P9-DGE-163

MILLENNIUM® WORLD ATLAS

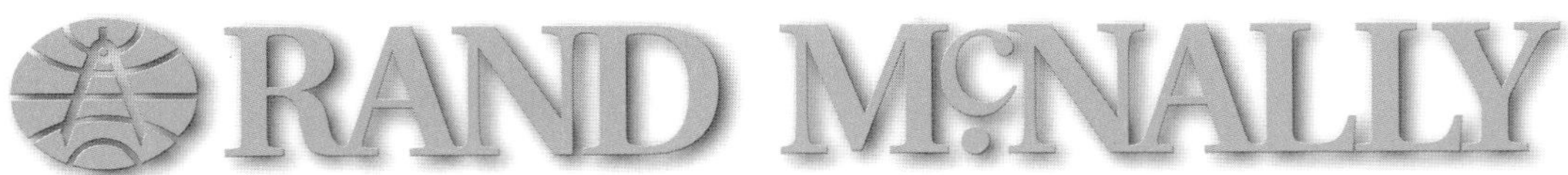

MILLENNIUM®
WORLD ATLAS

President and CEO, Rand McNally & Company
Richard J. Davis

Senior Vice President, Marketing
Margaret A. Stender

Director, Reference Publishing
Kendra L. Ensor

Editors
Kathryn Martin O'Neil
Brett R. Gover
Ann T. Natunewicz

Art Direction and Design
John C. Nelson
Peggy R. Hogan

Marketing
Leslie H. Hoadley
JoEllen A. Klein

Manufacturing
Terry D. Rieger

Cartography (U.S.)
Michael W. Dobson, V. Patrick Healy, Jeffrey J. Harris, David Lanter, Jon M. Leverenz

Chris Adomshick, Hans A. Anderson, Robert K. Argersinger, Gregory P. Babiak, Tim Bauserman, Barbara Benstead-Strassheim, David M. Bukala, Brian L. Cantwell, Kerry B. Chambers, Victor Collins, Laurence A. Disch, Marzee L. Eckhoff, Winifred V. Farbman, Charles C. Geraci, Julie A. Geyer, Michael B. Healy, Susan K. Hudson, Elizabeth A. Hunt, Nancy Jurus-Ottini, William R. Karbler, James B. Kierski, Gennadiy Kogan, Lisa Kunkle, Mary Lamb, Brian M. Lash, Felix A. Lopez, Nina Lusterman, John M. McAvoy, Erik A. Pedersen, Darren L. Raffel, Yvonne Rosenberg, Scott Rudy, Ty Rue, Emanuel Scotidis, Richard P. Slota, Jill M. Stift, Raymond T. Tobiaski, Thomas F. Vitacco, David R. Walters, Zewen Wang, Richard A. Wanzo, Bryan D. Weaver, Steven R. Wiertz, James A. Wooden, David C. Zapenski

Cartography (U.K.)
Craig Asquith

Cartography (Italy)
Giovanni Baselli
Ubaldo Uberti

Photo Credits (l=left, r=right, c=center, t=top, b=bottom)

Jacket
© European Space Agency/Science Photo Library (globe); © Digital Art/WestLight (starry background)

Front Section
© North Wind Picture Archives, vi (t)

Timeline (pages A2 - A3)
© North Wind Picture Archives/Leif Ericcson, Stanley & Livingstone, reaper, iron plough, corn, Adam Smith, Chaco Canyon, Nibelungenlied, King John, Bastille, Abraham Lincoln; © SuperStock/Astrolabe, Marco Polo, Christopher Columbus, Ortelius map, Jamestown, Neil Armstrong, Gutenberg, Galileo, Newton, Copernicus, Eli Whitney, Arab traders, Medici, Model T, Spanish Armada, dodo, Mt. Fuji, Giotto fresco, Dante, Chaucer, Sistine mural, Hamlet playbill, Picasso Cubist art, Normans, Saladin, Ming mask, Cortés, Louis XIV, Lenin, Pope Urban, Martin Luther

Thematic Material (pages A4 - A40)
© Istituto Geografico De Agostini
Designed by Siena Artworks Ltd.

© B&C Alexander, A22 (b l); © Tim Bedlow, A11 (t r); © Jeremy Burgess, A24 (b r); © Sarah Errington, A35 (t r); © Fred Espenak, A4 (t r); © Simon Fraser, A27 (c r); © Robert Frerck/Odyssey, A39 (b r); © Michael Giannechini, A17 (b c); © Herbert Giradet/Still Pictures, A38 (c l); © Hale Observatory, A6 (c l); © Robert Harding, A35 (c l), A38 (t r); © Peter Hendrie, A32 (c r); © Mark Henley, A33 (t l); © Robert Hessler, A1 (b r), A20 (t r); © Image Bank/Infocus International, A30 (t r); © Impact/Dagino/Cosmos, A40 (c l); © Adam Jones, A14 (t r); © Keith Kent, viii (c l), A19 (t r); © Paolo Koch, A35 (t l); © Barry Lewis, A31 (t r); © R. Ian Lloyd/WestLight, A34 (b l); © Eric Meola, A18 (b r); © Kaz Mari, A20 (b l); © NASA, A5 (c l), A7 (b l), A9 (t r), A10 (c l), A16 (c l); © Trevor Page, A40 (b r); © David Parker, A12 (b l), A23 (b r); © Gary Parker, A27 (b r); © Fram Petit, A31 (c l); © RHPL, A1 (c r), A29 (t r); © Roger Ressmeyer/Starlight, A9 (c), A13 (t l); © Rex Features/SIPA, A33 (b r), A37 (b r); © Peter Scoones, A25 (t l); © Simon Shepheard, A37 (c l); © Science Photo Library/Earth Satellite Corp., A26 (c l); © A. Tovy/TRIP, A37 (t r); © Luis Vega, viii (t l), A32 (c l); © Frank Zullo, A7 (c r)

Millennium® World Atlas

www.randmcnally.com

Published and printed in the United States of America.

Rand McNally & Company.
Millennium world atlas.
p. cm.
At head of title: Rand McNally.
Includes index and glossary.
ISBN 0-528-84175-0
1. Atlases. I. Title. II. Title: World atlas III. Title: Rand McNally millennium world atlas.
G1021 .R217 1999 <G&M>
912—DC21 99-27274
CIP
MAPS

10 9 8 7 6 5 4 3 2

Table of Contents

vi-vii .... How to Use the Atlas

"Our World at the Millennium"

A•1 .... Introduction
A•2 - A•3.... Timeline of the Millennium
A•4 - A•5.... The Universe
A•6 - A•7.... The Solar System
A•8 - A•9.... Earth and the Moon
A•10 - A•11 The Structure of Earth
A•12 - A•13 Volcanoes and Earthquakes
A•14 - A•15 Rocks and Minerals
A•16 - A•17 The Atmosphere
A•18 - A•19 Climate and Weather
A•20 - A•21 The Oceans
A•22 - A•23 Water
A•24 - A•25 Evolutionary Trails
A•26 - A•27 The Diversity of Life
A•28 - A•29 The Rise of Man
A•30 - A•31 The Population Explosion
A•32 - A•33 Population Patterns
A•34 - A•35 Wealth and Education
A•36 - A•37 Language and Religion
A•38 - A•39 The Environment
A•40 .... International Cooperation

Regional maps

1................. Map legend
2-3 .... World, Political
4-5 .... World, Physical

Europe

6-7 .... Europe, Political
8-9 .... Europe, Physical
10-11 .... British Isles
12-13 .... Northern Europe and Scandinavia
14-15 .... Northern Scandinavia
16-17 .... Southern Scandinavia
18-19 .... Southern Finland
20-21 .... Northern France, Belgium, and the Netherlands
22-23 .... Southern France and Switzerland
24-25 .... Germany, Czech Republic, Slovakia, and Poland
26-27 .... Baltic Regions and Moscow
28-29 .... Spain and Portugal
30-31 .... Northern Italy, Austria, and the Balkans
32-33 .... Southern Italy
34-35 .... Greece and Western Turkey
36-37 .... Hungary, Yugoslavia, Romania, and Bulgaria
38-39 .... Ukraine
40-41 .... Southwestern Russia, Belarus, and Ukraine
42-43 .... Turkey and the Caucasus

Asia

44-45 .... Asia, Political
46-47 .... Asia, Physical
48-49 .... Northwestern Asia
50-51 .... Northeastern Asia
52-53 .... China, Korea, and Japan
54-55 .... Japan, Korea, and Northeastern China
56-57 .... Central and Southern Japan
58-59 .... Eastern China
60-61 .... Southeast Asia
62-63 .... Southern Asia
64-65 .... Myanmar, Thailand, and Singapore
66-67 .... Borneo, Java, and Sumatra
68................ Philippines
69................ Southern India
70-71 .... Northern India
72-73 .... Southwestern Asia
74-75 .... The Middle East
76-77 .... Israel, Lebanon, and Jordan

Africa

78-79 .... Africa, Political
80-81 .... Africa, Physical
82-83 .... Northeastern Africa
84-85 .... Northwestern Africa
86-87 .... Central Africa
88-89 .... Southern Africa
90-91 .... South Africa

Australia and Oceania

92-93 .... Australia and Oceania, Political
94-95 .... Australia and Oceania, Physical
96-97 .... Australia
98-99 .... Eastern Australia
100-101 ...... Islands of the Pacific
102.............. New Zealand
103.............. Antarctica

North America

104-105 ...... North America, Political
106-107 ...... North America, Physical
108.............. Greenland
109.............. Alaska and Northwestern Canada
110-111 ...... Canada
112-113 ...... United States
114-115 ...... Northeastern United States and Southeastern Canada
116-117 ...... Southeastern United States
118-119 ...... Northwestern United States and Southwestern Canada
120-121 ...... Northern Mexico and Southwestern United States
122-123 ...... Northeastern United States
124-125 ...... Central Atlantic States
126-127 ...... Great Lakes
128-129 ...... Northern Midwestern United States
130-131 ...... Midwestern United States
132-133 ...... Coastal Southeastern United States
134-135 ...... Central Southern United States
136-137 ...... Southern Texas
138-139 ...... Southern Great Plains
140-141 ...... Central Great Plains
142-143 ...... Northern Great Plains
144-145 ...... Southwestern Canada
146-147 ...... Pacific Northwest States
148-149 ...... California, Nevada, and Hawaii
150-151 ...... Arizona and Utah
152-153 ...... Mexico, Central America, and the Caribbean
154-155 ...... Central Mexico
156-157 ...... Central America
158-159 ...... Islands of the Caribbean

South America

160-161 ...... South America, Political
162-163 ...... South America, Physical
164-165 ...... Northern South America
166-167 ...... Southern South America
168-169 ...... Venezuela and Colombia
170-171 ...... Eastern Brazil
172-173 ...... Central Argentina and Chile
174-175 ...... Pacific and Indian Oceans
176.............. Atlantic Ocean

Metropolitan area maps

177.............. Introduction
178.............. London
179.............. Paris
180.............. Manchester - Liverpool
181.............. Ruhr Area
182.............. Berlin • Vienna • Budapest
183.............. St. Petersburg • Moscow
184.............. Madrid • Milan • Lisbon • Barcelona
185.............. Rome • Athens • Istanbul • Tehran
186.............. Tokyo-Yokohama
187.............. Bangkok • Ho Chi Minh City (Saigon) • Jakarta • Shanghai • T'aipei • Manila
188.............. Osaka • Kobe • Kyoto
189.............. Beijing • Seoul • Singapore • Xianggang (Hong Kong)
190.............. Delhi • Mumbai (Bombay) • Calcutta
191.............. Lagos • Kinshasa - Brazzaville • Cairo • Johannesburg
192.............. Sydney • Melbourne
193.............. Montréal • Toronto
194-195 ...... New York
196.............. Chicago
197.............. Cleveland • Pittsburgh
198.............. Los Angeles
199.............. Detroit - Windsor
200.............. San Francisco - Oakland - San Jose
201.............. Boston
202.............. Buffalo - Niagara Falls • Baltimore • Washington
203.............. Philadelphia
204.............. Mexico City • Havana • Caracas • Lima • Santiago
205.............. Rio de Janeiro • São Paulo
206.............. Buenos Aires
207.............. World Metropolitan Areas Population Table

World Information Tables

209-212 ...... Political Information Table
213-224 ...... Populations of Cities and Towns

Index

I•1 .... Glossary
I•2 - I•160.. INDEX

How to Use the Atlas

What is an Atlas?

A set of maps bound together is called an atlas. Abraham Ortelius' *Theatrum orbis terrarum*, published in 1570, is considered to be the first modern "atlas," although it was not referred to as such for almost 20 years. In 1589, Gerardus Mercator *(figure 1)* coined the term when he named his collection of maps after Atlas, the mythological Titan who carried Earth on his shoulders as punishment for warring against Zeus.

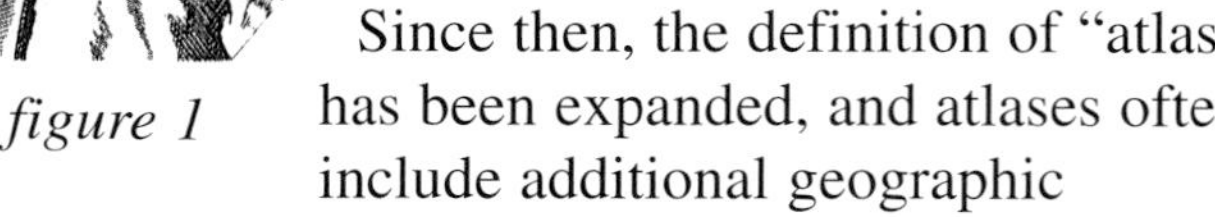

figure 1

Since then, the definition of "atlas" has been expanded, and atlases often include additional geographic information in diagrams, tables, and text.

Latitude and Longitude

The terms "latitude" and "longitude" refer to the grid of horizontal and vertical lines found on most maps and globes. Any point on Earth can be located by its precise latitude and longitude coordinates.

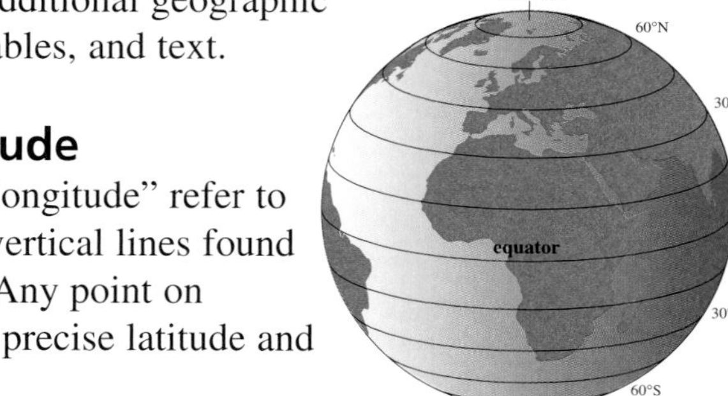

figure 2

The imaginary horizontal line that circles Earth halfway between the North and South poles is called the equator; it represents 0° latitude and lies 90° from either pole. The other lines of latitude, or parallels, measure distances north or south from the equator *(figure 2)*. The imaginary vertical line that measures 0° longitude runs through the Greenwich Observatory in the United Kingdom, and is called the Prime Meridian. The other lines of longitude, or meridians, measure distances east or west from the prime meridian *(figure 3)*, up to a maximum of 180°. Lines of latitude and longitude cross each other, forming a grid *(figure 4)*.

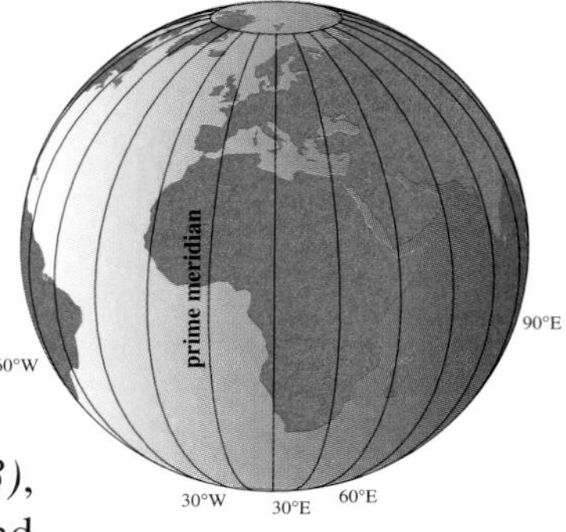

figure 3

Map Projections

Every cartographer is faced with the problem of transforming the curved surface of Earth onto a flat plane with a minimum of distortion. The systematic transformation of locations on Earth (a spherical surface) to locations on a map (a flat surface) is called projection.

figure 4

It is not possible to represent on a flat map the spatial relationships of angle, distance, direction, and area that only a globe can show faithfully. As a result, projections inevitably involve some distortion. On large-scale maps representing a few square miles, the distortion is generally negligible. But on maps depicting large countries, continents, or the entire world, the amount of distortion can be significant. On maps that use the Mercator Projection (*figure 5*), for example, distortion increases with distance from the equator. Thus the island of Greenland appears larger than the entire continent of South America, although South America is in fact nine time larger. In contrast, the Robinson Projection (*figure 6*) renders the world's major land areas in generally correct proportion to one another, although distortion is still apparent in areas such as Antarctica, which is actually smaller than all of the continents except Europe and Australia.

figure 5

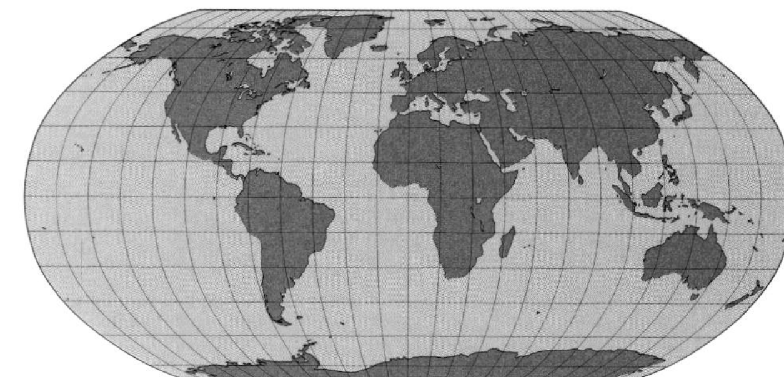

figure 6

There is an infinite number of possible map projections, all of which distort one or more of the characteristics of the globe in varying degrees. The projection that a cartographer chooses depends on the size and location of the area being projected and the purpose of the map. In this atlas, most of the maps are drawn on projections that give a consistent or only slightly distorted area scale, good land and ocean shape, parallels that are parallel, and as consistent a linear scale as possible throughout the projection.

Map Scale

The scale of a map is the relationship between distances or areas shown on the map and the corresponding distances or areas on Earth's surface. Large-scale maps show relatively small areas in greater detail than do small-scale maps, such as those of individual continents or of the world.

There are three different ways to express scale. Most often scale is given as a fraction, such as 1:10,000,000, which means that the ratio of distances on the map to actual distances on Earth is 1 to 10,000,000. Scale can also be expressed as a phrase, such as "One inch represents approximately ten million miles." Finally, scale can be illustrated via a bar scale on which various distances are labeled *(figure 7)*. Any of these three scale expressions can be used to calculate distances on a map.

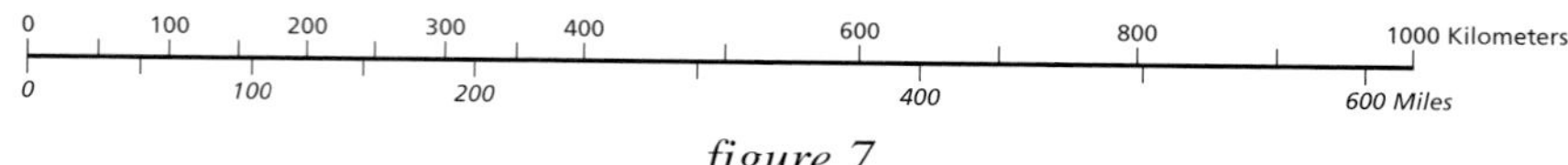

figure 7

Measuring Distances

Using a bar scale, it is possible to calculate the distance between any two points on a map. To find the approximate distance between São Paulo and Rio de Janeiro, Brazil, for example, follow these steps:

1) Lay a piece of paper on the right-hand page of the "Eastern Brazil" map found on pages 170-171, lining up its edge with the city dots for São Paulo and Rio de Janeiro. Make a mark on the paper next to each dot *(figure 8)*.

figure 8

2) Place the paper along the scale bar found below the map, and position the first mark at 0. The second mark falls about a quarter of the way between the 200-mile tick and the 300-mile tick, indicating that the distance separating the two cities is approximately 225 miles *(figure 9)*.

0 100 200 400 600 Miles
600 800 1000 Kilometers
Scale 1 : 10,000,000 Lambert Conformal Conic Projection

figure 9

3) To confirm this measurement, make a third pencil mark (shown in red in *figure 9*) at the 200-mile tick. Slide the paper to the left so that this mark lines up with 0. The Rio de Janeiro mark now falls about halfway between the 0 tick and the 50-mile tick. Thus, São Paulo and Rio de Janeiro are indeed approximately 225 (200 + 25) miles apart.

Using the Index to Find Places

One of the most important purposes of an atlas is to help the reader locate places on the maps. This atlas uses two types of indexing systems: map reference "bingo keys" and latitude/longitude coordinates. In the index, found on pages I•1 through I•160, every entry is assigned an alpha-numeric code that consists of a letter and a number. This code relates to the red letters and numbers that run along the perimeter of each map. Each entry also lists precise latitude/longitude coordinates for that particular feature. To locate places or features, follow the steps below for the city of Bratsk, Russia.

1) Look up Bratsk in the index. The entry *(figure 10)* contains the following information: the place name (Bratsk), the country name (Russia) in which Bratsk is located, the page number (48) of the map on which Bratsk can be found, the map reference key (C18) corresponding to Bratsk's location on the map grid, and the precise latitude/longitude coordinates (56.08 N, 101.38 E).

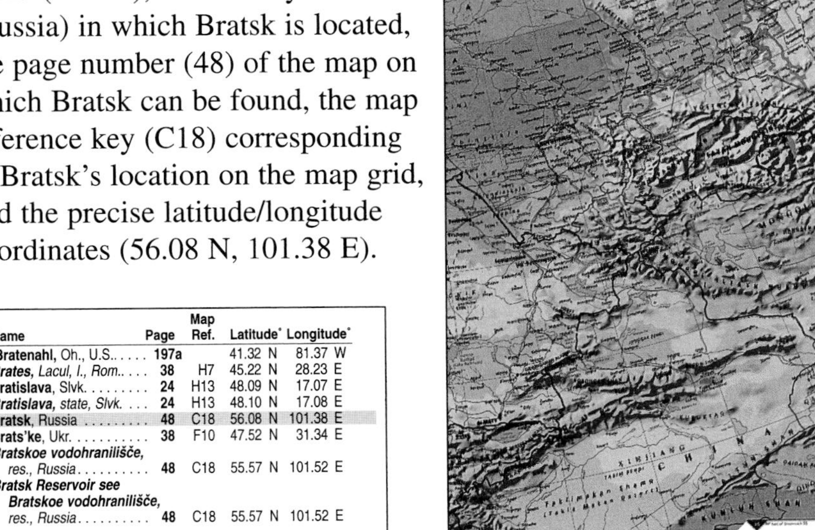

Name	Page	Map Ref.	Latitude°	Longitude°
Bratenahl, Oh., U.S.	**197a**		41.32 N	81.37 W
Brates, *Lacul, l., Rom.*	**38**	H7	45.22 N	28.23 E
Bratislava, Slvk.	**24**	H13	48.09 N	17.07 E
Bratislava, *state, Slvk.*	**24**	H13	48.10 N	17.08 E
Bratsk, Russia	**48**	C18	56.08 N	101.38 E
Brats'ke, Ukr.	**38**	F10	47.52 N	31.34 E
Bratskoe vodohranilišče, *res., Russia*	**48**	C18	55.57 N	101.52 E
Bratsk Reservoir see Bratskoe vodohranilišče, *res., Russia*	**48**	C18	55.57 N	101.52 E

figure 10

figure 11

2) Turn to the Northwestern Asia map on pages 48-49. Look along either the left or right-hand margin for the red letter "C"—the letter code given for Bratsk. The "C" denotes a band that arcs horizontally across the map, between the grid lines representing 55° and 60° North latitude. Then, look along either the top or bottom margin for the red number "18"—the numerical part of the code given for Bratsk. The "18" denotes a widening vertical band, between the grid lines representing 100° and 105° East longitude, which angles from the top center of the map to right-hand edge.

3) Using your finger, follow the horizontal "C" band and the vertical "18" band to the area where they overlap *(figure 11)*. Bratsk lies within this overlap area.

Physical Maps and Political Maps

Most of the maps in the *Millennium World Atlas* are physical maps, like the one shown in *figure 12*, emphasizing terrain, landforms, and elevation. Political maps, as in *figure 13*, emphasize countries and other political units over topography. The atlas includes political maps of the world and each of the continents except Antarctica.

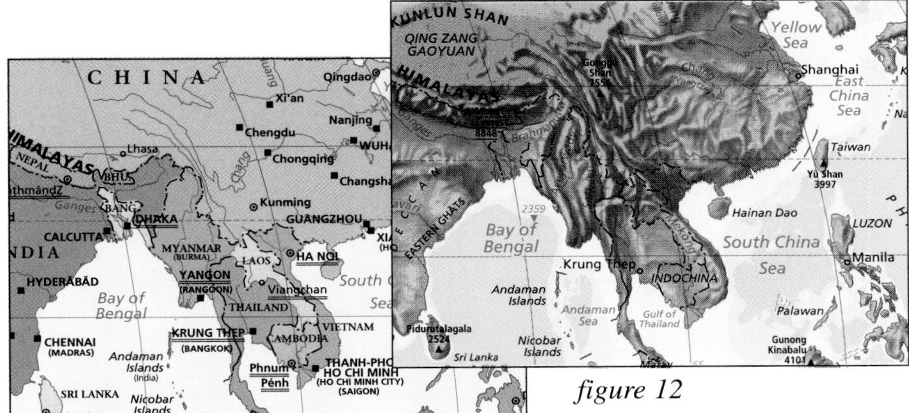

figure 12

figure 13

How Maps Show Topography

The physical maps in this atlas use two techniques to depict Earth's topography. Variations in elevation are shown through a series of colors called hypsometric tints. Areas below sea level appear as a dark green; as the elevation rises, the tints move successively through lighter green, yellow, and orange. Similarly, variations in ocean depth are represented by bathymetric tints. The shallowest areas appear as light blue; darker tints of blue indicate greater depths. The hypsometric/bathymetric scale that accompanies each map identifies, in feet and meters, all of the elevation and depth categories that appear on the map.

Principal landforms, such as mountain ranges and valleys, are rendered in shades of gray, a technique known as shaded relief. The combination of hypsometric tints and shaded relief provides the map reader with a three-dimensional picture of Earth's surface *(figure 14)*.

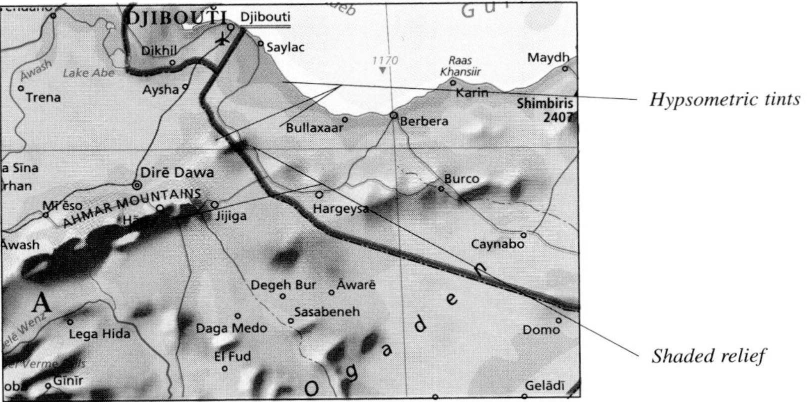

figure 14

Our World at the Millennium

Timeline of the Millennium

	1000-1100	1100-1200	1200-1300	1300-1400	1400-1500
Exploration and Mapping	c. 1000 — Leif Ericsson and the Vikings sail to North America. ► c. 1000 — Maoris settle present-day New Zealand. c. 1050 — Astrolabes introduced into Europe from Asia. ►	1120 — Welcher of Malvern uses degrees, minutes, and seconds to measure latitude and longitude. 1154 — Mohammed al-Idrisi produces world map for Roger II of Sicily, depicting the world as round. 1155 — Liu Ching Tha produces first printed map in China. 1159 — Spanish Jew Benjamin of Tudela travels to India.	1224 — Abdallah ur-Rūmī writes his Arabic geographical encyclopedia *Mu'jam ul-buldân*. c. 1290 — Arab sailors discover Comoros and Madagascar while conducting trade in Africa. 1298 — Marco Polo completes his *Description of the World*, describing his trip to Cathay (China). ►	1312 — Sailors from Genoa reach the Canary Islands. 1324-25 — Mali emperor Mansa Musa makes pilgrimage to Mecca. 1353 — Ibn Battuta begins to compose a travel narrative of his journeys from Morocco to India and China.	1405-1433 — Zheng He sails from China as far east as Africa. 1492 — Martin Behaim produces the first globe in Nürnberg. 1492 — Thinking he has arrived in the East Indies, Christopher Columbus lands in the Caribbean. ◄ 1498 — Portuguese sailor Vasco de Gama reaches India.
Science and Inventions	c. 1000 — Indian mathematician Sridhara recognizes the significance of the zero. c. 1000 — Chinese begin using gunpowder to make explosive weapons. c. 1025 — Arab physicist Alhazen studies optics and develops parabolic mirrors. 1037 — Arab physician Avicenna writes influential *Canon of Medicine*. 1041 — Chinese printer Pi Sheng invents moveable type.	c. 1100 — Chinese explain the causes of solar and lunar eclipses. 1121 — Al-Khazini speculates about Earth's gravitational force. 1175 — Gerard of Gremona translates Ptolemy's astronomical text *The Almagest* into Latin.	1202 — Leonardo Pisano Fibonacci's *Liber abaci* introduces Arabic numerals to Europe. 1259-1260 — Important astronomical observatories are built in Maragha, Iran, and Beijing, China. 1272 — Alphonsine Tables (planetary charts) completed in Castile. 1298 — English archers use longbows to defeat Scottish army.	c. 1300 — Sternpost rudder in European ships permits longer sailing distances. 1303 — Chinese mathematician Chu-Shi-Kié writes algebra book *Precious Mirror of the Four Elements.* 1316 — Mondino de Luzzi writes anatomy book based on human dissections. 1391 — Geoffrey Chaucer's *Treatise on the Astrolabe* describes how to accurately measure the positions of stars.	1430s — Mongol astronomer Ulugh Beg publishes star maps and tables. 1440 — Nicolas Cusanus claims that Earth is in constant motion and that space is infinite. c. 1450 — Johannes Gutenberg invents the printing press. ► 1491 — Joannes de Ketham publishes *Fasiculus medicinae*, the first anatomical book with printed illustrations.
Agriculture, Industry, and Trade	c. 1050 — Iron ploughs replace wooden ones in Europe. ▼ 1068 — Chinese emperor She-tsung nationalizes agricultural production. 1081 — Venice and Byzantine Empire sign trade treaty.	c. 1100 — Arab traders ► increasingly settle in Africa along the Indian Ocean coast. c. 1100 — Introduction of horse-collar harness in Europe permits replacement of oxen by horses as plough animals. 1173 — Pisa establishes trading post in Alexandria, Egypt. 1191 — Tea introduced to Japan from China.	1230 — Lübeck and Hamburg forge trading alliance (Hanseatic League). 1233 — Coal is mined in Newcastle, England, for the first time. 1277 — Genoese traders sail through the Strait of Gibraltar into the Atlantic Ocean for the first time.	c. 1300 — Europeans make increasing use of cargo and merchant galleys. 1340 — First blast furnace for smelting iron built in Belgium. 1378-1381 — Workers' Revolt in Florence (1378) and Peasants' Revolt in England (1381). 1397 — Medici establish themselves as bankers in Florence. ►	c. 1400 — Dutch use windmills to expand arable land by pumping water from coastal lowlands. 1441 — Portuguese revive African slave trade. 1450 — Arabian coffee trade becomes centered in the port town of Mocha.
Nature, Weather, and the Environment	1040 — Tabriz, Persia, leveled by earthquake that kills 50,000. 1064-72 — Nile River fails to flood for seven years due to drought, resulting in famine. c. 1080 — Chinese scientists theorize that climate has changed over time, pointing to fossilized plants as evidence.	1150-1200 — Droughts in the Gobi Desert pressure Huns to expand into new lands. 1160 — Drift ice begins to block passage of Norse ships to Iceland and Greenland. 1169 — Sicily's Mount Etna becomes active after centuries of dormancy, killing 15,000.	c. 1200 — Drought in Africa causes famine in Nile delta; 100,000 die. 1275-1300 – Severe drought in Chaco Canyon accelerates collapse of central Anasazi communities. ► 1281 — Mongol invasion of Japan fails due to typhoon that destroys fleet. c. 1297 — Moas hunted to extinction by Maoris of New Zealand.	1337 — William Merlee attempts first scientific weather forecasts at Oxford.	1410 — Iceland loses contact with Greenland colony, probably due to encroaching ice and glaciers. 1421 — Sea floods in Holland submerge 72 counties. c. 1430 — The beginning of the "Little Ice Age." 1470s — Aristotle's *Meteorologica*, about meteorology and other Earth sciences, is published.
Culture and the Arts	c. 1000 — *Thousand Stories*, a collection of Persian and Indian tales that forms the basis for *The One Thousand and One Nights*, is compiled. 1011 — Firdausi completes epic poem *The Book of Kings*, describing nearly 4,000 years of Persian history. c. 1019 — Murasaki Shikibu completes *Tale of Genji*, first Japanese novel. 1090s — Troubadors begin to popularize vernacular singing in Provence.	c. 1100 — French epic poem *Chanson de Roland* depicts ideal of knightly chivalry. c. 1120 — Chinese Emperor Huizong establishes Academy of Painting at Kaifeng. c. 1150 — Golden age of Buddhist art in Burma. c. 1195 — German epic poem *Nibelungenlied* composed. ►	1207 — The epic *Poem of the Cid* recounts the conquest of the Moors in Valencia. c. 1230 — Guillaume de Lorris composes the first part of the French poem *Romance of the Rose.* 1258 — Persian poet Saadi writes the *Rose Garden.* c. 1270 — The *Saga of the Volsungs*, a collection of Icelandic tales and legends, is composed.	c. 1300 — Renaissance begins in Europe. 1304 — Giotto's frescos in Padua introduce a realistic and naturalistic style ▲ to European painting. 1308 — Dante begins writing *The Divine Comedy.* ◄ 1368 — Persian poet Hafiz composes *The Diwan.* c. 1387 — Chaucer ► begins writing *The Canterbury Tales.*	c. 1400 — Zeami Motokiyo's plays signal rising popularity of Noh theater in Japan. c. 1430-1435 — Donatello sculpts *David*, the first nude statue in Europe since antiquity. 1480s — Persian painter Kamal Ud-din Bihzad illustrates manuscripts with his miniatures. 1497 — Leonardo da Vinci paints *The Last Supper.*
Population and Politics	1000 — World population estimate: 275 million. c. 1000 — Kingdom of Ghana at its zenith. c. 1043 — Mandingo Empire founded near Djenné in West Africa. 1066 — Norman conquest of England. ► 1071 — Seljuk Turks defeat Byzantines, take Asia Minor.	c. 1150 — Anasazi begin to abandon their settlements in the American Southwest. 1183 — Emperor Frederick Barbarossa forced to grant the city-states of Lombardy independence. 1187 — Saladin, sultan of Egypt, wrests Jerusalem away from European Christians. ► 1192 — Yoritomo establishes first shogunate in Kamakura, Japan.	1206 — Genghis Khan unites the Mongols and initiates eastward and westward expansion. 1215 — King John of England signs the Magna Carta, ► limiting royal power and conceding privileges to the nobility. c. 1235 — Sundiata Keita builds city of Mali, future capital of the Mali Empire. 1250 — Mamelukes overthrow the Ayyubid dynasty in Egypt.	1325 — Aztecs build their capital Tenochtitlán. 1337 — Beginning of the 100 Years' War between France and England. 1347-51 — Bubonic plague hits Europe, killing an estimated 75 million people. 1368 — Ming dynasty begins in China. ► 1369 — Tamerlane ascends to the throne in Samarkand; will later conquer much of Afghanistan, Persia, India, and Asia Minor.	1430s — Pachacutec begins to expand Inca territories in Peru. 1438 — Albert II becomes the first Hapsburg Holy Roman Emperor. 1453 — Ottoman Turks take Constantinople, leading to the collapse of the Byzantine Empire. 1468 — Sanghai Empire dominates central Sudan in Africa.
Philosophy, Religion, and Learning	c. 1000 — Practice of Yoga spreads throughout India. 1054 — Schism permanently divides Roman Catholic and Eastern Orthodox Churches. 1067 — Mosque-university of Mizamiyya founded in Baghdad. 1096 — Pope Urban II initiates first of numerous crusades to wrest Holy Land from the Turks. ►	1119 — First European university established in Bologna. c. 1180 — Islamic philosopher Averroës completes *The Incoherence of the Incoherence.* 1183 — Zhu Xi, Neo-Confucianist philosopher, founds academy in China. 1190 — Jewish philosopher Moses Maimonides builds on Aristotelian thought in *The Guide for the Perplexed.*	c. 1200 — Jewish mystical movement called Cabala develops in France and Spain. 1233 — Pope Gregory IX begins Inquisition to root out heresy. c. 1250 — Nasir al-Din Tusi's writings develop Shiite theology. 1273 — Thomas Aquinas completes *Summa Theologica*, synthesizing philosophy of Aristotle with Christian theology.	1324 — Political theorist Marsilius of Padua critiques power of the pope in his *Defensor Pacis.* 1360s — Ibn Khaldun begins writing seven volumes of *Universal History.* 1378 — The Great Schism divides the Roman Catholic Church. 1399 — Henry IV of England begins repression of religious reform movement known as the Lollards.	1403 — Chinese encyclopedia *Yung Lo Ta Tien* is compiled, containing more than 22,000 volumes. 1415-1418 — Council of Constance burns John Hus at the stake for heresy and ends the Great Schism. 1465 — Muhammad ibn Sulayman al-Jazuli composes *The Signs of the Blessings.* 1492 — Jews expelled from Spain.

1500-1600	1600-1700	1700-1800	1800-1900	1900-2000
1506-07 — First maps depicting the New World are printed in Europe. 1519 — Ferdinand Magellan sets sail from Spain to circumnavigate the globe. 1533 — Francisco Pizarro conquers the Inca Empire. 1569 — Gerard Mercator's world map permits more accurate plotting of navigational courses. 1570 — Abraham Ortelius publishes the first complete world atlas, *Theatrum orbis terrarum.* ► 	1607 — England's first permanent colony in North America is established at Jamestown, Virginia. ►  1608 — French explorer and geographer Samuel de Champlain founds Quebec. 1610 — English navigator Henry Hudson explores Hudson Bay. 1625 — Dutch found New Amsterdam (later called New York). 1672 — Dutch found Cape Town in southern Africa.	1735 — First reliable chronometer invented in England, permitting accurate determination of longitude. 1784 — Russians establish settlement in Alaska. 1788 — British begin to settle Australia as a penal colony.	1804 — Lewis and Clark depart to explore route across North America to the Pacific Ocean. 1830 — Founding of the Royal Geographical Society. 1871 — Stanley finds Livingstone in Ujiji, Africa. ▼ 1884 — Greenwich established as zero meridian for international time zones.	1946 — Azimuthal World Air Charts become cartographic standard for air navigation. 1960s — Seasat satellite used to map the ocean floor. 1969 — American astronaut Neil Armstrong steps on the moon.► 1990 — Hubble Space Telescope launched by NASA to map space. 1995 — Satellite-based Global Positioning System (GPS) becomes fully operational.
1527 — Paracelsus critiques traditional medicine based on Greek learning at University of Basel. 1543 — Copernicus argues that the Sun, not Earth, is the center of the universe. ► 1543 — Vesalius publishes *On the Structure of the Human Body.* 1590 — Dutch optician Zacharias Janssen invents the compound microscope.	1609 — Galileo makes astronomical observations using newly invented telescope. ► 1628 — William Harvey describes the circulation of blood in the body. 1687 — Isaac Newton's *Principia* describes fundamental laws of motion.◄	c. 1700 — Jethro Tull invents the seed drill, improving agricultural production. 1753 — Carolus Linnaeus describes plant and animal classification scheme. 1793 — Eli Whitney invents the cotton gin, making the U.S. the world's leading supplier of cotton. ►  1796 — Edward Jenner develops smallpox vaccination.	1827 — Joseph Niepce produces photographs on metal plate. 1831 — Cyrus McCormick invents the reaper, first mechanized harvesting machine. ► 1859 — Charles Darwin publishes "On the Origin of Species." 1860 — Etienne Lenoir develops first practical internal-combustion engine. 1876 — Bell invents the telephone. 1880 — Thomas Edison and Joseph Swan independently invent first practical light bulbs.	1916 — Einstein publishes "General Theory of Relativity." 1928 — British scientist Alexander Fleming discovers penicillin, the first antibiotic. 1939 — Television system demonstrated at New York World's Fair. 1946 — ENIAC, first general-purpose electronic digital computer, successfully tested. 1953 — Watson and Crick construct a molecular model of DNA. 1990 — Human Genome Project begins to map all genetic codes in human beings. 1990s — Internet gains widespread popularity.
1514-1565 — Pineapples, coffee, porcelain, chocolate, sweet potatoes, corn, and tobacco make their first appearances in Europe. ► 1531 — First stock exchange opened in Antwerp, followed by the Royal Exchange in London (1565). 1544 — Spanish begin mining silver in Potosi, Peru, a significant cause of worldwide inflation.	1609 — Dutch East India Company introduces tea from China into Europe. 1619 — First African slaves brought to North America. 1623 — Patents law introduced in England. 1630s — Japan expels most foreigners, allowing trade only with the Dutch and Chinese.	1730s — Experiments with four-field crop rotation improve agricultural yields. c. 1770 — Industrial Revolution begins in England. 1776 — Adam Smith publishes *Wealth of Nations.* ► 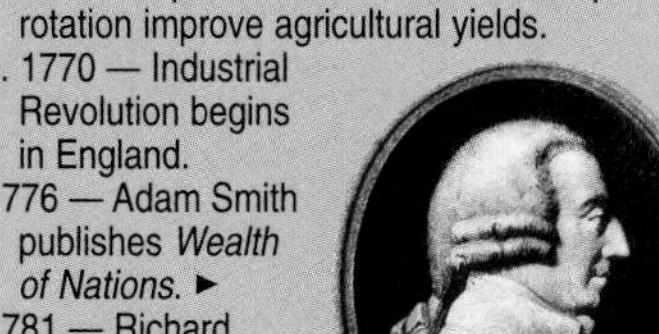 1781 — Richard Arkwright introduces factory system of production. 1792 — New York Stock Exchange is organized.	1839 — Illegal opium trade leads to First Opium War between Britain and China. 1854 — Commodore Perry forces Japan to trade with the United States. 1870 — John Rockefeller founds Standard Oil Company. 1886 — Samuel Gompers founds the American Federation of Labor.	1908 — Ford Motor Company begins producing Model "T" automobile. ► 1929 — U.S. stock market collapses, contributing to global depression. 1960s — "Green revolution" introduces new grains yielding more food for countries such as India and Mexico. 1980 — International Business Machines (IBM) markets first home computer.
1530 — Dikes burst in Holland; flooding causes 400,000 deaths. 1556 — Earthquake in Shaanxi, China, results in 830,000 deaths. 1588 — Legendary storm later called the "Protestant wind" helps English navy defeat Spanish Armada.► 1593 — Galileo invents thermometer to measure air temperature. c. 1599 — Alpine glaciers begin remarkable advance.	1624 — M.A. de Dominis argues that tides are created by magnetic pull of sun and moon. 1669 — Nicolaus Steno argues that rock strata correspond to their age. c. 1680 — Dodos on Mauritius become extinct due to the introduction of pigs by Portuguese sailors. ►	1707 — Mt. Fuji erupts.► 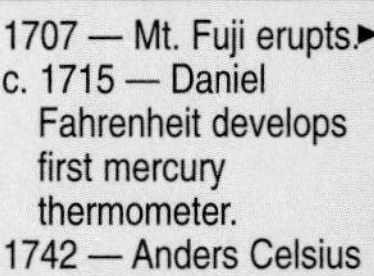 c. 1715 — Daniel Fahrenheit develops first mercury thermometer. 1742 — Anders Celsius creates thermometer marking 0° as freezing and 100° as boiling. 1755 — One of the most powerful earthquakes in recorded history (estimated at 8.75 on the Richter scale) hits Lisbon, Portugal.	c. 1830 — Swiss naturalist Louis Agassiz claims that glaciers once covered much of Europe. 1870 — Yellowstone is established as the first U.S. National Park. 1883 — Krakatoa volcano erupts in Indonesia with force of 26 hydrogen bombs. 1897 — Hluhluwe game reserve established, one of Africa's first.	1910 — Halley's Comet makes its closest approach to Earth, provoking panic. 1958 — Scientists warn of global temperature warming. 1985 — British Antarctic Survey discovers hole in Earth's ozone layer. 1986 — Chernobyl nuclear power plant explodes in Ukraine.
1508 — Michelangelo begins painting frescos in the Sistine Chapel, Rome. ► 1558 — Marguerite de Navarre's stories published posthumously in the *Heptameron.* c. 1574 — Hindu poet Tulsi Das writes *The Lake of the Deeds of Rama.* 1575 — Japanese woman Okuni founds first kabuki theater group.	1600 — The first opera, *Eurydice,* performed at Pitti Palace in Florence. 1601 — Shakespeare's *Hamlet* performed for the first time. ► 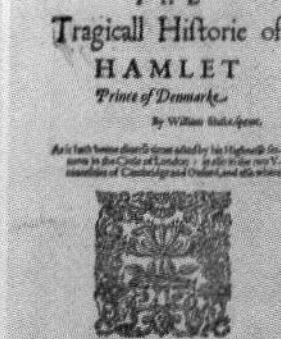 THE Tragicall Historie of HAMLET Prince of Denmarke 1642 — Rembrandt paints *The Night Watch.* 1682 — Ihara Saikaku writes novel *Koshoku ichidai otoko* (*Life of an Amorous Man*).	1715 — Chikamatsu Monzaemon's puppet play *The Battles of Coxinga* (*Kokusenya Kassen*) premiers in Japan. 1721 — First performance of Bach's *Brandenburg Concertos.* 1726 — Swift publishes his satire *Gulliver's Travels.* 1759 — Voltaire publishes *Candide.* 1791 — Mozart composes *The Magic Flute.*	1808 — Goethe publishes first part of *Faust.* 1840s — Wagner opens *Tannhauser* and *Lohengrin.* 1852 — Harriet Beecher Stowe publishes *Uncle Tom's Cabin.* 1866 — Dostoevsky publishes *Crime and Punishment.* 1870 — Monet paints *Impression: Sunrise.*	1907 — Picasso and Braque develop Cubism. ► 1913 — Premier of Stravinsky and Diaghilev's controversial ballet, *The Rite of Spring.* 1925 — Franz Kafka publishes *The Trial,* exemplifying literary surrealism. 1927 — "The Jazz Singer" is first film to synchronize moving images with sound. 1969 — Woodstock Music Festival attracts more than 500,000 people.
1519 — Charles V unites the Holy Roman Empire, Spain, and Burgundy under his rule. 1521 — Cortés conquers the Aztecs. ► 1526 — Mongols invade India, establishing Mogul Empire. 1533 — Ivan the Terrible rules as the first tsar of Russia.	1643 — Louis XIV ascends the throne of France. ►  1644 — Manchus invade China, establishing the Quing dynasty. 1648 — Peace of Westphalia ends Europe's devastating 30 Years' War. 1649 — King Charles I of England is beheaded. 1650 — World population estimate: 500 million.	c. 1710 — The 300-year-old African kingdom of Kongo collapses after Portuguese invasion. 1735-95 — Chinese Empire reaches furthest extent. 1772 — Austria, Prussia, and Russia partition Poland among themselves. 1776 — American Revolution begins. 1789 — French Revolution begins.▼ 	1810 — Simón Bolívar emerges as leader of Latin American revolutions. 1815 — Napoleon defeated at Waterloo. 1848 — Revolution sweeps Europe. 1863 — Abraham Lincoln issues Emancipation Proclamation, declaring slaves free. ► 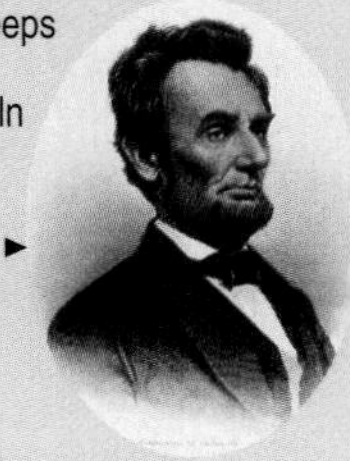 1866-1871 — Bismarck unifies Germany.	1914-1918 — World War I. 1917 — Russian revolutionaries overthrow Tsar Nicholas II, install Vladimir Lenin. ► 1939-1945 — World War II. 1945 — United Nations formed. 1989-1990 — Germans tear down Berlin Wall, erected in 1962. 1991 — South Africa ends Apartheid. 1999 — World population estimate: 5.9 billion.
1513 — Niccolo Machiavelli publishes *The Prince,* advising rulers that "It is better to be feared than loved." 1517 — German monk Martin Luther challenges Catholic Church with his 95 Theses, beginning Protestant Reformation. ► 1545 — The Council of Trent marks start of Counter-Reformation. 1578 — Leader of the Yellow Hat sect in Tibet receives the title Dalai Lama.	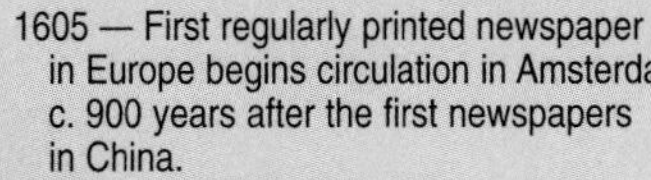 1605 — First regularly printed newspaper in Europe begins circulation in Amsterdam, c. 900 years after the first newspapers in China. 1637 — "I think, therefore I am." René Descartes publishes the *Discourse on Method.* 1651 — Thomas Hobbes defends royal absolutism in *Leviathan.* 1690 — John Locke's *Two Treatises on Government* justifies rebellion against tyrants.	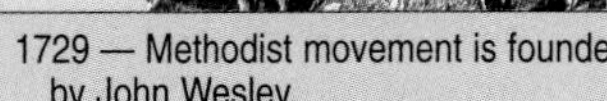 1729 — Methodist movement is founded by John Wesley. 1740s — Muhammed ibn Abd al-Wahhab founds the Islamic sect known as the Wahhabi. 1781 — Immanuel Kant publishes his *Critique of Pure Reason* and *Critique of Practical Reason.* 1792 — Mary Wollstonecraft publishes *A Vindication of the Rights of Women.*	1848 — Karl Marx and Friedrich Engels issue "Communist Manifesto." 1859 — John Stuart Mill, English philosopher of utilitarianism, publishes *On Liberty.* 1868 — Japanese government institutes State Shinto as official religion. 1883 — Nietzsche proclaims "God is dead" in *Thus Spoke Zarathustra.*	1901 — First Nobel Prizes awarded. 1903 — "The problem of the Twentieth Century is the problem of the color line," W.E.B. Dubois, *The Souls of Black Folk.* 1915 — Gandhi leads Indian nationalism movement using principles of non-violence. 1943 — Jean-Paul Sartre's *Being and Nothingness* becomes central text of existentialist philosophy. 1962 — Second Vatican Council initiates major reforms in Roman Catholic Church.

The Universe

The scientific view of the origins of the universe is based on the Big Bang, which occurred 10 to 15 billion years ago. This was the beginning of all space, time, and matter, which immediately expanded outward and eventually formed everything in the universe, including our solar system, the hundred billion stars that make up our galaxy, and the billions of other galaxies in the universe. The universe is still expanding outward. It is not yet known whether it will continue to grow, or whether the universe contains so much matter that, in many billions of years' time, gravitational attraction will have stopped its outward expansion and it will collapse back in upon itself in a "Big Crunch."

Active galaxies radiate vast amounts of energy from their cores. Centaurus A (above) is the nearest active galaxy to our own. A giant cluster of hot stars and gas lies at its center, which may contain a black hole – a massive star that has collapsed under its own gravitational pull.

After the Big Bang

Because space and time themselves began only at the Big Bang, it is meaningless to talk of a time – or to ask what happened – "before" the Big Bang occurred. Scientists do have information about events from almost immediately afterward, however, starting when the universe was only 10^{-43} seconds old (one ten-million billion billion billion billionth of a second after the Big Bang). Earlier than this the universe was in a state of "quantum uncertainty" – one about which nothing can be known, even theoretically. At this time the universe occupied a space less than a billion billionth the size of an atomic nucleus, but was expanding so rapidly that it took only 10^{-12} seconds (one million millionth of a second) to expand to the size of our solar system. As the universe expanded, it cooled.

In its early moments, most of the universe consisted not of matter but of a "sea" of high-energy radiation, where matched pairs of quarks (the basic building blocks of atomic nuclei) and antiquarks were created and annihilated. As temperatures fell and the universe continued to expand, the proportion of matter relative to radiation increased. Matter became dominant after around 10,000 years. The forces acting between the particles of the early universe developed more rapidly. The Grand Unified Force (a single force that existed immediately after the Big Bang) soon separated into the four fundamental forces that now govern the universe: the strong force (which holds the constituents of atomic nuclei particles together); gravity; the weak force (which is involved in radioactivity); and the electromagnetic force (the basis of electric and magnetic attraction and repulsion).

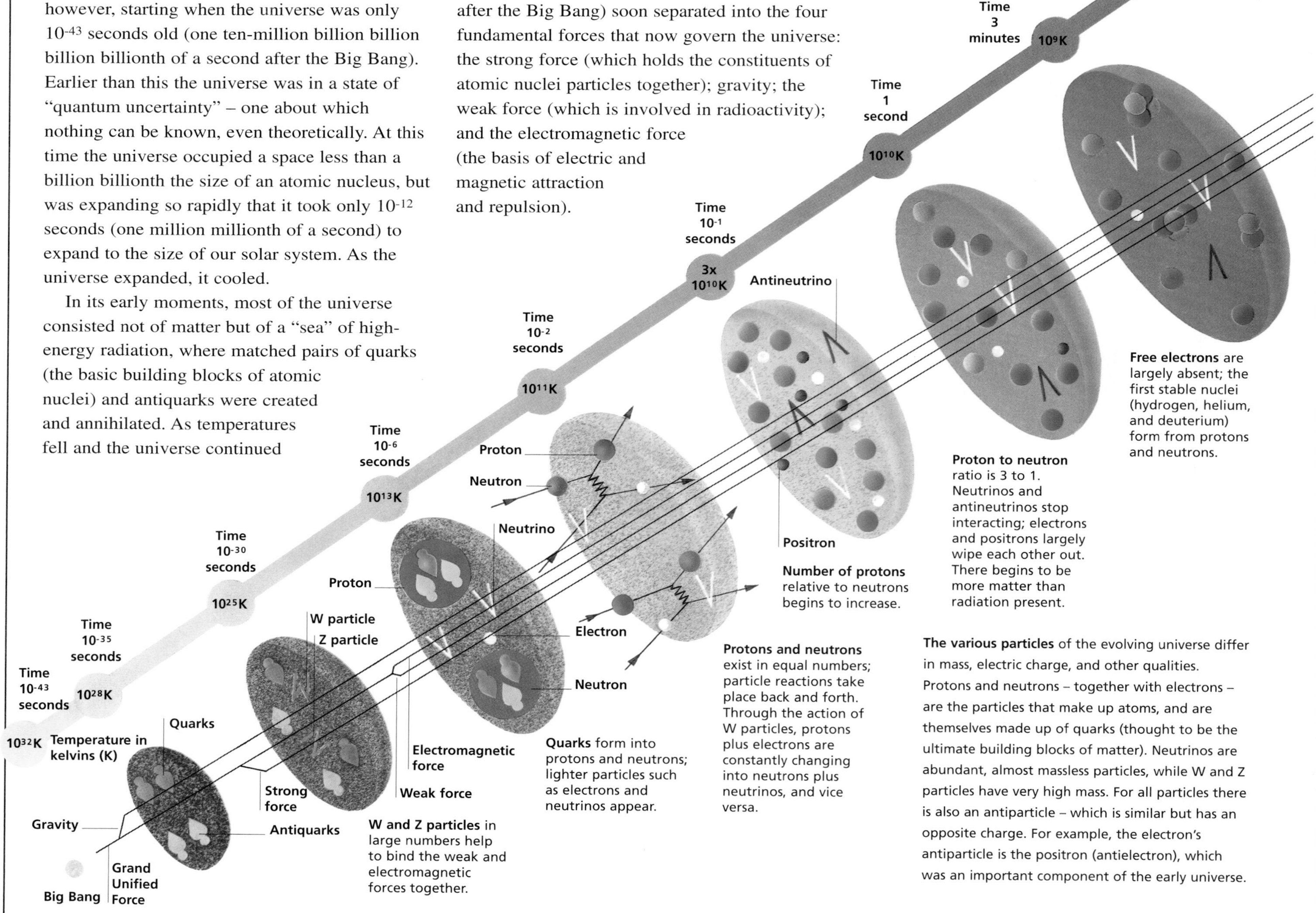

Big Bang

Grand Unified Force

Gravity

Quarks

Antiquarks

Strong force

W particle

Z particle

Electromagnetic force

Weak force

Time 10^{-43} seconds — 10^{32}K Temperature in kelvins (K)

Time 10^{-35} seconds — 10^{28}K

Time 10^{-30} seconds — 10^{25}K

Time 10^{-6} seconds — 10^{13}K

Time 10^{-2} seconds — 10^{11}K

Time 10^{-1} seconds — 3×10^{10}K

Time 1 second — 10^{10}K

Time 3 minutes — 10^{9}K

Proton

Neutrino

Electron

Neutron

Antineutrino

Positron

W and Z particles in large numbers help to bind the weak and electromagnetic forces together.

Quarks form into protons and neutrons; lighter particles such as electrons and neutrinos appear.

Protons and neutrons exist in equal numbers; particle reactions take place back and forth. Through the action of W particles, protons plus electrons are constantly changing into neutrons plus neutrinos, and vice versa.

Number of protons relative to neutrons begins to increase.

Proton to neutron ratio is 3 to 1. Neutrinos and antineutrinos stop interacting; electrons and positrons largely wipe each other out. There begins to be more matter than radiation present.

Free electrons are largely absent; the first stable nuclei (hydrogen, helium, and deuterium) form from protons and neutrons.

The various particles of the evolving universe differ in mass, electric charge, and other qualities. Protons and neutrons – together with electrons – are the particles that make up atoms, and are themselves made up of quarks (thought to be the ultimate building blocks of matter). Neutrinos are abundant, almost massless particles, while W and Z particles have very high mass. For all particles there is also an antiparticle – which is similar but has an opposite charge. For example, the electron's antiparticle is the positron (antielectron), which was an important component of the early universe.

Standard form is a method used by scientists to express the vast or infinitesimal quantities associated with the birth and development of the universe. For example, the number 4×10^9 means four followed by nine zeros – that is, four billion. Similarly, 10^{-6} means one divided by 10^6 (one followed by six zeros) – or one millionth (0.000001). Temperature is measured using the Kelvin temperature scale. The unit intervals of this scale are the same as those of the Celsius scale, but the zero point (0 K) is taken as -459.67°F or -273.15°C (absolute zero) – the lowest temperature that can be attained even in theory.

Time 3×10^5 years

3×10^3K

Primordial gases condense and cool.

Time 2×10^9 years

50K

Time 4×10^9 years

25K

Present day approximately 10^{10} years

3K

Atom

Stable atoms of hydrogen and helium form from protons, neutrons and electrons, creating primordial gases; chemical reactions start to occur.

The first galaxies form in regions where the primordial gas is denser than average. These regions result from fluctuations within the early Universe.

Death of a Star

Star with mass equal to that of the Sun

Star's hydrogen nearly exhausted

Star expands to red giant

Helium fusion starts; star contracts

White dwarf

Black dwarf

Star's outer layers are blown off, producing a white dwarf

Our galaxy

The death of stars

Stars collapse when the gravitational pull of the matter that composes them is no longer balanced by a sufficient outward force. During the star's life, this force is produced by vast amounts of electromagnetic radiation the star emits in various forms, including visible light, ultraviolet and infrared radiation, and X-rays. When the star has used up most of its hydrogen – the fuel from which radiant energy is generated by fusion – its core implodes.

As its hydrogen is exhausted, a star's outer layers expand, turning red as they cool to form a "red giant." In a small star, helium fusion begins at the core, but is soon exhausted. The star expands again, puffing off its outer layers and leaving its core as a "white dwarf," which cools to form a "black dwarf." In a more massive star, fusion may continue using heavier elements. When the core of such a massive star collapses, protons and electrons fuse to form neutrons, producing a superdense neutron star. This collapse creates a huge explosion – a supernova. The biggest stars fall in on themselves totally, leaving a "black hole" from which no matter or light can escape.

The Eagle Nebula (below) is a column of hydrogen gas and dust that acts as an incubator for stars. The visible finger-like protrusions are trails of gas drifting away from dense, gaseous globules within the nebula. Each "fingertip" is somewhat larger than our solar system. Some of the gaseous globules are thought to contain embryonic stars, which will become visible as the gas burns away.

Galaxies and nebulas

The galaxies were formed when clouds of gas, consisting mainly of hydrogen, condensed under the gravitational pull of the matter within them. In some cases, gravitational forces exerted by matter outside a condensing gas cloud caused the cloud to start rotating. As it collapsed, the gas cloud spun faster so that the spinning matter was flung outward with a force balanced by the inward pull of gravity. This process created stable, rotating, disk-like galaxies, such as the Milky Way. Other galaxies that did not acquire an overall rotation probably derive their stability from the movement of their parts around a common center in different, separate orbits. Galaxies are also known to have an overall movement away from one another – a fact that has provided evidence of the Big Bang.

Galaxies are made up of nebulas – clouds of dust or gas – as well as individual stars. "Bright" nebulas consist of interstellar gas clouds; "dark" nebulas are vast clouds of dust. Stars are formed when regions of gas become sufficiently concentrated to form globules that collapse under their own gravity. This causes a rise in temperature at their center, and when this temperature becomes high enough for nuclear fusion of hydrogen to occur, a star is formed. Shock waves from the birth of a star create eddies in the surrounding gas, which may in turn trigger the creation of more stars.

The Solar System

Around 4.6 billion years ago, the Sun condensed from a vast rotating cloud of gaseous material that contained hydrogen and helium, plus heavier elements from the debris of earlier stars. One percent of the gas cloud did not condense into the newly formed star, but instead became spread out in a thin disk called the solar nebula. As particles in the disk collided with each other, some coalesced, creating larger and larger bodies that were able to pull in surrounding matter by gravitational attraction. In this way, most of the material in the early solar system was swept up into a few very large bodies – the planetary system that we see today.

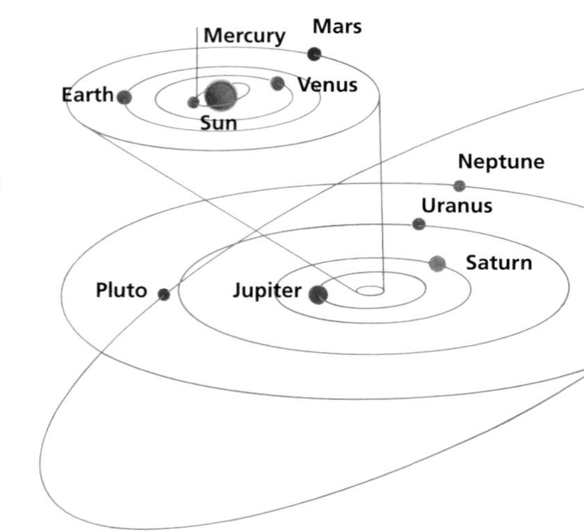

The planets (left) all move around the Sun in the same direction, in stable and elliptical orbits. Mercury has the most eccentric orbit of the inner planets. Planetary orbits are all in approximately the same plane, except for that of Pluto, which is inclined at 17°. This anomaly may result from Pluto being merely the brightest member of an outer asteroid and comet belt, called the Kuiper belt.

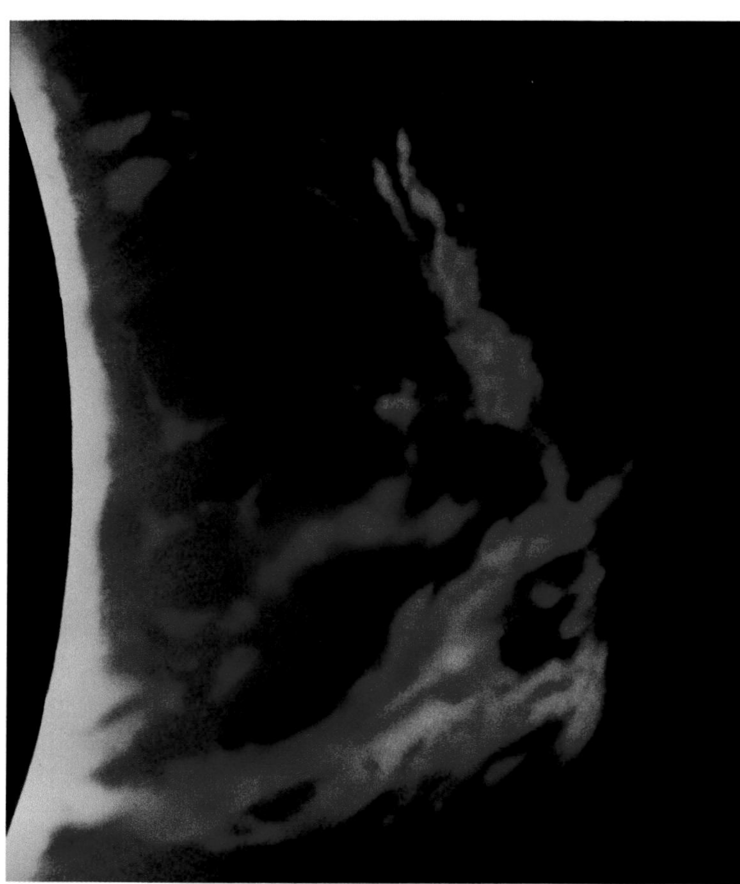

Solar prominences (left) are arcs of gas more than 62,000 miles (100,000 km) long with temperatures of 18,000°F (10,000°C). They can be held above the Sun's surface for months by its magnetic field.

Uranus (below) has several narrow rings, each only 6.2 miles (10 km) wide on average. It is the only planet that rotates (turns on its axis) in a retrograde (east to west, rather than west to east) direction.

Neptune (below left) is the outermost of the four gas giants. Its rings are less substantial than those of the other gas giants, and include a disk of tiny particles.

Inner and outer planets

The inner planets – Mercury, Venus, Earth, and Mars – are all small and rocky. These planets formed in regions that were swept free of light gases by the Sun. The outer planets include the four "gas giants" – Jupiter, Saturn, Uranus, and Neptune – which formed in those regions of the solar nebula that were still rich in gases. Pluto, the outermost planet, is only twice the size of its satellite, Charon.

Jupiter (above right) is the largest of the gas giants. It has a solid inner core of iron and silicates, surrounded by hydrogen that has become a metallic liquid under the great atmospheric pressure (45 million times that of Earth). Enormous storms rage on its surface. The Great Red Spot – a huge vortex with a tranquil center – has a diameter twice that of Earth.

Saturn (above left) has a spectacular ring system. At least 10,000 individual rings occupy concentric orbits from 4,350 miles (7,000 km) out to 46,000 miles (74,000 km) from the planet's surface. The rings were formed relatively recently, after a cosmic catastrophe in Saturn's orbit – such as the break-up of a comet. Over millions of years, Saturn's gravitational force will strip the material from the rings.

Planetary comparisons	Sun	Mercury	Venus	Earth	Mars	Jupiter	Saturn	Uranus	Neptune	Pluto
Distance from the Sun (millions of miles) (kilometers)	–	36.0 57.9	67.2 108.2	92.9 149.6	141.6 227.9	483.6 778.3	888.2 1,427.0	1,782.0 2,869.6	2,792.4 4,496.6	3,664.0 5,900.1
Period of orbit (in Earth days)	–	88	225	365	687	4,333	10,759	30,685	60,190	90,764
Period of rotation (in Earth hours)	–	1,404	5,816	23.9	24.6	9.9	10.7	16.8	16.1	152.9
Diameter (miles) (kilometers)	865,000 1,392,000	3,031 4,878	7,521 12,104	7,926 12,756	4,222 6,794	88,700 142,800	75,000 120,700	31,700 51,100	30,200 48,600	1,416 2,280
Mass (Earth=1)	333,000	0.06	0.06	1.00	0.11	317.83	95.16	14.50	17.20	0.002
Density (water=1)	1.40	5.43	5.24	5.52	3.94	1.33	0.70	1.30	1.76	about 2

The outermost layer of the Sun (below right) normally visible from Earth is the photosphere. Above this is a 6,200-mile- (10,000-km) thick layer of mainly hydrogen – the chromosphere – and a gas halo, or corona, that is very hot (3,600,000°F or 2,000,000°C). Both the chromosphere and corona are visible during solar eclipses. Sunspots occur when disturbances in the Sun's magnetic field lower the surface temperature. Solar flares – eruptions of hot gas that fire atomic particles into space at 600 miles (1,000 km) per second – are caused by the release of magnetic energy.

From red giant to white dwarf

The Sun is composed of some 70 percent hydrogen and 30 percent helium; heavier elements comprise less than 1 percent of its mass. The high temperature at its core – 27 million °F (15 million °C) – is produced by heat from nuclear reactions that fuse hydrogen into helium. At such a high temperature and pressure, these elements exist not as complete atoms, but as a "soup" of very high density, made up of atomic nuclei and stray electrons. Nuclear energy is released predominantly in the form of high-energy gamma rays and X-rays, which are repeatedly absorbed and re-emitted by the closely packed atomic nuclei of the core. This radiative energy may take up to a million years to reach the convection zone. Here, at a distance of 372,000 miles (600,000 km) from the center, the temperature has dropped sufficiently for the hydrogen and helium gases to exist as atoms with their electrons. Atoms are opaque to radiation, so energy is transferred by convection cells. Hot gas rises to the surface, the photosphere, where it radiates heat and light. As it cools, the gas sinks deeper into the Sun, where it is reheated.

The Sun revolves once every 25 days near its equator, and more slowly at the poles. No significant change in its brightness is expected to occur for another 1.5 billion years. Then, its fuel used up, the Sun will swell to become a "red giant" and swallow up Earth completely. Finally, it will blow off most of its atmosphere to become a "white dwarf" about the size of Earth.

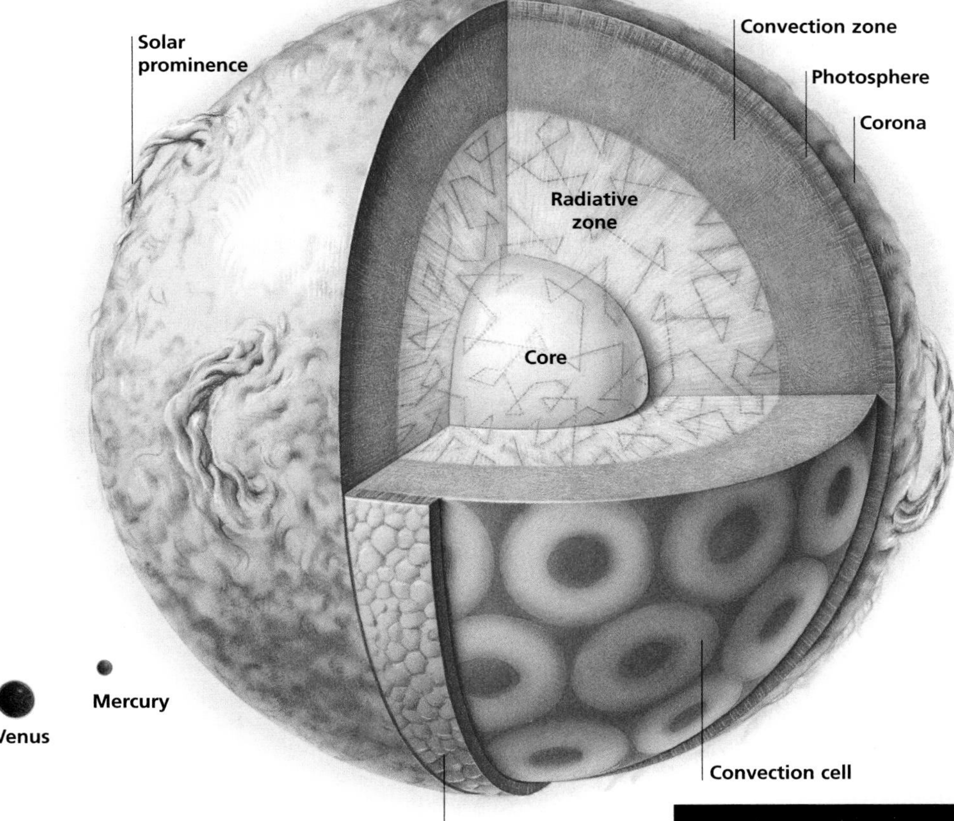

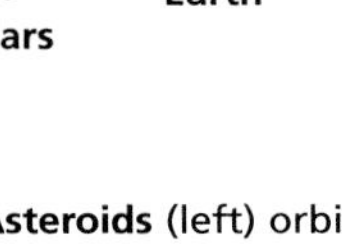

Comets

Most comets probably originate in the Oort cloud – a spherical shell of hundreds of billions of bodies made of ice and interstellar dust – which surrounds the Sun outward to a distance of about one light year. Collisions or the gravitational effects of passing stars may cause one of these bodies to fall into a highly elliptical orbit around the Sun, which heats it up as it approaches the Sun and creates the characteristically bright cometary tail of dust and gas.

Asteroids (left) orbit the Sun between Mars and Jupiter; they are composed of rocky material that did not coalesce into planets.

Comet Hale-Bopp (right) was discovered in July 1995. It passed the Sun at a distance of 77.6 million miles (125 million km) on April 1, 1997. Hale-Bopp is a "long-period" comet, and will not return to the inner solar system for another 2,400 years. Some "short-period" comets, such as Halley's, may have been long-period comets whose orbits were distorted by Jupiter's gravity.

Space probes transmit information to Earth from space using a variety of instruments, including infrared and ultraviolet detectors, and cameras. Space probes are not powered rockets: Once launched, they rely on gravitational pull and carefully calculated trajectories to carry them near to their target planet. The Viking 2 Lander (below) settled on Mars on September 3, 1976 and sent back photographs of the barren, rocky landscape.

Exploring the solar system

The planets as far as Saturn have been known since antiquity, but detailed knowledge of the entire solar system began with the development of the telescope in the 17th and 18th centuries. The observations of Copernicus (1473–1543) and Galileo (1564–1642) established that the planets revolve around the Sun, and not Earth; and Johannes Kepler (1571–1630) discovered that their orbits were not circular, but elliptical. Uranus was discovered by William Herschel (1738–1822) in 1781. Irregularities in its orbit suggested gravitational pull from another planet, Neptune, discovered in 1846. Perturbations in the orbit of Neptune suggested the existence of Pluto, first observed in 1930.

Modern telescopes use reflectors, rather than lenses, to collect and focus light. The Hubble Space Telescope, launched into orbit in 1990, obtains clearer pictures than any observatory on Earth.

Earth and the Moon

Earth is an oblate spheroid planet, bulging slightly at the equator. It orbits the Sun once a year at a mean distance of 92,900,000 miles (149,600,000 km). The planet Earth originally formed from the collision of many smaller planetisimals around 4.5 billion years ago. As these rocky bodies collided, the heat generated created a molten sphere in which the heaviest elements, such as iron, fell to the center. Earth's interior is kept molten today by the heat trapped during its formation and the energy released by radioactive elements beneath the thin solid crust. Early in its history, an atmosphere formed around Earth by gases escaping from inside. But plant and animal life have changed it over billions of years.

The Van Allen belts (below left) are two regions surrounding Earth in which high-energy particles from the Sun – the solar wind – are trapped by Earth's magnetic field. These particles spill out of the belts at the polar cusps of the magnetic field. As they flow out into Earth's atmosphere, they create spectacular auroras (light effects) in the sky.

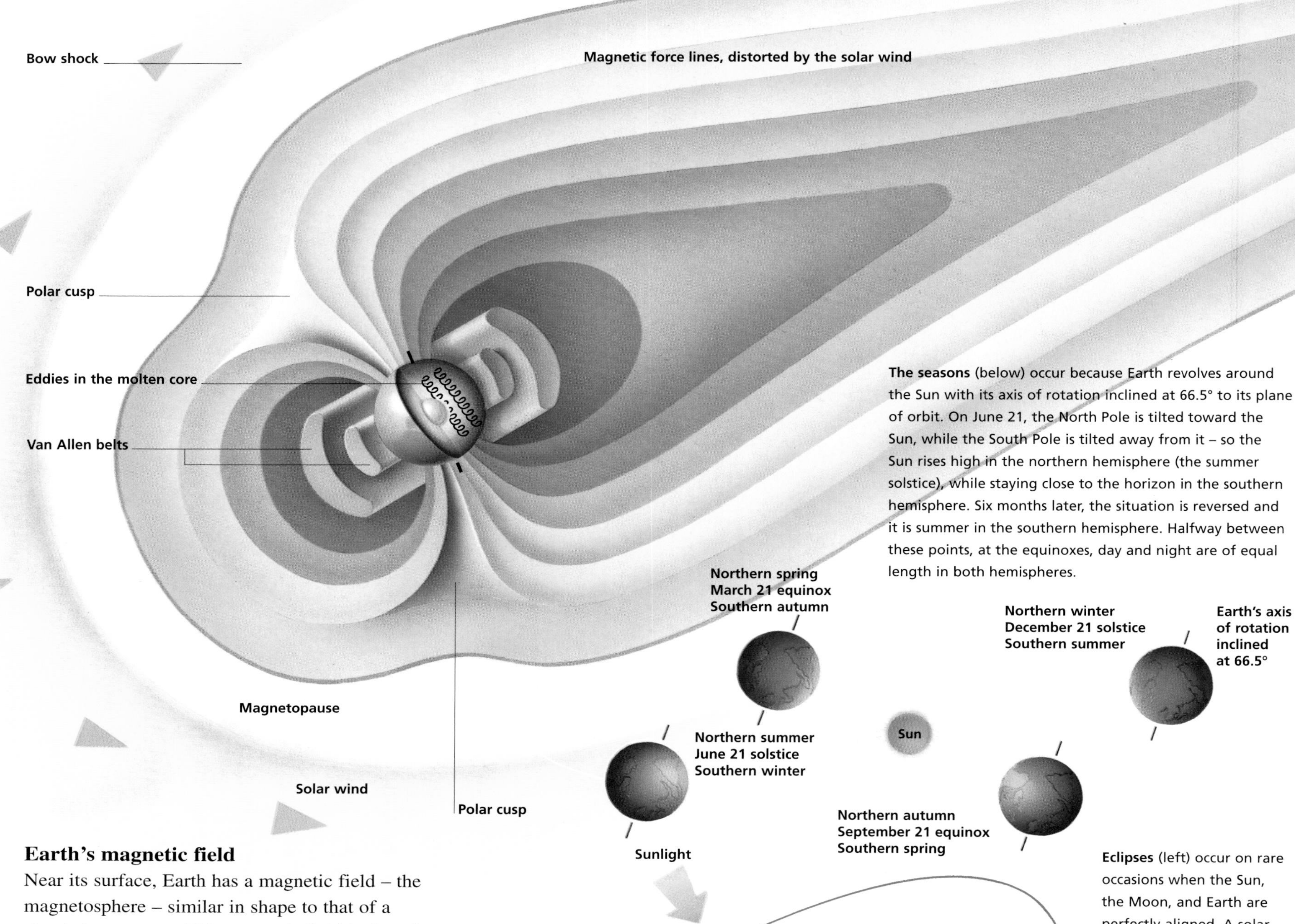

The seasons (below) occur because Earth revolves around the Sun with its axis of rotation inclined at 66.5° to its plane of orbit. On June 21, the North Pole is tilted toward the Sun, while the South Pole is tilted away from it – so the Sun rises high in the northern hemisphere (the summer solstice), while staying close to the horizon in the southern hemisphere. Six months later, the situation is reversed and it is summer in the southern hemisphere. Halfway between these points, at the equinoxes, day and night are of equal length in both hemispheres.

Earth's magnetic field

Near its surface, Earth has a magnetic field – the magnetosphere – similar in shape to that of a simple bar magnet. This magnetic field is thought to be generated in Earth's liquid iron core, where the very high temperatures break down iron atoms into electrically charged ions. A combination of heat convection and Earth's rotation causes these ions to move in twisting spirals, carrying a large electric current and generating a magnetic field. Changes in the direction and strength of the magnetic field are recorded by the magnetism of volcanic rocks forming on the seabed. Earth's magnetic poles are currently tilted at 11.5° to its axis of rotation, but the sea-floor record shows that they have wandered over time, and regularly reverse completely.

Eclipses (left) occur on rare occasions when the Sun, the Moon, and Earth are perfectly aligned. A solar eclipse occurs when the Moon is "new," and passes between the Sun and Earth. It appears total from only a small part of Earth's surface, within the umbra of the Moon's shadow. A lunar eclipse occurs when the Moon is '"full," and passes through Earth's shadow.

The magnetopause (below) is the boundary of Earth's magnetic field. On the side toward the Sun, charged particles in the solar wind hit the magnetic field, slow down, and compress the magnetosphere, forming the bow shock. On the other side, the solar wind pushes the magnetosphere into a teardrop shape that stretches far into space.

The Moon's crust (right) is covered by regolith – a loose debris of rocks, mineral fragments, beads of glass, and lunar dust – which may sometimes be only an inch or two (two to five cm) deep. In a light microscope image of a thin section of moon rock (below), the orange particles are glass beads, and the black dots are small fragments of crystallized material.

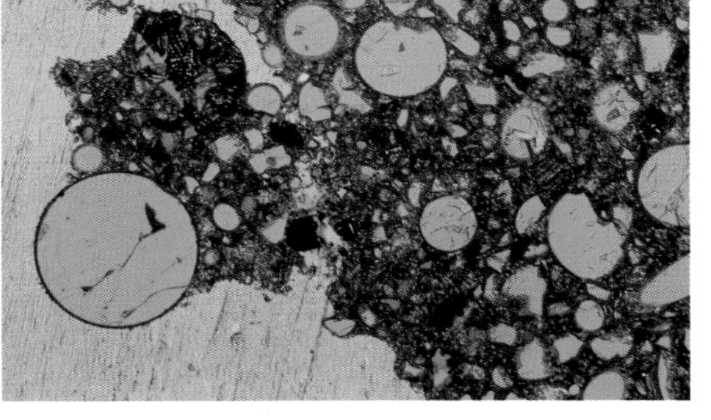

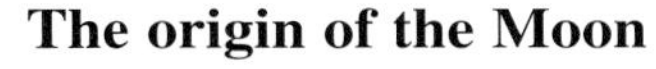

The origin of the Moon

The Moon's mass is less than one-eightieth that of Earth, although its diameter (2,160 miles or 3,476 km) is more than a quarter of Earth's. There are several theories about the Moon's origin. It may have broken away from Earth early in the history of the solar system, or it may be an independent body captured more recently by Earth's gravitational pull. One widely accepted theory is that an object the size of Mars collided with Earth early in its history, and the Moon was flung off as a result. This theory provides an explanation for Earth and the Moon having similarities in composition.

The Moon's small size and low mass give it a very small gravitational field, and it has no atmosphere of its own. It cooled much more rapidly than Earth, and became dormant more than three billion years ago. Occasional glows seen on its surface may be caused by the escape of trapped gas during "moonquakes."

The Moon's surface (left) was bombarded by meteors that produced deep craters soon after it was formed 4.5 billion years ago. Around 3.5 billion years ago, intense volcanic activity flooded the plains with lava, creating the comparatively smooth mare (lunar sea) features and the ghost craters partly smoothed by lava. Volcanic craters also formed with more symmetrical rims and smoother interiors than impact craters. More recently, craters have been formed only by infrequent meteor strikes.

The phase of the Moon (below) varies with the angle between the Sun, the Moon, and Earth. The Moon always has the same side facing Earth. It does not emit any light of its own, but reflects the light of the Sun. When the side of the Moon facing us has no sunlight on it, we cannot see it at all.

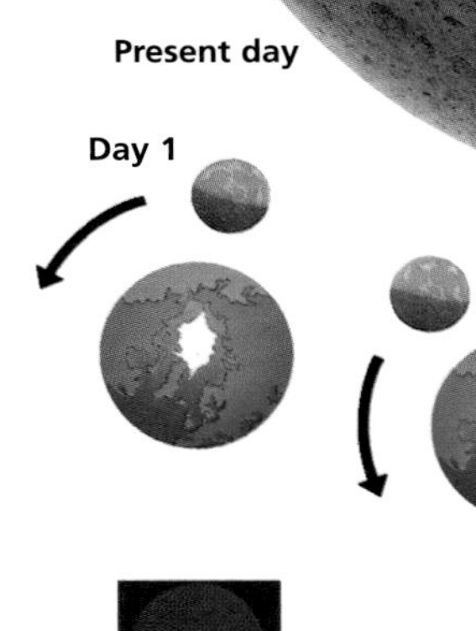

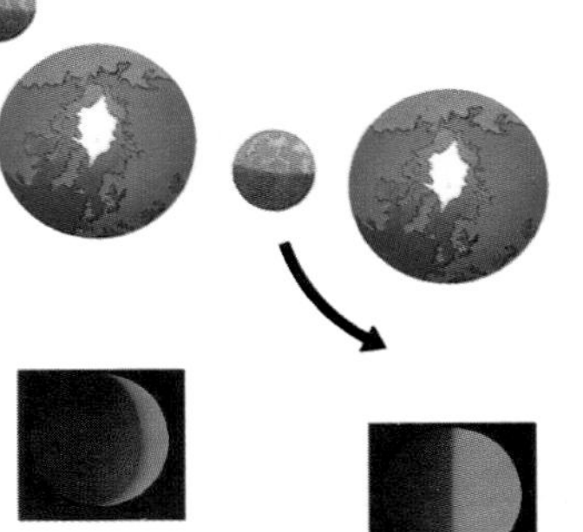

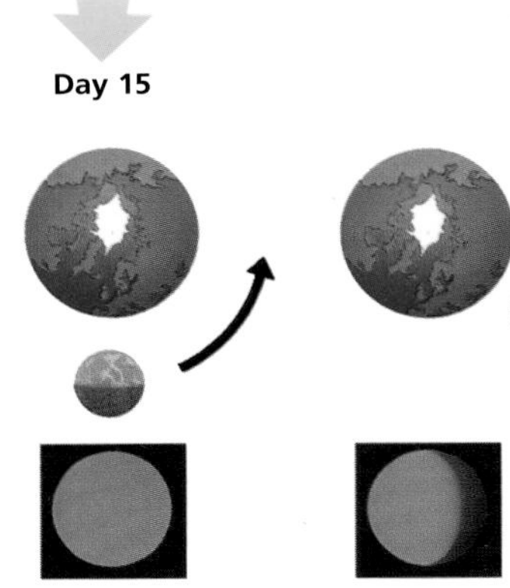

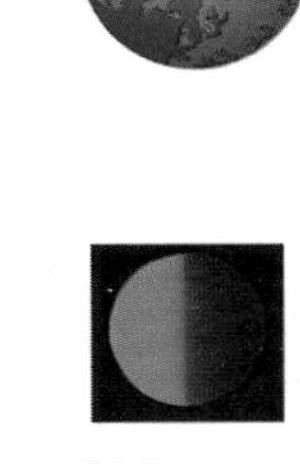

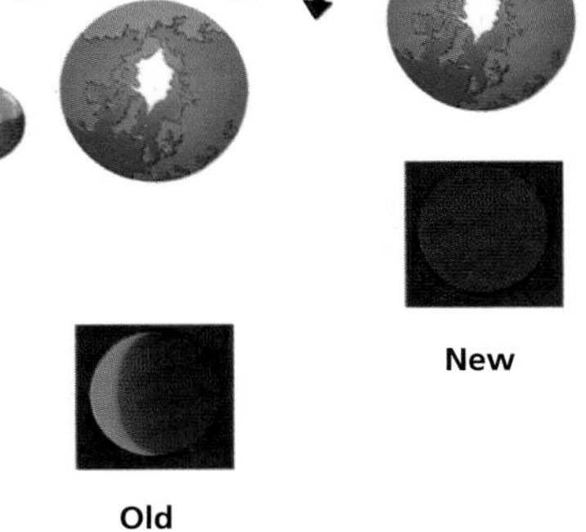

Time and motion

Earth rotates once on its axis every 23 hours, 56 minutes (a day). It orbits the Sun once every 365 days, 6 hours and 8 minutes (a year), at an average speed of 18.6 miles (30 km) per second. The leap year compensates for the fact that, at the end of the 365-day year, Earth still has to travel for about a quarter of a day before it completes its orbit. The eccentricity of Earth's orbit varies over a 90,000- to 100,000-year cycle: at the moment, Earth travels around the Sun in a nearly circular path, which will become an increasingly perfect circle over the next 10,000 years or so.

Earth and the Moon rotate around a common center of gravity, but because Earth is much more massive, this barycenter lies 1,050 miles (1,700 km) below Earth's surface. The Moon appears to orbit Earth, at a distance of between 223,500 miles (360,000 km) and 251,500 miles (405,000 km), once every 27 days, 7 hours and 41 minutes (the sidereal month). Because this period is longer than the time Earth takes to rotate on its axis, the Moon's gravitational pull has a braking effect on Earth's rotation. This slows down Earth minutely, so that a day increases by about 1.6 seconds every 100,000 years.

The Structure of Earth

Over the last few decades our understanding of Earth's structure and composition has been completely revolutionized. Fundamental differences in the structure and formation of the oceans and continents have become clear. The division of Earth's hard outer layers into crustal plates, and their role in the creation of oceans and mountains, is now also established. However, while Earth's internal heat is acknowledged as the ultimate source of the dynamic motion of the crustal plates, the way in which internal convection currents move the plates is still being investigated. The most widely held view is that heat is convected toward the surface by slow-moving currents of semi-molten rock; these well up in places, then cool and descend to the interior again.

Earth (below) is made up of three main layers – the crustal plates, the mantle, and the core. The thin outer plates of solid, brittle rocks make up the continents and ocean floor. The plates overlie a thick mantle layer of denser and hotter rocks, which in turn surrounds the metallic liquid outer core and its solid center. Movement of the plates generates energy in the form of heat and pressure, which is released at the surface by volcanoes and earthquakes – a reminder that not only is the interior of Earth hot, but it is also in constant motion.

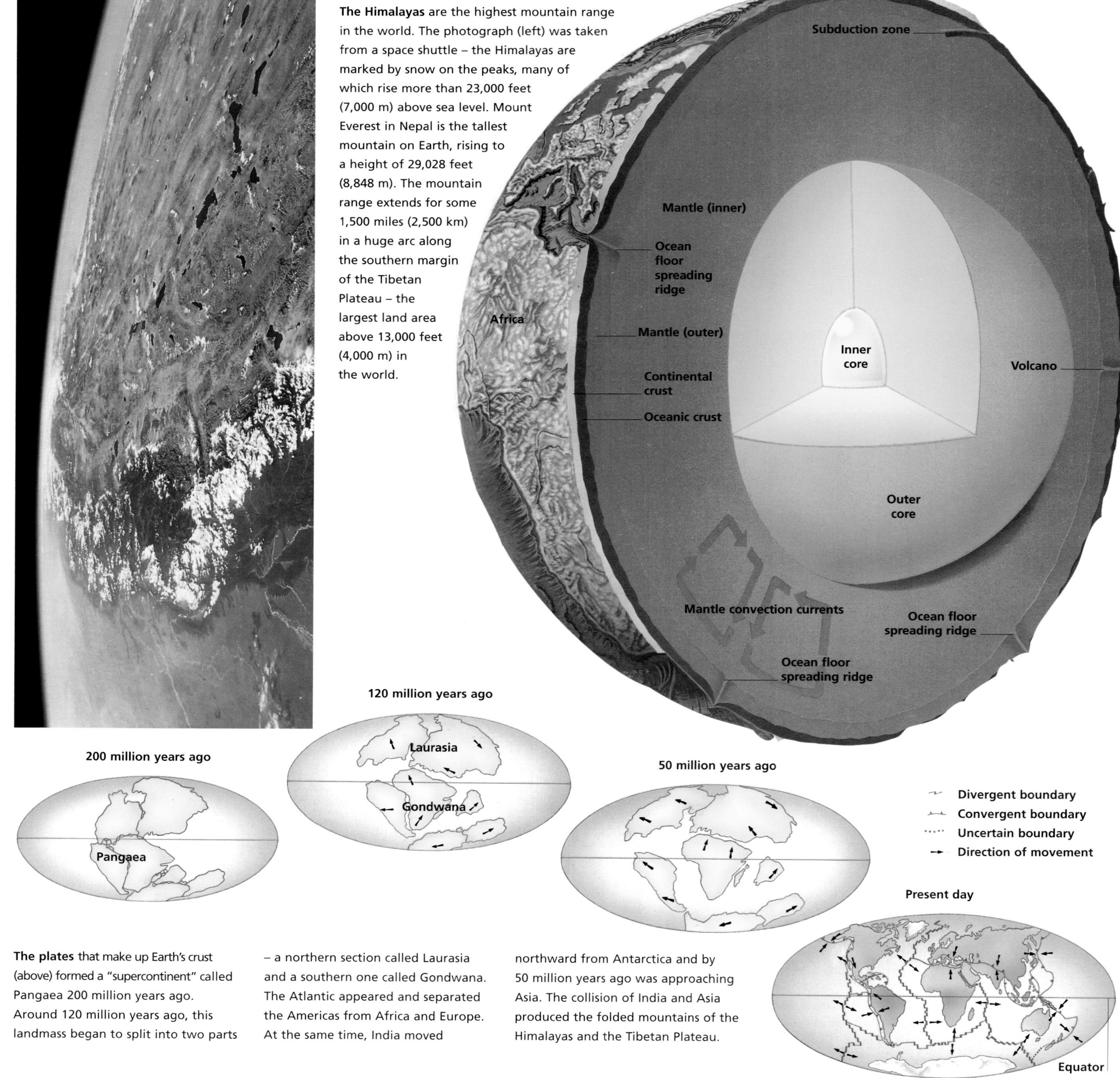

The Himalayas are the highest mountain range in the world. The photograph (left) was taken from a space shuttle – the Himalayas are marked by snow on the peaks, many of which rise more than 23,000 feet (7,000 m) above sea level. Mount Everest in Nepal is the tallest mountain on Earth, rising to a height of 29,028 feet (8,848 m). The mountain range extends for some 1,500 miles (2,500 km) in a huge arc along the southern margin of the Tibetan Plateau – the largest land area above 13,000 feet (4,000 m) in the world.

The plates that make up Earth's crust (above) formed a "supercontinent" called Pangaea 200 million years ago. Around 120 million years ago, this landmass began to split into two parts – a northern section called Laurasia and a southern one called Gondwana. The Atlantic appeared and separated the Americas from Africa and Europe. At the same time, India moved northward from Antarctica and by 50 million years ago was approaching Asia. The collision of India and Asia produced the folded mountains of the Himalayas and the Tibetan Plateau.

The continental jigsaw

The internal heat of Earth is circulated in slow-moving convection cells. Hot plumes of mantle material rise beneath the ocean ridges before diverging. This forces the crustal plates apart, causing the ocean floor to spread. The gaps are plugged with new crustal rock. As the oceans expand, the continents are pushed apart. Since Earth does not expand overall, as much ocean floor must be lost as is created. The loss occurs along convergent plate boundaries, where ocean floor rocks are pushed under the lighter rocks of the continental crust. Over time, internal heat circulation has been responsible for moving the global jigsaw puzzle of plates into different configurations.

Fault scarps and volcanoes mark the line of the East African Rift Valley (above).

Drifting and shifting of Earth's plates change the structure of oceans and continents (below). Over the last 20 million years, repeated volcanic eruptions and earthquakes have been associated with tension faults in East Africa. The movement of the African continental plate has opened a faulted rift valley (1), dotted with volcanoes, from Mozambique to Syria, via Kenya, the Red Sea, and the Dead Sea.

The Carlsberg Ridge in the Indian Ocean (2) marks a divergent plate boundary. Here, submerged chains of volcanic mountains and fissures throw out basalt magma, forming new ocean floor and causing the Indian Ocean to widen.

As the Indian continental plate moved toward Asia, the ocean floor that originally separated them was subducted (pushed down). Eventually, the two continents collided, crumpling the intervening rocks into the Himalaya mountains and pushing up the Tibetan Plateau (3).

Where the Pacific Ocean crust is subducted, a deep sea trench (4) is formed as the ocean floor is dragged down. The subduction process generates enormous energy, which is released on the surface as earthquakes, causing faults and melting the rocks at depth. The resulting molten rock rises and erupts through explosive volcanoes alongside the subduction zones.

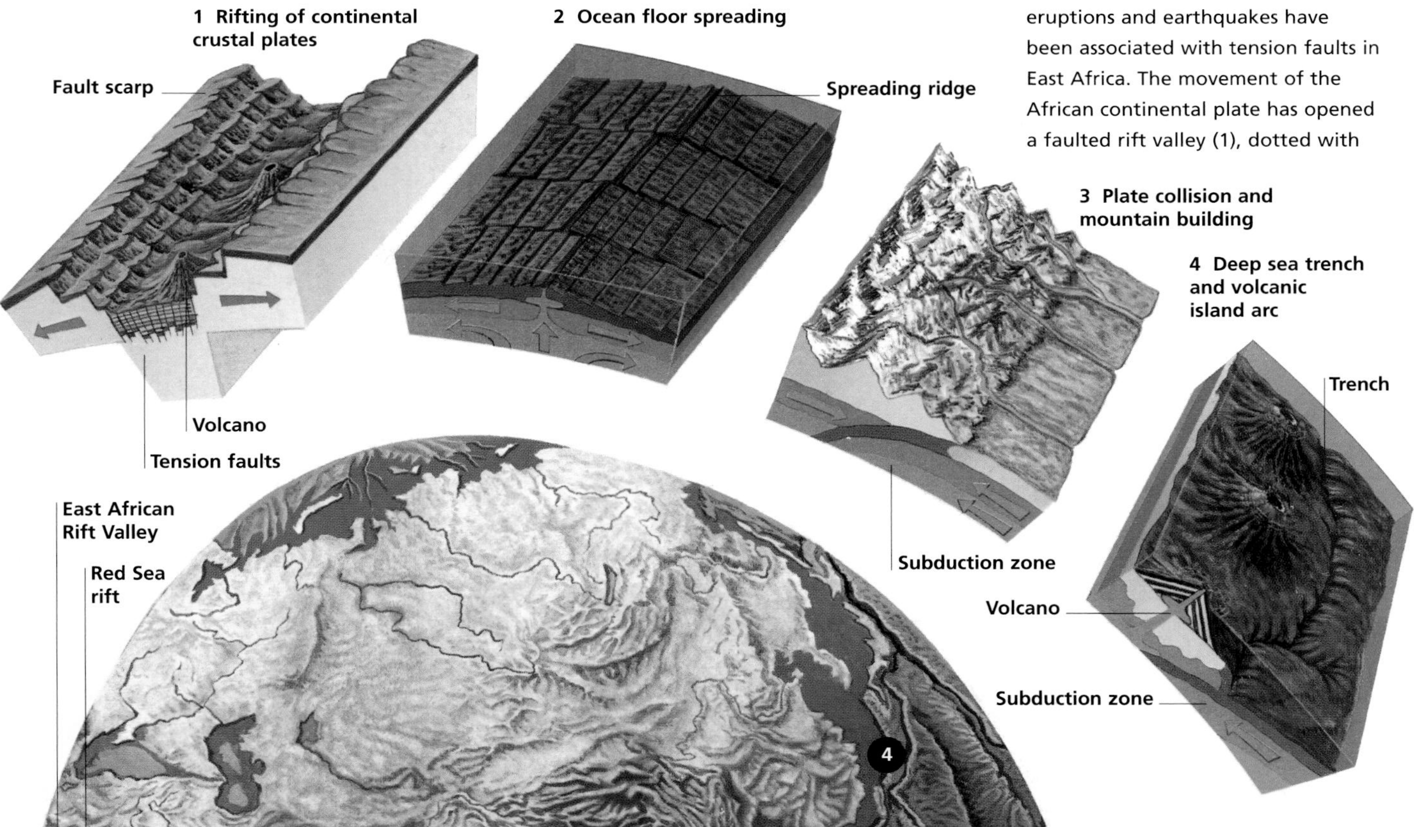

Plate tectonics

Earth's topography reflects a fundamental difference between the continents and oceans in structure and composition. The less dense rocks of the continents rise above sea level, while the denser volcanic rocks of the ocean floors lie well below sea level. The global distribution of earthquakes and volcanoes coincides with certain zones above and below sea level, indicating that all these brittle surface rocks are divided into plates.

The form of the plate boundaries reflects their dynamic relationships. Divergent plates stretch the rocks of the crust until they fracture and move apart, eventually generating new ocean floor from upwellings of volcanic basalt magma. Convergent plates move together, initially compressing and buckling the rocks and sediments at the plate edges into mountain ranges. Finally, one of the plates will override the other, which is subducted (pushed down), generating earthquakes and volcanic activity. Where plates slide past one another, intense earthquake activity occurs along the line of movement, called a transform fault.

Volcanoes and Earthquakes

Heat and pressure are the driving forces behind the dynamic processes of Earth's interior. Deep within Earth, heat-driven circulation moves the plates that make up Earth's outermost layers and causes pressure to build up within the rock. The pent-up energy can lead to rock fracture and earthquakes at the surface, or to rocks melting at depth, leading in turn to the formation of volcanoes.

Earthquake waves (below) are formed when energy is released in movements of Earth's plates. They radiate from the focus and are first felt at the epicenter (the point directly above the focus). Primary P-waves are fast, compressional "push and pull" waves. Secondary S-waves are slower, transverse "shaking" waves, which vibrate the rocks and structures on the surface.

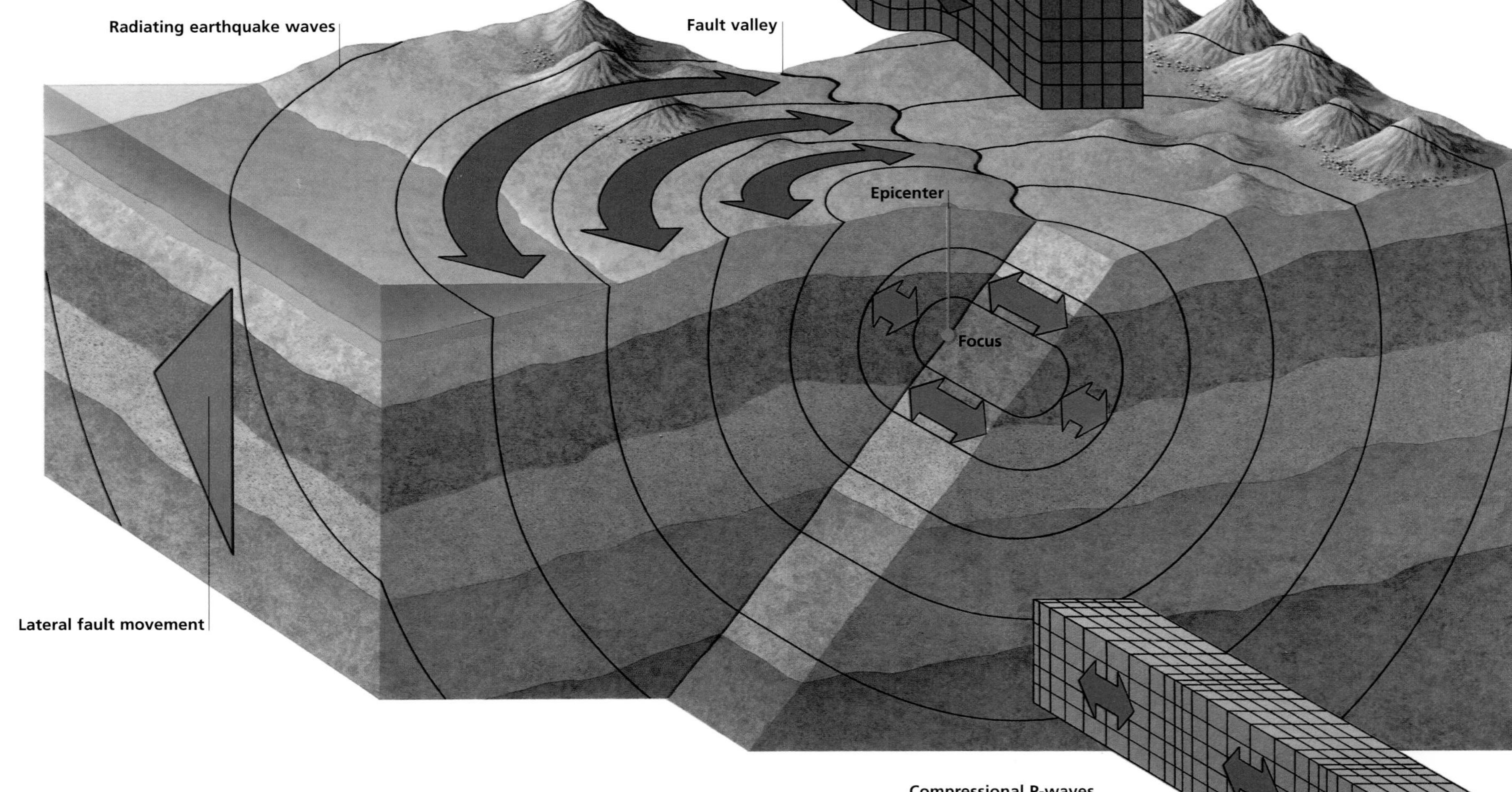

The San Andreas fault zone (below) occurs where the Pacific crustal plate slides northward relative to the North American plate. The Pacific plate has shifted about 350 miles (560 km) in the past 20 million years. Earthquakes occur as a result of plate movements.

Why earthquakes happen

The distribution of most major earthquakes is concentrated within well-defined zones around Earth, at the boundaries of the plates of Earth's crust and at the sites of active volcanoes. Movement of the plates builds up forces within the rocks of plate boundary zones. The brittle rocks eventually fracture along fault planes. At the focus (where the rocks first break), energy is released, sending out shock waves in all directions. The greater the initial energy, the farther the shock waves travel and the more violent they are. The magnitude of earthquakes is measured on the Richter scale of 1–10, with 2 being a tremor that can just be felt and 6 the threshold of damage to buildings. Shock waves can be detected and measured by seismographs. Analysis of the travel times of P- and S-waves has shown that Earth's interior has a layered structure of differing composition and properties.

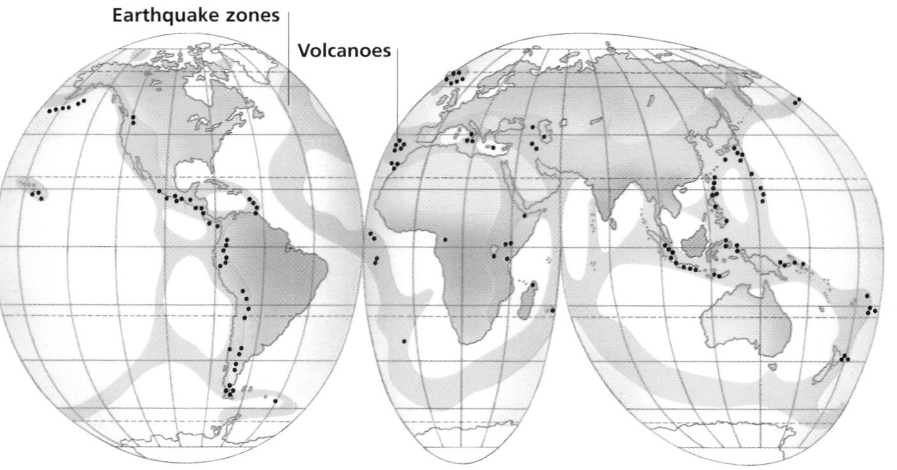

Volcanoes and earthquake zones (left) are linked to movement of plates along the following plate boundaries: divergent boundaries, where the crustal plates are forced apart; convergent boundaries, where they collide; and transform boundaries, where they slide past one another.

Mount Etna in Sicily (left) is the most active volcano in Europe and has erupted more than 90 times since 1500 B.C. In 1669, some 33 billion cubic feet (937 million cu m) of lava poured out at 3,178 cubic feet (90 cubic m) per second, covering around 15 square miles (38 sq km) of countryside. During an eruption in 1989, Etna's summit cone spouted fountains of lava for two weeks. The flanks of Etna are covered with more than 100 subsidiary cones, which are intermittently active.

Volcanic fires

Earth's active volcanoes provide the most dramatic evidence of a hot interior. Molten rock, hot gases, water, ash, and rock fragments are all products of volcanic activity. However, the type of eruption, material ejected, and cone shape vary depending on the site of the volcano. Where crustal plates collide and one slides under the other, as along the Pacific margin of South America, rocks are partially melted at great depth. As the lighter molten rock (called magma) rises through the denser rocks of continental plate margins, such as in the Andes, its composition is changed. The resulting volcanoes are dangerously explosive and can erupt violently, producing clouds of gas, ash, and rock fragments or thick, viscous lava.

Where plates are forced apart, new ocean floor is created as molten basaltic rock wells up from the interior through fissures and volcanic vents. Most of this volcanic activity is concentrated along mid-ocean ridges such as that in the Atlantic, but occasionally it surfaces, as in Iceland. Ocean-type volcanoes produce great volumes of flowing basalt lavas.

Clouds of gas, steam, rock, and magma fragments

Volcanic ash, lava bombs , and rain

Avalanching lava debris and mud

Feeder dike supplying magma to satellite vent

Lava flow

Vent

Lava flow

1 Composite steep cone of ash and lava layers

2 Wide cone of oceanic shield volcano built by free-flowing lavas

3 Steep-sided ash and cinder cone

Volcanic eruptions (above) are by far the most powerful single events on Earth. Most of the fragmented rock, ash, and lava ejected over a period of a few days piles up around the vent, building up a cone-shaped mountain, but fine ash may be spread across the world. The shape of the cone depends on the volcano's site and lava type. Eruptions within oceanic ridges are often from fissures and produce more elongated mountains.

Composite or stratovolcanoes (1), such as Stromboli, build up steep-sided cones with alternating layers of ash and lava. Low viscosity, free-flowing basalt lavas build oceanic shield volcanoes (2) with wide, gently sloping cones like those of Etna or Hawaii. Explosive volcanic activity produces tiny, angular rock fragments and viscous lava, which form steep-sided cones (3) like that of Vesuvius.

Rocks and Minerals

The geological study of the rocks that make up Earth reveals the extraordinarily dynamic history that has taken place over the last 4.5 billion years, with phases of large-scale violent upheaval and slow change. Life has evolved within a constantly changing environment on the surface of the planet Earth. Living organisms have had to adapt to a multitude of changes in climate, sea level, and topography. Two principal influences have shaped the terrain. Constructive processes have created new landscape features – continents have been split apart, mountain barriers have appeared where none existed before, and dramatic and hazardous volcanic activity has burst through the surface of Earth. Destructive forces – erosion and weathering – have gradually worn away exposed landforms.

Sandstones are sedimentary rocks formed from particles of sand or quartz. The alternating sloping and horizontal layers of the Paria Wilderness in Arizona (above), originally formed as desert sand dunes. Over millions of years they have been compacted and cemented into rock.

The rocks of Earth

The geological materials of Earth range from relatively soft sedimentary rocks, formed at Earth's surface from the accumulation of sediment, to hard, crystalline igneous and metamorphic rocks produced by the heat and pressure within Earth's crust. Over several thousand million years, the mineral components of these materials have been constantly broken down and recombined to give the extraordinary variety of rocks and minerals found on Earth's surface today.

When molten material (magma) cools and hardens within Earth, igneous rock is produced. Coarse-grained, mountain-sized granite plutons are formed at the greatest depths, while wall-like sheets of basalt, in the form of dikes and sills, are found relatively close to Earth's surface. Magma expelled through volcanoes and fissures reaches the surface and forms lavas. Heat and pressure metamorphose (transform) rock, causing it to melt and recrystallize in alignment with the confining force. This process, called regional metamorphism, affects wide areas. Contact metamorphism occurs when rock is in contact with a mass of magma at high temperature.

Magma reaches Earth's surface through fissures
Volcano
Formation of ring dike
Ring dike
Shield volcanoes
Volcano erodes to leave neck
Plateau basalts
Pluton
Coal seam
Sills
Magma chamber
Evaporation leaving mineral salts
Sand, silt, and mud from river mouth
Multiple dike (formed when magma cools around cracks)
Beds of sand and mud
Sea
Coral reef
Chemical sedimentary rock
Biogenic sedimentary rock
Oil deposit
Clastic sedimentary rock

Sedimentary rocks (left) are classified as clastic (consisting of fragments of pre-existing rocks), biogenic (made up of organic material such as coal, shell, and coral reef debris), or chemical (formed from evaporated mineral salts). Over the millennia, the deposits are compressed to form the characteristic layering pattern known as bedding.

Rock structure and composition

The dynamic processes of plate movements and mountain formation produce many geological structures, each made up of thousands of kinds of rocks containing many different component minerals. Mountain ranges are formed from folded piles of sedimentary rock, often mixed with volcanic materials. Deep down, the rocks are transformed by intense heat and pressure and intruded by molten magma, forming igneous rock bodies of various sizes, shapes, and composition. Common sedimentary rocks are shales, limestones, and sandstones. Igneous rocks range from deep-seated granites to basalts extruded at the surface. Metamorphic rocks vary from rocks such as slate that are only slightly altered by metamorphosis to rocks such as schists, gneisses, and marble that are recrystallized and greatly changed.

Most rocks are composed of a few common silicate minerals, such as quartz and feldspar, which consist mainly of silicon and oxygen. Important non-silicate rocks include limestone (calcium carbonate), coal (a hydrocarbon), and metal ore minerals.

Ore minerals occur naturally in rock and are mined for their metals and precious stones. The mineral iron pyrite, or "fool's gold" (above), is composed of iron sulfide, but its yellow, metallic appearance can be mistaken for true gold.

Igneous rock is formed when molten rock from magma chambers (below right) inside Earth cools and crystallizes. Within the crust, large pluton bodies and smaller sheet-like formations called dikes (including cylindrical ring dikes) and sills are formed. Where the magma reaches the surface, it is extruded as lava flows through fissures and volcanic vents. Where the activity is explosive, ash, rock and lava pile up to form steep-sided cones. Where it is quieter, extensive flows build up low-coned shield volcanoes and plateau basalt formations.

Metamorphic rocks (below) are formed when a rock is chemically changed by intense heat and pressure to form a new rock type. They may be produced from sedimentary or igneous rocks, or from pre-existing metamorphic rocks. Changes that take place during metamorphism can affect the structure of the rock and its composition.

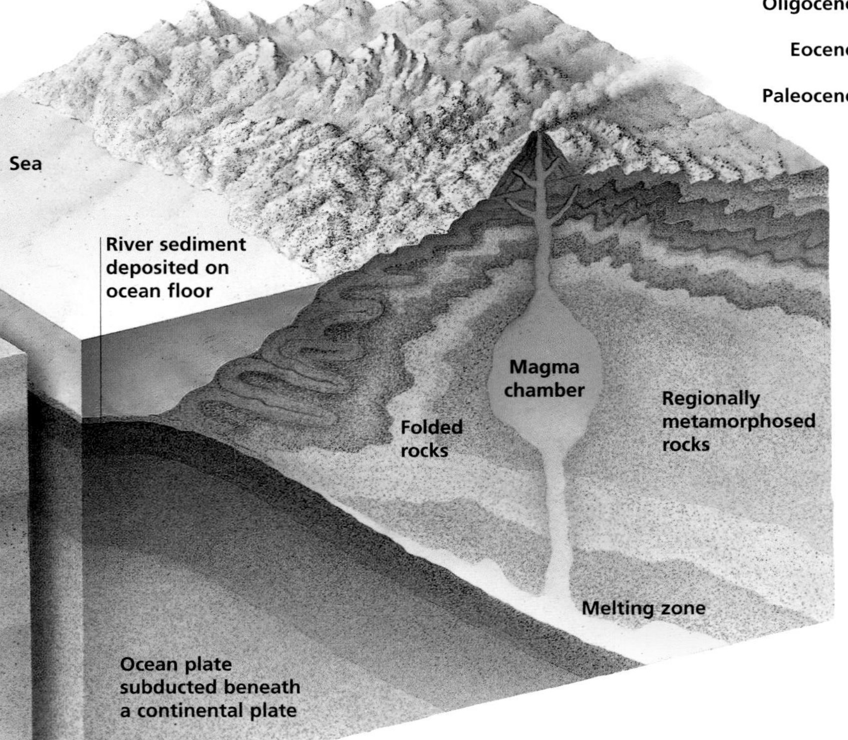

Epochs	Periods	Millions of years ago	Eras
Holocene	Quaternary	66	Cenozoic
Pleistocene		245	Mesozoic
Pliocene		570	Paleozoic
Miocene			
Oligocene	Tertiary		
Eocene			
Paleocene			
	Cretaceous		
	Jurassic		
	Triassic		
	Permian		
	Upper Carboniferous		Precambrian
	Lower Carboniferous		
	Devonian		
	Silurian		
	Ordovician		
	Cambrian		
	Proterozoic		
	Archean		
	Hadean	4,500	

The divisions of geological time (above) are characterized by changes in living organisms and the materials in which their remains are deposited. Radiometric dating has allowed specific dates to be associated with these named time periods.

The fossil skeleton of a straight-headed unicorn fish (left) was found in Italy. It dates from the Eocene epoch, around 40 million years ago.

The rock record

By studying the layers of sedimentary rock, igneous rock bodies, and metamorphic rock masses that form the rock record, geologists can work out the history of the formation of Earth and the development of life. Geological time – from the origin of Earth 4.5 billion years ago – is divided into periods depending on the life forms that existed, with these periods grouped together into four eras. The geological periods are further divided into epochs and ages. Fossils in sedimentary rocks give evidence of the evolution of life from its beginnings some 3.8 million years ago, and yield information on the emergence, diversification, and extinction of species over time.

The Atmosphere

Earth would be a barren, rocky world without the thin but complex layer of gases – the atmosphere – that surrounds it. The atmosphere filters out dangerous radiation from the Sun, regulates temperatures across Earth's surface, and provides oxygen for life. Over billions of years, the gases that originally accumulated around Earth have been greatly modified by volcanic eruptions, plant and animal life, and recently by industrial pollution. Although the outer reaches of the atmosphere stretch to a height of 1,200 miles (2,000 km), 75 percent of its gases are contained within six miles (10 km) of Earth's surface. This lowest region, the troposphere, is where the atmospheric systems that control Earth's weather patterns are located.

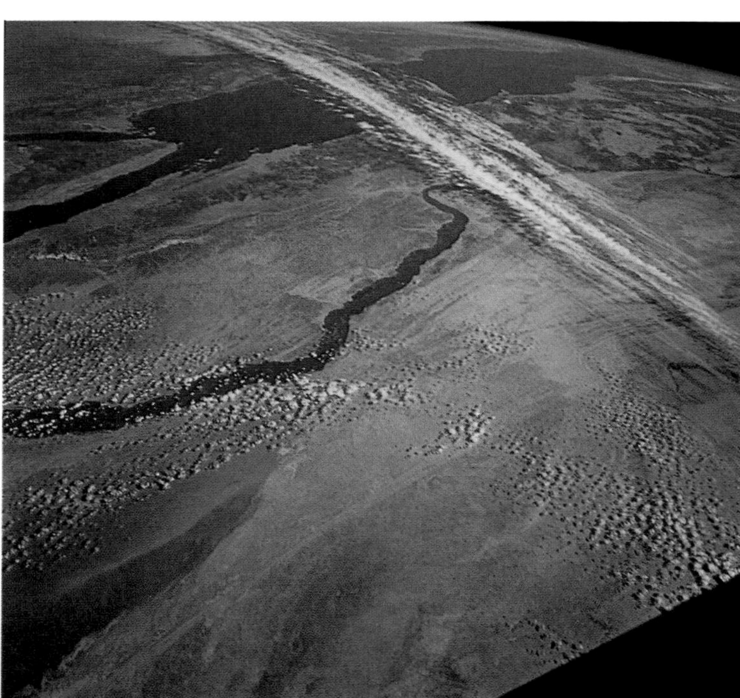

Jet streams (left) are created at the boundaries between different convection cells in the upper part of the troposphere. Clouds caught up in the jet stream become stretched out along it.

Atmospheric pressure falls steadily with increasing altitude, but temperature (right) varies depending on radiation from space and the density of the atmosphere.

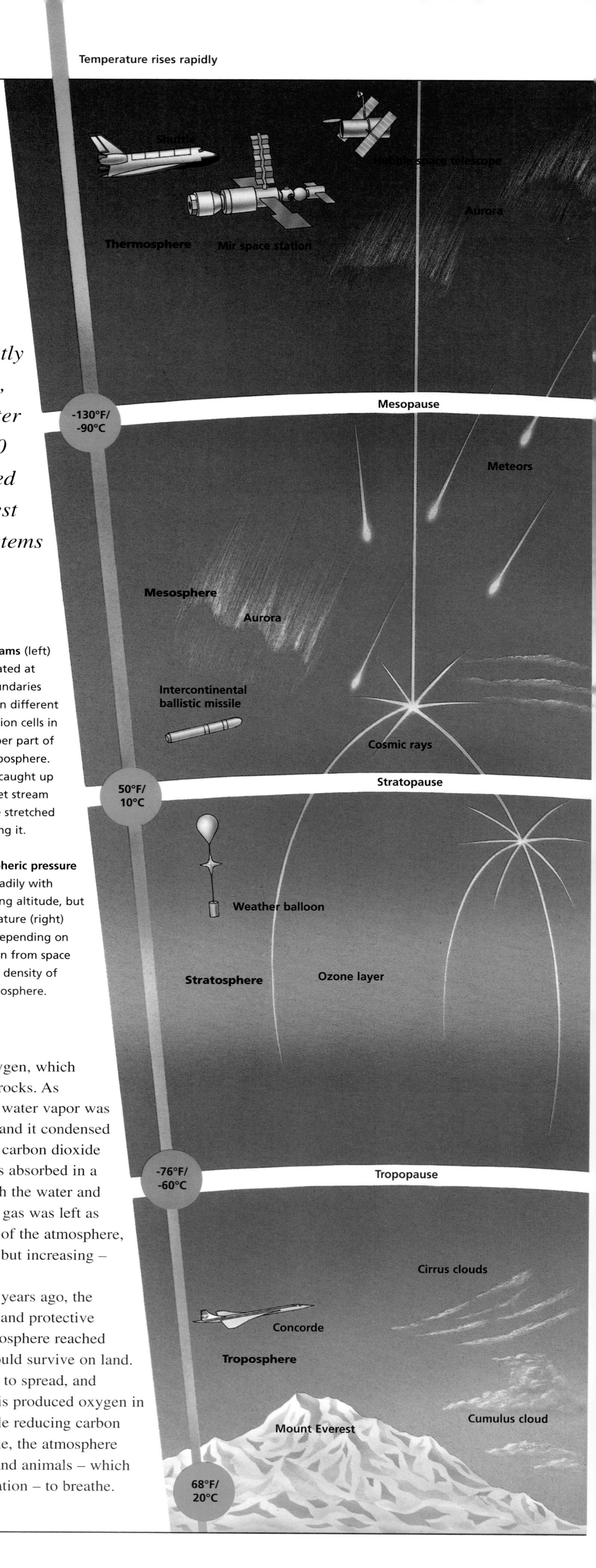

The origins of the atmosphere

The atmosphere's complex structure reveals a great deal about its history. The outermost region, the exosphere, contains traces of hydrogen and helium – light gases left over from the formation of Earth. The denser and lower layers of the atmosphere all have roughly the same composition, around 80 percent nitrogen, 20 percent oxygen, and small amounts of other gases including water vapor, carbon dioxide, and argon. The atmosphere's composition is the result of a variety of processes that have taken place on Earth since its formation 4.5 billion years ago.

Today's atmosphere had its origins in massive volcanic eruptions as the early Earth cooled. These eruptions released large amounts of nitrogen, carbon dioxide, and water vapor, which were trapped by Earth's gravity. High temperatures broke the water vapor down into hydrogen – most of which escaped from the atmosphere – and oxygen, which was absorbed by hot rocks. As temperatures fell, the water vapor was able to remain stable and it condensed into rain. Most of the carbon dioxide in the atmosphere was absorbed in a chemical reaction with the water and some rocks. Nitrogen gas was left as the major component of the atmosphere, together with small – but increasing – amounts of oxygen.

About 500 million years ago, the proportion of oxygen and protective ozone (O_3) in the atmosphere reached levels at which life could survive on land. The first plants began to spread, and through photosynthesis produced oxygen in massive amounts while reducing carbon dioxide further. In time, the atmosphere became suitable for land animals – which use oxygen for respiration – to breathe.

Temperature rises rapidly

Shuttle

Hubble space telescope

Aurora

Thermosphere

Mir space station

-130°F/ -90°C

Mesopause

Meteors

Mesosphere

Aurora

Intercontinental ballistic missile

Cosmic rays

50°F/ 10°C

Stratopause

Weather balloon

Stratosphere

Ozone layer

-76°F/ -60°C

Tropopause

Cirrus clouds

Concorde

Troposphere

Mount Everest

Cumulus cloud

68°F/ 20°C

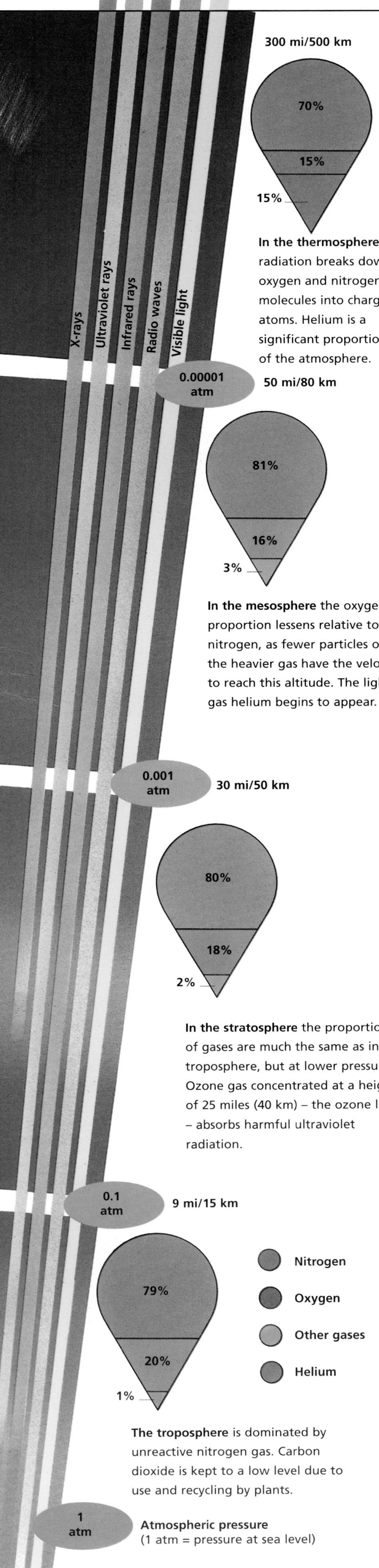

In the thermosphere radiation breaks down oxygen and nitrogen molecules into charged atoms. Helium is a significant proportion of the atmosphere.

In the mesosphere the oxygen proportion lessens relative to nitrogen, as fewer particles of the heavier gas have the velocity to reach this altitude. The light gas helium begins to appear.

In the stratosphere the proportions of gases are much the same as in the troposphere, but at lower pressure. Ozone gas concentrated at a height of 25 miles (40 km) – the ozone layer – absorbs harmful ultraviolet radiation.

The troposphere is dominated by unreactive nitrogen gas. Carbon dioxide is kept to a low level due to use and recycling by plants.

Atmospheric pressure
(1 atm = pressure at sea level)

Electromagnetic radiation and high-energy cosmic rays (left) constantly bombard Earth from space. The atmosphere filters out dangerous high-energy X-rays and ultraviolet light, but allows visible light and some radio and infrared rays through. Cosmic rays collide with atoms in the atmosphere, disintegrating into showers of harmless, low-energy particles.

The atmosphere is divided into several distinct zones (left), distinguished by changes in composition, temperature, and pressure. The lowermost zone, the troposphere, extends to about 9 miles (15 km) above sea level, and is where Earth's weather occurs. The stratosphere lies beyond this, and contains the ozone layer. The mesosphere stretches up to 50 miles (80 km), followed by the thermosphere, in which gas molecules are broken up by radiation from space. Beyond the thermosphere, traces of hydrogen and helium gas form the exosphere, stretching higher than 1,200 miles (2,000 km) from Earth. Atmospheric pressure drops with increasing altitude, while temperatures vary according to radiation absorption.

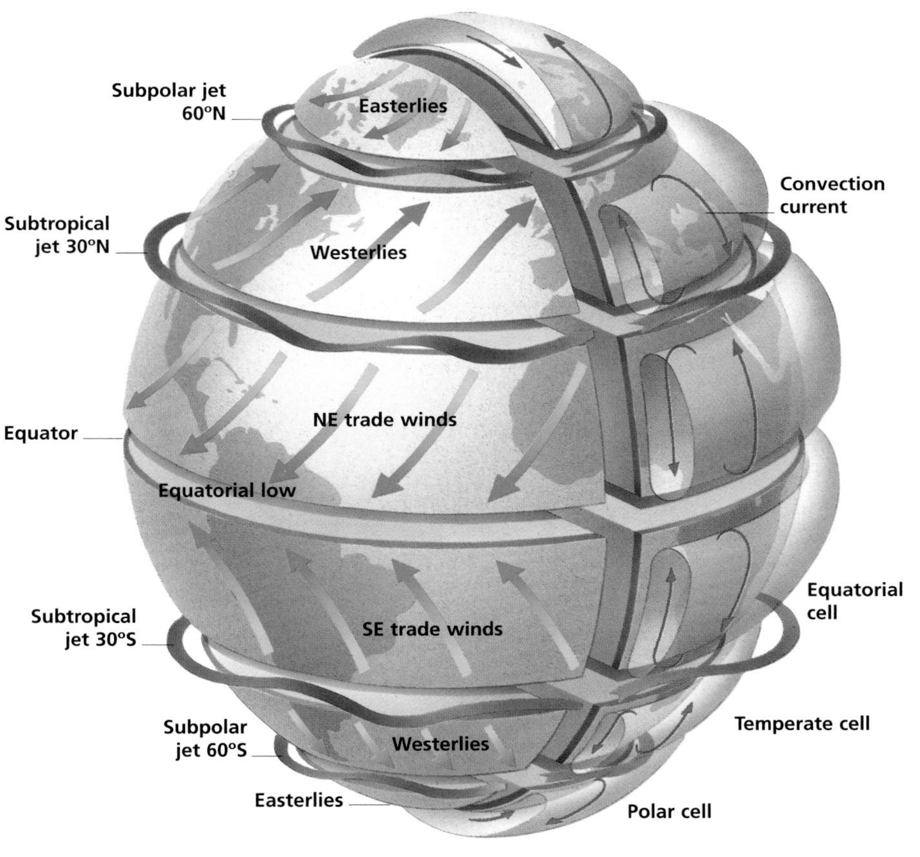

Three vast convection currents or "cells" in each of Earth's hemispheres (above) carry heat from the equator to the poles. The equatorial and polar cells rotate in one direction, while temperate cells rotate in the opposite direction. This pattern, combined with Earth's daily rotation, gives rise to prevailing winds in fixed general directions within each cell – polar easterlies, westerlies in the temperate regions, and trade winds near the equator. These determine long-term weather.

At boundaries between the cells are high-speed jet streams, where winds blow at hundreds of miles or kilometers per hour. Changes in air pressure on either side create kinks in the jet stream. Patterns of air flow determine the climate on the ground: Desert regions are zones of high pressure caused by air descending between the equatorial and temperate cells, while unpredictable weather in temperate regions is caused by low pressure air systems with warm rising air at around 60° latitude.

Auroras (above) occur near the magnetic poles, where high-energy particles from space are funnelled into the atmosphere and collide with gas molecules and atoms. Energy from these collisions is released as light, with different colors generated by different gases.

The dynamics of the atmosphere

Weather patterns are manifestations of global movements in Earth's atmosphere, driven by the general imbalance of heat around Earth. At the equator, the Sun shines down from high in the sky and heats Earth's surface for long periods of time. At the poles, the Sun always stays close to the horizon, so that its heating effect is weak and there is darkness for much of the year. This uneven heating sets up natural convection currents, which carry warm air up through the atmosphere above hot regions and drop it down in cooler areas.

Because of the complexity of the atmosphere and the delicate balance of its constituent gases, it can easily be upset from its equilibrium. However, scientists do not yet understand the atmosphere sufficiently to predict the effects of disruption – for example, the extent of global warming that is likely to result from changes in carbon dioxide levels is unclear. Some natural phenomena, although well documented, are also poorly understood. One example is El Niño – an unpredictable periodic reversal of currents in the South Pacific Ocean and atmosphere, which brings high pressure and drought to Southeast Asia in the rainy season, while creating violent rainstorms in South America.

Climate and Weather

The atmosphere is vital to life on Earth. More than 600 miles (1,000 km) thick, it protects the planet from harmful solar radiation and also acts as an insulating "blanket" by trapping the life-giving heat from the Sun. The lowest layer, which averages a mere six miles (10 km) in depth, contains most of the atmospheric water, and consequently – because weather patterns are strongly related to the water cycle – is where Earth's weather is generated. Solar heat evaporates water from the land and oceans into the atmosphere, where it is circulated by winds and moving air masses. The interaction of these air masses produces localized instability in the form of cyclones (spiraling winds) and ensuing storms, during which much of the atmospheric moisture returns to the surface as snow or rain. Many other factors contribute to a region's climate and weather patterns – for example, Earth's rotation and the tilt of its axis, the distribution of oceans and continents, and the terrain and its proximity to the sea.

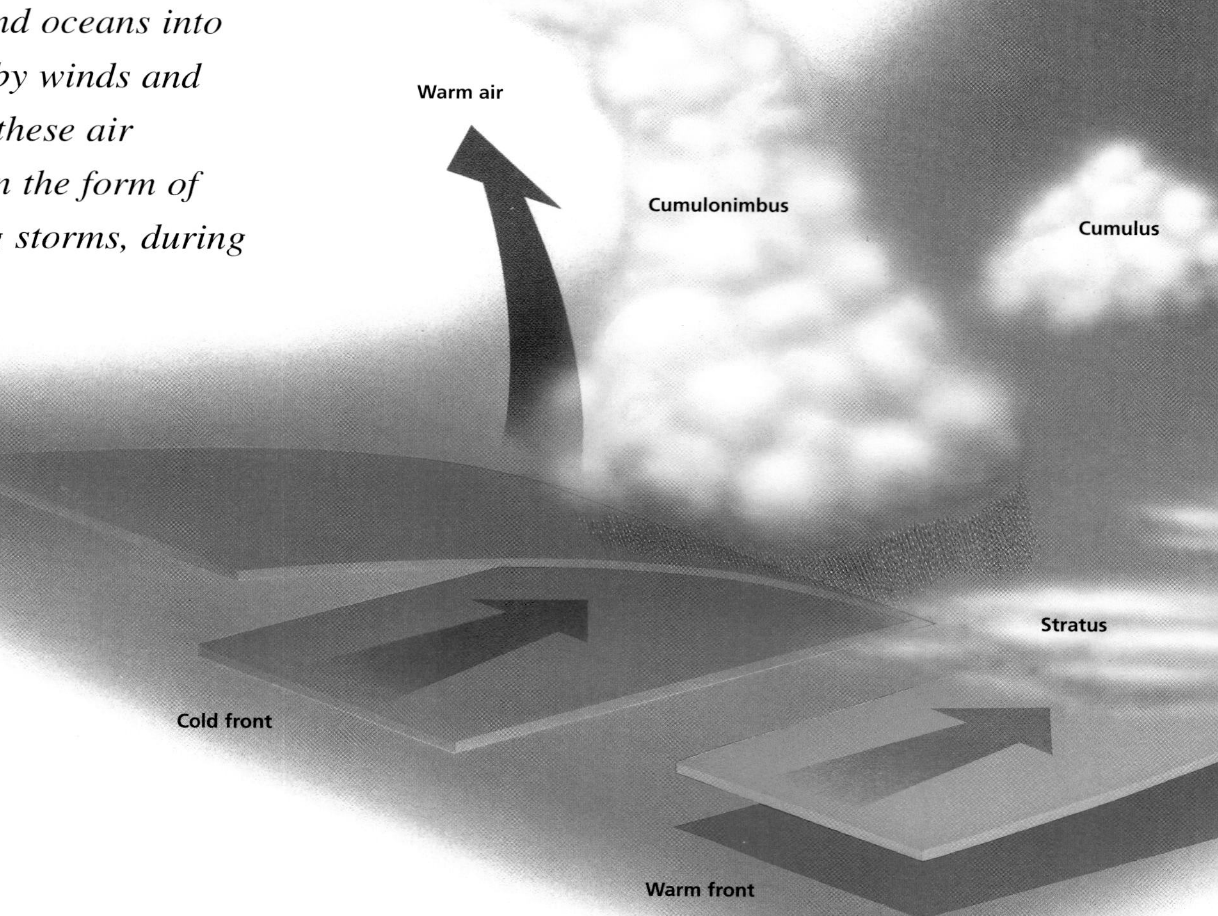

A cold front (right) is formed when cold air forces warm air to rise. The water vapor in the warm air condenses into billowing cumulonimbus clouds, causing heavy precipitation. The warm air continues to rise rapidly, forming towering thunder clouds. As the warm air rises through increasingly cold air, it passes through the freezing point and forms snow or hail, but this may melt before reaching the ground. High up, the wind sweeps the clouds into a characteristic flat-topped anvil shape.

A warm front (above right) moving into a cold area pushes the cold air forward, forcing the warm air to rise slowly over a vast area. The warm air cools and the water vapor condenses to form high clouds with a wispy or sheet-like form, which gradually thicken. Rain may begin to fall, warning of the approaching front. This front is preceded by thick rain clouds. Rain falls steadily until the warm front has passed.

Cloud formation

The formation of clouds is part of the water cycle and fundamentally affects the weather. Moisture evaporated by the heating of Earth's surface rises in warm, humid air. As the air rises and cools, its moisture condenses into myriad tiny droplets or ice crystals, forming clouds. The quantity of water droplets may increase to such an extent that the water precipitates from the clouds as rain, hail, or snow and returns to Earth's surface.

Clouds are named according to whether they are layered (stratus), wispy (cirrus), or heaped (cumulus). Cloud forms vary with altitude. The highest clouds (those above 20,000 feet or 6,000 m) are mainly wispy or made up of layers of ice crystals. At mid-altitude (6,500–20,000 feet or 2,000–6,000 m), clouds are layered or heaped, and may form continuous sheets that produce light rain. Below 6,500 feet (2,000 m), clouds tend to vary from heaped to thunderstorm (cumulonimbus) and blanket overcast (stratus).

Cloud formation at any one time indicates the prevailing atmospheric conditions and the likely weather in the short term. For example, cumulus clouds are indicative of stable, anticyclonic conditions in the atmosphere and presage fine weather. By contrast, the approach of towering anvil-shaped cumulonimbus clouds warns of unstable cyclonic conditions with thunder, lightning, high winds, and torrential rain.

A tornado (below) forms when a funnel of air sinks from a storm cloud. Warm air rises and rotates rapidly around the funnel. The winds can blow up to 500 miles (800 km) per hour and have great destructive power.

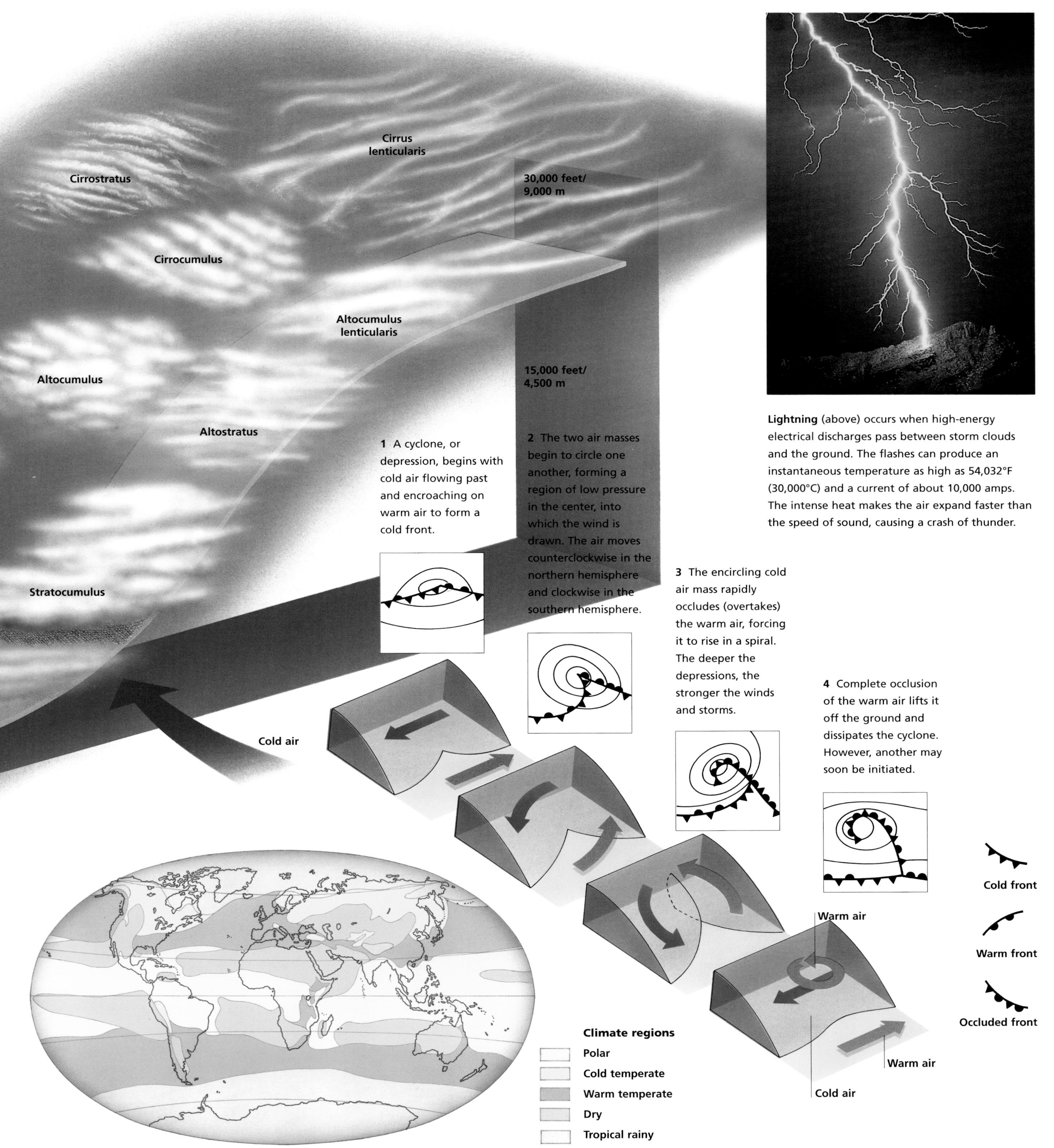

1 A cyclone, or depression, begins with cold air flowing past and encroaching on warm air to form a cold front.

2 The two air masses begin to circle one another, forming a region of low pressure in the center, into which the wind is drawn. The air moves counterclockwise in the northern hemisphere and clockwise in the southern hemisphere.

3 The encircling cold air mass rapidly occludes (overtakes) the warm air, forcing it to rise in a spiral. The deeper the depressions, the stronger the winds and storms.

4 Complete occlusion of the warm air lifts it off the ground and dissipates the cyclone. However, another may soon be initiated.

Lightning (above) occurs when high-energy electrical discharges pass between storm clouds and the ground. The flashes can produce an instantaneous temperature as high as 54,032°F (30,000°C) and a current of about 10,000 amps. The intense heat makes the air expand faster than the speed of sound, causing a crash of thunder.

Climate and weather forecasting

Climate regions are based mainly on rainfall and temperature. Average temperatures in the warmest month in cold polar climates are always less than 50ºF (10ºC). Cold temperate wet climates have more precipitation but warmer summers. In warm temperate climates, the average temperature is higher still. Desert climates have an average annual rainfall of less than 10 inches (25 cm) and may be hot or cold. In tropical rainy climates, average temperatures exceed 64ºF (18ºC) throughout the year. A sixth climate region, the mountain climate, which consists of climatic zones determined by altitude, is also sometimes recognized.

Many regions have fairly predictable seasonal changes in their climate, but with global warming these patterns are now changing in less predictable ways. Where the weather is characteristically unpredictable, it is controlled by successive depressions, or cyclones. These can cause a great deal of destruction, so weather forecasting can save lives. Today, radar provides a continuous warning system for forecasting, and satellite images provide larger-scale surveillance of the global development of major cyclonic storms such as hurricanes.

The Oceans

Oceans cover about 70 percent of Earth's surface and contain 97 percent of all its water, most of it in the southern hemisphere. The Pacific is by far the largest ocean, spreading across more than one-third of Earth's surface. The Atlantic Ocean, the second largest, is only half as large. Next in size is the Indian Ocean, and the Arctic is the smallest ocean.

Life could not exist on our planet without the oceans. They are a major source of food, energy, and minerals, and they help to maintain the world's climate. Warm currents transport heat toward the poles from the tropics, while cold currents flow back from the poles. The oceans thus regulate global temperatures, while their water supplies moisture for the rainfall that replenishes rivers, lakes, and ground water.

Waves (above) start as ripples caused by winds blowing across the sea surface. As they approach the shore, waves grow and may pile up to heights of ten feet (three m) and reach speeds of eight miles (13 km) per hour before the crests break.

High spring tides (below) are generated when the Moon is new or full, and its gravity and that of the Sun pull in the same, or opposite, direction. At other times, the Moon and Sun pull at right angles, producing smaller neap tides.

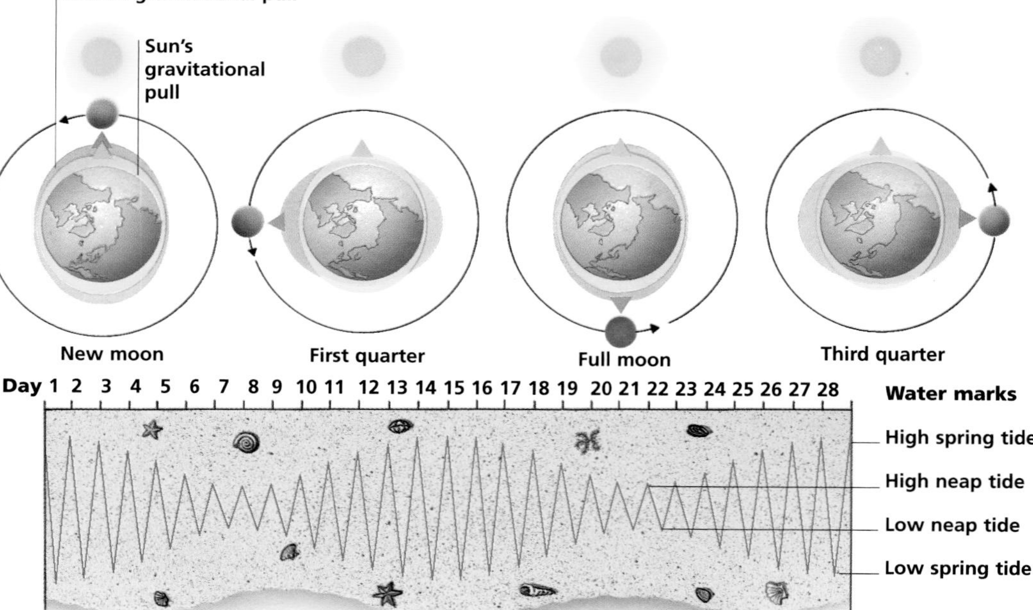

Hydrothermal vents, also known as black smokers, have been discovered along ocean ridges where the sea floor is spreading. These chimney-like structures shoot out boiling hot, mineral-laden water that supports communities of strange marine life. These include blind lobsters and crabs, eel-like fish, giant clams, and tube worms nearly 13 feet (4 m) long (below). Bacteria living inside the tube worms use energy derived from oxidation of the sulphur in seawater to make food. This is called chemosynthesis, and is the only food chain that does not start with plant life.

The ocean floor

The longest mountain ranges on Earth are under the sea, rising from the floors of the world's major oceans. These ocean ridges are formed as crustal plates are forced apart. In the deep valleys that slice through the ridges, volcanoes erupt and spew out molten magma. Their activity creates gigantic, cone-shaped underwater mountains called seamounts. Islands such as Hawaii started out as under-sea volcanoes.

Spread out across the ocean floor are huge, featureless regions called the abyssal plains, which lie 13,000 to 20,000 feet (4,000 to 6,000 m) beneath the ocean surface. These plains are the flattest places on Earth. They are covered with a layer of sediment up to 1,600 feet (500 m) thick, which has taken millions of years to accumulate. Here, deep-water currents moving just several feet each day are driven by differences in the density of the seawater.

The enormous weight of seawater creates astounding pressures on the ocean floor. For every 33 feet (10 m) of depth, the pressure increases by an amount equal to the whole atmosphere above the surface. Few marine creatures can survive these extreme conditions; those that do are very specialized.

Profiles of the ocean floor (right) show rises and falls that are just as steep as those on dry land. Modern imaging methods, which include sonar and satellite-borne sensors, show a system of oceanic ridges. For the most part these ridges are submerged, but in some places peaks appear above the surface. Deep trenches produced by the subduction of plates plunge down to a depth of seven miles (11 km).

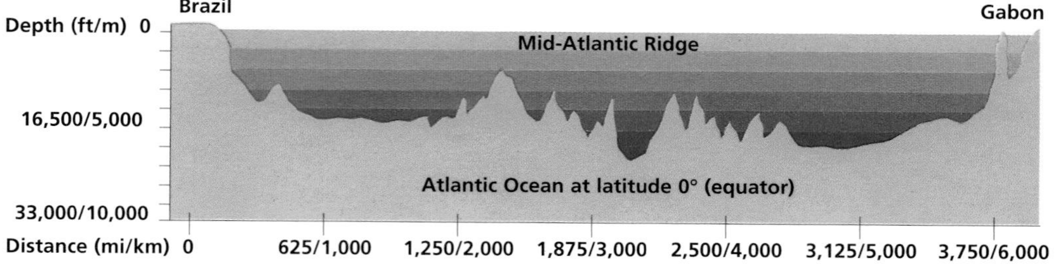

Moving waters

The regular rhythm of the tides, currents, and waves keeps the oceans in constant motion. Currents are created and driven mainly by the wind, but the difference in temperature – and therefore density – between the ocean's surface and its depths also has an effect. Earth's rotation subjects currents to a force that causes them to move clockwise in the northern hemisphere and counter-clockwise in the southern hemisphere; this is known as the Coriolis effect. As the main wind systems drive the currents east or west, the massive presence of major continents directs the currents north or south. The large circular currents that result, called gyres, cool the equatorial regions by transferring heat to cooler regions at high latitudes.

Tides are an observable effect of the Moon's gravitational pull as it orbits the Earth. The Moon's mass, one-eightieth that of Earth, exerts an enormous gravitational pull. This causes water in the oceans to heap up on the side of Earth nearest the Moon, and also causes the oceans to bulge on the opposite side due to the reduced gravitational pull there. This movement produces the tides in shallow coastal waters. Because of Earth's rotation, two high tides occur each day, about 12 hours apart. The Sun's gravitational pull adds to the tidal effect, although its influence is only half that of the Moon.

Life in the surface waters of the Pacific Ocean consists of two main habitats: the pelagic (open sea) and the benthic (ocean floor). The pelagic habitat has several distinct depth zones. The density of sea life off the coast of Chile and Peru (right) lessens with depth as food supplies decrease, but the diversity remains quite high.

The living sea

A huge variety of animal and plant species lives in the oceans. Here, almost every food chain starts with marine plants. The most abundant of these are microscopic phytoplankton that live at the surface: There may be as many as a million of these in a quart or liter of sea water. Like land plants, phytoplankton are photosynthetic – they need energy from the Sun, and they also need the minerals that are found in seawater. Phytoplankton are more numerous in cooler oceans where there are more nutrients, such as phosphorus and nitrogen compounds. Larger plants such as algae and seaweeds grow closer to the shore.

Phytoplankton provide food for the microscopic animals, called zooplankton, which are the main food of small carnivores such as shrimp and other crustaceans. These in turn are eaten by larger fish such as herrings, which are themselves an important part of the diet of dolphins, sharks, and whales.

Most marine plant and animal life occurs in the sunlit surface waters, called the euphotic zone, which is only about 330 feet (100 m) deep. Below 3,300 feet (1,000 m), the sea is permanently dark and there is no plant life. Deep-sea creatures depend on the constant drift of dead animal and plant material from above for food, as well as eating each other.

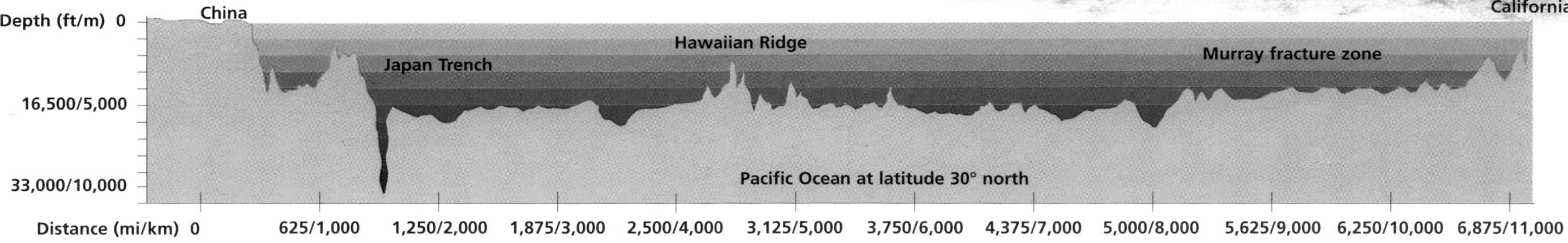

Water

Without water, Earth would be dead, like the Moon. The life processes of all plants and animals are dependent on water: The most lifeless places on Earth – deserts and frozen mountaintops – are those that do not have freely available water. Life evolved in water more than three and a half billion years ago, but living organisms did not emerge onto dry land until three billion years later. Since then, terrestrial life has been maintained by the constant recycling of fresh water, which passes from the saline water of the oceans into the atmosphere, then falls as rain onto the land, and finally flows back into the oceans.

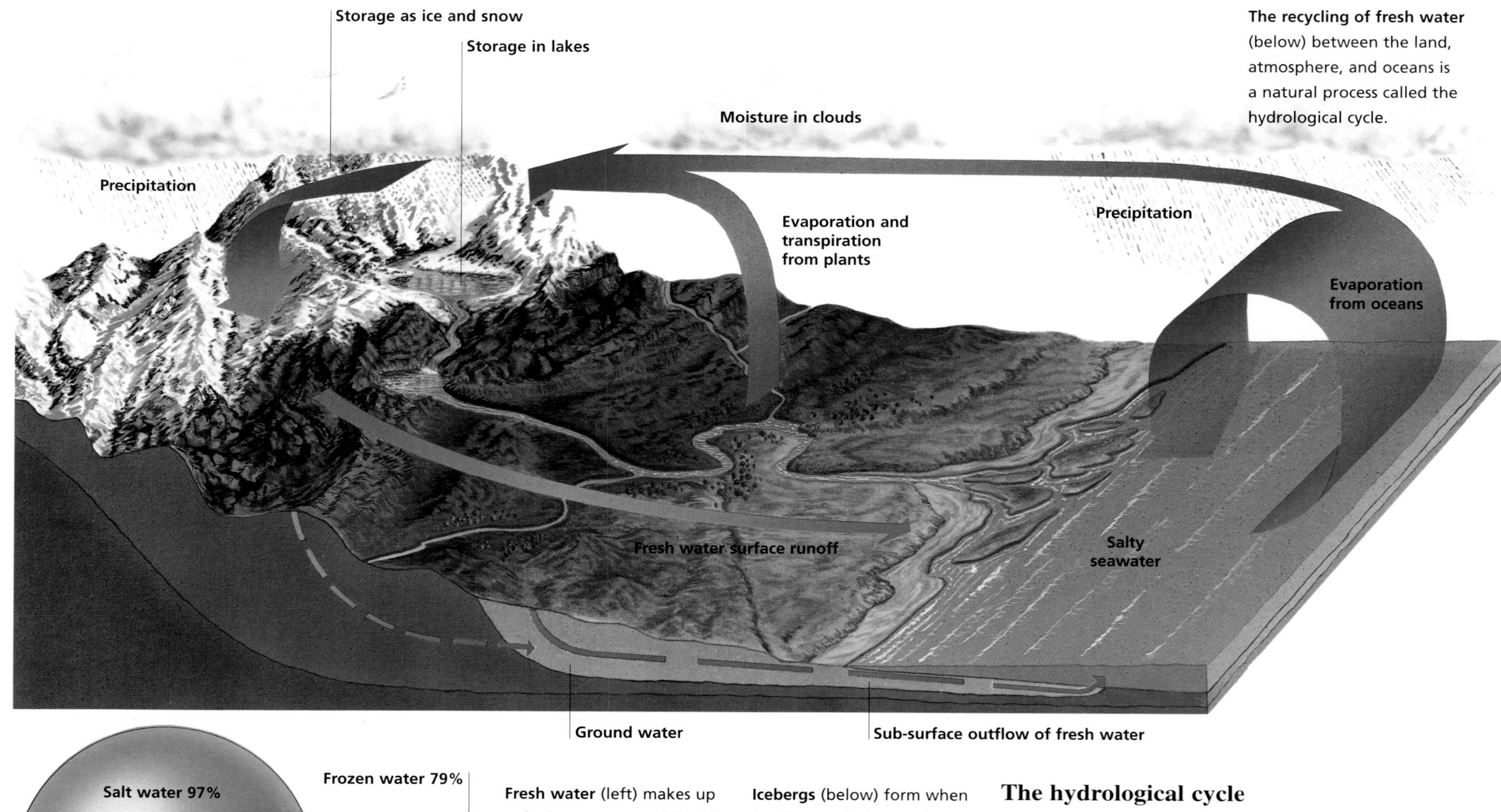

The recycling of fresh water (below) between the land, atmosphere, and oceans is a natural process called the hydrological cycle.

Salt water 97%
Fresh water 3%
Frozen water 79%
Ground water 20%
Easily accessible surface water 1%

Fresh water (left) makes up only three percent of Earth's water – the rest is seawater. Most of the 10 million cubic miles (42 million cu km) of fresh water is locked up in glaciers and ice sheets; only one percent of it is accessible on the surface.

Icebergs (below) form when ice sheets, glaciers, and ice caps meet the ocean and break up. Air bubbles make icebergs buoyant; currents may carry them a thousand miles (1,600 km) before they melt to release a reservoir of fresh water.

The hydrological cycle

The total volume of water on Earth is about 335 million cubic miles (1.4 billion cu km). Most of this is stored in the oceans, while water is continuously recycled between ocean and land. Water evaporates from the oceans into the atmosphere, and much of it returns directly to the oceans as rainfall. However, some ocean moisture is blown over the land and is joined by water transferred from the land surface through evaporation and transpiration from plants. This combined atmospheric water condenses to form clouds and returns to the land as snow and rain. Most of this precipitation is recycled through the processes of evaporation and transpiration, but a small amount is stored as ground water and the remainder runs off back to the sea. Globally this fresh water runoff amounts to some 9,500 cubic miles (40,000 cu km) a year.

Despite the seeming abundance and constant replenishment of fresh water, only about 2,100 cubic miles (9,000 cu km) are readily available each year for human use. This averages around 1,200 gallons (4,400 liters) per person per day. However, fresh water is not equally distributed around the globe.

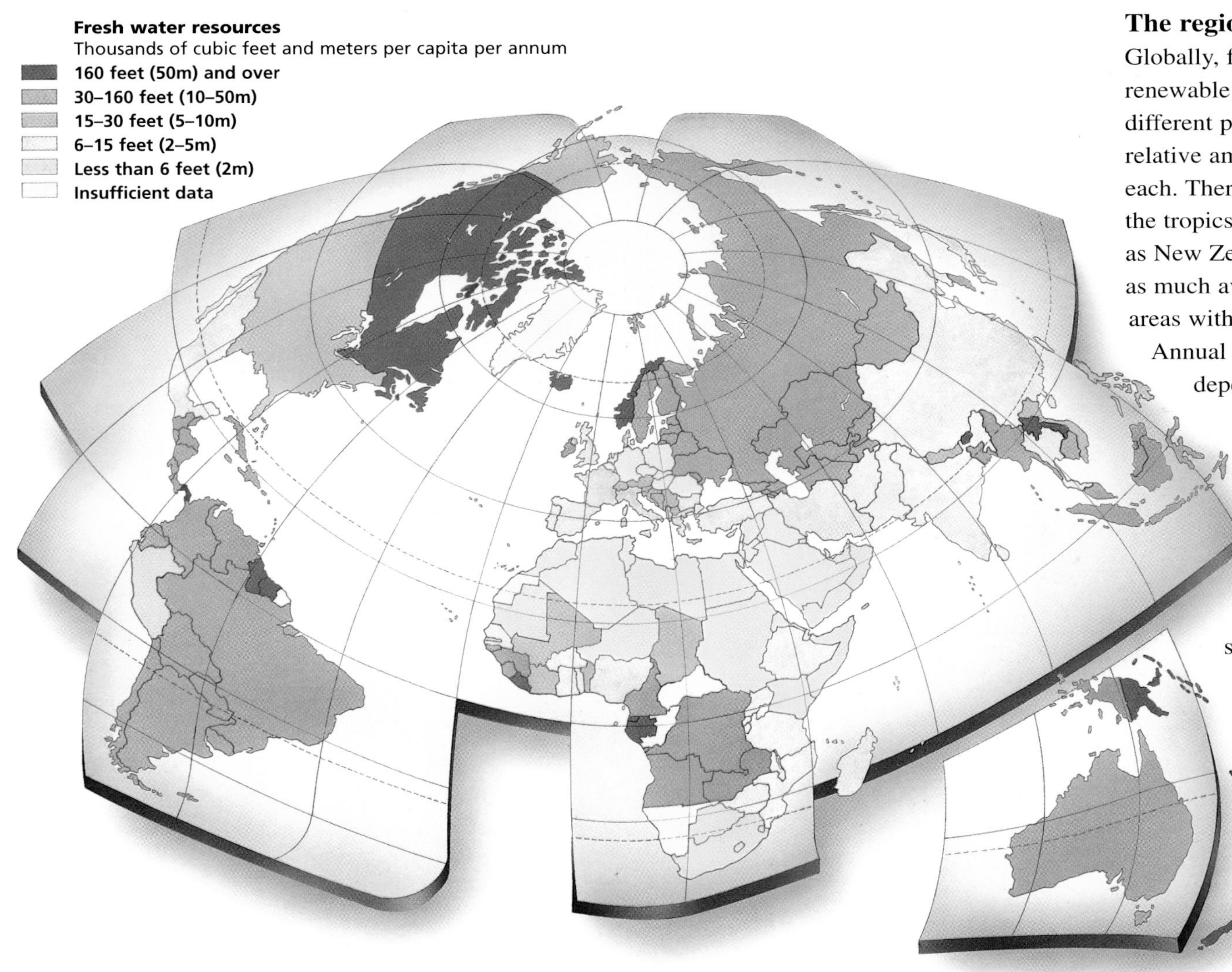

The regional distribution of water

Globally, fresh water is an abundant and renewable resource, but its distribution in different parts of the world is controlled by the relative amounts of rainfall and evaporation in each. There are large water surpluses in much of the tropics, and some high-latitude countries such as New Zealand and Iceland have 20,000 times as much available water per person per year as areas with deficiencies, such as the Middle East.

Annual precipitation is climate-driven and depends upon factors such as the interplay between ocean and atmosphere, and the topography and temperature of the land. However, much of this precipitation is reliable from year to year. In many semiarid areas, such as the Sahel, which borders the Sahara Desert, precipitation is seasonal and low overall. Populations here are highly dependent on rainfall for growth of staple crops, so any climate change puts these marginal areas at risk of drought and famine. Countries like Ethiopia – parts of which have rainfall figures as high as Britain – suffer frequent water shortages because there is little or no infrastructure to conserve and supply water.

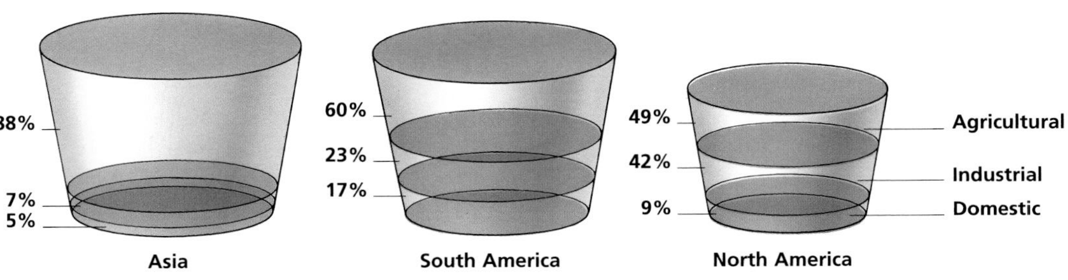

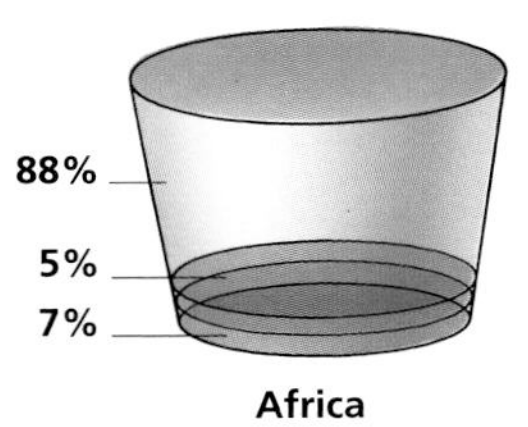

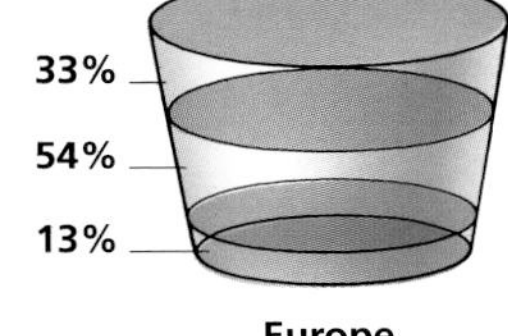

32%
4%
64%
Australasia

Fresh water consumption by use is shown for the six populated continents (above). For its size, South America has by far the most fresh water. Australia has a semiarid climate with the least fresh water overall – but its low population can afford to use most for domestic consumption. Africa and Asia are both largely dependent on subsistence farming, which uses the highest proportion of available fresh water.

Water management

Water management originated more than 5,000 years ago when the first dams for water storage were built in Egypt. Despite the long history and development of water management, lack of clean water still kills at least 25 million people a year. At subsistence level, each person requires at least 5.3 quarts (five liters) of water a day for drinking and cooking. Growing food adds considerably to the amount required, depending on the region and the type of agriculture. In the industrialized world, the average per capita consumption is around 130 gallons (500 liters) a day.

Globally, 69 percent of fresh water is used for agriculture, 23 percent for industry, and the remaining 8 percent goes toward domestic consumption. However, usage differs greatly among the various continents.

The Hoover Dam (below) was the world's highest dam when it was completed in 1936. It rises 725 feet (221 m) above the Colorado River between Nevada and Arizona, forming a 115-mile-long (185-km) reservoir called Lake Mead. The dam is a multipurpose structure providing flood control, drinking and irrigation water, and 1,345 megawatts of hydroelectric power.

Evolutionary Trails

Many scientists believe that Earth has been inhabited by living organisms since soon after it cooled sufficiently for complex organic compounds to form. The first fossil evidence of primitive life dates from about 3.8 billion years ago. Abundant fossils of marine invertebrates – the first multicellular life forms – date from some 550 million years ago. Life evolved rapidly over the following 300 million years, producing most of the major groups of living organisms known today. In the 19th century, Charles Darwin and Alfred Russel Wallace conceived the theory of an evolutionary process driven by natural selection. Since then, it has been recognized that life has evolved through many generations of genetic change, under the pressure of sexual and environmental selection.

Stromatolites (above) provide some of the earliest evidence of life on Earth. These mounds began forming 3.8 billion years ago, when densely packed colonies of primitive organisms, called cyanobacteria, trapped sediment as they grew.

Millions of years ago
4,500
4,000
3,000
2,500
1,000
570
510
438
400
360
286
245
213
140
66
58
37
24
Today
Precambrian
Paleozoic
Mesozoic
Cenozoic
•Prokaryotes
Bacteria
Cyanobacteria
Eubacteria
•Protoctistans
Slime molds
Dinoflagellates
Diatoms
Euglenids
Coccoliths
Radiolarians
Foraminiferans
Green algae
•Higher plants
Early vascular plants
Flowering plants
Cycads
Conifers
Ferns
Fungi
Sponges
Trilobites

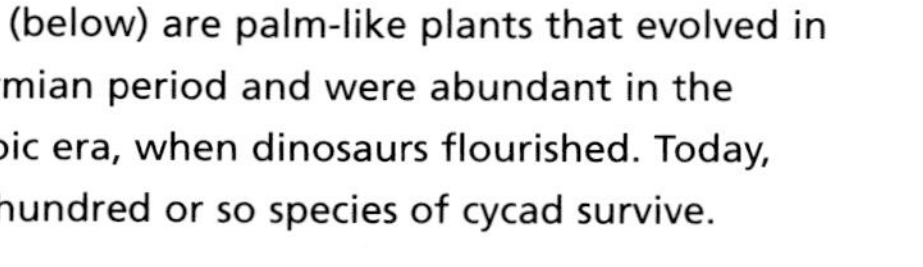

Cycads (below) are palm-like plants that evolved in the Permian period and were abundant in the Mesozoic era, when dinosaurs flourished. Today, only a hundred or so species of cycad survive.

Panderichthys

Acanthostega

Evolutionary change

Over the millennia, evolutionary changes in living species have resulted from the interplay of inherited characteristics and the environment. During reproduction, genetic information is transferred from one generation to the next. This process can produce mutations (changes) that are inherited, and some of these may result in advantageous adaptations to the environment. For example, a mutation may produce thicker hair or more fat under the skin, giving greater body insulation. In a cold climate, individuals with such mutated genes will have a better chance of survival, and are more likely to reproduce and pass on copies of their genes to their offspring. These genes will thus occur more frequently in future generations. The woolly mammoth evolved from less hairy elephants in this way, thereby withstanding the cold during the last Ice Age.

A group of bony fish with paired pectoral and pelvic fins (above) gave rise to the first tetrapod (four-limbed) animals around 370 million years ago. These later evolved the ability to lay a shell-covered egg, which finally gave them independence from water.

The coelacanth (above), a "living fossil," belongs to an ancient group of bony fish thought to have been extinct for 90 million years until 1938, when living specimens were found in the Indian Ocean.

The evolution of living and extinct organisms (below) can be traced using evidence from fossils (shown by colored lines), combined with the results of theoretical studies and other sources of evidence (shown in pale gray).

The fossil record

The evidence found in fossils gives us an incomplete view of the history of life on Earth. This is because only some organisms have body structures, such as shells or bones, that are preserved as fossils. Nevertheless, combining this evidence with the study of relationships between living and ancient organisms reveals a detailed picture of how life has evolved.

Eukaryotes (cells with nuclear membranes) evolved from prokaryotes (cells without nuclear membranes) about 1.8 billion years ago. This was the first step in the evolution of multi-cellular life forms. The long Precambrian phase of the early evolution of life produced multi-celled seaweeds and jellyfish-like animals by around 600 million years ago. The Paleozoic era began around 540 million years ago when an abundance of marine invertebrates – especially shellfish with hard, preservable parts – appeared. Within a hundred million years there was an enormous diversification in marine life, during which most of the main groups of marine invertebrates in existence today evolved. From them the first vertebrates – the extinct conodonts – soon evolved. These were tiny, eel-like creatures with elongated bodies. The first fish species appeared more than 470 million years ago; within a hundred million years of that date, some species had evolved paired limbs and an internal skeleton.

These four-limbed amphibian-like vertebrates moved onto land in late Devonian times. This followed the first ecosystems of soils and primitive plants in late Silurian times, when small arthropods became established on land. The early land vertebrates became truly independent of water only when they evolved amniote (shelled) eggs and scaly, reptilian skins in the Carboniferous period. The reptiles, plants, and insects went on to dominate life on land for well over 200 million years.

Mammals evolved from reptiles by a series of changes beginning in Permian times, and finally gained dominance over reptiles at the beginning of the Cenozoic era. Flowering plants and modern birds also developed during this period.

Two major extinction events have disturbed the evolutionary progression of life, one at the end of the Paleozoic era and the other at the end of the Mesozoic. The latter caused the demise of many groups of reptiles, including the dinosaurs.

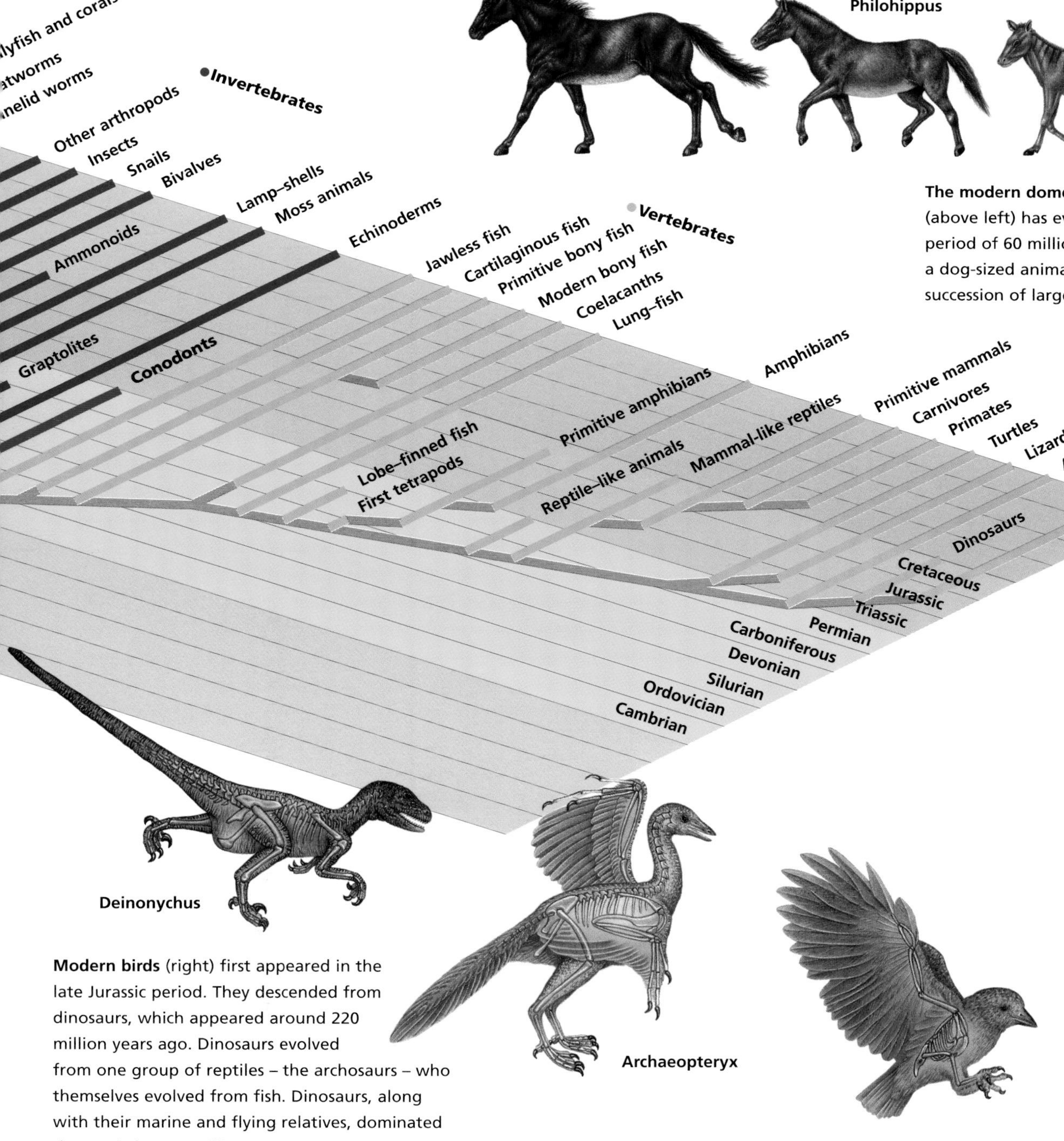

Equus

Philohippus

Merychippus

Mesohippus

Hydracotherium

The modern domesticated horse (above left) has evolved over a period of 60 million years from a dog-sized animal through a succession of larger, longer-legged forms. The earliest form, called Hydracotherium, had four toes on its front feet and three on the back. During evolution, contact with the ground has been gradually reduced, promoting faster running: modern horses have just a single "toe."

Expansion and extinction

Bursts of evolution have produced rapidly evolving groups of species that colonized new environments; life, for example, first invaded land in Silurian and Devonian times. There have also been reductions in biological diversity, when species unable to adapt to new conditions have been forced into extinction. These changes are generally driven by dynamic Earth processes – especially plate tectonics, which leads to mountain building and changes in sea level and climate. At the end of the Permian period, for example, more than 60 percent of existing species became extinct as a result of sea-level changes. Although rarer, there is also evidence of extinctions due to extraterrestrial events: At the end of the Cretaceous period, a meteorite impact probably helped push the dinosaurs to extinction.

Modern bird

Modern birds (right) first appeared in the late Jurassic period. They descended from dinosaurs, which appeared around 220 million years ago. Dinosaurs evolved from one group of reptiles – the archosaurs – who themselves evolved from fish. Dinosaurs, along with their marine and flying relatives, dominated the Earth for 150 million years.

The Diversity of Life

As far as we know, living organisms are confined to a thin layer on the surface of just one planet in the Universe – Earth. This layer of life, called the biosphere, extends from the bottom of the oceans to the atmosphere over the highest mountains. One of the most obvious features of the biosphere is that plants and animals are found only in particular places. There are many reasons for this: Over the land surface, for example, the climate, soils, and availability of water differ; and in aquatic habitats there are differences in the levels of salinity and the amount of water movement. These geographical variations restrict collections of plants and animals to certain places, where they form characteristic communities called biomes.

An oak tree (below) is an example of an ecosystem. It provides a habitat for a large number of animal and plant species that are dependent on each other.

Communities, ecosystems, and food chains

The collection of interacting plant and animal species in an area is called a community; the community and the non-living elements are together called an ecosystem. Energy, usually from the Sun, is trapped by the community's photosynthesizing plants. Some of this energy passes to herbivores when they eat plants, and is then passed on to their predators and parasites. These feeding relationships form food webs – the routes by which energy passes through the ecosystem. Energy is being lost from the ecosystem all the time as heat, so more energy must be added constantly for the ecosystem to persist. Inorganic elements are continuously recycled within the ecosystem. Uneaten plant material and dead animals are decomposed by invertebrates, fungi, and bacteria into simple molecules. These are then taken up by the roots of growing plants and turned into more complex substances, forming new plant tissue.

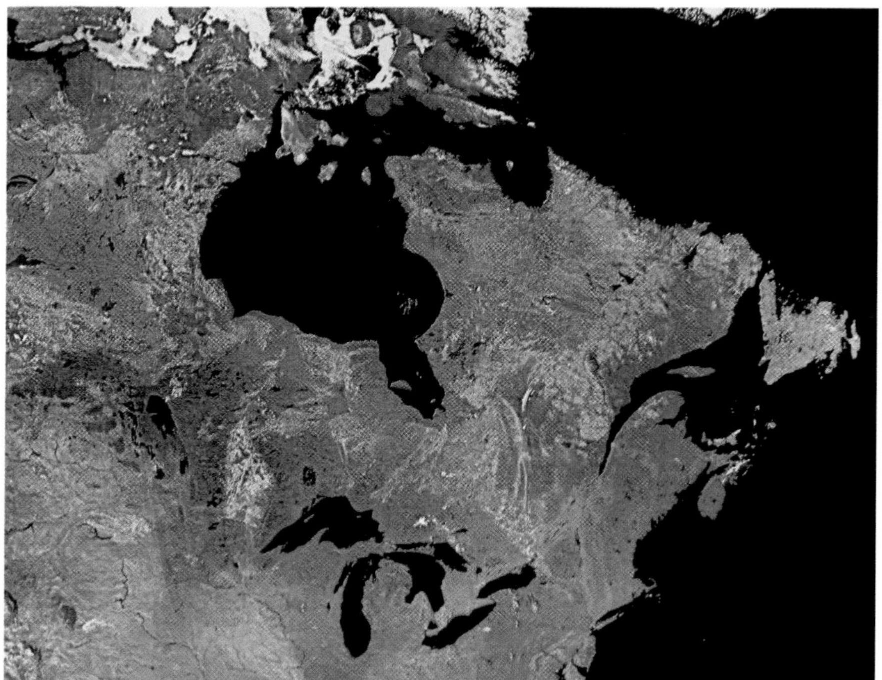

Vegetation zones can be clearly seen in this infrared satellite photograph (left) of eastern Canada and the northeastern United States – from tundra in the north, through boreal (coniferous) forest, also called taiga, to prairie at the bottom left.

Types of soil

In very cold climates, soils are frozen for much of the year and are usually permanently frozen not far beneath the surface. Water cannot drain away, instead leaving a waterlogged topsoil where organic decay is very slow and peat accumulates. In warmer climates, movement of water through the soil often generates a layered soil profile, called a podsol. Under deciduous trees, earthworms mix the upper layers and produce a brown soil that is rich in humus, but in coniferous forests a thick layer of needles builds up. Above limestone rocks, rendzinas (thin, calcium-rich soils) develop, which are often covered in grasses. In the tropics, decomposition of organic material is fast and water movements tend to concentrate aluminum and iron (which gives the soil a characteristic red color) in the surface layers.

Microscopic insect life

Bacteria

Fungi

Actinomycetes (filamentous bacteria)

Coniferous

Deciduous

World biomes

With the variations in climate, water, and soils around the world, it is not surprising that plant and animal communities also vary from place to place. As plants are especially sensitive to local conditions, they have been used to define a series of biomes around the world. In general, terrestrial biomes are linked to latitude. They range from the perpetually frozen regions at the poles and on high mountains, where there is no vegetation, to the hot areas with high rainfall near the equator, where there is dense tropical forest.

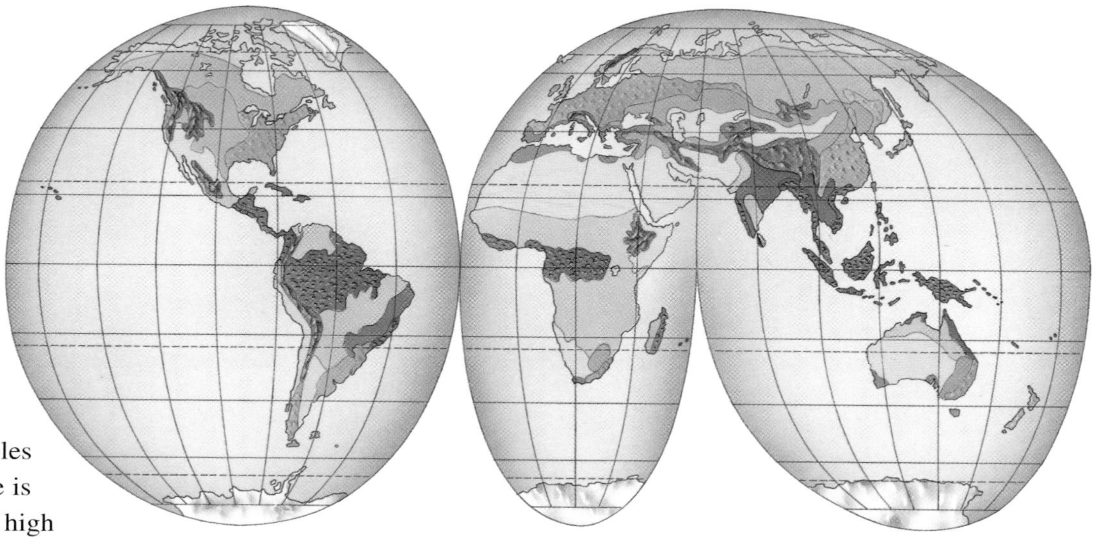

Distribution of world biomes

Monsoon
Tropical rain forest
Savanna
Desert
Mediterranean
Temperate grassland
Temperate forest
Mountain
Taiga
Tundra
Polar

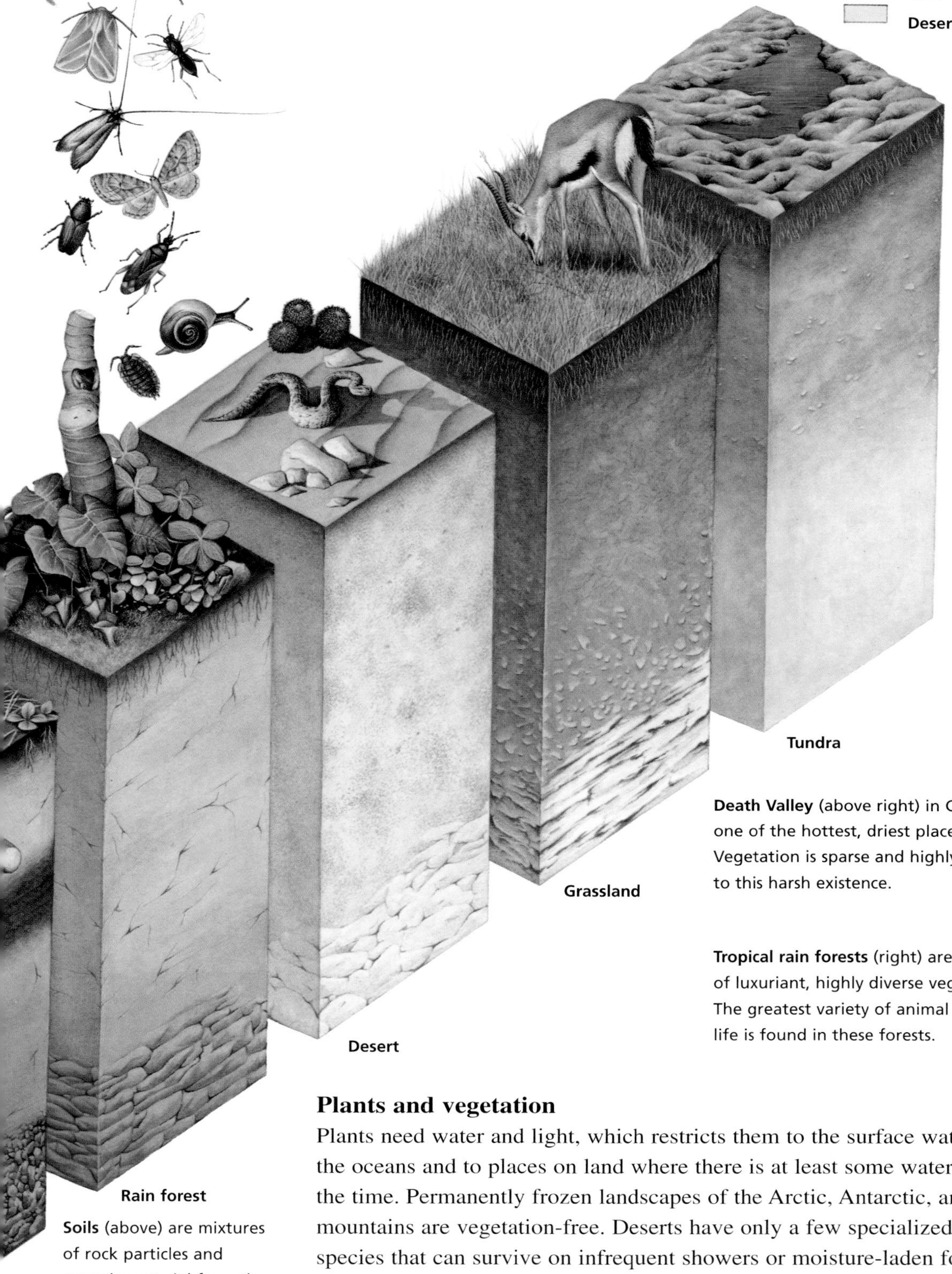

Tundra

Grassland

Desert

Rain forest

Soils (above) are mixtures of rock particles and organic material from the decomposition of plants and animals. Organic material adds to a soil's complexity and its ability to retain water and nutrients.

Death Valley (above right) in California is one of the hottest, driest places on Earth. Vegetation is sparse and highly adapted to this harsh existence.

Tropical rain forests (right) are composed of luxuriant, highly diverse vegetation. The greatest variety of animal and plant life is found in these forests.

Plants and vegetation

Plants need water and light, which restricts them to the surface waters of the oceans and to places on land where there is at least some water some of the time. Permanently frozen landscapes of the Arctic, Antarctic, and high mountains are vegetation-free. Deserts have only a few specialized plant species that can survive on infrequent showers or moisture-laden fogs. In temperate regions of the world (those with a moderate climate), vegetation is influenced by the seasons. Plant growth is limited to the spring and, more especially, summer, when there are long periods of daylight and the temperature is high. In equatorial regions where rainfall is plentiful, plants grow continuously throughout the year, forming tropical rain forests.

The Rise of Man

Charles Darwin predicted that the earliest human ancestors would be found in Africa. The fossil record and modern genetic studies suggest that Darwin was right: Modern humans almost certainly evolved from a group of ape-like ancestors that originated in Africa. Humans share a common ancestor and more than 98 percent of their genetic material with one group of higher apes: the chimpanzees. Over the last 50 million years, waves of anthropoids (monkeys, apes, ape-men, and humans) evolved in Africa and moved into other regions. Modern humans originated some 100,000 years ago and gradually spread around the world. Stone tools were sufficiently developed for a change from hunting-gathering to settled agriculture around 12,000 years ago, when the global climate became warmer after the last Ice Age.

A Neanderthal skull (above left) has a larger face and a more prominent brow ridge than Cro-Magnon (above right). The groups coexisted between 100,000 and 30,000 years ago. During this period, the Neanderthals became extinct while the Cro-Magnons gave rise to modern humans.

The family tree (below) of hominids (ape-men) shows how the *Homo* genus (group of species), which includes humans, evolved from one species of the genus *Australopithecus*.

Fossil footprints (above) from East Africa, dated at 3.6 million years old, are the earliest evidence for the evolution of upright walking on two legs by our ancestors, the early hominids.

The degree of hominization or likeness to modern humans (right) of successive hominid (ape-man) species can be traced via several important developments or attributes. Bipedalism freed hands for tasks requiring increased manual dexterity, such as making stone tools for hunting. Teeth became smaller as the protein value of food increased, and brain size grew as communication and intelligence evolved. Material culture – the use of tools, fire, writing, and other skills – developed alongside increases in hominization.

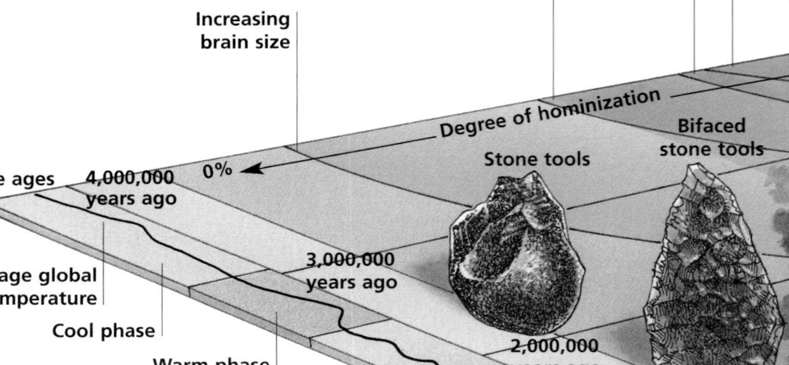

Climate change over the last four million years (above) has been marked by increasing fluctuations in average global temperatures. These culminated in the onset of the last Ice Age around two million years ago, with its alternating cool glacial and warm interglacial phases.

Mammal relatives

The possession of warm blood, hair, and milk-producing breasts characterizes humans as mammals – one of the major groups of vertebrate animals – whose evolution from reptiles began some 250 million years ago. Human ancestry began around 55 million years ago with the evolution of the first primate mammals – the ancestors of lemurs, tarsiers, monkeys, apes, and humans.

The early primates had well-developed brains, good eyesight, agility in climbing, a degree of manual dexterity, and gave good parental care. They exist in the fossil record throughout North America, Asia, Europe, and possibly Africa, as small, squirrel-like animals. The first anthropoids evolved from these primates, but exactly how this link was made is not clear.

The oldest known anthropoids are 37 million-year-old fossils from Egypt. Over the following 17 million years, these monkey and ape ancestors diverged into different forms. Many became large, plant-eating species, with pronounced differences in size between the sexes and increased social behavior. By around 20 million years ago, about 30 different species of apes had evolved. Most became extinct, but one group of species gave rise to the line that produced the modern higher apes. Fossils in Africa have shown that by 14 million years ago apes had evolved into tree-climbers that could hang from branches by their arms and occasionally walk semi-upright on their hind legs. The development of these capabilities was essential to the survival of this evolutionary line.

Rise of the ape-men

Recent genetic studies have estimated that humans and the living higher apes diverged from one another between 15 and five million years ago. This time scale is confirmed by fossils of the first group of ape-men to evolve, which date from some 4.5 million years ago. Over the following three million years, a succession of australopithecines (southern ape-men) evolved increasingly human characteristics. They began to walk upright instead of using their arms for knuckle-walking. Bipedalism allowed hominids to move greater distances over open ground and has been linked to a habitat change from forest to savanna.

Between three and two million years ago, australopithecines diversified into a number of coexisting species in Africa whose interrelationships are unclear. All were less than five feet (1.5 m) in height and their brain size was between 24 and 30 cubic inches (400 and 500 cu cm). Some had a relatively light build (66–132 pounds/30–60 kg in weight), while others were more robust and heavy (88–176 pounds/40–80 kg), with powerful jaws and massive teeth. Some species were the first ape-men to make stone tools around 2.6 million years ago. Around two million years ago, a new group of hominids with similar stature but larger brains (up to 49 cu inches/800 cu cm) appeared in Africa. These were the first examples of the *Homo* genus: Humans – though not in their modern form – had evolved.

Wall paintings (above) have been found in rock shelters and caves in many parts of the world, from Africa to Australia, Europe, and the Americas. Some of them date back as much as 40,000 years. These pictures of animal prey were drawn by early modern human hunters. Many images record animals that no longer live in these regions or have become extinct, such as mammoths. A combination of climate change and over-hunting were probably responsible for both eventualities.

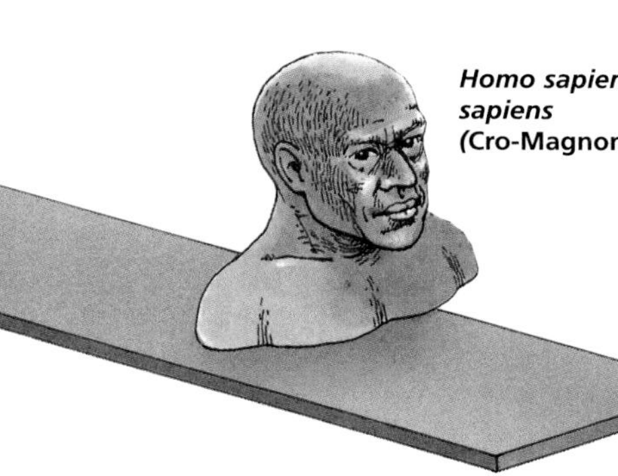

Human development

The first human species, *Homo habilis* (handy man) and the later *Homo erectus* (upright man) had relatively large brain capacities, flat faces, prominent brows, and big jaws. They coexisted with the more primitive australopithecine survivors and other apes and monkeys. As they spread beyond Africa to the Far East, they took their developing skills as nomadic hunters and gatherers of plant food with them. Their stature and brain size increased and their skull shape changed. The earliest *Homo sapiens* evolved in Africa around 400,000 years ago and spread into Europe and eventually Asia. The European group – known as Neanderthals – lived from around 200,000 until 30,000 years ago. They were tough, stocky individuals, well adapted to the cold since they had to contend with the Ice Age. Around 100,000 years ago another wave of humans – the Cro-Magnons – emerged in Africa and the Middle East. They spread rapidly throughout Asia, Australasia, Europe and, around 12,000 years ago, into North America. Cro-Magnons were the ancestors of today's humans, from whom they were virtually indistinguishable.

The success of the human ape as a species has been phenomenal. The global population around 12,000 years ago, at the transition from hunting and gathering to farming, is estimated to have been between five and ten million, compared with nearly six billion today. Life expectancy was around 20 years (compared to around 70 years now), and infant mortality was perhaps one in four, compared with less than one in 40 on average today. These dramatic changes have occurred alongside various revolutions in culture and behavior and ways of life, and owe much to the development of new food production methods and other technologies. The rate of change has accelerated in the last 5,000 years or so with inventions such as the plow and the potter's wheel.

The Population Explosion

One thousand years ago, the world was still a relatively empty place. Human numbers were small and their influence over the environment and other species was limited. The population of Europe, for example, was about 35 million, one-twentieth of the present total. Even 300 years ago, many of today's great cities – from New York to Sydney – were not even villages. Several factors, including industrialization and improvements in health and hygiene, have contributed to the world's population explosion, which continues today.

The population in most major cities today is a "melting pot" of first- or second-generation immigrants from a variety of ethnic backgrounds (above). Such cities gain benefits from the cultural enrichment that a mixed population brings. They may also face difficulties such as the problem of educating children whose first language is not that of the host country. Racial tensions sometimes also develop within such communities.

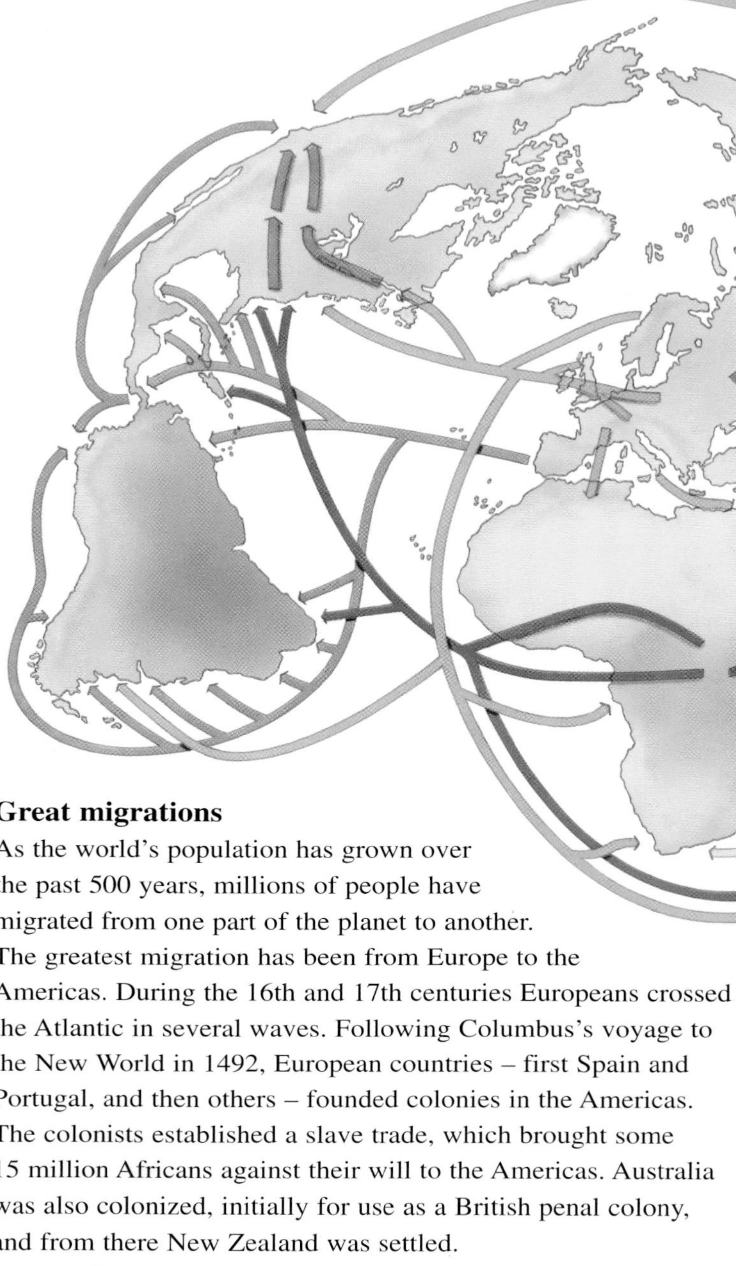

Great migrations

As the world's population has grown over the past 500 years, millions of people have migrated from one part of the planet to another. The greatest migration has been from Europe to the Americas. During the 16th and 17th centuries Europeans crossed the Atlantic in several waves. Following Columbus's voyage to the New World in 1492, European countries – first Spain and Portugal, and then others – founded colonies in the Americas. The colonists established a slave trade, which brought some 15 million Africans against their will to the Americas. Australia was also colonized, initially for use as a British penal colony, and from there New Zealand was settled.

The 19th century saw the movement of people from the eastern seaboard of North America to the central and western part of the continent, and similar migrations from European Russia eastward into Siberia. As a result of the growth of European empires in the 19th century, millions of European traders, farmers, administrators, and missionaries found new homes in Africa, Asia, and South America. Workers were often moved from one part of an empire to another: For example, Indians were brought by the British to East Africa, Malaya (Malaysia), and the islands of the Caribbean and Pacific.

In the first half of the 20th century, the expansion of the Soviet empire brought millions of Russians into central Asia, Siberia, and the far east of Russia, as well as into the Baltic region and central Europe. With the dissolution of European empires after the Second World War, many people from former colonies moved to live in the countries that had occupied them.

Until 10,000 years ago (below) the most important factor in population growth was the use of stone tools. From then until the Black Death in the 14th century A.D., settled agriculture supported a steady rise in population numbers.

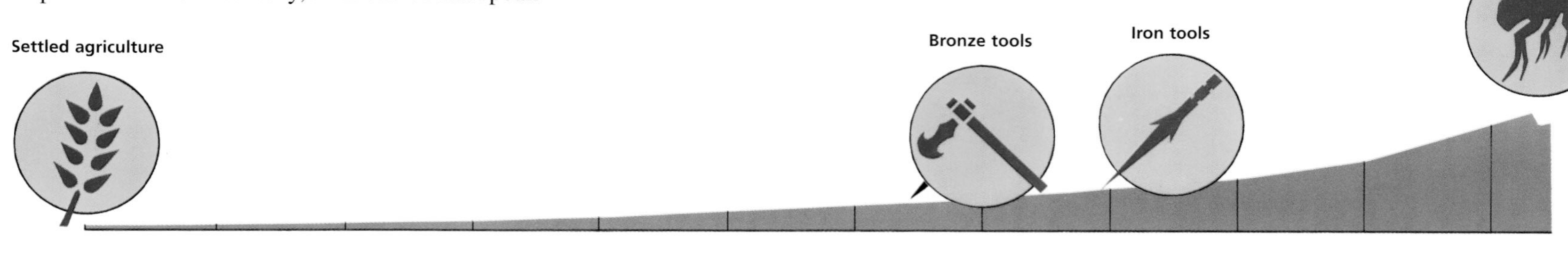

Family planning

For various reasons, the late 20th century has seen a rapid decline in birth rates worldwide. Modern methods of birth control are increasingly being used, and families have fewer children as improved health care and hygiene ensure that fewer die in infancy and more survive to adulthood. The move to smaller families also reflects social changes. In poor rural societies, children remain vital as laborers in fields and as caretakers for their parents in old age. But in richer urban societies they are an economic drain, costly to educate, clothe, and feed. Pensions and welfare provisions mean children are not essential for support in old age.

In rural areas of India (left), families are large as children are needed to work on the land and care for their parents in old age. The average Indian family has four children. India is the world's second most populous country (after China), with more than 975 million people.

China (above) has reduced its rate of population growth to about one percent a year – one of the lowest in the developing world – by restricting state benefits to a family's first child. It remains the most populous country in the world, with 1.2 billion people.

Population growth

For the past 900,000 or so years, the world population has grown almost continuously. This expansion has been driven by three great technological revolutions, each of which dramatically raised the number of people the world could sustain.

The first was the invention of tools, which spread around the world between one million and 100,000 years ago. The second revolution was the move to settled agriculture. This began at the end of the last Ice Age and spread outward from areas where settled agriculture was first established, such as the Middle East. Agriculture lifted the world population from less than ten million in 10000 B.C. to about 200 million around the year A.D. 1 and 350 million around A.D. 1000. There followed a partial collapse of Europe's population as a result of the Black Death plague, which killed up to one-third of the continent's population during the 14th century.

By the late 18th century, the third great demographic upheaval – caused by the Industrial Revolution – was under way in Europe and beginning to spread worldwide. This process continues today. A United Nations forecast predicts that industrialization will have sustained a rise in the world's population from about 700 million in the mid-18th century to some ten billion by the year 2100.

Since industrialization began in the late 18th century, the rate of increase in populations has been unevenly spread around the world (below). Europe was the first area to experience a rapid increase, while Africa's population was almost steady until the 20th century.

Europe's Industrial Revolution (below right) caused a world population boom. In the last hundred years, clean water and immunization programs have also boosted population figures. The annual increase peaked at around 90 million a year in the 1990s, but is now set to fall back to near zero towards the end of the 21st century.

Industrial Revolution
Clean water
Immunization
Asia
Americas
Africa
Oceania
Europe and Russia
World population (billions)
0 1 2 3 4 5 6
1450 1500 1550 1600 1650 1700 1750 1800 1850 1900 1950 2000

Population Patterns

Over the past half century, as health care has reduced death rates at all stages of life, the most dramatic demographic change has been the rising populations of the developing countries of Asia, Latin America, and Africa. By the mid-1990s, worldwide average life expectancy at birth was 66 years – seven years more than two decades before. Fertility rates had fallen to an average of fewer than three children for each woman, compared to five in 1950. By the year 2100, birth and death rates are likely to be equal, as they are already in most of Western Europe. The global population is expected to stabilize at close to ten billion people; before then, the dominant trends in many countries will be an aging population and the continuing movement of rural people into cities.

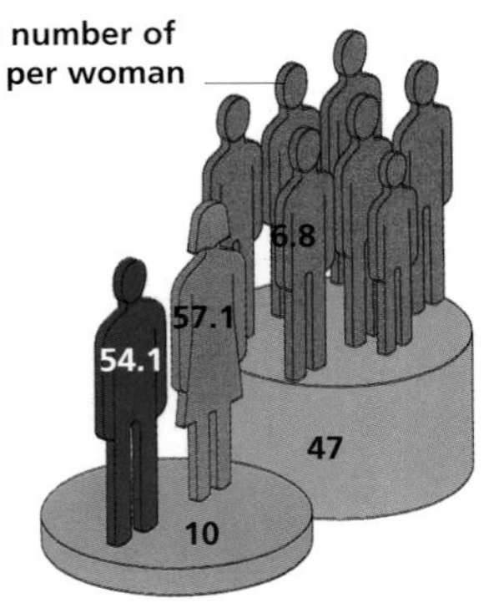

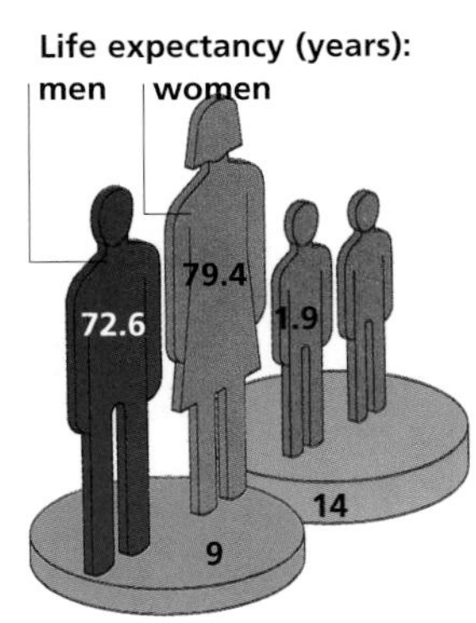

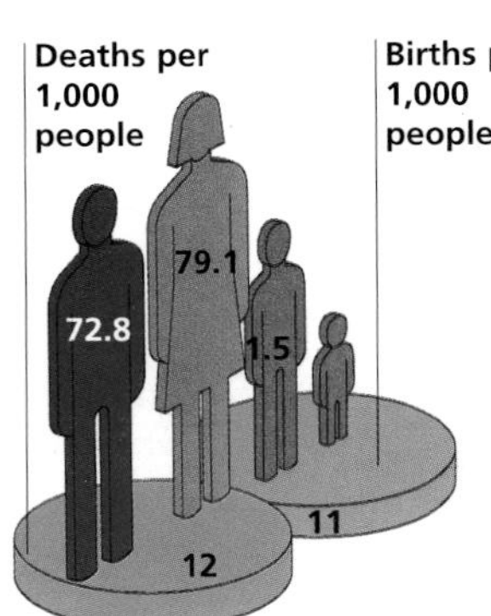

Population growth depends on the balance between births and deaths. In the past 200 years, most countries have progressed through a similar transition (above). First, improved life expectancy causes a fall in death rates, while births stay high. Thus, Kenya today has four times as many births as deaths. Later, birth rates start to fall, as they have in the U.S. In the final stage, as now in Germany, deaths may exceed births and the population may decrease. In all three countries, life expectancy for women exceeds that for men.

Hong Kong accommodates a high population density (15,000 people per square mile/6,000 per square km) by building upwards (above).

Brasilia (left) was built in the center of Brazil to encourage people to move away from the densely populated coast. The modernist high-rise architecture and wide boulevards have led to it being called "the city without street corners."

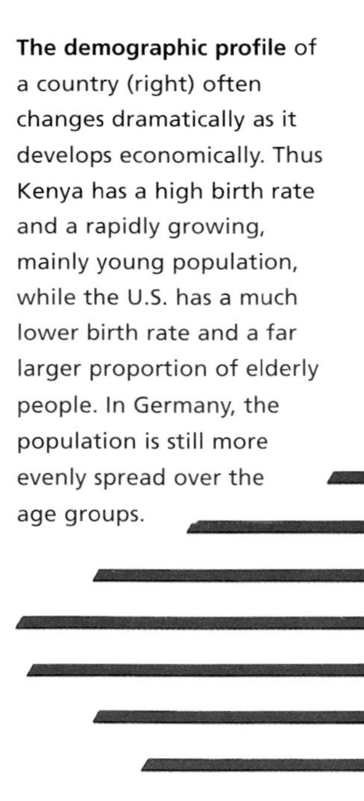

The demographic profile of a country (right) often changes dramatically as it develops economically. Thus Kenya has a high birth rate and a rapidly growing, mainly young population, while the U.S. has a much lower birth rate and a far larger proportion of elderly people. In Germany, the population is still more evenly spread over the age groups.

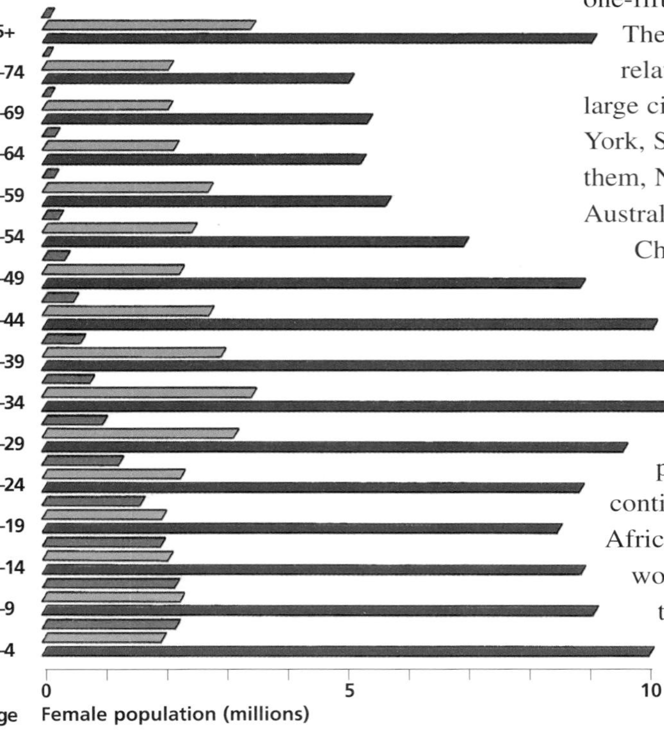

Population density

Despite the recent massive growth in world population, the highest population densities are still found in the same regions as before the industrial era – Europe and eastern and southern Asia. China, which for most of recorded history has been the country with the world's largest population, continues to hold that position with about 1.2 billion people – one-fifth of the global total.

The Americas and Australia are still relatively thinly populated outside large cities such as Los Angeles, New York, São Paulo, and Sydney. Between them, North and South America and Australia have fewer inhabitants than China, despite a land area more than five times greater. Much of Africa is still sparsely populated, but while the population of many countries is stabilizing, the number of people in Africa is expected to continue rising fast for some decades. Africa's population growth is now the world's fastest – by 1996, for the first time in recorded history, the continent was home to more people than Europe.

Bombay, or Mumbai, (above) is one of the world's fastest-growing cities. More than half of the population lives in squalid shanty towns.

The growth of megacities

By the year 2025, the majority of the world's population will live in urban areas. People are being driven from the countryside by the mechanization of farming or by the exhaustion of the soil, and are lured to towns and cities by their better resources and services, and the prospect of jobs in new industries.

Megacities – those cities with populations of more than ten million people – have formed rapidly in many developing countries. Mexico City, São Paulo, Shanghai, and Bombay, with around 16 million people apiece, are each more than twice the size of London. Tokyo, the largest urban complex in the world, has 26.5 million people. Even so, only three percent of the world's population live in a megacity. In the 1990s, the growth of these cities has slowed as services have become overburdened, causing traffic gridlock, pollution, urban decay, and the emergence of giant shanty towns. Now, second cities and smaller urban areas grow most rapidly. Many people live in areas that are part-urban and part-rural: One-third of the world's urban residents spend some time growing food.

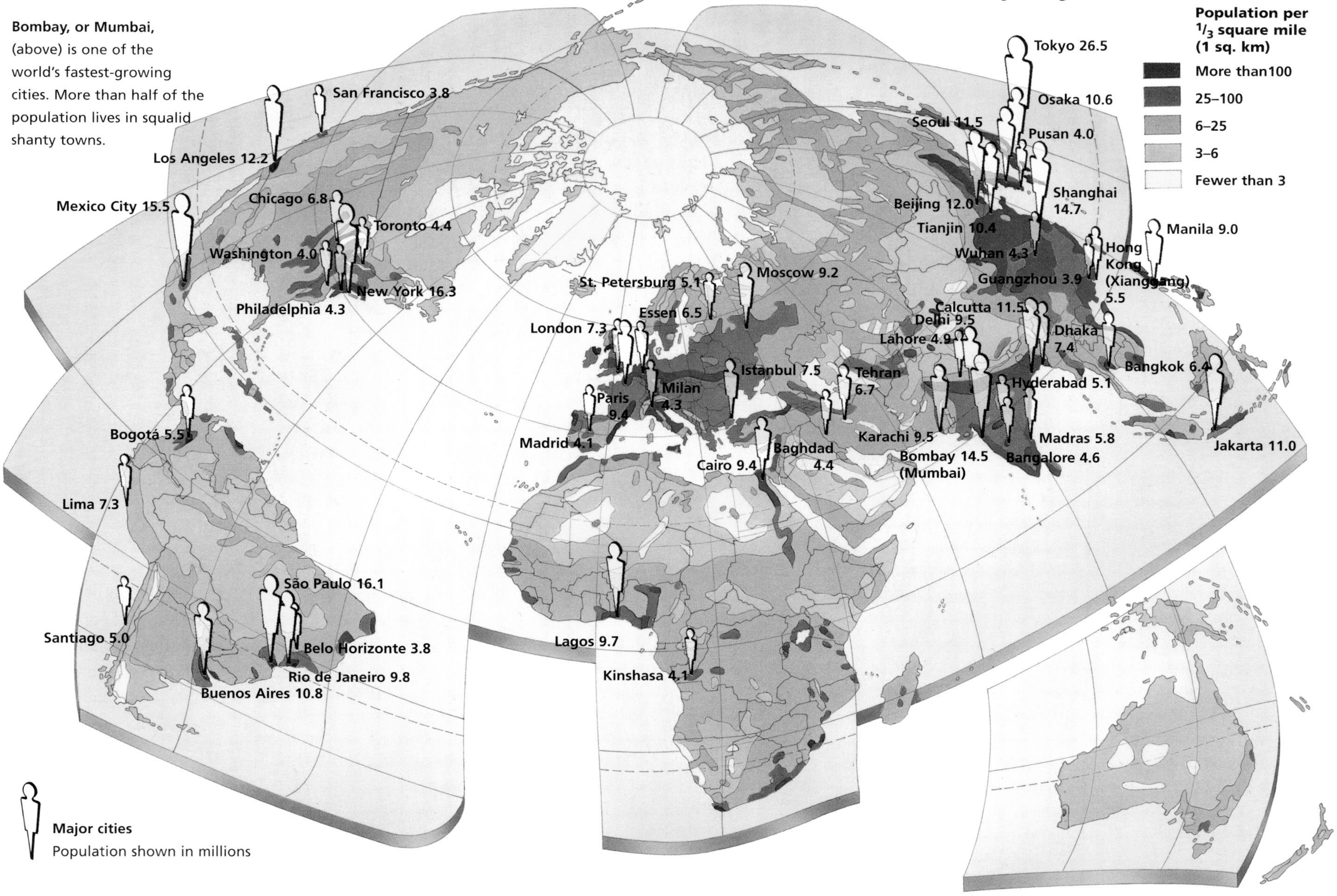

Population per $^{1}/_{3}$ square mile (1 sq. km)
More than100
25–100
6–25
3–6
Fewer than 3

Tokyo 26.5
Osaka 10.6
Seoul 11.5
Pusan 4.0
Shanghai 14.7
Beijing 12.0
Tianjin 10.4
Manila 9.0
Wuhan 4.3
Hong Kong (Xianggang) 5.5
Guangzhou 3.9
Calcutta 11.5
Delhi 9.5
Dhaka 7.4
Lahore 4.9
Bangkok 6.4
Hyderabad 5.1
Madras 5.8
Bangalore 4.6
Jakarta 11.0
Karachi 9.5
Bombay 14.5 (Mumbai)
Tehran 6.7
Baghdad 4.4
Istanbul 7.5
Cairo 9.4
Moscow 9.2
St. Petersburg 5.1
Essen 6.5
London 7.3
Paris 9.6
Milan 4.3
Madrid 4.1
Lagos 9.7
Kinshasa 4.1
San Francisco 3.8
Los Angeles 12.2
Mexico City 15.5
Chicago 6.8
Toronto 4.4
Washington 4.0
New York 16.3
Philadelphia 4.3
Bogotá 5.5
Lima 7.3
São Paulo 16.1
Santiago 5.0
Belo Horizonte 3.8
Rio de Janeiro 9.8
Buenos Aires 10.8

Major cities
Population shown in millions

International migration

Though still exceeded by migration within countries, international migration is at a record level. People move to find work, or to escape persecution, war, and famine. During the first half of the 1990s, people in Eastern Europe moved west following the break-up of the Soviet Union and the reunification of Germany. One million East Germans moved to West Germany as the country reunited. At the same time, around a million Soviet Jews emigrated to Israel. During the 1991 Gulf crisis, five million foreign workers in Iraq, Kuwait, and Saudi Arabia returned to homes in Egypt, Jordan, Yemen, and the Indian subcontinent. Since then, civil wars and persecution have caused major migrations of refugees from Rwanda into the Democratic Republic of the Congo (Zaire) and Tanzania, from Iraq into Turkey, and from Sudan into Ethiopia.

In the second half of the 20th century, many people from Mexico and Central America have moved to the United States, most taking low-paying jobs. However, some migrants, notably the Chinese in Asia and North America, have taken dominant places in their hosts' economies. Today, developed countries are increasingly anxious to restrict entry of "economic" refugees – those regarded as looking for a better life rather than fleeing persecution.

Kurdish refugees (below) fled from the army of Iraq's Saddam Hussein at the end of the Gulf War in 1991, taking the mountain passes from Iraq into Turkey. Most of them later returned home. In the mid-1990s, around 23 million refugees were living in foreign lands, often in poorly equipped camps and dependent on aid.

Wealth and Education

On average, people become richer, healthier, and better educated every year, but more progress is made in some countries than in others. By the start of the 1990s, the total output of the world economy exceeded $20 trillion U.S. dollars. Of this amount, 75 percent was in the hands of the quarter of the world's population living in the industrialized countries of Europe, North America, Australasia, and Japan. In the 1980s, economists argued that inequalities provided the incentives for creating the wealth that would benefit everyone. However, by the mid-1990s, many were saying that too much inequality was harmful for economic growth. The United Nations Development Program (UNDP) reported in 1996 that in the fastest-growing economies growth was stimulated by fair access to land and credit, along with good education and health services.

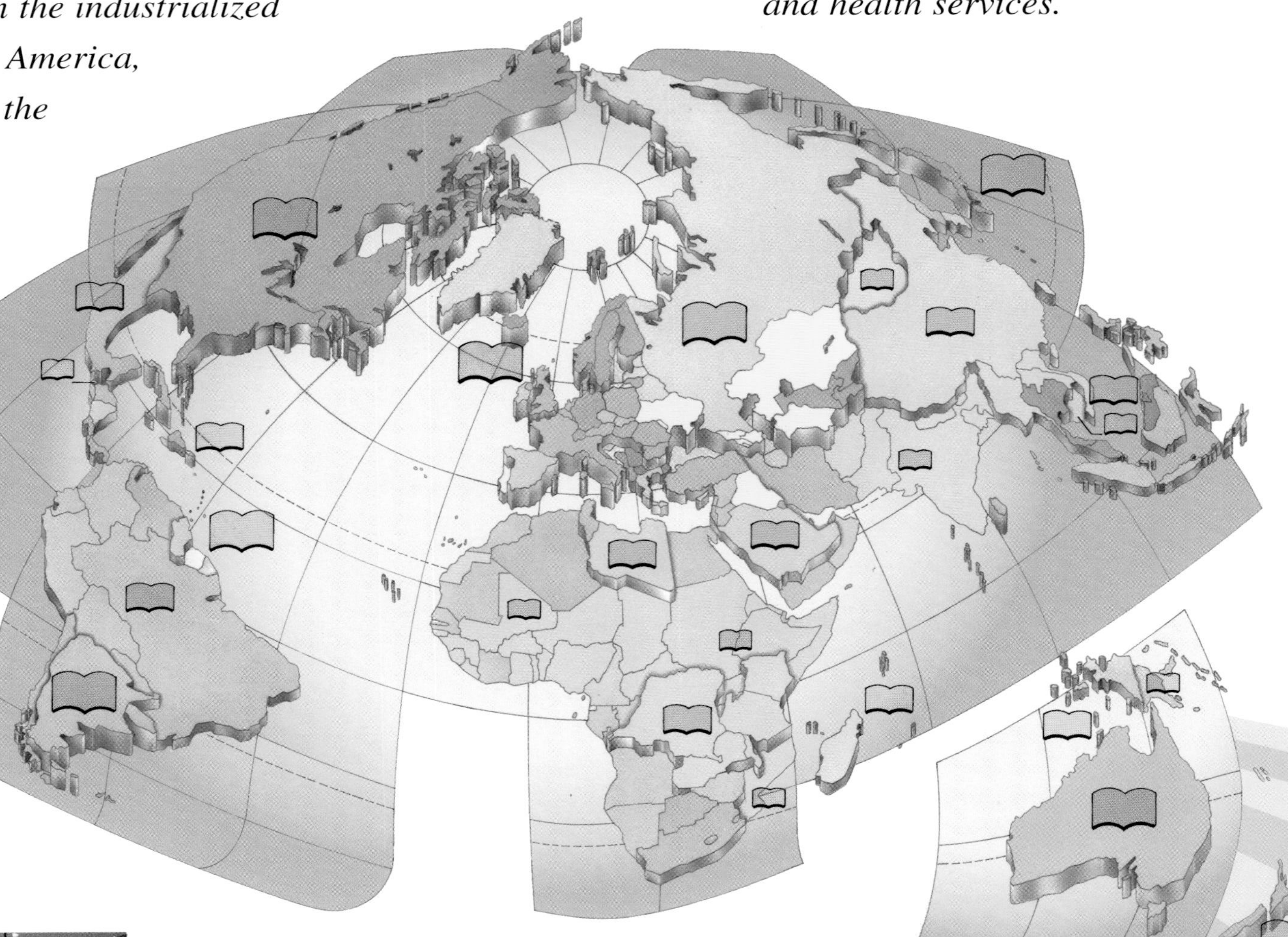

Kuala Lumpur and other Asian cities increasingly resemble their European counterparts, with shopping malls (above), elevated highways, high-rise hotels, and banking centers. Shopping has become an increasingly popular activity in cities all over the world.

The wealth gap

Since about 1980, the world's wealth gap has widened. By the mid-1990s, around half of the world's countries were economically worse off than a decade before, and 19 were worse off than they were in 1960. Many of these countries were in Eastern Europe and central Asia where, following the collapse of communism, industrial economies declined sharply and incomes fell by a fifth on average. Others were in Africa where economies burdened by foreign debts, corruption and sometimes civil war have declined. In Latin America, fast economic advance in countries such as Chile was matched by decline in others, including Nicaragua, which in the mid-1990s owed foreign banks the equivalent of around six years' income for all its citizens.

In contrast, the "tiger" economies of the Far East, such as South Korea, Thailand, Singapore, Malaysia, and China, grew very fast in the 1980s. In China and South Korea, growth exceeded eight percent annually from 1980 to 1995. But these Asian Tigers were also burdened with overvalued currencies, heavily indebted corporations, bad loans, and inflated stock and property prices. A 1997 currency crisis in Thailand spurred an economic crisis throughout the region; even the Japanese economy experienced its worst recession since World War II. But in early 1999 the economies of Japan, South Korea, and Hong Kong showed signs of recovery.

By the mid-1990s there were around 450 U.S.-dollar billionaires in the world – more than one-third of them in North America. Asia was just ahead of Europe, each with about 25 percent of the world's total. The Philippines, where average incomes are a twentieth of those in Britain, had more billionaires than Britain. The combined wealth of these super-rich people exceeded the combined annual incomes of half the population of the world – almost three billion people.

For the average citizen, Switzerland is the most affluent place to live, followed by Japan and Norway. The people of Africa and India are the poorest. Nonetheless, the consumerism of the industrialized way of life is spreading, especially in Asia and Latin America. Brazil, Malaysia, and Cuba have roughly one television per household. However, more expensive items are concentrated in wealthier countries. The United States has fewer than two people to each car, while Africa has one car for every 70 people and China – still the land of the bicycle – has one car for every 670 people.

Computer literacy (above) is a vital skill in the modern workplace. Some poorer places, such as India, run data-processing businesses for large multinational companies. However, these developing countries find it hard to afford a computer for every classroom.

Ethiopia's literacy rate in 1995 was 25 percent for women and 45 percent for men. Adult classes (right) aim to improve these rates, but Ethiopia allocates a relatively small proportion of its total expenditure to education. This amount will need to increase if Ethiopia is to join other countries such as South Korea, where economic advance is aided by substantial investment in education.

Asia's investment in education has meant that in the late 1990s there are more research scientists in Asia (above) than in either Europe or North America.

An increasingly educated population

A generation ago, in 1970, only three children in ten worldwide received secondary education. Now half of all children do, although the figure is fewer than one in ten for much of Africa. Apparently similar countries can vary drastically in their attitude to education. Sri Lanka educates all its children in primary schools; Morocco, which is twice as wealthy, educates only about two-thirds to this level. Standards of education are evident in a country's economic performance. In 1960, South Korea and Pakistan had similar-sized economies, but while the Koreans invested heavily in universal education, Pakistan did not. Pakistan spends ten times more on defense than on schools, and only half of Pakistani boys and one-third of its girls attend primary schools. By 1996 South Korea's economy had grown to be three times that of Pakistan. While investment in education does not guarantee economic success, some economists argue that Asia's economic miracle has been built on good education.

In many countries, women receive less education than men. Most of these are the world's poorest nations, but some are richer nations, such as Saudi Arabia, where cultural attitudes play a role. The greatest difference is in Afghanistan, where 14 percent of females are literate, compared to 45 percent of males.

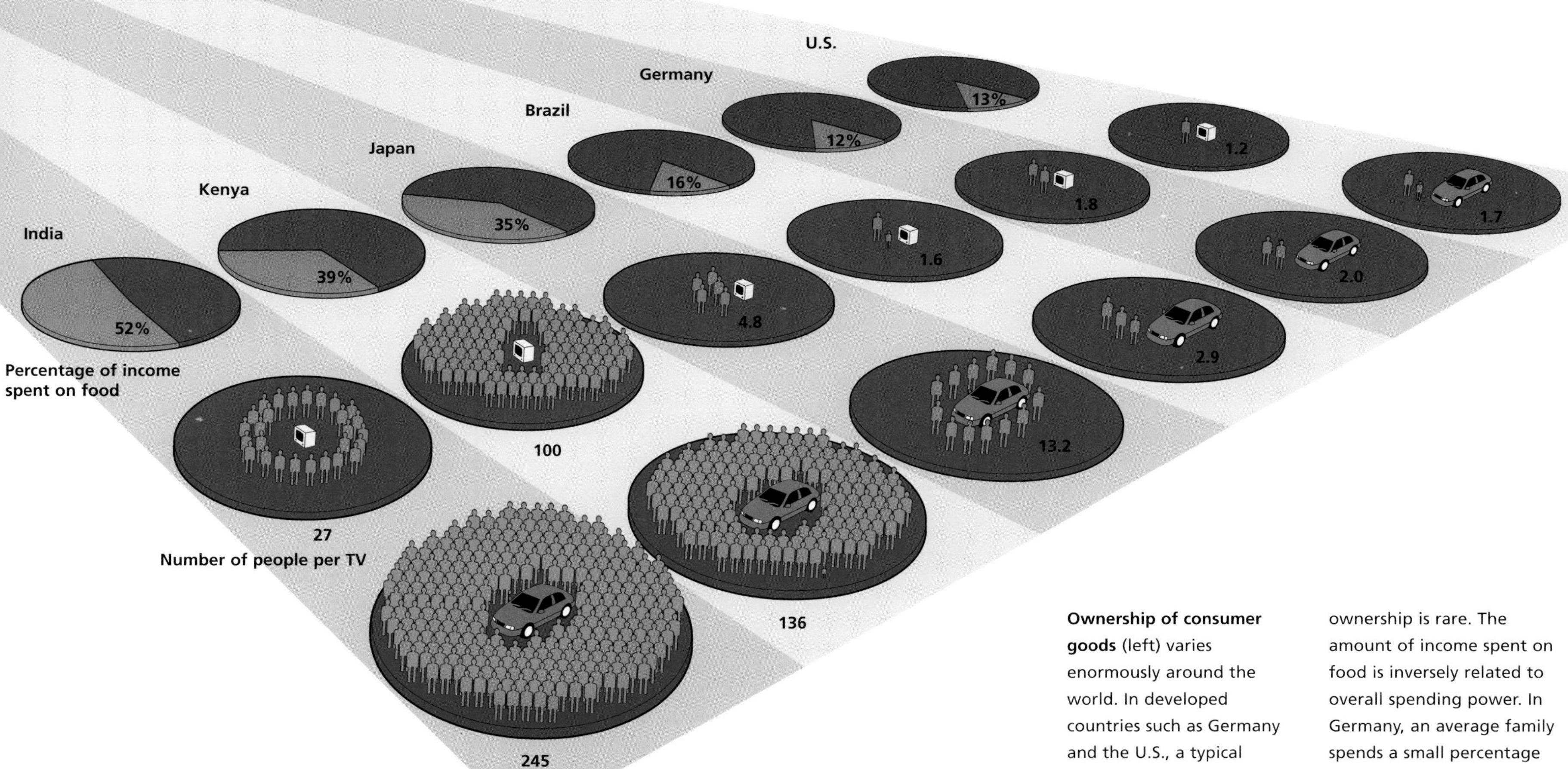

Ownership of consumer goods (left) varies enormously around the world. In developed countries such as Germany and the U.S., a typical family owns at least one car. In poorer countries such as India and Kenya, car ownership is rare. The amount of income spent on food is inversely related to overall spending power. In Germany, an average family spends a small percentage of its income on food, while in India this proportion is more than 50 percent.

Language and Religion

The total number of languages spoken in the world today is unknown, with estimates varying between 3,000 and 10,000. Of these, a handful of languages now dominate; several – such as English and Spanish – have mother-tongue speakers spread over a vast geographical area, far from the language's origin. Today, these dominant languages continue to spread, both as second languages to aid global communication and through people taking their language and customs with them in migrations from one country to another.

Migration has also been important in the spread of religions, along with dissemination by imperial conquests. Three of the world's great religions – Christianity, Islam, and Judaism – began in southwestern Asia. Although in an earlier age a country could be described as Christian or Muslim, for example, today national communities tend to be multi-faith.

A mother tongue is a speaker's native language. Many of the top 12 mother tongues (left) are far more widely used as second languages, while others, such as Hindi and Mandarin Chinese, are concentrated almost entirely in one area.

Punjabi 70 million

French 70 million

German 100 million

Japanese 120 million

Portuguese 135 million

Bengali 150 million

Arabic 150 million

Russian 150 million

Hindi 200 million

Spanish 250 million

English 350 million

World language groups
Number of speakers shown in millions

Speakers	Language group
1,900	Indo-European
797	Sino-Tibetan
198	Austronesian
c.150	African
137	Korean and Japanese
127	Dravidian
122	Hamito-Semitic
90	Uralic and Altaic
37	Austro-Asiatic
16	American Indian and Inuit-Aleut
6	Caucasian
3	Papuan and Australian Aboriginal
<1	Paleo-Asiatic

The world's major languages

Mandarin Chinese is the most widely spoken first language, or mother tongue, with some one billion speakers. However, English is the most widely used language in the world. It is the mother tongue for around 350 million people, and the second language for at least 100 million more. English is also the predominant language used for business and science.

Some major languages are confined more or less to one geographical area. The Indian languages – Hindi, Bengali, Gujerati, and several others – are largely restricted to the Indian subcontinent (together with some overseas Indian communities, notably in South Africa and the West Indies). Similarly, the Chinese languages are broadly confined to China itself, although they are also spoken in Chinese expatriate communities around the world. Other major languages are a legacy of imperialism, and have been spread over a wide area far from their starting point. The whole of Latin America, apart from Brazil (where Portuguese is spoken), is Spanish-speaking. French, English, and Portuguese are the three main second languages of sub-Saharan Africa, while Arabic is spoken from Western Sahara across North Africa and the Arabian Peninsula to Iraq.

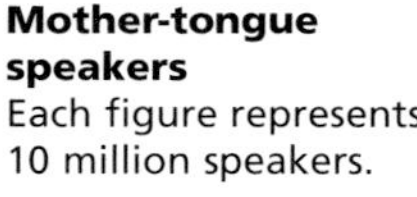

Mother-tongue speakers
Each figure represents 10 million speakers.

Mandarin Chinese 1 billion

Multi-faith societies

Religions act as a complement to nationalism and help to bind peoples together. They can also be divisive and a source of confrontation – as between Protestants and Roman Catholics in Ulster, or Jews and Muslims in Israel. Attempts to modernize established religions – for example, the introduction of women priests in the Church of England – have also led to fierce controversy.

Christians make up one third of the world's population. They divide between Protestant (with a variety of sects), Anglican, Roman Catholic, (whose adherents comprise slightly more than half the total), the Orthodox Church (which, since the collapse of communism in the former Soviet Bloc, has enjoyed a resurgence), and a wide range of often small groups that have moved away from the principal churches. In Islamic countries there has been a rise of fundamentalism in recent years, and this trend has been echoed in the U.S. among extreme Christian groups. Buddhists are found primarily in Asia, and in countries such as Myanmar and Vietnam they have come into growing conflict with authoritarian governments – as has Tibet's spiritual leader, the Dalai Lama, with the government in Beijing. Since the 1960s, as a result of migrations, societies that formerly saw themselves as belonging overwhelming to one faith, such as Christianity in Britain or France, have now become multi-faith societies. This is all the more striking where Christianity is on the wane, as appears to be the case in much of the Western world.

Despite confrontations between faiths, there have also been strong ecumenical efforts to bring faiths closer together. In June 1995, for example, Roman Catholic and Muslim officials announced the formation of a Joint Liaison Committee to explore together their positions on religious and social issues.

The Western Wall (above) is what remains of the wall that surrounded the Temple Mount built by Herod in the first century B.C. It is regarded by Jews as the most sacred ancient shrine of their faith. Judaism is a monotheistic religion which originated more than 3,000 years ago. Unlike both Christianity and Islam, Judaism does not seek to make converts. In 1995 there were just more than 14 million Jews worldwide, of whom less than one-third live in Israel.

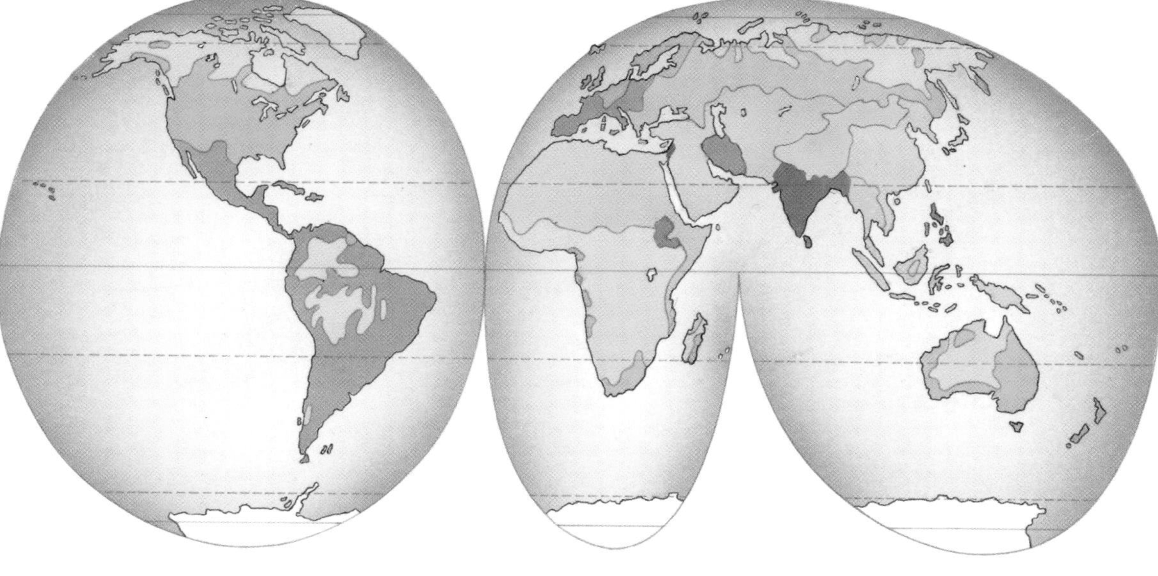

Major world religions
Number of adherents

Christianity (1.9 billion)
- Roman Catholicism
- Protestantism
- Orthodox Christian
- Coptic Christian

Islam (1.1 billion)
- Sunni Muslim
- Shia Muslim

Buddhism (324 million)
- Buddhism with Lamaism
- Buddhism with Confucianism and Taoism
- Buddhism with Shintoism

Other religions
- Hinduism (780 million)
- Judaism (14 million)
- Tribal religions

The Hindu temple at Neasden, London (above), is the largest Hindu temple in the world outside India. Completed in 1995, its construction was sponsored by the Swaminarayan sect, which has a large following in Britain.

Vatican City is the home of the Pope, head of the Roman Catholic Church. On special occasions conducted annually by the Pope, such as Easter Mass, huge crowds gather before St Peter's Church (right). The world's Roman Catholic population exceeds one billion.

The Environment

In the 1990s, environmental problems became part of international politics, reflecting the fact that human actions can now profoundly alter Earth's basic features. Changes to the chemistry of the atmosphere, the climate, the extent of forests and deserts, and the diversity of species that inhabit the Earth are now matters of global concern. The Earth Summit, held in Rio de Janeiro in 1992 to promote global consensus on such issues, resulted in treaties to limit the extent of climate change and decline of biodiversity; these were followed by other agreements dealing with deforestation and desertification. Fulfilling these treaties, however, requires implementing more sustainable forms of development that minimize damage to the environment and its resources.

The rise in sea levels is a particular problem for the Republic of Maldives in the Indian Ocean (right). The country consists of hundreds of islands, all less than six-and-a-half feet (two m) above sea level. Sandbags and sea walls are used to protect the shoreline.

The Amazon basin in Brazil contains the world's largest surviving rain forest. In the mid-1990s the rate of deforestation was still as high as in the late 1980s, when the destruction made headlines worldwide (below left).

Endangered species

Earth sustains between 15 million and 100 million species, although most of these are still to be identified by biologists. Dozens of species are believed to become extinct every day, as their habitats are destroyed to make way for human activity. The extinction of many species passes unnoticed, but some rare animal and plant species are closely monitored to check their remaining numbers. Mammals known to be under threat include the forest-dwelling Sumatran rhinoceros, the giant panda of China, and Rwanda's mountain gorilla. Rare birds include the Siberian crane, while in the ocean, turtles, the blue whale, and the great white shark are at risk. The green pitcher plant of the United States is just one of many endangered plants.

Deforestation

Tropical rain forests support about half the world's species. Economic development and population increases have forced people to colonize these wildernesses, which are disappearing faster than any other type of habitat. Natural forests are also threatened in the western United States and Canada, while in Europe remaining "old growth" forests are being replaced by commercial plantations of single species. Only the remote Siberian forests remain largely untouched. Besides destroying the wildlife, deforestation has other impacts on the environment. Deprived of vegetation cover, thin tropical soils are leached and eroded by heavy rains. This causes silting of rivers, and often leaves the land useless for farming. Large-scale deforestation can alter climate by reducing rainfall and by increasing the amount of carbon dioxide (a "greenhouse gas") in the atmosphere.

Major deforesting countries
Trees show total remaining forest area for each country in acres and hectares. Percentages indicate decrease in forest area, 1983–93.

The changing climate

Climate change is being brought about by increasing amounts of greenhouse gases (which trap solar heat) in the atmosphere. Human activity – mainly from burning coal and oil, but also from deforestation – has significantly raised the concentration of carbon dioxide. This concentration is expected to double from 1992 levels by the year 2100, creating an average global warming of four to seven degrees Fahrenheit (two to four degrees C), and leading to droughts in Europe, new deserts in the interior of continents, and "super-hurricanes" in coastal regions. As ice caps on land melt, scientists predict a 20-inch (50-cm) rise in sea level globally, causing floods in low-lying areas.

While there is still speculation, the United Nations' scientific advisers say that warming has probably already begun. Ten of the eleven warmest years on record have occurred since 1980, glaciers are retreating, and sea levels are rising. In 1992, world leaders agreed on the need to cut carbon dioxide emissions, which scientists say must be reduced to 50 percent of the 1992 level to stabilize the climate. Separately, the stratosphere's ozone layer has begun to thin, and an ozone "hole" forms each spring over Antarctica. The discovery of ozone depletion in the early 1980s resulted in a global ban on chemicals such as chlorofluorocarbons (CFCs) that are believed to destroy ozone. Even so, scientists predict it will be 2050 before the ozone layer over the Antarctic is restored.

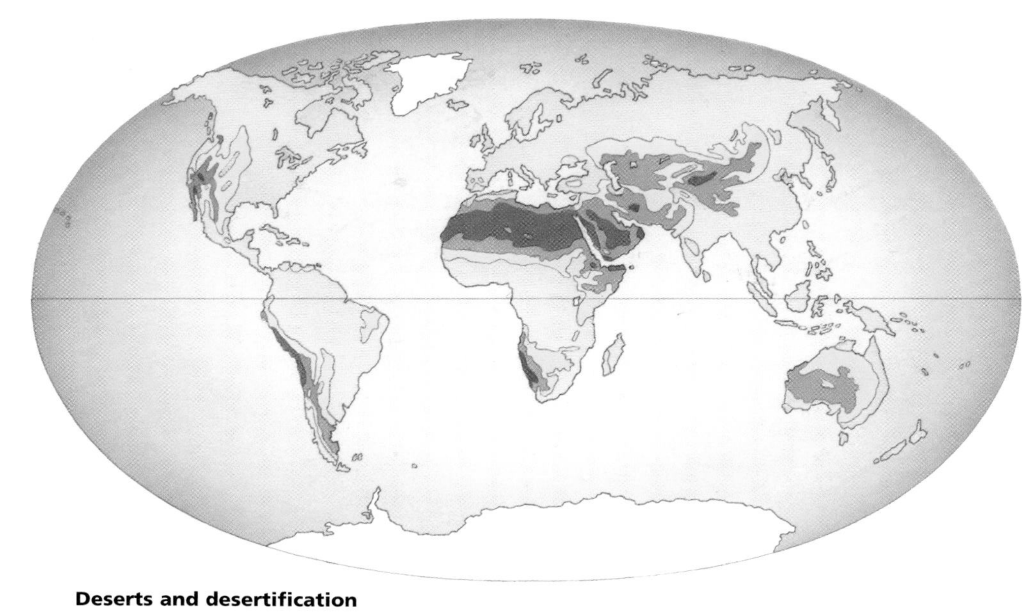

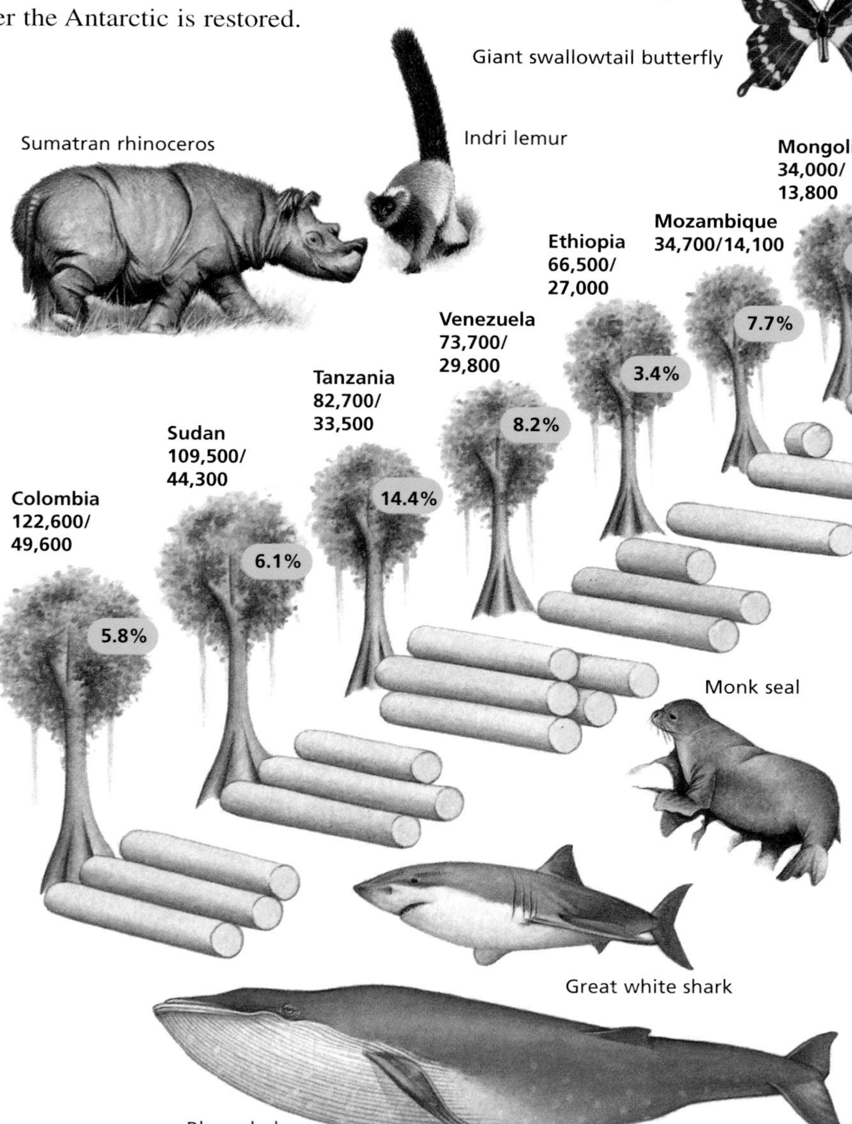

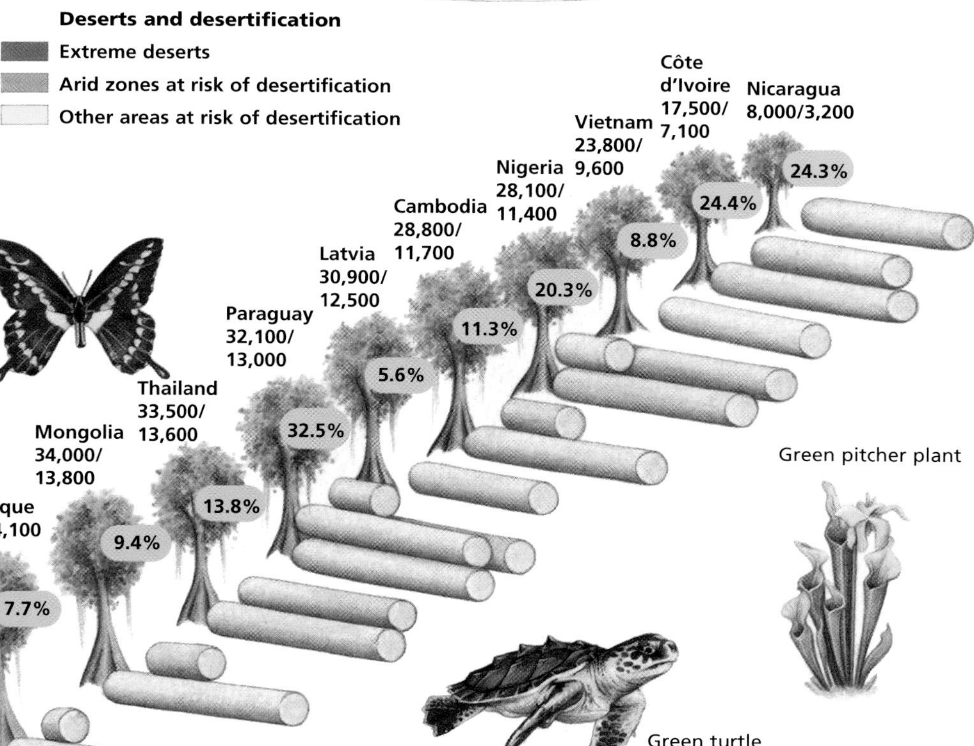

Deforestation rates vary widely from country to country (above). Over recent years, Brazil has lost the greatest area of forested land, while Paraguay has lost the largest proportion of its forest.

Many species of animals and plants are currently threatened with extinction (above). The major cause of extinction is loss of habitat; other causes include hunting, competition from introduced species, and pollution of land and sea.

Soil degradation and desertification

In 1992 the United Nations Environment Program (UNEP) estimated that two-thirds of the world's dry lands are affected by soil degradation and desertification. Increasing human populations – with the resulting extra demands on agriculture – together with the effects of drought years, place vegetation in arid areas under increasing stress. Ecosystems on the margins of deserts are usually resilient, and can remain dormant for several years before bursting into life when the rains return. Even so, these dry areas may be damaged by deforestation, excessive grazing, or cultivation by farmers who cannot afford to nourish the soil with fertilizer.

Planting trees or constructing fences can halt advancing dunes that threaten to bury oases, as in the Sahara (right). Desertification caused mainly by long droughts and poor farming occurs in arid regions bordering deserts.

International Cooperation

In the aftermath of the Second World War, people began to think of the world as a single community with shared problems. This belief persisted despite the divisions of the Cold War: If the countries of the world could not work together, then they would face disaster separately. In the quarter century after 1945 the United Nations emerged as a modern attempt at world government. Economically advanced countries accepted that they had a responsibility to assist in the development of the newly independent nations that emerged from the break-up of the old empires, and numerous regional groups were formed to promote cooperation, security, and economic growth.

Trusteeship Council

General Assembly

Secretariat

Economic and Social Council

Security Council

International Court of Justice

The General Assembly consists of all the UN members. It meets regularly once a year, and each member has one vote.

The Trusteeship Council is concerned with territories that are not yet fully self-governing. Since 1994 it has met only occasionally.

The Secretariat carries out the day-to-day work of the UN under the leadership of the Secretary-General.

The Economic and Social Council co-ordinates matters between the UN and the specialized agencies. It is a central policy-making body.

The International Court of Justice is the independent judicial organ of the UN, composed of 15 judges.

The Security Council holds ultimate power in the UN. Of the 15 members, five – the U.S., Russia, Britain, France, and China – are permanent and have the power to veto decisions.

The United Nations

The United Nations was created when representatives from 50 countries met in 1945 in San Francisco. By 1997 membership had grown to 185 countries, to include almost all the countries of the world. UN official languages are English, French, Chinese, Russian, Spanish, and Arabic.

The United Nations Charter established six main bodies. The Secretary-General is the chief administrative officer, elected for a five-year term by the General Assembly. In addition, there are 14 major programs and funds devoted to achieving economic and social progress in developing countries, as well as a number of specialized agencies.

During its first 40 years, the UN faced many problems, including Middle East conflicts, the Korean War, and the Congo crises. However, during this period, solutions were nearly always hampered by rivalries between the superpowers. The end of the Cold War raised expectations of a more active United Nations.

International aid

After 1945, aid – the flow of financial resources and technical assistance from developed to developing countries – became a significant aspect of international relations. In 1948 massive U.S. aid in the form of the Marshall Plan was provided to assist the recovery of war-torn Europe. This was followed by the Colombo Plan of 1950, which emphasized mutual cooperation by providing aid to developing countries within the British Commonwealth. When in 1956 the U.S.S.R. took over the financing of Egypt's Aswan High Dam from the United States and Britain, aid became an expression of Cold War hostility between the superpowers.

The end of the Cold War in 1989 saw a sharp drop in aid. Today most aid donors are rich Western nations; however, since the 1970s wealthy OPEC countries have also been important donors. The biggest recipients of aid are the least developed countries with huge populations, such as Bangladesh.

The principal aid donors (below) are Western European countries, the U.S. and Canada, and Japan. The main aid recipients include five of the world's most densely populated countries – China, India, Pakistan, Bangladesh, and Indonesia – as well as Mozambique, the world's poorest nation.

Denmark	Sweden	Canada	Netherlands	Italy	U.K.	Germany	France	U.S.	Japan
1,446	1,819	2,250	2,517	2,705	3,197	6,818	8,466	9,927	13,239

Top ten aid donors (U.S.$ millions)

UN troops (above left) from many countries were deployed during the civil war which led to the disintegration of former Yugoslavia during the 1990s. Attempts to safeguard supplies of humanitarian aid or to separate the combatants involved the European Union and NATO as well as the UN.

Somalia collapsed into violence between ethnic groups at the end of the 1980s. The famine in 1992 was the result of four years of civil war and two years of drought. International efforts (right) brought relief to the starving.

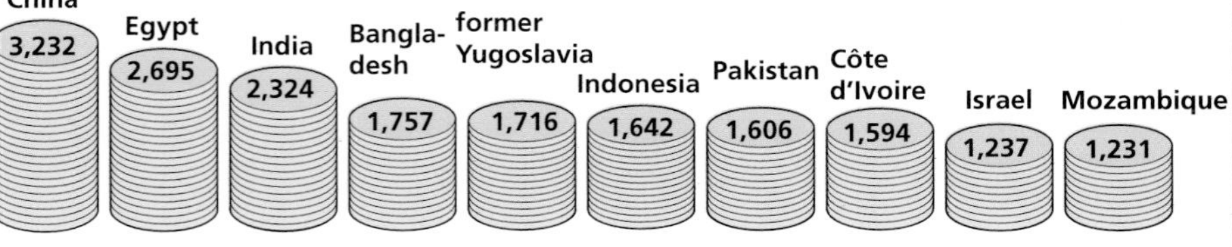

Top ten aid recipients (U.S.$ millions)

Map legend

Regional maps (pages 2-176)

Note: An asterisk (*) denotes symbols that appear on both the regional maps and the metropolitan area maps. Symbols that are unique to the metropolitan area maps are identified in the lower section.

Hydrographic Features

Perennial river *
Seasonal river *
Dam * (Aswan High Dam)
Falls (Salto Ángel)
Aqueduct * (Los Angeles Aqueduct)
Lake, reservoir *
Seasonal lake *
Salt lake
Seasonal salt lake
Dry lake *
Lake surface elevation (395)
Swamp, marsh
Reef *
Glacier/ice sheet

Cultural Features

National park, reservation
Point of interest
Wall
Ruins
Military installation
Polar research station
International date line (International Date Line)

Topographic Features

All elevations and depths are given in meters.

764 Depth of water
2278 Elevation above sea level
1700 Elevation below sea level
Mountain pass *
Huo Shan 1774 Mountain peak/elevation *

The highest elevation on each continent is underlined. *

The highest elevation in each country is shown in boldface.

HIMALAYAS / ALPS / EASTERN GHĀTS — Mountain range *
SUDAN / LIBYAN DESERT — Physical region
NEW GUINEA / Melville Island — Island
Cape York — Cape

Political Features

International boundaries (First-order political unit)

Demarcated
Disputed (de facto)
Disputed (de jure)
Indefinite/undefined
Demarcation line

Internal boundaries

State/province
Third-order (counties, oblasts, etc.)
NORMANDIE — Cultural/historic region
(Denmark) — Administering country

Transportation Features

Motorway/special highway
Major road *
Other road *
Trail *
Major railway
Other railway
Navigable canal *
Tunnel
Ferry
Bridge *
International airport
Other airport

Cities and Towns

The size of symbol and type indicates the relative importance of the locality.

LONDON
CHICAGO
Milwaukee
Tacna
Iquitos
Old Crow
Mettawa
Urban area

Capitals

MEXICO CITY / Bonn — Country, dependency
RIO DE JANEIRO / Perth — State/province
MANCHESTER / Chester — County

Metropolitan area maps (pages 178-206)

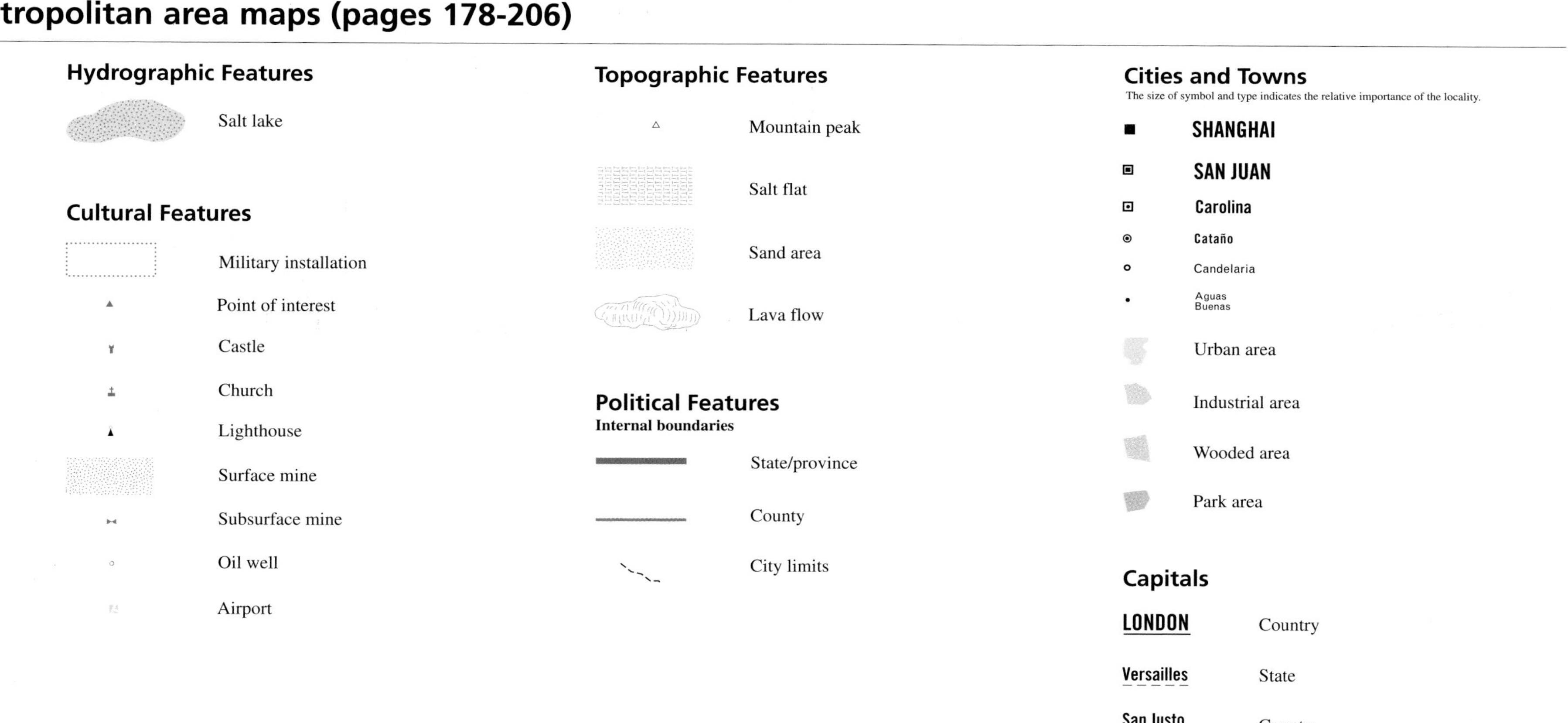

Hydrographic Features

Salt lake

Cultural Features

Military installation
Point of interest
Castle
Church
Lighthouse
Surface mine
Subsurface mine
Oil well
Airport

Topographic Features

Mountain peak
Salt flat
Sand area
Lava flow

Political Features

Internal boundaries

State/province
County
City limits

Cities and Towns

The size of symbol and type indicates the relative importance of the locality.

SHANGHAI
SAN JUAN
Carolina
Cataño
Candelaria
Aguas Buenas
Urban area
Industrial area
Wooded area
Park area

Capitals

LONDON — Country
Versailles — State
San Justo — County

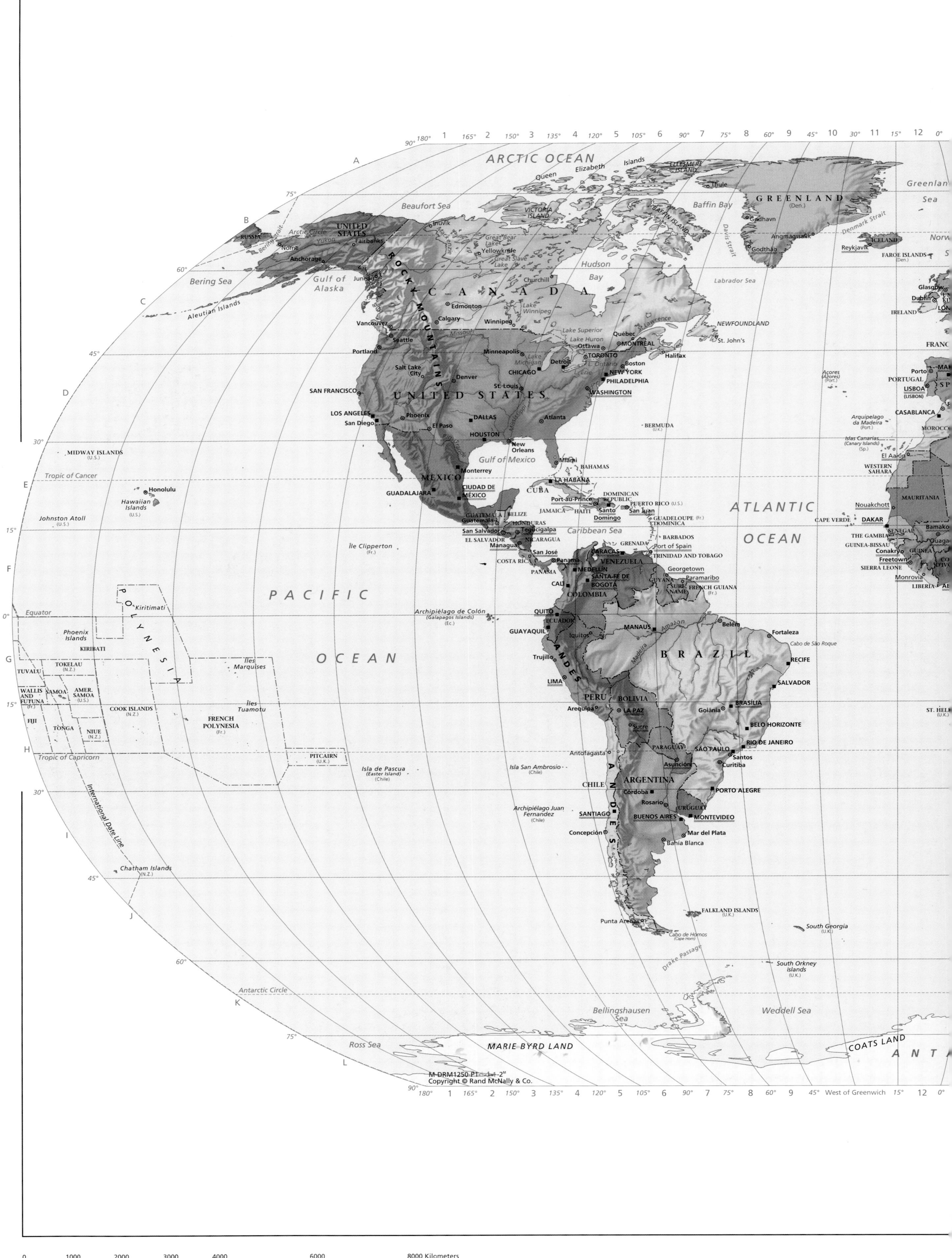

0 1000 2000 3000 4000 6000 8000 Kilometers

0 500 1000 1500 2000 3000 4000 5000 Miles

Scale 1 : 80,000,000 Robinson Projection

ARCTIC OCEAN
Zemlja Franca-Iosifa
Barents Sea
Novaja Zemlja
Karskoe more
more Laptevyh
Novosibirskie ostrova
Vostočno-Sibirskoe more
Hammerfest
Murmansk
Vorkuta
Igarka
Tiksi
Arhangel'sk
FINLAND
Helsinki
SANKT-PETERBURG (ST. PETERSBURG)
Stockholm
SWEDEN
ESTONIA
LATVIA
LITH.
POLAND
BELARUS
WARSZAWA
MOSKVA (MOSCOW)
NIŽNIJ NOVGOROD
Perm'
Ekaterinburg
Samara
Čeljabinsk
Omsk
Novosibirsk
Krasnojarsk
Jakutsk
Magadan
R U S S I A
Arctic Circle
Sea of Okhotsk
Bering Sea
Aleutian Is.
Petropavlovsk-Kamčatskij
ostrov Sahalin
Kuril'skie ostrova
KYIV
UKRAINE
Volgograd
BUDAPEST
ROMANIA
Beograd
Sofija
BULGARIA
Black Sea
ISTANBUL
ANKARA
TURKEY
GEORGIA
BAKI
Astana (Akmola)
KAZAKHSTAN
Aral Sea
Irkutsk
Čita
Ulaanbaatar
MONGOLIA
Habarovsk
Harbin
ALTAI
ALMATY
Ürümqi
UZBEKISTAN
KYRGYZSTAN
TAŠKENT
TURKMENISTAN
TIEN SHAN
GOBI DESERT
Hohhot
BEIJING
SHENYANG
Vladivostok
Sapporo
Hokkaidō
ITALY
ROMA
Napoli
GREECE
ATHINA (ATHENS)
Izmir
Mediterranean Sea
CYPRUS
SYRIA
LEBANON
ISRAEL
'Ammān
JORDAN
BAGHDĀD
IRAQ
TEHRAN
Eşfahān
IRAN
KĀBOL
AFGHANISTAN
Islamabad
Rawalpindi
LAHORE
PAKISTAN
TIANJIN
Dalian
NORTH KOREA
P'yongyang
SOUL
SOUTH KOREA
PUSAN
Sea of Japan
Sendai
JAPAN
HONSHU
TŌKYŌ
ŌSAKA
Fukuoka
C H I N A
Qingdao
Yellow Sea
Xi'an
Nanjing
SHANGHAI
WUHAN
Chengdu
Chongqing
Changsha
Lhasa
HIMALAYAS
NEPAL
Kāthmāndau
BHUTAN
DELHI
New Delhi
TUNISIA
Tarābulus
Banghāzī
EL-ISKANDARĪYA (ALEXANDRIA)
EL-QÂHIRA (CAIRO)
LIBYA
EGYPT
Nile
KUWAIT
BAHRAIN
QATAR
Abū Zaby
U.A.E.
Masqaţ
OMAN
AR-RIYĀD (RIYADH)
SAUDI ARABIA
Red Sea
KARĀCHI
Ahmadābād
INDIA
BANGL.
DHAKA
CALCUTTA
MYANMAR (BURMA)
Kunming
GUANGZHOU
XIANGGANG (HONG KONG)
T'AIPEI
TAIWAN
Nansei-shotō
PACIFIC OCEAN
Tropic of Cancer
NIGER
CHAD
Lake Chad
N'Djamena
SUDAN
Al-Kharţūm (Khartoum)
ERITREA
Asmera
YEMEN
San'a
Adan
DJIBOUTI
Djibouti
ETHIOPIA
ĀDĪS ĀBEBA
SOMALIA
Gees Gwardafuy
Arabian Sea
MUMBAI (BOMBAY)
Pune
HYDERĀBĀD
BANGALORE
CHENNAI (MADRAS)
Kochi
SRI LANKA
Colombo
Bay of Bengal
YANGON (RANGOON)
LAOS
Viangchan
THAILAND
KRUNG THEP (BANGKOK)
CAMBODIA
VIETNAM
HA NOI
South China Sea
Phnum Pénh
THANH-PHO HO CHI MINH (HO CHI MINH CITY) (SAIGON)
Andaman Islands (India)
Nicobar Islands (India)
LUZON
PHILIPPINES
MANILA
Philippine Sea
NORTHERN MARIANA ISLANDS (U.S.)
GUAM (U.S.)
WAKE ISLAND (U.S.)
MARSHALL ISLANDS
FEDERATED STATES OF MICRONESIA
MICRONESIA
Davao
MINDANAO
PALAU
Kano
NIGERIA
Abuja
CAMEROON
Yaoundé
CENTRAL AFRICAN REPUBLIC
Bangui
UGANDA
Kampala
KENYA
NAIROBI
Muqdisho
GABON
CONGO
Brazzaville
DEM. REP. OF THE CONGO
KINSHASA
RWANDA
Kigali
BURUNDI
Bujumbura
Lake Tanganyika
TANZANIA
Dodoma
Zanzibar
Dar es Salaam
MALDIVES
SEYCHELLES
BRITISH INDIAN OCEAN TERRITORY
Medan
Kuala Lumpur
MALAYSIA
SINGAPORE
BRUNEI
BORNEO (KALIMANTAN)
Banjarmasin
SULAWESI (CELEBES)
Ujungpandang
SUMATERA (SUMATRA)
JAKARTA
INDONESIA
Surabaya
JAWA (JAVA)
PAPUA NEW GUINEA
NEW GUINEA
Port Moresby
NAURU
KIRIBATI
Equator
SOLOMON ISLANDS
TUVALU
MELANESIA
LUANDA
ANGOLA
Lobito
Lubumbashi
ZAMBIA
Lusaka
MALAWI
Lilongwe
MOZAMBIQUE
Harare
ZIMBABWE
COMOROS
Mozambique Channel
MADAGASCAR
Antananarivo
MAURITIUS
RÉUNION (Fr.)
NAMIBIA
Windhoek
Walvis Bay
BOTSWANA
Gaborone
Pretoria
JOHANNESBURG
Maputo
SWAZILAND
Durban
SOUTH AFRICA
LESOTHO
Cape Town
Cape of Good Hope
Port Elizabeth
INDIAN OCEAN
Cape York
Darwin
Cairns
Coral Sea
VANUATU
FIJI
Suva
NEW CALEDONIA (Fr.)
Nouméa
Rockhampton
Tropic of Capricorn
Alice Springs
AUSTRALIA
Brisbane
Perth
Darling
Adelaide
SYDNEY
Canberra
MELBOURNE
Tasman Sea
TASMANIA
Hobart
Auckland
NORTH ISLAND
NEW ZEALAND
Wellington
SOUTH ISLAND
Christchurch
International Date Line
SOUTHERN OCEAN
Archipel de Kerguelen (Fr.)
Antarctic Circle
ENDERBY LAND
WILKES LAND
ICA
of Greenwich

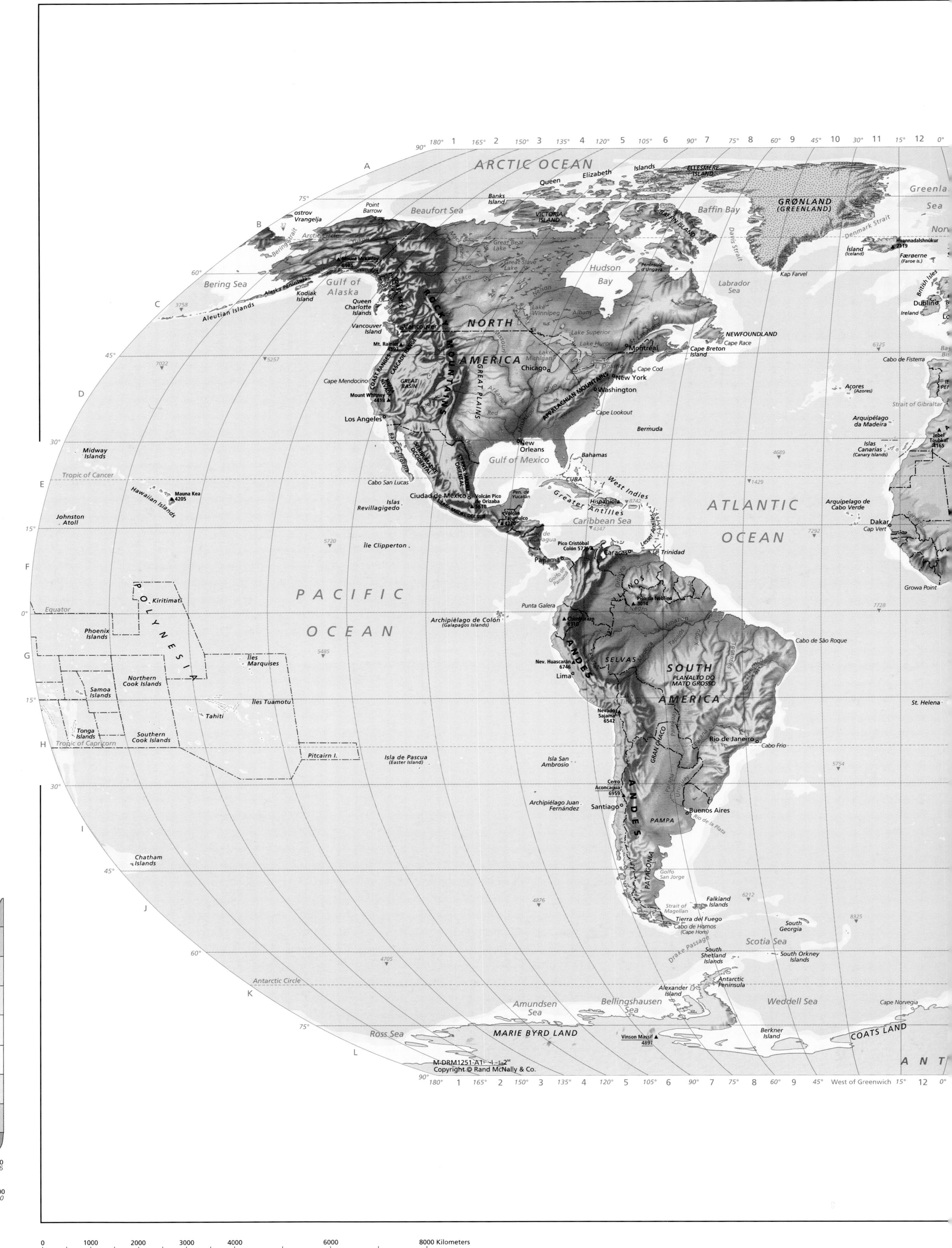

0 1000 2000 3000 4000 6000 8000 Kilometers
0 500 1000 1500 2000 3000 4000 5000 Miles

Scale 1 : 80,000,000 Robinson Projection

ARCTIC OCEAN
Barents Sea
Karskoe more
more Laptevyh
Vostočno-Sibirskoe more
Zemlja Franca-Iosifa
Severnaja Zemlja
Novosibirskie ostrova
SIBIR' (SIBERIA)
ZAPADNO-SIBIRSKAJA RAVNINA (WEST SIBERIAN PLAIN)
ASIA
Moskva (Moscow)
Ekaterinburg
Black Sea
Mediterranean Sea
Caspian Sea
Bering Sea
Sea of Okhotsk
Sea of Japan
Yellow Sea
East China Sea
South China Sea
Philippine Sea
Ulaanbaatar
Beijing
Shanghai
Tōkyō
Delhi
Mumbai (Bombay)
Krung Thep
Manila
Jakarta
GOBI DESERT
KUNLUN SHAN
QING ZANG GAOYUAN
HIMALAYAS
TIEN SHAN
HINDU KUSH
ALTAI
ARABIAN PENINSULA
Arabian Sea
Bay of Bengal
INDIAN OCEAN
PACIFIC OCEAN
SOUTHERN OCEAN
AFRICA
MICRONESIA
MELANESIA
AUSTRALIA
GREAT DIVIDING RANGE
Sydney
Melbourne
Tasman Sea
Coral Sea
NORTH ISLAND
SOUTH ISLAND
TASMANIA
ENDERBY LAND
WILKES LAND
VICTORIA LAND
Ross Sea
Antarctic Circle
Tropic of Cancer
Tropic of Capricorn
Equator

Scale 1 : 12,500,000 Conic Equidistant Projection

BARENTS SEA
FINLAND
ESTONIA
LATVIA
LITHUANIA
BELARUS
UKRAINE
MOLDOVA
ROMANIA
BULGARIA
RUSSIA
KAZAKHSTAN
UZBEKISTAN
TURKMENISTAN
GEORGIA
ARMENIA
AZERBAIJAN
TURKEY
SYRIA
IRAQ
IRAN
CYPRUS
NORTH CYPRUS
LEBANON
BLACK SEA
CASPIAN SEA
Sea of Azov
Gulf of Finland
Gulf of Riga
BELOE MORE (WHITE SEA)
KOL'SKIJ POLUOSTROV (KOLA PENINSULA)
POLUOSTROV KANIN
URAL'SKIE GORY (URAL MOUNTAINS)
ZAPADNO-SIBIRSKAJA RAVNINA (WEST SIBERIAN PLAIN)
CASPIAN DEPRESSION (PRIKASPIJSKAJA NIZMENNOST')
CAUCASUS
KRYMS'KYI PIVOSTRIV (CRIMEAN PENINSULA)
ANADOLU (ANATOLIA)
TOROS DAĞLARI (TAURUS MOUNTAINS)
KURDISTAN
MESOPOTAMIA
RESHTEH-YE KŪHHĀ-YE ALBORZ
KŪHHĀ-YE ZAGROS
BALKAN PENINSULA
CARPATHIAN MTS.
Murmansk
Arhangel'sk
SANKT-PETERBURG (ST. PETERSBURG)
MOSKVA (MOSCOW)
NIŽNIJ NOVGOROD
KAZAN'
SAMARA
PERM'
EKATERINBURG
ČELJABINSK
UFA
SARATOV
VOLGOGRAD
ROSTOV-NA-DONU
KHARKIV
KYÏV (KIEV)
DNIPROPETROVS'K
DONETS'K
ODESA
MINSK
Vilnius
Rīga
Tallinn
Chişinău
BUCUREŞTI (BUCHAREST)
SOFIJA (SOFIA)
İSTANBUL
ANKARA
İZMIR
ATHÍNA (ATHENS)
Tbilisi
Yerevan
BAKI (BAKU)
TEHRĀN
BAGHDĀD
ESFAHĀN
OMSK
Nicosia
gora El'brus 5642
Ağrı Dağı 5137
Qolleh-ye Damāvand 5604

GREENLAND SEA
ÍSLAND (ICELAND)
Reykjavík
Hvannadalshnúkur 2119
Arctic Circle
NORWEGIAN SEA
FÆRØERNE (FAROE ISLANDS)
SHETLAND ISLANDS
ORKNEY ISLANDS
Rockall
ATLANTIC OCEAN
BRITISH ISLES
HEBRIDES
Ben Nevis 1343
GRAMPIAN MTS.
Aberdeen
Edinburgh
Glasgow
Newcastle upon Tyne
PENNINES
IRELAND
Dublin
Belfast
Carrauntoohil 1038
Cork
IRISH SEA
Liverpool
Manchester
Snowdon 1085
CAMBRIAN MTS.
Birmingham
Bristol
London
GREAT BRITAIN
NORTH SEA
English Channel
Strait of Dover
CHANNEL ISLANDS
Isle of Wight
ISLES OF SCILLY
Land's End
Skagerrak
Kattegat
JYLLAND (JUTLAND)
København
Ålesund
Trondheim
Galdhøpiggen 2469
Bergen
Oslo
Stavanger
Kristiansand
Göteborg
Stockholm
Norrköping
Sundsvall
Kebnekaise 2111
Tromsø
Narvik
Bodø
LOFOTEN
VESTERÅLEN
GOTLAND
ÖLAND
Bornholm
Malmö
FRISIAN ISLANDS
Amsterdam
Rotterdam
Hamburg
Kiel
Rügen
VORPOMMERN
Berlin
Gdańsk
Bydgoszcz
Poznań
Wrocław
HARZ
Leipzig
Düsseldorf
Köln
Bonn
Bruxelles
ARDENNES
Luxembourg
Frankfurt am Main
ORE MTS.
SILESIA
SUDETES
Praha
ČECHY
MORAVA
BOHEMIAN FOREST
München
Wien
Bratislava
Le Havre
Brest
BRETAGNE
NORMANDIE
Paris
Orléans
Nantes
CHAMPAGNE
BOURGOGNE
VOSGES
SCHWARZWALD
JURA
Bern
Lake Constance
Danube
Loire
Seine
Rhine
Bay of Biscay
Bordeaux
MASSIF CENTRAL
Puy de Sancy 1885
Lyon
Mont Blanc 4807
ALPS
Grossglockner 3798
TAUERN
Piz Bernina 4049
DOLOMITI
Milano
Torino
Venézia
Trieste
Ljubljana
Zagreb
SLAVONIJA
Balaton
CÉVENNES
Barre des Écrins 4102
Toulouse
PYRENEES
Aneto 3404
Marseille
Nice
Genova
Golfe du Lion
LIGURIAN SEA
Bologna
Firenze
Ancona
APPENNINO
ADRIATIC SEA
DALMATIA
Sarajevo
Durmitor 2522
A Coruña
GALICIA
CORDILLERA CANTÁBRICA
Bilbao
Porto
CASTILLA LA VIEJA
SISTEMA IBÉRICO
SISTEMA CENTRAL
IBERIAN PENINSULA
Madrid
Lisboa (Lisbon)
Tagus
CASTILLA LA NUEVA
SIERRA MORENA
CATALUNYA
Barcelona
València
Sevilla
ANDALUCÍA
CORD. PENIBÉTICA
SIERRA NEVADA
Mulhacén 3482
Granada
Málaga
Cádiz
Murcia
Strait of Gibraltar
Gibraltar
Tanger
ILLES BALEARS (BALEARIC ISLANDS)
MALLORCA
Menorca
Palma de Mallorca
Eivissa
CORSE (CORSICA)
Monte Cinto 2706
Ajaccio
SARDEGNA (SARDINIA)
Punta La Marmora 1834
Cagliari
Roma (Rome)
Napoli (Naples)
Vesuvio 1277
Bari
TYRRHENIAN SEA
Golfo di Taranto
ISOLE EOLIE (ISOLE LIPARI)
Palermo
Messina
Monte Etna 3323
SICILIA (SICILY)
Malta
IONIAN SEA
MEDITERRANEAN
Tunis
Jebel Chambi 1544
El Djazaïr (Algiers)
Qacentina
Wahran
ATLAS TELLIEN
ATLAS SAHARIEN
ATLAS MOUNTAINS
MOYEN ATLAS
HAUT ATLAS
RIF
Jbel Tidirhin 2456
Rabat
Casablanca
Meknès
Fès
Oujda
Safi
Marrakech
Agadir
Jebel Toubkal 4165
Meters / Feet
4000 13120
3000 9840
2000 6560
1000 3280
500 1640
200 656
Sea Level
200 656
2000 6560
M-DRM3301-A1
Copyright © Rand McNally & Co.
West of Greenwich 0° East of Greenwich
0 200 400 800 1200 Kilometers
0 100 200 400 600 800 Miles
Scale 1 : 12,500,000
Conic Equidistant Projection

BARENTS SEA
ostrov Kolguev
mys Kanin Nos
mys Svjatoj Nos
POLUOSTROV KANIN
Češskaja guba
Nar'jan-Mar
Arctic Circle
Murmansk
Inarijärvi
Varangerfjorden
KOL'SKIJ POLUOSTROV (KOLA PENINSULA)
ozero Imandra
Kandalakša
BELOE MORE (WHITE SEA)
Dvinskaja guba
Arhangel'sk
Onežskaja guba
ozero Topozero
Kemi
Oulu
Oulujärvi
KARELIA
Kuopio
Saimaa
Päijänne
SALPAUSSELKÄ
Petrozavodsk
Onežskoe ozero
Ladožskoe ozero
Helsinki
Gulf of Finland
Tallinn
Sankt-Peterburg (St. Petersburg)
Lake Peipus
ozero Il'men'
Gulf of Riga
VIDZEME
Riga
VALDAJSKAJA VOZVYŠENNOST'
MOSKOVSKAJA VOZVYŠENNOST'
Moskva (Moscow)
Rybinskoe vodohranilišče
Rybinsk
Jaroslavl'
ozero Beloe
Vicebsk
Smolensk
SMOLENSKAJA-MOSKOVSKAJA VOZVYŠENNOST'
Vilnius
Minsk
Tula
SREDNERUSSKAJA VOZVYŠENNOST'
Voronež
PRIPET MARSHES
Kyiv (Kiev)
Kyivs'ke vodoskhovyshche
Kremenchuts'ke vodoskhovyshche
Kharkiv
VOLYN'
PRYDNIPROVS'KA VYSOCHYNA
PODIL'S'KA VYSOCHYNA
L'viv
Dnipropetrovs'k
Donets'k
CARPATHIAN MTS.
MOLDAVIA
Chişinău
Odesa
Vârful Pietrosu 2303
Cluj-Napoca
TRANSYLVANIA
CARPAŢII MERIDIONALI
Vârful Moldoveanu 2544
Iron Gate
WALACHIA
Bucureşti
Galaţi
DOBRUJA
Constanţa
Mouths of the Danube
Kakhovs'ke vodoskhovyshche
Sea of Azov
KRYMS'KYI PIVOSTRIV
KRYMS'KI HORY
Kerch
Kerch Strait
Sevastopol'
Rostov-na-Donu
Cimljanskoe vodohranilišče
Krasnodar
BLACK SEA
Varna
Burgas
Sofija
BALKAN PENINSULA
Musala 2925
Plovdiv
RHODOPE MTS.
THRACE
MACEDONIA
Thessaloniki
Ólympos 2917
İstanbul
İstanbul Boğazı (Bosporus)
Marmara Denizi
Bursa
Uludağ 2543
Çanakkale Boğazı (Dardanelles)
Lésvos
AEGEAN SEA
Chíos
EVVOIA
Athína (Athens)
PELOPÓNNISOS
KIKLÁDES (CYCLADES)
DODEKÁNISOS
RÓDOS
KRÍTI (CRETE)
Ídhi Óros 2454
İzmir
Afyon
KÜRE DAĞLARI
İnce Burun
Samsun
ANADOLU (ANATOLIA)
Ankara
Tuz Gölü
Konya
Kayseri
Erciyes Dağı 3917
Sivas
TOROS DAĞLARI (TAURUS MTS.)
Antalya
Antalya Körfezi
Adana
İskenderun
İskenderun Körfezi
Gaziantep
Halab (Aleppo)
Nicosia
CYPRUS
Ólimbos 1951
Qurnat as-Sawdā' 3083
Ḩimş
SYRIAN DESERT
Bahr al-Milh
Euphrates (Al-Furāt)
MESOPOTAMIA
Baghdād
Tigris (Dijlah)
Kirkūk
Al-Mawsil
KURDISTAN
Elazığ
Van Gölü
Trabzon
DOĞU KARADENİZ DAĞLARI
Erzurum
Ağrı Dağı 5137
Aragats Lerr 4090
Yerevan
Sevana Lich
Batumi
LESSER CAUCASUS
Tbilisi
TRANSCAUCASIA
CAUCASUS
gora El'brus 5642
gora Kazbek 5047
Bazardüzü dağ 4480
Groznyj
Mahačkala
Baki
Tabrīz
Daryācheh-ye Orūmīyeh (Lake Urmia)
Orūmīyeh
RESHTEH-YE KŪHHĀ-YE ALBORZ
Qolleh-ye Damāvand 5604
Tehrān
Daryācheh-ye Namak
Hamadān
Eşfahān
Zard Kūh 4547
KŪHHĀ-YE ZĀGROS
Ahvāz
Kāzerūn
Nā'īn
CASPIAN SEA
Turkmenbaši
zaliv Kara-Bogaz-Gol
Gyzylarbat
CASPIAN DEPRESSION (PRIKASPIJSKAJA NIZMENNOST')
Astrahan'
Atyrau
Volgograd
ERGENI
Volgogradskoe vodohranilišče
Saratov
Saratovskoe vodohranilišče
PRIVOLŽSKAJA VOZVYŠENNOST'
Samara
Kujbyševskoe vodohranilišče
Kazan'
Nižnij Novgorod
Gor'kovskoe vodohranilišče
Kirov
SEVERNYE UVALY
Kotlas
Syktyvkar
TIMANSKIJ KRJAŽ
Uhta
Perm'
Kamskoe vodohranilišče
gora Konžakovskij Kamen' 1569
Serov
URAL'SKIE GORY (URAL MOUNTAINS)
PRIPOLJARNYJ URAL
gora Narodnaja 1895
SEVERNYJ URAL
SREDNIJ URAL
JUŽNYJ URAL
Ekaterinburg
Čeljabinsk
Ufa
gora Jamantau 1640
Magnitogorsk
Orenburg
OBŠČIJ SYRT
Ural'sk
Aktjubinsk
GORY MUGODZHARY
ZAPADNO-SIBIRSKAJA RAVNINA (WEST SIBERIAN PLAIN)
Serginskij
Hanty-Mansijsk
Surgut
Ust'-Tym
Tobol'sk
Tjumen'
Kurgan
Išimskaja ravnina
Petropavlovsk
Omsk
Kokčetav
Atbasar
Arkalyk
Turgajskaja ložbina
TURGAJSKOE PLATO
Aral'sk
Novokazalinsk
Aral Sea
Kungrad
UST-URT PLATEAU

ATLANTIC OCEAN
NORTH SEA
SHETLAND ISLANDS
ORKNEY ISLANDS
Same scale as main map
OUTER HEBRIDES
INNER HEBRIDES
HEBRIDES
ISLE OF LEWIS
ISLAND OF SKYE
NORTHWEST HIGHLANDS
GRAMPIAN MOUNTAINS
CAIRNGORM MTS.
MONADHLIATH MOUNTAINS
BADENOCH
SCOTLAND
SOUTHERN UPLANDS
CHEVIOT HILLS
GALLOWAY
UNITED KINGDOM
NORTHERN IRELAND
DONEGAL
EDINBURGH
GLASGOW
Aberdeen
Dundee
Inverness
NEWCASTLE UPON TYNE
Sunderland
Carlisle
Stornoway
Fort William
Ben Nevis 1343
Perth
Stirling
Kirkcaldy
Dunfermline
Motherwell
Kilmarnock
Ayr
Londonderry (Derry)
Coleraine
Ballymena
Larne
Wick
Thurso
Kirkwall
Lerwick
Moray Firth
The Minch
The Little Minch
Sea of the Hebrides
North Channel
Firth of Forth
Firth of Clyde
Solway Firth
St. Kilda
Rona
Fair Isle

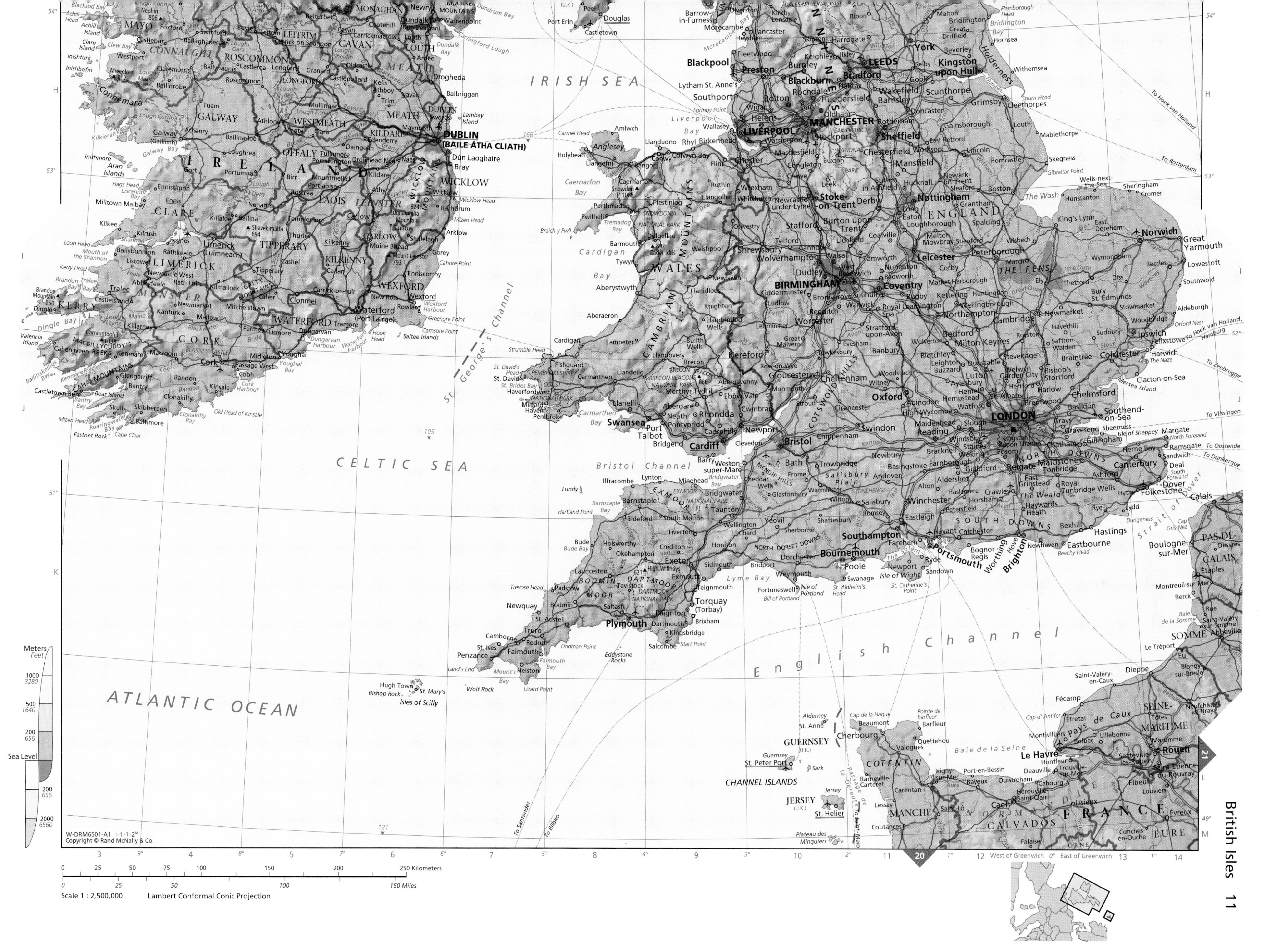
IRISH SEA
CELTIC SEA
ATLANTIC OCEAN
English Channel
St. George's Channel
Bristol Channel
Cardigan Bay
Lyme Bay
The Wash
Strait of Dover
IRELAND
ENGLAND
WALES
FRANCE
CAMBRIAN MOUNTAINS
COTSWOLD HILLS
NORTH DOWNS
SOUTH DOWNS
THE FENS
DARTMOOR
EXMOOR
BODMIN MOOR
CHANNEL ISLANDS
GUERNSEY
JERSEY
Isle of Wight
Isles of Scilly
DUBLIN (BAILE ÁTHA CLIATH)
LONDON
BIRMINGHAM
MANCHESTER
LIVERPOOL
LEEDS
Sheffield
Bristol
Cardiff
Swansea
Plymouth
Southampton
Portsmouth
Brighton
Norwich
Cork
Waterford
Wexford
Limerick
Galway
Le Havre
Rouen
Cherbourg
Calais
Boulogne-sur-Mer
Douglas
Land's End
Meters / Feet
1000 / 3280
500 / 1640
200 / 656
Sea Level
200 / 656
2000 / 6560
W-DRM6501-A1 -1-1-2M
Copyright © Rand McNally & Co.
0 25 50 75 100 150 200 250 Kilometers
0 25 50 100 150 Miles
Scale 1 : 2,500,000
Lambert Conformal Conic Projection

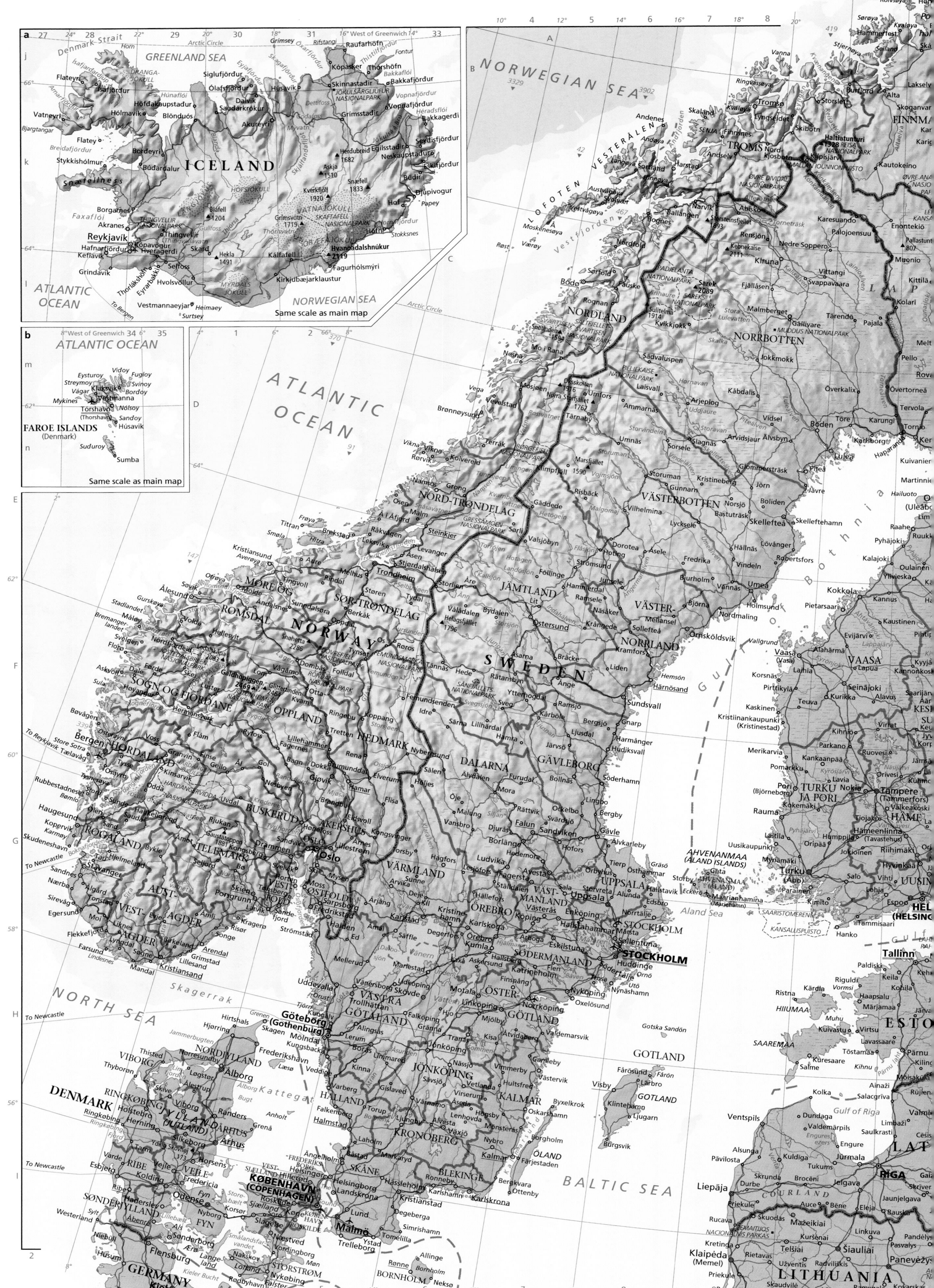
GREENLAND SEA
ICELAND
Reykjavík
ATLANTIC OCEAN
NORWEGIAN SEA
Same scale as main map
ATLANTIC OCEAN
FAROE ISLANDS
(Denmark)
Tórshavn
(Thorshavn)
Same scale as main map
NORWEGIAN SEA
ATLANTIC OCEAN
LOFOTEN
VESTERÅLEN
NORDLAND
NORRBOTTEN
TROMS
FINNMARK
NORD-TRØNDELAG
SØR-TRØNDELAG
MØRE OG ROMSDAL
NORWAY
SWEDEN
JÄMTLAND
VÄSTERBOTTEN
VÄSTERNORRLAND
SOGN OG FJORDANE
OPPLAND
HEDMARK
HORDALAND
BUSKERUD
AKERSHUS
ROGALAND
TELEMARK
VESTFOLD
ØSTFOLD
AUST-AGDER
VEST-AGDER
DALARNA
GÄVLEBORG
VÄRMLAND
UPPSALA
VÄSTMANLAND
ÖREBRO
SÖDERMANLAND
STOCKHOLM
ÖSTERGÖTLAND
VÄSTRA GÖTALAND
JÖNKÖPING
KALMAR
KRONOBERG
HALLAND
BLEKINGE
SKÅNE
GOTLAND
NORTH SEA
Skagerrak
Kattegat
BALTIC SEA
Gulf of Bothnia
Oslo
Trondheim
Bergen
Stavanger
Göteborg
(Gothenburg)
Malmö
KØBENHAVN
(COPENHAGEN)
DENMARK
NORDJYLLAND
VIBORG
RINGKØBING
ÅRHUS
RIBE
VEJLE
SØNDERJYLLAND
FYN
GERMANY
LITHUANIA
Riga
Tallinn
Gulf of Riga
Aland Sea
AHVENANMAA
(ÅLAND ISLANDS)
TURKU JA PORI
VAASA
HÄME
COURLAND

BARENTS SEA

BELOE MORE (WHITE SEA)

KOL'SKIJ POLUOSTROV (KOLA PENINSULA)

MURMANSKAJA OBLAST'

KARELIJA

ARHANGEL'SKAJA OBLAST'

VOLOGODSKAJA OBLAST'

LENINGRADSKAJA OBLAST'

NOVGORODSKAJA OBLAST'

PSKOVSKAJA OBLAST'

TVERSKAJA OBLAST'

JAROSLAVSKAJA OBLAST'

KOSTROMSKAJA OBLAST'

IVANOVSKAJA OBLAST'

VLADIMIRSKAJA OBLAST'

NIŽEGORODSKAJA OBLAST'

KIROVSKAJA OBLAST'

KOMI

NENECKIJ AVTONOMNYJ OKRUG

RUSSIA

Murmansk

Arhangel'sk

Severodvinsk (Molotovsk)

Petrozavodsk

Vologda

Čerepovec

Rybinsk

Jaroslavl'

Kostroma

Ivanovo

Vladimir

Tver'

Novgorod

Pskov

SANKT-PETERBURG (ST. PETERSBURG)

MOSKVA (MOSCOW)

NIŽNIJ NOVGOROD (GORKI)

Meters / Feet

2000 / 6560

1000 / 3280

500 / 1640

200 / 656

Sea Level

200 / 656

2000 / 6560

Scale 1 : 5,000,000

0 50 100 150 200 300 400 500 Kilometers

0 50 100 200 300 Miles

Lambert Conformal Conic Projection

W-DRM5502-A1-2

27

48

NORWEGIAN SEA
Gulf of Bothnia
NORWAY
SWEDEN
FINNMARK
TROMS
NORDLAND
NORRBOTTEN
VÄSTERBOTTEN
VÄSTERNORRLAND
JÄMTLAND
NORD-TRØNDELAG
POHJANMAA
LAPLAND
VESTERÅLEN
LOFOTEN
Vestfjorden
Finnmarksvidda
SALTEN
SALTFJELLET
BØRGEFJELL
BURGFJÄLLEN
HOTAGSFJÄLLENLEN
BJÖRKFJÄLLET
PÄRTEFJÄLLEN
BARTURTE
Kiruna
Gällivare
Luleå
Umeå
Skellefteå
Boden
Piteå
Haparanda
Tornio
Kemi
Rovaniemi
Oulu (Uleåborg)
Kokkola (Gamlakarleby)
VAASA
Tromsø
Alta
Narvik
Bodø
Mo i Rana
Mosjøen
Namsos
Östersund
Örnsköldsvik
Kebnekaise 2114
Sarek 2089
Haltiatunturi 1328
Meters
Feet
2000
6560
1000
3280
500
1640
200
656
Sea Level
Scale 1 : 2 500 000
Lambert Conformal Conic Projection
250 Kilometers
150 Miles

BARENTS SEA

MURMANSKAJA OBLAST'

KOL'SKIJ POLUOSTROV (KOLA PENINSULA)

BELOE MORE (WHITE SEA)

RUSSIA

KARELIJA

ARHANGEL'SKAJA OBLAST'

Murmansk

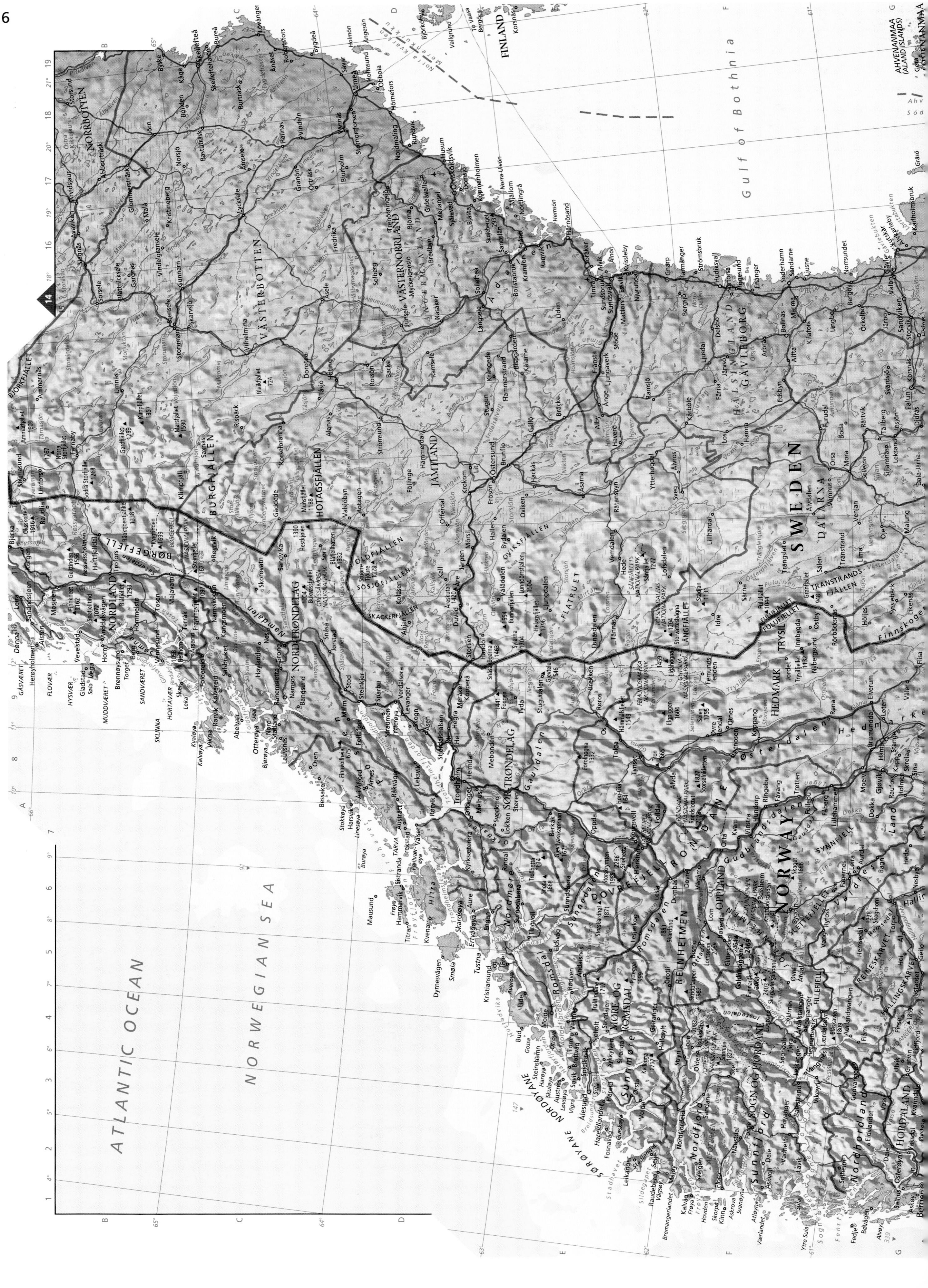
ATLANTIC OCEAN
NORWEGIAN SEA
Gulf of Bothnia
FINLAND
SWEDEN
NORWAY
NORRBOTTEN
VÄSTERBOTTEN
VÄSTERNORRLAND
JÄMTLAND
GÄVLEBORG
DALARNA
HEDMARK
OPPLAND
HORDALAND
NORDLAND
NORD-TRØNDELAG
SØR-TRØNDELAG
MØRE OG ROMSDAL
SOGN OG FJORDANE
BURGFJÄLLEN
HOTAGSFJÄLLEN
BØRGEFJELL
TRANSTRANDS-FJÄLLEN
SØRØYANE
NORDØYANE
AHVENANMAA (ÅLAND ISLANDS)
Trondheim
Östersund
Umeå
Sundsvall
Härnösand
Skellefteå
Falun
Lillehammer
Molde
Ålesund
Kristiansund

Scale 1 : 2 500 000

Lambert Conformal Conic Projection

0 25 50 75 100 150 200 250 Kilometers

0 25 50 100 150 Miles

Meters	Feet
2000	6560
1000	3280
500	1640
200	656
Sea Level	
200	656
2000	6560

0 25 50 75 100 150 200 250 Kilometers

0 25 50 100 150 Miles

Scale 1 : 2 500 000 Lambert Conformal Conic Projection

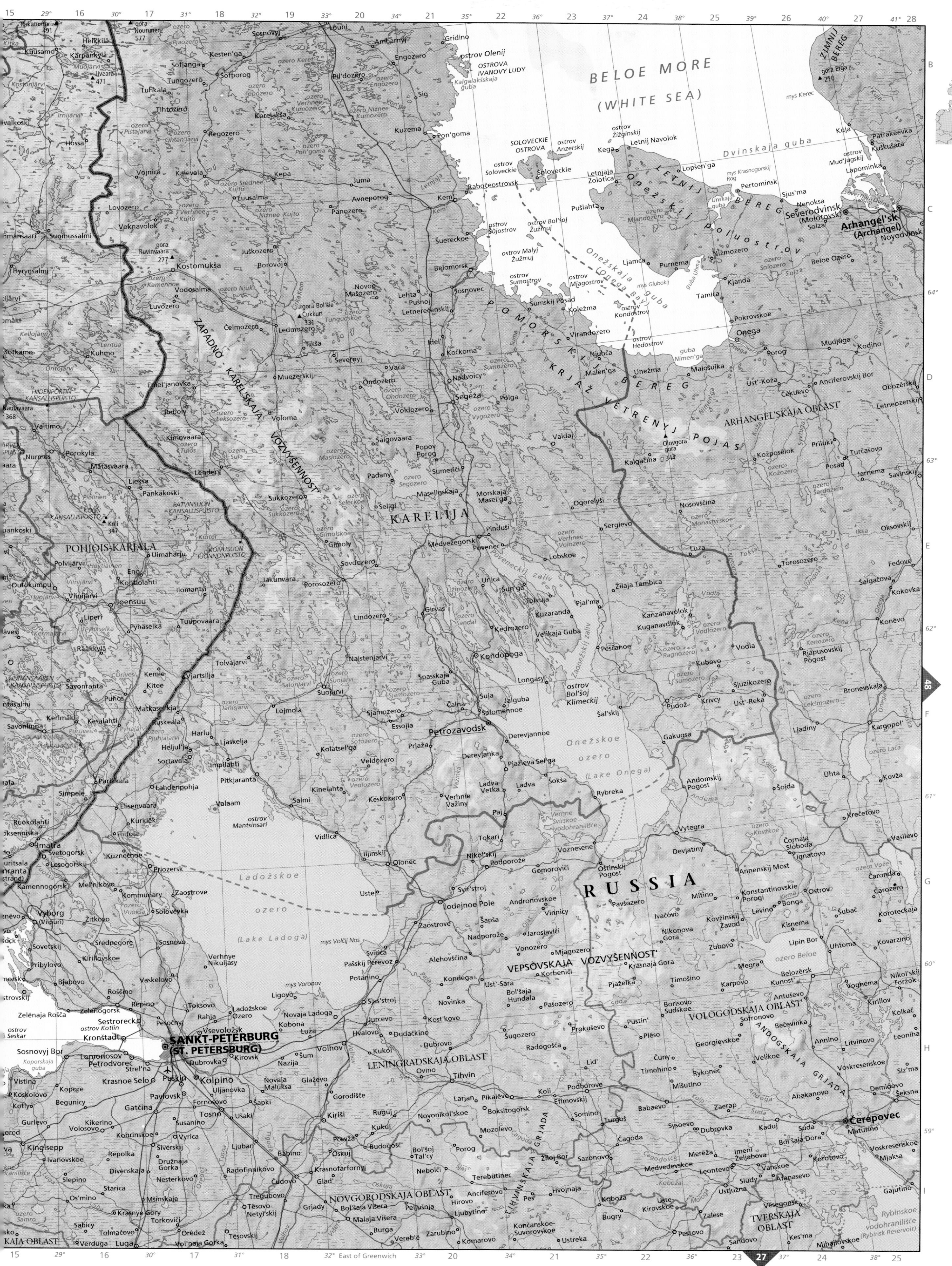

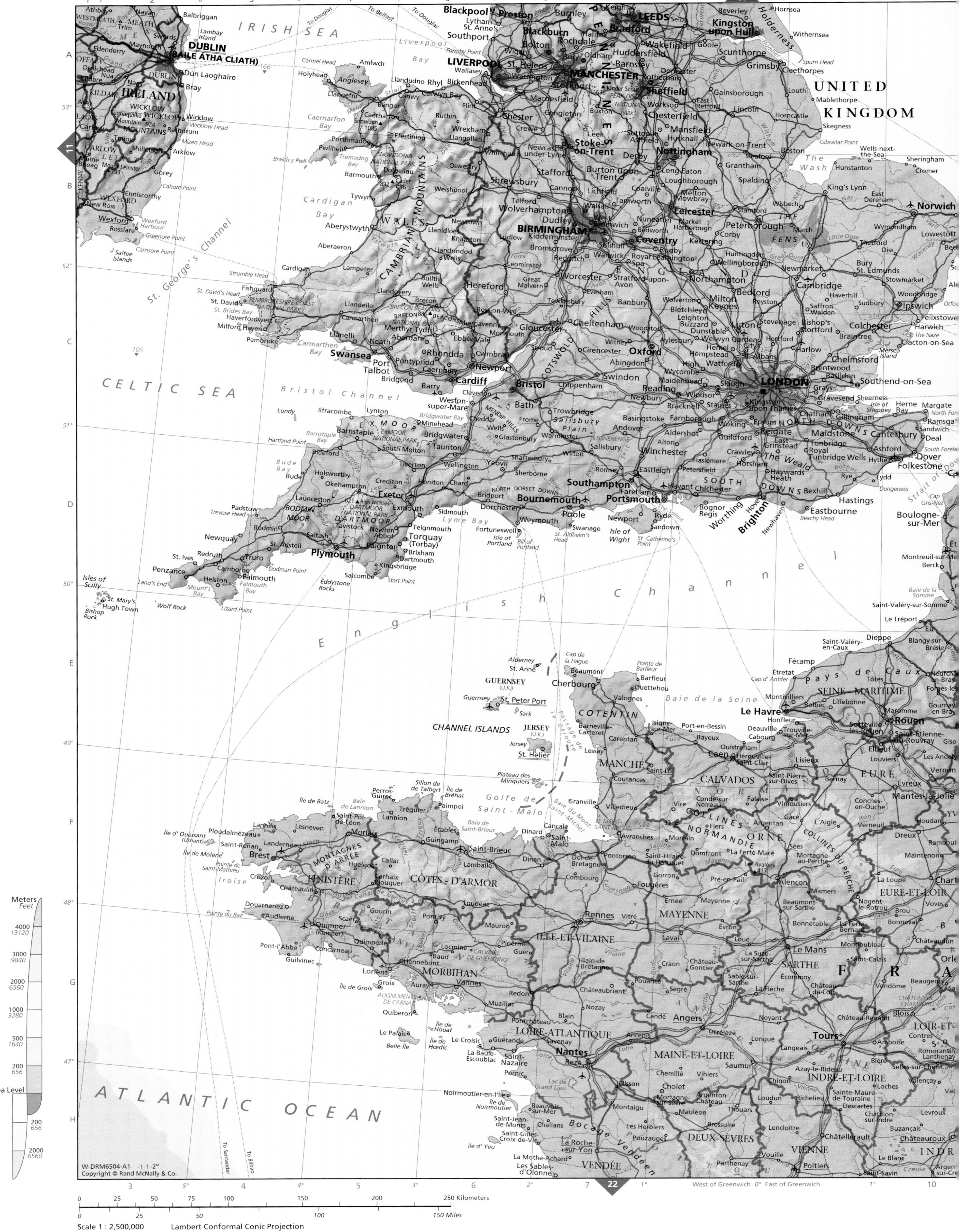

IRISH SEA
DUBLIN (BAILE ÁTHA CLIATH)
IRELAND
WICKLOW MOUNTAINS
St. George's Channel
CELTIC SEA
Bristol Channel
Cardigan Bay
WALES
CAMBRIAN MOUNTAINS
UNITED KINGDOM
Blackpool
Preston
LEEDS
Bradford
Kingston upon Hull
LIVERPOOL
MANCHESTER
Sheffield
Nottingham
Leicester
BIRMINGHAM
Coventry
Norwich
Cambridge
Oxford
LONDON
Bristol
Cardiff
Swansea
Southampton
Portsmouth
Bournemouth
Brighton
Exeter
Plymouth
The Wash
English Channel
CHANNEL ISLANDS
GUERNSEY (U.K.)
JERSEY (U.K.)
St. Peter Port
St. Helier
Cherbourg
Le Havre
Rouen
SEINE-MARITIME
MANCHE
CALVADOS
ORNE
EURE
EURE-ET-LOIR
Golfe de Saint-Malo
Brest
FINISTÈRE
CÔTES-D'ARMOR
ILLE-ET-VILAINE
MORBIHAN
Rennes
MAYENNE
Le Mans
SARTHE
Angers
LOIRE-ATLANTIQUE
Nantes
MAINE-ET-LOIRE
Tours
INDRE-ET-LOIRE
LOIR-ET-CHER
VENDÉE
DEUX-SÈVRES
VIENNE
ATLANTIC OCEAN
Meters
Feet
4000
13120
3000
9840
2000
6560
1000
3280
500
1640
200
656
Sea Level
200
656
2000
6560
W-DRM6504-A1 -1-1-2[M]
Copyright © Rand McNally & Co.
West of Greenwich 0° East of Greenwich
0 25 50 75 100 150 200 250 Kilometers
0 25 50 100 150 Miles
Scale 1 : 2,500,000
Lambert Conformal Conic Projection

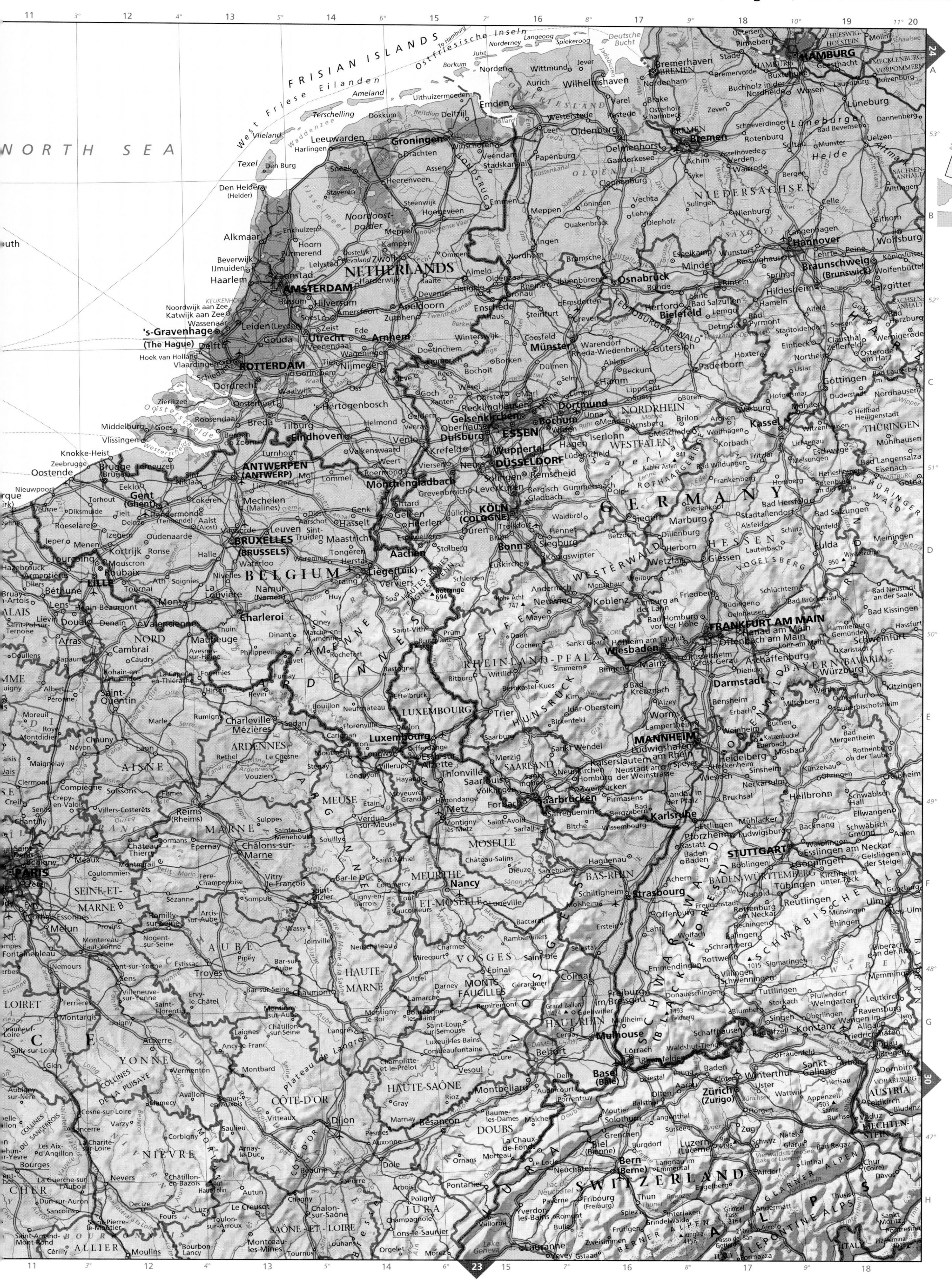
NORTH SEA
FRISIAN ISLANDS
West Friese Eilanden
Ostfriesische Inseln
NETHERLANDS
BELGIUM
LUXEMBOURG
GERMANY
SWITZERLAND
ALPS
AMSTERDAM
's-Gravenhage
(The Hague)
ROTTERDAM
Utrecht
Groningen
Leeuwarden
Eindhoven
ANTWERPEN
(ANTWERP)
BRUXELLES
(BRUSSELS)
Gent
(Ghent)
Brugge
(Bruges)
Liège (Luik)
Namur
Charleroi
LILLE
PARIS
Reims
Luxembourg
Metz
Nancy
Strasbourg
Mulhouse
Basel
(Bâle)
Zürich
(Zurigo)
Bern
(Berne)
Lausanne
Dijon
Besançon
HAMBURG
Bremen
Bremerhaven
Hannover
Braunschweig
(Brunswick)
Osnabrück
Münster
Bielefeld
Dortmund
ESSEN
Duisburg
DÜSSELDORF
Wuppertal
KÖLN
(COLOGNE)
Bonn
Aachen
Koblenz
Wiesbaden
FRANKFURT AM MAIN
MANNHEIM
Heidelberg
Karlsruhe
STUTTGART
Saarbrücken
Kassel
NIEDERSACHSEN
(LOWER SAXONY)
NORDRHEIN-WESTFALEN
HESSEN
RHEINLAND-PFALZ
SAARLAND
BADEN-WÜRTTEMBERG
BAYERN (BAVARIA)
THÜRINGEN
ARDENNES
EIFEL
HUNSRÜCK
WESTERWALD
SCHWARZWALD
(BLACK FOREST)
VOSGES
JURA
Lake Geneva

ATLANTIC OCEAN
Bay of Biscay
FRANCE
SPAIN
ANDORRA
Paris
Versailles
Brest
Quimper
Lorient
Vannes
Saint-Brieuc
Rennes
Nantes
Saint-Nazaire
Angers
Le Mans
Tours
Orléans
Blois
Poitiers
La Rochelle
Rochefort
Angoulême
Limoges
Périgueux
Bordeaux
Arcachon
Agen
Montauban
Toulouse
Bayonne
Biarritz
Pau
Tarbes
Lourdes
Carcassonne
Bilbao
Donostia (San Sebastián)
Gasteiz (Vitoria)
Pamplona
Logroño
Burgos
Santander
Zaragoza (Saragossa)
Huesca
Lleida
Barcelona
L'Hospitalet de Llobregat
Andorra la Vella
FINISTÈRE
CÔTES-D'ARMOR
MORBIHAN
ILLE-ET-VILAINE
LOIRE-ATLANTIQUE
MAYENNE
SARTHE
ORNE
MAINE-ET-LOIRE
INDRE-ET-LOIRE
LOIR-ET-CHER
LOIRET
EURE-ET-LOIR
VENDÉE
DEUX-SÈVRES
VIENNE
INDRE
CHER
CHARENTE-MARITIME
CHARENTE
HAUTE-VIENNE
CORRÈZE
DORDOGNE
GIRONDE
LANDES
LOT-ET-GARONNE
LOT
TARN-ET-GARONNE
GERS
HAUTE-GARONNE
TARN
AVEYRON
PYRÉNÉES-ATLANTIQUES
HAUTES-PYRÉNÉES
ARIÈGE
AUDE
CANTABRIA
CORDILLERA CANTÁBRICA
EUSKAL HERRIKO
NAVARRA
LA RIOJA
BURGOS
SORIA
ARAGON
CATALUNYA
LLEIDA
HUESCA
ZARAGOZA
CASTILLA Y LEÓN
SISTEMA IBÉRICO
PYRENEES
Plateau du Limousin
MÉDOC
Côte d'Argent
CHALOSSE
Meters
Feet
4000 13120
3000 9840
2000 6560
1000 3280
500 1640
200 656
Sea Level
200 656
2000 6560
0 25 50 75 100 150 200 250 Kilometers
0 25 50 100 150 Miles
Scale 1 : 2,500,000
Lambert Conformal Conic Projection
West of Greenwich
East of Greenwich

GERMANY
SWITZERLAND
AUSTRIA
ITALY
FRANCE
LIGURIAN SEA
MEDITERRANEAN SEA
Golfe du Lion
Golfo di Genova
Riviera di Ponente
Riviera di Levante
Côte d'Azur
ALPS
BERNER ALPEN
PENNINE ALPS
LEPONTINE ALPS
GLARNER ALPEN
RHAETIAN ALPS
GRAIAN ALPS
COTTIAN ALPS
MARITIME ALPS
JURA
VOSGES
SCHWARZWALD (BLACK FOREST)
SCHWÄBISCHE ALB
MASSIF CENTRAL
CÉVENNES
Camargue
APPENNINO LIGURE
APPENNINO TOSCO-EMILIANO
BADEN-WÜRTTEMBERG
BAYERN
VORARLBERG
TIROL
LIECHTENSTEIN
LOMBARDIA
PIEMONTE
VALLE D'AOSTA
EMILIA-ROMAGNA
HAUTE-SAVOIE
SAVOIE
ISÈRE
DRÔME
ARDÈCHE
VAUCLUSE
BOUCHES-DU-RHÔNE
VAR
ALPES-MARITIMES
ALPES-DE-HAUTE-PROVENCE
HAUTES-ALPES
RHÔNE
LOIRE
AIN
DOUBS
CÔTE-D'OR
SAÔNE-ET-LOIRE
NIÈVRE
HAUTE-SAÔNE
HAUTE-MARNE
AUBE
MARNE
YONNE
GARD
HÉRAULT
LOZÈRE
HAUTE-LOIRE
CORSE
(CORSICA)
HAUTE-CORSE
CORSE-DU-SUD
Strasbourg
Basel (Bâle)
Zürich (Zurigo)
Bern (Berne)
Luzern (Lucerne)
Genève (Geneva)
Lausanne
Lyon
Saint-Étienne
Grenoble
Marseille
Toulon
Nice
Monaco
Avignon
Montpellier
Dijon
Besançon
Mulhouse
Torino (Turin)
Milano (Milan)
Genova (Genoa)
Bergamo
Brescia
Parma
Livorno (Leghorn)
Bastia
Ajaccio
Bonifacio
Augsburg
Ulm
Konstanz
Chur (Coire)
Mont Blanc 4808
Monte Rosa
Matterhorn
Dufourspitze 4634
Jungfrau 4158
Isola d'Elba
SARDEGNA (SARDINIA)
W-DRM6508-A1 -1-1-2
Copyright © Rand McNally & Co.

21
30

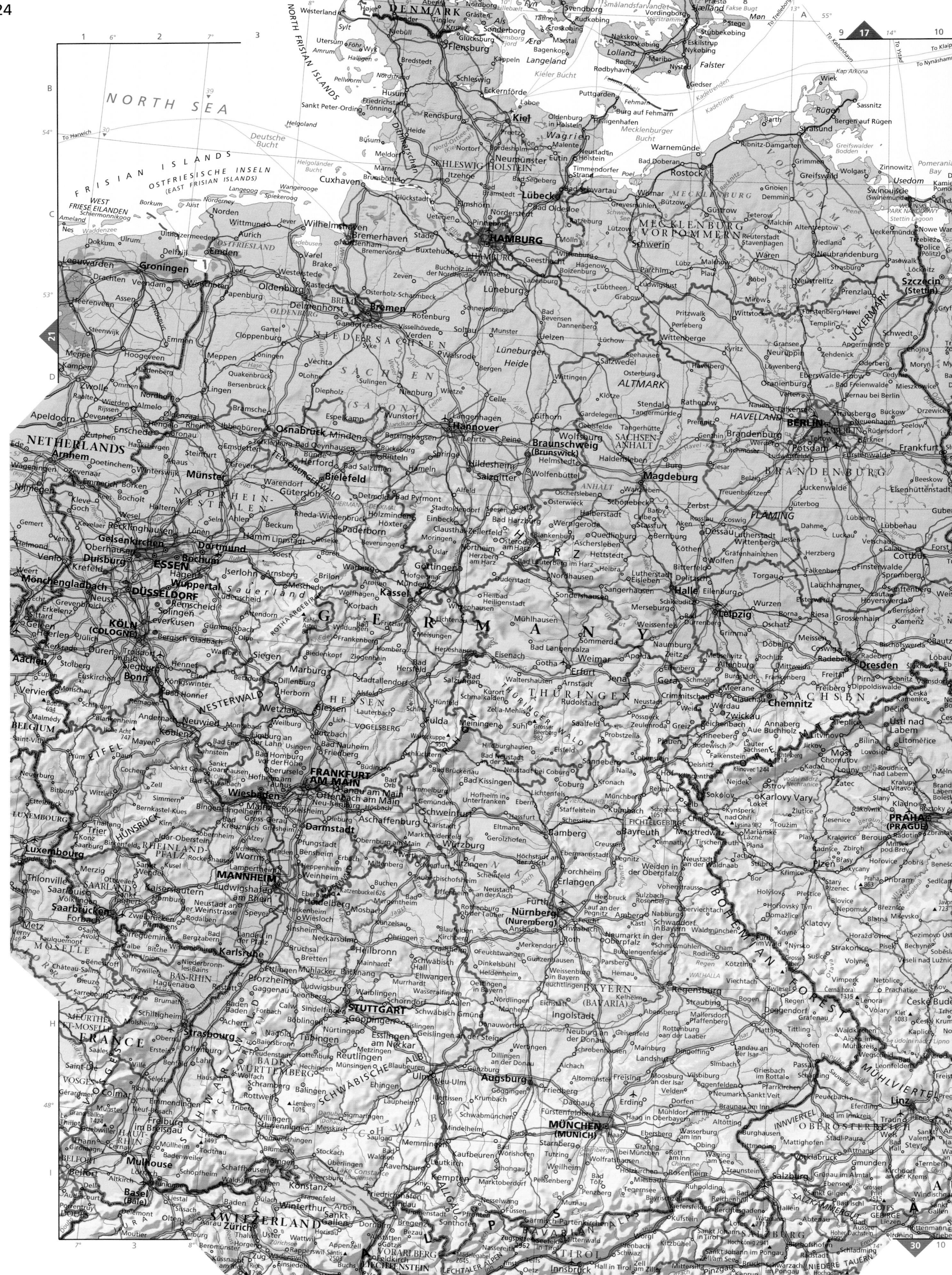
NORTH SEA
FRISIAN ISLANDS
OSTFRIESISCHE INSELN
(EAST FRISIAN ISLANDS)
WEST FRIESE EILANDEN
NORTH FRISIAN ISLANDS
DENMARK
NETHERLANDS
BELGIUM
LUXEMBOURG
FRANCE
SWITZERLAND
GERMANY
Deutsche Bucht
Kieler Bucht
Mecklenburger Bucht
Pomeranian Bay
SCHLESWIG-HOLSTEIN
MECKLENBURG-VORPOMMERN
NIEDERSACHSEN
(LOWER SAXONY)
SACHSEN-ANHALT
BRANDENBURG
NORDRHEIN-WESTFALEN
HESSEN
THÜRINGEN
SACHSEN
RHEINLAND-PFALZ
SAARLAND
BADEN-WÜRTTEMBERG
BAYERN
(BAVARIA)
HARZ
Lüneburger Heide
ALTMARK
HAVELLAND
FLÄMING
UCKERMARK
Sauerland
WESTERWALD
EIFEL
HUNSRÜCK
VOGELSBERG
THÜRINGER WALD
FICHTELGEBIRGE
BOHEMIAN FOREST
SCHWARZWALD
SCHWÄBISCHE ALB
ALLGÄU
ALPS
BAVARIAN ALPS
TIROL
SALZBURG
MÜHLVIERTEL
VOSGES
HAMBURG
Bremen
Kiel
Lübeck
Rostock
Schwerin
Hannover
BERLIN
Potsdam
Magdeburg
Braunschweig
(Brunswick)
Osnabrück
Münster
Bielefeld
Dortmund
ESSEN
Duisburg
DÜSSELDORF
Wuppertal
KÖLN
(COLOGNE)
Bonn
Aachen
Kassel
Göttingen
Erfurt
Weimar
Jena
Halle
Leipzig
Dresden
Chemnitz
Koblenz
Wiesbaden
FRANKFURT AM MAIN
Mainz
Darmstadt
MANNHEIM
Heidelberg
Karlsruhe
Saarbrücken
Trier
Luxembourg
Würzburg
Nürnberg
(Nuremberg)
Regensburg
STUTTGART
Augsburg
MÜNCHEN
(MUNICH)
Ulm
Freiburg im Breisgau
Strasbourg
Basel
(Bâle)
Zürich
Innsbruck
Salzburg
Linz
PRAHA
(PRAGUE)
Plzeň
Szczecin
(Stettin)
Groningen
Arnhem
Flensburg
Cuxhaven
Frankfurt
Cottbus

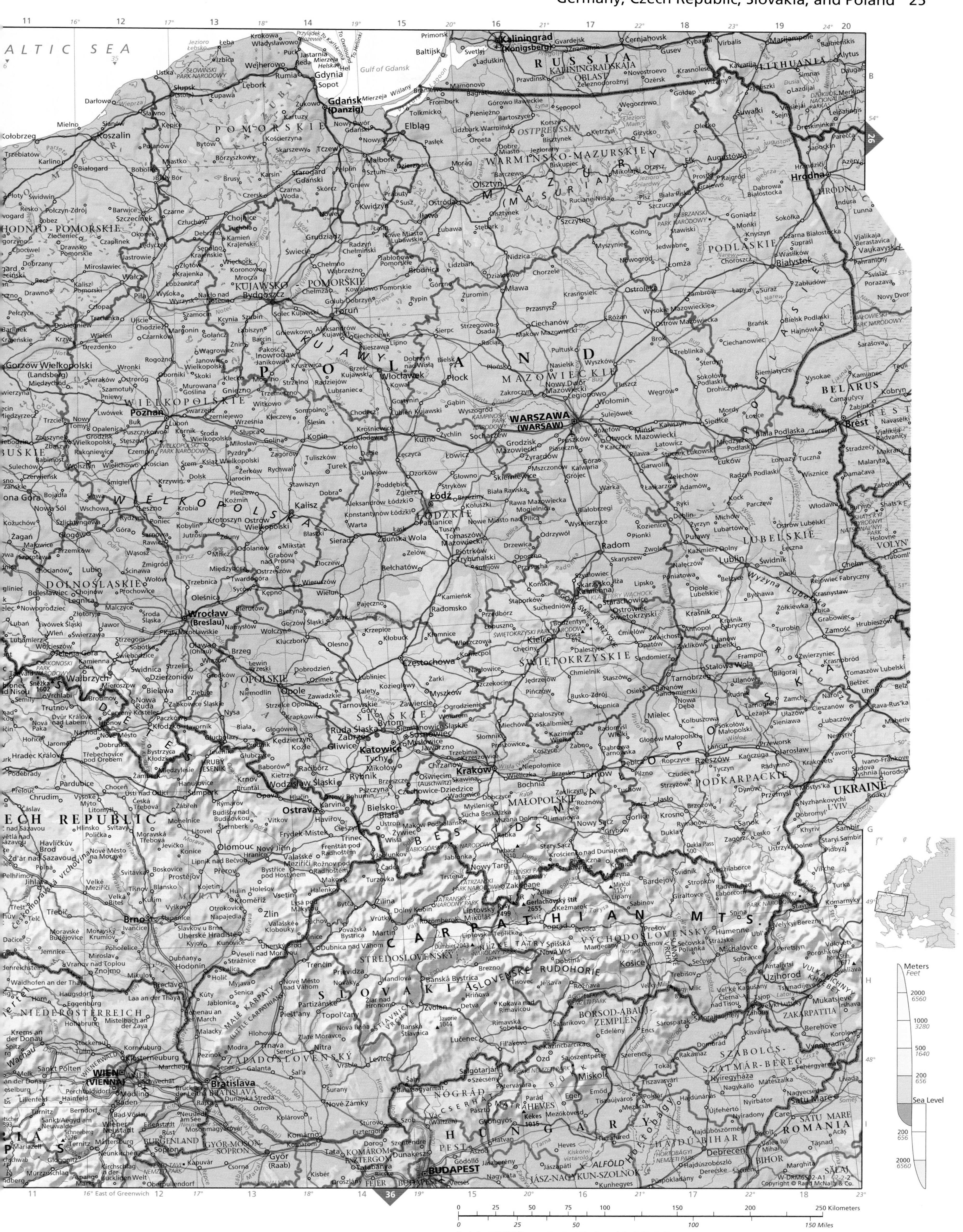
BALTIC SEA
Gulf of Gdansk
RUSSIA
KALININGRADSKAJA OBLAST
Kaliningrad (Königsberg)
LITHUANIA
POLAND
POMORSKIE
WARMIŃSKO-MAZURSKIE
KUJAWSKO-POMORSKIE
ZACHODNIO-POMORSKIE
PODLASKIE
MAZOWIECKIE
WIELKOPOLSKIE
ŁÓDZKIE
LUBELSKIE
DOLNOŚLĄSKIE
OPOLSKIE
ŚLĄSKIE
ŚWIĘTOKRZYSKIE
MAŁOPOLSKIE
PODKARPACKIE
WARSZAWA (WARSAW)
Gdańsk (Danzig)
Gdynia
Poznań
Łódź
Wrocław (Breslau)
Kraków
Katowice
Białystok
Lublin
Rzeszów
Szczecinek
Bydgoszcz
Toruń
Olsztyn
Kielce
Radom
Częstochowa
Opole
Tarnów
BELARUS
Hrodna
Brest
UKRAINE
L'VIV
CZECH REPUBLIC
Ostrava
Olomouc
Brno
SLOVAKIA
Bratislava
Košice
CARPATHIAN MTS.
BESKIDS
Gerlachovský štít 2655
HUNGARY
BUDAPEST
Miskolc
Debrecen
ROMANIA
Satu Mare
WIEN (VIENNA)
NIEDERÖSTERREICH
Győr (Raab)
Meters
Feet
Sea Level
0 25 50 75 100 150 200 250 Kilometers
0 25 50 100 150 Miles
Scale 1 : 2,500,000
Lambert Conformal Conic Projection
W-DRM6502-A1
Copyright © Rand McNally & Co.

BALTIC SEA
Gulf of Finland
Gulf of Riga
Gulf of Gdansk
ESTONIA
LATVIA
LITHUANIA
BELARUS
POLAND
RUSSIA
KALININGRADSKAJA OBLAST
SWEDEN
Tallinn
RIGA
Vilnius
MINSK
WARSZAWA (WARSAW)
Kaliningrad (Königsberg)
Tartu
Pärnu
Liepāja
Ventspils
Klaipėda (Memel)
Kaunas
Daugavpils
Šiauliai
Panevėžys
Hrodna
Białystok
Brèst
Pskov
Narva
HIIUMAA
SAAREMAA
COURLAND (KURZEME)
MAZURY (MASURIA)
Lake Peipus
Gotska Sandön (Sweden)
Fårön (Sweden)
Meters
Feet
Sea Level
200
656
2000
6560
0 25 50 100 Kilometers
0 25 50 Miles
Scale 1 : 2,500,000
Lambert Conformal Conic Projection
17
18
25

SANKT-PETERBURG (ST. PETERSBURG)

LENINGRADSKAJA OBLAST'

NOVGORODSKAJA OBLAST'

VOLOGODSKAJA OBLAST'

JAROSLAVSKAJA OBLAST'

TVERSKAJA OBLAST'

MOSKOVSKAJA OBLAST'

VLADIMIRSKAJA OBLAST'

SMOLENSKAJA OBLAST'

KALUŽSKAJA OBLAST'

TUL'SKAJA OBLAST'

BRJANSKAJA OBLAST'

ORLOVSKAJA OBLAST'

KURSKAJA OBLAST'

VORONEŽSKAJA OBLAST'

R U S S I A

VALDAJSKAJA VOZVYŠENNOST' (VALDAJ HILLS)

SMOLENSKAJA-MOSKOVSKAJA VOZVYŠENNOST'

SREDNERUSSKAJA VOZVYŠENNOST'

TIHVINSKAJA GRJADA

ANDOGSKAJA GRJADA

BEŽECKIJ VERH

KLINSKO-DMITROVSKAJA GRJADA

MOSKVA (MOSCOW)

Tver' (Kalinin)

Novgorod

Vologda

Čerepovec

Rybinsk

Rybinskoe vodohranilišče (Rybinsk Reservoir)

ozero Il'men'

ozero Seliger

Velikie Luki

Smolensk

Vicebsk

Orša

Mahilëu

MAHILËU

Homel'

Brjansk

Kaluga

Tula

Orel

Novomoskovsk (Stalinogorsk)

Serpuhov

Kolomna

Obninsk

Elec

UKRAINE

33° East of Greenwich

Copyright © Rand McNally & Co.

Meters
Feet
3000
9840
2000
6560
1000
3280
500
1640
200
656
Sea Level
200
656
2000
6560

Bay of Biscay

ATLANTIC OCEAN

ALBORAN SEA

PORTUGAL

SPAIN

MOROCCO

0 25 50 75 100 150 200 Kilometers
0 25 50 100 Miles
Scale 1 : 2,500,000 Lambert Conformal Conic Projection

CZECH REPUBLIC
CARPATHIAN MOUNTAINS
SLOVAKIA
AUSTRIA
NIEDERÖSTERREICH
STEIERMARK
KÄRNTEN
HUNGARY
SLOVENIA
CROATIA
BOSNIA AND HERZEGOVINA
YUGOSLAVIA
SRBIJA
(SERBIA)
CRNA GORA
(MONTENEGRO)
ROMANIA
ALBANIA
ADRIATIC SEA
BUDAPEST
WIEN
(VIENNA)
Bratislava
Ljubljana
Zagreb
Sarajevo
BEOGRAD
(BELGRADE)
Graz
Linz
Klagenfurt
Trieste
(Trst)
Rijeka
(Fiume)
Split
Dubrovnik
Novi Sad
Szeged
Pécs
Győr
(Raab)
Miskolc
Podgorica
(Titograd)
Pescara
Ancona
Manfredonia
Copyright © Rand McNally & Co.

FRANCE
CORSE (CORSICA)
HAUTE-CORSE
CORSE-DU-SUD
SARDEGNA (SARDINIA)
ITALY
SARDEGNA
TOSCANA
UMBRIA
MARCHE
LAZIO
ABRUZZO
ROMA (ROME)
NAPOLI (NAPLES)
TYRRHENIAN SEA
MEDITERRANEAN SEA
SICILIA (SICILY)
Palermo
ISOLE EGADI
ISOLE EOLIE (ISOLE LIPARI)
ISOLE PONZIANE (PONTINE ISLANDS)
Strait of Bonifacio
Strait of Sicily
TUNISIA
TUNIS
ALGERIA
MALTA
ISOLE PELAGIE (Italy)
Cagliari
Sassari
Bastia
Ajaccio
Bizerte (Binzert)
Sousse
Meters / Feet
3000 9840
2000 6560
1000 3280
500 1640
200 656
Sea Level
200 656
2000 6560
0 25 50 75 100 150 200 250 Kilometers
0 25 50 100 150 Miles
Scale 1 : 2,500,000
Lambert Conformal Conic Projection

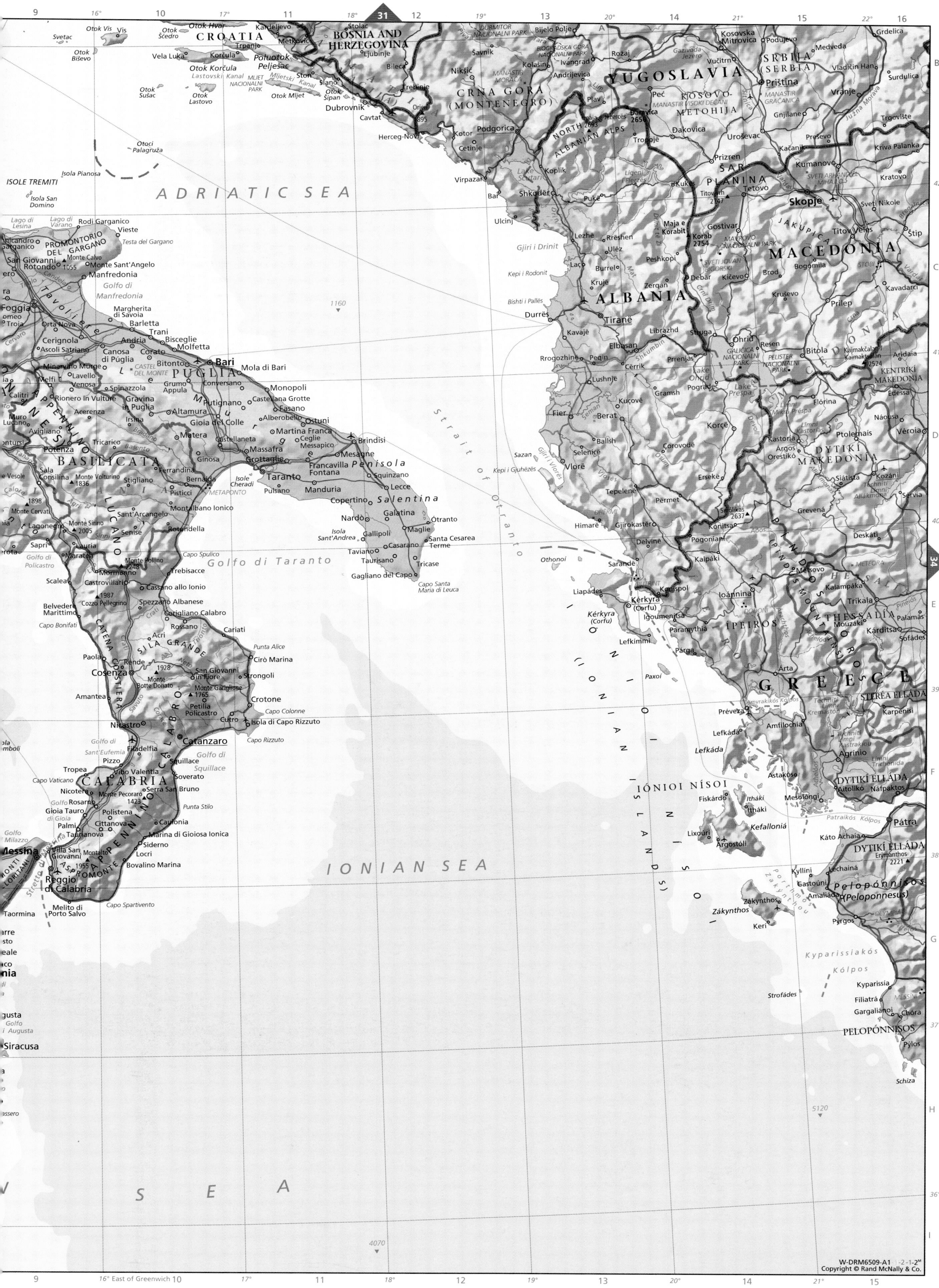

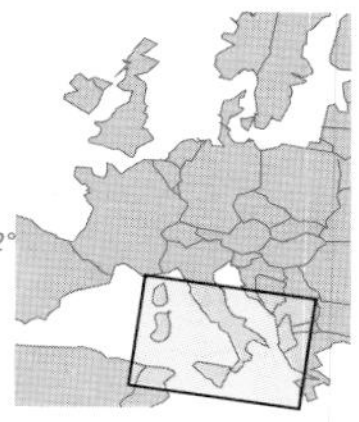

ADRIATIC SEA

IONIAN SEA

CROATIA

BOSNIA AND HERZEGOVINA

YUGOSLAVIA

CRNA GORA (MONTENEGRO)

SRBIJA (SERBIA)

KOSOVO-METOHIJA

ALBANIA

MACEDONIA

GREECE

PUGLIA

BASILICATA

CALABRIA

IÓNIOI NÍSOI (IONIAN ISLANDS)

Golfo di Taranto

Strait of Otranto

YUGOSLAVIA
CRNA GORA
(MONTENEGRO)
ADRIATIC SEA
ALBANIA
Tiranë
Durrës
Shkodër
Vlorë
MACEDONIA
Skopje
Bitola
Ohrid
BALKAN
SOFIJA
Plovdiv
PLOVDIV
RHODOPE MOUNTAINS
ANATOLIKÍ MAKEDONÍA KAI THRÁKI
KENTRIKÍ MAKEDONÍA
Thessaloníki
(Salonika)
DYTIKÍ MAKEDONÍA
THRAKIKÓ PÉLAGOS
Thermaïkós Kólpos
(Gulf of Salonika)
AGIO ÓROS
Olympos
(Mount Olympus)
2917
Lárisa
THESSALÍA
Vólos
ÍPEIROS
Ioánnina
Kérkyra
(Corfu)
Strait of Otranto
IÓNIOI NÍSOI
Ionian Islands
G R E E C E
Vóreioi Sporades
VÓREIO AIGAIO
Límnos
DYTIKÍ ELLÁDA
STEREÁ ELLÁDA
Lamía
Agrínio
Kefallonia
Zákynthos
Pátra
Korinthiakós Kólpos
(Gulf of Corinth)
ATHÍNA
(ATHENS)
Peiraiás
(Piraeus)
Évvoia
AEGEAN SEA
Pelopónnisos
(Peloponnesus)
PELOPÓNNISOS
Kalamáta
Trípoli
Kyparissiakós Kólpos
IONIAN SEA
ATTIKÍ
MYRTÓON PÉLAGOS
Kykládes
Lakonikós Kólpos
(Gulf of Laconia)
Kýthira
MEDITERRANEAN SEA
KRITIKÓN PÉLAGOS
(SEA OF CRETE)
KRÍTI
Kríti
(Crete)
Chania
Irákleio
Meters
Feet
3000
9840
2000
6560
1000
3280
500
1640
200
656
Sea Level
200
656
2000
6560
W-DRM6511-A1 -2-2-2
Copyright © Rand McNally & Co.
0 25 50 75 100 150 200 250 Kilometers
0 25 50 100 150 Miles
Scale 1 : 2,500,000
Lambert Conformal Conic Projection

BLACK SEA
Marmara Denizi (Sea of Marmara)
MEDITERRANEAN SEA
TURKEY
İSTANBUL
ANKARA
İZMİR (SMYRNA)
Bursa
Eskişehir
Konya
Antalya
Edirne
Tekirdağ
Çanakkale
Balıkesir
Manisa
Kütahya
Afyon
Uşak
Denizli
Aydın
Muğla
Isparta
Burdur
Bilecik
Sakarya
İzmit (Kocaeli)
Bolu
Zonguldak
Karabük
Bartın
Kastamonu
Çankırı
Kırklareli
BURGAS
BOZ DAĞLAR
AYDIN DAĞLARI
EMİR DAĞLARI
TOROS DAĞLARI (TAURUS MOUNTAINS)
BEY DAĞLARI
SAMANLI DAĞLARI
ALAÇAM DAĞLARI
YILDIZ DAĞLARI
Antalya Körfezi (Gulf of Antalya)
Gökova Körfezi (Gulf of Kerme)
Saros Körfezi
Edremit Körfezi
İzmit Körfezi
Kuşadası Körfezi
Finike Körfezi
Fethiye Körfezi
Reşadiye Yarımadası
Bozburun Yarımadası
Dodecanese (Dodekánisos)
AIGAÍO
Ródos (Rhodes)
Kárpathos
Kásos
Kos
Kálymnos
Sámos
Mytilini
Pátmos
Tílos
Nísyros
Sými
CYPRUS
Istanbul Boğazı (Bosporus)
Çanakkale Boğazı (Dardanelles)
Uludağ 2543
Kaz Dağı 1774
Murat Dağı 2309
Boz Dağ 2159
Boz Dağ 2419
Boncuk Dağı 2418
Dedegöl Tepesi 2992
Köroğlu Tepesi 2400
Elmadağ 1862
Sultan Dağı 1074
Kızıl Adalar
İmralı Adası
Türkeli Adası
Paşalimanı Adası
Kapıdağ Yarımadası
Gelibolu Yarımadası (Gallipoli Peninsula)
Alibey Adası
Megísti
To Lemesós
28° East of Greenwich
27° 28° 29° 30° 31° 32° 33°
42° 41° 40° 39° 38° 37° 36° 35°
9 10 11 12 13 14 15 16
A B C D E F G H I
38
42

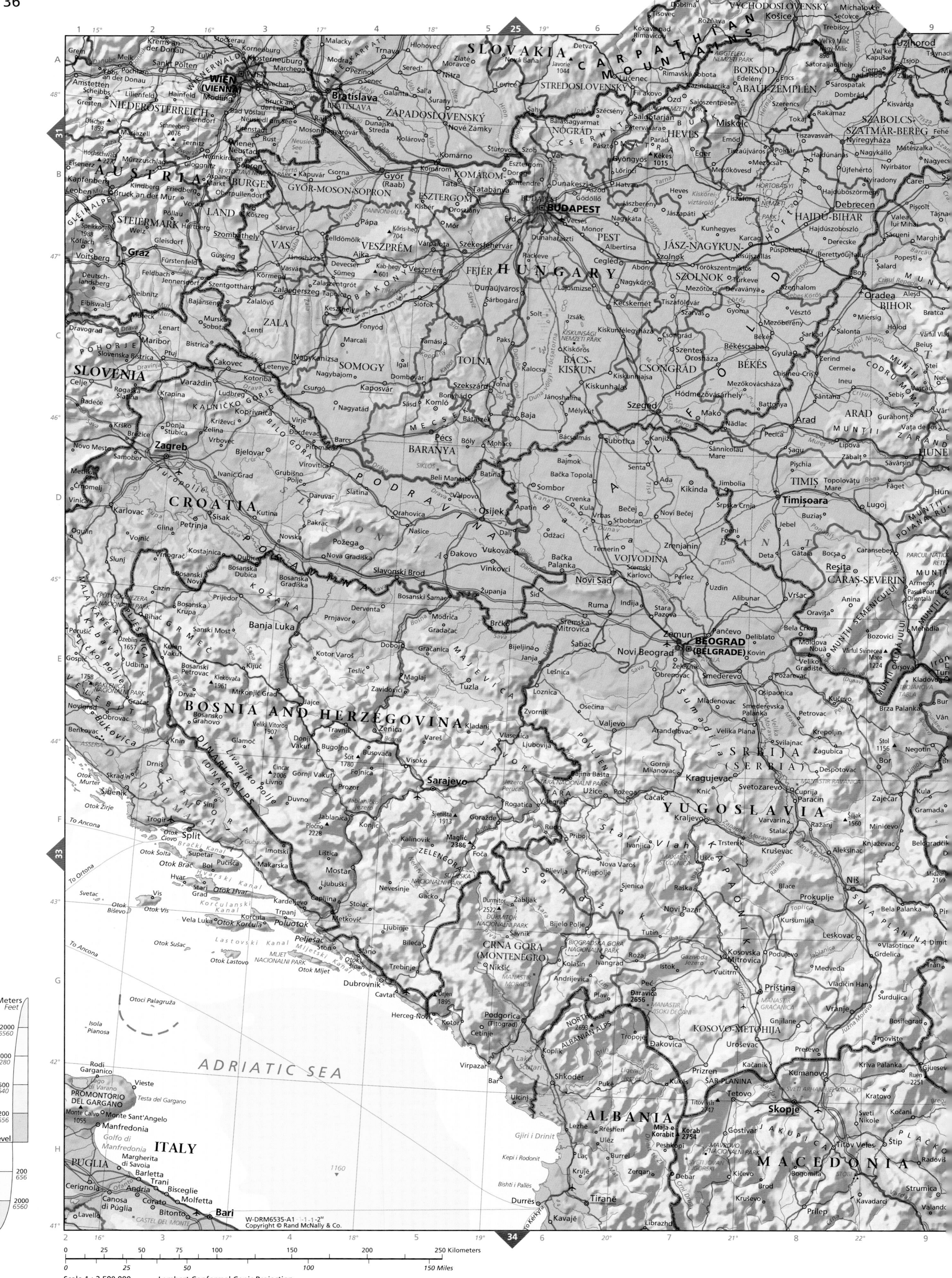
AUSTRIA
SLOVAKIA
HUNGARY
SLOVENIA
CROATIA
BOSNIA AND HERZEGOVINA
YUGOSLAVIA
SRBIJA (SERBIA)
CRNA GORA (MONTENEGRO)
ALBANIA
MACEDONIA
ITALY
ADRIATIC SEA
CARPATHIAN MOUNTAINS
DINARIC ALPS (DINARA)
WIEN (VIENNA)
Bratislava
BUDAPEST
Zagreb
Sarajevo
BEOGRAD (BELGRADE)
Skopje
Tiranë
Timișoara
Graz
Bari
To Ancona
To Ortona
W-DRM6535-A1 -1-1-2
Copyright © Rand McNally & Co.
Meters
Feet
Sea Level
0 25 50 75 100 150 200 250 Kilometers
0 25 50 100 150 Miles
Scale 1 : 2,500,000
Lambert Conformal Conic Projection

UKRAINE
ROMANIA
MOLDOVA
BULGARIA
TURKEY
GREECE
BLACK SEA
CARPATHIAN MOUNTAINS
TRANSYLVANIAN ALPS
RHODOPE MOUNTAINS
BUCUREȘTI
(BUCHAREST)
Chișinău
ODESA
Iași
Cluj-Napoca
Brașov
Galați
Brăila
Ploiești
Constanța
Craiova
Varna
Burgas
Plovdiv
Ruse
Pleven
Chernivtsi
Tulcea
Edirne
İSTANBUL
Mouths of the Danube
East of Greenwich

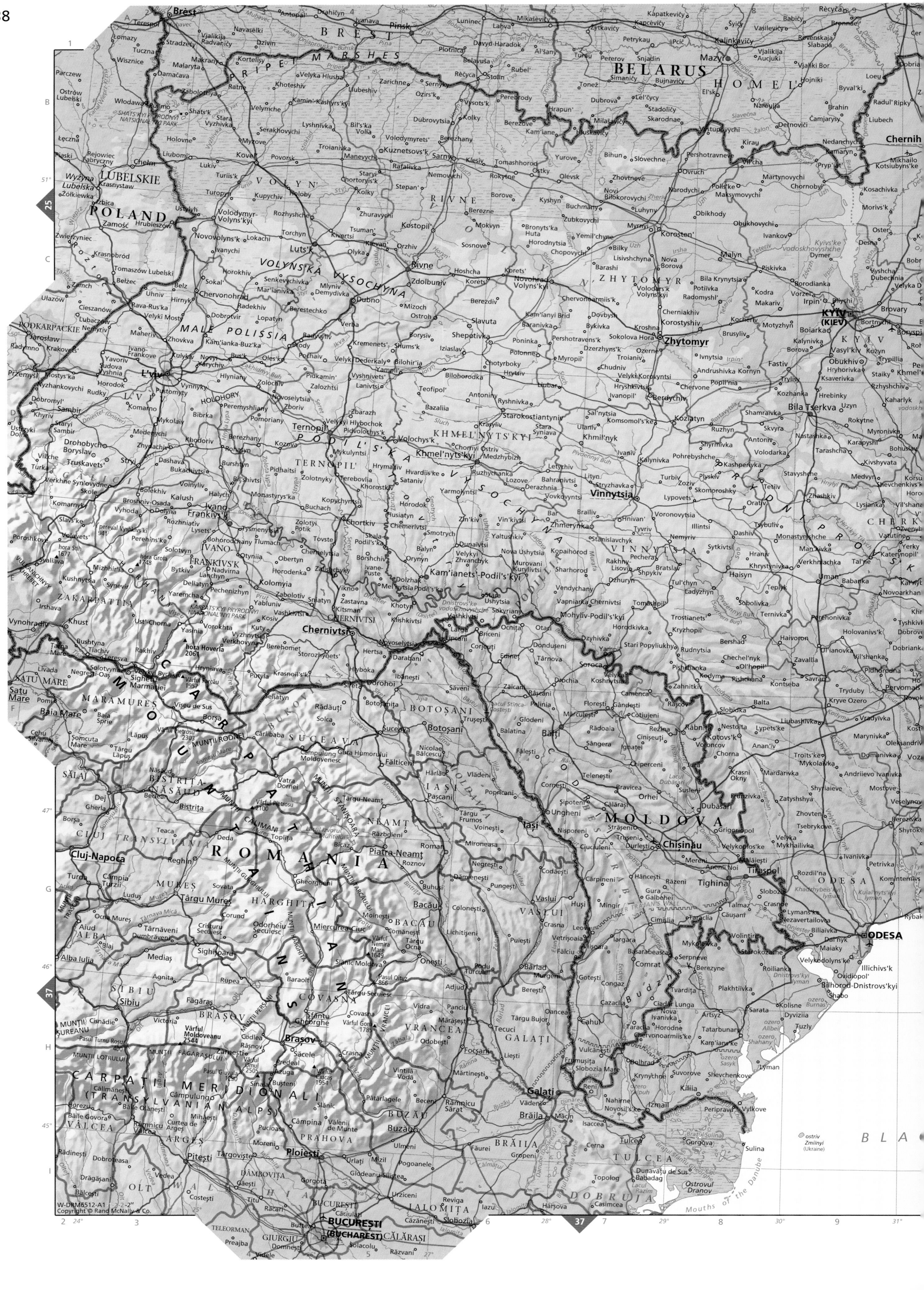

BELARUS

POLAND

ROMANIA

MOLDOVA

BREST

HOMEL'

PRIPET MARSHES

LUBELSKIE

PODKARPACKIE

VOLYN'

RIVNE

VOLYNS'KA VYSOCHYNA

MALE POLISSIA

L'VIV

TERNOPIL'

PODIL'S'KA VYSOCHYNA

KHMEL'NYTS'KYI

ZHYTOMYR

KYÏV (KIEV)

VINNYTSIA

IVANO-FRANKIVS'K

ZAKARPATTIA

CHERNIVTSI

CARPATHIAN MOUNTAINS

MARAMUREȘ

SATU MARE

SUCEAVA

BOTOȘANI

IAȘI

NEAMȚ

BISTRIȚA-NĂSĂUD

CLUJ

MUREȘ

HARGHITA

BACĂU

VASLUI

COVASNA

BRAȘOV

SIBIU

ALBA

VRANCEA

GALAȚI

BUZĂU

PRAHOVA

DÂMBOVIȚA

ARGEȘ

VÂLCEA

CARPAȚII MERIDIONALI (TRANSYLVANIAN ALPS)

BRĂILA

TULCEA

IALOMIȚA

CĂLĂRAȘI

TELEORMAN

GIURGIU

BUCUREȘTI (BUCHAREST)

ODESA

Chișinău

Tighina

Tiraspol

Budzhak

Mouths of the Danube

BLA[CK SEA]

ostriv Zmiinyi (Ukraine)

W-DRM6512-A1

Kursk
Voronež
Belgorod
Staryj Oskol
Sumy
KHARKIV
Poltava
Cherkasy
Kremenchuk
Lubny
Nizhyn
Konotop
Kirovohrad
Oleksandriia
Dniprodzerzhyns'k
DNIPROPETROVS'K
Kryvyi Rih
Nikopol'
Zaporizhzhia
Melitopol'
Berdians'k
Mariupol'
DONETS'K
Makiivka
Horlivka
Kramators'k
Slov'ians'k
Sieverodonets'k
Lysychans'k
Luhans'k
Alchevs'k
Stakhanov
Krasnyi Luch
Torez
Taganrog
ROSTOV-NA-DONU
Novošahtinsk
Mykolaïv
Kherson
Yevpatoriia
Simferopol'
Sevastopol'
Yalta
Alushta
Feodosiia
Kerch
Krasnodar
Novorossijsk
Anapa
Ejsk
R U S S I A
U K R A I N E
KURSKAJA OBLAST'
BELGORODSKAJA OBLAST'
VORONEŽSKAJA OBLAST'
ROSTOVSKAJA OBLAST'
KRASNODARSKIJ KRAJ
ADYGEJA
SREDNERUSSKAJA VOZVYŠENNOST'
Don Upland (Donskaja grjada)
RESPUBLIKA KRYM
KRYMS'KYI PIVOSTRIV (CRIMEAN PENINSULA)
Kerchens'kyi pivostriv
Sea of Azov
BLACK SEA
Gulf of Taganrog
Karkinits'ka zatoka
Kakhovs'ke vodoskhovyshche
Kremenchuts'ke vodoskhovyshche
Dnieper
Don
Meters
Feet
2000
6560
1000
3280
500
1640
200
656
Sea Level
200
656
2000
6560
0 25 50 75 100 150 200 250 Kilometers
0 25 50 100 150 Miles
Scale 1 : 2 500 000
Lambert Conformal Conic Projection
32° East of Greenwich
27
41
43

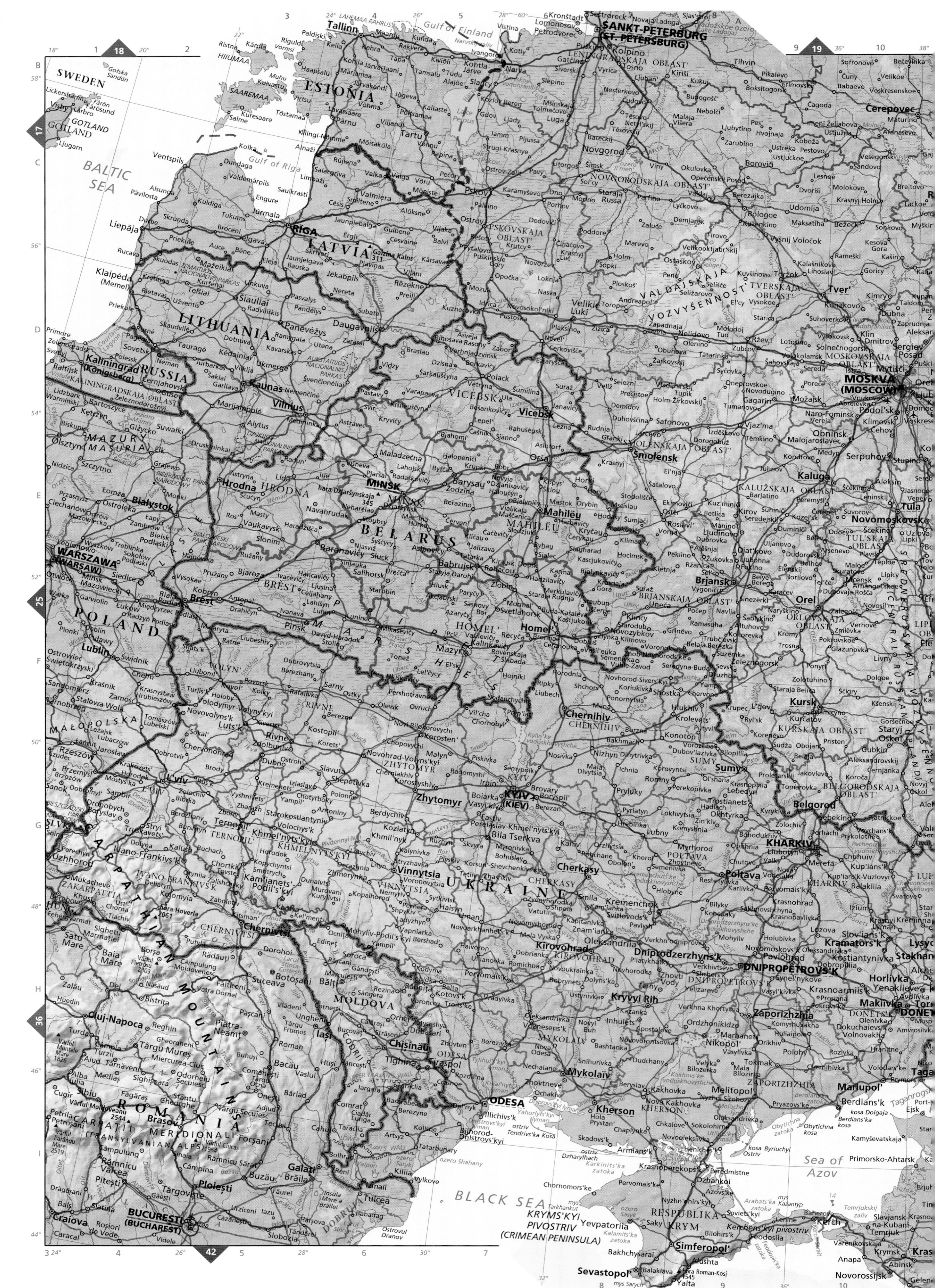
SWEDEN
ESTONIA
LATVIA
LITHUANIA
RUSSIA
BELARUS
POLAND
UKRAINE
MOLDOVA
ROMANIA
BALTIC SEA
Gulf of Riga
Gulf of Finland
BLACK SEA
Sea of Azov
GOTLAND
SAAREMAA
HIIUMAA
Tallinn
Riga
Vilnius
Kaunas
Kaliningrad (Königsberg)
KALININGRADSKAJA OBLAST'
Klaipėda (Memel)
Liepāja
Ventspils
Daugavpils
Šiauliai
Panevėžys
Tartu
Pärnu
Narva
SANKT-PETERBURG (ST. PETERSBURG)
LENINGRADSKAJA OBLAST'
Novgorod
NOVGORODSKAJA OBLAST'
Pskov
PSKOVSKAJA OBLAST'
Velikie Luki
VALDAJSKAJA VOZVYŠENNOST'
Tver'
TVERSKAJA OBLAST'
MOSKVA (MOSCOW)
MOSKOVSKAJA OBLAST'
Smolensk
SMOLENSKAJA OBLAST'
Kaluga
KALUŽSKAJA OBLAST'
Tula
Brjansk
BRJANSKAJA OBLAST'
Orel
ORLOVSKAJA OBLAST'
Kursk
KURSKAJA OBLAST'
Belgorod
BELGORODSKAJA OBLAST'
MINSK
Hrodna
HRODNA
Brest
BREST
Vicebsk
VICEBSK
Mahilëu
MAHILËU
Homel'
HOMEL'
Babrujsk
Pinsk
PRIPET MARSHES
WARSZAWA (WARSAW)
Białystok
Lublin
MAZURY (MASURIA)
MAŁOPOLSKA
Rzeszów
L'viv
Luts'k
Rivne
Zhytomyr
KYIV (KIEV)
Chernihiv
Sumy
Kharkiv
Poltava
Cherkasy
Vinnytsia
Chernivtsi
Ternopil'
Ivano-Frankivs'k
Uzhhorod
Khmel'nyts'kyi
Kirovohrad
Kremenchuk
Dniprodzerzhyns'k
DNIPROPETROVS'K
Zaporizhzhia
Kryvyi Rih
Mykolaiv
Kherson
ODESA
Melitopol'
Mariupol'
Berdians'k
Simferopol'
Sevastopol'
Yalta
Kerch
Yevpatoriia
RESPUBLIKA KRYM
KRYMS'KYI PIVOSTRIV (CRIMEAN PENINSULA)
Chişinău
Tiraspol
Bălţi
Iaşi
Suceava
Botoşani
Bacău
Galaţi
Brăila
Tulcea
Constanţa
Ploieşti
BUCUREŞTI (BUCHAREST)
Braşov
Cluj-Napoca
Sibiu
Craiova
Piteşti
CARPATHIAN MOUNTAINS
CARPAŢII MERIDIONALI (TRANSYLVANIAN ALPS)
Hoverla 2061
Moldoveanu 2544
Novorossijsk
Anapa
Krymsk
Horlivka
Kramators'k
Čerepovec
Tihvin
Vologda
Borovici
Rževˈ
Kalinin
Kursk
Galazina Kalns 311
Dzjaržynskaja 345

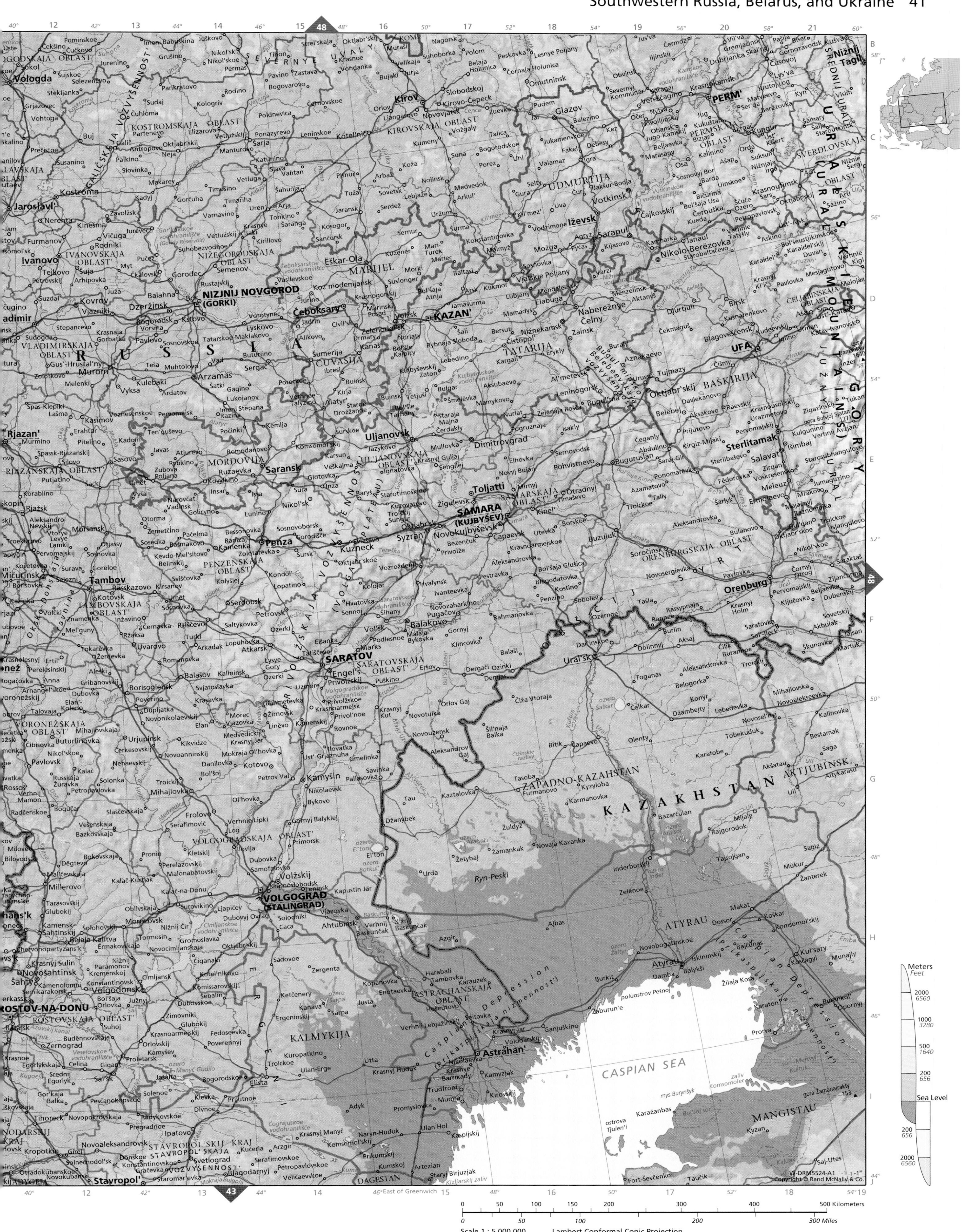

R U S S I A
K A Z A K H S T A N
CASPIAN SEA
VOLGOGRAD (STALINGRAD)
SARATOV
SAMARA (KUJBYŠEV)
KAZAN'
NIZNIJ NOVGOROD (GORKI)
PERM'
UFA
Orenburg
Astrahan'
ROSTOV-NA-DONU
Stavropol'
Uljanovsk
Penza
Tambov
Saransk
Toljatti
Ural'sk
Atyrau
Elista
Kirov
Ižjevsk
Vologda
Jaroslavl'
Kostroma
Ivanovo
Rjazan'
Caspian Depression
Meters
Feet
2000
6560
1000
3280
500
1640
200
656
Sea Level
Scale 1 : 5,000,000
Lambert Conformal Conic Projection
Kilometers
Miles
East of Greenwich
Copyright © Rand McNally & Co.

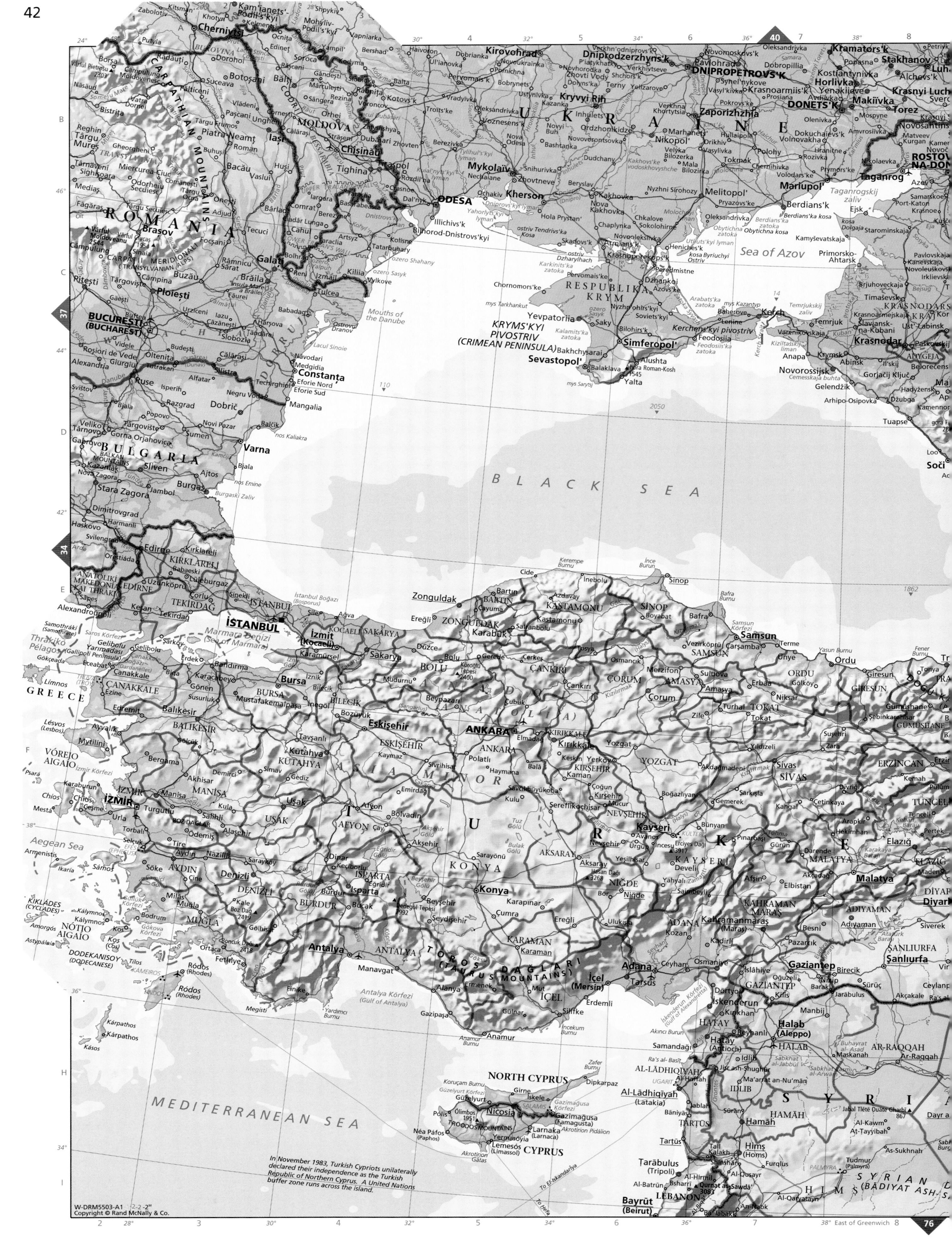

UKRAINE
ROMANIA
MOLDOVA
BULGARIA
GREECE
TURKEY
SYRIA
LEBANON
NORTH CYPRUS
CYPRUS
BLACK SEA
Sea of Azov
MEDITERRANEAN SEA
Aegean Sea
CARPATHIAN MOUNTAINS
MERIDIONALII (TRANSYLVANIAN ALPS)
BALKAN MOUNTAINS
TOROS DAĞLARI (TAURUS MOUNTAINS)
KRYMS'KYI PIVOSTRIV (CRIMEAN PENINSULA)
RESPUBLIKA KRYM
ANATOLIA
ASIA MINOR
Mouths of the Danube
BUCUREŞTI (BUCHAREST)
Chişinău
ODESA
Mykolaïv
Kherson
Kirovohrad
Dniprodzerzhyns'k
DNIPROPETROVS'K
Zaporizhzhia
Kryvyi Rih
DONETS'K
Mariupol'
Melitopol'
Nikopol'
Berdians'k
Taganrog
Simferopol'
Sevastopol'
Yevpatoriia
Kerch
Feodosiia
Yalta
Krasnodar
Novorossijsk
Soči
Chernivtsi
Iaşi
Galaţi
Brăila
Constanţa
Ploieşti
Braşov
Ruse
Varna
Burgas
Sliven
Stara Zagora
Edirne
İSTANBUL
İzmit (Kocaeli)
Bursa
Zonguldak
Samsun
Sinop
Ordu
Eskişehir
ANKARA
Kırıkkale
Yozgat
Sivas
Kayseri
Konya
İzmir
Manisa
Denizli
Isparta
Antalya
Adana
İçel (Mersin)
Kahramanmaraş
Gaziantep
Şanlıurfa
Malatya
Elazığ
İskenderun
Halab (Aleppo)
Al-Lādhiqīyah (Latakia)
Ḥamāh
Ḥimṣ (Homs)
Ṭarābulus (Tripoli)
Bayrūt (Beirut)
Nicosia
Lemesós (Limassol)
Larnaka (Larnaca)
Gazimağusa (Famagusta)
Ródos (Rhodes)
In November 1983, Turkish Cypriots unilaterally declared their independence as the Turkish Republic of Northern Cyprus. A United Nations buffer zone runs across the island.
W-DRM5503-A1
East of Greenwich

KAZAKHSTAN
ZAPADNO-KAZAHSTAN
ATYRAU
AKTJUBINSK
MANGISTAU
RUSSIA
KALMYKIJA
ASTRAHANSKAJA OBLAST'
VOLGOGRADSKAJA OBLAST'
ROSTOVSKAJA OBLAST'
STAVROPOL'SKIJ KRAJ
DAGESTAN
ČEČNJA (CHECHNYA)
GEORGIA
ARMENIA
AZERBAIJAN
TURKMENISTAN
BALKAN
IRAN
IRAQ
CASPIAN SEA
-28
Caspian Depression (Prikaspijskaja nizmennost')
CAUCASUS
BOL'ŠOJ KAVKAZ
LESSER CAUCASUS
TALISH MOUNTAINS
RESHTEH-YE KŪHHĀ-YE ALBORZ (ELBURZ MOUNTAINS)
MESOPOTAMIA
zaliv Kara-Bogaz-Gol (Kara-Bogaz-Gol Gulf)
Abşeron yarımadası (Apsheron Peninsula)
plato Mangyšlak
VOLGOGRAD (STALINGRAD)
Astrahan'
Atyrau
Aktau (Ševčenko)
Mahačkala
Groznyj
Vladikavkaz (Dzaudzhikau)
Nal'čik
Stavropol'
Tbilisi
Yerevan (Erivan)
BAKI (BAKU)
Sumqayıt
Gäncä
Batumi
Turkmenbaşy
Nebitdag
Tabrīz
Orūmīyeh (Urmia)
Rasht
Qazvīn
TEHRĀN (TEHERAN)
Qom
Hamadān
Arāk (Sultanabad)
Kermānshāh (Bākhtarān)
Sanandaj
Zanjān
Ardabīl
Erzurum
Van
Al-Mawsil (Mosul)
Irbil
Karkūk
As-Sulaymānīyah
BAGHDĀD
gora El'brus (Mount Elbrus) 5642
Ağrı Dağı (Mount Ararat) 5137
Qolleh-ye Damāvand (Mount Demavend) 5604
Meters
Feet
4000 13120
3000 9840
2000 6560
1000 3280
500 1640
200 656
Sea Level
200 656
2000 6560
0 50 100 150 200 300 400 500 Kilometers
0 50 100 200 300 Miles
Scale 1 : 5 000 000
Lambert Conformal Conic Projection

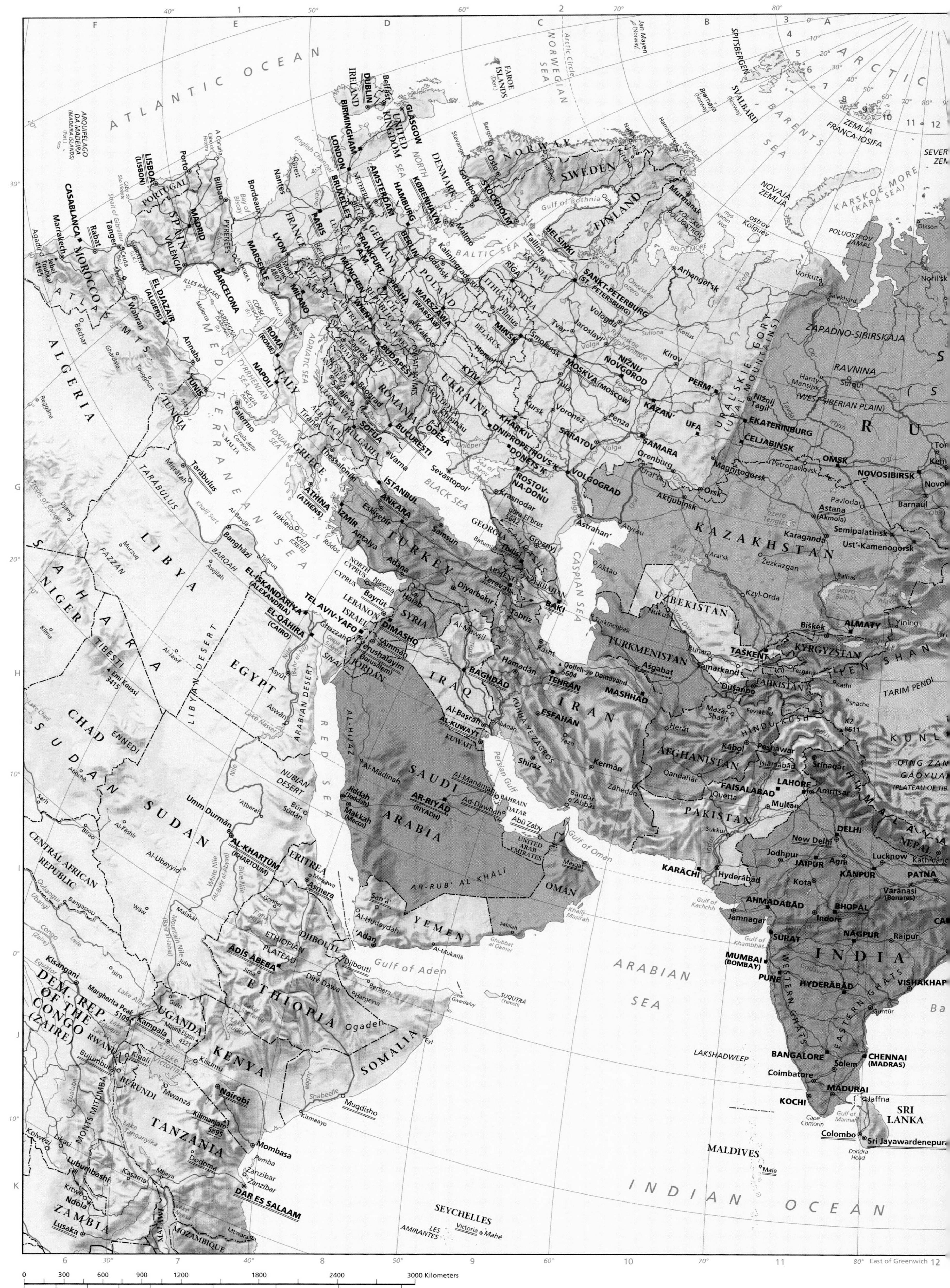
ATLANTIC OCEAN
ARCTIC
NORWEGIAN SEA
BARENTS SEA
KARSKOE MORE (KARA SEA)
NORTH SEA
BALTIC SEA
MEDITERRANEAN SEA
BLACK SEA
CASPIAN SEA
RED SEA
ARABIAN SEA
INDIAN OCEAN
Persian Gulf
Gulf of Oman
Gulf of Aden
IRELAND
UNITED KINGDOM
NORWAY
SWEDEN
FINLAND
DENMARK
PORTUGAL
SPAIN
FRANCE
GERMANY
POLAND
ITALY
GREECE
UKRAINE
ROMANIA
BULGARIA
TURKEY
SYRIA
IRAQ
IRAN
SAUDI ARABIA
YEMEN
OMAN
KAZAKHSTAN
UZBEKISTAN
TURKMENISTAN
AFGHANISTAN
PAKISTAN
INDIA
NEPAL
SRI LANKA
MALDIVES
SEYCHELLES
MOROCCO
ALGERIA
TUNISIA
LIBYA
EGYPT
SUDAN
CHAD
NIGER
ETHIOPIA
ERITREA
DJIBOUTI
SOMALIA
KENYA
UGANDA
TANZANIA
ZAMBIA
RWANDA
BURUNDI
CENTRAL AFRICAN REPUBLIC
DEM. REP. OF THE CONGO (ZAIRE)
SAHARA
LONDON
DUBLIN
PARIS
MADRID
LISBOA (LISBON)
ROMA (ROME)
BERLIN
WARSZAWA (WARSAW)
MOSKVA (MOSCOW)
SANKT-PETERBURG (ST. PETERSBURG)
KYIV
ISTANBUL
ANKARA
ATHINA (ATHENS)
EL-QAHIRA (CAIRO)
BAGHDAD
TEHRAN
AR-RIYAD (RIYADH)
AL-KHARTUM (KHARTOUM)
ADIS ABEBA
Nairobi
DAR ES SALAAM
New Delhi
MUMBAI (BOMBAY)
KARACHI
CHENNAI (MADRAS)
Colombo
Scale 1 : 30,000,000
Lambert Azimuthal Equal Area Projection
3000 Kilometers
1800 Miles
East of Greenwich

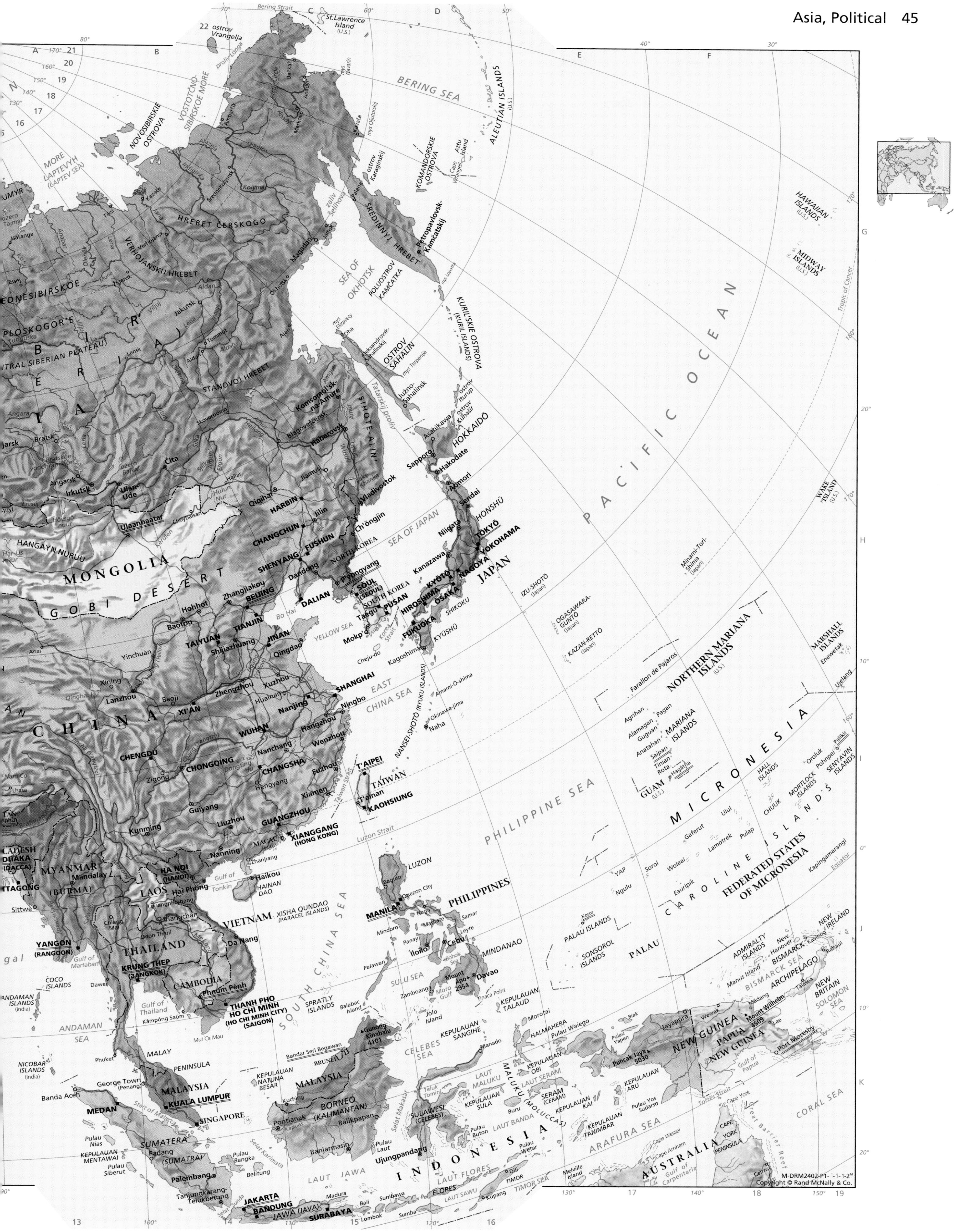

Meters / Feet: 6000 / 19680; 4000 / 13120; 3000 / 9840; 2000 / 6560; 1000 / 3280; 500 / 1640; 200 / 656; Sea Level; 200 / 656; 2000 / 6560

0 300 600 900 1200 1800 2400 3000 Kilometers

0 300 600 1200 1800 Miles

Scale 1 : 30,000,000 Lambert Azimuthal Equal Area Projection

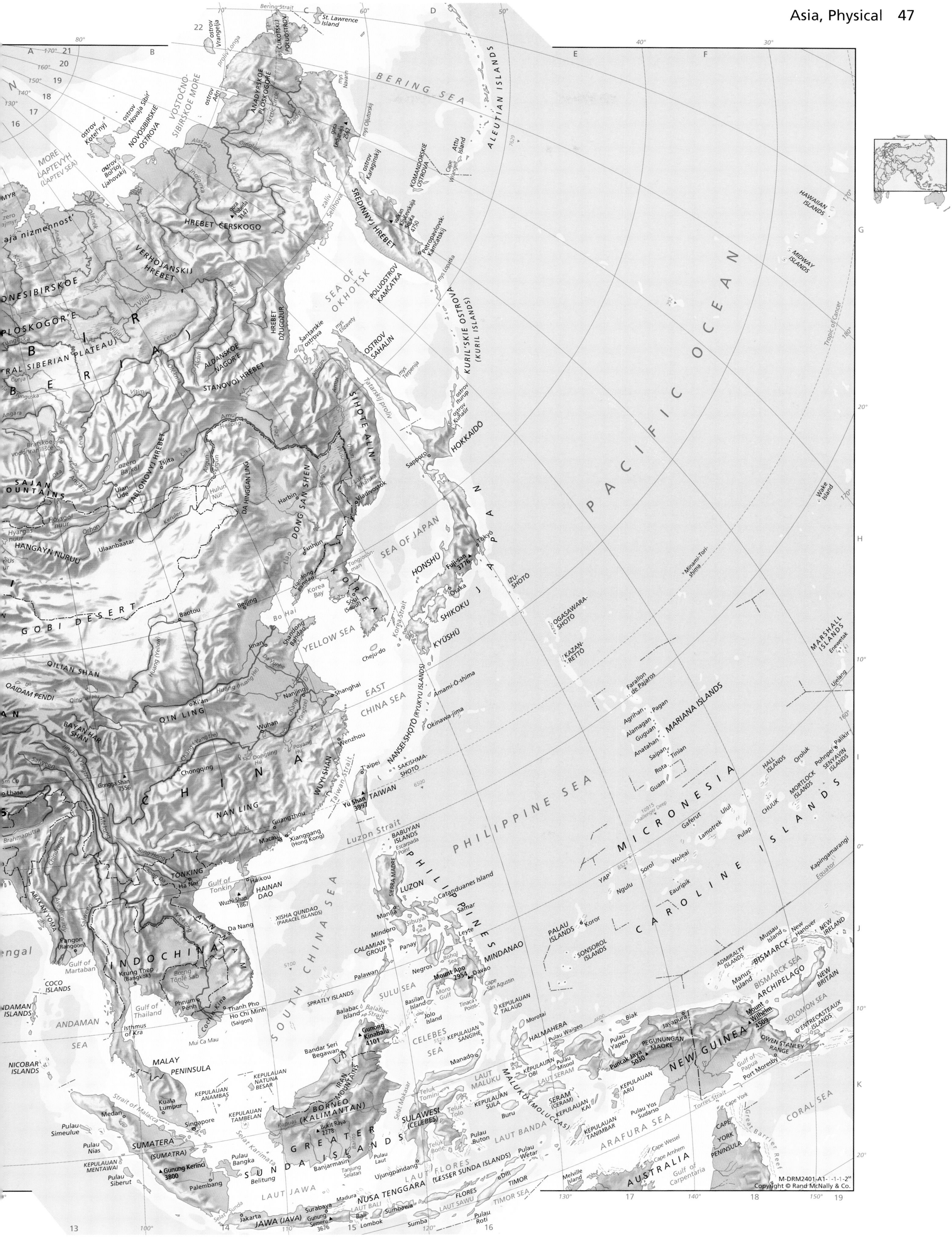

Bering Strait
St. Lawrence Island
BERING SEA
ALEUTIAN ISLANDS
KOMANDORSKIE OSTROVA
Attu Island
Cape Wrangell
ostrov Vrangelja
CUKOTSKIJ POLUOSTROV
ANADYRSKOE PLOSKOGOR'E
Arctic Circle
VOSTOČNO-SIBIRSKOE MORE
NOVOSIBIRSKIE OSTROVA
ostrov Kotel'nyj
ostrov Novaja Sibir'
ostrov Bol'šoj Ljahovskij
MORE LAPTEVYH (LAPTEV SEA)
ostrov Karaginskij
SREDINNYJ HREBET
POLUOSTROV KAMČATKA
Petropavlovsk-Kamčatskij
mys Lopatka
HREBET ČERSKOGO
VERHOJANSKIJ HREBET
SEA OF OKHOTSK
HREBET DŽUGDŽUR
ALDANSKOE NAGOR'E
STANOVOJ HREBET
CENTRAL SIBERIAN PLATEAU
SIBERIA
Šantarskie ostrova
OSTROV SAHALIN
KURIL'SKIE OSTROVA (KURIL ISLANDS)
Tatarskij proliv
SIHOTE-ALIN'
HOKKAIDŌ
Sapporo
Amur
ozero Bajkal
JABLONOVYJ HREBET
SAJAN MOUNTAINS
Ulan-Ude
Čita
DA HINGGAN LING
DONG SAN SHEN
Harbin
Vladivostok
Hövsgöl nuur
HANGAYN NURUU
Ulaanbaatar
GOBI DESERT
Baotou
Beijing
Fushun
Liaodong Bandao
Korea Bay
KOREA
Sŏul (Seoul)
SEA OF JAPAN
HONSHŪ
Fuji-san 3776
Tōkyō
Ōsaka
SHIKOKU
KYŪSHŪ
JAPAN
IZU-SHOTŌ
PACIFIC OCEAN
HAWAIIAN ISLANDS
MIDWAY ISLANDS
Tropic of Cancer
Wake Island
Minami-Tori-shima
OGASAWARA-SHOTŌ
KAZAN-RETTŌ
MARSHALL ISLANDS
Enewetak
Ujelang
Bo Hai
Shandong Bandao
Jinan
YELLOW SEA
Cheju-do
Korea Strait
QILIAN SHAN
QAIDAM PENDI
Xi'an
QIN LING
Nanjing
Shanghai
EAST CHINA SEA
Amami-Ō-shima
Okinawa-jima
NANSEI-SHOTŌ (RYUKYU ISLANDS)
Farallon de Pajaros
Agrihan
Pagan
Alamagan
Guguan
Anatahan
Saipan
Tinian
Rota
Guam
MARIANA ISLANDS
BAYAN HAR SHAN
Wuhan
Chongqing
Wenzhou
CHINA
WUYI SHAN
T'aipei
Taiwan Strait
SAKISHIMA-SHOTŌ
Yü Shan 3997
TAIWAN
Lhasa
Gongga Shan 7556
NAN LING
Guangzhou
Macau
Xianggang (Hong Kong)
Luzon Strait
BABUYAN ISLANDS
PHILIPPINE SEA
MICRONESIA
HALL ISLANDS
MORTLOCK ISLANDS
SENYAVIN ISLANDS
Pohnpei
Palikir
Oroluk
CHUUK
CAROLINE ISLANDS
Ulul
Gaferut
Lamotrek
Pulap
Woleai
Sorol
Eauripik
Ngulu
YAP
Kapingamarangi
Equator
Brahmaputra
Mekong
TONKING
Gulf of Tonkin
Ha Noi
Haikou
HAINAN DAO
Wuzhi Shan 1867
XISHA QUNDAO (PARACEL ISLANDS)
LUZON
SIERRA MADRE
Catanduanes Island
Samar
Leyte
Manila
Mindoro
Sibuyan Sea
PHILIPPINES
Panay
Negros
Bohol Sea
MINDANAO
Mount Apo 2954
Davao
Moro Gulf
Cape San Agustin
CALAMIAN GROUP
Palawan
SULU SEA
Da Nang
ANNAM
INDOCHINA
ARAKAN YOMA
Yangon (Rangoon)
Gulf of Martaban
Bay of Bengal
Krung Thep (Bangkok)
Bœng Tônlé Sab
Phnum Pénh
Thanh Pho Ho Chi Minh (Saigon)
Gulf of Thailand
Isthmus of Kra
Mui Ca Mau
COCO ISLANDS
ANDAMAN ISLANDS
ANDAMAN SEA
NICOBAR ISLANDS
MALAY PENINSULA
SOUTH CHINA SEA
SPRATLY ISLANDS
Balabac Island
Balabac Strait
Basilan Island
Jolo Island
Tinaca Point
PALAU ISLANDS
Koror
SONSOROL ISLANDS
KEPULAUAN TALAUD
KEPULAUAN SANGIHE
CELEBES SEA
Gunong Kinabalu 4101
Bandar Seri Begawan
Manado
Morotai
HALMAHERA
Pulau Waigeo
Biak
Pulau Yapen
Jayapura
PEGUNUNGAN MAOKE
Puncak Jaya 5030
NEW GUINEA
Mount Wilhelm 4509
OWEN STANLEY RANGE
Gulf of Papua
Port Moresby
ADMIRALTY ISLANDS
Manus Island
Mussau Island
New Hanover
NEW IRELAND
BISMARCK SEA
BISMARCK ARCHIPELAGO
NEW BRITAIN
SOLOMON SEA
D'ENTRECASTEAUX ISLANDS
CORAL SEA
Torres Strait
Cape York
CAPE YORK PENINSULA
Great Barrier Reef
Gulf of Carpentaria
ARAFURA SEA
AUSTRALIA
Melville Island
Cape Wessel
Cape Arnhem
KEPULAUAN NATUNA BESAR
KEPULAUAN ANAMBAS
Kuala Lumpur
Strait of Malacca
Singapore
Medan
Pulau Simeulue
Pulau Nias
SUMATERA (SUMATRA)
KEPULAUAN MENTAWAI
Pulau Siberut
Gunung Kerinci 3800
Palembang
KEPULAUAN TAMBELAN
Selat Karimata
Pulau Bangka
Belitung
BORNEO (KALIMANTAN)
IRAN MOUNTAINS
Bukit Raya 2278
Kapuas
Barito
Banjarmasin
Tanjung Selatan
GREATER SUNDA ISLANDS
Selat Makasar
Teluk Tomini
SULAWESI (CELEBES)
Teluk Tolo
Teluk Bone
Pulau Buton
Ujungpandang
KEPULAUAN SULA
Buru
LAUT MALUKU
MALUKU (MOLUCCAS)
KEPULAUAN OBI
Pulau Misool
LAUT SERAM
SERAM (CERAM)
KEPULAUAN KAI
KEPULAUAN ARU
KEPULAUAN TANIMBAR
Pulau Yos Sudarso
LAUT BANDA
Pulau Wetar
Dili
TIMOR
TIMOR SEA
Pulau Roti
LAUT FLORES
NUSA TENGGARA (LESSER SUNDA ISLANDS)
FLORES
LAUT SAWU
Sumba
Sumbawa
Lombok
Bali
LAUT BALI
Madura
Surabaya
LAUT JAWA
JAWA (JAVA)
Jakarta
Selat Sunda
Gunung Semeru 3676
M-DRM2401-A1- -1-1-2M
Copyright © Rand McNally & Co.

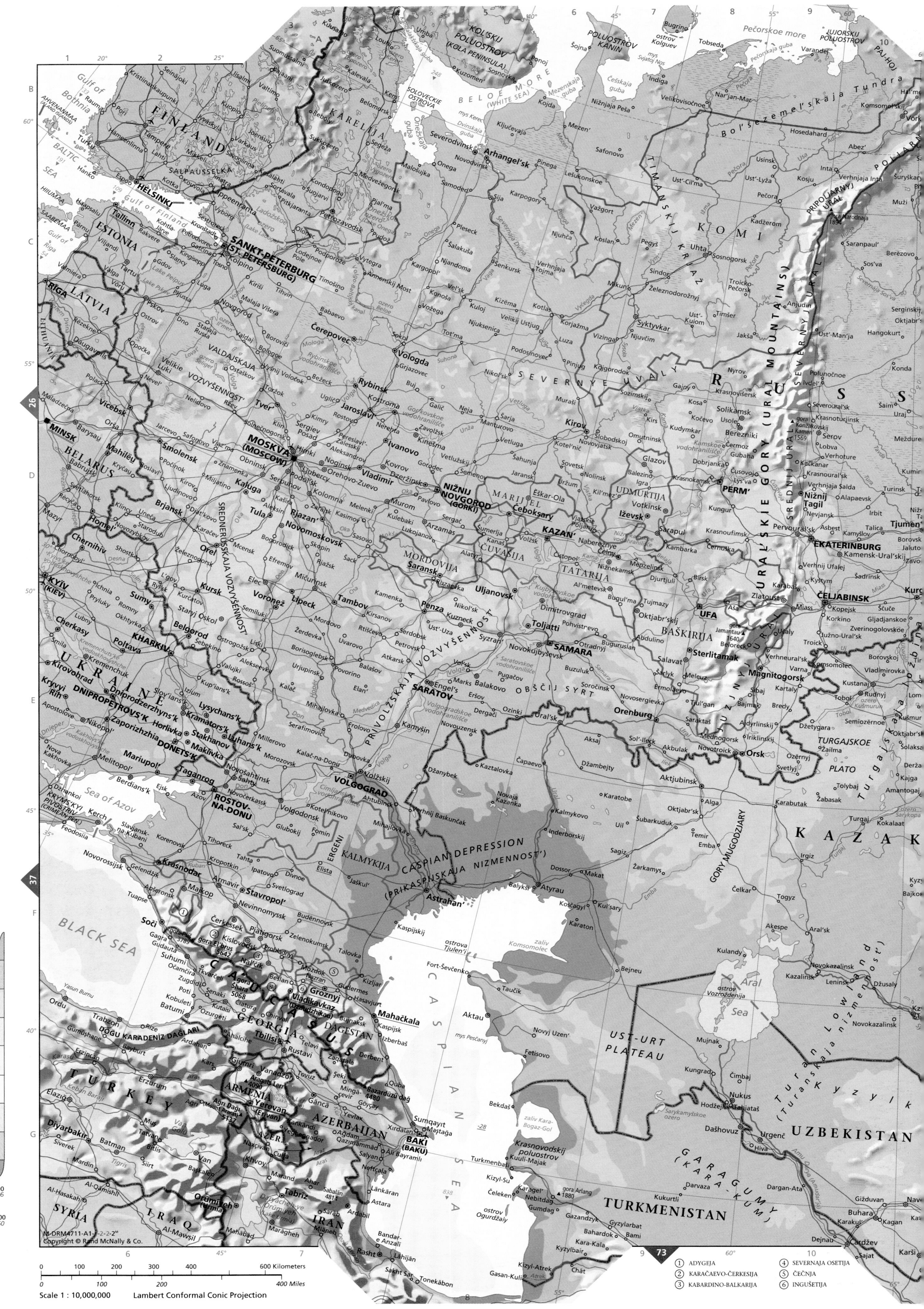
FINLAND
ESTONIA
LATVIA
LITHUANIA
BELARUS
UKRAINE
RUSSIA
KAZAK
UZBEKISTAN
TURKMENISTAN
GEORGIA
ARMENIA
AZERBAIJAN
TURKEY
SYRIA
IRAQ
IRAN
Gulf of Bothnia
BALTIC SEA
Gulf of Finland
Gulf of Riga
BELOE MORE (WHITE SEA)
Pečorskoe more
Sea of Azov
BLACK SEA
CASPIAN SEA
Aral Sea
KOL'SKIJ POLUOSTROV (KOLA PENINSULA)
POLUOSTROV KANIN
KARELIJA
KOMI
TIMANSKIJ KRJAŽ
Bol'šezemel'skaja Tundra
SEVERNYE UVALY
VALDAJSKAJA VOZVYŠENNOST'
SREDNERUSSKAJA VOZVYŠENNOST'
PRIVOLŽSKAJA VOZVYŠENNOST'
URAL'SKIE GORY (URAL MOUNTAINS)
SEVERNYJ URAL
SREDNIJ URAL
JUŽNYJ URAL
PRIPOLJARNYJ URAL
MARIJ EL
UDMURTIJA
ČUVAŠIJA
MORDOVIJA
TATARIJA
BAŠKIRIJA
KALMYKIJA
DAGESTAN
CASPIAN DEPRESSION (PRIKASPIJSKAJA NIZMENNOST')
OBŠČIJ SYRT
ERGENI
TURGAJSKOE PLATO
GORY MUGODŽARY
UST-URT PLATEAU
Turan Lowland (Turanskaja nizmennost')
GARAGUMY (KARA-KUM)
Kyzyl
CAUCASUS
DOĞU KARADENİZ DAĞLARI
HELSINKI
Tallinn
RIGA
MINSK
KYÏV (KIEV)
SANKT-PETERBURG (ST. PETERSBURG)
MOSKVA (MOSCOW)
NIŽNIJ NOVGOROD (GOR'KIJ)
KAZAN'
SAMARA
SARATOV
VOLGOGRAD
ROSTOV-NA-DONU
KHARKIV
DNIPROPETROVS'K
DONETS'K
PERM'
EKATERINBURG
ČELJABINSK
UFA
Tbilisi
Yerevan (Erivan)
BAKI (BAKU)
Arhangel'sk
Petrozavodsk
Vologda
Jaroslavl'
Tver'
Smolensk
Kaluga
Tula
Rjazan'
Vladimir
Ivanovo
Kirov
Izevsk
Čeboksary
Uljanovsk
Penza
Toljatti
Orenburg
Magnitogorsk
Orsk
Aktjubinsk
Atyrau
Astrahan'
Stavropol'
Krasnodar
Groznyj
Mahačkala
Syktyvkar
Uhta
Voronež
Lipeck
Tambov
Kursk
Belgorod
Brjansk
Orel
Mariupol'
Zaporizhzhia
Aktau
Nukus
Dašhovuz
Turkmenbaši
Tabriz
Meters
Feet
6000
19680
4000
13120
3000
9840
2000
6560
1000
3280
500
1640
200
656
Sea Level
200
656
2000
6560
0
100
200
300
400
600 Kilometers
0
100
200
400 Miles
Scale 1 : 10,000,000
Lambert Conformal Conic Projection
① ADYGEJA
② KARAČAEVO-ČERKESIJA
③ KABARDINO-BALKARIJA
④ SEVERNAJA OSETIJA
⑤ ČEČNJA
⑥ INGUŠETIJA
26
37
73
M-DRM4711-A1-2-2-2"
Copyright © Rand McNally & Co.

SREDNESIBIRSKOE PLOSKOGOR'E
(CENTRAL SIBERIAN PLATEAU)
(SIBERIA)
SIBIR'
ZAPADNO-SIBIRSKAJA RAVNINA
(WEST SIBERIAN PLAIN)
CENTRALNO-TUNGUSSKOE PLATO
ENISEJSKIJ KRJAŽ
VOSTOČNYJ SAJAN
SAYAN MOUNTAINS
ZAPADNYJ SAJAN
TUVA
TANNU-OLA HREBET
HREBET SANGILEN
ALTAJ
ALTAI
MONGOLIA
HANGAYN NURUU
MONGOL ALTAYN NURUU
Barabinskaja step'
Kulundinskaja ravnina
KAZAKHSKIJ MELKOSOPOČNIK
(KAZAKH HILLS)
HREBET TARBAGATAJ
JUNGGAR PENDI
DZHUNGARIAN ALATAU
BOROHORO SHAN
BOGDA SHAN
Turpan Pendi
(Turfan Depression)
KURUKTAG
TIEN SHAN
KYRGYZSTAN
TAJIKISTAN
PAMIR
XINJIANG
CHINA
TARIM PENDI
Taklimakan Shamo
(Takla Makan Desert)
ALTUN SHAN
KUNLUN SHAN
QAIDAM PENDI
QINGHAI
GANSU
BEI SHAN
PESKI MOJYNKUM
Betpak-Dala
ozero Balhaš
(Lake Balkhash)
Obskaja guba
JAMAL
Tazovskij poluostrov
Arctic Circle
NOVOSIBIRSK
OMSK
Tomsk
Kemerovo
Novokuzneck
Barnaul
Krasnojarsk
Irkutsk
Bratsk
Angarsk
Surgut
Pavlodar
Astana (Akmola)
Karaganda
Semipalatinsk
Ust'-Kamenogorsk
ALMATY
Biškek
TAŠKENT
Ürümqi
Mount Belukha 4374
pik Pobedy 7439
pik Kommunizma (Communism Peak) 7495
52
90° East of Greenwich
50

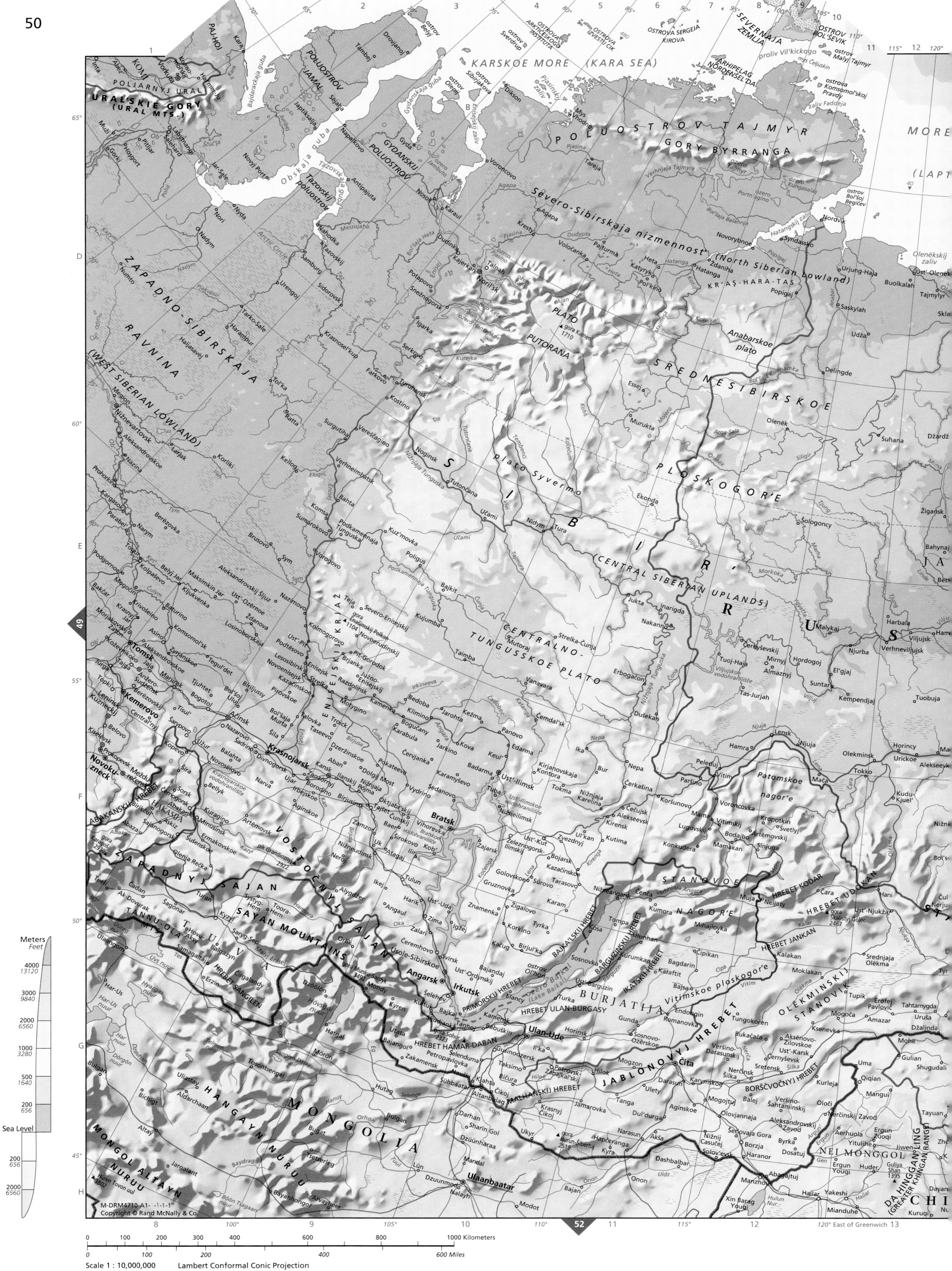
KARSKOE MORE (KARA SEA)
SEVERNAJA ZEMLJA
ARHIPELAG NORDENŠEL'DA
POLUOSTROV TAJMYR
GORY BYRRANGA
POLUOSTROV JAMAL
GYDANSKIJ POLUOSTROV
Tazovskij poluostrov
Obskaja guba
URAL'SKIE GORY (URAL MTS.)
POLJARNYJ URAL
Sevěro-Sibirskaja nizmennost' (North Siberian Lowland)
ZAPADNO-SIBIRSKAJA RAVNINA (WEST SIBERIAN LOWLAND)
PLATO PUTORANA
gora Kamen' 1710
Anabarskoe plato
SREDNESIBIRSKOE PLOSKOGOR'E (CENTRAL SIBERIAN UPLANDS)
plato Syverma
CENTRAL'NO-TUNGUSSKOE PLATO
S I B I R ' R U S
ENISEJSKIJ KRJAŽ
VOSTOČNYJ SAJAN
SAYAN MOUNTAINS
ZAPADNYJ SAJAN
TANNU-OLA
HREBET SANGILEN
Ozero Bajkal (Lake Baikal)
BAJKAL'SKIJ HREBET
BARGUZINSKIJ HREBET
PRIMORSKIJ HREBET
HREBET ULAN-BURGASY
HREBET HAMAR-DABAN
BURJATIJA
Vitimskoe ploskogor'e
JABLONOVYJ HREBET
STANOVOE NAGOR'E
Patomskoe nagor'e
HREBET KODAR
HREBET UDOKAN
HREBET JANKAN
OLEKMINSKIJ STANOVIK
BORŠČOVOČNYJ HREBET
MALHANSKIJ HREBET
MONGOLIA
HANGAYN NURUU
MONGOL ALTAYN NURUU
NEI MONGGOL
DA HINGGAN LING (GREATER KHINGAN RANGE)
Noril'sk
Dudinka
Krasnojarsk
Bratsk
Irkutsk
Angarsk
Ulan-Ude
Čita
Ulaanbaatar
Tomsk
Kemerovo
Novokuzneck
Abakan
Ust'-Ilimsk
Nižnevartovsk
Surgut
Salehard
Nadym
Urengoj
Dikson
Hatanga
Tura
Mirnyj
Lensk
Kyzyl
Meters / Feet
4000 13120
3000 9840
2000 6560
1000 3280
500 1640
200 656
Sea Level
200 656
2000 6560
0 100 200 300 400 600 800 1000 Kilometers
0 100 200 400 600 Miles
Scale 1 : 10,000,000
Lambert Conformal Conic Projection
120° East of Greenwich
M-DRM4710-A1-
Copyright © by Rand McNally & Co.

49
52

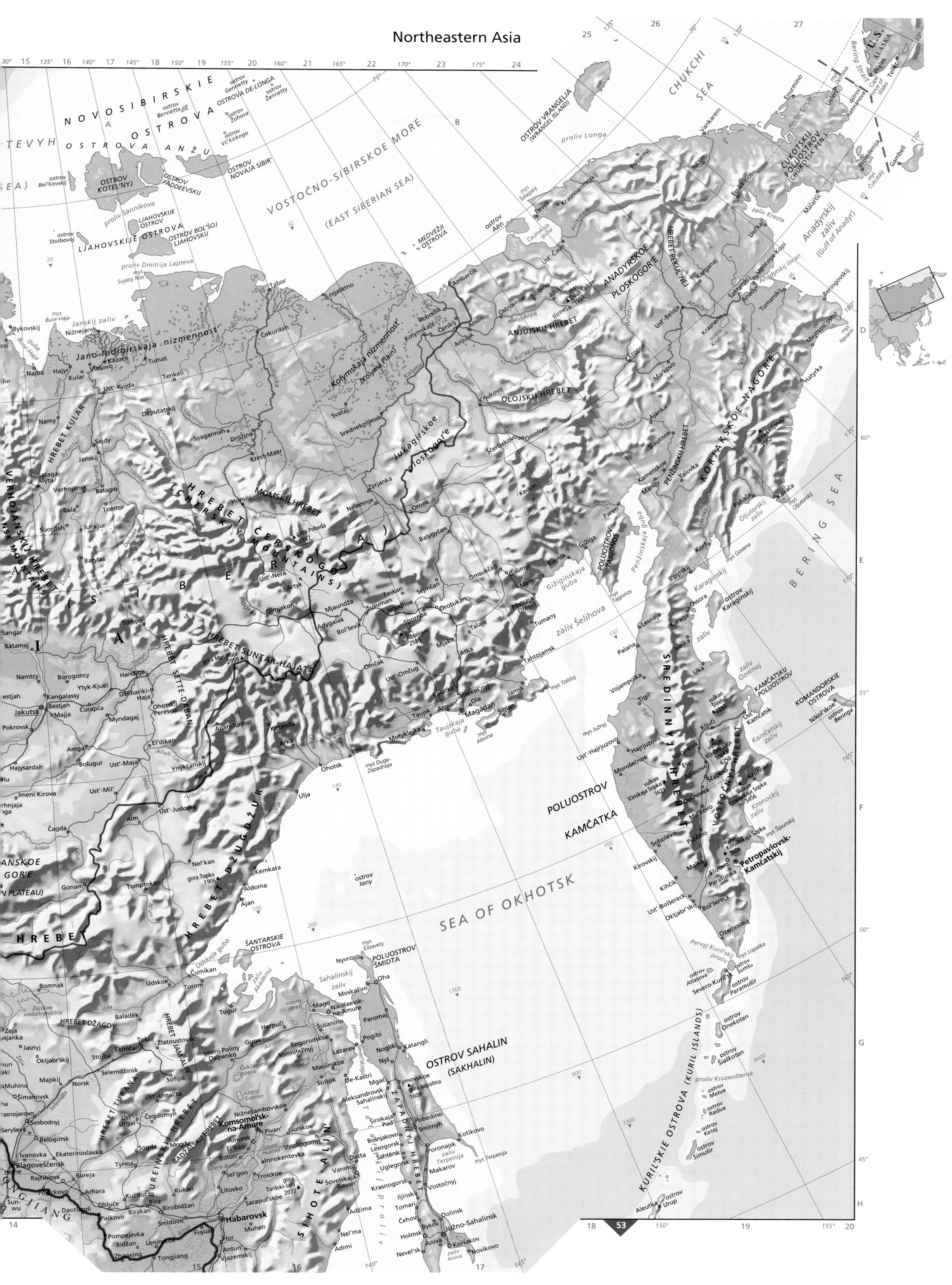
NOVOSIBIRSKIE OSTROVA
OSTROVA DE-LONGA
OSTROV KOTEL'NYJ
OSTROV FADDEEVSKIJ
OSTROV NOVAJA SIBIR'
LJAHOVSKIJE OSTROVA
VOSTOČNO-SIBIRSKOE MORE
(EAST SIBERIAN SEA)
MEDVEŽJI OSTROVA
OSTROV VRANGELJA
(WRANGEL ISLAND)
proliv Longa
CHUKCHI SEA
Bering Strait
U.S.
ALASKA
Arctic Circle
ČUKOTSKIJ POLUOSTROV
(CHUKOTSK PEN.)
Anadyrskij zaliv
(Gulf of Anadyr)
ANADYRSKOE PLOSKOGOR'E
HREBET PEKUL'NEJ
ANJUJSKIJ HREBET
Jano-Indigirskaja nizmennost'
Kolymskaja nizmennost'
(Kolyma Plain)
Jukagirskoe ploskogor'e
OLOJSKIJ HREBET
KORJAKSKOE NAGOR'E
PENŽINSKIJ HREBET
MOMSKIJ HREBET
HREBET ČERSKOGO
(CHERSKIY MOUNTAINS)
HREBET KULAR
VERHOJANSKIJ HREBET
HREBET SUNTAR-HAJATA
HREBET SETTE-DABAN
HREBET DŽUGDŽUR
HREBET DŽAGDY
BUREINSKIJ HREBET
SIHOTE-ALIN'
POLUOSTROV TAJGONOS
Penžinskaja guba
zaliv Šelihova
Tauiskaja guba
BERING SEA
KOMANDORSKIE OSTROVA
KAMČATSKIJ POLUOSTROV
SREDINNYJ HREBET
VOSTOČNYJ HREBET
POLUOSTROV KAMČATKA
Petropavlovsk-Kamčatskij
SEA OF OKHOTSK
ŠANTARSKIE OSTROVA
POLUOSTROV ŠMIDTA
OSTROV SAHALIN
(SAKHALIN)
ZAPADNYJ HREBET
zaliv Terpenija
KURIL'SKIE OSTROVA (KURIL ISLANDS)
Magadan
Ohotsk
Jakutsk
Komsomol'sk-na-Amure
Habarovsk
Blagoveščensk
Južno-Sahalinsk
Anadyr'
gora Pobeda 3147
gora Mus-Haja 2959
gora Lopatina 1609
Ključevskaja Sopka 4750
HREBET
SEA

RUSSIA
KAZAKHSTAN
MONGOLIA
CHINA
INDIA
BHUTAN
BANGLADESH
MYANMAR (BURMA)
VIETNAM
LAOS
XINJIANG
QINGHAI
XIZANG (TIBET)
GANSU
NINGXIA
NEI MONGGOL
SHAANXI
SHANXI
HENAN
HUBEI
HUNAN
SICHUAN
CHONGQING
GUIZHOU
YUNNAN
GUANGXI
GUANGDONG
ASSAM
MEGHALAYA
NAGALAND
MANIPUR
TRIPURA
MIZORAM
ARUNACHAL PRADESH
GOBI DESERT
MONGOL ALTAYN NURUU
HANGAYN NURUU
GURVAN SAYHAN UUL
ALTUN SHAN
KUNLUN SHAN
QILIAN SHAN
QAIDAM PENDI
HOH XIL SHAN
TANGGULA SHAN
QING ZANG GAOYUAN (PLATEAU OF TIBET)
BAYAN HAR SHAN
BOGDA SHAN
KURUKTAG
BEI SHAN
YIN SHAN
QIN LING
DABA SHAN
MIN SHAN
DAXUE SHAN
SHALULI SHAN
NU SHAN
YUN LING
AILAO SHAN
WULIANG SHAN
ARAKAN YOMA
CHIN HILLS
PATKAI RANGE
KUMON RANGE
MANGIN RANGE
Junggar Pendi
Tengger Shamo
MU US SHAMO
Sichuan Pendi
Ulaanbaatar
Ürümqi
Lanzhou
Xining
Lhasa
Chengdu
Chongqing
Kunming
Xi'an
Taiyuan
Hohhot
Baotou
Datong
Luoyang
Zhengzhou
Guiyang
Nanning
Liuzhou
Guilin
Hengyang
Zunyi
Zigong
Yibin
Hami
Dunhuang
Golmud
Yinchuan
Baoji
Hanzhong
Mandalay
Monywa
Taunggyi
Sittwe
Chittagong
Guwahati
Shillong
Imphal
Aizawl
Agartala
Kohima
Ha Noi
Hai Phong
Thai Nguyen
Lao Cai
Louangphrabang
Haikou
Zhanjiang
Maoming
Shenzhen
Jiangmen
Macau
Gulf of Tonkin
Bay of Bengal
Meters
Feet
6000
19680
4000
13120
3000
9840
2000
6560
1000
3280
500
1640
200
656
Sea Level
200
656
2000
6560
0 100 200 300 400 600 Kilometers
0 100 200 400 Miles
Scale 1 : 10,000,000
Lambert Conformal Conic Projection

RUSSIA
HEILONGJIANG
JILIN
LIAONING
NORTH KOREA
SOUTH KOREA
JAPAN
HONSHŪ
HOKKAIDO
SHIKOKU
KYŪSHŪ
TAIWAN
SHANDONG
JIANGSU
ZHEJIANG
FUJIAN
SEA OF JAPAN
(EAST SEA)
YELLOW SEA
EAST CHINA SEA
PACIFIC
OCEAN
SEA OF OKHOTSK
Korea Bay
Bo Hai
(Gulf of Chihli)
Korea Strait
Taiwan Strait
Bashi Channel
La Perouse Strait
Tropic of Cancer
HARBIN
CHANGCHUN
SHENYANG
FUSHUN
Jilin
Qiqihar
Mudanjiang
Vladivostok
Nahodka
Habarovsk
P'yŏngyang
SŎUL
(SEOUL)
INCH'ŎN
PUSAN
(FUSAN)
Taegu
Kwangju
TIANJIN
DALIAN
(DAIREN)
JINAN
Qingdao
(Tsingtao)
NANJING
SHANGHAI
Hangzhou
Ningbo
Fuzhou
Xiamen
T'AIPEI
KAOHSIUNG
Sapporo
Hakodate
Sendai
TŌKYŌ
YOKOHAMA
KAWASAKI
NAGOYA
KYŌTO
ŌSAKA
KŌBE
HIROSHIMA
KITAKYŪSHŪ
FUKUOKA
Nagasaki
Kagoshima
NANSEI-SHOTŌ (RYUKYU ISLANDS)
IZU-SHOTŌ
(IZU ISLANDS)
OSTROV SAHALIN
(SAHALIN)
KURIL'SKIE OSTROVA
(KURIL ISLANDS)
120° East of Greenwich
M-DRM4716-A1-·-2-2-2[M]
Copyright © Rand McNally & Co.

52
58
CHINA
NEI MONGGOL
DONG SAN SHENG
(MANCHURIA)
HEILONGJIANG
JILIN
LIAONING
HEBEI
SHANDONG
JIANGSU
ANHUI
ZHEJIANG
NORTH KOREA
SOUTH KOREA
HARBIN
CHANGCHUN
Jilin
SHENYANG
(MUKDEN)
FUSHUN
Anshan
Benxi
Fuxin
Jinzhou
Yingkou
Dandong
Sinŭiju
BEIJING
(PEKING)
TIANJIN
(TIENTSIN)
Tangshan
Qinhuangdao
DALIAN
(DAIREN)
Lüshun
(Port Arthur)
P'yŏngyang
Hamhŭng
Wŏnsan
Kaesŏng
SŎUL
(SEOUL)
INCH'ŎN
Taejŏn
Taegu
Kwangju
PUSAN
(FUSAN)
Ulsan
Mokp'o
Cheju
Halla-san 1950
CHEJU-DO
(QUELPART ISLAND)
TSUSHIMA
Korea Strait
KITAKYŪSHŪ
FUKUOKA
Nagasaki
Kagoshima
Qingdao (Tsingtao)
Yantai
Weihai
Weifang
Shandong Bandao
(Shantung Peninsula)
Liaodong Bandao
(Liaotung Peninsula)
Liaodong Wan
(Gulf of Liaotung)
Bo Hai
(Gulf of Chihli)
Bohai Wan
Laizhou Wan
(Laizhou Bay)
Korea Bay
YELLOW SEA
EAST CHINA SEA
Lianyungang
Nantong
NANJING
(NANKING)
Zhenjiang
Yangzhou
Changzhou
Wuxi
Suzhou
SHANGHAI
Hangzhou
Mudanjiang
Yanji
Meters
Feet
3000
9840
2000
6560
1000
3280
500
1640
200
656
Sea Level
200
656
2000
6560
500 Kilometers
300 Miles
Scale 1 : 5,000,000
Lambert Conformal Conic Projection

Japan, Korea, and Northeastern China

SEA OF JAPAN
(EAST SEA)
SOUTH KOREA
JAPA
KYŪSHŪ
SHIKOKU
EAST CHINA SEA
NORTH KOREA
PUSAN (FUSAN)
HIROSHIMA
FUKUOKA
KITAKYŪSHŪ
Korea Strait
Western Channel
Tsushima-kaikyō (Eastern Channel)
Tok-to ° Take-shima
(Claimed by S. Korea and Japan)
Ullŭng-do (S. Korea)
OKI-SHOTŌ
TSUSHIMA
GOTŌ-RETTŌ
Shimonoseki
Nagasaki
Kumamoto
Kagoshima
Miyazaki
Ōita
Matsuyama
Kōchi
Takamatsu
Okayama
Matsue
Taegu
Ulsan
Changwŏn
P'ohang
Kangnŭng
134° East of Greenwich

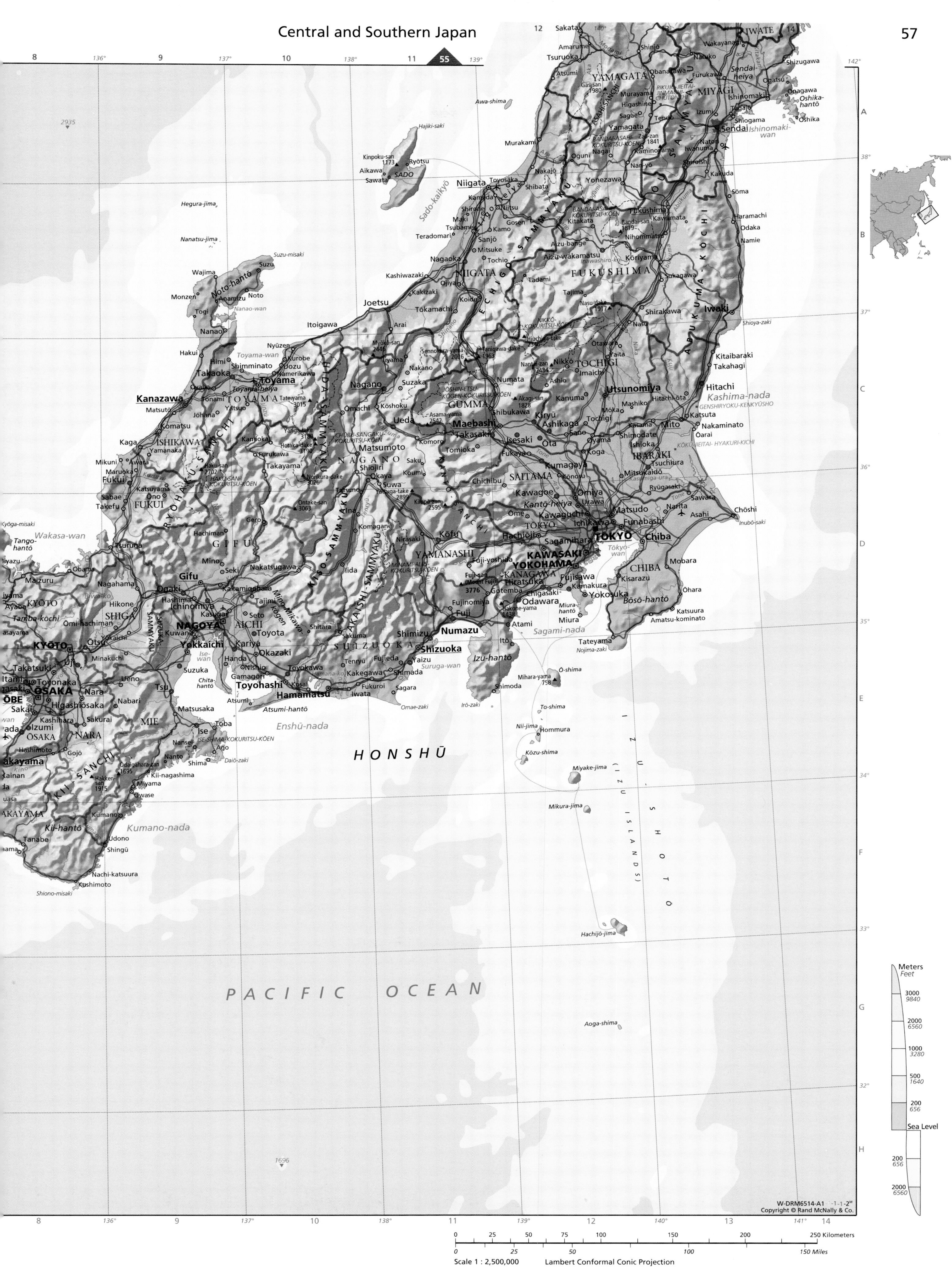
HONSHŪ
PACIFIC OCEAN
Enshū-nada
Kumano-nada
Sagami-nada
Kashima-nada
Wakasa-wan
Toyama-wan
Suruga-wan
Tōkyō-wan
Ise-wan
Nanao-wan
Sado-kaikyō
IZU-SHOTO (IZU ISLANDS)
TŌKYŌ
YOKOHAMA
KAWASAKI
NAGOYA
KYŌTO
ŌSAKA
Chiba
Sendai
Niigata
Kanazawa
Toyama
Nagano
Maebashi
Utsunomiya
Fukushima
Shizuoka
Hamamatsu
Numazu
Gifu
Fukui
Otsu
Nara
Tsu
Yamagata
Mito
Kōfu
Takasaki
Iwaki
Hitachi
Toyohashi
Okazaki
Toyota
Yokkaichi
Wakayama
Hachiōji
Sagamihara
Yokosuka
Fujisawa
Hiratsuka
Odawara
Funabashi
Ichikawa
Matsudo
Kawagoe
Kawaguchi
Urawa
Ōmiya
Kumagaya
Matsumoto
Ueda
Nagaoka
Joetsu
Aizu-wakamatsu
Kōriyama
Sado
Noto-hantō
Izu-hantō
Bōsō-hantō
Atsumi-hantō
Kii-hantō
Chita-hantō
Miura-hantō
Ō-shima
Miyake-jima
Hachijō-jima
Mikura-jima
Niï-jima
Kōzu-shima
Aoga-shima
Hida-sammyaku
Kiso-sammyaku
Akaishi-sammyaku
Echigo-sammyaku
Ōu-sammyaku
Abukuma-kōchi
Kii-sanchi
Fuji-san 3776
Kantō-heiya
YAMAGATA
MIYAGI
FUKUSHIMA
NIIGATA
TOCHIGI
GUMMA
IBARAKI
SAITAMA
CHIBA
TŌKYŌ
KANAGAWA
YAMANASHI
NAGANO
TOYAMA
ISHIKAWA
FUKUI
GIFU
SHIZUOKA
AICHI
MIE
SHIGA
KYŌTO
NARA
ŌSAKA
WAKAYAMA
Meters / Feet
3000 9840
2000 6560
1000 3280
500 1640
200 656
Sea Level
200 656
2000 6560
W-DRM6514-A1
Copyright © Rand McNally & Co.
0 25 50 75 100 150 200 250 Kilometers
0 25 50 100 150 Miles
Scale 1 : 2,500,000
Lambert Conformal Conic Projection

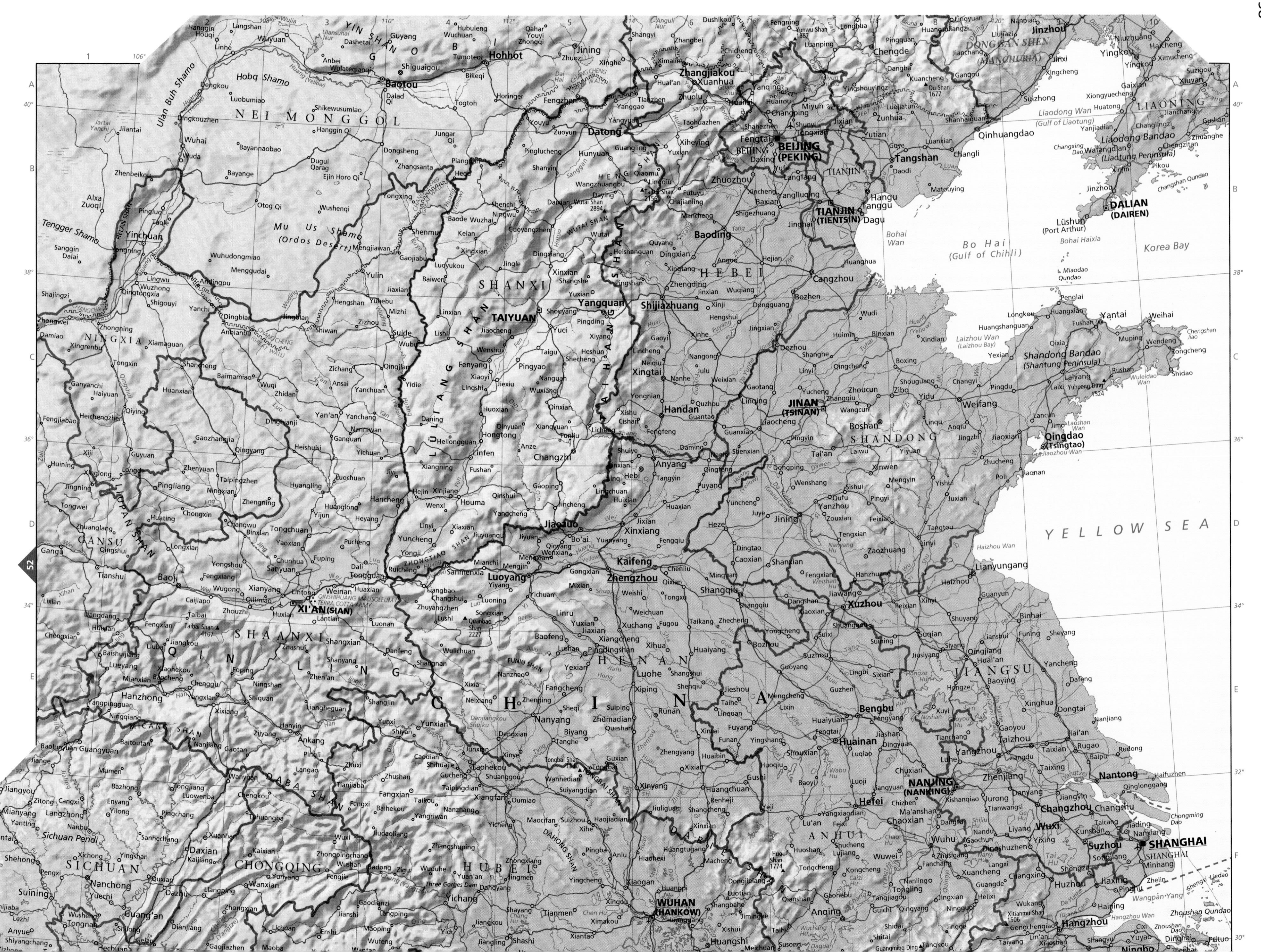
YELLOW SEA
Korea Bay
Bo Hai
(Gulf of Chihli)
Liaodong Wan
(Gulf of Liaotung)
Laizhou Wan
(Laizhou Bay)
Bohai Haixia
Liaodong Bandao
(Liaotung Peninsula)
Shandong Bandao
(Shantung Peninsula)
LIAONING
HEBEI
TIANJIN
SHANDONG
JIANGSU
SHANGHAI
ANHUI
HENAN
SHANXI
SHAANXI
NEI MONGGOL
NINGXIA
GANSU
HUBEI
CHONGQING
SICHUAN
C H I N A
BEIJING
(PEKING)
TIANJIN
(TIENTSIN)
DALIAN
(DAIREN)
Lüshun
(Port Arthur)
Qingdao
(Tsingtao)
JINAN
(TSINAN)
NANJING
(NANKING)
WUHAN
(HANKOW)
XI'AN (SIAN)
TAIYUAN
Shijiazhuang
Zhengzhou
Kaifeng
Luoyang
Hefei
Hangzhou
Suzhou
Wuxi
Changzhou
Nantong
Xuzhou
Bengbu
Huainan
Anqing
Datong
Baotou
Hohhot
Zhangjiakou
Tangshan
Qinhuangdao
Yantai
Weifang
Zibo
Handan
Anyang
Xinxiang
Jiaozuo
Yinchuan
Baoji
Tianshui
Hanzhong
Nanchong
Suining
Yichang
Lianyungang
YIN SHAN
LÜLIANG SHAN
TAIHANG SHAN
QINLING
DABA SHAN
LIUPAN SHAN
Mu Us Shamo
(Ordos Desert)
Hobq Shamo
Ulan Buh Shamo
Tengger Shamo
Sichuan Pendi
Three Gorges Dam
Huang (Yellow)
Grand Canal
40°
38°
36°
34°
32°
30°
106°
110°
112°
120°
A
B
C
D
E
F
52

EAST CHINA SEA
SOUTH CHINA SEA
Taiwan Strait
Luzon Strait
Bashi Channel
Gulf of Tonkin
ZHEJIANG
FUJIAN
JIANGXI
HUNAN
GUANGDONG
GUANGXI
GUIZHOU
HAINAN
HAINAN DAO (HAINAN ISLAND)
TAIWAN
PHILIPPINES
VIETNAM
BAC PHAN (TONKIN)
WENZHOU
Fuzhou
Xiamen (Amoy)
Shantou
Nanchang
CHANGSHA
Xiangtan
Zhuzhou
Hengyang
Ganzhou
Shaoguan
GUANGZHOU (CANTON)
Foshan
Shenzhen
Xinjiulong (New Kowloon)
XIANGGANG (HONG KONG)
Jiulong
Macau
MACAU (Port.)
Zhanjiang
Haikou
Nanning
Liuzhou
Guilin
Guiyang
Zunyi
Hai Phong
T'AIPEI
Chilung
T'aichung
T'ainan
KAOHSIUNG
Hsinchu
Hualien
P'enghu Ch'üntao (Pescadores)
Chinmen Tao (Quemoy)
Tungsha Tao (Pratas Island) (China/Taiwan)
WUYI SHAN
NAN LING
DAIYUN SHAN
LUZON
BATAN ISLANDS
BABUYAN ISLANDS
Tropic of Cancer
Scale 1 : 5,000,000
0 50 100 150 200 300 400 500 Kilometers
0 50 100 200 300 Miles
Lambert Conformal Conic Projection
114° East of Greenwich
Meters / Feet
3000 9840
2000 6560
1000 3280
500 1640
200 656
Sea Level
200 656
2000 6560
64

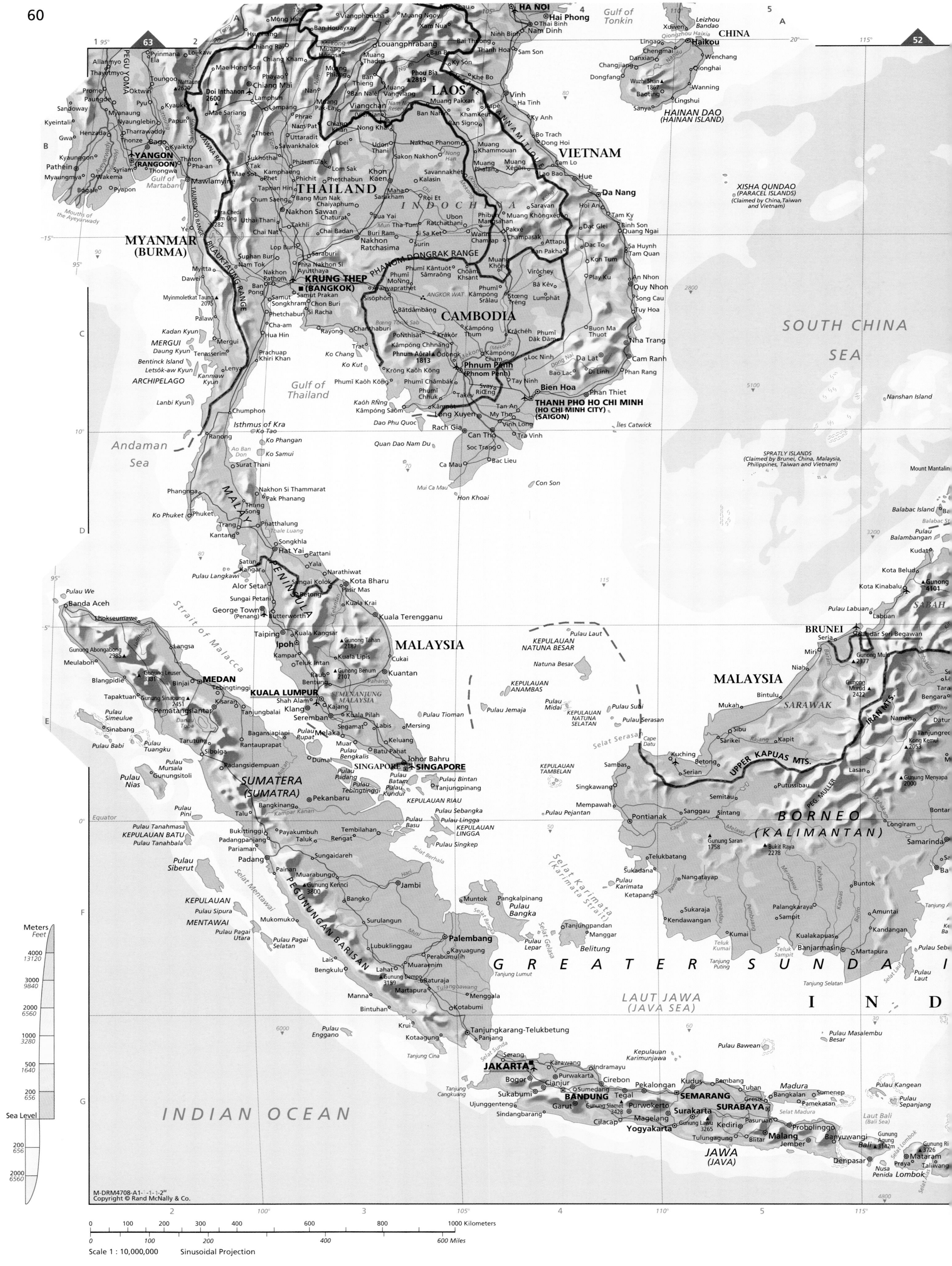
HA NOI
Hai Phong
Gulf of Tonkin
CHINA
Haikou
HAINAN DAO
(HAINAN ISLAND)
LAOS
Vientiane
Louangphrabang
VIETNAM
Da Nang
Hue
XISHA QUNDAO
(PARACEL ISLANDS)
(Claimed by China,Taiwan and Vietnam)
THAILAND
Chiang Mai
KRUNG THEP
(BANGKOK)
MYANMAR
(BURMA)
YANGON
(RANGOON)
Gulf of Martaban
CAMBODIA
Phnum Penh
(Phnom Penh)
THANH PHO HO CHI MINH
(HO CHI MINH CITY)
(SAIGON)
SOUTH CHINA
SEA
Gulf of Thailand
Andaman Sea
Isthmus of Kra
SPRATLY ISLANDS
(Claimed by Brunei, China, Malaysia, Philippines, Taiwan and Vietnam)
MALAY
PENINSULA
Strait of Malacca
MALAYSIA
KUALA LUMPUR
SINGAPORE
BRUNEI
Bandar Seri Begawan
SABAH
SARAWAK
KEPULAUAN NATUNA BESAR
KEPULAUAN ANAMBAS
MEDAN
SUMATERA
(SUMATRA)
Palembang
BORNEO
(KALIMANTAN)
Selat Karimata
(Karimata Strait)
GREATER SUNDA I
LAUT JAWA
(JAVA SEA)
I N D
JAKARTA
BANDUNG
SEMARANG
SURABAYA
Yogyakarta
JAWA
(JAVA)
Madura
Bali
Lombok
INDIAN OCEAN
Equator
Meters
Feet
4000
13120
3000
9840
2000
6560
1000
3280
500
1640
200
656
Sea Level
200
656
2000
6560
0
100
200
300
400
600
800
1000 Kilometers
0
100
200
400
600 Miles
Scale 1 : 10,000,000
Sinusoidal Projection

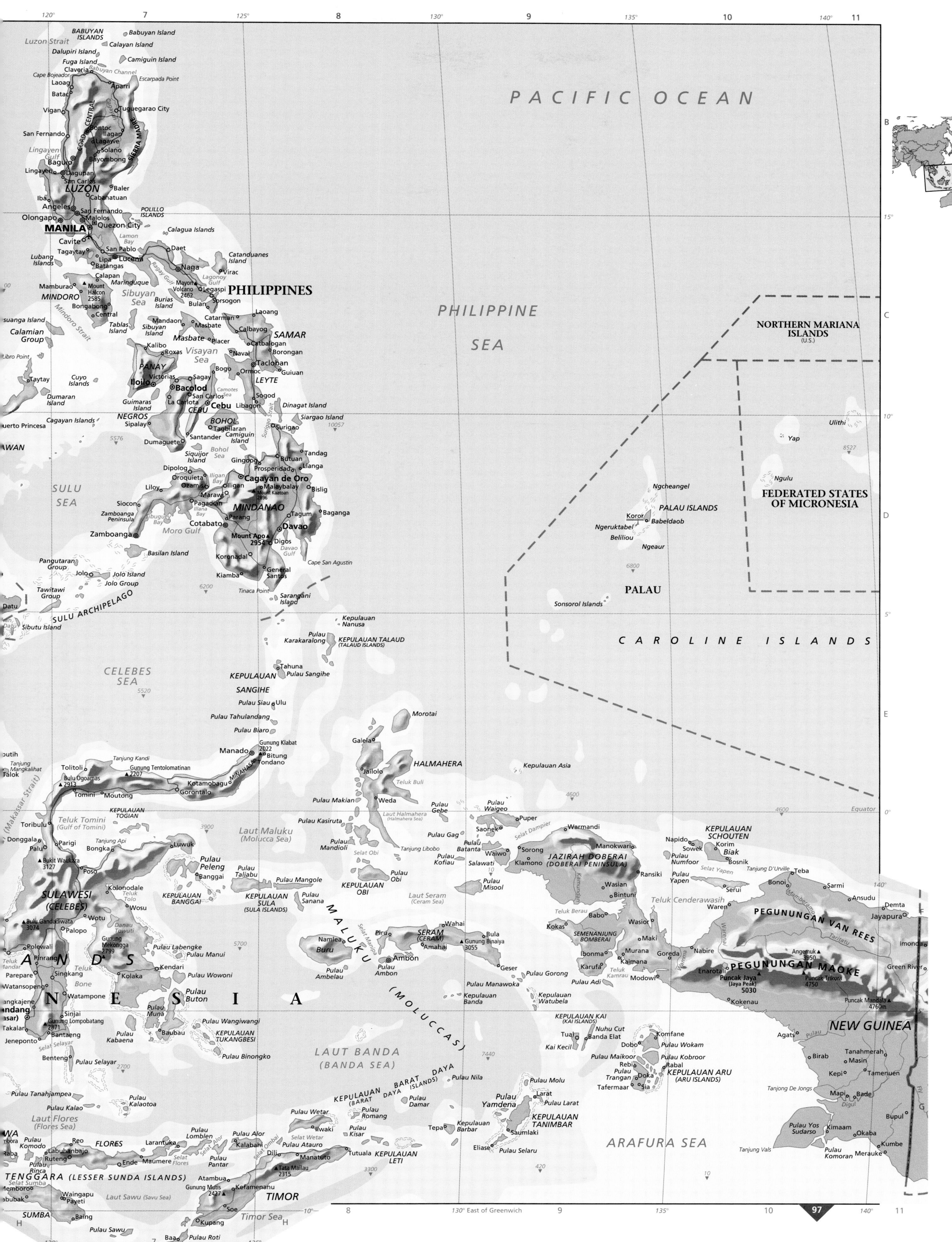
PACIFIC OCEAN
PHILIPPINE SEA
PHILIPPINES
NORTHERN MARIANA ISLANDS (U.S.)
FEDERATED STATES OF MICRONESIA
PALAU
PALAU ISLANDS
CAROLINE ISLANDS
Yap
Ulithi
Ngulu
Ngcheangel
Koror
Babeldaob
Ngeruktabel
Beliliou
Ngeaur
Sonsorol Islands
Luzon Strait
BABUYAN ISLANDS
Babuyan Island
Calayan Island
Dalupiri Island
Camiguin Island
Fuga Island
Claveria
Babuyan Channel
Cape Bojeador
Escarpada Point
Laoag
Aparri
Batac
Vigan
Tuguegarao City
San Fernando
Bontoc
Ilagan
Lagawe
Solano
Bayombong
Lingayen Gulf
Baguio
Lingayen
Dagupan
San Carlos
LUZON
Baler
Iba
Cabanatuan
Angeles
San Fernando
POLILLO ISLANDS
Olongapo
Malolos
MANILA
Quezon City
Calagua Islands
Cavite
Lamon Bay
Tagaytay
San Pablo
Daet
Lubang Islands
Lipa
Lucena
Batangas
Catanduanes Island
Naga
Calapan
Lagonoy Gulf
Virac
Mamburao
Mount Halcon 2585
Marinduque
Mayon Volcano 2462
Legaspi
MINDORO
Sibuyan Sea
Burias Island
Sorsogon
Bongabong
Bulan
Mindoro Strait
Central
Laoang
Busuanga Island
Tablas Island
Mandaon
Catarman
Calamian Group
Sibuyan Island
Masbate
Calbayog
SAMAR
Masbate
Placer
Catbalogan
Kalibo
Roxas
Visayan Sea
Naval
Borongan
PANAY
Victorias
Bogo
Ormoc
Tacloban
Guiuan
Taytay
Cuyo Islands
Sagay
LEYTE
Iloilo
Bacolod
Camotes Sea
Dumaran Island
Guimaras Island
San Carlos
Sogod
La Carlota
Cebu
Libagon
Dinagat Island
NEGROS
CEBU
Siargao Island
Cagayan Islands
BOHOL
Sipalay
Tagbilaran
Surigao
Puerto Princesa
Camiguin Island
Santander
Dumaguete
Siquijor Island
Bohol Sea
Butuan
Tandag
Gingoog
Lianga
Dipolog
Prosperidad
Cagayan de Oro
Oroquieta
Ozamis
Iligan Bay
Iligan
Malaybalay
Bislig
SULU SEA
Liloy
Marawi
Mount Kaatoan 2896
Siocon
Pagadian
MINDANAO
Illana Bay
Zamboanga Peninsula
Sibuguey Bay
Parang
Tagum
Baganga
Cotabato
Davao
Moro Gulf
Zamboanga
Mount Apo 2954
Digos
Basilan Island
Davao Gulf
Koronadal
Pangutaran Group
Cape San Agustin
Jolo
Jolo Island
General Santos
Jolo Group
Kiamba
Tawitawi Group
Tinaca Point
Sarangani Island
SULU ARCHIPELAGO
Sibutu Island
Kepulauan Nanusa
Pulau Karakaralong
KEPULAUAN TALAUD (TALAUD ISLANDS)
CELEBES SEA
Tahuna
KEPULAUAN SANGIHE
Pulau Sangihe
Pulau Siau
Ulu
Pulau Tahulandang
Pulau Biaro
Morotai
Gunung Klabat 2022
Manado
Galela
Bitung
Tondano
HALMAHERA
Tanjung Kandi
Gunung Tentolomatinan 2207
Tolitoli
Kepulauan Asia
Jailolo
Bulu Ogoamas 2913
Kotamobagu
MINAHASA
Teluk Buli
Gorontalo
Tomini
Moutong
Pulau Makian
Weda
KEPULAUAN TOGIAN
Laut Halmahera (Halmahera Sea)
Pulau Gebe
Pulau Waigeo
Puper
Toribulu
Teluk Tomini (Gulf of Tomini)
Pulau Kasiruta
Saonek
Selat Dampier
Warmandi
KEPULAUAN SCHOUTEN
Laut Maluku (Molucca Sea)
Pulau Gag
Napido
Donggala
Parigi
Tanjung Api
Korim
Palu
Bongka
Luwuk
Pulau Mandioli
Tanjung Libobo
Pulau Batanta
Sorong
Manokwari
Sowek
Biak
Waiwo
Bosnik
Bukit Waukara 3127
Pulau Peleng
Selat Obi
Pulau Kofiau
Salawati
Klamono
JAZIRAH DOBERAI (DOBERAI PENINSULA)
Pulau Numfoor
Tanjung D'Urville
Teba
Poso
Banggai
Pulau Taliabu
Pulau Mangole
Pulau Obi
Pulau Misool
Ransiki
Pulau Yapen
Selat Yapen
Kolonodale
KEPULAUAN BANGGAI
KEPULAUAN SULA (SULA ISLANDS)
Pulau Sanana
KEPULAUAN OBI
Laut Seram (Ceram Sea)
Wasian
Bintuni
Serui
Bonoi
Sarmi
SULAWESI (CELEBES)
Wosu
Teluk Cenderawasih
Ansudu
Demta
Wotu
Teluk Berau
Babo
Waren
Jayapura
Bulu Gandadiwata 3074
Palopo
Danau Towuti
Wahai
Kokas
Wasior
PEGUNUNGAN VAN REES
MALUKU
SERAM (CERAM)
Bula
SEMENANJUNG BOMBERAI
Maki
Piru
Gunung Binaiya 3055
Polewali
Gunung Mekongga 2799
Namlea
Amahai
Imonda
Pulau Labengke
Buru
Ambon
Geser
Murana
Goreda
Nabire
Pulau Manui
Angemuk 3950
Pinrang
Kaimana
Green River
Kendari
Selat Manipa
Karufa
Teluk Kamrau
Enarotali
PEGUNUNGAN MAOKE
Parepare
Kolaka
Pulau Ambelau
Pulau Ambon
Pulau Gorong
Pulau Adi
Modowi
Puncak Jaya (Jaya Peak) 5030
Puncak Trikora 4750
Singkang
Pulau Wowoni
Teluk Bone
Pulau Manawoka
Watansoppeng
Watampone
Pulau Buton
(MOLUCCAS)
Kepulauan Banda
Kepulauan Watubela
Puncak Mandala 4760m
Kokenau
Sinjai
Pulau Muna
Pulau Wangiwangi
KEPULAUAN KAI (KAI ISLANDS)
Gunung Lompobatang 2871
Baubau
KEPULAUAN TUKANGBESI
Nuhu Cut
Komfane
NEW GUINEA
Takalar
Bantaeng
Pulau Kabaena
Tual
Banda Elat
Agats
Jeneponto
Selat Selayar
Kai Kecil
Dobo
Pulau Wokam
Tanahmerah
Pulau Binongko
LAUT BANDA (BANDA SEA)
Pulau Maikoor
Pulau Kobroor
Masin
Benteng
Pulau Selayar
Rebi
Rabal
Birab
Pulau Trangan
Doka
KEPULAUAN ARU (ARU ISLANDS)
Kepi
Tamenuen
Pulau Nila
Pulau Molu
Tafermaar
Sia
KEPULAUAN BARAT DAYA (BARAT DAYA ISLANDS)
Tanjong De Jongs
Pulau Tanahjampea
Pulau Kalaotoa
Pulau Damar
Pulau Yamdena
Larat
Mapi
Bade
Pulau Larat
Digul
Pulau Kalao
Pulau Wetar
Pulau Romang
Laut Flores (Flores Sea)
KEPULAUAN TANIMBAR
Bupul
Pulau Lomblen
Pulau Alor
Ilwaki
Pulau Kisar
Tepa
Kepulauan Barbar
Saumlaki
Pulau Yos Sudarso
Kimaam
Okaba
Pulau Komodo
Reo
FLORES
Larantuka
Selat Alor
Kalabahi
Selat Wetar
Pulau Atauro
ARAFURA SEA
Labuhanbajo
Ruteng
Selat Ombai
Dili
Eliase
Pulau Selaru
Kumbe
Pulau Rinca
Ende
Maumere
Selat Flores
Pulau Pantar
Manatuto
Tutuala
KEPULAUAN LETI
Tanjung Vals
Pulau Komoran
Merauke
TENGGARA (LESSER SUNDA ISLANDS)
Tata Mailau 2315
Selat Sumba
Atambua
Kefamenanu
Gunung Mutis 2427
Waingapu
Payeti
Laut Sawu (Savu Sea)
TIMOR
Soe
SUMBA
Baing
Timor Sea
Kupang
Pulau Sawu
Baa
Pulau Roti
INDONESIA
130° East of Greenwich
Equator
97

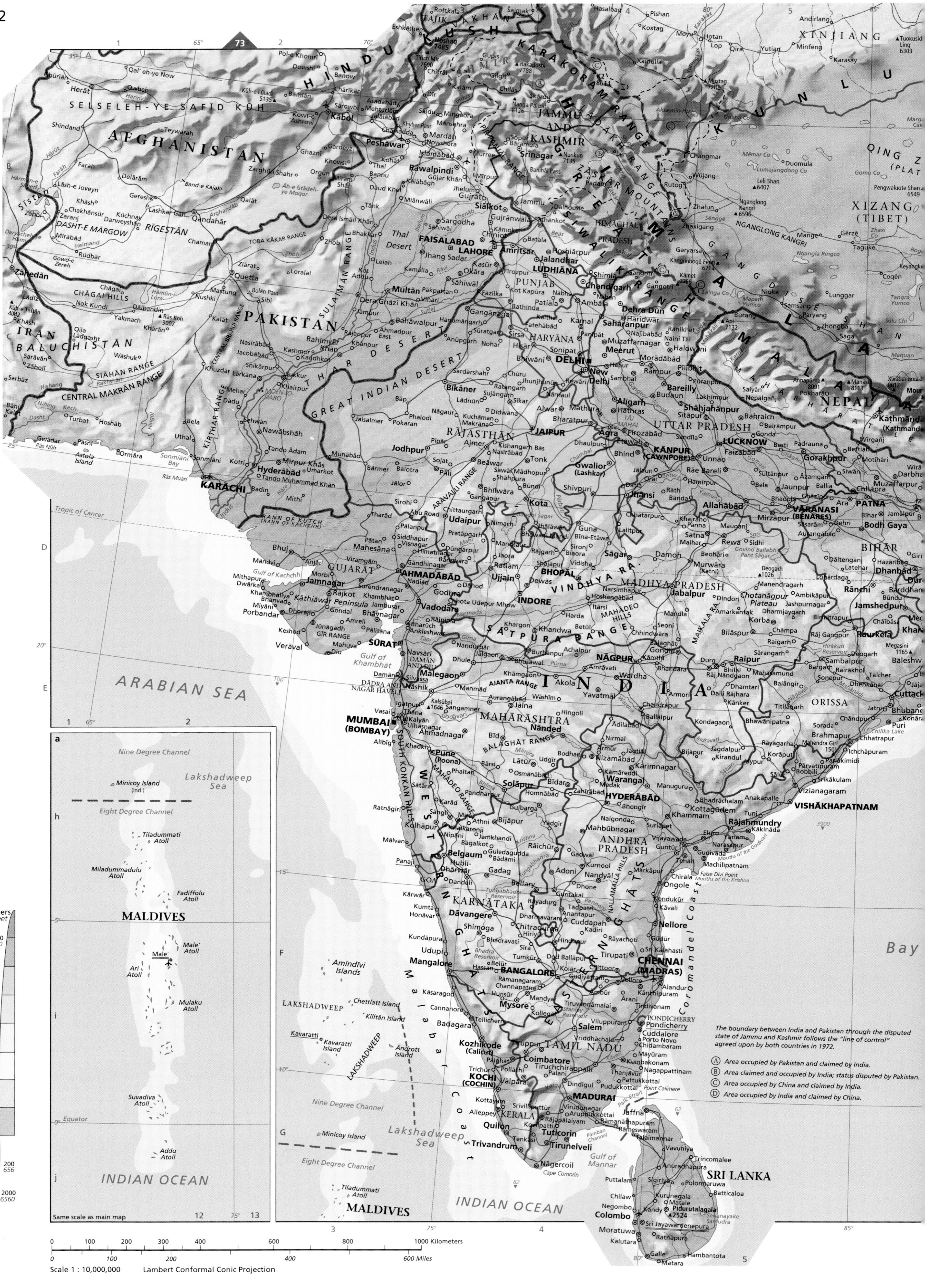

73

AFGHANISTAN

PAKISTAN

INDIA

NEPAL

SRI LANKA

MALDIVES

IRAN

XIZANG (TIBET)

XINJIANG

JAMMU AND KASHMIR

HINDU KUSH

KARAKORAM RANGE

HIMALAYA

KUNLUN

SELSELEH-YE SAFĪD KŪH

BALUCHISTĀN

GREAT INDIAN DESERT

THAR DESERT

VINDHYA RA.

SATPURA RANGE

WESTERN GHATS

EASTERN GHATS

ARABIAN SEA

INDIAN OCEAN

Lakshadweep Sea

Malabar Coast

Coromandel Coast

Bay

PUNJAB

HARYANA

RĀJASTHĀN

UTTAR PRADESH

GUJARĀT

MADHYA PRADESH

BIHAR

ORISSA

MAHĀRĀSHTRA

ANDHRA PRADESH

KARNĀTAKA

TAMIL NĀDU

KERALA

GOA

LAKSHADWEEP

KĀBOL

ISLĀMĀBĀD

NEW DELHI

KĀTHMĀNDU

COLOMBO

KARĀCHI

LAHORE

FAISALABAD

MUMBAI (BOMBAY)

CHENNAI (MADRAS)

BANGALORE

HYDERĀBĀD

AHMADĀBĀD

KĀNPUR (CAWNPORE)

LUCKNOW

JAIPUR

PATNA

VĀRĀNASI (BENARES)

NĀGPUR

INDORE

BHOPĀL

SŪRAT

PUNE (Poona)

VISHĀKHAPATNAM

MADURAI

KOCHI (COCHIN)

Tropic of Cancer

Equator

The boundary between India and Pakistan through the disputed state of Jammu and Kashmir follows the "line of control" agreed upon by both countries in 1972.

(A) Area occupied by Pakistan and claimed by India.

(B) Area claimed and occupied by India; status disputed by Pakistan.

(C) Area occupied by China and claimed by India.

(D) Area occupied by India and claimed by China.

Meters / Feet

6000 / 19680

4000 / 13120

3000 / 9840

2000 / 6560

1000 / 3280

500 / 1640

200 / 656

Sea Level

200 / 656

2000 / 6560

Same scale as main map

0 100 200 300 400 600 800 1000 Kilometers

0 100 200 400 600 Miles

Scale 1 : 10,000,000 Lambert Conformal Conic Projection

CHINA
MYANMAR (BURMA)
THAILAND
LAOS
CAMBODIA
VIETNAM
BANGLADESH
BHUTAN
MALAYSIA
Andaman Sea
Gulf of Thailand
Gulf of Tonkin
SOUTH CHINA SEA
KRUNG THEP (BANGKOK)
YANGON (RANGOON)
HA NOI
THANH PHO HO CHI MINH (HO CHI MINH CITY) (SAIGON)
DHAKA
Mandalay
Kunming
Chengdu
Chongqing
Guiyang
Nanning
Lhasa
Vientiane
Phnom Penh
ANDAMAN AND NICOBAR ISLANDS (India)
90° East of Greenwich
M-DRM4707-A1-1-1-1
Copyright © Rand McNally & Co.

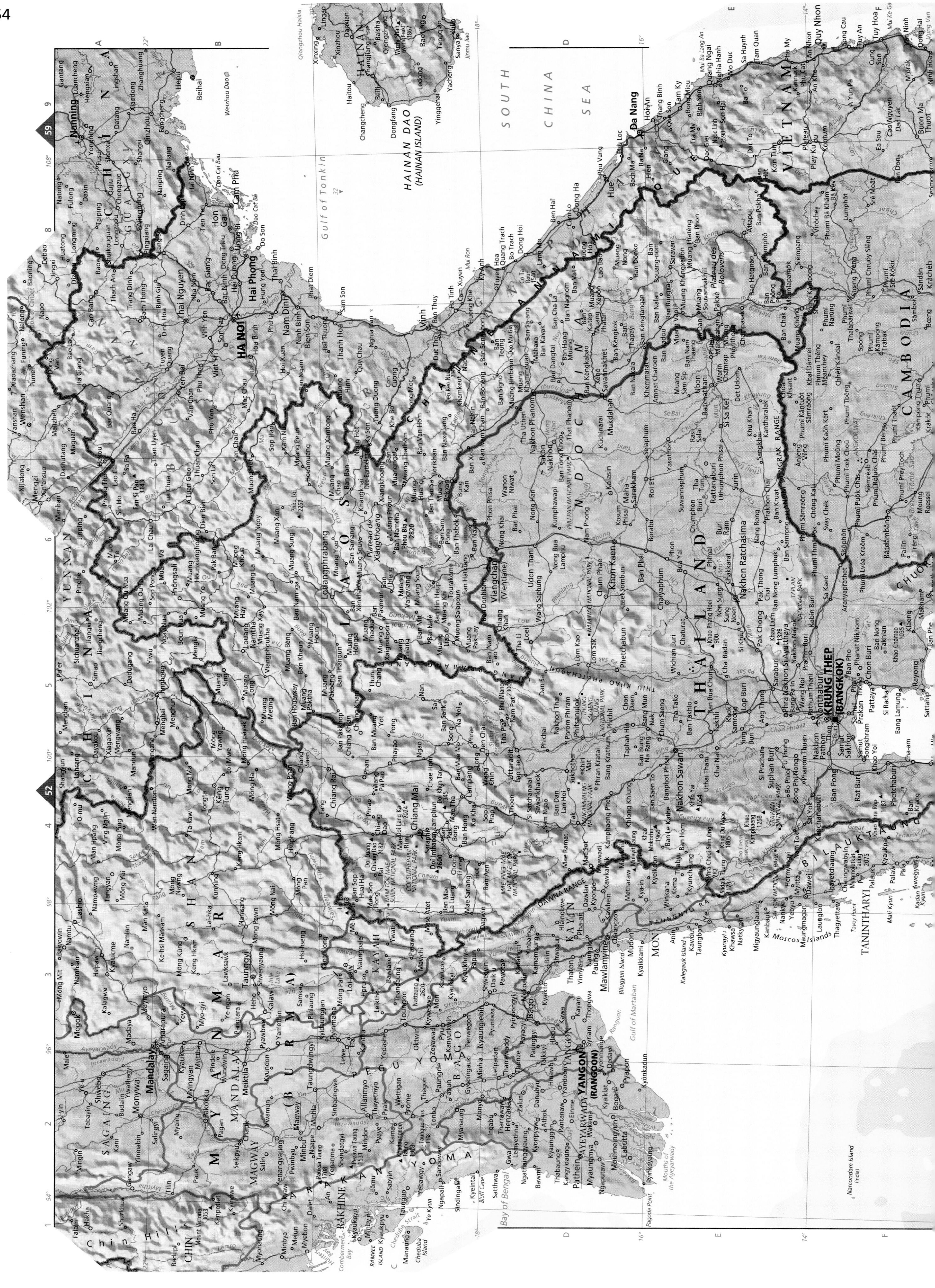

CHINA

YUNNAN

GUANGXI

HAINAN

HAINAN DAO (HAINAN ISLAND)

Gulf of Tonkin

SOUTH CHINA SEA

VIETNAM

LAOS

CAMBODIA

THAILAND

MYANMAR (BURMA)

INDOCHINA

Bay of Bengal

Gulf of Martaban

HA NOI

Hai Phong

Da Nang

Hue

Vinh

Viangchan (Vientiane)

Louangphrabang

KRUNG THEP (BANGKOK)

Nakhon Ratchasima

Chiang Mai

YANGON (RANGOON)

Mandalay

Mawlamyine

Nanning

Quy Nhon

Moscos Islands

TANINTHARYI

SHAN

KAYIN

KAYAH

MANDALAY

MAGWAY

SAGAING

BAGO

AYEYARWADY

RAKHINE

CHIN

MON

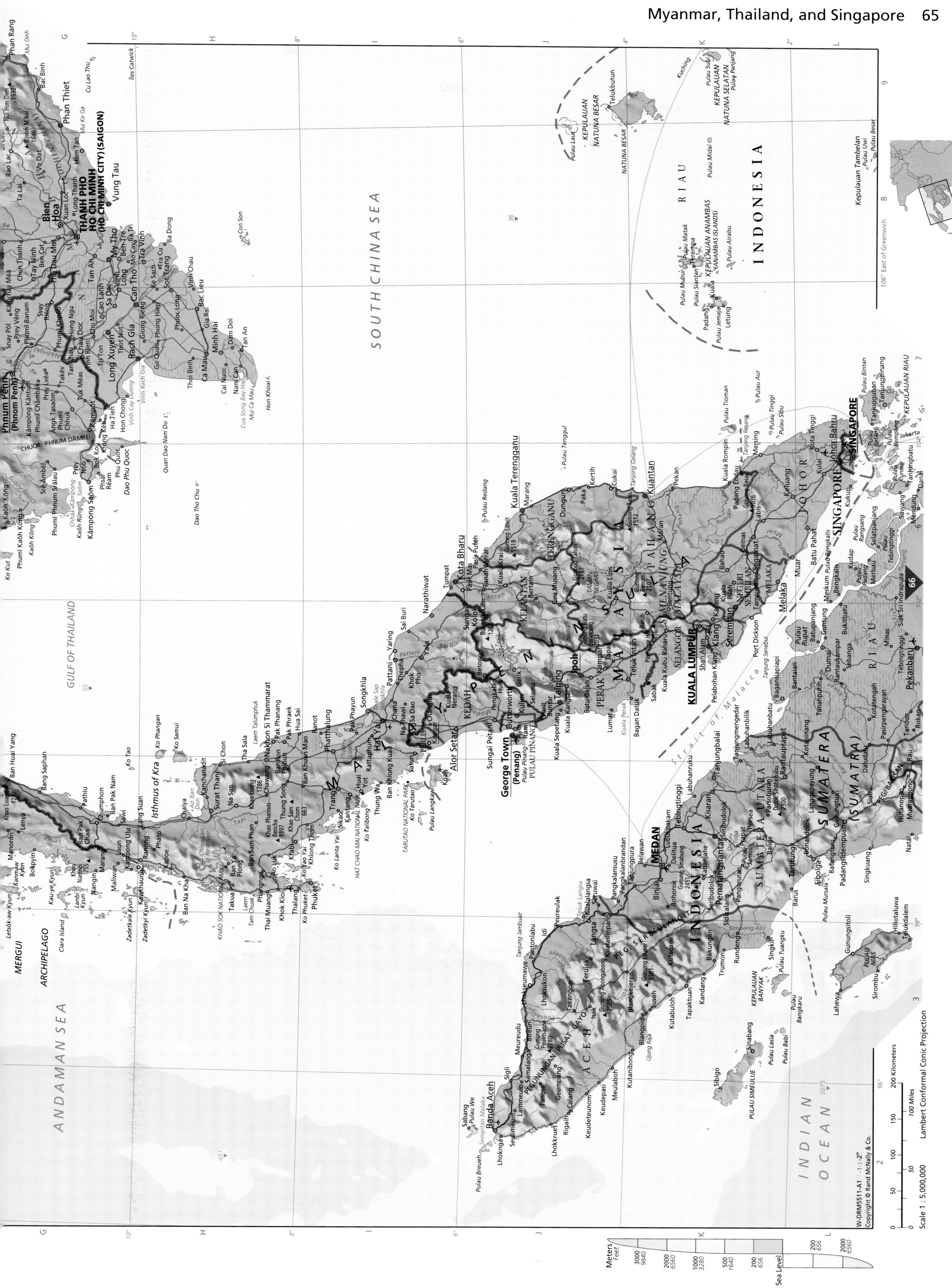
SOUTH CHINA SEA
GULF OF THAILAND
ANDAMAN SEA
INDIAN OCEAN
MERGUI ARCHIPELAGO
Isthmus of Kra
INDONESIA
MALAYSIA
SINGAPORE
KUALA LUMPUR
Kota Bharu
Kuala Terengganu
Kuantan
George Town (Penang)
Ipoh
Melaka
Medan
Banda Aceh
Pekanbaru
Phuket
Hat Yai
Songkhla
Surat Thani
Nakhon Si Thammarat
THANH PHO HO CHI MINH (HO CHI MINH CITY) (SAIGON)
Phnum Penh (Phnom Penh)
Vung Tau
Phan Thiet
Strait of Malacca
Scale 1 : 5,000,000
Lambert Conformal Conic Projection
Copyright © Rand McNally & Co.

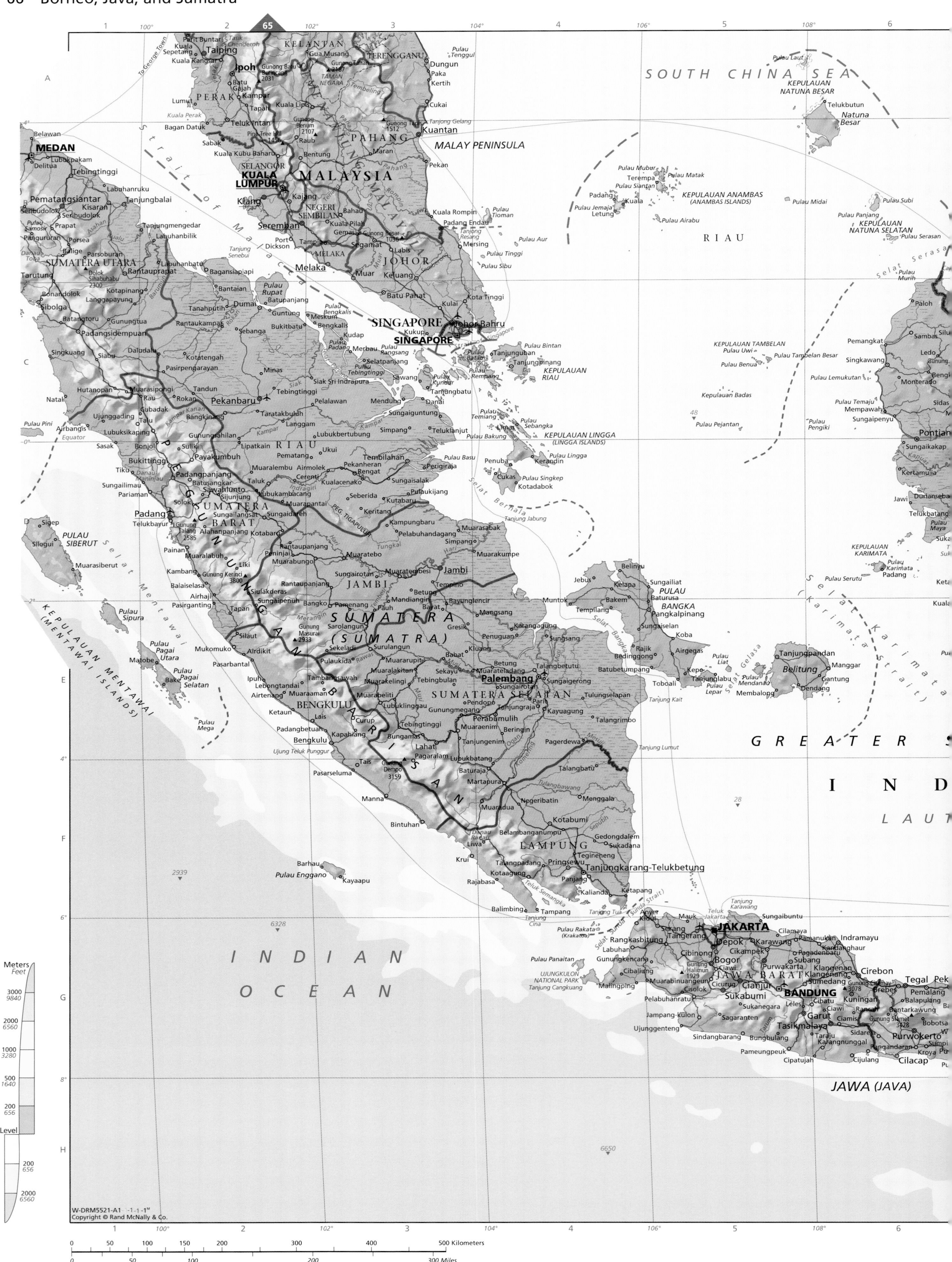
65
SOUTH CHINA SEA
MALAY PENINSULA
MALAYSIA
KUALA LUMPUR
SINGAPORE
Johor Bahru
Strait of Malacca
KELANTAN
TERENGGANU
PERAK
PAHANG
SELANGOR
NEGERI SEMBILAN
MELAKA
JOHOR
Ipoh
Taiping
Kuantan
Kelang
Seremban
Melaka
Muar
Kluang
Mersing
Batu Pahat
MEDAN
Belawan
Pematangsiantar
Tebingtinggi
Sibolga
Padangsidempuan
SUMATERA UTARA
RIAU
Pekanbaru
Dumai
Bengkalis
SUMATERA BARAT
Padang
Bukittinggi
Solok
Sawahlunto
JAMBI
Jambi
SUMATERA (SUMATRA)
SUMATERA SELATAN
Palembang
BENGKULU
Bengkulu
LAMPUNG
Tanjungkarang-Telukbetung
GUNUNG BARISAN
KEPULAUAN RIAU
KEPULAUAN LINGGA (LINGGA ISLANDS)
KEPULAUAN ANAMBAS (ANAMBAS ISLANDS)
KEPULAUAN NATUNA BESAR
Natuna Besar
KEPULAUAN NATUNA SELATAN
KEPULAUAN TAMBELAN
PULAU BANGKA
Pangkalpinang
Belitung
Tanjungpandan
Selat Karimata (Karimata Strait)
Selat Mentawai
KEPULAUAN MENTAWAI (MENTAWAI ISLANDS)
PULAU SIBERUT
Pulau Sipura
Pulau Pagai Utara
Pulau Pagai Selatan
Pulau Enggano
Equator
Selat Sunda (Sunda Strait)
JAKARTA
Bogor
BANDUNG
Cirebon
Tasikmalaya
Cilacap
JAWA BARAT
JAWA (JAVA)
UJUNGKULON NATIONAL PARK
INDIAN OCEAN
GREATER
LAUT
Pontianak
KEPULAUAN KARIMATA
Meters
Feet
3000
9840
2000
6560
1000
3280
500
1640
200
656
Sea Level
200
656
2000
6560
100°
102°
104°
106°
108°
4°
2°
0°
4°
6°
8°
0 50 100 150 200 300 400 500 Kilometers
0 50 100 200 300 Miles
Scale 1 : 5,000,000
Sinusoidal Projection

SULU SEA
SABAH
BRUNEI
Bandar Seri Begawan
PHILIPPINES
SULU ARCHIPELAGO
BANJARAN BRASSEY
MALAYSIA
SARAWAK
CELEBES SEA
KALIMANTAN TIMUR
BORNEO
(KALIMANTAN)
KALIMANTAN BARAT
PEGUNUNGAN SCHWANER
PEGUNUNGAN MULLER
UPPER KAPUAS MOUNTAINS
KALIMANTAN TENGAH
KALIMANTAN SELATAN
PEGUNUNGAN MERATUS
Samarinda
Balikpapan
Banjarmasin
Palangkaraya
Selat Makasar
(Makassar Strait)
Equator
Teluk Tomini
(Gulf of Tomini)
SULAWESI TENGAH
PEGUNUNGAN TAKOLEKAJU
SULAWESI SELATAN
SULAWESI
(CELEBES)
SULAWESI TENGGARA
Teluk Bone
(Gulf of Bone)
Ujungpandang
(Makasar)
DA ISLANDS
NESIA
WA (JAVA SEA)
MADURA
SURABAYA
SEMARANG
Surakarta
JAWA TIMUR
Malang
Laut Bali
(Bali Sea)
BALI
Denpasar
LOMBOK
Mataram
NUSA TENGGARA BARAT
SUMBAWA
Laut Flores
(Flores Sea)
FLORES
NUSA TENGGARA TIMUR
NUSA TENGGARA
(LESSER SUNDA ISLANDS)
Laut Sawu
(Savu Sea)
SUMBA
112° East of Greenwich
114°
116°
118°

PHILIPPINES

PHILIPPINE SEA

SOUTH CHINA SEA

SULU SEA

CELEBES SEA

LUZON

MINDANAO

MINDORO

PALAWAN

PANAY

NEGROS

CEBU

BOHOL

LEYTE

SAMAR

MASBATE

VISAYAN ISLANDS

SULU ARCHIPELAGO

MALAYSIA

BORNEO

SABAH

INDONESIA

MANILA

Meters / Feet

3000 / 9840

2000 / 6560

1000 / 3280

500 / 1640

200 / 656

Sea Level

200 / 656

2000 / 6560

0 50 100 150 200 300 400 500 Kilometers

0 50 100 200 300 Miles

Scale 1 : 5,000,000

Lambert Conformal Conic Projection

122° East of Greenwich

W-DRM5516-A1 -1-1-1[M]

67

MAHARASHTRA
KARNATAKA
ANDHRA PRADESH
ORISSA
MADHYA PRADESH
TAMIL NADU
KERALA
INDIA
DECCAN
SRI LANKA
HYDERĀBĀD
BANGALORE
CHENNAI (MADRAS)
VISHĀKHAPATNAM
KOCHI (COCHIN)
MADURAI
Colombo
Bay of Bengal
INDIAN OCEAN
LAKSHADWEEP SEA
LAKSHADWEEP
MALABAR COAST
COROMANDEL COAST
WESTERN GHATS
EASTERN GHATS
Gulf of Mannar
Palk Strait
Meters
Feet
Sea Level
W-DRM5520-A1
Copyright © Rand McNally & Co.
0 50 100 150 200 300 400 500 Kilometers
0 50 100 200 300 Miles
Scale 1 : 5,000,000
Lambert Conformal Conic Projection

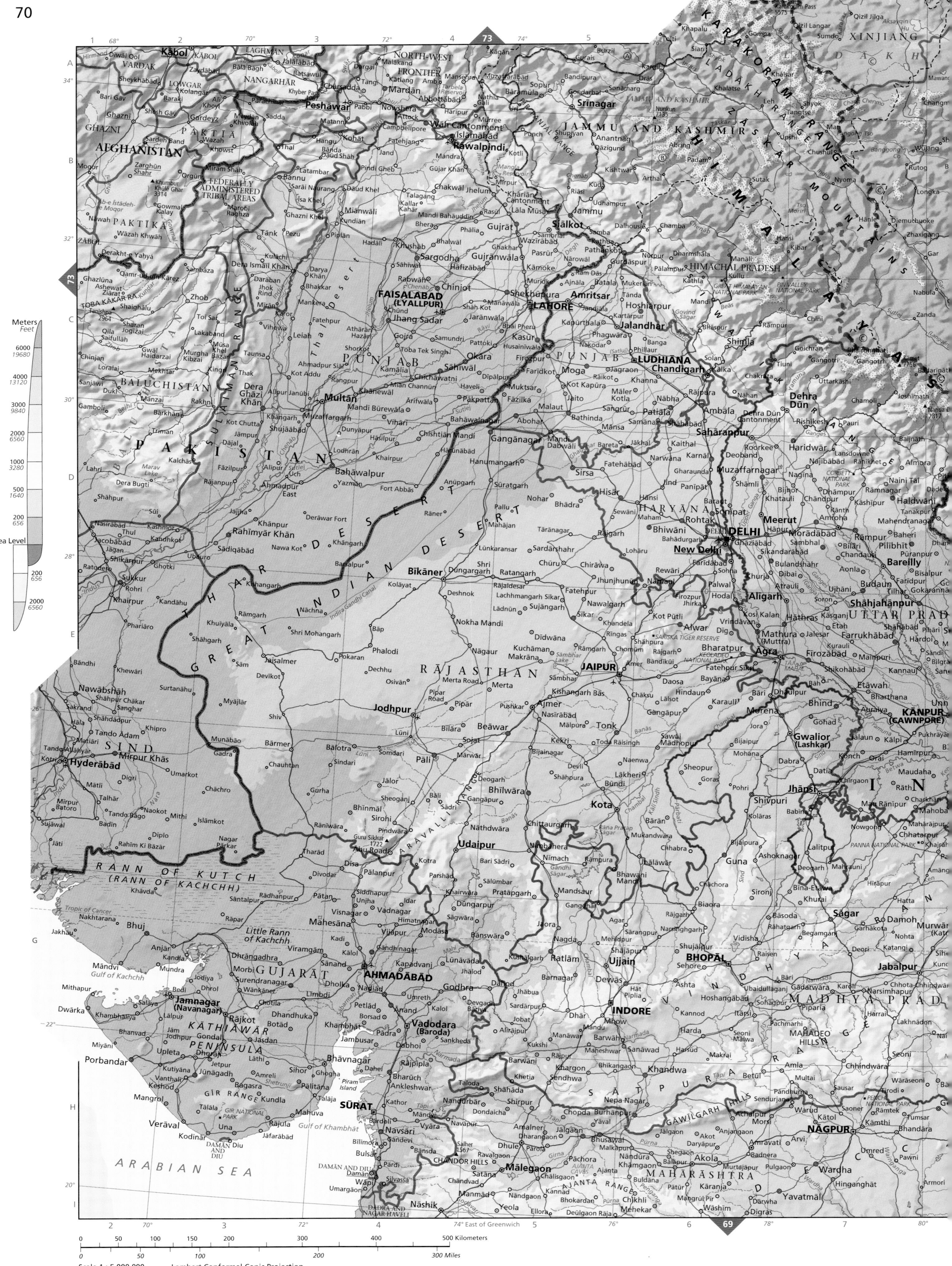
AFGHANISTAN
PAKISTAN
Kābol
Peshāwar
Rāwalpindi
Islāmābād
NORTH-WEST FRONTIER
FEDERALLY ADMINISTERED TRIBAL AREAS
BALUCHISTAN
SULAIMAN RANGE
PUNJAB
FAISALABAD (LYALLPUR)
LAHORE
Multān
Bahāwalpur
Sargodha
Gujrānwāla
Siālkot
Srīnagar
JAMMU AND KASHMIR
KARAKORAM RANGE
LADĀKH RANGE
ZASKAR MOUNTAINS
HIMALAYAS
XINJIANG
HIMACHAL PRADESH
Shimla
Amritsar
Jalandhar
LUDHIANA
Chandīgarh
HARYĀNA
DELHI
New Delhi
UTTAR PRADESH
Meerut
Bareilly
Alīgarh
Āgra
KĀNPUR (CAWNPORE)
Gwalior (Lashkar)
Jhānsi
SIND
Hyderābād
Sukkur
THAR DESERT
GREAT INDIAN DESERT
RĀJASTHAN
Bīkāner
Jodhpur
JAIPUR
Ajmer
Kota
Udaipur
ARAVALLI RANGE
RANN OF KUTCH (RANN OF KACHCHH)
Little Rann of Kachchh
Gulf of Kachchh
GUJARĀT
AHMADĀBĀD
Vadodara (Baroda)
SŪRAT
Rājkot
Jamnagar (Navanagar)
KĀTHIĀWĀR PENINSULA
GĪR RANGE
Gulf of Khambhāt
ARABIAN SEA
DAMĀN AND DIU
DADRA AND NAGAR HAVELI
MADHYA PRADESH
INDORE
BHOPĀL
Ujjain
Jabalpur
NĀGPUR
VINDHYA RANGE
SĀTPURA RANGE
MAHĀDEO HILLS
GĀWILGARH HILLS
AJANTA RANGE
MAHĀRĀSHTRA
Nāshik
Mālegaon
Akola
Tropic of Cancer
Meters / Feet
6000 19680
4000 13120
3000 9840
2000 6560
1000 3280
500 1640
200 656
Sea Level
200 656
2000 6560
74° East of Greenwich
0 50 100 150 200 300 400 500 Kilometers
0 50 100 200 300 Miles
Scale 1 : 5,000,000
Lambert Conformal Conic Projection

CHINA
QINGHAI
XIZANG (TIBET)
QING ZANG GAOYUAN (PLATEAU OF TIBET)
TANGGULA SHAN
NYAINQÊNTANGLHA SHAN
GANGDISÊ SHAN
HIMALAYAS
NEPAL
BHUTAN
SIKKIM
ARUNACHAL PRADESH
ASSAM
MEGHALAYA
NĀGĀLAND
MANIPUR
MIZORAM
TRIPURA
BANGLADESH
BIHĀR
WEST BENGAL
ORISSA
MYANMAR
CHIN
RAKHINE
Lhasa
Kāthmāndau (Kathmandu)
Thimphu
Mount Everest (Qomolangma Feng) 8848
Kānchenjunga 8598
Kula Kangri 7554
Gangtok
Dārjiling
Shillong
Guwāhāti
DHAKA (DACCA)
CHITTAGONG
CALCUTTA
Hāora
PATNA
VĀRĀNASI (BENARES)
Allahābād
Gorakhpur
Gaya
Rānchi
Jamshedpur
Dhanbād
Asānsol
Durgāpur
Cuttack
Bhubaneshwar
Puri
Raipur
Sambalpur
Raurkela
Kharagpur
Bhāgalpur
Muzaffarpur
Darbhanga
Khulna
Barisāl
Rājshāhi
Mymensingh
Sylhet
Āgartala
Āīzawl
Silchar
Imphal
Sittwe
Mouths of the Ganges
Bay of Bengal
SUNDARBANS
DEOGARH HILLS
KHONDMAL HILLS
Ⓐ Area occupied by Pakistan and claimed by India.
Ⓑ Area claimed and occupied by India; status disputed by Pakistan.
Ⓒ Area occupied by China and claimed by India.
Ⓓ Area occupied by India and claimed by China.
W-DRM5515-A1 -1-1-2M
Copyright © Rand McNally & Co.

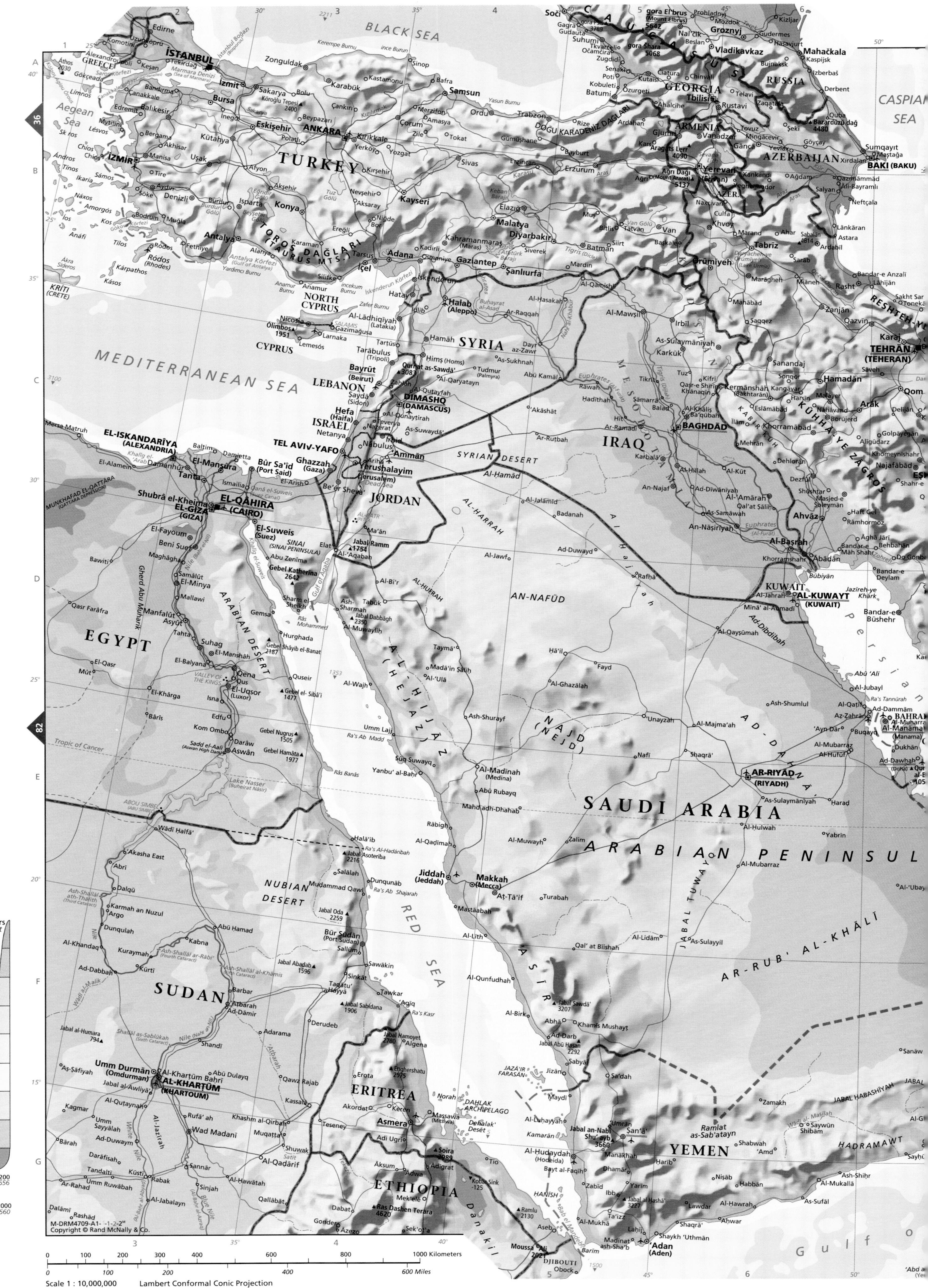

BLACK SEA
CASPIAN SEA
MEDITERRANEAN SEA
RED SEA
Aegean Sea
TURKEY
GEORGIA
ARMENIA
AZERBAIJAN
RUSSIA
SYRIA
LEBANON
ISRAEL
JORDAN
IRAQ
CYPRUS
NORTH CYPRUS
EGYPT
SUDAN
ERITREA
ETHIOPIA
DJIBOUTI
YEMEN
KUWAIT
SAUDI ARABIA
ARABIAN PENINSUL
GREECE
İSTANBUL
ANKARA
İzmir
Bursa
Eskişehir
Konya
Kayseri
Samsun
Trabzon
Erzurum
Sivas
Malatya
Diyarbakır
Gaziantep
Şanlıurfa
Adana
Antalya
İçel
İskenderun
Tbilisi
Yerevan
BAKI (BAKU)
Mahačkala
Groznyj
Vladikavkaz
Soči
gora El'brus (Mount Elbrus) 5642
gora Shara 5068
Bazardüzü dağ 4480
Aragats Lerr 4090
Ağrı Dağı (Mount Ararat) 5137
TOROS DAĞLARI (TAURUS MTS.)
Kahramanmaraş (Maraş)
Tabriz
Orūmīyeh
TEHRĀN (TEHERAN)
Hamadān
Kermānshāh (Bākhtarān)
Ahvāz
Ābādān
Halab (Aleppo)
Ḥimṣ (Homs)
Ḥamāh
DIMASHQ (DAMASCUS)
Bayrūt (Beirut)
Ṭarābulus (Tripoli)
Nicosia
Larnaka
Lemesós
Ólimbos 1951
Qurnat as-Sawdā' 3083
Ḥefa (Haifa)
TEL AVIV-YAFO
Yerushalayim (Jerusalem)
'Ammān
Ghazzah (Gaza)
Be'er Sheva'
Al-Mawṣil
Irbīl
Karkūk
BAGHDĀD
Karbalā'
An-Najaf
Al-Baṣrah
AL-KUWAYT (KUWAIT)
EL-ISKANDARÎYA (ALEXANDRIA)
EL-QÂHIRA (CAIRO)
EL-GÎZA (GIZA)
Bûr Sa'îd (Port Said)
El-Suweis (Suez)
SINAI (SINAI PENINSULA)
Gebel Katherina 2642
Jabal Ramm 1754
Al-'Aqabah
Elat
Qena
El-Uqṣor (Luxor)
Aswân
Lake Nasser
Tropic of Cancer
ARABIAN DESERT
NUBIAN DESERT
SYRIAN DESERT
AN-NAFŪD
AL-HIJĀZ (HEJAZ)
NAJD (NEJD)
AD-DAHNĀ'
AR-RUB' AL-KHĀLĪ
'ASĪR
AR-RIYĀD (RIYADH)
Makkah (Mecca)
Jiddah (Jeddah)
Al-Madīnah (Medina)
Tabūk
Ḥā'il
Yanbu' al-Baḥr
Aṭ-Ṭā'if
Wādī Ḥalfā'
Bûr Sûdân (Port Sudan)
Umm Durmān (Omdurman)
AL-KHARṬŪM (KHARTOUM)
Wad Madanī
Kassalā
Asmera
Ras Dashen Terara 4620
Ṣan'ā'
'Adan (Aden)
Al-Mukallā
HADRAMAWT
DAHLAK ARCHIPELAGO
Gulf of Aden
Persian Gulf
Meters / Feet
6000 19680
4000 13120
3000 9840
2000 6560
1000 3280
500 1640
200 656
Sea Level
200 656
2000 6560
M-DRM4709-A1- -1-2-2[M]
Copyright © Rand McNally & Co.
0 100 200 300 400 600 800 1000 Kilometers
0 100 200 400 600 Miles
Scale 1 : 10,000,000
Lambert Conformal Conic Projection

UZBEKISTAN
TURKMENISTAN
KAZAKHSTAN
KYRGYZSTAN
TAJIKISTAN
AFGHANISTAN
PAKISTAN
INDIA
CHINA
IRAN
OMAN
XINJIANG
Taklimakan Shamo
JAMMU AND KASHMIR
ARABIAN SEA
Gulf of Oman
Makran Coast
GARAGUMY (KARA KUM)
DASHT-E KAVĪR
DASHT-E LŪT
HINDU KUSH
KARAKORAM RANGE
PAMIR
TIEN SHAN
GREAT HIMALAYA RANGE
THAR DESERT
GREAT INDIAN DESERT
SULAIMAN RANGE
KIRTHAR RANGE
CENTRAL MAKRAN RANGE
BALUCHISTAN
RĪGESTĀN
SELSELEH-YE SAFĪD KŪH
WESTERN GHATS
ARAVALLI RANGE
RAJASTHAN
PUNJAB
GUJARAT
MAHARASHTRA
KARNATAKA
HARYANA
MADHYA PRADESH
UTTAR PRADESH
Taşkent
Samarkand
Dušanbe
Kābol
Islamabad
Lahore
Faisalabad
Karāchi
Hyderābād
Quetta
Peshāwar
Rāwalpindi
Srinagar
Delhi
New Delhi
Jaipur
Ahmadābād
Mumbai (Bombay)
Pune
Sūrat
Ludhiāna
Amritsar
Chandīgarh
Indore
Mashhad
Herāt
Kandahār
Zāhedān
Kermān
Ašgabat
Mary
Dubayy (Dubai)
Abū Zaby (Abu Dhabi)
Masqaţ (Muscat)
Strait of Hormuz
Bandar-e 'Abbās
Suquţrá (Socotra) (Yemen)
60° East of Greenwich
The boundary between India and Pakistan through the disputed state of Jammu and Kashmir follows the "line of control" agreed upon by both countries in 1972.
Ⓐ Area occupied by Pakistan and claimed by India.
Ⓑ Area claimed and occupied by India; status disputed by Pakistan.
Ⓒ Area occupied by China and claimed by India.

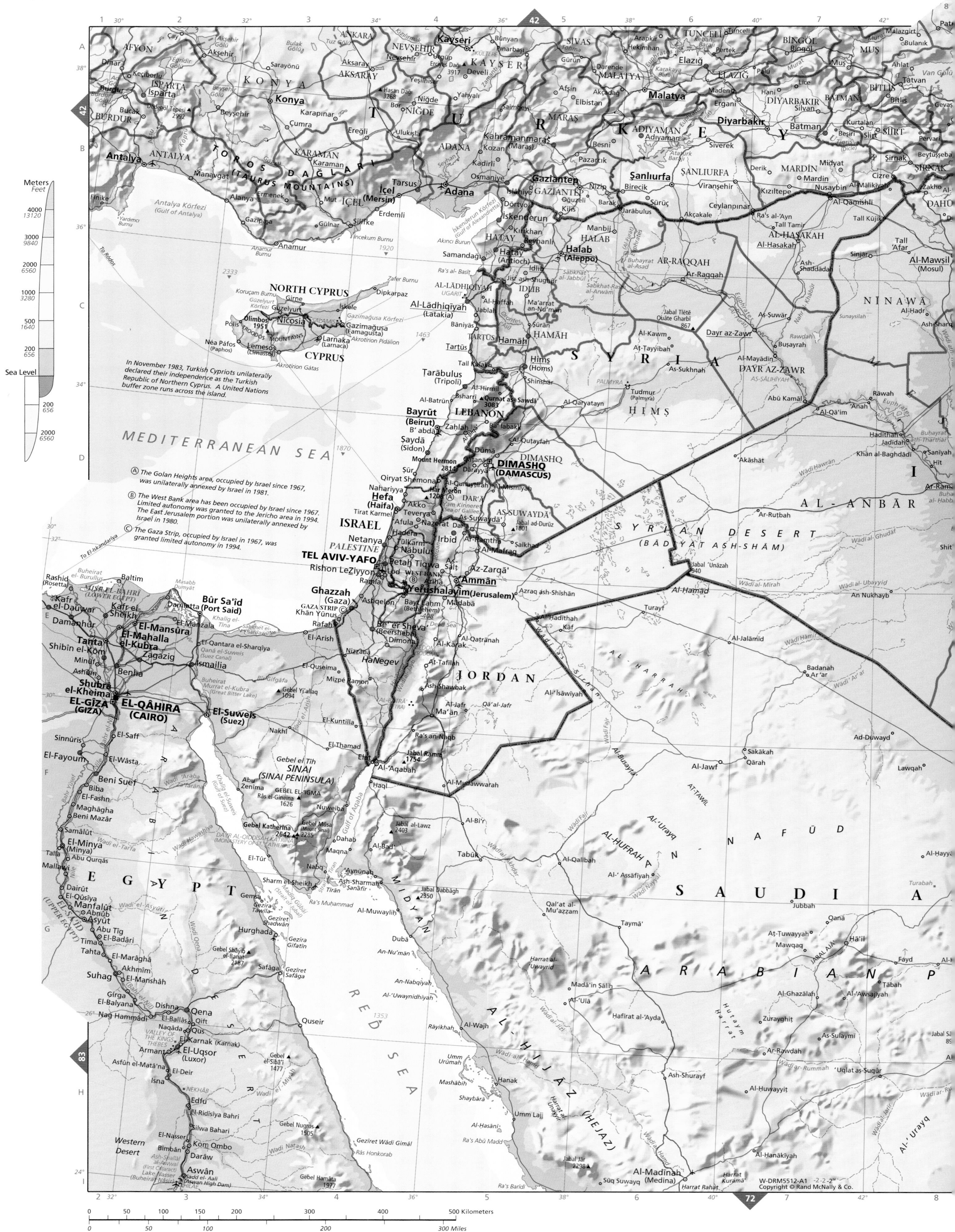

0 50 100 150 200 300 400 500 Kilometers

0 50 100 200 300 Miles

Scale 1 : 5 000 000 Lambert Conformal Conic Projection

TURKEY
SYRIA
LEBANON
IRAQ
NORTH CYPRUS
CYPRUS
MEDITERRANEAN SEA
TOROS DAĞLARI (TAURUS MOUNTAINS)
SYRIAN DESERT (BĀDIYAT ASH-SHĀM)
Halab (Aleppo)
DIMASHQ (DAMASCUS)
Bayrūt (Beirut)
Nicosia (Lefkoşa) (Levkosía)
Adana
Antalya
İçel (Mersin)
İskenderun (Alexandretta)
Al-Lādhiqīyah (Latakia)
Ḥimṣ (Homs)
Ḥamāh
Ṭarābulus (Tripoli)
Ṣaydā (Sidon)
Ṣūr (Tyre)
Hefa (Haifa)
Gaziantep
Şanlıurfa (Urfa)
Kahramanmaraş (Maraş)
Antalya Körfezi (Gulf of Antalya)
İskenderun Körfezi
In November 1983, Turkish Cypriots unilaterally declared their independence as the Turkish Republic of Northern Cyprus. A United Nations buffer zone runs across the island.
Ⓐ Golan Heights area. occupied by Israel since 1967, was unilaterally annexed by Israel in 1981.
Ⓑ West Bank area has been occupied by Israel since 1967. Limited autonomy was granted to the Jericho area in 1994. The East Jerusalem portion was unilaterally annexed by Israel in 1980.
Ⓒ The Gaza Strip. occupied by Israel in 1967,

Meters / Feet

3000 9840

2000 6560

1000 3280

500 1640

200 656

Sea Level

200 656

2000 6560

Scale 1 : 2,500,000

Lambert Conformal Conic Projection

0 25 50 75 100 150 200 250 Kilometers

0 25 50 100 150 Miles

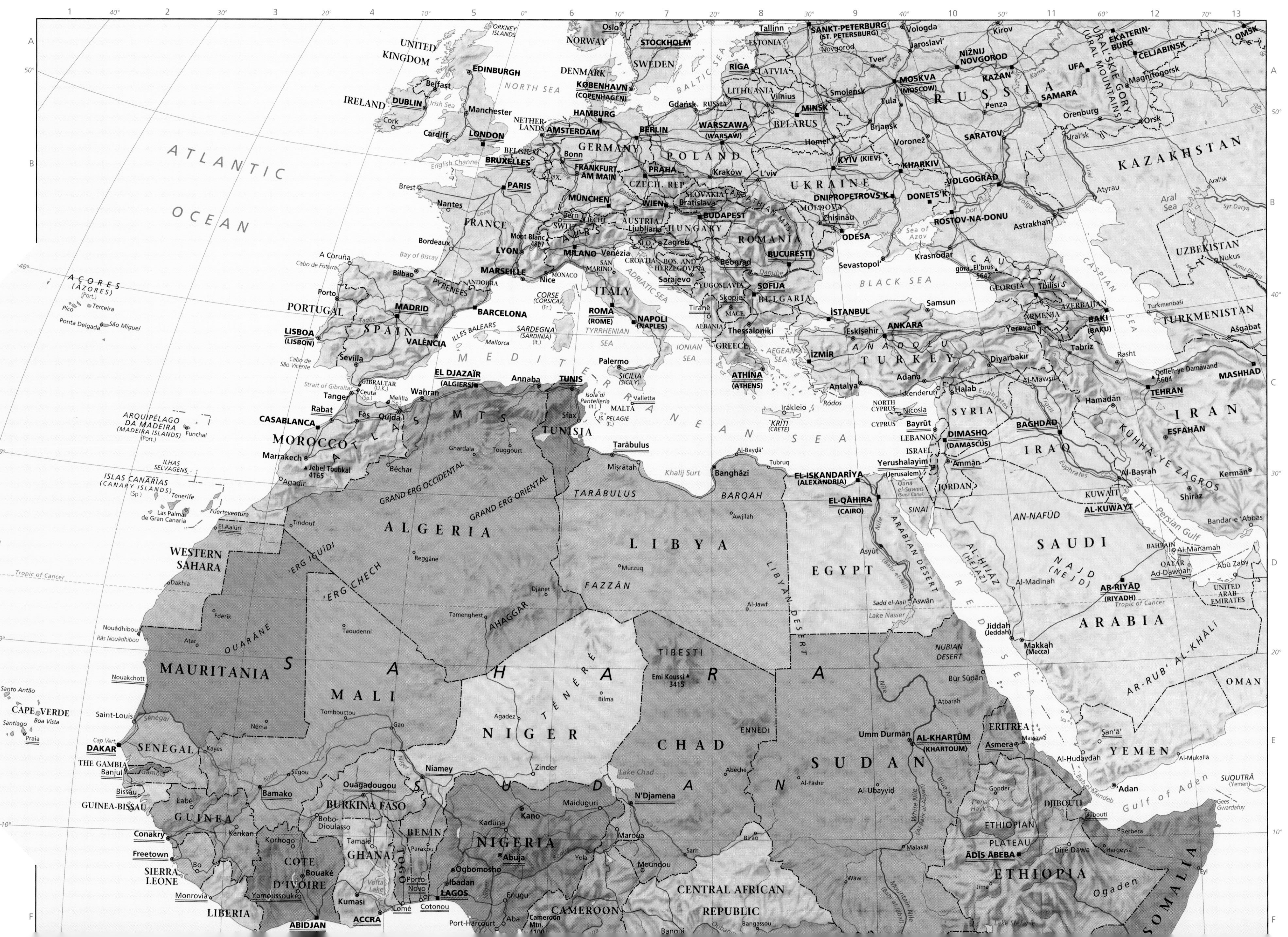
ATLANTIC
OCEAN
UNITED KINGDOM
IRELAND
NORWAY
SWEDEN
DENMARK
NORTH SEA
BALTIC SEA
GERMANY
POLAND
FRANCE
SPAIN
PORTUGAL
ITALY
BELARUS
UKRAINE
RUSSIA
KAZAKHSTAN
UZBEKISTAN
TURKMENISTAN
IRAN
IRAQ
SYRIA
TURKEY
SAUDI
ARABIA
YEMEN
OMAN
EGYPT
LIBYA
ALGERIA
MOROCCO
TUNISIA
SAHARA
MAURITANIA
MALI
NIGER
CHAD
SUDAN
ETHIOPIA
SOMALIA
NIGERIA
CAMEROON
CENTRAL AFRICAN REPUBLIC
SENEGAL
GUINEA
SIERRA LEONE
LIBERIA
GHANA
BENIN
BURKINA FASO
WESTERN SAHARA
CASPIAN SEA
BLACK SEA
MEDITERRANEAN SEA
RED SEA
Persian Gulf
Gulf of Aden
LIBYAN DESERT
ARABIAN DESERT
URAL'SKIE GORY (URAL MOUNTAINS)
KŪHHA-YE ZAGROS
AR-RUB' AL-KHĀLĪ
MOSKVA (MOSCOW)
SANKT-PETERBURG (ST. PETERSBURG)
KYÏV (KIEV)
WARSZAWA (WARSAW)
BERLIN
PARIS
LONDON
MADRID
LISBOA (LISBON)
ROMA (ROME)
İSTANBUL
ANKARA
TEHRĀN
BAGHDĀD
AR-RIYĀD (RIYADH)
EL-QĀHIRA (CAIRO)
AL-KHARṬŪM (KHARTOUM)
ĀDIS ĀBEBA
Ṭarābulus
TUNIS
EL DJAZAÏR (ALGIERS)
Rabat
DAKAR
LAGOS
ACCRA
ABIDJAN
N'Djamena
Niamey
Bamako
Ouagadougou
Tropic of Cancer

M-DRM2502-P1- -1-1-2"

Scale 1 : 25,000,000

0 250 500 1000 1500 2000 2500 Kilometers

0 250 500 1000 1500 Miles

Lambert Azimuthal Equal Area Projection

ATLANTIC
OCEAN
BRITISH ISLES
GREAT BRITAIN
IRELAND
NORTH SEA
BALTIC SEA
URAL'SKIE GORY (URAL MOUNTAINS)
SREDNERUSSKAJA VOZVYŠENNOST'
PRIVOLŽSKAJA VOZVYŠENNOST'
CASPIAN DEPRESSION
CASPIAN SEA
TURAN LOWLAND
BLACK SEA
CAUCASUS
gora El'brus 5642
MEDITERRANEAN SEA
ALPS
Mont Blanc 4807
APPENNINO
PYRENEES
IBERIAN PENINSULA
BALKAN PENINSULA
CARPATHIAN MOUNTAINS
CARPAŢII MERIDIONALI
SUDETES
ANADOLU (ANATOLIA)
TOROS DAĞLARI
MESOPOTAMIA
KŪHHĀ-YE ZAGROS
DASHT-E KAVIR
KOPET MOUNTAINS
ARABIAN PENINSULA
AN-NAFŪD
NAJD (NEJD)
AD-DAHNĀ'
AR-RUB' AL-KHĀLĪ
AL-HIJĀZ (HEJAZ)
ASIR
HADRAMAWT
RED SEA
Persian Gulf
Gulf of Aden
ATLAS MOUNTAINS
ATLAS TELLIEN
ATLAS SAHARIEN
Jebel Toubkal 4165
GRAND ERG OCCIDENTAL
GRAND ERG ORIENTAL
PLATEAU DU TADEMAÏT
PLATEAU DU TINGHERT
HAMĀDAT TINGHERT
TASSILI-N-AJJER
AHAGGAR
Tahat 2908
ERG IGUIDI
ERG CHECH
Tanezrouft
ADRAR DES IFÔGHAS
MASSIF DE L'AÏR
Idoukâl-en-Taghès 2022
TÉNÉRÉ
Grand Erg de Bilma
TIBESTI
Emi Koussi 3415
SAHARA
SUDAN
FAZZĀN
ṬARĀBULUS
BARQAH
LIBYAN DESERT
WESTERN DESERT
ARABIAN DESERT
NUBIAN DESERT
SINAI
Munkhafaḑ el-Qaţţāra
ETHIOPIAN PLATEAU
Ras Dashen Terara 4620
Tropic of Cancer
ISLAS CANARIAS (CANARY ISLANDS)
ARQUIPÉLAGO DE CABO VERDE
AÇORES (AZORES)
ARQUIPÉLAGO DA MADEIRA (MADEIRA ISLANDS)
ILHAS SELVAGENS
ARQUIPÉLAGO DOS BIJAGÓS
FOUTA DJALON
Bintimani 1945
Mount Nimba 1752
ADAMAOUA
CONGO
Bight of Benin
Bay of Biscay
Strait of Gibraltar
English Channel
Adriatic Sea
Tyrrhenian Sea
Ionian Sea
Aegean Sea
Sea of Azov
Aral Sea
London
Paris
Madrid
Lisboa (Lisbon)
Roma
Berlin
Warszawa
Moskva (Moscow)
Kyiv (Kiev)
Istanbul
Ankara
Baghdād
Tehrān
Ar-Riyāḍ
Makkah (Mecca)
El-Qâhira (Cairo)
Al-Kharṭūm (Khartoum)
Ādīs Ābeba
Dakar
Bamako
Niamey
Lagos
Accra
Abidjan
Ṭarābulus
Tunis
El Djazaïr (Algiers)
Rabat
Casablanca

ATLANTIC OCEAN
INDIAN OCEAN
MADAGASCAR
Mozambique Channel
KALAHARI DESERT
NAMIB DESERT
KAOKO VELD
GREAT NAMAQUALAND
BUSHMAN LAND
GREAT KARROO
LITTLE KARROO
DRAKENSBERG
KATANGA
MUCHINGA MTS.
MONTS MITUMBA
Serengeti Plain
Masai Steppe
Tropic of Capricorn
SEYCHELLES
Mahé
LES AMIRANTES
Groupe d'Aldabra
Farquhar Group
Agalega Islands
ARCHIPEL DES COMORES
Njazidja
Nzwani
Mwali
Mayotte
Îles Glorieuses
Tanjona Bobaomby
Île Tromelin
MASCARENE IS.
Port Louis
Mauritius
Réunion
Île Juan de Nova
Bassas da India
Île Europa
Tanjona Vohimena
PRINCE EDWARD ISLANDS
ÎLES DE CROZET
ÎLES KERGUELEN
TRISTAN DA CUNHA GROUP
Gough Island
St. Helena
Ascension
Annobón
Cap Lopez
Kilimanjaro 5895
Maromokotro 2876
Tsiafajavona 2642
Boby 2658
Morro de Môco 2620
Brandberg 2579
Thabana-Ntlenyana 3482
Monte Binga 2437
Inyangani 2592
Serra Namúli 2419
Nairobi
Mombasa
Pemba
Zanzibar
Dar es Salaam
Mafia Island
Mtwara
Dodoma
Kigali
Bujumbura
Lusaka
Harare
Bulawayo
Lilongwe
Beira
Maputo
Baía de Maputo
Mbabane
Pretoria
Johannesburg
Maseru
Durban
Gaborone
Windhoek
Walvis Bay
Cape Fria
Sint Helenabaai
Cape Town
Cape of Good Hope
Kaap Agulhas
Port Elizabeth
Luanda
Lobito
Kinshasa
Brazzaville
Pointe-Noire
Cabinda
Kananga
Lubumbashi
Antananarivo
Antsiranana
Toliara
Lake Victoria
Lake Eyasi
Lake Tanganyika
Lake Rukwa
Lake Mweru
Lake Bangweulu
Lake Nyasa
Lac Kivu
Lac Mai-Ndombe
Lake Kariba
Cahora Bassa
Victoria Falls
Livingstone Falls
Zambezi
Limpopo
Orange
Vaal
Okavango
Okavango Delta
Makgadikgadi
Etosha Pan
Cuando
Cuito
Cubango
Cuanza
Cunene
Kasai
Lualaba
Lomami
Lukenie
Kafue
Nossob
Rovuma
Tana
5759
5157
649
5536
5340
4406
Equator
M-DRM2501-A1-·1·1-1™
Copyright © Rand McNally & Co.
West of Greenwich 0° East of Greenwich
0 250 500 750 1000 1500 2000 2500 Kilometers
0 250 500 1000 1500 Miles
Scale 1 : 25,000,000
Lambert Azimuthal Equal Area Projection
Meters Feet
4000 13120
3000 9840
2000 6560
1000 3280
500 1640
200 656
Sea Level
200 656
2000 6560

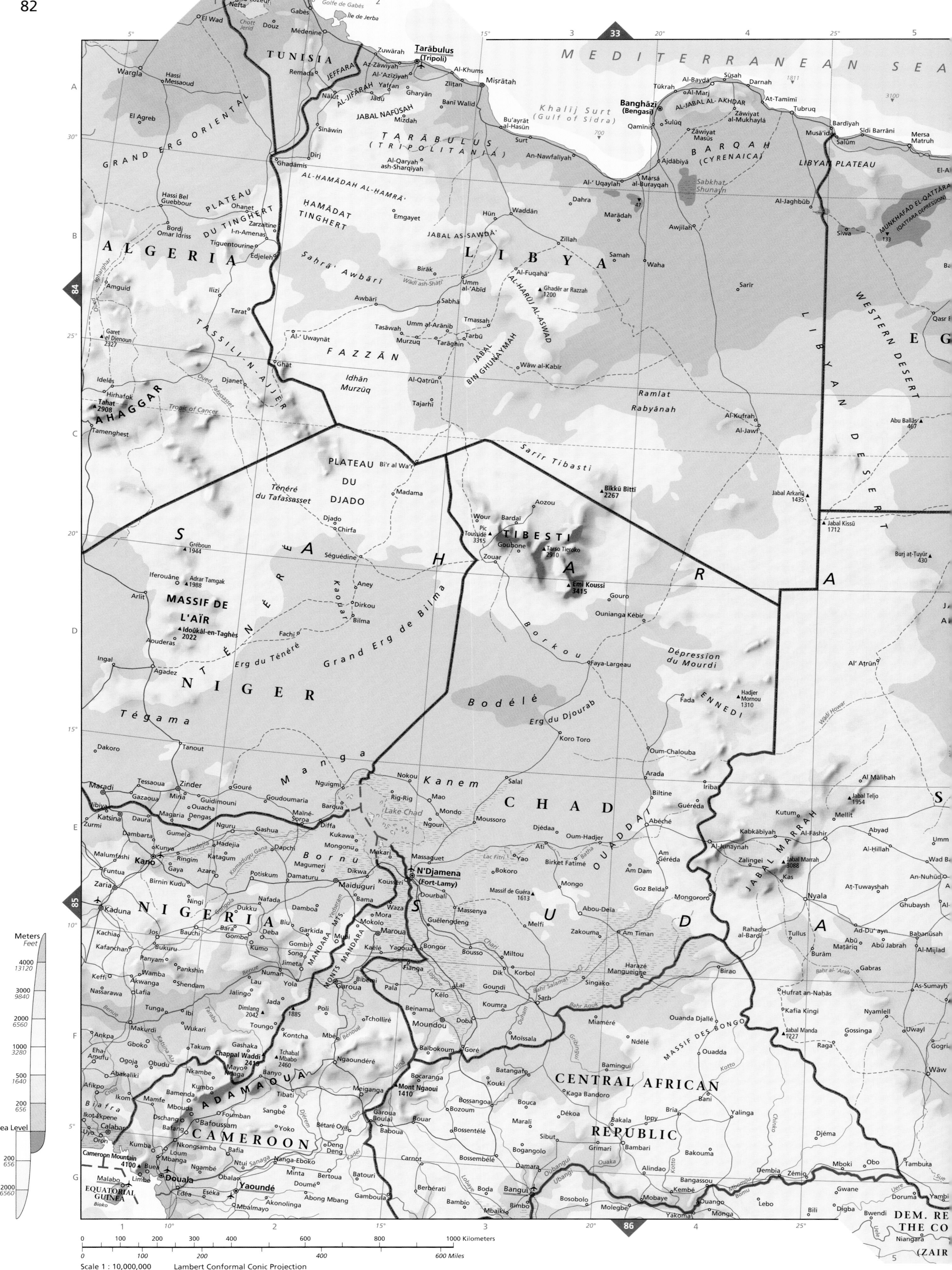
MEDITERRANEAN SEA
TUNISIA
ALGERIA
LIBYA
NIGER
CHAD
NIGERIA
CAMEROON
CENTRAL AFRICAN REPUBLIC
SUDAN
EQUATORIAL GUINEA
Tarābulus (Tripoli)
Banghāzī (Bengasi)
N'Djamena (Fort-Lamy)
Yaoundé
Bangui
Khalīj Surt (Gulf of Sidra)
GRAND ERG ORIENTAL
PLATEAU DU TINGHERT
HAMĀDAT TINGHERT
AL-HAMĀDAH AL-HAMRĀ'
TARĀBULUS (TRIPOLITANIA)
BARQAH (CYRENAICA)
LIBYAN PLATEAU
LIBYAN DESERT
WESTERN DESERT
FAZZĀN
TASSILI-N-AJJER
AHAGGAR
JABAL AS-SAWDĀ'
AL-HARŪJ AL-ASWAD
JABAL BIN GHUNAYMAH
Ṣaḥrā' Awbārī
Idhān Murzūq
Ramlat Rabyānah
Sarīr Tibasti
PLATEAU DU DJADO
Ténéré du Tafassasset
TIBESTI
SAHARA
MASSIF DE L'AÏR
TÉNÉRÉ
Erg du Ténéré
Grand Erg de Bilma
Kaouar
Borkou
Dépression du Mourdi
ENNEDI
Bodélé
Erg du Djourab
Tégama
Manga
Kanem
Lake Chad
Bornu
OUADDAÏ
JABAL MARRAH
ADAMAOUA
MANDARA MTS.
MONTS MANDARA
MASSIF DES BONGO
Tropic of Cancer
Emi Koussi 3415
Pic Toussidé 3315
Tarso Tieroko 2910
Bikkū Bittī 2267
Adrar Tamgak 1988
Gréboun 1944
Idoukâl-en-Taghès 2022
Tahat 2908
Garet el Djenoun 2327
Jabal Marrah 3088
Jabal Teljo 1954
Chappal Waddi 2419
Mont Ngaoui 1410
Cameroon Mountain 4100
Jabal Arkanū 1435
Jabal Kissū 1712
Ghadīr ar Razzah 1200
Hadjer Mornou 1310
Agadez
Zinder
Maradi
Kano
Kaduna
Maiduguri
Garoua
Maroua
Douala
Faya-Largeau
Abéché
Sabhā
Ghadāmis
Ghāt
Murzuq
Al-Kufrah
Miṣrātah
Ouargla
Nyala
Al-Fāshir
Moundou
Bilma
Aozou
Scale 1 : 10,000,000 Lambert Conformal Conic Projection
0 100 200 300 400 500 600 700 800 900 1000 Kilometers
0 100 200 300 400 500 600 Miles
Meters Feet
4000 13120
3000 9840
2000 6560
1000 3280
500 1640
200 656
Sea Level
200 656
2000 6560

LEBANON
SYRIA
DIMASHQ
(DAMASCUS)
Hefa (Haifa)
TEL AVIV-YAFO
ISRAEL
Ghazzah (Gaza)
JORDAN
'Ammān
Yerushalayim (Jerusalem)
SYRIAN DESERT
IRAQ
BAGHDĀD
MESOPOTAMIA
Karbalā'
Al-Ḥillah
Al-Kūt
Al-'Amārah
An-Najaf
Ad-Dīwānīyah
An-Nāṣirīyah
As-Samāwah
Al-Baṣrah
Abādān
Ahvāz
Dezfūl
Shūshtar
IRAN
ESFAHĀN
Shīrāz
KŪHHĀ-YE ZĀGROS
Bandar-e Būshehr
KUWAIT
AL-KUWAYT
(KUWAIT)
Persian Gulf
BAHRAIN
Al-Manāmah
(Manama)
QATAR
Ad-Dawḥah
(Doha)
UNITED ARAB EMIRATES
Tropic of Cancer
Būr Sa'īd
(Port Said)
El-Manṣūra
Ismailia
EL-QÂHIRA (CAIRO)
EL-GÎZA
(GIZA)
El-Suweis (Suez)
SINAI
(SINAI PENINSULA)
Gebel Katherina 2642
Beni Suef
Sharm el-Sheikh
Hurghada
ARABIAN DESERT
Qena
Qus
El-Uqṣor
(Luxor)
Isna
Edfu
Kom Ombo
Aswân
Sadd el-Aali
(Aswan High Dam)
Lake Nasser
(Buheirat Nâṣir)
Wādī Ḥalfā'
NUBIAN DESERT
Abū Ḥamad
Būr Sūdān
(Port Sudan)
Sawākin
Kassalā
Umm Durmān
(Omdurman)
AL-KHARṬŪM
(KHARTOUM)
Wad Madanī
Al-Qaḍārif
Kūstī
Sennar
Malakāl
Juba
AL-ḤIJĀZ
(HEJAZ)
AN-NAFŪD
AN-NEJD
Ḥā'il
Tabūk
Taymā'
Al-Madīnah
(Medina)
Yanbu' al-Bahr
Jiddah
(Jeddah)
Makkah
(Mecca)
Aṭ-Ṭā'if
'ASĪR
Abhā
Khamīs Mushayt
Jīzān
RED SEA
SAUDI ARABIA
AR-RIYĀḌ
(RIYADH)
Buraydah
'Unayzah
Al-Hufūf
Ad-Dammām
AD-DAHNĀ'
JABAL TUWAYQ
ARABIAN PENINSULA
AR-RUB' AL-KHĀLĪ
OMAN
YEMEN
Ṣan'ā'
Al-Ḥudaydah
(Hodeida)
Ta'izz
'Adan
(Aden)
Al-Mukallā
HADRAMAWT
Gulf of Aden
Bab el Mandeb
DAHLAK ARCHIPELAGO
ERITREA
Asmera
Massawa
Keren
DJIBOUTI
Djibouti
ETHIOPIAN PLATEAU
ETHIOPIA
ĀDĪS ĀBEBA
(ADDIS ABABA)
Ras Dashen Terara 4620
T'ana Hāyk'
Gonder
Bahir Dar
Dīrē Dawa
Harer
RIFT VALLEY
Danakil
Ogaden
SOMALIA
Hargeysa
Berbera
Boosaaso
INDIAN OCEAN
Lake Rudolf
(Lake Turkana)
KENYA
UGANDA
Sudd
ÉT
Copyright © Rand McNally & Co.

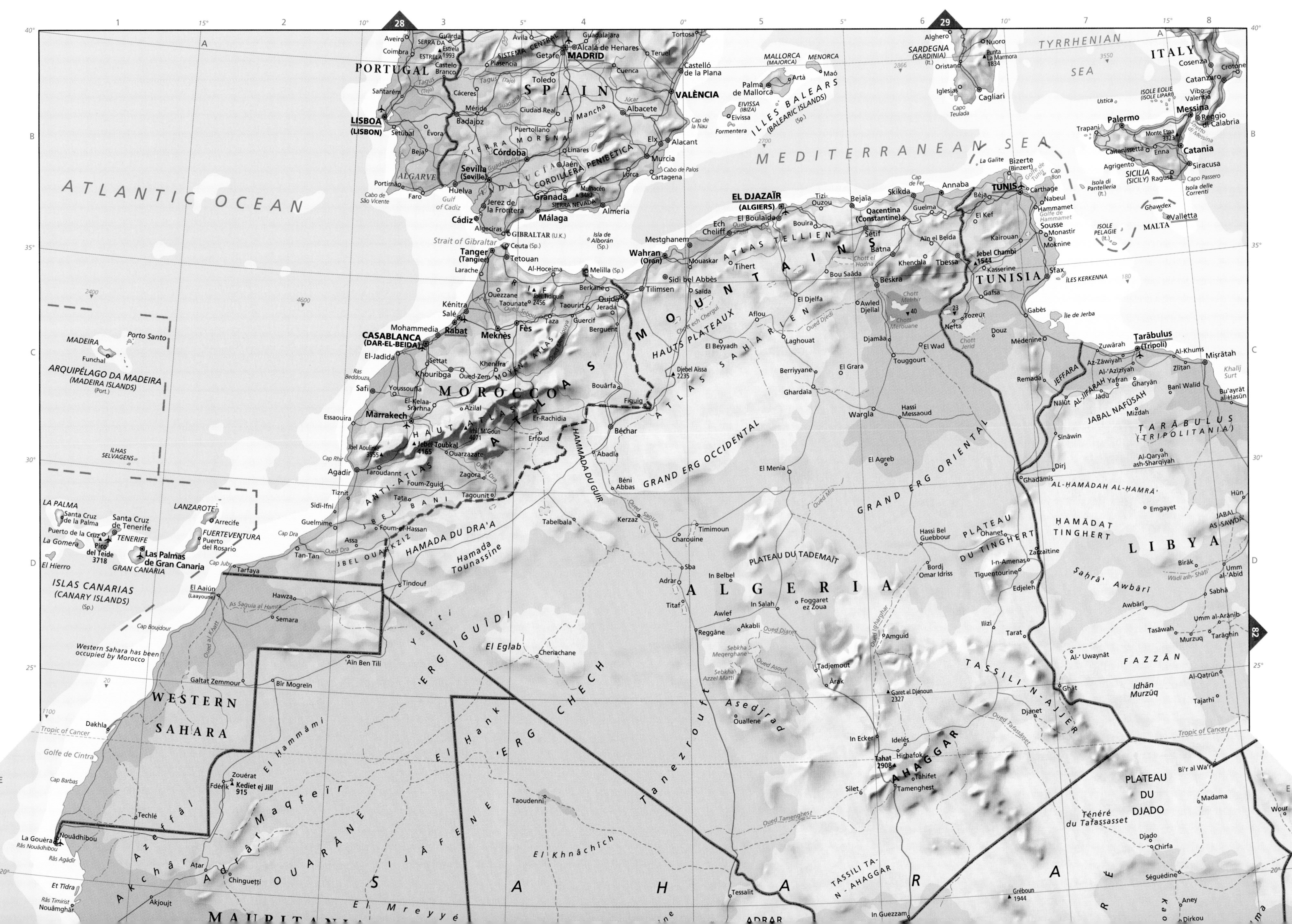
ATLANTIC OCEAN
MEDITERRANEAN SEA
TYRRHENIAN SEA
PORTUGAL
SPAIN
ITALY
MALTA
TUNISIA
MOROCCO
ALGERIA
LIBYA
WESTERN SAHARA
MAURITANIA
LISBOA (LISBON)
MADRID
VALÈNCIA
Sevilla (Seville)
Córdoba
Granada
Málaga
Cádiz
GIBRALTAR (U.K.)
Ceuta (Sp.)
Melilla (Sp.)
Tanger (Tangier)
Rabat
CASABLANCA (DAR-EL-BEIDA)
Marrakech
Fès
Meknès
Agadir
Wahran (Oran)
EL DJAZAÏR (ALGIERS)
Qacentina (Constantine)
Annaba
TUNIS
Sfax
Țarābulus (Tripoli)
Palermo
Catania
Messina
Cagliari
SARDEGNA (SARDINIA) (It.)
SICILIA (SICILY)
ILLES BALEARS (BALEARIC ISLANDS) (Sp.)
MADEIRA
ARQUIPÉLAGO DA MADEIRA (MADEIRA ISLANDS) (Port.)
ISLAS CANARIAS (CANARY ISLANDS) (Sp.)
Las Palmas de Gran Canaria
Santa Cruz de Tenerife
El Aaiún (Laayoune)
Western Sahara has been occupied by Morocco
ATLAS SAHARIEN
GRAND ERG OCCIDENTAL
GRAND ERG ORIENTAL
PLATEAU DU TADEMAÏT
HAMMADA DU GUIR
HAMADA DU DRA'A
AHAGGAR
TASSILI-N-AJJER
PLATEAU DU DJADO
Tropic of Cancer
Strait of Gibraltar

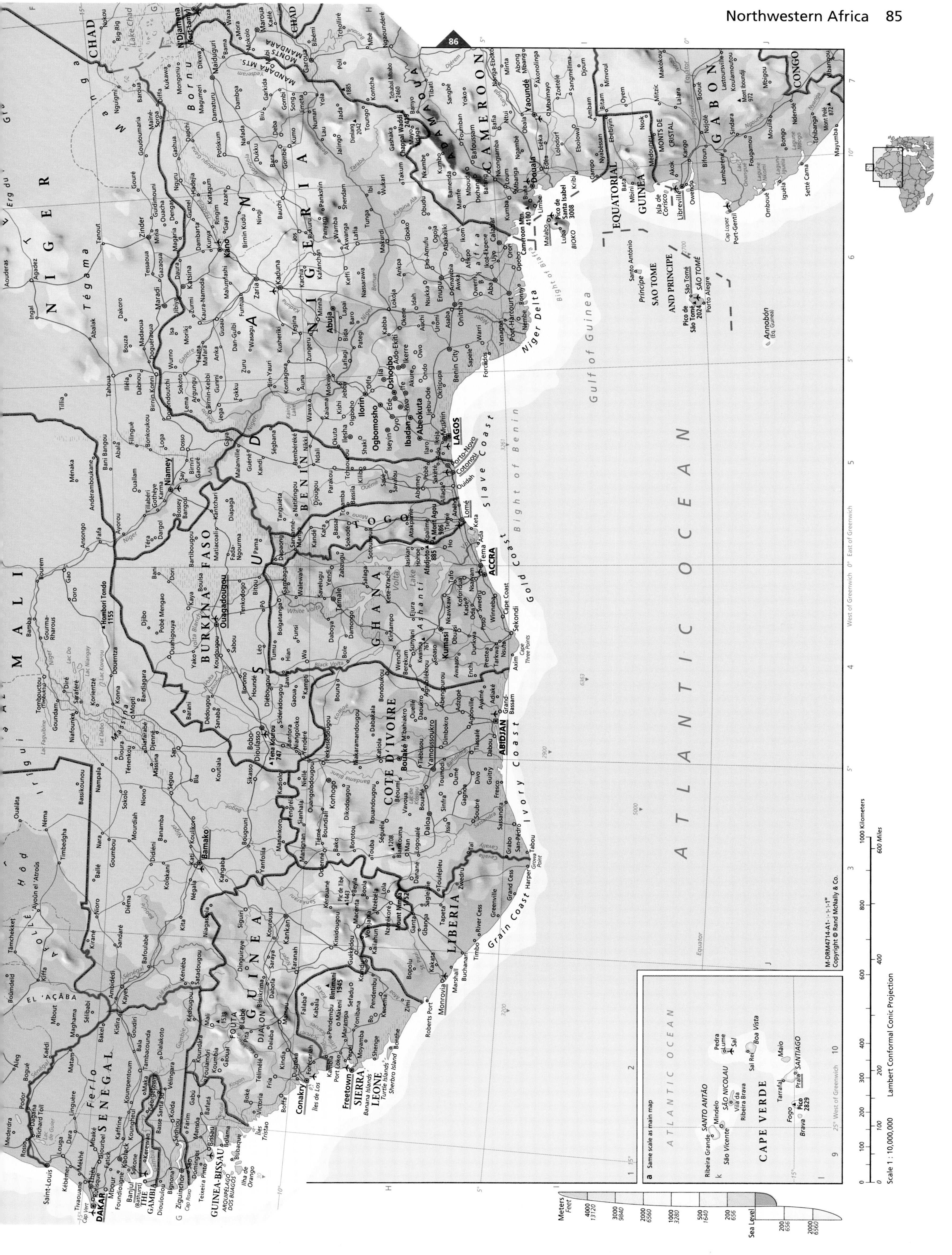

Meters / Feet: 4000 13120; 3000 9840; 2000 6560; 1000 3280; 500 1640; 200 656; Sea Level; 200 656; 2000 6560

Scale 1 : 10,000,000

Lambert Conformal Conic Projection

0 100 200 300 400 600 800 1000 Kilometers

0 100 200 400 600 Miles

a Same scale as main map

NIGER
CHAD
NIGERIA
CAMEROON
CENTRAL AFRICAN REPUBLIC
EQUATORIAL GUINEA
SAO TOME AND PRINCIPE
GABON
CONGO
DEMOCRATIC REPUBLIC OF THE CONGO (ZAIRE)
ANGOLA
ATLANTIC OCEAN
Gulf of Guinea
Bight of Biafra
Lake Chad
Kanem
Manga
Bornu
OUADDAI
JABAL MARRAH
MASSIF DES BONGO
ADAMAOUA
MANDARA MTS.
CONGO BASIN
PLATEAUX BATÉKÉ
KATANGA
MONTS MULUMBA
BIOKO
N'Djamena (Fort-Lamy)
Bangui
Yaoundé
Douala
Libreville
São Tomé
Malabo
Brazzaville
KINSHASA (LÉOPOLDVILLE)
LUANDA
Kisangani (Stanleyville)
Mbandaka (Coquilhatville)
Kananga (Luluabourg)
Mbuji-Mayi (Bakwanga)
Lubumbashi (Élisabethville)
Likasi (Jadotville)
Kolwezi
Kano
Kaduna
Maiduguri
Maroua
Garoua
Ngaoundéré
Moundou
Sarh
Abéché
Nyala
Al-Fāshir
Port-Gentil
Pointe-Noire
Cabinda
Matadi
Boma
Benguela
Lobito
Huambo
Kitwe
Cameroon Mtn. 4100
Pico de Santa Isabel 3008
Jabal Marrah 3088
Morro de Moco 2620
Chappal Waddi 2419
Mont Ngaoui 1410
Equator
PARQUE NACIONAL DA QUIÇAMA
PARC NATIONAL DE LA SALONGA
Meters / Feet
4000 13120
3000 9840
2000 6560
1000 3280
500 1640
200 656
Sea Level
200 656
2000 6560
M-DRM4712-A1-1-1-1-M
Copyright © Rand McNally & Co.
0 100 200 300 400 600 800 1000 Kilometers
0 100 200 400 600 Miles
Scale 1 : 10,000,000
Sinusoidal Projection

RED SEA
ERITREA
Asmera
YEMEN
San'a'
Adan (Aden)
Gulf of Aden
DJIBOUTI
Djibouti
ETHIOPIAN PLATEAU
ETHIOPIA
ĀDĪS ĀBEBA (ADDIS ABABA)
Danakil
Ogaden
SOMALIA
Muqdisho (Mogadiscio)
KENYA
NAIROBI
Mombasa
Lake Rudolf (Lake Turkana)
Chalbi Desert
UGANDA
Kampala
Lake Victoria
TANZANIA
DAR ES SALAAM
Dodoma
Zanzibar
Kilimanjaro 5895
Serengeti Plain
Masai Steppe
INDIAN OCEAN
SEYCHELLES
COMOROS
Moroni
ARCHIPEL DES COMORES
MAYOTTE (Fr.)
MADAGASCAR
MOZAMBIQUE
MALAWI
Lake Nyasa
Lilongwe
RIFT VALLEY
KIPENGERE RANGE
Equator

0 100 200 300 400 600 800 1000 Kilometers
0 100 200 400 600 Miles

Scale 1 : 10,000,000 Lambert Conformal Conic Projection

20° East of Greenwich

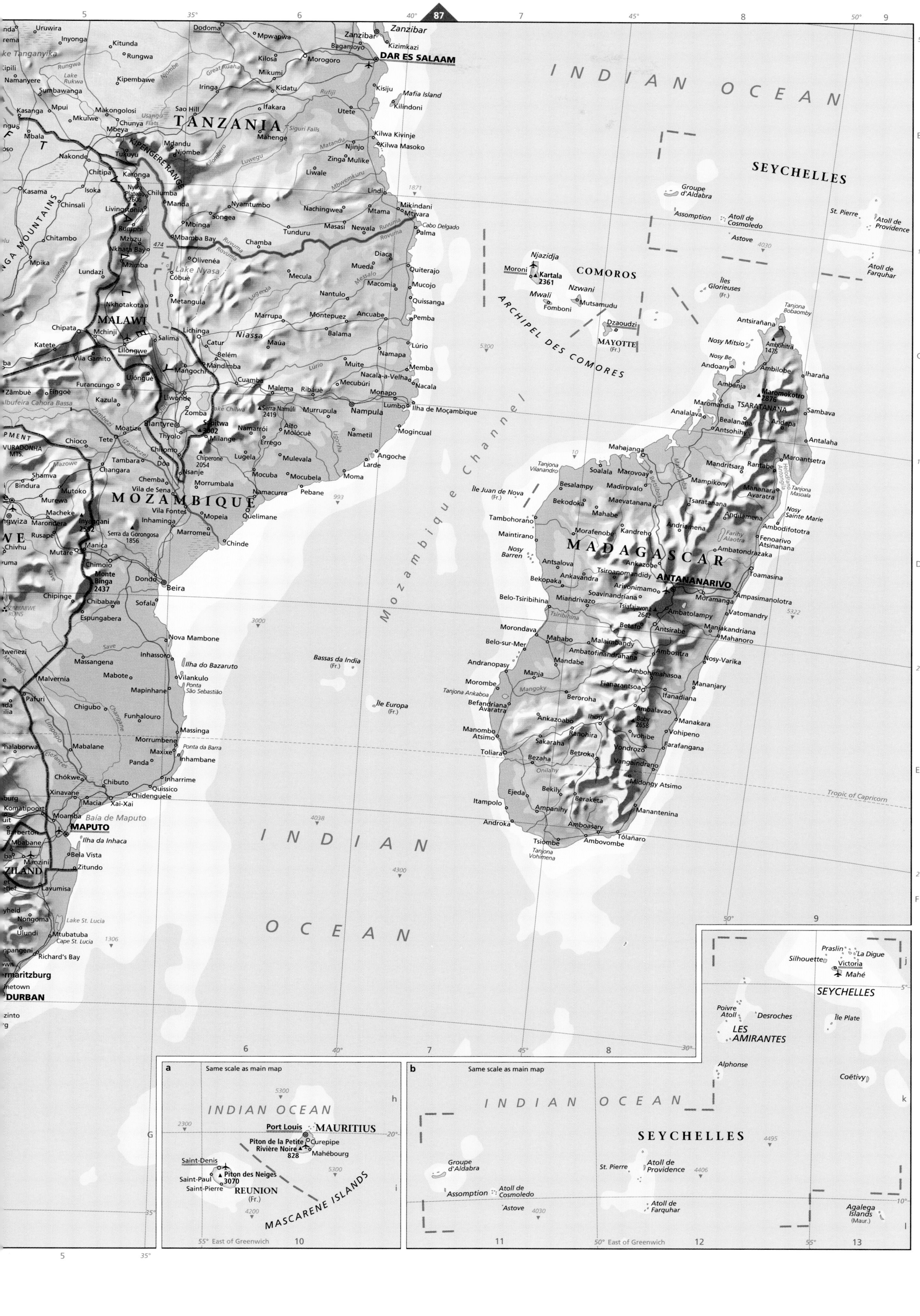

87
INDIAN OCEAN
TANZANIA
DAR ES SALAAM
Zanzibar
Kizimkazi
Bagamoyo
Dodoma
Mpwapwa
Morogoro
Kilosa
Mikumi
Kidatu
Iringa
Kitunda
Rungwa
Kipembawe
Uruwira
Inyonga
Lake Tanganyika
Sumbawanga
Namanyere
Lake Rukwa
Kasanga
Mpui
Mkulwe
Makongolosi
Chunya
Mbeya
Sao Hill
Ifakara
Mahenge
Kisiju
Mafia Island
Kilindoni
Utete
Kilwa Kivinje
Kilwa Masoko
Njinjo
Zinga Mulike
Liwale
Lindi
Mikindani
Mtwara
Mtama
Nachingwea
Masasi
Newala
Tunduru
Songea
Nyamtumbo
Mbinga
Mbamba Bay
Cabo Delgado
Palma
Kipengere Range
Mdandu
Njombe
Tukuyu
Karonga
Nakonde
Chitipa
Isoka
Kasama
Chinsali
Chilumba
Manda
Nyika Plateau 2606
Livingstonia
Rumphi
Mzuzu
Nkhata Bay
Mzimba
Chitambo
Mpika
Lundazi
Lake Nyasa
Likoma
Olivenéa
Cóbuè
Metangula
Nkhotakota
MALAWI
Mchinji
Lilongwe
Chipata
Katete
Vila Gamito
Salima
Lichinga
Niassa
Catur
Belém
Mandimba
Mangochi
Ulongwe
Cuamba
Liwonde
Zomba
Blantyre
Thyolo
Sapitwa 3002
Milange
Chiperone 2054
Mulanje
Namarrói
Erego
Alto Molócuè
Serra Namúli 2419
Malema
Ribáuè
Mecubúri
Murrupula
Nampula
Marrupa
Maúa
Montepuez
Balama
Ancuabe
Pemba
Mueda
Macomia
Quiterajo
Mucojo
Quissanga
Mecula
Nantulo
Diaca
Lúrio
Namapa
Memba
Muite
Nacala-a-Velha
Nacala
Monapo
Lumbo
Ilha de Moçambique
Nametil
Mogincual
Angoche
Larde
Moma
Mulevala
Mocuba
Mocubela
Pebane
Namacurra
Quelimane
Mopeia
Marromeu
Chinde
Vila Fontes
Inhaminga
Serra da Gorongosa 1856
MOZAMBIQUE
Furancungo
Fingoè
Zâmbuè
Kazula
Albufeira Cahora Bassa
Moatize
Tete
Chioco
Tambara
Changara
Chemba
Vila de Sena
Chiromo
Dôa
Nsanje
Morrumbala
Mazowe
Shamva
Bindura
Mutoko
Murewa
Macheke
Marondera
Inyangani 2592
Rusape
Chivhu
Mutare
Manica
Chimoio
Monte Binga 2437
Dondo
Beira
Chipinge
Chibabava
Sofala
Espungabera
Save
Nova Mambone
Inhassoro
Ilha do Bazaruto
Vilankulo
Ponta São Sebastião
Massangena
Mabote
Mapinhane
Malvernia
Pafuri
Chigubo
Funhalouro
Massinga
Limpopo
Changane
Mabalane
Morrumbene
Maxixe
Ponta da Barra
Inhambane
Panda
Chókwè
Chibuto
Inharrime
Xinavane
Quissico
Chidenguele
Macia
Xai-Xai
Komatipoort
Moamba
Baía de Maputo
MAPUTO
Ilha da Inhaca
Mbabane
Manzini
Bela Vista
Zitundo
Lavumisa
Nongoma
Ulundi
Lake St. Lucia
Mtubatuba
Cape St. Lucia
Richard's Bay
Pietermaritzburg
DURBAN
Mozambique Channel
Bassas da India (Fr.)
Île Europa (Fr.)
Île Juan de Nova (Fr.)
COMOROS
Njazidja
Moroni
Kartala 2361
Mwali
Fomboni
Nzwani
Mutsamudu
Dzaoudzi
MAYOTTE (Fr.)
ARCHIPEL DES COMORES
SEYCHELLES
Groupe d'Aldabra
Assomption
Atoll de Cosmoledo
Astove
St. Pierre
Atoll de Providence
Atoll de Farquhar
Îles Glorieuses (Fr.)
MADAGASCAR
ANTANANARIVO
Antsirañana
Tanjona Bobaomby
Nosy Mitsio
Nosy Be
Andoany
Ambohitra 1475
Ambilobe
Iharaña
Ambanja
Maromokotro 2876
TSARATANANA
Maromandia
Analalava
Bealanana
Andapa
Sambava
Antsohihy
Antalaha
Mahajanga
Tanjona Vilanandro
Soalala
Marovoay
Mandritsara
Maroantsetra
Mampikony
Rantabe
Mananara Avaratra
Tanjona Masoala
Besalampy
Madirovalo
Maevatanana
Bekodoka
Mahabe
Tsaratanana
Andilamena
Nosy Sainte Marie
Ambodifototra
Tambohorano
Morafenobe
Kandreho
Andriamena
Farihy Alaotra
Fenoarivo Atsinanana
Maintirano
Nosy Barren
Ambatondrazaka
Antsalova
Ankazobe
Tsiroanomandidy
Toamasina
Bekopaka
Ankavandra
Arivonimamo
Soavinandriana
Ampasimanolotra
Belo-Tsiribihina
Miandrivazo
Tsiafajavona 2642
Moramanga
Vatomandry
Ambatolampy
Betafo
Antsirabe
Manjakandriana
Mahanoro
Morondava
Mahabo
Malaimbandy
Belo-sur-Mer
Ambatofinandrahana
Ambositra
Nosy-Varika
Andranopasy
Mandabe
Ambohimahasoa
Manja
Mananjary
Fianarantsoa
Morombe
Tanjona Ankaboa
Befandriana Avaratra
Mangoky
Beroroha
Ifanadiana
Ambalavao
Ihosy
Boby 2658
Manakara
Ankazoabo
Vohipeno
Manombo Atsimo
Ranohira
Ivohibe
Sakaraha
Farafangana
Toliara
Betroka
Vondrozo
Bezaha
Onilahy
Vangaindrano
Midongy Atsimo
Ejeda
Bekily
Beraketa
Itampolo
Ampanihy
Manantenina
Androka
Amboasary
Tôlañaro
Tsiombe
Ambovombe
Tanjona Vohimena
Tropic of Capricorn
INDIAN OCEAN
a
Same scale as main map
INDIAN OCEAN
Port Louis
MAURITIUS
Piton de la Petite Rivière Noire 828
Curepipe
Mahébourg
Saint-Denis
Piton des Neiges 3070
Saint-Paul
Saint-Pierre
REUNION (Fr.)
MASCARENE ISLANDS
55° East of Greenwich
b
Same scale as main map
INDIAN OCEAN
SEYCHELLES
Praslin
La Digue
Silhouette
Victoria
Mahé
Poivre Atoll
Desroches
LES AMIRANTES
Île Plate
Alphonse
Coëtivy
Groupe d'Aldabra
St. Pierre
Atoll de Providence
Assomption
Atoll de Cosmoledo
Astove
Atoll de Farquhar
Agalega Islands (Maur.)
50° East of Greenwich

88
KAOKO VELD
KUNENE
Skeleton Coast
Fransfontein
Khorixas
Outjo
Otjiwarongo
WATERBERG PLATOPARK
OTJOZONDJUPA
Sorris-Sorris
Kalkfeld
Sukses
Osire Süd
Otjinene
Brandberg 2579
Uis
Okombahe
Omaruru
Etjo 2085
Omatako 2289
Ombotozo 1916
Hochfeld
Epukiro
Erongo 2305
DAMARALAND
Steinhausen
Rietfontein
Karibib
Okahandja
Usakos
Wilhelmstal
OMAHEKE
Tshootsha
Mamuno
Cape Cross (Kaap Kruis)
Hentiesbaai
ERONGO
Otjimbingwe
Omitara
Witvlei
Seeis
Gobabis
Arandis
Khomas Hochland
Windhoek
Swakopmund
Walvis Bay
KHOMAS
Dordabis
Walvis Bay (Walvisbaai)
NAMIBIA
Rehoboth
Leonardville
Aminuis
Sandwich Bay
Ilhea Point
Tropic of Capricorn
Uhlenhorst
Kalkrand
Aranos
Conception Bay
NAMIB-NAUKLUFT PARK
Nomtsas
Stampriet
HARDAP
Mariental
GREAT NAMAQUALAND
(GROOT NAMALAND)
Maltahöhe
Gochas
Gibeon
Witbooisvlei
Meobbaai
Hollandsbird Island
NAMIB DESERT
Schwarz-rand
Tses
Berseba
Koës
Helmeringhausen
Hottentotsbaai
Bethanien
Keetmanshoop
Aroab
Diaz Point
Lüderitz
Aus
Seeheim
Gawachab
Schroffenstein 2202
GROOT KARASBERGE
Possession Island
HUIB-HOCH PLATEAU
KARAS
Holoog
HUNSBERGE
1654
Grünau
Kanus
Karasburg
Sendelingsdrif
Warmbad
Oranjemund
Alexander Bay
Noordoewer
Vioolsdrif
LITTLE NAMAQUALAND
(KLEIN NAMALAND)
Goodhouse
AUGRABIES FALLS NATIONAL PARK
Onseepkans
Kakamas
Keimoes
Upington
Grobblershoop
Pofadder
Bladgrond-Noord
Aggeneys
Namies
Port Nolloth
Steinkopf
BUSHMAN LAND
Kenhardt
Nababeep
Okiep
Springbok
Gamoep
Grootvloer
NORTHERN CAPE
Kamieskroon
Vanwyksvlei
Hondeklipbaai
Brandvlei
Garies
Loeriesfontein
Sakrivier
Carnarvon
Bitterfontein
Nuwerus
Nieuwoudtville
Calvinia
Williston
Lutzville
Vredendal
Vanrhynsdorp
Klawer
ROGGEVELDBERGE
Bastersberge 1596
Fraserburg
ATLANTIC OCEAN
Lambert's Bay
Clanwilliam
Elandsvlei
Wuppertal
Bontberg 1922
Sutherland
Citrusdal
Bo-Wadrif
Aurora
Velddrif
Cape Columbine
Vredenburg
Saldanha
Piketberg
Porterville
Hopefield
Moorreesburg
WESTERN CAPE
Tulbagh
Darling
Malmesbury
Ceres
Wellington
Worcester
Paarl
Bellville
CAPE TOWN (KAAPSTAD)
Stellenbosch
Somerset West
Strand
Simon's Town
False Bay
Cape of Good Hope (Kaap die Goeie Hoop)
Caledon
Hermanus
Walker Bay
Danger Point
Gansbaai
Elim
Bredasdorp
Kaap Agulhas
Robertson
Ashton
Montagu
Swellendam
BONTEBOK NATIONAL PARK
Touwsrivier
De Doorns
LANGEBERG
Laingsburg
Ladismith
Zoar
Calitzdorp
LITTLE KARROO (KLEIN KAROO)
Van Wyksdorp
Oudtshoorn
Riversdale
Albertinia
Witsand
Stilbaai
St. Sebastian Bay
Herbertsdale
Groot-Brakrivier
George
Mosselbaai (Mossel Bay)
Knysna
Plettenbergbaai
Cape Seal
GROOT-SWARTBERGE
KOUGABERGE
Uniondale
Avontuur
Joubertina
Stormsrivier
Prince Albert
Willowmore
Steytlerville
Leeu-Gamka
Merweville
GREAT KARROO (GROOT KARROO)
Beaufort West
NUWEVELDBERGE
Nelspoort
Murraysburg
Graaff-Reinet
KAROO NATIONAL PARK
Aberdeen
Kendrew
Jansenville
Loxton
Victoria West
Hutchinson
Richmond
Hanover
Mynfontein
De Aar
Britstown
Vosburg
Philipstown
Petrusville
Strydenburg
Hopetown
Prieska
Niekerkshoop
SOUTH A
Marydale
Putsonderwater
Douglas
Griekwastad
Campbell
GRIQUALAND WEST
ASBESBERGE
Postmasburg
Daniëlskuil
Olifantshoek
Sishen
Gakarosa 1855
KURUMANHEUWELS
Dibeng
Hotazel
Kuruman
Tsineng
Sonstraal
Van Zylsrus
Askham
BECHUANALAND
Khuis
Twee Rivieren
Tshabong
Maralaleng
Pomfret
Morokweng
Werda
KALAHARI GEMSBOK NATIONAL PARK
GEMSBOK NATIONAL PARK
MABUASEHUBE GAME RESERVE
KGALAGADI DESERT
KALAHARI
Lehututu
Hukuntsi
Tshane
Kang
Kokong
Khakhea
Sekoma
KWENEN
Kule
Takachu
Tswaane
GHANZI
CENTRAL KALAHARI GAME RESERVE
BOTS
Khomodimo
KUTSE GAME RESERVE
Ghanzi
NGAMILAND
Mabeleapodi
Sehithwa
Lake Ngami
Toteng
MAKGADIKGADI PANS GAME RESERVE
Khasebake
Rakops
Scale 1 : 5,000,000
Lambert Conformal Conic Projection
1000 Kilometer
600 Miles
East of Greenwich
ATLANTIC OCEAN
Meters Feet
Sea Level

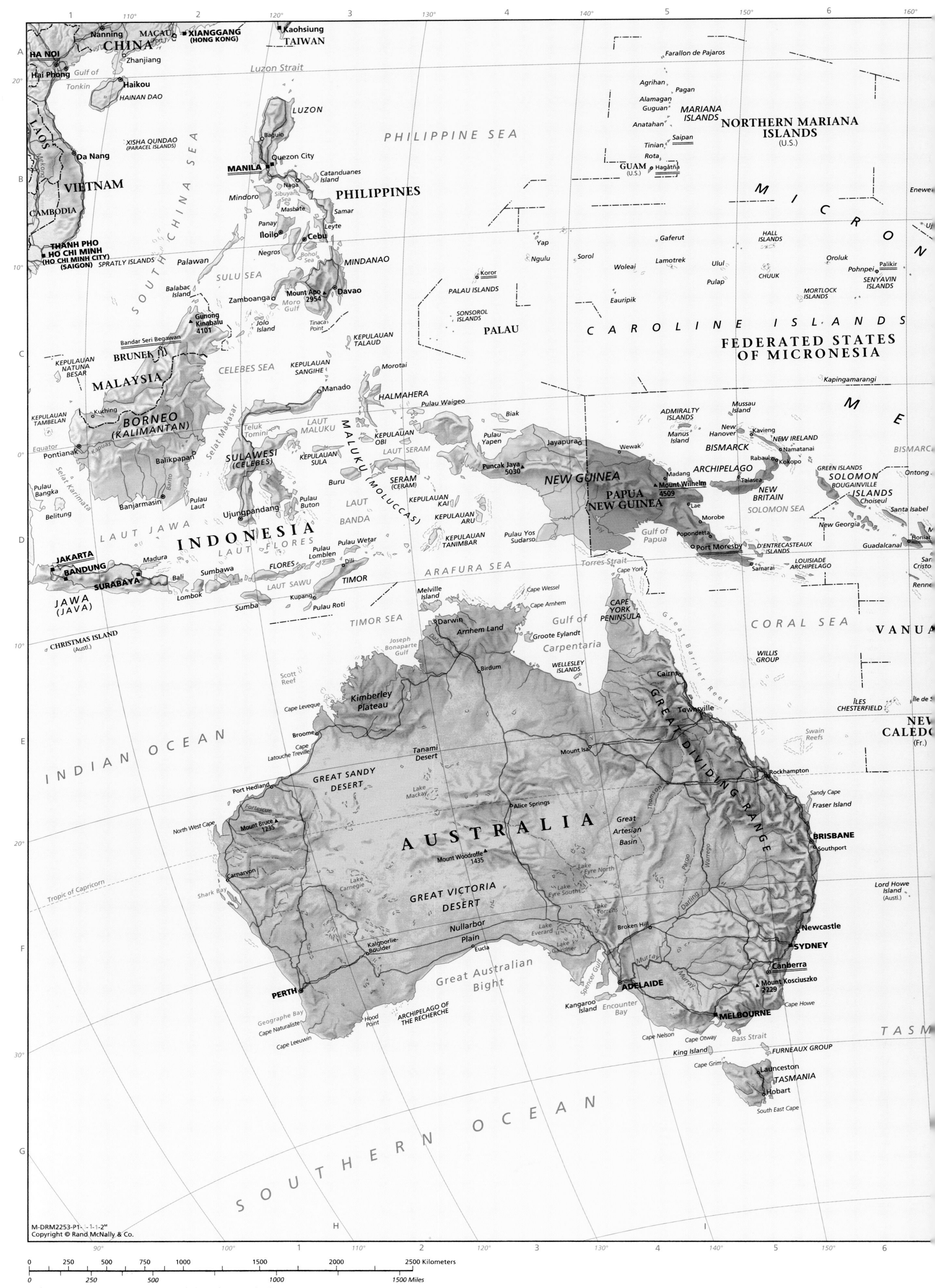

CHINA
XIANGGANG (HONG KONG)
MACAU
Nanning
Kaohsiung
TAIWAN
HA NOI
Hai Phong
Zhanjiang
Gulf of Tonkin
Luzon Strait
Haikou
HAINAN DAO
LAOS
LUZON
XISHA QUNDAO (PARACEL ISLANDS)
PHILIPPINE SEA
Baguio
Da Nang
Quezon City
MANILA
VIETNAM
CAMBODIA
PHILIPPINES
Mindoro
Samar
Leyte
Panay
Iloilo
Cebu
Negros
THANH PHO HO CHI MINH (HO CHI MINH CITY) (SAIGON)
SPRATLY ISLANDS
Palawan
SULU SEA
MINDANAO
Davao
Mount Apo 2954
Zamboanga
Balabac Island
Gunong Kinabalu 4101
Jolo Island
SOUTH CHINA SEA
Bandar Seri Begawan
BRUNEI
KEPULAUAN NATUNA BESAR
MALAYSIA
CELEBES SEA
KEPULAUAN SANGIHE
Manado
Morotai
HALMAHERA
Kuching
BORNEO (KALIMANTAN)
KEPULAUAN TAMBELAN
Pontianak
Equator
Balikpapan
SULAWESI (CELEBES)
LAUT MALUKU
MALUKU (MOLUCCAS)
KEPULAUAN OBI
KEPULAUAN SULA
LAUT SERAM
SERAM (CERAM)
Buru
Pulau Bangka
Belitung
Banjarmasin
Pulau Laut
Ujungpandang
Pulau Buton
LAUT BANDA
KEPULAUAN KAI
KEPULAUAN ARU
LAUT JAWA
INDONESIA
LAUT FLORES
JAKARTA
BANDUNG
Madura
SURABAYA
Bali
Lombok
Sumbawa
FLORES
Pulau Lomblen
Pulau Wetar
Dili
TIMOR
LAUT SAWU
Kupang
Pulau Roti
Sumba
JAWA (JAVA)
KEPULAUAN TANIMBAR
ARAFURA SEA
TIMOR SEA
CHRISTMAS ISLAND (Austl.)
Farallon de Pajaros
Agrihan
Pagan
Alamagan
Guguan
MARIANA ISLANDS
NORTHERN MARIANA ISLANDS (U.S.)
Anatahan
Saipan
Tinian
Rota
GUAM (U.S.)
Hagåtña
MICRONESIA
Yap
Ngulu
Sorol
Gaferut
Woleai
Lamotrek
Ulul
Pulap
HALL ISLANDS
CHUUK
Oroluk
Pohnpei
Palikir
SENYAVIN ISLANDS
MORTLOCK ISLANDS
Eauripik
Koror
PALAU ISLANDS
SONSOROL ISLANDS
PALAU
CAROLINE ISLANDS
FEDERATED STATES OF MICRONESIA
Kapingamarangi
Pulau Waigeo
Biak
Pulau Yapen
Jayapura
Wewak
ADMIRALTY ISLANDS
Manus Island
Mussau Island
New Hanover
Kavieng
NEW IRELAND
Namatanai
BISMARCK ARCHIPELAGO
Rabaul
Kokopo
Madang
Mount Wilhelm 4509
Puncak Jaya 5030
NEW GUINEA
PAPUA NEW GUINEA
Talasea
NEW BRITAIN
SOLOMON SEA
GREEN ISLANDS
SOLOMON ISLANDS
BOUGAINVILLE
Choiseul
Santa Isabel
New Georgia
Guadalcanal
Lae
Morobe
Gulf of Papua
Popondetta
Port Moresby
D'ENTRECASTEAUX ISLANDS
LOUISIADE ARCHIPELAGO
Samarai
Pulau Yos Sudarso
Torres Strait
Cape York
CAPE YORK PENINSULA
Melville Island
Cape Wessel
Cape Arnhem
Darwin
Arnhem Land
Gulf of Carpentaria
Groote Eylandt
WELLESLEY ISLANDS
Joseph Bonaparte Gulf
Birdum
Scott Reef
Kimberley Plateau
Cape Leveque
Broome
Cape Latouche Treville
CORAL SEA
WILLIS GROUP
Great Barrier Reef
Cairns
Townsville
GREAT DIVIDING RANGE
ÎLES CHESTERFIELD
Swain Reefs
Mount Isa
Rockhampton
INDIAN OCEAN
GREAT SANDY DESERT
Tanami Desert
Port Hedland
Lake Mackay
Alice Springs
Sandy Cape
Fraser Island
North West Cape
Fortescue
Mount Bruce 1235
AUSTRALIA
Thomson
Great Artesian Basin
BRISBANE
Southport
Mount Woodroffe 1435
Paroo
Warrego
Lake Eyre North
Lake Eyre South
Carnarvon
Shark Bay
Tropic of Capricorn
Lake Carnegie
GREAT VICTORIA DESERT
Lord Howe Island (Austl.)
Lake Torrens
Darling
Broken Hill
Newcastle
Nullarbor Plain
Lake Everard
Kalgoorlie-Boulder
Eucla
Lake Gairdner
SYDNEY
Canberra
Great Australian Bight
Spencer Gulf
Murray
ADELAIDE
Mount Kosciuszko 2229
PERTH
Geographe Bay
Cape Naturaliste
Cape Leeuwin
Hood Point
ARCHIPELAGO OF THE RECHERCHE
Kangaroo Island
Encounter Bay
Cape Howe
MELBOURNE
Cape Nelson
Cape Otway
Bass Strait
King Island
FURNEAUX GROUP
Cape Grim
Launceston
TASMANIA
Hobart
South East Cape
SOUTHERN OCEAN
M-DRM2253-P1-1-1-2M
Copyright © Rand McNally & Co.
Scale 1 : 25,000,000
Lambert Azimuthal Equal Area Projection
0 250 500 750 1000 1500 2000 2500 Kilometers
0 250 500 1000 1500 Miles

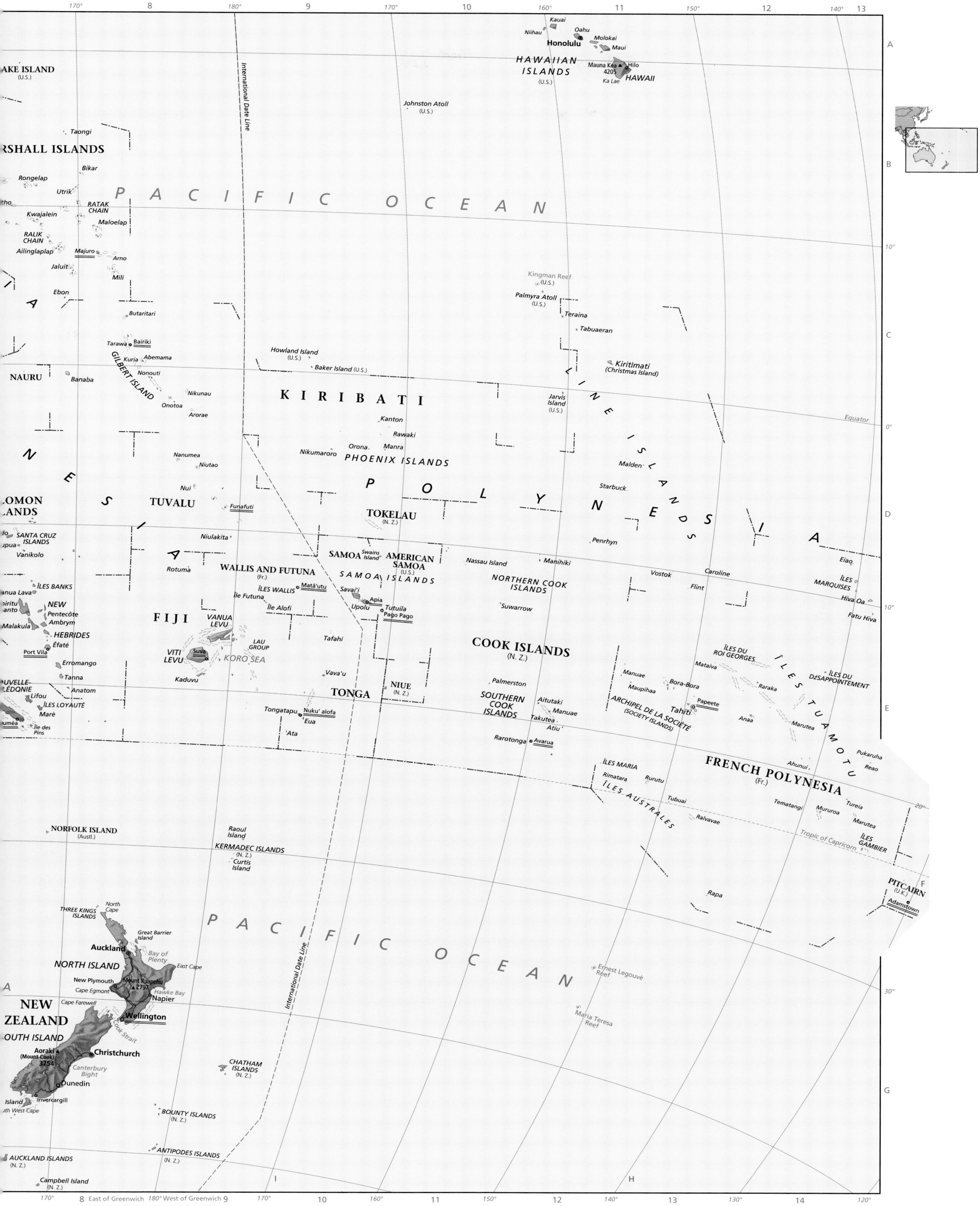

HAWAIIAN ISLANDS (U.S.)
Kauai
Niihau
Oahu
Honolulu
Molokai
Maui
Mauna Kea 4205
Hilo
HAWAII
Ka Lae
Johnston Atoll (U.S.)
WAKE ISLAND (U.S.)
MARSHALL ISLANDS
Taongi
Bikar
Rongelap
Utrik
RATAK CHAIN
Kwajalein
Maloelap
RALIK CHAIN
Ailinglaplap
Majuro
Arno
Jaluit
Mili
Ebon
PACIFIC OCEAN
Kingman Reef (U.S.)
Palmyra Atoll (U.S.)
Teraina
Tabuaeran
Kiritimati (Christmas Island)
Butaritari
Tarawa
Bairiki
Kuria
Abemama
Nonouti
GILBERT ISLANDS
NAURU
Banaba
Nikunau
Onotoa
Arorae
Howland Island (U.S.)
Baker Island (U.S.)
KIRIBATI
Jarvis Island (U.S.)
LINE ISLANDS
Equator
Kanton
Rawaki
Orona
Manra
Nikumaroro
PHOENIX ISLANDS
Malden
Starbuck
Nanumea
Niutao
Nui
TUVALU
Funafuti
POLYNESIA
TOKELAU (N. Z.)
Penrhyn
SOLOMON ISLANDS
SANTA CRUZ ISLANDS
Vanikolo
Niulakita
Rotuma
SAMOA
Swains Island
AMERICAN SAMOA (U.S.)
SAMOA ISLANDS
Savai'i
Apia
Upolu
Tutuila
Pago Pago
WALLIS AND FUTUNA (Fr.)
ÎLES WALLIS
Matā'utu
Île Futuna
Île Alofi
Nassau Island
Manihiki
NORTHERN COOK ISLANDS
Vostok
Caroline
Flint
Eiao
ÎLES MARQUISES
Hiva Oa
Fatu Hiva
ÎLES BANKS
NEW HEBRIDES
Pentecôte
Ambrym
Malakula
Éfaté
Port Vila
Erromango
Tanna
Anatom
FIJI
VANUA LEVU
VITI LEVU
Suva
KORO SEA
LAU GROUP
Kaduvu
Suwarrow
Tafahi
COOK ISLANDS (N. Z.)
ÎLES DU ROI GEORGES
Mataiva
ÎLES TUAMOTU
ÎLES DU DÉSAPPOINTEMENT
Raraka
Vava'u
TONGA
NIUE (N. Z.)
Palmerston
SOUTHERN COOK ISLANDS
Aitutaki
Manuae
Takutea
Atiu
Manuae
Maupihaa
Bora-Bora
Tahiti
Papeete
ARCHIPEL DE LA SOCIÉTÉ (SOCIETY ISLANDS)
Anaa
Marutea
NOUVELLE-CALÉDONIE
Lifou
ÎLES LOYAUTÉ
Maré
Nouméa
Île des Pins
Tongatapu
Nuku'alofa
'Eua
'Ata
Rarotonga
Avarua
Pukaruha
Reao
ÎLES MARIA
Rimatara
Rurutu
ÎLES AUSTRALES
Tubuai
Raivavae
FRENCH POLYNESIA (Fr.)
Ahunui
Tematangi
Mururoa
Tureia
Marutea
ÎLES GAMBIER
Tropic of Capricorn
NORFOLK ISLAND (Austl.)
Raoul Island
KERMADEC ISLANDS (N. Z.)
Curtis Island
Rapa
PITCAIRN (U.K.)
Adamstown
THREE KINGS ISLANDS
North Cape
Great Barrier Island
Auckland
Bay of Plenty
NORTH ISLAND
East Cape
New Plymouth
Mount Ruapehu 2797
Cape Egmont
Hawke Bay
Napier
Cape Farewell
NEW ZEALAND
Wellington
Cook Strait
SOUTH ISLAND
Aoraki (Mount Cook) 3754
Christchurch
Canterbury Bight
Dunedin
Stewart Island
Invercargill
South West Cape
PACIFIC OCEAN
International Date Line
Ernest Legouvé Reef
Maria Teresa Reef
CHATHAM ISLANDS (N. Z.)
BOUNTY ISLANDS (N. Z.)
ANTIPODES ISLANDS (N. Z.)
AUCKLAND ISLANDS (N. Z.)
Campbell Island (N. Z.)
East of Greenwich 180° West of Greenwich

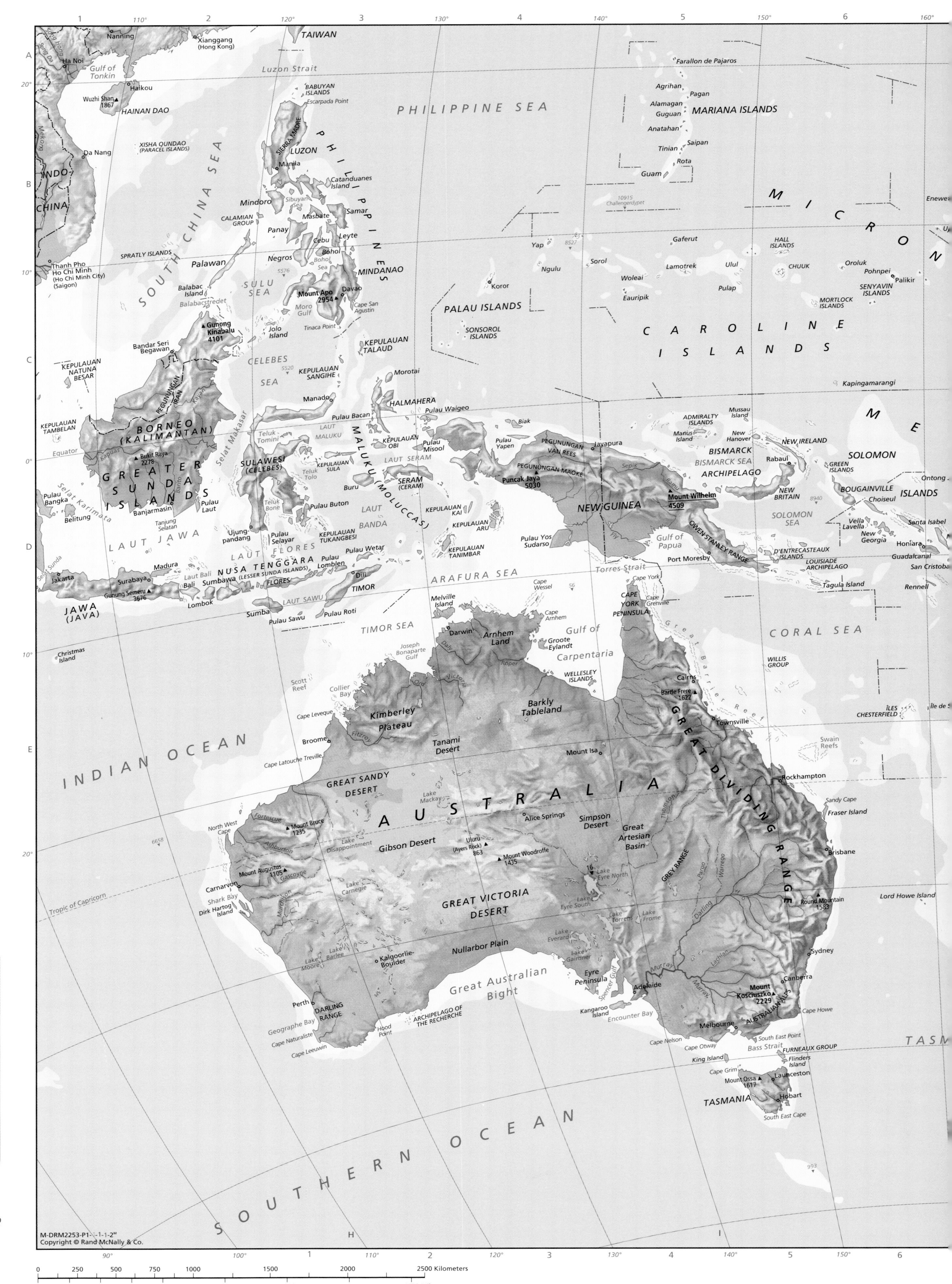

0 250 500 750 1000 1500 2000 2500 Kilometers

0 250 500 1000 1500 Miles

Scale 1 : 25,000,000 Lambert Azimuthal Equal Area Projection

PACIFIC OCEAN
POLYNESIA
HAWAIIAN ISLANDS
Kauai
Niihau
Oahu
Honolulu
Molokai
Maui
Lanai
Mauna Kea 4205
HAWAII
Johnston Atoll
Wake Island
Taongi
Bikar
Rongelap
Utrik
MARSHALL ISLANDS
RATAK CHAIN
RALIK CHAIN
Kwajalein
Maloelap
Ailinglaplap
Arno
Majuro
Mili
Jaluit
Ebon
Butaritari
GILBERT ISLANDS
Tarawa
Abemama
Kuria
Nonouti
Banaba
Nikunau
Onotoa
Arorae
Howland Island
Baker Island
PHOENIX ISLANDS
Kanton
Rawaki
Orona
Manra
Nikumaroro
Nanumea
Niutao
Nui
TUVALU
Funafuti
Niulakita
TOKELAU ISLANDS
Swains Island
SAMOA ISLANDS
Savai'i
Apia
Upolu
Tutuila
Pago Pago
ÎLES WALLIS
Île Futuna
Île Alofi
Rotuma
FIJI ISLANDS
VANUA LEVU
VITI LEVU
Suva
KORO SEA
LAU GROUP
Kaduvu
Ono-I-Lau
TONGA ISLANDS
Vava'u
Tafahi
Niue
Tongatapu
Nuku' alofa
'Eua
'Ata
Kingman Reef
Palmyra Atoll
Teraina
Tabuaeran
LINE ISLANDS
Kiritimati (Christmas Island)
Jarvis Island
Equator
Malden
Starbuck
Penrhyn
Manihiki
Nassau Island
NORTHERN COOK ISLANDS
Suwarrow
Vostok
Caroline
Flint
Palmerston
SOUTHERN COOK ISLANDS
Aitutaki
Manuae
Takutea
Mitiaro
Atiu
Rarotonga
Mangaia
ÎLES DU ROI GEORGES
Mataiva
Manuae
Maupihaa
Bora-Bora
ARCHIPEL DE LA SOCIÉTÉ (SOCIETY ISLANDS)
Tahiti
Anaa
Raraka
ÎLES TUAMOTU
ÎLES DU DÉSAPPOINTEMENT
Marutea
Pukaruha
Reao
Ahunui
Tematangi
Tureia
Marutea
Mururoa
ÎLES GAMBIER
Oeno
Pitcairn Island
Tropic of Capricorn
ÎLES MARIA
Rimatara
Rurutu
ÎLES AUSTRALES
Tubuai
Raivavae
Rapa
Eiao
ÎLES MARQUISES
Hiva Oa
Fatu Hiva
Utupua
Vanikolo
Vanua Lava
NEW HEBRIDES
Pentecôte
Ambrym
Malakula
Port Vila
Éfaté
Erromango
Tanna
Anatom
Lifou
ÎLES LOYAUTÉ
Maré
Île des Pins
Norfolk Island
Raoul Island
KERMADEC ISLANDS
Curtis Island
Three Kings Islands
North Cape
Great Barrier Island
Auckland
Bay of Plenty
East Cape
NORTH ISLAND
Mount Ruapehu 2797
Cape Egmont
Hawke Bay
NEW ZEALAND
Cape Farewell
Wellington
Cook Strait
Cape Palliser
SOUTH ISLAND
Aoraki (Mount Cook) 3754
SOUTHERN ALPS
Christchurch
Canterbury Bight
Dunedin
CHATHAM ISLANDS
Bounty Islands
ANTIPODES ISLANDS
AUCKLAND ISLANDS
Campbell Island
Ernest Legouvé Reef
Maria Teresa Reef
East of Greenwich
West of Greenwich

INDONESIA
SUMBA
TIMOR
Kupang
Baing
Seba
Pulau Sawu
Baa
Pulau Roti
Sedah
Nembrala
TIMOR SEA
INDIAN OCEAN
Ashmore Islands
Cartier Islands
Scott Reef
Browse Island
Adèle Island
BUCCANEER ARCHIPELAGO
Cape Leveque
Beagle Bay
Cape Londonderry
Admiralty Gulf
Kalumburu
Joseph Bonaparte Gulf
Cape Van Diemen
Bathurst Island
Melville Island
Dundas Strait
Coburg Peninsula
Cape Croker
Croker Island
Van Diemen Gulf
Clarence Strait
Beagle Gulf
Charles Point
Darwin
Humpty Doo
Oenpelli
Jabiru
Rum Jungle
Batchelor
Adelaide River
Arnhem Land
Anson Bay
Tipperary
Pine Creek
Katherine
Mataranka
Larrimah
Birdum
Willeroo
Daly Waters
Top Springs
Dunmarra
Wyndham
Kununurra
Auvergne
Kildurk
Victoria River Downs
Montejinni
Waterloo
Camfield
Newcastle
Wave Hill
Gibb River
Karunjie
Kimberley Plateau
KING LEOPOLD RANGES
Mount Ord 947
Mount Lush 781
Mount Wells 983
Ord River
Mount Napier 487
Inverway
Hooker Creek
Derby
Yeeda
Kimberley Downs
Liveringa
Fitzroy Crossing
Halls Creek
Turner
Gordon Downs
Christmas Creek
Noonkanbah
Broome
Roebuck Bay
Thangoo
Cape Latouche Treville
Lagrange Bay
LaGrange
Anna Plains
EDGAR RANGES
Billiluna
Tanami
Tanami Desert
The Granites 436
NORTHERN TERRITORY
Banka Banka
Mount Samuel 433
Wauchope
Willowra
Eighty Mile Beach
Mandora
Wallal Downs
GREAT SANDY DESERT
Lake Gregory
Lake White
Lake Hazlett
Percival Lakes
Port Hedland
Goldsworthy
Shay Gap
Warrawagine
Marble Bar
Lake Waukarlycarly
Mount Singleton 808
AUSTRALIA
Dampier
Wickham
Karratha
Roebourne
Barrow Island
Millstream
Nullagine
Lake Auld
Lake Dora
Lake Mackay
Mount Cockburn 846
Aileron
Onslow
Yarraloola
Pannawonica
North West Cape
Glenroy
Exmouth
Minderoo
Learmonth
HAMERSLEY RANGE
Mount Brockman 1132
Wittenoom
Mount Bruce 1235
Mount Meharry 1253
Boolaloo
Tom Price
Ethel Creek
Lake George
Mount Liebig 1274
Narwietooma
Mount Zeil 1531
Mount Leisler 897
MACDONNELL RANGES
Lake Macdonald
Ningaloo
Giralia
Paraburdoo
Newman
Lake Disappointment
Gibson Desert
Lake Neale
Hermannsburg
Chabjuwardoo Bay
Winning
BARLEE RANGE
WESTERN AUSTRALIA
Lake Amadeus
Angas Downs
Henbury
PETERMANN RANGES
Mount Olga 1066
Uluru (Ayers Rock) 863
Curtin Springs
Erldunda
Tropic of Capricorn
Cape Farquhar
Gnaraloo
Minilya
Gifford Creek
Mount Vernon
Mount Augustus 1105
Mount Augustus
Mount Essendon 910
Mount Salvado 738
Mount Jenkins
Lake Burnside
Mount Aloysius 982
Mount Cockburn 1134
Kulgera
Cape Cuvier
Lake Macleod
Boologooro
Gascoyne Junction
Granite Peak
Carnegie
Lake Carnegie
Lake Gillen
Mount Squires 705
TOMKINSON RANGES
Mount Woodroffe 1435
Sundown
Bernier Island
Carnarvon
Mount Fraser 770
Peak Hill
Lake Gregory
Lake Nabberu
Baker Lake
Dorre Island
Shark Bay
Carey Downs
Karalundi
Wiluna
Lake Way
Lake Wells
Cape Inscription
Dirk Hartog Island
Wooramel
Byro
Denham
Hamelin
Mount Murchison 520
Meekatharra
Nannine
Mount Sir Thomas 805
Wintinna
Mount Willoughby
Tamala
Meeberrie
Tuckanarra
Cue
Lake Darlot
Mount Shenton 520
Lake Throssel
Yeo Lake
GREAT VICTORIA DESERT
Serpentine Lakes
Lake Meramangye
Lake Austin
Wondinong
Agnew
Melrose
White Cliffs
Lennonville
Mount Magnet
Sandstone
Mount Redcliffe 562
Laverton
Leonora
Lake Carey
Rason Lake
Lake Gidgi
Lake Dey-Dey
Lake Maurice
Coob
SOUTH AUSTRALIA
Kalbarri
Bluff Point
Murchison
Greenough
Northampton
Yalgoo
Youanmi
Gwalia
Malcolm
Lake Ballard
Kookynie
Lake Miniqwal
Plumridge Lakes
Maralinga
Houtman Abrolhos
Geelvink Channel
Mullewa
Geraldton
Mingenew
Morawa
Monger Lake
Paynes Find
Lake Barlee
Menzies
Mount Singleton 678
Dongara
Three Springs
Lake Moore
Goongarrie
Lake Rebecca
Nullarbor Plain
Ooldea
Malbooma
Carnamah
Coorow
Mount Jackson 617
Seemore Downs
Forrest
Deakin
Cook
Dalwallinu
Beacon
Bonnie Rock
Lake Deborah West
Kalgoorlie-Boulder
Karonie
Zanthus
Rawlinna
Haig
Loongana
Mount Lesueur 313
Watheroo
Pithara
Coolgardie
Mount Monger
Lake Seabrook
Kambalda
Nullarbor
Colona
Head of Bight
Penong
Moora
Bencubbin
Mukinbudin
Bullfinch
Southern Cross
Lake Lefroy
Widgiemooltha
Hampton Tableland
Eucla
Mundrabilla
Madura
Fowlers Bay
Lancelin
New Norcia
Trayning
Higginsville
Lake Cowan
Fraser Range
Eyre
Gingin
DARLING RANGE
Toodyay
Merredin
Kellerberrin
Lake Johnston
Streaky Bay
Wanneroo
Stirling
Northam
York
Bruce Rock
Norseman
Balladonia
PERTH
Fremantle
Gosnells
Armadale
Corrigin
Hyden
Peak Charles 651
Lake Dundas
Salmon Gums
Rockingham
Pingelly
Kondinin
Great Australian Bight
Pinjarra
Wickepin
Lake King
RUSSELL RANGE
Yarloop
Narrogin
Lake Grace
Newdegate
Ravensthorpe
Gibson
Point Dempster
Wagin
Esperance
Bunbury
Collie
Darkan
Nyabing
Geographe Bay
Donnybrook
Katanning
Hopetoun
Cape Arid
Cape Naturaliste
Busselton
Kojonup
Gnowangerup
Nannup
Bridgetown
Cranbrook
Hood Point
Bremer Bay
ARCHIPELAGO OF THE RECHERCHE
Margaret River
Augusta
Pemberton
Mount Barker
Cheyne Bay
Cape Leeuwin
Northcliffe
Denmark
Albany
Flinders Bay
King George Sound
Point D'Entrecasteaux
Walpole
West Cape Howe
Bald Head
SOUTHERN OCEAN
Meters
Feet
2000
6560
1000
3280
500
1640
200
656
Sea Level
200
656
2000
6560
M-DRM4717-A1-
Copyright © Rand McNally & Co.
0 100 200 300 400 600 800 1000 Kilometers
0 100 200 400 600 Miles
Scale 1 : 10,000,000
Lambert Conformal Conic Projection

A.C.T. = AUSTRALIAN CAPITAL TERRITORY

CORAL SEA ISLANDS TERRITORY (Austl.)
CORAL SEA
PACIFIC OCEAN
GREAT BARRIER REEF MARINE PARK
GREAT BARRIER REEF
Capricorn Channel
Gulf of Carpentaria
QUEENSLAND
GREAT DIVIDING RANGE
GREGORY RANGE
LEICHHARDT RANGE
CONNORS RANGE
DAWSON RA.
EXPEDITION RANGE
AUBURN RANGE
WARREGO RA.
GOWAN RA.
FORSYTH RA.
SELWYN RA.
Channel Country
Great Artesian Basin
Darling Downs
AUSTRALIA
BRISBANE
Townsville
Cairns
Mackay
Rockhampton
Gladstone
Bundaberg
Maryborough
Toowoomba
Mount Isa
Cloncurry
Longreach
Emerald
Charleville
Roma
Normanton
Hughenden
Charters Towers
Winton
Fraser Island
Diamond Islets
Tregosse Islets
Flinders Reefs
Lihou Reefs and Cays
Marion Reef
Saumarez Reef
Frederick Reef
Swain Reefs
Capricorn Group
Bunker Group
Whitsunday Island
Magnetic Island
Hinchinbrook Island
Wellesley Islands
Tropic of Capricorn

NEW SOUTH WALES
VICTORIA
SOUTH AUSTRALIA
TASMANIA
TASMAN SEA
SOUTHERN OCEAN
Bass Strait
Great Australian Bight
RIVERINA
GREAT DIVIDING RANGE
AUSTRALIAN CAPITAL TERRITORY
JERVIS BAY TERRITORY
SYDNEY
MELBOURNE
ADELAIDE
Canberra
Hobart
Newcastle
Wollongong
Geelong
Launceston
Same scale as main map
W-DRM5517-A1 -1-1-2"
Copyright © Rand McNally & Co.
Scale 1 : 5,000,000
Lambert Conformal Conic Projection
400 Kilometers
200 Miles
Meters
Feet
Sea Level

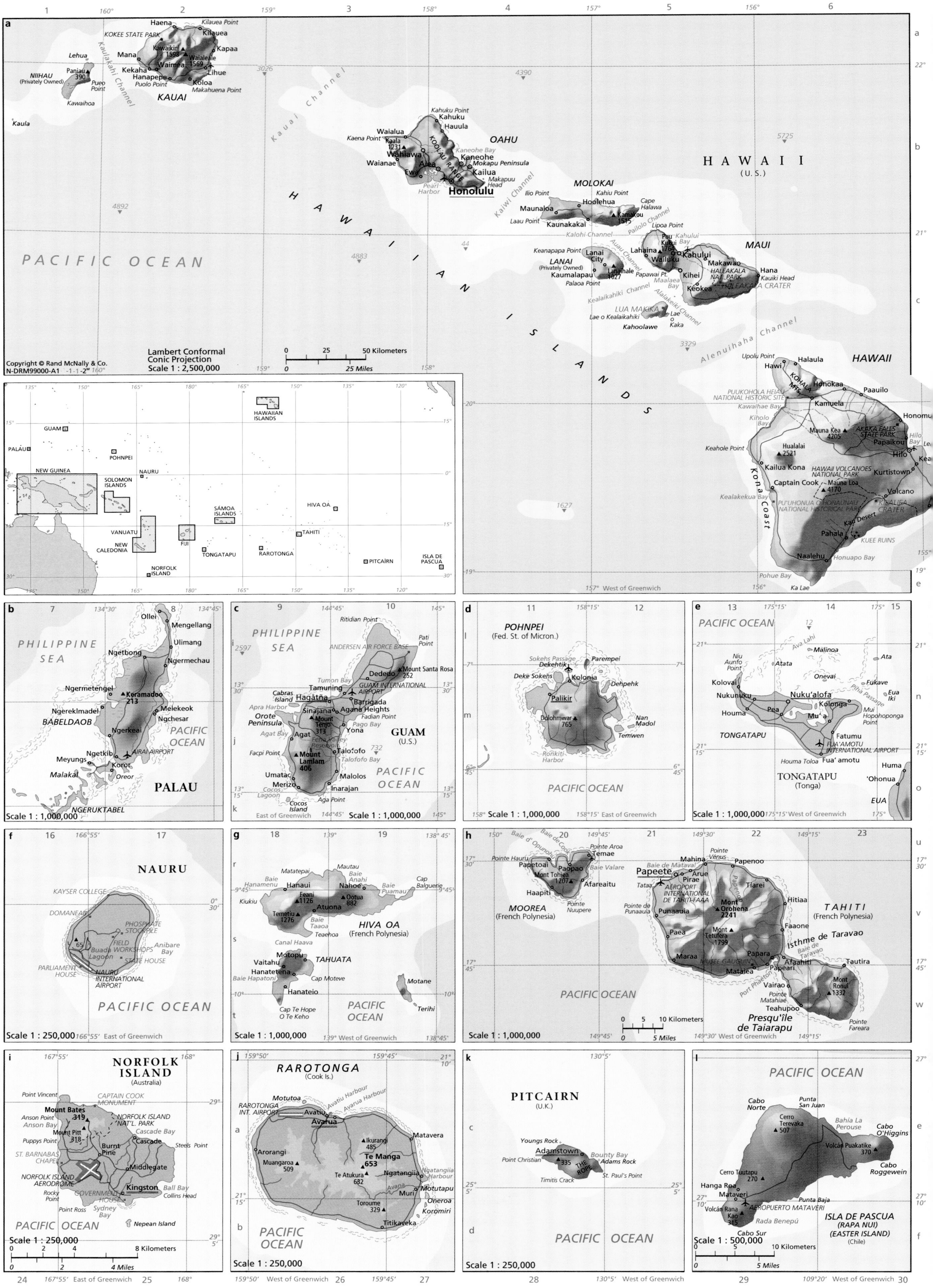

a — Hawaiian Islands

HAWAII (U.S.)

HAWAIIAN ISLANDS

PACIFIC OCEAN

NIIHAU (Privately Owned)
Lehua
Paniau 390
Pueo Point
Kawaihoa
Kaula
Kaulakahi Channel

KAUAI
KOKEE STATE PARK
Haena
Kilauea Point
Kilauea
Kapaa
Mana
Kawaikini 1598
Waialeale 1569
Waimea
Kekaha
Hanapepe
Lihue
Puolo Point
Koloa
Makahuena Point

Kauai Channel

OAHU
Kahuku Point
Kahuku
Hauula
Waialua
Kaena Point
Kaala 1231
Wahiawa
Waianae
KOOLAU RANGE
Kaneohe Bay
Kaneohe
Mokapu Peninsula
Ewa
Aiea
Kailua
Pearl Harbor
Makapuu Head
Honolulu

Kaiwi Channel

MOLOKAI
Ilio Point
Kahiu Point
Hoolehua
Cape Halawa
Maunaloa
Kamakou 1515
Laau Point
Kaunakakai
Pailolo Channel
Kalohi Channel
Lipoa Point

LANAI (Privately Owned)
Keanapapa Point
Lanai City
Lanaihale 1027
Kaumalapau
Palaoa Point
Auau Channel

MAUI
Puu Kukui 1764
Kahului Bay
Kahului
Lahaina
Wailuku
Papawai Pt.
Maalaea Bay
Kihei
Makawao
HALEAKALA NAT. PARK
HALEAKALA CRATER
Hana
Kauiki Head
Keokea

Kealaikahiki Channel
LUA MAKIKA
Lae o Kealaikahiki
Lae
Kaka
Kahoolawe
Alalakeiki Channel
Alenuihaha Channel

HAWAII
Upolu Point
Hawi
Halaula
KOHALA MTS.
Honokaa
Paauilo
PUUKOHOLA HEIAU NATIONAL HISTORIC SITE
Kawaihae Bay
Kamuela
Honomu
Kiholo Bay
Mauna Kea 4205
AKAKA FALLS STATE PARK
Papaikou
Hilo Bay
Hilo
Keahole Point
Hualalai 2521
Kailua Kona
HAWAII VOLCANOES NATIONAL PARK
Kurtistown
Captain Cook
Mauna Loa 4170
Volcano
Kona Coast
Kealakekua Bay
PU'UHONUA O HONAUNAU NATIONAL HISTORICAL PARK
KILAUEA CRATER
Kau Desert
Pahala
KUEE RUINS
Naalehu
Honuapo Bay
Pohue Bay
Ka Lae

3026
4390
5725
4892
4883
44
3329
1627

157° West of Greenwich

Lambert Conformal Conic Projection
Scale 1 : 2,500,000
0 25 50 Kilometers
0 25 Miles

Locator map

HAWAIIAN ISLANDS
GUAM
PALAU
POHNPEI
NEW GUINEA
NAURU
SOLOMON ISLANDS
SAMOA ISLANDS
HIVA OA
VANUATU
NEW CALEDONIA
FIJI
TONGATAPU
RAROTONGA
TAHITI
PITCAIRN
ISLA DE PASCUA
NORFOLK ISLAND

b — Palau

PALAU
PHILIPPINE SEA
PACIFIC OCEAN
Ollei
Mengellang
Ulimang
Ngetbong
Ngermechau
Ngermetengel
Keramadoo 213
Ngereklmadel
Melekeok
Ngchesar
BABELDAOB
Ngerkeai
Ngetkib
AIRAI AIRPORT
Meyungs
Koror
Malakal
Oreor
NGERUKTABEL
Scale 1 : 1,000,000

c — Guam

GUAM (U.S.)
PHILIPPINE SEA
PACIFIC OCEAN
Ritidian Point
Pati Point
ANDERSEN AIR FORCE BASE
2597
Mount Santa Rosa 252
Dededo
Tumon Bay
Tamuning
GUAM INTERNATIONAL AIRPORT
Cabras Island
Hagåtña
Barrigada
Apra Harbor
Sinajana
Agana Heights
Orote Peninsula
Mount Tenjo 313
Fadian Point
Pago Bay
Agat Bay
Agat
Yona
Fena Valley Reservoir
Facpi Point
Talofofo
732
Talofofo Bay
Mount Lamlam 406
Umatac
Malolos
Merizo
Inarajan
Cocos Lagoon
Cocos Island
Aga Point
East of Greenwich
Scale 1 : 1,000,000

d — Pohnpei

POHNPEI (Fed. St. of Micron.)
Sokehs Passage
Dekehtik
Parempei
Deke Sokehs
Kolonia
Dehpehk
Palikir
Dolohmwar 765
Nan Madol
Temwen
Ronkiti Harbor
PACIFIC OCEAN
Scale 1 : 1,000,000
158°15' East of Greenwich

e — Tongatapu

PACIFIC OCEAN
TONGATAPU (Tonga)
Ava Lahi
Malinoa
Niu Aunfo Point
Atata
Ata
Onevai
Kolovai
Fukave
Piha Passage
Eua Iki
Nukunuku
Nuku'alofa
Kolonga
Houma
Pea
Mu'a
Mui Hopohoponga Point
TONGATAPU
Fatumu
FUA'AMOTU INTERNATIONAL AIRPORT
Houma Toloa
Fua' amotu
Huma
'Ohonua
EUA
Scale 1 : 1,000,000
175°15' West of Greenwich

f — Nauru

NAURU
KAYSER COLLEGE
DOMANEAB
PHOSPHATE STOCKPILE
65
FIELD WORKSHOPS
Anibare Bay
Buada Lagoon
STATE HOUSE
PARLIAMENT HOUSE
NAURU INTERNATIONAL AIRPORT
PACIFIC OCEAN
Scale 1 : 250,000
166°55' East of Greenwich

g — Hiva Oa

Matatepai
Mautau
Baie Hanamenu
Baie Anahi
Cap Balguerie
Hanaui
Nahoe
Baie Puamau
Feani 1126
Ootua 882
Kiukiu
Temetiu 1276
Atuona
Baie Taaoa
Teaehoa
HIVA OA (French Polynesia)
Canal Haava
Motopu
TAHUATA
Vaitahu
Hanatetena
Baie Hapatoni
Cap Moteve
Hanateio
Motane
Terihi
Cap Te Hope O Te Keho
PACIFIC OCEAN
Scale 1 : 1,000,000
139° West of Greenwich

h — Tahiti and Moorea

Baie d' Opunohu
Baie de Cook
Pointe Aroa
Temae
Pointe Hauru
Papetoai
Paopao
Baie Valare
Mont Tohiea 1207
Afareaitu
Haapiti
Pointe Nuupere
MOOREA (French Polynesia)
Pointe Venus
Mahina
Papenoo
Baie de Matavai
Papeete
Arue
Pirae
Tataa
AEROPORT INTERNATIONAL DE TAHITI-FAAA
Tiarei
Pointe de Punaauia
Punaauia
Hitiaa
Mont Orohena 2241
TAHITI (French Polynesia)
Paea
Mont Tetufera 1799
Faaone
Isthme de Taravao
Baie de Taravao
Maraa
Papara
Afaahiti
Tautira
Mataiea
Papeari
Port Phaeton
Vairao
Mont Ronui 1332
Pointe Matahiae
Teahupoo
Presqu'ile de Taiarapu
Pointe Fareara
PACIFIC OCEAN
0 5 10 Kilometers
0 5 Miles
Scale 1 : 1,000,000
149°30' West of Greenwich

i — Norfolk Island

NORFOLK ISLAND (Australia)
Point Vincent
CAPTAIN COOK MONUMENT
Mount Bates 319
Anson Point
Anson Bay
NORFOLK ISLAND 'NAT'L. PARK
Mount Pitt 318
Cascade Bay
Puppys Point
Cascade
Steels Point
ST. BARNABAS CHAPEL
Burnt Pine
Middlegate
NORFOLK ISLAND AERODROME
Kingston
Ball Bay
Rocky Point
GOVERNMENT HOUSE
Collins Head
Point Ross
Sydney Bay
Nepean Island
PACIFIC OCEAN
Scale 1 : 250,000
0 2 4 8 Kilometers
0 2 4 Miles
167°55' East of Greenwich

j — Rarotonga

RAROTONGA (Cook Is.)
Motutoa
Avatiu Harbour
Avarua Harbour
RAROTONGA INT. AIRPORT
Avatiu
Avarua
Matavera
Ikurangi 485
Arorangi
Muangaroa 509
Te Manga 653
Te Atukura 682
Ngatangiia
Ngatangiia Harbour
Motutapu
Muri
Avana
Oneroa
Koromiri
Toroume 329
Titikaveka
PACIFIC OCEAN
Scale 1 : 250,000
159°50' West of Greenwich

k — Pitcairn

PITCAIRN (U.K.)
Youngs Rock
Adamstown
Bounty Bay
Point Christian
335
THE ROPE
Adams Rock
Timitis Crack
St. Paul's Point
PACIFIC OCEAN
Scale 1 : 250,000
130°5' West of Greenwich

l — Isla de Pascua

PACIFIC OCEAN
Cabo Norte
Punta San Juan
Cerro Terevaka 507
Bahía La Perouse
Cabo O'Higgins
Volcán Puakatike 370
Cerro Tuutapu 270
Cabo Roggewein
Hanga Roa
Mataveri
AEROPUERTO MATAVERI
Punta Baja
Volcán Rana Kao 315
Rada Benepú
Cabo Sur
ISLA DE PASCUA (RAPA NUI) (EASTER ISLAND) (Chile)
Scale 1 : 500,000
0 5 10 Kilometers
0 5 Miles
109°20' West of Greenwich

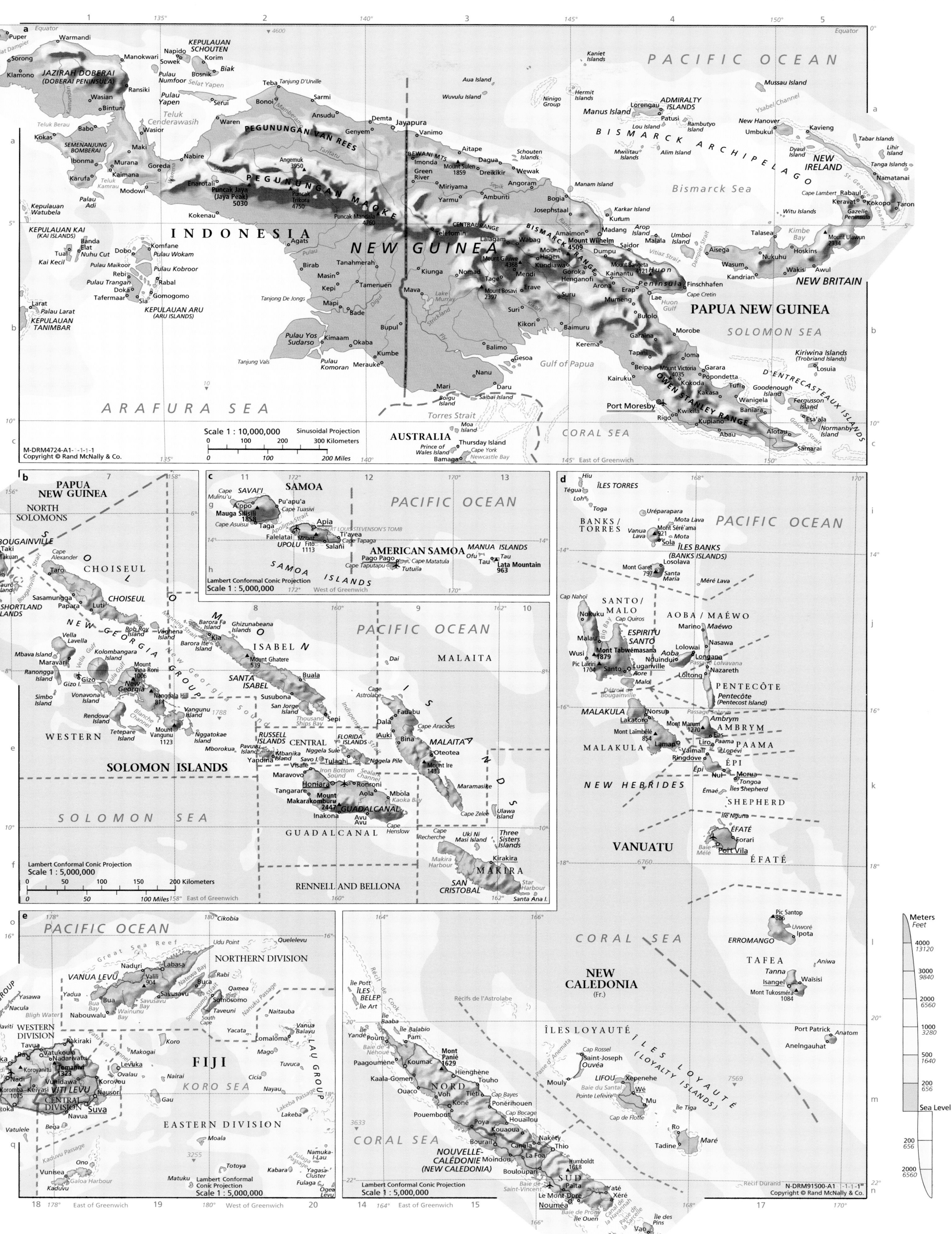
PACIFIC OCEAN
INDONESIA
NEW GUINEA
PAPUA NEW GUINEA
ARAFURA SEA
CORAL SEA
SOLOMON SEA
Bismarck Sea
BISMARCK ARCHIPELAGO
ADMIRALTY ISLANDS
NEW IRELAND
NEW BRITAIN
Gulf of Papua
Torres Strait
AUSTRALIA
PEGUNUNGAN MAOKE
PEGUNUNGAN VAN REES
OWEN STANLEY RANGE
D'ENTRECASTEAUX ISLANDS
JAZIRAH DOBERAI (DOBERAI PENINSULA)
KEPULAUAN ARU (ARU ISLANDS)
KEPULAUAN TANIMBAR
KEPULAUAN KAI (KAI ISLANDS)
Puncak Jaya (Jaya Peak) 5030
Mount Wilhelm 4509
Port Moresby
Jayapura
Scale 1 : 10,000,000
Sinusoidal Projection
M-DRM4724-A1- -1-1-1
Copyright © Rand McNally & Co.
PAPUA NEW GUINEA
NORTH SOLOMONS
BOUGAINVILLE
CHOISEUL
NEW GEORGIA GROUP
ISABEL
MALAITA
SANTA ISABEL
CENTRAL
GUADALCANAL
Honiara
WESTERN
SOLOMON ISLANDS
SOLOMON SEA
RENNELL AND BELLONA
MAKIRA
SAN CRISTOBAL
Lambert Conformal Conic Projection
Scale 1 : 5,000,000
SAMOA
SAVAI'I
UPOLU
Apia
AMERICAN SAMOA
MANUA ISLANDS
Pago Pago
Tutuila
SAMOA ISLANDS
ROBERT LOUIS STEVENSON'S TOMB
ÎLES TORRES
BANKS / TORRES
ÎLES BANKS (BANKS ISLANDS)
SANTO / MALO
ESPIRITU SANTO
AOBA / MAÉWO
PENTECÔTE
MALAKULA
AMBRYM
PAAMA
ÉPI
SHEPHERD
NEW HEBRIDES
VANUATU
ÉFATÉ
Port Vila
ERROMANGO
TAFEA
Tanna
CORAL SEA
NEW CALEDONIA (Fr.)
ÎLES LOYAUTÉ
ÎLES LOYAUTÉ (LOYALTY ISLANDS)
NORD
SUD
NOUVELLE-CALÉDONIE (NEW CALEDONIA)
Nouméa
N-DRM91500-A1 -1-1-1
Copyright © Rand McNally & Co.
PACIFIC OCEAN
NORTHERN DIVISION
VANUA LEVU
WESTERN DIVISION
VITI LEVU
CENTRAL DIVISION
Suva
FIJI
KORO SEA
EASTERN DIVISION
LAU GROUP
Meters
Feet
Sea Level

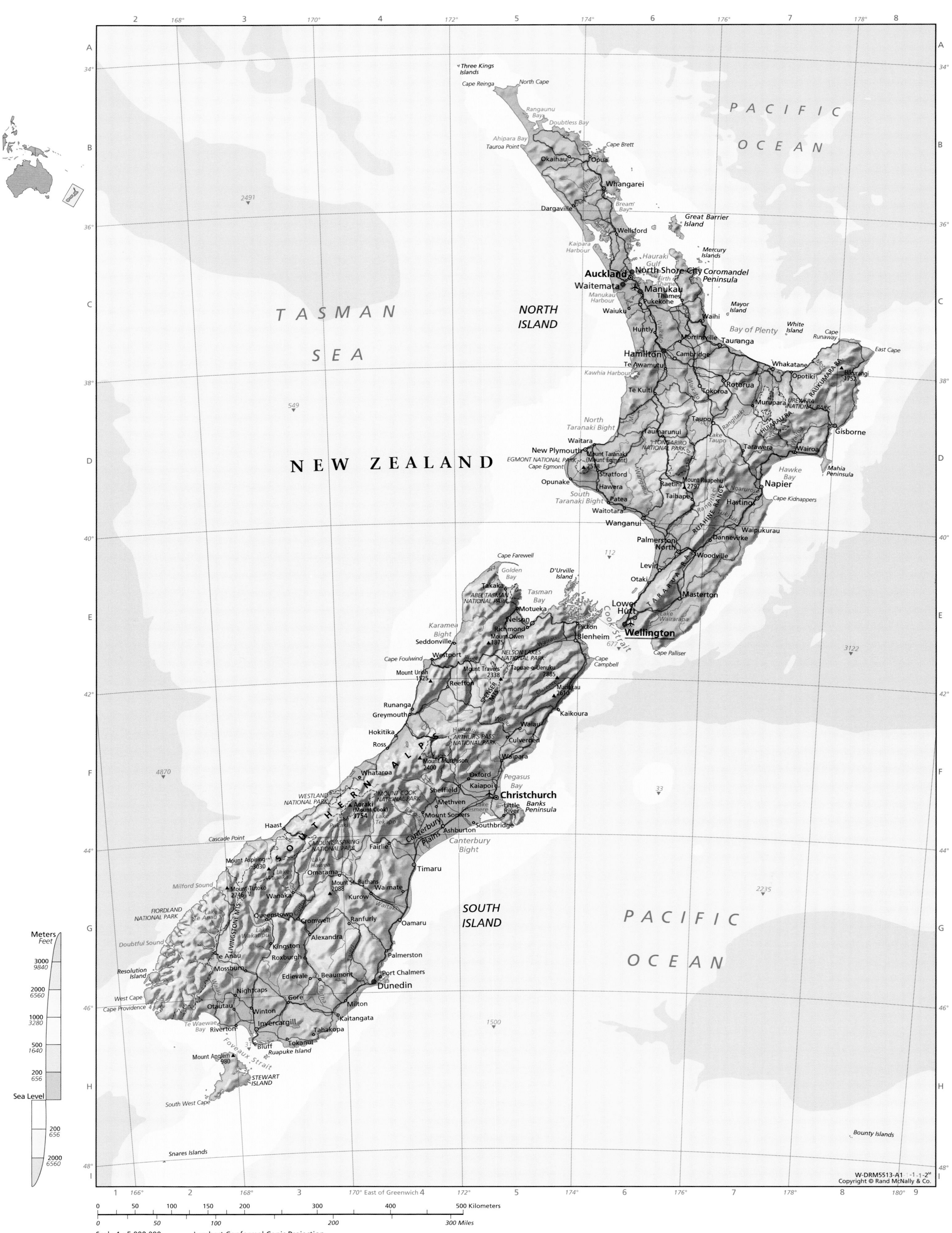

PACIFIC OCEAN
TASMAN SEA
NEW ZEALAND
NORTH ISLAND
SOUTH ISLAND
STEWART ISLAND
Three Kings Islands
Cape Reinga
North Cape
Auckland
North Shore City
Manukau
Waitemata
Hamilton
Tauranga
Rotorua
Taupo
Gisborne
Napier
Hastings
New Plymouth
Wanganui
Palmerston North
Lower Hutt
Wellington
Whangarei
Great Barrier Island
Coromandel Peninsula
Bay of Plenty
East Cape
Cook Strait
Nelson
Blenheim
Picton
Westport
Greymouth
Hokitika
Kaikoura
Christchurch
Banks Peninsula
Canterbury Bight
Timaru
Oamaru
Dunedin
Invercargill
Bluff
Queenstown
Te Anau
Milford Sound
Foveaux Strait
SOUTHERN ALPS
Aoraki (Mount Cook) 3754
Mount Ruapehu 2797
Mount Taranaki (Mount Egmont) 2518
Snares Islands
Bounty Islands
Meters Feet
3000 9840
2000 6560
1000 3280
500 1640
200 656
Sea Level
200 656
2000 6560
170° East of Greenwich
0 50 100 150 200 300 400 500 Kilometers
0 50 100 200 300 Miles
Scale 1 : 5,000,000
Lambert Conformal Conic Projection
W-DRM5513-A1

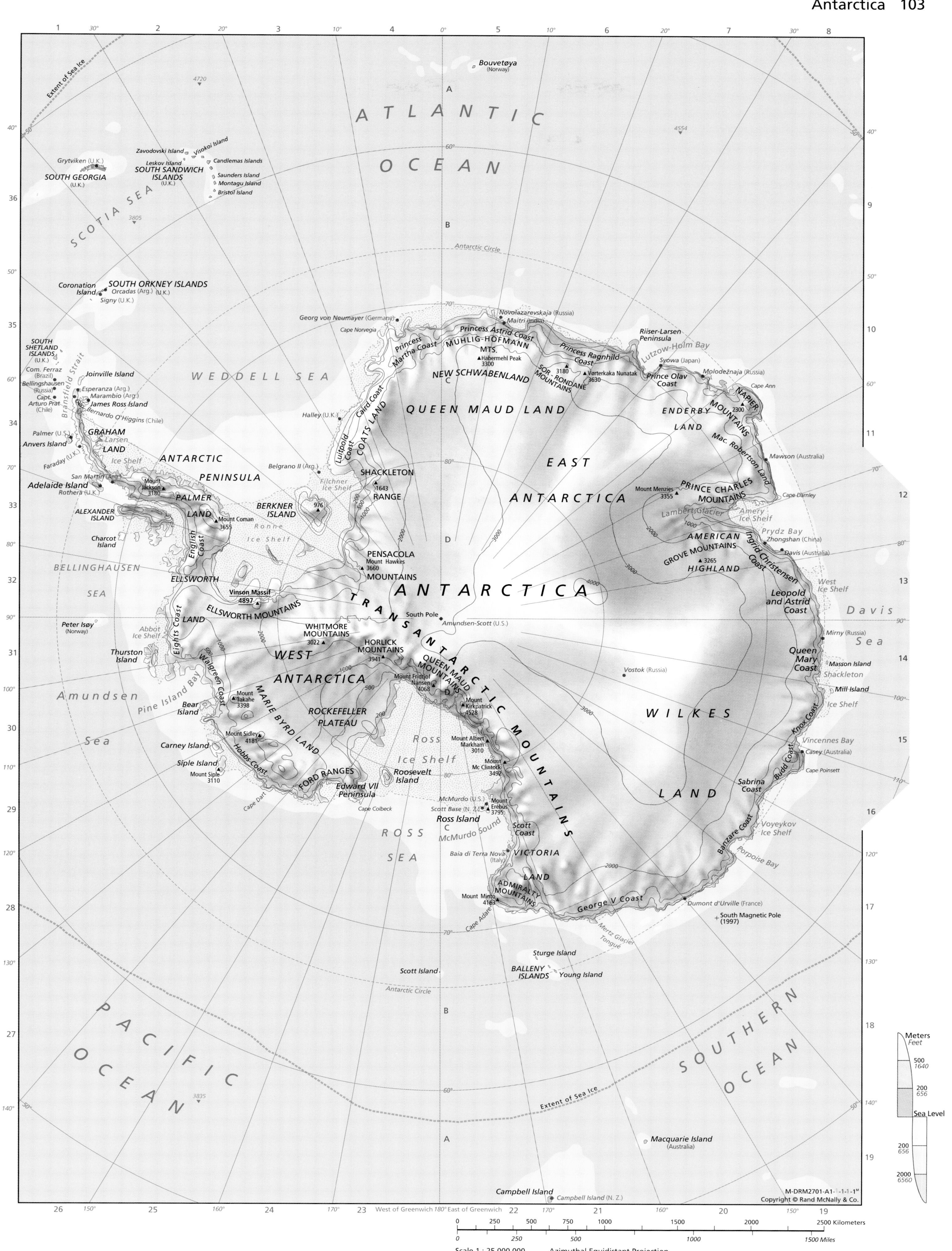
ATLANTIC OCEAN
PACIFIC OCEAN
SOUTHERN OCEAN
SCOTIA SEA
WEDDELL SEA
BELLINGHAUSEN SEA
Amundsen Sea
ROSS SEA
Davis Sea
ANTARCTICA
EAST ANTARCTICA
WEST ANTARCTICA
QUEEN MAUD LAND
WILKES LAND
TRANSANTARCTIC MOUNTAINS
ANTARCTIC PENINSULA
ENDERBY LAND
VICTORIA LAND
MARIE BYRD LAND
ELLSWORTH LAND
PALMER LAND
GRAHAM LAND
AMERICAN HIGHLAND
PRINCE CHARLES MOUNTAINS
NEW SCHWABENLAND
Ross Ice Shelf
Ronne Ice Shelf
Bouvetøya (Norway)
SOUTH GEORGIA (U.K.)
SOUTH SANDWICH ISLANDS (U.K.)
SOUTH ORKNEY ISLANDS (U.K.)
SOUTH SHETLAND ISLANDS (U.K.)
Vinson Massif 4897
South Pole
Amundsen-Scott (U.S.)
Vostok (Russia)
McMurdo (U.S.)
Scott Base (N. Z.)
Ross Island
Mount Erebus 3795
Macquarie Island (Australia)
Campbell Island
Campbell Island (N. Z.)
Scott Island
BALLENY ISLANDS
Peter Isøy (Norway)
Extent of Sea Ice
Antarctic Circle
South Magnetic Pole (1997)
M-DRM2701-A1-1-1-1-1M
Copyright © Rand McNally & Co.
Scale 1 : 25,000,000
Azimuthal Equidistant Projection
0 250 500 750 1000 1500 2000 2500 Kilometers
0 250 500 1000 1500 Miles
West of Greenwich 180° East of Greenwich
Meters Feet
500 1640
200 656
Sea Level
200 656
2000 6560

ARCTIC OCEAN
ATLANTIC OCEAN
PACIFIC OCEAN
NORWEGIAN SEA
GREENLAND SEA
LABRADOR SEA
BERING SEA
Beaufort Sea
Chukchi Sea
Baffin Bay
Hudson Bay
Davis Strait
Denmark Strait
Gulf of Alaska
GREENLAND
(Denmark)
ICELAND
Reykjavík
SVALBARD
(Nor.)
SWEDEN
NORWAY
DENMARK
UNITED KINGDOM
Oslo
Göteborg
Bergen
Stavanger
Trondheim
FAROE ISLANDS
(Den.)
Shetland Islands
(U.K.)
Jan Mayen
(Nor.)
RUSSIA
CANADA
ELLESMERE ISLAND
BAFFIN ISLAND
VICTORIA ISLAND
BANKS ISLAND
QUEEN ELIZABETH ISLANDS
ALEUTIAN ISLANDS
North Pole
International Date Line
Arctic Circle
BROOKS RANGE
MACKENZIE MOUNTAINS
COAST MOUNTAINS
ROCKY MOUNTAINS
CASCADE RANGE
GREAT PLAINS
ALASKA RANGE
Mount McKinley
6194
Mount Logan
5959
Gunnbjørn Fjeld
3700
Hvannadalshnúkur
2119
Galdhøpiggen
2469
Anchorage
Fairbanks
Juneau
Nome
Barrow
VANCOUVER
Victoria
SEATTLE
PORTLAND
SACRAMENTO
SAN FRANCISCO
Edmonton
Calgary
Saskatoon
Regina
Winnipeg
Churchill
Yellowknife
TORONTO
Ottawa
MONTREAL
Quebec
Halifax
St. John's
BOSTON
NEW YORK
PHILADELPHIA
BUFFALO
CLEVELAND
PITTSBURGH
DETROIT
CHICAGO
MILWAUKEE
MINNEAPOLIS
St. Paul
Lake Michigan
Lake Winnipeg
Great Bear Lake
Great Slave Lake
Spokane
Boise
Salt Lake City
Bismarck
Fargo
Omaha
Des Moines
Duluth
ST. PIERRE AND MIQUELON
(Fr.)
Gulf of St. Lawrence
Bering Strait
Seward Peninsula
Alaska Peninsula
Bristol Bay
Kodiak Island
VANCOUVER ISLAND
Queen Charlotte Islands
POLUOSTROV KAMČATKA
ČUKOTSKIJ POLUOSTROV
ostrov Vrangelja

ATLANTIC OCEAN
PACIFIC OCEAN
CARIBBEAN SEA
GULF OF MEXICO
WEST INDIES
GREATER ANTILLES
LESSER ANTILLES
BAHAMAS
CUBA
LA HABANA (HAVANA)
HAITI
Port-au-Prince
DOMINICAN REPUBLIC
SANTO DOMINGO
PUERTO RICO (U.S.)
SAN JUAN
JAMAICA
Kingston
HISPANIOLA
MEXICO
CIUDAD DE MÉXICO
GUADALAJARA
MONTERREY
SIERRA MADRE ORIENTAL
SIERRA MADRE OCCIDENTAL
BAJA CALIFORNIA
Golfo de California
PENÍNSULA DE YUCATÁN
BELIZE
Belmopan
GUATEMALA
HONDURAS
Tegucigalpa
EL SALVADOR
San Salvador
NICARAGUA
Managua
COSTA RICA
SAN JOSÉ
PANAMA
Panamá
COLOMBIA
SANTA FE DE BOGOTÁ
VENEZUELA
CARACAS
ECUADOR
QUITO
GUAYAQUIL
PERU
LIMA
BRAZIL
BOLIVIA
LA PAZ
GUYANA
Archipiélago de Colón (Galápagos Islands) (Ec.)
HOUSTON
DALLAS
NEW ORLEANS
ATLANTA
MIAMI
PHOENIX
SAN DIEGO
Tropic of Cancer
Equator
M-DRM2241-P1- -1-1-1*
Copyright © Rand McNally & Co.
Scale 1 : 25,000,000
Lambert Azimuthal Equal Area Projection
2500 Kilometers
1500 Miles

ARCTIC OCEAN
ATLANTIC OCEAN
PACIFIC OCEAN
NORWEGIAN SEA
GREENLAND SEA
LABRADOR SEA
BERING SEA
Beaufort Sea
Chuckchi Sea
Baffin Bay
Hudson Bay
Davis Strait
Denmark Strait
Hudson Strait
Gulf of Alaska
Bristol Bay
Arctic Circle
North Pole
International Date Line
POLUOSTROV KAMČATKA
SREDINNYJ HREBET
ostrov Karaginskij
ostrov Aën
ostrov Vrangelja (Wrangel Island)
NOVOSIBIRSKIE OSTROVA
Anadyr'
Uel'kal'
ČUKOTSKIJ POLUOSTROV
SVALBARD
Spitsbergen
Edgeøya
Nordaustlandet
Trondheim
Oslo
Göteborg
Galdhøpiggen 2469
Bergen
Stavanger
Jan Mayen
Shetland Islands
Færøerne (Faroe Islands)
BRITISH ISLES
ÍSLAND (ICELAND)
Hvannadalshnúkur 2119
Reykjavík
GRØNLAND (GREENLAND)
PEARYLAND
Gunnbjørn Fjeld 3700
Kap Brewster
Angmagssalik
Godthåb
Godhavn
Disko
Thule
Kap York
Etah
Kap Farvel
ELLESMERE ISLAND
Alert
Cape Columbia
Axel Heiberg Island
Ellef Ringnes Island
Prince Patrick Island
QUEEN ELIZABETH ISLANDS
North Magnetic Pole
Melville Island
Bathurst Island
Devon Island
Lancaster Sound
Parry Channel
Viscount Melville Sound
BANKS ISLAND
VICTORIA ISLAND
Prince of Wales Island
Somerset Island
Bylot Island
BAFFIN ISLAND
Gulf of Boothia
King William Island
Ikaluktutiak
Naujaat
Prince Charles Island
Foxe Basin
Cumberland Sound
Iqaluit
Southampton Island
Coats Island
Mansel Island
PENINSULE D'UNGAVA
Ungava Bay
Churchill
Belcher Islands
James Bay
Akimiski Island
Moosonee
Labrador
Happy Valley-Goose Bay
Smallwood Reservoir
NEWFOUNDLAND
Gander
St. John's
Cape Race
Cape Bauld
Île d'Anticosti
Gulf of St. Lawrence
Prince Edward Island
Cape Breton Island
Sable Island
Cape Sable
Bay of Fundy
Les Laurentides
MONTS NOTRE-DAME
Québec
Montréal
Ottawa
Mount Washington 1917
ADIRONDACK MTS.
Portland
Gulf of Maine
Boston
Cape Cod
Long Island
New York
Philadelphia
Pittsburgh
Cleveland
Buffalo
Toronto
Lake Ontario
Lake Erie
Lake Huron
Georgian Bay
Lake Michigan
Lake Superior
Lake Nipigon
Lake of the Woods
Detroit
Chicago
Milwaukee
Des Moines
Minneapolis
Fargo
Winnipeg
Lake Winnipeg
Lake Winnipegosis
Lake Manitoba
Regina
Reindeer Lake
Lake Athabasca
Uranium City
Great Slave Lake
Great Bear Lake
Yellowknife
Horn Plateau
Norman Wells
Inuvik
CARIBOU MTS.
Calgary
Great Falls
Fort Peck Lake
Lake Sakakawea
Lake Oahe
BLACK HILLS
Gannett Peak 4207
Kings Peak 4123
Salt Lake City
Great Salt Lake
Boise
SALMON RIVER MOUNTAINS
BITTERROOT RANGE
BLUE MTS.
ROCKY MOUNTAINS
MACKENZIE MTS.
SELWYN MOUNTAINS
OGILVIE MOUNTAINS
PELLY MOUNTAINS
STIKINE RANGES
COAST MOUNTAINS
COLUMBIA MOUNTAINS
Mount Robson 3954
Mount Assiniboine 3618
Mount Waddington 3994
CASCADE RANGE
Mount Rainier 4392
Mount Hood 3426
Mount Shasta 4317
COAST RANGES
SIERRA
Cape Mendocino
Cape Flattery
Seattle
Portland
Vancouver
VANCOUVER ISLAND
Queen Charlotte Islands
Ketchikan
Baranof Island
Juneau
Skagway
Whitehorse
Fairweather Mountain 4663
Mount Logan 5959
WRANGELL MOUNTAINS
Mount McKinley 6194
ALASKA RANGE
BROOKS RANGE
Barrow
Point Barrow
Point Hope
Bering Strait
Seward Peninsula
Nome
Norton Sound
Bethel
Anchorage
Seward
Kodiak Island
Alaska Peninsula
Unalaska
ALEUTIAN ISLANDS
St. Lawrence Island
St. Matthew Island
Nunivak Island

ATLANTIC
OCEAN
PACIFIC
OCEAN
GULF OF MEXICO
CARIBBEAN SEA
WEST INDIES
GREATER ANTILLES
LESSER ANTILLES
LEEWARD ISLANDS
WINDWARD IS.
BAHAMAS
CUBA
HISPANIOLA
Bermuda
Puerto Rico
Jamaica
Kingston
Port-au-Prince
Santo Domingo
Pico Duarte 3175
La Habana
Nassau
Trinidad
Tobago
Barbados
Caracas
Maracaibo
Pico Bolívar 5007
Pico Cristóbal Colón 5775
Barranquilla
Cartagena
Medellín
Santa Fe de Bogotá
Quito
Chimborazo 6310
Guayaquil
Lima
Nevado Huascarán 6746
Pico da Neblina 3014
LLANOS
SELVAS
ANDES
CORDILLERA ORIENTAL
CORDILLERA CENTRAL
CORDILLERA OCCIDENTAL
CORDILLERA REAL
DESIERTO DE ATACAMA
GRAN CHACO
Nevado Sajama 6542
Iquique
Arica
Panamá
Volcán Barú 3475
Cerro Chirripó 3819
Managua
Tegucigalpa
San Salvador
Guatemala
Volcán Tajumulco 4220
Belmopan
PENÍNSULA DE YUCATÁN
Mérida
Villahermosa
Istmo de Tehuantepec
Golfo de Tehuantepec
Bahía de Campeche
Ciudad de México
Volcán Pico de Orizaba 5610
SIERRA MADRE DEL SUR
SIERRA MADRE ORIENTAL
SIERRA MADRE OCCIDENTAL
Desierto de Chihuahua
Guadalajara
Monterrey
Tampico
Brownsville
Matamoros
Houston
San Antonio
Dallas
Shreveport
New Orleans
Mobile
Birmingham
Memphis
Atlanta
Charleston
Jacksonville
Tampa
Miami
El Paso
Albuquerque
Wheeler Peak 4011
Phoenix
San Diego
BAJA CALIFORNIA
Golfo de California
Desierto de Sonora
Mazatlán
Islas Revillagigedo
Isla Guadalupe
Isla de Malpelo
Isla del Coco
ARCHIPIÉLAGO DE COLÓN (GALÁPAGOS ISLANDS)
Isla Isabela
Isla Fernandina
Isla Santiago
Isla Santa Cruz
Isla San Cristóbal
Tropic of Cancer
Equator
90° West of Greenwich
2500 Kilometers
1500 Miles
Scale 1 : 25,000,000
Lambert Azimuthal Equal Area Projection
Meters
Feet
6000 19680
4000 13120
3000 9840
2000 6560
1000 3280
500 1640
200 656
Sea Level
200 656
2000 6560
M-DRM2241-P1-1-1-1

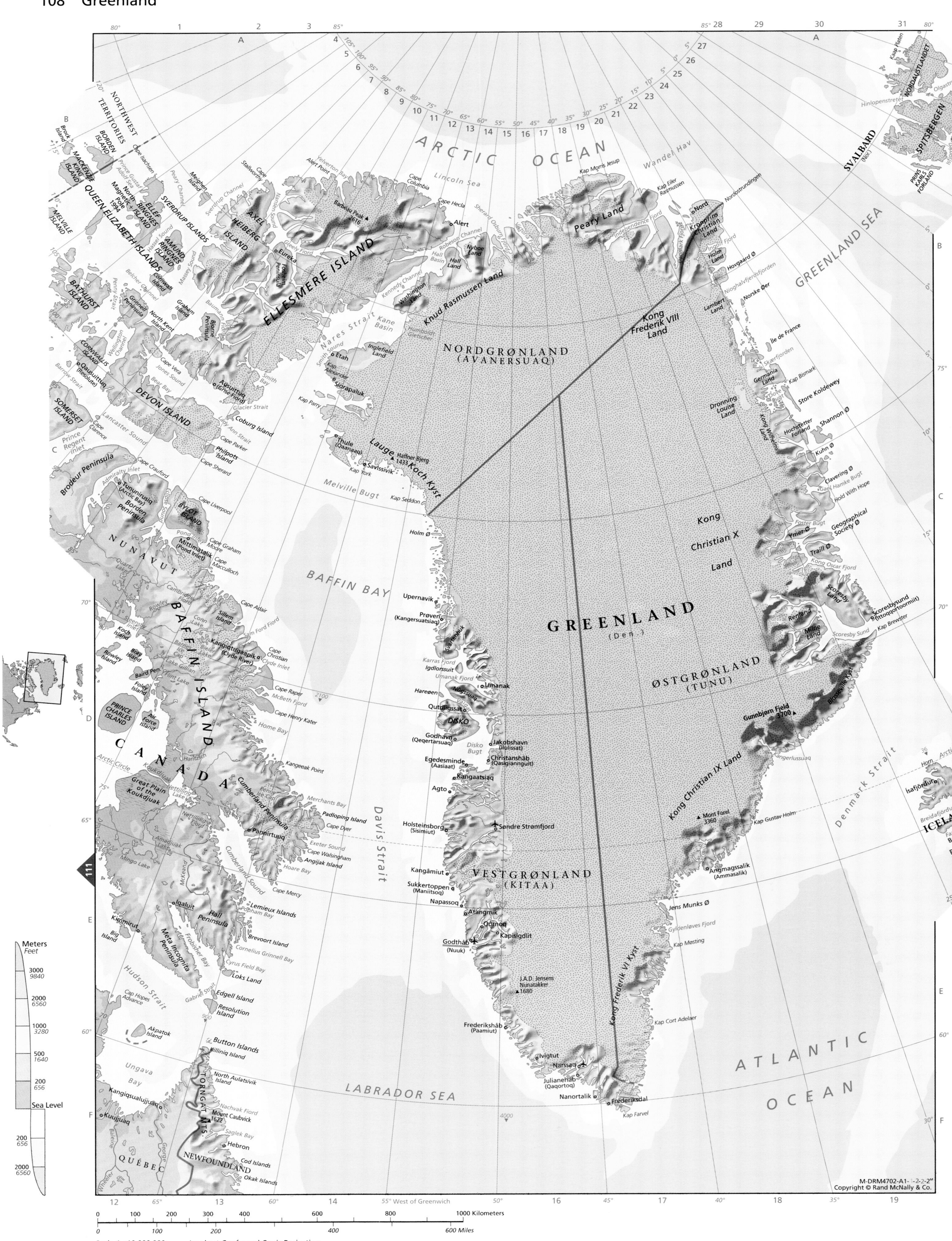

111

0 100 200 300 400 600 800 1000 Kilometers

0 100 200 400 600 Miles

Scale 1 : 10,000,000 Lambert Conformal Conic Projection

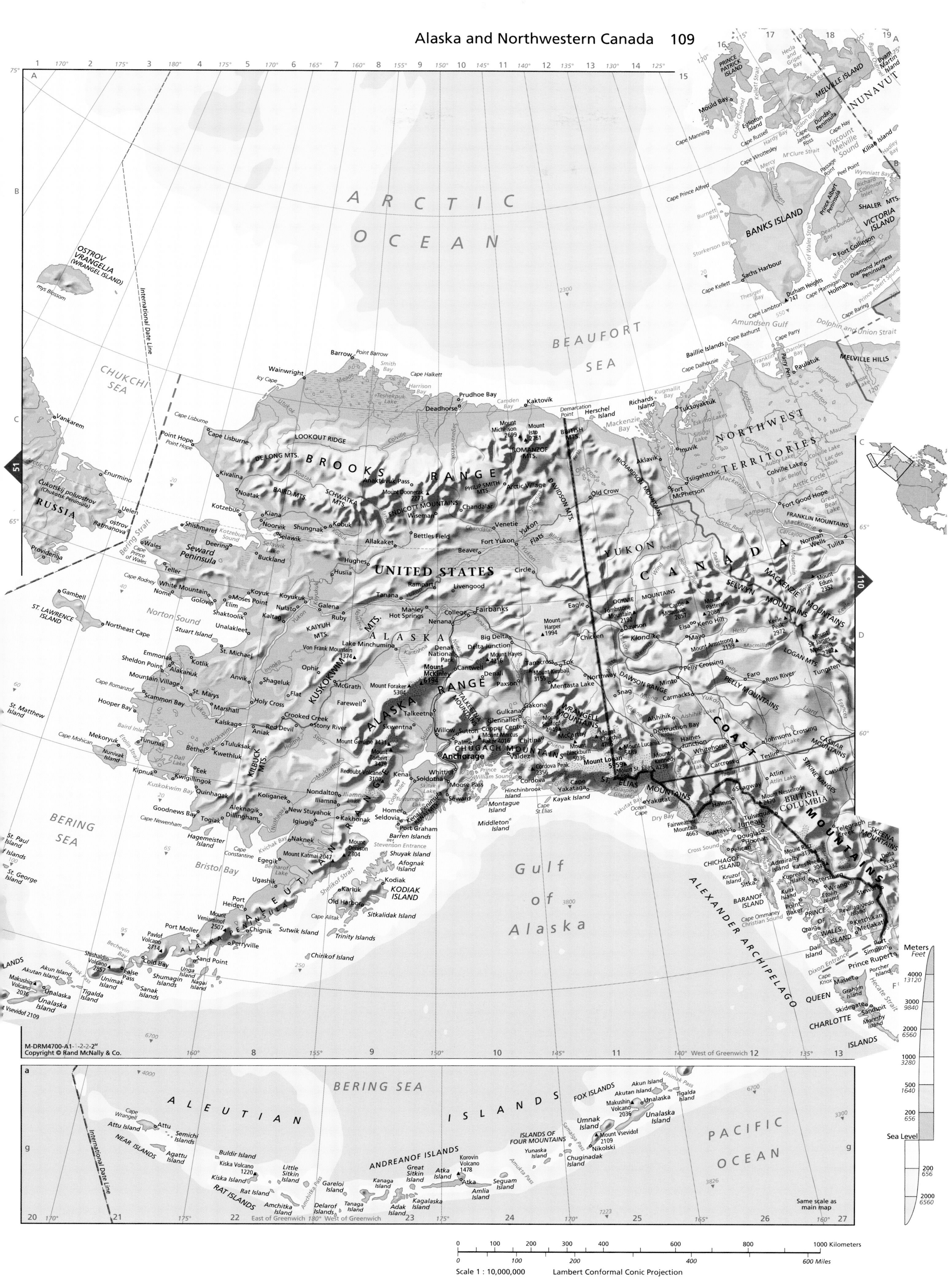
ARCTIC OCEAN
BEAUFORT SEA
CHUKCHI SEA
BERING SEA
Gulf of Alaska
Norton Sound
Bristol Bay
OSTROV VRANGELJA (WRANGEL ISLAND)
RUSSIA
International Date Line
UNITED STATES
CANADA
YUKON
NORTHWEST TERRITORIES
BRITISH COLUMBIA
NUNAVUT
BROOKS RANGE
ALASKA RANGE
ALEUTIAN RANGE
CHUGACH MOUNTAINS
ST. ELIAS MOUNTAINS
COAST MOUNTAINS
MACKENZIE MOUNTAINS
SELWYN MOUNTAINS
ALEXANDER ARCHIPELAGO
KODIAK ISLAND
BANKS ISLAND
VICTORIA ISLAND
MELVILLE ISLAND
PRINCE PATRICK ISLAND
ST. LAWRENCE ISLAND
Seward Peninsula
Anchorage
Fairbanks
Juneau
Mount McKinley 6194
Mount Logan 5959
Barrow
Prudhoe Bay
Nome
Kotzebue
Whitehorse
Dawson
Inuvik
Kodiak
Valdez
Sitka
Ketchikan
BERING SEA
ALEUTIAN ISLANDS
PACIFIC OCEAN
FOX ISLANDS
ANDREANOF ISLANDS
RAT ISLANDS
NEAR ISLANDS
ISLANDS OF FOUR MOUNTAINS
Attu Island
Kiska Island
Adak Island
Atka Island
Umnak Island
Unalaska Island
Same scale as main map
Meters
Feet
4000 13120
3000 9840
2000 6560
1000 3280
500 1640
200 656
Sea Level
200 656
2000 6560
0 100 200 300 400 600 800 1000 Kilometers
0 100 200 400 600 Miles
Scale 1 : 10,000,000
Lambert Conformal Conic Projection
M-DRM4700-A1-1-2-2-2M

Meters
Feet
4000 13120
3000 9840
2000 6560
1000 3280
500 1640
200 656
Sea Level
200 656
2000 6560

0 100 200 300 400 600 800 1000 Kilometers
0 100 200 400 600 Miles
Scale 1 : 10,000,000 Lambert Conformal Conic Projection

109
112

BAFFIN ISLAND
Davis Strait
GREENLAND (Den.)
Cumberland Peninsula
Foxe Basin
Foxe Peninsula
Hall Peninsula
Meta Incognita Peninsula
Iqaluit
Hudson Strait
SOUTHAMPTON ISLAND
COATS ISLAND
MANSEL ISLAND
Melville Peninsula
PRINCE CHARLES ISLAND
Air Force Island
Borden Peninsula
Brodeur Peninsula
BYLOT ISLAND
Arctic Circle
Hudson Bay
James Bay
Ungava Bay
PÉNINSULE D'UNGAVA
LABRADOR SEA
ATLANTIC OCEAN
Labrador
NEWFOUNDLAND
LONG RANGE MOUNTAINS
QUÉBEC
ONTARIO
ÎLE D'ANTICOSTI
Gulf of St. Lawrence
PRINCE EDWARD ISLAND
NEW BRUNSWICK
NOVA SCOTIA
CAPE BRETON ISLAND
MAINE
VERMONT
N.H.
MASS.
NEW YORK
MICHIGAN
Lake Superior
Lake Huron
Lake Ontario
Lake Erie
Gulf of Maine
MONTRÉAL
Québec
Ottawa
TORONTO
BOSTON
BUFFALO
DETROIT
Windsor
Halifax
Fredericton
St. John's
Saint-Pierre
SAINT PIERRE AND MIQUELON (Fr.)
Same scale as main map
All islands within Hudson Bay, James Bay, and Ungava Bay lie within Nunavut
West of Greenwich
M-DRM4701-A1-2-2-2
113

0 100 200 300 400 600 800 1000 Kilometer
0 100 200 400 600 Miles
Scale 1 : 10,000,000 Lambert Conformal Conic Projection

111
153
95° West of Greenwich
James Bay
Hudson Bay
ONTARIO
QUÉBEC
Lake Nipigon
Lake Superior
Lake Michigan
Lake Huron
Georgian Bay
Lake Erie
Lake Ontario
Thunder Bay
International Falls
Duluth
Sault Sainte Marie
Sudbury
North Bay
Timmins
Kapuskasing
Moosonee
Chibougamau
Chicoutimi
Québec
Trois-Rivières
MONTRÉAL
Ottawa
Kingston
TORONTO
Hamilton
London
Windsor
Les Laurentides
MONTS NOTRE-DAME
NEW BRUNSWICK
Fredericton
Saint John
Moncton
NOVA SCOTIA
PRINCE EDWARD ISLAND
ÎLE D'ANTICOSTI
Gulf of St. Lawrence
Bay of Fundy
Gulf of Maine
MAINE
Bangor
Augusta
Portland
VERMONT
N.H.
Mount Washington 1917
MASS.
BOSTON
Worcester
Springfield
Providence
Hartford
CONN.
New Haven
Bridgeport
LONG ISLAND
NEW YORK
Albany
Syracuse
Rochester
BUFFALO
Niagara Falls
ADIRONDACK MTS.
NEW JERSEY
Trenton
Newark
PENNSYLVANIA
PHILADELPHIA
PITTSBURGH
Harrisburg
Allentown
Scranton
Erie
MARYLAND
BALTIMORE
DELAWARE
Dover
WASHINGTON
VIRGINIA
Richmond
Norfolk
Virginia Beach
WEST VIRGINIA
Charleston
Spruce Knob 1482
NORTH CAROLINA
Raleigh
Greensboro
Charlotte
Wilmington
Cape Hatteras
Cape Fear
SOUTH CAROLINA
Columbia
Charleston
GEORGIA
ATLANTA
Savannah
Augusta
Macon
FLORIDA
Jacksonville
Tallahassee
Orlando
Tampa
St. Petersburg
MIAMI
Fort Lauderdale
Key West
Florida Keys
Straits of Florida
APPALACHIAN MOUNTAINS
BLUE RIDGE
Mount Mitchell 2037
TENNESSEE
Nashville
Knoxville
Memphis
Chattanooga
KENTUCKY
Louisville
Lexington
OHIO
Columbus
CLEVELAND
CINCINNATI
Toledo
Akron
Dayton
INDIANA
INDIANAPOLIS
Fort Wayne
MICHIGAN
DETROIT
Lansing
Grand Rapids
WISCONSIN
MILWAUKEE
Madison
Green Bay
MINNESOTA
MINNEAPOLIS
St. Paul
IOWA
Des Moines
ILLINOIS
CHICAGO
Springfield
Peoria
MISSOURI
ST. LOUIS
KANSAS CITY
Jefferson City
Ozark Plateau
BOSTON MTS.
OUACHITA MTS.
ARKANSAS
Little Rock
MISSISSIPPI
Jackson
ALABAMA
Birmingham
Montgomery
Mobile
LOUISIANA
Baton Rouge
NEW ORLEANS
Shreveport
Mississippi Delta
Tulsa
Beaumont
HOUSTON
Galveston
UNITED STATES
CANADA
Gulf of Mexico
ATLANTIC OCEAN
BAHAMAS
Nassau
Grand Bahama
Andros
CUBA
LA HABANA (HAVANA)
Tropic of Cancer

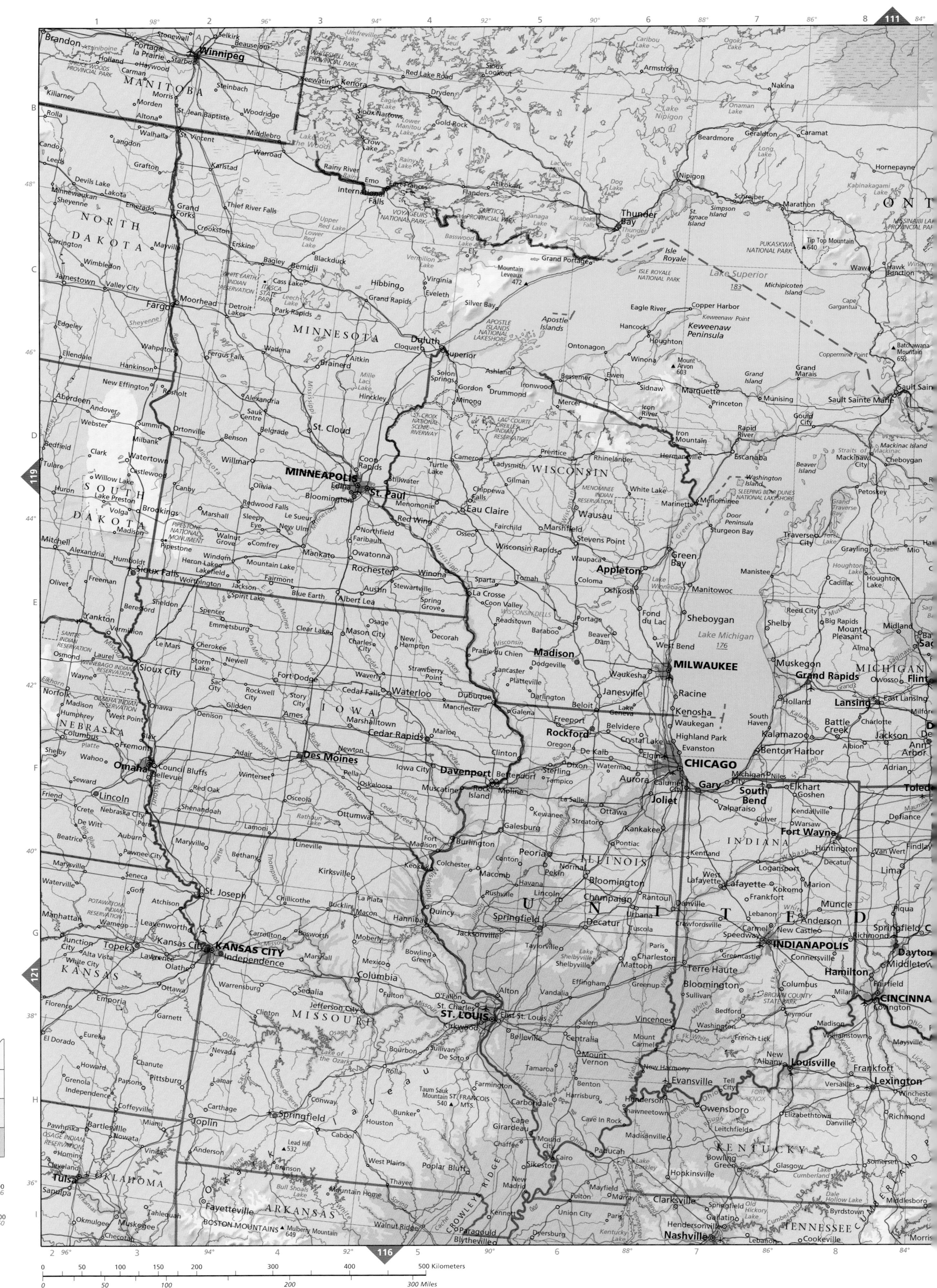

Scale 1 : 5 000 000 — Lambert Conformal Conic Projection

0 50 100 150 200 300 400 500 Kilometers

0 50 100 200 300 Miles

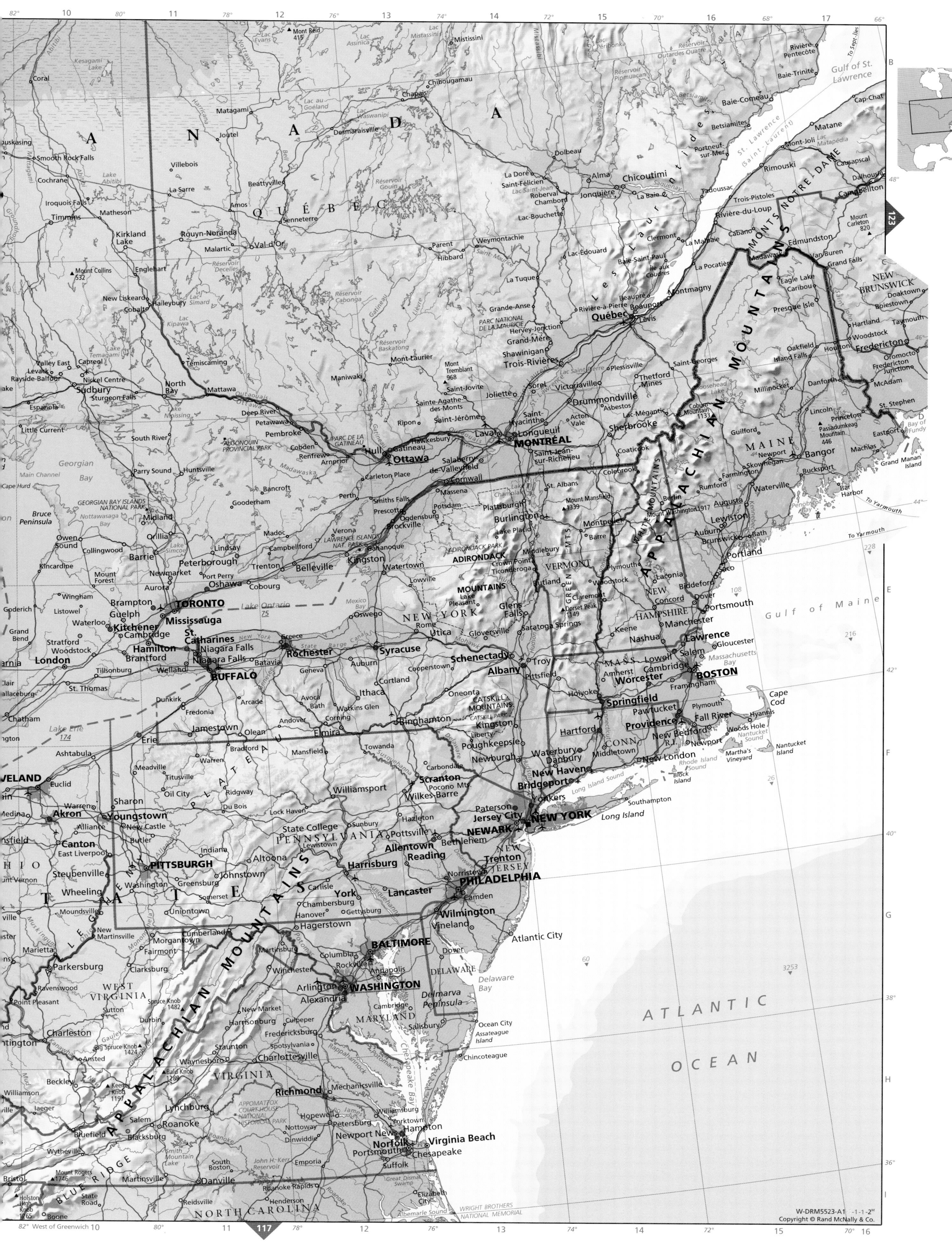

C A N A D A
QUÉBEC
Mont Reid 415
Mistissini
Chibougamau
Chapais
Matagami
Joutel
Desmaraisville
Coral
Smooth Rock Falls
Cochrane
Iroquois Falls
Timmins
Matheson
Kirkland Lake
Villebois
La Sarre
Beattyville
Amos
Senneterre
Rouyn-Noranda
Val-d'Or
Malartic
Mount Collins 532
Englehart
New Liskeard
Haileybury
Cobalt
Témiscaming
North Bay
Mattawa
Sudbury
Sturgeon Falls
Valley East
Capreol
Levack
Rayside-Balfour
Nickel Centre
Espanola
Little Current
South River
Deep River
Petawawa
Pembroke
Cobden
Renfrew
Arnprior
ALGONQUIN PROVINCIAL PARK
Georgian Bay
Parry Sound
Huntsville
Bancroft
Gooderham
GEORGIAN BAY ISLANDS NATIONAL PARK
Bruce Peninsula
Midland
Orillia
Owen Sound
Collingwood
Barrie
Lindsay
Peterborough
Campbellford
Madoc
Trenton
Belleville
Kincardine
Mount Forest
Newmarket
Port Perry
Oshawa
Cobourg
Aurora
Wingham
Goderich
Listowel
Brampton
TORONTO
Guelph
Mississauga
Kitchener
Cambridge
Waterloo
Grand Bend
Stratford
Woodstock
Hamilton
St. Catharines
Niagara Falls
Brantford
London
Tillsonburg
Welland
St. Thomas
Chatham
Lake Ontario
Lake Erie
Ottawa
Gatineau
Hull
Hawkesbury
Carleton Place
Perth
Smiths Falls
Prescott
Ogdensburg
Brockville
Kingston
Gananoque
ST. LAWRENCE ISLANDS NAT. PARK
Cornwall
Massena
Potsdam
Salaberry-de-Valleyfield
Parent
Weymontachie
Hibbard
Mont-Laurier
Maniwaki
Mont Tremblant 968
Saint-Jovite
Sainte-Agathe-des-Monts
Saint-Jérôme
Ripon
Joliette
Laval
Longueuil
MONTRÉAL
Saint-Jean-sur-Richelieu
Saint-Hyacinthe
Sorel
La Tuque
Grande-Anse
PARC NATIONAL DE LA MAURICIE
Hervey-Jonction
Grand-Mère
Shawinigan
Trois-Rivières
Victoriaville
Drummondville
Plessisville
Thetford Mines
Asbestos
Acton Vale
Sherbrooke
Lac-Mégantic
Coaticook
Dolbeau
La Doré
Saint-Félicien
Roberval
Chambord
Lac-Bouchette
Alma
Chicoutimi
Jonquière
La Baie
Lac-Édouard
Québec
Lévis
Beauport
Beaupré
Rivière-à-Pierre
Baie-Saint-Paul
Clermont
La Malbaie
Montmagny
La Pocatière
Saint-Georges
Tadoussac
Trois-Pistoles
Rivière-du-Loup
Cabano
Baie-Comeau
Betsiamites
Portneuf-sur-Mer
Rimouski
Mont-Joli
Matane
Causapscal
Cap-Chat
Rivière-Pentecôte
Baie-Trinité
Gulf of St. Lawrence
St. Lawrence
Les Laurentides
MONTS NOTRE-DAME
Dalhousie
Campbellton
Mount Carleton 820
Edmundston
Madawaska
Van Buren
Grand Falls
NEW BRUNSWICK
Doaktown
Boiestown
Eagle Lake
Caribou
Presque Isle
Hartland
Woodstock
Fredericton
Oromocto
Fredericton Junction
McAdam
St. Stephen
Houlton
Oakfield
Island Falls
Millinocket
Danforth
Lincoln
Princeton
Passadumkeag Mountain 446
Eastport
Machias
Bay of Fundy
Grand Manan Island
MAINE
Newport
Bangor
Guilford
Skowhegan
Farmington
Bucksport
Bar Harbor
Waterville
Rumford
Augusta
Lewiston
Auburn
Brunswick
Bath
Portland
Saco
Biddeford
Berlin
Mount Washington 1917
WHITE MOUNTAINS
APPALACHIAN MOUNTAINS
Coburn Mountain 1133
Colebrook
St. Albans
Mount Mansfield 1339
Plattsburgh
Burlington
Montpelier
Barre
Lake Placid
Middlebury
VERMONT
GREEN MTS.
Rutland
Plymouth
Woodstock
Laconia
NEW HAMPSHIRE
Concord
Dover
Portsmouth
Claremont
Dorset Peak 1149
Keene
Manchester
Nashua
Lawrence
Gloucester
Lowell
Salem
BOSTON
Cambridge
Framingham
Amherst
Worcester
Springfield
Holyoke
Pittsfield
MASS.
Massachusetts Bay
Cape Cod
Plymouth
Fall River
Hyannis
Woods Hole
Nantucket Sound
Nantucket Island
Martha's Vineyard
New Bedford
Newport
Pawtucket
Providence
R.I.
Hartford
CONN.
Middletown
Waterbury
Danbury
New Haven
Bridgeport
New London
Block Island
Rhode Island Sound
Long Island Sound
Southampton
Long Island
Gulf of Maine
To Yarmouth
ADIRONDACK MOUNTAINS
Crown Point
Ticonderoga
Lake Pleasant
Glens Falls
Saratoga Springs
Lowville
Watertown
Oswego
NEW YORK
Rome
Utica
Gloversville
Schenectady
Troy
Albany
Syracuse
Rochester
Greece
Batavia
BUFFALO
Auburn
Geneva
Cooperstown
Cortland
Ithaca
Oneonta
CATSKILL MOUNTAINS
CATSKILL PARK
Kingston
Poughkeepsie
Newburgh
Liberty
Avoca
Bath
Watkins Glen
Corning
Elmira
Binghamton
Andover
Olean
Jamestown
Dunkirk
Fredonia
Arcade
Erie
Ashtabula
Bradford
Warren
Mansfield
Towanda
Carbondale
Scranton
Pocono Mts.
Wilkes-Barre
Williamsport
Lock Haven
Hazleton
Sunbury
State College
PENNSYLVANIA
Pottsville
Allentown
Bethlehem
Reading
Harrisburg
Lewistown
Altoona
Johnstown
Indiana
Lancaster
York
Carlisle
Chambersburg
Gettysburg
Hanover
Hagerstown
Norristown
PHILADELPHIA
Camden
Trenton
NEW JERSEY
Wilmington
Vineland
Atlantic City
Paterson
Jersey City
Yonkers
NEW YORK
NEWARK
Meadville
Titusville
Oil City
Ridgway
Du Bois
Sharon
Youngstown
New Castle
Butler
PITTSBURGH
Washington
Greensburg
Somerset
Uniontown
CLEVELAND
Euclid
Warren
Akron
Alliance
Canton
East Liverpool
Steubenville
Wheeling
Moundsville
New Martinsville
Mount Vernon
OHIO
ALLEGHENY PLATEAU
UNITED STATES
Marietta
Parkersburg
Ravenswood
Point Pleasant
WEST VIRGINIA
Clarksburg
Morgantown
Fairmont
Cumberland
Martinsburg
Winchester
Columbia
Rockville
BALTIMORE
Annapolis
Dover
DELAWARE
Delaware Bay
Delmarva Peninsula
MARYLAND
Cambridge
Salisbury
Ocean City
Assateague Island
Chincoteague
Arlington
Alexandria
WASHINGTON
Spruce Knob 1482
Sutton
Durbin
Charleston
Big Spruce Knob 1424
Ansted
New Market
Harrisonburg
Culpeper
Fredericksburg
Staunton
Spotsylvania
Charlottesville
Waynesboro
Bald Knob 1289
VIRGINIA
Beckley
Keeney Knob 1191
Williamson
Jaeger
Lynchburg
APPOMATTOX COURT HOUSE NATIONAL HISTORICAL PARK
Salem
Roanoke
Bluefield
Blacksburg
Wytheville
Smith Mountain Lake
Mount Rogers 1746
Bristol
Martinsville
South Boston
Danville
John H. Kerr Reservoir
Emporia
Richmond
Mechanicsville
Hopewell
Petersburg
Williamsburg
Yorktown
Hampton
Newport News
Nottoway
Dinwiddie
Norfolk
Portsmouth
Virginia Beach
Chesapeake
Suffolk
Chesapeake Bay
Great Dismal Swamp
Roanoke Rapids
Henderson
Reidsville
Elizabeth City
Albemarle Sound
WRIGHT BROTHERS NATIONAL MEMORIAL
NORTH CAROLINA
Holston High Knob 1285
State Road
Boone
BLUE RIDGE
APPALACHIAN MOUNTAINS
ATLANTIC OCEAN
West of Greenwich
W-DRM5523-A1 -1-1-2"

123
117

119
121
155
COLORADO
KANSAS
MISSOURI
OKLAHOMA
ARKANSAS
TEXAS
LOUISIANA
MISSISSIPPI
COAHUILA
NUEVO LEÓN
TAMAULIPAS
MEXICO
GREAT PLAINS
OZARK PLATEAU
BOSTON MOUNTAINS
OUACHITA MOUNTAINS
WICHITA MTS.
CROWLEY'S RIDGE
Edwards Plateau
Balcones Escarpment
Nueces Plains
SIERRA MADRE ORIENTAL
GULF
KANSAS CITY
Independence
Topeka
Wichita
ST. LOUIS
Springfield
Joplin
Tulsa
Oklahoma City
Amarillo
Lubbock
Wichita Falls
Fort Smith
Little Rock
Memphis
Abilene
Fort Worth
DALLAS
Shreveport
Jackson
Waco
Austin
SAN ANTONIO
HOUSTON
Beaumont
Baton Rouge
NEW ORLEANS
Galveston
Corpus Christi
Laredo
Nuevo Laredo
McAllen
Reynosa
Brownsville
Matamoros
MONTERREY
Saltillo
Meters
Feet
3000
9840
2000
6560
1000
3280
500
1640
200
656
Sea Level
200
656
2000
6560
0
50
100
150
200
300
400
500 Kilometers
0
50
100
200
300 Miles
Scale 1 : 5 000 000
Lambert Conformal Conic Projection

114
115
CINCINNATI
OHIO
INDIANA
Bloomington
Columbus
Louisville
Frankfort
Lexington
Evansville
Owensboro
KENTUCKY
WEST VIRGINIA
Charleston
Huntington
Portsmouth
VIRGINIA
WASHINGTON
Arlington
Alexandria
DELAWARE
MARYLAND
Delmarva Peninsula
Chincoteague
Ocean City
Salisbury
Fredericksburg
Harrisonburg
Staunton
Charlottesville
Waynesboro
Richmond
Lynchburg
Roanoke
Blacksburg
Bluefield
Beckley
Danville
Norfolk
Virginia Beach
Chesapeake
Portsmouth
Newport News
Hampton
Williamsburg
Yorktown
Suffolk
Elizabeth City
A P P A L A C H I A N   M O U N T A I N S
BLUE RIDGE
C U M B E R L A N D   P L A T E A U
A L L E G H E N Y   P L A T E A U
GREAT SMOKY MTS.
Bowling Green
Hopkinsville
Clarksville
Nashville
Murfreesboro
TENNESSEE
Knoxville
Johnson City
Kingsport
Bristol
Chattanooga
Cleveland
Asheville
NORTH CAROLINA
Winston-Salem
Greensboro
Durham
Raleigh
High Point
Charlotte
Gastonia
Hickory
Fayetteville
Wilson
Goldsboro
Jacksonville
Wilmington
Hatteras Island
Cape Hatteras
Cape Lookout
Onslow Bay
Cape Fear
Pamlico Sound
Albemarle Sound
WRIGHT BROTHERS NATIONAL MEMORIAL
Huntsville
Florence
Decatur
Birmingham
Tuscaloosa
Gadsden
Anniston
ALABAMA
Montgomery
Mobile
Dothan
Auburn
Opelika
ATLANTA
Marietta
Athens
Rome
Columbus
Macon
Augusta
GEORGIA
Albany
Valdosta
Savannah
Brunswick
SOUTH CAROLINA
Columbia
Greenville
Spartanburg
Anderson
Sumter
Florence
Myrtle Beach
Long Bay
Charleston
FORT SUMTER NATIONAL MONUMENT
SEA ISLANDS
TRAIL RIDGE
Okefenokee Swamp
Tallahassee
Pensacola
Fort Walton Beach
Panama City
Jacksonville
Jacksonville Beach
St. Augustine
Amelia Island
Gainesville
Ocala
Daytona Beach
FLORIDA
Orlando
Sanford
Titusville
JOHN F. KENNEDY SPACE CENTER
Cape Canaveral
Cocoa Beach
Melbourne
Lakeland
Tampa
St. Petersburg
Clearwater
Bradenton
Sarasota
Vero Beach
Fort Pierce
Port St. Lucie
Fort Myers
Cape Coral
Naples
West Palm Beach
Boca Raton
Fort Lauderdale
Hollywood
Hialeah
Miami Beach
MIAMI
Homestead
EVERGLADES NATIONAL PARK
BISCAYNE NATIONAL PARK
Lake Okeechobee
Florida Bay
FLORIDA KEYS
Key Largo
Key West
Dry Tortugas
Straits of Florida
ATLANTIC OCEAN
MEXICO
BAHAMAS
GRAND BAHAMA
Freeport
West End
ABACO
Marsh Harbour
Bimini Islands
Berry Islands
ANDROS
Andros Town
Nassau
New Providence
Northwest Providence Channel
Northeast Providence Channel
W-DRM5518-A1
Copyright © Rand McNally & Co.

144
120
PACIFIC OCEAN
BRITISH COLUMBIA
ALBERTA
WASHINGTON
OREGON
IDAHO
MONTANA
CALIFORNIA
NEVADA
UTAH
COAST MOUNTAINS
PACIFIC RANGES
ROCKY MOUNTAINS
COLUMBIA MOUNTAINS
MONASHEE MOUNTAINS
FRASER PLATEAU
CASCADE RANGE
COAST RANGE
BLUE MOUNTAINS
BITTERROOT RANGE
SALMON RIVER MOUNTAINS
KLAMATH MTS.
SIERRA NEVADA
COAST RANGES
GREAT BASIN
HARNEY BASIN
Great Salt Lake
Great Salt Lake Desert
VANCOUVER ISLAND
Edmonton
Calgary
Red Deer
Lethbridge
Medicine Hat
VANCOUVER
Burnaby
New Westminster
Victoria
Nanaimo
Kamloops
Kelowna
Vernon
Penticton
Prince George
Williams Lake
Bellingham
Everett
SEATTLE
Tacoma
Olympia
Bremerton
Yakima
Spokane
Richland
Kennewick
Pasco
Walla Walla
Lewiston
Coeur d'Alene
PORTLAND
Vancouver
Salem
Eugene
Corvallis
Medford
Klamath Falls
Bend
Pendleton
Boise
Nampa
Idaho Falls
Pocatello
Twin Falls
Missoula
Helena
Butte
Kalispell
Salt Lake City
Ogden
Provo
Reno
Carson City
Redding
Chico
Eureka
Santa Rosa
SACRAMENTO
SAN FRANCISCO
OAKLAND
Stockton
Mount Rainier 4392
Mount Hood 3426
Mount St. Helens 2250
Mount Adams 3742
Mount Shasta 4317
Mount Baker 3285
Mount Olympus 2428
Lassen Peak 3187
Borah Peak 3859
Meters
Feet
4000 13120
3000 9840
2000 6560
1000 3280
500 1640
200 656
Sea Level
200 656
2000 6560
W-DRM5514-A1
Copyright © Rand McNally & Co.
0 50 100 150 200 300 400 500 Kilometers
0 50 100 200 300 Miles
Scale 1 : 5 000 000
Lambert Conformal Conic Projection

SASKATCHEWAN
MANITOBA
ONTARIO
CANADA
NORTH DAKOTA
SOUTH DAKOTA
MONTANA
WYOMING
NEBRASKA
COLORADO
KANSAS
MINNESOTA
IOWA
MISSOURI
UNITED STATES
GREAT PLAINS
ROCKY MOUNTAINS
BIGHORN MOUNTAINS
LARAMIE MOUNTAINS
FRONT RANGE
BLACK HILLS
SAND HILLS
Shoshone Basin
Great Divide Basin
Saskatoon
Regina
Moose Jaw
Swift Current
North Battleford
Yorkton
Melville
Estevan
Weyburn
Winnipeg
Brandon
Portage la Prairie
Dauphin
Kenora
Lake Winnipeg
Lake Manitoba
Lake Winnipegosis
Lake of the Woods
Billings
Miles City
Glendive
Williston
Minot
Bismarck
Mandan
Dickinson
Jamestown
Fargo
Moorhead
Grand Forks
Valley City
Devils Lake
Aberdeen
Watertown
Brookings
Pierre
Rapid City
Mitchell
Sioux Falls
Yankton
Sioux City
Sheridan
Casper
Cheyenne
Laramie
Rawlins
Rock Springs
Fort Collins
Greeley
Boulder
Lakewood
DENVER
Aurora
Colorado Springs
Pueblo
Grand Junction
North Platte
Kearney
Grand Island
Hastings
Lincoln
Omaha
Council Bluffs
Norfolk
Columbus
Scottsbluff
Alliance
Salina
Topeka
Lawrence
Manhattan
Junction City
Emporia
Hutchinson
Wichita
Hays
Great Bend
Garden City
Dodge City
Missouri
Yellowstone
North Platte
South Platte
Arkansas
Red
Souris
Assiniboine
THEODORE ROOSEVELT NATIONAL PARK
BADLANDS NATIONAL PARK
WIND CAVE NATIONAL PARK
MOUNT RUSHMORE NATIONAL MEMORIAL
ROCKY MOUNTAIN NATIONAL PARK
GRASSLANDS NATIONAL PARK
RIDING MOUNTAIN NATIONAL PARK
PINE RIDGE INDIAN RESERVATION
STANDING ROCK INDIAN RESERVATION
CHEYENNE RIVER INDIAN RESERVATION
FORT PECK INDIAN RESERVATION
WIND RIVER INDIAN RESERVATION
Pikes Peak 4301
Wind River Peak 4021
108° West of Greenwich
110
114
121

0 50 100 150 200 300 400 500 Kilometers

0 50 100 200 300 Miles

Scale 1 : 5,000,000 Lambert Conformal Conic Projection

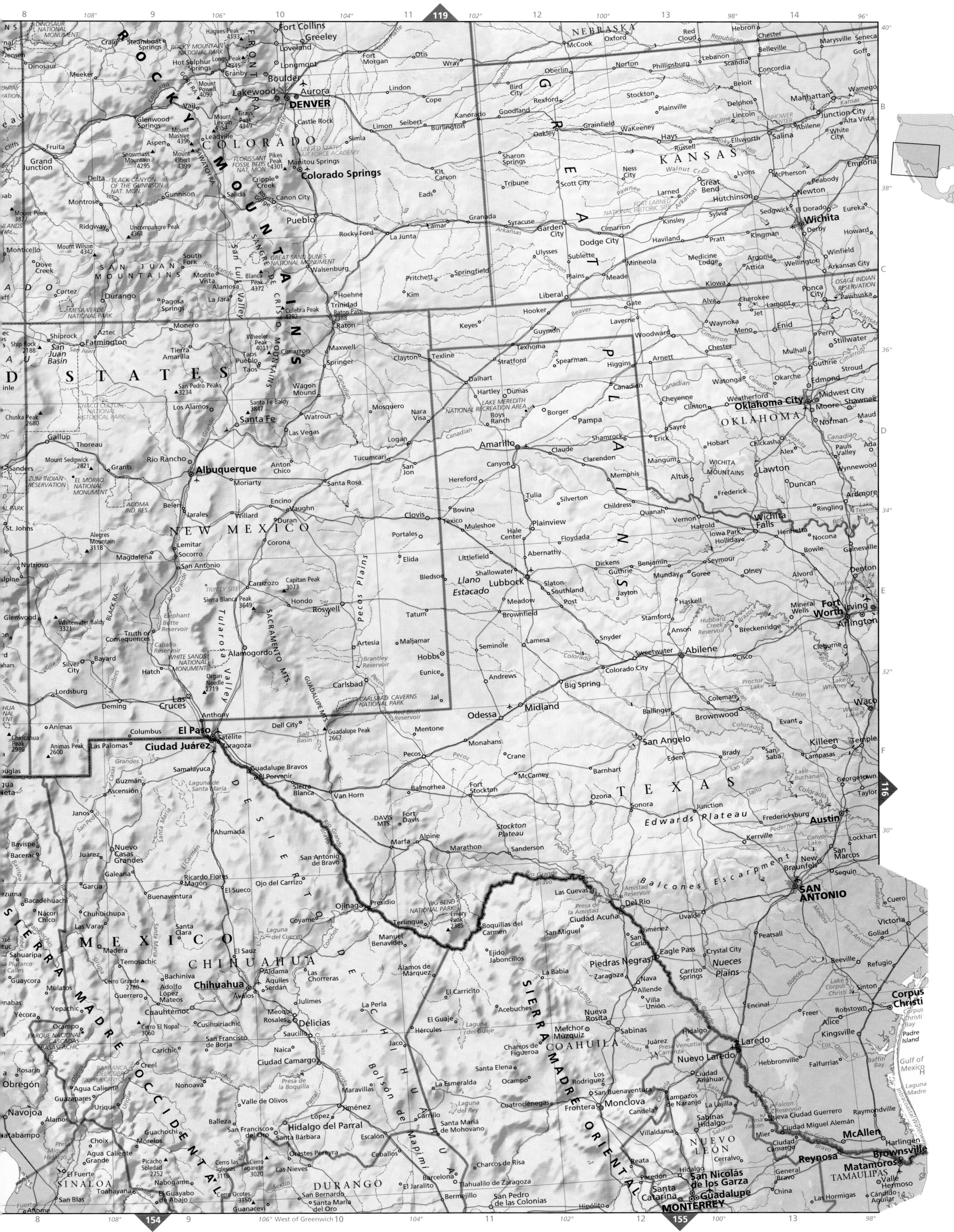

119
116
154
155
ROCKY MOUNTAINS
GREAT PLAINS
COLORADO
KANSAS
NEBRASKA
OKLAHOMA
NEW MEXICO
TEXAS
MEXICO
CHIHUAHUA
COAHUILA
NUEVO LEÓN
TAMAULIPAS
DURANGO
SINALOA
SIERRA MADRE OCCIDENTAL
SIERRA MADRE ORIENTAL
DESIERTO DE CHIHUAHUA
Bolsón de Mapimí
Llano Estacado
Edwards Plateau
Balcones Escarpment
Pecos Plains
Nueces Plains
Stockton Plateau
SANGRE DE CRISTO MOUNTAINS
SAN JUAN MOUNTAINS
FRONT RANGE
SACRAMENTO MTS.
GUADALUPE MTS.
DAVIS MTS.
WICHITA MOUNTAINS
Tularosa Valley
San Luis Valley
Fort Collins
Greeley
Loveland
Longmont
Boulder
Aurora
Lakewood
DENVER
Castle Rock
Colorado Springs
Manitou Springs
Pueblo
Cañon City
Grand Junction
Gunnison
Montrose
Durango
Cortez
Trinidad
Walsenburg
Alamosa
Lamar
La Junta
Rocky Ford
Goodland
Colby
Oakley
Hays
Salina
Abilene
Junction City
Manhattan
Emporia
Hutchinson
Newton
Wichita
Dodge City
Garden City
Liberal
Great Bend
Farmington
Gallup
Grants
Albuquerque
Rio Rancho
Santa Fe
Los Alamos
Las Vegas
Taos
Raton
Clayton
Tucumcari
Santa Rosa
Clovis
Portales
Roswell
Artesia
Carlsbad
Hobbs
Alamogordo
Las Cruces
Deming
Lordsburg
Silver City
Socorro
Truth or Consequences
Amarillo
Dalhart
Lubbock
Plainview
Midland
Odessa
Big Spring
Abilene
San Angelo
Wichita Falls
Fort Worth
Arlington
Irving
Waco
Austin
SAN ANTONIO
Del Rio
Eagle Pass
Laredo
Corpus Christi
McAllen
Harlingen
Brownsville
Oklahoma City
Norman
Moore
Enid
Stillwater
Lawton
El Paso
Ciudad Juárez
Chihuahua
Delicias
Ciudad Camargo
Hidalgo del Parral
Nuevo Casas Grandes
Ojinaga
Ciudad Acuña
Piedras Negras
Nuevo Laredo
Monclova
Reynosa
Matamoros
MONTERREY
San Nicolás de los Garza
Guadalupe
Santa Catarina
Navojoa
Obregón
Los Mochis
Gulf of Mexico
Rio Grande
Pecos
Canadian
Red
Arkansas
Colorado
Brazos
Conchos
106° West of Greenwich

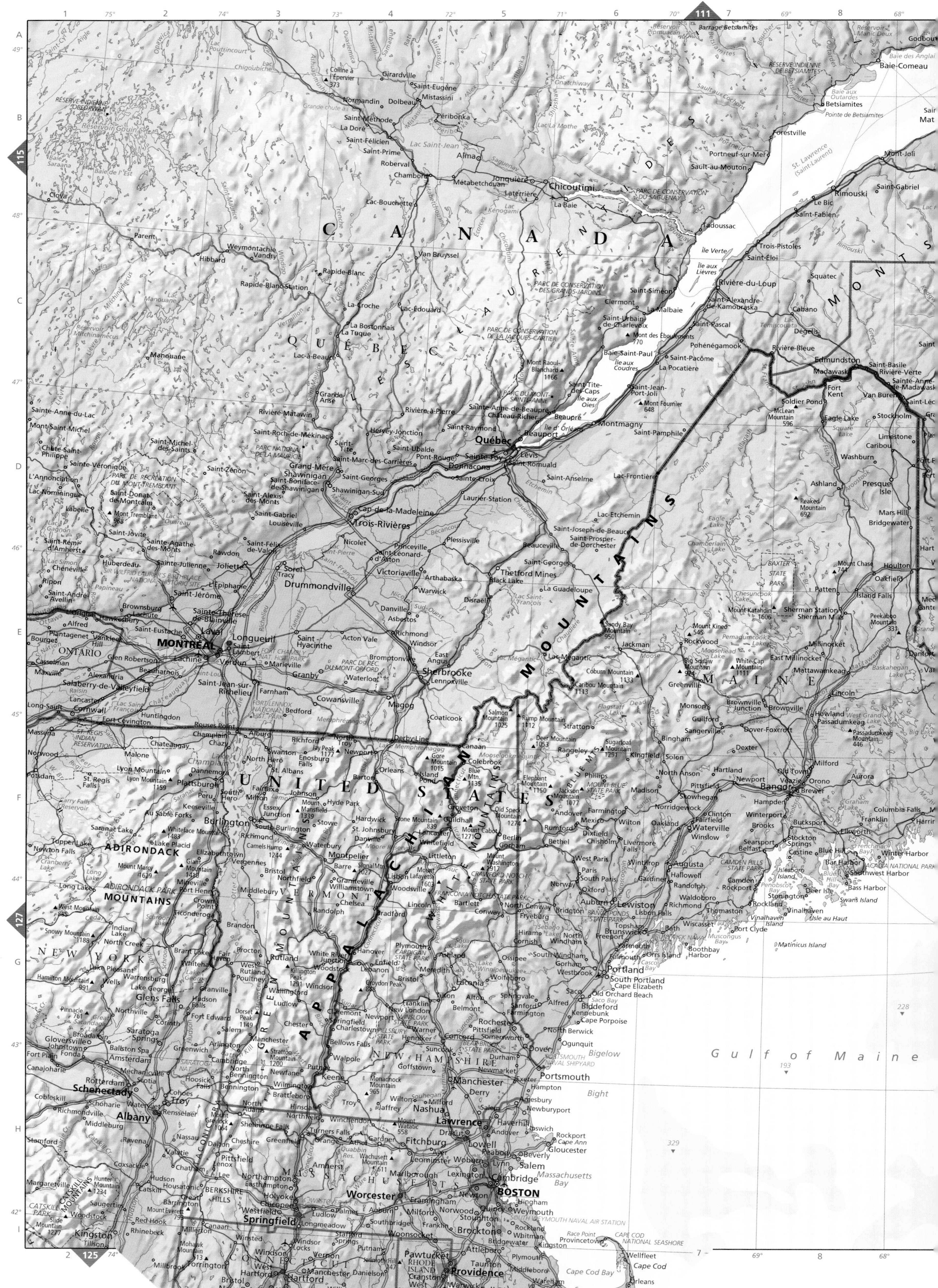

Gulf of St. Lawrence
ATLANTIC OCEAN
NEW BRUNSWICK
NOVA SCOTIA
PRINCE EDWARD ISLAND
NEWFOUNDLAND
ÎLE D'ANTICOSTI
ÎLES DE LA MADELEINE
PÉNINSULE DE LA GASPÉSIE (GASPE PENINSULA)
CAPE BRETON ISLAND
Bay of Fundy
Cabot Strait
Northumberland Strait
Chaleur Bay
Halifax
Saint John
Fredericton
Moncton
Charlottetown
Sydney
Sable Island (N.S.)
Meters Feet
1000 3280
500 1640
200 656
Sea Level
200 656
2000 6560
Scale 1 : 2,500,000
Lambert Conformal Conic Projection
250 Kilometers
150 Miles
West of Greenwich
W-DRM6518-A1 -1-1-2

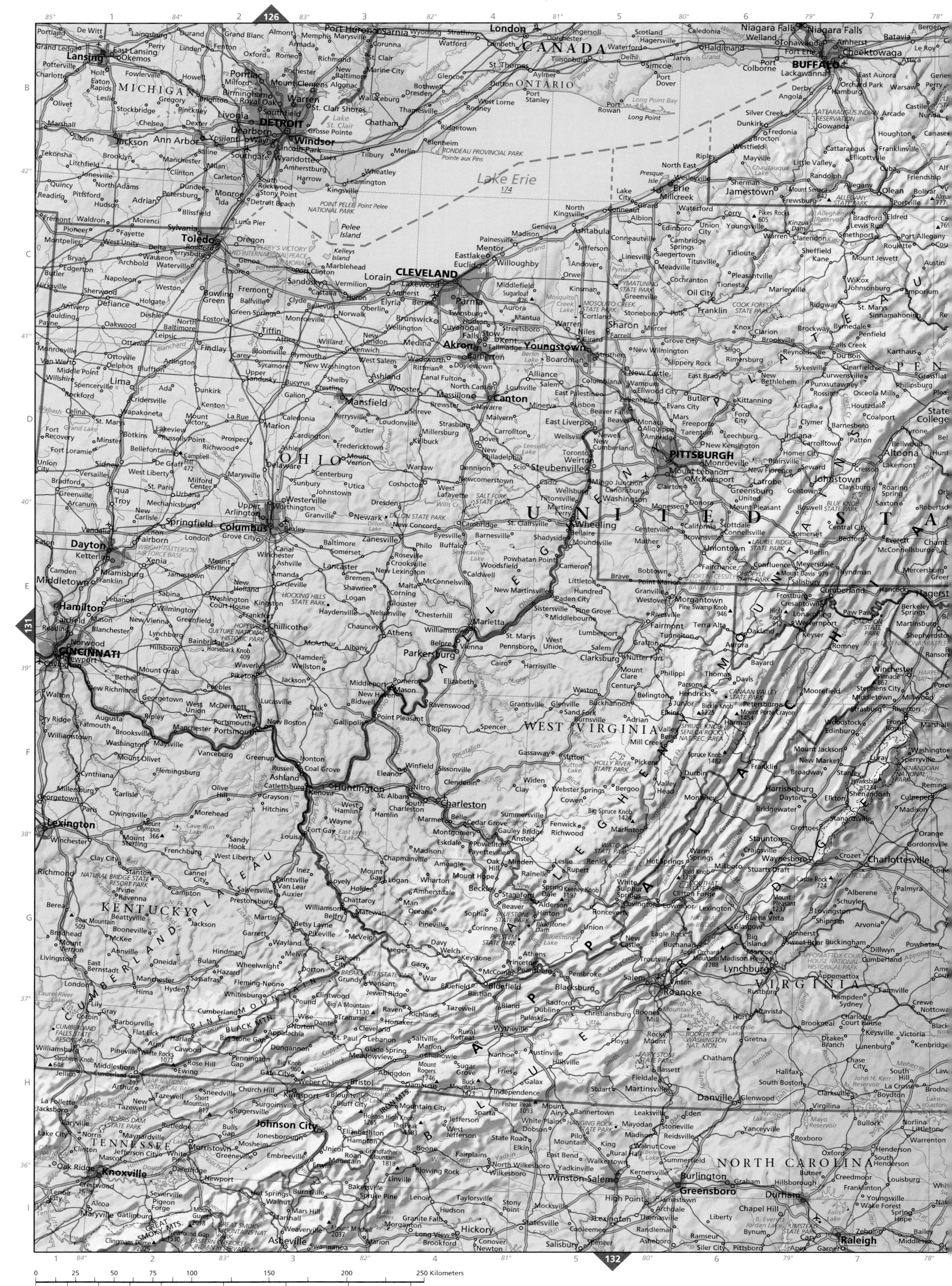

0 25 50 75 100 150 200 250 Kilometers

0 25 50 100 150 Miles

Scale 1 : 2,500,000 Lambert Conformal Conic Projection

127
122
NEW YORK
MASSACHUSETTS
NEW HAMPSHIRE
VERMONT
CONNECTICUT
RHODE ISLAND
NEW JERSEY
DELAWARE
CATSKILL MOUNTAINS
Syracuse
Schenectady
Albany
Binghamton
Scranton
Wilkes-Barre
Allentown
Reading
Harrisburg
Lancaster
York
Trenton
PHILADELPHIA
Wilmington
BALTIMORE
WASHINGTON
Alexandria
NEWARK
NEW YORK
Jersey City
Paterson
Yonkers
Bridgeport
New Haven
Hartford
Springfield
Worcester
BOSTON
Lawrence
Providence
Pawtucket
Fall River
New Bedford
Poughkeepsie
Newburgh
Danbury
Waterbury
Stamford
Atlantic City
Vineland
Norfolk
Virginia Beach
Portsmouth
Chesapeake
Newport News
Hampton
Gulf of Maine
Cape Cod
Cape Cod Bay
Long Island Sound
LONG ISLAND
Delaware Bay
Delmarva Peninsula
Chesapeake Bay
Albemarle Sound
Rhode Island Sound
Nantucket Sound
Martha's Vineyard
Nantucket Island
Block Island
ATLANTIC OCEAN
West of Greenwich
W-DRM6521-A1-1-1-1
Copyright © Rand McNally & Co.

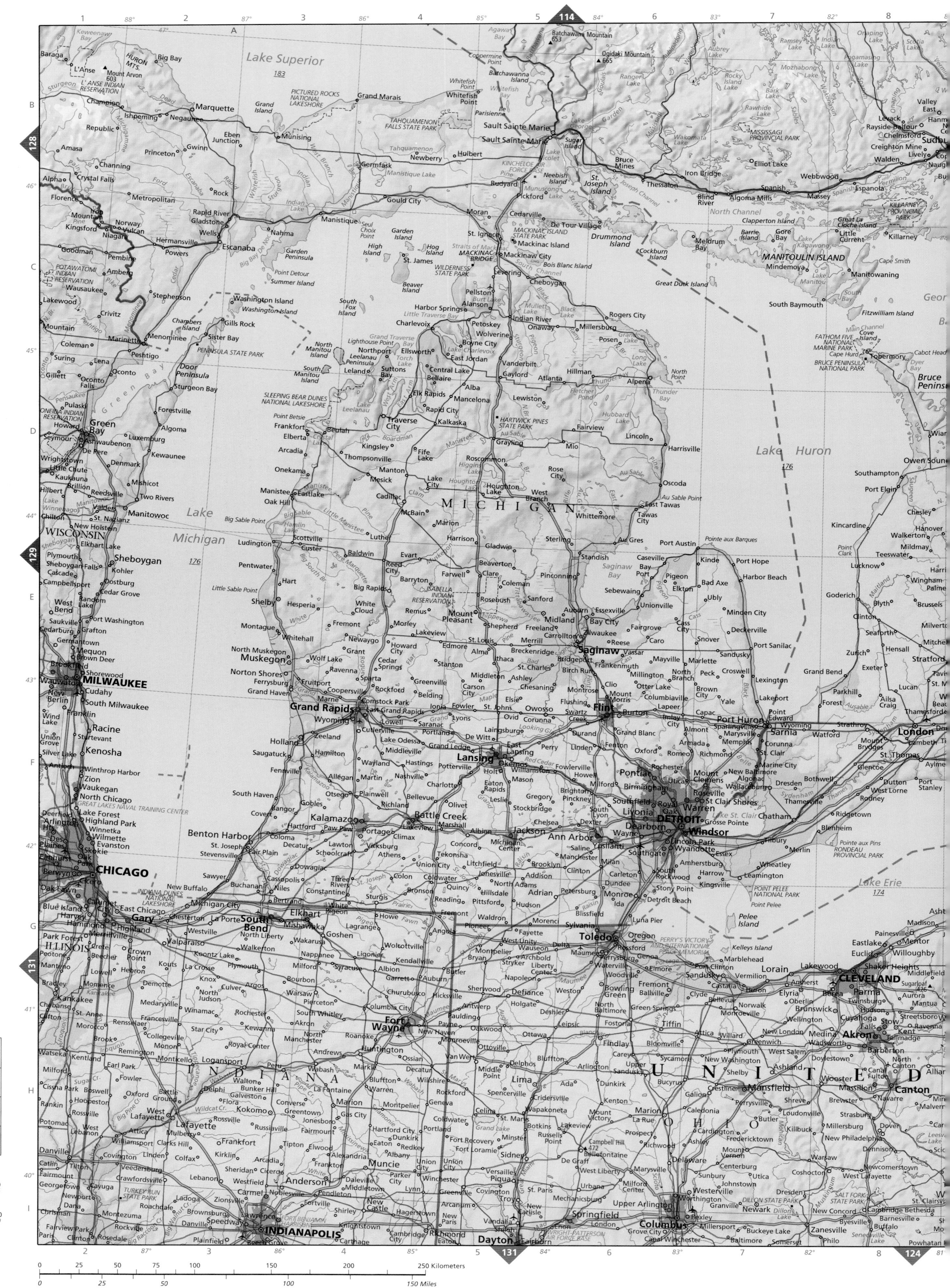
Lake Superior
183
Lake Michigan
176
Lake Huron
176
Lake Erie
174
Green Bay
Saginaw Bay
Georgian Bay
North Channel
MANITOULIN ISLAND
MICHIGAN
WISCONSIN
ILLINOIS
INDIANA
OHIO
UNITED
MILWAUKEE
CHICAGO
DETROIT
Windsor
INDIANAPOLIS
CLEVELAND
Columbus
Toledo
Dayton
Akron
Canton
Grand Rapids
Lansing
Flint
Saginaw
Kalamazoo
Fort Wayne
South Bend
Gary
Ann Arbor
Battle Creek
Muskegon
Green Bay
Marquette
Sault Sainte Marie
Sudbury
London
Sarnia
Port Huron
PICTURED ROCKS NATIONAL LAKESHORE
SLEEPING BEAR DUNES NATIONAL LAKESHORE
INDIANA DUNES NATIONAL LAKESHORE
TAHQUAMENON FALLS STATE PARK
MACKINAC ISLAND STATE PARK
HARTWICK PINES STATE PARK
FATHOM FIVE NATIONAL MARINE PARK
BRUCE PENINSULA NATIONAL PARK
POINT PELEE NATIONAL PARK
RONDEAU PROVINCIAL PARK
KILLARNEY PROVINCIAL PARK
MISSISSAGI PROVINCIAL PARK
Meters
Feet
1000
3280
500
1640
200
656
Sea Level
200
656
2000
6560
0 25 50 75 100 150 200 250 Kilometers
0 25 50 100 150 Miles
Scale 1 : 2,500,000
Lambert Conformal Conic Projection
114
124
128
129
131

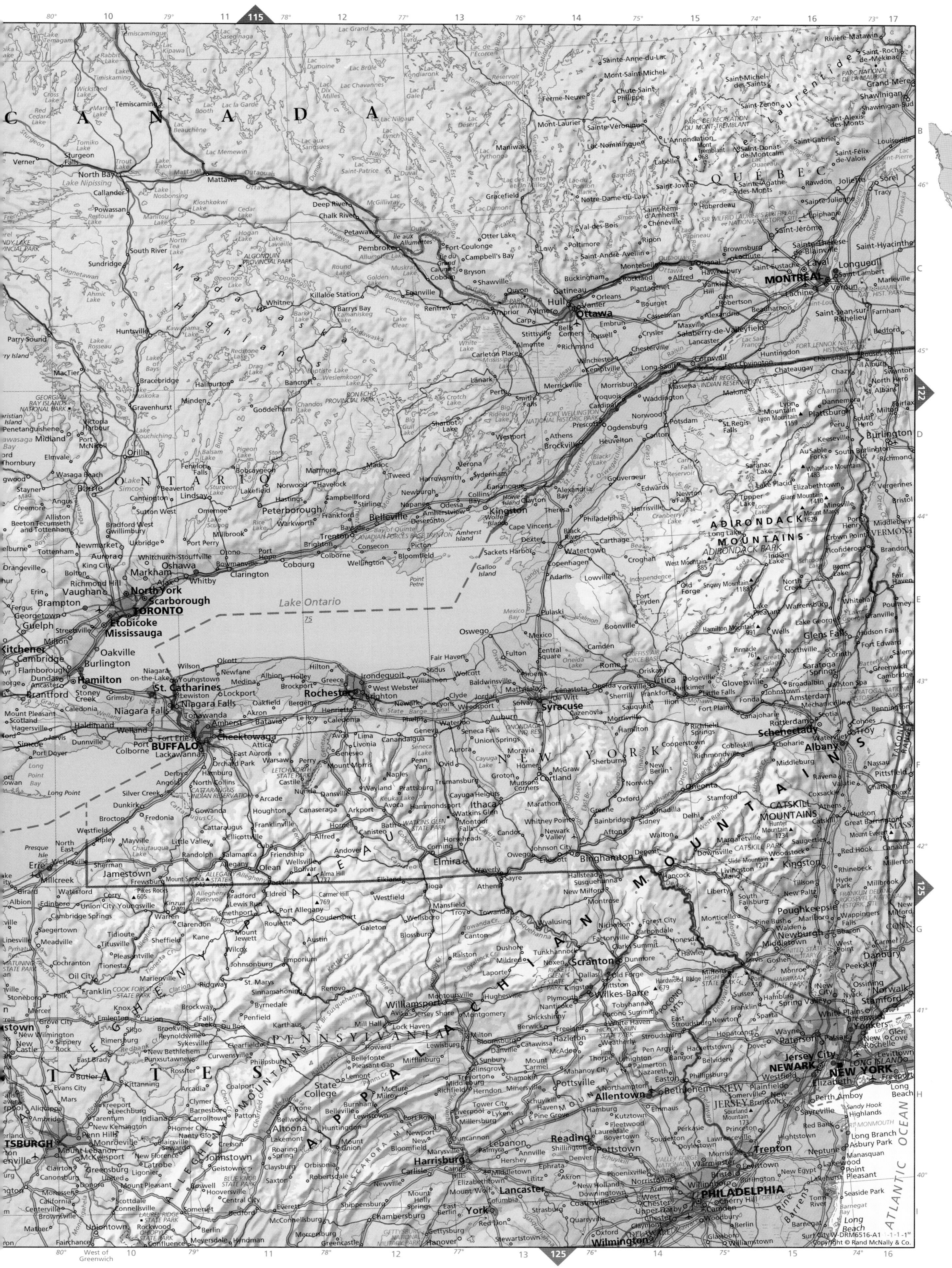
CANADA
ONTARIO
QUÉBEC
NEW YORK
PENNSYLVANIA
NEW JERSEY
VERMONT
MASS.
CONN.
UNITED STATES
ADIRONDACK MOUNTAINS
CATSKILL MOUNTAINS
APPALACHIAN MOUNTAINS
ALLEGHENY MOUNTAINS
ALLEGHENY PLATEAU
Lake Ontario
Lake Erie
ATLANTIC OCEAN
MONTREAL
Ottawa
Hull
Kingston
Peterborough
Oshawa
Markham
North York
Scarborough
TORONTO
Etobicoke
Mississauga
Oakville
Burlington
Hamilton
St. Catharines
Niagara Falls
BUFFALO
Cheektowaga
Rochester
Syracuse
Utica
Rome
Schenectady
Albany
Troy
Binghamton
Elmira
Ithaca
Scranton
Wilkes-Barre
Williamsport
Allentown
Bethlehem
Reading
Harrisburg
Lancaster
York
Altoona
State College
Erie
Jamestown
PITTSBURGH
Trenton
PHILADELPHIA
Wilmington
NEWARK
Jersey City
NEW YORK
Yonkers
Paterson
Stamford
Danbury
Poughkeepsie
Kingston
Burlington
Plattsburgh
Longueuil
Laval
Sorel
Saint-Jérôme
Cornwall
Brockville
Belleville
Oswego
Watertown
Gloversville
Long Island
Copyright © Rand McNally & Co.

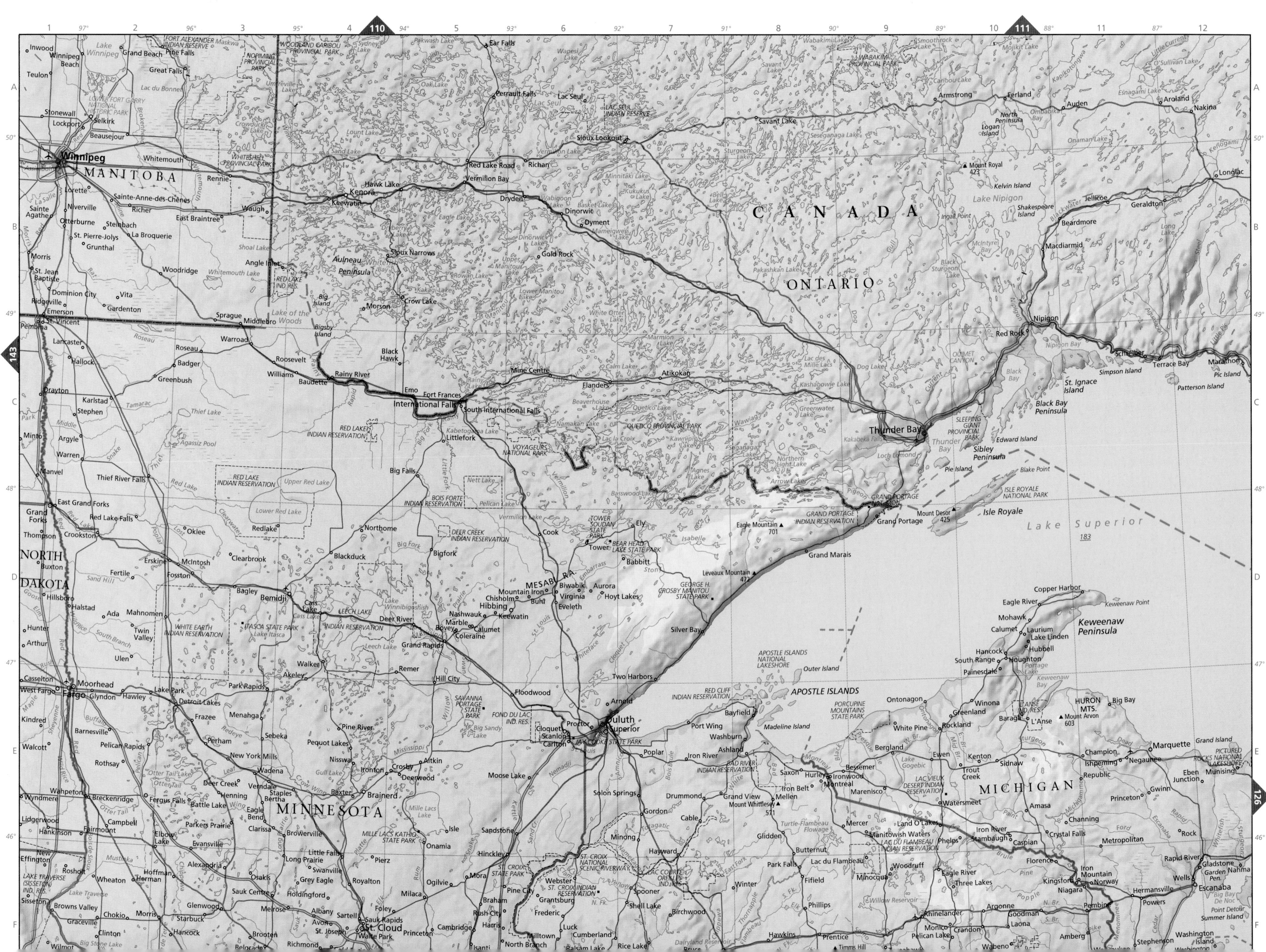

CANADA
ONTARIO
MANITOBA
MINNESOTA
MICHIGAN
NORTH DAKOTA
Lake Superior
Isle Royale
Keweenaw Peninsula
APOSTLE ISLANDS
Lake Nipigon
Lake of the Woods
Thunder Bay
Duluth
Superior
Winnipeg
International Falls
Fort Frances
Kenora
Dryden
Nipigon
Marathon
Grand Marais
Two Harbors
Hibbing
Bemidji
Grand Forks
Fargo
Moorhead
St. Cloud
Brainerd
Marquette
Escanaba
Ashland
110
111
143
126

WISCONSIN
IOWA
ILLINOIS
MISSOURI
INDIANA
NEBRASKA
KANSAS
SOUTH DAKOTA
UNITED STATES

Lake Michigan
CHICAGO
MILWAUKEE
Madison
Des Moines
St. Paul
Omaha
Springfield

Scale 1 : 2,500,000
0 25 50 75 100 150 200 250 Kilometers
0 25 50 100 150 Miles
Lambert Conformal Conic Projection

Meters / Feet
Sea Level
200 / 656
500 / 1640
2000 / 6560

W-DRM6517-A1 -1-1-2

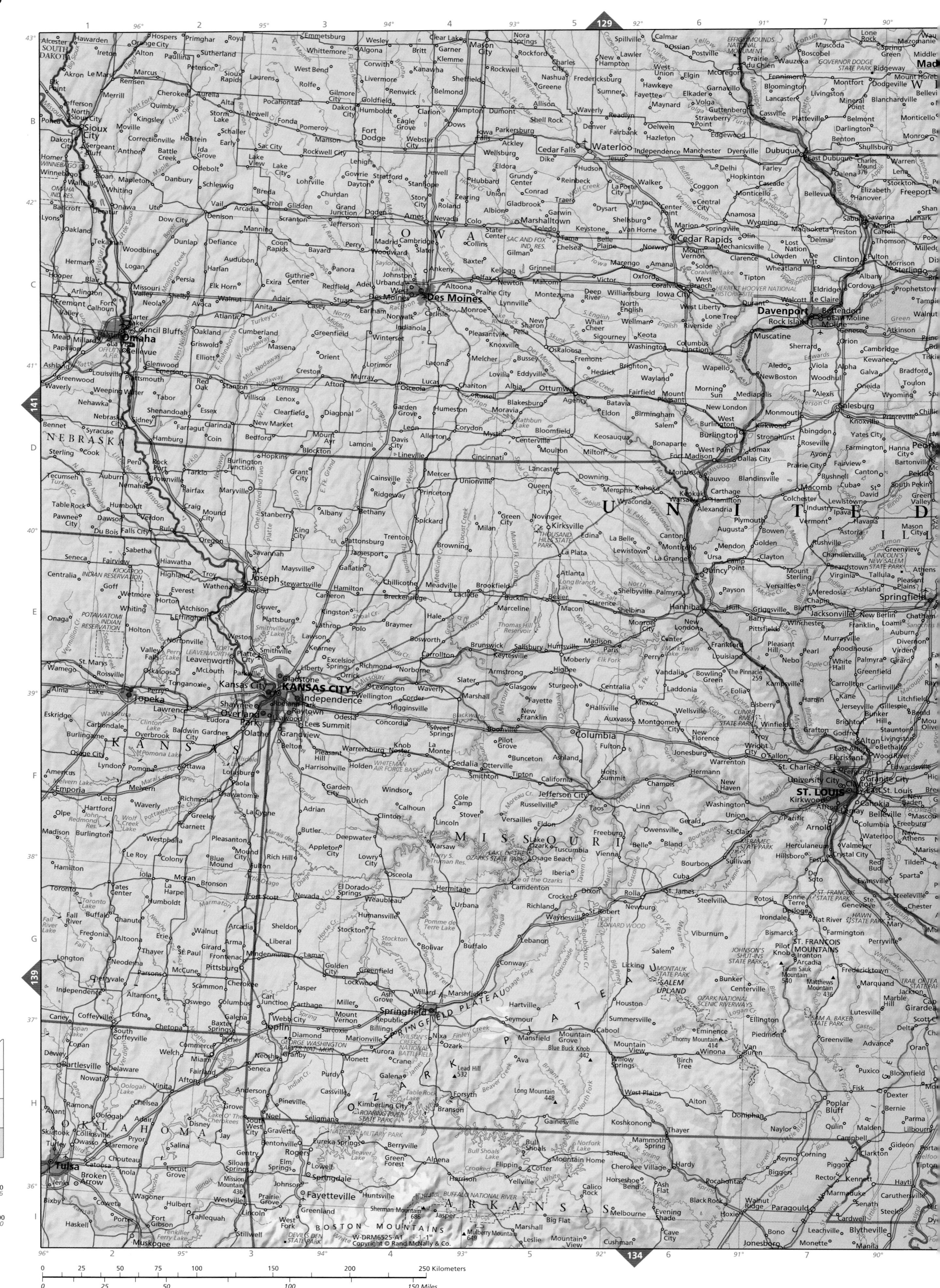

0 25 50 75 100 150 200 250 Kilometers

0 25 50 100 150 Miles

Scale 1 : 2,500,000 Lambert Conformal Conic Projection

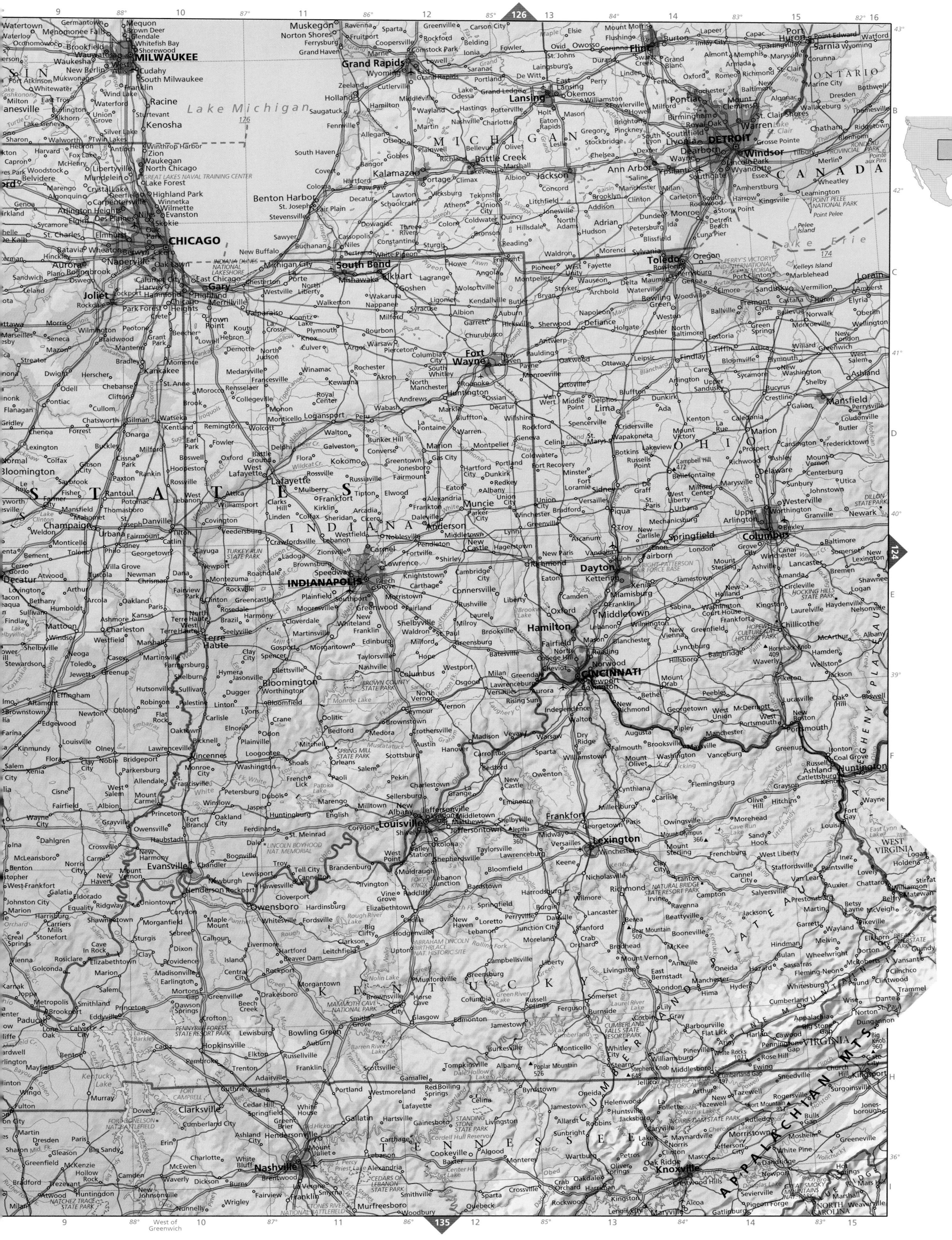
MILWAUKEE
CHICAGO
INDIANAPOLIS
CINCINNATI
DETROIT
Louisville
Nashville
Knoxville
Lexington
Dayton
Columbus
Toledo
Fort Wayne
South Bend
Grand Rapids
Lansing
Flint
Windsor
Evansville
Terre Haute
Kalamazoo
Battle Creek
Jackson
Ann Arbor
Springfield
Hamilton
Frankfort
Gary
Joliet
Lake Michigan
Lake Erie
MICHIGAN
INDIANA
OHIO
KENTUCKY
TENNESSEE
CANADA
ONTARIO
WEST VIRGINIA
VIRGINIA
APPALACHIAN MTS.
CUMBERLAND PLATEAU
ALLEGHENY PLATEAU
126
124
135
West of Greenwich

ATLANTIC
OCEAN
NORTH CAROLINA
SOUTH CAROLINA
GEORGIA
TENNESSEE
UNITED STATES
APPALACHIAN MOUNTAINS
BLUE RIDGE
GREAT SMOKY MTS.
SEA ISLANDS
Charlotte
Raleigh
Columbia
Charleston
Savannah
Atlanta
Augusta
Macon
Greenville
Asheville
Wilmington
Fayetteville
Goldsboro
Jacksonville
Myrtle Beach
North Myrtle Beach
Florence
Sumter
Athens
Anderson
Albany
Valdosta
Brunswick
Hickory
Pamlico Sound
Onslow Bay
Long Bay
Cape Hatteras
Cape Lookout
Cape Fear
Cape Romain
Hatteras Island
Ocracoke Island
Hilton Head Island
Okefenokee Swamp
124
125
135

FLORIDA

BAHAMAS

Gulf of Mexico

Straits of Florida

FLORIDA KEYS

GRAND BAHAMA

ABACO

ELEUTHERA

NEW PROVIDENCE

ANDROS

Northwest Providence Channel

Northeast Providence Channel

Orlando

Tampa

St. Petersburg

Lakeland

Gainesville

Ocala

Daytona Beach

Melbourne

Fort Pierce

West Palm Beach

Fort Lauderdale

MIAMI

Miami Beach

Hialeah

Fort Myers

Naples

Key West

Freeport

Nassau

Scale 1 : 2,500,000

Lambert Conformal Conic Projection

0 25 50 75 100 Miles

0 50 100 150 200 Kilometers

Meters / Feet: 1000 3280; 500 1640; 200 656; Sea Level; 200 656; 2000 6560

84° West of Greenwich

W-DRM6515-A1 -1-1-1"

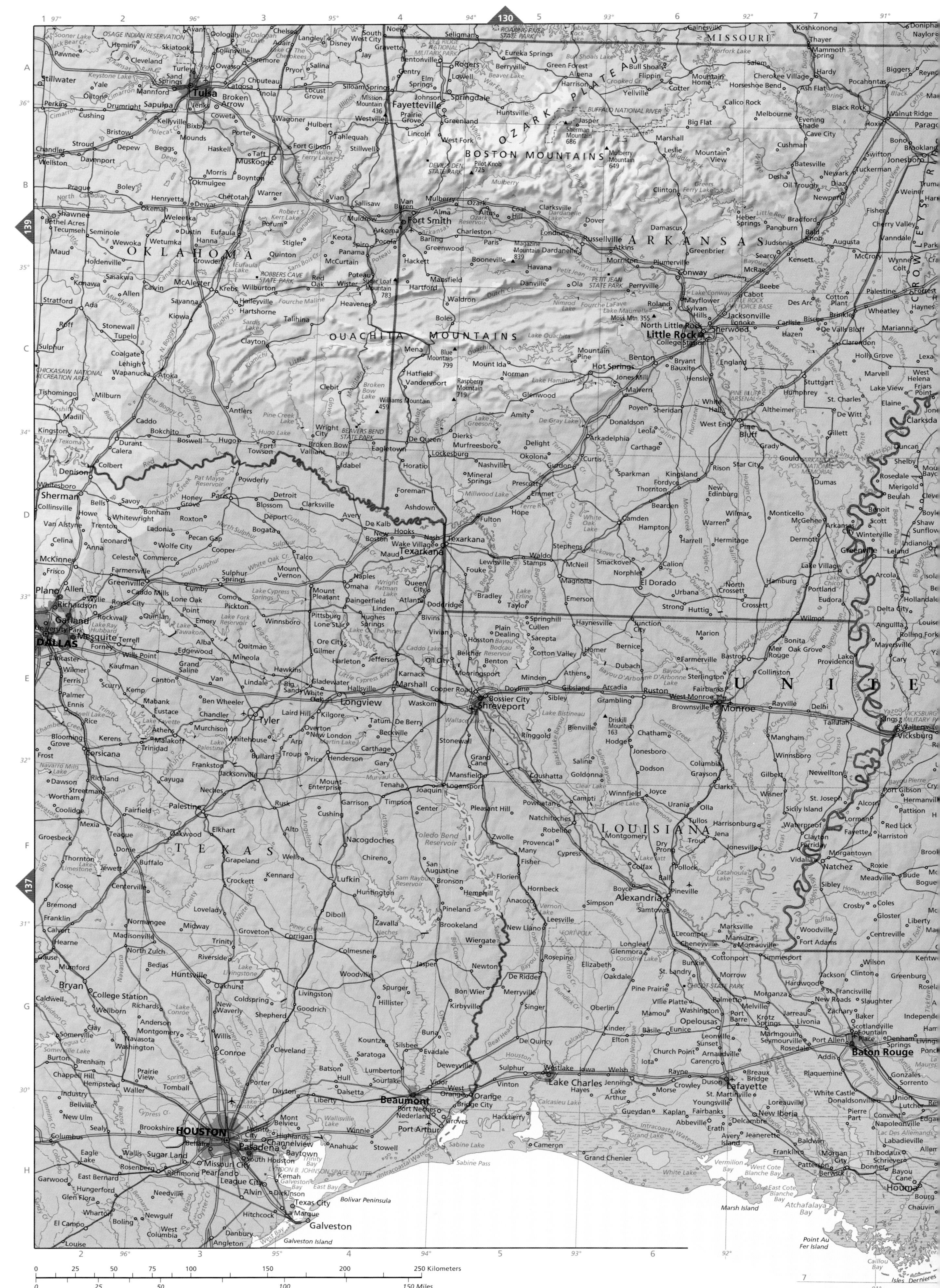

Scale 1 : 2,500,000 Lambert Conformal Conic Projection

KENTUCKY
TENNESSEE
MISSISSIPPI
STATES
ALABAMA
GEORGIA
FLORIDA
NORTH CAROLINA
APPALACHIAN MOUNTAINS
CUMBERLAND PLATEAU
WALDEN RIDGE
LOOKOUT MOUNTAIN
BLUE RIDGE
Dahlonega Plateau
Nashville
Knoxville
Chattanooga
Memphis
Huntsville
Birmingham
Tuscaloosa
Montgomery
Columbus
ATLANTA
Mobile
Pensacola
Biloxi
Pascagoula
Panama City
Tallahassee
Dothan
Albany
Meridian
Gadsden
Anniston
Florence
Decatur
Clarksville
Murfreesboro
Jackson
Tupelo
Hattiesburg
NEW ORLEANS
Gulf of Mexico
Mississippi Sound
Chandeleur Sound
Chandeleur Islands
Breton Sound
Apalachee Bay
Mississippi Delta
Kentucky Lake
Lake Barkley
GULF ISLANDS NATIONAL SEASHORE
TYNDALL AIR FORCE BASE
87° West of Greenwich
W-DRM6529-A1 -1-1-1M
Copyright © Rand McNally & Co.

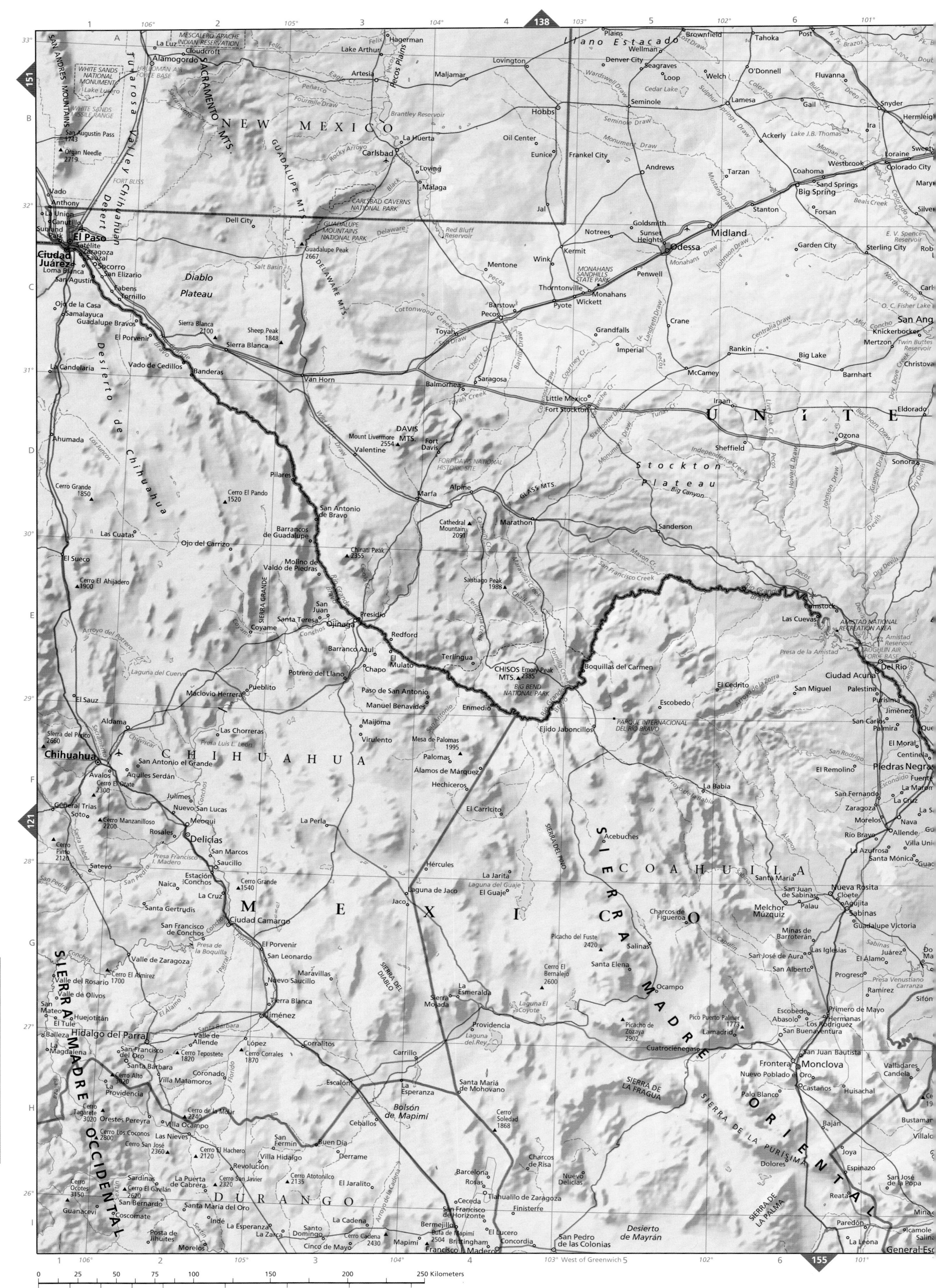

138
151
121
155
N E W   M E X I C O
Llano Estacado
U N I T E
C H I H U A H U A
M E X I C O
C O A H U I L A
D U R A N G O
SIERRA MADRE OCCIDENTAL
SIERRA MADRE ORIENTAL
SAN ANDRES MOUNTAINS
SACRAMENTO MTS.
GUADALUPE MTS.
DELAWARE MTS.
DAVIS MTS.
GLASS MTS.
CHISOS MTS.
SIERRA GRANDE
SIERRA DEL PINO
SIERRA DEL DIABLO
SIERRA DE LA FRAGUA
SIERRA DE LA PURISIMA
SIERRA DE LA PALMA
Tularosa Valley
Chihuahuan Desert
Desierto de Chihuahua
Diablo Plateau
Stockton Plateau
Bolsón de Mapimí
Desierto de Mayrán
WHITE SANDS NATIONAL MONUMENT
WHITE SANDS MISSILE RANGE
HOLLOMAN AIR FORCE BASE
MESCALERO APACHE INDIAN RESERVATION
FORT BLISS
CARLSBAD CAVERNS NATIONAL PARK
GUADALUPE MOUNTAINS NATIONAL PARK
MONAHANS SANDHILLS STATE PARK
FORT DAVIS NATIONAL HISTORIC SITE
BIG BEND NATIONAL PARK
PARQUE INTERNACIONAL DEL RIO BRAVO
AMISTAD NATIONAL RECREATION AREA
LAUGHLIN AIR FORCE BASE
San Augustin Pass 1743
Organ Needle 2719
Guadalupe Peak 2667
Sierra Blanca 2100
Sheep Peak 1848
Mount Livermore 2554
Cathedral Mountain 2091
Chinati Peak 2355
Santiago Peak 1988
Emory Peak 2385
Cerro Grande 1850
Cerro El Pando 1520
Cerro El Ahijadero 1900
Sierra del Perico 2660
Mesa de Palomas 1995
Cerro El Otate 2300
Cerro Manzanilloso 2200
Cerro Pimo 2120
Cerro Grande 1540
Picacho del Fuste 2420
Cerro El Bernalejo 2600
Picacho de Zozaya 2902
Pico Puerto Palmer 1773
Cerro El Almirez 1700
Cerro Tepestete 1820
Cerro Corrales 1870
Cerro Alto 3020
Cerro Tagarete 3020
Cerro de la Mula 2240
Cerro Los Coconos 2800
Cerro San José 2360
Cerro El Hachero 2120
Cerro Ocotes 3150
Cerro El Gavilán 2620
Cerro San Javier 2320
Cerro Atotonilco 2135
Cerro Soledad 1868
Cerro Cadena 2430
Bufa de Mapimí 2504
El Paso
Ciudad Juárez
Alamogordo
La Luz
Cloudcroft
Hagerman
Lake Arthur
Artesia
Carlsbad
La Huerta
Loving
Malaga
Hobbs
Lovington
Maljamar
Eunice
Oil Center
Jal
Plains
Wellman
Denver City
Seagraves
Loop
Seminole
Welch
Lamesa
O'Donnell
Tahoka
Brownfield
Post
Fluvanna
Gail
Snyder
Hermleigh
Ira
Ackerly
Andrews
Tarzan
Frankel City
Westbrook
Coahoma
Colorado City
Loraine
Big Spring
Sand Springs
Forsan
Stanton
Midland
Odessa
Goldsmith
Notrees
Sunset Heights
Kermit
Wink
Mentone
Penwell
Thorntonville
Monahans
Wickett
Pyote
Barstow
Pecos
Toyah
Grandfalls
Imperial
Crane
Rankin
McCamey
Big Lake
Mertzon
Knickerbocker
Barnhart
Christoval
Sterling City
Garden City
Balmorhea
Saragosa
Fort Stockton
Iraan
Sheffield
Ozona
Sonora
Eldorado
Valentine
Fort Davis
Marfa
Alpine
Marathon
Sanderson
Van Horn
Sierra Blanca
Dell City
Anthony
Vado
La Union
Canutillo
Sunland Park
Satélite
Zaragoza
Sauzal
Socorro
San Elizario
Loma Blanca
San Agustín
Fabens
Tornillo
Ojo de la Casa
Samalayuca
Guadalupe Bravos
El Porvenir
Vado de Cedillos
Banderas
La Candelaria
Ahumada
Las Cuatas
El Sueco
Ojo del Carrizo
Pilares
San Antonio de Bravo
Barrancos de Guadalupe
Molino de Valdo de Piedras
Presidio
Ojinaga
San Juan
Santa Teresa
Coyame
Redford
Barranco Azul
El Mulato
Chapo
Terlingua
Potrero del Llano
Paso de San Antonio
Manuel Benavides
Enmedio
Boquillas del Carmen
Ejido Jaboncillos
Comstock
Las Cuevas
Del Rio
Ciudad Acuña
Palestina
Purisima
Jiménez
San Miguel
El Cedrito
Escobedo
San Carlos
Palmira
El Moral
Centinela
Piedras Negras
El Remolino
San Fernando
La Cruz
Zaragoza
Morelos
Nava
Allende
Río Bravo
La Azufrosa
Santa Mónica
Villa Unión
Guadalupe Victoria
Nueva Rosita
Cloete
Agujita
Sabinas
San Juan de Sabinas
Palau
Melchor Múzquiz
Santa María
Minas de Barroterán
Las Iglesias
San José de Aura
San Alberto
El Álamo
Juárez
Progreso
Ramírez
Primero de Mayo
Escobedo
Abasolo
Hermanas
Los Rodríguez
San Buenaventura
San Juan Bautista
Frontera
Monclova
Nuevo Poblado el Oro
Castaños
Palo Blanco
Candela
Valladares
Huisachal
Bajan
Joya
Espinazo
San José de la Popa
Reata
Paredón
La Leona
Dolores
Acebuches
La Babia
Charcos de Figueroa
Salinas
Santa Elena
Ocampo
Lamadrid
Cuatrociénegas
La Jarita
El Guaje
Laguna de Jaco
Jaco
Hércules
El Carricito
Hechiceros
Álamos de Márquez
Palomas
Maijoma
Virulento
Pueblito
Maclovio Herrera
El Sauz
Aldama
Las Chorreras
Chihuahua
San Antonio el Grande
Aquiles Serdán
Avalos
Julimes
General Trias
Soto
Nuevo San Lucas
Meoqui
Rosales
Delicias
San Marcos
Saucillo
Satevó
Naica
Estación Conchos
La Cruz
Santa Gertrudis
Ciudad Camargo
San Francisco de Conchos
El Porvenir
San Leonardo
Valle de Zaragoza
Maravillas
Nuevo Saucillo
Valle del Rosario
Valle de Olivos
San Mateo
El Tule
Huejotitán
Tierra Blanca
Jiménez
Balleza
Hidalgo del Parral
La Magdalena
Valle de Allende
San Francisco del Oro
Santa Bárbara
López
Corralitos
Coronado
Villa Matamoros
La Providencia
Escalón
Carrillo
Sierra Mojada
La Esmeralda
Providencia
La Esperanza
Santa María de Mohovano
Orestes Pereyra
Villa Ocampo
Las Nieves
Ceballos
San Fermín
Buen Día
Villa Hidalgo
Derrame
Revolución
Sardinas
La Puerta de Cabrera
El Jaralito
Barcelona
Rosas
Charcos de Risa
Nuevo Delicias
Ceceda
Tlahualilo de Zaragoza
San Francisco de Horizonte
Finisterre
Bermejillo
El Lucero
Brittingham
Concordia
San Pedro de las Colonias
Madero
Mapimí
Francisco
La Cadena
Santo Domingo
Cinco de Mayo
La Esperanza
La Zarca
Indé
Santa María del Oro
Coscomate
San Bernardo
Guanaceví
Posta de Jihuites
Morelos
Pecos
Rio Grande
Bravo
Conchos
Salt Basin
Red Bluff Reservoir
Brantley Reservoir
Lake J.B. Thomas
Amistad Reservoir
Presa de la Amistad
Presa Luis L. León
Presa Francisco I. Madero
Presa de la Boquilla
Laguna del Cuervo
Laguna del Guaje
Laguna El Coyote
Laguna del Rey
Presa Venustiano Carranza
Meters
Feet
4000 13120
3000 9840
2000 6560
1000 3280
500 1640
200 656
Sea Level
200 656
2000 6560
33°
32°
31°
30°
29°
28°
27°
26°
106°
105°
104°
103°
102°
101°
103° West of Greenwich
0 25 50 75 100 150 200 250 Kilometers
0 25 50 100 150 Miles
Scale 1 : 2,500,000
Lambert Conformal Conic Projection

139
134
TEXAS
UNITED STATES
LOUISIANA
EDWARDS PLATEAU
BALCONES ESCARPMENT
NUECES PLAINS
BRADY MOUNTAINS
TAMAULIPAS
Gulf of Mexico
DALLAS
Fort Worth
Arlington
Irving
Garland
Plano
Mesquite
Abilene
Waco
Killeen
Temple
Austin
SAN ANTONIO
HOUSTON
Pasadena
Baytown
Galveston
Texas City
Beaumont
Port Arthur
Orange
Tyler
Longview
Shreveport
Lufkin
Nacogdoches
Bryan
College Station
Victoria
Corpus Christi
Laredo
Nuevo Laredo
McAllen
Reynosa
Brownsville
Matamoros
Harlingen
Edinburg
Padre Island
Matagorda Island
Mustang Island
San Jose Island
Galveston Island
Bolivar Peninsula
Matagorda Peninsula
Laguna Madre
PADRE ISLAND NATIONAL SEASHORE
Intracoastal Waterway
W-DRM6530-A1
Copyright © Rand McNally & Co.

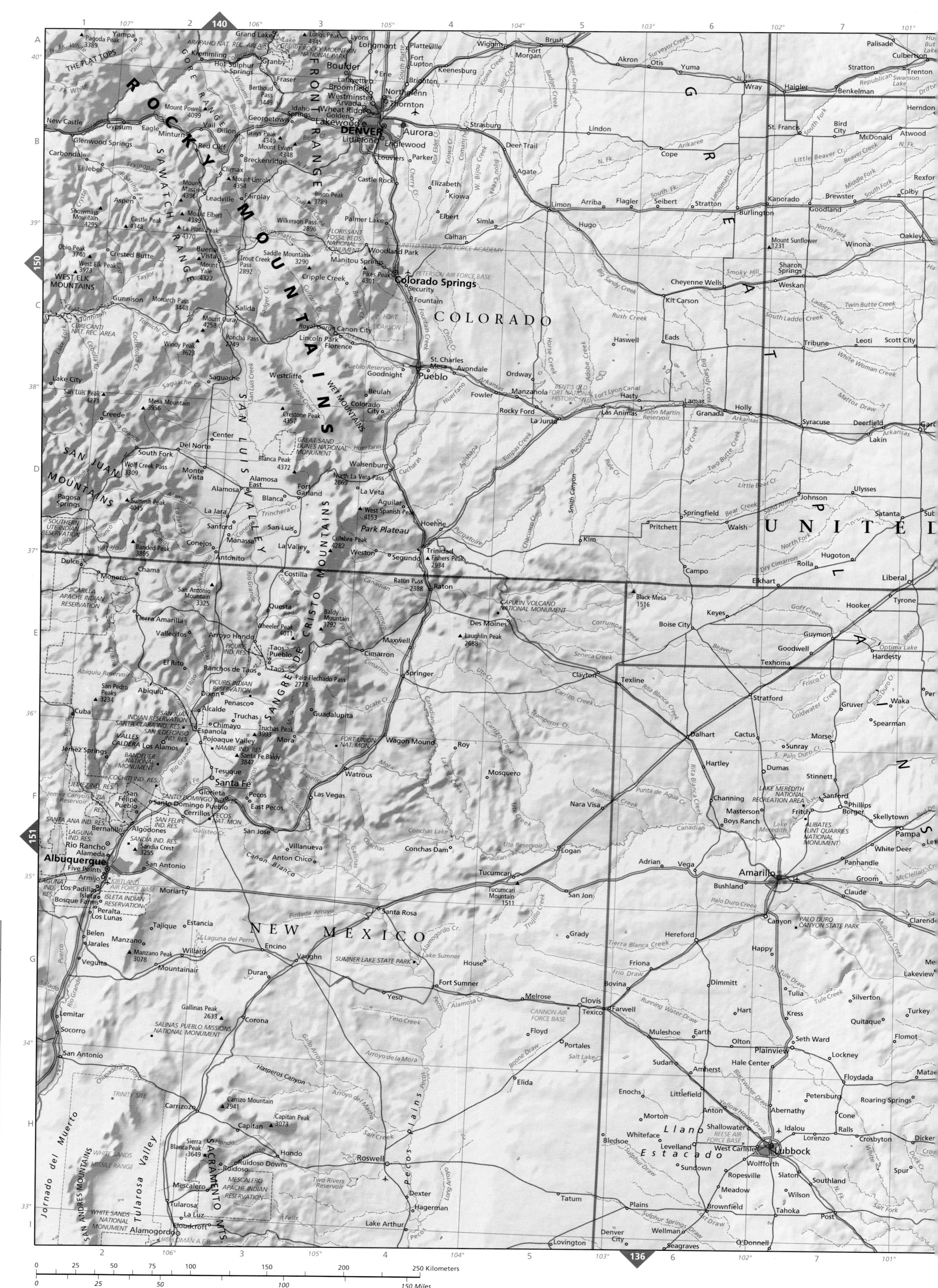

0 25 50 75 100 150 200 250 Kilometers

0 25 50 100 150 Miles

Scale 1 : 2,500,000 Lambert Conformal Conic Projection

NEBRASKA

KANSAS

MISSOURI

OKLAHOMA

TEXAS

ARKANSAS

LOUISIANA

OZARK PLATEAU

BOSTON MOUNTAINS

OUACHITA MOUNTAINS

WICHITA MOUNTAINS

FLINT HILLS

ARBUCKLE MTS.

Kansas City

Topeka

Wichita

Tulsa

Oklahoma City

Fort Smith

Fayetteville

Joplin

Springfield

Wichita Falls

Dallas

Fort Worth

Lawton

St. Joseph

0 25 50 75 100 150 200 250 Kilometers

0 25 50 100 150 Miles

Scale 1 : 2,500,000 Lambert Conformal Conic Projection

NORTH DAKOTA
SOUTH DAKOTA
NEBRASKA
KANSAS
MINNESOTA
IOWA
SAND HILLS
COTEAU DU MISSOURI
COTEAU DES PRAIRIES
BADLANDS
Bismarck
Mandan
Dickinson
Richardton
Glen Ullin
New Salem
FORT LINCOLN STATE PARK
Lake Tschida
New England
Regent
Mott
Elgin
Carson
Flasher
New Leipzig
Hazelton
Cannon Ball
Solen
Moffit
Linton
Strasburg
Hague
Napoleon
Wishek
Lehr
Fredonia
Kulm
Edgeley
Streeter
Gackle
Litchville
Marion
Enderlin
Kindred
Walcott
Lisbon
La Moure
Gwinner
Milnor
Wyndmere
Wahpeton
Breckenridge
Barnesville
Rothsay
Pelican Rapids
Fergus Falls
Campbell
Hankinson
Fairmount
Oakes
Forman
Lidgerwood
Cogswell
Rutland
Havana
Ellendale
Monango
Ashley
Zeeland
Venturia
Fort Yates
Selfridge
Scranton
Reeder
Hettinger
Lemmon
Morristown
McIntosh
McLaughlin
Bullhead
Pollock
Herreid
Mound City
Eureka
Leola
Frederick
Hecla
Britton
Veblen
New Effington
Rosholt
Wheaton
Herman
Elbow Lake
Claremont
Sisseton
Browns Valley
Graceville
Chokio
Langford
Pierpont
Groton
Andover
Aberdeen
Ipswich
Roscoe
Bowdle
Hosmer
Java
Selby
Mobridge
STANDING ROCK INDIAN RESERVATION
Shadehill Reservoir
Bison
Isabel
Timber Lake
Thunder Butte 840
CHEYENNE RIVER INDIAN RESERVATION
Lake Oahe
Hoven
Lebanon
Gettysburg
Faulkton
Redfield
Mellette
Conde
Bristol
Webster
Waubay
Wilmot
Summit
Milbank
Big Stone City
Ortonville
Clinton
Appleton
Bellingham
Madison
Dawson
Marietta
Revillo
Clear Lake
Gary
Canby
Watertown
Henry
Clark
Doland
Frankfort
Tulare
Bradley
Castlewood
Vienna
Hayti
Willow Lake
Bryant
Lake Norden
Estelline
Toronto
Hendricks
Ivanhoe
Bruce
White
Brookings
Lake Benton
Arlington
Lake Preston
Volga
De Smet
Iroquois
Huron
Wolsey
Wessington
Miller
Highmore
Blunt
Onida
Pierre
Fort Pierre
Oahe Dam
Faith
Dupree
North Eagle Butte
Eagle Butte
Castle Rock Butte 1148
Newell
Bear Butte 1349
Rapid City
Keystone
MOUNT RUSHMORE NATIONAL MEMORIAL
CUSTER STATE PARK
WIND CAVE NATIONAL PARK
ELLSWORTH AIR FORCE BASE
Wall
Philip
Midland
Kadoka
BADLANDS NATIONAL PARK
Murdo
Presho
Kennebec
Chamberlain
Oacoma
Kimball
White Lake
Plankinton
Mount Vernon
Mitchell
Alexandria
Emery
Canistota
Salem
Montrose
Hartford
Brandon
Sioux Falls
Humboldt
Bridgewater
Parker
Lennox
Canton
Marion
Freeman
Menno
Hurley
Viborg
Centerville
Irene
Beresford
Alcester
Hawarden
Wakonda
Vermillion
Akron
Elk Point
Yankton
Gavins Point Dam
Tabor
Tyndall
Avon
Springfield
Pickstown
Fort Randall Dam
Wagner
Lake Andes
Geddes
Armour
Delmont
Parkston
Tripp
Olivet
Scotland
Corsica
Platte
Stickney
Ethan
Lake Francis Case
LOWER BRULE INDIAN RESERVATION
CROW CREEK INDIAN RESERVATION
Fort Thompson
Gannvalley
Wessington Springs
Woonsocket
Artesian
Howard
Carthage
Alpena
Letcher
Madison
Flandreau
Pipestone
PIPESTONE NATIONAL MONUMENT
Jasper
Dell Rapids
Garretson
Valley Springs
Colman
Elkton
Oldham
Ramona
Canova
Colton
Wanblee
PINE RIDGE INDIAN RESERVATION
Eagle Nest Butte 1039
Kyle
Allen
Martin
Wounded Knee
Pine Ridge
White River
Wood
Mission
Winner
Colome
Gregory
Burke
Bonesteel
Fairfax
Rosebud
St. Francis
ROSEBUD INDIAN RESERVATION
Angostura Reservoir
Hot Springs
Chadron
Crawford
Hay Springs
Rushville
Gordon
Merriman
Cody
Valentine
Springview
Butte
Spencer
Lynch
Niobrara
Verdigre
Center
Bloomfield
Crofton
Wynot
Newcastle
Hartington
Coleridge
Ponca
Sioux City
South Sioux City
Dakota City
Laurel
Allen
Wausa
Creighton
Randolph
Osmond
Plainview
Wood Lake
Ainsworth
Bassett
Long Pine
Stuart
Atkinson
O'Neill
Orchard
Ewing
Chambers
Clearwater
Neligh
Oakdale
Tilden
Norfolk
Pierce
Wayne
Wakefield
Emerson
Winnebago
WINNEBAGO IND. RES.
OMAHA IND. RES.
Pender
Walthill
Bancroft
Lyons
Pilger
Wisner
Stanton
Beemer
West Point
Oakland
Carroll
Winside
Hemingford
Alliance
Hyannis
Mullen
Thedford
Halsey
Brewster
Dunning
Taylor
Burwell
Sargent
Comstock
Ord
Ericson
Bartlett
Elgin
Petersburg
Albion
Newman Grove
Madison
Humphrey
Spalding
Greeley
Cedar Rapids
Scotia
North Loup
Arcadia
Belgrade
Genoa
Columbus
Schuyler
North Bend
Fremont
Clarkson
Howells
Dodge
Scribner
Hooper
Platte Center
St. Edward
Lindsay
Bayard
Bridgeport
Broadwater
Arthur
Tryon
Stapleton
Anselmo
Merna
Broken Bow
Arnold
Callaway
Ansley
Mason City
Litchfield
Loup City
Ashton
Dannebrog
St. Paul
Cairo
Grand Island
Central City
Chapman
Palmer
Fullerton
Wolbach
Silver Creek
Clarks
Osceola
Polk
Stromsburg
Shelby
Bellwood
David City
Prague
Wahoo
Cedar Bluffs
Brainard
Ulysses
Valparaiso
Ceresco
Seward
Utica
York
Bradshaw
Lincoln
Oshkosh
Dalton
Lewellen
Lake McConaughy
Kingsley Dam
Potter
Sidney
Lodgepole
Chappell
Big Springs
Ogallala
Paxton
Brule
Sutherland
Hershey
North Platte
BUFFALO BILL RANCH STATE HISTORICAL PARK
Maxwell
Brady
Gothenburg
Cozad
Lexington
Overton
Elm Creek
Kearney
Gibbon
Shelton
Wood River
Aurora
Hampton
Henderson
Giltner
Doniphan
Beaver Crossing
Friend
Dorchester
Crete
Hickman
Julesburg
Peetz
Sedgwick
Crook
Iliff
Sterling
Fleming
Haxtun
Holyoke
Madrid
Grant
Wallace
Imperial
Hayes Center
Wauneta
Palisade
Maywood
Curtis
Farnam
Eustis
Stockville
Elwood
Bertrand
Loomis
Axtell
Holdrege
Wilcox
Hildreth
Minden
Kenesaw
Juniata
Hastings
Harvard
Clay Center
Fairmont
Sutton
Exeter
Geneva
Milligan
Wilber
De Witt
Cortland
Firth
Shickley
Tobias
Western
Plymouth
Beatrice
Fairfield
Edgar
Davenport
Carleton
Alexandria
Hebron
Deshler
Fairbury
Diller
Odell
HOMESTEAD NATIONAL MONUMENT OF AMERICA
Blue Springs
Blue Hill
Campbell
Upland
Lawrence
Nelson
Red Cloud
Guide Rock
Superior
Hardy
Chester
Republic
Hanover
Belleville
Haddam
Washington
Cuba
Greenleaf
Waterville
Linn
Clifton
Scandia
Mankato
Jewell
Lebanon
Smith Center
Kensington
Kirwin
Phillipsburg
Logan
Kirwin Reservoir
Downs
Osborne
Cawker City
Glen Elder
Beloit
Concordia
Jamestown
Glasco
Miltonvale
Clay Center
Riley
Alton
Stockton
Waconda Lake
Holbrook
Arapahoe
Oxford
Cambridge
Bartley
Indianola
Culbertson
McCook
Beaver City
Orleans
Alma
Franklin
Riverton
Harlan County Lake
Wilsonville
Danbury
Trenton
Stratton
Benkelman
Haigler
Wray
Yuma
Otis
Akron
Herndon
Oberlin
Norcatur
Norton
Almena
McDonald
Atwood
St. Francis
Bird City
Lindon
Cope
Selden
Rexford
Hugh Butler Lake
Swanson Lake
CHIMNEY ROCK NATIONAL HISTORIC SITE
Missouri
Platte
Niobrara
Cheyenne
White
Republican
Elkhorn
Loup
Big Blue
Little Blue
James
Bad
Moreau
Grand
Cannonball
Heart
Sheyenne
Red
Minnesota
Big Sioux
143
129
130
139
103°
102°
101°
100°
99°
98°
97°
96°
46°
45°
44°
43°
42°
41°
40°
West of Greenwich
10
11
12
13
14
15
16
17
A
B
C
D
E
F
G
H

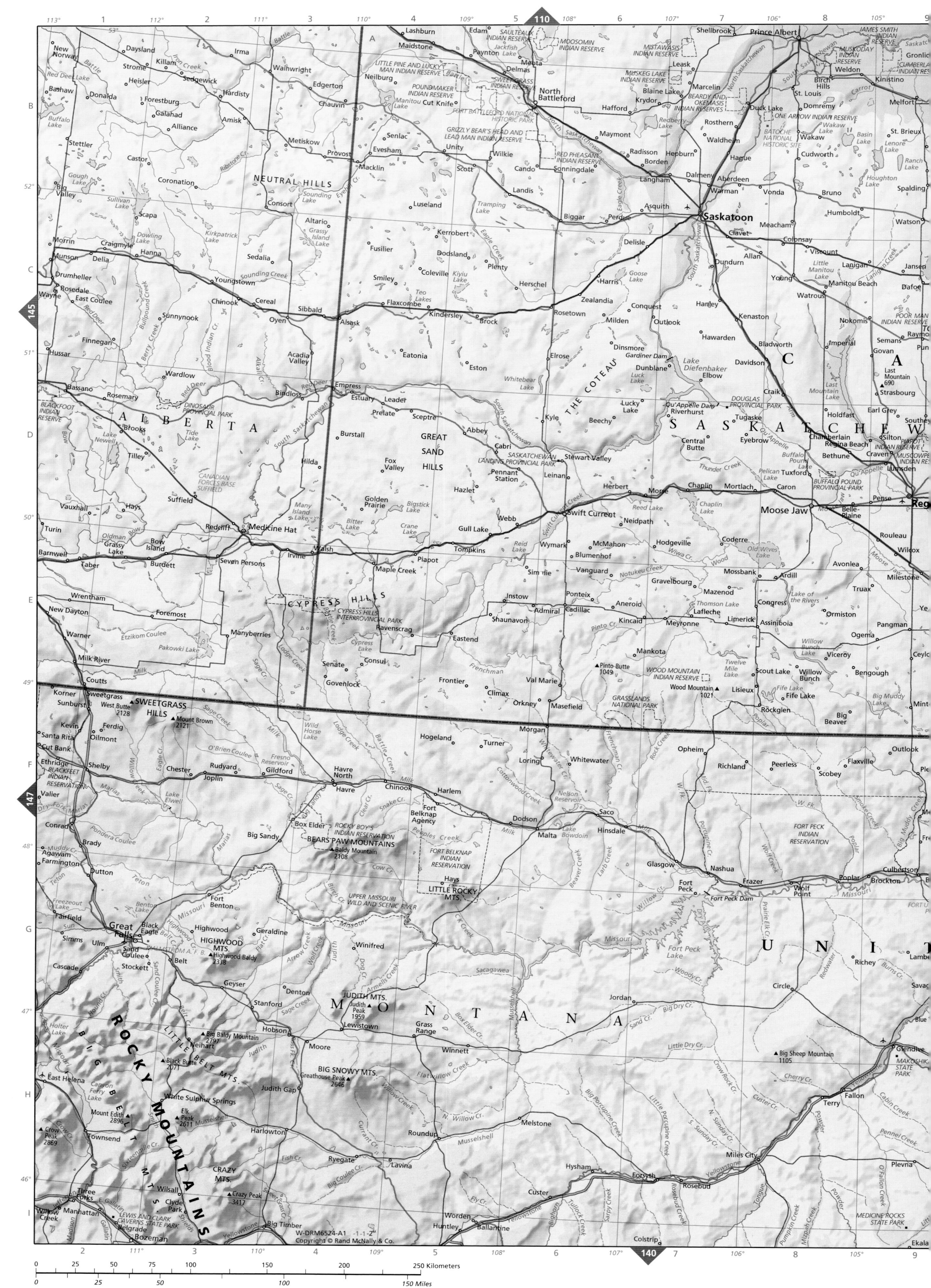

ALBERTA
SASKATCHEWAN
CANADA
MONTANA
UNITED
ROCKY MOUNTAINS
NEUTRAL HILLS
GREAT SAND HILLS
CYPRESS HILLS
CYPRESS HILLS INTERPROVINCIAL PARK
THE COTEAU
SWEETGRASS HILLS
BEARS PAW MOUNTAINS
LITTLE ROCKY MTS.
HIGHWOOD MTS.
JUDITH MTS.
BIG SNOWY MTS.
LITTLE BELT MTS.
BIG BELT MTS.
CRAZY MTS.
Lashburn
Maidstone
Edam
Paynton
Meota
Delmas
North Battleford
Neilburg
Cut Knife
Unity
Wilkie
Scott
Cando
Sonningdale
Landis
Luseland
Kerrobert
Biggar
Perdue
Asquith
Saskatoon
Langham
Dalmeny
Warman
Aberdeen
Vonda
Bruno
Humboldt
Meacham
Colonsay
Clavet
Allan
Dundurn
Delisle
Hanley
Kenaston
Bladworth
Davidson
Craik
Outlook
Conquest
Milden
Dinsmore
Zealandia
Rosetown
Harris
Elrose
Kyle
Beechy
Lucky Lake
Dunblane
Elbow
Riverhurst
Tugaske
Eyebrow
Central Butte
Chamberlain
Bethune
Prince Albert
Shellbrook
Leask
Marcelin
Blaine Lake
Krydor
Hafford
Maymont
Radisson
Borden
Hepburn
Hague
Rosthern
Waldheim
Duck Lake
St. Louis
Domremy
Birch Hills
Weldon
Kinistino
Melfort
St. Brieux
Wakaw
Cudworth
Spalding
Watson
Lanigan
Viscount
Young
Watrous
Manitou Beach
Nokomis
Imperial
Semans
Strasbourg
Holdfast
Earl Grey
Craven
Lumsden
Buffalo Pound
Tuxford
Moose Jaw
Pense
Belle Plaine
Caron
Mortlach
Chaplin
Morse
Herbert
Swift Current
Neidpath
Webb
Gull Lake
Tompkins
Piapot
Maple Creek
Walsh
Irvine
Medicine Hat
Redcliff
Seven Persons
Bow Island
Burdett
Grassy Lake
Taber
Barnwell
Turin
Vauxhall
Hays
Suffield
Tilley
Brooks
Bassano
Rosemary
Wardlow
Hussar
Finnegan
Sunnynook
Drumheller
Rosedale
Wayne
East Coulee
Munson
Morrin
Craigmyle
Delia
Hanna
Youngstown
Chinook
Cereal
Sibbald
Oyen
Alsask
Kindersley
Brock
Flaxcombe
Eatonia
Eston
Acadia Valley
Empress
Bindloss
Estuary
Leader
Prelate
Sceptre
Abbey
Cabri
Burstall
Hilda
Fox Valley
Golden Prairie
Hazlet
Pennant Station
Leinan
Stewart Valley
Wymark
Blumenhof
McMahon
Hodgeville
Coderre
Vanguard
Gravelbourg
Mossbank
Ardill
Avonlea
Rouleau
Wilcox
Milestone
Truax
Mazenod
Ponteix
Aneroid
Instow
Admiral
Cadillac
Shaunavon
Kincaid
Meyronne
Lafleche
Limerick
Assiniboia
Congress
Ormiston
Pangman
Ogema
Viceroy
Bengough
Willow Bunch
Scout Lake
Fife Lake
Rockglen
Big Beaver
Lisieux
Mankota
Pinto Butte 1049
Wood Mountain 1021
Val Marie
Masefield
Orkney
Climax
Frontier
Eastend
Ravenscrag
Consul
Senate
Govenlock
Manyberries
Foremost
Wrentham
New Dayton
Warner
Milk River
Coutts
Sweetgrass
Sunburst
Kevin
Ferdig
Oilmont
Santa Rita
Cut Bank
Ethridge
Shelby
Valier
Conrad
Brady
Agawam
Farmington
Dutton
Chester
Rudyard
Joplin
Gildford
Havre
Havre North
Chinook
Harlem
Hogeland
Turner
Loring
Morgan
Whitewater
Opheim
Richland
Peerless
Scobey
Flaxville
Outlook
Dodson
Malta
Saco
Hinsdale
Glasgow
Nashua
Fort Peck
Frazer
Wolf Point
Poplar
Brockton
Culbertson
Box Elder
Big Sandy
Fort Belknap Agency
Hays
Fort Benton
Great Falls
Black Eagle
Highwood
Geraldine
Winifred
Fairfield
Simms
Ulm
Sand Coulee
Belt
Stockett
Cascade
Geyser
Denton
Stanford
Hobson
Lewistown
Moore
Grass Range
Winnett
Jordan
Circle
Richey
Glendive
Terry
Fallon
Neihart
White Sulphur Springs
Judith Gap
Harlowton
Roundup
Melstone
Ryegate
Lavina
Hysham
Forsyth
Rosebud
Miles City
Plevna
Custer
Worden
Huntley
Ballantine
Colstrip
Big Timber
Wilsall
Clyde Park
Bozeman
Belgrade
Manhattan
Three Forks
Willow Creek
Townsend
East Helena
West Butte 2128
Mount Brown 2121
Baldy Mountain 2108
Highwood Baldy 2338
Judith Peak 1959
Big Baldy Mountain 2797
Black Butte 2071
Greathouse Peak 2646
Mount Edith 2896
Elk Peak 2611
Crow Peak 2869
Crazy Peak 3417
Big Sheep Mountain 1105
Last Mountain 690
DINOSAUR PROVINCIAL PARK
BLACKFOOT INDIAN RESERVE
CANADIAN FORCES BASE SUFFIELD
SASKATCHEWAN LANDING PROVINCIAL PARK
DOUGLAS PROVINCIAL PARK
BUFFALO POUND PROVINCIAL PARK
GRASSLANDS NATIONAL PARK
WOOD MOUNTAIN INDIAN RESERVE
FORT BATTLEFORD NATIONAL HISTORIC PARK
BATOCHE NATIONAL HISTORIC SITE
MOOSOMIN INDIAN RESERVE
RED PHEASANT INDIAN RESERVE
POUNDMAKER INDIAN RESERVE
ONE ARROW INDIAN RESERVE
POOR MAN INDIAN RESERVE
BLACKFEET INDIAN RESERVATION
ROCKY BOY'S INDIAN RESERVATION
FORT BELKNAP INDIAN RESERVATION
FORT PECK INDIAN RESERVATION
UPPER MISSOURI WILD AND SCENIC RIVER
LEWIS AND CLARK CAVERNS STATE PARK
MAKOSHIKA STATE PARK
MEDICINE ROCKS STATE PARK
MALMSTROM A.F.B.
Lake Diefenbaker
Gardiner Dam
Qu'Appelle Dam
Fort Peck Lake
Fort Peck Dam
Old Wives Lake
Missouri
Milk
Yellowstone
Musselshell
South Saskatchewan
North Saskatchewan
Red Deer
Bow
Oldman
Marias
Teton
Meters / Feet
4000 13120
3000 9840
2000 6560
1000 3280
500 1640
200 656
Sea Level
200 656
2000 6560
110
145
147
140
W-DRM6524-A1 -1-1-2
Copyright © Rand McNally & Co.
0 25 50 75 100 150 200 250 Kilometers
0 25 50 100 150 Miles
Scale 1 : 2,500,000
Lambert Conformal Conic Projection

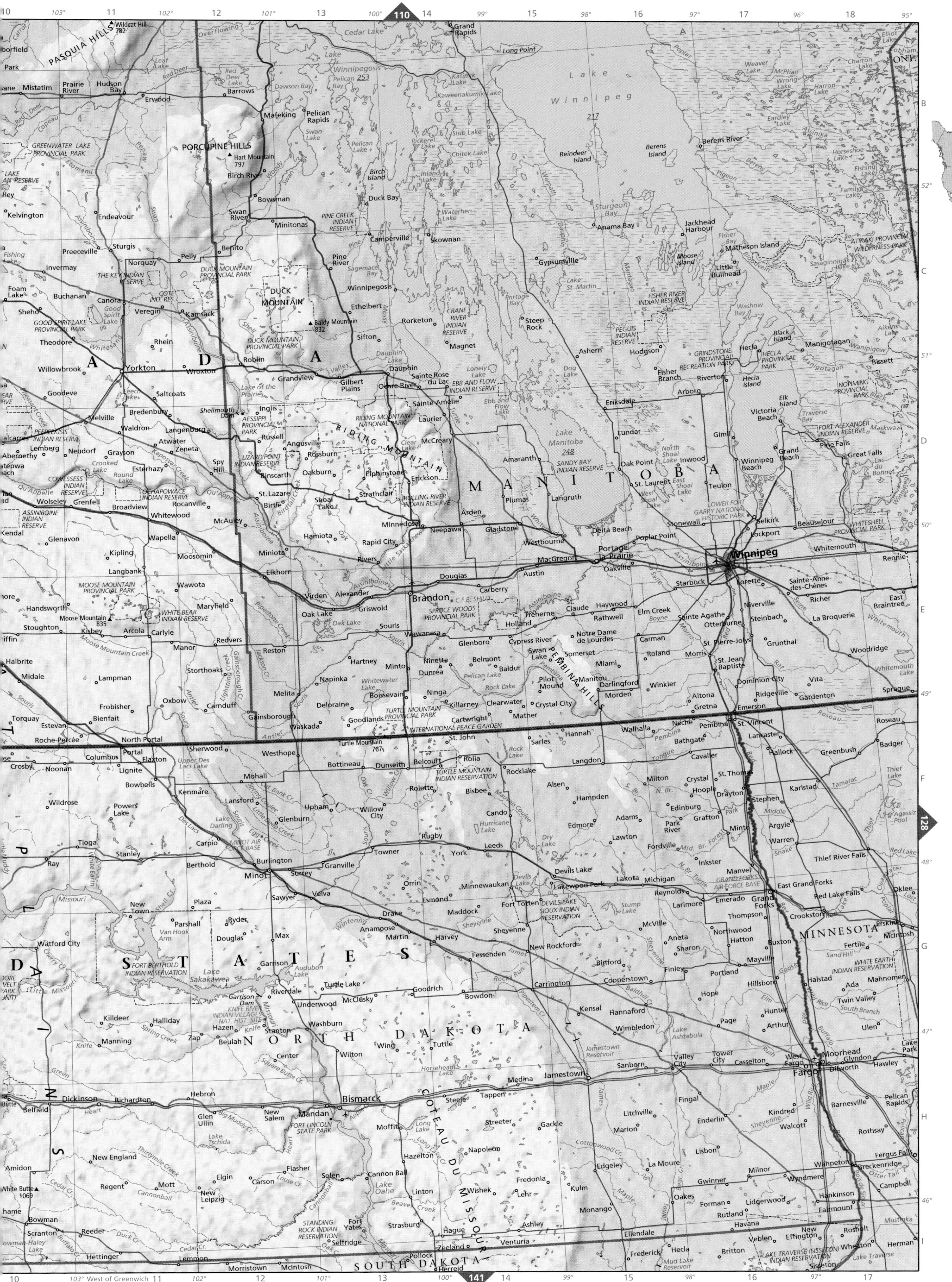

0 25 50 75 100 150 200 250 Kilometers
0 25 100 150 Miles
Scale 1 : 2,500,000 Lambert Conformal Conic Projection

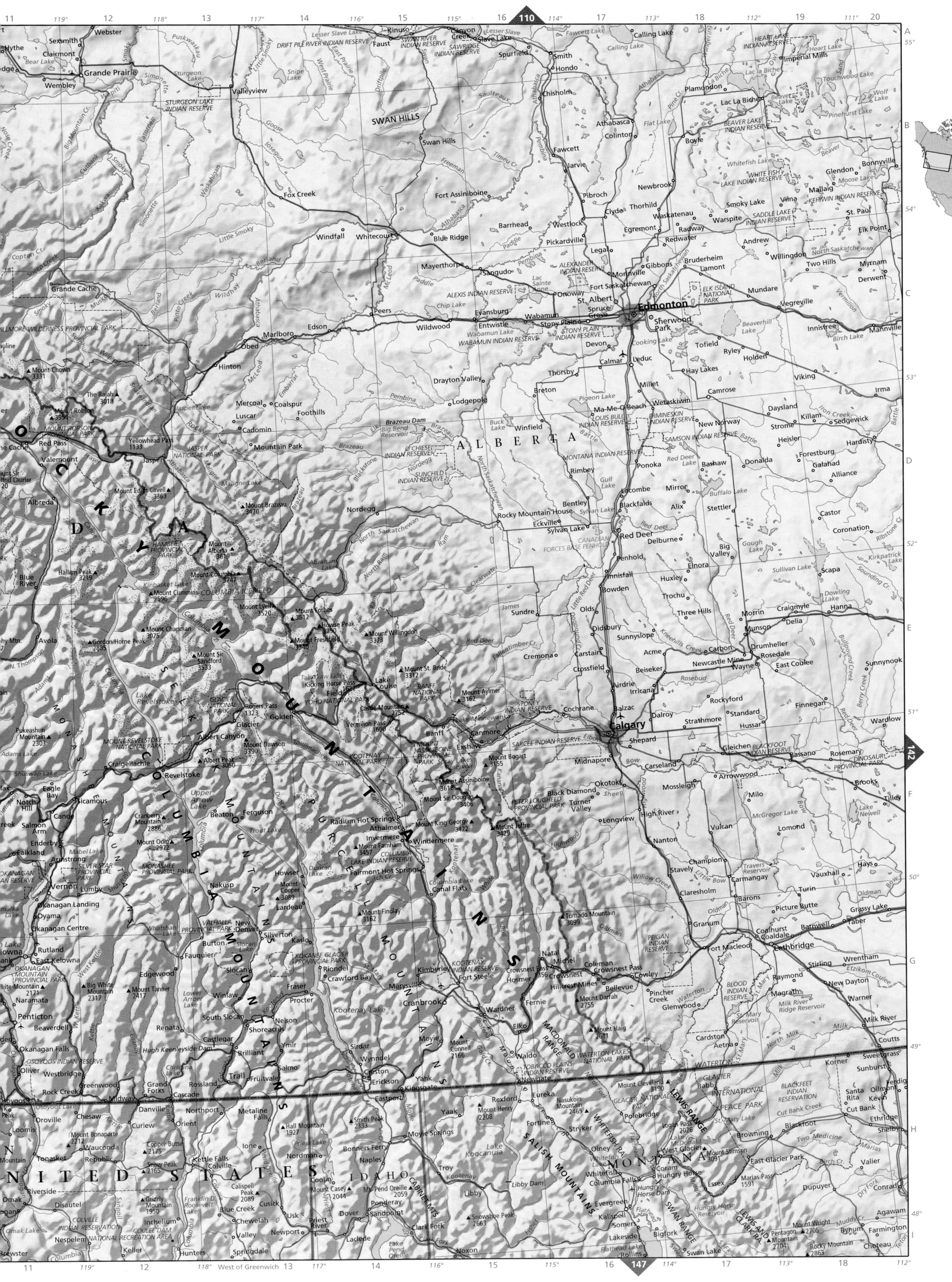
ALBERTA
ROCKY MOUNTAINS
COLUMBIA MOUNTAINS
SELKIRK MOUNTAINS
PURCELL MOUNTAINS
MONASHEE MOUNTAINS
MONTANA
IDAHO
UNITED STATES
SWAN HILLS
Edmonton
Calgary
Red Deer
Lethbridge
Grande Prairie
Medicine Hat
Kamloops
Vernon
Kelowna
Penticton
Revelstoke
Banff
Jasper
Canmore
Cranbrook
Nelson
Fort Macleod
Drumheller
Camrose
Kalispell
West of Greenwich
110
142
147

Meters / Feet
6000 / 19680
4000 / 13120
3000 / 9840
2000 / 6560
1000 / 3280
500 / 1640
200 / 656
Sea Level
200 / 656
2000 / 6560

0 25 50 75 100 150 200 250 Kilometers
0 50 100 150 Miles

Scale 1 : 2,500,000 Lambert Conformal Conic Projection

ALBERTA
SASKATCHEWAN
MONTANA
IDAHO
WYOMING
UTAH
ROCKY MOUNTAINS
BITTERROOT RANGE
SALMON RIVER MOUNTAINS
CLEARWATER MOUNTAINS
LEMHI RANGE
LOST RIVER RANGE
BEAVERHEAD MOUNTAINS
MADISON RANGE
GALLATIN RANGE
ABSAROKA RANGE
BIG BELT MOUNTAINS
LITTLE BELT MTS.
SWAN RANGE
MISSION RA.
LEWIS RANGE
SALISH MOUNTAINS
PURCELL MOUNTAINS
CABINET MOUNTAINS
GARNET RANGE
SAPPHIRE MTS.
ANACONDA RANGE
PIONEER MTS.
TOBACCO ROOT MTS.
CENTENNIAL MTS.
CARIBOU RANGE
TETON RANGE
BEARTOOTH MTS.
CRAZY MTS.
HIGHWOOD MOUNTAINS
BEARS PAW MOUNTAINS
JUDITH MTS.
BIG SNOWY MTS.
Snake River
Great Falls
Helena
Missoula
Butte
Bozeman
Kalispell
Havre
Lewistown
Livingston
Dillon
Salmon
Boise
Nampa
Caldwell
Idaho Falls
Pocatello
Twin Falls
Mountain Home
Coeur d'Alene
Sandpoint
YELLOWSTONE NATIONAL PARK
GRAND TETON NATIONAL PARK
IDAHO NATIONAL ENGINEERING LABORATORY
CRATERS OF THE MOON NATIONAL MONUMENT
FORT HALL INDIAN RESERVATION
BLACKFEET INDIAN RESERVATION
FLATHEAD INDIAN RESERVATION
NEZ PERCE INDIAN RESERVATION
COEUR D'ALENE INDIAN RESERVATION
DUCK VALLEY INDIAN RESERVATION
Granite Peak 3901
Borah Peak 3859
Grand Teton 4197
West of Greenwich
Copyright © Rand McNally & Co.

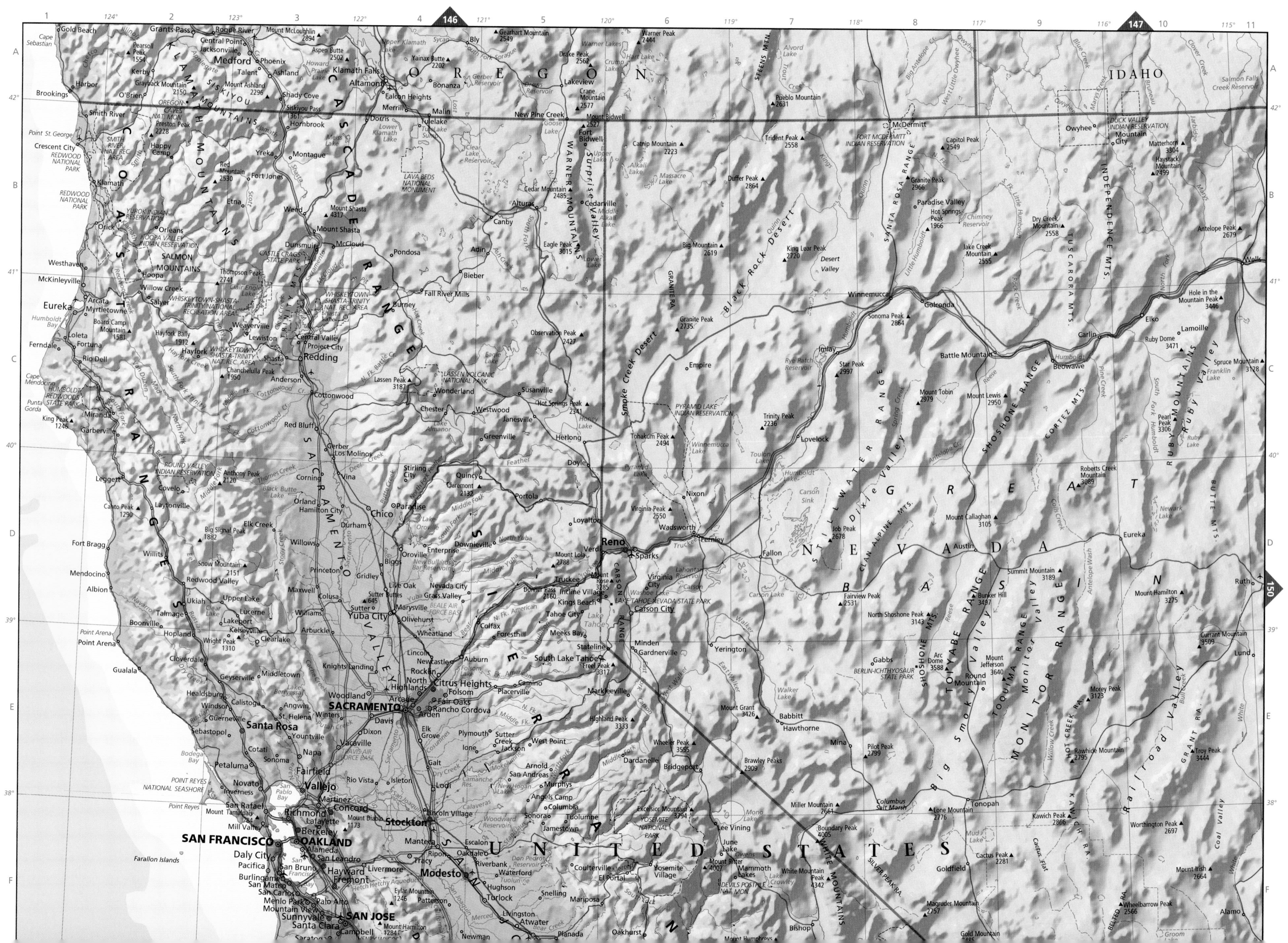
IDAHO
OREGON
NEVADA
GREAT BASIN
UNITED STATES
SIERRA NEVADA
SACRAMENTO
SAN FRANCISCO
OAKLAND
SAN JOSE
Reno
Carson City
Stockton
Modesto
Redding
Eureka
Medford
Elko
Winnemucca
Lovelock
Fallon
Tonopah
Austin
Chico
Yuba City
Santa Rosa
Vallejo
Berkeley
Fremont
INDEPENDENCE MTS.
TUSCARORA MTS.
SHOSHONE RANGE
TOIYABE RANGE
MONITOR RANGE
WHITE MOUNTAINS
WARNER MOUNTAINS
CARSON RANGE
CASCADE RANGE
COAST RANGES
KLAMATH MOUNTAINS
SACRAMENTO VALLEY
Black Rock Desert
Smoke Creek Desert
Surprise Valley
Big Smoky Valley
Railroad Valley

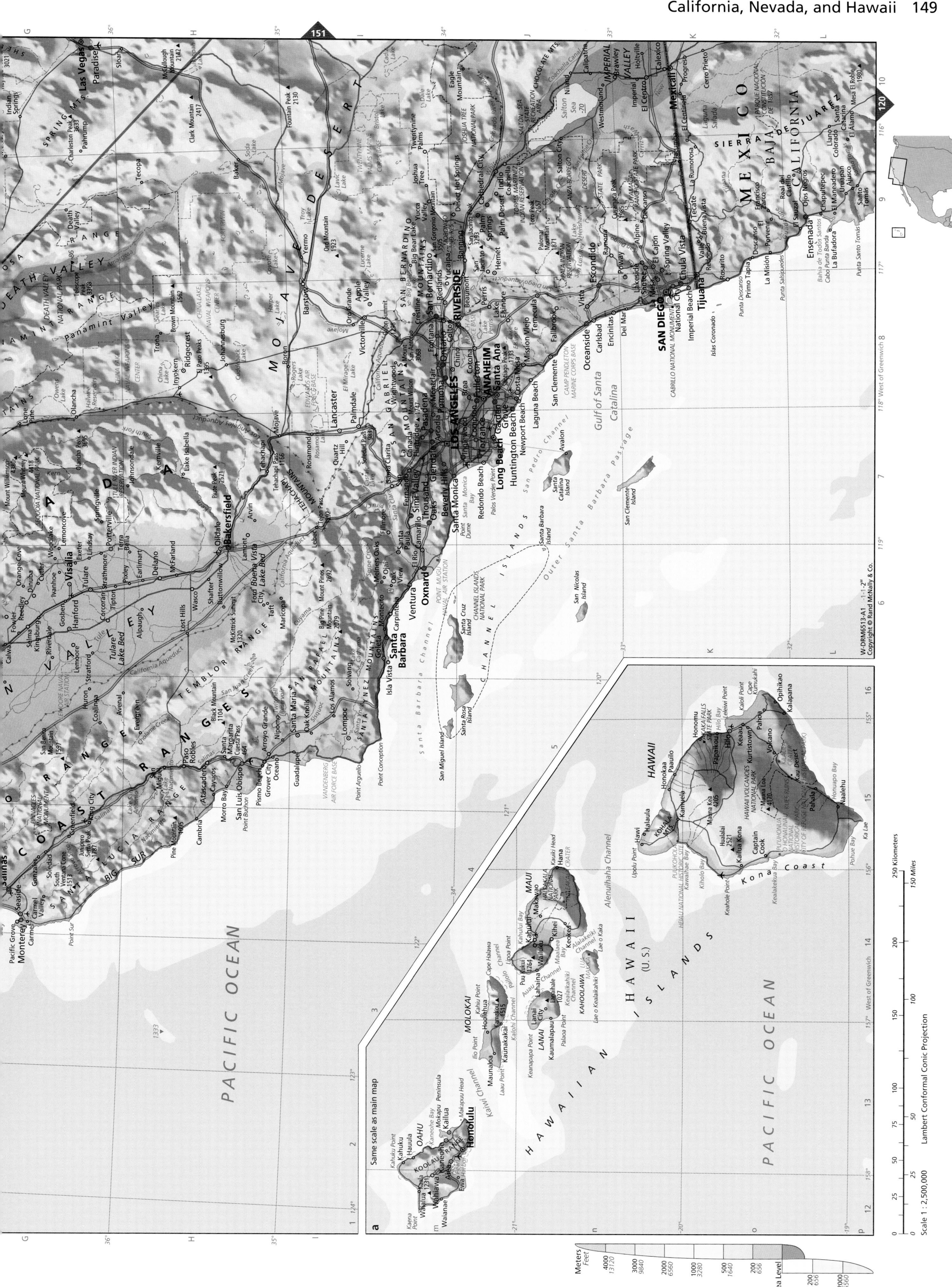
PACIFIC OCEAN
MOJAVE DESERT
DEATH VALLEY
COAST RANGES
SAN JOAQUIN VALLEY
LOS ANGELES
ANAHEIM
SAN DIEGO
RIVERSIDE
Bakersfield
Las Vegas
Santa Barbara
Ventura
Oxnard
Long Beach
Tijuana
Mexicali
MEXICO
BAJA CALIFORNIA
CHANNEL ISLANDS
Gulf of Santa Catalina
HAWAIIAN ISLANDS
HAWAII (U.S.)
OAHU
Honolulu
MOLOKAI
LANAI
MAUI
KAHOOLAWE
HAWAII
Hilo
Same scale as main map
Scale 1 : 2,500,000
Lambert Conformal Conic Projection
W-DRM6513-A1 1-1-2"
Copyright © Rand McNally & Co.
Meters
Feet
Sea Level

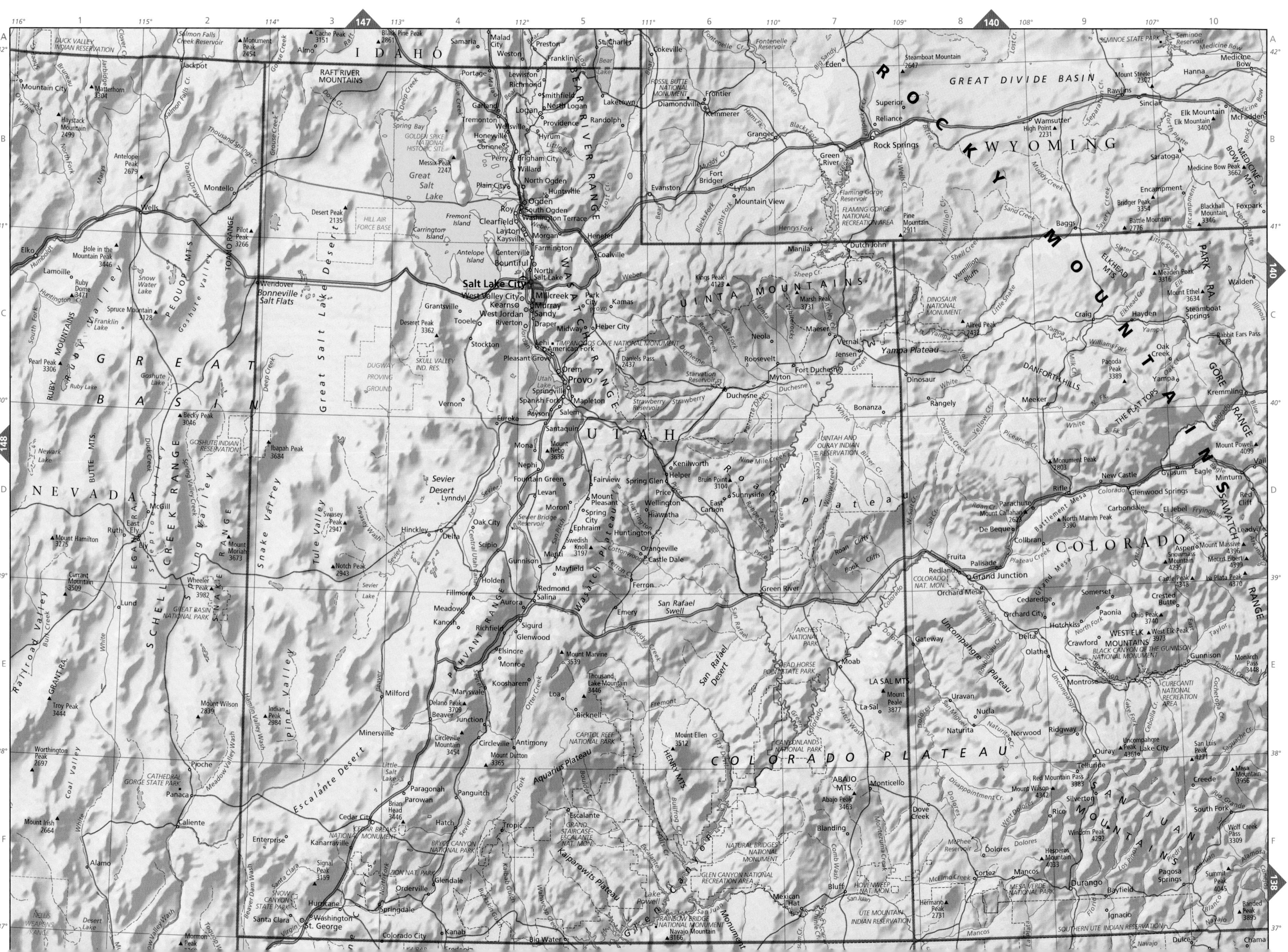
ROCKY MOUNTAINS
WYOMING
GREAT DIVIDE BASIN
COLORADO
UTAH
IDAHO
NEVADA
COLORADO PLATEAU
UINTA MOUNTAINS
WASATCH RANGE
BEAR RIVER RANGE
GREAT BASIN
SAN JUAN MOUNTAINS
Great Salt Lake
Great Salt Lake Desert
Bonneville Salt Flats
Sevier Desert
San Rafael Desert
Escalante Desert
Salt Lake City
Provo
Ogden
Grand Junction
Rock Springs
147
140
148
138

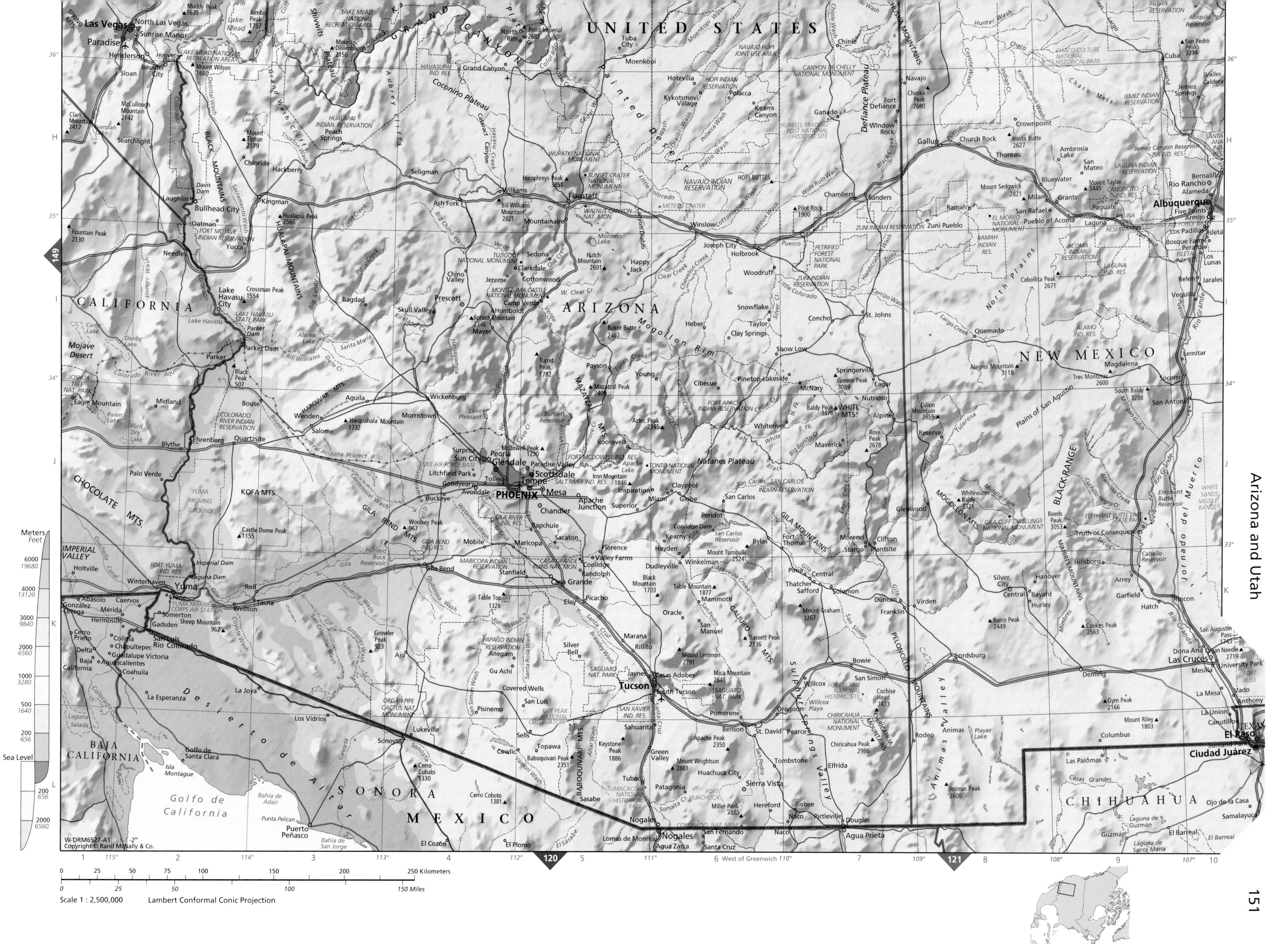
UNITED STATES
ARIZONA
NEW MEXICO
CALIFORNIA
MEXICO
SONORA
CHIHUAHUA
BAJA CALIFORNIA
PHOENIX
Tucson
Albuquerque
Ciudad Juárez
El Paso
Las Vegas
Flagstaff
Yuma
Golfo de California
Desierto de Altar
West of Greenwich
0 25 50 75 100 150 200 250 Kilometers
0 25 50 100 150 Miles
Scale 1 : 2,500,000
Lambert Conformal Conic Projection
Meters Feet
6000 19680
4000 13120
3000 9840
2000 6560
1000 3280
500 1640
200 656
Sea Level
200 656
2000 6560
W-DRM6527-A1
Copyright © Rand McNally & Co.

Meters / Feet: 4000 / 13120; 3000 / 9840; 2000 / 6560; 1000 / 3280; 500 / 1640; 200 / 656; Sea Level; 200 / 656; 2000 / 6560

0 100 200 300 400 600 800 1000 Kilometers
0 100 200 400 600 Miles

Scale 1 : 10,000,000 Lambert Conformal Conic Projection

113
ATLANTIC OCEAN
Huntsville
Decatur
Rome
Gainesville
Anderson
Hartsville
Newberry
Columbia
Florence
N. C.
Wilmington
Cape Fear
Conway
Myrtle Beach
Long Bay
Oxford
Tupelo
Clarksdale
Grenada
Gadsden
Marietta
Athens
ATLANTA
Greenwood
Sumter
SOUTH CAROLINA
Georgetown
Jasper
Birmingham
Bessemer
Anniston
Talladega
Covington
Augusta
Aiken
Orangeburg
Columbus
Tuscaloosa
Griffin
Milledgeville
Charleston
Hamilton
BERMUDA
(U.K.)
Yazoo City
MISSISSIPPI
Canton
Jackson
Meridian
ALABAMA
La Grange
Macon
GEORGIA
Walterboro
Beaufort
Demopolis
Selma
Auburn
Opelika
Phenix City
Columbus
Dublin
Statesboro
Montgomery
Eastman
Savannah
Eufaula
Greenville
Troy
Cordele
Jesup
Laurel
Hattiesburg
McComb
Albany
Tifton
Brunswick
Sea Islands
Andalusia
Ozark
Dothan
Valdosta
Atmore
Mobile
Thomasville
Biloxi
Gulfport
Pascagoula
Pensacola
Fort Walton Beach
Tallahassee
Lake City
Jacksonville
Jacksonville Beach
NEW ORLEANS
Mobile Bay
Panama City
Perry
Port St. Joe
Cape San Blas
Apalachee Bay
Gainesville
Palatka
St. Augustine
Chandeleur Islands
Mississippi Delta
Daytona Beach
Ocala
De Land
Leesburg
Sanford
Titusville
Orlando
FLORIDA
Cocoa
Cape Canaveral
Melbourne
Tampa
Lakeland
Winter Haven
Clearwater
St. Petersburg
Tampa Bay
Vero Beach
Bradenton
Avon Park
Fort Pierce
Sarasota
Lake Okeechobee
Little Abaco
Port Charlotte
Fort Myers
West Palm Beach
Marsh Harbour
Charlotte Harbor
Lake Worth
Freeport
Grand Bahama
Cape Coral
Boca Raton
Abaco
Fort Lauderdale
Naples
Hialeah
Hollywood
Miami Beach
Everglades City
MIAMI
Berry Islands
Eleuthera
Governor's Harbour
Homestead
Bimini Islands
Nicholl's Town
Nassau
New Providence
BAHAMAS
Cape Sable
Key Largo
Arthur's Town
Cat Island
Mount Alvernia
63
San Salvador
Dry Tortugas
Florida Keys
Key West
Straits of Florida
Andros
Exuma Cays
Exuma Sound
Kemps Bay
Tongue of the Ocean
Great Exuma
Rum Cay
Long Island
Tropic of Cancer
Clarence Town
Crooked Island
TURKS AND CAICOS ISLANDS
(U.K.)
Ragged Island Range
Acklins
Mayaguana
Caicos Islands
Grand Turk
Turks Islands
Kew
Little Inagua
Matthew Town
Great Inagua
LA HABANA
(HAVANA)
Matanzas
Cárdenas
Colón
Artemisa
Güines
Sagua la Grande
Caibarién
Cayo Romano
Los Palacios
Santo Domingo
Santa Clara
Placetas
Pinar del Río
Cienfuegos
Morón
Sancti Spíritus
Ciego de Ávila
Guane
Cabo de San Antonio
Nueva Gerona
Trinidad
Florida
Nuevitas
Archipiélago de los Canarreos
Cabo Corrientes
Isla de la Juventud
Camagüey
CUBA
Gibara
Banes
Las Tunas
Holguín
Sagua de Tánamo
Baracoa
Arrecife Alacrán
Rio Lagartos
Cabo Catoche
Yucatan Channel
Puerto Juárez
Cancún
Progreso
Temax
Tizimin
Izamal
Mérida
Valladolid
YUCATÁN
PENÍNSULA DE YUCATÁN
Ticul
Peto
Tulum
Isla Cozumel
Hopelchén
Felipe Carrillo Puerto
QUINTANA ROO
Chetumal
Bahía Chetumal
Corozal
Orange Walk
BELIZE
Belize City
Belmopan
Dangriga
Victoria Peak
1120
La Libertad
San Luis
Punta Gorda
Livingston
Puerto Barrios
Puerto Cortés
Tela
La Ceiba
Pico Bonito
2435
Olanchito
Yoro
El Progreso
San Pedro Sula
Santa Rosa de Copán
Cerro Las Minas
2849
GUATEMALA
HONDURAS
Juticalpa
Comayagua
Tegucigalpa
Cerro El Pital
2730
EL SALVADOR
San Salvador
San Miguel
La Unión
Choluteca
Danlí
Mogoton
2107
Cerro Kilambé
1750
Bonanza
Siuna
Gulf of Honduras
Islas de la Bahía
Roatán
Isla de Roatán
Trujillo
Balfate
Cabo Camarón
Laguna de Caratasca
Cabo Gracias a Dios
Waspam
Cayos Miskitos
Puerto Cabezas
Prinzapolka
Golfo de Fonseca
Chinandega
Estelí
Jinotega
Matagalpa
León
Boaco
NICARAGUA
Managua
Juigalpa
Masaya
Jinotepe
Granada
Santo Tomás
El Rama
Bluefields
Laguna de Perlas
Islas del Maíz
Lago de Nicaragua
Rivas
San Juan del Sur
Isla de Ometepe
San Carlos
Punta Gorda
San Juan del Norte
Cabo Santa Elena
Golfo de Papagayo
La Cruz
Volcán Miravalles
2028
Liberia
COSTA RICA
Santa Cruz
Nicoya
Quesada
Puntarenas
Alajuela
SAN JOSÉ
3432
Cartago
Puerto Limón
Península de Nicoya
Golfo de Nicoya
San Isidro del General
Cerro Chirripó
3819
Bocas del Toro
Ciudad Cortés
Península de Osa
Golfito
Volcán Barú
3475
Puerto Armuelles
Punta Burica
David
Boquete
Cerro Santiago
2121
Almirante
Golfo de los Mosquitos
Penonomé
Santiago
Chitré
Las Tablas
Golfo de Chiriquí
Isla de Coiba
Isla de Cebaco
Península de Azuero
Punta Mala
Punta Mariato
Colón
Portobelo
Canal de Panamá
PANAMA
Panamá
La Chorrera
Aguadulce
San Carlos
Golfo de Panamá
La Palma
Isla del Rey
Yaviza
Jaqué
Serranía del Darién
Isla del Coco
(Costa Rica)
George Town
Grand Cayman
CAYMAN ISLANDS
(U.K.)
Little Cayman
Cayman Brac
Cabo Cruz
Pico Turquino
1972
Santiago de Cuba
SIERRA MAESTRA
Bayamo
Palma Soriano
Guantánamo
Caimanera
Manzanillo
Golfo de Guacanayabo
Santa Cruz del Sur
Archipiélago de los Jardines de la Reina
Golfo de Ana María
Windward Passage
GREATER ANTILLES
WEST INDIES
Île de la Tortue
Port-de-Paix
Monte Cristi
Puerto Plata
Cap-Haïtien
Santiago de los Caballeros
Cabo Samaná
San Francisco de Macorís
La Vega
Mao
Gonaïves
Saint-Marc
Pico Duarte
3175
HISPANIOLA
HAITI
SANTO DOMINGO
La Romana
Cabo Engaño
PUERTO RICO
(U.S.)
Mayagüez
Isla de Mona
Cabo Rojo
Mona Passage
Île de la Gonâve
Golfe de la Gonâve
Port-au-Prince
San Cristóbal
Azua
Baní
San Pedro de Macorís
Jérémie
Pic Macaya
2347
Les Cayes
Morne La Selle
2674
Jacmel
Barahona
Île à Vache
DOMINICAN REPUBLIC
Isla Beata
Cabo Beata
Navassa Island
(U.S.)
Jamaica Channel
Montego Bay
Mount Denham
986
St. Ann's Bay
Savanna-la-Mar
Spanish Town
Blue Mountain Peak
2256
Kingston
JAMAICA
Morant Cays
Cayo de Serranilla
(Col.)
Bayo Nuevo
(Col.)
Cayo de Serrana
Quitasueño
Cayos de Roncador
Isla de Providencia (Col.)
Isla de San Andrés (Col.)
San Andrés
Cayos de Albuquerque
CARIBBEAN SEA
ARUBA
(Neth.)
Oranjestad
NETH. ANT.
Curaçao
Punta Gallinas
Cabo de La Vela
Península de La Guajira
Península de Paraguaná
Punto Fijo
Riohacha
Uribia
Maicao
Golfo de Venezuela
Coro
Santa Marta
Barranquilla
Ciénaga
Pico Cristóbal Colón
5775
Soledad
Fundación
Cartagena
Turbaco
Valledupar
MARACAIBO
Cabimas
Ciudad Ojeda
Barquisimeto
VENEZUELA
Lago de Maracaibo
Plato
El Carmen de Bolívar
San Jacinto
San Onofre
Magangué
Mompós
Sincelejo
Lorica
Cereté
Montería
Sahagún
El Banco
Majagual
Aguachica
Acandí
Turbo
Apartadó
Chigorodó
Riosucio
Ayapel
Caucasia
Nechí
Cúcuta
San Cristóbal
Mérida
Pico Bolívar
5007
CORD. DE MÉRIDA
Barinas
Guasdualito
COLOMBIA
CORDILLERA OCCIDENTAL
CORDILLERA CENTRAL
Bucaramanga
Floridablanca
Barrancabermeja
Arauquita
Arauca
Pamplona
Rionegro
Puerto Wilches
MEDELLÍN
Frontino
Páramo Frontino
4080
Urrao
Itagüí
Envigado
Bello
Quibdó
Nuquí
Cabo Corrientes
Golfo de Cupica
Punta Marzo
Istmina
Condoto
Manizales
Pereira
Armenia
Cartago
Ibagué
Nevado del Tolima
5215
Honda
La Dorada
Tunja
Sogamoso
Duitama
Yopal
Zipaquirá
SANTA FE DE BOGOTÁ
Villavicencio
Fusagasugá
Cabuyaro
Chaviva
LLANOS
Paz de Ariporo
Trinidad
Tame
Cravo Norte
Puerto Rondón
Orocué
164
90° West of Greenwich
85°
80°
75°
70°
65°
30°
25°
20°
15°
10°
5°

PACIFIC OCEAN
Gulf of California (Golfo de California)
BAJA CALIFORNIA
BAJA CALIFORNIA SUR
SONORA
CHIHUAHUA
SINALOA
DURANGO
NAYARIT
JALISCO
COLIMA
SIERRA MADRE OCCIDENTAL
SIERRA DE LA GIGANTA
Hermosillo
Chihuahua
Culiacán
La Paz
Mazatlán
Durango
Tepic
Los Mochis
Guaymas
Ciudad Obregón
Navojoa
Puerto Vallarta
San José del Cabo
Cabo San Lucas
Isla Cedros
Desierto de Vizcaíno
Isla Tiburón
ISLAS TRES MARÍAS
ISLAS REVILLAGIGEDO
Tropic of Cancer
W-DRM5507-A1-1-1-1
Copyright © Rand McNally & Co.
Scale 1 : 5,000,000
Lambert Conformal Conic Projection
West of Greenwich
0 50 100 150 200 300 400 500 Kilometers
0 50 100 200 300 Miles
Meters Feet
4000 13120
3000 9840
2000 6560
1000 3280
500 1640
200 656
Sea Level
200 656
2000 6560

UNITED STATES
TEXAS
SAN ANTONIO
Corpus Christi
Laredo
Nuevo Laredo
Brownsville
Matamoros
McAllen
Reynosa
MONTERREY
San Nicolás de los Garza
Guadalupe
Saltillo
Monclova
Piedras Negras
Ciudad Acuña
Del Rio
NUEVO LEÓN
TAMAULIPAS
Ciudad Victoria
Ciudad Madero
Tampico
SAN LUIS POTOSÍ
San Luis Potosí
Aguascalientes
León
Irapuato
Querétaro
GUANAJUATO
QUERÉTARO
HIDALGO
Pachuca de Soto
Morelia
CIUDAD DE MÉXICO (MEXICO CITY)
Tlalnepantla
Ciudad Netzahualcoyotl
Toluca
Cuernavaca
PUEBLA
Tlaxcala de Xicohténcatl
Xalapa (Jalapa)
Veracruz
VERACRUZ
Orizaba
Córdoba
Poza Rica de Hidalgo
Chilpancingo de los Bravo
Acapulco
GUERRERO
MORELOS
OAXACA
Oaxaca de Juárez
Salina Cruz
Coatzacoalcos
Minatitlán
Villahermosa
TABASCO
CAMPECHE
Ciudad del Carmen
CHIAPAS
Tuxtla Gutiérrez
Tapachula
GUATEMALA
GULF OF MEXICO
Bahía de Campeche
Golfo de Tehuantepec
ISTMO DE TEHUANTEPEC
SIERRA MADRE ORIENTAL
SIERRA MADRE DEL SUR
SIERRA MADRE DE CHIAPAS
Tropic of Cancer
Nueces Plains
Laguna Madre
Padre Island
Cayo Arenas
Cayo Nuevo
Cayos Arcas

Gulf of Mexico
Yucatan Channel
LA HABANA (HAVANA)
Matanzas
San Antonio de los Baños
San José de las Lajas
Artemisa
Güines
Unión de Reyes
La Esperanza
Minas de Matahambre
Los Palacios
Pinar del Río
Consolación del Sur
Mantua
Guane
Golfo de Batabanó
Golfo de Guanahacabibes
Cabo de San Antonio
Bahía de Corrientes
Cabo Corrientes
Cayos de San Felipe
Nueva Gerona
La Fe
Archipiélago de los Canarreos
Isla de la Juventud (Isle of Pines)
Cayo Largo
Jagüey Grande
Península de Zapata
Bahía de Cochinos (Bay of Pigs)
CAYMAN
George Town
Grand Cayman
Cayo Arenas
Río Lagartos
Punta Holohit
Cabo Catoche
Progreso
Dzilam González
Motul de Felipe Carrillo Puerto
Panabá
Tizimín
Temax
Puerto Juárez
Isla Mujeres
Punta Cancún
Cancún
Kantunilkin
Celestún
Umán
Mérida
Izamal
Espita
X-Can
Valladolid
Playa del Carmen
Puerto Morelos
Cozumel
Isla Cozumel
Maxcanú
Muna
Halachó
Becal
Ticul
YUCATÁN
Oxkutzcab
Dzitbalché
Hecelchakán
Tenabo
Tekax
Peto
Chikindzonot
Tulum
TULUM
COBÁ
CHICHÉN ITZÁ
Bahía de Campeche
Campeche
Bolonchén de Rejón
Hopelchén
PENÍNSULA DE YUCATÁN
(YUCATAN PENINSULA)
Seybaplaya
Punta Morro
Champotón
Dzibalchén
Iturbide
Chunhuhux
Felipe Carrillo Puerto
MEXICO
QUINTANA ROO
Sabancuy
Isla del Carmen
Ciudad del Carmen
Laguna de Términos
CAMPECHE
Escárcega
Bahía Chetumal
Chetumal
Corozal
Caledonia
Orange Walk
Xcalak
Ambergris Cay
San Pedro
Emiliano Zapata
San Pedro Tabasco
TABASCO
Tenosique
Indian Church
Hill Bank
Belize City
Turneffe Islands
Chuntuqui
UAXACTÚN
Sierra de Agua
El Encanto
PARQUE NACIONAL TIKAL
Belmopan
BELIZE
Piedras Negras
Lago Petén Itzá
Benque Viejo del Carmen
Middlesex
Dangriga
CHIAPAS
La Libertad
La Florida
Victoria Peak 1120
MAYA MOUNTAINS
Dolores
Sayaxché
Palmar Carpp
Las Margaritas
Comitán de Domínguez
San Luis
Punta Negra
Punta Gorda
Gulf of Honduras
ISLAS DE LA BAHÍA
Isla de Guanaja
Guanaja
Roatán
Isla de Roatán
Isla de Utila
Utila
Cabo de Honduras
Trujillo
Cabo Camarón
La Delicias
Barillas
GUATEMALA
Chahal
Livingston
Puerto Cortés
Puerto Barrios
Colorado
La Ceiba
Balfate
Limón
Punta Patuca
Cerro Payas 1128
Brus Laguna
Paya
Tocoa
El Pacayal
Concepción Huista
Cobán
El Estor
Lago de Izabal
San Pedro Sula
Pico Bonito 2435
Olanchito
Huehuetenango
San Pedro Carchá
Panzós
Volcán Tacaná 4093
SIERRA MADRE
San Andrés Sajcabajá
Cerro San Ildefonso 2228
La Lima
El Progreso
El Negrito
Volcán Tajumulco 4220
San Jerónimo
Santa Cruz del Quiché
Santa Rita
Yoro
Pico Pijol 2282
Laguna de Caratasca
Arrecifes de la Media Luna
Quetzaltenango
Chiquimula
Zacapa
Santa Rosa de Copán
Santa Bárbara
HONDURAS
Catacamas
Wampú
Cabo Gracias a Dios
Chimaltenango
Mazatenango
Jalapa
San Luis Jilotepeque
Siguatepeque
Salamá
Juticalpa
Minas de Oro
Guaimaca
Retalhuleu
GUATEMALA
Volcán de Fuego 3763
Barberena
Cerro El Pital 2730
Cerro Las Minas 2849
Comayagua
Montaña El Chile 2256
Waspam
Bilwaskarma
Champerico
Escuintla
Cuilapa
Metapán
La Esperanza
La Paz
Bocay
Cayos Miskitos
Quitasueño
Santa Ana
Chalatenango
Tegucigalpa
Yablis
Puerto San José
Sonsonate
Nueva San Salvador
Cojutepeque
Sabanagrande
Yuscarán
Danlí
Bonanza
COSTA DE MOSQUITOS
Puerto Cabezas
San Salvador
San Vicente
San Francisco
Güinope
Cerro Saslaya 1650
Punta Remedios
EL SALVADOR
San Miguel
Ocotal
Mogotón 2107
Cerro Kilambé 1750
Siuna
Somoto
Condega
Wouhnta
Usulután
Choluteca
La Unión
El Corpus
San Rafael del Norte
CORDILLERA ISABELIA
Tungla
Prinzapolka
Golfo de Fonseca
Estelí
Jinotega
La Cruzde Río Grande
Isla de Providencia
Punta Cosigüina
Volcán Cosigüina 859
Volcán San Cristóbal 1745
La Trinidad
Matagalpa
CORDILLERA DARIENSE
Barra de Río Grande
El Viejo
Chinandega
Río Grande
Ciudad Darío
Sébaco
NICARAGUA
León
Volcán Momotombo 1280
Boaco
Isla de San Andrés
San Andrés
Cayos del Este Sudeste
La Paz Centro
Nagarote
Tipitapa
Santo Domingo
Cayos de Albuquerque
Managua
Masaya
Granada
Juigalpa
Santo Tomás
El Rama
Muelle de los Bueyes
Bluefields
El Bluff
Islas del Maíz
SAN ANDRÉS Y PROVIDENCIA (Col.)
Jinotepe
Masatepe
Nandaime
CORDILLERA CHONTALEÑA
Volcán Concepción 1610
Isla de Ometepe
Belén
Rivas
Lago de Nicaragua
Punta Gorda
San Juan del Sur
San Carlos
Bahía de Punta Gorda
Cabo Santa Elena
Volcán Miravalles 2028
San Juan del Norte
Golfo de Papagayo
CORDILLERA DE GUANACASTE
Liberia
Bagaces
Cañas
Barra del Colorado
Puerto Viejo
Fortuna
Cabo Velas
Santa Cruz
Nicoya
Cerro Azul 1018
Puntarenas
Alajuela
Heredia
Guápiles
Siquirres
Puerto Limón
Península de Nicoya
Golfo de Nicoya
SAN JOSÉ
Cartago
Juan Viñas
Cabo Blanco
Punta Mona
CORDILLERA DE TALAMANCA
PARQUE INTERNACIONAL DE LA AMISTAD
Bocas del Toro
San Isidro del General
Cerro Chirripó 3819
Cerro Kámuk 3554
COSTA RICA
Almirante
Península Valiente
Buenos Aires
Ciudad Cortés
Volcán Barú 3475
Bajo Boquete
Golfo de los Mosquitos
Bahía de Coronado
Península de Osa
PARQUE NACIONAL CORCOVADO
Golfito
Golfo Dulce
La Concepción
Dolega
Gualaca
Cerro Santiago 2121
David
Pedregal
Puerto Armuelles
Punta Burica
Golfo de Chiriquí
Remedios
Soná
PACIFIC OCEAN
Isla de Coiba
Isla de Cebaco
Isla Jicarón
Punta Mariato
Golfo de Montijo
Meters
Feet
3000 9840
2000 6560
1000 3280
500 1640
200 656
Sea Level
200 656
2000 6560
5578
3493
W-DRM5505-A1 -1-1-2
Copyright © Rand McNally & Co.
0 50 100 150 200 300 400 500 Kilometers
0 50 100 200 300 Miles
Scale 1 : 5,000,000
Lambert Conformal Conic Projection

BAHAMAS
Deadman's Cay
Long Island
Clarence Town
Cape Verde
Crooked Island Passage
Crooked Island
Samana Cay
North East Point
Long Cay
Bight of Acklins
Acklins
Ragged Island Range
Ragged Island
Salina Point
Mayaguana Passage
Mayaguana
Canal Viejo de Bahama
Canal de San Nicolás
Cay Lobos
Cay Coco
Caibarién
Yaguajay
Bahía de Perros
Placetas
Morón
Cayo Romano
Sancti Spíritus
Ciego de Avila
Bahía de Jigüey
Esmeralda
Cayo Guajaba
Cayo Sabinal
CUBA
Júcaro
Nuevitas
Minas
Florida
Puerto Manatí
Camagüey
Golfo de Ana María
Vertientes
Jesús Menéndez
Puerto Padre
Martí
Rafael Freyre
Punta de Mulas
Gibara
Las Tunas
Holguín
Antilla
Banes
Bahía de Nipe
Archipiélago de los Jardines de la Reina
Guayabal
Cueto
Mayarí
Sagua de Tánamo
Santa Cruz del Sur
Golfo de Guacanayabo
Bayamo
Alto Cedro
Baracoa
Jiguaní
Palma Soriano
San Luis
Tiguabos
Campechuela
Manzanillo
Guantánamo
Punta de Quemado
SIERRA MAESTRA
Niquero
Santiago de Cuba
Caimanera
Imías
GUANTANAMO BAY NAVAL STATION (U.S.)
Cabo Cruz
Marea de Portillo
Pico Turquino 1972

WEST INDIES
TURKS AND CAICOS ISLANDS (U.K.)
Caicos Passage
Providenciales
Kew
North Caicos
Middle Caicos
East Caicos
West Caicos
Grand Turk
CAICOS ISLANDS
TURKS ISLANDS
Turks Island Passage
Mouchoir Passage
Silver Bank Passage
ATLANTIC OCEAN
Little Inagua
North East Point
Palacca Point
Lake Rosa
Great Inagua
Matthew Town
Seal Cays

HISPANIOLA
Île de la Tortue
Windward Passage
Port-de-Paix
Cap du Môle
Cap-Haïtien
Manzanillo Bay
Monte Cristi
Cabo Isabela
Puerto Plata
Cabo Macorís
Cabo Francés Viejo
Cap à Foux
Limbé
SANS SOUCI
LA CITADELLE
Fort-Liberté
Dajabón
Mao
Pico Diego de Ocampo 1249
Moca
Nagua
Bahía Escocesa
Cabo Samaná
Santiago de los Caballeros
Gonaïves
Desdunes
HAITI
Golfe de la Gonâve
Pico Duarte 3175
La Vega
San Francisco de Macorís
Samaná
Bahía de Samaná
Yuna
Saint-Marc
Morne Bonhomme 1788
Île de la Gonâve
Canal de Saint-Marc
Artibonite
Bonao
Cotuí
Sabana de la Mar
Miches
Comendador
Alto Bandera 2630
Hato Mayor del Rey
El Seibo
Higüey
Cabo Engaño
Jérémie
Grande Cayemite
Canal du Sud
Baie de Port-au-Prince
Port-au-Prince
San Juan de la Maguana
SANTO DOMINGO
Anse-d'Hainault
Léogâne
Pétion-Ville
Neiba
Lago Enriquillo
Azua
San Cristóbal
La Romana
San Pedro de Macorís
Bahía de Yuma
Mona Passage
Pointe Fanchon
Pic Macaya 2347
Aquin
Petit-Goâve
Jacmel
Morne La Selle 2674
Bahía de Ocoa
Baní
Punta Palenque
Isla Saona
Coteaux
Les Cayes
Pointe Abacou
Île à Vache
Barahona
Pedernales
Enriquillo
DOMINICAN REPUBLIC
Cabo Falso
Isla Beata
Cabo Beata

GREATER ANTILLES
Jamaica Channel
Navassa Island (U.S.)
JAMAICA
Montego Bay
Falmouth
Ocho Rios
Saint Ann's Bay
Port Maria
South Negril Point
Savanna-la-Mar
Mount Denham 986
Port Antonio
Kingston
Blue Mountain Peak 2256
Mandeville
Spanish Town
Morant Point
Portland Bight
Morant Bay
Portland Point
Morant Cays
Pedro Cays
Cayo de Serranilla (Col.)
Bajo Nuevo (Col.)
Roncador
CARIBBEAN SEA

LESSER ANTILLES
ARUBA (Neth.)
Oranjestad
NETHERLANDS ANTILLES (Neth.)
Bonaire
Curaçao
Willemstad
Bahía Honda
Punta Gallinas
Puerto Bolívar
Bahía Portete
Cabo de La Vela
Península de La Guajira
Punta Espada
Cabo San Román
Pueblo Nuevo
Península de Paraguaná
Los Taques
Punto Fijo
Golfo de Venezuela
Punta Cardón
Golfete de Coro
Puerto Cumarebo
Punta Zamuro
Uribia
Ensenada de Calabozo
Riohacha
Coro
La Vela de Coro
Cabo de La Aguja
Maicao
Paraguaipoa
Capatárida
San Luis
Cabure
Santa Marta
LA GUAJIRA
Sinamaica
Pedregal
Dabajuro
FALCÓN
Churuguara
Barranquilla
Ciénaga
Pico Cristóbal Colón 5775
Albania
San Rafael
Soledad
Barrancas
Fonseca
Altagracia
Yumare
YARACUY
ATLÁNTICO
Malambo
Ciénaga Grande de Santa Marta
San Juan del Cesar
Villanueva
MARACAIBO
Mene de Mauroa
Siquisique
Baranoa
Aracataca
Santa Rita
Cabimas
PARQUE NACIONAL YURUBÍ
Cartagena
Sabanalarga
Pivijay
Fundación
Valledupar
Cerro Cerrón 1900
VENEZUELA
San Felipe
Islas del Rosario
Manatí
Turbaco
El Piñón
La Paz
Tía Juana
Ciudad Ojeda
LARA
Yaritagua
Carora
Barquisimeto
Arjona
Calamar
Agustín Codazzi
Villa del Rosario
Bachaquero
Quíbor
Mahates
El Guamo
Pedraza
Machiques
Lago de Maracaibo
Mene Grande
Sarare
Istmo de Panamá (Isthmus of Panama)
María La Baja
San Juan Nepomuceno
CESAR
San Timoteo
Acarigua
Araure
Islas de San Bernardo
San Onofre
San Jacinto
MAGDALENA
ZULIA
TRUJILLO
Carache
Trujillo
Guárico
Biscucuy
Píritu
Punta Manzanillo
Nombre de Dios
El Carmen de Bolívar
Ovejas
Cerro Mu 2610
La Ceiba
Sabana de Mendoza
Bobures
Valera
Boconó
Ospino
El Porvenir
Golfo de San Blas
Nusagandi
Golfo de Morrosquillo
Tolú
San Antero
San Pedro
Magangué
Chiriguaná
Niatupo
SERRANÍA DE SAN BLAS
Chepo
Lago Alajuela
Sincelejo
Corozal
Mompós
Guamal
Chimichagua
San Carlos del Zulia
Guanare
PORTUGUESA
Panamá
Punta Mosquito
Mansucum
Lorica
Chinú
COLOMBIA
Encontrados
Timotes
Barrancas
Guanarito
Lago Bayano
San Pelayo
Sahagún
Pinillos
El Banco
Pailitas
San Pedro
Mucuchíes
Barinitas
Cereté
Ciénaga de Oro
SUCRE
Sucre
Tamalameque
Casigua
El Vigía
Mérida
Barinas
Santa Rosa
Arboletes
Montería
San Marcos
BOLÍVAR
La Gloria
Ejido
PARQUE NAC. SIERRA NEVADA
Bahía de Panamá
Chimán
Cabo Tiburón
Punta Caribaná
Achí
Majagual
El Carmen
Petrólea
Pico Bolívar (La Columna) 5007
Dolores
San Miguel
Acandí
Planeta Rica
Río de Oro
NORTE DE SANTANDER
Ciudad Bolivia
Libertad
Ciudad de Nutrias
Carlos
La Palma
Golfo de Urabá
ANTIOQUIA
CÓRDOBA
Gamarra
Aguachica
Tovar
Bailadores
CORDILLERA DE MÉRIDA
BARINAS
ARCHIPIÉLAGO DE LAS PERLAS
Isla del Rey
CHOCÓ
Alto de Quimarí 2000
Tierralta
Ayapel
Ocaña
La Grita
MÉRIDA
Bruzual
Golfo de San Miguel
Yaviza
Nechí
Ábrego
Sardinata
San Juan de Colón
TÁCHIRA
Isla San José
Garachiné
El Real de Santa María
Turbo
Montelíbano
Caucasia
Cúcuta
Santa Bárbara
LLANOS
Golfo de Panamá
PARQUE NACIONAL DARIÉN
Apartadó
ANTIOQUIA
Simití
San Antonio del Táchira
Rubio
San Cristóbal
Palmarito
APURE
Serranía del Perijá
Cordillera de Mérida
Serranía de Abibe
Serranía del Darién

A B C D E F G H I
8 9 10 11 12 13
78° West of Greenwich 76° 74° 72° 70°
22° 18° 16° 14° 12° 10° 8°

168
169

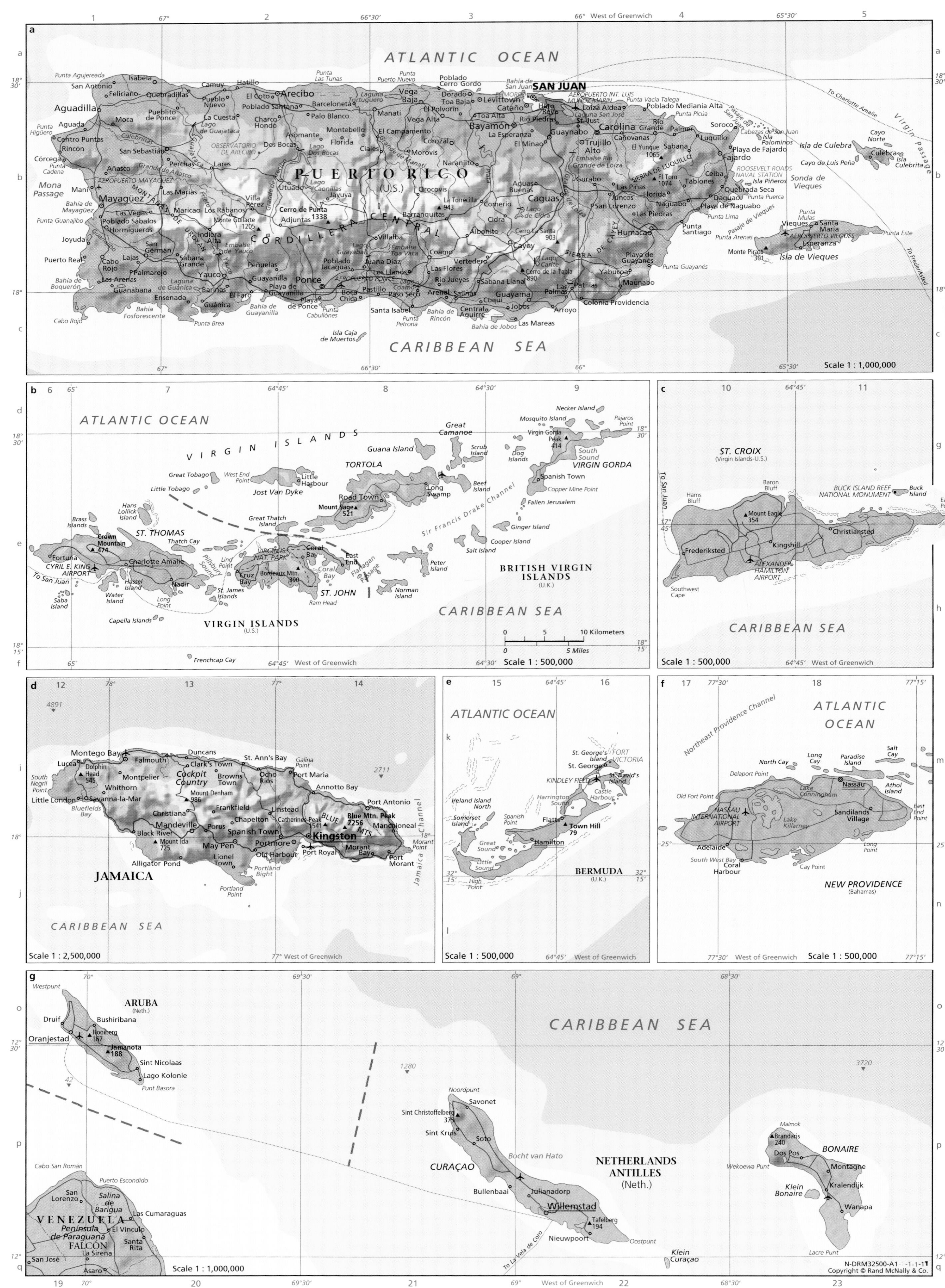

ATLANTIC OCEAN
PUERTO RICO
(U.S.)
SAN JUAN
CORDILLERA CENTRAL
CARIBBEAN SEA
Scale 1 : 1,000,000
VIRGIN ISLANDS
ST. THOMAS
ST. JOHN
TORTOLA
VIRGIN GORDA
BRITISH VIRGIN ISLANDS
(U.K.)
Scale 1 : 500,000
ST. CROIX
(Virgin Islands-U.S.)
JAMAICA
Kingston
Scale 1 : 2,500,000
BERMUDA
(U.K.)
NEW PROVIDENCE
(Bahamas)
ARUBA
(Neth.)
CURAÇAO
BONAIRE
NETHERLANDS ANTILLES
(Neth.)
VENEZUELA
N-DRM32500-A1

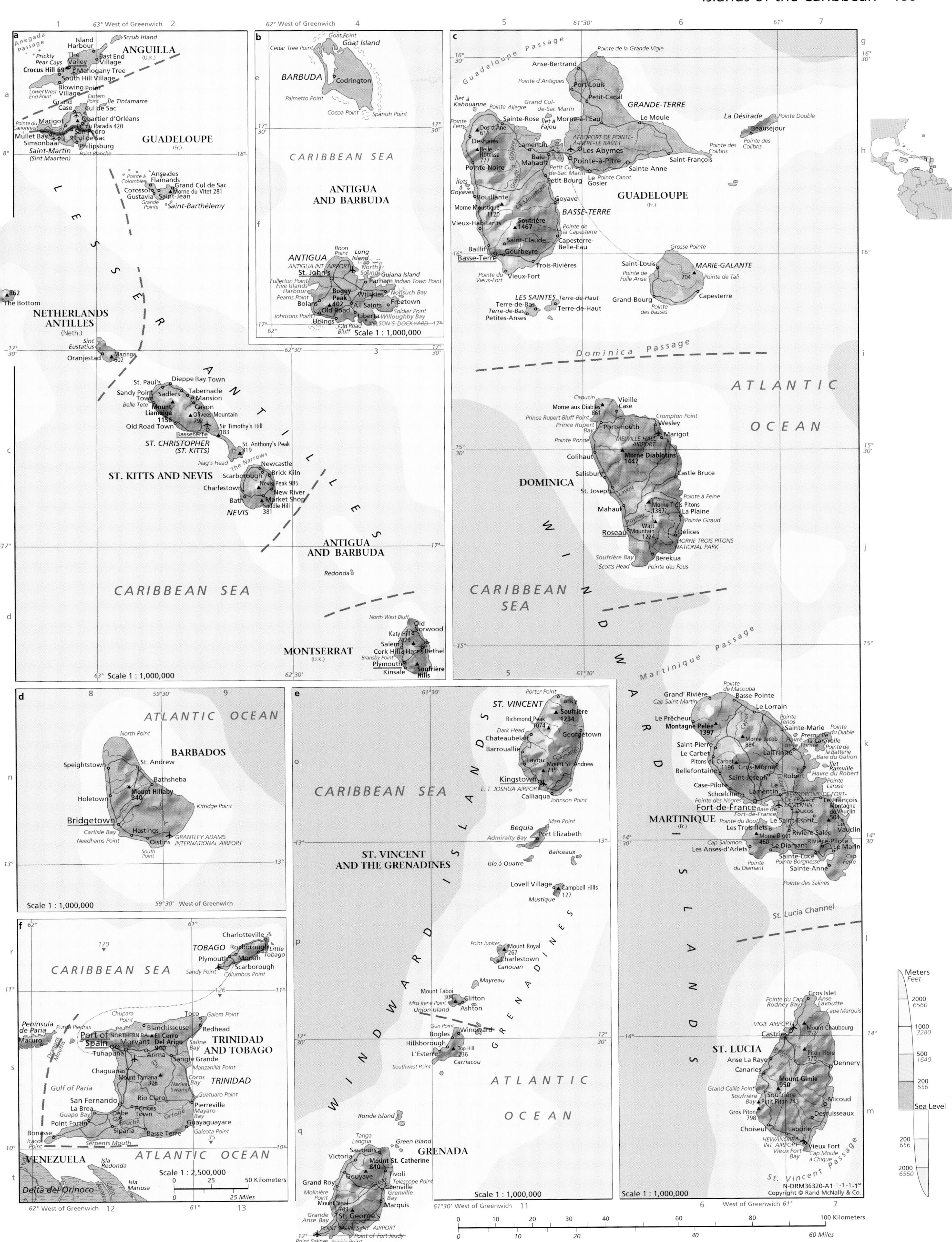

ATLANTIC OCEAN
AÇORES (AZORES) (Port.)
São Miguel
BERMUDA (U.K.)
UNITED STATES
APPALACHIAN MOUNTAINS
CHICAGO
CLEVELAND
PITTSBURGH
Hartford
Providence
NEW YORK
PHILADELPHIA
BALTIMORE
WASHINGTON
Richmond
Norfolk
Cape Hatteras
Cape Lookout
Cape Fear
Omaha
Des Moines
INDIANAPOLIS
CINCINNATI
Charleston
KANSAS CITY
ST. LOUIS
Louisville
Wichita
Raleigh
Charlotte
Columbia
Chattanooga
Oklahoma City
Little Rock
Birmingham
ATLANTA
Charleston
Savannah
DALLAS
Fort Worth
Shreveport
Jackson
Montgomery
Baton Rouge
Mobile
Tallahassee
Jacksonville
Austin
HOUSTON
NEW ORLEANS
Daytona Beach
Orlando
Cape Canaveral
SAN ANTONIO
Tampa
Lake Okeechobee
Corpus Christi
GULF OF MEXICO
MIAMI
Brownsville
Matamoros
Grand Bahama
Abaco
Eleuthera
Nassau
Cat Island
Cape Sable
Straits of Florida
Andros
BAHAMAS
Tropic of Cancer
LA HABANA (HAVANA)
Matanzas
Cienfuegos
CUBA
WEST INDIES
Acklins
Long Island
Mayaguana
TURKS AND CAICOS ISLANDS (U.K.)
Great Inagua
DOMINICAN REPUBLIC
Yucatan Channel
Cabo Catoche
Cancún
Isla de la Juventud
Camagüey
Holguín
Santiago de Cuba
Mérida
Isla Cozumel
CAYMAN ISLANDS (U.K.)
GREATER ANTILLES
HAITI
Port-au-Prince
Pico Duarte 3175
SANTO DOMINGO
PUERTO RICO (U.S.)
SAN JUAN
ANGUILLA (U.K.)
LEEWARD ISLANDS
Bahía de Campeche
Campeche
PENÍNSULA DE YUCATÁN
JAMAICA
Kingston
HISPANIOLA
ANTIGUA AND BARBUDA
GUADELOUPE (Fr.)
MONTSERRAT (U.K.)
Veracruz
Villahermosa
Belize City
BELIZE
Belmopan
DOMINICA
MARTINIQUE (Fr.)
Lesser Antilles
WINDWARD ISLANDS
MEXICO
Tuxtla Gutiérrez
CARIBBEAN SEA
ST. LUCIA
BARBADOS
Volcán Tajumulco 4220
GUATEMALA
San Pedro Sula
HONDURAS
ST. VINCENT AND THE GRENADINES
Golfo de Tehuantepec
Guatemala
Tegucigalpa
Punta Gallinas
ARUBA (Neth.)
NETHERLANDS ANTILLES
GRENADA
San Salvador
EL SALVADOR
NICARAGUA
Isla de San Andrés (Col.)
Riohacha
Punto Fijo
Port of Spain
Tobago
TRINIDAD AND TOBAGO
Lago de Nicaragua
Managua
Barranquilla
Pico Cristóbal Colón 5775
MARACAIBO
CARACAS
Puerto la Cruz
Trinidad
Cartagena
Barquisimeto
Maracay
Maturín
SAN JOSÉ
Cerro Chirripó 3819
Colón
Panamá
Sincelejo
Barinas
El Tigre
COSTA RICA
Volcán Barú 3475
Montería
Lago de Maracaibo
Pico Bolívar 5007
San Fernando de Apure
Orinoco
Ciudad Guayana
Ciudad Bolívar
Golfo de Panamá
Cúcuta
San Cristóbal
VENEZUELA
Georgetown
Isla de Coiba
PANAMA
Bucaramanga
LLANOS
Paramaribo
GUYANA
Roraima 2875
MEDELLÍN
Puerto Ayacucho
Cayenne
Quibdó
Manizales
PAKARAIMA MTS.
SURINAME
FRENCH GUIANA (Fr.)
Isla del Coco (C.R.)
SANTA FE DE BOGOTÁ
Ibagué
CORDILLERA OCCIDENTAL
CORDILLERA CENTRAL
CORDILLERA ORIENTAL
Boa Vista
Isla de Malpelo (Col.)
Buenaventura
CALI
COLOMBIA
Branco
TUMAC-HUMAC MOUNTAINS
Amapá
Ilha de Maracá
Tumaco
Pasto
Mitú
Pico da Neblina 3014
Ilha Caviana de Fora
Macapá
Esmeraldas
Punta Galera
ARCHIPIÉLAGO DE COLÓN (GALÁPAGOS ISLANDS) (Ec.)
QUITO
Cayambe 5790
Ilha Grande do Gurupá
Ilha de Marajó
Bragança
Isla Santiago
Isla Santa Cruz
Portoviejo
ECUADOR
Chimborazo 6310
Putumayo
Negro
Óbidos
Amazon (Amazonas)
BELÉM
Equator
Isla Fernandina
Isla Isabela
Isla San Cristóbal
GUAYAQUIL
Fonte Boa
Manacapuru
MANAUS
Itacoatiara
Santarém
Altamira
Xingu
Tocantins
São Luís
Parnaíba
Isla Puná
Cuenca
Iquitos
Amazon
Leticia
Itaituba
Bacabal
Sobral
FORTALEZA
Atol das Rocas
Ilha Fernando de Noronha (Brazil)
Talara
ANDES
PERU
Caxias
Marabá
Imperatriz
Teresina
Mossoró
Cabo de São Roque
Piura
Purus
Tapajós
Natal
Chiclayo
Cajamarca
Cruzeiro do Sul
SELVAS
BRAZIL
Carolina
Juazeiro do Norte
Campina Grande
Trujillo
Nevado Huascarán 6746
Pucallpa
São Manuel
Paulistana
João Pessoa
Madeira
Porto Velho
Palmas
Caruaru
Chimbote
Huánuco
Rio Branco
Petrolina
Represa de Sobradinho
Juazeiro
São Francisco
RECIFE
Nevado Yerupajá 6634
Cerro de Pasco
SERRA FORMOSA
Ilha do Bananal
Porto Nacional
Senhor do Bonfim
Maceió
Cobija
Riberalta
Gurupi
Barra
Xique-Xique
Aracaju
LIMA
Huancayo
Puerto Maldonado
Barreiras
Feira de Santana

PACIFIC
OCEAN
ATLANTIC
OCEAN
ANTARCTICA
CHILE
ARGENTINA
PARAGUAY
URUGUAY
PAMPA
PATAGONIA
ANDES
GRAN CHACO
FALKLAND ISLANDS (U.K.)
SOUTH GEORGIA AND THE SOUTH SANDWICH ISLANDS (U.K.)
SOUTH ORKNEY ISLANDS (U.K.)
SOUTH SHETLAND ISLANDS (U.K.)
SOUTH SANDWICH ISLANDS
SCOTIA SEA
Drake Passage
Antarctic Peninsula
TIERRA DEL FUEGO
ARCHIPIÉLAGO JUAN FERNÁNDEZ (Chile)
Isla Róbinson Crusoe
Isla Alejandro Selkirk
Isla San Félix (Chile)
Isla San Ambrosio (Chile)
Trindade (Brazil)
Ilhas Martin Vaz (Brazil)
Bouvetøya (Nor.)
SANTIAGO
BUENOS AIRES
MONTEVIDEO
Asunción
RIO DE JANEIRO
SÃO PAULO
BELO HORIZONTE
SANTOS
CURITIBA
PORTO ALEGRE
CÓRDOBA
Rosario
Mendoza
Mar del Plata
Bahía Blanca
Valparaíso
Concepción
Antofagasta
Iquique
Punta Arenas
Stanley
South Georgia
Tropic of Capricorn
Antarctic Circle
West of Greenwich
East of Greenwich
M-DRM2202-P1- -1-1-1
Copyright © Rand McNally & Co.
0 250 500 750 1000 1500 2000 2500 Kilometers
0 250 500 1000 1500 Miles
Scale 1 : 25,000,000
Lambert Azimuthal Equal Area Projection

ATLANTIC OCEAN
AÇORES (AZORES)
São Miguel
Bermuda
Tropic of Cancer
Equator
GULF OF MEXICO
CARIBBEAN SEA
Gulf of Honduras
Bahía de Campeche
Golfo de Tehuantepec
Golfo de Panamá
Golfo de Guayaquil
Golfo de Venezuela
BAHAMAS
WEST INDIES
GREATER ANTILLES
LESSER ANTILLES
LEEWARD ISLANDS
WINDWARD ISLANDS
CUBA
HISPANIOLA
APPALACHIAN MOUNTAINS
Ozark Plateau
PENÍNSULA DE YUCATÁN
Istmo de Tehuantepec
LLANOS
CORDILLERA OCCIDENTAL
CORDILLERA CENTRAL
CORDILLERA ORIENTAL
ANDES
SELVAS
SERRA FORMOSA
PAKARAIMA MTS.
TUMUC-HUMAC MTS.
ARCHIPIÉLAGO DE COLÓN (GALÁPAGOS ISLANDS)
Isla Isabela
Isla Fernandina
Isla Santiago
Isla Santa Cruz
Isla San Cristóbal
Isla del Coco
Isla de Malpelo
Isla de San Andrés
Isla de Coiba
Pen. de Azuero
Cayman Islands
Isla de la Juventud
Isla Cozumel
Yucatan Channel
Straits of Florida
Florida Keys
Mona Passage
Grand Bahama
Abaco
Eleuthera
Andros
Cat Island
Long Island
Great Inagua
Virgin Islands
Puerto Rico
Barbuda
Antigua
Guadeloupe
Dominica
Martinique
St. Lucia
Barbados
St. Vincent
Grenada
Tobago
Trinidad
Isla de Margarita
Aruba
Bonaire
Curaçao
Delta del Orinoco
Ilha de Maracá
Ilha Caviana de Fora
Ilha de Marajó
Ilha Grande do Gurupá
Ilha do Bananal
Atol das Rocas
Ilha Fernando de Noronha
Cabo de São Roque
Cape Hatteras
Cape Lookout
Cape Fear
Cape Canaveral
Cape Sable
Cabo Catoche
Punta Gallinas
Punta Galera
Cabo San Lorenzo
Punta Pariñas
Lake Okeechobee
Laguna Madre
Lago de Nicaragua
Lago de Maracaibo
Represa de Tucuruí
Represa de Sobradinho
Represa Balbina
Salto Angel (Angel Falls)
Brokopondo Stuwmeer
Mississippi
Missouri
Illinois
Ohio
Arkansas
Red
Brazos
Colorado
Alabama
Savannah
Orinoco
Apure
Meta
Amazon
Negro
Branco
Japurá
Caquetá
Putumayo
Vaupés
Uaupés
Içá
Ucayali
Marañón
Madeira
Purus
Juruá
Tapajós
Xingu
Tocantins
Araguaia
Parnaíba
São Francisco
São Manuel
Mamoré
Madre de Dios
Pico Duarte 3175
Pico Cristóbal Colón 5775
Pico Bolívar 5007
Roraima 2875
Juliana Top 1230
Pico da Neblina 3014
Nevado del Tolima 5215
Cayambe 5790
Chimborazo 6310
Nevado Huascarán 6746
Nevado Yerupajá 6634
Volcán Tajumulco 4220
Cerro Las Minas 2849
Cerro Chirripó 3819
Volcán Barú 3475
Mount Mitchell 2037
Chicago
Des Moines
Omaha
Kansas City
Wichita
Indianapolis
Cincinnati
Cleveland
Pittsburgh
New York
Philadelphia
Washington
Charleston
Richmond
Norfolk
Raleigh
Charlotte
Columbia
Atlanta
Birmingham
St. Louis
Dallas
Shreveport
Mobile
Jacksonville
New Orleans
Houston
San Antonio
Tampa
Miami
Nassau
Brownsville
Matamoros
La Habana
Camagüey
Santiago de Cuba
Port-au-Prince
Santo Domingo
Jamaica
Kingston
Mérida
Villahermosa
Belmopan
Guatemala
San Salvador
Tegucigalpa
Managua
San José
Panamá
Barranquilla
Cartagena
Sincelejo
Montería
Maracaibo
Maracay
Caracas
Barquisimeto
Port of Spain
Maturín
Ciudad Bolívar
Ciudad Guayana
Cúcuta
San Cristóbal
Bucaramanga
Medellín
Manizales
Ibagué
Santa Fe de Bogotá
Buenaventura
Puerto Ayacucho
Georgetown
Paramaribo
Cayenne
Boa Vista
Amapá
Macapá
Mitú
Pasto
Quito
Portoviejo
Guayaquil
Cuenca
Piura
Chiclayo
Trujillo
Chimbote
Cerro de Pasco
Lima
Iquitos
Leticia
Pucallpa
Fonte Boa
Manaus
Óbidos
Santarém
Belém
São Luís
Parnaíba
Fortaleza
Teresina
Marabá
Imperatriz
Carolina
Mossoró
Natal
Campina Grande
João Pessoa
Caruaru
Recife
Maceió
Aracaju
Juazeiro do Norte
Petrolina
Porto Nacional
Barra
Porto Velho
Rio Branco
Riberalta

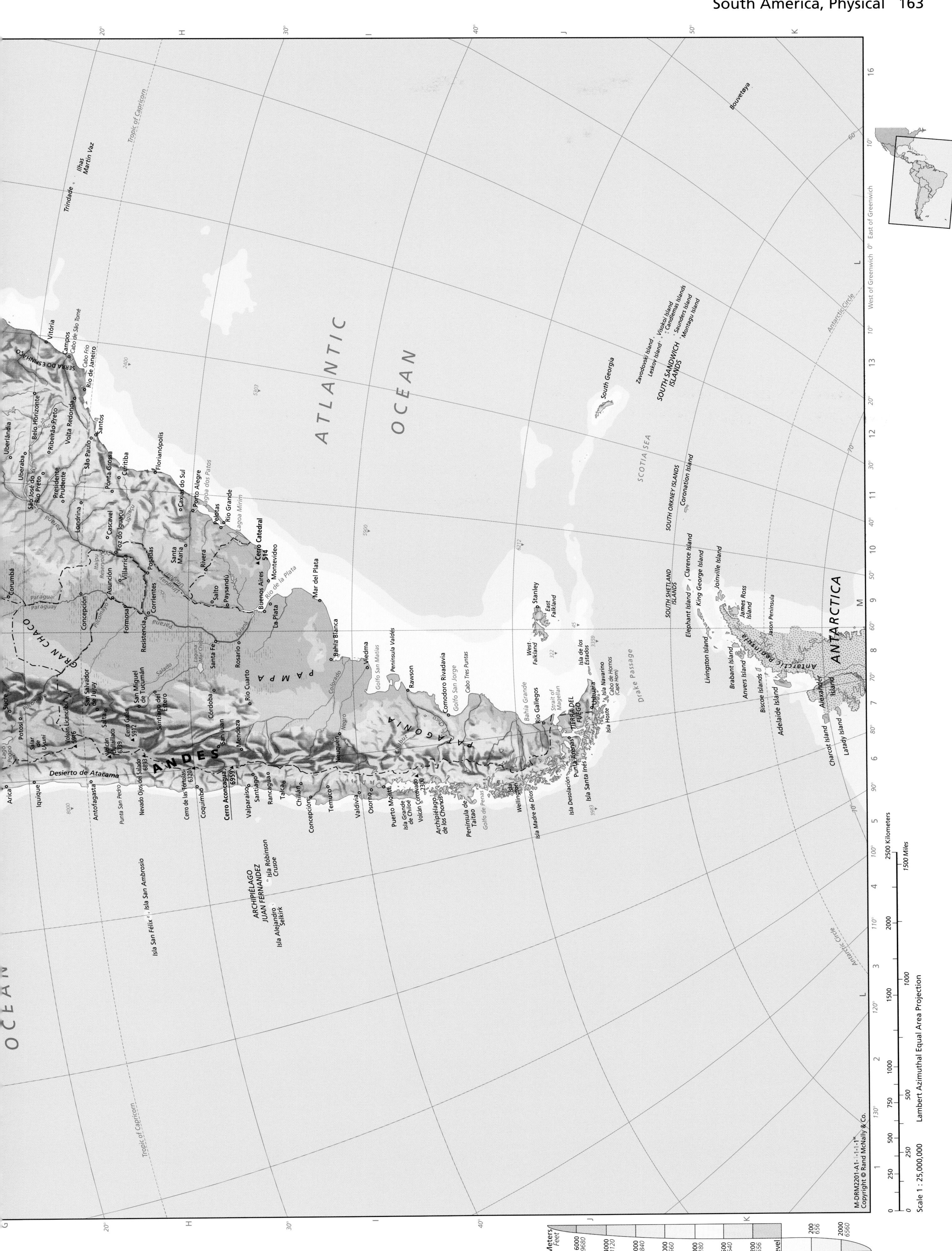
ATLANTIC
OCEAN
OCEAN
ANTARCTICA
ANDES
PAMPA
PATAGONIA
GRAN CHACO
SERRA DO ESPINHAÇO
TIERRA DEL FUEGO
SCOTIA SEA
Drake Passage
Tropic of Capricorn
Antarctic Circle
Antarctic Peninsula
Desierto de Atacama
Trindade
Ilhas Martin Vaz
Bouvetøya
South Georgia
SOUTH SANDWICH ISLANDS
Zavodovski Island
Leskov Island
Visokoi Island
Candlemas Islands
Saunders Island
Montagu Island
SOUTH ORKNEY ISLANDS
Coronation Island
SOUTH SHETLAND ISLANDS
Elephant Island
Clarence Island
King George Island
Joinville Island
James Ross Island
Jason Peninsula
Livingston Island
Brabant Island
Anvers Island
Biscoe Islands
Adelaide Island
Alexander Island
Charcot Island
Latady Island
West Falkland
East Falkland
Stanley
Isla de los Estados
Isla Navarino
Cabo de Hornos (Cape Horn)
Isla Hoste
Ushuaia
Strait of Magellan
Punta Arenas
Isla Santa Inés
Isla Desolación
Isla Madre de Dios
Isla Wellington
Golfo de Penas
Península de Taitao
Archipiélago de los Chonos
Volcán Corcovado 2300
Isla Grande de Chiloé
Puerto Montt
Osorno
Valdivia
Temuco
Concepción
Chillán
Talca
Rancagua
Santiago
Valparaíso
Cerro Aconcagua 6959
Coquimbo
Cerro de las Tórtolas 6320
Nevado Ojos del Salado 6893
Antofagasta
Punta San Pedro
Iquique
Arica
Salar de Uyuni
Potosí
Sucre
Volcán Llullaillaco 6739
Volcán Licancabur 5916
Cerro Galán 5912
Salta
San Salvador de Jujuy
San Miguel de Tucumán
Santiago del Estero
Córdoba
San Juan
Mendoza
Río Cuarto
Neuquén
Comodoro Rivadavia
Golfo San Jorge
Cabo Tres Puntas
Río Gallegos
Bahía Grande
Rawson
Península Valdés
Golfo San Matías
Viedma
Bahía Blanca
Mar del Plata
La Plata
Buenos Aires
Río de la Plata
Montevideo
Cerro Catedral 514
Rosario
Santa Fe
Laguna Mar Chiquita
Resistencia
Corrientes
Formosa
Asunción
Concepción
Corumbá
Posadas
Villarrica
Foz do Iguaçu
Itaipu Reservoir
Salto
Paysandú
Rivera
Santa Maria
Pelotas
Rio Grande
Lagoa Mirim
Lagoa dos Patos
Porto Alegre
Caxias do Sul
Florianópolis
Curitiba
Ponta Grossa
Cascavel
Londrina
Presidente Prudente
São José do Rio Preto
Uberaba
Uberlândia
Ribeirão Preto
São Paulo
Santos
Volta Redonda
Belo Horizonte
Rio de Janeiro
Cabo Frio
Campos
Cabo de São Tomé
Vitória
Paraná
Paraguay
Uruguay
Salado
Colorado
Negro
Pilcomayo
Iguaçu
ARCHIPIÉLAGO JUAN FERNÁNDEZ
Isla Robinson Crusoe
Isla Alejandro Selkirk
Isla San Félix
Isla San Ambrosio
West of Greenwich 0° East of Greenwich
Meters Feet
6000 19680
4000 13120
3000 9840
2000 6560
1000 3280
500 1640
200 656
Sea Level
200 656
2000 6560
2500 Kilometers
1500 Miles
Scale 1 : 25,000,000
Lambert Azimuthal Equal Area Projection
M-DRM2201-A1- -1-1-1"
Copyright © Rand McNally & Co.

CARIBBEAN SEA
PANAMA
Panamá
Barranquilla
Cartagena
MARACAIBO
CARACAS
Barquisimeto
Valencia
Maracay
ARUBA
NETHERLANDS ANTILLES
Willemstad
Oranjestad
TRINIDAD AND TOBAGO
Port of Spain
VENEZUELA
Ciudad Guayana
Ciudad Bolívar
LLANOS
Cúcuta
Bucaramanga
MEDELLÍN
SANTA FE DE BOGOTÁ
CALI
COLOMBIA
Villavicencio
CORDILLERA OCCIDENTAL
CORDILLERA CENTRAL
CORDILLERA ORIENTAL
CORD. DE MÉRIDA
Pico Cristóbal Colón 5775
Pico Bolívar 5007
Pico da Neblina 3014
Mount Roraima 2875
SIERRA PARIMA
SERRA PARIMA
PAKARAIMA MTS.
LA GRAN SABANA
RORAIMA
Boa Vista
QUITO
ECUADOR
GUAYAQUIL
Chimborazo 6310
Cotopaxi 5897
Cayambe 5790
ANDES
Equator
AMAZONAS
SELVAS
MANAUS
Amazon
Negro
Iquitos
Leticia
PERU
CORDILLERA ORIENTAL
CORDILLERA CENTRAL
CORDILLERA OCCIDENTAL
Nevado Huascarán 6746
Trujillo
Chiclayo
Chimbote
Callao
LIMA
Huancayo
Cusco
Arequipa
Lake Titicaca
LA PAZ
Cochabamba
Santa Cruz de la Sierra
BOLIVIA
CORDILLERA REAL
ALTIPLANO
CHILE
Arica
ACRE
Rio Branco
Porto Velho
RONDÔNIA
SERRA DOS PACAÁS NOVOS
SERRA DO DIVISOR
PACIFIC OCEAN
Meters
Feet
6000
19680
4000
13120
3000
9840
2000
6560
1000
3280
500
1640
200
656
Sea Level
200
656
2000
6560
ARCHIPIÉLAGO DE COLÓN (GALAPAGOS ISLANDS) (Ec.)
Isla Pinta
Isla Marchena
Volcán Wolf 1646
Isla Santiago
Isla Santa Cruz
Isla Fernandina
Isla San Cristobal
Isla Isabela
Puerto Villamil
Puerto Baquerizo Moreno
Isla Santa Maria
Same scale as main map
0 100 200 300 400 600 Kilometers
0 100 200 400 Miles
Scale 1 : 10,000,000
Sinusoidal Projection

ATLANTIC
OCEAN
Equator
SURINAME
FRENCH GUIANA
AMAPÁ
PARÁ
MARANHÃO
PIAUÍ
CEARÁ
RIO GRANDE DO NORTE
PARAÍBA
PERNAMBUCO
ALAGOAS
SERGIPE
BAHIA
TOCANTINS
GOIÁS
DISTRITO FEDERAL
MINAS GERAIS
MATO GROSSO
MATO GROSSO DO SUL
BRAZIL
PLANALTO DO MATO GROSSO
TUMUC-HUMAC MOUNTAINS
ORANJE GEBERGTE
SERRA DOS CARAJÁS
SERRA DO ESTRONDO
CHAPADA DAS MANGABEIRAS
SERRA GERAL DE GOIÁS
SERRA GRANDE
CHAPADA DO ARARIPE
SERRA DO RONCADOR
SERRA FORMOSA
SERRA DOURADA
SERRA DO ESPINHAÇO
SERRA DO CAIAPÓ
SERRA DE SÃO JERÔNIMO
SA. DO PENITENTE
Juliana Top 1230
Paramaribo
Cayenne
Île du Diable
Cabo Orange
Cabo Norte
Ilha de Maracá
Ilha Caviana de Fora
Ilha Mexiana
ILHA DE MARAJÓ
Macapá
BELÉM
Santarém
Altamira
Marabá
Imperatriz
São Luís
Teresina
Parnaíba
FORTALEZA
Natal
João Pessoa
Campina Grande
RECIFE
Maceió
Aracaju
SALVADOR
Feira de Santana
Petrolina
Juazeiro
Juazeiro do Norte
Ilhéus
Vitória da Conquista
Montes Claros
BRASÍLIA
GOIÂNIA
Anápolis
Cuiabá
Cabo de São Roque
Ilha de Tinharé
Ponta da Baleia
Represa de Tucuruí
Represa de Sobradinho
Represa Boa Esperança
Ilha do Bananal
Amazon
Xingu
Tocantins
Araguaia
55° West of Greenwich

3
4
5
6
7
8
B
C
D
E
164
165
BRAZIL
BOLIVIA
PARAGUAY
PERU
ANDES
ACRE
RONDÔNIA
PLANALTO DO MATO GROSSO
MATO GROSSO
MATO GROSSO DO SUL
TOCANTINS
GOIÁS
BAHIA
MINAS GERAIS
ESPÍRITO SANTO
RIO DE JANEIRO
SÃO PAULO
PARANÁ
SANTA CATARINA
RIO GRANDE DO SUL
MISIONES
CORRIENTES
SANTA FE
CÓRDOBA
FORMOSA
CHACO
CHACO BOREAL
Chaco Austral
Chaco Central
SANTIAGO DEL ESTERO
JUJUY
SALTA
TUCUMÁN
CATAMARCA
LA RIOJA
SAN JUAN
ALTIPLANO
CORDILLERA REAL
CORDILLERA OCCIDENTAL
CORDILLERA DE CHICHAS
CORDILLERA DOMEYKO
DESIERTO DE ATACAMA
Salar de Uyuni
Pantanal
SERRA DOS PACAÁS NOVOS
SERRANÍA DE HUANCHACA
SERRA DO NORTE
SERRA DO TOMBADOR
SERRA FORMOSA
SERRA DO RONCADOR
SERRA DE SÃO JERÔNIMO
SERRA DOURADA
SERRA GERAL DE GOIÁS
SERRA DO ESPINHAÇO
SERRA DA MANTIQUEIRA
SERRA DO MAR
SERRA GERAL
SERRA DA BODOQUENA
SERRA DE MARACAJU
SERRA DO CAIAPÓ
COXILHA DE SANTANA
Tropic of Capricorn
BRASÍLIA
DISTRITO FEDERAL
GOIÂNIA
BELO HORIZONTE
RIO DE JANEIRO
Niterói
SÃO PAULO
SANTOS
CAMPINAS
CURITIBA
Florianópolis
PORTO ALEGRE
Vitória
Campo Grande
Cuiabá
Uberlândia
Ribeirão Preto
Londrina
Joinville
Caxias do Sul
Pelotas
Asunción
LA PAZ
Cochabamba
Santa Cruz de la Sierra
Sucre
Potosí
Oruro
Salta
San Salvador de Jujuy
San Miguel de Tucumán
Corrientes
Resistencia
Posadas
Santa Fe
CÓRDOBA
Antofagasta
Iquique
Arica
Coquimbo
La Serena
Rio Branco

ATLANTIC OCEAN
PACIFIC OCEAN
ARGENTINA
CHILE
ANDES
PATAGONIA
PAMPA
TIERRA DEL FUEGO
FALKLAND ISLANDS
(U.K.)
WEST FALKLAND
EAST FALKLAND
Stanley
SOUTH GEORGIA AND THE
SOUTH SANDWICH ISLANDS
(U.K.)
SOUTH GEORGIA
BUENOS AIRES
MONTEVIDEO
SANTIAGO
Valparaíso
Mar del Plata
Bahía Blanca
Comodoro Rivadavia
Río Gallegos
Punta Arenas
Ushuaia
M-DRM4706-A1-
Copyright © Rand McNally & Co.
Scale 1 : 10,000,000
Lambert Conformal Conic Projection
600 Kilometers
400 Miles
50° West of Greenwich
Meters
Feet
Sea Level

CARIBBEAN SEA
PACIFIC OCEAN
PANAMA
Istmo de Panamá (Isthmus of Panama)
Golfo de Panamá
PENÍNSULA DE AZUERO
Panamá
Colón
ARCHIPIÉLAGO DE LAS PERLAS
COLOMBIA
ECUADOR
PERU
Península de La Guajira
Lago de Maracaibo
MARACAIBO
Cabimas
ZULIA
LA GUAJIRA
Riohacha
Santa Marta
Barranquilla
Soledad
Cartagena
Valledupar
MAGDALENA
BOLÍVAR
SUCRE
CÓRDOBA
Montería
Sincelejo
CESAR
NORTE DE SANTANDER
Cúcuta
San Cristóbal
TÁCHIRA
Mérida
MÉRIDA
SERRANÍA DE PERIJÁ
Bucaramanga
Floridablanca
SANTANDER
Barrancabermeja
ANTIOQUIA
MEDELLÍN
Bello
Itagüí
Envigado
CHOCÓ
Quibdó
RISARALDA
CALDAS
Manizales
Pereira
Armenia
QUINDÍO
Ibagué
TOLIMA
CUNDINAMARCA
SANTA FE DE BOGOTÁ
Soacha
Zipaquirá
Tunja
BOYACÁ
CASANARE
ARAUCA
Villavicencio
META
CORDILLERA OCCIDENTAL
CORDILLERA CENTRAL
CORDILLERA ORIENTAL
VALLE DEL CAUCA
CALI
Palmira
Buenaventura
Tuluá
CAUCA
Popayán
HUILA
Neiva
NARIÑO
Pasto
Ipiales
Tumaco
PUTUMAYO
CAQUETÁ
Florencia
GUAVIARE
San José del Guaviare
AMAZONAS
VAUPÉS
LORETO
Esmeraldas
ESMERALDAS
CARCHI
IMBABURA
Ibarra
PICHINCHA
QUITO
Santo Domingo de los Colorados
MANABÍ
Manta
Portoviejo
COTOPAXI
Latacunga
Ambato
TUNGURAHUA
Chimborazo 6310
Riobamba
CHIMBORAZO
BOLÍVAR
LOS RÍOS
GUAYAS
GUAYAQUIL
Golfo de Guayaquil
CAÑAR
AZUAY
Cuenca
MORONA SANTIAGO
PASTAZA
NAPO
SUCUMBÍOS
Nueva Loja
ANDES
Equator
72° West of Greenwich
W-DRM5522-A1 -1-1-2M
Copyright © Rand McNally & Co.
Meters / Feet
4000 / 13120
3000 / 9840
2000 / 6560
1000 / 3280
500 / 1640
200 / 656
Sea Level
200 / 656
2000 / 6560
500 Kilometers
300 Miles
Scale 1 : 5,000,000
Sinusoidal Projection

NETHERLANDS ANTILLES
Willemstad
Kralendijk
Bonaire
Curaçao
L E S S E R   A N T I L L E S
Isla de Margarita
La Asunción
Porlamar
TRINIDAD AND TOBAGO
Tobago
Charlotteville
Scarborough
Port of Spain
Arima
Sangre Grande
San Fernando
Princes Town
TRINIDAD
Point Fortin
Gulf of Paria
ATLANTIC OCEAN
DISTRITO FEDERAL
Maiquetía
CARACAS
Petare
Guarenas
Los Teques
Maracay
Valencia
Puerto Cabello
Morón
San Felipe
YARACUY
CARABOBO
ARAGUA
MIRANDA
Puerto la Cruz
Barcelona
Cumaná
Carúpano
SUCRE
Maturín
MONAGAS
ANZOÁTEGUI
GUÁRICO
El Tigre
Calabozo
Delta del Orinoco
Tucupita
DELTA AMACURO
V E N E Z U E L A
Ciudad Guayana
Ciudad Bolívar
San Fernando de Apure
APURE
Acarigua
COJEDES
Puerto Carreño
Puerto Ayacucho
B O L Í V A R
Canaima
Auyán Tepuy 2950
PARQUE NACIONAL CANAIMA
LA GRAN SABANA
G U I A N A   H I G H L A N D S
(M A C I Z O   D E   G U A Y A N A)
Santa Elena de Uairén
Mount Roraima 2875
PAKARAIMA MOUNTAINS
G U Y A N A
CUYUNI-MAZARUNI
BARIMA-WAINI
POTARO-SIPARUNI
UPPER TAKUTU-UPPER ESSEQUIBO
Lethem
A M A Z O N A S
San Fernando de Atabapo
Puerto Inírida
GUAINÍA
SIERRA PARIMA
Pico da Neblina 3014
R O R A I M A
Boa Vista
B R A Z I L
A M A Z O N A S
Barcelos
Novo Airão
PARQUE NACIONAL DO JAÚ
MANAUS
Manacapuru

ATLANTIC
OCEAN
B R A Z I L
BAHIA
P A R Á
M A R A N H Ã O
P I A U Í
C E A R Á
RIO GRANDE DO NORTE
P A R A Í B A
P E R N A M B U C O
A L A G O A S
S E R G I P E
T O C A N T I N S
SERRA GRANDE
CHAPADA DO ARARIPE
CHAPADA DAS MANGABEIRAS
SERRA DA URUÇUÍ
SERRA DO PENITENTE
SERRA DO ESTRONDO
SERRA GERAL
SA. DO BOQUEIRÃO
BELÉM
São Luís
Teresina
FORTALEZA
Natal
João Pessoa
RECIFE
Maceió
Aracaju
Feira de Santana
Petrolina
Juazeiro
Juazeiro do Norte
Campina Grande
Mossoró
Imperatriz
Marabá
Parnaíba
Caxias
Sobral
Crato
Caruaru
Arapiraca
Araguaína
Palmas
Olinda
Jaboatão dos Guararapes
Maracanaú
165

ATLANTIC
OCEAN
MINAS GERAIS
ESPÍRITO SANTO
RIO DE JANEIRO
SÃO PAULO
GOIÁS
DISTRITO FEDERAL
BRASÍLIA
BELO HORIZONTE
RIO DE JANEIRO
SÃO PAULO
Vitória
GOIÂNIA
CAMPINAS
SANTOS
Niterói
Uberlândia
Tropic of Capricorn
42° West of Greenwich
Scale 1 : 5,000,000
500 Kilometers
300 Miles
Lambert Conformal Conic Projection
W-DRM5508-A1
Copyright © Rand McNally & Co.
Meters
Feet
Sea Level

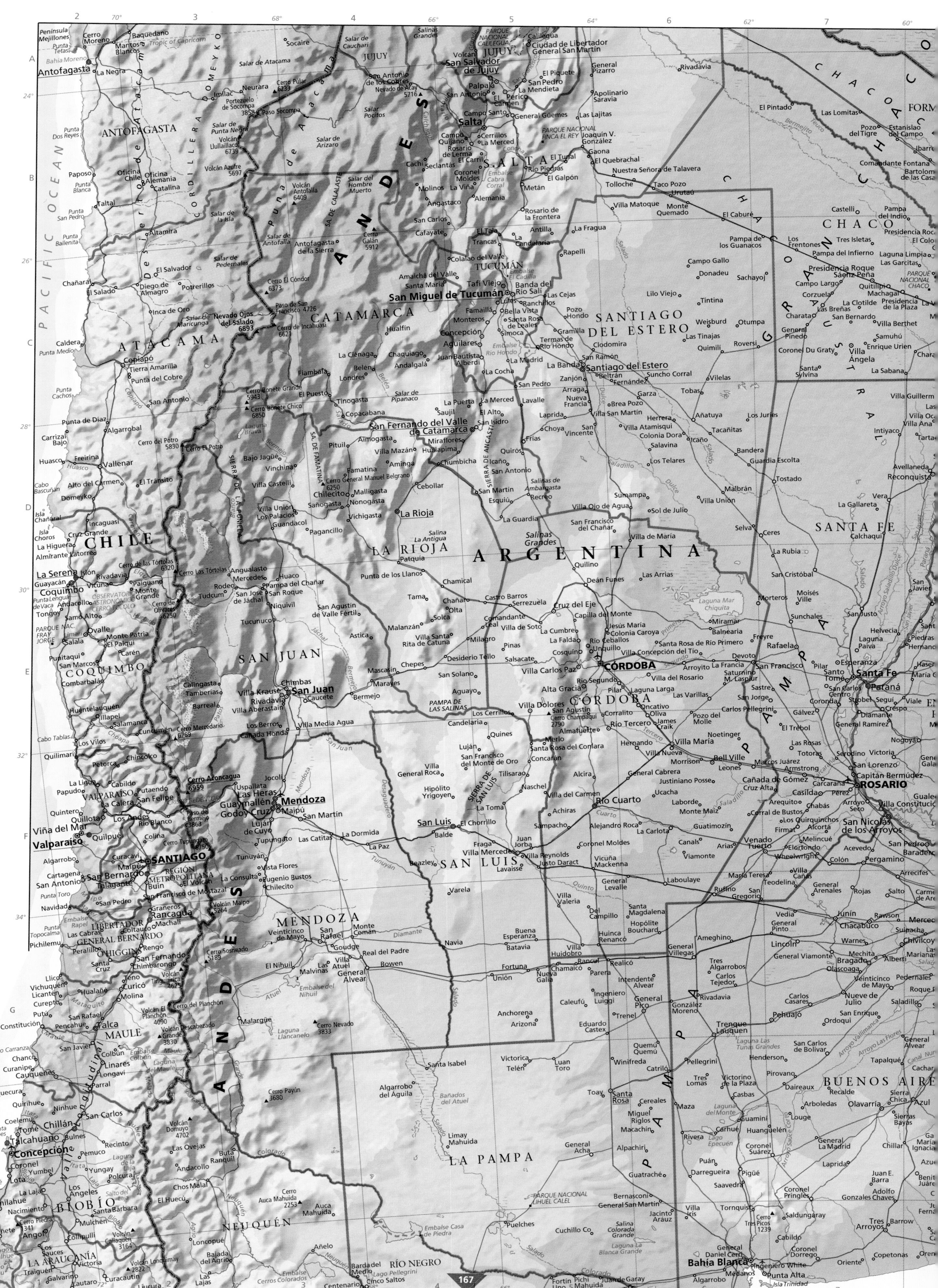
PACIFIC OCEAN
A N D E S
CHILE
ARGENTINA
ANTOFAGASTA
ATACAMA
COQUIMBO
VALPARAÍSO
REGIÓN METROPOLITANA
LIBERTADOR GENERAL BERNARDO O'HIGGINS
MAULE
BIOBÍO
LA ARAUCANÍA
JUJUY
SALTA
TUCUMÁN
CATAMARCA
SANTIAGO DEL ESTERO
LA RIOJA
SAN JUAN
CÓRDOBA
SAN LUIS
MENDOZA
LA PAMPA
NEUQUÉN
RÍO NEGRO
SANTA FE
BUENOS AIRES
CHACO
GRAN CHACO
PAMPA
CORDILLERA DOMEYKO
Desierto de Atacama
Puna de Atacama
Tropic of Capricorn
Antofagasta
Copiapó
La Serena
Coquimbo
Valparaíso
Viña del Mar
SANTIAGO
Rancagua
Talca
Chillán
Talcahuano
Concepción
Los Angeles
San Salvador de Jujuy
Salta
San Miguel de Tucumán
Santiago del Estero
San Fernando del Valle de Catamarca
La Rioja
San Juan
Mendoza
San Luis
CÓRDOBA
Santa Fe
Paraná
ROSARIO
Río Cuarto
San Rafael
Santa Rosa
Bahía Blanca
Cerro Aconcagua 6959
Nevado Ojos del Salado 6893
Salinas Grandes
Laguna Mar Chiquita
PAMPA DE LAS SALINAS
SIERRA DE SAN LUIS
167

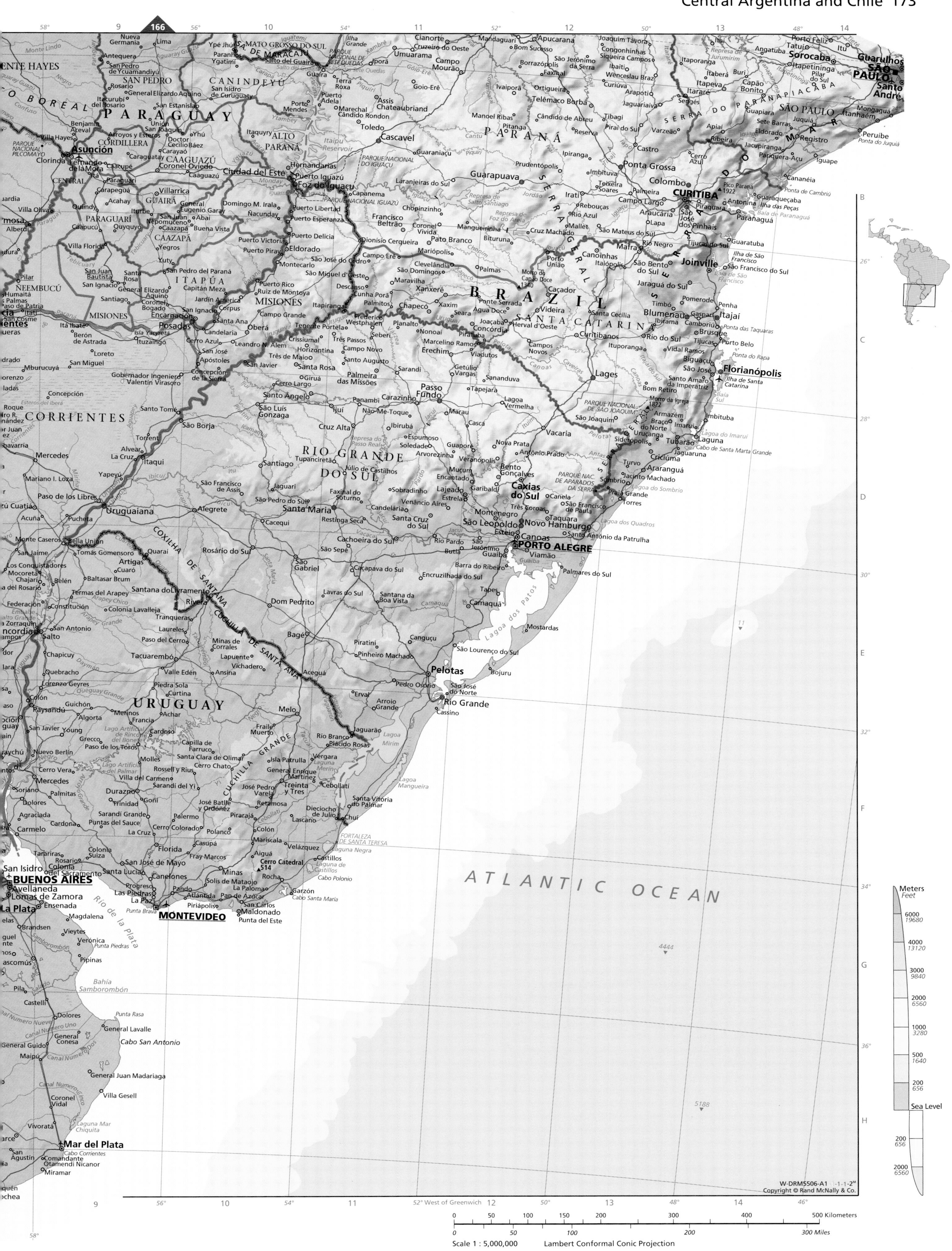
166
PARAGUAY
BRAZIL
URUGUAY
PARANÁ
SANTA CATARINA
RIO GRANDE DO SUL
CORRIENTES
MISIONES
ITAPÚA
CANINDEYÚ
SÃO PAULO
Asunción
Ciudad del Este
Foz do Iguaçu
Posadas
Encarnación
Curitiba
Florianópolis
Joinville
Blumenau
Ponta Grossa
Cascavel
Guarapuava
Passo Fundo
Santa Maria
Caxias do Sul
Novo Hamburgo
PORTO ALEGRE
Pelotas
Rio Grande
Uruguaiana
Alegrete
Rivera
Tacuarembó
Melo
Salto
Paysandú
MONTEVIDEO
BUENOS AIRES
La Plata
Mar del Plata
Maldonado
Punta del Este
Río de la Plata
Lagoa dos Patos
Lagoa Mirim
COXILHA DE SANTANA
CUCHILLA GRANDE
SERRA GERAL
SERRA DO MAR
ATLANTIC OCEAN
Meters
Feet
Sea Level
Scale 1 : 5,000,000
Lambert Conformal Conic Projection
500 Kilometers
300 Miles
52° West of Greenwich
W-DRM5506-A1
Copyright © Rand McNally & Co.

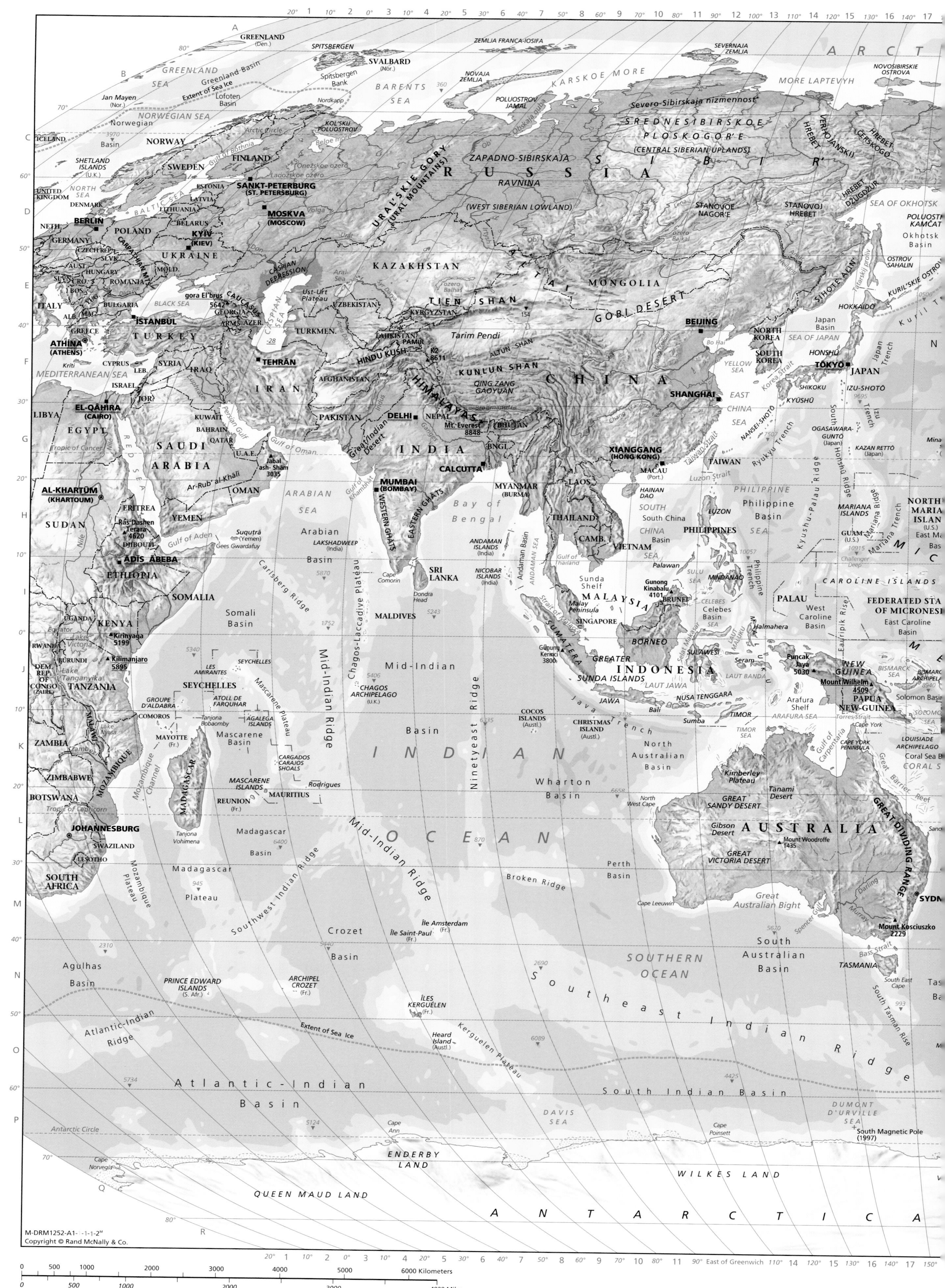

Scale 1 : 60,000,000 Robinson Projection

Canada Basin
North Magnetic Pole (1994)
ELLESMERE ISLAND
QUEEN ELIZABETH ISLANDS
GREENLAND (Den.)
Baffin Bay
Baffin Basin
BAFFIN ISLAND
VICTORIA ISLAND
Banks Island
BEAUFORT SEA
CHUKCHI SEA
ostrov Vrangelja
Point Barrow
BROOKS RANGE
ALASKA (U.S.)
Mount McKinley 6194
ALASKA RANGE
Mount Logan 5959
MACKENZIE MOUNTAINS
Great Bear Lake
Great Slave Lake
Southampton Island
Hudson Bay
Hudson Strait
Péninsule d'Ungava
Davis Strait
Gunnbjørn Fjeld 3700
Arctic Circle
Irminger Basin
LABRADOR SEA
LABRADOR
Labrador Basin
Extent of Sea Ice
BERING SEA
Aleutian Basin
Alaska Peninsula
Kodiak Island
Gulf of Alaska
ALEUTIAN ISLANDS
Aleutian Trench
International Date Line
Emperor Seamounts
COAST MTS.
QUEEN CHARLOTTE ISLANDS
Mount Waddington 3994
ROCKY MOUNTAINS
CANADA
Lake Athabasca
Lake Winnipeg
VANCOUVER ISLAND
CASCADE RANGE
COAST RANGES
Lake Superior
Lake Huron
Lake Michigan
Ottawa
Montreal
NEWFOUNDLAND
ST. PIERRE AND MIQUELON (Fr.)
CHICAGO
GREAT PLAINS
UNITED STATES
APPALACHIAN MTS.
NEW YORK
Washington
Cape Cod
Cape Mendocino
Mendocino Fracture Zone
GREAT BASIN
Great Salt Lake
Mount Whitney 4418
LOS ANGELES
Cape Lookout
ATLANTIC
North American Basin
OCEAN
BERMUDA (U.K.)
Blake Plateau
PACIFIC OCEAN
Musicians Seamounts
Murray Fracture Zone
HOUSTON
Gulf of Mexico
Mexico Basin
Isla Guadalupe (Mex.)
Baja California
Golfo de California
SIERRA MADRE OCCIDENTAL
SIERRA MADRE ORIENTAL
MIDWAY ISLANDS (U.S.)
Hawaiian Ridge
HAWAIIAN ISLANDS (U.S.)
Oahu
Hawaii
Molokai Fracture Zone
Cabo San Lucas
CIUDAD DE MÉXICO
MEXICO
Volcán Pico de Orizaba 5610
SIERRA MADRE DEL SUR
Pen. de Yucatán
BAHAMAS
Tropic of Cancer
WEST INDIES
CUBA
GREATER ANTILLES
HAITI
DOM. REP.
JAMAICA
PUERTO RICO (U.S.)
BELIZE
GUAT.
HONDURAS
EL SALV.
NICARAGUA
CARIBBEAN SEA
COSTA RICA
PANAMA
Istmo de Panamá
VENEZUELA
Lago de Maracaibo
SANTA FE DE BOGOTÁ
COLOMBIA
WAKE ISLAND (U.S.)
Johnston Atoll (U.S.)
Clarion Fracture Zone
ISLAS REVILLAGIGEDO (Mex.)
Middle America Trench
Guatemala Basin
Île Clipperton (Fr.)
Central Pacific Basin
Christmas Ridge
POLYNESIA
LINE ISLANDS
Clipperton Fracture Zone
Isla del Coco (C.R.)
Cocos Ridge
Panama Basin
RATAK CHAIN
GILBERT ISLANDS
Howland Island (U.S.)
Baker Island (U.S.)
Kiritimati
Jarvis Island (U.S.)
PHOENIX ISLANDS
ARCHIPIÉLAGO DE COLÓN (Ec.)
Chimborazo 6310
ECUADOR
Equator
Punta Pariñas
PERU
BRAZIL
Amazon
SOLOMON ISLANDS
TUVALU
KIRIBATI
TOKELAU (N.Z.)
ÎLES MARQUISES
Nevado Huascarán 6746
Lima
ANDES
WALLIS AND FUTUNA (Fr.)
SAMOA
AMERICAN SAMOA (U.S.)
NORTHERN COOK ISLANDS
COOK ISLANDS (N.Z.)
FRENCH POLYNESIA (Fr.)
ÎLES TUAMOTU
Tuamotu Ridge
ARCHIPEL DE LA SOCIÉTÉ
Tahiti
North Fiji Basin
FIJI
Suva
TONGA
Tonga Ridge
Tonga Trench
NEW HEBRIDES
New Hebrides Trench
NIUE (N.Z.)
SOUTHERN COOK ISLANDS
Austral Seamounts
ÎLES AUSTRALES
ÎLES GAMBIER
PITCAIRN (U.K.)
Pitcairn Island
Peru Basin
La Paz
BOLIVIA
Nazca Ridge
Peru-Chile Trench
Tropic of Capricorn
East Pacific Ridge
Isla Sala y Gómez (Chile)
Sala y Gomez Ridge
Isla de Pascua (Chile)
South Fiji Basin
Lau Ridge
NORFOLK ISLAND (Austl.)
Norfolk Ridge
KERMADEC ISLANDS (N.Z.)
Kermadec Ridge
Kermadec Trench
Louisville Ridge
Southwest PACIFIC OCEAN
ARCHIPIÉLAGO JUAN FERNÁNDEZ (Chile)
Cerro Aconcagua 6959
SANTIAGO
PAMPA
CHILE
ARGENTINA
North Cape
NORTH ISLAND
NEW ZEALAND
Cook Strait
Chatham Rise
CHATHAM ISLANDS (N.Z.)
Aoraki (Mount Cook) 3754
Pacific Basin
Chile Rise
Isla Grande de Chiloé
Golfo San Matías
PATAGONIA
Golfo San Jorge
Argentine Basin
Bounty Trough
BOUNTY ISLANDS (N.Z.)
Campbell Plateau
ANTIPODES ISLANDS (N.Z.)
Campbell Island (N.Z.)
ATLANTIC OCEAN
FALKLAND ISLANDS (U.K.)
Strait of Magellan
TIERRA DEL FUEGO
Cabo de Hornos (Cape Horn)
Extent of Sea Ice
Drake Passage
SCOTIA SEA
Pacific-Antarctic Ridge
Southeast Pacific Basin
SOUTH SHETLAND ISLANDS (U.K.)
SOUTH ORKNEY ISLANDS (U.K.)
Antarctic Circle
ANTARCTIC PENINSULA
Atlantic-Indian Basin
Scott Island
AMUNDSEN SEA
Thurston Island
BELLINGSHAUSEN SEA
ALEXANDER ISLAND
WEDDELL SEA
Cape Adare
ROSS SEA
MARIE BYRD LAND
Vinson Massif 5140
Ronne Ice Shelf
BERKNER ISLAND
Ross Ice Shelf
Roosevelt Island
West of Greenwich

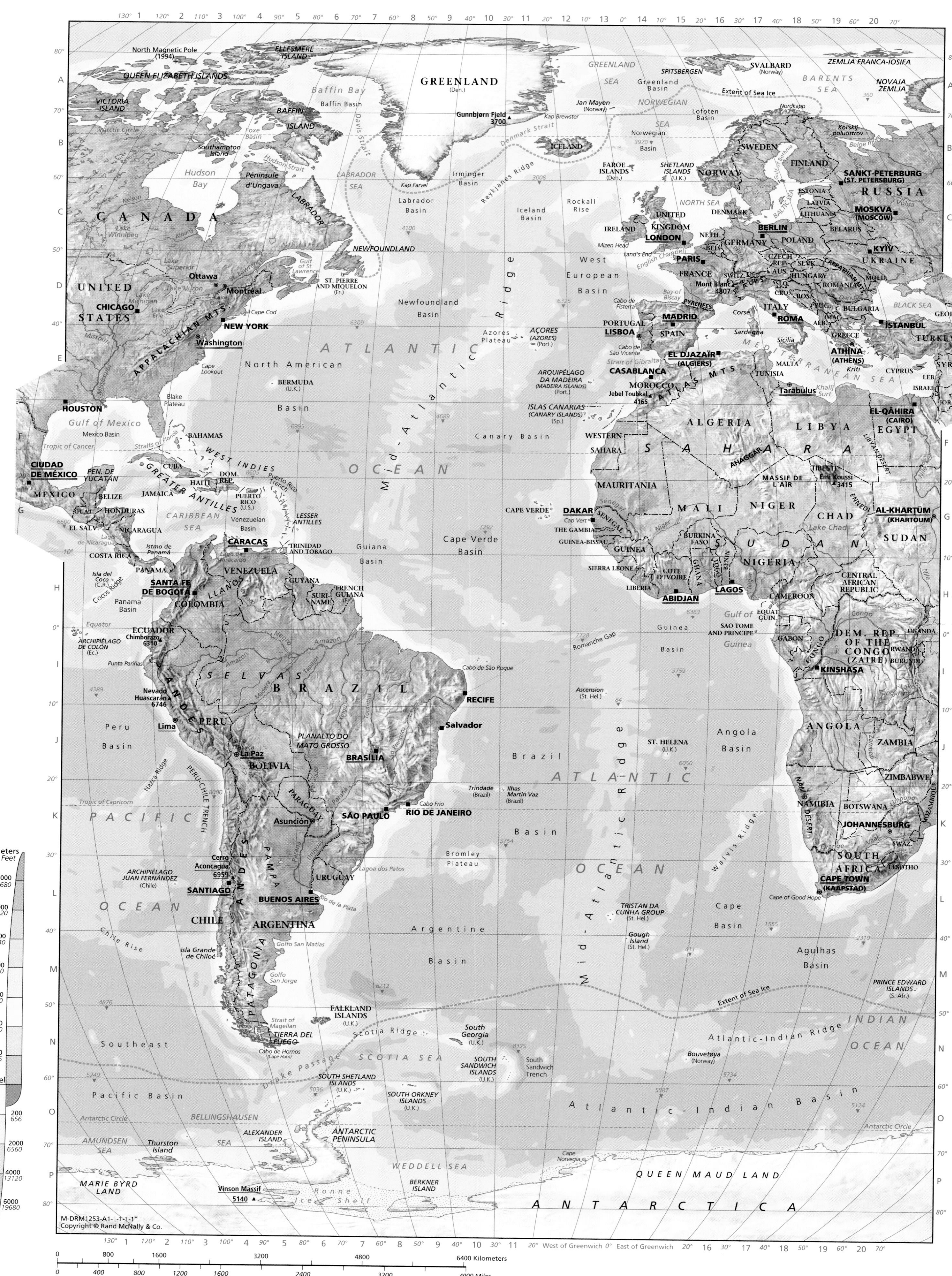
GREENLAND
CANADA
UNITED STATES
ATLANTIC OCEAN
North American Basin
Mid-Atlantic Ridge
BRAZIL
ARGENTINA
CHILE
PACIFIC OCEAN
ANTARCTICA
RUSSIA
ALGERIA
LIBYA
EGYPT
SAHARA
West European Basin
Canary Basin
Cape Verde Basin
Brazil Basin
Argentine Basin
Angola Basin
Cape Basin
Agulhas Basin
Atlantic-Indian Basin
Atlantic-Indian Ridge
INDIAN OCEAN
SCOTIA SEA
WEDDELL SEA
QUEEN MAUD LAND
Scale 1 : 60,000,000
Robinson Projection
M-DRM1253-A1- -1-1-1M
Copyright © Rand McNally & Co.

World Metropolitan Areas

This section consists of 60 maps of the world's major metropolitan areas, shown at a scale of 1:300,000. The maps illustrate the generalized land-use patterns in and around each city—the total urban extent, major industrial areas, parks and preserves, and wooded areas. Airports are labeled, as are many details of the highway and rail transportation networks. Also included are selected points of interest, such as Fisherman's Wharf and Chinatown in San Francisco, the Welcome monument in Jakarta, the Temple of the Jade Buddha in Shanghai, and the Cristo Redentor statue in Rio de Janeiro.

The maps name and locate a great number of towns, villages, and suburbs or neighborhoods within limits of the larger cities. Prominent physical features, including named and unnamed elevations, have been indicated to give a general impression of the local typography. Shaded relief has been omitted, however, to permit display of such details as streams, parks, airport runways, important public buildings and monuments, and the names of major streets. The corporate limits of major cities are also outlined. To identify the symbols used on these maps, refer to the Map Legend on page 1.

Maps of major world cities usually vary widely in scale and and are inconsistent in design and coverage. For this section, a special effort has been made to portray these varied metropolitan areas in as standard and comparable a fashion as possible. However, for a few cities (notably several in Asia) there has not been adequate source material to include certain information, such as major industrial areas and corporate limits.

The order of presentation is generally regional, with some exceptions where major capitals, industrial centers, or cities located in similar physical surroundings have been juxtaposed for ease of comparison. Many American and European cities, with their lower population densities and more extensive land areas, require larger maps than do Asiatic cities of comparable population.

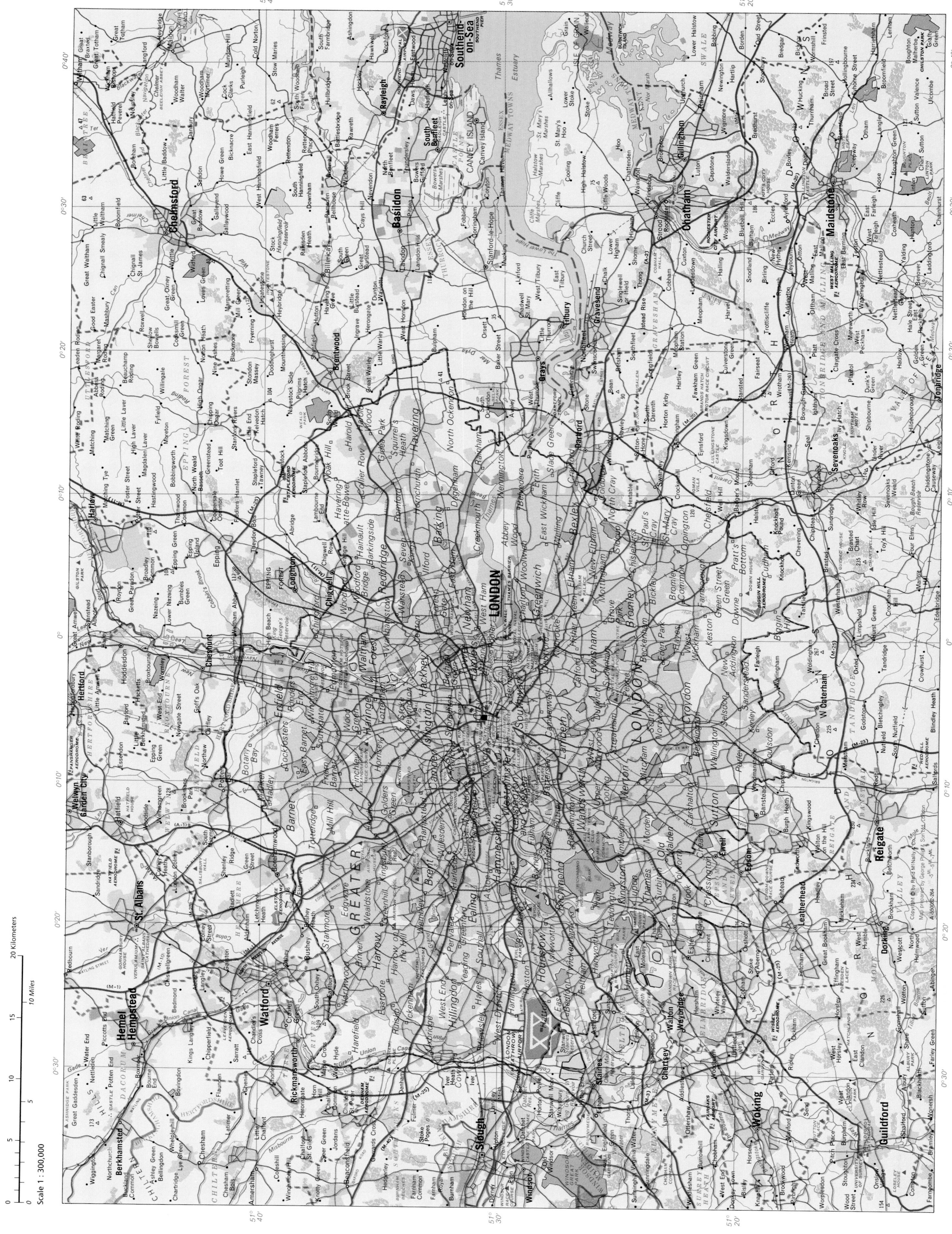

Scale 1 : 300,000
10 Miles
20 Kilometers
LONDON
GREATER LONDON
Chelmsford
Southend-on-Sea
Basildon
Brentwood
Chatham
Gillingham
Maidstone
Gravesend
Tilbury
Grays
Dartford
Sevenoaks
Tonbridge
Reigate
Dorking
Guildford
Woking
Leatherhead
Epsom
Staines
Chertsey
Weybridge
Slough
Windsor
Watford
Hemel Hempstead
St. Albans
Berkhamsted
Rickmansworth
Welwyn Garden City
Hertford
Harlow
Cheshunt
Chigwell
Loughton
Rayleigh
Thames Estuary
CANVEY ISLAND

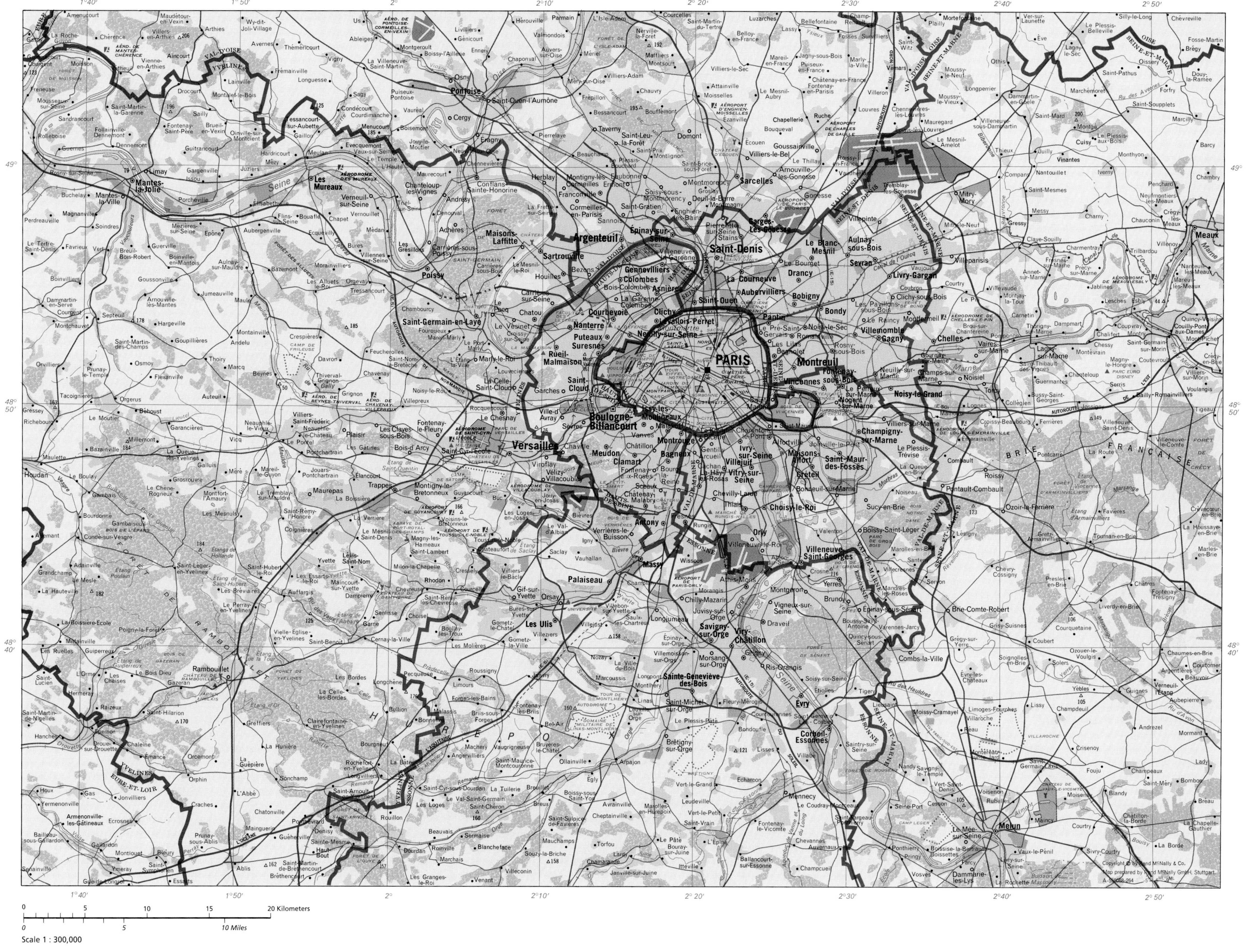
PARIS
Saint-Denis
Versailles
Argenteuil
Montreuil
Melun
Meaux
Pontoise
Copyright © by Rand McNally & Co.
Map prepared by Rand McNally GmbH, Stuttgart
20 Kilometers
10 Miles
Scale 1 : 300,000

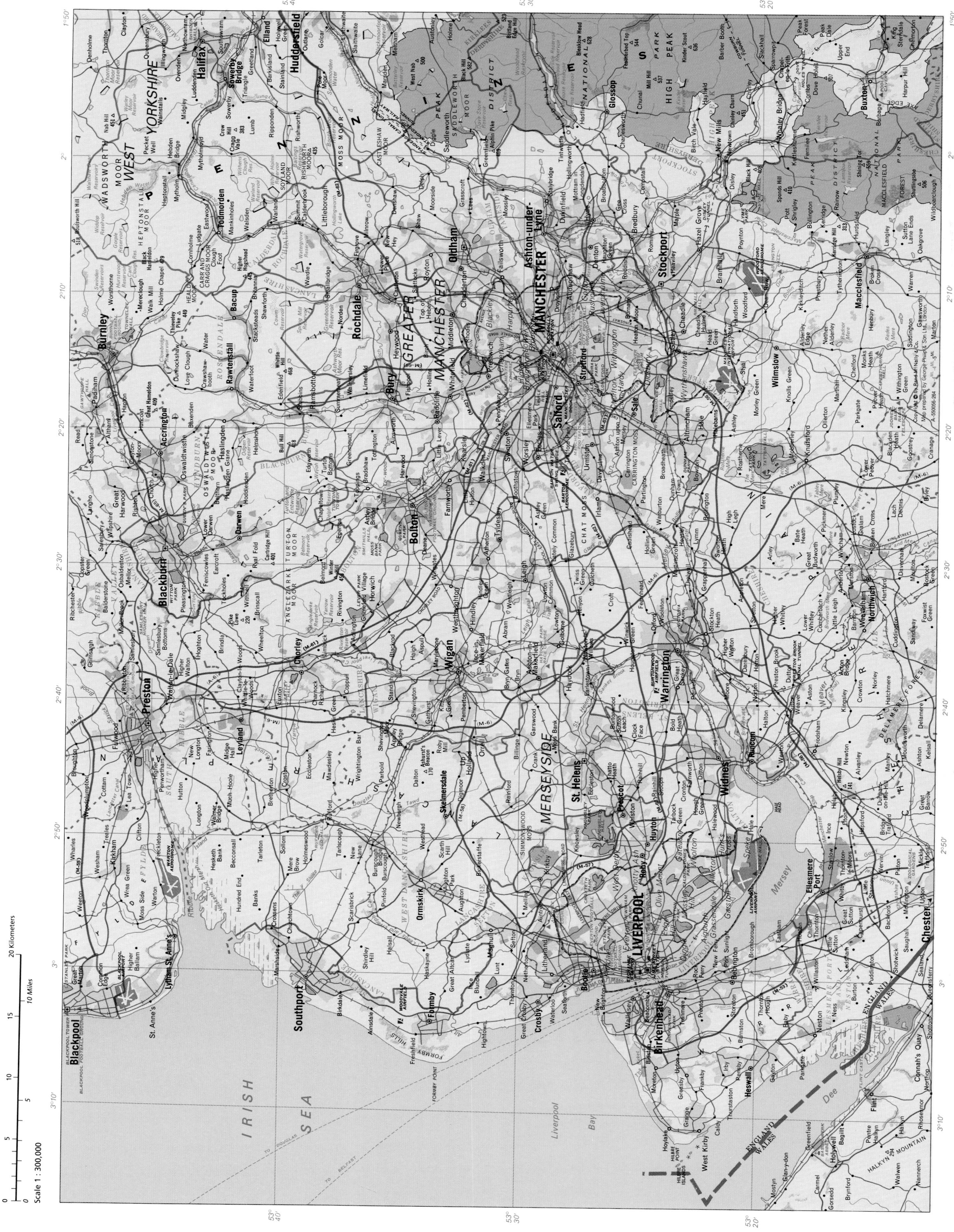
Scale 1 : 300,000
20 Kilometers
10 Miles
MANCHESTER
LIVERPOOL
GREATER MANCHESTER
MERSEYSIDE
WEST YORKSHIRE
IRISH SEA
Liverpool Bay
Blackpool
Preston
Blackburn
Burnley
Southport
Bolton
Wigan
Rochdale
Oldham
Stockport
Salford
Warrington
Widnes
Runcorn
Birkenhead
Chester
Halifax
Huddersfield
Macclesfield
Northwich
St. Helens
Ormskirk
Formby
Bootle
Bury
Ellesmere Port

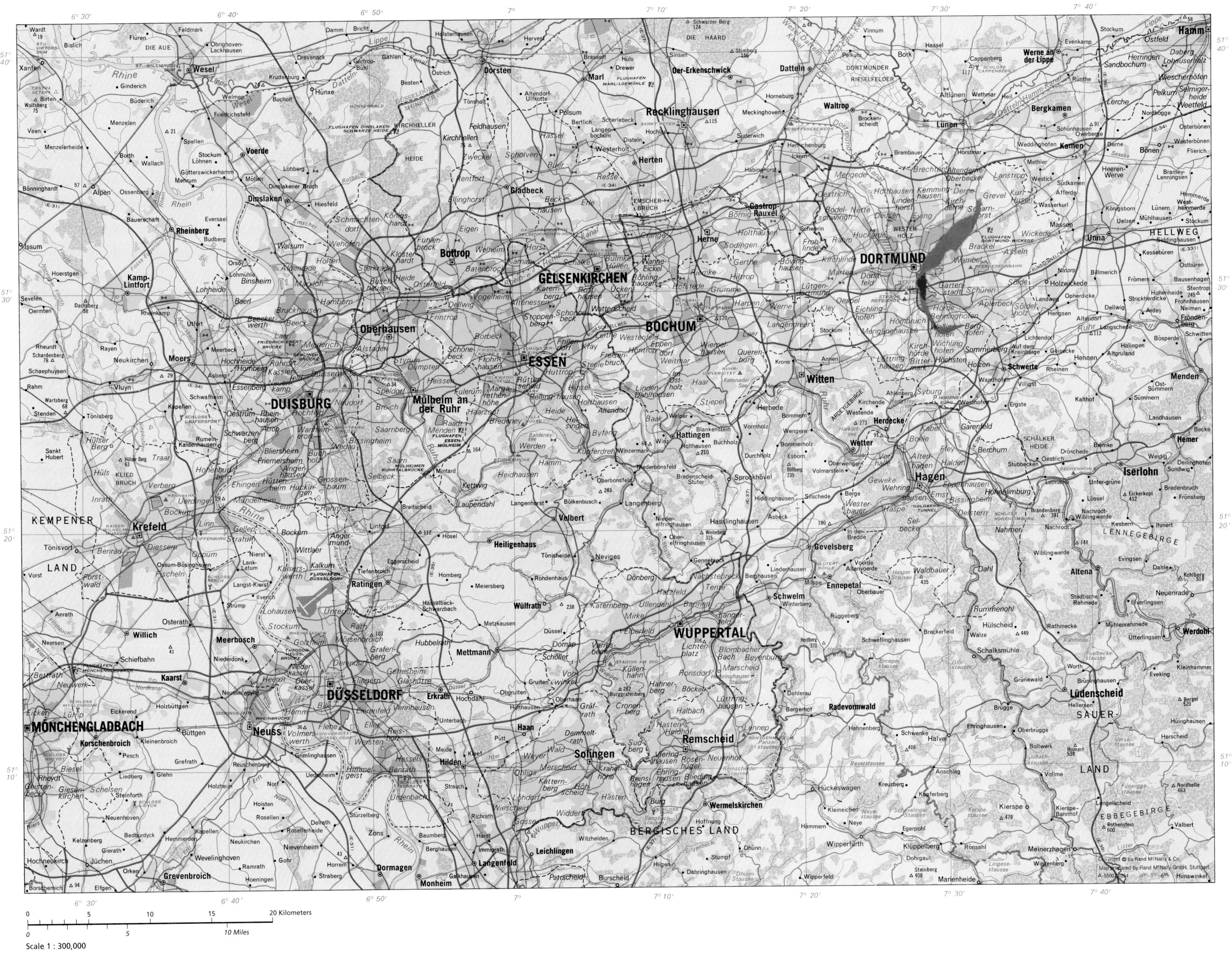
Hamm
DORTMUND
BOCHUM
GELSENKIRCHEN
ESSEN
DUISBURG
DÜSSELDORF
WUPPERTAL
Hagen
Witten
Herne
Recklinghausen
Bottrop
Oberhausen
Mülheim an der Ruhr
Remscheid
Solingen
Neuss
Krefeld
MÖNCHENGLADBACH
Moers
Wesel
Iserlohn
Lüdenscheid
Ratingen
Velbert
BERGISCHES LAND
KEMPENER LAND
Scale 1 : 300,000
20 Kilometers
10 Miles

a

b

c

0 5 10 15 20 Kilometers

0 5 10 Miles

Scale 1 : 300,000

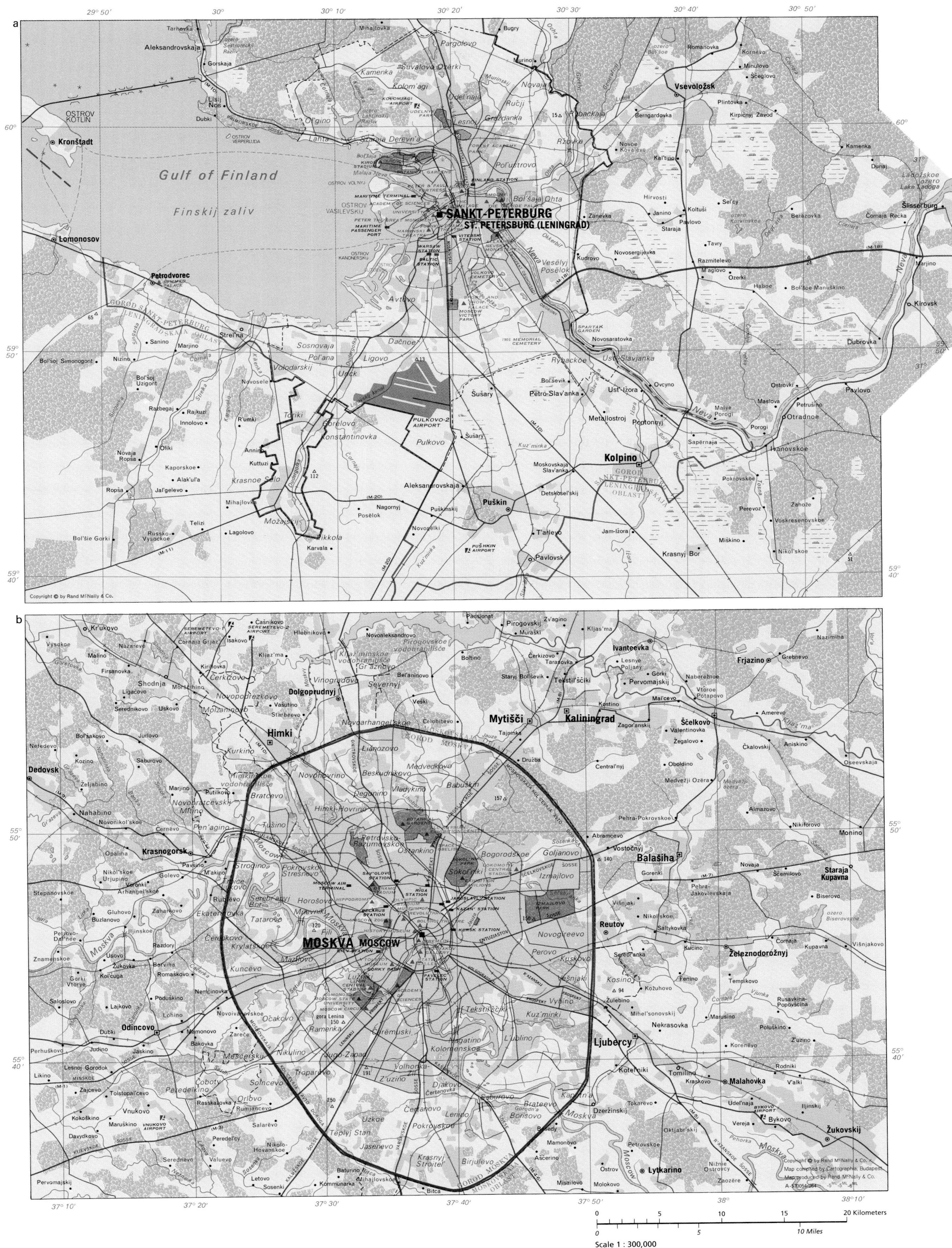
a
Gulf of Finland
Finskij zaliv
SANKT-PETERBURG
ST. PETERSBURG (LENINGRAD)
Kronštadt
Lomonosov
Petrodvorec
Strel'na
Puškin
Pavlovsk
Kolpino
Vsevoložsk
Šlissel'burg
Kirovsk
Otradnoe
PULKOVO-2 AIRPORT
Copyright © by Rand McNally & Co.
b
MOSKVA MOSCOW
Himki
Dolgoprudnyj
Mytišči
Kaliningrad
Ščelkovo
Balašiha
Reutov
Krasnogorsk
Odincovo
Ljubercy
Dzeržinskij
Lytkarino
Železnodorožnyj
Žukovskij
Malahovka
Frjazino
Ivanteevka
Dedovsk
Staraja Kupavna
Copyright © by Rand McNally & Co.
Map compiled by Cartographia, Budapest
Map produced by Rand McNally & Co.
0 5 10 15 20 Kilometers
0 5 10 Miles
Scale 1 : 300,000

Scale 1 : 300,000
20 Kilometers
10 Miles
a
MADRID
Alcobendas
San Sebastián de los Reyes
Torrejón de Ardoz
Coslada
Alcorcón
Móstoles
Leganés
Getafe
Fuenlabrada
Arganda
b
MILANO
MILAN
Monza
Busto Arsizio
Gallarate
Legnano
Saronno
Novara
Rho
Magenta
Abbiategrasso
Sesto San Giovanni
c
LISBOA
LISBON
Amadora
Odivelas
Sacavém
Moscavide
Queluz
Oeiras
Cascais
Almada
Barreiro
Montijo
Tagus
Tejo
ATLANTIC OCEAN
d
BARCELONA
Badalona
Terrassa
Sabadell
Rubí
Ripollet
Mataró
L'Hospitalet de Llobregat
Cornellà de Llobregat
Sant Boi de Llobregat
El Prat de Llobregat
Viladecans
Gavà
MEDITERRANEAN SEA
Copyright © by Rand McNally & Co.
Map prepared by Rand McNally GmbH, Stuttgart.

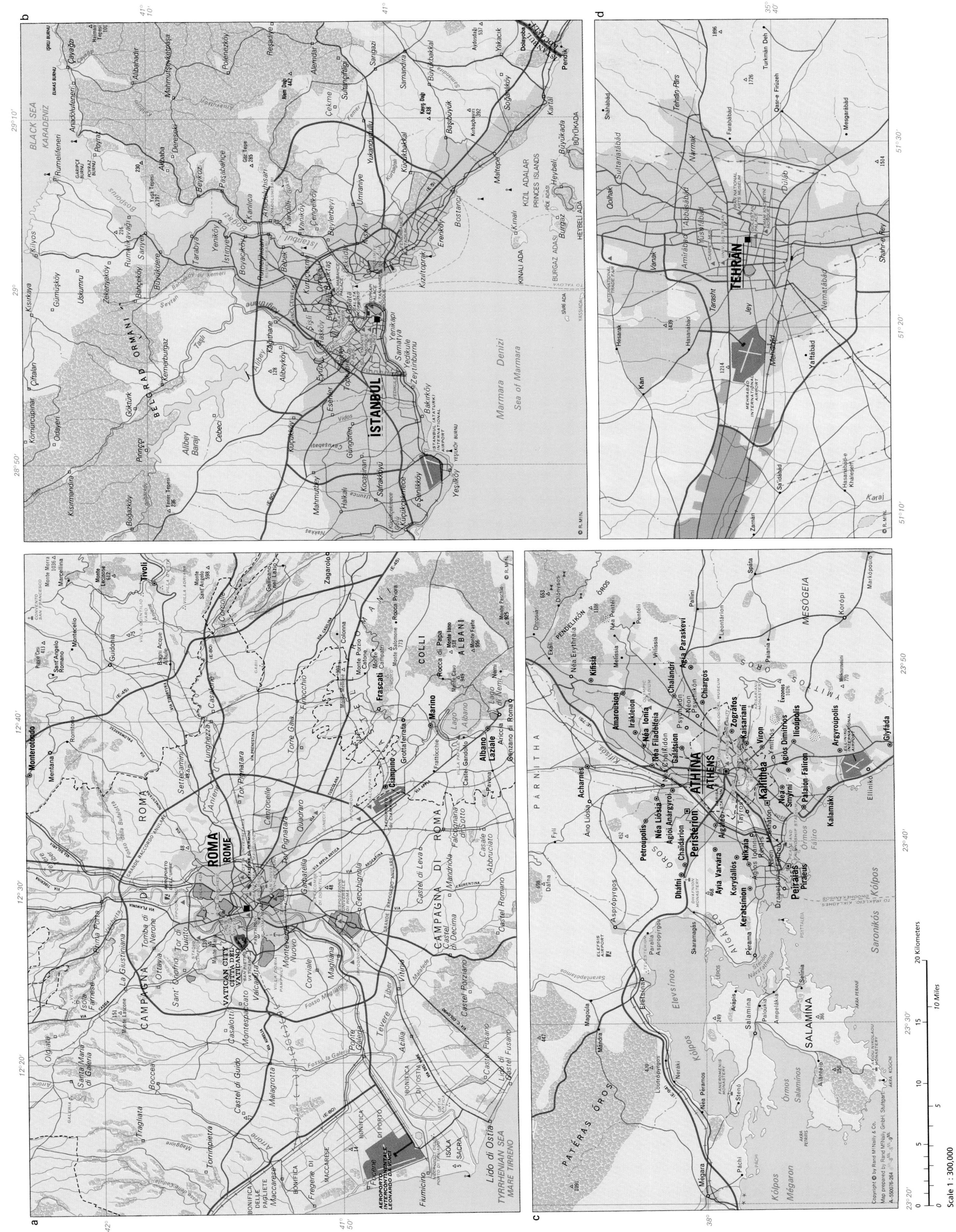

a
b
c
d
ROMA
ROME
VATICAN CITY
CITTÀ DEL VATICANO
TYRRHENIAN SEA
MARE TIRRENO
İSTANBUL
BLACK SEA
KARADENİZ
Marmara Denizi
Sea of Marmara
ATHÍNA
ATHENS
Piraiévs
Piraeus
TEHRĀN
Scale 1 : 300,000
20 Kilometers
10 Miles

Map prepared by Teikoku-Shoin Co., Ltd., Tokyo.
A-560076-264

0 5 10 15 20 Kilometers

0 5 10 Miles

Scale 1 : 300,000

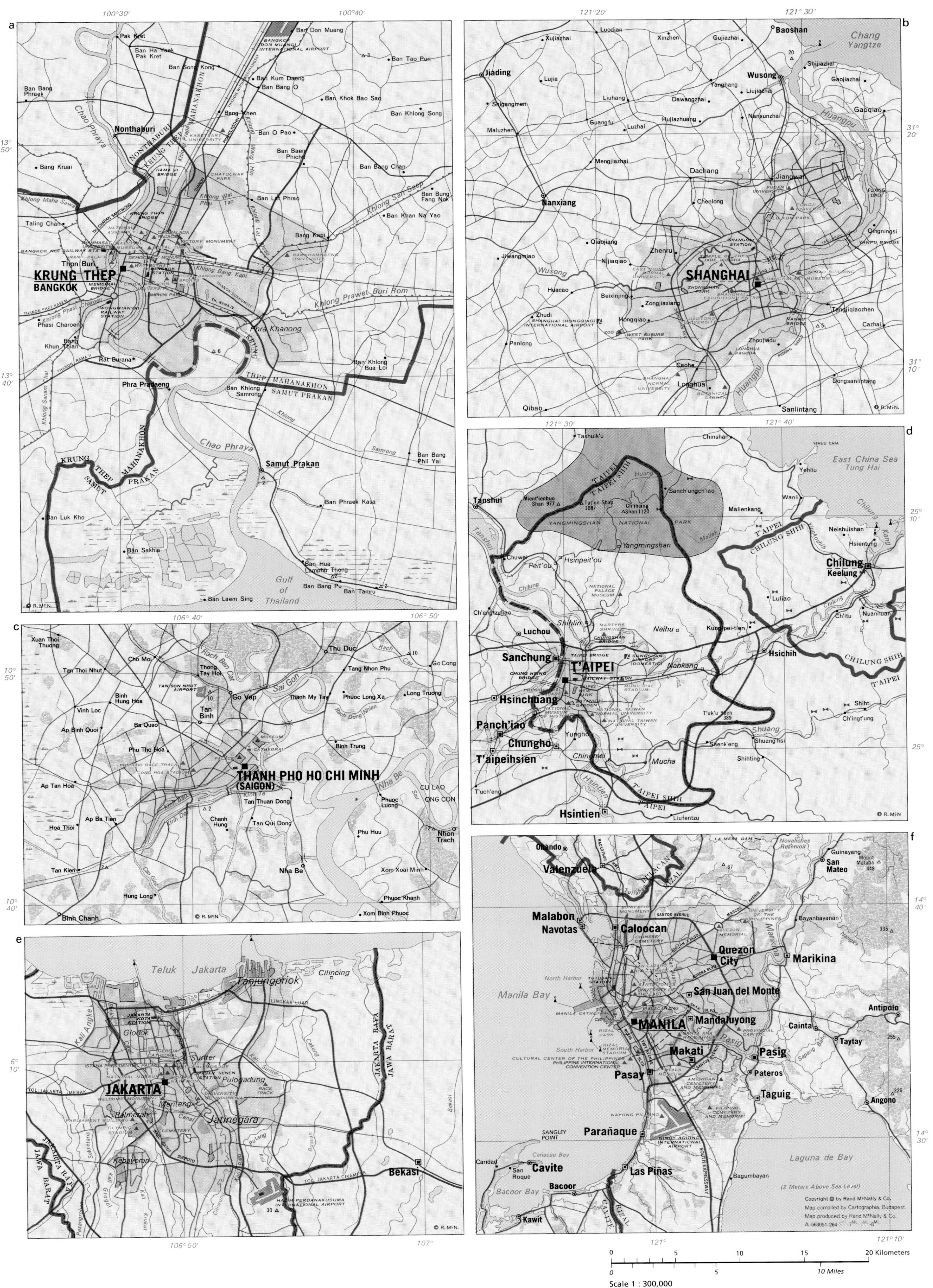
a
KRUNG THEP
BANGKOK
Nonthaburi
Thon Buri
Pak Kret
Bang Kruai
Taling Chan
Phasi Charoen
Rat Burana
Phra Pradaeng
Samut Prakan
Ban Sakhla
Ban Laem Sing
Gulf of Thailand
Chao Phraya
Phra Khanong
Bang Kapi
Ban Don Muang
Ban Tao Pun
Ban Khlong Song
Ban Bang Chan
Ban Khan Na Yao
Ban Phraek Kasa
Ban Luk Kho
Ban Bang Pu
Ban Tamru
Khlong Prawet Buri Rom
Khlong San Saep
KRUNG THEP MAHANAKHON
SAMUT PRAKAN
b
SHANGHAI
Baoshan
Jiading
Wusong
Nanxiang
Zhenru
Jiangwan
Dachang
Gaoqiao
Huacao
Beixinjing
Hongqiao
Panlong
Qibao
Caohe
Longhua
Sanlintang
Dongsanlintang
Cazhai
Chang Yangtze
Huangpu
Wusong
Luodian
Xinzhen
Gujiazhai
c
THANH PHO HO CHI MINH (SAIGON)
Thu Duc
Go Vap
Tan Binh
Binh Hung Hoa
Vinh Loc
Ba Queo
Phu Tho Hoa
Tan Thuan Dong
Chanh Hung
Tan Qui Dong
Nha Be
Binh Chanh
Hung Long
Tan Kien
Hoa Thoi
Phu Huu
Nhon Trach
Phuoc Khanh
Xom Binh Phuoc
Sai Gon
Nha Be
CU LAO ONG CON
d
T'AIPEI
Tanshui
Chilung
Keelung
Sanchung
Hsinchuang
Panch'iao
Chungho
T'aipeihsien
Yungho
Hsintien
Luchou
Shihlin
Neihu
Nankang
Hsichih
Mucha
Shenk'eng
Shuang'hsi
Shihting
Yangmingshan
East China Sea
Tung Hai
YANGMINGSHAN NATIONAL PARK
T'AIPEI SHIH
CHILUNG SHIH
e
JAKARTA
Teluk Jakarta
Tanjungpriok
Cilincing
Glodok
Sunter
Pulogadung
Menteng
Jatinegara
Kebayoran
Bekasi
JAKARTA RAYA
JAWA BARAT
f
MANILA
Quezon City
Caloocan
Malabon
Navotas
Valenzuela
Marikina
San Mateo
San Juan del Monte
Mandaluyong
Makati
Pasig
Pasay
Pateros
Taguig
Cainta
Taytay
Antipolo
Angono
Parañaque
Las Piñas
Cavite
Bacoor
Kawit
Manila Bay
Bacoor Bay
Laguna de Bay
(2 Meters Above Sea Level)
Copyright © by Rand McNally & Co.
Map compiled by Cartographia, Budapest.
Map produced by Rand McNally & Co.
Scale 1 : 300,000
0 5 10 15 20 Kilometers
0 5 10 Miles

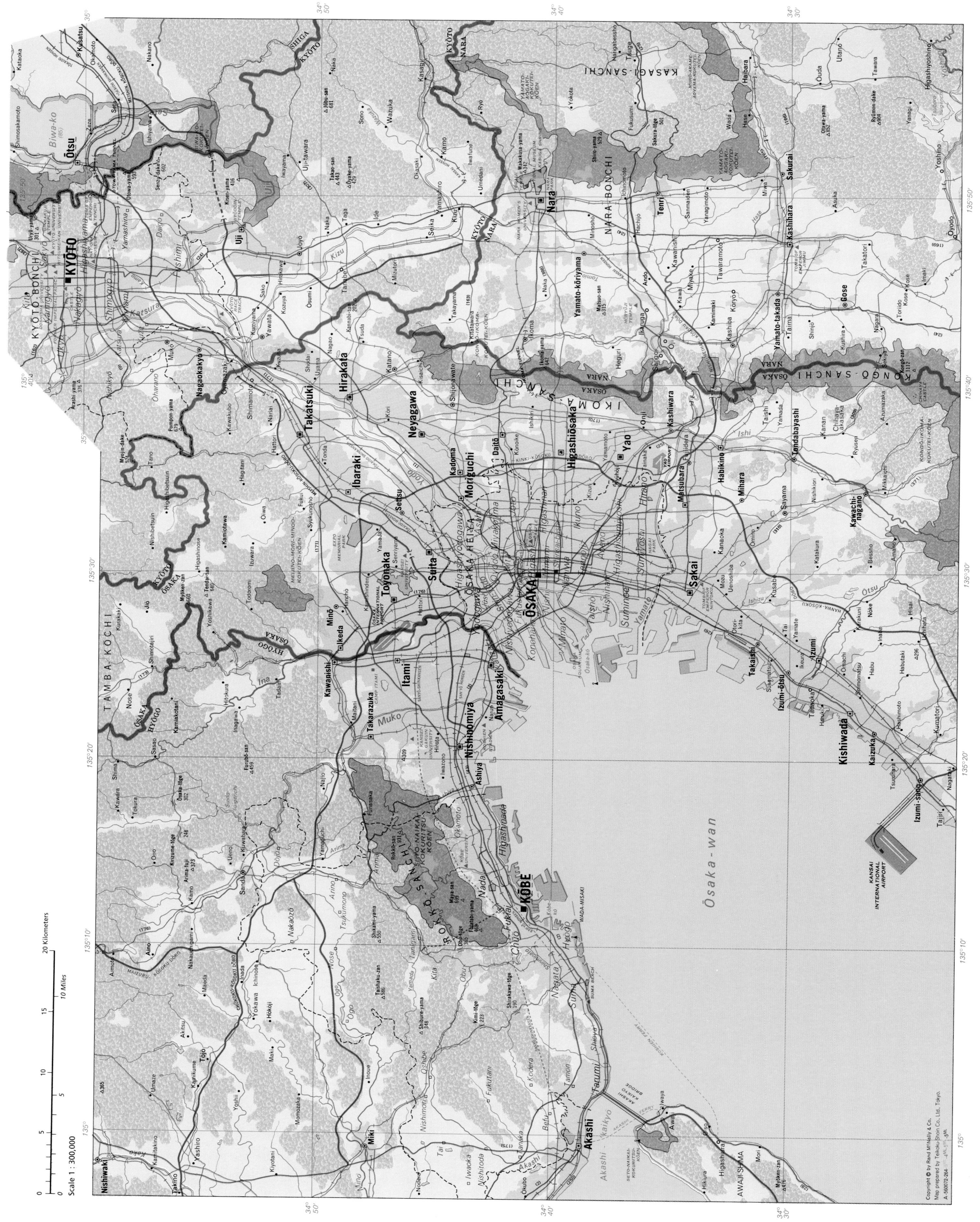
KYŌTO
ŌSAKA
KŌBE
Nara
Ōtsu
Biwa-ko
Uji
Takatsuki
Hirakata
Neyagawa
Ibaraki
Suita
Toyonaka
Itami
Amagasaki
Nishinomiya
Ashiya
Takarazuka
Kawanishi
Ikeda
Minō
Moriguchi
Kadoma
Daitō
Higashiōsaka
Yao
Matsubara
Sakai
Habikino
Mihara
Kashiwara
Tondabayashi
Kawachi-nagano
Takaishi
Izumi
Izumi-ōtsu
Kishiwada
Kaizuka
Izumi-sano
Akashi
Miki
Sanda
Nishiwaki
Yamato-kōriyama
Tenri
Kashihara
Sakurai
Gose
Yamato-takada
Ōsaka-wan
KANSAI INTERNATIONAL AIRPORT
KYŌTO-BONCHI
NARA-BONCHI
ŌSAKA-HEIYA
IKOMA-SANCHI
KONGŌ-SANCHI
KASAGI-SANCHI
TAMBA-KŌCHI
ROKKŌ-SANCHI
AWAJI-SHIMA
Yodo
Kizu
Muko
Ina
Scale 1 : 300,000
0 5 10 15 20 Kilometers
0 5 10 Miles
Copyright © by Rand McNally & Co.
Map prepared by Teikoku-Shoin Co., Ltd., Tokyo.

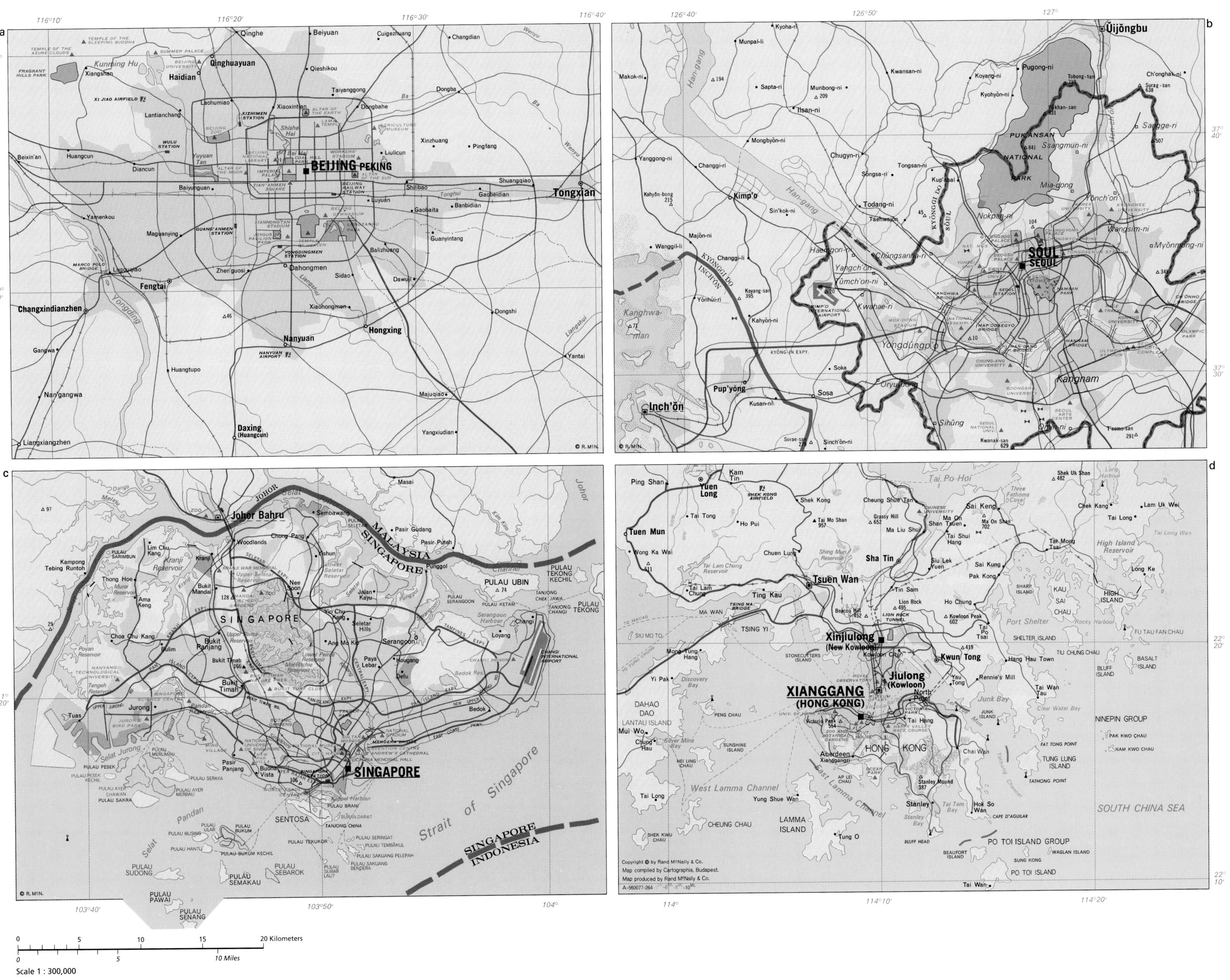
a
BEIJING PEKING
Haidian
Qinghuayuan
Tongxian
Fengtai
Changxindianzhen
Nanyuan
Hongxing
Daxing (Huangcun)
Kunming Hu
Yongding
b
SŎUL SEOUL
Ŭijŏngbu
Inch'ŏn
Kimp'o
Pup'yŏng
Kangnam
Yŏngdŭngp'o
Han-gang
PUK'ANSAN NATIONAL PARK
c
SINGAPORE
Johor Bahru
MALAYSIA
SINGAPORE
INDONESIA
Strait of Singapore
PULAU UBIN
SENTOSA
Jurong
Tuas
Changi
Woodlands
d
XIANGGANG (HONG KONG)
Jiulong (Kowloon)
Xinjiulong (New Kowloon)
Kwun Tong
Sha Tin
Tsuen Wan
Tuen Mun
Yuen Long
LANTAU ISLAND
LAMMA ISLAND
HONG KONG
SOUTH CHINA SEA
Copyright © by Rand McNally & Co.
Map compiled by Cartographia, Budapest.
Map produced by Rand McNally & Co.
Scale 1 : 300,000
20 Kilometers
10 Miles

Scale 1 : 300,000

0 5 10 15 20 Kilometers

0 5 10 Miles

a DELHI

b CALCUTTA

c MUMBAI (BOMBAY)

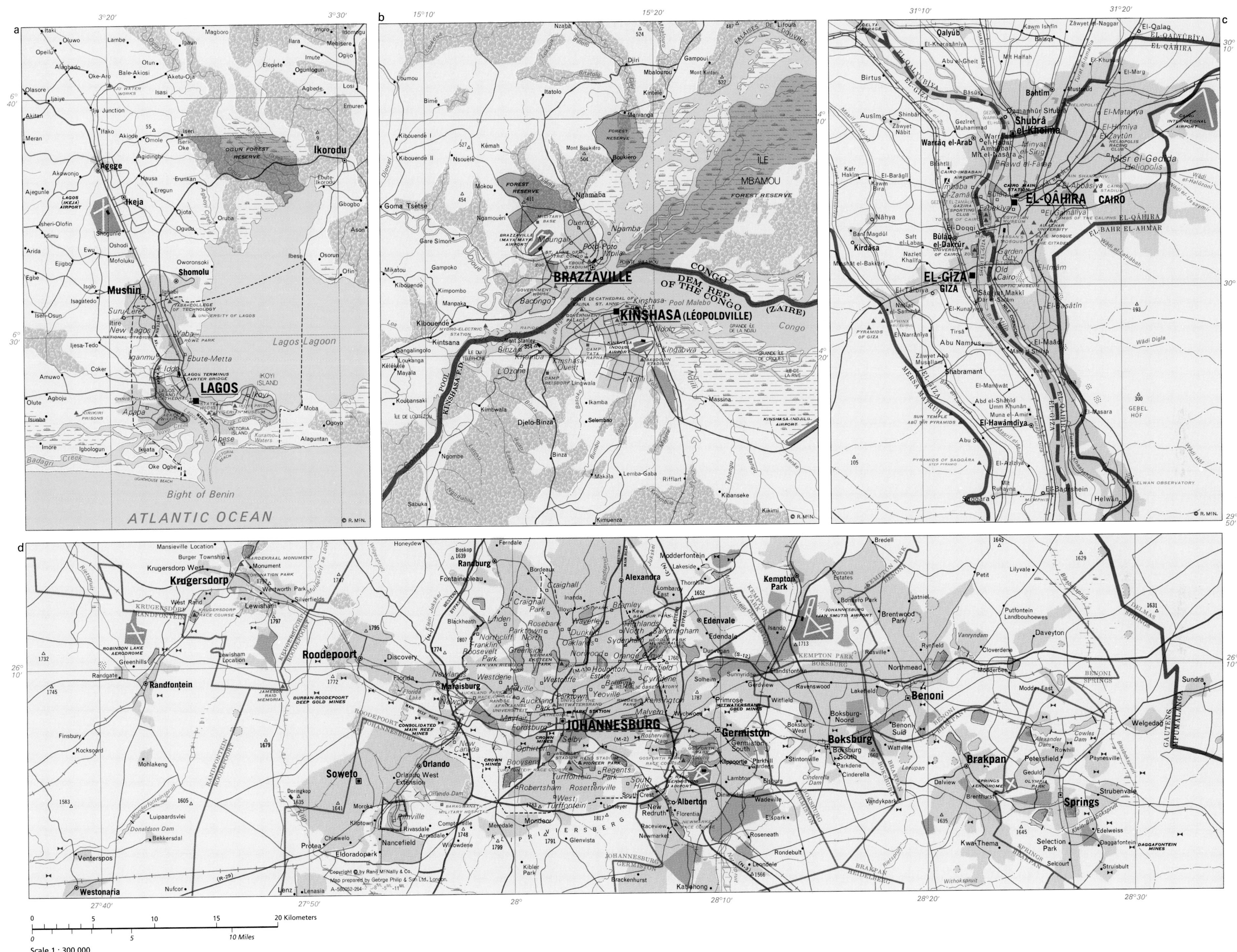
a
b
c
d
ATLANTIC OCEAN
Bight of Benin
Lagos Lagoon
LAGOS
Ikeja
Agege
Mushin
Shomolu
Ikorodu
BRAZZAVILLE
KINSHASA (LÉOPOLDVILLE)
CONGO
DEM. REP. OF THE CONGO (ZAIRE)
ÎLE MBAMOU
EL-QÂHIRA
CAIRO
EL-GÎZA
GIZA
Shubrâ el-Kheima
JOHANNESBURG
Soweto
Roodepoort
Krugersdorp
Randfontein
Germiston
Boksburg
Benoni
Brakpan
Springs
Alberton
Randburg
Kempton Park
Alexandra
Scale 1 : 300,000
20 Kilometers
10 Miles
© R. MᶜN.

a
150° 40′
150° 50′
151°
151° 10′
151° 20
33° 40′
33° 50′
34°
Riverstone
Schofields
Rouse Hill
Kenthurst
Dural
Mount Colah
Bobbin Head
Bayview
Newport
Terry Hills
Mona Vale
Asquith
Hornsby
Waitara
Wahroonga
Turramurra
Saint Ives
Narrabeen
Collaroy
Dee Why
Manly
Penrith
Kingswood
Emu Plains
Saint Marys
Mount Druitt
Rooty Hill
Blacktown
Seven Hills
Castle Hill
Baulkham Hills
Parramatta
Holroyd
Granville
Auburn
Fairfield
Liverpool
Bankstown
Strathfield
Burwood
Ashfield
Leichhardt
SYDNEY
North Sydney
Mosman
Chatswood
Willoughby
Lane Cove
Ryde
Epping
Pymble
Lindfield
Roseville
Marrickville
Canterbury
Rockdale
Hurstville
Kogarah
Botany
Randwick
Waverley
Woollahra
Maroubra
Mascot
Kingsford
La Perouse
Botany Bay
Sylvania
Sutherland
Miranda
Caringbah
Cronulla
Kurnell
KURNELL PENINSULA
Engadine
Heathcote
Bundeena
ROYAL NATIONAL PARK
Campbelltown
Camden
Narellan
Leppington
Macquarie Fields
Glenfield
Ingleburn
Minto
Long Point
Mulgoa
Wallacia
Luddenham
Greendale
Bringelly
Rossmore
Austral
Cobbitty
Theresa Park
PACIFIC
OCEAN
Copyright © by Rand McNally & Co.
b
37° 40′
37° 50′
38°
Broadmeadows
Tullamarine
Campbellfield
Thomastown
Keilor
Coburg
Preston
Brunswick
Essendon
Northcote
Heidelberg
Templestowe
Doncaster
Eltham
Greensborough
Sunshine
Footscray
MELBOURNE
Fitzroy
Collingwood
Richmond
Kew
Hawthorn
Camberwell
Box Hill
Nunawading
Ringwood
Croydon
Lilydale
Prahran
Malvern
Caulfield
Saint Kilda
Brighton
Oakleigh
Glen Waverley
Knoxfield
Moorabbin
Sandringham
Springvale
Dandenong
Mordialloc
Chelsea
Berwick
Williamstown
Altona
Laverton
Werribee
Point Cook
Port Phillip Bay
Hobsons Bay
Altona Bay
Yarra Glen
Olinda
Belgrave
Carrum
Carrum Downs
Copyright © by Rand McNally & Co.
Map prepared by George Philip & Son Ltd., London.
144° 40′
144° 50′
145°
145° 10′
145° 20′
0 5 10 15 20 Kilometers
0 5 10 Miles
Scale 1 : 300,000

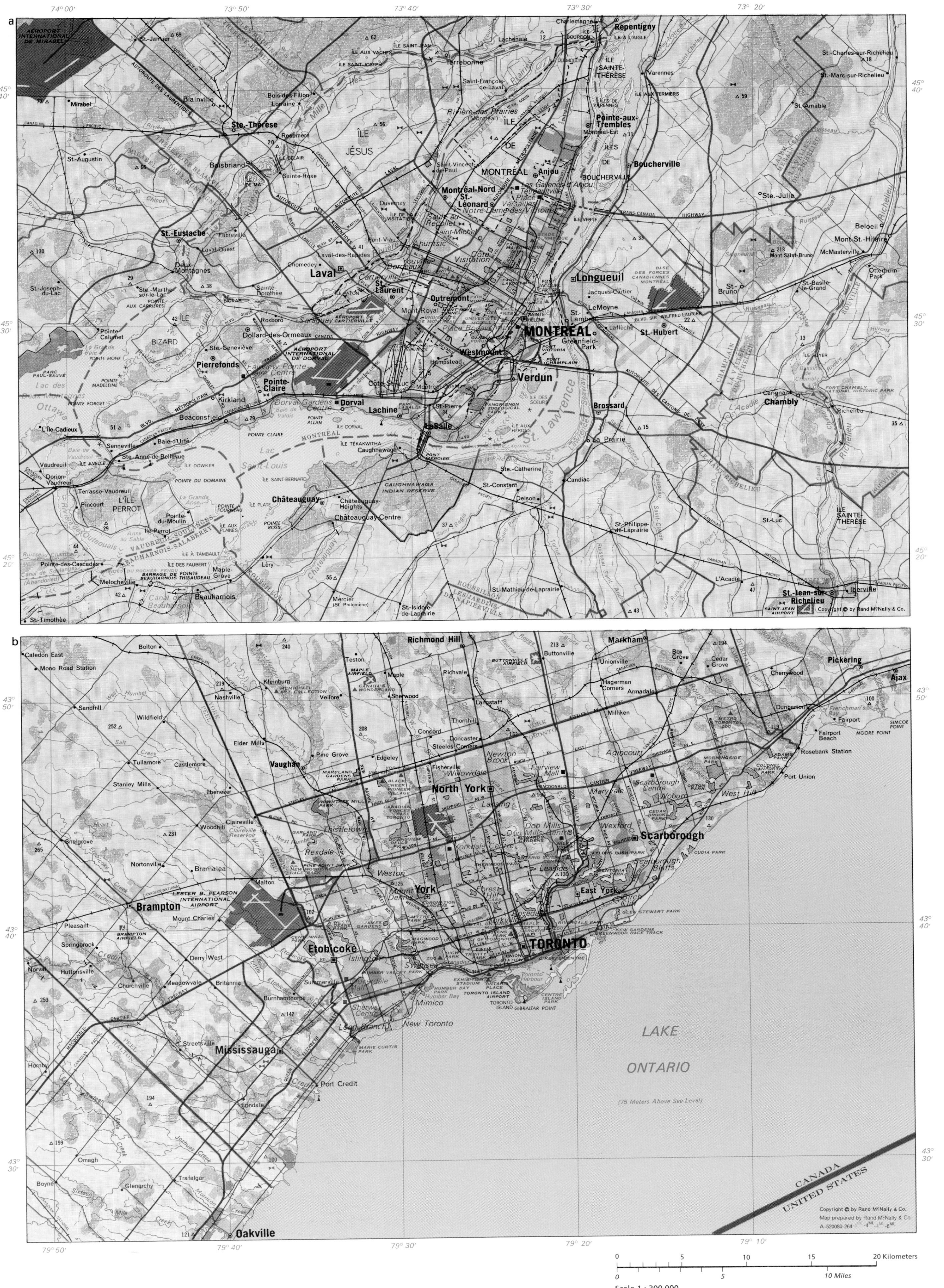
a
MONTREAL
Laval
Longueuil
Verdun
Lachine
Dorval
LaSalle
Pointe-Claire
Pierrefonds
Outremont
Westmount
St.-Laurent
Brossard
Chambly
St.-Hubert
Châteauguay
Boucherville
Repentigny
St.-Jean-sur-Richelieu
Copyright © by Rand McNally & Co.
b
TORONTO
North York
Scarborough
Etobicoke
York
East York
Mississauga
Brampton
Oakville
Markham
Richmond Hill
Pickering
Ajax
LAKE
ONTARIO
(75 Meters Above Sea Level)
CANADA
UNITED STATES
Copyright © by Rand McNally & Co.
Map prepared by Rand McNally & Co.
Scale 1 : 300,000
20 Kilometers
10 Miles

0 5 10 15 20 Kilometers

0 5 10 Miles

Scale 1 : 300,000

73°40'
73°30'
73°20'
73°10'
41° 10'
41°
40° 50'
40° 40'
40° 30'
40° 20'
NEW YORK
CONNECTICUT
Long Island Sound
Bridgeport
Fairfield
Westport
Norwalk
New Canaan
Darien
Stamford
Greenwich
Port Chester
Rye
White Plains
Scarsdale
New Rochelle
Mamaroneck
Larchmont
Chappaqua
Pleasantville
Valhalla
Harrison
Glen Cove
Oyster Bay
Huntington
Huntington Station
Northport
Commack
Smithtown
Port Jefferson
Centereach
Coram
Selden
Lake Ronkonkoma
Ronkonkoma
Holbrook
Medford
Patchogue
Bayport
Sayville
Oakdale
Bay Shore
Central Islip
Brentwood
Deer Park
West Islip
Babylon
West Babylon
Lindenhurst
Amityville
Massapequa
Seaford
Wantagh
Bellmore
Merrick
Freeport
Baldwin
Oceanside
Rockville Centre
Valley Stream
Lynbrook
Hempstead
West Hempstead
Franklin Square
Elmont
Garden City
Mineola
Levittown
East Meadow
Hicksville
Plainview
Farmingdale
Bethpage
Westbury
Jericho
Syosset
Manhasset
Great Neck
Port Washington
Long Beach
LONG ISLAND
JOHN F. KENNEDY INTERNATIONAL AIRPORT
FIRE ISLAND NATIONAL SEASHORE
JONES BEACH STATE PARK
ROBERT MOSES STATE PARK
Great South Bay
ATLANTIC OCEAN
QUEENS
NASSAU
Copyright © by Rand McNally & Co.
Map prepared by Rand McNally & Co.
A-520060-264

88°
87° 50′
87° 40′
87° 30′
87° 20′
42° 20′
42° 10′
42°
41° 50′
41° 40′
41° 30′
LAKE
MICHIGAN
(176 Meters Above Sea Level)
ILLINOIS
INDIANA
Waukegan
North Chicago
GREAT LAKES NAVAL TRAINING CENTER
Round Lake Park
Round Lake
Highland Lake
Grayslake
Gages Lake
Wildwood
Hainesville
Wilson
Park City
CAMPBELL'S AIRPORT
Countryside Manor
Green Oaks
North Hills
Libertyville
Mundelein
Ivanhoe
Knollwood
Lake Bluff
Rondout
Wauconda
Lake Forest
Sylvan Lake
Diamond Lake
Mettawa
Gilmer
Indian Creek
Timber Lake
Hawthorn Woods
Vernon Hills
Highwood
Half Day
Lake Zurich
Prairie View
Bannockburn
Highland Park
Lincolnshire
Kildeer
Aptakisic
Long Grove
Horatio Gardens
Deerfield
Deer Park
Barrington
Barrington Woods
Riverwoods
RAVINIA PARK
Buffalo Grove
Wheeling
Glencoe
Northbrook
Inverness
Palatine
PAL-WAUKEE AIRPORT
Prospect Heights
Northfield
Winnetka
South Barrington
Arlington Heights
Kenilworth
Wilmette
Rolling Meadows
Mount Prospect
Glenview
Plum Grove Estates
Hoffman Estates
Schaumburg
Des Plaines
Evanston
NORTHWESTERN UNIVERSITY
Morton Grove
Skokie
Niles
Elk Grove Village
Park Ridge
CHICAGO-O'HARE INTERNATIONAL AIRPORT
Lincolnwood
LOYOLA UNIVERSITY
Roselle
SCHAUMBURG AIRPORT
Keeneyville
Medinah
Itasca
Bloomingdale
Wood Dale
Bensenville
Harwood Heights
Norridge
Schiller Park
Franklin Park
Stratford Square
Cloverdale
Glendale Heights
Addison
River Grove
Elmwood Park
Carol Stream
Glen Ellyn Countryside
Northlake
Stone Park
Melrose Park
Lombard
Elmhurst
Villa Park
River Forest
Oak Park
North Glen Ellyn
Glen Ellyn
Glen Oak
Berkeley
Hillside
Bellwood
Maywood
Forest Park
Wheaton
NAVY PIER
CHICAGO
Brandywine
Yorkfield
York Center
Oakbrook Terrace
Westchester
Broadview
Berwyn
Cicero
Highland Hills
North Riverside
Butterfield
Oak Brook
La Grange Park
Riverside
Valley View
Brookfield
Stickney
ILLINOIS INSTITUTE OF TECHNOLOGY
Downers Grove
Lisle
Westmont
Hinsdale
Western Springs
La Grange
Lyons
Forest View
Clarendon Hills
Golfview Hills
Countryside
Indian Head Park
McCook
CHICAGO MIDWAY AIRPORT
Summit
Bedford Park
MUSEUM OF SCIENCE AND INDUSTRY
Woodridge
Willowbrook
Darien
Burr Ridge
Hodgkins
Justice
Nottingham Park
Bridgeview
Burbank
Tristate Village
Willow Springs
Roberts Park
Hickory Hills
Oak Lawn
Hometown
Evergreen Park
Bolingbrook
Palos Hills
Chicago Ridge
Worth
Hastings
Lemont
Merrionette Park
Palos Park
Palos Heights
Alsip
Whiting
Blue Island
Romeoville
Creekwood
Robbins
Orland Park
Riverdale
Dolton
East Chicago
Crestwood
Midlothian
Posen
Dixmoor
LEWIS-LOCKPORT AIRPORT
Oak Forest
Harvey
Phoenix
Calumet City
Hammond
Gary
Markham
South Holland
Lockport
Westhaven
Hazel Crest
Tinley Park
East Hazel Crest
Thornton
Lansing
Munster
Highland
Dellwood Highlands
Fairmont
Crest Hill
Homewood
Homewood Acres
Marley
Country Club Hills
Flossmoor
Glenwood
Joliet
Arbury Hills
Sunny Crest
Mokena
Ross
Ingalls Park
Cherry Hill
Crawford Countryside
Olympia Fields
Lynwood
Griffith
New Lenox
Lincolnwood Hills
Lincoln Estates
Frankfort
Matteson
Chicago Heights
East Chicago Heights
Dyer
Schererville
Merrillville
Copyright by Rand McNally & Co.
Map prepared by Rand McNally & Co.
0 5 10 15 20 Kilometers
0 5 10 Miles
Scale 1 : 300,000

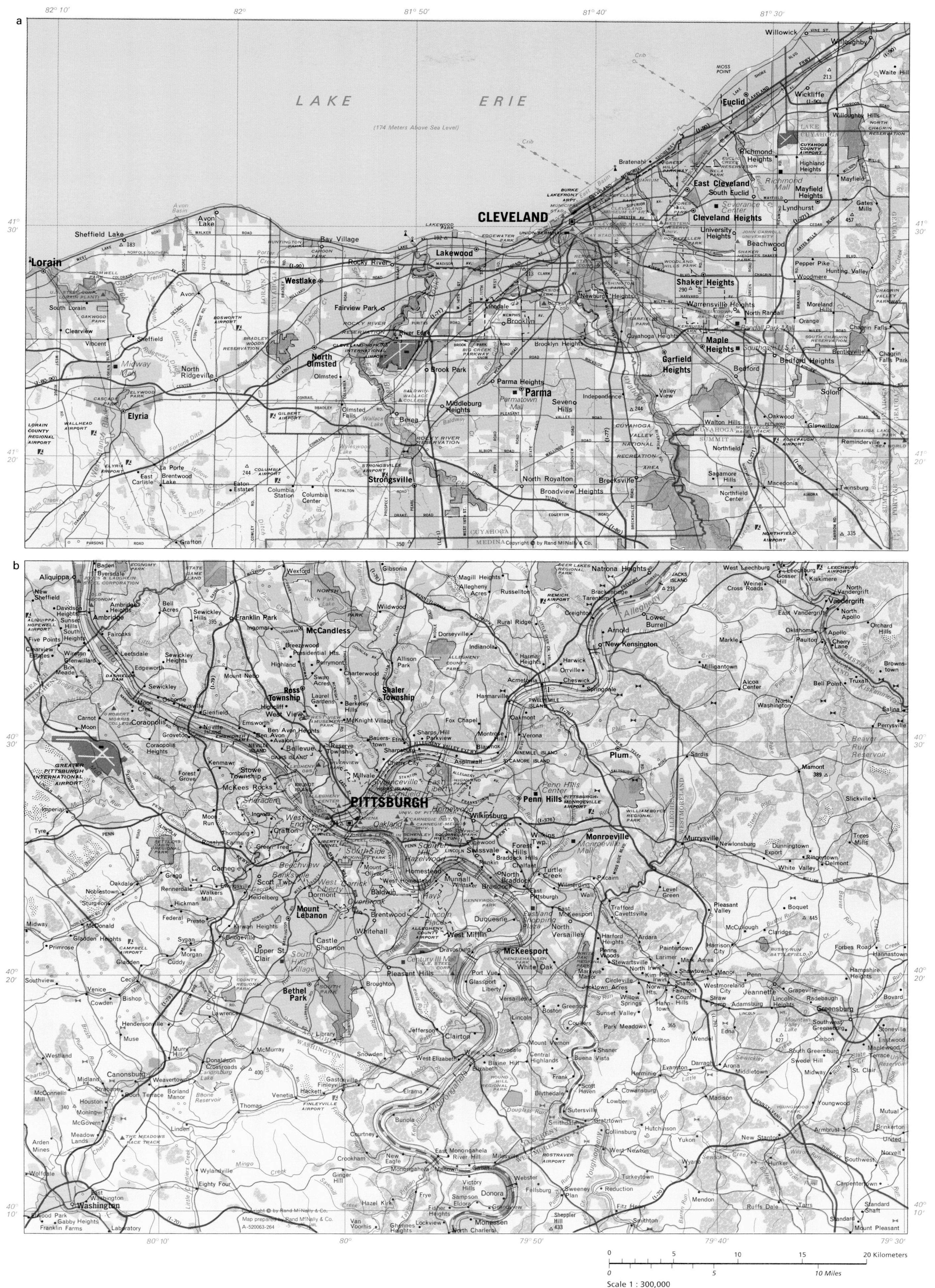
a
82° 10'
82°
81° 50'
81° 40'
81° 30'
41° 30'
41° 20'
LAKE
ERIE
(174 Meters Above Sea Level)
Crib
CLEVELAND
Lorain
Sheffield Lake
Avon Lake
Bay Village
Lakewood
Rocky River
Westlake
Fairview Park
Avon
South Lorain
Clearview
Vincent
Sheffield
North Ridgeville
Elyria
North Olmsted
Olmsted
Olmsted Falls
Berea
Brook Park
Middleburg Heights
Parma Heights
Parma
Seven Hills
Independence
Brooklyn
Linndale
Brooklyn Heights
Cuyahoga Heights
Garfield Heights
Maple Heights
Valley View
Strongsville
North Royalton
Broadview Heights
Brecksville
Columbia Station
Columbia Center
Eaton Estates
La Porte
Brentwood Lake
East Carlisle
Grafton
Euclid
Wickliffe
Willowick
Willoughby
Willoughby Hills
Waite Hill
Richmond Heights
Highland Heights
Mayfield Heights
Mayfield
Gates Mills
Lyndhurst
East Cleveland
South Euclid
Cleveland Heights
University Heights
Beachwood
Shaker Heights
Warrensville Heights
North Randall
Pepper Pike
Hunting Valley
Woodmere
Moreland Hills
Orange
Chagrin Falls
Bentleyville
Bedford
Bedford Heights
Solon
Oakwood
Walton Hills
Glenwillow
Northfield
Sagamore Hills
Macedonia
Northfield Center
Twinsburg
Reminderville
Bratenahl
CUYAHOGA
MEDINA
SUMMIT
GEAUGA
PORTAGE
Copyright © by Rand McNally & Co.
b
Aliquippa
Baden
Ambridge
Sewickley
Coraopolis
Franklin Park
McCandless
Wexford
Gibsonia
Ross Township
Shaler Township
West View
Bellevue
Avalon
Stowe Township
McKees Rocks
Crafton
PITTSBURGH
Oakland
Wilkinsburg
Penn Hills
Plum
Monroeville
Murrysville
Natrona Heights
Tarentum
Lower Burrell
Arnold
New Kensington
Vandergrift
Apollo
Carnegie
Bridgeville
Mount Lebanon
Castle Shannon
Upper St. Clair
Bethel Park
Pleasant Hills
Homestead
West Mifflin
McKeesport
White Oak
Duquesne
Clairton
Canonsburg
Washington
Jeannette
Greensburg
Irwin
North Irwin
Donora
Monessen
GREATER PITTSBURGH INTERNATIONAL AIRPORT
80° 10'
80°
79° 50'
79° 40'
79° 30'
40° 30'
40° 20'
40° 10'
Copyright © by Rand McNally & Co.
Map prepared by Rand McNally & Co.
0
5
10
15
20 Kilometers
0
5
10 Miles
Scale 1 : 300,000

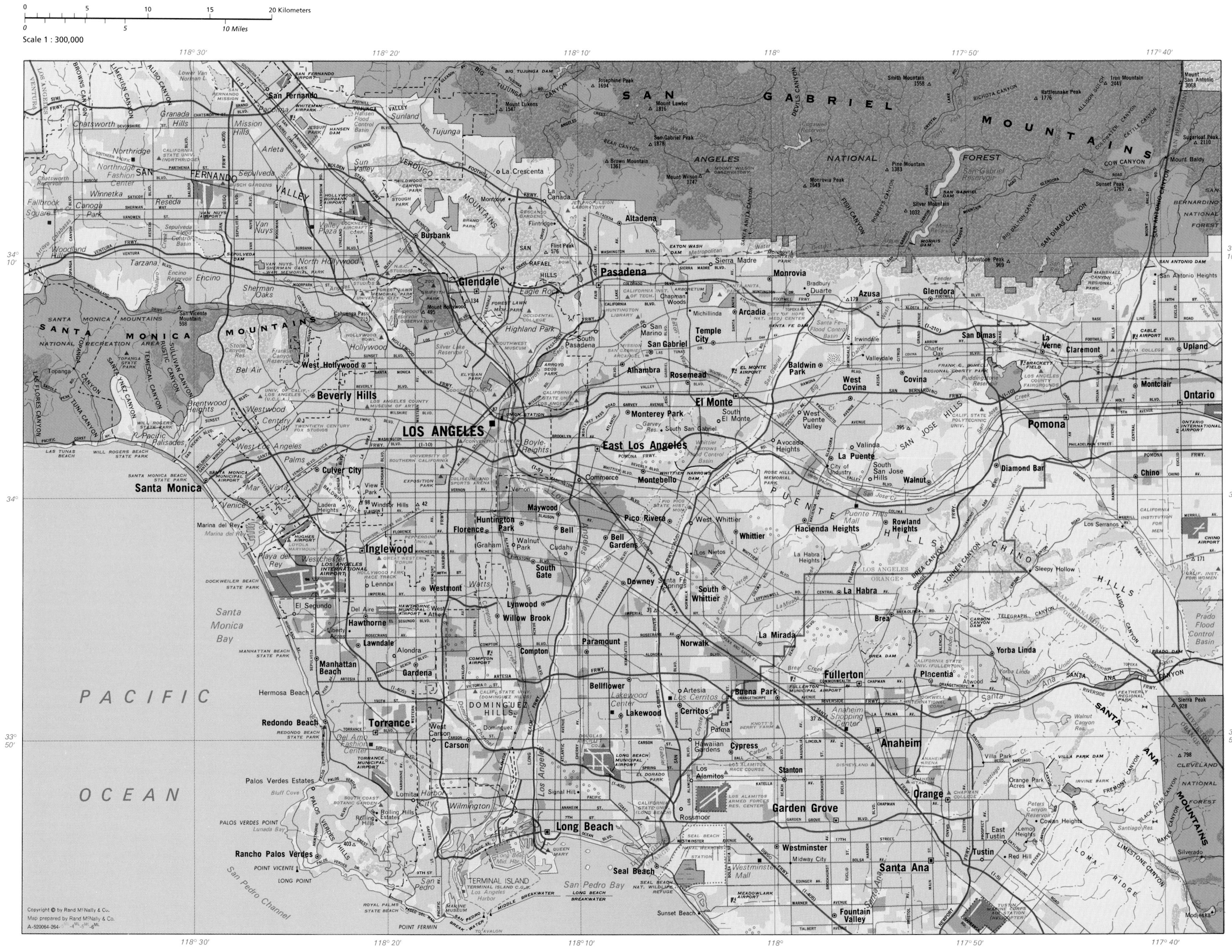

0 5 10 15 20 Kilometers
0 5 10 Miles
Scale 1 : 300,000
SAN GABRIEL MOUNTAINS
ANGELES NATIONAL FOREST
SANTA MONICA MOUNTAINS
SAN FERNANDO VALLEY
PACIFIC OCEAN
Santa Monica Bay
San Pedro Bay
San Pedro Channel
LOS ANGELES
Pasadena
Glendale
Burbank
Santa Monica
Beverly Hills
West Hollywood
Culver City
Inglewood
Hawthorne
Torrance
Redondo Beach
Manhattan Beach
Hermosa Beach
El Segundo
Gardena
Compton
Long Beach
Seal Beach
Carson
Lakewood
Downey
Norwalk
Whittier
East Los Angeles
Montebello
Monterey Park
Alhambra
El Monte
Arcadia
Monrovia
Azusa
Glendora
Covina
West Covina
San Dimas
Pomona
Claremont
Upland
Ontario
Chino
Diamond Bar
Walnut
La Puente
Hacienda Heights
La Habra
Fullerton
Brea
Placentia
Yorba Linda
Anaheim
Orange
Santa Ana
Tustin
Garden Grove
Westminster
Buena Park
Cypress
Cerritos
Bellflower
Paramount
Fountain Valley
Rancho Palos Verdes
San Fernando
Altadena
Sierra Madre
Temple City
Rosemead
San Gabriel
Pico Rivera
Bell Gardens
Bell
Maywood
Huntington Park
South Gate
Lynwood
Willow Brook
Westmont
Lawndale
Venice
Marina del Rey
SANTA ANA MOUNTAINS
CLEVELAND NATIONAL FOREST
PUENTE HILLS
Copyright © by Rand McNally & Co.
Map prepared by Rand McNally & Co.

Lake Saint Clair
(175 Meters Above Sea Level)
UNITED STATES
CANADA
MICHIGAN
ONTARIO
DETROIT
Windsor
Warren
Sterling Heights
Troy
Pontiac
Southfield
Livonia
Dearborn
Royal Oak
Farmington Hills
Rochester Hills
Clinton Township
St. Clair Shores
Roseville
Eastpointe
Madison Heights
Ferndale
Hamtramck
Highland Park
Oak Park
Redford Township
Dearborn Heights
Westland
Garden City
Inkster
Taylor
Wyandotte
Lincoln Park
Allen Park
Southgate
Romulus
Wayne
Plymouth
Novi
Ypsilanti
Ann Arbor
Tecumseh
Belle River
Essex
Amherstburg
La Salle
Mount Clemens
Waterford
Anchor Bay
Scale 1 : 300,000
0 5 10 15 20 Kilometers
0 5 10 Miles
Copyright © by Rand McNally & Co.
Map prepared by Rand McNally & Co.
A-520065-264

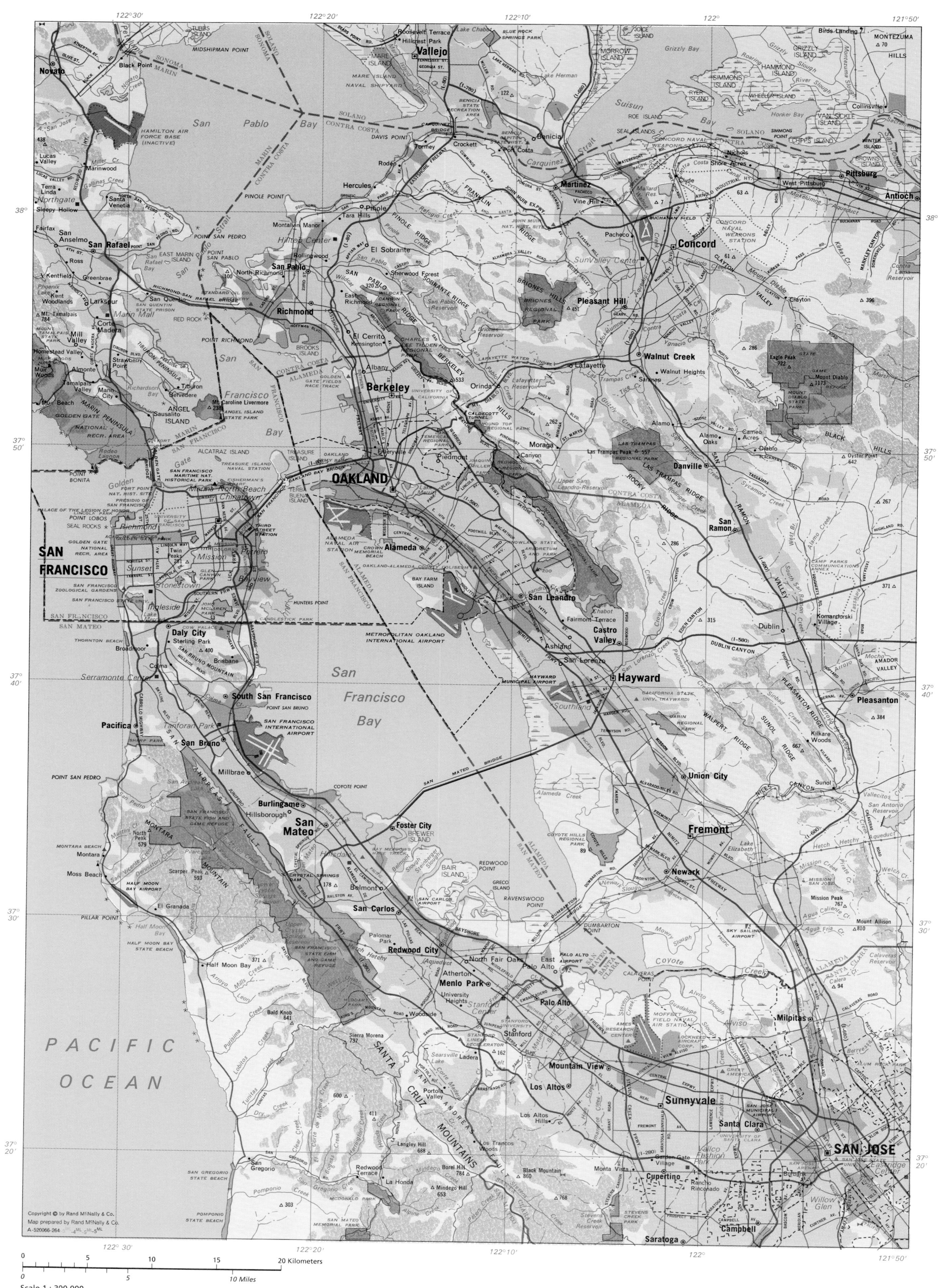
122°30′
122°20′
122°10′
122°
121°50′
38°
37° 50′
37° 40′
37° 30′
37° 20′
San Pablo Bay
Vallejo
Benicia
Martinez
Suisun Bay
Pittsburg
Antioch
Concord
Pleasant Hill
Walnut Creek
Novato
San Rafael
Richmond
Berkeley
OAKLAND
Alameda
San Leandro
Hayward
Castro Valley
Danville
San Ramon
Dublin
Pleasanton
SAN FRANCISCO
Daly City
South San Francisco
Pacifica
San Bruno
Millbrae
Burlingame
San Mateo
Foster City
San Carlos
Redwood City
Menlo Park
Palo Alto
Mountain View
Los Altos
Sunnyvale
Santa Clara
SAN JOSE
Cupertino
Saratoga
Campbell
Milpitas
Fremont
Newark
Union City
Half Moon Bay
San Francisco Bay
PACIFIC OCEAN
SANTA CRUZ MOUNTAINS
SAN ANDREAS FAULT
Mount Diablo
METROPOLITAN OAKLAND INTERNATIONAL AIRPORT
SAN FRANCISCO INTERNATIONAL AIRPORT
Copyright © by Rand McNally & Co.
Map prepared by Rand McNally & Co.
0 5 10 15 20 Kilometers
0 5 10 Miles
Scale 1 : 300,000

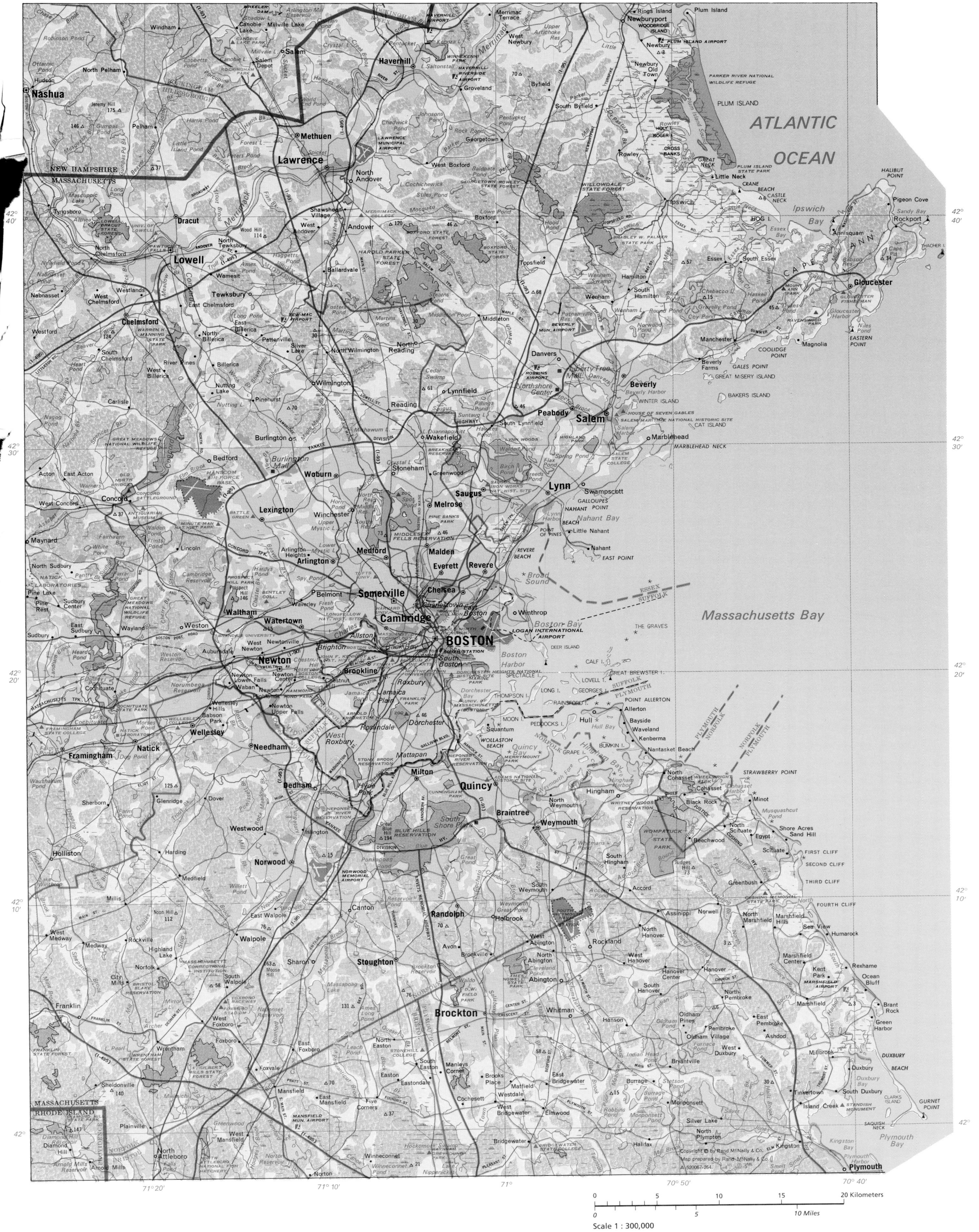
ATLANTIC
OCEAN
Massachusetts Bay
Ipswich Bay
Boston Bay
Boston Harbor
Nahant Bay
Plymouth Bay
NEW HAMPSHIRE
MASSACHUSETTS
RHODE ISLAND
BOSTON
Cambridge
Somerville
Newton
Quincy
Lynn
Salem
Lowell
Lawrence
Nashua
Haverhill
Methuen
Brockton
Gloucester
Newburyport
Plymouth
Framingham
Natick
Wellesley
Needham
Dedham
Norwood
Waltham
Watertown
Lexington
Woburn
Medford
Malden
Melrose
Everett
Revere
Chelsea
Saugus
Peabody
Beverly
Danvers
Weymouth
Braintree
Milton
Randolph
Stoughton
Walpole
Canton
Hingham
Hull
Winthrop
Marblehead
Swampscott
Arlington
Belmont
Brookline
Concord
Chelmsford
Dracut
Andover
North Andover
Ipswich
Rockport
Manchester
Marshfield
Duxbury
Scituate
Cohasset
Wakefield
Reading
Burlington
Bedford
Wilmington
Tewksbury
Billerica
Franklin
Foxboro
Mansfield
North Attleboro
Plum Island
PLUM ISLAND
CAPE ANN
LOGAN INTERNATIONAL AIRPORT
71° 20'
71° 10'
71°
70° 50'
70° 40'
42° 40'
42° 30'
42° 20'
42° 10'
42°
Copyright © by Rand McNally & Co.
Map prepared by Rand McNally & Co.
0
5
10
15
20 Kilometers
10 Miles
Scale 1 : 300,000

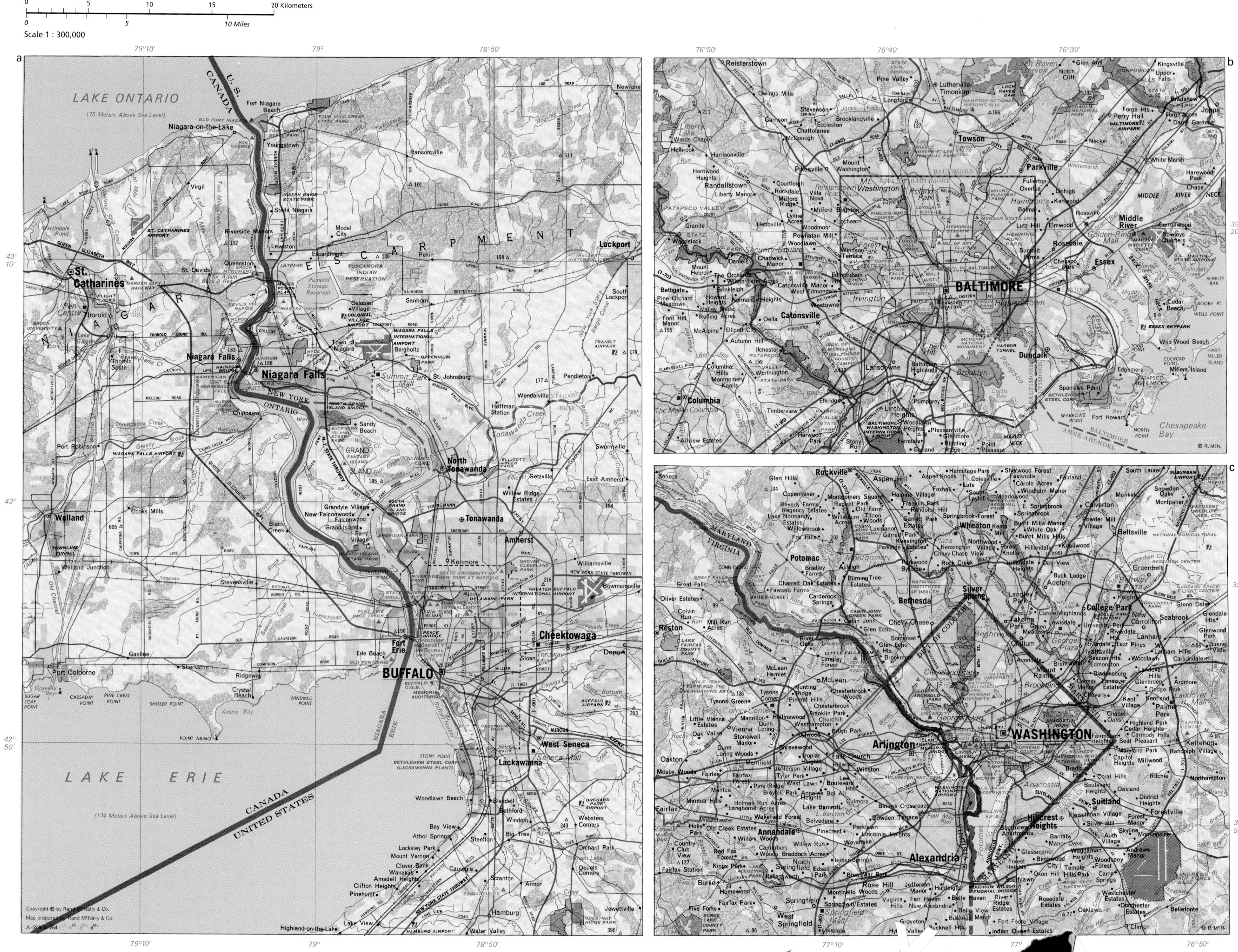
a
b
c
Scale 1 : 300,000
20 Kilometers
10 Miles
LAKE ONTARIO
(75 Meters Above Sea Level)
LAKE ERIE
(174 Meters Above Sea Level)
NIAGARA ESCARPMENT
St. Catharines
Niagara-on-the-Lake
Niagara Falls
Welland
Port Colborne
Fort Erie
BUFFALO
Tonawanda
North Tonawanda
Lockport
Amherst
Cheektowaga
Lackawanna
West Seneca
Hamburg
CANADA
UNITED STATES
BALTIMORE
Towson
Catonsville
Dundalk
Essex
Columbia
Parkville
Middle River
Chesapeake Bay
WASHINGTON
Arlington
Alexandria
Bethesda
Silver Spring
Rockville
College Park
Potomac
Reston
Annandale
Suitland
MARYLAND
VIRGINIA
DISTRICT OF COLUMBIA
Copyright © by Rand McNally & Co.

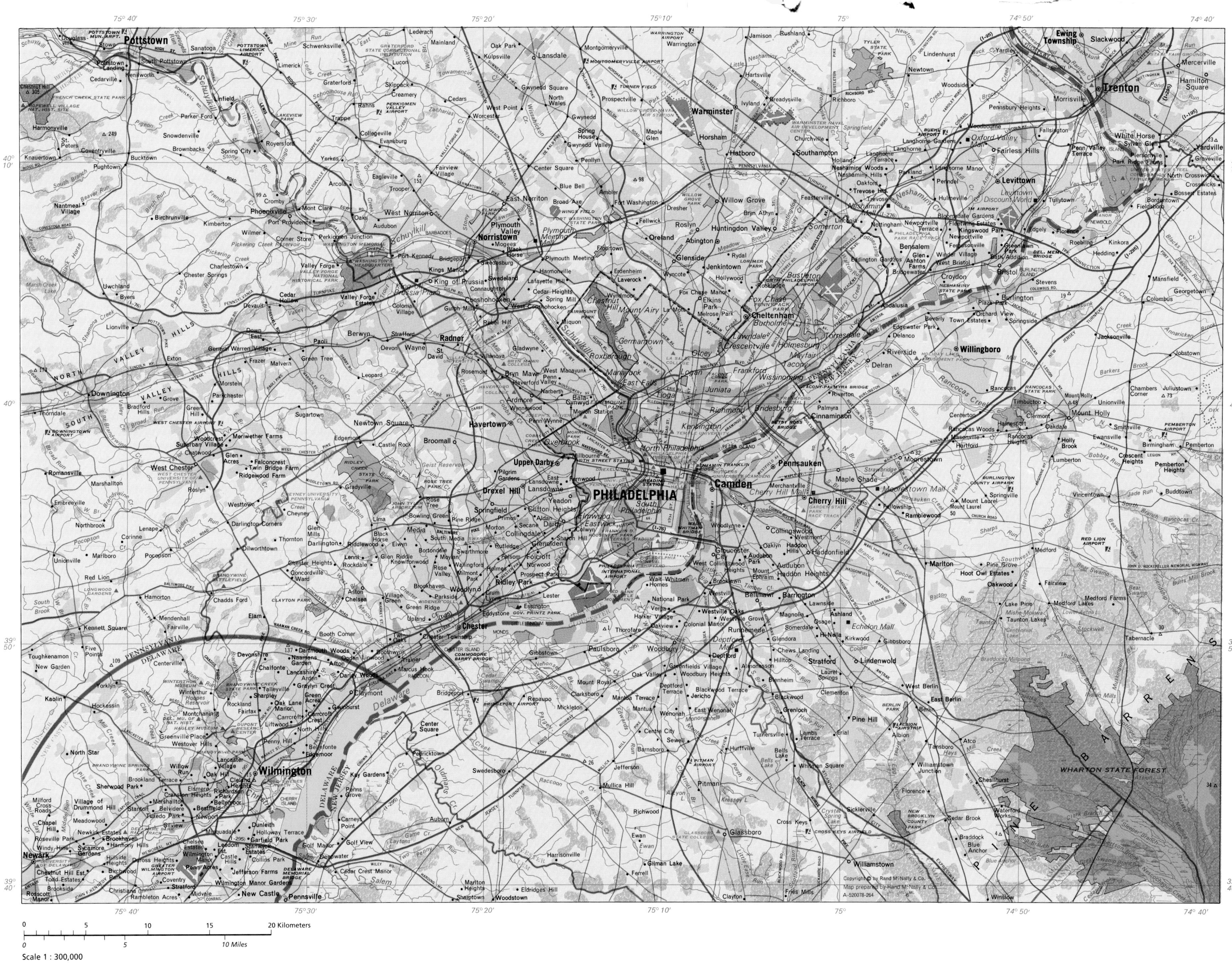
PHILADELPHIA
Trenton
Camden
Wilmington
Norristown
Chester
Pottstown
Levittown
Cherry Hill
WHARTON STATE FOREST
PINE BARRENS
Scale 1 : 300,000
10 Miles
20 Kilometers
Copyright © by Rand McNally & Co.

a

CIUDAD DE MÉXICO
MEXICO CITY

b

LA HABANA
HAVANA

GULF OF MEXICO

c

CARACAS

CARIBBEAN SEA

d

LIMA

PACIFIC OCEAN

e

SANTIAGO

0 5 10 15 20 Kilometers

0 5 10 Miles

Scale 1 : 300,000

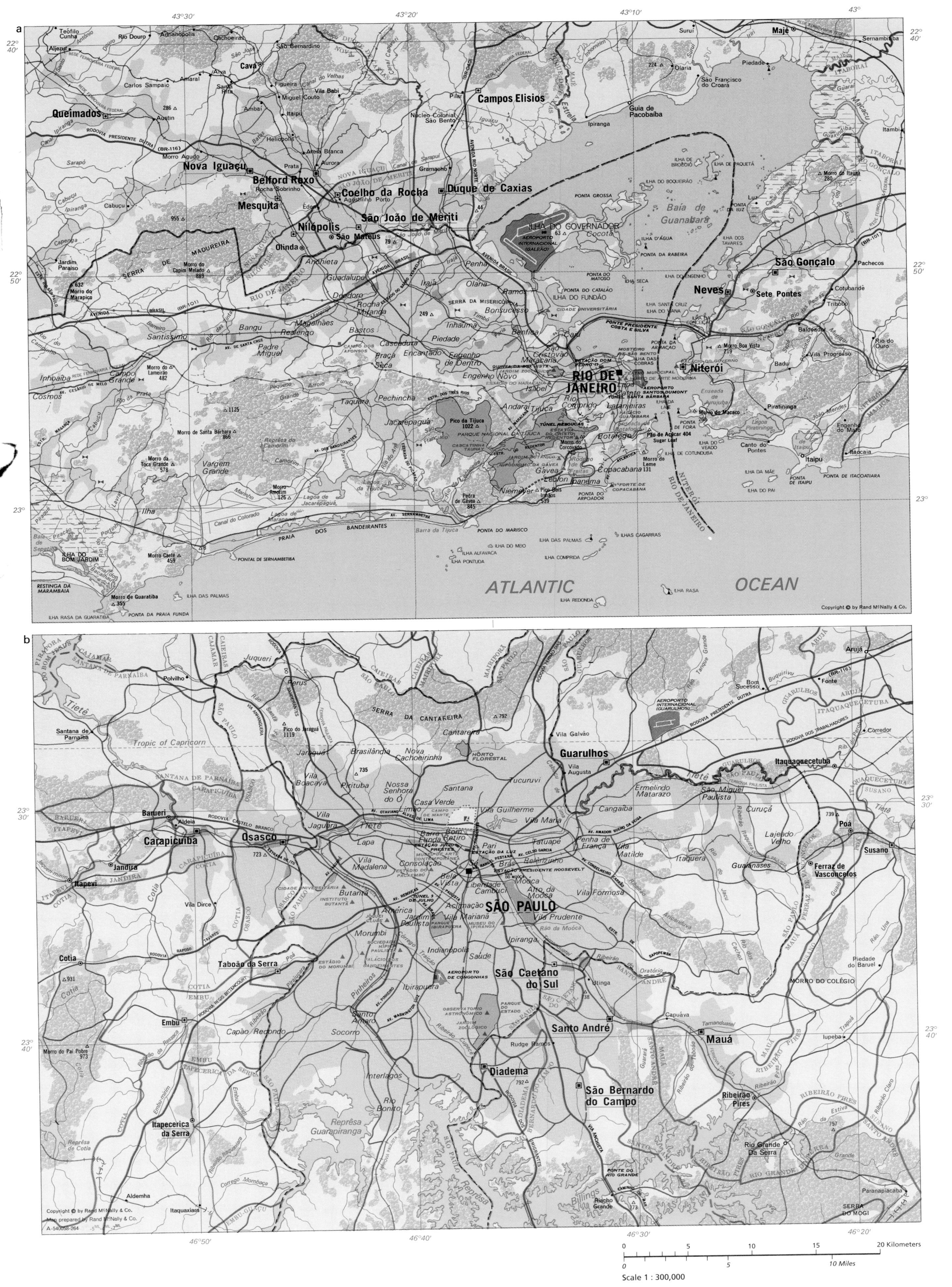
a
ATLANTIC
OCEAN
Rio de Janeiro
Niterói
Duque de Caxias
Nova Iguaçu
Belford Roxo
Nilópolis
São João de Meriti
São Gonçalo
Queimados
Campos Elisios
Baía de Guanabara
Copyright © by Rand McNally & Co.
b
São Paulo
Guarulhos
Osasco
Carapicuíba
Barueri
Santo André
São Bernardo do Campo
São Caetano do Sul
Diadema
Mauá
Taboão da Serra
Itaquaquecetuba
Poá
Susano
Cotia
Embu
Itapecerica da Serra
Ribeirão Pires
Tropic of Capricorn
Copyright © by Rand McNally & Co.
Map prepared by Rand McNally & Co.
A-540058-264
0 5 10 15 20 Kilometers
0 5 10 Miles
Scale 1 : 300,000

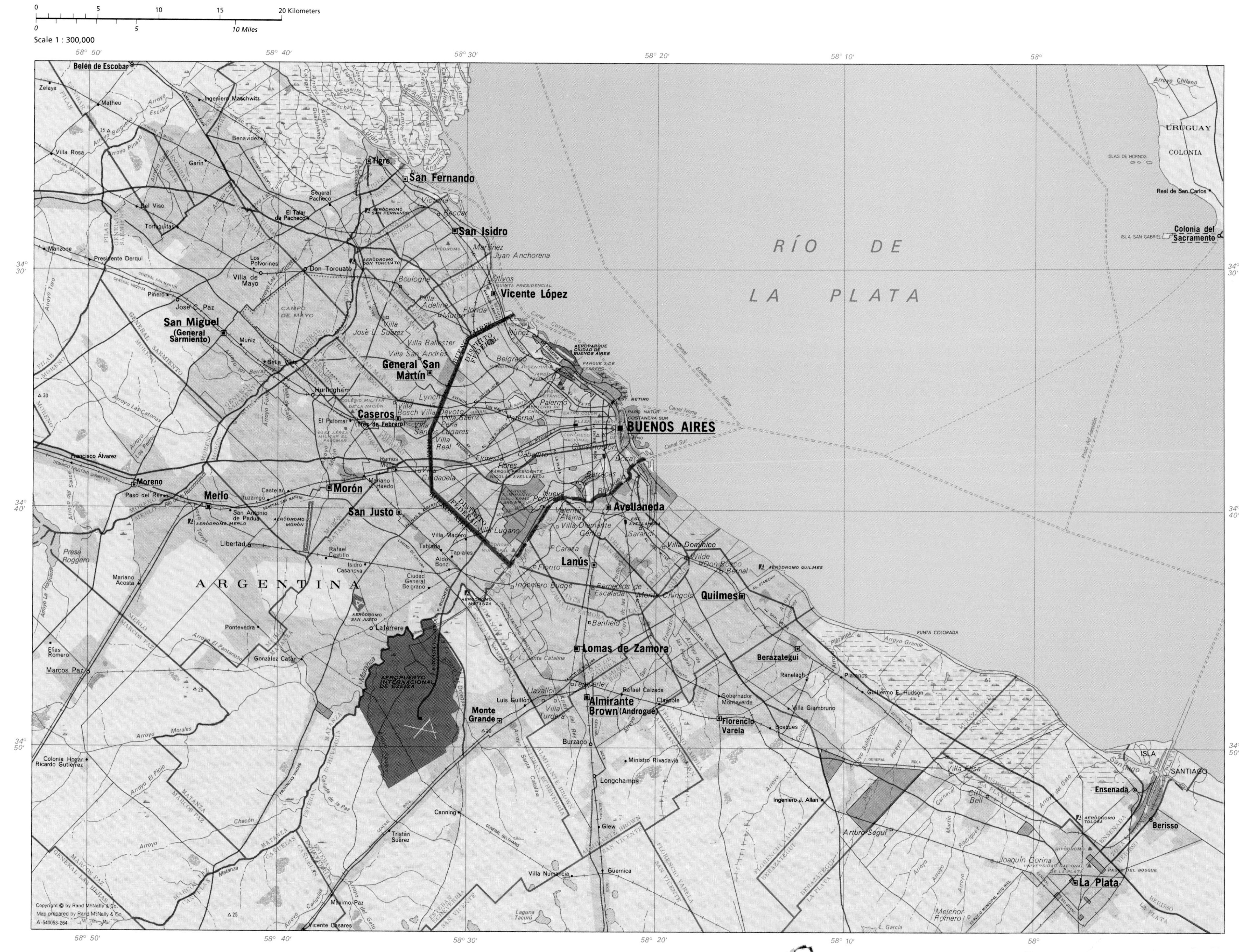
0 5 10 15 20 Kilometers
0 5 10 Miles
Scale 1 : 300,000
RÍO DE LA PLATA
URUGUAY
COLONIA
Colonia del Sacramento
Real de San Carlos
ISLA SAN GABRIEL
ISLAS DE HORNOS
ARGENTINA
BUENOS AIRES
DISTRITO FEDERAL
AEROPARQUE CIUDAD DE BUENOS AIRES
AEROPUERTO INTERNACIONAL DE EZEIZA
Belén de Escobar
Tigre
San Fernando
San Isidro
Vicente López
San Miguel (General Sarmiento)
General San Martín
Caseros (Tres de Febrero)
Moreno
Merlo
Morón
San Justo
Avellaneda
Lanús
Quilmes
Lomas de Zamora
Almirante Brown (Adrogué)
Monte Grande
Florencio Varela
Berazategui
Ensenada
Berisso
La Plata
ISLA SANTIAGO
PUNTA COLORADA
Copyright © by Rand McNally & Co.
Map prepared by Rand McNally & Co.
A-540053-264

This table lists the major metropolitan areas of the world according to their estimated populations on January 1, 1999. For convenience in reference, these areas are classified in broadly defined population categories: more than 25 million; 15,000,000 – 25,000,000; 10,000,000 – 14,999,999; 5,000,000 – 9,999,999; and 4,500,000 – 4,999,999.

For ease of comparison, each metropolitan area has been defined by Rand McNally according to consistent rules. A metropolitan area includes a central city, neighboring communities linked to it by built-up areas, and more distant communities if the bulk of their population is supported by commuters to the central city. Some metropolitan areas have more than one central city; in such cases each central city is listed.

Metropolitan Areas of 4.5 Million or More, 1999

Rank	Name	Country	Estimated Population 1/1/99
1	Tōkyō-Yokohama	Japan	31,500,000
2	Sŏul (Seoul)	South Korea	19,800,000
3	Ciudad de México (Mexico City)	Mexico	19,100,000
4	New York	United States	18,400,000
5	Jakarta	Indonesia	17,300,000
6	Ōsaka-Kōbe-Kyōto	Japan	17,225,000
7	São Paulo	Brazil	17,200,000
8	Mumbai (Bombay)	India	16,800,000
9	Delhi-New Delhi	India	15,600,000
10	Los Angeles	United States	14,600,000
11	Calcutta	India	14,550,000
12	Manila	Philippines	14,400,000
13	Buenos Aires	Argentina	13,400,000
14	El-Qâhira (Cairo)	Egypt	13,250,000
15	Moskva (Moscow)	Russia	13,000,000
16	London	United Kingdom	12,400,000
17	Beijing (Peking)	China	11,600,000
18	Tehrān (Teheran)	Iran	11,050,000
19	Paris	France	11,000,000
20	Shanghai	China	10,900,000
21	Rio de Janeiro	Brazil	10,750,000
22	İstanbul	Turkey	10,400,000
23	Karāchi	Pakistan	9,650,000
24	Xianggang (Hong Kong)-Shenzhen	China	9,000,000
25	Chicago	United States	8,375,000
26	Dhaka (Dacca)	Bangladesh	7,400,000
27	Krung Thep (Bangkok)	Thailand	7,300,000
28	Lima	Peru	7,250,000
29	Lagos	Nigeria	6,800,000
30	T'aipei	Taiwan	6,750,000
31	Tianjin (Tientsin)	China	6,700,000
32	Chennai (Madras)	India	6,600,000
33	Santa Fe de Bogotá	Colombia	6,500,000
34	Hyderābād	India	6,100,000
35	San Francisco-Oakland-San Jose	United States	6,000,000
36	Santiago	Chile	5,700,000
37	Philadelphia-Trenton-Wilmington	United States	5,650,000
38	Toronto-Hamilton	Canada	5,625,000
39	Essen-Dortmund-Duisburg (Ruhr Area)	Germany	5,500,000
40	Lahore	Pakistan	5,325,000
41	Kinshasa (Léopoldville)	Dem. Rep. of the Congo	5,300,000
42	Sankt-Peterburg (Saint Petersburg)	Russia	5,275,000
43	Johannesburg	South Africa	5,250,000
44	Bangalore	India	5,200,000
45	Nagoya	Japan	5,150,000
46	Detroit-Windsor	United States-Canada	5,000,000
47	Shenyang (Mukden)	China	4,985,000
48	Madrid	Spain	4,800,000
49	Wuhan (Hankow)	China	4,800,000
50	Baghdād	Iraq	4,700,000
51	Miami-Fort Lauderdale	United States	4,650,000
52	Boston	United States	4,535,000

This table gives the area, population, population density, capital, and political status for every country in the world. The political units listed are categorized by political status as follows: A - independent countries; B - internally independent political entities that are under the protection of another country in matters of defense and foreign affairs; C - colonies and other dependent political units; and D - the major administrative subdivisions of Australia, Canada, China, the United Kingdom, and the United States. For units categorized B, the names of protecting countries are specified in the political status column. For units categorized C, the names of administering countries are given in parentheses in the first column.

The populations are estimates for January 1, 1999, made by Rand McNally on the basis of official data, United Nations estimates, and other available information.

NAME		AREA		POPULATION	DENSITY PER		CAPITAL	POLITICAL STATUS
English	Local	sq. km.	sq. mi.		sq. km.	sq. mi.		
† Afghanistan	Afghānestān	652,225	251,826	25,315,000	39	101	Kābol (Kabul)	A
Africa	. . .	30,300,000	11,700,000	770,300,000	25	66	. . .	. . .
Alabama, U.S.	Alabama	135,293	52,237	4,344,000	32	83	Montgomery	D
Alaska, U.S.	Alaska	1,593,444	615,232	625,000	0.4	1.0	Juneau	D
† Albania	Shqipëria	28,748	11,100	3,347,000	116	302	Tiranë	A
Alberta, Can.	Alberta	661,190	255,287	2,929,000	4.4	11	Edmonton	D
† Algeria	El Djazaïr	2,381,741	919,595	30,805,000	13	33	El Djazaïr (Algiers)	A
American Samoa (U.S.)	American Samoa (English) / Amerika Samoa (Samoan)	199	77	63,000	317	818	Pago Pago	C
† Andorra	Andorra	453	175	65,000	143	371	Andorra-la-Vella	B(Sp., Fr.)
† Angola	Angola	1,246,700	481,354	11,020,000	8.8	23	Luanda	A
Anguilla	Anguilla	91	35	11,000	121	314	The Valley	B(U.K.)
Anhui, China	Anhui	139,000	53,668	61,610,000	443	1,148	Hefei	D
Antarctica	. . .	14,000,000	5,400,000	(1)	. . .	. . .	. . .	. . .
† Antigua and Barbuda	Antigua and Barbuda	442	171	64,000	145	374	St. John's	A
† Argentina	Argentina	2,780,400	1,073,519	36,500,000	13	34	Buenos Aires and Viedma(4)	A
Arizona, U.S.	Arizona	295,276	114,007	4,697,000	16	41	Phoenix	D
Arkansas, U.S.	Arkansas	137,742	53,183	2,552,000	19	48	Little Rock	D
† Armenia	Hayastan	29,800	11,506	3,416,000	115	297	Jerevan	A
Aruba	Aruba	193	75	68,000	352	907	Oranjestad	B(Neth.)
Asia	. . .	44,900,000	17,300,000	3,629,100,000	81	210	. . .	. . .
† Australia	Australia	7,682,300	2,966,155	18,735,000	2.4	6.3	Canberra	A
Australian Capital Territory, Austl.	Australian Capital Territory	2,400	927	315,000	131	340	Canberra	D
† Austria	Österreich	83,856	32,377	8,136,000	97	251	Wien (Vienna)	A
† Azerbaijan	Azärbaycan	86,600	33,436	7,883,000	91	236	Bakı (Baku)	A
† Bahamas	Bahamas	13,939	5,382	282,000	20	52	Nassau	A
† Bahrain	Al-Baḥrayn	691	267	622,000	900	2,330	Al-Manāmah	A
† Bangladesh	Bangladesh	143,998	55,598	126,110,000	876	2,268	Dhaka (Dacca)	A
† Barbados	Barbados	430	166	259,000	602	1,560	Bridgetown	A
Beijing, China	Beijing	16,800	6,486	12,790,000	761	1,972	Beijing (Peking)	D
† Belarus	Belarus'	207,600	80,155	10,405,000	50	130	Minsk	A
† Belgium	Belgique (French) / België (Flemish)	30,518	11,783	10,180,000	334	864	Bruxelles (Brussels)	A
† Belize	Belize	22,963	8,866	233,000	10	26	Belmopan	A
† Benin	Bénin	112,600	43,475	6,202,000	55	143	Porto-Novo and Cotonou	A
Bermuda (U.K.)	Bermuda	54	21	62,000	1,148	2,952	Hamilton	C
† Bhutan	Druk-Yul	46,500	17,954	1,930,000	42	107	Thimphu	B(India)
† Bolivia	Bolivia	1,098,581	424,165	7,904,000	7.2	19	La Paz and Sucre	A
† Bosnia and Herzegovina	Bosna i Hercegovina	51,129	19,741	3,427,000	67	174	Sarajevo	A
† Botswana	Botswana	582,000	224,711	1,456,000	2.5	6.5	Gaborone	A
† Brazil	Brasil	8,547,404	3,300,172	170,860,000	20	52	Brasília	A
British Columbia, Can.	British Columbia (English) / Colombie-Britannique (French)	947,800	365,948	4,043,000	4.3	11	Victoria	D
British Indian Ocean Territory (U.K.)	British Indian Ocean Territory	60	23	(1)	. . .	. . .	. . .	C
British Virgin Islands (U.K.)	British Virgin Islands	153	59	19,000	124	322	Road Town	C
† Brunei	Brunei	5,765	2,226	319,000	55	143	Bandar Seri Begawan	A
† Bulgaria	Bălgarija	110,994	42,855	8,215,000	74	192	Sofija (Sofia)	A
† Burkina Faso	Burkina Faso	274,200	105,869	11,420,000	42	108	Ouagadougou	A
† Burundi	Burundi	27,830	10,745	5,634,000	202	524	Bujumbura	A
California, U.S.	California	411,470	158,869	33,340,000	81	210	Sacramento	D
† Cambodia	Kâmpŭchéa	181,035	69,898	11,485,000	63	164	Phnum Pénh (Phnom Penh)	A
† Cameroon	Cameroon (English) / Cameroun (French)	475,440	183,568	15,240,000	32	83	Yaoundé	A
† Canada	Canada	9,970,610	3,849,674	30,450,000	3.1	7.9	Ottawa	A
† Cape Verde	Cabo Verde	4,033	1,557	403,000	100	259	Praia	A
Cayman Islands (U.K.)	Cayman Islands	259	100	39,000	151	390	George Town	C
† Central African Republic	République centrafricaine	622,984	240,535	3,410,000	5.5	14	Bangui	A
† Chad	Tchad	1,284,000	495,755	7,458,000	5.8	15	N'Djamena	A
† Chile	Chile	756,626	292,135	14,880,000	20	51	Santiago	A
† China (excl. Taiwan)	Zhongguo	9,557,172	3,690,045	1,242,070,000	130	337	Beijing (Peking)	A
Chongqing, China	Chongqing	82,400	31,815	36,120,000	438	1,135	Chongqing	D
Christmas Island (Austl.)	Christmas Island	135	52	2,300	17	44	Settlement	C
Cocos Islands (Austl.)	Cocos (Keeling) Islands	14	5.4	600	43	111	West Island	C
† Colombia	Colombia	1,141,748	440,831	38,950,000	34	88	Santa Fe de Bogotá	A
Colorado, U.S.	Colorado	269,618	104,100	3,937,000	15	38	Denver	D
† Comoros (excl. Mayotte)	Al-Qumur							
† Congo	Congo	342,000	132,047	2,688,000	7.9	20	Brazzaville	A
† Congo, Democratic Republic of the (Zaire)	Congo, République démocratique du	2,345,095	905,446	49,735,000	21	55	Kinshasa	A
Connecticut, U.S.	Connecticut	14,358	5,544	3,260,000	227	588	Hartford	D
Cook Islands	Cook Islands	236	91	20,000	85	220	Avarua	B(N.Z.)
† Costa Rica	Costa Rica	51,100	19,730	3,639,000	71	184	San José	A
† Cote d'Ivoire	Côte d'Ivoire	322,500	124,518	15,630,000	48	126	Abidjan and Yamoussoukro	A
† Croatia	Hrvatska	56,538	21,829	4,675,000	83	214	Zagreb	A
† Cuba	Cuba	110,861	42,804	11,075,000	100	259	La Habana (Havana)	A
† Cyprus (excl. North Cyprus)	Kípros (Greek) / Kıbrıs (Turkish)	5,896	2,277	615,000	104	270	Nicosia (Levkosía)	A
Cyprus, North(2)	Kuzey Kıbrıs	3,355	1,295	137,000	41	106	Nicosia (Lefkoşa)	A
† Czech Republic	Česká Republika	78,864	30,450	10,280,000	130	338	Praha (Prague)	A
Delaware, U.S.	Delaware	6,206	2,396	738,000	119	308	Dover	D
† Denmark	Danmark	43,094	16,639	5,347,000	124	321	København (Copenhagen)	A
District of Columbia, U.S.	District of Columbia	177	68	516,000	2,915	7,588	Washington	D
† Djibouti	Djibouti	23,200	8,958	444,000	19	50	Djibouti	A
† Dominica	Dominica	790	305	66,000	84	216	Roseau	A
† Dominican Republic	República Dominicana	48,442	18,704	8,064,000	166	431	Santo Domingo	A
† Ecuador	Ecuador	272,045	105,037	12,450,000	46	119	Quito	A
† Egypt	Mişr	1,001,449	386,662	66,660,000	67	172	Al-Qāhirah (Cairo)	A
† El Salvador	El Salvador	21,041	8,124	5,797,000	276	714	San Salvador	A

England, U.K.	England	130,410	50,352	49,240,000	378	978	London	D
† Equatorial Guinea	Guinea Ecuatorial	28,051	10,831	460,000	16	42	Malabo	A
† Eritrea	Ērtra	93,679	36,170	3,907,000	42	108	Asmera	A
† Estonia	Eesti	45,100	17,413	1,414,000	31	81	Tallinn	A
† Ethiopia	Ītyop'iya	1,157,603	446,953	59,040,000	51	132	Adis Abeba	A
Europe	. . .	9,900,000	3,800,000	709,300,000	72	187	. . .	. . .
Falkland Islands (U.K.)[3]	Falkland Islands	12,173	4,700	2,900	0.2	0.6	Stanley	C
Faroe Islands	Føroyar	1,399	540	42,000	30	78	Tórshavn	B(Den.)
† Fiji	Fiji (French) / Viti (Fijian)	18,274	7,056	808,000	44	115	Suva	A
† Finland	Suomi (Finnish) / Finland (Swedish)	338,145	130,559	5,154,000	15	39	Helsinki (Helsingfors)	A
Florida, U.S.	Florida	155,214	59,928	15,065,000	97	251	Tallahassee	D
† France (excl. Overseas Departments)	France	547,026	211,208	58,890,000	108	279	Paris	A
French Guiana (Fr.)	Guyane	83,534	32,253	166,000	2.0	5.1	Cayenne	C
French Polynesia (Fr.)	Polynésie française	3,521	1,360	228,000	65	168	Papeete	C
Fujian, China	Fujian	120,000	46,332	33,160,000	276	716	Fuzhou	D
† Gabon	Gabon	267,667	103,347	1,217,000	4.5	12	Libreville	A
† Gambia, The	Gambia, The	10,689	4,127	1,314,000	123	318	Banjul	A
Gansu, China	Gansu	450,000	173,746	24,970,000	55	144	Lanzhou	D
Gaza Strip	. . .	360	139	1,094,000	3,039	7,871	. . .	. . .
† Georgia	Sakart'velo	69,700	26,911	5,085,000	73	189	Tbilisi	A
Georgia, U.S.	Georgia	152,750	58,977	7,600,000	50	129	Atlanta	D
† Germany	Deutschland	356,955	137,822	82,700,000	232	600	Berlin and Bonn	A
† Ghana	Ghana	238,533	92,098	18,695,000	78	203	Accra	A
Gibraltar (U.K.)	Gibraltar	6.0	2.3	29,000	4,833	12,609	Gibraltar	C
Golan Heights	. . .	1,176	454	33,000	28	73	. . .	. . .
† Greece	Ellás	131,957	50,949	10,685,000	81	210	Athína (Athens)	A
Greenland	Kalaallit Nunaat (Inuit) / Grønland (Danish)	2,175,600	840,004	59,000	. . .	0.1	Godthåb (Nuuk)	B(Den.)
† Grenada	Grenada	344	133	96,000	279	722	St. George's	A
Guadeloupe (incl. Dependencies) (Fr.)	Guadeloupe	1,702	657	418,000	246	636	Basse-Terre	C
Guam (U.S.)	Guam	541	209	150,000	277	718	Hagåtña	C
Guangdong, China	Guangdong	177,800	68,649	70,430,000	396	1,026	Guangzhou (Canton)	D
Guangxi, China	Guangxi Zhuangzu	236,300	91,236	46,580,000	197	511	Nanning	D
† Guatemala	Guatemala	108,889	42,042	12,170,000	112	289	Guatemala	A
Guernsey (incl. Dependencies)	Guernsey	78	30	65,000	833	2,167	St. Peter Port	B(U.K.)
† Guinea	Guinée	245,857	94,926	7,508,000	31	79	Conakry	A
† Guinea-Bissau	Guiné-Bissau	36,125	13,948	1,220,000	34	87	Bissau	A
Guizhou, China	Guizhou	170,000	65,637	36,020,000	212	549	Guiyang	D
† Guyana	Guyana	214,969	83,000	706,000	3.3	8.5	Georgetown	A
Hainan, China	Hainan	34,200	13,205	7,452,000	218	564	Haikou	D
† Haiti	Haïti	27,750	10,714	6,833,000	246	638	Port-au-Prince	A
Hawaii, U.S.	Hawaii	16,729	6,459	1,195,000	71	185	Honolulu	D
Hebei, China	Hebei	190,000	73,359	65,950,000	347	899	Shijiazhuang	D
Heilongjiang, China	Heilongjiang	469,000	181,082	38,005,000	81	210	Harbin	D
Henan, China	Henan	167,000	64,479	93,280,000	559	1,447	Zhengzhou	D
† Honduras	Honduras	112,088	43,277	5,931,000	53	137	Tegucigalpa	A
Hubei, China	Hubei	187,400	72,356	59,250,000	316	819	Wuhan	D
Hunan, China	Hunan	210,000	81,081	65,580,000	312	809	Changsha	D
† Hungary	Magyarország	93,030	35,919	10,195,000	110	284	Budapest	A
† Iceland	Ísland	103,000	39,769	272,000	2.6	6.8	Reykjavík	A
Idaho, U.S.	Idaho	216,456	83,574	1,230,000	5.7	15	Boise	D
Illinois, U.S.	Illinois	150,007	57,918	12,025,000	80	208	Springfield	D
† India (incl. part of Jammu and Kashmir)	India (English) / Bharat (Hindi)	3,203,975	1,237,061	992,470,000	310	802	New Delhi	A
Indiana, U.S.	Indiana	94,328	36,420	5,919,000	63	163	Indianapolis	D
† Indonesia	Indonesia	1,948,732	752,409	214,530,000	110	285	Jakarta	A
Iowa, U.S.	Iowa	145,754	56,276	2,878,000	20	51	Des Moines	D
† Iran	Īrān	1,633,189	630,578	64,830,000	40	103	Tehrān	A
† Iraq	Al-'Irāq	438,317	169,235	22,070,000	50	130	Baghdād	A
† Ireland	Ireland (English) / Éire (Gaelic)	70,285	27,137	3,626,000	52	134	Dublin (Baile Átha Cliath)	A
Isle of Man	Isle of Man	572	221	75,000	131	339	Douglas	B(U.K.)
† Israel	Yisra'el (Hebrew) / Isrā'īl (Arabic)	20,770	8,019	5,353,000	258	668	Yerushalayim (Jerusalem)	A
† Italy	Italia	301,309	116,336	56,760,000	188	488	Roma (Rome)	A
† Jamaica	Jamaica	10,991	4,244	2,644,000	241	623	Kingston	A
† Japan	Nihon	377,750	145,850	126,060,000	334	864	Tōkyō	A
Jersey	Jersey	116	45	89,000	767	1,978	St. Helier	B(U.K.)
Jiangsu, China	Jiangsu	102,600	39,614	72,410,000	706	1,828	Nanjing (Nanking)	D
Jiangxi, China	Jiangxi	166,600	64,325	41,610,000	250	647	Nanchang	D
Jilin, China	Jilin	187,000	72,201	26,580,000	142	368	Changchun	D
† Jordan	Al-Urdun	91,000	35,135	4,491,000	49	128	'Ammān	A
Kansas, U.S.	Kansas	213,110	82,282	2,606,000	12	32	Topeka	D
† Kazakhstan	Kazahstan	2,717,300	1,049,155	16,835,000	6.2	16	Astana (Akmola)	A
Kentucky, U.S.	Kentucky	104,665	40,411	3,937,000	38	97	Frankfort	D
† Kenya	Kenya	582,646	224,961	28,580,000	49	127	Nairobi	A
Kiribati	Kiribati	811	313	85,000	105	272	Bairiki	A
† Korea, North	Chosŏn minjujuŭi-inmīn-konghwaguk	120,538	46,540	21,230,000	176	456	P'yŏngyang	A
† Korea, South	Taehan-min'guk	99,016	38,230	46,650,000	471	1,220	Sŏul (Seoul)	A
† Kuwait	Al-Kuwayt	17,818	6,880	1,952,000	110	284	Al-Kuwayt (Kuwait)	A
† Kyrgyzstan	Kirgizija	198,500	76,641	4,531,000	23	59	Biškek	A
† Laos	Lao	236,800	91,429	5,334,000	23	58	Viangchan (Vientiane)	A
† Latvia	Latvija	63,700	24,595	2,368,000	37	96	Rīga	A
† Lebanon	Lubnān	10,400	4,016	3,534,000	340	880	Bayrūt (Beirut)	A
† Lesotho	Lesotho	30,355	11,720	2,110,000	70	180	Maseru	A
Liaoning, China	Liaoning	145,700	56,255	41,980,000	288	746	Shenyang (Mukden)	D
† Liberia	Liberia	99,067	38,250	2,852,000	29	75	Monrovia	A
† Libya	Lībiyā	1,759,540	679,362	4,934,000	2.8	7.3	Ṭarābulus (Tripoli)	A
† Liechtenstein	Liechtenstein	160	62	32,000	200	516	Vaduz	A
† Lithuania	Lietuva	65,300	25,213	3,592,000	55	142	Vilnius	A
Louisiana, U.S.	Louisiana	128,595	49,651	4,371,000	34	88	Baton Rouge	D
† Luxembourg	Luxembourg (French) / Luxemburg (German)	2,586	999	427,000	165	427	Luxembourg	A
Macau (Port.)	Macau	17	6.6	433,000	25,471	65,606	Macau	C
† Macedonia	Makedonija	25,713	9,928	2,016,000	78	203	Skopje	A
† Madagascar	Madagasikara	587,041	226,658	14,665,000	25	65	Antananarivo	A
Maine, U.S.	Maine	87,388	33,741	1,249,000	14	37	Augusta	D
† Malawi	Malaŵi	118,484	45,747	9,922,000	84	217	Lilongwe	A
† Malaysia	Malaysia	329,758	127,320	21,155,000	64	166	Kuala Lumpur	A
† Maldives	Maldives	298	115	295,000	990	2,565	Male'	A
† Mali	Mali	1,248,574	482,077	10,275,000	8.2	21	Bamako	A
† Malta	Malta	316	122	381,000	1,206	3,123	Valletta	A
Manitoba, Can.	Manitoba	649,950	250,947	1,148,000	1.8	4.6	Winnipeg	D
† Marshall Islands	Marshall Islands	181	70	64,000	354	914	Majuro (island)	A
Martinique (Fr.)	Martinique	1,128	436	409,000	363	938	Fort-de-France	C
Maryland, U.S.	Maryland	31,849	12,297	5,158,000	162	419	Annapolis	D
Massachusetts, U.S.	Massachusetts	23,934	9,241	6,163,000	258	667	Boston	D

† **Mauritania**	Mūrītāniyā (Arabic) / Mauritanie (French)	1,030,700	397,955	2,543,000	2.5	6.4	Nouakchott	A
† **Mauritius (incl. Dependencies)**	Mauritius	2,040	788	1,175,000	576	1,491	Port Louis	A
Mayotte (Fr.)[5]	Mayotte	374	144	146,000	390	1,014	Dzaoudzi and Mamoudzou[4]	C
† **Mexico**	México	1,967,183	759,533	99,430,000	51	131	Ciudad de México (Mexico City)	A
Michigan, U.S.	Michigan	250,465	96,705	9,882,000	39	102	Lansing	D
† **Micronesia, Federated States of**	Federated States of Micronesia	702	271	132,000	188	487	Palikir	A
Midway Islands (U.S.)	Midway Islands	5.2	2.0	140	27	70	. . .	C
Minnesota, U.S.	Minnesota	225,182	86,943	4,734,000	21	54	St. Paul	D
Mississippi, U.S.	Mississippi	125,060	48,286	2,742,000	22	57	Jackson	D
Missouri, U.S.	Missouri	180,546	69,709	5,457,000	30	78	Jefferson City	D
† **Moldova**	Moldova	33,700	13,012	4,459,000	132	343	Chişinău (Kishinev)	A
† **Monaco**	Monaco	2.0	0.8	32,000	16,000	40,000	Monaco	A
† **Mongolia**	Mongol Ard Uls	1,566,500	604,829	2,599,000	1.7	4.3	Ulaanbaatar (Ulan Bator)	A
Montana, U.S.	Montana	10,607	4,095	896,000	84	219	Helena	D
Montserrat (U.K.)	Montserrat	102	39	13,000	127	333	Plymouth	C
† **Morocco (excl. Western Sahara)**	Al-Maghrib	446,550	172,414	29,390,000	66	170	Rabat	A
† **Mozambique**	Moçambique	799,380	308,642	19,895,000	25	64	Maputo	A
† **Myanmar (Burma)**	Myanmar	676,578	261,228	47,700,000	71	183	Yangon (Rangoon)	A
† **Namibia**	Namibia	823,144	317,818	1,635,000	2.0	5.1	Windhoek	A
Nauru	Nauru (English) / Naoero (Nauruan)	21	8.1	11,000	524	1,358	Yaren District	A
Nebraska, U.S.	Nebraska	200,358	77,359	1,656,000	8.3	21	Lincoln	D
Nei Monggol, China	Nei Monggol	1,183,000	456,759	23,475,000	20	51	Hohhot	D
† **Nepal**	Nepāl	147,181	56,827	23,995,000	163	422	Kāthmāṇḍāu (Kathmandu)	A
† **Netherlands**	Nederland	41,864	16,164	15,770,000	377	976	Amsterdam and 's-Gravenhage (The Hague)	
Netherlands Antilles	Nederlandse Antillen	800	309	207,000	259	670	Willemstad	B(Neth.)
Nevada, U.S.	Nevada	286,367	110,567	1,846,000	6.4	17	Carson City	D
New Brunswick, Can.	New Brunswick (English) / Nouveau-Brunswick (French)	73,440	28,355	752,000	10	27	Fredericton	D
New Caledonia (Fr.)	Nouvelle-Calédonie	18,575	7,172	196,000	11	27	Nouméa	C
New Hampshire, U.S.	New Hampshire	24,044	9,283	1,195,000	50	129	Concord	D
New Jersey, U.S.	New Jersey	21,277	8,215	8,118,000	382	988	Trenton	D
New Mexico, U.S.	New Mexico	314,939	121,599	1,742,000	5.5	14	Santa Fe	D
New South Wales, Austl.	New South Wales	801,600	309,499	6,348,000	7.9	21	Sydney	D
New York, U.S.	New York	139,833	53,990	18,270,000	131	338	Albany	D
† **New Zealand**	New Zealand	270,534	104,454	3,644,000	13	35	Wellington	A
Newfoundland, Can.	Newfoundland (English) / Terre-Neuve (French)	405,720	156,649	535,000	1.3	3.4	St. John's	D
† **Nicaragua**	Nicaragua	129,640	50,054	4,650,000	36	93	Managua	A
† **Niger**	Niger	1,267,000	489,191	9,815,000	7.7	20	Niamey	A
† **Nigeria**	Nigeria	923,768	356,669	112,170,000	121	314	Lagos and Abuja	A
Ningxia, China	Ningxia Huizu	66,400	25,637	5,216,000	79	203	Yinchuan	D
Niue	Niue	259	100	1,600	6.2	16	Alofi	B(N.Z.)
Norfolk Island (Austl.)	Norfolk Island	36	14	2,200	61	157	Kingston	C
North America	. . .	24,700,000	9,500,000	472,600,000	19	50	. . .	. . .
North Carolina, U.S.	North Carolina	136,421	52,672	7,530,000	55	143	Raleigh	D
North Dakota, U.S.	North Dakota	183,123	70,704	652,000	3.6	9.2	Bismarck	D
Northern Ireland, U.K.	Northern Ireland	14,160	5,467	1,652,000	117	302	Belfast	D
Northern Mariana Islands	Northern Mariana Islands	477	184	68,000	143	370	Saipan (island)	B(U.S.)
Northern Territory, Austl.	Northern Territory	1,346,200	519,771	185,000	0.1	0.4	Darwin	D
Northwest Territories, Can.	Northwest Territories (English) / Territoires du Nord-Ouest (French)	1,526,320	589,315	41,000	. . .	0.1	Yellowknife	D
† **Norway (incl. Svalbard and Jan Mayen)**	Norge	386,958	149,405	4,430,000	11	30	Oslo	A
Nova Scotia, Can.	Nova Scotia (English) / Nouvelle-Écosse (French)	55,490	21,425	941,000	17	44	Halifax	D
Nunavut, Can.	Nunavut	1,900,000	733,594	25,000	. . .	. . .	Iqaluit	D
Oceania (incl. Australia)	. . .	8,500,000	3,300,000	29,900,000	3.5	9.1	. . .	. . .
Ohio, U.S.	Ohio	116,103	44,828	11,250,000	97	251	Columbus	D
Oklahoma, U.S.	Oklahoma	181,048	69,903	3,339,000	18	48	Oklahoma City	D
† **Oman**	'Umān	212,457	82,030	2,405,000	11	29	Masqat (Muscat)	A
Ontario, Can.	Ontario	1,068,580	412,581	11,465,000	11	28	Toronto	D
Oregon, U.S.	Oregon	251,571	97,132	3,286,000	13	34	Salem	D
† **Pakistan (incl. part of Jammu and Kashmir)**	Pākistān	879,902	339,732	136,620,000	155	402	Islāmābād	A
† **Palau**	Palau (English) / Belau (Palauan)	508	196	18,000	35	92	Koror and Melekeok[4]	A
† **Panama**	Panamá	75,517	29,157	2,757,000	37	95	Panamá	A
† **Papua New Guinea**	Papua New Guinea	462,840	178,703	4,652,000	10	26	Port Moresby	A
† **Paraguay**	Paraguay	406,752	157,048	5,362,000	13	34	Asunción	A
Pennsylvania, U.S.	Pennsylvania	119,291	46,059	12,110,000	102	263	Harrisburg	D
† **Peru**	Perú	1,285,216	496,225	26,365,000	21	53	Lima	A
† **Philippines**	Pilipinas (Pilipino) / Philippines (English)	300,000	115,831	78,530,000	262	678	Manila	A
Pitcairn (incl. Dependencies) (U.K.)	Pitcairn	49	19	400	8.2	21	Adamstown	C
† **Poland**	Polska	313,895	121,196	38,600,000	123	318	Warszawa (Warsaw)	A
† **Portugal**	Portugal	91,985	35,516	9,925,000	108	279	Lisboa (Lisbon)	A
Prince Edward Island, Can.	Prince Edward Island (English) / Île-du Prince-Édouard (French)	5,660	2,185	136,000	24	62	Charlottetown	D
Puerto Rico (U.S.)	Puerto Rico	9,104	3,515	3,870,000	425	1,101	San Juan	B(U.S.)
† **Qatar**	Qatar	11,427	4,412	710,000	62	161	Ad-Dawḥah (Doha)	A
Qinghai, China	Qinghai	720,000	277,993	4,968,000	6.9	18	Xining	D
Quebec, Can.	Québec	1,540,680	594,860	7,376,000	4.8	12	Québec	D
Queensland, Austl.	Queensland	1,727,200	666,875	3,416,000	2.0	5.1	Brisbane	D
Reunion (Fr.)	Réunion	2,504	967	711,000	284	735	Saint-Denis	C
Rhode Island, U.S.	Rhode Island	3,189	1,231	970,000	304	788	Providence	D
† **Romania**	România	237,500	91,699	22,360,000	94	244	Bucureşti (Bucharest)	A
† **Russia**	Rossija	17,075,400	6,592,849	146,630,000	8.6	22	Moskva (Moscow)	A
† **Rwanda**	Rwanda	26,338	10,169	8,055,000	306	792	Kigali	A
St. Helena (incl. Dependencies) (U.K.)	St. Helena	314	121	7,000	22	58	Jamestown	C
† **St. Kitts and Nevis**	St. Kitts and Nevis	269	104	42,000	156	404	Basseterre	A
† **St. Lucia**	St. Lucia	616	238	153,000	248	643	Castries	A
St. Pierre and Miquelon (Fr.)	Saint-Pierre-et-Miquelon	242	93	7,000	29	75	Saint-Pierre	C
† **St. Vincent and the Grenadines**	St. Vincent and the Grenadines	388	150	120,000	309	800	Kingstown	A
† **Samoa**	Samoa	2,831	1,093	228,000	81	209	Apia	A
† **San Marino**	San Marino	61	24	25,000	410	1,042	San Marino	A
† **Sao Tome and Principe**	São Tomé e Príncipe	964	372	152,000	158	409	São Tomé	A
Saskatchewan, Can.	Saskatchewan	652,330	251,866	1,029,000	1.6	4.1	Regina	D
† **Saudi Arabia**	Al-'Arabīyah as-Su'ūdīyah	2,149,690	830,000	21,140,000	9.8	25	Ar-Riyāḍ (Riyadh)	A
Scotland, U.K.	Scotland	78,789	30,421	5,196,000	66	171	Edinburgh	D
† **Senegal**	Sénégal	196,712	75,951	9,885,000	50	130	Dakar	A
† **Seychelles**	Seychelles	453	175	79,000	174	451	Victoria	A
Shaanxi, China	Shaanxi	205,000	79,151	36,020,000	176	455	Xi'an (Sian)	D
Shandong, China	Shandong	153,000	59,074	89,310,000	584	1,512	Jinan	D
Shanghai, China	Shanghai	6,200	2,394	14,530,000	2,344	6,069	Shanghai	D
Shanxi, China	Shanxi	156,000	60,232	31,550,000	202	524	Taiyuan	D

	Sichuan, China	Sichuan	487,600	188,263	80,010,000	164	425	Chengdu	D
†	Sierra Leone	Sierra Leone	72,325	27,925	5,182,000	72	186	Freetown	A
†	Singapore	Singapore	636	246	3,511,000	5,520	14,272	Singapore	A
†	Slovakia	Slovensko	49,035	18,933	5,395,000	110	285	Bratislava	A
†	Slovenia	Slovenija	20,253	7,820	1,971,000	97	252	Ljubljana	A
†	Solomon Islands	Solomon Islands	28,370	10,954	448,000	16	41	Honiara	A
†	Somalia	Soomaaliya	637,657	246,201	6,993,000	11	28	Muqdisho (Mogadishu)	A
†	South Africa	South Africa (English) / Suid-Afrika (Afrikaans)	1,219,909	471,009	43,140,000	35	92	Pretoria, Cape Town (Kaapstad), and Bloemfontein	A
	South America	. . .	17,800,000	6,900,000	340,800,000	19	49	. . .	. . .
	South Australia, Austl.	South Australia	984,000	379,924	1,510,000	1.5	4.0	Adelaide	D
	South Carolina, U.S.	South Carolina	80,779	31,189	3,801,000	47	122	Columbia	D
	South Dakota, U.S.	South Dakota	199,744	77,122	740,000	3.7	9.6	Pierre	D
	South Georgia and the South Sandwich Islands (U.K.)(3)	South Georgia and the South Sandwich Islands	3,755	1,450	(1)	. . .	. . .	. . .	C
†	Spain	España	504,750	194,885	39,150,000	78	201	Madrid	A
	Spanish North Africa (Sp.)(6)	Plazas de Soberanía en el Norte de África	32	12	153,000	4,781	12,750	. . .	C
†	Sri Lanka	Sri Lanka	64,652	24,962	19,040,000	295	763	Colombo and Sri Jayawardenepura (Kotte)	A
†	Sudan	As-Sūdān	2,505,813	967,499	34,010,000	14	35	Al-Kharṭūm (Khartoum)	A
†	Suriname	Suriname	163,820	63,251	430,000	2.6	6.8	Paramaribo	A
†	Swaziland	Swaziland	17,364	6,704	975,000	56	145	Mbabane and Lobamba	A
†	Sweden	Sverige	449,964	173,732	8,899,000	20	51	Stockholm	A
	Switzerland	Schweiz (German) / Suisse (French) / Svizzera (Italian)	41,293	15,943	7,268,000	176	456	Bern (Berne)	A
†	Syria	Sūrīyah	185,180	71,498	16,955,000	92	237	Dimashq (Damascus)	A
	Taiwan	T'aiwan	36,002	13,900	22,010,000	611	1,583	T'aipei	A
†	Tajikistan	Tadžikistan	143,100	55,251	6,059,000	42	110	Dušanbe	A
†	Tanzania	Tanzania	945,087	364,900	30,935,000	33	85	Dar es Salaam and Dodoma	A
	Tasmania, Austl.	Tasmania	67,800	26,178	485,000	7.2	19	Hobart	D
	Tennessee, U.S.	Tennessee	109,158	42,146	5,435,000	50	129	Nashville	D
	Texas, U.S.	Texas	692,248	267,278	19,710,000	28	74	Austin	D
†	Thailand	Prathet Thai	513,115	198,115	60,330,000	118	305	Krung Thep (Bangkok)	A
	Tianjin, China	Tianjin	11,300	4,363	9,688,000	857	2,220	Tianjin (Tientsin)	D
†	Togo	Togo	56,785	21,925	4,992,000	88	228	Lomé	A
	Tokelau (N.Z.)	Tokelau	12	4.6	1,400	117	304	. . .	C
	Tonga	Tonga	747	288	108,000	145	375	Nuku' alofa	A
†	Trinidad and Tobago	Trinidad and Tobago	5,128	1,980	1,110,000	216	561	Port of Spain	A
†	Tunisia	Tunisie (French) / Tunis (Arabic)	163,610	63,170	9,448,000	58	150	Tunis	A
†	Turkey	Türkiye	779,452	300,948	65,090,000	84	216	Ankara	A
†	Turkmenistan	Turkmenija	488,100	188,456	4,332,000	8.9	23	Aŝchabad (Ashgabat)	A
	Turks and Caicos Islands (U.K.)	Turks and Caicos Islands	500	193	16,000	32	83	Grand Turk	C
	Tuvalu	Tuvalu	26	10	10,000	385	1,000	Funafuti	A
†	Uganda	Uganda	241,139	93,104	22,485,000	93	242	Kampala	A
†	Ukraine	Ukraïna	603,700	233,090	49,965,000	83	214	Kyïv (Kiev)	A
†	United Arab Emirates	Al-Imārāt al-' Arabīyah al-Muttaḥidah	83,600	32,278	2,323,000	28	72	Abū Ẓaby (Abu Dhabi)	A
†	United Kingdom	United Kingdom	244,101	94,249	59,040,000	242	626	London	A
†	United States	United States	9,809,431	3,787,425	271,490,000	28	72	Washington	A
†	Uruguay	Uruguay	177,414	68,500	3,297,000	19	48	Montevideo	A
	Utah, U.S.	Utah	219,902	84,905	2,091,000	9.5	25	Salt Lake City	D
†	Uzbekistan	Uzbekiston	447,400	172,742	23,940,000	54	139	Taškent (Toshkent)	A
†	Vanuatu	Vanuatu	12,190	4,707	187,000	15	40	Port Vila	A
	Vatican City	Città del Vaticano	0.4	0.2	1,000	2,500	5,000	Città del Vaticano (Vatican City)	A
†	Venezuela	Venezuela	912,050	352,144	23,005,000	25	65	Caracas	A
	Vermont, U.S.	Vermont	24,903	9,615	597,000	24	62	Montpelier	D
	Victoria, Austl.	Victoria	227,600	87,877	4,669,000	21	53	Melbourne	D
†	Vietnam	Viet Nam	330,036	127,428	76,790,000	233	603	Ha Noi	A
	Virgin Islands (U.S.)	Virgin Islands	344	133	119,000	346	895	Charlotte Amalie	C
	Virginia, U.S.	Virginia	109,625	42,326	6,787,000	62	160	Richmond	D
	Wake Island (U.S.)	Wake Island	7.8	3.0	200	26	67	. . .	C
	Wales, U.K.	Wales	20,758	8,015	2,952,000	142	368	Cardiff	D
	Wallis and Futuna (Fr.)	Wallis et Futuna	255	99	15,000	59	152	Mata-Utu	C
	Washington, U.S.	Washington	182,949	70,637	5,701,000	31	81	Olympia	D
	West Bank (incl. Jericho)	. . .	5,860	2,262	1,911,000	326	845	. . .	. . .
	West Virginia, U.S.	West Virginia	62,759	24,231	1,819,000	29	75	Charleston	D
	Western Australia, Austl.	Western Australia	2,525,500	975,101	1,807,000	0.7	1.9	Perth	D
	Western Sahara	. . .	266,000	102,703	237,000	0.9	2.3	El Aaiún (Laayoune)	. . .
	Wisconsin, U.S.	Wisconsin	169,643	65,500	5,240,000	31	80	Madison	D
	Wyoming, U.S.	Wyoming	253,349	97,819	489,000	1.9	5.0	Cheyenne	D
	Xianggang (Hong Kong), China	Xianggang	1,100	425	6,782,000	6,165	15,958	Xianggang (Hong Kong)	D
	Xinjiang, China	Xinjiang Uygur	1,600,000	617,763	17,015,000	11	28	Ürümqi	D
	Xizang (Tibet), China	Xizang	1,220,000	471,044	2,484,000	2.0	5.3	Lhasa	D
†	Yemen	Al-Yaman	527,968	203,850	16,660,000	32	82	San' ā'	A
†	Yugoslavia	Jugoslavija	102,173	39,449	11,205,000	110	284	Beograd (Belgrade)	A
	Yukon Territory, Can.	Yukon Territory	483,450	186,661	30,000	0.1	0.2	Whitehorse	D
	Yunnan, China	Yunnan	394,000	152,124	40,865,000	104	269	Kunming	D
†	Zambia	Zambia	752,614	290,586	9,561,000	13	33	Lusaka	A
	Zhejiang, China	Zhejiang	101,800	39,305	44,340,000	436	1,128	Hangzhou	D
†	Zimbabwe	Zimbabwe	390,759	150,873	11,105,000	28	74	Harare (Salisbury)	A
	WORLD	. . .	150,100,000	57,900,000	5,952,000,000	40	103	. . .	. . .

† Member of the United Nations.
. . . None, or not applicable
(1) No permanent population
(2) North Cyprus unilaterally declared its independence from Cyprus in 1983
(3) Claimed by Argentina
(4) Future capital
(5) Claimed by Comoros
(6) Comprises Ceuta, Melilla, and several small islands

The following table lists all urban centers of 50,000 or more population, along with many other important or well-known cities and towns. The populations have been obtained from either recent censuses (designated C) or official estimates (designated E) for the dates specified. For a few cities, only unofficial estimates are available (designated U). For comparison, the total population of each country is also given. The year listed for each country's total population also applies to the cities, unless another date is specified.

Country population estimates for 1999 may be found in the Political Information Table, pages 209–212.

A population figure in parentheses and preceded by a star (★) is the population of the entire metropolitan area in which a city is located. To permit meaningful comparisons, these metropolitan areas have been defined by Rand McNally according to consistent rules (see introduction to World Metropolitan Area Population Table, page 207). In some cases, they may differ somewhat from the officially recognized metropolitan area of another city; that city's name is then given in parentheses preceded by the star (★). City entries in all-capital letters are national capitals.

AFGHANISTAN / Afghānestān

1988 E	17,672,000
Herāt	177,300
Jalālābād (1982 E)	58,000
• KĀBOL	1,424,400
Kandahār	225,500
Kondoz (1982 E)	57,000
Mazār-e Sharīf	130,600

ALBANIA / Shqipëria

1990 E	3,250,000
Durrës	85,400
Elbasan	83,300
Korçë	65,300
Shkodër	81,800
• TIRANË	243,000
Vlorë	73,800

ALGERIA / El Djazaïr

1987 C	23,038,942
Aïn el Beïda	61,997
Annaba	305,526
Bab Ezzouar (★65,000) (★El Djazaïr)	55,211
Barika	56,488
Batna	181,601
Béchar	107,311
Bejaïa	114,534
Beskra	128,281
Bordj Bou Arreridj	84,264
Bordj el Kiffan (★El Djazaïr)	61,035
Bou Saâda	66,688
Ech Cheliff	129,976
El Boulaïda	170,935
• EL DJAZAÏR (ALGIERS) (★2,547,983)	1,507,241
El Djelfa	84,207
El Eulma	67,933
El Wad	70,073
Ghardaïa	89,415
Ghilizane	80,091
Guelma	77,821
Jijel	62,793
Khemis Melyana	55,335
Khenchla	69,743
Laghouat	67,214
Lemdiyya	85,195
Maghniyya	52,275
Mestghanem	114,037
Mouaskar	64,691
M'Sila	65,805
Qacentina	440,842
Saïda	80,825
Sétif	170,182
Sidi bel Abbès	152,778
Skikda	128,747
Souq Ahras	83,015
Tbessa	107,559
Tihert	95,821
Tilimsen	126,882
Tizi-Ouzou	61,163
Touggourt	70,645
Wahran	628,558
Wargla	81,721

AMERICAN SAMOA / Amerika Samoa

1990 C	46,773
• Nu'uuli (▲18,379)	3,893
PAGO PAGO (▲14,295)	3,519

ANDORRA

1991 E	54,507
• ANDORRA-LA-VELLA	20,437

ANGOLA

1989 E	9,739,100
Benguela (1983 E)	155,000
Huambo (1983 E)	203,000
Lobito (1983 E)	150,000
• LUANDA	1,459,900
Lubango (1984 E)	95,915
Namibe (1981 E)	100,000

ANGUILLA

1992 C	8,960
• THE VALLEY	1,462

ANTIGUA AND BARBUDA

1977 E	72,000
• SAINT JOHN'S	24,359

ARGENTINA

1991 C	32,608,560
Almirante Brown (★Buenos Aires)	449,105
Avellaneda (★Buenos Aires)	346,620
Bahía Blanca	271,467
Banda del Río Salí (★San Miguel de Tucumán)	50,282
Belén de Escobar (★Buenos Aires)	116,675
Berazategui (★Buenos Aires)	244,881
Berisso (★Buenos Aires)	74,012
• BUENOS AIRES (★11,000,000)	2,960,976
Campana (★Buenos Aires)	71,360
Caseros (★Buenos Aires)	349,221
Chimbas (★San Juan)	52,415
Cipolletti	60,089
Comodoro Rivadavia	124,151
Concepción del Uruguay	55,942
Concordia	116,491
Córdoba (★1,260,000)	1,179,067
Corrientes	257,766
Empalme San Vicente (★Buenos Aires)	74,890
Florencio Varela (★Buenos Aires)	249,006
Formosa	153,855
General Roca	61,896
General San Martín (★Buenos Aires)	407,506
Godoy Cruz	179,502
Goya	56,720
Gualeguaychú	64,620
Guaymallén (★Mendoza)	200,595
Junín	70,138
La Banda	73,136
La Plata	542,567
La Rioja	104,494
Lanús (★Buenos Aires)	466,755
Las Heras (★Mendoza)	145,823
Lomas de Zamora (★Buenos Aires)	572,769
Luján (★Buenos Aires)	66,226
Luján de Cuyo (★Mendoza)	54,241
Maipú (★Mendoza)	71,693
Mar del Plata	519,707
Mendoza (★770,000)	121,739
Merlo	386,304
Monte Grande (★Buenos Aires)	274,303
Moreno (★Buenos Aires)	285,964
Morón (★Buenos Aires)	641,541
Necochea	59,775
Neuquén	167,078
Olavarría	72,821
Paraná	206,848
Pergamino	78,200
Pilar (★Buenos Aires)	113,428
Posadas	201,943
Presidencia Roque Sáenz Peña	64,476
Punta Alta	56,165
Quilmes (★Buenos Aires)	509,445
Rafaela	67,086
Reconquista	50,284
Resistencia (★291,083)	228,199
Río Cuarto	134,677
Río Gallegos	64,628
Rivadavia (★San Juan)	56,426
Rosario (★1,190,000)	894,645
Salta	367,099
San Carlos de Bariloche	77,750
San Fernando (★Buenos Aires)	141,496
San Fernando del Valle de Catamarca (★133,050)	110,269
San Francisco (★58,536)	55,828
San Isidro (★Buenos Aires)	299,022
San Juan (★353,476)	119,492
San Justo (★Buenos Aires)	1,111,811
San Luis	110,353
San Martín	64,821
San Miguel (★Buenos Aires)	646,891
San Miguel de Tucumán (★622,348)	470,604
San Nicolás de los Arroyos	114,752
San Pedro	49,816
San Rafael	94,776
San Ramón de la Nueva Orán	50,717
San Salvador de Jujuy	181,318
Santa Fe (★394,888)	342,796
Santa Rosa	75,103
Santiago del Estero (★255,000)	189,490
Tandil	90,427
Tigre (★Buenos Aires)	253,748
Trelew	78,089
Venado Tuerto	58,678
Vicente López (★Buenos Aires)	289,142
Villa Krause (★San Juan)	83,266
Villa María	64,763
Villa Mercedes	77,137
Zárate	77,877

ARMENIA / Hayastan

1989 C	3,283,000
Abovjan (1987 E)	53,000
Echmiadzin (1987 E)	53,000
Gjumri	120,000
Hrazdan (1987 E)	56,000
Vanadzor (1987 E)	169,000
• YEREVAN (★1,315,000)	1,199,000

ARUBA

1991 C	66,687
• ORANJESTAD	20,054

AUSTRALIA

1996 C	18,311,000
Adelaide (★1,045,854)	16,115
Albury (★77,818)	41,796
Auburn (★Sydney)	50,959
Bankstown	157,735
Bendigo (★81,338)	40,336
Berwick (★Melbourne)	89,327
Blacktown (★Sydney)	232,219
Blue Mountains (★Sydney)	72,506
Brisbane (★1,488,883)	806,746
Broadmeadows	116,030
Cairns	121,036
Camberwell (★Melbourne)	85,476
Campbelltown	143,773
CANBERRA (★324,536)	298,847
Canning (★Perth)	68,374
Canterbury	132,360
Caulfield (★Melbourne)	70,326
Cockburn (★Perth)	57,335
Coffs Harbour	58,337
Croydon (★Melbourne)	50,160
Dandenong (★Melbourne)	55,817
Darwin (★80,000)	72,622
Doncaster (★Melbourne)	90,474
Enfield (★Adelaide)	59,901
Essendon (★Melbourne)	63,991
Fairfield (★Sydney)	181,785
Frankston (★Melbourne)	74,522
Geelong (★125,382)	12,091
Gosford	144,840
Gosnells	73,705
Heidelberg (★Melbourne)	59,871
Hobart (★189,944)	46,676
Holroyd (★Sydney)	80,470
Hurstville (★Sydney)	65,392
Ipswich	114,481
Keilor (★Melbourne)	73,202
Knox (★Melbourne)	130,794
Lake Macquarie (★Newcastle)	170,495
Launceston (★95,982)	62,421
Leichhardt (★Sydney)	58,304
Liverpool (★Sydney)	120,197
Logan (★Brisbane)	158,459
Mackay (★71,894)	44,880
Maitland	49,941
Maribyrnong	59,029
Marion (★Adelaide)	74,317
Marrickville (★Sydney)	76,017
Melbourne (★3,040,000)	48,560
Melville (★Perth)	89,238
Mitcham (★Adelaide)	59,289
Moorabbin (★Melbourne)	84,738
Newcastle (★449,772)	133,686
Noarlunga (★Adelaide)	89,377
North Sydney (★Sydney)	53,790
Nunawading (★Melbourne)	88,938
Parramatta	139,157
Penrith (★Sydney)	163,122
Perth (★1,244,320)	10,095
Preston (★Melbourne)	77,838
Randwick (★Sydney)	118,905
Rockdale (★Sydney)	84,847
Rockhampton (★64,233)	59,732
Rockingham	58,167
Ryde (★Sydney)	92,675
Salisbury (★Adelaide)	108,465
Shellharbour	52,080
Shoalhaven	76,726
South Sydney (★Sydney)	82,960
Southport (Gold Coast) (★375,175)	274,157
Springvale (★Melbourne)	70,362
Stirling (★Perth)	174,088
Sunshine (★Melbourne)	75,929
• Sydney (★3,741,290)	11,115
Tea Tree Gully (★Adelaide)	92,187
Toowoomba	83,633
Townsville (★109,914)	88,348
Wagga Wagga	55,519
Wanneroo (★Perth)	202,919
Waverley (★Melbourne)	112,934
Waverley (★Sydney)	61,674
Werribee	73,897
Whittlesea	101,894
Willoughby (★Sydney)	53,735
Wollongong (★219,761)	177,009
Woodville (★85,157) (★Adelaide)	78,000
Woollahra (★Sydney)	50,159

AUSTRIA / Österreich

1991 C	7,795,786
Bregenz (★77,000)	27,097
Bruck an der Mur (★50,000)	14,046
Feldkirch (★56,000)	26,730
Graz (★265,000)	237,810
Innsbruck (★200,000)	118,112
Klagenfurt (★118,000)	89,415
Knittelfeld (★58,000)	12,873
Linz (★352,000)	203,044
Salzburg (★185,000)	143,978
Sankt Pölten (★69,500)	50,026
Steyr (★58,000)	39,337
Villach (★66,500)	54,640
Wels (★68,000)	52,594
• WIEN (VIENNA) (★1,900,000)	1,539,848
Wiener Neustadt (★64,000)	35,134

AZERBAIJAN / Azărbaycan

1991 E	7,136,600
Äli Bayramlı	61,500
• BAKI (★2,020,000)	1,080,500
Gäncä	282,200
Mingäçevir	90,900
Naxçıvan	61,700
Şeki	63,200
Şumqayıt (★Bakı)	236,200
Xankändi	55,200

BAHAMAS

1990 C	254,685
• NASSAU	141,000

BAHRAIN / Al-Baḥrayn

1991 C	508,037
• AL-MANĀMAH (★290,000)	127,578
Al-Muharraq (★Al-Manāmah)	73,760

BANGLADESH

1991 C	104,766,143
Barisāl	180,014
Begamganj (1981 C)	69,623
Bhairab Bāzār	75,747
Bogra	93,114
Brāhmanbāria	114,297
Chāndpur	84,067
Chittagong (★2,342,662)	1,566,070
Chuādanga	65,222
Comilla (1981 C)	184,132
• DHAKA (DACCA) (★6,537,308)	3,637,892
Dinājpur	136,657
Farīdpur	72,927
Gulshan (★Dhaka) (1981 C)	215,444
Jamālpur	108,416
Jessore	176,398
Jhenida	69,501
Khulna (★966,096)	601,051
Kishorganj	64,676
Kurīgrām	62,075
Kushtia	71,706
Mīrpur (★Dhaka) (1981 C)	349,031
Mymensingh (Nasirābād)	138,662
Naogaon	109,156
Nārāyanganj (★Dhaka)	288,008
Narsinghdi	100,120
Nawābganj	131,260
Noākhāli	73,766
Pābna	113,146
Patuākhāli	50,344
Rājshāhi (★560,013)	324,532
Rangpur	220,849
Saidpur	110,494
Sātkhira	81,199
Sherpur	63,030
Sirājganj	100,003
Sītākunda (★Chittagong) (1981 C)	237,520
Sylhet	114,284
Tangail	111,783
Tongi (★Dhaka)	165,099

BARBADOS

1990 C	260,491
• BRIDGETOWN (★125,000)	5,928

BELARUS / Belarus'

1993 E	10,188,000
Babrujsk	226,000
Baranavičy	171,000
Barysaŭ	154,000
Brėst	289,000
Homel'	506,000
Hrodna	296,000
Lida (1991 E)	95,000
Mahilëu	366,000
Maladzečna (1991 E)	93,500
Mazyr	105,000
• MINSK (★1,722,000)	1,661,000
Navapolack (1991 E)	96,600
Orša	126,000
Pinsk	129,000
Polack (1991 E)	78,700
Rėčyca (1991 E)	69,400
Salihorsk (1991 E)	96,000
Sluck (1991 E)	60,100
Svetlahorsk (1991 E)	71,600
Vicebsk	368,000
Žlobin (1991 E)	60,800
Žodzina (1991 E)	56,000

BELGIUM / België / Belgique

1991 C	9,978,681
Aalst (Alost) (★Bruxelles)	76,382
Anderlecht (★Bruxelles)	87,884
Antwerpen (Antwerp) (★1,140,000)	467,518
Brugge (Bruges) (★223,000)	117,063
• BRUXELLES (BRUSSELS) (★2,385,000)	136,424
Charleroi (★480,000)	206,214
Genk (★Hasselt)	61,339
Gent (Ghent) (★467,000)	230,246
Hasselt (★295,000)	66,611
Ixelles (★Bruxelles)	72,610
Kortrijk (★204,000)	76,141
La Louvière (★150,000)	76,432
Leuven (★178,000)	85,018
Liège (Luik) (★747,000)	194,596
Mechelen (Malines) (★122,000)	75,313
Molenbeek-Saint-Jean (★Bruxelles)	68,759
Mons (★247,000)	91,726
Mouscron (★Lille, France)	53,513
Namur (Namen) (★149,000)	130,443
Oostende (★124,000)	68,500
Roeselare	52,872
Schaerbeek (★Bruxelles)	102,702
Seraing (★Liège)	60,838
Sint-Niklaas	68,203
Uccle (★Bruxelles)	73,721
Verviers (★104,000)	53,482

BELIZE

1991 C	189,392
• Belize City	42,887
BELMOPAN	5,256

BENIN / Bénin

1992 C	4,915,555
• COTONOU (★605,000)	536,827
Djougou	▲49,769
Parakou	103,577
PORTO-NOVO	179,138

BERMUDA

1991 C	58,460
• HAMILTON (★15,200)	1,100

BHUTAN / Druk-Yul

1982 E	1,333,000
• THIMPHU	12,000

BOLIVIA

1992 C	6,420,792
Cochabamba (▲446,000)	407,825
El Alto (★La Paz)	405,492
• LA PAZ (★1,120,000)	713,378
Montero	52,021
Oruro	183,422
Potosí	112,078
Quillacollo	70,965
Santa Cruz de la Sierra	697,278
Sucre	131,769
Tarija	90,113
Tiraque Chico (1990 E)	74,600
Trinidad	57,328

BOSNIA AND HERZEGOVINA / Bosna i Hercegovina

1987 E	4,400,464
Banja Luka (▲193,890)	130,900
• SARAJEVO (▲479,688)	341,200
Tuzla (▲129,967)	67,300
Zenica (▲144,869)	67,500

BOTSWANA

1991 C	1,326,796
Francistown	65,244
• GABORONE	133,468

BRAZIL / Brasil

1991 C	146,825,475
Abaetetuba (▲100,016)	55,442
Abreu e Lima (▲76,568)	70,099
Alagoinhas (▲116,740)	97,819
Alegrete (▲78,879)	67,505
Almirante Tamandaré (▲66,090)	51,240
Alvorada (▲142,020) (★Porto Alegre)	132,582
Americana	153,592
Ananindeua (▲88,035)	73,941
Anápolis (▲239,047)	222,400
Anil (▲695,199)	81,879
Antônio Bezerra (▲1,765,794) (★Fortaleza)	193,682
Apucarana (▲94,914)	80,048
Aracaju	401,676
Araçatuba (▲159,499)	146,977
Araguaína (▲103,396)	81,729
Araguari (▲91,202)	80,568
Arapiraca (▲165,379)	131,449
Arapongas (▲64,531)	59,996
Araraquara (▲166,732)	101,302
Araras (▲87,355)	79,002
Araucária (▲61,767)	53,522
Araxá	67,919
Arcoverde (▲55,790)	49,479
Assis (▲85,265)	72,004
Atibaia (▲86,193)	74,658
Avaré (▲61,063)	56,232
Bacabal (▲98,875)	64,844
Bagé (▲118,736)	89,372
Barbacena (▲99,895)	80,682
Barra Alegre (▲179,710)	58,445
Barra do Piraí (▲78,426)	59,202
Barra Mansa (▲171,671)	145,112
Barreiras (▲92,439)	70,701
Barreiros (▲139,318) (★Florianópolis)	58,694
Barretos (▲95,538)	88,935
Barueri (▲130,383)	66,722
Bauru	254,690
Bayeux (★João Pessoa)	77,047
Bebedouro (▲67,752)	60,792
Belém (★1,355,000)	765,476
Belford Roxo (▲1,293,611) (★Rio de Janeiro)	337,698
Belo Horizonte (★3,340,000)	1,526,566
Bento Gonçalves (▲78,652)	63,594

▲ Population of an entire municipality, commune, or district, including rural areas
• Largest city in country
★ Population or designation of the metropolitan area, including suburbs
★★ Population of metropolitan agglomeration
C Census E Official estimate U Unofficial estimate

Betim (★Belo Horizonte) 162,462
Birigui 70,547
Blumenau (▲211,862) 185,200
Boa Vista (▲142,902) 118,928
Botucatu (▲90,620) 81,528
Bragança Paulista (▲108,602) 88,336
Brás Cubas (▲273,255) 65,538
BRASÍLIA 1,513,470
Brusque 53,438
Cabo (▲126,756) 68,594
Cabo Frio (▲84,635) 70,251
Caçapava (▲65,889) 58,145
Cáceres (▲77,475) 51,891
Cachoeira do Sul (▲89,148) 69,780
Cachoeirinha (★Porto Alegre) 87,976
Cachoeiro de Itapemirim (▲143,763) 112,099
Camaçari (▲113,615) 88,302
Camarajibe 99,431
Cambé (▲73,803) 66,767
Campina Grande 298,331
Campinas (★1,290,000) 759,032
Campo Comprido (▲1,313,094) (★Curitiba) 105,631
Campo Grande 516,403
Campo Mourão (▲82,280) 69,966
Campos (▲388,747) 277,482
Campos Elísios (▲665,343) (★Rio de Janeiro) 197,833
Candeias (▲67,936) 61,432
Canoas (★Porto Alegre) 269,234
Capuava (▲615,112) 92,950
Carapicuíba (▲283,653) (★São Paulo) 207,264
Carapina (▲221,510) (★Vitória) 141,234
Cariacica (▲274,455) (★Vitória) 91,888
Carpina (▲65,949) 50,962
Caruaru (▲213,573) 180,654
Cascatinha (▲255,261) 56,890
Cascavel (▲192,884) 175,332
Castanhal (▲101,963) 90,364
Cataguazes (▲58,167) 51,000
Catanduva 88,024
Caucaia (▲165,015) (★Fortaleza) 66,379
Cava (▲1,293,611) 59,506
Cavaleiro (▲486,774) (★Recife) 120,065
Caxias (▲146,730) 85,332
Caxias do Sul (▲290,969) 262,983
Chapecó (▲122,889) 93,697
Codó (▲111,679) 58,163
Coelho da Rocha (▲424,689) (★Rio de Janeiro) 152,045
Colatina (▲106,712) 71,094
Colombo (▲117,658) (★Curitiba) 110,161
Conselheiro Lafaiete (▲88,843) 82,619
Contagem (▲448,991) (★Belo Horizonte) 195,705
Corumbá (▲88,290) 75,235
Cotia (▲106,822) 90,469
Coxipó da Ponte (▲401,303) 140,130
Crato (▲91,413) 56,374
Criciúma (▲146,162) 99,375
Cruz Alta (▲68,784) 61,860
Cruzeiro 65,935
Cubatão (★Santos) 90,572
Cuiabá (▲401,303) 252,784
Curitiba (★1,815,000) 841,882
Diadema (★São Paulo) 305,068
Divinópolis (▲151,382) 141,984
Dourados (▲135,786) 116,817
Duque de Caxias (▲665,343) (★Rio de Janeiro) 325,903
Embu (★São Paulo) 155,851
Erechim (▲72,292) 61,509
Esteio (★Porto Alegre) 70,449
Eunápolis (▲70,561) 63,553
Feira de Santana (▲405,848) 340,034
Fernandópolis (▲56,125) 51,216
Ferraz de Vasconcelos (▲95,973) (★São Paulo) 65,319
Florianópolis (★420,000) 191,664
Fortaleza (★2,040,000) 743,335
Foz do Iguaçu 186,362
Franca 227,613
Francisco Morato 83,361
Franco da Rocha 79,534
Garanhuns (▲103,365) 86,593
Goiabeiras (▲258,243) (★Vitória) 74,086
Goiânia (★1,130,000) 912,136
Governador Valadares (▲230,403) 210,396
Gravataí (▲181,019) (★Porto Alegre) 166,954
Guaíba (▲83,119) 72,739
Guarapari (▲61,594) 54,994
Guarapuava (▲159,692) 107,046
Guaratinguetá (▲102,005) 84,660
Guarujá (▲209,814) (★Santos) 98,918
Guarulhos (▲786,355) 546,417
Gurupi (▲56,741) 51,005
Hortolândia (▲226,225) 78,011
Ibes (▲265,251) (★Vitória) 91,071
Icoraci (▲1,244,688) (★Belém) 67,458
Igapó (▲606,681) 117,251
Ijuí (▲75,169) 58,627
Ilhéus (▲223,482) 135,117
Imbariê (▲665,343) 100,687
Imperatriz (▲276,440) 209,970
Indaiatuba (▲100,816) 91,752
Inhomirim (▲191,249) 76,031
Ipatinga (★179,710) 120,025
Ipiíba (▲778,831) (★Rio de Janeiro) 121,785
Itabira (▲85,284) 71,287
Itaboraí (▲161,398) 72,410
Itabuna (▲185,165) 170,434
Itaituba (▲116,541) 62,278
Itajaí 114,558
Itajubá (▲74,618) 68,469
Itapecerica da Serra (▲92,854) (★São Paulo) 84,479
Itaperuna (▲78,017) 55,484
Itapetininga (▲105,071) 84,703
Itapeva (▲81,858) 55,658
Itapevi (★São Paulo) 107,983
Itaquaquecetuba (★São Paulo) 164,665
Itaquari (▲274,455) (★Vitória) 169,145
Itatiba (▲61,587) 54,044
Itaúna 61,891
Itu (▲107,176) 88,838
Ituiutaba (▲84,581) 78,211
Itumbiara (▲79,457) 68,673
Jaboatão (▲486,774) (★Recife) 81,178
Jaboticabal (▲59,130) 53,037
Jacareí (▲163,843) 144,141
Jandira 62,573
Japeri (▲1,293,611) 65,576
Jaraguá do Sul (▲76,994) 62,578
Jardim Presidente Dutra (▲786,355) (★São Paulo) 229,987
Jataí (▲65,921) 53,431
Jaú (▲94,138) 80,331
Jequié (▲144,572) 114,542
Ji-Paraná (▲97,719) 75,384
João Monlevade 57,413
João Pessoa (★670,000) 497,308
Joinville 326,208
Juazeiro (★Petrolina) 95,676
Juazeiro do Norte 163,527
Juiz de Fora 377,538
Jundiaí (▲288,644) 265,599
Jurema (▲165,015) (★Fortaleza) 75,463
Justinópolis (▲143,696) (★Belo Horizonte) 85,452
Lages (▲151,100) 137,169
Lavras (▲65,857) 60,690
Leme 64,525
Limeira (▲207,416) 177,591
Linhares (▲119,501) 73,082
Lins (▲59,218) 54,868
Londrina (▲389,959) 355,062
Lorena (▲73,167) 67,766
Luziânia (▲207,425) 194,128
Macaé (▲100,642) 57,581
Macapá (▲179,252) 146,523
Maceió (▲628,241) 554,727
Manaus 1,005,634
Marabá (▲22,231) 102,364
Maracanaú (▲157,029) 133,206
Marília (▲160,872) 144,906
Maringá 225,516
Matão 59,694
Mauá (★São Paulo) 294,631
Mesquita (▲1,293,611) (★Rio de Janeiro) 141,326
Messejana (▲1,765,794) (★Fortaleza) 229,507
Moji das Cruzes (▲273,255) (★São Paulo) 138,995
Moji-Guaçu (▲107,440) 92,440
Moji-Mirim (▲64,750) 57,395
Mondubim (▲1,765,794) (★Fortaleza) 331,591
Monjolo (▲778,831) (★Rio de Janeiro) 137,974
Montes Claros (▲249,565) 223,046
Mossoró (▲191,959) 177,020
Muriaé (▲84,507) 65,406
Muribeca dos Guararapes (▲486,774) (★Recife) 217,905
Natal (▲606,681) 459,827
Neves (▲778,831) (★Rio de Janeiro) 151,067
Nilópolis (▲157,936) (★Rio de Janeiro) 104,671
Niterói (▲435,658) (★Rio de Janeiro) 400,586
Nossa Senhora do Socorro 67,443
Nova Brasília (▲178,326) (★Goiânia) 126,701
Nova Friburgo (▲166,975) 111,020
Nova Iguaçu (▲1,293,611) (★Rio de Janeiro) 562,062
Nova Veneza (▲226,225) 82,203
Novo Hamburgo (★Porto Alegre) 201,334
Novo Mundo (▲1,313,094) (★Curitiba) 71,508
Olinda (★Recife) 341,059
Olinda (▲157,936) 53,265
Osasco (★São Paulo) 566,949
Ourinhos (▲76,912) 70,690
Palhoça (▲68,298) (★Florianópolis) 58,097
Pará de Minas (▲61,066) 51,679
Paranaguá (▲107,601) 88,110
Paranavaí (▲71,173) 61,043
Parangaba (▲1,765,794) (★Fortaleza) 267,679
Parnaíba (▲127,992) 105,131
Parque Industrial (▲448,991) (★Belo Horizonte) 223,660
Passo do Sabão (▲169,079) (★Porto Alegre) 63,140
Passo Fundo (▲147,239) 135,158
Passos (▲84,618) 74,218
Patos (▲81,292) 76,378
Patos de Minas (▲102,766) 83,670
Paulista (▲211,017) (★Recife) 53,566
Paulo Afonso (▲86,594) 74,326
Pelotas (▲290,660) 260,510
Petrolina (★300,000) 123,857
Petrópolis (▲255,261) (★Rio de Janeiro) 164,849
Pindamonhangaba (▲101,939) 71,449
Pinhais (▲106,764) (★Curitiba) 71,973
Pinheirinho (▲1,313,094) (★Curitiba) 117,516
Piracicaba (▲283,634) 223,170
Poá (★São Paulo) 72,151
Poços de Caldas 105,223
Ponta Grossa 219,955
Porto Alegre (★2,850,000) 1,247,352
Porto Velho (▲286,471) 226,196
Porto Velho (▲161,611) 56,973
Pouso Alegre (▲81,776) 73,875
Praia da Conceição (▲211,017) (★Recife) 97,635
Praia Grande (▲123,494) 97,173
Presidente Prudente 157,618
Queimados (▲1,293,611) (★Rio de Janeiro) 124,121
Recife (★2,880,000) 1,296,995
Resende (▲91,605) 52,261
Ribeirão Pires 62,240
Ribeirão Preto 416,186
Rio Branco (▲196,871) 136,457
Rio Claro 130,364
Rio de Janeiro (★11,050,000) 5,473,909
Rio Grande (▲172,408) 157,608
Rio Verde (▲95,894) 76,818
Rondonópolis (▲126,082) 87,307
Salto 72,076
Salvador (★2,340,000) 2,070,296
Santa Bárbara d'Oeste 141,230
Santa Cruz do Sul (▲117,779) 74,295
Santa Felicidade (▲1,313,094) (★Curitiba) 53,560
Santa Inês (▲64,655) 54,006
Santa Maria (▲217,604) 193,294
Santa Rita (▲94,412) (★João Pessoa) 74,396
Santana do Livramento (▲80,145) 72,950
Santarém (▲264,779) 168,153
Santo André (▲615,112) (★São Paulo) 518,272
Santo Ângelo (▲76,461) 59,688
Santo Antônio de Jesus (▲64,198) 52,770
Santos (★1,165,000) 415,554
São Benedito (▲137,686) (★Belo Horizonte) 91,733
São Bernardo do Campo (★São Paulo) 550,030
São Borja (▲63,766) 52,493
São Caetano do Sul (★São Paulo) 149,203
São Carlos (▲158,186) 100,502
São Gonçalo (▲778,831) (★Rio de Janeiro) 296,021
São João da Boa Vista (▲69,090) 60,845
São João de Meriti (▲424,689) (★Rio de Janeiro) 220,742
São João Del Rei (▲72,741) 63,680
São José do Rio Preto 263,454
São José dos Campos (▲442,009) 385,879
São José dos Pinhais (▲128,170) (★Curitiba) 99,154
São Leopoldo (★Porto Alegre) 160,228
São Lourenço da Mata (▲85,889) (★Recife) 68,479
São Luís (★710,000) 164,334
São Mateus (▲424,689) 51,902
•São Paulo (★16,925,000) 9,393,753
São Vicente (★Santos) 268,467
Sapiranga (▲58,522) 51,387
Sapucaia do Sul (★Porto Alegre) 104,626
Serra (▲221,510) 62,398
Sertãozinho (▲78,753) 68,874
Sete Lagoas 139,910
Sete Pontes (▲778,831) (★Rio de Janeiro) 71,984
Sobral (▲127,459) 92,805
Sorocaba 348,952
Sumaré (▲226,225) 64,673
Suzano (▲159,142) (★São Paulo) 110,414
Taboão da Serra (★São Paulo) 159,894
Tatuí (▲76,662) 68,808
Taubaté (▲206,416) 185,790
Teixeira de Freitas (▲85,227) 73,107
Telêmaco Borba (▲64,854) 50,774
Teófilo Otoni (▲140,676) 96,382
Teresina (★665,000) 556,073
Teresópolis (▲120,712) 96,516
Timon (▲107,394) (★Teresina) 90,577
Toledo (▲94,857) 67,343
Três Lagoas (▲68,067) 60,716
Três Rios (▲81,163) 60,201
Tubarão (▲95,058) 83,262
Tupã (▲61,290) 53,282
Ubá (▲66,422) 52,673
Uberaba (▲211,356) 198,565
Uberlândia 255,191
Umbará (▲1,313,094) (★Curitiba) 64,523
Umuarama (▲100,185) 66,995
Uruguaiana (▲117,437) 103,160
Valinhos (▲67,867) 59,896
Varginha (▲88,045) 82,263
Várzea Grande (▲161,611) 96,379
Várzea Paulista 67,911
Venda Nova (▲2,017,127) (★Belo Horizonte) 481,470
Viamão (▲169,079) 75,782
Vicente de Carvalho (▲209,814) (★Santos) 110,881
Vila Velha (▲265,251) (★Vitória) 113,664
Vila Xavier (▲166,732) 50,922
Vitória (★810,000) 184,157
Vitória da Conquista (▲224,896) 179,868
Vitória de Santo Antão (▲106,661) 84,116
Volta Redonda (★430,000) 219,988
Votorantim 79,150
Votuporanga (▲66,037) 59,604

BRITISH VIRGIN ISLANDS

1980 C 12,034
•ROAD TOWN 2,479

BRUNEI

1991 C 260,482
•BANDAR SERI BEGAWAN (★120,000) 45,867

BULGARIA / Bălgarija

1992 C 8,487,317
Asenovgrad 52,360
Blagoevgrad 71,476
Burgas 198,093
Dimitrovgrad 53,579
Dobrič 104,494
Gabrovo 76,522
Haskovo 80,700
Jambol 91,497
Kazanlăk 61,829
Kjustendil 54,431
Montana 52,476
Pazardžik 82,578
Pernik 93,502
Pleven 136,077
Plovdiv 341,058
Ruse 170,038
Sliven 108,722
•SOFIJA (SOFIA) (★1,280,000) 1,190,126
Stara Zagora 150,518
Šumen 93,390
Varna 308,432
Veliko Tărnovo 75,020
Vidin 66,056
Vraca 75,518

BURKINA FASO

1985 C 7,964,705
Bobo-Dioulasso 228,668
Koudougou 51,926
•OUAGADOUGOU 441,514

BURUNDI

1990 C 5,356,266
•BUJUMBURA 226,628

CAMBODIA / Kâmpŭchéa

1990 E 8,567,582
Bătdâmbâng 94,412
Kâmpóng Saôm 67,452
•PHNUM PENH (PHNOM PENH) 620,000
Siĕmréab 76,434

CAMEROON / Cameroun

1987 C 9,312,429
Bafoussam 92,331
Bamenda 95,445
•Douala 712,251
Garoua 122,584
Kumba 63,911
Loum 50,005
Maroua 111,630
Ngaoundéré 62,468
Nkongsamba 76,887
YAOUNDÉ 560,785

CANADA

1996 C 28,846,761

CANADA: ALBERTA

1996 C 2,696,826
Calgary (★821,628) 768,082
Edmonton (★862,597) 616,306
Lethbridge 63,053
Medicine Hat (★56,570) 46,783
Red Deer 60,075

CANADA: BRITISH COLUMBIA

1996 C 3,724,500
Abbotsford (★136,480) 105,403
Burnaby (★Vancouver) 179,209
Chilliwack (★66,254) 60,186
Coquitlam (★Vancouver) 101,820
Courtenay (★54,912) 17,335
Delta (★Vancouver) 95,411
Kamloops (★84,914) 76,394
Kelowna (★136,541) 89,442
Maple Ridge 56,173
Nanaimo (★85,585) 70,130
Prince George 75,150
Richmond (★Vancouver) 148,867
Saanich (★Victoria) 101,388
Surrey (★Vancouver) 304,477
Vancouver (★1,831,665) 514,008
Vernon (★55,359) 31,817
Victoria (★304,287) 73,504

CANADA: MANITOBA

1996 C 1,113,898
Winnipeg (★667,209) 618,477

CANADA: NEW BRUNSWICK

1996 C 738,133
Fredericton (★78,950) 46,507
Moncton (★113,491) 59,313
Saint John (★125,705) 72,494

CANADA: NEWFOUNDLAND

1996 C 551,792
Saint John's (★174,051) 101,936

CANADA: NORTHWEST TERRITORIES

1996 C 39,672
Yellowknife 17,275

CANADA: NOVA SCOTIA

1996 C 909,282
Dartmouth 65,629
Halifax (★332,518) 113,910

CANADA: NUNAVUT

1996 C 24,730
Iqaluit 4,220

CANADA: ONTARIO

1996 C 10,753,573
Ajax (★Toronto) 64,430
Barrie (★118,695) 79,191
Belleville (★93,442) 37,083
Brampton (★Toronto) 268,251
Brantford (★100,238) 84,764
Burlington (★Hamilton) 136,976
Cambridge (★Kitchener) 101,429
Chatham (★67,068) 43,409
Clarington 60,615
Cornwall (★62,183) 47,403
Gloucester (★Ottawa) 104,022
Guelph (★105,420) 95,821
Hamilton (★624,360) 322,352
Kingston (★143,416) 55,947
Kitchener (★382,940) 178,420
London (★398,616) 325,646
Markham (★Toronto) 173,383
Mississauga (★Toronto) 544,382
Nepean (★Ottawa) 115,100
Newmarket (★Toronto) 57,125
Niagara Falls (★Saint Catharines) 76,917
North Bay (★64,785) 54,332
Oakville (★Toronto) 128,405
Oshawa (★268,773) 134,364
OTTAWA (★1,010,498) 323,340
Peterborough (★100,193) 69,535
Pickering (★Toronto) 78,989
Richmond Hill (★Toronto) 101,725
Saint Catharines (★372,406) 130,926
Sarnia (★86,480) 72,738
Sault Sainte Marie 80,054
Stoney Creek (★Hamilton) 54,318
Sudbury (★160,488) 92,059
Thunder Bay (★125,562) 113,662
•Toronto (★4,263,757) 2,385,421
Vaughan (★Toronto) 132,549
Waterloo (★Kitchener) 77,949
Whitby (★Oshawa) 73,794
Windsor (★278,685) 197,694

CANADA: PRINCE EDWARD ISLAND

1996 C 134,557
Charlottetown (★57,224) 32,531

CANADA: QUÉBEC

1996 C 7,138,795
Beauport (★Québec) 72,920
Brossard (★Montréal) 65,927
Charlesbourg (★Québec) 70,942
Chicoutimi (★160,454) 63,061
Drummondville (★65,119) 44,882
Gatineau (★Ottawa) 100,702
Granby (★58,872) 43,316
Hull (★Ottawa) 62,339
Jonquière (★Chicoutimi) 56,503
LaSalle (★Montréal) 72,029
Laval (★Montréal) 330,393
Longueuil (★Montréal) 127,977
Montréal (★3,326,510) 1,016,376
Montréal-Nord (★Montréal) 81,581
Pierrefonds (★Montréal) 52,986
Québec (★671,889) 167,264
Repentigny (★Montréal) 53,824
Saint-Hubert (★Montréal) 77,042
Saint-Hyacinthe (★50,027) 38,981
Saint-Jean-sur-Richelieu (★76,461) 36,435
Saint-Laurent (★Montréal) 74,240
Saint-Léonard (★Montréal) 71,327
Sainte-Foy 72,330
Shawinigan (★59,851) 18,678
Sherbrooke (★147,384) 76,786
Trois-Rivières (★139,956) 48,419
Verdun (★Montréal) 59,714

CANADA: SASKATCHEWAN

1996 C 990,237
Regina (★193,652) 180,400
Saskatoon (★219,056) 193,647

CANADA: YUKON

1996 C 30,766
Whitehorse (★21,808) 19,157

CAPE VERDE / Cabo Verde

1990 C 341,491
•PRAIA 61,644

CAYMAN ISLANDS

1989 C 25,355
•GEORGE TOWN 12,921

CENTRAL AFRICAN REPUBLIC / République centrafricaine

1988 C 2,463,616
•BANGUI 451,690

CHAD / Tchad

1993 C 6,288,261
Abéché 55,715
Moundou 99,607
•N'DJAMENA 546,572
Sarh 77,605

CHILE

1992 C 13,348,401
Antofagasta 225,316
Arica 161,333
Calama 106,970
Chillán 145,759
Concepción (★735,000) 326,784
Copiapó 98,188
Coquimbo 110,879
Coronel (★Concepción) 79,677
Curicó 77,733
Iquique 145,139
La Serena 109,293
Linares 59,658
Los Angeles 94,716
Lota (★Concepción) 50,123
Osorno 114,239
Ovalle 53,515
Puerto Montt 110,139
Punta Arenas 109,110
Quillota 53,765
Quilpué (★Valparaíso) 102,233
Rancagua 179,638
San Antonio 74,742
San Bernardo (★Santiago) 179,398
•SANTIAGO (★4,740,000) 4,295,593
Talca 159,711
Talcahuano (★Concepción) 244,034
Temuco 210,587
Valdivia 112,712
Valparaíso (★690,000) 274,228
Villa Alemana (★Valparaíso) 70,663
Viña del Mar (★Valparaíso) 303,589

CHINA / Zhongguo

1994 E 1,185,170,000
Acheng (1985 E) 100,304
Aksu (▲345,900) (1986 E) 143,100
Altay (▲141,700) (1986 E) 62,800
Anda (▲425,500) (1986 E) 130,200
Ankang (1985 E) 89,188
Anqing (▲433,900) (1986 E) 213,200
Anshan (1988 E) 1,330,000
Anshun (▲214,700) (1986 E) 128,800
Anyang (▲541,900) (1986 E) 361,200
Baicheng (▲282,000) (1986 E) 198,600
Baiquan (1985 E) 50,996
Baiyin (▲301,900) (1986 E) 157,100
Baoding (▲535,100) (1986 E) 423,200
Baoji (▲359,500) (1986 E) 286,200
Baoshan (▲688,400) (1986 E) 52,300
Baotou (1988 E) 1,130,000
Baoying (1985 E) 50,479
Bei'an (▲440,500) (1986 E) 199,500
Beihai (▲175,900) (1986 E) 119,000
BEIJING (PEKING) (★7,320,000) 6,690,000
Beipiao (▲603,700) (1986 E) 180,900
Bengbu (▲612,600) (1986 E) 403,900
Benxi (1988 E) 860,000
Bijie (1985 E) 54,871
Binxian (1982 C) 127,326
Binxian (▲177,900) (1986 E) 86,700
Boli (1985 E) 61,990
Bose (▲271,400) (1986 E) 82,000
Boshan (1975 U) 100,000
Boxing (1982 C) 57,554
Boyang (1985 E) 60,688
Bozhou (1985 E) 63,222
Cangshan (1982 C) 79,334
Cangzhou (▲293,600) (1986 E) 196,700
Changchun 2,470,000
Changde (▲220,800) (1986 E) 178,200
Changge (1982 C) 67,002
Changji (▲233,400) (1986 E) 110,500
Changqing (1982 C) 65,094
Changsha 1,510,000
Changshou (1985 E) 51,923
Changshu (▲998,000) (1986 E) 281,300
Changtu (1985 E) 49,937
Changyi (1982 C) 64,513
Changzhi (▲463,400) (1986 E) 273,000
Changzhou (1986 E) 522,700
Chao'an (▲1,214,500) (1986 E) 265,400
Chaoxian (▲739,500) (1986 E) 116,800
Chaoyang (1985 E) 85,968
Chaoyang (▲318,900) (1986 E) 180,300
Chengde (▲330,400) (1986 E) 226,600
Chengdu 2,760,000
Chenghai (1985 E) 50,631
Chenzhou (▲191,900) (1986 E) 143,500

▲ Population of an entire municipality, commune, or district, including rural areas
• Largest city in country
★ Population or designation of the metroplitan area, including suburbs
★★ Population of metropolitan agglomeration
C Census E Official estimate U Unofficial estimate

Chifeng (▲882,900) (1986 E)	299,000
Chongqing (Chungking)	3,870,000
Chuxian (▲365,000) (1986 E)	113,300
Chuxiong (▲379,400) (1986 E)	67,700
Da'an (1985 E)	70,552
Dachangzhen (1975 U)	50,000
Dali (▲395,800) (1986 E)	112,100
Dalian (Dairen)	2,400,000
Dandong (1986 E)	579,800
Daqing (1988 E)	640,000
Dashiqiao (1985 E)	68,898
Datong (1985 E)	55,529
Datong (▲1,040,000) (1988 E)	810,000
Dawa (1985 E)	142,581
Daxian (▲209,400) (1986 E)	142,000
Dehui (1985 E)	60,247
Deyang (▲753,400) (1986 E)	184,800
Dezhou (▲276,200) (1986 E)	161,300
Didao (1975 U)	50,000
Dinghai (1985 E)	50,161
Dongchuan (▲275,100) (1986 E)	67,400
Dongguan (▲1,208,500) (1986 E)	254,900
Dongsheng (▲121,300) (1986 E)	57,500
Dongtai (1985 E)	65,788
Dongying (▲514,400) (1986 E)	178,100
Dukou (▲551,200) (1986 E)	380,200
Dunhua (▲448,000) (1986 E)	217,100
Duyun (▲386,600) (1986 E)	123,800
Echeng (▲938,000) (1986 E)	217,400
Enshi (▲679,000) (1986 E)	84,300
Ergun Zuoqi (1985 E)	55,970
Feixian (1982 C)	73,246
Fengcheng (1985 E)	66,745
Foshan (▲312,700) (1986 E)	243,500
Fujin (1985 E)	60,948
Fuling (▲973,500) (1986 E)	166,300
Fushun (1988 E)	1,290,000
Fuxin (1988 E)	700,000
Fuyang (▲195,200) (1986 E)	143,400
Fuyu (1985 E)	98,373
Fuzhou	1,380,000
Fuzhou (▲171,800) (1986 E)	106,700
Gaixian (1985 E)	67,587
Ganzhou (▲346,000) (1986 E)	191,600
Gaoqing (1982 C)	70,411
Gaoyou (1985 E)	57,844
Gejiu (▲341,700) (1986 E)	193,600
Golmud (1986 E)	60,300
Gongzhuling (▲899,400) (1986 E)	187,600
Guangyuan (▲805,500) (1986 E)	162,200
Guangzhou (Canton)	3,750,000
Guanxian (1985 E)	65,039
Guilin (▲457,500) (1986 E)	324,200
Guixian (1985 E)	61,970
Guiyang	1,080,000
Haicheng (▲984,800) (1986 E)	210,700
Haifeng (1985 E)	50,401
Haikou	340,000
Hailar (▲163,549) (1986 E)	180,000
Hailin (1985 E)	58,909
Hailun (1985 E)	83,448
Haiyang (1982 C)	77,098
Hami (▲270,300) (1986 E)	146,400
Hancheng (▲304,200) (1986 E)	66,600
Handan (▲1,030,000) (1988 E)	870,000
Hangu (1975 U)	100,000
Hangzhou	1,790,000
Hanzhong (▲415,000) (1986 E)	151,700
Harbin	3,120,000
Hebi (▲321,600) (1986 E)	158,500
Hechi (▲266,800) (1986 E)	74,400
Hechuan (1985 E)	65,237
Hefei	1,110,000
Hegang (▲576,159) (1986 E)	588,300
Heihe (▲135,000) (1986 E)	76,700
Helong (1985 E)	62,665
Hengshui (▲286,500) (1986 E)	83,100
Hengyang (▲601,300) (1986 E)	419,200
Heze (▲1,001,500) (1986 E)	115,400
Hohhot	730,000
Hongjiang (▲67,000) (1986 E)	54,300
Hotan (▲122,800) (1986 E)	71,700
Houma (▲158,500) (1986 E)	67,000
Huadian (1985 E)	75,183
Huai'an (1985 E)	65,673
Huaibei (▲447,200) (1986 E)	252,100
Huaihua (▲427,100) (1986 E)	102,000
Huainan (▲1,110,000) (1988 E)	700,000
Huaiyin (▲382,500) (1986 E)	201,700
Huanan (1985 E)	66,596
Huanggang (1982 C)	65,961
Huangshan (▲104,500) (1986 E)	61,800
Huangshi (1986 E)	451,900
Huaying (▲313,500) (1986 E)	81,000
Huinan (1985 E)	52,429
Huizhou (▲182,100) (1986 E)	117,000
Hulan (1985 E)	74,989
Hunjiang (▲687,700) (1986 E)	442,600
Huzhou (▲964,400) (1986 E)	208,500
Jiading (1985 E)	60,718
Jiamusi (▲557,700) (1986 E)	429,800
Ji'an (▲184,300) (1986 E)	132,200
Jiangling (1985 E)	77,887
Jiangmen (▲231,700) (1986 E)	168,800
Jiangyin (1985 E)	66,476
Jiangyou (1985 E)	72,663
Jian'ou (1985 E)	55,180
Jiaohe (1985 E)	51,504
Jiaoxian (1985 E)	51,869
Jiaozuo (▲509,900) (1986 E)	335,400
Jiawang (1975 U)	50,000
Jiaxing (▲686,500) (1986 E)	210,200
Jiayuguan (▲102,100) (1986 E)	73,800
Jiexiu (1985 E)	51,300
Jieyang (1985 E)	98,531
Jilin (▲1,114,100) (1988 E)	1,200,000
Jinan (Tsinan)	2,150,000
Jinchang (▲136,000) (1986 E)	90,500
Jincheng (▲612,700) (1986 E)	99,900
Jingdezhen (▲569,700) (1986 E)	304,000
Jingmen (▲946,500) (1986 E)	227,000
Jinhua (▲799,900) (1986 E)	147,800
Jining (▲765,700) (1986 E)	222,600
Jining (▲156,800) (1986 C)	163,300
Jinshi (▲219,700) (1986 E)	73,700
Jinxi (▲634,300) (1986 E)	223,100
Jinzhou (1985 E)	95,761
Jinzhou (▲810,000) (1988 E)	710,000
Jishou (▲194,500) (1986 E)	59,500
Jishu (1985 E)	75,587
Jiujiang (▲382,300) (1986 E)	248,500
Jiulong (Kowloon) (1986 C)	774,781
Jiuquan (▲269,900) (1986 E)	56,300
Jiutai (1985 E)	63,021
Jixi (▲820,000) (1988 E)	700,000
Jixian (1985 E)	59,725
Juancheng (1982 C)	54,110
Junan (1982 C)	90,222
Junxian (▲423,400) (1986 E)	97,000
Juxian (1982 C)	51,666
Kaifeng (▲629,100) (1986 E)	458,800
Kaili (▲342,100) (1986 E)	96,600
Kaiping (1985 E)	54,145
Kaiyuan (1985 E)	85,762
Kaiyuan (▲342,100) (1986 E)	96,600
Karamay (▲168,868) (1986 E)	185,300
Kashi (▲194,500) (1986 E)	146,300
Keshan (1985 E)	65,088
Korla (▲219,000) (1986 E)	129,400
Kunming	1,500,000
Kuqa (1985 E)	63,847
Kuytun (1986 E)	60,200
Kwai Chung (★Xianggang) (1986 C)	131,362
Laiwu (▲1,041,800) (1986 E)	143,500
Langfang (▲522,800) (1986 E)	122,100
Langxiang (1985 E)	64,658
Lanxi (▲606,800) (1986 E)	70,500
Lanxi (1985 E)	53,236
Lanzhou	1,340,000
Laohekou (▲420,000) (1986 E)	104,400
Lechang (1986 E)	56,913
Lengshuijiang (▲277,600) (1986 E)	101,700
Lengshuitan (▲362,000) (1986 E)	60,900
Leshan (▲972,300) (1986 E)	307,300
Lhasa (▲107,700) (1986 E)	84,400
Lianyungang (▲459,400) (1986 E)	288,000
Liaocheng (▲724,300) (1986 E)	119,000
Liaoyang (▲576,900) (1986 E)	442,600
Liaoyuan (1986 E)	370,400
Liling (▲856,300) (1986 E)	107,100
Linfen (▲530,100) (1986 E)	157,600
Lingyuan (1985 E)	66,825
Linhai (1985 E)	52,653
Linhe (▲365,900) (1986 E)	99,800
Linkou (1985 E)	52,936
Linqing (▲603,000) (1986 E)	87,000
Linqu (1982 C)	84,196
Linxia (▲150,200) (1986 E)	72,900
Linyi (▲1,365,000) (1986 E)	190,000
Liuzhou (1988 E)	680,000
Longjiang (1985 E)	51,156
Longyan (▲378,500) (1986 E)	114,500
Loudi (▲254,300) (1986 E)	84,200
Lu'an (▲163,400) (1986 E)	122,600
Lufeng (1985 E)	53,015
Luohe (▲159,100) (1986 E)	102,300
Luoyang (▲1,090,000) (1988 E)	760,000
Lupanshui (▲2,216,500) (1986 E)	363,500
Luzhou (▲360,300) (1986 E)	237,800
Ma'anshan (▲367,000) (1986 E)	258,900
Manzhouli (1986 E)	116,600
Maoming (▲434,900) (1986 E)	118,600
Meihekou (▲534,200) (1986 E)	117,500
Meizhou (▲740,600) (1986 E)	169,000
Mengyin (1982 C)	70,602
Mianyang (▲848,500) (1986 E)	233,900
Minhang (1975 U)	60,000
Mishan (1985 E)	54,919
Mixian (1982 C)	64,776
Mudanjiang (1988 E)	650,000
Naizishan (1985 E)	51,982
Nancha (1975 U)	50,000
Nanchang	1,440,000
Nanchong (▲238,100) (1986 E)	158,000
Nanjing (Nanking)	2,490,000
Nanning	960,000
Nanpiao (1982 C)	67,274
Nanping (▲420,800) (1986 E)	157,100
Nantong (▲411,000) (1986 E)	308,800
Nanyang (▲294,800) (1986 E)	199,400
Neihuang (1982 C)	56,039
Neijiang (▲298,500) (1986 E)	191,100
Ningbo	1,100,000
Ningyang (1982 C)	55,424
Nong'an (1985 E)	55,966
Nunjiang (1985 E)	59,276
Panshan (▲343,100) (1986 E)	248,100
Panshi (1985 E)	59,270
Pingdingshan (▲819,900) (1986 E)	363,200
Pingliang (▲362,500) (1986 E)	85,400
Pingxiang (▲1,286,700) (1986 E)	368,700
Pingyi (1982 C)	89,373
Pingyin (1982 C)	62,827
Potou (▲456,100) (1986 E)	59,000
Puqi (1985 E)	65,239
Putian (▲265,400) (1986 E)	64,600
Putuo (1985 E)	50,962
Puyang (▲1,086,100) (1986 E)	131,000
Qian Gorlos (1985 E)	79,494
Qingdao (Tsingtao)	2,300,000
Qingjiang (▲382,500) (1986 E)	201,700
Qingyuan (1985 E)	51,756
Qinhuangdao (▲436,000) (1986 E)	307,500
Qinzhou (▲923,400) (1986 E)	97,100
Qiqihar (▲1,330,000) (1988 E)	1,180,000
Qitaihe (▲309,900) (1986 E)	166,400
Qixia (1982 C)	54,158
Qixian (1982 C)	53,041
Quanzhou (▲436,000) (1986 E)	157,000
Qujing (▲758,000) (1986 E)	135,000
Quzhou (▲704,800) (1986 E)	124,000
Raoping (1985 E)	54,831
Rizhao (▲970,300) (1986 E)	93,300
Rongcheng (1982 C)	52,878
Rugao (1985 E)	50,643
Rui'an (1985 E)	57,993
Sanmenxia (▲150,000) (1986 E)	79,000
Sanming (▲214,300) (1986 E)	144,900
Sanya (▲321,700) (1986 E)	70,500
Sha Tin (★Xianggang) (1986 C)	355,810
•Shanghai (★11,010,000)	8,930,000
Shangqiu (▲199,400) (1986 E)	135,400
Shangrao (▲142,500) (1986 E)	113,000
Shangshui (1982 C)	50,191
Shantou (▲790,000) (1988 E)	560,000
Shanwei (1985 E)	61,234
Shaoguan (1986 E)	363,100
Shaowu (▲266,700) (1986 E)	81,400
Shaoxing (▲250,900) (1986 E)	167,100
Shaoyang (▲465,900) (1986 E)	218,600
Shashi (1986 E)	253,700
Shenxian (1982 C)	50,208
Shenyang (Mukden)	4,050,000
Shenzhen	640,000
Sheung Shui (1986 C)	87,206
Shiguaigou (1975 U)	50,000
Shihezi (▲549,300) (1987 E)	304,700
Shijiazhuang	1,610,000
Shiyan (▲332,600) (1986 E)	227,300
Shizuishan (▲317,400) (1986 E)	225,500
Shouguang (1982 C)	83,400
Shuangcheng (1985 E)	91,163
Shuangliao (1985 E)	67,326
Shuangyashan (1986 E)	427,300
Shulan (1986 E)	50,582
Shunde (1985 E)	50,262
Siping (▲357,800) (1986 E)	280,100
Sishui (1982 C)	82,990
Songjiang (1985 E)	71,864
Songjianghe (1985 E)	53,023
Suihua (▲732,100) (1986 E)	200,400
Suileng (1985 E)	68,399
Suining (▲1,174,900) (1986 E)	118,500
Suixian (▲132,814) (1982 C)	60,000
Suizhou (▲1,281,600) (1986 E)	187,700
Suqian (1985 E)	50,742
Suzhou (▲218,600) (1986 E)	123,300
Suzhou (▲681,000) (1988 E)	740,000
Tai Po (1986 C)	119,679
Tai'an (▲1,325,400) (1986 E)	215,900
Taiyuan	1,720,000
Taizhou (▲210,800) (1987 E)	143,200
Taizhou (▲385,200) (1986 E)	82,300
Tancheng (1982 C)	61,857
Tangshan (▲1,440,000) (1988 E)	1,080,000
Taonan (1985 E)	76,269
Tengxian (1985 E)	53,254
Tianjin (Tientsin)	5,000,000
Tianshui (▲953,200) (1986 E)	209,500
Tiefa (▲146,367) (1982 C)	60,000
Tieli (1985 E)	102,527
Tieling (▲454,100) (1986 E)	326,100
Tongchuan (▲393,200) (1986 E)	268,900
Tonghua (▲367,400) (1986 E)	290,200
Tongliao (▲253,100) (1986 E)	190,100
Tongling (▲216,400) (1986 E)	182,900
Tongren (1985 E)	50,307
Tongxian (1985 E)	97,168
Tsuen Wan (★Xianggang) (1986 C)	514,241
Tuen Mun (★Xianggang) (1986 C)	262,458
Tumen (▲99,700) (1986 E)	77,600
Turpan (▲196,800) (1986 E)	52,300
Ulanhot (▲192,100) (1986 E)	129,100
Ürümqi	1,130,000
Wafangdian (▲960,700) (1986 E)	246,200
Wangkui (1985 E)	52,021
Wangqing (1985 E)	61,237
Wanxian (▲280,800) (1986 E)	138,700
Weifang (▲1,042,200) (1986 E)	312,500
Weihai (▲220,800) (1986 E)	83,000
Weinan (▲699,400) (1986 E)	111,300
Weishan (1982 C)	57,932
Weixian (1982 C)	50,180
Wenzhou (Wenchow) (▲530,600) (1986 E)	372,200
Wuchang (1985 E)	64,403
Wuhai (1986 E)	266,000
Wuhan (Hankow)	3,870,000
Wuhu (▲502,200) (1986 E)	396,000
Wulian (1982 C)	51,718
Wusong (1982 C)	64,017
Wuwei (▲804,000) (1986 E)	115,500
Wuxi (1988 E)	880,000
Wuzhou (▲261,500) (1986 E)	194,800
Xiamen (Amoy)	470,000
Xi'an (Sian)	2,410,000
Xiangfan (▲421,200) (1986 E)	314,900
Xianggang (Hong Kong) (★4,770,000) (1991C)	1,250,993
Xiangtan (▲511,100) (1986 E)	389,500
Xianning (▲402,200) (1986 E)	122,200
Xianyang (▲641,800) (1986 E)	285,900
Xiaogan (▲1,204,400) (1986 E)	125,500
Xiaoshan (1985 E)	63,074
Xichang (▲161,000) (1986 E)	105,000
Xilinhot (▲100,700) (1986 E)	71,700
Xinghua (1985 E)	75,573
Xinglongzhen (1982 C)	52,961
Xingtai (▲350,800) (1986 E)	265,600
Xinhui (1985 E)	77,381
Xining (1988 E)	620,000
Xinjiulong (New Kowloon) (1986 C)	1,526,910
Xintai (▲1,157,300) (1986 E)	171,400
Xinwen (1975 U)	50,000
Xinxian (▲398,600) (1986 E)	74,200
Xinxiang (▲540,500) (1986 E)	411,000
Xinyang (▲234,200) (1986 E)	169,100
Xinyu (▲610,600) (1986 E)	140,200
Xuancheng (1985 E)	52,387
Xuanhua (1975 U)	140,000
Xuanwei (1982 C)	70,081
Xuchang (▲247,200) (1986 E)	167,800
Xuzhou (▲793,000) (1988 E)	860,000
Yaan (▲277,600) (1986 E)	89,200
Yakeshi (1986 E)	390,000
Yan'an (▲259,800) (1986 E)	86,700
Yancheng (▲1,251,400) (1986 E)	258,400
Yangcheng (1982 C)	57,255
Yangjiang (1986 E)	91,433
Yangquan (▲478,900) (1986 E)	295,100
Yangzhou (▲417,300) (1986 E)	321,500
Yanji (1985 E)	55,035
Yanji (▲216,900) (1986 E)	175,000
Yanling (1982 C)	52,679
Yantai (▲717,300) (1986 E)	327,000
Yi'an (1986 E)	54,253
Yibin (▲636,500) (1986 E)	218,800
Yichang (▲363,578) (1986 E)	410,500
Yichuan (1982 C)	58,914
Yichun (▲770,200) (1986 E)	132,600
Yichun (1988 E)	840,000
Yidu (1985 E)	54,838
Yilan (1985 E)	50,436
Yima (▲84,800) (1986 E)	53,700
Yinan (1982 C)	67,803
Yinchuan	430,000
Yingchengzi (1985 E)	59,072
Yingkou (▲480,000) (1986 E)	366,900
Yingtan (▲116,200) (1986 E)	64,500
Yining (▲232,000) (1986 E)	153,200
Yiyang (▲365,000) (1986 E)	155,300
Yiyuan (1982 C)	53,800
Yong'an (▲269,000) (1986 E)	105,100
Yongchuan (1985 E)	70,444
Yongzhou (▲515,300) (1986 E)	72,700
Yuci (▲420,700) (1986 E)	171,000
Yuen Long (1986 C)	75,740
Yueyang (▲411,300) (1986 E)	239,500
Yulin (▲1,228,800) (1986 E)	115,600
Yulin (1985 E)	51,610
Yumen (▲160,100) (1986 E)	84,300
Yuncheng (▲434,900) (1986 E)	87,000
Yuncheng (1982 C)	54,262
Yunyang (1982 C)	54,903
Yushu (1985 E)	57,222
Yuyao (▲772,700) (1986 E)	169,700
Zalantun (▲389,500) (1986 E)	111,300
Zaozhuang (▲1,592,000) (1986 E)	292,200
Zhangjiakou (▲640,000) (1988 E)	500,000
Zhangye (▲394,200) (1986 E)	73,000
Zhangzhou (▲310,400) (1986 E)	159,400
Zhanjiang (▲920,900) (1986 E)	335,500
Zhaodong (1985 E)	99,836
Zhaoqing (▲187,600) (1986 E)	145,700
Zhaotong (▲546,600) (1986 E)	77,500
Zhaoyuan (1982 C)	56,389
Zhengzhou	1,690,000
Zhenjiang (1986 E)	412,400
Zhongshan (▲1,059,700) (1986 E)	238,700
Zhoucun (1975 U)	50,000
Zhoukou (▲220,400) (1986 E)	110,500
Zhuhai (▲155,000) (1986 E)	88,800
Zhumadian (▲149,500) (1986 E)	99,400
Zhuozhou (1985 E)	54,523
Zhuzhou (▲499,600) (1986 E)	344,800
Zibo (▲2,370,000) (1988 E)	840,000
Zigong (▲909,300) (1986 E)	361,700
Zixing (▲334,300) (1986 E)	97,100
Ziyang (1985 E)	57,349
Zouxian (1985 E)	61,578
Zunyi (▲347,600) (1986 E)	236,600

COLOMBIA

1993 C	33,109,840
Aguachica	50,001
Apartadó	56,330
Armenia	216,467
Barrancabermeja	144,769
Barranquilla (★1,260,000)	990,547
Bello (★Medellín)	257,707
Bucaramanga (★660,000)	410,065
Buenaventura	194,727
Buga	94,840
Cali (★1,735,000)	1,641,498
Cartagena	616,231
Cartago	100,946
Ciénaga	66,236
Cúcuta (★575,000)	459,640
Dos Quebradas (★Pereira)	129,572
Duitama	71,444
Envigado (★Medellín)	107,402
Facatativá	63,237
Florencia	82,708
Floridablanca (★Bucaramanga)	187,197
Fusagasugá	57,915
Girardot	81,380
Girón	71,618
Ibagué	340,191
Ipiales	59,351
Itagüí (★Medellín)	175,626
La Dorada	58,736
Magangué	61,452
Maicao	80,770
Malambo (★Barranquilla)	68,714
Manizales (★365,000)	303,136
Medellín (★2,290,000)	1,551,160
Montería	210,297
Neiva	237,239
Ocaña	59,574
Palmira	196,213
Pasto	261,368
Pereira (★580,000)	348,023
Piedecuesta	60,057
Popayán	169,423
Quibdó	65,904
Riohacha	77,083
•SANTA FE DE BOGOTÁ (★5,290,000)	4,931,796
Santa Marta	270,253
Sincelejo	168,410
Soacha (★Santa Fe de Bogotá)	222,565
Sogamoso	83,152
Soledad (★Barranquilla)	236,521
Tuluá	125,137
Tumaco	58,436
Tunja	101,622
Valledupar	202,404
Villavicencio	219,976
Yumbo (★Cali)	55,236
Zipaquirá	60,585

COMOROS / Comores

1990 E	452,742
•MORONI	23,432

CONGO

1989 E	2,188,367
•BRAZZAVILLE	693,712
Loubomo	57,991
Pointe-Noire	350,139

CONGO, DEMOCRATIC REPUBLIC OF THE / Congo, République démocratique du

1984 C	30,729,443
Bandundu	63,642
Boma	197,617
Bukavu	167,950
Bumba	51,197
Bunia	59,598
Butembo	73,312
Gandajika	64,878
Gemena	63,052
Goma	77,908
Ilebo	53,877
Isiro	78,268
Kalemie	73,528
Kamina	62,789
Kananga	298,693
Kikwit	149,296
Kindu	66,812
•KINSHASA (1986 E)	3,000,000
Kipushi	53,207
Kisangani	317,581
Kolwezi	416,122
Likasi	213,862
Lubumbashi	564,830
Matadi	138,798
Mbandaka	137,291
Mbuji-Mayi	486,235
Mwene-Ditu	94,560
Tshikapa	116,016
Uvira	74,432

COOK ISLANDS

1991 C	18,617
•AVARUA	10,886

COSTA RICA

1995 E	3,301,210
Puerto Limón (▲75,427)	48,600
•SAN JOSÉ (★1,549,700)	318,765

COTE D'IVOIRE (Ivory Coast)

1988 C	10,815,694
Abengourou	59,114
•ABIDJAN	1,929,079
Anyama	56,690
Bouaké	329,850
Daloa	121,842
Divo	72,350
Gagnoa	85,563
Korhogo	109,445
Man	89,575
San-Pédro	70,611
YAMOUSSOUKRO	106,786

CROATIA / Hrvatska

1991 C	4,784,265
Dubrovnik	55,638
Karlovac	70,729
Osijek	129,792
Pula	69,690
Rijeka (Fiume)	167,964
Šibenik	55,842
Sisak	60,564
Slavonski Brod	58,531
Split	200,459
Zadar (Zara)	80,355
•ZAGREB	867,865

CUBA

1991 E	10,694,465
Bayamo	139,061
Camagüey	286,404
Cárdenas (▲84,590)	69,800
Ciego de Ávila	101,620
Cienfuegos	136,233
Florida	51,442
Guantánamo	215,864
Holguín	236,967
•LA HABANA (HAVANA) (★2,210,000)	2,119,059
Las Tunas	126,678
Manzanillo	108,668
Matanzas	119,510
Morón	49,793
Palma Soriano (▲124,543)	66,600
Pinar del Río	136,303
Sancti Spíritus	97,522
Santa Clara	203,753
Santiago de Cuba	434,541

CYPRUS / Kípros

1992 C	602,025
Larnaka (Larnaca) (★60,500)	43,586
Lemesós (Limassol) (★137,000)	87,136
•LEVKOSÍA (NICOSIA) (★177,500)	47,036
Strovolos	51,499

CYPRUS, NORTH / Kuzey Kıbrıs

1985 E	160,287
•LEFKOŞA	37,400

CZECH REPUBLIC / Česká Republika

1991 C	10,302,215
Brno (★450,000)	387,986
České Budějovice (★114,000)	97,243
Chomutov (★80,000)	53,107
Děčín (★72,000)	54,341
Frýdek-Místek (★Ostrava)	63,808
Havířov (★Ostrava)	86,297
Hradec Králové (★113,000)	99,917
Jihlava	51,831
Karlovy Vary	56,222
Karviná (★Ostrava)	68,405
Kladno (★88,500)	71,753
Liberec (★175,000)	101,162
Most (★135,000)	70,670
Olomouc (★126,000)	103,993
Opava (★78,000)	62,815
Ostrava (★760,000)	327,371
Pardubice	94,636
Plzeň (★210,000)	173,008
•PRAHA (PRAGUE) (★1,328,000)	1,214,174
Přerov	51,300
Prostějov	50,074
Tábor (★55,500)	36,342
Teplice (★94,000)	53,004
Třinec (★87,500)	45,210
Ústí nad Labem (★115,000)	100,002
Zlín (★124,000)	82,869

DENMARK / Danmark

1995 E	5,228,000
Aalborg (▲159,056)	117,000
Århus (▲277,477)	214,700
Esbjerg (▲82,579)	72,900
Frederiksberg (★København)	88,002
Gentofte (★København)	66,508
Gladsakse (★København)	61,369
Helsingør (★København)	56,855
•KØBENHAVN (COPENHAGEN) (★1,780,000)	471,300
Odense (▲182,617)	145,300
Randers	61,435

DJIBOUTI

1991 E	508,541
•DJIBOUTI	329,337

DOMINICA

1984 E	77,000
•ROSEAU	9,348

DOMINICAN REPUBLIC / República Dominicana

1993 C	7,293,390
Bajos de Haina	69,260
Barahona	62,354
Bonao	69,672
Higüey	54,832
La Romana	140,204
La Vega	87,162
Moca	50,449
Puerto Plata	89,423
San Cristóbal	88,605
San Francisco de Macorís	108,485
San Juan de la Maguana	61,690
San Pedro de Macorís	124,735
Santiago de los Caballeros	365,463
•SANTO DOMINGO	1,609,966

▲ Population of an entire municipality, commune, or district, including rural areas
• Largest city in country
★ Population or designation of the metropolitan area, including suburbs
★★ Population of metropolitan agglomeration
C Census E Official estimate U Unofficial estimate

ECUADOR

1990 C	9,648,189
Ambato	124,166
Babahoyo	50,285
Cuenca	194,981
Eloy Alfaro	82,359
Esmeraldas	98,558
•Guayaquil	1,508,444
Ibarra	80,991
La Libertad	50,108
Loja	94,305
Machala	144,197
Manta	125,505
Milagro	93,637
Portoviejo	132,937
Quevedo	86,910
QUITO (★1,300,000)	1,100,847
Riobamba	94,505
Santo Domingo de los Colorados	114,422

EGYPT / Mişr

1986 C	48,205,049
Abu Kebir	68,394
Akhmīm	70,494
Al-'Akrīshah	67,337
Armant	54,618
Ashûm	54,450
Aswân	190,579
Asyût	272,986
Bahtīm (★El-Qâhira)	275,807
Benha	115,701
Beni Suef	152,476
Bilbeis	96,511
Bilqas Qism Awwal	73,040
Būlāq ad-Dakrūr (★El-Qâhira)	148,787
Bûr Sa'îd (Port Said)	401,172
Bûsh	54,655
Damanhûr	188,939
Damietta	89,069
Dis Ûq	78,316
El-Arish	67,337
El-Fayoum	213,070
El-Gîza (Giza) (★El-Qâhira)	1,883,189
El-Hawâmdîya (★El-Qâhira)	73,298
El-Iskandarîya (★3,350,000)	2,926,859
El-Mahalla el-Kubra	306,509
El-Mansûra (★375,000)	317,508
El-Manzala	54,918
El-Matariya	73,315
El-Minya (Minya)	179,060
•EL-QÂHIRA (CAIRO) (★9,300,000)	6,068,695
El-Simbillawein	60,159
El-Suweis (Suez)	327,717
El-Uqsor	126,160
Girga	71,564
Hosh Isa	53,619
Idku	70,724
Ismailia (★235,000)	158,045
Kafr el-Dauwar (★El-Iskandarîya)	198,244
Kafr el-Sheikh	103,301
Kafr el-Zaiyât	58,276
Kom Ombo	52,506
Maghâgha	50,916
Mallawi	98,632
Manfalût	52,281
Minûf	69,673
Mît Ghamr (★100,000)	91,927
Qalyûb	84,413
Qena	119,917
Rashid (Rosetta)	51,789
Samâlût	62,404
Sâqiyat Makkī	51,062
Shibîn el-Kôm	132,209
Shubrâ el-Kheima (★El-Qâhira)	714,594
Sinnûris	55,187
Suhag	132,649
Tahta	58,457
Talkha (★El-Mansûra)	54,923
Tanta	336,517
Warrāq al-'Arab (★El-Qâhira)	127,108
Zagazig	244,354
Zifta	69,253

EL SALVADOR

1992 C	5,118,599
Apopa	88,827
Delgado (★San Salvador)	56,701
Ilopango (★San Salvador)	79,069
Mejicanos (★San Salvador)	131,972
Nueva San Salvador (★San Salvador)	98,392
San Miguel	127,696
•SAN SALVADOR (★1,250,000)	415,346
Santa Ana	139,389
Soyapango (★San Salvador)	261,122

EQUATORIAL GUINEA / Guinea Ecuatorial

1983 C	300,000
•MALABO	31,630

ERITREA / Ērtra

1990 E	2,951,000
•ASMERA	358,100

ESTONIA / Eesti

1991 E	1,581,800
Kohtla-Järve	74,700
Narva (1992E)	82,900
Pärnu (1992E)	52,600
•TALLINN (1993E)	452,665
Tartu (1992E)	113,400

ETHIOPIA / Ītyop'iya

1986 E	44,927,000
•ĀDĪS ĀBEBA (★1,990,000) (1990 E)	1,912,500
Āk'ak'ī Besek'a (★Ādīs Ābeba)	58,977
Bahir Dar	59,951
Debre Zeyit	55,706
Desē	77,459
Dirē Dawa (1990 E)	127,400
Gonder	88,000
Hārer	68,000
Jīma	67,470
Mek'elē	66,640
Nazrēt	83,091

FALKLAND ISLANDS

1991 C	2,050
•STANLEY	1,557

FAROE ISLANDS / Færøerne / Føroyar

1990 E	47,946
•TÓRSHAVN	14,767

FIJI

1996 C	775,077
•SUVA (★167,975)	77,366

FINLAND / Suomi

1995 C	5,116,826
Espoo (★Helsinki)	187,499
•HELSINKI (HELSINGFORS) (★1,075,000)	512,686
Jyväskylä (★100,000)	73,096
Kotka	53,712
Kouvola (★55,500)	31,529
Kuopio	78,100
Lahti (★109,000)	93,110
Lappeenranta	50,329
Oulu (Uleåborg) (★125,000)	106,983
Pori (Björneborg)	72,121
Tampere (Tammerfors) (★250,000)	175,335
Turku (Åbo) (★228,500)	158,527
Vaasa (Vasa)	54,067
Vantaa (★Helsinki)	162,946

FRANCE

1990 C	56,614,493
Agen (★67,960)	30,553
Aix-en-Provence (★Marseille)	123,842
Ajaccio	58,315
Albi (★54,359)	46,579
Alès (★76,856)	41,037
Amiens (★156,120)	131,872
Angers (★208,282)	141,404
Angoulême (★102,908)	42,876
Annecy (★126,729)	49,644
Antibes (★Cannes)	70,005
Antony (★Paris)	57,771
Argenteuil (★Paris)	93,096
Arles (★54,309)	52,058
Armentières (★57,738)	25,219
Arras (★79,607)	38,983
Asnières-sur-Seine (★Paris)	71,850
Aubervilliers (★Paris)	67,557
Aulnay-sous-Bois (★Paris)	82,314
Avignon (★181,136)	86,939
Bastia (★52,446)	37,845
Bayonne (★164,378)	40,051
Beauvais (★57,704)	54,190
Belfort (★77,844)	50,125
Besançon (★122,623)	113,828
Béthune (★261,535)	24,556
Béziers (★76,304)	70,996
Blois (★65,132)	49,318
Bordeaux (★760,000)	210,336
Boulogne-Billancourt (★Paris)	101,743
Boulogne-sur-Mer (★91,249)	43,678
Bourg-en-Bresse (★55,784)	40,972
Bourges (★94,731)	75,609
Brest (★201,480)	147,956
Brive-la-Gaillarde (★64,379)	49,765
Caen (★191,490)	112,846
Calais (★101,768)	75,309
Cannes (★335,647)	68,676
Chalon-sur-Saône (★77,764)	54,575
Châlons-sur-Marne (★61,452)	48,423
Chambéry (★103,283)	54,120
Champigny-sur-Marne (★Paris)	79,486
Charleville-Mézières (★67,213)	57,008
Chartres (★85,933)	39,595
Châteauroux (★67,090)	50,969
Cherbourg (★92,045)	27,121
Cholet	55,132
Clermont-Ferrand (★254,416)	136,181
Colmar (★83,816)	63,498
Colombes (★Paris)	78,513
Compiègne (★67,057)	41,896
Courbevoie (★Paris)	65,389
Creil (★97,119)	31,956
Créteil (★Paris)	82,088
Dijon (★230,451)	146,703
Douai (★199,562)	42,175
Drancy (★Paris)	60,707
Dunkerque (Dunkirk) (★190,879)	70,331
Elbeuf (★53,886)	16,604
Épinal (★62,140)	36,732
Évreux (★57,968)	49,103
Fontenay-sous-Bois (★Paris)	51,868
Forbach (★98,758)	27,076
Fréjus (★73,967)	41,486
Grenoble (★404,733)	150,758
Hagondange (★112,061)	8,222
Ivry-sur-Seine (★Paris)	53,619
La Rochelle (★100,264)	71,094
La Seyne-sur-Mer (★Toulon)	59,968
Laval (★56,855)	50,473
Le Havre (★253,627)	195,854
Le Mans (★189,107)	145,502
Lens (★323,174)	35,017
Lille (★1,050,000)	172,142
Limoges (★170,065)	133,464
Lorient (★115,488)	59,271
Lyon (★1,335,000)	415,487
Maisons-Alfort (★Paris)	53,375
Marseille (★1,225,000)	800,550
Maubeuge (★102,772)	34,989
Meaux (★63,006)	48,305
Melun (★107,705)	35,319
Mérignac (★Bordeaux)	57,273
Metz (★193,117)	119,594
Montargis (★52,804)	15,020
Montauban	51,224
Montbéliard (★117,510)	29,005
Montluçon (★63,018)	44,248
Montpellier (★248,303)	207,996
Montreuil (★Paris)	94,754
Mulhouse (★223,856)	108,357
Nancy (★329,447)	99,351
Nanterre (★Paris)	84,565
Nantes (★496,078)	244,995
Neuilly-sur-Seine (★Paris)	61,768
Nevers (★58,915)	41,968
Nice (★516,740)	342,439
Nîmes (★138,527)	128,471
Niort (★65,792)	57,012
Noisy-le-Grand (★Paris)	54,032
Orléans (★243,153)	105,111
•PARIS (★10,275,000)	2,152,423
Pau (★144,674)	82,157
Périgueux (★63,322)	30,280
Perpignan (★157,873)	105,983
Pessac (★Bordeaux)	51,055
Poitiers (★107,625)	78,894
Quimper (Kemper) (★65,954)	59,437
Reims (Rheims) (★206,437)	180,620
Rennes (★245,065)	197,536
Roanne (★77,160)	41,756
Roubaix (★Lille)	97,746
Rouen (★380,161)	102,723
Rueil-Malmaison (★Paris)	66,401
Saint-Brieuc (★83,861)	44,752
Saint-Chamond (★81,795)	38,878
Saint-Denis (★Paris)	89,988
Saint-Étienne (★313,338)	199,396
Saint-Malo	48,057
Saint-Maur-des-Fossés (★Paris)	77,206
Saint-Nazaire (★131,511)	64,812
Saint-Quentin (★71,113)	60,644
Sarcelles (★Paris)	56,833
Sartrouville (★Paris)	50,329
Sète (★63,833)	41,510
Strasbourg (★415,000)	252,338
Tarbes (★77,787)	47,566
Thionville (★132,413)	39,712
Thonon-les-Bains (★54,000)	29,677
Toulon (★437,553)	167,619
Toulouse (★650,000)	358,688
Tourcoing (★Lille)	93,765
Tours (★282,152)	129,509
Troyes (★122,763)	59,255
Valence (★107,965)	63,437
Valenciennes (★338,392)	38,441
Vénissieux (★Lyon)	60,444
Versailles (★Paris)	87,789
Vichy (★61,566)	27,714
Villefranche-sur-Saône (★55,249)	29,542
Villeneuve-d'Ascq (★Lille)	65,320
Villeurbanne (★Lyon)	116,872
Vitry-sur-Seine	82,400

FRENCH GUIANA / Guyane

1990 C	114,808
•CAYENNE	41,067

FRENCH POLYNESIA / Polynésie française

1996 C	219,521
•PAPEETE (★95,000)	25,553

GABON

1990 E	1,365,000
•LIBREVILLE	337,700
Port-Gentil	78,000

GAMBIA, THE

1993 C	1,025,867
•BANJUL (★280,000)	42,407

GAZA STRIP / Qiṭā'Ghazzah

1992 E	667,000
Dayr al-Balah (★55,000)	29,200
•Ghazzah (Gaza) (★390,000)	238,905
Khān Yūnus (★130,000)	76,194
Rafah (★95,000)	41,096

GEORGIA / Gruzija / Sakart'velo

1991 E	5,464,200
Batumi	137,500
Gori	70,100
Kutaisi	238,200
Poti	51,100
Rustavi (★Tbilisi)	161,900
Suhumi	120,000
•TBILISI (★1,460,000)	1,279,000
Zugdidi	50,600

GERMANY / Deutschland

1994 E	81,410
Aachen (★550,000)	246,671
Aalen (★80,000)	66,333
Ahlen	55,657
Albstadt	50,057
Arnsberg	77,847
Aschaffenburg	65,650
Augsburg (★430,000)	264,764
Bad Homburg vor der Höhe (★Frankfurt am Main)	51,455
Bad Salzuflen	54,979
Baden-Baden	52,712
Bamberg (★122,000)	70,770
Bayreuth (★88,000)	73,393
Bergheim (★Köln)	60,121
Bergisch Gladbach (★Köln)	104,991
Bergkamen (★Essen)	51,054
BERLIN (★4,200,000)	3,475,392
Bielefeld (★540,000)	324,674
Bitterfeld (★105,000)	17,027
Bocholt	70,272
Bochum (★Essen)	401,058
BONN (★580,000)	296,859
Bottrop (★Essen)	119,676
Brandenburg	89,208
Braunschweig (Brunswick) (★320,000)	256,267
Bremen (★790,000)	551,604
Bremerhaven (★180,000)	131,492
Castrop-Rauxel (★Essen)	79,101
Celle	73,671
Chemnitz (★500,000)	279,520
Cottbus	128,121
Cuxhaven	56,003
Darmstadt (★315,000)	139,754
Delmenhorst (★Bremen)	77,127
Dessau (★138,000)	93,287
Detmold	72,109
Dinslaken (★Essen)	67,619
Dormagen (★Köln)	59,915
Dorsten (★Essen)	79,941
Dortmund (★Essen)	601,966
Dresden (★870,000)	479,273
Duisburg (★Essen)	536,797
Düren (★110,000)	89,852
Düsseldorf (★1,225,000)	574,936
Eberswalde-Finow	50,730
Emden	52,216
Erfurt	200,799
Erlangen (★Nürnberg)	102,383
Eschweiler (★Aachen)	55,791
•Essen (★5,050,000)	622,380
Esslingen am Neckar (★Stuttgart)	91,388
Euskirchen	51,247
Flensburg (★98,000)	87,994
Frankfurt	83,850
Frankfurt am Main (★1,950,000)	659,803
Freiburg im Breisgau (★235,400)	197,384
Friedrichshafen	56,047
Fulda (★76,000)	58,711
Fürth (★Nürnberg)	108,097
Garbsen (★Hannover)	62,196
Gelsenkirchen (★Essen)	295,037
Gera	122,974
Giessen (★155,000)	73,705
Gladbeck (★Essen)	79,931
Göppingen (★155,000)	56,771
Görlitz	67,647
Goslar (★72,000)	46,191
Gotha	52,265
Göttingen	128,419
Greifswald	63,941
Grevenbroich (★Düsseldorf)	62,737
Gummersbach	52,374
Gütersloh (★Bielefeld)	91,634
Hagen (★Essen)	214,877
Halle (★455,000)	295,372
Hamburg (★2,440,000)	1,702,887
Hameln (★65,000)	59,209
Hamm	182,390
Hanau am Main (★Frankfurt am Main)	89,156
Hannover (★1,015,000)	524,823
Hattingen (★Essen)	58,481
Heidelberg (★Mannheim)	139,429
Heidenheim an der Brenz (★83,000)	52,670
Heilbronn (★250,000)	122,396
Herford (★123,000)	65,682
Herne (★Essen)	180,539
Herten (★Essen)	69,592
Hilden (★Düsseldorf)	55,296
Hildesheim (★126,000)	106,303
Hof	52,724
Hoyerswerda	60,894
Hürth (★Köln)	51,974
Ingolstadt (★150,000)	109,666
Iserlohn	98,478
Jena	100,093
Kaiserslautern (★133,000)	102,370
Karlsruhe (★508,000)	277,998
Kassel (★385,000)	202,158
Kempten (Allgäu)	61,669
Kerpen (★Köln)	60,395
Kiel (★330,000)	248,931
Kleve	47,869
Koblenz (★170,000)	109,807
Köln (Cologne) (★1,820,000)	962,517
Konstanz	75,891
Krefeld (★Essen)	249,565
Landshut	59,637
Langenfeld (★Düsseldorf)	56,153
Leipzig (★720,000)	490,851
Leverkusen (★Köln)	161,761
Lingen	51,338
Lippstadt	65,822
Lübeck (★255,000)	217,269
Lüdenscheid	80,277
Ludwigsburg (★Stuttgart)	86,216
Ludwigshafen am Rhein (★Mannheim)	168,130
Lüneburg	63,299
Lünen (★Essen)	89,741
Lutherstadt Wittenberg	53,374
Magdeburg (★400,000)	270,546
Mainz (★Wiesbaden)	185,487
Mannheim (★1,530,000)	318,025
Marburg	76,582
Marl (★Essen)	92,590
Meerbusch (★Düsseldorf)	53,249
Menden	57,538
Minden (★124,000)	80,423
Moers (★Essen)	106,631
Mönchengladbach (★420,000)	265,312
Mülheim an der Ruhr (★Essen)	177,175
München (Munich) (★1,930,000)	1,255,623
Münster	267,367
Neu-Ulm (★Ulm)	51,068
Neubrandenburg	85,540
Neumünster	82,014
Neunkirchen (★125,000)	51,997
Neuss (★Düsseldorf)	148,560
Neustadt an der Weinstrasse	53,782
Neuwied (★160,000)	65,740
Norderstedt (★Hamburg)	69,916
Nordhorn	50,835
Nürnberg (★1,070,000)	498,945
Oberhausen (★Essen)	226,254
Offenbach am Main (★Frankfurt am Main)	116,870
Offenburg	54,963
Oldenburg	147,701
Osnabrück (★275,000)	168,078
Paderborn	130,130
Passau	51,041
Pforzheim (★235,000)	117,450
Plauen	69,387
Potsdam (★Berlin)	139,262
Pulheim (★Köln)	50,474
Ratingen (★Düsseldorf)	90,443
Ravensburg (★75,000)	47,099
Recklinghausen (★Essen)	127,150
Regensburg (★185,000)	125,337
Remscheid (★Wuppertal)	123,610
Reutlingen (★175,000)	107,607
Rheine	73,543
Rosenheim	58,553
Rostock	237,307
Rüsselsheim (★Wiesbaden)	60,361
Saarbrücken (★365,000)	190,902
Saarlouis (★115,000)	38,347
Salzgitter	117,684
Sankt Augustin (★Bonn)	53,969
Schwäbisch Gmünd	63,701
Schweinfurt (★105,000)	55,284
Schwerin	122,189
Schwerte (★Essen)	50,955
Siegburg (★175,000)	36,628
Siegen (★195,000)	111,845
Sindelfingen (★Stuttgart)	59,930
Solingen (★Wuppertal)	166,064
Stolberg (★Aachen)	58,028
Stralsund	69,230
Stuttgart (★2,020,000)	594,406
Suhl	52,386
Trier (★122,000)	99,183
Troisdorf (★Siegburg)	67,584
Tübingen	83,553
Ulm (★220,000)	114,839
Unna (★Essen)	64,327
Velbert (★Essen)	89,643
Viersen (★Mönchengladbach)	77,204
Villingen-Schwenningen	81,315
Waiblingen (★Stuttgart)	50,259
Weimar	58,807
Wesel	61,111
Wetzlar (★100,000)	54,188
Wiesbaden (★800,000)	270,873
Wilhelmshaven (★122,000)	91,680
Wismar	53,149
Witten (★Essen)	105,807
Wolfenbüttel (★Braunschweig)	53,812
Wolfsburg	128,032
Worms (★Mannheim)	79,155
Wuppertal (★850,000)	386,625
Würzburg (★195,000)	128,875
Zweibrücken (★105,000)	35,704
Zwickau (★180,000)	107,988

GHANA

1987 E	13,577,538
•ACCRA (★1,390,000)	949,113
Cape Coast (1984 C)	86,620
Koforidua (1984 C)	54,400
Kumasi (★540,000)	385,192
Obuasi (1984 C)	60,146
Sekondi (★175,352) (1984 C)	32,355
Tafo (★Kumasi) (1984 C)	50,432
Takoradi (★Sekondi) (1984 C)	61,527
Tamale (★171,661)	151,069
Tema (★179,076) (★Accra)	109,975
Teshie (★Accra) (1984 C)	62,954

GIBRALTAR

1997 E	27,086
•GIBRALTAR	27,086

GREECE / Ellás

1991 C	10,259,900
Acharnés	59,698
Aiyáleo (★Athína)	78,563
Amaroúsion (★Athína)	64,092
•ATHÍNA (ATHENS) (★3,150,000)	772,072
Ayía Varvára (★Athína)	68,134
Áyios Dhimítrios (★Athína)	57,547
Chalandri (★Athína)	66,285
Chalkída	51,646
Chaniá (★65,500)	50,077
Galátsion (★Athína)	57,230
Glifádha (★Athína)	63,306
Ilioúpolis (★Athína)	75,037
Ioánnina	56,699
Irákleio (★127,600)	115,124
Kalamariá (★Thessaloníki)	80,698
Kallithéa (★Athína)	114,233
Kavála	56,571
Keratsínion (★Athína)	71,982
Koridhallós (★Athína)	63,184
Lárisa (★125,600)	112,777
Néa Ionía (★Athína)	60,635
Néa Liósia (★Athína)	78,326
Néa Smírni (★Athína)	69,749
Níkaia (★Athína)	87,597
Palaión Fáliron (★Athína)	61,371
Pátra (★172,800)	152,570
Peiraiás (Piraeus) (★Athína)	182,671
Peristérion (★Athína)	137,288
Sérres	49,380
Thessaloníki (Salonika) (★755,000)	383,967
Víron (★Athína)	58,523
Vólos (★106,200)	77,192
Zográfos (★Athína)	80,492

GREENLAND / Grønland / Kalaallit Nunaat

1998 E	56,076
•GODTHÅB	13,024

GRENADA

1991 C	90,691
•SAINT GEORGE'S (★25,000)	4,439

GUADELOUPE

1990 C	387,034
BASSE-TERRE (★27,500)	14,003
Les Abymes (★Pointe-à-Pitre)	62,605
•Pointe-à-Pitre (★84,000)	26,029

GUAM

1990 C	133,152
•HAGÅTÑA (★50,000)	1,139

GUATEMALA

1994 C	8,331,874
•GUATEMALA (★1,500,000)	823,301
Mixco (★Guatemala)	209,791
Quetzaltenango	90,801
Villa Nueva (★Guatemala)	101,295

GUERNSEY

1991 C	58,867
•SAINT PETER PORT (★36,000)	16,648

GUINEA / Guinée

1992 E	6,116,000
•CONAKRY	950,000
Kankan	70,000
Kindia (1986 E)	80,000
Labé (1986 E)	110,000
Nzérékoré (1983C)	55,356

GUINEA-BISSAU / Guiné-Bissau

1988 E	945,000
•BISSAU	125,000

GUYANA

1983 E	918,000
•GEORGETOWN (★188,000)	78,500

HAITI / Haïti

1995 E	7,180,294
Cap-Haïtien	100,638
Gonaïves	59,049
Pétion-Ville (★Port-au-Prince)	69,543
•PORT-AU-PRINCE (★1,425,594)	846,247

HONDURAS

1988 C	4,443,721
Choluteca	54,481
El Progreso	60,058
La Ceiba	68,764
San Pedro Sula (★375,000)	287,350
•TEGUCIGALPA	576,661

▲ Population of an entire municipality, commune, or district, including rural areas
• Largest city in country
★ Population or designation of the metroplitan area, including suburbs
★★ Population of metropolitan agglomeration
C Census E Official estimate U Unofficial estimate

HUNGARY / Magyarország

City	Population
1996 E	10,212,300
Békéscsaba	65,039
•BUDAPEST (★2,450,000)	1,906,798
Debrecen	210,143
Dunaújváros	57,438
Eger	59,308
Győr (Raab)	127,404
Hódmezővásárhely	49,901
Kaposvár	68,485
Kecskemét	105,058
Miskolc	180,005
Nagykanizsa	52,976
Nyíregyháza	113,136
Pécs	162,216
Sopron	53,762
Szeged	167,170
Székesfehérvár	107,181
Szolnok	78,398
Szombathely	83,425
Tatabánya	72,510
Veszprém	64,345
Zalaegerszeg	61,678

ICELAND / Ísland

City	Population
1992 E	262,193
•REYKJAVÍK (★151,779)	100,850

INDIA / Bharat

City	Population
1991 C	846,302,688
Abohar	107,163
Achalpur	96,229
Ādilābād	84,255
Adityapur (★Jamshedpur)	77,803
Ādoni	136,182
Agartala	157,358
Āgra (★948,063)	891,790
Ahmadābād (★3,312,216)	2,876,710
Ahmadnagar (★222,088)	181,339
Āizawl	155,240
Ajmer	402,700
Akola	328,034
Akot	65,681
Alandur (★Chennai)	125,244
Alīgarh	480,520
Ālīpur Duār (★102,815)	65,241
Allahābād (★844,546)	792,858
Alleppey (★264,969)	174,666
Allinagaram	60,050
Alwal (★Hyderābād)	66,471
Alwar (★210,146)	205,086
Amalner	76,442
Ambājogāi	57,159
Ambāla (★259,227)	119,338
Ambāla Sadar	90,872
Ambattur (★Chennai)	215,424
Ambikāpur (★53,227)	50,277
Āmbūr	75,911
Amrāvati	421,576
Amreli (★69,366)	67,827
Amritsar	708,835
Amroha	137,061
Anakāpalle	84,356
Ānand (★174,480)	110,266
Anantapur	174,924
Anjār	51,209
Ankleshwar (★78,100)	51,739
Ara	157,082
Arakkonam	71,928
Ārani	54,898
Arcot (★114,760)	45,205
Aruppukkottai	78,976
Āsansol (★763,939)	262,188
Ashoknagar-Kalyangarh (★Hābra)	96,747
Āttūr	55,667
Auraiya	50,772
Aurangābād (★592,709)	573,272
Avadi (★Chennai)	183,215
Āzamgarh	78,567
Badagara (★102,430)	72,434
Bagaha	64,627
Bāgalkot	76,903
Bahādurgarh	56,524
Baharampur (★126,400)	115,144
Bahraich	135,400
Baidyabāti (★Calcutta)	90,081
Bālāghāt (★67,151)	62,178
Balāngīr	69,920
Baleshwar (★101,829)	85,442
Ballālpur (★92,436)	83,511
Ballia	84,063
Bālly (★Calcutta)	184,474
Bālly (★Calcutta)	73,322
Balrāmpur	59,619
Bālurghāt (★126,225)	119,796
Bānda	96,795
Bangalore (★4,130,288)	2,660,088
Bangaon	79,571
Bānkura	114,876
Bansberia (★Calcutta)	93,520
Bānswāra (★67,908)	66,632
Bāpatla	62,536
Bārākpur (★Calcutta)	133,265
Bārān	57,719
Baranagar (★Calcutta)	224,821
Bārāsat (★Calcutta)	102,660
Barauni	60,685
Baraut	67,705
Barddhamān	245,079
Bareilly (★617,350)	587,211
Bargarh	51,205
Bārmer	68,625
Barnāla	75,430
Bārsi	88,810
Basīrhāt	101,409
Basti	87,371
Batala (★103,367)	86,006
Bathinda	159,114
Beāwar (★106,721)	105,363
Begusarai (★84,018)	71,424
Bela	65,945
Belampalli	66,780
Belgaum (★402,412)	326,399
Bellary	245,391
Bettiah	92,653
Betūl	63,534
Beypore	56,505
Bhadohi	64,010
Bhadrak	76,435
Bhadrāvati (★149,257)	55,475
Bhadrāvati New Town (★Bhadrāvati)	74,928
Bhadreswar (★Calcutta)	72,474
Bhāgalpur (★260,119)	253,225
Bhandāra	71,813
Bharatpur (★156,880)	148,519
Bharūch (★139,029)	133,102
Bhātpāra	304,952
Bhavāni (★97,160)	35,198
Bhāvnagar (★405,225)	402,338
Bhawānipatna	51,062
Bhilai (★685,474)	386,159
Bhīlwāra	183,965
Bhīmavaram	121,314
Bhind	109,755
Bhiwandi (★392,214)	379,070
Bhiwāni	121,629
Bhopāl	1,062,771
Bhubaneshwar	411,542
Bhuj (★121,009)	102,176
Bhusāwal (★159,799)	145,143
Bīd	112,434
Bīdar (★132,408)	108,016
Bihar	201,323
Bijāpur (★193,131)	186,939
Bijnor (★73,900)	66,486
Bīkāner	416,289
Bilāspur (★229,615)	179,833
Birnagar (★92,208)	20,015
Bishnupur	56,128
Bodhan	64,406
Bodināyakkanūr	66,500
Bokāro Steel City (★398,890)	333,683
Bolpur	52,760
Botād	64,603
Brahmapur	210,418
Brajrajnagar	69,667
Budaun	116,695
Budge Budge (★Calcutta)	72,951
Bulandshahr	127,201
Buldāna	52,767
Bulsār (★111,775)	57,909
Būndi	65,047
Burhānpur	172,710
Burhar (★82,226)	16,515
Burnpur (★Āsansol)	174,933
Buxar	55,753
Calcutta (★11,021,918)	4,399,819
Cannanore (★Tellicherry)	65,238
Chāībāsa	56,729
Chākdaha	74,769
Chālisgaon	77,420
Champdāni (★Calcutta)	101,067
Chandannagar (★Calcutta)	120,378
Chandausi	82,748
Chandīgarh (★575,829)	504,094
Chāndpur	55,825
Chandrapur	226,105
Changanācheri	52,445
Channapatna	55,209
Chās	65,207
Chennai (Madras) (★5,421,985)	3,841,396
Chhapra	136,877
Chhatarpur (★75,594)	72,824
Chhindwāra (★96,858)	93,650
Chidambaram (★67,949)	58,740
Chikmagalūr	60,816
Chilakalūrupet	79,142
Chingleput	54,127
Chintāmani	50,394
Chīrāla (★142,778)	80,861
Chitradurga (★103,435)	87,069
Chittaurgarh	71,569
Chittoor	133,462
Chūru	82,464
Coimbatore (Koyambattur) (★1,100,746)	816,321
Contai	53,484
Coonoor (★100,687)	48,003
Cuddalore	144,561
Cuddapah (★215,866)	121,463
Cumbum	54,435
Cuttack (★440,295)	403,418
Dabgram	147,217
Dabhoi	50,641
Dāhod (★96,632)	66,500
Dalli Rājhara	55,996
Dāltenganj	56,323
Damoh (★105,043)	95,661
Dānāpur (★Pātan)	84,616
Dandeli	52,701
Darbhanga	218,391
Dārjiling	73,062
Datia	64,477
Dāvangere (★287,233)	266,082
Dehra Dūn (★368,053)	270,159
Dehri	93,694
Delhi (★8,419,084)	7,206,704
Delhi Cantonment (★Delhi)	94,393
Deoband	66,208
Deoghar (★85,902)	76,380
Deoria	82,168
Dewās	164,364
Dhamtari	69,357
Dhanbād (★815,005)	151,789
Dhār	59,246
Dharmapuri	59,318
Dharmavaram	78,961
Dhaulpur	68,533
Dholka (★54,352)	49,860
Dhorāji (★79,479)	77,748
Dhrāngadhra	57,961
Dhuburi	66,216
Dhule	278,317
Dibrugarh (★125,667)	120,127
Dimāpur	57,182
Dindigul	182,477
Dīsa	62,435
Dishergarh (★Āsansol)	86,832
Dod Ballāpur	54,609
Durg (★Bhilai)	150,645
Durgāpur	425,836
Elūru	212,866
Emmiganūru	65,089
Erode (★361,755)	159,323
Etah	78,458
Etāwah	124,072
Faizābād (★176,922)	124,437
Farīdābād (★Delhi)	617,717
Farīdkot	58,244
Farrukhābād (★208,727)	194,657
Fatehpur	117,675
Fatehpur	66,387
Fāzilka	58,028
Firozābād (★270,536)	215,128
Firozpur	78,738
Firozpur Cantonment	53,094
Gadag	134,051
Gāndhidham	104,585
Gāndhinagar	123,359
Ganga Ghat	50,260
Gangānagar	161,482
Gangāpur (★68,886)	53,689
Gangāwati (★85,515)	64,843
Gārulia (★Calcutta)	80,918
Gaya (★294,427)	219,675
Ghāziābād (★511,759)	454,156
Ghāzīpur	76,547
Girīdīh	78,097
Godhra (★100,662)	96,813
Gokāk	52,080
Gonda	95,553
Gondal (★81,611)	80,584
Gondia	109,470
Gopichettipālaiyam	48,364
Gorakhpur	505,566
Gudivāda	101,656
Gudiyāttam (★90,557)	83,232
Gūdūr	55,984
Gulbarga (★310,920)	304,099
Guna	100,490
Guntakal	107,592
Guntūr	471,051
Gurdāspur	54,733
Gurgaon (★135,884)	121,486
Guruvayur (★118,632)	20,216
Guwāhāti	584,342
Gwalior (Lashkar) (★717,780)	690,765
Hābra (★196,970)	100,223
Hājīpur	87,687
Haldwāni	104,195
Hālisahar (★Calcutta)	114,028
Hānsi	59,653
Hanumangarh (★82,733)	78,525
Hāora (★Calcutta)	950,435
Hāpur	146,262
Hardoi	88,651
Haridwār (★187,392)	147,305
Harihar	66,647
Hassan (★108,706)	90,803
Hāthras	113,285
Hazārībāg	97,824
Himatnagar	51,461
Hindaun	60,780
Hindupur	104,651
Hinganghāt	78,715
Hingoli	54,457
Hisār (★181,255)	172,677
Hoshangābād	70,914
Hoshiārpur	122,705
Hospet (★134,799)	96,322
Hubli-Dhārwār	648,298
Hugli-Chinsurah	151,806
Hyderābād (★4,344,437)	3,043,896
Ichalkaranji (★235,979)	214,950
Imphāl (★202,839)	198,535
Indore (★1,109,056)	1,091,674
Ingrāj Bāzār (★177,164)	139,204
Itārsi (★84,626)	77,334
Jabalpur (★888,916)	741,927
Jabalpur Cantonment (★Jabalpur)	56,124
Jagādhri (★Yamunānagar)	67,386
Jagdalpur (★84,578)	66,154
Jagtiāl	67,591
Jahānābād	52,332
Jaipur (★1,518,235)	1,458,483
Jalandhar	509,510
Jālgaon	242,193
Jālna	174,985
Jalpāiguri	68,732
Jamālpur	86,112
Jammu (★223,361) (1981 C)	206,135
Jamnagar (Navanagar) (★381,646)	341,637
Jamshedpur (★829,171)	460,577
Jangīpur	55,981
Jaora (★56,023)	54,997
Jaunpur	136,062
Jaypur	65,246
Jetpur (★95,397)	73,560
Jhānsi (★368,154)	300,850
Jharia (★Dhanbād)	69,641
Jhārsuguda	65,054
Jhunjhunūn	72,187
Jīnd	85,315
Jodhpur	666,279
Jorhāt (★112,030)	58,358
Jūnāgadh (★167,110)	130,484
Kadaiyanallūr	68,819
Kadiri	63,378
Kagaznagar	57,535
Kairāna	56,079
Kaithal	71,142
Kākināda (Cocanada) (★327,541)	279,980
Kalamassery (★Kochi)	54,342
Kālol (★92,550)	82,137
Kalyān (★Mumbai)	1,014,557
Kāmārhāti (★Calcutta)	266,889
Kambam	52,435
Kāmthi (★127,151)	78,612
Kānchipuram (★171,129)	144,955
Kānchrāpāra (★Calcutta)	100,194
Kānnangād (★118,214)	57,165
Kannauj	58,932
Kānpur (Cawnpore) (★2,029,889)	1,874,409
Kānpur Cantonment (★Kānpur)	95,021
Kapra (★Hyderābād)	87,747
Kapūrthala	64,567
Karād	56,819
Kāraikāl	61,804
Kāraikkudi (★110,926)	71,965
Karīmnagar	148,583
Karnāl (★176,131)	173,751
Karūr (★113,669)	73,418
Kārwār	51,022
Kāsaragod	50,126
Kāsganj	75,634
Kāshīpur	69,870
Katihār (★154,367)	135,436
Kātwa	55,541
Kāvali	65,910
Kāyankulam	67,151
Keshod	50,172
Khadki (★Pune)	78,323
Khambhāt (★89,834)	76,746
Khāmgaon	79,692
Khammam (★149,077)	127,992
Khandwa	145,133
Khanna	71,990
Kharagpur (★264,842)	177,989
Kharagpur Railway Settlement (★Kharagpur)	84,252
Khardaha	88,358
Khargon	66,786
Khurja	80,305
Kishanganj	64,568
Kishangarh Bās	81,948
Koch Bihār (★92,820)	71,215
Kochi (Cochin) (★1,140,605)	564,589
Kodarma	53,577
Kohīma	51,418
Kolār	83,287
Kolār Gold Fields (★156,746)	72,485
Kolhāpur (★418,538)	406,370
Konnagar (★Calcutta)	62,200
Korba	124,501
Kot Kapūra	62,430
Kota	537,371
Kottagūdem (★102,137)	80,440
Kottayam (★166,552)	63,155
Kovilpatti	78,834
Kozhikode (Calicut) (★801,190)	419,831
Krishnagiri	60,315
Krishnanagar	121,110
Kukatpalle (★Hyderābād)	186,963
Kulti (★Āsansol)	108,518
Kumārapālaiyam (★Bhavāni)	57,672
Kumbakonam (★150,540)	139,483
Kundla (★65,785)	64,815
Kurasia (★71,708)	15,898
Kurichi (★Coimbatore)	64,796
Kurnool (★275,360)	236,800
Lakhīmpur	79,951
Lalbahadur Nagar (★Hyderābād)	155,514
Lalitpur	79,870
Lātūr	197,408
Luckeesarai	53,360
Lucknow (★1,669,204)	1,619,115
Lucknow Cantonment (★Lucknow)	50,089
Ludhiāna	1,042,740
Machilīpatnam (Bandar)	159,110
Madanapalle	73,820
Madgaon (★72,400)	58,951
Madhubani	53,747
Madhyamgrām (★Calcutta)	69,252
Madurai (★1,085,914)	940,989
Mahbūbnagar	116,833
Mahesāna (★109,950)	88,201
Mahoba	56,247
Mahuva (★64,144)	59,912
Mainpuri	76,735
Makrāna (★66,720)	59,714
Malappuram (★142,204)	49,692
Malaut	56,868
Mālegaon	342,595
Māler Kotla	88,600
Malkajgiri (★Hyderābād)	127,178
Malkāpur	51,311
Mancherāl	52,657
Mandsaur	95,907
Mandya	120,265
Mangalagiri	59,152
Mangalore (★426,341)	273,304
Mango (★Jamshedpur)	108,100
Manjeri	69,334
Manmād	61,312
Mannārgudi	56,552
Mānsa	55,089
Mathura (Muttra) (★235,922)	226,691
Maunath Bhanjan	136,697
Mawāna	51,701
Māyūram	76,837
Medinīpur	125,498
Meerut (★849,799)	753,778
Meerut Cantonment (★Meerut)	96,021
Melappālaiyam (★Tirunelveli)	68,347
Mettuppālaiyam	63,479
Mhow (★83,796)	74,987
Mira Bhayandar (★Mumbai)	175,605
Miraj (★Sāngli)	121,593
Miryalaguda	65,879
Mirzāpur	169,336
Modinagar (★123,279)	101,660
Moga (★110,958)	108,304
Mokāma	59,528
Morādābād (★443,701)	429,214
Morbi (★120,117)	90,357
Morena	147,124
Mormugao (★90,429)	83,367
Motihāri (★83,255)	77,432
Mughal Sarāi (★91,505)	66,529
Muktsar	66,383
•Mumbai (Bombay) (★12,596,243)	9,925,891
Munger	150,112
Murwāra (Katni)	163,431
Muzaffarnagar (★247,624)	240,609
Muzaffarpur	241,107
Mysore (★653,345)	480,692
Nābha	54,421
Nadiād (★170,217)	167,051
Nagaon	93,350
Nāgappattinam (★99,745)	86,489
Nāgaur	68,194
Nagda	79,622
Nāgercoil	190,084
Nagīna	58,513
Nāgpur (★1,664,006)	1,624,752
Naihāti (★Calcutta)	132,701
Najībābād	66,860
Nalasopara (★Mumbai)	67,732
Nalgonda	84,910
Nānded (★309,316)	275,083
Nandurbār	78,378
Nandyāl	119,813
Nangi (★Calcutta)	52,958
Narasapur	56,362
Narasaraopet	88,726
Nārnaul	51,976
Nāshik (★725,341)	656,925
Navadwīp (★155,905)	125,037
Navsāri (★190,946)	126,089
Nawābganj (★77,234)	64,582
Nawāda	53,174
Nawalgarh	51,190
Nedumangād	49,875
Neemuch (★90,474)	86,439
Nellore	316,606
New Bārākpur (★Calcutta)	63,795
New Bombay (★Mumbai)	304,724
NEW DELHI	301,297
Neyveli (★126,889)	118,080
Nīmach (★90,474)	86,439
Nipāni	51,624
Nirmal	57,761
Nizāmābād	241,034
North Bārākpur (★Calcutta)	100,606
North Dum Dum (★Calcutta)	149,965
Ongole (★128,648)	100,836
Orai	98,716
Osmānābād	68,019
Pālakodu	56,969
Palani (★76,209)	68,907
Pālanpur (★90,269)	80,657
Pālayankottai (★Tirunelveli)	98,399
Pālghāt (★180,033)	123,289
Pāli	136,842
Pallavaram (★Chennai)	111,866
Palwal	59,168
Palwancha	53,102
Panaji (★85,515)	43,349
Pānchur (★Calcutta)	77,547
Pandharpur	79,902
Pānihāti (★Calcutta)	275,990
Panīpāt	191,212
Panruti	51,394
Panvel	58,986
Paramakkudi	72,321
Parāsia (★94,725)	33,797
Parbhani	190,255
Parli	72,670
Pātan (★97,025)	96,112
Pathānkot (★128,198)	123,930
Patiāla (★253,706)	238,368
Patna (★1,099,647)	917,243
Pattukkottai	58,062
Payyannūr	64,032
Phagwāra (★88,316)	83,163
Pīlībhīt	106,605
Pilkhua	51,162
Pimpri-Chinchwad (★Pune)	517,083
Pollāchi (★127,132)	86,897
Pondicherry (Puducheri) (★401,437)	203,065
Ponmalai (★Tiruchchirāppalli)	69,639
Ponnāni	51,770
Ponnūru Nidubrolu	54,363
Porbandar (★160,167)	116,671
Port Blair	74,955
Proddatūr	133,914
Pudukkottai	99,058
Puliyangudi	53,287
Pune (Poona) (★2,493,987)	1,566,651
Pune Cantonment (★Pune)	82,139
Puri	125,199
Pūrnia (★136,918)	114,912
Puruliya	92,386
Pusad	55,931
Quilon (★362,572)	139,852
Qutubullapur (★Hyderābād)	106,591
Rabkavi Banhatti	60,609
Rāe Bareli	129,904
Rāichūr (★170,577)	157,551
Raiganj (★159,266)	151,045
Raigarh (★90,265)	86,767
Raipur (★462,694)	438,639
Rāj Nāndgaon	125,371
Rājahmundry (★401,397)	324,851
Rājapālaiyam	114,202
Rajendranagar (★Hyderābād)	84,520
Rajhara-Jharandalli	55,996
Rājkot (★654,490)	559,407
Rājpur (★86,451)	60,175
Rājpura	70,983
Rāmanagaram	50,437
Rāmanāthapuram	52,879
Rāmgarh (★82,328)	51,264
Rāmpur	243,742
Rānāghāt (★127,035)	62,532
Rānchi (★614,795)	599,306
Rānībennur	67,442
Rānīganj (★155,823)	61,997
Ratangarh	55,079
Ratlām (★195,776)	183,375
Ratnāgiri	56,529
Raurkela (★398,864)	215,509
Raurkela Civil Township (★Raurkela)	142,408
Rāyachoti	51,931
Rewa	128,981
Rewāri	75,342
Rishra (★Calcutta)	102,815
Robertson Pet (★Kolār Gold Fields)	68,230
Rohtak	216,096
Roorkee (★91,139)	80,262
Rudrapur	61,280
Sāgar (★257,119)	195,346
Sahāranpur	374,945
Saharsa	80,149
Sahaswān	51,080
Salem (★578,291)	366,712
Sambalpur (★193,297)	131,138
Sambhal	150,869
Sangareddi	50,123
Sāngli (★363,751)	193,197
Sangrūr	56,419
Sardārshahr	67,954
Sarni	84,379
Sāsarām	98,122
Sātāra	95,180
Satna (★160,500)	156,630
Saunda (★109,822)	76,691
Sawāi Mādhopur (★77,690)	72,165
Secunderābād Cantonment (★Hyderābād)	171,148
Sehore	71,456
Seoni	64,532
Serampore (★Calcutta)	137,026
Serilungampalle (★Hyderābād)	72,320
Shāhābād	53,657
Shahdol (★60,529)	55,508
Shāhjahānpur (★260,403)	237,713
Shāmli	70,853
Shāntipur	109,956
Shertallai (★132,883)	43,326
Shikohābād	62,829
Shiliguri	216,950
Shillong (★223,366)	131,719
Shimla (★110,360)	82,054
Shimoga (★193,028)	179,258
Shivpuri	108,277
Siddhapur (★51,794)	50,770
Siddipet	54,091
Sikandarābād	60,992
Sīkar	148,272
Silchar	115,483
Sindri (★Dhanbād)	72,333
Sirsa	112,841
Sirsilla	50,048
Sītāpur	121,842
Siuri	54,298
Sivakāsi (★102,175)	65,593
Siwān	63,125
Solāpur (★620,846)	604,215
Sonīpat	143,922
South Dum Dum (★Calcutta)	232,811
Srī Kālahasti	61,278
Srīkākulam	88,883
Srikalahasti	61,578
Srīnagar (★606,002) (1981 C)	594,775
Srīrampur (★79,052)	71,368
Srīrangam (★Tiruchchirāppalli)	70,109
Srivilliputtūr	68,644
Sujāngarh	70,843
Sultānpur	76,533
Sūrat (★1,518,950)	1,498,817
Surendranagar (★166,466)	106,110
Suriāpet	60,630
Tādepallegūdem	88,878
Tādpatri	71,068

▲ Population of an entire municipality, commune, or district, including rural areas
• Largest city in country
★ Population or designation of the metropolitan area, including suburbs
★★ Population of metropolitan agglomeration
C Census E Official estimate U Unofficial estimate

Taliparamba 60,226
Tāmbaram (★Chennai) 107,187
Tānda 70,605
Tanuku 62,913
Tellicherry (★463,962) 103,579
Tenāli 143,726
Tenkāsi 55,189
Tezpur 55,064
Thāna (★Mumbai) 803,369
Thānesar 61,255
Thanjāvūr 202,013
Theni-Allinagaram 60,050
Thrippunithura (★Cochin) 51,078
Tīkamgarh 54,173
Tindivanam 61,579
Tinsukia 73,918
Tiruchchirāppalli (★711,862) 387,223
Tiruchengodu 63,027
Tirunelveli (★366,869) 135,825
Tirupati (★188,904) 174,369
Tiruppattūr 55,282
Tiruppur (★306,237) 235,661
Tiruvalla 54,780
Tiruvannāmalai 109,196
Tiruvottiyūr (★Chennai) 168,642
Titāgarh (★Calcutta) 114,085
Tonk 100,079
Trichūr (★275,053) 74,604
Trivandrum (★826,225) 524,006
Tumkūr (★179,877) 138,903
Tuticorin (★280,091) 199,854
Udagamandalam 81,763
Udaipur 308,571
Udamalpet 58,678
Udgīr 70,453
Udupi (★117,674) 33,913
Ujjain 362,266
Ulhāsnagar (★Mumbai) 369,077
Ulubāria 155,172
Unjha 51,003
Unnāo 107,425
Upleta 51,801
Uppal Kalan (★Hyderābād) 75,644
Uttarpara-Kotrung (★Calcutta) 101,268
Vadodara (Baroda) (★1,126,824) 1,031,346
Vālpārai 106,523
Vāniyambādi (★92,307) 72,426
Vārānasi (Benares) (★1,030,863) 929,270
Vasai (★83,734) 39,781
Veerappanchattiram (★Erode) 61,649
Vejalpur (★Ahmadābād) 92,116
Vellore (★310,776) 175,061
Verāval (★120,178) 93,976
Vidisha 92,922
Vijayawāda (★845,756) 701,827
Vikramasingapuram 49,834
Viluppuram 88,788
Viramgām 50,788
Virār (★Mumbai) 57,600
Virudunagar 70,971
Vishākhapatnam (★1,057,118) 752,037
Visnagar (★59,647) 57,869
Vizianagaram (★177,022) 160,359
Vriddhāchalam 52,819
Warangal (★467,757) 447,657
Wardha 102,985
Yamunānagar (★219,754) 144,346
Yavatmāl (★121,816) 108,578
Yemmiganur 65,089

INDONESIA

1990 C 179,378,946
Ambon (▲275,888) 205,193
Balikpapan 344,147
Banda Aceh (▲184,650) 143,360
Bandung (★2,220,000) 2,058,122
Banjarmasin 480,737
Banyuwangi (▲1,455,010) 92,800
Batang (▲591,647) 55,200
Bekasi (▲951,509) (★Jakarta) 146,400
Bengkulu 170,183
Binjai (▲181,866) 127,184
Blitar (★150,000) 118,933
Bogor (★620,000) 271,341
Bojonegoro (▲1,104,031) 63,700
Bukittinggi 83,753
Cianjur (▲1,420,228) 108,700
Cibinong (▲1,812,734) 264,100
Cikampek (▲1,152,405) 91,200
Cilacap (▲1,487,308) 141,900
Ciledug (▲1,244,151) 293,000
Cimahi (▲1,909,459) (★Bandung) 196,900
Ciparay (▲1,909,456) 135,300
Cirebon (★315,000) 254,477
Denpasar (▲663,390) 209,500
Depok (▲1,812,734) (★Jakarta) 382,000
Dumai (▲904,375) 71,500
Garut (▲1,478,757) 145,900
Genteng (▲1,455,010) 60,900
Gorontalo (▲119,745) 94,058
Gresik (▲856,853) 102,000
•JAKARTA (★10,200,000) 8,227,746
Jambi 339,786
Jayapura (▲246,389) 101,200
Jember (▲2,062,554) 190,000
Jombang (▲1,048,805) 65,700
Karawang (▲1,152,405) 143,300
Kediri 249,538
Kendari (▲488,471) 70,700
Kisaran (▲884,594) 66,600
Klangenang (▲1,035,575) 291,200
Klaten (▲1,056,135) 120,400
Kotabaru 53,753
Kotabumi (▲1,643,485) 76,700
Kudus (▲631,322) 182,600
Kupang (▲522,944) 111,300
Lumajang (▲924,894) 62,100
Madiun (★200,000) 170,050
Magelang (★180,000) 123,156
Majalaya (▲1,909,459) 176,600
Malang 695,089
Manado 320,600
Mataram (▲859,273) 276,300
Medan 1,730,052
Mojokerto 99,707
Padang (▲631,263) 477,064
Padangsidempuan (▲954,184) 72,100
Palangkaraya 112,511
Palembang 1,144,047
Palopo (▲683,893) 60,800
Palu (▲784,647) 56,500
Pangkalpinang 113,129
Pare (▲1,343,125) 51,400
Parepare (★101,421) 84,093
Pasuruan (★190,000) 152,075
Pati (▲1,064,115) 54,900
Payakumbuh (▲90,838) 50,475
Pekalongan (★430,000) 242,714
Pekanbaru 398,621
Pemalang (▲1,114,228) 86,200
Pematangsiantar (★250,000) 219,316
Perabumulih (▲582,396) 59,500
Ponorogo (▲837,055) 59,500
Pontianak 396,658
Pringsewu (▲1,825,040) 58,300
Probolinggo (▲176,906) 131,077
Purwakarta (▲437,327) 62,300
Purwokerto (▲1,348,825) 158,300
Salatiga 98,012
Samarinda (▲407,174) 334,851
Semarang 1,249,230
Serang (▲1,201,742) 84,900
Sibolga 71,559
Sidoarjo (▲1,167,467) 76,800
Singaraja (▲540,150) 59,200
Singkawang (▲574,156) 64,000
Situbondo (▲574,156) 63,800
Sorong (▲199,085) 77,900
Subang (▲1,037,394) 52,700
Sukabumi (★250,000) 119,938
Sumenep (▲933,746) 53,300
Surabaya 2,473,272
Surakarta (★590,000) 503,827
Taman (▲1,167,467) 88,100
Tangerang (▲1,244,151) 99,100
Tanjungbalai 107,751
Tanjungkarang-Telukbetung (▲636,418) 457,927
Tanjungpinang 105,820
Tarakan (▲232,494) 61,300
Tasikmalaya (▲1,444,242) 194,000
Tebingtinggi 116,749
Tegal (★510,000) 229,553
Tembilahan (▲4,878,066) 62,700
Tuban (▲977,716) 54,700
Tulungagung (▲890,032) 97,000
Ujungpandang (Makasar) 944,372
Yogyakarta (★540,000) 412,059

IRAN / Īrān

1991 E 56,825,000
Ābādān 84,774
Abhar 49,908
Ahar 71,633
Ahvāz 724,653
Alīgūdarz 58,648
Āmol 139,923
Andīmeshk 73,759
Arāk 331,354
Ārān 54,766
Ardabīl 311,022
Bābol 137,348
Bam 59,007
Bandar-e 'Abbās 249,504
Bandar-e Anzalī 94,697
Bandar-e Būshehr 132,824
Bandar-e Khomeynī 56,988
Bandar-e Māh Shahr 74,248
Behbahān 85,846
Behshahr 61,825
Benāb 57,047
Bīrjand 101,177
Bojnūrd 112,426
Borāzjān 75,841
Borūjerd 201,016
Būkān 83,041
Dezfūl 181,309
Do Gonbadān 62,230
Do Rūd 77,299
Emāmshahr 92,195
Eşfahān (★1,375,000) 1,127,030
Eslāmābād 77,412
Eslāmshahr (★Tehrān) 230,183
Fasā 74,487
Gonbad-e Qābūs 102,768
Gorgān 162,468
Hamadān 349,653
Harsīn 52,544
Īlām 116,428
Īrānshahr 56,581
Īzeh 64,072
Jahrom 88,693
Karaj (★Tehrān) 442,387
Kāshān 155,188
Kāshmar 58,522
Kāzerūn 74,048
Kermānshāh 624,084
Khomeynīshahr (★Eşfahān) 118,348
Khorramābād 249,258
Khvorāsgān 55,705
Khvoy 137,885
Kūhdasht 61,935
Langarūd 52,518
Mahābād 81,987
Malāyer 130,458
Marāgheh 117,388
Marand 85,253
Marv Dasht 92,013
Mashhad 1,759,155
Masjed-e Soleymān 107,539
Miāndoāb 71,273
Mīāneh 72,712
Nahāvand 59,307
Najafābād 160,004
Naqadeh 61,286
Neyshābūr 135,681
Orūmīyeh 357,399
Qā'emshahr 123,684
Qazvīn 278,826
Qom 681,253
Qomsheh 84,666
Qorveh 51,247
Qūchān 74,919
Rafsanjān 79,926
Rasht 340,637
Sabzevār 148,065
Salmās 57,441
Sanandaj 244,039
Saqqez 98,933
Sārī 167,602
Sāveh 87,621
Semnān 75,131
Shahr-e Kord 89,253
Shīrāz 965,117
Shīrvān 58,940
Shūshtar 70,294
Sīrjān 107,887
Tabrīz 1,088,985
•TEHRĀN (★8,000,000) 6,475,527
Torbat-e Heydarīyeh 81,781
Torbat-e Jām 82,970
Varāmīn 77,624
Yazd 275,298
Zābol 91,041
Zāhedān 361,623
Zanjān 254,100

IRAQ / Al-'Irāq

1985 E 15,584,987
Ad-Dīwānīyah (1970 E) 62,300
Al-'Amārah 131,785
Al-Başrah 616,700
Al-Ḩillah 215,249
Al-Kūt 73,022
Al-Mawşil 570,926
An-Najaf 242,603
An-Nāşirīyah 138,842
Ar-Ramādī 137,388
As-Samāwah 75,293
As-Sulaymānīyah 279,424
•BAGHDĀD (1987 C) 3,841,268
Ba'qūbah 114,516
Irbīl 333,903
Karbalā' 184,574
Karkūk (1970 E) 207,900

IRELAND / Éire

1996 C 3,626,087
Cork (★179,954) 127,187
•DUBLIN (BAILE ÁTHA CLIATH) (★1,175,000) 481,854
Dún Laoghaire (★184,829) (★Dublin) 57,000
Galway (Gaillimh) 57,241
Limerick (Luimneach) (★75,729) 52,039

ISLE OF MAN

1996 C 74,680
•Douglas (★33,000) 23,487

ISRAEL / Yisra'el

1996 E 5,696,000
Ashdod 128,400
Ashqelon 84,200
Bat Yam (★Tel Aviv-Yafo) 142,300
Be'ér Sheva' (Beersheba) 152,600
Bene Beraq (★Tel Aviv-Yafo) 128,600
Hadera 62,800
Hefa (Haifa) (★470,000) 252,300
Herzliyya (★Tel Aviv-Yafo) 84,100
Holon (★Tel Aviv-Yafo) 163,900
Kefar Sava (★Tel Aviv-Yafo) 69,000
Lod (Lydda) (★Tel Aviv-Yafo) 52,600
Nazerat (Nazareth) (★78,000) 54,900
Netanya (★Tel Aviv-Yafo) 148,400
Petah Tiqwa (★Tel Aviv-Yafo) 153,100
Ra'anana (★Tel Aviv-Yafo) 58,600
Ramat Gan (★Tel Aviv-Yafo) 121,700
Ramla (★Tel Aviv-Yafo) 58,600
Rehovot (★Tel Aviv-Yafo) 86,700
Rishon LeZiyyon (★Tel Aviv-Yafo) 165,300
•Tel Aviv-Yafo (★1,888,000) 355,900
YERUSHALAYIM (JERUSALEM) (★635,000) 591,400

ITALY / Italia

1996 E 57,380,894
Acireale (1995 E) 51,469
Afragola (★Napoli) (1995 E) 60,755
Agrigento 55,761
Alessandria 89,034
Altamura (1995 E) 60,463
Ancona 99,639
Andria (1995 E) 92,321
Aprilia (1995 E) 54,359
Arezzo 90,821
Ascoli Piceno 52,516
Asti 73,532
Avellino 55,982
Aversa (★Napoli) (1995 E) 54,218
Bagheria (1995 E) 51,198
Bari (★480,000) 335,947
Barletta (1995 E) 90,079
Battipaglia (1995 E) 50,049
Benevento 63,664
Bergamo (★365,000) 117,096
Bitonto (1995 E) 55,880
Bologna (★530,000) 385,813
Bolzano (Bozen) 96,913
Brescia 190,059
Brindisi 94,820
Busto Arsizio (★Milano) (1995 E) 77,427
Cagliari (★310,000) 173,564
Caltanissetta 62,841
Campobasso 51,888
Carpi (1995 E) 60,187
Carrara (★Massa) (1995 E) 66,416
Caserta 72,408
Casoria (★Napoli) (1995 E) 83,250
Castellammare di Stabia (★Napoli) (1995 E) 66,985
Catania (★580,000) 341,685
Catanzaro 97,059
Cava de' Tirreni (★Salerno) (1995 E) 53,235
Cerignola (1995 E) 55,716
Cesena (1995 E) 89,307
Chieti 56,912
Chioggia (1995 E) 52,805
Cinisello Balsamo (★Milano) (1995 E) 75,284
Civitavecchia (1995 E) 51,562
Cologno Monzese (★Milano) (1995 E) 50,293
Como (★168,000) 84,603
Cosenza 77,659
Cremona 72,449
Crotone 59,425
Cuneo (Coni) 54,763
Ercolano (★Napoli) (1995 E) 59,695
Faenza (1995 E) 53,565
Fano (1995 E) 54,884
Ferrara 134,703
Firenze (Florence) (★640,000) 381,762
Foggia 156,327
Foligno (1995 E) 52,930
Forlì 107,909
Gela (1995 E) 75,321
Genova (Genoa) (★800,000) 655,704
Giugliano in Campania (★Napoli) (1995 E) 80,219
Grosseto 72,048
Guidonia-Montecelio (★Roma) (1995 E) 63,037
Imola (1995 E) 63,699
La Spezia (★185,000) 98,060
L'Aquila 69,213
Latina 111,047
Lecce 99,951
Legnano (★Milano) (1995 E) 52,698
Livorno (Leghorn) 164,371
Lucca 85,612
Manfredonia (1995 E) 58,408
Mántova 49,800
Marano di Napoli (1995 E) 54,444
Marsala (1995 E) 80,475
Massa (★145,000) 68,014
Matera 56,105
Mazara del Vallo (1995 E) 50,846
Messina 262,524
•Milano (Milan) (★3,790,000) 1,305,591
Módena 174,686
Modica (1995 E) 51,517
Molfetta (1995 E) 65,801
Moncalieri (★Torino) (1995 E) 58,789
Monza (★Milano) (1995 E) 119,658
Napoli (Naples) (★3,150,000) 1,046,987
Nicastro (1995 E) 71,274
Novara 102,327
Pádova (Padua) (★275,000) 213,072
Palermo 689,349
Parma 167,685
Pavia 74,815
Perugia 152,379
Pesaro 87,932
Pescara 118,473
Piacenza 99,799
Pisa 93,907
Pistoia 86,219
Portici (★Napoli) (1995 E) 64,180
Potenza 65,999
Pozzuoli (★Napoli) (1995 E) 79,977
Prato (★220,000) 168,683
Quartu Sant'Elena (1995 E) 66,344
Ragusa 69,253
Ravenna 137,129
Reggio di Calabria 179,829
Reggio nell'Emilia 136,675
Rho (★Milano) (1995 E) 51,997
Rimini 129,720
Rivoli (★Torino) (1995 E) 52,548
ROMA (ROME) (★3,235,000) 2,649,765
Rovigo 51,077
Salerno (★265,000) 143,580
San Giorgio a Cremano (★Napoli) (1995 E) 60,854
San Remo (1995 E) 56,507
San Severo (1995 E) 55,389
Sassari 121,455
Savona (★110,000) 64,539
Scandicci (★Firenze) (1995 E) 51,773
Sesto San Giovanni (★Milano) (1995 E) 83,756
Siena 55,094
Siracusa 127,345
Taranto 212,381
Teramo 52,217
Terni 108,521
Tivoli (1995 E) 52,616
Torino (Turin) (★1,550,000) 921,485
Torre Annunziata (★Napoli) (1995 E) 50,105
Torre del Greco (★Napoli) (1995 E) 98,749
Trani (1995 E) 52,606
Trapani 69,881
Trento (Trent) 103,269
Treviso 81,230
Trieste 222,589
Udine (★130,000) 95,374
Varese 84,595
Venézia (Venice) (★420,000) 297,743
Verona 254,146
Viareggio (1995 E) 57,765
Vicenza 108,041
Vigevano (1995 E) 60,003
Viterbo 60,458
Vittoria (1995 E) 57,969

JAMAICA

1991 C 2,314,479
•KINGSTON (★830,000) 516,500
Montego Bay 82,002
Portmore (★Kingston) 93,799
Spanish Town (★Kingston) 110,379

JAPAN / Nihon

1990 C 123,611,167
Abiko (★Tōkyō) 120,628
Ageo (★Tōkyō) 194,947
Aizu-wakamatsu 119,080
Akashi (★Ōsaka) 270,722
Akigawa (★Tōkyō) 50,387
Akishima (★Tōkyō) 105,372
Akita 302,362
Akō 51,131
Amagasaki (★Ōsaka) 498,999
Anjō 142,251
Aomori 287,808
Arao (★Ōmuta) 59,507
Asahikawa 359,071
Asaka (★Tōkyō) 103,617
Ashikaga 167,686
Ashiya (★Ōsaka) 87,524
Atsugi (★Tōkyō) 197,282
Ayase (★Tōkyō) 77,926
Beppu 130,334
Bisai (★Nagoya) 55,880
Chiba (★Tōkyō) 829,455
Chichibu 60,915
Chigasaki (★Tōkyō) 201,675
Chikushino (★Fukuoka) 70,303
Chiryū (★Nagoya) 54,059
Chita (★Nagoya) 75,433
Chitose 78,946
Chōfu (★Tōkyō) 197,677
Chōshi 85,138
Daitō (★Ōsaka) 126,460
Dazaifu (★Fukuoka) 62,402
Ebetsu (★Sapporo) 97,201
Ebina (★Tōkyō) 105,822
Eniwa 55,615
Fuchū 50,060
Fuchū (★Tōkyō) 209,396
Fuji (★370,000) 222,490
Fuji-yoshida 54,804
Fujieda (★Shizuoka) 119,815
Fujiidera (★Ōsaka) 65,922
Fujimi (★Tōkyō) 94,864
Fujinomiya (★Fuji) 117,092
Fujioka (▲60,981) 50,100
Fujisawa (★Tōkyō) 350,330
Fukaya (▲94,017) 75,600
Fukuchiyama (▲66,506) 56,700
Fukui 252,743
Fukuoka (★1,750,000) 1,237,062
Fukushima 277,528
Fukuyama 365,612
Funabashi (★Tōkyō) 533,270
Furukawa (▲64,230) 51,200
Fussa (★Tōkyō) 58,062
Gamagōri 84,819
Gifu 410,324
Ginowan 75,905
Gotemba 79,557
Gushikawa 54,018
Gyōda 83,181
Habikino (★Ōsaka) 115,049
Hachinohe 241,057
Hachiōji (★Tōkyō) 466,347
Hadano (★Tōkyō) 155,620
Hagi 50,618
Hakodate 307,249
Hamakita 81,157
Hamamatsu 534,620
Hanamaki (▲70,514) 55,000
Handa (★Nagoya) 99,550
Hannō (★Tōkyō) 73,214
Hashima 61,460
Hasuda (★Tōkyō) 59,706
Hatogaya (★Tōkyō) 56,440
Hatsukaichi (★Hiroshima) 63,441
Hekinan 65,899
Higashihiroshima (★Hiroshima) 94,209
Higashikurume (★Tōkyō) 113,818
Higashimatsuyama 84,394
Higashimurayama (★Tōkyō) 134,002
Higashiōsaka (★Ōsaka) 518,319
Higashiyamato (★Tōkyō) 75,132
Hikone 99,519
Himeji (★660,000) 454,360
Himi (▲60,766) 51,400
Hino (★Tōkyō) 165,928
Hirakata (★Ōsaka) 390,788
Hiratsuka (★Tōkyō) 245,950
Hirosaki (▲174,704) 133,800
Hiroshima (★1,575,000) 1,085,705
Hita (▲64,695) 57,100
Hitachi 202,141
Hōfu 117,634
Honjō 59,098
Hōya (★Tōkyō) 95,146
Hyūga 58,442
Ibaraki (★Ōsaka) 254,078
Ichihara (★Tōkyō) 257,716
Ichikawa (★Tōkyō) 436,596
Ichinomiya (★Nagoya) 262,434
Ichinoseki (▲61,967) 50,100
Iida (▲91,859) 64,700
Iizuka (★110,000) 83,131
Ikeda (★Ōsaka) 104,218
Ikoma (★Ōsaka) 99,604
Imabari 123,114
Imari (▲60,882) 50,000
Inagi (★Tōkyō) 58,635
Inazawa (★Nagoya) 96,274
Inuyama (★Nagoya) 69,801
Iruma (★Tōkyō) 137,585
Isahaya 90,683
Ise 104,164
Isehara (★Tōkyō) 89,567
Isesaki 115,938
Ishinomaki 121,976
Itami (★Ōsaka) 186,134
Itō 71,223
Iwaki 355,812
Iwakuni 109,530
Iwamizawa 80,417
Iwata 83,521
Iwatsuki (★Tōkyō) 106,462
Izumi (★Ōsaka) 146,127
Izumi (★Sendai) 124,216
Izumi-ōtsu (★Ōsaka) 67,035
Izumi-sano (★Ōsaka) 88,866
Izumo (▲82,679) 69,600
Joetsu 130,116
Jōyō (★Ōsaka) 84,770
Kadoma (★Ōsaka) 142,297
Kaga 69,196
Kagoshima 536,752
Kaizuka (★Ōsaka) 79,234
Kakamigahara 129,680
Kakegawa (▲72,795) 59,000
Kakogawa (★Ōsaka) 239,803
Kamagaya (★Tōkyō) 95,052
Kamaishi 52,484
Kamakura (★Tōkyō) 174,307
Kameoka 85,283
Kamifukuoka (★Tōkyō) 58,761
Kanazawa 442,868
Kani (★Nagoya) 80,012
Kanoya (▲77,655) 61,500
Kanuma (▲90,043) 74,900
Karatsu (▲79,207) 70,500
Kariya (★Nagoya) 120,126
Kasai 51,784
Kasaoka (▲59,619) 52,700
Kashihara (★Ōsaka) 115,554
Kashiwa (★Tōkyō) 305,058
Kashiwara (★Ōsaka) 76,819
Kashiwazaki (▲88,309) 75,300
Kasuga (★Fukuoka) 88,699
Kasugai (★Nagoya) 266,599
Kasukabe (★Tōkyō) 188,823
Katano (★Ōsaka) 65,308
Katsuta 109,825
Kawachi-nagano (★Ōsaka) 108,767
Kawagoe (★Tōkyō) 304,854
Kawaguchi (★Tōkyō) 438,680
Kawanishi (★Ōsaka) 141,253
Kawasaki (★Tōkyō) 1,173,603
Kesennuma 65,578
Kimitsu (▲89,242) 76,100
Kiryū 126,446
Kisarazu 123,433
Kishiwada (★Ōsaka) 188,563
Kitaibaraki 51,093
Kitakyūshū (★1,525,000) 1,026,455
Kitami 107,247
Kitamoto (★Tōkyō) 63,929
Kiyose (★Tōkyō) 67,539
Kōbe (★Ōsaka) 1,477,410
Kōchi 317,069
Kodaira (★Tōkyō) 164,013
Kōfu 200,626
Koga (★Tōkyō) 58,231
Koganei (★Tōkyō) 105,899
Kokubunji (★Tōkyō) 100,982
Komae (★Tōkyō) 74,189
Komaki (★Nagoya) 124,441
Komatsu 106,075
Kōnan (★Nagoya) 93,837
Kōnosu (★Tōkyō) 72,435
Kōriyama 314,642
Koshigaya (★Tōkyō) 285,259
Kudamatsu (★Tokuyama) 53,030
Kuki (★Tōkyō) 66,852

▲ Population of an entire municipality, commune, or district, including rural areas
• Largest city in country
★ Population or designation of the metropolitan area, including suburbs
★★ Population of metropolitan agglomeration
C Census E Official estimate U Unofficial estimate

City	Population
Kumagaya	152,124
Kumamoto	579,306
Kunitachi (★Tōkyō)	65,833
Kurashiki	414,693
Kure (★Hiroshima)	216,723
Kurume	228,347
Kusatsu (★Ōsaka)	94,767
Kushiro	205,639
Kuwana (★Nagoya)	97,909
Kyōto (★Ōsaka)	1,461,103
Machida (★Tōkyō)	349,050
Maebashi	286,261
Maizuru	96,333
Marugame	75,606
Matsubara (★Ōsaka)	135,919
Matsudo (★Tōkyō)	456,210
Matsue	142,956
Matsumoto	200,715
Matsusaka	118,725
Matsuyama	443,322
Mihara	85,518
Miki (★Ōsaka)	76,501
Minō (★Ōsaka)	122,120
Misato (★Tōkyō)	128,376
Mishima (★Numazu)	105,418
Mitaka (★Tōkyō)	165,564
Mito	234,968
Miura (★Tōkyō)	52,440
Miyako	58,503
Miyakonojō (▲130,153)	106,200
Miyazaki	287,352
Mobara	83,437
Moriguchi (★Ōsaka)	157,372
Morioka	235,434
Moriyama	58,561
Mukō (★Ōsaka)	52,928
Munakata	68,265
Muroran (★195,000)	117,855
Musashimurayama (★Tōkyō)	65,562
Musashino (★Tōkyō)	139,077
Nabari	68,933
Nagahama	55,485
Nagano	347,026
Nagaoka	185,938
Nagaokakyō (★Ōsaka)	77,191
Nagareyama (★Tōkyō)	140,059
Nagasaki	444,599
Nagoya (★4,800,000)	2,154,793
Naha	304,836
Nakatsu	66,388
Nakatsugawa	53,722
Nanao	50,103
Nara (★Ōsaka)	349,349
Narashino (★Tōkyō)	151,471
Narita	86,708
Naruto	64,575
Neyagawa (★Ōsaka)	256,524
Niigata	486,097
Niihama	129,149
Niitsu (▲63,999)	55,700
Niiza (★Tōkyō)	138,919
Nishinomiya (★Ōsaka)	426,909
Nishio	95,197
Nobeoka	130,624
Noboribetsu (★Muroran)	55,571
Noda (★Tōkyō)	114,475
Nōgata	62,530
Numazu (★495,000)	211,732
Obihiro	167,384
Ōbu (★Nagoya)	69,720
Ōdate (▲68,195)	58,500
Odawara	193,417
Ōgaki	148,281
Ōita	408,501
Okaya	59,849
Okayama	593,730
Okazaki	306,822
Okegawa (★Tōkyō)	69,029
Okinawa	105,845
Ōme (★Tōkyō)	125,960
Ōmi-hachiman (★Ōsaka)	66,066
Ōmiya (★Tōkyō)	403,776
Ōmura	73,435
Ōmuta (★225,000)	150,453
Ōnojō (★Fukuoka)	75,214
Onomichi	97,103
Ōsaka (★16,900,000)	2,623,801
Ōta	139,801
Otaru (★Sapporo)	163,211
Ōtsu (★Ōsaka)	260,018
Owariashi (★Nagoya)	65,675
Oyama (▲142,262)	120,000
Sabae	62,283
Saga	169,963
Sagamihara (★Tōkyō)	531,542
Saijō	56,821
Saiki	52,323
Sakado (★Tōkyō)	95,740
Sakai (★Ōsaka)	807,765
Sakaide	63,876
Sakata	100,811
Saku (▲62,003)	50,000
Sakura (★Tōkyō)	144,688
Sakurai	60,262
Sanda (▲64,560) (★Ōsaka)	54,500
Sanjō	85,823
Sano	83,484
Sapporo (★1,900,000)	1,671,742
Sasebo	244,677
Satte	54,342
Sayama (★Ōsaka)	54,319
Sayama (★Tōkyō)	157,309
Seki	68,386
Sendai (▲71,735)	58,000
Sendai (★1,175,000)	918,398
Sennan (★Ōsaka)	60,065
Seto	126,340
Settsu (★Ōsaka)	87,453
Shibata (▲78,170)	63,600
Shijōnawate (★Ōsaka)	50,035
Shiki (★Tōkyō)	63,491
Shimada (▲73,810)	64,500
Shimizu (★Shizuoka)	241,523
Shimodate (▲66,028)	54,100
Shimonoseki (★Kitakyūshū)	262,635
Shiogama (★Sendai)	62,025
Shizuoka (★975,000)	472,196
Sōka (★Tōkyō)	206,132
Suita (★Ōsaka)	345,206
Suwa	52,464
Suzuka	174,105
Tachikawa (★Tōkyō)	152,824
Tagajō (★Sendai)	58,456
Tagawa	57,700
Tajimi (★Nagoya)	94,036
Takaishi (★Ōsaka)	65,086
Takamatsu	329,684
Takaoka (★220,000)	175,466
Takarazuka (★Ōsaka)	201,862
Takasago (★Ōsaka)	93,273
Takasaki	236,461
Takatsuki (★Ōsaka)	359,867
Takayama	65,243
Takefu	70,187
Tama (★Tōkyō)	144,489
Tamano	73,238
Tanabe (▲69,859)	59,100
Tanashi (★Tōkyō)	75,144
Tatebayashi	76,221
Tenri	68,815
Tochigi	86,216
Toda (★Tōkyō)	87,599
Tōkai (★Nagoya)	97,358
Toki	64,946
Tokoname (★Nagoya)	51,784
Tokorozawa (★Tōkyō)	303,040
Tokushima	263,356
Tokuyama (★250,000)	110,900
•TŌKYŌ (★30,300,000)	8,163,573
Tomakomai	160,118
Tondabayashi (★Ōsaka)	110,447
Toride (★Tōkyō)	81,665
Tosu	55,877
Tottori	142,467
Toyama	321,254
Toyoake (★Nagoya)	62,160
Toyohashi	337,982
Toyokawa	111,730
Toyonaka (★Ōsaka)	409,837
Toyota	332,336
Tsu	157,177
Tsuchiura	127,471
Tsuruga	68,041
Tsuruoka	99,889
Tsushima (★Nagoya)	59,343
Tsuyama	89,400
Ube (★230,000)	175,053
Ueda	119,435
Ueno (▲60,242)	51,400
Uji (★Ōsaka)	177,010
Urasoe	89,994
Urawa (★Tōkyō)	418,271
Urayasu (★Tōkyō)	115,675
Ushiku	60,693
Utsunomiya	426,795
Uwajima	68,034
Wakayama (★495,000)	396,553
Wakō (★Tōkyō)	56,890
Warabi (★Tōkyō)	73,620
Yachiyo (★Tōkyō)	148,615
Yaizu (★Shizuoka)	112,186
Yakumo (▲104,500) (1986 E)	61,800
Yamagata	249,487
Yamaguchi	129,461
Yamato (★Tōkyō)	194,866
Yamato-kōriyama (★Ōsaka)	92,949
Yamato-takada (★Ōsaka)	68,237
Yao (★Ōsaka)	277,568
Yashio (★Tōkyō)	72,473
Yatsushiro (▲108,135)	88,300
Yawata (★Ōsaka)	75,758
Yokkaichi	274,180
Yokohama (★Tōkyō)	3,220,331
Yokosuka (★Tōkyō)	433,358
Yonago	131,453
Yonezawa	94,760
Yono (★Tōkyō)	79,060
Yotsukaidō (★Tōkyō)	72,157
Yukuhashi	65,711
Zama (★Tōkyō)	112,102
Zushi (★Tōkyō)	56,704

JERSEY

City	Population
1991 C	84,082
•SAINT HELIER (★46,500)	28,123

JORDAN / Al-Urdun

City	Population
1994 C	4,095,579
Al-'Aqabah	61,673
•'AMMĀN (★1,500,000)	963,490
Ar-Rusayfah (★'Ammān)	131,130
As-Salt	56,296
Az-Zarqā'	344,524
Irbid	208,201
Mādabā	55,156
Mukhayyam al-Baq'ah (★'Ammān)	58,166
Suwaylih	53,083
Wādī as-Sīr	87,980

KAZAKHSTAN / Kazahstan

City	Population
1991 E	16,793,100
Aktau	169,000
Aktjubinsk	266,600
•Almaty (★1,190,000)	1,156,200
Arkalyk	64,900
ASTANA	286,000
Atyrau	156,700
Balhaš	87,600
Ekibastuz	138,900
Karaganda	608,600
Kentau	65,100
Kokčetav	143,300
Kustanaj	233,900
Kzyl-Orda	158,200
Leninogorsk	69,500
Leninsk	73,000
Pavlodar	342,500
Petropavlovsk	248,300
Rudnyj	128,800
Šahtinsk	65,300
Šaran'	62,600
Šatpaev	61,400
Ščučinsk	56,000
Semipalatinsk	344,700
Šymkent	438,800
Taldykorgan	136,100
Temirtau	213,100
Turkestan	81,200
Ural'sk	214,000
Ust'-Kamenogorsk	332,900
Žambyl	312,300
Žanatas	53,000
Žezkazgan	111,100
Zyrjanovsk	53,800

KENYA

City	Population
1989 C	21,397,000
Eldoret	104,900
Kisumu	185,100
Kitale	53,000
Machakos	116,100
Meru	78,100
Mombasa (1990 E)	537,000
•NAIROBI (1990 E)	1,505,000
Nakuru	162,800
Nyeri	88,600
Thika	57,100

KIRIBATI

City	Population
1990 C	72,298
BAIRIKI	2,226
•Bikenibeu	5,055

KOREA, NORTH / Chosŏn minjujuŭi-inmīn-konghwaguk

City	Population
1981 E	18,317,000
Ch'ŏngjin	490,000
Haeju (1983 E)	213,000
Hamhŭng (1970 E)	150,000
Hŭngdŏki-dong (1976 E)	260,000
Kaesŏng	259,000
Kanggye (1967 E)	130,000
Kimch'aek (1967 E)	265,000
Namp'o	241,000
•P'YŎNGYANG	2,355,000
Sinŭiju	305,000
Songnim (1944 C)	53,035
Wŏnsan	398,000

KOREA, SOUTH / Taehan-min'guk

City	Population
1990 C	43,520,199
Andong	116,932
Ansan (★Sŏul)	252,157
Anyang (★Sŏul)	480,668
Bucheon (★Sŏul)	667,777
Changwŏn (★Masan)	323,138
Chech'on	102,037
Cheju	232,687
Chinhae	120,207
Chinju	258,365
Ch'ŏnan	211,382
Ch'ŏngju	497,429
Chŏngŭp	86,850
Chŏnju	517,104
Ch'unch'ŏn	174,153
Ch'ungju	129,994
Ch'ungmu	92,159
Hanam (★Sŏul)	101,278
Inch'ŏn (★Sŏul)	1,818,293
Iri	203,401
Kangnŭng	152,605
Kimch'ŏn	81,349
Kimhae	106,166
Kimje	55,136
Kongju	65,195
Kumi	206,101
Kunp'o (★Sŏul)	99,956
Kunsan	218,216
Kwach'ŏn (★Sŏul)	72,328
Kwangju	1,144,695
Kwangmyŏng (★Sŏul)	328,803
Kyŏngju	141,895
Kyŏngsan	60,524
Masan (★625,000)	496,639
Mikŭm (★Sŏul)	74,688
Miryang	52,995
Mokp'o	253,423
Naju	55,306
Namwŏn	63,121
Ŏnyang	66,379
Osan	59,492
P'ohang	318,595
Pusan (Fusan) (★3,800,000)	3,797,566
P'yŏngt'aek	79,238
Samch'ŏnp'o	62,824
Sangju	51,875
Shihŭng (★Sŏul)	107,190
Sŏgwipo	88,292
Sokch'o	73,796
Sŏngnam (★Sŏul)	540,764
Songtan	77,460
Sŏsan	55,930
•SŎUL (SEOUL) (★15,850,000)	10,627,790
Sunch'ŏn	167,209
Suwŏn	644,968
T'aebaek	89,770
Taech'ŏn	56,922
Taegu	2,228,834
Taejŏn	1,062,084
Tongduchŏn	71,448
Tonghae	89,162
Tongkwang	70,118
Ŭijŏngbu (★Sŏul)	212,368
Ŭiwang	96,892
Ulsan	682,978
Wŏnju	173,013
Yŏch'ŏn	63,802
Yŏngju	84,335
Yŏsu	173,164

KUWAIT / Al-Kuwayt

City	Population
1995 C	1,575,983
Al-Ahmadī (★450,000)	21,504
Al-Farwānīyah (★Al-Kuwayt)	53,100
•AL-KUWAYT (★1,126,000)	28,859
As-Sālimīyah (★Al-Kuwayt)	130,215
Aș-Şulaybīyah (★Al-Kuwayt)	53,587
El-Kreem (★Al-Kuwayt)	50,338
Hawallī (★Al-Kuwayt)	82,238
Qalīb ash-Shuyūkh (★Al-Kuwayt)	102,178
South Khītān (★Al-Kuwayt)	63,628
Subahiya (★Al-Ahmadī)	50,535
Subbah al-Salem (★Al-Kuwayt)	54,400

KYRGYZSTAN / Kirgizija

City	Population
1991 E	4,422,200
•BIŠKEK	631,300
Džalal-Abad	79,900
Kara-Balta	55,000
Karakol	64,300
Oš	238,200
Tokmak	71,200

LAOS / Lao

City	Population
1990 E	4,139,000
Louangphrabang (1985 C)	68,000
Savannakhét (1985 C)	97,000
•VIANGCHAN (VIENTIANE)	464,000

LATVIA / Latvija

City	Population
1993 E	2,577,000
Daugavpils	124,900
Jelgava	72,300
Jūrmala (★Rīga)	60,100
Liepāja	108,300
•RĪGA (★1,000,000)	874,200

LEBANON / Lubnān

City	Population
1982 E	2,637,000
•BAYRŪT (BEIRUT) (★1,675,000)	509,000
Şaydā (Sidon)	105,000
Tarābulus (Tripoli) (★950,000)	198,000

LESOTHO

City	Population
1986 C	1,577,536
•MASERU	98,017

LIBERIA

City	Population
1986 E	2,221,000
•MONROVIA	465,000

LIBYA / Lībiyā

City	Population
1988 E	3,772,500
Ajdābiyā (1984 C)	65,276
Al-Bayḍā' (1984 C)	67,120
Al-Marj (1984C)	54,010
Az-Zāwiyah (1984 C)	91,603
Banghāzī (★472,000)	446,250
Darnah (1984 C)	62,179
Mişrātah (★160,000)	121,669
Sabhā (1984 C)	70,905
Tājūrā' (1984C)	59,674
•TARĀBULUS (★960,000)	591,062
Tubruq (1984 C)	75,282

LIECHTENSTEIN

City	Population
1995 E	30,923
•Schaan	5,106
VADUZ	5,085

LITHUANIA / Lietuva

City	Population
1994 E	3,723,970
Alytus	77,414
Kaunas	418,964
Klaipėda (Memel)	203,415
Marijampolė	52,280
Panevėžys	131,630
Šiauliai	147,324
•VILNIUS	578,639

LUXEMBOURG / Luxemburg

City	Population
1991 C	384,062
Esch-sur-Alzette (★83,000)	24,012
•LUXEMBOURG (★136,000)	75,377

MACAU

City	Population
1991 C	355,693
•MACAU	342,548

MACEDONIA / Makedonija

City	Population
1994 C	1,936,877
Bitola	75,386
Kumanovo	66,237
Prilep	67,371
•SKOPJE	440,577
Tetovo	50,376

MADAGASCAR / Madagasikara

City	Population
1988 E	11,238,000
•ANTANANARIVO	1,250,000
Antsirabe	100,000
Antsiranana	220,000
Fianarantsoa	300,000
Mahajanga	200,000
Toamasina	230,000
Toliara	150,000

MALAWI / Malaŵi

City	Population
1987 C	7,988,507
•Blantyre	333,120
LILONGWE	223,318
Mzuzu	51,904

MALAYSIA

City	Population
1991 C	17,566,982
Alor Setar (★165,113)	125,026
Batu Pahat (★84,538)	71,132
Bukit Mertajam (★122,044)	25,732
Butterworth (★94,231)	78,672
George Town (Penang) (★520,000)	219,376
Ipoh (★468,765)	382,633
Johor Bahru (★442,250)	328,646
Kajang (★99,914)	46,269
Keluang (★98,837)	49,043
Klang (★368,228)	243,698
Kota Bharu (★234,604)	219,713
Kota Kinabalu (★160,122)	75,787
•KUALA LUMPUR (★1,800,000)	1,145,075
Kuala Terengganu	228,659
Kuantan	198,356
Kuching	147,729
Melaka (★112,873)	74,962
Miri (★102,969)	87,230
Muar (★70,637)	63,123
Petaling Jaya (★351,719) (★Kuala Lumpur)	254,849
Sandakan (★157,180)	126,092
Seremban (★193,009)	182,584
Shah Alam (★Kuala Lumpur)	101,733
Sibu (★133,471)	126,384
Sungai Petani	115,519
Taiping	183,165
Tawau (★124,683)	85,999

MALDIVES

City	Population
1990 C	213,215
•MALE'	55,130

MALI

City	Population
1987 C	7,696,348
•BAMAKO	658,275
Gao	55,266
Kayes	50,993
Mopti	74,771
Ségou	88,135
Sikasso	73,859

MALTA

City	Population
1995 C	378,132
•VALLETTA (★235,000)	7,262

MARSHALL ISLANDS

City	Population
1988 C	43,380
•Jarej-Uliga-Delap	14,649

MARTINIQUE

City	Population
1990 C	359,579
•FORT-DE-FRANCE (★116,400)	100,080

MAURITANIA / Mūrītāniyā

City	Population
1988 C	1,864,236
Nouâdhibou	59,198
•NOUAKCHOTT	393,325

MAURITIUS

City	Population
1990 C	1,056,660
Curepipe (★Port Louis)	65,414
•PORT LOUIS (★420,000)	132,460
Quatre Bornes (★Port Louis)	68,398
Vacoas (★Port Louis)	56,452

MAYOTTE

City	Population
1991 C	94,385
•MAMOUDZOU	20,274

MEXICO / México

City	Population
1995 C	91,158,290
Acámbaro	54,523
Acapulco de Juárez	592,528
Agua Prieta	54,681
Aguascalientes	537,523
Apatzingán de la Constitución	89,834
Apizaco	50,593
Apodaca	212,118
Atlixco	79,556
Buenavista	160,596
Campeche	178,160
Cancún	297,183
Cárdenas	72,739
Celaya	251,724
Chalco (★Ciudad de México)	96,978
Chetumal	115,152
Chicoloapan de Juárez	70,959
Chihuahua	613,722
Chilpancingo de los Bravo	123,475
Chimalhuacán	410,031
Cholula de Rivadabia (★Puebla)	62,259
Ciudad Acuña	79,221
•CIUDAD DE MÉXICO (MEXICO CITY) (★14,530,000)	8,489,007
Ciudad del Carmen	114,360
Ciudad Hidalgo	55,225
Ciudad Juárez (★El Paso, U.S.A.)	995,770
Ciudad López Mateos	427,192
Ciudad Madero (★Tampico)	171,091
Ciudad Mante	81,128
Ciudad Netzahualcóyotl (★Ciudad de México)	1,233,681
Ciudad Obregón	244,028
Ciudad Valles	102,226
Ciudad Victoria	230,304
Coacalco	202,778
Coatzacoalcos	222,027
Colima	110,977
Comitán de Domínguez	62,292
Córdoba	132,091
Cortazar	51,617
Cozumel	47,841
Cuauhtémoc	80,428
Cuautitlán Izcalli	401,119
Cuautla	128,781
Cuernavaca	311,095
Culiacán	505,518
Delicias	94,001
Durango	397,687
Ecatepec de Morelos (★Ciudad de México)	1,455,909
Ensenada	192,550
Fresnillo	89,338
Frontera	60,434
Garza García (★Monterrey)	120,868
General Escobedo	174,486
Gómez Palacio (★Torreón)	192,888
Guadalajara (★2,400,000)	1,633,053
Guadalupe	65,726
Guadalupe (★Monterrey)	618,610
Guamúchil	56,091
Guanajuato	69,970
Guasave	57,581
Guaymas	90,964
Guzmán	81,720
Hermosillo	504,009
Heroica Zitácuaro	74,824
Hidalgo del Parral	96,267
Iguala	98,276
Irapuato	299,604
Ixtapaluca	153,138
Jiutepec	125,148
Juchitán de Zaragoza	62,065
La Paz	154,314
La Piedad de Cabadas	72,041
Lagos de Moreno	75,220
Lázaro Cárdenas	63,723
León	941,626
Lerdo (★Torreón)	54,570
Linares	49,921
Los Mochis	188,349
Los Reyes la Paz	178,534
Manzanillo	80,568
Matamoros (★Brownsville, U.S.A.)	323,794
Matehuala	60,726
Mazatlán	302,808
Mérida	612,261
Metepec	147,360
Mexicali (★530,000)	505,016
Minatitlán	145,795
Miramar	51,462
Monclova	188,850
Monterrey (★2,050,000)	1,088,023
Morelia	512,169
Naucalpan de Juárez (★Ciudad de México)	915,992
Navojoa	94,837
Nogales	131,578
Nuevo Laredo (★Laredo, U.S.A.)	273,797
Oaxaca de Juárez	242,247
Ocotlán	70,537
Ojo de Agua (★Ciudad de México)	65,106
Orizaba (★220,000)	114,341
Pachuca de Soto	209,996
Papantla de Olarte	49,916
Piedras Negras	114,384
Poza Rica de Hidalgo	153,585

▲ Population of an entire municipality, commune, or district, including rural areas
• Largest city in country
★ Population or designation of the metroplitan area, including suburbs
★★ Population of metropolitan agglomeration
C Census E Official estimate U Unofficial estimate

Puebla de Zaragoza (★1,380,000) 1,157,625
Puerto Vallarta 121,844
Querétaro 469,542
Reynosa 320,458
Río Bravo 74,913
Sahuayo de José María Morelos 57,612
Salamanca 135,874
Salina Cruz 71,464
Saltillo 510,131
San Andrés Tuxtla 54,043
San Cristóbal de las Casas 99,254
San Francisco del Rincón 64,577
San Juan del Río 84,532
San Luis Potosí (★720,000) 586,585
San Luis Río Colorado 115,596
San Martín Texmelucan 65,855
San Miguel de Allende 52,966
San Nicolás de los Garza (★Monterrey) 487,924
San Pablo de las Salinas 126,659
Santa Catarina (★Monterrey) 201,233
Silao 58,457
Soledad de Graciano Sánchez 147,188
Tampico (★450,000) 278,933
Tapachula 163,253
Tecomán 68,847
Tehuacán 172,510
Temixco 82,441
Tepatitlán de Morelos 65,930
Tepic 254,551
Texcoco de Mora (★Ciudad de México) 89,524
Teziutlán 50,415
Tijuana (★San Diego, U.S.A.) 966,097
Tlalnepantla (★Ciudad de México) 708,013
Tlaquepaque (★Guadalajara) 434,710
Tlaxcala de Xicohténcatl 63,335
Toluca de Lerdo 368,384
Tonalá 250,058
Torreón (★760,000) 481,493
Tulancingo 87,458
Tuxpan de Rodríguez Cano 74,692
Tuxtepec 77,467
Tuxtla Gutiérrez 378,079
Uruapan del Progreso 215,449
Valle de Santiago 56,517
Veracruz (★620,000) 505,015
Villa de Álvarez 63,982
Villa Nicolás Romero 192,534
Villahermosa 301,238
Xalapa (Jalapa) 324,081
Xico (★Ciudad de México) 286,839
Zacatecas 109,109
Zamora de Hidalgo 121,181
Zapopan (★Guadalajara) 850,315
Zihuatanejo 54,537

MICRONESIA, FEDERATED STATES OF

1994 C 105,506
•Kolonia (1985 E) 6,306
PALIKIR (1985 E) 5,047

MOLDOVA

1991 E 4,366,300
Bălţi 164,900
•CHIŞINĂU 676,700
Râbniţa 62,900
Tighina 141,500
Tiraspol 186,000

MONACO

1990 C 29,972
•MONACO (★87,000) 29,972

MONGOLIA / Mongol Ard Uls

1995 E 2,410,000
Darhan 89,400
Ulaan-Uul (1991 E) 58,200
•ULAANBAATAR 616,900

MONTSERRAT

1980 C 11,606
•PLYMOUTH 1,568

MOROCCO / Al-Maghrib

1994 E 26,590,000
Agadir 155,244
Aït-Melloul 82,825
Al-Hoceima 55,216
Beni-Mellal 154,000
Berkane 77,026
•Casablanca (★3,400,000) 3,022,000
El-Jadida 130,000
Er-Rachidia 65,842
Fès (★670,000) 576,000
Kénitra 244,000
Khemisset (1982 C) 58,925
Khouribga 187,000
Ksar-el-Kebir (1982 C) 73,541
Larache (1982 C) 63,893
Marrakech (★700,000) 602,000
Meknès (★470,000) 399,000
Mohammedia (★Casablanca) 162,000
Nador (1982 C) 62,040
Oued-Zem (1982 C) 58,744
Oujda 337,000
RABAT (★1,200,000) 717,000
Safi 255,000
Salé (★Rabat) 456,000
Settat (1982 C) 65,203
Sidi-Kacem (1982 C) 55,833
Sidi-Slimane (1982 C) 50,457
Tanger (★450,000) 327,000
Taza 92,704
Tetouan 274,000
Youssoufia 60,451

MOZAMBIQUE / Moçambique

1989 E 15,326,476
Beira 291,604
Chimoio (1986 E) 86,928
Inhambane (1986 E) 64,274
•MAPUTO 1,069,727
Nacala 101,615
Nampula 197,379
Pemba (1986 E) 50,215
Quelimane 78,520
Tete (1986 E) 56,178
Xai-Xai (1986 E) 51,620

MYANMAR (Burma)

1983 C 34,124,908
Bago 150,528
Chauk 51,437
Dawei 69,882
Henzada 82,005
Kale 52,628
Lashio 88,590
Magway 54,881
Mandalay 532,949
Mawlamyine 219,961
Maymyo 63,782
Meiktila 96,496
Mergui 88,600
Monywa 106,843
Myingyan 77,060
Myitkyinā 56,427
Nyaunglebin 55,194
Pakokku 71,860
Pathein 144,096
Prome 83,332
Pyinmana 52,962
Shwebo 52,185
Sittwe 107,621
Taunggyi 108,231
Thaton 61,790
Toungoo 65,861
•YANGON (RANGOON) (★2,800,000) 2,705,039
Yenangyaung 62,582

NAMIBIA

1991 C 1,409,920
Walvis Bay (★22,999) 12,383
•WINDHOEK 147,056

NEPAL / Nepāl

1991 C 18,491,097
Bhaktapur (Bhādgāon) 61,405
Bharatpur 54,670
Dharān 66,457
Hetauṇḍā 53,836
Janakpur 54,710
•KĀTHMĀNDAU (KATHMANDU) (★520,000) 421,258
Lalitpur 115,865
Mahendranagar 62,050
Pokharā 95,286
Wirātnagar 129,388
Wirgañj 69,005

NETHERLANDS / Nederland

1998 E 15,700,000
Alkmaar (★124,000) 92,881
Almelo 65,545
Almere 126,382
Alphen aan den Rijn 65,335
Amersfoort 119,908
Amstelveen (★Amsterdam) 77,615
•AMSTERDAM (★1,104,000) 717,304
Apeldoorn (1995 E) 130,730
Arnhem (★305,000) 136,017
Assen 55,339
Bijlmermeer (1995 E) 88,600
Breda (★157,000) (1995 E) 127,870
Capelle aan de IJssel 63,108
Delft (★'s-Gravenhage) 94,433
Deventer 70,804
Dordrecht 117,969
Ede (1995 E) 65,930
Eindhoven (★409,000) 198,299
Enschede (★256,000) 136,541
Gouda 71,539
Groningen (★210,000) 160,877
Haarlem (★212,000) 147,729
Heerlen (★267,500) 95,746
Helmond 77,507
Hengelo (★Enschede) 76,017
Hilversum (★101,000) 76,032
Hoek van Holland 62,864
Hoofddorp (★Amsterdam) (1995 E) 51,700
Hoorn 62,864
Kerkrade (★Heerlen) 52,026
Leeuwarden 84,291
Leiden (Leyden) (★209,000) 117,036
Lelystad 59,985
Maastricht (★166,000) 117,206
Nieuwegein (★Utrecht) 61,205
Nijmegen (★253,000) 150,493
Oss 54,680
Purmerend (★Amsterdam) 66,667
Roosendaal (1995 E) 61,820
Rotterdam (★1,080,000) 590,436
'S-GRAVENHAGE (THE HAGUE) (★698,000) 441,561
's-Hertogenbosch (★187,000) (1995 E) 96,390
Schiedam 74,766
Spijkenisse (★Rotterdam) 71,387
Tilburg (★245,000) (1995 E) 163,720
Utrecht (★552,000) 232,983
Veenendaal 57,047
Venlo (★88,000) (▲64,274) 35,844
Vlaardingen (★Rotterdam) 74,188
Zaandam (★Amsterdam) (1995 E) 70,210
Zeist (1995 E) (★Utrecht) 49,968
Zoetermeer (★'s-Gravenhage) 107,591
Zwolle 100,277

NETHERLANDS ANTILLES / Nederlandse Antillen

1992 C 189,474
•WILLEMSTAD (★130,000) (1981 C) 31,883

NEW CALEDONIA / Nouvelle-Calédonie

1996 C 196,836
•NOUMÉA (★120,000) 76,293

NEW ZEALAND

1991 C 3,434,950
•Auckland (★855,571) 315,668
Christchurch (★307,179) 292,858
Dunedin 116,577
Hamilton (★148,625) 101,448
Invercargill 56,148
Lower Hutt (★Wellington) 94,540
Manukau (★Auckland) 226,147
Napier (★110,216) 51,645
North Shore City (★Auckland) 152,134
Palmerston North (★70,951) 70,318
Tauranga (★70,803) 46,308
Waitemata (★Auckland) 136,716
WELLINGTON (★375,000) 150,301

NICARAGUA

1995 C 4,357,099
Chinandega 97,387
Estelí 71,550
Granada 71,783
León 123,865
•MANAGUA 864,201
Masaya 88,971
Matagalpa 59,397
Tipitapa 67,925

NIGER

1988 C 7,220,089
Agadez 49,361
Maradi 104,386
•NIAMEY 392,165
Tahoua 49,948
Zinder 119,838

NIGERIA

1987 E 101,907,000
Aba 239,800
Abakaliki 56,800
Abeokuta 341,300
ABUJA (1993 U) 250,000
Ado-Ekiti 287,000
Afikpo 65,790
Agege 83,810
Akure 129,600
Amaigbo 53,690
Amawbia Awka 88,800
Azare 50,020
Bauchi 68,840
Benin City 183,200
Bida 100,200
Calabar 139,800
Deba 110,600
Dukku 52,880
Ede 245,200
Effon-Alaiye 122,300
Ejigbo 84,570
Emure-Ekiti 58,750
Enugu 252,500
Epe 80,560
Erin-Oshogbo 59,940
Gbongan 53,990
Gombe 86,120
Gusau 126,200
Ibadan 1,144,000
Idah 50,550
Idanre 56,080
Ife 237,000
Ifon-Oshogbo 65,980
Igbo-Ora 68,060
Igboho 85,230
Igede-Ekiti 56,570
Ihiala 73,240
Ijebu-Igbo 78,680
Ijebu-Ode 124,900
Ijero-Ekiti 76,420
Ikare 112,500
Ikerre 195,400
Ikire 94,450
Ikirun 144,900
Ikole 71,860
Ikorodu 147,700
Ikot Ekpene 69,440
Ila 210,800
Ilawe 147,300
Ilesha 302,100
Ilobu 159,000
Ilorin 380,000
Inisa 95,630
Ipoti-Ekiti 53,220
Ise-Ekiti 82,580
Iseyin 173,500
Iwo 289,100
Jimeta 66,130
Jos 164,700
Kaduna 273,200
Kano 538,300
Katsina 165,000
Kaura-Namoda 52,910
Keffi 57,790
Kishi 77,210
Kumo 118,200
Lafia 97,810
Lafiagi 57,580
•LAGOS (★3,800,000) 1,213,000
Lalupon 56,130
Maiduguri 255,100
Makurdi 98,350
Minna 109,300
Mubi 51,190
Mushin (★Lagos) 266,100
Nguru 78,770
Offa 157,500
Ogbomosho 582,900
Oka 114,400
Oke-Mesi 55,040
Okwe 52,550
Olupona 65,720
Ondo 135,300
Onitsha 298,200
Opobo 64,620
Oron 62,260
Oshogbo 380,800
Owo 146,600
Oyan 50,930
Oyo 204,700
Pindiga 64,130
Port-Harcourt 327,300
Potiskum 56,490
Sapele 111,200
Shagamu 93,610
Shaki 139,000
Shomolu (★Lagos) 120,700
Sokoto 163,700
Ugep 81,910
Umuahia 52,550
Uyo 60,500
Warri 100,700
Zaria 302,800

NIUE

1991 C 2,239
•ALOFI 682

NORTHERN MARIANA ISLANDS

1995 C 58,846
•Garapan 6,634

NORWAY / Norge

1993 E 4,312,000
Bærum (★Oslo) 89,774
Bergen (▲218,105) 192,747
Fredrikstad 50,077
Kristiansand (▲67,113) 55,129
•OSLO (★703,896) 470,204
Stavanger (★102,267) 97,721
Trondheim (▲140,718) 132,301

OMAN / 'Umān

1993 C 2,018,074
As-Sīb 149,801
Bawshar 105,941
•MASQAT (★210,000) 34,683
Maṭraḥ 173,908
Nazwá 58,582
Ṣalālah 116,087
Ṣuḥār 83,011

PAKISTAN / Pākistān

1981 C 84,253,644
Ahmadpur East 56,979
Bahāwalnagar 74,533
Bahāwalpur (★180,263) 152,009
Chārsadda 62,530
Chīchāwatni 50,241
Chiniot 105,559
Chishtiān Mandi 61,959
Daska 55,555
Dera Ghāzi Khān 102,007
Dera Ismāīl Khān (★68,145) 64,358
Drigh Road Cantonment (★Karāchi) 56,742
Faisalabad (Lyallpur) 1,104,209
Gojra 68,000
Gujrānwāla (★658,753) 600,993
Gujrānwāla Cantonment (★Gujrānwāla) 57,760
Gujrāt 155,058
Hāfizābād 83,464
Hyderābād (★800,000) 702,539
ISLĀMĀBĀD (★Rāwalpindi) 204,364
Jacobābād 79,365
Jarānwāla 69,459
Jhang Sadar 195,558
Jhelum (★106,462) 92,646
Kamālia 61,107
Kāmoke 71,097
•Karāchi (★5,300,000) 4,901,627
Karāchi Cantonment (★Karāchi) 181,981
Kasūr 155,523
Khairpur 61,447
Khānewāl 89,090
Khānpur 70,589
Khushāb 56,274
Kohāt (★77,604) 55,832
Lahore (★3,025,000) 2,707,215
Lahore Cantonment (★Lahore) 245,474
Lārkāna 123,890
Leiah 51,482
Mandi Būrewāla 86,311
Mardān (★147,977) 141,842
Miānwāli 59,159
Mingāora 88,078
Mirpur Khās 124,371
Multān (★732,070) 696,316
Muzaffargarh 53,000
Nawābshāh 102,139
Okāra (★153,483) 127,455
Pākpattan 69,820
Peshāwar (★566,248) 506,896
Peshāwar Cantonment (★Peshāwar) 59,352
Quetta (★285,719) 244,842
Rahīmyār Khān (★132,635) 119,036
Rāwalpindi (★1,040,000) 457,091
Rāwalpindi Cantonment (★Rāwalpindi) 337,752
Sādiqābād 63,935
Sāhīwāl 150,954
Sargodha (★291,362) 231,895
Sargodha Cantonment (★Sargodha) 59,467
Shekhūpura 141,168
Shikārpur 88,138
Siālkot (★302,009) 258,147
Sukkur 190,551
Tando Ādam 62,744
Turbat 52,337
Vihāri 53,799
Wāh Cantonment 122,335
Wazīrābād 62,725

PALAU

1990 C 15,122
•KOROR 9,018

PANAMA / Panamá

1990 C 2,315,047
Colón (★96,000) 54,469
David 65,635
•PANAMÁ (★770,000) 411,549
San Miguelito (★Panamá) 242,529

PAPUA NEW GUINEA

1995 E 4,074,000
Lae 106,154
•PORT MORESBY 246,664

PARAGUAY

1992 C 4,123,550
•ASUNCIÓN (★700,000) 502,426
Capiatá 83,189
Ciudad del Este 133,893
Encarnación 55,359
Fernando de la Mora (★Asunción) 95,287
Lambaré (★Asunción) 99,681
Luque (★Asunción) 83,591
Pedro Juan Caballero 53,601
San Lorenzo (★Asunción) 133,311

PERU / Perú

1981 C 17,031,221
Arequipa (★446,942) 108,023
Ayacucho (★69,533) 57,432
Breña (★Lima) 112,398
Cajamarca 62,259
Callao (★Lima) 264,133
Castilla (★207,934) 144,609
Cerro de Pasco (★66,373) 55,597
Chiclayo (★279,527) 213,095
Chimbote 223,341
Chorrillos (★Lima) 141,881
Chosica 65,139
Cusco (★184,550) 89,563
Huancayo (★164,954) 84,845
Huánuco 61,812
Ica 114,786
Iquitos 178,738
Jesús María (★Lima) 83,179
Juliaca 87,651
La Victoria (★Lima) 270,778
•LIMA (★4,608,010) 371,122
Lince (★Lima) 80,456
Magdalena (★Lima) 55,535
Miraflores (★Lima) 103,453
Pisco 55,604
Piura (★207,934) 144,609
Pucallpa 112,263
Pueblo Libre (★Lima) 83,985
Puno 67,397
Rímac (★Lima) 184,484
San Isidro (★Lima) 71,203
San Martín de Porras (★Lima) 404,856
Sullana 89,037
Surco (★Lima) 146,636
Surquillo (★Lima) 134,158
Tacna 97,173
Talara 57,351
Trujillo (★354,301) 202,469
Vitarte (★Lima) 145,504

PHILIPPINES / Pilipinas

1995 C 68,616,536
Angeles 234,011
Antipolo (▲207,842) (1990 C) 83,641
Bacolod 402,345
Bacoor (★Manila) (1990 C) 159,685
Baguio 226,883
Baliuag (1990 C) 89,719
Biñan (★Manila) (1990 C) 134,553
Binangonan (1990 C) 127,561
Bocaue (1990 C) 67,243
Butuan 247,074
Cabanatuan (▲173,065) (1990 C) 74,966
Cagayan de Oro 428,314
Cainta (★Manila) (1990 C) 126,839
Calamba (▲173,453) (1990 C) 97,623
Caloocan 1,023,159
Calumpit (1990 C) 59,042
Cavite (★195,000) (1990 C) 91,641
Cebu (★900,000) 662,299
Cotabato (1990 C) 127,065
Dagupan (1990 C) 122,247
Davao 1,006,840
Dumaguete (1990 C) 80,262
General Santos 327,173
Guagua (1990 C) 88,290
Iligan 273,004
Iloilo 334,539
Jolo (1990 C) 53,055
Lapu-Lapu (1990 C) 146,194
Las Piñas (★Manila) 413,086
Legaspi (▲121,116) (1990 C) 62,974
Lucena 177,750
Mabalacat (▲121,115) (1990 C) 64,261
Macabebe (1990 C) 55,505
Makati (★Manila) 484,176
Malabon (★Manila) 347,484
Malolos (1990 C) 125,178
Mandaluyong (★Manila) 286,870
Mandaue (★Cebu) 194,745
Mangaldan (1990 C) 65,947
•MANILA (★11,200,000) 1,654,761
Marawi (1990 C) 92,000
Marikina (★Manila) 357,231
Mariveles (▲60,761) (1990 C) 52,000
Meycauayan (★Manila) (1990 C) 123,982
Muntinglupa (★Manila) 399,846
Naga (1990 C) 115,329
Navotas (★Manila) 229,039
Olongapo 179,754
Parañaque (★Manila) 391,296
Pasay (★Manila) 408,610
Pasig (★Manila) 471,075
Pateros (★Manila) 55,286
Quezon City (★Manila) 1,989,419
San Fernando (1990 C) 157,851
San Juan del Monte (★Manila) 124,187
San Pablo (▲161,630) (1990 C) 80,671
San Pedro (1990 C) 156,486
Santa Cruz (1990 C) 76,603
Santa Rosa (★Manila) (1990 C) 94,719
Tacloban (1990 C) 137,190
Tagbilaran (1990 C) 56,363
Taguig (★Manila) 381,350
Tagum (▲135,440) (1990 C) 60,865
Taytay (★Manila) (1990 C) 112,403
Valenzuela (★Manila) 437,165
Zamboanga 511,139

PITCAIRN

1988 C 59
•ADAMSTOWN 59

POLAND / Polska

1993 E 38,505,000
Będzin (★Katowice) 63,385
Bełchatów 60,183
Biała Podlaska 55,620
Białystok 276,045
Bielsko-Biała 180,953
Bydgoszcz 384,830
Bytom (★Katowice) 229,605
Chełm 68,569
Chorzów (★Katowice) 127,049
Częstochowa 259,864
Dąbrowa Górnicza (★Katowice) 132,784
Dzierżoniów (★90,000) 38,401
Elbląg 127,828
Ełk 54,190
Gdańsk (Danzig) (★892,000) 463,058
Gdynia 250,590
Gliwice 214,494
Głogów 74,347
Gniezno 70,765
Gorzów Wielkopolski (Landsberg) 124,998
Grudziądz 103,733
Inowrocław 79,259
Jastrzębie-Zdrój 103,629
Jaworzno (★Katowice) 98,437
Jelenia Góra 93,213
Kalisz 106,680
•Katowice (★2,770,000) 359,408
Kędzierzyn-Koźle 71,170
Kielce 214,086
Konin 82,137

▲ Population of an entire municipality, commune, or district, including rural areas
• Largest city in country
★ Population or designation of the metroplitan area, including suburbs
★★ Population of metropolitan agglomeration
C Census E Official estimate U Unofficial estimate

Koszalin	111,140
Kraków (★823,000)	745,101
Kutno	51,053
Legionowo (★Warszawa)	50,582
Legnica	107,108
Leszno	60,490
Łódź (★950,000)	833,698
Łomża	62,250
Lubin	83,352
Lublin (★390,000)	351,646
Mielec	64,128
Mysłowice (★Katowice)	93,646
Nowy Sőcz	81,238
Olsztyn	166,142
Opole	129,978
Ostrołęka	53,337
Ostrów Wielkopolski	74,397
Ostrowiec Świętokrzyski	79,541
Pabianice (★Łódź)	75,968
Piekary Śląskie	67,532
Piła	75,170
Piotrków Trybunalski	81,403
Płock	125,894
Poznań (★666,000)	582,813
Pruszków (★Warszawa)	53,503
Przemyśl	68,657
Puławy	54,654
Racibórz	64,875
Radom	231,626
Radomsko	51,014
Ruda Śląska (★Katowice)	167,971
Rybnik	143,793
Rzeszów	158,510
Siedlce	73,545
Siemianowice Śląskie (★Katowice)	79,086
Skarżysko-Kamienna	51,370
Słupsk (Stolp)	102,449
Sosnowiec (★Katowice)	250,398
Stalowa Wola	72,019
Starachowice	57,299
Stargard Szczeciński	72,547
Starogard Gdański	50,370
Suwałki	64,923
Świdnica	64,618
Świętochłowice (★Katowice)	60,155
Szczecin (Stettin) (★449,000)	417,747
Tarnobrzeg	50,334
Tarnów	122,219
Tarnowskie Góry (★Katowice)	75,548
Tczew	60,046
Tomaszów Mazowiecki	69,898
Toruń	203,147
Tychy (★Katowice)	136,754
Wałbrzych (★207,000)	140,294
WARSZAWA (WARSAW) (★2,312,000)	1,642,694
Włocławek	122,882
Wodzisław Śląski	88,528
Wrocław (Breslau)	642,332
Zabrze (★Katowice)	203,950
Zamość	65,421
Zawiercie	56,564
Zgierz (★Łódź)	59,047
Zielona Góra	115,557
Żory	66,558

PORTUGAL

1991 E	9,862,540
Agualva-Cacém (★Lisboa)	56,779
Amadora (★Lisboa)	140,001
Barreiro (★Lisboa)	59,449
Braga	102,665
Carnaxide	79,081
Coimbra	118,856
•LISBOA (LISBON) (★2,350,000)	663,394
Odivelas (★Lisboa)	53,531
Porto (★1,230,000)	302,472
Queluz (★Lisboa)	60,370
Setúbal	85,289

PUERTO RICO

1990 C	3,522,037
Aguadilla (★150,000)	18,347
Arecibo (★160,500)	49,545
Bayamón (▲220,262) (★San Juan)	202,103
Caguas (▲133,447) (★San Juan)	92,429
Carolina (▲177,806) (★San Juan)	162,404
Guaynabo (▲92,886) (★San Juan)	73,385
Mayagüez (★200,600)	83,010
Ponce (★232,700)	159,151
•SAN JUAN (★1,877,000)	426,832

QATAR / Qaṭar

1994 E	593,007
•AD-DAWHAH (★500,000)	361,540
Ar-Rayyān (★Ad-Dawḥah)	152,246

REUNION / Réunion

1990 C	597,213
•SAINT-DENIS	121,999
Saint-Paul	71,669
Saint-Pierre	58,846

ROMANIA / România

1992 C	22,810,035
Alba Iulia	71,168
Alexandria	58,478
Arad	190,144
Bacău	205,029
Baia Mare	149,205
Bârlad	77,518
Bistrița	87,710
Botoșani	126,145
Brăila	234,110
Brașov	323,736
•BUCUREȘTI (BUCHAREST) (★2,300,000)	2,067,545
Buzău	148,087
Călărași	76,952
Cluj-Napoca	328,602
Constanța	350,581
Craiova	303,959
Deva	78,438
Drobeta-Turnu Severin	115,259
Focșani	101,335
Galați	326,141
Giurgiu	74,191
Hunedoara	81,337
Iași	344,425
Lugoj	50,939
Mediaș	64,484
Onești	58,810
Oradea	222,741
Petroșani	52,390
Piatra-Neamț	123,360
Pitești	179,337
Ploiești (★312,000)	252,715
Râmnicu Vâlcea	113,624
Reșița	96,918
Roman	80,328
Satu Mare	131,987
Sfântu Gheorghe	68,359
Sibiu	169,656
Slatina	85,168
Slobozia	56,048
Suceava	114,462
Târgoviște	98,117
Târgu Jiu	98,238
Târgu Mureș	164,445
Timișoara	334,115
Tulcea	97,904
Turda	61,200
Vaslui	80,614
Zalău	68,404

RUSSIA / Rossija

1992 E	148,700,000
Abakan	158,000
Ačinsk	122,000
Ahtubinsk (1991 E)	50,800
Alapaevsk (1991 E)	50,300
Aleksandrov (1991 E)	68,600
Aleksin (1991 E)	74,200
Al'metevsk	133,000
Amursk (1991 E)	59,600
Anapa (1991 E)	55,900
Angarsk	269,000
Anžero-Sudžensk	106,000
Apatity (1991 E)	88,600
Arhangel'sk	414,000
Armavir	163,000
Arsenev (1991 E)	71,200
Art'em (1991 E)	70,100
Arzamas	112,000
Asbest (1991 E)	84,900
Astrahan'	512,000
Azov (1991 E)	80,700
Balakovo	203,000
Balašiha (★Moskva)	138,000
Balašov (1991 E)	97,300
Barnaul (★673,000)	606,000
Batajsk (★Rostov-na-Donu) (1991 E)	93,300
Belebej (1991 E)	54,500
Belgorod	314,000
Belogorsk (1991 E)	74,300
Belorečensk (1991 E)	51,900
Beloreck (1991 E)	73,100
Belovo	92,900
Berdsk (★Novosibirsk) (1991 E)	80,400
Berezniki	197,000
Berëzovskij (1991 E)	51,900
Bijsk	235,000
Birobidžan (1991 E)	86,300
Blagoveščensk	214,000
Bol'šoj Kamen' (1991 E)	67,600
Bor (★Nižnij Novgorod) (1991 E)	64,500
Borisoglebsk (1991 E)	72,100
Boroviči (1991 E)	62,800
Bratsk	259,000
Brjansk	461,000
Budënnovsk (1991 E)	57,500
Bugul'ma (1991 E)	91,100
Buguruslan (1991 E)	54,100
Bujnaksk (1991 E)	57,900
Buzuluk (1991 E)	85,100
Čajkovskij (1991 E)	88,300
Čapaevsk (1991 E)	96,000
Čebarkul' (1991 E)	50,700
Čeboksary	442,000
Čehov (1991 E)	60,200
Čeljabinsk (★1,325,000)	1,143,000
Čeremhovo (1991 E)	73,600
Čerepovec	317,000
Čerkessk	119,000
Černogorsk (1991 E)	79,700
Čistopol' (1991 E)	66,600
Čita	377,000
Čusovoj (1991 E)	58,000
Dal'negorsk (1991 E)	50,300
Derbent (1991 E)	81,500
Dimitrovgrad	129,000
Dmitrov (1991 E)	65,600
Dolgoprudnyj (★Moskva) (1991 E)	71,100
Domodedovo (★Moskva) (1991 E)	56,300
Dubna (1991 E)	67,200
Dzeržinsk (★Nižnij Novgorod)	287,000
Efremov (1991 E)	56,600
Egorevsk (1991 E)	74,200
Ejsk (1991 E)	79,400
Ekaterinburg (★1,620,000)	1,371,000
Elabuga (1991 E)	60,500
Elec	121,000
Elektrostal'	153,000
Elista (1991 E)	92,700
Engel's (★Saratov)	183,000
Ermolaevo (1991 E)	65,600
Ëškar-Ola	249,000
Essentuki (1991 E)	86,300
Frjazino (1991 E)	54,000
Gatčina (★Sankt-Peterburg) (1991 E)	80,600
Georgievsk (1991 E)	63,700
Glazov	107,000
Groznyj	388,000
Gubkin (1991 E)	76,400
Gukovo (1991 E)	67,700
Gus'-Hrustal'nyj (1991 E)	77,000
Habarovsk	615,000
Hasavjurt (1991 E)	72,800
Himki (★Moskva)	135,000
Holmsk (1991 E)	51,800
Inta (1991 E)	60,900
Irbit (1991 E)	51,300
Irkutsk	639,000
Išim (1991 E)	65,900
Išimbaj (1991 E)	71,000
Iskitim (1991 E)	68,700
Ivanovo	480,000
Ivanteevka (★Moskva) (1991 E)	53,200
Iževsk	651,000
Jakutsk	198,000
Jarcevo (1991 E)	54,000
Jaroslavl'	637,000
Jurga (1991 E)	94,000
Južno-Sahalinsk	165,000
Kaliningrad (Königsberg)	411,000
Kaliningrad (★Moskva)	162,000
Kaluga	347,000
Kamensk-Šahtinskij (1991 E)	73,100
Kamensk-Ural'skij	209,000
Kamyšin	125,000
Kanaš (1991 E)	56,100
Kandalakša (1991 E)	54,300
Kansk	110,000
Kaspijsk (1991 E)	61,900
Kazan' (★1,165,000)	1,104,000
Kemerovo	521,000
Kimry (1991 E)	62,000
Kinešma	104,000
Kingisepp (1991 E)	50,600
Kiriši (1991 E)	53,100
Kirov	493,000
Kirovo-Čepeck (1991 E)	95,600
Kiselëvsk (★Prokopevsk)	126,000
Kislovodsk	118,000
Klimovsk (★Moskva) (1991 E)	57,600
Klin (1991 E)	95,100
Klincy (1991 E)	71,200
Kolomna	164,000
Kolpino (★Sankt-Peterburg)	145,000
Komsomol'sk-na-Amure	319,000
Kopejsk (★Čeljabinsk) (1991 E)	78,300
Kostroma	282,000
Kotlas (1991 E)	68,900
Kovrov	162,000
Krasnodar	635,000
Krasnogorsk (★Moskva) (1991 E)	91,700
Krasnojarsk	925,000
Krasnokamensk (1991 E)	57,800
Krasnokamsk (1991 E)	67,000
Krasnoturjinsk (1991 E)	67,200
Kropotkin (1991 E)	76,600
Krymsk (1991 E)	51,100
Kstovo (★Nižnij Novgorod) (1991 E)	65,300
Kujbyšev (1991 E)	51,600
Kungur (1991 E)	81,800
Kurgan	365,000
Kursk	435,000
Kuzneck	101,000
Kyzyl (1991 E)	88,000
Labinsk (1991 E)	58,600
Leninogorsk (1991 E)	63,300
Leninsk-Kuzneckij	132,000
Lesosibirsk (1991 E)	69,300
Lipeck	464,000
Liski (1991 E)	54,600
Livny (1991 E)	52,600
Ljubercy (★Moskva)	164,000
Lobnja (★Moskva) (1991 E)	61,000
Lys'va (1991 E)	77,800
Lytkarino (★Moskva) (1991 E)	51,700
Magadan	152,000
Magnitogorsk	441,000
Mahačkala	339,000
Majkop	155,000
Meleuz (1991 E)	55,200
Meždurečensk	108,000
Miass	170,000
Mičurinsk	109,000
Mihajlovka (1991 E)	58,700
Mineral'nye Vody (1991 E)	72,500
Minusinsk (1991 E)	74,200
Mončegorsk (1991 E)	68,100
Moršansk (1991 E)	50,500
•MOSKVA (MOSCOW) (★13,170,000)	8,747,000
Murmansk	468,000
Murom	127,000
Mytišči (★Moskva)	154,000
Naberežnye Čelny	514,000
Nadym (1991 E)	52,200
Nahodka	166,000
Nal'čik	242,000
Naro-Fominsk (1991 E)	58,800
Nazarovo (1991 E)	65,200
Neftejugansk (1991 E)	65,500
Nerjungri (1991 E)	77,200
Nevinnomyssk	125,000
Nikolo-Berëzovka	113,000
Nižnekamsk	199,000
Nižnevartovsk	243,000
Nižnij Novgorod (Gorki) (★2,025,000)	1,441,000
Nižnij Tagil	437,000
Njagan (1991 E)	59,800
Noginsk	122,000
Nojabr'sk (1991 E)	88,900
Noril'sk	165,000
Novgorod	235,000
Novoaltajsk (★Barnaul) (1991 E)	55,200
Novočeboksarsk	121,000
Novočerkassk	188,000
Novodvinsk (1991 E)	50,300
Novokujbyševsk (★Samara)	113,000
Novokuzneck	600,000
Novomoskovsk (Stalinogorsk) (★365,000)	145,000
Novorossijsk	190,000
Novošahtinsk	107,000
Novosibirsk (★1,600,000)	1,442,000
Novotroick	107,000
Novyj Urengoj (1991 E)	93,600
Obninsk	105,000
Odincovo (★Moskva)	129,000
Oktjabr'skij	107,000
Omsk (★1,195,000)	1,169,000
Orehovo-Zuevo (★205,000)	136,000
Orel	347,000
Orenburg	557,000
Orsk	273,000
Osinniki (1991 E)	63,200
Partizansk (1991 E)	50,000
Pavlovo (1991 E)	72,200
Pavlovskij Posad (1991 E)	70,800
Pečora (1991 E)	65,500
Penza	552,000
Perm' (★1,180,000)	1,099,000
Pervoural'sk	144,000
Petrodvorec (★Sankt-Peterburg) (1991 E)	83,800
Petropavlovsk-Kamčatskij	273,000
Petrozavodsk	280,000
Pjatigorsk	132,000
Podol'sk (★Moskva)	208,000
Polevskoj (1991 E)	71,900
Prohladnyj (1991 E)	58,500
Prokopevsk (★410,000)	272,000
Pskov	209,000
Puškin (★Sankt-Peterburg) (1991 E)	95,300
Puškino (★Moskva) (1991 E)	75,800
Ramenskoe (1991 E)	88,800
Reutov (★Moskva) (1991 E)	68,900
Revda (1991 E)	66,000
Rjazan'	529,000
Roslavl' (1991 E)	60,700
Rossoš' (1991 E)	58,900
Rostov-na-Donu (★1,165,000)	1,027,000
Rubcovsk	172,000
Ruzaevka (1991 E)	52,100
Rybinsk	252,000
Ržev (1991 E)	70,900
Šadrinsk (1991 E)	87,500
Šafonovo (1991 E)	56,300
Šahty	228,000
Sajanogorsk (1991 E)	53,000
Salavat	152,000
Sal'sk (1991 E)	61,700
Samara (★1,505,000)	1,239,000
Sankt-Peterburg (Saint Petersburg) (★5,525,000)	4,437,000
Saransk	322,000
Sarapul	111,000
Saratov (★1,155,000)	909,000
Šatka (1991 E)	51,100
Ščekino (1991 E)	68,800
Ščelkovo (★Moskva)	109,000
Sergiev Posad	116,000
Serov	106,000
Serpuhov	141,000
Severodvinsk (Molotovsk)	250,000
Severomorsk (1991 E)	66,200
Slavjansk-na-Kubani (1991 E)	58,500
Smolensk	352,000
Soči	344,000
Solikamsk	110,000
Solnečnogorsk (★Moskva) (1991 E)	56,700
Sosnovyj Bor (1991 E)	56,700
Spassk-Dal'nij (1991 E)	61,100
Staryj Oskol	184,000
Stavropol'	332,000
Sterlitamak	254,000
Stupino (1991 E)	74,600
Šuja (1991 E)	69,000
Surgut	260,000
Svetlogorsk (1991 E)	71,600
Svobodnyj (1991 E)	80,900
Syktyvkar	226,000
Syzran'	175,000
Taganrog	293,000
Talnah (1991 E)	65,600
Tambov	311,000
Tihoreck (1991 E)	67,600
Tihvin (1991 E)	71,800
Tjumen'	496,000
Tobol'sk (1991 E)	96,800
Toljatti	666,000
Tomsk	505,000
Toržok (1991 E)	50,500
Troick (1991 E)	89,800
Tuapse (1991 E)	63,800
Tujmazy (1991 E)	59,800
Tula (★640,000)	541,000
Tulun (1991 E)	53,700
Tver' (Kalinin)	456,000
Tynda (1991 E)	64,700
Ufa (★1,118,000)	1,097,000
Uhta	112,000
Ulan-Ude	366,000
Uljanovsk	656,000
Usinsk (1991 E)	52,300
Usole-Sibirskoe	107,000
Ussurijsk	161,000
Ust'-Ilimsk	114,000
Ust'-Kut (1991 E)	61,800
Uzlovaja (★Novomoskovsk) (1991 E)	64,000
Velikie Luki	116,000
Verhnjaja Pyšma (★Sverdlovsk) (1991 E)	53,500
Verhnjaja Salda (1991 E)	55,100
Vidnoe (★Moskva) (1991 E)	56,900
Vjaz'ma (1991 E)	59,900
Vladikavkaz	325,000
Vladimir	356,000
Vladivostok	648,000
Volgodonsk	182,000
Volgograd (★1,360,000)	1,006,000
Volhov (1991 E)	50,100
Vologda	290,000
Vol'sk (1991 E)	65,500
Volžsk (1991 E)	62,000
Volžskij (★Volgograd)	281,000
Vorkuta	116,000
Voronež	902,000
Voskresensk (1991 E)	81,400
Votkinsk	105,000
Vyborg (Viipuri) (1991 E)	81,100
Vyksa (1991 E)	62,200
Vyšnij Voloček (1991 E)	64,600
Zarinsk (1991 E)	51,800
Zarinskaja (1991 E)	51,800
Zelenodol'sk (1991 E)	97,000
Zelenograd (★Moskva)	170,000
Železnodorožnyj (★Moskva) (1991 E)	99,300
Železnogorsk (1991 E)	89,200
Zlatoust	208,000
Žukovskij	101,000

RWANDA

1991 C	6,762,145
•KIGALI	232,733

SAINT HELENA

1987 C	5,644
•JAMESTOWN	1,413

SAINT KITTS AND NEVIS

1980 C	44,404
•BASSETERRE	14,725

SAINT LUCIA

1991 C	133,308
•CASTRIES (★13,138)	11,147

SAINT PIERRE AND MIQUELON

1990 C	6,277
•SAINT-PIERRE	5,580

SAINT VINCENT AND THE GRENADINES

1991 C	106,499
•KINGSTOWN (★26,223)	15,466

SAMOA

1991 C	161,298
•APIA	34,126

SAN MARINO

1989 E	23,000
•SAN MARINO	2,794

SAO TOME AND PRINCIPE / São Tomé e Príncipe

1991 C	117,504
•SÃO TOMÉ	5,245

SAUDI ARABIA / Al-'Arabīyah as-Su'ūdīyah

1980 E	9,229,000
Ad-Dammām	200,000
Al-Hufūf (1974 C)	101,271
Al-Madīnah	290,000
Al-Mubarraz (1974 C)	54,325
AR-RIYĀḌ	1,250,000
At-Ṭā'if	300,000
Buraydah (1974 C)	69,940
•Jiddah	1,300,000
Makkah	550,000
Tabūk (1974 C)	74,825

SENEGAL / Sénégal

1988 C	6,892,720
•DAKAR	1,490,450
Diourbel	77,548
Kaolack	152,007
Louga	52,763
Mbour	95,754
Rufisque	95,000
Saint-Louis	160,689
Thiès	184,902
Ziguinchor	124,283

SEYCHELLES

1994 C	74,331
•VICTORIA	24,907

SIERRA LEONE

1985 C	3,515,812
Bo	59,768
•FREETOWN (★525,000)	469,776
Kenema	52,473
Koidu-Sefagu	82,474

SINGAPORE

1990 C	2,690,100
•SINGAPORE (★3,025,000)	2,690,100

SLOVAKIA / Slovensko

1994 E	5,347,000
Banská Bystrica	84,575
•BRATISLAVA	441,453
Košice	238,886
Martin	60,155
Nitra	86,679
Poprad	54,505
Prešov	90,963
Prievidza	54,264
Trenčín	57,748
Trnava	71,624
Žilina	85,686

SLOVENIA / Slovenija

1991 C	1,974,839
•LJUBLJANA	292,589
Maribor	124,650

SOLOMON ISLANDS

1986 C	285,176
•HONIARA	30,413

SOMALIA / Soomaaliya

1984 E	5,423,000
Berbera	65,000
Hargeysa	70,000
Kismaayo	70,000
Marka	60,000
•MUQDISHO	600,000

SOUTH AFRICA / Suid-Afrika

1991 C	30,986,920
Alberton (★Johannesburg)	76,642
Alexandra (★Johannesburg)	124,586
Atteridgeville (★Pretoria)	92,008
Bellville (★Cape Town)	78,822
Benoni (★Johannesburg)	113,501
Bloemfontein (★280,000)	126,867
Blue Downs	60,781
Boksburg (★Johannesburg)	119,890
Botshabelo (★Bloemfontein)	117,926
Brakpan (★Johannesburg)	53,522
CAPE TOWN (KAAPSTAD) (★1,900,000)	854,616
Carletonville (★175,000)	118,699
Daveyton (★Johannesburg)	151,659
Diepmeadow (★Johannesburg)	241,099
Dobsonville (★Johannesburg)	53,091
Durban (★1,740,000)	715,669
East London (Oos-Londen) (★365,000)	102,325
Edendale	72,063
Elsiesrivier (★Cape Town)	82,045
eMbalenhle	56,502
Evaton (★Vereeniging)	201,026
Ezakheni	55,532
Galeshewe (★Kimberley)	72,118
Germiston (★Johannesburg)	134,005
Grassy Park (★Cape Town)	52,675
Guguletu (★Cape Town)	54,635
Ibhayi (★Port Elizabeth)	257,054
Ikageng (★Potchefstroom)	54,545
•Johannesburg (★4,000,000)	712,507
Jouberton (★Klerksdorp)	74,377
Kagiso (★Johannesburg)	61,680
Katlehong (★Johannesburg)	201,785
Kempton Park (★Johannesburg)	106,606
Khayelitsha (★Cape Town)	189,586
Kimberley (★160,000)	80,082
Klerksdorp (★275,000)	58,923
Krugersdorp (★Johannesburg)	81,584
Kwaguqa (★Witbank)	66,673
KwaMashu (★Durban)	156,679
KwaNgendezi (★Durban)	50,835
KwaNobuhle (★Port Elizabeth)	92,381
KwaThema (★Johannesburg)	81,345
Lekoa (★Vereeniging)	217,582
Madadeni (★Newcastle)	95,931
Mamelodi (★Pretoria)	154,845

▲ Population of an entire municipality, commune, or district, including rural areas
• Largest city in country
★ Population or designation of the metroplitan area, including suburbs
★★ Population of metropolitan agglomeration
C Census E Official estimate U Unofficial estimate

City	Population
Mangaung (★Bloemfontein)	125,545
Maokeng (★Kroonstad)	55,064
Mdantsana (★East London) (1986 E)	242,823
Motherwell (★Port Elizabeth)	72,999
Mpumalanga (★Durban)	62,140
Newcastle (★170,000)	38,767
Newtown (★Durban)	60,696
Ntuzuma (★Durban)	102,310
Nyanga (★Cape Town)	92,896
Orange Farm	49,838
Osizweni (★Durban)	78,079
Paarl	73,415
Parow (★Cape Town)	68,081
Pietermaritzburg (★265,000)	156,473
Pinetown (★Durban)	70,001
Port Elizabeth (★810,000)	303,353
Potchefstroom (★102,000)	46,538
PRETORIA (★1,100,000)	525,583
Randburg (★Johannesburg)	90,557
Randfontein (★Johannesburg)	51,940
Roodepoort (★Johannesburg)	162,632
Soshanguve (★Pretoria)	146,334
Soweto (★Johannesburg)	596,632
Springs (★Johannesburg)	72,647
Tembisa (★Johannesburg)	209,238
Thabong (★Welkom)	88,547
Tokoza (★Johannesburg)	74,071
Tsakane (★Johannesburg)	76,858
Uitenhage	67,581
Umlazi (★Durban)	299,275
Vanderbijlpark (★Vereeniging)	67,291
Vereeniging (★675,000)	71,255
Verwoerdburg (★Pretoria)	80,552
Vosloosrus (★Johannesburg)	76,015
Welkom (★156,658)	68,111
Westonaria (★Johannesburg)	57,177
Witbank (★114,612)	47,939
Worcester (★63,077)	54,371

SPAIN / España

City	Population
1988 E	39,217,804
A Coruña (Corunna)	248,862
Alacant (Alicante)	261,051
Albacete	125,997
Alcalá de Guadaira	50,935
Alcalá de Henares (★Madrid)	150,021
Alcobendas (★Madrid)	73,455
Alcoi	66,074
Alcorcón (★Madrid)	139,796
Algeciras	99,528
Almería	157,644
Avilés (★131,000)	87,811
Badajoz (▲122,407)	106,400
Badalona (★Barcelona)	225,229
Barakaldo (★Bilbao)	113,502
Barcelona (★4,040,000)	1,714,355
Bilbao (★985,000)	384,733
Burgos	160,561
Cáceres	71,598
Cádiz (★240,000)	156,591
Cartagena (▲172,710)	70,000
Castelló de la Plana	131,809
Ciudad Real	56,300
Córdoba (Cordova)	302,301
Coslada (★Madrid)	68,765
Donostia (★285,000)	177,622
Dos Hermanas (▲68,456)	60,600
El Prat de Llobregat (★Barcelona)	64,193
El Puerto de Santa María (▲62,285)	49,900
Elda	56,756
Elx (▲180,256)	158,300
Ferrol (★129,000)	86,503
Fuenlabrada (★Madrid)	128,872
Gasteiz (Vitoria)	204,264
Getafe (★Madrid)	135,367
Gijón	262,156
Granada	263,334
Guadalajara	61,309
Huelva	137,826
Irún	54,886
Jaén	106,435
Jerez de la Frontera (▲183,007)	156,200
La Línea de la Concepción	60,956
Las Palmas de Gran Canaria (▲366,347)	319,000
Leganés (★Madrid)	168,403
León (★159,000)	136,558
L'Hospitalet de Llobregat (★Barcelona)	278,449
Linares	58,622
Lleida (Lérida) (▲109,795)	91,500
Logroño	119,038
Lugo (▲78,795)	68,700
•MADRID (★4,650,000)	3,102,846
Málaga	574,456
Manresa	65,607
Mataró	100,817
Mérida	52,368
Móstoles (★Madrid)	181,648
Murcia (▲314,124)	149,800
Ourense	106,042
Oviedo (▲190,073)	168,900
Palencia	76,692
Palma de Mallorca (▲314,608)	249,000
Pamplona	180,598
Parla (★Madrid)	66,253
Portugalete (★Bilbao)	57,813
Puertollano	52,284
Reus	83,800
Sabadell (★Barcelona)	189,489
Salamanca	159,342
San Fernando (★Cádiz)	81,975
San Sebastián de los Reyes (★Madrid)	51,653
Sant Boi de Llobregat (★Barcelona)	77,502
Santa Coloma de Gramenet (★Barcelona)	136,042
Santa Cruz de Tenerife	215,228
Santander (▲190,795)	166,800
Santiago de Compostela (▲88,110)	68,800
Santurce-Antiguo (★Bilbao)	52,334
Segovia	54,402
Sevilla (Seville) (★945,000)	663,132
Talavera de la Reina	68,158
Tarragona (▲109,586)	63,500
Terrassa (Tarrasa)	161,410
Toledo	59,551
Torrejón de Ardoz (★Madrid)	83,267
Torrent (★València)	55,751
València (★1,270,000)	743,933
Valladolid	331,461
Vigo (▲271,128)	179,500
Zamora	62,047
Zaragoza (Saragossa)	582,239

SPANISH NORTH AFRICA / Plazas de Soberanía en el Norte de África

City	Population
1988 E	122,905
•Ceuta	67,188
Melilla	55,717

SRI LANKA

City	Population
1989 E	16,806,000
Battaramulla (★Colombo) (1981 C)	56,535
Batticaloa	50,000
•COLOMBO (★2,050,000)	612,000
Dehiwala-Mount Lavinia (★Colombo)	193,000
Galle	83,000
Jaffna	128,000
Kandy	103,000
Moratuwa (★Colombo)	166,000
Negombo	64,000
SRI JAYAWARDENEPURA (KOTTE) (★Colombo)	108,000

SUDAN / As-Sūdān

City	Population
1983 C	20,594,197
Al-Fāshir	84,298
Al-Junaynah	55,460
•AL-KHARTŪM (★1,450,000)	473,597
Al-Kharṭūm Baḥrī (★Al-Kharṭūm)	340,857
Al-Qaḍārif	116,876
Al-Ubayyid	137,582
'Aṭbarah	72,836
Būr Sūdān	206,038
Juba	84,377
Kassalā	141,429
Kūstī	89,135
Nyala	111,693
Umm Durmān (★Al-Kharṭūm)	526,192
Wad Madanī	145,015
Wāw	90,960

SURINAME

City	Population
1988 E	392,000
•PARAMARIBO (★296,000)	241,000
Wanica (★Paramaribo)	55,000

SWAZILAND

City	Population
1986 C	712,131
LOBAMBA	
Manzini (★30,000)	18,084
•MBABANE	38,290

SWEDEN / Sverige

City	Population
1990 C	8,587,353
Borås	59,817
Eskilstuna	59,899
Gävle	67,320
Göteborg (Gothenburg)	398,682
Helsingborg	81,769
Huddinge (★Stockholm)	73,785
Järfälla (★Stockholm)	56,270
Jönköping	76,443
Karlstad	53,025
Linköping	82,450
Lund	62,918
Malmö	223,691
Nacka (★Stockholm)	63,959
Norrköping	82,693
Örebro	85,970
Södertälje (★Stockholm)	57,906
Solna (★Stockholm)	51,718
•STOCKHOLM (★1,491,726)	674,452
Sundsvall	50,440
Täby (★Stockholm)	54,550
Umeå	60,371
Uppsala	109,551
Västerås	98,269

SWITZERLAND / Helvetia / Schweiz / Suisse / Svizzera

City	Population
1990 C	6,873,687
Basel (Bâle) (★587,000)	178,428
BERN (BERNE) (★300,400)	136,338
Biel (Bienne) (★83,100)	51,893
Genève (Geneva) (★470,000)	171,042
Lausanne (★265,000)	128,112
Lugano (★94,700)	25,344
Luzern (Lucerne) (★165,000)	61,034
Sankt Gallen (★127,000)	75,237
Thun (★79,500)	38,211
Winterthur (★110,500)	86,959
•Zürich (★870,000)	365,043

SYRIA / Sūrīyah

City	Population
1994 E	13,844,000
Al-Hasakah (1981 C)	73,426
Al-Kiswah	99,050
Al-Lādhiqīyah (Latakia)	306,535
Al-Qāmishlī (1988 E)	126,236
Ar-Raqqah	219,016
At-Tall	66,248
Dar'ā	180,093
Dārayyā (★Dimashq) (1988 E)	53,204
Dayr az-Zawr	174,085
•DIMASHQ (DAMASCUS) (★2,230,000)	1,549,932
Dūmā (★Dimashq)	131,158
Halab (Aleppo) (★1,640,000)	1,591,400
Hamāh (1988 E)	222,000
Ḥimṣ (Homs)	644,204
Idlib	113,360
Jaramānah (★Dimashq)	138,469
Tartūs	136,812

TAIWAN / T'aiwan

City	Population
1992 E	20,752,500
Changhua (▲215,224) (1991 E)	165,000
Chiai	258,713
Chilung	357,000
Chungho (★T'aipei) (1991 E)	374,339
Chungli (1991 E)	269,804
Chutung (1988 E)	104,797
Fangshan (★Kaohsiung) (1991 E)	290,777
Fengyüan (▲151,642) (1991 E)	121,100
Hsichih (★T'aipei) (1980 C)	70,031
Hsinchu	330,576
Hsinchuang (★T'aipei) (1991 E)	299,174
Hsintien (★T'aipei) (1991 E)	225,517
Hualien (1991 E)	107,552
Ilan (▲81,751) (1980 C)	70,900
Kangshan (1980 C)	78,049
Kaohsiung (★1,845,000)	1,401,239
Lotung (1980 C)	57,925
Lukang (1980 C)	72,019
Miaoli (1980 C)	81,500
Nant'ou (1980 C)	84,038
P'ingchen (★T'aipei) (1991 E)	147,030
P'ingtung (▲210,801) (1991 E)	172,400
Sanchung (★T'aipei) (1991 E)	375,996
Shulin (★T'aipei) (1991 E)	111,993
Tach'i (1980 C)	67,209
T'aichung	785,182
T'ainan	692,116
•T'AIPEI (★6,200,000)	2,706,453
T'aipeihsien (★T'aipei) (1991 E)	538,954
T'aitung (▲108,196) (1991 E)	79,100
Taoyüan (1991 E)	241,263
T'oufen (1980 C)	66,536
T'uch'eng (▲136,928) (★T'aipei) (1991 E)	80,300
Yangmei (1980 C)	84,353
Yüanlin (▲121,251) (1991 E)	53,200
Yungho (★T'aipei) (1991 E)	249,736
Yungkang (▲136,705) (1991 E)	70,900

TAJIKISTAN / Tadžikistan

City	Population
1991 E	5,358,300
•DUŠANBE (★700,000)	582,400
Hudžand (★363,000)	164,500
Isfara (★103,000)	35,500
Kuljab	79,300
Kurgan-Tjube (★90,000)	58,400
Ura-Tjube (★95,000)	47,700

TANZANIA

City	Population
1985 E	21,733,000
Arusha (1984 E)	69,000
•DAR ES SALAAM	1,096,000
DODOMA	85,000
Iringa (1984 E)	67,000
Kigoma (1978 C)	50,044
Mbeya	194,000
Morogoro (1984 E)	72,000
Moshi (1984 E)	62,000
Mwanza	252,000
Tabora	214,000
Tanga	172,000
Zanzibar	133,000

THAILAND / Prathet Thai

City	Population
1991 E	56,961,030
Chiang Mai	161,541
Hat Yai	142,351
Khon Kaen	131,478
•KRUNG THEP (BANGKOK) (★7,060,000)	5,620,591
Nakhon Ratchasima	202,503
Nakhon Sawan	108,569
Nakhon Si Thammarat	74,219
Nonthaburi (★Krung Thep)	264,201
Pattaya	64,731
Phitsanulok	77,672
Phra Nakhon Si Ayutthaya	60,561
Samut Prakan (★Krung Thep)	71,538
Samut Sakhon	55,509
Saraburi	64,915
Songkhla	82,167
Ubon Ratchathani	98,950
Udon Thani	78,489
Yala	68,834

TOGO

City	Population
1987 E	3,148,000
•LOMÉ	500,000
Sokodé	55,000

TONGA

City	Population
1986 C	94,535
•NUKU'ALOFA	21,265

TRINIDAD AND TOBAGO

City	Population
1990 C	1,234,388
•PORT OF SPAIN (★370,000)	50,878
San Fernando (★75,000)	30,092

TUNISIA / Tunis

City	Population
1994 C	8,785,364
Ariana (★Tunis)	152,694
Bardo (★Tunis)	72,707
Béja	53,224
Ben Arous (★Tunis)	67,158
Bizerte (Binzert)	98,865
Gabès (★98,935)	65,725
Gafsa	71,107
Kairouan	102,634
Kasserine	68,258
La Goulette (★Tunis)	66,488
La Marsa (★Tunis)	54,611
Mohammedia Fouchana	50,897
Moknine	341,656
M'Saken	50,603
Sfax (★325,000)	230,855
Sousse (★210,000)	124,990
Tataouine	50,352
•TUNIS (★1,300,000)	674,142

TURKEY / Türkiye

City	Population
1990 C	56,473,035
Adana	916,150
Adıyaman	100,045
Afyon	95,643
Ağrı	58,038
Akhisar	73,944
Aksaray	90,698
Akşehir	51,746
Alanya	52,460
Amasya	57,288
ANKARA (★2,650,000)	2,559,471
Antalya	378,208
Aydın	107,011
Bafra	65,600
Balıkesir	170,589
Bandırma	77,444
Batman	147,347
Bolu	60,789
Burdur	56,432
Bursa	834,576
Çanakkale	53,995
Ceyhan	85,308
Cizre	50,023
Çorlu	74,681
Çorum	116,810
Darıca	53,560
Denizli	204,118
Diyarbakır	381,144
Düzce	61,878
Edirne	102,345
Elazığ	204,603
Elbistan	54,741
Ereğli	74,283
Ereğli	63,987
Erzincan	91,772
Erzurum	242,391
Esenyurt (★İstanbul)	70,280
Eskişehir	413,082
Gaziantep	603,434
Gebze (★İstanbul)	159,116
Gemlik	50,237
Giresun	67,604
Gölcük	64,911
Hatay (Antioch)	123,871
İçel (Mersin)	422,357
İnegöl	71,120
İskenderun (Alexandretta)	154,807
Isparta	112,117
•İstanbul (★7,550,000)	6,620,241
İzmir (Smyrna) (★1,900,000)	1,757,414
İzmit (Kocaeli)	256,882
Kadirli	55,061
Kahramanmaraş (Maraş)	228,129
Karabük	105,373
Karaman	76,525
Kars	78,455
Kastamonu	51,560
Kayseri	421,362
Kilis	82,882
Kırıkhan	68,601
Kırıkkale	185,431
Kırşehir	73,538
Kızıltepe	60,134
Konya	513,346
Körfez	65,786
Kozan	54,451
Kütahya	130,994
Lüleburgaz	52,384
Malatya	281,776
Manisa	158,928
Mardin	53,005
Nazilli	80,277
Nevşehir	52,719
Niğde	55,035
Nizip	58,604
Ödemiş	51,620
Ordu	102,107
Osmaniye	123,307
Polatlı	60,158
Rize	52,031
Sakarya	171,225
Salihli	70,861
Samsun	303,979
Şanlıurfa (Urfa)	276,528
Siirt	68,320
Silvan	59,865
Sivas	221,512
Siverek	63,049
Söke	50,866
Soma	49,977
Sultanbeyli (★İstanbul)	82,298
Tarsus	187,508
Tatvan	54,071
Tekirdağ	80,442
Tokat	83,058
Trabzon	143,941
Turgutlu	73,634
Turhal	68,384
Uşak	105,270
Van	153,111
Viranşehir	57,461
Yalova	65,823
Yozgat (★İstanbul)	50,335
Zonguldak (★220,000)	116,725

TURKMENISTAN / Turkmenija

City	Population
1991 E	3,714,100
•AŠGABAT	412,200
Čardžev	166,400
Dašhovuz	117,000
Mary	94,900
Nebitdag	89,100
Turkmenbaši	59,500

TURKS AND CAICOS ISLANDS

City	Population
1990 C	11,465
•GRAND TURK	3,691

TUVALU

City	Population
1979 C	7,349
•FUNAFUTI	2,191

UGANDA

City	Population
1991 C	16,582,700
Jinja	60,979
•KAMPALA	773,463
Mbale	53,634

UKRAINE / Ukraïna

City	Population
1992 E	52,200,000
Alchevs'k	127,000
Antratsyt (★Krasnyi Luch)	73,000
Artemivs'k	91,000
Berdians'k	137,000
Berdychiv	95,000
Bila Tserkva	209,000
Bilhorod-Dnistrovs'kyi	57,000
Boryspil' (★Kyïv)	53,000
Brianka (★Stachanov)	65,000
Brovary (★Kyïv)	86,000
Cherkasy	308,000
Chernihiv	311,000
Chernivtsi	261,000
Chervonohrad	75,000
Dniprodzerzhyns'k (★Dnipropetrovs'k)	286,000
Dnipropetrovs'k (★1,615,000)	1,190,000
Donets'k (★2,125,000)	1,121,000
Drohobych	80,000
Druzhkivka (★Kramators'k)	74,000
Dymytrov (★Krasnoarmiis'k)	64,000
Dzerzhyns'k (★Horlivka)	50,000
Dzhankoi	55,000
Enerhodar	54,000
Fastiv	55,000
Feodosiia	86,000
Horlivka (★700,000)	336,000
Illichivs'k (★Odesa)	57,000
Ivano-Frankivs'k	230,000
Izium	65,000
Izmaïl	95,000
Kalush	71,000
Kam'ianets'-Podil's'kyi	106,000
Kerch	181,000
Kharkiv (★2,050,000)	1,622,000
Khartsyz'k (★Donets'k)	70,000
Kherson	368,000
Khmel'nyts'kyi	250,000
Kirovohrad	280,000
Kolomyia	68,000
Komsomol's'k	54,000
Konotop	99,000
Korosten'	67,000
Kostiantynivka	107,000
Kovel'	71,000
Kramators'k (★517,000)	203,000
Krasnoarmiis'k (★180,000)	74,000
Krasnodon (★165,000)	55,000
Krasnyi Luch (★321,000)	114,000
Kremenchuk	245,000
Kryvyi Rih	729,000
•KYÏV (KIEV) (★3,260,000)	2,643,000
Lozova	74,000
Lubny	61,000
Luhans'k (★651,000)	505,000
Luts'k	215,000
L'viv	807,000
Lysychans'k (★415,000)	127,000
Makiïvka (★Donets'k)	426,000
Marhanets'	55,000
Mariupol'	523,000
Melitopol'	178,000
Mukacheve	90,000
Mykolaïv	515,000
Nikopol'	160,000
Nizhyn	83,000
Nova Kakhovka	60,000
Novohrad-Volyns'kyi	57,000
Novomoskovs'k	77,000
Novovolyns'k	57,000
Odesa (★1,190,000)	1,096,000
Okhtyrka	53,000
Oleksandriia	106,000
Pavlohrad	136,000
Pervomais'k	85,000
Pervomais'k (★Stakhanov)	52,000
Poltava	324,000
Pryluky	74,000
Rivne	244,000
Romny	57,000
Roven'ky	59,000
Rubizhne (★Lysychans'k)	76,000
Sevastopol'	371,000
Shakhtars'k (★Torez)	73,000
Shepetivka	53,000
Shostka	96,000
Sieverodonets'k (★Lysychans'k)	134,000
Simferopol'	357,000
Slov'ians'k (★Kramators'k)	138,000
Smila	82,000
Snizhne (★Torez)	69,000
Stakhanov (★703,000)	113,000
Stryi	70,000
Sumy	305,000
Sverdlovs'k (★145,000)	84,000
Svitlovods'k	59,000
Ternopil'	225,000
Torez (★320,000)	88,000
Uman'	93,000
Uzhhorod	125,000
Vinnytsia	384,000
Yalta	90,000
Yenakiieve (★Horlivka)	120,000
Yevpatoriia	113,000
Zaporizhzhia	898,000
Zhovti Vody	64,000
Zhytomyr	299,000

UNITED ARAB EMIRATES / Al-Imārāt al-'Arabīyah al-Muttaḥidah

City	Population
1980 C	980,000
ABŪ ZABY	242,975
Al-'Ayn	101,663
Ash-Shāriqah	125,149
•Dubayy	265,702

UNITED KINGDOM

City	Population
1991 C	56,352,200

UNITED KINGDOM: ENGLAND

City	Population
1991 C	48,208,000
Aldershot (★London) (★231,194)	51,356
Ashford	52,002
Aylesbury	58,058
Barnsley (★228,000)	75,120
Basildon (★London)	100,924
Basingstoke	77,837
Bath	85,202
Bebington (★Liverpool)	60,148
Bedford	73,917
Birkenhead (★Liverpool)	93,087
Birmingham (★2,705,000)	965,928
Blackburn (★255,000)	105,994
Blackpool (★275,000)	146,262
Bognor Regis	56,744
Bolton (★Manchester)	139,020
Bootle	65,454
Bournemouth (★360,000)	155,488
Bracknell (★London)	60,895
Bradford (★Leeds)	289,376
Brighton (★435,000)	124,851
Bristol (★650,000)	407,992
Burnley (★160,000)	74,661
Burton upon Trent	60,525
Bury (★Manchester)	62,633
Cambridge (★113,500)	95,682
Cannock (★Birmingham)	60,106
Carlisle	72,439
Chatham (★London)	71,691
Chelmsford (★London)	97,451
Cheltenham	91,301
Cheshunt (★London)	51,998
Chester (★89,629)	80,110
Chesterfield (★125,000)	71,945
Colchester	96,063
Coventry (★635,000)	299,316
Crawley (★116,000) (★London)	88,203
Crewe	63,351
Crosby (★Liverpool)	52,869
Darlington	86,767
Dartford	59,411
Derby (★285,000)	223,836
Dewsbury (★Leeds)	50,168
Doncaster (★128,847)	71,595
Dudley (★Birmingham)	192,171
Eastbourne	94,793
Eastleigh	49,934

▲ Population of an entire municipality, commune, or district, including rural areas
• Largest city in country
★ Population or designation of the metroplitan area, including suburbs
★★ Population of metropolitan agglomeration
C Census E Official estimate U Unofficial estimate

Ellesmere Port (★Liverpool) 64,504
Exeter 94,717
Fareham (★Portsmouth) 54,866
Farnborough (★London) 52,535
Gateshead (★Newcastle) 83,159
Gillingham (★London) 94,923
Gloucester (★130,000) 114,003
Gosport (★Portsmouth) 67,802
Gravesend (★London) 51,345
Grays (★London) 50,145
Great Yarmouth (★65,000) 56,190
Grimsby (★137,000) 90,703
Guildford (★London) 65,998
Halesowen (★Birmingham) 57,918
Halifax (★197,000) 91,069
Haltemprice (★Hull) (1981 C) 53,633
Harlow (★London) 74,629
Harrogate 66,178
Hartlepool (★Middlesbrough) 87,310
Hastings (★120,000) 81,139
Hemel Hempstead (★London) 79,235
Hereford 54,326
High Wycombe (★116,500) 71,718
Hove (★Brighton) 67,602
Huddersfield (★377,400) 143,726
Huyton-with-Roby (★Liverpool) 56,500
Ipswich 130,157
Kidderminster 54,664
Kingston upon Hull (★380,000) 310,636
Kingston upon Thames 132,206
Kingswood (★Bristol) 60,192
Leeds (★1,530,000) 424,194
Leicester (★540,000) 318,518
Lincoln (★98,000) 80,281
Littlehampton 50,408
Liverpool (★1,515,000) 481,786
•LONDON (★12,000,000) 7,650,944
Lowestoft 62,907
Luton (★230,000) 171,671
Macclesfield 50,270
Maidenhead (★London) 59,605
Maidstone 90,878
Manchester (★2,760,000) 402,889
Mansfield (★210,000) 71,858
Margate 56,734
Middlesbrough (★580,000) 147,430
Newcastle upon Tyne (★1,350,000) 189,150
Newcastle-under-Lyme (★Stoke-on-Trent) 73,731
Northampton 179,596
Norwich (★250,000) 171,304
Nottingham (★640,000) 270,222
Nuneaton (★Coventry) 66,715
Oldbury (★Birmingham) (▲145,542) 65,500
Oldham (★Manchester) 103,931
Oxford (★250,000) 118,795
Peterborough 134,788
Plymouth (★290,000) 245,295
Poole (★Bournemouth) 138,479
Portsmouth (★490,000) 174,690
Preston (★260,000) 177,660
Reading (★230,000) 213,474
Redditch (★Birmingham) 73,372
Rochdale (★Manchester) 94,313
Rotherham (★Sheffield) 121,380
Royal Leamington Spa (★Coventry) 55,396
Royal Tunbridge Wells 60,272
Rugby 61,106
Runcorn (★Liverpool) 64,154
Saint Albans (★London) 80,376
Saint Helens (★200,000) 106,293
Sale (★Manchester) 56,052
Salford (★Manchester) 79,755
Scunthorpe 75,982
Sheffield (★690,000) 431,607
Shrewsbury 64,219
Slough (★127,000) (★London) 110,708
Smethwick (★Birmingham) (1981 C) 153,268
Solihull (★Birmingham) 94,531
South Shields (★Newcastle) 83,704
Southampton (★420,000) 210,138
Southend-on-Sea (★London) (★277,000) 158,517
Southport (★Liverpool) 90,959
Stafford 61,885
Staines (★London) 51,167
Stapleford (▲66,626) 53,000
Stevenage 76,064
Stockport (★Manchester) 132,813
Stockton-on-Tees (★Middlesbrough) 83,576
Stoke-on-Trent (★458,000) 266,543
Stourbridge (★Birmingham) 55,624
Sunderland (★Newcastle upon Tyne) 183,310
Sutton Coldfield (★Birmingham) 106,001
Swindon 145,236
Tamworth (★73,000) 68,440
Taunton 55,855
Torquay (Torbay) (★112,400) 59,587
Wakefield (★Leeds) 73,955
Wallasey (★Liverpool) 60,895
Walsall (★Birmingham) 174,739
Warrington (★170,000) 82,812
Washington (★Newcastle upon Tyne) 56,848
Waterlooville (★Portsmouth) 65,473
Watford (★London) 113,080
West Bromwich (★Birmingham) 146,386
Weston-super-Mare 69,372
Widnes 57,162
Wigan (★Manchester) 85,819
Woking (★London) 98,138
Wolverhampton (★Birmingham) 257,943
Worcester 82,661
Worthing (★Brighton) 95,732
York (★158,000) 124,609

UNITED KINGDOM: NORTHERN IRELAND

1991 C 1,601,000

Bangor (▲71,832) 51,300
Belfast (★Belfast) (★685,000) 279,237
Castlereagh (★Belfast) (1990 E) 58,100
Londonderry (Derry) (▲95,371) 72,200
Newtownabbey (★Belfast) (▲74,035) 58,400

UNITED KINGDOM: SCOTLAND

1991 C 4,998,567

Aberdeen (★200,000) 189,707
Ayr (★100,000) 47,962
Dundee 158,981
Dunfermline (★130,000) 55,089
East Kilbride (★Glasgow) 70,422
Edinburgh (★640,000) 401,910
Falkirk (★148,200) 35,610
Glasgow (★1,870,000) 662,954
Greenock (★99,800) 50,013
Hamilton (★Glasgow) 49,991
Irvine (★90,000) 32,988
Kilmarnock (★80,000) 44,307
Kirkcaldy (★149,000) 47,155
Paisley (★Glasgow) 75,526

UNITED KINGDOM: WALES

1991 C 2,891,000

Barry 49,887
Cardiff (★645,000) 272,129
Newport (★311,000) 115,522
Port Talbot (★130,000) 37,647
Rhondda (★Cardiff) 59,947
Swansea (★280,000) 171,038

UNITED STATES

1990 C 248,709,873

UNITED STATES: ALABAMA

1990 C 4,040,587

Anniston (★116,034) 26,623
Birmingham (★907,810) 265,968
Decatur (★131,556) 48,761
Dothan (★130,964) 53,589
Florence (★131,327) 36,426
Gadsden (★99,840) 42,523
Huntsville (★238,912) 159,789
Mobile (★476,923) 196,278
Montgomery (★292,517) 187,106
Tuscaloosa (★150,522) 77,759

UNITED STATES: ALASKA

1990 C 550,043

Anchorage (★248,400) 226,338
Fairbanks (★59,500) 30,843
Juneau 26,751

UNITED STATES: ARIZONA

1990 C 3,665,228

Chandler (★Phoenix) 90,533
Glendale (★Phoenix) 148,134
Lakeside (1991C) 78,563
Mesa (★Phoenix) 288,091
Peoria 50,618
Phoenix (★2,122,101) 983,403
Scottsdale (★Phoenix) 130,069
Tempe (★Phoenix) 141,865
Tucson (★666,880) 405,390
Yuma (★106,895) 54,923

UNITED STATES: ARKANSAS

1990 C 2,350,725

Fayetteville (★113,409) 42,099
Fort Smith (★175,911) 72,798
Little Rock (★513,117) 175,795
North Little Rock (★Little Rock) 61,741
Pine Bluff (★85,487) 57,140

UNITED STATES: CALIFORNIA

1990 C 29,760,021

Alameda (★Oakland) 76,459
Alhambra (★Los Angeles) 82,106
Anaheim (★Los Angeles) (★2,410,556) 266,406
Antioch (★Oakland) 62,195
Arden (★Sacramento) 62,900
Bakersfield (★543,477) 174,820
Baldwin Park (★Los Angeles) 69,330
Bellflower (★Los Angeles) 61,815
Berkeley (★Oakland) 102,724
Buena Park (★Anaheim) 68,784
Burbank (★Los Angeles) 93,643
Camarillo (★Oxnard) 52,303
Carlsbad (★San Diego) 63,126
Carson (★Los Angeles) 83,995
Cerritos (★Los Angeles) 53,240
Chico (★182,120) 40,079
Chino (★Riverside) 59,682
Chula Vista (★San Diego) 135,163
Citrus Heights (★Sacramento) 107,439
Clovis (★Fresno) 50,323
Compton (★Los Angeles) 90,454
Concord (★Oakland) 111,348
Corona (★Riverside) 76,095
Costa Mesa (★Anaheim) 96,357
Cucamonga (★Riverside) 101,409
Daly City (★San Francisco) 92,311
Diamond Bar (★Los Angeles) 53,672
Downey (★Los Angeles) 91,444
East Los Angeles (★Los Angeles) 126,379
El Cajon (★San Diego) 88,693
El Monte (★Los Angeles) 106,209
El Toro (★Anaheim) 62,685
Encinitas (★San Diego) 55,386
Escondido (★San Diego) 108,635
Eureka (★89,800) 27,025
Fairfield (★Vallejo) 77,211
Fontana (★Riverside) 87,535
Fountain Valley (★Anaheim) 53,691
Fremont (★Oakland) 173,339
Fresno (★667,490) 354,202
Fullerton (★Anaheim) 114,144
Garden Grove (★Anaheim) 143,050
Gardena (★Los Angeles) 49,847
Glendale (★Los Angeles) 180,038
Hacienda Heights (★Los Angeles) 52,354
Hawthorne (★Los Angeles) 71,349
Hayward (★Oakland) 111,498
Hesperia 50,418
Huntington Beach (★Los Angeles) 181,519
Huntington Park (★Los Angeles) 56,065
Inglewood (★Los Angeles) 109,602
Irvine (★Anaheim) 110,330
La Habra (★Anaheim) 51,266
La Mesa (★San Diego) 52,931
Lakewood (★Los Angeles) 73,557
Lancaster (★Los Angeles) (★189,300) 97,291
Livermore (★Oakland) 56,741
Lodi (★Stockton) 51,874
Long Beach (★Los Angeles) 429,433
Los Angeles (★★14,531,529) 3,485,398
Lynwood (★Los Angeles) 61,945
Merced (★178,403) 56,216
Milpitas (★San Jose) 50,686
Mission Viejo (★Anaheim) 72,820
Modesto (★370,522) 164,730
Montebello (★Los Angeles) 59,564
Monterey Park (★Los Angeles) 60,738
Moreno Valley (★Riverside) 118,779
Mountain View (★San Jose) 67,460
Napa (★Vallejo) 61,842
National City (★San Diego) 54,249
Newport Beach (★Anaheim) 66,643
Norwalk (★Los Angeles) 94,279
Oakland (★San Francisco) (★2,082,914) 372,242
Oceanside (★San Diego) 128,398
Ontario (★Riverside) 133,179
Orange (★Anaheim) 110,658
Oxnard (★Los Angeles) (★669,016) 142,216
Palmdale (★Los Angeles) 68,842
Palo Alto (★San Jose) 55,900
Pasadena (★Los Angeles) 131,591
Pico Rivera (★Los Angeles) 59,177
Pleasanton (★Oakland) 50,553
Pomona (★Los Angeles) 131,723
Redding (★147,036) 66,462
Redlands (★Riverside) 60,394
Redondo Beach (★Los Angeles) 60,167
Redwood City (★San Francisco) 66,072
Rialto (★Riverside) 72,388
Richmond (★Oakland) 87,425
Riverside (★Los Angeles) (★2,588,793) 226,505
Rosemead (★Los Angeles) 51,638
Sacramento (★1,481,102) 369,365
Salinas (★355,660) 108,777
San Bernardino (★Riverside) 164,164
San Diego (★2,949,000) 1,110,549
San Francisco (★★6,253,311) 723,959
San Jose (★San Francisco) (★1,497,577) 782,248
San Leandro (★Oakland) 68,223
San Mateo (★San Francisco) 85,486
Santa Ana (★Anaheim) 293,742
Santa Barbara (★369,608) 85,571
Santa Clara (★San Jose) 93,613
Santa Cruz (★San Francisco) (★229,734) 49,040
Santa Maria (★Santa Barbara) 61,284
Santa Monica (★Los Angeles) 86,905
Santa Rosa (★388,222) 113,313
Santee (★San Diego) 52,902
Simi Valley (★Oxnard) 100,217
South Gate (★Los Angeles) 86,284
South San Francisco (★San Francisco) 54,312
South Whittier (★Los Angeles) 51,100
Spring Valley (★San Diego) 54,600
Stockton (★480,628) 210,943
Sunnyvale (★San Jose) 117,229
Thousand Oaks (★Oxnard) 104,352
Torrance (★Los Angeles) 133,107
Tustin (★Anaheim) 50,689
Union City (★Oakland) 53,762
Upland (★Riverside) 63,374
Vacaville (★Vallejo) 71,479
Vallejo (★San Francisco) (★451,186) 109,199
Ventura (★Oxnard) 92,575
Visalia (★311,921) 75,636
Vista (★San Diego) 71,872
Walnut Creek (★Oakland) 60,569
West Covina (★Los Angeles) 96,086
Westminster (★Anaheim) 78,118
Whittier (★Los Angeles) 77,671
Yorba Linda (★Anaheim) 52,422
Yuba City (★122,643) 27,437

UNITED STATES: COLORADO

1990 C 3,294,394

Arvada (★Denver) 89,235
Aurora (★Denver) 222,103
Boulder (★Denver) (★225,339) 83,312
Colorado Springs (★397,014) 281,140
Denver (★★1,848,319) 467,610
Fort Collins (★186,136) 87,758
Grand Junction (★85,200) 29,034
Greeley (★131,821) 60,536
Lakewood (★Denver) 126,481
Longmont (★Boulder) 51,555
Pueblo (★123,051) 98,640
Thornton (★Denver) 55,031
Westminster (★Denver) 74,625

UNITED STATES: CONNECTICUT

1990 C 3,287,116

Bridgeport (★New York, N.Y.) (★443,722) 141,686
Bristol (★79,488) (★Hartford) 60,640
Danbury (★187,867) (★New York, N.Y.) 65,585
East Hartford (★Hartford) 50,452
Fairfield (★Bridgeport) 53,418
Greenwich (★Stamford) 58,441
Hamden (★New Haven) 52,434
Hartford (★★1,085,837) 139,739
Manchester (★Hartford) 51,618
Meriden (★New Haven) 59,479
Middletown (★90,320) (★Hartford) 42,762
New Britain (★148,188) (★Hartford) 75,491
New Haven (★530,180) 130,474
New London (★266,819) 28,540
Norwalk (★127,378) (★New York, N.Y.) 78,331
Stamford (★202,557) (★New York, N.Y.) 108,056
Waterbury (★221,629) 108,961
West Hartford (★Hartford) 60,110
West Haven (★New Haven) 54,021

UNITED STATES: DELAWARE

1990 C 666,168

Dover (★78,900) 27,630
Wilmington (★Philadelphia, Pa.) 71,529

UNITED STATES: DISTRICT OF COLUMBIA

1990 C 606,900

WASHINGTON (★3,923,574) 606,900

UNITED STATES: FLORIDA

1990 C 12,937,926

Boca Raton (★West Palm Beach) 61,492
Bradenton (★211,707) 43,779
Brandon (★Tampa) 57,985
Cape Coral (★Fort Myers) 74,991
Carol City (★Miami) 53,331
Clearwater (★Tampa) 98,784
Coral Springs (★Miami) 79,443
Daytona Beach (★370,712) 61,921
Deltona 50,828
Fort Lauderdale (★Miami) (★1,255,488) 149,377
Fort Myers (★335,113) 45,206
Fort Pierce (★251,071) 36,830
Fort Walton Beach (★143,776) 21,471
Gainesville (★204,111) 84,770
Hialeah (★Miami) 188,004
Hollywood (★Fort Lauderdale) 121,697
Jacksonville (★906,727) 635,230
Kendall (★Miami) 87,271
Lakeland (★405,382) 70,576
Largo (★Tampa) 65,674
Lauderhill (★Fort Lauderdale) 49,708
Melbourne (★398,978) 59,646
Miami (★★3,192,582) 358,548
Miami Beach (★Miami) 92,639
Naples (★152,099) 19,505
North Miami (★Miami) 49,998
Ocala (★194,833) 42,045
Orlando (★1,072,748) 164,693
Palm Bay (★Melbourne) 62,632
Palm Harbor (★Tampa) 50,256
Panama City (★126,994) 34,378
Pembroke Pines (★Fort Lauderdale) 65,452
Pensacola (★344,406) 58,165
Plantation (★Fort Lauderdale) 66,692
Pompano Beach (★Fort Lauderdale) 72,411
Port Saint Lucie (★Fort Pierce) 55,866
Saint Petersburg (★Tampa) 238,629
Sarasota (★277,776) 50,961
Sunrise (★Fort Lauderdale) 64,407
Tallahassee (★233,598) 124,773
Tampa (★2,067,959) 280,015
Town 'n Country (★Tampa) 60,946
West Palm Beach (★863,518) 67,643

UNITED STATES: GEORGIA

1990 C 6,478,216

Albany (★112,561) 78,122
Athens (★156,267) 45,734
Atlanta (★2,833,511) 394,017
Augusta (★396,809) 44,639
Columbus (★243,072) 178,681
Macon (★281,103) 106,612
Sandy Springs (★Atlanta) 67,842
Savannah (★242,622) 137,560

UNITED STATES: HAWAII

1990 C 1,108,229

Honolulu (★836,231) 365,272

UNITED STATES: IDAHO

1990 C 1,006,749

Boise (★205,775) 125,738
Idaho Falls (★72,700) 43,929
Nampa (★70,500) 28,365
Pocatello (★56,700) 46,080

UNITED STATES: ILLINOIS

1990 C 11,430,602

Arlington Heights (★Chicago) 75,460
Aurora (★356,884) (★Chicago) 99,581
Bloomington (★129,180) 51,972
Champaign (★173,025) 63,502
Chicago (★★8,065,633) 2,783,726
Cicero (★Chicago) 67,436
Danville (★68,000) 33,828
De Kalb (★52,200) 34,925
Decatur (★117,206) 83,885
Des Plaines (★Chicago) 53,223
Elgin (★Aurora) 77,010
Evanston (★Chicago) 73,233
Joliet (★Chicago) (★389,650) 76,836
Kankakee (★96,255) 27,575
Mount Prospect (★Chicago) 53,170
Naperville (★Chicago) 85,351
Oak Lawn (★Chicago) 56,182
Oak Park (★Chicago) 53,648
Peoria (★339,172) 113,504
Rockford (★283,719) 139,426
Schaumburg (★Chicago) 68,586
Skokie (★Chicago) 59,432
Springfield (★189,550) 105,227
Waukegan (★Chicago) 69,392
Wheaton (★Chicago) 51,464

UNITED STATES: INDIANA

1990 C 5,544,159

Anderson (★130,669) 59,459
Bloomington (★108,978) 60,633
Elkhart (★156,198) 43,627
Evansville (★278,990) 126,272
Fort Wayne (★363,811) 173,072
Gary (★Chicago, Ill.) (★604,526) 116,646
Hammond (★Gary) 84,236
Indianapolis (★1,249,822) 731,327
Kokomo (★96,946) 44,962
Lafayette (★130,598) 43,764
Muncie (★119,659) 71,035
South Bend (★247,052) 105,511
Terre Haute (★130,812) 57,483

UNITED STATES: IOWA

1990 C 2,776,755

Ames (★65,400) 47,198
Cedar Rapids (★168,767) 108,751
Council Bluffs (★Omaha, Neb.) 54,315
Davenport (★350,861) 95,333
Des Moines (★392,928) 193,187
Dubuque (★86,403) 57,546
Iowa City (★96,119) 59,738
Sioux City (★115,018) 80,505
Waterloo (★146,611) 66,467

UNITED STATES: KANSAS

1990 C 2,477,574

Kansas City (★Kansas City, Mo.) 149,767
Lawrence (★81,798) 65,608
Olathe (★Kansas City, Mo.) 63,352
Overland Park (★Kansas City, Mo.) 111,790
Topeka (★160,976) 119,883
Wichita (★485,270) 304,011

UNITED STATES: KENTUCKY

1990 C 3,685,296

Frankfort 25,968
Lexington (★348,428) 225,366
Louisville (★952,662) 269,063
Owensboro (★87,189) 53,549

UNITED STATES: LOUISIANA

1990 C 4,219,973

Alexandria (★131,556) 49,188
Baton Rouge (★528,264) 219,531
Bossier City (★Shreveport) 52,721
Houma (★182,842) 96,982
Kenner (★New Orleans) 72,033
Lafayette (★208,740) 94,440
Lake Charles (★168,134) 70,580
Metairie (★New Orleans) 149,428
Monroe (★142,191) 54,909
New Orleans (★1,238,816) 496,938
Shreveport (★334,341) 198,525

UNITED STATES: MAINE

1990 C 1,227,928

Augusta (★56,700) 21,325
Bangor (★88,745) 33,181
Lewiston (★88,141) 39,757
Portland (★215,281) 64,358

UNITED STATES: MARYLAND

1990 C 4,781,468

Annapolis (★Baltimore) 33,187
Baltimore (★2,382,172) 736,014
Bethesda (★Washington, D.C.) 62,936
Columbia (★Baltimore) 75,883
Cumberland (★101,643) 23,706
Dundalk (★Baltimore) 65,800
Hagerstown (★121,393) 35,445
Silver Spring (★Washington, D.C.) 76,046
Wheaton (★Washington, D.C.) (1989E) 58,300

UNITED STATES: MASSACHUSETTS

1990 C 6,016,425

Boston (★★4,171,643) 574,283
Brockton (★Boston) (★189,478) 92,788
Brookline (★Boston) 54,718
Cambridge (★Boston) 95,802
Chicopee (★Springfield) 56,632
Fall River (★Providence, R.I.) (★157,272) 92,703
Fitchburg (★102,797) 41,194
Framingham (★Boston) 64,994
Haverhill (★Lawrence) 51,418
Lawrence (★Boston) (★393,516) 70,207
Lowell (★Boston) (★273,067) 103,439
Lynn (★Salem) 81,245
Malden (★Boston) 53,884
Medford (★Boston) 57,407
New Bedford (★175,641) 99,922
Newton (★Boston) 82,585
Pittsfield (★79,250) 48,622
Quincy (★Boston) 84,985
Salem (★264,356) 38,091
Somerville (★Boston) 76,210
Springfield (★529,519) 156,983
Taunton (★59,700) 49,832
Waltham (★Boston) 57,878
Weymouth (★Boston) 54,063
Worcester (★436,905) 169,759

UNITED STATES: MICHIGAN

1990 C 9,295,297

Ann Arbor (★Detroit) (★282,937) 109,592
Battle Creek (★135,982) 53,540
Benton Harbor (★161,378) 12,818
Canton (★Detroit) 57,047
Clinton Township (★Detroit) 85,866
Dearborn (★Detroit) 89,286
Dearborn Heights (★Detroit) 60,838
Detroit (★★4,665,236) 1,027,974
East Lansing (★Lansing) 50,677
Farmington Hills (★Detroit) 74,652
Flint (★430,459) 140,761
Grand Rapids (★688,399) 189,126
Jackson (★149,756) 37,446
Kalamazoo (★223,411) 80,277
Lansing (★432,674) 127,321
Livonia (★Detroit) 100,850
Muskegon (★158,983) 40,283
Pontiac (★Detroit) 71,166
Redford (★Detroit) 54,387
Rochester Hills (★Detroit) 61,766
Roseville (★Detroit) 51,412
Royal Oak (★Detroit) 65,410
Saginaw (★399,320) 69,512
Saint Clair Shores (★Detroit) 68,107
Southfield (★Detroit) 75,728
Sterling Heights (★Detroit) 117,810
Taylor (★Detroit) 70,811
Troy (★Detroit) 72,884
Warren (★Detroit) 144,864
Waterford (★Detroit) 66,692
Westland (★Detroit) 84,724
Wyoming (★Grand Rapids) 63,891

UNITED STATES: MINNESOTA

1990 C 4,375,099

Bloomington (★Minneapolis) 86,335
Brooklyn Park (★Minneapolis) 56,381
Burnsville (★Minneapolis) 51,288
Coon Rapids (★Minneapolis) 52,978
Duluth (★239,971) 85,493
Minneapolis (★2,464,124) 368,383
Plymouth (★Minneapolis) 50,889
Rochester (★106,470) 70,745
Saint Cloud (★190,921) 48,812
Saint Paul (★Minneapolis) 272,235

UNITED STATES: MISSISSIPPI

1990 C 2,573,216

Biloxi (★197,125) 46,319
Jackson (★395,396) 196,637
Pascagoula (★115,243) 25,899

UNITED STATES: MISSOURI

1990 C 5,117,073

Columbia (★112,379) 69,101
Florissant (★Saint Louis) 51,206
Independence (★Kansas City) 112,301
Jefferson City (★60,100) 35,481

▲ Population of an entire municipality, commune, or district, including rural areas
• Largest city in country
★ Population or designation of the metroplitan area, including suburbs
★★ Population of metropolitan agglomeration
C Census E Official estimate U Unofficial estimate

Joplin (★134,910)	40,961
Kansas City (★1,566,280)	435,146
Saint Charles (★Saint Louis)	54,555
Saint Joseph (★83,083)	71,852
Saint Louis (★2,444,099)	396,685
Springfield (★240,593)	140,494

UNITED STATES: MONTANA

1990 C	799,065
Billings (★113,419)	81,151
Great Falls (★77,691)	55,097
Helena	24,569
Missoula (★65,700)	42,918

UNITED STATES: NEBRASKA

1990 C	1,578,385
Lincoln (★213,641)	191,972
Omaha (★618,262)	335,795

UNITED STATES: NEVADA

1990 C	1,201,833
Carson City	40,443
Henderson (★Las Vegas)	64,942
Las Vegas (★741,459)	258,295
Paradise (★Las Vegas)	124,682
Reno (★254,667)	133,850
Sparks (★Reno)	53,367
Sunrise Manor (★Las Vegas)	95,362

UNITED STATES: NEW HAMPSHIRE

1990 C	1,109,252
Concord (★73,300)	36,006
Manchester (★147,809)	99,567
Nashua (★180,557) (★Boston, Ma.)	79,662
Portsmouth (★223,578)	25,925

UNITED STATES: NEW JERSEY

1990 C	7,730,188
Atlantic City (★319,416)	37,986
Bayonne (★Jersey City)	61,444
Brick Township (★New York, N.Y.)	66,473
Camden (★Philadelphia, Pa.)	87,492
Cherry Hill (★Philadelphia, Pa.)	69,319
Clifton (★New York, N.Y.)	71,742
East Orange (★Newark)	73,552
Edison (★New York, N.Y.)	88,680
Elizabeth (★Newark)	110,002
Irvington (★Newark)	59,774
Jersey City (★New York, N.Y.) (★553,099)	228,537
Middletown (★New York, N.Y.)	62,298
Newark (★1,824,321)	275,221
Passaic (★New York, N.Y.)	58,041
Paterson (★New York, N.Y.)	140,891
Trenton (★Philadelphia, Pa.) (★325,824)	88,675
Union (★Newark)	50,024
Union City (★Jersey City)	58,012
Vineland (★Philadelphia, Pa.) (★138,053)	54,780

UNITED STATES: NEW MEXICO

1990 C	1,515,069
Albuquerque (★480,577)	384,736
Las Cruces (★135,510)	62,126
Santa Fe (★117,043)	55,859

UNITED STATES: NEW YORK

1990 C	17,990,455
Albany (★874,304)	101,082
Binghamton (★264,497)	53,008
Buffalo (★★1,189,288)	328,123
Cheektowaga (★Buffalo)	84,387
Elmira (★95,195)	33,724
Glens Falls (★118,539)	15,023
Irondequoit (★Rochester)	52,322
Ithaca (★82,700)	29,541
Jamestown (★141,895)	34,681
Kingston (★88,200)	23,095
Levittown (★New York)	53,286
Middletown (★85,400)	24,160
Mount Vernon (★New York)	67,153
New Rochelle (★New York)	67,265
• New York (★★18,087,251)	7,322,564
Newburgh (★102,300)	26,454
Niagara Falls (★Buffalo) (★220,756)	61,840
Poughkeepsie (★259,462)	28,844
Rochester (★1,002,410)	231,636
Schenectady (★Albany)	65,566
Syracuse (★659,864)	163,860
Troy (★Albany)	54,269
Utica (★316,633)	68,637
Yonkers (★New York)	188,082

UNITED STATES: NORTH CAROLINA

1990 C	6,628,637
Asheville (★174,821)	61,607
Burlington (★108,213)	39,498
Charlotte (★1,162,093)	395,934
Durham (★Raleigh)	136,611
Fayetteville (★274,566)	75,695
Gastonia (★Charlotte)	54,732
Goldsboro (★94,200)	40,709
Greensboro (★942,091)	183,521
Hickory (★221,700)	28,301
High Point (★Greensboro)	69,496
Jacksonville (★149,838)	30,013
Raleigh (★735,480)	207,951
Rocky Mount (★83,400)	48,997
Wilmington (★120,284)	55,530
Winston-Salem (★Greenboro)	143,485

UNITED STATES: NORTH DAKOTA

1990 C	638,800
Bismarck (★83,831)	49,256
Fargo (★153,296)	74,111
Grand Forks (★70,683)	49,425

UNITED STATES: OHIO

1990 C	10,847,115
Akron (★Cleveland) (★657,575)	223,019
Canton (★394,106)	84,161
Cincinnati (★★1,744,124)	364,040
Cleveland (★★2,759,823)	505,616
Cleveland Heights (★Cleveland)	54,052
Columbus (★1,377,419)	632,910
Dayton (★951,270)	182,044
Elyria (★Lorain)	56,746
Euclid (★Cleveland)	54,875
Hamilton (★Cincinnati) (★291,479)	61,368
Kettering (★Dayton)	60,569
Lakewood (★Cleveland)	59,718
Lima (★154,340)	45,549
Lorain (★Cleveland) (★271,126)	71,245
Mansfield (★126,137)	50,627
Middletown (★Cincinnati) (★107,200)	46,022
Parma (★Cleveland)	87,876
Sandusky (★79,800)	29,764
Springfield	70,487
Steubenville (★142,523)	22,125
Toledo (★614,128)	332,943
Warren (★Youngstown)	50,793
Youngstown (★492,619)	95,732
Zanesville (★67,800)	26,778

UNITED STATES: OKLAHOMA

1990 C	3,145,585
Broken Arrow (★Tulsa)	58,043
Edmond (★Oklahoma City)	52,315
Lawton (★111,486)	80,561
Midwest City (★Oklahoma City)	52,267
Norman (★Oklahoma City)	80,071
Oklahoma City (★958,839)	444,719
Tulsa (★708,954)	367,302

UNITED STATES: OREGON

1990 C	2,842,321
Beaverton (★Portland)	53,310
Corvallis (★98,700)	44,757
Eugene (★282,912)	112,669
Gresham (★Portland)	68,235
Medford (★146,389)	46,951
Portland (★★1,477,895)	437,319
Salem (★278,024)	107,786

UNITED STATES: PENNSYLVANIA

1990 C	11,881,643
Abington (★Philadelphia)	59,300
Allentown (★686,688)	105,090
Altoona (★130,542)	51,881
Bensalem (★Philadelphia)	56,788
Bethlehem (★Allentown)	71,428
Bristol (★Philadelphia)	57,129
Coatesville (★Philadelphia) (★93,400)	11,038
Erie (★275,572)	108,718
Harrisburg (★587,986)	52,376
Haverford (★Philadelphia)	49,848
Johnstown (★241,247)	28,134
Lancaster (★422,822)	55,551
Levittown (★Philadelphia)	55,362
Lower Merion Township (★Philadelphia)	58,003
Penn Hills (★Pittsburgh)	51,430
Philadelphia (★★5,899,345)	1,585,577
Pittsburgh (★★2,242,798)	369,879
Pottstown (★Philadelphia) (★88,300)	21,831
Reading (★336,523)	78,380
Scranton (★734,175)	81,805
Sharon (★121,003)	17,493
State College (★123,786)	38,923
Upper Darby (★Philadelphia)	84,054
Williamsport (★118,710)	31,933
York (★417,848)	42,192

UNITED STATES: RHODE ISLAND

1990 C	1,003,464
Cranston (★Providence)	76,060
East Providence (★Providence)	50,380
Newport (★64,500)	28,227
Pawtucket (★329,384) (★Providence)	72,644
Providence (★★1,141,510)	160,728
Warwick (★Providence)	85,427

UNITED STATES: SOUTH CAROLINA

1990 C	3,486,703
Anderson (★145,196)	26,184
Charleston (★506,875)	80,414
Columbia (★453,331)	98,052
Florence (★114,344)	29,813
Greenville (★640,861)	58,282
Myrtle Beach (★95,200)	24,848
North Charleston (★Charleston)	70,218
Sumter (★90,300)	41,943

UNITED STATES: SOUTH DAKOTA

1990 C	696,004
Pierre	12,906
Rapid City (★81,343)	54,523
Sioux Falls (★123,809)	100,814

UNITED STATES: TENNESSEE

1990 C	4,877,185
Chattanooga (★433,210)	152,466
Clarksville (★169,439)	75,494
Johnson City (★436,047)	49,381
Knoxville (★604,816)	165,121
Memphis (★981,747)	610,337
Nashville (★985,026)	487,969

UNITED STATES: TEXAS

1990 C	16,986,510
Abilene (★119,655)	106,654
Amarillo (★187,547)	157,615
Arlington (★Fort Worth)	261,721
Austin (★781,572)	465,622
Baytown (★Houston)	63,850
Beaumont (★361,226)	114,323
Brownsville (★469,000)	98,962
Bryan (★121,862)	55,002
Carrollton (★Dallas)	82,169
College Station (★Bryan)	52,456
Corpus Christi (★349,894)	257,453
Dallas (★★3,885,415)	1,006,877
Denton (★Dallas)	66,270
El Paso (★1,211,300)	515,342
Fort Worth (★Dallas) (★1,332,053)	447,619
Freeport (★Houston) (★88,600)	11,389
Galveston (★Houston) (★217,399)	59,070
Garland (★Dallas)	180,650
Grand Prairie (★Dallas)	99,616
Houston (★★3,711,043)	1,630,553
Hunters Creek Village (★Houston)	174,013
Irving (★Dallas)	155,037
Killeen (★255,301)	63,535
Laredo (★354,000)	122,899
Longview (★162,431)	70,311
Lubbock (★222,636)	186,206
McAllen (★383,545)	84,021
Mesquite (★Dallas)	101,484
Midland (★106,611)	89,443
Odessa (★118,934)	89,699
Pasadena (★Houston)	119,363
Plano (★Dallas)	128,713
Port Arthur (★Beaumont)	58,724
Richardson (★Dallas)	74,840
San Angelo (★98,458)	84,474
San Antonio (★1,302,099)	935,933
Sherman (★95,021)	31,601
Texarkana (★120,132)	31,656
Tyler (★151,309)	75,450
Victoria (★74,361)	55,076
Waco (★189,123)	103,590
Wichita Falls (★122,378)	96,259

UNITED STATES: UTAH

1990 C	1,722,850
Ogden (★Salt Lake City)	63,909
Orem (★Provo)	67,561
Provo (★263,590)	86,835
Salt Lake City (★1,072,227)	159,936
Sandy (★Salt Lake City)	75,058
West Valley City (★Salt Lake City)	86,976

UNITED STATES: VERMONT

1990 C	562,758
Burlington (★131,439)	39,127
Montpelier (★52,800)	8,247

UNITED STATES: VIRGINIA

1990 C	6,187,358
Alexandria (★Washington, D.C.)	111,183
Annandale (★Washington, D.C.)	50,975
Arlington (★Washington, D.C.)	170,936
Burke (★Washington, D.C.)	57,734
Charlottesville (★131,107)	40,341
Chesapeake (★Norfolk)	151,976
Danville (★108,711)	53,056
Hampton (★Norfolk)	133,793
Lynchburg (★142,199)	66,049
Newport News (★Norfolk)	170,045
Norfolk (★1,396,107)	261,229
Portsmouth (★Norfolk)	103,907
Richmond (★865,640)	203,056
Roanoke (★224,477)	96,397
Suffolk (★Norfolk)	52,141
Virginia Beach (★Norfolk)	393,069

UNITED STATES: WASHINGTON

1990 C	4,866,692
Bellevue (★Seattle)	86,874
Bellingham (★127,780)	52,179
Bremerton (★189,731)	38,142
Everett (★Seattle)	69,961
Federal Way	67,554
Lakewood	58,412
Longview (★67,100)	31,499
Olympia (★161,238)	33,840
Richland (★150,033)	32,315
Seattle (★★2,559,164)	516,259
Spokane (★361,364)	177,196
Tacoma (★Seattle) (★586,203)	176,664
Vancouver (★238,053)	46,380
Yakima (★188,823)	54,827

UNITED STATES: WEST VIRGINIA

1990 C	1,793,477
Charleston (★250,454)	57,287
Huntington (★312,529)	54,844
Morgantown (★71,500)	25,879
Parkersburg (★149,169)	33,862
Wheeling (★159,301)	34,882

UNITED STATES: WISCONSIN

1990 C	4,891,769
Appleton (★315,121)	65,695
Eau Claire (★137,543)	56,856
Fond du Lac (★52,400)	37,757
Green Bay (★194,594)	96,466
Janesville (★139,510)	52,133
Kenosha (★Chicago, Ill.) (★128,181)	80,352
La Crosse (★97,904)	51,003
Madison (★367,085)	191,262
Manitowoc (★57,300)	32,520
Milwaukee (★★1,607,183)	628,088
Oshkosh (★Appleton)	55,006
Racine (★Milwaukee) (★175,034)	84,298
Sheboygan (★103,877)	49,676
Waukesha (★Milwaukee)	56,958
Wausau (★115,400)	37,060
West Allis (★Milwaukee)	63,221

UNITED STATES: WYOMING

1990 C	453,588
Casper (★61,226)	46,742
Cheyenne (★73,142)	50,008

URUGUAY

1985 C	2,955,241
Las Piedras (★Montevideo)	58,288
• MONTEVIDEO (★1,550,000)	1,251,647
Paysandú	76,191
Rivera	57,316
Salto	80,823

UZBEKISTAN / Uzbekiston

1991 E	20,708,200
Almalyk	116,400
Andižan	298,300
Angren	132,600
Bekabad	82,800
Buhara	249,600
Čirčik (★Taškent)	158,400
Džizak	110,900
Fergana	226,500
Gulistan	56,900
Hodžejli	61,200
Jangijul'	56,900
Kagan	49,800
Karši	168,000
Kattakurgan	59,600
Kokand	175,000
Margilan	124,900
Namangan	319,200
Navoi	111,600
Nukus	179,600
Šahrisabz	53,200
Samarkand	370,500
• TAŠKENT (★2,325,000)	2,113,300
Termez	90,400
Urgenč	130,400

VANUATU

1989 C	142,944
• PORT VILA (★23,000)	19,311

VATICAN CITY / Vaticano, Città del

1997 E	770

VENEZUELA

1990 C	18,105,265
Acarigua	116,551
Anaco	61,386
Araure	55,299
Barcelona	221,792
Barinas	153,630
Barquisimeto	625,450
Baruta (★Caracas)	182,941
Cabimas	165,755
Cagua	73,465
Calabozo	79,578
• CARACAS (★4,000,000)	1,822,465
Carora	70,715
Carúpano	92,333
Catia La Mar (★Caracas)	100,104
Chacao (★Caracas)	66,897
Ciudad Bolívar	225,340
Ciudad Guayana	453,047
Ciudad Ojeda	73,473
Coro	124,506
Cúa	62,836
Cumaná	212,432
El Limón	90,030
El Tigre	93,229
Guacara	100,766
Guanare	84,904
Guarenas (★Caracas)	134,158
La Victoria	77,326
Los Dos Caminos (★Caracas)	59,141
Los Teques (★Caracas)	140,617
Maiquetía (★Caracas)	62,834
Maracaibo	1,249,670
Maracay	354,196
Mariara	69,404
Maturín	206,654
Mérida	170,902
Ocumare del Tuy	76,880
Palo Negro	50,718
Petare (★Caracas)	338,417
Porlamar	62,732
Pozuelos (1981 C)	80,342
Puerto Cabello	128,825
Puerto la Cruz	155,731
Punto Fijo	88,681
San Carlos	50,708
San Cristóbal	220,675
San Felipe	65,509
San Fernando de Apure	72,716
San Juan de los Morros	67,791
Turmero	174,280
Valencia	903,621
Valera	97,012
Valle de la Pascua	67,100
Villa de Cura	51,096

VIETNAM / Viet Nam

1989 C	64,411,668
Bac Giang	50,879
Bac Lieu	83,483
Bien Hoa	273,879
Buon Ma Thuot	97,044
Ca Mau	81,901
Cam Pha	105,336
Cam Ranh (1973E)	118,111
Can Tho	208,078
Cao Lanh	54,349
Chau Doc	50,935
Da Lat	102,583
Da Nang	369,734
HA NOI (★1,275,000)	905,939
Hai Duong	53,370
Hai Phong (▲1,447,523)	351,919
Hoa Binh	69,323
Hon Gai	123,102
Hue	211,718
Long Xuyen	128,814
Minh Hai (1979 C)	72,517
My Tho	104,724
Nam Dinh	165,629
Nha Trang	213,460
Phan Rang	71,111
Phan Thiet	114,236
Play Ku	76,991
Quy Nhon	159,852
Rach Gia	137,784
Sa Dec	50,733
Soc Trang	87,899
Tan An	50,288
Thai Binh	57,640
Thai Nguyen	124,871
Thanh Hoa	84,951
• Thanh Pho Ho Chi Minh (Ho Chi Minh City) (★3,300,000)	2,796,229
Tuy Hoa	54,081
Viet Tri	73,347
Vinh	110,793
Vinh Long	81,620
Vung Tau	123,528
Yen Bai	58,645

VIRGIN ISLANDS (U.S.) / Virgin Islands

1990 C	101,809
• CHARLOTTE AMALIE (★32,000)	12,331

WALLIS AND FUTUNA / Wallis et Futuna

1990 C	13,705
• MATĀ'UTU	1,222

WEST BANK

1992 E	1,653,000
Al-Khalīl (Hebron)	78,358
• Al-Quds (★Yerushalayim)	285,000
Nābulus	84,881

WESTERN SAHARA

1982 C	142,000
• EL AAIÚN	93,875

YEMEN / Al-Yaman

1990 E	15,267,000
'Adan (★318,000) (1984 E)	176,100
Al-Hudaydah (1986 C)	155,110
Al-Mukallā (1984 E)	58,000
• ṢAN'Ā' (1986 C)	427,150
Ta'izz (1986 C)	178,043

YUGOSLAVIA / Jugoslavija

1991 C	10,337,920
• BEOGRAD (BELGRADE) (★1,554,826)	1,136,786
Čačak	72,392
Kosovska Mitrovica (1981 C)	52,866
Kragujevac	146,607
Kraljevo	56,616
Kruševac	58,114
Leskovac	61,963
Nikšić	56,483
Niš	175,555
Novi Pazar	51,906
Novi Sad	178,896
Pančevo (★Beograd)	72,717
Peć (1981 C)	54,497
Podgorica (Titograd)	118,059
Priština (▲244,830) (1987 E)	125,400
Prizren	61,801
Šabac	54,829
Smederevo	64,257
Subotica	100,219
Užice	53,666
Valjevo	58,324
Vranje	51,695
Zrenjanin	81,382

ZAMBIA

1990 C	7,818,447
Chingola	167,954
Kabwe	166,519
Kalulushi	75,197
Kitwe (★338,207)	247,100
Livingstone	82,218
Luanshya (★146,275)	79,500
• LUSAKA	982,362
Mufulira (★152,944)	85,000
Ndola	376,311

ZIMBABWE

1992 C	10,412,548
Bulawayo	621,742
Chitungwiza (★Harare)	274,912
Gweru	128,037
• HARARE (★1,470,000)	1,189,103
Kadoma	67,750
Kwekwe	75,425
Masvingo	51,743
Mutare	131,367

▲ Population of an entire municipality, commune, or district, including rural areas
• Largest city in country
★ Population or designation of the metroplitan area, including suburbs
★★ Population of metropolitan agglomeration
C Census E Official estimate U Unofficial estimate

Index to the World Reference Maps

Introduction

This index is an alphabetical listing of approximately 92,000 names of places and geographic features that appear on the reference maps and the metropolitan area maps. Each entry includes the name of the country or continent in which it is located, an alpha-numeric map reference key, and a page reference.

Names City and town names appear in the index in regular type. The names of all other features appear in *italics*, followed by descriptive terms (hill, mtn., state) to indicate their nature.

Abbreviations on the maps have been standardized as much as possible. Names that are abbreviated on the maps are generally spelled out in the index.

Country and feature names that cross international boundaries are followed by the name of the continent in which each is located. Country designations follow the names of all other places. The locations of places in the United States, Canada, and the United Kingdom are further defined by abbreviations indicating the state, province, or other political division in which each is located.

All abbreviations used in the index are defined in the List of Abbreviations to the right.

Alphabetization Names are alphabetized in the order of the letters of the English alphabet. Spanish *ll* and *ch*, for example, are not treated as distinct letters. This alphabetization also disregards diacritical marks—German or Scandinavian *ä* or *ö* are treated as *a* or *o*.

The names of physical features may appear inverted, since they are always alphabetized under the proper—not the generic—part of the name, such as: "Gibraltar, Strait of." Otherwise every entry, whether consisting of one word or more, is alphabetized as a single continuous entity. "Lakeland," for example, appears after "La Crosse" and before "La Salle." Names beginning with articles (Le Havre, Den Helder, Al-Manāma) are not inverted. Names beginning "St.," "Ste.," and "Sainte" are alphabetized as though spelled "Saint." In the case of identical names, towns are listed first, followed by political divisions and physical features. Entries that are completely identical are listed alphabetically by country name.

Map Reference Keys and Page References The map reference keys and page references are found in the last two columns of each entry. Each map reference key consists of a letter and number. The letters correspond to letters that run along the sides of the maps; lowercase letters refer to inset maps. The numbers correspond to numbers that appear across the tops and bottoms of the maps. Map reference keys for point features, such as cities and mountain peaks, indicate the locations of the symbols for these features. The page number generally refers to the main map for the country in which the feature is located. Page references to two-page maps always refer to the left-hand page.

List of Abbreviations

Abbreviation	Meaning
Ab., Can.	Alberta, Can.
Afg.	Afghanistan
Afr.	Africa
Ak., U.S.	Alaska, U.S.
Al., U.S.	Alabama, U.S.
Alb.	Albania
Alg.	Algeria
Am. Sam.	American Samoa
anch.	anchorage
And.	Andorra
Ang.	Angola
Ant.	Antarctica
Antig.	Antigua and Barbuda
aq.	aqueduct
Ar., U.S.	Arkansas, U.S.
Arg.	Argentina
Arm.	Armenia
at.	atoll
Aus.	Austria
Austl.	Australia
Az., U.S.	Arizona, U.S.
Azer.	Azerbaijan
b.	bay, gulf, inlet, lagoon
B.C., Can.	British Columbia, Can.
Bah.	Bahamas
Bahr.	Bahrain
Barb.	Barbados
bas.	basin
Bdi.	Burundi
Bel.	Belgium
Bela.	Belarus
Ber.	Bermuda
Bhu.	Bhutan
B.I.O.T.	British Indian Ocean Territory
Blg.	Bulgaria
Bngl.	Bangladesh
Bol.	Bolivia
Bos.	Bosnia and Hercegovina
Bots.	Botswana
Braz.	Brazil
Bru.	Brunei
Br. Vir. Is.	British Virgin Islands
Burkina	Burkina Faso
c.	cape, point
Ca., U.S.	California, U.S.
Cam.	Cameroon
Camb.	Cambodia
Can.	Canada
can.	canal
C.A.R.	Central African Republic
Cay. Is.	Cayman Islands
Christ. I.	Christmas Island
C. Iv.	Cote d'Ivoire
clf.	cliff, escarpment
Co., U.S.	Colorado, U.S.
co.	county, district, etc.
Cocos Is.	Cocos (Keeling) Islands
Col.	Colombia
Com.	Comoros
cont.	continent
Cook Is.	Cook Islands
C.R.	Costa Rica
crat.	crater
Cro.	Croatia
cst.	coast, beach
Ct., U.S.	Connecticut, U.S.
ctry.	independent country
C.V.	Cape Verde
cv.	cave
Cyp.	Cyprus
Czech Rep.	Czech Republic
D.C., U.S.	District of Columbia, U.S.
De., U.S.	Delaware, U.S.
Den.	Denmark
dep.	dependency, colony
depr.	depression
des.	desert
Dji.	Djibouti
Dom.	Dominica
Dom. Rep.	Dominican Republic
D.R.C.	Congo, Democratic Republic of the
Ec.	Ecuador
El Sal.	El Salvador
Eng., U.K.	England, U.K.
Eq. Gui.	Equatorial Guinea
Erit.	Eritrea
Est.	Estonia
est.	estuary
Eth.	Ethiopia
Eur.	Europe
Falk. Is.	Falkland Islands
Far. Is.	Faroe Islands
Fin.	Finland
Fl., U.S.	Florida, U.S.
for.	forest, moor
Fr.	France
Fr. Gu.	French Guiana
Fr. Poly.	French Polynesia
Ga., U.S.	Georgia, U.S.
Gam.	Gambia
Gaza	Gaza Strip
Geor.	Georgia
Ger.	Germany
Gib.	Gibraltar
Golan	Golan Heights
Grc.	Greece
Gren.	Grenada
Grnld.	Greenland
Guad.	Guadeloupe
Guat.	Guatemala
Guern.	Guernsey
Gui.	Guinea
Gui.-B.	Guinea-Bissau
Guy.	Guyana
gysr.	geyser
Hi., U.S.	Hawaii, U.S.
hist.	historic site, ruins
hist. reg.	historic region
Hond.	Honduras
Hung.	Hungary
i.	island
Ia., U.S.	Iowa, U.S.
Ice.	Iceland
ice	ice feature, glacier
Id., U.S.	Idaho, U.S.
Il., U.S.	Illinois, U.S.
In., U.S.	Indiana, U.S.
Indon.	Indonesia
I. of Man	Isle of Man
Ire.	Ireland
is.	islands
Isr.	Israel
isth.	isthmus
Jam.	Jamaica
Jord.	Jordan
Kaz.	Kazakhstan
Kir.	Kiribati
Kor., N.	Korea, North
Kor., S.	Korea, South
Ks., U.S.	Kansas, U.S.
Kuw.	Kuwait
Ky., U.S.	Kentucky, U.S.
Kyrg.	Kyrgyzstan
l.	lake, pond
La., U.S.	Louisiana, U.S.
Lat.	Latvia
lav.	lava flow
Leb.	Lebanon
Leso.	Lesotho
Lib.	Liberia
Liech.	Liechtenstein
Lith.	Lithuania
Lux.	Luxembourg
Ma., U.S.	Massachusetts, U.S.
Mac.	Macedonia
Madag.	Madagascar
Malay.	Malaysia
Mald.	Maldives
Marsh. Is.	Marshall Islands
Mart.	Martinique
Maur.	Mauritania
May.	Mayotte
Mb., Can.	Manitoba, Can.
Md., U.S.	Maryland, U.S.
Me., U.S.	Maine, U.S.
Mex.	Mexico
Mi., U.S.	Michigan, U.S.
Micron.	Micronesia, Federated States of
Mid. Is.	Midway Islands
misc. cult.	miscellaneous cultural
Mn., U.S.	Minnesota, U.S.
Mo., U.S.	Missouri, U.S.
Mol.	Moldova
Mon.	Monaco
Mong.	Mongolia
Monts.	Montserrat
Mor.	Morocco
Moz.	Mozambique
Mrts.	Mauritius
Ms., U.S.	Mississippi, U.S.
Mt., U.S.	Montana, U.S.
mth.	river mouth or channel
mtn.	mountain
mts.	mountains
Mwi.	Malawi
Mya.	Myanmar
N.A.	North America
N.B., Can.	New Brunswick, Can.
N.C., U.S.	North Carolina, U.S.
N. Cal.	New Caledonia
N. Cyp.	Cyprus, North
N.D., U.S.	North Dakota, U.S.
Ne., U.S.	Nebraska, U.S.
Neth.	Netherlands
Neth. Ant.	Netherlands Antilles
Nf., Can.	Newfoundland, Can.
ngh.	neighborhood
N.H., U.S.	New Hampshire, U.S.
Nic.	Nicaragua
Nig.	Nigeria
N. Ire., U.K.	Northern Ireland, U.K.
N.J., U.S.	New Jersey, U.S.
N.M., U.S.	New Mexico, U.S.
N. Mar. Is.	Northern Mariana Islands
Nmb.	Namibia
Nor.	Norway
Norf. I.	Norfolk Island
N.S., Can.	Nova Scotia, Can.
N.T., Can.	Northwest Territories, Can.
Nu., Can.	Nunavut, Can.
Nv., U.S.	Nevada, U.S.
N.Y., U.S.	New York, U.S.
N.Z.	New Zealand
Oc.	Oceania
Oh., U.S.	Ohio, U.S.
Ok., U.S.	Oklahoma, U.S.
On., Can.	Ontario, Can.
Or., U.S.	Oregon, U.S.
p.	pass
Pa., U.S.	Pennsylvania, U.S.
Pak.	Pakistan
Pan.	Panama
Pap. N. Gui.	Papua New Guinea
Para.	Paraguay
P.E., Can.	Prince Edward Island, Can.
pen.	peninsula
Phil.	Philippines
Pit.	Pitcairn
pl.	plain, flat
plat.	plateau, highland
p.o.i.	point of interest
Pol.	Poland
Port.	Portugal
P.R.	Puerto Rico
Qc., Can.	Quebec, Can.
r.	rock, rocks
reg.	physical region
res.	reservoir
Reu.	Reunion
rf.	reef, shoal
R.I., U.S.	Rhode Island, U.S.
Rom.	Romania
Rw.	Rwanda
S.A.	South America
S. Afr.	South Africa
sand	sand area
Sau. Ar.	Saudi Arabia
S.C., U.S.	South Carolina, U.S.
sci.	scientific station
Scot., U.K.	Scotland, U.K.
S.D., U.S.	South Dakota, U.S.
Sen.	Senegal
Sey.	Seychelles
S. Geor.	South Georgia
Sing.	Singapore
Sk., Can.	Saskatchewan, Can.
S.L.	Sierra Leone
Slvk.	Slovakia
Slvn.	Slovenia
S. Mar.	San Marino
Sol. Is.	Solomon Islands
Som.	Somalia
Sp. N. Afr.	Spanish North Africa
Sri L.	Sri Lanka
state	state, province, etc.
St. Hel.	St. Helena
St. K./N.	St. Kitts and Nevis
St. Luc.	St. Lucia
stm.	stream (river, creek)
S. Tom./P.	Sao Tome and Principe
St. P./M.	St. Pierre and Miquelon
strt.	strait, channel, etc.
St. Vin.	St. Vincent and the Grenadines
Sur.	Suriname
sw.	swamp, marsh
Swaz.	Swaziland
Swe.	Sweden
Switz.	Switzerland
Tai.	Taiwan
Taj.	Tajikistan
Tan.	Tanzania
T./C. Is.	Turks and Caicos Islands
Thai.	Thailand
Tn., U.S.	Tennessee, U.S.
Tok.	Tokelau
Trin.	Trinidad and Tobago
Tun.	Tunisia
Tur.	Turkey
Turkmen.	Turkmenistan
Tx., U.S.	Texas, U.S.
U.A.E.	United Arab Emirates
Ug.	Uganda
U.K.	United Kingdom
Ukr.	Ukraine
unds.	undersea feature
Ur.	Uruguay
U.S.	United States
Ut., U.S.	Utah, U.S.
Uzb.	Uzbekistan
Va., U.S.	Virginia, U.S.
val.	valley, watercourse
Vat.	Vatican City
Ven.	Venezuela
Viet.	Vietnam
V.I.U.S.	Virgin Islands (U.S.)
vol.	volcano
Vt., U.S.	Vermont, U.S.
Wa., U.S.	Washington, U.S.
Wake I.	Wake Island
Wal./F.	Wallis and Futuna
W.B.	West Bank
well	well, spring, oasis
Wi., U.S.	Wisconsin, U.S.
W. Sah.	Western Sahara
wtfl.	waterfall, rapids
W.V., U.S.	West Virginia, U.S.
Wy., U.S.	Wyoming, U.S.
Yk., Can.	Yukon Territory, Can.
Yugo.	Yugoslavia
Zam.	Zambia
Zimb.	Zimbabwe

A

Name	Page	Map Ref.	Latitude	Longitude
Allegheny County Park, p.o.i., Pa., U.S.	197b		40.34 N	79.55 W
Allegheny Mountains, mts., U.S.	124	F5	39.20 N	79.38 W
Allegheny Observatory, sci., Pa., U.S.	197b		40.29 N	80.01 W
Allegheny Plateau, plat., U.S.	124	C7	41.30 N	78.00 W
Allegheny Reservoir, res., U.S.	124	C7	42.00 N	78.57 W
Allègre, Pointe, c., Guad.	159c	h5	16.21 N	61.44 W
Allemands, Lac des, l., La., U.S.	134	H8	29.55 N	90.35 W
Allemant, Fr.	179		48.45 N	1.37 E
Allen, Ne., U.S.	128	I2	42.25 N	96.51 W
Allen, Ok., U.S.	134	C2	34.52 N	96.25 W
Allen, S.D., U.S.	140	D11	43.16 N	101.55 W
Allen, Tx., U.S.	136	A11	33.06 N	96.40 W
Allen, Lough, l., Ire.	10	G4	54.07 N	8.02 W
Allendale, Il., U.S.	130	F10	38.31 N	87.42 W
Allendale, N.J., U.S.	194		41.02 N	74.07 W
Allendale, S.C., U.S.	132	C4	33.00 N	81.18 W
Allende, Mex.	154	A8	28.20 N	100.50 W
All England Lawn Tennis Club, p.o.i., Eng., U.K.	178		51.26 N	0.13 W
Allenstein see Olsztyn, Pol.	24	C16	53.46 N	20.28 E
Allentown, Pa., U.S.	124	D10	40.36 N	75.29 W
Allentsteig, Aus.	24	H11	48.42 N	15.19 E
Allenwood, N.Y., U.S.	194		40.48 N	73.44 W
Alleppey, India	69	G3	9.29 N	76.20 E
Aller, stm., Ger.	24	D5	52.56 N	9.11 E
Allerton, Ia., U.S.	130	D4	40.42 N	93.21 W
Allerton, ngh., Eng., U.K.	180		53.22 N	2.53 W
Allevard, Fr.	22	D12	45.24 N	6.04 E
Alley Park, p.o.i., N.Y., U.S.	194		40.45 N	73.44 W
Allgäu see Kempten, Ger.	24	I6	47.43 N	10.18 E
Allgäu, reg., Ger.	24	I6	47.36 N	10.11 E
Allhallows, Eng., U.K.	178		51.28 N	0.39 E
Alliance, Ab., Can.	144	D19	52.26 N	111.45 W
Alliance, Ne., U.S.	140	E10	42.06 N	102.52 W
Alliance, Oh., U.S.	124	D4	40.54 N	81.06 W
Al-Lidām, Sau. Ar.	72	E5	20.29 N	44.47 E
Allier, state, Fr.	22	C9	46.25 N	3.00 E
Allier, stm., Fr.	22	C9	46.58 N	3.04 E
Alligator, stm., N.C., U.S.	132	A10	35.46 N	75.58 W
Alligator Pond, Jam.	158d	j13	17.52 N	77.33 W
Allinagaram, India	69	F3	10.00 N	77.29 E
Allinge, Den.	16	L12	55.16 N	14.47 E
Allington Castle, hist., Eng., U.K.	178		51.17 N	0.31 E
Allison, Ia., U.S.	130	B5	42.45 N	92.47 W
Allison, Mount, mtn., Ca., U.S.	200		37.30 N	121.52 W
Allison Gulch, val., Ca., U.S.	198		34.16 N	117.44 W
Alliston see New Tecumseth, On., Can.	126	D10	44.08 N	79.51 W
Al-Līth, Sau. Ar.	72	E5	20.09 N	40.16 E
Alloa, Scot., U.K.	10	E9	56.07 N	3.48 W
Allora, Austl.	98	F8	28.02 S	151.58 E
Allos, Fr.	22	E12	44.13 N	6.37 E
Allouez, Wi., U.S.	128	G11	44.28 N	88.01 W
Allred Peak, mtn., Co., U.S.	150	C8	40.32 N	108.33 W
All Russian Exhibition Center, bldg., Russia	183b		55.50 N	37.37 E
All Saints, Antig.	159b	f4	17.03 N	61.47 W
Allston, ngh., Ma., U.S.	201		42.22 N	71.08 W
Al-Lubnān see Lebanon, ctry., Asia	76	E6	34.00 N	36.00 E
Alluets, Forêt des, p.o.i., Fr.	179		48.55 N	1.55 E
Al-Luḥayyah, Yemen	72	F5	15.42 N	42.41 E
Allumette Lake, l., Can.	126	C12	45.51 N	77.09 W
Allumettes, Île aux, i., Qc., Can.	126	C12	45.52 N	77.02 W
Allyn, Wa., U.S.	146	C4	47.23 N	122.50 W
Alm, stm., Aus.	30	C10	48.05 N	13.55 E
Alma, N.B., Can.	122	E12	45.36 N	64.57 W
Alma, Qc., Can.	122	B5	48.33 N	71.39 W
Alma, Ar., U.S.	134	B4	35.28 N	94.13 W
Alma, Ga., U.S.	132	E3	31.32 N	82.27 W
Alma, Ks., U.S.	130	E1	39.01 N	96.17 W
Alma, Mi., U.S.	126	E5	43.22 N	84.39 W
Alma, Ne., U.S.	138	A9	40.06 N	99.21 W
Alma, Wi., U.S.	128	G7	44.19 N	91.54 W
Alma-Ata see Almaty, Kaz.	48	F13	43.17 N	76.56 E
Alma Center, Wi., U.S.	128	G7	44.25 N	90.54 W
Almada, Port.	28	F1	38.41 N	9.09 W
Almaden, Austl.	98	A5	17.20 S	144.41 E
Almadén, Spain	28	F6	38.46 N	4.49 W
Almadén de la Plata, Spain	28	G4	37.52 N	6.04 W
Al-Madīnah (Medina), Sau. Ar.	72	E4	24.27 N	39.36 E
Al-Mafraq, Jord.	76	F7	32.20 N	36.12 E
Al-Mafraq, state, Jord.	76	F8	32.15 N	37.30 E
Almafuerte, Arg.	172	F5	32.12 S	64.15 W
Al-Maghrib see Morocco, ctry., Afr.	84	C4	32.00 N	5.00 W
Almagro, Spain	28	F7	38.53 N	3.42 W
Alma Hill, hill, N.Y., U.S.	124	B8	42.03 N	78.01 W
Al-Majma'ah, Sau. Ar.	72	D6	25.54 N	45.20 E
Almăjului, Munţii, mts., Rom.	36	E9	44.43 N	22.12 E
Al-Makhā' see Al-Mukhā, Yemen	72	G5	13.18 N	43.15 E
Al-Mālihah, Sudan	82	D5	15.07 N	26.10 E
Al-Mālikīyah, Syria	74	B7	37.10 N	42.09 E
Almalyk, Uzb.	48	F11	40.50 N	69.35 E
Al-Manāmah (Manama), Bahr.	74	G12	26.13 N	50.35 E
Almanor, Lake, res., Ca., U.S.	148	C4	40.14 N	121.07 W
Almansa, Spain	28	F9	38.51 N	1.05 W
Almanza, Spain	28	B5	42.39 N	5.02 W
Almanzor, mtn., Spain	28	D5	40.15 N	5.18 W
Almanzora, stm., Spain	28	G8	37.16 N	1.49 W
Almar, stm., Spain	28	D5	40.53 N	5.28 W
Almargem do Bispo, Port.	184c		38.51 N	9.16 W
Al-Marj, Libya	82	A4	32.30 N	20.53 E
Almas, Braz.	170	F2	11.33 S	47.13 W
Almas, Pico das, mtn., Braz.	170	G4	13.33 S	41.56 W
Al-Mashrafah, Syria	76	D7	34.50 N	36.52 E
Almaty, Kaz.	48	F13	43.17 N	76.56 E
Al-Mawṣil (Mosul), Iraq	74	B8	36.20 N	43.07 E
Al-Mayādīn, Syria	74	C7	35.01 N	40.27 E
Almazán, Spain	28	C8	41.29 N	2.31 W
Al-Mazār, Jord.	76	G6	31.03 N	35.42 E
Almazovo, Russia	183b		55.51 N	38.02 E
Almeida, Port.	28	D4	40.43 N	6.54 W
Almejas, Bahía, b., Mex.	154	C3	24.27 N	111.40 W
Almelo, Neth.	20	B15	52.21 N	6.39 E
Almena, Ks., U.S.	138	B9	39.53 N	99.42 W
Almenara, Braz.	170	I5	16.12 S	40.40 W
Almenar de Soria, Spain	28	C8	41.41 N	2.12 W
Almendares, stm., Cuba	204b		23.08 N	82.25 W
Almendra, Embalse de, res., Spain	28	C4	41.14 N	6.13 W
Almendralejo, Spain	28	F4	38.41 N	6.24 W
Almería, Spain	28	H8	36.50 N	2.27 W
Almería, co., Spain	28	G8	37.10 N	2.25 W
Almería, Golfo de, b., Spain	28	H8	36.46 N	2.30 W
Al'metevsk, Russia	40	D18	54.53 N	52.18 E
Al'mež, Russia	12	F22	60.02 N	48.02 E
Älmhult, Swe.	16	K12	56.33 N	14.09 E
Al-Midhnab, Sau. Ar.	74	H9	25.54 N	44.14 E
Al-Mijlad, Sudan	82	E5	11.01 N	27.45 E
Al-Mīnā', Leb.	76	D6	34.27 N	35.49 E
Almina, Punta de, c., Sp. N. Afr.	28	I5	35.54 N	5.16 W
Almino Afonso, Braz.	170	D7	6.09 S	37.46 W
Al-Miqdādīyah, Iraq	74	D9	33.58 N	44.55 E
Almira, Wa., U.S.	146	C7	47.42 N	118.56 W
Almirante, Pan.	156	H6	9.17 N	82.23 W
Almirante Brown, state, Arg.	206		34.50 S	58.20 W
Almirante Guillermo Brown, Parque, p.o.i., Arg.	206		34.40 S	58.28 W
Almirante Latorre, Chile	172	D2	29.37 S	70.57 W
Al-Mismīyah, Syria	76	E7	33.07 N	36.23 E
Almo, Id., U.S.	146	H13	42.06 N	113.37 W
Almoçageme, Port.	184c		38.48 N	9.28 W
Almodôvar, Port.	28	G2	37.30 N	8.03 W
Almodóvar del Campo, Spain	28	F6	38.43 N	4.10 W
Almond, Wi., U.S.	128	G9	44.15 N	89.24 W
Almont, Mi., U.S.	124	B2	42.54 N	83.03 W
Almont, stm., Fr.	179		48.32 N	2.40 E
Almonte, On., Can.	126	C13	45.13 N	76.11 W
Almonte, Spain	28	G4	37.15 N	6.30 W
Almonte, Ca., U.S.	200		37.53 N	122.32 W
Almonte, stm., Spain	28	E4	39.42 N	6.28 W
Almora, India	70	D7	29.36 N	79.39 E
Al-Mubarraz, Sau. Ar.	72	E6	22.17 N	46.43 E
Al-Mubarraz, Sau. Ar.	72	D6	25.25 N	49.35 E
Al-Mudawwarah, Jord.	76	I6	29.19 N	35.59 E
Almudévar, Spain	28	B10	42.03 N	0.35 W
Al-Muglad see Al-Mijlad, Sudan	82	E5	11.01 N	27.45 E
Al-Muḥarraq, Bahr.	74	G12	26.16 N	50.37 E
Al-Mukallā, Yemen	72	G6	14.32 N	49.07 E
Al-Mukhā, Yemen	72	G5	13.18 N	43.15 E
Almuñécar, Spain	28	H7	36.44 N	3.40 W
Al-Musayyib, Iraq	74	D9	32.46 N	44.18 E
Al-Muthannā, state, Iraq	74	E9	30.30 N	45.15 E
Al-Muwayh, Sau. Ar.	72	E5	22.45 N	41.36 E
Al-Muwayliḥ, Sau. Ar.	72	D4	27.40 N	35.28 E
Almyrós, Grc.	34	D5	39.10 N	22.45 E
Almyroú, Órmos, b., Grc.	34	H7	35.23 N	24.20 E
Alnön, i., Swe.	16	E15	62.25 N	17.26 E
Alnwick, Eng., U.K.	10	F11	55.24 N	1.43 W
Alofi, Île, i., Wal./F.	94	E9	14.21 S	178.02 W
Aloja, Lat.	26	C7	57.46 N	24.53 E
Alondra, Ca., U.S.	198		33.55 N	118.15 W
Alónnisos, Grc.	34	D6	39.09 N	23.50 E
Alónnisos, i., Grc.	34	D6	39.13 N	23.55 E
Alor, Pulau, i., Indon.	60	G7	8.15 S	124.45 E
Alor, Selat, strt., Indon.	60	G7	8.20 S	123.48 E
Álora, Spain	28	H6	36.48 N	4.42 W
Alor Setar, Malay.	64	I5	6.06 N	100.22 E
Alor Star see Alor Setar, Malay.	64	I5	6.06 N	100.22 E
Alosno, Spain	28	G3	37.33 N	7.07 W
Alost see Aalst, Bel.	20	D13	50.56 N	4.02 E
Alotau, Pap. N. Gui.	101a	c5	10.18 S	150.27 E
Aloysius, Mount, mtn., Austl.	96	E5	26.00 S	128.36 E
Alpachiri, Arg.	172	H6	37.21 S	63.47 W
Alpaugh, Ca., U.S.	134	B6	35.53 N	119.29 W
Alpen see Alps, mts., Eur.	8	F10	46.24 N	10.00 E
Alpena, Ar., U.S.	130	H4	36.17 N	93.17 W
Alpena, Mi., U.S.	126	C6	45.03 N	83.26 W
Alpena, S.D., U.S.	140	C14	44.10 N	98.21 W
Alpercatas, stm., Braz.	170	D3	6.02 S	44.19 W
Alpes see Alps, mts., Eur.	8	F10	46.24 N	10.00 E
Alpes-de-Haute-Provence, state, Fr.	22	E12	44.10 N	6.00 E
Alpes-Maritimes, state, Fr.	22	F13	44.00 N	7.10 E
Alpes Valaisannes see Pennine Alps, mts., Eur.	30	D4	46.05 N	7.49 E
Alpha, Austl.	98	D6	23.39 S	146.38 E
Alpha, Il., U.S.	130	C7	41.11 N	90.23 W
Alpha, Mi., U.S.	126	B1	46.02 N	88.24 W
Alpharetta, Ga., U.S.	132	B1	34.04 N	84.17 W
Alphin Pike, hill, Eng., U.K.	180		53.31 N	2.00 W
Alphonse, i., Sey.	89b	k12	7.00 S	52.45 E
Alpi see Alps, mts., Eur.	8	F10	46.24 N	10.00 E
Alpine, Az., U.S.	150	J7	33.50 N	109.08 W
Alpine, Ca., U.S.	148	K9	32.51 N	116.48 W
Alpine, N.J., U.S.	194		40.57 N	73.55 W
Alpine, Tx., U.S.	136	D4	30.21 N	103.39 W
Alpine Creek, stm., Ca., U.S.	200		37.19 N	122.17 W
Alpine National Park, p.o.i., Austl.	98	K6	36.56 S	147.12 E
Alpinópolis, Braz.	170	K2	20.51 S	46.23 W
Alps, mts., Eur.	8	F10	46.24 N	10.00 E
Al-Qābil, Oman	74	I14	23.58 N	55.50 E
Al-Qaḍārif, Sudan	82	E7	14.01 N	35.22 E
Al-Qaḍīmah, Sau. Ar.	74	E4	22.25 N	39.11 E
Al-Qādisīyah, state, Iraq	74	E9	31.55 N	45.00 E
Al-Qā'im, Iraq	74	C7	34.21 N	41.07 E
Al-Qā'īyah, well, Sau. Ar.	74	G9	26.27 N	45.35 E
Al-Qalībah, Sau. Ar.	74	F5	28.24 N	37.40 E
Al-Qāmishlī, Syria	74	B7	37.03 N	41.14 E
Al-Qaryah ash-Sharqīyah, Libya	82	A2	30.24 N	13.36 E
Al-Qaryatayn, Syria	76	D8	34.15 N	37.19 E
Al-Qaṣr, Jord.	76	G6	31.18 N	35.45 E
Al-Qaṭīf, Sau. Ar.	72	D6	26.33 N	50.00 E
Al-Qaṭrānah, Jord.	76	G7	31.15 N	36.03 E
Al-Qaṭrūn, Libya	82	C2	24.56 N	14.38 E
Al-Qayṣūmah, Sau. Ar.	82	D6	28.25 N	45.58 E
Al-Quds see Yerushalayim, Isr.	76	G6	31.46 N	35.13 E
Al-Qunayṭirah, Syria	76	E6	33.07 N	35.49 E
Al-Qunayṭirah, state, Syria	76	E6	33.00 N	35.50 E
Al-Qunfudhah, Sau. Ar.	72	F5	19.07 N	41.05 E
Al-Qurnah, Iraq	74	E10	31.00 N	47.26 E
Al-Quṣayr, Syria	76	D7	34.29 N	36.35 E
Al-Quṭayfah, Syria	76	E7	33.44 N	36.36 E
Al-Quṭaynah, Sudan	82	E6	14.50 N	32.21 E
Als, i., Den.	16	M7	54.59 N	9.55 E
Alsace, hist. reg., Fr.	20	F16	48.30 N	7.30 E
Al'šany, Bela.	26	H10	52.04 N	27.20 E
Alsask, Sk., Can.	142	C4	51.23 N	109.59 W
Alsasua, Spain	28	B8	42.54 N	2.10 W
Alsea, Or., U.S.	146	F3	44.23 N	123.35 W
Alsea, stm., Or., U.S.	146	F2	44.25 N	124.05 W
Alsek, stm., N.A.	109	D12	59.11 N	138.27 W
Alsen, N.D., U.S.	142	F15	48.37 N	98.42 W
Alsensjön, l., Swe.	16	D11	63.22 N	14.03 E
Alsfeld, Ger.	24	F5	50.44 N	9.16 E
Alsina, Arg.	172	F8	33.54 S	59.23 W
Alsónémedi, Hung.	182c		47.19 N	19.10 E
Alstaden, ngh., Ger.	181		51.28 N	6.50 E
Alsten, i., Nor.	16	B10	65.57 N	12.34 E
Alsterbro, Swe.	16	K13	56.56 N	15.56 E
Alsunga, Lat.	26	D4	56.59 N	21.34 E
Alta, Nor.	14	C14	69.56 N	23.13 E
Alta, Ia., U.S.	130	B2	42.40 N	95.18 W
Altadammen, dam., Nor.	14	C14	69.42 N	23.49 E
Altaelva, stm., Nor.	14	C14	69.58 N	23.22 E
Altafjorden, strt., Nor.	14	B14	70.07 N	23.06 E
Alta Gracia, Arg.	172	E5	31.40 S	64.26 W
Altagracia, Ven.	168	B6	10.43 N	71.30 W
Altagracia de Orituco, Ven.	168	C8	9.52 N	66.23 W
Altai, mts., Asia	48	E15	48.00 N	90.00 E
Altaj, state, Russia	48	D15	51.00 N	86.00 E
Altaj see Altai, mts., Asia	48	E15	48.00 N	90.00 E
Altajskij, Russia	48	D14	51.57 N	85.19 E
Altamaha, stm., Ga., U.S.	132	E4	31.19 N	81.17 W
Altamira, Braz.	164	D7	3.10 S	52.14 W
Altamira, Chile	172	B3	25.47 S	69.51 W
Altamira, Las Cuevas de, cv., Spain	28	A6	43.23 N	4.07 W
Altamirano, Mex.	136	I10	25.53 N	97.49 W
Altamont, Il., U.S.	130	E9	39.03 N	88.45 W
Altamont, Ks., U.S.	130	G2	37.11 N	95.17 W
Altamont, Or., U.S.	148	A4	42.12 N	121.45 W
Altamont, Tn., U.S.	134	B13	35.25 N	85.43 W
Altamura, Italy	32	D10	40.49 N	16.32 E
Altamura, Isla, i., Mex.	154	C4	24.52 N	108.07 W
Altanbulag, Mong.	52	A6	50.19 N	106.29 E
Altar, Mex.	120	F7	30.43 N	111.49 W
Altar, stm., Mex.	120	F7	30.38 N	111.58 W
Altar, Desierto de, des., Mex.	120	F6	31.50 N	114.15 W
Altar de Los Sacrificios, hist., Guat.	156	D2	16.28 N	90.32 W
Altario, Ab., Can.	142	C3	51.55 N	110.09 W
Altar of the Earth, rel., China	189a		39.57 N	116.24 E
Altar of the Moon, rel., China	189a		39.55 N	116.20 E
Altar of the Sun, rel., China	189a		39.54 N	116.27 E
Altar Wash, stm., Az., U.S.	150	L5	32.04 N	111.20 W
Altata, Mex.	154	C4	24.38 N	107.55 W
Alta Vista, Ks., U.S.	138	C12	38.51 N	96.30 W
Altavista, Va., U.S.	124	G6	37.06 N	79.17 W
Altay, China	48	E15	47.50 N	88.07 E
Altay, Mong.	52	B4	46.23 N	96.15 E
Altay, Russia	48	B11	60.20 N	68.57 E
Altay see Altaj, state, Russia	48	D15	51.00 N	86.00 E
Altay Mountains see Altai, mts., Asia	48	E15	48.00 N	90.00 E
Altay Shan see Altai, mts., Asia	48	E15	48.00 N	90.00 E
Alt Buchhorst, Ger.	182a		52.26 N	13.51 E
Altdorf, Switz.	30	D5	46.53 N	8.38 E
Alte Donau, l., Aus.	182b		48.14 N	16.26 E
Alte Grund, Ger.	182a		52.28 N	13.47 E
Altenburg, Ger.	24	E8	50.59 N	12.25 E
Altenderne Oberbecker, ngh., Ger.	181		51.35 N	7.33 E
Altendorf, Ger.	181		51.29 N	7.40 E
Altendorf, ngh., Ger.	181		51.25 N	7.06 E
Altendorf-Ulfkotte, Ger.	181		51.38 N	7.00 E
Altenessen, ngh., Ger.	181		51.29 N	7.00 E
Altenhagen, ngh., Ger.	181		51.22 N	7.28 E
Altentreptow, Ger.	24	C9	53.42 N	13.14 E
Altenvoerde, Ger.	181		51.18 N	7.22 E
Alter do Chão, Port.	28	E3	39.12 N	7.40 W
Alter Rhein, stm., Ger.	181		51.35 N	6.36 E
Altevatnet, l., Nor.	14	D9	68.32 N	19.31 E
Alt-Glienicke, ngh., Ger.	182a		52.25 N	13.32 E
Altgruland, Ger.	181		51.27 N	7.41 E
Altha, Fl., U.S.	134	G13	30.34 N	85.08 W
Altham, Eng., U.K.	180		53.47 N	2.21 W
Alt-Hartmannsdorf, Ger.	182a		52.21 N	13.50 E
Althea Lake, l., Ma., U.S.	201		42.40 N	71.23 W
Altheimer, Ar., U.S.	134	C7	34.19 N	91.50 W
Althofen, Aus.	30	D11	46.53 N	14.26 E
Altınekin, Tur.	34	E15	38.18 N	32.53 E
Altinho, Braz.	170	E7	8.29 S	36.04 W
Altınoluk, Tur.	34	D9	39.34 N	26.43 E
Altınova, Tur.	34	D9	39.13 N	26.47 E
Altınözü, Tur.	76	B7	36.05 N	36.15 E
Altıntaş, Tur.	34	D13	39.04 N	30.08 E
Altınyaka, Tur.	76	B1	36.33 N	30.19 E
Altiplano, plat., S.A.	166	C3	18.00 S	68.00 W
Altkirch, Fr.	24	I3	47.37 N	7.12 E
Altlangerwisch, Ger.	182a		52.19 N	13.04 E
Altmannsdorf, ngh., Aus.	182b		48.10 N	16.20 E
Altmark, reg., Ger.	24	D7	52.40 N	11.20 E
Altmühl, stm., Ger.	24	G6	48.54 N	11.53 E
Alto, Tx., U.S.	136	C12	31.38 N	95.04 W
Alto, Cerro, mtn., Mex.	136	H2	26.44 N	105.53 W
Alto Araguaia, Braz.	166	C6	17.18 S	53.12 W
Alto Cedro, Cuba	156	B10	20.31 N	75.57 W
Alto Chicapa, Ang.	88	C2	10.56 S	19.09 E
Alto da Moóca, ngh., Braz.	205b		23.34 S	46.35 W
Alto de las Vizcachas, Cerro, mtn., Chile	204e		33.25 S	70.26 W
Alto del Carmen, Chile	172	D2	28.48 S	70.30 W
Alto de Ña Paula, Ven.	204c		10.24 N	66.48 W
Alto Garças, Braz.	166	C6	16.56 S	53.32 W
Alto Longá, Braz.	170	C4	5.15 S	42.12 W
Alto Molócuè, Moz.	88	D6	15.38 S	37.40 E
Altomünster, Ger.	24	H7	48.23 N	11.15 E
Alton, Eng., U.K.	10	J11	51.09 N	0.58 W
Alton, Il., U.S.	130	F7	38.55 N	90.11 W
Alton, Ia., U.S.	130	B1	42.59 N	96.00 W
Alton, Ks., U.S.	138	B10	39.28 N	98.56 W
Alton, Mo., U.S.	130	H6	36.41 N	91.24 W
Alton, N.H., U.S.	122	G5	43.27 N	71.13 W
Altona, Mb., Can.	142	E16	49.05 N	97.35 W
Altona Bay, b., Austl.	192b		37.53 S	144.51 E
Altona North, Austl.	192b		37.50 S	144.51 E
Altona Sports Park, p.o.i., Austl.	192b		37.52 S	144.52 E
Altoona, Al., U.S.	134	C12	34.01 N	86.19 W
Altoona, Ia., U.S.	130	C4	41.39 N	93.27 W
Altoona, Ks., U.S.	130	G2	37.31 N	95.39 W
Altoona, Pa., U.S.	124	D7	40.29 N	78.23 W
Altoona, Wi., U.S.	128	G7	44.48 N	91.25 W
Alto Paraguai, Braz.	166	B5	14.30 S	56.31 W
Alto Paraíso de Goiás, Braz.	170	G2	14.07 S	47.31 W
Alto Paraná, state, Para.	172	B10	25.30 S	54.50 W
Alto Parnaíba, Braz.	170	E2	9.06 S	45.57 W
Alto Rio Doce, Braz.	170	K4	21.02 S	43.25 W
Alto Río Mayo, Arg.	166	I2	45.03 S	71.02 W
Alto Río Senguer, Arg.	166	I2	45.03 S	70.51 W
Altos, Braz.	170	C5	5.03 S	42.28 W
Alto Santo, Braz.	170	C6	5.31 S	38.15 W
Altötting, Ger.	24	H8	48.12 N	12.39 E
Alt Rüdersdorf, Ger.	182a		52.28 N	13.49 E
Alt Stahnsdorf, Ger.	182a		52.17 N	13.53 E
Altstätten, Switz.	24	I5	47.22 N	9.32 E
Alt Töplitz, Ger.	182a		52.26 N	12.55 E
Altuhovo, Russia	26	H17	52.40 N	34.22 E
Altun Kupri, Iraq	74	C9	35.45 N	44.13 E
Altun Shan, mts., China	52	D2	38.00 N	88.00 E
Alturas, Ca., U.S.	148	B5	41.29 N	120.31 W
Altus, Ar., U.S.	134	B5	35.26 N	93.45 W
Altus, Ok., U.S.	138	G9	34.38 N	99.20 W
Altus, Lake, res., Ok., U.S.	138	G9	34.55 N	99.18 W
Altus Air Force Base, mil., Ok., U.S.	138	G9	34.40 N	99.16 W
Altynkarasu, Kaz.	40	G19	49.11 N	55.51 E
Altynivka, Ukr.	38	B12	51.27 N	33.11 E
Alu see Shortland Island, i., Sol. Is.	101b	d6	7.03 S	155.42 E
Al-ʿUbaylah, Sau. Ar.	72	E7	21.59 N	50.57 E
Al-Ubayyiḍ, Sudan	82	E6	13.11 N	30.13 E
Alubijid, Phil.	68	F5	8.34 N	124.28 E
Al-Udayyah, Sudan	82	E5	12.03 N	28.15 E
Alūksne, Lat.	26	C9	57.25 N	27.03 E
Al-ʿUlā, Sau. Ar.	72	D4	26.37 N	37.52 E
Alula see Caluula, Som.	86	B10	11.57 N	50.45 E
Alum Rock Park, p.o.i., Ca., U.S.	200		37.24 N	121.49 W
Alunda, Swe.	16	G16	60.04 N	18.05 E
Al-ʿUqaylah, Libya	82	A3	30.15 N	19.11 E
Al-ʿUqayr, Sau. Ar.	74	H12	25.39 N	50.12 E
Al-ʿUrayq, sand, Sau. Ar.	74	F6	29.10 N	39.15 E
Al-ʿUrayq, reg., Sau. Ar.	74	H8	24.50 N	42.40 E
Al-Urdun see Jordan, ctry., Asia	76	H7	31.00 N	36.00 E
Al-Urdunn see Jordan, stm., Asia	76	F6	31.45 N	35.33 E
Alushta, Ukr.	38	I13	44.41 N	34.24 E
Al-ʿUwaynāt, Libya	82	B2	25.47 N	10.33 E
Al-ʿUwaynidhīyah, i., Sau. Ar.	74	G4	26.37 N	36.04 E
Al-ʿUyaynah, Sau. Ar.	74	H10	24.54 N	46.23 E
Alva, Ok., U.S.	138	E10	36.48 N	98.39 W
Alva, stm., Port.	28	D3	40.17 N	8.14 W
Alvaiázere, Port.	28	E2	39.49 N	8.23 W
Älvängen, Swe.	16	I10	58.00 N	12.09 E
Alvanley, Eng., U.K.	180		53.16 N	2.45 W
Alvarado, Mex.	154	F11	18.46 N	95.45 W
Alvarado, Tx., U.S.	136	B10	32.24 N	97.12 W
Alvarães, Braz.	164	D5	3.11 S	64.49 W
Alvarinhos, Port.	184c		38.54 N	9.22 W
Alvaro Obregón, ngh., Mex.	204a		19.21 N	99.12 W
Álvaro Obregón, Presa, res., Mex.	154	B4	27.51 N	109.51 W
Alvastra, hist., Swe.	16	I12	58.18 N	14.39 E
Alvdal, Nor.	16	E8	62.06 N	10.38 E
Älvdalen, Swe.	16	F12	61.14 N	14.02 E
Alvear, Arg.	172	D9	29.03 S	56.33 W
Alverca, Port.	28	F1	38.53 N	9.02 W
Alverca do Ribatejo see Alverca, Port.	28	F1	38.53 N	9.02 W
Alvernia, Mount, hill, Bah.	152	C10	24.15 N	75.22 W
Alvesta, Swe.	16	K12	56.53 N	14.33 E
Ålvik, Nor.	16	G4	60.26 N	6.26 E
Alvik, Swe.	16	E15	62.25 N	17.25 E
Alvin, Tx., U.S.	136	E12	29.25 N	95.14 W
Alvinópolis, Braz.	170	K4	20.06 S	43.03 W
Alviso, ngh., Ca., U.S.	200		37.26 N	121.58 W
Alviso Slough, stm., Ca., U.S.	200		37.27 N	122.02 W
Alvito, Port.	28	F2	38.15 N	7.59 W
Älvkarleby, Swe.	16	G15	60.34 N	17.26 E
Alvord, Tx., U.S.	138	H11	33.22 N	97.42 W
Alvord Desert, des., Or., U.S.	146	H8	42.32 N	118.26 W
Alvord Lake, l., Or., U.S.	148	A7	42.23 N	118.36 W
Alvøy, i., Nor.	16	G2	60.36 N	4.50 E
Älvros, Swe.	16	E12	62.03 N	14.39 E
Älvsbyn, Swe.	14	G11	65.40 N	20.59 E
Al-Wajh, Sau. Ar.	72	D4	26.13 N	36.28 E
Al-Wakrah, Qatar	74	H12	25.10 N	51.36 E
Alwar, India	70	E6	27.33 N	76.36 E
Alwaye, India	69	F3	10.06 N	76.21 E
Alxa Zuoqi, China	58	B1	38.49 N	105.34 E
Al-Yaman see Yemen, ctry., Asia	72	F6	15.00 N	44.00 E
Alygdžer, Russia	48	D17	53.37 N	98.14 E
Alyn and Deeside, mun., Wales, U.K.	180		53.16 N	3.02 W
Alytus, Lith.	26	F6	54.23 N	24.03 E
Alz, stm., Ger.	30	B9	48.16 N	12.48 E
Alzey, Ger.	24	G4	49.44 N	8.07 E
Alzira, Spain	28	E10	39.09 N	0.26 W
Amacuro (Amakura), stm., S.A.	168	C11	8.31 N	60.27 W
Amadeus, Lake, l., Austl.	96	D6	24.41 S	130.50 E
Amadjuak Lake, l., Nu., Can.	110	B16	65.00 N	71.00 W
Amadora, Port.	184c		38.45 N	9.14 W
Amador Valley, val., Ca., U.S.	200		37.41 N	121.51 W
Amagansett, N.Y., U.S.	124	D13	40.58 N	72.08 W
Amagasaki, Japan	56	E8	34.43 N	135.25 E
Amager, i., Den.	16	L10	55.36 N	12.36 E
Amagi, Japan	56	F3	33.25 N	130.39 E
Amahai, Indon.	60	F8	3.19 S	128.56 E
Amaichá del Valle, Arg.	172	C4	26.36 S	65.51 W
Amaimon, Pap. N. Gui.	101a	b4	5.07 S	145.24 E
Amajac, stm., Mex.	154	E9	21.15 N	98.46 W
Ama Keng, Sing.	189c		1.24 N	103.42 E
Amakura (Amacuro), stm., S.A.	168	C11	8.31 N	60.27 W
Amakusa-nada, s., Japan	56	G2	32.35 N	130.01 E
Amakusa-shotō, is., Japan	56	G2	32.20 N	130.15 E
Amakuso-Shimo-shima, i., Japan	56	G2	32.20 N	130.05 E
Åmål, Swe.	16	H10	59.03 N	12.42 E
Amalāpuram, India	69	C6	16.35 N	82.01 E
Amalfi, Col.	164	B2	6.54 N	75.04 W
Amaliáda, Grc.	34	F4	37.47 N	21.21 E
Amalner, India	70	H5	21.02 N	75.04 E
Amambaí, Braz.	166	D5	23.06 S	55.13 W
Amami Islands see Amami-Ō-shima, i., Japan	55a	k19	28.15 N	129.20 E
Amami-Ō-shima, i., Japan	55a	k19	28.15 N	129.20 E
Amami-shotō, is., Japan	55a	k19	27.58 N	129.02 E
Amana, Ia., U.S.	130	C6	41.47 N	91.52 W
Amana, stm., Ven.	168	C10	9.44 N	62.38 W
Amanã, Lago, l., Braz.	168	I9	2.35 S	64.40 W
Amanda, Oh., U.S.	124	E3	39.38 N	82.44 W
Amānganj, India	70	F8	24.24 N	80.02 E
Ämänningen, l., Swe.	16	H13	59.56 N	15.58 E
Amano, Japan	188		34.26 N	135.33 E
Amantea, Italy	32	E9	39.08 N	16.05 E
Amantogaj, Kaz.	48	D10	50.27 N	65.37 E
Amapá, Braz.	164	C7	2.02 N	50.46 W
Amapá, state, Braz.	164	C7	1.00 N	52.00 W
Amaral, Braz.	205a		22.42 S	43.29 W
Amarante, Braz.	170	D4	6.14 S	42.50 W
Amarante do Maranhão, Braz.	170	C2	5.30 S	46.45 W
Amaranth, Mb., Can.	142	D15	50.35 N	98.44 W
Amarapura, Mya.	64	B3	21.55 N	96.04 E
Amărăştii de Jos, Rom.	36	F11	43.59 N	24.10 E
Amarāvati, stm., India	69	F3	10.56 N	78.13 E
Amardalay, Mong.	52	B6	46.07 N	106.22 E
Amares, Port.	28	C2	41.38 N	8.21 W
Amargosa, Braz.	170	G6	13.01 S	39.35 W
Amargosa, stm., U.S.	148	G9	36.12 N	116.49 W
Amargosa Range, mts., Ca., U.S.	148	G9	36.28 N	116.44 W
Amarillo, Tx., U.S.	138	F7	35.13 N	101.49 W
Amarkantak, India	70	G8	22.40 N	81.45 E
Amaro, Monte, mtn., Italy	30	H11	42.05 N	14.05 E
Amaroúsion, Grc.	185c		38.03 N	23.49 E
Amarume, Japan	56	A12	38.49 N	139.54 E
Amasa, Mi., U.S.	126	B1	46.13 N	88.29 W
Amasia, Arm.	42	E10	40.58 N	43.46 E
Amasija see Amasia, Arm.	42	E10	40.58 N	43.46 E
Amasra, Tur.	34	B15	41.44 N	32.22 E
Amasya, Tur.	42	E6	40.39 N	35.49 E
Amasya, state, Tur.	42	E6	40.45 N	35.30 E
aMatikulu, S. Afr.	90	F10	29.02 S	31.32 E
Amatrice, Italy	30	H10	42.37 N	13.17 E
Amatsu-kominato, Japan	56	D13	35.07 N	140.09 E
Amawbia Awka, Nig.	84	H6	6.12 N	7.04 E
Amazar, Russia	50	F13	53.51 N	120.51 E
Amazon (Amazonas) (Solimões), stm., S.A.	164	D7	0.03 S	49.15 W
Amazonas, state, Braz.	164	D4	5.00 S	63.00 W
Amazonas, state, Col.	168	H6	1.28 S	71.01 W
Amazonas, state, Ven.	168	F9	3.30 N	66.00 W
Amazonas see Amazon, stm., S.A.	164	D7	0.03 S	49.15 W
Amb, Pak.	70	A4	34.19 N	72.51 E
Ambaí, Braz.	205a		22.43 S	43.28 W
Ambājogāi, India	69	B3	18.44 N	76.23 E
Ambāla, India	70	C6	30.21 N	76.49 E
Ambalangoda, Sri L.	69	H4	6.14 N	80.03 E
Ambalavao, Madag.	88	E8	21.50 S	46.58 E
Ambam, Cam.	86	D2	2.23 N	11.16 E
Ambanja, Madag.	88	C8	13.40 S	48.27 E
Ambarčik, Russia	50	C21	69.38 N	162.27 E
Ambargasta, Salinas de, pl., Arg.	172	D5	29.15 S	64.30 W
Ambarnyj, Russia	18	B20	65.54 N	33.39 E
Ambassador Bridge, trans., N.A.	199		42.20 N	83.05 W
Ambato, Ec.	168	H2	1.14 S	78.37 W
Ambatofinandrahana, Madag.	88	E8	20.33 S	46.48 E
Ambatolampy, Madag.	88	D8	19.22 S	47.27 E
Ambatondrazaka, Madag.	88	D8	17.51 S	48.24 E
Ambelau, Pulau, i., Indon.	60	F8	3.51 S	127.12 E
Amberg, Ger.	24	G7	49.26 N	11.51 E
Amberg, Wi., U.S.	126	C2	45.30 N	88.00 W
Ambergris Cay, i., Belize	156	C4	18.03 N	87.55 W
Ambérieu-en-Bugey, Fr.	22	D11	45.57 N	5.22 E
Ambert, Fr.	22	D9	45.33 N	3.45 E
Ambidédi, Mali	84	G2	14.34 N	11.47 W
Ambikāpur, India	70	G9	23.07 N	83.12 E
Ambilobe, Madag.	88	C8	13.11 S	49.02 E
Ambjörby, Swe.	16	G11	60.29 N	13.11 E
Ambla, Est.	26	A8	59.11 N	25.50 E
Amble, Eng., U.K.	10	F11	55.20 N	1.35 W
Ambléve, stm., Bel.	20	D14	50.28 N	5.35 E
Ambo, Peru	164	F2	10.07 S	76.10 W
Amboasary, Madag.	88	E8	25.02 S	46.23 E
Ambodifototra, Madag.	88	D8	17.00 S	49.51 E
Ambohimahasoa, Madag.	88	E8	21.06 S	47.13 E
Ambohitra, mtn., Madag.	88	C8	12.33 S	49.10 E
Amboina see Ambon, Indon.	60	F8	3.43 S	128.11 E
Amboise, Fr.	22	G10	47.24 N	0.59 E
Ambon, Indon.	60	F8	3.43 S	128.11 E
Ambon, Pulau, i., Indon.	60	F8	3.39 S	128.05 E
Amboseli, Lake, l., Afr.	86	E7	2.37 S	37.08 E
Amboseli National Park, p.o.i., Kenya	86	E7	2.36 S	37.11 E
Amboshe, India	190c		19.09 N	73.08 E
Ambositra, Madag.	88	E8	20.31 S	47.15 E
Ambovombe, Madag.	88	F8	25.11 S	46.05 E
Amboy, Il., U.S.	130	C8	41.42 N	89.19 W
Amboy, Mn., U.S.	128	H4	43.53 N	94.09 W
Ambre, Cap d' see Bobaomby, Tanjona, c., Madag.	88	C8	11.57 S	49.15 E
Ambridge, Pa., U.S.	124	D5	40.36 N	80.13 W
Ambridge Heights, Pa., U.S.	197b		40.36 N	80.13 W
Ambriz, Ang.	88	B1	7.51 S	13.10 E
Ambrose, N.D., U.S.	142	F10	48.57 N	103.29 W
Ambrose Brook, stm., N.J., U.S.	194		40.33 N	74.32 W
Ambrose Channel, strt., U.S.	194		40.32 N	74.02 W
Ambrosia Lake, N.M., U.S.	150	H9	35.25 N	107.49 W
Ambrym, i., Vanuatu	101d	k17	16.15 S	168.10 E
Ambuntentimur, Indon.	66	G8	6.53 S	113.48 E
Ambunti, Pap. N. Gui.	101a	a3	4.12 S	142.51 E
Āmbūr, India	69	E4	12.47 N	78.43 E
Amburambur, Indon.	66	H10	8.15 S	116.17 E
Amchitka Island, i., Ak., U.S.	109a	g22	51.31 N	179.01 E
Amchitka Pass, strt., Ak., U.S.	109a	g22	51.30 N	179.30 W
'Amd, Yemen	72	F6	15.17 N	47.57 E
Am Dam, Chad	82	E4	12.45 N	20.27 E
Āmdānga, India	190b		22.49 N	88.31 E
Amdo, China	52	E3	32.16 N	91.43 E
Ameagle, W.V., U.S.	124	G4	37.56 N	81.25 W
Ameca, Mex.	154	E6	20.33 N	104.02 W
Ameca, stm., Mex.	154	E6	20.41 N	105.17 W
Ameghino, Arg.	172	G6	34.50 S	62.28 W
Ameixoeira, ngh., Port.	184c		38.47 N	9.10 W
Ameland, i., Neth.	20	A14	53.27 N	5.44 E
Amelia Court House, Va., U.S.	124	G8	37.20 N	77.58 W
Amelia Island, i., Fl., U.S.	132	F4	30.37 N	81.27 W
Amenucourt, Fr.	179		49.06 N	1.39 E
Amer, India	70	E5	26.59 N	75.52 E
Amerevo, Russia	183b		55.55 N	38.03 E
American, North Fork, stm., Ca., U.S.	148	D5	38.43 N	121.09 W
American, South Fork, stm., Ca., U.S.	148	E5	38.43 N	121.08 W
Americana, Braz.	170	L2	22.45 S	47.19 W
American Cemetery and Memorial, misc. cult., Phil.	187l		14.33 N	121.03 E
American Falls, Id., U.S.	146	H14	42.47 N	112.51 W
American Falls, wtfl., N.Y., U.S.	202a		43.05 N	79.04 W
American Falls Reservoir, res., Id., U.S.	146	H13	42.56 N	112.44 W
American Fork, Ut., U.S.	150	C5	40.23 N	111.47 W
American Highland, plat., Ant.	103	C12	72.30 S	78.00 E
American Museum of Natural History, bldg., N.Y., U.S.	194		40.47 N	73.59 W
Americanos, Barra de los, i., Mex.	154	C10	24.52 N	97.35 W
American Samoa, dep., Oc.	101c	h12	14.20 S	170.00 W
American University, educ., D.C., U.S.	202c		38.56 N	77.05 W
Américas, Hipódromo de las, p.o.i., Mex.	204a		19.26 N	99.13 W
Americus, Ga., U.S.	132	D1	32.04 N	84.13 W
Americus, Ks., U.S.	130	F1	38.30 N	96.15 W
Amerika Samoa see American Samoa, dep., Oc.	101c	h12	14.20 S	170.00 W

Name	Page	Map Ref.	Latitude	Longitude
Anpu, China	58	K3	21.27 N	110.01 E
Anqing, China	58	F7	30.30 N	117.02 E
Anqiu, China	58	C8	36.25 N	119.11 E
Anren, China	58	H5	26.41 N	113.15 E
Ansai, China	58	C3	36.51 N	109.18 E
Ansbach, Ger.	24	G6	49.18 N	10.34 E
Anschlag, Ger.	181		51.10 N	7.29 E
Anse-Bertrand, Guad.	159c	h5	16.28 N	61.30 W
Anse-d'Hainault, Haiti	156	C10	18.29 N	74.26 W
Anse La Raye, St. Luc.	159c	m6	13.56 N	61.02 W
Anselmo, Ne., U.S.	140	F13	41.37 N	99.51 W
Anserma, Col.	168	E4	5.14 N	75.47 W
Anshan, China	52	C9	41.08 N	122.59 E
Anshun, China	58	H1	26.15 N	105.56 E
Ansina, Ur.	172	E10	31.52 S	55.26 W
Ansley, Ne., U.S.	140	F13	41.17 N	99.23 W
Anson, Tx., U.S.	136	B8	32.44 N	99.53 W
Anson Bay, b., Austl.	96	B5	13.23 S	130.03 E
Anson Bay, b., Norf. I.	100i	y24	29.00 S	167.55 E
Ansongo, Mali	84	F5	15.40 N	0.30 E
Anson Point, c., Norf. I.	100i	y24	29.00 S	167.54 E
Ansonville, N.C., U.S.	132	A5	35.05 N	80.06 W
Ansted, W.V., U.S.	124	F4	38.07 N	81.06 W
Ansudu, Indon.	60	F10	2.07 S	139.15 E
Antakya see Hatay, Tur.	42	G7	36.12 N	36.10 E
Antalaha, Madag.	88	C9	14.54 S	50.16 E
Antalieptė, Lith.	26	E8	55.40 N	25.51 E
Antalivtsi, Ukr.	24	H18	48.37 N	22.31 E
Antalya, Tur.	34	G13	36.53 N	30.41 E
Antalya, state, Tur.	34	F14	37.00 N	31.00 E
Antalya, Gulf of see Antalya Körfezi, b., Tur.	34	G14	36.30 N	31.00 E
Antalya Körfezi (Antalya, Gulf of), b., Tur.	34	G14	36.30 N	31.00 E
Antananarivo, Madag.	88	D8	18.55 S	47.31 E
An tAonach see Nenagh, Ire.	10	I4	52.51 N	8.11 W
Antarctica, cont.	103	D11	87.00 S	60.00 E
Antarctic Peninsula, pen., Ant.	103	C35	70.14 S	65.55 W
Antas, Braz.	170	F6	10.22 S	38.20 W
Antas, stm., Braz.	172	D12	29.01 S	51.28 W
Antelope Creek, stm., Nv., U.S.	148	C8	40.00 N	117.25 W
Antelope Creek, stm., S.D., U.S.	140	B10	45.19 N	102.26 W
Antelope Creek, stm., Wy., U.S.	140	D7	43.29 N	105.14 W
Antelope Island, i., Ut., U.S.	150	C4	40.57 N	112.12 W
Antelope Mine, Zimb.	90	B9	21.02 S	28.27 E
Antelope Peak, mtn., Nv., U.S.	148	B10	41.19 N	114.58 W
Antelope Reservoir, res., Or., U.S.	146	H9	42.54 N	117.13 W
Antelope Wash, stm., Nv., U.S.	148	D9	39.32 N	116.16 W
Antenor Navarro, Braz.	170	D6	6.44 S	38.27 W
Antequera, Para.	172	A9	24.03 S	57.13 W
Antequera, Spain	28	H6	37.01 N	4.33 W
Anthon, Ia., U.S.	130	B2	42.22 N	95.52 W
Anthony, Fl., U.S.	132	G3	29.17 N	82.06 W
Anthony, Ks., U.S.	138	D10	37.09 N	98.01 W
Anthony, N.M., U.S.	136	B1	32.00 N	106.36 W
Anthony, Tx., U.S.	120	E9	31.59 N	106.35 W
Anthony Chabot Regional Park, p.o.i., Ca., U.S.	200		37.45 N	122.06 W
Anthony Creek, stm., W.V., U.S.	124	F5	37.53 N	80.19 W
Anthony Peak, mtn., Ca., U.S.	148	D3	39.51 N	122.58 W
Anti-Atlas, mts., Mor.	84	D3	30.00 N	8.30 W
Antibes, Fr.	22	F13	43.35 N	7.07 E
Anticosti, Île d', i., Qc., Can.	106	E16	49.30 N	63.00 W
Antietam National Battlefield, p.o.i., Md., U.S.	124	E7	39.24 N	77.47 W
Antifer, Cap d', c., Fr.	20	E8	49.41 N	0.10 E
Antigo, Wi., U.S.	128	F9	45.08 N	89.08 W
Antigonish, N.S., Can.	122	E14	45.37 N	61.59 W
Antigua, i., Antig.	159b	f4	17.04 N	61.49 W
Antigua and Barbuda, ctry., N.A.	152a	h15	17.03 N	61.48 W
Antigua International Airport, arpt., Antig.	159b	f4	17.08 N	61.47 W
Antigues, Pointe d', c., Guad.	159c	h5	16.26 N	61.32 W
Antiguo Morelos, Mex.	154	D9	22.33 N	99.05 W
Antikýthira, i., Grc.	34	H6	35.52 N	23.18 E
Anti-Lebanon (Sharqī, Al-Jabal ash-), mts., Asia	76	E7	34.00 N	36.30 E
Antilla, Arg.	172	C5	26.07 S	64.36 W
Antilla, Cuba	156	B10	20.50 N	75.43 W
Antillas, Archipiélago de las see West Indies, is.	106	G15	19.00 N	70.00 W
Antillas, Mar de las see Caribbean Sea, s.	106	H15	15.00 N	73.00 W
Antillas Mayores see Greater Antilles, is., N.A.	106	H15	20.00 N	74.00 W
Antillen, Nederlandse see Netherlands Antilles, dep., N.A.	158g	p22	12.15 N	68.45 W
Antilles, Grandes see Greater Antilles, is., N.A.	106	H15	20.00 N	74.00 W
Antilles, Mer des see Caribbean Sea, s.	106	H15	15.00 N	73.00 W
Antilles, Petites see Lesser Antilles, is.	106	H16	15.00 N	61.00 W
Antímano, ngh., Ven.	204c		10.28 N	66.59 W
Antimony, Ut., U.S.	150	E5	38.07 N	112.00 W
An tInbhear Mór see Arklow, Ire.	10	I6	52.48 N	6.09 W
Antioch see Hatay, Tur.	42	G7	36.12 N	36.10 E
Antioch, Il., U.S.	130	B9	42.28 N	88.05 W
Antioquia, Col.	168	D4	6.33 N	75.49 W
Antioquia, state, Col.	168	D4	7.00 N	75.30 W
Antipajuta, Russia	50	C4	69.06 N	76.48 E
Antíparos, i., Grc.	34	G8	37.00 N	25.03 E
Antipino, Russia	26	E16	55.54 N	33.17 E
Antipodes Islands, is., N.Z.	94	H8	49.40 S	178.47 E
Antiquarian Museum, bldg., Ma., U.S.	201		42.27 N	71.20 W
Antisana, vol., Ec.	168	H2	0.28 S	78.08 W
Antler, stm., N.A.	142	E12	49.07 N	101.00 W
Antlers, Ok., U.S.	134	C3	34.13 N	95.36 W
Antofagasta, Chile	172	A2	23.39 S	70.23 W
Antofagasta, state, Chile	172	B3	24.31 S	69.51 W
Antofagasta de la Sierra, Arg.	172	C4	26.04 S	67.23 W
Antofalla, Salar de, pl., Arg.	172	C3	25.52 S	67.50 W
Antofalla, Volcán, vol., Arg.	172	B4	25.34 S	67.55 W
Antón, Pan.	156	H7	8.24 N	80.14 W
Anton, Tx., U.S.	138	H6	33.48 N	102.10 W
Anton Chico, N.M., U.S.	138	F3	35.12 N	105.09 W
Antongil, Baia d' see Antongila, Helodrano, b., Madag.	88	D8	15.45 S	49.50 E
Antongila, Helodrano, b., Madag.	88	D8	15.45 S	49.50 E
Antonina, Braz.	172	B13	25.26 S	48.43 W
Antonina do Norte, Braz.	170	D5	6.43 S	39.58 W
Antoniny, Ukr.	38	D5	49.48 N	26.53 E
Antonio Amaro, Mex.	154	C6	24.16 N	104.01 W
Antonio de Biedma, Arg.	166	I3	47.29 S	66.30 W
António Enes see Angoche, Moz.	88	D6	16.13 S	39.55 E
Antônio Prado, Braz.	172	D12	28.51 S	51.16 W
Antonito, Co., U.S.	138	D2	37.04 N	106.01 W
Antoniv, Ukr.	38	D8	49.36 N	29.47 E
Antón Lizardo, Punta, c., Mex.	154	F10	19.02 N	96.02 W
Antopal', Bela.	26	H7	52.12 N	24.47 E
Antou, China	58	H8	26.07 N	118.11 E
Antratsyt, Ukr.	38	E18	48.07 N	39.06 E
Antrim, N. Ire., U.K.	10	G6	54.43 N	6.13 W
Antrodoco, Italy	32	B7	42.25 N	13.04 E
Antropologia, Museo Nacional de, bldg., Mex.	204a		19.25 N	99.11 W
Antropovo, Russia	40	B13	58.23 N	42.58 E
Antsalova, Madag.	88	D7	18.41 S	44.37 E
Antsirabe, Madag.	88	D8	19.52 S	47.01 E
Antsiranana, Madag.	88	C8	12.16 S	49.17 E
Antsirane see Antsiranana, Madag.	88	C8	12.16 S	49.17 E
Antsla, Est.	26	C9	57.50 N	26.32 E
Antsohihy, Madag.	88	C8	14.48 S	48.03 E
Anttis, Swe.	14	E13	67.14 N	22.54 E
Antulai, Gunong, mtn., Malay.	66	A10	4.40 N	116.21 E
Antun', Russia	50	G16	47.36 N	135.45 E
Antung see Dandong, China	52	C9	40.06 N	124.21 E
Antuševo, Russia	18	H24	59.54 N	37.40 E
Antwerp see Antwerpen, Bel.	20	C13	51.13 N	4.24 E
Antwerp, Oh., U.S.	124	C1	41.10 N	84.44 W
Antwerpen (Antwerp), Bel.	20	C13	51.13 N	4.24 E
An Uaimh see Navan, Ire.	10	H6	53.39 N	6.41 W
Anučino, Russia	54	C10	43.57 N	133.02 E
Anugul, India	70	H10	20.51 N	85.06 E
Anūpgarh, India	70	D4	29.11 N	73.13 E
Anuradhapura, Sri L.	69	G5	8.20 N	80.23 E
Anvers see Antwerpen, Bel.	20	C13	51.13 N	4.24 E
Anvers Island, i., Ant.	103	B34	64.33 S	63.35 W
Anvik, Ak., U.S.	109	D7	62.40 N	160.12 W
Anxi, China	52	C4	40.28 N	95.46 E
Anxi, China	58	I8	25.03 N	118.10 E
Anxiang, China	58	G5	29.23 N	112.09 E
Anxious Bay, b., Austl.	96	F6	33.25 S	134.35 E
Anyang, China	58	C6	36.05 N	114.20 E
Anyang, Kor., S.	54	F7	37.23 N	126.55 E
Anyang, stm., China	58	C6	35.59 N	114.47 E
A'nyêmaqên Shan, mts., China	52	E4	34.49 N	99.45 E
Anyer Kidul, Indon.	66	F5	6.04 S	105.53 E
Anykščiai, Lith.	26	E8	55.31 N	25.06 E
Anyuan, China	58	I6	25.08 N	115.23 E
Anyuanyi see Tianzhu, China	52	D5	36.59 N	103.06 E
Anyue, China	58	F1	30.06 N	105.19 E
Anza-Borrego Desert State Park, p.o.i., Ca., U.S.	148	J9	33.04 N	116.17 W
Anze, China	58	C5	36.11 N	112.16 E
Anžero-Sudžensk, Russia	48	C15	56.04 N	86.01 E
Anzerskij, ostrov, i., Russia	18	B23	65.09 N	36.02 E
Anzio, Italy	32	C6	41.26 N	12.37 E
Anzoátegui, state, Ven.	168	C9	9.00 N	64.30 W
Anžu, ostrova, is., Russia	50	A17	75.31 N	142.54 E
Aoba, i., Vanuatu	101d	j16	15.25 S	167.50 E
Aoga-shima, i., Japan	56	G12	32.28 N	139.46 E
Aohan Qi, China	54	C3	42.16 N	119.54 E
Aoiz, Spain	28	B9	42.47 N	1.22 W
Aojiang, China	58	H9	27.36 N	120.32 E
Aoji-ri, Kor., N.	54	C9	42.31 N	130.20 E
Aola, Sol. Is.	101b	e9	9.32 S	160.28 E
Ao Luk, Thai.	64	H4	8.23 N	98.44 E
Aomar, Alg.	28	H14	36.30 N	3.45 E
Aomen see Macau, Macao	58	J5	22.12 N	113.32 E
Aomen see Macau, dep., Asia	58	J5	22.10 N	113.33 E
Aomori, Japan	54	D14	40.49 N	140.45 E
Aonla, India	70	D7	28.16 N	79.07 E
Aóös (Vjosës), stm., Eur.	32	D13	40.39 N	19.19 E
A'opo, Samoa	101c	g11	13.32 S	172.30 W
Aoraki (Cook, Mount), mtn., N.Z.	102	F4	43.36 S	170.10 E
Aôral, Phnum, mtn., Camb.	64	F7	12.02 N	104.09 E
Aore, i., Vanuatu	101d	j16	15.35 S	167.10 E
Aosta (Aoste), Italy	30	E4	45.44 N	7.19 E
Aoste see Aosta, Italy	30	E4	45.44 N	7.19 E
'Aouâna see 'Aklé 'Aouâna, reg., Afr.	84	F3	18.00 N	5.30 W
Aouderas, Niger	84	F6	17.36 N	8.24 E
Aouk, Bahr, stm., Afr.	82	F3	8.51 N	18.51 E
Aoukâr, reg., Maur.	84	F3	18.00 N	9.30 W
Aoulime, Jbel, mtn., Mor.	84	C3	30.48 N	8.50 W
Aoya, Japan	56	D7	35.31 N	133.59 E
Aoyama University, educ., Japan	186		35.39 N	139.43 E
Aozou, Chad	82	C3	21.49 N	17.25 E
Apache, Ok., U.S.	138	G10	34.53 N	98.22 W
Apache Junction, Az., U.S.	150	J5	33.26 N	111.34 W
Apache Lake, res., Az., U.S.	150	J5	33.35 N	111.14 W
Apache Peak, mtn., Az., U.S.	150	L6	31.49 N	110.25 W
Apalachee, stm., Ga., U.S.	132	C2	33.32 N	83.17 W
Apalachee Bay, b., Fl., U.S.	112	F11	30.01 N	84.13 W
Apalaches see Appalachian Mountains, mts., N.A.	112	D12	41.00 N	77.00 W
Apalachicola, Fl., U.S.	134	H13	29.43 N	84.59 W
Apalachicola, stm., Fl., U.S.	134	H14	29.43 N	84.58 W
Apalachicola Bay, b., Fl., U.S.	134	H13	29.39 N	85.02 W
Apapa, ngh., Nig.	191a		6.27 N	3.22 E
Apapa Wharf, trans., Nig.	191a		6.23 N	3.23 E
Apaporis, stm., S.A.	168	H7	1.21 S	69.25 W
Aparados da Serra, Parque Nacional de, p.o.i., Braz.	172	D12	29.15 S	50.07 W
Aparime see Riverton, N.Z.	102	H2	46.21 S	168.01 E
Aparri, Phil.	68	A3	18.20 N	121.39 E
Apartadó, Col.	168	D3	7.55 N	76.38 W
Apatin, Yugo.	36	D5	45.40 N	18.58 E
Apatity, Russia	14	E24	67.33 N	33.23 E
Apatzingán de la Constitución, Mex.	154	F7	19.05 N	102.21 W
Apaxtla de Castrejón, Mex.	154	F9	18.08 N	99.53 W
Ap Ba Tien, Viet.	187c		10.44 N	106.36 E
Ap Binh Quoi, Viet.	187c		10.48 N	106.36 E
Ape, Lat.	26	C9	57.32 N	26.40 E
Apelação, Port.	184c		38.49 N	9.08 W
Apeldoorn, Neth.	20	B15	52.12 N	5.57 E
Apennines see Appennino, mts., Italy	8	G11	43.00 N	13.00 E
Apese, ngh., Nig.	191a		6.25 N	3.25 E
Apex, N.C., U.S.	124	I7	35.43 N	78.51 W
Api, mtn., Nepal	70	D8	30.00 N	80.57 E
Api, Tanjung, c., Indon.	60	F7	0.48 S	121.38 E
Apía, Col.	168	E4	5.05 N	75.57 W
Apia, Samoa	101c	g12	13.50 S	171.45 W
Apiacás, Serra dos, plat., Braz.	164	E6	10.15 S	57.15 W
Apiaí, Braz.	172	B13	24.31 S	48.50 W
Apiaú, stm., Braz.	168	F11	2.40 N	61.12 W
Apishapa, stm., Co., U.S.	138	D4	38.08 N	103.57 W
Apizaco, Mex.	154	F9	19.25 N	98.08 W
Apizolaya, Mex.	154	C7	24.50 N	102.15 W
Ap Lei Chau, i., China	189d		22.15 N	114.09 E
Aplerbeck, ngh., Ger.	181		51.29 N	7.33 E
Apo, Mount, mtn., Phil.	68	G5	6.59 N	125.16 E
Apodi, Braz.	170	C7	5.39 S	37.48 W
Apodi, stm., Braz.	170	C7	4.56 S	37.08 W
Apolakkiá, Grc.	34	G10	36.05 N	27.46 E
Apolda, Ger.	24	E7	51.01 N	11.31 E
Apolima Strait, strt., Samoa	101c	g11	13.47 S	172.07 W
Apolinario Saravia, Arg.	172	B6	24.25 S	64.00 W
Apollo Bay, Austl.	98	L4	38.45 S	143.40 E
Apolo, Bol.	166	B3	14.43 S	68.31 W
Apón, stm., Ven.	168	B5	10.00 N	72.16 W
Aponguao, stm., Ven.	168	E11	4.49 N	61.34 W
Apopka, Lake, l., Fl., U.S.	132	H4	28.37 N	81.38 W
Apoquindo, Chile	204e		33.24 S	70.32 W
Aporá, Braz.	170	F6	11.39 S	38.04 W
Aporé, Braz.	166	C6	18.57 S	52.00 W
Aporema, Braz.	164	C7	1.14 N	50.48 W
Apostle Islands, is., Wi., U.S.	128	E8	46.50 N	90.30 W
Apostle Islands National Lakeshore, p.o.i., Wi., U.S.	128	D8	46.55 N	90.45 W
Apóstoles, Arg.	172	C10	27.54 S	55.47 W
Apostolove, Ukr.	38	F12	47.39 N	33.43 E
Appalaches, Les see Appalachian Mountains, mts., N.A.	112	D12	41.00 N	77.00 W
Appalachia, Va., U.S.	124	H3	36.54 N	82.48 W
Appalachian Mountains, mts., N.A.	112	D12	41.00 N	77.00 W
Äppelbo, Swe.	16	G11	60.29 N	13.59 E
Appennino (Apennines), mts., Italy	8	G11	43.00 N	13.00 E
Appennino, Calabro, mts., Italy	32	F10	39.00 N	16.30 E
Appennino Abruzzese, mts., Italy	32	B7	42.00 N	14.00 E
Appennino Ligure, mts., Italy	30	F5	44.30 N	9.00 E
Appennino Lucano, mts., Italy	32	D9	40.42 N	15.37 E
Appennino Tosco-Emiliano, mts., Italy	30	G8	44.00 N	11.30 E
Appennino Umbro-Marchigiano, mts., Italy	30	G9	43.20 N	12.45 E
Appenzell, Switz.	30	C6	47.19 N	9.24 E
Apple, stm., U.S.	130	B7	42.09 N	90.13 W
Apple, stm., Wi., U.S.	128	F6	45.08 N	92.44 W
Appleby, Eng., U.K.	10	G10	54.35 N	2.30 W
Apple Creek, stm., Il., U.S.	130	E7	39.21 N	90.36 W
Apple Creek, stm., N.D., U.S.	142	H13	46.41 N	100.46 W
Applegate, stm., Or., U.S.	148	A2	42.26 N	123.27 W
Apple Orchard Mountain, mtn., Va., U.S.	124	G6	37.31 N	79.31 W
Appleton, Eng., U.K.	180		53.21 N	2.33 W
Appleton, Mn., U.S.	128	F3	45.12 N	96.01 W
Appleton, Wi., U.S.	128	G10	44.16 N	88.23 W
Appleton City, Mo., U.S.	130	F3	38.11 N	94.01 W
Apple Valley, Ca., U.S.	148	I8	34.30 N	117.11 W
Appley Bridge, Eng., U.K.	180		53.35 N	2.43 W
Appomattox, Va., U.S.	124	G7	37.20 N	78.49 W
Appomattox, stm., Va., U.S.	124	G7	37.18 N	77.15 W
Appomattox Court House National Historical Park, p.o.i., Va., U.S.	124	G7	37.23 N	78.48 W
Apra Harbor, b., Guam	100c	j9	13.26 N	144.39 E
Aprelevka, Russia	26	E20	55.32 N	37.04 E
Aprilia, Italy	32	C6	41.35 N	12.38 E
Apšeronsk, Russia	42	C8	44.27 N	39.43 E
Apšeronskij poluostrov see Abşeron yarımadası, pen., Azer.	42	E14	40.27 N	50.08 E
Apshawa, N.J., U.S.	194		41.01 N	74.22 W
Apsheron Peninsula see Abşeron yarımadası, pen., Azer.	42	E14	40.27 N	50.08 E
Apt, Fr.	22	F11	43.52 N	5.23 E
Aptakisic, Il., U.S.	196		42.12 N	87.56 W
Ap Tan Hoa, Viet.	187c		10.45 N	106.35 E
Apuane, Alpi, mts., Italy	30	F7	44.03 N	10.27 E
Apuaú, stm., Braz.	168	I11	2.32 S	60.47 W
Apucarana, Braz.	172	A12	23.32 S	51.27 W
Apulia see Puglia, state, Italy	32	C11	41.00 N	16.30 E
Apure, state, Ven.	168	D7	7.10 N	68.50 W
Apure, stm., Ven.	168	D8	7.37 N	66.22 W
Apurímac, stm., Peru	164	F3	11.51 S	73.57 W
Apurito, Ven.	168	D7	7.55 N	68.28 W
Aqaba, Gulf of, b.	76	J5	29.05 N	34.44 E
Āqchah, Afg.	72	B10	36.55 N	66.09 E
'Aqīq, Sudan	82	D7	18.10 N	38.10 E
Aq Qal'eh, Iran	74	B14	37.01 N	54.27 E
'Aqrah, Iraq	74	B8	36.44 N	43.57 E
Aqtaū see Aktau, Kaz.	48	F8	43.38 N	51.10 E
Aqtöbe see Aktjubinsk, Kaz.	48	D9	50.17 N	57.09 E
Aquarium, bldg., India	190c		18.57 N	72.49 E
Aquarius Plateau, plat., Ut., U.S.	150	E5	38.01 N	111.39 W
Aqueduct Race Track, p.o.i., N.Y., U.S.	194		40.40 N	73.50 W
Aquidabã, Braz.	170	F7	10.16 S	37.02 W
Aquidauana, Braz.	166	D5	20.28 S	55.47 W
Aquila see L'Áquila, Italy	30	H10	42.21 N	13.23 E
Aquila, Mex.	154	F7	18.36 N	103.30 W
Aquiles Serdán, Mex.	154	A6	28.35 N	105.53 W
Aquiles Serdán, Mex.	154	C9	25.34 N	97.55 W
Aquilla, Tx., U.S.	136	C10	31.51 N	97.13 W
Aquilla Creek, stm., Tx., U.S.	136	C10	31.40 N	97.11 W
Aquin, Haiti	156	C11	18.17 N	73.24 W
Aquincum Museum, bldg., Hung.	182c		47.34 N	19.03 E
Aquio, stm., Col.	168	F7	2.43 N	67.34 W
Ara, India	70	F10	25.34 N	84.40 E
Ara, stm., Japan	56	D12	35.40 N	139.51 E
Ara, stm., Japan	56	A12	38.08 N	139.25 E
Ara, stm., Spain	28	B11	42.24 N	0.08 E
Arab, Al., U.S.	134	C12	34.19 N	86.29 W
'Arab, Baḥr al-, stm., Sudan	82	E5	9.02 N	29.28 E
'Arab, Khalîg el-, b., Egypt	72	C2	30.55 N	29.05 E
'Arab, Shaṭṭ al-, stm., Asia	74	E11	29.57 N	48.32 E
'Araba, Wadi, stm., Egypt	76	I3	29.07 N	32.41 E
'Arabah, Wādī al- (Ha'Arava), val., Asia	76	H6	30.34 N	35.12 E
Arabako, co., Spain	28	B8	42.50 N	2.45 W
Araban, Tur.	76	A8	37.25 N	37.41 E
Arabats'ka zatoka, b., Ukr.	38	H14	45.26 N	35.21 E
Arabelo, Ven.	168	E9	4.55 N	64.11 W
Arabian Basin, unds.	174	H9	11.30 N	65.00 E
Arabian Desert, des., Egypt	74	F2	28.00 N	32.00 E
Arabian Gulf see Persian Gulf, b., Asia	72	D7	27.00 N	51.00 E
Arabian Peninsula, pen., Asia	72	E6	25.00 N	45.00 E
Arabian Sea, s.	62	E2	15.00 N	65.00 E
Araçá, stm., Braz.	168	G10	0.25 S	62.54 W
Aracaju, Braz.	170	F7	10.54 S	37.03 W
Aracataca, Col.	168	B4	10.35 N	74.11 W
Aracati, Braz.	170	C7	4.34 S	37.46 W
Araçatuba, Braz.	166	D6	21.12 S	50.27 W
Aracena, Spain	28	G4	37.53 N	6.33 W
Árachthos, stm., Grc.	34	D3	39.00 N	21.03 E
Araci, Braz.	170	F6	11.19 S	38.57 W
Aracides, Cape, c., Sol. Is.	101b	e9	8.38 S	161.00 E
Aracoiaba, Braz.	170	C6	4.23 S	38.49 W
Aracruz, Braz.	170	J5	19.49 S	40.16 W
Araçuaí, Braz.	170	I4	16.53 S	42.04 W
Araçuaí, stm., Braz.	170	I4	16.46 S	42.02 W
'Arad, Isr.	76	G6	31.15 N	35.13 E
Arad, Rom.	36	C8	46.11 N	21.19 E
Arad, state, Rom.	36	C8	46.20 N	21.40 E
Arada, Chad	82	D4	15.01 N	20.39 E
Aradhíppou, Cyp.	76	D4	34.56 N	33.35 E
Arafura, Laut see Arafura Sea, s.	46	J17	9.00 S	133.00 E
Arafura Sea, s.	46	J17	9.00 S	133.00 E
Arafura Shelf, unds.	174	K16	10.00 S	137.00 E
Aragac, gora see Aragats Lerr, mtn., Arm.	42	E11	40.32 N	44.14 E
Aragarças, Braz.	166	C6	15.55 S	52.15 W
Aragats Lerr, mtn., Arm.	42	E11	40.32 N	44.14 E
Arago, Cape, c., Or., U.S.	146	G2	43.18 N	124.22 W
Aragón, state, Spain	28	C10	41.30 N	0.30 W
Aragón, stm., Spain	28	B9	42.13 N	1.45 W
Aragona, Italy	32	G7	37.24 N	13.37 E
Aragua, state, Ven.	168	B8	10.00 N	67.10 W
Araguacema, Braz.	164	E8	8.50 S	49.33 W
Araguaçu, Braz.	166	B7	12.49 S	49.51 W
Aragua de Barcelona, Ven.	168	C9	9.27 N	64.49 W
Araguaia, stm., Braz.	164	E8	5.20 S	48.42 W
Araguaína, Braz.	170	D1	7.11 S	48.12 W
Araguao, Caño, stm., Ven.	168	C11	9.11 N	60.58 W
Araguari, Braz.	170	J1	18.38 S	48.12 W
Araguari, stm., Braz.	164	C7	1.13 N	50.01 W
Araguari, stm., Braz.	170	J1	18.21 S	48.40 W
Araguatins, Braz.	170	C1	5.38 S	48.06 W
Arahal, Spain	28	G5	37.15 N	5.32 W
Arai, Japan	56	B11	37.01 N	138.15 E
Araioses, Braz.	170	B4	2.53 S	41.55 W
Ârak, Alg.	84	D5	25.17 N	3.42 E
Arāk (Sultanabad), Iran	74	C11	34.05 N	49.41 E
Arakan see Rakhine, state, Mya.	64	C1	19.39 N	93.55 E
Arakan Yoma, mts., Mya.	64	C2	19.00 N	94.40 E
Arakawa, ngh., Japan	186		35.47 N	139.47 E
Arakkonam, India	69	E4	13.05 N	79.40 E
Arakpur, ngh., India	190a		28.35 N	77.10 E
Araks (Aras) (Araz), stm., Asia	42	F12	40.01 N	48.27 E
Aral Sea, l., Asia	48	E9	45.00 N	60.00 E
Aral'sk, Kaz.	48	E10	46.48 N	61.40 E
Aral'skoe more see Aral Sea, l., Asia	48	E9	45.00 N	60.00 E
Aralsor, ozero, l., Kaz.	40	G18	48.42 N	52.24 E
Aralsor, ozero, l., Kaz.	40	G16	49.04 N	48.12 E
Aramac, Austl.	98	D5	22.58 S	145.14 E
Aramac, stm., Austl.	98	D5	23.01 S	144.31 E
Aramari, Braz.	170	G6	12.04 S	38.30 W
Ārāmbāg, India	70	G11	22.53 N	87.47 E
Aramberri, Mex.	154	C9	24.05 N	99.49 W
Ārān, Iran	74	C12	34.03 N	51.29 E
Aranda de Duero, Spain	28	C7	41.40 N	3.41 W
Arandas, Mex.	154	E7	20.42 N	102.20 W
Aranđelovac, Yugo.	36	E7	44.18 N	20.34 E
Arandis, Nmb.	90	C2	22.24 S	15.00 E
Arang, India	70	H8	21.11 N	81.58 E
Aranhegyi-patak, stm., Hung.	182c		47.34 N	19.04 E
Ārani, India	69	E4	12.40 N	79.17 E
Aran Island, i., Ire.	10	F4	54.59 N	8.32 W
Aran Islands, is., Ire.	10	H3	53.06 N	9.42 W
Aranjuez, Spain	28	D7	40.01 N	3.36 W
Aranos, Nmb.	90	D4	24.09 S	19.07 E
Aransas, stm., Tx., U.S.	136	F10	28.04 N	97.12 W
Aransas Pass, Tx., U.S.	136	G10	27.54 N	97.08 W
Arantāngi, India	69	F4	10.09 N	78.59 E
Aranyaprathet, Thai.	64	F6	13.41 N	102.30 E
Arao, Japan	56	G3	32.58 N	130.26 E
Araouane, Mali	84	F4	18.54 N	3.31 W
Arapaho, Ok., U.S.	138	F9	35.34 N	98.57 W
Arapahoe, Ne., U.S.	138	A9	40.18 N	99.53 W
Arapaho National Recreation Area, p.o.i., Co., U.S.	138	A2	40.07 N	105.48 W
Arāpānja, India	190b		22.26 N	88.28 E
Arapey Chico, stm., Ur.	172	E9	30.57 S	57.30 W
Arapey Grande, stm., Ur.	172	E9	30.55 S	57.49 W
Arapiraca, Braz.	170	E7	9.45 S	36.39 W
Arápis, Grc.	185c		37.59 N	23.32 E
Arapkir, Tur.	42	F8	39.02 N	38.30 E
Arapongas, Braz.	166	D6	23.24 S	51.25 W
Arapoti, Braz.	172	B13	24.07 S	49.50 W
Araquil, stm., Spain	28	B9	42.48 N	1.46 W
Ar'ar, Sau. Ar.	74	E7	30.56 N	41.04 E
'Ar'ar, Wādī, stm., Asia	74	E7	31.24 N	42.24 E
Araracuara, Col.	168	H5	0.37 S	72.14 W
Araranguá, Braz.	172	D13	28.56 S	49.29 W
Araraquara, Braz.	170	K1	21.47 S	48.10 W
Araras, Braz.	170	L2	22.22 S	47.22 W
Araras, Açude, res., Braz.	170	C5	4.14 S	40.26 W
Ararat, Arm.	42	F11	39.50 N	44.42 E
Ararat, Austl.	98	K4	37.16 S	142.55 E
Ararat, Mount see Ağrı Dağı, vol., Tur.	74	A9	39.42 N	44.18 E
Arari, Braz.	170	B3	3.28 S	44.47 W
Arāria, India	70	E11	26.07 N	87.25 E
Araripe, Braz.	170	D5	7.12 S	40.08 W
Araripe, Chapada do, plat., Braz.	170	D6	7.22 S	39.49 W
Araripina, Braz.	170	D5	7.33 S	40.34 W
Ararirá, stm., Braz.	168	H10	0.32 S	63.27 W
Araruama, Lagoa de, b., Braz.	170	L4	22.53 S	42.12 W
Araruna, Braz.	170	D8	6.32 S	35.44 W
Aras (Araks) (Araz), stm., Asia	42	F12	40.01 N	48.27 E
Arashi-yama, hill, Japan	188		35.01 N	135.40 E
Aratuípe, Braz.	170	G6	13.07 S	38.59 W
Arauca, Col.	168	D6	7.03 N	70.45 W
Arauca, state, Col.	168	D6	6.40 N	71.00 W
Arauca, stm., S.A.	168	D8	7.25 N	66.31 W
Araucária, Braz.	172	B13	25.35 S	49.24 W
Araújos, Braz.	170	J3	19.56 S	45.09 W
Arauquita, Col.	168	D6	7.00 N	71.26 W
Araure, Ven.	168	C7	9.35 N	69.13 W
Aravaca, ngh., Spain	184a		40.28 N	3.46 W
Aravaipa Creek, stm., Az., U.S.	150	K6	32.50 N	110.43 W
Arāvalli Range, mts., India	70	F4	24.42 N	73.19 E
Arawa, Pap. N. Gui.	101b	d6	6.13 S	155.33 E
Araxá, Braz.	170	J2	19.36 S	46.55 W
Araya, Ven.	168	B9	10.35 N	64.16 W
Araya, Punta de, c., Ven.	168	B9	10.37 N	64.17 W
Araz (Araks) (Aras), stm., Asia	42	F12	40.01 N	48.27 E
Arba de Luesia, stm., Spain	28	C9	41.52 N	1.18 W
Ārba Minch', Eth.	82	F7	6.01 N	37.33 E
Arbatax, Italy	32	E3	39.56 N	9.42 E
Arbaž, Russia	40	C16	57.41 N	48.18 E
Arboga, Swe.	16	H13	59.24 N	15.51 E
Arbois, Fr.	20	H14	46.54 N	5.46 E
Arboledas, Arg.	172	H7	36.53 S	61.29 W
Arboletes, Col.	168	C3	8.50 N	76.25 W
Arbolito, Cerro, hill, Peru	204d		12.10 S	76.57 W
Arbon, Switz.	30	C6	47.30 N	9.25 E
Arboréa, Italy	32	E2	39.46 N	8.35 E
Arborea, reg., Italy	32	E2	39.50 N	8.46 E
Arborfield, Sk., Can.	142	A10	53.06 N	103.39 W
Arborg, Mb., Can.	142	D16	50.53 N	97.13 W
Arbrå, Swe.	16	F14	61.29 N	16.23 E
Arbroath, Scot., U.K.	10	E10	56.33 N	2.35 W
Arbuckle, Ca., U.S.	148	D3	39.01 N	122.03 W
Arbuckle, Lake, l., Fl., U.S.	132	I4	27.41 N	81.23 W
Arbuckle Mountains, mts., Ok., U.S.	138	G11	34.25 N	97.20 W
Arbuckles, Lake of the, res., Ok., U.S.	138	G12	34.26 N	97.01 W
Arbutus Lake, l., N.Y., U.S.	194		40.31 N	74.10 W
Arbuzovo, Russia	26	D15	56.22 N	32.26 E
Arbuzynka, Ukr.	38	F10	47.54 N	31.18 E
Arc, stm., Fr.	22	D12	45.34 N	6.12 E
Arc, stm., Fr.	22	F11	43.29 N	5.03 E
Arc, Bayou des, stm., Ar., U.S.	134	B7	35.00 N	91.29 W
Arcachon, Fr.	22	E4	44.39 N	1.10 W
Arcachon, Bassin d', b., Fr.	22	E4	44.42 N	1.10 W
Arcade, Ca., U.S.	148	E4	34.02 N	118.15 W
Arcade, N.Y., U.S.	124	B7	42.31 N	78.24 W
Arcadia, Ca., U.S.	148	I7	34.08 N	118.01 W
Arcadia, Fl., U.S.	132	I4	27.12 N	81.51 W
Arcadia, In., U.S.	130	D11	40.10 N	86.01 W
Arcadia, Ia., U.S.	130	B2	42.04 N	95.02 W
Arcadia, Ks., U.S.	130	G3	37.38 N	94.37 W
Arcadia, La., U.S.	134	E6	32.33 N	92.55 W
Arcadia, Mi., U.S.	126	D3	44.29 N	86.13 W
Arcadia, Mo., U.S.	130	G7	37.35 N	90.37 W
Arcadia, Ne., U.S.	140	F13	41.25 N	99.07 W
Arcadia, Pa., U.S.	124	D7	40.47 N	78.51 W
Arcadia, S.C., U.S.	132	B3	34.57 N	82.00 W
Arcadia, Wi., U.S.	128	G7	44.15 N	91.29 W
Arcanum, Oh., U.S.	124	D1	39.59 N	84.32 W
Arcas, Cayos, is., Mex.	154	E12	20.09 N	91.58 W
Arcata, Ca., U.S.	148	C1	40.52 N	124.04 W
Arc de Triomphe, hist., Fr.	179		48.53 N	2.17 E
Arc Dome, mtn., Nv., U.S.	148	E8	38.50 N	117.21 W
Arcelia, Mex.	154	F8	18.18 N	100.16 W
Arcevia, Italy	30	G9	43.30 N	12.56 E
Archangel see Arhangel'sk, Russia	18	C27	64.32 N	40.25 E
Archángelos, Grc.	34	G11	36.12 N	28.07 E
Archbold, Oh., U.S.	124	C1	41.30 N	84.18 W
Archdale, N.C., U.S.	124	I6	35.54 N	79.58 W
Archer, Fl., U.S.	132	G3	29.32 N	82.31 W
Archer, stm., Austl.	96	B8	13.27 S	141.41 E
Archer, Lake, l., Ma., U.S.	201		42.04 N	71.20 W
Archer, Mount, mtn., Austl.	98	D8	23.20 S	150.34 E
Archer City, Tx., U.S.	138	H10	33.35 N	98.37 W
Archer's Post, Kenya	86	D7	0.37 N	37.40 E
Arches National Park, p.o.i., Ut., U.S.	150	E7	38.43 N	109.35 W
Archiac, Fr.	22	D5	45.31 N	0.17 W
Archidona, Spain	28	G6	37.05 N	4.23 W
Archville, N.Y., U.S.	194		41.07 N	73.52 W
Arcidosso, Italy	30	H8	42.52 N	11.32 E
Arcis-sur-Aube, Fr.	20	F13	48.32 N	4.08 E
Arco, Id., U.S.	146	G13	43.38 N	113.18 W
Arco de Baúlhe, Port.	28	C2	41.29 N	7.58 W
Arcola, Sk., Can.	142	E11	49.38 N	102.28 W
Arcola, Il., U.S.	130	E9	39.41 N	88.18 W
Arcola, Ms., U.S.	134	D8	33.16 N	90.53 W
Arcola, Pa., U.S.	203		40.09 N	75.27 W
Arconate, Italy	184b		45.32 N	8.51 E
Arconce, stm., Fr.	22	C10	46.27 N	4.00 E
Arcore, Italy	184b		45.38 N	9.19 E
Arcos, Braz.	170	K3	20.17 S	45.32 W
Arcos de la Frontera, Spain	28	H5	36.44 N	5.48 W
Arcot, India	69	E4	12.54 N	79.19 E
Arcoverde, Braz.	170	E7	8.25 S	37.04 W
Arctic Bay, Nu., Can.	110	A14	73.02 N	85.10 W
Arctic Ocean, oc.	4	A21	85.00 N	170.00 E
Arctic Red, stm., N.T., Can.	110	B4	67.27 N	133.45 W
Arctic Red River see Tsiigehtchic, N.T., Can.	110	B4	67.27 N	133.34 W
Arctic Village, Ak., U.S.	109	C10	68.05 N	145.31 W
Arcueil, Fr.	179		48.48 N	2.20 E
Arḍ, Ra's al-, c., Kuw.	74	F11	29.19 N	48.05 E
Arda, stm., Eur.	36	H12	41.40 N	26.29 E
Arda, stm., Italy	30	F6	45.02 N	10.04 E
Ardabīl, Iran	74	A11	38.15 N	48.17 E
Ardahan, Tur.	42	E10	41.06 N	42.42 E
Ardahan, state, Tur.	42	E10	41.05 N	43.00 E
Ardakān, Iran	74	E12	30.16 N	52.01 E
Ardakān, Iran	74	D13	32.20 N	53.56 E
Ardal, Iran	74	E12	32.01 N	50.37 E
Årdalstangen, Nor.	16	F5	61.14 N	7.42 E
Ardara, Pa., U.S.	197b		40.22 N	79.44 W
Árdas see Arda, stm., Eur.	36	H12	41.40 N	26.29 E
Ardatov, Russia	40	D13	55.14 N	43.06 E
Ardebil see Ardabīl, Iran	74	A11	38.15 N	48.17 E
Ardèche, state, Fr.	22	E10	44.40 N	4.20 E
Ardee, Ire.	10	H6	53.51 N	6.32 W
Arden, Mb., Can.	142	D14	50.16 N	99.16 W
Arden, Ca., U.S.	148	E4	38.35 N	121.22 W
Arden Mines, Pa., U.S.	197b		40.12 N	80.17 W
Ardennen see Ardennes, reg., Eur.	20	E13	50.10 N	5.45 E
Ardennes, state, Fr.	20	E13	49.40 N	4.40 E
Ardennes, reg., Eur.	20	E13	50.10 N	5.45 E
Ardennes, Canal des, can., Fr.	20	E13	49.25 N	4.02 E
Ardestān, Iran	74	D13	33.22 N	52.22 E
Ardey, Ger.	181		51.28 N	7.43 E
Ardeygebirge, hills, Ger.	181		51.25 N	7.23 E
Ardila, stm., Eur.	28	F3	38.10 N	7.29 W
Ardill, Sk., Can.	142	E8	49.56 N	105.50 W
Ardlethan, Austl.	98	J6	34.21 S	146.53 E
Ardmore, Al., U.S.	134	B12	34.59 N	86.50 W
Ardmore, Md., U.S.	202c		38.56 N	76.51 W
Ardmore, Ok., U.S.	138	G11	34.10 N	97.08 W
Ardmore, Pa., U.S.	124	D10	40.00 N	75.17 W
Ardnamurchan, Point of, c., Scot., U.K.	10	E6	56.43 N	6.13 W
Ardoch, Austl.	98	F5	27.25 S	144.07 E

Name	Page	Map Ref.	Latitude	Longitude
Ashton, Il., U.S.	130	C8	41.51 N	89.13 W
Ashton, Ia., U.S.	128	H3	43.18 N	95.48 W
Ashton, Ne., U.S.	140	F14	41.15 N	98.47 W
Ashton upon Mersey, Eng., U.K.	180		53.26 N	2.19 W
Ashuanipi Lake, l., Nf., Can.	110	E17	52.32 N	66.06 W
Ashuapmushuan, stm., Qc., Can.	122	B4	48.53 N	72.58 W
Ashuelot, stm., N.H., U.S.	122	H4	42.46 N	72.29 W
Ashūm, Egypt	76	H1	30.17 N	30.58 E
Ashurst's Beacon, hill, Eng., U.K.	180		53.34 N	2.45 W
Ashville, Al., U.S.	134	D12	33.49 N	86.15 W
Ashville, Oh., U.S.	124	E3	39.42 N	82.57 W
Ashwaubenon, Wi., U.S.	126	D1	44.28 N	88.03 W
Ashworth Moor Reservoir, res., Eng., U.K.	180		53.38 N	2.16 W
'Āṣī see Orontes, stm., Asia	76	B7	36.02 N	35.58 E
Asi see Orontes, stm., Asia	76	B7	36.02 N	35.58 E
Asia, cont.	4	C19	50.00 N	100.00 E
Asia, Kepulauan, is., Indon.	60	E9	1.03 N	131.18 E
Asiago, Italy	30	E8	45.52 N	11.30 E
Asia Minor, hist. reg., Tur.	34	E12	39.00 N	32.00 E
Āsika, India	70	I10	19.36 N	84.38 E
Asinara, Golfo dell', b., Italy	32	D2	41.00 N	8.32 E
Asinara, Isola, i., Italy	32	C2	41.04 N	8.16 E
Asíni, hist., Grc.	34	F5	37.31 N	22.53 E
Asino, Russia	48	C15	56.59 N	86.08 E
Asintorf, Bela.	26	F13	54.42 N	30.39 E
Asipovičy, Bela.	26	G11	53.17 N	28.38 E
'Asīr, reg., Sau. Ar.	72	F5	19.00 N	42.00 E
Aska, Fin.	14	E17	67.17 N	26.41 E
Aşkale, Tur.	42	F9	39.55 N	40.42 E
Askaniia-Nova, Ukr.	38	G12	46.27 N	33.53 E
Asker, Nor.	16	H8	59.50 N	10.23 E
Askersund, Swe.	16	I12	58.53 N	14.54 E
Askham, S. Afr.	90	E5	26.59 S	20.46 E
Askim, Nor.	16	H9	59.35 N	11.09 E
Askino, Russia	40	C20	56.05 N	56.35 E
Askiz, Russia	48	D16	53.07 N	90.31 E
Askja, vol., Ice.	12a	k31	64.59 N	16.47 W
Askøy, Nor.	16	G3	60.24 N	5.13 E
Askrova, i., Nor.	16	F2	61.31 N	4.57 E
Askvoll, Nor.	16	F3	61.21 N	5.05 E
Aslanapa, Tur.	34	D12	39.13 N	29.52 E
Aslantaş Barajı, res., Tur.	76	A7	37.20 N	36.17 E
Asleigh, Md., U.S.	202c		39.01 N	77.10 W
Asmara see Asmera, Erit.	82	D7	15.20 N	38.55 E
Asmera, Erit.	82	D7	15.20 N	38.55 E
Ašmjanskae uzvyšša, plat., Eur.	26	F9	54.22 N	26.08 E
Ašmjany, Bela.	26	F8	54.25 N	25.56 E
Asnæs, Den.	16	L9	55.48 N	11.29 E
Åsnen, l., Swe.	16	K12	56.37 N	14.44 E
Aso, stm., Italy	32	B7	43.06 N	13.50 E
Asola, Italy	30	E7	45.13 N	10.23 E
Asomante, P.R.	158a	b2	18.21 N	66.37 W
Ason, Nig.	191a		6.34 N	3.31 E
Āsosa, Eth.	82	E6	10.03 N	34.32 E
Aso-san, mtn., Japan	56	G4	32.53 N	131.06 E
Asoteriba, Jabal, mtn., Sudan	82	C7	21.51 N	36.30 E
Asotin, Wa., U.S.	146	D9	46.19 N	117.02 W
Asouf, Oued, stm., Alg.	84	D5	25.52 N	1.27 E
Asp, Spain	28	F10	38.20 N	0.46 W
Aspang Markt, Aus.	30	C13	47.32 N	16.05 E
Aspe see Asp, Spain	28	F10	38.20 N	0.46 W
Aspe, Gave d', stm., Fr.	28	A10	43.11 N	0.36 W
Aspen, Co., U.S.	138	B2	39.11 N	106.49 W
Aspen Butte, mtn., Or., U.S.	148	A3	42.19 N	122.05 W
Aspendale, Austl.	192b		38.02 S	145.07 E
Aspendos, hist., Tur.	34	G14	37.00 N	31.10 E
Aspen Hill, Md., U.S.	202c		39.04 N	77.04 W
Aspen Knolls, Md., U.S.	202c		39.05 N	77.05 W
Aspen Lake, l., Or., U.S.	146	H4	42.17 N	122.00 W
Aspermont, Tx., U.S.	136	A7	33.08 N	100.13 W
Aspern, ngh., Aus.	182b		48.13 N	16.29 E
Aspinwall, Pa., U.S.	197b		40.29 N	79.54 W
Aspiring, Mount, mtn., N.Z.	102	G3	44.23 S	168.44 E
Aspromonte, mts., Italy	32	F9	38.11 N	15.54 E
Asprópyrgos, Grc.	185c		38.04 N	23.35 E
Aspull, Eng., U.K.	180		53.34 N	2.35 W
Aspy Bay, b., N.S., Can.	122	D16	46.56 N	60.24 W
Asquith, Austl.	192a		33.41 S	151.06 E
Asquith, Sk., Can.	142	B6	52.08 N	107.12 W
Assa, Mor.	84	D3	28.36 N	9.25 W
Assab see Aseb, Erit.	82	E8	12.57 N	42.42 E
Assabet, stm., Ma., U.S.	201		42.28 N	71.21 W
As-Sa'dīyah, Iraq	74	C9	34.11 N	45.08 E
As-Saffānīyah, Sau. Ar.	74	F11	28.00 N	48.45 E
As-Safīrah, Syria	76	B8	36.04 N	37.23 E
Aş-Şāfiyah, Sudan	82	D6	15.30 N	30.07 E
Assago, Italy	184b		45.24 N	9.08 E
Aş-Şāliḥīyah, hist., Syria	74	C7	34.45 N	40.43 E
As-Salmān, Iraq	74	E9	30.29 N	44.32 E
As-Salt, Jord.	76	F6	32.02 N	35.43 E
Assam, state, India	62	C7	26.00 N	93.00 E
As-Samāwah, Iraq	74	E9	31.18 N	45.16 E
'Assān, Syria	76	B8	36.05 N	37.13 E
Aş-Şanamayn, Syria	76	E7	33.05 N	36.10 E
Aş-Şaqlabiyah, Syria	76	C7	35.22 N	36.24 E
Aş-Şarafand, Leb.	76	E6	33.26 N	35.18 E
Assaré, Braz.	170	D6	6.52 S	39.52 W
Aş-Şarīḥ, Jord.	76	F6	32.30 N	35.53 E
Assateague Island, i., U.S.	124	F10	38.05 N	75.12 W
Assateague Island National Seashore, p.o.i., U.S.	124	F10	37.59 N	75.17 W
Asse, stm., Fr.	22	F12	43.52 N	5.52 E
Assegaai see Mkhondvo, stm., Afr.	90	E10	26.40 S	31.26 E
Asseln, ngh., Ger.	181		51.32 N	7.35 E
Assembleia Nacional, Palacio da, bldg., Port.	184c		38.43 N	9.09 W
Assemini, Italy	32	E2	39.17 N	9.00 E
Assen, Neth.	20	A15	52.59 N	6.34 E
Assens, Den.	16	L7	55.16 N	9.55 E
Asseria, hist., Cro.	30	F12	44.02 N	15.39 E
Assiniboia, Sk., Can.	142	E8	49.38 N	105.59 W
Assiniboine, stm., Can.	142	E16	49.52 N	97.08 W
Assiniboine, Mount, mtn., Can.	144	F15	50.52 N	115.39 W
Assiniboine Indian Reserve, ind. res., Sk., Can.	142	D10	50.21 N	103.28 W
Assinica, Lac, l., Qc., Can.	114	A13	50.30 N	75.16 W
Assinika, stm., Mb., Can.	142	B17	52.36 N	96.09 W
Assinippi, Ma., U.S.	201		42.09 N	70.51 W
Assis, Braz.	166	D6	22.40 S	50.25 W
Assis Chateaubriand, Braz.	172	B11	24.24 S	53.30 W
Assisi, Italy	30	G9	43.04 N	12.36 E
Assomption, i., Sey.	89b	k11	9.44 S	46.29 E
Assu, Braz.	170	C7	5.34 S	36.54 W
As-Sūdān see Sudan, ctry., Afr.	82	E5	15.00 N	30.00 E
As-Sudd, reg., Sudan	82	F6	8.00 N	31.00 E
As-Sufāl, Yemen	72	G6	14.06 N	48.42 E
As-Sukhnah, Syria	76	D9	34.52 N	38.52 E
As-Sulaymānīyah, Iraq	74	C9	35.33 N	45.26 E
As-Sulaymānīyah, Sau. Ar.	72	E6	24.08 N	47.18 E
As-Sulaymānīyah, state, Iraq	74	C9	35.30 N	45.25 E
As-Sulaymī, Sau. Ar.	74	G7	26.17 N	41.21 E
As-Sulayyil, Sau. Ar.	72	E6	20.26 N	45.32 E
As-Sumayh, Sudan	82	F5	9.48 N	27.39 E
Aş-Şummān, reg., Sau. Ar.	74	G10	25.00 N	47.00 E
Assumption, Il., U.S.	130	E8	39.30 N	89.03 W
Assunpink Creek, stm., N.J., U.S.	203		40.13 N	74.46 W
As-Sūrīyah see Syria, ctry., Asia	74	C6	35.00 N	38.00 E
Aş-Şuwār, Syria	74	C7	35.30 N	40.39 E
As-Suwaydā', Syria	76	F7	32.42 N	36.34 E
As-Suwaydā', state, Syria	76	F7	32.45 N	36.45 E
Assynt, Loch, l., Scot., U.K.	10	C7	58.10 N	5.04 W
Astakós, Grc.	34	E4	38.32 N	21.04 E
Astana (Akmola), Kaz.	48	D12	51.11 N	71.27 E
Āstāneh, Iran	74	D11	33.53 N	49.22 E
Āstāneh, Iran	74	B11	37.16 N	49.57 E
Astara, Azer.	42	F13	38.28 N	48.52 E
Āstārā, Iran	74	A11	38.26 N	48.52 E
Asterābād see Gorgān, Iran	74	B14	36.50 N	54.25 E
Asti, Italy	30	F5	44.54 N	8.12 E
Astica, Arg.	172	E4	30.56 S	67.18 W
Astico, stm., Italy	30	E8	45.37 N	11.37 E
Astley Bridge, Eng., U.K.	180		53.36 N	2.26 W
Astley Green, Eng., U.K.	180		53.29 N	2.27 W
Astley Hall, hist., Eng., U.K.	180		53.39 N	2.38 W
Astola Island, i., Pak.	62	C1	25.07 N	63.51 E
Aston, Eng., U.K.	180		53.18 N	2.40 W
Aston, Pa., U.S.	203		39.52 N	75.26 W
Astor, Pak.	72	B11	35.22 N	74.51 E
Astorga, Spain	28	B4	42.27 N	6.02 W
Astoria, Il., U.S.	130	D7	40.13 N	90.20 W
Astoria, Or., U.S.	146	D3	46.11 N	123.49 W
Astoria, ngh., N.Y., U.S.	194		40.46 N	73.55 W
Åstorp, Swe.	16	K10	56.08 N	12.57 E
Astove, i., Sey.	89b	I11	10.06 S	47.45 E
Astrachanskaja oblast', co., Russia	40	H16	47.00 N	47.30 E
Astrahan', Russia	40	H16	46.21 N	48.02 E
Astrahanskaja oblast', co., Russia	42	B12	47.41 N	46.28 E
Astrašyckì Haradok, Bela.	26	F10	54.03 N	27.41 E
Astravec, Bela.	26	F8	54.37 N	25.57 E
Astrolabe, Cape, c., Sol. Is.	101b	e9	8.20 S	160.33 E
Astrolabe, Récifs de l', rf., N. Cal.	101d	I15	19.48 S	165.37 E
Astrolabe Reefs see Astrolabe, Récifs de l', rf., N. Cal.	101d	I15	19.48 S	165.37 E
Astrouna, Bela.	26	E12	55.08 N	29.52 E
Astryna, Bela.	26	G7	53.44 N	24.32 E
Astudillo, Spain	28	B6	42.11 N	4.17 W
Asturias, state, Spain	28	A4	43.20 N	6.00 W
Astypálaia, Grc.	34	G9	36.33 N	26.20 E
Astypálaia, i., Grc.	34	G9	36.35 N	26.25 E
Asuisui, Cape, c., Samoa	101c	g11	13.47 S	172.31 W
Asunción, Para.	172	B9	25.16 S	57.38 W
Asunción, Bahía la, b., Mex.	154	B1	27.06 N	114.10 W
Asunción Nochixtlán, Mex.	154	G10	17.28 N	97.14 W
Åsunden, l., Swe.	16	J11	57.44 N	13.23 E
Åsunden, l., Swe.	16	I13	57.58 N	15.50 E
Åsværet, is., Nor.	14	F3	66.14 N	12.15 E
Asveja, Bela.	26	E11	56.00 N	28.06 E
Asvejskae, vozera, l., Bela.	26	D10	56.02 N	28.09 E
Aswa see Achwa, stm., Afr.	86	D6	3.44 N	31.55 E
Aswān, Egypt	74	H3	24.05 N	32.54 E
Aswan High Dam see Aali, Sadd el-, dam., Egypt	74	H3	23.58 N	32.52 E
Aswatthaberia, India	190b		22.26 N	88.32 E
Asyūt, Egypt	76	K2	27.11 N	31.11 E
Asyūt, Wadi el-, stm., Egypt	76	K2	27.10 N	31.17 E
Aszód, Hung.	36	B6	47.39 N	19.30 E
'Ata, i., Tonga	94	F9	22.20 S	176.12 W
'Ata, i., Tonga	100e	n15	21.02 S	175.00 W
Atabapo, stm., S.A.	168	F8	4.02 N	67.42 W
Atabey, Tur.	34	F13	37.57 N	30.39 E
Atacama, state, Chile	172	C3	27.30 S	70.00 W
Atacama, Desierto de, des., Chile	166	E2	20.07 S	69.53 W
Atacama, Puna de, plat., S.A.	172	A4	23.51 S	67.18 W
Atacama, Salar de, pl., Chile	166	D3	23.32 S	68.14 W
Atacama Desert see Atacama, Desierto de, des., Chile	166	E2	20.07 S	69.53 W
Ataco, Col.	168	F4	3.35 N	75.23 W
Atagaj, Russia	48	C17	55.06 N	99.24 E
'Aṭā'itah, Jabal al-, mtn., Jord.	76	H6	30.40 N	35.39 E
Atakpamé, Togo	84	H5	7.31 N	1.08 E
Atalaia, Braz.	170	E7	9.31 S	36.02 W
Atalaia, Port.	184c		38.42 N	8.55 W
Atalánti, Grc.	34	E5	38.39 N	22.59 E
Atalaya, Peru	164	F3	10.43 S	73.47 W
Atambua, Indon.	60	G7	9.05 S	124.53 E
Atami, Japan	56	D12	35.05 N	139.04 E
Atangmik, Grnld.	108	E15	64.48 N	52.13 W
Atar, Maur.	84	E2	20.32 N	13.02 W
Atarés, Castillo de, hist., Cuba	204b		23.08 N	82.21 W
Atas Bogd uul, mtn., Mong.	52	C4	43.18 N	96.36 E
Atascadero, Ca., U.S.	148	H5	35.29 N	120.39 W
Atascosa, stm., Tx., U.S.	136	F9	28.26 N	98.11 W
Atasu, Kaz.	48	E12	48.40 N	71.38 E
Atata, i., Tonga	100e	n13	21.02 S	175.15 W
Atatürk Barajı, res., Tur.	42	G8	37.30 N	38.30 E
Ataturk Tower, hist., Tur.	185b		41.00 N	28.59 E
Ataur, India	190a		28.43 N	77.24 E
Atauro, Pulau, i., Indon.	60	G8	8.13 S	125.35 E
'Aṭbarah, Sudan	82	D6	17.42 N	33.59 E
Atbarah, stm., Afr.	80	E9	17.40 N	33.58 E
'Aṭbarah, stm., Afr.	82	D7	17.40 N	33.58 E
Atbasar, Kaz.	48	D11	51.48 N	68.20 E
Atchafalaya, stm., La., U.S.	134	G7	29.28 N	91.16 W
Atchafalaya Bay, b., La., U.S.	134	H7	29.29 N	91.23 W
Atchison, Ks., U.S.	130	E2	39.33 N	95.07 W
Ate, Peru	204d		12.03 S	76.58 W
Ateca, Spain	28	C9	41.20 N	1.47 W
Atenguillo, Mex.	154	E6	20.24 N	104.30 W
Aterno, stm., Italy	30	H10	42.08 N	13.49 E
Aṭfīḥ, Egypt	76	I2	29.24 N	31.15 E
Ath, Bel.	20	D12	50.38 N	3.47 E
Athabasca, Ab., Can.	144	B17	54.42 N	113.17 W
Athabasca, stm., Ab., Can.	110	D8	58.40 N	110.55 W
Athabasca, Lake, l., Can.	110	D9	59.07 N	109.58 W
Athalmer, B.C., Can.	144	F14	50.32 N	116.02 W
Athārān Hazārī, Pak.	70	C3	31.10 N	72.05 E
Athboy, Ire.	10	H6	53.37 N	6.55 W
Athena, Or., U.S.	146	E8	45.48 N	118.29 W
Athenry, Ire.	10	H4	53.18 N	8.45 W
Athens, On., Can.	126	D14	44.37 N	75.57 W
Athens see Athína, Grc.	34	E6	37.58 N	23.43 E
Athens, Al., U.S.	134	C11	34.48 N	86.58 W
Athens, Ga., U.S.	132	C2	33.57 N	83.22 W
Athens, Il., U.S.	130	E8	39.57 N	89.42 W
Athens, La., U.S.	134	E5	32.39 N	93.01 W
Athens, Mi., U.S.	130	B12	42.04 N	85.14 W
Athens, N.Y., U.S.	124	B12	42.16 N	73.48 W
Athens, Oh., U.S.	124	E3	39.19 N	82.06 W
Athens, Pa., U.S.	124	C9	41.57 N	76.31 W
Athens, Tn., U.S.	134	B14	35.26 N	84.35 W
Athens, Tx., U.S.	136	B12	32.12 N	95.51 W
Athens, W.V., U.S.	124	G5	37.25 N	80.59 W
Athens, Wi., U.S.	128	F8	45.01 N	90.04 W
Athens University, educ., Grc.	185c		37.59 N	23.44 E
Atherton, Austl.	98	A5	17.16 S	145.30 E
Athi, stm., Kenya	86	E7	2.57 S	38.30 E
Athiaínou, Cyp.	76	C4	35.04 N	33.32 E
Athína (Athens), Grc.	34	E6	37.58 N	23.43 E
Athína (Athens), Grc.	185c		37.58 N	23.43 E
Athis-Mons, Fr.	179		48.43 N	2.24 E
Athlone, Ire.	10	H4	53.25 N	7.56 W
Athni, India	69	C2	16.43 N	75.03 E
Athok, Mya.	64	D2	17.12 N	95.04 E
Athol, Ma., U.S.	124	B13	42.36 N	72.13 W
Athol Island, i., Bah.	158f	m18	25.04 N	77.16 W
Áthos, mtn., Grc.	34	C7	40.09 N	24.19 E
Athos, Mount see Áthos, mtn., Grc.	34	C7	40.09 N	24.19 E
Athy, Ire.	10	H6	52.59 N	6.58 W
Ati, Chad	82	E3	13.11 N	18.19 E
Atiak, Ug.	86	D6	3.16 N	32.06 E
Atico, Peru	164	G3	16.12 S	73.37 W
Atienza, Spain	28	C8	41.12 N	2.52 W
Atikaki Provincial Wilderness Park, p.o.i., Mb., Can.	142	C18	51.40 N	95.30 W
Atikokan, On., Can.	128	C7	48.45 N	91.37 W
Atiparaná, stm., Braz.	168	I9	1.50 S	65.40 W
Atirāmpattinam, India	69	F4	10.20 N	79.23 E
Atiu, i., Cook Is.	94	F11	20.02 S	158.07 W
Atjurevo, Russia	40	D13	54.20 N	43.19 E
Atka, Russia	50	D19	60.45 N	151.45 E
Atka, Ak., U.S.	109a	g24	52.12 N	174.12 W
Atka Island, i., Ak., U.S.	109a	g24	52.15 N	174.07 W
Atkarsk, Russia	40	F14	51.52 N	45.00 E
Atkins, Ar., U.S.	134	B6	35.14 N	92.56 W
Atkinson, Il., U.S.	130	C8	41.24 N	90.00 W
Atkinson, Ne., U.S.	140	E14	42.32 N	98.58 W
Atkinson, N.C., U.S.	132	B7	34.31 N	78.10 W
Atlanta, Ga., U.S.	134	D14	33.45 N	84.23 W
Atlanta, Il., U.S.	130	D8	40.15 N	89.13 W
Atlanta, Mi., U.S.	126	C5	45.00 N	84.08 W
Atlanta, Mo., U.S.	130	E5	39.53 N	92.29 W
Atlanta, Tx., U.S.	134	D4	33.06 N	94.10 W
Atlantic, Ia., U.S.	130	C2	41.24 N	95.00 W
Atlantic, N.C., U.S.	132	B9	34.53 N	76.20 W
Atlantic Beach, Fl., U.S.	132	F4	30.20 N	81.25 W
Atlantic Beach, N.Y., U.S.	194		40.35 N	73.44 W
Atlantic City, N.J., U.S.	124	E11	39.21 N	74.25 W
Atlantic-Indian Basin, unds.	174	O5	60.00 S	14.59 E
Atlantic-Indian Ridge, unds.	176	N15	53.00 S	15.00 E
Atlántico, state, Col.	168	B4	10.45 N	75.00 W
Atlantic Ocean, oc.	176	E9	5.00 S	25.00 W
Atlantic Peak, mtn., Wy., U.S.	140	E3	42.37 N	109.00 W
Atlántida, Ur.	172	G10	34.46 S	55.45 W
Atlantique, N.Y., U.S.	194		40.39 N	73.10 W
Atlas Mountains, mts., Afr.	84	C4	33.00 N	2.00 W
Atlasova, ostrov, i., Russia	50	F20	50.52 N	155.32 E
Atlas Saharien, mts., Alg.	84	C4	33.36 N	0.45 E
Atlas Tellien, mts., Alg.	80	C6	36.00 N	3.00 E
Atlin, B.C., Can.	110	D4	59.34 N	133.41 W
Atlin Lake, l., Can.	110	D4	59.22 N	133.46 W
'Atlit, Isr.	76	F5	32.41 N	34.56 E
Atløyna, i., Nor.	16	F2	61.21 N	4.57 E
Ātmakūr, India	69	D4	15.52 N	78.35 E
Atmore, Al., U.S.	134	F11	31.01 N	87.29 W
Atna, stm., Nor.	16	F8	61.44 N	10.49 E
Atna Peak, mtn., B.C., Can.	144	C2	53.57 N	128.03 W
Atnarko, stm., B.C., Can.	144	D5	52.22 N	126.05 W
Atnosen, Nor.	16	F8	61.43 N	10.49 E
Atocha, Bol.	166	D3	20.57 S	66.12 W
Atocha, Estación de, trans., Spain	184a		40.24 N	3.41 W
Atocongo, Peru	204d		12.08 S	76.56 W
Atocongo, hist., Peru	204d		12.12 S	76.55 W
Atoka, Ok., U.S.	134	C2	34.22 N	96.08 W
Atotonilco, Mex.	154	C7	24.16 N	102.45 W
Atotonilco, Cerro, mtn., Mex.	136	H3	26.08 N	104.43 W
Atoyac, stm., Mex.	154	F9	18.06 N	98.44 W
Atoyac de Álvarez, Mex.	154	G8	17.11 N	100.25 W
Atoyaquillo, stm., Mex.	154	G10	16.36 N	97.36 W
Atpur, India	190b		22.50 N	88.23 E
Atrå, Nor.	16	G6	59.59 N	8.45 E
Atrak (Atrek), stm., Asia	72	B7	37.26 N	53.53 E
Ätran, stm., Swe.	16	J10	56.53 N	12.29 E
Atrato, stm., Col.	168	D3	8.11 N	76.56 W
Atrauli, India	70	D7	28.01 N	78.17 E
Atrek (Atrak), stm., Asia	72	B7	37.26 N	53.53 E
Atri, Italy	30	H10	42.35 N	13.58 E
Atrop, ngh., Ger.	181		51.24 N	6.43 E
Atsion Lake, l., N.J., U.S.	203		39.44 N	74.44 W
Atsumi, Japan	56	A12	38.37 N	139.36 E
Atsumi, Japan	56	E10	34.37 N	137.06 E
Atsumi-hantō, pen., Japan	56	E10	34.39 N	137.15 E
Atta, India	190a		28.34 N	77.20 E
Aṭ-Ṭafīlah, Jord.	76	H6	30.50 N	35.36 E
Aṭ-Ṭafīlah, state, Jord.	76	H6	30.45 N	35.45 E
Aṭ-Ṭā'if, Sau. Ar.	72	E5	21.16 N	40.24 E
Attainville, Fr.	179		49.03 N	2.21 E
At-Tall, Syria	76	E7	33.36 N	36.19 E
Attalla, Al., U.S.	134	C12	34.01 N	86.05 W
At-Ta'mīm, state, Iraq	74	C9	35.25 N	44.20 E
At-Tamīmī, Libya	82	A4	32.20 N	23.03 E
At-Tanf, Syria	76	E9	33.29 N	38.40 E
Attapu, Laos	64	E8	14.48 N	106.50 E
Attávyros, mtn., Grc.	34	G10	36.12 N	27.52 E
Attawapiskat, On., Can.	110	E14	52.55 N	82.24 W
Attawapiskat, stm., On., Can.	110	E13	52.57 N	82.18 W
Attawapiskat Lake, l., On., Can.	110	E13	52.17 N	87.55 W
Aṭ-Ṭawīl, mts., Sau. Ar.	72	D4	29.20 N	39.29 E
Aṭ-Ṭaysīyah, pl., Sau. Ar.	74	G9	28.00 N	44.00 E
Aṭ-Ṭayyibah, Syria	76	C9	35.06 N	38.54 E
Attendorn, Ger.	24	E3	51.08 N	7.54 E
Attersee, l., Aus.	30	C10	47.52 N	13.32 E
Attica, In., U.S.	130	D10	40.17 N	87.13 W
Attica, Ks., U.S.	138	D10	37.14 N	98.13 W
Attica, N.Y., U.S.	124	B7	42.51 N	78.16 W
Attica, Oh., U.S.	124	C3	41.03 N	82.53 W
Attica see Attikí, hist. reg., Grc.	34	E6	38.10 N	23.20 E
Attikí, state, Grc.	34	F6	38.00 N	23.45 E
Attikí, hist. reg., Grc.	34	E6	38.10 N	23.20 E
Attleboro, Ma., U.S.	124	C14	41.56 N	71.17 W
Attnang, Aus.	24	H9	48.01 N	13.42 E
Attock, Pak.	70	B4	33.54 N	72.15 E
Attoyac, stm., Tx., U.S.	136	C13	31.13 N	94.19 W
Attu, Ak., U.S.	109a	g21	52.56 N	173.14 E
Attu Island, i., Ak., U.S.	109a	g21	52.55 N	173.00 E
Āttūr, India	69	F4	11.35 N	78.37 E
Aṭ-Ṭuwayshah, Sudan	82	E5	12.21 N	26.32 E
Aṭ-Ṭuwayyah, Sau. Ar.	74	G7	27.38 N	41.12 E
Atuel, stm., Arg.	172	G3	36.16 S	66.50 W
Atuel, Bañados del, sw., Arg.	172	H4	36.30 S	66.55 W
Atuntaqui, Ec.	168	G2	0.20 N	78.13 W
Atuona, Fr. Poly.	100g	s18	9.48 S	139.02 W
Åtvidaberg, Swe.	16	I14	58.12 N	16.00 E
Atwater, Sk., Can.	142	D11	50.46 N	102.10 W
Atwater, Ca., U.S.	148	F5	37.21 N	120.36 W
Atwater, Mn., U.S.	128	F4	45.08 N	94.46 W
Atwood, Ca., U.S.	198		33.52 N	117.50 W
Atwood, Il., U.S.	130	E9	39.48 N	88.28 W
Atwood, Ks., U.S.	138	B7	39.48 N	101.02 W
Atwood, Tn., U.S.	130	I9	35.58 N	88.41 W
Atyraū see Atyrau, Kaz.	48	E8	47.07 N	51.55 E
Atyrau, Kaz.	48	E8	47.07 N	51.55 E
Atyrau, state, Kaz.	40	H17	47.38 N	52.27 E
Atzalpur, India	190a		28.43 N	77.21 E
Atzgersdorf, ngh., Aus.	182b		48.09 N	16.18 E
Aua Island, i., Pap. N. Gui.	101a	a3	1.28 S	143.03 E
Auari, stm., Braz.	168	F9	3.33 N	63.46 W
Auau Channel, strt., Hi., U.S.	100a	c5	20.51 N	156.45 W
Aubagne, Fr.	22	F11	43.17 N	5.34 E
Aube, state, Fr.	20	F13	48.15 N	4.05 E
Aube, stm., Fr.	20	G14	48.33 N	3.43 E
Aubepierre, Fr.	179		48.38 N	2.53 E
Aubergenville, Fr.	179		48.58 N	1.51 E
Aubette, stm., Fr.	179		49.00 N	1.54 E
Aubigny-sur-Nère, Fr.	20	G11	47.29 N	2.26 E
Aubin, Fr.	22	E8	44.31 N	2.14 E
Aubinadong, stm., On., Can.	126	A6	47.10 N	83.17 W
Aubrey Cliffs, clf., Az., U.S.	150	H3	35.45 N	113.02 W
Aubrey Lake, res., On., Can.	126	A6	46.54 N	83.01 W
Aubry Lake, l., N.T., Can.	110	B5	67.22 N	126.26 W
Auburn, Austl.	192a		33.51 S	151.02 E
Auburn, Al., U.S.	134	E13	32.36 N	85.28 W
Auburn, Ca., U.S.	148	E4	38.53 N	121.03 W
Auburn, Il., U.S.	130	E8	39.35 N	89.44 W
Auburn, In., U.S.	130	C12	41.21 N	85.02 W
Auburn, Ky., U.S.	130	H11	36.52 N	86.43 W
Auburn, Me., U.S.	122	F6	44.06 N	70.13 W
Auburn, Ma., U.S.	124	B14	42.11 N	71.49 W
Auburn, Mi., U.S.	126	E5	43.36 N	84.04 W
Auburn, Ne., U.S.	130	D2	40.23 N	95.50 W
Auburn, N.J., U.S.	203		39.42 N	75.22 W
Auburn, N.Y., U.S.	124	B9	42.56 N	76.34 W
Auburn, Wa., U.S.	146	C4	47.18 N	122.13 W
Auburn, stm., Austl.	98	E8	25.38 S	151.12 E
Auburndale, Ma., U.S.	201		42.21 N	71.22 W
Auburn Hills, Palace of, p.o.i., Mi., U.S.	199		42.41 N	83.14 W
Auburn Range, mts., Austl.	98	E8	25.10 S	150.30 E
Aubusson, Fr.	22	D8	45.57 N	2.09 E
Auca Mahuida, Arg.	172	H3	37.55 S	68.27 W
Auca Mahuida, Cerro, mtn., Arg.	172	H3	37.44 S	68.55 W
Auce, Lat.	26	D5	56.27 N	22.53 E
Auch, Fr.	22	F6	43.38 N	0.35 E
Auchi, Nig.	84	H6	7.04 N	6.15 E
Aucilla, stm., U.S.	132	F2	30.06 N	83.59 W
Auckland, N.Z.	102	C6	36.51 S	174.44 E
Auckland Islands, is., N.Z.	94	I7	50.45 S	166.11 E
Auckland Park, ngh., S. Afr.	191d		26.11 S	28.00 E
Auckland Park Race Course, p.o.i., S. Afr.	191d		26.11 S	28.00 E
Aude, state, Fr.	22	F8	43.05 N	2.30 E
Aude, stm., Fr.	22	F9	43.12 N	3.13 E
Auden, On., Can.	128	A11	50.14 N	87.53 W
Audenarde see Oudenaarde, Bel.	20	D12	50.50 N	3.36 E
Audenge, Fr.	22	E5	44.40 N	1.00 W
Audenshaw, Eng., U.K.	180		53.28 N	2.08 W
Audenshaw Reservoirs, res., Eng., U.K.	180		53.28 N	2.08 W
Audierne, Fr.	20	F4	48.01 N	4.32 W
Audincourt, Fr.	20	G15	47.29 N	6.50 E
Audubon, Ia., U.S.	130	C2	41.43 N	94.56 W
Audubon, Pa., U.S.	203		40.07 N	75.27 W
Audubon Lake, res., N.D., U.S.	142	G12	47.35 N	101.13 W
Audubon Park, N.J., U.S.	203		39.54 N	75.05 W
Aue, Ger.	24	F8	50.35 N	12.42 E
Auf dem Kreinberge, Ger.	181		51.27 N	7.36 E
Auffargis, Fr.	179		48.42 N	1.53 E
Augarten, p.o.i., Aus.	182b		48.14 N	16.23 E
Augathella, Austl.	98	E6	25.48 S	146.34 E
Aughton, Eng., U.K.	180		53.32 N	2.56 W
Aughton Park, Eng., U.K.	180		53.33 N	2.53 W
Auglaize, stm., Oh., U.S.	130	C13	41.16 N	84.22 W
Augrabies Falls National Park, p.o.i., S. Afr.	90	F4	28.35 S	20.19 E
Augrabiesvalle, wtfl., S. Afr.	90	F5	28.35 S	20.19 E
Au Gres, Mi., U.S.	126	D6	44.03 N	83.40 W
Au Gres, stm., Mi., U.S.	126	D6	44.01 N	83.40 W
Au Gres, East Branch, stm., Mi., U.S.	126	D6	44.05 N	83.40 W
Augsburg, Ger.	24	H6	48.22 N	10.53 E
Augšlīgatne, Lat.	26	C8	57.10 N	25.02 E
Augusta, Austl.	96	F2	34.19 S	115.09 E
Augusta, Italy	32	G9	37.13 N	15.13 E
Augusta, Ar., U.S.	134	B7	35.16 N	91.21 W
Augusta, Ga., U.S.	132	C3	33.27 N	82.01 W
Augusta, Il., U.S.	130	D6	40.13 N	90.57 W
Augusta, Ks., U.S.	138	D10	37.41 N	97.58 W
Augusta, Ky., U.S.	124	F1	38.45 N	84.00 W
Augusta, Me., U.S.	122	F7	44.18 N	69.46 W
Augusta, Mt., U.S.	146	C14	47.29 N	112.24 W
Augusta, Wi., U.S.	128	G7	44.41 N	91.07 W
Augusta, Golfo di, b., Italy	32	G9	37.12 N	15.13 E
Augusto Severo, Braz.	170	C7	5.52 S	37.19 W
Augustów, Pol.	24	C18	53.50 N	22.59 E
Augustowski, Kanał, can., Eur.	24	C19	53.54 N	23.26 E
Augustus, Mount, mtn., Austl.	96	D3	24.19 S	116.50 E
Augustus Downs, Austl.	98	B2	18.32 S	139.53 E
Auki, Sol. Is.	101b	e9	8.46 S	160.42 E
Aukstaitijos nacionalnis parkas, p.o.i., Lith.	26	E8	55.24 N	26.00 E
Auktsjaur, Swe.	14	G10	65.44 N	19.24 E
Aulander, N.C., U.S.	124	H8	36.13 N	77.07 W
Aulanko, Fin.	18	F11	61.01 N	24.25 E
Auld, Lake, l., Austl.	96	D4	22.24 S	123.50 E
Aulla, Italy	30	F6	44.11 N	9.57 E
Aulnay-sur-Mauldre, Fr.	179		48.56 N	1.51 E
Aulne, stm., Fr.	20	F5	48.17 N	4.16 W
Aulneau Peninsula, pen., On., Can.	128	B4	49.23 N	94.29 W
Ault, Co., U.S.	140	G8	40.34 N	104.44 W
Aumale, Fr.	20	E10	49.46 N	1.45 E
Auna, Nig.	84	G5	10.11 N	4.43 E
Auning, Den.	16	K8	56.25 N	10.22 E
Auob, stm., Afr.	90	E5	26.25 S	20.36 E
Aur, Pulau, i., Malay.	64	K7	2.27 N	104.31 E
Aura, Fin.	18	G9	60.38 N	22.35 E
Auraiya, India	70	E7	26.28 N	79.31 E
Aurangābād, India	69	B2	19.53 N	75.19 E
Aurangābād, India	70	F10	24.44 N	84.22 E
Auray, Fr.	20	G5	47.39 N	2.58 W
Aurdal, Nor.	16	G7	60.56 N	9.24 E
Aure, Nor.	16	D6	63.16 N	8.32 E
Aure, stm., Fr.	20	E8	49.19 N	1.07 W
Aurelia, Ia., U.S.	130	B2	42.42 N	95.25 W
Aurich, Ger.	24	C3	53.28 N	7.29 E
Aurilândia, Braz.	166	C6	16.44 S	50.28 W
Aurillac, Fr.	22	E8	44.55 N	2.25 E
Aurine, Alpi (Zillertaler Alpen), mts., Eur.	30	C8	46.54 N	11.49 E
Aurlandsvangen, Nor.	16	G5	60.54 N	7.11 E
Auron, stm., Fr.	20	H11	47.05 N	2.23 E
Aurora, Braz.	205a		22.46 S	43.24 W
Aurora, On., Can.	126	D10	44.00 N	79.28 W
Aurora, S. Afr.	90	H4	32.42 S	18.28 E
Aurora, Co., U.S.	138	B4	39.44 N	104.49 W
Aurora, Il., U.S.	130	C9	41.45 N	88.18 W
Aurora, In., U.S.	130	E13	39.03 N	84.54 W
Aurora, Me., U.S.	122	F8	44.51 N	68.20 W
Aurora, Mn., U.S.	128	D6	47.31 N	92.14 W
Aurora, Mo., U.S.	130	H4	36.58 N	93.43 W
Aurora, Ne., U.S.	140	G14	40.51 N	98.00 W
Aurora, N.Y., U.S.	124	B9	42.45 N	76.41 W
Aurora, N.C., U.S.	132	A9	35.18 N	76.47 W
Aurora, Oh., U.S.	124	C4	41.19 N	81.20 W
Aurora, Ut., U.S.	150	E4	38.55 N	111.56 W
Aurora, W.V., U.S.	124	E6	39.18 N	79.32 W
Aurora, bldg., Russia	183a		59.57 N	30.21 E
Aurora do Norte, Braz.	170	G2	12.43 S	46.24 W
Aurora Pond, l., Oh., U.S.	197a		41.20 N	81.23 W
Aursjøen, l., Nor.	16	E6	62.21 N	8.39 E
Aursunden, l., Nor.	16	E9	62.40 N	11.40 E
Aurukun, Austl.	96	B8	13.21 S	141.44 E
Aurunci, Monti, mts., Italy	32	C7	41.22 N	13.40 E
Aus, Nmb.	90	E3	26.40 S	16.15 E
Ausable, stm., On., Can.	126	E8	43.18 N	81.45 W
Au Sable, stm., Mi., U.S.	126	D6	44.24 N	83.19 W
Au Sable, North Branch, stm., Mi., U.S.	126	D5	44.39 N	84.23 W
Au Sable, South Branch, stm., Mi., U.S.	126	D5	44.38 N	84.28 W
Au Sable Forks, N.Y., U.S.	126	D16	44.26 N	73.40 W
Au Sable Point, c., Mi., U.S.	126	D6	44.20 N	83.20 W
Auschwitz see Oświęcim, Pol.	24	F15	50.03 N	19.13 E
Ausîm, Egypt	191c		30.07 N	31.08 E
Aussig see Ústí nad Labem, Czech Rep.	24	F10	50.39 N	14.02 E
Aust-Agder, state, Nor.	16	I6	58.50 N	8.00 E
Austerlitz see Slavkov u Brna, Czech Rep.	24	G12	49.09 N	16.52 E
Austerlitz, Gare, trans., Fr.	179		48.50 N	2.22 E
Austin, Braz.	205a		22.43 S	43.32 W
Austin, Mb., Can.	142	E15	49.56 N	98.57 W
Austin, In., U.S.	130	F12	38.45 N	85.48 W
Austin, Mn., U.S.	128	H6	43.40 N	92.58 W
Austin, Nv., U.S.	148	D8	39.30 N	117.06 W
Austin, Pa., U.S.	124	C7	41.37 N	78.04 W
Austin, Tx., U.S.	136	D10	30.16 N	97.44 W
Austin, ngh., Il., U.S.	196		41.54 N	87.45 W
Austin, Lake, l., Austl.	96	E3	27.40 S	118.00 E
Austinville, Va., U.S.	124	H5	36.51 N	80.55 W
Austnes, Nor.	16	E4	62.38 N	6.15 E
Austonley, Eng., U.K.	180		53.34 N	1.50 W
Austral, Austl.	192a		33.56 S	150.48 E
Australes, Îles, is., Fr. Poly.	94	F11	23.00 S	150.00 W
Australia, ctry., Oc.	96	D5	25.00 S	135.00 E
Australia, i., Austl.	94	F4	25.00 S	135.00 E
Australian Capital Territory, state, Austl.	98	J7	35.30 S	149.00 E
Austral Islands see Australes, Îles, is., Fr. Poly.	94	F11	23.00 S	150.00 W
Austral Seamounts, unds.	174	L24	23.31 S	151.39 W
Austrått, Nor.	16	D7	63.43 N	9.45 E
Austria, ctry., Eur.	30	C11	47.20 N	13.20 E
Austvågøya, i., Nor.	14	D5	68.20 N	14.37 E
Auteuil, Fr.	179		48.50 N	1.49 E
Authie, stm., Fr.	20	D10	50.22 N	1.37 E
Auth Village, Md., U.S.	202c		38.49 N	76.55 W
Autlán de Navarro, Mex.	154	F6	19.46 N	104.22 W
Autumn Hill, Md., U.S.	202b		39.16 N	76.48 W
Autun, Fr.	20	H13	46.57 N	4.18 E
Auvergne, hist. reg., Fr.	22	D8	45.25 N	2.30 E
Auvernaux, Fr.	179		48.32 N	2.30 E
Auxerre, Fr.	20	G12	47.47 N	3.33 E
Auxier, Ky., U.S.	124	G3	37.43 N	82.46 W
Auxi-le-Château, Fr.	20	D11	50.13 N	2.07 E
Auxonne, Fr.	20	G14	47.11 N	5.23 E
Auxvasse, Mo., U.S.	130	E6	39.01 N	91.52 W
Auyamita, Quebrada, stm., Ven.	204c		10.30 N	66.46 W
Auyán Tepuy, mtn., Ven.	168	E10	5.50 N	62.24 W
Auzances, Fr.	22	C8	46.02 N	2.30 E
Auzangate, Nevado, mtn., Peru	164	F3	13.48 S	71.14 W
Ava, Il., U.S.	130	G8	37.52 N	89.29 W
Ava, Mo., U.S.	130	H5	36.57 N	92.39 W
Avadhara, Geor.	42	D9	43.31 N	40.39 E
Avaí, Braz.	170	L1	22.09 S	49.23 W
Āvaj, Iran	74	C11	35.34 N	49.13 E
Avala, hist., Yugo.	36	E7	44.45 N	20.35 E
Avaldsnes, Nor.	16	H3	59.21 N	5.16 E
Avallon, Fr.	20	G12	47.29 N	3.53 E
Avaloirs, Les, hill, Fr.	20	F8	48.28 N	0.07 W
Avalon, Ca., U.S.	148	J7	33.20 N	118.19 W
Ávalos, Mex.	154	A5	28.36 N	106.00 W
Avana, stm., Cook Is.	100j	a27	21.14 S	159.43 W
Avanersuaq see Nordgrønland, state, Grnld.	108	B14	79.56 N	49.59 W
Avanos, Tur.	42	F6	38.43 N	34.51 E
Avant, Ok., U.S.	130	H1	36.29 N	96.03 W
Avaré, Braz.	170	L1	23.07 S	48.55 W
Avarua, Cook Is.	100j	a26	21.12 S	159.46 W
Avarua Harbour, b., Cook Is.	100j	a26	21.11 S	159.45 W
Avatiu, Cook Is.	100j	a26	21.12 S	159.47 W
Avatiu Harbour, b., Cook Is.	100j	a26	21.11 S	159.46 W
Avaviken, Swe.	16	B16	65.36 N	18.39 E
Avdiïvka, Ukr.	38	E16	48.08 N	37.46 E
Ave, stm., Port.	28	C2	41.20 N	8.44 W
'Avedat, Ḥorvot, hist., Isr.	76	H5	30.48 N	34.46 E
Aveiro, Port.	28	D2	40.38 N	8.38 W
Aveiro, state, Port.	28	D2	40.45 N	8.30 W
Aveiro, Ria de, mth., Port.	28	D1	40.38 N	8.44 W
Aveley, Eng., U.K.	178		51.30 N	0.16 E
Avellaneda, Arg.	172	D8	29.06 S	59.39 W
Avellaneda, Arg.	172	G8	34.40 S	58.23 W

Name	Page	Map Ref.	Latitude	Longitude
Avellaneda, state, Arg.	206		34.40 S	58.20 W
Avellaneda, Estacion, trans., Arg.	206		34.41 S	58.22 W
Avelle, Île, i., Qc., Can.	193a		45.24 N	74.00 W
Avellino, Italy	32	D8	40.54 N	14.47 E
Avenal, Ca., U.S.	148	G5	36.00 N	120.07 W
Aven Armand, cv., Fr.	22	E9	44.15 N	3.22 E
Avenel, N.J., U.S.	194		40.34 N	74.17 W
Avernes, Fr.	179		49.05 N	1.52 E
Avernes, Ru des, stm., Fr.	179		49.04 N	2.51 E
Averøya, i., Nor.	16	D5	63.01 N	7.34 E
Aversa, Italy	32	D8	40.58 N	14.11 E
Avery, Id., U.S.	146	C11	47.15 N	115.47 W
Avery, Tx., U.S.	134	D4	33.33 N	94.46 W
Avery Island, La., U.S.	134	H7	29.54 N	91.54 W
Aves, Islas de, is., Ven.	168	B8	12.00 N	67.30 W
Avesnes-sur-Helpe, Fr.	20	D12	50.07 N	3.56 E
Avesta, Swe.	16	G14	60.09 N	16.11 E
Aveyron, state, Fr.	22	E8	44.15 N	2.40 E
Aveyron, stm., Fr.	22	E7	44.05 N	1.15 E
Avezzano, Italy	30	H10	42.02 N	13.25 E
Aviemore, Scot., U.K.	10	D9	57.12 N	3.50 W
Avigliano, Italy	32	D9	40.44 N	15.44 E
Avignon, Fr.	22	F10	43.57 N	4.48 E
Ávila, Spain	28	D6	40.39 N	4.41 W
Ávila, co., Spain	28	D6	40.35 N	5.00 W
Ávila, Sierra de, mts., Spain	28	D6	40.38 N	4.57 W
Avilés, Spain	28	A5	43.33 N	5.53 W
Aviño, Spain	28	A2	43.36 N	8.08 W
Avinurme, Est.	26	B9	58.59 N	26.51 E
Avis, Pa., U.S.	124	C8	41.10 N	77.18 W
Avispa, Cerro, mtn., Ven.	168	G9	1.16 N	65.51 W
Aviz, Port.	28	E3	39.03 N	7.53 W
Avlan Gölü, l., Tur.	34	G12	36.34 N	29.56 E
Avlum, Den.	16	K6	56.16 N	8.48 E
Avneporog, Russia	18	B20	65.08 N	33.46 E
Avoca, Austl.	98	K4	37.05 S	143.28 E
Avoca, Ia., U.S.	130	C2	41.28 N	95.20 W
Avoca, N.Y., U.S.	124	B8	42.25 N	77.25 W
Avoca, stm., Austl.	98	K4	35.42 S	143.44 E
Avocado Heights, Ca., U.S.	198		34.08 N	117.54 W
Avola, B.C., Can.	144	E11	51.48 N	119.19 W
Avola, Italy	32	H9	36.54 N	15.08 E
Avon, Il., U.S.	130	D7	40.39 N	90.25 W
Avon, Mn., U.S.	128	F4	45.35 N	94.26 W
Avon, Mt., U.S.	146	D14	46.35 N	112.36 W
Avon, N.Y., U.S.	124	B8	42.54 N	77.44 W
Avon, N.C., U.S.	132	A10	35.20 N	75.30 W
Avon, S.D., U.S.	140	D14	43.00 N	98.03 W
Avon, stm., N.S., Can.	122	F12	45.10 N	64.15 W
Avon, stm., Eng., U.K.	10	K11	50.44 N	1.46 W
Avon, stm., Eng., U.K.	10	I11	51.59 N	2.10 W
Avon, stm., Eng., U.K.	10	J10	51.29 N	2.41 W
Avon, stm., Scot., U.K.	10	D9	57.25 N	3.22 W
Avon, Ru d', stm., Fr.	179		48.39 N	2.46 E
Avon Basin, b., Oh., U.S.	197a		41.30 N	82.03 W
Avondale, Az., U.S.	150	J4	33.25 N	112.20 W
Avondale, Co., U.S.	138	C4	38.14 N	104.20 W
Avondale, Md., U.S.	202c		38.56 N	76.59 W
Avondale Heights, Austl.	192b		37.46 S	144.51 E
Avon Downs, Austl.	96	D7	20.04 S	137.29 E
Avonlea, Sk., Can.	142	D8	50.00 N	105.03 W
Avon Park, Fl., U.S.	132	I4	27.35 N	81.30 W
Avontuur, S. Afr.	90	H6	33.43 S	23.10 E
Avrainville, Fr.	179		48.34 N	2.15 E
Avranches, Fr.	20	F7	48.41 N	1.22 W
Avre, stm., Fr.	20	F9	48.47 N	1.22 E
Avre, stm., Fr.	20	E11	49.53 N	2.20 E
Avtovo, ngh., Russia	183a		59.52 N	30.15 E
Avu Avu, Sol. Is.	101b	e9	9.50 S	160.23 E
Awaaso, Ghana	84	H4	6.13 N	2.17 W
Awaji, Japan	56	E8	34.35 N	135.00 E
Awaji-shima, i., Japan	56	E7	34.20 N	134.51 E
Awara, Japan	56	C9	36.13 N	136.12 E
Āwarē, Eth.	82	F8	8.15 N	44.08 E
Āwasa, Eth.	82	F7	6.56 N	38.31 E
Āwash, Eth.	82	F8	8.59 N	40.10 E
Āwash, stm., Eth.	82	E8	11.09 N	41.41 E
Awa-shima, i., Japan	56	A12	38.27 N	139.14 E
Awat, China	48	F14	40.38 N	80.22 E
Awbārī, Libya	82	B2	26.40 N	12.43 E
Awbārī, Ṣaḥrā', reg., Libya	82	B2	27.56 N	11.06 E
Awe, Loch, l., Scot., U.K.	10	E7	56.22 N	5.04 W
Awegyun, Mya.	64	F4	12.44 N	98.44 E
Awjilah, Libya	82	B4	29.07 N	21.18 E
Awled Djellal, Alg.	84	C6	34.25 N	5.04 E
Awlef, Alg.	84	D5	26.58 N	1.04 E
Awosting, N.J., U.S.	194		41.09 N	74.20 W
Awul, Pap. N. Gui.	101a	b5	6.00 S	151.00 E
Axat, Fr.	28	B13	42.48 N	2.14 E
Axe Edge, hills, Eng., U.K.	180		53.14 N	1.57 W
Axel Heiberg Island, i., Nu., Can.	106	B13	79.45 N	91.00 W
Axim, Ghana	84	I4	4.52 N	2.14 W
Axinim, Braz.	164	D6	4.01 S	59.22 W
Axiós (Vardar), stm., Eur.	34	B5	40.31 N	22.43 E
Axis, Al., U.S.	134	G10	30.53 N	88.02 W
Axixá, Braz.	170	B3	2.51 S	44.04 W
Ax-les-Thermes, Fr.	22	G7	42.43 N	1.50 E
Axtell, Ks., U.S.	128	L2	39.52 N	96.15 W
Axtell, Ne., U.S.	140	G13	40.29 N	99.07 W
Ayabe, Japan	56	D8	35.18 N	135.15 E
Ayacucho, Arg.	172	H8	37.09 S	58.29 W
Ayacucho, Peru	164	F3	13.08 S	74.13 W
Ayakkum Hu, l., China	52	D2	37.32 N	89.23 E
Ayakoz see Ajaguz, Kaz.	48	E13	47.57 N	80.26 E
Ayala Museum, bldg., Phil.	187f		14.33 N	121.01 E
Ayamé, C. Iv.	84	H4	5.37 N	3.08 W
Ayamonte, Spain	28	G3	37.13 N	7.24 W
Āyān, India	190b		22.43 N	88.09 E
Ayapel, Col.	168	C4	8.19 N	75.09 W
Ayaş, Tur.	34	C15	40.02 N	32.18 E
Ayase, stm., Japan	186		35.45 N	139.49 E
Ayaviri, Peru	164	F3	14.53 S	70.35 W
Ayden, N.C., U.S.	132	A8	35.28 N	77.25 W
Aydın, Tur.	34	F10	37.51 N	27.50 E
Aydın, state, Tur.	34	F11	37.45 N	28.00 E
Aydıncık, Tur.	76	B4	36.08 N	33.18 E
Aydın Dağları, mts., Tur.	34	E11	38.00 N	28.00 E
Aydınkent, Tur.	34	F14	37.05 N	31.35 E
Aydosdağı, mtn., Tur.	185b		40.56 N	29.15 E
Ayer, Ma., U.S.	124	B14	42.33 N	71.35 W
Ayer Chawan, Pulau, i., Sing.	189c		1.17 N	103.42 E
Ayer Itam, Malay.	64	J5	5.23 N	100.16 E
Ayer Merbau, Pulau, i., Sing.	189c		1.16 N	103.43 E
Ayers Rock see Uluru, mtn., Austl.	96	E6	25.19 S	130.59 E
Ayeyarwady, state, Mya.	64	D2	16.45 N	95.06 E
Ayeyarwady (Irrawaddy), stm., Mya.	62	E8	15.50 N	95.04 E
Ayeyarwady, Mouths of the, mth., Mya.	64	E2	15.39 N	94.44 E
Ayía Varvára, Grc.	185c		37.59 N	23.39 E
Ayiou Nikolaou Monastery, rel., Grc.	185c		37.53 N	23.27 E
Aylesbury, Eng., U.K.	10	J12	51.49 N	0.49 W
Aylmer, On., Can.	126	F8	42.46 N	80.58 W
Aylmer, Qc., Can.	126	C14	45.23 N	75.50 W
Aylmer, Mount, mtn., Ab., Can.	144	E15	51.19 N	115.26 W
Aylmer Lake, l., N.T., Can.	110	C9	64.05 N	108.30 W
Aylsham, Sk., Can.	142	A10	53.10 N	103.48 W
'Ayn al-'Arab, Syria	76	B9	36.52 N	38.22 E
'Ayn Dār, Sau. Ar.	72	D6	25.59 N	49.23 E
Aynor, S.C., U.S.	132	B6	33.59 N	79.11 W
'Aynūnah, Sau. Ar.	74	F4	28.04 N	35.07 E
Ayod, Sudan	82	F6	8.07 N	31.24 E
Ayon Island see Aën, ostrov, i., Russia	50	B22	69.46 N	168.40 E
Ayora see Aiora, Spain	28	E9	39.02 N	1.03 W
Ayorou, Niger	84	G5	14.44 N	0.55 E
'Ayoûn el 'Atroûs, Maur.	84	F3	16.40 N	9.37 W
Ayr, Austl.	98	B6	19.34 S	147.24 E
Ayr, On., Can.	126	E9	43.17 N	80.27 W
Ayr, Scot., U.K.	10	F8	55.28 N	4.38 W
Ayr, stm., Scot., U.K.	10	F8	55.28 N	4.38 W
Ayrag nuur, l., Mong.	48	E16	48.54 N	93.28 E
Ayrancı, Tur.	76	A4	37.19 N	33.46 E
Ayre, Point of, c., I. of Man	10	G8	54.24 N	4.22 W
Ayrum, Arm.	42	E11	41.13 N	44.55 E
Āysha, Eth.	82	E8	10.44 N	42.34 E
Ayton, Austl.	96	C9	15.55 S	145.20 E
Aytos see Ajtos, Blg.	36	G14	42.42 N	27.16 E
Ayulhai, China	54	B1	44.34 N	115.39 E
Ayun see A Dun, stm., Viet.	64	F9	13.23 N	108.27 E
A Yun Pa, Viet.	64	F9	13.24 N	108.26 E
Ayutla, Mex.	154	E6	20.07 N	104.21 W
Ayutla de los Libres, Mex.	154	G9	16.53 N	99.13 W
Ayvacık, Tur.	34	D9	39.34 N	26.23 E
Ayvalık, Tur.	34	D9	39.19 N	26.42 E
Azādpur, ngh., India	190a		28.43 N	77.11 E
Azaila, Spain	28	C10	41.17 N	0.29 W
Azamatovo, Russia	40	E18	53.16 N	53.28 E
Azambuja, Port.	28	E2	39.04 N	8.52 W
Āzamgarh, India	70	E9	26.03 N	83.11 E
Azángaro, Peru	164	F3	14.55 S	70.12 W
Azaouâd, reg., Mali	84	F4	19.00 N	3.00 W
Azärbaycan see Azerbaijan, ctry., Asia	42	E12	40.30 N	47.30 E
Āzārbāyjān-e Gharbī, state, Iran	74	A9	37.40 N	45.00 E
Āzārbāyjān-e Sharqī, state, Iran	74	A10	38.00 N	47.00 E
Azare, Nig.	84	G6	11.40 N	10.11 E
Āzar Shahr, Iran	74	B10	37.45 N	45.59 E
Azaryčy, Bela.	26	H12	52.28 N	29.14 E
Azay-le-Rideau, Fr.	20	G9	47.15 N	0.27 E
A'zāz, Syria	76	B8	36.35 N	37.03 E
Azdavay, Tur.	34	B16	41.38 N	33.16 E
Azdzjacičy, Bela.	26	F11	54.06 N	28.50 E
Azeffâl, sand, Afr.	84	E2	21.16 N	14.20 W
Azenhas do Mar, Port.	184c		38.50 N	9.28 W
Azerbaijan see Āzārbāyjān-e Sharqī, state, Iran	74	A10	38.00 N	47.00 E
Azerbaijan, ctry., Asia	42	E12	40.30 N	47.30 E
Azerbajdžan see Azerbaijan, ctry., Asia	42	E12	40.30 N	47.30 E
Azëry, Bela.	26	G7	53.43 N	24.11 E
Āzezo, Eth.	82	E7	12.32 N	37.25 E
Azgir, Kaz.	40	H15	47.50 N	47.55 E
Azhikode, India	69	F2	11.58 N	75.19 E
Azilal, Mor.	84	C3	31.58 N	6.34 W
Aznakaevo, Russia	40	D18	54.51 N	53.04 E
Aznapuquio, Peru	204d		11.59 S	77.04 W
Azogues, Ec.	168	I2	2.44 S	78.50 W
Azoia, Port.	184c		38.46 N	9.29 W
Azores see Açores, is., Port.	80	C3	38.30 N	28.00 W
Azores Plateau, unds.	176	E10	39.00 N	30.00 W
Azov, Russia	40	H11	47.06 N	39.25 E
Azov, Sea of, s., Eur.	38	G15	46.00 N	36.00 E
Azovs'ke, Ukr.	38	H13	45.35 N	34.34 E
Azovs'ke more see Azov, Sea of, s., Eur.	38	G15	46.00 N	36.00 E
Azovskij kanal, can., Russia	40	H12	47.07 N	39.26 E
Azovskoe more see Azov, Sea of, s., Eur.	38	G15	46.00 N	36.00 E
Azpeitia, Spain	22	F3	43.11 N	2.16 W
Azraq, Al-Bahr al- see Blue Nile, stm., Afr.	82	E6	15.37 N	32.30 E
Azraq ash-Shīshān, Jord.	76	G7	31.50 N	36.49 E
Aztec, N.M., U.S.	150	G9	36.49 N	108.00 W
Azteca, Estadio, p.o.i., Mex.	204a		19.18 N	99.09 W
Aztec Peak, mtn., Az., U.S.	150	J6	33.48 N	110.55 W
Aztec Ruins National Monument, p.o.i., N.M., U.S.	150	G8	36.52 N	108.01 W
Azua, Dom. Rep.	156	C12	18.27 N	70.44 W
Azuaga, Spain	28	F5	38.15 N	5.40 W
Azuay, state, Ec.	168	I2	2.50 S	79.15 W
Azucena, Arg.	172	H8	37.30 S	59.19 W
Azuer, stm., Spain	28	F7	39.07 N	3.35 W
Azuero, Península de, pen., Pan.	168	D1	7.40 N	80.35 W
Azufre, Volcán, vol., S.A.	172	B3	25.11 S	68.31 W
Azufre, Volcán del see Azufre, Volcán, vol., S.A.	172	B3	25.11 S	68.31 W
Azuga, Rom.	36	D12	45.27 N	25.33 E
Azul, Arg.	172	H8	36.47 S	59.51 W
Azul, Cerro, mtn., C.R.	156	G5	9.54 N	85.14 W
Azumazaka, Japan	188		34.26 N	135.39 E
Azur, Côte d', cst., Fr.	22	F13	43.30 N	7.00 E
Azurduy, Bol.	166	C4	19.59 S	64.29 W
Azure Clouds, Temple of the, rel., China	189a		40.00 N	116.11 E
Azure Lake, l., B.C., Can.	144	D10	52.23 N	119.58 W
Az-Zāb al-Kabīr see Great Zab, stm., Asia	74	B9	36.00 N	43.21 E
Az-Zāb aṣ-Ṣaghīr see Little Zab, stm., Asia	74	C9	35.14 N	43.25 E
Az-Zahrān, Sau. Ar.	72	D6	26.18 N	50.08 E
Az-Zarbah, Syria	76	B7	36.04 N	36.58 E
Az-Zarqā', Jord.	76	F7	32.03 N	36.05 E
Az-Zarqā', state, Jord.	76	G8	31.50 N	36.45 E
Az-Zāwiyah, Libya	82	A2	32.46 N	12.44 E
Azzel Matti, Sebkha, pl., Alg.	84	D5	25.55 N	0.56 E
Az-Zilfī, Sau. Ar.	74	G9	26.17 N	44.48 E
Az-Zubayr, Iraq	74	E10	30.23 N	47.42 E

B

Name	Page	Map Ref.	Latitude	Longitude
Ba, Fiji	101e	p18	17.33 S	177.41 E
Ba, stm., China	58	F6	30.25 N	115.00 E
Ba, stm., China	58	F2	31.02 N	107.09 E
Ba, stm., China	189a		39.57 N	116.38 E
Ba, stm., Viet.	64	F9	13.01 N	108.58 E
Baa, Indon.	60	H7	10.44 S	123.02 E
Baaba, Île, i., N. Cal.	101d	I15	20.03 S	163.57 E
Baak, Ger.	181		51.25 N	7.10 E
Baao, Phil.	68	D4	13.26 N	123.23 E
Baarbach, stm., Ger.	181		51.27 N	7.39 E
Baardheere, Som.	86	D8	2.19 N	42.17 E
Baba Burnu, c., Tur.	34	B14	41.18 N	31.24 E
Baba Burnu, c., Tur.	34	D9	39.29 N	26.05 E
Babaçulândia, Braz.	170	D2	7.13 S	47.45 W
Babadag, Rom.	36	E15	44.54 N	28.43 E
Babadağ, Tur.	34	F11	37.48 N	28.51 E
Babaeski, Tur.	34	B10	41.26 N	27.06 E
Babaevo, Russia	26	A18	59.23 N	35.56 E
Babahoyo, Ec.	168	H2	1.48 S	79.31 W
Babaikivka, Ukr.	38	D13	49.01 N	34.32 E
Babak, Phil.	68	G5	7.08 N	125.41 E
Babanango, S. Afr.	90	F10	28.21 S	31.02 E
Babanka, Ukr.	38	E9	48.42 N	30.27 E
Babanūsah, Sudan	82	E5	11.18 N	27.47 E
Babar, Kepulauan, is., Indon.	60	G8	7.50 S	129.45 E
Bābarpur, ngh., India	190a		28.41 N	77.17 E
Babat, Indon.	66	E3	2.44 S	103.38 E
Babb, Mt., U.S.	146	B13	48.52 N	113.26 W
Babbitt, Mn., U.S.	128	D7	47.43 N	91.57 W
Babbitt, Nv., U.S.	148	E7	38.32 N	118.38 W
B'abdā, Leb.	76	E6	33.50 N	35.32 E
Babeldaob, i., Palau	100b	g7	7.29 N	134.34 E
Babelsberg, ngh., Ger.	182a		52.24 N	13.05 E
Babelsberg, Schloss, hist., Ger.	182a		52.24 N	13.05 E
Babelthuap see Babeldaob, i., Palau	100b	g7	7.29 N	134.34 E
Babi, Pulau, i., Indon.	64	K3	2.05 N	96.39 E
Babia, Arroyo de la, stm., Mex.	136	F5	28.24 N	101.43 W
Babian, stm., China	64	A5	23.03 N	101.39 E
Babičy, Bela.	26	H12	52.17 N	30.00 E
Bābil, state, Iraq	74	D9	32.40 N	44.35 E
Bābil, Aṭlāl (Babylon), hist., Iraq	74	D9	32.33 N	44.24 E
Babimost, Pol.	24	D11	52.10 N	15.51 E
Babīna, India	70	F7	25.14 N	78.27 E
Babinda, Austl.	98	A5	17.20 S	145.55 E
Babine, stm., B.C., Can.	110	D5	55.41 N	127.41 W
Babine Lake, l., B.C., Can.	110	D5	54.45 N	126.00 W
Babine Range, mts., B.C., Can.	144	A3	54.39 N	126.07 W
Babino, Russia	26	D17	56.44 N	34.17 E
Babino, Russia	26	A14	59.14 N	31.28 E
Babiogórski Park Narodowy, p.o.i., Pol.	24	G15	49.35 N	19.30 E
Babje, ozero, l., Russia	14	F30	66.39 N	39.52 E
Babo, Indon.	60	F9	2.31 S	133.27 E
Bābol, Iran	74	B13	36.32 N	52.40 E
Bābol Sar, Iran	74	B13	36.41 N	52.39 E
Baboquivari Mountains, mts., Az., U.S.	150	L5	31.45 N	111.35 W
Baboquivari Peak, mtn., Az., U.S.	150	L5	31.46 N	111.35 W
Babórów, Pol.	24	F13	50.09 N	17.59 E
Baboua, C.A.R.	86	C2	5.48 N	14.49 E
Babozero, ozero, l., Russia	14	F28	66.28 N	37.22 E
Babrujsk, Bela.	26	G12	53.08 N	29.14 E
Babson Park, Ma., U.S.	201		42.18 N	71.23 W
Babson Reservoir, res., Ma., U.S.	201		42.38 N	70.40 W
Bābu Bheri, India	190b		22.51 N	88.14 E
Bābūpur, India	190a		28.30 N	76.59 E
Babuškin, Russia	50	F10	51.42 N	105.56 E
Babuškin, ngh., Russia	183b		55.52 N	37.42 E
Babuyan Channel, strt., Phil.	68	A3	18.44 N	121.40 E
Babuyan Island, i., Phil.	68	A3	19.32 N	121.57 E
Babuyan Islands, is., Phil.	60	B7	19.15 N	121.40 E
Babylon see Bābil, Aṭlāl, hist., Iraq	74	D9	32.33 N	44.24 E
Babynino, Russia	26	F18	54.22 N	35.44 E
Bacabal, Braz.	170	C3	4.14 S	44.47 W
Bacadéhuachi, Mex.	120	G8	29.44 N	109.10 W
Bacalhau, Canal do, can., Braz.	205a		23.03 S	43.35 W
Bacan, Pulau, i., Indon.	94	C3	0.35 S	127.30 E
Bacatuba, Braz.	170	C4	5.40 S	43.42 W
Bacău, Rom.	36	C13	46.34 N	26.55 E
Bacău, state, Rom.	36	C13	46.30 N	26.45 E
Bac Binh, Viet.	64	G9	11.11 N	108.33 E
Bac Bo, Vinh see Tonkin, Gulf of, b., Asia	52	G6	20.00 N	108.00 E
Baccarat, Fr.	20	F15	48.26 N	6.44 E
Bačėjkava, Bela.	26	F12	55.01 N	29.09 E
Bacerac, Mex.	120	F8	30.21 N	108.57 W
Bacevičy, Bela.	26	G12	53.24 N	29.13 E
Bac Giang, Viet.	64	B8	21.16 N	106.11 E
Bachaquero, Ven.	168	B6	9.57 N	71.07 W
Bachiniva, Mex.	154	A5	28.46 N	107.15 W
Bach Ma, Viet.	64	D8	16.11 N	107.51 E
Bachten-Berg, hill, Ger.	182a		52.20 N	12.54 E
Bach Thong, Viet.	64	A7	22.09 N	105.50 E
Bachu, China	48	G13	39.50 N	78.20 E
Back, stm., Nu., Can.	110	B11	67.09 N	95.21 W
Bačka, reg., Eur.	30	E16	45.49 N	19.30 E
Bačka Palanka, Yugo.	36	D6	45.15 N	19.23 E
Bačka Topola, Yugo.	36	D6	45.48 N	19.38 E
Back Bay, b., ngh., Ma., U.S.	201		42.21 N	71.05 W
Back Bay, b., India	190c		18.56 N	72.49 E
Back Branch, stm., Md., U.S.	202c		38.50 N	76.48 W
Back Brook, stm., N.J., U.S.	194		40.26 N	74.39 W
Back Channel, mth., Pa., U.S.	197b		40.30 N	80.05 W
Back Creek, stm., Va., U.S.	124	F6	38.01 N	79.54 W
Backe, Swe.	16	D14	63.49 N	16.24 E
Bäckefors, Swe.	16	I10	58.48 N	12.10 E
Backford, Eng., U.K.	180		53.15 N	2.54 W
Backnang, Ger.	24	H5	48.56 N	9.26 E
Back River Neck, pen., Md., U.S.	202b		39.18 N	76.26 W
Backstairs Passage, strt., Austl.	98	J1	35.42 S	138.05 E
Bac Lieu, Viet.	64	H7	9.17 N	105.43 E
Bac Ninh, Viet.	64	B8	21.11 N	106.05 E
Baco, Mount, mtn., Phil.	68	D3	12.49 N	121.10 E
Bacoachi, Mex.	120	F8	30.38 N	109.56 W
Bacolod, Phil.	68	E4	10.40 N	122.57 E
Baconga, ngh., Congo	191b		4.18 S	15.16 E
Bacons Run, stm., N.J., U.S.	203		40.06 N	74.41 W
Baconton, Ga., U.S.	132	E1	31.22 N	84.09 W
Bacoor, Phil.	68	C3	14.27 N	120.57 E
Bacoor Bay, b., Phil.	187f		14.28 N	120.54 E
Bac Phan (Tonkin), hist. reg., Viet.	64	A7	22.00 N	105.00 E
Bac Quang, Viet.	64	A7	22.29 N	104.52 E
Bácsalmás, Hung.	36	C6	46.07 N	19.20 E
Bacska see Bačka, reg., Eur.	30	E16	45.49 N	19.30 E
Bács-Kiskun, state, Hung.	36	C6	46.30 N	19.25 E
Bâcu, stm., Mol.	36	C15	46.54 N	29.28 E
Bácum, Mex.	120	H7	27.33 N	110.05 W
Bacuranao, stm., Cuba	204b		23.10 N	82.14 W
Bacuranao, Presa, res., Cuba	204b		23.07 N	82.13 W
Bacuri, Lago do, l., Braz.	170	B4	3.14 S	42.10 W
Bād, Iran	74	D13	33.39 N	52.02 E
Bad, stm., Mi., U.S.	126	E5	43.19 N	84.03 W
Bad, stm., S.D., U.S.	140	C12	44.20 N	100.21 W
Bad, stm., Wi., U.S.	128	E8	46.37 N	90.38 W
Badagara, India	69	F2	11.37 N	75.34 E
Badagri Creek, b., Nig.	191a		6.25 N	3.18 E
Badajós, Lago, l., Braz.	164	D5	3.14 S	62.46 W
Badajoz, Spain	28	F4	38.52 N	6.57 W
Badajoz, co., Spain	28	F4	38.40 N	6.00 W
Badalona, Spain	28	C13	41.28 N	2.15 E
Bādāmi, India	69	D2	15.55 N	75.41 E
Badanah, Sau. Ar.	72	C5	30.59 N	41.01 E
Badarīnāth, India	70	C7	30.46 N	79.51 E
Badarma, Russia	48	C18	57.46 N	102.34 E
Badas, Bru.	66	A9	4.33 N	114.24 E
Badas, Kepulauan, is., Indon.	66	C5	0.35 N	107.06 E
Bad Aussee, Aus.	30	C10	47.35 N	13.46 E
Bad Axe, Mi., U.S.	126	E7	43.48 N	82.59 W
Bad Bergzabern, Ger.	24	G3	49.05 N	7.59 E
Bad Bevensen, Ger.	24	C6	53.05 N	10.34 E
Bad Bramstedt, Ger.	24	C5	53.55 N	9.53 E
Bad Brückenau, Ger.	24	F5	50.18 N	9.47 E
Baddeck, N.S., Can.	122	D16	46.07 N	60.45 W
Bad Doberan, Ger.	24	B7	54.06 N	11.54 E
Bad Dürrenberg, Ger.	24	E8	51.17 N	12.04 E
Bade, Indon.	60	G10	7.09 S	139.34 E
Bad Ems, Ger.	24	F3	50.20 N	7.43 E
Baden, Aus.	24	H12	48.00 N	16.14 E
Baden, Switz.	30	C5	47.29 N	8.18 E
Baden-Baden, Ger.	24	H4	48.45 N	8.14 E
Baden bei Wien see Baden, Aus.	24	H12	48.00 N	16.14 E
Badenoch, hist. reg., Scot., U.K.	10	E8	56.57 N	4.19 W
Badenweiler, Ger.	24	I3	47.47 N	7.39 E
Baden-Württemberg, state, Ger.	24	H4	48.30 N	9.00 E
Bad Freienwalde, Ger.	24	D9	52.47 N	14.02 E
Badgastein, Aus.	30	C10	47.07 N	13.08 E
Badger, Mn., U.S.	128	C3	48.45 N	95.59 W
Badger Creek, stm., Co., U.S.	138	C3	38.27 N	105.51 W
Badger Creek, stm., Co., U.S.	138	A5	40.17 N	103.42 W
Badger's Mount, Eng., U.K.	178		51.20 N	0.09 E
Badgerys Creek, Austl.	192a		33.53 S	150.44 E
Badgerys Creek, stm., Austl.	192a		33.51 S	150.46 E
Bad Hall, Aus.	30	B11	48.01 N	14.13 E
Bad Harzburg, Ger.	24	E6	51.53 N	10.34 E
Badhela, ngh., India	190a		28.38 N	77.04 E
Bad Hersfeld, Ger.	24	F5	50.52 N	9.42 E
Bad Homburg vor der Höhe, Ger.	24	F4	50.14 N	8.36 E
Bad Honnef, Ger.	24	F3	50.38 N	7.14 E
Badīn, Pak.	70	F2	24.40 N	68.51 E
Bādinan, India	190b		22.54 N	88.14 E
Badin Lake, res., N.C., U.S.	132	A5	35.26 N	80.05 W
Badiraguato, Mex.	154	C5	25.22 N	107.31 W
Bad Ischl, Aus.	30	C10	47.42 N	13.37 E
Bad Kissingen, Ger.	24	F6	50.12 N	10.05 E
Bad Kreuznach, Ger.	24	G3	49.51 N	7.52 E
Badlands, hills, U.S.	140	A9	46.14 N	103.36 W
Badlands, hills, S.D., U.S.	140	D10	43.36 N	102.09 W
Badlands National Park, p.o.i., S.D., U.S.	140	D10	43.49 N	102.20 W
Bad Langensalza, Ger.	24	E6	51.06 N	10.39 E
Bad Lauterberg im Harz, Ger.	24	E6	51.37 N	10.27 E
Bad Leonfelden, Aus.	24	H10	48.31 N	14.17 E
Bādli, ngh., India	190a		28.45 N	77.09 E
Bad Mergentheim, Ger.	24	G5	49.29 N	9.46 E
Bad Muskau, Ger.	24	E10	51.32 N	14.43 E
Bad Nauheim, Ger.	24	F4	50.21 N	8.44 E
Badnera, India	70	H6	20.51 N	77.43 E
Badner Lindkogel, mtn., Aus.	182b		48.01 N	16.11 E
Bad Neustadt an der Saale, Ger.	24	F6	50.19 N	10.13 E
Bad Oeynhausen, Ger.	24	D4	52.12 N	8.48 E
Bad Oldesloe, Ger.	24	C6	53.48 N	10.23 E
Badong, China	58	F4	31.02 N	110.19 E
Ba Dong, Viet.	64	H8	9.40 N	106.33 E
Bad Orb, Ger.	24	F5	50.13 N	9.21 E
Bad Pyrmont, Ger.	24	E5	51.59 N	9.15 E
Bad Ragaz, Switz.	30	C6	46.59 N	9.29 E
Bad Reichenhall, Ger.	24	I8	47.43 N	12.53 E
Bad River Indian Reservation, ind. res., Wi., U.S.	128	E7	46.33 N	90.40 W
Bad Salzuflen, Ger.	24	D4	52.05 N	8.44 E
Bad Salzungen, Ger.	24	F6	50.49 N	10.11 E
Bad Schönfliess see Trzcińsko-Zdrój, Pol.	24	C10	52.57 N	14.35 E
Bad Schwalbach, Ger.	24	F3	50.07 N	8.03 E
Bad Schwartau, Ger.	24	C6	53.54 N	10.41 E
Bad Segeberg, Ger.	24	C6	53.55 N	10.18 E
Bādshāhpur, India	70	F9	25.46 N	82.49 E
Bad Tölz, Ger.	24	I7	47.45 N	11.34 E
Badu, Braz.	205a		22.54 S	43.04 W
Badulla, Sri L.	69	H5	6.59 N	81.03 E
Badupi, Mya.	64	B1	21.36 N	93.25 E
Badvel, India	69	D4	14.44 N	79.04 E
Bad Vöslau, Aus.	30	C13	47.58 N	16.14 E
Bad Waldsee, Ger.	24	I5	47.55 N	9.44 E
Bad Wildungen, Ger.	24	E5	51.06 N	9.08 E
Bad Wörishofen, Ger.	24	I6	48.00 N	10.36 E
Badžalskij hrebet, mts., Russia	50	F15	50.40 N	134.50 E
Baena, Spain	28	G6	37.37 N	4.19 W
Baependi, Braz.	170	K3	21.57 S	44.53 W
Baer, Russia	48	C17	55.44 N	99.27 E
Baerl, ngh., Ger.	181		51.29 N	6.41 E
Baeza, Ec.	168	H3	0.28 S	77.53 W
Baeza, Spain	28	G7	37.59 N	3.28 W
Baezaeko, stm., B.C., Can.	144	D7	53.08 N	123.40 W
Bafang, Cam.	86	C1	5.09 N	10.11 E
Bafatá, Gui.-B.	84	G2	12.09 N	14.41 W
Baffin Basin, unds.	176	A7	73.15 N	67.00 W
Baffin Bay, b., N.A.	108	C12	73.00 N	66.00 W
Baffin Bay, b., Tx., U.S.	136	G10	27.15 N	97.33 W
Baffin Bugt see Baffin Bay, b., N.A.	108	C12	73.00 N	66.00 W
Baffin Island, i., Nu., Can.	110	B16	68.00 N	70.00 W
Bafia, Cam.	86	D2	4.45 N	11.15 E
Bafing, stm., Afr.	84	G2	13.47 N	10.50 W
Bafoulabé, Mali	84	G2	13.47 N	10.50 W
Bafoussam, Cam.	86	C2	5.29 N	10.24 E
Bāfq, Iran	74	E14	31.35 N	55.24 E
Bafra, Tur.	42	E6	41.33 N	35.53 E
Bafra Burnu, c., Tur.	42	E7	41.42 N	35.58 E
Bāft, Iran	72	D8	29.14 N	56.36 E
Bafwaboli, D.R.C.	86	D5	0.40 N	26.05 E
Bafwasende, D.R.C.	86	D5	1.05 N	27.16 E
Bagaces, C.R.	156	G5	10.30 N	85.15 W
Bagagem, stm., Braz.	170	F1	11.37 S	48.12 W
Bagagem, stm., Braz.	170	H1	13.58 S	48.20 W
Bagaha, India	70	E9	27.06 N	84.05 E
Bāgalkot, India	69	C2	16.11 N	75.41 E
Bagamoyo, Tan.	86	F7	6.26 S	38.53 E
Bagan Datuk, Malay.	64	K5	3.58 N	100.47 E
Baganga, Phil.	68	G6	7.33 N	126.33 E
Bagansiapiapi, Indon.	66	B2	2.08 N	100.48 E
Bağarası, Tur.	34	F10	37.42 N	27.32 E
Bagasra, India	70	H3	21.29 N	70.57 E
Bagdad see Baghdād, Iraq	74	D9	33.21 N	44.25 E
Bagdad, Az., U.S.	150	I3	34.32 N	113.13 W
Bagdad, Fl., U.S.	134	G11	30.36 N	87.01 W
Bagdarin, Russia	50	F11	54.26 N	113.36 E
Bagé, Braz.	172	E10	31.19 S	54.06 W
Bagenkop, Den.	16	M8	54.45 N	10.41 E
Bāgerhāt, Bngl.	70	G12	22.38 N	89.48 E
Bages et de Sigean, Étang de, l., Fr.	22	F9	43.04 N	3.03 E
Bāgevādi, India	69	C2	16.34 N	75.58 E
Baggio, ngh., Italy	184b		45.27 N	9.06 E
Baggs, Wy., U.S.	150	B9	41.02 N	107.39 W
Baghdād, Iraq	74	D9	33.21 N	44.25 E
Baghdād, state, Iraq	74	D9	33.20 N	44.25 E
Bāgh-e Malek, Iran	74	E11	31.28 N	49.55 E
Bagheria, Italy	32	F7	38.04 N	13.30 E
Baghlān, Afg.	72	B10	36.08 N	68.42 E
Bagillt, Wales, U.K.	180		53.16 N	3.10 W
Bağırsak (Sājūr), stm., Asia	76	B8	36.40 N	38.06 E
Bagley, Mn., U.S.	128	D3	47.30 N	95.22 W
Bāgmāri, ngh., India	190b		22.34 N	88.25 E
Bagn, Nor.	16	G7	60.49 N	9.32 E
Bagnères-de-Luchon, Fr.	22	G6	42.47 N	0.35 E
Bagneux, Fr.	179		48.48 N	2.18 E
Bagni di Lucca, Italy	30	F7	44.01 N	10.34 E
Bagno di Romagna, Italy	30	G8	43.50 N	11.57 E
Bagnolet, Fr.	179		48.52 N	2.25 E
Bagnols-sur-Cèze, Fr.	22	E10	44.10 N	4.37 E
Bago, Mya.	64	D3	17.20 N	96.29 E
Bago, state, Mya.	64	C2	18.00 N	96.00 E
Bagodar, India	70	F10	24.04 N	85.50 E
Bagoé, stm., Afr.	84	G3	12.35 N	6.34 W
Bagolino, Italy	30	E7	45.49 N	10.27 E
Bağpınar, Tur.	76	A9	37.36 N	38.20 E
Bagrationovsk, Russia	26	F3	54.23 N	20.38 E
Bagraula, ngh., India	190a		28.34 N	77.04 E
Bag Tal, China	54	C5	43.20 N	122.13 E
Bāguiati, India	190b		22.36 N	88.26 E
Baguio, Phil.	68	B3	16.24 N	120.35 E
Bagumbayan, Phil.	187f		14.28 N	121.03 E
Bāh, India	70	E7	26.53 N	78.36 E
Bahādurgarh, India	70	D6	28.41 N	76.55 E
Bahai Temple, rel., India	190a		28.33 N	77.15 E
Baha'i Temple, rel., Il., U.S.	196		42.05 N	87.41 W
Bahama, Canal Viejo de, strt., N.A.	156	A9	22.39 N	78.40 W
Bahamas, ctry., N.A.	152	C9	24.15 N	76.00 W
Bahamas, is., Bah.	106	G15	24.15 N	76.00 W
Bahār, Iran	42	H13	34.55 N	48.32 E
Baharampur, India	70	F11	24.06 N	88.15 E
Baharden, Turkmen.	74	A15	38.25 N	57.26 E
Bahardok, Turkmen.	72	B8	38.45 N	58.28 E
Bahata Cherneshchyna, Ukr.	38	D14	48.59 N	35.34 E
Bahau, Malay.	64	K6	2.49 N	102.24 E
Bahau, stm., Indon.	66	B9	2.33 N	116.26 E
Bahāwalnagar, Pak.	70	C4	29.59 N	73.15 E
Bahāwalpur, Pak.	70	D3	29.23 N	71.40 E
Bahçe, Tur.	76	A7	37.12 N	36.35 E
Bahçeköy, ngh., Tur.	185b		41.11 N	28.59 E
Bahçeköy su kemeri, aq., Tur.	185b		41.03 N	28.59 E
Baheri, India	70	D7	28.47 N	79.30 E
Baherove, Ukr.	38	H15	45.21 N	36.17 E
Bahi, Phil.	68	D4	13.53 N	123.37 E
Bahia see Salvador, Braz.	170	G6	12.59 S	38.30 W
Bahia, state, Braz.	170	G4	12.00 S	42.00 W
Bahía, Islas de la, is., Hond.	156	D4	16.20 N	86.30 W
Bahía Blanca, Arg.	172	I6	38.43 S	62.17 W
Bahía Bustamante, Arg.	166	I3	45.07 S	66.32 W
Bahía de Caráquez, Ec.	168	H1	0.36 S	80.25 W
Bahía Kino, Mex.	154	A3	28.50 N	111.55 W
Bahía Laura, Arg.	166	I3	48.23 S	66.29 W
Bahir Dar, Eth.	82	E7	11.35 N	37.23 E
Bahlolpur, India	190a		28.37 N	77.24 E
Bahmetevka, Russia	40	F14	51.06 N	44.46 E
Bahmutovo, Russia	26	D17	56.21 N	34.03 E
Bahn see Banie, Pol.	24	C10	53.06 N	14.40 E
Bahraich, India	70	E8	27.34 N	81.35 E
Bahrain, ctry., Asia	74	G12	26.00 N	50.30 E
Bahrain, Gulf of see Baḥrayn, Khalīj al-, b., Asia	74	H12	25.45 N	50.40 E
Baḥrānī, Ḥālat al-, i., U.A.E.	74	H14	24.27 N	54.21 E
Bahranivtsi, Ukr.	38	D6	49.18 N	27.56 E
Baḥrayn, Khalīj al-, b., Asia	74	H12	25.45 N	50.40 E
Bahr el-Nîl see Nile, stm., Afr.	191c		30.10 N	31.06 E
Bahta, Russia	48	B15	62.28 N	89.00 E
Bahtîm, Egypt	76	H2	30.08 N	31.17 E
Bahtîm, Egypt	191c		30.08 N	31.17 E
Bahty, Kaz.	48	E14	46.39 N	82.40 E
Bāhū Kalāt, Iran	72	D9	25.41 N	61.25 E
Bahušèusk, Bela.	26	F13	54.50 N	30.12 E
Bai, stm., China	58	E5	32.02 N	112.09 E
Bai, stm., China	58	A7	40.33 N	116.51 E
Baia de Aramă, Rom.	36	E9	44.59 N	22.48 E
Baia di Terra Nova, sci., Ant.	103	C21	74.40 S	163.30 E
Baía Farta, Ang.	88	C1	12.36 S	13.11 E
Baia Mare, Rom.	36	B10	47.39 N	23.35 E
Baião, Braz.	170	B1	2.46 S	49.38 W
Baia Sprie, Rom.	36	B10	47.40 N	23.41 E
Baïbokoum, Chad	82	F3	7.45 N	15.41 E
Baicheng, China	48	F14	41.46 N	81.52 E
Baicheng, China	52	B9	45.36 N	122.50 E
Baidoa see Baydhabo, Som.	86	D8	3.07 N	43.39 E
Baie-Comeau, Qc., Can.	122	A8	49.13 N	68.10 W
Baie-Mahault, Guad.	159c	h5	16.15 N	61.35 W
Baiersbronn, Ger.	24	H4	48.30 N	8.23 E
Baie-Saint-Paul, Qc., Can.	122	C6	47.26 N	70.29 W
Baie-Trinité, Qc., Can.	122	A9	49.26 N	67.16 W
Baie Verte, Nf., Can.	111a	j22	49.56 N	56.12 W
Baihe, China	62	B11	32.17 N	110.02 E
Baihekou, China	58	F4	31.46 N	110.13 E
Baijala, India	190b		22.51 N	88.16 E
Baijnāth, India	70	D7	29.55 N	79.37 E
Baikal, Lake see Bajkal, ozero, l., Russia	50	F10	53.00 N	107.40 E
Baikal Mountains see Bajkal'skij hrebet, mts., Russia	50	F10	55.36 N	108.44 E
Baikonur see Bajkonur, Kaz.	48	E11	47.50 N	66.03 E
Baikunthapur, India	190b		22.59 N	88.13 E
Baikunthpur, India	70	G9	23.15 N	82.33 E
Bailadores, Ven.	168	C6	8.13 N	71.49 W
Baile Átha Cliath see Dublin, Ire.	10	H6	53.20 N	6.14 W
Baile Átha Luain see Athlone, Ire.	10	H4	53.25 N	7.56 W

Name	Page	Map Ref.	Latitude	Longitude
Baile Chaisleáin Bhéarra see Castletown Bere, Ire.	10	J2	51.39 N	9.55 W
Băile Govora, Rom.	36	D11	45.05 N	24.11 E
Bailén, Spain	28	F7	38.06 N	3.46 W
Băile Olănești, Rom.	36	D11	45.11 N	24.15 E
Băilești, Rom.	36	F10	44.01 N	23.21 E
Bailey, N.C., U.S.	124	I7	35.46 N	78.07 W
Bailey Run, stm., Pa., U.S.	197b		40.35 N	79.47 W
Baileys Crossroads, Va., U.S.	202c		38.51 N	77.07 W
Bail Hongal, India	69	D2	15.48 N	74.51 E
Bailicun, China	58	I4	25.45 N	110.33 E
Bailique, Ilha, i., Braz.	164	C8	1.02 N	49.58 W
Bailleau-sous-Gallardon, Fr.	179		48.32 N	1.39 E
Baillie Islands, is., N.T., Can.	109	B14	70.30 N	128.17 W
Baillif, Guad.	159c	h5	16.01 N	61.44 W
Bailly-Romainvilliers, Fr.	179		48.50 N	2.49 E
Bailong, stm., China	58	E1	32.29 N	105.32 E
Bailu Hu, l., China	58	G5	28.50 N	112.32 E
Bailundo, Ang.	88	C2	12.11 S	15.51 E
Baimachang, China	58	G2	29.23 N	107.31 E
Baimamiao, China	58	C2	36.57 N	108.05 E
Baima Shan, mtn., China	58	H4	27.12 N	110.32 E
Baimashi, China	58	G8	29.15 N	118.42 E
Baimuru, Pap. N. Gui.	101a	b3	7.31 S	144.49 E
Bainang, China	70	D12	29.09 N	89.11 E
Bainbridge, Ga., U.S.	134	G14	30.53 N	84.34 W
Bainbridge, N.Y., U.S.	124	B10	42.18 N	75.28 W
Bainbridge, Oh., U.S.	124	E2	39.13 N	83.16 W
Bainchipota, India	190b		22.52 N	88.16 E
Bain-de-Bretagne, Fr.	20	G7	47.50 N	1.41 W
Baing, Indon.	66	I12	10.13 S	120.33 E
Bainville, Mt., U.S.	142	F9	48.08 N	104.12 W
Baio Grande, Spain	28	A2	43.09 N	8.57 W
Baiona, Spain	28	B2	42.07 N	8.50 W
Baipeng, China	58	I3	24.06 N	109.15 E
Baipu, China	58	E9	32.15 N	120.44 E
Baiquan, China	52	B10	47.35 N	126.05 E
Baird, Tx., U.S.	136	B8	32.24 N	99.23 W
Baird, Mount, mtn., Id., U.S.	146	G15	43.22 N	111.06 W
Baird Inlet, b., Ak., U.S.	109	D6	60.49 N	164.03 W
Baird Mountains, mts., Ak., U.S.	109	C7	67.35 N	161.30 W
Baird Peninsula, pen., Nu., Can.	110	B15	68.55 N	76.04 W
Bairiki, Kir.	92	C8	1.01 N	173.00 E
Bairin Youqi, China	54	C3	43.31 N	118.39 E
Bairin Zuoqi, China	52	C8	43.58 N	119.23 E
Bair Island, i., Ca., U.S.	200		37.32 N	122.13 W
Bairnsdale, Austl.	98	K6	37.49 S	147.37 E
Bairoil, Wy., U.S.	140	E5	42.14 N	107.33 W
Baïse, stm., Fr.	22	F6	44.16 N	0.19 E
Baisha, China	58	L3	19.14 N	109.27 E
Baisha, China	58	H6	26.57 N	115.25 E
Baisha, China	58	G2	29.03 N	106.06 E
Baisha, China	58	I8	25.40 N	118.59 E
Baishe, China	58	H7	27.03 N	116.26 E
Baishi, China	58	J4	22.34 N	110.58 E
Baishuijiang, China	58	E2	33.28 N	106.01 E
Baisley Pond, l., N.Y., U.S.	194		40.41 N	73.47 W
Baisogala, Lith.	26	E6	55.38 N	23.42 E
Baita, India	190b		22.27 N	88.11 E
Bai Thuong, Viet.	64	C7	19.53 N	105.23 E
Baitings Reservoir, res., Eng., U.K.	180		53.40 N	1.59 W
Baitou Shan see Paektu-san, mtn., Asia	54	D8	41.59 N	128.06 E
Baitoutan, China	58	E2	32.29 N	106.53 E
Baiwang, China	58	I3	24.09 N	108.36 E
Baiwen, China	58	B4	38.15 N	111.03 E
Baixa da Banheira, Port.	184c		38.39 N	9.03 W
Baixa Grande, Braz.	170	F5	11.57 S	40.09 W
Baixingt, China	54	C4	43.08 N	120.56 E
Baixio, Braz.	170	D6	6.44 S	38.43 W
Baiyan Shan, mtn., China	58	H8	26.05 N	118.25 E
Baiyin, China	52	D5	36.33 N	104.11 E
Baiyinheshuo, China	54	B3	44.31 N	119.51 E
Baiyü, China	52	E4	31.18 N	98.49 E
Baiyunguan, China	189a		39.54 N	116.19 E
Baja, Hung.	36	C5	46.10 N	18.57 E
Baja, Punta, c., Chile	100l	e29	27.10 S	109.21 W
Baja, Punta, c., Mex.	120	G4	29.58 N	115.49 W
Baja California, Mex.	120	K1	32.18 N	115.12 W
Baja California, state, Mex.	120	F5	30.00 N	115.00 W
Baja California, pen., Mex.	152	B2	27.53 N	113.27 W
Baja California Norte see Baja California, state, Mex.	120	F5	30.00 N	115.00 W
Baja California Sur, state, Mex.	152	C2	26.00 N	112.00 W
Bajada del Agrio, Arg.	172	I2	38.23 S	70.02 W
Baján, Mex.	136	H6	26.32 N	101.14 W
Bajan, Mong.	52	B7	48.33 N	111.04 E
Bajanaul, Kaz.	48	D13	50.47 N	75.44 E
Bajandaj, Russia	48	D19	53.03 N	105.30 E
Bajangol, Russia	50	F9	50.41 N	103.27 E
Bajánsenye, Hung.	36	C3	46.48 N	16.23 E
Bajawa, Indon.	66	H12	8.48 S	120.57 E
Bajčunas, Kaz.	48	H18	47.15 N	52.55 E
Bajdaracskaja guba, b., Russia	50	C2	69.00 N	67.30 E
Bājegūn, Kūh-e, mtn., Iran	74	E14	31.28 N	55.51 E
Bajestān, Iran	72	C8	34.31 N	58.10 E
Bajghera, India	190a		28.32 N	77.01 E
Bajimba, Mount, mtn., Austl.	98	G9	29.18 S	152.07 E
Bajina Bašta, Yugo.	36	F6	43.57 N	19.33 E
Bajkal, Russia	50	F9	51.52 N	104.47 E
Bajkal, ozero (Baikal, Lake), l., Russia	50	F10	53.00 N	107.40 E
Bajkalovo, Russia	48	C11	57.45 N	67.38 E
Bajkal'skij hrebet, mts., Russia	50	F10	55.36 N	108.44 E
Bajkit, Russia	48	B17	61.41 N	96.25 E
Bajkonur, Kaz.	48	E11	47.50 N	66.03 E
Bajmak, Russia	48	D9	52.35 N	58.19 E
Bajmok, Yugo.	36	D6	45.58 N	19.25 E
Bajo, Indon.	66	C12	0.27 N	120.50 E
Bajo, Indon.	66	H11	8.35 S	119.00 E
Bajo, Canal, can., Spain	184a		40.27 N	3.43 W
Bajo Boquete, Pan.	156	H6	8.46 N	82.26 W
Bajo Jagüé, Arg.	172	D3	28.40 S	68.22 W
Bajool, Austl.	98	D8	23.39 S	150.39 E
Bajramaly, Turkmen.	72	B9	37.36 N	62.09 E
Bajsa, Russia	50	F11	53.59 N	113.34 E
Bajsun, Uzb.	48	G11	38.12 N	67.12 E
Bakacak, Tur.	34	C10	40.12 N	27.06 E
Bakala, C.A.R.	86	C4	6.12 N	20.24 E
Bakanas, Kaz.	48	F13	44.48 N	76.16 E
Bakau, Pulau, i., Sing.	189c		1.16 N	103.43 E
Bakčar, Russia	48	C14	57.01 N	82.03 E
Bake, Indon.	66	E2	3.03 S	100.16 E
Bakel, Sen.	84	G2	14.54 N	12.26 W
Bakem, Indon.	66	E4	1.58 S	105.52 E
Baker, Ca., U.S.	148	H9	35.15 N	116.04 W
Baker, Fl., U.S.	134	G12	30.47 N	86.40 W
Baker, La., U.S.	134	G7	30.35 N	91.10 W
Baker, Mt., U.S.	140	A8	46.21 N	104.16 W
Baker, Or., U.S.	146	F9	44.46 N	117.49 W
Baker, Mount, vol., Wa., U.S.	146	B5	48.47 N	121.49 W
Baker Butte, mtn., Az., U.S.	150	I5	34.27 N	111.22 W
Baker Canyon, val., Ca., U.S.	198		33.47 N	117.38 W
Baker Creek, stm., B.C., Can.	144	D8	52.58 N	122.30 W
Baker Creek, stm., Oh., U.S.	197a		41.21 N	81.54 W
Baker Island, i., Oc.	94	C9	0.12 N	176.28 W
Baker Lake, Nu., Can.	110	C11	64.18 N	95.55 W
Baker Lake, l., Austl.	96	E5	26.49 S	126.04 E
Baker Lake, l., Nu., Can.	110	C11	64.10 N	95.30 W
Baker Lake, l., Il., U.S.	196		42.08 N	88.07 W
Bakersfield, Ca., U.S.	148	H7	35.22 N	119.01 W
Bakers Island, i., Ma., U.S.	201		42.32 N	70.47 W
Baker Street, Eng., U.K.	178		51.30 N	0.21 E
Bakersville, N.C., U.S.	124	I4	36.00 N	82.09 W
Bakerville, S. Afr.	90	E8	25.59 S	26.06 E
Bâ Kêv, Camb.	64	F8	13.41 N	107.11 E
Bakhchysarai, Ukr.	38	I12	44.45 N	33.51 E
Bakhmach, Ukr.	38	B11	51.10 N	32.49 E
Bākhtarān see Kermānshāh, Iran	74	C10	34.18 N	47.03 E
Bākhtarān see Kermānshāh, state, Iran	74	C10	34.30 N	47.00 E
Bakhtegān, Daryācheh-ye, l., Iran	74	F14	29.20 N	54.05 E
Bakı (Baku), Azer.	42	F13	40.23 N	49.51 E
Bakır, stm., Tur.	34	D10	38.56 N	26.58 E
Bakkafjörður, Ice.	12a	j32	66.02 N	14.47 W
Bakkaflói, b., Ice.	12a	j32	66.10 N	14.45 W
Bakkagerdi, Ice.	12a	k33	65.30 N	13.48 W
Bakkeswar, India	190b		22.25 N	88.22 E
Baklan, Tur.	34	F12	37.57 N	29.32 E
Bako, C. Iv.	84	H3	9.08 N	7.35 W
Bako, Eth.	82	F7	5.49 N	36.39 E
Bakony, mts., Hung.	36	C4	47.00 N	17.44 E
Bakouma, C.A.R.	86	C4	5.42 N	22.47 E
Bakovka, Russia	183b		55.41 N	37.20 E
Baksan, Russia	42	D10	43.40 N	43.32 E
Bakšty, Bela.	26	G9	53.56 N	26.12 E
Baku see Bakı, Azer.	42	E13	40.23 N	49.51 E
Bakumpai, Indon.	66	D8	1.26 S	113.03 E
Bakun, China	70	B8	32.32 N	80.26 E
Bakung, Pulau, i., Indon.	66	C4	0.04 N	104.27 E
Bakungan, Indon.	64	K3	2.56 N	97.30 E
Bakwanga see Mbuji-Mayi, D.R.C.	86	F4	6.07 S	23.39 E
Bala, Sen.	84	G2	14.01 N	13.10 W
Balâ, Tur.	34	D16	39.33 N	33.07 E
Balabac, Phil.	68	F1	7.58 N	117.03 E
Balabac, Selat see Balabac Strait, strt., Asia	68	G1	7.35 N	117.00 E
Balabac Island, i., Phil.	68	G1	7.57 N	117.01 E
Balabac Strait, strt., Asia	68	G1	7.35 N	117.00 E
Balā Bāgh, Afg.	70	A3	34.23 N	70.15 E
Ba'labakk, Leb.	76	D7	34.00 N	36.13 E
Balabalagan, Kepulauan, is., Indon.	66	E10	2.20 S	117.25 E
Balabanovo, Russia	26	E19	55.10 N	36.40 E
Balabio, Île, i., N. Cal.	101d	m15	20.06 S	164.10 E
Balabyne, Ukr.	38	F14	47.43 N	35.12 E
Balaci, Rom.	36	E11	44.20 N	24.55 E
Bala-Cynwyd, Pa., U.S.	203		40.00 N	75.14 W
Balad, Iraq	74	C9	34.00 N	44.09 E
Baladbandh, India	190b		22.52 N	88.07 E
Baladeh, Iran	74	B12	36.12 N	51.48 E
Baladëk, Russia	50	F15	53.40 N	133.04 E
Bālāghāt, India	70	H8	21.48 N	80.11 E
Bālāghāt Range, mts., India	69	B3	18.49 N	76.29 E
Balagne, reg., Fr.	22	G14	42.35 N	8.53 E
Balaguer, Spain	28	C11	41.47 N	0.49 E
Balahna, Russia	40	C13	56.29 N	43.35 E
Balahta, Russia	48	C16	55.23 N	91.36 E
Balaikarangan, Indon.	66	C7	0.50 N	110.25 E
Balaiselasa, Indon.	66	D2	1.47 S	100.47 E
Balaisepuah, Indon.	66	C7	0.25 N	111.13 E
Balakirevo, Russia	26	D21	56.30 N	38.50 E
Balaklava, Austl.	98	J2	34.08 S	138.24 E
Balaklava, Ukr.	38	I12	44.33 N	33.36 E
Balakliia, Ukr.	38	D10	49.13 N	31.43 E
Balakliia, Ukr.	38	D15	49.27 N	36.52 E
Balakovo, Russia	40	F16	52.00 N	47.46 E
Balama, Moz.	88	C6	13.20 S	38.34 E
Balambangan, Pulau, i., Malay.	68	G1	7.15 N	116.55 E
Bālā Morghāb, Afg.	72	B9	35.36 N	63.21 E
Balandi, India	190b		22.58 N	88.32 E
Balanga, Phil.	68	C3	14.40 N	120.33 E
Ba Lang An, Mui, c., Viet.	64	E9	15.14 N	108.56 E
Balangiga, Phil.	68	E5	11.06 N	125.22 E
Balāngīr, India	70	H9	20.43 N	83.29 E
Bālān Şafar 'Alī, Iran	74	A10	38.59 N	47.27 E
Balapulang, Indon.	66	G6	7.03 S	109.05 E
Bālāpur, India	70	H6	20.39 N	76.46 E
Balaqs, Egypt	191c		30.10 N	31.17 E
Balarāmbāti, India	190b		22.48 N	88.13 E
Balarāmpota, India	190b		22.31 N	88.08 E
Balarāmpur, India	70	G11	23.06 N	86.14 E
Balaši, Russia	40	F16	51.24 N	49.55 E
Balašiha, Russia	26	E20	55.48 N	37.57 E
Balasore see Bāleshwar, India	70	H11	21.29 N	86.57 E
Balašov, Russia	40	F13	51.32 N	43.10 E
Balassagyarmat, Hung.	36	A6	48.04 N	19.19 E
Balatina, Mol.	38	F6	47.41 N	27.21 E
Balaton, Mn., U.S.	128	G3	44.14 N	95.52 W
Balaton, l., Hung.	36	C4	46.50 N	17.45 E
Balayan, Phil.	68	D3	13.56 N	120.44 E
Balazote, Spain	28	F8	38.53 N	2.08 W
Balbieriškis, Lith.	26	F6	54.32 N	23.54 E
Balbina, Represa, res., Braz.	168	H12	1.20 S	59.40 W
Balbriggan, Ire.	10	H6	53.36 N	6.11 W
Balcad, Som.	86	D9	2.21 N	45.23 E
Balcanoona, Austl.	98	H2	30.32 S	139.18 E
Balcarce, Arg.	172	H8	37.50 S	58.15 W
Balcarres, Sk., Can.	142	D10	50.48 N	103.33 W
Bălcești, Rom.	36	E10	44.38 N	23.56 E
Balčik, Blg.	36	F15	43.25 N	28.10 E
Balcones Escarpment, clf., Tx., U.S.	136	E8	29.35 N	99.11 W
Balde, Arg.	172	F4	33.21 S	66.37 W
Baldeador, Braz.	205a		22.53 S	43.02 W
Bald Eagle Creek, stm., Pa., U.S.	126	H12	41.07 N	77.28 W
Baldeneysee, l., Ger.	181		51.24 N	7.03 E
Balderstone, Eng., U.K.	180		53.47 N	2.34 W
Bald Hill, hill, Austl.	98	C5	20.17 S	144.06 E
Bald Hill Branch, stm., Md., U.S.	202c		38.55 N	76.49 W
Baldhill Creek, stm., N.D., U.S.	142	G15	47.07 N	98.02 W
Bald Knob, Ar., U.S.	134	B7	35.18 N	91.34 W
Bald Knob, mtn., Ca., U.S.	200		37.25 N	122.21 W
Bald Knob, mtn., Va., U.S.	124	G6	37.56 N	79.51 W
Bald Knoll, mtn., Wy., U.S.	146	H16	42.24 N	110.29 W
Bald Mountain, mtn., Or., U.S.	146	F3	44.48 N	123.33 W
Bald Mountain, mtn., Or., U.S.	146	G5	43.16 N	121.21 W
Bald Mountain, mtn., Or., U.S.	146	F9	44.36 N	117.53 W
Baldock Lake, l., Mb., Can.	110	D11	56.33 N	97.57 W
Baldone, Lat.	26	D7	56.44 N	24.23 E
Baldovino, Arroyo, stm., Arg.	206		34.46 S	58.07 W
Baldpate Pond, l., Ma., U.S.	201		42.42 N	71.00 W
Baldur, Mb., Can.	142	E14	49.23 N	99.15 W
Baldwin, La., U.S.	134	H7	29.50 N	91.33 W
Baldwin, Mi., U.S.	126	E4	43.53 N	85.50 W
Baldwin, Wi., U.S.	128	G6	44.58 N	92.22 W
Baldwin Bay, b., N.Y., U.S.	194		40.38 N	73.35 W
Baldwin City, Ks., U.S.	130	F2	38.46 N	95.10 W
Baldwin Creek, stm., Oh., U.S.	197a		41.22 N	81.51 W
Baldwin Hills, hills, Ca., U.S.	198		34.00 N	118.22 W
Baldwin Lake, l., Oh., U.S.	197a		41.21 N	81.51 W
Baldwinsville, N.Y., U.S.	126	E13	43.09 N	76.20 W
Baldwin-Wallace College, educ., Oh., U.S.	197a		41.23 N	81.51 W
Baldwyn, Ms., U.S.	134	C10	34.31 N	88.38 W
Baldy Mountain, mtn., B.C., Can.	144	E11	51.28 N	120.02 W
Baldy Mountain, mtn., Mb., Can.	142	C13	51.28 N	100.44 W
Baldy Mountain, mtn., Mt., U.S.	146	B17	48.09 N	109.39 W
Baldy Mountain, mtn., N.M., U.S.	138	E3	36.38 N	105.13 W
Baldy Peak, mtn., Az., U.S.	150	J7	33.55 N	109.35 W
Bale, India	190c		19.08 N	73.06 E
Bâle see Basel, Switz.	30	C4	47.33 N	7.35 E
Bale-Akiosi, Nig.	191a		6.41 N	3.21 E
Baleares see Balears, state, Spain	28	E13	39.30 N	3.00 E
Baleares, Islas see Balears, Illes, is., Spain	28	E12	39.28 N	3.00 E
Balearic Islands see Balears, state, Spain	28	E13	39.30 N	3.00 E
Balearic Islands see Balears, Illes, is., Spain	28	E12	39.28 N	3.00 E
Balears, Illes, is., Spain	28	E12	39.28 N	3.00 E
Balears, state, Spain	28	E13	39.30 N	3.00 E
Balears, Illes (Balearic Islands), is., Spain	28	E12	39.28 N	3.00 E
Balease, Gunung, mtn., Indon.	66	E12	2.24 S	120.33 E
Baleh, stm., Malay.	66	C8	2.01 N	113.01 E
Baleia, Ponta da, c., Braz.	170	I6	17.41 S	39.08 W
Baleine, stm., Qc., Can.	110	D17	57.55 N	67.42 W
Baleine, Grande rivière de la, stm., Qc., Can.	110	D15	55.15 N	77.48 W
Baleine, Petite rivière de la, stm., Qc., Can.	110	D15	56.00 N	76.47 W
Balej, Russia	50	F12	51.33 N	116.38 E
Baler, Phil.	68	C3	15.45 N	121.33 E
Baler Bay, b., Phil.	68	C3	15.50 N	121.35 E
Bāleshwar, India	70	H11	21.29 N	86.57 E
Balestrand, Nor.	16	F4	61.11 N	6.30 E
Balezino, Russia	40	B18	57.58 N	53.00 E
Balfate, Hond.	156	E4	15.46 N	86.23 W
Balfes Creek, Austl.	98	C5	20.13 S	145.54 E
Balfour, N.C., U.S.	124	A3	35.20 N	82.28 W
Balfour Park, p.o.i., S. Afr.	191d		26.08 S	28.06 E
Bălgarija see Bulgaria, ctry., Eur.	36	G12	43.00 N	25.00 E
Bâlgarovo, Blg.	36	G14	42.47 N	27.18 E
Balgazyn, Russia	48	D17	50.57 N	95.11 E
Balgowlah, Austl.	192a		33.48 S	151.16 E
Balguerie, Cap, c., Fr. Poly.	100g	r19	9.44 S	138.48 W
Balhaš, Kaz.	48	E13	46.51 N	74.57 E
Balhaš, ozero (Balkhash, Lake), l., Kaz.	48	E13	46.00 N	74.00 E
Bāli, India	70	F4	25.11 N	73.17 E
Bali, state, Indon.	66	G9	8.30 S	115.00 E
Bali, i., Indon.	66	G9	8.20 S	115.00 E
Bali, Laut (Bali Sea), s., Indon.	66	G9	7.45 S	115.30 E
Bali, Selat, strt., Indon.	66	H9	8.18 S	114.25 E
Bali Barat National Park, p.o.i., Indon.	66	H9	8.22 S	114.58 E
Baliceaux, i., St. Vin.	159e	p11	12.56 N	61.08 W
Balidianzi, China	54	D6	41.14 N	124.53 E
Balige, Indon.	66	B1	2.20 N	99.04 E
Bālihāti, India	190b		22.44 N	88.19 E
Balıkesir, Tur.	34	D10	39.38 N	27.53 E
Balıkesir, state, Tur.	34	D11	39.45 N	27.50 E
Balīkh, stm., Syria	76	B10	35.52 N	39.12 E
Balikpapan, Indon.	66	D10	1.15 S	116.50 E
Balimbing, Indon.	66	F4	5.55 S	104.33 E
Balimbing, Phil.	68	H2	5.05 N	119.57 E
Balimo, Pap. N. Gui.	101a	b3	8.03 S	142.56 E
Balingasag, Phil.	68	F5	8.44 N	124.47 E
Balingen, Ger.	24	H4	48.16 N	8.51 E
Balingian, Malay.	66	B8	2.56 N	112.31 E
Balintang Channel, strt., Phil.	58	K9	19.57 N	121.38 E
Bali Sea see Bali, Laut, s., Indon.	66	G9	7.45 S	115.30 E
Bali Strait see Bali, Selat, strt., Indon.	66	H9	8.18 S	114.25 E
Baliza, Braz.	166	C6	16.15 S	52.25 W
Balizhuang, China	189a		39.52 N	116.28 E
Balkan, state, Turkmen.	42	F15	39.50 N	53.58 E
Balkan Mountains, mts., Eur.	36	F10	42.45 N	25.00 E
Balkan Peninsula, pen., Eur.	8	G13	43.00 N	23.00 E
Balkaria see Kabardino-Balkarija, state, Russia	42	D10	43.30 N	43.30 E
Balkašino, Kaz.	48	D11	52.31 N	68.43 E
Balkh, Afg.	72	B10	36.44 N	66.53 E
Balkhash, Lake see Balhaš, ozero, l., Kaz.	48	E13	46.00 N	74.00 E
Balkon-Myl'k, gora, hill, Russia	14	D28	68.05 N	37.12 E
Balky, Ukr.	38	F13	47.23 N	34.56 E
Ball, La., U.S.	134	F6	31.24 N	92.24 W
Ballabhpur, India	190b		22.44 N	88.21 E
Ballachulish, Scot., U.K.	10	E7	56.40 N	5.09 W
Balladonia, Austl.	96	F4	32.27 S	123.51 E
Ballaghaderreen, Ire.	10	H4	53.55 N	8.36 W
Ballālpur, India	69	B4	19.53 N	79.20 E
Ballangen, Nor.	14	D7	68.20 N	16.48 E
Ballantine, Mt., U.S.	140	B4	45.57 N	108.11 W
Ballantrae, Scot., U.K.	10	F7	55.05 N	5.00 W
Ballarat, Austl.	98	K4	37.34 S	143.51 E
Ballard, Lake, l., Austl.	96	E4	29.27 S	120.55 E
Ballater, Scot., U.K.	10	D9	57.03 N	3.03 W
Ball Bay, b., Norf. I.	100i	y25	29.03 S	167.59 E
Ballé, Mali	84	F3	15.20 N	8.35 W
Ballenas, Bahía de, b., Mex.	154	B2	26.46 N	113.26 W
Ballenato, Punta, c., Cuba	204b		23.06 N	82.30 W
Ballenita, Punta, c., Chile	172	B2	25.47 S	70.42 W
Balleny Islands, is., Ant.	103	B21	66.35 S	162.49 E
Balleza, Mex.	154	B5	26.57 N	106.21 W
Balleza, stm., Mex.	154	B5	27.23 N	106.17 W
Ball Ground, Ga., U.S.	132	B1	34.18 N	84.26 W
Ballı, Tur.	34	C10	40.50 N	27.03 E
Ballia, India	70	F10	25.45 N	84.09 E
Ballina, Austl.	98	G9	28.52 S	153.33 E
Ballina, Ire.	10	I4	52.49 N	8.24 W
Ballina, Ire.	10	G3	54.07 N	9.09 W
Ballinasloe, Ire.	10	H4	53.20 N	8.13 W
Ballinger, Tx., U.S.	136	C8	31.44 N	99.56 W
Ballinrobe, Ire.	10	H3	53.38 N	9.13 W
Ballinskelligs Bay, b., Ire.	10	J2	51.50 N	10.15 W
Ballona Creek, stm., Ca., U.S.	198		33.58 N	118.27 W
Ballsfjorden, b., Nor.	14	C9	69.23 N	19.03 E
Ballsh, Alb.	32	D13	40.35 N	19.44 E
Ballston Spa, N.Y., U.S.	126	E16	43.00 N	73.51 W
Ballville, Oh., U.S.	124	C2	41.18 N	83.07 W
Bālly, India	190b		22.38 N	88.21 E
Bālly, ngh., India	190b		22.39 N	88.21 E
Ballybunnion, Ire.	10	I3	52.31 N	9.40 W
Ballycastle, N. Ire., U.K.	10	F6	55.12 N	6.15 W
Ballygunge, ngh., India	190b		22.31 N	88.21 E
Ballyhaunis, Ire.	10	H4	53.46 N	8.46 W
Ballymena, N. Ire., U.K.	10	G6	54.52 N	6.17 W
Ballymoney, N. Ire., U.K.	10	F6	55.04 N	6.29 W
Ballyrogan, Lake, l., Austl.	98	I6	33.28 S	145.57 E
Ballyshannon, Ire.	10	G4	54.30 N	8.11 W
Balmaceda, Chile	166	I2	45.54 S	71.48 W
Balmain, Austl.	192a		33.51 S	151.11 E
Balmoral, Austl.	98	K3	37.14 S	141.50 E
Balmoral Castle, hist., Scot., U.K.	10	D9	57.01 N	3.12 W
Balmorhea, Tx., U.S.	136	C4	30.58 N	103.44 W
Balnearia, Arg.	172	E6	31.00 S	62.39 W
Baloda Bāzār, India	70	H9	21.39 N	82.10 E
Balombo, Ang.	88	C1	12.20 S	14.45 E
Balong, Indon.	66	G7	7.57 S	111.25 E
Balonne, stm., Austl.	98	G7	28.37 S	148.09 E
Bālotra, India	70	F4	25.50 N	72.14 E
Baloži, Lat.	26	D7	56.53 N	24.04 E
Balphakram National Park, p.o.i., India	70	F13	25.35 N	90.35 E
Balqash see Balhaš, Kaz.	48	E13	46.51 N	74.57 E
Balqash Köli see Balhaš, ozero, l., Kaz.	48	E13	46.00 N	74.00 E
Balrāmpur, India	70	E8	27.25 N	82.11 E
Balranald, Austl.	98	J4	34.38 S	143.33 E
Balș, Rom.	36	E11	44.21 N	24.07 E
Balsam Lake, Wi., U.S.	128	F6	45.27 N	92.27 W
Balsam Lake, l., On., Can.	126	D11	44.35 N	78.50 W
Balsas, Braz.	170	D2	7.32 S	46.03 W
Balsas, stm., Braz.	170	D3	7.14 S	44.33 W
Balsas, stm., Braz.	170	E2	9.52 S	47.50 W
Balsas, stm., Mex.	154	F8	17.54 N	102.10 W
Balsas, stm., Pan.	168	D3	8.14 N	77.59 W
Balsas Sur, Mex.	154	F9	18.00 N	99.47 W
Bal'šavik, Bela.	26	H13	52.34 N	30.53 E
Bålsta, Swe.	16	H15	59.34 N	17.30 E
Balsthal, Switz.	30	C4	47.18 N	7.41 E
Balta, Ukr.	38	F8	47.55 N	29.39 E
Baltanás, Spain	28	C6	41.56 N	4.15 W
Baltasar Brum, Ur.	172	E9	30.41 S	57.19 W
Baltasi, Russia	40	C17	56.20 N	50.16 E
Bălți, Mol.	38	F6	47.45 N	27.55 E
Baltic Sea, s., Eur.	8	D12	57.00 N	19.00 E
Baltic Station, trans., Russia	183a		59.55 N	30.18 E
Baltijas jūra see Baltic Sea, s., Eur.	8	D12	57.00 N	19.00 E
Baltijos jūra see Baltic Sea, s., Eur.	8	D12	57.00 N	19.00 E
Baltijsk, Russia	26	F2	54.38 N	19.55 E
Baltijskaja kosa, spit, Eur.	26	F2	54.38 N	19.48 E
Baltijskoe more see Baltic Sea, s., Eur.	8	D12	57.00 N	19.00 E
Baltim, Egypt	76	G2	31.33 N	31.05 E
Baltimore, Ire.	10	J3	51.28 N	9.22 W
Baltimore, S. Afr.	90	C9	23.15 S	28.25 E
Baltimore, Md., U.S.	124	E9	39.17 N	76.36 W
Baltimore, Md., U.S.	202b		39.17 N	76.36 W
Baltimore, Oh., U.S.	124	E3	39.51 N	82.36 W
Baltimore, City of, mun., Md., U.S.	202b		39.18 N	76.35 W
Baltimore, University of, educ., Md., U.S.	202b		39.18 N	76.37 W
Baltimore Airpark, arpt., Md., U.S.	202b		39.24 N	76.25 W
Baltimore Highlands, Md., U.S.	202b		39.13 N	76.38 W
Baltoji Vokė, Lith.	26	F8	54.27 N	25.10 E
Bałtyckie, Morze see Baltic Sea, s., Eur.	8	D12	57.00 N	19.00 E
Ba Lu, stm., Viet.	64	E9	14.21 N	107.52 E
Baluarte, stm., Mex.	154	D6	22.49 N	106.01 W
Baluarte, Arroyo, stm., Tx., U.S.	136	G9	27.09 N	98.06 W
Balūchestān see Balūchistān, hist. reg., Asia	46	G10	28.00 N	63.00 E
Balūchestān see Baluchistān, hist. reg., Asia	62	C1	28.00 N	63.00 E
Baluchistān, state, Pak.	70	C2	30.15 N	69.47 E
Balūchistān, hist. reg., Asia	46	G10	28.00 N	63.00 E
Baluchistān, hist. reg., Asia	62	C1	28.00 N	63.00 E
Bāluhāti, India	190b		22.39 N	88.16 E
Balui, stm., Malay.	66	B8	2.42 N	113.46 E
Balupe, stm., Lat.	26	C10	56.57 N	26.56 E
Bālurghāt, India	70	F12	25.13 N	88.46 E
Balvatnet, l., Nor.	14	F6	66.57 N	15.55 E
Balvi, Lat.	26	C10	57.07 N	27.16 E
Balwyn, Austl.	192b		37.49 S	145.05 E
Balxuca, Arroyo de la, stm., Spain	184d		41.31 N	2.06 E
Balya, Tur.	34	D10	39.43 N	27.35 E
Balygyčan, Russia	50	D19	63.55 N	154.08 E
Balykši, Kaz.	48	E8	47.05 N	51.54 E
Balyn, Ukr.	38	E5	48.52 N	26.40 E
Balzac, Ab., Can.	144	E16	51.10 N	114.01 W
Balzar, Ec.	168	H2	1.22 S	79.53 W
Bam, Iran	72	D8	29.06 N	58.21 E
Bama, China	58	I2	24.20 N	107.07 E
Bama, Nig.	84	G7	11.31 N	13.40 E
Bamaga, Austl.	96	B8	10.50 S	142.25 E
Bamako, Mali	84	G3	12.39 N	8.00 W
Bāmangāchi, India	190b		22.46 N	88.31 E
Bāmanghāra, India	190b		22.31 N	88.28 E
Bāmanmura, India	190b		22.42 N	88.31 E
Bamba, Mali	84	F4	17.02 N	1.23 W
Bambamarca, Peru	164	E2	6.39 S	78.31 W
Bambana, stm., Nic.	156	F6	13.27 N	83.50 W
Bambari, C.A.R.	86	C4	5.45 N	20.39 E
Bambaroo, Austl.	98	B6	18.53 S	146.13 E
Bambāvi, India	190c		18.58 N	73.03 E
Bamberg, Ger.	24	G6	49.54 N	10.54 E
Bamberg, S.C., U.S.	132	C4	33.17 N	81.02 W
Bambesi, Eth.	82	F6	9.44 N	34.43 E
Bambio, C.A.R.	86	D3	3.56 N	16.58 E
Bambuí, Braz.	170	K2	20.00 S	45.58 W
Bam Co, l., China	70	C13	31.29 N	90.58 E
Bamenda, Cam.	86	C1	5.57 N	10.09 E
Bamfield, B.C., Can.	144	H5	48.49 N	125.08 W
Bami, Turkmen.	72	B8	38.43 N	56.48 E
Bāmīān, Afg.	72	C10	34.49 N	67.49 E
Bamiancheng, China	54	C6	43.12 N	124.02 E
Bamingui, C.A.R.	86	C4	7.34 N	20.11 E
Bamndali, ngh., India	190a		28.33 N	77.03 E
Bampūr, Iran	72	D9	27.11 N	60.26 E
Bāmra Hills, hills, India	70	H10	21.30 N	84.30 E
Bamumo, China	70	B14	32.31 N	93.13 E
Ba Na, Viet.	64	D8	15.59 N	107.59 E
Banaba, i., Kir.	94	D7	0.51 S	169.32 E
Banabuiú, stm., Braz.	170	C6	5.07 S	38.05 W
Banabuiú, Açude, l., Braz.	170	C6	5.21 S	38.57 W
Ban Aen, Thai.	64	D4	18.01 N	98.35 E
Banalia, D.R.C.	86	D5	1.33 N	25.19 E
Banamba, Mali	84	G3	13.33 N	7.27 W
Banana, Austl.	98	E8	24.28 S	150.07 E
Banana Islands, is., S.L.	84	H2	8.07 N	13.13 W
Bananal, stm., Braz.	170	E1	8.51 S	48.45 W
Bananal, Ilha do, i., Braz.	166	B6	11.30 S	50.15 W
Bananga, India	62	G7	6.56 N	93.53 E
Banaras see Vārānasi, India	70	F9	25.20 N	82.59 E
Banarlı, Tur.	34	B10	41.03 N	27.20 E
Banās, stm., India	70	E6	25.55 N	76.43 E
Banâs, Râs, c., Egypt	82	C7	23.54 N	35.47 E
Banat, hist. reg., Eur.	36	D7	45.20 N	20.40 E
Banaz, Tur.	34	E12	38.46 N	29.45 E
Ban Baen Phichit, Thai.	187a		13.50 N	100.40 E
Ban Ban, Laos	64	C6	19.37 N	103.33 E
Ban Bang Chan, Thai.	187a		13.49 N	100.42 E
Ban Bang O, Thai.	187a		13.53 N	100.36 E
Ban Bang Phli Yai, Thai.	187a		13.36 N	100.42 E
Ban Bang Phraek, Thai.	187a		13.53 N	100.26 E
Ban Bang Pu, Thai.	187a		13.31 N	100.39 E
Banbidian, China	189a		39.54 N	116.32 E
Ban Bonèng, Laos	64	C7	17.58 N	104.35 E
Ban Bouang-nom, Laos	64	E8	15.49 N	106.44 E
Banbridge, N. Ire., U.K.	10	G6	54.21 N	6.16 W
Ban Bua Chum, Thai.	64	E5	15.15 N	101.11 E
Ban Bung Fang Nok, Thai.	187a		13.48 N	100.43 E
Ban Bung Na Rang, Thai.	64	D4	16.11 N	100.09 E
Ban Bungxai, Laos	64	E8	15.42 N	106.14 E
Banbury, Eng., U.K.	10	I11	52.04 N	1.20 W
Ban Chak, Laos	64	E7	14.17 N	105.25 E
Ban Cha La, Laos	64	D7	17.11 N	106.05 E
Banchory, Scot., U.K.	10	D10	57.03 N	2.30 W
Bancroft, On., Can.	126	C12	45.03 N	77.50 W
Bancroft, Id., U.S.	146	H15	42.43 N	111.53 W
Bancroft, Ia., U.S.	128	H4	43.17 N	94.13 W
Bancroft, Ne., U.S.	130	C1	42.00 N	96.34 W
Bancroft see Chililabombwe, Zam.	88	C4	12.21 S	27.49 E
Bānda, India	70	F8	25.28 N	80.20 E
Banda, Kepulauan, is., Indon.	60	F9	4.35 S	129.55 E
Banda, Laut (Banda Sea), s., Indon.	60	G8	5.00 S	128.00 E
Banda Aceh, Indon.	64	J2	5.33 N	95.19 E
Bānda Dāūd Shāh, Pak.	70	B3	33.16 N	71.11 E
Banda del Río Salí, Arg.	172	C5	26.49 S	65.09 W
Banda Elat, Indon.	60	G9	5.39 S	133.00 E
Bandai-Asahi-kokuritsu-kōen, p.o.i., Japan	56	B12	37.53 N	139.33 E
Bandai-san, vol., Japan	56	B13	37.36 N	140.04 E
Bandak, l., Nor.	16	H6	59.24 N	8.15 E
Bandama, stm., C. Iv.	84	H3	5.07 N	4.59 W
Bandama Blanc, stm., C. Iv.	84	H3	6.54 N	5.31 W
Ban Dan, Thai.	64	E7	15.18 N	105.29 E
Ban Dangtai, Laos	64	D7	17.06 N	104.56 E
Ban Dan Lan Hoi, Thai.	64	D4	16.59 N	99.34 E
Bandar see Machilīpatnam, India	69	C5	16.11 N	81.08 E
Bandar Beheshtī, Iran	72	D9	25.17 N	60.38 E
Bandarbeyla, Som.	86	C10	9.29 N	50.48 E
Bandar-e 'Abbās, Iran	74	G14	27.11 N	56.15 E
Bandar-e Anzalī, Iran	74	B11	37.28 N	49.28 E
Bandar-e Būshehr, Iran	74	F12	28.58 N	50.50 E
Bandar-e Chārak, Iran	74	G14	26.44 N	54.16 E
Bandar-e Deylam, Iran	74	E11	30.03 N	50.09 E
Bandar-e Gaz, Iran	74	B13	36.46 N	53.57 E
Bandar-e Khomeynī (Bandar-e Shāhpūr), Iran	74	E11	30.25 N	49.05 E
Bandar-e Lengeh, Iran	74	G14	26.33 N	54.52 E
Bandar-e Māh Shahr, Iran	74	E11	30.32 N	49.09 E
Bandar-e Moghūyeh, Iran	74	G14	26.36 N	54.30 E
Bandar-e Pahlavī see Bandar-e Anzalī, Iran	74	B11	37.28 N	49.28 E
Bandar-e Rīg, Iran	74	F12	29.29 N	50.38 E
Bandar-e Shāhpūr see Bandar-e Khomeynī, Iran	74	E11	30.25 N	49.05 E
Bandar-e Torkeman, Iran	74	B13	36.54 N	54.04 E
Bandar Maharani see Muar, Malay.	64	L6	2.02 N	102.34 E
Bandar Penggaram see Batu Pahat, Malay.	64	L6	1.51 N	102.56 E
Bandar Seri Begawan, Bru.	66	A9	4.56 N	114.56 E
Banda Sea see Banda, Laut, s., Indon.	60	G8	5.00 S	128.00 E
Bande, Spain	28	B3	42.02 N	7.58 W
Banded Peak, mtn., Co., U.S.	138	D2	37.06 N	106.38 W
Bandeira, Pico da, mtn., Braz.	170	K5	20.26 S	41.47 W
Bandeirantes, Braz.	166	C6	19.53 S	54.23 W
Bandeirantes, Braz.	166	B6	13.41 S	50.48 W
Bandeirantes, Palácio dos, bldg., Braz.	205b		23.36 S	46.43 W
Bandeirantes, Praia dos, cst., Braz.	205a		23.01 S	43.25 W
Bāndel, India	190b		22.56 N	88.22 E
Bandelier National Monument, p.o.i., N.M., U.S.	138	F2	35.45 N	106.20 W
Bandera, Arg.	172	D6	28.53 S	62.16 W
Bandera, Tx., U.S.	136	E8	29.43 N	99.04 W
Bandera, Alto, mtn., Dom. Rep.	156	C12	18.49 N	70.37 W
Banderas, Mex.	136	C2	31.01 N	105.35 W
Banderas, Bahía de, b., Mex.	154	E6	20.38 N	105.26 W
Bandhavgarh National Park, p.o.i., India	70	G8	23.37 N	81.07 E
Bāndhi, Pak.	70	E2	26.35 N	68.18 E
Bandiagara, Mali	84	G4	14.20 N	3.36 W
Bandiantaolehai, China	52	C5	41.46 N	104.04 E
Bāndīkūi, India	70	E6	27.02 N	76.34 E
Bandipur, India	190b		22.44 N	88.26 E
Bandipur, India	190b		22.51 N	88.10 E
Bandipura, India	70	A5	34.24 N	74.38 E
Bandipur Tiger Reserve, ind. res., India	69	F3	11.35 N	76.35 E
Bandırma, Tur.	34	C11	40.20 N	27.59 E
Bandırma Körfezi, b., Tur.	34	C11	40.25 N	28.00 E
Bandon, Ire.	10	J4	51.45 N	8.44 W

Name	Page	Map Ref.	Latitude	Longitude
Ban Don see Surat Thani, Thai.	64	H4	9.06 N	99.18 E
Bandon, Or., U.S.	146	G2	43.06 N	124.23 W
Ban Don, Viet.	64	F8	12.53 N	107.47 E
Bandon, stm., Ire.	10	J4	51.41 N	8.30 W
Ban Don, Ao, b., Thai.	64	H4	9.18 N	99.19 E
Ban Donhiang, Laos	64	C5	18.04 N	101.46 E
Ban Dônko, Laos	64	D8	16.12 N	106.17 E
Ban Don Muang, Thai.	187a		13.55 N	100.36 E
Bāndra, ngh., India	190c		19.03 N	72.49 E
Bāndra Point, c., India	190c		19.03 N	72.49 E
Bandundu, D.R.C.	86	E3	3.16 S	17.21 E
Bandung, Indon.	66	G5	6.54 S	107.36 E
Bāneh, Iran	74	B10	35.59 N	45.53 E
Banehra, India	190a		28.44 N	77.23 E
Banes, Cuba	156	B10	20.58 N	75.42 W
Banff, Ab., Can.	144	E15	51.09 N	115.35 W
Banff, Scot., U.K.	10	D10	57.39 N	2.31 W
Banff National Park, p.o.i., Ab., Can.	144	E15	51.38 N	116.22 W
Banfora, Burkina	84	G4	10.38 N	4.44 W
Banga, D.R.C.	86	F4	5.27 S	20.28 E
Banga, India	70	C6	31.10 N	75.59 E
Banga, stm., Phil.	68	G5	6.42 N	124.34 E
Bangalore, India	69	E3	12.59 N	77.35 E
Bangaon, India	70	G12	23.03 N	88.49 E
Bangassou, C.A.R.	86	D4	4.44 N	22.49 E
Bangdag Co, l., China	70	A8	34.52 N	81.36 E
Bangeluo, China	70	B13	32.27 N	90.35 E
Bangeta, Mount, mtn., Pap. N. Gui.	101a	b4	6.15 S	147.03 E
Banggai, Indon.	60	F7	1.35 S	123.30 E
Banggai, Kepulauan, is., Indon.	60	F7	1.30 S	123.15 E
Banggi, Pulau, i., Malay.	68	G1	7.17 N	117.12 E
Banggong Co see Pangong Tso, l., Asia	70	B7	33.44 N	78.41 E
Banggong Co, l., China	70	B7	33.44 N	79.31 E
Banghāzī (Bengasi), Libya	82	A3	32.06 N	20.04 E
Banghiang, stm., Laos	64	D7	16.02 N	105.14 E
Bangholme, Austl.	192b		38.02 S	145.11 E
Bangil, Indon.	66	G8	7.35 S	112.47 E
Bangka, Pulau, i., Indon.	66	E5	2.15 S	106.00 E
Bangka, Selat, strt., Indon.	66	E4	2.20 S	105.45 E
Bangkalan, Indon.	66	G8	7.02 S	112.44 E
Bang Kapi, Thai.	187a		13.46 N	100.39 E
Bang Kapi, Khlong, can., Thai.	187a		13.45 N	100.36 E
Bangkaru, Pulau, i., Indon.	64	L3	2.04 N	97.07 E
Bang Khen, Thai.	187a		13.52 N	100.36 E
Bang Khun Thian, Thai.	187a		13.42 N	100.28 E
Bangkinang, Indon.	66	C2	0.21 N	101.02 E
Bangkir, Indon.	66	C12	0.46 N	120.12 E
Bangko, Indon.	66	E3	2.04 S	102.16 E
Bangkog Co, l., China	70	C12	31.42 N	89.28 E
Bangkok see Krung Thep, Thai.	64	F5	13.45 N	100.31 E
Bangkok (Don Muang) International Airport, arpt., Thai.	187a		13.56 N	100.37 E
Bangkok Noi Railway Station, trans., Thai.	187a		13.45 N	100.29 E
Bangkok Station, trans., Thai.	187a		13.44 N	100.32 E
Bang Krathum, Thai.	64	D5	16.34 N	100.18 E
Bang Kruai, Thai.	187a		13.48 N	100.29 E
Bangkulua, Indon.	66	H11	8.40 S	118.14 E
Bangladesh, ctry., Asia	70	G13	24.00 N	90.00 E
Bang Lamung, Thai.	64	F5	12.57 N	100.54 E
Bang Mun Nak, Thai.	64	D5	16.02 N	100.23 E
Bangor, N. Ire., U.K.	10	G7	54.39 N	5.41 W
Bangor, Wales, U.K.	10	H8	53.13 N	4.08 W
Bangor, Me., U.S.	122	F8	44.48 N	68.46 W
Bangor, Mi., U.S.	130	B11	42.18 N	86.06 W
Bangor, Pa., U.S.	124	D10	40.51 N	75.12 W
Bang Pa In, Thai.	64	E5	14.17 N	100.33 E
Bangriposi, India	70	G11	22.10 N	86.32 E
Bangs, Tx., U.S.	136	C8	31.42 N	99.07 W
Bangs, Mount, mtn., Az., U.S.	150	G3	36.48 N	113.51 W
Bang Saphan, Thai.	64	G4	11.12 N	99.30 E
Bangsjøan, l., Nor.	16	C9	64.19 N	12.02 E
Bangs Lake, l., Il., U.S.	196		42.16 N	88.08 W
Bangsri, Indon.	66	G7	6.30 S	110.45 E
Bangsund, Nor.	16	C9	64.23 N	11.23 E
Bangued, Phil.	68	B3	17.36 N	120.37 E
Bangui, C.A.R.	86	D3	4.22 N	18.33 E
Bangweulu, Lake, l., Zam.	88	C4	11.03 S	29.53 E
Bangweulu Swamps, sw., Zam.	88	C5	11.30 S	30.15 E
Bangxu, China	58	J2	23.45 N	107.36 E
Ban Hatgnao, Laos	64	E8	14.40 N	106.33 E
Ban Hatkiang, Laos	64	C6	18.10 N	102.40 E
Ban Hat Yai see Hat Yai, Thai.	64	I5	7.00 N	100.28 E
Ban Ha Yaek Pak Kret, Thai.	187a		13.54 N	100.31 E
Ban Hèt, Laos	64	E8	14.39 N	107.30 E
Ban Hin Heup, Laos	64	C6	18.38 N	102.18 E
Ban Hom, Thai.	64	E5	15.33 N	98.46 E
Ban Hong, Thai.	64	C4	18.18 N	98.49 E
Ban Hong Muang, Laos	64	D7	17.03 N	105.10 E
Ban Houayxay, Laos	64	B5	20.15 N	100.24 E
Ban Huai Yang, Thai.	64	G4	11.36 N	99.40 E
Ban Hua Lamphu Thong, Thai.	187a		13.32 N	100.38 E
Bani, Burkina	84	G4	13.43 N	0.11 W
Bani, C.A.R.	86	C4	7.09 N	22.47 E
Baní, Dom. Rep.	156	C12	18.16 N	70.19 W
Bani, Jbel, mts., Mor.	84	D3	29.26 N	7.52 W
Baniara, Pap. N. Gui.	101a	b4	9.45 S	149.52 E
Bani Bangou, Niger	84	F5	15.03 N	2.42 E
Banie, Pol.	24	C10	53.06 N	14.40 E
Banihāl Pass, p., India	62	B4	33.32 N	75.11 E
Banī Magdûl, Egypt	191c		30.02 N	31.07 E
Banister, stm., Va., U.S.	124	H6	36.41 N	78.47 W
Banī Walīd, Libya	82	A2	31.44 N	14.01 E
Bāniyās, Golan	76	E6	33.15 N	35.41 E
Bāniyās, Syria	76	C6	35.11 N	35.57 E
Banja Luka, Bos.	36	E4	44.46 N	17.11 E
Banjarmasin, Indon.	66	E9	3.19 S	114.34 E
Banjir Kanal, can., Indon.	187e		6.07 S	106.45 E
Banjul (Bathurst), Gam.	84	G1	13.26 N	16.35 W
Bānka, India	70	F11	24.52 N	86.55 E
Ban'ka, stm., Russia	183b		55.49 N	37.22 E
Banka Banka, Austl.	96	C6	18.42 S	133.57 E
Ban Katêp, Laos	64	D7	16.48 N	105.52 E
Ban Kavak, Laos	64	D7	17.19 N	105.43 E
Ban Kèngkabao, Laos	64	D7	16.47 N	104.45 E
Ban Kèngkok, Laos	64	D7	16.26 N	105.11 E
Ban Kèngtangan, Laos	64	D7	16.03 N	105.22 E
Bankeryd, Swe.	16	J12	57.51 N	14.07 E
Ban Khamphô, Laos	64	E8	14.36 N	106.17 E
Ban Khan Na Yao, Thai.	187a		13.47 N	100.41 E
Ban Kheun, Laos	64	B5	20.11 N	101.04 E
Ban Khlong Bua Loi, Thai.	187a		13.41 N	100.41 E
Ban Khlong Kua, Thai.	64	I4	6.57 N	100.08 E
Ban Khlong Samrong, Thai.	187a		13.39 N	100.36 E
Ban Khlong Song, Thai.	187a		13.51 N	100.43 E
Ban Khok Bao Sao, Thai.	187a		13.52 N	100.39 E
Ban Khuan Mao, Thai.	64	I4	7.58 N	99.37 E
Bānkipur, India	190b		22.48 N	88.14 E
Bankja, Blg.	36	G10	42.42 N	23.08 E
Ban Krang, Thai.	64	F4	12.52 N	99.18 E
Ban Kruat, Thai.	64	E6	14.24 N	103.05 E
Banks, Al., U.S.	134	F13	31.48 N	85.51 W
Banks, Cape, c., Austl.	192a		34.00 S	151.15 E
Banks, Îles (Banks Islands), is., Vanuatu	101d	i16	13.25 S	167.41 E
Banks Island, i., B.C., Can.	110	E4	53.25 N	130.10 W
Banks Island, i., N.T., Can.	109	B15	73.15 N	121.30 W
Banks Islands see Banks, Îles, is., Vanuatu	101d	i16	13.25 S	167.41 E
Banks Lake, res., Wa., U.S.	146	C7	47.43 N	119.15 W
Banksmeadow, Austl.	192a		33.58 S	151.13 E
Banks Peninsula, pen., N.Z.	102	F5	43.45 S	173.00 E
Banks Strait, strt., Austl.	99a	n13	40.40 S	148.07 E
Bankstown Aerodrome, arpt., Austl.	192a		33.55 S	150.59 E
Banksville, N.Y., U.S.	194		41.09 N	73.38 W
Banksville, ngh., Pa., U.S.	197b		40.24 N	80.03 W
Ban Kum Daeng, Thai.	187a		13.53 N	100.36 E
Bānkura, India	70	G11	23.15 N	87.04 E
Ban Laem Sing, Thai.	187a		13.30 N	100.34 E
Ban Lat Phrao, Thai.	187a		13.47 N	100.36 E
Ban Le Kathe, Thai.	64	E4	15.50 N	98.49 E
Ban Luk Kho, Thai.	187a		13.34 N	100.27 E
Ban Mae La Luang, Thai.	64	C3	18.31 N	97.56 E
Ban Mae Mo, Thai.	64	C4	18.16 N	99.42 E
Ban Mit, Laos	64	C5	18.51 N	101.55 E
Ban Muangngat, Laos	64	C6	19.04 N	104.04 E
Ban Muang Yot, Thai.	64	C5	19.24 N	100.34 E
Bann, stm., N. Ire., U.K.	10	F6	55.10 N	6.46 W
Ban Nadou, Laos	64	E7	15.51 N	105.38 E
Ban Nagnom, Laos	64	D7	17.03 N	105.44 E
Ban Nahin, Laos	64	C7	18.12 N	104.13 E
Ban Nakala, Laos	64	D7	16.14 N	105.12 E
Ban Na Kha, Thai.	64	H4	9.25 N	98.26 E
Ban Nalan, Laos	64	E7	15.50 N	106.04 E
Ban Nalè, Laos	64	C5	18.41 N	101.31 E
Ban Namcha, Laos	64	C6	19.09 N	102.53 E
Ban Nam Chan, Thai.	64	C6	18.01 N	103.52 E
Ban Namnga, Laos	64	B6	20.21 N	102.19 E
Ban Nam Tao, Laos	64	D5	17.51 N	101.14 E
Ban Nam Thaeng, Thai.	64	E7	15.34 N	105.27 E
Ban Naxon, Laos	64	C6	18.11 N	103.03 E
Ban Naxouang, Laos	64	C7	18.25 N	104.31 E
Banner Park, p.o.i., Md., U.S.	202b		39.19 N	76.42 W
Bannertown, N.C., U.S.	124	H5	36.29 N	80.34 W
Ban Ngam, Laos	64	B7	20.09 N	104.52 E
Banning, Ca., U.S.	148	J9	33.55 N	116.52 W
Banningville see Bandundu, D.R.C.	86	E3	3.16 S	17.21 E
Bannister Ditch, can., Oh., U.S.	197a		41.18 N	82.01 W
Bannockburn, Il., U.S.	196		42.12 N	87.52 W
Bannockburn, Zimb.	90	B9	20.17 S	29.52 E
Bannock Creek, stm., Id., U.S.	146	H14	42.53 N	112.45 W
Bannock Peak, mtn., Id., U.S.	146	H14	42.36 N	112.42 W
Ban Nong Lumphuk, Thai.	64	E6	14.26 N	102.43 E
Ban Nong Takhian, Thai.	64	F5	13.08 N	101.23 E
Bannu, Pak.	70	B3	32.59 N	70.36 E
Bañolas see Banyoles, Spain	28	B13	42.06 N	2.46 E
Ban O Pao, Thai.	187a		13.50 N	100.38 E
Baños, Ec.	168	H2	1.24 S	78.25 W
Banow, Afg.	72	B10	35.37 N	69.13 E
Ban Pak Bong, Thai.	64	C4	18.31 N	98.54 E
Ban Pak Chan, Thai.	64	G4	10.34 N	98.49 E
Ban Pakha, Laos	64	E8	14.39 N	107.22 E
Ban Pakkhop, Laos	64	C5	19.47 N	100.36 E
Ban Pak Nam, Thai.	64	G4	10.22 N	99.13 E
Ban Pakneun, Laos	64	C5	19.14 N	101.50 E
Ban Phai, Thai.	64	D6	17.35 N	102.58 E
Ban Phai, Thai.	64	D6	16.03 N	102.42 E
Ban Phe, Thai.	64	F5	12.38 N	101.25 E
Ban Pho, Thai.	64	F5	13.37 N	101.04 E
Ban Phon, Laos	64	E8	15.24 N	106.41 E
Ban Phông Pho, Laos	64	E7	14.35 N	105.53 E
Banphot Phisai, Thai.	64	E4	15.52 N	99.54 E
Ban Phraek Kasa, Thai.	187a		13.34 N	100.38 E
Ban Pong, Thai.	64	F4	13.48 N	99.53 E
Ban Ron Phibun, Thai.	64	H4	8.09 N	99.51 E
Ban Sa-ang, Laos	64	D7	17.24 N	105.44 E
Ban Saen To, Thai.	64	E4	16.01 N	99.46 E
Ban Sakhla, Thai.	187a		13.32 N	100.30 E
Ban Salik, Thai.	64	C5	18.30 N	100.44 E
Ban Samang, Laos	64	C6	19.41 N	102.34 E
Ban Sam Phan, Thai.	64	H4	8.33 N	99.09 E
Ban Sam Pong, Laos	64	C6	18.34 N	102.47 E
Ban Samrong, Thai.	64	E6	14.23 N	102.49 E
Bānsda, India	70	H4	20.46 N	73.21 E
Banshadhāra, stm., India	69	B6	18.20 N	84.08 E
Banshi, China	58	I6	25.18 N	115.21 E
Ban Signo, Laos	64	D7	17.50 N	105.02 E
Banská Bystrica, Slvk.	24	H15	48.44 N	19.09 E
Banská Štiavnica, Slvk.	24	H14	48.27 N	18.55 E
Bansko, Blg.	36	H10	41.50 N	23.29 E
Ban Songkhon, Laos	64	C7	17.59 N	105.11 E
Ban Song Kong, Thai.	187a		13.53 N	100.34 E
Ban Sop Huai Hai, Thai.	64	C4	19.33 N	98.05 E
Banstala, India	190b		22.32 N	88.25 E
Bānswāra, India	70	G5	23.32 N	74.26 E
Bantaeng, Indon.	66	F11	5.32 S	119.56 E
Bantaian, Indon.	66	C2	1.56 N	100.55 E
Ban Takhlo, Thai.	64	E5	15.27 N	100.44 E
Ban Tamru, Thai.	187a		13.31 N	100.41 E
Ban Tao Pun, Thai.	187a		13.53 N	100.41 E
Bantarkawung, Indon.	66	G6	7.13 S	108.55 E
Bantayan, Phil.	68	E4	11.10 N	123.43 E
Bantenan, Tanjung, c., Indon.	66	H9	8.45 S	114.32 E
Ban Teung, Laos	64	D7	17.54 N	105.29 E
Ban Thabôk, Laos	64	C6	18.22 N	103.11 E
Ban Thanoun, Laos	64	C5	19.48 N	101.29 E
Ban Thapayi, Laos	64	D7	16.19 N	105.40 E
Ban Thieng, Laos	64	C6	19.08 N	102.11 E
Ban Tian Sa, Laos	64	C6	18.43 N	103.12 E
Banton, Phil.	68	D4	12.57 N	122.05 E
Ban Tong Khop, Thai.	64	D7	17.03 N	104.16 E
Bāntra, India	190b		22.35 N	88.19 E
Bantry, Ire.	10	J3	51.41 N	9.27 W
Bantry Bay, b., Ire.	10	J3	51.38 N	9.48 W
Ban Van Hom, Laos	64	C7	18.44 N	104.00 E
Ban Vat, Laos	64	D8	16.53 N	106.26 E
Ban Xènkhalôk, Laos	64	C5	19.40 N	101.55 E
Ban Xot, Laos	64	C6	18.12 N	104.05 E
Banya, Testa de la, c., Spain	28	D11	40.34 N	0.39 E
Banyak, Kepulauan, is., Indon.	64	K3	2.10 N	97.15 E
Ban Ya Plong, Thai.	64	H4	8.52 N	98.37 E
Banyo, Cam.	86	C2	6.45 N	11.49 E
Banyoles, Spain	28	B13	42.06 N	2.46 E
Banyuwangi, Indon.	66	H9	8.12 S	114.21 E
Banyuwedang, Indon.	66	H9	8.08 S	114.36 E
Banzare Coast, cst., Ant.	103	B17	67.00 S	126.00 E
Baocheng, China	58	E2	33.12 N	106.57 E
Baode, China	58	B4	39.00 N	111.05 E
Baoding, China	58	B6	38.51 N	115.29 E
Baofeng, China	58	E5	33.54 N	113.01 E
Bao Ha, Viet.	64	A7	22.10 N	104.22 E
Baoji, China	58	D2	34.23 N	107.08 E
Baojing, China	58	G3	28.43 N	109.25 E
Bao Lac, Viet.	64	A7	22.57 N	105.40 E
Bao Loc, Viet.	64	G8	11.32 N	107.46 E
Baolunyuan, China	58	E1	32.22 N	105.36 E
Baoning, China	58	J2	23.31 N	106.24 E
Baoqing, China	52	B11	46.19 N	132.12 E
Baoshan, China	52	F4	25.07 N	99.09 E
Baoting, China	58	L3	18.38 N	109.47 E
Baotou, China	52	A4	40.35 N	109.57 E
Baoulé, stm., Mali	84	G3	13.33 N	9.54 W
Baowei, China	64	A8	22.38 N	106.49 E
Baoxikou, China	58	J6	23.13 N	115.12 E
Baoyi, China	58	E7	32.13 N	116.43 E
Baoying, China	58	E8	33.13 N	119.18 E
Bāp, India	70	E4	27.23 N	72.21 E
Bāpatla, India	69	D5	15.54 N	80.28 E
Bapaume, Fr.	20	D11	50.06 N	2.50 E
Bapchule, Az., U.S.	150	J5	33.10 N	111.54 W
Baptiste Lake, res., On., Can.	126	C12	45.06 N	78.02 W
Bāqa el Gharbiyya, Isr.	76	F6	32.25 N	35.03 E
Baqên, China	52	E3	31.54 N	94.00 E
Baqing, China	70	B14	32.15 N	93.30 E
Ba'qūbah, Iraq	74	D9	33.45 N	44.39 E
Baquedano, Chile	172	A3	23.20 S	69.50 W
Ba Queo, Viet.	187c		10.48 N	106.38 E
Bar, Ukr.	38	D6	49.04 N	27.41 E
Bar, Yugo.	36	G6	42.05 N	19.06 E
Bara, India	190b		22.43 N	88.31 E
Bara, India	190b		22.46 N	88.17 E
Bara, Nig.	84	G7	10.22 N	10.43 E
Baraawe, Som.	86	D8	1.06 N	44.01 E
Barabai, Indon.	66	E9	2.36 S	115.21 E
Barabinsk, Russia	48	C13	55.21 N	78.21 E
Barabinskaja step', pl., Russia	48	C13	55.00 N	79.00 E
Baraboo, Wi., U.S.	128	H9	43.28 N	89.43 W
Baraboo, stm., Wi., U.S.	128	H8	43.28 N	89.25 W
Baracaldo see Barakaldo, Spain	28	A8	43.18 N	2.59 W
Baracoa, Cuba	156	B10	20.20 N	74.29 W
Baradero, Arg.	172	F8	33.48 S	59.31 W
Baradine, Austl.	98	H7	30.57 S	149.04 E
Baraga, Mi., U.S.	126	B1	46.46 N	88.29 W
Baragaon see Nālanda, India	70	F10	25.07 N	85.24 E
Baragoi, Kenya	86	D7	1.47 N	36.47 E
Baragwanath Military Hospital, bldg., S. Afr.	191d		26.16 S	27.56 E
Bārah, Sudan	82	E6	13.42 N	30.22 E
Barahona, Dom. Rep.	156	C12	18.12 N	71.05 W
Barajas, Aeropuerto, arpt., Spain	184a		40.28 N	3.34 W
Barajas de Madrid, ngh., Spain	184a		40.28 N	3.35 E
Barak, Tur.	42	G7	36.51 N	37.59 E
Barāk, stm., India	70	F14	24.52 N	92.29 E
Barakaldo, Spain	28	A8	43.18 N	2.59 W
Barakī Barak, Afg.	70	B2	33.55 N	68.55 E
Bārākpur Cantonment, India	190b		22.46 N	88.22 E
Barakula, Austl.	98	F8	26.26 S	150.30 E
Barāl, India	190b		22.27 N	88.22 E
Baralaba, Austl.	98	E7	24.11 S	149.49 E
Baram, stm., Malay.	66	A9	4.34 N	114.00 E
Baram, Tanjong, c., Malay.	66	A8	4.35 N	113.59 E
Barama, stm., Guy.	168	D12	7.39 N	59.14 W
Bārāmati, India	69	B2	18.09 N	74.36 E
Bārāmūla, India	70	A5	34.12 N	74.20 E
Baran', Bela.	26	F13	54.28 N	30.21 E
Baran', Bela.	26	F11	54.28 N	28.39 E
Bārān, India	70	F6	25.06 N	76.31 E
Baranagar, India	70	G12	22.37 N	88.22 E
Baranavičy, Bela.	26	G9	53.07 N	26.01 E
Barangbarang, Indon.	66	G12	6.24 S	120.27 E
Barani, Burkina	84	G4	13.10 N	3.53 W
Baranivka, Ukr.	38	C6	50.18 N	27.40 E
Baran'ja Iolga, gora, mtn., Russia	14	E24	67.11 N	33.10 E
Baranoa, Col.	168	B4	10.48 N	74.55 W
Baranof Island, i., Ak., U.S.	109	E12	57.00 N	135.00 W
Baranoviči see Baranavičy, Bela.	26	G9	53.07 N	26.01 E
Baranów Sandomierski, Pol.	24	F17	50.30 N	21.33 E
Barany, Russia	26	C12	57.20 N	29.07 E
Baranya, state, Hung.	36	D5	46.05 N	18.15 E
Baranykivka, Ukr.	38	D18	49.10 N	39.50 E
Barão de Grajaú, Braz.	170	D4	6.45 S	43.01 W
Barão de Melgaço, Braz.	166	C5	16.13 S	55.58 W
Barão de Tromaí, Braz.	170	A3	1.36 S	45.37 W
Baraolt, Rom.	36	C12	46.05 N	25.36 E
Bārasat, India	190b		22.51 N	88.22 E
Barashi, Ukr.	38	C7	50.43 N	28.01 E
Baraški, Russia	12	D24	65.41 N	52.09 E
Baratā, Port.	184c		38.48 N	9.19 W
Barataria, La., U.S.	134	H8	29.43 N	90.07 W
Barataria Bay, b., La., U.S.	134	H8	29.22 N	89.55 W
Barat Daya, Kepulauan (Barat Daya Islands), is., Indon.	60	G8	7.25 S	128.00 E
Barat Daya Islands see Barat Daya, Kepulauan, is., Indon.	60	G8	7.25 S	128.00 E
Baratta, Austl.	98	H2	31.58 S	139.06 E
Barauana, stm., Braz.	168	G11	1.05 N	60.52 W
Baraula, India	190a		28.34 N	77.22 E
Barauni, India	70	F10	25.28 N	85.58 E
Baraut, India	70	D6	29.05 N	77.15 E
Baravuha, Bela.	26	E11	55.35 N	28.36 E
Baraya, Col.	168	F4	3.10 N	75.04 W
Barbacena, Braz.	170	K4	21.13 S	43.44 W
Barbacoas, Col.	168	G2	1.41 N	78.09 W
Barbadillo del Mercado, Spain	28	B7	42.02 N	3.21 W
Barbadoes Island, i., Pa., U.S.	203		40.07 N	75.22 W
Barbados, ctry., N.A.	159d	n9	13.10 N	59.32 W
Barbagia, mts., Italy	32	E3	39.56 N	9.13 E
Barbalha, Braz.	170	D6	7.19 S	39.17 W
Barbar, Sudan	82	D6	18.00 N	34.00 E
Barbaria, Cap de, c., Spain	28	F12	38.38 N	1.23 E
Barbaros, Tur.	34	C10	40.54 N	27.27 E
Barbas, Cap, c., W. Sah.	84	E1	22.17 N	16.39 W
Barbaši, Russia	26	C11	57.42 N	28.20 E
Barbastro, Spain	28	B11	42.01 N	0.08 E
Barbate, Spain	28	H5	36.11 N	5.55 W
Barbeau Peak, mtn., Nu., Can.	108	A10	81.54 N	75.00 W
Barberà del Vallès, Spain	184d		41.31 N	2.08 E
Barber Booth, Eng., U.K.	180		53.22 N	1.50 W
Barberena, Guat.	156	E2	14.18 N	90.22 W
Barberton, S. Afr.	90	D10	25.48 S	31.03 E
Barberton, Oh., U.S.	124	C4	41.01 N	81.35 W
Barbezieux, Fr.	22	D5	45.28 N	0.09 W
Barbil, India	70	G10	22.05 N	85.21 E
Barbosa, Col.	168	E5	5.56 N	73.37 W
Barbosa, Col.	168	D4	6.26 N	75.20 W
Barbourville, Ky., U.S.	124	H2	36.52 N	83.53 W
Barbuda, i., Antig.	159b	e4	17.38 N	61.48 W
Barby, Ger.	24	E7	51.58 N	11.53 E
Bârca, Rom.	36	F10	43.58 N	23.37 E
Barcaldine, Austl.	98	D5	23.33 S	145.17 E
Barcarena, Port.	184c		38.44 N	9.17 W
Barcarena, Ribeira de, stm., Port.	184c		38.42 N	9.27 W
Barcarrota, Spain	28	F4	38.31 N	6.51 W
Barcău (Berettyó), stm., Eur.	36	B8	46.59 N	21.07 E
Barce see Al-Marj, Libya	82	A4	32.30 N	20.53 E
Barcellona Pozzo di Gotto, Italy	32	F9	38.09 N	15.13 E
Barcelona, Mex.	154	B7	26.12 N	103.25 W
Barcelona, Spain	28	C13	41.24 N	2.10 E
Barcelona, Spain	184d		41.23 N	2.11 E
Barcelona, Ven.	168	B9	10.07 N	64.40 W
Barcelona, co., Spain	28	C13	41.40 N	2.00 E
Barcelona, Aeropuerto Transoceánico de, arpt., Spain	184d		41.18 N	2.05 E
Barceloneta, P.R.	158a	b2	18.26 N	66.32 W
Barcelos, Braz.	168	H10	0.59 S	62.54 W
Barcelos, Port.	28	C2	41.32 N	8.36 W
Barcin, Pol.	24	D13	52.51 N	17.55 E
Barclay Brook, stm., N.J., U.S.	194		40.19 N	74.22 W
Barcoo, stm., Austl.	98	E4	25.12 S	142.49 E
Barcroft, Lake, res., Va., U.S.	202c		38.51 N	77.09 W
Barcs, Hung.	36	D4	45.57 N	17.27 E
Barcy, Fr.	179		49.01 N	2.53 E
Barczewo, Pol.	24	C16	53.50 N	20.41 E
Bärdä, Azer.	42	E12	40.22 N	47.10 E
Barda, Russia	40	C19	56.55 N	55.35 E
Barda del Medio, Arg.	172	I3	38.42 S	68.09 W
Bardaï, Chad	82	C3	21.22 N	16.59 E
Bardawīl, Sabkhet el-, b., Egypt	76	G3	31.10 N	33.10 E
Barddhamān, India	70	G11	23.14 N	87.52 E
Bardejov, Slvk.	24	G17	49.17 N	21.16 E
Bardenas Reales, plat., Spain	28	B9	42.10 N	1.25 W
Bardera see Baardheere, Som.	86	D8	2.19 N	42.17 E
Bardeskan, Iran	72	B8	35.14 N	57.57 E
Bardīyah, Libya	82	A5	31.45 N	25.04 E
Bardo, Tun.	32	H4	36.50 N	10.06 E
Bārdoli, India	70	H4	21.06 N	73.06 E
Bardonecchia, Italy	30	E3	45.05 N	6.42 E
Bardonia, N.Y., U.S.	194		41.07 N	74.00 W
Bardstown, Ky., U.S.	130	G12	37.48 N	85.28 W
Bardwell, Ky., U.S.	130	H9	36.52 N	89.01 W
Bardwell Lake, res., Tx., U.S.	136	B11	32.16 N	96.39 W
Bareggio, Italy	184b		45.29 N	9.00 E
Bareilly, India	70	D7	28.20 N	79.24 E
Barencevo more see Barents Sea, s., Eur.	46	B7	74.00 N	36.00 E
Barentsburg, Nor.	108	B29	78.04 N	14.13 E
Barentshavet see Barents Sea, s., Eur.	46	B7	74.00 N	36.00 E
Barentsøya, i., Nor.	108	B30	78.27 N	21.15 E
Barents Sea, s., Eur.	46	B7	74.00 N	36.00 E
Bareo, Malay.	66	B9	3.44 N	115.27 E
Bareta, India	70	D5	29.51 N	75.41 E
Barfleur, Fr.	20	E7	49.40 N	1.16 W
Barfleur, Pointe de, c., Fr.	20	E7	49.42 N	1.16 W
Bargaal, Som.	86	B10	11.17 N	51.04 E
Bargāchia, India	190b		22.48 N	88.27 E
Bargara, Austl.	98	E9	24.49 S	152.27 E
Bargarh, India	62	D5	21.19 N	83.37 E
Bargas, Spain	28	E6	39.55 N	4.01 W
Barguzin, stm., Russia	50	F11	53.25 N	108.58 E
Barguzinskij hrebet, mts., Russia	50	F11	54.30 N	110.20 E
Bar Harbor, Me., U.S.	122	F8	44.23 N	68.12 W
Barharwa, India	70	F11	24.51 N	87.46 E
Barhau, Indon.	66	F2	5.21 S	102.07 E
Barhi, India	70	F10	24.18 N	85.25 E
Bāri, India	70	G7	23.02 N	78.04 E
Bāri, India	70	E6	26.39 N	77.36 E
Bari, Italy	32	C10	41.07 N	16.51 E
Baria, stm., Ven.	168	G8	1.54 N	66.36 W
Barīdī, Ra's, c., Sau. Ar.	74	H5	24.16 N	37.31 E
Barī Gāv, Afg.	70	B1	33.52 N	67.52 E
Barigua, Salina de, pl., Ven.	158g	p20	12.06 N	69.57 W
Barillas, Guat.	156	E2	15.48 N	91.17 W
Bariloche see San Carlos de Bariloche, Arg.	166	H2	41.09 S	71.17 W
Barīm, i., Yemen	72	G5	12.39 N	43.23 E
Barima, stm., S.A.	168	C12	8.34 N	60.23 W
Barima-Waini, state, Guy.	168	D12	7.25 N	59.40 W
Barinas, P.R.	158a	b2	18.00 N	66.50 W
Barinas, Ven.	168	C6	8.37 N	70.12 W
Barinas, state, Ven.	168	C7	8.10 N	69.50 W
Baring, Cape, c., N.T., Can.	110	A7	70.02 N	117.16 W
Baringo, Lake, l., Kenya	86	D7	0.38 N	36.05 E
Barinitas, Ven.	168	C6	8.44 N	70.23 W
Bāripada, India	70	H11	21.56 N	86.43 E
Bariri, Braz.	170	L1	22.04 S	48.44 W
Bârîs, Egypt	82	C6	24.47 N	30.34 E
Bari Sādri, India	70	F5	24.25 N	74.28 E
Barisāl, Bngl.	70	G13	22.41 N	90.22 E
Barisāl, state, Bngl.	70	G13	22.30 N	90.30 E
Barisan, Pegunungan, mts., Indon.	66	E3	3.00 S	102.15 E
Bariti Bil, l., India	190b		22.48 N	88.26 E
Barito, stm., Indon.	66	E9	3.20 S	114.32 E
Barjatino, Russia	26	F17	54.18 N	34.32 E
Barjols, Fr.	22	F11	43.34 N	6.00 E
Bark, stm., Wi., U.S.	128	I10	42.55 N	88.49 W
Barkal, Bngl.	70	G14	22.42 N	92.24 E
Barkam, China	52	E5	31.50 N	102.33 E
Barkava, Lat.	26	D9	56.43 N	26.36 E
Barker Point, c., N.Y., U.S.	194		40.51 N	73.44 W
Barkers Brook, stm., N.J., U.S.	203		40.03 N	74.45 W
Barkerville, B.C., Can.	144	C9	53.04 N	121.31 W
Barkerville Historic Park, p.o.i., B.C., Can.	144	C9	53.04 N	121.30 W
Bārkhān, Pak.	70	D2	29.52 N	69.30 E
Barkingside, ngh., Eng., U.K.	178		51.36 N	0.05 E
Barkisland, Eng., U.K.	180		53.41 N	1.55 W
Bark Lake, l., On., Can.	126	C12	45.27 N	77.50 W
Bark Lake, l., On., Can.	126	B7	46.51 N	82.29 W
Barkley, Lake, res., U.S.	130	H10	36.44 N	87.57 W
Barkley Sound, strt., B.C., Can.	144	H5	48.53 N	125.20 W
Barkly East, S. Afr.	90	G8	30.57 S	27.35 E
Barkly Tableland, plat., Austl.	96	C7	18.00 S	136.00 E
Barkly West, S. Afr.	90	F7	28.05 S	24.31 E
Barkol, China	52	C3	43.32 N	93.01 E
Barksdale, Tx., U.S.	136	E7	29.43 N	100.01 W
Bârlad, Rom.	36	C14	46.13 N	27.40 E
Bârlad, stm., Rom.	36	D14	45.37 N	27.31 E
Barlassina, Italy	184b		45.39 N	9.08 E
Bar-le-Duc, Fr.	20	F14	48.46 N	5.10 E
Barlee, Lake, l., Austl.	96	E3	29.10 S	119.30 E
Barlee Range, mts., Austl.	96	D3	23.43 S	116.19 E
Barletta, Italy	32	C10	41.19 N	16.16 E
Barlinek, Pol.	24	D11	52.59 N	15.12 E
Barling, Ar., U.S.	134	B4	35.19 N	94.18 W
Barlow, Ky., U.S.	130	G8	37.03 N	89.03 W
Barmashove, Ukr.	38	F11	47.05 N	32.27 E
Barmedman, Austl.	98	J6	34.08 S	147.23 E
Barmen, ngh., Ger.	181		51.17 N	7.13 E
Bārmer, India	70	F3	25.44 N	71.23 E
Barmera, Austl.	98	J3	34.15 S	140.27 E
Barmouth, Wales, U.K.	10	I8	52.44 N	4.03 W
Barnaby Manor Oaks, Md., U.S.	202c		38.50 N	76.58 W
Barnagar, India	70	G5	23.02 N	75.22 E
Barnard Castle, Eng., U.K.	10	G11	54.32 N	1.55 W
Barnaul, Russia	48	D14	53.21 N	83.45 E
Barn Bluff, mtn., Austl.	99a	n12	41.43 S	145.56 E
Barnegat, N.J., U.S.	124	E11	39.44 N	74.13 W
Barnegat Bay, b., N.J., U.S.	124	E11	39.52 N	74.07 W
Barnes, ngh., Eng., U.K.	178		51.28 N	0.15 W
Barnesboro, Pa., U.S.	124	D7	40.39 N	78.47 W
Barnes Ice Cap, ice, Nu., Can.	110	A16	69.58 N	73.28 W
Barnesville, Ga., U.S.	132	C1	33.03 N	84.09 W
Barnesville, Mn., U.S.	128	E2	46.39 N	96.25 W
Barnesville, Oh., U.S.	124	E4	39.58 N	81.10 W
Barneville-Carteret, Fr.	20	E7	49.23 N	1.47 W
Barnhart, Tx., U.S.	136	C6	31.08 N	101.10 W
Barnówko, Pol.	24	D10	52.47 N	14.46 E
Barnsboro, N.J., U.S.	203		39.46 N	75.09 W
Barnsdall, Ok., U.S.	138	E12	36.33 N	96.09 W
Barnsley, Eng., U.K.	10	H11	53.33 N	1.28 W
Barnstable, Ma., U.S.	124	C15	41.42 N	70.17 W
Barnstaple, Eng., U.K.	10	J8	51.04 N	4.03 W
Barnstaple Bay, b., Eng., U.K.	10	J8	51.05 N	4.20 W
Barnston, Eng., U.K.	180		53.21 N	3.05 W
Barnton, Eng., U.K.	180		53.16 N	2.33 W
Barnum Island, N.Y., U.S.	194		40.36 N	73.39 W
Barnwell, Ab., Can.	144	G18	49.45 N	112.14 W
Barnwell, S.C., U.S.	132	C4	33.14 N	81.21 W
Baro, Nig.	84	H6	8.36 N	6.25 E
Baro, stm., Afr.	82	F7	8.25 N	33.13 E
Baroda see Vadodara, India	70	G4	22.18 N	73.11 E
Baron'ki, Bela.	26	G15	53.09 N	32.08 E
Barons, Ab., Can.	144	G18	50.00 N	113.04 W
Barora Fa Island, i., Sol. Is.	101b	d8	7.29 S	158.18 E
Barora Ite Island, i., Sol. Is.	101b	d8	7.35 S	158.24 E
Baroua, Niger	84	G7	13.52 N	13.10 E
Barpeta, India	70	E13	26.18 N	91.00 E
Barqa, China	70	C8	30.57 N	81.20 E
Barqah (Cyrenaica), hist. reg., Libya	82	A4	31.00 N	22.30 E
Barques, Pointe aux, c., Mi., U.S.	126	D7	44.03 N	82.57 W
Barquisimeto, Ven.	168	B7	10.04 N	69.19 W
Barra, Braz.	170	F4	11.05 S	43.08 W
Barra, i., Scot., U.K.	10	D5	56.58 N	7.29 W
Barra, Ponta da, c., Moz.	90	C12	23.47 S	35.30 E
Barra, Sound of, strt., Scot., U.K.	10	D5	57.05 N	7.25 W
Barraba, Austl.	98	H8	30.23 S	150.36 E
Barracas, ngh., Arg.	206		34.38 S	58.22 W
Barrackpore Airport, arpt., India	190b		22.47 N	88.22 E
Barra da Estiva, Braz.	170	G5	13.37 S	41.19 W
Barra del Colorado, C.R.	156	G6	10.45 N	83.35 W
Barra de Rio Grande, Nic.	156	F6	12.54 N	83.31 W
Barra do Corda, Braz.	170	C3	5.30 S	45.15 W
Barra do Cuanza, Ang.	88	B1	9.19 S	13.09 E
Barra do Dande, Ang.	88	B1	8.28 S	13.22 E
Barra do Garças, Braz.	166	C6	15.50 S	52.15 W
Barra do Mendes, Braz.	170	F4	11.43 S	42.04 W
Barra do Piraí, Braz.	170	L4	22.28 S	43.49 W
Barra do Ribeiro, Braz.	172	E12	30.18 S	51.18 W
Barra dos Coqueiros, Braz.	170	F7	10.54 S	37.00 W
Barra Falsa, Ponta da, c., Moz.	90	C12	22.54 S	35.34 E
Barra Funda, ngh., Braz.	205b		23.31 S	46.39 W
Barra Mansa, Braz.	170	L3	22.33 S	44.09 W
Barranca, Peru	164	F2	10.45 S	77.46 W
Barrancabermeja, Col.	168	D5	7.03 N	73.51 W
Barrancas, Col.	168	B5	10.57 N	72.47 W
Barrancas, Ven.	168	C10	8.43 N	62.10 W
Barrancas, Ven.	168	C7	8.45 N	70.05 W
Barrancas, stm., Arg.	172	H2	36.52 S	69.45 W
Barranco, Peru	204d		12.09 S	77.02 W
Barranco Azul, Mex.	136	E3	29.21 N	104.16 W
Barranco do Velho, Port.	28	G3	37.14 N	7.56 W
Barrancos de Guadalupe, Mex.	136	D3	30.02 N	104.44 W
Barranqueras, Arg.	172	C8	27.29 S	58.56 W
Barranquilla, Col.	168	B4	10.58 N	74.47 W
Barranquitas, P.R.	158a	b3	18.10 N	66.18 W
Barras, Braz.	170	C4	4.15 S	42.18 W
Barrax, Spain	28	E8	39.02 N	2.11 W
Barre, Vt., U.S.	122	F4	44.11 N	72.30 W
Barreal, Arg.	172	E3	31.37 S	69.29 W
Barreiras, Braz.	170	G3	12.08 S	45.00 W
Barreirinha, Braz.	164	D6	2.47 S	57.03 W
Barreirinhas, Braz.	170	B4	2.45 S	42.50 W
Barreiro, Port.	28	F1	38.39 N	9.03 W
Barreiro, stm., Braz.	205a		22.52 S	43.34 W
Barreiros, Braz.	170	E8	8.49 S	35.12 W
Barren, stm., Ky., U.S.	130	H11	37.10 N	86.37 W
Barren, Nosy, is., Madag.	88	D7	18.29 S	43.53 E
Barren Islands, is., Ak., U.S.	109	E9	58.55 N	152.15 W
Barren River Lake, res., Ky., U.S.	130	H11	36.53 N	86.05 W
Barren Run, stm., Pa., U.S.	197b		40.09 N	79.42 W
Barretos, Braz.	170	K1	20.33 S	48.33 W
Barrhead, Ab., Can.	144	B16	54.07 N	114.23 W
Barrie, On., Can.	126	D10	44.22 N	79.41 W
Barrie Island, i., On., Can.	126	C7	45.55 N	82.40 W
Barrière, B.C., Can.	144	E10	51.11 N	120.07 W
Barrier Range, mts., Austl.	98	H3	31.25 S	141.25 E
Barrigada, Guam	100c	j10	13.28 N	144.47 E
Barrilla Draw, stm., Tx., U.S.	136	C4	31.22 N	103.23 W
Barrington, N.S., Can.	122	G11	43.34 N	65.34 W
Barrington, N.J., U.S.	203		39.51 N	75.03 W
Barrington Tops, mtn., Austl.	98	I8	32.00 S	151.28 E
Barrington Tops National Park, p.o.i., Austl.	98	I8	32.06 S	151.30 E
Barrington Woods, Il., U.S.	196		42.09 N	88.04 W
Barringun, Austl.	98	G5	29.00 S	145.42 E
Barro Alto, Braz.	170	H1	15.02 S	48.58 W
Barron, Wi., U.S.	128	F7	45.24 N	91.50 W

Name	Page	Map Ref.	Latitude	Longitude
Barron Creek, stm., Ca., U.S.	200		37.27 N	122.05 W
Barrouallie, St. Vin.	159e	o11	13.13 N	61.16 W
Barrow, Arg.	172	I7	38.17 S	60.13 W
Barrow, Ak., U.S.	109	B8	71.18 N	156.38 W
Barrow, stm., Ire.	10	I5	52.17 N	7.00 W
Barrow, Point, c., Ak., U.S.	109	B8	71.23 N	156.28 W
Barrow Creek, Austl.	96	D6	21.31 S	133.54 E
Barrow-in-Furness, Eng., U.K.	10	G9	54.06 N	3.13 W
Barrow Island, i., Austl.	96	D2	20.48 S	115.23 E
Barrows, Mb., Can.	142	B12	52.50 N	101.26 W
Barrow Strait, strt., Nu., Can.	108	C6	74.21 N	94.10 W
Barry, Wales, U.K.	10	J9	51.24 N	3.17 W
Barry, Il., U.S.	130	E6	39.41 N	91.02 W
Barrys Bay, On., Can.	126	C12	45.28 N	77.39 W
Barryton, Mi., U.S.	126	E4	43.45 N	85.08 W
Barsalpur, India	70	D4	28.11 N	72.14 E
Bārsi, India	69	B2	18.14 N	75.41 E
Barsinghausen, Ger.	24	D5	52.18 N	9.28 E
Baršino, Kaz.	48	E11	49.41 N	69.32 E
Barstow, Ca., U.S.	148	I8	34.53 N	117.01 W
Barstow, Tx., U.S.	136	C4	31.28 N	103.24 W
Bar-sur-Aube, Fr.	20	F13	48.14 N	4.42 E
Bar-sur-Seine, Fr.	20	F13	48.07 N	4.22 E
Bārta (Bartuva), stm., Eur.	26	D4	56.21 N	21.05 E
Bartala, India	190b		22.33 N	88.16 E
Bartang, Taj.	72	B11	38.04 N	71.51 E
Barth, Ger.	24	B8	54.21 N	12.43 E
Barthélemy, Deo, p., Viet.	64	C7	19.24 N	104.08 E
Bartholomew, Bayou, stm., U.S.	134	E6	32.40 N	92.02 W
Bartibougou, Burkina	84	G5	12.52 N	0.47 E
Bartica, Guy.	164	B6	6.24 N	58.37 W
Bartın, Tur.	34	B15	41.38 N	32.20 E
Bartın, state, Tur.	34	B15	41.35 N	32.30 E
Bartle Frere, mtn., Austl.	98	A5	17.23 S	145.49 E
Bartlesville, Ok., U.S.	130	H2	36.44 N	95.59 W
Bartlett, Ne., U.S.	140	F14	41.53 N	98.33 W
Bartlett, N.H., U.S.	122	F5	44.04 N	71.18 W
Bartlett, Tn., U.S.	134	B9	35.12 N	89.52 W
Bartlett, Tx., U.S.	136	D10	30.47 N	97.25 W
Bartlett Brook, stm., Ma., U.S.	201		42.42 N	71.13 W
Bartlett Reservoir, res., Az., U.S.	150	J5	33.51 N	111.36 W
Bartley, Ne., U.S.	138	A8	40.14 N	100.18 W
Bartolomé de las Casas, Arg.	172	B8	25.23 S	59.34 W
Barton, Vt., U.S.	122	F4	44.45 N	72.12 W
Barton Aerodrome, arpt., Eng., U.K.	180		53.28 N	2.23 W
Barton Park, p.o.i., Austl.	192a		33.57 S	151.09 E
Barton Run, stm., N.J., U.S.	203		39.53 N	74.51 W
Bartonville, Il., U.S.	130	D8	40.38 N	89.38 W
Barton Water Swing Bridge, trans., Eng., U.K.	180		53.28 N	2.21 W
Bartoszyce, Pol.	24	B16	54.14 N	20.49 E
Bartow, Fl., U.S.	132	I4	27.54 N	81.50 W
Bartow, Ga., U.S.	132	D3	32.52 N	82.28 W
Barturte, mts., Swe.	14	F7	66.40 N	17.11 E
Bartuva (Bārta), stm., Eur.	26	D4	56.21 N	21.05 E
Bārū see Baro, stm., Afr.	82	F7	8.25 N	33.13 E
Baru, Kali, can., Indon.	187e		6.10 S	106.51 E
Barú, Volcán, vol., Pan.	156	H6	8.48 N	82.33 W
Barueri, mun., Braz.	205b		23.30 S	46.54 W
Bāruipāra, India	190b		22.46 N	88.14 E
Bārūk, Jabal al-, mtn., Leb.	76	E6	33.44 N	35.45 E
Barumini, Italy	32	E2	39.41 N	9.00 E
Barumun, stm., Indon.	66	C2	2.31 N	100.08 E
Barung, Nusa, i., Indon.	66	H8	8.28 S	113.20 E
Barun Su, China	52	C7	42.26 N	111.04 E
Barus, Indon.	64	L4	2.00 N	98.24 E
Baruta, Ven.	204c		10.26 N	66.53 W
Baruunharaa, Mong.	50	G10	48.53 N	106.06 E
Baruun-Urt, Mong.	52	B7	46.40 N	113.17 E
Barvas, Scot., U.K.	10	C6	58.21 N	6.31 W
Barview, Or., U.S.	146	G2	43.21 N	124.18 W
Barviha, Russia	183b		55.44 N	37.16 E
Barvinkove, Ukr.	38	E16	48.54 N	37.01 E
Barwāh, India	70	G5	22.15 N	76.02 E
Barwāla, ngh., India	190a		28.46 N	77.04 E
Bärwalde see Mieszkowice, Pol.	24	D10	52.46 N	14.29 E
Barwāni, India	70	H5	22.01 N	74.55 E
Barwice, Pol.	24	C12	53.44 N	16.21 E
Barwick, Ga., U.S.	132	F2	30.54 N	83.44 W
Barwon, stm., Austl.	98	H6	30.07 S	147.23 E
Barybino, Russia	26	E20	55.15 N	37.54 E
Barycz, stm., Pol.	24	E13	51.41 N	16.15 E
Baryš, Russia	40	E15	53.38 N	47.06 E
Barysau, Bela.	26	F11	54.13 N	28.30 E
Baryshivka, Ukr.	38	C10	50.21 N	31.20 E
Basai Dārāpur, ngh., India	190a		28.40 N	77.08 E
Bāsa' īdū, Iran	74	G14	26.39 N	55.17 E
Basail, Arg.	172	C8	27.52 S	59.18 W
Basalt, stm., Austl.	98	B5	19.38 S	145.52 E
Basalt Island, i., China	189d		22.19 N	114.22 E
Basankusu, D.R.C.	86	D3	1.12 N	19.48 E
Basarabeasca, Mol.	38	G7	46.19 N	28.58 E
Basarabi, Rom.	36	E15	44.11 N	28.26 E
Basarabia see Bessarabia, hist. reg., Eur.	38	G7	46.52 N	28.43 E
Basatongwula Shan, mtn., China	52	E3	33.05 N	91.30 E
Basavakalyān, India	69	C3	17.52 N	76.56 E
Basavilbaso, Arg.	172	F8	32.22 S	58.52 W
Bāsawul, Afg.	70	A3	34.15 N	70.52 E
Bascuñán, Cabo, c., Chile	172	D2	28.51 S	71.29 W
Basel (Bâle), Switz.	30	C4	47.33 N	7.35 E
Basella see Bassella, Spain	28	B12	42.01 N	1.18 E
Basento, stm., Italy	32	D10	40.20 N	16.48 E
Başeu, stm., Rom.	36	B14	47.48 N	27.14 E
Basey, Phil.	68	E5	11.17 N	125.03 E
Bashaw, Ab., Can.	144	D18	52.35 N	112.58 W
Bashi Channel, strt., Asia	52	G9	22.00 N	121.00 E
Bashkortostan see Baškirija, state, Russia	48	D9	54.00 N	56.00 E
Bashtanka, Ukr.	38	F11	47.24 N	32.27 E
Bashtīl, Egypt	191c		30.05 N	31.11 E
Başıbüyük, ngh., Tur.	185b		40.57 N	29.08 E
Basilan see Isabela, Phil.	68	G3	6.41 N	121.57 E
Basilan Island, i., Phil.	68	G4	6.34 N	122.03 E
Basilan Strait, strt., Phil.	68	G3	6.49 N	122.05 E
Basildon, Eng., U.K.	10	J13	51.34 N	0.25 E
Basildon, mun., Eng., U.K.	178		51.35 N	0.29 E
Basile, La., U.S.	134	G6	30.28 N	92.35 W
Basilicata, state, Italy	32	D10	40.30 N	16.10 E
Basin, Mt., U.S.	146	D14	46.16 N	112.15 W
Basin, Wy., U.S.	140	C4	44.22 N	108.02 W
Basin, The, Austl.	192b		37.51 S	145.19 E
Basingstoke, Eng., U.K.	10	J11	51.15 N	1.06 W
Basingstoke Canal, can., Eng., U.K.	178		51.21 N	0.29 W
Basingwerk Abbey, rel., Wales, U.K.	180		53.17 N	3.12 W
Basin Lake, l., Sk., Can.	142	B8	52.36 N	105.14 W
Basīrhāt, India	70	G12	22.39 N	88.52 E
Basīt, Ra's al-, c., Syria	76	C6	35.50 N	35.50 E
Basja, stm., Bela.	26	F13	53.46 N	31.00 E
Baška, Cro.	30	F11	44.58 N	14.45 E
Baskahegan Lake, l., Me., U.S.	122	E8	45.29 N	67.50 W
Baskakovka, Russia	26	F17	54.36 N	34.20 E
Başkale, Tur.	42	F10	38.03 N	44.01 E
Baskatong, Réservoir, res., Qc., Can.	114	C13	46.46 N	75.49 W
Basket Lake, l., On., Can.	128	B6	49.43 N	92.00 W
Basking Ridge, N.J., U.S.	194		40.42 N	74.32 W
Baškirija, state, Russia	48	D9	54.00 N	56.00 E
Baskomutan Milli Parkı, p.o.i., Tur.	34	E13	38.50 N	30.05 E
Baskunčak, ozero, l., Russia	40	G15	48.12 N	46.54 E
Baskuntsjak, ozero, l., Russia	42	A12	48.12 N	46.54 E
Bašmakovo, Russia	40	E13	53.12 N	43.02 E
Basmat, India	69	B3	19.19 N	77.08 E
Bāsoda, India	70	G6	23.51 N	77.55 E
Basoko, D.R.C.	86	D4	1.14 N	23.36 E
Basoko, stm., D.R.C.	191b		4.19 S	15.16 E
Basongo, D.R.C.	86	E4	4.23 S	20.18 E
Basora, Punt, c., Aruba	158g	p20	12.25 N	69.52 W
Bas Qafqaz Silsilasi see Caucasus, mts.	42	D11	42.37 N	45.00 E
Basque Provinces see Euskal Herriko, state, Spain	28	A8	43.00 N	2.30 W
Basra see Al-Başrah, Iraq	74	E10	30.30 N	47.48 E
Bas-Rhin, state, Fr.	20	F16	48.35 N	7.40 E
Bassano, Ab., Can.	144	F18	50.47 N	112.27 W
Bassano del Grappa, Italy	30	E8	45.46 N	11.44 E
Bassari, Togo	84	H5	9.16 N	0.46 E
Bassas da India, rf., Reu.	88	E6	21.25 S	39.42 E
Bassein see Vasai, India	62	E3	19.21 N	72.48 E
Bassein see Pathein, Mya.	64	D2	16.46 N	94.43 E
Bassein, stm., Mya.	64	D2	16.00 N	94.22 E
Bassella, Spain	28	B12	42.01 N	1.18 E
Basse-Pointe, Mart.	159c	k6	14.51 N	61.07 W
Basses, Pointe des, c., Guad.	159c	i6	15.52 N	61.17 W
Basse Santa Su, Gam.	84	G2	13.18 N	14.12 W
Basse-Terre, Guad.	159c	i5	16.00 N	61.43 W
Basseterre, St. K./N.	159a	c2	17.17 N	62.44 W
Basse Terre, Trin.	159f	s12	10.07 N	61.17 W
Basse-Terre, i., Guad.	159c	h5	16.10 N	61.40 W
Bassett, Ne., U.S.	140	E13	42.35 N	99.32 W
Bassett, Va., U.S.	124	H6	36.45 N	79.59 W
Bassett Creek, stm., Al., U.S.	134	F11	31.25 N	87.56 W
Bassett Peak, mtn., Az., U.S.	150	K6	32.30 N	110.17 W
Bassfield, Ms., U.S.	134	F9	31.30 N	89.44 W
Bass Harbor, Me., U.S.	122	F8	44.14 N	68.20 W
Bass Hill, Austl.	192a		33.54 S	151.00 E
Bassikounou, Maur.	84	F3	15.52 N	5.57 W
Bassila, Benin	84	H5	9.00 N	1.40 E
Bass River, N.S., Can.	122	E13	45.24 N	63.47 W
Bass Strait, strt., Austl.	96	G9	39.20 S	145.30 E
Basswood Lake, l., N.A.	128	C6	48.05 N	91.37 W
Båstad, Swe.	16	K10	56.25 N	12.51 E
Bastak, Iran	74	G14	27.14 N	54.22 E
Bastām, Iran	74	B14	36.31 N	55.01 E
Bastenaken see Bastogne, Bel.	20	D14	49.59 N	5.43 E
Bastersberge, hill, S. Afr.	90	G5	31.58 S	20.38 E
Basti, India	70	E9	26.47 N	82.44 E
Bastia, Fr.	22	G15	42.42 N	9.27 E
Bastian, Va., U.S.	124	G4	37.10 N	81.09 W
Bastogne, Bel.	20	D14	49.59 N	5.43 E
Bastrop, La., U.S.	134	E7	32.46 N	91.54 W
Bastrop, Tx., U.S.	136	D10	30.06 N	97.18 W
Bastuträsk, Swe.	16	C17	64.47 N	20.02 E
Basu, Pulau, i., Indon.	66	D3	0.18 S	103.36 E
Basubāti, India	190b		22.47 N	88.12 E
Bāsudebpur, India	190b		22.49 N	88.25 E
Bāsūs, Egypt	191c		30.08 N	31.13 E
Basutoland see Lesotho, ctry., Afr.	90	F9	29.30 S	28.30 E
Bata, Eq. Gui.	84	I6	1.51 N	9.46 E
Bataan Peninsula, pen., Phil.	68	C3	14.40 N	120.25 E
Batabanó, Golfo de, b., Cuba	156	A6	22.15 N	82.30 W
Batac, Phil.	68	A3	18.03 N	120.33 E
Batagaj, Russia	50	C15	67.39 N	134.40 E
Batagaj-Alyta, Russia	50	C15	67.48 N	130.25 E
Batajsk, Russia	40	H11	47.08 N	39.45 E
Batak, Blg.	36	H11	41.56 N	24.14 E
Batak, Jazovir, res., Blg.	36	H10	41.57 N	24.11 E
Batakan, Indon.	66	F9	4.04 S	114.36 E
Batala, India	70	C5	31.49 N	75.12 E
Batalha, Braz.	170	E7	9.41 S	37.08 W
Batalha, Braz.	170	C4	4.01 S	42.05 W
Batalha, Port.	28	E2	39.39 N	8.50 W
Batam, Pulau, i., Indon.	66	C4	1.05 N	104.03 E
Batamaj, Russia	50	D14	63.29 N	129.33 E
Batang, China	52	E5	30.02 N	99.10 E
Batangafo, C.A.R.	86	C3	7.18 N	18.17 E
Batangas, Phil.	68	D3	13.46 N	121.03 E
Batangbatangdaya, Indon.	66	G9	6.56 S	114.00 E
Batangtoru, Indon.	66	C1	1.29 N	99.03 E
Batan Islands, is., Phil.	58	K9	20.24 N	121.40 E
Batanta, Pulau, i., Indon.	60	F9	0.51 S	130.39 E
Batas, stm., Braz.	205a		22.44 S	43.24 W
Bátaszék, Hung.	36	C5	46.12 N	18.43 E
Batatais, Braz.	170	K2	20.54 S	47.35 W
Batavia, Arg.	172	G5	34.46 S	65.41 W
Batavia see Jakarta, Indon.	66	G5	6.10 S	106.50 E
Batavia, Il., U.S.	130	C9	41.51 N	88.17 W
Batavia, Ia., U.S.	130	D5	40.59 N	92.10 W
Batavia, N.Y., U.S.	124	A7	42.59 N	78.10 W
Batchawana, stm., On., Can.	126	B5	47.09 N	84.27 W
Batchawana Mountain, mtn., On., Can.	126	A5	47.03 N	84.23 W
Batchawana Island, i., On., Can.	126	B5	46.53 N	84.30 W
Batchelor, Austl.	96	B6	13.03 S	131.01 E
Bătdâmbâng, Camb.	64	F6	13.05 N	103.12 E
Bateckij, Russia	26	B13	58.39 N	30.19 E
Bate Heath, Eng., U.K.	180		53.19 N	2.28 W
Batéké, Plateaux, plat., Congo	84	E2	3.42 S	15.29 E
Batemans Bay, Austl.	98	J8	35.43 S	150.10 E
Batenbrock, ngh., Ger.	181		51.31 N	6.57 E
Bates, Mount, mtn., Norf. I.	100i	y24	29.01 S	167.56 E
Batesburg, S.C., U.S.	132	C4	33.54 N	81.32 W
Bates Creek, stm., Wy., U.S.	140	E6	42.41 N	106.36 W
Batesville, Ar., U.S.	134	B7	35.46 N	91.38 W
Batesville, In., U.S.	130	E12	39.18 N	85.13 W
Batesville, Ms., U.S.	134	C9	34.19 N	89.57 W
Batesville, Tx., U.S.	136	F8	28.57 N	99.36 W
Bath, N.B., Can.	122	D9	46.30 N	67.34 W
Bath, St. K./N.	159a	c2	17.07 N	62.37 W
Bath, Eng., U.K.	10	J10	51.23 N	2.22 W
Bath, Me., U.S.	122	G7	43.55 N	69.49 W
Bath, N.Y., U.S.	124	B8	42.19 N	77.18 W
Batha, stm., Chad	82	E3	12.47 N	17.34 E
Bath Addition, Pa., U.S.	203		40.06 N	74.52 W
Bathgate, N.D., U.S.	142	F16	48.52 N	97.29 W
Bathinda, India	70	C5	30.12 N	74.56 E
Bathsheba, Barb.	159d	n8	13.12 N	59.31 W
Bathurst, Austl.	98	I7	33.25 S	149.34 E
Bathurst, N.B., Can.	122	C11	47.36 N	65.39 W
Bathurst see Banjul, Gam.	84	G1	13.26 N	16.35 W
Bathurst, S. Afr.	90	H8	33.30 S	26.50 E
Bathurst, Cape, c., N.T., Can.	110	A5	70.35 N	128.00 W
Bathurst Inlet, Nu., Can.	110	B9	66.50 N	108.02 W
Bathurst Island, i., Austl.	96	B5	11.36 S	130.16 E
Bathurst Island, i., Nu., Can.	106	B13	75.49 N	99.08 W
Bāţin, Wādī al-, stm., Asia	74	F10	29.41 N	47.01 E
Batina, Cro.	30	E15	45.50 N	18.51 E
Batlow, Austl.	98	J6	35.32 S	148.07 E
Batman, Tur.	42	G9	37.52 N	41.07 E
Batman, state, Tur.	42	F9	38.00 N	41.15 E
Batna, Alg.	84	B6	35.34 N	6.11 E
Ba To, Viet.	64	E9	14.47 N	108.45 E
Batoche National Historic Site, p.o.i., Sk., Can.	142	B7	52.41 N	106.02 W
Baton Rouge, La., U.S.	134	G7	30.26 N	91.10 W
Batouri, Cam.	86	D2	4.26 N	14.22 E
Ba Tri, Viet.	64	G8	10.02 N	106.36 E
Båtsfjord, Nor.	14	B20	70.36 N	29.40 E
Batson, Tx., U.S.	136	D13	30.14 N	94.36 W
Batsto, stm., N.J., U.S.	203		39.39 N	74.39 W
Batsto, Skit Branch, stm., N.J., U.S.	203		39.46 N	74.41 W
Battambang see Bătdâmbâng, Camb.	64	F6	13.05 N	103.12 E
Batten Kill, stm., U.S.	122	G3	43.06 N	73.34 W
Batterie, Pointe de la, c., Mart.	159c	k7	14.44 N	60.54 W
Battersea, ngh., Eng., U.K.	178		51.28 N	0.10 W
Battersea Park, p.o.i., Eng., U.K.	178		51.29 N	0.09 W
Batticaloa, Sri L.	69	H5	7.42 N	81.42 E
Battipaglia, Italy	32	D8	40.37 N	14.58 E
Battle, stm., Can.	144	D19	52.42 N	108.15 W
Battle Creek, Ia., U.S.	130	B2	42.18 N	95.35 W
Battle Creek, Mi., U.S.	130	B12	42.18 N	85.10 W
Battle Creek, Ne., U.S.	140	F15	42.00 N	97.36 W
Battle Creek, stm., N.A.	142	F4	48.36 N	109.10 W
Battle Creek, stm., Id., U.S.	146	H10	42.14 N	116.31 W
Battle Creek, stm., Tx., U.S.	136	B8	32.48 N	99.00 W
Battle Creek, North Fork, stm., Ca., U.S.	148	C4	40.25 N	121.59 W
Battle Green, hist., Ma., U.S.	201		42.27 N	71.14 W
Battle Ground, In., U.S.	130	D11	40.30 N	86.49 W
Battle Ground, Wa., U.S.	146	E4	45.46 N	122.31 W
Battle Harbour, Nf., Can.	111a	i22	52.16 N	55.35 W
Battle Lake, Mn., U.S.	118	E3	46.16 N	95.42 W
Battlement Mesa, mtn., Co., U.S.	150	D8	39.20 N	108.00 W
Battle Mountain, Nv., U.S.	148	C8	40.39 N	116.55 W
Battle Mountain, mtn., Wy., U.S.	150	B9	41.02 N	107.16 W
Battlesbridge, Eng., U.K.	178		51.37 N	0.34 E
Battonya, Hung.	36	C8	46.17 N	21.01 E
Battuello, Italy	184b		45.27 N	8.56 E
Batu, mtn., Eth.	82	F7	6.55 N	39.46 E
Batu, Bukit, mtn., Malay.	66	B8	2.16 N	113.43 E
Batu, Kepulauan, is., Indon.	60	F2	0.18 S	98.28 E
Batu-Batu, Indon.	66	F11	4.08 S	119.53 E
Batu Berincang, Gunong, mtn., Malay.	64	J5	4.30 N	101.24 E
Batubetumpang, Indon.	66	E4	2.51 S	106.08 E
Batubrok, Bukit, mtn., Indon.	66	C9	1.05 N	114.22 E
Batu Gajah, Malay.	64	J5	4.28 N	101.02 E
Batukelau, Indon.	66	C9	0.48 N	115.01 E
Batulicin, Indon.	66	E10	3.27 S	115.59 E
Batumi, Geor.	42	E9	41.38 N	41.38 E
Batu Pahat, Malay.	64	L6	1.51 N	102.56 E
Batupanjang, Indon.	66	C2	1.43 N	101.30 E
Batuputih, Indon.	66	C11	1.21 N	118.27 E
Baturaja, Indon.	66	F4	4.07 S	104.09 E
Baturino, Russia	48	C15	57.45 N	85.10 E
Baturino, Russia	183b		55.35 N	37.31 E
Baturité, Braz.	170	C6	4.20 S	38.53 W
Baturotok, Indon.	66	H10	8.42 S	117.10 E
Batusura, Indon.	66	D5	2.02 S	106.06 E
Baturyn, Ukr.	38	B11	51.20 N	32.53 E
Batusangkar, Indon.	66	D2	0.29 S	100.36 E
Batutinggi, Indon.	66	D8	1.52 S	113.18 E
Batz, Île de, i., Fr.	20	F4	48.45 N	4.01 W
Bau, Malay.	66	C7	1.25 N	110.08 E
Baubau, Indon.	60	G7	5.28 S	122.37 E
Bauchi, Nig.	84	G6	10.18 N	9.50 E
Baud, Fr.	20	G6	47.51 N	3.00 W
Bauda, India	70	H10	20.50 N	84.20 E
Baudette, Mn., U.S.	128	C4	48.42 N	94.36 W
Baudó, stm., Col.	168	E3	4.58 N	77.19 W
Baudouin Stadium, p.o.i., D.R.C.	191b		4.20 S	15.20 E
Bauernschaft, Ger.	181		51.34 N	6.33 E
Bauerstown, Pa., U.S.	197b		40.30 N	79.59 W
Baúl, Cerro, mtn., Mex.	154	G8	17.38 N	100.19 W
Bauld, Cape, c., Nf., Can.	111a	i22	51.38 N	55.25 W
Baulkham Hills, Austl.	192a		33.46 S	151.00 E
Bauman Fiord, b., Nu., Can.	108	B8	77.40 N	85.35 W
Baumberg, Ger.	181		51.07 N	6.54 E
Baume-les-Dames, Fr.	20	G15	47.21 N	6.22 E
Baumschulenweg, ngh., Ger.	182a		52.28 N	13.29 E
Baunei, Italy	32	D3	40.01 N	9.39 E
Baures, Bol.	166	B4	13.35 S	63.35 W
Bauru, Braz.	170	L1	22.19 S	49.04 W
Bausenhagen, Ger.	181		51.31 N	7.48 E
Bauska, Lat.	26	D7	56.24 N	24.13 E
Bauta, mun., Cuba	204b		22.59 N	82.33 W
Bautzen, Ger.	24	E10	51.11 N	14.26 E
Bauxite, Ar., U.S.	134	C6	34.33 N	92.31 W
Bavaria see Bayern, state, Ger.	24	H7	49.00 N	11.30 E
Bavarian Alps, mts., Eur.	24	I7	47.30 N	11.00 E
Båven, l., Swe.	16	I14	59.00 N	16.56 E
Bavispe, Mex.	120	F8	30.27 N	108.56 W
Bavispe, stm., Mex.	120	F8	29.32 N	109.14 W
Bawal, Pulau, i., Indon.	66	E6	2.44 S	110.06 E
Bāwāli, India	190b		22.25 N	88.12 E
Bawang, Indon.	66	G6	7.06 S	109.55 E
Bawdwin, Mya.	64	A3	23.07 N	97.14 E
Bawean, Pulau, i., Indon.	66	F8	5.46 S	112.40 E
Bawiti, Egypt	82	B5	28.21 N	28.52 E
Bawlake, Mya.	64	C3	19.11 N	97.21 E
Bawmi, Mya.	62	D2	17.19 N	94.35 E
Baxaya, mtn., Som.	86	B9	11.20 N	49.45 E
Baxenden, Eng., U.K.	180		53.44 N	2.20 W
Baxian, China	58	B7	39.05 N	116.23 E
Baxian, China	62	G9	29.24 N	106.30 E
Baxley, Ga., U.S.	132	E3	31.46 N	82.20 W
Baxter, Ia., U.S.	130	C4	41.49 N	93.09 W
Baxter, Mn., U.S.	128	E4	46.19 N	94.17 W
Baxter, Tn., U.S.	130	H12	36.09 N	85.38 W
Baxter Estates, N.Y., U.S.	194		40.50 N	73.42 W
Baxter Springs, Ks., U.S.	130	G3	37.01 N	94.43 W
Baxter State Park, p.o.i., Me., U.S.	122	D8	46.00 N	68.58 W
Baxterville, Ms., U.S.	134	F9	31.05 N	89.35 W
Bay, Ar., U.S.	134	B8	35.44 N	90.33 W
Bay, Laguna de, l., Phil.	68	C3	14.23 N	121.15 E
Bayamo, Cuba	156	B9	20.22 N	76.38 W
Bayamón, P.R.	158a	b3	18.23 N	66.09 W
Bayan, China	52	B10	46.04 N	127.24 E
Bayan, Indon.	66	H10	8.16 S	116.26 E
Bayāna, India	70	E6	26.54 N	77.17 E
Bayanbayanan, Phil.	187f		14.39 N	121.06 E
Bayandelger, Mong.	50	G10	47.43 N	108.06 E
Bayanga, C.A.R.	86	D3	2.50 N	16.24 E
Bayange, China	58	B2	39.19 N	107.31 E
Bayan Har Shan, mts., China	52	E4	33.47 N	97.54 E
Bayanhongor, Mong.	52	B5	46.10 N	100.41 E
Bayannaobao, China	58	B2	39.44 N	107.40 E
Bayano, Lago, res., Pan.	156	H8	9.12 N	78.43 W
Bayan Obo, China	52	C7	41.59 N	110.07 E
Bayard, Ia., U.S.	130	C3	41.51 N	94.32 W
Bayard, Ne., U.S.	140	F9	41.45 N	103.19 W
Bayard, N.M., U.S.	150	K8	32.45 N	108.07 W
Bayard, W.V., U.S.	124	E6	39.15 N	79.22 W
Bayard Cutting Arboretum State Park, p.o.i., N.Y., U.S.	194		40.45 N	73.10 W
Bayas, stm., Spain	22	G3	42.40 N	2.55 W
Bayat, Indon.	66	E3	2.07 S	103.37 E
Bayawan, Phil.	68	F4	9.22 N	122.48 E
Baybay, Phil.	68	E5	10.40 N	124.49 E
Bayboro, N.C., U.S.	132	A9	35.08 N	76.46 W
Bayburt, Tur.	42	E9	40.15 N	40.13 E
Bayburt, state, Tur.	42	E8	40.15 N	40.00 E
Bay City, Mi., U.S.	126	E6	43.35 N	83.52 W
Bay City, Or., U.S.	146	E3	45.31 N	123.52 W
Bay City, Tx., U.S.	136	F12	28.58 N	95.58 W
Bay Creek, stm., Il., U.S.	130	G9	37.15 N	88.30 W
Bay Creek, stm., Il., U.S.	130	E7	39.19 N	90.46 W
Bay de Verde, Nf., Can.	111a	j23	48.05 N	52.54 W
Baydhabo (Baidoa), Som.	86	D8	3.07 N	43.39 E
Baydrag, stm., Mong.	52	B4	45.37 N	99.15 E
Bayerische Alpen see Bavarian Alps, mts., Eur.	24	I7	47.30 N	11.00 E
Bayern (Bavaria), state, Ger.	24	H7	49.00 N	11.30 E
Bayes, Cap, c., N. Cal.	101d	m15	20.57 S	165.23 E
Bayeux, Braz.	170	D8	7.08 S	34.56 W
Bayeux, Fr.	20	E8	49.16 N	0.42 W
Bay Farm Island, i., Ca., U.S.	200		37.43 N	122.14 W
Bayfield, Co., U.S.	150	F9	37.13 N	107.37 W
Bayfield, Wi., U.S.	128	E8	46.48 N	90.49 W
Bayford, Eng., U.K.	178		51.46 N	0.06 W
Bayındır, Tur.	34	E10	38.13 N	27.39 E
Baykonur see Bajkonur, Kaz.	48	E11	47.50 N	66.03 E
Bay Meadows Race Track, p.o.i., Ca., U.S.	200		37.32 N	122.18 W
Bay Minette, Al., U.S.	134	G11	30.52 N	87.47 W
Baynūnah, reg., U.A.E.	74	I13	23.50 N	52.50 E
Bayo see Baio Grande, Spain	28	A2	43.09 N	8.57 W
Bayombong, Phil.	68	B3	16.29 N	121.08 E
Bayona see Baiona, Spain	28	B2	42.07 N	8.50 W
Bayonne, Fr.	22	F4	43.29 N	1.28 W
Bayonne Bridge, trans., U.S.	194		40.38 N	74.09 W
Bayou Bodcau Reservoir, res., La., U.S.	134	E5	32.48 N	93.26 W
Bayou Cane, La., U.S.	134	H8	29.37 N	90.45 W
Bayou D'Arbonne Lake, res., La., U.S.	134	E6	32.45 N	92.25 W
Bayou La Batre, Al., U.S.	134	G10	30.24 N	88.14 W
Bayovar, Peru	164	E1	5.49 S	81.02 W
Bay Park, N.Y., U.S.	194		40.38 N	73.40 W
Bay Port, Mi., U.S.	126	E6	43.50 N	83.22 W
Bayport, Mn., U.S.	128	F6	45.01 N	92.46 W
Bayramiç, Tur.	34	D9	39.48 N	26.36 E
Bayreuth, Ger.	24	G7	49.56 N	11.34 E
Bay Ridge, ngh., N.Y., U.S.	194		40.37 N	74.02 W
Bay Ridge Channel, strt., N.Y., U.S.	194		40.39 N	74.02 W
Bayrischzell, Ger.	24	I8	47.40 N	12.00 E
Bayrūt (Beirut), Leb.	76	E6	33.53 N	35.29 E
Bays, Lake of, l., On., Can.	126	C10	45.14 N	79.00 W
Bay Saint Louis, Ms., U.S.	134	G9	30.18 N	89.19 W
Bay Shore, N.Y., U.S.	124	D12	40.43 N	73.14 W
Bayside, On., Can.	126	D12	44.07 N	77.27 W
Bayside, Ma., U.S.	201		42.18 N	70.53 W
Bayside, ngh., N.Y., U.S.	194		40.46 N	73.46 W
Bay Springs, Ms., U.S.	134	F9	31.58 N	89.17 W
Bay Springs Lake, res., Ms., U.S.	134	C10	34.35 N	88.17 W
Bayswater, Austl.	192b		37.51 S	145.16 E
Bayswater North, Austl.	192b		37.49 S	145.17 E
Bayt ad-Dīn, Leb.	76	E6	33.41 N	35.34 E
Bayt al-Faqīh, Yemen	72	G5	14.30 N	43.19 E
Bayt Laḩm (Bethlehem), W.B.	76	G6	31.42 N	35.11 E
Baytown, Tx., U.S.	136	E13	29.44 N	94.58 W
Bayunglencir, Indon.	66	E3	2.03 S	103.40 E
Bayview, Austl.	192a		33.40 S	151.18 E
Bayview, ngh., Ca., U.S.	200		37.44 N	122.23 W
Bayyā'īyah al-Kabīrah, Syria	76	C8	35.42 N	37.09 E
Baza, Spain	28	G8	37.29 N	2.46 W
Baza, Sierra de, mts., Spain	28	G8	37.18 N	2.46 W
Bazainville, Fr.	179		48.48 N	1.40 E
Bazaliia, Ukr.	38	D5	49.43 N	26.28 E
Bazarčulan, Kaz.	40	G18	49.04 N	51.56 E
Bazardjuzju, gora see Bazardüzü dağ, mtn., Azer.	42	E12	41.13 N	47.51 E
Bazardüzü dağ, mtn., Azer.	42	E12	41.13 N	47.51 E
Bazargic see Dobrič, Blg.	36	F14	43.34 N	27.49 E
Bazaruto, Ilha do, i., Moz.	90	B12	21.40 S	35.27 E
Bazas, Fr.	22	E5	44.25 N	0.12 W
Bazavluk, stm., Ukr.	38	E13	47.32 N	34.03 E
Bazemont, Fr.	179		48.56 N	1.52 E
Bazhong, China	58	F2	31.50 N	106.45 E
Bazièges, Fr.	22	F7	43.27 N	1.36 E
Bazin, stm., Qc., Can.	122	C2	47.28 N	75.22 W
Bazine, Ks., U.S.	138	C9	38.26 N	99.41 W
Bazkovskaja, Russia	40	G12	49.35 N	41.44 E
Be, stm., Viet.	64	G8	11.06 N	106.57 E
Be, Nosy, i., Madag.	88	C8	13.20 S	48.15 E
Beach, N.D., U.S.	142	H9	46.55 N	104.00 W
Beach Channel, strt., N.Y., U.S.	194		40.35 N	73.50 W
Beach Glen, N.J., U.S.	194		40.56 N	74.29 W
Beach Haven, N.J., U.S.	124	E11	39.33 N	74.14 W
Beach Lake, l., Mi., U.S.	199		42.33 N	83.43 W
Beachport, Austl.	98	K3	37.29 S	140.00 E
Beachville, On., Can.	126	E9	43.05 N	80.50 W
Beachy Head, c., Eng., U.K.	10	K13	50.44 N	0.14 E
Beacon, Austl.	96	F3	30.26 S	117.49 E
Beacon, N.Y., U.S.	124	C12	41.30 N	73.58 W
Beacon Heights, Md., U.S.	202c		38.57 N	76.54 W
Beacon Hill, Austl.	192a		33.45 S	151.15 E
Beacon Hill, Wa., U.S.	146	D4	46.09 N	122.55 W
Beacon Hill, hill, China	189d		22.21 N	114.09 E
Beacon Rock State Park, p.o.i., Wa., U.S.	146	E4	45.38 N	122.03 W
Beaconsfield, Austl.	99a	n13	41.11 S	146.48 E
Beaconsfield, Austl.	192b		38.03 S	145.22 E
Beagle Bay, Austl.	96	C4	16.58 S	122.39 E
Beagle Gulf, b., Austl.	96	B5	12.00 S	130.20 E
Beahcegealháldi, mtn., Nor.	14	C12	69.32 N	21.52 E
Bealanana, Madag.	88	C8	14.33 S	48.44 E
Beale, Cape, c., B.C., Can.	144	H5	48.47 N	125.12 W
Beale Air Force Base, mil., Ca., U.S.	148	D4	39.07 N	121.22 W
Beals Creek, stm., Tx., U.S.	136	B6	32.10 N	100.51 W
Beam, stm., Eng., U.K.	178		51.31 N	0.10 E
Bean, Eng., U.K.	178		51.25 N	0.17 E
Bear, stm., U.S.	118	F10	41.31 N	112.06 W
Bear, stm., Ca., U.S.	148	D4	38.56 N	121.34 W
Bear Bay, b., Nu., Can.	108	B8	75.47 N	87.04 W
Bear Brook, stm., N.J., U.S.	194		41.02 N	74.03 W
Bear Brook State Park, p.o.i., N.H., U.S.	122	G5	43.07 N	71.21 W
Bear Butte, mtn., S.D., U.S.	140	C9	44.27 N	103.26 W
Bear Canyon, val., Ca., U.S.	198		34.14 N	118.07 W
Bear Cove, B.C., Can.	144	F3	50.43 N	127.26 W
Bear Creek, stm., U.S.	134	C11	34.53 N	88.05 W
Bear Creek, stm., U.S.	138	D6	37.45 N	101.23 W
Bear Creek, stm., Al., U.S.	134	D11	33.11 N	88.05 W
Bear Creek, stm., Ca., U.S.	148	F5	37.16 N	120.49 W
Bear Creek, stm., Ca., U.S.	198		34.14 N	117.53 W
Bear Creek, stm., Co., U.S.	138	B3	39.48 N	104.58 W
Bear Creek, stm., Md., U.S.	202b		39.13 N	76.30 W
Bear Creek, stm., N.D., U.S.	140	A15	46.09 N	98.06 W
Bear Creek, stm., Or., U.S.	146	G6	44.06 N	120.46 W
Bear Creek, stm., Or., U.S.	148	A3	42.26 N	122.58 W
Bear Creek, stm., Wy., U.S.	140	F8	41.42 N	104.13 W
Bear Creek, West Fork, stm., Ca., U.S.	198		34.16 N	117.53 W
Bearden, Ar., U.S.	134	D6	33.43 N	92.37 W
Beardmore, On., Can.	128	B11	49.36 N	87.57 W
Beardstown, Il., U.S.	130	E7	40.00 N	90.25 W
Beardy and Okemasis Indian Reserves, ind. res., Sk., Can.	142	B7	52.48 N	106.20 W
Bearfort Mountain, mtn., N.J., U.S.	194		41.09 N	74.23 W
Bear Head Creek, stm., La., U.S.	134	G5	30.18 N	93.31 W
Bear Head Lake State Park, p.o.i., Mn., U.S.	128	D6	47.49 N	92.04 W
Bear-in-the-Lodge Creek, stm., S.D., U.S.	140	D11	43.41 N	101.50 W
Bear Island, i., Ant.	103	C29	74.30 S	110.45 W
Bear Island, i., Ire.	10	J3	51.38 N	9.51 W
Bear Island, i., Va., U.S.	202c		38.59 N	77.14 W
Bear Lake, l., Ab., Can.	144	A11	55.15 N	119.00 W
Bear Lake, l., U.S.	146	H15	42.00 N	111.20 W
Bear Mountain, mtn., Ky., U.S.	124	G1	37.32 N	84.16 W
Bear Mountain, mtn., Or., U.S.	146	G4	43.51 N	122.53 W
Béarn, hist. reg., Fr.	22	F5	43.20 N	0.45 W
Béarn, hist. reg., Fr.	28	A10	43.20 N	0.45 W
Bear Pond, l., N.J., U.S.	194		40.58 N	74.40 W
Bear River, N.S., Can.	122	F11	44.34 N	65.38 W
Bear River Range, mts., U.S.	118	G10	41.29 N	111.41 W
Bear Run, stm., Pa., U.S.	197b		40.33 N	80.04 W
Bears Paw Mountains, mts., Mt., U.S.	146	B17	48.13 N	109.30 W
Bearstead, Eng., U.K.	178		51.16 N	0.35 E
Bear Swamp, stm., N.J., U.S.	203		39.54 N	74.47 W
Bear Swamp, sw., N.J., U.S.	203		39.53 N	74.45 W
Bear Swamp Brook, stm., N.J., U.S.	194		41.04 N	74.13 W
Bear Swamp Lake, l., N.J., U.S.	194		41.06 N	74.13 W
Beartooth Mountains, mts., U.S.	140	B3	45.00 N	109.30 W
Beartooth Pass, p., Wy., U.S.	140	C3	44.58 N	109.29 W
Bear Town, Ms., U.S.	134	F8	31.13 N	90.27 W
Beās, stm., India	70	C6	31.10 N	74.58 E
Beasain, Spain	28	A8	43.03 N	2.10 W
Beas de Segura, Spain	28	F8	38.15 N	2.53 W
Beata, Cabo, c., Dom. Rep.	156	D12	17.37 N	71.24 W
Beata, Isla, i., Dom. Rep.	156	D12	17.35 N	71.31 W
Beato, ngh., Port.	184c		38.44 N	9.06 W
Beaton, B.C., Can.	144	F13	50.43 N	117.43 W
Beatrice, Al., U.S.	134	F11	31.44 N	87.12 W
Beatrice, Ne., U.S.	138	A12	40.15 N	96.45 W
Beatrice, Cape, c., Austl.	96	B7	14.17 S	136.56 E
Beattie, Ks., U.S.	128	L2	39.51 N	96.25 W
Beatton, stm., B.C., Can.	110	D6	56.05 N	120.22 W
Beatton River, B.C., Can.	110	D6	57.23 N	121.25 W
Beatty, Nv., U.S.	148	G9	36.54 N	116.45 W
Beattyville, Qc., Can.	114	B12	48.52 N	77.08 W
Beattyville, Ky., U.S.	124	G2	37.34 N	83.43 W
Beaucaire, Fr.	22	F10	43.48 N	4.38 E
Beauce, reg., Fr.	20	F10	48.21 N	1.51 E
Beauceville, Qc., Can.	122	D6	46.12 N	70.46 W
Beauchamp, Fr.	179		49.01 N	2.12 E
Beauchamp Roding, Eng., U.K.	178		51.46 N	0.18 E
Beauchêne, Lac, l., Qc., Can.	126	B11	46.38 N	78.55 W
Beauchêne Island, i., Falk. Is.	166	J5	52.53 S	59.12 W
Beaudesert, Austl.	98	F9	27.59 S	152.59 E
Beaufort, Malay.	66	A9	5.21 N	115.43 E
Beaufort, N.C., U.S.	132	B9	34.43 N	76.39 W
Beaufort, S.C., U.S.	132	D5	32.24 N	80.43 W
Beaufort Castle see Qal'at ash-Shaqīf, hist., Leb.	76	E6	33.19 N	35.32 E
Beaufort Island, i., China	189d		22.11 N	114.15 E
Beaufort Marine Corps Air Station, mil., S.C., U.S.	132	D5	32.30 N	80.44 W
Beaufort Sea, s., N.A.	109	B12	73.00 N	140.00 W
Beaufort West, S. Afr.	90	H6	32.21 S	22.34 E
Beaugency, Fr.	20	G10	47.46 N	1.37 E
Beauharnois, Qc., Can.	126	C16	45.18 N	73.52 W
Beauharnois, Barrage de, dam., Qc., Can.	193a		45.19 N	73.55 W
Beaujolais, hist. reg., Fr.	22	C10	46.13 N	4.19 E
Beauly, Scot., U.K.	10	D8	57.28 N	4.29 W
Beauly, stm., Scot., U.K.	10	D8	57.28 N	4.28 W
Beaumaris, Austl.	192b		37.59 S	145.02 E
Beaumaris Bay, b., Austl.	192b		38.00 S	145.03 E
Beaumont, Fr.	20	E7	49.40 N	1.50 W

Name	Page	Map Ref.	Latitude	Longitude
Beaumont, N.Z.	102	G3	45.49 S	169.32 E
Beaumont, Ca., U.S.	148	J8	33.56 N	116.58 W
Beaumont, Ms., U.S.	134	F9	31.10 N	88.55 W
Beaumont, Tx., U.S.	136	D13	30.04 N	94.07 W
Beaumont Hill, hill, Austl.	98	H5	31.32 S	145.12 E
Beaumont-sur-Sarthe, Fr.	20	F9	48.13 N	0.07 E
Beaune, Fr.	20	G13	47.01 N	4.49 E
Beauport, Qc., Can.	122	D5	46.52 N	71.10 W
Beaupré, Qc., Can.	122	C6	47.02 N	70.53 W
Beaurepaire, Fr.	22	D11	45.19 N	5.03 E
Beausejour, Mb., Can.	142	D17	50.03 N	96.31 W
Beauséjour, Guad.	159c	h6	16.18 N	61.04 W
Beauvais, Fr.	20	E11	49.25 N	2.05 E
Beauvais, Fr.	179		48.32 N	2.03 E
Beauvais Creek, stm., Mt., U.S.	140	B4	45.29 N	107.44 W
Beauville, Fr.	22	E6	44.17 N	0.52 E
Beauvoir, Fr.	179		48.39 N	2.52 E
Beauvoir-sur-Mer, Fr.	20	H6	46.54 N	2.02 W
Beaver, Ak., U.S.	109	C10	66.22 N	147.22 W
Beaver, Ok., U.S.	138	E8	36.49 N	100.31 W
Beaver, Pa., U.S.	124	D5	40.41 N	80.17 W
Beaver, Ut., U.S.	150	E4	38.16 N	112.38 W
Beaver, W.V., U.S.	124	G4	37.44 N	81.09 W
Beaver, stm., Can.	110	C6	59.42 N	124.19 W
Beaver, stm., Can.	110	D9	55.26 N	107.47 W
Beaver, stm., U.S.	138	E9	36.35 N	99.30 W
Beaver, stm., N.Y., U.S.	126	E14	43.53 N	75.30 W
Beaver, stm., Pa., U.S.	126	H9	40.41 N	80.17 W
Beaver, stm., Ut., U.S.	150	E3	39.09 N	112.56 W
Beaver Brook, stm., Ma., U.S.	201		42.03 N	70.58 W
Beaver Brook, stm., Ma., U.S.	201		42.36 N	71.21 W
Beaver Brook, stm., Ma., U.S.	201		42.23 N	71.14 W
Beaver Brook, stm., N.J., U.S.	194		40.54 N	74.30 W
Beaver Brook, stm., N.J., U.S.	194		40.58 N	74.35 W
Beaver City, Ne., U.S.	138	A9	40.08 N	99.48 W
Beaver Creek, stm., On., Can.	193b		43.51 N	79.20 W
Beaver Creek, stm., On., Can.	202a		42.58 N	79.01 W
Beaver Creek, stm., U.S.	138	B8	40.07 N	99.28 W
Beaver Creek, stm., U.S.	140	D8	43.25 N	103.59 W
Beaver Creek, stm., U.S.	142	G9	47.19 N	103.39 W
Beaver Creek, stm., Co., U.S.	138	C3	38.22 N	104.58 W
Beaver Creek, stm., Co., U.S.	140	G9	40.20 N	103.33 W
Beaver Creek, stm., Mo., U.S.	130	H5	36.38 N	93.02 W
Beaver Creek, stm., Mt., U.S.	142	F6	48.25 N	107.17 W
Beaver Creek, stm., Ne., U.S.	140	G14	40.46 N	97.18 W
Beaver Creek, stm., Ne., U.S.	140	F14	41.26 N	97.43 W
Beaver Creek, stm., N.J., U.S.	203		39.45 N	75.23 W
Beaver Creek, stm., N.D., U.S.	140	A12	46.14 N	100.33 W
Beaver Creek, stm., Ok., U.S.	138	G10	33.59 N	97.57 W
Beaver Creek, stm., Pa., U.S.	203		40.00 N	75.42 W
Beaver Creek, stm., Tx., U.S.	138	H9	33.53 N	98.49 W
Beaver Creek, stm., Wy., U.S.	140	E4	42.57 N	108.27 W
Beaver Crossing, Ne., U.S.	140	G15	40.46 N	97.16 W
Beaver Dam, Ky., U.S.	130	G11	37.24 N	86.52 W
Beaver Dam, Wi., U.S.	128	H9	43.27 N	88.49 W
Beaverdam Brook, stm., N.J., U.S.	194		40.26 N	74.28 W
Beaverdam Creek, stm., U.S.	202c		38.55 N	76.57 W
Beaverdam Creek, stm., Md., U.S.	202c		39.01 N	76.54 W
Beaverdam Creek, stm., N.J., U.S.	203		39.56 N	74.45 W
Beaver Dams Creek, stm., On., Can.	202a		43.06 N	79.11 W
Beaver Dam Wash, stm., U.S.	150	F3	36.53 N	113.55 W
Beaverdell, B.C., Can.	144	G11	49.26 N	119.05 W
Beaver Falls, Pa., U.S.	124	D5	40.45 N	80.19 W
Beaverhead, stm., Mt., U.S.	146	E14	45.31 N	112.21 W
Beaverhead Mountains, mts., U.S.	146	F13	44.57 N	113.26 W
Beaverhill Lake, l., Ab., Can.	144	C18	53.27 N	112.32 W
Beaverhouse Lake, l., On., Can.	128	C6	48.32 N	92.06 W
Beaver Island, i., Mi., U.S.	126	C4	45.39 N	85.31 W
Beaver Lake, l., Ab., Can.	144	B19	54.43 N	111.50 W
Beaver Lake, l., N.J., U.S.	194		41.05 N	74.33 W
Beaver Lake, l., N.Y., U.S.	194		40.53 N	73.34 W
Beaver Lake, res., Ar., U.S.	130	H4	36.20 N	93.55 W
Beaver Lake Indian Reserve, ind. res., Ab., Can.	144	B18	54.39 N	111.53 W
Beaverlodge, Ab., Can.	144	A11	55.12 N	119.26 W
Beaver Run, stm., N.J., U.S.	194		41.11 N	74.36 W
Beaver Run, stm., Pa., U.S.	197b		40.34 N	79.33 W
Beaver Run, stm., Pa., U.S.	203		40.10 N	75.40 W
Beavers Bend State Park, p.o.i., Ok., U.S.	134	C4	34.08 N	94.42 W
Beaver Swamp Brook, stm., N.Y., U.S.	194		40.57 N	73.43 W
Beaverton, On., Can.	126	D10	44.25 N	79.08 W
Beaverton, Mi., U.S.	126	E5	43.52 N	84.29 W
Beaverton, Or., U.S.	146	E4	45.29 N	122.49 W
Beāwar, India	70	E5	26.06 N	74.19 E
Beazley, Arg.	172	F4	33.45 S	66.38 W
Bebedouro, Braz.	170	K1	20.56 S	48.28 W
Bebek, ngh., Tur.	185b		41.04 N	29.02 E
Bebeli, Tur.	76	B6	36.39 N	35.29 E
Beberibe, Braz.	170	C6	4.11 S	38.08 W
Becal, Mex.	156	B2	20.27 N	90.02 W
Bécancour, stm., Qc., Can.	122	D5	46.22 N	72.27 W
Beccar, ngh., Arg.	206		34.28 S	58.31 W
Beccles, Eng., U.K.	10	I14	52.27 N	1.34 E
Becconsall, Eng., U.K.	180		53.42 N	2.50 W
Bečej, Yugo.	36	D6	45.37 N	20.02 E
Beceni, Rom.	36	D13	45.22 N	26.48 E
Becerra Creek, stm., Tx., U.S.	136	G8	27.57 N	98.58 W
Becerreá, Spain	28	B3	42.51 N	7.09 W
Bečevinka, Russia	18	H24	59.44 N	37.40 E
Béchar, Alg.	84	C4	31.37 N	2.13 W
Becharof Lake, l., Ak., U.S.	109	E8	58.00 N	156.30 W
Bechet, Rom.	36	F10	43.46 N	23.58 E
Bechevin Bay, b., Ak., U.S.	109	E7	54.57 N	163.22 W
Bechuanaland, hist. reg., S. Afr.	90	E5	27.17 S	21.08 E
Bechuanaland see Botswana, ctry., Afr.	88	E3	22.00 S	24.00 E
Bechyně, Czech Rep.	24	G10	49.18 N	14.29 E
Becke, Ger.	181		51.24 N	7.47 E
Beckenham, ngh., Eng., U.K.	178		51.24 N	0.02 W
Beckhausen, ngh., Ger.	181		51.34 N	7.02 E
Beck Lake, l., Il., U.S.	196		42.04 N	87.52 W
Beckley, W.V., U.S.	124	G4	37.47 N	81.10 W
Beck Pond, l., Ma., U.S.	201		42.36 N	70.49 W
Beckum, Ger.	24	E4	51.45 N	8.02 E
Beckville, Tx., U.S.	136	B13	32.15 N	94.27 W
Becky Peak, mtn., Nv., U.S.	150	D2	39.58 N	114.36 W
Beclean, Rom.	36	B11	47.11 N	24.11 E
Bédarieux, Fr.	22	F9	43.37 N	3.09 E
Beddington, ngh., Eng., U.K.	178		51.22 N	0.08 W
Beddouza, Ras, c., Mor.	84	C3	32.32 N	9.16 W
Bedelē, Eth.	82	F7	8.34 N	36.20 E
Beden Brook, stm., N.J., U.S.	194		40.25 N	74.38 W
Bedeque Bay, b., P.E., Can.	122	D12	46.22 N	63.53 W
Bedford, Qc., Can.	126	C16	45.07 N	72.59 W
Bedford, S. Afr.	90	H8	32.41 S	26.05 E
Bedford, Eng., U.K.	10	I12	52.08 N	0.29 W
Bedford, In., U.S.	130	F11	38.51 N	86.29 W
Bedford, Ia., U.S.	130	D3	40.40 N	94.43 W
Bedford, Ky., U.S.	130	F12	38.35 N	85.18 W
Bedford, Pa., U.S.	124	D7	40.01 N	78.30 W
Bedford, Tx., U.S.	136	B10	32.50 N	97.08 W
Bedford Heights, Oh., U.S.	197a		41.25 N	81.31 W
Bedford Park, Il., U.S.	196		41.46 N	87.49 W
Bedford Park, ngh., N.Y., U.S.	194		40.52 N	73.53 W
Bedford-Stuyvesant, ngh., N.Y., U.S.	194		40.41 N	73.55 W
Bedi, India	70	G3	22.29 N	70.02 E
Bedias, Tx., U.S.	136	D12	30.46 N	95.57 W
Bedinggong, Indon.	66	E4	2.41 S	106.10 E
Bedminster, N.J., U.S.	194		40.40 N	74.38 W
Bedmond, Eng., U.K.	178		51.43 N	0.25 W
Bedoba, Russia	48	C17	58.47 N	97.13 E
Bedok, Sing.	189c		1.19 N	103.57 E
Bedok Reservoir, res., Sing.	189c		1.21 N	103.56 E
Bedourie, Austl.	98	E2	24.20 S	139.27 E
Bedworth, Eng., U.K.	10	I11	52.28 N	1.29 W
Beebe, Ar., U.S.	134	B7	35.04 N	91.53 W
Beech, stm., Tn., U.S.	134	B10	35.37 N	88.02 W
Beechal Creek, stm., Austl.	98	F5	27.24 S	145.12 E
Beech Brook, stm., N.J., U.S.	194		41.08 N	74.18 W
Beech Creek, Ky., U.S.	130	G10	37.10 N	87.03 W
Beecher, Il., U.S.	130	C10	41.20 N	87.37 W
Beech Fork, stm., Ky., U.S.	130	G12	37.45 N	85.42 W
Beech Grove, In., U.S.	130	E11	39.42 N	86.05 W
Beechview, ngh., Pa., U.S.	197b		40.25 N	80.02 W
Beechwood, Ma., U.S.	201		42.12 N	70.49 W
Beechworth, Austl.	98	K6	36.22 S	146.40 E
Beechy, Sk., Can.	142	D6	50.52 N	107.22 W
Beeck, ngh., Ger.	181		51.29 N	6.44 E
Beeckerwerth, ngh., Ger.	181		51.29 N	6.41 E
Beecroft, Austl.	192a		33.45 S	151.04 E
Beecroft Head, c., Austl.	98	J8	35.00 S	150.50 E
Beef Island, i., Br. Vir. Is.	158b	e8	18.26 N	64.31 W
Beeleigh Abbey, rel., Eng., U.K.	178		51.44 N	0.40 E
Beemer, Ne., U.S.	128	J2	41.55 N	96.49 W
Beenleigh, Austl.	98	F9	27.43 S	153.12 E
Bee Ridge, Fl., U.S.	132	I3	27.16 N	82.29 W
Beersheba see Be'ér Sheva', Isr.	76	G6	30.47 N	34.35 E
Beersheba Springs, Tn., U.S.	134	B13	35.27 N	85.38 W
Be'ér Sheva' (Beersheba), Isr.	76	G6	30.47 N	34.35 E
Beeskow, Ger.	24	D10	52.10 N	14.15 E
Beestekraal, S. Afr.	90	D8	25.22 S	27.35 E
Beeville, Tx., U.S.	136	F10	28.24 N	97.44 W
Befale, D.R.C.	86	D4	0.23 N	20.48 E
Befandriana Avaratra, Madag.	88	E7	15.15 S	48.32 E
Befu, ngh., Japan	188		34.40 N	135.02 E
Bega, Austl.	98	K7	36.40 S	149.50 E
Bega, stm., Eur.	36	D8	45.12 N	20.19 E
Begamganj, India	70	G7	23.35 N	78.20 E
Begampur, ngh., India	190a		28.44 N	77.04 E
Begej see Bega, stm., Eur.	36	D8	45.12 N	20.19 E
Beggs, Ok., U.S.	134	B2	35.45 N	96.04 W
Begna, stm., Nor.	16	G8	60.10 N	10.16 E
Begovat see Bekabad, Uzb.	48	F11	40.12 N	69.10 E
Begunicy, Russia	26	A12	59.35 N	29.19 E
Begur, Cap de, c., Spain	28	C14	41.58 N	3.13 E
Begusarai, India	70	F11	25.25 N	86.08 E
Behbahān, Iran	74	E12	30.35 N	50.14 E
Béhoust, Fr.	179		48.50 N	1.43 E
Behrāmpur, India	190a		28.38 N	77.24 E
Behshahr, Iran	74	B13	36.41 N	53.32 E
Bei, stm., China	58	J5	23.09 N	112.48 E
Bei'an, China	52	B10	48.14 N	126.31 E
Beibei, China	58	G2	29.49 N	106.26 E
Beibu Wan see Tonkin, Gulf of, b., Asia	52	G6	20.00 N	108.00 E
Beicheng, China	52	G5	24.21 N	102.32 E
Beida see Al-Bayḍā', Libya	82	A4	32.45 N	21.36 E
Beiersdorf, Ger.	182a		52.42 N	13.47 E
Beigi, Eth.	82	F6	9.23 N	34.37 E
Beihai, China	58	K3	21.27 N	109.05 E
Bei Hai, l., China	189a		39.56 N	116.22 E
Beijing (Peking), China	58	B7	39.55 N	116.22 E
Beijing (Peking), China	189a		39.55 N	116.25 E
Beijing, state, China	58	B6	40.15 N	116.30 E
Beijing Gymnasium, bldg., China	189a		39.53 N	116.25 E
Beijing National Library, bldg., China	189a		39.56 N	116.22 E
Beijing Railway Station, trans., China	189a		39.54 N	116.26 E
Beijing University, educ., China	189a		39.59 N	116.18 E
Beijing Zoo, p.o.i., China	189a		39.56 N	116.19 E
Beili, China	58	L3	19.10 N	108.43 E
Beiliu, China	58	J4	22.43 N	110.21 E
Beinamar, Chad	82	F3	8.39 N	15.25 E
Beipa, Pap. N. Gui.	101a	b4	8.30 S	146.35 E
Beipan, stm., China	58	I1	25.09 N	105.57 E
Beipiao, China	52	C9	41.48 N	120.46 E
Beipo, China	58	K3	21.14 N	109.53 E
Beira, Moz.	90	A12	19.49 S	34.50 E
Beira, hist. reg., Port.	28	E3	40.15 N	8.25 W
Beira Alta see Viseu, state, Port.	28	D3	40.45 N	7.45 W
Beiru, stm., China	58	D5	33.42 N	113.35 E
Beirut see Bayrūt, Leb.	76	E6	33.53 N	35.29 E
Beiseker, Ab., Can.	144	E17	51.23 N	113.30 W
Beishan, China	58	I3	24.28 N	108.38 E
Bei Shan, mts., China	52	C4	41.30 N	96.00 E
Beitbridge, Zimb.	88	E5	22.12 S	30.00 E
Beitstadfjorden, b., Nor.	16	D8	63.50 N	11.04 E
Beiuş, Rom.	36	C9	46.40 N	22.23 E
Beixin'an, China	189a		39.55 N	116.08 E
Beizhen, China	52	C9	41.35 N	121.47 E
Beja, Braz.	170	A1	1.34 S	48.45 W
Beja, Port.	28	G3	38.00 N	7.51 W
Béja, Tun.	84	B6	36.43 N	9.11 E
Beja, state, Port.	28	G3	37.50 N	8.00 W
Bejaïa, Alg.	84	B6	36.45 N	5.04 E
Béjar, Spain	28	D5	40.23 N	5.46 W
Bejhi, stm., Pak.	70	D2	29.58 N	68.47 E
Bejneu, Kaz.	48	E9	45.25 N	55.08 E
Bejsug, stm., Russia	40	H11	46.02 N	38.35 E
Bejsugskij liman, b., Russia	38	G17	46.07 N	38.25 E
Bejucal, mun., Cuba	204b		22.56 N	82.23 W
Bejuco, Pan.	156	H8	8.36 N	79.53 W
Bekaa Valley see Al-Biqā', val., Leb.	76	D7	34.00 N	36.07 E
Bekabad, Uzb.	48	F11	40.12 N	69.10 E
Bekasi, stm., Indon.	187e		6.10 S	107.02 E
Békásmegyer, ngh., Hung.	182c		47.36 N	19.03 E
Bekdaš, Turkmen.	72	A7	41.32 N	52.34 E
Bekdaš, mys, c., Turkmen.	42	E15	41.32 N	52.34 E
Békés, Hung.	36	C8	46.46 N	21.08 E
Békés, state, Hung.	36	C7	46.46 N	21.08 E
Békéscsaba, Hung.	36	C7	46.40 N	21.05 E
Bekilli, Tur.	34	E12	38.12 N	29.26 E
Bekily, Madag.	88	E8	24.13 S	45.18 E
Bekkersdal, S. Afr.	191d		26.18 S	27.42 E
Bekmurad, gora, hill, Turkmen.	42	E16	41.04 N	54.52 E
Bekodoka, Madag.	88	D7	16.58 S	45.06 E
Bekopaka, Madag.	88	D7	19.09 S	44.47 E
Bela, India	70	F9	25.55 N	82.00 E
Bela, Pak.	62	C2	26.13 N	66.17 E
Belaazërsk, Bela.	26	H8	52.28 N	25.11 E
Bela Crkva, Yugo.	36	E8	44.54 N	21.26 E
Bela Cruz, Braz.	170	B5	3.03 S	40.11 W
Belaga, Malay.	66	B8	2.42 N	113.46 E
Bel-Air, Fr.	179		48.37 N	2.10 E
Bel Air, Md., U.S.	124	E9	39.31 N	76.21 W
Bel Air, Va., U.S.	202c		38.52 N	77.10 W
Bel Air, ngh., Ca., U.S.	198		34.05 N	118.27 W
Bélair, Île, i., Qc., Can.	193a		45.37 N	73.48 W
Belaja, Russia	40	F9	51.03 N	35.43 E
Belaja, stm., Russia	40	D19	55.47 N	54.03 E
Belaja, stm., Russia	42	C8	45.05 N	39.28 E
Belaja Berëzka, Russia	26	H16	52.23 N	33.29 E
Belaja Cerkov' see Bila Tserkva, Ukr.	38	D9	49.47 N	30.08 E
Belaja Gora, Russia	26	B14	58.32 N	31.48 E
Belaja Holunica, Russia	40	B17	58.52 N	50.50 E
Belaja Kalitva, Russia	40	G12	48.10 N	40.46 E
Belalcázar, Spain	28	F5	38.34 N	5.09 W
Belambanganumpu, Indon.	66	F4	4.53 S	105.02 E
Belampalli, India	69	B4	19.02 N	79.29 E
Bel'aninovo, Russia	183b		55.57 N	37.39 E
Bela Palanka, Yugo.	36	F9	43.13 N	22.18 E
Belapurpāda, India	190c		19.01 N	73.02 E
Belarus, ctry., Eur.	40	E5	53.50 N	28.00 E
Belarus' see Belarus, ctry., Eur.	40	E5	53.50 N	28.00 E
Belaruskaja hrada, mts., Bela.	26	G10	53.40 N	27.00 E
Belarus Station, trans., Russia	183b		55.47 N	37.35 E
Belas, Port.	184c		38.47 N	9.16 W
Belau see Palau, ctry., Oc.	60	D9	5.00 N	137.00 E
Bela Vista, Braz.	166	D5	22.06 S	56.31 W
Bela Vista, Moz.	90	E11	26.19 S	32.40 E
Bela Vista, ngh., Braz.	205b		23.33 S	46.38 W
Belavuša, Bela.	38	B5	51.56 N	26.55 E
Belawan, Indon.	66	B1	3.47 N	98.40 E
Belayan, stm., Indon.	66	C10	0.13 S	116.35 E
Belchatów, Pol.	24	E15	51.22 N	19.21 E
Belcher, La., U.S.	136	B14	32.44 N	93.50 W
Belcherāgh, Afg.	72	B10	35.51 N	65.14 E
Belcher Channel, strt., Nu., Can.	108	B6	77.15 N	94.04 W
Belcher Creek, stm., N.J., U.S.	194		41.08 N	74.23 W
Belcher Islands, is., Nu., Can.	110	D14	56.20 N	79.30 W
Belchite, Spain	28	C10	41.18 N	0.44 W
Belcourt, N.D., U.S.	142	F14	48.48 N	99.46 W
Bel'cy see Bălţi, Mol.	38	F6	47.45 N	27.55 E
Belding, Mi., U.S.	130	A12	43.05 N	85.13 W
Bel'djažki, Russia	26	H18	52.39 N	35.42 E
Belebej, Russia	40	D18	54.06 N	54.07 E
Belebelka, Russia	26	C13	57.34 N	30.55 E
Beledweyne, Som.	86	D8	4.43 N	45.11 E
Belém, Braz.	170	A1	1.26 S	48.28 W
Belém, Moz.	88	C6	14.11 S	35.58 E
Belém, ngh., Port.	184c		38.42 N	9.12 W
Belém, Torre de, hist., Port.	184c		38.42 N	9.13 W
Belém de São Francisco, Braz.	170	E6	8.46 S	38.58 W
Belén, Arg.	172	C4	27.39 S	67.02 W
Belén, Col.	168	D5	6.00 N	72.55 W
Belén, Nic.	156	G5	11.29 N	85.53 W
Belén, Para.	166	D5	23.28 S	57.15 W
Belen, Tur.	76	B7	36.30 N	36.11 E
Belen, N.M., U.S.	138	G2	34.39 N	106.45 W
Belén, Ur.	172	E9	30.47 S	57.47 W
Belén, stm., Arg.	172	C4	27.59 S	66.51 W
Belene, Blg.	36	F12	43.38 N	25.08 E
Belenihino, Russia	38	C15	50.56 N	36.37 E
Belènzinho, ngh., Braz.	205b		23.32 S	46.35 W
Belep, Îles, is., N. Cal.	101d	I14	19.45 S	163.40 E
Belesar, Embalse de, res., Spain	28	B3	42.44 N	7.39 W
Belet Uen see Beledweyne, Som.	86	D8	4.43 N	45.11 E
Belëv, Russia	26	G19	53.47 N	36.09 E
Belews Lake, res., N.C., U.S.	124	H5	36.17 N	80.03 W
Belfast, S. Afr.	90	D9	25.42 S	30.03 E
Belfast, N. Ire., U.K.	10	G6	54.35 N	5.55 W
Belfast, Me., U.S.	122	F7	44.25 N	69.00 W
Belfast Lough, b., N. Ire., U.K.	10	G7	54.41 N	5.48 W
Belfield, Austl.	192a		33.54 S	151.05 E
Belfield, N.D., U.S.	142	H10	46.53 N	103.11 W
Belford, Eng., U.K.	10	F11	55.36 N	1.49 W
Belford, N.J., U.S.	194		40.25 N	74.05 W
Belfort, Fr.	20	G15	47.38 N	6.50 E
Belfort, state, Fr.	24	I2	47.38 N	6.55 E
Belfry, Ky., U.S.	124	G3	37.38 N	82.16 W
Belfry, Mt., U.S.	140	B3	45.07 N	109.00 W
Belgard see Białogard, Pol.	24	B12	54.00 N	15.59 E
Belgaum, India	69	D2	15.51 N	74.30 E
België see Belgium, ctry., Eur.	20	D13	50.50 N	4.00 E
Belgique see Belgium, ctry., Eur.	20	D13	50.50 N	4.00 E
Belgium, ctry., Eur.	20	D13	50.50 N	4.00 E
Belgorod, Russia	40	F10	50.36 N	36.35 E
Belgorodskaja oblast', co., Russia	40	F10	50.45 N	37.30 E
Belgrade, Mn., U.S.	128	F3	45.26 N	95.00 W
Belgrade, Mt., U.S.	146	E15	45.47 N	111.11 W
Belgrade, Ne., U.S.	140	F14	41.28 N	98.04 W
Belgrade see Beograd, Yugo.	36	E7	44.49 N	20.27 E
Belgrad Ormanı, for., Tur.	185b		41.10 N	28.55 E
Belgrano, ngh., Arg.	206		34.34 S	58.28 W
Belgrano II, sci., Ant.	103	C36	77.45 S	38.11 W
Belgrave, Austl.	192b		37.55 S	145.21 E
Belhaven, N.C., U.S.	132	A9	35.32 N	76.37 W
Belhus Park, p.o.i., Eng., U.K.	178		51.31 N	0.17 E
Belica, Russia	38	B14	51.07 N	35.34 E
Belice, stm., Italy	32	G7	37.34 N	12.51 E
Belick, Bela.	26	H13	52.55 N	30.27 E
Beliliou, i., Palau	60	D9	7.00 N	134.14 E
Beli Manastir, Cro.	30	E15	45.46 N	18.36 E
Belin, Fr.	22	E5	44.30 N	0.47 W
Belin-Béliet see Belin, Fr.	22	E5	44.30 N	0.47 W
Belington, W.V., U.S.	124	E5	39.01 N	79.56 W
Belinskij, Russia	40	E13	52.57 N	43.25 E
Belinyu, Indon.	66	D4	1.39 S	105.45 E
Belitung, i., Indon.	66	E5	2.50 S	107.55 E
Belize, ctry., N.A.	156	D3	17.15 N	88.45 W
Belize, stm., Belize	156	D3	17.30 N	88.10 W
Belize City, Belize	156	D3	17.30 N	88.11 W
Belize Inlet, b., B.C., Can.	144	E3	51.07 N	127.14 W
Beljaevka, Russia	40	F20	51.27 N	56.25 E
Beljaevka, Russia	40	C19	57.28 N	55.28 E
Beljaevo, Russia	26	E14	55.28 N	31.07 E
Belkovskij, ostrov see Bel'kovskij, ostrov, i., Russia	50	A16	75.32 N	135.44 E
Bel'kovskij, ostrov, i., Russia	50	A16	75.32 N	135.44 E
Bell, Austl.	192b		37.45 S	145.00 E
Bell, Ca., U.S.	198		33.58 N	118.11 W
Bell, stm., Qc., Can.	114	B12	49.50 N	77.40 W
Bella Bella, B.C., Can.	144	D2	52.08 N	128.06 W
Bellac, Fr.	22	C7	46.07 N	1.01 E
Bella Coola, B.C., Can.	144	D4	52.21 N	126.46 W
Bella Coola, stm., B.C., Can.	144	D4	52.22 N	126.46 W
Bell Acres, Pa., U.S.	197b		40.36 N	80.10 W
Bellagio, Italy	30	E6	45.58 N	9.14 E
Bellair, Fl., U.S.	132	F4	30.10 N	81.44 W
Bellaire, Mi., U.S.	126	C4	44.58 N	85.12 W
Bellaire, Oh., U.S.	124	D5	40.00 N	80.45 W
Bellaire, Tx., U.S.	136	E12	29.42 N	95.28 W
Bellamy, Al., U.S.	134	E10	32.26 N	88.08 W
Bellaria, Italy	30	F9	44.09 N	12.27 E
Bellary, India	69	D3	15.08 N	76.55 E
Bellas Artes, Museo de, bldg., Ven.	204c		10.30 N	66.53 W
Bellas Artes, Palacio de, bldg., Mex.	204a		19.26 N	99.08 W
Bellata, Austl.	98	G7	29.55 S	149.47 E
Bella Unión, Ur.	172	E9	30.15 S	57.35 W
Bella Vista, Arg.	172	C5	27.02 S	65.18 W
Bella Vista, Arg.	172	D8	28.30 S	59.02 W
Bellavista, Chile	204e		33.31 S	70.37 W
Bellavista, Peru	164	E2	7.03 S	76.35 W
Bellavista, Peru	204d		12.04 S	77.08 W
Bellbrook, Austl.	98	H9	30.49 S	152.31 E
Bell Creek, stm., Ca., U.S.	198		34.12 N	118.36 W
Belle, Mo., U.S.	130	F6	38.17 N	91.43 W
Belle, W.V., U.S.	124	F4	38.13 N	81.32 W
Belle, stm., Mi., U.S.	130	B15	42.44 N	82.28 W
Belledonne, Chaîne de, mts., Fr.	22	D11	45.16 N	6.06 E
Bellefontaine, Fr.	179		49.06 N	2.28 E
Bellefontaine, Mart.	159c	k6	14.40 N	61.09 W
Bellefontaine, Oh., U.S.	124	D2	40.21 N	83.44 W
Bellefonte, Md., U.S.	202c		38.47 N	76.52 W
Bellefonte, Pa., U.S.	124	D8	40.54 N	77.46 W
Belle Fourche, S.D., U.S.	140	C9	44.40 N	103.51 W
Belle Fourche, stm., U.S.	140	C10	44.26 N	102.18 W
Belle Fourche Reservoir, res., S.D., U.S.	140	C9	44.44 N	103.42 W
Bellegarde-sur-Valserine, Fr.	22	C11	46.06 N	5.49 E
Belle Glade, Fl., U.S.	132	J5	26.41 N	80.40 W
Belle Haven, Va., U.S.	202c		38.47 N	77.04 W
Belle Hôtesse, mtn., Guad.	159c	h5	16.16 N	61.46 W
Belle-Île, i., Fr.	20	G5	47.20 N	3.10 W
Belle Isle, i., Nf., Can.	111a	i22	51.56 N	55.21 W
Belle Isle, i., Mi., U.S.	199		42.20 N	82.58 W
Belle Isle, Strait of, strt., Nf., Can.	111a	i22	51.36 N	56.27 W
Belle Isle Park, p.o.i., Mi., U.S.	199		42.20 N	82.59 W
Bellemoor, De., U.S.	203		39.43 N	75.35 W
Bellenden Ker National Park, p.o.i., Austl.	98	A5	17.20 S	145.50 E
Belle-Plaine, Sk., Can.	142	D8	50.24 N	105.09 W
Belle Plaine, Ia., U.S.	130	C5	41.53 N	92.17 W
Belle Plaine, Ks., U.S.	138	D11	37.23 N	97.16 W
Belle Plaine, Mn., U.S.	128	G5	44.37 N	93.46 W
Bellerose, N.Y., U.S.	194		40.44 N	73.43 W
Bellerose, ngh., N.Y., U.S.	194		40.45 N	73.43 W
Bellerose Terrace, N.Y., U.S.	194		40.43 N	73.43 W
Belle Terre, N.Y., U.S.	194		40.58 N	73.04 W
Belle Tete, c., St. K./N.	159a	c2	17.22 N	62.52 W
Belleview, Fl., U.S.	134	G11	30.28 N	87.18 W
Belleville, On., Can.	126	D12	44.09 N	77.22 W
Belleville, Il., U.S.	130	F8	38.30 N	89.59 W
Belleville, Ks., U.S.	138	B11	39.49 N	97.37 W
Belleville, Pa., U.S.	124	D8	40.35 N	77.43 W
Belleville, Wi., U.S.	130	B8	42.51 N	89.31 W
Belleville Lake, l., Mi., U.S.	199		42.12 N	83.29 W
Belleville-sur-Saône, Fr.	22	C10	46.06 N	4.45 E
Bellevue, Ab., Can.	144	G16	49.33 N	114.19 W
Bellevue, Id., U.S.	146	G12	43.28 N	114.16 W
Bellevue, Ia., U.S.	130	B7	42.15 N	90.25 W
Bellevue, Mi., U.S.	130	B12	42.26 N	85.00 W
Bellevue, Ne., U.S.	130	C2	41.08 N	95.55 W
Bellevue, Oh., U.S.	124	C3	41.16 N	82.49 W
Bellevue, Tx., U.S.	138	H10	33.38 N	98.00 W
Bellevue, Wa., U.S.	146	C4	47.36 N	122.11 W
Bellevue, ngh., S. Afr.	191d		26.11 S	28.05 E
Belle Vue Zoological Gardens, p.o.i., Eng., U.K.	180		53.28 N	2.11 W
Belley, Fr.	22	D11	45.45 N	5.41 E
Bellingdon, Eng., U.K.	178		51.44 N	0.38 W
Bellingen, Austl.	98	H9	30.27 S	152.54 E
Bellingham, Eng., U.K.	10	F10	55.08 N	2.16 W
Bellingham, Mn., U.S.	128	F2	45.08 N	96.16 W
Bellingham, Wa., U.S.	146	B4	48.45 N	122.28 W
Bellingshausen, sci., Ant.	103	B35	62.12 S	58.58 W
Bellingshausen Sea, s., Ant.	176	O5	71.00 S	85.00 W
Bellinzona, Switz.	30	D6	46.10 N	9.00 E
Bell Lake, l., On., Can.	128	B7	49.48 N	90.58 W
Bellmead, Tx., U.S.	136	C10	31.35 N	97.06 W
Bellmore, N.Y., U.S.	194		40.40 N	73.31 W
Bello, Col.	168	D4	6.19 N	75.34 W
Bello, Cuba	204b		23.07 N	82.24 W
Bellot Strait, strt., Nu., Can.	110	A12	72.00 N	94.40 W
Bellows Falls, Vt., U.S.	122	G4	43.08 N	72.26 W
Belloy-en-France, Fr.	179		49.05 N	2.22 E
Bell Peninsula, pen., Nu., Can.	110	C14	63.50 N	82.00 W
Bell Point, Pa., U.S.	197b		40.33 N	79.33 W
Bells, Tn., U.S.	134	B9	35.43 N	89.04 W
Bells, Tx., U.S.	134	D2	33.37 N	96.25 W
Bells Corners, On., Can.	126	C14	45.19 N	75.50 W
Bells Lake, l., N.J., U.S.	203		39.44 N	75.02 W
Bells Lake, l., N.J., U.S.	203		39.45 N	75.04 W
Belluno, Italy	30	D9	46.08 N	12.13 E
Bell Ville, Arg.	172	F6	32.38 S	62.41 W
Bellville, S. Afr.	90	H4	33.53 S	18.36 E
Bellville, Tx., U.S.	136	E11	29.57 N	96.15 W
Bellwood, Il., U.S.	196		41.52 N	87.52 W
Bellwood, Ne., U.S.	140	F15	41.19 N	97.13 W
Bellwood, Pa., U.S.	124	D7	40.35 N	78.19 W
Belly, stm., N.A.	144	G17	49.46 N	113.03 W
Bellyk, Russia	48	D16	54.31 N	91.16 E
Belmar, Md., U.S.	202b		39.21 N	76.32 W
Bélmez, Spain	28	F5	38.16 N	5.11 W
Belmond, Ia., U.S.	130	B4	42.51 N	93.37 W
Belmont, Mb., Can.	142	E14	49.24 N	99.27 W
Belmont, N.S., Can.	122	E13	45.24 N	63.23 W
Belmont, S. Afr.	90	F7	29.24 S	24.21 E
Belmont, Eng., U.K.	180		53.38 N	2.30 W
Belmont, Ma., U.S.	201		42.23 N	71.10 W
Belmont, Ms., U.S.	134	C10	34.30 N	88.12 W
Belmont, N.H., U.S.	122	G5	43.26 N	71.28 W
Belmont, Wi., U.S.	130	B7	42.44 N	90.20 W
Belmonte, Braz.	170	H6	15.53 S	38.52 W
Belmonte, Port.	28	D3	40.21 N	7.21 W
Belmonte, Spain	28	A4	43.17 N	6.13 W
Belmonte, Spain	28	E8	39.33 N	2.42 W
Belmont Harbor, b., Il., U.S.	196		41.57 N	87.38 W
Belmont Lake, l., N.Y., U.S.	194		40.44 N	73.20 W
Belmont Lake State Park, p.o.i., N.Y., U.S.	194		40.43 N	73.20 W
Belmont Park Race Track, p.o.i., N.Y., U.S.	194		40.43 N	73.43 W
Belmont Reservoir, res., Eng., U.K.	180		53.39 N	2.30 W
Belmont Slough, stm., Ca., U.S.	200		37.33 N	122.14 W
Belmopan, Belize	156	D3	17.14 N	88.46 W
Belmore, Austl.	192a		33.55 S	151.05 E
Belmullet, Ire.	10	G3	54.13 N	9.59 W
Belmuri, India	190b		22.57 N	88.09 E
Beloe, Russia	26	B22	58.23 N	39.24 E
Beloe, ozero, l., Russia	18	G24	60.11 N	37.37 E
Beloeil, Ruisseau, stm., Qc., Can.	193a		45.39 N	73.12 W
Beloe More, Russia	14	E23	67.05 N	32.12 E
Beloe more (White Sea), s., Russia	14	G27	65.36 N	37.52 E
Beloe Ozero, Russia	18	C26	64.16 N	39.48 E
Belogore, Russia	38	C18	50.30 N	40.04 E
Belogorka, Kaz.	40	F18	50.42 N	53.27 E
Belogorsk, Russia	50	F14	50.54 N	128.29 E
Belogradčik, Blg.	36	F9	43.38 N	22.40 E
Belo Horizonte, Braz.	170	J3	19.55 S	43.56 W
Beloit, Ks., U.S.	138	B10	39.27 N	98.06 W
Beloit, Wi., U.S.	130	B8	42.30 N	89.02 W
Belo Jardim, Braz.	170	E7	8.20 S	36.26 W
Belomestnaja, Russia	26	H20	52.24 N	37.36 E
Belomorsk, Russia	18	C21	64.32 N	34.45 E
Belomorsko-Baltijskij kanal, can., Russia	18	D22	62.48 N	34.48 E
Belorado, Spain	28	B7	42.25 N	3.10 W
Belorečensk see Beloretsjensk, Russia	42	C8	44.46 N	39.52 E
Beloreck, Russia	48	D9	53.58 N	58.24 E
Belören, Tur.	34	F15	37.12 N	32.33 E
Belören, Tur.	76	A8	37.39 N	37.34 E
Beloretsjensk, Russia	42	C8	44.46 N	39.52 E
Belorussia see Belarus, ctry., Eur.	40	E5	53.50 N	28.00 E
Belorussija see Belarus, ctry., Eur.	40	E5	53.50 N	28.00 E
Belorusskaja grjada see Belaruskaja hrada, mts., Bela.	26	G10	53.40 N	27.00 E
Belosčele, Russia	12	D22	64.55 N	46.52 E
Belo sur Mer, Madag.	88	E7	20.44 S	44.01 E
Belot, Lac, l., N.T., Can.	110	B5	66.55 N	126.18 W
Belo Tsiribihina, Madag.	88	D7	19.42 S	44.32 E
Belousovo, Russia	26	E19	55.05 N	36.40 E
Belo Vale, Braz.	170	K3	20.25 S	44.01 W
Belovo, Russia	48	D15	54.25 N	86.19 E
Belozërsk, Russia	18	G24	60.02 N	37.48 E
Belpāda, India	190c		19.02 N	73.03 E
Belpre, Oh., U.S.	124	E4	39.17 N	81.34 W
Belrose, Austl.	192a		33.44 S	151.13 E
Belson Run, stm., Pa., U.S.	197b		40.12 N	79.37 W
Belt, Mt., U.S.	146	C16	47.23 N	110.57 W
Beltana, Austl.	98	H2	30.48 S	138.24 E
Belt Creek, stm., Mt., U.S.	146	C16	47.35 N	111.03 W
Belted Range, mts., Nv., U.S.	148	F9	37.23 N	116.07 W
Belthorn, Eng., U.K.	180		53.43 N	2.26 W
Belton, Mo., U.S.	130	F3	38.48 N	94.32 W
Belton, S.C., U.S.	132	B3	34.31 N	82.29 W
Belton, Tx., U.S.	136	C10	31.03 N	97.27 W
Belton Lake, res., Tx., U.S.	136	C10	31.06 N	97.30 W
Beltrán, Arg.	172	C5	27.51 S	64.05 W
Belts see Bălţi, Mol.	38	F6	47.45 N	27.55 E
Beltsville, Md., U.S.	202c		39.02 N	76.54 W
Belturbet, Ire.	10	G5	54.06 N	7.26 W
Beltway Plaza, shp. cen., Md., U.S.	202c		39.00 N	76.54 W
Beluha, gora see Belukha, Mount, mtn., Asia	48	E15	49.50 N	86.29 E
Belukha, Mount, mtn., Asia	48	E15	49.50 N	86.29 E
Belūr, India	69	E2	13.09 N	75.51 E
Belur, India	190b		22.38 N	88.18 E
Beluran, Malay.	68	H1	5.52 N	117.33 E
Belur Math, rel., India	190b		22.38 N	88.22 E
Beluše, Russia	12	C22	66.53 N	47.33 E
Belvedere, Va., U.S.	202c		38.50 N	77.10 W
Belvedere, ngh., Eng., U.K.	178		51.29 N	0.09 E
Belvedere, bldg., Aus.	182b		48.11 N	16.23 E
Belvedere Marittimo, Italy	32	E9	39.37 N	15.52 E
Belvidere, Il., U.S.	130	B9	42.15 N	88.49 W
Belvidere, N.J., U.S.	124	D10	40.49 N	75.04 W
Belview, Mn., U.S.	128	G3	44.36 N	95.19 W
Belvis, Spain	184a		40.33 N	3.33 E
Belvís de la Jara, Spain	28	E6	39.45 N	4.57 W
Belvoir see Kokhav HaYarden, hist., Isr.	76	F6	32.36 N	35.31 E
Belyando, stm., Austl.	98	D6	21.38 S	146.50 E
Belye Berega, Russia	26	G17	53.12 N	34.41 E
Belye Stolby, Russia	26	E20	55.19 N	37.51 E
Belyj, Russia	26	E15	55.50 N	32.57 E
Belyj Gorodok, Russia	26	C20	56.58 N	37.30 E
Belyj Jar, Russia	48	C15	58.26 N	85.03 E
Belyj Kalodez', Russia	38	D18	50.01 N	38.39 E
Belz, Ukr.	38	C3	50.23 N	24.01 E
Bełżec, Pol.	24	F19	50.23 N	23.26 E

Name	Page	Map Ref.	Latitude	Longitude
Belzig, Ger.	24	D8	52.08 N	12.35 E
Belzoni, Ms., U.S.	134	D8	33.11 N	90.29 W
Bełżyce, Pol.	24	E18	51.11 N	22.18 E
Bembèrèkè, Benin	84	G5	10.13 N	2.39 E
Bembézar, stm., Spain	28	F5	37.45 N	5.12 W
Bembezi see Mbembesi, Zimb.	90	A9	19.59 S	28.55 E
Bement, Il., U.S.	130	E9	39.55 N	88.34 W
Bemidji, Mn., U.S.	128	D4	47.28 N	94.53 W
Bemidji, Lake, l., Mn., U.S.	112	B9	47.29 N	94.51 W
Bemis, Tn., U.S.	134	B10	35.34 N	88.49 W
Ben, Kinh, can., Viet.	187c		10.43 N	106.37 E
Benāb, Iran	74	B9	37.19 N	46.03 E
Benaco see Garda, Lago di, l., Italy	30	E7	45.40 N	10.41 E
Bena-Dibele, D.R.C.	86	E4	4.05 S	22.49 E
Benagerie, Austl.	98	H3	31.25 S	140.24 E
Benalla, Austl.	98	K6	36.33 S	145.58 E
Benamejí, Spain	28	G6	37.15 N	4.31 W
Benares see Vārānasi, India	70	F9	25.20 N	82.59 E
Ben Arous, Tun.	32	H4	36.45 N	10.13 E
Benavarri, Spain	28	B11	42.06 N	0.28 E
Benavente, Port.	28	E2	38.59 N	8.47 W
Benavente, Spain	28	B5	42.00 N	5.40 W
Benavides, Tx., U.S.	136	G9	27.35 N	98.24 W
Ben Avon, Pa., U.S.	197b		40.31 N	80.05 W
Ben Avon Heights, Pa., U.S.	197b		40.31 N	80.04 W
Benbecula, i., Scot., U.K.	10	D5	57.26 N	7.22 W
Ben Bolt, Tx., U.S.	136	G9	27.39 N	98.04 W
Benbonyathe Hill, mtn., Austl.	98	H2	30.24 S	139.11 E
Benbrook Lake, res., Tx., U.S.	136	B10	32.37 N	97.28 W
Ben Cat, Viet.	64	G8	11.08 N	106.35 E
Ben Cat, Rach, stm., Viet.	187c		10.50 N	106.42 E
Bencha, Khao Phanom, mtn., Thai.	64	H4	8.17 N	98.56 E
Ben-Chicao, Col de, p., Alg.	28	H13	36.11 N	2.44 E
Bencubbin, Austl.	96	F3	30.48 S	117.51 E
Bend, Or., U.S.	146	F5	44.03 N	121.18 W
Bendemeer, Austl.	98	H8	30.53 S	151.09 E
Bender see Tighina, Mol.	38	G8	46.50 N	29.28 E
Bender Cassim see Boosaaso, Som.	86	B9	11.16 N	49.10 E
Bendigo, Austl.	98	K5	36.45 S	144.16 E
Bēne, Lat.	26	D6	56.28 N	23.03 E
Beneditinos, Braz.	170	C4	5.27 S	42.22 W
Benedito Leite, Braz.	170	D3	7.13 S	44.34 W
Benepú, Rada, anch., Chile	1001	f29	27.10 S	109.23 W
Benešov, Czech Rep.	24	G10	49.47 N	14.43 E
Bénestroff, Fr.	24	H2	48.53 N	6.46 E
Benevento, Italy	32	C8	41.07 N	14.46 E
Benfeld, Fr.	24	H3	48.22 N	7.36 E
Benfica, ngh., Braz.	205a		22.53 S	43.15 W
Benfica, ngh., Port.	184c		38.45 N	9.12 W
Benfica, Estádio, p.o.i., Port.	184c		38.45 N	9.11 W
Bèng, stm., Laos	64	B5	19.53 N	101.08 E
Bengal, Bay of, b., Asia	46	H12	15.00 N	90.00 E
Bengara, Indon.	66	B10	3.08 N	117.11 E
Bengasi see Banghāzī, Libya	82	A3	32.06 N	20.04 E
Bengbu, China	58	E7	32.56 N	117.21 E
Benghazi see Banghāzī, Libya	82	A3	32.06 N	20.04 E
Bengkalis, Indon.	66	C3	1.28 N	102.06 E
Bengkalis, Pulau, i., Indon.	66	C3	1.30 N	102.15 E
Bengkayang, Indon.	66	C6	0.49 N	109.28 E
Bengkulu, Indon.	66	E3	3.48 S	102.16 E
Bengkulu, state, Indon.	66	E3	4.00 S	102.30 E
Bengough, Sk., Can.	142	E8	49.24 N	105.07 W
Bengtsfors, Swe.	16	H10	59.02 N	12.14 E
Benguela, Ang.	88	C1	12.34 S	13.24 E
Benguerua, Ilha, i., Moz.	90	B12	21.53 S	35.26 E
Bengut, Cap, c., Alg.	28	H14	36.55 N	3.53 E
Benha, Egypt	76	H2	30.27 N	31.11 E
Ben Hai, Viet.	64	D8	17.04 N	107.02 E
Beni, D.R.C.	86	D5	0.29 N	29.28 E
Beni, stm., Bol.	166	B3	10.59 S	66.07 W
Béni Abbas, Alg.	84	C4	30.07 N	2.09 W
Beni 'Adi el-Bahariya, Egypt	76	K1	27.14 N	30.55 E
Beni Ahmad, Egypt	76	J1	28.03 N	30.46 E
Benicarló, Spain	28	D11	40.25 N	0.25 E
Benicia Capitol State Historic Park, p.o.i., Ca., U.S.	200		38.03 N	122.09 W
Benicia State Recreation Area, p.o.i., Ca., U.S.	200		38.05 N	122.13 W
Benidorm, Spain	28	F10	38.32 N	0.08 W
Beni Mazâr, Egypt	76	J1	28.29 N	30.47 E
Beni Muhammadîyat, Egypt	76	K2	27.17 N	31.05 E
Bénin see Benin, ctry., Afr.	84	G5	9.30 N	2.15 E
Benin, ctry., Afr.	84	G5	9.30 N	2.15 E
Benin, Bight of, b., Afr.	84	I5	5.30 N	3.00 E
Bénin, Golfe de see Benin, Bight of, b., Afr.	84	I5	5.30 N	3.00 E
Benin City, Nig.	84	H6	6.20 N	5.37 E
Benisa see Benissa, Spain	28	F11	38.42 N	0.02 E
Benissa, Spain	28	F11	38.42 N	0.02 E
Beni Suef, Egypt	82	I2	29.04 N	31.05 E
Benito, Mb., Can.	142	C12	51.54 N	101.32 W
Benito Juárez, Arg.	172	H8	37.40 S	59.48 W
Benito Juárez, Aeropuerto Internacional, arpt., Mex.	204a		19.26 N	99.04 W
Benito Juárez, Presa, res., Mex.	154	G10	16.29 N	95.28 W
Benjakoni, Bela.	26	F8	54.14 N	25.21 E
Benjamin, Tx., U.S.	138	H9	33.35 N	99.47 W
Benjamín, Isla, i., Chile	166	H2	44.40 S	74.08 W
Benjamín Aceval, Para.	172	B9	25.00 S	57.34 W
Benjamin Constant, Braz.	164	D3	4.28 S	70.01 W
Benjamin Franklin Bridge, trans., U.S.	203		39.57 N	75.08 W
Benjamín Hill, Mex.	120	F7	30.10 N	111.06 W
Benkelman, Ne., U.S.	138	A7	40.03 N	101.32 W
Benkovac, Cro.	30	F12	44.02 N	15.36 E
Benld, Il., U.S.	130	E8	39.06 N	89.48 W
Ben Lomond, Ca., U.S.	148	F3	37.04 N	122.05 W
Ben Lomond National Park, p.o.i., Austl.	99a	n13	41.36 S	147.41 E
Benndale, Ms., U.S.	134	G10	30.52 N	88.48 W
Bennet, Ne., U.S.	130	D1	40.40 N	96.30 W
Bennetta, ostrov, i., Russia	50	A18	76.40 N	149.05 E
Bennett Island see Bennetta, ostrov, i., Russia	50	A18	76.40 N	149.05 E
Bennettsville, S.C., U.S.	132	B6	34.37 N	79.41 W
Bennettswood, Austl.	192b		37.51 S	145.07 E
Benninghofen, ngh., Ger.	181		51.29 N	7.31 E
Bennington, Ks., U.S.	138	B11	39.01 N	97.35 W
Bennington, Vt., U.S.	124	B12	42.53 N	73.12 W
Benoit, Ms., U.S.	134	D7	33.39 N	91.01 W
Benoni, S. Afr.	90	E9	26.11 S	28.19 E
Benoni, state, S. Afr.	191d		26.08 S	28.22 E
Benoni-Suid, S. Afr.	191d		26.13 S	28.18 E
Bénoué see Benue, stm., Afr.	84	H6	7.47 N	6.45 E
Benover, Eng., U.K.	178		51.13 N	0.26 E
Benque Viejo Del Carmen, Belize	156	D3	17.05 N	89.08 W
Benrad, ngh., Ger.	181		51.20 N	6.30 E
Benrath, Schloss, hist., Ger.	181		51.10 N	6.52 E
Bensalem, Pa., U.S.	203		40.04 N	74.56 W
Ben Sekka, Rass, c., Tun.	32	G3	37.20 N	9.45 E
Bensenville, Il., U.S.	196		41.57 N	87.56 W
Bensheim, Ger.	24	G4	49.40 N	8.37 E
Benson, Az., U.S.	150	L6	31.57 N	110.17 W
Benson, Mn., U.S.	128	F3	45.18 N	95.36 W
Benson, N.C., U.S.	132	A7	35.22 N	78.33 W
Bensonhurst, ngh., N.Y., U.S.	194		40.35 N	73.59 W
Bens Run, stm., Md., U.S.	202b		39.19 N	76.48 W
Benteng, Indon.	66	G12	6.10 S	120.26 E
Ben Thuy, Viet.	64	C7	18.38 N	105.43 E
Bentinck Island, i., Austl.	96	C7	17.04 S	139.30 E
Bentinck Island, i., Mya.	64	G3	11.45 N	98.03 E
Bentiu, Sudan	82	F6	9.10 N	29.45 E
Bentleigh, Austl.	192b		37.55 S	145.02 E
Bentley, Ab., Can.	144	D16	52.28 N	114.04 W
Bentley College, educ., Ma., U.S.	201		42.23 N	71.13 W
Bentleyville, Oh., U.S.	197a		41.25 N	81.26 W
Bento Gonçalves, Braz.	172	D12	29.10 S	51.30 W
Benton, Ar., U.S.	134	C6	34.34 N	92.36 W
Benton, Il., U.S.	130	F9	37.59 N	88.55 W
Benton, Ky., U.S.	130	H9	36.51 N	88.20 W
Benton, La., U.S.	136	B14	32.42 N	93.44 W
Benton, Ms., U.S.	134	E8	32.49 N	90.15 W
Benton, Mo., U.S.	130	G8	37.05 N	89.34 W
Benton, Tn., U.S.	134	B14	35.10 N	84.39 W
Benton, Wi., U.S.	130	B7	42.34 N	90.22 W
Benton City, Wa., U.S.	146	D7	46.15 N	119.29 W
Benton Harbor, Mi., U.S.	130	B11	42.07 N	86.26 W
Bentonia, Ms., U.S.	134	E8	32.39 N	90.22 W
Benton Lake, l., Mt., U.S.	146	C15	47.40 N	111.20 W
Bentonville, Ar., U.S.	130	H3	36.22 N	94.12 W
Ben Tre, Viet.	64	G8	10.14 N	106.22 E
Bent's Old Fort National Historic Site, p.o.i., Co., U.S.	138	C5	38.05 N	103.28 W
Bentung, Malay.	64	K5	3.32 N	101.55 E
Benua, Pulau, i., Indon.	66	C5	0.57 N	107.27 E
Benue, stm., Afr.	84	H6	7.47 N	6.45 E
Benum, Gunong, mtn., Malay.	64	K6	3.49 N	102.05 E
Ben Wheeler, Tx., U.S.	136	B12	32.27 N	95.41 W
Benxi, China	52	C9	41.18 N	123.45 E
Beograd (Belgrade), Yugo.	36	E7	44.49 N	20.27 E
Beohāri, India	70	F8	24.02 N	81.22 E
Beonta, India	190b		22.31 N	88.31 E
Béoumi, C. Iv.	84	H3	7.40 N	5.34 W
Beowawe, Nv., U.S.	148	C9	40.35 N	116.28 W
Beppu, Japan	56	F4	33.16 N	131.29 E
Beqa, i., Fiji	101e	q18	18.23 S	178.08 E
Bequia, i., St. Vin.	159e	o11	13.01 N	61.13 W
Bequimão, Braz.	170	B3	2.26 S	44.47 W
Bera, Bngl.	70	F12	24.03 N	89.39 E
Berābāria, India	190b		22.52 N	88.34 E
Beraberi, India	190b		22.46 N	88.27 E
Berāberi, India	190b		22.51 N	88.12 E
Beraketa, Madag.	88	E8	24.10 S	45.40 E
Berat, Alb.	32	D13	40.42 N	19.57 E
Berati see Berat, Alb.	32	D13	40.42 N	19.57 E
Berau, stm., Indon.	66	B10	2.10 N	117.41 E
Berau, Teluk, b., Indon.	60	F9	2.30 S	132.30 E
Berazategui, state, Arg.	206		34.50 S	58.10 W
Berazino, Bela.	26	G11	53.50 N	28.59 E
Berazino, Bela.	26	F11	54.54 N	28.12 E
Berbera, Som.	86	B9	10.26 N	45.00 E
Berbérati, C.A.R.	86	D3	4.14 N	15.47 E
Berchtesgaden, Ger.	24	I8	47.38 N	13.00 E
Berchum, ngh., Ger.	181		51.23 N	7.32 E
Berck, Fr.	20	D10	50.24 N	1.34 E
Berclair, Tx., U.S.	136	F10	28.31 N	97.35 W
Berdians'k, Ukr.	38	G15	46.44 N	36.48 E
Berdians'ka kosa, spit, Ukr.	38	G15	46.39 N	36.47 E
Berdians'ka zatoka, b., Ukr.	38	G15	46.40 N	36.30 E
Berdigestjah, Russia	50	D14	62.06 N	126.41 E
Berdjansk see Berdians'k, Ukr.	38	G15	46.44 N	36.48 E
Berdsk, Russia	48	D14	54.45 N	83.04 E
Berdychiv, Ukr.	38	D7	49.53 N	28.36 E
Berea, Ky., U.S.	124	G1	37.33 N	84.18 W
Berea, Oh., U.S.	124	C4	41.22 N	81.51 W
Berea, S.C., U.S.	132	B3	34.53 N	82.26 W
Berehomet, Ukr.	38	E4	48.12 N	25.21 E
Berehove, Ukr.	36	A9	48.12 N	22.38 E
Bereka, stm., Ukr.	38	D15	49.10 N	37.00 E
Berekua, Dom.	159c	j6	15.14 N	61.19 W
Berekum, Ghana	84	H4	7.27 N	2.34 W
Berendeevo, Russia	26	D21	56.35 N	39.00 E
Berens, stm., Can.	142	B17	52.25 N	97.17 W
Berens Island, i., Mb., Can.	142	B16	52.19 N	97.18 W
Berens River, Mb., Can.	142	B16	52.22 N	97.01 W
Beresford, N.B., Can.	122	C11	47.42 N	65.42 W
Beresford, S.D., U.S.	128	H2	43.04 N	96.46 W
Berestechko, Ukr.	38	C4	50.21 N	25.07 E
Bereşti, Rom.	36	C14	46.06 N	27.53 E
Berettyó (Barcău), stm., Eur.	36	B8	46.59 N	21.07 E
Berettyóújfalu, Hung.	36	B8	47.13 N	21.32 E
Berëza see Bjaroza, Bela.	26	H7	52.32 N	24.59 E
Berezajka, Russia	26	C16	57.59 N	33.55 E
Berezan', Ukr.	38	C10	50.18 N	31.29 E
Berezans'kyi lyman, est., Ukr.	38	G10	46.43 N	31.30 E
Berezdiv, Ukr.	38	C6	50.28 N	27.07 E
Bereze, Ukr.	38	B12	51.44 N	33.52 E
Berezhany, Ukr.	38	D3	49.26 N	24.57 E
Berezhany, Ukr.	38	B5	51.26 N	26.27 E
Berezivka, Ukr.	38	H12	45.34 N	33.20 E
Berezivka, Ukr.	38	F9	47.12 N	30.55 E
Berezivka, Ukr.	38	F11	47.48 N	32.27 E
Berezna, Ukr.	38	B10	51.34 N	31.47 E
Berezne, Ukr.	38	B5	51.00 N	26.46 E
Bereznehuvate, Ukr.	38	F11	47.18 N	32.52 E
Berezniaky, Ukr.	38	D10	49.08 N	31.57 E
Berezniaky, Ukr.	38	D12	49.51 N	33.00 E
Bereznik, Russia	12	E20	62.51 N	42.42 E
Berezniki, Russia	48	C9	59.24 N	56.45 E
Berezova Rudka, Ukr.	38	C11	50.19 N	32.14 E
Berezove, Ukr.	38	B6	51.36 N	28.12 E
Berëzovka, Russia	40	C20	57.36 N	57.19 E
Berëzovka, Russia	48	C14	59.22 N	82.48 E
Berëzovka, Russia	183a		59.56 N	30.49 E
Berëzovo, Russia	48	B10	63.55 N	65.03 E
Berëzovskij, Russia	48	C15	55.35 N	86.12 E
Berëzovskij Rjadok, Russia	26	B17	58.05 N	34.27 E
Berezyne, Ukr.	38	G8	46.14 N	29.12 E
Berg, Nor.	16	B10	65.22 N	12.11 E
Berga, Spain	28	B12	42.06 N	1.51 E
Bergama, Tur.	34	D10	39.07 N	27.10 E
Bergamasker Alpen see Orobie, Alpi, mts., Italy	30	D6	46.00 N	10.00 E
Bergamasque Alps see Orobie, Alpi, mts., Italy	30	D6	46.00 N	10.00 E
Bergamo, Italy	30	E6	45.41 N	9.40 E
Bergan Point, c., N.Y., U.S.	194		40.40 N	73.20 W
Bergantín, Ven.	168	C9	10.00 N	64.21 W
Bergara, Spain	22	F3	43.07 N	2.24 W
Bergbau Museum, bldg., Ger.	181		51.29 N	7.13 E
Bergby, Swe.	16	G14	60.55 N	17.02 E
Berge, Ger.	181		51.21 N	7.22 E
Bergei, hill, Ger.	181		51.13 N	7.46 E
Bergen see Mons, Bel.	20	D12	50.27 N	3.56 E
Bergen, Ger.	24	D5	52.48 N	9.58 E
Bergen, Nor.	16	G3	60.22 N	5.20 E
Bergen, N.Y., U.S.	124	A7	43.04 N	77.56 W
Bergen auf Rügen, Ger.	24	B9	54.25 N	13.26 E
Bergen Basin, b., N.Y., U.S.	194		40.39 N	73.49 W
Bergen Mall, shp. cen., N.J., U.S.	194		40.55 N	74.04 W
Bergen op Zoom, Neth.	20	C13	51.30 N	4.17 E
Bergerac, Fr.	22	E6	44.51 N	0.29 E
Bergerhof, Ger.	181		51.12 N	7.21 E
Berghausen, Ger.	181		51.18 N	7.17 E
Berghausen, Ger.	181		51.07 N	6.55 E
Berghofen, ngh., Ger.	181		51.29 N	7.32 E
Bergholtz Creek, stm., N.Y., U.S.	202a		43.05 N	78.57 W
Bergisch Gladbach, Ger.	24	F3	50.59 N	7.05 E
Bergkvara, Swe.	16	K14	56.23 N	16.05 E
Bergland, Mi., U.S.	128	E9	46.34 N	89.37 W
Bergö, i., Fin.	18	E8	62.59 N	21.09 E
Bergoo, W.V., U.S.	124	F5	38.28 N	80.21 W
Bergsjö, Swe.	16	F14	61.58 N	17.03 E
Bergslagen, hist. reg., Swe.	16	H13	59.58 N	15.20 E
Berguent, Mor.	84	C4	34.00 N	2.01 W
Bergville, S. Afr.	90	F9	28.43 S	29.21 E
Berhala, Selat, strt., Indon.	66	D4	0.48 S	104.25 E
Beringa, ostrov, i., Russia	50	F22	54.54 N	166.24 E
Bering Glacier, ice, Ak., U.S.	109	D11	60.15 N	143.30 W
Beringin, Indon.	66	E4	3.41 S	104.19 E
Beringovo more see Bering Sea, s.	44	D22	60.00 N	175.00 W
Beringov proliv see Bering Strait, strt.	50	C27	65.30 N	169.00 W
Beringovskij, Russia	50	D24	63.03 N	179.21 E
Bering Sea, s.	44	D22	60.00 N	175.00 W
Bering Strait, strt.	50	C27	65.30 N	169.00 W
Berisso, state, Arg.	206		34.55 S	57.53 W
Berja, Spain	28	H8	36.51 N	2.57 W
Berkåk, Nor.	16	E7	62.49 N	9.57 E
Berkakit, Russia	50	E14	56.34 N	124.47 E
Berkane, Mor.	84	C4	34.55 N	2.19 W
Berkel, stm., Eur.	20	B15	52.08 N	6.11 E
Berkeley, Ca., U.S.	148	F3	37.52 N	122.16 W
Berkeley, Il., U.S.	196		41.53 N	87.54 W
Berkeley Hills, Pa., U.S.	197b		40.32 N	80.00 W
Berkeley Hills, hills, Ca., U.S.	200		37.54 N	122.16 W
Berkeley Springs, W.V., U.S.	124	E7	39.36 N	78.14 W
Berkley, Mi., U.S.	199		42.30 N	83.11 W
Berkner Island, i., Ant.	103	C35	79.30 S	49.30 W
Berkshire, co., Eng., U.K.	178		51.29 N	0.37 W
Berkshire Hills, hills, Ma., U.S.	124	B12	42.20 N	73.10 W
Berland, stm., Ab., Can.	144	B13	53.59 N	116.51 W
Berlanga de Duero, Spain	28	C8	41.28 N	2.51 W
Berlenga, i., Port.	28	E1	39.25 N	9.30 W
Berlengas, stm., Braz.	170	C4	5.39 S	42.18 W
Berlevåg, Nor.	14	B20	70.51 N	29.06 E
Berlin, Ger.	24	D9	52.30 N	13.25 E
Berlin, Ger.	182a		52.31 N	13.24 E
Berlin, Md., U.S.	124	F10	38.19 N	75.12 W
Berlin, N.H., U.S.	122	F5	44.28 N	71.10 W
Berlin, N.J., U.S.	124	E11	39.47 N	74.55 W
Berlin, Pa., U.S.	124	E7	39.54 N	78.56 W
Berlin, Wi., U.S.	128	H10	43.58 N	88.56 W
Berliner Brücke, trans., Ger.	181		51.27 N	6.47 E
Berlinguet Inlet, b., Nu., Can.	110	A14	71.10 N	85.35 W
Berlin-Hauptbahnhof, trans., Ger.	182a		52.30 N	13.26 E
Berlin-Ichthyosaur State Park, p.o.i., Nv., U.S.	148	E8	38.51 N	117.35 W
Berlin Lake, res., Oh., U.S.	124	C4	41.00 N	81.00 W
Berlin Park, p.o.i., N.J., U.S.	203		39.47 N	74.57 W
Bermagui, Austl.	98	K8	36.25 S	150.03 E
Bermejillo, Mex.	154	C7	25.53 N	103.36 W
Bermejito, stm., Arg.	172	B7	24.57 S	61.13 W
Bermejo, Arg.	172	E4	31.36 S	67.38 W
Bermejo, stm., Arg.	172	E4	32.16 S	67.22 W
Bermejo, stm., S.A.	172	C8	26.52 S	58.22 W
Bermejo, Paso del, p., S.A.	172	F2	32.49 S	70.04 W
Bermen, Lac, l., Qc., Can.	110	E17	53.37 N	68.48 W
Bermeo, Spain	28	A8	43.25 N	2.43 W
Bermillo de Sayago, Spain	28	C4	41.22 N	6.06 W
Bermondsey, ngh., Eng., U.K.	178		51.30 N	0.04 W
Bermuda, dep., N.A.	158e	k16	32.20 N	64.45 W
Bermuda, is., Ber.	106	F16	32.21 N	64.45 W
Bern (Berne), Switz.	30	C4	46.57 N	7.26 E
Bernabéu, Estadio, p.o.i., Spain	184a		40.27 N	3.41 W
Bernalda, Italy	32	D10	40.23 N	16.40 E
Bernalillo, N.M., U.S.	138	F2	35.18 N	106.33 W
Bernardo O'Higgins, Parque, p.o.i., Chile	204e		33.28 S	70.40 W
Bernasconi, Arg.	172	H6	37.53 S	63.44 W
Bernate, Italy	184b		45.29 N	8.49 E
Bernau bei Berlin, Ger.	24	D9	52.40 N	13.35 E
Bernauer Heide, for., Ger.	182a		52.43 N	13.30 E
Bernay, Fr.	20	E9	49.05 N	0.36 E
Bernburg, Ger.	24	E7	51.47 N	11.44 E
Berndorf, Aus.	30	C13	47.57 N	16.06 E
Berne see Bern, Switz.	30	C4	46.57 N	7.26 E
Berner Alpen, mts., Switz.	30	D4	46.29 N	7.44 E
Berneray, i., Scot., U.K.	10	D5	57.43 N	7.10 W
Bernese Alps see Berner Alpen, mts., Switz.	30	D4	46.29 N	7.44 E
Berneuchen see Barnówko, Pol.	24	D10	52.47 N	14.46 E
Berngardovka, Russia	183a		60.01 N	30.36 E
Bernice, La., U.S.	134	E6	32.49 N	92.39 W
Bernie, Mo., U.S.	130	H8	36.40 N	89.58 W
Bernier Bay, b., Nu., Can.	110	A12	71.00 N	87.30 W
Bernier Island, i., Austl.	96	D2	24.52 S	113.08 E
Bernina see Bernina, Piz, mtn., Eur.	20	H18	46.21 N	9.51 E
Bernina, Piz, mtn., Eur.	20	H18	46.21 N	9.51 E
Bernkastel-Kues, Ger.	24	G3	49.54 N	7.04 E
Bernsdorf, Ger.	24	E10	51.21 N	14.03 E
Beromünster, Switz.	24	I4	47.12 N	8.11 E
Berón de Astrada, Arg.	172	C9	27.33 S	57.33 W
Beroroha, Madag.	88	E8	21.40 S	45.10 E
Beroun, Czech Rep.	24	G9	49.58 N	14.04 E
Berounka, stm., Czech Rep.	24	F9	49.59 N	14.24 E
Berovo, Mac.	34	B5	41.42 N	22.51 E
Berras, Arroyo los, stm., Arg.	206		34.34 S	58.40 W
Berre, Étang de, l., Fr.	22	F11	43.27 N	5.08 E
Berri, Austl.	98	J3	34.17 S	140.35 E
Berrigan, Austl.	98	J5	35.39 S	145.48 E
Berriyyane, Alg.	84	C5	32.50 N	3.46 E
Berry, Al., U.S.	134	D11	33.39 N	87.35 W
Berry, hist. reg., Fr.	20	H11	46.52 N	2.07 E
Berry, Canal du, can., Fr.	20	G10	47.16 N	1.23 E
Berry Creek, stm., Ab., Can.	144	E19	50.50 N	111.36 W
Berryessa, Lake, res., Ca., U.S.	148	E3	38.35 N	122.14 W
Berryessa Creek, stm., Ca., U.S.	200		37.24 N	121.53 W
Berry Islands, is., Bah.	132	K8	25.39 N	77.46 W
Berrys Creek, stm., N.J., U.S.	194		40.47 N	74.05 W
Berryville, Ar., U.S.	130	H4	36.22 N	93.34 W
Berseba, Nmb.	90	D3	26.00 S	17.46 E
Bersenbrück, Ger.	24	D3	52.33 N	7.57 E
Bershad', Ukr.	38	E8	48.22 N	29.33 E
Bersut, Russia	40	D17	55.30 N	50.50 E
Bertam, Malay.	64	J6	5.09 N	102.02 E
Bertha, Mn., U.S.	128	E3	46.16 N	95.04 W
Berthold, N.D., U.S.	142	F12	48.18 N	101.44 W
Berthoud, Co., U.S.	140	G7	40.18 N	105.06 W
Berthoud Pass, p., Co., U.S.	138	B3	39.49 N	105.46 W
Bertlich, Ger.	181		51.37 N	7.04 E
Bertolínia, Braz.	170	D3	7.38 S	43.57 W
Bertoua, Cam.	86	D2	4.35 N	13.41 E
Bertram, Tx., U.S.	136	D9	30.44 N	98.03 W
Bertrand, Mi., U.S.	130	C11	41.46 N	86.15 W
Bertrand, Ne., U.S.	140	G13	40.31 N	99.38 W
Beruri, Braz.	164	D5	3.52 S	61.20 W
Berwick, N.S., Can.	122	E12	45.03 N	64.44 W
Berwick, La., U.S.	134	H7	29.41 N	91.13 W
Berwick, Pa., U.S.	124	C9	41.03 N	76.14 W
Berwick-upon-Tweed, Eng., U.K.	10	F11	55.46 N	2.00 W
Berwyn, Il., U.S.	130	C10	41.50 N	87.47 W
Berwyn Heights, Md., U.S.	202c		38.59 N	76.54 W
Beryslav, Ukr.	38	G12	46.50 N	33.26 E
Bērze, stm., Lat.	26	D6	56.40 N	23.37 E
Berz-Macomb Airport, arpt., Mi., U.S.	199		42.40 N	82.58 W
Besalampy, Madag.	88	D7	16.45 S	44.29 E
Besançon, Fr.	20	G15	47.15 N	6.01 E
Bešankovičy, Bela.	26	E12	55.03 N	29.27 E
Besar, Gunong, mtn., Malay.	64	K6	2.31 N	103.09 E
Besar, Gunung, vol., Indon.	66	E9	2.43 S	115.37 E
Besaya, stm., Spain	28	A6	43.21 N	4.03 W
Besbre, stm., Fr.	22	C9	46.32 N	3.42 E
Besed' see Besedz', stm., Eur.	26	H14	52.37 N	31.09 E
Besedino, Russia	38	B15	51.42 N	36.29 E
Besedy, Russia	183b		55.37 N	37.47 E
Besedz', stm., Eur.	26	H14	52.37 N	31.09 E
Beşiktaş, ngh., Tur.	185b		41.03 N	29.01 E
Beşiri, Tur.	42	G9	37.55 N	41.17 E
Beskid Mountains see Beskids, mts., Eur.	24	G15	49.39 N	20.14 E
Beskids, mts., Eur.	24	G15	49.39 N	20.14 E
Beskidy see Beskids, mts., Eur.	24	G15	49.39 N	20.14 E
Beşkonak, Tur.	76	A2	37.08 N	31.13 E
Beskra, Alg.	84	C6	34.50 N	5.42 E
Beskudnikovo, ngh., Russia	183b		55.52 N	37.34 E
Beskydy see Beskids, mts., Eur.	24	G15	49.39 N	20.14 E
Beslan, Russia	42	D11	43.11 N	44.31 E
Besni, Tur.	42	G7	37.41 N	37.52 E
Besor, Nahal, stm., Asia	76	G5	31.27 N	34.22 E
Besós, stm., Spain	184d		41.25 N	2.04 E
Bessaker, Nor.	16	C8	64.14 N	10.20 E
Bessancourt, Fr.	179		49.02 N	2.13 E
Bessarabia, hist. reg., Eur.	38	G7	46.52 N	28.43 E
Bessemer, Al., U.S.	134	D11	33.24 N	86.58 W
Bessemer, Mi., U.S.	128	E8	46.28 N	90.03 W
Bessemer City, N.C., U.S.	132	A4	35.17 N	81.16 W
Bessheim, Nor.	16	F6	61.31 N	8.52 E
Bessho, Japan	188		34.27 N	135.31 E
Bessonovka, Russia	40	E14	53.18 N	45.02 E
Bestamak, Kaz.	40	G19	49.44 N	55.05 E
Besten, Ger.	181		51.39 N	6.54 E
Bestfield, De., U.S.	203		39.43 N	75.36 W
Bestjah, Russia	50	D15	61.56 N	129.54 E
Bestobe, Kaz.	48	D12	52.29 N	73.05 E
Bestuževo, Russia	12	F20	61.35 N	43.56 E
Betā, India	190b		22.55 N	88.14 E
Betafo, Madag.	88	D8	19.50 S	46.51 E
Betanzos, Spain	28	A2	43.17 N	8.12 W
Betanzos, Ría de, est., Spain	28	A2	43.23 N	8.15 W
Bétaré Oya, Cam.	86	C2	5.35 N	14.05 E
Betarsjön, l., Swe.	16	D14	63.44 N	16.52 E
Betchworth, Eng., U.K.	178		51.14 N	0.16 W
Bétera, Spain	28	E10	39.35 N	0.27 W
Bethal, S. Afr.	90	E9	26.26 S	29.27 E
Bethalto, Il., U.S.	130	F7	38.53 N	90.02 W
Bethanien, Nmb.	90	E3	26.32 S	17.10 E
Bethany, Il., U.S.	130	E9	39.38 N	88.44 W
Bethany, Mo., U.S.	130	D3	40.16 N	94.02 W
Bethany, Ok., U.S.	138	F11	35.31 N	97.36 W
Bethel, Monts.	159a	d3	16.44 N	62.09 W
Bethel, Ak., U.S.	109	D7	60.48 N	161.46 W
Bethel, Me., U.S.	122	F6	44.25 N	70.47 W
Bethel, N.C., U.S.	124	I8	35.48 N	77.22 W
Bethel, Oh., U.S.	124	F1	38.57 N	84.05 W
Bethel Acres, Ok., U.S.	134	B2	35.19 N	97.00 W
Bethel Springs, Tn., U.S.	134	B10	35.14 N	88.36 W
Bethesda, Oh., U.S.	126	H8	40.00 N	81.04 W
Bethford, N.Y., U.S.	202a		42.48 N	78.48 W
Bethgate, Md., U.S.	202b		39.18 N	76.51 W
Bethlehem, S. Afr.	90	F9	28.13 S	28.18 E
Bethlehem, Pa., U.S.	124	D10	40.37 N	75.23 W
Bethlehem, W.V., U.S.	126	H9	40.03 N	80.40 W
Bethlehem see Bayt Lahm, W.B.	76	G6	31.42 N	35.11 E
Bethlehem Steel Corporation, sci., Md., U.S.	202b		39.13 N	76.29 W
Bethlehem Steel Corporation (Lackawanna Plant), sci., N.Y., U.S.	202a		42.49 N	78.52 W
Bethnal Green, ngh., Eng., U.K.	178		51.32 N	0.03 W
Bethulie, S. Afr.	90	G7	30.30 S	25.59 E
Bethune, Sk., Can.	142	D8	50.42 N	105.11 W
Béthune, Fr.	20	D11	50.31 N	2.38 E
Bethune, S.C., U.S.	132	B5	34.24 N	80.20 W
Béthune, stm., Fr.	20	E10	49.56 N	1.05 E
Betlica, Russia	26	F16	54.01 N	33.57 E
Betong, Malay.	66	C7	1.24 N	111.32 E
Betong, Thai.	64	J5	5.46 N	101.03 E
Betoota, Austl.	98	E3	25.41 S	140.44 E
Betpak-Dala, des., Kaz.	48	E11	46.00 N	70.00 E
Betroka, Madag.	88	E8	23.16 S	46.05 E
Betsham, Eng., U.K.	178		51.25 N	0.19 E
Bet She'arim, Horbat, hist., Isr.	76	F6	32.42 N	35.08 E
Betsiamites, Qc., Can.	122	B8	48.56 N	68.39 W
Betsiamites, stm., Qc., Can.	114	B16	49.17 N	69.14 W
Betsiamites, Barrage, dam., Qc., Can.	122	A7	49.23 N	69.45 W
Betsiamites, Pointe de, c., Qc., Can.	122	B8	48.54 N	68.37 W
Betsiamites, Réserve indienne de, ind. res., Qc., Can.	122	A8	49.05 N	68.37 W
Betsiboka, stm., Madag.	88	D8	16.03 S	46.34 E
Betsie, Point, c., Mi., U.S.	126	D3	44.41 N	86.13 W
Betsy Layne, Ky., U.S.	124	G3	37.32 N	82.39 W
Betsy Ross Bridge, trans., U.S.	203		39.59 N	75.04 W
Bettendorf, Ia., U.S.	130	C7	41.31 N	90.30 W
Bettiah, India	70	E10	26.48 N	84.30 E
Bettles Field, Ak., U.S.	109	C9	66.55 N	151.28 W
Bettola, Italy	30	F6	44.47 N	9.36 E
Bettrath, ngh., Ger.	181		51.13 N	6.26 E
Betūl, India	70	H6	21.54 N	77.54 E
Betung, Indon.	66	D3	1.53 S	103.15 E
Betung, Indon.	66	E4	2.51 S	104.13 E
Betwa, stm., India	70	F7	25.54 N	80.12 E
Betzdorf, Ger.	24	F3	50.47 N	7.52 E
Beulah, Austl.	98	J4	35.55 S	142.25 E
Beulah, Co., U.S.	138	C4	38.04 N	104.59 W
Beulah, Mi., U.S.	126	D3	44.38 N	86.04 W
Beulah, Ms., U.S.	134	D8	33.47 N	90.58 W
Beulah, N.D., U.S.	142	G12	47.15 N	101.46 W
Beulah Reservoir, res., Or., U.S.	146	G8	43.56 N	118.09 W
Beulaville, N.C., U.S.	132	B8	34.55 N	77.46 W
Beuthen see Bytom, Pol.	24	F14	50.21 N	18.55 E
Beuvron, stm., Fr.	20	G11	47.29 N	1.15 E
Beuvron, stm., Fr.	20	G12	47.27 N	3.31 E
Beuvronne, stm., Fr.	179		48.56 N	2.44 E
Bever, stm., Ger.	20	B17	52.00 N	7.46 E
B. Everett Jordan Lake, res., N.C., U.S.	132	A7	35.46 N	78.52 W
Beverley, Eng., U.K.	10	H12	53.50 N	0.26 W
Beverly, Ma., U.S.	124	B15	42.33 N	70.52 W
Beverly, ngh., Il., U.S.	196		41.43 N	87.41 W
Beverly Farms, Md., U.S.	202c		39.04 N	77.11 W
Beverly Farms, Ma., U.S.	201		42.34 N	70.49 W
Beverly Harbor, b., Ma., U.S.	201		42.32 N	70.53 W
Beverly Hills, Austl.	192a		33.57 S	151.05 E
Beverly Hills, Ca., U.S.	148	I7	34.04 N	118.23 W
Beverly Lake, l., Nu., Can.	110	C10	64.36 N	100.30 W
Beverly Municipal Airport, arpt., Ma., U.S.	201		42.35 N	70.55 W
Beverstausee, res., Ger.	181		51.09 N	7.23 E
Beverungen, Ger.	24	E5	51.39 N	9.22 E
Beverwijk, Neth.	20	B13	52.29 N	4.39 E
Bevier, Mo., U.S.	130	E5	39.44 N	92.33 W
Bewani Mountains, mts., Pap. N. Gui.	101a	a3	3.11 S	141.23 E
Bexhill, Eng., U.K.	10	K13	50.50 N	0.28 E
Bexley, Austl.	192a		33.57 S	151.08 E
Bexley, Oh., U.S.	124	E3	39.58 N	82.55 W
Bey Dağları, mts., Tur.	34	G13	36.40 N	30.15 E
Beydagları Olimpos Milli Parkı, p.o.i., Tur.	34	G13	36.29 N	30.24 E
Beydili, Tur.	34	C14	40.09 N	31.00 E
Beyenburg, ngh., Ger.	181		51.15 N	7.18 E
Beykoz, ngh., Tur.	185b		41.08 N	29.05 E
Beyla, Gui.	84	H3	8.41 N	8.39 W
Beylerbeyi, ngh., Tur.	185b		41.03 N	29.03 E
Beynes, Fr.	179		48.51 N	1.53 E
Beynes-Thiverval, Aérodrome de, arpt., Fr.	179		48.51 N	1.54 E
Beyoğlu, ngh., Tur.	185b		41.02 N	28.59 E
Beypazarı, Tur.	34	C14	40.10 N	31.55 E
Beypore, India	69	F2	11.10 N	75.48 E
Beyra, Som.	86	C9	6.57 N	47.19 E
Beyşehir, Tur.	34	F14	37.43 N	31.43 E
Beyşehir Gölü, l., Tur.	34	F14	37.40 N	31.30 E
Beytüşşebap, Tur.	42	G10	37.34 N	43.10 E
Bezaha, Madag.	88	E7	23.30 S	44.31 E
Bežanickaja vozvyšennost', plat., Russia	26	D12	56.48 N	29.35 E
Bežanicy, Russia	26	D12	56.58 N	29.53 E
Bezau, Aus.	24	I5	47.23 N	9.54 E
Bezdzež, Bela.	26	H8	52.19 N	25.18 E
Bežeck, Russia	26	C19	57.47 N	36.42 E
Bežeckij Verh, mts., Russia	26	C19	57.36 N	36.54 E
Bezenčuk, Russia	40	E16	52.59 N	49.24 E
Béziers, Fr.	22	F9	43.20 N	3.13 E
Bezmein, Turkmen.	72	B8	38.03 N	58.09 E
Bezons, Fr.	179		48.56 N	2.13 E
Bezwada see Vijayawāda, India	69	C5	16.30 N	80.37 E
Bhabānipur, India	190b		22.57 N	88.27 E
Bhabānipur, India	190b		22.56 N	88.13 E
Bhādgāon see Bhaktapur, Nepal	70	E10	27.40 N	85.25 E
Bhadohi, India	70	F9	25.24 N	82.34 E
Bhādra, India	70	D5	29.06 N	75.10 E
Bhadrāchalam, India	69	C5	17.39 N	80.56 E
Bhadrak, India	70	H11	21.03 N	86.30 E
Bhadra Reservoir, res., India	69	E2	13.41 N	75.34 E
Bhadrāvati, India	69	E2	13.50 N	75.41 E
Bhādua, India	190b		22.41 N	88.12 E
Bhāgalpur, India	70	F11	25.14 N	86.58 E
Bhainsa, India	69	B3	19.07 N	77.58 E
Bhāi Pheru, Pak.	70	C4	31.12 N	73.56 E
Bhairab Bāzār, Bngl.	70	F13	24.03 N	90.58 E
Bhaironghāti, India	70	C7	31.01 N	78.54 E
Bhakkar, Pak.	70	C3	31.37 N	71.03 E
Bhaktapur (Bhādgāon), Nepal	70	E10	27.40 N	85.25 E
Bhal, India	190c		19.11 N	73.08 E
Bhālki, India	69	C3	18.03 N	77.12 E
Bhalswa, ngh., India	190a		28.44 N	77.10 E
Bhalwāl, Pak.	70	B4	32.15 N	72.53 E
Bhamdūn, Leb.	76	E6	33.48 N	35.40 E
Bhamo, Mya.	62	D8	24.16 N	97.15 E
Bhandāra, India	70	H7	21.09 N	79.39 E
Bhandārdaha, India	190b		22.37 N	88.13 E
Bhāndup, ngh., India	190c		19.09 N	72.57 E
Bhāngar Kāta Khāl, stm., India	190b		22.31 N	88.33 E
Bhanvad, India	70	H2	21.55 N	69.48 E
Bharat see India, ctry., Asia	62	D4	20.00 N	77.00 E
Bharatpur, India	70	E6	27.12 N	77.29 E
Bharatpur, Nepal	70	E10	27.14 N	84.21 E
Bharthana, India	70	E7	26.45 N	79.13 E
Bharūch, India	70	H4	21.42 N	72.59 E

Name	Page	Map Ref.	Latitude	Longitude
Bhātāpāra, India	70	H8	21.44 N	81.56 E
Bhatgaon see Bhaktapur, Nepal	70	E10	27.40 N	85.25 E
Bhātghar Lake, res., India	69	B1	18.10 N	73.50 E
Bhatkal, India	69	E2	13.59 N	74.32 E
Bhātpāra, India	70	G12	22.52 N	88.24 E
Bhātpur, India	190b		22.43 N	88.25 E
Bhattiprolu, India	69	C5	16.05 N	80.47 E
Bhātua, India	190b		22.57 N	88.22 E
Bhaunja, India	190a		28.40 N	77.25 E
Bhavāni, India	69	F3	11.27 N	77.26 E
Bhāvnagar, India	70	H4	21.46 N	72.08 E
Bhawani Mandi, India	70	F5	24.25 N	75.50 E
Bhawānipatna, India	70	I9	19.54 N	83.10 E
Bhendkhal, India	190c		18.53 N	72.59 E
Bhera, Pak.	70	B4	32.28 N	72.54 E
Bhikampur, India	190a		28.45 N	77.27 E
Bhikangaon, India	70	H5	21.51 N	75.57 E
Bhilai, India	70	H8	21.13 N	81.26 E
Bhilainagar see Bhilai, India	70	H8	21.13 N	81.26 E
Bhilwāra, India	70	F5	25.20 N	74.38 E
Bhīma, stm., India	69	B1	16.24 N	77.17 E
Bhīmavaram, India	69	C5	16.32 N	81.32 E
Bhimpur, India	190b		22.46 N	88.08 E
Bhind, India	70	E7	26.34 N	78.46 E
Bhīnmāl, India	70	F4	24.58 N	72.14 E
Bhiwandi, India	69	B1	19.16 N	73.01 E
Bhiwāni, India	70	D6	28.47 N	76.08 E
Bhoāgāchi, India	190b		22.57 N	88.20 E
Bhojpur, Nepal	70	E11	27.10 N	87.03 E
Bhokardan, India	70	H5	20.15 N	75.46 E
Bhongīr, India	69	C4	17.30 N	78.53 E
Bhopāl, India	70	G6	23.15 N	77.24 E
Bhopar, India	190c		19.12 N	73.05 E
Bhopura, India	190a		28.42 N	77.20 E
Bhuāpur, India	190a		28.43 N	77.26 E
Bhuban, India	70	H10	20.53 N	85.50 E
Bhubaneshwar, India	70	H10	20.14 N	85.50 E
Bhuj, India	70	G2	23.15 N	69.39 E
Bhusāwal, India	70	H5	21.02 N	75.47 E
Bhutali, India	190c		19.07 N	73.04 E
Bhutan, ctry., Asia	70	E13	27.30 N	90.30 E
Bia, Phou, mtn., Laos	64	C6	18.58 N	103.08 E
Biafra, Bahía de see Biafra, Bight of, b., Afr.	84	I6	4.00 N	8.00 E
Biafra, Bight of, b., Afr.	84	I6	4.00 N	8.00 E
Biafra, Golfe de see Biafra, Bight of, b., Afr.	84	I6	4.00 N	8.00 E
Biak, i., Indon.	60	F10	1.00 S	136.00 E
Biała, Pol.	24	F13	50.23 N	17.40 E
Biała, stm., Pol.	24	G16	50.02 N	20.55 E
Biała Piska, Pol.	24	C18	53.37 N	22.04 E
Biała Podlaska, Pol.	24	D19	52.01 N	23.07 E
Biała Rawska, Pol.	24	E16	51.49 N	20.29 E
Białobrzegi, Pol.	24	E16	51.39 N	20.57 E
Białogard, Pol.	24	B12	54.00 N	15.59 E
Białowieski Park Narodowy, p.o.i., Pol.	24	D19	52.46 N	23.51 E
Biały Bór, Pol.	24	C12	53.54 N	16.50 E
Białystok, Pol.	24	C19	53.07 N	23.09 E
Bianco, Monte see Blanc, Mont, mtn., Eur.	30	E3	45.50 N	6.52 E
Biankouma, C. Iv.	84	H3	7.44 N	7.37 W
Biaora, India	70	F6	23.56 N	76.55 E
Biaro, Pulau, i., Indon.	60	E8	2.05 N	125.21 E
Biarritz, Fr.	22	F4	43.28 N	1.33 W
Biasca, Switz.	30	D5	46.21 N	8.58 E
Biba, Egypt	76	J2	28.55 N	30.59 E
Bibala, Ang.	88	C1	14.44 S	13.19 E
Bibân el-Mulûk see Valley of the Kings, hist., Egypt	74	H3	25.45 N	32.37 E
Bibb City, Ga., U.S.	134	E14	32.29 N	84.58 W
Bibbiena, Italy	30	G8	43.42 N	11.49 E
Bibei, stm., Spain	28	B3	42.23 N	7.12 W
Bibémi, Cam.	86	C2	9.19 N	13.53 E
Biberach an der Riss, Ger.	20	F18	48.05 N	9.47 E
Biberonne, stm., Fr.	179		48.59 N	2.41 E
Bibey see Bibei, stm., Spain	28	B3	42.23 N	7.12 W
Bibirëvo, Russia	26	F16	54.28 N	33.08 E
Bibrka, Ukr.	38	D3	49.38 N	24.17 E
Bicas, Braz.	170	K4	21.43 S	43.01 W
Bicaz, Rom.	36	C13	46.55 N	26.05 E
Biche, Lac la, l., Ab., Can.	144	B18	54.50 N	111.58 W
Bicheno, Austl.	99a	n14	41.53 S	148.17 E
Bichigt, Mong.	52	B4	47.06 N	95.04 E
Bichota Canyon, val., Ca., U.S.	198		34.16 N	117.48 W
Bickerstaffe, Eng., U.K.	180		53.32 N	2.50 W
Bickle Knob, mtn., W.V., U.S.	124	F6	38.56 N	79.44 W
Bickley, ngh., Eng., U.K.	178		51.24 N	0.03 E
Bicknacre, Eng., U.K.	178		51.41 N	0.35 E
Bicknell, In., U.S.	130	F10	38.45 N	87.18 W
Bicknell, Ut., U.S.	150	E5	38.20 N	111.32 W
Bicknor, Eng., U.K.	178		51.18 N	0.40 E
Bicol, stm., Phil.	68	D4	13.44 N	123.07 E
Bicske, Hung.	24	I14	47.29 N	18.36 E
Bicudo, stm., Braz.	170	J3	18.04 S	44.33 W
Bičura, Russia	50	F10	50.34 N	107.35 E
Bičurina, Russia	40	C19	56.50 N	55.25 E
Bīd, India	69	B2	18.59 N	75.45 E
Bida, Nig.	84	H6	9.04 N	5.59 E
Bīdar, India	69	C3	17.54 N	77.31 E
Biddeford, Me., U.S.	122	G6	43.29 N	70.27 W
Bideford, Eng., U.K.	10	J8	51.00 N	4.12 W
Bidston, Eng., U.K.	180		53.24 N	3.05 W
Bidwell, Oh., U.S.	124	F3	38.54 N	82.20 W
Bidyādhari, stm., India	190b		22.23 N	88.35 E
Bidyādharpur, India	190b		22.50 N	88.24 E
Bidžan, Russia	50	G15	47.58 N	131.56 E
Bieber, Ca., U.S.	148	B4	41.07 N	121.07 W
Biebrza, stm., Pol.	24	C18	53.13 N	22.25 E
Biebrzański Park Narodowy, p.o.i., Pol.	24	C18	53.28 N	22.34 E
Biecz, Pol.	24	G17	49.44 N	21.13 E
Biedenkopf, Ger.	24	F4	50.55 N	8.32 E
Biedermannsdorf, Aus.	182b		48.05 N	16.21 E
Biel (Bienne), Switz.	30	C4	47.08 N	7.15 E
Bielawa, Pol.	24	F12	50.40 N	16.37 E
Bielefeld, Ger.	24	D4	52.01 N	8.32 E
Bieler Lake, l., Nu., Can.	110	A15	70.21 N	73.05 W
Biella, Italy	30	E5	45.34 N	8.03 E
Bielsk, Pol.	24	D15	52.40 N	19.48 E
Bielsko-Biała, Pol.	24	G14	49.48 N	19.02 E
Bielsk Podlaski, Pol.	24	D19	52.46 N	23.11 E
Bien Dong see South China Sea, s., Asia	46	I15	10.00 N	113.00 E
Bienfait, Sk., Can.	142	E11	49.08 N	102.48 W
Bien Hoa, Viet.	64	G8	10.56 N	106.49 E
Bienne see Biel, Switz.	30	C4	47.08 N	7.15 E
Bien Son, Viet.	64	B7	20.04 N	105.51 E
Bienville, La., U.S.	134	E3	32.22 N	92.58 W
Bienville, Lac, l., Qc., Can.	110	D16	55.05 N	72.40 W
Bierdnačokka, mtn., Nor.	14	F6	66.49 N	15.53 E
Bierutów, Pol.	24	E13	51.08 N	17.32 E
Biesdorf, ngh., Ger.	182a		52.31 N	13.33 E
Biesel, ngh., Ger.	181		51.10 N	6.29 E
Bieszczadzki Park Narodowy, p.o.i., Pol.	24	G18	49.05 N	22.45 E
Bièvre, stm., Fr.	179		48.47 N	2.20 E
Bièvres, Fr.	179		48.45 N	2.13 E
Biferno, stm., Italy	32	C8	41.59 N	15.01 E
Bifoun, Gabon	86	E2	0.17 S	10.22 E
Big, stm., Mo., U.S.	130	F7	38.27 N	90.36 W
Biga, Tur.	34	C10	40.14 N	27.14 E
Bigadiç, Tur.	34	D11	39.23 N	28.08 E
Big A Mountain, mtn., Va., U.S.	124	G3	37.03 N	82.02 W
Big Antelope Creek, stm., Or., U.S.	148	A8	42.27 N	117.12 W
Big Bald Mountain, mtn., N.B., Can.	122	C10	47.12 N	66.25 W
Big Bald Mountain, mtn., Ga., U.S.	132	B1	34.45 N	84.19 W
Big Baldy, mtn., Id., U.S.	146	F11	44.47 N	115.13 W
Big Baldy Mountain, mtn., Mt., U.S.	146	D16	46.58 N	110.37 W
Big Bar Creek, B.C., Can.	144	E8	51.10 N	122.06 W
Big Basin Redwoods State Park, p.o.i., Ca., U.S.	148	F3	37.09 N	122.17 W
Big Bay, Mi., U.S.	126	B2	46.48 N	87.43 W
Big Bay, b., Vanuatu	101d	j16	15.06 S	166.54 E
Big Bay De Noc, b., Mi., U.S.	126	C3	45.46 N	86.43 W
Big Bear Lake, Ca., U.S.	148	I9	34.15 N	116.54 W
Big Bear Lake, res., Ca., U.S.	148	I8	34.15 N	116.55 W
Big Beaver, Sk., Can.	142	E8	49.08 N	105.08 W
Big Beaver Airport, arpt., Mi., U.S.	199		42.33 N	83.06 W
Big Beaver Creek, stm., Mi., U.S.	199		42.32 N	83.01 W
Big Belt Mountains, mts., Mt., U.S.	146	D16	46.40 N	111.25 W
Big Bend, Swaz.	90	E10	26.48 S	32.04 E
Big Bend National Park, p.o.i., Tx., U.S.	136	E4	29.12 N	103.12 W
Big Bend Reservoir, res., Ab., Can.	144	D15	52.58 N	115.37 W
Big Black, stm., Ms., U.S.	134	E8	32.02 N	91.03 W
Big Blue, stm., U.S.	114	F2	39.11 N	96.32 W
Big Blue, West Fork, stm., Ne., U.S.	140	G14	40.42 N	96.59 W
Big Bonito Creek, stm., Az., U.S.	150	J7	33.34 N	109.56 W
Big Brook, stm., N.J., U.S.	194		40.19 N	74.10 W
Big Cabin Creek, stm., Ok., U.S.	138	E13	36.26 N	95.08 W
Big Canyon, val., Tx., U.S.	136	D5	30.23 N	102.11 W
Big Chino Wash, stm., Az., U.S.	150	H4	34.52 N	112.28 W
Big Clifty, Ky., U.S.	130	G11	37.32 N	86.09 W
Big Coulee Creek, stm., Mt., U.S.	140	A3	46.16 N	108.56 W
Big Cow Creek, stm., Tx., U.S.	136	D14	30.33 N	93.43 W
Big Creek, B.C., Can.	144	E7	51.44 N	123.03 W
Big Creek, Ca., U.S.	148	F6	37.12 N	119.13 W
Big Creek, stm., B.C., Can.	144	E7	51.50 N	122.41 W
Big Creek, stm., On., Can.	126	F9	42.35 N	80.26 W
Big Creek, stm., Ar., U.S.	134	C8	34.20 N	91.05 W
Big Creek, stm., Id., U.S.	146	E11	45.06 N	114.44 W
Big Creek, stm., Ks., U.S.	138	C9	38.47 N	98.55 W
Big Creek, stm., La., U.S.	134	E7	32.08 N	91.53 W
Big Creek, stm., Mo., U.S.	130	D3	40.01 N	94.07 W
Big Creek, stm., Oh., U.S.	197a		41.27 N	81.41 W
Big Creek, stm., Tx., U.S.	136	C11	31.09 N	96.51 W
Big Creek, East Fork, stm., U.S.	128	K5	40.16 N	94.03 W
Big Creek, West Fork, stm., U.S.	128	K4	40.16 N	94.03 W
Big Creek Parkway, p.o.i., Oh., U.S.	197a		41.24 N	81.45 W
Big Creek Peak, mtn., Id., U.S.	146	F13	44.28 N	113.32 W
Big Crow Island, i., N.Y., U.S.	194		40.37 N	73.33 W
Big Cypress Indian Reservation, ind. res., Fl., U.S.	132	J5	26.17 N	80.59 W
Big Cypress National Preserve, ind. res., Fl., U.S.	132	J4	25.55 N	81.10 W
Big Cypress Swamp, sw., Fl., U.S.	132	J4	26.10 N	81.38 W
Big Dalton Canyon, val., Ca., U.S.	198		34.10 N	117.48 W
Big Dalton Wash, val., Ca., U.S.	198		34.04 N	117.58 W
Big Delta, Ak., U.S.	109	D10	64.09 N	145.47 W
Big Desert, des., Austl.	98	J3	35.40 S	141.00 E
Big Diomede Island see Ratmanova, ostrov, i., Russia	50	C27	65.47 N	169.04 W
Big Dry Creek, stm., Mt., U.S.	142	G7	47.56 N	106.28 W
Big Eau Pleine, stm., Wi., U.S.	128	G8	44.43 N	89.42 W
Big Elm Creek, stm., Tx., U.S.	136	D10	30.52 N	96.55 W
Bigelow Bight, b., U.S.	122	H6	43.17 N	70.32 W
Big Escambia Creek, stm., U.S.	134	F11	30.58 N	87.14 W
Big Falls, Mn., U.S.	128	C5	48.10 N	93.46 W
Big Flat, Ar., U.S.	130	I5	36.00 N	92.24 W
Bigflat see Big Flat, Ar., U.S.	130	I5	36.00 N	92.24 W
Big Flat Creek, stm., Al., U.S.	134	F11	31.34 N	87.31 W
Bigfork, Mn., U.S.	128	D5	47.45 N	93.38 W
Bigfork, Mt., U.S.	146	B12	48.04 N	114.04 W
Big Fork, stm., Mn., U.S.	128	C5	48.31 N	93.42 W
Big Frog Mountain, mtn., Tn., U.S.	134	C14	34.58 N	84.32 W
Biggar, Sk., Can.	142	B6	52.03 N	107.58 W
Biggar, Scot., U.K.	10	F9	55.37 N	3.30 W
Biggers, Ar., U.S.	130	H7	36.19 N	90.48 W
Biggin Hill Aerodrome, arpt., Eng., U.K.	178		51.19 N	0.03 E
Biggs, Ca., U.S.	148	D4	39.25 N	121.41 W
Big Gull Lake, l., On., Can.	126	D12	44.49 N	76.58 W
Big Hole, stm., Mt., U.S.	146	E14	45.33 N	112.20 W
Big Hole National Battlefield, p.o.i., Mt., U.S.	146	E13	45.35 N	113.35 W
Bighorn, stm., U.S.	140	A5	46.09 N	107.28 W
Bighorn Basin, bas., U.S.	140	C4	44.15 N	108.10 W
Bighorn Canyon National Recreation Area, p.o.i., U.S.	140	B5	45.00 N	108.15 W
Bighorn Lake, res., U.S.	140	B4	45.06 N	108.11 W
Bighorn Mountains, mts., U.S.	140	D6	43.59 N	107.04 W
Bight, Head of, b., Austl.	96	F6	31.34 S	131.03 E
Big Island, Va., U.S.	124	G6	37.31 N	79.21 W
Big Island, i., Nu., Can.	110	C17	62.43 N	70.43 W
Big Island, i., On., Can.	128	B4	49.08 N	94.37 W
Big Knob, mtn., Va., U.S.	124	H3	36.40 N	82.31 W
Big Lake, Mn., U.S.	128	F5	45.19 N	93.44 W
Big Lake, Tx., U.S.	136	C6	31.11 N	101.27 W
Big Lake, l., Me., U.S.	122	E9	45.10 N	67.41 W
Big Lookout Mountain, mtn., Or., U.S.	146	F9	44.37 N	117.17 W
Big Lost, stm., Id., U.S.	146	G13	43.50 N	112.43 W
Big Mountain, mtn., Nv., U.S.	148	B6	41.17 N	119.04 W
Big Mountain Creek, stm., Ab., Can.	144	B12	55.03 N	118.39 W
Big Muddy, stm., Il., U.S.	130	G8	37.34 N	89.31 W
Big Muddy Creek, stm., Mt., U.S.	142	F9	48.08 N	104.37 W
Big Muddy Creek, stm., N.D., U.S.	142	H12	46.36 N	101.23 W
Big Muddy Lake, l., Sk., Can.	142	E9	49.08 N	104.54 W
Big Muscamoot Bay, b., Mi., U.S.	199		42.33 N	82.40 W
Big Nasty Creek, stm., S.D., U.S.	140	B9	45.40 N	102.51 W
Big Nemaha, North Fork, stm., Ne., U.S.	128	K3	40.10 N	95.59 W
Bignona, Sen.	84	G1	12.48 N	16.14 W
Bigot, Morne, hill, Mart.	159c	k6	14.31 N	61.04 W
Big Otter, stm., Va., U.S.	124	G6	37.06 N	79.22 W
Big Otter Creek, stm., On., Can.	126	F9	42.38 N	80.48 W
Big Pine, Ca., U.S.	148	F7	37.09 N	118.16 W
Big Pine Creek, stm., In., U.S.	130	D10	40.17 N	87.14 W
Big Pine Mountain, mtn., Ca., U.S.	148	I6	34.42 N	119.39 W
Big Piney, Wy., U.S.	146	H16	42.31 N	110.05 W
Big Piney, stm., Mo., U.S.	130	G6	37.52 N	92.03 W
Big Piney Creek, stm., Ar., U.S.	134	B5	35.20 N	93.19 W
Bigpoint, Ms., U.S.	134	G10	30.35 N	88.28 W
Big Porcupine Creek, stm., Mt., U.S.	142	H6	46.16 N	106.42 W
Big Prairie Creek, stm., Al., U.S.	134	E11	32.31 N	87.51 W
Big Quill Lake, l., Sk., Can.	142	B8	51.55 N	104.22 W
Big Raccoon Creek, stm., In., U.S.	130	E11	39.45 N	87.22 W
Big Rapids, Mi., U.S.	126	E4	43.41 N	85.28 W
Bigras, Île, i., Qc., Can.	193a		45.31 N	73.51 W
Big Rib, stm., Wi., U.S.	128	F9	44.55 N	89.38 W
Big Rideau Lake, l., On., Can.	126	D13	44.45 N	76.14 W
Big River, Sk., Can.	110	E9	53.50 N	107.00 W
Big Sable, stm., Mi., U.S.	126	D3	44.02 N	86.30 W
Big Sable Point, c., Mi., U.S.	126	D3	44.03 N	86.29 W
Big Sand Lake, l., Mb., Can.	110	D11	57.46 N	99.43 W
Big Sandy, Mt., U.S.	146	B16	48.10 N	110.06 W
Big Sandy, Tn., U.S.	130	H9	36.14 N	88.04 W
Big Sandy, Tx., U.S.	136	B12	32.35 N	95.06 W
Big Sandy, stm., U.S.	124	F3	38.24 N	82.36 W
Big Sandy, stm., Az., U.S.	150	I3	34.19 N	113.30 W
Big Sandy, stm., Tn., U.S.	134	A10	36.26 N	88.03 W
Big Sandy, stm., Wy., U.S.	140	F3	41.51 N	109.47 W
Big Sandy Creek, stm., Co., U.S.	138	C6	38.06 N	102.29 W
Big Sandy Creek, stm., Ga., U.S.	132	D2	32.42 N	82.57 W
Big Sandy Creek, stm., Mt., U.S.	146	B16	48.34 N	109.48 W
Big Sandy Creek, stm., Ne., U.S.	140	G14	40.12 N	97.18 W
Big Sandy Creek, stm., Tx., U.S.	136	B12	32.33 N	95.04 W
Big Sandy Creek, stm., Tx., U.S.	138	H11	33.11 N	97.40 W
Big Sandy Lake, res., Mn., U.S.	128	E5	46.45 N	93.17 W
Big Sandy Reservoir, res., Wy., U.S.	140	E3	42.16 N	109.26 W
Big Satilla Creek, stm., Ga., U.S.	132	E3	31.27 N	82.03 W
Bigsby Island, i., On., Can.	128	B4	49.04 N	94.35 W
Big Sewickley Creek, stm., Pa., U.S.	197b		40.35 N	80.13 W
Big Sheep Mountain, mtn., Mt., U.S.	142	G8	47.03 N	105.43 W
Big Signal Peak, mtn., Ca., U.S.	148	D2	39.31 N	123.06 W
Big Sioux, stm., U.S.	140	E16	42.29 N	96.28 W
Big Sixmile Creek, stm., N.Y., U.S.	202a		43.02 N	79.01 W
Big Sky, Mt., U.S.	146	E15	45.16 N	111.17 W
Big Slough, stm., Ga., U.S.	134	F14	30.56 N	84.33 W
Big Smoky Valley, val., Nv., U.S.	148	E8	38.30 N	117.15 W
Big Snowy Mountains, mts., Mt., U.S.	142	H4	46.49 N	109.25 W
Big Southern Butte, mtn., Id., U.S.	146	G13	43.23 N	113.01 W
Big Spring, Tx., U.S.	136	B6	32.15 N	101.28 W
Big Springs, Ne., U.S.	140	F10	41.04 N	102.04 W
Big Spruce Knob, mtn., W.V., U.S.	124	F5	38.16 N	80.12 W
Big Squaw Mountain, mtn., Me., U.S.	122	E7	45.30 N	69.45 W
Bigstick Lake, l., Sk., Can.	142	D4	50.16 N	109.20 W
Big Stone City, S.D., U.S.	128	F2	45.17 N	96.28 W
Big Stone Gap, Va., U.S.	124	H3	36.51 N	82.47 W
Big Stone Lake, l., U.S.	128	F2	45.24 N	96.40 W
Big Sunflower, stm., Ms., U.S.	134	D8	32.39 N	90.40 W
Big Sur, reg., Ca., U.S.	148	G4	35.44 N	121.18 W
Big Swamp Creek, stm., Al., U.S.	134	E12	32.19 N	86.49 W
Big Swan Creek, stm., Tn., U.S.	134	B11	35.46 N	87.24 W
Big Thompson, stm., Co., U.S.	140	G7	40.21 N	104.45 W
Big Timber, Mt., U.S.	146	E16	45.50 N	109.57 W
Big Timber Creek, stm., N.J., U.S.	203		39.53 N	75.08 W
Big Timber Creek, North Branch, stm., N.J., U.S.	203		39.50 N	75.05 W
Big Timber Creek, South Branch, stm., N.J., U.S.	203		39.50 N	75.05 W
Big Trout Lake, l., On., Can.	110	E12	53.44 N	89.57 W
Big Tujunga Dam, dam., Ca., U.S.	198		34.18 N	118.12 W
Biguaçu, Braz.	172	C13	27.30 S	48.40 W
Big Valley, Ab., Can.	144	D18	52.02 N	112.46 W
Big Walnut Creek, stm., In., U.S.	130	E11	39.29 N	86.56 W
Big Water, Ut., U.S.	150	F5	37.01 N	111.36 W
Big Wells, Tx., U.S.	136	F8	28.34 N	99.34 W
Big White Mountain, mtn., B.C., Can.	144	G12	49.42 N	118.58 W
Big Wills Creek, stm., Al., U.S.	134	C12	34.00 N	85.59 W
Big Wood, stm., Id., U.S.	146	G12	42.52 N	114.54 W
Bihać, Bos.	36	E2	44.49 N	15.52 E
Bīhar, India	70	F10	25.12 N	85.31 E
Bihār, state, India	70	F10	25.00 N	86.00 E
Biharamulo, Tan.	86	E6	2.38 S	31.20 E
Bihor, state, Rom.	36	C9	47.00 N	22.15 E
Bihor, Vârful, mtn., Rom.	36	C9	46.27 N	22.42 E
Bihoro, Japan	54	C16	43.49 N	144.06 E
Bihosava, Bela.	26	E10	55.50 N	27.44 E
Bihu, China	58	G8	28.20 N	119.48 E
Bihun, Ukr.	38	B7	51.24 N	28.17 E
Biiuk-Karasu (Biyuk-Karasu), stm., Ukr.	38	H13	45.28 N	34.47 E
Bija, stm., Russia	48	D15	52.25 N	85.00 E
Bijagós, Arquipélago dos, is., Gui.-B.	84	G1	11.21 N	16.18 W
Bijainagar, India	70	F5	25.56 N	74.38 E
Bijaipur, India	70	E6	26.03 N	77.22 E
Bijaipura, India	70	F6	24.45 N	77.47 E
Bijāpur, India	69	C2	16.49 N	75.42 E
Bījāpur, India	69	B5	18.48 N	80.49 E
Bījār, Iran	74	C10	35.52 N	47.36 E
Bijeljina, Bos.	36	E6	44.45 N	19.13 E
Bijelo Polje, Yugo.	36	F6	43.01 N	19.44 E
Bijie, China	52	F6	27.18 N	105.16 E
Bijlikol', ozero, l., Kaz.	48	F12	43.01 N	70.41 E
Bijna, India	190b		22.55 N	88.27 E
Bijnor, India	70	D7	29.22 N	78.08 E
Bijōki, Japan	186		35.49 N	139.39 E
Bijou Creek, stm., Co., U.S.	138	B4	40.17 N	103.52 W
Bijsk, Russia	48	D15	52.33 N	85.14 E
Bijwāsan, ngh., India	190a		28.32 N	77.03 E
Bīkāner, India	70	D4	28.01 N	73.19 E
Bikar, at., Marsh. Is.	94	B7	12.13 N	170.07 E
Bikeqi, China	58	A4	40.43 N	111.16 E
Bikeru, Indon.	66	F12	5.15 S	120.08 E
Bikin, Russia	52	B11	46.49 N	134.17 E
Bikini, at., Marsh. Is.	94	B7	11.35 N	165.23 E
Bīkkū Bīttī, mtn., Libya	82	C3	22.00 N	19.12 E
Bikoro, D.R.C.	86	E3	0.45 S	18.07 E
Bila Krynytsia, Ukr.	38	F12	47.21 N	33.10 E
Bila Krynytsia, Ukr.	38	C8	50.38 N	29.29 E
Bilāra, India	70	E4	26.10 N	73.42 E
Bilāri, India	70	D7	28.37 N	78.48 E
Bilāsipāra, India	70	E13	26.14 N	90.14 E
Bilāspur, India	70	G9	22.04 N	82.09 E
Bilāspur, India	70	C6	31.18 N	76.46 E
Biläsuvar, Azer.	42	F13	39.27 N	48.33 E
Bila Tserkva, Ukr.	38	D9	49.47 N	30.08 E
Bilauktaung Range, mts., Asia	64	F4	13.00 N	99.00 E
Bilbao, Spain	28	A7	43.15 N	2.56 W
Bilbeis, Egypt	76	H2	30.25 N	31.33 E
Bilbilis, hist., Spain	28	C9	41.25 N	1.39 W
Bileća, Bos.	36	G5	42.52 N	18.25 E
Bilecik, Tur.	34	C12	40.10 N	29.58 E
Bilecik, state, Tur.	34	C13	40.10 N	30.10 E
Bilen'ke, Ukr.	38	F13	47.37 N	35.01 E
Biles Island, i., Pa., U.S.	203		40.10 N	74.45 W
Biłgoraj, Pol.	24	F18	50.33 N	22.42 E
Bilgrām, India	70	E8	27.10 N	80.02 E
Bilhorod-Dnistrovs'kyi, Ukr.	38	G9	46.11 N	30.18 E
Bili, D.R.C.	86	D5	4.08 N	25.10 E
Biliaïvka, Ukr.	38	G9	46.28 N	30.13 E
Bīlimora, India	70	H4	20.45 N	72.57 E
Bilin, Mya.	64	D3	17.12 N	97.14 E
Bilin, stm., Mya.	64	D3	17.04 N	97.08 E
Bílina, Czech Rep.	24	F9	50.32 N	13.45 E
Biliran Island, i., Phil.	68	E5	11.35 N	124.28 E
Bilk, ngh., Ger.	181		51.12 N	6.47 E
Bilky, Ukr.	38	C7	50.49 N	28.10 E
Billabong Creek, stm., Austl.	98	J5	35.05 S	144.02 E
Billiluna, Austl.	96	C5	19.34 S	127.39 E
Billinge, Eng., U.K.	180		53.30 N	2.42 W
Billingen, hills, Swe.	16	I11	58.24 N	13.45 E
Billings, Mo., U.S.	130	G4	37.04 N	93.33 W
Billings, Mt., U.S.	140	B4	45.46 N	108.32 W
Billings, Ok., U.S.	138	E11	36.31 N	97.26 W
Billingsfors, Swe.	16	H10	59.00 N	12.17 E
Billings Heights, Mt., U.S.	140	B4	45.45 N	108.34 W
Billiton see Belitung, i., Indon.	66	E5	2.50 S	107.55 E
Billmerich, Ger.	181		51.30 N	7.41 E
Billolo, stm., Congo	191b		4.07 S	15.19 E
Bill Williams, stm., Az., U.S.	150	I3	34.18 N	114.08 W
Bill Williams Mountain, mtn., Az., U.S.	150	H4	35.12 N	112.12 W
Billy Chinook, Lake, res., Or., U.S.	146	F5	44.38 N	121.16 W
Bilma, Niger	84	F7	18.41 N	12.56 E
Biloela, Austl.	98	E8	24.24 S	150.30 E
Bilo Gora, mts., Cro.	30	E14	46.01 N	16.54 E
Bilohir'ia, Ukr.	38	C5	50.00 N	26.24 E
Bilohirs'k, Ukr.	38	H13	45.03 N	34.35 E
Bilohorodka, Ukr.	38	D5	49.59 N	26.39 E
Bilokurakine, Ukr.	38	D17	49.31 N	38.43 E
Biloluts'k, Ukr.	38	D17	49.41 N	39.00 E
Bilopillia, Ukr.	38	B13	51.09 N	34.16 E
Bilousivka, Ukr.	38	D11	49.56 N	32.22 E
Bilovods'k, Ukr.	38	D18	49.12 N	39.35 E
Biloxi, Ms., U.S.	134	G10	30.23 N	88.53 W
Biloxi, stm., Ms., U.S.	134	G9	30.26 N	89.00 W
Bilozers'ke, Ukr.	38	E16	48.32 N	37.04 E
Bilozir'ia, Ukr.	38	D10	49.18 N	31.54 E
Bilpa Morea Claypan, l., Austl.	98	E2	25.00 S	140.00 E
Bilqas Qism Awwal, Egypt	76	G2	31.13 N	31.21 E
Bil'sha Kam'ianka, stm., Eur.	38	E18	48.22 N	40.03 E
Bil'shivtsi, Ukr.	38	D3	49.11 N	24.44 E
Bil's'ka Volia, Ukr.	38	B4	51.27 N	25.49 E
Biltine, Chad	82	E4	14.32 N	20.55 E
Biltmore Forest, N.C., U.S.	132	A3	35.33 N	82.32 W
Bilugyun Island, i., Mya.	64	D3	16.24 N	97.32 E
Bilüü, Mong.	48	E15	49.03 N	89.27 E
Bilwaskarma, Nic.	156	E6	14.45 N	83.52 W
Bilychi, Ukr.	38	C9	50.29 N	30.20 E
Bilyi Kolodiaz', Ukr.	38	C16	50.12 N	37.07 E
Bilyky, Ukr.	38	D13	49.15 N	34.17 E
Bilyts'ke, Ukr.	38	E16	48.25 N	37.14 E
Bimbân, Egypt	74	H3	24.26 N	32.52 E
Bimbo, C.A.R.	86	D3	4.20 N	18.34 E
Bimbowrie, Austl.	98	H3	32.03 S	140.09 E
Bimé, Congo	191b		4.09 S	15.11 E
Bimini Islands, is., Bah.	132	K6	25.42 N	79.15 W
Bin, stm., China	58	I5	23.41 N	112.59 E
Bina, Sol. Is.	101b	e9	8.55 S	160.46 E
Bīna-Etāwa, India	70	F7	24.10 N	78.11 E
Binaiya, Gunung, mtn., Indon.	60	F9	3.09 S	129.27 E
Binalbagan, Phil.	68	E4	10.12 N	122.52 E
Bin'an, China	54	B7	45.50 N	127.43 E
Binchuan, China	52	F5	25.47 N	100.34 E
Bindalsfjorden, b., Nor.	16	B9	65.12 N	12.07 E
Bindki, India	70	E8	26.02 N	80.35 E
Bindloss, Ab., Can.	142	D3	50.52 N	110.15 W
Bindow, Ger.	182a		52.17 N	13.45 E
Bindura, Zimb.	88	D5	17.18 S	31.19 E
Binéfar, Spain	28	C11	41.51 N	0.18 E
Binford, N.D., U.S.	142	G15	47.33 N	98.20 W
Binga, D.R.C.	86	D4	2.22 N	20.30 E
Binga, Monte, mtn., Afr.	88	D5	19.46 S	33.02 E
Binga, Mount see Binga, Monte, mtn., Afr.	88	D5	19.46 S	33.02 E
Bingara, Austl.	98	G8	29.52 S	150.34 E
Bingen, Ger.	24	G3	49.57 N	7.53 E
Binger, Ok., U.S.	138	F10	35.18 N	98.21 W
Bingham, Me., U.S.	122	E7	45.04 N	69.53 W
Bingham Farms, Mi., U.S.	199		42.32 N	83.16 W
Binghamton, N.Y., U.S.	124	B10	42.06 N	75.55 W
Bin Ghunaymah, Jabal, mts., Libya	82	B3	25.31 N	15.49 E
Bingöl, Tur.	42	F9	38.52 N	40.29 E
Bingöl, state, Tur.	42	F9	39.00 N	40.40 E
Binhai, China	58	D8	34.00 N	119.49 E
Binh Chanh, Viet.	187c		10.40 N	106.34 E
Binh Gia, Viet.	64	B8	21.57 N	106.22 E
Binh Hung Hoa, Viet.	187c		10.49 N	106.37 E
Binh Son, Viet.	64	E9	15.17 N	108.45 E
Binh Trung, Viet.	187c		10.47 N	106.46 E
Binjai, Indon.	64	K4	3.36 N	98.30 E
Binnaway, Austl.	98	H7	31.33 S	149.23 E
Binongko, Pulau, i., Indon.	60	G7	5.57 S	124.02 E
Binscarth, Mb., Can.	142	D12	50.36 N	101.15 W
Binsheim, ngh., Ger.	181		51.31 N	6.42 E
Bintan, Pulau, i., Indon.	66	C4	1.05 N	104.30 E
Bintimani, mtn., S.L.	84	H2	9.13 N	11.07 W
Bintuhan, Indon.	66	F3	4.47 S	103.20 E
Bintulu, Malay.	66	B8	3.09 N	113.02 E
Bintuni, Indon.	60	F9	2.06 S	133.32 E
Binxian, China	52	B10	45.45 N	127.29 E
Binxian, China	58	C7	37.28 N	117.58 E
Binxian, China	58	D3	35.01 N	108.05 E
Binyang, China	58	J3	23.14 N	108.49 E
Bin-Yauri, Nig.	84	G5	10.47 N	4.48 E
Binza, D.R.C.	191b		4.21 S	15.14 E
Binza, ngh., D.R.C.	191b		4.20 S	15.14 E
Binza, stm., D.R.C.	191b		4.21 S	15.14 E
Binzert see Bizerte, Tun.	84	B6	37.16 N	9.52 E
Biobío, state, Chile	172	H1	37.31 S	71.43 W
Biobío, stm., Chile	166	G2	36.49 S	73.10 W
Biogradska Gora Nacionalni Park, p.o.i., Yugo.	36	G6	42.53 N	19.36 E
Bioko, i., Eq. Gui.	84	I6	3.30 N	8.40 E
Bira, India	190b		22.47 N	88.34 E
Bira, Russia	50	G15	48.59 N	132.27 E
Birab, Indon.	60	G10	6.10 S	138.24 E
Birac, Phil.	68	B3	16.22 N	120.39 E
Birāk, Libya	82	B2	27.32 N	14.16 E
Birakan, Russia	50	G15	49.00 N	131.43 E
Bi'r al Wa'r, Libya	82	C2	22.31 N	14.08 E
Birao, C.A.R.	86	B4	10.16 N	22.47 E
Birati, India	190b		22.39 N	88.27 E
Bircao see Buur Gaabo, Som.	86	E8	1.12 S	41.50 E
Birch, Eng., U.K.	180		53.34 N	2.13 W
Birch, stm., Ab., Can.	110	D8	58.26 N	112.21 W
Birch, stm., W.V., U.S.	124	F5	38.35 N	80.53 W
Birch Cliff, ngh., On., Can.	193b		43.41 N	79.17 W
Birch Creek, stm., Id., U.S.	146	F14	43.56 N	112.44 W
Birch Creek, stm., Mt., U.S.	146	C17	47.44 N	109.40 W
Birch Creek, stm., Mt., U.S.	146	B14	48.26 N	112.16 W
Birch Hills, Sk., Can.	142	B8	52.59 N	105.25 W
Birch Island, B.C., Can.	144	E11	51.35 N	119.55 W
Birch Island, i., Mb., Can.	142	B13	52.25 N	99.55 W
Birch Lake, l., Ab., Can.	144	C19	53.19 N	111.35 W
Birch Lake, l., On., Can.	112	A9	51.24 N	92.20 W
Birch Mountains, hills, Ab., Can.	110	D8	57.33 N	113.06 W
Birch Pond, l., Ma., U.S.	201		42.28 N	71.00 W
Birch River, Mb., Can.	142	B12	52.23 N	101.06 W
Birch Run, Mi., U.S.	126	E6	43.15 N	83.47 W
Birch Run, stm., Pa., U.S.	203		40.09 N	75.37 W
Birchrunville, Pa., U.S.	203		40.08 N	75.39 W
Birch Tree, Mo., U.S.	130	H6	36.59 N	91.29 W
Birch Vale, Eng., U.K.	180		53.23 N	1.57 W
Birchwood, Wi., U.S.	128	F7	45.39 N	91.33 W
Birchwood City, Md., U.S.	202c		38.49 N	76.59 W
Birchwood Park, De., U.S.	203		39.22 N	75.39 W
Bird City, Ks., U.S.	138	B7	39.45 N	101.32 W
Bird Creek, stm., Ok., U.S.	138	E13	36.13 N	95.44 W
Bird Island, Mn., U.S.	128	G4	44.46 N	94.53 W
Bird Island, sci., S. Geor.	166	J9	54.00 S	38.03 W
Bird River, b., Md., U.S.	202b		39.23 N	76.23 W
Birds Landing, Ca., U.S.	200		38.08 N	121.52 W
Birdsville, Austl.	98	E2	25.53 S	139.21 E
Birdtail Creek, stm., Mb., Can.	142	D12	50.15 N	101.12 W
Birdum, Austl.	96	C6	15.39 S	133.12 E
Birecik, Tur.	42	G8	37.02 N	38.02 E
Bireun, Indon.	64	J3	5.12 N	96.41 E
Bir Ghbalou, Alg.	28	H14	36.15 N	3.34 E
Birigui, Braz.	166	D6	21.16 S	50.20 W
Birikčul', Russia	48	D15	53.19 N	89.52 E
Biriljussy, Russia	48	C16	57.07 N	90.33 E
Bīrjand, Iran	72	C8	32.52 N	59.12 E
Birjulëvo, ngh., Russia	183b		55.35 N	37.40 E
Birjul'ka, Russia	48	D19	53.52 N	106.18 E
Birjusa, stm., Russia	48	C17	57.42 N	95.27 E
Birjusinsk, Russia	48	C17	55.57 N	97.49 E
Birkdale, Eng., U.K.	180		53.37 N	3.02 W
Birkeland, Nor.	16	I6	58.20 N	8.14 E
Birken, B.C., Can.	144	F8	50.29 N	122.37 W
Birkenfeld, Ger.	24	G3	49.38 N	7.09 E
Birkenhead, Eng., U.K.	10	H9	53.24 N	3.01 W
Birkenhead Park, p.o.i., Eng., U.K.	180		53.24 N	3.02 W
Birkerød, Den.	16	L10	55.50 N	12.26 E
Birket, The, stm., Eng., U.K.	180		53.24 N	3.01 W
Birket Fatimé, Chad	82	E3	12.54 N	19.04 E
Birkholz, Ger.	182a		52.38 N	13.34 E
Birky, Ukr.	38	D15	49.42 N	36.01 E
Birla Museum, bldg., India	190b		22.32 N	88.22 E
Birling, Eng., U.K.	178		51.19 N	0.25 E
Birling, hill, Austl.	192a		33.57 S	150.43 E
Birmingham, Eng., U.K.	10	I10	52.28 N	1.52 W
Birmingham, Al., U.S.	134	D12	33.31 N	86.48 W
Birmingham, Ia., U.S.	130	D6	40.52 N	91.56 W
Birmingham, Mi., U.S.	124	B2	42.32 N	83.13 W
Birmingham, N.J., U.S.	203		39.58 N	74.42 W
Birmitrapur, India	70	G10	22.24 N	84.44 E
Bîr Mogreïn, Maur.	84	D2	25.14 N	11.35 W
Birnamwood, Wi., U.S.	128	G9	44.56 N	89.12 W
Birnin Gaouré, Niger	84	G5	13.04 N	2.54 E
Birnin-Kebbi, Nig.	84	G5	12.27 N	4.11 E
Birnin Konni, Niger	84	G5	13.48 N	5.15 E
Birnin Kudu, Nig.	84	G6	11.27 N	9.30 E
Birobidžan, Russia	50	G15	48.47 N	132.54 E
Birr, Ire.	10	H5	53.05 N	7.54 W
Birrie, stm., Austl.	98	G6	29.43 S	146.37 E
Birsk, Russia	40	D19	55.25 N	55.33 E
Birštonas, Lith.	26	F7	54.35 N	24.02 E
Birten, Ger.	181		51.38 N	6.29 E
Birtle, Mb., Can.	142	D12	50.25 N	101.03 W
Birtus, Egypt	191c		30.09 N	31.08 E
Biru, China	52	E3	31.29 N	93.50 E
Birūr, India	69	E2	13.35 N	75.58 E

Name	Page	Map Ref.	Latitude	Longitude
Biržai, Lith.	26	D7	56.11 N	24.45 E
Birżebbuġa, Malta	32	I8	35.49 N	14.32 E
Bisaccia, Italy	32	C9	41.01 N	15.22 E
Bīsalpur, India	70	D7	28.17 N	79.48 E
Bisamberg, Aus.	182b		48.20 N	16.22 E
Bisamberg, hill, Aus.	182b		48.19 N	16.22 E
Bisbee, Az., U.S.	150	L7	31.26 N	109.54 W
Bisbee, N.D., U.S.	142	F14	48.37 N	99.22 W
Biscarrosse, Fr.	22	E4	44.23 N	1.09 W
Biscarrosse et de Parentis, Étang de, l., Fr.	22	E4	44.20 N	1.10 W
Biscay, Bay of, b., Eur.	8	G8	44.00 N	4.00 W
Biscayne Bay, b., Fl., U.S.	132	K5	25.33 N	80.15 W
Biscayne National Park, p.o.i., Fl., U.S.	132	K5	25.25 N	80.12 W
Bisceglie, Italy	32	C10	41.14 N	16.30 E
Bischofshofen, Aus.	30	C10	47.25 N	13.13 E
Bischofswerda, Ger.	24	E10	51.07 N	14.10 E
Biscoe, Ar., U.S.	134	C7	34.49 N	91.24 W
Biscoe, N.C., U.S.	132	A6	35.21 N	79.47 W
Biscucuy, Ven.	168	C7	9.22 N	69.59 W
Biser, Russia	40	B21	58.51 N	58.53 E
Biserovo, Russia	183b		55.47 N	38.07 E
Biserovskoe, ozero, l., Russia	183b		55.46 N	38.07 E
Bisert', stm., Russia	40	C21	56.39 N	57.55 E
Biševo, Otok, i., Cro.	30	H12	42.58 N	16.00 E
Bishnupur, India	70	G11	23.05 N	87.19 E
Bishnupur, India	190b		22.37 N	88.31 E
Bisho, S. Afr.	90	H8	32.48 S	27.27 E
Bishop, Ca., U.S.	148	F7	37.22 N	118.23 W
Bishop, Pa., U.S.	197b		40.19 N	80.12 W
Bishop, Tx., U.S.	136	G10	27.34 N	97.47 W
Bishop Auckland, Eng., U.K.	10	G11	54.40 N	1.40 W
Bishop Rock, r., Eng., U.K.	10	L6	49.52 N	6.27 W
Bishop's Falls, Nf., Can.	111a	j22	49.02 N	55.29 W
Bishop's Stortford, Eng., U.K.	10	J13	51.52 N	0.09 E
Bishopville, S.C., U.S.	132	B5	34.12 N	80.15 W
Biškek, Kyrg.	48	F12	42.52 N	74.34 E
Biskupiec, Pol.	24	C16	53.51 N	20.57 E
Bisley, Eng., U.K.	178		51.20 N	0.38 W
Bislich, Ger.	181		51.41 N	6.29 E
Bislig, Phil.	68	F6	8.12 N	126.18 E
Bismarck, Mo., U.S.	130	G7	37.46 N	90.37 W
Bismarck, N.D., U.S.	140	A12	46.48 N	100.47 W
Bismarck Archipelago, is., Pap. N. Gui.	101a	a4	5.00 S	150.00 E
Bismarck Range, mts., Pap. N. Gui.	101a	b3	5.30 S	144.45 E
Bismarck Sea, s., Pap. N. Gui.	101a	a4	4.00 S	148.00 E
Bismark, Kap, c., Grnld.	108	B22	76.43 N	18.27 W
Bismo, Nor.	16	F6	61.52 N	8.16 E
Bison, S.D., U.S.	140	B10	45.31 N	102.27 W
Bison Peak, mtn., Co., U.S.	138	B3	39.14 N	105.30 W
Bispgården, Swe.	16	D14	63.01 N	16.37 E
Bisrakh, India	190a		28.34 N	77.26 E
Bissa, Djebel, mtn., Alg.	28	H12	36.26 N	1.27 E
Bissagos see Bijagós, Arquipélago dos, is., Gui.-B.	84	G1	11.21 N	16.18 W
Bissau, Gui.-B.	84	G1	11.51 N	15.36 W
Bissett, Mb., Can.	142	C18	51.01 N	95.40 W
Bissikrima, Gui.	84	G2	10.51 N	10.56 W
Bissingheim, ngh., Ger.	181		51.21 N	7.31 E
Bistcho Lake, l., Ab., Can.	110	D7	59.43 N	118.45 W
Bistineau, Lake, res., La., U.S.	134	E5	32.25 N	93.22 W
Bistreț, Rom.	36	F10	43.54 N	23.30 E
Bistrica, Slvn.	30	D13	46.32 N	16.16 E
Bistrița, Rom.	36	B11	47.08 N	24.30 E
Bistrița, stm., Rom.	36	C13	46.27 N	26.57 E
Bistrița-Năsăud, state, Rom.	36	B11	47.15 N	24.30 E
Biswān, India	70	E8	27.30 N	81.00 E
Bisztynek, Pol.	24	B16	54.05 N	20.54 E
Bitam, Gabon	86	D2	2.07 N	11.28 E
Bitatolo, stm., Congo	191b		4.09 S	15.19 E
Bitburg, Ger.	24	G2	49.58 N	6.31 E
Bitca, Russia	183b		55.34 N	37.37 E
Bitca, stm., Russia	183b		55.34 N	37.37 E
Bitche, Fr.	20	E16	49.03 N	7.25 E
Bitik, Kaz.	40	F17	50.08 N	50.29 E
Bitjug, stm., Russia	40	F12	50.37 N	39.55 E
Bitlis, Tur.	42	F10	38.22 N	42.06 E
Bitlis, state, Tur.	42	F10	38.30 N	42.10 E
Bitola, Mac.	34	B4	41.01 N	21.20 E
Bitolj see Bitola, Mac.	34	B4	41.01 N	21.20 E
Bitonto, Italy	32	C10	41.06 N	16.41 E
Bitou, Burkina	84	G4	11.16 N	0.18 W
Bitter Creek, stm., Ut., U.S.	150	D7	39.58 N	109.24 W
Bitter Creek, stm., Wy., U.S.	150	B8	41.31 N	109.27 W
Bitterfeld, Ger.	24	E8	51.37 N	12.18 E
Bitterfontein, S. Afr.	90	G4	31.00 S	18.15 E
Bitter Lake, l., Sk., Can.	142	D4	50.08 N	109.48 W
Bittermark, ngh., Ger.	181		51.27 N	7.28 E
Bitterroot, stm., Mt., U.S.	146	D12	46.51 N	114.07 W
Bitterroot, East Fork, stm., Mt., U.S.	146	E13	45.56 N	114.07 W
Bitterroot, West Fork, stm., Mt., U.S.	146	E12	45.56 N	114.08 W
Bitterroot Range, mts., U.S.	146	D12	47.06 N	115.10 W
Bitti, Italy	32	D3	40.28 N	9.22 E
Bitung, Indon.	60	E8	1.26 N	125.08 E
Bitupitá, Braz.	170	B5	2.54 S	41.16 W
Bituruna, Braz.	172	C12	26.09 S	51.33 W
Biu, Nig.	84	G7	10.35 N	12.13 E
Bivins, Tx., U.S.	136	B13	33.01 N	94.12 W
Biwabik, Mn., U.S.	128	D6	47.31 N	92.20 W
Biwa-ko, l., Japan	56	D8	35.15 N	136.05 E
Bixby, Ok., U.S.	130	I2	35.56 N	95.52 W
Biyala, Egypt	76	G2	31.10 N	31.13 E
Biyang, China	58	E5	32.42 N	113.19 E
Biyuk-Karasu (Biiuk-Karasu), stm., Ukr.	38	H13	45.28 N	34.47 E
Bizana, S. Afr.	90	G9	30.53 S	29.52 E
Bizard, Île, i., Qc., Can.	193a		45.29 N	73.54 W
Bizen, Japan	56	E7	34.44 N	134.11 E
Bizerte (Binzert), Tun.	84	B6	37.16 N	9.52 E
Bizerte, Lac de, l., Tun.	32	G3	37.12 N	9.48 E
Bizjar, Russia	40	C20	57.31 N	56.08 E
Bizkaiko, co., Spain	28	A8	43.20 N	2.45 W
Bjøbovo, Russia	18	G16	60.20 N	28.59 E
Bjahoml', Bela.	26	F10	54.43 N	28.03 E
Bjala, Blg.	36	F12	43.28 N	25.44 E
Bjala, Blg.	36	G14	42.53 N	27.53 E
Bjala Slatina, Blg.	36	F10	43.28 N	23.57 E
Bjalyničy, Bela.	26	F12	54.00 N	29.43 E
Bjalynkavičy, Bela.	26	F15	53.15 N	32.08 E
Bjarèzina, stm., Bela.	26	G12	52.33 N	30.14 E
Bjarèzina, stm., Bela.	26	G9	53.45 N	26.04 E
Bjargtangar, c., Ice.	12a	k27	65.30 N	24.30 W
Bjärnum, Swe.	16	K11	56.17 N	13.42 E
Bjaroza, Bela.	26	H7	52.32 N	24.59 E
Bjarozauka, Bela.	26	G8	53.42 N	25.28 E
Bjästa, Swe.	16	D16	63.12 N	18.30 E
Bjelovar, Cro.	30	E13	45.54 N	16.50 E
Bjerka, Nor.	16	A11	66.08 N	13.49 E
Bjerkvik, Nor.	14	D8	68.33 N	17.33 E
Bjerringbro, Den.	16	K7	56.23 N	9.40 E
Bjørkelangen, Nor.	16	H9	59.53 N	11.33 E
Björkfjället, mts., Swe.	14	F6	66.06 N	16.20 E
Björkliden, Swe.	14	D9	68.23 N	18.41 E
Björköby, Fin.	18	D8	63.21 N	21.19 E
Björna, Swe.	16	D16	63.34 N	18.33 E
Bjørnafjorden, b., Nor.	16	G3	60.05 N	5.29 E
Björneborg see Pori, Fin.	18	F8	61.29 N	21.47 E
Bjorne Peninsula, pen., Nu., Can.	108	B8	77.37 N	86.50 W
Bjørnesfjorden, l., Nor.	16	G5	60.10 N	7.40 E
Bjørnevatn, Nor.	14	C20	69.39 N	29.57 E
Bjørntoppen, mtn., Nor.	14	D7	67.58 N	16.51 E
Bjørøya, i., Nor.	16	C8	64.34 N	10.49 E
Bjurholm, Swe.	16	D17	63.56 N	19.13 E
Bjuv, Swe.	16	K10	56.04 N	12.55 E
Bla, Mali	84	G3	12.57 N	5.46 W
Bla see Ba Lu, stm., Viet.	64	D8	14.21 N	107.52 E
Blace, Yugo.	36	F8	43.18 N	21.17 E
Black (Da, Song) (Lixian), stm., Asia	64	B7	21.14 N	105.21 E
Black, stm., Mb., Can.	142	D18	50.47 N	95.36 W
Black, stm., On., Can.	126	D12	44.31 N	77.21 W
Black, stm., On., Can.	126	C11	44.41 N	79.18 W
Black, stm., Ak., U.S.	109	C11	66.40 N	144.43 W
Black, stm., Az., U.S.	150	J6	33.44 N	110.13 W
Black, stm., Ar., U.S.	130	I6	36.29 N	90.22 W
Black, stm., La., U.S.	134	F7	31.15 N	91.49 W
Black, stm., Mi., U.S.	126	E7	42.58 N	82.24 W
Black, stm., Mi., U.S.	126	C5	45.35 N	84.27 W
Black, stm., Mi., U.S.	128	E8	46.39 N	90.02 W
Black, stm., N.M., U.S.	136	B3	32.14 N	104.01 W
Black, stm., N.Y., U.S.	126	E14	44.00 N	76.03 W
Black, stm., N.C., U.S.	132	B7	34.20 N	78.03 W
Black, stm., Vt., U.S.	122	F4	44.55 N	72.13 W
Black, stm., Vt., U.S.	122	G4	43.15 N	72.25 W
Black, stm., Wi., U.S.	128	G7	43.56 N	91.22 W
Black, East Fork, stm., Wi., U.S.	128	G8	44.25 N	90.41 W
Blackall, Austl.	98	E5	24.25 S	145.27 E
Black Bay, b., On., Can.	128	C10	48.34 N	88.32 W
Black Bay Peninsula, pen., On., Can.	128	C10	48.43 N	88.12 W
Black Bear Creek, stm., Ok., U.S.	138	E11	36.25 N	96.38 W
Black Brook, stm., Ma., U.S.	201		42.38 N	71.21 W
Black Brook, stm., Ma., U.S.	201		41.59 N	71.03 W
Black Brook, stm., N.J., U.S.	194		40.42 N	74.31 W
Blackburn, Austl.	192b		37.49 S	145.09 E
Blackburn, Eng., U.K.	10	H10	53.45 N	2.28 W
Blackburn, mun., Eng., U.K.	180		53.42 N	2.28 W
Blackburn, mun., Eng., U.K.	180		53.42 N	2.28 W
Blackburn, Mount, mtn., Ak., U.S.	109	D11	61.44 N	143.26 W
Black Butte, mtn., Mt., U.S.	146	F15	44.54 N	111.51 W
Black Butte, mtn., Mt., U.S.	146	D16	46.47 N	110.56 W
Black Butte Lake, res., Ca., U.S.	148	D3	39.46 N	122.22 W
Black Canyon of the Gunnison National Monument, p.o.i., Co., U.S.	150	E9	38.34 N	107.43 W
Black Creek, B.C., Can.	144	G5	49.49 N	125.08 W
Black Creek, On., Can.	202a		43.00 N	79.01 W
Black Creek, stm., On., Can.	193b		43.41 N	79.32 W
Black Creek, stm., On., Can.	202a		42.59 N	79.01 W
Black Creek, stm., Az., U.S.	150	H7	35.16 N	109.13 W
Black Creek, stm., Ms., U.S.	134	F9	30.43 N	88.39 W
Black Creek, stm., Ms., U.S.	134	D8	33.01 N	90.20 W
Black Creek, stm., N.Y., U.S.	202a		43.03 N	78.42 W
Black Creek, stm., N.Y., U.S.	202a		43.05 N	78.57 W
Black Creek, stm., S.C., U.S.	132	B5	34.18 N	79.37 W
Black Creek Park, p.o.i., On., Can.	193b		43.46 N	79.31 W
Black Creek Pioneer Village, p.o.i., On., Can.	193b		43.47 N	79.32 W
Blackden Heath, Eng., U.K.	180		53.14 N	2.20 W
Black Diamond, Ab., Can.	144	F16	50.41 N	114.13 W
Black Diamond, Wa., U.S.	146	C5	47.18 N	122.00 W
Blackdown Tableland National Park, p.o.i., Austl.	98	D7	23.44 S	149.00 E
Blackduck, Mn., U.S.	128	D4	47.43 N	94.32 W
Black Eagle, Mt., U.S.	146	C15	47.31 N	111.14 W
Blackfalds, Ab., Can.	144	D17	52.23 N	113.47 W
Blackfeet Indian Reservation, ind. res., Mt., U.S.	146	B14	48.40 N	113.00 W
Blackfoot, Id., U.S.	146	G14	43.11 N	112.21 W
Blackfoot, Mt., U.S.	146	B14	48.34 N	112.53 W
Blackfoot, stm., Id., U.S.	146	G15	43.08 N	112.30 W
Blackfoot, stm., Mt., U.S.	146	D13	46.52 N	113.53 W
Blackfoot, North Fork, stm., Mt., U.S.	146	C14	46.58 N	113.08 W
Blackfoot Indian Reserve, ind. res., Ab., Can.	144	F18	50.45 N	113.00 W
Blackfoot Reservoir, res., Id., U.S.	146	H15	42.53 N	111.35 W
Black Forest see Schwarzwald, mts., Ger.	24	H4	48.20 N	8.10 E
Blackhall Mountain, mtn., Wy., U.S.	150	B10	41.02 N	106.41 W
Black Hameldon, hill, Eng., U.K.	180		53.44 N	2.08 W
Black Hawk, On., Can.	128	C4	48.48 N	93.57 W
Blackheath, S. Afr.	191d		26.08 S	27.58 E
Blackheath, Eng., U.K.	178		51.12 N	0.31 W
Black Hill, hill, Eng., U.K.	180		53.33 N	1.53 W
Black Hill, hill, Eng., U.K.	180		53.20 N	2.01 W
Black Hills, mts., U.S.	140	C9	44.00 N	104.00 W
Black Hills, hills, Ca., U.S.	200		37.50 N	121.52 W
Black Horse, Pa., U.S.	203		39.55 N	75.25 W
Black Horse, Pa., U.S.	203		40.06 N	75.19 W
Black Horse Creek, stm., Pa., U.S.	203		40.05 N	75.43 W
Black Island, i., Mb., Can.	142	C17	51.12 N	96.30 W
Black Lake, Qc., Can.	122	D5	46.02 N	71.22 W
Black Lake, l., Sk., Can.	110	D10	59.12 N	105.04 W
Black Lake, l., Mi., U.S.	126	C5	45.28 N	84.15 W
Black Lake, l., N.Y., U.S.	126	D14	44.32 N	75.34 W
Black Lake Bayou, stm., La., U.S.	134	E5	32.00 N	93.09 W
Blackley, ngh., Eng., U.K.	180		53.31 N	2.13 W
Black Mesa, mtn., U.S.	138	E6	36.56 N	102.56 W
Black Mesa, mtn., Az., U.S.	150	G6	36.35 N	110.20 W
Blackmoorfoot Reservoir, res., Eng., U.K.	180		53.37 N	1.51 W
Blackmore, Eng., U.K.	178		51.41 N	0.19 E
Blackmore, Mount, mtn., Mt., U.S.	146	E15	45.27 N	111.01 W
Black Mountain, N.C., U.S.	132	A3	35.37 N	82.19 W
Black Mountain, mtn., Az., U.S.	150	K6	32.46 N	110.57 W
Black Mountain, mtn., Ca., U.S.	148	H5	35.24 N	120.21 W
Black Mountain, mtn., Ca., U.S.	200		37.19 N	122.09 W
Black Mountain, mtn., Id., U.S.	146	D11	46.53 N	115.33 W
Black Mountain, mtn., Mt., U.S.	146	D14	46.44 N	112.31 W
Black Mountain, mtn., Or., U.S.	146	E7	45.13 N	119.17 W
Black Mountain, mtn., Wy., U.S.	140	C5	44.45 N	107.22 W
Black Mountain, hill, Austl.	98	C2	21.07 S	139.41 E
Black Mountains, mts., Az., U.S.	150	H2	35.18 N	114.23 W
Black Nossob, stm., Nmb.	90	C4	23.06 S	18.41 E
Black Peak, mtn., Az., U.S.	150	I2	34.08 N	114.13 W
Black Pine Peak, mtn., Id., U.S.	146	H13	42.08 N	113.08 W
Black Pipe Creek, stm., S.D., U.S.	140	D11	43.47 N	101.14 W
Blackpool, Eng., U.K.	10	H9	53.49 N	3.02 W
Blackpool, mun., Eng., U.K.	180		53.47 N	3.02 W
Blackpool Airport, arpt., Eng., U.K.	180		53.47 N	3.02 W
Blackpool Football Ground, p.o.i., Eng., U.K.	180		53.49 N	3.03 W
Blackpool Tower, bldg., Eng., U.K.	180		53.49 N	3.03 W
Black Range, mts., N.M., U.S.	150	J9	33.20 N	107.50 W
Black River, Jam.	158d	i13	18.01 N	77.50 W
Black River, N.Y., U.S.	126	D14	44.00 N	75.49 W
Black River Falls, Wi., U.S.	128	G8	44.17 N	90.50 W
Black Rock, Austl.	192b		37.59 S	145.01 E
Black Rock, Ar., U.S.	130	H6	36.06 N	91.06 W
Black Rock, Ma., U.S.	201		42.14 N	70.49 W
Black Rock, r., Ire.	10	G2	54.05 N	10.22 W
Black Rock, r., S. Geor.	166	J8	53.39 S	41.48 W
Black Rock Desert, des., Nv., U.S.	148	B7	41.05 N	118.51 W
Blackrod, Eng., U.K.	180		53.35 N	2.35 W
Blacksburg, S.C., U.S.	132	A4	35.07 N	81.31 W
Blacksburg, Va., U.S.	124	G5	37.13 N	80.25 W
Blacks Creek, stm., N.J., U.S.	203		40.08 N	74.43 W
Black Sea, s.	42	D5	43.00 N	35.00 E
Black Sea Lowland see Prychornomors'ka nyzovyna, pl., Ukr.	38	G12	47.00 N	33.00 E
Blacks Fork, stm., U.S.	150	B7	41.22 N	109.37 W
Blackshear, Ga., U.S.	132	E3	31.17 N	82.14 W
Blackshear, Lake, res., Ga., U.S.	132	D2	31.55 N	83.55 W
Blacksod Bay, b., Ire.	10	G2	54.08 N	10.02 W
Black Springs, Austl.	192b		37.46 S	145.19 E
Black Springs Hill, hill, Austl.	192b		37.46 S	145.19 E
Black Star Canyon, val., Ca., U.S.	198		33.47 N	117.39 W
Blackstone, Va., U.S.	124	G8	37.04 N	77.59 W
Blackstone, stm., Ab., Can.	144	D14	52.49 N	116.04 W
Black Sturgeon Lake, l., On., Can.	128	B9	49.20 N	88.53 W
Black Sugarloaf, mtn., Austl.	98	H8	31.20 S	151.33 E
Black Thunder Creek, stm., Wy., U.S.	140	D7	43.33 N	104.41 W
Blackville, S.C., U.S.	132	C4	33.21 N	81.16 W
Black Volta (Volta Noire) (Mouhoun), stm., Afr.	84	H4	8.40 N	0.59 W
Blackwall Tunnel, trans., Eng., U.K.	178		51.30 N	0.01 E
Black Warrior, stm., Al., U.S.	134	E11	32.34 N	87.45 W
Blackwater, Austl.	98	D7	23.34 S	148.52 E
Blackwater, stm., On., Can.	128	B10	49.30 N	88.08 W
Blackwater, stm., Eur.	10	G6	54.30 N	6.34 W
Blackwater, stm., Ire.	10	I4	52.00 N	7.51 W
Blackwater, stm., Ire.	10	H6	53.39 N	6.40 W
Blackwater, stm., U.S.	134	G12	30.36 N	87.02 W
Blackwater, stm., Mo., U.S.	136	E4	38.56 N	92.56 W
Blackwater Creek, stm., Austl.	98	E5	25.57 S	144.27 E
Blackwater Draw, stm., Tx., U.S.	138	G6	33.37 N	101.50 W
Blackwater Lake, l., N.T., Can.	110	C6	64.00 N	123.05 W
Blackwell, Ok., U.S.	138	E11	36.48 N	97.17 W
Blackwell, Tx., U.S.	138	B7	32.05 N	100.19 W
Blackwood, N.J., U.S.	203		39.48 N	75.03 W
Blackwood, Mount, mtn., Austl.	98	K5	37.33 S	144.20 E
Blackwood Terrace, N.J., U.S.	203		39.48 N	75.05 W
Bladenboro, N.C., U.S.	132	B7	34.32 N	78.47 W
Bladensburg, Md., U.S.	202c		38.56 N	76.56 W
Bladensburg National Park, p.o.i., Austl.	98	D4	22.42 S	143.02 E
Bladgrond-Noord, S. Afr.	90	F4	28.52 S	19.54 E
Bladworth, Sk., Can.	142	C7	51.19 N	106.04 W
Bláfell, mtn., Ice.	12a	k30	64.29 N	19.52 W
Blåfjellet, mtn., Nor.	16	B11	65.27 N	13.16 E
Blåfjellhatten, mtn., Nor.	16	C11	64.07 N	13.29 E
Blagodarnyj, Russia	40	I13	45.06 N	43.25 E
Blagodatnoe, Russia	38	B13	51.32 N	34.54 E
Blagoevgrad, Blg.	36	G10	42.01 N	23.06 E
Blagoščatovka, Russia	42	F12	52.13 N	50.25 E
Blagoveščensk, Russia	40	D19	55.02 N	56.00 E
Blagoveščensk, Russia	50	D16	50.16 N	127.32 E
Blaikfjället, mtn., Swe.	16	C14	64.33 N	16.12 E
Blain, Fr.	20	G7	47.29 N	1.46 W
Blaine, Mn., U.S.	128	F5	45.09 N	93.14 W
Blaine, Wa., U.S.	144	B4	48.59 N	122.44 W
Blaine Creek, stm., Ky., U.S.	130	F15	38.11 N	82.37 W
Blaine Hill, Pa., U.S.	197b		40.16 N	79.53 W
Blaine Lake, Sk., Can.	142	B7	52.50 N	106.52 W
Blair, Ne., U.S.	130	C1	41.32 N	96.08 W
Blair, Ok., U.S.	138	G9	34.46 N	99.20 W
Blair, Wi., U.S.	128	G7	44.17 N	91.13 W
Blair Athol, Austl.	98	D6	22.42 S	147.33 E
Blairstown, Ia., U.S.	128	J6	41.54 N	92.04 W
Blairsville, Ga., U.S.	132	B2	34.52 N	83.57 W
Blairsville, Pa., U.S.	124	D6	40.25 N	79.15 W
Blaise, stm., Fr.	20	F13	48.37 N	4.42 E
Blaj, Rom.	36	C10	46.10 N	23.55 E
Blakehurst, Austl.	192a		33.59 S	151.07 E
Blakely, Ga., U.S.	134	F14	31.22 N	84.56 W
Blake Plateau, unds.	176	E6	31.00 N	79.00 W
Blake Point, c., Mi., U.S.	128	C10	48.10 N	88.26 W
Blakesburg, Ia., U.S.	130	D5	40.57 N	92.38 W
Blalock Island, i., Wa., U.S.	146	E7	45.54 N	119.37 W
Blåmannsisen, ice, Nor.	14	E6	67.15 N	16.07 E
Blanc, Cap see Nouâdhibou, Râs, c., Afr.	84	E1	20.46 N	17.03 W
Blanc, Cap, c., Tun.	32	G3	37.20 N	9.51 E
Blanc, Mont, mtn., Qc., Can.	122	B10	48.47 N	66.52 W
Blanc, Mont, mtn., Eur.	30	E3	45.50 N	6.52 E
Blanca, Co., U.S.	138	D3	37.25 N	105.32 W
Blanca, Bahía, b., Arg.	166	G4	38.55 S	62.10 W
Blanca, Laguna, l., Chile	166	J2	52.24 S	71.12 W
Blanca, Punta, c., Chile	172	B2	25.06 S	70.30 W
Blanca, Sierra, mtn., Tx., U.S.	136	C2	31.15 N	105.26 W
Blanca Peak, mtn., Co., U.S.	138	D3	37.35 N	105.29 W
Blanchard, Ok., U.S.	138	F11	35.08 N	97.39 W
Blanchard, stm., Oh., U.S.	124	D2	41.02 N	84.17 W
Blanchardville, Wi., U.S.	130	B8	42.48 N	89.51 W
Blanche, Lake, l., Austl.	98	G2	29.15 S	139.39 E
Blanche Channel, strt., Sol. Is.	101b	e7	8.30 S	157.30 E
Blancheface, Fr.	179		48.32 N	2.06 E
Blanchester, Oh., U.S.	124	E1	39.17 N	83.59 W
Blanchisseuse, Trin.	159f	s12	10.47 N	61.18 W
Blanco, Tx., U.S.	136	D9	30.06 N	98.25 W
Blanco, stm., Arg.	172	D3	30.11 S	69.04 W
Blanco, stm., Ec.	168	G2	0.27 N	79.22 W
Blanco, stm., Tx., U.S.	136	D9	29.51 N	97.54 W
Blanco, Cabo see Nouâdhibou, Râs, c., Afr.	84	E1	20.46 N	17.03 W
Blanco, Cabo, c., C.R.	156	H5	9.34 N	85.07 W
Blanco, Cañon, val., N.M., U.S.	138	F3	35.10 N	105.26 W
Blanco, Cape, c., Or., U.S.	146	H2	42.50 N	124.32 W
Blanco, Lago, l., Chile	166	J3	54.02 S	68.59 W
Blanco Creek, stm., Tx., U.S.	136	F10	28.18 N	97.18 W
Blanc-Sablon, Qc., Can.	111a	i22	51.25 N	57.06 W
Bland, Mo., U.S.	130	F6	38.18 N	91.38 W
Bland, Va., U.S.	124	G4	37.06 N	81.07 W
Blanda, stm., Ice.	12a	k30	65.39 N	20.17 W
Blanding, Ut., U.S.	150	F7	37.37 N	109.31 W
Blandinsville, Il., U.S.	130	D7	40.33 N	90.51 W
Blandy, Fr.	179		48.34 N	2.47 E
Blanes, Spain	28	C13	41.40 N	2.47 E
Blangkejeren, Indon.	64	K3	3.59 N	97.20 E
Blangpidie, Indon.	64	K3	3.44 N	96.50 E
Blangy-sur-Bresle, Fr.	20	E10	49.55 N	1.37 E
Blankenburg, Ger.	24	E6	51.48 N	10.58 E
Blankenburg, ngh., Ger.	182a		52.35 N	13.28 E
Blankenfelde, ngh., Ger.	182a		52.37 N	13.23 E
Blankenheim, Ger.	24	F2	50.26 N	6.36 E
Blankenstein, Ger.	181		51.24 N	7.14 E
Blanket, Tx., U.S.	136	C9	31.49 N	98.47 W
Blanquilla, Isla, i., Ven.	168	B9	11.51 N	64.37 W
Blansko, Czech Rep.	24	G12	49.22 N	16.39 E
Blantyre, Mwi.	88	D6	15.47 S	35.00 E
Blarney Castle, hist., Ire.	10	J4	51.56 N	8.34 W
Blåsjø, l., Nor.	16	H4	59.22 N	6.53 E
Blåskavlen, mtn., Nor.	16	F5	61.00 N	7.08 E
Błaszki, Pol.	24	E14	51.39 N	18.26 E
Blatná, Czech Rep.	24	G9	49.25 N	13.52 E
Blattnicksele, Swe.	16	B15	65.21 N	17.34 E
Blaubeuren, Ger.	24	H5	48.24 N	9.47 E
Blaufelden, Ger.	24	G5	49.18 N	9.57 E
Blauvelt, N.Y., U.S.	194		41.03 N	73.57 W
Blauvelt State Park, p.o.i., N.Y., U.S.	194		41.04 N	73.56 W
Blavet, stm., Fr.	20	G5	47.47 N	3.17 W
Blawenburg, N.J., U.S.	194		40.24 N	74.42 W
Blawnox, Pa., U.S.	197b		40.29 N	79.51 W
Blaxland Creek, stm., Austl.	192a		33.48 S	150.46 E
Blaye-et-Sainte-Luce, Fr.	22	D5	45.08 N	0.39 W
Blayney, Austl.	98	I7	33.32 S	149.15 E
Bleaklow Head, mtn., Eng., U.K.	180		53.28 N	1.50 W
Bled, Slvn.	30	D11	46.21 N	14.06 E
Bledsoe, Tx., U.S.	138	H5	33.37 N	103.01 W
Blega, Indon.	66	G8	7.07 S	113.03 E
Blekinge, state, Swe.	16	K13	56.20 N	15.20 E
Blenheim, On., Can.	126	F8	42.20 N	81.59 W
Blenheim, N.Z.	102	E5	41.30 S	173.57 E
Blenheim, N.J., U.S.	203		39.48 N	75.05 W
Bléré, Fr.	20	G9	47.19 N	0.59 E
Blesbokspruit, stm., S. Afr.	191d		26.14 S	28.29 E
Blessing, Tx., U.S.	136	F11	28.52 N	96.13 W
Bletchingley, Eng., U.K.	178		51.14 N	0.06 W
Bletchley, Eng., U.K.	10	J12	51.59 N	0.45 W
Bletoppen, mtn., Nor.	16	H7	59.48 N	9.10 E
Bleury, Fr.	179		48.31 N	1.45 E
Blewett Falls Lake, res., N.C., U.S.	132	A6	35.03 N	79.54 W
Blidinje jezero, l., Bos.	30	G14	43.06 N	17.30 E
Blidö, i., Swe.	16	H16	59.36 N	18.54 E
Bliedinghausen, ngh., Ger.	181		51.09 N	7.12 E
Bliersheim, ngh., Ger.	181		51.23 N	6.43 E
Bligh Water, strt., Fiji	101e	p18	17.00 S	178.00 E
Bliksvær, i., Nor.	14	E4	67.16 N	13.58 E
Blind, stm., N.Y., U.S.	194		40.57 N	73.42 W
Blind Creek, stm., Austl.	192b		37.54 S	145.12 E
Blindley Heath, Eng., U.K.	178		51.12 N	0.04 W
Blind River, On., Can.	126	B6	46.11 N	82.56 W
Blissfield, Mi., U.S.	124	C2	41.49 N	83.51 W
Blitar, Indon.	66	H8	8.06 S	112.09 E
Block Island, R.I., U.S.	124	C14	41.09 N	71.33 W
Block Island, i., R.I., U.S.	124	C14	41.10 N	71.35 W
Blockton, Ia., U.S.	130	D3	40.37 N	94.29 W
Bloedel, B.C., Can.	144	F5	50.06 N	125.22 W
Bloemfontein, S. Afr.	90	F8	29.07 S	26.12 E
Bloemhof, S. Afr.	90	E7	27.38 S	25.36 E
Bloemhofdam, res., S. Afr.	90	E7	27.40 S	25.40 E
Blois, Fr.	20	G10	47.34 N	1.19 E
Blokhus, Den.	16	J7	57.15 N	9.35 E
Blombacher Bach, ngh., Ger.	181		51.15 N	7.14 E
Blommestein Meer see Brokopondo Stuwmeer, res., Sur.	164	C6	4.48 N	55.04 W
Blomstermåla, Swe.	16	J14	56.59 N	16.20 E
Blönduós, Ice.	12a	k29	65.39 N	20.16 W
Blood Indian Creek, stm., Ab., Can.	142	C2	50.55 N	111.02 W
Blood Indian Reserve, ind. res., Ab., Can.	144	G17	49.30 N	113.10 W
Blood Mountain, mtn., Ga., U.S.	132	B2	34.44 N	83.56 W
Bloodvein, stm., Can.	118	B17	51.47 N	96.52 W
Bloody Foreland, c., Ire.	10	F4	55.09 N	8.17 W
Bloomer, Wi., U.S.	128	F7	45.06 N	91.29 W
Bloomfield, On., Can.	126	E12	43.59 N	77.14 W
Bloomfield, In., U.S.	130	E11	39.01 N	86.56 W
Bloomfield, Ia., U.S.	130	D5	40.45 N	92.25 W
Bloomfield, Ky., U.S.	130	G12	37.54 N	85.18 W
Bloomfield, Mo., U.S.	130	H8	36.53 N	89.56 W
Bloomfield, Ne., U.S.	140	E15	42.36 N	97.38 W
Bloomfield, N.M., U.S.	150	G9	36.42 N	107.59 W
Bloomfield, ngh., Pa., U.S.	197b		40.27 N	79.56 W
Bloomfield Glens, Mi., U.S.	199		42.33 N	83.20 W
Bloomfield Highlands, Mi., U.S.	199		42.36 N	83.16 W
Bloomingdale, Il., U.S.	196		41.57 N	88.04 W
Blooming Grove, Tx., U.S.	136	B11	32.05 N	96.43 W
Blooming Prairie, Mn., U.S.	128	H5	43.52 N	93.03 W
Bloomington, Il., U.S.	130	D9	40.28 N	88.59 W
Bloomington, In., U.S.	130	E11	39.10 N	86.31 W
Bloomington, Mn., U.S.	128	G5	44.50 N	93.17 W
Bloomington, Tx., U.S.	136	F11	28.38 N	96.53 W
Bloomington, Wi., U.S.	130	B7	42.53 N	90.55 W
Bloomsburg, Pa., U.S.	124	C9	40.59 N	76.27 W
Bloomsbury, Austl.	98	C7	20.42 S	148.36 E
Bloomsdale Gardens, Pa., U.S.	203		40.07 N	74.52 W
Bloomville, Oh., U.S.	124	C2	41.02 N	83.00 W
Blora, Indon.	66	G7	6.57 S	111.25 E
Blossburg, Pa., U.S.	124	C8	41.40 N	77.04 W
Blosseville Kyst, cst., Grnld.	108	D20	68.49 N	28.27 W
Blossom, Tx., U.S.	134	D3	33.40 N	95.22 W
Blouberg, mtn., S. Afr.	90	C9	23.01 S	28.59 E
Blountstown, Fl., U.S.	134	G13	30.26 N	85.02 W
Blountsville, Al., U.S.	134	C12	34.04 N	86.35 W
Blountville, Tn., U.S.	124	H3	36.32 N	82.19 W
Blovice, Czech Rep.	24	G9	49.34 N	13.31 E
Blowering Reservoir, res., Austl.	98	J6	35.29 S	148.15 E
Blowing Point Village, Anguilla	159a	a1	18.11 N	63.05 W
Blowing Rock, N.C., U.S.	124	H4	36.08 N	81.40 W
Bludenz, Aus.	30	C6	47.09 N	9.49 E
Blue, stm., Az., U.S.	150	J7	33.12 N	109.11 W
Blue, stm., Co., U.S.	138	B2	40.02 N	106.24 W
Blue, stm., In., U.S.	130	F11	38.10 N	86.19 W
Blue, stm., Ok., U.S.	134	C2	33.52 N	95.56 W
Blue Anchor, N.J., U.S.	203		39.41 N	74.52 W
Blue Anchor Brook, stm., N.J., U.S.	203		39.42 N	74.49 W
Bluebell Hill, Eng., U.K.	178		51.20 N	0.30 E
Blue Bonnets, Champ de Course, p.o.i., Qc., Can.	193a		45.29 N	73.39 W
Blue Brook, stm., N.J., U.S.	194		40.40 N	74.25 W
Blue Buck Knob, hill, Mo., U.S.	130	G5	36.57 N	92.07 W
Blue Creek, Wa., U.S.	146	B9	48.18 N	117.50 W
Blue Creek, stm., Id., U.S.	146	H10	42.02 N	116.12 W
Blue Creek, stm., Ne., U.S.	140	F10	41.20 N	102.10 W
Blue Creek, stm., Ut., U.S.	150	B4	41.31 N	112.24 W
Blue Cypress Lake, l., Fl., U.S.	132	I5	27.44 N	80.45 W
Blue Earth, Mn., U.S.	128	H4	43.38 N	94.06 W
Blue Earth, stm., U.S.	128	H4	44.08 N	94.04 W
Bluefield, Va., U.S.	124	G4	37.14 N	81.19 W
Bluefield, W.V., U.S.	124	G4	37.15 N	81.13 W
Bluefields, Nic.	156	F6	12.00 N	83.45 W
Bluefields Bay, b., Jam.	158d	i12	18.10 N	78.04 W
Blue Hill, Me., U.S.	122	F8	44.24 N	68.35 W
Blue Hill, Ne., U.S.	138	A10	40.20 N	98.27 W
Blue Hill Bay, b., Me., U.S.	122	F8	44.15 N	68.30 W
Blue Hills Reservation, p.o.i., Ma., U.S.	201		42.13 N	71.05 W
Blue Island, Il., U.S.	126	G2	41.39 N	87.40 W
Bluejoint Lake, l., Or., U.S.	146	H6	42.39 N	119.40 W
Blue Knob State Park, p.o.i., Pa., U.S.	124	D7	40.16 N	78.35 W
Blue Mosque, rel., Egypt	191c		30.02 N	31.15 E
Blue Mound, Ks., U.S.	130	F3	38.04 N	95.00 W
Blue Mountain, Ms., U.S.	134	C9	34.40 N	89.03 W
Blue Mountain, mtn., N.B., Can.	122	C10	47.48 N	66.19 W
Blue Mountain, mtn., Ar., U.S.	134	C4	34.41 N	94.03 W
Blue Mountain, mtn., Mt., U.S.	142	G9	47.16 N	104.10 W
Blue Mountain, mtn., N.H., U.S.	122	F5	44.47 N	71.29 W
Blue Mountain, mts., Pa., U.S.	124	D10	40.14 N	77.29 W
Blue Mountain Peak, mtn., Jam.	158d	i14	18.03 N	76.35 W
Blue Mountains, mts., Jam.	158d	i14	18.06 N	76.40 W
Blue Mountains, mts., U.S.	146	E9	45.15 N	118.41 W
Blue Mountains, mts., Me., U.S.	122	E6	44.50 N	70.35 W
Blue Mountains National Park, p.o.i., Austl.	98	J8	33.48 S	150.23 E
Blue Mud Bay, b., Austl.	96	B7	13.25 S	136.02 E
Blue Nile (Ābay) (Azraq, Al-Bahr al-), stm., Afr.	82	E6	15.37 N	32.30 E
Bluenose Lake, l., Nu., Can.	110	B6	68.25 N	119.45 W
Blue Point, N.Y., U.S.	194		40.45 N	73.02 W
Blue Point, c., N.Y., U.S.	194		40.44 N	73.02 W
Blue Rapids, Ks., U.S.	138	B12	39.40 N	96.39 W
Blue Ridge, Ab., Can.	144	B15	54.07 N	115.22 W
Blue Ridge, Ga., U.S.	132	B1	34.52 N	84.19 W
Blue Ridge, mts., U.S.	112	D11	37.00 N	82.00 W
Blue River, B.C., Can.	144	D11	52.06 N	119.19 W
Blue Rock Springs Park, p.o.i., Ca., U.S.	200		38.08 N	122.12 W
Blue Springs, Ne., U.S.	128	K2	40.08 N	96.40 W
Bluestone Dam, dam., W.V., U.S.	124	G5	37.38 N	80.53 W
Bluestone Lake, res., W.V., U.S.	124	G5	37.31 N	80.52 W
Bluestone State Park, p.o.i., W.V., U.S.	124	G4	37.37 N	80.56 W
Bluewater, N.M., U.S.	150	H9	35.16 N	107.57 W
Bluff, N.Z.	102	H3	46.36 S	168.20 E
Bluff, Ut., U.S.	150	F7	37.17 N	109.32 W
Bluff Cape, c., Mya.	64	D2	17.58 N	94.27 E
Bluff City, Tn., U.S.	124	H3	36.27 N	82.16 W
Bluff Cove, b., Ca., U.S.	198		33.48 N	118.24 W
Bluff Creek, stm., U.S.	138	D10	36.58 N	97.26 W
Bluff Creek, stm., Ks., U.S.	138	D9	37.02 N	99.29 W
Bluff Dale, Tx., U.S.	136	B9	32.21 N	98.01 W
Bluff Head, c., China	189d		22.11 N	114.12 E
Bluff Island, i., China	189d		22.19 N	114.21 E
Bluff Park, Al., U.S.	134	D12	33.24 N	86.51 W
Bluff Point, c., Austl.	96	E2	27.50 S	114.06 E
Bluffs, Il., U.S.	130	E7	39.44 N	90.31 W
Bluffton, In., U.S.	130	D12	40.44 N	85.10 W
Bluffton, Oh., U.S.	124	D2	40.52 N	83.53 W
Bluffton, S.C., U.S.	132	D5	32.14 N	80.51 W
Blumberg, Ger.	24	I4	47.50 N	8.32 E
Blumenau, Braz.	172	C13	26.55 S	49.04 W
Blumenhof, Sk., Can.	142	D6	50.01 N	107.41 W
Blunt, S.D., U.S.	140	C13	44.30 N	99.59 W
Bly, Or., U.S.	148	A4	42.26 N	121.06 W
Blyth, On., Can.	126	E8	43.44 N	81.26 W
Blyth, Eng., U.K.	10	F11	55.07 N	1.31 W
Blythe, Ca., U.S.	150	J2	33.36 N	114.35 W
Blytheville, Ar., U.S.	130	I8	35.55 N	89.55 W
Blyzniuky, Ukr.	38	E15	48.51 N	36.34 E
Bø, Nor.	16	H7	59.25 N	9.04 E
Bo, S.L.	84	H2	7.59 N	11.43 W
Boac, Phil.	68	D3	13.27 N	121.50 E
Boaco, Nic.	156	F5	12.28 N	85.39 W
Boadilla del Monte, Spain	184a		40.24 N	3.53 W
Boa Esperança, Braz.	170	K3	21.05 S	45.33 W

Name	Page	Map Ref.	Latitude	Longitude
Boa Esperança, Represa, res., Braz.	170	D3	6.45 S	44.03 W
Bo'ai, China	58	D5	35.09 N	113.03 E
Boane, Moz.	90	E11	26.00 S	32.28 E
Boa Nova, Braz.	170	H5	14.22 S	40.11 W
Bo'ao, China	58	L4	19.10 N	110.34 E
Board Camp Mountain, mtn., Ca., U.S.	148	C2	40.42 N	123.43 W
Boardman, Oh., U.S.	124	C5	41.00 N	80.40 W
Boardman, stm., Mi., U.S.	126	D4	44.46 N	85.38 W
Boat Basin, B.C., Can.	144	G4	49.28 N	126.26 W
Boatman, Austl.	98	F6	27.16 S	146.55 E
Boa Viagem, Braz.	170	C6	5.07 S	39.44 W
Boa Vista, Braz.	168	F11	2.49 N	60.40 W
Boa Vista, i., C.V.	85a	k10	16.05 N	22.50 W
Boa Vista, Morro, hill, Braz.	205a		22.53 S	43.06 W
Boavita, Col.	168	D5	6.20 N	72.35 W
Bobawai, Indon.	66	H12	8.45 S	121.10 E
Boaz, Al., U.S.	134	C12	34.12 N	86.10 W
Bobai, China	58	J3	22.12 N	109.52 E
Bobaomby, Tanjona, c., Madag.	88	C8	11.57 S	49.15 E
Bobbili, India	69	B6	18.34 N	83.21 E
Bobbing, Eng., U.K.	178		51.21 N	0.43 E
Bobbingworth, Eng., U.K.	178		51.44 N	0.13 E
Bobbin Head, Austl.	192a		33.39 S	151.08 E
Bobbio, Italy	30	F6	44.46 N	9.22 E
Bobbys Run, stm., N.J., U.S.	203		39.58 N	74.48 W
Bobcaygeon, On., Can.	126	D11	44.31 N	78.32 W
Bobigny, Fr.	20	F11	48.54 N	2.27 E
Böblingen, Ger.	24	H4	48.41 N	9.00 E
Boblo Island Amusement Park, p.o.i., On., Can.	199		42.06 N	83.07 W
Bobo-Dioulasso, Burkina	84	G4	11.10 N	4.18 W
Bobolice, Pol.	24	C12	53.57 N	16.35 E
Bobonaza, stm., Ec.	168	H3	2.36 S	76.38 W
Bobonong, Bots.	90	B9	21.57 S	28.25 E
Bobotsari, Indon.	66	G6	7.16 S	109.20 E
Bobr, Bela.	26	F12	54.20 N	29.18 E
Bobr, stm., Bela.	26	F11	54.02 N	28.51 E
Bobrov, Russia	40	F11	51.06 N	40.02 E
Bobrovytsia, Ukr.	38	C10	50.44 N	31.23 E
Bobrujsk see Babrujsk, Bela.	26	G12	53.08 N	29.14 E
Bobryk, stm., Bela.	26	H9	52.08 N	26.46 E
Bobrynets', Ukr.	38	E11	48.03 N	32.10 E
Bobtown, Pa., U.S.	124	E5	39.45 N	79.58 W
Bobures, Ven.	168	C6	9.14 N	71.09 W
Boby, mtn., Madag.	88	E8	22.13 S	46.54 E
Boca, ngh., Arg.	206		34.38 S	58.21 W
Boca Chica, P.R.	158a	c2	17.59 N	66.31 W
Bôca da Mata, Braz.	170	E7	9.41 S	36.11 W
Boca de Pozo, Ven.	168	B9	11.00 N	64.22 W
Boca do Acre, Braz.	164	E4	8.45 S	67.22 W
Boca do Jari, Braz.	164	D7	1.06 S	51.58 W
Bocage, Cap, c., N. Cal.	101d	m15	21.11 S	165.35 E
Boca Grande, Fl., U.S.	132	J3	26.44 N	82.15 W
Bocaiúva, Braz.	170	I4	17.07 S	43.49 W
Bocanegra, Peru	204d		12.01 S	77.07 W
Bocaranga, C.A.R.	86	C3	7.00 N	15.39 E
Boca Raton, Fl., U.S.	132	J5	26.21 N	80.05 W
Bocas del Toro, Pan.	156	H6	9.19 N	82.15 W
Bocay, Nic.	156	E5	14.18 N	85.08 W
Boccea, ngh., Italy	185a		41.58 N	12.19 E
Bochnia, Pol.	24	G16	49.58 N	20.25 E
Bocholt, Ger.	24	E2	51.50 N	6.36 E
Bochum, Ger.	24	E3	51.28 N	7.13 E
Bochum, Ger.	181		51.28 N	7.13 E
Bochum, S. Afr.	90	C9	23.17 S	29.07 E
Böckel, ngh., Ger.	181		51.13 N	7.12 E
Bockum, ngh., Ger.	181		51.21 N	6.38 E
Bockum, ngh., Ger.	181		51.20 N	6.44 E
Bocognano, Fr.	22	G14	42.05 N	9.03 E
Bocón, Caño, stm., Col.	168	F7	3.42 N	67.52 W
Boconó, Ven.	168	C6	9.14 N	70.16 W
Bocşa, Rom.	36	D8	45.23 N	21.47 E
Boda, C.A.R.	86	D3	4.19 N	17.28 E
Böda, Swe.	16	J15	57.15 N	17.03 E
Boda, Swe.	16	F13	61.01 N	15.13 E
Bodafors, Swe.	16	J12	57.30 N	14.42 E
Boda Glasbruk, Swe.	16	K13	56.44 N	15.40 E
Bodāi, India	190b		22.48 N	88.29 E
Bodajbo, Russia	50	E11	57.51 N	114.11 E
Bodalla, Austl.	98	K8	36.05 S	150.03 E
Bodcau Creek, stm., Ar., U.S.	134	D5	32.35 N	93.37 W
Bode, Ia., U.S.	128	I4	42.52 N	94.17 W
Bodega Bay, b., Ca., U.S.	148	E2	38.16 N	123.00 W
Bodélé, reg., Chad	82	D3	16.30 N	16.30 E
Bodelschwingh, ngh., Ger.	181		51.33 N	7.22 E
Boden, Swe.	14	G12	65.49 N	21.43 E
Bodensee see Constance, Lake, I., Eur.	24	I5	47.39 N	8.54 E
Bodhan, India	69	B3	18.39 N	77.53 E
Bodh Gaya, India	70	F10	24.41 N	84.58 E
Bodināyakkanūr, India	69	G3	10.00 N	77.21 E
Bodmin, Eng., U.K.	10	K8	50.29 N	4.43 W
Bodmin Moor, for., Eng., U.K.	10	K8	50.36 N	4.31 W
Bodø, Nor.	14	E5	67.16 N	14.23 E
Bodocó, Braz.	170	D6	7.47 S	39.55 W
Bodoquena, Serra da, plat., Braz.	166	D5	21.00 S	56.50 W
Bodrog, stm., Eur.	24	H17	48.07 N	21.25 E
Bodrum, Tur.	34	F10	37.02 N	27.26 E
Bodträskfors, Swe.	14	F11	66.05 N	20.56 E
Bodzentyn, Pol.	24	F16	50.56 N	20.58 E
Boele, ngh., Ger.	181		51.24 N	7.28 E
Boende, D.R.C.	86	E4	0.13 S	20.51 E
Bœng Lvea, Camb.	64	F7	12.36 N	105.34 E
Boën-sur-Lignon, Fr.	22	D9	45.44 N	3.59 E
Boeo, Capo, c., Italy	32	G6	37.48 N	12.26 E
Boerne, Tx., U.S.	136	E9	29.46 N	98.43 W
Boesmans, stm., S. Afr.	90	H7	33.40 S	26.37 E
Boeuf, stm., U.S.	134	E7	31.53 N	91.46 W
Boevo, Russia	38	B18	51.24 N	39.19 E
Boffa, Gui.	84	G2	10.10 N	14.02 W
Boffalora, Italy	184b		45.28 N	8.50 E
Bofors, Swe.	16	H12	59.19 N	14.33 E
Bōfu see Hōfu, Japan	56	E4	34.02 N	131.34 E
Bogachiel, stm., Wa., U.S.	146	C2	47.55 N	124.28 W
Bogale, Mya.	64	D2	16.17 N	95.23 E
Bogalusa, La., U.S.	134	G9	30.47 N	89.50 W
Bogan, stm., Austl.	98	H6	29.58 S	146.19 E
Bog and Vly Meadows, sw., N.J., U.S.	194		40.56 N	74.19 W
Bogan Gate, Austl.	98	I6	33.06 S	147.47 E
Bogangolo, C.A.R.	86	C3	5.34 N	18.14 E
Bogantungan, Austl.	98	D6	23.39 S	147.18 E
Bogart, Mount, mtn., Ab., Can.	144	F15	50.55 N	115.14 W
Bogastow Brook, stm., Ma., U.S.	201		42.12 N	71.22 W
Bogata, Tx., U.S.	134	D3	33.28 N	95.12 W
Boğazköy, ngh., Tur.	185b		41.11 N	28.46 E
Boğazköy, stm., Tur.	185b		41.10 N	28.49 E
Boğazlıyan, Tur.	42	F6	39.12 N	35.15 E
Bogcang, stm., China	70	C11	31.52 N	87.24 E
Bogda Shan, mts., China	52	C2	43.30 N	89.45 E
Bogen, Ger.	24	H8	48.55 N	12.43 E
Bogen, Nor.	14	D8	68.31 N	16.59 E
Bogense, Den.	16	L8	55.34 N	10.05 E
Boger City, N.C., U.S.	132	A4	35.29 N	81.12 W
Bogess Creek, stm., Ca., U.S.	200		37.18 N	122.19 W
Boggabilla, Austl.	98	G8	28.36 S	150.21 E
Boggabri, Austl.	98	H7	30.42 S	150.02 E
Boggs Run, stm., Pa., U.S.	197b		40.32 N	80.14 W
Boggy Peak, mtn., Antig.	159b	f4	17.03 N	61.51 W
Bogia, Pap. N. Gui.	101a	a3	4.14 S	144.55 E
Bogie Lake, I., Mi., U.S.	199		42.37 N	83.31 W
Bogles, Gren.	159e	p11	12.30 N	61.26 W
Bognes, Nor.	14	D6	68.12 N	16.00 E
Bognor Regis, Eng., U.K.	10	K12	50.47 N	0.41 W
Bogo, Phil.	68	E5	11.02 N	124.00 E
Bogoljubovo, Russia	26	E15	55.29 N	32.58 E
Bogomila, Mac.	34	B4	41.35 N	21.29 E
Bogong, Mount, mtn., Austl.	98	K6	36.44 S	147.18 E
Bogor, Indon.	66	G5	6.35 S	106.47 E
Bogorodick, Russia	26	G21	53.46 N	38.07 E
Bogorodsk, Russia	40	C13	56.06 N	43.31 E
Bogorodskoe, Russia	40	H13	46.20 N	43.53 E
Bogorodskoe, Russia	40	C17	57.50 N	50.44 E
Bogorodskoe, Russia	50	F17	52.22 N	140.26 E
Bogorodskoe, ngh., Russia	183b		55.49 N	37.44 E
Bogotá see Santa Fe de Bogotá, Col.	168	E5	4.36 N	74.05 W
Bogota, N.J., U.S.	194		40.52 N	74.01 W
Bogotol, Russia	48	C15	56.11 N	89.31 E
Bogovarovo, Russia	40	B15	58.58 N	47.01 E
Bogra, Bngl.	70	F12	24.50 N	89.22 E
Bogučany, Russia	48	C17	58.22 N	97.29 E
Bogučar, Russia	40	G12	49.56 N	40.34 E
Bogučar, stm., Russia	38	D19	49.56 N	40.15 E
Bogué, Maur.	84	F2	16.35 N	14.15 W
Bogue Chitto, Ms., U.S.	134	F8	31.26 N	90.27 W
Bogue Chitto, stm., U.S.	134	G8	30.35 N	89.49 W
Bogue Chitto Creek, stm., Al., U.S.	134	E11	32.10 N	87.14 W
Bogue Phalia, stm., Ms., U.S.	134	D8	33.15 N	90.43 W
Böğürtlen, Tur.	76	A8	37.10 N	38.04 E
Bo Hai (Chihli, Gulf of), b., China	58	B8	38.29 N	120.01 E
Bohai Haixia, strt., China	58	B9	38.15 N	121.00 E
Bohain-en-Vermandois, Fr.	20	D12	49.59 N	3.27 E
Bohai Wan, b., China	58	B8	38.42 N	118.18 E
Bohemia see Čechy, hist. reg., Czech Rep.	24	G10	49.50 N	14.00 E
Bohemian Forest, mts., Eur.	24	G8	48.53 N	13.51 E
Bohemian-Moravian Highlands see Českomoravská vrchovina, plat., Czech Rep.	24	G11	49.20 N	15.30 E
Böhmer Wald see Bohemian Forest, mts., Eur.	24	G8	48.53 N	13.51 E
Böhnsdorf, ngh., Ger.	182a		52.24 N	13.33 E
Bohodukhiv, Ukr.	38	C14	50.09 N	35.31 E
Bohol, I., Phil.	68	F4	9.54 N	123.43 E
Bohol Sea, s., Phil.	68	F5	9.10 N	124.25 E
Bohol Strait see Cebu Strait, strt., Phil.	68	F4	9.47 N	123.39 E
Bohorodchany, Ukr.	38	E3	48.48 N	24.32 E
Bohorok, Indon.	64	K4	3.30 N	98.09 E
Bohuslav, Ukr.	38	D9	49.32 N	30.53 E
Boiaçu, Braz.	168	H11	0.26 S	61.45 W
Boiano, Italy	32	C8	41.28 N	14.28 E
Boiarka, Ukr.	38	C9	50.19 N	30.17 E
Boiestown, N.B., Can.	122	D10	46.27 N	66.24 W
Boinville-en-Mantois, Fr.	179		48.56 N	1.46 E
Boinvilliers, Fr.	179		48.55 N	1.40 E
Boipeba, Ilha de, i., Braz.	170	G6	13.37 S	38.56 W
Bois, stm., Braz.	166	C6	18.36 S	50.01 W
Bois, Lac des, I., N.T., Can.	110	B6	66.46 N	125.08 W
Bois Blanc Island, i., Mi., U.S.	126	C5	45.45 N	84.28 W
Boisbriand, Qc., Can.	193a		45.37 N	73.51 W
Bois Brule, stm., Wi., U.S.	128	E7	46.44 N	91.36 W
Bois-Colombes, Fr.	179		48.55 N	2.16 E
Bois d'Arc Creek, stm., Tx., U.S.	134	D3	33.50 N	95.50 W
Bois-d'Arcy, Fr.	179		48.48 N	2.01 E
Bois de Sioux, stm., U.S.	128	E2	46.16 N	96.36 W
Boise, Id., U.S.	146	G10	43.37 N	116.12 W
Boise, stm., Id., U.S.	146	G10	43.49 N	117.01 W
Boise, Middle Fork, stm., Id., U.S.	146	G11	43.43 N	115.36 W
Boise, North Fork, stm., Id., U.S.	146	G11	43.44 N	115.37 W
Boise, South Fork, stm., Id., U.S.	146	G11	43.36 N	115.51 W
Boise City, Ok., U.S.	138	E6	36.44 N	102.30 W
Boisemont, Fr.	179		49.01 N	2.00 E
Bois Forte Indian Reservation, ind. res., Mn., U.S.	128	C5	48.06 N	93.10 W
Boissettes, Fr.	179		48.31 N	2.37 E
Boissevain, Mb., Can.	142	E13	49.13 N	100.02 W
Boissise-la-Bertrand, Fr.	179		48.32 N	2.35 E
Boissy-l'Aillerie, Fr.	179		49.05 N	2.02 E
Boissy-sous-Saint-Yon, Fr.	179		48.34 N	2.13 E
Boistfort Peak, mtn., Wa., U.S.	146	D3	46.30 N	123.13 W
Boizenburg, Ger.	24	C6	53.22 N	10.43 E
Boja, Indon.	66	G7	7.06 S	110.16 E
Bojadła, Pol.	24	E11	51.56 N	15.50 E
Bojarsk, Russia	48	C19	56.20 N	106.04 E
Bojayá, stm., Col.	168	D3	6.34 N	76.53 W
Bojeador, Cape, c., Phil.	68	A3	18.29 N	120.34 E
Bojnūrd, Iran	74	B15	37.28 N	57.19 E
Bojonegoro, Indon.	66	G7	7.09 S	111.52 E
Bojuru, Braz.	172	E12	31.38 S	51.26 W
Bokad, India	190c		18.53 N	72.58 E
Bokāro Steel City, India	70	G10	23.45 N	86.07 E
Bokatola, D.R.C.	86	E3	0.38 S	18.46 E
Bokchito, Ok., U.S.	134	C2	34.01 N	96.09 W
Boké, Gui.	84	G2	10.56 N	14.18 W
Bokes Creek, stm., Oh., U.S.	124	D2	40.19 N	83.10 W
Bokhara, stm., Austl.	98	G6	29.55 S	146.42 E
Bok Koŭ, Camb.	64	G6	10.34 N	104.02 E
Bokn, I., Nor.	16	H3	59.12 N	5.26 E
Boknafjorden, strt., Nor.	16	H3	59.10 N	5.35 E
Boko, Congo	86	E2	4.46 S	14.37 E
Bokoro, Chad	82	E3	12.22 N	17.03 E
Bokote, D.R.C.	86	E4	0.03 S	20.08 E
Bokovskaja, Russia	40	G12	49.13 N	41.49 E
Bokpyin, Mya.	64	G4	11.16 N	98.46 E
Boksburg, state, S. Afr.	191d		26.12 S	28.14 E
Boksburg-Noord, S. Afr.	191d		26.12 S	28.15 E
Boksburg-South, S. Afr.	191d		26.14 S	28.15 E
Boksburg-West, S. Afr.	191d		26.13 S	28.14 E
Boksitogorsk, Russia	26	A16	59.27 N	33.52 E
Bokungu, D.R.C.	86	E4	0.39 S	22.18 E
Bol, Cro.	30	G13	43.15 N	16.39 E
Bolama, Gui.-B.	84	G1	11.35 N	15.29 W
Bolangum, Austl.	98	K4	36.44 S	142.53 E
Bolaños, stm., Mex.	154	E7	21.11 N	104.05 W
Bolaños de Calatrava, Spain	28	F7	38.53 N	3.39 W
Bolān Pass, p., Pak.	62	C2	29.57 N	67.02 E
Bolans, Antig.	159b	f4	17.03 N	61.52 W
Bolayır, Tur.	34	C9	40.30 N	26.45 E
Bolbec, Fr.	20	E9	49.33 N	0.29 E
Bold Heath, Eng., U.K.	180		53.24 N	2.42 W
Bole, China	48	F14	44.54 N	82.03 E
Bole, Ghana	84	H4	9.01 N	2.29 W
Bolekhiv, Ukr.	38	D2	49.03 N	23.52 E
Boles, Ar., U.S.	134	C4	34.46 N	94.02 W
Bolesławiec, Pol.	24	E11	51.15 N	15.35 E
Boley, Ok., U.S.	134	B2	35.30 N	96.28 W
Bolgatanga, Ghana	84	G4	10.47 N	0.50 W
Bolhov, Russia	26	G18	53.26 N	36.00 E
Bolhrad, Ukr.	38	H7	45.41 N	28.36 E
Boli, China	52	B11	45.44 N	130.34 E
Boliden, Swe.	16	C18	64.51 N	20.23 E
Boligee, Al., U.S.	134	E10	32.45 N	88.01 W
Boling, Tx., U.S.	136	E12	29.15 N	95.56 W
Bolingbrook, Il., U.S.	130	C9	41.40 N	88.04 W
Bolinger Creek, stm., Ca., U.S.	200		37.47 N	122.00 W
Bolishan, China	54	C5	43.48 N	123.28 E
Bolívar, Col.	164	C2	4.21 N	76.10 W
Bolívar, Col.	168	G3	1.50 N	76.58 W
Bolívar, Col.	168	E4	5.50 N	76.01 W
Bolivar, Mo., U.S.	130	G4	37.36 N	93.24 W
Bolivar, N.Y., U.S.	124	B7	42.03 N	78.09 W
Bolivar, Tn., U.S.	134	B9	35.15 N	88.59 W
Bolívar, state, Col.	168	C4	9.00 N	74.40 W
Bolívar, state, Ec.	168	H2	1.35 S	79.00 W
Bolívar, state, Ven.	168	D10	6.20 N	63.30 W
Bolívar, Cerro, mtn., Ven.	168	D10	7.28 N	63.25 W
Bolívar, Pico, mtn., Ven.	168	C6	8.32 N	71.00 W
Bolivar Peninsula, pen., Tx., U.S.	136	E13	29.27 N	94.39 W
Bolivia, ctry., S.A.	166	C4	17.00 S	65.00 W
Bolkar Dağları, mts., Tur.	76	A5	37.15 N	34.20 E
Bölkenbusch, Ger.	181		51.21 N	7.06 E
Bolladello, Italy	184b		45.41 N	8.50 E
Böllberg, hill, Ger.	181		51.23 N	7.19 E
Bollène, Fr.	22	E10	44.17 N	4.44 E
Bollensdorf, Ger.	182a		52.31 N	13.43 E
Bolling Air Force Base, mil., D.C., U.S.	202c		38.51 N	77.02 W
Bollington, Eng., U.K.	180		53.22 N	2.25 W
Bollnäs, Swe.	16	F14	61.20 N	16.24 E
Bollon, Austl.	98	G6	28.01 S	147.24 E
Bollstabruk, Swe.	16	E15	62.59 N	17.40 E
Bollwerk, Ger.	181		51.10 N	7.35 E
Bolmen, I., Swe.	16	K11	56.55 N	13.40 E
Bolnisi, Geor.	42	E11	41.26 N	44.32 E
Bolobo, D.R.C.	86	E3	2.10 S	16.15 E
Bologna, Italy	30	F8	44.30 N	11.20 E
Bolognesi, Peru	164	F3	6.32 S	73.18 W
Bologoe, Russia	26	C17	57.53 N	34.03 E
Bologovo, Russia	26	D14	56.54 N	31.41 E
Bolohovo, Russia	26	F20	54.05 N	37.50 E
Bol'oj Anjuj, stm., Russia	50	C21	68.31 N	160.40 E
Bolomba, D.R.C.	86	D3	0.20 N	19.11 E
Bolon', Russia	50	G16	49.52 N	136.07 E
Bolon', ozero, I., Russia	50	G16	49.51 N	136.22 E
Bolonchén de Rejón, Mex.	156	C3	20.00 N	89.49 W
Bolos, Deir Mar (Saint Paul, Monastery of), rel., Egypt	76	J3	28.52 N	32.33 E
Bolotnoe, Russia	48	C14	55.39 N	84.24 E
Bolovens, Plateau des, plat., Laos	64	E8	15.14 N	106.16 E
Bol'šaja Atnja, Russia	40	C16	56.15 N	49.27 E
Bol'šaja Balahnja, stm., Russia	50	B9	73.38 N	106.07 E
Bol'šaja Dora, Russia	26	A20	59.05 N	37.38 E
Bol'šaja Glušica, Russia	40	E17	52.23 N	50.28 E
Bol'šaja Halan', Russia	38	C16	50.55 N	37.26 E
Bol'šaja Heta, stm., Russia	50	C5	69.34 N	84.17 E
Bol'šaja Hobda, stm., Kaz.	40	F19	50.56 N	54.34 E
Bol'šaja Hundala, Russia	18	G21	60.04 N	34.15 E
Bol'šaja Ižorka, stm., Russia	183a		59.48 N	30.36 E
Bol'šaja Kamenka see Bil'sha Kam'ianka, stm., Eur.	38	E18	48.22 N	40.03 E
Bol'šaja Kinel', stm., Russia	40	E18	53.13 N	50.31 E
Bol'šaja Kuonamka, stm., Russia	50	C10	70.45 N	113.20 E
Bol'šaja Lica, stm., Russia	14	C23	69.24 N	32.12 E
Bol'šaja Murta, Russia	48	C16	56.54 N	93.09 E
Bol'šaja Neva, stm., Russia	183a		59.58 N	30.13 E
Bol'šaja Ohta, ngh., Russia	183a		59.57 N	30.25 E
Bol'šaja Orlovka, Russia	40	H12	47.19 N	41.16 E
Bol'šaja Usa, Russia	40	C19	56.44 N	55.05 E
Bol'šaja Ussurka, stm., Russia	54	B11	44.49 N	135.34 E
Bol'šaja Varzuga, stm., Russia	14	F27	66.57 N	36.21 E
Bol'šaja Višera, Russia	26	B15	58.54 N	32.06 E
Bol'šaja Vladimirovka, Kaz.	48	D14	50.53 N	79.29 E
Bol'šakovo, Russia	26	F4	54.53 N	21.39 E
Bol'šakovo, Russia	183b		55.54 N	37.17 E
Bolsena, Italy	30	H8	42.39 N	11.59 E
Bolsena, Lago di, I., Italy	30	H9	42.36 N	11.56 E
Bol'šereče, Russia	48	C13	56.05 N	74.37 E
Bol'šereck, Russia	50	F20	52.27 N	156.21 E
Bol'šetroickoe, Russia	38	C16	50.32 N	37.17 E
Bol'šeustjikinskoe, Russia	40	D20	55.56 N	58.16 E
Bol'ševik, Russia	50	D18	62.41 N	147.35 E
Bol'ševik, Russia	183a		59.49 N	30.30 E
Bol'ševik, ostrov, i., Russia	50	A10	78.40 N	102.30 E
Bol'šezemel'skaja Tundra, reg., Russia	48	A9	67.30 N	56.00 E
Bolshevik see Bol'ševik, ostrov, i., Russia	50	A10	78.40 N	102.30 E
Bolshoi Theatre, bldg., Russia	183b		55.46 N	37.37 E
Bol'šie Čukkuri, gora, hill, Russia	18	C19	64.19 N	32.22 E
Bol'šie Gorki, Russia	183a		59.42 N	29.51 E
Bol'šie Kajbicy, Russia	40	D16	55.24 N	48.10 E
Bol'šie Saly, Russia	38	F18	47.23 N	39.41 E
Bol'šie Tarhany, Russia	40	D16	54.42 N	48.33 E
Bol'šie Uki, Russia	48	C12	56.57 N	72.37 E
Bolsjoj Sjatan, gora, mtn., Russia	40	E20	53.41 N	57.36 E
Bol'šoe, ozero, I., Russia	183a		60.04 N	30.39 E
Bol'šoe Gorodišče, Russia	26	C13	57.17 N	30.31 E
Bol'šoe Gorodišče, Russia	38	C16	50.37 N	37.03 E
Bol'šoe Manuškino, Russia	183a		59.53 N	30.49 E
Bol'šoe Mihajlovskoe, Russia	26	D21	56.47 N	38.04 E
Bol'šoe Ogarëvo, Russia	26	G20	53.33 N	37.43 E
Bol'šoe Polpino, Russia	26	G17	53.14 N	34.30 E
Bol'šoe Ramene, Russia	26	B19	58.21 N	36.39 E
Bol'šoe Selo, Russia	26	C21	57.43 N	38.57 E
Bol'šoe Soldatskoe, Russia	38	B14	51.19 N	35.30 E
Bol'šoe Zagore, Russia	26	C11	57.51 N	28.57 E
Bol'šoj, Russia	40	F13	50.13 N	43.26 E
Bol'šoj Begičev, ostrov, i., Russia	50	B11	74.20 N	112.30 E
Bol'šoj Irgiz, stm., Russia	40	E16	52.01 N	47.23 E
Bol'šoj Jugan, stm., Russia	48	B12	61.03 N	73.10 E
Bol'šoj Kamen', Russia	54	C10	43.06 N	132.21 E
Bol'šoj Kavkaz see Caucasus, mts.	42	D11	42.37 N	45.00 E
Bol'šoj Klimeckij, ostrov, i., Russia	18	F22	61.58 N	35.16 E
Bol'šoj Ljahovskij, ostrov, i., Russia	50	B17	73.35 N	142.00 E
Bol'šoj Šatan, gora see Bolsjoj Sjatan, gora, mtn., Russia	40	E20	53.41 N	57.36 E
Bol'šoj Simonogont, Russia	183a		59.50 N	29.49 E
Bol'šoj sor, I., Kaz.	40	I17	45.10 N	51.45 E
Bol'šoj Tal'cy, Russia	26	A15	59.12 N	33.00 E
Bol'šoj Tjuters, ostrov, i., Russia	18	H14	59.51 N	27.11 E
Bol'šoj Uluj, Russia	48	C16	56.39 N	90.35 E
Bol'šoj Uzen', stm., Eur.	40	G16	48.59 N	49.59 E
Bol'šoj Uzigont, Russia	183a		59.48 N	29.53 E
Bol'šoj Žužmuj, ostrov, i., Russia	18	C22	64.41 N	35.33 E
Boltaña, Spain	28	B11	42.27 N	0.04 E
Boltino, Russia	183b		55.58 N	37.41 E
Bolton, On., Can.	126	E10	43.52 N	79.43 W
Bolton, Eng., U.K.	10	H10	53.35 N	2.26 W
Bolton, Ms., U.S.	134	E8	32.21 N	90.27 W
Bolton, N.C., U.S.	132	B7	34.19 N	78.24 W
Bolton, mun., Eng., U.K.	180		53.34 N	2.28 W
Bolton, mun., Eng., U.K.	180		53.34 N	2.28 W
Bolton Wanderers Football Ground, p.o.i., Eng., U.K.	180		53.34 N	2.25 W
Bolu, Tur.	34	C14	40.44 N	31.36 E
Bolu, state, Tur.	34	C14	40.40 N	31.30 E
Bolva, stm., Russia	26	G17	53.16 N	34.20 E
Bolvadin, Tur.	34	E13	38.41 N	31.02 E
Bolwarra, Austl.	98	A5	17.23 S	144.10 E
Bóly, Hung.	36	C5	45.59 N	18.32 E
Bolzano (Bozen), Italy	30	D8	46.29 N	11.21 E
Boma, D.R.C.	86	F2	5.50 S	13.03 E
Bomaderry, Austl.	98	J8	34.51 S	150.36 E
Bomarsund, Fin.	18	G7	60.13 N	20.13 E
Bombala, Austl.	98	K7	36.54 S	149.14 E
Bombarral, Port.	28	E1	39.15 N	9.09 W
Bombay see Mumbai, India	69	B1	18.57 N	72.50 E
Bombay see Mumbai, India	190c		18.58 N	72.50 E
Bombay Harbour, b., India	190c		18.57 N	72.53 E
Bomberai, Semenanjung, pen., Indon.	60	F9	3.00 S	133.00 E
Bomboma, D.R.C.	86	D3	2.25 N	18.54 E
Bombon, Fr.	179		48.34 N	2.52 E
Bom Conselho, Braz.	170	E7	9.10 S	36.41 W
Bom Despacho, Braz.	170	J3	19.44 S	45.14 W
Bomdila, India	70	E14	27.27 N	92.17 E
Bomili, D.R.C.	86	D5	1.39 N	27.00 E
Bom Jardim, Ilha do, i., Braz.	205a		23.02 S	43.35 W
Bom Jesus, Braz.	170	E3	9.04 S	44.22 W
Bom Jesus da Lapa, Braz.	170	G4	13.15 S	43.25 W
Bømlafjorden, strt., Nor.	16	H3	59.39 N	5.20 E
Bømlo, i., Nor.	16	H3	59.47 N	5.11 E
Bommerholz, Ger.	181		51.23 N	7.18 E
Bommern, Ger.	181		51.25 N	7.20 E
Bomnak, Russia	50	F14	54.45 N	128.50 E
Bomokandi, stm., D.R.C.	86	D5	3.38 N	26.08 E
Bomongo, D.R.C.	86	D3	1.25 N	18.23 E
Bom Retiro, Braz.	172	C13	27.49 S	49.33 W
Bom Retiro, ngh., Braz.	205b		23.32 S	46.38 W
Bom Sucesso, Braz.	172	A12	23.40 S	51.45 W
Bom Sucesso, Braz.	205b		23.25 S	46.24 W
Bomu (Mbomou), stm., Afr.	82	G4	4.08 N	22.29 E
Bon, Cap, c., Tun.	84	B7	37.05 N	11.03 E
Bonaero Park, S. Afr.	191d		26.07 S	28.16 E
Bonaigarh, India	70	H10	21.48 N	84.57 E
Bon Air, Va., U.S.	124	G8	37.31 N	77.33 W
Bonaire, i., Neth. Ant.	158g	p23	12.10 N	68.14 W
Bonampak, hist., Mex.	156	D2	16.44 N	91.05 W
Bonandolok, Indon.	66	C1	1.47 N	98.49 E
Bonanza, Nic.	156	E5	14.00 N	84.33 W
Bonanza, Or., U.S.	148	A4	42.12 N	121.24 W
Bonanza, Ut., U.S.	150	C7	40.01 N	109.10 W
Bonanza Peak, mtn., Wa., U.S.	146	B6	48.14 N	120.52 W
Bonao, Dom. Rep.	156	C12	18.56 N	70.25 W
Bonaparte, Ia., U.S.	130	D6	40.41 N	91.48 W
Bonaparte, stm., B.C., Can.	144	E9	50.44 N	121.15 W
Bonaparte, Mount, mtn., Wa., U.S.	146	B7	48.45 N	119.08 W
Bonaparte Lake, I., B.C., Can.	144	E10	51.16 N	120.35 W
Bonar Bridge, Scot., U.K.	10	D8	57.53 N	4.21 W
Bonasse, Trin.	159f	s12	10.04 N	61.52 W
Bonaventure, Qc., Can.	122	B11	48.02 N	65.29 W
Bonaventure, stm., Qc., Can.	122	B11	48.01 N	65.29 W
Bonaventure, Île, i., Qc., Can.	122	B12	48.29 N	64.10 W
Bonavista, Nf., Can.	111a	j23	48.38 N	53.07 W
Bonavista Bay, b., Nf., Can.	111a	j23	48.50 N	53.21 W
Bonawon, Phil.	68	F4	9.07 N	122.56 E
Bonbeach, Austl.	192b		38.04 S	145.08 E
Boncuk Dağı, mtn., Tur.	34	G12	36.53 N	29.17 E
Bond, Ms., U.S.	134	G9	30.53 N	89.11 W
Bondeno, Italy	30	F8	44.53 N	11.24 E
Bondi, Austl.	192a		33.53 S	151.17 E
Bondo, D.R.C.	86	D4	3.49 N	23.40 E
Bondo, D.R.C.	86	E4	1.21 S	23.53 E
Bondoc Peninsula, pen., Phil.	68	D4	13.30 N	122.30 E
Bondoc Point, c., Phil.	68	D4	13.10 N	122.35 E
Bondoufle, Fr.	179		48.37 N	2.23 E
Bondoukou, C. Iv.	84	H4	8.02 N	2.48 W
Bondowoso, Indon.	66	G8	7.54 S	113.49 E
Bonduel, Wi., U.S.	128	G10	44.44 N	88.26 W
Bondy, Fr.	179		48.54 N	2.28 E
Bondy, Forêt de, p.o.i., Fr.	179		48.55 N	2.35 E
Bône see Annaba, Alg.	84	B6	36.54 N	7.45 E
Bone see Watampone, Indon.	66	F12	4.32 S	120.19 E
Bone, Teluk, b., Indon.	66	F7	4.00 S	120.40 E
Bonebone, Indon.	66	E12	2.40 S	120.33 E
Bon Echo Provincial Park, p.o.i., On., Can.	126	D12	44.55 N	77.16 W
Bonelohe, Indon.	66	F12	5.49 S	120.27 E
Boneogeh, Indon.	66	G12	7.17 S	120.49 E
Bonerate, Pulau, i., Indon.	66	G12	7.21 S	121.06 E
Bonesteel, S.D., U.S.	140	D13	43.04 N	98.59 W
Bonete Chico, Cerro, mtn., Arg.	172	D3	28.01 S	68.45 W
Bonete Grande, Cerro, mtn., Arg.	172	C3	27.56 S	68.44 W
Bonfinópolis de Minas, Braz.	170	I2	16.29 S	45.58 W
Bonga, Russia	18	G24	60.30 N	37.32 E
Bongabong, Phil.	68	D3	12.45 N	121.28 E
Bongaigaon, India	70	E13	26.26 N	90.34 E
Bongandanga, D.R.C.	86	D4	1.30 N	21.03 E
Bongao, Phil.	68	H2	5.01 N	119.46 E
Bongka, Indon.	60	F7	0.59 S	121.24 E
Bong Mieu, Viet.	64	E9	15.26 N	108.23 E
Bongo, Gabon	86	E2	2.08 S	10.13 E
Bongo, Massif des, mts., C.A.R.	86	C4	8.44 N	22.58 E
Bongor, Chad	82	E3	10.17 N	15.22 E
Bonham, Tx., U.S.	134	D2	33.35 N	96.10 W
Bonhomme, Morne, mtn., Haiti	156	C11	19.05 N	72.18 W
Bonifacio, Fr.	22	H15	41.23 N	9.10 E
Bonifacio, Phil.	68	F4	8.03 N	123.37 E
Bonifacio, Bouches de see Bonifacio, Strait of, strt., Eur.	22	H15	41.18 N	9.15 E
Bonifacio, Strait of, strt., Eur.	22	H15	41.18 N	9.15 E
Bonifacio Monument, hist., Phil.	187f		14.39 N	120.59 E
Bonifati, Capo, c., Italy	32	E9	39.35 N	15.52 E
Bonifay, Fl., U.S.	134	G13	30.47 N	85.40 W
Bonin Islands see Ogasawara-guntō, is., Japan	44	G18	26.57 N	142.14 E
Bonita, La., U.S.	134	E7	32.55 N	91.41 W
Bonita, Point, c., Ca., U.S.	200		37.49 N	122.32 W
Bonita Springs, Fl., U.S.	132	J4	26.20 N	81.47 W
Bonito, Braz.	166	D5	21.10 S	56.26 W
Bonito, Braz.	170	E8	8.29 S	35.44 W
Bonito, Pico, mtn., Hond.	156	E4	15.38 N	86.55 W
Bonito de Santa Fé, Braz.	170	D6	7.19 S	38.31 W
Bonjol, Indon.	66	D2	0.01 S	100.13 E
Bonkoukou, Niger	84	G5	14.00 N	3.12 E
Bon Meade, Pa., U.S.	197b		40.33 N	80.14 W
Bonn, Ger.	24	F2	50.44 N	7.05 E
Bonnechere, stm., On., Can.	126	C12	45.31 N	76.32 W
Bonnelles, Fr.	179		48.37 N	2.02 E
Bonners Ferry, Id., U.S.	146	B10	48.41 N	116.19 W
Bonnet, Lac du, res., Mb., Can.	142	D18	50.22 N	95.55 W
Bonnétable, Fr.	20	F9	48.10 N	0.25 E
Bonne Terre, Mo., U.S.	130	G7	37.55 N	90.33 W
Bonnet Plume, stm., Yk., Can.	110	B3	65.56 N	134.55 W
Bonneuil-sur-Marne, Fr.	179		48.46 N	2.29 E
Bonneval, Fr.	20	F10	48.11 N	1.24 E
Bonneville, Fr.	22	C12	46.04 N	6.24 E
Bonneville Peak, mtn., Id., U.S.	146	H14	42.46 N	112.08 W
Bonneville Salt Flats, pl., Ut., U.S.	132	C3	40.45 N	113.52 W
Bonney SE, Lake, I., Austl.	98	K3	37.48 S	140.22 E
Bonnie Doone, N.C., U.S.	132	A6	35.05 N	78.57 W
Bonnie Rock, Austl.	96	F3	30.32 S	118.21 E
Bönninghardt, Ger.	181		51.35 N	6.28 E
Bonny, Nig.	84	I6	4.26 N	7.10 E
Bonnyrigg, Austl.	192a		33.54 S	150.54 E
Bonnyville, Ab., Can.	144	B20	54.16 N	110.44 W
Bono, Italy	32	D2	40.25 N	9.01 E
Bono, Ar., U.S.	130	I7	35.55 N	90.48 W
Bonoi, Indon.	60	F10	1.51 S	137.48 E
Bonorva, Italy	32	D2	40.25 N	8.45 E
Bonsari, India	190c		19.04 N	73.02 E
Bon Secour, Al., U.S.	134	G11	30.17 N	87.42 W
Bonshaw, P.E., Can.	122	D13	46.12 N	63.23 W
Bonsucesso, ngh., Braz.	205a		22.52 S	43.15 W
Bontang, Indon.	66	C10	0.07 N	117.29 E
Bontberg, mtn., S. Afr.	90	H5	32.21 S	21.04 E
Bontebok National Park, p.o.i., S. Afr.	90	I5	34.07 S	20.23 E
Bonthe, S.L.	84	H2	7.31 N	12.30 W
Bontoc, Phil.	68	B3	17.04 N	120.59 E
Bon Wier, Tx., U.S.	136	D14	30.44 N	93.38 W
Bonyhád, Hung.	36	C5	46.18 N	18.32 E
Booby Point, c., Md., U.S.	202b		39.17 N	76.23 W
Boohatnie Indian Reserve, ind. res., B.C., Can.	144	F9	50.24 N	121.33 W
Book Cliffs, clf., U.S.	150	D7	39.11 N	109.19 W
Booker, Tx., U.S.	138	E8	36.27 N	100.32 W
Booker T. Washington National Monument, p.o.i., Va., U.S.	124	H6	37.01 N	79.45 W
Boola, Gui.	84	H3	8.22 N	8.43 W
Boolaloo, Austl.	96	D3	22.35 S	115.52 E
Booleroo Centre, Austl.	98	I2	32.52 S	138.20 E
Booligal, Austl.	98	I5	33.52 S	144.53 E
Boologooro, Austl.	96	D2	24.21 S	114.02 E
Boomarra, Austl.	98	B3	19.27 S	140.20 E
Boomi, Austl.	98	G7	28.44 S	149.35 E
Boonah, Austl.	98	F9	28.00 S	152.40 E
Boone, Ia., U.S.	128	I5	42.03 N	93.52 W
Boone, N.C., U.S.	124	H4	36.12 N	81.41 W
Boone, stm., Ia., U.S.	130	A4	42.19 N	93.56 W
Boone Draw, stm., N.M., U.S.	138	G5	33.51 N	103.42 W
Boone Lake, res., Tn., U.S.	126	H3	36.25 N	82.24 W
Boone Reservoir, res., Pa., U.S.	197b		40.15 N	80.08 W
Boones Mill, Va., U.S.	124	G5	37.07 N	79.57 W
Booneville, Ar., U.S.	134	B5	35.08 N	93.55 W
Booneville, Ky., U.S.	124	G2	37.27 N	83.41 W
Booneville, Ms., U.S.	134	C10	34.39 N	88.34 W
Boon Point, c., Antig.	159b	f4	17.10 N	61.50 W
Boonsboro, Md., U.S.	124	E8	39.30 N	77.39 W
Boonton Reservoir, res., N.J., U.S.	194		40.53 N	74.25 W
Böön Tsagaan nuur, I., Mong.	52	B4	45.35 N	99.09 E
Boonville, Ca., U.S.	148	D2	39.00 N	123.21 W
Boonville, In., U.S.	130	F10	38.02 N	87.16 W
Boonville, Mo., U.S.	130	F5	38.58 N	92.44 W
Boonville, N.Y., U.S.	126	E14	43.29 N	75.20 W
Boorindal, Austl.	98	H6	30.20 S	146.07 E
Booroorban, Austl.	98	J5	34.56 S	144.46 E
Boorowa, Austl.	98	J7	34.27 S	148.42 E
Boosaaso, Som.	86	B9	11.16 N	49.10 E
Booth, Al., U.S.	134	E12	32.30 N	86.34 W
Booth, Lac, res., Qc., Can.	126	B11	46.45 N	78.37 W
Boothbay Harbor, Me., U.S.	122	G7	43.51 N	69.37 W
Booth Corner, Pa., U.S.	203		39.51 N	75.29 W
Boothia, Gulf of, b., Nu., Can.	110	A12	71.00 N	91.00 W
Boothia Peninsula, pen., Nu., Can.	110	A12	70.30 N	95.00 W
Boothstown, Eng., U.K.	180		53.30 N	2.25 W
Boothville, La., U.S.	134	H9	29.19 N	89.24 W
Booth Wood Reservoir, res., Eng., U.K.	180		53.38 N	1.58 W
Boothwyn, Pa., U.S.	203		39.49 N	75.26 W
Booué, Gabon	86	E2	0.06 S	11.56 E
Booysens, ngh., S. Afr.	191d		26.14 S	28.01 E
Booze Creek, stm., Md., U.S.	202c		38.59 N	77.07 W
Bo Phloi, Thai.	64	E4	14.18 N	99.31 E
Bophuthatswana, hist. reg., S. Afr.	90	D7	26.00 S	25.35 E
Boping Ling, mts., China	58	I7	25.00 N	117.00 E
Bopolu, Lib.	84	H2	7.04 N	10.29 W

Name	Page	Map Ref.	Latitude	Longitude
Boqueirão, Ilha do, i., Braz.	205a		22.46 S	43.09 W
Boqueirão, Serra do, hills, Braz.	170	F4	11.30 S	43.45 W
Boquerón, Bahía de, b., P.R.	158a	b1	18.01 N	67.12 W
Boquerón, Túnel, trans., Ven.	204c		10.34 N	67.00 W
Boquet, Pa., U.S.	197b		40.23 N	79.36 W
Boquilla, Presa de la, res., Mex.	154	B6	27.31 N	105.30 W
Boquillas del Carmen, Mex.	154	A7	29.17 N	102.52 W
Boquim, Braz.	170	F7	11.09 S	37.37 W
Bor, Czech Rep.	24	G8	49.43 N	12.47 E
Bor, Russia	12	E20	62.57 N	42.36 E
Bor, Russia	40	C13	56.21 N	44.04 E
Bor, Sudan	82	F6	6.12 N	31.33 E
Bor, Tur.	42	G6	37.54 N	34.34 E
Bor, Yugo.	36	E9	44.04 N	22.06 E
Bor, Lak, stm., Kenya	86	D7	1.18 N	40.39 E
Bora-Bora, i., Fr. Poly.	94	E11	16.30 S	151.45 W
Borabu, Thai.	64	E6	16.02 N	103.07 E
Borah Peak, mtn., Id., U.S.	146	F13	44.08 N	113.48 W
Borås, Swe.	16	J10	57.43 N	12.56 E
Borāzjān, Iran	74	F12	29.15 N	51.12 E
Borba, Braz.	164	D6	4.23 S	59.34 W
Borba, Port.	28	F3	38.48 N	7.27 W
Borbeck, ngh., Ger.	181		51.29 N	6.57 E
Bordeaux, Fr.	22	E5	44.50 N	0.34 W
Bordeaux, S. Afr.	191d		26.06 S	28.01 E
Bordeaux, ngh., Qc., Can.	193a		45.33 N	73.41 W
Bordeaux Mountain, hill, V.I.U.S.	158b	e8	18.20 N	64.44 W
Borden, Sk., Can.	142	B6	52.25 N	107.13 W
Borden, Eng., U.K.	178		51.20 N	0.42 E
Borden Island, i., Can.	108	B3	78.30 N	111.30 W
Borden Peninsula, pen., Nu., Can.	110	A14	73.00 N	83.00 W
Bordertown, Austl.	98	K3	36.18 S	140.46 E
Bordesholm, Ger.	24	B6	54.10 N	10.02 E
Borðeyri, Ice.	12a	k29	65.13 N	21.09 W
Bordighera, Italy	30	G4	43.47 N	7.39 E
Bordj Menaïel, Alg.	28	H14	36.44 N	3.42 E
Bordj Omar Idriss, Alg.	84	D6	28.08 N	6.49 E
Borðoy, i., Far. Is.	12b	m34	62.17 N	6.32 W
Boreham, Eng., U.K.	178		51.46 N	0.33 E
Borel Hill, mtn., Ca., U.S.	200		37.19 N	122.12 W
Borensberg, Swe.	16	I13	58.33 N	15.17 E
Borgå see Porvoo, Fin.	18	G12	60.23 N	25.40 E
Borgarnes, Ice.	12a	k28	64.33 N	21.54 W
Børgefjell, mts., Nor.	16	B11	65.20 N	13.47 E
Børgefjell Nasjonalpark, p.o.i., Nor.	16	B11	65.10 N	14.00 E
Borger, Tx., U.S.	138	F7	35.39 N	101.24 W
Borgholm, Swe.	16	K14	56.52 N	16.40 E
Borgne, Lake, b., La., U.S.	134	G9	30.05 N	89.35 W
Borgnesse, Pointe, c., Mart.	159c	l7	14.27 N	60.54 W
Borgomanero, Italy	30	E5	45.42 N	8.28 E
Borgo San Dalmazzo, Italy	30	F4	44.19 N	7.28 E
Borgosesia, Italy	30	E5	45.43 N	8.16 E
Borgo Val di Taro, Italy	30	F6	44.29 N	9.46 E
Borgo Valsugana, Italy	30	D8	46.03 N	11.27 E
Borgsdorf, Forst, for., Ger.	182a		52.42 N	13.19 E
Borgworm see Waremme, Bel.	20	D14	50.41 N	5.16 E
Borikhan, Laos	64	C6	18.33 N	103.43 E
Borilovo, Russia	26	G18	53.22 N	35.58 E
Borisoglebsk, Russia	40	F13	51.21 N	42.05 E
Borisoglebskij, Russia	26	C22	57.15 N	39.09 E
Borisovka, Russia	38	C14	50.35 N	36.01 E
Borisovka, Russia	40	E11	52.50 N	39.58 E
Borisovo, ngh., Russia	183b		55.38 N	37.45 E
Borisovo-Sudskoe, Russia	18	H23	59.54 N	36.00 E
Borja, Spain	28	C9	41.50 N	1.31 W
Borjas Blancas see Les Borges Blanques, Spain	28	C11	41.31 N	0.52 E
Borkavičy, Bela.	26	E11	55.40 N	28.20 E
Borken, Ger.	24	E2	51.51 N	6.51 E
Borkou, reg., Chad	82	D3	18.01 N	18.25 E
Borkum, i., Ger.	24	C2	53.35 N	6.41 E
Borland Manor, Pa., U.S.	197b		40.15 N	80.09 W
Borlänge, Swe.	16	G13	60.29 N	15.27 E
Borle, ngh., India	190c		19.02 N	72.55 E
Borlu, Tur.	34	E11	38.44 N	28.24 E
Bormes, Fr.	22	F12	43.09 N	6.20 E
Bormes-les-Mimosas see Bormes, Fr.	22	F12	43.09 N	6.20 E
Bormida di Millesimo, stm., Italy	30	F5	44.39 N	8.21 E
Bormio, Italy	30	D7	46.28 N	10.22 E
Borna, Ger.	24	E9	51.19 N	13.12 E
Borneo (Kalimantan), i., Asia	60	E5	0.30 N	114.00 E
Bornholm, state, Den.	16	L13	55.10 N	15.00 E
Bornholm, i., Den.	16	L12	55.08 N	14.54 E
Börnicke, Ger.	182a		52.40 N	13.38 E
Börnig, ngh., Ger.	181		51.33 N	7.16 E
Bornim, ngh., Ger.	182a		52.26 N	13.00 E
Bornos, Embalse de, res., Spain	28	H5	36.49 N	5.41 W
Bornstedt, ngh., Ger.	182a		52.25 N	13.02 E
Borocay Island, i., Phil.	68	D3	11.59 N	121.55 E
Borodianka, Ukr.	38	D4	50.38 N	29.56 E
Borodino, Russia	26	E18	55.31 N	35.50 E
Borodino, Russia	44	C17	55.54 N	94.54 E
Borogoncy, Russia	50	D15	62.40 N	131.09 E
Borohoro Shan, mts., China	48	F14	44.06 N	83.10 E
Boromlia, Ukr.	38	C13	50.37 N	34.58 E
Boromo, Burkina	84	G4	11.45 N	2.56 W
Boron, Ca., U.S.	148	H8	34.59 N	117.38 W
Boronga Islands, is., Mya.	70	H14	19.56 N	92.49 E
Borongan, Phil.	68	E5	11.37 N	125.26 E
Boronia, Austl.	192b		37.52 S	145.17 E
Borotou, C. Iv.	84	H3	8.43 N	7.30 W
Borough Park, ngh., N.Y., U.S.	194		40.38 N	74.00 W
Borova, Ukr.	38	D16	49.23 N	37.38 E
Borova, Ukr.	38	C9	50.13 N	30.08 E
Borovan, Blg.	36	F10	43.26 N	23.46 E
Borove, Ukr.	38	B6	51.06 N	27.13 E
Borovići, Russia	26	B16	58.23 N	33.54 E
Borovljanka, Russia	48	D14	52.37 N	84.25 E
Borovoj, Russia	18	C19	64.38 N	32.13 E
Borovsk, Russia	26	E19	55.12 N	36.29 E
Borovskaja, Russia	12	F19	60.45 N	41.06 E
Borovskij, Russia	48	C11	57.02 N	65.43 E
Borovskoj, Kaz.	48	D10	53.47 N	64.10 E
Borrachudo, stm., Braz.	170	J3	18.12 S	45.16 W
Borrazópolis, Braz.	172	A12	23.54 S	51.37 W
Borrby, Swe.	16	L12	55.26 N	14.10 E
Borriana, Spain	28	E10	39.53 N	0.05 W
Borroloola, Austl.	96	C7	16.05 S	136.17 E
Borş, Rom.	36	B8	47.07 N	21.49 E
Borşa, Rom.	36	C10	46.56 N	23.40 E
Borşa, Rom.	36	B11	47.39 N	24.39 E
Borsad, India	70	G4	22.24 N	72.53 E
Borsano, Italy	184b		45.35 N	8.51 E
Borschemich, Ger.	181		51.04 N	6.25 E
Borščovočnyj hrebet, mts., Russia	50	F12	52.00 N	117.00 E
Børselva, stm., Nor.	14	B16	70.18 N	25.32 E
Borshchiv, Ukr.	38	E5	48.48 N	26.03 E
Borskoe, Russia	40	E17	53.02 N	51.41 E
Borsod-Abaúj-Zemplén, state, Hung.	36	A8	48.15 N	21.00 E
Bort-les-Orgues, Fr.	22	D8	45.24 N	2.29 E
Bortnychi, Ukr.	38	C9	50.21 N	30.42 E
Bortondale, Pa., U.S.	203		39.54 N	79.24 W
Borūjen, Iran	74	D12	31.57 N	51.17 E
Borūjerd, Iran	74	D11	33.53 N	48.45 E
Borysiv, Ukr.	38	C5	50.11 N	26.31 E
Boryslav, Ukr.	38	D2	49.17 N	23.25 E
Boryspil', Ukr.	38	C9	50.21 N	30.57 E
Borzja, Russia	50	F12	50.22 N	116.31 E
Borzna, Ukr.	38	B11	51.15 N	32.26 E
Borzyszkowy, Pol.	24	B13	54.03 N	17.22 E
Bosa, Italy	32	D2	40.18 N	8.30 E
Bosaga, Kaz.	48	E12	47.54 N	72.57 E
Bosanska Dubica, Bos.	36	D3	45.10 N	16.49 E
Bosanska Gradiška, Bos.	36	D4	45.09 N	17.15 E
Bosanska Krupa, Bos.	36	E3	44.53 N	16.09 E
Bosanski Novi, Bos.	36	D3	45.03 N	16.23 E
Bosanski Petrovac, Bos.	36	E3	44.33 N	16.21 E
Bosanski Šamac, Bos.	36	D5	45.03 N	18.27 E
Bosansko Grahovo, Bos.	36	E3	44.10 N	16.21 E
Bosavi, Mount, mtn., Pap. N. Gui.	101a	b3	6.35 S	142.50 E
Boscobel, Wi., U.S.	130	A7	43.07 N	90.41 W
Bose, China	58	J2	23.54 N	106.38 E
Boshan, China	58	C7	36.29 N	117.50 E
Boshof, S. Afr.	90	F7	28.32 S	25.14 E
Bosilegrad, Yugo.	36	G9	42.29 N	22.30 E
Boskop, mtn., S. Afr.	191d		26.05 S	27.57 E
Boskovice, Czech Rep.	24	G12	49.28 N	16.39 E
Bosna, India	190b		22.37 N	88.30 E
Bosna, stm., Bos.	36	E5	45.04 N	18.28 E
Bosna i Hercegovina see Bosnia and Herzegovina, ctry., Eur.	36	E3	44.15 N	17.50 E
Bosnia and Hercegovina see Bosnia and Herzegovina, ctry., Eur.	36	E3	44.15 N	17.50 E
Bosnia and Herzegovina, ctry., Eur.	36	E3	44.15 N	17.50 E
Bosnik, Indon.	60	F10	1.07 S	136.20 E
Bošnjakovo, Russia	50	G17	49.38 N	142.10 E
Boso, India	190b		22.58 N	88.08 E
Bosobolo, D.R.C.	86	D3	4.10 N	19.52 E
Bōsō-kyūryō, hills, Japan	186		35.08 N	139.56 E
Bösperde, Ger.	181		51.28 N	7.46 E
Bosporus see İstanbul Boğazı, strt., Tur.	34	B12	41.06 N	29.04 E
Bosque, Paseo del, p.o.i., Arg.	206		34.55 S	57.56 W
Bosque Farms, N.M., U.S.	138	G2	34.53 N	106.40 W
Bosques, Arg.	206		34.49 S	58.14 W
Bossangoa, C.A.R.	86	C3	6.29 N	17.27 E
Bossembélé, C.A.R.	86	C3	5.15 N	17.38 E
Bossentélé, C.A.R.	86	C3	5.41 N	16.38 E
Bossert Estates, N.J., U.S.	203		40.09 N	74.44 W
Bossey Bangou, Niger	84	G5	13.20 N	1.17 E
Bossier City, La., U.S.	134	E5	32.31 N	93.43 W
Bossley Park, Austl.	192a		33.52 S	150.54 E
Bostān, Iran	74	E11	31.43 N	48.00 E
Bostancı, ngh., Tur.	185b		40.57 N	29.05 E
Bosten Hu, l., China	52	C2	42.00 N	87.00 E
Bostock Green, Eng., U.K.	180		53.13 N	2.30 W
Boston, Eng., U.K.	10	H12	52.58 N	0.02 W
Boston, Ga., U.S.	132	F2	30.47 N	83.47 W
Boston, Ma., U.S.	124	B14	42.22 N	71.03 W
Boston, Ma., U.S.	201		42.21 N	71.03 W
Boston, Pa., U.S.	197b		40.18 N	79.49 W
Boston Bar, B.C., Can.	144	G9	49.51 N	121.26 W
Boston Bay, b., Ma., U.S.	201		42.22 N	70.54 W
Boston Brook, stm., Ma., U.S.	201		42.37 N	71.00 W
Boston College, educ., Ma., U.S.	201		42.20 N	71.10 W
Boston Common, p.o.i., Ma., U.S.	201		42.21 N	71.05 W
Boston Harbor, b., Ma., U.S.	201		42.20 N	70.58 W
Boston Mountains, mts., Ar., U.S.	134	B5	35.50 N	93.20 W
Bostonnais, stm., Qc., Can.	122	C4	47.27 N	72.47 W
Boston University, educ., Ma., U.S.	201		42.21 N	71.07 W
Boswell, In., U.S.	130	D10	40.31 N	87.21 W
Boswell, Ok., U.S.	134	C3	34.02 N	95.52 W
Boswell, Pa., U.S.	124	D6	40.09 N	79.01 W
Bosworth, Mo., U.S.	130	E4	39.28 N	93.20 W
Bosworth Airport, arpt., Oh., U.S.	197a		41.26 N	82.00 W
Botād, India	70	G3	22.10 N	71.39 E
Botafogo, ngh., Braz.	205a		22.57 S	43.11 W
Botafogo, Enseada de, b., Braz.	205a		22.57 S	43.10 W
Botanical Garden, p.o.i., China	187b		31.09 N	121.26 E
Botany, Austl.	192a		33.57 S	151.12 E
Botany Bay, ngh., Eng., U.K.	178		51.41 N	0.07 W
Botany Bay, b., Austl.	98	J8	33.58 S	151.10 E
Boteti, stm., Bots.	88	E3	20.08 S	23.22 E
Botev, mtn., Blg.	36	G11	42.43 N	24.55 E
Botevgrad, Blg.	36	G10	42.54 N	23.48 E
Bothaville, S. Afr.	90	E8	27.23 S	26.37 E
Bothnia, Gulf of, b., Eur.	18	D8	63.00 N	20.00 E
Bothwell, Austl.	99a	o13	42.23 S	147.00 E
Bothwell, On., Can.	126	F8	42.37 N	81.51 W
Boticas, Port.	28	C3	41.41 N	7.40 W
Botiieve, Ukr.	38	G14	46.40 N	35.50 E
Botkins, Oh., U.S.	124	D1	40.28 N	84.10 W
Botkul', ozero, l.	40	G15	48.46 N	46.40 E
Botlih, Russia	42	D12	42.39 N	46.10 E
Botna, stm., Mol.	38	G7	46.48 N	29.35 E
Botoşani, Rom.	36	B13	47.44 N	26.40 E
Botoşani, state, Rom.	36	B13	48.00 N	26.45 E
Botoşaniţa, Rom.	36	B13	47.53 N	26.07 E
Bo Trach, Viet.	64	D8	17.35 N	106.32 E
Botrange, mtn., Bel.	20	D15	50.30 N	6.08 E
Botswana, ctry., Afr.	88	E3	22.00 S	24.00 E
Botte Donato, Monte, mtn., Italy	32	E10	39.17 N	16.26 E
Bottineau, N.D., U.S.	142	F13	48.49 N	100.27 W
Bottniska Viken see Bothnia, Gulf of, b., Eur.	18	D8	63.00 N	20.00 E
Bottoms Reservoir, res., Eng., U.K.	180		53.28 N	1.58 W
Botucatu, Braz.	170	L1	22.52 S	48.26 W
Botwood, Nf., Can.	111a	j22	49.08 N	55.21 W
Bötzsee, l., Ger.	182a		52.34 N	13.50 E
Bouaflé, C. Iv.	84	H3	6.59 N	5.45 W
Bouafle, Fr.	179		48.58 N	1.54 E
Bouaké, C. Iv.	84	H3	7.41 N	5.02 W
Bouandougou, C. Iv.	84	H3	8.13 N	5.40 W
Bouar, C.A.R.	86	C3	5.56 N	15.36 E
Bouârfa, Mor.	84	C4	32.31 N	1.56 W
Bouca, C.A.R.	86	C3	6.30 N	18.17 E
Boucher, stm., Qc., Can.	122	A7	49.25 N	69.06 W
Boucherville, Îles de, is., Qc., Can.	193a		45.37 N	73.28 W
Bouches-du-Rhône, state, Fr.	22	F11	43.30 N	5.00 E
Bouctouche, N.B., Can.	122	D12	46.28 N	64.43 W
Boufarik, Alg.	28	H13	36.34 N	2.54 E
Bouffémont, Fr.	179		49.03 N	2.18 E
Bou Ficha, Tun.	32	H4	36.18 N	10.29 E
Bougainville see North Solomons, state, Pap. N. Gui.	101b	c7	6.03 S	156.22 E
Bougainville, i., Pap. N. Gui.	94	D6	6.00 S	155.00 E
Bougainville, Détroit de, strt., Vanuatu	101d	j16	15.47 S	167.03 E
Bougainville Strait, strt., Oc.	101b	d7	6.45 S	155.59 E
Bough Beech Reservoir, res., Eng., U.K.	178		51.13 N	0.08 E
Boughton Green, Eng., U.K.	178		51.14 N	0.32 E
Boughton Malherbe, Eng., U.K.	178		51.13 N	0.42 E
Boughton Place, bldg., Eng., U.K.	178		51.13 N	0.32 E
Bougie see Bejaïa, Alg.	84	B6	36.45 N	5.04 E
Bougouni, Mali	84	G3	11.25 N	7.29 W
Bouillante, Guad.	159c	h5	16.08 N	61.46 W
Bouillon, Bel.	20	E14	49.48 N	5.04 E
Bouïra, Alg.	84	B5	36.22 N	3.53 E
Bouisy, Ru de, stm., Fr.	179		48.34 N	2.45 E
Boujdour, Cap, c., W. Sah.	84	D2	26.08 N	14.29 W
Boukiéro, Congo	191b		4.12 S	15.18 E
Boukiéro, Mont, hill, Congo	191b		4.11 S	15.17 E
Boulardérie Island, i., N.S., Can.	122	D16	46.12 N	60.29 W
Boulder, Co., U.S.	138	A3	40.02 N	105.16 W
Boulder, Mt., U.S.	146	D14	46.13 N	112.07 W
Boulder, stm., Mt., U.S.	146	D15	45.52 N	111.56 W
Boulder City, Nv., U.S.	150	H2	35.58 N	114.49 W
Boulder Creek, stm., Ut., U.S.	150	F5	37.45 N	111.20 W
Bouleaux, Lac des, l., Qc., Can.	193a		45.33 N	73.19 W
Boulia, Austl.	98	D2	22.55 S	139.54 E
Boullay-les-Troux, Fr.	179		48.41 N	2.03 E
Boulogne, Bois de, p.o.i., Fr.	179		48.50 N	2.15 E
Boulogne-sur-Gesse, Fr.	22	F6	43.17 N	0.39 E
Boulogne-sur-Mer, Fr.	20	D10	50.43 N	1.36 E
Bouloupari, N. Cal.	101d	m15	21.52 S	166.02 E
Boulsa, Burkina	84	G4	12.39 N	0.34 W
Bou Maad, Djebel, mtn., Alg.	28	H13	36.26 N	2.08 E
Boûmdeïd, Maur.	84	F2	17.26 N	11.20 W
Bou Medfaa, Alg.	28	H13	36.21 N	2.28 E
Bouna, C. Iv.	84	H4	9.16 N	2.59 W
Boundary Peak, mtn., Nv., U.S.	148	F7	37.51 N	118.21 W
Bound Brook, stm., Ma., U.S.	201		42.13 N	70.47 W
Bound Brook, stm., N.J., U.S.	194		40.35 N	74.30 W
Boundiali, C. Iv.	84	H3	9.31 N	6.29 W
Boun Nua, Laos	64	B5	21.38 N	101.54 E
Bountiful, Ut., U.S.	150	C5	40.52 N	111.52 W
Bounty Bay, b., Pit.	100k	c28	25.03 S	130.05 W
Bounty Islands, is., N.Z.	102	H8	47.42 S	179.04 E
Bounty Trough, unds.	174	N20	46.00 S	178.00 E
Bouqueval, Fr.	179		49.01 N	2.26 E
Bourail, N. Cal.	101d	m15	21.33 S	165.27 E
Bouray-sur-Juine, Fr.	179		48.31 N	2.18 E
Bourbeuse, stm., Mo., U.S.	130	F6	38.23 N	90.53 W
Bourbon, In., U.S.	130	C11	41.17 N	86.05 W
Bourbon, Mo., U.S.	130	F6	38.08 N	91.16 W
Bourbon-Lancy, Fr.	20	H12	46.37 N	3.46 E
Bourbonnais, hist. reg., Fr.	22	C9	46.20 N	3.00 E
Bourbonne-les-Bains, Fr.	20	G14	47.56 N	5.44 E
Bourbre, stm., Fr.	22	D11	45.46 N	5.11 E
Bourdon, Île, i., Qc., Can.	193a		45.43 N	73.29 W
Bourdonné, Fr.	179		48.45 N	1.40 E
Beurem, Mali	84	F4	16.58 N	0.20 W
Bourg, La., U.S.	134	H8	29.33 N	90.36 W
Bourganeuf, Fr.	22	D7	45.57 N	1.45 E
Bourg-en-Bresse, Fr.	22	C11	46.12 N	5.12 E
Bourges, Fr.	22	B8	47.04 N	2.24 E
Bourget, On., Can.	126	C14	45.26 N	75.09 W
Bourget, Lac du, l., Fr.	22	D11	45.43 N	5.51 E
Bourg-la-Reine, Fr.	179		48.47 N	2.19 E
Bourgneuf, Fr.	179		48.36 N	2.00 E
Bourgogne (Burgundy), hist. reg., Fr.	22	C10	47.00 N	4.30 E
Bourgogne, Canal de, can., Fr.	20	G13	47.58 N	3.30 E
Bourgoin-Jallieu, Fr.	22	D11	45.36 N	5.16 E
Bourke, Austl.	98	H5	30.05 S	145.56 E
Bourne, The, stm., Eng., U.K.	178		51.22 N	0.29 W
Bournebridge, Eng., U.K.	178		51.38 N	0.11 E
Bourne End, Eng., U.K.	178		51.45 N	0.32 W
Bournemouth, Eng., U.K.	10	K11	50.44 N	1.51 W
Bou Saâda, Alg.	84	B5	35.12 N	4.11 E
Bou Salem, Tun.	32	H2	36.36 N	8.59 E
Bouse, Az., U.S.	150	J2	33.55 N	114.00 W
Bouse Wash, stm., Az., U.S.	150	J3	34.02 N	114.19 W
Bou Smail, Alg.	28	H13	36.38 N	2.41 E
Boussac, Fr.	22	C8	46.21 N	2.13 E
Bousso, Chad	82	E3	10.29 N	16.42 E
Boussy-Saint-Antoine, Fr.	179		48.41 N	2.32 E
Bout, Pointe du, c., Mart.	159c	k6	14.33 N	61.03 W
Boutilimit, Maur.	84	F2	17.33 N	14.41 W
Bouvetøya, i., Ant.	103	A5	54.26 S	3.24 E
Bouvier Bay, b., Mi., U.S.	199		42.39 N	82.38 W
Bouza, Niger	84	G6	14.24 N	6.02 E
Bov, Den.	24	B5	54.50 N	9.22 E
Bøvågen, Nor.	16	G2	60.40 N	4.58 E
Bovalino Marina, Italy	32	F10	38.10 N	16.11 E
Bovard, Pa., U.S.	197b		40.19 N	79.30 W
Bovec, Slvn.	30	D10	46.20 N	13.32 E
Boven Slinge see Schlinge, stm., Eur.	20	C15	51.55 N	6.19 E
Bøverdal, Nor.	16	F6	61.43 N	8.20 E
Bovey, Mn., U.S.	128	D5	47.17 N	93.25 W
Bovill, Id., U.S.	146	D10	46.51 N	116.23 W
Bovina, Tx., U.S.	138	G6	34.31 N	102.53 W
Bövinghausen, ngh., Ger.	181		51.31 N	7.19 E
Bovisio Masciago, Italy	184b		45.37 N	9.09 E
Bovril, Arg.	172	E8	31.19 S	59.26 W
Bow, stm., Ab., Can.	144	G19	49.56 N	111.41 W
Bo-Wadrif, S. Afr.	90	H4	32.24 S	20.06 E
Bowbells, N.D., U.S.	142	F11	48.47 N	102.14 W
Bow Creek, stm., Ks., U.S.	138	B9	39.35 N	99.14 W
Bowden, Ab., Can.	144	E16	51.56 N	114.02 W
Bowdle, S.D., U.S.	140	B13	45.25 N	99.38 W
Bowdoin, Lake, l., Mt., U.S.	142	F6	48.24 N	107.41 W
Bowdon, Eng., U.K.	180		53.23 N	2.22 W
Bowdon, Ga., U.S.	134	D13	33.32 N	85.15 W
Bowdon, N.D., U.S.	142	G13	47.27 N	99.42 W
Bowen, Arg.	172	G4	35.00 S	67.31 W
Bowen, Austl.	98	C7	20.00 S	148.13 E
Bowen, Il., U.S.	130	D7	40.13 N	91.03 W
Bowen, stm., Austl.	98	C6	20.23 S	147.20 E
Bowers Gifford, Eng., U.K.	178		51.34 N	0.32 E
Bowers Marshes, sw., Eng., U.K.	178		51.33 N	0.32 E
Bowie, Az., U.S.	150	K7	32.19 N	109.29 W
Bowie, Md., U.S.	124	F9	39.00 N	76.45 W
Bowie, Tx., U.S.	138	H11	33.33 N	97.50 W
Bowie Creek, stm., Ms., U.S.	134	F9	31.26 N	89.24 W
Bow Island, Ab., Can.	142	E2	49.52 N	111.22 W
Bowley Bar, spit, Md., U.S.	202b		39.18 N	76.23 W
Bowleys Quarters, Md., U.S.	202b		39.19 N	76.24 W
Bowling Green, Fl., U.S.	132	I4	27.38 N	81.49 W
Bowling Green, Ky., U.S.	130	H11	36.59 N	86.26 W
Bowling Green, Mo., U.S.	130	E6	39.20 N	91.12 W
Bowling Green, Oh., U.S.	124	C2	41.22 N	83.38 W
Bowling Green, Pa., U.S.	203		39.55 N	75.23 W
Bowling Green, Va., U.S.	124	F8	38.02 N	77.20 W
Bowling Green, Cape, c., Austl.	98	B6	19.19 S	147.25 E
Bowling Green Bay National Park, p.o.i., Austl.	98	B7	19.27 S	147.12 E
Bowman, Ga., U.S.	132	B2	34.12 N	83.01 W
Bowman, N.D., U.S.	140	A9	46.10 N	103.24 W
Bowman, S.C., U.S.	132	C5	33.20 N	80.40 W
Bowman, Mount, mtn., B.C., Can.	144	E9	51.10 N	121.55 W
Bowman-Haley Lake, res., N.D., U.S.	140	A9	45.59 N	103.15 W
Bowmanville, On., Can.	126	E11	43.55 N	78.41 W
Bowral, Austl.	98	J8	34.28 S	150.25 E
Bowraville, Austl.	98	H9	30.39 S	152.51 E
Bowron, stm., B.C., Can.	144	C9	54.03 N	121.49 W
Bowron Lake Provincial Park, p.o.i., B.C., Can.	144	C9	53.10 N	121.06 W
Bowsman, Mb., Can.	142	B12	52.14 N	101.11 W
Box Butte Creek, stm., Ne., U.S.	140	E10	42.28 N	102.38 W
Box Elder, Mt., U.S.	146	B16	48.19 N	110.00 W
Boxelder Creek, stm., U.S.	140	B8	45.58 N	103.56 W
Box Elder Creek, stm., Co., U.S.	140	G8	40.22 N	104.28 W
Boxelder Creek, stm., Co., U.S.	140	G7	40.32 N	105.00 W
Box Elder Creek, stm., Mt., U.S.	142	G5	46.57 N	108.04 W
Boxelder Creek, stm., S.D., U.S.	140	C10	44.00 N	102.28 W
Boxford State Forest, p.o.i., Ma., U.S.	201		42.39 N	71.02 W
Box Grove, On., Can.	193b		43.51 N	79.14 W
Boxholm, Swe.	16	I13	58.11 N	15.03 E
Boxing, China	58	C8	37.08 N	118.07 E
Boxley, Eng., U.K.	178		51.18 N	0.33 E
Boxmoor, Eng., U.K.	178		51.45 N	0.29 W
Boyabat, Tur.	42	E6	41.28 N	34.47 E
Boyacá, state, Col.	168	E5	5.30 N	73.30 W
Boyacıköy, ngh., Tur.	185b		41.06 N	29.02 E
Boyang, China	58	G7	28.59 N	116.40 E
Boyce, La., U.S.	134	F6	31.23 N	92.40 W
Boyceville, Wi., U.S.	128	F6	45.02 N	92.02 W
Boyd, Mn., U.S.	128	G3	44.50 N	95.54 W
Boyd, Tx., U.S.	136	A10	33.04 N	97.33 W
Boyd, stm., Austl.	98	G9	29.50 S	152.35 E
Boydton, Va., U.S.	124	H7	36.39 N	78.23 W
Boyer, stm., Ia., U.S.	130	C2	41.25 N	95.56 W
Boyer Aḩmadī va Kohkīlūyeh see Kohkīlūyeh va Boyer Aḩmadī, state, Iran	74	E12	30.40 N	50.40 E
Boyer Run, stm., Pa., U.S.	197b		40.13 N	79.32 W
Boyer's Creek, stm., On., Can.	202a		43.00 N	79.02 W
Boyertown, Pa., U.S.	124	D10	40.20 N	75.38 W
Boykins, Va., U.S.	124	H8	36.35 N	77.12 W
Boyle, Ab., Can.	144	B18	54.35 N	112.48 W
Boyle, Ire.	10	G4	53.58 N	8.18 W
Boyle, Ms., U.S.	134	D8	33.41 N	90.43 W
Boyle Heights, ngh., Ca., U.S.	198		34.02 N	118.13 W
Boylston, Al., U.S.	134	E12	32.26 N	86.17 W
Boyne, On., Can.	193b		43.29 N	79.50 W
Boyne, stm., Austl.	98	E8	23.59 S	151.19 E
Boyne, stm., Mb., Can.	142	E16	49.34 N	97.34 W
Boyne, stm., On., Can.	126	D9	44.10 N	79.49 W
Boyne, stm., Ire.	10	H5	53.43 N	6.20 W
Boyne City, Mi., U.S.	126	C5	45.12 N	85.00 W
Boynton, Ok., U.S.	134	B3	35.38 N	95.38 W
Boynton Beach, Fl., U.S.	132	J5	26.31 N	80.04 W
Boyoma Falls see Stanley Falls, wtfl., D.R.C.	86	D4	0.28 N	25.13 E
Boysen Reservoir, res., Wy., U.S.	140	D4	43.21 N	108.11 W
Boysen State Park, p.o.i., Wy., U.S.	140	D4	43.23 N	108.08 W
Boys Ranch, Tx., U.S.	138	F6	35.32 N	102.15 W
Boyuibe, Bol.	166	D4	20.25 S	63.17 W
Bozburun, Tur.	34	G11	36.40 N	28.05 E
Boz Burun, c., Tur.	34	C11	40.32 N	28.48 E
Bozburun Yarımadası, pen., Tur.	34	G11	36.49 N	28.07 E
Bozcaada, Tur.	34	D9	39.50 N	26.03 E
Bozca Ada, i., Tur.	34	D8	39.49 N	26.03 E
Boz Dağ, mtn., Tur.	34	E11	38.19 N	28.08 E
Boz Dağ, mtn., Tur.	34	F12	37.18 N	29.12 E
Bozdağ, mtn., Tur.	76	B7	36.50 N	36.22 E
Boz Dağlar, mts., Tur.	34	E10	38.20 N	27.45 E
Bozdoğan, Tur.	34	F11	37.40 N	28.18 E
Bozeman, Mt., U.S.	146	E15	45.41 N	111.02 W
Bozen see Bolzano, Italy	30	D8	46.29 N	11.21 E
Bozhen, China	58	B7	38.04 N	116.33 E
Bozhou, China	58	E6	33.52 N	115.46 E
Bozkır, Tur.	34	F15	37.11 N	32.14 E
Bozkurt, Tur.	34	F12	37.50 N	29.40 E
Bozoum, C.A.R.	86	C3	6.19 N	16.23 E
Bozova, Tur.	76	A9	37.21 N	38.32 E
Bozova, Tur.	76	A1	37.13 N	30.17 E
Bozovici, Rom.	36	E9	44.55 N	21.59 E
Bozšakol', Kaz.	48	D12	51.51 N	74.20 E
Bozüyük, Tur.	34	D13	39.54 N	30.03 E
Bra, Italy	30	F4	44.40 N	7.51 E
Braås, Swe.	16	J13	57.03 N	15.03 E
Brač, Otok, i., Cro.	30	G13	43.20 N	16.40 E
Bracadale, Loch, b., Scot., U.K.	10	D6	57.21 N	6.32 W
Bracciano, Italy	30	H9	42.06 N	12.10 E
Bracciano, Lago di, l., Italy	30	H9	42.07 N	12.14 E
Bracebridge, On., Can.	126	C10	45.02 N	79.17 W
Bräcke, Swe.	16	E13	62.44 N	15.27 E
Brackel, ngh., Ger.	181		51.32 N	7.33 E
Brackendale, B.C., Can.	144	G7	49.45 N	123.07 W
Brackenhurst, S. Afr.	191d		26.19 S	28.06 E
Brackett Field, arpt., Ca., U.S.	198		34.05 N	117.47 W
Brackettville, Tx., U.S.	136	E7	29.18 N	100.24 W
Bračiki Kanal, strt., Cro.	30	G13	43.24 N	16.40 E
Bracknell, Eng., U.K.	10	J12	51.25 N	0.45 W
Braço do Norte, Braz.	172	D13	28.17 S	49.10 W
Brad, Rom.	36	C9	46.07 N	22.47 E
Bradano, stm., Italy	32	D10	40.23 N	16.51 E
Bradbury, Ca., U.S.	198		34.08 N	117.59 W
Bradbury Heights, Md., U.S.	202c		38.52 N	76.56 W
Braddock, N.J., U.S.	203		39.42 N	74.53 W
Braddock Acres, Va., U.S.	202c		38.49 N	77.10 W
Braddock Hills, Pa., U.S.	197b		40.25 N	79.51 W
Braddocks Millpond, l., N.J., U.S.	203		39.49 N	74.51 W
Bradenton, Fl., U.S.	132	I3	27.29 N	82.33 W
Bradford see Bradford West Gwillimbury, On., Can.	126	D10	44.07 N	79.33 W
Bradford, Eng., U.K.	10	H11	53.47 N	1.45 W
Bradford, Ar., U.S.	134	B7	35.25 N	91.27 W
Bradford, Il., U.S.	130	C8	41.10 N	89.39 W
Bradford, Oh., U.S.	124	D1	40.08 N	84.26 W
Bradford, Pa., U.S.	124	C7	41.57 N	78.37 W
Bradford, Tn., U.S.	130	H9	36.04 N	88.48 W
Bradford, Vt., U.S.	122	G4	43.59 N	72.09 W
Bradford, mun., Eng., U.K.	180		53.47 N	1.52 W
Bradford, mun., Eng., U.K.	180		53.47 N	1.52 W
Bradford Hills, Pa., U.S.	203		40.01 N	75.39 W
Bradford West Gwillimbury, On., Can.	126	D10	44.07 N	79.33 W
Bradley, Ar., U.S.	134	D5	33.05 N	93.39 W
Bradley, Fl., U.S.	132	I3	27.48 N	81.59 W
Bradley, Il., U.S.	130	C10	41.08 N	87.50 W
Bradley, S.D., U.S.	140	B15	45.05 N	97.38 W
Bradley Farms, Md., U.S.	202c		39.00 N	77.11 W
Bradley Gardens, N.J., U.S.	194		40.34 N	74.39 W
Bradley Woods Reservation, p.o.i., Oh., U.S.	197a		41.25 N	81.58 W
Bradley W. Palmer State Park, p.o.i., Ma., U.S.	201		42.39 N	70.54 W
Bradshaw, Eng., U.K.	180		53.36 N	2.24 W
Bradshaw, Ne., U.S.	140	G15	40.52 N	97.44 W
Brady, Mt., U.S.	146	B15	48.02 N	111.50 W
Brady, Ne., U.S.	140	F12	41.01 N	100.22 W
Brady, Tx., U.S.	136	C8	31.08 N	99.19 W
Brady Creek, stm., Tx., U.S.	136	C8	31.07 N	98.59 W
Brady Mountains, mts., Tx., U.S.	136	C8	31.20 N	99.40 W
Brædstrup, Den.	16	L7	55.58 N	9.37 E
Braeside, Austl.	192b		37.59 S	145.07 E
Braga, Port.	28	C2	41.32 N	8.25 W
Braga, state, Port.	28	C2	41.30 N	8.20 W
Bragado, Arg.	172	G7	35.07 S	60.30 W
Bragança, Braz.	164	D8	1.02 S	46.45 W
Bragança, Port.	28	C4	41.48 N	6.45 W
Bragança, state, Port.	28	C4	41.30 N	6.50 W
Bragança Paulista, Braz.	170	L2	22.57 S	46.32 W
Braham, Mn., U.S.	128	F5	45.43 N	93.10 W
Brahetrolleborg, hist., Den.	16	L8	55.09 N	10.22 E
Brahin, Bela.	38	B9	51.46 N	30.14 E
Brahinka, stm., Bela.	38	B9	51.14 N	30.27 E
Brāhmanbāria, Bngl.	70	F13	23.59 N	91.07 E
Brāhmani, stm., India	70	H10	20.46 N	87.00 E
Brahmapur, India	69	B7	19.18 N	84.48 E
Brahmapur, India	190b		22.28 N	88.22 E
Brahmaputra (Yarlung), stm., Asia	62	C7	24.01 N	91.00 E
Brahynivka, Ukr.	38	E15	48.29 N	36.22 E
Braich y Pwll, c., Wales, U.K.	10	I8	52.47 N	4.45 W
Braidwood, Austl.	98	J7	35.26 S	149.48 E
Braidwood, Il., U.S.	130	C9	41.15 N	88.12 W
Brăila, Rom.	36	D14	45.16 N	27.57 E
Brăila, state, Rom.	36	D14	45.00 N	27.40 E
Brailiv, Ukr.	38	D7	49.06 N	28.10 E
Brainard, Ne., U.S.	140	F15	41.11 N	97.00 W
Brainerd, Mn., U.S.	128	E4	46.21 N	94.11 W
Braintree, Eng., U.K.	10	J13	51.53 N	0.32 E
Braintree, mun., Eng., U.K.	178		51.47 N	0.36 E
Brak, stm., S. Afr.	90	G6	29.35 S	22.54 E
Brak, stm., S. Afr.	90	G5	31.39 S	21.49 E
Brake, Ger.	24	C4	53.19 N	8.29 E
Brakpan, state, S. Afr.	191d		26.16 S	28.21 E
Brålanda, Swe.	16	I10	58.34 N	12.22 E
Bralorne, B.C., Can.	144	F8	50.46 N	122.49 W
Bramall Hall, hist., Eng., U.K.	180		53.23 N	2.09 W
Braman, Ok., U.S.	138	E11	36.56 N	97.21 W
Brambauer, Ger.	181		51.35 N	7.27 E
Bramey-Lenningsen, Ger.	181		51.34 N	7.46 E
Bramhall, Eng., U.K.	180		53.22 N	2.10 W
Bramley, Eng., U.K.	178		51.12 N	0.34 W
Bramley, ngh., S. Afr.	191d		26.08 S	28.05 E
Bramming, Den.	16	L6	55.28 N	8.42 E
Brampton, On., Can.	126	E10	43.41 N	79.45 W
Brampton Airfield, arpt., On., Can.	193b		43.40 N	79.47 W
Bramsche, Ger.	24	D3	52.24 N	7.58 E
Branch Brook Park, p.o.i., N.J., U.S.	194		40.46 N	74.10 W
Branchville, S.C., U.S.	132	C5	33.15 N	80.48 W
Branco, stm., Braz.	168	H11	1.23 S	61.52 W
Branco, stm., Braz.	170	F3	12.00 S	44.56 W
Brandaris, hill, Neth. Ant.	158g	p23	12.17 N	68.24 W
Brandberg, mtn., Nmb.	90	B2	21.10 S	14.33 E
Brandbu, Nor.	16	G8	60.28 N	10.28 E
Brande, Den.	16	L7	55.57 N	9.07 E
Brandeis University, educ., Ma., U.S.	201		42.22 N	71.16 W
Brandenberg, hill, Ger.	181		51.20 N	7.37 E
Brandenburg, Ger.	24	D8	52.24 N	12.33 E
Brandenburg, Ky., U.S.	130	G11	38.00 N	86.10 W
Brandenburger Tor, hist., Ger.	182a		52.31 N	13.23 E
Brandfort, S. Afr.	90	F8	28.41 S	26.28 E
Brandon, Mb., Can.	142	E14	49.50 N	99.57 W
Brandon, Fl., U.S.	132	I3	27.56 N	82.17 W
Brandon, Ms., U.S.	134	E9	32.16 N	89.59 W
Brandon, S.D., U.S.	128	H2	43.35 N	96.34 W
Brandon, Vt., U.S.	126	E16	43.48 N	73.05 W
Brandon, Wi., U.S.	128	H10	43.43 N	88.46 W
Brandon Bay, b., Ire.	10	I2	52.15 N	10.06 W
Brandon Mountain, mtn., Ire.	10	I2	52.14 N	10.15 W
Brandon Road Lock and Dam, trans., Il., U.S.	196		41.30 N	88.06 W
Brand Park, p.o.i., Ca., U.S.	198		34.11 N	118.16 W
Brandsen, Arg.	172	G8	35.10 S	58.14 W
Brands Hatch Motor Race Circuit, p.o.i., Eng., U.K.	178		51.22 N	0.16 E
Brandval, Nor.	16	G10	60.19 N	12.02 E
Brandvlei, S. Afr.	90	G5	30.27 S	20.29 E
Brandy Peak, mtn., Or., U.S.	146	H3	42.36 N	123.53 W
Brandýs nad Labem see Brandýs nad Labem-Stará Boleslav, Czech Rep.	24	F10	50.11 N	14.39 E
Brandýs nad Labem-Stará Boleslav, Czech Rep.	24	F10	50.11 N	14.39 E

Name	Page	Map Ref.	Latitude	Longitude
Brandywine Creek, stm., U.S.	203		39.44 N	75.32 W
Brandywine Creek, stm., Oh., U.S.	197a		41.17 N	81.34 W
Brandywine Creek State Park, p.o.i., De., U.S.	203		39.48 N	75.35 W
Brandywine Park, p.o.i., De., U.S.	203		39.45 N	75.33 W
Brandywine Springs Park, p.o.i., De., U.S.	203		39.45 N	75.38 W
Branford, Fl., U.S.	132	G3	29.57 N	82.55 W
Brani, Pulau, i., Sing.	189c		1.15 N	103.50 E
Braniewo, Pol.	24	B15	54.23 N	19.49 E
Bransby, Austl.	98	G4	28.13 S	142.03 E
Bransby Point, c., Monts.	159a	d3	16.43 N	62.14 W
Bransfield Strait, strt., Ant.	103	B35	63.00 S	59.00 W
Brańsk, Pol.	24	D18	52.44 N	22.50 E
Branson, Mo., U.S.	130	H4	36.38 N	93.13 W
Brantford, On., Can.	126	E9	43.08 N	80.15 W
Brant Lake, N.Y., U.S.	126	E16	43.40 N	73.45 W
Brantley, Al., U.S.	134	F12	31.34 N	86.15 W
Brantley Tank, res., N.M., U.S.	136	B3	32.40 N	104.20 W
Brantôme, Fr.	22	D6	45.22 N	0.39 E
Brant Rock, Ma., U.S.	201		42.05 N	70.38 W
Brantville, N.B., Can.	122	C12	47.22 N	64.58 W
Branxholme, Austl.	98	K3	37.51 S	141.47 E
Brasøya, i., Nor.	14	D6	68.21 N	16.06 E
Brás, ngh., Braz.	205b		23.32 S	46.36 W
Bras d'Or Lake, l., N.S., Can.	122	E16	45.52 N	60.50 W
Brasil see Brazil, ctry., S.A.	160	F9	10.00 S	55.00 W
Brasilândia, ngh., Braz.	205b		23.28 S	46.41 W
Brasiléia, Braz.	166	B3	10.59 S	68.44 W
Brasília, Braz.	170	H1	15.47 S	47.52 W
Brasília, Parque Nacional de, p.o.i., Braz.	170	H1	15.36 S	48.08 W
Brasília de Minas, Braz.	170	I3	16.12 S	44.25 W
Braslau, Bela.	26	E9	55.38 N	27.02 E
Brașov, Rom.	36	D12	45.39 N	25.37 E
Brașov, state, Rom.	36	D12	45.45 N	25.15 E
Brassert, Ger.	181		51.40 N	7.05 E
Brassey, Banjaran, mts., Malay.	66	A10	4.54 N	117.30 E
Brassey, Mount, mtn., Austl.	96	D6	23.05 S	134.56 E
Brass Islands, is., V.I.U.S.	158b	e7	18.24 N	64.58 W
Brassó see Brașov, Rom.	36	D12	45.39 N	25.37 E
Brasstown Bald, mtn., Ga., U.S.	132	B2	34.52 N	83.48 W
Brastad, Swe.	16	I9	58.23 N	11.29 E
Brasted, Eng., U.K.	178		51.16 N	0.06 E
Brasted Chart, Eng., U.K.	178		51.16 N	0.06 E
Břasy, Czech Rep.	24	G9	49.50 N	13.33 E
Bratca, Rom.	36	C9	46.55 N	22.37 E
Bratcevo, ngh., Russia	183b		55.51 N	37.24 E
Brateevo, ngh., Russia	183b		55.38 N	37.45 E
Bratenahl, Oh., U.S.	197a		41.32 N	81.37 W
Brateș, Lacul, l., Rom.	38	H7	45.22 N	28.23 E
Bratislava, Slvk.	24	H13	48.09 N	17.07 E
Bratislava, state, Slvk.	24	H13	48.10 N	17.08 E
Bratsk, Russia	48	C18	56.08 N	101.38 E
Brats'ke, Ukr.	38	F10	47.52 N	31.34 E
Bratskoe vodohranilišče, res., Russia	48	C18	55.57 N	101.52 E
Bratsk Reservoir see Bratskoe vodohranilišče, res., Russia	48	C18	55.57 N	101.52 E
Bratslav, Ukr.	38	E7	48.49 N	28.57 E
Brattleboro, Vt., U.S.	124	B13	42.51 N	72.34 W
Brattvåg, Nor.	16	E4	62.36 N	6.26 E
Braulio Carrillo, Parque Nacional, p.o.i., C.R.	156	G5	10.10 N	84.00 W
Braúnas, Braz.	170	J4	19.04 S	42.43 W
Braunau am Inn, Aus.	30	B10	48.15 N	13.02 E
Braunschweig (Brunswick), Ger.	24	D6	52.16 N	10.31 E
Brava, i., C.V.	85a	I10	14.52 N	24.43 W
Brava, Costa, cst., Spain	28	B14	41.46 N	3.01 E
Brava, Laguna, l., Arg.	172	D3	28.18 S	68.51 W
Brava, Punta, c., Ur.	172	G9	34.56 S	56.09 W
Brave, Pa., U.S.	124	E5	39.43 N	80.16 W
Bravicea, Mol.	38	F7	47.21 N	28.26 E
Bråviken, b., Swe.	16	I14	58.38 N	16.32 E
Bravo (Grande, Rio) (Rio Grande), stm., N.A.	120	H13	25.56 N	97.08 W
Bravo, Cerro, mtn., Peru	164	E2	5.32 S	79.15 W
Bravo del Norte see Rio Grande, stm., N.A.	120	H13	25.56 N	97.08 W
Bravo del Norte see Bravo, stm., N.A.	120	H13	25.56 N	97.08 W
Bravo del Norte see Grande, Rio, stm., N.A.	120	H13	25.56 N	97.08 W
Brawley, Ca., U.S.	148	K10	32.59 N	115.32 W
Brawley Peaks, mtn., Nv., U.S.	148	E7	38.15 N	118.55 W
Brawley Wash, stm., Az., U.S.	150	K5	32.33 N	111.25 W
Bray, Ire.	10	H6	53.12 N	6.06 W
Braybrook, Austl.	192b		37.47 S	144.51 E
Bray Island, i., Nu., Can.	110	B15	69.19 N	76.59 W
Braymer, Mo., U.S.	130	E4	39.35 N	93.47 W
Brazeau, stm., Ab., Can.	144	D15	52.54 N	115.13 W
Brazeau, Mount, mtn., Ab., Can.	144	D13	52.33 N	117.21 W
Brazeau Dam, dam., Ab., Can.	144	C15	52.45 N	115.30 W
Brazil, In., U.S.	130	E10	39.31 N	87.07 W
Brazil, ctry., S.A.	160	F9	10.00 S	55.00 W
Brazil Basin, unds.	176	J11	15.00 S	25.00 W
Brazoria, Tx., U.S.	136	E12	29.02 N	95.34 W
Brazos, stm., Tx., U.S.	116	E4	33.15 N	100.00 W
Brazos, Clear Fork, stm., Tx., U.S.	136	B8	33.00 N	98.40 W
Brazos, Double Mountain Fork, stm., Tx., U.S.	138	H8	33.15 N	99.59 W
Brazos, North Fork, stm., Tx., U.S.	116	D3	33.00 N	98.40 W
Brazzaville, Congo	86	E2	4.16 S	15.17 E
Brazzaville, Congo	191b		4.16 S	15.17 E
Brazzaville (Maya Maya) Airport, arpt., Congo	191b		4.15 S	15.15 E
Brčko, Bos.	36	E5	44.52 N	18.48 E
Brda, stm., Pol.	24	C13	53.07 N	17.57 E
Bré see Bray, Ire.	10	H6	53.12 N	6.06 W
Brea, Ca., U.S.	148	J8	33.55 N	117.53 W
Brea, Punta, c., P.R.	158a	c2	17.56 N	66.55 W
Brea Canyon, val., Ca., U.S.	198		33.55 N	117.55 W
Brea Creek, stm., Ca., U.S.	198		33.53 N	117.59 W
Breadalbane, Austl.	98	D2	23.48 S	139.33 E
Brea Dam, dam., Ca., U.S.	198		33.54 N	117.56 W
Breadysville, Pa., U.S.	203		40.13 N	75.04 W
Breakenridge, Mount, mtn., B.C., Can.	144	G9	49.43 N	121.56 W
Breakheart Reservation, p.o.i., Ma., U.S.	201		42.29 N	71.02 W
Breaks Interstate Park, p.o.i., U.S.	124	G3	37.17 N	82.18 W
Bream Bay, b., N.Z.	102	B6	35.55 S	174.30 E
Brea Pozo, Arg.	172	D6	28.14 S	63.56 W
Bréau, Fr.	179		48.34 N	2.53 E
Breaux Bridge, La., U.S.	134	G7	30.16 N	91.53 W
Brebes, Indon.	66	G6	6.52 S	109.02 E
Brechin, Scot., U.K.	10	E10	56.43 N	2.40 W
Brechten, ngh., Ger.	181		51.35 N	7.28 E
Breckenridge, Co., U.S.	138	B2	39.29 N	106.01 W
Breckenridge, Mi., U.S.	126	E5	43.24 N	84.28 W
Breckenridge, Mn., U.S.	128	E2	46.15 N	96.34 W
Breckenridge, Mo., U.S.	130	E4	39.45 N	93.48 W
Breckenridge, Tx., U.S.	136	B9	32.45 N	98.54 W
Brecknock, Peninsula, pen., Chile	166	J2	54.34 S	71.50 W
Břeclav, Czech Rep.	24	H12	48.45 N	16.53 E
Brecon, Wales, U.K.	10	J9	51.57 N	3.23 W
Brecon Beacons, hills, Wales, U.K.	10	J9	51.53 N	3.25 W
Brecon Beacons National Park, p.o.i., Wales, U.K.	10	J9	51.52 N	3.27 W
Breda, Neth.	20	C13	51.35 N	4.46 E
Breda, Ia., U.S.	130	B3	42.10 N	94.59 W
Bredaryd, Swe.	16	J11	57.10 N	13.44 E
Bredasdorp, S. Afr.	90	I5	34.32 S	20.02 E
Bredbury, Eng., U.K.	180		53.25 N	2.06 W
Bredbyn, Swe.	16	D15	63.27 N	18.07 E
Bredell, S. Afr.	191d		26.05 S	28.17 E
Bredenbruch, Ger.	181		51.21 N	7.45 E
Bredenbury, Sk., Can.	142	D11	50.57 N	102.02 W
Bredeney, ngh., Ger.	181		51.24 N	6.59 E
Bredenscheid-Stüter, Ger.	181		51.22 N	7.11 E
Bredgar, Eng., U.K.	178		51.18 N	0.42 E
Bredhurst, Eng., U.K.	178		51.20 N	0.35 E
Bredsel, Swe.	14	G11	65.55 N	20.20 E
Bredstedt, Ger.	24	B4	54.37 N	8.59 E
Bredy, Russia	48	D9	52.25 N	60.21 E
Breë, stm., S. Afr.	90	I5	34.23 S	20.45 E
Breeds Pond, l., Ma., U.S.	201		42.28 N	70.59 W
Breese, Il., U.S.	130	F8	38.36 N	89.31 W
Breezewood, Pa., U.S.	197b		40.34 N	80.03 W
Bregalnica, stm., Mac.	34	A5	41.36 N	21.55 E
Bregenz, Aus.	30	C6	47.29 N	9.46 E
Bregovo, Blg.	36	E9	44.09 N	22.38 E
Brégy, Fr.	179		49.05 N	2.52 E
Bréhat, Île de, i., Fr.	20	F6	48.50 N	3.00 W
Breiðafjörður, b., Ice.	12a	k27	65.15 N	23.15 W
Breidsundet, strt., Nor.	16	E3	62.27 N	6.00 E
Breidvikeidet, Nor.	14	C10	69.39 N	19.38 E
Breimsvatnet, l., Nor.	16	F4	61.42 N	6.24 E
Breitenlee, ngh., Aus.	182b		48.15 N	16.30 E
Breivika, Nor.	14	D7	68.45 N	16.33 E
Breivikbotn, Nor.	14	B13	70.36 N	22.20 E
Brejinho de Nazaré, Braz.	170	F1	11.00 S	48.34 W
Brejo, Braz.	170	B4	3.41 S	42.47 W
Brejões, Braz.	170	G5	13.06 S	39.55 W
Brejo Grande, Braz.	170	F7	10.26 S	36.26 W
Brejo Santo, Braz.	170	D6	7.29 S	39.00 W
Brejtovo, Russia	26	B20	58.17 N	37.52 E
Brekken, Nor.	16	E9	62.39 N	11.52 E
Brekstad, Nor.	16	D7	63.42 N	9.40 E
Bremangerlandet, i., Nor.	16	F2	61.51 N	5.02 E
Brembo, stm., Italy	30	E6	45.34 N	9.32 E
Bremen, Ger.	24	C4	53.04 N	8.51 E
Bremen, Ga., U.S.	134	D13	33.43 N	85.08 W
Bremen, Oh., U.S.	124	E3	39.41 N	82.26 W
Bremen, state, Ger.	24	C4	53.05 N	8.50 E
Bremer Bay, Austl.	96	F3	34.23 S	119.23 E
Bremer Bay, b., Austl.	96	F3	34.24 S	119.26 E
Bremerhaven, Ger.	24	C4	53.31 N	8.35 E
Bremerton, Wa., U.S.	146	C4	47.33 N	122.38 W
Bremervörde, Ger.	24	C5	53.29 N	9.09 E
Bremke, Ger.	181		51.23 N	7.41 E
Bremond, Tx., U.S.	136	C11	31.09 N	96.40 W
Brem River, B.C., Can.	144	F6	50.26 N	124.39 W
Breña, Peru	204d		12.04 S	77.04 W
Brendel Lake, l., Mi., U.S.	199		42.38 N	83.30 W
Brenham, Tx., U.S.	136	D11	30.09 N	96.24 W
Bren Mar Park, Va., U.S.	202c		38.48 N	77.09 W
Brennero, Passo del see Brenner Pass, p., Eur.	30	C8	47.00 N	11.29 E
Brennerpass see Brenner Pass, p., Eur.	30	C8	47.00 N	11.29 E
Brenner Pass, p., Eur.	30	C8	47.00 N	11.29 E
Brent, Al., U.S.	134	E11	32.56 N	87.09 W
Brent, Fl., U.S.	134	G11	30.27 N	87.13 W
Brent, stm., Eng., U.K.	178		51.28 N	0.18 W
Brenta, stm., Italy	30	D8	45.11 N	12.14 E
Brentford, ngh., Eng., U.K.	178		51.29 N	0.18 W
Brenthurst, S. Afr.	191d		26.16 S	28.23 E
Brent Reservoir, res., Eng., U.K.	178		51.35 N	0.15 W
Brentwood, Eng., U.K.	10	J13	51.37 N	0.18 E
Brentwood, Eng., U.K.	178		51.38 N	0.18 E
Brentwood, N.Y., U.S.	124	D12	40.46 N	73.14 W
Brentwood, Tn., U.S.	130	H11	36.02 N	86.46 W
Brentwood, mun., Eng., U.K.	178		51.37 N	0.20 E
Brentwood Heights, ngh., Ca., U.S.	198		34.04 N	118.30 W
Brentwood Park, S. Afr.	191d		26.08 S	28.18 E
Brenz, stm., Ger.	30	B7	48.33 N	10.24 E
Breo, Italy	30	F4	44.23 N	7.48 E
Bréon, Ruisseau du, stm., Fr.	179		48.40 N	2.49 E
Brera, Palazzo di, bldg., Italy	184b		45.28 N	9.11 E
Brescia, Italy	30	E7	45.32 N	10.13 E
Breslau see Wrocław, Pol.	24	E13	51.06 N	17.01 E
Bresle, stm., Fr.	20	E10	50.03 N	1.22 E
Bressanone, Italy	30	D8	46.43 N	11.38 E
Bressay, i., Scot., U.K.	10	A11	60.08 N	1.05 W
Bresse, reg., Fr.	22	C11	46.33 N	5.12 E
Bresso, Italy	184b		45.32 N	9.11 E
Bressuire, Fr.	20	H8	46.50 N	0.29 W
Brèst, Bela.	26	H6	52.06 N	23.41 E
Brest, Blg.	36	F11	43.38 N	24.36 E
Brest, Fr.	20	F4	48.23 N	4.29 W
Brèst, state, Bela.	40	E4	52.30 N	25.30 E
Brest-Litovsk see Brèst, Bela.	26	H6	52.06 N	23.41 E
Bretagne (Brittany), hist. reg., Fr.	20	F5	48.00 N	3.00 W
Bretenoux, Fr.	22	E7	44.55 N	1.50 E
Breteuil, Fr.	20	E11	49.38 N	2.18 E
Bréthencourt, Fr.	179		48.30 N	1.55 E
Bretherton, Eng., U.K.	180		53.41 N	2.48 W
Brétigny, mil., Fr.	179		48.35 N	2.20 E
Breton, Ab., Can.	144	C16	53.06 N	114.29 W
Breton, Pertuis, strt., Fr.	22	C4	46.17 N	1.31 W
Breton Islands, is., La., U.S.	134	H9	29.29 N	89.08 W
Breton Sound, strt., La., U.S.	134	H9	29.33 N	89.16 W
Brett, Cape, c., N.Z.	102	B6	35.11 S	174.20 E
Bretten, Ger.	24	G4	49.02 N	8.42 E
Breueh, Pulau, i., Indon.	64	J2	5.41 N	95.05 E
Breuil-Bois-Robert, Fr.	179		48.57 N	1.43 E
Breuil-Cervinia, Italy	30	E4	45.56 N	7.38 E
Breuillet, Fr.	179		48.34 N	2.10 E
Breux, Fr.	179		48.34 N	2.11 E
Brevard, N.C., U.S.	132	A3	35.13 N	82.44 W
Breves, Braz.	164	D7	1.40 S	50.29 W
Brevik, Nor.	16	H7	59.03 N	9.41 E
Brevoort Island, i., Nu., Can.	108	E13	63.30 N	64.20 W
Brewarrina, Austl.	98	G6	29.57 S	146.52 E
Brewer, Me., U.S.	122	F8	44.47 N	68.45 W
Brewer Island, i., Ca., U.S.	200		37.33 N	122.16 W
Brewster, Ks., U.S.	138	B7	39.21 N	101.22 W
Brewster, Mn., U.S.	128	H3	43.42 N	95.28 W
Brewster, Ne., U.S.	140	F13	41.55 N	99.51 W
Brewster, Oh., U.S.	124	D4	40.42 N	81.37 W
Brewster, Wa., U.S.	146	B7	48.06 N	119.46 W
Brewster, Kap, c., Grnld.	108	C21	70.08 N	22.05 W
Brewton, Al., U.S.	134	F11	31.06 N	87.04 W
Breyten, S. Afr.	90	E10	26.15 S	30.00 E
Brežice, Slvn.	30	E12	45.54 N	15.37 E
Březnice, Czech Rep.	24	G9	49.32 N	13.57 E
Breznik, Blg.	36	G9	42.44 N	22.54 E
Brezno, Slvk.	24	H15	48.48 N	19.40 E
Bria, C.A.R.	86	C4	6.33 N	21.57 E
Brian Boru Peak, mtn., B.C., Can.	144	A3	55.05 N	127.35 W
Briançon, Fr.	22	E12	44.53 N	6.37 E
Brian Head, mtn., Ut., U.S.	150	F4	37.41 N	112.50 W
Briare, Canal de, can., Fr.	20	G11	48.01 N	2.43 E
Briarwood Center, shp. cen., Mi., U.S.	199		42.14 N	83.45 W
Bribie Island, i., Austl.	98	F9	27.00 S	153.08 E
Bricelyn, Mn., U.S.	128	H5	43.33 N	93.48 W
Briceni, Mol.	38	E6	48.21 N	27.06 E
Brice Run, stm., Md., U.S.	202b		39.19 N	76.50 W
Brices Cross Roads National Battlefield Site, p.o.i., Ms., U.S.	134	C10	34.26 N	88.40 W
Briceville, Tn., U.S.	134	A14	36.10 N	84.10 W
Bricht, Ger.	181		51.41 N	6.51 E
Bri Chualtan see Bray, Ire.	10	H6	53.12 N	6.06 W
Brick Kiln, St. K./N.	159a	c2	17.10 N	62.33 W
Bride, stm., Ire.	10	I4	52.04 N	7.52 W
Bridesburg, ngh., Pa., U.S.	203		40.00 N	75.04 W
Bridge, stm., B.C., Can.	144	F7	50.45 N	121.55 W
Bridge City, Tx., U.S.	134	D14	30.01 N	93.50 W
Bridge Lake, B.C., Can.	144	E10	51.28 N	120.44 W
Bridgend, Wales, U.K.	10	J9	51.30 N	3.35 W
Bridgeport, Al., U.S.	134	C13	34.56 N	85.42 W
Bridgeport, Ca., U.S.	148	E6	38.15 N	119.13 W
Bridgeport, Ct., U.S.	124	C12	41.11 N	73.13 W
Bridgeport, Il., U.S.	130	F10	38.42 N	87.45 W
Bridgeport, Mi., U.S.	126	E6	43.21 N	83.52 W
Bridgeport, Ne., U.S.	140	F9	41.39 N	103.05 W
Bridgeport, N.J., U.S.	203		39.48 N	75.20 W
Bridgeport, Pa., U.S.	203		40.06 N	75.21 W
Bridgeport, Tx., U.S.	138	H11	33.12 N	97.45 W
Bridgeport, Wa., U.S.	146	C7	48.00 N	119.40 W
Bridgeport, ngh., Il., U.S.	196		41.51 N	87.39 W
Bridgeport, Lake, res., Tx., U.S.	138	H10	33.12 N	97.51 W
Bridgeport, University of, educ., Ct., U.S.	194		41.10 N	73.12 W
Bridgeport Airport, arpt., N.J., U.S.	203		39.47 N	75.20 W
Bridgeport Harbor, b., Ct., U.S.	194		41.10 N	73.11 W
Bridgeport Municipal Airport, arpt., Ct., U.S.	194		41.10 N	73.08 W
Bridger, Mt., U.S.	140	B4	45.17 N	108.55 W
Bridge River Indian Reserve, ind. res., B.C., Can.	144	F8	50.48 N	122.03 W
Bridger Peak, mtn., Wy., U.S.	150	B9	41.12 N	107.02 W
Bridgeton, N.J., U.S.	124	E10	39.25 N	75.14 W
Bridgetown, Austl.	96	F3	33.57 S	116.08 E
Bridgetown, Barb.	159d	n8	13.06 N	59.36 W
Bridgetown, N.S., Can.	122	F11	44.51 N	65.15 W
Bridge Trafford, Eng., U.K.	180		53.14 N	2.49 W
Bridgeview, Il., U.S.	196		41.45 N	87.48 W
Bridgeville, De., U.S.	124	F10	38.44 N	75.36 W
Bridgewater, Austl.	99a	o13	42.44 S	147.14 E
Bridgewater, N.S., Can.	122	F12	44.22 N	64.30 W
Bridgewater, Me., U.S.	122	D9	46.23 N	67.50 W
Bridgewater, Ma., U.S.	124	B15	41.58 N	70.59 W
Bridgewater, Pa., U.S.	203		40.05 N	74.55 W
Bridgewater, S.D., U.S.	140	D15	43.33 N	97.30 W
Bridgewater, Va., U.S.	124	F6	38.22 N	78.58 W
Bridgewater Canal, can., Eng., U.K.	180		53.20 N	2.45 W
Bridgewater State College, educ., Ma., U.S.	201		41.59 N	70.58 W
Bridgton, Me., U.S.	122	F6	44.03 N	70.42 W
Bridgwater, Eng., U.K.	10	J9	51.07 N	3.00 W
Bridgwater Bay, b., Eng., U.K.	10	J9	51.14 N	3.12 W
Bridlington, Eng., U.K.	10	G12	54.05 N	0.12 W
Bridlington Bay, b., Eng., U.K.	10	H12	54.01 N	0.10 W
Bridport, Eng., U.K.	10	K10	50.44 N	2.45 W
Brie, reg., Fr.	20	F12	48.40 N	3.20 E
Brie Française, reg., Fr.	179		48.48 N	2.46 E
Brieg see Brzeg, Pol.	24	F13	50.51 N	17.28 E
Brien Run, stm., Md., U.S.	202b		39.20 N	76.28 W
Brienzer See, l., Switz.	30	D4	46.43 N	7.57 E
Brier Creek, stm., Ga., U.S.	132	C4	32.47 N	81.26 W
Brier Island, i., N.S., Can.	122	F10	44.15 N	66.22 W
Briese, Ger.	182a		52.42 N	13.18 E
Briese, stm., Ger.	182a		52.41 N	13.15 E
Brig, Switz.	30	D5	46.19 N	8.00 E
Briggs, Tx., U.S.	136	D10	30.52 N	97.56 W
Brigham City, Ut., U.S.	150	B4	41.31 N	112.00 W
Bright, Austl.	98	K6	36.44 S	146.57 E
Brightmoor, ngh., Mi., U.S.	199		42.24 N	83.14 W
Brighton, On., Can.	126	D12	44.01 N	77.43 W
Brighton, Eng., U.K.	10	K12	50.50 N	0.08 W
Brighton, Co., U.S.	138	A4	39.59 N	104.48 W
Brighton, Il., U.S.	130	E7	39.03 N	90.08 W
Brighton, Ia., U.S.	130	C6	41.10 N	91.49 W
Brighton, Md., U.S.	202b		39.21 N	76.43 W
Brighton, Mi., U.S.	124	B2	42.31 N	83.46 W
Brighton, N.Y., U.S.	126	E12	43.08 N	77.33 W
Brighton, ngh., Ma., U.S.	201		42.21 N	71.08 W
Brighton Airport, arpt., Mi., U.S.	199		42.34 N	83.47 W
Brighton Downs, Austl.	98	D3	23.22 S	141.33 E
Brighton Indian Reservation, ind. res., Fl., U.S.	132	I4	27.04 N	81.05 W
Brighton-Le-Sands, Austl.	192a		33.58 S	151.09 E
Brighton Park, ngh., Il., U.S.	196		41.49 N	87.42 W
Brightwaters, N.Y., U.S.	194		40.43 N	73.16 W
Brightwood, ngh., D.C., U.S.	202c		38.58 N	77.02 W
Brigittenau, ngh., Aus.	182b		48.14 N	16.22 E
Brignoles, Fr.	22	F12	43.24 N	6.04 E
Brihuega, Spain	28	D8	40.45 N	2.52 W
Briis-sous-Forges, Fr.	179		48.38 N	2.07 E
Brijuni, i., Cro.	30	F10	44.55 N	13.46 E
Brilliant, B.C., Can.	144	G13	49.18 N	117.37 W
Brilliant, Al., U.S.	134	C11	34.01 N	87.45 W
Brillion, Wi., U.S.	126	D1	44.10 N	88.04 W
Brilon, Ger.	24	E4	51.24 N	8.34 E
Brilyn Park, Va., U.S.	202c		38.54 N	77.10 W
Brindisi, Italy	32	D11	40.38 N	17.56 E
Brindle, Eng., U.K.	180		53.43 N	2.36 W
Bringelly Creek, stm., Austl.	192a		33.58 S	150.38 E
Brinkerton, Pa., U.S.	197b		40.13 N	79.32 W
Brinkleigh, Md., U.S.	202b		39.18 N	76.50 W
Brinkley, Ar., U.S.	134	C7	34.53 N	91.11 W
Brinkworth, Austl.	98	I2	33.42 S	138.23 E
Brinscall, Eng., U.K.	180		53.41 N	2.34 W
Brion, Île, i., Qc., Can.	122	C15	47.48 N	61.28 W
Briones Hills, hills, Ca., U.S.	200		37.56 N	122.08 W
Briones Regional Park, p.o.i., Ca., U.S.	200		37.56 N	122.08 W
Briones Reservoir, res., Ca., U.S.	200		37.55 N	122.12 W
Brioude, Fr.	22	D9	45.17 N	3.22 E
Brisbane, Austl.	98	F9	27.27 S	153.02 E
Brisighella, Italy	30	F8	44.13 N	11.45 E
Bristol, Eng., U.K.	10	J10	51.27 N	2.35 W
Bristol, Ct., U.S.	124	C13	41.40 N	72.56 W
Bristol, Fl., U.S.	134	G14	30.25 N	84.58 W
Bristol, N.H., U.S.	122	G5	43.35 N	71.44 W
Bristol, Pa., U.S.	124	D11	40.06 N	74.51 W
Bristol, R.I., U.S.	124	C14	41.40 N	71.16 W
Bristol, S.D., U.S.	140	B15	45.20 N	97.45 W
Bristol, Tn., U.S.	124	H3	36.35 N	82.10 W
Bristol, Vt., U.S.	126	D16	44.08 N	73.04 W
Bristol Bay, b., Ak., U.S.	109	E7	58.00 N	159.00 W
Bristol-Blake Reservation, p.o.i., Ma., U.S.	201		42.06 N	71.19 W
Bristol Channel, strt., U.K.	10	J8	51.22 N	4.01 W
Bristol Island, i., S. Geor.	103	A2	59.02 S	26.34 W
Bristol Lake, l., Ca., U.S.	148	I10	34.28 N	115.41 W
Bristow, Ok., U.S.	134	B2	35.50 N	96.23 W
Britânia, Braz.	166	C6	15.14 S	51.09 W
Britannia, On., Can.	193b		43.37 N	79.41 W
Britannia, Eng., U.K.	180		53.41 N	2.11 W
Britannia Beach, B.C., Can.	144	G7	49.37 N	123.11 W
British Columbia, state, Can.	110	E5	54.00 N	125.00 W
British Guiana see Guyana, ctry., S.A.	164	C6	5.00 N	59.00 W
British Honduras see Belize, ctry., N.A.	156	D3	17.15 N	88.45 W
British Indian Ocean Territory, dep., Afr.	2	G17	7.00 S	72.00 E
British Isles, is., Eur.	8	E6	54.00 N	4.00 W
British Mountains, mts., N.A.	109	C11	69.02 N	140.21 W
British Museum, bldg., Eng., U.K.	178		51.31 N	0.08 W
British Solomon Islands see Solomon Islands, ctry., Oc.	92	D7	8.00 S	159.00 E
British Virgin Islands, dep., N.A.	158b	e9	18.30 N	64.30 W
Britland Edge Hill, hill, Eng., U.K.	180		53.31 N	1.50 W
Brits, S. Afr.	90	D8	25.38 S	27.47 E
Britstown, S. Afr.	90	G6	30.34 S	23.30 E
Britt, Ia., U.S.	130	A4	43.05 N	93.48 W
Brittany see Bretagne, hist. reg., Fr.	20	F5	48.00 N	3.00 W
Brittingham, Mex.	136	I4	25.46 N	103.24 W
Britton, S.D., U.S.	140	B15	45.47 N	97.45 W
Britz, ngh., Ger.	182a		52.27 N	13.26 E
Brive-la-Gaillarde, Fr.	22	D7	45.09 N	1.31 E
Briviesca, Spain	28	B7	42.32 N	3.19 W
Brixen see Bressanone, Italy	30	D8	46.43 N	11.38 E
Brixham, Eng., U.K.	10	K9	50.23 N	3.30 W
Brixton, Austl.	98	D5	23.32 S	144.57 E
Brjanka, Russia	48	C16	59.06 N	93.25 E
Brjansk, Russia	26	G17	53.14 N	34.21 E
Brjanskaja oblast', co., Russia	40	E8	53.00 N	34.00 E
Brjuhoveckaja, Russia	40	I11	45.48 N	39.00 E
Brno, Czech Rep.	24	G12	49.12 N	16.36 E
Broa, Ensenada de la, b., Cuba	156	A6	22.35 N	82.00 W
Broad, stm., U.S.	132	B4	34.00 N	81.03 W
Broad, stm., Ga., U.S.	132	B2	33.57 N	82.34 W
Broadalbin, N.Y., U.S.	126	E15	43.04 N	74.11 W
Broad Axe, Pa., U.S.	203		40.10 N	75.15 W
Broad Bay, b., Scot., U.K.	10	C6	58.15 N	6.15 W
Broadbottom, Eng., U.K.	180		53.26 N	2.01 W
Broadford, Scot., U.K.	10	D7	57.14 N	5.52 W
Broad Haven, b., Ire.	10	G2	54.18 N	9.55 W
Broadheath, Eng., U.K.	180		53.24 N	2.21 W
Broad Law, mtn., Scot., U.K.	10	F9	55.30 N	3.22 W
Broadley Common, Eng., U.K.	178		51.45 N	0.04 E
Broad Run, stm., Pa., U.S.	203		39.59 N	75.40 W
Broad Run, stm., Pa., U.S.	203		39.56 N	75.41 W
Broad Sound, b., Austl.	98	D7	22.10 S	149.45 E
Broad Sound, strt., Ma., U.S.	201		42.25 N	70.58 W
Broad Sound Channel, strt., Austl.	98	C7	21.57 S	150.17 E
Broad Street, Eng., U.K.	178		51.17 N	0.38 E
Broadus, Mt., U.S.	140	B7	45.26 N	105.24 W
Broadview, Sk., Can.	142	D11	50.22 N	102.35 W
Broadwater, Ne., U.S.	140	F10	41.35 N	102.50 W
Broadway, Va., U.S.	124	F7	38.36 N	78.47 W
Brocēni, Lat.	26	D5	56.41 N	22.34 E
Brochet, Mb., Can.	110	D10	57.53 N	101.40 W
Brock, Sk., Can.	142	C5	51.27 N	108.42 W
Brock Creek, stm., Pa., U.S.	203		40.15 N	74.50 W
Brockenscheidt, Ger.	181		51.38 N	7.25 E
Brockham, Eng., U.K.	178		51.14 N	0.17 W
Brock Island, i., N.T., Can.	108	B2	77.52 N	114.19 W
Brockman, Mount, mtn., Austl.	96	D3	22.28 S	117.18 E
Brock Monument, hist., On., Can.	202a		43.09 N	79.04 W
Brockport, N.Y., U.S.	126	E11	43.12 N	77.55 W
Brockton, Ma., U.S.	124	B14	42.05 N	71.01 W
Brockton, Mt., U.S.	142	F9	48.08 N	104.56 W
Brockton Reservoir, res., Ma., U.S.	201		42.07 N	71.03 W
Brock University, educ., On., Can.	202a		43.07 N	79.15 W
Brockville, On., Can.	126	D14	44.36 N	75.41 W
Brockway, Pa., U.S.	124	C7	41.14 N	78.47 W
Brocoió, Ilha de, i., Braz.	205a		22.45 S	43.07 W
Brocton, N.Y., U.S.	124	B6	42.23 N	79.26 W
Brod, Mac.	34	B4	41.30 N	21.12 E
Brodeur Peninsula, pen., Nu., Can.	110	A13	73.00 N	88.00 W
Brodhead, Ky., U.S.	124	G1	37.23 N	84.25 W
Brodhead, Wi., U.S.	130	B8	42.37 N	89.22 W
Brodick, Scot., U.K.	10	F7	55.35 N	5.10 W
Brodnax, Va., U.S.	124	H7	36.42 N	78.02 W
Brodnica, Pol.	24	C15	53.15 N	19.24 E
Brody, Pol.	24	E10	51.46 N	14.48 E
Brody, Ukr.	38	C4	50.05 N	25.09 E
Brogan, Or., U.S.	146	F9	44.15 N	117.31 W
Broich, ngh., Ger.	181		51.25 N	6.51 E
Brok, Pol.	24	D17	52.42 N	21.51 E
Broken Arrow, Ok., U.S.	130	H2	36.02 N	95.47 W
Broken Bay, b., Austl.	98	I8	33.34 S	151.18 E
Broken Bow, Ne., U.S.	140	F13	41.24 N	99.38 W
Broken Bow, Ok., U.S.	134	C4	34.02 N	94.44 W
Broken Bow Lake, res., Ok., U.S.	134	C4	34.10 N	94.41 W
Broken Cross, Eng., U.K.	180		53.15 N	2.10 W
Broken Cross, Eng., U.K.	180		53.15 N	2.29 W
Brokenhead, stm., Mb., Can.	142	D17	50.33 N	96.40 W
Broken Hill, Austl.	98	H3	31.57 S	141.26 E
Broken Hill see Kabwe, Zam.	88	C4	14.26 S	28.26 E
Broken Ridge, unds.	174	M12	31.30 S	95.00 E
Brokopondo, Sur.	164	B6	5.03 N	54.59 W
Brokopondo Stuwmeer, res., Sur.	164	C6	4.48 N	55.04 W
Bromberg see Bydgoszcz, Pol.	24	C14	53.07 N	18.00 E
Bromborough, Eng., U.K.	180		53.19 N	2.59 W
Bromley Common, ngh., Eng., U.K.	178		51.22 N	0.03 E
Bromley Plateau, unds.	176	K10	30.52 S	35.00 W
Brommö, i., Swe.	16	I11	58.50 N	13.41 E
Bromölla, Swe.	16	K12	56.04 N	14.28 E
Brompton, Eng., U.K.	178		51.23 N	0.33 E
Bromptonville, Qc., Can.	122	E4	45.28 N	71.57 W
Bromsgrove, Eng., U.K.	10	I10	52.20 N	2.03 W
Brønderslev, Den.	16	J8	57.16 N	9.58 E
Bronevskaja, Russia	18	F26	61.41 N	39.13 E
Bronkhorstspruit, S. Afr.	90	D9	25.47 S	28.45 E
Bronlund Peak, mtn., B.C., Can.	110	D5	57.26 N	126.38 W
Bronnae, Bela.	26	H13	52.19 N	30.28 E
Bronnicy, Russia	26	E21	55.25 N	38.15 E
Brønnøysund, Nor.	16	B10	65.30 N	12.15 E
Bronson, Fl., U.S.	132	G3	29.26 N	82.38 W
Bronson, Ks., U.S.	130	G2	37.54 N	95.04 W
Bronson, Mi., U.S.	130	C12	41.51 N	85.12 W
Bronson, Tx., U.S.	136	C13	31.21 N	94.01 W
Bronte, Italy	32	G8	37.47 N	14.50 E
Bronte, Tx., U.S.	136	C7	31.53 N	100.17 W
Bronwood, Ga., U.S.	132	E1	31.50 N	84.20 W
Bronx, ngh., N.Y., U.S.	194		40.49 N	73.54 W
Bronx, stm., N.Y., U.S.	194		40.49 N	73.52 W
Bronx Park, p.o.i., N.Y., U.S.	194		40.52 N	73.53 W
Bronxville, N.Y., U.S.	194		40.56 N	73.49 W
Bronx-Whitestone Bridge, trans., N.Y., U.S.	194		40.48 N	73.50 W
Bronx Zoo, p.o.i., N.Y., U.S.	194		40.51 N	73.53 W
Bronyts'ka Huta, Ukr.	38	C6	50.56 N	27.19 E
Brook, In., U.S.	130	D10	40.51 N	87.21 W
Brookeland, Tx., U.S.	136	C14	31.09 N	94.00 W
Brooker, Fl., U.S.	132	G3	29.53 N	82.20 W
Brookfield, N.S., Can.	122	E13	45.15 N	63.17 W
Brookfield, Mo., U.S.	130	E4	39.47 N	93.04 W
Brookfield, Wi., U.S.	130	A9	43.03 N	88.06 W
Brookfield Zoo, p.o.i., Il., U.S.	196		41.50 N	87.50 W
Brookford, N.C., U.S.	124	I4	35.42 N	81.20 W
Brookhaven, De., U.S.	203		39.42 N	75.41 W
Brookhaven, Ms., U.S.	134	F8	31.34 N	90.26 W
Brookhaven, Pa., U.S.	203		39.52 N	75.22 W
Brookings, Or., U.S.	148	A1	42.03 N	124.17 W
Brookings, S.D., U.S.	128	G2	44.18 N	96.47 W
Brookland, Ar., U.S.	134	B8	35.54 N	90.34 W
Brookland, ngh., D.C., U.S.	202c		38.56 N	76.59 W
Brookland Terrace, De., U.S.	203		39.44 N	75.37 W
Brooklandville, Md., U.S.	202b		39.25 N	76.40 W
Brooklawn, N.J., U.S.	203		39.52 N	75.07 W
Brooklet, Ga., U.S.	132	D4	32.23 N	81.39 W
Brooklyn, N.S., Can.	122	F12	44.03 N	64.40 W
Brooklyn, Ia., U.S.	128	J6	41.43 N	92.26 W
Brooklyn, Mi., U.S.	124	B1	42.06 N	84.15 W
Brooklyn, Ms., U.S.	134	F9	31.03 N	89.12 W
Brooklyn, ngh., Md., U.S.	202b		39.14 N	76.36 W
Brooklyn Battery Tunnel, trans., N.Y., U.S.	194		40.42 N	74.01 W
Brooklyn Bridge, trans., N.Y., U.S.	194		40.42 N	74.00 W
Brooklyn Center, Mn., U.S.	128	F5	45.04 N	93.19 W
Brooklyn Heights, Oh., U.S.	197a		41.24 N	81.40 W
Brooklyn Marine Park, p.o.i., N.Y., U.S.	194		40.35 N	73.55 W
Brooklyn Museum, bldg., N.Y., U.S.	194		40.40 N	73.58 W
Brookmans Park, Eng., U.K.	178		51.43 N	0.12 W
Brookmere, B.C., Can.	144	G10	49.49 N	120.53 W
Brookmont, Md., U.S.	202c		38.57 N	77.07 W
Brookneal, Va., U.S.	124	G7	37.02 N	78.56 W
Brookport, Il., U.S.	130	G9	37.07 N	88.37 W
Brooks, Ab., Can.	144	F19	50.34 N	111.53 W
Brooks, Me., U.S.	122	F7	44.33 N	69.07 W
Brooks Air Force Base, mil., Tx., U.S.	136	E9	29.21 N	98.25 W
Brooks Bay, b., B.C., Can.	144	F2	50.13 N	127.55 W
Brookshire, Tx., U.S.	136	E12	29.47 N	95.57 W
Brookside, De., U.S.	203		39.40 N	75.43 W
Brookside, N.J., U.S.	194		40.48 N	74.34 W
Brookside Park, p.o.i., Oh., U.S.	197a		41.27 N	81.43 W
Brooks Island, i., Ca., U.S.	200		37.54 N	122.21 W
Brooks Peninsula Recreation Area, p.o.i., B.C., Can.	144	F2	50.10 N	127.45 W
Brooks Place, Ma., U.S.	201		42.02 N	71.01 W
Brooks Range, mts., Ak., U.S.	109	C8	68.00 N	154.00 W
Brook Street, Eng., U.K.	178		51.37 N	0.17 E
Brooksville, Fl., U.S.	132	H3	28.33 N	82.23 W
Brooksville, Ky., U.S.	124	F1	38.41 N	84.03 W
Brooksville, Ms., U.S.	134	D10	33.14 N	88.34 W
Brookvale, Austl.	192a		33.46 S	151.17 E
Brookville, In., U.S.	130	E12	39.25 N	85.00 W
Brookville, N.Y., U.S.	194		40.48 N	73.34 W
Brookville, Pa., U.S.	124	C6	41.09 N	79.04 W
Brookville Lake, res., In., U.S.	130	E13	39.30 N	84.59 W
Brookwood, Eng., U.K.	178		51.18 N	0.38 W
Brooloo, Austl.	98	F9	26.29 S	152.41 E
Broom, Loch, b., Scot., U.K.	10	D7	57.57 N	5.17 W
Broomall, Pa., U.S.	203		39.58 N	75.21 W
Broome, Austl.	96	C4	17.57 S	122.14 E
Broomfield, Eng., U.K.	178		51.14 N	0.38 E
Broomfield, Eng., U.K.	178		51.46 N	0.28 E
Broomfield, Co., U.S.	138	B3	39.55 N	105.04 W
Brooten, Mn., U.S.	128	F3	45.29 N	95.08 W
Brora, Scot., U.K.	10	C9	58.01 N	3.51 W
Brora, stm., Scot., U.K.	10	C8	58.00 N	3.51 W
Brørup, Den.	16	L7	55.29 N	9.01 E
Brosewere Bay, b., N.Y., U.S.	194		40.37 N	73.42 W

Name	Page	Map Ref.	Latitude	Longitude
Broshniv-Osada, Ukr.	38	D3	49.00 N	24.11 E
Brosna, stm., Ire.	10	H5	53.13 N	7.58 W
Brotas de Macaúbas, Braz.	170	G4	12.00 S	42.37 W
Brothers Brook, stm., Ct., U.S.	194		41.02 N	73.36 W
Broto, Spain	28	B10	42.35 N	0.08 W
Brou, Fr.	20	F10	48.12 N	1.10 E
Brough, Eng., U.K.	10	G10	54.31 N	2.19 W
Broughton, Eng., U.K.	180		53.49 N	2.44 W
Broughton, Mount, mtn., Austl.	98	K5	37.08 S	145.25 E
Broughty Ferry, Scot., U.K.	10	E10	56.28 N	2.52 W
Broumov, Czech Rep.	24	F12	50.35 N	16.20 E
Brou-sur-Chantereine, Fr.	179		48.53 N	2.38 E
Brovary, Ukr.	38	C9	50.30 N	30.46 E
Brovst, Den.	16	J7	57.06 N	9.32 E
Browerville, Mn., U.S.	128	E4	46.05 N	94.52 W
Brown, Mount, mtn., Mt., U.S.	146	B15	48.52 N	111.09 W
Brown, Point, c., Wa., U.S.	146	D2	46.56 N	124.10 W
Brownbacks, Pa., U.S.	203		40.11 N	75.37 W
Brown City, Mi., U.S.	126	E7	43.12 N	82.59 W
Brown County State Park, p.o.i., In., U.S.	130	E11	39.07 N	86.16 W
Brown Creek, stm., N.Y., U.S.	194		40.43 N	73.04 W
Brown Deer, Wi., U.S.	130	A10	43.09 N	87.57 W
Browne Bay, b., Nu., Can.	110	A11	73.08 N	97.30 W
Brownfield, Tx., U.S.	136	A5	33.10 N	102.16 W
Browning, Mo., U.S.	130	D4	40.02 N	93.09 W
Browning, Mt., U.S.	146	B13	48.33 N	112.59 W
Brownlee Reservoir, res., U.S.	146	F9	44.40 N	117.05 W
Brown Mountain, mtn., Ca., U.S.	148	H8	35.41 N	117.01 W
Brown Mountain, mtn., Ca., U.S.	198		34.14 N	118.08 W
Brown Point, c., N.Y., U.S.	194		40.43 N	73.04 W
Browns Brook, stm., Ct., U.S.	194		41.09 N	73.17 W
Brownsburg, Qc., Can.	126	C15	45.41 N	74.24 W
Brownsburg, In., U.S.	130	E11	39.50 N	86.23 W
Browns Canyon, val., Ca., U.S.	198		34.18 N	118.35 W
Brownsdale, Mn., U.S.	128	H5	43.44 N	92.53 W
Browns Island, i., Ca., U.S.	200		38.02 N	121.52 W
Browns Town, Jam.	158d	i13	18.23 N	77.21 W
Brownstown, Il., U.S.	130	F9	38.59 N	88.56 W
Brownstown, In., U.S.	130	F11	38.52 N	86.02 W
Brownstown Creek, stm., Mi., U.S.	199		42.06 N	83.13 W
Browns Valley, Mn., U.S.	128	F2	45.35 N	96.50 W
Brownsville, Ky., U.S.	130	G11	37.11 N	86.15 W
Brownsville, La., U.S.	134	E6	32.29 N	92.10 W
Brownsville, Or., U.S.	146	F4	44.24 N	122.59 W
Brownsville, Pa., U.S.	124	E6	40.01 N	79.53 W
Brownsville, Tn., U.S.	134	B9	35.35 N	89.16 W
Brownsville, Tx., U.S.	136	I10	25.54 N	97.29 W
Brownton, Mn., U.S.	128	G4	44.43 N	94.21 W
Browntown, N.J., U.S.	194		40.24 N	74.19 W
Brownville, Al., U.S.	134	D11	33.23 N	87.47 W
Brownville, Me., U.S.	122	E7	45.18 N	69.02 W
Brownville, Ne., U.S.	130	D2	40.23 N	95.39 W
Brownville Junction, Me., U.S.	122	E7	45.20 N	69.03 W
Brownwood, Tx., U.S.	136	C8	31.42 N	98.58 W
Brownwood, Lake, res., Tx., U.S.	136	C9	31.49 N	99.03 W
Browse Island, i., Austl.	96	B4	14.07 S	123.33 E
Broxbourne, Eng., U.K.	178		51.45 N	0.01 W
Broxbourne, mun., Eng., U.K.	178		51.44 N	0.04 W
Broxton, Ga., U.S.	132	E3	31.37 N	82.53 W
Broyhill Park, Va., U.S.	202c		38.51 N	77.11 W
Broža, Bela.	26	H12	52.57 N	29.07 E
Bruay-en-Artois, Fr.	20	D11	50.28 N	2.33 E
Bruce, Ms., U.S.	134	C9	33.59 N	89.20 W
Bruce, S.D., U.S.	128	G2	44.26 N	96.54 W
Bruce, Wi., U.S.	128	F7	45.27 N	91.16 W
Bruce, Mount, mtn., Austl.	96	D3	22.35 S	118.07 E
Bruce Creek, stm., On., Can.	193b		43.52 N	79.18 W
Bruce Mines, On., Can.	126	B6	46.18 N	83.47 W
Bruce Museum, bldg., Ct., U.S.	194		41.01 N	73.37 W
Bruce Peninsula, pen., On., Can.	126	C8	44.51 N	81.12 W
Bruce Peninsula National Park, p.o.i., On., Can.	126	C7	45.12 N	81.40 W
Bruce Rock, Austl.	96	F3	31.52 S	118.08 E
Bruchmühle, Ger.	182a		52.33 N	13.47 E
Bruchsal, Ger.	24	G4	49.07 N	8.35 E
Bruck, Aus.	24	I8	47.17 N	12.49 E
Bruck an der Leitha, Aus.	30	B13	48.02 N	16.49 E
Bruck an der Mur, Aus.	30	C12	47.25 N	15.16 E
Bruckhausen, ngh., Ger.	181		51.29 N	6.44 E
Bruderheim, Ab., Can.	144	C18	53.48 N	112.55 W
Brue, stm., Eng., U.K.	10	J10	51.13 N	3.00 W
Brueil-en-Vexin, Fr.	179		49.02 N	1.49 E
Bruges see Brugge, Bel.	20	C12	51.13 N	3.14 E
Brugg, Switz.	30	C5	47.28 N	8.12 E
Brugge (Bruges), Bel.	20	C12	51.13 N	3.14 E
Brügge, Ger.	181		51.13 N	7.34 E
Brühl, Ger.	24	F2	50.49 N	6.56 E
Bruin Point, mtn., Ut., U.S.	150	D6	39.39 N	110.22 W
Bruit, Pulau, i., Malay.	66	B7	2.35 N	111.20 E
Brule, Ne., U.S.	140	F11	41.05 N	101.53 W
Brule, stm., U.S.	128	F10	45.57 N	88.12 W
Brûlé, Lac, l., Qc., Can.	126	B12	46.56 N	77.11 W
Brumadinho, Braz.	170	K3	20.07 S	44.12 W
Brumado, Braz.	170	H5	14.12 S	41.40 W
Brumath, Fr.	24	H3	48.44 N	7.42 E
Brumunddal, Nor.	16	G8	60.52 N	10.56 E
Brundidge, Al., U.S.	134	F13	31.43 N	85.48 W
Bruneau, Id., U.S.	146	H11	42.53 N	115.48 W
Bruneau, stm., U.S.	118	G8	42.57 N	115.57 W
Bruneck see Brunico, Italy	30	D8	46.48 N	11.56 E
Brunei see Bandar Seri Begawan, Bru.	66	A9	4.56 N	114.56 E
Brunei, ctry., Asia	66	A9	4.30 N	114.40 E
Brunflo, Swe.	16	D12	63.05 N	14.49 E
Brunico, Italy	30	D8	46.48 N	11.56 E
Brüninghausen, Ger.	181		51.13 N	7.41 E
Brunkeberg, Nor.	16	H6	59.26 N	8.29 E
Brünn see Brno, Czech Rep.	24	G12	49.12 N	16.36 E
Bruno, Sk., Can.	142	B8	52.15 N	105.30 W
Brunot Island, i., Pa., U.S.	197b		40.28 N	80.03 W
Brunow, Ger.	182a		52.44 N	13.52 E
Brunsbüttel, Ger.	24	C4	53.54 N	9.05 E
Brunson, S.C., U.S.	132	D4	32.55 N	81.11 W
Brunswick, Austl.	192b		37.46 S	144.58 E
Brunswick see Braunschweig, Ger.	24	D6	52.16 N	10.31 E
Brunswick, Ga., U.S.	132	E4	31.11 N	81.29 W
Brunswick, Me., U.S.	122	G6	43.54 N	69.57 W
Brunswick, Md., U.S.	124	E8	39.18 N	77.38 W
Brunswick, Mo., U.S.	130	E4	39.25 N	93.07 W
Brunswick, Oh., U.S.	124	C4	41.14 N	81.49 W
Brunswick, Península, pen., Chile	166	J2	53.11 S	71.10 W
Brunswick Naval Air Station, mil., Me., U.S.	122	G7	43.54 N	69.56 W
Brunswick Square, shp. cen., N.J., U.S.	194		40.25 N	74.23 W
Bruntál, Czech Rep.	24	F13	49.59 N	17.27 E
Brus, Laguna de, b., Hond.	156	E5	15.49 N	84.35 W
Brusendorf, Ger.	182a		52.19 N	13.31 E
Brush, Co., U.S.	138	A5	40.15 N	103.37 W
Brush Creek, stm., Pa., U.S.	197b		40.23 N	79.46 W
Brush Run, stm., Pa., U.S.	197b		40.16 N	80.10 W
Brush Run, stm., Pa., U.S.	197b		40.18 N	80.07 W
Brushy Creek, stm., Austl.	192b		37.43 S	145.17 E
Brushy Creek, stm., Ok., U.S.	134	C3	34.54 N	95.34 W
Brushy Creek, stm., Tx., U.S.	136	D10	30.43 N	97.03 W
Brus Laguna, Hond.	156	E5	15.45 N	84.30 W
Brusovo, Russia	26	C18	57.51 N	35.24 E
Brusque, Braz.	172	C13	27.07 S	48.55 W
Brussel see Bruxelles, Bel.	20	D13	50.50 N	4.22 E
Brussels see Bruxelles, Bel.	20	D13	50.50 N	4.22 E
Brussels, On., Can.	126	E8	43.44 N	81.14 W
Brusy, Pol.	24	C13	53.53 N	17.43 E
Brusyliv, Ukr.	38	C8	50.17 N	29.31 E
Bruthen, Austl.	98	K6	37.42 S	147.49 E
Brüx see Most, Czech Rep.	24	F9	50.30 N	13.38 E
Bruxelles (Brussels), Bel.	20	D13	50.50 N	4.22 E
Bruyères-le-Châtel, Fr.	179		48.36 N	2.11 E
Bruzual, Ven.	168	D7	8.02 N	69.20 W
Bryan, Oh., U.S.	124	C1	41.28 N	84.33 W
Bryan, Tx., U.S.	136	D11	30.40 N	96.22 W
Bryan, Mount, mtn., Austl.	98	I2	33.26 S	138.59 E
Bryant, Ar., U.S.	134	C6	34.36 N	92.29 W
Bryant, S.D., U.S.	140	C15	44.35 N	97.28 W
Bryant Creek, stm., Mo., U.S.	130	H5	36.35 N	92.17 W
Bryce Canyon National Park, p.o.i., Ut., U.S.	150	F4	37.28 N	112.14 W
Bryli, Bela.	26	G13	53.55 N	30.33 E
Bryn, Eng., U.K.	180		53.30 N	2.39 W
Bryn Athyn, Pa., U.S.	203		40.08 N	75.04 W
Bryne, Nor.	16	I3	58.44 N	5.39 E
Brynford, Wales, U.K.	180		53.16 N	3.14 W
Bryn Gates, Eng., U.K.	180		53.30 N	2.37 W
Bryn'kovskaja, Russia	38	G17	46.01 N	38.35 E
Bryn Mawr College, educ., Pa., U.S.	203		40.02 N	75.19 W
Bryson, Qc., Can.	126	C13	45.40 N	76.36 W
Bryson, Tx., U.S.	136	A9	33.08 N	98.23 W
Bryson City, N.C., U.S.	132	A2	35.26 N	83.26 W
Brza Palanka, Yugo.	36	E9	44.28 N	22.26 E
Brzeg, Pol.	24	F13	50.51 N	17.28 E
Brześć Kujawski, Pol.	24	D14	52.37 N	18.58 E
Brzesko, Pol.	24	F16	49.58 N	20.36 E
Brzeszcze, Pol.	24	F15	49.59 N	19.07 E
Brzeziny, Pol.	24	E15	51.48 N	19.45 E
Brzozów, Pol.	24	G17	49.42 N	22.02 E
Bsharrī, Leb.	76	D6	34.15 N	36.01 E
Bua, Fiji	101e	p19	16.48 S	178.37 E
Bua Bay, b., Fiji	101e	p19	16.49 S	178.35 E
Buada Lagoon, b., Nauru	100f	q17	0.31 S	166.54 E
Buala, Sol. Is.	101b	e8	8.07 S	159.33 E
Buaran, stm., Indon.	187e		6.17 S	106.55 E
Bua Yai, Thai.	64	E6	15.34 N	102.26 E
Bu'ayrat al-Hasun, Libya	82	A3	31.24 N	15.43 E
Bubai, Japan	186		35.40 N	139.29 E
Bubanza, Bdi.	86	E5	3.06 S	29.23 E
Bubaque, Gui.-B.	84	G1	11.17 N	15.50 W
Bubi, stm., Zimb.	90	B10	22.20 S	31.07 E
Būbiyān, i., Kuw.	74	F11	29.45 N	48.15 E
Bubuduo, China	70	C10	30.06 N	84.36 E
Buc, Fr.	179		48.46 N	2.08 E
Bucak, Tur.	34	F13	37.29 N	30.35 E
Bucakkışla, Tur.	76	B4	36.57 N	33.01 E
Bucaramanga, Col.	168	D5	7.03 N	73.04 W
Buccaneer Archipelago, is., Austl.	96	C4	16.17 S	123.20 E
Buccinasco, Italy	184b		45.24 N	9.07 E
Bucelas, Port.	184c		38.54 N	9.07 W
Bucelas, hill, Port.	184c		38.53 N	9.07 W
Buch, ngh., Ger.	182a		52.38 N	13.30 E
Buchach, Ukr.	38	D4	49.03 N	25.24 E
Buchanan, Sk., Can.	142	C11	51.41 N	102.45 W
Buchanan, Lib.	84	H2	5.52 N	10.01 W
Buchanan, Ga., U.S.	134	D13	33.48 N	85.11 W
Buchanan, Mi., U.S.	130	C11	41.49 N	86.21 W
Buchanan, Va., U.S.	124	G6	37.31 N	79.41 W
Buchanan, Lake, l., Austl.	98	C5	21.34 S	145.52 E
Buchanan, Lake, l., Tx., U.S.	136	D9	30.48 N	98.25 W
Buchanan Field, arpt., Ca., U.S.	200		37.59 N	122.03 W
Buchan Ness, c., Scot., U.K.	10	D11	57.28 N	1.46 W
Buchans, Nf., Can.	111a	j22	48.49 N	56.52 W
Bucharest see București, Rom.	36	E13	44.26 N	26.06 E
Buchelay, Fr.	179		48.59 N	1.40 E
Buchen, Ger.	24	G5	49.31 N	9.20 E
Buchholz, Ger.	181		51.23 N	7.15 E
Buchholz, Ger.	182a		52.35 N	13.47 E
Buchholz, ngh., Ger.	181		51.23 N	6.46 E
Buchholz, ngh., Ger.	182a		52.36 N	13.26 E
Buchholz in der Nordheide, Ger.	24	C5	53.19 N	9.52 E
Buchloe, Ger.	24	H6	48.02 N	10.43 E
Buchmany, Ukr.	38	B6	51.04 N	28.04 E
Bucholt, Ger.	181		51.39 N	6.43 E
Buchon, Point, c., Ca., U.S.	148	H4	35.15 N	120.54 W
Buchow-Karpzow, Ger.	182a		52.31 N	12.57 E
Buchs, Switz.	30	C6	47.09 N	9.27 E
Buckatunna, Ms., U.S.	134	F10	31.32 N	88.31 W
Buckatunna Creek, stm., Ms., U.S.	134	F10	31.30 N	88.32 W
Buck Branch, stm., Md., U.S.	202b		39.01 N	77.10 W
Buck Creek, stm., U.S.	138	G8	34.34 N	99.57 W
Buck Creek, stm., Ky., U.S.	130	G13	36.59 N	84.30 W
Buck Creek, stm., Pa., U.S.	203		40.15 N	74.50 W
Bückeburg, Ger.	24	D5	52.15 N	9.03 E
Buckeye, Az., U.S.	150	J4	33.22 N	112.35 W
Buckeye Lake, Oh., U.S.	126	I7	39.54 N	82.29 W
Buckhannon, W.V., U.S.	124	F5	38.59 N	80.13 W
Buckhaven, Scot., U.K.	10	E9	56.10 N	3.02 W
Buckholts, Tx., U.S.	136	D10	30.52 N	97.07 W
Buckhorn Draw, stm., Tx., U.S.	136	D6	30.38 N	100.51 W
Buckhorn Island State Park, p.o.i., N.Y., U.S.	202a		43.03 N	78.59 W
Buckie, Scot., U.K.	10	D10	57.40 N	2.59 W
Buckingham, Qc., Can.	126	C14	45.34 N	75.23 W
Buckingham, Va., U.S.	124	G7	37.32 N	78.32 W
Buckingham Bay, b., Austl.	96	B7	12.10 S	135.46 E
Buckingham Palace, bldg., Eng., U.K.	178		51.30 N	0.08 W
Buck Island Reef National Monument, p.o.i., V.I.U.S.	158c	g11	17.48 N	64.37 W
Buck Lake, l., Ab., Can.	144	D16	52.59 N	114.46 W
Buckland, Austl.	99a	o13	42.37 S	147.43 E
Buckland, Eng., U.K.	178		51.15 N	0.15 W
Buckland, Ak., U.S.	109	C7	65.58 N	161.12 W
Buckland Common, Eng., U.K.	178		51.45 N	0.39 W
Buckley, Il., U.S.	130	D9	40.35 N	88.01 W
Buckley, Wa., U.S.	146	C4	47.09 N	122.01 W
Bucklin, Ks., U.S.	138	D9	37.32 N	99.38 W
Bucklin, Mo., U.S.	130	E5	39.46 N	92.53 W
Buck Lodge, Md., U.S.	202c		39.01 N	76.58 W
Buck Mountain, mtn., Va., U.S.	124	H4	36.40 N	81.15 W
Buck Mountain, mtn., Wa., U.S.	146	B7	48.26 N	119.50 W
Bucknell Heights, Va., U.S.	202c		38.46 N	77.04 W
Buckner Creek, stm., Ks., U.S.	138	C8	38.11 N	99.34 W
Buckow, Ger.	24	D10	52.34 N	14.04 E
Buckow, ngh., Ger.	182a		52.25 N	13.26 E
Buckskin Gulch, stm., Ut., U.S.	150	F4	37.01 N	111.51 W
Buckskin Gulch, stm., Ut., U.S.	150	F4	37.00 N	111.52 W
Bucksport, Me., U.S.	122	F8	44.34 N	68.47 W
Bucktown, Pa., U.S.	203		40.10 N	75.43 W
Buc-Louis-Blériot, Aérodrome de, arpt., Fr.	179		48.45 N	2.05 E
Bucovăț, Mol.	36	B15	47.12 N	28.26 E
Bucovina see Bukovina, hist. reg., Eur.	38	F4	47.56 N	25.33 E
Buco Zau, Ang.	88	A1	4.46 S	12.33 E
București (Bucharest), Rom.	36	E13	44.26 N	26.06 E
București, state, Rom.	36	E13	44.30 N	26.15 E
Bucyrus, Oh., U.S.	124	D3	40.48 N	82.58 W
Bud, Nor.	16	E4	62.54 N	6.56 E
Buda, Il., U.S.	130	C8	41.19 N	89.40 W
Buda, Tx., U.S.	136	D10	30.05 N	97.50 W
Buda, ngh., Hung.	182c		47.30 N	19.02 E
Buda Castle, hist., Hung.	182c		47.30 N	19.02 E
Budafok, ngh., Hung.	182c		47.26 N	19.02 E
Budai-hegység, mts., Hung.	182c		47.31 N	18.58 E
Budakalász, Hung.	182c		47.37 N	19.03 E
Buda-Kašalëva, Bela.	26	H13	52.42 N	30.34 E
Budakeszi, Hung.	182c		47.31 N	18.56 E
Budalin, Mya.	64	A2	22.23 N	95.08 E
Budaörs, Hung.	182c		47.27 N	18.58 E
Budapest, Hung.	36	B6	47.29 N	19.04 E
Budapest, Hung.	182c		47.30 N	19.05 E
Budapest, state, Hung.	36	B6	47.30 N	19.05 E
Budapest, mun., Hung.	182c		47.30 N	19.05 E
Búðardalur, Ice.	12a	k29	65.06 N	21.45 W
Budatétény, ngh., Hung.	182c		47.25 N	19.01 E
Budaun, India	70	D7	28.02 N	79.07 E
Budberg, Ger.	181		51.32 N	6.38 E
Budd Coast, cst., Ant.	103	B16	66.54 S	112.10 E
Buddha Jayanti Park, p.o.i., India	190a		28.37 N	77.10 E
Buddh Gaya see Bodh Gaya, India	70	F10	24.41 N	84.58 E
Buddtown, N.J., U.S.	203		39.56 N	74.42 W
Buddusò, Italy	32	D3	40.35 N	9.15 E
Bude, Eng., U.K.	10	K8	50.50 N	4.32 W
Bude, Ms., U.S.	134	F8	31.27 N	90.51 W
Bude Bay, b., Eng., U.K.	10	K8	50.48 N	4.35 W
Budënnovsk, Russia	42	C11	44.47 N	44.09 E
Budënnovskaja, Russia	40	H12	46.55 N	41.33 E
Budești, Rom.	36	E13	44.14 N	26.28 E
Büdingen, Ger.	24	F5	50.17 N	9.07 E
Búðir, Ice.	12a	k32	64.55 N	14.04 W
Budišov nad Budišovkou, Czech Rep.	24	G13	49.47 N	17.36 E
Budjala, D.R.C.	86	D3	2.38 N	19.42 E
Budogošč', Russia	26	A15	59.16 N	32.28 E
Budogovišči, Russia	26	G19	53.35 N	36.18 E
Bu Dop, Viet.	64	F8	11.57 N	106.47 E
Budrio, Italy	30	F8	44.32 N	11.32 E
Budslau, Bela.	26	F10	54.47 N	27.27 E
Budweis see České Budějovice, Czech Rep.	24	H10	48.58 N	14.28 E
Budworth Mere, l., Eng., U.K.	180		53.17 N	2.31 W
Budy, Ukr.	38	D15	49.54 N	35.59 E
Budyłka, Ukr.	38	C13	50.30 N	34.26 E
Budzhak, plat., Eur.	38	D15	46.07 N	28.49 E
Buea, Cam.	86	D1	4.09 N	9.14 E
Buehl Airport, arpt., Pa., U.S.	203		40.11 N	74.54 W
Buena Esperanza, Arg.	172	G5	34.45 S	65.15 W
Buenaventura, Col.	168	F3	3.53 N	77.03 W
Buenaventura, Mex.	120	G9	29.51 N	107.27 W
Buena Vista, Bol.	166	C4	17.27 S	63.40 W
Buena Vista, Mex.	148	K9	32.30 N	116.44 W
Buena Vista, Para.	172	C10	26.08 S	55.56 W
Buenavista, Phil.	68	G4	7.17 N	122.15 E
Buena Vista, Co., U.S.	138	C2	38.50 N	106.08 W
Buena Vista, Ga., U.S.	134	E14	32.19 N	84.31 W
Buena Vista, Md., U.S.	202c		38.57 N	76.50 W
Buena Vista, Ms., U.S.	134	D10	33.53 N	88.45 W
Buena Vista, Pa., U.S.	197b		40.17 N	79.48 W
Buena Vista, Va., U.S.	124	G6	37.44 N	79.21 W
Buena Vista Lake Bed, reg., Ca., U.S.	148	H6	35.11 N	119.17 W
Buen Día, Mex.	136	H3	26.21 N	104.32 W
Buendía, Embalse de, res., Spain	28	D8	40.25 N	2.43 W
Buenópolis, Braz.	170	I3	17.54 S	44.07 W
Buenos Aires, Arg.	172	G8	34.37 S	58.23 W
Buenos Aires, Arg.	206		34.36 S	58.27 W
Buenos Aires, C.R.	156	H6	9.09 N	83.20 W
Buenos Aires, state, Arg.	166	G5	36.00 S	60.00 W
Buenos Aires, Lago see General Carrera, Lago, l., S.A.	166	I2	46.26 S	71.39 W
Buen Pasto, Arg.	166	I3	45.05 S	69.28 W
Buer, ngh., Ger.	181		51.36 N	7.03 E
Buerarema, Braz.	170	H6	14.57 S	39.15 W
Buesaco, Col.	168	G3	1.23 N	77.09 W
Bufalotta, Fosso della, stm., Italy	185a		41.59 N	12.30 E
Buffalo, Ks., U.S.	130	G2	37.41 N	95.41 W
Buffalo, Mn., U.S.	128	F5	45.10 N	93.53 W
Buffalo, Mo., U.S.	130	G4	37.38 N	93.05 W
Buffalo, N.Y., U.S.	124	B7	42.53 N	78.52 W
Buffalo, N.Y., U.S.	202a		42.53 N	78.52 W
Buffalo, Oh., U.S.	124	E4	39.54 N	81.31 W
Buffalo, Ok., U.S.	138	E9	36.50 N	99.37 W
Buffalo, S.C., U.S.	132	B4	34.43 N	81.40 W
Buffalo, S.D., U.S.	140	B9	45.34 N	103.32 W
Buffalo, Tx., U.S.	136	C11	31.27 N	96.03 W
Buffalo, Wy., U.S.	140	C6	44.21 N	106.42 W
Buffalo, stm., Can.	110	C8	60.52 N	115.02 W
Buffalo, stm., Ar., U.S.	130	H4	36.09 N	92.25 W
Buffalo, stm., Mn., U.S.	128	E2	47.05 N	96.49 W
Buffalo, stm., Ms., U.S.	134	F7	31.04 N	91.34 W
Buffalo, stm., N.Y., U.S.	202a		42.53 N	78.53 W
Buffalo, stm., Tn., U.S.	134	B11	35.59 N	87.50 W
Buffalo, stm., Wi., U.S.	128	G7	44.20 N	91.55 W
Buffalo, State University College at, educ., N.Y., U.S.	202a		42.56 N	78.53 W
Buffalo Airpark, arpt., N.Y., U.S.	202a		42.52 N	78.43 W
Buffalo Bill Ranch State Historical Park, p.o.i., Ne., U.S.	140	F12	41.10 N	100.48 W
Buffalo Bill State Park, p.o.i., Wy., U.S.	140	C3	44.30 N	109.14 W
Buffalo Center, Ia., U.S.	128	H5	43.22 N	93.57 W
Buffalo Coast Guard Base, mil., N.Y., U.S.	202a		42.52 N	78.54 W
Buffalo Creek, stm., U.S.	140	B10	45.56 N	102.52 W
Buffalo Creek, stm., Il., U.S.	196		42.08 N	87.55 W
Buffalo Creek, stm., Ia., U.S.	130	B6	42.05 N	91.17 W
Buffalo Creek, stm., Ks., U.S.	138	B10	39.35 N	97.43 W
Buffalo Creek, stm., Mn., U.S.	128	G4	44.51 N	94.00 W
Buffalo Creek, stm., Ok., U.S.	138	E9	36.47 N	99.15 W
Buffalo Harbor, b., N.Y., U.S.	202a		42.51 N	78.52 W
Buffalo Lake, Mn., U.S.	128	G4	44.44 N	94.37 W
Buffalo Lake, l., Ab., Can.	144	D18	52.29 N	112.54 W
Buffalo Lake, l., N.T., Can.	110	C7	60.10 N	115.30 W
Buffalo Museum of Science, bldg., N.Y., U.S.	202a		42.54 N	78.51 W
Buffalo Narrows, Sk., Can.	110	D8	55.50 N	108.28 W
Buffalo National River, p.o.i., Ar., U.S.	130	H5	35.58 N	92.53 W
Buffalo Pound Lake, l., Sk., Can.	142	D8	50.39 N	105.30 W
Buffalo Pound Provincial Park, p.o.i., Sk., Can.	142	D8	50.34 N	105.23 W
Buffalo Run, stm., Pa., U.S.	197b		40.12 N	79.37 W
Buffalo Zoo, p.o.i., N.Y., U.S.	202a		42.56 N	78.51 W
Buffels, stm., S. Afr.	90	F10	28.42 S	30.38 E
Buffels, stm., S. Afr.	90	H5	33.14 S	20.56 E
Buffels, stm., S. Afr.	90	F3	29.40 S	17.03 E
Buffington Harbor, b., In., U.S.	196		41.38 N	87.25 W
Buford, Ga., U.S.	132	B2	34.07 N	84.00 W
Buford Dam, dam., Ga., U.S.	132	B1	34.09 N	84.04 W
Buftea, Rom.	36	E12	44.30 N	26.00 E
Bug, stm., Eur.	8	E13	52.25 N	20.41 E
Buga, Col.	168	F3	3.54 N	76.18 W
Bugala Island, i., Ug.	86	E6	0.39 S	32.19 E
Bugat, Mong.	58	B5	47.55 N	101.18 E
Bugeac see Budzhak, plat., Eur.	36	D15	46.07 N	28.49 E
Bugeat, Fr.	22	D7	45.35 N	1.59 E
Bugio, i., Port.	184c		38.39 N	9.18 W
Bugojno, Bos.	36	E4	44.03 N	17.27 E
Bugøynes, Nor.	14	C20	69.58 N	29.36 E
Bugrino, Russia	12	B23	68.48 N	49.09 E
Bugry, Russia	26	B18	58.45 N	35.17 E
Bugry, Russia	183a		60.04 N	30.24 E
Bugsuk Island, i., Phil.	68	F1	8.15 N	117.18 E
Bugt, China	54	C4	42.19 N	120.41 E
Bugul'ma, Russia	40	D18	54.31 N	52.47 E
Bugul'minsko-Belebeevskaja vozvyšennost', plat., Russia	40	D18	54.43 N	52.28 E
Buguruslan, Russia	40	E18	53.38 N	52.26 E
Buh, stm., China	52	D4	37.00 N	99.50 E
Buh (Bug) (Zakhidnyi Buh), stm., Eur.	40	E3	52.15 N	23.21 E
Buhaivka, Ukr.	38	D16	49.28 N	37.23 E
Buhara, Uzb.	48	G10	39.46 N	64.25 E
Buhl, Id., U.S.	146	H12	42.36 N	114.45 W
Buhl, Mn., U.S.	128	D6	47.29 N	92.46 W
Buhler, Ks., U.S.	138	C11	38.08 N	97.45 W
Buhuai, China	70	B8	33.22 N	80.36 E
Buhuşi, Rom.	36	C13	46.43 N	26.44 E
Buies Creek, N.C., U.S.	132	A7	35.24 N	78.44 W
Buile Hill Park, p.o.i., Eng., U.K.	180		53.29 N	2.18 W
Builth Wells, Wales, U.K.	10	I9	52.09 N	3.24 W
Buin, Chile	172	F2	33.42 S	70.42 W
Buin, Pap. N. Gui.	101b	d6	6.49 S	155.43 E
Buinsk, Russia	40	D15	55.11 N	47.03 E
Buinsk, Russia	40	D16	54.57 N	48.17 E
Buique, Braz.	170	E7	8.37 S	37.09 W
Buir Nur see Buyr nuur, l., Asia	52	B8	47.48 N	117.42 E
Buitenzorg see Bogor, Indon.	66	G5	6.35 S	106.47 E
Buitsivango (Rietfontein), stm., Afr.	90	B4	22.25 S	22.13 E
Buj, Russia	40	B12	58.28 N	41.33 E
Bujaki, Russia	40	B16	59.02 N	48.43 E
Bujalance, Spain	28	G6	37.54 N	4.22 W
Bujaraloz, Spain	28	C10	41.30 N	0.09 W
Buje, Cro.	30	E10	45.24 N	13.39 E
Bujnaksk, Russia	42	D12	42.49 N	47.05 E
Bujnavičy, Bela.	38	B7	51.52 N	28.33 E
Bujumbura, Bdi.	86	E5	3.23 S	29.22 E
Buk, Pol.	24	D12	52.21 N	16.30 E
Bukačača, Russia	50	F12	52.59 N	116.54 E
Bukachivtsi, Ukr.	38	D3	49.14 N	24.29 E
Bukama, D.R.C.	86	F5	9.12 S	25.51 E
Būkān, Iran	42	G12	36.31 N	46.12 E
Bukan', Russia	26	G17	53.55 N	34.43 E
Bukavu, D.R.C.	86	E5	2.30 S	28.51 E
Bukene, Tan.	86	E6	4.13 S	32.52 E
Bukeya, D.R.C.	86	G5	10.23 S	26.58 E
Bukitbatu, Indon.	66	C2	1.26 N	101.59 E
Bukit Mandai, Sing.	189c		1.25 N	103.45 E
Bukit Panjang, Sing.	189c		1.23 N	103.46 E
Bukit Timah, Sing.	189c		1.20 N	103.47 E
Bukit Timah Nature Preserve, p.o.i., Sing.	189c		1.21 N	103.47 E
Bukittinggi, Indon.	66	D2	0.18 S	100.22 E
Bukit Turf Club, p.o.i., Sing.	189c		1.20 N	103.48 E
Bükk, mts., Hung.	36	A7	48.02 N	20.26 E
Bükki Nemzeti Park, p.o.i., Hung.	36	A7	48.08 N	20.30 E
Bukoba, Tan.	86	E6	1.18 S	31.48 E
Bukovica, reg., Cro.	30	F12	44.10 N	15.40 E
Bukovina, hist. reg., Eur.	38	F4	47.56 N	25.33 E
Bukovyna see Bukovina, hist. reg., Eur.	38	F4	47.56 N	25.33 E
Bukum, Pulau, i., Sing.	189c		1.14 N	103.47 E
Bukum Kechil, Pulau, i., Sing.	189c		1.14 N	103.46 E
Bukuru, Nig.	84	H6	9.47 N	8.51 E
Bukvassfjellet, mtn., Nor.	16	C11	64.21 N	13.09 E
Bula, Indon.	60	F9	3.06 S	130.30 E
Bülach, Switz.	24	I4	47.31 N	8.32 E
Bulaevo, Kaz.	48	C12	54.53 N	70.27 E
Bulak Gölü, l., Tur.	34	E15	38.31 N	32.55 E
Bulan, Phil.	68	D4	12.40 N	123.53 E
Bulan, Ky., U.S.	124	G2	37.16 N	83.11 W
Bulandshahr, India	70	D6	28.24 N	77.51 E
Bulanık, Tur.	42	F10	39.05 N	42.17 E
Bulanovo, Russia	40	E19	52.27 N	55.10 E
Būlāq, ngh., Egypt	191c		30.04 N	31.14 E
Būlāq el-Dakrūr, Egypt	191c		30.02 N	31.11 E
Bulawayo, Zimb.	88	E4	20.09 S	28.34 E
Bulbul, Syria	76	B7	36.46 N	36.49 E
Buldan, Tur.	34	E11	38.03 N	28.50 E
Buldāna, India	70	H6	20.31 N	76.11 E
Buldir Island, i., Ak., U.S.	109a	g22	52.21 N	175.54 E
Bulgakovo, Russia	26	E15	55.14 N	32.07 E
Bulgan, Mong.	52	B5	48.48 N	103.33 E
Bulgan, Mong.	52	B3	46.57 N	93.34 E
Bulgan, Mong.	52	C4	44.48 N	98.39 E
Bulgar, Russia	40	D16	54.58 N	49.01 E
Bulgaria, ctry., Eur.	36	G12	43.00 N	25.00 E
Bulgroo, Austl.	98	E5	25.48 S	143.59 E
Bulim, Sing.	189c		1.22 N	103.43 E
Bulkley, stm., B.C., Can.	144	B3	54.29 N	126.23 W
Bulkley Ranges, mts., B.C., Can.	144	B3	54.30 N	127.30 W
Bull, stm., B.C., Can.	144	G15	49.27 N	115.27 W
Bullaque, stm., Spain	28	E6	38.58 N	4.17 W
Bullard, Tx., U.S.	136	B12	32.08 N	95.19 W
Bulla Regia, hist., Tun.	32	H2	36.34 N	8.45 E
Bullas, Spain	28	F9	38.02 N	1.39 W
Bullaxaar, Som.	86	B8	10.23 N	44.23 E
Bull Creek, stm., Nv., U.S.	148	E10	38.36 N	115.35 W
Bull Creek, stm., N.Y., U.S.	202a		43.03 N	78.50 W
Bull Creek, stm., S.D., U.S.	140	B9	45.39 N	103.17 W
Bull Creek, stm., S.D., U.S.	140	D13	43.40 N	99.28 W
Bull Creek, stm., Tx., U.S.	136	B6	32.36 N	101.10 W
Bulle, Switz.	30	D4	46.36 N	7.03 E
Bullenbaai, Neth. Ant.	158g	p21	12.09 N	69.00 W
Buller, stm., N.Z.	102	E5	41.44 S	171.35 E
Buller, Mount, mtn., Austl.	98	K6	37.09 S	146.26 E
Bullfinch, Austl.	96	F3	30.59 S	119.06 E
Bullfrog Creek, stm., Ut., U.S.	150	F6	37.28 N	110.42 W
Bull Harbour, B.C., Can.	144	F2	50.54 N	127.54 W
Bullhead, S.D., U.S.	140	B11	45.46 N	101.06 W
Bullhead City, Az., U.S.	150	H2	35.08 N	114.33 W
Bull Hill, hill, Eng., U.K.	180		53.40 N	2.21 W
Bullion, Fr.	179		48.37 N	2.00 E
Bull Lake, res., Wy., U.S.	140	D3	43.11 N	109.07 W
Bull Lake Creek, stm., Wy., U.S.	140	D3	43.13 N	109.00 W
Bull Mountain, mtn., Mt., U.S.	146	D14	46.05 N	112.04 W
Bullock, N.C., U.S.	124	H7	36.29 N	78.31 W
Bullock Creek, Austl.	98	A5	17.43 S	144.31 E
Bullock Creek, stm., Austl.	98	C5	21.50 S	145.14 E
Bulloo, stm., Austl.	98	G4	28.39 S	142.31 E
Bulloo Downs, Austl.	98	G4	28.31 S	142.57 E
Bullpound Creek, stm., Ab., Can.	144	E19	51.04 N	111.58 W
Bullrun Rock, mtn., Or., U.S.	146	F8	44.21 N	118.17 W
Bulls Bay, b., S.C., U.S.	132	D6	32.59 N	79.33 W
Bulls Gap, Tn., U.S.	124	H2	36.15 N	83.04 W
Bull Shoals, Ar., U.S.	130	H5	36.22 N	92.34 W
Bull Shoals Lake, res., U.S.	130	H5	36.28 N	92.47 W
Bully Creek, stm., Or., U.S.	146	F9	43.59 N	117.22 W
Bulmke-Hüllen, ngh., Ger.	181		51.31 N	7.06 E
Bulnes, Chile	172	H1	36.44 S	72.18 W
Bulolo, Pap. N. Gui.	101a	b4	7.11 S	146.38 E
Bulpham, Eng., U.K.	178		51.33 N	0.22 E
Bulsār, India	70	H4	20.36 N	72.55 E
Bultfontein, S. Afr.	90	F8	28.17 S	26.09 E
Buluan, Phil.	68	G5	6.46 N	124.48 E
Bulukumba, Indon.	66	F12	5.33 S	120.11 E
Bululawang, Indon.	66	H8	8.05 S	112.38 E
Bulusan, Phil.	68	D5	12.44 N	124.07 E
Bumba, D.R.C.	86	D4	2.11 N	22.28 E
Bumbles Green, Eng., U.K.	178		51.44 N	0.02 E
Bumbu, stm., D.R.C.	191b		4.23 S	15.18 E
Bumbun, Pulau, i., Malay.	66	A11	4.27 N	118.40 E
Bumkin Island, i., Ma., U.S.	201		42.17 N	70.54 W
Bumpus, Mount, hill, Nu., Can.	110	B8	69.33 N	112.40 W
Bumu Hu, l., China	70	C13	31.13 N	91.08 E
Buna, Kenya	86	D7	2.47 N	39.29 E
Buna, Tx., U.S.	136	D13	30.26 N	93.57 W
Bunawan, Phil.	68	F5	8.11 N	125.59 E
Bunbury, Austl.	96	F3	33.19 S	115.38 E
Bunceton, Mo., U.S.	130	F5	38.47 N	92.47 W
Buncrana, Ire.	10	F5	55.08 N	7.27 W
Bundaberg, Austl.	98	E9	24.52 S	152.20 E
Bundarra, Austl.	98	H8	30.11 S	151.04 E
Bünde, Ger.	24	D4	52.11 N	8.35 E
Bundeena, Austl.	192a		34.05 S	151.09 E
Būndi, India	70	F5	25.26 N	75.38 E
Bundick Creek, stm., La., U.S.	134	G5	30.36 N	92.56 W
Bundoora, Austl.	192b		37.42 S	145.04 E
Bundoran, Ire.	10	G4	54.28 N	8.17 W
Būndu, India	70	G10	23.10 N	85.34 E
Bungamas, Indon.	66	E3	3.41 S	103.22 E
Bungbulang, Indon.	66	G5	7.27 S	107.34 E
Bunge, Swe.	16	J17	57.50 N	19.00 E
Bung Kan, Thai.	64	C6	18.21 N	103.38 E
Bungoma, Kenya	86	D6	0.34 N	34.34 E
Bungo-suidō, strt., Japan	56	G5	33.00 N	132.13 E
Bungo-takada, Japan	56	F4	33.33 N	131.27 E
Bungtlang, India	70	G14	22.20 N	92.46 E
Bunia, D.R.C.	86	D6	1.31 N	30.15 E
Bunker, Mo., U.S.	130	G6	37.27 N	91.12 W
Bunker Group, is., Austl.	98	D9	23.48 S	152.20 E
Bunker Hill, Il., U.S.	130	E7	39.02 N	89.57 W
Bunker Hill, In., U.S.	130	D11	40.39 N	86.05 W
Bunker Hill, Or., U.S.	146	G2	43.20 N	124.11 W
Bunker Hill, mtn., Nv., U.S.	148	D8	39.15 N	117.08 W
Bunker Hill Monument, hist., Ma., U.S.	201		42.22 N	71.04 W
Bunkie, La., U.S.	134	G6	30.56 N	92.10 W
Bunkyō, ngh., Japan	186		35.43 N	139.45 E
Bunnell, Fl., U.S.	132	G4	29.28 N	81.15 W
Bunnerfjällen, mtn., Swe.	16	D10	63.07 N	12.34 E
Buñol see Bunyolo, Spain	28	E10	39.25 N	0.47 W
Buntok, Indon.	66	D9	1.44 S	114.49 E
Bunut, Indon.	66	C8	0.43 N	112.29 E
Bünyan, Tur.	42	F6	38.51 N	35.52 E
Bunyolo, Spain	28	E10	39.25 N	0.47 W
Bunyu, Pulau, i., Indon.	66	B10	3.30 N	117.50 E
Bunzlau see Bolesławiec, Pol.	24	E11	51.15 N	15.35 E
Buolkalah, Russia	50	B12	72.54 N	119.56 E
Buona Vista, Sing.	189c		1.16 N	103.47 E
Buon Ma Thuot, Viet.	64	F9	12.40 N	108.02 E
Buor-Haja, guba, b., Russia	50	B15	71.30 N	131.00 E
Buor-Haja, mys, c., Russia	50	B15	71.56 N	132.40 E
Bupul, Indon.	60	G11	7.30 S	140.52 E
Buqayq, Sau. Ar.	72	D6	25.56 N	49.40 E
Buquirivu, stm., Braz.	205b		23.28 S	46.28 W
Bur, Russia	48	C19	58.47 N	107.03 E

Name	Page	Map Ref.	Latitude	Longitude
Bura, Kenya	86	E7	1.05 S	39.56 E
Buraly, Russia	40	D18	55.04 N	52.49 E
Burām, Sudan	82	E5	10.48 N	25.10 E
Buran Darat, i., Sing.	189c		1.15 N	103.51 E
Burang, China	70	C8	30.14 N	81.11 E
Buranhém, stm., Braz.	170	I5	16.27 S	39.04 W
Burankol', Kaz.	40	H19	46.15 N	54.12 E
Burannoe, Russia	40	F19	50.59 N	54.28 E
Burāq, Syria	76	E7	33.10 N	36.29 E
Burāri, ngh., India	190a		28.46 N	77.12 E
Buras, La., U.S.	134	H9	29.21 N	89.32 W
Buraševo, Russia	26	D18	56.44 N	35.52 E
Burauen, Phil.	68	E5	10.58 N	124.54 E
Buraydah, Sau. Ar.	74	G9	26.19 N	43.58 E
Burbage, Eng., U.K.	180		53.15 N	1.56 W
Burbank, Il., U.S.	196		41.45 N	87.46 W
Burbank, Wa., U.S.	146	D8	46.12 N	119.01 W
Burbank Studios, sci., Ca., U.S.	198		34.09 N	118.21 W
Burç, Tur.	76	A8	37.00 N	37.10 E
Burcher, Austl.	98	I6	33.31 S	147.15 E
Burco, Som.	86	C9	9.31 N	45.32 E
Burdekin, stm., Austl.	98	C6	19.38 S	147.27 E
Burdekin Falls, wtfl., Austl.	98	C6	20.38 S	147.09 E
Burden, Ks., U.S.	138	D12	37.18 N	96.44 W
Burdeos, Phil.	68	C3	14.51 N	121.58 E
Burdett, Ab., Can.	142	E2	49.49 N	111.31 W
Burdett, Ks., U.S.	138	C9	38.11 N	99.31 W
Burdul, India	190c		19.07 N	73.07 E
Burdur, Tur.	34	F13	37.43 N	30.16 E
Burdur, state, Tur.	34	F13	37.30 N	30.00 E
Burdur Gölü, l., Tur.	34	F12	37.44 N	30.12 E
Bureå, Swe.	16	C19	64.37 N	21.12 E
Bureälven, stm., Swe.	16	C18	64.37 N	21.13 E
Bureinskij hrebet, mts., Russia	50	G15	51.03 N	133.48 E
Bureja, Russia	50	G15	49.49 N	129.48 E
Bureja, stm., Russia	50	F15	49.25 N	129.32 E
Büren, Ger.	24	E4	51.32 N	8.34 E
Bürenhayrhan, Mong.	52	B3	46.53 N	91.05 E
Bures, Fr.	179		48.57 N	1.58 E
Bures-sur-Yvette, Fr.	179		48.42 N	2.10 E
Burfjord, Nor.	14	C12	69.52 N	21.58 E
Burford, On., Can.	126	E9	43.05 N	80.25 W
Burg, Ger.	24	D7	52.16 N	11.51 E
Burg, ngh., Ger.	181		51.08 N	7.09 E
Burg, Den see Den Burg, Neth.	20	A13	53.03 N	4.47 E
Burg, Schloss, hist., Ger.	181		51.08 N	7.10 E
Burga, Russia	26	B15	58.45 N	32.29 E
Burgas, Blg.	36	G14	42.31 N	27.28 E
Burgas, state, Blg.	36	G13	42.30 N	27.00 E
Burgas, Gulf of see Burgaski Zaliv, b., Blg.	36	G14	42.30 N	27.33 E
Burgaski Zaliv, b., Blg.	36	G14	42.30 N	27.33 E
Burg auf Fehmarn, Ger.	24	B7	54.26 N	11.11 E
Burgaw, N.C., U.S.	132	B8	34.33 N	77.55 W
Burgaz, ngh., Tur.	185b		40.53 N	29.03 E
Burgaz Adası, i., Tur.	185b		40.53 N	29.04 E
Burgdorf, Switz.	30	C4	47.03 N	7.37 E
Burgenland, state, Aus.	30	C13	47.30 N	16.20 E
Burgeo, Nf., Can.	111a	j22	47.37 N	57.38 W
Burgersdorp, S. Afr.	90	G8	30.59 S	26.19 E
Burger Township, S. Afr.	191d		26.05 S	27.46 E
Burgess, Va., U.S.	124	G9	37.52 N	76.21 W
Burgfjällen, mts., Swe.	16	C12	64.56 N	14.54 E
Burggrafenberg, hill, Ger.	181		51.13 N	7.07 E
Burghausen, Ger.	24	H8	48.09 N	12.49 E
Burghead, Scot., U.K.	10	D9	57.42 N	3.29 W
Burgh Heath, Eng., U.K.	178		51.18 N	0.13 W
Burgin, Ky., U.S.	130	G13	37.42 N	84.47 W
Burglengenfeld, Ger.	24	G7	49.12 N	12.02 E
Burgo de Osma, Spain	28	C7	41.35 N	3.04 W
Burgos, Mex.	154	C9	24.56 N	98.47 W
Burgos, Phil.	68	C3	15.29 N	120.23 E
Burgos, Spain	28	B7	42.20 N	3.41 W
Burgos, co., Spain	28	B7	42.20 N	3.40 W
Burgstädt, Ger.	24	F8	50.55 N	12.48 E
Burgsvik, Swe.	16	J16	57.01 N	18.18 E
Burgueño, Arroyo, stm., Arg.	206		34.24 S	58.47 W
Burgundy see Bourgogne, hist. reg., Fr.	22	C10	47.00 N	4.30 E
Burham, Eng., U.K.	178		51.20 N	0.29 E
Burhan Budai Shan, mts., China	52	D4	36.00 N	96.00 E
Burhaniye, Tur.	34	D9	39.30 N	26.58 E
Burhānpur, India	70	H6	21.18 N	76.13 E
Burholme, ngh., Pa., U.S.	203		40.03 N	75.05 W
Buri, Braz.	170	L1	23.47 S	48.35 W
Burias Island, i., Phil.	68	D4	12.57 N	123.08 E
Burica, Punta, c., N.A.	156	I6	8.02 N	82.52 W
Burien, Wa., U.S.	146	C4	47.27 N	122.19 W
Burila Mare, Rom.	36	E9	44.28 N	22.33 E
Buri Ram, Thai.	64	E6	14.59 N	103.06 E
Buriti, Braz.	170	B4	3.55 S	42.57 W
Buriti Bravo, Braz.	170	C4	5.50 S	43.50 W
Buriticupu, stm., Braz.	170	C2	4.12 S	46.28 W
Buriti dos Lopes, Braz.	170	B5	3.10 S	41.52 W
Buritizeiro, Braz.	170	I3	17.21 S	44.58 W
Burjassot see Burjassot, Spain	28	E10	39.30 N	0.24 W
Burjassot, Spain	28	E10	39.30 N	0.24 W
Burjatija, state, Russia	50	F11	53.00 N	109.00 E
Burj Islām, Syria	76	C6	35.41 N	35.48 E
Burkburnett, Tx., U.S.	138	G10	34.06 N	98.34 W
Burke, S.D., U.S.	140	D13	43.10 N	99.17 W
Burke, Va., U.S.	202c		38.47 N	77.16 W
Burke, stm., Austl.	98	D2	23.12 S	139.33 E
Burke Channel, strt., B.C., Can.	144	E3	52.06 N	127.38 W
Burke Lake, res., Va., U.S.	202c		38.46 N	77.18 W
Burke Lake County Park, p.o.i., Va., U.S.	202c		38.45 N	77.18 W
Burke Lakefront Airport, arpt., Oh., U.S.	197a		41.31 N	81.41 W
Burkesville, Ky., U.S.	130	H12	36.47 N	85.22 W
Burketown, Austl.	98	A2	17.44 S	139.32 E
Burkina Faso, ctry., Afr.	84	G4	13.00 N	1.30 W
Burkit, Kaz.	40	H17	47.03 N	50.42 E
Burleson, Tx., U.S.	136	B10	32.32 N	97.19 W
Burley, Id., U.S.	146	H13	42.32 N	113.47 W
Burlin, Kaz.	40	F18	51.25 N	52.43 E
Burlingame, Ca., U.S.	148	F3	37.35 N	122.22 W
Burlingame, Ks., U.S.	130	F2	38.45 N	95.49 W
Burlington, On., Can.	126	E10	43.19 N	79.47 W
Burlington, Co., U.S.	138	B6	39.18 N	102.15 W
Burlington, Ia., U.S.	130	D6	40.48 N	91.06 W
Burlington, Ks., U.S.	130	F2	38.11 N	95.44 W
Burlington, N.J., U.S.	124	D11	40.04 N	74.51 W
Burlington, N.C., U.S.	124	H6	36.05 N	79.26 W
Burlington, N.D., U.S.	142	F12	48.16 N	101.25 W
Burlington, Vt., U.S.	126	D16	44.28 N	73.11 W
Burlington, Wa., U.S.	146	B4	48.28 N	122.20 W
Burlington, Wi., U.S.	130	B9	42.40 N	88.15 W
Burlington, Wy., U.S.	140	C4	44.26 N	108.25 W
Burlington County Airpark, arpt., N.J., U.S.	203		39.56 N	74.50 W
Burlington Island, i., N.J., U.S.	203		40.05 N	74.51 W
Burlington Junction, Mo., U.S.	130	D2	40.26 N	95.04 W
Burlington Mall, shp. cen., Ma., U.S.	201		42.29 N	71.13 W
Burma see Myanmar, ctry., Asia	62	D8	22.00 N	98.00 E
Burnaby, B.C., Can.	144	G7	49.14 N	122.59 W
Burnage, Eng., U.K.	180		53.26 N	2.12 W
Burnas, ozero, l., Ukr.	38	G9	45.59 N	30.19 E
Burnet, Tx., U.S.	136	D9	30.45 N	98.13 W
Burnett, stm., Austl.	98	E8	24.46 S	152.22 E
Burnett Bay, b., N.T., Can.	109	B14	73.46 N	123.58 W
Burnett Brook, stm., N.J., U.S.	194		40.46 N	74.38 W
Burnett Heads, Austl.	98	E9	24.50 S	152.24 E
Burney, Ca., U.S.	148	C4	40.52 N	121.39 W
Burnham, Il., U.S.	196		41.39 N	87.34 W
Burnham, Pa., U.S.	124	D8	40.38 N	77.34 W
Burnham Beeches, for., Eng., U.K.	178		51.34 N	0.38 W
Burnhamthorpe, On., Can.	193b		43.37 N	79.36 W
Burnie, Austl.	99a	n12	41.04 S	145.53 E
Burning Tree Estates, Md., U.S.	202c		39.01 N	77.12 W
Burnley, Eng., U.K.	10	H10	53.47 N	2.15 W
Burnley, mun., Eng., U.K.	180		53.46 N	2.15 W
Burnley Football Ground, p.o.i., Eng., U.K.	180		53.48 N	2.14 W
Burns, Ks., U.S.	138	C12	38.05 N	96.53 W
Burns, Or., U.S.	146	G7	43.35 N	119.03 W
Burns, Tn., U.S.	130	H10	36.02 N	87.18 W
Burns, Wy., U.S.	140	F8	41.11 N	104.21 W
Burns Creek, stm., Mt., U.S.	142	G9	47.22 N	104.23 W
Burns Flat, Ok., U.S.	138	F9	35.20 N	99.10 W
Burnside, Ky., U.S.	130	G13	36.59 N	84.36 W
Burnside, stm., Nu., Can.	110	B8	66.51 N	108.11 W
Burnside, Lake, l., Austl.	96	E4	25.18 S	122.58 E
Burns Lake, B.C., Can.	144	B5	54.13 N	125.46 W
Burnsville, Al., U.S.	134	E12	32.28 N	86.53 W
Burnsville, Ms., U.S.	134	C10	34.50 N	88.18 W
Burnsville, N.C., U.S.	124	I3	35.55 N	82.18 W
Burnsville, W.V., U.S.	124	F5	38.50 N	80.40 W
Burnt, stm., On., Can.	126	D11	44.34 N	78.47 W
Burnt, stm., Or., U.S.	146	F9	44.21 N	117.13 W
Burnt Corn Creek, stm., Al., U.S.	134	F11	31.06 N	87.04 W
Burnt Meadow Brook, stm., N.J., U.S.	194		41.05 N	74.18 W
Burnt Mills Hills, Md., U.S.	202c		39.02 N	77.00 W
Burnt Mills Manor, Md., U.S.	202c		39.02 N	77.00 W
Burnt Pine, Norf. I.	100i	y25	29.02 S	167.56 E
Burntwick Island, i., Eng., U.K.	178		51.25 N	0.41 E
Burntwood, stm., Mb., Can.	110	D11	56.07 N	96.19 W
Bureya, i., Nor.	16	D7	63.58 N	9.03 E
Burpham, Eng., U.K.	178		51.15 N	0.33 W
Burqin, China	52	B2	47.42 N	86.53 E
Burra, Austl.	98	I2	33.40 S	138.54 E
Burrage, Ma., U.S.	201		42.02 N	70.51 W
Burrage Pond, l., Ma., U.S.	201		42.01 N	70.52 W
Burragorang, Lake, res., Austl.	98	J7	33.57 S	150.26 E
Burrel, Alb.	32	C13	41.37 N	20.00 E
Burreli see Burrel, Alb.	32	C13	41.37 N	20.00 E
Burrendong, Lake, res., Austl.	98	I7	32.37 S	149.09 E
Burren Junction, Austl.	98	H7	30.06 S	148.57 E
Burriana see Borriana, Spain	28	E10	39.53 N	0.05 W
Burrinjuck Reservoir, res., Austl.	98	J7	34.57 S	148.45 E
Burr Oak, Ks., U.S.	138	B10	39.51 N	98.18 W
Burro Creek, stm., Az., U.S.	150	I3	34.32 N	113.34 W
Burro Peak, mtn., N.M., U.S.	150	K8	32.35 N	108.26 W
Burrowhill, Eng., U.K.	178		51.21 N	0.36 W
Burr Ridge, Il., U.S.	196		41.46 N	87.55 W
Burrs Mill Brook, stm., N.J., U.S.	203		39.53 N	74.42 W
Burrton, Ks., U.S.	138	C11	38.01 N	97.40 W
Burruyacú, Arg.	166	E4	26.29 S	64.44 W
Burrwood, La., U.S.	134	I9	28.58 N	89.23 W
Bursa, Tur.	34	C12	40.11 N	29.04 E
Bursa, state, Tur.	34	C12	40.10 N	29.00 E
Būr Sa'īd (Port Said), Egypt	76	G3	31.15 N	32.17 E
Burscough, Eng., U.K.	180		53.35 N	2.51 W
Burshtyn, Ukr.	38	D3	49.17 N	24.37 E
Burstall, Sk., Can.	142	D4	50.39 N	109.54 W
Būr Sūdān (Port Sudan), Sudan	82	D7	19.37 N	37.12 E
Burt, Ia., U.S.	130	H4	43.11 N	94.13 W
Burt Lake, l., Mi., U.S.	126	C5	45.27 N	84.40 W
Burtnieks ezers, l., Lat.	26	C8	57.43 N	25.15 E
Burton, B.C., Can.	144	G13	49.58 N	117.53 W
Burton, Eng., U.K.	180		53.16 N	3.01 W
Burton, Mi., U.S.	130	A14	43.00 N	83.35 W
Burton, S.C., U.S.	130	D11	30.10 N	96.35 W
Burton, Tx., U.S.	136	E15	54.45 N	78.25 W
Burton, Lac, l., Qc., Can.	110	E15	54.45 N	78.25 W
Burton, Lake, res., Ga., U.S.	132	B2	34.50 N	83.33 W
Burton upon Trent, Eng., U.K.	10	I11	52.48 N	1.38 W
Burtonwood, Eng., U.K.	180		53.26 N	2.39 W
Burtonwood Airfield, arpt., Eng., U.K.	180		53.24 N	2.39 W
Burträsk, Swe.	16	C18	64.30 N	20.38 E
Burtundy, Austl.	98	I4	33.44 S	142.16 E
Buru, i., Indon.	60	F8	3.24 S	126.40 E
Burullus, Buheirat el-, l., Egypt	76	G1	31.28 N	30.52 E
Burundi, ctry., Afr.	86	E6	3.15 S	30.00 E
Burun-Šibertuj, gora, mtn., Russia	50	G10	49.42 N	109.57 E
Bururi, Bdi.	86	E5	3.56 S	29.38 E
Burwash, On., Can.	126	B9	46.18 N	80.49 W
Burwell, Ne., U.S.	140	F13	41.46 N	99.07 W
Burwood, Austl.	192a		33.53 S	151.06 E
Burwood, Austl.	192b		37.51 S	145.06 E
Bury, Eng., U.K.	10	H10	53.36 N	2.17 W
Bury, mun., Eng., U.K.	180		53.35 N	2.19 W
Bury, mun., Eng., U.K.	180		53.35 N	2.19 W
Buryatia see Burjatija, state, Russia	50	F11	53.00 N	109.00 E
Buryn', Ukr.	38	B12	51.12 N	33.51 E
Buryns'kyi, mys, c., Kaz.	40	I17	45.26 N	51.44 E
Bury Saint Edmunds, Eng., U.K.	10	I13	52.14 N	0.42 E
Burzil, Pak.	70	A5	34.51 N	75.06 E
Busa, Mount, mtn., Phil.	68	G5	6.08 N	124.39 E
Busalla, Italy	30	F5	44.34 N	8.56 E
Busambra, Rocca, mtn., Italy	32	G7	37.51 N	13.24 E
Busan see Pusan, Kor., S.	54	G8	35.05 N	129.02 E
Busan see Pusan-jikhalsi, state, Kor., S.	54	D2	35.10 N	129.05 E
Busanga, D.R.C.	86	E4	0.50 S	22.04 E
Buşayrah, Syria	74	C7	35.08 N	40.27 E
Busby, Austl.	192a		33.54 S	150.53 E
Busby, Mt., U.S.	140	B5	45.33 N	106.58 W
Buscate, Italy	184b		45.32 N	8.49 E
Busch Gardens, p.o.i., Ca., U.S.	198		34.13 N	118.28 W
Buschhausen, ngh., Ger.	181		51.30 N	6.51 E
Būsh, Egypt	76	I2	29.09 N	31.08 E
Bush, stm., S.C., U.S.	132	B4	34.07 N	81.36 W
Būshehr, state, Iran	74	F12	28.50 N	51.20 E
Bushey Heath, Eng., U.K.	178		51.38 N	0.20 W
Bushi, Japan	186		35.50 N	139.22 E
Bushire see Bandar-e Būshehr, Iran	74	F12	28.58 N	50.50 E
Bushiribana, Aruba	158g	o20	12.32 N	69.58 W
Bushland, Tx., U.S.	138	F6	35.11 N	102.04 W
Bushman Land, reg., S. Afr.	90	F4	29.25 S	19.15 E
Bushnell, Fl., U.S.	132	H3	28.39 N	82.06 W
Bushnell, Il., U.S.	130	D7	40.33 N	90.30 W
Bushton, Ks., U.S.	138	C10	38.30 N	98.23 W
Bushtyna, Ukr.	38	E2	48.04 N	23.27 E
Bushwick, ngh., N.Y., U.S.	194		40.42 N	73.55 W
Bushy Park, Austl.	98	C2	21.17 S	139.44 E
Bushy Park, p.o.i., Eng., U.K.	178		51.25 N	0.20 W
Bushy Run, stm., Pa., U.S.	197b		40.20 N	79.40 W
Bushy Run Battlefield, hist., Pa., U.S.	197b		40.21 N	79.38 W
Busia, Ug.	86	D6	0.28 N	34.05 E
Busing, Pulau, i., Sing.	189c		1.14 N	103.45 E
Businga, D.R.C.	86	D4	3.20 N	20.53 E
Busira, stm., D.R.C.	86	E3	0.15 S	18.58 E
Bus'k, Ukr.	38	C3	49.58 N	24.37 E
Buskerud, state, Nor.	16	G7	60.25 N	9.12 E
Busko-Zdrój, Pol.	24	F16	50.28 N	20.44 E
Busovača, Bos.	36	E4	44.05 N	17.52 E
Buṣrá ash-Shām, Syria	76	F7	32.31 N	36.29 E
Busselton, Austl.	96	F3	33.39 S	115.20 E
Bussey, Ia., U.S.	130	C5	41.12 N	92.52 W
Bussum, Neth.	20	B14	52.17 N	5.10 E
Bussy-Saint-Georges, Fr.	179		48.51 N	2.42 E
Bustamante, Mex.	154	B8	26.32 N	100.30 W
Buşteni, Rom.	36	D12	45.25 N	25.32 E
Bustleton, ngh., Pa., U.S.	203		40.05 N	75.02 W
Busto Arsizio, Italy	30	E5	45.37 N	8.51 E
Busuanga Island, i., Phil.	68	D2	12.05 N	120.05 E
Busu-Djanoa, D.R.C.	86	D4	1.44 N	21.27 E
Büsum, Ger.	24	B4	54.08 N	8.51 E
Buta, D.R.C.	86	D4	2.48 N	24.44 E
Butan, Blg.	36	F10	43.39 N	23.46 E
Butantã, ngh., Braz.	205b		23.34 S	46.43 W
Butantã, Instituto, sci., Braz.	205b		23.34 S	46.43 W
Buta Ranquil, Arg.	172	H3	37.03 S	69.50 W
Butare, Rw.	86	E5	2.36 S	29.44 E
Butaritari, at., Kir.	94	C8	3.05 N	172.49 E
Butarque, Arroyo de, stm., Spain	184a		40.19 N	3.39 W
Butcher Island (Dia Deva), i., India	190c		18.58 N	72.54 E
Bute, Island of, i., Scot., U.K.	10	F7	55.50 N	5.06 W
Bute, Sound of, strt., Scot., U.K.	10	F7	55.44 N	5.12 W
Bute Inlet, b., B.C., Can.	144	F6	50.37 N	124.53 W
Butembo, D.R.C.	86	D5	0.07 N	29.17 E
Butera, Italy	32	G8	37.11 N	14.11 E
Butere, Kenya	86	D6	0.12 N	34.29 E
Butha-Buthe, Leso.	90	F9	28.45 S	28.15 E
Butha Qi see Zalantun, China	52	B9	47.59 N	122.44 E
Buthidaung, Mya.	70	H14	20.50 N	92.32 E
Butiá, Braz.	172	E11	30.06 S	51.57 W
Butiaba, Ug.	86	D6	1.48 N	31.19 E
Butler, Al., U.S.	134	E10	32.05 N	88.13 W
Butler, Ga., U.S.	132	D1	32.33 N	84.14 W
Butler, In., U.S.	124	C1	41.25 N	84.52 W
Butler, Mo., U.S.	130	F3	38.15 N	94.20 W
Butler, Oh., U.S.	124	D3	40.35 N	82.25 W
Butler, Ok., U.S.	138	F9	35.38 N	99.11 W
Butler, Pa., U.S.	124	D6	40.51 N	79.53 W
Butler Lake, l., Il., U.S.	196		42.17 N	87.58 W
Butler Reservoir, res., N.J., U.S.	194		40.59 N	74.23 W
Butner, N.C., U.S.	124	H7	36.08 N	78.45 W
Buto, hist., Egypt	76	G1	31.11 N	30.45 E
Buton, Pulau, i., Indon.	60	F7	5.02 S	122.53 E
Butong, Indon.	66	D9	1.06 S	114.51 E
Butrint, hist., Alb.	32	E14	39.45 N	20.01 E
Butru, Austl.	98	C2	21.30 S	139.43 E
Butte, Mt., U.S.	146	D14	46.01 N	112.32 W
Butte, Ne., U.S.	140	E14	42.55 N	98.50 W
Butte Creek, stm., Ca., U.S.	148	D4	39.12 N	121.55 W
Butte Falls, Or., U.S.	146	H4	42.32 N	122.33 W
Butte Mountains, mts., Nv., U.S.	148	D10	39.43 N	115.16 W
Butter Brook, stm., Ma., U.S.	201		42.31 N	71.24 W
Butter Creek, stm., Or., U.S.	146	E7	45.45 N	119.20 W
Butterfield, Il., U.S.	196		41.50 N	88.02 W
Butterfield, Mn., U.S.	128	H4	43.57 N	94.47 W
Butterfield Creek, stm., Il., U.S.	196		41.33 N	87.37 W
Butterley Reservoir, res., Eng., U.K.	180		53.35 N	1.56 W
Butternut, Wi., U.S.	128	E8	46.00 N	90.29 W
Butterworth, Malay.	64	J5	5.23 N	100.23 E
Butterworth, S. Afr.	90	H9	32.20 S	28.06 E
Buttle Lake, l., B.C., Can.	144	G5	49.46 N	125.36 W
Button Islands, is., Nu., Can.	110	C17	60.35 N	64.45 W
Buttonville, On., Can.	193b		43.52 N	79.22 W
Buttonville Airfield, arpt., On., Can.	193b		43.52 N	79.23 W
Buttonwillow, Ca., U.S.	148	H6	35.24 N	119.28 W
Butuan, Phil.	68	F5	8.56 N	125.31 E
Buturlino, Russia	40	D14	55.34 N	44.54 E
Buturlinovka, Russia	40	F12	50.50 N	40.35 E
Butwal, Nepal	70	E9	27.42 N	83.28 E
Butzbach, Ger.	24	F4	50.26 N	8.40 E
Bützow, Ger.	24	C7	53.50 N	11.58 E
Buulobarde, Som.	86	D9	3.51 N	45.34 E
Buur Gaabo, Som.	86	E8	1.12 S	41.50 E
Buurgplaatz, mtn., Lux.	20	D15	50.10 N	6.01 E
Buurhakaba, Som.	86	D8	2.48 N	44.05 E
Buxtehude, Ger.	24	C5	53.28 N	9.41 E
Buxton, S. Afr.	90	E7	27.30 S	24.40 E
Buxton, Eng., U.K.	10	H11	53.15 N	1.55 W
Buxton, N.C., U.S.	132	A10	35.15 N	75.32 W
Buxton, N.D., U.S.	128	D1	47.35 N	97.07 W
Buxton, Mount, mtn., B.C., Can.	144	E2	51.35 N	127.55 W
Buyant-Ovoo, Mong.	52	C6	44.59 N	107.08 E
Buyat, Mong.	52	G8	47.12 N	97.35 E
Buyr nuur, l., Asia	52	B8	47.48 N	117.42 E
Büyükada, Tur.	34	C12	40.51 N	29.07 E
Büyükada, i., Tur.	185b		40.52 N	29.07 E
Büyük Ağrı Dağı see Ağrı Dağı, vol., Tur.	74	A9	39.42 N	44.18 E
Büyükbakkal, ngh., Tur.	185b		40.59 N	29.11 E
Büyükçekmece, Tur.	34	B11	41.02 N	28.36 E
Büyükdere, ngh., Tur.	185b		41.09 N	29.02 E
Büyükeceli, Tur.	76	B4	36.11 N	33.40 E
Büyükkarıştıran, Tur.	34	B10	41.18 N	27.33 E
Büyükkemikli Burnu, c., Tur.	34	C9	40.19 N	26.15 E
Büyükmenderes, stm., Tur.	34	F10	37.29 N	27.13 E
Büyükzap see Great Zab, stm., Asia	74	B9	36.00 N	43.21 E
Buzançais, Fr.	20	H10	46.53 N	1.25 E
Buzău, Rom.	36	D13	45.09 N	26.49 E
Buzău, state, Rom.	36	D13	45.15 N	26.45 E
Buzău, stm., Rom.	36	D13	45.31 N	27.40 E
Buzen, Japan	56	F4	33.36 N	131.08 E
Búzi, stm., Moz.	90	A12	19.52 S	34.44 E
Buziaș, Rom.	36	D8	45.38 N	21.36 E
Búzios, Ponta dos, c., Braz.	170	L5	22.44 S	41.52 W
Buz'kyi lyman, est., Ukr.	38	G10	46.45 N	31.55 E
Buzlanovo, Russia	183b		55.46 N	37.13 E
Buzuluk, Russia	40	E18	52.47 N	52.15 E
Buzuluk, stm., Russia	40	F13	50.12 N	42.11 E
Byādgi, India	69	D2	14.42 N	75.29 E
Byam Channel, strt., Nu., Can.	109	A19	75.20 N	105.20 W
Byam Martin Channel, strt., Nu., Can.	108	B4	75.45 N	104.00 W
Byam Martin Island, i., Nu., Can.	109	B19	75.13 N	104.13 W
Byberry Creek, stm., Pa., U.S.	203		40.04 N	74.59 W
Byblos see Jubayl, Leb.	76	D6	34.07 N	35.39 E
Bycen', Bela.	26	H8	52.54 N	25.29 E
Bychawa, Pol.	24	E18	51.01 N	22.32 E
Byčki, Russia	26	F17	54.14 N	34.39 E
Byculla, ngh., India	190c		18.58 N	72.49 E
Byčyha, Bela.	26	E12	55.41 N	29.58 E
Byczyna, Pol.	24	E14	51.07 N	18.12 E
Bydalen, Swe.	16	D11	63.06 N	13.47 E
Bydgoszcz, Pol.	24	C14	53.07 N	18.00 E
Byelarus' see Belarus, ctry., Eur.	40	E5	53.50 N	28.00 E
Byelorussia see Belarus, ctry., Eur.	40	E5	53.50 N	28.00 E
Byers, Pa., U.S.	203		40.05 N	75.41 W
Byers, Tx., U.S.	138	G10	34.04 N	98.11 W
Byersdale, Pa., U.S.	197b		40.37 N	80.13 W
Byers Run, stm., Pa., U.S.	197b		40.24 N	79.42 W
Byesville, Oh., U.S.	124	E4	39.57 N	81.32 W
Byfang, ngh., Ger.	181		51.24 N	7.06 E
Byforde, Md., U.S.	202c		39.01 N	77.05 W
Bygdeå, Swe.	16	C18	64.03 N	20.54 E
Bygdeträsket, l., Swe.	16	C18	64.24 N	20.27 E
Bygdin, Nor.	16	F6	61.20 N	8.48 E
Bygdin, l., Nor.	16	F6	61.21 N	8.36 E
Byglandsfjord, Nor.	16	I5	58.41 N	7.48 E
Byglandsfjorden, l., Nor.	16	I5	58.47 N	7.49 E
Byhalia, Ms., U.S.	134	C9	34.52 N	89.41 W
Byhau, Bela.	26	G13	53.31 N	30.14 E
Bykivka, Ukr.	38	C6	50.17 N	27.58 E
Bykle, Nor.	16	H5	59.21 N	7.20 E
Bykov, Russia	50	G17	47.20 N	142.33 E
Bykovo, Russia	40	G14	49.46 N	45.23 E
Bykovo Airport, arpt., Russia	183b		55.36 N	38.05 E
Bylas, Az., U.S.	150	J6	33.07 N	110.06 W
Byley, Eng., U.K.	180		53.13 N	2.25 W
Bylnice, Czech Rep.	24	G14	49.03 N	18.01 E
Bylot Island, i., Nu., Can.	110	A15	73.13 N	78.34 W
Byng Inlet, On., Can.	126	C9	45.45 N	80.32 W
Bynum, Mt., U.S.	146	C14	47.58 N	112.17 W
Bynum, N.C., U.S.	124	I6	35.46 N	79.08 W
Byōdōin Temple, rel., Japan	188		34.53 N	135.48 E
Byram, stm., U.S.	194		40.59 N	73.39 W
Byram Lake Reservoir, res., N.Y., U.S.	194		41.10 N	73.41 W
Byrd, Lac, l., Qc., Can.	126	A13	47.01 N	76.56 W
Byrdstown, Tn., U.S.	130	H12	36.34 N	85.07 W
Byriuchyi Ostriv, kosa, spit, Ukr.	38	G14	46.08 N	35.05 E
Byrka, Russia	50	F12	50.38 N	118.33 E
Byrne Arena, p.o.i., N.J., U.S.	194		40.49 N	74.05 W
Byrnedale, Pa., U.S.	124	C7	41.17 N	78.30 W
Byro, Austl.	96	E3	26.06 S	116.09 E
Byrock, Austl.	98	H6	30.39 S	146.24 E
Byron, Ga., U.S.	132	D2	32.38 N	83.45 W
Byron, Il., U.S.	130	B8	42.07 N	89.15 W
Byron, Wy., U.S.	140	C4	44.48 N	108.31 W
Byron, Cape, c., Austl.	98	G9	28.38 S	153.37 E
Byron Bay, Austl.	98	G9	28.39 S	153.37 E
Byrranga, gory, mts., Russia	50	B8	75.00 N	104.00 E
Bysjön, l., Swe.	16	G12	60.23 N	14.30 E
Byske, Swe.	16	C19	64.57 N	21.11 E
Bystřice pod Hostýnem, Czech Rep.	24	G13	49.24 N	17.40 E
Bystrij Tanyp, stm., Russia	40	D19	55.42 N	54.33 E
Bystrzyca Kłodzka, Pol.	24	F12	50.17 N	16.39 E
Bytantaj, stm., Russia	50	C15	68.45 N	134.27 E
Bytča, Bela.	26	F11	54.18 N	28.25 E
Bytča, Slvk.	24	G14	49.13 N	18.34 E
Bytkiv, Ukr.	38	E3	48.38 N	24.26 E
Bytom, Pol.	24	F14	50.21 N	18.55 E
Bytoš', Russia	26	G17	53.49 N	34.05 E
Bytów, Pol.	24	B13	54.10 N	17.29 E
Byumba see Butare, Rw.	86	E5	2.36 S	29.44 E
Byval'ki, Bela.	38	B9	51.51 N	30.37 E
Byxelkrok, Swe.	16	J15	57.20 N	17.02 E

C

Name	Page	Map Ref.	Latitude	Longitude
Ca, stm., Asia	64	C7	18.44 N	105.44 E
Caacupé, Para.	172	B9	25.22 S	57.08 W
Caaguazú, Para.	172	B9	25.27 S	56.01 W
Caaguazú, state, Para.	172	B9	25.05 S	56.00 W
Caála, Ang.	88	C2	12.50 S	15.33 E
Caapiranga, Braz.	168	I11	3.18 S	61.12 W
Caapucú, Para.	172	C9	26.14 S	57.11 W
Caatinga, Braz.	170	I3	17.10 S	45.53 W
Caazapá, Para.	172	C9	26.10 S	56.22 W
Caazapá, state, Para.	172	C9	26.10 S	56.00 W
Cabaiguán, Cuba	156	A8	22.05 N	79.29 W
Cabaliana, Lago, l., Braz.	168	I11	3.20 S	60.50 W
Caballero Creek, stm., Ca., U.S.	198		34.11 N	118.32 W
Caballito, ngh., Arg.	206		34.37 S	58.27 W
Caballococha, Peru	164	D3	3.54 S	70.30 W
Caballo Reservoir, res., N.M., U.S.	150	K9	32.56 N	107.17 W
Cabanatuan, Phil.	68	C3	15.29 N	120.58 E
Cabano, Qc., Can.	122	C8	47.40 N	68.52 W
Cabarroguis, Phil.	68	B3	16.32 N	121.35 E
Cabeceiras, Braz.	170	H2	15.48 S	46.59 W
Cabeço de Montachique, Port.	184c		38.54 N	9.11 W
Cabedelo, Braz.	170	D8	6.58 S	34.49 W
Cabeza del Buey, Spain	28	F5	38.43 N	5.13 W
Cabeza de Tigre, Ven.	204c		10.28 N	66.46 W
Cabezas, Bol.	166	C4	18.48 S	63.20 W
Cabiate, Italy	184b		45.40 N	9.10 E
Cabildo, Arg.	172	I7	38.29 S	61.53 W
Cabildo, Chile	172	F2	32.26 S	71.05 W
Cabimas, Ven.	168	B6	10.23 N	71.26 W
Cabin Branch, stm., Md., U.S.	202b		39.13 N	76.35 W
Cabin Branch, stm., Md., U.S.	202c		38.51 N	76.48 W
Cabin Creek, stm., Mt., U.S.	142	H9	46.55 N	104.52 W
Cabinda, Ang.	88	B1	5.33 S	12.12 E
Cabinet Mountains, mts., U.S.	146	B10	48.18 N	116.12 W
Cabin John Creek, stm., Md., U.S.	202b		38.58 N	77.09 W
Cabin John Creek Park, p.o.i., Md., U.S.	202c		38.59 N	77.09 W
Cabin John Regional Park, p.o.i., Md., U.S.	202c		39.02 N	77.09 W
Cable, Wi., U.S.	128	E7	46.12 N	91.17 W
Cable Airport, arpt., Ca., U.S.	198		34.08 N	117.41 W
Cabo, Braz.	170	E8	8.17 S	35.02 W
Cabo Blanco, Arg.	166	I3	47.12 S	65.46 W
Cabo Frio, Braz.	170	L4	22.52 S	42.01 W
Cabonga, Réservoir, res., Qc., Can.	114	C12	47.17 N	76.32 W
Cabool, Mo., U.S.	130	G5	37.07 N	92.06 W
Caboolture, Austl.	98	F9	27.05 S	152.57 E
Caborca, Mex.	120	F6	30.42 N	112.08 W
Cabo Rojo, P.R.	158a	b1	18.05 N	67.08 W
Cabot, Ar., U.S.	134	C7	34.58 N	92.00 W
Cabot, Mount, mtn., N.H., U.S.	122	F5	44.31 N	71.24 W
Cabot Head, c., On., Can.	126	C8	45.14 N	81.17 W
Cabot Strait, strt., Can.	111a	j21	47.20 N	59.30 W
Cabourg, Fr.	20	E8	49.17 N	0.07 W
Cabo Verde see Cape Verde, ctry., Afr.	85a	k9	16.00 N	24.00 W
Cabo Verde, Arquipélago de, is., C.V.	80	E3	16.00 N	24.00 W
Cabra Corral, Embalse, res., Arg.	172	B5	25.18 S	65.24 W
Cabramatta, Austl.	192a		33.54 S	150.56 E
Cabramatta Creek, stm., Austl.	192a		33.54 S	150.57 E
Cabramurra, Austl.	98	J7	35.57 S	148.23 E
Cabras, Italy	32	E2	39.56 N	8.32 E
Cabras, Stagno di, l., Italy	32	D2	39.57 N	8.29 E
Cabras Island, i., Guam	100c	j9	13.27 N	144.39 E
Cabrayıl, Azer.	42	F12	39.26 N	47.00 E
Cabrera, stm., Col.	168	F4	3.21 N	75.11 W
Cabrera, stm., Spain	28	B4	42.24 N	6.49 W
Cabrera, Illa de, i., Spain	28	E13	39.08 N	2.56 E
Cabrera, Isla de see Cabrera, Illa de, i., Spain	28	E13	39.08 N	2.56 E
Cabrera, Sierra de la, mts., Spain	28	B4	42.12 N	6.40 W
Cabrera de Mar, Spain	184d		41.32 N	2.24 E
Cabri, Sk., Can.	142	D5	50.37 N	108.26 W
Cabriel, stm., Spain	28	E9	39.14 N	1.03 W
Cabrillo National Monument, p.o.i., Ca., U.S.	148	K8	32.40 N	117.14 W
Cabrils, Spain	184d		41.32 N	2.22 E
Cabrobó, Braz.	170	E6	8.31 S	39.19 W
Cabruta, Ven.	168	D8	7.39 N	66.14 W
Cabuçu, stm., Braz.	205a		22.59 S	43.37 W
Cabuçu, stm., Braz.	205a		22.48 S	43.37 W
Cabuçu de Cima, stm., Braz.	205b		23.31 S	46.33 W
Cabullónes, Punta, c., P.R.	158a	c2	17.58 N	66.34 W
Cabure, Ven.	168	B7	11.08 N	69.38 W
Čabusy, Bela.	26	H11	52.49 N	28.06 E
Cabuyaro, Col.	168	E5	4.17 N	72.48 W
Caca, Russia	40	G14	48.11 N	44.40 E
Caçador, Braz.	172	C12	26.47 S	51.00 W
Čačak, Yugo.	36	F7	43.53 N	20.20 E
Caçapava, Braz.	170	L3	23.06 S	45.42 W
Caçapava do Sul, Braz.	172	E11	30.29 S	53.28 W
Cacapon, stm., W.V., U.S.	124	E7	39.36 N	78.16 W
Cacapon State Park, p.o.i., W.V., U.S.	124	E7	39.32 N	78.23 W
Caccamo, Italy	32	G7	37.56 N	13.40 E
Caccia, Capo, c., Italy	32	D2	40.34 N	8.09 E
Čačenka, stm., Russia	183b		55.46 N	37.18 E
Cacequi, Braz.	172	D10	29.53 S	54.48 W
Cáceres, Braz.	166	C5	16.03 S	57.41 W
Cáceres, Col.	168	D4	7.34 N	75.19 W
Cáceres, Spain	28	E4	39.28 N	6.22 W
Cáceres, co., Spain	28	E4	39.40 N	6.05 E
Čačèrsk, Bela.	26	H13	52.54 N	30.55 E
Čačèvičy, Bela.	26	G12	53.30 N	29.48 E
Cachan, Fr.	179		48.48 N	2.20 E
Cacharí, Arg.	172	H8	36.22 S	59.30 W
Cache, Ok., U.S.	138	G10	34.38 N	98.37 W
Cache, stm., Ar., U.S.	134	B7	34.42 N	91.19 W
Cache, stm., Il., U.S.	130	G8	37.03 N	89.09 W
Cache Creek, B.C., Can.	144	F9	50.48 N	121.18 W
Cache Creek, stm., Ca., U.S.	148	E3	38.41 N	121.41 W
Cache la Poudre, stm., Co., U.S.	140	G7	40.25 N	104.35 W
Cache la Poudre, North Fork, stm., Co., U.S.	140	G7	40.41 N	105.14 W
Cache Peak, mtn., Id., U.S.	146	H13	42.11 N	113.40 W
Cachi, Arg.	172	B4	25.07 S	66.11 W
Cachimbo, Braz.	164	E7	9.24 S	54.49 W
Cachimbo, Serra do, mts., Braz.	164	E6	8.25 S	55.45 W
Cachingues, Ang.	88	C2	13.04 S	16.44 E
Cachoeira, Rio da, stm., Braz.	205a		23.00 S	43.18 W
Cachoeira Alta, Braz.	166	C6	18.48 S	50.58 W
Cachoeira de Manteiga, Braz.	170	I3	16.38 S	45.06 W
Cachoeira do Sul, Braz.	172	E11	30.02 S	52.54 W
Cachoeiras, Braz.	205a		22.39 S	43.28 W
Cachoeirinha, Braz.	170	E7	8.29 S	36.14 W
Cachoeiro de Itapemirim, Braz.	170	K5	20.51 S	41.08 W
Cachos, Punta, c., Chile	172	C2	27.40 S	71.01 W
Cachos, Rio dos, stm., Braz.	205b		23.36 S	46.26 W
Cachuela Esperanza, Bol.	166	B3	10.34 S	65.34 W
Cachuma, Lake, res., Ca., U.S.	148	I6	34.34 N	119.55 W
Cacilhas, Port.	184c		38.41 N	9.09 W
Caciporé, Cabo, c., Braz.	164	C7	3.53 N	51.07 W
Căciulați, Rom.	36	E13	44.37 N	26.10 E
Cacolo, Ang.	88	C2	10.08 S	19.16 E
Caconda, Ang.	88	C2	13.43 S	15.03 E
Cacongo see Lândana, Ang.	88	B1	5.12 S	12.08 E
Cactus, Tx., U.S.	138	E6	36.04 N	102.00 W
Cactus Flat, pl., Nv., U.S.	148	F9	37.43 N	116.41 W

Name	Page	Map Ref.	Latitude	Longitude
Campo de Mayo, mil., Arg.	206		34.32 S	58.38 W
Campo Erê, Braz.	172	C11	26.26 S	53.05 W
Campo Florido, Braz.	170	J1	19.46 S	48.33 W
Campo Formoso, Braz.	170	F5	10.31 S	40.19 W
Campo Gallo, Arg.	172	C6	26.34 S	62.50 W
Campo Grande, Arg.	172	C10	27.12 S	54.58 W
Campo Grande, Braz.	166	D6	20.27 S	54.37 W
Campo Grande, ngh., Port.	184c		38.45 N	9.09 W
Campo Largo, Arg.	172	C7	26.47 S	60.50 W
Campo Largo, Braz.	172	B13	25.27 S	49.32 W
Campo Libertad, mil., Cuba	204b		23.05 N	82.26 W
Campo Maior, Braz.	170	C4	4.49 S	42.10 W
Campo Maior, Port.	28	F3	39.01 N	7.04 W
Campo Militar Número Uno, mil., Mex.	204a		19.27 N	99.14 W
Campo Mourão, Braz.	172	A11	24.01 S	52.24 W
Campo Novo, Braz.	172	C11	27.41 S	53.47 W
Campo Pequeno, p.o.i., Port.	184c		38.44 N	9.08 W
Campo Quijano, Arg.	172	B5	24.55 S	65.39 W
Campos, Braz.	170	K5	21.45 S	41.20 W
Campos Altos, Braz.	170	J2	19.42 S	46.11 W
Campo Santo, Arg.	172	B5	24.40 S	65.06 W
Campos Belos, Braz.	170	G2	13.02 S	46.47 W
Campos do Jordão, Braz.	170	L3	22.44 S	45.35 W
Campos Gerais, Braz.	170	K3	21.13 S	45.45 W
Campos Novos, Braz.	172	C12	27.23 S	51.13 W
Campos Sales, Braz.	170	D5	7.04 S	40.23 W
Campo Túres, Italy	30	D8	46.55 N	11.58 E
Camp Parks Communications Annex, mil., Ca., U.S.	200		37.44 N	121.54 W
Camp Pendleton Marine Corps Base, mil., Ca., U.S.	148	J8	33.19 N	117.18 W
Camp Point, Il., U.S.	130	D6	40.02 N	91.04 W
Campsie, Austl.	192a		33.55 S	151.06 E
Campti, La., U.S.	134	F5	31.53 N	93.07 W
Campton, Ky., U.S.	124	G2	37.44 N	83.34 W
Câmpulung, Rom.	36	D11	45.16 N	25.03 E
Câmpulung Moldovenesc, Rom.	36	B12	47.32 N	25.35 E
Campuya, stm., Peru	168	H4	1.43 S	73.32 W
Camp Verde, Az., U.S.	150	I5	34.34 N	111.51 W
Camp Wood, Tx., U.S.	136	E7	29.40 N	100.01 W
Cam Ranh, Viet.	64	G9	11.53 N	109.15 E
Cam Ranh, Vinh, b., Viet.	64	G9	11.53 N	109.10 E
Cam Ranh Bay see Cam Ranh, Vinh, b., Viet.	64	G9	11.53 N	109.10 E
Camrose, Ab., Can.	144	C18	53.01 N	112.50 W
Camsell, stm., N.T., Can.	110	B7	65.41 N	118.19 W
Camurí Chiquito, Quebrada, stm., Ven.	204c		10.37 N	66.52 W
Camuy, P.R.	158a	b2	18.28 N	66.50 W
Cam Xuyen, Viet.	64	C8	18.15 N	105.59 E
Çan, Tur.	34	C10	40.02 N	27.03 E
Canaan, Ct., U.S.	124	B12	42.01 N	73.19 W
Canaan, Vt., U.S.	122	E5	44.59 N	71.32 W
Canaan, stm., N.B., Can.	122	D11	45.55 N	65.46 W
Canaan Lake, l., N.Y., U.S.	194		40.47 N	73.01 W
Canaan Valley State Park, p.o.i., W.V., U.S.	124	E6	39.02 N	79.32 W
Cana-brava, stm., Braz.	170	G1	12.13 S	48.43 W
Cana-brava, stm., Braz.	170	G1	13.11 S	48.11 W
Cañacao Bay, b., Phil.	187f		14.29 N	120.55 E
Canada, ctry., N.A.	104	D13	60.00 N	95.00 W
Canada Basin, unds.	174	A25	80.00 N	145.00 W
Cañada de Gómez, Arg.	172	F7	32.49 S	61.24 W
Cañada Honda, Arg.	172	F3	31.59 S	68.33 W
Canada's Wonderland, p.o.i., On., Can.	193b		43.51 N	79.33 W
Canadian, Tx., U.S.	138	F8	35.54 N	100.22 W
Canadian, stm., U.S.	138	F13	35.27 N	95.05 W
Canadian, Deep Fork, stm., Ok., U.S.	138	F12	35.28 N	95.50 W
Canaguá, stm., Ven.	168	D6	7.56 N	69.34 W
Canaima, Ven.	168	D10	6.15 N	62.50 W
Canaima, Parque Nacional, p.o.i., Ven.	168	E10	5.20 N	62.01 W
Canajoharie, N.Y., U.S.	124	B11	42.54 N	74.34 W
Çanakkale, Tur.	34	C9	40.09 N	26.25 E
Çanakkale, state, Tur.	34	D9	40.10 N	26.45 E
Çanakkale Boğazi (Dardanelles), strt., Tur.	34	C9	40.17 N	26.32 E
Canala, N. Cal.	101d	m15	21.32 S	165.58 E
Canal Flats, B.C., Can.	144	F15	50.09 N	115.48 W
Canal Fulton, Oh., U.S.	124	D4	40.53 N	81.35 W
Canal Point, Fl., U.S.	132	J5	26.51 N	80.37 W
Canals, Arg.	172	F6	33.34 S	62.52 W
Canal Winchester, Oh., U.S.	124	E3	39.51 N	82.48 W
Canandaigua, N.Y., U.S.	124	B8	42.53 N	77.16 W
Cananea, Mex.	120	F7	30.58 N	110.17 W
Cananéia, Braz.	172	B14	25.00 S	47.56 W
Canápolis, Braz.	170	J1	18.44 S	49.13 W
Cañar, Ec.	168	I2	2.33 S	78.56 W
Cañar, state, Ec.	168	I2	2.30 S	79.00 W
Canarias, Islas (Canary Islands), is., Spain	84	D1	28.00 N	15.34 W
Canaries, St. Luc.	159c	m6	13.54 N	61.03 W
Canarreos, Archipiélago de los, is., Cuba	156	B6	21.39 N	82.23 W
Canarsie, ngh., N.Y., U.S.	194		40.38 N	73.53 W
Canarsie Park, p.o.i., N.Y., U.S.	194		40.38 N	73.53 W
Canarsie Polder, i., N.Y., U.S.	194		40.37 N	73.52 W
Canary Basin, unds.	176	F11	30.00 N	25.00 W
Canary Islands see Canarias, Islas, is., Spain	84	D1	28.00 N	15.34 W
Cañas, C.R.	156	G5	10.25 N	85.05 W
Canaseraga, N.Y., U.S.	124	B8	42.27 N	77.47 W
Canastota, N.Y., U.S.	126	E14	43.04 N	75.45 W
Canatlán, Mex.	154	C6	24.31 N	104.46 W
Canaveral, Cape, c., Fl., U.S.	132	H5	28.27 N	80.32 W
Canaveral National Seashore, p.o.i., Fl., U.S.	132	H5	28.45 N	80.42 W
Cañaveras, Spain	28	D8	40.22 N	2.24 W
Canavese, hist. reg., Italy	30	E4	45.20 N	7.40 E
Canavieiras, Braz.	170	H6	15.38 S	38.57 W
Cañazas, Pan.	156	H7	8.19 N	81.13 W
Canbelego, Austl.	98	H6	31.31 S	146.16 E
Canberra, Austl.	98	J7	35.17 S	149.07 E
Canby, Ca., U.S.	148	B5	41.26 N	120.53 W
Canby, Mn., U.S.	128	G2	44.42 N	96.16 W
Canby, Or., U.S.	146	E4	45.15 N	122.41 W
Cancale, Fr.	20	F7	48.40 N	1.51 W
Cancon, Fr.	22	E6	44.32 N	0.38 E
Cancún, Mex.	156	B4	21.07 N	86.51 W
Cancún, Punta, c., Mex.	156	B4	21.08 N	86.45 W
Candala see Qandala, Som.	86	B9	11.27 N	49.52 E
Çandarlı, Tur.	34	E9	38.56 N	26.56 E
Çandarlı Körfezi, b., Tur.	34	E9	38.52 N	26.55 E
Candé, Fr.	20	G7	47.33 N	1.02 W
Candeias, Braz.	170	G6	12.40 S	38.32 W
Candeias, Braz.	170	K3	20.46 S	45.16 W
Candela, Mex.	154	B8	26.50 N	100.40 W
Candela, stm., Mex.	154	B8	27.16 N	100.18 W
Candelaria, Arg.	172	F5	32.04 S	65.49 W
Candelaria, Arg.	172	C10	27.27 S	55.44 W
Candelária, Braz.	172	D11	29.40 S	52.47 W
Candelaria, stm., Mex.	156	C2	18.37 N	91.17 W
Candelaro, stm., Italy	32	C9	41.35 N	15.53 E
Candeleda, Spain	28	D5	40.09 N	5.14 W
Candelo, Austl.	98	K7	36.46 S	149.41 E
Cândido Aguilar, Mex.	154	C9	25.30 N	97.59 W
Cândido de Abreu, Braz.	172	B12	24.34 S	51.20 W
Cândido Mendes, Braz.	170	A3	1.27 S	45.42 W
Candies Creek, stm., Tn., U.S.	134	B14	35.18 N	84.50 W
Candlemas Islands, is., S. Geor.	103	A2	57.10 S	26.42 W
Candlestick, Ms., U.S.	134	E8	32.15 N	90.19 W
Candlestick Park, p.o.i., Ca., U.S.	200		37.43 N	122.23 W
Candlewood, Lake, res., Ct., U.S.	124	C12	41.29 N	73.26 W
Cando, Sk., Can.	142	B5	52.22 N	108.13 W
Cando, N.D., U.S.	142	F14	48.29 N	99.12 W
Candon, Phil.	68	B3	17.11 N	120.26 E
Candor, N.Y., U.S.	124	B9	42.14 N	76.20 W
Candor, N.C., U.S.	132	A6	35.17 N	79.44 W
Cane, stm., La., U.S.	134	F6	31.30 N	92.43 W
Canea see Chaniá, Grc.	34	H7	35.30 N	24.01 E
Caneças, Port.	184c		38.49 N	9.14 W
Cane Creek, stm., U.S.	130	H7	36.28 N	90.28 W
Canegrate, Italy	184b		45.34 N	8.56 E
Canela, Braz.	172	D12	29.21 S	50.48 W
Canelas, Mex.	154	C5	25.06 N	106.34 W
Canelles, Embalse de, res., Spain	28	C11	41.59 N	0.37 E
Canelli, Italy	30	F5	44.43 N	8.16 E
Canelones, Ur.	172	G9	34.32 S	56.16 W
Cañete, Chile	172	H1	37.47 S	73.23 W
Cañete, Spain	28	D9	40.03 N	1.35 W
Caney, Ks., U.S.	130	G1	37.01 N	95.56 W
Caney, stm., U.S.	138	E13	36.20 N	95.42 W
Caney Brook, stm., N.Y., U.S.	194		41.07 N	73.50 W
Caney Creek, stm., Ar., U.S.	134	D5	33.46 N	93.06 W
Caney Creek, stm., Tx., U.S.	136	F12	28.45 N	95.38 W
Caney Creek, stm., Tx., U.S.	136	D12	30.07 N	95.10 W
Canfield Island, i., Ct., U.S.	194		41.06 N	73.23 W
Canfranc, Spain	28	B10	42.43 N	0.32 W
Cangaíba, ngh., Braz.	205b		23.30 S	46.31 W
Cangandala, Ang.	86	F3	9.47 S	16.25 E
Cangas, Spain	28	B2	42.16 N	8.46 W
Cangas de Narcea, Spain	28	A4	43.11 N	6.33 W
Cangas de Onís, Spain	28	A5	43.21 N	5.07 W
Can Gioc, stm., Viet.	187c		10.42 N	106.37 E
Cangkuang, Tanjung, c., Indon.	66	G4	6.49 S	105.14 E
Cangombe, Ang.	88	C2	14.26 S	19.59 E
Canguaretama, Braz.	170	D8	6.24 S	35.08 W
Canguçu, Braz.	172	E11	31.21 S	52.37 W
Cangumbe, Ang.	88	C2	11.57 S	19.12 E
Cangwu, China	58	J4	23.24 N	111.14 E
Cangxi, China	58	F1	31.44 N	105.55 E
Cangzhou, China	58	B7	38.18 N	116.51 E
Canhotinho, Braz.	170	E7	8.53 S	36.12 W
Caniapiscau, stm., Qc., Can.	110	D17	57.40 N	69.29 W
Caniapiscau, Lac, res., Qc., Can.	110	E17	54.08 N	69.51 W
Canicattì, Italy	32	G7	37.21 N	13.51 E
Canigou, Pic du, mtn., Fr.	22	G8	42.31 N	2.27 E
Canillas, ngh., Spain	184a		40.28 N	3.38 W
Canillejas, ngh., Spain	184a		40.27 N	3.37 W
Canim Lake, B.C., Can.	144	E10	51.45 N	120.55 W
Canim Lake, l., B.C., Can.	144	E9	51.51 N	120.41 W
Canim Lake Indian Reserve, ind. res., B.C., Can.	144	E10	51.47 N	121.00 W
Canindé, Braz.	170	C6	4.22 S	39.19 W
Canindé, stm., Braz.	170	D4	6.14 S	42.51 W
Canindeyú, state, Para.	172	B10	24.16 S	54.49 W
Canisius College, educ., N.Y., U.S.	202a		42.55 N	78.52 W
Canisteer Reservoir, res., N.J., U.S.	194		41.08 N	74.29 W
Canisteo, N.Y., U.S.	124	B8	42.16 N	77.35 W
Canisteo, stm., N.Y., U.S.	126	F12	42.06 N	77.08 W
Canistota, S.D., U.S.	140	D15	43.35 N	97.17 W
Cañitas de Felipe Pescador, Mex.	154	D7	23.36 N	102.42 W
Canjáyar, Spain	28	G8	37.00 N	2.43 W
Çankırı, Tur.	42	E5	40.36 N	33.37 E
Çankırı, state, Tur.	42	E5	40.45 N	33.25 E
Canley Vale, Austl.	192a		33.53 S	150.57 E
Canmore, Ab., Can.	144	E15	51.05 N	115.21 W
Canna, i., Scot., U.K.	10	D6	57.03 N	6.32 W
Cannanore, India	69	F1	11.51 N	75.22 E
Cannel City, Ky., U.S.	124	G2	37.46 N	83.17 W
Cannelton, In., U.S.	130	G11	37.54 N	86.44 W
Cannes, Fr.	22	F13	43.33 N	7.00 E
Canning, Arg.	206		34.53 S	58.30 W
Canning, N.S., Can.	122	E12	45.09 N	64.25 W
Cannington, On., Can.	126	D10	44.20 N	79.02 W
Cannobio, Italy	30	D5	46.04 N	8.40 E
Cannock, Eng., U.K.	10	I10	52.42 N	2.02 W
Cannon, stm., Mn., U.S.	128	G5	44.35 N	92.33 W
Cannon Air Force Base, mil., N.M., U.S.	138	G5	34.23 N	103.18 W
Cannon Ball, N.D., U.S.	140	A12	46.23 N	100.35 W
Cannonball, stm., N.D., U.S.	140	A11	46.25 N	100.35 W
Cannon Beach, Or., U.S.	146	E2	45.53 N	123.57 W
Cannon Falls, Mn., U.S.	128	G6	44.30 N	92.53 W
Cannonvale, Austl.	98	C7	20.18 S	148.40 E
Cann River, Austl.	98	K7	37.34 S	149.09 E
Canoas, Braz.	172	D12	29.55 S	51.10 W
Canoas, stm., Braz.	172	C12	27.36 S	51.26 W
Canobie Lake, N.H., U.S.	201		42.48 N	71.14 W
Canobie Lake, l., Ma., U.S.	201		42.49 N	71.15 W
Canobie Lake Park, p.o.i., N.H., U.S.	201		42.48 N	71.15 W
Canoe, B.C., Can.	144	F11	50.45 N	119.13 W
Canoe, stm., B.C., Can.	144	D12	52.09 N	118.26 W
Canoe, stm., Ma., U.S.	201		41.58 N	71.08 W
Canoe Brook, stm., N.J., U.S.	194		40.45 N	74.22 W
Canoe Brook Reservoirs, res., N.J., U.S.	194		40.45 N	74.21 W
Canoe Creek Indian Reserve, ind. res., B.C., Can.	144	E8	51.32 N	122.15 W
Canoga Park, ngh., Ca., U.S.	198		34.12 N	118.35 W
Canoinhas, Braz.	172	C12	26.10 S	50.23 W
Canon, Ga., U.S.	132	B2	34.21 N	83.07 W
Canoncito Indian Reservation, ind. res., N.M., U.S.	150	H9	35.05 N	107.05 W
Canon City, Co., U.S.	138	C3	38.26 N	105.14 W
Cañon de Río Blanco, Parque Nacional, p.o.i., Mex.	154	F10	18.45 N	97.10 W
Canonsburg, Pa., U.S.	124	D5	40.15 N	80.10 W
Canonsburg Lake, l., Pa., U.S.	197b		40.16 N	80.07 W
Canoochee, stm., Ga., U.S.	132	D4	31.59 N	81.18 W
Canora, Sk., Can.	142	C11	51.37 N	102.26 W
Canosa di Púglia, Italy	32	C10	41.13 N	16.03 E
Canossa, hist., Italy	30	F7	44.35 N	10.27 E
Canot, Pointe, c., Guad.	159c	h6	16.12 N	61.27 W
Canouan, i., St. Vin.	159e	p11	12.43 N	61.19 W
Canova, S.D., U.S.	140	D15	43.52 N	97.30 W
Canova Beach, Fl., U.S.	132	H5	28.09 N	80.35 W
Cañovanas, P.R.	158a	b4	18.22 N	65.53 W
Cánoves, stm., Spain	184d		41.37 N	2.22 E
Canowindra, Austl.	98	I7	33.34 S	148.39 E
Can Quer, Torrente de, stm., Spain	184d		41.31 N	2.11 E
Cansanção, Braz.	170	F6	10.40 S	39.29 W
Canso, N.S., Can.	122	E16	45.20 N	61.00 W
Canso, Strait of, strt., N.S., Can.	122	E15	45.33 N	61.20 W
Cantabria, state, Spain	28	A6	43.15 N	4.00 W
Cantabrian Mountains see Cantábrica, Cordillera, mts., Spain	28	A6	43.00 N	5.00 W
Cantábrica, Cordillera, mts., Spain	28	A6	43.00 N	5.00 W
Cantagalo, Braz.	170	K4	21.58 S	42.22 W
Cantal, state, Fr.	22	D8	45.05 N	2.45 E
Cantalejo, Spain	28	C7	41.15 N	3.55 W
Cantanhede, Braz.	170	B3	3.39 S	44.24 W
Cantanhede, Port.	28	D2	40.20 N	8.35 W
Cantareira, ngh., Braz.	205b		23.27 S	46.37 W
Cantareira, Serra da, mtn., Braz.	205b		23.25 S	46.39 W
Cantaura, Ven.	168	C9	9.18 N	64.21 W
Cant Clough Reservoir, res., Eng., U.K.	180		53.46 N	2.09 W
Canterbury, Austl.	192a		33.55 S	151.07 E
Canterbury, Austl.	192b		37.49 S	145.05 E
Canterbury, N.B., Can.	122	E9	45.53 N	67.27 W
Canterbury, Eng., U.K.	10	J14	51.17 N	1.05 E
Canterbury Bight, b., N.Z.	102	G5	44.15 S	171.38 E
Canterbury Park Racecourse, p.o.i., Austl.	192a		33.54 S	151.07 E
Canterbury Plains, pl., N.Z.	102	G4	44.00 S	171.45 E
Canterbury Woods, Va., U.S.	202c		38.49 N	77.15 W
Can Tho, Viet.	64	G7	10.02 N	105.47 E
Canto do Buriti, Braz.	170	E4	8.07 S	42.58 W
Canto do Pontes, Braz.	205a		22.58 S	43.04 W
Canto Grande, Quebrada, val., Peru	204d		11.59 S	77.01 W
Canton see Guangzhou, China	58	J5	23.08 N	113.16 E
Canton, Ga., U.S.	134	C14	34.13 N	84.29 W
Canton, Il., U.S.	130	D7	40.33 N	90.01 W
Canton, Ks., U.S.	138	C11	38.23 N	97.25 W
Canton, Mn., U.S.	128	H7	43.31 N	91.57 W
Canton, Ms., U.S.	134	E8	32.36 N	90.01 W
Canton, Mo., U.S.	130	D6	40.08 N	91.31 W
Canton, N.Y., U.S.	126	D14	44.35 N	75.10 W
Canton, N.C., U.S.	132	A3	35.32 N	82.50 W
Canton, Oh., U.S.	124	D4	40.47 N	81.23 W
Canton, Ok., U.S.	138	E10	36.03 N	98.35 W
Canton, Pa., U.S.	124	C9	41.39 N	76.50 W
Canton, S.D., U.S.	128	H2	43.18 N	96.35 W
Canton, Tx., U.S.	136	B12	32.33 N	95.52 W
Canton see Kanton, i., Kir.	94	D9	2.48 S	171.40 W
Canton Lake, res., Ok., U.S.	138	E10	36.08 N	98.36 W
Canton Lake State Recreational Area, p.o.i., Ok., U.S.	138	E9	36.08 N	98.39 W
Cantonment, Fl., U.S.	134	G11	30.37 N	87.19 W
Cantribana, Port.	184c		38.53 N	9.25 W
Cantù, Italy	30	E6	45.44 N	9.07 E
Cantu, stm., Braz.	172	B11	24.45 S	52.51 W
Cantwell, Ak., U.S.	109	D10	63.23 N	148.56 W
Cañuelas, Arg.	172	G8	35.03 S	58.45 W
Cañuelas, state, Arg.	206		34.56 S	58.41 W
Canumã, Braz.	164	D6	4.00 S	59.03 W
Canumã, stm., Braz.	164	D6	3.59 S	59.05 W
Canutama, Braz.	164	E5	6.30 S	64.21 W
Canutillo, Tx., U.S.	136	C1	31.55 N	106.35 W
Čany, Russia	48	C13	55.18 N	76.45 E
Čany, ozero, l., Russia	48	D13	54.50 N	77.30 E
Canyon, Ca., U.S.	200		37.49 N	122.09 W
Canyon, Tx., U.S.	138	G7	34.58 N	101.55 W
Canyon City, Or., U.S.	146	F8	44.23 N	118.57 W
Canyon Creek, Ab., Can.	144	A15	55.21 N	115.02 W
Canyon Creek, stm., Az., U.S.	150	J6	33.48 N	110.39 W
Canyon Creek, stm., Id., U.S.	146	G11	42.59 N	115.57 W
Canyon de Chelly National Monument, p.o.i., Az., U.S.	150	G7	36.07 N	109.26 W
Canyon Ferry Lake, res., Mt., U.S.	146	D15	46.33 N	111.37 W
Canyon Lake, res., Tx., U.S.	136	D9	29.53 N	98.14 W
Canyonlands National Park, p.o.i., Ut., U.S.	150	E7	38.10 N	110.00 W
Canyonville, Or., U.S.	146	H3	42.56 N	123.16 W
Cao, stm., China	54	D5	40.26 N	124.11 E
Cao Bang, Viet.	64	A8	22.40 N	106.14 E
Caodian, China	58	E4	32.29 N	111.09 E
Caohe, China	187b		31.09 N	121.25 E
Cao Lanh, Viet.	64	G7	10.26 N	105.38 E
Caombo, Ang.	88	B2	8.45 S	16.52 E
Caonillas, Lago, l., P.R.	158a	b2	18.15 N	66.39 W
Caorle, Italy	30	E9	45.36 N	12.53 E
Caoxian, China	58	D6	34.49 N	115.32 E
Cap, Pointe du, c., St. Luc.	159c	I7	14.04 N	60.57 W
Capac, Mi., U.S.	130	A15	43.00 N	82.55 W
Čapaevo, Kaz.	48	D8	50.11 N	51.09 E
Čapaevsk, Russia	40	E16	52.58 N	49.41 E
Capanaparo, stm., S.A.	168	D8	7.03 N	67.04 W
Capanema, Braz.	164	D8	1.11 S	47.10 W
Capanema, Braz.	172	B11	25.40 S	53.48 W
Capão Bonito, Braz.	170	L1	24.00 S	48.20 W
Capão Doce, Morro do, mtn., Braz.	172	C12	26.43 S	51.25 W
Capão Redondo, ngh., Braz.	205b		23.40 S	46.46 W
Caparaó, Parque Nacional do, p.o.i., Braz.	170	K4	20.29 S	41.46 W
Caparica, Port.	184c		38.40 N	9.12 W
Caparo Viejo, stm., Ven.	168	D6	7.48 N	70.18 W
Capatárida, Ven.	168	B6	11.11 N	70.37 W
Cap-aux-Meules, Qc., Can.	122	C15	47.23 N	61.52 W
Cap aux Meules, Île du, i., Qc., Can.	122	C14	47.23 N	61.54 W
Cap-Chat, Qc., Can.	122	A10	49.04 N	66.41 W
Cap-de-la-Madeleine, Qc., Can.	122	D4	46.22 N	72.31 W
Cape, stm., Austl.	98	C5	20.49 S	146.50 E
Cape Barren Island, i., Austl.	99a	n13	40.25 S	148.12 E
Cape Basin, unds.	176	L14	37.00 S	7.00 E
Cape Breton Highlands National Park, p.o.i., N.S., Can.	122	D16	46.45 N	60.45 W
Cape Breton Island, i., N.S., Can.	122	D16	46.03 N	60.29 W
Cape Canaveral, Fl., U.S.	132	H5	28.24 N	80.36 W
Cape Charles, Va., U.S.	124	G9	37.15 N	76.00 W
Cape Coast, Ghana	84	H4	5.07 N	1.15 W
Cape Cod Bay, b., Ma., U.S.	124	C15	41.52 N	70.22 W
Cape Cod National Seashore, p.o.i., Ma., U.S.	124	B16	41.58 N	70.01 W
Cape Comorin see Kanniyākumari, India	69	G3	8.05 N	77.32 E
Cape Coral, Fl., U.S.	132	J4	26.33 N	81.57 W
Cape Dorset, Nu., Can.	110	C15	64.13 N	76.32 W
Cape Elizabeth, Me., U.S.	122	G6	43.34 N	70.12 W
Cape Fear, stm., N.C., U.S.	132	C8	33.53 N	78.00 W
Cape Girardeau, Mo., U.S.	130	G8	37.17 N	89.31 W
Cape Hatteras National Seashore, p.o.i., N.C., U.S.	132	A10	35.14 N	75.32 W
Capelinha, Braz.	170	I4	17.41 S	42.31 W
Cape Lisburne, Ak., U.S.	109	C6	68.52 N	166.05 W
Capel'ka, Russia	26	B11	58.03 N	28.58 E
Capella, Austl.	98	D7	23.05 S	148.02 E
Capelongo, Ang.	88	C2	14.53 S	15.04 E
Cape Lookout National Seashore, p.o.i., N.C., U.S.	132	B9	34.40 N	76.29 W
Cape May, N.J., U.S.	124	F10	38.55 N	74.55 W
Cape May Court House, N.J., U.S.	124	E11	39.05 N	74.49 W
Capenga, stm., Braz.	205a		22.49 S	43.37 W
Capenhurst, Eng., U.K.	180		53.15 N	2.57 W
Cape Pond, l., Ma., U.S.	201		42.38 N	70.38 W
Cape Porpoise, Me., U.S.	122	G6	43.21 N	70.28 W
Capernaum see Kefar Naḥum, hist., Isr.	76	F6	32.53 N	35.34 E
Cape Sable Island, i., N.S., Can.	122	G11	43.27 N	65.36 W
Cape Scott Provincial Park, p.o.i., B.C., Can.	144	F2	50.45 N	128.20 W
Capesterre, Guad.	159c	i6	15.54 N	61.13 W
Capesterre, Pointe de la, c., Guad.	159c	h5	16.03 N	61.33 W
Capesterre-Belle-Eau, Guad.	159c	h5	16.02 N	61.33 W
Capesthorne Hall, hist., Eng., U.K.	180		53.15 N	2.14 W
Cape Tormentine, N.B., Can.	122	D13	46.07 N	63.49 W
Cape Town (Kaapstad), S. Afr.	90	H4	33.54 S	18.29 E
Cape Verde, ctry., Afr.	85a	k9	16.00 N	24.00 W
Cape Verde Basin, unds.	176	G10	15.00 N	29.59 W
Cape Vincent, N.Y., U.S.	126	D13	44.07 N	76.20 W
Cape Yakataga, Ak., U.S.	109	D11	60.05 N	142.32 W
Cape York Peninsula, pen., Austl.	96	B8	14.00 S	142.30 E
Cap-Haïtien, Haiti	156	C11	19.45 N	72.12 W
Capilla de Farruco, Ur.	172	F10	32.53 S	55.24 W
Capilla del Monte, Arg.	172	E5	30.51 S	64.31 W
Capim, stm., Braz.	170	B1	1.40 S	47.46 W
Capim Melado, Morro do, mtn., Braz.	205a		22.50 S	43.29 W
Capinota, Bol.	166	C3	17.42 S	66.15 W
Capira, Pan.	156	H8	8.45 N	79.52 W
Capistrano, Braz.	170	C6	4.28 S	38.55 W
Capital, The, bldg., D.C., U.S.	202c		38.53 N	77.00 W
Capital Centre, p.o.i., Md., U.S.	202c		38.54 N	76.51 W
Capitan, N.M., U.S.	138	H3	33.32 N	105.34 W
Capitán Arturo Prat, sci., Ant.	103	B34	62.30 S	59.41 W
Capitán Bado, Para.	166	D5	23.14 S	55.32 W
Capitán Bermúdez, Arg.	172	F7	32.49 S	60.43 W
Capitán Meza, Para.	172	C10	26.59 S	55.26 W
Capitan Peak, mtn., N.M., U.S.	138	H3	33.35 N	105.21 W
Capitão de Campos, Braz.	170	C5	4.28 S	41.57 W
Capitão Enéas, Braz.	170	I4	16.20 S	43.41 W
Capitola, Ca., U.S.	148	G4	36.58 N	121.57 W
Capitol Peak, mtn., Nv., U.S.	148	B8	41.50 N	117.18 W
Capitol Reef National Park, p.o.i., Ut., U.S.	150	E5	38.15 N	111.10 W
Capivara, Represa de, res., Braz.	166	D6	22.43 S	51.11 W
Capivari, Braz.	170	L2	23.00 S	47.30 W
Capivari, stm., Braz.	170	G5	12.30 S	39.55 W
Capivari, Canal, can., Braz.	205a		22.42 S	43.21 W
Capiz see Roxas, Phil.	68	E4	11.35 N	122.45 E
Caplan, Qc., Can.	122	B11	48.06 N	65.41 W
Čapljina, Bos.	36	F4	43.07 N	17.42 E
Čaplygin, Russia	40	E11	53.14 N	39.58 E
Čapoma, stm., Russia	14	F29	66.05 N	38.50 E
Capot, stm., Mart.	159c	k6	14.50 N	61.05 W
Cap-Pelé, N.B., Can.	122	D12	46.12 N	64.16 W
Cappella Islands, is., V.I.U.S.	158b	e7	18.17 N	64.54 W
Cappenberg, Ger.	181		51.39 N	7.32 E
Cappenberg, Schloss, hist., Ger.	181		51.39 N	7.32 E
Capraia, Italy	30	G6	43.03 N	9.49 E
Capraia, Isola di, i., Italy	30	G6	43.02 N	9.49 E
Caprara, Punta, c., Italy	32	C2	41.07 N	8.19 E
Caprarola, Italy	32	B6	42.19 N	12.13 E
Capreol, On., Can.	126	B9	46.42 N	80.54 W
Caprera, Isola, i., Italy	32	C3	41.12 N	9.27 E
Capri, Italy	32	D8	40.33 N	14.14 E
Capri, Isola di, i., Italy	32	D8	40.33 N	14.13 E
Capricorn, Cape, c., Austl.	98	D8	23.30 S	151.13 E
Capricorn Channel, strt., Austl.	98	D9	22.35 S	152.18 E
Capricorn Group, is., Austl.	98	D9	23.28 S	152.00 E
Caprivi Strip, hist. reg., Nmb.	88	D3	17.59 S	23.00 E
Capron, Il., U.S.	130	B9	42.23 N	88.44 W
Cap Saint Jacques see Vung Tau, Viet.	64	G8	10.21 N	107.04 E
Capstone, Eng., U.K.	178		51.21 N	0.34 E
Captain Cook, Hi., U.S.	100a	d6	19.30 N	155.54 W
Captain Cook Bridge, trans., Austl.	192a		34.00 S	151.08 E
Captain Cook Landing Place Park, p.o.i., Austl.	192a		34.00 S	151.14 E
Captain Cook Monument, hist., Norf. I.	100i	x25	29.00 S	167.56 E
Captain Daniel Wright Woods, p.o.i., Il., U.S.	196		42.13 N	87.56 W
Captain Harbor, b., Ct., U.S.	194		41.00 N	73.36 W
Captain Pond, l., N.H., U.S.	201		42.48 N	71.10 W
Captains Flat, Austl.	98	J7	35.35 S	149.26 E
Captieux, Fr.	22	E5	44.18 N	0.15 W
Captree Island, i., N.Y., U.S.	194		40.39 N	73.16 W
Captree State Park, p.o.i., N.Y., U.S.	194		40.39 N	73.16 W
Capua, Italy	32	C8	41.06 N	14.12 E
Capuáva, Braz.	205b		23.39 S	46.29 W
Capucapu, stm., Braz.	168	H12	1.11 S	59.09 W
Capucin, c., Dom.	159c	i5	15.38 N	61.28 W
Capulín, stm., Mex.	136	G6	27.28 N	101.38 W
Capulin Volcano National Monument, p.o.i., N.M., U.S.	138	E5	36.47 N	103.56 W
Capunda Cabilongo, Ang.	88	C2	14.57 S	13.59 E
Caquetá, state, Col.	168	G5	1.00 N	74.00 W
Caquetá (Japurá), stm., S.A.	164	D3	3.08 S	64.46 W
Čara, Russia	50	E12	56.53 N	118.15 E
Čara, stm., Russia	50	E12	60.19 N	120.53 E
Caraballeda, Ven.	204c		10.37 N	66.50 W
Caraballeda, Punta, c., Ven.	204c		10.37 N	66.50 W
Carabanchel Alto, ngh., Spain	184a		40.22 N	3.45 W
Carabanchel Bajo, ngh., Spain	184a		40.23 N	3.47 W
Carabayllo, Peru	204d		11.52 S	77.02 W
Carabinani, stm., Braz.	168	I10	1.57 S	61.30 W
Carabobo, state, Ven.	168	B7	10.10 N	68.05 W
Caracal, Rom.	36	E11	44.07 N	24.21 E
Caracalla, Terme di, hist., Italy	185a		41.53 N	12.29 E
Caracaraí, Braz.	168	G11	1.50 N	61.08 W
Caracas, Ven.	168	B8	10.30 N	66.55 W
Caracas, Ven.	204c		10.30 N	66.56 W
Carache, Ven.	156	H12	9.38 N	70.14 W
Caracol, Braz.	170	E4	9.17 S	43.20 W
Caraguata, Arroyo, stm., Arg.	206		34.24 S	58.38 W
Caraguatatuba, Braz.	170	L3	23.37 S	45.25 W
Caraguatay, Para.	172	B9	25.14 S	56.50 W
Caraí, Braz.	170	I5	17.12 S	41.43 W
Caraïbes, Îles des see West Indies, is.	106	G15	19.00 N	70.00 W
Caraïbes, Mer des see Caribbean Sea, s.	106	H15	15.00 N	73.00 W
Caraíva, stm., Braz.	170	I6	16.48 S	39.08 W
Carajás, Braz.	164	E7	6.06 S	50.23 W
Carajás, Serra dos, hills, Braz.	164	E7	6.15 S	51.20 W
Carakol, hist., Belize	156	D3	16.56 N	89.07 W
Caramat, On., Can.	114	B7	49.37 N	86.09 W
Caranavi, Bol.	166	C3	15.46 S	67.37 W
Carandaí, Braz.	170	K4	20.57 S	43.47 W
Carangola, Braz.	170	K4	20.42 S	42.01 W
Caransebeș, Rom.	36	D9	45.24 N	22.13 E
Carapá, stm., Para.	172	B10	24.26 S	54.17 W
Carapachay, mth., Arg.	206		34.25 S	58.35 W
Carapajó, Braz.	170	B1	2.16 S	49.21 W
Cara-Paraná, stm., Col.	168	H5	1.46 S	73.12 W
Carapeguá, Para.	172	B9	25.45 S	57.15 W
Carapicuíba, mun., Braz.	205b		23.31 S	46.53 W
Carapina, Braz.	170	K5	20.12 S	40.16 W
Carapo, stm., Ven.	168	D10	7.28 N	64.01 W
Caraquet, N.B., Can.	122	C11	47.47 N	64.56 W
Carare, stm., Col.	168	D4	6.45 N	74.07 W
Caraș-Severin, state, Rom.	36	D8	45.00 N	22.00 E
Caratasca, Laguna de, b., Hond.	156	E5	15.23 N	83.54 W
Caratinga, Braz.	170	J4	19.47 S	42.08 W
Carauari, Braz.	164	D4	4.52 S	66.52 W
Caraúbas, Braz.	170	C7	5.47 S	37.34 W
Caravaca de la Cruz, Spain	28	F9	38.06 N	1.51 W
Čáravárri, mtn., Nor.	14	C13	69.21 N	22.50 E
Caravelas, Braz.	170	I6	17.44 S	39.15 W
Caravelí, Peru	164	G3	15.46 S	73.22 W
Caravelle, Presqu'île la, pen., Mart.	159c	k7	14.45 N	60.55 W
Caraway, Ar., U.S.	134	B8	35.45 N	90.19 W
Carayaó, Para.	172	B9	25.11 S	56.24 W
Caraz, Peru	164	E2	9.03 S	77.47 W
Caraza, ngh., Arg.	206		34.42 S	58.26 W
Carazinho, Braz.	172	D11	28.16 S	52.46 W
Carballiño, Spain	28	B2	42.26 N	8.04 W
Carballo, Spain	28	A2	43.13 N	8.41 W
Carberry, Mb., Can.	142	E14	49.51 N	99.21 W
Carbet, Pitons du, mtn., Mart.	159c	k6	14.42 N	61.07 W
Carbo, Mex.	120	G7	29.41 N	110.58 W
Carbon, Ab., Can.	144	E17	51.29 N	113.06 W
Carbon, Pa., U.S.	197b		40.17 N	79.34 W
Carbon, Tx., U.S.	136	B9	32.16 N	98.49 W
Carbon, stm., Wa., U.S.	146	C5	47.07 N	122.13 W
Carbonara, Capo, c., Italy	32	E3	39.06 N	9.30 E
Carbonate, Italy	184b		45.41 N	8.56 E
Carbon Canyon Dam, dam., Ca., U.S.	198		33.55 N	117.50 W
Carbon Creek, stm., Ca., U.S.	198		33.49 N	118.04 W
Carbondale, Co., U.S.	138	B1	39.24 N	107.11 W
Carbondale, Il., U.S.	130	G8	37.43 N	89.13 W
Carbondale, Ks., U.S.	130	F2	38.49 N	95.41 W
Carbondale, Pa., U.S.	124	C10	41.34 N	75.30 W
Carbonear, Nf., Can.	111a	j23	47.45 N	53.13 W
Carboneras de Guadazaón, Spain	28	E9	39.53 N	1.48 W
Carbon Hill, Al., U.S.	134	D11	33.53 N	87.31 W
Carbonia, Italy	32	E2	39.10 N	8.31 E
Carcagente see Carcaixent, Spain	28	E10	39.08 N	0.27 W
Carcaixent, Spain	28	E10	39.08 N	0.27 W
Carcajou, stm., N.T., Can.	110	B5	65.37 N	128.42 W
Carcans, Lac de, b., Fr.	22	D4	45.05 N	1.06 W
Carcarañá, Arg.	172	F7	32.52 S	61.08 W
Carcarañá, stm., Arg.	172	F7	32.26 S	60.48 W
Carcassonne, Fr.	22	F8	43.13 N	2.21 E
Carcastillo, Spain	28	B9	42.22 N	1.26 W
Carcavelos, Port.	184c		38.53 N	9.14 W
Carcavelos, Port.	184c		38.41 N	9.20 W
Carchi, state, Ec.	168	G3	0.45 N	78.00 W
Carcross, Yk., Can.	110	C3	60.10 N	134.42 W
Çardak, Tur.	34	F12	38.06 N	36.49 E
Cardano al Campo, Italy	184b		45.39 N	8.47 E
Čardara, Kaz.	48	F11	41.17 N	67.56 E
Čardarinskoe vodohranilišče, res., Asia	72	A10	41.08 N	68.12 E
Cardeña, Spain	28	F6	38.13 N	4.19 W
Cárdenas, Cuba	156	A7	23.02 N	81.12 W
Cárdenas, Mex.	154	F12	18.00 N	93.22 W
Cárdenas, Mex.	154	D9	21.59 N	99.38 W
Cárdenas, Bahía de, b., Cuba	156	A7	23.05 N	81.10 W
Cardener, stm., Spain	28	C12	41.41 N	1.50 E
Carderock Springs, Md., U.S.	202c		38.59 N	77.10 W
Cardiel, Lago, l., Arg.	166	I2	48.55 S	71.15 W
Cardiff, Wales, U.K.	10	J9	51.29 N	3.11 W
Cardigan, P.E., Can.	122	D14	46.14 N	62.38 W

Name Page Map Ref. Latitude Longitude

Cardigan, Wales, U.K. 10 I8 52.05 N 4.39 W
Cardigan Bay, b., P.E., Can. 122 D14 46.09 N 62.29 W
Cardigan Bay, b., Wales, U.K. 10 I8 52.27 N 4.35 W
Cardigan State Park, p.o.i., N.H., U.S. 122 G5 43.39 N 71.54 W
Cardinal, On., Can. 126 D14 44.48 N 75.23 W
Cardington, Oh., U.S. 124 D3 40.29 N 82.53 W
Cardinia Creek, stm., Austl. 192b 38.12 S 145.23 E
Cardona, Ur. 172 F9 33.52 S 57.21 W
Cardonal, Punta, c., Mex. 154 A2 28.27 N 111.42 W
Cardoso, Ur. 172 F9 32.41 S 56.19 W
Cardston, Ab., Can. 144 G17 49.12 N 113.18 W
Cardwell, Austl. 98 B5 18.16 S 146.01 E
Cardwell, Mo., U.S. 130 H7 36.03 N 90.17 W
Cardwell Mountain, mtn., Tn., U.S. 134 B13 35.41 N 85.41 W
Čardžev, Turkmen. 72 B9 39.05 N 63.34 E
Carei, Rom. 36 B9 47.40 N 22.28 E
Careiro, Braz. 168 I12 3.13 S 59.46 W
Careiro, Ilha do, i., Braz. 168 I12 3.09 S 59.48 W
Čarėja, Bela. 26 F12 54.36 N 29.18 E
Carelia see Karelia, hist. reg., Eur. 18 E18 63.00 N 32.00 E
Carén, Chile 172 E2 30.50 S 70.45 W
Carencro, La., U.S. 134 G6 30.19 N 92.02 W
Carentan, Fr. 20 E7 49.18 N 1.15 W
Cares, stm., Spain 28 A6 43.19 N 4.36 W
Carey, Oh., U.S. 124 D2 40.56 N 83.22 W
Carey, Lake, l., Austl. 96 E4 29.04 S 122.18 E
Carey Downs, Austl. 96 E3 25.37 S 115.26 E
Cargados Carajos Shoals, is., Mrts. 174 K9 16.38 S 59.38 E
Carhaix-Plouguer, Fr. 20 F5 48.17 N 3.35 W
Carhué, Arg. 172 H6 37.10 S 62.45 W
Cariacica, Braz. 170 K5 20.16 S 40.24 W
Cariaco, Ven. 168 B10 10.29 N 63.33 W
Cariaco, Golfo de, b., Ven. 168 B9 10.30 N 64.00 W
Cariati, Italy 32 E10 39.30 N 16.56 E
Caribana, Punta, c., Col. 168 C3 8.37 N 76.52 W
Caribbean Sea, s. 106 H15 15.00 N 73.00 W
Caribe, Mar see Caribbean Sea, s. 106 H15 15.00 N 73.00 W
Caribische Zee see Caribbean Sea, s. 106 H15 15.00 N 73.00 W
Cariboo, stm., B.C., Can. 144 D9 52.39 N 121.40 W
Cariboo Mountains, mts., B.C., Can. 144 D10 53.00 N 121.00 W
Caribou, N.S., Can. 122 E14 45.44 N 62.41 W
Caribou, Me., U.S. 122 D8 46.51 N 68.00 W
Caribou Lake, l., On., Can. 128 A9 50.26 N 89.05 W
Caribou Mountain, mtn., Id., U.S. 146 G15 43.06 N 111.18 W
Caribou Mountain, mtn., Me., U.S. 122 E6 45.26 N 70.38 W
Caribou Mountains, mts., Ab., Can. 110 D7 59.06 N 115.10 W
Caribou Range, mts., U.S. 146 G15 43.10 N 111.22 W
Caribrod see Dimitrovgrad, Yugo. 36 G9 43.01 N 22.48 E
Carichic, Mex. 154 B5 27.55 N 107.03 W
Caricuao, Ven. 204c 10.27 N 66.59 W
Caricuao, Quebrada, stm., Ven. 204c 10.26 N 66.59 W
Caridad, Phil. 187f 14.29 N 120.53 E
Caridade, Braz. 170 C6 4.13 S 39.12 W
Carigara, Phil. 68 E5 11.17 N 124.42 E
Carignan, Qc., Can. 193a 45.27 N 73.18 W
Carignan, Fr. 20 E14 49.38 N 5.10 E
Carinda, Austl. 98 H6 30.27 S 147.40 E
Cariñena, Spain 28 C9 41.20 N 1.13 W
Caringbah, Austl. 192a 34.03 S 151.08 E
Carinhanha, Braz. 170 H4 14.19 S 43.47 W
Carinhanha, stm., Braz. 170 H3 14.20 S 43.47 W
Carini, Italy 32 F7 38.08 N 13.11 E
Carinthia see Kärnten, state, Aus. 30 D10 46.50 N 13.50 E
Caripe, Ven. 168 B10 10.10 N 63.28 W
Caripito, Ven. 168 B10 10.06 N 63.05 W
Carira, Braz. 170 F7 10.20 S 37.41 W
Cariré, Braz. 170 C5 3.57 S 40.27 W
Caririaçu, Braz. 170 D6 7.02 S 39.17 W
Carite, Ven. 204c 10.24 N 67.01 W
Carite, Lago, l., P.R. 158a b3 18.04 N 66.06 W
Cariús, Braz. 170 D6 6.32 S 39.30 W
Carle Place, N.Y., U.S. 194 40.45 N 73.36 W
Carleton, Mi., U.S. 124 B2 42.03 N 83.23 W
Carleton, Ne., U.S. 138 A11 40.18 N 97.40 W
Carleton, Mount, mtn., N.B., Can. 122 C10 47.22 N 66.53 W
Carleton Place, On., Can. 126 C13 45.08 N 76.08 W
Carletonville, S. Afr. 90 E8 26.21 S 27.24 E
Cârlibaba, Rom. 36 B12 47.34 N 25.08 E
Carlin, Nv., U.S. 148 C9 40.43 N 116.06 W
Carlingford, Austl. 192a 33.47 S 151.03 E
Carlingford Lough, b., Eur. 10 G6 54.03 N 6.10 W
Carlinville, Il., U.S. 130 E8 39.16 N 89.52 W
Carlisle, Eng., U.K. 10 G9 54.53 N 2.56 W
Carlisle, Ar., U.S. 134 C7 34.47 N 91.44 W
Carlisle, In., U.S. 130 F10 38.57 N 87.24 W
Carlisle, Ia., U.S. 130 C4 41.30 N 93.29 W
Carlisle, Ky., U.S. 124 F1 38.18 N 84.01 W
Carlisle, Ma., U.S. 201 42.31 N 71.21 W
Carlisle, Pa., U.S. 124 D8 40.11 N 77.11 W
Carlisle Bay, b., Barb. 159d n8 13.05 N 59.37 W
Carl Junction, Mo., U.S. 130 G3 37.11 N 94.33 W
Carlls, stm., N.Y., U.S. 194 40.41 N 73.20 W
Carloforte, Italy 32 E2 39.08 N 8.18 E
Carlos, Isla, i., Chile 166 J2 54.03 S 73.18 W
Carlos Casares, Arg. 172 G7 35.37 S 61.21 W
Carlos Chagas, Braz. 170 I5 17.43 S 40.44 W
Carlos Pellegrini, Arg. 172 E7 32.02 S 61.48 W
Carlos Sampaio, Braz. 205a 22.42 S 43.31 W
Carlos Tejedor, Arg. 172 G6 35.23 S 62.25 W
Carlow, Ire. 10 I5 52.50 N 6.55 W
Carlow, state, Ire. 10 I6 52.40 N 6.50 W
Carloway, Scot., U.K. 10 C6 58.16 N 6.47 W
Carl Sandburg Home National Historic Site, p.o.i., N.C., U.S. 132 A3 35.16 N 82.27 W
Carlsbad see Karlovy Vary, Czech Rep. 24 F8 50.13 N 12.52 E
Carlsbad, Ca., U.S. 148 J8 33.09 N 117.20 W
Carlsbad, N.M., U.S. 136 B3 32.25 N 104.14 W
Carlsbad, Tx., U.S. 136 C7 31.36 N 100.38 W
Carlsbad Caverns National Park, p.o.i., N.M., U.S. 136 B3 32.08 N 104.35 W
Carlsberg Ridge, unds. 174 I9 6.00 N 61.00 E
Carlstadt, N.J., U.S. 194 40.50 N 74.05 W
Carlton, Austl. 192a 33.58 S 151.08 E
Carlton, Mn., U.S. 128 E6 46.39 N 92.25 W
Carlton, Or., U.S. 146 E3 45.17 N 123.09 W
Carlton, Tx., U.S. 136 C9 31.55 N 98.10 W
Carlton Gardens, p.o.i., Austl. 192b 37.48 S 144.59 E
Carlyle, Sk., Can. 142 E11 49.38 N 102.16 W
Carlyle, Il., U.S. 130 F8 38.36 N 89.22 W
Carlyle Lake, res., Il., U.S. 130 F8 38.40 N 89.18 W
Carmacks, Yk., Can. 110 C3 62.04 N 136.15 W
Carmagnola, Italy 30 F4 44.50 N 7.42 E
Carman, Mb., Can. 142 E16 49.30 N 97.58 W
Carmangay, Ab., Can. 144 F17 50.07 N 113.07 W
Carmarthen, Wales, U.K. 10 J8 51.51 N 4.18 W
Carmarthen Bay, b., Wales, U.K. 10 J8 51.40 N 4.30 W
Carmaux, Fr. 22 E8 44.02 N 2.09 E
Carmel, Wales, U.K. 180 53.17 N 3.15 W
Carmel, Ca., U.S. 148 G4 36.33 N 121.54 W
Carmel, In., U.S. 130 E11 39.58 N 86.07 W
Carmel, N.Y., U.S. 126 G16 41.25 N 73.40 W
Carmel Head, c., Wales, U.K. 10 H8 53.24 N 4.34 W
Carmelo, Ur. 172 F8 33.59 S 58.16 W
Carmel Valley, Ca., U.S. 148 G4 36.27 N 121.42 W
Carmen see Ciudad del Carmen, Mex. 154 F12 18.38 N 91.49 W
Carmen, Ok., U.S. 138 E10 36.34 N 98.27 W
Carmen, stm., Chile 172 D2 28.45 S 70.29 W
Carmen, Isla, i., Mex. 154 C3 26.00 N 111.08 W
Carmen, Isla del, i., Mex. 154 F13 18.42 N 91.39 W
Carmen de Areco, Arg. 172 G8 34.23 S 59.50 W
Carmen de Huechuraba, Chile 204e 33.21 S 70.40 W
Carmen de Patagones, Arg. 166 H4 40.48 S 62.57 W
Carmer Hill, hill, Pa., U.S. 124 C8 41.52 N 77.58 W
Carmi, Il., U.S. 130 F9 38.04 N 88.09 W
Carmila, Austl. 98 C7 21.55 S 149.25 E
Carmine, Tx., U.S. 136 D11 30.08 N 96.41 W
Carmo, stm., Braz. 170 C7 5.04 S 37.14 W
Carmo do Paranaíba, Braz. 170 J2 18.58 S 46.20 W
Carmody Hills, Md., U.S. 202c 38.54 N 76.54 W
Carmona, Spain 28 G5 37.27 N 5.38 W
Carmópolis de Minas, Braz. 170 K3 20.32 S 44.38 W
Carnamah, Austl. 96 E3 29.41 S 115.53 E
Carnarvon, Austl. 96 D2 24.51 S 113.39 E
Carnarvon, S. Afr. 90 G5 30.58 S 22.07 E
Carnarvon see Caernarfon, Wales, U.K. 10 H8 53.08 N 4.16 W
Carnarvon National Park, p.o.i., Austl. 98 E6 24.42 S 147.54 E
Čarnaučycy, Bela. 26 H6 52.12 N 23.44 E
Carnaval, Arroyo, stm., Arg. 206 34.52 S 58.02 W
Carnaxide, Port. 184c 38.43 N 9.15 W
Carndonagh, Ire. 10 F5 55.15 N 7.15 W
Carnduff, Sk., Can. 142 E12 49.11 N 101.47 W
Carnegie, Austl. 96 E4 25.43 S 122.59 E
Carnegie, Ok., U.S. 138 F10 35.06 N 98.35 W
Carnegie, Lake, l., Austl. 96 E4 26.10 S 122.30 E
Carnegie Institute, educ., Pa., U.S. 197b 40.27 N 79.57 W
Carnegie-Mellon University, educ., Pa., U.S. 197b 40.27 N 79.57 W
Carnetin, Fr. 179 48.54 N 2.42 E
Carnia, reg., Italy 30 D9 46.27 N 12.59 E
Carnic Alps, mts., Eur. 30 D10 46.35 N 13.02 E
Carniche, Alpi see Carnic Alps, mts., Eur. 30 D10 46.35 N 13.02 E
Car Nicobar Island, i., India 62 G7 9.10 N 92.47 E
Carnide, ngh., Port. 184c 38.46 N 9.11 W
Carnot, C.A.R. 86 D3 4.56 N 15.52 E
Carnoustie, Scot., U.K. 10 E10 56.29 N 2.43 W
Carnsore Point, c., Ire. 10 I6 52.10 N 6.22 W
Carnwath, stm., N.T., Can. 110 B5 68.26 N 128.50 W
Caro, Mi., U.S. 126 E6 43.29 N 83.23 W
Carol City, Fl., U.S. 132 K5 25.56 N 80.14 W
Carole Acres, Md., U.S. 202c 39.04 N 77.00 W
Carole Highlands, Md., U.S. 202c 38.58 N 76.59 W
Carolina, Braz. 170 D2 7.20 S 47.24 W
Carolina, Col. 168 D4 6.43 N 75.17 W
Carolina, P.R. 158a b4 18.22 N 65.57 W
Carolina, S. Afr. 90 E10 26.03 S 30.07 E
Carolina Beach, N.C., U.S. 132 B8 34.02 N 77.54 W
Caroline, at., Kir. 94 D11 9.58 S 150.13 W
Caroline Islands, is., Oc. 94 C5 8.00 N 147.00 E
Caroline Livermore, Mount, hill, Ca., U.S. 200 37.52 N 122.26 W
Caron, Sk., Can. 142 D8 50.28 N 105.52 W
Čaronda, Russia 18 G25 60.34 N 38.59 E
Caroní, stm., Ven. 168 D10 8.20 N 62.47 W
Caronie see Nebrodi, Monti, mts., Italy 32 G8 37.54 N 14.35 E
Caronno Pertusella, Italy 184b 45.36 N 9.03 E
Carora, Ven. 168 B6 10.10 N 70.04 W
Čarozero, Russia 18 G25 60.27 N 38.39 E
Carp, On., Can. 126 C13 45.20 N 76.01 W
Carpathian Mountains, mts., Eur. 8 F13 48.00 N 24.00 E
Carpații see Carpathian Mountains, mts., Eur. 8 F13 48.00 N 24.00 E
Carpații Meridionali (Transylvanian Alps), mts., Rom. 36 D10 45.25 N 23.32 E
Carpentaria, Gulf of, b., Austl. 96 B7 14.00 S 139.00 E
Carpenter, Wy., U.S. 140 F8 41.02 N 104.22 W
Carpenter Lake, res., B.C., Can. 144 F8 50.50 N 122.26 W
Carpentersville, Il., U.S. 130 B9 42.07 N 88.15 W
Carpentertown, Pa., U.S. 197b 40.11 N 79.31 W
Carpentras, Fr. 22 E11 44.03 N 5.02 E
Carpet Museum, bldg., Iran 185d 35.43 N 51.24 E
Carpi, Italy 30 F7 44.47 N 10.53 E
Carpina, Braz. 170 D8 7.51 S 35.15 W
Cărpineni, Mol. 38 G7 46.46 N 28.21 E
Carpinteria, Ca., U.S. 148 I6 34.23 N 119.31 W
Carpio, N.D., U.S. 142 F12 48.25 N 101.43 W
Carp Lake, l., B.C., Can. 144 B7 54.45 N 123.20 W
Carpolac, Austl. 98 K3 36.44 S 141.18 E
Carquinez Bridge, trans., Ca., U.S. 200 38.04 N 122.14 W
Carquinez Strait, strt., Ca., U.S. 200 38.02 N 122.12 W
Carrabelle, Fl., U.S. 134 H14 29.51 N 84.39 W
Carramar, Austl. 192a 33.53 S 150.58 E
Carr and Craggs Moor, for., Eng., U.K. 180 53.43 N 2.09 W
Carranglan, Phil. 68 C3 15.58 N 121.04 E
Carranza, Cabo, c., Chile 172 G1 35.35 S 72.37 W
Carrao, stm., Ven. 168 D10 6.16 N 62.52 W
Carrara, Italy 30 F7 44.04 N 10.06 E
Carrathool, Austl. 98 J5 34.24 S 145.25 E
Carrauntoohil, mtn., Ire. 10 I3 51.59 N 9.45 W
Carrazedo, Braz. 164 D7 1.34 S 52.15 W
Carrcroft, De., U.S. 203 39.47 N 75.30 W
Carrcroft Crest, De., U.S. 203 39.47 N 75.30 W
Carrefour Pompadour, p.o.i., Fr. 179 48.46 N 2.26 E
Carregueira, Serra da, hills, Port. 184c 38.48 N 9.15 W
Carreta, Punta, c., Peru 164 F2 14.10 S 76.16 W
Carriacou, i., Gren. 159e q11 12.29 N 61.26 W
Carrick, ngh., Pa., U.S. 197b 40.23 N 79.59 W
Carrickmacross, Ire. 10 H6 53.58 N 6.43 W
Carrick on Shannon, Ire. 10 H4 53.57 N 8.05 W
Carrick-on-suir, Ire. 10 I5 52.21 N 7.25 W
Carrie, Mount, mtn., Wa., U.S. 146 C3 47.53 N 123.39 W
Carriere, Ms., U.S. 134 G9 30.37 N 89.40 W
Carrières, Pointe aux, c., Qc., Can. 193a 45.31 N 73.54 W
Carrières-sous-Bois, Fr. 179 48.57 N 2.07 E
Carrières-sous-Poissy, Fr. 179 48.57 N 2.03 E
Carrières-sur-Seine, Fr. 179 48.55 N 2.11 E
Carriers Mills, Il., U.S. 130 G9 37.41 N 88.38 W
Carrieton, Austl. 98 I2 32.25 S 138.30 E
Carrillo, Mex. 154 B7 26.54 N 103.54 W
Carrington, Eng., U.K. 180 53.26 N 2.24 W
Carrington, N.D., U.S. 142 G14 47.26 N 99.07 W
Carrington Island, i., Ut., U.S. 150 B4 41.00 N 112.34 W
Carrington Moss, for., Eng., U.K. 180 53.25 N 2.23 W
Carrión, stm., Spain 28 B6 41.52 N 4.31 W
Carrión de los Condes, Spain 28 B6 42.20 N 4.35 W
Carrizal, Cerro, mtn., Mex. 136 H7 26.43 N 100.36 W
Carrizal Bajo, Chile 172 D2 28.06 S 71.09 W
Carrizo Creek, stm., U.S. 138 E5 36.04 N 102.35 W
Carrizo de la Ribera, Spain 28 B5 42.35 N 5.50 W
Carrizo Mountain, mtn., N.M., U.S. 138 H3 33.41 N 105.42 W
Carrizo Mountains, mts., U.S. 150 G7 36.47 N 109.12 W
Carrizo Springs, Tx., U.S. 136 F8 28.31 N 99.51 W
Carrizo Wash, stm., U.S. 150 I7 34.36 N 109.25 W
Carrizo Wash, stm., Ca., U.S. 148 K9 33.05 N 115.55 W
Carrizozo, N.M., U.S. 138 H3 33.38 N 105.52 W
Carroll, Ia., U.S. 130 B3 42.03 N 94.52 W
Carroll, Ne., U.S. 140 E15 42.16 N 97.12 W
Carroll Park, p.o.i., Md., U.S. 202b 39.17 N 76.39 W
Carrollton, Al., U.S. 134 D10 33.12 N 88.06 W
Carrollton, Ga., U.S. 134 D13 33.35 N 85.04 W
Carrollton, Il., U.S. 130 E7 39.18 N 90.24 W
Carrollton, Ky., U.S. 130 F12 38.40 N 85.10 W
Carrollton, Mi., U.S. 126 E5 43.26 N 83.56 W
Carrollton, Ms., U.S. 134 D9 33.30 N 89.55 W
Carrollton, Mo., U.S. 130 E4 39.21 N 93.29 W
Carrollton, Oh., U.S. 124 D4 40.34 N 81.04 W
Carrollton, Tx., U.S. 136 A11 32.57 N 96.53 W
Carrolltown, Pa., U.S. 124 D7 40.35 N 78.41 W
Carrollwood, Md., U.S. 202b 39.20 N 76.23 W
Carron, stm., Austl. 98 A3 17.42 S 141.06 E
Carron, Loch, b., Scot., U.K. 10 D7 57.23 N 5.28 W
Carrot, stm., Can. 110 E10 53.49 N 101.19 W
Carrot River, Sk., Can. 142 A10 53.16 N 103.34 W
Carrowmore Lake, l., Ire. 10 G3 54.12 N 9.47 W
Carrum Downs, Austl. 192b 38.06 S 145.11 E
Carrum North, Austl. 192b 38.03 S 145.09 E
Carrville, Al., U.S. 134 E13 32.32 N 85.52 W
Carry Falls Reservoir, res., N.Y., U.S. 126 D15 44.25 N 74.45 W
Çarşamba, Tur. 42 E7 41.11 N 36.45 E
Carseland, Ab., Can. 144 F17 50.51 N 113.28 W
Carshalton, ngh., Eng., U.K. 178 51.22 N 0.10 W
Čarsk, Kaz. 48 E14 49.35 N 81.03 E
Carson, N.D., U.S. 140 A11 46.25 N 101.33 W
Carson, Wa., U.S. 146 E5 45.44 N 121.49 W
Carson, East Fork, stm., U.S. 148 E6 38.59 N 119.49 W
Carson City, Mi., U.S. 130 A13 43.10 N 84.50 W
Carson City, Nv., U.S. 148 D6 39.10 N 119.46 W
Carsondale, Md., U.S. 202c 38.57 N 76.50 W
Carson Lake, res., Nv., U.S. 148 D7 39.18 N 118.42 W
Carson Range, mts., U.S. 148 D6 39.10 N 119.52 W
Carson Sink, l., Nv., U.S. 148 D7 39.53 N 118.25 W
Carstairs, Ab., Can. 144 E16 51.34 N 114.04 W
Cartagena, Chile 172 F2 33.33 S 71.36 W
Cartagena, Col. 168 B4 10.24 N 75.30 W
Cartagena, Spain 28 G9 37.36 N 0.59 W
Cartago, Col. 168 E3 4.45 N 75.55 W
Cartago, C.R. 156 H6 9.51 N 83.55 W
Cartaxo, Port. 28 E2 39.09 N 8.47 W
Cartaxos, hill, Port. 184c 38.54 N 9.20 W
Cartaya, Spain 28 G3 37.17 N 7.09 W
Carter, Ok., U.S. 138 F9 35.13 N 99.30 W
Carter Bridge, trans., Nig. 191a 6.28 N 3.23 E
Carter Lake, Ia., U.S. 130 C2 41.16 N 95.53 W
Carter Mountain, mtn., Wy., U.S. 140 C3 44.12 N 109.25 W
Carters Lake, res., Ga., U.S. 134 C14 34.36 N 84.38 W
Cartersville, Ga., U.S. 134 C14 34.10 N 84.48 W
Carthage, Tun. 84 B7 36.51 N 10.19 E
Carthage, Ar., U.S. 134 C6 34.04 N 92.33 W
Carthage, Il., U.S. 130 D6 40.24 N 91.07 W
Carthage, In., U.S. 130 E12 39.43 N 85.33 W
Carthage, Ms., U.S. 134 E9 32.43 N 89.32 W
Carthage, Mo., U.S. 130 G3 37.10 N 94.18 W
Carthage, N.Y., U.S. 126 E14 43.58 N 75.36 W
Carthage, N.C., U.S. 132 A6 35.20 N 79.25 W
Carthage, S.D., U.S. 140 C15 44.10 N 97.42 W
Carthage, Tn., U.S. 130 H11 36.15 N 85.57 W
Carthage, Tx., U.S. 136 B13 32.08 N 94.21 W
Carthage, hist., Tun. 32 H4 36.52 N 10.20 E
Cartier Islands, is., Austl. 96 B4 12.32 S 123.32 E
Cartierville, ngh., Qc., Can. 193a 45.32 N 73.42 W
Cartierville, Aéroport de, arpt., Qc., Can. 193a 45.31 N 73.43 W
Cartridge Hill, hill, Eng., U.K. 180 53.41 N 2.30 W
Cartwright, Mb., Can. 142 E14 49.06 N 99.20 W
Caruaru, Braz. 170 E8 8.17 S 35.58 W
Carúpano, Ven. 168 B10 10.39 N 63.15 W
Caruray, Phil. 68 E2 10.19 N 119.01 E
Carutapera, Braz. 164 D8 1.13 S 46.00 W
Caruthersville, Mo., U.S. 130 H8 36.11 N 89.39 W
Carutu, stm., Ven. 168 E10 5.05 N 63.27 W
Carvoeiro, Braz. 168 H10 1.26 S 61.59 W
Carvoeiro, Cabo, c., Port. 28 E1 39.21 N 9.24 W
Cary, Ms., U.S. 134 E8 32.48 N 90.55 W
Cary, N.C., U.S. 124 I7 35.46 N 78.47 W
Čaryšskoe, Russia 48 D14 51.23 N 83.33 E
Caryville, Fl., U.S. 134 G13 30.46 N 85.48 W
Caryville, Tn., U.S. 124 H1 36.17 N 84.13 W
Casablanca (Dar-el-Beida), Mor. 84 C3 33.35 N 7.35 W
Casablanca, ngh., Cuba 204b 23.09 N 82.20 W
Casa Branca, Braz. 170 K2 21.47 S 47.04 W
Casa de la Torrecilla, Spain 184a 40.19 N 3.37 W
Casa del Campo, p.o.i., Spain 184a 40.32 N 3.47 W
Casa de Piedra, Embalse, res., Arg. 172 I4 38.14 S 67.27 W
Casa Grande, Az., U.S. 150 K5 32.52 N 111.45 W
Casa Grande Ruins National Monument, p.o.i., Az., U.S. 150 K5 32.59 N 111.32 W
Casainhos, Port. 184c 38.53 N 9.10 W
Casalbordino, Italy 30 H11 42.09 N 14.35 E
Casale Abbruciato, ngh., Italy 185a 41.44 N 12.33 E
Casale Monferrato, Italy 30 E5 45.08 N 8.27 E
Casa Loma, bldg., On., Can. 193b 43.41 N 79.25 W
Casalone, ngh., Italy 185a 41.56 N 12.41 E
Casalotti, ngh., Italy 185a 41.55 N 12.22 E
Casanare, state, Col. 168 E6 5.45 N 72.00 W
Casanare, stm., Col. 168 D6 6.02 N 69.50 W
Casa Nova, Braz. 170 E5 9.09 S 40.55 W
Casar, N.C., U.S. 132 A4 35.30 N 81.37 W
Casarano, Italy 32 D12 40.00 N 18.09 E
Casar de Cáceres, Spain 28 E4 39.34 N 6.25 W
Casas Adobes, Az., U.S. 150 K6 32.14 N 110.58 W
Casas Grandes, stm., Mex. 120 F9 31.31 N 107.28 W
Casas-Ibáñez, Spain 28 E9 39.17 N 1.28 W
Casa Verde, ngh., Braz. 205b 23.30 S 46.39 W
Casavieja, Spain 28 D6 40.17 N 4.46 W
Casbas, Arg. 172 H6 36.45 S 62.30 W
Casca, Braz. 172 D12 28.32 S 51.59 W
Cascadas Basaseachic, Parque Nacional, p.o.i., Mex. 154 B4 28.10 N 108.22 W
Cascade, B.C., Can. 144 G12 49.00 N 118.13 W
Cascade, Norf. I. 100i y25 29.02 S 167.58 E
Cascade, Id., U.S. 146 F10 44.31 N 116.02 W
Cascade, Ia., U.S. 130 B6 42.17 N 91.01 W
Cascade, Mt., U.S. 146 C15 47.16 N 111.43 W
Cascade, Wi., U.S. 126 E1 43.39 N 88.00 W
Cascade Bay, b., Norf. I. 100i y25 29.01 S 167.58 E
Cascade Locks, Or., U.S. 146 E5 45.39 N 121.52 W
Cascade Mountains see Cascade Range, mts., N.A. 118 D5 45.13 N 121.55 W
Cascade Park, p.o.i., Oh., U.S. 197a 41.23 N 82.06 W
Cascade Point, c., N.Z. 102 F3 44.00 S 168.22 E
Cascade Range, mts., N.A. 118 D5 45.13 N 121.55 W
Cascade Reservoir, res., Id., U.S. 146 F10 44.35 N 116.06 W
Cascadura, ngh., Braz. 205a 22.53 S 43.20 W
Cascais, Port. 28 F1 38.41 N 9.25 W
Cascalho Rico, Braz. 170 J1 18.33 S 47.52 W
Cascapédia, stm., Qc., Can. 122 B10 48.10 N 65.55 W
Cascavel, Braz. 170 C6 4.07 S 38.14 W
Cascavel, Braz. 172 B11 24.57 S 53.27 W
Casciana Terme, Italy 30 G7 43.31 N 10.36 E
Cascina, Italy 30 G7 43.40 N 10.31 E
Casco Bay, b., Me., U.S. 122 G7 43.40 N 70.01 W
Cascumpec Bay, b., P.E., Can. 122 D12 46.45 N 64.03 W
Casenuove, Italy 184b 45.38 N 8.42 E
Case-Pilote, Mart. 159c k6 14.38 N 61.07 W
Caserta, Italy 32 C8 41.04 N 14.18 E
Caseville, Mi., U.S. 126 E6 43.56 N 83.16 W
Case Western Reserve University, educ., Oh., U.S. 197a 41.30 N 81.36 W
Casey, Il., U.S. 130 E9 39.17 N 87.59 W
Casey, Ia., U.S. 130 C3 41.30 N 94.31 W
Casey, sci., Ant. 103 B16 66.17 S 110.32 E
Casey, Mount, mtn., Id., U.S. 146 B10 48.26 N 116.42 W
Caseyr see Gwardafuy, Gees, c., Som. 86 B10 11.49 N 51.16 E
Cashel, Ire. 10 I5 52.31 N 7.53 W
Cashie, stm., N.C., U.S. 124 H8 35.53 N 76.48 W
Cashiers, N.C., U.S. 132 A2 35.07 N 83.06 W
Cashmere, Wa., U.S. 146 C6 47.31 N 120.27 W
Cashton, Wi., U.S. 128 H8 43.44 N 90.46 W
Casigua, Ven. 168 C5 8.46 N 72.30 W
Casilda, Arg. 172 F7 33.02 S 61.10 W
Casimcea, Rom. 36 E15 44.43 N 28.23 E
Casino, Austl. 98 G9 28.52 S 153.03 E
Casiquiare, stm., Ven. 168 F8 1.59 N 67.07 W
Čáslav, Czech Rep. 24 G11 49.55 N 15.23 E
Casma, Peru 164 E2 9.28 S 78.18 W
Časniki, Bela. 26 F12 54.51 N 29.09 E
Časnikovo, Russia 183b 55.59 N 37.25 E
Časnočor, gora, mtn., Russia 12 C15 67.43 N 33.22 E
Casoli, Italy 30 H11 42.07 N 14.16 E
Casorezzo, Italy 184b 45.31 N 8.54 E
Caspe, Spain 28 C10 41.14 N 0.02 W
Casper, Wy., U.S. 140 E6 42.50 N 106.18 W
Casper Creek, Middle Fork, stm., Wy., U.S. 140 D6 43.01 N 106.30 W
Caspian, Mi., U.S. 128 E10 46.03 N 88.37 W
Caspian Depression (Prikaspijskaja nizmennost'), pl. 48 E7 48.00 N 52.00 E
Caspian Sea, s. 48 F7 41.18 N 50.59 E
Cass, stm., Mi., U.S. 126 E6 43.22 N 83.58 W
Cassaday Point, c., On., Can. 202a 42.52 N 79.13 W
Cassai (Kasai), stm., Afr. 86 G4 3.01 S 16.56 E
Cassano allo Ionio, Italy 32 E10 39.47 N 16.20 E
Cass Benton Parkway, p.o.i., Mi., U.S. 199 42.25 N 83.28 W
Cass City, Mi., U.S. 126 E6 43.36 N 83.09 W
Casselman, On., Can. 126 C14 45.19 N 75.05 W
Casselton, N.D., U.S. 128 E1 46.54 N 97.13 W
Cássia, Braz. 170 K2 20.32 S 46.55 W
Cassiar, B.C., Can. 110 D5 59.16 N 129.43 W
Cassiar Mountains, mts., Can. 110 D5 59.00 N 129.00 W
Cassilândia, Braz. 166 C6 19.06 S 51.43 W
Cassinetta di Lugagnano, Italy 184b 45.25 N 8.54 E
Cassinga, Ang. 88 D2 15.06 S 16.05 E
Cassino, Braz. 172 F11 32.11 S 52.10 W
Cassino, Italy 32 C7 41.29 N 13.50 E
Cassipore, ngh., India 190b 22.37 N 88.22 E
Cass Lake, Mn., U.S. 128 D4 47.22 N 94.37 W
Cass Lake, l., Mi., U.S. 199 42.36 N 83.22 W
Cass Lake, res., Mn., U.S. 128 D4 47.25 N 94.33 W
Cassongue, Ang. 88 C1 11.51 S 15.03 E
Cassopolis, Mi., U.S. 130 C11 41.54 N 86.00 W
Cassumba, Ilha, i., Braz. 170 I6 17.48 S 39.16 W
Cassville, Mo., U.S. 130 H4 36.40 N 93.52 W
Cassville, Wi., U.S. 130 B7 42.43 N 90.58 W
Castagniccia, reg., Fr. 22 G15 42.22 N 9.21 E
Castaic Lagoon, res., Ca., U.S. 148 I7 34.32 N 118.36 W
Castalia, Oh., U.S. 124 C3 41.24 N 82.48 W
Castanheira de Pêra, Port. 28 E2 40.01 N 7.53 W
Castaños, Mex. 136 H6 26.47 N 101.25 W
Castelbuono, Italy 32 G8 37.56 N 14.05 E
Castel di Decima, ngh., Italy 185a 41.45 N 12.26 E
Castel di Guido, ngh., Italy 185a 41.54 N 12.17 E
Castel di Leva, ngh., Italy 185a 41.47 N 12.32 E
Castelfranco Veneto, Italy 30 E8 45.40 N 11.56 E
Castel Fusano, ngh., Italy 185a 41.44 N 12.19 E
Castellammare, Golfo di, b., Italy 32 F6 38.08 N 12.54 E
Castellammare del Golfo, Italy 32 F6 38.01 N 12.53 E
Castellammare di Stabia, Italy 32 D7 40.41 N 14.28 E
Castellana Grotte, Italy 32 D11 40.52 N 17.09 E
Castellane, Fr. 22 F12 43.51 N 6.30 E
Castellaneta, Italy 32 D10 40.37 N 16.55 E
Castellbisbal, Spain 184d 41.29 N 1.59 E
Castelldefels, Spain 184d 41.17 N 1.59 E
Castelletto, Italy 184b 45.30 N 8.48 E
Castelli, Arg. 172 H9 36.05 S 57.48 W
Castelli, Arg. 172 B7 25.57 S 60.37 W
Castelli Romani, reg., Italy 185a 41.48 N 12.42 E
Castelló, co., Spain 28 D10 40.10 N 0.10 W
Castelló de la Plana, Spain 28 E11 39.59 N 0.02 W
Castellón de la Plana see Castelló de la Plana, Spain 28 E11 39.59 N 0.02 W
Castellón de la Plana see Castelló, co., Spain 28 D10 40.10 N 0.10 W
Castellote, Spain 28 D10 40.48 N 0.19 W
Castelnaudary, Fr. 22 F7 43.19 N 1.57 E
Castelnau-Montratier, Fr. 22 E7 44.16 N 1.21 E
Castelnovo ne'Monti, Italy 30 F7 44.25 N 10.23 E
Castelo, Braz. 170 K5 20.35 S 41.13 W
Castelo Branco, Port. 28 E3 39.48 N 7.28 W
Castelo Branco, state, Port. 28 E3 40.00 N 7.30 W
Castelo de Paiva, Port. 28 C2 41.02 N 8.16 W
Castelo do Piauí, Braz. 170 C5 5.20 S 41.33 W
Castel Porziano, ngh., Italy 185a 41.44 N 12.24 E
Castel Romano, ngh., Italy 185a 41.44 N 12.27 E
Castel San Giovanni, Italy 30 E6 45.04 N 9.26 E
Castelsardo, Italy 32 D2 40.55 N 8.42 E
Castelsarrasin, Fr. 22 E7 44.02 N 1.06 E
Casteltermini, Italy 32 G7 37.32 N 13.39 E
Castelvetrano, Italy 32 G6 37.41 N 12.47 E
Casterton, Austl. 98 K3 37.35 S 141.24 E
Castets, Fr. 22 F4 43.53 N 1.09 W
Castiglione del Lago, Italy 30 G8 43.07 N 12.02 E
Castiglion Fiorentino, Italy 30 G8 43.21 N 11.54 E
Castile, N.Y., U.S. 124 B7 42.37 N 78.03 W
Castilla, Peru 164 E1 5.12 S 80.36 W
Castilla, Playa de, cst., Spain 28 H4 37.00 N 6.33 W
Castilla-La Mancha, state, Spain 28 E9 39.30 N 3.00 W
Castilla la Nueva, hist. reg., Spain 28 E7 40.00 N 3.40 W
Castilla-La Nueva, hist. reg., Spain 84 B4 39.59 N 3.45 W
Castilla la Vieja (Old Castille), hist. reg., Spain 28 C7 41.30 N 4.00 W
Castilla y León, state, Spain 28 C6 41.30 N 5.00 W
Castillo de San Marcos National Monument, p.o.i., Fl., U.S. 132 F4 29.44 N 81.20 W
Castillo Incaico de Ingapirca, hist., Ec. 168 I2 2.34 S 78.50 W
Castillon-la-Bataille, Fr. 22 E5 44.51 N 0.02 W
Castillos, Ur. 172 G11 34.13 S 53.50 W
Castillos, Laguna de, l., Ur. 172 G11 34.20 S 53.54 W
Castine, Me., U.S. 122 F8 44.23 N 68.48 W
Castlebar, Ire. 10 H3 53.51 N 9.17 W
Castleberry, Al., U.S. 134 F11 31.17 N 87.01 W
Castle Bruce, Dom. 159c j6 15.25 N 61.16 W
Castlecrag, Austl. 192a 33.48 S 151.13 E
Castle Crags State Park, p.o.i., Ca., U.S. 148 B3 41.10 N 122.20 W
Castle Creek, stm., Id., U.S. 146 H10 43.06 N 116.16 W
Castle Dale, Ut., U.S. 150 D6 39.23 N 110.27 W
Castle Dome Peak, mtn., Az., U.S. 150 J2 33.05 N 114.08 W
Castle Douglas, Scot., U.K. 10 G9 54.56 N 3.55 W
Castlegar, B.C., Can. 144 G13 49.19 N 117.39 W
Castle Harbour, strt., Ber. 158e k16 32.21 N 64.41 W
Castle Hill, Austl. 192a 33.44 S 151.00 E
Castle Hills, Tx., U.S. 136 E9 29.32 N 98.31 W
Castleisland, Ire. 10 I3 52.14 N 9.27 W
Castlemaine, Austl. 98 K5 37.04 S 144.12 E
Castlemore, On., Can. 193b 43.47 N 79.41 W
Castle Mountain, mtn., Ab., Can. 144 E15 51.18 N 115.55 W
Castle Mountain, mtn., Yk., Can. 110 C3 64.32 N 135.25 W
Castle Neck, pen., Ma., U.S. 201 42.41 N 70.45 W
Castle Neck, stm., Ma., U.S. 201 42.40 N 70.44 W
Castle Peak, mtn., Co., U.S. 138 B2 39.01 N 106.52 W
Castle Peak, mtn., Id., U.S. 146 F12 44.02 N 114.35 W
Castle Point, mun., Eng., U.K. 178 51.33 N 0.35 E
Castlepollard, Ire. 10 H5 53.40 N 7.17 W
Castlerea, Ire. 10 H4 53.45 N 8.28 W
Castlereagh, stm., Austl. 98 H7 30.12 S 147.30 E
Castle Rock, Co., U.S. 138 B4 39.22 N 104.50 W
Castle Rock, Pa., U.S. 203 39.58 N 75.26 W
Castle Rock, Wa., U.S. 146 D4 46.16 N 122.53 W
Castle Rock, mtn., Or., U.S. 146 F8 44.02 N 118.11 W
Castle Rock, stm., Va., U.S. 124 G7 37.57 N 78.44 W
Castle Rock Butte, mtn., S.D., U.S. 140 B9 45.02 N 103.25 W
Castle Rock Lake, res., Wi., U.S. 128 H8 43.55 N 89.57 W
Castle Shannon, Pa., U.S. 197b 40.21 N 80.01 W
Castleshaw Moor, for., Eng., U.K. 180 53.36 N 2.00 W
Castleton, Eng., U.K. 180 53.35 N 2.11 W
Castletown, I. of Man 10 G8 54.04 N 4.39 W
Castletown, Scot., U.K. 10 C9 58.35 N 3.22 W
Castletown Bere, Ire. 10 J2 51.39 N 9.55 W
Castlewood, S.D., U.S. 128 G1 44.43 N 97.02 W
Castor, Ab., Can. 144 D19 52.13 N 111.54 W
Castor, stm., Mo., U.S. 130 G7 36.51 N 89.44 W
Castor Creek, stm., La., U.S. 134 E6 31.47 N 92.21 W
Castra Vetera, hist., Ger. 181 51.39 N 6.28 E
Castres, Fr. 22 F8 43.36 N 2.15 E
Castries, St. Luc. 159c l7 14.00 N 60.59 W
Castro, Braz. 172 B13 24.47 S 49.59 W
Castro, Chile 166 H2 42.28 S 73.46 W
Castro Barros, Arg. 172 E5 30.35 S 65.44 W
Castro Daire, Port. 28 D3 40.54 N 7.56 W
Castro del Río, Spain 28 G6 37.41 N 4.28 W
Castrojeriz, Spain 28 B6 42.17 N 4.09 W
Castro Marim, Port. 28 G3 37.13 N 7.26 W
Castronuño, Spain 28 C5 41.23 N 5.15 W
Castropol, Spain 28 A4 43.30 N 7.00 W
Castro Verde, Port. 28 G2 37.41 N 8.05 W
Castrovillari, Italy 32 E10 39.49 N 16.13 E
Castroville, Ca., U.S. 148 G4 36.45 N 121.45 W
Castroville, Tx., U.S. 136 E9 29.21 N 98.52 W
Casupá, Ur. 172 G10 34.05 S 55.38 W
Catacamas, Hond. 156 E5 14.50 N 85.53 W
Catacaos, Peru 164 E1 5.16 S 80.41 W
Catacocha, Ec. 164 D2 4.03 S 79.38 W

Name	Page	Map Ref.	Latitude	Longitude
Cataguazes, Braz.	170	K4	21.23 S	42.41 W
Catahoula Lake, l., La., U.S.	134	F6	31.29 N	92.07 W
Çatak, Tur.	42	G10	38.00 N	43.02 E
Çatalan, Tur.	76	A6	37.13 N	35.20 E
Catalão, Braz.	170	J2	18.10 S	47.56 W
Catalão, Ponta do, c., Braz.	205a		22.51 S	43.13 W
Çatalca, Tur.	34	B11	41.07 N	28.27 E
Catalina, Chile	172	B3	25.13 S	69.43 W
Catalina see Santa Catalina Island, i., Ca., U.S.	148	J7	33.23 N	118.24 W
Catalina, Punta, c., Chile	166	J3	52.31 S	68.46 W
Catalonia see Catalunya, state, Spain	28	C12	41.40 N	1.30 E
Cataluña see Catalunya, state, Spain	28	C12	41.40 N	1.30 E
Catalunya, state, Spain	28	C12	41.40 N	1.30 E
Catalunya, hist. reg., Spain	8	G9	42.00 N	1.30 E
Catamarca, state, Arg.	172	C4	27.00 S	67.00 W
Catamare, Ven.	204c		10.36 N	67.02 W
Catamayo, Ec.	164	D2	3.59 S	79.21 W
Catanauan, Phil.	68	D4	13.36 N	122.19 E
Catanduanes Island, i., Phil.	68	D5	13.45 N	124.15 E
Catanduva, Braz.	170	K1	21.07 S	48.57 W
Catania, Italy	32	G9	37.30 N	15.05 E
Catania, Golfo di, b., Italy	32	G9	37.24 N	15.09 E
Catania, Piana di, pl., Italy	32	G8	37.25 N	14.51 E
Cataño, P.R.	158a	b3	18.26 N	66.07 W
Catanzaro, Italy	32	F10	38.54 N	16.36 E
Cataract Canyon, val., Az., U.S.	150	H4	35.34 N	112.17 W
Catarina, Braz.	170	D6	6.12 S	39.54 W
Catarino Rodríguez, Mex.	154	C8	24.50 N	100.18 W
Catarman, Phil.	68	F5	9.07 N	124.41 E
Catarman, Phil.	68	D5	12.30 N	124.38 E
Catarroja, Spain	28	E10	39.24 N	0.24 W
Catatumbo, stm., Ven.	168	C5	9.22 N	71.44 W
Catawba, stm., U.S.	132	B5	34.35 N	80.53 W
Catawissa, Pa., U.S.	124	D9	40.57 N	76.27 W
Cat Ba, Dao, i., Viet.	64	B8	20.50 N	107.00 E
Catbalogan, Phil.	68	E5	11.50 N	124.50 E
Catedral, Cerro, hill, Ur.	172	G10	34.22 S	54.38 W
Catembe, Moz.	90	E11	26.00 S	32.33 E
Catete, Ang.	88	B1	9.05 S	13.41 E
Catete, ngh., Braz.	205a		22.55 S	43.10 W
Catfish Creek, stm., Tx., U.S.	136	C12	31.46 N	95.56 W
Catford, ngh., Eng., U.K.	178		51.27 N	0.01 W
Cathcart, S. Afr.	90	H8	32.18 S	27.09 E
Cathedral City, Ca., U.S.	148	J9	33.46 N	116.27 W
Cathedral Gorge State Park, p.o.i., Nv., U.S.	150	F2	37.50 N	114.30 W
Cathedral Mountain, mtn., Tx., U.S.	136	D4	30.10 N	103.40 W
Cathedral Provincial Park, p.o.i., B.C., Can.	144	H10	49.05 N	120.10 W
Catherine, Mount see Katherîna, Gebel, mtn., Egypt	76	J4	28.31 N	33.57 E
Catherines Peak, mtn., Jam.	158d	i14	18.04 N	76.42 W
Cathlamet, Wa., U.S.	146	D3	46.12 N	123.22 W
Catholic University, educ., D.C., U.S.	202c		38.56 N	77.00 W
Catia, ngh., Ven.	204c		10.31 N	66.57 W
Catia La Mar, Ven.	204c		10.36 N	67.02 W
Cat Island, i., Bah.	152	C9	24.26 N	75.31 W
Cat Island, i., Ma., U.S.	201		42.31 N	70.49 W
Cat Island, i., Ms., U.S.	134	G9	30.13 N	89.06 W
Čatkal, stm., Asia	48	F12	41.38 N	70.02 E
Čatkal'skij hrebet see Chatkal Range, mts., Asia	48	F12	41.40 N	71.05 E
Cat Lake, l., On., Can.	118	E12	51.41 N	91.52 W
Catlettsburg, Ky., U.S.	124	F3	38.24 N	82.37 W
Catlin, Il., U.S.	130	D10	40.03 N	87.42 W
Catnip Mountain, mtn., Nv., U.S.	148	B6	41.52 N	119.23 W
Catoche, Cabo, c., Mex.	156	B4	21.36 N	87.06 W
Catolé do Rocha, Braz.	170	D7	6.21 S	37.45 W
Católica, Universidad, educ., Chile	204e		33.27 S	70.39 W
Católica, Universidad, educ., Peru	204d		12.04 S	77.05 W
Catonsville Manor, Md., U.S.	202b		39.18 N	76.44 W
Catoosa, Ok., U.S.	130	H2	36.11 N	95.44 W
Catorce, Mex.	154	D8	23.42 N	100.56 W
Catriló, Arg.	172	H6	36.24 S	63.25 W
Catrimani, stm., Braz.	168	G11	0.28 N	61.42 W
Catskill, N.Y., U.S.	124	B12	42.13 N	73.52 W
Catskill Aqueduct, stm., N.Y., U.S.	194		41.11 N	73.48 W
Catskill Creek, stm., N.Y., U.S.	122	H2	42.12 N	73.51 W
Catskill Mountains, mts., N.Y., U.S.	124	B11	42.10 N	74.30 W
Catskill Park, p.o.i., N.Y., U.S.	124	B11	42.00 N	74.30 W
Catt, Mount, mtn., B.C., Can.	144	B2	54.21 N	128.47 W
Cattai Creek, stm., Austl.	192a		33.40 S	150.56 E
Cattaraugus, N.Y., U.S.	124	B7	42.19 N	78.51 W
Cattaraugus Creek, stm., N.Y., U.S.	126	F11	42.34 N	79.07 W
Cattaraugus Indian Reservation, ind. res., N.Y., U.S.	124	B7	42.32 N	78.58 W
Cattle Canyon, val., Ca., U.S.	198		34.14 N	117.46 W
Cattolica, Italy	30	G9	43.58 N	12.44 E
Cattolica del Sacro Cuore, Università, educ., Italy	184b		45.27 N	9.11 E
Catu, Braz.	170	G6	12.23 S	38.21 W
Catuane, Moz.	90	E11	26.49 S	32.16 E
Catur, Moz.	88	C6	13.45 S	35.34 E
Catwick, Îles, is., Viet.	64	G9	10.00 N	109.00 E
Čatyrtaš, Kyrg.	48	F13	40.55 N	76.28 E
Cau, stm., Viet.	64	B7	21.07 N	106.18 E
Cau, Rach, stm., Viet.	187c		10.51 N	106.49 E
Cauaburi, stm., Braz.	168	G8	0.18 S	65.54 W
Caubvick, Mount, mtn., Can.	108	F13	58.53 N	63.43 W
Cauca, state, Col.	168	F3	2.30 N	76.50 W
Cauca, stm., Col.	168	D4	8.53 N	74.28 W
Caucaia, Braz.	170	B6	3.42 S	38.39 W
Caucasia, Col.	168	D4	8.00 N	75.12 W
Caucasus (Bol'šoj Kavkaz), mts.	42	D11	42.37 N	45.00 E
Caucete, Arg.	172	E3	31.39 S	68.17 W
Cauchari, Salar de, pl., Arg.	166	D3	23.31 S	66.44 W
Caudry, Fr.	20	D12	50.07 N	3.24 E
Caughnawaga, Qc., Can.	193a		45.25 N	73.41 W
Caulfield Racecourse, p.o.i., Austl.	192b		37.53 S	145.02 E
Caulonia, Italy	32	F10	38.23 N	16.25 E
Caumsett State Park, p.o.i., N.Y., U.S.	194		40.55 N	73.28 W
Caungula, Ang.	88	B2	8.26 S	18.37 E
Čaunskaja guba, b., Russia	50	C22	69.19 N	169.41 E
Cauquenes, Chile	172	G1	35.57 S	72.18 W
Caura, stm., Ven.	168	D9	7.38 N	64.53 W
Caurés, stm., Braz.	168	H10	1.21 S	62.20 W
Caurimare, stm., Ven.	204c		10.28 N	66.48 W
Căuşani, Mol.	38	G8	46.38 N	29.24 E
Causapscal, Qc., Can.	122	B9	48.20 N	67.14 W
Caussade, Fr.	22	E7	44.10 N	1.32 E
Caution, Cape, c., B.C., Can.	144	E3	51.09 N	127.45 W
Cauto, stm., Cuba	156	B9	20.33 N	77.14 W
Cauvery see Kāveri, stm., India	69	E3	11.08 N	79.50 E
Caux, Pays de, reg., Fr.	20	E10	49.40 N	0.40 E
Cávado, stm., Port.	28	C3	41.30 N	8.44 W
Cavaillon, Fr.	22	F11	43.50 N	5.02 E
Cavalaire-sur-Mer, Fr.	22	F12	43.10 N	6.31 E
Cavalcante, Braz.	170	G2	13.47 S	47.29 W
Cavalese, Italy	30	D8	46.17 N	11.30 E
Cavalheiro, Braz.	170	I2	17.15 S	48.00 W
Cavalier, N.D., U.S.	142	F16	48.47 N	97.37 W
Cavalla (Cavally), stm., Afr.	84	H3	4.21 N	7.31 W
Cavalleria, Cap de, c., Spain	28	D15	40.05 N	4.05 E
Cavally (Cavalla), stm., Afr.	84	H3	4.21 N	7.31 W
Cavan, Ire.	10	G5	53.59 N	7.21 W
Cavan, state, Ire.	10	H5	53.55 N	7.15 W
Čavan'ga, Russia	14	F28	66.06 N	37.43 E
Cavarzere, Italy	30	E9	45.08 N	12.04 E
Çavdır, Tur.	34	F12	37.08 N	29.40 E
Cave City, Ar., U.S.	130	I6	35.56 N	91.33 W
Cave City, Ky., U.S.	130	G11	37.07 N	85.58 W
Cave Creek, stm., Az., U.S.	150	J5	33.34 N	112.07 W
Cave In Rock, Il., U.S.	130	G9	37.28 N	88.10 W
Caveiras, stm., Braz.	172	C12	27.34 S	50.53 W
Cavendish, Austl.	98	K4	37.31 S	142.02 E
Cave Run Lake, res., Ky., U.S.	124	F2	38.03 N	83.30 W
Cave Spring, Ga., U.S.	134	C13	34.14 N	85.19 W
Cavettsville, Pa., U.S.	197b		40.22 N	79.46 W
Caviana, Ilha see Caviana de Fora, Ilha, i., Braz.	164	C8	0.10 N	50.10 W
Caviana de Fora, Ilha, i., Braz.	164	C8	0.10 N	50.10 W
Cavinzas, Isla, i., Peru	204d		12.07 S	77.13 W
Cavite, Phil.	68	C3	14.29 N	120.54 E
Cavo, Monte, mtn., Italy	185a		41.45 N	12.42 E
Cavour, Canale, can., Italy	30	E5	45.11 N	7.53 E
Cavtat, Cro.	30	H15	42.35 N	18.13 E
Çavuş, Tur.	76	A2	37.36 N	31.55 E
Çavuşbaşı, stm., Tur.	185b		40.58 N	28.51 E
Çavuşçu Gölü, l., Tur.	34	E14	38.21 N	31.53 E
Čavusy, Bela.	26	G14	53.48 N	30.59 E
Cawker City, Ks., U.S.	138	B10	39.30 N	98.25 W
Cawnpore see Kānpur, India	70	E7	26.27 N	80.19 E
Cawood, Ky., U.S.	124	H2	36.47 N	83.14 W
Cawston, B.C., Can.	144	G11	49.10 N	119.46 W
Caxambu, Braz.	170	K3	21.58 S	44.55 W
Caxias, Braz.	170	C4	4.50 S	43.21 W
Caxias, Port.	184c		38.42 N	9.16 W
Caxias do Sul, Braz.	172	D12	29.10 S	51.11 W
Caxito, Ang.	88	B1	8.33 S	13.36 E
Çay, Tur.	34	E13	38.35 N	31.01 E
Caya see Caia, stm., Eur.	28	E3	38.50 N	7.04 W
Çayağzı, ngh., Tur.	185b		41.13 N	29.12 E
Çayağzı, stm., Tur.	185b		41.14 N	29.12 E
Cayambe, Ec.	168	G2	0.03 N	78.08 W
Cayambe, vol., Ec.	168	G3	0.02 N	77.59 W
Cayce, S.C., U.S.	132	C4	33.58 N	81.03 W
Çaycuma, Tur.	34	B14	41.25 N	32.03 E
Cay Duong, Vinh, b., Viet.	64	G7	10.10 N	104.45 E
Cayenne, Fr. Gu.	164	C7	4.55 N	52.19 W
Cayey, P.R.	158a	b3	18.07 N	66.09 W
Cayey, Sierra de, mts., P.R.	158a	b4	18.06 N	65.59 W
Çaylarbaşı, Tur.	76	A10	37.41 N	39.01 E
Caylus, Fr.	22	E7	44.14 N	1.45 E
Cayman Brac, i., Cay. Is.	156	C8	19.43 N	79.49 W
Cayman Islands, dep., N.A.	152	D8	19.30 N	80.40 W
Caynaba, Som.	86	C9	8.56 N	46.24 E
Cayon, St. K./N.	159a	c2	17.22 N	62.45 W
Cay Point, c., Bah.	158l	n18	24.59 N	77.25 W
Cayucos, Ca., U.S.	148	H5	35.27 N	120.54 W
Cayuga, In., U.S.	130	E10	39.56 N	87.28 W
Cayuga, Tx., U.S.	136	C11	31.55 N	95.57 W
Cayuga Creek, stm., N.Y., U.S.	202a		43.04 N	78.57 W
Cayuga Heights, N.Y., U.S.	124	B9	42.27 N	76.29 W
Cayuga Lake, res., N.Y., U.S.	124	B9	42.45 N	76.45 W
Çayuma, Tur.	42	E5	41.25 N	32.05 E
Cayuta Creek, stm., U.S.	124	B9	41.59 N	76.30 W
Cazaclia, Mol.	38	G7	46.00 N	28.37 E
Cazalla de la Sierra, Spain	28	G5	37.56 N	5.46 W
Căzănești, Rom.	36	E13	44.37 N	27.03 E
Cazaux et de Sanguinet, Étang de, l., Fr.	22	E4	44.29 N	1.09 W
Cazenovia, N.Y., U.S.	124	B10	42.56 N	75.51 W
Cazenovia Park, p.o.i., N.Y., U.S.	202a		42.51 N	78.48 W
Cazères, Fr.	22	F7	43.13 N	1.05 E
Cazhai, China	187b		31.12 N	121.34 E
Cazin, Bos.	36	E2	44.57 N	15.57 E
Cazombo, Ang.	88	C3	11.53 S	22.54 E
Cazorla, Spain	28	G7	37.55 N	3.01 W
Cazorla, Ven.	168	D8	8.01 N	67.00 W
Cazula see Kazula, Moz.	88	D5	15.23 S	33.37 E
Cea, stm., Spain	28	B5	42.00 N	5.35 W
Ceanannas see Kells, Ire.	10	H6	53.44 N	6.52 W
Ceará see Fortaleza, Braz.	170	B6	3.43 S	38.29 W
Ceará, state, Braz.	170	C6	5.00 S	40.00 W
Ceará-Mirim, Braz.	170	C8	5.38 S	35.26 W
Ceará-Mirim, stm., Braz.	170	C8	5.40 S	35.12 W
Ceatharlach see Carlow, Ire.	10	I5	52.50 N	6.55 W
Cebaco, Isla de, i., Pan.	156	I7	7.32 N	81.09 W
Ceballos, Mex.	154	B6	26.31 N	104.09 W
Cebeci, ngh., Tur.	185b		41.07 N	28.52 E
Čeboksarskoe vodohranilišče, res., Russia	40	C14	56.10 N	46.00 E
Čeboksary, Russia	40	C15	56.07 N	47.15 E
Cebolla Creek, stm., Co., U.S.	150	E9	38.27 N	107.18 W
Cebollar, Arg.	172	D4	29.04 S	66.33 W
Cebollas, Mex.	154	D6	23.22 N	104.50 W
Cebollatí, Ur.	172	F11	33.14 S	53.48 W
Cebollatí, stm., Ur.	172	F10	33.08 S	53.36 W
Cebolleta Peak, mtn., N.M., U.S.	150	I9	34.43 N	107.51 W
Céboruco, Volcán, vol., Mex.	154	E6	21.09 N	104.30 W
Čebsara, Russia	26	A21	59.12 N	38.50 E
Cebu, Phil.	68	E4	10.19 N	123.53 E
Cebu, i., Phil.	68	E4	10.20 N	123.45 E
Čeburgol', Russia	38	H17	45.33 N	38.06 E
Cebu Strait, strt., Phil.	68	F4	9.47 N	123.39 E
Cecchignola, ngh., Italy	185a		41.49 N	12.29 E
Ceceda, Mex.	136	H4	26.01 N	103.24 W
Čečen', ostrov, i., Russia	42	D12	43.58 N	47.45 E
Čechtice, Czech Rep.	24	G11	49.37 N	15.03 E
Čechy, hist. reg., Czech Rep.	24	G10	49.50 N	14.00 E
Cecil, Ga., U.S.	132	E2	31.02 N	83.23 W
Cecil Field Naval Air Station, mil., Fl., U.S.	132	F4	30.12 N	81.52 W
Cecilia, Ky., U.S.	130	G12	37.39 N	85.57 W
Cecil Park, Austl.	192a		33.52 S	150.51 E
Cecil Plains, Austl.	98	F8	27.32 S	151.12 E
Cecina, Italy	30	G7	43.18 N	10.31 E
Cecina, stm., Italy	30	G7	43.18 N	10.29 E
Čečnja (Chechnya), state, Russia	42	D11	43.20 N	45.45 E
Čečujsk, Russia	48	C19	58.06 N	108.44 E
Cedar, stm., U.S.	128	J7	41.17 N	91.20 W
Cedar, stm., Mi., U.S.	126	C2	45.24 N	87.20 W
Cedar, stm., Ne., U.S.	140	F14	41.21 N	97.57 W
Cedar, stm., N.Y., U.S.	126	E15	43.51 N	74.11 W
Cedar, West Fork, stm., Ia., U.S.	130	B5	42.38 N	92.30 W
Cedar Beach, Md., U.S.	202b		39.17 N	76.25 W
Cedar Bluff Reservoir, res., Ks., U.S.	138	C9	38.47 N	99.47 W
Cedar Bluffs, Ne., U.S.	128	J2	41.24 N	96.36 W
Cedar Breaks National Monument, p.o.i., Ut., U.S.	150	F4	37.38 N	112.50 W
Cedar Brook, stm., N.J., U.S.	194		40.19 N	74.33 W
Cedar Brook, stm., N.J., U.S.	194		40.23 N	74.23 W
Cedar Brook, stm., N.J., U.S.	203		39.40 N	74.43 W
Cedar Brook Park, p.o.i., On., Can.	193b		43.45 N	79.14 W
Cedarburg, Wi., U.S.	126	E1	43.17 N	87.57 W
Cedar City, Ut., U.S.	150	F3	37.40 N	113.03 W
Cedar Creek, stm., Al., U.S.	134	E11	32.13 N	87.06 W
Cedar Creek, stm., Az., U.S.	150	J6	33.47 N	110.19 W
Cedar Creek, stm., Ct., U.S.	194		41.09 N	73.13 W
Cedar Creek, stm., Ga., U.S.	134	C13	34.11 N	85.24 W
Cedar Creek, stm., Id., U.S.	146	H12	42.17 N	114.51 W
Cedar Creek, stm., Ia., U.S.	130	C5	40.58 N	91.40 W
Cedar Creek, stm., Ia., U.S.	130	B3	42.24 N	94.59 W
Cedar Creek, stm., N.D., U.S.	140	A11	46.07 N	101.18 W
Cedar Creek, stm., Pa., U.S.	197b		40.10 N	79.47 W
Cedar Creek, stm., Tx., U.S.	136	B9	32.53 N	98.31 W
Cedar Creek, stm., Tx., U.S.	136	D10	30.01 N	97.17 W
Cedar Creek Reservoir, res., Tx., U.S.	136	B11	32.17 N	96.09 W
Cedar Crest Manor, N.J., U.S.	203		39.41 N	75.28 W
Cedaredge, Co., U.S.	150	E8	38.54 N	107.55 W
Cedar Falls, Ia., U.S.	130	B5	42.31 N	92.26 W
Cedar Grove, On., Can.	193b		43.52 N	79.12 W
Cedar Grove, N.J., U.S.	194		40.51 N	74.13 W
Cedar Grove, W.V., U.S.	124	F4	38.13 N	81.26 W
Cedar Grove, Wi., U.S.	126	E2	43.33 N	87.49 W
Cedar Grove Reservoir, res., N.J., U.S.	194		40.52 N	74.13 W
Cedar Heights, Md., U.S.	202c		38.54 N	76.54 W
Cedar Heights, Pa., U.S.	203		40.05 N	75.17 W
Cedar Hill, Tn., U.S.	130	H11	36.33 N	86.59 W
Cedar Hollow, Pa., U.S.	203		40.04 N	75.31 W
Cedarhurst, N.Y., U.S.	194		40.37 N	73.43 W
Cedar Island, i., N.Y., U.S.	194		40.38 N	73.21 W
Cedar Island Lake, l., Mi., U.S.	199		42.38 N	83.28 W
Cedar Key, Fl., U.S.	132	G2	29.08 N	83.02 W
Cedar Knolls, N.J., U.S.	194		40.49 N	74.26 W
Cedar Lake, In., U.S.	128	J11	41.21 N	87.26 W
Cedar Lake, l., On., Can.	126	B11	46.01 N	78.28 W
Cedar Lake, l., N.J., U.S.	194		40.55 N	74.28 W
Cedar Lake, l., Tx., U.S.	136	B5	32.49 N	102.17 W
Cedar Lake, res., Mb., Can.	110	E10	53.15 N	100.10 W
Cedar Mountain, mtn., Ca., U.S.	148	B5	41.36 N	120.16 W
Cedar Point, c., Ct., U.S.	194		41.06 N	73.22 W
Cedar Pond, l., N.J., U.S.	194		41.07 N	74.06 W
Cedar Rapids, Ia., U.S.	130	C6	41.59 N	91.39 W
Cedar Rapids, Ne., U.S.	140	F14	41.34 N	98.10 W
Cedars, Pa., U.S.	203		40.13 N	75.22 W
Cedars of Lebanon see Arz Lubnān, for., Leb.	76	D7	34.14 N	36.03 E
Cedars of Lebanon State Park, p.o.i., Tn., U.S.	130	H11	36.03 N	86.18 W
Cedar Springs, Mi., U.S.	126	E4	43.13 N	85.32 W
Cedar Swamp, sw., Ma., U.S.	201		42.33 N	71.05 W
Cedar Swamp, sw., N.J., U.S.	203		39.48 N	75.20 W
Cedartown, Ga., U.S.	134	C13	34.02 N	85.14 W
Cedar Tree Point, c., Antig.	159b	e4	17.41 N	61.52 W
Cedarvale, B.C., Can.	144	A2	55.01 N	128.20 W
Cedar Vale, Ks., U.S.	138	D12	37.06 N	96.30 W
Cedarville, S. Afr.	90	G9	30.23 S	29.02 E
Cedarville, Ca., U.S.	148	B5	41.31 N	120.10 W
Cedarville, Mi., U.S.	126	B5	45.59 N	84.22 W
Cedarville, N.J., U.S.	124	E10	39.20 N	75.12 W
Cedarville, Pa., U.S.	203		40.14 N	75.40 W
Cedar Wash, stm., Az., U.S.	150	H5	35.52 N	111.25 W
Cedeira, Spain	28	A2	43.39 N	8.02 W
Cedillo, Embalse de, res., Eur.	28	E3	39.39 N	7.25 W
Cedrino, stm., Italy	32	D3	40.22 N	9.43 E
Cedro, Braz.	170	D6	6.36 S	39.03 W
Cedros, Mex.	154	C8	24.41 N	101.46 W
Cedros, Isla, i., Mex.	154	A1	28.11 N	115.12 W
Ceduna, Austl.	96	F6	32.06 S	133.41 E
Cedynia, Pol.	24	D10	52.51 N	14.11 E
Ceelbuur, Som.	86	D9	4.40 N	46.37 E
Ceeldheere, Som.	86	D9	3.51 N	47.12 E
Ceepeecee, B.C., Can.	144	G4	49.52 N	126.41 W
Ceerigaabo, Som.	86	B9	10.37 N	47.22 E
Cefalonia see Kefallonía, i., Grc.	34	E3	38.13 N	20.34 E
Cefalù, Italy	32	F8	38.02 N	14.01 E
Cega, stm., Spain	28	C7	41.33 N	4.46 W
Čeganly, Russia	40	E18	53.53 N	53.34 E
Čegdomyn, Russia	50	F15	51.07 N	133.04 E
Cegléd, Hung.	36	B6	47.10 N	19.47 E
Ceglie Messapico, Italy	32	D11	40.39 N	17.30 E
Cehegín, Spain	28	F9	38.06 N	1.48 W
Čehov, Russia	26	E20	55.08 N	37.27 E
Čehov, Russia	50	G17	47.26 N	141.59 E
Cehu Silvaniei, Rom.	36	B10	47.25 N	23.11 E
Ceiba, P.R.	158a	b4	18.16 N	65.38 W
Čekalin, Russia	26	F19	54.05 N	36.15 E
Čekišljar, Turkmen.	42	G15	37.33 N	53.55 E
Čekmaguš, Russia	40	D19	55.08 N	54.40 E
Çekme, ngh., Tur.	185b		41.03 N	29.10 E
Čekšino, Russia	40	B12	59.39 N	40.38 E
Čekuevo, Russia	18	D25	63.34 N	38.56 E
Čelákovice, Czech Rep.	24	F10	50.09 N	14.44 E
Celano, Italy	30	H10	42.05 N	13.32 E
Celanova, Spain	28	B3	42.09 N	7.56 W
Celaya, Mex.	154	E8	20.31 N	100.48 W
Čelbas, stm., Russia	38	G18	46.08 N	39.12 E
Célé, stm., Fr.	22	E7	44.29 N	1.38 E
Celebes see Sulawesi, i., Indon.	60	F7	2.00 S	121.00 E
Celebes Basin, unds.	174	I15	4.00 N	122.00 E
Celebes Sea, s., Asia	60	E7	3.00 N	122.00 E
Čeleken, Turkmen.	72	B7	39.26 N	53.07 E
Celeste, Tx., U.S.	134	D2	33.17 N	96.11 W
Celestún, Mex.	156	B2	20.51 N	90.23 W
Celina, Russia	40	H12	46.32 N	41.02 E
Celina, Oh., U.S.	124	D1	40.32 N	84.33 W
Celina, Tn., U.S.	130	H12	36.31 N	85.30 W
Celina, Tx., U.S.	134	D2	33.19 N	96.47 W
Celinograd see Astana, Kaz.	48	D12	51.11 N	71.27 E
Čeljabinsk, Russia	48	C10	55.09 N	61.25 E
Čeljabinskaja oblast', co., Russia	40	D20	55.07 N	57.23 E
Celjahany, Bela.	26	H8	52.30 N	25.50 E
Celje, Slvn.	30	D12	46.14 N	15.16 E
Čeljuskin, mys, c., Russia	50	A9	77.45 N	104.20 E
Čelkar, Kaz.	40	F17	50.32 N	51.50 E
Čelkar, Kaz.	48	E9	47.49 N	59.36 E
Celldömölk, Hung.	36	B4	47.15 N	17.09 E
Celle, Ger.	24	D6	52.37 N	10.04 E
Celle, Ruisseau la, stm., Fr.	179		48.35 N	2.01 E
Cellina, stm., Italy	30	D9	46.00 N	12.47 E
Čelmozero, Russia	18	C18	64.15 N	31.50 E
Čelobitevo, Russia	183b		55.55 N	37.40 E
Celone, stm., Italy	32	C9	41.36 N	15.40 E
Celorico da Beira, Port.	28	D3	40.38 N	7.23 W
Celtic Sea, s., Eur.	10	J6	51.00 N	6.30 W
Çeltikçi, Tur.	34	C15	40.19 N	32.26 E
Çeltikçi, Tur.	76	A1	37.31 N	30.29 E
Čemal, Russia	48	D15	51.23 N	86.01 E
Cement, Ok., U.S.	138	G10	34.56 N	98.08 W
Cemesskaja buhta, b., Russia	42	C7	44.40 N	37.50 E
Cenajo, Embalse del, res., Spain	28	F9	38.24 N	1.53 W
Čenča, Russia	50	E11	55.58 N	110.57 E
Cenderawasih, Teluk, b., Indon.	60	F10	2.30 S	135.20 E
Çengelköy, ngh., Tur.	185b		41.03 N	29.03 E
Ceno, stm., Italy	30	F6	44.42 N	10.05 E
Cenovo, Blg.	36	F12	43.32 N	25.40 E
Cenrana, Indon.	66	E11	3.17 S	118.51 E
Centenario, Arg.	172	I3	38.49 S	68.07 W
Centennial Lake, l., N.J., U.S.	203		39.50 N	74.51 W
Centennial Mountains, mts., U.S.	146	F15	44.32 N	111.58 W
Centennial Park, p.o.i., Austl.	192a		33.54 S	151.14 E
Centennial Park, p.o.i., On., Can.	193b		43.39 N	79.35 W
Centennial Wash, stm., Az., U.S.	150	J3	33.16 N	112.48 W
Center, Co., U.S.	138	D2	37.45 N	106.06 W
Center, Mo., U.S.	130	E6	39.30 N	91.31 W
Center, Ne., U.S.	140	E15	42.36 N	97.52 W
Center, N.D., U.S.	142	G12	47.06 N	101.18 W
Center, Tx., U.S.	136	C13	31.47 N	94.10 W
Centerburg, Oh., U.S.	124	D3	40.18 N	82.42 W
Center City, Mn., U.S.	128	F6	45.23 N	92.48 W
Center Hill, Fl., U.S.	132	H8	28.38 N	81.59 W
Center Hill Lake, res., Tn., U.S.	130	H12	36.02 N	85.46 W
Center Moriches, N.Y., U.S.	124	D13	40.47 N	72.47 W
Center Mountain, mtn., Id., U.S.	146	E11	45.06 N	115.13 W
Center Point, Al., U.S.	134	D12	33.37 N	86.41 W
Center Point, Ia., U.S.	130	B6	42.11 N	91.47 W
Center Point, Tx., U.S.	136	E8	29.56 N	99.02 W
Center Square, N.J., U.S.	203		39.46 N	75.23 W
Centerton, N.J., U.S.	203		39.31 N	75.10 W
Centerville, De., U.S.	203		39.49 N	75.37 W
Centerville, Ia., U.S.	130	D5	40.43 N	92.52 W
Centerville, Mo., U.S.	130	G7	37.26 N	90.57 W
Centerville, Pa., U.S.	124	D5	40.02 N	79.58 W
Centerville, S.D., U.S.	140	D15	43.06 N	96.59 W
Centerville, Tn., U.S.	134	B11	35.46 N	87.27 W
Centerville, Tx., U.S.	136	C11	31.14 N	95.58 W
Centerville, Ut., U.S.	150	C5	40.55 N	111.53 W
Centinela, Mex.	136	F7	28.46 N	100.33 W
Centocelle, ngh., Italy	185a		41.53 N	12.34 E
Central, Braz.	170	F4	11.07 S	42.06 W
Central, Phil.	68	D3	12.21 N	121.04 E
Central, Az., U.S.	150	K7	32.52 N	109.47 W
Central, N.M., U.S.	150	K8	32.46 N	108.09 W
Central, state, Bots.	90	C8	22.07 S	26.36 E
Central, state, Para.	172	B9	25.30 S	57.30 W
Central, state, Sol. Is.	101b	e8	9.10 S	159.50 E
Central, Cordillera, mts., Col.	168	E4	5.00 N	75.00 W
Central, Cordillera, mts., Peru	164	E2	8.00 S	77.00 W
Central, Cordillera, mts., Phil.	68	B3	17.01 N	120.52 E
Central, Cordillera, mts., P.R.	158a	b3	18.09 N	66.29 W
Central, Massif, mts., Fr.	22	D9	44.41 N	3.19 E
Central, Sistema, mts., Spain	28	D6	40.34 N	4.28 W
Central African Republic, ctry., Afr.	82	F4	7.00 N	21.00 E
Central Aguirre, P.R.	158a	c3	17.57 N	66.13 W
Central Arizona Project Aqueduct, aq., U.S.	150	J3	32.25 N	111.10 W
Central Borneo see Kalimantan Tengah, state, Indon.	66	D8	2.00 S	113.30 E
Central Brāhui Range, mts., Pak.	62	C2	28.48 N	66.34 E
Central Butte, Sk., Can.	142	D7	50.47 N	106.30 W
Central Celebes see Sulawesi Tengah, state, Indon.	66	D12	1.11 S	120.12 E
Central City, Il., U.S.	130	F8	38.32 N	89.07 W
Central City, Ia., U.S.	130	B6	42.11 N	91.30 W
Central City, Ky., U.S.	130	G10	37.17 N	87.07 W
Central City, Ne., U.S.	140	F14	41.07 N	97.59 W
Central City, Pa., U.S.	124	D7	40.05 N	78.47 W
Central Division, state, Fiji	101e	q19	18.05 S	178.30 E
Centrale, Stazione, trans., Italy	184b		45.29 N	9.12 E
Central Highlands, Pa., U.S.	197b		40.16 N	79.50 W
Centralia, Il., U.S.	130	F8	38.31 N	89.08 W
Centralia, Ks., U.S.	130	E1	39.43 N	96.07 W
Centralia, Mo., U.S.	130	E5	39.12 N	92.08 W
Centralia, Wa., U.S.	146	D4	46.42 N	122.57 W
Centralia Draw, stm., Tx., U.S.	136	C6	31.25 N	101.17 W
Centralina, Braz.	170	J1	18.33 S	49.13 W
Central Intelligence Agency, bldg., Va., U.S.	202c		38.57 N	77.09 W
Central Java see Jawa Tengah, state, Indon.	66	G6	7.30 S	110.00 E
Central Kalahari Game Reserve, ind. res., Bots.	90	C6	22.15 S	23.45 E
Central Lake, Mi., U.S.	126	C4	45.04 N	85.16 W
Central Makrān Range, mts., Pak.	62	C1	26.46 N	64.07 E
Central Nyack, N.Y., U.S.	194		41.06 N	73.57 W
Central'nyj, Russia	48	C15	55.13 N	87.38 E
Central'nyj, Russia	183b		55.53 N	37.52 E
Central Pacific Basin, unds.	174	I21	5.00 N	175.00 W
Central Park, N.J., U.S.	194		40.26 N	74.18 W
Central Park, p.o.i., N.Y., U.S.	194		40.47 N	73.58 W
Central Point, Or., U.S.	148	A3	42.22 N	122.54 W
Central Range, mts., Leso.	90	F9	29.35 S	28.35 E
Central Range, mts., Pap. N. Gui.	101a	a3	4.57 S	142.31 E
Central Russian Upland see Srednerusskaja vozvyšennost', plat., Russia	40	F11	52.00 N	38.00 E
Central Siberian Uplands see Srednesibirskoe ploskogor'e, plat., Russia	50	C10	65.00 N	105.00 E
Central Slovakia see Stredoslovenský, state, Slvk.	24	H15	48.50 N	19.10 E
Central Square, N.Y., U.S.	126	E13	43.17 N	76.08 W
Central Terminus, trans., India	190c		18.58 N	72.49 E
Central Utah Canal, can., Ut., U.S.	150	D4	39.34 N	112.12 W
Central Valley, Ca., U.S.	148	C3	40.40 N	122.23 W
Central Valley see Longitudinal, Valle, val., Chile	172	H1	36.00 S	72.00 W
Centre, Al., U.S.	134	C13	34.09 N	85.40 W
Centre, Canal du, can., Fr.	22	C10	46.29 N	4.00 E
Centre City, N.J., U.S.	203		39.46 N	75.10 W
Centre Island, N.Y., U.S.	194		40.54 N	73.32 W
Centre Island Park, p.o.i., On., Can.	193b		43.37 N	79.23 W
Centreville, Al., U.S.	134	E11	32.56 N	87.08 W
Centreville, Md., U.S.	124	E9	39.02 N	76.04 W
Centreville, Ms., U.S.	134	F7	31.05 N	91.04 W
Centro Puntas, P.R.	158a	b1	18.22 N	67.15 W
Centro Simón Bolívar, shp. cen., Ven.	204c		10.30 N	66.55 W
Century, Fl., U.S.	134	G11	30.58 N	87.15 W
Century, W.V., U.S.	124	E5	39.05 N	80.11 W
Century City, ngh., Ca., U.S.	198		34.03 N	118.26 W
Century III Mall, shp. cen., Pa., U.S.	197b		40.21 N	79.57 W
Cenxi, China	58	J4	23.02 N	111.03 E
Ceos see Kéa, i., Grc.	34	F7	37.38 N	24.20 E
Čepca, stm., Russia	40	B17	58.33 N	50.04 E
Čepelare, Blg.	36	H11	41.44 N	24.41 E
Cephalonia see Kefallonía, i., Grc.	34	E3	38.13 N	20.34 E
Cepu, Indon.	66	G7	7.08 S	111.36 E
Cerahoŭka, Bela.	26	H14	52.12 N	31.26 E
Ceram see Seram, i., Indon.	60	F8	3.00 S	129.00 E
Ceram Sea see Seram, Laut, s., Indon.	60	F8	2.30 S	128.00 E
Čerčany, Czech Rep.	24	G10	49.51 N	14.43 E
Čerdakly, Russia	40	D16	54.21 N	48.49 E
Cerdanyola del Vallès, Spain	184d		41.30 N	2.09 E
Cerdas, Bol.	166	D3	20.49 S	66.23 W
Cereal, Ab., Can.	142	C3	51.25 N	110.47 W
Cereales, Arg.	172	H6	36.48 S	63.52 W
Čereha, stm., Russia	26	C11	57.45 N	28.21 E
Čeremhovo, Russia	48	D18	53.08 N	103.04 E
Čeremisinovo, Russia	38	B16	51.53 N	37.15 E
Čeremšany, Russia	54	B11	44.41 N	135.44 E
Čerëmuški, ngh., Russia	183b		55.41 N	37.35 E
Cerenti, Indon.	66	D2	0.30 S	101.52 E
Čerepanovo, Russia	48	D14	54.13 N	83.20 E
Čerepet', Russia	26	F19	54.06 N	36.23 E
Čerepkovo, ngh., Russia	183b		55.46 N	37.23 E
Čerepovec, Russia	26	A20	59.08 N	37.54 E
Ceres, Arg.	172	D7	29.53 S	61.57 W
Ceres, Braz.	166	C7	15.17 S	49.35 W
Ceres, S. Afr.	90	H4	33.21 S	19.18 E
Ceresco, Ne., U.S.	128	J2	41.03 N	96.39 W
Ceresio see Lugano, Lago di, l., Eur.	30	E5	46.00 N	9.00 E
Ceresole Reale, Italy	30	E4	45.26 N	7.13 E
Céret, Fr.	28	B13	42.29 N	2.44 E
Cereté, Col.	168	C4	8.53 N	75.48 W
Čerevkovo, Russia	12	F21	61.47 N	45.15 E
Cereweh, Indon.	66	H10	8.51 S	116.49 E
Cergy, Fr.	179		49.02 N	2.04 E
Ceriano, Italy	184b		45.38 N	9.05 E
Cerignola, Italy	32	C9	41.16 N	15.53 E
Cérilly, Fr.	20	H11	46.37 N	2.49 E
Čerkašina, Russia	48	C19	58.37 N	108.29 E
Čerkassy see Cherkasy, Ukr.	38	D11	49.26 N	32.04 E
Çerkeş, Tur.	34	C15	40.49 N	32.53 E
Čerkesovskij, Russia	40	F13	50.41 N	42.34 E
Čerkessk, Russia	42	C10	44.13 N	42.04 E
Çerkezköy, Tur.	34	B10	41.17 N	27.59 E
Čerkizovo, Russia	183b		55.58 N	37.48 E
Čerkizovo, ngh., Russia	183b		55.57 N	37.22 E
Čerkovišče, Russia	26	E13	55.54 N	30.50 E
Čerlak, Russia	48	D12	54.08 N	74.48 E
Cermei, Rom.	36	C8	46.32 N	21.50 E
Čermoz, Russia	40	B19	58.47 N	56.09 E
Čern', Russia	26	G19	53.27 N	36.54 E
Cerna, Rom.	36	D15	45.05 N	28.18 E
Černá hora, mtn., Czech Rep.	24	G9	48.58 N	13.48 E
Cernăuţi see Chernivtsi, Ukr.	38	E4	48.17 N	25.57 E
Černavka, Russia	40	E13	52.11 N	42.25 E
Cernavodă, Rom.	36	E15	44.20 N	28.02 E
Cernay, Fr.	20	G16	47.48 N	7.10 E
Cernei, Munţii, mts., Rom.	36	D9	45.05 N	22.34 E
Černëvo, Russia	26	B11	58.39 N	28.14 E
Černëvo, Russia	183b		55.50 N	37.18 E
Černigov see Chernihiv, Ukr.	38	B10	51.30 N	31.17 E
Černigovka, Russia	54	B10	44.20 N	132.33 E
Černi Vrăh, mtn., Blg.	36	G10	42.34 N	23.17 E
Černjahovsk, Russia	26	F4	54.38 N	21.49 E
Černjanka, Russia	40	F10	50.56 N	37.48 E
Černobyl' see Chornobyl', Ukr.	38	B9	51.16 N	30.14 E

Name	Page	Map Ref.	Latitude	Longitude
Černogorsk, Russia	48	D16	53.49 N	91.17 E
Černo more see Black Sea, s.	42	D5	43.00 N	35.00 E
Černovcy see Chernivtsi, Ukr.	38	E4	48.17 N	25.57 E
Černovskoe, Russia	40	B15	58.41 N	47.22 E
Černuška, Russia	40	C19	56.30 N	56.04 E
Černyševsk, Russia	50	F12	52.31 N	116.59 E
Černyševskij, Russia	50	D11	63.00 N	112.29 E
Cérou, stm., Fr.	22	E8	44.08 N	1.51 E
Cerralvo, Mex.	154	B9	26.05 N	99.36 W
Cerralvo, Isla, i., Mex.	154	C4	24.14 N	109.51 W
Cërrik, Alb.	32	C14	41.02 N	19.59 E
Cërriku see Cërrik, Alb.	32	C14	41.02 N	19.59 E
Cerrillos, Arg.	172	B5	24.54 S	65.29 W
Cerrillos, Chile	204e		33.30 S	70.43 W
Cerrillos, N.M., U.S.	138	F2	35.26 N	106.07 W
Cerritos, Mex.	154	D8	22.26 N	100.17 W
Cerritos, Ca., U.S.	198		33.52 N	118.05 W
Cerro Azul, Arg.	172	C10	27.38 S	55.30 W
Cerro Azul, Braz.	172	B13	24.49 S	49.15 W
Cerro Azul, Mex.	154	E10	21.12 N	97.44 W
Cerro Azul, Peru	164	F2	13.01 S	76.28 W
Cerro Chato, Ur.	172	F10	33.06 S	55.07 W
Cerro Colorado, Ur.	172	F10	33.51 S	55.32 W
Cerro de las Mesas, hist., Mex.	154	F10	18.47 N	96.05 W
Cerro de los Angeles, rel., Spain	184a		40.19 N	3.41 W
Cerro de Pasco, Peru	164	F2	10.41 S	76.16 W
Cerro Gordo, Il., U.S.	130	E9	39.53 N	88.43 W
Cerro Grande, stm., Ven.	204c		10.37 N	66.49 W
Cerro Largo, Braz.	172	D10	28.08 S	54.44 W
Cerro Maggiore, Italy	184b		45.36 N	8.58 E
Cerro Moreno, Chile	172	A2	23.28 S	70.25 W
Cerrón, Cerro, mtn., Ven.	168	B6	10.19 N	70.39 W
Cerro Navia, Chile	204e		33.25 S	70.43 W
Cerrón Grande, Embalse, res., El Sal.	156	E3	14.00 N	89.00 W
Cerro Prieto, Mex.	148	K10	32.27 N	115.22 W
Cerros Colorados, Embalse, res., Arg.	172	I3	38.34 S	68.48 W
Cerro Tololo, Observatorio Astronómico, sci., Chile	172	E2	30.05 S	71.00 W
Cerro Vera, Ur.	172	F9	33.11 S	57.27 W
Čerskij, Russia	50	C21	68.46 N	161.24 E
Čerskogo, hrebet (Cherskiy Mountains), mts., Russia	50	C17	65.00 N	144.00 E
Čertanovka, stm., Russia	183b		55.38 N	37.47 E
Čertanovo, ngh., Russia	183b		55.38 N	37.37 E
Čertkovo, Russia	38	D19	49.22 N	40.10 E
Čertolino, Russia	26	D16	56.12 N	33.57 E
Cervaro, stm., Italy	32	C9	41.30 N	15.52 E
Cervati, Monte, mtn., Italy	32	D9	40.17 N	15.29 E
Cervelló, Spain	184d		41.24 N	1.57 E
Cervelló, Riera de, stm., Spain	184d		41.24 N	2.01 E
Čërven', Bela.	26	G11	53.42 N	28.26 E
Červen Brjag, Blg.	36	F11	43.16 N	24.06 E
Červený Kostelec, Czech Rep.	24	F12	50.30 N	16.13 E
Cervera, Spain	28	C12	41.40 N	1.17 E
Cervera del Río Alhama, Spain	28	B9	42.01 N	1.57 W
Cervera de Pisuerga, Spain	28	B6	42.52 N	4.29 W
Cervia, Italy	30	F9	44.15 N	12.22 E
Cervialto, Monte, mtn., Italy	32	D9	40.47 N	15.08 E
Cervino see Matterhorn, mtn., Eur.	30	D4	45.59 N	7.43 E
Cervione, Fr.	22	G15	42.20 N	9.30 E
Červjanka, Russia	48	C17	57.41 N	99.32 E
Červlënnaja, Russia	42	D11	43.29 N	45.52 E
Cervo, Spain	28	A3	43.40 N	7.24 W
Čèrykaŭ, Bela.	26	G14	53.34 N	31.23 E
Cesano, stm., Italy	30	G10	43.45 N	13.10 E
Cesano Boscone, Italy	184b		45.27 N	9.06 E
Cesar, state, Col.	168	C5	9.20 N	73.30 W
Cesar, stm., Col.	168	B5	8.59 N	73.58 W
Cesate, Italy	184b		45.36 N	9.05 E
Cesena, Italy	30	F9	44.08 N	12.14 E
Cesenatico, Italy	30	F9	44.12 N	12.24 E
Cesi, Poggio, hill, Italy	185a		42.02 N	12.44 E
Cēsis, Lat.	26	C8	57.18 N	25.17 E
Česká Kamenice, Czech Rep.	24	F10	50.48 N	14.25 E
Česká Lípa, Czech Rep.	24	F10	50.41 N	14.32 E
Česká Republika see Czech Republic, ctry., Eur.	24	G12	49.40 N	15.10 E
Česká Třebová, Czech Rep.	24	G12	49.53 N	16.27 E
České Budějovice, Czech Rep.	24	H10	48.58 N	14.28 E
Českomoravská vrchovina, plat., Czech Rep.	24	G11	49.20 N	15.30 E
Československo see Czech Republic, ctry., Eur.	24	G12	49.40 N	15.10 E
Český Brod, Czech Rep.	24	F10	50.04 N	14.51 E
Český Krumlov, Czech Rep.	24	H10	48.48 N	14.18 E
Český les see Bohemian Forest, mts., Eur.	24	G8	48.53 N	13.51 E
Çeşme, Tur.	34	E9	38.17 N	26.18 E
Češskaja guba (Chesha Bay), b., Russia	12	C21	67.30 N	46.30 E
Cessnock, Austl.	98	I8	32.50 S	151.20 E
Cesson, Fr.	179		48.34 N	2.36 E
Cesvaine, Lat.	26	D9	56.58 N	26.19 E
Cetate, Rom.	36	E10	44.06 N	23.03 E
Cetatea Albă see Bilhorod-Dnistrovs'kyi, Ukr.	38	G9	46.11 N	30.18 E
Cetina, stm., Cro.	30	G13	43.26 N	16.41 E
Cetinje, Yugo.	36	G5	42.23 N	18.55 E
Çetinkaya, Tur.	42	F7	39.15 N	37.37 E
Ceuta, Sp. N. Afr.	84	B3	35.53 N	5.19 W
Cévennes, reg., Fr.	22	E9	44.07 N	3.31 E
Cévennes, Parc National des, p.o.i., Fr.	22	E9	44.15 N	3.40 E
Cevizli, Tur.	34	F14	37.12 N	31.45 E
Ceyhan, Tur.	42	G6	37.02 N	35.49 E
Ceyhan, stm., Tur.	76	B6	37.40 N	36.48 E
Ceylanpınar, Tur.	42	G8	36.52 N	40.03 E
Ceylon, Sk., Can.	142	E9	49.27 N	104.36 W
Ceylon, Mn., U.S.	128	H4	43.32 N	94.37 W
Ceylon see Sri Lanka, ctry., Asia	69	G5	7.00 N	81.00 E
Cèze, stm., Fr.	22	E10	44.06 N	4.42 E
Cha-am, Thai.	64	F4	12.47 N	99.58 E
Chabanais, Fr.	22	D6	45.52 N	0.42 E
Chabás, Arg.	172	F7	33.15 S	61.22 W
Chabjuwardoo Bay, b., Austl.	96	D2	22.57 S	113.48 E
Chablais, reg., Fr.	22	C12	46.18 N	6.39 E
Chabogongba, China	70	C8	31.48 N	81.11 E
Chabot, Lake, l., Ca., U.S.	200		37.43 N	122.07 W
Chabot, Lake, l., Ca., U.S.	200		38.08 N	122.14 W
Chacabuco, Arg.	172	G7	34.38 S	60.29 W
Chacaito, Quebrada, stm., Ven.	204c		10.29 N	66.52 W
Chacao, Ven.	204c		10.30 N	66.51 W
Chacarita, Cementerio de la, misc. cult., Arg.	206		34.33 S	58.28 W
Chachani, Nevado, vol., Peru	164	G3	16.12 S	71.33 W
Chachapoyas, Peru	164	E2	6.13 S	77.52 W
Chāchora, India	70	F6	24.12 N	76.57 E
Chāchro, Pak.	70	F3	25.06 N	70.15 E
Chachu, China	70	B8	33.16 N	81.41 E
Chaco, state, Arg.	172	C7	26.00 S	60.30 W
Chaco, stm., N.M., U.S.	150	G8	36.46 N	108.39 W
Chaco, Parque Nacional, p.o.i., Arg.	172	C8	26.54 S	59.41 W
Chaco Austral, reg., Arg.	172	C7	26.30 S	61.30 W
Chaco Boreal, reg., Para.	166	D4	23.00 S	60.00 W
Chaco Central, reg., Arg.	166	D4	26.33 S	59.41 W
Chaco Culture National Historical Park, p.o.i., N.M., U.S.	150	G9	36.03 N	107.59 W
Chaco Mesa, mtn., N.M., U.S.	150	H9	35.47 N	107.35 W
Chacón, Arroyo, stm., Arg.	206		34.53 S	58.39 W
Chacra Cerro, Peru	204d		11.55 S	77.04 W
Chacuaco Creek, stm., Co., U.S.	138	D5	37.34 N	103.38 W
Chad, ctry., Afr.	82	E3	15.00 N	19.00 E
Chad, Lake, l., Afr.	82	E2	13.20 N	14.00 E
Chadbourn, N.C., U.S.	132	B7	34.19 N	78.49 W
Chadds Ford, Pa., U.S.	203		39.52 N	75.35 W
Chādegān, Iran	74	D12	32.49 N	50.26 E
Chadian, China	58	H1	26.54 N	105.46 E
Chadileuvu see Salado, stm., Arg.	172	G4	38.49 S	64.59 W
Chadron, Ne., U.S.	140	E10	42.49 N	103.00 W
Chadstone, Austl.	192b		37.53 S	145.05 E
Chadwell Saint Mary, Eng., U.K.	178		51.29 N	0.22 E
Chadwick, Il., U.S.	128	I9	42.01 N	89.53 W
Chadwick Manor, Md., U.S.	202b		39.19 N	76.46 W
Chadwick Pond, l., Ma., U.S.	201		42.44 N	71.05 W
Chae Hom, Thai.	64	C4	18.42 N	99.34 E
Chaem, stm., Thai.	64	C4	18.11 N	98.38 E
Chaffee, Mo., U.S.	130	G8	37.10 N	89.39 W
Chāgai, Pak.	62	C1	29.18 N	64.42 E
Chāgai Hills, hills, Asia	62	C1	29.30 N	63.47 E
Chagny, Fr.	20	H13	46.54 N	4.44 E
Chagos Archipelago, is., B.I.O.T.	174	J10	6.00 S	72.00 E
Chagos-Laccadive Plateau, unds.	174	J10	3.00 N	73.00 E
Chagrin, Aurora Branch, stm., Oh., U.S.	197a		41.25 N	81.25 W
Chagrin Valley Parkway, p.o.i., Oh., U.S.	197a		41.26 N	81.25 W
Chaguanas, Trin.	159f	s12	10.30 N	61.24 W
Chaguaramas, Ven.	168	C8	9.20 N	66.15 W
Chahal, Guat.	156	E3	15.45 N	89.33 W
Chahanwusu see Dulan, China	52	D4	36.09 N	98.22 E
Chahār Borjak, Afg.	72	C9	30.17 N	62.01 E
Chahār Mahāl va Bakhtīārī, state, Iran	74	D12	32.00 N	51.00 E
Chahe, China	52	E4	33.51 N	97.08 E
Chāh Gay see Chāgai Hills, hills, Asia	62	C1	29.30 N	63.47 E
Chai Badan, Thai.	64	E5	15.04 N	101.04 E
Chāībāsa, India	70	G10	22.32 N	85.48 E
Chaïdárion, Grc.	185c		38.01 N	23.38 E
Chaihe, China	54	B8	44.46 N	129.41 E
Chai Nat, Thai.	64	E5	15.11 N	100.08 E
Chainhurst, Eng., U.K.	178		51.12 N	0.29 E
Chai Wan, China	189d		22.16 N	114.13 E
Chaiya, Thai.	64	H4	9.22 N	99.12 E
Chaiyaphum, Thai.	64	E6	15.48 N	102.02 E
Chajarí, Arg.	172	E8	30.44 S	57.58 W
Chajianling, China	58	B6	39.14 N	114.36 E
Chakari, Zimb.	88	D4	18.04 S	29.51 E
Chakaria, Bngl.	70	H14	21.46 N	92.05 E
Chākdaha, India	70	G12	23.05 N	88.31 E
Chakdaha, India	190b		22.20 N	88.20 E
Chake Chake, Tan.	86	F7	5.13 S	39.45 E
Chakhānsūr, Afg.	72	C9	31.14 N	62.01 E
Chākia, India	70	E10	26.25 N	85.03 E
Chakkarat, Thai.	64	E6	14.59 N	102.16 E
Chakradharpur, India	70	G10	22.40 N	85.38 E
Chakrāta, India	70	C6	30.42 N	77.51 E
Chāksu, India	70	E5	26.36 N	75.57 E
Chakwāl, Pak.	70	B4	32.55 N	72.51 E
Chal, India	190c		19.06 N	73.08 E
Chala, Peru	164	G3	15.49 S	74.17 W
Chalais, Fr.	22	D6	45.16 N	0.02 E
Chālakuda, India	69	F3	10.16 N	76.21 E
Chalándri, Grc.	185c		38.01 N	23.48 E
Chalatenango, El Sal.	156	F3	14.02 N	88.56 W
Chalaxung, China	54	E4	34.10 N	97.42 E
Chalbi Desert, des., Kenya	86	D7	3.00 N	37.20 E
Chalcidice see Chalkidikí, hist. reg., Grc.	34	C6	40.25 N	23.27 E
Chalcis see Chalkída, Grc.	34	E6	38.28 N	23.36 E
Chalco, stm., Mex.	204a		19.19 N	99.08 W
Chaldon, Eng., U.K.	178		51.17 N	0.07 W
Chaleine, Fr.	179		48.36 N	1.43 E
Chaleur Bay, b., Can.	122	C11	48.00 N	65.45 W
Chaleurs, Baie des see Chaleur Bay, b., Can.	122	C11	48.00 N	65.45 W
Chalfant, Pa., U.S.	197b		40.25 N	79.52 W
Chalfant Run, stm., Pa., U.S.	197b		40.25 N	79.48 W
Chalfont Common, Eng., U.K.	178		51.38 N	0.33 W
Chalfonte, De., U.S.	203		39.49 N	75.31 W
Chalfont Saint Giles, Eng., U.K.	178		51.38 N	0.34 W
Chalhuanca, Peru	164	F3	14.17 S	73.14 W
Chalía, stm., Arg.	166	I2	49.34 S	69.30 W
Chalifert, Fr.	179		48.53 N	2.46 E
Chālisgaon, India	70	H5	20.27 N	75.00 E
Chalk, Eng., U.K.	178		51.26 N	0.25 E
Chalk Draw, stm., Tx., U.S.	136	E4	29.35 N	103.13 W
Chalke see Chálki, i., Grc.	34	G10	36.13 N	27.32 E
Chálki, i., Grc.	34	G10	36.13 N	27.32 E
Chalkída, Grc.	34	E6	38.28 N	23.36 E
Chalkidikí, hist. reg., Grc.	34	C6	40.25 N	23.27 E
Chalk River, On., Can.	126	B12	46.01 N	77.26 W
Challakere, India	69	D3	14.18 N	76.39 E
Challans, Fr.	20	H7	46.50 N	1.52 W
Challapata, Bol.	166	C3	18.54 S	66.46 W
Challenger Deep, unds.	46	H18	11.21 N	142.12 E
Challis, Id., U.S.	146	F12	44.30 N	114.15 W
Chalmette, La., U.S.	134	H9	29.56 N	89.57 W
Châlons-sur-Marne, Fr.	20	F13	48.57 N	4.21 E
Chalon-sur-Saône, Fr.	20	H13	46.47 N	4.50 E
Chalosse, reg., Fr.	22	F5	43.40 N	0.30 W
Chaltel, Cerro (Fitz Roy, Monte), mtn., S.A.	166	I2	49.17 S	73.05 W
Chaluhe, China	54	C6	43.42 N	125.59 E
Châlus, Fr.	22	D6	45.39 N	0.59 E
Chālūs, Iran	74	B12	36.39 N	51.25 E
Cham, Ger.	24	G8	49.13 N	12.40 E
Chama, N.M., U.S.	138	E2	36.54 N	106.35 W
Chama, stm., U.S.	138	E2	36.03 N	106.05 W
Chama, stm., Ven.	168	C6	9.02 N	71.41 W
Chamaicó, Arg.	172	G5	35.03 S	64.58 W
Chaman, Pak.	62	B2	30.55 N	66.26 E
Chamao, Khao, mtn., Thai.	64	F5	12.57 N	101.45 E
Chamarande, Fr.	179		48.31 N	2.13 E
Chāmārpāra, India	190b		22.35 N	88.08 E
Chamba, India	70	B6	32.33 N	76.08 E
Chamba, Tan.	86	G7	11.34 S	36.55 E
Chambal, stm., India	70	F5	26.29 N	79.14 E
Chamberlain, Sk., Can.	142	D8	50.50 N	105.34 W
Chamberlain, S.D., U.S.	140	D13	43.48 N	99.18 W
Chamberlain, stm., Austl.	96	C5	15.10 S	128.07 E
Chamberlain Lake, l., Me., U.S.	122	D7	46.13 N	69.18 W
Chamberry, Ruisseau, stm., Qc., Can.	193a		45.20 N	73.58 W
Chambers, Az., U.S.	150	H7	35.12 N	109.25 W
Chambers, Ne., U.S.	140	E14	42.13 N	98.46 W
Chambers Brook, stm., N.J., U.S.	194		40.35 N	74.41 W
Chambersburg, Pa., U.S.	124	E8	39.56 N	77.39 W
Chambers Corner, N.J., U.S.	203		40.01 N	74.44 W
Chambers Creek, stm., Tx., U.S.	136	B11	31.57 N	96.11 W
Chambers Island, i., Wi., U.S.	126	C2	45.11 N	87.21 W
Chambéry, Fr.	22	D11	45.34 N	5.54 E
Chambi, Jebel, mtn., Tun.	84	B6	35.12 N	8.40 E
Chamblee, Ga., U.S.	134	D14	33.54 N	84.17 W
Chambly, Canal de, can., Qc., Can.	193a		45.25 N	73.15 W
Chambon-sur-Voueize, Fr.	22	C8	46.11 N	2.24 E
Chambord, Qc., Can.	122	B4	48.26 N	72.04 W
Chambord, Château de, hist., Fr.	20	G10	47.37 N	1.31 E
Chambourcy, Fr.	179		48.54 N	2.03 E
Chambry, Fr.	179		49.00 N	2.54 E
Chamdo see Qamdo, China	52	E4	31.10 N	97.08 E
Chamical, Arg.	172	E4	30.21 S	66.18 W
Chamo, Lake see Ch'amo Häyk', l., Eth.	82	F7	5.49 N	37.34 E
Ch'amo Häyk', l., Eth.	82	F7	5.49 N	37.34 E
Chamois, Mo., U.S.	130	F6	38.40 N	91.45 W
Chamoli, India	70	C7	30.24 N	79.19 E
Chamonix-Mont-Blanc, Fr.	22	D13	45.55 N	6.52 E
Chāmpa, India	70	G9	22.03 N	82.39 E
Champagne, hist. reg., Fr.	20	F13	49.00 N	4.30 E
Champagne Castle, mtn., S. Afr.	90	F9	29.06 S	29.20 E
Champagner-Berg, hill, Ger.	182a		52.31 N	13.05 E
Champagnole, Fr.	20	H14	46.45 N	5.53 E
Champaign, Il., U.S.	130	D9	40.06 N	88.14 W
Champaquí, Cerro, mtn., Arg.	172	F5	32.01 S	64.55 W
Champasak, Laos	64	E7	14.50 N	105.52 E
Champcueil, Fr.	179		48.31 N	2.27 E
Champdeuil, Fr.	179		48.37 N	2.44 E
Champdoré, Lac, l., Qc., Can.	110	D17	55.55 N	65.48 W
Champerico, Guat.	156	E2	14.17 N	91.54 W
Champigny-sur-Marne, Fr.	179		48.49 N	2.31 E
Champion, Ab., Can.	144	F17	50.13 N	113.08 W
Champion, Mi., U.S.	126	B1	46.31 N	87.58 W
Champion, Oh., U.S.	126	G9	41.18 N	80.51 W
Champlain, N.Y., U.S.	126	C16	44.59 N	73.26 W
Champlain, Lac see Champlain, Lake, l., N.A.	126	D16	44.45 N	73.15 W
Champlain, Lake, l., N.A.	126	D16	44.45 N	73.15 W
Champlan, Fr.	179		48.43 N	2.16 E
Champlin Creek, stm., N.Y., U.S.	194		40.43 N	73.12 W
Champlitte-et-le-Prélot, Fr.	20	G14	47.36 N	5.30 E
Champotón, Mex.	156	C2	19.21 N	90.43 W
Champs-sur-Marne, Fr.	179		48.51 N	2.36 E
Chāmrāil, India	190b		22.38 N	88.18 E
Chāmrājnagar Rāmasamudram, India	69	F3	11.55 N	76.56 E
Chamusca, Port.	28	E2	39.20 N	8.28 W
Chana, Thai.	64	I5	6.54 N	100.44 E
Chanakyapuri, hist. reg., India	190a		28.36 N	77.11 E
Chañar, Arg.	172	E4	30.32 S	65.57 W
Chañaral, Chile	172	C2	26.20 S	70.37 W
Chañaral, Isla, i., Chile	172	D2	29.02 S	71.35 W
Chancay, Peru	164	F2	11.34 S	77.15 W
Chances Peak, vol., Monts.	159a	d3	16.42 N	62.11 W
Chanchelulla Peak, mtn., Ca., U.S.	148	C3	40.28 N	122.59 W
Chanco, Chile	172	G1	35.43 S	72.33 W
Chanda see Chandrapur, India	69	B4	19.57 N	79.18 E
Chandalar, Ak., U.S.	109	C10	67.29 N	148.29 W
Chandalar, stm., Ak., U.S.	109	C10	66.38 N	146.01 W
Chandan Chauki, India	70	D8	28.31 N	80.46 E
Chandannagar, India	70	G12	22.51 N	88.21 E
Chandausi, India	70	D7	28.26 N	78.46 E
Chāndbāli, India	70	H11	20.47 N	86.46 E
Chandeleur Islands, is., La., U.S.	134	H10	29.48 N	88.53 W
Chandeleur Sound, strt., La., U.S.	134	H9	29.52 N	89.05 W
Chandernagore see Chandannagar, India	70	G12	22.51 N	88.21 E
Chandīgarh, India	70	C6	30.44 N	76.53 E
Chandil, India	70	G11	22.57 N	86.03 E
Chanditala, India	190b		22.41 N	88.16 E
Chandler, Qc., Can.	122	B12	48.20 N	64.41 W
Chandler, Az., U.S.	150	J5	33.18 N	111.50 W
Chandler, In., U.S.	130	F10	38.02 N	87.22 W
Chandler, Ok., U.S.	130	B2	35.42 N	96.52 W
Chandler, Tx., U.S.	136	B12	32.18 N	95.30 W
Chandler Park, p.o.i., Mi., U.S.	199		42.24 N	82.58 W
Chandler's Cross, Eng., U.K.	178		51.40 N	0.27 W
Chandlerville, Il., U.S.	130	D7	40.02 N	90.08 W
Chāndor Hills, hills, India	70	H5	20.36 N	74.01 E
Chandos Lake, l., On., Can.	126	D12	44.49 N	77.58 W
Chāndpur, Bngl.	70	G13	23.13 N	90.39 E
Chāndpur, Bngl.	70	G14	22.09 N	92.00 E
Chāndpur, India	70	D7	29.08 N	78.16 E
Chāndpur, ngh., India	190a		28.45 N	77.01 E
Chandrapur, India	69	B4	19.57 N	79.18 E
Chāndvad, India	70	H5	20.20 N	74.17 E
Chang, stm., China	58	G1	29.07 N	105.57 E
Chang, Ko, i., Thai.	64	F6	12.05 N	102.20 E
Chang'an, China	58	I3	26.00 N	109.34 E
Changan see Xi'an, China	58	D3	34.15 N	108.52 E
Changanācheri, India	69	G3	9.27 N	76.33 E
Changane, stm., Moz.	90	D11	24.43 S	33.32 E
Changara, Moz.	88	D5	16.50 S	33.16 E
Changcheng, China	58	L3	19.20 N	108.40 E
Chang Cheng (Great Wall), misc. cult., China	52	D6	40.00 N	112.30 E
Chang Chenmo, stm., Asia	70	A7	34.16 N	78.17 E
Changchow see Changzhou, China	58	F8	31.46 N	119.56 E
Changchow see Zhangzhou, China	58	I7	24.31 N	117.39 E
Changchun, China	52	C10	43.52 N	125.19 E
Changde, China	58	G4	29.01 N	111.41 E
Changgi-ap, c., Kor., S.	54	F8	36.05 N	129.34 E
Changgi-li, Kor., S.	189b		37.35 N	126.44 E
Changgi-ri, Kor., S.	189b		37.38 N	126.41 E
Changgyong Palace, bldg., Kor., S.	189b		37.36 N	127.00 E
Chang Hu, l., China	58	F5	30.25 N	112.26 E
Changhua, Tai.	58	I9	24.04 N	120.30 E
Changhŭng, Kor., S.	54	G7	34.40 N	126.53 E
Changi, Sing.	189c		1.23 N	103.59 E
Changi, Tanjong, c., Sing.	189c		1.23 N	104.00 E
Changi International Airport, arpt., Sing.	189c		1.22 N	103.59 E
Changi Prison, bldg., Sing.	189c		1.22 N	103.58 E
Changji, China	52	C2	44.01 N	87.17 E
Changjiang, China	58	L3	19.16 N	109.01 E
Changkiakow see Zhangjiakou, China	58	A6	40.49 N	114.52 E
Changli, China	58	B8	39.42 N	119.10 E
Changling, China	52	C9	44.16 N	123.59 E
Changlingzi, China	58	B10	39.47 N	122.44 E
Changlun, Malay.	64	I5	6.25 N	100.26 E
Changmar, China	70	A7	34.16 N	79.56 E
Changmong-ni, Kor., S.	56	E1	34.58 N	128.40 E
Changning, China	52	G4	24.57 N	99.42 E
Changning, China	58	H5	26.19 N	112.21 E
Ch'angnyŏng, Kor., S.	56	D1	35.31 N	128.29 E
Changping, China	58	A7	40.13 N	116.14 E
Changsa, China	58	L4	19.45 N	110.53 E
Changsan-got, c., Kor., N.	54	E6	38.07 N	124.40 E
Changsha, China	58	I7	24.12 N	116.07 E
Changsha, China	58	G5	28.11 N	112.58 E
Changshan Qundao, is., China	58	B10	38.57 N	122.40 E
Changshou, China	58	G2	29.50 N	107.04 E
Changshu, China	58	F9	31.38 N	120.44 E
Changshui, China	58	D4	34.21 N	111.29 E
Changtien see Zibo, China	58	C8	36.47 N	118.02 E
Changting, China	54	B8	44.30 N	128.48 E
Changting, China	58	I7	25.50 N	116.21 E
Changwŏn, Kor., S.	54	G8	35.16 N	128.37 E
Changwu, China	58	D2	35.12 N	107.47 E
Changxing, China	58	F8	30.59 N	119.54 E
Changxing Dao, i., China	58	B9	39.34 N	121.23 E
Changyi, China	58	C8	36.51 N	119.24 E
Changyŏn-ŭp, Kor., N.	54	E6	38.15 N	125.06 E
Changzhi, China	58	C5	36.11 N	113.06 E
Changzhou, China	58	F8	31.46 N	119.56 E
Chanh Hung, Viet.	187c		10.44 N	106.41 E
Chaniá, Grc.	34	H7	35.30 N	24.01 E
Chanión, Kólpos, b., Grc.	34	H6	35.34 N	23.57 E
Chankiang see Zhanjiang, China	58	K4	21.12 N	110.22 E
Channagiri, India	69	D2	14.01 N	75.55 E
Channapatna, India	69	E3	12.39 N	77.12 E
Channel Country, reg., Austl.	98	E3	24.45 S	141.00 E
Channel Islands, is., Eur.	10	L10	49.20 N	2.20 W
Channel Islands, is., Ca., U.S.	148	J6	34.00 N	120.00 W
Channel Islands National Park, p.o.i., Ca., U.S.	148	J6	33.28 N	119.02 W
Channel-Port aux Basques, Nf., Can.	111a	j22	47.34 N	59.10 W
Channelview, Tx., U.S.	136	E12	29.46 N	95.06 W
Channing, Mi., U.S.	126	B1	46.08 N	88.08 W
Channing, Tx., U.S.	138	F6	35.41 N	102.20 W
Chantada, Spain	28	B3	42.37 N	7.45 W
Chanteloup, Fr.	179		48.51 N	2.44 E
Chanteloup-les-Vignes, Fr.	179		48.59 N	2.02 E
Chanthaburi, Thai.	64	F6	12.36 N	102.06 E
Chantilly, Fr.	20	E11	49.12 N	2.28 E
Chantrey Inlet, b., Nu., Can.	110	B11	67.52 N	95.52 W
Chanumla, India	62	G7	8.18 N	93.05 E
Chanute, Ks., U.S.	130	G2	37.40 N	95.27 W
Chao, stm., China	58	A7	40.30 N	117.00 E
Chao'an, China	58	J7	23.40 N	116.38 E
Chaochow see Chao'an, China	58	J7	23.40 N	116.38 E
Chao Hu, l., China	58	F7	31.31 N	117.33 E
Chao Phraya, stm., Thai.	64	E5	13.31 N	100.36 E
Chaor, stm., China	52	B9	46.48 N	123.35 E
Chaoxian, China	58	F7	31.35 N	117.51 E
Chaoyang, China	52	C9	41.34 N	120.27 E
Chaoyang, China	54	B7	44.34 N	126.20 E
Chaoyang, China	58	J7	23.15 N	116.35 E
Chaoyangpo, China	54	C6	43.38 N	124.42 E
Chaoyangshan, China	54	C6	43.02 N	125.40 E
Chapa see Sa Pa, Viet.	64	A6	22.21 N	103.48 E
Chapada dos Veadeiros, Parque Nacional da, p.o.i., Braz.	170	H2	13.57 S	47.37 W
Chapadinha, Braz.	170	B4	3.44 S	43.21 W
Chapaievka, Ukr.	38	F15	47.28 N	36.20 E
Chapais, Qc., Can.	114	B13	49.47 N	74.51 W
Chapala, Mex.	154	E7	20.17 N	103.10 W
Chapala, Laguna de, l., Mex.	154	E7	20.15 N	103.00 W
Chāparmukh, India	70	E14	26.12 N	92.31 E
Chaparral, Col.	168	F4	3.43 N	75.28 W
Chapecó, Braz.	172	C11	27.06 S	52.37 W
Chapel Hill, De., U.S.	203		39.42 N	75.44 W
Chapel Hill, N.C., U.S.	124	I6	35.54 N	79.03 W
Chapel Hill, Tn., U.S.	134	B12	35.37 N	86.41 W
Chapel Hill Channel, strt., U.S.	194		40.32 N	74.02 W
Chapelle Creek, stm., S.D., U.S.	140	C13	44.15 N	99.55 W
Chapellerie, Fr.	179		49.02 N	2.26 E
Chapel Oaks, Md., U.S.	202c		38.54 N	76.55 W
Chapelton, Jam.	158d	i13	18.04 N	77.15 W
Chapeltown, Eng., U.K.	180		53.38 N	2.24 W
Chapet, Fr.	179		48.58 N	1.56 E
Chapéu, Morro do, mtn., Braz.	170	H4	14.55 S	42.31 W
Chapicuy, Ur.	172	E9	31.38 S	57.53 W
Chapin, Il., U.S.	130	E7	39.45 N	90.24 W
Chapleau, On., Can.	114	C9	47.50 N	83.24 W
Chaplíivka, Ukr.	38	B12	51.43 N	33.13 E
Chaplin, Sk., Can.	142	D7	50.27 N	106.40 W
Chaplin, stm., Ky., U.S.	130	G12	37.50 N	85.17 W
Chaplin Lake, l., Sk., Can.	142	D7	50.18 N	106.35 W
Chaplyne, Ukr.	38	E15	48.08 N	36.14 E
Chaplynka, Ukr.	38	G12	46.21 N	33.32 E
Chapman, Ks., U.S.	138	C11	38.58 N	97.01 W
Chapman, Ne., U.S.	140	F14	41.01 N	98.09 W
Chapman, Cape, c., Nu., Can.	110	B13	69.12 N	88.59 W
Chapman, Mount, mtn., B.C., Can.	144	E12	51.50 N	118.20 W
Chapman College, educ., Ca., U.S.	198		33.47 N	117.51 W
Chapman Creek, stm., Ks., U.S.	138	B11	38.58 N	97.00 W
Chapman's see Okwa, stm., Afr.	90	C6	22.14 S	23.59 E
Chapmanville, W.V., U.S.	124	G3	37.57 N	82.01 W
Chapman Woods, Ca., U.S.	198		34.08 N	118.05 W
Chapo, Mex.	136	E3	29.17 N	104.20 W
Chaponval, Fr.	179		49.04 N	2.09 E
Chappal, Waddi, mtn., Afr.	82	F2	7.02 N	11.43 E
Chappell, Ne., U.S.	140	F10	41.06 N	102.28 W
Chappell Hill, Tx., U.S.	136	D11	30.08 N	96.16 W
Chapultepec, Mex.	148	L9	31.46 N	116.35 W
Chapultepec, Mex.	150	K1	32.22 N	115.03 W
Chapultepec, Bosque de, p.o.i., Mex.	204a		19.25 N	99.12 W
Chapultepec, Castillo de, hist., Mex.	204a		19.25 N	99.11 W
Chaquiago, Arg.	172	C4	27.32 S	66.21 W
Charadai, Arg.	172	C8	27.39 S	59.51 W
Charagua, Bol.	166	C4	19.48 S	63.13 W
Charalá, Col.	168	D5	6.17 N	73.08 W
Charām, Iran	74	E12	30.44 N	50.44 E
Charata, Arg.	172	C7	27.13 S	61.11 W
Charcas, Mex.	154	D8	23.08 N	101.08 W
Charco Hondo, P.R.	158a	b2	18.25 N	66.43 W
Charcos de Figueroa, Mex.	154	B7	27.45 N	102.09 W
Charcos de Risa, Mex.	154	B7	26.15 N	103.09 W
Charcot Island, i., Ant.	103	B33	69.41 S	75.08 W
Chard, Eng., U.K.	10	K10	50.52 N	2.57 W
Chārduār, India	70	E14	26.49 N	92.42 E
Charente, state, Fr.	22	D6	45.40 N	0.10 E
Charente, stm., Fr.	22	C6	45.57 N	1.04 W
Charente-Maritime, state, Fr.	22	C5	45.30 N	0.45 W
Charenton-le-Pont, Fr.	179		48.49 N	2.25 E
Chari, stm., Afr.	82	E3	12.54 N	14.33 E
Chariāl Canal, can., India	190b		22.28 N	88.11 E
Chārīkār, Afg.	72	B10	35.00 N	69.10 E
Chariton, Ia., U.S.	130	C4	41.01 N	93.19 W
Chariton, stm., U.S.	130	D4	39.18 N	92.57 W
Chariton, Mussel Fork, stm., Mo., U.S.	130	E5	39.23 N	92.54 W
Charity, Guy.	164	B6	7.24 N	58.34 W
Charkhāri, India	70	F7	25.23 N	79.45 E
Charkhlik see Ruoqiang, China	52	D2	39.01 N	88.10 E
Charkop, ngh., India	190c		19.13 N	72.49 E
Charleroi, Bel.	20	D13	50.25 N	4.26 E
Charles, Cape, c., Va., U.S.	124	G10	37.07 N	75.57 W
Charles, Lake, l., Il., U.S.	196		42.15 N	87.58 W
Charles, Peak, mtn., Austl.	96	F4	32.52 S	121.09 E
Charles Branch, stm., Md., U.S.	202c		38.47 N	76.48 W
Charles City, Ia., U.S.	130	A5	43.03 N	92.40 W
Charles City, Va., U.S.	124	G8	37.20 N	77.04 W
Charles de Gaulle, Aéroport de, arpt., Fr.	179		49.01 N	2.33 E
Charles Island, i., Nu., Can.	110	C16	62.40 N	74.15 W
Charles Lee Tilden Regional Park, p.o.i., Ca., U.S.	200		37.54 N	122.15 W
Charles Mound, hill, Il., U.S.	130	B7	42.30 N	90.14 W
Charles Point, c., Austl.	96	B6	12.24 S	130.37 E
Charleston, Ar., U.S.	134	B4	35.18 N	94.02 W
Charleston, Il., U.S.	130	E9	39.29 N	88.10 W
Charleston, Ms., U.S.	134	C8	34.00 N	90.03 W
Charleston, Mo., U.S.	130	H8	36.55 N	89.20 W
Charleston, S.C., U.S.	132	D6	32.46 N	79.56 W
Charleston, W.V., U.S.	124	F4	38.21 N	81.38 W
Charleston Air Force Base, mil., S.C., U.S.	132	D6	32.57 N	79.57 W
Charleston Peak, mtn., Nv., U.S.	148	G10	36.16 N	115.42 W
Charlestown, St. K./N.	159a	c2	17.08 N	62.37 W
Charlestown, St. Vin.	159e	p11	12.41 N	61.20 W
Charlestown, S. Afr.	90	E9	27.24 S	29.53 E
Charlestown, In., U.S.	130	F12	38.26 N	85.39 W
Charlestown, N.H., U.S.	122	G4	43.14 N	72.25 W
Charlestown, Pa., U.S.	203		40.06 N	75.33 W
Charles Town, W.V., U.S.	124	E8	39.17 N	77.51 W
Charlestown, ngh., Ma., U.S.	201		42.23 N	71.04 W
Charlesworth, Eng., U.K.	180		53.26 N	1.59 W
Charleville, Austl.	98	F6	26.23 S	146.13 E
Charleville-Mézières, Fr.	20	E13	49.46 N	4.43 E
Charlevoix, Mi., U.S.	126	C4	45.18 N	85.15 W
Charlevoix, Lake, l., Mi., U.S.	126	C5	45.16 N	85.09 W
Charlie Creek, stm., Fl., U.S.	132	I4	27.21 N	81.49 W
Charlieu, Fr.	22	C10	46.09 N	4.09 E
Charlotte, Mi., U.S.	124	B1	42.33 N	84.49 W
Charlotte, N.C., U.S.	132	A5	35.13 N	80.50 W
Charlotte, Tn., U.S.	130	H10	36.10 N	87.20 W
Charlotte, Tx., U.S.	136	F9	28.51 N	98.42 W
Charlotte Amalie, V.I.U.S.	158b	e7	18.20 N	64.55 W
Charlotte Court House, Va., U.S.	124	G7	37.02 N	78.38 W
Charlotte Harbor, b., Fl., U.S.	132	J3	26.44 N	82.11 W
Charlotte Lake, l., B.C., Can.	144	D5	52.11 N	125.19 W
Charlottenberg, Swe.	16	H10	59.53 N	12.18 E
Charlottenburg, ngh., Ger.	182a		52.31 N	13.16 E
Charlottenburg, Schloss, hist., Ger.	182a		52.31 N	13.14 E
Charlottesburg Reservoir, res., N.J., U.S.	194		41.02 N	74.26 W
Charlottesville, Va., U.S.	124	F7	38.01 N	78.28 W
Charlottetown, P.E., Can.	122	D13	46.14 N	63.07 W
Charlotteville, Trin.	159f	r13	11.19 N	60.32 W
Charlton, Austl.	98	K4	36.16 S	143.21 E
Charlton, ngh., Eng., U.K.	178		51.29 N	0.02 E
Charlton Island, i., Nu., Can.	110	E14	52.00 N	79.30 W
Charmentray, Fr.	179		48.57 N	2.47 E
Charmes, Fr.	20	F15	48.22 N	6.17 E
Charneca, Port.	184c		38.44 N	9.27 W
Charneca, ngh., Port.	184c		38.47 N	9.08 W
Charnock Richard, Eng., U.K.	180		53.38 N	2.41 W
Charny, Fr.	179		48.58 N	2.46 E
Charouine, Alg.	84	D4	29.01 N	0.16 W
Charred Oak Estates, Md., U.S.	202c		39.00 N	77.10 W
Charron Lake, l., Mb., Can.	142	B18	52.43 N	95.15 W
Charroux, Fr.	22	C6	46.09 N	0.24 E
Chārsadda, Pak.	70	A3	34.09 N	71.44 E
Charter Oak, Ca., U.S.	198		34.06 N	117.52 W
Charter Oak, Ia., U.S.	128	I3	42.03 N	95.35 W
Charters Towers, Austl.	98	C6	20.04 S	146.15 E
Charterwood, Pa., U.S.	197b		40.33 N	80.00 W
Chartiers Run, stm., Pa., U.S.	197b		40.36 N	79.43 W
Chartiers Run, stm., Pa., U.S.	197b		40.15 N	80.12 W
Chartres, Fr.	20	F10	48.26 N	1.29 E
Chartridge, Eng., U.K.	178		51.44 N	0.39 W
Chart Sutton, Eng., U.K.	178		51.13 N	0.35 E
Chartwell, hist., Eng., U.K.	178		51.14 N	0.05 E
Chascomús, Arg.	172	G8	35.34 S	58.01 W

Name	Page	Map Ref.	Latitude	Longitude
Chase, B.C., Can.	144	F11	50.49 N	119.41 W
Chase, Ks., U.S.	138	C10	38.20 N	98.20 W
Chase, Mount, mtn., Me., U.S.	122	D8	46.07 N	68.29 W
Chase Brook, stm., N.H., U.S.	201		42.48 N	71.27 W
Chase City, Va., U.S.	124	H7	36.47 N	78.27 W
Chasiv Yar, Ukr.	38	E16	48.35 N	37.48 E
Chaska, Mn., U.S.	128	G5	44.47 N	93.36 W
Chāt, Iran	74	B14	37.58 N	55.16 E
Châteaubelair, St. Vin.	159e	o11	13.16 N	61.14 W
Châteaubriant, Fr.	20	G7	47.42 N	1.22 W
Château-du-Loir, Fr.	20	G9	47.41 N	0.25 E
Châteaudun, Fr.	20	F10	48.04 N	1.20 E
Châteaufort, Fr.	179		48.44 N	2.06 E
Chateaugay, N.Y., U.S.	126	D15	44.55 N	74.04 W
Chateaugay (Châteauguay), stm., N.A.	126	D15	45.24 N	73.45 W
Château-Gontier, Fr.	20	G8	47.49 N	0.42 W
Châteauguay (Chateaugay), stm., N.A.	126	D15	45.24 N	73.45 W
Châteauguay Heights, Qc., Can.	193a		45.23 N	73.44 W
Châteaulin, Fr.	20	F4	48.11 N	4.05 W
Châteauneuf-de-Randon, Fr.	22	E9	44.39 N	3.40 E
Châteauneuf-sur-Charente, Fr.	22	D5	45.36 N	0.03 W
Châteauneuf-sur-Loire, Fr.	20	G11	47.51 N	2.13 E
Château-Renault, Fr.	20	G9	47.35 N	0.54 E
Château-Richer, Qc., Can.	122	C11	46.58 N	71.01 W
Châteauroux, Fr.	22	C7	46.48 N	1.41 E
Château-Salins, Fr.	20	F15	48.49 N	6.30 E
Château-Thierry, Fr.	20	E12	49.02 N	3.24 E
Châtellerault, Fr.	20	H9	46.48 N	0.32 E
Châtenay-en-France, Fr.	179		49.04 N	2.27 E
Châtenay-Malabry, Fr.	179		48.46 N	2.17 E
Chatfield, Mn., U.S.	128	H6	43.51 N	92.12 W
Chatham, N.B., Can.	122	C11	47.02 N	65.28 W
Chatham, On., Can.	126	F7	42.23 N	82.10 W
Chatham, Eng., U.K.	10	J13	51.22 N	0.30 E
Chatham, Il., U.S.	130	E8	39.40 N	89.42 W
Chatham, La., U.S.	134	E6	32.18 N	92.27 W
Chatham, Ma., U.S.	124	C15	41.41 N	69.57 W
Chatham, N.Y., U.S.	124	B12	42.21 N	73.35 W
Chatham, Va., U.S.	124	H6	36.49 N	79.24 W
Chatham, ngh., Il., U.S.	196		41.45 N	87.37 W
Chatham see San Cristóbal, Isla, i., Ec.	164a	i12	0.49 S	89.26 W
Chatham, Isla, i., Chile	166	J2	50.37 S	74.26 W
Chatham Head, N.B., Can.	122	D11	46.59 N	65.32 W
Chatham Islands, is., N.Z.	94	H9	43.57 S	176.22 W
Chatham Rise, unds.	174	N20	43.26 S	178.01 W
Chatham Strait, strt., Ak., U.S.	109	E13	57.30 N	134.45 W
Châtillon, Fr.	179		48.48 N	2.17 E
Châtillon-en-Bazois, Fr.	20	G12	47.03 N	3.40 E
Châtillon-la-Borde, Fr.	179		48.33 N	2.49 E
Châtillon-sur-Indre, Fr.	20	H10	46.58 N	1.10 E
Châtillon-sur-Seine, Fr.	20	G13	47.51 N	4.33 E
Chatkal Range, mts., Asia	48	F12	41.40 N	71.05 E
Chat Moss, for., Eng., U.K.	180		53.27 N	2.27 W
Chatom, Al., U.S.	134	F10	31.27 N	88.15 W
Chatonville, Fr.	179		48.33 N	1.52 E
Chatou, Fr.	179		48.54 N	2.09 E
Chatpur, ngh., India	190b		22.36 N	88.22 E
Chatra, India	70	F10	24.12 N	84.52 E
Chatra, India	190b		22.46 N	88.20 E
Châtres, Fr.	179		48.43 N	2.49 E
Chatsquot Mountain, mtn., B.C., Can.	144	C3	53.08 N	127.30 W
Chatswood, Austl.	192a		33.48 S	151.12 E
Chatsworth, Austl.	98	C3	21.58 S	140.17 E
Chatsworth, Ga., U.S.	134	C14	34.47 N	84.46 W
Chatsworth, Il., U.S.	130	D9	40.45 N	88.17 W
Chatsworth, ngh., Ca., U.S.	198		34.15 N	118.36 W
Chattahoochee, Fl., U.S.	134	G14	30.41 N	84.50 W
Chattahoochee, stm., U.S.	116	E10	30.45 N	84.51 W
Chattanooga, Tn., U.S.	134	B13	35.01 N	85.19 W
Chattaroy, W.V., U.S.	124	G3	37.41 N	82.17 W
Chattenden, Eng., U.K.	178		51.25 N	0.32 E
Chattolanee, Md., U.S.	202b		39.24 N	76.45 W
Chatuchak Park, p.o.i., Thai.	187a		13.48 N	100.33 E
Chaturat, Thai.	64	E5	15.33 N	101.50 E
Chaubourg, Mount, hill, St. Luc.	159c	I7	14.02 N	60.57 W
Chauconin, Fr.	179		48.58 N	2.51 E
Chaudière, stm., Qc., Can.	122	E6	46.44 N	71.16 W
Chau Doc, Viet.	64	G7	10.42 N	105.07 E
Chauhtan, India	70	F3	25.29 N	71.04 E
Chauk, Mya.	64	B2	20.53 N	94.49 E
Chaukhandi, India	190a		28.37 N	77.24 E
Chaumes-en-Brie, Fr.	179		48.40 N	2.51 E
Chaumont, Fr.	20	F13	48.06 N	5.08 E
Chaumua, India	190b		22.39 N	88.33 E
Chauncey, Oh., U.S.	124	E3	39.23 N	82.07 W
Chaungwabyin, Mya.	64	F4	13.40 N	98.22 E
Chaungzon, Mya.	64	D3	16.22 N	97.32 E
Chauny, Fr.	20	E12	49.37 N	3.13 E
Chaupāran, India	70	F10	24.22 N	85.15 E
Chautārā, Nepal	70	E10	27.45 N	85.42 E
Chautauqua Lake, l., N.Y., U.S.	124	B6	42.12 N	79.26 W
Chauvin, Ab., Can.	142	B3	52.42 N	110.05 W
Chauvin, La., U.S.	134	H8	29.26 N	90.36 W
Chauvry, Fr.	179		49.03 N	2.16 E
Chavakkad, India	69	F2	10.32 N	76.05 E
Chaval, Braz.	170	B5	3.02 S	41.15 W
Chavannes, Lac, l., Qc., Can.	126	B12	46.51 N	77.10 W
Chavarría, Arg.	172	D8	28.57 S	58.33 W
Chavarría, Peru	204d		12.01 S	77.05 W
Chavenay, Fr.	179		48.51 N	1.59 E
Chavenay-Villepreux, Aérodrome de, arpt., Fr.	179		48.51 N	1.58 E
Chaves, Port.	28	C3	41.44 N	7.27 W
Chaville, Fr.	179		48.48 N	2.10 E
Cháviva, Col.	168	E5	4.21 N	72.18 W
Chavuma, Zam.	88	C3	13.04 S	22.41 E
Chawa'nanake, China	70	C12	31.34 N	89.38 E
Chawang, Thai.	64	H4	8.25 N	99.30 E
Chay, stm., Viet.	64	A7	21.38 N	105.11 E
Chayuan, China	58	G9	29.18 N	121.34 E
Chazy, N.Y., U.S.	126	D16	44.54 N	73.25 W
Chbar, stm., Camb.	64	F8	13.18 N	107.05 E
Cheadle Hulme, Eng., U.K.	180		53.22 N	2.12 W
Cheaha Mountain, mtn., Al., U.S.	134	D13	33.30 N	85.47 W
Cheakamus Indian Reserve, ind. res., B.C., Can.	144	G7	49.47 N	123.15 W
Cheam, ngh., Eng., U.K.	178		51.21 N	0.13 W
Cheat, stm., U.S.	124	E6	39.44 N	79.54 W
Cheat, Shavers Fork see Shavers Fork, stm., W.V., U.S.	124	F6	39.05 N	79.41 W
Cheb, Czech Rep.	24	F8	50.04 N	12.22 E
Chebacco Lake, l., Ma., U.S.	201		42.37 N	70.48 W
Chebanse, Il., U.S.	130	D9	41.00 N	87.54 W
Chebogue Point, c., N.S., Can.	122	G10	43.44 N	66.07 W
Cheboygan, Mi., U.S.	126	C5	45.38 N	84.29 W
Chech, 'Erg, des., Afr.	84	E4	24.42 N	2.30 W
Chechel'nyk, Ukr.	38	E8	48.13 N	29.22 E
Chechnya see Čečnja, state, Russia	42	D11	43.20 N	45.45 E
Chech'on, Kor., S.	54	F8	37.08 N	128.12 E
Chęciny, Pol.	24	F16	50.48 N	20.28 E
Checleset Bay, b., B.C., Can.	144	F3	50.03 N	127.40 W
Checotah, Ok., U.S.	134	B3	35.28 N	95.31 W
Chedabucto Bay, b., N.S., Can.	122	E15	45.23 N	61.10 W
Cheddar, Eng., U.K.	10	J10	51.16 N	2.47 W
Cheduba Island, i., Mya.	64	C1	18.48 N	93.38 E
Cheduba Strait, strt., Mya.	64	C1	18.56 N	93.45 E
Cheektowaga, N.Y., U.S.	124	B7	42.54 N	78.44 W
Cheepie, Austl.	98	F5	26.38 S	145.01 E
Cheesequake, N.J., U.S.	194		40.25 N	74.17 W
Cheesequake Creek, stm., N.J., U.S.	194		40.28 N	74.16 W
Cheesequake State Park, p.o.i., N.J., U.S.	194		40.26 N	74.16 W
Cheetham Hill, ngh., Eng., U.K.	180		53.31 N	2.15 W
Chef-Boutonne, Fr.	22	C5	46.07 N	0.04 W
Chefoo see Yantai, China	58	C9	37.32 N	121.21 E
Chehalis, Wa., U.S.	146	D4	46.39 N	122.57 W
Chehalis, stm., Wa., U.S.	146	D3	46.57 N	123.50 W
Chehe, China	58	I2	25.00 N	107.38 E
Cheiron, Cime du, mtn., Fr.	22	F12	43.49 N	6.58 E
Cheju, Kor., S.	54	H7	33.30 N	126.31 E
Cheju-do (Quelpart Island), i., Kor., S.	54	H7	33.22 N	126.29 E
Chekiang see Zhejiang, state, China	52	F8	29.00 N	120.00 E
Chek Jawa, Tanjong, c., Sing.	189c		1.24 N	104.00 E
Chek Kang, China	189d		22.26 N	114.21 E
Chela, Serra da, mts., Ang.	88	D1	15.52 S	13.30 E
Chelan, Wa., U.S.	136	C6	47.50 N	120.00 W
Chelan, Lake, res., Wa., U.S.	146	B6	48.05 N	120.29 W
Chelas, ngh., Port.	184c		38.45 N	9.07 W
Cheleiros, Port.	184c		38.53 N	9.20 W
Cheleiros, Ribeira de, stm., Port.	184c		38.54 N	9.22 W
Chelford, Eng., U.K.	180		53.16 N	2.16 W
Chéliff, Oued, stm., Alg.	84	B5	36.02 N	0.08 E
Chelles-le-Pin, Aérodrome de, arpt., Fr.	179		48.55 N	2.35 E
Chelm, Pol.	24	E19	51.08 N	23.29 E
Chelmer and Blackwater Navigation, can., Eng., U.K.	178		51.44 N	0.43 E
Chelmno, Pol.	24	C14	53.20 N	18.26 E
Chelmorton, Eng., U.K.	180		53.13 N	1.50 W
Chelmsford, On., Can.	126	B8	46.33 N	81.11 W
Chelmsford, Eng., U.K.	10	J13	51.44 N	0.28 E
Chelmsford, mun., Eng., U.K.	178		51.44 N	0.30 E
Chelmża, Pol.	24	C14	53.10 N	18.36 E
Chelsea, Ia., U.S.	130	C5	41.55 N	92.23 W
Chelsea, Mi., U.S.	124	B1	42.19 N	84.01 W
Chelsea, Ok., U.S.	130	H2	36.32 N	95.25 W
Chelsea, Pa., U.S.	203		39.52 N	75.28 W
Chelsea, Vt., U.S.	122	F4	43.59 N	72.27 W
Chelsfield, ngh., Eng., U.K.	178		51.21 N	0.08 E
Cheltenham, Austl.	192a		33.46 S	151.05 E
Cheltenham, Austl.	192b		37.58 S	145.03 E
Cheltenham, Eng., U.K.	10	J10	51.54 N	2.04 W
Chelva see Xelva, Spain	28	E9	39.45 N	0.59 W
Chelvand, Iran	74	A11	38.18 N	48.51 E
Chelyuskin, Cape see Čeljuskin, mys, c., Russia	50	A9	77.45 N	104.20 E
Chemainus, B.C., Can.	144	H7	48.55 N	123.42 W
Chemba, Moz.	88	D5	17.07 S	34.51 E
Chembūr, ngh., India	190c		19.04 N	72.54 E
Chemer, Ukr.	38	B10	51.05 N	31.13 E
Chemerivtsi, Ukr.	38	E5	49.00 N	26.20 E
Chemillé, Fr.	20	G8	47.12 N	0.43 W
Chemnitz, Ger.	24	F8	50.49 N	12.55 E
Chemulpo see Inch'ŏn, Kor., S.	54	F7	37.28 N	126.38 E
Chemult, Or., U.S.	146	G5	43.12 N	121.46 W
Chena, Cerro, mtn., Chile	204e		33.36 S	70.45 W
Chenāb, stm., Asia	70	D3	29.21 N	71.01 E
Chenachane, Alg.	84	D4	26.01 N	4.12 W
Chenango, stm., N.Y., U.S.	124	B10	42.05 N	75.55 W
Chendauli, ngh., India	190c		19.07 N	72.54 E
Chenderoh, Tasik, l., Malay.	64	J5	4.59 N	100.58 E
Chénéville, Qc., Can.	126	C14	45.52 N	75.02 W
Cheney, Ks., U.S.	138	D11	37.37 N	97.46 W
Cheney, Wa., U.S.	146	C9	47.28 N	117.34 W
Cheney Reservoir, res., Ks., U.S.	138	D10	37.45 N	97.50 W
Cheneyville, La., U.S.	134	F6	31.00 N	92.17 W
Chengbu, China	58	H4	26.18 N	110.13 E
Chengchow see Zhengzhou, China	58	D5	34.45 N	113.38 E
Chengde, China	58	A7	40.58 N	117.56 E
Chengdu, China	52	E5	30.39 N	104.04 E
Chenggu, China	58	E2	33.09 N	107.23 E
Chenghai, China	58	J7	23.29 N	116.47 E
Chengkou, China	58	F3	31.56 N	108.39 E
Chengmai, China	58	L3	19.45 N	110.00 E
Chengshan Jiao, c., China	58	C10	37.24 N	122.42 E
Chengteh see Chengde, China	58	A7	40.58 N	117.56 E
Ch'engtzuliao, Tai.	187d		25.06 N	121.27 E
Chengxian, China	58	E1	33.43 N	105.41 E
Chengyang, China	58	G7	29.57 N	119.44 E
Chengzitan, China	58	B10	39.32 N	122.30 E
Chen Hu, l., China	58	F5	30.39 N	113.40 E
Chenies, Eng., U.K.	178		51.41 N	0.32 W
Chenjiahe, China	58	G3	29.28 N	109.59 E
Chenliu, China	58	D6	34.43 N	114.31 E
Chenlong, China	187b		31.17 N	121.25 E
Chennai (Madras), India	69	E5	13.05 N	80.15 E
Chennevières, Fr.	179		49.00 N	2.07 E
Chennevières-lès-Louvres, Fr.	179		49.03 N	2.33 E
Chenoa, Il., U.S.	130	D9	40.44 N	88.42 W
Chentang, China	58	J4	23.52 N	110.40 E
Chenxi, China	58	H3	27.51 N	109.59 E
Chenxian see Chenzhou, China	58	I5	25.48 N	112.59 E
Chenxiangtun, China	54	D5	41.35 N	123.29 E
Chenyang see Shenyang, China	52	C9	41.48 N	123.27 E
Chenzhou, China	58	I5	25.48 N	112.59 E
Cheonan see Ch'ŏnan, Kor., S.	54	F7	36.48 N	127.09 E
Cheongju see Ch'ŏngju, Kor., S.	54	F7	36.38 N	127.29 E
Chepén, Peru	164	E2	7.13 S	79.24 W
Chepes, Arg.	172	E4	31.20 S	66.36 W
Chepil', Ukr.	38	D15	49.19 N	36.56 E
Chepkotet, mtn., Kenya	86	D7	1.15 N	35.26 E
Chepo, Pan.	156	H8	9.10 N	79.05 W
Cheptainville, Fr.	179		48.33 N	2.16 E
Cher, state, Fr.	22	B8	47.05 N	2.30 E
Cher, stm., Fr.	22	B7	47.20 N	0.28 E
Cheradi, Isole, i., Italy	32	D11	40.27 N	17.09 E
Cheraw, S.C., U.S.	132	B6	34.41 N	79.53 W
Cheraw State Park, p.o.i., S.C., U.S.	132	B5	34.36 N	79.55 W
Cherbourg, Fr.	20	E7	49.38 N	1.37 W
Cherchell, Alg.	28	H13	36.36 N	2.12 E
Chère, stm., Fr.	20	G7	47.42 N	1.49 W
Cheremosh, stm., Ukr.	38	F3	48.23 N	25.37 E
Chérence, Fr.	179		49.05 N	1.41 E
Chergui, Chott ech, l., Alg.	84	C5	34.13 N	0.25 E
Cheribon see Cirebon, Indon.	66	G6	6.44 S	108.33 E
Cheriton, Va., U.S.	124	G10	37.16 N	75.57 W
Cheriyam Island, i., India	69	F1	10.08 N	73.39 E
Cherkas'ke, Ukr.	38	E16	48.50 N	37.23 E
Cherkas'ke, Ukr.	38	E14	48.42 N	35.23 E
Cherkassy see Cherkasy, Ukr.	38	D11	49.26 N	32.04 E
Cherkasy, Ukr.	38	D11	49.26 N	32.04 E
Cherkasy, co., Ukr.	38	D10	49.30 N	31.30 E
Cherkessia see Karačaevo-Čerkesija, state, Russia	42	D9	44.00 N	42.00 E
Chernelytsia, Ukr.	38	E4	48.48 N	25.25 E
Cherniakhiv, Ukr.	38	C7	50.27 N	28.40 E
Chernihiv, Ukr.	38	B10	51.30 N	31.17 E
Chernihiv, co., Ukr.	38	B11	51.15 N	32.00 E
Chernihivka, Ukr.	38	F15	47.11 N	36.13 E
Chernivtsi, Ukr.	38	E7	48.32 N	28.07 E
Chernivtsi, Ukr.	38	E4	48.17 N	25.57 E
Chernivtsi, co., Ukr.	38	E4	43.30 N	26.00 E
Chernobyl see Chornobyl', Ukr.	38	B9	51.16 N	30.14 E
Cherokee, Al., U.S.	134	C11	34.45 N	87.57 W
Cherokee, Ia., U.S.	130	B2	42.45 N	95.33 W
Cherokee, Ks., U.S.	130	G3	37.20 N	94.48 W
Cherokee, Ok., U.S.	138	E10	36.45 N	98.21 W
Cherokee, Tx., U.S.	136	C9	30.59 N	98.42 W
Cherokee Lake, res., Tn., U.S.	124	H2	36.15 N	83.23 W
Cherokee Point, c., Bah.	132	J8	26.16 N	77.03 W
Cherokees, Lake O' The, res., Ok., U.S.	130	H3	36.37 N	94.49 W
Cherokee Sound, Bah.	132	J8	26.18 N	77.01 W
Cherokee Village, Ar., U.S.	130	H6	36.17 N	91.31 W
Cherrapunji, India	70	F13	25.12 N	91.42 E
Cherry Brook, stm., Ma., U.S.	201		42.23 N	71.17 W
Cherry Brook, stm., N.J., U.S.	194		41.01 N	74.00 W
Cherry City, Pa., U.S.	197b		40.29 N	79.58 W
Cherry Creek, stm., Az., U.S.	150	J6	33.40 N	110.48 W
Cherry Creek, stm., Co., U.S.	138	B4	39.44 N	105.00 W
Cherry Creek, stm., Mt., U.S.	142	H8	46.48 N	105.15 W
Cherry Creek, stm., N.D., U.S.	142	G10	47.40 N	103.02 W
Cherry Creek, stm., S.D., U.S.	140	C11	44.35 N	101.29 W
Cherry Creek, stm., Tx., U.S.	136	C4	31.14 N	103.32 W
Cherry Hill, Il., U.S.	196		41.32 N	88.02 W
Cherry Hill, N.J., U.S.	124	E10	39.56 N	75.01 W
Cherry Hill, ngh., Md., U.S.	202b		39.15 N	76.38 W
Cherry Hill Mall, shp. cen., N.J., U.S.	203		39.56 N	75.02 W
Cherry Island, i., De., U.S.	203		39.43 N	75.31 W
Cherry Lane, Pa., U.S.	197b		40.34 N	79.33 W
Cherry Point Marine Corps Air Station, mil., N.C., U.S.	132	B9	34.54 N	76.54 W
Cherryvale, Ks., U.S.	130	G2	37.16 N	95.33 W
Cherry Valley, Ar., U.S.	134	B8	35.24 N	90.45 W
Cherryville, N.C., U.S.	132	A4	35.22 N	81.22 W
Cherrywood, On., Can.	193b		43.52 N	79.08 W
Cherskiy Mountains see Čerskogo, hrebet, mts., Russia	50	C17	65.00 N	144.00 E
Chervona Kam'ianka, Ukr.	38	E12	48.38 N	33.27 E
Chervone, Ukr.	38	D7	49.58 N	28.52 E
Chervone, Ukr.	38	B13	51.46 N	34.04 E
Chervonoarmiis'k, Ukr.	38	C7	50.28 N	28.16 E
Chervonoarmiis'ke, Ukr.	38	H7	45.47 N	28.45 E
Chervonohrad, Ukr.	38	C3	50.23 N	24.13 E
Chervonooskil's'ke vodoskhovyshche, res., Ukr.	38	D16	49.23 N	37.34 E
Chervonopartyzans'k, Ukr.	40	G11	48.04 N	39.48 E
Chervonyi Donets', Ukr.	38	D15	49.30 N	36.34 E
Chervonyi Perekop, Ukr.	38	G12	46.40 N	33.47 E
Chesaco Park, Md., U.S.	202b		39.19 N	76.30 W
Chesaning, Mi., U.S.	126	E5	43.10 N	84.07 W
Chesapeake, Va., U.S.	124	H9	36.48 N	76.16 W
Chesapeake Bay, b., U.S.	124	G9	38.38 N	76.26 W
Chesapeake Bay Bridge-Tunnel, trans., Va., U.S.	124	H10	37.01 N	76.04 W
Chesapeake Beach, Md., U.S.	124	F9	38.40 N	76.32 W
Chesaw, Wa., U.S.	146	B7	48.56 N	119.03 W
Chesdin, Lake, res., Va., U.S.	124	G8	37.15 N	77.39 W
Chesha Bay see Češskaja guba, b., Russia	12	C21	67.30 N	46.30 E
Chesham Bois, Eng., U.K.	178		51.41 N	0.37 W
Cheshire, Ma., U.S.	124	B12	42.33 N	73.10 W
Chesilhurst, N.J., U.S.	203		39.43 N	74.52 W
Cheslatta Lake, l., B.C., Can.	144	C5	53.44 N	125.18 W
Chesley, On., Can.	126	D8	44.17 N	81.05 W
Chesnee, S.C., U.S.	132	A4	35.08 N	81.52 W
Chess, stm., Eng., U.K.	178		51.38 N	0.27 W
Chessington, ngh., Eng., U.K.	178		51.21 N	0.18 W
Chessy, Fr.	179		48.53 N	2.46 E
Chest Creek, stm., Pa., U.S.	124	D7	40.52 N	78.43 W
Chester, Eng., U.K.	10	H10	53.12 N	2.53 W
Chester, Ca., U.S.	148	C4	40.17 N	121.13 W
Chester, Il., U.S.	130	G8	37.54 N	89.49 W
Chester, Mt., U.S.	146	B15	48.32 N	110.56 W
Chester, Ne., U.S.	138	A11	40.00 N	97.37 W
Chester, Ok., U.S.	138	E10	36.12 N	98.55 W
Chester, Pa., U.S.	124	E10	39.51 N	75.21 W
Chester, S.C., U.S.	132	B4	34.42 N	81.12 W
Chester, Vt., U.S.	122	G4	43.15 N	72.35 W
Chester, Va., U.S.	124	G8	37.21 N	77.25 W
Chester, mun., Eng., U.K.	180		53.16 N	2.52 W
Chester Basin, N.S., Can.	122	F12	44.34 N	64.15 W
Chesterbrook, Va., U.S.	202c		38.55 N	77.09 W
Chester Brook, stm., Ma., U.S.	201		42.23 N	71.14 W
Chesterbrook Woods, Va., U.S.	202c		38.56 N	77.08 W
Chester Creek, East Branch, stm., Pa., U.S.	203		39.56 N	75.32 W
Chester Creek, West Branch, stm., Pa., U.S.	203		39.54 N	75.27 W
Chesterfield, Eng., U.K.	10	H11	53.14 N	1.25 W
Chesterfield, S.C., U.S.	132	B5	34.44 N	80.05 W
Chesterfield, Îles, is., N. Cal.	94	E6	19.30 S	158.00 E
Chesterfield Inlet, Nu., Can.	110	C12	63.21 N	90.43 W
Chesterfield Inlet, b., Nu., Can.	110	C12	63.25 N	90.45 W
Chesterfield Islands see Chesterfield, Îles, is., N. Cal.	94	E6	19.30 S	158.00 E
Chester Heights, Pa., U.S.	203		39.53 N	75.28 W
Chester Hill, Austl.	192a		33.53 S	151.00 E
Chesterhill, Oh., U.S.	124	E4	39.29 N	81.52 W
Chester Island, i., N.J., U.S.	203		39.50 N	75.21 W
Chester-le-Street, Eng., U.K.	10	G11	54.51 N	1.35 W
Chester Springs, Pa., U.S.	203		40.06 N	75.37 W
Chesterton, In., U.S.	130	C10	41.36 N	87.02 W
Chesterton Range, mts., Austl.	98	E6	25.30 S	147.27 E
Chestertown, Md., U.S.	124	E9	39.12 N	76.04 W
Chesterville, On., Can.	126	C14	45.07 N	75.14 W
Chestnut Hill, Ma., U.S.	201		42.20 N	71.10 W
Chestnut Hill, ngh., Pa., U.S.	203		40.04 N	75.13 W
Chestnut Hill, hill, Pa., U.S.	203		40.13 N	75.45 W
Chestnut Hill Estates, De., U.S.	203		39.40 N	75.42 W
Chestnut Hill Reservoir, res., Ma., U.S.	201		42.20 N	71.10 W
Chestnut Ridge Park, p.o.i., N.Y., U.S.	202a		42.43 N	78.46 W
Chesuncook Lake, l., Me., U.S.	122	E7	45.59 N	69.20 W
Chetco, stm., Or., U.S.	148	A1	42.02 N	124.16 W
Chetek, Wi., U.S.	128	F7	45.18 N	91.39 W
Chéticamp, N.S., Can.	122	D16	46.38 N	60.58 W
Chetopa, Ks., U.S.	130	G2	37.02 N	95.05 W
Chettlatt Island, i., India	62	F3	11.41 N	72.42 E
Chetumal, Mex.	156	C3	18.29 N	88.17 W
Chetumal, Bahía, b., N.A.	152	D7	18.38 N	88.05 W
Chetumal, Bahía, b., N.A.	156	C3	18.38 N	88.05 W
Cheung Chau, i., China	189d		22.12 N	114.01 E
Cheung Shue Tan, China	189d		22.26 N	114.12 E
Chevannes, Fr.	179		48.32 N	2.27 E
Chevelon Creek, stm., Az., U.S.	150	I6	34.57 N	110.31 W
Chevening, Eng., U.K.	178		51.18 N	0.08 E
Cheverly, Md., U.S.	202c		38.55 N	76.54 W
Chevilly-Larue, Fr.	179		48.46 N	2.21 E
Cheviot, Oh., U.S.	130	E13	39.09 N	84.36 W
Cheviot Hills, hills, U.K.	10	F10	55.22 N	2.22 W
Chèvreville, Fr.	179		49.07 N	2.51 E
Chevry-Cossigny, Fr.	179		48.43 N	2.40 E
Chevy Chase, Md., U.S.	202c		38.58 N	77.04 W
Chevy Chase View, Md., U.S.	202c		39.01 N	77.05 W
Chewaucan, stm., Or., U.S.	146	H6	42.31 N	120.16 W
Ch'ew Bahir see Stefanie, Lake, l., Afr.	82	G7	4.40 N	36.50 E
Chewelah, Wa., U.S.	146	B9	48.16 N	117.42 W
Chew Reservoir, res., Eng., U.K.	180		53.31 N	1.56 W
Chews Landing, N.J., U.S.	203		39.50 N	75.04 W
Cheyenne, Ok., U.S.	138	F9	35.37 N	99.40 W
Cheyenne, Wy., U.S.	140	F8	41.08 N	104.49 W
Cheyenne, stm., U.S.	140	C11	44.46 N	100.43 W
Cheyenne, Dry Fork, stm., Wy., U.S.	140	D7	43.25 N	105.03 W
Cheyenne River Indian Reservation, ind. res., S.D., U.S.	140	B11	45.00 N	100.40 W
Cheyenne Wells, Co., U.S.	138	C6	38.49 N	102.20 W
Cheyne Bay, b., Austl.	96	F3	34.34 S	118.46 E
Cheyney, Pa., U.S.	203		39.56 N	75.31 W
Cheyney University of Pennsylvania, educ., Pa., U.S.	203		39.56 N	75.32 W
Chhabra, India	70	F6	24.40 N	76.51 E
Chhajārsi, India	190a		28.38 N	77.23 E
Chhalera Bāngar, India	190a		28.33 N	77.20 E
Chhapra, India	70	F10	25.46 N	84.44 E
Chhātak, Bngl.	70	F13	25.02 N	91.40 E
Chhatarpur, India	70	F10	24.22 N	84.13 E
Chhatarpur, India	70	F7	24.55 N	79.36 E
Chhatrapur, India	62	E6	19.21 N	84.59 E
Chhattīsgarh, pl., India	70	H9	21.15 N	82.00 E
Chhay Arĕng, stm., Camb.	64	G6	11.27 N	103.06 E
Chhĕb Khândal, Camb.	64	F7	13.45 N	105.24 E
Chhināmor, India	190b		22.48 N	88.18 E
Chhindwāra, India	70	H7	22.03 N	78.57 E
Chhlong, stm., Camb.	64	F8	12.15 N	105.59 E
Chhota-Chhindwāra, India	70	G7	23.02 N	79.29 E
Chhota Udepur Mhow, India	62	D3	22.18 N	74.01 E
Chhukha Dzong, Bhu.	70	E12	27.08 N	89.32 E
Chi, stm., China	58	E7	32.51 N	117.59 E
Chi, stm., Thai.	64	E7	15.10 N	104.42 E
Chi, stm., Thai.	64	E6	15.17 N	103.30 E
Chía, Col.	168	E4	4.52 N	74.02 W
Chiai, Tai.	58	J9	23.28 N	120.26 E
Chianciano Terme, Italy	30	G8	43.02 N	11.48 E
Chiang Dao, Thai.	64	C4	19.22 N	98.58 E
Chiange, Ang.	88	D1	15.43 S	13.54 E
Chiang Kham, Thai.	64	C5	19.31 N	100.19 E
Chiang Khan, Thai.	64	D5	17.53 N	101.39 E
Chiang Khian, Thai.	64	C5	19.36 N	99.59 E
Chiang Mai, Thai.	64	C4	18.47 N	99.00 E
Chiang Rai, Thai.	64	C4	19.54 N	99.49 E
Chiang Saen, Thai.	64	B4	20.16 N	100.05 E
Chiani, stm., Italy	30	H9	42.43 N	12.07 E
Chiapa, Chile	166	C3	19.31 S	69.10 W
Chiapas, state, Mex.	152	D6	16.30 N	92.30 W
Chiargós, Grc.	185c		38.00 N	23.48 E
Chiasso, Switz.	30	E6	45.50 N	9.01 E
Chiavari, Italy	30	F6	44.19 N	9.19 E
Chiavenna, Italy	30	D6	46.19 N	9.23 E
Chiawelo, S. Afr.	191d		26.17 S	27.52 E
Chiba, Japan	56	D13	35.35 N	140.07 E
Chiba, state, Japan	56	D13	35.30 N	140.20 E
Chibabava, Moz.	90	B11	20.17 S	33.39 E
Chiba-kō, b., Japan	186		35.35 N	140.06 E
Chiba University, educ., Japan	186		35.38 N	140.06 E
Chibemba, Ang.	88	D1	15.45 S	14.05 E
Chibia, Ang.	88	D1	15.08 S	13.42 E
Chibougamau, Qc., Can.	114	B13	49.54 N	74.21 W
Chibuto, Moz.	90	D11	24.41 S	33.34 E
Chibuzhangchu Hu, l., China	70	B13	33.28 N	90.21 E
Chicago, Il., U.S.	130	C10	41.51 N	87.38 W
Chicago, Il., U.S.	196		41.51 N	87.39 W
Chicago, North Branch, West Fork, stm., Il., U.S.	196		42.03 N	87.54 W
Chicago, South Branch, stm., Il., U.S.	196		41.53 N	87.38 W
Chicago, University of, educ., Il., U.S.	196		41.47 N	87.36 W
Chicago Botanic Garden, p.o.i., Il., U.S.	196		42.09 N	87.47 W
Chicago Heights, Il., U.S.	130	C10	41.30 N	87.38 W
Chicago-Hinsdale Airport, arpt., Il., U.S.	196		41.46 N	87.56 W
Chicago Lawn, ngh., Il., U.S.	196		41.47 N	87.41 W
Chicago-O'Hare International Airport, arpt., Il., U.S.	196		41.59 N	87.54 W
Chicago Portage National Historic Site, hist., Il., U.S.	196		41.48 N	87.49 W
Chicapa, stm., Afr.	86	F4	6.24 S	20.47 E
Chic-Chocs, Monts, mts., Qc., Can.	122	B10	48.55 N	66.00 W
Chichagof Island, i., Ak., U.S.	109	E12	57.06 N	135.11 W
Chichas, Cordillera de, mts., Bol.	166	D3	20.32 S	66.14 W
Chīchāwatni, Pak.	70	C4	30.32 N	72.42 E
Chicheng, China	58	A6	40.54 N	115.46 E
Chichén Itzá, hist., Mex.	156	B3	20.40 N	88.35 W
Chichester, Eng., U.K.	10	K12	50.50 N	0.47 W
Chichibu, Japan	56	C12	35.59 N	139.05 E
Chichiriviche, Ven.	168	B7	10.55 N	68.16 W
Chickahominy, stm., Va., U.S.	124	G8	37.13 N	76.53 W
Chickamauga, Ga., U.S.	134	C13	34.52 N	85.17 W
Chickamauga Lake, res., Tn., U.S.	134	B14	35.22 N	85.02 W
Chickasaw, Al., U.S.	134	G10	30.45 N	88.04 W
Chickasaw Bogue, stm., Al., U.S.	134	E11	32.17 N	87.55 W
Chickasawhatchee Creek, stm., Ga., U.S.	134	F14	31.19 N	84.29 W
Chickasawhay, stm., Ms., U.S.	134	F10	31.00 N	88.45 W
Chickasaw National Recreation Area, p.o.i., Ok., U.S.	134	C2	34.25 N	96.59 W
Chickasaw State Park, p.o.i., Tn., U.S.	134	B10	35.24 N	88.51 W
Chickasha, Ok., U.S.	138	F11	35.02 N	97.57 W
Chicken, Ak., U.S.	109	D11	64.04 N	141.54 W
Chicken Brook, stm., Ma., U.S.	201		42.08 N	71.25 W
Chiclana de la Frontera, Spain	28	H4	36.25 N	6.08 W
Chiclayo, Peru	164	E2	6.46 S	79.50 W
Chico, Ca., U.S.	148	D4	39.44 N	121.48 W
Chico, Tx., U.S.	138	H11	33.17 N	97.47 W
Chico, stm., Arg.	166	I2	49.52 S	68.34 W
Chico, stm., Arg.	166	I3	43.48 S	66.25 W
Chico, stm., Cuba	204b		23.02 N	82.17 W
Chico, stm., Phil.	68	B3	17.57 N	121.36 E
Chico Creek, stm., Co., U.S.	138	C4	38.14 N	104.21 W
Chicomba, Ang.	88	C2	14.08 S	14.54 E
Chicomo, Moz.	90	D12	24.30 S	34.14 E
Chicomuselo, Mex.	154	H12	15.44 N	92.17 W
Chiconautla, Cerro, mtn., Mex.	204a		19.39 N	98.58 W
Chicopee, Ga., U.S.	132	B2	34.15 N	83.50 W
Chicopee, Ma., U.S.	124	B13	42.08 N	72.36 W
Chicot, Lake, l., Ar., U.S.	134	D7	33.20 N	91.16 W
Chicot, Rivière du, stm., Qc., Can.	193a		45.35 N	73.51 W
Chicot State Park, p.o.i., La., U.S.	134	G6	30.47 N	92.19 W
Chicoutimi, Qc., Can.	122	B5	48.25 N	71.03 W
Chicoutimi, stm., Qc., Can.	122	B5	48.26 N	71.04 W
Chicuma, Ang.	88	C1	13.25 S	14.51 E
Chidambaram, India	69	F4	11.24 N	79.41 E
Chiddingstone Causeway, Eng., U.K.	178		51.12 N	0.10 E
Chidenguele, Moz.	90	D12	24.54 S	34.10 E
Chidralada Palace, bldg., Thai.	187a		13.46 N	100.32 E
Chief Justice William Cushing Memorial State Park, p.o.i., Ma., U.S.	201		42.10 N	70.45 W
Chiefland, Fl., U.S.	132	G3	29.28 N	82.51 W
Chiemsee, l., Ger.	24	I8	47.53 N	12.26 E
Chien, Bayou de, stm., Ky., U.S.	130	H9	36.34 N	89.11 W
Chiens, Rivière aux, stm., Qc., Can.	193a		45.39 N	73.46 W
Chienti, stm., Italy	30	G10	43.17 N	13.44 E
Chieo Lan Reservoir, res., Thai.	64	H4	9.04 N	98.38 E
Chieri, Italy	30	F4	45.01 N	7.49 E
Chiese, stm., Italy	30	E7	45.09 N	10.26 E
Chieti, Italy	30	H11	42.20 N	14.10 E
Chifeng, China	52	C8	42.15 N	118.57 E
Chigasaki, Japan	56	D12	35.18 N	139.24 E
Chignahuapan, Mex.	154	F9	19.50 N	98.02 W
Chignall Saint James, Eng., U.K.	178		51.46 N	0.25 E
Chignall Smealy, Eng., U.K.	178		51.47 N	0.25 E
Chignecto, Cape, c., N.S., Can.	122	E11	45.20 N	64.55 W
Chignecto Bay, b., Can.	122	E12	45.35 N	64.45 W
Chignik, Ak., U.S.	109	E8	56.17 N	158.22 W
Chigorodó, Col.	168	D3	7.40 N	76.41 W
Chigoubiche, Lac, l., Qc., Can.	122	A3	49.05 N	73.32 W
Chigubo, Moz.	90	C11	22.52 S	33.30 E
Chigu Co, l., China	70	D13	28.40 N	91.40 E
Chigwell Row, Eng., U.K.	178		51.37 N	0.07 E
Chihaya-akasaka, Japan	188		34.24 N	135.38 E
Chihaya Castle, hist., Japan	188		34.24 N	135.40 E
Chihli, Gulf of see Bo Hai, b., China	58	B8	38.29 N	120.01 E
Ch'ihsing Shan, mtn., Tai.	187d		25.10 N	121.33 E
Chihuahua, Mex.	154	A5	28.38 N	106.05 W
Chihuahua, state, Mex.	152	B3	28.30 N	106.00 W
Chihuahua, Desierto de, des., N.A.	120	G10	30.00 N	105.00 W
Chihuahuan Desert (Chihuahua, Desierto de), des., N.A.	136	B1	30.00 N	105.00 W
Chii-san, mtn., Kor., S.	54	G7	35.20 N	127.44 E
Chikaskia, stm., U.S.	138	E11	36.37 N	97.15 W
Chik Ballāpur, India	69	E3	13.26 N	77.44 E
Chikhli, India	70	H6	20.20 N	76.15 E
Chikindzonot, Mex.	156	B3	20.20 N	88.29 W
Chikmagalūr, India	69	E2	13.18 N	75.46 E
Chiknāyakanhalli, India	69	E3	13.24 N	76.37 E
Chikodi, India	69	C2	16.25 N	74.34 E
Chikrêng, stm., Camb.	64	F7	12.52 N	104.14 E

Name Page Map Ref. Latitude Longitude

Chikugo, stm., Japan 56 F3 33.08 N 130.21 E
Chikujō-kichi, Kōkū-jieitai-, mil., Japan 56 F4 33.41 N 131.03 E
Chikuma, stm., Japan 56 C11 36.59 N 138.35 E
Chi-kyaw, Mya. 64 B1 20.17 N 93.54 E
Chilakalūrupet, India 69 C4 16.05 N 80.10 E
Chilako, stm., B.C., Can. 144 C6 53.52 N 122.58 W
Chilanko Forks, B.C., Can. 144 D6 52.06 N 124.10 W
Chilapa de Álvarez, Mex. 154 G9 17.36 N 99.10 W
Chilās, Pak. 62 A3 35.25 N 74.03 E
Chilaw, Sri L. 69 H4 7.34 N 79.48 E
Chilcotin, stm., B.C., Can. 144 E8 51.44 N 122.24 W
Childers, Austl. 98 E9 25.14 S 152.16 E
Childersburg, Al., U.S. 134 D12 33.16 N 86.21 W
Childer Thornton, Eng., U.K. 180 53.17 N 2.57 W
Childress, Tx., U.S. 138 G8 34.25 N 100.12 W
Chile, ctry., S.A. 166 F2 30.00 S 71.00 W
Chile, Hipódromo, p.o.i., Chile 204e 33.24 S 70.41 W
Chile, Universidad de, educ., Chile 204e 33.27 S 70.40 W
Chile Chico, Chile 166 I2 46.33 S 71.44 W
Chilecito, Arg. 172 F3 33.52 S 69.04 W
Chilecito, Arg. 172 D4 29.10 S 67.30 W
Chileno, Arroyo, stm., Ur. 206 34.22 S 57.54 W
Chile Rise, unds. 176 M5 40.00 S 90.00 W
Chilhowie, Va., U.S. 124 H4 36.48 N 81.40 W
Chilia, Brațul, stm., Eur. 36 D16 45.23 N 29.35 E
Chilika Lake, l., India 70 I10 19.45 N 85.25 E
Chililabombwe, Zam. 88 C4 12.21 S 27.49 E
Chilko, stm., B.C., Can. 144 E7 52.05 N 123.27 W
Chilko Lake, l., B.C., Can. 144 E6 51.16 N 124.04 W
Chilko Lake Indian Reserve, ind. res., B.C., Can. 144 E6 51.25 N 124.07 W
Chillagoe, Austl. 96 C8 17.08 S 144.31 E
Chillán, Chile 172 H1 36.36 S 72.07 W
Chillar, Arg. 172 H7 37.18 S 59.59 W
Chilla Saroda, ngh., India 190a 28.36 N 77.18 E
Chillicothe, Il., U.S. 130 D8 40.55 N 89.28 W
Chillicothe, Mo., U.S. 130 E4 39.47 N 93.33 W
Chillicothe, Oh., U.S. 124 E3 39.19 N 82.58 W
Chillicothe, Tx., U.S. 138 G9 34.15 N 99.30 W
Chilliwack, B.C., Can. 144 G9 49.09 N 121.57 W
Chillón, Peru 204d 11.55 S 77.05 W
Chillon, Château de, hist., Switz. 30 D3 46.25 N 6.56 E
Chillum, Md., U.S. 202c 38.58 N 76.59 W
Chilly-Mazarin, Fr. 179 48.42 N 2.19 E
Chiloé, Isla Grande de, i., Chile 166 H2 42.30 S 73.55 W
Chilón, Mex. 154 G12 17.14 N 92.25 W
Chiloquin, Or., U.S. 146 H5 42.34 N 121.52 W
Chilpancingo de los Bravo, Mex. 154 G9 17.33 N 99.30 W
Chilston Park, p.o.i., Eng., U.K. 178 51.12 N 0.42 E
Chiltern, mun., Eng., U.K. 178 51.40 N 0.37 W
Chilton, Wi., U.S. 126 D1 44.01 N 88.09 W
Chiluage, Ang. 88 B3 9.31 S 21.47 E
Chilumba, Mwi. 88 C5 10.26 S 34.12 E
Chilung, Tai. 58 I9 25.07 N 121.43 E
Chilung, stm., Tai. 187d 25.07 N 121.27 E
Chilung Kang, b., Tai. 187d 25.09 N 121.45 E
Chilung Shih, mun., Tai. 187d 25.08 N 121.45 E
Chilwa, Lake, l., Afr. 88 D6 15.23 S 35.41 E
Chimaltenango, Guat. 156 E2 14.39 N 90.49 W
Chimán, Pan. 156 H8 8.42 N 78.37 W
Chimayo, N.M., U.S. 138 E3 36.00 N 105.58 W
Chimbarongo, Chile 172 G2 34.41 S 71.02 W
Chimbas, Arg. 172 E3 31.29 S 68.32 W
Chimborazo, state, Ec. 168 H2 2.00 S 78.40 W
Chimborazo, vol., Ec. 168 H2 1.28 S 78.48 W
Chimbote, Peru 164 E2 9.04 S 78.35 W
Chimichagua, Col. 168 C5 9.15 N 73.49 W
Chimney Dam Reservoir, res., Nv., U.S. 148 B8 41.24 N 117.10 W
Chimney Rock National Historic Site, p.o.i., Ne., U.S. 140 F9 41.39 N 103.20 W
Chimoio, Moz. 88 D5 19.09 S 33.29 E
Chimon Island, i., Ct., U.S. 194 41.04 N 73.23 W
Chimpay, Arg. 166 G3 39.10 S 66.08 W
Chin, state, Mya. 64 B1 21.29 N 93.18 E
China, Mex. 154 C9 25.42 N 99.14 W
China, ctry., Asia 44 F14 35.00 N 105.00 E
China, Tanjong, c., Sing. 189c 1.14 N 103.51 E
China Grove, N.C., U.S. 132 A5 35.34 N 80.34 W
China Lake, l., Ca., U.S. 148 H8 35.43 N 117.37 W
China Lake Naval Weapons Center, mil., Ca., U.S. 148 H8 35.35 N 117.10 W
Chinandega, Nic. 156 F4 12.37 N 87.07 W
China Sea see South China Sea, s., Asia 46 I15 10.00 N 113.00 E
Chinati Peak, mtn., Tx., U.S. 136 E3 29.57 N 104.29 W
Chinatown, ngh., Ca., U.S. 200 37.48 N 122.26 W
Chincha Alta, Peru 164 F2 13.25 S 76.08 W
Chinchaga, stm., Can. 110 D7 58.52 N 118.18 W
Chinchilla, Austl. 98 F8 26.44 S 150.37 E
Chinchilla de Monte-Aragón, Spain 28 F9 38.55 N 1.43 W
Chinchiná, Col. 168 E4 4.58 N 75.36 W
Chincholi, India 190c 19.10 N 73.08 E
Chinchón, Spain 28 D7 40.08 N 3.25 W
Chinchorro, Banco, unds., Mex. 152 D7 18.35 N 87.22 W
Chinchow see Jinzhou, China 58 A9 41.07 N 121.08 E
Chincolco, Chile 172 F2 32.12 S 70.49 W
Chincoteague, Va., U.S. 124 G10 37.55 N 75.22 W
Chinde, Moz. 88 D6 18.37 S 36.25 E
Chindo, Kor., S. 54 G7 34.27 N 126.16 E
Chin-do, i., Kor., S. 54 G7 34.26 N 126.14 E
Chindong, Kor., S. 56 D1 35.07 N 128.29 E
Chindwinn, stm., Mya. 62 D7 21.24 N 95.15 E
Chinese Cemetery, misc. cult., Phil. 187f 14.38 N 120.59 E
Chinese University, educ., China 189d 22.26 N 114.12 E
Chingarora Creek, stm., N.J., U.S. 194 40.27 N 74.12 W
Chingford, ngh., Eng., U.K. 178 51.38 N 0.01 E
Chingleput, India 69 E4 12.41 N 79.58 E
Chingmei, ngh., Tai. 187d 24.59 N 121.32 E
Chingola, Zam. 88 C4 12.32 S 27.51 E
Ch'ing'tung, Tai. 187d 25.02 N 121.43 E
Chinguetti, Maur. 84 E2 20.31 N 12.23 W
Chingune, Moz. 90 B12 20.37 S 34.53 E
Chinhae, Kor., S. 56 D1 35.08 N 128.40 E
Chinhae-man, b., Kor., S. 56 D1 35.01 N 128.34 E
Chin Hills, hills, Mya. 62 D7 22.30 N 93.30 E
Chinhoyi, Zimb. 88 D5 17.21 S 30.11 E
Chīni, India 70 C7 31.31 N 78.16 E
Chiniot, Pak. 70 C4 31.42 N 72.59 E
Chinīt, stm., Camb. 64 F7 13.02 N 105.35 E
Chinjan, Pak. 70 C1 30.33 N 67.59 E
Chinju, Kor., S. 54 G7 35.10 N 128.05 E
Chinkiang see Zhenjiang, China 58 E8 32.12 N 119.25 E
Chinko, stm., C.A.R. 86 C4 4.50 N 23.53 E
Chinle, Az., U.S. 150 G7 36.09 N 109.32 W
Chinle Creek, stm., U.S. 150 F7 37.12 N 109.42 W
Chinle Wash, stm., Az., U.S. 150 G7 36.53 N 109.43 W
Chinley, Eng., U.K. 180 53.20 N 1.56 W
Chinley Churn, hill, Eng., U.K. 180 53.21 N 1.57 W
Chinmen Tao (Quemoy), i., Tai. 58 I8 24.27 N 118.23 E
Chinnampo see Namp'o, Kor., N. 54 E6 38.45 N 125.23 E
Chino, Ca., U.S. 148 J8 34.00 N 117.41 W
Chino Airport, arpt., Ca., U.S. 198 33.59 N 117.38 W
Chino Creek, stm., Ca., U.S. 198 33.53 N 117.38 W
Chino Hills, hills, Ca., U.S. 198 33.56 N 117.45 W
Chinon, Fr. 20 G9 47.10 N 0.14 E
Chinook, Ab., Can. 142 C2 51.27 N 110.56 W
Chinook, Mt., U.S. 146 B17 48.35 N 109.13 W
Chinook Cove, B.C., Can. 144 E10 51.14 N 120.10 W
Chino Valley, Az., U.S. 150 I4 34.45 N 112.27 W
Chinquapin, N.C., U.S. 132 B8 34.49 N 77.49 W
Chinsali, Zam. 88 C5 10.32 S 32.04 E
Chintāmani, India 69 E4 13.23 N 78.03 E
Chinú, Col. 168 C4 9.05 N 75.23 W
Chinvali, Geor. 42 D10 42.11 N 43.58 E
Chinwangtao see Qinhuangdao, China 58 B8 39.56 N 119.36 E
Chioco, Moz. 88 D5 16.24 S 32.50 E
Chioggia, Italy 30 E9 45.13 N 12.16 E
Chíos, Grc. 34 E9 38.22 N 26.08 E
Chíos see Chíos, Grc. 34 E9 38.22 N 26.08 E
Chios see Khíos, Grc. 72 B2 38.22 N 26.08 E
Chíos, i., Grc. 34 E8 38.23 N 26.01 E
Chipata, Zam. 88 C5 13.37 S 32.38 E
Chiperceni, Mol. 38 F7 47.30 N 28.52 E
Chiperone, mtn., Moz. 88 D6 16.29 S 35.41 E
Chipinge, Zimb. 88 E5 20.12 S 32.36 E
Chip Lake, l., Ab., Can. 144 C15 53.39 N 115.23 W
Chipley, Fl., U.S. 134 G13 30.46 N 85.32 W
Chiplūn, India 69 C1 17.32 N 73.31 E
Chipman, N.B., Can. 122 D11 46.09 N 65.53 W
Chipola, stm., Fl., U.S. 134 G13 30.01 N 85.05 W
Chippawa, ngh., On., Can. 202a 43.04 N 79.03 W
Chippawa Channel, mth., N.A. 202a 43.04 N 79.01 W
Chippenham, Eng., U.K. 10 J10 51.27 N 2.07 W
Chipperfield, Eng., U.K. 178 51.42 N 0.29 W
Chippewa, stm., Mi., U.S. 126 E5 43.36 N 84.17 W
Chippewa, stm., Mn., U.S. 128 F3 44.56 N 95.44 W
Chippewa, stm., Wi., U.S. 128 G6 44.24 N 92.04 W
Chippewa, East Branch, stm., Mn., U.S. 128 F3 45.19 N 95.37 W
Chippewa, East Fork, stm., Wi., U.S. 128 F7 45.53 N 91.03 W
Chippewa, Lake, l., Wi., U.S. 112 B9 45.55 N 91.11 W
Chippewa Falls, Wi., U.S. 128 G7 44.56 N 91.22 W
Chipps Island, i., Ca., U.S. 200 38.03 N 121.55 W
Chipstead, Eng., U.K. 178 51.17 N 0.09 E
Chipstead, Eng., U.K. 178 51.18 N 0.10 W
Chiquimula, Guat. 156 E3 14.48 N 89.32 W
Chiquinquirá, Col. 168 E5 5.36 N 73.48 W
Chiquito, stm., Mex. 154 F8 18.31 N 101.05 W
Chirad, India 190c 19.09 N 73.07 E
Chirāgh Delhi, ngh., India 190a 28.32 N 77.14 E
Chīrāla, India 69 D5 15.49 N 80.21 E
Chirāwa, India 70 D5 28.14 N 75.38 E
Chire see Shire, stm., Afr. 88 D5 17.41 S 35.19 E
Chiredzi, Zimb. 90 B10 21.04 S 31.40 E
Chireno, Tx., U.S. 136 C13 31.29 N 94.20 W
Chirfa, Niger 84 E7 20.56 N 12.20 E
Chirgaon, India 70 F7 25.35 N 78.49 E
Chiribiquete, Parque Nacional, p.o.i., Col. 168 G5 0.45 N 72.58 W
Chiricahua Mountains, mts., Az., U.S. 150 L7 31.50 N 109.15 W
Chiricahua National Monument, p.o.i., Az., U.S. 150 K7 31.59 N 109.22 W
Chiricahua Peak, mtn., Az., U.S. 150 L7 31.52 N 109.20 W
Chiriguaná, Col. 168 C5 9.22 N 73.35 W
Chirikof Island, i., Ak., U.S. 109 E8 55.50 N 155.35 W
Chiriquí, Golfo de, b., Pan. 156 H6 8.04 N 82.05 W
Chiriquí, Laguna de, b., Pan. 156 H6 9.03 N 82.00 W
Chirle, India 190c 18.56 N 73.02 E
Chiromo, Mwi. 88 D5 16.33 S 35.08 E
Chirpan see Čirpan, Blg. 36 G12 42.11 N 25.20 E
Chirripó, stm., C.R. 156 G6 10.41 N 83.43 W
Chirripó, Cerro, mtn., C.R. 156 H6 9.29 N 83.30 W
Chirripó, Parque Nacional, p.o.i., C.R. 156 H6 9.30 N 83.30 W
Chirua, Lago see Chilwa, Lake, l., Afr. 88 D6 15.23 S 35.41 E
Chisago City, Mn., U.S. 128 F6 45.22 N 92.53 W
Chisamba, Zam. 88 C4 14.58 S 28.23 E
Chisasibi, Qc., Can. 110 E15 53.48 N 79.01 W
Chiscas, Col. 168 D5 6.33 N 72.29 W
Chisep'o, Kor., S. 56 E1 34.50 N 128.41 E
Ch'ishan, Tai. 58 J9 22.53 N 120.28 E
Chishima-rettō see Kuril'skie ostrova, is., Russia 46 E19 47.14 N 152.17 E
Chisholm, Ab., Can. 144 B16 54.53 N 114.11 W
Chisholm, Al., U.S. 134 E12 32.25 N 86.15 W
Chisholm, Me., U.S. 122 F6 44.29 N 70.12 W
Chisholm, Mn., U.S. 128 D6 47.29 N 92.53 W
Chisholm Mills see Chisholm, Ab., Can. 144 B16 54.53 N 114.11 W
Chishtiān Mandi, Pak. 70 D4 29.47 N 72.51 E
Chishui, China 58 G1 28.35 N 105.41 E
Chishui, stm., China 52 F6 28.48 N 105.51 E
Chishuihe, China 58 H1 27.43 N 105.34 E
Chisimaio see Kismaayo, Som. 86 E8 0.21 S 42.32 E
Chisimayu see Kismaayo, Som. 86 E8 0.21 S 42.32 E
Chişinău, Mol. 38 F7 47.01 N 28.50 E
Chişineu-Criş, Rom. 36 C8 46.31 N 21.31 E
Chislehurst, ngh., Eng., U.K. 178 51.25 N 0.04 E
Chisone, stm., Italy 30 E4 44.49 N 7.24 E
Chisos Mountains, mts., Tx., U.S. 136 E4 29.13 N 103.21 W
Chiswellgreen, Eng., U.K. 178 51.44 N 0.22 W
Chiswick, ngh., Eng., U.K. 178 51.29 N 0.16 W
Chita, Col. 168 D5 6.11 N 72.28 W
Chitado, Ang. 88 D1 17.19 S 13.55 E
Chitagá, Col. 168 D5 7.09 N 72.40 W
Chita-hantō, pen., Japan 56 E9 34.50 N 136.53 E
Chitambo, Zam. 88 C5 12.51 S 30.47 E
Chitato, Ang. 88 B3 7.20 S 20.45 E
Chitek Lake, l., Mb., Can. 142 B14 52.26 N 99.25 W
Chitembo, Ang. 88 C2 13.32 S 16.45 E
Chitina, Ak., U.S. 109 D11 61.30 N 144.28 W
Chitina, stm., Ak., U.S. 109 D11 61.30 N 144.25 W
Chitipa, Mwi. 88 B5 9.42 S 33.16 E
Chitokoloki, Zam. 88 C3 13.50 S 23.13 E
Chitose, Japan 54 C14 42.46 N 141.38 E
Chitradurga, India 69 D3 14.13 N 76.24 E
Chitrakūt Dham, India 70 F8 25.13 N 80.50 E
Chitrāl, Pak. 62 A3 35.52 N 71.49 E
Chitrasāli, India 190b 22.52 N 88.09 E
Chitrāvati, stm., India 69 D3 14.47 N 78.13 E
Chitré, Pan. 156 H7 7.57 N 80.26 W
Chittagong, Bngl. 70 G13 22.20 N 91.49 E
Chittagong, state, Bngl. 70 G13 23.00 N 91.00 E
Chittāpur, India 69 C3 17.07 N 77.05 E
Chittaurgarh, India 70 F5 24.53 N 74.37 E
Chittoor, India 69 E4 13.12 N 79.06 E
Chittūr, India 69 F3 10.41 N 76.44 E
Ch'itu, Tai. 187d 25.06 N 121.43 E
Chitungwiza, Zimb. 88 D5 18.01 S 31.03 E
Chiumbe (Tshumbe), stm., Afr. 86 F4 6.59 S 21.11 E
Chiume, Ang. 88 D3 15.01 S 21.15 E
Chiusi, Italy 30 G8 43.00 N 11.57 E
Chiva see Xiva, Spain 28 E10 39.28 N 0.43 W
Chivacoa, Ven. 168 B7 10.10 N 68.50 W
Chivasso, Italy 30 E4 45.12 N 7.53 E
Chivato, Punta, c., Mex. 154 B3 27.05 N 111.56 W
Chivhu, Zimb. 88 D5 19.01 S 30.53 E
Chivi, Zimb. 90 B10 20.18 S 30.30 E
Chivilcoy, Arg. 172 G7 34.54 S 60.02 W
Chivirira Falls, wtfl., Zimb. 90 B11 21.14 S 32.20 E
Chiwawa, stm., Wa., U.S. 146 B6 47.46 N 120.39 W
Chiyoda, ngh., Japan 186 35.41 N 139.44 E
Chizhen, China 58 F8 31.55 N 118.11 E
Chizu, Japan 56 D7 35.16 N 134.14 E
Chkalove, Ukr. 38 G13 46.27 N 34.11 E
Chloride, Az., U.S. 150 H2 35.25 N 114.11 W
Chmielnik, Pol. 24 F16 50.37 N 20.45 E
Choa Chu Kang, Sing. 189c 1.22 N 103.41 E
Choāli, India 190b 22.24 N 88.24 E
Chŏâm Khsant, Camb. 64 E7 14.12 N 104.56 E
Choapa, stm., Chile 172 E2 31.37 S 71.33 W
Chobham, Eng., U.K. 178 51.21 N 0.36 W
Chobham Common, p.o.i., Eng., U.K. 178 51.23 N 0.37 W
Choccolocco Creek, stm., Al., U.S. 134 D13 33.33 N 86.11 W
Choceň, Czech Rep. 24 F12 49.59 N 16.13 E
Chochis, Cerro, mtn., Bol. 166 C5 18.08 S 59.53 W
Choch'iwŏn, Kor., S. 54 F7 36.36 N 127.18 E
Chocianów, Pol. 24 E11 51.24 N 15.54 E
Chociwel, Pol. 24 C11 53.27 N 15.19 E
Chocó, state, Col. 168 E3 6.00 N 77.00 W
Chocolate Mountains, mts., U.S. 150 J2 33.09 N 114.54 W
Chocontá, Col. 168 E5 5.08 N 73.40 W
Chocope, Peru 164 E2 7.46 S 79.12 W
Choctawhatchee, East Fork, stm., Al., U.S. 134 F13 31.21 N 85.33 W
Choctawhatchee, West Fork, stm., Al., U.S. 134 G13 31.20 N 85.32 W
Choctawhatchee Bay, b., Fl., U.S. 134 G12 30.25 N 86.21 W
Chodecz, Pol. 24 D14 52.24 N 19.01 E
Ch'o-do, i., Kor., N. 54 E6 38.32 N 124.50 E
Chodzież, Pol. 24 D12 52.59 N 16.55 E
Choele Choel, Arg. 166 G3 39.17 S 65.39 W
Chofu Airport, arpt., Japan 186 35.40 N 139.32 E
Choisel, Fr. 179 48.41 N 2.01 E
Choiseul, St. Luc. 159c m6 13.46 N 61.02 W
Choiseul, state, Sol. Is. 101b d7 7.00 S 157.00 E
Choiseul, i., Sol. Is. 101b d7 7.05 S 157.00 E
Choisy-le-Roi, Fr. 179 48.46 N 2.25 E
Choix, Mex. 154 B4 26.43 N 108.17 W
Chojna, Pol. 24 D10 52.57 N 14.25 E
Chojnice, Pol. 24 C13 53.41 N 17.33 E
Chojnów, Pol. 24 E11 51.16 N 15.56 E
Ch'ok'ē, mts., Eth. 82 E7 10.43 N 37.47 E
Choke Canyon Reservoir, res., Tx., U.S. 136 F9 28.30 N 98.20 W
Chokio, Mn., U.S. 128 F2 45.34 N 96.11 W
Chókwe, Moz. 90 D11 24.32 S 32.59 E
Cholame Creek, stm., Ca., U.S. 148 H5 35.39 N 120.22 W
Cholet, Fr. 20 G8 47.03 N 0.53 W
Choluteca, Hond. 156 F4 13.18 N 87.11 W
Choluteca, stm., Hond. 156 F4 13.06 N 87.19 W
Choma, Zam. 88 D4 16.48 S 26.59 E
Chomedey, ngh., Qc., Can. 193a 45.32 N 73.44 W
Cho Moi, Viet. 64 G7 10.33 N 105.22 E
Cho Moi, Viet. 187c 10.51 N 106.38 E
Chomo Lhāri, mtn., Asia 70 E12 27.50 N 89.15 E
Chom Thong, Thai. 64 C4 18.25 N 98.40 E
Chomūm, India 70 E5 27.10 N 75.43 E
Chomutov, Czech Rep. 24 F9 50.28 N 13.25 E
Ch'ŏnan, Kor., S. 54 F7 36.48 N 127.09 E
Chon Buri, Thai. 64 F5 13.22 N 101.00 E
Chon Daen, Thai. 64 D5 16.11 N 100.51 E
Chone, Ec. 168 H1 0.41 S 80.05 W
Chong'an, China 58 H8 27.45 N 118.01 E
Ch'ŏngdo, Kor., S. 56 D1 35.38 N 128.43 E
Ch'ŏngha, Kor., S. 56 C2 36.12 N 129.20 E
Ch'onghak-ni, Kor., S. 189b 37.43 N 127.05 E
Chonghe, China 54 B7 44.43 N 127.45 E
Ch'ŏngjin, Kor., N. 54 D8 41.46 N 129.48 E
Ch'ŏngju, Kor., S. 54 F7 36.38 N 127.29 E
Chŏng Kal, Camb. 64 E6 13.59 N 103.33 E
Chongming, China 54 I4 31.37 N 121.24 E
Chongming Dao, i., China 58 F9 31.36 N 121.33 E
Chongmyo Shrine, rel., Kor., S. 189b 37.35 N 127.00 E
Chongoene, Moz. 90 D11 25.00 S 33.47 E
Chongoroi, Ang. 88 C1 13.34 S 13.56 E
Chong Pang, Sing. 189c 1.26 N 103.50 E
Chongqing (Chungking), China 58 G2 29.33 N 106.34 E
Chongqing, state, China 52 F6 30.00 N 108.00 E
Ch'ŏngsŏn, Kor., S. 58 B1 37.22 N 128.35 E
Chŏngŭp, Kor., S. 54 G7 35.36 N 126.51 E
Chongxin, China 58 D2 35.19 N 107.08 E
Chongzuo, China 64 A8 22.23 N 107.21 E
Ch'ŏnho Bridge, trans., Kor., S. 189b 37.33 N 127.05 E
Chŏnju, Kor., S. 54 G7 35.49 N 127.09 E
Chonos, Archipiélago de los, is., Chile 166 I1 45.00 S 74.00 W
Ch'ŏnsu-ri, Kor., N. 54 D8 41.43 N 128.48 E
Chontaleña, Cordillera, mts., Nic. 156 G5 11.50 N 84.50 W
Chon Thanh, Viet. 64 G8 11.26 N 106.36 E
Cho Oyu see Chopu, mtn., Asia 70 D11 28.06 N 86.39 E
Cho Oyu see Qowowuyag, mtn., Asia 70 D11 28.06 N 86.39 E
Chop see Tsjop, Ukr. 36 A9 48.26 N 22.13 E
Chopda, India 70 H5 21.15 N 75.18 E
Chopim, stm., Braz. 172 C11 25.34 S 53.04 W
Chopinzinho, Braz. 172 B11 25.51 S 52.32 W
Chopovychi, Ukr. 38 C6 50.49 N 27.58 E
Chopu (Qowowuyag), mtn., Asia 70 D11 28.06 N 86.39 E
Chóra, Grc. 34 F4 37.03 N 21.42 E
Chora Saādatpur, India 190a 28.36 N 77.21 E
Chorley, mun., Eng., U.K. 180 53.38 N 2.38 W
Chorleywood, Eng., U.K. 178 51.39 N 0.31 W
Chorlton-cum-Hardy, ngh., Eng., U.K. 180 53.27 N 2.17 W
Chorna, Ukr. 38 F8 47.36 N 29.19 E
Chorne more see Black Sea, s. 42 D5 43.00 N 35.00 E
Chornobai, Ukr. 38 D11 49.40 N 32.20 E
Chornobaïvka, Ukr. 38 G11 46.41 N 32.33 E
Chornobyl', Ukr. 38 B9 51.16 N 30.14 E
Chornomors'ke, Ukr. 38 H14 45.03 N 35.55 E
Chornomors'ke, Ukr. 38 H11 45.30 N 32.43 E
Chornukhy, Ukr. 38 C11 50.16 N 32.56 E
Chornyi Ostriv, Ukr. 38 D5 49.31 N 26.46 E
Chornyi Tashlyk, stm., Ukr. 38 E10 48.11 N 30.51 E
Čhorocku, Geor. 42 D10 42.31 N 42.10 E
Chorolque, Cerro, mtn., Bol. 166 D3 20.56 S 66.01 W
Choros, Isla, i., Chile 172 D2 29.16 S 71.33 W
Choroszcz, Pol. 24 C18 53.10 N 22.58 E
Chorrillos, Peru 204d 12.10 S 77.02 W
Chorrochó, Braz. 170 E6 8.59 S 39.06 W
Chortkiv, Ukr. 38 D4 49.01 N 25.48 E
Ch'ŏrwŏn, Kor., S. 54 E7 38.17 N 127.14 E
Chorzele, Pol. 24 C16 53.15 N 20.54 E
Chosen, Fl., U.S. 132 J5 26.42 N 80.41 W
Chōshi, Japan 56 D13 35.44 N 140.49 E
Chosica, Peru 164 F2 11.54 S 76.40 W
Chos Malal, Arg. 172 H2 37.23 S 70.16 W
Chosŏn minjujuŭi-inmin-konghwaguk see Korea, North, ctry., Asia 54 D7 40.00 N 127.00 E
Choszczno, Pol. 24 C11 53.10 N 15.25 E
Chotanāgpur Plateau, plat., India 62 D5 23.30 N 84.30 E
Choteau, Mt., U.S. 146 C14 47.48 N 112.11 W
Choteau Creek, stm., S.D., U.S. 140 D14 42.50 N 98.09 W
Chotila, India 70 G3 22.25 N 71.11 E
Chotyrboky, Ukr. 38 C6 50.01 N 27.01 E
Chouchiak'ou see Shangshui, China 58 E6 33.33 N 114.33 E
Chouk'ou see Shangshui, China 58 E6 33.33 N 114.33 E
Choushan Islands see Zhoushan Qundao, is., China 58 F10 30.21 N 122.21 E
Chouteau, Ok., U.S. 130 H2 36.10 N 95.20 W
Chowan, stm., N.C., U.S. 124 H9 36.01 N 76.40 W
Chowchilla, Ca., U.S. 148 F5 37.07 N 120.15 W
Chowchilla, stm., Ca., U.S. 148 F5 37.06 N 120.31 W
Chown, Mount, mtn., Ab., Can. 144 C11 53.24 N 119.22 W
Choya, Arg. 172 D5 28.30 S 64.50 W
Choybalsan, Mong. 52 B7 48.04 N 114.31 E
Choyr, Mong. 52 B6 46.21 N 108.20 E
Chrapun' see Hrapun', Bela. 38 B6 51.42 N 27.29 E
Chrisman, Il., U.S. 130 E10 39.48 N 87.40 W
Christanshåb (Qasigiannguit), Grnld. 108 D15 68.50 N 51.12 W
Christchurch, N.Z. 102 F5 43.31 S 172.38 E
Christ Church Cathedral, rel., Nig. 191a 6.27 N 3.23 E
Christian, Cape, c., Nu., Can. 110 A17 70.32 N 68.20 W
Christian, Point, c., Pit. 100k c28 25.04 S 130.07 W
Christiana, Jam. 158d i13 18.09 N 77.31 W
Christiana, S. Afr. 90 E7 27.55 S 25.09 E
Christiana, De., U.S. 203 39.39 N 75.39 W
Christian Island, i., On., Can. 126 D9 44.50 N 80.13 W
Christiansburg, Va., U.S. 124 G5 37.07 N 80.24 W
Christiansfeld, Den. 16 L7 55.21 N 9.29 E
Christianse, i., Den. 16 L13 55.19 N 15.12 E
Christian Sound, strt., Ak., U.S. 109 E12 56.00 N 134.25 W
Christianstad, V.I.U.S. 158c h11 17.45 N 64.42 W
Christina, stm., De., U.S. 203 39.43 N 75.31 W
Christina Lake, l., B.C., Can. 144 G12 49.05 N 118.14 W
Christmas Creek, Austl. 96 C5 18.56 S 125.55 E
Christmas Island, dep., Oc. 174 K13 10.30 S 105.40 E
Christmas Island, i., Christ. I. 94 E1 10.30 S 105.40 E
Christmas Island see Kiritimati, at., Kir. 94 C11 1.48 N 157.19 W
Christmas Ridge, unds. 174 I22 4.49 N 159.51 W
Christ of the Andes see Cristo Redentor, misc. cult., S.A. 172 F2 32.50 S 70.05 W
Christopher, Il., U.S. 130 G8 37.58 N 89.03 W
Christoval, Tx., U.S. 136 C7 31.11 N 100.30 W
Chrudim, Czech Rep. 24 G11 49.57 N 15.47 E
Chrysoúpoli, Grc. 34 C7 40.58 N 24.42 E
Chrzanów, Pol. 24 F15 50.07 N 19.25 E
Chu (Xam), stm., Asia 64 B7 19.53 N 105.45 E
Chuādanga, Bngl. 70 G12 23.38 N 88.51 E
Chubbuck, Id., U.S. 146 H14 42.55 N 112.28 W
Chūbu-Sangaku-kokuritsu-kōen, p.o.i., Japan 56 C10 36.30 N 137.41 E
Chubut, state, Arg. 166 H3 44.00 S 69.00 W
Chubut, stm., Arg. 166 H3 43.20 S 65.03 W
Chuchi Lake, l., B.C., Can. 144 A6 55.10 N 124.33 W
Chuchow see Zhuzhou, China 58 H5 27.50 N 113.08 E
Chu Chua, B.C., Can. 144 E10 51.21 N 120.09 W
Chuchuwayha Indian Reserve, ind. res., B.C., Can. 144 G10 49.21 N 120.06 W
Chucunaque, stm., Pan. 156 H9 8.08 N 77.44 W
Chudniv, Ukr. 38 C7 50.03 N 28.07 E
Chuen Lung, China 189d 22.24 N 114.06 E
Chugach Mountains, mts., Ak., U.S. 109 D10 61.00 N 145.00 W
Chuginadak Island, i., Ak., U.S. 109a g25 52.49 N 169.46 W
Chūgoku-sanchi, mts., Japan 56 D6 34.58 N 132.57 E
Chugwater, Wy., U.S. 140 F8 41.46 N 104.50 W
Chugwater Creek, stm., Wy., U.S. 140 F8 42.07 N 104.51 W
Chugyn-ri, Kor., S. 189b 37.39 N 126.50 E
Chuhuichupa, Mex. 120 G8 29.38 N 108.22 W
Chuhuïv, Ukr. 38 D15 49.50 N 36.42 E
Chuí, Braz. 172 F11 33.41 S 53.27 W
Chuius Mountain, mtn., B.C., Can. 144 B6 54.51 N 124.30 W
Chukchi Sea, s. 106 B5 69.00 N 171.00 W
Chuke Hu, l., China 70 C11 31.42 N 87.57 E
Chukotsk Peninsula see Čukotskij poluostrov, pen., Russia 50 C26 66.00 N 175.00 W
Chulalongkorn University, educ., Thai. 187a 13.44 N 100.33 E
Chula Vista, Ca., U.S. 148 K8 32.37 N 117.04 W
Chullora, Austl. 192a 33.54 S 151.04 E
Chulucanas, Peru 164 E1 5.05 S 80.09 W
Chumbicha, Arg. 172 D4 28.51 S 66.14 W
Chum Phae, Thai. 64 D6 16.32 N 102.06 E
Chumphon, Thai. 64 G4 10.30 N 99.07 E
Chumphon Buri, Thai. 64 E6 15.20 N 103.24 E
Chum Saeng, Thai. 64 E5 15.53 N 100.14 E
Chumunjin, Kor., S. 54 F8 37.53 N 128.47 E
Chunal, Eng., U.K. 180 53.25 N 1.57 W
Chun'an, China 58 G8 29.35 N 118.57 E
Chunan, Tai. 58 I9 24.41 N 120.53 E
Chuncheon see Ch'unch'ŏn, Kor., S. 54 F7 37.51 N 127.43 E
Chunchi, Ec. 168 I2 2.17 S 78.54 W
Ch'unch'ŏn, Kor., S. 54 F7 37.51 N 127.43 E
Chunchula, Al., U.S. 134 G10 30.55 N 88.12 W
Chūnd, Pak. 70 C4 31.25 N 72.16 E
Chung-ang University, educ., Kor., S. 189b 37.30 N 126.58 E
Ch'ungch'ŏng-bukto, state, Kor., S. 56 B1 37.00 N 128.20 E
Chung Hau, China 189d 22.16 N 114.00 E
Chungho, Tai. 187d 25.00 N 121.30 E
Chung Hsing Bridge, trans., Tai. 187d 25.03 N 121.29 E
Ch'ungju, Kor., S. 54 F7 36.58 N 127.56 E
Chungking see Chongqing, China 58 G2 29.33 N 106.34 E
Ch'ungmu, Kor., S. 54 G8 34.50 N 128.25 E
Chŭngsanha-ri, ngh., Kor., S. 189b 37.35 N 126.54 E
Chungshan Bridge, trans., Tai. 187d 25.05 N 121.31 E
Chungyang Shanmo, mts., Tai. 58 J9 23.30 N 121.00 E
Chunhua, China 58 D3 34.48 N 108.34 E
Chunhuhux, Mex. 156 C3 19.34 N 88.36 W
Chuntuquí, Guat. 156 D2 17.31 N 90.09 W
Chunya, Tan. 86 F6 8.31 S 33.25 E
Chunyang, China 54 C8 43.42 N 129.27 E
Ch'unyang, Kor., S. 56 C1 36.55 N 128.52 E
Chūō, ngh., Japan 186 35.40 N 139.47 E
Chūō, ngh., Japan 188 34.42 N 135.11 E
Chupadera Arroyo, stm., N.M., U.S. 138 H2 33.48 N 106.36 W
Chupakhivka, Ukr. 38 C13 50.22 N 34.35 E
Chupara Point, c., Trin. 159f s12 10.48 N 61.22 W
Chuquibamba, Peru 164 G3 15.50 S 72.39 W
Chuquicamata, Chile 166 D3 22.19 S 68.55 W
Chuquitanta, Peru 204d 11.58 S 77.06 W
Chur (Coire), Switz. 30 D6 46.51 N 9.31 E
Church, Eng., U.K. 180 53.45 N 2.24 W
Church Hill, Tn., U.S. 124 H3 36.31 N 82.42 W
Churchill, Mb., Can. 110 D12 58.46 N 94.10 W
Churchill, Pa., U.S. 197b 40.27 N 79.51 W
Churchill, Va., U.S. 202c 38.54 N 77.10 W
Churchill, stm., Can. 110 D11 58.48 N 94.11 W
Churchill, stm., Nf., Can. 110 E18 53.19 N 60.09 W
Churchill, Mount, mtn., B.C., Can. 144 G7 49.58 N 123.51 W
Churchill, Mount, vol., Ak., U.S. 109 D11 61.25 N 141.43 W
Churchill Falls, wtfl., Nf., Can. 110 E17 53.31 N 64.30 W
Churchill Lake, l., Sk., Can. 110 D9 55.55 N 108.20 W
Church Point, La., U.S. 134 G6 30.24 N 92.13 W
Church Rock, N.M., U.S. 150 H8 35.32 N 108.35 W
Church Street, Eng., U.K. 178 51.26 N 0.28 E
Churchtown, Eng., U.K. 180 53.40 N 2.58 W
Churchville, On., Can. 193b 43.38 N 79.45 W
Churchville, Pa., U.S. 203 40.11 N 75.01 W
Churdan, Ia., U.S. 130 B3 42.09 N 94.28 W
Churn Creek, stm., B.C., Can. 144 E8 51.30 N 122.17 W
Chūru, India 70 D5 28.17 N 74.58 E
Churubusco, In., U.S. 130 C12 41.13 N 85.18 W
Churuguara, Ven. 168 B7 10.48 N 69.32 W
Chushul, India 70 B7 33.36 N 78.39 E
Chuska Mountains, mts., U.S. 150 G8 36.13 N 108.59 W
Chuska Peak, mtn., N.M., U.S. 150 H8 35.53 N 108.50 W
Chute-Saint-Philippe, Qc., Can. 126 B14 46.40 N 75.13 W
Chutove, Ukr. 38 D14 49.42 N 35.09 E
Chutung, Tai. 58 I9 24.44 N 121.05 E
Chuuk, is., Micron. 94 C6 7.16 N 151.44 E
Chuvashia see Čuvašija, state, Russia 40 D15 55.30 N 47.00 E
Chuviscar, stm., Mex. 136 F2 28.33 N 105.25 W
Chuwei, Tai. 187d 25.08 N 121.27 E
Chuxian, China 58 E8 32.19 N 118.18 E
Chuxiong, China 52 F5 25.02 N 101.32 E
Chychykliia, stm., Ukr. 38 F9 47.22 N 31.33 E
Chyhyryn, Ukr. 38 D11 49.04 N 32.41 E
Chynadiieve see Tsjynadijeve, Ukr. 36 A9 48.30 N 22.50 E
Ci, stm., China 58 E6 33.00 N 115.46 E
Ci, stm., China 58 B6 38.18 N 115.27 E
Ciadâr Lunga, Mol. 38 G7 46.03 N 28.50 E
Ciales, P.R. 158a b3 18.20 N 66.28 W
Ciamis, Indon. 66 G6 7.20 S 108.19 E
Ciampino, Aeroporto di, arpt., Italy 185a 41.48 N 12.36 E
Cianjur, Indon. 66 G5 6.48 S 107.08 E
Cianorte, Braz. 172 A11 23.39 S 52.36 W
Čiatura, Geor. 42 D10 42.17 N 43.17 E
Ciawi, Indon. 66 G5 6.39 S 106.50 E
Ciawi, Indon. 66 G6 7.10 S 108.08 E
Cibaliung, Indon. 66 G4 6.43 S 105.42 E
Cibatu, Indon. 66 G6 7.05 S 107.59 E
Cibecue, Az., U.S. 150 I6 34.02 N 110.29 W
Cibinong, Indon. 66 G5 6.26 S 106.51 E
Čibisovka, Russia 40 F12 50.48 N 40.04 E
Cibolo Creek, stm., Tx., U.S. 136 F8 28.26 N 98.53 W
Cibolo Creek, stm., Tx., U.S. 136 E3 29.33 N 104.23 W
Cibolo Creek, stm., Tx., U.S. 136 E10 28.56 N 97.52 W
Ćićarija, mts., Cro. 30 E11 45.27 N 14.07 E
Cicero, Il., U.S. 130 C10 41.50 N 87.45 W
Cicero, In., U.S. 130 D11 40.07 N 86.00 W
Cicero Dantas, Braz. 170 F6 10.35 S 38.22 W
Cicia, i., Fiji 101e p20 17.45 S 179.18 W
Cicurug, Indon. 66 G5 6.47 S 106.47 E
Cidacos, stm., Spain 28 B8 42.18 N 1.54 W
Cidade Universitária, educ., Braz. 205a 22.52 S 43.14 W
Cidade Universitária, educ., Braz. 205b 23.33 S 46.43 W
Cide, Tur. 34 B15 41.54 N 33.00 E
Cidra, P.R. 158a b3 18.10 N 66.10 W
Cidra, Lago de, res., P.R. 158a b3 18.11 N 66.08 W
Ciechanów, Pol. 24 D16 52.52 N 20.36 E
Ciechanowiec, Pol. 24 D18 52.40 N 22.29 E
Ciechocinek, Pol. 24 D14 52.54 N 18.48 E
Ciego de Ávila, Cuba 156 A8 21.50 N 78.46 W
Ciempozuelos, Spain 28 D7 40.09 N 3.37 W
Ciénaga, Col. 168 B4 11.00 N 74.14 W

Name	Page	Map Ref.	Latitude	Longitude
Ciénaga de Oro, Col.	168	C4	8.53 N	75.37 W
Ciénega de Flores, Mex.	136	H7	25.56 N	100.09 W
Cienfuegos, Cuba	156	A7	22.09 N	80.25 W
Čierna nad Tisou, Slvk.	24	H18	48.24 N	22.04 E
Čierny Balog, Slvk.	30	B16	48.45 N	19.40 E
Cíes, Illas, is., Spain	28	B2	42.13 N	8.54 W
Cíes, Islas see Cíes, Illas, is., Spain	28	B2	42.13 N	8.54 W
Cieszanów, Pol.	24	F19	50.14 N	23.07 E
Cieszyn, Pol.	24	G14	49.45 N	18.38 E
Cieza, Spain	28	F9	38.14 N	1.25 W
Çiftalan, ngh., Tur.	185b		41.15 N	28.54 E
Çiftehan, Tur.	76	A5	37.31 N	34.45 E
Çifteler, Tur.	34	D13	39.24 N	31.02 E
Cifuentes, Spain	28	D8	40.47 N	2.38 W
Čiganaki, Russia	40	H13	47.56 N	43.05 E
Cigüela, stm., Spain	28	E7	39.07 N	3.43 W
Čihačovo, Russia	26	C12	57.17 N	29.54 E
Cihanbeyli, Tur.	34	E15	38.39 N	32.56 E
Čiili, Kaz.	48	F11	44.09 N	66.44 E
Cijara, Embalse de, res., Spain	28	E6	39.19 N	4.51 W
Cijulang, Indon.	66	G6	7.43 S	108.28 E
Cikampek, Indon.	66	G5	6.24 S	107.28 E
Cikobia, i., Fiji	101e	o20	15.43 S	179.58 W
Čikoj, Russia	50	F10	50.16 N	106.54 E
Čikoj see Cöch, stm., Asia	52	B6	51.02 N	106.38 E
Cilacap, Indon.	66	G6	7.44 S	109.00 E
Cilamaya, Indon.	66	G5	6.14 S	107.35 E
Çıldır Gölü, l., Tur.	42	E10	41.04 N	43.15 E
Cilento, reg., Italy	32	D9	40.15 N	15.15 E
Cili, China	58	G4	29.17 N	111.00 E
Cilician Gates see Gülek Boğazı, p., Tur.	76	A5	37.18 N	34.46 E
Čilik, Kaz.	40	F19	51.05 N	54.04 E
Čilik, Kaz.	48	F13	43.35 N	78.15 E
Cilincing, ngh., Indon.	187e		6.06 S	106.56 E
Ciliwung, stm., Indon.	187e		6.08 S	106.49 E
Cill Airne see Killarney, Ire.	10	I3	52.03 N	9.30 W
Cill Chainnigh see Kilkenny, Ire.	10	I5	52.39 N	7.14 W
Cilleruelo de Bezana, Spain	28	B7	42.58 N	3.51 W
Cil'ma, stm., Russia	12	D24	65.26 N	52.03 E
Čilov ada, i., Azer.	42	E14	40.19 N	50.35 E
Čiltal'd, gora, mtn., Russia	14	D22	68.15 N	30.59 E
Cimarron, Ks., U.S.	138	D8	37.48 N	100.20 W
Cimarron, N.M., U.S.	138	E4	36.30 N	104.54 W
Cimarron, stm., U.S.	138	F12	36.10 N	96.17 W
Cimarron, stm., N.M., U.S.	138	E4	36.20 N	104.31 W
Cimarron, North Fork, stm., U.S.	138	D7	37.25 N	101.07 W
Čimbaj, Uzb.	48	F9	42.56 N	59.46 E
Cimino see Vico, Lago di, l., Italy	30	H9	42.19 N	12.10 E
Cimișlia, Mol.	38	G7	46.31 N	28.47 E
Cimkavičy, Bela.	26	G10	53.03 N	27.00 E
Cimljansk, Russia	40	H13	47.38 N	42.05 E
Cimljanskoe vodohranilišče, res., Russia	40	G13	48.00 N	43.00 E
Cimone, Monte, mtn., Italy	30	F7	44.12 N	10.42 E
Cîmpina see Câmpina, Rom.	36	D12	45.07 N	25.44 E
Cimpu, Indon.	66	E12	3.25 S	120.21 E
Cîmpulung see Câmpulung, Rom.	36	D11	45.16 N	25.03 E
Cîmpulung Moldovenesc see Câmpulung Moldovenesc, Rom.	36	B12	47.32 N	25.35 E
Cina, Tanjung, c., Indon.	66	G4	5.54 S	104.41 E
Çınarcık, Tur.	34	C12	40.39 N	29.06 E
Cinaruco, stm., Ven.	168	D7	6.41 N	67.06 W
Cina Selatan, Laut see South China Sea, s., Asia	46	I15	10.00 N	113.00 E
Cinca, stm., Spain	28	C11	41.26 N	0.20 E
Cincar, mtn., Bos.	36	F4	43.54 N	17.04 E
Cincinnati, Ia., U.S.	130	D5	40.37 N	92.55 W
Cincinnati, Oh., U.S.	124	E1	39.10 N	84.28 W
Cinco, Canal Numero, can., Arg.	172	H9	37.31 S	57.17 W
Cinco de Mayo, Mex.	136	I3	25.46 N	104.17 W
Cinco Saltos, Arg.	172	I3	38.49 S	68.02 W
Cinderella, S. Afr.	191d		26.15 S	28.16 E
Cinderella Dam, res., S. Afr.	191d		26.15 S	28.14 E
Cinder Island, i., N.Y., U.S.	194		40.36 N	73.36 W
Çine, Tur.	34	F11	37.36 N	28.03 E
Cinecittà, sci., Italy	185a		41.51 N	12.34 E
Cinema, B.C., Can.	144	C8	53.13 N	122.26 W
Ciney, Bel.	20	D14	50.18 N	5.05 E
Cinfães, Port.	28	C2	41.04 N	8.05 W
Cingoli, Italy	30	G10	43.22 N	13.12 E
Cinișeuți, Mol.	38	F7	47.41 N	28.52 E
Cinkota, ngh., Hung.	182c		47.31 N	19.14 E
Cinnaminson, N.J., U.S.	203		40.00 N	74.59 W
Cintalapa, Mex.	154	G12	16.41 N	93.42 W
Cinto, Monte, mtn., Fr.	22	G14	42.23 N	8.56 E
Cintra see Sintra, Port.	28	F1	38.47 N	9.22 W
Cintra, Golfe de, b., W. Sah.	84	E1	22.58 N	16.12 W
Ciocănești, Rom.	36	E14	44.12 N	27.03 E
Ciociaria, reg., Italy	30	I10	41.47 N	13.05 E
Čiovo, Otok, i., Cro.	30	G13	43.30 N	16.20 E
Cipa, stm., Russia	50	F11	55.22 N	115.55 E
Cipatujah, Indon.	66	G5	7.44 S	108.00 E
Cipikan, Russia	50	F11	54.55 N	113.21 E
Cipó, Braz.	170	F6	11.06 S	38.31 W
Cipó, stm., Braz.	170	J4	18.40 S	43.59 W
Cipolletti, Arg.	166	G3	38.56 S	67.59 W
Čir, stm., Russia	40	G13	48.21 N	43.10 E
Circeo, Parco Nazionale del, p.o.i., Italy	32	C6	41.18 N	13.01 E
Čirčik, Uzb.	48	F11	41.27 N	69.35 E
Circle, Ak., U.S.	109	C11	65.49 N	144.04 W
Circle, Mt., U.S.	142	G8	47.26 N	105.35 W
Circleville, Oh., U.S.	124	E3	39.35 N	82.56 W
Circleville, Pa., U.S.	197b		40.20 N	79.44 W
Circleville, Ut., U.S.	150	E4	38.10 N	112.16 W
Circleville Mountain, mtn., Ut., U.S.	150	E4	38.12 N	112.24 W
Cirebon, Indon.	66	G6	6.44 S	108.33 E
Ciremay, Gunung, vol., Indon.	66	G6	6.54 S	108.24 E
Cirencester, Eng., U.K.	10	J11	51.43 N	1.57 W
Čirgalandy, Russia	48	D17	50.36 N	97.10 E
Ciriè, Italy	30	E4	45.14 N	7.35 E
Čirka Kem, stm., Russia	18	C19	64.45 N	32.07 E
Cirò Marina, Italy	32	E11	39.22 N	17.08 E
Ciron, stm., Fr.	22	E5	44.36 N	0.18 W
Čirpan, Blg.	36	G12	42.11 N	25.20 E
Cisco, Tx., U.S.	136	B9	32.23 N	98.59 W
Cishan, China	58	C6	36.34 N	114.06 E
Ciskei, hist. reg., S. Afr.	90	H8	32.52 S	26.54 E
Cisliano, Italy	184b		45.27 N	8.59 E
Čišmy, Russia	40	D19	54.34 N	55.21 E
Cisnădie, Rom.	36	D11	45.42 N	24.09 E
Cisne, Il., U.S.	130	F9	38.29 N	88.26 W
Cisne, Islas del see Santanilla, Islas, is., Hond.	156	D6	17.25 N	83.55 W
Cisneros, Col.	168	D4	6.33 N	75.04 W
Cisolok, Indon.	66	G5	6.56 S	106.25 E
Cispus, stm., Wa., U.S.	146	D5	46.28 N	122.05 W
Cissna Park, Il., U.S.	130	D10	40.33 N	87.53 W
Cistierna, Spain	28	B5	42.48 N	5.07 W
Čistoozërnoe, Russia	48	D13	54.42 N	76.34 E
Čistopol', Russia	40	D17	55.21 N	50.37 E
Čita, Russia	50	F11	52.02 N	113.28 E
Cité Universitaire, educ., Fr.	179		48.49 N	2.20 E
Citlaltépetl, Volcán see Pico de Orizaba, Volcán, vol., Mex.	154	F10	19.01 N	97.16 W
Citra, Fl., U.S.	132	G3	29.24 N	82.06 W
Citronelle, Al., U.S.	134	F10	31.05 N	88.14 W
Citrusdal, S. Afr.	90	H4	32.35 S	19.00 E
Citrus Heights, Ca., U.S.	148	E4	38.42 N	121.16 W
Città di Castello, Italy	30	G9	43.27 N	12.14 E
Cittanova, Italy	32	F10	38.21 N	16.05 E
Città Universitaria, educ., Italy	185a		41.55 N	12.31 E
City Hall, bldg., Sing.	189c		1.17 N	103.51 E
City Island, ngh., N.Y., U.S.	194		40.51 N	73.47 W
City Mills, Ma., U.S.	201		42.06 N	71.21 W
City of Hope National Medical Center, bldg., Ca., U.S.	198		34.08 N	117.58 W
City Of Industry, Ca., U.S.	198		34.01 N	117.57 W
City of London, ngh., Eng., U.K.	178		51.31 N	0.05 W
City of Refuge National Historical Park see Pu'uhonua o Honaunau National Histori, p.o.i., Hi., U.S.	100a	d6	19.25 N	155.54 W
City of Sunrise see Sunrise, Fl., U.S.	132	J5	26.08 N	80.16 W
City Point, Fl., U.S.	132	H5	28.24 N	80.45 W
City University of New York Brooklyn College, educ., N.Y., U.S.	194		40.38 N	73.57 W
City University of New York City College, educ., N.Y., U.S.	194		40.49 N	73.57 W
City University of New York Queens College, educ., N.Y., U.S.	194		40.44 N	73.49 W
City University of New York York College, educ., N.Y., U.S.	194		40.42 N	73.48 W
Ciucaș, Vârful, mtn., Rom.	36	D12	45.31 N	25.55 E
Ciuciuleni, Mol.	38	F7	47.02 N	28.25 E
Ciudad Acuña, Mex.	154	A8	29.19 N	100.55 W
Ciudad Altamirano, Mex.	154	F8	18.20 N	100.39 W
Ciudad Anáhuac, Mex.	154	B8	27.14 N	100.08 W
Ciudad Bolívar, Ven.	168	D10	8.07 N	63.32 W
Ciudad Bolivia, Ven.	168	C6	8.22 N	70.34 W
Ciudad Camargo, Mex.	154	B6	27.41 N	105.10 W
Ciudad Camargo, Mex.	154	B9	26.18 N	98.50 W
Ciudad Constitución, Mex.	154	C3	25.01 N	111.40 W
Ciudad Cortés, C.R.	156	H6	8.57 N	83.31 W
Ciudad Darío, Nic.	156	F4	12.43 N	86.07 W
Ciudad del Carmen, Mex.	154	F12	18.38 N	91.49 W
Ciudad del Este, Para.	172	B10	25.29 S	54.38 W
Ciudad de Libertador General San Martín, Arg.	172	A5	23.48 S	64.47 W
Ciudad del Maíz, Mex.	154	D9	22.23 N	99.36 W
Ciudad de los Deportes, p.o.i., Mex.	204a		19.23 N	99.11 W
Ciudad de México (Mexico City), Mex.	154	F9	19.24 N	99.09 W
Ciudad de México (Mexico City), Mex.	204a		19.24 N	99.09 W
Ciudad de Nutrias, Ven.	168	C7	8.05 N	69.17 W
Ciudad Deportiva, p.o.i., Cuba	204b		23.07 N	82.22 W
Ciudad Deportiva, p.o.i., Mex.	204a		19.24 N	99.06 W
Ciudadela see Ciutadella de Menorca, Spain	28	D14	40.00 N	3.48 E
Ciudadela, Parque de la, p.o.i., Spain	184d		41.23 N	2.11 E
Ciudad General Belgrano, Arg.	206		34.43 S	58.32 W
Ciudad Guayana, Ven.	168	C10	8.21 N	62.39 W
Ciudad Hidalgo, Mex.	154	F8	19.41 N	100.34 W
Ciudad Jiménez see Jiménez, Mex.	154	B6	27.07 N	104.55 W
Ciudad Juárez, Mex.	120	F9	31.44 N	106.28 W
Ciudad Lerdo see Lerdo, Mex.	154	C7	25.32 N	103.31 W
Ciudad Lineal, ngh., Spain	184a		40.27 N	3.40 W
Ciudad López Mateos, Mex.	204a		19.33 N	99.15 W
Ciudad Madero, Mex.	154	D10	22.15 N	97.50 W
Ciudad Mante, Mex.	154	D9	22.44 N	98.57 W
Ciudad Miguel Alemán, Mex.	154	B9	26.23 N	99.01 W
Ciudad Morelos, Mex.	120	E5	32.27 N	114.53 W
Ciudad Netzahualcóyotl, Mex.	154	F9	19.27 N	99.03 W
Ciudad Obregón, Mex.	154	B4	27.28 N	109.56 W
Ciudad Ojeda, Ven.	168	B6	10.12 N	71.18 W
Ciudad Piar, Ven.	168	D10	7.28 N	63.17 W
Ciudad Real, Spain	28	F6	38.58 N	3.55 W
Ciudad Real, co., Spain	28	E6	38.50 N	3.45 W
Ciudad Rodrigo, Spain	28	D4	40.36 N	6.31 W
Ciudad Universitaria, ngh., Spain	184a		40.27 N	3.44 W
Ciudad Universitaria, educ., Mex.	204a		19.20 N	99.11 W
Ciudad Universitaria, educ., Spain	184a		40.27 N	3.43 W
Ciudad Universitaria, educ., Ven.	204c		10.29 N	66.53 W
Ciudad Valles, Mex.	154	E9	21.59 N	99.00 W
Ciudad Victoria, Mex.	154	D9	23.44 N	99.08 W
Ciutadella de Menorca, Spain	28	D14	40.00 N	3.48 E
Civil Air Terminal see Kindley Field, arpt., Ber.	158e	k16	32.22 N	64.41 W
Civil'sk, Russia	40	D15	55.52 N	47.29 E
Civita Castellana, Italy	30	H9	42.16 N	12.25 E
Civitanova Marche, Italy	30	G10	43.18 N	13.43 E
Civitavecchia, Italy	30	H8	42.05 N	11.47 E
Çivril, Tur.	34	E12	38.17 N	29.44 E
Cixerri, stm., Italy	32	E2	39.16 N	9.00 E
Cixi, China	58	F9	30.10 N	121.16 E
Čiža, Russia	12	C21	67.05 N	44.17 E
Čiža Vtoraja, Kaz.	40	F16	50.52 N	49.38 E
Čižinskie razlivy, sw., Kaz.	40	F16	50.01 N	49.54 E
Cizre, Tur.	42	G10	37.20 N	42.11 E
Cjahcin, Bela.	26	G12	53.51 N	29.44 E
Cjaluša, Bela.	26	G12	53.02 N	29.28 E
C.J. Strike Reservoir, res., Id., U.S.	146	H10	42.56 N	115.46 W
Čkalov see Orenburg, Russia	40	F19	51.48 N	55.05 E
Čkalovsk, Russia	40	C13	56.45 N	43.14 E
Čkalovskij, Russia	183b		55.54 N	38.04 E
C K Creek, stm., Mt., U.S.	142	G5	47.35 N	108.11 W
Clackamas, stm., Or., U.S.	146	E4	45.22 N	122.36 W
Clacton-on-Sea, Eng., U.K.	10	J14	51.47 N	1.09 E
Claflin, Ks., U.S.	138	C10	38.31 N	98.32 W
Claiborne, Al., U.S.	134	F11	31.32 N	87.31 W
Clain, stm., Fr.	22	C6	46.46 N	0.32 E
Claire, Lake, l., Ab., Can.	110	D8	58.35 N	112.05 W
Claire, Pointe, c., Qc., Can.	193a		45.25 N	73.50 W
Clair Engle Lake, res., Ca., U.S.	148	C3	40.50 N	122.47 W
Claireville, On., Can.	193b		43.45 N	79.38 W
Claireville Reservoir, res., On., Can.	193b		43.44 N	79.39 W
Clairmont, Ab., Can.	144	A12	55.15 N	118.49 W
Clairton, Pa., U.S.	124	D6	40.17 N	79.52 W
Clallam Bay, Wa., U.S.	146	B2	48.14 N	124.16 W
Clam, stm., Mi., U.S.	126	D4	44.05 N	84.59 W
Clam, stm., Wi., U.S.	128	F6	45.57 N	92.32 W
Clam, North Fork, stm., Wi., U.S.	128	F6	45.46 N	92.17 W
Clamart, Fr.	179		48.48 N	2.16 E
Clamecy, Fr.	20	G12	47.27 N	3.30 E
Clan Alpine Mountains, mts., Nv., U.S.	148	D8	39.36 N	117.53 W
Clandon Park, p.o.i., Eng., U.K.	178		51.15 N	0.30 W
Clanton, Al., U.S.	134	E12	32.51 N	86.38 W
Clanwilliam, S. Afr.	90	H4	32.09 S	18.53 E
Clapperton Island, i., On., Can.	126	B7	46.01 N	82.13 W
Clara, Ire.	10	H5	53.20 N	7.37 W
Clara, Ms., U.S.	134	F10	31.34 N	88.41 W
Clara, stm., Austl.	98	B4	18.27 S	141.18 E
Clara, Punta, c., Arg.	166	H4	43.58 S	65.13 W
Clara City, Mn., U.S.	128	G3	44.55 N	95.24 W
Clara Island, i., Mya.	64	G3	10.54 N	97.55 E
Claraz, Arg.	172	H8	37.53 S	59.17 W
Clare, Austl.	98	I4	33.25 S	143.55 E
Clare, Austl.	98	I2	33.50 S	138.36 E
Clare, Mi., U.S.	126	E5	43.49 N	84.45 W
Clare, state, Ire.	10	I3	52.49 N	9.01 W
Clare, stm., Ire.	10	H4	53.19 N	9.06 W
Clare Island, i., Ire.	10	H2	53.48 N	10.00 W
Claremont, Eng., U.K.	178		51.21 N	0.22 W
Claremont, N.H., U.S.	122	G4	43.22 N	72.20 W
Claremont, S.D., U.S.	140	B15	45.41 N	97.59 W
Claremont, mtn., Ca., U.S.	148	D4	39.53 N	120.57 W
Claremore, Ok., U.S.	132	H2	36.18 N	95.36 W
Claremorris, Ire.	10	H3	53.43 N	8.59 W
Clarence, Ia., U.S.	130	C6	41.53 N	91.02 W
Clarence, Mo., U.S.	130	E5	39.44 N	92.15 W
Clarence, stm., Austl.	98	G9	29.25 S	153.16 E
Clarence, stm., N.Z.	102	F5	42.09 S	173.55 E
Clarence, Cape, c., Nu., Can.	110	A13	73.54 N	90.10 W
Clarence, Isla, i., Chile	166	J2	54.10 S	71.49 W
Clarence Strait, strt., Austl.	96	B6	12.00 S	131.00 E
Clarence Strait, strt., Ak., U.S.	109	E13	55.25 N	132.00 W
Clarence Town, Bah.	155	A10	23.04 N	74.56 W
Clarenceville, Mi., U.S.	199		42.27 N	83.19 W
Clarendon, Ar., U.S.	134	C7	34.41 N	91.18 W
Clarendon, Pa., U.S.	124	C6	41.46 N	79.05 W
Clarendon, Tx., U.S.	138	G8	34.56 N	100.53 W
Clarendon Hills, Il., U.S.	196		41.47 N	87.57 W
Clarenville, Nf., Can.	111a	j23	48.09 N	53.57 W
Claresholm, Ab., Can.	144	F17	50.01 N	113.34 W
Clarinda, Ia., U.S.	130	D2	40.44 N	95.02 W
Clarines, Ven.	168	C9	9.57 N	65.09 W
Clarington, On., Can.	126	E11	43.54 N	78.35 W
Clarion, Ia., U.S.	130	B4	42.43 N	93.43 W
Clarion, Pa., U.S.	124	C6	41.12 N	79.22 W
Clarion, stm., Pa., U.S.	124	C6	41.06 N	79.40 W
Clarion Fracture Zone, unds.	174	H25	18.00 N	122.00 W
Clarissa, Mn., U.S.	128	E3	46.07 N	94.58 W
Clark, N.J., U.S.	194		40.38 N	74.18 W
Clark, S.D., U.S.	140	C15	44.52 N	97.44 W
Clark, Mount, mtn., N.T., Can.	110	C6	64.25 N	124.12 W
Clark, Point, c., On., Can.	126	D8	44.04 N	81.45 W
Clark Branch, stm., N.J., U.S.	203		39.43 N	74.45 W
Clark Canyon Reservoir, res., Mt., U.S.	146	E14	44.58 N	112.52 W
Clarkdale, Az., U.S.	150	I4	34.46 N	112.03 W
Clarke, stm., Austl.	98	B5	19.12 S	145.28 E
Clarke Island, i., Austl.	99a	n14	40.33 S	148.10 E
Clarke Range, mts., Austl.	98	C7	20.43 S	148.17 E
Clarkesville, Ga., U.S.	132	B2	34.37 N	83.31 W
Clarkfield, Mn., U.S.	128	G3	44.47 N	95.48 W
Clark Fork, Id., U.S.	146	B10	48.08 N	116.10 W
Clark Fork, stm., U.S.	146	C11	48.08 N	116.11 W
Clark Mountain, mtn., Ca., U.S.	148	H10	35.32 N	115.35 W
Clarks, La., U.S.	134	E6	32.01 N	92.08 W
Clarks, Ne., U.S.	140	F15	41.12 N	97.49 W
Clarks, stm., Ky., U.S.	130	H9	37.02 N	88.32 W
Clarksboro, N.J., U.S.	203		39.47 N	75.13 W
Clarksburg, W.V., U.S.	124	E5	39.16 N	80.19 W
Clarks Creek, stm., Ks., U.S.	138	C12	39.05 N	96.42 W
Clarksdale, Ms., U.S.	134	C8	34.12 N	90.34 W
Clark's Harbour, N.S., Can.	122	G11	43.28 N	65.38 W
Clarks Hill, In., U.S.	130	D11	40.14 N	86.43 W
Clarks Island, i., Ma., U.S.	201		42.01 N	70.38 W
Clarkson, On., Can.	193b		43.31 N	79.37 W
Clarkson, Ky., U.S.	130	G11	37.29 N	86.13 W
Clarkson, Ne., U.S.	140	F15	41.43 N	97.07 W
Clarks Summit, Pa., U.S.	124	C10	41.29 N	75.41 W
Clarkston, Wa., U.S.	146	D9	46.24 N	117.03 W
Clark's Town, Jam.	158d	I13	18.25 N	77.31 W
Clarksville, Ar., U.S.	134	B5	35.28 N	93.27 W
Clarksville, Ia., U.S.	128	I6	42.47 N	92.40 W
Clarksville, Tn., U.S.	130	H10	36.31 N	87.20 W
Clarksville, Tx., U.S.	134	D3	33.37 N	95.03 W
Clarksville, Va., U.S.	124	H7	36.37 N	78.33 W
Clarkton, Mo., U.S.	130	H8	36.27 N	89.58 W
Clarkton, N.C., U.S.	132	B7	34.29 N	78.39 W
Claro, stm., Braz.	166	C6	15.25 S	51.42 W
Claro, stm., Braz.	170	J2	19.06 S	47.52 W
Claro, Arroyo, stm., Arg.	206		34.25 S	58.41 W
Claro, Ribeirão, stm., Braz.	205b		23.40 S	46.17 W
Clatskanie, Or., U.S.	146	D3	46.06 N	123.12 W
Clatskanie, stm., Or., U.S.	146	D3	46.08 N	123.13 W
Claude, Tx., U.S.	138	F7	35.07 N	101.22 W
Clausthal-Zellerfeld, Ger.	24	E6	51.48 N	10.20 E
Claveria, Phil.	68	B7	18.36 N	121.05 E
Clavering Ø, i., Grnld.	108	C22	74.16 N	21.00 W
Clavet, Sk., Can.	142	B7	52.00 N	106.23 W
Clawson, Mi., U.S.	199		42.32 N	83.08 W
Claxton, Ga., U.S.	132	D4	32.09 N	81.53 W
Clay, Ky., U.S.	130	G10	37.28 N	87.49 W
Clay, Tx., U.S.	136	D11	30.23 N	96.21 W
Clay, W.V., U.S.	124	F4	38.27 N	81.04 W
Claybank Creek, stm., Al., U.S.	134	F13	31.10 N	85.44 W
Clay Center, Ks., U.S.	138	B11	39.22 N	97.07 W
Clay Center, Ne., U.S.	140	G14	40.31 N	98.03 W
Clay City, Il., U.S.	130	F9	38.41 N	88.21 W
Clay City, In., U.S.	130	E10	39.16 N	87.06 W
Clay City, Ky., U.S.	124	G1	37.51 N	83.56 W
Clay Creek, stm., Co., U.S.	138	D6	38.06 N	102.31 W
Claygate, Eng., U.K.	178		51.22 N	0.20 W
Claygate Cross, Eng., U.K.	178		51.16 N	0.19 E
Clayhole Wash, stm., Az., U.S.	150	G3	36.58 N	113.16 W
Claymont, De., U.S.	124	E10	39.47 N	75.27 W
Clayoquot Sound, strt., B.C., Can.	144	G4	49.13 N	126.07 W
Claypole, Arg.	206		34.48 S	58.20 W
Claypool, Az., U.S.	150	J6	33.24 N	110.50 W
Claysburg, Pa., U.S.	124	D7	40.17 N	78.27 W
Clay Springs, Az., U.S.	150	I6	34.21 N	110.24 W
Clayton, Austl.	192b		37.56 S	145.07 E
Clayton, Eng., U.K.	180		53.47 N	1.50 W
Clayton, Al., U.S.	134	F13	31.52 N	85.27 W
Clayton, Ca., U.S.	200		37.57 N	121.56 W
Clayton, De., U.S.	124	E10	39.17 N	75.37 W
Clayton, Ga., U.S.	132	B2	34.53 N	83.23 W
Clayton, Il., U.S.	130	D7	40.01 N	90.57 W
Clayton, La., U.S.	134	F7	31.43 N	91.31 W
Clayton, Mo., U.S.	130	F7	38.39 N	90.17 W
Clayton, N.M., U.S.	138	E5	36.26 N	103.10 W
Clayton, N.Y., U.S.	126	D13	44.14 N	76.05 W
Clayton, N.C., U.S.	132	A7	35.39 N	78.27 W
Clayton, Ok., U.S.	134	C3	34.36 N	95.21 W
Clayton, Wa., U.S.	146	B9	48.00 N	117.33 W
Clayton-le-Moors, Eng., U.K.	180		53.47 N	2.23 W
Clayton-le-Woods, Eng., U.K.	180		53.41 N	2.38 W
Clayton Park, p.o.i., Pa., U.S.	203		39.52 N	75.29 W
Clayton Valley, val., Ca., U.S.	200		37.58 N	121.58 W
Clear, Cape, c., Ire.	10	J3	51.25 N	9.31 W
Clear, Lake, l., On., Can.	126	C12	45.26 N	77.12 W
Clear Boggy Creek, stm., Ok., U.S.	134	C3	34.02 N	95.47 W
Clearbrook, Mn., U.S.	128	D3	47.41 N	95.25 W
Clear Creek, stm., Al., U.S.	134	C11	34.01 N	87.14 W
Clear Creek, stm., Az., U.S.	150	I6	34.59 N	110.38 W
Clear Creek, stm., Ca., U.S.	148	C3	40.30 N	122.21 W
Clear Creek, stm., Ca., U.S.	198		34.17 N	118.12 W
Clear Creek, stm., Ca., U.S.	200		37.20 N	122.21 W
Clear Creek, stm., Mo., U.S.	130	G3	37.59 N	93.55 W
Clear Creek, stm., Mt., U.S.	146	B17	48.35 N	109.24 W
Clear Creek, stm., Ne., U.S.	140	F13	41.08 N	99.06 W
Clear Creek, stm., Tn., U.S.	138	H13	36.05 N	84.43 W
Clear Creek, stm., Tx., U.S.	138	H11	33.16 N	97.02 W
Clear Creek, stm., Wy., U.S.	140	C6	44.52 N	106.04 W
Clearfield, Ia., U.S.	130	D3	40.48 N	94.28 W
Clearfield, Pa., U.S.	124	C7	41.01 N	78.26 W
Clearfield, Ut., U.S.	150	B4	41.07 N	112.01 W
Clearfield Creek, stm., Pa., U.S.	126	H11	41.01 N	78.24 W
Clearing, ngh., Il., U.S.	196		41.47 N	87.47 W
Clearlake, Ca., U.S.	148	E3	38.56 N	122.38 W
Clear Lake, Ia., U.S.	130	A4	43.08 N	93.22 W
Clear Lake, S.D., U.S.	128	G2	44.45 N	96.41 W
Clear Lake, Wi., U.S.	128	F6	45.15 N	92.16 W
Clear Lake, l., Mb., Can.	142	D14	50.40 N	100.01 W
Clear Lake, l., Ca., U.S.	148	D2	39.02 N	122.50 W
Clear Lake, res., La., U.S.	134	F5	31.54 N	93.00 W
Clear Lake Reservoir, res., Ca., U.S.	148	B4	41.51 N	121.10 W
Clearmont, Wy., U.S.	140	C6	44.38 N	106.23 W
Clearview Estates, Pa., U.S.	197b		40.34 N	80.16 W
Clearwater, B.C., Can.	144	E10	51.39 N	120.02 W
Clearwater, Mb., Can.	142	E14	49.07 N	99.01 W
Clearwater, Fl., U.S.	132	I3	27.58 N	82.47 W
Clearwater, Ks., U.S.	138	D11	37.30 N	97.30 W
Clearwater, Ne., U.S.	140	E14	42.09 N	98.10 W
Clearwater, stm., Can.	110	D8	56.44 N	111.23 W
Clearwater, stm., Ab., Can.	144	D15	52.21 N	114.57 W
Clearwater, stm., B.C., Can.	144	D10	51.38 N	120.04 W
Clearwater, stm., Id., U.S.	146	D10	46.25 N	117.02 W
Clearwater, stm., Mn., U.S.	128	D3	47.53 N	96.17 W
Clearwater, stm., Mt., U.S.	146	C13	46.58 N	113.23 W
Clearwater, Middle Fork, stm., Id., U.S.	146	D11	46.08 N	115.59 W
Clearwater, North Fork, stm., Id., U.S.	146	D11	46.30 N	116.19 W
Clearwater, South Fork, stm., Id., U.S.	146	E11	46.09 N	115.59 W
Clear Water Bay, b., China	189d		22.17 N	114.18 E
Clearwater Lake, l., B.C., Can.	144	D10	52.15 N	120.13 W
Clearwater Mountains, mts., Id., U.S.	146	D11	46.00 N	115.30 W
Clebit, Ok., U.S.	134	C4	34.20 N	94.49 W
Cleburne, Tx., U.S.	136	B10	32.21 N	97.24 W
Cle Elum, Wa., U.S.	146	C6	47.11 N	120.56 W
Cle Elum, stm., Wa., U.S.	146	C5	47.10 N	121.00 W
Cle Elum Lake, res., Wa., U.S.	146	C5	47.16 N	121.05 W
Cleethorpes, Eng., U.K.	10	H12	53.33 N	0.02 W
Cleland Heights, De., U.S.	203		39.44 N	75.34 W
Clementon, N.J., U.S.	203		39.48 N	74.59 W
Clementsport, N.S., Can.	122	F11	44.39 N	65.36 W
Clemson, S.C., U.S.	132	B3	34.41 N	82.49 W
Clendenin, W.V., U.S.	124	F4	38.28 N	81.21 W
Clermont, Austl.	98	D6	22.49 S	147.39 E
Clermont, Qc., Can.	122	C6	47.41 N	70.13 W
Clermont, Fr.	20	E11	49.22 N	2.25 E
Clermont, N.J., U.S.	203		39.59 N	74.48 W
Clermont-Ferrand, Fr.	22	D9	45.46 N	3.05 E
Cles, Italy	30	D8	46.22 N	11.01 E
Clevedon, Eng., U.K.	10	J10	51.26 N	2.51 W
Cleveland, Al., U.S.	134	D12	33.59 N	86.35 W
Cleveland, Ga., U.S.	132	B2	34.36 N	83.45 W
Cleveland, Ms., U.S.	134	D8	33.44 N	90.43 W
Cleveland, N.C., U.S.	132	A5	35.43 N	80.40 W
Cleveland, Oh., U.S.	124	C4	41.29 N	81.41 W
Cleveland, Oh., U.S.	197a		41.29 N	81.41 W
Cleveland, Ok., U.S.	134	A2	36.18 N	96.27 W
Cleveland, Tn., U.S.	134	B14	35.09 N	84.52 W
Cleveland, Tx., U.S.	136	D12	30.20 N	95.05 W
Cleveland, Va., U.S.	124	H3	36.56 N	82.09 W
Cleveland, Cape, c., Austl.	98	B6	19.13 S	147.02 E
Cleveland, Mount, mtn., Austl.	99a	n12	41.25 S	145.23 E
Cleveland, Mount, mtn., Mt., U.S.	146	B13	48.56 N	113.51 W
Cleveland-Hopkins International Airport, arpt., Oh., U.S.	197a		41.25 N	81.51 W
Clevelândia, Braz.	172	C11	26.29 S	52.21 W
Clevelândia do Norte, Braz.	164	C7	3.48 N	51.51 W
Cleveland Museum of Art, bldg., Oh., U.S.	197a		41.31 N	81.37 W
Cleveland National Forest, p.o.i., Ca., U.S.	198		33.47 N	117.38 W
Cleveland Park, ngh., D.C., U.S.	202c		38.56 N	77.04 W
Cleveland Pond, l., Ma., U.S.	201		42.07 N	70.58 W
Cleveland State University, educ., Oh., U.S.	197a		41.30 N	81.40 W
Cleveland Zoo, p.o.i., Oh., U.S.	197a		41.27 N	81.43 W
Cleves see Kleve, Ger.	24	E2	51.47 N	6.08 E
Clew Bay, b., Ire.	10	H3	53.50 N	9.50 W
Clewiston, Fl., U.S.	132	J5	26.45 N	80.54 W
Clichy-sous-Bois, Fr.	179		48.55 N	2.33 E
Cliffe Marshes, sw., Eng., U.K.	178		51.28 N	0.30 E
Cliffe Woods, Eng., U.K.	178		51.26 N	0.30 E
Clifford Park, p.o.i., Austl.	192b		37.43 S	145.16 E
Cliffside Park, N.J., U.S.	194		40.48 N	73.59 W
Cliffwood, N.J., U.S.	194		40.26 N	74.14 W
Cliffwood Beach, N.J., U.S.	194		40.26 N	74.13 W
Clifton, St. Vin.	159e	p11	12.35 N	61.25 W
Clifton, Eng., U.K.	180		53.46 N	2.49 W
Clifton, Az., U.S.	150	J7	33.04 N	109.18 W
Clifton, Il., U.S.	130	D10	40.56 N	87.55 W
Clifton, Ks., U.S.	138	B11	39.34 N	97.16 W
Clifton, Tn., U.S.	134	B11	35.22 N	87.59 W
Clifton, Tx., U.S.	136	C10	31.46 N	97.34 W
Clifton Forge, Va., U.S.	124	G6	37.48 N	79.49 W
Clifton Heights, N.Y., U.S.	202a		42.44 N	78.56 W
Clifton Heights, Pa., U.S.	203		39.55 N	75.17 W
Clifton Hills, Austl.	98	F2	26.52 S	138.50 E
Clifton Park, p.o.i., Md., U.S.	202b		39.19 N	76.35 W
Clifton Point, c., Bah.	132	K8	25.01 N	77.33 W
Climax, Sk., Can.	142	E5	49.12 N	108.23 W
Climax, Co., U.S.	138	B2	39.22 N	106.10 W
Climax, Mi., U.S.	130	B12	42.14 N	85.19 W
Clinch, stm., U.S.	130	I13	35.53 N	84.29 W
Clinchco, Va., U.S.	130	G15	37.09 N	82.21 W
Clingmans Dome, mtn., U.S.	124	I2	35.35 N	83.30 W
Clinton, B.C., Can.	144	E9	51.04 N	121.37 W
Clinton, On., Can.	126	E8	43.37 N	81.31 W
Clinton, Al., U.S.	134	E11	32.55 N	88.00 W
Clinton, Ar., U.S.	134	B6	35.35 N	92.27 W
Clinton, Il., U.S.	130	D8	40.09 N	88.56 W
Clinton, In., U.S.	130	E10	39.38 N	87.24 W
Clinton, Ia., U.S.	130	C7	41.50 N	90.11 W
Clinton, Ky., U.S.	130	H9	36.39 N	89.00 W
Clinton, La., U.S.	134	G7	30.51 N	91.00 W
Clinton, Me., U.S.	122	F7	44.38 N	69.30 W
Clinton, Mi., U.S.	124	B2	42.04 N	83.58 W
Clinton, Mn., U.S.	128	F2	45.27 N	96.26 W
Clinton, Ms., U.S.	134	E8	32.20 N	90.19 W
Clinton, Mo., U.S.	130	F4	38.22 N	93.46 W
Clinton, N.C., U.S.	132	A7	34.59 N	78.18 W
Clinton, Ok., U.S.	138	F9	35.30 N	98.58 W
Clinton, S.C., U.S.	132	B4	34.28 N	81.52 W
Clinton, Tn., U.S.	124	H1	36.06 N	84.08 W
Clinton, Wi., U.S.	130	B9	42.33 N	88.51 W
Clinton, Cape, c., Austl.	98	D8	22.32 S	150.47 E
Clinton, Lake, res., Il., U.S.	130	D9	40.10 N	88.50 W
Clinton, Middle Branch, stm., Mi., U.S.	199		42.36 N	82.54 W
Clinton-Colden Lake, l., N.T., Can.	110	C9	63.58 N	107.27 W
Clinton Lake, res., Ks., U.S.	130	F2	38.55 N	95.25 W
Clinton Reservoir, res., N.J., U.S.	194		41.05 N	74.27 W
Clintonville, Mi., U.S.	199		42.43 N	83.22 W
Clintonville, Wi., U.S.	128	G10	44.36 N	88.46 W
Clintwood, Va., U.S.	124	G3	37.07 N	82.28 W
Clio, Al., U.S.	134	F13	31.42 N	85.36 W
Clio, Mi., U.S.	126	E6	43.10 N	83.43 W
Clio, S.C., U.S.	132	B6	34.35 N	79.32 W
Clipperton, Île, at., Oc.	174	H28	10.17 N	109.13 W
Clipperton Fracture Zone, unds.	174	I25	10.00 N	115.00 W
Clipperton Island see Clipperton, Île, at., Oc.	174	H28	10.17 N	109.13 W
Clisham, mtn., Scot., U.K.	10	C6	57.58 N	6.48 W
Clisson, Fr.	20	G7	47.05 N	1.17 W
Clitunno, stm., Italy	32	B6	42.59 N	12.35 E
Clock Face, Eng., U.K.	180		53.25 N	2.43 W
Clodomira, Arg.	172	C5	27.33 S	64.07 W
Cloete, Mex.	136	G6	27.55 N	101.10 W
Cloisters, The, bldg., N.Y., U.S.	194		40.52 N	73.56 W
Clonakilty, Ire.	10	J4	51.37 N	8.53 W
Clonakilty Bay, b., Ire.	10	J4	51.35 N	8.50 W
Cloncurry, Austl.	98	C3	20.42 S	140.30 E
Cloncurry, stm., Austl.	98	B3	18.35 S	140.41 E
Clonmel, Ire.	10	I5	52.21 N	7.42 W
Clontarf, Austl.	192a		33.48 S	151.16 E
Clo-oose, B.C., Can.	144	H6	48.40 N	124.49 W
Cloppenburg, Ger.	24	D3	52.50 N	8.03 E
Cloquet, Mn., U.S.	128	E6	46.43 N	92.27 W
Cloquet, stm., Mn., U.S.	128	D6	46.51 N	92.34 W
Clorinda, Arg.	172	B9	25.17 S	57.42 W
Closter, N.J., U.S.	194		40.58 N	73.57 W
Cloudcroft, N.M., U.S.	136	B2	32.57 N	105.44 W
Cloud Peak, mtn., Wy., U.S.	140	C5	44.25 N	107.10 W
Clough Foot, Eng., U.K.	180		53.43 N	2.08 W
Clova, Qc., Can.	122	B1	48.07 N	75.22 W
Clove Lakes Park, p.o.i., N.Y., U.S.	194		40.37 N	74.07 W
Clovelly, Austl.	192a		33.55 S	151.16 E
Clover, S.C., U.S.	132	A4	35.06 N	81.13 W
Clover Creek, stm., Id., U.S.	146	H11	42.34 N	115.37 W
Clover Creek, stm., Id., U.S.	146	H11	42.59 N	115.10 W
Cloverdale, Al., U.S.	134	C11	34.56 N	87.46 W
Cloverdale, Ca., U.S.	148	E2	38.48 N	123.01 W
Cloverdale, Il., U.S.	196		41.56 N	88.07 W
Cloverdale, In., U.S.	130	E11	39.29 N	86.47 W
Cloverdale Mall, shp. cen., On., Can.	193b		43.38 N	79.34 W
Cloverdene, S. Afr.	191d		26.09 S	28.22 E
Cloverport, Ky., U.S.	130	G11	37.49 N	86.38 W
Clovis, Ca., U.S.	148	G6	36.49 N	119.42 W
Clovis, N.M., U.S.	138	G5	34.24 N	103.13 W
Clowbridge Reservoir, res., Eng., U.K.	180		53.45 N	2.16 W
Cluain Meala see Clonmel, Ire.	10	I5	52.21 N	7.42 W
Cluj, state, Rom.	36	C10	46.45 N	23.45 E
Cluj-Napoca, Rom.	36	C10	46.46 N	23.36 E
Clunes, Austl.	98	K4	37.17 S	143.46 E
Cluny, Austl.	98	E2	24.31 S	139.34 E
Cluny, Fr.	22	C10	46.26 N	4.38 E
Cluses, Fr.	22	C12	46.03 N	6.35 E
Clusone, Italy	30	E7	45.54 N	10.00 E
Clute, Tx., U.S.	136	E12	29.01 N	95.24 W
Clutha, stm., N.Z.	102	G3	46.19 S	169.49 E
Clwyd, co., Wales, U.K.	180		53.15 N	3.10 W
Clyde, Austl.	192a		33.50 S	151.00 E

Name	Page	Map Ref.	Latitude	Longitude
Clyde, Ab., Can.	144	B17	54.09 N	113.39 W
Clyde, Ks., U.S.	138	B11	39.35 N	97.23 W
Clyde, Mi., U.S.	199		42.41 N	83.37 W
Clyde, N.Y., U.S.	126	E13	43.05 N	76.52 W
Clyde, N.C., U.S.	132	A3	35.31 N	82.54 W
Clyde, Oh., U.S.	124	C3	41.18 N	82.58 W
Clyde, Tx., U.S.	136	B8	32.24 N	99.29 W
Clyde, stm., N.S., Can.	122	G11	43.31 N	65.20 W
Clyde, stm., Scot., U.K.	10	F9	55.55 N	4.29 W
Clyde, stm., Vt., U.S.	122	F4	44.55 N	72.13 W
Clyde, Firth of, b., Scot., U.K.	10	F7	55.31 N	5.01 W
Clyde Inlet, b., Nu., Can.	110	A17	70.15 N	68.45 W
Clyde Park, Mt., U.S.	146	E16	45.53 N	110.37 W
Clyde Potts Reservoir, res., N.J., U.S.	194		40.48 N	74.35 W
Clyde River, Nu., Can.	110	A16	70.23 N	68.40 W
Clymer, Pa., U.S.	124	D6	40.39 N	79.00 W
Ćmielów, Pol.	24	F17	50.53 N	21.31 E
Cna, stm., Bela.	26	H9	52.09 N	27.01 E
Cna, stm., Russia	26	C16	57.31 N	34.23 E
Cna, stm., Russia	26	D13	54.28 N	42.01 E
Cnossus see Knosós, hist., Grc.	34	H8	35.16 N	25.12 E
Côa, stm., Port.	28	D3	41.05 N	7.05 W
Coacalco, Mex.	204a		19.37 N	99.05 W
Coachella, Ca., U.S.	148	J9	33.40 N	116.09 W
Coachella Canal, can., Ca., U.S.	150	J1	33.43 N	116.15 W
Coacoyole, Mex.	154	C5	24.31 N	106.34 W
Coahoma, Tx., U.S.	136	B6	32.18 N	101.18 W
Coahuila, Mex.	150	K2	32.11 N	114.59 W
Coahuila, state, Mex.	154	B8	27.20 N	102.00 W
Coal City, Il., U.S.	128	J10	41.16 N	88.16 W
Coalcomán de Matamoros, Mex.	154	F7	18.47 N	103.09 W
Coal Creek, stm., Co., U.S.	140	G8	40.30 N	104.25 W
Coal Creek, stm., Wa., U.S.	146	C8	47.19 N	118.36 W
Coaldale, Ab., Can.	144	G18	49.43 N	112.37 W
Coal Fire Creek, stm., U.S.	134	D10	33.15 N	88.18 W
Coalgate, Ok., U.S.	134	C2	34.31 N	96.14 W
Coal Grove, Oh., U.S.	124	F3	38.29 N	82.39 W
Coal Harbour, B.C., Can.	144	F3	50.36 N	127.35 W
Coal Hill, Ar., U.S.	134	B5	35.26 N	93.40 W
Coal Hill Park, p.o.i., China	189a		39.56 N	116.23 E
Coalhurst, Ab., Can.	144	G18	49.45 N	112.56 W
Coalinga, Ca., U.S.	148	G5	36.08 N	120.21 W
Coalmont, B.C., Can.	144	G10	49.31 N	120.41 W
Coalport, Pa., U.S.	124	D7	40.44 N	78.31 W
Coal River, B.C., Can.	110	D5	59.39 N	126.57 W
Coal Run, stm., Pa., U.S.	197b		40.21 N	80.07 W
Coalspur, Ab., Can.	144	C13	53.09 N	117.02 W
Coal Valley, val., Nv., U.S.	148	F10	37.57 N	115.19 W
Coalville, Eng., U.K.	10	I11	52.42 N	1.22 W
Coalville, Ut., U.S.	150	C5	40.55 N	111.23 W
Coamo, P.R.	158a	b3	18.04 N	66.21 W
Coamo, Lago, res., P.R.	158a	b3	18.01 N	66.23 W
Coaraci, Braz.	170	H6	14.39 S	39.32 W
Coari, Braz.	164	D5	4.05 S	63.07 W
Coari, stm., Braz.	164	D5	4.26 S	63.28 W
Coast Mountains, mts., N.A.	110	D4	55.00 N	129.00 W
Coast Ranges, mts., U.S.	112	C3	40.00 N	123.38 W
Coatbridge, Scot., U.K.	10	F9	55.52 N	4.01 W
Coatesville, Pa., U.S.	124	E10	39.58 N	75.48 W
Coaticook, Qc., Can.	122	E5	45.08 N	71.48 W
Coats Island, i., Nu., Can.	110	C13	62.30 N	83.00 W
Coats Land, reg., Ant.	103	C2	77.00 S	28.00 W
Coatzacoalcos, Mex.	154	F11	18.08 N	94.26 W
Cobá, hist., Mex.	156	B4	20.36 N	87.35 W
Cobadin, Rom.	36	E15	44.04 N	28.14 E
Cobalt, On., Can.	114	C11	47.23 N	79.40 W
Cobán, Guat.	156	E2	15.27 N	90.22 W
Cobar, Austl.	98	H5	31.29 S	145.49 E
Cobargo, Austl.	98	K7	36.23 S	149.53 E
Cobb Creek, stm., Ok., U.S.	138	F10	35.05 N	98.25 W
Cobberas, Mount, mtn., Austl.	98	K6	36.51 S	148.08 E
Cobbetts Pond, l., N.H., U.S.	201		42.48 N	71.17 W
Cobbin's Brook, stm., Eng., U.K.	178		51.41 N	0.01 W
Cobbitty, Austl.	192a		34.01 S	150.41 E
Cobbitty, hill, Austl.	192a		33.59 S	150.42 E
Cobbs Creek, stm., Pa., U.S.	203		39.54 N	75.15 W
Cobbs Creek Park, p.o.i., Pa., U.S.	203		39.58 N	75.16 W
Cobden, On., Can.	126	C13	45.37 N	76.52 W
Cobeña, Spain	184a		40.34 N	3.30 W
Cobequid Bay, b., N.S., Can.	122	E13	45.21 N	63.45 W
Cobequid Mountains, mts., N.S., Can.	122	E13	45.31 N	64.05 W
Cobh, Ire.	10	J4	51.51 N	8.17 W
Cobham, Eng., U.K.	178		51.23 N	0.24 E
Cobham, stm., Can.	142	B18	52.49 N	94.57 W
Cobham Hall, hist., Eng., U.K.	178		51.23 N	0.25 E
Cobija, Bol.	166	B3	11.02 S	68.44 W
Coblence see Koblenz, Ger.	24	F3	50.21 N	7.35 E
Coblenz see Koblenz, Ger.	24	F3	50.21 N	7.35 E
Cobleskill, N.Y., U.S.	124	B11	42.40 N	74.29 W
Cobo Hall, bldg., Mi., U.S.	199		42.19 N	83.03 W
Coboto, Cerro, mtn., Mex.	150	L4	31.29 N	112.05 W
Čoboty, ngh., Russia	183b		55.39 N	37.21 E
Cobourg, On., Can.	126	E11	43.57 N	78.09 W
Cobquecura, Chile	172	H1	36.08 S	72.47 W
Cobram, Austl.	98	J5	35.55 S	145.39 E
Cobras, Ilha das, i., Braz.	205a		22.54 S	43.10 W
Cobre, Barranca del (Copper Canyon), misc. cult., Mex.	154	B5	27.26 N	107.32 W
Cóbuè, Moz.	88	C5	12.05 S	34.50 E
Coburg, Ger.	24	F6	50.15 N	10.58 E
Coburg Island, i., Nu., Can.	108	B10	76.01 N	79.10 W
Coburg Peninsula, pen., Austl.	96	B6	11.22 S	132.16 E
Coburn Mountain, mtn., Me., U.S.	122	E6	45.28 N	70.06 W
Coca, stm., Ec.	168	H3	0.28 S	76.57 W
Coca, Laguna, l., Cuba	204b		22.57 N	82.27 W
Cocachacra, Peru	164	G3	17.04 S	71.45 W
Cocal, Braz.	170	B5	3.28 S	41.34 W
Cocanada see Kākināda, India	69	C6	16.56 N	82.14 E
Cocentaina, Spain	28	F10	38.45 N	0.26 W
Cöch, stm., Asia	52	B6	51.02 N	106.38 E
Cochabamba, Bol.	166	C3	17.23 S	66.09 W
Cochato, stm., Ma., U.S.	201		42.10 N	71.01 W
Coche, Isla, i., Ven.	168	B10	10.45 N	63.55 W
Cochem, Ger.	24	F3	50.08 N	7.09 E
Cochesett, Ma., U.S.	201		42.01 N	71.02 W
Cochetopa Creek, stm., Co., U.S.	138	C2	38.31 N	106.47 W
Cochichewick, Lake, l., Ma., U.S.	201		42.42 N	71.06 W
Cochin see Kochi, India	69	G3	9.56 N	76.15 E
Cochin China see Nam Phan, hist. reg., Viet.	64	G8	11.00 N	107.00 E
Cochinos, Bahía de (Pigs, Bay of), b., Cuba	156	A7	22.07 N	81.10 W
Cochise Head, mtn., Az., U.S.	150	K7	32.03 N	109.18 W
Cochiti Indian Reservation, ind. res., N.M., U.S.	138	F2	35.37 N	106.20 W
Cochituate, Lake, l., Ma., U.S.	201		42.17 N	71.22 W
Cochran, Ga., U.S.	132	D2	32.23 N	83.20 W
Cochrane, Ab., Can.	144	E16	51.11 N	114.28 W
Cochrane, On., Can.	114	B10	49.03 N	81.01 W
Cochrane, Wi., U.S.	128	G7	44.14 N	91.50 W
Cochrane, Cerro (San Lorenzo, Monte), mtn., S.A.	166	I2	47.37 S	72.19 W
Cochrane, Lago (Pueyrredón, Lago), l., S.A.	166	I2	47.20 S	71.56 W
Cochranton, Pa., U.S.	124	C5	41.31 N	80.02 W
Cockburn, Austl.	98	I3	32.04 S	140.59 E
Cockburn, Mount, mtn., Austl.	96	D5	22.47 S	130.30 E
Cockburn, Mount, mtn., Austl.	96	E5	25.57 S	129.27 E
Cockburn Island, i., On., Can.	126	C6	45.55 N	83.22 W
Cock Clarks, Eng., U.K.	178		51.42 N	0.37 E
Cockenoe Island, i., Ct., U.S.	194		41.05 N	73.21 W
Cockermouth, Eng., U.K.	10	G9	54.39 N	3.21 W
Cockfosters, ngh., Eng., U.K.	178		51.39 N	0.09 W
Cockpit Country, reg., Jam.	158d	i13	18.21 N	77.33 W
Côco, stm., Braz.	170	F1	10.10 S	49.10 W
Coco, stm., N.A.	156	E6	14.59 N	83.10 W
Coco, Cayo, i., Cuba	156	A8	22.29 N	78.27 W
Coco, Isla del, i., C.R.	152	F7	5.32 N	87.04 W
Cocoa, Fl., U.S.	132	H5	28.21 N	80.44 W
Cocoa Beach, Fl., U.S.	132	H5	28.19 N	80.36 W
Cocoa Point, c., Antig.	159b	e4	17.36 N	61.44 W
Coco Channel, strt., Asia	62	F7	13.45 N	93.01 E
Cococi, Braz.	170	D5	6.25 S	40.30 W
Cocodrie Lake, res., La., U.S.	134	G6	30.58 N	92.25 W
Coco Islands, is., Mya.	62	F7	14.08 N	93.25 E
Coconino Plateau, plat., Az., U.S.	150	H4	35.50 N	112.30 W
Cocos, Braz.	170	H3	14.11 S	44.32 W
Cocos Bay, b., Trin.	159f	s12	10.26 N	61.01 W
Cocos Island, i., Guam	100c	k9	13.14 N	144.39 E
Cocos Islands, dep., Oc.	174	K12	12.10 S	96.55 E
Cocos Lagoon, b., Guam	100c	j9	13.14 N	144.38 E
Cocos Ridge, unds.	176	H5	5.30 N	86.00 W
Cocotá, ngh., Braz.	205a		22.49 S	43.11 W
Cocuiza, stm., Ven.	168	B6	10.58 N	71.17 W
Cocula, Mex.	154	E7	20.23 N	103.50 W
Cod, Cape, pen., Ma., U.S.	124	C15	41.42 N	70.15 W
Codăești, Rom.	36	C14	46.51 N	27.47 E
Codajás, Braz.	164	D5	3.49 S	62.05 W
Codera, Cabo, c., Ven.	168	B8	10.34 N	66.03 W
Coderre, Sk., Can.	142	D7	50.08 N	106.20 W
Coderre, Ruisseau, stm., Qc., Can.	193a		45.43 N	73.19 W
Codigoro, Italy	30	F9	44.50 N	12.06 E
Cod Island, i., Nf., Can.	108	F13	57.45 N	61.45 W
Codlea, Rom.	36	D12	45.41 N	25.26 E
Codó, Braz.	170	C4	4.29 S	43.53 W
Codogno, Italy	30	E6	45.09 N	9.42 E
Codózinho, Braz.	170	C3	4.46 S	44.10 W
Codrii, hills, Mol.	38	F6	47.22 N	28.07 E
Codrington, Antig.	159b	e4	17.38 N	61.50 W
Codroy, Nf., Can.	122	C17	47.52 N	59.23 W
Codru-Moma, Munții, mts., Rom.	36	C9	46.30 N	22.20 E
Cody, Ne., U.S.	140	E11	42.54 N	101.14 W
Cody, Wy., U.S.	140	C3	44.32 N	109.02 W
Coelemu, Chile	172	H1	36.29 S	72.42 W
Coelho Neto, Braz.	170	C4	4.15 S	43.00 W
Coen, Austl.	96	B8	13.56 S	143.13 E
Coeroeni (Corentyne), stm., S.A.	164	C6	5.50 N	57.05 W
Coesfeld, Ger.	20	C16	51.56 N	7.10 E
Coëtivy, i., Sey.	89b	k13	7.08 S	56.16 E
Coeur d'Alene, Id., U.S.	146	C10	47.40 N	116.46 W
Coeur d'Alene, stm., Id., U.S.	146	C10	47.26 N	116.47 W
Coeur d'Alene Indian Reservation, ind. res., Id., U.S.	146	C10	47.18 N	116.45 W
Coeur d'Alene Lake, res., Id., U.S.	146	C10	47.32 N	116.48 W
Coeur d'Alene Mountains, mts., Id., U.S.	146	C10	47.49 N	116.23 W
Coffeen, Il., U.S.	130	E8	39.05 N	89.24 W
Coffeeville, Ms., U.S.	134	D9	33.58 N	89.39 W
Coffeyville, Ks., U.S.	130	G2	37.02 N	95.36 W
Coffs Harbour, Austl.	98	H9	30.18 S	153.08 E
Cofre de Perote, Cerro, mtn., Mex.	154	F10	19.29 N	97.08 W
Cofre de Perote, Parque Nacional, p.o.i., Mex.	154	F10	19.32 N	97.10 W
Cofrentes see Cofrents, Spain	28	E9	39.13 N	1.04 W
Cofrents, Spain	28	E9	39.13 N	1.04 W
Cogâlnic (Kohyl'nyk), stm., Eur.	36	C15	45.49 N	29.38 E
Coggon, Ia., U.S.	130	B6	42.16 N	91.32 W
Coghinas, stm., Italy	32	D2	40.56 N	8.49 E
Coghinas, Lago del, res., Italy	32	D3	40.45 N	9.02 E
Cogliate, Italy	184b		45.39 N	9.05 E
Cognac, Fr.	22	D5	45.41 N	0.19 W
Cogolludo, Spain	28	D7	40.57 N	3.05 W
Cogoon, stm., Austl.	98	F7	27.19 S	148.49 E
Čograjskoe vodohranilišče, res., Russia	40	I14	45.33 N	44.20 E
Cogswell, N.D., U.S.	140	A15	46.06 N	97.47 W
Cogswell Reservoir, res., Ca., U.S.	198		34.14 N	117.58 W
Çoğun, Tur.	42	F6	39.19 N	34.07 E
Cohasset Harbor, b., Ma., U.S.	201		42.15 N	70.47 W
Čohkarášša, mtn., Nor.	14	C15	69.57 N	24.32 E
Cohocton, stm., N.Y., U.S.	126	F12	42.09 N	77.05 W
Cohoes, N.Y., U.S.	124	B12	42.46 N	73.42 W
Cohuna, Austl.	98	J5	35.48 S	144.12 E
Coiba, Isla de, i., Pan.	156	I7	7.27 N	81.45 W
Coig, stm., Arg.	166	J3	50.57 S	69.08 W
Coignières, Fr.	179		48.45 N	1.55 E
Coihaique, Chile	166	I2	45.34 S	72.04 W
Coils Creek, stm., Nv., U.S.	148	D9	39.32 N	116.15 W
Coimbatore (Koyambattur), India	69	F3	10.59 N	76.58 E
Coimbra, Braz.	170	K4	20.51 S	42.48 W
Coimbra, Port.	28	D2	40.12 N	8.25 W
Coimbra, state, Port.	28	D2	40.15 N	8.20 W
Coín, Spain	28	H6	36.39 N	4.45 W
Coin, Ia., U.S.	130	D2	40.39 N	95.14 W
Coina, stm., Port.	184c		38.38 N	9.03 W
Coipasa, Lago, l., Bol.	166	C3	19.12 S	68.07 W
Coipasa, Salar de, pl., S.A.	166	C3	19.25 S	68.10 W
Coire see Chur, Switz.	30	D6	46.51 N	9.31 E
Cojedes, state, Ven.	168	C7	9.20 N	68.20 W
Cojímar, ngh., Cuba	204b		23.10 N	82.18 W
Cojímar, stm., Cuba	204b		23.10 N	82.17 W
Cojudo Blanco, Cerro, mtn., Arg.	166	I3	47.05 S	69.20 W
Cojutepeque, El Sal.	156	F3	13.42 N	88.56 W
Çokak, Tur.	76	A7	37.45 N	36.19 E
Čokato, Mn., U.S.	128	F4	45.04 N	94.12 W
Coker, Nig.	191a		6.29 N	3.20 E
Cokeville, Wy., U.S.	146	H16	42.04 N	110.57 W
Čokpar, Kaz.	48	F12	43.49 N	74.22 E
Čokurdah, Russia	50	B18	70.37 N	147.53 E
Colāba, ngh., India	190c		18.54 N	72.48 E
Colāba Point, c., India	190c		18.53 N	72.48 E
Colac, Austl.	98	L4	38.20 S	143.35 E
Colalao del Valle, Arg.	172	C5	26.21 S	65.57 W
Colares, Port.	184c		38.48 N	9.27 W
Colares, Ribeira de, stm., Port.	184c		38.49 N	9.28 W
Colatina, Braz.	170	J5	19.31 S	40.38 W
Colbeck, Cape, c., Ant.	103	C25	77.04 S	157.32 W
Colberry Park, Mi., U.S.	199		42.36 N	83.16 W
Colbert, Ok., U.S.	134	D2	33.51 N	96.30 W
Colbinabbin, Austl.	98	K5	36.35 S	144.47 E
Colborne, On., Can.	126	E12	44.00 N	77.51 W
Colbún, Chile	172	G2	35.42 S	71.24 W
Colbún, Embalse, res., Chile	172	G2	35.40 S	71.15 W
Colby, Ks., U.S.	138	B7	39.23 N	101.02 W
Colby, Wi., U.S.	128	G8	44.54 N	90.19 W
Colchester, Eng., U.K.	10	J13	51.53 N	0.54 E
Colchester, Ct., U.S.	124	C13	41.34 N	72.19 W
Colchester, Il., U.S.	130	D7	40.25 N	90.46 W
Cold Bay, Ak., U.S.	109	E7	55.11 N	162.30 W
Coldblow, ngh., Eng., U.K.	178		51.26 N	0.10 E
Cold Lake, Ab., Can.	110	E8	54.27 N	110.10 W
Cold Norton, Eng., U.K.	178		51.40 N	0.40 E
Cold Spring, Mn., U.S.	128	F4	45.27 N	94.26 W
Coldspring, Tx., U.S.	136	D12	30.35 N	95.06 W
Cold Spring Harbor, N.Y., U.S.	194		40.52 N	73.27 W
Cold Spring Harbor, b., N.Y., U.S.	194		40.53 N	73.28 W
Cold Spring Terrace, N.Y., U.S.	194		40.50 N	73.26 W
Coldstream, Scot., U.K.	10	F10	55.39 N	2.15 W
Coldwater, Ks., U.S.	138	D9	37.16 N	99.19 W
Coldwater, Mi., U.S.	130	C12	41.56 N	85.00 W
Coldwater, Ms., U.S.	134	C8	34.42 N	89.58 W
Coldwater, Oh., U.S.	130	D13	40.29 N	84.37 W
Coldwater, stm., Ms., U.S.	134	C8	34.10 N	90.12 W
Coldwater Canyon, val., Ca., U.S.	198		34.14 N	117.44 W
Coldwater Creek, stm., U.S.	138	E7	36.40 N	101.08 W
Coldwater Indian Reserve, ind. res., B.C., Can.	144	F9	50.02 N	120.52 W
Coleambally, Austl.	98	J5	34.48 S	145.52 E
Colebrook, N.H., U.S.	122	F5	44.53 N	71.29 W
Cole Camp, Mo., U.S.	130	F4	38.27 N	93.12 W
Colégio, Morro do, mtn., Braz.	205b		23.38 S	46.21 W
Coleman, Ab., Can.	144	G16	49.38 N	114.29 W
Coleman, Fl., U.S.	132	H3	28.48 N	82.04 W
Coleman, Mi., U.S.	126	E5	43.45 N	84.35 W
Coleman, Tx., U.S.	136	C8	31.49 N	99.25 W
Coleman, Wi., U.S.	126	C1	45.03 N	88.02 W
Coleman, stm., Austl.	96	B8	15.05 S	141.39 E
Coleman, Lake, res., Tx., U.S.	136	B8	32.02 N	99.29 W
Colenso, S. Afr.	90	F9	28.44 S	29.49 E
Coleraine, Austl.	98	K3	37.36 S	141.41 E
Coleraine, N. Ire., U.K.	10	F6	55.08 N	6.40 W
Coleraine, Mn., U.S.	128	D5	47.17 N	93.25 W
Coleridge, Ne., U.S.	140	E15	42.30 N	97.13 W
Coles, Ms., U.S.	134	F7	31.16 N	91.01 W
Colesberg, S. Afr.	90	G7	30.43 S	25.06 E
Coles Brook, stm., N.J., U.S.	194		40.55 N	74.02 W
Coleshill, Eng., U.K.	178		51.39 N	0.38 W
Colesville, Md., U.S.	202c		39.05 N	77.00 W
Coleto Creek, stm., Tx., U.S.	136	F10	28.41 N	97.00 W
Coleville, Sk., Can.	142	C4	51.43 N	109.16 W
Colfax, Ca., U.S.	148	D5	39.05 N	120.56 W
Colfax, Il., U.S.	130	D9	40.33 N	88.36 W
Colfax, In., U.S.	130	D11	40.11 N	86.39 W
Colfax, Ia., U.S.	130	C4	41.40 N	93.14 W
Colfax, La., U.S.	134	F6	31.31 N	92.42 W
Colfax, Wa., U.S.	146	D9	46.52 N	117.21 W
Colfax, Wi., U.S.	128	F7	44.59 N	91.43 W
Colgate Creek, stm., Md., U.S.	202b		39.15 N	76.32 W
Colgong, India	70	F11	25.15 N	87.14 E
Colhué Huapi, Lago, l., Arg.	166	I3	45.32 S	68.46 W
Colibris, Pointe des, c., Guad.	159c	h6	16.14 N	61.10 W
Colibris, Pointe des, c., Guad.	159c	h6	16.17 N	61.05 W
Colico, Italy	30	D6	46.08 N	9.21 E
Coligny, S. Afr.	90	E8	26.19 S	26.18 E
Colihaut, Dom.	159c	j6	15.29 N	61.28 W
Colima, Mex.	154	K1	32.26 N	115.03 W
Colima, Mex.	154	F7	19.14 N	103.43 W
Colima, state, Mex.	152	D4	19.10 N	104.00 W
Colima, Nevado de, vol., Mex.	154	F7	19.33 N	103.38 W
Colimes, stm., Ec.	168	H1	1.32 S	80.00 W
Colina, Chile	172	F2	33.12 S	70.41 W
Colinas, Braz.	170	H1	14.12 S	48.04 W
Colinas, Braz.	170	D3	6.02 S	44.14 W
Colinton, Ab., Can.	144	B17	54.36 N	113.16 W
Coliseum see Colosseo, hist., Italy	185a		41.54 N	12.29 E
Coll, i., Scot., U.K.	10	E6	56.38 N	6.34 W
Collarenebri, Austl.	98	G7	29.31 S	148.37 E
Collaroy, Austl.	192a		33.44 S	151.18 E
Collbran, Co., U.S.	150	D8	39.15 N	107.59 W
Colleen Bawn, Zimb.	90	B9	21.00 S	29.13 E
College, Ak., U.S.	109	D10	64.50 N	147.46 W
Collegedale, Tn., U.S.	134	B13	35.03 N	85.03 W
College Park, Ga., U.S.	134	D14	33.38 N	84.27 W
College Park Airport, arpt., Md., U.S.	202c		38.58 N	76.55 W
College Place, Wa., U.S.	146	D8	46.02 N	118.23 W
College Point, ngh., N.Y., U.S.	194		40.47 N	73.51 W
College Station, Ar., U.S.	134	C6	34.42 N	92.14 W
College Station, Tx., U.S.	136	D11	30.37 N	96.20 W
Collegeville, In., U.S.	130	D10	40.54 N	87.08 W
Collégien, Fr.	179		48.50 N	2.40 E
Collerina, Austl.	98	G6	29.41 S	146.38 E
Colleymount, B.C., Can.	144	B4	54.02 N	126.08 W
Collie, Austl.	96	F3	33.21 S	116.09 E
Collier Bay, b., Austl.	96	C4	16.10 S	124.15 E
Collier Row, ngh., Eng., U.K.	178		51.36 N	0.10 E
Collier-Seminole State Park, p.o.i., Fl., U.S.	132	K4	25.59 N	81.36 W
Collierville, Tn., U.S.	134	B9	35.03 N	89.40 W
Collingswood, N.J., U.S.	203		39.55 N	75.04 W
Collingwood, Austl.	192b		37.48 S	145.00 E
Collingwood, On., Can.	126	D9	44.29 N	80.12 W
Collins, Ga., U.S.	132	D3	32.10 N	82.06 W
Collins, Ia., U.S.	130	C4	41.54 N	93.18 W
Collins, Ms., U.S.	134	F9	31.38 N	89.33 W
Collins, stm., Tn., U.S.	134	B13	35.48 N	85.37 W
Collins, Mount, hill, On., Can.	114	C10	47.51 N	80.59 W
Collins Bay, On., Can.	126	D13	44.14 N	76.37 W
Collins Head, c., Norf. I.	100i	y25	29.03 S	167.58 E
Collinston, La., U.S.	134	E7	32.42 N	91.52 W
Collinsville, Austl.	98	C6	20.34 S	147.51 E
Collinsville, Al., U.S.	134	C13	34.15 N	85.52 W
Collinsville, Ca., U.S.	200		38.05 N	121.51 W
Collinsville, Ms., U.S.	134	E10	32.29 N	88.50 W
Collinsville, N.J., U.S.	194		40.49 N	74.28 W
Collinsville, Ok., U.S.	130	H2	36.21 N	95.50 W
Collinsville, Tx., U.S.	134	D2	33.32 N	96.55 W
Collinwood, Tn., U.S.	134	B11	35.10 N	87.44 W
Collipulli, Chile	172	H1	37.57 S	72.26 W
Collister, Id., U.S.	146	G10	43.38 N	116.14 W
Collooney, Ire.	10	G4	54.10 N	8.29 W
Collserola, Serra de, mts., Spain	184d		41.26 N	2.07 E
Colma Creek, stm., Ca., U.S.	200		37.38 N	122.23 W
Colman, S.D., U.S.	128	H2	43.58 N	96.48 W
Colmar, Fr.	20	F16	48.04 N	7.21 E
Colmar Manor, Md., U.S.	202c		38.55 N	76.56 W
Colmenar, Spain	28	H6	36.54 N	4.20 W
Colmenar Viejo, Spain	28	D7	40.40 N	3.46 W
Colmeneros, Mex.	154	F8	18.06 N	101.41 W
Colmesneil, Tx., U.S.	136	D13	30.54 N	94.25 W
Colnbrook, Eng., U.K.	178		51.29 N	0.31 W
Colne, stm., Eng., U.K.	178		51.26 N	0.30 W
Colnett, Punta, c., Mex.	120	F4	30.58 N	116.19 W
Colney Heath, Eng., U.K.	178		51.44 N	0.15 W
Colney Street, Eng., U.K.	178		51.42 N	0.20 W
Colo, Ia., U.S.	130	B4	42.01 N	93.18 W
Cologne see Köln, Ger.	24	E2	50.55 N	6.57 E
Cologne, Mn., U.S.	128	G5	44.46 N	93.47 W
Cologno Monzese, Italy	184b		45.32 N	9.17 E
Cololo, Nevado, mtn., Bol.	166	B3	14.53 S	69.06 W
Coloma, Mi., U.S.	130	B11	42.11 N	86.18 W
Coloma, Wi., U.S.	128	G9	44.01 N	89.30 W
Colomb-Béchar see Béchar, Alg.	84	C4	31.37 N	2.13 W
Colômbia, Braz.	170	K1	20.10 S	48.41 W
Colombia, Col.	168	F4	3.23 N	74.48 W
Colombia, Mex.	136	G8	27.41 N	99.45 W
Colombia, ctry., S.A.	164	C3	4.00 N	72.00 W
Colombie-Britannique see British Columbia, state, Can.	110	E5	54.00 N	125.00 W
Colombier, Pointe à, c., Guad.	159a	b2	17.55 N	62.52 W
Colombo, Braz.	172	B13	25.14 S	49.13 W
Colombo, Sri L.	69	H4	6.54 N	79.51 E
Colome, S.D., U.S.	140	D13	43.15 N	99.41 W
Colomiers, Fr.	22	F7	43.37 N	1.20 E
Colón, Arg.	172	F7	33.54 S	61.03 W
Colón, Arg.	172	F8	32.16 S	58.07 W
Colón, Cuba	156	A7	22.43 N	80.54 W
Colón, Pan.	156	H8	9.21 N	79.54 W
Colon, Mi., U.S.	130	C12	41.57 N	85.19 W
Colón, Ur.	172	F10	33.53 S	54.44 W
Colón, Archipiélago de (Galapagos Islands), is., Ec.	164a	h12	0.42 N	91.30 W
Colón, Cementerio, misc. cult., Cuba	204b		23.08 N	82.23 W
Colón, Teatro, p.o.i., Arg.	206		34.36 S	58.23 W
Colona, Austl.	96	F6	31.37 S	132.04 E
Colonarie, stm., St. Vin.	159e	o11	13.14 N	61.07 W
Colonel Danforth Park, p.o.i., On., Can.	193b		43.47 N	79.10 W
Colonelganj, India	70	E8	27.07 N	81.42 E
Colonești, Rom.	36	C14	46.34 N	27.18 E
Colônia, stm., Braz.	170	H6	14.48 S	39.02 W
Colonia Alvear Norte see General Alvear, Arg.	172	G4	34.58 S	67.41 W
Colonia Caroya, Arg.	172	E5	31.01 S	64.04 W
Colonia del Sacramento, Ur.	172	G9	34.28 S	57.50 W
Colonia Dora, Arg.	172	D6	28.36 S	62.57 W
Colonia Elisa, Arg.	172	C8	26.55 S	59.32 W
Colonia Hogar Ricardo Gutiérrez, Arg.	206		34.51 S	58.51 W
Colonia Lavalleja, Ur.	172	E9	31.05 S	57.01 W
Colônia Leopoldina, Braz.	170	E8	8.57 S	35.39 W
Colonial Heights, Va., U.S.	124	G8	37.14 N	77.24 W
Colonial Manor, N.J., U.S.	203		39.51 N	75.09 W
Colonial Village, Pa., U.S.	203		40.04 N	75.24 W
Colonial Village Airport, arpt., N.Y., U.S.	202a		43.08 N	78.58 W
Colonia Providencia, P.R.	158a	c4	17.58 N	65.59 W
Colonia Suiza, Ur.	172	G9	34.17 S	57.13 W
Colonias Unidas, Arg.	172	C8	26.42 S	59.37 W
Colonia Vicente Guerrero, Mex.	120	F4	30.43 N	115.59 W
Colonna, Italy	185a		41.50 N	12.45 E
Colonne, Capo, c., Italy	32	E11	39.01 N	17.12 E
Colonsay, Sk., Can.	142	B8	51.57 N	105.51 W
Colonsay, i., Scot., U.K.	10	E6	56.04 N	6.13 W
Colony, Ks., U.S.	130	F2	38.04 N	95.21 W
Colorada, Punta, c., Arg.	206		34.45 S	58.06 W
Colorada Grande, Salina, pl., Arg.	172	I5	38.17 S	63.44 W
Coloradas, Lomas, hills, Arg.	166	H3	43.24 S	67.24 W
Colorado, Hond.	156	E4	15.48 N	87.18 W
Colorado, state, U.S.	112	D6	39.00 N	105.30 W
Colorado, stm., Arg.	166	G4	39.51 S	62.08 W
Colorado, stm., N.A.	120	E5	31.54 N	114.57 W
Colorado, stm., Tx., U.S.	136	F11	28.35 N	95.58 W
Colorado, Canal do, can., Braz.	205a		23.00 S	43.25 W
Colorado, Cerro, mtn., Arg.	166	H3	45.02 S	69.38 W
Colorado, Cerro, mtn., Chile	204e		33.24 S	70.45 W
Colorado, Cerro, mtn., Peru	204d		12.07 S	76.55 W
Colorado, Williams Fork, stm., Co., U.S.	138	B3	40.00 N	106.30 W
Colorado City, Az., U.S.	150	F4	36.59 N	112.58 W
Colorado City, Co., U.S.	138	D4	37.58 N	104.51 W
Colorado City, Tx., U.S.	136	B7	32.23 N	100.51 W
Colorado Kolonie see Lago Kolonie, Aruba	158g	p20	12.26 N	69.52 W
Colorado National Monument, p.o.i., Co., U.S.	150	D8	39.02 N	108.41 W
Colorado Plateau, plat., U.S.	150	E8	38.00 N	109.00 W
Colorado River Aqueduct, aq., Ca., U.S.	120	E5	33.50 N	117.23 W
Colorado River Indian Reservation, ind. res., U.S.	150	J2	34.00 N	114.25 W
Colorado Springs, Co., U.S.	138	C4	38.50 N	104.49 W
Colosseo, hist., Italy	185a		41.54 N	12.29 E
Colotepec, stm., Mex.	154	H10	15.47 N	97.00 W
Colotlán, Mex.	154	D7	22.06 N	103.14 W
Colquechaca, Bol.	166	C3	18.41 S	66.01 W
Colquitt, Ga., U.S.	134	F14	31.10 N	84.43 W
Colstrip, Mt., U.S.	140	B6	45.52 N	106.38 W
Colt, Ar., U.S.	134	B8	35.07 N	90.49 W
Coltauco, Chile	172	G2	34.17 S	71.08 W
Colton, Ca., U.S.	148	I8	34.03 N	117.19 W
Colton, S.D., U.S.	128	H2	43.47 N	96.55 W
Columbia, Al., U.S.	134	F13	31.17 N	85.06 W
Columbia, Ca., U.S.	148	E5	38.02 N	120.24 W
Columbia, Il., U.S.	130	F7	38.26 N	90.11 W
Columbia, Ky., U.S.	130	G12	37.06 N	85.18 W
Columbia, La., U.S.	134	E6	32.06 N	92.04 W
Columbia, Md., U.S.	124	E9	39.14 N	76.50 W
Columbia, Ms., U.S.	134	F9	31.15 N	89.50 W
Columbia, Mo., U.S.	130	F5	38.57 N	92.20 W
Columbia, N.C., U.S.	124	I9	35.54 N	76.15 W
Columbia, Pa., U.S.	124	D9	40.02 N	76.30 W
Columbia, S.C., U.S.	132	C4	33.59 N	81.02 W
Columbia, Tn., U.S.	134	B11	35.36 N	87.02 W
Columbia, stm., N.A.	118	D4	46.13 N	124.05 W
Columbia, Cape, c., Nu., Can.	108	A11	83.08 N	70.35 W
Columbia, Mount, mtn., Ab., Can.	144	D13	52.09 N	117.25 W
Columbia Airport, arpt., Oh., U.S.	197a		41.19 N	81.58 W
Columbia Basin, bas., Wa., U.S.	146	C8	46.45 N	119.05 W
Columbia Center, Oh., U.S.	197a		41.19 N	81.56 W
Columbia City, In., U.S.	130	C12	41.08 N	85.28 W
Columbia Falls, Me., U.S.	122	F9	44.39 N	67.43 W
Columbia Falls, Mt., U.S.	146	B12	48.22 N	114.10 W
Columbia Hills, Md., U.S.	202b		39.15 N	76.50 W
Columbia Icefield, ice, Can.	144	D13	52.07 N	117.26 W
Columbia Lake, l., B.C., Can.	144	F15	50.14 N	115.51 W
Columbia Lake Indian Reserve, ind. res., B.C., Can.	144	F14	50.25 N	115.53 W
Columbia Mountains, mts., N.A.	110	D6	52.00 N	119.00 W
Columbiana, Al., U.S.	134	D12	33.10 N	86.36 W
Columbiana, Oh., U.S.	124	D5	40.53 N	80.41 W
Columbia Road Reservoir, res., S.D., U.S.	140	B14	45.44 N	98.15 W
Columbia University, educ., N.Y., U.S.	194		40.48 N	73.58 W
Columbiaville, Mi., U.S.	126	E6	43.09 N	83.24 W
Columbine, Cape, c., S. Afr.	90	H3	32.45 S	17.56 E
Columbrets, Illes, is., Spain	28	E11	39.52 N	0.40 E
Columbus, Ga., U.S.	134	E14	32.28 N	84.58 W
Columbus, In., U.S.	130	E12	39.11 N	85.55 W
Columbus, Ks., U.S.	130	G3	37.10 N	94.50 W
Columbus, Ms., U.S.	134	D10	33.29 N	88.25 W
Columbus, Mt., U.S.	140	B3	45.38 N	109.15 W
Columbus, Ne., U.S.	140	F15	41.26 N	97.21 W
Columbus, N.M., U.S.	150	L9	31.49 N	107.37 W
Columbus, N.C., U.S.	132	A3	35.15 N	82.11 W
Columbus, N.D., U.S.	142	F11	48.53 N	102.47 W
Columbus, Oh., U.S.	124	E2	39.57 N	82.59 W
Columbus, Tx., U.S.	136	E11	29.42 N	96.32 W
Columbus, Wi., U.S.	128	H9	43.20 N	89.00 W
Columbus Air Force Base, mil., Ms., U.S.	134	D10	33.38 N	88.26 W
Columbus Junction, Ia., U.S.	130	C6	41.16 N	91.21 W
Columbus Lake, res., Ms., U.S.	134	D10	33.31 N	88.30 W
Columbus Park, p.o.i., Il., U.S.	196		41.53 N	87.47 W
Columbus Point, c., Trin.	159f	r13	11.08 N	60.48 W
Columbus Salt Marsh, pl., Nv., U.S.	148	E8	38.05 N	117.58 W
Coluna, Braz.	170	J4	18.14 S	42.50 W
Colusa, Ca., U.S.	148	D3	39.12 N	122.00 W
Colville, Wa., U.S.	146	B9	48.32 N	117.53 W
Colville, stm., Ak., U.S.	109	C9	70.27 N	150.18 W
Colville, stm., Wa., U.S.	146	B9	48.34 N	118.07 W
Colville Indian Reservation, ind. res., Wa., U.S.	146	B8	48.15 N	119.00 W
Colville Lake, l., N.T., Can.	110	B5	67.10 N	126.00 W
Colvin Run, Va., U.S.	202c		38.58 N	77.18 W
Colwyn, Pa., U.S.	203		39.55 N	75.15 W
Colwyn Bay, Wales, U.K.	10	H9	53.17 N	3.44 W
Colyton, Austl.	192a		33.47 S	150.48 E
Comacchio, Italy	30	F9	44.42 N	12.11 E
Comacchio, Valli di, l., Italy	30	F9	44.36 N	12.09 E
Comala, Mex.	154	F7	19.19 N	103.45 W
Comalcalco, Mex.	154	F12	18.16 N	93.12 W
Comales, Mex.	136	H9	26.11 N	98.55 W
Coman, Mount, mtn., Ant.	103	C34	74.02 S	65.04 W
Comana, Rom.	36	F15	43.54 N	28.17 E
Comanche, Ok., U.S.	138	G10	34.21 N	97.57 W
Comanche, Tx., U.S.	136	C9	31.53 N	98.36 W
Comanche Creek, stm., Co., U.S.	138	B4	40.00 N	104.17 W
Comanche Creek, stm., Tx., U.S.	136	C5	31.05 N	102.42 W
Comandante Ferraz, sci., Ant.	103	B35	62.03 S	58.22 W
Comandante Fontana, Arg.	172	B8	25.19 S	59.40 W
Comandante Leal, Arg.	172	E5	30.53 S	65.47 W
Comandante Luis Piedra Buena, Arg.	166	I3	49.57 S	68.54 W
Comandante Nicanor Otamendi, Arg.	172	I9	38.07 S	57.51 W
Comănești, Rom.	36	C13	46.25 N	26.27 E
Comas, Peru	204d		11.57 S	77.04 W
Comayagua, Hond.	156	E4	14.26 N	87.38 W
Comayagua, Montañas de, mts., Hond.	156	E4	14.23 N	87.26 W
Combahee, stm., S.C., U.S.	132	D5	32.30 N	80.31 W
Combarbalá, Chile	172	E2	31.11 S	71.02 W
Combault, Fr.	179		48.48 N	2.36 E
Combeaufontaine, Fr.	20	G14	47.42 N	5.52 E
Comberbach, Eng., U.K.	180		53.17 N	2.32 W
Combermere Bay, b., Mya.	64	C1	19.37 N	93.34 E
Combourg, Fr.	20	F7	48.25 N	1.45 W
Comboyne, Austl.	98	H9	31.33 S	152.30 E
Combs, Eng., U.K.	180		53.18 N	1.57 W
Combs Reservoir, res., Eng., U.K.	180		53.19 N	1.57 W
Comb Wash, stm., Ut., U.S.	150	F7	37.12 N	109.42 W
Comendador, Dom. Rep.	156	C12	18.53 N	71.42 W
Comer, Ga., U.S.	132	B2	34.03 N	83.07 W
Comercinho, Braz.	170	I5	16.20 S	41.49 W
Comerío, P.R.	158a	b3	18.12 N	66.13 W
Comet, Austl.	98	D7	23.35 S	148.33 E
Comet, stm., Austl.	98	E7	23.33 S	148.32 E
Cometela, Moz.	90	B12	21.50 S	34.28 E

Name	Page	Map Ref.	Latitude	Longitude
Comfort, N.C., U.S.	132	B8	35.00 N	77.30 W
Comfort, Tx., U.S.	136	E9	29.58 N	98.54 W
Comfort, Cape, c., Nu., Can.	110	B14	65.07 N	83.24 W
Comfort, Point, c., N.J., U.S.	194		40.27 N	74.08 W
Comfrey, Mn., U.S.	128	G4	44.06 N	94.54 W
Comilla, Bngl.	70	G13	23.27 N	91.12 E
Comino see Kemmuna, i., Malta	32	H8	36.00 N	14.20 E
Comino, Capo, c., Italy	32	D3	40.32 N	9.49 E
Comiskey Park, p.o.i., Il., U.S.	196		41.50 N	87.38 W
Comiso, Italy	32	H8	36.56 N	14.36 E
Comitán de Domínguez, Mex.	154	G12	16.14 N	92.07 W
Commentry, Fr.	22	C8	46.16 N	2.43 E
Commerce, Ca., U.S.	198		34.00 N	118.09 W
Commerce, Ga., U.S.	132	B2	34.12 N	83.27 W
Commerce, Ok., U.S.	130	H3	36.56 N	94.52 W
Commerce, Tx., U.S.	134	D2	33.15 N	95.54 W
Commerciale Luigi Bocconi, Università, educ., Italy	184b		45.26 N	9.11 E
Commercy, Fr.	20	F14	48.45 N	5.34 E
Comminges, reg., Fr.	22	F6	43.02 N	0.37 E
Committee Bay, b., Nu., Can.	110	B13	68.30 N	86.30 W
Commodore Barry Bridge, trans., U.S.	203		39.49 N	75.22 W
Common Edge, Eng., U.K.	180		53.47 N	3.02 W
Communism Peak see Kommunizma, pik, mtn., Taj.	72	B11	38.57 N	72.01 E
Como, Austl.	192a		34.00 S	151.04 E
Como, Italy	30	E6	45.47 N	9.05 E
Como, Ms., U.S.	134	C9	34.31 N	89.56 W
Como, Tx., U.S.	136	A12	33.03 N	95.27 W
Como, Lago di, l., Italy	30	D6	46.01 N	9.15 E
Comodoro Rivadavia, Arg.	166	I3	45.52 S	67.30 W
Comores see Comoros, ctry., Afr.	86	G8	12.10 S	44.15 E
Comores, Archipel des, is., Afr.	86	G8	12.06 S	44.03 E
Comorin, Cape, c., India	69	G3	8.06 N	77.33 E
Comoros, ctry., Afr.	86	G8	12.10 S	44.15 E
Comox, B.C., Can.	144	G6	49.40 N	124.55 W
Comox, Canadian Forces Base, mil., B.C., Can.	144	G6	49.43 N	124.54 W
Compans, Fr.	179		49.00 N	2.40 E
Compiègne, Fr.	20	E11	49.24 N	2.49 E
Compo Cove, b., Ct., U.S.	194		41.07 N	73.21 W
Compostela, Mex.	154	E6	21.14 N	104.53 W
Comprida, Ilha, i., Braz.	205a		23.02 S	43.12 W
Compstall, Eng., U.K.	180		53.25 N	2.03 W
Compton, Eng., U.K.	178		51.13 N	0.38 W
Compton, Ca., U.S.	148	J7	33.52 N	118.12 W
Compton Airport, arpt., Ca., U.S.	198		33.53 N	118.15 W
Compton Creek, stm., Ca., U.S.	198		33.50 N	118.12 W
Compton Creek, stm., N.J., U.S.	194		40.26 N	74.05 W
Comptonville, S. Afr.	191d		26.17 S	27.58 E
Comrat, Mol.	38	G7	46.18 N	28.39 E
Comstock, Ne., U.S.	140	F13	41.33 N	99.15 W
Comstock, Tx., U.S.	136	E6	29.40 N	101.11 W
Comstock Park, Mi., U.S.	130	A12	43.02 N	85.39 W
Con, stm., Russia	26	G18	52.53 N	36.01 E
Con, stm., Viet.	64	C7	19.02 N	104.58 E
Čona, stm., Russia	48	B19	62.54 N	111.06 E
Co Nag, l., China	70	C13	32.01 N	91.28 E
Conakry, Gui.	84	H2	9.30 N	13.42 W
Conambo, stm., Ec.	168	H3	2.08 S	76.02 W
Cona Niyeo, Arg.	166	H3	41.53 S	66.58 W
Conara Junction, Austl.	99a	n13	41.50 S	147.26 E
Conasauga, stm., U.S.	134	C14	34.33 N	84.54 W
Conaskonk Point, c., N.J., U.S.	194		40.27 N	74.11 W
Concarán, Arg.	172	F5	32.33 S	65.14 W
Concarneau, Fr.	20	G5	47.52 N	3.54 W
Conceição, Braz.	170	D6	7.33 S	38.31 W
Conceição, Ilha da, i., Braz.	205a		22.52 S	43.07 W
Conceição da Barra, Braz.	170	J6	18.34 S	39.44 W
Conceição das Alagoas, Braz.	170	J1	19.54 S	48.23 W
Conceição de Ipanema, Braz.	170	J5	19.55 S	41.41 W
Conceição do Araguaia, Braz.	170	E1	8.15 S	49.18 W
Conceição do Canindé, Braz.	170	D5	7.54 S	41.34 W
Conceição do Coité, Braz.	170	F6	11.33 S	39.15 W
Conceição do Mato Dentro, Braz.	170	J4	19.01 S	43.26 W
Conceição do Maú, Braz.	168	F11	3.35 N	59.52 W
Conceição do Norte, Braz.	170	G2	12.13 S	47.18 W
Concepción, Arg.	172	C5	27.20 S	65.35 W
Concepción, Arg.	172	D9	28.23 S	57.53 W
Concepción, Bol.	166	B3	11.29 S	66.35 W
Concepción, Bol.	166	C4	16.15 S	62.04 W
Concepción, Chile	172	H1	36.49 S	73.04 W
Concepción, Col.	168	D5	6.46 N	72.42 W
Concepción, Para.	166	D5	23.24 S	57.25 W
Concepción, Bahía, b., Mex.	154	B3	26.39 N	111.48 W
Concepción, Canal, strt., Chile	166	J2	50.30 S	74.55 W
Concepción, Laguna, l., Bol.	166	C4	17.30 S	61.22 W
Concepción, Volcán, vol., Nic.	156	G5	11.34 N	85.37 W
Concepción de la Sierra, Arg.	172	D10	27.57 S	55.30 W
Concepción del Oro, Mex.	154	C8	24.37 N	101.24 W
Concepción del Uruguay, Arg.	172	F8	32.29 S	58.14 W
Concepción Huista, Guat.	156	E2	15.37 N	91.40 W
Conception, Point, c., Ca., U.S.	148	I5	34.27 N	120.27 W
Conception Bay, b., Nf., Can.	111a	j23	47.44 N	52.58 W
Conception Bay, b., Nmb.	90	C2	23.53 S	14.29 E
Conchalí, Chile	204e		33.24 S	70.39 W
Conchalí, Cerros de, mts., Chile	204e		33.20 S	70.38 W
Conchas, stm., Arg.	172	B5	25.15 S	65.21 W
Conchas, stm., N.M., U.S.	138	F4	35.23 N	104.18 W
Conchas Dam, N.M., U.S.	138	F4	35.20 N	104.11 W
Conchas Lake, res., N.M., U.S.	138	F4	35.22 N	104.13 W
Conches-en-Ouche, Fr.	20	F9	48.57 N	0.56 E
Conchitas, Arroyo, stm., Arg.	206		34.45 S	58.09 W
Concho, Az., U.S.	150	I7	34.27 N	109.36 W
Concho, stm., Tx., U.S.	136	C8	31.33 N	99.43 W
Conchos, stm., Mex.	154	C10	24.55 N	97.38 W
Conchos, stm., Mex.	154	A6	29.34 N	104.24 W
Conconully, Wa., U.S.	146	B7	48.33 N	119.45 W
Concord, Austl.	192a		33.52 S	151.06 E
Concord, On., Can.	193b		43.48 N	79.29 W
Concord, Ca., U.S.	148	E4	37.58 N	122.01 W
Concord, Ga., U.S.	134	D14	33.05 N	84.26 W
Concord, Mi., U.S.	130	B13	42.09 N	84.38 W
Concord, N.H., U.S.	122	G5	43.12 N	71.32 W
Concord, N.C., U.S.	132	A5	35.24 N	80.35 W
Concord, stm., Ma., U.S.	201		42.39 N	71.18 W
Concord Battleground, hist., Ma., U.S.	201		42.28 N	71.21 W
Concordia, Arg.	172	E8	31.23 S	58.01 W
Concórdia, Braz.	164	D4	4.35 S	66.35 W
Concórdia, Braz.	172	C11	27.13 S	52.01 W
Concordia, Mex.	136	I4	25.47 N	103.06 W
Concordia, Mex.	154	D5	23.16 N	106.03 W
Concordia, Ks., U.S.	138	B11	39.34 N	97.39 W
Concordia, Mo., U.S.	130	F4	38.58 N	93.34 W
Concord Naval Weapons Station, mil., Ca., U.S.	200		38.03 N	122.02 W
Concordville, Pa., U.S.	203		39.53 N	75.31 W
Concord West, Austl.	192a		33.51 S	151.05 E
Concrete, Wa., U.S.	146	B5	48.32 N	121.45 W
Con Cuong, Viet.	64	C7	19.02 N	104.54 E
Conda, Ang.	88	C1	11.06 S	14.20 E
Condamine, Austl.	98	F7	26.55 S	150.07 E
Condamine, stm., Austl.	98	F8	27.07 S	149.47 E
Condat, Fr.	22	D8	45.21 N	2.46 E
Conde, Braz.	170	F7	11.49 S	37.35 W
Conde, S.D., U.S.	140	B14	45.09 N	98.06 W
Condécourt, Fr.	179		49.02 N	1.57 E
Condega, Nic.	156	F4	13.21 N	86.23 W
Condé-sur-Noireau, Fr.	20	F8	48.51 N	0.33 W
Condé-sur-Vesgre, Fr.	179		48.45 N	1.40 E
Condeúba, Braz.	170	H5	14.52 S	41.58 W
Condevilla, Peru	204d		12.02 S	77.05 W
Condobolin, Austl.	98	I6	33.05 S	147.08 E
Condom, Fr.	22	F6	43.57 N	0.22 E
Condon, Or., U.S.	146	E6	45.14 N	120.10 W
Condoto, Col.	168	E3	5.05 N	76.38 W
Condroz, hist. reg., Bel.	20	D13	50.26 N	5.07 E
Cone, Tx., U.S.	138	H7	33.48 N	101.23 W
Conecuh, stm., U.S.	134	F12	30.58 N	87.14 W
Conegliano, Italy	30	E9	45.53 N	12.18 E
Conejos, Co., U.S.	138	D2	37.05 N	106.02 W
Conejos, stm., Co., U.S.	138	D3	37.18 N	105.44 W
Coney Island, ngh., N.Y., U.S.	194		40.34 N	74.00 W
Confluence, Pa., U.S.	124	E6	39.48 N	79.21 W
Confolens, Fr.	22	C6	46.01 N	0.41 E
Confraternidad, Parque, p.o.i., Peru	204d		12.09 S	77.02 W
Confuso, stm., Para.	172	B8	25.07 S	57.32 W
Congaree Swamp National Monument, p.o.i., S.C., U.S.	132	C4	33.48 N	80.47 W
Congaz, Mol.	38	G7	46.06 N	28.35 E
Congers Lake, l., N.Y., U.S.	194		41.09 N	73.57 W
Cong Hoa Stadium, p.o.i., Viet.	187c		10.45 N	106.40 E
Conghua, China	58	J5	23.32 N	113.35 E
Congjiang, China	58	I3	25.45 N	108.52 E
Congleton, Eng., U.K.	10	H10	53.10 N	2.12 W
Congo, ctry., Afr.	86	E3	1.00 S	15.00 E
Congo (Zaïre), stm., Afr.	86	F2	5.58 S	12.44 E
Congo, Democratic Republic of the (Zaïre), ctry., Afr.	86	E4	4.00 S	25.00 E
Congo, Le Bassin du see Congo Basin, bas., Afr.	86	E4	0.00 N	19.59 E
Congo, République démocratique du see Congo, Democratic Republic of the, ctry., Afr.	86	E4	4.00 S	25.00 E
Congo Basin, bas., Afr.	86	E4	0.00 N	19.59 E
Congonhinhas, Braz.	172	A12	23.33 S	50.33 W
Congost, stm., Spain	184d		41.33 N	2.15 E
Congress, Sk., Can.	142	E8	49.45 N	106.00 W
Coni see Cuneo, Italy	30	F4	44.23 N	7.32 E
Conitaca, Mex.	154	C5	24.09 N	106.43 W
Conjeeveram see Kānchipuram, India	69	E4	12.50 N	79.42 E
Conklin Point, c., N.Y., U.S.	194		40.41 N	73.17 W
Conn, Lough, l., Ire.	10	G3	54.03 N	9.15 W
Connacht see Connaught, hist. reg., Ire.	10	H3	53.45 N	9.00 W
Connaught, hist. reg., Ire.	10	H3	53.45 N	9.00 W
Connaughton, Pa., U.S.	203		40.05 N	75.19 W
Connaught Place, p.o.i., India	190a		28.38 N	77.12 E
Conneaut, Oh., U.S.	124	C5	41.56 N	80.33 W
Conneautville, Pa., U.S.	124	C5	41.45 N	80.22 W
Connecticut, state, U.S.	124	C13	41.45 N	72.45 W
Connecticut, stm., U.S.	114	F14	41.15 N	72.20 W
Connell, Wa., U.S.	146	D8	46.39 N	118.51 W
Connell, Mount, mtn., B.C., Can.	144	G15	49.18 N	115.38 W
Connellsville, Pa., U.S.	124	D6	40.00 N	79.35 W
Connemara, Austl.	98	E4	24.13 S	142.17 E
Connemara, reg., Ire.	10	H3	53.31 N	9.44 W
Conner, Phil.	52	B3	17.47 N	121.17 E
Connersville, In., U.S.	130	E12	39.38 N	85.08 W
Connetquot, stm., N.Y., U.S.	194		40.43 N	73.08 W
Connetquot Brook, stm., N.Y., U.S.	194		40.45 N	73.09 W
Conn Island, i., Md., U.S.	202c		39.00 N	77.16 W
Conn Lake, l., Nu., Can.	110	A15	70.32 N	73.41 W
Connors Range, mts., Austl.	98	C7	21.40 S	149.10 E
Cononaco, stm., Ec.	168	H3	1.33 S	75.34 W
Conorochite, stm., Ven.	168	F8	2.40 N	67.29 W
Conover, N.C., U.S.	124	I4	35.42 N	81.13 W
Conquest, Sk., Can.	142	C6	51.32 N	107.17 W
Conquista, Braz.	170	J2	19.56 S	47.33 W
Conrad, Ia., U.S.	130	B5	42.13 N	92.52 W
Conrad, Mt., U.S.	146	B15	48.10 N	111.56 W
Conroe, Tx., U.S.	136	D12	30.18 N	95.27 W
Conroe, Lake, res., Tx., U.S.	136	D12	30.23 N	95.34 W
Conscience Bay, b., N.Y., U.S.	194		40.57 N	73.07 W
Consecon, On., Can.	126	D12	43.59 N	77.30 W
Conselheiro Lafaiete, Braz.	170	K4	20.39 S	43.46 W
Conselheiro Pena, Braz.	170	J5	19.11 S	41.30 W
Conselice, Italy	30	F8	44.31 N	11.49 E
Consett, Eng., U.K.	10	G11	54.50 N	1.51 W
Consolação, ngh., Braz.	205b		23.33 S	46.39 W
Consolación del Sur, Cuba	156	A6	22.30 N	83.30 W
Consolidated Main Reef Mines, mine, S. Afr.	191d		26.11 S	27.56 E
Con Son, is., Viet.	64	H8	8.43 N	106.36 E
Consort, Ab., Can.	142	B3	52.01 N	110.45 W
Constance see Konstanz, Ger.	24	I5	47.39 N	9.10 E
Constance, Lake (Bodensee), l., Eur.	24	I5	47.39 N	8.54 E
Constância, Port.	28	E2	39.28 N	8.20 W
Constanța, Rom.	36	E15	44.11 N	28.38 E
Constanța, state, Rom.	36	E15	44.20 N	28.20 E
Constantina, Spain	28	G5	37.52 N	5.37 W
Constantine see Qacentina, Alg.	84	B6	36.21 N	6.36 E
Constantine, Mi., U.S.	130	C12	41.50 N	85.39 W
Constantine, Cape, c., Ak., U.S.	109	E8	58.23 N	158.53 W
Constantinople see İstanbul, Tur.	34	B12	41.01 N	28.59 E
Constitución, Chile	172	G1	35.19 S	72.24 W
Constitución, Ur.	172	E9	31.04 S	57.49 W
Constitución, ngh., Arg.	206		34.37 S	58.23 W
Constitución de 1857, Parque Nacional, p.o.i., Mex.	148	K10	32.05 N	115.55 W
Consuegra, Spain	28	E7	39.27 N	3.36 W
Consul, Sk., Can.	142	E4	49.17 N	109.31 W
Contai, India	70	H11	21.47 N	87.45 E
Contas, stm., Braz.	170	H6	14.17 S	39.01 W
Contendas do Sincorá, Braz.	170	G5	13.45 S	41.02 W
Contentnea Creek, stm., N.C., U.S.	132	A8	35.26 N	77.30 W
Continental Peak, mtn., Wy., U.S.	140	E4	42.16 N	108.43 W
Contra Costa Canal, can., Ca., U.S.	200		38.02 N	121.58 W
Contra Loma Reservoir, res., Ca., U.S.	200		37.58 N	121.49 W
Contratación, Col.	168	D5	6.17 N	73.27 W
Contre Island, pen., N.Y., U.S.	194		40.54 N	73.32 W
Contreras, Embalse de, res., Spain	28	E9	39.33 N	1.29 W
Contreras, Isla, i., Chile	166	J1	51.52 S	74.56 W
Contres, Fr.	20	G10	47.25 N	1.26 E
Contursi, Italy	32	D9	40.39 N	15.14 E
Contwoyto Lake, l., Can.	110	B8	65.42 N	110.50 W
Convent, La., U.S.	134	G8	30.01 N	90.49 W
Convention Centre, bldg., Sing.	189c		1.18 N	103.52 E
Convent Station, N.J., U.S.	194		40.47 N	74.26 W
Conversano, Italy	32	D11	40.57 N	17.06 E
Converse, In., U.S.	130	D12	40.34 N	85.52 W
Converse Lake, l., U.S.	194		41.08 N	73.39 W
Converse Pond Brook, stm., Ct., U.S.	194		41.03 N	73.40 W
Conway, P.E., Can.	122	D13	46.39 N	64.00 W
Conway, Ar., U.S.	134	B6	35.05 N	92.27 W
Conway, Mo., U.S.	130	G5	37.30 N	92.49 W
Conway, N.H., U.S.	122	F5	43.58 N	71.07 W
Conway, N.C., U.S.	124	H8	36.26 N	77.13 W
Conway, S.C., U.S.	132	C6	33.50 N	79.03 W
Conway, Cape, c., Austl.	98	C7	20.31 S	148.54 E
Conway, Lake, res., Ar., U.S.	134	C6	35.00 N	92.23 W
Conway National Park, p.o.i., Austl.	98	C7	20.22 S	148.47 E
Conway Springs, Ks., U.S.	138	D11	37.23 N	97.38 W
Conwy, Wales, U.K.	10	H9	53.17 N	3.50 W
Conwy, stm., Wales, U.K.	20	A5	53.13 N	3.49 W
Conyers, Ga., U.S.	132	C1	33.40 N	84.01 W
Coober Pedy, Austl.	96	E6	29.01 S	134.44 E
Coogee, Austl.	192a		33.55 S	151.16 E
Coogee Bay, b., Austl.	192a		33.55 S	151.16 E
Cook, Austl.	96	F6	30.37 S	130.25 E
Cook, Mn., U.S.	128	D6	47.51 N	92.41 W
Cook, Ne., U.S.	130	D1	40.30 N	96.11 W
Cook, Baie de, b., Fr. Poly.	100h	u20	17.29 S	149.49 W
Cook, Cape, c., B.C., Can.	144	F2	50.07 N	127.54 W
Cook, Mount see Aoraki, mtn., N.Z.	102	F4	43.36 S	170.10 E
Cook, Point, c., Austl.	192b		37.55 S	144.48 E
Cook, Récif de, rf., N. Cal.	101d	I14	19.50 S	164.12 E
Cookes Peak, mtn., N.M., U.S.	150	K9	32.32 N	107.44 W
Cookeville, Tn., U.S.	130	H12	36.09 N	85.31 W
Cook Forest State Park, p.o.i., Pa., U.S.	124	C6	41.21 N	79.13 W
Cookhouse, S. Afr.	90	H7	32.45 S	25.48 E
Cooking Lake, l., Ab., Can.	144	C17	53.25 N	113.02 W
Cook Inlet, b., Ak., U.S.	109	D9	60.31 N	151.40 W
Cook Islands, dep., Oc.	92	E10	20.00 S	158.00 W
Cooks, stm., Austl.	192a		33.56 S	151.10 E
Cooksmill Green, Eng., U.K.	178		51.44 N	0.22 E
Cooks Mills, On., Can.	202a		43.00 N	79.11 W
Cookstown, N. Ire., U.K.	10	G6	54.39 N	6.44 W
Cook Strait, strt., N.Z.	102	E6	41.15 S	174.30 E
Cooksville Creek, stm., On., Can.	193b		43.34 N	79.34 W
Cooktown, Austl.	96	C9	15.28 S	145.15 E
Coolabah, Austl.	98	H6	31.01 S	146.42 E
Cooladdi, Austl.	98	F5	26.38 S	145.27 E
Coolah, Austl.	98	H7	31.50 S	149.42 E
Coolamon, Austl.	98	J6	34.49 S	147.12 E
Coolangatta, Austl.	98	G9	28.10 S	153.32 E
Cooleemee, N.C., U.S.	124	I5	35.49 N	80.33 W
Cooley Lake, l., Mi., U.S.	199		42.37 N	83.27 W
Coolgardie, Austl.	96	F4	30.57 S	121.10 E
Coolidge, Az., U.S.	150	K5	32.58 N	111.31 W
Coolidge, Ga., U.S.	132	E2	31.00 N	83.51 W
Coolidge, Tx., U.S.	136	C11	31.44 N	96.39 W
Coolidge, Mount, mtn., S.D., U.S.	140	D9	43.44 N	103.29 W
Coolidge Dam, dam., Az., U.S.	150	J6	33.10 N	110.30 W
Coolidge Point, c., Ma., U.S.	201		42.34 N	70.44 W
Coolin, Id., U.S.	146	B10	48.28 N	116.50 W
Cooling, Eng., U.K.	178		51.27 N	0.32 E
Cooloola National Park, p.o.i., Austl.	98	F9	26.05 S	153.00 E
Cooma, Austl.	98	K7	36.14 S	149.07 E
Coombe Cottage, hist., Austl.	192b		37.43 S	145.23 E
Coonabarabran, Austl.	98	H7	31.16 S	149.16 E
Coonalpyn, Austl.	98	J2	35.41 S	139.50 E
Coonamble, Austl.	98	H7	30.57 S	148.23 E
Coondambo, Austl.	96	F7	31.04 S	135.50 E
Coonoor, India	69	F3	11.20 N	76.48 E
Coon Rapids, Ia., U.S.	130	C3	41.52 N	94.41 W
Coon Rapids, Mn., U.S.	128	F5	45.10 N	93.19 W
Coontown, N.J., U.S.	194		40.37 N	74.31 W
Coon Valley, Wi., U.S.	128	H8	43.41 N	91.00 W
Cooper, Tx., U.S.	134	D3	33.22 N	95.41 W
Cooper, stm., N.J., U.S.	203		39.57 N	75.07 W
Cooper, Mount, mtn., B.C., Can.	144	F13	50.11 N	117.12 W
Cooper, North Branch, stm., N.J., U.S.	203		39.55 N	75.02 W
Cooper Creek, stm., Austl.	98	F3	28.18 S	137.29 E
Cooper Island, i., Br. Vir. Is.	158b	e9	18.22 N	64.30 W
Cooper River Parkway, p.o.i., Pa., U.S.	203		39.55 N	75.03 W
Cooper Road, La., U.S.	136	B14	32.32 N	93.48 W
Coopers, Al., U.S.	134	E12	32.46 N	86.33 W
Coopersale Common, Eng., U.K.	178		51.42 N	0.08 E
Cooperstown, N.Y., U.S.	124	B11	42.42 N	74.56 W
Cooperstown, N.D., U.S.	142	G15	47.26 N	98.07 W
Coopersville, Mi., U.S.	130	A12	43.03 N	85.56 W
Coopracambra National Park, p.o.i., Austl.	98	K7	37.18 S	149.23 E
Coorong National Park, p.o.i., Austl.	98	K2	36.01 S	139.30 E
Coorow, Austl.	96	E3	29.53 S	116.01 E
Cooroy, Austl.	98	F9	26.25 S	152.55 E
Coosa, stm., U.S.	134	E12	32.30 N	86.16 W
Coosawhatchie, stm., S.C., U.S.	132	D5	32.27 N	80.49 W
Coos Bay, Or., U.S.	146	G2	43.22 N	124.12 W
Coos Bay, b., Or., U.S.	146	G2	43.24 N	124.17 W
Cootamundra, Austl.	98	J7	34.38 S	148.01 E
Cootehill, Ire.	10	G5	54.05 N	7.04 W
Cooyar, Austl.	98	F8	26.59 S	151.50 E
Copacabana, Arg.	172	D4	28.12 S	67.29 W
Copacabana, Col.	168	D4	6.21 N	75.29 W
Copacabana, ngh., Braz.	205a		22.58 S	43.11 W
Copacabana, Forte de, hist., Braz.	205a		22.59 S	43.11 W
Copainalá, Mex.	154	G12	17.06 N	93.11 W
Copan, Ok., U.S.	130	H2	36.53 N	95.56 W
Copán, hist., Hond.	156	E3	14.50 N	89.09 W
Copan Lake, res., Ok., U.S.	130	H2	36.54 N	95.57 W
Copano Bay, b., Tx., U.S.	136	F10	28.06 N	97.06 W
Copatana, Braz.	168	I8	2.51 S	67.10 W
Cope, Co., U.S.	138	B6	39.39 N	102.51 W
Copeau, stm., Sk., Can.	142	B10	52.44 N	102.58 W
Copeland, Fl., U.S.	132	K4	25.57 N	81.21 W
Copenhagen see København, Den.	16	L10	55.40 N	12.33 E
Copenhagen, N.Y., U.S.	126	E14	43.53 N	75.40 W
Copenhaver, Md., U.S.	202c		39.04 N	77.11 W
Copertino, Italy	32	D11	40.16 N	18.02 E
Copetonas, Arg.	172	I7	38.43 S	60.27 W
Copiague Neck, pen., N.Y., U.S.	194		40.40 N	73.22 W
Copiapó, Chile	172	C2	27.21 S	70.19 W
Copiapó, stm., Chile	172	C2	27.18 S	70.55 W
Copley, Austl.	98	H2	30.33 S	138.25 E
Copparo, Italy	30	F8	44.53 N	11.48 E
Copper, stm., Ak., U.S.	109	D11	60.33 N	144.52 W
Copperas Cove, Tx., U.S.	136	C9	31.07 N	97.54 W
Copperas Mountain, mtn., N.J., U.S.	194		41.02 N	74.28 W
Copper Butte, mtn., Wa., U.S.	146	B8	48.42 N	118.28 W
Copper Canyon see Cobre, Barranca del, misc. cult., Mex.	154	B5	27.26 N	107.32 W
Copper Center, Ak., U.S.	109	D10	61.57 N	145.21 W
Copper Cliff, On., Can.	126	B8	46.27 N	81.04 W
Copper Creek, stm., Va., U.S.	124	H3	36.39 N	82.45 W
Copper Harbor, Mi., U.S.	128	D10	47.27 N	87.54 W
Coppermine see Kugluktuk, Nu., Can.	110	B8	67.47 N	115.10 W
Coppermine, stm., Can.	110	B7	67.47 N	115.08 W
Copper Mine Point, c., Br. Vir. Is.	158b	e9	18.26 N	64.25 W
Coppermine Point, c., On., Can.	126	B5	46.59 N	84.47 W
Copper Mountain, B.C., Can.	144	G10	49.19 N	120.32 W
Copper Mountain, mtn., Wy., U.S.	140	D5	43.27 N	107.57 W
Coppin State College, educ., Md., U.S.	202b		39.19 N	76.40 W
Coppull, Eng., U.K.	180		53.37 N	2.40 W
Copster Green, Eng., U.K.	180		53.48 N	2.30 W
Coptic Museum, bldg., Egypt	191c		30.00 N	31.13 E
Copton Creek, stm., Ab., Can.	144	B11	54.15 N	119.16 W
Coptos see Qift, Egypt	74	G3	26.00 N	32.49 E
Coqên, China	70	C10	31.06 N	85.09 E
Coquet, stm., Eng., U.K.	10	F11	55.20 N	1.36 W
Coquí, P.R.	158a	c3	17.58 N	66.14 W
Coquilhatville see Mbandaka, D.R.C.	86	D3	0.01 N	18.14 E
Coquille, Or., U.S.	146	G2	43.11 N	124.11 W
Coquille, stm., Or., U.S.	146	G2	43.07 N	124.26 W
Coquille, East Fork, stm., Or., U.S.	146	G3	43.06 N	124.04 W
Coquille, Middle Fork, stm., Or., U.S.	146	G3	43.05 N	124.09 W
Coquille, South Fork, stm., Or., U.S.	146	H2	43.02 N	124.07 W
Coquimbo, Chile	172	E2	29.57 S	71.19 W
Coquimbo, state, Chile	172	E2	31.02 S	70.30 W
Corabia, Rom.	36	F11	43.46 N	24.31 E
Coração de Jesus, Braz.	170	I3	16.41 S	44.22 W
Corace, stm., Italy	32	F10	38.48 N	16.37 E
Coradi, Isole see Cheradi, Isole, i., Italy	32	D11	40.27 N	17.09 E
Corail, Mer de see Coral Sea, s., Oc.	94	E6	20.00 S	158.00 E
Coral, On., Can.	114	A10	50.13 N	81.41 W
Coral Bay, b., V.I.U.S.	158b	e8	18.20 N	64.41 W
Coral Gables, Fl., U.S.	132	K5	25.45 N	80.15 W
Coral Harbour, Nu., Can.	110	C14	64.07 N	83.12 W
Coral Hills, Md., U.S.	202c		38.52 N	76.55 W
Coral Sea, s., Oc.	94	E6	20.00 S	158.00 E
Coral Sea Basin, unds.	174	K18	14.00 S	152.00 E
Coralville, Ia., U.S.	130	C6	41.40 N	91.34 W
Coralville Lake, res., Ia., U.S.	130	C6	41.47 N	91.33 W
Coram, Mt., U.S.	146	B12	48.25 N	114.02 W
Corangamite, Lake, l., Austl.	98	K4	38.10 S	143.25 E
Corantijn see Coeroeni, stm., S.A.	164	C6	5.50 N	57.05 W
Corantijn see Corentyne, stm., S.A.	164	C6	5.50 N	57.05 W
Coraopolis Heights, Pa., U.S.	197b		40.29 N	80.10 W
Corato, Italy	32	C10	41.09 N	16.24 E
Corbeil-Essonnes, Fr.	20	F11	48.36 N	2.28 E
Corbera, Riera de, stm., Spain	184d		41.27 N	1.59 E
Corbett National Park, p.o.i., India	70	D7	29.31 N	78.58 E
Corbigny, Fr.	20	G12	47.15 N	3.39 E
Corbin, Ky., U.S.	124	H1	36.56 N	84.05 W
Corbones, stm., Spain	28	G5	37.36 N	5.39 W
Corbu, Rom.	36	E11	44.29 N	24.41 E
Corby, Eng., U.K.	10	I12	52.29 N	0.39 W
Corcaigh see Cork, Ire.	10	J4	51.54 N	8.28 W
Córcega, P.R.	158a	b1	18.18 N	67.14 W
Corcelle, ngh., Italy	185a		41.55 N	12.46 E
Corcoran, Ca., U.S.	148	G6	36.05 N	119.34 W
Corcovado see Palena, stm., S.A.	166	H2	43.46 S	72.59 W
Corcovado, Golfo, b., Chile	166	H2	43.30 S	73.30 W
Corcovado, Morro do, mtn., Braz.	205a		22.57 S	43.13 W
Corcovado, Parque Nacional, p.o.i., C.R.	156	H6	8.35 N	83.40 W
Corcovado, Volcán, vol., Chile	166	H2	43.12 S	72.48 W
Corcubión, Spain	28	B1	42.56 N	9.11 W
Cordeiro, Braz.	170	L4	22.01 S	42.22 W
Cordele, Ga., U.S.	132	E2	31.58 N	83.46 W
Cordell, Ok., U.S.	138	F10	35.18 N	98.59 W
Cordell Hull Reservoir, res., Tn., U.S.	130	H12	36.23 N	85.40 W
Corder, Mo., U.S.	130	E4	39.06 N	93.38 W
Cordes, Fr.	22	E7	44.03 N	1.57 E
Cordevole, stm., Italy	30	D9	46.05 N	12.05 E
Cordillera, state, Para.	172	B9	25.15 S	57.00 W
Cordillo Downs, Austl.	98	F3	26.43 S	140.38 E
Cordisburgo, Braz.	170	J3	19.05 S	44.20 W
Córdoba, Arg.	172	E5	31.23 S	64.11 W
Córdoba, Mex.	154	F10	18.53 N	96.56 W
Córdoba (Cordova), Spain	28	G6	37.53 N	4.46 W
Córdoba, state, Arg.	172	E6	32.00 S	64.00 W
Córdoba, state, Col.	168	C4	8.20 N	75.40 W
Córdoba, co., Spain	28	F6	38.00 N	4.50 W
Córdova, Peru	164	F2	14.02 S	75.11 W
Cordova see Córdoba, Spain	28	G6	37.53 N	4.46 W
Cordova, Al., U.S.	134	D11	33.45 N	87.11 W
Cordova, Ak., U.S.	109	D10	60.32 N	145.44 W
Cordova, Il., U.S.	130	C7	41.40 N	90.18 W
Cordova Peak, mtn., Ak., U.S.	109	D10	60.51 N	145.16 W
Coreaú, Braz.	170	B5	3.33 S	40.39 W
Coreaú, stm., Braz.	170	B5	2.53 S	40.50 W
Core Creek, stm., Pa., U.S.	203		40.11 N	74.55 W
Coremas, Braz.	170	D7	7.01 S	37.58 W
Corentyne (Coeroeni), stm., S.A.	164	c6	5.50 N	57.05 W
Corerepe, Mex.	154	C4	25.40 N	108.40 W
Corfield, Austl.	98	C4	21.43 S	143.22 E
Corfu see Kérkyra, Grc.	34	D2	39.37 N	19.55 E
Corfu see Kérkyra, i., Grc.	34	D2	39.40 N	19.45 E
Corhanwarrabul Creek, stm., Austl.	192b		37.55 S	145.12 E
Coria, Spain	28	D4	39.59 N	6.32 W
Coria del Río, Spain	28	G4	37.15 N	6.02 W
Coribe, Braz.	170	G3	13.50 S	44.28 W
Coricudgy, Mount, mtn., Austl.	98	I8	32.50 S	150.22 E
Corigliano Calabro, Italy	32	E10	39.36 N	16.31 E
Corinda, Austl.	96	C7	17.53 S	138.35 E
Corinne, Pa., U.S.	203		39.54 N	75.40 W
Corinne, Ut., U.S.	150	B4	41.33 N	112.07 W
Corinne, W.V., U.S.	124	G4	37.34 N	81.21 W
Corinth see Kórinthos, Grc.	34	F5	37.56 N	22.57 E
Corinth, Ms., U.S.	134	C10	34.56 N	88.31 W
Corinth, N.Y., U.S.	126	E16	43.14 N	73.49 W
Corinth, Gulf of see Korinthiakós Kólpos, b., Grc.	34	E5	38.12 N	22.35 E
Corinto, Braz.	170	J3	18.22 S	44.26 W
Corisco, Isla de, i., Eq. Gui.	84	I6	0.53 N	9.19 E
Corjeuți, Mol.	38	E6	48.13 N	27.03 E
Cork, Ire.	10	J4	51.54 N	8.28 W
Cork, state, Ire.	10	I4	51.58 N	8.35 W
Cork Harbour, b., Ire.	10	J4	51.45 N	8.15 W
Cork Hill, Monts.	159a	d3	16.43 N	62.13 W
Corleone, Italy	32	G7	37.49 N	13.18 E
Çorlu, Tur.	34	B10	41.09 N	27.48 E
Cormano, Italy	184b		45.33 N	9.10 E
Čornaja, stm., Russia	183a		59.47 N	30.10 E
Čornaja, stm., Russia	183a		59.55 N	30.59 E
Čornaja, stm., Russia	183a		60.01 N	30.10 E
Čornaja, stm., Russia	183a		59.50 N	30.00 E
Čornaja, stm., Russia	183b		55.41 N	37.58 E
Čornaja Grjaz', Russia	183b		55.58 N	37.19 E
Čornaja Holunica, Russia	40	B17	58.51 N	51.42 E
Čornaja Rečka, Russia	183a		59.56 N	30.58 E
Čornaja rečka, stm., Russia	183a		59.55 N	30.22 E
Čornaja rečka, stm., Russia	183a		59.46 N	30.45 E
Čornaja Sloboda, Russia	18	G24	60.47 N	37.45 E
Cornaredo, Italy	184b		45.30 N	9.02 E
Cornelia, Ga., U.S.	132	B2	34.31 N	83.31 W
Cornélio Procópio, Braz.	166	D6	23.10 S	50.38 W
Cornelius, N.C., U.S.	132	A5	35.29 N	80.51 W
Cornelius Grinnell Bay, b., Nu., Can.	108	E13	63.20 N	64.50 W
Cornell, Wi., U.S.	128	F7	45.10 N	91.08 W
Cornellà de Llobregat, Spain	184d		41.21 N	2.05 E
Corner Brook, Nf., Can.	111a	j22	48.57 N	57.57 W
Corner Store, Pa., U.S.	203		40.07 N	75.30 W
Cornersville, Tn., U.S.	134	B12	35.21 N	86.50 W
Cornești, Mol.	38	F6	47.21 N	28.00 E
Corneta, Punta, c., Mex.	154	H10	15.39 N	96.29 W
Cornholme, Eng., U.K.	180		53.44 N	2.08 W
Cornia, stm., Italy	30	G7	42.57 N	10.33 E
Corning, Ar., U.S.	130	H7	36.24 N	90.35 W
Corning, Ca., U.S.	148	D3	39.55 N	122.10 W
Corning, Ia., U.S.	130	D3	40.59 N	94.44 W
Corning, Ks., U.S.	138	B12	39.39 N	96.01 W
Corning, N.Y., U.S.	124	B8	42.09 N	77.03 W
Corning, Oh., U.S.	124	E3	39.36 N	82.05 W
Cornish, Me., U.S.	122	G6	43.48 N	70.48 W
Čornoe more see Black Sea, s.	42	D5	43.00 N	35.00 E
Corno Grande, mtn., Italy	30	H10	42.28 N	13.34 E
Cornwall, On., Can.	126	C15	45.02 N	74.44 W
Cornwallis Island, i., Nu., Can.	108	B7	75.15 N	94.30 W
Cornwall Island, i., Nu., Can.	108	B6	77.37 N	94.38 W
Čornyj Mys, Russia	14	D29	68.20 N	38.38 E
Čornyj Otrog, Russia	40	F19	51.53 N	55.58 E
Coro, Ven.	168	B7	11.26 N	69.40 W
Coro, Golfete de, b., Ven.	168	B7	11.30 N	69.55 W
Coroaci, Braz.	170	J4	18.37 S	42.17 W
Coroatá, Braz.	170	C3	4.08 S	44.08 W
Corocoro, Bol.	166	C3	17.11 S	68.27 W
Corocoro, Isla, i., S.A.	168	C11	8.34 N	60.12 W
Corocoro Island see Corocoro, Isla, i., S.A.	168	C11	8.34 N	60.12 W
Čoroh see Çoruh, stm., Asia	42	E9	41.36 N	41.35 E
Coroico, Bol.	166	C3	16.10 S	67.42 W
Coromandel, Braz.	170	J2	18.28 S	47.11 W
Coromandel Coast, cst., India	69	E5	13.30 N	80.30 E
Coromandel Peninsula, pen., N.Z.	102	C6	36.50 S	175.35 E
Corona, Ca., U.S.	148	J8	33.52 N	117.32 W
Corona, N.M., U.S.	138	G3	34.13 N	105.35 W
Corona, ngh., N.Y., U.S.	194		40.45 N	73.52 W
Coronado, Mex.	136	H2	26.44 N	105.09 W
Coronado, Mex.	154	D8	22.55 N	100.56 W
Coronado, Bahía de, b., C.R.	156	H6	9.00 N	83.50 W
Coronado, Islas, is., Mex.	148	K8	32.25 N	117.16 W
Coronado National Memorial, p.o.i., Az., U.S.	150	L6	31.10 N	110.29 W
Coronation, Ab., Can.	144	D19	52.06 N	111.26 W
Coronation Gardens, p.o.i., On., Can.	193b		43.41 N	79.29 W

Name Page Map Ref. Latitude Longitude

Coronation Gulf, b., Nu., Can. 110 B8 68.24 N 109.56 W
Coronation Island, i., Ant. 103 B36 60.35 S 45.34 W
Coronation Park, p.o.i., S. Afr. 191d 26.06 S 27.47 E
Coronda, Arg. 172 E7 31.58 S 60.54 W
Coronel, Chile 172 H1 37.01 S 73.07 W
Coronel Bogado, Para. 172 C9 27.09 S 56.14 W
Coronel Dorrego, Arg. 172 I7 38.42 S 61.16 W
Coronel Du Graty, Arg. 172 C7 27.40 S 60.54 W
Coronel Fabriciano, Braz. 170 J4 19.31 S 42.39 W
Coronel Moldes, Arg. 172 B5 25.16 S 65.29 W
Coronel Moldes, Arg. 172 F5 33.38 S 64.36 W
Coronel Murta, Braz. 170 I4 16.37 S 42.11 W
Coronel Oviedo, Para. 172 B9 25.27 S 56.25 W
Coronel Pringles, Arg. 172 H7 37.58 S 61.22 W
Coronel Suárez, Arg. 172 H6 37.26 S 61.55 W
Coronel Vidal, Arg. 172 H9 37.27 S 57.44 W
Coronel Vivida, Braz. 172 C11 25.59 S 52.33 W
Corongo, Peru 164 E2 8.34 S 77.54 W
Coropuna, Nevado, vol., Peru 164 G3 15.31 S 72.42 W
Corossol, Guad. 159a b2 17.55 N 62.51 W
Çorovodë, Alb. 32 D14 40.30 N 20.15 E
Corowa, Austl. 98 J6 36.00 S 146.23 E
Corozal, Belize 156 C3 18.24 N 88.24 W
Corozal, Col. 168 C4 9.19 N 75.17 W
Corozal, P.R. 158a b3 18.21 N 66.18 W
Corpus, Arg. 172 C10 27.07 S 55.32 W
Corpus Christi, Tx., U.S. 136 G10 27.48 N 97.23 W
Corpus Christi, Lake, res., Tx., U.S. 136 F9 28.10 N 97.54 W
Corpus Christi Bay, b., Tx., U.S. 136 G10 27.48 N 97.20 W
Corpus Christi Naval Air Station, mil., Tx., U.S. 136 G10 27.41 N 97.16 W
Corral, Chile 166 H2 39.52 S 73.27 W
Corral de Almaguer, Spain 28 E7 39.45 N 3.09 W
Corral de Bustos, Arg. 172 F6 33.17 S 62.11 W
Corrales, Cerro, mtn., Mex. 136 H2 26.55 N 105.03 W
Corralito, Arg. 172 F5 32.01 S 64.11 W
Corralitos, Mex. 136 H3 26.57 N 104.39 W
Correas, Arroyo, stm., Arg. 206 34.24 S 58.32 W
Correctionville, Ia., U.S. 130 B2 42.28 N 95.47 W
Corredor, Braz. 205b 23.27 S 46.19 W
Corregidor Island, i., Phil. 68 C3 14.23 N 120.35 E
Córrego Rico, Braz. 170 H2 15.05 S 47.55 W
Corrente, Braz. 170 F3 10.27 S 45.10 W
Corrente, stm., Braz. 170 G4 13.08 S 43.28 W
Correntes, Cabo das, c., Moz. 90 D12 24.07 S 35.29 E
Correnti, Isola delle, i., Italy 32 H9 36.38 N 15.05 E
Correntina, Braz. 170 G3 13.20 S 44.38 W
Corrèze, state, Fr. 22 D7 45.20 N 1.50 E
Corrèze, stm., Fr. 22 D7 45.09 N 1.27 E
Correzzana, Italy 184b 45.40 N 9.18 E
Corrib, Lough, I., Ire. 10 H3 53.26 N 9.14 W
Corrientes, Arg. 172 C8 27.28 S 58.50 W
Corrientes, state, Arg. 172 D8 29.00 S 58.00 W
Corrientes, stm., Arg. 172 D8 30.25 S 59.35 W
Corrientes, stm., S.A. 168 I3 3.43 S 74.33 W
Corrientes, Bahía de, b., Cuba 156 B5 21.51 N 84.36 W
Corrientes, Cabo, c., Arg. 172 I9 38.01 S 57.31 W
Corrientes, Cabo, c., Col. 168 E3 5.29 N 77.31 W
Corrientes, Cabo, c., Cuba 156 B5 21.48 N 84.30 W
Corrientes, Cabo, c., Mex. 154 E6 20.24 N 105.41 W
Corrigan, Tx., U.S. 136 C13 30.59 N 94.49 W
Corrigin, Austl. 96 F3 32.20 S 117.52 E
Corringham, Eng., U.K. 178 51.31 N 0.28 E
Corriverton, Guy. 164 B6 5.53 N 57.08 W
Corroios, Port. 184c 38.38 N 9.09 W
Corrumpa Creek, stm., U.S. 138 E6 36.36 N 102.52 W
Corry, Pa., U.S. 124 C6 41.55 N 79.38 W
Corse (Corsica), i., Fr. 22 G14 42.00 N 9.00 E
Corse, Cap, c., Fr. 22 F15 43.01 N 9.25 E
Corse-du-Sud, state, Fr. 22 H15 41.50 N 9.00 E
Corsica, S.D., U.S. 140 D14 43.25 N 98.24 W
Corsica see Corse, i., Fr. 22 G14 42.00 N 9.00 E
Corsicana, Tx., U.S. 136 B11 32.06 N 96.28 W
Cort Adelaer, Kap, c., Grnld. 108 E17 62.00 N 42.00 W
Cortazar, Mex. 154 E8 20.29 N 100.56 W
Corte, Fr. 22 G15 42.18 N 9.08 E
Cortegana, Spain 28 G4 37.55 N 6.49 W
Corte Madera Creek, stm., Ca., U.S. 200 37.23 N 122.14 W
Cortes, bldg., Spain 184a 40.25 N 3.41 W
Cortés, Mar de see California, Golfo de, b., Mex. 152 B2 28.00 N 112.00 W
Cortez, Co., U.S. 150 F8 37.20 N 108.35 W
Cortez, Sea of see California, Golfo de, b., Mex. 152 B2 28.00 N 112.00 W
Cortez Mountains, mts., Nv., U.S. 148 C9 40.21 N 116.20 W
Cortina d'Ampezzo, Italy 30 D9 46.32 N 12.08 E
Cortland, Ne., U.S. 128 K2 40.30 N 96.43 W
Cortland, N.Y., U.S. 124 B9 42.36 N 76.11 W
Cortland, Oh., U.S. 124 C5 41.19 N 80.43 W
Cortona, Italy 30 G8 43.16 N 11.58 E
Corubal, stm., Afr. 84 G2 11.56 N 15.02 W
Coruche, Port. 28 F2 38.57 N 8.31 W
Çoruh, stm., Asia 42 E9 41.36 N 41.35 E
Çorum, Tur. 42 E6 40.33 N 34.57 E
Çorum, state, Tur. 42 E6 40.30 N 34.40 E
Corumbá, Braz. 166 C5 19.01 S 57.39 W
Corumbá, stm., Braz. 170 I1 18.18 S 48.53 W
Corumbá de Goiás, Braz. 170 H1 15.55 S 48.48 W
Corumbaíba, Braz. 170 J1 18.09 S 48.34 W
Corumbataí, stm., Braz. 172 B12 23.54 S 51.56 W
Corumbaú, Ponta do, c., Braz. 170 I6 16.53 S 39.08 W
Corumo, stm., Ven. 168 D11 6.48 N 60.51 W
Corund, Rom. 36 C12 46.28 N 25.12 E
Corunna, On., Can. 126 F7 42.52 N 82.26 W
Corunna see A Coruña, Spain 28 A2 43.21 N 8.24 W
Corunna, Mi., U.S. 130 A14 42.58 N 84.06 W
Coruripe, Braz. 170 F7 10.08 S 36.10 W
Corvallis, Mt., U.S. 146 D12 46.18 N 114.06 W
Corvallis, Or., U.S. 146 F3 44.35 N 123.16 W
Corviale, ngh., Italy 185a 41.52 N 12.25 E
Corwith, Ia., U.S. 130 B3 42.59 N 93.57 W
Corydon, In., U.S. 130 F11 38.12 N 86.07 W
Corydon, Ia., U.S. 130 D4 40.45 N 93.19 W
Corydon, Ky., U.S. 130 G10 37.44 N 87.42 W
Coryton, Eng., U.K. 178 51.31 N 0.31 E
Corzu, Rom. 36 E10 44.27 N 23.10 E
Corzuela, Arg. 172 C7 26.56 S 60.57 W
Cos see Kos, i., Grc. 34 G10 36.50 N 27.10 E
Cosamaloapan de Carpio, Mex. 154 F10 18.23 N 95.46 W
Cos Cob, Ct., U.S. 194 41.02 N 73.36 W
Cos Cob Harbor, b., Ct., U.S. 194 41.01 N 73.36 W
Coscomate, Mex. 136 I2 25.54 N 105.50 W
Cosenza, Italy 32 E10 39.17 N 16.15 E
Cosgroves Creek, stm., Austl. 192a D4 33.50 S 150.46 E
Coshocton, Oh., U.S. 124 D4 40.16 N 81.51 W
Cosigüina, Punta, c., Nic. 156 F4 12.54 N 87.41 W
Cosigüina, Volcán, vol., Nic. 156 F4 12.59 N 87.34 W
Coslada, Spain 184a 40.26 N 3.34 W
Cosmoledo, Atoll de, i., Sey. 89b k11 9.42 S 47.30 E
Cosmos, Mn., U.S. 128 G4 44.56 N 94.41 W
Cosmos, ngh., Braz. 205a 22.55 S 44.37 W
Cosne-sur-Loire, Fr. 20 G11 47.24 N 2.55 E
Cosquín, Arg. 172 E5 31.14 S 64.27 W
Cossato, Italy 30 E5 45.34 N 8.10 E
Cossatot, stm., Ar., U.S. 134 C4 33.46 N 94.08 W
Cosson, stm., Fr. 20 G10 47.29 N 1.15 E
Costa, Cordillera de la, mts., Ven. 204c 10.33 N 66.52 W
Costa de Caparica, Port. 184c 38.38 N 9.14 W
Costa Mesa, Ca., U.S. 148 J8 33.38 N 117.54 W
Costanera Sur, Parque Natural, p.o.i., Arg. 206 34.37 S 58.21 W
Costanero, Canal de, can., Arg. 206 34.28 S 58.28 W
Costa Rica, Mex. 154 C5 24.32 N 107.18 W
Costa Rica, ctry., N.A. 156 H5 10.00 N 84.00 W
Costermansville see Bukavu, D.R.C. 86 E5 2.30 S 28.51 E
Costești, Rom. 36 E11 44.40 N 24.55 E
Costiera, Catena, mts., Italy 32 E10 39.20 N 16.05 E
Costilla, N.M., U.S. 138 E3 36.58 N 105.31 W
Costilla Creek, stm., U.S. 138 E3 37.00 N 105.43 W
Cosumnes, stm., Ca., U.S. 148 E4 38.15 N 121.26 W
Cosumnes, Middle Fork, stm., Ca., U.S. 148 E5 38.33 N 120.49 W
Cosumnes, North Fork, stm., Ca., U.S. 148 E5 38.33 N 120.50 W
Coswig, Ger. 24 E9 51.07 N 13.34 E
Coswig, Ger. 24 E8 51.53 N 12.26 E
Cotabato, Phil. 68 G5 7.12 N 124.14 E
Cotagaita, Bol. 166 D3 20.49 S 65.39 W
Cotahuasi, Peru 164 G3 15.13 S 72.53 W
Cotão, hill, Port. 184c 38.45 N 9.18 W
Cotati, Ca., U.S. 148 E3 38.18 N 122.40 W
Coteaux, Haiti 156 C10 18.12 N 74.02 W
Cote d'Ivoire, ctry., Afr. 84 H3 8.00 N 5.00 W
Côte d'Ivoire see Cote d'Ivoire, ctry., Afr. 84 H3 8.00 N 5.00 W
Côte d'Ivoire see Ivory Coast, cst., C. Iv. 84 I3 5.04 N 5.15 W
Côte-d'Or, state, Fr. 20 G13 47.30 N 4.50 E
Cotegipe, Braz. 170 F3 12.02 S 44.15 W
Cote Indian Reserve, ind. res., Sk., Can. 142 C11 51.38 N 101.53 W
Cotentin, pen., Fr. 20 E7 49.29 N 1.34 W
Côte-Saint-Luc, Qc., Can. 193a 45.28 N 73.40 W
Côtes-d'Armor, state, Fr. 20 F6 48.25 N 2.40 W
Côte Visitation, ngh., Qc., Can. 193a 45.33 N 73.36 W
Cotia, mun., Braz. 205b 23.38 S 46.56 W
Cotia, Represa de, res., Braz. 205b 23.44 S 46.57 W
Cotingo, stm., Braz. 168 E11 3.54 N 60.29 W
Cotiujeni, Mol. 38 F7 47.50 N 28.33 E
Cotmeana, stm., Rom. 36 E11 44.24 N 24.45 E
Cotonou, Benin 84 H5 6.22 N 2.26 E
Cotopaxi, state, Ec. 168 H2 0.55 S 78.55 W
Cotopaxi, vol., Ec. 168 H2 0.41 S 78.26 W
Cotopaxi, Parque Nacional, p.o.i., Ec. 168 H2 0.38 S 78.28 W
Cotorro, ngh., Cuba 204b 23.03 N 82.16 W
Cotswold Hills, hills, Eng., U.K. 10 J10 51.48 N 1.57 W
Cottage Grove, Or., U.S. 146 G3 43.47 N 123.02 W
Cottageville, S.C., U.S. 132 D5 32.56 N 80.29 W
Cottam, Eng., U.K. 180 53.47 N 2.46 W
Cottbus, Ger. 24 E10 51.45 N 14.19 E
Cotter, Ar., U.S. 130 H5 36.16 N 92.31 W
Cottian Alps, mts., Eur. 22 E12 44.45 N 7.00 E
Cottiennes, Alpes see Cottian Alps, mts., Eur. 30 F3 44.45 N 7.00 E
Cottondale, Al., U.S. 134 D11 33.11 N 87.26 W
Cottondale, Fl., U.S. 134 G13 30.47 N 85.22 W
Cotton Plant, Ar., U.S. 134 C7 35.00 N 91.15 W
Cottonport, La., U.S. 134 G6 30.59 N 92.03 W
Cotton Valley, La., U.S. 134 E5 32.49 N 93.24 W
Cottonwood, Az., U.S. 150 I5 34.44 N 112.00 W
Cottonwood, Ca., U.S. 148 C3 40.24 N 122.16 W
Cottonwood, Id., U.S. 146 D10 46.03 N 116.21 W
Cottonwood, Mn., U.S. 128 G3 44.36 N 95.40 W
Cottonwood, stm., Ks., U.S. 138 C12 38.23 N 96.03 W
Cottonwood, stm., Mn., U.S. 128 G3 44.17 N 94.26 W
Cottonwood Creek, stm., Mt., U.S. 142 F6 48.32 N 107.45 W
Cottonwood Creek, stm., N.D., U.S. 140 A14 46.15 N 98.15 W
Cottonwood Creek, stm., Or., U.S. 146 G9 43.58 N 117.14 W
Cottonwood Creek, stm., Tx., U.S. 136 C4 31.20 N 103.42 W
Cottonwood Creek, stm., Tx., U.S. 136 B7 32.47 N 100.22 W
Cottonwood Creek, stm., Ut., U.S. 150 D6 39.09 N 110.54 W
Cottonwood Creek, Middle Fork, stm., Ca., U.S. 148 C3 40.23 N 122.21 W
Cottonwood Creek, South Fork, stm., Ca., U.S. 148 C3 40.22 N 122.20 W
Cottonwood Falls, Ks., U.S. 138 C12 38.22 N 96.32 W
Cottonwood Wash, stm., Az., U.S. 150 H6 35.00 N 110.39 W
Cottonwood Wash, stm., Az., U.S. 150 G3 36.19 N 113.59 W
Cotubandê, Braz. 205a 22.51 S 43.01 W
Cotulla, Tx., U.S. 136 F8 28.26 N 99.14 W
Cotunduba, Ilha de, i., Braz. 205a 22.58 S 43.09 W
Coubert, Fr. 179 48.40 N 2.42 E
Coubre, Pointe de la, c., Fr. 22 D4 45.40 N 1.13 W
Coubron, Fr. 179 48.55 N 2.35 E
Couchiching, Lake, I., On., Can. 126 D10 44.39 N 79.22 W
Coudersport, Pa., U.S. 124 C8 41.46 N 78.00 W
Coudres, Île aux, i., Qc., Can. 122 C6 47.24 N 70.23 W
Couedic, Cape du, c., Austl. 96 G7 36.03 S 136.42 E
Couesnon, stm., Fr. 20 F7 48.37 N 1.30 W
Cougar Reservoir, res., Or., U.S. 146 F4 44.05 N 122.13 W
Couhé, Fr. 22 C6 46.18 N 0.11 E
Couilly-Pont-aux-Dames, Fr. 179 48.53 N 2.52 E
Coulee City, Wa., U.S. 146 C7 47.36 N 119.17 W
Coulee Dam, Wa., U.S. 146 B8 47.59 N 118.56 W
Coulee Dam National Recreation Area, p.o.i., Wa., U.S. 146 B8 48.10 N 118.15 W
Coulommiers, Fr. 20 F12 48.49 N 3.05 E
Coulonge, stm., Qc., Can. 126 B13 45.51 N 76.45 W
Coulonge Est, stm., Qc., Can. 126 B13 46.06 N 76.42 W
Coulsdon, ngh., Eng., U.K. 178 51.19 N 0.08 W
Coulters, Pa., U.S. 197b 40.18 N 79.48 W
Coulterville, Ca., U.S. 148 F5 37.42 N 120.11 W
Coulterville, Il., U.S. 130 F8 38.11 N 89.36 W
Counce, Tn., U.S. 134 B10 35.02 N 88.16 W
Council, Id., U.S. 146 F10 44.44 N 116.26 W
Council Bluffs, Ia., U.S. 130 C2 41.15 N 95.51 W
Council Grove, Ks., U.S. 138 C12 38.39 N 96.28 W
Council Grove Lake, res., Ks., U.S. 138 C12 38.42 N 96.31 W
Country Club Hills, Il., U.S. 196 41.34 N 87.43 W
Country Club View, Va., U.S. 202c 38.49 N 77.19 W
Country Hills, Pa., U.S. 197b 40.19 N 79.42 W
Country Homes, Wa., U.S. 146 C9 47.44 N 117.23 W
Country Ridge Estates, N.Y., U.S. 194 41.02 N 73.41 W
Countryside, Il., U.S. 196 41.46 N 87.52 W
Countryside Lake, I., Il., U.S. 196 42.15 N 88.03 W
Countryside Manor, Il., U.S. 196 42.18 N 87.56 W
Coupeville, Wa., U.S. 146 B4 48.12 N 122.41 W
Coupvray, Fr. 179 48.54 N 2.48 E
Courantyne see Coeroeni, stm., S.A. 164 C6 5.50 N 57.05 W
Courantyne see Corentyne, stm., S.A. 164 C6 5.50 N 57.05 W
Courcelle, Fr. 179 48.42 N 2.06 E
Courcelles, Fr. 179 49.07 N 2.18 E
Courcouronnes, Fr. 179 48.37 N 2.24 E
Courdimanche, Fr. 179 49.02 N 2.00 E
Courgent, Fr. 179 48.54 N 1.40 E
Courgent, Fr. 179 49.04 N 1.35 E
Courland (Kurzeme), hist. reg., Lat. 26 C5 56.50 N 22.30 E
Courland Lagoon, b., Eur. 26 E3 55.00 N 21.00 E
Courmayeur, Italy 30 E3 45.47 N 6.58 E
Courquetaine, Fr. 179 48.41 N 2.45 E
Course Brook, stm., Ma., U.S. 201 42.17 N 71.22 W
Courtenay, B.C., Can. 144 G5 49.41 N 124.59 W
Courtland, Al., U.S. 134 C11 34.40 N 87.18 W
Courtland, Va., U.S. 124 H8 36.43 N 77.04 W
Courtleigh, Md., U.S. 202b 39.22 N 76.46 W
Courtney, Pa., U.S. 197b 40.13 N 79.58 W
Courtney Creek, stm., Tx., U.S. 136 C5 31.16 N 102.50 W
Courtomer, Fr. 179 48.39 N 2.54 E
Courtrai see Kortrijk, Bel. 20 D12 50.50 N 3.16 E
Courtry, Fr. 179 48.55 N 2.36 E
Courtry, Fr. 179 48.33 N 2.46 E
Coushatta, La., U.S. 134 E5 32.00 N 93.20 W
Cousiño Macul, Parque, p.o.i., Chile 204e 33.30 S 70.35 W
Coutances, Fr. 20 E7 49.03 N 1.26 W
Coutevroult, Fr. 179 48.52 N 2.51 E
Coutras, Fr. 22 D5 45.02 N 0.08 W
Coutts, Ab., Can. 144 G19 49.01 N 111.58 W
Couture, Lac, I., Qc., Can. 110 C16 60.07 N 75.20 W
Cova da Piedade, Port. 184c 38.40 N 9.10 W
Covane, Moz. 90 B11 21.21 S 33.57 E
Covasna, Rom. 36 D13 45.51 N 26.11 E
Covasna, state, Rom. 36 C12 46.00 N 26.00 E
Cove, Or., U.S. 146 E9 45.17 N 117.49 W
Cove Harbor, b., Ct., U.S. 194 41.03 N 73.30 W
Cove Island, i., On., Can. 126 C8 45.17 N 81.43 W
Covelo, Ca., U.S. 148 D2 39.47 N 123.14 W
Cove Neck, N.Y., U.S. 194 40.53 N 73.31 W
Cove Neck, pen., N.Y., U.S. 194 40.53 N 73.30 W
Coventry, Eng., U.K. 10 I11 52.25 N 1.30 W
Coventry, De., U.S. 203 39.40 N 75.38 W
Coventryville, Pa., U.S. 203 40.10 N 75.41 W
Cove Palisades State Park, p.o.i., Or., U.S. 146 F5 44.34 N 121.15 W
Covered Wells, Az., U.S. 150 K4 32.09 N 112.07 W
Covert, Mi., U.S. 130 B11 42.17 N 86.15 W
Covilhã, Port. 28 D3 40.17 N 7.30 W
Covington, Ga., U.S. 132 C2 33.36 N 83.51 W
Covington, In., U.S. 130 D10 40.08 N 87.23 W
Covington, Ky., U.S. 124 E1 39.04 N 84.30 W
Covington, La., U.S. 134 G8 30.28 N 90.06 W
Covington, Oh., U.S. 126 H5 40.06 N 84.20 W
Covington, Ok., U.S. 138 E11 36.18 N 97.34 W
Covington, Tn., U.S. 134 B9 35.33 N 89.38 W
Covington, Va., U.S. 124 G5 37.47 N 79.59 W
Covões, Port. 184c 38.50 N 9.20 W
Cowal, pen., Scot., U.K. 10 F7 56.05 N 5.08 W
Cowal, Lake, I., Austl. 98 I6 33.38 S 147.27 E
Cowan, Tn., U.S. 134 B13 35.09 N 86.00 W
Cowan, Lake, I., Austl. 96 F4 31.50 S 121.50 E
Cowan Creek, stm., Austl. 192a 33.40 S 151.10 E
Cowan Heights, Ca., U.S. 198 33.47 N 117.47 W
Cowansburg, Pa., U.S. 197b 40.15 N 79.46 W
Cowansville, Qc., Can. 122 E4 45.12 N 72.44 W
Coward, S.C., U.S. 132 C6 33.58 N 79.45 W
Cowarie, Austl. 96 E7 27.43 S 138.20 E
Cowburn Tunnel, trans., Eng., U.K. 180 53.21 N 1.52 W
Cow Canyon, val., Ca., U.S. 198 34.01 N 120.06 W
Cow Creek, stm., Ks., U.S. 138 C10 38.02 N 97.56 W
Cow Creek, stm., Mt., U.S. 142 F4 47.46 N 108.57 W
Cow Creek, stm., Ok., U.S. 138 G11 34.09 N 98.01 W
Cow Creek, stm., Or., U.S. 146 H3 42.57 N 123.20 W
Cow Creek, stm., Wa., U.S. 146 D8 46.45 N 118.09 W
Cowden, Pa., U.S. 197b 40.19 N 80.13 W
Cowdenbeath, Scot., U.K. 10 E9 56.06 N 3.20 W
Cowell, Austl. 96 F7 33.41 S 136.54 E
Cowen, W.V., U.S. 124 F5 38.24 N 80.33 W
Cowen, Mount, mtn., Mt., U.S. 146 E16 45.23 N 110.29 W
Cowessess Indian Reserve, ind. res., Sk., Can. 142 D10 50.31 N 102.42 W
Coweta, Ok., U.S. 130 I2 35.57 N 95.39 W
Cow Gulch, stm., Mt., U.S. 140 A4 46.01 N 107.50 W
Cowhouse Creek, stm., Tx., U.S. 136 C10 31.07 N 97.30 W
Cowichan Bay, B.C., Can. 144 H7 48.43 N 123.38 W
Cowichan Lake, I., B.C., Can. 144 H6 48.54 N 124.20 W
Cowies Dam, res., S. Afr. 191d 26.13 S 28.28 E
Cowley, Austl. 98 F5 26.54 S 144.49 E
Cowley, Ab., Can. 144 G16 49.34 N 114.04 W
Cowley, Wy., U.S. 140 C4 44.53 N 108.28 W
Cowley, ngh., Eng., U.K. 178 51.32 N 0.29 W
Cowlic, Az., U.S. 150 L4 31.48 N 111.59 W
Cowlitz, stm., Wa., U.S. 146 D4 46.05 N 122.54 W
Cowm Reservoir, res., Eng., U.K. 180 53.40 N 2.11 W
Cow Palace, bldg., Ca., U.S. 200 37.42 N 122.25 W
Cowpasture, stm., Va., U.S. 124 F6 37.47 N 79.46 W
Cowpens, S.C., U.S. 132 A4 35.00 N 81.48 W
Cowpens National Battlefield, p.o.i., S.C., U.S. 132 A4 35.06 N 81.46 W
Cowra, Austl. 98 I7 33.50 S 148.41 E
Coxá, stm., Braz. 170 H3 14.16 S 44.11 W
Coxim, Braz. 166 C6 18.30 S 54.45 W
Coxsackie, N.Y., U.S. 124 B12 42.21 N 73.48 W
Cox's Bāzār, Bngl. 70 H13 21.26 N 91.58 E
Coyaguaima, Cerro, mtn., Arg. 166 D3 22.55 S 66.35 W
Coyame, Mex. 154 A6 29.27 N 105.06 W
Coyame, stm., Mex. 136 E2 29.24 N 104.54 W
Coyanosa Draw, stm., Tx., U.S. 136 D4 31.15 N 103.05 W
Coyle see Coig, stm., Arg. 166 J3 50.57 S 69.08 W
Coyoacán, ngh., Mex. 204a 19.20 N 99.10 W
Coyote, stm., Mex. 120 F6 30.49 N 112.35 W
Coyote Creek, stm., Ca., U.S. 148 J9 33.13 N 116.13 W
Coyote Creek, stm., Ca., U.S. 198 33.47 N 118.05 W
Coyote Hills, hills, Ca., U.S. 200 37.33 N 122.05 W
Coyote Hills Regional Park, p.o.i., Ca., U.S. 200 37.33 N 122.06 W
Coyote Lake, I., Ca., U.S. 148 H9 35.04 N 116.45 W
Coyote Point, c., Ca., U.S. 200 37.35 N 122.19 W
Coyote Wash, stm., Az., U.S. 150 K2 32.39 N 114.08 W
Coyote Wash, stm., N.M., U.S. 150 G8 36.10 N 108.32 W
Coy Pond, I., Ma., U.S. 201 42.36 N 70.49 W
Coyuca de Benítez, Mex. 154 G8 17.01 N 100.04 W
Coyuca de Catalán, Mex. 154 F8 18.19 N 100.41 W
Cozad, Ne., U.S. 140 G13 40.51 N 99.58 W
Cozie, Alpi see Cottian Alps, mts., Eur. 30 F3 44.45 N 7.00 E
Cozumel, Mex. 156 B4 20.31 N 86.54 W
Cozumel, Isla, i., Mex. 156 B4 20.25 N 86.55 W
Cozy Lake, N.J., U.S. 194 41.01 N 74.30 W
Crab Creek, stm., Wa., U.S. 146 D7 46.48 N 119.55 W
Crab Meadow, sw., N.Y., U.S. 194 40.55 N 73.20 W
Crab Orchard, Ky., U.S. 130 G13 37.27 N 84.30 W
Crab Orchard, Tn., U.S. 130 I13 35.54 N 84.51 W
Crab Orchard Lake, res., Il., U.S. 130 G8 37.43 N 89.05 W
Crabtree Creek, stm., Pa., U.S. 197b 40.21 N 79.30 W
Craches, Fr. 179 48.34 N 1.49 E
Cracow see Kraków, Pol. 24 F15 50.03 N 19.57 E
Cradle Mountain-Lake Saint Clair National Park, p.o.i., Austl. 99a n12 41.50 S 145.56 E
Cradock, Austl. 98 I2 32.04 S 138.29 E
Cradock, S. Afr. 90 H7 32.10 S 25.36 E
Crafts Creek, stm., N.J., U.S. 203 40.07 N 74.46 W
Cragg Vale, Eng., U.K. 180 53.42 N 2.00 W
Craig, Ak., U.S. 109 E13 55.28 N 133.05 W
Craig, Co., U.S. 150 C9 40.31 N 107.32 W
Craig, Mo., U.S. 130 D2 40.11 N 95.22 W
Craig, Ne., U.S. 128 J2 41.47 N 96.21 W
Craig Creek, stm., Va., U.S. 124 G5 37.38 N 79.49 W
Craigellachie, B.C., Can. 144 E12 51.00 N 118.43 W
Craighall, ngh., S. Afr. 191d 26.07 S 28.02 E
Craighall Park, ngh., S. Afr. 191d 26.08 S 28.01 E
Craigmont, Id., U.S. 146 D10 46.14 N 116.28 W
Craigmyle, Ab., Can. 144 E18 51.40 N 112.14 W
Craigsville, Va., U.S. 124 F6 38.04 N 79.23 W
Craik, Sk., Can. 142 C8 51.03 N 105.49 W
Crailsheim, Ger. 24 G6 49.08 N 10.04 E
Craiova, Rom. 36 E10 44.19 N 23.48 E
Cranage, Eng., U.K. 180 53.12 N 2.22 W
Cranberry Brook, stm., Ma., U.S. 201 42.11 N 71.01 W
Cranberry Lake, I., N.Y., U.S. 126 D15 44.10 N 74.50 W
Cranberry Mountain, mtn., B.C., Can. 144 F12 50.42 N 118.12 W
Cranberry Pond, I., N.Y., U.S. 194 41.08 N 74.12 W
Cranbrook, Austl. 96 F3 34.17 S 117.32 E
Cranbrook, B.C., Can. 144 G15 49.30 N 115.45 W
Cranbrook Academy of Art, bldg., Mi., U.S. 199 42.34 N 83.14 W
Cranbury, N.J., U.S. 194 40.18 N 74.30 W
Cranbury Brook, stm., N.J., U.S. 194 40.19 N 74.37 W
Crandon, Wi., U.S. 128 F10 45.33 N 88.53 W
Crane, Az., U.S. 150 K2 32.42 N 114.39 W
Crane, In., U.S. 130 F11 38.53 N 86.53 W
Crane, Mo., U.S. 130 H4 36.54 N 93.34 W
Crane, Tx., U.S. 136 C5 31.23 N 102.20 W
Crane Beach, cst., Ma., U.S. 201 42.41 N 70.46 W
Cranebrook, Austl. 192a 33.43 S 150.42 E
Crane Creek, stm., Ia., U.S. 128 H6 43.00 N 91.57 W
Crane Lake, I., Sk., Can. 142 D4 50.05 N 109.05 W
Crane Mountain, mtn., Or., U.S. 148 A5 42.04 N 120.13 W
Crane River Indian Reserve, ind. res., Mb., Can. 142 C14 51.30 N 99.14 W
Crange, ngh., Ger. 181 51.32 N 7.11 E
Crângeni, Rom. 36 E11 44.01 N 24.49 E
Crank, Eng., U.K. 180 53.29 N 2.45 W
Cranston, R.I., U.S. 124 C14 41.47 N 71.26 W
Cranston Heights, De., U.S. 203 39.38 N 75.38 W
Craon, Fr. 20 G8 47.50 N 0.56 W
Crasna, Rom. 36 D13 45.36 N 26.08 E
Crasna, Rom. 36 C14 46.31 N 27.50 E
Crasna, stm., Eur. 24 I18 48.03 N 22.20 E
Crasnoe, Mol. 38 G8 46.38 N 29.48 E
Crater Lake, I., Or., U.S. 146 H4 42.56 N 122.06 W
Crater Lake National Park, p.o.i., Or., U.S. 146 G5 42.52 N 122.10 W
Craters of the Moon National Monument, p.o.i., Id., U.S. 146 G13 43.25 N 113.33 W
Crateús, Braz. 170 C5 5.10 S 40.40 W
Crati, stm., Italy 32 E10 39.43 N 16.31 E
Crato, Braz. 170 D6 7.14 S 39.23 W
Crauford, Cape, c., Nu., Can. 110 A14 73.43 N 84.56 W
Craven, Sk., Can. 142 D9 50.42 N 104.48 W
Cravo Norte, Col. 168 D6 6.18 N 70.11 W
Cravo Norte, stm., Col. 168 D6 6.17 N 70.12 W
Cravo Sur, stm., Col. 168 E6 4.40 N 71.31 W
Crawford, Co., U.S. 150 E9 38.42 N 107.35 W
Crawford, Ms., U.S. 134 D10 33.18 N 88.36 W
Crawford, Ne., U.S. 140 E9 42.40 N 103.24 W
Crawford, Tx., U.S. 136 C10 31.32 N 97.27 W
Crawford Bay, B.C., Can. 144 G14 49.42 N 116.48 W
Crawford Countryside, Il., U.S. 196 41.32 N 87.43 W
Crawford Notch State Park, p.o.i., N.H., U.S. 122 F5 44.12 N 71.24 W
Crawfordsville, Ar., U.S. 134 B8 35.13 N 90.20 W
Crawfordsville, In., U.S. 130 D11 40.01 N 86.53 W
Crawfordville, Fl., U.S. 134 G14 30.10 N 84.22 W
Crawfordville, Ga., U.S. 132 C3 33.33 N 82.53 W
Crawley, Eng., U.K. 10 J12 51.07 N 0.12 W
Crawshawbooth, Eng., U.K. 180 53.43 N 2.17 W
Crayford, ngh., Eng., U.K. 178 51.27 N 0.11 E
Crays Hill, Eng., U.K. 178 51.36 N 0.28 E
Crazy Mountains, mts., Mt., U.S. 146 D16 46.08 N 110.20 W
Crazy Peak, mtn., Mt., U.S. 146 D16 46.01 N 110.16 W
Crazy Woman Creek, stm., Wy., U.S. 140 C6 44.29 N 106.08 W
Creal Springs, Il., U.S. 130 G9 37.36 N 88.50 W
Creamery, Pa., U.S. 203 40.13 N 75.25 W
Crécy, Forêt de, p.o.i., Fr. 179 48.48 N 2.53 E
Crediton, Eng., U.K. 10 K9 50.47 N 3.39 W
Cree, stm., Sk., Can. 110 D9 58.55 N 105.45 W
Creede, Co., U.S. 138 D2 37.50 N 106.56 W
Creedmoor, N.C., U.S. 124 H7 36.07 N 78.41 W
Creek Brook, stm., Ma., U.S. 201 42.47 N 71.08 W
Creekmouth, ngh., Eng., U.K. 178 51.31 N 0.06 E
Creekwood, Il., U.S. 196 41.39 N 87.59 W
Creel, Mex. 154 B5 27.44 N 107.37 W
Cree Lake, I., Sk., Can. 110 D9 57.30 N 106.30 W
Creemore, On., Can. 126 D9 44.19 N 80.05 W
Crégy-lès-Meaux, Fr. 179 48.58 N 2.52 E
Creighton, Ne., U.S. 140 E15 42.28 N 97.54 W
Creighton Mine, On., Can. 126 B8 46.28 N 81.11 W
Creil, Fr. 20 E11 49.16 N 2.28 E
Crema, Italy 30 E6 45.22 N 9.41 E
Cremona, Ab., Can. 144 E16 51.32 N 114.30 W
Cremona, Italy 30 E7 45.08 N 10.01 E
Crenshaw, Ms., U.S. 134 C8 34.30 N 90.11 W
Creporí, stm., Braz. 164 E6 5.44 S 57.20 W
Crépy-en-Valois, Fr. 20 E11 49.13 N 2.53 E
Cres, Cro. 30 E11 44.58 N 14.24 E
Cres, Otok, i., Cro. 30 F11 44.50 N 14.25 E
Cresaptown, Md., U.S. 124 E7 39.35 N 78.49 W
Crescent, Ok., U.S. 138 F11 35.57 N 97.35 W
Crescent, Or., U.S. 146 G5 43.28 N 121.41 W
Crescent City, Ca., U.S. 148 B1 41.45 N 124.11 W
Crescent City, Fl., U.S. 132 G4 29.25 N 81.30 W
Crescent Heights, N.J., U.S. 203 39.58 N 74.43 W
Crescent Lake Estates, Mi., U.S. 199 42.38 N 83.25 W
Crescent Spur, B.C., Can. 144 C10 53.34 N 120.43 W
Crescentville, ngh., Pa., U.S. 203 40.02 N 75.05 W
Crescenzago, ngh., Italy 184b 45.30 N 9.15 E
Cresco, Ia., U.S. 128 H6 43.22 N 92.06 W
Crespières, Fr. 179 48.53 N 1.55 E
Crespo, Arg. 172 F7 32.01 S 60.18 W
Cressely, Fr. 179 48.43 N 2.05 E
Cresskill, N.J., U.S. 194 40.56 N 73.57 W
Cresskill Brook, stm., N.J., U.S. 194 40.57 N 73.58 W
Cresson, Pa., U.S. 124 D7 40.26 N 78.36 W
Cresson, Tx., U.S. 136 B10 32.32 N 97.37 W
Cressy, Austl. 98 K4 38.02 S 143.38 E
Crest, Fr. 22 E11 44.44 N 5.00 E
Crested Butte, Co., U.S. 138 C2 38.51 N 106.59 W
Crestline, Ca., U.S. 148 I8 34.14 N 117.16 W
Crestline, Oh., U.S. 124 D3 40.46 N 82.43 W
Creston, B.C., Can. 144 G14 49.05 N 116.30 W
Creston, Ia., U.S. 130 C3 41.03 N 94.22 W
Crestone Peak, mtn., Co., U.S. 138 D3 37.58 N 105.36 W
Crestview, Fl., U.S. 134 G12 30.45 N 86.34 W
Crestwood, Il., U.S. 196 41.39 N 87.45 W
Crestwood Hills, Tn., U.S. 124 I1 35.55 N 84.04 W
Creswell, Or., U.S. 146 G3 43.55 N 123.00 W
Creswell Bay, b., Nu., Can. 110 A12 72.35 N 93.25 W
Creswick, Austl. 98 K4 37.25 S 143.53 E
Crete, Il., U.S. 130 C10 41.26 N 87.37 W
Crete, Ne., U.S. 140 G16 40.37 N 96.58 W
Crete see Kriti, i., Grc. 34 H7 35.12 N 25.00 E
Crete, Sea of see Kritikón Pélagos, s., Grc. 34 H8 35.54 N 25.01 E
Créteil, Fr. 20 F11 48.47 N 2.27 E
Cretin, Cape, c., Pap. N. Gui. 101a b4 6.36 S 147.50 E
Creus, Cabo de see Creus, Cap de, c., Spain 28 B14 42.19 N 3.18 E
Creus, Cap de, c., Spain 28 B14 42.19 N 3.18 E
Creuse, state, Fr. 22 C8 46.05 N 2.00 E
Creuse, stm., Fr. 22 C6 47.00 N 0.34 E
Creussen, Ger. 24 G7 49.51 N 11.37 E
Creve Coeur, Il., U.S. 128 K9 40.38 N 89.35 W
Crèvecœur-en-Brie, Fr. 179 48.45 N 2.55 E
Crevillent, Spain 28 F10 38.15 N 0.48 W
Crevillente see Crevillent, Spain 28 F10 38.15 N 0.48 W
Crewe, Eng., U.K. 10 H10 53.05 N 2.27 W
Crewe, Va., U.S. 124 G7 37.10 N 78.07 W
Cricaré, stm., Braz. 170 J5 18.40 S 40.05 W
Criciúma, Braz. 172 D13 28.41 S 49.24 W
Cridersville, Oh., U.S. 124 D1 40.39 N 84.08 W
Crieff, Scot., U.K. 10 E9 56.22 N 3.50 W
Crikvenica, Cro. 30 E11 45.11 N 14.42 E
Crimea see Kryms'kyi pivostriv, pen., Ukr. 38 H12 45.00 N 34.00 E
Crimean Mountains see Kryms'ki hory, mts., Ukr. 38 I13 44.45 N 34.25 E
Crimean Peninsula see Kryms'kyi pivostriv, pen., Ukr. 38 H12 45.00 N 34.00 E
Crimmitschau, Ger. 24 F8 50.49 N 12.23 E
Cripple Creek, Co., U.S. 138 C3 38.45 N 105.10 W
Crisenoy, Fr. 179 48.36 N 2.45 E
Crisfield, Md., U.S. 124 F10 37.58 N 75.50 W
Criss Creek, B.C., Can. 144 E10 51.03 N 120.44 W
Crissiumal, Braz. 172 C10 27.30 S 54.06 W
Cristal, Monts de, mts., Afr. 84 I7 3.53 S 13.47 E
Cristalândia, Braz. 170 F1 10.35 S 49.11 W
Cristália, Braz. 170 I4 16.43 S 42.52 W
Cristalina, Braz. 170 I2 16.46 S 47.36 W
Cristianópolis, Braz. 170 I1 17.10 S 48.43 W
Cristinápolis, Braz. 170 F7 11.32 S 37.41 W
Cristino Castro, Braz. 170 E3 8.49 S 44.13 W
Cristóbal, Pan. 168 C2 9.20 N 79.54 W
Cristóbal Colón, Pico, mtn., Col. 168 B5 10.50 N 73.41 W
Cristo Redentor, misc. cult., S.A. 172 F2 32.50 S 70.05 W
Cristo Redentor, Estatua do, rel., Braz. 205a 22.57 S 43.13 W
Cristuru Secuiesc, Rom. 36 C12 46.17 N 25.02 E
Crișul Alb, stm., Eur. 36 C8 46.42 N 21.16 E
Crișul Negru, stm., Eur. 36 C8 46.42 N 21.16 E
Crișul Repede (Sebes Körös), stm., Eur. 36 B8 46.55 N 20.58 E
Crivitz, Wi., U.S. 126 C1 45.14 N 88.00 W
Crixalândia, Braz. 170 H2 15.18 S 47.16 W
Crixás, stm., Braz. 170 F1 11.02 S 48.34 W
Crna, stm., Mac. 34 B4 41.33 N 21.59 E
Crna Gora (Montenegro), state, Yugo. 36 G6 42.30 N 19.18 E
Crni Drim (Drinit të Zi), stm., Eur. 32 C14 42.05 N 20.24 E

Name Page Map Ref. Latitude Longitude

Črnomelj, Slvn. 30 E12 45.33 N 15.11 E
Croajingolong National Park, p.o.i., Austl. 98 K7 37.42 S 149.28 E
Croal, stm., Eng., U.K. 180 53.33 N 2.23 W
Croatia, ctry., Eur. 30 E13 45.10 N 15.30 E
Croche, stm., Qc., Can. 122 C4 47.30 N 72.46 W
Crockenhill, Eng., U.K. 178 51.23 N 0.10 E
Crocker, Mo., U.S. 130 G5 37.56 N 92.16 W
Crocker, Banjaran, mts., Malay. 68 H1 6.27 N 116.48 E
Crockett, Tx., U.S. 136 C12 31.18 N 95.27 W
Crockham Hill, Eng., U.K. 178 51.14 N 0.04 E
Crocodilopolis, hist., Egypt 76 I1 29.19 N 30.50 E
Crocus Hill, hill, Anguilla 159a a1 18.13 N 63.04 W
Croft, Eng., U.K. 180 53.26 N 2.33 W
Crofton, Ky., U.S. 130 G10 37.02 N 87.28 W
Crofton, Ne., U.S. 140 E15 42.43 N 97.29 W
Croft State Park, p.o.i., S.C., U.S. 132 B4 34.49 N 81.52 W
Croghan, N.Y., U.S. 126 E14 43.53 N 75.23 W
Croissy-Beaubourg, Fr. 179 48.50 N 2.40 E
Croissy-sur-Seine, Fr. 179 48.53 N 2.09 E
Croix, Lac la, l., N.A. 128 C6 48.21 N 92.05 W
Croker, Cape, c., Austl. 96 B6 10.58 S 132.34 E
Croker, Cape, c., On., Can. 126 D9 44.57 N 80.58 W
Croker Island, i., Austl. 96 B6 11.12 S 132.32 E
Cromarty, Scot., U.K. 10 D8 57.40 N 4.02 W
Cromby, Pa., U.S. 203 40.09 N 75.32 W
Cromer, Austl. 192a 33.44 S 151.17 E
Cromer, Eng., U.K. 10 I14 52.56 N 1.17 E
Crominia, Braz. 170 I1 17.16 S 49.22 W
Crompton Point, c., Dom. 159c i6 15.35 N 61.19 W
Cromwell, N.Z. 102 G3 45.02 S 169.11 E
Cromwell, Al., U.S. 134 E10 32.13 N 88.16 W
Cromwell Park, p.o.i., Oh., U.S. 197a 41.28 N 82.08 W
Cronenberg, ngh., Ger. 181 51.12 N 7.08 E
Cronin, Mount, mtn., B.C., Can. 144 B4 54.54 N 126.52 W
Cronton, Eng., U.K. 180 53.23 N 2.46 W
Cronulla Beach, cst., Austl. 192a 34.02 S 151.11 E
Crook, Co., U.S. 140 G10 40.51 N 102.48 W
Crooked, stm., B.C., Can. 144 B8 54.49 N 122.53 W
Crooked, stm., Or., U.S. 146 F5 44.34 N 121.16 W
Crooked Creek, Ak., U.S. 109 D8 61.52 N 158.08 W
Crooked Creek, stm., U.S. 138 D8 36.57 N 100.06 W
Crooked Creek, stm., Ar., U.S. 130 H5 36.13 N 92.28 W
Crooked Island, i., Bah. 156 A10 22.45 N 74.13 W
Crooked Island Passage, strt., Bah. 156 A10 22.43 N 74.34 W
Crooked Lake, l., Sk., Can. 142 D11 50.36 N 102.45 W
Crooked Lake, l., Fl., U.S. 132 I4 27.49 N 81.34 W
Crooked River, Sk., Can. 142 B10 52.51 N 103.43 W
Crookes Point, c., N.Y., U.S. 194 40.32 N 74.08 W
Crookham, Pa., U.S. 197b 40.12 N 79.59 W
Crookston, Mn., U.S. 128 D2 47.46 N 96.36 W
Crooksville, Oh., U.S. 124 E3 39.46 N 82.06 W
Crookwell, Austl. 98 J7 34.27 S 149.27 E
Crosby, Mn., U.S. 128 E5 46.28 N 93.57 W
Crosby, Ms., U.S. 134 F7 31.17 N 91.04 W
Crosby, N.D., U.S. 142 F10 48.54 N 103.17 W
Crosby, Mount, mtn., Wy., U.S. 140 D3 43.53 N 109.20 W
Crosbyton, Tx., U.S. 138 H7 33.39 N 101.14 W
Crosne, Fr. 179 48.43 N 2.28 E
Cross, stm., Afr. 82 F1 4.49 N 8.15 E
Cross, Cape (Kruis, Kaap), c., Nmb. 90 B1 21.46 S 13.57 E
Cross Banks, is., Ma., U.S. 201 42.43 N 70.49 W
Cross Bay Bridge, trans., N.Y., U.S. 194 40.35 N 73.49 W
Cross City, Fl., U.S. 132 G2 29.38 N 83.06 W
Cross County Center, shp. cen., N.Y., U.S. 194 40.56 N 73.51 W
Crossens, Eng., U.K. 180 53.41 N 2.57 W
Crossett, Ar., U.S. 134 D7 33.08 N 91.58 W
Cross Fell, mtn., Eng., U.K. 10 G10 54.42 N 2.29 W
Crossfield, Ab., Can. 144 E16 51.25 N 114.02 W
Cross Island, i., India 190c 18.57 N 72.51 E
Cross Keys, N.J., U.S. 203 39.42 N 75.01 W
Cross Keys Airfield, arpt., N.J., U.S. 203 39.42 N 75.02 W
Cross Lake, l., On., Can. 126 B9 46.51 N 79.57 W
Cross Lake, res., Mb., Can. 110 E11 54.45 N 97.30 W
Crossman Peak, mtn., Az., U.S. 150 I2 34.32 N 114.09 W
Cross Plains, Tx., U.S. 136 B8 32.07 N 99.10 W
Cross Plains, Wi., U.S. 128 H9 43.06 N 89.39 W
Cross Sound, strt., Ak., U.S. 109 E12 58.10 N 136.30 W
Crossville, Il., U.S. 130 F9 38.09 N 88.04 W
Crossville, Tn., U.S. 132 I12 35.56 N 85.01 W
Crosswicks, N.J., U.S. 203 40.09 N 74.38 W
Croswell, Mi., U.S. 126 E7 43.16 N 82.37 W
Crotch Lake, l., On., Can. 126 D13 44.55 N 76.48 W
Crothersville, In., U.S. 130 F12 38.47 N 85.50 W
Crotona Park, p.o.i., N.Y., U.S. 194 40.50 N 73.54 W
Croton Creek, stm., Tx., U.S. 138 H8 33.17 N 100.24 W
Crotone, Italy 32 E11 39.05 N 17.07 E
Croton Point, c., N.Y., U.S. 194 41.10 N 73.54 W
Crouse Run, stm., Pa., U.S. 197b 40.35 N 79.58 W
Crow, stm., Mn., U.S. 128 F5 45.14 N 93.31 W
Crow, North Fork, stm., Mn., U.S. 128 F5 45.04 N 93.45 W
Crow, South Fork, stm., Mn., U.S. 128 G4 45.04 N 93.45 W
Crow Agency, Mt., U.S. 140 B5 45.36 N 107.28 W
Crow Creek, stm., U.S. 140 G8 40.22 N 104.28 W
Crow Creek, stm., Ca., U.S. 200 37.42 N 122.03 W
Crow Creek, stm., Il., U.S. 128 K9 40.55 N 89.27 W
Crow Creek, stm., Mt., U.S. 140 B7 45.44 N 105.06 W
Crow Creek, stm., Mt., U.S. 146 D15 46.11 N 111.29 W
Crow Creek, stm., Wy., U.S. 140 D3 43.19 N 109.08 W
Crow Creek Indian Reservation, ind. res., S.D., U.S. 140 C13 44.11 N 99.30 W
Crowder, Ms., U.S. 134 C8 34.10 N 90.08 W
Crowder, Ok., U.S. 134 B3 35.07 N 95.42 W
Crowduck Lake, l., Mb., Can. 128 A3 50.08 N 95.15 W
Crowdy Head, c., Austl. 98 H9 31.50 S 152.43 E
Crowe, stm., On., Can. 126 D12 44.22 N 77.45 W
Crowell, Tx., U.S. 138 H9 33.59 N 99.43 W
Crow Hill, hill, Eng., U.K. 180 53.42 N 1.58 W
Crowhurst, Eng., U.K. 178 51.12 N 0.01 W
Crow Indian Reservation, ind. res., Mt., U.S. 140 B5 45.27 N 108.00 W
Crow Lake, On., Can. 128 B5 49.11 N 93.57 W
Crowley, La., U.S. 134 G6 30.12 N 92.22 W
Crowley, Lake, res., Ca., U.S. 148 F7 37.37 N 118.44 W
Crowleys Ridge, mts., U.S. 116 C7 35.45 N 90.45 W
Crown Memorial Beach, p.o.i., Ca., U.S. 200 37.46 N 122.16 W
Crown Mines, mine, S. Afr. 191d 26.13 S 28.00 E
Crown Mountain, mtn., V.I.U.S. 158b e7 18.22 N 64.58 W
Crown Point, In., U.S. 130 C10 41.25 N 87.21 W
Crownpoint, N.M., U.S. 150 H8 35.40 N 108.09 W
Crown Point, N.Y., U.S. 126 E16 43.56 N 73.25 W
Crown Prince Frederik Island, i., Nu., Can. 110 A13 70.02 N 86.50 W
Crown Village, N.Y., U.S. 194 40.40 N 73.27 W
Crow Peak, mtn., Mt., U.S. 146 D15 46.18 N 111.54 W
Crow Rock Creek, stm., Mt., U.S. 142 H7 47.05 N 106.14 W
Crows Nest, Austl. 192a 33.50 S 151.12 E
Crowsnest, Ab., Can. 144 G16 49.38 N 114.41 W
Crowsnest Pass, Ab., Can. 144 G16 49.36 N 114.25 W
Crowsnest Pass, p., Can. 144 G16 49.40 N 114.46 W
Crows Nest Peak, mtn., S.D., U.S. 140 C8 44.03 N 103.58 W
Crowton, Eng., U.K. 180 53.16 N 2.38 W
Crow Wing, stm., Mn., U.S. 128 E4 46.16 N 94.21 W
Croxteth Park, p.o.i., Eng., U.K. 180 53.26 N 2.53 W
Croydon, Austl. 98 B4 18.12 S 142.14 E
Croydon, Austl. 192a 33.53 S 151.07 E
Croydon Park, Austl. 192a 33.54 S 151.07 E
Croydon Peak, mtn., N.H., U.S. 122 G4 43.29 N 72.13 W
Croydon Station, B.C., Can. 144 C11 53.03 N 119.41 W
Crozet, Va., U.S. 124 F7 38.04 N 78.41 W
Crozet, Îles de, is., Afr. 80 K11 46.00 S 52.00 E
Crozet Basin, unds. 174 M9 39.00 S 60.00 E
Crozon, Fr. 20 F4 48.15 N 4.29 W
Crucea, Rom. 36 E15 44.32 N 28.14 E
Cruces, Cuba 156 A7 22.20 N 80.17 W
Cruger, Ms., U.S. 134 D8 33.19 N 90.14 W
Cruillas, Mex. 154 C9 24.44 N 98.32 W
Crum Creek, stm., Pa., U.S. 203 39.51 N 75.19 W
Crum Lynne, Pa., U.S. 203 39.52 N 75.20 W
Crump Lake, l., Or., U.S. 148 A5 42.17 N 119.50 W
Cruser Brook, stm., N.J., U.S. 194 40.27 N 74.39 W
Cruz, Cabo, c., Cuba 156 C9 19.51 N 77.44 W
Cruz Alta, Arg. 172 F7 32.59 S 61.48 W
Cruz Alta, Braz. 172 D11 28.37 S 53.35 W
Cruz Bay, V.I.U.S. 158b e7 18.20 N 64.47 W
Cruz del Eje, Arg. 172 E5 30.43 S 64.48 W
Cruz del Marquez, Cerro, mtn., Mex. 204a 19.12 N 99.15 W
Cruzeiro, Braz. 170 L3 22.34 S 44.57 W
Cruzeiro do Oeste, Braz. 172 A11 23.46 S 53.04 W
Cruzeiro do Sul, Braz. 164 E3 7.38 S 72.41 W
Cruzeta, Braz. 170 D7 6.25 S 36.47 W
Cruz Grande, Chile 172 D2 29.25 S 71.17 W
Cruz Machado, Braz. 172 B12 26.01 S 51.21 W
Crvenka, Yugo. 36 D6 45.39 N 19.27 E
Crysler, On., Can. 126 C14 45.13 N 75.09 W
Crystal, Mn., U.S. 128 F5 45.01 N 93.21 W
Crystal, N.D., U.S. 142 F16 48.35 N 97.40 W
Crystal, stm., Co., U.S. 138 B1 39.25 N 107.14 W
Crystal Beach, On., Can. 202a 42.52 N 79.04 W
Crystal Beach, Fl., U.S. 132 H3 28.05 N 82.46 W
Crystal Brook, Austl. 98 I2 33.21 S 138.11 E
Crystal City, Mb., Can. 142 E15 49.08 N 98.57 W
Crystal City, Mo., U.S. 130 F7 38.13 N 90.22 W
Crystal City, Tx., U.S. 136 F8 28.40 N 99.49 W
Crystal Creek, stm., Il., U.S. 196 41.58 N 87.51 W
Crystal Falls, Mi., U.S. 126 B1 46.05 N 88.18 W
Crystal Lake, Il., U.S. 130 B9 42.14 N 88.17 W
Crystal Lake, l., Ma., U.S. 201 42.48 N 71.09 W
Crystal Lake, l., Ma., U.S. 201 42.29 N 71.05 W
Crystal Lake, l., Mi., U.S. 126 D3 44.39 N 86.09 W
Crystal Lake, l., N.J., U.S. 194 41.02 N 74.15 W
Crystal Palace National Sports Centre, p.o.i., Eng., U.K. 178 51.25 N 0.04 W
Crystal River, Fl., U.S. 132 H3 28.54 N 82.35 W
Crystal Spring Lake, l., N.J., U.S. 203 39.43 N 75.01 W
Crystal Springs, Ms., U.S. 134 E8 31.59 N 90.21 W
Crystal Springs Dam, dam., Ca., U.S. 200 37.32 N 122.22 W
Csepel, ngh., Hung. 182c 47.24 N 19.14 E
Cserhát, mts., Hung. 36 A6 47.55 N 19.30 E
Csobánka, Hung. 182c 47.38 N 18.58 E
Csomád, Hung. 182c 47.40 N 19.15 E
Csömör, Hung. 182c 47.33 N 19.14 E
Csömöri-patak, stm., Hung. 182c 47.36 N 19.07 E
Csongrád, Hung. 36 C7 46.42 N 20.09 E
Csongrád, state, Hung. 36 C7 46.25 N 20.15 E
Csorna, Hung. 36 B4 47.37 N 17.16 E
Csurgó, Hung. 36 C4 46.16 N 17.05 E
Ču, stm., Asia 48 F11 45.00 N 67.44 E
Cúa, Ven. 168 B8 10.09 N 66.52 W
Cuajimalpa, ngh., Mex. 204a 19.21 N 99.18 W
Cuajinicuilapa, Mex. 154 G9 16.28 N 98.25 W
Cuamba, Moz. 88 C6 14.47 S 36.32 E
Cuando (Kwando), stm., Afr. 88 D3 18.29 S 23.36 E
Cuangar, Ang. 88 D2 17.35 S 18.37 E
Cuango, Ang. 88 B2 6.17 S 16.41 E
Cuango, Ang. 88 B2 9.08 S 18.03 E
Cuango (Kwango), stm., Afr. 86 F3 3.12 S 17.23 E
Cuanza, stm., Ang. 88 C2 9.20 S 13.09 E
Cuao, stm., Ven. 168 E8 4.56 N 67.41 W
Cuareim (Quaraí), stm., S.A. 172 E9 30.11 S 57.36 W
Cuaró, Ur. 172 E9 30.35 S 56.53 W
Cuarto, stm., Arg. 172 F5 33.24 S 62.54 W
Cuatro Caminos, Cuba 204b 22.54 N 82.23 W
Cuatrociénegas, Mex. 154 B7 26.59 N 102.04 W
Cuauhtémoc, Mex. 154 A5 28.24 N 106.51 W
Cuautepec el Alto, ngh., Mex. 204a 19.34 N 99.08 W
Cuautitlán, Mex. 154 F6 19.27 N 104.21 W
Cuautitlán, stm., Mex. 204a 19.41 N 99.13 W
Cuautitlán Izcalli, Mex. 204a 19.39 N 99.13 W
Cuautzin, Volcán, vol., Mex. 204a 19.09 N 99.06 W
Cuba, Port. 28 F3 38.09 N 7.53 W
Cuba, Al., U.S. 134 E10 32.25 N 88.22 W
Cuba, Il., U.S. 130 D7 40.29 N 90.12 W
Cuba, Ks., U.S. 138 B11 39.48 N 97.27 W
Cuba, Mo., U.S. 130 F6 38.03 N 91.24 W
Cuba, N.M., U.S. 138 E2 36.01 N 106.58 W
Cuba, N.Y., U.S. 124 B7 42.12 N 78.16 W
Cuba, ctry., N.A. 152 C9 21.30 N 80.00 W
Cuba, i., Cuba 106 G15 21.38 N 79.40 W
Cubabi, Cerro, mtn., Mex. 150 L4 31.42 N 112.46 W
Cubadak, Indon. 66 C2 0.20 N 100.00 E
Cubagua, Isla, i., Ven. 168 B9 10.48 N 64.10 W
Cuba Island, i., N.Y., U.S. 194 40.38 N 73.32 W
Cubal, Ang. 88 C1 13.02 S 14.16 E
Cubango (Okavango), stm., Afr. 88 D2 18.56 S 22.24 E
Cubatí, Braz. 170 D7 6.51 S 36.21 W
Čublas, Russia 12 D21 64.40 N 45.01 E
Çubuk, Tur. 34 C15 40.14 N 33.02 E
Cucamonga Creek, stm., Ca., U.S. 198 33.57 N 117.37 W
Cucharas, stm., Co., U.S. 138 D4 37.55 N 104.32 W
Cuchi, Ang. 88 C2 14.39 S 16.53 E
Cuchi, stm., Ang. 88 C2 15.27 S 17.20 E
Cuchillo Co, Arg. 172 I5 38.20 S 64.38 W
Cuchillo Negro Creek, stm., N.M., U.S. 150 J9 33.08 N 107.13 W
Cuchivero, stm., Ven. 168 D9 7.40 N 65.57 W
Cuchumatanes, Sierra los, mts., Guat. 152 D6 15.35 N 91.25 W
Cuckels Brook, stm., N.J., U.S. 194 40.33 N 74.33 W
Cuckold Point, c., Md., U.S. 202b 39.14 N 76.24 W
Čučkovo, Russia 40 B12 59.36 N 41.14 E
Cucuí, Braz. 168 G8 1.12 N 66.50 W
Cucumbi, Ang. 88 C2 10.17 S 19.02 E
Cucurpe, Mex. 120 F7 30.19 N 110.41 W
Cúcuta, Col. 168 D5 7.53 N 72.29 W
Cucuy, Piedra de, hill, Ven. 168 G8 1.15 N 66.45 W
Cudahy, Ca., U.S. 198 33.57 N 118.11 W
Cudahy, Wi., U.S. 130 B10 42.57 N 87.52 W
Cuddalore, India 69 F4 11.44 N 79.46 E
Cuddapah, India 69 D4 14.28 N 78.49 E
Cuddeback Lake, l., Ca., U.S. 148 H8 35.18 N 117.28 W
Cuddy, Pa., U.S. 197b 40.21 N 80.09 W
Cuddy Mountain, mtn., Id., U.S. 146 F10 44.46 N 116.47 W
Cudham, ngh., Eng., U.K. 178 51.19 N 0.05 E
Cudia Park, p.o.i., On., Can. 193b 43.43 N 79.13 W
Čudovo, Russia 26 A14 59.07 N 31.41 E
Čudskoe ozero see Peipus, Lake, l., Eur. 26 B10 58.45 N 27.25 E
Cudworth, Sk., Can. 142 B8 52.29 N 105.43 W
Čudzin, Bela. 26 H9 52.44 N 26.57 E
Čudzjavr, ozero, l., Russia 14 D25 68.13 N 34.29 E
Cue, Austl. 96 E3 27.25 S 117.54 E
Cuéllar, Spain 28 C6 41.24 N 4.18 W
Cuemba, Ang. 88 C2 12.08 S 18.06 E
Cuenca, Ec. 168 I2 2.53 S 79.00 W
Cuenca, Spain 28 D8 40.04 N 2.08 W
Cuenca, co., Spain 28 E9 39.55 N 2.10 W
Cuencamé de Ceniceros, Mex. 154 C7 24.51 N 103.41 W
Cuerda del Pozo, Embalse de la, res., Spain 22 H2 41.51 N 2.44 W
Cuernavaca, Mex. 154 F9 18.55 N 99.13 W
Cuero, Tx., U.S. 136 E10 29.05 N 97.17 W
Cuers, Fr. 22 F12 43.13 N 6.04 E
Cuervo, Laguna del, l., Mex. 154 A6 29.16 N 105.55 W
Cuervos, Mex. 150 K2 32.37 N 114.51 W
Cuesta Pass, p., Ca., U.S. 148 H5 35.21 N 120.38 W
Cueto, Cuba 156 B9 20.39 N 75.56 W
Cuevas del Almanzora, Spain 28 G9 37.18 N 1.53 W
Cugir, Rom. 36 D10 45.50 N 23.22 E
Čuguevka, Russia 50 B10 44.09 N 133.51 E
Čuguš, gora, mtn., Russia 42 D9 43.47 N 40.16 E
Čuhloma, Russia 40 B13 58.45 N 42.42 E
Čuhlomskoe, ozero, l., Russia 12 G19 58.47 N 42.38 E
Cuiabá, Braz. 166 C5 15.36 S 56.05 W
Cuiabá, stm., Braz. 166 C5 17.54 S 57.27 W
Cuiari, Braz. 168 G7 1.30 N 68.10 W
Cuiari see Cuyarí, stm., S.A. 168 G7 1.30 N 68.11 W
Cuicatlán, Mex. 154 G10 17.46 N 96.57 W
Cuieiras, stm., Braz. 168 I11 2.50 S 60.30 W
Cuilapa, Guat. 156 E2 14.17 N 90.18 W
Cuilco, stm., N.A. 156 E1 15.27 N 91.52 W
Cuilo (Kwilu), stm., Afr. 86 F3 3.22 S 17.22 E
Cuisy, Fr. 179 49.01 N 2.46 E
Cuité, Braz. 170 D7 6.29 S 36.09 W
Cuíto, stm., Ang. 88 D2 18.00 S 20.47 E
Cuito Cuanavale, Ang. 88 D2 15.10 S 19.10 E
Cuitzeo, Lago de, l., Mex. 154 F8 19.55 N 101.05 W
Cuiuni, stm., Braz. 168 H10 0.46 S 63.03 W
Cuivre, North Fork, stm., Mo., U.S. 130 E6 39.00 N 90.59 W
Cuivre, West Fork, stm., Mo., U.S. 130 E6 39.00 N 90.59 W
Cuivre River State Park, p.o.i., Mo., U.S. 130 E6 39.02 N 90.57 W
Cuji, Ven. 204c 10.28 N 67.02 W
Cukai, Malay. 64 J6 4.14 N 103.25 E
Cukas, Indon. 66 D4 0.25 S 104.16 E
Čukčagirskoe ozero, l., Russia 50 F16 52.00 N 136.36 E
Čukotskij, mys, c., Russia 50 D26 64.15 N 173.06 W
Čukotskij poluostrov (Chukotsk Peninsula), pen., Russia 50 C26 66.00 N 175.00 W
Čukotskoe more see Chukchi Sea, s. 106 B5 69.00 N 171.00 W
Çukurca, Tur. 42 G10 37.15 N 43.37 E
Čulakkurgan, Kaz. 48 F11 43.45 N 69.11 E
Culaman, Phil. 68 H5 5.58 N 125.40 E
Culbertson, Mt., U.S. 142 F9 48.08 N 104.30 W
Culbertson, Ne., U.S. 138 A8 40.13 N 100.50 W
Culbertson Run, stm., Pa., U.S. 203 40.03 N 75.45 W
Culcairn, Austl. 98 J6 35.40 S 147.02 E
Culcheth, Eng., U.K. 180 53.27 N 2.32 W
Cul de Sac, Guad. 159a a1 18.06 N 63.01 W
Cul de Sac, Neth. Ant. 159a a1 18.02 N 63.03 W
Culebra, P.R. 158a b5 18.18 N 65.17 W
Culebra, Isla de, i., P.R. 158a b5 18.19 N 65.17 W
Culebra, Sierra de la, mts., Spain 28 C4 41.53 N 6.20 W
Culebra Peak, mtn., Co., U.S. 138 D3 37.07 N 105.11 W
Culebrinas, stm., P.R. 158a b1 18.24 N 67.10 W
Culebrita, Isla, i., P.R. 158a b5 18.19 N 65.13 W
Culebro, Arroyo del, stm., Spain 184a 40.19 N 3.34 W
Culfa, Azer. 48 G7 38.57 N 45.37 E
Culgoa, stm., Austl. 98 G6 29.58 S 146.06 E
Culiacán, Mex. 154 C5 24.04 N 107.05 W
Culiacán, Mex. 154 C5 24.48 N 107.24 W
Culiacancito, Mex. 154 C5 24.49 N 107.32 W
Culijón, Nevado, mtn., Peru 164 F4 14.38 S 69.14 W
Culion Island, i., Phil. 68 E2 11.51 N 119.56 E
Cúllar, Spain 28 G8 37.35 N 2.34 W
Cull Creek, stm., Ca., U.S. 200 37.42 N 122.03 W
Cullen, La., U.S. 134 E5 32.58 N 93.27 W
Culleoka, Tn., U.S. 134 B12 35.28 N 86.58 W
Cullera, Spain 28 E10 39.10 N 0.14 W
Cullman, Al., U.S. 134 C12 34.10 N 86.50 W
Cullom, Il., U.S. 130 D9 40.52 N 88.15 W
Cullowhee, N.C., U.S. 132 A2 35.18 N 83.10 W
Čul'man, Russia 50 E13 56.51 N 124.53 E
Çülmen, Tur. 76 A9 37.18 N 38.47 E
Culmore, Va., U.S. 202c 38.51 N 77.08 W
Culpeper, Va., U.S. 124 F7 38.27 N 77.59 W
Culpina, Bol. 166 D4 20.50 S 64.54 W
Culuene, stm., Braz. 166 B6 12.55 S 52.49 W
Culver, In., U.S. 130 C11 41.12 N 86.24 W
Culver, Or., U.S. 146 F5 44.31 N 121.12 W
Culverden, N.Z. 102 F5 42.45 S 172.50 E
Culverstone Green, Eng., U.K. 178 51.20 N 0.21 E
Čulym, Russia 48 C14 55.08 N 80.59 E
Čulym, stm., Russia 48 C14 57.42 N 83.51 E
Čum, Russia 50 C1 67.05 N 63.04 E
Cumaná, Ven. 168 B9 10.27 N 64.10 W
Cumanacoa, Ven. 168 B10 10.14 N 63.55 W
Cumaovası, Tur. 34 E10 38.14 N 27.09 E
Cumare, Cerro, hill, Col. 168 G5 0.28 N 73.52 W
Cumari, Braz. 170 J1 18.16 S 48.09 W
Cumbal, Nevado, vol., Col. 168 G2 0.57 N 77.52 W
Cumbe, Braz. 170 F7 10.21 S 37.15 W
Cumberland, B.C., Can. 144 G5 49.37 N 125.00 W
Cumberland, Ia., U.S. 130 C3 41.16 N 94.52 W
Cumberland, Ky., U.S. 124 G2 36.58 N 83.00 W
Cumberland, Md., U.S. 124 E7 39.39 N 78.45 W
Cumberland, Va., U.S. 124 G7 37.29 N 78.14 W
Cumberland, Wi., U.S. 128 F6 45.31 N 92.01 W
Cumberland, stm., U.S. 124 H2 37.08 N 88.25 W
Cumberland, Lake, res., Ky., U.S. 130 H12 36.56 N 84.55 W
Cumberland, South Fork, stm., U.S. 130 H13 36.58 N 84.37 W
Cumberland City, Tn., U.S. 130 H10 36.22 N 87.38 W
Cumberland Falls State Resort Park, p.o.i., Ky., U.S. 124 H1 36.50 N 84.20 W
Cumberland Gap, p., U.S. 124 H2 36.35 N 83.40 W
Cumberland Gap National Historical Park, p.o.i., U.S. 124 H2 36.36 N 83.40 W
Cumberland Indian Reserve, ind. res., Sk., Can. 142 A9 53.04 N 104.50 W
Cumberland Island National Seashore, p.o.i., Ga., U.S. 132 F4 30.50 N 81.27 W
Cumberland Islands, is., Austl. 98 C7 20.40 S 149.09 E
Cumberland Lake, l., Sk., Can. 110 E10 54.02 N 102.17 W
Cumberland Peninsula, pen., Nu., Can. 110 B17 66.31 N 64.13 W
Cumberland Plateau, plat., U.S. 116 B11 36.00 N 85.00 W
Cumberland Sound, strt., Nu., Can. 110 B17 65.10 N 65.30 W
Cumbernauld, Scot., U.K. 10 F9 55.57 N 3.58 W
Cumborah, Austl. 98 G6 29.44 S 147.46 E
Cumbrian Mountains, mts., Eng., U.K. 10 G9 54.32 N 3.10 W
Cumby, Tx., U.S. 136 A12 33.08 N 95.50 W
Čumikan, Russia 50 F16 54.42 N 135.19 E
Cuminá see Paru de Oeste, stm., Braz. 164 C6 1.31 S 56.02 W
Cumming, Ga., U.S. 132 B1 34.12 N 84.08 W
Cummins, Austl. 96 F7 34.15 S 135.43 E
Cummins, Mount, mtn., B.C., Can. 144 D12 52.03 N 118.15 W
Cummins Creek, stm., Tx., U.S. 136 E11 29.43 N 96.30 W
Cumnock, Scot., U.K. 10 F8 55.27 N 4.16 W
Cumpas, Mex. 120 F8 30.00 N 109.47 W
Çumra, Tur. 34 F15 37.33 N 32.49 E
Cumuripa, Mex. 154 A3 28.08 N 109.53 W
Čumyš, stm., Russia 48 D15 53.31 N 83.09 E
Čuna, stm., Russia 48 C17 57.44 N 95.27 E
Cunani, Braz. 164 C7 2.52 N 51.06 W
Cunaviche, Ven. 168 D8 7.22 N 67.25 W
Cunco, Chile 166 G2 38.55 S 72.01 W
Cuncumén, Chile 172 E2 31.53 S 70.38 W
Cundinamarca, state, Col. 168 E4 5.00 N 74.00 W
Čundža, Kaz. 48 F13 43.31 N 79.28 E
Cunene (Kunene), stm., Afr. 88 D1 17.15 S 11.45 E
Cuneo (Coni), Italy 30 F4 44.23 N 7.32 E
Cung Hau, Cua, mth., Viet. 62 G10 9.47 N 106.33 E
Cung Son, Viet. 64 F9 13.03 N 108.58 E
Cunha Porã, Braz. 172 C11 26.53 S 53.10 W
Čunja, stm., Russia 48 B17 61.36 N 96.32 E
Cunnamulla, Austl. 98 G5 28.04 S 145.40 E
Cunningham, Ks., U.S. 138 D10 37.38 N 98.25 W
Cunningham, Lake, l., Bah. 158f m18 25.03 N 77.24 W
Cunningham Park, p.o.i., Ma., U.S. 201 42.15 N 71.03 W
Cunningham Park, p.o.i., N.Y., U.S. 194 40.44 N 73.46 W
Čunskij, Russia 48 C17 56.04 N 99.39 E
Cunucunuma, stm., Ven. 168 F8 3.12 N 66.00 W
Čuny, Russia 18 H22 59.39 N 36.04 E
Cuorgnè, Italy 30 E4 45.23 N 7.38 E
Čupa, Russia 14 F24 66.15 N 33.01 E
Cupar, Sk., Can. 142 D9 50.57 N 104.11 W
Cupar, Scot., U.K. 10 E9 56.19 N 3.01 W
Cupecê, Ribeirão, stm., Braz. 205b 23.37 S 46.42 W
Cupica, Golfo de, b., Col. 168 D3 6.31 N 77.27 W
Ćuprija, Yugo. 36 F8 43.56 N 21.23 E
Čuprovo, Russia 12 D22 64.13 N 46.26 E
Cupsaw Lake, l., N.J., U.S. 194 41.07 N 74.15 W
Cuquenán, stm., Ven. 168 E11 4.44 N 61.28 W
Čur, Russia 40 C18 57.06 N 52.59 E
Curaçá, Braz. 170 E6 8.59 S 39.54 W
Curaçao, i., Neth. Ant. 158g p21 12.11 N 69.00 W
Curacautín, Chile 172 I2 38.25 S 71.55 W
Curacaví, Chile 172 F2 33.24 S 71.09 W
Curacó see Salado, stm., Arg. 172 G4 38.49 S 64.59 W
Curanilahue, Chile 172 H1 37.28 S 73.21 W
Curanipe, Chile 172 G1 35.50 S 72.37 W
Čurapča, Russia 50 D15 61.59 N 132.29 E
Curaray, stm., S.A. 168 H4 2.25 S 74.03 W
Curcani, Rom. 36 E13 44.12 N 26.35 E
Cure, stm., Fr. 20 G12 47.40 N 3.40 E
Curecanti National Recreation Area, p.o.i., Co., U.S. 150 E9 38.26 N 107.28 W
Curepipe, Mrts. 89a i10 20.19 S 57.31 E
Curepto, Chile 172 G1 35.05 S 72.07 W
Curiapo, Ven. 168 C11 8.32 N 61.00 W
Curicó, Chile 172 G2 34.59 S 71.14 W
Curicuriari, stm., Braz. 168 H8 0.12 S 66.46 W
Curimatá, Braz. 170 E3 10.02 S 44.17 W
Curitiba, Braz. 172 B13 25.25 S 49.15 W
Curitibanos, Braz. 172 C12 27.16 S 50.34 W
Curiuaú, stm., Braz. 168 H11 1.50 S 61.14 W
Curiúva, Braz. 172 B12 24.00 S 50.29 W
Curl Curl, Austl. 192a 33.46 S 151.18 E
Curlew, Wa., U.S. 146 B8 48.52 N 118.35 W
Curlewis, Austl. 98 H8 31.07 S 150.16 E
Curnamona, Austl. 98 H2 31.39 S 139.32 E
Čurovići, Russia 26 H15 52.10 N 32.00 E
Currais Novos, Braz. 170 D7 6.15 S 36.31 W
Curralinho, Braz. 164 D8 1.48 S 49.47 W
Currant Creek, stm., Co., U.S. 138 C3 38.29 N 105.22 W
Currant Creek, stm., Mt., U.S. 140 A3 46.21 N 108.38 W
Currant Mountain, mtn., Nv., U.S. 148 E10 38.55 N 115.25 W
Current, stm., On., Can. 128 C9 48.27 N 89.12 W
Current, stm., U.S. 130 H7 36.14 N 90.54 W
Currie, Austl. 98 L4 39.56 S 143.51 E
Currie, Mn., U.S. 128 G3 44.03 N 95.41 W
Currituck, N.C., U.S. 124 H9 36.26 N 76.01 W
Currituck Sound, strt., N.C., U.S. 124 H10 36.20 N 75.52 W
Curtea de Argeș, Rom. 36 D11 45.08 N 24.43 E
Curtina, Ur. 172 F9 32.10 S 56.06 W
Curtin Springs, Austl. 96 E6 25.18 S 131.44 E
Curtis see Teixeiro, Spain 28 A2 43.06 N 8.02 W
Curtis, Ar., U.S. 134 D5 33.59 N 93.06 W
Curtis, Ne., U.S. 140 G12 40.37 N 100.30 W
Curtis, Port, b., Austl. 98 D8 23.51 S 151.20 E
Curtis Bay, b., Md., U.S. 202b 39.13 N 76.35 W
Curtis Channel, strt., Austl. 98 D8 23.31 S 151.30 E
Curtis Creek, b., Md., U.S. 202b 39.12 N 76.35 W
Curtis Island, i., Austl. 98 D8 23.38 S 151.09 E
Curtis Island, i., N.Z. 94 G9 30.30 S 178.34 W
Curu, stm., Braz. 170 C6 3.24 S 39.03 W
Curuá, stm., Braz. 164 D7 1.57 S 55.07 W
Curuá, stm., Braz. 164 E7 5.20 S 54.28 W
Curuá, Ilha do, i., Braz. 164 C7 0.48 N 50.10 W
Curuá-Una, stm., Braz. 164 D7 2.22 S 54.04 W
Curuçá, Braz. 164 D8 0.43 S 47.51 W
Curuçá, ngh., Braz. 205b 23.30 S 46.25 W
Curuçambaba, Braz. 170 B1 2.08 S 49.18 W
Curumo, Ven. 204c 10.27 N 66.52 W
Curumu, Braz. 164 D7 1.00 S 51.03 W
Curup, Indon. 66 E3 3.27 S 102.31 E
Curupá, Braz. 170 E2 9.52 S 45.53 W
Cururupu, Braz. 170 A3 1.50 S 44.52 W
Curuzú Cuatiá, Arg. 172 D8 29.47 S 58.03 W
Curva Grande, Braz. 170 B3 2.36 S 45.27 W
Curvelo, Braz. 170 J3 18.45 S 44.26 W
Curwensville, Pa., U.S. 124 D7 40.58 N 78.31 W
Cusago, Italy 184b 45.27 N 9.02 E
Cusco, Peru 164 F3 13.31 S 71.58 W
Cushing, Ok., U.S. 134 B2 35.59 N 96.46 W
Cushing, Tx., U.S. 136 C13 31.48 N 94.50 W
Cushing Memorial State Park, p.o.i., Ma., U.S. 201 42.10 N 70.45 W
Cushman, Ar., U.S. 130 I6 35.52 N 91.45 W
Cushman, Lake, res., Wa., U.S. 146 C3 47.28 N 123.15 W
Cusiana, stm., Col. 168 E5 4.31 N 71.51 W
Cusick, Wa., U.S. 146 B9 48.20 N 117.18 W
Cusihuiriachic, Mex. 154 A5 28.14 N 106.50 W
Cusio see Orta, Lago d', l., Italy 30 E5 45.49 N 8.24 E
Cusna, Monte, mtn., Italy 30 F7 44.15 N 10.24 E
Čusovaja, stm., Russia 40 C21 58.08 N 57.02 E
Čusovoj, Russia 40 B20 58.17 N 57.48 E
Cusset, Fr. 22 C9 46.07 N 3.28 E
Cusseta, Ga., U.S. 134 E14 32.18 N 84.47 W
Čust, Uzb. 48 F12 41.00 N 71.14 E
Custer, Mi., U.S. 126 E3 43.57 N 86.13 W
Custer, Mt., U.S. 140 A5 46.07 N 107.34 W
Custer, Ok., U.S. 138 F10 35.40 N 98.52 W
Custer, S.D., U.S. 140 D9 43.44 N 103.35 W
Custer Creek, stm., Mt., U.S. 140 A7 46.42 N 105.28 W
Custer State Park, p.o.i., S.D., U.S. 140 D9 43.43 N 103.23 W
Custódia, Braz. 170 E7 8.07 S 37.39 W
Cut, Nuhu, i., Indon. 60 G9 5.28 S 133.05 E
Cut Bank, Mt., U.S. 146 B14 48.38 N 112.19 W
Cutbank, stm., Ab., Can. 144 B12 54.41 N 118.32 W
Cut Bank Creek, stm., U.S. 142 F12 48.21 N 100.47 W
Cut Bank Creek, stm., Mt., U.S. 146 B14 48.38 N 112.21 W
Cutervo, Peru 164 E2 6.22 S 78.49 W
Cuthand Creek, stm., Tx., U.S. 134 D4 33.23 N 94.56 W
Cuthbert, Ga., U.S. 134 F14 31.45 N 84.47 W
Cut Knife, Sk., Can. 142 B4 52.44 N 109.02 W
Cutler, Ca., U.S. 148 G6 36.31 N 119.17 W
Cutler, Me., U.S. 122 F9 44.40 N 67.12 W
Cutlerville, Mi., U.S. 130 B12 42.50 N 85.39 W
Cutral-Có, Arg. 166 G3 38.56 S 69.14 W
Cutro, Italy 32 E10 39.02 N 16.59 E
Cuttack, India 70 H10 20.30 N 85.50 E
Cutzamalá, stm., Mex. 154 F8 18.22 N 100.40 W
Čuvašija, state, Russia 40 D15 55.30 N 47.00 E
Cuvier, Cape, c., Austl. 96 D2 24.04 S 113.25 E
Cuvo, stm., Ang. 88 C1 10.51 S 13.47 E
Cuxhaven, Ger. 24 C4 53.52 N 8.42 E
Cuxton, Eng., U.K. 178 51.22 N 0.27 E
Cuyabá see Cuiabá, Braz. 166 C5 15.36 S 56.05 W
Cuyahoga County Airport, arpt., Oh., U.S. 197a 41.34 N 81.29 W
Cuyahoga Falls, Oh., U.S. 124 C4 41.08 N 81.29 W
Cuyahoga Heights, Oh., U.S. 197a 41.26 N 81.39 W
Cuyama, stm., Ca., U.S. 148 I6 34.59 N 120.19 W
Cuyamaca Peak, mtn., Ca., U.S. 148 J9 32.57 N 116.36 W
Cuyamaca Rancho State Park, p.o.i., Ca., U.S. 148 K9 32.56 N 116.33 W
Cuyapo, Phil. 68 C3 15.43 N 120.42 E
Cuyarí, stm., S.A. 168 G7 1.30 N 68.11 W
Cuyo, Phil. 68 E3 10.50 N 121.01 E
Cuyo East Pass, strt., Phil. 68 E3 11.00 N 121.28 E
Cuyo Islands, is., Phil. 68 E3 11.04 N 120.57 E
Cuyo West Pass, strt., Phil. 68 E3 11.00 N 120.30 E
Cuyubini, stm., Ven. 168 D11 8.23 N 60.19 W
Cuyuni, stm., S.A. 164 B6 6.23 N 58.40 W
Cuyuni-Mazaruni, state, Guy. 168 D11 6.07 N 59.17 W
Cuzna, stm., Spain 28 F6 38.04 N 4.40 W
Cwmbran, Wales, U.K. 10 J10 51.39 N 3.02 W
Cybinka, Pol. 24 D10 52.11 N 14.47 E
Cyclades see Kykládes, is., Grc. 34 F7 37.30 N 25.00 E
Cylburn Park, p.o.i., Md., U.S. 202b 39.21 N 76.39 W
Cynthiana, Ky., U.S. 124 F1 38.22 N 84.18 W
Cypress, Ca., U.S. 198 33.49 N 118.02 W
Cypress, La., U.S. 134 F5 31.36 N 93.02 W
Cypress Bayou, stm., Ar., U.S. 134 B6 35.03 N 91.39 W
Cypress Creek, stm., Tx., U.S. 136 D12 30.02 N 95.18 W
Cypress Creek, stm., Tx., U.S. 136 D14 30.18 N 93.44 W
Cypress Hills, hills, Can. 142 E3 49.41 N 109.36 W
Cypress Hills Interprovincial Park, p.o.i., Sk., Can. 142 E4 49.39 N 109.30 W
Cypress Lake, l., Sk., Can. 142 E4 49.28 N 109.29 W
Cypress River, Mb., Can. 142 E14 49.33 N 99.06 W
Cypress Springs, Lake, res., Tx., U.S. 136 A12 33.03 N 95.09 W
Cyprus, ctry., Asia 76 C4 35.00 N 33.00 E
Cyprus, i., Asia 46 F7 35.00 N 33.00 E
Cyprus, North, cty., Asia 76 C4 35.15 N 33.40 E
Cyrenaica see Barqah, hist. reg., Libya 82 A4 31.00 N 22.30 E
Cyril, Ok., U.S. 138 G10 34.53 N 98.12 W
Cyrildene, ngh., S. Afr. 191d 26.11 S 28.06 E

Name Page Map Ref. Latitude Longitude

Cyrus Field Bay, b., Nu., Can. 108 E13 62.50 N 64.55 W
Čyrvonae, vozero, l., Bela. 26 H10 52.24 N 27.58 E
Cythera see Kýthira, i., Grc. 34 G5 36.17 N 22.57 E
Czaplinek, Pol. 24 C12 53.33 N 16.14 E
Czarna Białostocka, Pol. 24 C19 53.18 N 23.16 E
Czarna Woda, Pol. 24 C14 53.51 N 18.07 E
Czarne, Pol. 24 C12 53.40 N 16.54 E
Czarnków, Pol. 24 D12 52.54 N 16.34 E
Czechoslovakia see Czech Republic, ctry., Eur. 24 G12 49.40 N 15.10 E
Czechowice-Dziedzice, Pol. 24 G15 49.54 N 19.00 E
Czech Republic, ctry., Eur. 24 G12 49.40 N 15.10 E
Czempiń, Pol. 24 D12 52.10 N 16.47 E
Czerniejewo, Pol. 24 D13 52.25 N 17.29 E
Czernowitz see Chernivtsi, Ukr. 38 E4 48.17 N 25.57 E
Czersk, Pol. 24 C13 53.47 N 17.58 E
Czerwieńsk, Pol. 24 D11 52.00 N 15.25 E
Częstochowa, Pol. 24 F15 50.48 N 19.07 E
Człopa, Pol. 24 C12 53.05 N 16.07 E
Człuchów, Pol. 24 C13 53.40 N 17.21 E
Czudec, Pol. 24 G17 49.56 N 21.51 E

D

Da, stm., China 58 G8 28.11 N 120.13 E
Da, Song see Black, stm., Asia 64 B7 21.14 N 105.21 E
Da'an, China 58 J4 23.19 N 110.32 E
Daawo see Daua, stm., Afr. 82 G8 4.09 N 42.05 E
Daawo see Dawa, stm., Afr. 82 G8 4.09 N 42.05 E
Dabajuro, Ven. 168 B6 11.00 N 70.40 W
Dabakala, C. Iv. 84 H4 8.22 N 4.26 W
Daba Ling, mtn., China 58 I5 24.28 N 113.17 E
Daba Shan, mts., China 58 E3 32.03 N 109.09 E
Dabat, Eth. 82 E7 12.58 N 37.45 E
Dabbāgh, Jabal, mtn., Sau. Ar. 72 D4 27.50 N 35.44 E
Dabeiba, Col. 168 D3 7.00 N 76.15 W
Daberg, ngh., Ger. 181 51.40 N 7.47 E
Dabhoi, India 70 G4 22.08 N 73.25 E
Dābhol, India 69 C1 17.36 N 73.10 E
Dąbie, Pol. 24 D14 52.05 N 18.50 E
Dabie Shan, mts., China 58 F6 31.06 N 115.55 E
Dabnou, Niger 84 G5 14.09 N 5.22 E
Dabola, Gui. 84 G2 10.45 N 11.06 W
Daborow, Som. 86 C9 6.21 N 48.43 E
Dabou, C. Iv. 84 H4 5.18 N 4.20 W
Daboya, Ghana 84 H4 9.31 N 1.23 W
Dabra, India 70 F7 25.53 N 78.19 E
Dabrasiauka, Bela. 26 H9 52.23 N 26.14 E
Dābri, ngh., India 190a 28.37 N 77.05 E
Dąbrowa Białostocka, Pol. 24 C19 53.39 N 23.20 E
Dąbrowa Tarnowska, Pol. 24 F17 50.10 N 20.59 E
Dabu, China 58 I7 24.19 N 116.43 E
Dacca see Dhaka, Bngl. 70 G13 23.43 N 90.25 E
Dac Glei, Viet. 64 E8 15.11 N 107.48 E
Dachang Airport, arpt., China 187b 31.18 N 121.25 E
Dachau, Ger. 24 H7 48.15 N 11.26 E
Dachsberg, hill, Ger. 181 51.30 N 6.30 E
Dačice, Czech Rep. 24 G11 49.05 N 15.26 E
Dac Lac, Cao Nguyen, plat., Viet. 64 F9 12.50 N 108.05 E
Dačnoe, ngh., Russia 183a 59.50 N 30.16 E
Dacoma, Ok., U.S. 138 E10 36.39 N 98.33 W
Dacorum, mun., Eng., U.K. 178 51.45 N 0.30 W
Dac To, Viet. 64 E8 14.39 N 107.50 E
Dadanawa, Guy. 168 F12 2.50 N 59.30 W
Dadar, ngh., India 190c 19.01 N 72.50 E
Daddys Creek, stm., Tn., U.S. 134 B14 36.04 N 84.46 W
Dade City, Fl., U.S. 132 H3 28.22 N 82.11 W
Dadeldhurā, Nepal 70 D8 29.17 N 80.33 E
Dadeville, Al., U.S. 132 E13 32.49 N 85.45 W
Dadiangas see General Santos, Phil. 68 G5 6.07 N 125.10 E
Dadnah, U.A.E. 74 H15 25.32 N 56.20 E
Dadou, stm., Fr. 22 F8 43.44 N 1.47 E
Dādpur, India 190b 22.54 N 88.31 E
Dādpur, India 190b 22.42 N 88.33 E
Dādra and Nagar Haveli, state, India 70 I4 20.05 N 73.00 E
Dādu, Pak. 62 C2 26.43 N 67.46 E
Dadugang, China 64 A5 22.22 N 100.57 E
Daegu see Taegu, Kor., S. 54 G8 35.52 N 128.35 E
Daejeon see Taejŏn, Kor., S. 54 F7 36.20 N 127.26 E
Daerhanwangfu, China 54 B5 44.13 N 122.13 E
Daet, Phil. 68 C4 14.07 N 122.57 E
Dafan, China 58 G6 29.40 N 114.39 E
Dafang, China 52 F6 27.08 N 105.36 E
Dafeng, China 58 E9 33.12 N 120.30 E
Dāfna, mtn., Grc. 185c 38.07 N 23.38 E
Dáfni, Grc. 34 F5 37.46 N 22.01 E
Dafoe, Sk., Can. 142 C9 51.44 N 104.31 W
Dafu, stm., China 58 F5 30.47 N 113.36 E
Dagā, stm., Mya. 64 D2 16.55 N 94.45 E
Daga Medo, Eth. 82 F8 7.59 N 43.01 E
Dagana, Sen. 84 F1 16.30 N 15.30 W
Daganzo de Arriba, Spain 184a 40.33 N 3.27 W
Daga Post, Sudan 82 F6 9.12 N 33.57 E
Dağardı, Tur. 34 D12 39.26 N 29.00 E
Dağbeli, Tur. 34 F13 37.12 N 30.30 E
Dagda, Lat. 26 D10 56.05 N 27.32 E
Dagenham, ngh., Eng., U.K. 178 51.32 N 0.10 E
Dagestan, state, Russia 42 D12 43.00 N 47.00 E
Daggafontein, S. Afr. 191d 26.18 S 28.28 E
Daggafontein Mines, mine, S. Afr. 191d 26.18 S 28.29 E
Dağkızılca, Tur. 34 E10 38.18 N 27.23 E
Daglung, China 70 D13 28.46 N 90.29 E
Dagongtun, China 54 C4 42.48 N 121.58 E
Dagu, China 58 B7 38.59 N 117.41 E
Dagua, Pap. N. Gui. 101a a3 3.24 S 143.18 E
Daguan, China 52 F5 27.48 N 104.01 E
Daguan Hu, l., China 58 F7 30.02 N 116.21 E
Daguao, P.R. 158a b4 18.13 N 65.40 W
D'Aguilar, Cape, c., China 189d 22.14 N 114.15 E
Dagujia, China 54 C6 42.22 N 124.52 E
Da Guokui Shan, mtn., China 54 B8 45.12 N 129.54 E
Dagupan, Phil. 68 B3 16.02 N 120.21 E
Dagwin, Mya. 64 C3 18.04 N 97.41 E
Dagzê Co, l., China 70 C11 31.54 N 87.31 E
Dahab, Egypt 76 J5 28.29 N 34.30 E
Dahao Dao (Lantau Island), i., China 189d 22.17 N 113.59 E
Dahei, India 70 H4 21.42 N 72.37 E
Daheiding Shan, mtn., China 52 B10 47.57 N 129.09 E
Da Hinggan Ling (Greater Khingan Range), mts., China 52 B9 49.00 N 122.00 E
Dahīrpur, ngh., India 190a 28.43 N 77.12 E
Dahlak Archipelago, is., Erit. 82 D8 15.45 N 40.30 E
Dahlak Kebir see Dehalak' Desēt, i., Erit. 82 D8 15.39 N 40.06 E
Dahle, Ger. 181 51.18 N 7.45 E
Dahlem, ngh., Ger. 182a 52.28 N 13.17 E
Dahlem, Museum, bldg., Ger. 182a 52.27 N 13.18 E
Dahlerau, Ger. 181 51.13 N 7.19 E
Dahlgren, Il., U.S. 130 F9 38.12 N 88.41 W
Dahlonega, Ga., U.S. 132 B1 34.32 N 83.59 W
Dahlonega Plateau, plat., U.S. 134 C14 34.26 N 83.55 W
Dahlwitz, Ger. 182a 52.30 N 13.38 E
Dahmani, Tun. 32 I2 35.57 N 8.50 E
Dahmarū, Egypt 76 J1 28.40 N 30.48 E
Dahme, Ger. 24 E9 51.52 N 13.25 E
Dāhod, India 70 G5 22.49 N 74.15 E
Dahomey see Benin, ctry., Afr. 84 G5 9.30 N 2.15 E
Dahong Shan, mts., China 58 F5 31.30 N 113.00 E
Dahra, Libya 82 B3 29.31 N 17.57 E
Dahra, mts., Alg. 28 H11 36.24 N 1.08 E
Dahshur, Pyramides de (Dashur, Pyramids of), hist., Egypt 76 I1 29.48 N 31.13 E
Dahua, China 58 J2 23.43 N 107.53 E
Dahūk, Iraq 74 B8 36.51 N 42.59 E
Dahūk, state, Iraq 74 B8 37.00 N 43.00 E
Dahuofang Shuiku, res., China 54 D6 41.56 N 124.18 E
Dai, i., Sol. Is. 101b d9 7.53 S 160.37 E
Daia, Rom. 36 E12 44.01 N 25.57 E
Daigo, ngh., Japan 188 34.57 N 135.50 E
Dai Hai, l., China 58 A5 40.34 N 112.40 E
Daik-u, Mya. 64 D3 17.51 N 96.54 E
Dā'il, Syria 76 F7 32.45 N 36.08 E
Dailekh, Nepal 70 D8 28.49 N 81.43 E
Daimanji-san, mtn., Japan 56 C6 36.15 N 133.20 E
Daimiel, Spain 28 E7 39.04 N 3.36 W
Daimon, Japan 186 35.53 N 139.44 E
Daingean, Ire. 10 H5 53.18 N 7.17 W
Daingerfield, Tx., U.S. 136 A13 33.02 N 94.43 W
Dainkog, China 52 E4 32.29 N 97.59 E
Daiō-zaki, c., Japan 56 E9 34.16 N 136.53 E
Dairago, Italy 184b 45.34 N 8.52 E
Daireaux, Arg. 172 H7 36.36 S 61.45 W
Dairen see Dalian, China 58 B9 38.53 N 121.34 E
Dairūt, Egypt 76 K1 27.33 N 30.49 E
Dairy City see Cypress, Ca., U.S. 198 33.50 N 118.01 W
Dairyland see La Palma, Ca., U.S. 198 33.51 N 118.02 W
Dairyland Reservoir, res., Wi., U.S. 128 F7 45.29 N 91.01 W
Dairy Valley see Cerritos, Ca., U.S. 198 33.51 N 118.05 W
Dai-sen, vol., Japan 56 D6 35.22 N 133.33 E
Daisetta, Tx., U.S. 136 D13 30.06 N 94.38 W
Daixian, China 58 B5 39.06 N 113.02 E
Daiyun Shan, mts., China 58 I8 25.46 N 118.16 E
Dajabón, Dom. Rep. 156 C12 19.33 N 71.42 W
Dājal, Pak. 70 D3 29.33 N 70.22 E
Dajarra, Austl. 98 C2 21.42 S 139.30 E
Dajian Shan, mtn., China 52 F5 26.42 N 103.34 E
Dakar, Sen. 84 G1 14.40 N 17.26 W
Dakeng, China 58 H6 26.17 N 115.28 E
Dakengkou, China 58 I5 24.33 N 113.37 E
Dakhin Shāhbāzpur Island, i., Bngl. 70 G13 22.30 N 90.45 E
Dakhla, W. Sah. 84 E1 23.42 N 15.56 W
Dākoānk, India 62 G7 7.01 N 93.40 E
Dakoro, Niger 84 G6 14.30 N 6.46 E
Dakota City, Ia., U.S. 130 B3 42.43 N 94.12 W
Dakota City, Ne., U.S. 130 B1 42.25 N 96.25 W
Đakovica, Yugo. 36 G7 42.22 N 20.27 E
Đakovo, Cro. 30 E15 45.18 N 18.24 E
Dal, Nor. 16 G9 60.15 N 11.12 E
Dala, Sol. Is. 101b e9 8.36 S 160.40 E
Dalaba, Gui. 84 G2 10.42 N 12.15 W
Dalad Qi, China 58 A4 40.27 N 110.00 E
Dalai Nur, l., China 52 C8 43.17 N 116.38 E
Dala-Järna, Swe. 16 G12 60.33 N 14.22 E
Dalälven, stm., Swe. 12 F7 60.37 N 17.26 E
Dalaman, stm., Tur. 34 G11 36.42 N 28.43 E
Dalāmī, Sudan 82 E6 11.51 N 30.28 E
Dalandzadgad, Mong. 52 C5 43.34 N 104.25 E
Dalane, reg., Nor. 16 I4 58.35 N 6.20 E
Dalarna, state, Swe. 16 F12 61.00 N 14.30 E
Dalarö, Swe. 16 H16 59.08 N 18.24 E
Dalat, Malay. 66 B7 2.44 N 111.56 E
Da Lat, Viet. 64 G9 11.57 N 108.26 E
Dālbandin, Pak. 62 C1 28.52 N 64.25 E
Dalbosjön, b., Swe. 16 I10 58.45 N 12.48 E
Dalboslätten, hills, Swe. 16 I10 58.33 N 12.27 E
Dalby, Austl. 98 F8 27.11 S 151.16 E
Dalby, Swe. 16 L11 55.39 N 13.21 E
Dale, Nor. 16 F3 61.21 N 5.24 E
Dale, Nor. 16 G3 60.35 N 5.48 E
Dale, In., U.S. 130 F10 38.09 N 86.59 W
Dale Hollow Lake, res., U.S. 130 H12 36.36 N 85.20 W
Dale Lake, l., Ca., U.S. 148 I10 34.08 N 115.42 W
Dalen, Nor. 16 H5 59.27 N 8.00 E
Daleszyce, Pol. 24 F16 50.48 N 20.48 E
Dalet, Mya. 64 B1 19.58 N 93.50 E
Daleville, Al., U.S. 134 F13 31.20 N 85.42 W
Daleville, In., U.S. 130 D12 40.07 N 85.32 W
Dalga, Egypt 76 K1 27.38 N 30.42 E
Dalhart, Tx., U.S. 138 E6 36.04 N 102.31 W
Dalhousie, N.B., Can. 122 B10 48.03 N 66.24 W
Dalhousie, India 70 B5 32.33 N 75.57 E
Dalhousie, Cape, c., N.T., Can. 109 B14 70.14 N 129.42 W
Dalhousie Square, p.o.i., India 190b 22.33 N 88.22 E
Dali, China 52 F5 25.35 N 100.12 E
Dali, China 58 D3 34.47 N 109.57 E
Dalian (Dairen), China 58 B9 38.53 N 121.34 E
Daliang Shan, mts., China 52 F5 28.00 N 103.00 E
Dalias, Spain 28 H8 36.49 N 2.52 W
Dalin, China 54 C5 43.43 N 122.48 E
Daling, stm., China 54 D4 40.50 N 121.34 E
Dalj, Cro. 30 E15 45.29 N 18.58 E
Dālkola, India 70 F11 25.52 N 87.50 E
Dallas, Al., U.S. 134 D12 33.49 N 86.38 W
Dallas, Ga., U.S. 134 D14 33.55 N 84.50 W
Dallas, Or., U.S. 146 F3 44.55 N 123.18 W
Dallas, Pa., U.S. 124 C10 41.20 N 75.57 W
Dallas, Tx., U.S. 136 B11 32.47 N 96.47 W
Dallas, Wi., U.S. 128 F7 45.15 N 91.48 W
Dallas Center, Ia., U.S. 128 J4 41.41 N 93.58 W
Dallas City, Il., U.S. 130 D6 40.37 N 91.09 W
Dalli Rājhara, India 70 H8 20.34 N 81.04 E
Dall Island, i., Ak., U.S. 109 F13 54.57 N 133.01 W
Dall Lake, l., Ak., U.S. 109 D7 60.16 N 163.38 W
Dalmā, i., U.A.E. 74 H13 24.30 N 52.19 E
Dalmacija see Dalmatia, hist. reg., Eur. 30 G14 43.00 N 17.00 E
Dalmally, Scot., U.K. 10 E8 56.24 N 4.57 W
Dalmatia (Dalmacija), hist. reg., Eur. 30 G14 43.00 N 17.00 E
Dalmau, India 70 E8 26.04 N 81.03 E
Dalmeny, Sk., Can. 142 B7 52.20 N 106.46 W
Dal'negorsk, Russia 54 B11 44.32 N 135.33 E
Dal'nerečensk, Russia 52 B11 45.56 N 133.43 E
Dal'nije Zelency, Russia 14 C27 69.05 N 36.05 E
Dal'njaja, Russia 52 B13 45.54 N 142.04 E
Dal'nyk, Ukr. 38 G9 46.28 N 30.33 E
Daloa, C. Iv. 84 H3 6.53 N 6.27 W
Dalqū, Sudan 82 C6 20.09 N 30.35 E
Dalroy, Ab., Can. 144 E17 51.06 N 113.41 W
Dalrymple, Mount, mtn., Austl. 98 C7 21.02 S 148.38 E
Dalsbruk see Taalintehdas, Fin. 18 G9 60.01 N 22.30 E
Dalsingpara, India 70 E12 26.47 N 89.21 E
Dalsing Sarai, India 70 F10 25.39 N 85.50 E
Dalsjöfors, Swe. 16 J11 57.43 N 13.04 E
Dalslands Kanal, can., Swe. 16 I10 58.46 N 12.31 E
Dals-Långed, Swe. 16 I10 58.55 N 12.18 E
Dāltenganj, India 70 F10 24.02 N 84.04 E
Dalton, Eng., U.K. 180 53.34 N 2.46 W
Dalton, Ga., U.S. 134 C13 34.46 N 84.57 W
Dalton, Ma., U.S. 124 B12 42.28 N 73.09 W
Dalton, Ne., U.S. 140 F10 41.23 N 102.58 W
Dalton Gardens, Id., U.S. 146 C10 47.43 N 116.47 W
Daludalu, Indon. 66 C2 1.05 N 100.14 E
Dalu Dao, i., China 54 E5 39.44 N 123.44 E
Dalupiri Island, i., Phil. 68 A3 19.05 N 121.14 E
Dalview, S. Afr. 191d 26.15 S 28.21 E
Dalvík, Ice. 12a k30 65.57 N 18.32 W
Dalwallinu, Austl. 96 F3 30.17 S 116.39 E
Daly, stm., Austl. 96 B6 13.19 S 130.16 E
Daly Bay, b., Nu., Can. 110 C13 64.00 N 89.40 W
Daly City, Ca., U.S. 148 F3 37.42 N 122.27 W
Daly Lake, l., Sk., Can. 110 D9 56.33 N 105.40 W
Daly Waters, Austl. 96 C6 16.14 S 133.22 E
Dam, stm., China 70 B14 32.53 N 93.45 E
Damačava, Bela. 38 B2 51.44 N 23.37 E
Damaia, Port. 28 F1 38.44 N 9.13 W
Damān, India 70 H4 20.25 N 72.50 E
Damān and Diu, state, India 70 H3 20.25 N 72.50 E
Damanhûr, Egypt 76 G1 31.02 N 30.28 E
Damanhûr Shubrâ, Egypt 191c 30.07 N 31.14 E
Damar, Pulau, i., Indon. 68 G8 7.07 S 128.35 E
Damara, C.A.R. 86 D3 4.57 N 18.41 E
Damaraland, hist. reg., Nmb. 88 E2 22.11 S 17.34 E
Damas see Dimashq, Syria 76 E7 33.30 N 36.18 E
Damascus see Dimashq, Syria 76 E7 33.30 N 36.18 E
Damascus, Ar., U.S. 134 B6 35.21 N 92.25 W
Damascus, Ga., U.S. 134 F14 31.17 N 84.43 W
Damascus, Md., U.S. 124 E8 39.17 N 77.12 W
Damascus, Va., U.S. 124 H4 36.38 N 81.47 W
Damaturu, Nig. 84 G7 11.45 N 11.58 E
Damāvand, Qolleh-ye (Demavend, Mount), vol., Iran 42 H15 35.56 N 52.08 E
Damba, Ang. 88 B2 6.41 S 15.08 E
Damba, Kaz. 40 H17 46.58 N 51.47 E
Dambarta, Nig. 84 G6 12.25 N 8.30 E
Damboa, Nig. 84 G7 11.09 N 12.45 E
Dâmbovița, state, Rom. 36 E12 45.00 N 25.30 E
Dâmbovița, stm., Rom. 36 D12 44.14 N 26.26 E
Dam Doi, Viet. 64 H7 8.51 N 105.13 E
Damen Dao, i., China 58 H9 27.58 N 121.06 E
Dämeritzsee, l., Ger. 182a 52.25 N 13.45 E
Dāmghān, Iran 74 B14 36.10 N 54.20 E
Damiao, China 58 C1 37.19 N 104.42 E
Dămienești, Rom. 36 C14 46.45 N 27.00 E
Damietta, Egypt 76 G2 31.25 N 31.48 E
Damietta Mouth see Dumyât, Masabb, mth., Egypt 76 G2 31.31 N 31.50 E
Daming, China 58 C6 36.16 N 115.08 E
Damm, Ger. 181 51.40 N 6.48 E
Dāmodar, stm., India 70 G11 22.16 N 88.05 E
Damoh, India 70 G7 23.50 N 79.27 E
Damongo, Ghana 84 H4 9.04 N 1.48 W
Damotapāda, India 190c 19.03 N 73.04 E
Damous, Alg. 28 H12 36.32 N 1.41 E
Dampier, Austl. 96 D3 20.38 S 116.44 E
Dampier, Selat, strt., Indon. 60 F9 0.40 S 130.40 E
Dampier Land, pen., Austl. 96 C4 17.30 S 122.55 E
Dampierre, Château de, hist., Fr. 179 48.42 N 1.59 E
Dampier Strait, strt., Pap. N. Gui. 101a b4 5.36 S 148.12 E
Dampmart, Fr. 179 48.53 N 2.44 E
Dâmrei, Chuŏr Phnum, mts., Camb. 64 G6 11.00 N 104.05 E
Damxung, China 52 E3 30.31 N 91.08 E
Dan, stm., China 58 E4 33.00 N 111.19 E
Dan, stm., U.S. 124 H6 36.41 N 78.38 W
Dana, In., U.S. 130 E10 39.48 N 87.29 W
Danai, Indon. 66 C3 0.30 N 103.24 E
Danakil, reg., Afr. 82 E8 13.00 N 41.00 E
Danané, C. Iv. 84 H3 7.16 N 8.09 W
Da Nang, Viet. 64 D9 16.03 N 108.11 E
Danao, Phil. 68 E5 10.31 N 124.01 E
Dānāpur, India 70 F10 25.38 N 85.02 E
Danba, China 52 E5 30.54 N 101.52 E
Danbury, Ct., U.S. 124 C12 41.23 N 73.26 W
Danbury, Ia., U.S. 130 B2 42.13 N 95.42 W
Danbury, Ne., U.S. 138 A8 40.02 N 100.24 W
Danbury, Tx., U.S. 136 E12 29.14 N 95.21 W
Danby Lake, l., Ca., U.S. 150 I1 34.14 N 115.07 W
Dandeli, India 69 D2 15.15 N 74.37 E
Dandenong, Austl. 98 K5 38.00 S 145.13 E
Dandenong, Mount, mtn., Austl. 192b 37.50 S 145.21 E
Dandenong Creek, stm., Austl. 192b 38.01 S 145.05 E
Dandong, China 52 C9 40.06 N 124.21 E
Dandridge, Tn., U.S. 132 H2 36.00 N 83.24 W
Danewitz, Ger. 182a 52.44 N 13.40 E
Danfeng, China 58 E4 33.40 N 110.17 E
Danforth, Me., U.S. 122 E9 45.39 N 67.52 W
Danforth Hills, mts., Co., U.S. 150 C9 40.15 N 108.00 W
Dang, stm., China 48 F16 40.26 N 94.34 E
Dānga, India 190b 22.47 N 88.28 E
Danga, stm., Malay. 189c 1.27 N 103.43 E
Dangan Liedao, is., China 58 K6 22.00 N 114.14 E
Dangara, Taj. 72 B10 38.05 N 69.20 E
Dangba, China 58 A8 40.44 N 118.34 E
Dangchang, China 52 E5 34.03 N 104.23 E
Danger Point, c., S. Afr. 90 I4 34.37 S 19.18 E
Danggali Conservation Park, ind. res., Austl. 98 I3 33.27 S 140.29 E
Dangila, Eth. 82 E7 11.13 N 36.50 E
Dângrêk, Chuŏr Phnum see Phanom Dongrak Range, mts., Asia 64 E6 14.25 N 103.30 E
Dangriga, Belize 156 D3 16.58 N 88.13 W
Dangshan, China 58 D7 34.25 N 116.20 E
Dangtu, China 58 F8 31.34 N 118.29 E
Dan-Gulbi, Nig. 84 G6 11.39 N 6.17 E
Dangyang, China 58 F4 30.51 N 111.45 E
Daniel, Wy., U.S. 146 H16 42.52 N 110.05 W
Daniel-Johnson, Barrage, dam., Qc., Can. 110 E17 50.39 N 68.44 W
Daniels, Md., U.S. 202b 39.26 N 77.03 W
Daniel's Harbour, Nf., Can. 111a i22 50.14 N 57.33 W
Daniëlskuil, S. Afr. 90 F6 28.11 S 23.32 E
Danielson, Ct., U.S. 124 C14 41.48 N 71.53 W
Daniels Pass, p., Ut., U.S. 150 C5 40.18 N 111.15 W
Daniels Run, stm., Va., U.S. 202c 38.51 N 77.17 W
Danielsville, Ga., U.S. 132 B2 34.08 N 83.13 W
Danilov, Russia 40 B11 58.11 N 40.11 E
Danilovka, Kaz. 48 D12 52.24 N 70.38 E
Danilovka, Russia 40 F10 50.21 N 44.07 E
Daning, China 58 I4 24.41 N 111.55 E
Daning, China 58 C4 36.28 N 110.44 E
Dänizkänarı, Azer. 42 E13 40.13 N 49.33 E
Danjiangkou Shuiku, res., China 58 E4 32.37 N 111.30 E
Danjo-guntō, is., Japan 56 G1 32.02 N 128.23 E
Dankov, Russia 40 E11 53.15 N 39.09 E
Danlí, Hond. 156 F4 14.01 N 86.34 W
Danmark see Denmark, ctry., Eur. 6 D10 56.00 N 10.00 E
Danmark Fjord, b., Grnld. 108 A22 81.14 N 21.32 W
Danmarksstrædet see Denmark Strait, strt. 106 C20 67.00 N 25.00 W
Dannebrog, Ne., U.S. 140 F14 41.07 N 98.32 W
Dannemora, Swe. 16 G15 60.11 N 17.48 E
Dannemora, N.Y., U.S. 126 D16 44.43 N 73.43 W
Dannenberg, Ger. 24 C6 53.06 N 11.07 E
Dannenreich, Ger. 182a 52.19 N 13.45 E
Dannevirke, N.Z. 102 E7 40.12 S 176.07 E
Dannhauser, S. Afr. 90 E10 28.01 S 30.04 E
Danompari, Indon. 66 C9 0.09 N 115.00 E
Dan Ryan Woods, p.o.i., Il., U.S. 196 41.45 N 87.39 W
Dan Sai, Thai. 64 D5 17.16 N 101.08 E
Danshui, China 58 J6 22.47 N 114.28 E
Dansville, N.Y., U.S. 124 B8 42.33 N 77.41 W
Dante, Va., U.S. 124 H3 36.58 N 82.18 W
Dantewāra, India 69 B5 18.52 N 81.18 E
Danube, stm., Eur. 8 G14 45.23 N 29.35 E
Danube, Mouths of the, mth., Eur. 36 D16 45.12 N 29.41 E
Danubyu, Mya. 64 D2 17.15 N 95.35 E
Danvers, Il., U.S. 130 D8 40.31 N 89.10 W
Danvers, stm., Ma., U.S. 201 42.32 N 70.53 W
Danville, Qc., Can. 122 E4 45.46 N 72.01 W
Danville, Ar., U.S. 134 B5 35.03 N 93.23 W
Danville, Ga., U.S. 132 D2 32.35 N 83.15 W
Danville, Il., U.S. 130 D10 40.07 N 87.37 W
Danville, In., U.S. 126 I3 39.45 N 86.31 W
Danville, Ky., U.S. 130 G13 37.38 N 84.46 W
Danville, Pa., U.S. 124 D9 40.57 N 76.36 W
Danville, Vt., U.S. 122 F4 44.25 N 72.07 W
Danville, Va., U.S. 124 H6 36.34 N 79.24 W
Danville, Wa., U.S. 146 B8 48.59 N 118.30 W
Danxian, China 58 L3 19.31 N 109.33 E
Danyang, China 58 F8 31.59 N 119.33 E
Danzig see Gdańsk, Pol. 24 B14 54.21 N 18.38 E
Danzig, Gulf of see Gdansk, Gulf of, b., Eur. 8 D12 54.40 N 19.15 E
Dao, stm., China 58 F6 30.37 N 114.35 E
Dão, stm., Port. 28 D3 40.20 N 8.11 W
Daocheng, China 52 F5 29.04 N 100.35 E
Daodemiao, China 52 C9 43.44 N 120.17 E
Daodi, China 58 B8 39.32 N 118.10 E
Daohu, China 58 G7 29.41 N 117.27 E
Daolin, China 58 G5 27.59 N 112.42 E
Daosa, India 70 E6 26.53 N 76.20 E
Daotiandi, China 52 B10 48.53 N 130.01 E
Daoukro, C. Iv. 84 H4 7.03 N 3.57 W
Daoxian, China 58 I4 25.35 N 111.27 E
Daozhen, China 58 G2 28.42 N 107.56 E
Daozi, China 54 B5 44.59 N 123.43 E
Dapaong, Togo 84 G5 10.52 N 0.12 E
Dapchi, Nig. 84 G7 12.27 N 11.32 E
Daphnae, hist., Egypt 76 H3 30.52 N 32.11 E
Daphne, Al., U.S. 134 G11 30.36 N 87.54 W
Dapingshan, China 58 I3 25.30 N 109.39 E
Da Qaidam, China 52 D4 37.52 N 95.19 E
Daqiaozhai, China 58 I2 25.21 N 106.15 E
Daqing Shan, mtn., China 54 B7 45.35 N 127.51 E
Daqiu, China 58 H8 25.24 N 119.38 E
Dara, Sen. 84 F1 15.21 N 15.29 W
Dar'ā, Syria 76 F7 32.37 N 36.07 E
Dar'ā, state, Syria 76 F7 33.00 N 36.10 E
Dārāb, Iran 74 F12 28.45 N 54.34 E
Darāban, Pak. 70 C3 31.44 N 70.20 E
Darabani, Rom. 36 A13 48.11 N 26.36 E
Darāfīsah, Sudan 82 E6 13.22 N 31.57 E
Dārān, Iran 74 D12 32.59 N 50.24 E
Daraoli, ngh., India 190c 19.11 N 72.48 E
Darap, Indon. 66 D8 1.13 S 112.00 E
Darasun, Russia 50 F11 51.38 N 113.55 E
Darave, India 190c 19.02 N 73.01 E
Đaravica, mtn., Yugo. 36 G7 42.33 N 20.07 E
Darâw, Egypt 74 H3 24.23 N 32.55 E
Darāyyā, Syria 76 E7 33.26 N 36.14 E
Darb al-Ḥajj, Jabal, mtn., Jord. 76 H6 30.05 N 35.26 E
Darbāsīyah, Syria 42 G9 37.03 N 40.38 E
Darbėnai, Lith. 26 D4 56.01 N 21.16 E
Darbhanga, India 70 E10 26.09 N 85.53 E
D'Arbonne, Bayou, stm., La., U.S. 134 E6 32.33 N 92.07 W
Darby, Mt., U.S. 146 D12 46.01 N 114.10 W
Darby Creek, stm., Pa., U.S. 203 39.52 N 75.18 W
D'Arcy, B.C., Can. 144 F8 50.32 N 122.28 W
Dardanelle, Ar., U.S. 134 B5 35.13 N 93.09 W
Dardanelle, Ca., U.S. 148 E6 38.20 N 119.49 W
Dardanelle Lake, res., Ar., U.S. 134 B5 35.20 N 93.20 W
Dardanelles see Çanakkale Boğazı, strt., Tur. 34 C9 40.17 N 26.32 E
Darebin Creek, stm., Austl. 192b 37.47 S 145.02 E
Dar-el-Beida see Casablanca, Mor. 84 C3 33.35 N 7.35 W
Dâr el-Salâm, Egypt 191c 29.59 N 31.13 E
Darende, Tur. 42 F7 38.33 N 37.30 E
Daresbury, Eng., U.K. 180 53.21 N 2.38 W
Dar es Salaam, Tan. 86 F7 6.48 S 39.16 E
Darfo, Italy 30 E7 45.52 N 10.10 E
Dargai, Pak. 70 A3 34.30 N 71.52 E
Dargan-Ata, Turkmen. 72 A9 40.29 N 62.10 E
Dargaville, N.Z. 102 B5 35.56 S 173.51 E
Dargol, Niger 84 G5 13.55 N 1.14 E
Darhan, Mong. 52 B6 49.28 N 105.55 E
Darıca, Tur. 34 C12 40.47 N 29.23 E
Darién, Col. 168 F3 3.55 N 76.30 W
Darien, Ga., U.S. 132 E4 31.22 N 81.26 W
Darien, Il., U.S. 196 41.45 N 87.58 W
Darien, Parque Nacional, p.o.i., Pan. 168 D2 7.49 N 77.39 W
Darién, Serranía del, mts. 156 H9 8.20 N 77.22 W
Dariense, Cordillera, mts., Nic. 156 F5 12.55 N 85.30 W
Dar'inskoe, Kaz. 40 F17 51.21 N 51.44 E
Dārjiling, India 70 E12 27.02 N 88.15 E
Darkan, Austl. 96 F3 33.20 S 116.44 E
Dark Head, c., St. Vin. 159e o11 13.17 N 61.16 W
Darkūsh, Syria 76 B7 35.59 N 36.25 E
Darlag, China 52 E4 33.45 N 99.39 E
Darley Woods, De., U.S. 203 39.49 N 75.28 W
Darling, S. Afr. 90 H4 33.22 S 18.22 E
Darling, Ms., U.S. 134 C8 34.21 N 90.16 W
Darling, stm., Austl. 98 I4 34.06 S 141.55 E
Darling, Lake, res., N.D., U.S. 142 F12 48.32 N 101.34 W
Darling Downs, reg., Austl. 98 F8 27.30 S 150.30 E
Darlingford, Mb., Can. 142 E15 49.12 N 98.22 W
Darling Range, mts., Austl. 96 F3 32.30 S 116.21 E
Darlington, Eng., U.K. 10 G11 54.31 N 1.33 W
Darlington, Pa., U.S. 203 39.54 N 75.28 W
Darlington, S.C., U.S. 132 B6 34.17 N 79.52 W
Darlington, Wi., U.S. 130 B7 42.40 N 90.07 W
Darlington Brook, stm., N.J., U.S. 194 41.05 N 74.11 W
Darlington Corners, Pa., U.S. 203 39.55 N 75.34 W
Darlington Dam, res., S. Afr. 90 H7 33.10 S 25.09 E
Darlot, Lake, l., Austl. 96 E4 27.45 S 121.31 E
Darłowo, Pol. 24 B12 54.25 N 16.24 E
Darmstadt, Ger. 24 G4 49.52 N 8.38 E
Darnah, Libya 82 A4 32.45 N 22.38 E
Darnall, S. Afr. 90 F10 29.21 S 31.17 E
Darney, Fr. 20 F15 48.04 N 6.02 E
Darnick, Austl. 98 I4 32.51 S 143.37 E
Darnley, Cape, c., Ant. 103 B11 67.43 S 69.30 E
Darnley Bay, b., N.T., Can. 110 B6 69.35 N 123.30 W
Daroca, Spain 28 C9 41.07 N 1.25 W
Darr, stm., Austl. 98 D4 23.41 S 143.50 E
Darragh, Pa., U.S. 197b 40.16 N 79.41 W
Darrah, Mount, mtn., Can. 144 G16 49.28 N 114.35 W
Darregueira, Arg. 172 H6 37.41 S 63.09 W
Darreh Gaz, Iran 72 B8 37.26 N 59.06 E
Darrington, Wa., U.S. 146 B5 48.15 N 121.36 W
Darrouzett, Tx., U.S. 138 E8 36.27 N 100.20 W
Darryl Gardens, Md., U.S. 202b 39.25 N 76.25 W
Dart, Cape, c., Ant. 103 C27 73.06 S 126.20 W
Darta, Turkmen. 42 E15 40.01 N 52.49 E
Dār Ta'izzah, Syria 76 B7 36.16 N 36.51 E
Dartford, mun., Eng., U.K. 178 51.26 N 0.15 E
Dartford Tunnel, trans., Eng., U.K. 178 51.28 N 0.16 E
Dartmoor, Austl. 98 K3 37.56 S 141.17 E
Dartmoor, for., Eng., U.K. 10 K8 50.35 N 3.55 W
Dartmoor National Park, p.o.i., Eng., U.K. 10 K9 50.33 N 3.50 W
Dartmouth, N.S., Can. 122 F13 44.40 N 63.34 W
Dartmouth, Eng., U.K. 10 K9 50.21 N 3.35 W
Dartmouth, stm., Qc., Can. 122 A12 48.46 N 64.19 W
Dartmouth, Lake, l., Austl. 98 E5 26.04 S 145.18 E
Dartmouth Reservoir, res., Austl. 98 K6 36.34 S 147.34 E
Dartmouth Woods, De., U.S. 203 39.50 N 75.31 W
Daru, Pap. N. Gui. 101a b3 9.04 S 143.13 E
Daruvar, Cro. 30 E14 45.36 N 17.12 E
Darvaza, Turkmen. 72 A8 40.09 N 58.29 E
Darwen, stm., Eng., U.K. 180 53.45 N 2.41 W
Dārwha, India 70 H6 20.18 N 77.46 E
Darwin, Austl. 96 B6 12.26 S 130.50 E
Darwin, Bahía, b., Chile 166 I2 45.27 S 74.40 W
Darya Khān, Pak. 70 C3 31.47 N 71.06 E
Daryāpur, India 70 H6 20.55 N 77.19 E
Dās, i., U.A.E. 74 H13 25.08 N 52.52 E
Dase see Desē, Eth. 82 E7 11.08 N 39.38 E
Dashava, Ukr. 38 D3 49.16 N 24.01 E
Dashbalbar, Mong. 52 B7 49.33 N 114.19 E
Dashetai, China 58 A3 40.56 N 109.17 E
Dashitou, China 54 C8 43.19 N 128.28 E
Dashiv, Ukr. 38 D8 49.00 N 29.26 E
Dašhovuz, Turkmen. 72 A8 41.50 N 59.58 E
Dasht, stm., Pak. 62 C1 25.13 N 61.41 E
Dashur, Pyramids of see Dahshur, Pyramides de, hist., Egypt 76 I1 29.48 N 31.13 E
Dashutang, China 64 A6 23.02 N 103.45 E
Daškauka, Bela. 26 G13 53.44 N 30.14 E
Dasol Bay, b., Phil. 68 C2 15.53 N 119.51 E
Dassel, Mn., U.S. 128 F4 45.04 N 94.18 W
Dastgardān, Iran 74 C15 34.18 N 56.54 E
Dastjerd, Iran 74 C12 34.32 N 50.15 E
Datagenoyang, Indon. 66 B9 2.03 N 115.10 E
Datang, China 58 J3 22.23 N 108.22 E
Datang, China 58 I3 24.07 N 108.54 E
Datça, Tur. 34 G10 36.45 N 27.40 E
Datchet, Eng., U.K. 178 51.29 N 0.34 W
Datchet Reservoir, res., Eng., U.K. 178 51.29 N 0.33 W
Date, Japan 54 C14 42.27 N 140.51 E
Date Creek, stm., Az., U.S. 150 I3 34.15 N 113.33 W
Datia, India 70 F7 25.40 N 78.27 E
Datian, China 58 I7 25.39 N 117.49 E
Datian Ding, mtn., China 58 J4 22.17 N 111.13 E
Dativli, India 190c 19.11 N 73.03 E
Datong, China 52 D5 37.02 N 101.36 E
Datong, China 58 B9 46.01 N 124.48 E
Datong, China 58 A5 40.05 N 113.17 E
Datong Shan, mts., China 52 D4 37.49 N 100.27 E
Dātra, India 190b 22.58 N 88.16 E
Datta, Russia 50 G17 49.16 N 140.21 E
Datteln-Hamm-Kanal, can., Ger. 181 51.39 N 7.21 E
Datu, Cape, c., Asia 60 E4 2.05 N 109.39 E
Datu, Tanjong see Datu, Cape, c., Asia 60 E4 2.05 N 109.39 E
Datu, Tanjung see Datu, Cape, c., Asia 60 E4 2.05 N 109.39 E
Datumakuta, Indon. 66 B10 2.32 N 117.52 E
Datu Piang, Phil. 68 G5 7.01 N 124.29 E
Daua (Dawa), stm., Afr. 82 G8 4.09 N 42.05 E
Dāud Khel, Pak. 70 B3 32.53 N 71.33 E
Daudnagar, India 70 F10 25.01 N 84.24 E
Daugai, Lith. 26 F7 54.21 N 24.21 E
Daugava see Western Dvina, stm., Eur. 26 D7 57.03 N 24.02 E
Daugavpils, Lat. 26 E9 55.53 N 26.31 E
Dauhinava, Bela. 26 F10 54.38 N 27.28 E
Daulatpur, India 190b 22.26 N 88.18 E
Daulatpur, ngh., India 190a 28.44 N 77.06 E
Daule, Ec. 168 G2 0.24 N 79.59 W
Daule, Ec. 168 H2 1.50 S 79.57 W
Daule, India 190c 19.10 N 73.03 E
Daule, stm., Ec. 168 H1 2.18 S 79.50 W
Daun, Ger. 24 F2 50.11 N 6.50 E
Daund, India 69 B2 18.27 N 74.34 E
Daung Kyun, i., Mya. 64 F3 12.14 N 98.05 E
Dauphin, Mb., Can. 142 C13 51.09 N 100.03 W
Dauphin, stm., Mb., Can. 142 C15 52.09 N 97.55 W
Dauphiné, hist. reg., Fr. 22 E11 44.50 N 6.00 E
Dauphin Island, Al., U.S. 134 G10 30.14 N 88.07 W
Dauphin Island, i., Al., U.S. 134 G10 30.14 N 88.12 W

Name	Page	Map Ref.	Latitude	Longitude
Dauphin Lake, l., Mb., Can.	142	C14	51.17 N	99.48 W
Daura, Nig.	84	G6	13.01 N	8.19 E
Däväçi, Azer.	42	E13	41.11 N	48.58 E
Dävangere, India	69	D2	14.27 N	75.55 E
Davant, La., U.S.	134	H9	29.37 N	89.53 W
Davao, Phil.	68	G5	7.04 N	125.35 E
Davao Gulf, b., Phil.	68	G5	6.40 N	125.55 E
Dävarzan, Iran	74	B15	36.21 N	56.49 E
Davenham, Eng., U.K.	180		53.14 N	2.31 W
Davenport, Fl., U.S.	132	H4	28.09 N	81.36 W
Davenport, Ia., U.S.	130	C7	41.31 N	90.34 W
Davenport, Ne., U.S.	138	A11	40.18 N	97.48 W
Davenport, Ok., U.S.	134	B2	35.42 N	96.45 W
Davenport, Wa., U.S.	146	C8	47.39 N	118.08 W
Davenport Downs, Austl.	98	E3	24.09 S	141.06 E
Davey, Port, b., Austl.	99a	o12	43.19 S	145.55 E
Daveyton, S. Afr.	191d		26.09 S	28.25 E
David, Pan.	156	H6	8.26 N	82.26 W
David City, Ne., U.S.	140	F15	41.15 N	97.07 W
Davids Island, i., N.Y., U.S.	194		40.53 N	73.46 W
Davidson, Sk., Can.	142	C7	51.16 N	105.59 W
Davidson, Ok., U.S.	138	G9	34.14 N	99.04 W
Davidson Creek, stm., Tx., U.S.	136	D11	30.20 N	96.27 W
Davidson Mountains, mts., Ak., U.S.	109	C11	68.45 N	142.10 W
Davidson Park, p.o.i., Austl.	192a		33.45 S	151.12 E
Davie, Fl., U.S.	132	J5	26.04 N	80.14 W
Davis, Ca., U.S.	148	E4	38.32 N	121.44 W
Davis, N.C., U.S.	132	B9	34.48 N	76.28 W
Davis, Ok., U.S.	138	G11	34.30 N	97.07 W
Davis, W.V., U.S.	124	E6	39.07 N	79.28 W
Davis, stm., Austl.	96	D4	21.38 S	121.08 E
Davis, sci., Ant.	103	B12	68.35 S	78.15 E
Davis, Mount, mtn., Pa., U.S.	124	E6	39.47 N	79.10 W
Davisboro, Ga., U.S.	132	C3	32.59 N	82.38 W
Davis City, Ia., U.S.	130	D4	40.38 N	93.48 W
Davis Creek, stm., Mi., U.S.	199		42.27 N	83.43 W
Davis Dam, dam, U.S.	150	H2	35.12 N	114.33 W
Davis Inlet, Nf., Can.	110	D18	55.55 N	60.58 W
Davis Island, i., Pa., U.S.	197b		40.29 N	80.05 W
Davis Lake, l., Il., U.S.	196		42.16 N	88.05 W
Davis Mountains, mts., Tx., U.S.	136	D3	30.41 N	104.10 W
Davis Point, c., Ca., U.S.	200		38.03 N	122.15 W
Davis Sea, s., Ant.	174	P11	66.00 S	92.00 E
Davisstrædet see Davis Strait, strt., N.A.	108	D14	67.00 N	57.00 W
Davis Strait, strt., N.A.	108	D14	67.00 N	57.00 W
Davlekanovo, Russia	40	D19	54.12 N	55.02 E
Davos, Switz.	30	D6	46.48 N	9.49 E
Davron, Fr.	179		48.52 N	1.57 E
Davutlar, Tur.	34	F10	37.43 N	27.15 E
Davy, W.V., U.S.	124	G4	37.28 N	81.39 W
Davyd-Haradok, Bela.	26	H10	52.03 N	27.13 E
Davydiv Brid, Ukr.	38	F12	47.14 N	33.12 E
Davydkovo, Russia	183b		55.35 N	37.12 E
Davyhulme, Eng., U.K.	180		53.27 N	2.22 W
Dawa (Daua), stm., Afr.	82	G7	4.09 N	42.05 E
Dawan, China	58	J3	23.52 N	109.25 E
Dawangzhai, China	187b		31.22 N	121.25 E
Dawei, Mya.	64	E4	14.05 N	98.12 E
Dawen, stm., China	58	D7	35.35 N	116.21 E
Dawes Park, p.o.i., Il., U.S.	196		42.03 N	87.40 W
Dawlan, Mya.	64	D4	16.43 N	98.00 E
Dawna Range, mts., Mya.	64	D4	16.50 N	98.15 E
Daws Heath, Eng., U.K.	178		51.34 N	0.37 E
Dawson, Yk., Can.	110	C3	64.02 N	139.23 W
Dawson, Ga., U.S.	134	F14	31.46 N	84.26 W
Dawson, Mn., U.S.	128	G2	44.55 N	96.03 W
Dawson, Ne., U.S.	130	D2	40.07 N	95.49 W
Dawson, Tx., U.S.	136	C11	31.53 N	96.42 W
Dawson, stm., Austl.	98	D7	23.37 S	149.45 E
Dawson, Isla, i., Chile	166	J2	53.55 S	70.43 W
Dawson, Mount, mtn., B.C., Can.	144	E13	51.09 N	117.25 W
Dawson Bay, b., Mb., Can.	142	B13	52.55 N	100.50 W
Dawson Creek, B.C., Can.	110	D7	55.47 N	120.19 W
Dawson Inlet, b., Nu., Can.	110	C12	61.49 N	93.19 W
Dawson Range, mts., Austl.	98	E7	24.20 S	149.45 E
Dawson Range, mts., Yk., Can.	110	C3	62.40 N	139.00 W
Dawson Springs, Ky., U.S.	130	G10	37.10 N	87.41 W
Dawsonville, Ga., U.S.	132	B1	34.28 N	84.11 W
Dawuji, China	189a		39.51 N	116.30 E
Dax, Fr.	22	F4	43.43 N	1.03 W
Daxian, China	52	F2	31.13 N	107.29 E
Daxin, China	58	J2	22.50 N	107.26 E
Daxing, China	58	B7	39.43 N	116.19 E
Daxu, China	58	I4	25.09 N	110.21 E
Daxue Shan, mts., China	52	F5	30.29 N	101.45 E
Dayakou, China	64	A5	22.40 N	100.20 E
Dayang, stm., China	55	D5	39.50 N	123.39 E
Dayangshu, China	52	B9	49.44 N	124.36 E
Dayao, China	52	F5	25.44 N	101.18 E
Dayaoshan, China	58	I4	24.05 N	110.17 E
Dayboro, Austl.	98	F9	27.12 S	152.49 E
Daye, China	58	F6	30.05 N	114.57 E
Dayghar, India	190c		19.09 N	73.03 E
Daying, China	58	B5	39.17 N	113.45 E
Daylesford, Austl.	98	K5	37.20 S	144.08 E
Daymán, stm., Ur.	172	E9	31.30 S	58.02 W
Dayong, China	58	G4	29.06 N	110.29 E
Dayr 'Afiyah, Syria	76	D7	34.06 N	36.46 E
Dayr az-Zawr, Syria	74	C6	35.20 N	40.08 E
Dayr az-Zawr, state, Syria	74	C7	35.00 N	40.30 E
Dayr Hāfir, Syria	76	B8	36.09 N	37.42 E
Days Island, i., Md., U.S.	202b		39.24 N	76.22 W
Daysland, Ab., Can.	144	D18	52.52 N	112.16 W
Day Star Indian Reserve, ind. res., Sk., Can.	142	C9	51.31 N	104.15 W
Dayton, Ia., U.S.	130	B3	42.15 N	94.03 W
Dayton, N.J., U.S.	194		40.22 N	74.30 W
Dayton, Oh., U.S.	124	E1	39.45 N	84.12 W
Dayton, Or., U.S.	146	E3	45.13 N	123.03 W
Dayton, Tn., U.S.	134	B13	35.29 N	85.01 W
Dayton, Tx., U.S.	136	D13	30.02 N	94.53 W
Dayton, Va., U.S.	124	F6	38.24 N	78.56 W
Dayton, Wa., U.S.	146	D9	46.19 N	117.58 W
Dayton, Wy., U.S.	140	C5	44.52 N	107.14 W
Daytona Beach, Fl., U.S.	132	G5	29.12 N	81.01 W
Dayu, China	58	I6	25.24 N	114.22 E
Dayu, Indon.	66	D9	1.59 S	115.04 E
Dayu Ling, mts., China	58	I6	25.20 N	114.16 E
Da Yunhe (Grand Canal), can., China	58	E8	32.10 N	119.33 E
Dayville, Or., U.S.	146	F7	44.28 N	119.31 W
Dazhu, China	58	F2	30.43 N	107.12 E
Dazkırı, Tur.	34	F12	37.55 N	29.51 E
De Aar, S. Afr.	90	G7	30.39 S	24.01 E
Dead, stm., Me., U.S.	122	E6	45.20 N	69.58 W
Dead, stm., Mi., U.S.	126	B2	46.34 N	87.24 W
Dead, stm., N.J., U.S.	194		40.39 N	74.31 W
Deadhorse, Ak., U.S.	109	B10	70.13 N	148.27 W
Dead Horse Point State Park, p.o.i., Ut., U.S.	150	E7	38.30 N	109.44 W
Deadman, stm., B.C., Can.	144	E10	50.44 N	120.54 W
Deadman Brook, stm., Ct., U.S.	194		41.08 N	73.22 W
Deadman's Cay, Bah.	156	A10	23.09 N	75.05 W
Deadmans Creek, stm., Austl.	192a		33.58 S	151.00 E
Deadman's Creek Indian Reserve, ind. res., B.C., Can.	144	F10	50.49 N	120.58 W
Dead Run, stm., Va., U.S.	202c		38.57 N	77.11 W
Dead Sea, l., Asia	76	G6	31.30 N	35.30 E
Deadwood, S.D., U.S.	140	C9	44.22 N	103.43 W
Deadwood, stm., Id., U.S.	146	F11	44.04 N	115.39 W
Deakin, Austl.	96	F5	30.46 S	128.58 E
Deal, Eng., U.K.	10	J14	51.13 N	1.23 E
Deale, Md., U.S.	124	F9	38.46 N	76.33 W
Dealesville, S. Afr.	90	F7	28.40 S	25.45 E
Deal Island, Md., U.S.	124	F10	38.09 N	75.56 W
De'an, China	58	G6	29.19 N	115.45 E
Dean, stm., B.C., Can.	144	D4	52.47 N	126.59 W
Dean, stm., Eng., U.K.	180		53.20 N	2.14 W
Dean Channel, strt., B.C., Can.	144	D3	52.33 N	127.13 W
Deane, Eng., U.K.	180		53.34 N	2.28 W
Deán Funes, Arg.	172	E5	30.25 S	64.20 W
Dean Row, Eng., U.K.	180		53.20 N	2.11 W
Deans, N.J., U.S.	194		40.24 N	74.30 W
Deans Dundas Bay, b., N.T., Can.	109	B16	72.15 N	118.25 W
Dearborn, Mi., U.S.	124	B2	42.18 N	83.09 W
Dearborn, stm., Mt., U.S.	146	C14	47.07 N	111.54 W
Dearg, Beinn, mtn., Scot., U.K.	10	D8	57.47 N	4.56 W
Dease, stm., B.C., Can.	110	D5	59.55 N	128.28 W
Dease Arm, b., N.T., Can.	110	B6	66.52 N	119.37 W
Dease Strait, strt., Nu., Can.	110	B9	68.44 N	108.06 W
Death Valley, Ca., U.S.	148	G9	36.18 N	116.24 W
Death Valley, val., Ca., U.S.	148	G9	36.30 N	117.00 W
Death Valley National Park, p.o.i., U.S.	148	G8	36.24 N	116.55 W
Deatsville, Al., U.S.	134	E12	32.36 N	86.23 W
Deauville, Fr.	20	E8	49.21 N	0.03 E
Deba, Nig.	84	G7	10.08 N	11.17 E
Debal'tseve, Ukr.	38	E17	48.19 N	38.24 E
Debānāndapur, India	190b		22.56 N	88.22 E
Debao, China	58	J2	23.20 N	106.36 E
Debar, Mac.	34	B3	41.32 N	20.30 E
De Bary, Fl., U.S.	132	H4	28.53 N	81.18 W
Debe, Trin.	159f	s12	10.12 N	61.27 W
De Beque, Co., U.S.	150	D8	39.20 N	108.13 W
De Berry, Tx., U.S.	136	B13	32.17 N	94.09 W
Debesy, Russia	40	C18	57.39 N	53.47 E
Dębica, Pol.	24	F17	50.03 N	21.25 E
Dęblin, Pol.	24	E17	51.34 N	21.52 E
Dębno, Pol.	24	D10	52.44 N	14.42 E
Débo, Lac, l., Mali	84	F4	15.18 N	4.08 W
Deborah West, Lake, l., Austl.	96	F3	30.46 S	119.04 E
Deboyne Islands, is., Pap. N. Gui.	96	B10	10.45 S	152.25 E
Debra Sīna, Eth.	82	F7	9.50 N	39.44 E
Debre Birhan, Eth.	82	F7	9.40 N	39.32 E
Debrecen, Hung.	36	B8	47.32 N	21.38 E
Debre Mark'os, Eth.	82	E7	10.20 N	37.43 E
Debre Tabor, Eth.	82	E7	11.51 N	38.01 E
Debre Zeyit, Eth.	82	F7	8.44 N	38.59 E
Debrzno, Pol.	24	C13	53.32 N	17.13 E
Decatur, Al., U.S.	134	C11	34.36 N	86.59 W
Decatur, Ga., U.S.	132	C1	33.46 N	84.18 W
Decatur, Il., U.S.	130	E9	39.50 N	88.57 W
Decatur, In., U.S.	130	D13	40.49 N	84.55 W
Decatur, Mi., U.S.	130	B11	42.06 N	85.58 W
Decatur, Ms., U.S.	134	E9	32.26 N	89.06 W
Decatur, Ne., U.S.	130	C1	42.00 N	96.15 W
Decatur, Tn., U.S.	134	B14	35.30 N	84.47 W
Decatur, Tx., U.S.	138	H11	33.14 N	97.35 W
Decaturville, Tn., U.S.	134	B10	35.35 N	88.07 W
Decazeville, Fr.	22	E8	44.33 N	2.14 E
Deccan, plat., India	62	E4	17.00 N	78.00 E
Decelles, Réservoir, res., Qc., Can.	114	C11	47.41 N	78.10 W
Deception, stm., Bots.	90	B6	21.01 S	24.12 E
Deception, Mount, mtn., Wa., U.S.	146	C3	47.49 N	123.14 W
Dechang, China	52	F5	27.24 N	102.10 E
Dechenhöhle, cv., Ger.	181		51.22 N	7.39 E
Decherd, Tn., U.S.	134	B12	35.12 N	86.04 W
Dechhu, India	70	E4	26.47 N	72.20 E
Děčín, Czech Rep.	24	F10	50.46 N	14.13 E
Decize, Fr.	20	H12	46.50 N	3.27 E
Decker Lake, B.C., Can.	144	B5	54.17 N	125.49 W
Deckerville, Mi., U.S.	126	E7	43.31 N	82.44 W
Decorah, Ia., U.S.	128	H7	43.17 N	91.46 W
Deda, Rom.	36	C11	46.57 N	24.53 E
Dedaye, Mya.	64	D2	16.24 N	95.53 E
Dededo, Guam	100c	i10	13.31 N	144.50 E
Dedeğöl Dağları, mts., Tur.	34	F14	37.47 N	31.13 E
Dedeğöl Tepesi, mtn., Tur.	34	F14	37.39 N	31.17 E
De Doorns, S. Afr.	90	H4	33.28 S	19.39 E
Dédougou, Burkina	84	G4	12.25 N	3.30 W
Dedoviči, Russia	26	C12	57.32 N	29.57 E
Dedovsk, Russia	26	E20	55.50 N	37.09 E
Deduru, stm., Sri L.	69	H5	7.36 N	79.48 E
Dee, stm., U.K.	10	I9	53.13 N	3.03 W
Dee, stm., Scot., U.K.	10	D10	57.08 N	2.05 W
Deenwood, Ga., U.S.	132	E3	31.13 N	82.25 W
Deep, stm., N.C., U.S.	148	A6	35.32 N	79.37 W
Deepavaal Brook, stm., N.J., U.S.	194		40.53 N	74.16 W
Deep Brook, stm., Ma., U.S.	201		42.38 N	71.22 W
Deep Brook, stm., N.J., U.S.	194		40.58 N	74.09 W
Deep Creek, stm., U.S.	146	H14	42.13 N	112.39 W
Deep Creek, stm., Id., U.S.	146	H10	42.16 N	116.38 W
Deep Creek, stm., Md., U.S.	202b		39.17 N	76.28 W
Deep Creek, stm., Tx., U.S.	136	B8	32.39 N	99.11 W
Deep Creek, stm., Tx., U.S.	136	B7	32.31 N	100.55 W
Deep Creek, stm., Ut., U.S.	150	C3	40.00 N	114.01 W
Deep Creek Indian Reserve, ind. res., B.C., Can.	144	D8	52.16 N	122.07 W
Deep Red Creek, stm., Ok., U.S.	138	G10	34.12 N	98.23 W
Deep River, On., Can.	112	B12	46.05 N	77.30 W
Deep River, Ia., U.S.	130	C5	41.34 N	92.22 W
Deep Run, stm., Md., U.S.	202b		39.13 N	76.42 W
Deep Run, stm., Md., U.S.	202b		39.25 N	76.40 W
Deep Run, stm., N.J., U.S.	194		40.26 N	74.22 W
Deep Run, stm., N.J., U.S.	203		39.44 N	74.41 W
Deepwater, Austl.	98	G8	29.27 S	151.50 E
Deepwater, Mo., U.S.	130	F4	38.15 N	93.46 W
Deep Well, Austl.	96	D6	24.24 S	134.02 E
Deer, stm., N.Y., U.S.	126	D15	44.55 N	74.43 W
Deer Creek, Mn., U.S.	128	E3	46.23 N	95.17 W
Deer Creek, stm., U.S.	124	E9	39.36 N	76.08 W
Deer Creek, stm., Ca., U.S.	148	C4	39.55 N	122.05 W
Deer Creek, stm., Ca., U.S.	200		37.24 N	122.09 W
Deer Creek, stm., Il., U.S.	196		41.32 N	87.37 W
Deer Creek, stm., In., U.S.	130	D11	40.34 N	86.41 W
Deer Creek, stm., Ks., U.S.	138	B9	39.40 N	99.06 W
Deer Creek, stm., Ms., U.S.	134	D8	32.32 N	90.47 W
Deer Creek, stm., Ne., U.S.	140	G13	40.17 N	99.53 W
Deer Creek, stm., Oh., U.S.	130	E14	39.27 N	83.01 W
Deer Creek, stm., Ok., U.S.	138	F10	35.33 N	98.27 W
Deer Creek, stm., Pa., U.S.	197b		40.32 N	79.51 W
Deer Creek, stm., Wy., U.S.	140	E5	43.08 N	107.42 W
Deer Creek, stm., Wy., U.S.	140	E6	42.52 N	105.52 W
Deer Creek Indian Reservation, ind. res., Mn., U.S.	128	D5	47.51 N	93.30 W
Deerfield, Il., U.S.	130	B10	42.10 N	87.50 W
Deerfield, Ks., U.S.	138	C7	37.58 N	101.07 W
Deerfield Beach, Fl., U.S.	132	J5	26.19 N	80.06 W
Deer Grove, p.o.i., Il., U.S.	196		42.09 N	88.04 W
Deering, Ak., U.S.	109	C7	66.03 N	162.44 W
Deer Island, pen., Ma., U.S.	201		42.21 N	70.58 W
Deer Island, i., N.B., Can.	122	F10	44.58 N	66.59 W
Deer Isle, Me., U.S.	122	F8	44.13 N	68.40 W
Deer Lake, Nf., Can.	111a	j22	49.11 N	57.26 W
Deer Lakes Regional Park, p.o.i., Pa., U.S.	197b		40.38 N	79.49 W
Deer Lodge, Mt., U.S.	146	D14	46.23 N	112.44 W
Deer Mountain, mtn., Me., U.S.	122	E6	45.01 N	70.56 W
Deer Park, Austl.	192b		37.47 S	144.47 E
Deer Park, Al., U.S.	134	F10	31.13 N	88.19 W
Deer Park, Il., U.S.	196		42.09 N	88.04 W
Deer Park, Wa., U.S.	146	C9	47.56 N	117.28 W
Deer Park, p.o.i., India	190a		28.33 N	77.11 E
Deer Park Airport, arpt., N.Y., U.S.	194		40.46 N	73.19 W
Deerpass Bay, b., N.T., Can.	110	B6	65.56 N	122.25 W
Deer Pond, l., N.J., U.S.	194		40.57 N	74.24 W
Deer River, Mn., U.S.	128	D5	47.19 N	93.47 W
Deer Trail, Co., U.S.	138	B4	39.36 N	104.02 W
Deerwood, Mn., U.S.	128	E5	46.27 N	93.53 W
Dee Why Head, c., Austl.	192a		33.46 S	151.19 E
Dee Why Lagoon, b., Austl.	192a		33.45 S	151.18 E
Deex Nugaaleed see Eyl, val., Som.	86	C9	7.57 N	49.50 E
Defiance, Ia., U.S.	130	C2	41.49 N	95.20 W
Defiance, Oh., U.S.	124	C1	41.16 N	84.21 W
Defiance, Mount, mtn., Or., U.S.	146	E5	45.38 N	121.43 W
Defiance Plateau, plat., Az., U.S.	150	H7	35.50 N	109.18 W
De Forest, Wi., U.S.	128	H9	43.15 N	89.19 W
De Forest Lake, l., N.Y., U.S.	194		41.08 N	73.58 W
Defu, Sing.	189c		1.21 N	103.54 E
De Funiak Springs, Fl., U.S.	134	G12	30.43 N	86.06 W
Dêgê, China	52	E4	31.50 N	98.40 E
Degeberga, Swe.	16	L12	55.50 N	14.05 E
Degeh Bur, Eth.	82	F8	8.13 N	43.33 E
Dégelis, Qc., Can.	122	C8	47.32 N	68.38 W
Degerby, Fin.	18	G7	60.01 N	20.25 E
Degerfors, Swe.	16	H12	59.14 N	14.26 E
Degerhamn, Swe.	16	K14	56.20 N	16.25 E
Deggendorf, Ger.	24	H8	48.50 N	12.57 E
Degh, stm., Asia	70	B5	31.35 N	74.08 E
Değirmendere, Tur.	34	E10	38.07 N	27.09 E
Değirmenlik, N. Cyp.	76	C4	35.14 N	33.28 E
De Graff, Oh., U.S.	124	D2	40.18 N	83.54 W
De Gray Reservoir, res., Ar., U.S.	134	C5	34.14 N	93.12 W
De Grey, stm., Austl.	96	D3	20.01 S	119.13 E
Degt'arka, stm., Russia	183a		59.57 N	30.52 E
Degtevo, Russia	40	G12	49.09 N	40.39 E
Degunino, ngh., Russia	183b		55.52 N	37.33 E
Dehalak' Desēt, i., Erit.	82	D8	15.39 N	40.06 E
Deh Bīd, Iran	74	E13	30.37 N	53.11 E
Dehdez, Iran	74	E12	31.42 N	50.19 E
Dehgolān, Iran	74	C10	35.17 N	47.25 E
Dehiwala-Mount Lavinia, Sri L.	69	H4	6.52 N	79.51 E
Deh Kord, Iran	74	D11	33.49 N	48.53 E
Dehlorān, Iran	74	D10	32.41 N	47.16 E
Dehpehk, i., Micron.	100d	m12	6.56 N	158.17 E
Dehra Dūn, India	70	C7	30.18 N	78.01 E
Dehra Dūn Cantonment, India	70	C6	30.20 N	77.58 E
Dehri, India	70	F10	24.54 N	84.11 E
Dehu, India	69	B1	18.35 N	73.51 E
Dehua, China	58	I8	25.30 N	118.14 E
Dehui, China	52	C10	44.31 N	125.42 E
Deilbach, stm., Ger.	181		51.23 N	7.05 E
Deinze, Bel.	20	D12	50.59 N	3.32 E
Deir Mawās, Egypt	76	K1	27.38 N	30.51 E
Dej, Rom.	36	B10	47.09 N	23.53 E
Deje, Swe.	16	H11	59.36 N	13.27 E
Dejnau, Turkmen.	72	B9	39.15 N	63.10 E
De Jongs, Tanjong, c., Indon.	60	G10	6.55 S	138.32 E
De Kalb, Il., U.S.	130	C9	41.55 N	88.44 W
De Kalb, Ms., U.S.	134	E10	32.46 N	88.39 W
De Kalb, Tx., U.S.	134	D4	33.31 N	94.36 W
De-Kastri, Russia	50	F17	51.28 N	140.46 E
Dekehtik, i., Micron.	100d	l11	6.59 N	158.12 E
Dekese, D.R.C.	86	E4	3.25 S	21.22 E
Deke Sokehs, i., Micron.	100d	m11	6.58 N	158.10 E
Dékoa, C.A.R.	86	C3	6.18 N	19.04 E
Del Aire, Ca., U.S.	198		33.55 N	118.21 W
Delamere, Eng., U.K.	180		53.13 N	2.39 W
Del Amo Fashion Center, shp. cen., Ca., U.S.	198		33.50 N	118.21 W
De Land, Fl., U.S.	132	G4	29.01 N	81.18 W
Delanggu, Indon.	66	G7	7.36 S	110.42 E
Delano, Ca., U.S.	148	H6	35.47 N	119.14 W
Delano, Mn., U.S.	128	F5	45.02 N	93.47 W
Delano Peak, mtn., Ut., U.S.	150	E4	38.22 N	112.23 W
Delaport Point, c., Bah.	158f	m18	25.04 N	77.26 W
Delapu, China	70	C13	31.35 N	90.35 E
Delārām, Afg.	72	C9	32.09 N	63.25 E
Delareyville, S. Afr.	90	E7	26.42 S	25.27 E
Delarof Islands, is., Ak., U.S.	109a	g23	51.28 N	178.45 W
Delavan, Il., U.S.	130	D8	40.21 N	89.32 W
Delaware, Oh., U.S.	124	D2	40.17 N	83.04 W
Delaware, Ok., U.S.	138	H2	36.46 N	95.38 W
Delaware, state, U.S.	124	F10	39.10 N	75.30 W
Delaware, stm., U.S.	124	D10	39.19 N	75.24 W
Delaware, stm., U.S.	136	C3	32.02 N	104.01 W
Delaware, stm., Ks., U.S.	130	E2	39.03 N	95.24 W
Delaware, East Branch, stm., N.Y., U.S.	124	B10	41.56 N	75.17 W
Delaware, University of, educ., De., U.S.	203		39.41 N	75.45 W
Delaware, West Branch, stm., U.S.	124	B10	41.56 N	75.17 W
Delaware Bay, b., U.S.	124	E10	39.05 N	75.15 W
Delaware City, De., U.S.	124	E10	39.34 N	75.36 W
Delaware Memorial Bridge, trans., U.S.	203		40.07 N	74.50 W
Delaware Mountains, mts., Tx., U.S.	136	C3	31.35 N	104.40 W
Delaware Museum of Natural History, bldg., De., U.S.	203		39.47 N	75.36 W
Delaware Park, p.o.i., N.Y., U.S.	202a		42.56 N	78.52 W
Delaware Park Race Track, p.o.i., De., U.S.	203		39.42 N	75.40 W
Delburne, Ab., Can.	144	D17	52.10 N	113.14 W
Delcambre, La., U.S.	134	H7	29.57 N	91.59 W
Del Campillo, Arg.	172	G5	34.22 S	64.29 W
Del City, Ok., U.S.	138	F11	35.26 N	97.28 W
Delegate, Austl.	98	K7	37.02 S	148.56 E
Delémont, Switz.	30	C4	47.22 N	7.21 E
De Leon, Tx., U.S.	136	B9	32.06 N	98.32 W
De Leon Springs, Fl., U.S.	132	G4	29.07 N	81.21 W
Delet, strt., Fin.	18	G7	60.15 N	20.35 E
Delfinópolis, Braz.	170	K2	20.20 S	46.50 W
Délfoi, hist., Grc.	34	E5	38.30 N	22.29 E
Delft, Neth.	20	B13	52.00 N	4.21 E
Delft Island, i., Sri L.	69	G4	9.30 N	79.42 E
Delfzijl, Neth.	20	A15	53.20 N	6.55 E
Delgado, Cabo, c., Moz.	88	C7	10.41 S	40.37 E
Delger, stm., Mong.	50	G9	49.16 N	100.41 E
Delgerhet, Mong.	52	B7	45.50 N	110.21 E
Delhi, On., Can.	126	F9	42.51 N	80.29 W
Delhi, India	70	D6	28.40 N	77.13 E
Delhi, India	190a		28.40 N	77.13 E
Delhi, Ia., U.S.	130	B6	42.25 N	91.20 W
Delhi, La., U.S.	134	E7	32.28 N	91.29 W
Delhi, N.Y., U.S.	124	B11	42.16 N	74.55 W
Delhi, state, India	70	D6	28.37 N	77.10 E
Delhi Cantonment, India	190a		28.36 N	77.08 E
Delhi Railroad Station, trans., India	190a		28.40 N	77.13 E
Delhi Tail Distributary, can., India	190a		28.41 N	77.10 E
Delhi University, educ., India	190a		28.42 N	77.13 E
Delia, Ab., Can.	144	E18	51.38 N	112.21 W
Deliatyn, Ukr.	38	E3	48.32 N	24.37 E
Deliblato, Yugo.	36	E8	44.50 N	21.02 E
Délices, Dom.	159c	j6	15.17 N	61.16 W
Delicias, Mex.	154	A6	28.11 N	105.28 W
Delight, Ar., U.S.	134	C5	34.02 N	93.30 W
Delījān, Iran	74	C12	33.59 N	50.40 E
Deline, N.T., Can.	110	B6	65.11 N	123.30 W
Delingde, Russia	50	B11	70.07 N	113.56 E
Delingha, China	52	D4	37.14 N	97.11 E
Dēliņkalns, hill, Lat.	26	C9	57.31 N	26.55 E
Déli Pályaudvar, trans., Hung.	182c		47.30 N	19.01 E
Delisle, Sk., Can.	142	C6	51.55 N	107.08 W
Delitua, Indon.	66	B1	3.30 N	98.41 E
Delitzsch, Ger.	24	E8	51.31 N	12.19 E
Dell City, Tx., U.S.	136	C2	31.55 N	105.12 W
Delle, Fr.	20	G16	47.30 N	6.59 E
Dellenbaugh, Mount, mtn., Az., U.S.	150	G3	36.07 N	113.32 W
Delles see Dellys, Alg.	28	H14	36.55 N	3.53 E
Dell Rapids, S.D., U.S.	128	H2	43.49 N	96.43 W
Dellwig, Ger.	181		51.29 N	7.41 E
Dellwig, ngh., Ger.	181		51.29 N	6.56 E
Dellwood Highlands, Il., U.S.	196		41.34 N	88.03 W
Dellys, Alg.	28	H14	36.55 N	3.53 E
Del Mar, Ca., U.S.	148	K8	32.57 N	117.15 W
Delmar, Ia., U.S.	130	C7	42.00 N	90.36 W
Delmar, Md., U.S.	124	F10	38.27 N	75.34 W
Del Mar Hills, Tx., U.S.	136	G8	27.37 N	99.26 W
Delmarva Peninsula, pen., U.S.	124	F11	38.30 N	75.30 W
Del Mar Woods, Il., U.S.	196		42.12 N	87.51 W
Delmas, Sk., Can.	142	B5	52.56 N	108.35 W
Delmas, state, S. Afr.	191d		26.10 S	28.33 E
Delme, stm., Ger.	20	B17	53.05 N	8.40 E
Delmenhorst, Ger.	24	C4	53.03 N	8.38 E
Delmiro Gouveia, Braz.	170	E7	9.23 S	37.59 W
Delmont, S.D., U.S.	140	D14	43.16 N	98.09 W
Delnice, Cro.	30	E11	45.24 N	14.48 E
Del Norte, Co., U.S.	138	D2	37.40 N	106.21 W
Del Norte Coast Redwood State Park, p.o.i., Ca., U.S.	146	I3	41.48 N	123.54 W
De-Longa, ostrova, is., Russia	50	A19	76.30 N	153.00 E
De Long Mountains, mts., Ak., U.S.	109	C7	68.20 N	162.00 W
Deloraine, Austl.	99a	n13	41.31 S	146.39 E
Deloraine, Mb., Can.	142	E13	49.10 N	100.31 W
Delorme, Lac, l., Qc., Can.	110	E16	54.38 N	69.41 W
Delos see Dílos, hist., Grc.	34	F8	37.23 N	25.16 E
Delphi, In., U.S.	130	D11	40.34 N	86.40 W
Delphi see Délfoi, hist., Grc.	34	E5	38.30 N	22.29 E
Delphos, Ks., U.S.	138	B11	39.16 N	97.46 W
Delphos, Oh., U.S.	124	D1	40.50 N	84.20 W
Delph Reservoir, res., Eng., U.K.	180		53.38 N	2.27 W
Delportshoop, S. Afr.	90	F7	28.24 S	24.18 E
Delran, N.J., U.S.	203		40.01 N	74.57 W
Delrath, Ger.	181		51.08 N	6.47 E
Delray, ngh., Mi., U.S.	199		42.18 N	83.08 W
Delray Beach, Fl., U.S.	132	J5	26.27 N	80.04 W
Del Rio, Tx., U.S.	136	E7	29.21 N	100.53 W
Delsbo, Swe.	16	F14	61.47 N	16.33 E
Delstern, ngh., Ger.	181		51.20 N	7.31 E
Delta, Mex.	150	K1	32.21 N	115.11 W
Delta, Co., U.S.	150	E8	38.44 N	108.04 W
Delta, Mo., U.S.	130	G8	37.11 N	89.44 W
Delta, Oh., U.S.	124	C1	41.34 N	84.00 W
Delta, Ut., U.S.	150	D4	39.21 N	112.34 W
Delta Amacuro, state, Ven.	168	C11	8.30 N	61.30 W
Delta Beach, Mb., Can.	142	D15	50.10 N	98.19 W
Delta City, Ms., U.S.	134	D8	33.04 N	90.47 W
Delta Downs, Austl.	96	C8	16.59 S	141.18 E
Delta Junction, Ak., U.S.	109	D10	64.02 N	145.44 W
Delta Peak, mtn., B.C., Can.	110	D4	56.39 N	129.34 W
Delungra, Austl.	98	G8	29.39 S	150.49 E
Del Valle, Tx., U.S.	136	D10	30.11 N	97.39 W
Del Verme Falls, wtfl., Eth.	82	F8	5.22 N	40.19 E
Delvina see Delvinë, Alb.	32	E14	39.57 N	20.06 E
Delvinë, Alb.	32	E14	39.57 N	20.06 E
Delyn, mun., Wales, U.K.	180		53.16 N	3.11 W
Dëma, stm., Russia	40	D19	54.44 N	55.54 E
Demak, Indon.	66	G7	6.52 S	110.38 E
Demarcation Point, c., Ak., U.S.	109	C11	69.40 N	141.10 W
Demarest, N.J., U.S.	194		40.57 N	73.57 W
Demarest Brook, stm., N.J., U.S.	194		40.57 N	73.58 W
Demavend, Mount see Damāvand, Qolleh-ye, vol., Iran	42	H15	35.56 N	52.08 E
Demba, D.R.C.	86	F4	5.27 S	22.16 E
Dembī, Eth.	82	F7	8.04 N	36.27 E
Dembia, C.A.R.	86	C4	5.08 N	24.29 E
Dembia, D.R.C.	86	D5	3.30 N	25.50 E
Dembī Dolo, Eth.	82	F6	8.31 N	34.48 E
Demer, stm., Bel.	20	C13	50.58 N	4.42 E
Demidov, Russia	26	E14	55.15 N	31.31 E
Demidovo, Russia	26	A21	59.16 N	38.16 E
Deming, N.M., U.S.	150	K9	32.16 N	107.45 W
Deming, Wa., U.S.	146	B4	48.49 N	122.14 W
Demini, stm., Braz.	168	H10	0.46 S	62.56 W
Demirci, Tur.	34	D11	39.03 N	28.39 E
Demirköprü Barajı, res., Tur.	34	E11	38.39 N	28.22 E
Demirköy, Tur.	34	B10	41.49 N	27.45 E
Demirtaş, Tur.	34	C12	40.15 N	29.05 E
Demjanka, stm., Russia	48	C12	59.31 N	69.04 E
Demjanovo, Russia	12	F22	60.21 N	47.02 E
Demjansk, Russia	26	C15	57.38 N	32.28 E
Demjanskoe, Russia	48	C11	59.35 N	69.19 E
Demjas, Russia	40	F16	51.12 N	49.06 E
Demmeltrath, ngh., Ger.	181		51.11 N	7.03 E
Demmin, Ger.	24	C8	53.54 N	13.02 E
Demmitt, Ab., Can.	144	A11	55.26 N	119.53 W
Democracy Monument, hist., Thai.	187a		13.45 N	100.30 E
Democrat Point, c., N.Y., U.S.	194		40.37 N	73.18 W
Demopolis, Al., U.S.	134	E11	32.31 N	87.50 W
Demorest, Ga., U.S.	132	B2	34.34 N	83.32 W
Demotte, In., U.S.	130	C10	41.11 N	87.11 W
Dempo, Gunung, vol., Indon.	66	F3	4.00 S	103.08 E
Dempster, Point, c., Austl.	96	F4	33.39 S	123.52 E
Demta, Indon.	60	F11	2.20 S	140.06 E
Demuryne, Ukr.	38	E15	48.10 N	36.28 E
Demydivka, Ukr.	38	C4	50.25 N	25.20 E
Denain, Fr.	20	D12	50.19 N	3.23 E
Denakil see Danakil, reg., Afr.	82	E8	13.00 N	41.00 E
Denali, Ak., U.S.	109	D10	63.11 N	147.28 W
Denali National Park, Ak., U.S.	109	D10	63.44 N	148.54 W
Denan, Eth.	82	F8	6.33 N	43.30 E
Denau, Uzb.	48	G11	38.16 N	67.53 E
Den Burg, Neth.	20	A13	53.03 N	4.47 E
Den Chai, Thai.	64	C5	17.59 N	100.02 E
Dendang, Indon.	66	E5	3.05 S	107.54 E
Dender, stm., Bel.	20	D12	51.02 N	4.06 E
Dendermonde (Termonde), Bel.	20	C12	51.01 N	4.06 E
Dendre see Dender, stm., Bel.	20	D12	51.02 N	4.06 E
Dendy Park, p.o.i., Austl.	192b		37.56 S	145.00 E
Denenchōfu, ngh., Japan	186		35.35 N	139.41 E
Dengas, Niger	84	G6	13.03 N	9.20 E
Deng Deng, Cam.	86	C2	5.11 N	13.31 E
Dengkou, China	58	A2	40.19 N	107.00 E
Dêngqên, China	52	E4	31.27 N	95.27 E
Dengta, China	58	I6	24.00 N	114.47 E
Dengxian, China	58	E5	32.42 N	112.01 E
Denham, Austl.	96	E2	25.55 S	113.32 E
Denham, Eng., U.K.	178		51.34 N	0.30 W
Denham, Mount, mtn., Jam.	158d	i13	18.13 N	77.32 W
Denham Aerodrome, arpt., Eng., U.K.	178		51.36 N	0.31 W
Denham Place, bldg., Eng., U.K.	178		51.34 N	0.30 W
Denham Range, mts., Austl.	98	C7	21.40 S	147.55 E
Denham Springs, La., U.S.	134	G8	30.28 N	90.57 W
Den Helder (Helder), Neth.	20	B13	52.57 N	4.46 E
Denholme, Eng., U.K.	180		53.48 N	1.54 W
Dénia, Spain	28	F11	38.50 N	0.06 E
Deniliquin, Austl.	98	J5	35.32 S	144.57 E
Deniskoviči, Russia	26	H14	52.18 N	31.42 E
Denison, Ia., U.S.	130	C2	42.01 N	95.21 W
Denison, Tx., U.S.	134	D2	33.45 N	96.32 W
Denison, Mount, vol., Ak., U.S.	109	E9	58.25 N	154.27 W
Denisy, Fr.	179		48.33 N	1.56 E
Denizli, Tur.	34	F12	37.46 N	29.05 E
Denizli, state, Tur.	34	F12	37.40 N	29.15 E
Denkanikota, India	69	E3	12.31 N	77.47 E
Denmark, Austl.	96	F3	34.57 S	117.22 E
Denmark, S.C., U.S.	132	C4	33.19 N	81.08 W
Denmark, Wi., U.S.	126	D2	44.20 N	87.49 W
Denmark, ctry., Eur.	6	D10	56.00 N	10.00 E
Denmark, Lake, l., N.J., U.S.	194		40.58 N	74.31 W
Denmark Strait, strt.	106	C20	67.00 N	25.00 W
Dennemont, Fr.	179		49.01 N	1.42 E
Dennery, St. Luc.	159c	m7	13.55 N	60.53 W
Dennison, Oh., U.S.	124	D4	40.23 N	81.20 W
Denniston Creek, stm., Ca., U.S.	200		37.30 N	122.28 W
Denouval, Fr.	179		48.58 N	2.03 E
Denpasar, Indon.	66	H9	8.39 S	115.13 E
Denshaw, Eng., U.K.	180		53.35 N	2.02 W
Dent Ditch, can., Oh., U.S.	197a		41.18 N	82.08 W
Denton, Md., U.S.	124	F10	38.52 N	75.49 W
Denton, Mi., U.S.	199		42.15 N	83.31 W
Denton, Mt., U.S.	146	C17	47.17 N	109.57 W
Denton, N.C., U.S.	132	A5	35.37 N	80.06 W
Denton, Tx., U.S.	138	H11	33.13 N	97.08 W
Denton Creek, stm., Tx., U.S.	138	H11	32.57 N	96.56 W
Dentonia Park, p.o.i., On., Can.	193b		43.42 N	79.17 W
D'Entrecasteaux, Point, c., Austl.	96	F3	34.50 S	116.00 E
D'Entrecasteaux Islands, is., Pap. N. Gui.	94	D6	9.27 S	150.31 E
Denver, Co., U.S.	138	B3	39.43 N	104.58 W
Denver, Ia., U.S.	130	B5	42.40 N	92.20 W
Denver, Pa., U.S.	124	D9	40.14 N	76.08 W
Denver City, Tx., U.S.	136	A5	32.57 N	102.49 W
Deoband, India	70	D6	29.41 N	77.40 E
Deodoro, ngh., Braz.	205a		22.51 S	43.23 W
Deogarh, India	70	F4	25.32 N	73.54 E
Deogarh, India	70	F7	24.32 N	78.15 E
Deogarh, India	70	H10	21.32 N	84.44 E
Deogarh, mtn., India	70	G9	23.32 N	82.16 E
Deogarh Hills, hills, India	70	G9	23.35 N	82.30 E
Deoghar, India	70	F11	24.29 N	86.41 E
Deogsu Palace, bldg., Kor., S.	189b		37.35 N	126.58 E
Deoli, ngh., India	190a		28.30 N	77.14 E
Deori, India	70	G7	23.24 N	79.01 E
Deoria, India	70	E9	26.30 N	83.47 E
Deosil, India	70	G9	23.46 N	82.27 E
Depāra, India	190b		22.53 N	88.34 E
DePaul University, educ., Il., U.S.	196		41.56 N	87.39 W
De Pere, Wi., U.S.	126	D1	44.26 N	88.03 W
Depew, Ok., U.S.	134	B2	35.48 N	96.30 W
Depoe Bay, Or., U.S.	146	F2	44.48 N	124.03 W
Depok, Indon.	66	G5	6.23 S	106.49 E
Deport, Tx., U.S.	134	D3	33.32 N	95.19 W
Deposit, N.Y., U.S.	124	B10	42.04 N	75.25 W
Deptford, N.J., U.S.	203		39.50 N	75.07 W
Deptford, ngh., Eng., U.K.	178		51.28 N	0.02 W
Deptford Mall, shp. cen., N.J., U.S.	203		39.50 N	75.06 W
Deptford Terrace, N.J., U.S.	203		39.48 N	75.09 W
Depue, Il., U.S.	130	C8	41.19 N	89.18 W

Name	Page	Map Ref.	Latitude	Longitude
Dêqên, China	52	F4	28.38 N	98.52 E
Deqing, China	58	J4	23.09 N	111.46 E
De Queen, Ar., U.S.	134	C4	34.02 N	94.20 W
De Quincy, La., U.S.	134	G5	30.26 N	93.26 W
Dera, stm., Hung.	182c		47.39 N	19.05 E
Dera, Lach, stm., Afr.	86	D8	0.13 N	42.17 E
Dera, Lak see Dera, Lach, stm., Afr.	86	D8	0.13 N	42.17 E
Dera Bugti, Pak.	70	D2	29.02 N	69.09 E
Dera Ghāzi Khān, Pak.	70	C3	30.03 N	70.38 E
Dera Ismāīl Khān, Pak.	70	C3	31.49 N	70.54 E
Derakht-e Yahyā, Afg.	70	C2	31.49 N	68.07 E
Derāwar Fort, Pak.	70	D3	28.46 N	71.20 E
Derazhnia, Ukr.	38	D6	49.15 N	27.27 E
Derbent, Russia	42	D13	42.03 N	48.17 E
Derby, Austl.	96	C4	17.19 S	123.38 E
Derby, Austl.	99a	n13	41.09 S	147.47 E
Derby, Eng., U.K.	10	I11	52.55 N	1.29 W
Derby, Ks., U.S.	138	D11	37.33 N	97.16 W
Derby, N.Y., U.S.	124	B6	42.40 N	78.58 W
Derby Line, Vt., U.S.	122	E4	45.00 N	72.05 W
Derecske, Hung.	36	B8	47.21 N	21.34 E
Dereköy, Tur.	34	B10	41.55 N	27.22 E
Derendorf, ngh., Ger.	181		51.15 N	6.48 E
Dereseki, ngh., Tur.	185b		41.08 N	29.08 E
Derevjanka, Russia	18	F21	61.34 N	34.27 E
Derevjannoe, Russia	18	F21	61.39 N	34.32 E
Derg, Lough, l., Ire.	10	I4	52.55 N	8.19 W
Dergači, Russia	40	F16	51.13 N	48.45 E
Derhachi, Ukr.	38	C15	50.06 N	36.06 E
De Ridder, La., U.S.	134	G5	30.50 N	93.17 W
Derik, Tur.	42	G9	37.21 N	40.17 E
Dermott, Ar., U.S.	134	D7	33.32 N	91.26 W
Derne, Ger.	181		51.35 N	7.41 E
Derne, ngh., Ger.	181		51.34 N	7.31 E
Dernieres, Isles, is., La., U.S.	134	H8	29.02 N	90.47 W
Dernovići, Bela.	38	B8	51.37 N	29.45 E
Dêrong, China	52	F4	28.47 N	99.14 E
Déroute, Passage de la, strt., Eur.	10	L11	49.21 N	1.57 W
Derrame, Mex.	136	H3	26.19 N	104.23 W
Derry see Londonderry, N. Ire., U.K.	10	F6	54.59 N	7.20 W
Derry, N.H., U.S.	124	B14	42.53 N	71.19 W
Derry West, On., Can.	193b		43.39 N	79.42 W
Der Sārāi, ngh., India	190a		28.33 N	77.11 E
Derudeb, Sudan	82	D7	17.31 N	36.04 E
Derventa, Bos.	36	E4	44.58 N	17.54 E
Derwent, Ab., Can.	144	C19	53.38 N	110.58 W
Derwent, stm., Austl.	99a	o13	43.03 S	147.22 E
Derwent, stm., Eng., U.K.	10	G12	53.45 N	0.58 W
Derwent Bridge, Austl.	99a	o13	42.08 S	146.13 E
Derwent Water, l., Eng., U.K.	10	G9	54.34 N	3.08 W
Deržavinsk, Kaz.	48	D11	51.06 N	66.19 E
Desaguadero, stm., Arg.	172	F4	34.13 S	66.45 W
Desaguadero, stm., S.A.	166	C3	18.04 S	67.06 W
Desagüe, Canal de, can., Mex.	204a		19.29 N	99.05 W
Des Allemands, La., U.S.	134	H8	29.49 N	90.27 W
Désappointement, Îles du, is., Fr. Poly.	94	E12	14.10 S	141.20 W
Des Arc, Ar., U.S.	134	C7	34.58 N	91.29 W
Descabezado Grande, Volcán, vol., Chile	172	G2	35.36 S	70.45 W
Descanso, Braz.	172	C11	26.49 S	53.30 W
Descanso, Mex.	120	E4	32.11 N	116.53 W
Descanso, Ca., U.S.	148	K9	32.51 N	116.36 W
Descanso, Punta, c., Mex.	148	K8	32.16 N	117.00 W
Descanso Gardens, p.o.i., Ca., U.S.	198		34.12 N	118.13 W
Descartes, Fr.	20	G9	46.58 N	0.42 E
Deschambault Lake, l., Sk., Can.	110	E10	54.40 N	103.35 W
Deschutes, stm., Or., U.S.	146	E6	45.38 N	120.54 W
Deschutes, stm., Wa., U.S.	146	C4	47.00 N	122.54 W
Desdunes, Haiti	156	C11	19.17 N	72.39 W
Desē, Eth.	82	E7	11.08 N	39.38 E
Deseado, stm., Arg.	166	I3	47.45 S	65.52 W
Deseado, Cabo, c., Chile	166	J1	52.44 S	74.42 W
Desengaño, Punta, c., Arg.	166	I3	49.15 S	67.37 W
Desenzano del Garda, Italy	30	E7	45.28 N	10.31 E
Deseret Peak, mtn., Ut., U.S.	150	C4	40.28 N	112.38 W
Deseronto, On., Can.	126	D12	44.11 N	77.03 W
Désert, stm., Qc., Can.	126	B13	46.23 N	75.58 W
Désert, Lac, l., Qc., Can.	126	B13	46.35 N	76.19 W
Desert Hot Springs, Ca., U.S.	148	J9	33.58 N	116.31 W
Desert Lake, l., Nv., U.S.	148	F10	36.58 N	115.15 W
Desert Peak, mtn., Ut., U.S.	150	B3	41.11 N	113.22 W
Desert Valley, val., Nv., U.S.	148	B7	41.14 N	118.11 W
Desha, Ar., U.S.	134	B7	35.44 N	91.40 W
Deshaies, Guad.	159c	h5	16.18 N	61.47 W
Desheng, China	58	I3	24.42 N	108.25 E
Deshler, Ne., U.S.	138	A11	40.08 N	97.43 W
Deshler, Oh., U.S.	124	C2	41.12 N	83.54 W
Deshnok, India	70	E4	27.47 N	73.21 E
Desiderio Tello, Arg.	172	E4	31.13 S	66.19 W
Deskáti, Grc.	34	D4	39.55 N	21.49 E
Des Lacs, stm., N.A.	142	F11	48.17 N	101.25 W
Desloge, Mo., U.S.	130	G7	37.52 N	90.31 W
Desmaraisville, Qc., Can.	114	B12	49.30 N	76.11 W
De Smet, S.D., U.S.	140	C15	44.22 N	97.32 W
De Smet, Lake, l., Wy., U.S.	140	C6	44.28 N	106.45 W
Des Moines, Ia., U.S.	130	C4	41.36 N	93.38 W
Des Moines, N.M., U.S.	138	E5	36.44 N	103.51 W
Des Moines, stm., U.S.	128	K7	40.22 N	91.25 W
Des Moines, East Fork, stm., U.S.	128	H4	42.40 N	94.12 W
Desna, Ukr.	38	C9	50.54 N	30.46 E
Desna, stm., Eur.	40	F7	50.32 N	30.34 E
Desna, stm., Russia	26	E19	55.26 N	37.30 E
Desolación, Isla, i., Chile	166	J2	53.00 S	74.09 W
Desor, Mount, hill, Mi., U.S.	128	D9	47.58 N	89.01 W
De Soto, Il., U.S.	130	G8	37.48 N	89.13 W
De Soto, Mo., U.S.	130	F7	38.08 N	90.33 W
De Soto National Memorial, p.o.i., Fl., U.S.	132	I2	27.31 N	82.40 W
De Soto State Park, p.o.i., Al., U.S.	134	C13	34.28 N	85.36 W
Despatch, S. Afr.	90	H7	33.46 S	25.30 E
Despeñaperros, Desfiladero de, p., Spain	28	F7	38.25 N	3.30 W
Des Plaines, Il., U.S.	130	B10	42.02 N	87.53 W
Des Plaines, stm., U.S.	130	C9	41.24 N	88.12 W
Despotovac, Yugo.	36	E8	44.02 N	21.35 E
Desroches, i., Sey.	89b	k12	5.41 S	53.41 E
Desruisseaux, St. Luc.	159c	m7	13.47 N	60.55 W
Dessau, Ger.	24	E8	51.49 N	12.14 E
Desterro, Braz.	170	D7	7.17 S	37.06 W
Destin, Fl., U.S.	134	G12	30.23 N	86.29 W
Destruction Bay, Yk., Can.	110	C3	61.14 N	138.50 W
Desvres, Fr.	20	D10	50.40 N	1.50 E
Deta, Rom.	36	D8	45.24 N	21.13 E
Detčino, Russia	26	F19	54.48 N	36.19 E
Dete, Zimb.	88	D4	18.36 S	26.51 E
Detling, Eng., U.K.	178		51.18 N	0.34 E
Detmold, Ger.	24	E4	51.56 N	8.52 E
Detour, Point, c., Mi., U.S.	126	C3	45.36 N	86.36 W
De Tour Village, Mi., U.S.	126	C6	45.59 N	83.54 W
Detrital Wash, stm., Az., U.S.	150	H2	36.02 N	114.28 W
Detroit, Mi., U.S.	126	F6	42.20 N	83.03 W
Detroit, Mi., U.S.	199		42.20 N	83.03 W
Detroit, Or., U.S.	146	F4	44.44 N	122.08 W
Detroit, Tx., U.S.	134	D3	33.40 N	95.16 W
Detroit Beach, Mi., U.S.	124	C2	41.55 N	83.19 W
Detroit City Airport, arpt., Mi., U.S.	199		42.25 N	83.01 W
Detroit Institute of Arts, bldg., Mi., U.S.	199		42.22 N	83.04 W
Detroit Lakes, Mn., U.S.	128	E3	46.49 N	95.51 W
Detroit Mercy, University of, educ., Mi., U.S.	199		42.25 N	83.08 W
Detroit Metropolitan-Wayne County Airport, arpt., Mi., U.S.	199		42.13 N	83.22 W
Detroit Race Course, p.o.i., Mi., U.S.	199		42.23 N	83.19 W
Detroit Reservoir, res., Or., U.S.	146	F4	44.43 N	122.10 W
Detroit-Windsor Tunnel, trans., N.A.	199		42.20 N	83.02 W
Detroit Zoological Park, p.o.i., Mi., U.S.	199		42.29 N	83.09 W
Detskosel'skij, Russia	183a		59.44 N	30.28 E
Dettifoss, wtfl., Ice.	12a	k31	65.49 N	16.22 W
Det Udom, Thai.	64	E7	14.53 N	105.04 E
Detva, Slvk.	24	H15	48.31 N	19.28 E
Deua National Park, p.o.i., Austl.	98	J7	35.54 S	149.45 E
Deuels Corners, N.Y., U.S.	202a		42.45 N	78.45 W
Deuil-la-Barre, Fr.	179		48.59 N	2.20 E
Deūlgaon Rāja, India	70	H5	20.02 N	76.01 E
Deulpur, India	190b		22.36 N	88.10 E
Deusen, ngh., Ger.	181		51.33 N	7.26 E
Deutsche Bucht, b., Ger.	24	B3	53.59 N	8.04 E
Deutsche Demokratische Republik see Germany, ctry., Eur.	6	E11	51.00 N	10.00 E
Deutsch Eylau see Iława, Pol.	24	C15	53.35 N	19.33 E
Deutsch Krone see Wałcz, Pol.	24	C12	53.16 N	16.28 E
Deutschland see Germany, ctry., Eur.	6	E11	51.00 N	10.00 E
Deutschlandsberg, Aus.	30	D12	46.49 N	15.12 E
Deutsch Wusterhausen, Ger.	182a		52.18 N	13.35 E
Deux-Sèvres, state, Fr.	22	C5	46.30 N	0.20 W
Deva, Rom.	36	D9	45.52 N	22.54 E
Devakottai, India	69	G4	9.56 N	78.49 E
De Valls Bluff, Ar., U.S.	134	C7	34.47 N	91.27 W
Devault, Pa., U.S.	203		40.05 N	75.32 W
Dévaványa, Hung.	36	B7	47.01 N	21.02 E
Devecser, Hung.	36	B4	47.06 N	17.26 E
Deventer, Neth.	20	B15	52.15 N	6.09 E
Deveron, stm., Scot., U.K.	10	D10	57.39 N	2.31 W
Devgadh Bāriya, India	70	G4	22.41 N	73.55 E
De View, Bayou, stm., Ar., U.S.	134	B7	34.47 N	91.17 W
Devīkot, India	70	E3	26.42 N	71.12 E
Devils, stm., Tx., U.S.	136	E6	29.32 N	100.58 W
Devils Brook, stm., N.J., U.S.	194		40.20 N	74.37 W
Devils Canyon, val., Ca., U.S.	198		34.16 N	117.58 W
Devil's Den State Park, p.o.i., Ar., U.S.	130	I3	35.46 N	94.16 W
Devils Hole Rapids, wtfl., N.Y., U.S.	202a		43.08 N	79.03 W
Devils Island see Diable, Île du, i., Fr. Gu.	164	B7	5.17 N	52.35 W
Devils Lake, N.D., U.S.	142	F15	48.06 N	98.52 W
Devils Lake, l., N.D., U.S.	142	F14	48.02 N	98.57 W
Devils Lake Sioux Indian Reservation, ind. res., N.D., U.S.	142	G15	47.53 N	98.50 W
Devils Lake State Park, p.o.i., Wi., U.S.	128	H8	43.24 N	89.44 W
Devils Postpile National Monument, p.o.i., Ca., U.S.	148	F6	37.37 N	119.05 W
Devils Tower National Monument, p.o.i., Wy., U.S.	140	C8	44.36 N	104.43 W
Devin, Blg.	36	H11	41.44 N	24.24 E
Devine, B.C., Can.	144	F8	50.30 N	122.29 W
Devine, Tx., U.S.	136	E9	29.08 N	98.54 W
Devjatiny, Russia	18	G23	60.54 N	36.45 E
Devladove, Ukr.	38	E12	48.05 N	33.43 E
Devli, India	70	F5	25.45 N	75.23 E
De Voe Lake, l., N.J., U.S.	194		40.23 N	74.23 W
Devoll, stm., Alb.	32	D14	40.48 N	19.52 E
Devon, Ab., Can.	144	C17	53.22 N	113.44 W
Devon, Pa., U.S.	203		40.02 N	75.25 W
Devon Island, i., Nu., Can.	106	B14	75.00 N	87.00 W
Devonport, Austl.	99a	n13	41.11 S	146.20 E
Devonshire, De., U.S.	203		39.49 N	75.32 W
Devonshire Plaza, shp. cen., On., Can.	199		42.17 N	83.00 W
Devoto, Arg.	172	E6	31.24 S	62.19 W
Devrek, Tur.	34	B14	41.13 N	31.57 E
Dewakang-lompo, Pulau, i., Indon.	66	F11	5.24 S	118.25 E
Dewar, Ok., U.S.	134	B3	35.26 N	95.56 W
Dewās, India	70	G5	22.57 N	76.03 E
Dewdney, B.C., Can.	144	G8	49.09 N	122.12 W
Dewetsdorp, S. Afr.	90	F8	29.34 S	26.41 E
Dewey, Ok., U.S.	130	H1	36.47 N	95.56 W
Deweyville, Tx., U.S.	136	D14	30.17 N	93.44 W
De Witt, Ar., U.S.	134	C7	34.17 N	91.20 W
De Witt, Ia., U.S.	130	C7	41.49 N	90.31 W
De Witt, Mi., U.S.	124	B1	42.50 N	84.34 W
De Witt, Ne., U.S.	140	G16	40.23 N	96.54 W
De Witt, N.Y., U.S.	124	A9	43.02 N	76.03 W
Dexing, China	58	G7	28.53 N	117.38 E
Dexter, Me., U.S.	122	F7	45.01 N	69.17 W
Dexter, Mi., U.S.	124	B2	42.19 N	83.52 W
Dexter, Mo., U.S.	130	H8	36.48 N	89.57 W
Dexter, N.M., U.S.	138	H4	33.11 N	104.22 W
Dexter, N.Y., U.S.	126	D13	44.00 N	76.02 W
Dexterity Fiord, b., Nu., Can.	110	A16	71.13 N	73.11 W
Deyang, China	52	E5	31.08 N	104.23 E
Dey-Dey, Lake, l., Austl.	96	E6	29.11 S	131.02 E
Deyhūk, Iran	72	C8	33.17 N	57.30 E
Deyyer, Iran	74	G12	27.50 N	51.55 E
Dez, stm., Iran	74	D11	31.38 N	48.52 E
Dezfūl, Iran	74	D11	32.23 N	48.24 E
Dez Gerd, Iran	74	E12	30.45 N	51.57 E
Dezhou, China	58	C7	37.26 N	116.17 E
Dežneva, mys, c., Russia	50	C27	66.07 N	169.41 W
Dezong, China	70	B13	32.05 N	90.17 E
Dháfni, Grc.	185c		38.01 N	23.38 E
Dhafnion Monastery, rel., Grc.	185c		38.01 N	23.38 E
Dhahran see Az-Zahrān, Sau. Ar.	72	D6	26.18 N	50.08 E
Dhaka (Dacca), Bngl.	70	G13	23.43 N	90.25 E
Dhaka, state, Bngl.	70	F13	24.15 N	90.15 E
Dhakuria Lake, l., India	190b		22.31 N	88.22 E
Dháli, Cyp.	76	C4	35.01 N	33.25 E
Dhamār, Yemen	72	G5	14.33 N	44.23 E
Dhāmpur, India	70	D7	29.19 N	78.31 E
Dhamtari, India	70	H8	20.42 N	81.33 E
Dhanbād, India	70	G11	23.47 N	86.26 E
Dhandhuka, India	70	G3	22.23 N	71.58 E
Dhangadhī, Nepal	70	D8	28.41 N	80.36 E
D'Hanis, Tx., U.S.	136	E8	29.19 N	99.16 W
Dhankuta, Nepal	70	E11	26.58 N	87.18 E
Dhansar, India	190c		19.07 N	73.05 E
Dhānyahānā, India	190b		22.48 N	88.11 E
Dhār, India	70	G5	22.36 N	75.18 E
Dharān, Nepal	70	E11	26.48 N	87.16 E
Dharangaon, India	70	H5	21.00 N	75.16 E
Dhārāpuram, India	69	F3	10.43 N	77.32 E
Dharmābād, India	69	B3	18.53 N	77.50 E
Dharmapuri, India	69	E4	12.08 N	78.10 E
Dharmavaram, India	69	D3	14.25 N	77.42 E
Dharmjaygarh, India	70	G9	22.27 N	83.13 E
Dharmshāla, India	70	B6	32.12 N	76.19 E
Dhaulpur, India	70	E6	26.41 N	77.52 E
Dhawalāgiri, mtn., Nepal	70	D9	28.42 N	83.30 E
Dhenkānāl, India	70	H10	20.40 N	85.36 E
Dherinia, Cyp.	76	C4	35.03 N	33.57 E
Dhērmi, rel., Alb.	32	D13	40.08 N	19.42 E
Dhī Qār, state, Iraq	74	E10	31.00 N	46.15 E
Dhofar see Zufar, reg., Oman	72	F7	17.01 N	54.06 E
Dhokra, India	190b		22.40 N	88.34 E
Dholka, India	70	G4	22.43 N	72.26 E
Dhone, India	69	D3	15.23 N	77.53 E
Dhoomadheere, Som.	86	D8	1.48 N	41.11 E
Dhorāji, India	70	H3	21.44 N	70.26 E
Dhrāngadhra, India	70	G3	22.59 N	71.27 E
Dhrol, India	70	G3	22.33 N	70.25 E
Dhuburi, India	70	E13	26.01 N	89.58 E
Dhulāgarh, India	190b		22.35 N	88.11 E
Dhule, India	70	H5	20.54 N	74.46 E
Dhulia see Dhule, India	70	H5	20.54 N	74.46 E
Dhuliān, India	70	F12	24.41 N	87.58 E
Dhūlsirās, ngh., India	190a		28.33 N	77.02 E
Dhünn-Stausee, res., Ger.	181		51.05 N	7.16 E
Dhupgāri, India	70	E12	26.35 N	89.00 E
Dhutumkhar, stm., India	190c		18.54 N	73.00 E
Dhusamarreeb, Som.	86	C9	5.31 N	46.24 E
Día, i., Grc.	34	H8	35.27 N	25.13 E
Diable, Île du, i., Fr. Gu.	164	B7	5.17 N	52.35 W
Diable, Pointe du, c., Mart.	159c	k7	14.45 N	60.52 W
Diables, Morne aux, vol., Dom.	159c	i6	15.37 N	61.27 W
Diablo, Canyon, val., Az., U.S.	150	H5	35.03 N	111.04 W
Diablo, Mount, mtn., Ca., U.S.	148	F4	37.53 N	121.55 W
Diablo, Pico del, mtn., Mex.	120	F5	30.59 N	115.45 W
Diablo, Sierra, plat., Tx., U.S.	136	C2	31.30 N	105.30 W
Diablo, Sierra del, mts., Mex.	136	G3	27.20 N	104.05 W
Diablo Range, mts., Ca., U.S.	148	F4	37.00 N	121.20 W
Diablotins, Morne, vol., Dom.	159c	j6	15.30 N	61.24 W
Diaca, Moz.	88	C6	11.31 S	39.56 E
Diadema, mun., Braz.	205b		23.42 S	46.36 W
Diafarabé, Mali	84	G4	14.10 N	5.02 W
Diagonal, Ia., U.S.	130	D3	40.48 N	94.21 W
Diakove, Ukr.	38	F18	47.56 N	39.07 E
Dialakoto, Sen.	84	G2	13.17 N	13.16 W
Diamant, Pointe du, c., Mart.	159c	l6	14.27 N	61.03 W
Diamante, Arg.	172	F7	32.04 S	60.38 W
Diamante, stm., Arg.	172	G4	34.27 S	66.44 W
Diamantina, Braz.	170	J4	18.14 S	43.36 W
Diamantina, stm., Austl.	98	E2	26.58 S	138.49 E
Diamantina Lakes, Austl.	98	D3	23.45 S	141.08 E
Diamantino, Braz.	166	B5	14.25 S	56.27 W
Diamond, Mo., U.S.	130	G3	36.59 N	94.19 W
Diamond Brook, stm., N.J., U.S.	194		40.56 N	74.08 W
Diamond Creek, Austl.	192b		37.41 S	145.09 E
Diamond Harbour, India	70	G12	22.12 N	88.12 E
Diamond Hill Reservoir, res., R.I., U.S.	201		42.00 N	71.24 W
Diamond Hill State Park, p.o.i., R.I., U.S.	201		42.00 N	71.26 W
Diamond Islets, is., Austl.	98	A8	17.25 S	150.58 E
Diamond Lake, Il., U.S.	196		42.15 N	88.00 W
Diamond Lake, l., Il., U.S.	196		42.15 N	88.00 W
Diamond Lake, l., Or., U.S.	146	G4	43.10 N	122.09 W
Diamond Peak, mtn., Id., U.S.	146	F13	44.09 N	113.05 W
Diamond Peak, mtn., Or., U.S.	146	G4	43.33 N	122.09 W
Diamond Peak, mtn., Wa., U.S.	146	D9	46.07 N	117.32 W
Diamondville, Wy., U.S.	150	B6	41.46 N	110.31 W
Diana, Baie see Diana Bay, b., Can.	110	C16	60.55 N	69.52 W
Diana Bay, b., Can.	110	C16	60.55 N	69.52 W
Dianalund, Den.	16	L9	55.32 N	11.29 E
Dianbai, China	58	K4	21.30 N	111.00 E
Dian Chi, l., China	58	G5	24.50 N	102.42 E
Dianjiang, China	58	F2	30.19 N	107.20 E
Dianópolis, Braz.	170	F2	11.37 S	46.49 W
Diapaga, Burkina	84	G5	12.04 N	1.47 E
Diaz, Ar., U.S.	134	B7	35.38 N	91.15 W
Diaz Point, c., Nmb.	90	E2	26.39 S	15.06 E
Dibai, India	70	D7	28.12 N	78.15 E
Dibaya, D.R.C.	86	F4	6.29 S	22.56 E
Dibaya-Lubwe, D.R.C.	86	E3	4.09 S	19.52 E
Dibeng, S. Afr.	90	E6	27.35 S	22.53 E
D'Iberville, Ms., U.S.	134	G10	30.25 N	88.53 W
d' Iberville, Mont see Caubvick, Mount, mtn., Can.	108	F13	58.53 N	63.43 W
Dibete, Bots.	90	C8	23.45 S	26.27 E
Diboll, Tx., U.S.	136	C13	31.10 N	94.47 W
Dibrugarh, India	62	C7	27.28 N	94.54 E
Dichāon Kalān, ngh., India	190a		28.39 N	76.59 E
Dickelsbach, stm., Ger.	181		51.24 N	6.45 E
Dickens, Tx., U.S.	138	H8	33.37 N	100.50 W
Dickinson, N.D., U.S.	140	A10	46.52 N	102.47 W
Dickinson, Tx., U.S.	136	E12	29.27 N	95.03 W
Dickinson Island, i., Mi., U.S.	199		42.37 N	82.38 W
Dickson, Ok., U.S.	138	G12	34.10 N	96.59 W
Dickson, Tn., U.S.	130	H10	36.04 N	87.22 W
Dicle see Tigris, stm., Asia	74	B7	30.59 N	47.26 E
Didao, China	52	B11	45.21 N	130.49 E
Didsbury, Ab., Can.	144	E16	51.39 N	114.09 W
Didsbury, ngh., Eng., U.K.	180		53.25 N	2.14 W
Dīdwāna, India	70	E5	27.24 N	74.34 E
Didymóteicho, Grc.	34	B9	41.21 N	26.30 E
Die, Fr.	22	E11	44.45 N	5.22 E
Die Aue, reg., Ger.	181		51.40 N	6.35 E
Die Berg, mtn., S. Afr.	90	D10	25.12 S	30.09 E
Diébougou, Burkina	84	G4	10.57 N	3.15 W
Dieburg, Ger.	24	G4	49.54 N	8.50 E
Dieciocho de Julio, Ur.	172	F11	33.41 S	53.33 W
Diedersdorf, Ger.	182a		52.20 N	13.21 E
Die Erpe, stm., Ger.	182a		52.27 N	13.38 E
Diefenbaker, Lake, res., Sk., Can.	142	C7	51.00 N	106.55 W
Diego de Almagro, Chile	172	C2	26.24 S	70.02 W
Diego de Almagro, Isla, i., Chile	166	J1	51.27 S	75.10 W
Diego de Ocampo, Pico, mtn., Dom. Rep.	156	C12	19.35 N	70.45 W
Diégo-Suarez see Antsirañana, Madag.	88	C8	12.16 S	49.17 E
Die Haard, reg., Ger.	181		51.41 N	7.15 E
Diéma, Mali	84	G3	14.32 N	9.12 W
Diemel, stm., Ger.	20	C17	51.38 N	9.26 E
Diemuchuoke, China	70	B7	32.41 N	79.27 E
Dien Bien, Viet.	64	B6	21.22 N	103.00 E
Dien Bien Phu see Dien Bien, Viet.	64	B6	21.22 N	103.00 E
Dien Khanh, Viet.	64	F9	12.14 N	109.05 E
Diepensee, Ger.	182a		52.22 N	13.31 E
Diepholz, Ger.	24	D4	52.36 N	8.22 E
Dieppe, N.B., Can.	122	D12	46.06 N	64.43 W
Dieppe, Fr.	20	E10	49.55 N	1.05 E
Dieppe Bay Town, St. K./N.	159a	c2	17.25 N	62.48 W
Dierks, Ar., U.S.	134	C4	34.07 N	94.02 W
Di'er Songhua, stm., China	54	B6	45.25 N	124.39 E
Diessem, ngh., Ger.	181		51.20 N	6.35 E
Diest, Bel.	20	D14	50.59 N	5.03 E
Dietrich, Id., U.S.	146	H12	42.54 N	114.15 W
Dieulefit, Fr.	22	E11	44.31 N	5.03 E
Dieuze, Fr.	20	F15	48.48 N	6.43 E
Dievenišķės, Lith.	26	F8	54.11 N	25.37 E
Dievenow see Dziwnów, Pol.	24	B10	54.01 N	14.46 E
Diez de Octubre, Mex.	154	C6	24.43 N	104.38 W
Dif, Kenya	86	D8	0.59 N	40.57 E
Diffa, Niger	84	G7	13.19 N	12.36 E
Differdange, Lux.	20	E14	49.31 N	5.54 E
Difficult Run, stm., Va., U.S.	202c		38.58 N	77.14 W
Dīg, India	70	E6	27.28 N	77.19 E
Digambar Jain Temple, rel., India	190b		22.36 N	88.23 E
Digba, D.R.C.	86	D5	4.22 N	25.46 E
Digboi, India	62	C8	27.23 N	95.38 E
Digby, N.S., Can.	122	F11	44.37 N	65.45 W
Digby Neck, pen., N.S., Can.	122	F10	44.28 N	66.05 W
Digges Islands, is., Nu., Can.	110	C15	62.35 N	77.50 W
Diggle, Eng., U.K.	180		53.34 N	1.59 W
Dighode, India	190c		18.54 N	73.02 E
Dighra, India	190b		22.47 N	88.32 E
Dighton, Ks., U.S.	138	C8	38.28 N	100.28 W
Dijla, Wādī, val., Egypt	191c		29.58 N	31.18 E
Diglūr, India	69	B3	18.32 N	77.35 E
Digmoor, Eng., U.K.	180		53.32 N	2.45 W
Digne-les-Bains, Fr.	22	E12	44.05 N	6.14 E
Digoin, Fr.	22	C9	46.29 N	3.59 E
Digos, Phil.	68	G5	6.45 N	125.20 E
Digra, India	190b		22.50 N	88.20 E
Digras, India	70	H6	20.06 N	77.43 E
Digri, Pak.	70	F2	25.09 N	69.06 E
Digul, stm., Indon.	60	G10	7.10 S	138.40 E
Dihtiari, Ukr.	38	C11	50.34 N	32.46 E
Diinsor, Som.	86	D8	2.25 N	42.57 E
Dijlah see Tigris, stm., Asia	74	E10	30.59 N	47.26 E
Dijon, Fr.	20	G14	47.19 N	5.02 E
Dik, Chad	82	F3	9.57 N	17.31 E
Dikaja, Russia	26	A22	59.14 N	39.30 E
Dike, Ia., U.S.	130	B5	42.27 N	92.37 W
Dikhil, Dji.	82	E8	11.05 N	42.22 E
Dikili, Tur.	34	D9	39.04 N	26.53 E
Dikirnis, Egypt	76	G2	31.04 N	31.35 E
Dikli, Lat.	26	C8	57.35 N	25.06 E
Dikodougou, C. Iv.	84	H3	9.03 N	5.46 W
Diksmuide, Bel.	20	C11	51.02 N	2.52 E
Dikson, Russia	50	B5	73.30 N	80.32 E
Díkti, mtn., Grc.	34	H8	35.08 N	25.30 E
Dikwa, Nig.	84	G7	12.02 N	13.56 E
Dīla, Eth.	82	F7	6.18 N	38.14 E
Dilek Milli Parkı, p.o.i., Tur.	34	F10	37.45 N	27.16 E
Dilerpur, India	190b		22.51 N	88.10 E
Dili, Indon.	60	G8	8.34 S	125.35 E
Di Linh, Viet.	64	G9	11.35 N	108.03 E
Dill City, Ok., U.S.	138	F9	35.16 N	99.09 W
Dillenburg, Ger.	24	F4	50.44 N	8.17 E
Diller, Ne., U.S.	138	A12	40.06 N	96.58 W
Dilley, Tx., U.S.	136	F8	28.40 N	99.09 W
Dilling, Sudan	82	E5	12.01 N	29.39 E
Dillingen an der Donau, Ger.	24	H6	48.34 N	10.30 E
Dillingham, Ak., U.S.	109	E8	59.02 N	158.28 W
Dillon, Co., U.S.	138	B2	39.36 N	106.05 W
Dillon, Mt., U.S.	146	E14	45.12 N	112.38 W
Dillon, S.C., U.S.	132	B6	34.25 N	79.22 W
Dillon Lake, l., Sk., Can.	124	D3	55.45 N	109.30 W
Dillon Lake, l., Oh., U.S.	126	H7	40.01 N	82.07 W
Dillon Mountain, mtn., N.M., U.S.	150	J8	33.51 N	108.48 W
Dillon State Park, p.o.i., Oh., U.S.	124	D3	40.03 N	82.08 W
Dillwyn, Va., U.S.	124	G7	37.32 N	78.27 W
Dilolo, D.R.C.	86	G4	10.41 S	22.20 E
Dílos, hist., Grc.	34	F8	37.23 N	25.16 E
Dilworth, Mn., U.S.	142	H17	46.52 N	96.42 W
Dilworthtown, Pa., U.S.	203		39.54 N	75.34 W
Dimāpur, India	62	C7	25.54 N	93.43 E
Dimashq (Damascus), Syria	76	E7	33.30 N	36.18 E
Dimashq, state, Syria	76	E7	33.30 N	37.00 E
Dimbelenge, D.R.C.	86	F4	5.33 S	23.06 E
Dimbokro, C. Iv.	84	H4	6.39 N	4.42 W
Dimboola, Austl.	98	K4	36.27 S	142.01 E
Dimbulah, Austl.	98	A5	17.07 S	145.07 E
Dime Box, Tx., U.S.	136	D11	30.20 N	96.49 W
Dimitrovgrad, Blg.	36	G12	42.03 N	25.37 E
Dimitrovgrad, Russia	40	D16	54.13 N	49.36 E
Dimitrovgrad, Yugo.	36	G9	43.01 N	22.48 E
Dimitrovo see Pernik, Blg.	36	G10	42.37 N	23.02 E
Dimitsána, Grc.	34	F4	37.36 N	22.03 E
Dimlang, mtn., Nig.	84	H7	8.24 N	11.47 E
Dimmitt, Tx., U.S.	138	G6	34.33 N	102.19 W
Dimona, Isr.	76	G6	31.03 N	35.01 E
Dinagat, Phil.	68	E5	9.57 N	125.36 E
Dinagat Island, i., Phil.	68	E5	10.12 N	125.35 E
Dinājpur, Bngl.	70	F12	25.38 N	88.38 E
Dinan, Fr.	20	F6	48.27 N	2.03 W
Dinant, Bel.	20	D13	50.15 N	4.55 E
Dinar, Tur.	34	E13	38.04 N	30.10 E
Dinara Planina see Dinaric Alps, mts., Eur.	30	G13	43.55 N	16.37 E
Dinard, Fr.	20	F6	48.38 N	2.03 W
Dinaric Alps (Dinara Planina), mts., Eur.	30	G13	43.55 N	16.37 E
Dinariche, Alpi see Dinaric Alps, mts., Eur.	30	G13	43.55 N	16.37 E
Dīndārpur, ngh., India	190a		28.36 N	76.59 E
Dindi, stm., India	69	C4	16.21 N	79.12 E
Dindigul, India	69	F4	10.21 N	77.59 E
Dindori, India	70	G8	22.56 N	81.05 E
Dineksaray, Tur.	76	A3	37.23 N	32.37 E
Dingalan Bay, b., Phil.	68	C3	15.18 N	121.25 E
Ding'an, China	58	L4	19.42 N	110.19 E
Dingbian, China	58	C2	37.36 N	107.35 E
Dingbianji, China	58	C3	36.30 N	108.49 E
Dinggyê, China	70	D11	28.34 N	86.37 E
Dinghai, China	58	F9	30.00 N	122.05 E
Dingkouzhen, China	58	A2	39.55 N	106.39 E
Dingle, Ire.	10	I2	52.08 N	10.16 W
Dingle, Swe.	16	I9	58.33 N	11.33 E
Dingle, ngh., Eng., U.K.	180		53.23 N	2.57 W
Dingle Bay, b., Ire.	10	I2	52.05 N	10.15 W
Dingley, Austl.	192b		37.58 S	145.07 E
Dingnan, China	58	I6	24.46 N	115.01 E
Dingo, Austl.	98	D7	23.39 S	149.20 E
Dingolfing, Ger.	24	H8	48.37 N	12.30 E
Dingshuzhen, China	58	F8	31.16 N	119.48 E
Dingtao, China	58	D6	35.04 N	115.34 E
Dinguiraye, Gui.	84	G2	11.17 N	10.43 W
Dingwall, N.S., Can.	122	D16	46.53 N	60.29 W
Dingwall, Scot., U.K.	10	D8	57.35 N	4.26 W
Dingxian, China	58	B6	38.30 N	114.59 E
Dingxiang, China	58	B5	38.28 N	112.57 E
Dingyuan, China	58	E7	32.31 N	117.40 E
Dinh, Mui, c., Viet.	64	G9	11.21 N	109.01 E
Dinhāta, India	70	E12	26.07 N	89.28 E
Dinh Hoa, Viet.	64	B7	21.55 N	105.38 E
Dinh Lap, Viet.	64	B8	21.32 N	107.06 E
Dinkel, stm., Eur.	20	C16	52.30 N	6.58 E
Dinkelsbühl, Ger.	24	G6	49.04 N	10.19 E
Dinnebito Wash, stm., Az., U.S.	150	H5	35.28 N	111.13 W
Dinokwe, Bots.	90	C8	23.23 S	26.41 E
Dinorwic, On., Can.	128	B6	49.41 N	92.30 W
Dinorwic Lake, l., On., Can.	128	B6	49.37 N	92.33 W
Dinosaur, Co., U.S.	150	C8	40.14 N	109.00 W
Dinosaur National Monument, p.o.i., U.S.	150	C8	40.32 N	108.58 W
Dinosaur Provincial Park, p.o.i., Ab., Can.	142	D2	50.46 N	111.30 W
Dinslakener Bruch, Ger.	181		51.35 N	6.43 E
Dinslaken-Schwarze Heide, Flughafen, arpt., Ger.	181		51.37 N	6.51 E
Dinsmore, Sk., Can.	142	C6	51.20 N	107.26 W
Dinuba, Ca., U.S.	148	G6	36.32 N	119.23 W
Dinwiddie, S. Afr.	191d		26.16 S	28.10 E
Dinwiddie, Va., U.S.	132	G8	37.04 N	77.34 W
Diö, Swe.	16	K12	56.37 N	14.13 E
Dionísio Cerqueira, Braz.	172	C11	26.15 S	53.38 W
Diónysos, Grc.	185c		38.06 N	23.53 E
Diósd, Hung.	182c		47.25 N	18.57 E
Diouloulou, Sen.	84	G1	13.02 N	16.36 W
Dioura, Mali	84	G3	14.50 N	5.15 W
Diourbel, Sen.	84	G1	14.39 N	16.14 W
Dīpālpur, Pak.	70	C4	30.40 N	73.39 E
Dipkarpaz, N. Cyp.	76	C5	35.36 N	34.23 E
Diplo, Pak.	70	F2	24.28 N	69.35 E
Dipolog, Phil.	68	F4	8.35 N	123.21 E
Dippoldiswalde, Ger.	24	F9	50.53 N	13.40 E
Dīr, Pak.	62	A3	35.12 N	71.52 E
Dira, Djebel, mtn., Alg.	28	H14	36.05 N	3.38 E
Diré, Mali	84	F4	16.16 N	3.24 W
Dirē Dawa, Eth.	82	F8	9.35 N	41.51 E
Dirico, Ang.	88	D3	17.59 S	20.46 E
Dirj, Libya	82	A2	30.09 N	10.27 E
Dirk Hartog Island, i., Austl.	96	E2	25.48 S	113.00 E
Dirkou, Niger	84	F7	19.06 N	12.52 E
Dirranbandi, Austl.	98	G7	28.35 S	148.14 E
Dirschau see Tczew, Pol.	24	B14	54.05 N	18.47 E
Dirty Devil, stm., Ut., U.S.	150	E6	37.53 N	110.24 W
Dīsa, India	70	F4	24.15 N	72.11 E
Disappointment, Cape, c., S. Geor.	166	J9	54.53 S	36.07 W
Disappointment, Cape, c., Wa., U.S.	146	D2	46.16 N	124.04 W
Disappointment, Lake, l., Austl.	96	D4	23.30 S	122.50 E
Disappointment Creek, stm., Co., U.S.	150	F8	38.01 N	108.50 W
Disaster Bay, b., Austl.	98	K8	37.17 S	149.58 E
Disautel, Wa., U.S.	146	B7	48.22 N	119.15 W
Disbrow Drain, can., Mi., U.S.	199		42.06 N	83.27 W
Discovery, S. Afr.	191d		26.10 S	27.54 E
Discovery Bay, b., Austl.	98	L3	38.12 S	141.07 E
Discovery Bay, b., China	189d		22.18 N	114.01 E
Discovery Passage, strt., B.C., Can.	144	F5	50.04 N	125.15 W
Dishman, Wa., U.S.	146	C9	47.38 N	117.15 W
Dishna, Egypt	74	G3	26.07 N	32.28 E
Disko, i., Grnld.	108	D15	69.50 N	53.30 W
Disko Bugt, b., Grnld.	108	D15	69.15 N	52.00 W
Disley, Eng., U.K.	180		53.21 N	2.02 W
Disley Tunnel, trans., Eng., U.K.	180		53.22 N	2.03 W
Dismal, stm., Ne., U.S.	140	F12	41.49 N	100.05 W
Disna see Dysna, stm., Eur.	26	E9	55.34 N	28.13 E
Disna see Dzisna, stm., Eur.	26	E9	55.34 N	28.13 E
Disney, Ok., U.S.	130	H2	36.28 N	95.00 W
Dispur, India	70	E13	26.08 N	91.48 E
Disraëli, Qc., Can.	122	E5	45.54 N	71.20 W
Diss, Eng., U.K.	10	I14	52.22 N	1.06 E
Disteln, Ger.	181		51.36 N	7.09 E
District Heights, Md., U.S.	202c		38.51 N	76.53 W
Distrito Capital, state, Col.	168	E4	4.15 N	74.15 W
Distrito Federal, state, Braz.	170	H2	15.45 S	47.45 W
Distrito Federal, state, Mex.	154	F9	19.15 N	99.10 W
Distrito Federal, state, Ven.	168	B8	10.30 N	66.55 W
Dis Ûq, Egypt	76	G1	31.08 N	30.39 E
Dithmarschen, reg., Ger.	24	B4	54.05 N	9.00 E
Ditton, Eng., U.K.	178		51.18 N	0.27 E
Ditton, Eng., U.K.	180		53.22 N	2.45 W
Diu, India	70	H3	20.42 N	70.59 E
Dīva, India	190c		19.09 N	72.59 E
Dīvāndarreh, Iran	74	C10	35.55 N	47.02 E
Dive, India	190c		19.11 N	73.02 E
Dive, can., Fr.	22	B5	47.11 N	0.04 W
Divenskaja, Russia	26	A12	59.11 N	30.01 E
Divernon, Il., U.S.	130	E8	39.33 N	89.40 W
Divignano, Italy	184b		45.40 N	8.36 E
Divinhe, Moz.	90	B12	20.42 S	34.47 E
Divino, Braz.	170	K4	20.37 S	42.09 W
Divinópolis, Braz.	170	K3	20.09 S	44.53 W
Divi Point, c., India	69	D5	15.58 N	81.08 E
Divisor, Serra do, plat., S.A.	164	E3	8.20 S	73.30 W
Divnoe, Russia	40	I13	45.54 N	43.21 E
Divnogorsk, Russia	48	C16	55.56 N	92.24 E

Name	Page	Map Ref.	Latitude	Longitude
Divo, C. Iv.	84	H3	5.50 N	5.22 W
Divodar, India	70	F3	24.07 N	71.46 E
Divriği, Tur.	42	F8	39.22 N	38.07 E
Dīwāl Qol, Afg.	70	A1	34.18 N	67.56 E
Dix, Ne., U.S.	140	F9	41.14 N	103.29 W
Dix, stm., Ky., U.S.	130	G13	37.48 N	84.43 W
Dixfield, Me., U.S.	122	F6	44.32 N	70.27 W
Dix Hills, N.Y., U.S.	194		40.49 N	73.22 W
Dixie, On., Can.	193b		43.36 N	79.36 W
Dixie Valley, val., Nv., U.S.	148	D7	39.50 N	117.55 W
Dix Milles, Lac, l., Qc., Can.	126	B12	46.47 N	77.44 W
Dixmoor, Il., U.S.	196		41.38 N	87.40 W
Dixmude see Diksmuide, Bel.	20	C11	51.02 N	2.52 E
Dixon, Ca., U.S.	148	E4	38.26 N	121.49 W
Dixon, Il., U.S.	130	C8	41.50 N	89.28 W
Dixon, Ky., U.S.	130	G10	37.31 N	87.41 W
Dixon, Mo., U.S.	130	G5	37.59 N	92.05 W
Dixon, N.M., U.S.	138	E3	36.12 N	105.54 W
Dixon Entrance, strt., N.A.	109	F13	54.25 N	132.30 W
Dixons Mills, Al., U.S.	134	E11	32.03 N	87.47 W
Dixons Pond, l., N.J., U.S.	194		40.56 N	74.27 W
Diyālá, state, Iraq	74	C9	34.00 N	45.00 E
Diyālá (Sīrvān), stm., Asia	74	C9	33.13 N	44.30 E
Diyarbakır, Tur.	42	F8	37.55 N	40.13 E
Diyarbakır, state, Tur.	42	F8	38.05 N	40.15 E
Dizhou, China	58	J2	23.00 N	106.20 E
Djado, Niger	84	E7	21.01 N	12.18 E
Djado, Plateau du, plat., Niger	84	E7	21.45 N	12.50 E
Djajapura see Jayapura, Indon.	60	F11	2.32 S	140.42 E
Djakarta see Jakarta, Indon.	66	G5	6.10 S	106.50 E
Djakarta see Jakarta, Indon.	187e		6.10 S	106.48 E
Djakovo, ngh., Russia	183b		55.39 N	37.40 E
Djamâa, Alg.	84	C6	33.31 N	5.59 E
Djambala, Congo	86	E2	2.33 S	14.46 E
Djambi see Jambi, Indon.	66	D3	1.36 S	103.36 E
Djanet, Alg.	84	E6	24.28 N	9.29 E
Djaret, Oued, stm., Alg.	84	D5	26.29 N	1.25 E
Djat'kovo, Russia	26	G17	53.35 N	34.21 E
Djédaa, Chad	82	E3	13.30 N	18.35 E
Djedi, Oued, stm., Alg.	84	C5	34.28 N	6.05 E
Djelo-Binza, D.R.C.	191b		4.23 S	15.16 E
Djéma, C.A.R.	86	C5	6.03 N	25.17 E
Djember see Jember, Indon.	66	H8	8.10 S	113.41 E
Djenné, Mali	84	G4	13.53 N	4.33 W
Djenoun, Garet el, mtn., Alg.	84	D6	25.05 N	5.25 E
Djérem, stm., Cam.	86	C2	5.19 N	13.23 E
Djibo, Burkina	84	G4	14.06 N	1.37 W
Djibouti, Dji.	82	E8	11.33 N	43.08 E
Djibouti, ctry., Afr.	82	E8	11.30 N	43.00 E
Djiri, Congo	191b		4.08 S	15.19 E
Djiri, stm., Congo	191b		4.11 S	15.20 E
Djokjakarta see Yogyakarta, Indon.	66	G7	7.47 S	110.22 E
Djoku-Punda, D.R.C.	86	F4	5.27 S	20.59 E
Djolu, D.R.C.	86	D4	0.39 N	22.28 E
Djouari, stm., Congo	191b		4.13 S	15.08 E
Djoué, stm., Congo	191b		4.19 S	15.14 E
Djougou, Benin	84	H5	9.42 N	1.40 E
Djougou see Cavalla, stm., Afr.	84	H3	4.21 N	7.31 W
Djougou see Cavally, stm., Afr.	84	H3	4.21 N	7.31 W
Djoum, Cam.	86	D2	2.40 N	12.40 E
Djourab, Erg du, sand, Chad	82	D3	16.40 N	18.50 E
Djugu, D.R.C.	86	D6	1.58 N	30.29 E
Djúpivogur, Ice.	12a	k32	64.38 N	14.17 W
Djupsvatnet, l., Nor.	16	G5	60.48 N	8.00 E
Djurås, Swe.	16	G13	60.33 N	15.07 E
Djursholm, Swe.	16	H16	59.24 N	18.04 E
Djurtjuli, Russia	40	D19	55.29 N	54.52 E
Dmitrija Lapteva, proliv, strt., Russia	50	B16	73.00 N	142.00 E
Dmitrivka, Ukr.	38	H13	45.28 N	35.03 E
Dmitrov, Russia	26	D20	56.20 N	37.31 E
Dmitrovsk-Orlovskij, Russia	26	H18	52.30 N	35.08 E
Dmukhailivka, Ukr.	38	D13	49.03 N	34.45 E
Dmytrivka, Ukr.	38	C11	50.56 N	32.58 E
Dmytrivka, Ukr.	38	E18	48.55 N	39.09 E
Dmytrivka, Ukr.	38	E11	48.47 N	32.43 E
Dmytrivka, Ukr.	38	G15	46.50 N	36.34 E
Dnepr see Dnieper, stm., Eur.	40	D8	46.31 N	32.21 E
Dnepropetrovsk see Dnipropetrovs'k, Ukr.	38	E14	48.28 N	34.57 E
Dneprovskoe, Russia	26	E16	55.39 N	33.54 E
Dnepr Upland see Prydniprovs'ka vysochyna, plat., Ukr.	38	E9	49.00 N	32.00 E
Dnestr see Dniester, stm., Eur.	24	G19	46.19 N	30.16 E
Dnieper (Dnepr) (Dnipro) (Dnjapro), stm., Eur.	40	H8	46.31 N	32.21 E
Dniester (Dnister), stm., Eur.	24	G19	46.19 N	30.16 E
Dnipro see Dnieper, stm., Eur.	40	H8	46.31 N	32.21 E
Dniprodzerzhyns'k, Ukr.	38	E13	48.29 N	34.40 E
Dniprodzerzhyns'ke vodoskhovyshche, res., Ukr.	38	E12	48.48 N	34.13 E
Dnipropetrovs'k, Ukr.	38	E14	48.28 N	34.57 E
Dnipropetrovs'k, co., Ukr.	38	E14	48.30 N	35.00 E
Dniprovka, Ukr.	38	F13	47.25 N	34.36 E
Dniprovs'kyi lyman, est., Ukr.	38	G10	46.35 N	31.55 E
Dnister see Dniester, stm., Eur.	24	G19	46.19 N	30.16 E
Dnistrovs'ke vodoskhovyshche, res., Ukr.	38	E5	48.29 N	26.43 E
Dnistrovs'kyi lyman, l., Ukr.	38	G8	46.13 N	30.21 E
Dnjapro see Dnieper, stm., Eur.	40	E7	46.31 N	32.21 E
Dnjaproŭska Buhski, kanal, can., Bela.	26	H8	52.01 N	25.33 E
Dno, Russia	26	C12	57.49 N	29.58 E
Do, Lac, l., Mali	84	F4	15.54 N	2.45 W
Dôa, Moz.	88	D5	16.37 S	34.40 E
Doaktown, N.B., Can.	122	D10	46.33 N	66.09 W
Doangdoangan-Besar, Pulau, i., Indon.	66	F10	5.23 S	117.56 E
Doba, Chad	82	F3	8.39 N	16.51 E
Dobbiaco, Italy	30	D9	46.43 N	12.13 E
Dobbins Air Force Base, mil., Ga., U.S.	134	D14	33.54 N	84.30 W
Dobczyce, Pol.	26	G16	49.53 N	20.06 E
Dobele, Lat.	26	D6	56.37 N	23.17 E
Döbeln, Ger.	24	E9	51.07 N	13.06 E
Doberai, Jazirah (Doberai Peninsula), pen., Indon.	60	F9	1.30 S	132.30 E
Doberai Peninsula see Doberai, Jazirah, pen., Indon.	60	F9	1.30 S	132.30 E
Döberitz, Ger.	182a		52.33 N	13.03 E
Dobiegniew, Pol.	24	C12	52.58 N	15.46 E
Döbling, ngh., Aus.	182b		48.15 N	16.22 E
Dobo, Indon.	60	G9	5.45 S	134.13 E
Doboj, Bos.	36	E5	44.44 N	18.05 E
Dobra, Pol.	24	E14	51.54 N	18.37 E
Dobra, Pol.	24	C11	53.35 N	15.18 E
Dobre Miasto, Pol.	24	B16	53.59 N	20.24 E
Dobrianka, Ukr.	38	A10	52.03 N	31.11 E
Dobrianka, Ukr.	38	E9	48.21 N	30.54 E
Dobrič, Blg.	36	F14	43.34 N	27.49 E
Dobříš, Czech Rep.	24	G10	49.47 N	14.11 E
Dobrjanka, Russia	40	B20	58.28 N	56.25 E
Dobrodzień, Pol.	24	F14	50.44 N	18.26 E
Dobroe, Russia	26	C15	57.05 N	32.00 E
Dobroe, Russia	40	E11	52.51 N	39.49 E
Dobrogea see Dobruja, hist. reg., Eur.	36	E15	44.00 N	28.00 E
Dobromyl', Ukr.	38	D1	49.34 N	22.46 E
Dobropillia, Ukr.	38	E16	48.28 N	37.05 E
Dobroteasa, Rom.	36	E11	44.47 N	24.23 E
Dobrotvir, Ukr.	38	C3	50.14 N	24.22 E
Dobrovelychkivka, Ukr.	38	E10	48.23 N	31.10 E
Dobrovillia, Ukr.	38	E15	48.41 N	36.37 E
Dobrovol'sk, Russia	26	F5	54.46 N	22.30 E
Dobrudža see Dobruja, hist. reg., Eur.	36	E15	44.00 N	28.00 E
Dobrudžansko plato, plat., Blg.	36	F14	43.28 N	27.54 E
Dobruja, hist. reg., Eur.	36	E15	44.00 N	28.00 E
Dobruš, Bela.	26	H14	52.25 N	31.19 E
Dobruška, Czech Rep.	24	F12	50.17 N	16.08 E
Dobrzany, Pol.	24	C11	53.21 N	15.26 E
Dobrzyń nad Wisłą, Pol.	24	D15	52.38 N	19.19 E
Dobšiná, Slvk.	24	H16	48.49 N	20.23 E
Dobson, N.C., U.S.	124	H5	36.23 N	80.43 W
Dobzha, China	70	D12	28.28 N	88.14 E
Doce, stm., Braz.	170	J5	19.39 S	39.48 W
Dock Junction, Ga., U.S.	132	E4	31.13 N	81.30 W
Dockweiler Beach State Park, p.o.i., Ca., U.S.	198		33.55 N	118.26 W
Doctor Arroyo, Mex.	154	D8	23.41 N	100.11 W
Doctor Cecilio Báez, Para.	172	B9	24.59 S	56.18 W
Doctor Coss, Mex.	136	I8	25.55 N	99.10 W
Doctor González, Mex.	136	I8	25.51 N	99.56 W
Dod Ballāpur, India	69	E3	13.18 N	77.32 E
Doddridge, Ar., U.S.	134	D5	33.05 N	93.54 W
Dodecanese see Dodekanisoy, is., Grc.	34	G9	36.30 N	27.00 E
Dodekanisoy (Dodecanese), is., Grc.	34	G9	36.30 N	27.00 E
Dodge, Ne., U.S.	140	F16	41.43 N	96.52 W
Dodge Brothers State Park Number 08, p.o.i., Mi., U.S.	199		42.36 N	83.01 W
Dodge Brothers State Park Number 04, p.o.i., Mi., U.S.	199		42.37 N	83.22 W
Dodge Center, Mn., U.S.	128	G5	44.01 N	92.52 W
Dodge City, Ks., U.S.	138	D9	37.45 N	100.01 W
Dodge Park, Md., U.S.	202c		38.56 N	76.53 W
Dodger Stadium, p.o.i., Ca., U.S.	198		34.04 N	118.14 W
Dodgeville, Wi., U.S.	130	B7	42.57 N	90.07 W
Dodman Point, c., Eng., U.K.	10	K8	50.13 N	4.48 W
Dodoma, Tan.	86	F7	6.11 S	35.45 E
Dodoni, hist., Grc.	34	D3	39.34 N	20.47 E
Dodsland, Sk., Can.	142	C5	51.48 N	108.49 W
Dodson, La., U.S.	134	E6	32.04 N	92.40 W
Dodson, Mt., U.S.	142	F5	48.22 N	108.06 W
Dodson, Tx., U.S.	138	G8	34.46 N	100.02 W
Dodurga, Tur.	34	D12	39.48 N	29.55 E
Doerun, Ga., U.S.	132	E2	31.19 N	83.55 W
Doetinchem, Neth.	20	C15	51.58 N	6.17 E
Dog, stm., On., Can.	128	B9	48.49 N	89.33 W
Doğāchia, India	190b		22.58 N	88.31 E
Dogai Coring, l., China	52	E2	34.34 N	88.59 E
Doğanbey, Tur.	34	E9	38.04 N	26.52 E
Doğanbey, Tur.	76	A2	37.47 N	31.53 E
Doğanhisar, Tur.	34	E14	38.09 N	31.41 E
Doğankent, Tur.	76	B6	36.51 N	35.20 E
Dog Creek, B.C., Can.	144	E8	51.35 N	122.16 W
Dog Creek, stm., B.C., Can.	144	E9	51.34 N	122.17 W
Dog Creek, stm., Mt., U.S.	146	C17	47.44 N	109.37 W
Dog Ear Creek, stm., S.D., U.S.	140	D12	43.41 N	100.00 W
Dog Island, i., Fl., U.S.	134	H14	29.48 N	84.35 W
Dog Islands, is., Br. Vir. Is.	158b	e9	18.29 N	64.28 W
Dog Lake, l., Mb., Can.	142	C15	51.02 N	98.30 W
Dog Lake, l., On., Can.	128	C9	48.46 N	89.32 W
Dogliani, Italy	30	F4	44.31 N	7.56 E
Dōgo, i., Japan	56	C6	36.15 N	133.16 E
Do Gonbadān, Iran	74	E12	30.21 N	50.47 E
Dogondoutchi, Niger	84	G5	13.38 N	4.02 E
Dogpound Creek, stm., Ab., Can.	144	E16	51.49 N	114.21 W
Dogs, Isle of, i., Eng., U.K.	178		51.29 N	0.01 W
Doğubayazıt, Tur.	42	F10	39.33 N	44.04 E
Dogueraoua, Niger	84	G6	13.57 N	5.35 E
Doğu Karadeniz Dağları, mts., Tur.	72	A5	40.30 N	40.30 E
Doha see Ad-Dawḥah, Qatar	74	H12	25.17 N	51.32 E
Dohhi, India	70	F10	24.31 N	84.54 E
Dohrgaul, Ger.	181		51.06 N	7.27 E
Dohrighāt, India	70	E9	26.15 N	83.30 E
Doi, Kinh, can., Viet.	187c		10.43 N	106.37 E
Doilungdêqên, China	62	C6	29.47 N	90.46 E
Doiran, Lake, l., Eur.	34	B5	41.13 N	22.44 E
Doïránis, Límni see Doiran, Lake, l., Eur.	34	B5	41.13 N	22.44 E
Doiras, Embalse de, res., Spain	28	A4	43.17 N	6.50 W
Dois Irmãos, Pico, mtn., Braz.	205a		22.59 S	43.14 W
Dois Irmãos de Goiás, Braz.	170	E1	9.15 S	49.04 W
Doi Suthep-Pui National Park, p.o.i., Thai.	64	C4	18.50 N	98.50 E
Dōjō, Japan	186		35.51 N	139.37 E
Dōjō, ngh., Japan	188		34.52 N	135.14 E
Dojransko Ezero see Doiran, Lake, l., Eur.	34	B5	41.13 N	22.44 E
Doka, Indon.	60	G9	6.35 S	134.15 E
Dokka, Nor.	16	G8	60.50 N	10.05 E
Dokka, stm., Nor.	16	F8	60.49 N	10.04 E
Dokkum, Neth.	20	A14	53.19 N	6.00 E
Dokkumer Ee, stm., Neth.	20	A14	53.21 N	6.10 E
Dokšicy see Dokšycy, Bela.	26	F10	54.53 N	27.46 E
Doksy, Czech Rep.	24	F10	50.34 N	14.39 E
Dokšycy, Bela.	26	F10	54.53 N	27.46 E
Dokuchaievs'k, Ukr.	38	F16	47.44 N	37.40 E
Doland, S.D., U.S.	140	C14	44.52 N	98.06 W
Dolayoba, Tur.	185b		40.54 N	29.15 E
Dolbeau, Qc., Can.	122	B4	48.53 N	72.13 W
Dol-de-Bretagne, Fr.	20	F7	48.33 N	1.45 W
Dole, Fr.	20	G14	47.06 N	5.29 E
Dolega, Pan.	156	H6	8.34 N	82.25 W
Dolgaja, kosa, spit, Russia	40	H10	46.41 N	37.43 E
Dolgellau, Wales, U.K.	10	I9	52.44 N	3.53 W
Dolgeville, N.Y., U.S.	126	E15	43.06 N	74.47 W
Dolgij Most, Russia	40	C17	56.45 N	96.48 E
Dolgoe, Russia	40	E10	52.03 N	37.32 E
Dolgorukovo, Russia	26	H21	52.19 N	38.21 E
Dolgoščele, Russia	12	C20	66.02 N	43.27 E
Dolianova, Italy	32	E3	39.21 N	9.09 E
Dolinnyj, Kaz.	40	F18	51.16 N	52.11 E
Dolinsk, Russia	50	G17	47.19 N	142.48 E
Dolisie see Loubomo, Congo	86	E2	4.11 S	12.40 E
Dolj, state, Rom.	36	E10	44.15 N	23.45 E
Dollard, b., Eur.	20	A16	53.17 N	7.10 E
Dollart see Dollard, b., Eur.	20	A16	53.17 N	7.10 E
Dolmabahçe Palace, bldg., Tur.	185b		41.02 N	29.00 E
Dolmativka, Ukr.	38	G11	46.13 N	32.27 E
Dolni Dăbnik, Blg.	36	F11	43.23 N	24.24 E
Dolni Lom, Blg.	36	F9	43.30 N	22.46 E
Dolnośląskie, state, Pol.	24	E12	51.00 N	16.30 E
Dolný Kubín, Slvk.	24	G15	49.12 N	19.18 E
Dolohmwar, mtn., Micron.	100d	m11	6.52 N	158.13 E
Dolomites see Dolomiti, mts., Italy	30	D8	46.20 N	11.58 E
Dolomiti, mts., Italy	30	D8	46.20 N	11.58 E
Doloon, Mong.	52	C6	44.24 N	105.18 E
Dolores, Arg.	172	H9	36.19 S	57.40 W
Dolores, Col.	168	F4	3.33 N	74.54 W
Dolores, Guat.	156	D3	16.31 N	89.25 W
Dolores, Mex.	136	H6	26.20 N	101.29 W
Dolores, Co., U.S.	150	F8	37.28 N	108.30 W
Dolores, Ur.	172	F8	33.32 S	58.12 W
Dolores, Ven.	168	C7	8.18 N	69.34 W
Dolores, stm., U.S.	150	E7	38.49 N	109.17 W
Dolores, Mission, rel., Ca., U.S.	200		37.46 N	122.26 W
Dolores Hidalgo, Mex.	154	E8	21.09 N	100.56 W
Dolphin, Cape, c., Falk. Is.	166	J5	51.14 S	58.57 W
Dolphin and Union Strait, strt., Nu., Can.	110	B7	69.05 N	114.45 W
Dolphin Head, mtn., Jam.	158d	i12	18.22 N	78.10 W
Dolsk, Pol.	24	D13	51.59 N	17.06 E
Dolyna, Ukr.	38	E3	48.58 N	24.01 E
Dolyns'ka, Ukr.	38	E11	48.06 N	32.46 E
Dolžanskaja, Russia	38	G16	46.38 N	37.48 E
Dolzhak, Ukr.	38	E5	48.40 N	26.33 E
Dolžicy, Russia	26	C12	58.00 N	29.51 E
Dolžicy, Russia	26	B12	58.30 N	29.06 E
Domaha, Russia	26	H17	52.29 N	34.58 E
Domaine, Pointe du, c., Qc., Can.	193a		45.23 N	73.54 W
Domaneab, bldg., Nauru	100f	q16	0.31 S	166.55 E
Domaniči, Russia	26	G16	53.02 N	33.25 E
Domanivka, Ukr.	38	F9	47.37 N	30.59 E
Domažlice, Czech Rep.	24	G8	49.26 N	12.55 E
Dombaj-Ul'gen, gora, mtn.	42	D9	43.14 N	41.41 E
Dombås, Nor.	16	E6	62.04 N	9.07 E
Dombe, Moz.	90	B11	19.58 S	33.25 E
Dombes, reg., Fr.	22	D11	46.00 N	5.03 E
Dombóvár, Hung.	36	C5	46.22 N	18.08 E
Dombrád, Hung.	36	A8	48.13 N	21.55 E
Dom Cavati, Braz.	170	J4	19.21 S	42.05 W
Dôme, Puy de, mtn., Fr.	22	D8	45.47 N	2.58 E
Dome Creek, B.C., Can.	144	C9	53.44 N	121.00 W
Domeyko, Chile	172	D2	28.57 S	70.54 W
Domeyko, Cordillera, mts., Chile	166	D3	24.44 S	69.09 W
Domfront, Fr.	20	F8	48.35 N	0.38 W
Domiciano Ribeiro, Braz.	170	I2	16.55 S	47.43 W
Domingo M. Irala, Para.	172	B10	25.52 S	54.45 W
Domingos Martins, Braz.	170	K5	20.24 S	40.39 W
Dominguez, Ca., U.S.	198		33.50 N	118.13 W
Dominguez Channel, strt., Ca., U.S.	198		33.47 N	118.15 E
Dominguez Hills, hills, Ca., U.S.	198		33.52 N	118.14 W
Dominica, ctry., N.A.	159c	j6	15.30 N	61.20 W
Dominica Channel see Martinique Passage, strt., N.A.	159c	k6	15.10 N	61.15 W
Dominicana, República see Dominican Republic, ctry., N.A.	152	D10	19.00 N	70.40 W
Dominican Republic, ctry., N.A.	152	D10	19.00 N	70.40 W
Dominica Passage, strt., N.A.	159c	i5	15.45 N	61.30 W
Dominion, N.S., Can.	122	D17	46.13 N	59.59 W
Dominion, Cape, c., Nu., Can.	110	B15	66.08 N	74.27 W
Dominion City, Mb., Can.	142	E16	49.09 N	97.10 W
Dominique, Canal de la see Martinique Passage, strt., N.A.	159c	k6	15.10 N	61.15 W
Domitilla, Catacombe di, hist., Italy	185a		41.52 N	12.31 E
Dom Joaquim, Braz.	170	J4	18.57 S	43.16 W
Domneşti, Rom.	36	E12	44.24 N	25.55 E
Domo, Eth.	82	F9	7.51 N	46.51 E
Domodedovo, Russia	26	E20	55.26 N	37.46 E
Domodossola, Italy	30	D5	46.06 N	8.17 E
Domont, Fr.	179		49.02 N	2.20 E
Dom Pedrito, Braz.	172	E10	30.58 S	54.39 W
Dom Pedro, Braz.	170	C3	4.29 S	44.27 W
Dom Pedro II, Estação, trans., Braz.	205a		23.54 S	43.12 W
Dompu, Indon.	66	H11	8.32 S	118.27 E
Domremy, Sk., Can.	142	B8	52.47 N	105.43 W
Domsjö, Swe.	16	D16	63.15 N	18.44 E
Domuyo, Volcán, vol., Arg.	172	H2	36.38 S	70.26 W
Dom Yai, stm., Thai.	64	E7	15.18 N	105.09 E
Don, stm., India	69	C2	16.16 N	76.27 E
Don, stm., Laos	64	E7	15.07 N	105.47 E
Don, stm., Russia	40	H11	47.05 N	39.14 E
Don, stm., Eng., U.K.	180		53.47 N	2.14 W
Don, stm., Scot., U.K.	10	D10	57.10 N	2.05 W
Don, East Branch, stm., On., Can.	193b		43.43 N	79.20 W
Don, West Branch, stm., On., Can.	193b		43.43 N	79.20 W
Dona Ana, N.M., U.S.	150	K10	32.22 N	106.49 W
Donadeu, Arg.	172	C6	26.43 S	62.42 W
Donaghadee, N. Ire., U.K.	10	G7	54.38 N	5.32 W
Donald, Austl.	98	K4	36.22 S	142.58 E
Donalda, Ab., Can.	144	D18	52.34 N	112.34 W
Donaldson, Ar., U.S.	134	C6	34.14 N	92.55 W
Donaldson Crossroads, Pa., U.S.	197b		40.16 N	80.07 W
Donaldson Dam, res., S. Afr.	191d		26.17 S	27.41 E
Donaldsonville, La., U.S.	134	G7	30.05 N	90.59 W
Donalsonville, Ga., U.S.	134	F14	31.02 N	84.52 W
Doñana, Parque Nacional de, p.o.i., Spain	28	H4	37.00 N	6.30 W
Donau see Danube, stm., Eur.	8	G14	45.23 N	29.35 E
Donaueschingen, Ger.	24	I4	47.57 N	8.29 E
Donaufeld, ngh., Aus.	182b		48.15 N	16.25 E
Donaukanal, can., Aus.	182b		48.10 N	16.30 E
Donaupark, p.o.i., Aus.	182b		48.14 N	16.25 E
Donaustadt, ngh., Aus.	182b		48.13 N	16.30 E
Donauturm, bldg., Aus.	182b		48.14 N	16.25 E
Donauwörth, Ger.	24	H6	48.43 N	10.46 E
Don Benito, Spain	28	F5	38.57 N	5.52 W
Dönberg, ngh., Ger.	181		51.18 N	7.10 E
Doncaster, Austl.	192b		37.47 S	145.08 E
Doncaster, On., Can.	193b		43.48 N	79.25 W
Doncaster, Eng., U.K.	10	H11	53.31 N	1.08 W
Doncaster East, Austl.	192b		37.47 S	145.10 E
Dondaicha, India	70	H5	21.19 N	74.33 E
Dondo, Ang.	88	B1	9.40 S	14.25 E
Dondo, Moz.	90	A12	19.35 S	34.43 E
Dondo, Teluk, b., Indon.	66	C12	0.54 N	120.32 E
Dondra Head, c., Sri L.	69	I5	5.55 N	80.35 E
Donduşeni, Mol.	38	E6	48.14 N	27.36 E
Doneck, Russia	40	G11	48.21 N	40.01 E
Doneck see Donets'k, Ukr.	38	F16	47.59 N	37.47 E
Donegal, Ire.	10	G4	54.39 N	8.06 W
Donegal, state, Ire.	10	G4	54.50 N	8.00 W
Donegal Bay, b., Ire.	10	G4	54.30 N	8.30 W
Doneraile, S.C., U.S.	132	B6	34.19 N	79.53 W
Donets'k, Ukr.	38	F16	47.59 N	37.47 E
Donets'k, co., Ukr.	38	E16	48.00 N	37.30 E
Dong, stm., China	58	J6	23.05 N	113.59 E
Dong'an, China	52	B11	47.21 N	134.12 E
Dong'an, China	58	H4	26.17 N	111.07 E
Dongara, Austl.	96	E3	29.14 S	114.58 E
Dongargarh, India	70	H8	21.11 N	80.46 E
Dongchuan, China	52	F5	26.10 N	103.08 E
Dongfang, China	58	L3	19.05 N	108.38 E
Dongfeng, China	52	C10	42.40 N	125.32 E
Donggala, Indon.	66	D11	0.40 S	119.44 E
Donggi Cona, l., China	52	D4	37.07 N	96.55 E
Donggong Shan, mts., China	58	H8	27.36 N	119.26 E
Dongguan, China	58	J5	23.02 N	113.44 E
Dongguang, China	58	C7	37.51 N	116.30 E
Dong Ha, Viet.	64	D8	16.49 N	107.08 E
Dong Hai, Viet.	64	F9	12.32 N	109.11 E
Dong Hai see East China Sea, s., Asia	52	F9	30.00 N	126.00 E
Donghai Dao, i., China	58	K4	21.02 N	110.25 E
Dong Hoi, Viet.	64	D8	17.28 N	106.37 E
Dong Hu, l., China	70	B10	32.10 N	84.43 E
Dongjielang, China	58	F6	31.01 N	115.56 E
Dongjingcheng, China	54	B8	44.06 N	129.13 E
Dongkalang, Indon.	66	C12	0.08 N	120.07 E
Donglan, China	58	I2	24.40 N	107.16 E
Dongli, China	58	K4	20.48 N	110.22 E
Dongliao, stm., China	54	C5	42.59 N	123.32 E
Dong Nai, stm., Viet.	64	G8	10.44 N	106.45 E
Dong Nhien, Rach, stm., Viet.	187c		10.49 N	106.46 E
Dongning, China	52	C11	44.03 N	131.07 E
Dongo, Ang.	88	C2	14.33 S	15.47 E
Dongo, D.R.C.	86	D3	2.43 N	18.24 E
Dongola see Dunqulah, Sudan	82	D5	19.10 N	30.28 E
Dongou, Congo	86	D3	2.00 N	18.03 E
Dongping, China	58	K5	21.43 N	112.15 E
Dongping, China	58	D7	35.54 N	116.18 E
Dong San Shen (Manchuria), hist. reg., China	52	B10	47.00 N	125.00 E
Dongshaer, China	70	D12	28.41 N	89.09 E
Dongshan, China	58	L4	19.46 N	110.14 E
Dongshan Dao, i., China	58	J7	23.40 N	117.25 E
Dongsheng, China	58	B4	39.48 N	109.59 E
Dongshi, China	189a		39.49 N	116.34 E
Dongtai, China	58	E9	32.50 N	120.18 E
Dongting Hu, l., China	58	G5	29.20 N	112.54 E
Dong Trieu, Viet.	64	B8	21.05 N	106.31 E
Dong Van, Viet.	64	A7	23.16 N	105.21 E
Dongwangfu, China	54	B4	44.46 N	120.43 E
Dongwe, stm., Zam.	88	C3	13.59 S	23.52 E
Dongxi, China	58	G2	28.47 N	106.39 E
Dongxiang, China	58	G7	28.14 N	116.35 E
Dongyang, China	58	G9	29.16 N	120.14 E
Dongzhang, China	58	I8	25.42 N	119.17 E
Dongzhi, China	58	F7	30.06 N	117.01 E
Donie, Tx., U.S.	136	C11	31.27 N	96.13 W
Doniphan, Mo., U.S.	130	H7	36.37 N	90.49 W
Doniphan, Ne., U.S.	140	G14	40.46 N	98.22 W
Donja Stubica, Cro.	30	D13	45.59 N	15.55 E
Donjek, stm., Yk., Can.	110	C3	62.35 N	140.00 W
Donji Vakuf, Bos.	36	E4	44.09 N	17.23 E
Donkey Creek, stm., Wy., U.S.	140	C7	44.17 N	104.58 W
Donkey Town, Eng., U.K.	178		51.20 N	0.39 W
Don Martín, Mex.	136	G7	27.32 N	100.36 W
Don Mills, ngh., On., Can.	193b		43.44 N	79.20 W
Don Mills Centre, shp. cen., On., Can.	193b		43.44 N	79.21 W
Donna, Tx., U.S.	136	H9	26.10 N	98.03 W
Dønna, i., Nor.	14	F3	66.05 N	12.31 E
Donnacona, Qc., Can.	122	D5	46.39 N	71.46 W
Donnelly, Id., U.S.	146	F10	44.44 N	116.05 W
Donner, La., U.S.	134	H7	29.41 N	90.56 W
Donner Pass, p., Ca., U.S.	148	D5	39.18 N	120.20 W
Donner und Blitzen, stm., Or., U.S.	146	G8	43.17 N	118.52 W
Donnybrook, Austl.	96	F3	33.35 S	115.48 E
Donnybrook, S. Afr.	90	F9	29.55 S	29.52 E
Donora, Pa., U.S.	124	D6	40.10 N	79.51 W
Donostia, Spain	6	G8	43.18 N	1.59 W
Donoússa, i., Grc.	34	F8	37.06 N	25.49 E
Don Pedro Reservoir, res., Ca., U.S.	148	F5	37.43 N	120.23 W
Don Peninsula, pen., B.C., Can.	144	D2	52.30 N	128.10 W
Donskaja grjada see Don Upland, hills, Eur.	38	D19	49.39 N	40.22 E
Dons'ke, Ukr.	38	F16	47.31 N	37.33 E
Donskoe, Russia	40	I12	45.19 N	41.57 E
Donskoe belogor'e, plat., Russia	38	C18	50.30 N	39.45 E
Donskoj, Russia	26	G21	53.58 N	38.19 E
Don Torcuato, Arg.	206		34.30 S	58.38 W
Don Torcuato, Aeródromo, arpt., Arg.	206		34.30 S	58.36 W
Don Upland (Donskaja grjada), hills, Eur.	38	D19	49.45 N	40.13 E
Donuzlav, ozero, l., Ukr.	38	H12	45.17 N	33.04 E
Doolow, Som.	86	D8	4.09 N	42.05 E
Doon, Ia., U.S.	128	H2	43.17 N	96.13 W
Doon, stm., Scot., U.K.	10	F8	55.26 N	4.39 W
Doonerak, Mount, mtn., Ak., U.S.	109	C9	67.56 N	150.37 W
Doonside, Austl.	192a		33.46 S	150.52 E
Doornik see Tournai, Bel.	20	D12	50.36 N	3.23 E
Door Peninsula, pen., Wi., U.S.	126	D2	44.55 N	87.20 W
Dopping Brook, stm., Ma., U.S.	201		42.12 N	71.23 W
Dor, Isr.	76	F5	32.37 N	34.55 E
Dora, Al., U.S.	134	D11	33.44 N	87.05 W
Dora, Lake, l., Austl.	96	D4	22.05 S	122.55 E
Dora Baltea, stm., Italy	30	E4	45.10 N	8.05 E
Dorado, P.R.	158a	b3	18.28 N	66.15 W
Dora Riparia, stm., Italy	30	E4	45.05 N	7.43 E
Doraville, Ga., U.S.	134	D14	33.55 N	84.15 W
Dorbod, China	52	B9	46.50 N	124.24 E
Dorcheat, Bayou, stm., U.S.	134	D5	32.14 N	93.25 W
Dorchester, N.B., Can.	122	E12	45.53 N	64.30 W
Dorchester, On., Can.	126	F8	42.59 N	81.05 W
Dorchester, Eng., U.K.	10	K10	50.43 N	2.26 W
Dorchester, Ne., U.S.	140	G15	40.38 N	97.07 W
Dorchester, Wi., U.S.	128	F8	45.00 N	90.19 W
Dorchester, ngh., Ma., U.S.	201		42.17 N	71.04 W
Dorchester, Cape, c., Nu., Can.	110	B15	65.27 N	77.26 W
Dorchester Bay, b., Ma., U.S.	201		42.19 N	71.02 W
Dorchester Estates, Md., U.S.	202c		38.47 N	76.55 W
Dorchester Heights National Historic Site, hist., Ma., U.S.	201		42.20 N	71.03 W
Dordabis, Nmb.	90	C3	22.57 S	17.40 E
Dordogne, state, Fr.	22	D6	45.10 N	0.45 E
Dordogne, stm., Fr.	22	E5	45.02 N	0.34 W
Dordrecht, Neth.	20	C13	51.48 N	4.40 E
Dordrecht, S. Afr.	90	G8	31.22 S	27.02 E
Dore, stm., Fr.	22	D9	46.00 N	3.28 E
Dore Lake, l., Sk., Can.	110	E9	54.46 N	107.17 W
Dorena, Or., U.S.	146	G4	43.41 N	122.50 W
Dores do Indaiá, Braz.	170	J3	19.27 S	45.36 W
Dorfen, Ger.	24	H8	48.16 N	12.09 E
Dorgali, Italy	32	D3	40.17 N	9.34 E
Dörgön nuur, l., Mong.	52	B3	47.40 N	93.30 E
Dori, Burkina	84	G4	14.02 N	0.02 W
Doring, stm., S. Afr.	90	G4	31.52 S	18.39 E
Doringkop, mtn., S. Afr.	191d		26.15 S	27.50 E
Dormans, Fr.	20	E12	49.04 N	3.38 E
Dormont, Pa., U.S.	197b		40.23 N	80.02 W
Dornap, ngh., Ger.	181		51.15 N	7.04 E
Dornbach, ngh., Aus.	182b		48.14 N	16.18 E
Dornbirn, Aus.	30	C6	47.24 N	9.44 E
Dorney, Eng., U.K.	178		51.30 N	0.40 W
Dornoch, Scot., U.K.	10	D8	57.52 N	4.02 W
Dornoch Firth, b., Scot., U.K.	10	D9	57.53 N	4.00 W
Doro, Mali	84	F4	16.09 N	0.51 W
Dorog, Hung.	36	B5	47.43 N	18.43 E
Dorogobuž, Russia	26	F16	54.55 N	33.18 E
Dorohoi, Rom.	36	A13	47.57 N	26.24 E
Dorohovo, Russia	26	E19	55.33 N	36.25 E
Dorokempo, Indon.	66	H11	8.33 S	118.15 E
Dorotea, Swe.	16	C14	64.15 N	16.24 E
Dorotockeys Run, stm., U.S.	194		40.59 N	73.58 W
Dorpat see Tartu, Est.	26	B9	58.22 N	26.42 E
Dorrance, Ks., U.S.	138	C10	38.50 N	98.34 W
Dorre Island, i., Austl.	96	E2	25.07 S	113.05 E
Dorrigo, Austl.	98	H9	30.20 S	152.42 E
Dorris, Ca., U.S.	148	B4	41.58 N	121.54 W
Dorsale, mts., Tun.	32	H3	36.07 N	9.48 E
Dorset Peak, mtn., Vt., U.S.	122	G3	43.18 N	73.01 W
Dorsey Run, stm., Md., U.S.	202b		39.11 N	76.48 W
Dorseyville, Pa., U.S.	197b		40.35 N	79.53 W
Dorsten, Ger.	20	C15	51.39 N	6.58 E
Dorstfeld, ngh., Ger.	181		51.31 N	7.25 E
Dort see Dordrecht, Neth.	20	C13	51.48 N	4.40 E
Dortmund, Ger.	24	E3	51.31 N	7.28 E
Dortmund, Ger.	181		51.31 N	7.28 E
Dortmunder Rieselfelder, reg., Ger.	181		51.39 N	7.25 E
Dortmund-Wickede, Flughafen, arpt., Ger.	181		51.32 N	7.35 E
Dorton, Ky., U.S.	124	G3	37.16 N	82.35 W
Dörtyol, Tur.	42	G7	36.51 N	36.13 E
Do Rūd, Iran	74	D11	33.28 N	49.04 E
Doruma, D.R.C.	86	D5	4.43 N	27.40 E
Dorval, Île, i., Qc., Can.	193a		45.26 N	73.45 W
Dorval Gardens Centre, shp. cen., Qc., Can.	193a		45.27 N	73.44 W
Dos, Canal Numero, can., Arg.	172	H9	36.23 S	56.56 W
Dosatuj, Russia	52	A8	50.21 N	118.33 E
Dos Bahías, Cabo, c., Arg.	166	H3	44.55 S	65.33 W
Dos Bocas, P.R.	158a	b2	18.20 N	66.40 W
Dos Bocas, Lago, res., P.R.	158a	b2	18.19 N	66.40 W
Döşemealtı, Tur.	34	F13	37.02 N	30.34 E
Dos Hermanas, Spain	28	G4	37.17 N	5.55 W
Doshisha University, educ., Japan	188		35.02 N	135.46 E
Do Son, Viet.	64	B8	20.42 N	106.47 E
Dosoris Island, pen., N.Y., U.S.	194		40.53 N	73.38 W
Dosoris Pond, l., N.Y., U.S.	194		40.54 N	73.38 W
Dos Palos, Ca., U.S.	148	G5	36.59 N	120.37 W
Dos Pos, Neth. Ant.	158g	p23	12.13 N	68.19 W
Dos Quebradas, Col.	168	E4	4.51 N	75.40 W
Dos Reyes, Punta, c., Chile	172	B2	24.32 S	70.34 W
Dossin Great Lakes Museum, bldg., Mi., U.S.	199		42.20 N	82.59 W
Dosso, Niger	84	G5	13.02 N	3.12 E
Dossor, Kaz.	48	E8	47.31 N	52.59 E
Dothan, Al., U.S.	134	F13	31.13 N	85.23 W
Dotnuva, Lith.	26	E6	55.21 N	23.54 E
Dou, stm., China	58	B8	39.13 N	118.03 E
Douai, Fr.	20	D11	50.22 N	3.05 E
Douala, Cam.	86	D1	4.02 N	9.42 E
Douarnenez, Fr.	20	F4	48.05 N	4.20 W
Doublé, Pointe, c., Guad.	159c	h7	16.20 N	61.00 W
Double Island Point, c., Austl.	98	E9	25.56 S	153.11 E
Double Point, c., Austl.	98	A6	17.39 S	146.07 E
Double Springs, Al., U.S.	134	C11	34.08 N	87.24 W
Doubletop Peak, mtn., Wy., U.S.	146	G16	43.21 N	110.17 W
Doubs, state, Fr.	20	G15	47.10 N	6.25 E
Doubs, stm., Eur.	20	H14	46.54 N	5.02 E
Doubtful Sound, strt., N.Z.	102	G2	45.15 S	166.52 E
Doubtless Bay, b., N.Z.	102	B5	34.55 S	173.27 E
Douentza, Mali	84	F4	15.00 N	2.57 W
Dougga, hist., Tun.	32	H3	36.25 N	9.13 E
Douglas, Mb., Can.	142	E14	49.54 N	99.42 W
Douglas, I. of Man	10	G8	54.09 N	4.29 W
Douglas, S. Afr.	90	F6	29.03 S	23.46 E
Douglas, Ak., U.S.	109	E13	58.18 N	134.27 W
Douglas, Az., U.S.	150	L7	31.20 N	109.33 W
Douglas, Ga., U.S.	132	E3	31.30 N	82.51 W
Douglas, N.D., U.S.	142	G12	47.51 N	101.31 W
Douglas, Wy., U.S.	140	E7	42.45 N	105.22 W
Douglas Aircraft Company, sci., Ca., U.S.	198		33.50 N	118.09 W
Douglas Channel, strt., B.C., Can.	144	C1	53.30 N	129.12 W
Douglas Creek, stm., Co., U.S.	150	D8	40.05 N	108.46 W
Douglas Lake, B.C., Can.	144	F10	50.09 N	120.12 W
Douglas Lake, res., Tn., U.S.	124	H2	35.59 N	83.23 W

Name Page Map Ref. Latitude Longitude

Douglas Lake Indian Reserve, ind. res., B.C., Can. 144 F10 50.10 N 120.17 W
Douglas Park, p.o.i., Il., U.S. 196 41.52 N 87.42 W
Douglas Provincial Park, p.o.i., Sk., Can. 142 C7 50.58 N 106.20 W
Douglass, Ks., U.S. 138 D12 37.30 N 96.59 W
Douglass Run, stm., Pa., U.S. 197b 40.15 N 79.48 W
Douglas Station see Douglas, Mb., Can. 142 E14 49.54 N 99.42 W
Douglasville, Ga., U.S. 134 D14 33.45 N 84.39 W
Doullens, Fr. 20 D11 50.09 N 2.20 E
Doumé, Cam. 86 D2 4.14 N 13.26 E
Dourada, Serra, plat., Braz. 170 G1 13.10 S 48.34 W
Dourados, Braz. 166 D6 22.13 S 54.48 W
Dourbali, Chad 82 E3 11.48 N 15.51 E
Dourdan, Fr. 20 F11 48.32 N 2.00 E
Douro, stm., Braz. 205a 22.42 S 43.35 W
Douro (Duero), stm., Eur. 28 C2 41.08 N 8.40 W
Dousk, Bela. 26 G13 53.10 N 30.25 E
Douthat State Park, p.o.i., Va., U.S. 124 G6 37.53 N 79.48 W
Douvres, Falaises de, clf., Congo 191b 4.06 S 15.25 E
Douy-la-Ramée, Fr. 179 49.04 N 2.53 E
Douz, Tun. 84 C6 33.22 N 8.59 E
Douze, stm., Fr. 22 F6 43.53 N 0.30 W
Dovadola, Italy 30 F8 44.07 N 11.53 E
Dovbysh, Ukr. 38 C7 50.22 N 28.00 E
Dove, stm., Eng., U.K. 10 I11 52.49 N 1.36 W
Dove Bugt, strt., Grnld. 108 B21 76.30 N 20.00 W
Dove Creek, Co., U.S. 150 F8 37.46 N 108.54 W
Dove Creek, stm., Tx., U.S. 136 C7 31.20 N 100.36 W
Dove Creek, stm., Ut., U.S. 150 B3 41.38 N 113.15 W
Dove Holes, Eng., U.K. 180 53.18 N 1.53 W
Dove Holes Tunnel, trans., Eng., U.K. 180 53.18 N 1.53 W
Dover, Austl. 99a o13 43.18 S 147.00 E
Dover, Eng., U.K. 10 J14 51.07 N 1.18 E
Dover, Ar., U.S. 134 B5 35.23 N 93.07 W
Dover, De., U.S. 124 E10 39.09 N 75.31 W
Dover, Id., U.S. 146 B10 48.15 N 116.37 W
Dover, Ma., U.S. 201 42.14 N 71.17 W
Dover, N.H., U.S. 122 G6 43.12 N 70.52 W
Dover, N.J., U.S. 124 D11 40.53 N 74.32 W
Dover, N.C., U.S. 132 A8 35.12 N 77.25 W
Dover, Oh., U.S. 124 D4 40.31 N 81.28 W
Dover, Ok., U.S. 138 E11 35.58 N 97.54 W
Dover, Tn., U.S. 130 H10 36.28 N 87.50 W
Dover, Strait of, strt., Eur. 10 J14 50.58 N 1.30 E
Dover Air Force Base, mil., De., U.S. 124 E10 39.08 N 75.28 W
Dover-Foxcroft, Me., U.S. 122 E7 45.11 N 69.13 W
Dover Heights, Austl. 192a 33.53 S 151.17 E
Dover Hills, N.J., U.S. 194 40.52 N 74.33 W
Dove Stone Reservoir, res., Eng., U.K. 180 53.32 N 1.58 W
Doveton, Austl. 192b 38.00 S 145.14 E
Dovre, Nor. 16 F7 61.59 N 9.15 E
Dovrefjell, mts., Nor. 16 E6 62.06 N 9.25 E
Dovrefjell Nasjonalpark, p.o.i., Nor. 16 E7 62.18 N 9.36 E
Dovzhyk, Ukr. 38 C14 50.11 N 35.57 E
Dowagiac, Mi., U.S. 130 C11 41.58 N 86.06 W
Dowagiac, stm., Mi., U.S. 126 G3 41.50 N 86.15 W
Dow City, Ia., U.S. 130 C2 41.55 N 95.29 W
Dowden Terrace, Va., U.S. 202c 38.50 N 77.08 W
Dowker, Île, i., Qc., Can. 193a 45.24 N 73.54 W
Dowlatābād, Iran 74 F15 28.18 N 56.40 E
Dowling Lake, l., Ab., Can. 144 E19 51.44 N 112.00 W
Downe, ngh., Eng., U.K. 178 51.20 N 0.03 E
Down East, Pa., U.S. 203 40.03 N 75.32 W
Downey, Id., U.S. 146 H14 42.26 N 112.07 W
Downham, Eng., U.K. 178 51.38 N 0.30 E
Down House, hist., Eng., U.K. 178 51.20 N 0.03 E
Downieville, Ca., U.S. 148 D5 39.33 N 120.49 W
Downing, Mo., U.S. 130 D5 40.29 N 92.21 W
Downingtown, Pa., U.S. 124 D10 40.00 N 75.42 W
Downingtown Airport, arpt., Pa., U.S. 203 39.59 N 75.45 W
Downpatrick, N. Ire., U.K. 10 G7 54.19 N 5.43 W
Downpatrick Head, c., Ire. 10 G3 54.19 N 9.20 W
Downs, Ks., U.S. 138 B10 39.30 N 98.32 W
Downs Mountain, mtn., Wy., U.S. 140 D3 43.18 N 109.40 W
Downsview Dells Park, p.o.i., On., Can. 193b 43.44 N 79.30 W
Downsville, N.Y., U.S. 124 B10 42.05 N 74.59 W
Downton, Mount, mtn., B.C., Can. 144 D6 52.42 N 124.51 W
Downton Lake, l., B.C., Can. 144 F7 50.50 N 122.58 W
Downwind Acres Airfield, arpt., Mi., U.S. 199 42.09 N 83.34 W
Dows, Ia., U.S. 130 B4 42.39 N 93.29 W
Dowshī, Afg. 72 B10 35.36 N 68.41 E
Doxáto, Grc. 34 B7 41.05 N 24.13 E
Doyle, Ca., U.S. 148 C5 40.00 N 120.06 W
Doyles, Nf., Can. 122 C17 47.50 N 59.11 W
Doylestown, Oh., U.S. 124 D4 40.58 N 81.41 W
Doylestown, Pa., U.S. 124 D10 40.18 N 75.07 W
Doyline, La., U.S. 134 E5 32.32 N 93.25 W
Dōzen, is., Japan 56 C5 36.05 N 133.05 E
Dozier, Al., U.S. 134 F12 31.29 N 86.22 W
Dozois, Réservoir, res., Qc., Can. 110 F15 47.29 N 77.05 W
Dra, Cap, c., Mor. 84 D2 28.44 N 11.04 W
Dra, Oued, stm., Afr. 84 D2 28.40 N 11.07 W
Dra'a, Hamada du, des., Alg. 84 D3 29.00 N 6.45 W
Draa, Oued see Dra, Oued, stm., Afr. 84 D2 28.40 N 11.07 W
Drabiv, Ukr. 38 D11 49.57 N 32.09 E
Drac, stm., Fr. 30 E2 45.12 N 5.40 E
Dracena, Braz. 166 D6 21.28 S 51.31 W
Drachten, Neth. 20 A15 53.06 N 6.06 E
Dracut, Ma., U.S. 124 B14 42.40 N 71.18 W
Dragalina, Rom. 36 E14 44.25 N 27.20 E
Drăgănești-Olt, Rom. 36 E11 44.09 N 24.32 E
Drăgănești-Vlașca, Rom. 36 E12 44.06 N 25.35 E
Drăgășani, Rom. 36 E11 44.40 N 24.16 E
Drag Lake, l., On., Can. 126 C11 45.05 N 78.24 W
Dragón, Bocas del see Dragons Mouths, strt. 159f s12 10.40 N 61.43 W
Dragonera, Sa, i., Spain 28 E13 39.34 N 2.19 E
Dragons Mouths, strt. 159f s12 10.40 N 61.43 W
Dragoon, Az., U.S. 150 K6 32.01 N 110.02 W
Draguignan, Fr. 22 F12 43.32 N 6.28 E
Drahičyn, Bela. 26 H8 52.11 N 25.09 E
Drain, Or., U.S. 146 G3 43.39 N 123.19 W
Drake, N.D., U.S. 142 G13 47.55 N 100.22 W
Drake, Pasaje de see Drake Passage, strt. 162 K8 58.00 S 70.00 W
Drakensberg, mts., Afr. 90 G8 27.00 S 30.00 E
Drake Passage, strt. 162 K8 58.00 S 70.00 W
Drake Peak, mtn., Or., U.S. 148 A5 42.19 N 120.07 W
Drakesboro, Ky., U.S. 130 G10 37.13 N 87.02 W
Drakes Branch, Va., U.S. 124 H7 36.59 N 78.36 W
Drakes Brook, stm., N.J., U.S. 194 40.49 N 74.43 W
Dráma, Grc. 34 B7 41.09 N 24.09 E
Drammen, Nor. 16 H8 59.44 N 10.13 E
Drang, stm., Asia 64 F8 13.18 N 107.20 E
Drangajökull, ice, Ice. 12a j28 66.11 N 22.15 W
Dranov, Ostrovul, i., Rom. 36 E16 44.52 N 29.16 E
Draper, Ut., U.S. 150 C5 40.34 N 111.52 W
Drapetsóna, Grc. 185c 37.57 N 23.37 E
Drās, India 70 A5 34.25 N 75.45 E
Drau (Drava) (Dráva), stm., Eur. 30 D11 45.32 N 18.55 E
Drava (Drau) (Dráva), stm., Eur. 30 D11 45.32 N 18.55 E
Dráva (Drau) (Drava), stm., Eur. 30 D11 45.32 N 18.55 E
Dravinja, stm., Slvn. 30 D12 46.22 N 15.54 E
Dravograd, Slvn. 30 D12 46.35 N 15.01 E
Dravosburg, Pa., U.S. 197b 40.21 N 79.51 W
Drawno, Pol. 24 C11 53.13 N 15.44 E
Drawsko Pomorskie, Pol. 24 C11 53.31 N 15.49 E
Drayton, N.D., U.S. 128 C1 48.32 N 97.11 W
Drayton, S.C., U.S. 132 B4 34.58 N 81.53 W
Drayton Valley, Ab., Can. 144 C15 53.13 N 114.58 W
Dreikikir, Pap. N. Gui. 101a a3 3.32 S 142.44 E
Drenovec, Blg. 36 F9 43.42 N 22.59 E
Drépano, Ákra, c., Grc. 34 D6 39.56 N 23.55 E
Dresden, On., Can. 126 F7 42.35 N 82.10 W
Dresden, Ger. 24 E9 51.03 N 13.44 E
Dresden, Oh., U.S. 124 D3 40.06 N 82.02 W
Dresden, Tn., U.S. 130 H9 36.17 N 88.42 W
Dresher, Pa., U.S. 203 40.08 N 75.10 W
Drètun', Bela. 26 E12 55.41 N 29.13 E
Dreux, Fr. 20 F10 48.44 N 1.22 E
Drevenack, Ger. 181 51.40 N 6.45 E
Drew, Ms., U.S. 134 D8 33.49 N 90.32 W
Drewer, Ger. 181 51.40 N 7.07 E
Drewitz see Drzewice, Pol. 24 D10 52.36 N 14.36 E
Drewitz, ngh., Ger. 182a 52.22 N 13.08 E
Drews Reservoir, res., Or., U.S. 148 A5 42.10 N 120.40 W
Drew University, educ., N.J., U.S. 194 40.46 N 74.25 W
Drexel Hill, Pa., U.S. 203 39.56 N 75.17 W
Drexel University, educ., Pa., U.S. 203 39.57 N 75.11 W
Drezdenko, Pol. 24 D12 52.53 N 16.02 E
Drienov, Slvk. 24 H17 48.53 N 21.15 E
Driftpile, stm., Ab., Can. 144 A15 55.22 N 115.38 W
Drift Pile River Indian Reserve, ind. res., Ab., Can. 144 A14 55.19 N 116.12 W
Driftwood, B.C., Can. 110 D5 55.49 N 126.25 W
Driftwood, stm., In., U.S. 130 E12 39.11 N 85.56 W
Driftwood Creek, stm., Ne., U.S. 138 A8 40.10 N 100.39 W
Driggs, Id., U.S. 146 G15 43.43 N 111.06 W
Drin, stm., Alb. 32 C13 41.45 N 19.34 E
Drina, stm., Eur. 30 F16 44.53 N 19.21 E
Drinit, Gjiri i, b., Alb. 32 C13 41.45 N 19.28 E
Drinit të Zi (Crni Drim), stm., Eur. 32 C14 42.05 N 20.24 E
Driscoll, Tx., U.S. 136 G10 27.39 N 97.44 W
Driskill Mountain, hill, La., U.S. 134 E6 32.25 N 92.54 W
Drissa (Drysa), stm., Eur. 26 E11 55.47 N 27.55 E
Drisvjaty, ozero see Drūkšiai, l., Eur. 26 E9 55.38 N 26.35 E
Driva, stm., Nor. 16 E7 62.40 N 8.33 E
Drjanovo, Blg. 36 G12 42.56 N 25.27 E
Drniš, Cro. 30 G13 43.51 N 16.09 E
Drøbak, Nor. 16 H8 59.39 N 10.38 E
Drobeta-Turnu Severin, Rom. 36 E9 44.38 N 22.39 E
Drochia, Mol. 38 E6 48.02 N 27.50 E
Drocourt, Fr. 179 49.03 N 1.46 E
Droë Harts, stm., S. Afr. 90 E7 27.34 S 24.42 E
Drogheda, Ire. 10 H6 53.43 N 6.21 W
Drohiczyn, Pol. 24 D18 52.23 N 22.39 E
Drohobych, Ukr. 38 D2 49.21 N 23.31 E
Drohobycz see Drohobych, Ukr. 38 D2 49.21 N 23.31 E
Droichead Átha see Drogheda, Ire. 10 H6 53.43 N 6.21 W
Droichead Nua, Ire. 10 H6 53.11 N 6.48 W
Drôme, state, Fr. 22 E11 44.35 N 5.10 E
Drôme, stm., Fr. 22 E10 44.46 N 4.45 E
Dronero, Italy 30 F4 44.28 N 7.22 E
Dronne, stm., Fr. 22 D6 45.02 N 0.08 W
Dronning Louise Land, reg., Grnld. 108 B20 76.17 N 29.11 W
Dronninglund, Den. 16 J8 57.08 N 10.18 E
Dropt, stm., Fr. 22 E6 44.34 N 0.08 W
Dröschede, Ger. 181 51.22 N 7.39 E
Drosiá, Grc. 185c 38.07 N 23.52 E
Droskovo, Russia 26 H19 52.30 N 37.03 E
Drossen see Ośno Lubuskie, Pol. 24 D10 52.28 N 14.50 E
Droue-sur-Drouette, Fr. 179 48.36 N 1.42 E
Drouette, stm., Fr. 179 48.37 N 1.37 E
Droylsden, Eng., U.K. 180 53.29 N 2.10 W
Druc', stm., Bela. 26 F12 53.04 N 30.02 E
Druid Hill Park, p.o.i., Md., U.S. 202b 39.19 N 76.39 W
Druif, Aruba 158g o19 12.33 N 70.03 W
Druja, Bela. 26 E10 55.47 N 27.27 E
Drūkšiai, l., Eur. 26 E9 55.38 N 26.35 E
Druk-Yul see Bhutan, ctry., Asia 70 E13 27.30 N 90.30 E
Drumheller, Ab., Can. 144 E18 51.27 N 112.41 W
Drummond, Mt., U.S. 146 D13 46.40 N 113.09 W
Drummond, Wi., U.S. 128 E7 46.20 N 91.15 W
Drummond Island, i., Mi., U.S. 126 C6 46.00 N 83.40 W
Drummond Range, mts., Austl. 98 D6 23.30 S 147.15 E
Drummondville, Qc., Can. 122 E4 45.53 N 72.29 W
Drummoyne, Austl. 192a 33.51 S 151.09 E
Drumright, Ok., U.S. 134 A2 35.59 N 96.36 W
Druskininkai, Lith. 26 F7 54.01 N 23.58 E
Družba, Kaz. 48 E14 45.15 N 82.28 E
Družba, Russia 183b 55.53 N 37.45 E
Druzhba see Družba, Kaz. 48 E14 45.15 N 82.28 E
Druzhba, Ukr. 38 A12 52.02 N 33.56 E
Druzhkivka, Ukr. 38 E18 48.37 N 37.32 E
Družina, Russia 50 C18 68.13 N 145.17 E
Družnaja Gorka, Russia 26 A13 59.16 N 30.07 E
Drvar, Bos. 36 E3 44.22 N 16.22 E
Drwęca, stm., Pol. 24 C14 52.59 N 18.41 E
Dry Arm, b., Mt., U.S. 142 G7 47.53 N 106.23 W
Dry Bay, b., Ak., U.S. 109 E12 59.08 N 138.33 W
Dryberry Lake, l., On., Can. 128 B4 49.33 N 93.53 W
Drybin, Bela. 26 F14 54.07 N 31.04 E
Dry Cimarron, stm., U.S. 134 B2 36.54 N 102.58 W
Dry Creek, stm., Ca., U.S. 148 E4 38.13 N 121.24 W
Dry Creek, stm., Ca., U.S. 148 E2 38.35 N 122.51 W
Dry Creek, stm., Ca., U.S. 200 37.22 N 122.23 W
Dry Creek, stm., Or., U.S. 146 G9 43.34 N 117.21 W
Dry Creek, stm., Wy., U.S. 140 D3 43.13 N 108.55 W
Dry Creek, stm., Wy., U.S. 140 C4 44.30 N 108.03 W
Dry Creek Mountain, mtn., Nv., U.S. 148 B9 41.22 N 116.22 W
Dryden, On., Can. 128 B6 49.47 N 92.50 W
Dry Devils, stm., Tx., U.S. 136 E7 29.47 N 100.59 W
Dry Devils, stm., Tx., U.S. 136 D7 30.19 N 100.56 W
Dry Fork, stm., Mo., U.S. 130 G6 37.58 N 91.31 W
Dry Frio, stm., Tx., U.S. 136 E8 29.16 N 99.38 W
Dry Lake, l., N.D., U.S. 142 F15 48.16 N 98.59 W
Dry Prong, La., U.S. 134 F6 31.34 N 92.31 W
Dry Ridge, Ky., U.S. 124 F1 38.40 N 84.35 W
Drysa see Drissa, stm., Eur. 26 E11 55.47 N 27.55 E
Drysdale, stm., Austl. 96 C5 13.59 S 126.55 E
Drysvjaty, vozero see Drūkšiai, l., Eur. 26 E9 55.38 N 26.35 E
Dry Tortugas, is., Fl., U.S. 116 H11 24.37 N 82.55 W
Dry Tortugas National Park, p.o.i., Fl., U.S. 132 L3 24.37 N 82.54 W
Drzewica, Pol. 24 E16 51.27 N 20.29 E
Drzewice, Pol. 24 D10 52.36 N 14.36 E
Dschang, Cam. 86 C1 5.27 N 10.04 E
Du, stm., China 58 E4 32.46 N 110.38 E
Duala see Douala, Cam. 86 D1 4.02 N 9.42 E
Du'an, China 58 I3 24.06 N 108.10 E
Duaringa, Austl. 98 D7 23.43 S 149.40 E
Duarte, Pico, mtn., Dom. Rep. 156 C12 19.02 N 70.59 W
Duartina, Braz. 170 L1 22.24 S 49.25 W
Dubā, Sau. Ar. 74 G4 27.21 N 35.41 E
Dubach, La., U.S. 134 E6 32.41 N 92.39 W
Dubai see Dubayy, U.A.E. 74 H14 25.15 N 55.18 E
Dubăsari, Mol. 38 F8 47.14 N 29.10 E
Dubăsari, Lacul, res., Mol. 38 F8 47.22 N 29.09 E
Dubawnt, stm., Can. 110 C10 64.30 N 100.05 W
Dubawnt Lake, l., Can. 110 C10 63.08 N 101.30 W
Dubayy (Dubai), U.A.E. 74 H14 25.15 N 55.18 E
Dubbo, Austl. 98 I7 32.15 S 148.35 E
Dubenskij, Russia 40 F20 51.27 N 56.38 E
Dubesar' see Dubăsari, Mol. 38 F8 47.14 N 29.10 E
Dubh Artach, r., Scot., U.K. 10 E6 56.08 N 6.40 W
Dubi Bheri, India 190b 22.53 N 88.17 E
Dubica, Cro. 30 E13 45.11 N 16.49 E
Dubki, Russia 183a 60.00 N 30.00 E
Dubki, Russia 183b 55.41 N 37.14 E
Dublin (Baile Átha Cliath), Ire. 10 H6 53.20 N 6.14 W
Dublin, Ga., U.S. 132 D3 32.32 N 82.54 W
Dublin, Tx., U.S. 136 B9 32.05 N 98.20 W
Dublin, Va., U.S. 124 G5 37.06 N 80.41 W
Dublin, state, Ire. 10 H6 53.20 N 6.15 W
Dublin Canyon, val., Ca., U.S. 200 37.42 N 121.59 W
Dubna, Russia 26 F19 54.09 N 36.59 E
Dubna, Russia 26 D20 56.44 N 37.10 E
Dubna, stm., Lat. 26 D9 56.21 N 26.09 E
Dubna, stm., Russia 26 D21 56.47 N 37.14 E
Dubňany, Czech Rep. 24 H12 48.55 N 17.04 E
Dubnica nad Váhom, Slvk. 24 H14 48.58 N 18.11 E
Dubno, Ukr. 38 C4 50.23 N 25.45 E
Dubois, Id., U.S. 146 F14 44.10 N 112.14 W
Dubois, In., U.S. 130 F11 38.26 N 86.48 W
Du Bois, Ne., U.S. 130 D1 40.03 N 96.03 W
Du Bois, Pa., U.S. 124 C7 41.07 N 78.45 W
Dubois, Wy., U.S. 140 D3 43.31 N 109.37 W
Dubossary Reservoir see Dubăsari, Lacul, res., Mol. 38 F8 47.22 N 29.09 E
Dubovaja Rošča, Russia 26 G19 53.11 N 36.05 E
Dubov'iazivka, Ukr. 38 B12 51.08 N 33.22 E
Dubovka, Russia 40 G14 49.03 N 44.49 E
Dubovka, Russia 40 F12 51.26 N 41.25 E
Dubovskoe, Russia 40 H13 47.24 N 42.44 E
Dubovychi, Ukr. 38 B12 51.38 N 33.34 E
Dubovyj Ovrag, Russia 40 G14 48.19 N 44.33 E
Dubrājpur, India 70 G11 23.46 N 87.23 E
Dubréka, Gui. 84 H2 9.48 N 13.29 W
Dubrouna, Bela. 26 F13 54.34 N 30.41 E
Dubrova, Bela. 26 H12 52.25 N 29.58 E
Dubrova, Ukr. 38 B7 51.46 N 28.11 E
Dubrovka, Russia 18 H17 59.51 N 30.56 E
Dubrovka, Russia 26 G16 53.41 N 33.30 E
Dubrovka, Russia 26 A19 59.12 N 36.14 E
Dubrovnik, Cro. 30 H15 42.38 N 18.05 E
Dubrovnoe, Russia 48 C11 57.57 N 69.26 E
Dubrovo, Russia 18 H20 59.50 N 33.32 E
Dubrovytsia, Ukr. 38 B5 51.34 N 26.34 E
Dubuque, Ia., U.S. 130 B7 42.30 N 90.40 W
Dubysa, stm., Lith. 26 E6 55.04 N 23.25 E
Duchang, China 58 G7 29.15 N 116.13 E
Duchesne, Ut., U.S. 150 C6 40.10 N 110.24 W
Duchesne, stm., Ut., U.S. 150 C7 40.05 N 109.41 W
Duchess, Austl. 98 C2 21.21 S 139.53 E
Duck, stm., Austl. 192a 33.50 S 151.02 E
Duck, stm., Tn., U.S. 134 B11 35.56 N 87.56 W
Duck Bay, Mb., Can. 142 B13 52.09 N 100.09 W
Duck Creek, stm., On., Can. 199 42.18 N 82.41 W
Duck Creek, stm., Nv., U.S. 150 D2 40.06 N 114.43 W
Duck Creek, stm., N.D., U.S. 140 A10 46.02 N 102.13 W
Duck Creek, stm., Tx., U.S. 138 H8 33.14 N 100.41 W
Duck Hill, Ms., U.S. 134 D9 33.36 N 89.42 W
Duck Island Harbor, b., N.Y., U.S. 194 40.55 N 73.23 W
Duck Lake, Sk., Can. 142 B7 52.48 N 106.13 W
Duck Lake, l., Mi., U.S. 199 42.40 N 83.35 W
Duck Mountain, mts., Mb., Can. 142 C13 51.35 N 101.00 W
Duck Mountain Provincial Park, p.o.i., Mb., Can. 142 C12 51.36 N 100.55 W
Ducktown, Tn., U.S. 134 B14 35.01 N 84.22 W
Duck Valley Indian Reservation, ind. res., U.S. 148 B10 42.00 N 116.10 W
Ducos, Mart. 159c k7 14.34 N 60.58 W
Duc Tho, Viet. 64 C7 18.32 N 105.34 E
Duda, stm., Col. 168 F4 2.34 N 74.01 W
Dudačkino, Russia 26 A15 59.57 N 32.51 E
Dudchany, Ukr. 38 F12 47.10 N 33.46 E
Dudelange, Lux. 24 G2 49.28 N 6.05 E
Dudergofka, stm., Russia 183a 59.52 N 30.12 E
Duderstadt, Ger. 24 E6 51.31 N 10.15 E
Dudhnai, India 70 E13 25.59 N 90.44 E
Dudinka, Russia 50 C6 69.24 N 86.10 E
Dudley, Eng., U.K. 10 I10 52.30 N 2.05 W
Dudley Pond, l., Ma., U.S. 201 42.20 N 71.22 W
Dudleyville, Az., U.S. 150 K6 32.58 N 110.46 W
Dudna, stm., India 69 B2 19.18 N 76.53 E
Dudorovskij, Russia 26 G18 53.39 N 35.20 E
Dudwa National Park, p.o.i., India 70 D8 28.30 N 80.40 E
Dueré, Braz. 170 F1 11.19 S 49.15 W
Dueré, stm., Braz. 170 F1 11.28 S 48.55 W
Duerna, stm., Spain 28 B4 42.17 N 5.51 W
Duero (Douro), stm., Eur. 28 C2 41.08 N 8.40 W
Due West, S.C., U.S. 132 B3 34.18 N 82.22 W
Duffer Peak, mtn., Nv., U.S. 148 B7 41.40 N 118.44 W
Dufourspitze, mtn., Eur. 30 E4 45.55 N 7.52 E
Dufur, Or., U.S. 146 E5 45.27 N 121.07 W
Duga-Zapadnaja, mys, c., Russia 50 E18 59.09 N 146.00 E
Dugdemona, stm., La., U.S. 134 F6 31.47 N 92.21 W
Dugede, China 70 C13 30.54 N 90.48 E
Dugger, In., U.S. 130 E10 39.04 N 87.15 W
Dugi Otok, i., Cro. 30 F11 43.59 N 15.04 E
Dugna, Russia 26 F19 54.25 N 36.51 E
Dug Pond, l., Ma., U.S. 201 42.17 N 71.22 W
Du Gué, stm., Qc., Can. 110 D16 57.21 N 70.45 W
Dugui Qarag, China 58 B3 39.36 N 108.48 E
Dugway Proving Ground, mil., Ut., U.S. 150 C3 40.10 N 113.15 W
Duhernal Lake, l., N.J., U.S. 194 40.24 N 74.22 W
Duhovščina, Russia 26 E15 55.11 N 32.25 E
Duida, Cerro, mtn., Ven. 168 F9 3.23 N 65.40 W
Duisburg, Ger. 24 E2 51.25 N 6.46 E
Duisburg, Ger. 181 51.25 N 6.46 E
Duissern, ngh., Ger. 181 51.26 N 6.47 E
Duitama, Col. 168 E5 5.50 N 73.02 W
Duiwelskloof, S. Afr. 90 C10 23.41 S 30.08 E
Dujuuma, Som. 86 D8 1.15 N 42.34 E
Dukazi, China 70 C14 30.49 N 92.44 E
Duke, Ok., U.S. 138 G9 34.39 N 99.34 W
Duke of York Bay, b., Nu., Can. 110 B13 65.25 N 84.50 W
Dukes Brook, stm., N.J., U.S. 194 40.33 N 74.37 W
Duk Fadiat, Sudan 82 F6 7.44 N 31.24 E
Dukhān, Qatar 74 H12 25.25 N 50.48 E
Duki, Pak. 70 C2 30.10 N 68.35 E
Dukielska, Przełęcze see Dukla Pass, p., Eur. 24 G17 49.25 N 21.42 E
Dukinfield, Eng., U.K. 180 53.29 N 2.05 W
Dukku, Nig. 84 G7 10.49 N 10.46 E
Dukla, Pol. 24 G17 49.34 N 21.41 E
Dukla Pass, p., Eur. 24 G17 49.25 N 21.42 E
Dukliansky priesmyk see Dukla Pass, p., Eur. 24 G17 49.25 N 21.42 E
Dukou, China 52 F5 26.37 N 101.47 E
Dūkštas, Lith. 26 E9 55.31 N 26.20 E
Dūlāb, ngh., Iran 185d 35.39 N 51.27 E
Dulan, China 52 D4 36.09 N 98.22 E
Dulce, N.M., U.S. 138 E1 36.56 N 106.59 W
Dulce, stm., Arg. 172 D6 30.29 S 62.31 W
Dulce, Golfo, b., C.R. 156 H6 8.32 N 83.14 W
Dul'durga, Russia 50 F11 50.40 N 113.35 E
Dulgalah, stm., Russia 50 C15 67.28 N 133.14 E
Dullstroom, S. Afr. 90 D10 25.27 S 30.06 E
Dülmen, Ger. 20 C16 51.50 N 7.16 E
Dulovka, Russia 26 C11 57.31 N 28.19 E
Dulovo, Blg. 36 F14 43.49 N 27.09 E
Dulq Maghār, Syria 76 B9 36.23 N 38.39 E
Duluth, Ga., U.S. 134 C14 34.00 N 84.08 W
Duluth, Mn., U.S. 128 E6 46.45 N 92.07 W
Dulwich, ngh., Eng., U.K. 178 51.26 N 0.05 W
Dūmā, Leb. 76 D6 34.12 N 35.50 E
Dūmā, Syria 76 E7 33.34 N 36.24 E
Dumaguete, Phil. 68 F4 9.18 N 123.18 E
Dumai, Indon. 66 C2 1.40 N 101.26 E
Dumalag, Phil. 68 E4 11.18 N 122.37 E
Dumali Point, c., Phil. 68 D3 13.06 N 121.32 E
Dumaran Island, i., Phil. 68 E2 10.33 N 119.51 E
Dumaresq, stm., Austl. 98 G8 28.39 S 150.29 E
Dumaring, Indon. 66 C11 1.31 N 118.12 E
Dumas, Ar., U.S. 134 D7 33.53 N 91.29 W
Dumas, Tx., U.S. 138 F7 35.52 N 101.57 W
Dumayr, Syria 76 E7 33.38 N 36.41 E
Dumbarton, Scot., U.K. 10 F8 55.56 N 4.33 W
Dumbarton Bridge, trans., Ca., U.S. 200 37.31 N 122.07 W
Dumbarton Point, c., Ca., U.S. 200 37.30 N 122.06 W
Ďumbier, mtn., Slvk. 24 H15 48.56 N 19.38 E
Dumbrăveni, Rom. 36 C11 46.14 N 24.34 E
Dume, Point, c., Ca., U.S. 148 J7 34.00 N 118.48 W
Dumfries, Scot., U.K. 10 F9 55.04 N 3.37 W
Duminiči, Russia 26 G18 53.55 N 35.08 E
Dumjor, India 190b 22.38 N 88.13 E
Dumka, India 70 F11 24.16 N 87.15 E
Dumlupınar, Tur. 34 E12 38.51 N 29.58 E
Dummar, Syria 76 E7 33.32 N 36.14 E
Dumoine, stm., Qc., Can. 126 B12 46.12 N 77.50 W
Dumoine, Lac, l., Qc., Can. 126 B12 46.53 N 77.54 W
Dumont, Ia., U.S. 130 B4 42.45 N 92.58 W
Dumont, Lac, l., Qc., Can. 126 B13 46.04 N 76.26 W
Dumont d'Urville, sci., Ant. 103 B18 66.35 S 140.00 E
Dümpten, ngh., Ger. 181 51.27 N 6.54 E
Dumpu, Pap. N. Gui. 101a b4 5.52 S 145.42 E
Dumraon, India 70 F10 25.33 N 84.09 E
Dumyât, Masabb (Damietta Mouth), mth., Egypt 76 G2 31.31 N 31.50 E
Duna see Danube, stm., Eur. 8 G14 45.23 N 29.35 E
Dünaburg see Daugavpils, Lat. 26 E9 55.53 N 26.31 E
Dunaharaszti, Hung. 36 B6 47.20 N 19.05 E
Dunai see Danube, stm., Eur. 8 G14 45.23 N 29.35 E
Dunaïvtsi, Ukr. 38 E5 48.53 N 26.52 E
Dunaj, Russia 183a 59.58 N 30.56 E
Dunaj see Danube, stm., Eur. 8 G14 45.23 N 29.35 E
Dunajec, stm., Eur. 24 F16 50.14 N 20.44 E
Dunajská Streda, Slvk. 24 H13 48.00 N 17.35 E
Dunakeszi, Hung. 36 B6 47.38 N 19.08 E
Dunărea see Danube, stm., Eur. 8 G14 45.23 N 29.35 E
Dunărea Veche, Brațul, stm., Rom. 36 E15 45.17 N 27.59 E
Duna-Tisza-csatorna, can., Hung. 182c 47.21 N 19.05 E
Dunaújváros, Hung. 36 C5 46.58 N 18.56 E
Dunav see Danube, stm., Eur. 8 G14 45.23 N 29.35 E
Dunavățu de Sus, Rom. 36 E16 44.58 N 29.13 E
Duna-völgyi-főcsatorna, can., Hung. 36 C6 46.11 N 18.55 E
Dunav-Tisa-Dunav, Kanal, can., Yugo. 36 D6 45.51 N 18.51 E
Dunbar, Scot., U.K. 10 E10 55.59 N 2.30 W
Dunbarton, On., Can. 193b 43.49 N 79.06 W
Dunblane, Sk., Can. 142 C6 51.12 N 106.52 W
Dunblane, Scot., U.K. 10 E8 56.11 N 3.57 W
Duncan, B.C., Can. 144 H7 48.46 N 123.41 W
Duncan, Az., U.S. 150 K7 32.43 N 109.06 W
Duncan, Ms., U.S. 134 C8 34.02 N 90.44 W
Duncan, Ok., U.S. 138 G11 34.30 N 97.57 W
Duncan, stm., B.C., Can. 144 F13 50.11 N 116.57 W
Duncan Lake, res., B.C., Can. 144 F13 50.22 N 116.57 W
Duncannon, Pa., U.S. 124 D8 40.23 N 77.01 W
Duncan Passage, strt., India 62 F7 10.58 N 92.25 E
Duncans, Jam. 158d i13 18.28 N 77.32 W
Duncansby Head, c., Scot., U.K. 10 C9 58.38 N 3.01 W
Duncans Creek, stm., Austl. 192a 33.53 S 150.39 E
Dundaga, Lat. 26 C5 57.30 N 22.20 E
Dundāhera, India 190a 28.38 N 77.26 E
Dundalk, On., Can. 126 D9 44.09 N 80.23 W
Dundalk (Dún Dealgan), Ire. 10 G6 54.00 N 6.24 W
Dundalk, Md., U.S. 124 E9 39.15 N 76.31 W
Dundalk Bay, b., Ire. 10 H6 53.57 N 6.17 W
Dundas, Austl. 192a 33.48 S 151.02 E
Dundas, On., Can. 126 E9 43.15 N 79.57 W
Dundas, Mn., U.S. 128 G5 44.25 N 93.12 W
Dundas, Lake, l., Austl. 96 F4 32.35 S 121.50 E
Dundas Peninsula, pen., Can. 109 B17 74.50 N 111.30 W
Dundas Strait, strt., Austl. 96 B6 11.20 S 131.35 E
Dún Dealgan see Dundalk, Ire. 10 G6 54.00 N 6.24 W
Dundee, S. Afr. 90 F10 28.09 S 30.14 E
Dundee, Scot., U.K. 10 E10 56.28 N 2.59 W
Dundee, Fl., U.S. 132 H4 28.01 N 81.37 W
Dundee, Mi., U.S. 124 C2 41.57 N 83.39 W
Dundee Creek, b., Md., U.S. 202b 39.21 N 76.22 W
Dunderlandsdalen, val., Nor. 14 F5 66.25 N 14.45 E
Dundoo, Austl. 98 F5 27.38 S 144.39 E
Dundret, mtn., Swe. 14 E11 67.06 N 20.30 E
Dundrum Bay, b., N. Ire., U.K. 10 G7 54.13 N 5.45 W
Dundurn, Sk., Can. 142 C7 51.49 N 106.31 W
Dunedin, N.Z. 102 G4 45.52 S 170.29 E
Dunedin, Fl., U.S. 132 H3 28.01 N 82.46 W
Dunedoo, Austl. 98 I7 32.00 S 149.23 E
Dunellen, N.J., U.S. 194 40.35 N 74.28 W
Dunewood, N.Y., U.S. 194 40.38 N 73.11 W
Dunfanaghy, Ire. 10 F5 55.10 N 7.59 W
Dunfermline, Scot., U.K. 10 E9 56.04 N 3.29 W
Du Ngae, Khao, mtn., Thai. 64 E4 15.10 N 98.47 E
Dungannon, N. Ire., U.K. 10 G6 54.30 N 6.46 W
Dungannon, Va., U.S. 124 H3 36.49 N 82.28 W
Dūngarpur, India 70 G4 23.49 N 73.43 E
Dungarvan, Ire. 10 I5 52.05 N 7.37 W
Dungarvan Harbour, b., Ire. 10 I5 52.05 N 7.31 W
Dungeness, c., Eng., U.K. 10 K13 50.55 N 0.58 E
Dungog, Austl. 98 I8 32.24 S 151.45 E
Dungu, D.R.C. 86 D5 3.37 N 28.34 E
Dungun, Malay. 64 J6 4.44 N 103.24 E
Dunham Lake, l., Mi., U.S. 199 42.39 N 83.41 W
Dunham-on-the-Hill, Eng., U.K. 180 53.15 N 2.47 W
Dunham Park, p.o.i., Eng., U.K. 180 53.23 N 2.24 W
Dunham Town, Eng., U.K. 180 53.23 N 2.24 W
Dunheved, Austl. 192a 33.45 S 150.47 E
Dunhua, China 52 C10 43.21 N 128.14 E
Dunhuang, China 52 C3 40.08 N 94.40 E
Dunilovo, Russia 26 C21 57.45 N 38.55 E
Dunkeld, ngh., S. Afr. 191d 26.09 S 28.03 E
Dunkerque (Dunkirk), Fr. 20 C11 51.02 N 2.23 E
Dunkirk see Dunkerque, Fr. 20 C11 51.02 N 2.23 E
Dunkirk, In., U.S. 130 D12 40.22 N 85.12 W
Dunkirk, N.Y., U.S. 124 B6 42.29 N 79.19 W
Dunkirk, Oh., U.S. 124 D2 40.47 N 83.38 W
Dunk's Green, Eng., U.K. 178 51.15 N 0.19 E
Dunkwa, Ghana 84 H4 5.57 N 1.47 W
Dún Laoghaire, Ire. 10 H6 53.17 N 6.08 W
Dunlap, Ia., U.S. 130 C2 41.51 N 95.36 W
Dunlap, Tn., U.S. 134 B13 35.22 N 85.23 W
Dunleary see Dún Laoghaire, Ire. 10 H6 53.17 N 6.08 W
Dunleith, De., U.S. 203 39.42 N 75.33 W
Dunmarra, Austl. 96 C6 16.37 S 133.21 E
Dunmore, Pa., U.S. 124 C10 41.26 N 75.38 W
Dunmore Town, Bah. 132 K9 25.30 N 76.38 W
Dunn, N.C., U.S. 132 A7 35.18 N 78.36 W
Dunnellon, Fl., U.S. 132 G3 29.02 N 82.28 W
Dunnet Head, c., Scot., U.K. 10 C9 58.39 N 3.24 W
Dunning, Ne., U.S. 140 F12 41.49 N 100.06 W
Dunningtown, Pa., U.S. 197b 40.25 N 79.35 W
Dunn Loring, Va., U.S. 202c 38.53 N 77.14 W
Dunn Loring Woods, Va., U.S. 202c 38.52 N 77.14 W
Dunnockshaw, Eng., U.K. 180 53.45 N 2.17 W
Dunnville, On., Can. 126 F10 42.54 N 79.36 W
Dunoon, Scot., U.K. 10 F8 55.57 N 4.55 W
Dunqulah, Sudan 82 D5 19.10 N 30.28 E
Dunqunāb, Sudan 82 C7 21.05 N 37.06 E
Dunrea, Mb., Can. 142 E14 49.23 N 99.43 W
Duns, Scot., U.K. 10 F10 55.47 N 2.20 W
Dunseith, N.D., U.S. 142 F13 48.48 N 100.03 W
Dunsmuir, Ca., U.S. 148 B3 41.13 N 122.16 W
Dunstable, Eng., U.K. 10 J12 51.53 N 0.31 W
Dunster, B.C., Can. 144 C11 53.08 N 119.50 W
Dun-sur-Auron, Fr. 20 H11 46.53 N 2.34 E
Dunton Wayletts, Eng., U.K. 178 51.35 N 0.24 E
Dunvegan, S. Afr. 191d 26.09 S 28.09 E
Dunvegan, Scot., U.K. 10 D6 57.26 N 6.35 W
Dunyāpur, Pak. 70 D3 29.48 N 71.44 E
Duolbagáisá, mtn., Nor. 14 B18 70.33 N 27.51 E
Duolun, China 52 C8 42.11 N 116.27 E
Duolundabohuer, China 70 B14 33.24 N 93.36 E
Duomo, rel., Italy 184b 45.27 N 9.11 E
Duomula, China 70 A9 34.07 N 82.30 E
Duozhu, China 58 J6 22.58 N 114.43 E
Du Page, stm., Il., U.S. 128 J10 41.25 N 88.13 W
Du Page, East Branch, stm., Il., U.S. 196 41.42 N 88.09 W
Dupang Ling, mts., China 58 I4 25.29 N 111.15 E
Duping, China 58 H3 27.11 N 108.20 E
Dupljatka, Russia 40 F13 51.06 N 42.21 E
Dupnica, Blg. 36 G10 42.16 N 23.08 E
Dupont Research Center, sci., De., U.S. 203 39.46 N 75.34 W
Düppel, Berliner Forst, for., Ger. 182a 52.25 N 13.08 E
Dupree, S.D., U.S. 140 B11 45.02 N 101.36 W
Dupuyer, Mt., U.S. 146 B14 48.11 N 112.30 W
Duque Bacelar, Braz. 170 C4 4.09 S 42.57 W
Duque de Caxias, Braz. 170 L4 22.47 S 43.17 W
Duque de Caxias, mun., Braz. 205a 22.45 S 43.16 W
Duque de York, Isla, i., Chile 166 J1 50.39 S 75.19 W
Duquesne University, educ., Pa., U.S. 197b 40.26 N 79.59 W
Du Quoin, Il., U.S. 130 F8 38.00 N 89.14 W
Duran, N.M., U.S. 138 G3 34.29 N 105.26 W
Durance, stm., Fr. 22 F11 43.55 N 4.44 E
Durand, Il., U.S. 130 B8 42.26 N 89.19 W
Durand, Mi., U.S. 124 B2 42.54 N 83.58 W
Durand, Wi., U.S. 128 G7 44.37 N 91.57 W
Durand, Récif, rf., N. Cal. 101d n17 22.03 S 168.39 E
Durand Reef see Durand, Récif, rf., N. Cal. 101d n17 22.03 S 168.39 E
Durango, Mex. 154 C6 24.01 N 104.40 W
Durango, Spain 28 A8 43.10 N 2.37 W
Durango, Co., U.S. 150 F9 37.16 N 107.52 W
Durango, state, Mex. 154 C6 24.50 N 104.50 W
Duranka, Egypt 76 K2 27.08 N 31.10 E
Durant, Ia., U.S. 130 C7 41.36 N 90.55 W

Name	Page	Map Ref.	Latitude	Longitude
Durant, Ms., U.S.	134	D9	33.05 N	89.51 W
Durant, Ok., U.S.	134	D2	33.59 N	96.22 W
Duras, Fr.	22	E6	44.41 N	0.11 E
Duratón, stm., Spain	28	C7	41.37 N	4.06 W
Durazno, Ur.	172	F9	33.25 S	56.30 W
Durazzo see Durrës, Alb.	32	C13	41.19 N	19.27 E
Durban, S. Afr.	90	F10	29.55 S	30.56 E
Durban Roodepoort Deep Gold Mines, mine, S. Afr.	191d		26.10 S	27.51 E
Durbe, Lat.	26	D4	56.34 N	21.21 E
Durbin, W.V., U.S.	124	F6	38.32 N	79.50 W
Durchholz, Ger.	181		51.23 N	7.17 E
Đurđevac, Cro.	30	D14	46.03 N	17.02 E
Düren, Ger.	24	F2	50.48 N	6.28 E
Durg, India	70	H8	21.11 N	81.17 E
Durgāpur, India	70	G11	23.29 N	87.20 E
Durham, On., Can.	126	D9	44.10 N	80.48 W
Durham, Eng., U.K.	10	G11	54.47 N	1.34 W
Durham, Ca., U.S.	148	D4	39.38 N	121.47 W
Durham, N.H., U.S.	122	G5	43.08 N	70.56 W
Durham, N.C., U.S.	124	H6	35.59 N	78.53 W
Durham Downs, Austl.	98	F3	27.05 S	141.54 E
Durham Heights, mtn., N.T., Can.	110	A6	71.08 N	122.56 W
Durham Pond, l., N.J., U.S.	194		41.00 N	74.27 W
Duriansebatang, Indon.	66	D6	0.47 S	109.55 E
Durlabhpur, India	190b		22.47 N	88.29 E
Durlas éile see Thurles, Ire.	10	I5	52.41 N	7.49 W
Durleşti, Mol.	38	F7	47.00 N	28.47 E
Durmitor, mtn., Yugo.	36	F6	43.08 N	19.01 E
Durmitor Nacionalni Park, p.o.i., Yugo.	36	F6	43.06 N	19.03 E
Durness, Scot., U.K.	10	C8	58.33 N	4.45 W
Dürnkrut, Aus.	30	B13	48.29 N	16.52 E
Durón, Spain	28	D8	40.38 N	2.43 W
Duross Heights, De., U.S.	203		39.40 N	75.37 W
Dürre Liesing, stm., Aus.	182b		48.08 N	16.16 E
Durrës, Alb.	32	C13	41.19 N	19.27 E
Durrësi see Durrës, Alb.	32	C13	41.19 N	19.27 E
Durrie, Austl.	98	E3	25.38 S	140.16 E
Dursunbey, Tur.	34	D11	39.33 N	28.39 E
Duru Gölü, l., Tur.	34	B11	41.20 N	28.34 E
Durūz, Jabal ad-, mtn., Syria	76	F7	32.39 N	36.43 E
D'Urville, Tanjung, c., Indon.	60	F10	1.28 S	137.54 E
D'Urville Island, i., N.Z.	102	E5	40.50 S	173.52 E
Dušak, Turkmen.	72	B9	37.11 N	59.59 E
Dusa Marreb see Dhuusamarreeb, Som.	86	C9	5.31 N	46.24 E
Dušanbe, Taj.	72	B10	38.34 N	68.46 E
Dušekan, Russia	48	B19	60.39 N	109.05 E
Dusetos, Lith.	26	E8	55.44 N	25.50 E
Dushan, China	58	I2	25.49 N	107.32 E
Du Shan, mtn., China	58	A8	40.29 N	118.47 E
Dushanzi, China	52	C1	44.19 N	84.51 E
Dushikou, China	58	A6	41.17 N	115.41 E
Dushore, Pa., U.S.	124	C9	41.31 N	76.23 W
Dusia, l., Lith.	26	F6	54.17 N	23.42 E
Duson, La., U.S.	134	G6	30.14 N	92.11 W
Düssel, Ger.	181		51.16 N	7.03 E
Düssel, stm., Ger.	181		51.13 N	6.45 E
Düsseldorf, Ger.	24	E2	51.14 N	6.48 E
Düsseldorf, Ger.	181		51.12 N	6.47 E
Düsseldorf, Universität, educ., Ger.	181		51.12 N	6.48 E
Dustin, Ok., U.S.	134	B2	35.16 N	96.01 W
Dutch Creek, stm., B.C., Can.	144	F14	50.17 N	115.51 W
Dutch Creek, stm., Ar., U.S.	134	C5	35.03 N	93.24 W
Dutch John, Ut., U.S.	150	C7	40.57 N	109.25 W
Dutton, On., Can.	126	F8	42.39 N	81.29 W
Dutton, Eng., U.K.	180		53.19 N	2.38 W
Dutton, Mt., U.S.	146	C15	47.51 N	111.44 W
Dutton, stm., Austl.	98	C4	20.43 S	143.09 E
Dutton, Mount, mtn., Ut., U.S.	150	E4	38.01 N	112.13 W
Duval, Lac, l., Qc., Can.	126	B12	46.19 N	76.55 W
Duvan, Russia	40	D20	55.40 N	57.53 E
Duved, Swe.	16	D10	63.24 N	12.52 E
Duvernay, ngh., Qc., Can.	193a		45.35 N	73.40 W
Duvno, Bos.	36	F4	43.42 N	17.13 E
Duxbury Beach, cst., Ma., U.S.	201		42.03 N	70.38 W
Duxun, China	58	J7	23.54 N	117.36 E
Duyagan Point, c., Phil.	68	D3	12.37 N	121.32 E
Duyang, China	58	J2	23.57 N	107.42 E
Duyfken Point, c., Austl.	96	B8	12.34 S	141.37 E
Duyun, China	58	H2	26.15 N	107.30 E
Düzce, Tur.	34	C14	40.50 N	31.09 E
Dve Mogili, Blg.	36	F12	43.36 N	25.52 E
Dvine, ozero, l., Russia	26	D14	56.08 N	31.12 E
Dvinsk see Daugavpils, Lat.	26	E9	55.53 N	26.31 E
Dvinskaja guba, b., Russia	18	B24	64.55 N	39.17 E
Dvorichna, Ukr.	38	D16	49.51 N	37.41 E
Dvoriši, Russia	26	B18	58.12 N	35.12 E
Dvuh Cirkov, gora, mtn., Russia	50	C22	67.31 N	168.08 E
Dvulučnoe, Russia	40	F11	50.02 N	38.01 E
Dvůr Králové nad Labem, Czech Rep.	24	F11	50.25 N	15.48 E
Dwarbasini, India	190b		22.59 N	88.14 E
Dwārka, India	70	G2	22.14 N	68.59 E
Dwarli, India	190c		19.12 N	73.08 E
Dwars Kill, stm., N.J., U.S.	194		40.58 N	73.58 W
D.W. Field Park, p.o.i., Ma., U.S.	201		42.06 N	71.03 W
Dwight, Il., U.S.	130	C9	41.05 N	88.25 W
Dworshak Reservoir, res., Id., U.S.	146	D11	46.40 N	116.00 W
Dwyka, stm., S. Afr.	90	H5	33.17 S	21.37 E
Dyaul Island, i., Pap. N. Gui.	101a	a5	2.56 S	150.53 E
Dyck, Schloss, hist., Ger.	181		51.09 N	6.34 E
Dyer, Tn., U.S.	130	H8	36.04 N	88.59 W
Dyer, Cape, c., Nu., Can.	108	D13	66.37 N	61.18 W
Dyer Bay, b., On., Can.	126	C8	45.10 N	81.18 W
Dyersburg, Tn., U.S.	130	H8	36.02 N	89.23 W
Dyersville, Ia., U.S.	130	B6	42.29 N	91.07 W
Dyess Air Force Base, mil., Tx., U.S.	136	B8	32.25 N	99.51 W
Dyhtau, gora, mtn., Russia	42	D10	43.03 N	43.08 E
Dyje (Thaya), stm., Eur.	24	H12	48.36 N	16.56 E
Dykan'ka, Ukr.	38	D13	49.49 N	34.32 E
Dykes Pond, l., Ma., U.S.	201		42.36 N	70.44 W
Dylym, Russia	42	D12	43.05 N	46.34 E
Dyment, On., Can.	128	B6	49.37 N	92.19 W
Dymer, Ukr.	38	C9	50.47 N	30.18 E
Dymytrove, Ukr.	38	E12	48.34 N	33.02 E
Dynamo Stadium, p.o.i., Russia	183b		55.48 N	37.34 E
Dynów, Pol.	24	G18	49.49 N	22.15 E
Dyrnesvågen, Nor.	16	D5	63.26 N	7.51 E
Dyrotz, Ger.	182a		52.33 N	12.58 E
Dyrøya, i., Nor.	14	D8	69.03 N	17.25 E
Dysart, Austl.	98	D7	22.27 S	148.14 E
Dysart, Sk., Can.	142	D9	50.57 N	104.02 W
Dysart, Ia., U.S.	130	B5	42.10 N	92.18 W
Dysna (Dzisna), stm., Eur.	26	E9	55.34 N	28.13 E
Dytikí Elláda, state, Grc.	34	E4	38.00 N	21.30 E
Dytikí Makedonía, state, Grc.	34	C4	40.30 N	21.30 E
Dyviziia, Ukr.	38	H9	45.57 N	29.59 E
Džagdy, hrebet, mts., Russia	50	F15	53.49 N	130.40 E
Džalal-Abad, Kyrg.	48	F12	40.55 N	73.00 E
Džalinda, Russia	50	F13	53.29 N	123.53 E
Džambejty, Kaz.	48	D8	50.15 N	52.36 E
Džanybek, Kaz.	48	E7	49.25 N	46.50 E
Dzaoudzi, May.	88	C8	12.47 S	45.17 E
Džardžan, Russia	50	C13	68.43 N	124.02 E
Dzaudzhikau see Vladikavkaz, Russia	42	D11	43.02 N	44.39 E
Dzavhan, stm., Mong.	52	B3	48.52 N	93.25 E
Džebel, Turkmen.	42	F16	39.37 N	54.13 E
Džermuk see Jermuk, Arm.	48	G7	39.51 N	45.41 E
Dzerzhyns'k, Ukr.	38	E16	48.24 N	37.51 E
Dzerzhyns'k, Ukr.	38	C6	50.08 N	27.56 E
Dzeržinsk, Russia	40	C13	56.15 N	43.24 E
Dzeržinskoe, Russia	48	C16	56.49 N	95.14 E
Džetygara, Kaz.	48	D10	52.11 N	61.12 E
Dzhankoi, Ukr.	38	H13	45.42 N	34.23 E
Dzharylhach, ostriv, i., Ukr.	38	H11	46.02 N	32.55 E
Dzharylhats'ka zatoka, b., Ukr.	38	G11	46.05 N	32.50 E
Dzhugdzhur Mountains see Džugdžur, hrebet, mts., Russia	50	E16	58.00 N	136.00 E
Dzhungarian Alatau Mountains, mts., Asia	48	E14	45.00 N	81.00 E
Dzhuryn, Ukr.	38	E7	48.40 N	28.17 E
Działdowo, Pol.	24	C16	53.14 N	20.11 E
Działoszyce, Pol.	24	F16	50.21 N	20.20 E
Dzibalchén, Mex.	156	C3	19.28 N	89.43 W
Dzibilchaltún, hist., Mex.	156	B3	21.05 N	89.36 W
Dzierzgoń, Pol.	24	C15	53.55 N	19.20 E
Dzierżoniów, Pol.	24	F12	50.43 N	16.39 E
Dzilam González, Mex.	156	B3	21.17 N	88.56 W
Dzisna, Bela.	26	E11	55.34 N	28.11 E
Dzisna (Dysna), stm., Eur.	26	E9	55.34 N	28.13 E
Dzitbalché, Mex.	156	B2	20.19 N	90.03 W
Dzivin, Bela.	26	I7	51.57 N	24.35 E
Dziwnów, Pol.	24	B10	54.01 N	14.46 E
Džizak, Uzb.	48	F11	40.08 N	67.50 E
Dzjaniskavičy, Bela.	26	H9	52.44 N	26.41 E
Dzjarèčyn, Bela.	26	G7	53.15 N	24.55 E
Dzjaršynskaja, hara, hill, Bela.	26	G9	53.51 N	27.03 E
Dzjaržynsk, Bela.	26	G10	53.41 N	27.08 E
Dzjatlava, Bela.	26	G8	53.27 N	25.24 E
Dzjatlavičy, Bela.	26	H9	52.19 N	26.49 E
Dzmitravičy, Bela.	26	G12	53.58 N	29.07 E
Dzöölön, Mong.	48	D17	51.06 N	99.40 E
Džubga, Russia	42	C8	44.18 N	38.42 E
Džugdžur, hrebet, mts., Russia	50	E16	58.00 N	136.00 E
Dzūkijos nacionalinis parkas, p.o.i., Lith.	26	F7	54.10 N	24.17 E
Džūkste, Lat.	26	D6	56.46 N	23.14 E
Dzungarian Basin see Junggar Pendi, bas., China	52	B2	45.00 N	88.00 E
Dzungarian Gate, p., Asia	48	E14	45.23 N	82.24 E
Džungarskie vorota see Dzungarian Gate, p., Asia	48	E14	45.23 N	82.24 E
Džungarskij Alatau, hrebet see Dzhungarian Alatau Mountains, mts., Asia	48	E14	45.00 N	81.00 E
Džusaly, Kaz.	48	E10	45.29 N	64.05 E
Dzüünharaa, Mong.	52	B6	48.51 N	106.27 E
Dzuunmod, Mong.	52	B6	47.42 N	106.57 E
Dzyhivka, Ukr.	38	E7	48.21 N	28.19 E

E

Name	Page	Map Ref.	Latitude	Longitude
Eads, Co., U.S.	138	C6	38.28 N	102.47 W
Eagar, Az., U.S.	150	I7	34.05 N	109.17 W
Eagle, Ak., U.S.	109	D11	64.47 N	141.12 W
Eagle, Co., U.S.	138	B2	39.39 N	106.49 W
Eagle, stm., Co., U.S.	138	B2	39.38 N	107.03 W
Eagle, Mount, hill, V.I.U.S.	158c	g10	17.46 N	64.49 W
Eagle Bay, B.C., Can.	144	F11	50.55 N	119.12 W
Eagle Bend, Mn., U.S.	118	E3	46.09 N	95.02 W
Eagle Butte, S.D., U.S.	140	C11	44.58 N	101.16 W
Eagle Chief Creek, stm., Ok., U.S.	138	E10	36.22 N	98.27 W
Eagle Creek, stm., Sk., Can.	142	B6	52.19 N	107.24 W
Eagle Creek, stm., Az., U.S.	150	J7	32.57 N	109.24 W
Eagle Creek, stm., Ky., U.S.	130	F13	38.35 N	85.04 W
Eagle Creek, stm., Mt., U.S.	146	B15	48.21 N	111.10 W
Eagle Creek, stm., N.M., U.S.	136	B3	32.52 N	104.20 W
Eagle Creek, stm., Or., U.S.	146	F9	44.45 N	117.11 W
Eagle Grove, Ia., U.S.	130	B4	42.40 N	93.54 W
Eaglehawk, Austl.	98	K5	36.43 S	144.15 E
Eagle Hill, stm., Ma., U.S.	201		42.42 N	70.49 W
Eagle Lake, Me., U.S.	122	C8	47.01 N	68.36 W
Eagle Lake, Tx., U.S.	136	E11	29.34 N	96.20 W
Eagle Lake, l., B.C., Can.	144	E6	51.54 N	124.23 W
Eagle Lake, l., On., Can.	128	B5	49.42 N	93.13 W
Eagle Lake, l., Ca., U.S.	148	C5	40.39 N	120.44 W
Eagle Lake, l., Me., U.S.	122	D7	46.20 N	69.22 W
Eagle Mountain, Ca., U.S.	148	J10	33.53 N	115.26 W
Eagle Mountain, mtn., Id., U.S.	146	D11	46.20 N	115.07 W
Eagle Mountain, mtn., Mn., U.S.	128	D8	47.54 N	90.33 W
Eagle Mountain Lake, res., Tx., U.S.	136	A10	32.55 N	97.30 W
Eagle Nest Butte, mtn., S.D., U.S.	140	D11	43.27 N	101.39 W
Eagle Pass, Tx., U.S.	136	F7	28.42 N	100.28 W
Eagle Peak, mtn., Ca., U.S.	148	B5	41.17 N	120.12 W
Eagle Peak, mtn., Ca., U.S.	200		37.54 N	121.54 W
Eagle River, Mi., U.S.	128	D10	47.24 N	88.17 W
Eagle River, Wi., U.S.	128	F9	45.54 N	89.14 W
Eagle Rock, Va., U.S.	124	G6	37.37 N	79.47 W
Eagle Rock, ngh., Ca., U.S.	198		34.09 N	118.12 W
Eagle Rock Reservation, p.o.i., N.J., U.S.	194		40.49 N	74.14 W
Eagletown, Ok., U.S.	134	C4	34.02 N	94.34 W
Eagleville, Pa., U.S.	203		40.10 N	75.24 W
Earcroft, Eng., U.K.	180		53.43 N	2.29 W
Eardley Lake, l., Mb., Can.	142	B17	52.22 N	96.05 W
Ear Falls, On., Can.	118	A5	50.38 N	93.13 W
Earle, Ar., U.S.	134	B8	35.16 N	90.27 W
Earlestown, Eng., U.K.	180		53.27 N	2.39 W
Earl Grey, Sk., Can.	142	D9	50.56 N	104.43 W
Earlham, Ia., U.S.	130	C3	41.29 N	94.07 W
Earlimart, Ca., U.S.	148	H6	35.53 N	119.15 W
Earlington, Ky., U.S.	130	G10	37.16 N	87.30 W
Earl Park, In., U.S.	130	D10	40.41 N	87.24 W
Earlville, Il., U.S.	130	C9	41.35 N	88.55 W
Earlwood, Austl.	192a		33.56 S	151.08 E
Early, Ia., U.S.	130	B2	42.28 N	95.08 W
Early, Tx., U.S.	136	C9	31.44 N	98.56 W
Earn, stm., Scot., U.K.	10	E9	56.21 N	3.18 W
Earn, Loch, l., Scot., U.K.	10	E8	56.23 N	4.14 W
Earth, Tx., U.S.	136	G6	34.14 N	102.24 W
Eas, Vanuatu	101d	k17	16.21 S	168.13 E
Easley, S.C., U.S.	132	B3	34.49 N	82.35 W
Ea Sou, Viet.	64	F8	13.05 N	107.52 E
East, stm., On., Can.	126	C10	45.19 N	79.16 W
East, stm., Co., U.S.	138	C2	38.39 N	106.51 W
East, stm., N.Y., U.S.	194		40.48 N	73.48 W
East, University of the, educ., Phil.	187f		14.36 N	120.59 E
East Acton, Ma., U.S.	201		42.28 N	71.24 W
East Alligator, stm., Austl.	96	B6	12.09 S	132.46 E
East Alton, Il., U.S.	130	F7	38.52 N	90.06 W
East Angus, Qc., Can.	122	E5	45.28 N	71.40 W
East Antarctica, reg., Ant.	103	C8	80.00 S	79.59 E
East Atlantic Beach, N.Y., U.S.	194		40.35 N	73.43 W
East Aurora, N.Y., U.S.	124	B7	42.45 N	78.36 W
East Barming, Eng., U.K.	178		51.16 N	0.28 E
East Barnet, ngh., Eng., U.K.	178		51.38 N	0.09 W
East Basin, b., Oh., U.S.	197a		41.32 N	81.40 W
East Bay, b., Fl., U.S.	134	G13	30.05 N	85.32 W
East Bay, b., Tx., U.S.	136	E13	29.30 N	94.38 W
East Bedfont, ngh., Eng., U.K.	178		51.27 N	0.26 W
East Bend, N.C., U.S.	124	H5	36.12 N	80.29 W
East Berlin, N.J., U.S.	203		39.48 N	74.55 W
East Berlin, Pa., U.S.	124	E8	39.56 N	76.58 W
East Bernard, Tx., U.S.	136	E11	29.32 N	96.04 W
East Bernstadt, Ky., U.S.	124	G1	37.11 N	84.07 W
East Bijou Creek, stm., Co., U.S.	138	B4	39.50 N	104.07 W
East Billerica, Ma., U.S.	201		42.34 N	71.14 W
East Borneo see Kalimantan Timur, state, Indon.	66	C10	1.30 N	116.30 E
East Boston, ngh., Ma., U.S.	201		42.23 N	71.02 W
Eastbourne, Eng., U.K.	10	K13	50.46 N	0.17 E
East Brady, Pa., U.S.	124	D6	40.58 N	79.36 W
East Braintree, Mb., Can.	142	E18	49.37 N	95.37 W
East Brewton, Al., U.S.	134	F11	31.05 N	87.03 W
East Burwood, Austl.	192b		37.51 S	145.09 E
Eastbury, Eng., U.K.	178		51.37 N	0.25 W
East Cache Creek, stm., Ok., U.S.	138	G10	34.11 N	98.18 W
East Caicos, i., T./C. Is.	156	B12	21.41 N	71.28 W
East Canada Creek, stm., N.Y., U.S.	126	E15	43.00 N	74.44 W
East Cape, c., N.Z.	102	C8	37.41 S	178.33 E
East Cape, c., Fl., U.S.	132	K4	25.07 N	81.05 W
East Carbon, Ut., U.S.	150	D6	39.32 N	110.24 W
East Caroline Basin, unds.	174	I17	4.00 N	146.45 E
Eastchester Bay, b., N.Y., U.S.	194		40.51 N	73.48 W
East Chicago, In., U.S.	130	C10	41.38 N	87.26 W
East Chicago Heights, Il., U.S.	196		41.30 N	87.35 W
East China Normal University, educ., China	187b		31.14 N	121.24 E
East China Sea, s., Asia	52	F9	30.00 N	126.00 E
East Clandon, Eng., U.K.	178		51.15 N	0.29 W
Eastcote, ngh., Eng., U.K.	178		51.35 N	0.24 W
East Cote Blanche Bay, b., La., U.S.	134	H7	29.35 N	91.40 W
East Coulee, Ab., Can.	144	E18	51.20 N	112.29 W
East Creek, stm., N.J., U.S.	194		40.27 N	74.09 W
East Dereham, Eng., U.K.	10	I13	52.40 N	0.56 E
East Dismal Swamp, sw., N.C., U.S.	132	A9	35.42 N	76.24 W
East Ditch, can., N.J., U.S.	194		40.56 N	74.19 W
East Dublin, Ga., U.S.	132	D3	32.32 N	82.51 W
East Dubuque, Il., U.S.	130	B7	42.29 N	90.37 W
East Ely, Nv., U.S.	150	D2	39.16 N	114.52 W
Eastend, Sk., Can.	142	E5	49.30 N	108.44 W
East End, V.I.U.S.	158b	e8	18.20 N	64.40 W
East End Point, c., Bah.	132	K8	25.02 N	77.15 W
East End Village, Anguilla	159a	a2	18.14 N	62.59 W
Easter Island see Pascua, Isla de, i., Chile	100l	f30	27.07 S	109.22 W
Eastern Cape, state, S. Afr.	90	G7	32.30 S	26.30 E
Eastern Channel see Tsushima-kaikyō, strt., Japan	56	E2	34.00 N	129.00 E
Eastern Cherokee Indian Reservation, ind. res., N.C., U.S.	132	A2	35.25 N	83.24 W
Eastern Creek, stm., Austl.	98	C3	20.14 S	141.08 E
Eastern Creek, stm., Austl.	192a		33.39 S	150.51 E
Eastern Desert see Arabian Desert, des., Egypt	74	F2	28.00 N	32.00 E
Eastern Division, state, Fiji	101e	q19	18.23 S	179.08 W
Eastern Ghāts, mts., India	69	D4	14.00 N	78.50 E
Eastern Michigan University, educ., Mi., U.S.	199		42.15 N	83.37 W
Eastern Point, c., Guad.	159a	a1	18.07 N	63.01 W
Eastern Point, c., Ma., U.S.	201		42.35 N	70.40 W
Eastern Sayans see Vostočnyj Sajan, mts., Russia	48	D17	53.00 N	97.00 E
Eastern Transvaal see Mpumalanga, state, S. Afr.	90	E9	26.00 S	30.30 E
Eastern Yamuna Canal, can., India	190a		28.40 N	77.15 E
East Falkland, i., Falk. Is.	166	J5	51.52 S	59.10 W
East Falls, ngh., Pa., U.S.	203		40.01 N	75.11 W
East Farleigh, Eng., U.K.	178		51.15 N	0.29 E
East Farmingdale, N.Y., U.S.	194		40.44 N	73.26 W
East Fayetteville, N.C., U.S.	132	A7	35.03 N	78.50 W
East Foxboro, Ma., U.S.	201		42.03 N	71.12 W
East Frisian Islands see Ostfriesische Inseln, is., Ger.	24	C3	53.44 N	7.25 E
East Gaffney, S.C., U.S.	132	A4	35.04 N	81.37 W
East Gallatin, stm., Mt., U.S.	146	E15	45.53 N	111.20 W
East Germany see Germany, ctry., Eur.	6	E11	51.00 N	10.00 E
East Glacier Park, Mt., U.S.	146	B13	48.26 N	113.13 W
East Grand Forks, Mn., U.S.	118	D2	47.55 N	97.00 W
East Grand Rapids, Mi., U.S.	130	B12	42.56 N	85.36 W
East Grinstead, Eng., U.K.	10	J12	51.07 N	0.00 W
East Half Hollow Hills, N.Y., U.S.	194		40.47 N	73.19 W
Eastham, Eng., U.K.	180		53.19 N	2.58 W
East Ham, ngh., Eng., U.K.	178		51.32 N	0.03 E
Easthampton, Ma., U.S.	124	B13	42.16 N	72.39 W
East Hanningfield, Eng., U.K.	178		51.41 N	0.34 E
East Hanover, N.J., U.S.	194		40.48 N	74.22 W
East Hazel Crest, Il., U.S.	196		41.35 N	87.39 W
East Helena, Mt., U.S.	146	D15	46.35 N	111.54 W
East Hertfordshire, mun., Eng., U.K.	178		51.46 N	0.02 W
East Hills, Austl.	192a		33.58 S	150.59 E
East Hills, N.Y., U.S.	194		40.47 N	73.37 W
East Huntington, N.Y., U.S.	194		40.52 N	73.24 W
East Irvington, N.Y., U.S.	194		41.03 N	73.51 W
East Island, pen., N.Y., U.S.	194		40.54 N	73.38 W
East Islip, N.Y., U.S.	194		40.43 N	73.11 W
East Java see Jawa Timur, state, Indon.	66	G8	8.00 S	113.00 E
East Jordan, Mi., U.S.	126	C4	45.09 N	85.06 W
East Keansburg, N.J., U.S.	194		40.26 N	74.07 W
East Kelowna, B.C., Can.	144	G11	49.50 N	119.24 W
East Kilbride, Scot., U.K.	10	F8	55.46 N	4.10 W
Eastlake, Mi., U.S.	126	D3	44.15 N	86.17 W
Eastlake, Oh., U.S.	124	C4	41.38 N	81.27 W
East Lake, l., N.J., U.S.	194		40.58 N	74.21 W
East Lamma Channel, strt., China	189d		22.14 N	114.09 E
Eastland, Tx., U.S.	136	B9	32.24 N	98.49 W
Eastland Center, shp. cen., Mi., U.S.	199		42.27 N	82.56 W
Eastland Shopping Plaza, shp. cen., Pa., U.S.	197b		40.22 N	79.50 W
East Lansdowne, Pa., U.S.	203		39.56 N	75.16 W
East Lansing, Mi., U.S.	124	B1	42.44 N	84.29 W
East Laurinburg, N.C., U.S.	132	B6	34.45 N	79.26 W
Eastleigh, Eng., U.K.	10	K11	50.58 N	1.22 W
East Liberty, ngh., Pa., U.S.	197b		40.27 N	79.55 W
East Lindfield, Austl.	192a		33.46 S	151.11 E
East Liverpool, Oh., U.S.	124	D5	40.37 N	80.34 W
East London (Oos-Londen), S. Afr.	90	H8	33.00 S	27.54 E
East Lynn Lake, res., W.V., U.S.	124	F3	38.05 N	82.22 W
Eastmain, Qc., Can.	110	E15	52.13 N	78.32 W
Eastmain, stm., Qc., Can.	110	E15	52.14 N	78.34 W
Eastmain-Opinaca, Réservoir, res., Qc., Can.	110	E15	52.23 N	76.34 W
East Malling, Eng., U.K.	178		51.17 N	0.26 E
Eastman, Ga., U.S.	132	D2	32.12 N	83.10 W
East Mansfield, Ma., U.S.	201		42.01 N	71.10 W
East Mariana Basin, unds.	174	H18	12.00 N	153.00 E
East Marin Island, i., Ca., U.S.	200		37.58 N	122.27 W
East Matagorda Bay, b., Tx., U.S.	136	F11	28.35 N	96.20 W
East McKeesport, Pa., U.S.	197b		40.23 N	79.48 W
East Meadow, stm., Ma., U.S.	201		42.47 N	71.02 W
East Meadow Brook, stm., N.Y., U.S.	194		40.39 N	73.34 W
East Millinocket, Me., U.S.	122	E8	45.37 N	68.34 W
East Millstone, N.J., U.S.	194		40.30 N	74.35 W
East Missoula, Mt., U.S.	146	D13	46.52 N	113.56 W
East Molesey, Eng., U.K.	178		51.24 N	0.21 W
East Moline, Il., U.S.	130	C7	41.30 N	90.26 W
East Monongahela, Pa., U.S.	197b		40.12 N	79.55 W
East Naples, Fl., U.S.	132	J4	26.06 N	81.45 W
East Newark, N.J., U.S.	194		40.48 N	73.59 W
East New York, ngh., N.Y., U.S.	194		40.40 N	73.53 W
East Nishnabotna, stm., Ia., U.S.	130	C2	40.38 N	95.38 W
East Nodaway, stm., Ia., U.S.	130	D3	40.38 N	95.01 W
East Nusa Tenggara see Nusa Tenggara Timur, state, Indon.	66	H12	9.04 S	120.29 E
East Olympia, Wa., U.S.	146	D4	46.57 N	122.49 W
Easton, Md., U.S.	124	F9	38.46 N	76.04 W
Easton, Ma., U.S.	201		42.02 N	71.06 W
Easton, Pa., U.S.	124	D10	40.41 N	75.13 W
Eastondale, Ma., U.S.	201		42.02 N	71.04 W
Eastover, S.C., U.S.	132	C5	33.52 N	80.41 W
East Pacific Rise, unds.	174	N27	20.00 S	115.00 W
East Pakistan see Bangladesh, ctry., Asia	70	G13	24.00 N	90.00 E
East Palatka, Fl., U.S.	132	G4	29.39 N	81.35 W
East Palestine, Oh., U.S.	124	D5	40.50 N	80.32 W
East Pecos, N.M., U.S.	138	F3	35.33 N	105.39 W
East Pembroke, Ma., U.S.	201		42.05 N	70.46 W
East Peoria, Il., U.S.	130	D8	40.39 N	89.34 W
East Pines, Md., U.S.	202c		38.57 N	76.55 W
East Pittsburgh, Pa., U.S.	197b		40.23 N	79.50 W
Eastpoint, Fl., U.S.	134	H14	29.44 N	84.53 W
East Point, Ga., U.S.	134	D14	33.40 N	84.26 W
East Point, c., P.E., Can.	122	D15	46.27 N	61.59 W
Eastpoint, shp. cen., Md., U.S.	202b		39.18 N	76.31 W
Eastport, Id., U.S.	146	B10	48.59 N	116.10 W
Eastport, Me., U.S.	122	F9	44.54 N	66.59 W
East Potomac Park, p.o.i., D.C., U.S.	202c		38.52 N	77.01 W
East Prairie, Mo., U.S.	130	H8	36.47 N	89.23 W
East Prairie, stm., Ab., Can.	144	A14	55.09 N	116.04 W
East Prussia see Ostpreussen, hist. reg., Eur.	26	F4	54.19 N	21.10 E
East Pryor Mountain, mtn., Mt., U.S.	140	B4	45.09 N	108.18 W
East Retford, Eng., U.K.	10	H12	53.19 N	0.56 W
East Richmond, Ca., U.S.	200		37.57 N	122.19 W
Eastridge Center, shp. cen., Ca., U.S.	200		37.20 N	121.49 W
East Rockaway, N.Y., U.S.	194		40.38 N	73.40 W
East Rosebud Creek, stm., Mt., U.S.	146	E17	45.29 N	109.27 W
East Rutherford, N.J., U.S.	194		40.50 N	74.05 W
East Saint Louis, Il., U.S.	130	F7	38.37 N	90.08 W
East Salt Creek, stm., Co., U.S.	150	D8	39.14 N	108.53 W
East Sea see Japan, Sea of, s., Asia	52	C11	40.00 N	135.00 E
East Shoal Lake, l., Mb., Can.	142	D16	50.23 N	97.37 W
East Siberian Sea see Vostočno-Sibirskoe more, s., Russia	46	B20	74.00 N	166.00 E
East Sister Island, i., Austl.	98	L6	39.39 S	147.59 E
East Sixteen Mile Creek, stm., On., Can.	193b		43.28 N	79.48 W
East Slovakia see Východoslovenský, state, Slvk.	24	H16	49.00 N	21.15 E
East Springbrook, Md., U.S.	202c		39.04 N	77.00 W
East Stroudsburg, Pa., U.S.	124	D11	41.00 N	75.10 W
East Sudbury, Ma., U.S.	201		42.24 N	71.24 W
East Tawas, Mi., U.S.	126	D6	44.16 N	83.28 W
East Tilbury, Eng., U.K.	178		51.28 N	0.26 E
East Troy, Wi., U.S.	130	B9	42.47 N	88.23 W
East Tustin, Ca., U.S.	198		33.46 N	117.49 W
Eastville, Va., U.S.	124	G10	37.21 N	75.57 W
East Walker, stm., U.S.	148	E6	38.53 N	119.10 W
East Wenatchee, Wa., U.S.	146	C6	47.25 N	120.17 W
East Wenonah, N.J., U.S.	203		39.47 N	75.08 W
East White Plains, N.Y., U.S.	194		41.03 N	73.47 W
Eastwick, ngh., Pa., U.S.	203		39.55 N	75.14 W
East Wickham, ngh., Eng., U.K.	178		51.28 N	0.07 E
East Williston, N.Y., U.S.	194		40.46 N	73.38 W
East Wilmington, N.C., U.S.	132	B8	34.14 N	77.57 W
Eastwood, Austl.	192a		33.48 S	151.05 E
Eastwood, Eng., U.K.	178		51.34 N	0.40 E
Eastwood, Eng., U.K.	180		53.43 N	2.03 W
Eastwood, Pa., U.S.	197b		40.17 N	79.31 W
East Yegua Creek, stm., Tx., U.S.	136	D11	30.18 N	96.44 W
East Yellow Creek, stm., Mo., U.S.	128	L6	39.39 N	93.03 W
Eaton, Co., U.S.	140	G8	40.31 N	104.42 W
Eaton, In., U.S.	130	D12	40.20 N	85.20 W
Eaton, Oh., U.S.	124	E1	39.44 N	84.38 W
Eatonia, Sk., Can.	142	C4	51.13 N	109.23 W
Eaton Rapids, Mi., U.S.	124	B1	42.30 N	84.38 W
Eatons Neck, N.Y., U.S.	194		40.56 N	73.24 W
Eatons Neck, pen., N.Y., U.S.	194		40.57 N	73.23 W
Eatonton, Ga., U.S.	132	C2	33.19 N	83.23 W
Eatonville, Wa., U.S.	146	D4	46.52 N	122.15 W
Eaton Wash, val., Ca., U.S.	198		34.04 N	118.03 W
Eaton Wash Dam, dam., Ca., U.S.	198		34.10 N	118.06 W
Eaubonne, Fr.	179		49.00 N	2.17 E
Eau Claire, Wi., U.S.	128	G7	44.48 N	91.29 W
Eau Claire, stm., Wi., U.S.	128	F9	44.54 N	89.37 W
Eau Claire, stm., Wi., U.S.	128	G7	44.48 N	91.29 W
Eau Claire, Lac à l', l., Qc., Can.	110	D16	56.10 N	74.26 W
Eau Galle, stm., Wi., U.S.	128	G6	44.36 N	91.59 W
Eauripik, at., Micron.	94	C5	6.41 N	143.03 E
Eauripik Rise, unds.	174	I17	3.00 N	142.00 E
Eauze, Fr.	22	F6	43.52 N	0.06 E
Ebano, Mex.	154	D9	22.12 N	98.23 W
Ebb and Flow Indian Reserve, ind. res., Mb., Can.	142	C14	51.01 N	99.00 W
Ebb and Flow Lake, l., Mb., Can.	142	D14	51.03 N	98.57 W
Ebben Creek, stm., Ma., U.S.	201		42.38 N	70.45 W
Ebbw Vale, Wales, U.K.	10	J9	51.46 N	3.12 W
Ebebiyín, Eq. Gui.	84	I7	2.09 N	11.19 E
Ebeltoft, Den.	16	K8	56.09 N	10.41 E
Ebenezer, On., Can.	193b		43.46 N	79.40 W
Eben Junction, Mi., U.S.	126	B2	46.20 N	86.57 W
Ebensee, Aus.	30	C10	47.48 N	13.46 E
Eberbach, Ger.	24	G4	49.27 N	8.58 E
Ebergassing, Aus.	182b		48.03 N	16.31 E
Eber Gölü, l., Tur.	34	E14	38.39 N	31.10 E
Ebermannstadt, Ger.	24	G7	49.46 N	11.10 E
Ebern, Ger.	24	F6	50.05 N	10.47 E
Ebersbach, Ger.	24	E10	51.00 N	14.35 E
Ebersberg, Ger.	24	H7	48.04 N	11.56 E
Eberswalde-Finow, Ger.	24	D9	52.50 N	13.49 E
Ebetsu, Japan	54	C14	43.06 N	141.33 E
Ebino, Japan	56	G3	32.02 N	130.49 E
Ebinur Hu, l., China	48	F14	44.55 N	82.52 E
Eboli, Italy	32	D9	40.37 N	15.03 E
Ebolowa, Cam.	86	D2	2.55 N	11.09 E
Ebon, at., Marsh. Is.	94	C7	4.35 N	168.44 E
Eboué Stadium, p.o.i., Congo	191b		4.17 S	15.18 E
Éboulements, Mont des, mtn., Qc., Can.	122	C6	47.31 N	70.17 W
Ebre (Ebro), stm., Spain	28	C11	40.43 N	0.35 E
Ebre, Delta de l', del., Spain	28	D11	40.41 N	0.44 E
Ebro (Ebre), stm., Spain	28	C11	40.43 N	0.35 E
Ebro, Delta del see Ebre, Delta de l', del., Spain	28	D11	40.41 N	0.44 E
Ebro, Embalse del, res., Spain	28	A7	43.00 N	3.58 W
Ebute-Ikorodu, Nig.	191a		6.37 N	3.30 E
Ebute-Metta, ngh., Nig.	191a		6.29 N	3.23 E
Ecatepec, Mex.	204a		19.35 N	99.04 W
Eccles, Eng., U.K.	178		51.19 N	0.29 E
Eccleston, Eng., U.K.	180		53.27 N	2.47 W
Eccleston, Md., U.S.	202b		39.24 N	76.44 W
Eceabat, Tur.	34	C9	40.11 N	26.21 E
Echague, Phil.	68	B3	16.41 N	121.39 E
Echarcon, Fr.	179		48.34 N	2.24 E
Ech Cheliff, Alg.	84	B5	36.10 N	1.20 E
Echeconnee Creek, stm., Ga., U.S.	132	D2	32.39 N	83.36 W
Echelon Mall, shp. cen., N.J., U.S.	203		39.51 N	75.00 W
Echeng, China	52	E7	30.24 N	114.52 E
Echigo-sammyaku, mts., Japan	56	B12	37.44 N	139.18 E
Echínos, Grc.	34	B7	41.17 N	24.59 E
Echmiadzin, Arm.	42	E11	40.10 N	44.18 E
Echo, Mn., U.S.	128	G3	44.37 N	95.25 W
Echo Bay, b., N.Y., U.S.	194		40.54 N	73.46 W
Echo Lake, l., Il., U.S.	196		42.13 N	88.05 W
Echo Lake, l., N.J., U.S.	194		41.04 N	74.25 W
Echt, Neth.	24	E1	51.06 N	5.52 E
Echuca, Austl.	98	K5	36.08 S	144.45 E
Écija, Spain	28	G5	37.32 N	5.05 W
Eckernförde, Ger.	24	B5	54.28 N	9.50 E
Eckerö, i., Fin.	18	G6	60.14 N	19.35 E
Eckville, Ab., Can.	144	D16	52.21 N	114.22 W
Eclectic, Al., U.S.	134	E12	32.38 N	86.02 W
Ecleto Creek, stm., Tx., U.S.	136	E10	28.52 N	97.45 W
Eclipse Sound, strt., Nu., Can.	110	A14	72.38 N	79.00 W
Ečmiadzin see Echmiadzin, Arm.	42	E11	40.10 N	44.18 E
Ècole, stm., Fr.	179		48.32 N	2.33 E
École Militaire (Saint-Cyr), mil., Fr.	179		48.48 N	2.04 E
Écommoy, Fr.	20	G9	47.50 N	0.16 E
Econfina, stm., Fl., U.S.	132	F2	30.02 N	83.55 W
Economy Park, p.o.i., Pa., U.S.	197b		40.37 N	80.12 W
Ecoporanga, Braz.	170	J5	18.21 S	40.50 W
Écorce, Lac de l', res., Qc., Can.	126	B13	47.05 N	76.21 W
Écorces, stm., Qc., Can.	122	B5	48.17 N	71.29 W
Ecorse, stm., Mi., U.S.	199		42.14 N	83.09 W
Ecorse, South Branch, stm., Mi., U.S.	199		42.14 N	83.09 W
Écouen, Château d', hist., Fr.	179		49.01 N	2.23 E
Ecoute, Ru d', stm., Fr.	179		48.39 N	2.26 E
Ecquevilly, Fr.	179		48.57 N	1.55 E
Écrins, Barre des, mtn., Fr.	22	E12	44.55 N	6.22 E
Écrins, Massif des, plat., Fr.	22	E12	44.52 N	6.20 E

Name	Page	Map Ref.	Latitude	Longitude
Écrosnes, Fr.	179		48.33 N	1.44 E
Ecru, Ms., U.S.	134	C9	34.21 N	89.01 W
Ecser, Hung.	182c		47.27 N	19.20 E
Ecstall, stm., B.C., Can.	144	C1	53.56 N	129.13 W
Ecuador, ctry., S.A.	164	D2	2.00 S	77.30 W
Ecum Secum, N.S., Can.	122	F14	44.59 N	62.12 W
Ed, Swe.	16	I9	58.55 N	11.55 E
Eda, ngh., Japan	186		35.34 N	139.34 E
Edam, Sk., Can.	142	A5	53.12 N	108.46 W
Edane, Swe.	16	H10	59.37 N	12.49 E
Edarma, Russia	48	C18	58.44 N	102.35 E
Eday, i., Scot., U.K.	10	B10	59.10 N	2.47 W
Eddington Gardens, Pa., U.S.	203		40.06 N	74.57 W
Eddrachillis Bay, b., Scot., U.K.	10	C7	58.18 N	5.15 W
Eddystone Point, c., Austl.	99a	n14	40.59 S	148.20 E
Eddystone Rocks, r., Eng., U.K.	10	K8	50.12 N	4.15 W
Eddyville, Ia., U.S.	130	C5	41.09 N	92.38 W
Eddyville, Ky., U.S.	130	G9	37.05 N	88.05 W
Ede, Neth.	20	B14	52.02 N	5.40 E
Ede, Nig.	84	H5	7.43 N	4.25 E
Edéa, Cam.	86	D2	3.47 N	10.07 E
Edefors, Swe.	14	F11	66.13 N	20.53 E
Edehon Lake, l., Nu., Can.	110	C11	60.24 N	97.20 W
Edelény, Hung.	36	A7	48.18 N	20.45 E
Edelweiss, S. Afr.	191d		26.16 S	28.28 E
Eden, Austl.	98	K7	37.03 S	149.53 E
Éden, Braz.	205a		22.48 S	43.24 W
Eden, Ms., U.S.	134	D8	32.59 N	90.20 W
Eden, N.C., U.S.	124	H6	36.29 N	79.46 W
Eden, Tx., U.S.	136	C8	31.13 N	99.50 W
Eden, Wy., U.S.	150	A7	42.02 N	109.26 W
Eden, stm., Eng., U.K.	10	G10	54.56 N	3.02 W
Edenburg, S. Afr.	90	F7	29.44 S	25.56 E
Eden Canyon, val., Ca., U.S.	200		37.42 N	122.01 W
Edendale, S. Afr.	90	F10	29.39 S	30.18 E
Edendale, S. Afr.	191d		26.09 S	28.09 E
Edenderry, Ire.	10	H5	53.20 N	7.03 W
Edenfield, Eng., U.K.	180		53.40 N	2.18 W
Eden Park, ngh., Eng., U.K.	178		51.23 N	0.02 W
Edenton, N.C., U.S.	124	H9	36.03 N	76.36 W
Edenvale, S. Afr.	191d		26.08 S	28.09 E
Eden Valley, Mn., U.S.	128	F4	45.19 N	94.33 W
Edenville, S. Afr.	90	E8	27.33 S	27.40 E
Eder, stm., Ger.	24	E4	51.13 N	9.27 E
Édessa, Grc.	34	C5	40.48 N	22.01 E
Edfu, Egypt	74	H3	24.58 N	32.52 E
Edgar, Ne., U.S.	140	G14	40.22 N	97.58 W
Edgar, Wi., U.S.	128	G8	44.55 N	89.57 W
Edgard, La., U.S.	134	H8	30.02 N	90.34 W
Edgar Ranges, mts., Austl.	96	C4	18.42 S	123.23 E
Edgars Creek, stm., Austl.	192b		37.44 S	144.58 E
Edgartown, Ma., U.S.	124	C15	41.23 N	70.31 W
Edgefield, S.C., U.S.	132	C3	33.47 N	81.56 W
Edge Hill, ngh., Eng., U.K.	180		53.24 N	2.57 W
Edge Island see Edgeøya, i., Nor.	106	B25	77.44 N	22.29 E
Edgeley, On., Can.	193b		43.48 N	79.31 W
Edgeley, N.D., U.S.	140	A14	46.21 N	98.42 W
Edgell Island, i., Grnld.	108	E13	61.48 N	65.00 W
Edgely, Pa., U.S.	203		40.07 N	74.50 W
Edgemont, Pa., U.S.	203		39.57 N	75.27 W
Edgemont, S.D., U.S.	140	D9	43.17 N	103.48 W
Edgemoor, De., U.S.	203		39.45 N	75.30 W
Edgeøya, i., Nor.	106	B25	77.44 N	22.29 E
Edgeroi, Austl.	98	H7	30.07 S	149.48 E
Edgerton, Ab., Can.	142	B3	52.45 N	110.26 W
Edgerton, Mn., U.S.	128	H2	43.52 N	96.07 W
Edgerton, Oh., U.S.	124	C1	41.26 N	84.44 W
Edgerton, Wi., U.S.	130	B8	42.50 N	89.04 W
Edgerton, Wy., U.S.	140	D6	43.26 N	106.15 W
Edgewater, Fl., U.S.	132	H5	28.59 N	80.54 W
Edgewater, N.J., U.S.	194		40.50 N	73.58 W
Edgewater Park, N.J., U.S.	203		40.04 N	74.54 W
Edgewater Park, p.o.i., Oh., U.S.	197a		41.29 N	81.43 W
Edgewater Point, c., N.Y., U.S.	194		40.55 N	73.44 W
Edgewood, B.C., Can.	144	G12	49.47 N	118.08 W
Edgewood, Il., U.S.	130	F9	38.55 N	88.40 W
Edgewood, Ia., U.S.	130	B6	42.38 N	91.24 W
Edgewood, Md., U.S.	124	E9	39.24 N	76.17 W
Edgewood, Pa., U.S.	197b		40.25 N	79.52 W
Edgewood, Tx., U.S.	136	B12	32.42 N	95.52 W
Edgware, ngh., Eng., U.K.	178		51.37 N	0.17 W
Edgworth, Eng., U.K.	180		53.39 N	2.24 W
Edievale, N.Z.	102	G3	45.48 S	169.22 E
Edina, Mn., U.S.	128	G5	44.53 N	93.21 W
Edina, Mo., U.S.	130	D5	40.10 N	92.10 W
Edinboro, Pa., U.S.	124	C5	41.52 N	80.07 W
Edinburg, Il., U.S.	130	E8	39.39 N	89.23 W
Edinburg, In., U.S.	130	E11	39.21 N	85.57 W
Edinburg, Ms., U.S.	134	E9	32.47 N	89.20 W
Edinburg, N.D., U.S.	142	F16	48.29 N	97.51 W
Edinburg, Tx., U.S.	136	H9	26.18 N	98.09 W
Edinburg, Va., U.S.	124	F7	38.49 N	78.33 W
Edinburgh, Scot., U.K.	10	F9	55.57 N	3.13 W
Edincik, Tur.	34	C10	40.20 N	27.54 E
Edineț, Mol.	38	E6	48.09 N	27.19 E
Edirne, Tur.	34	B9	41.41 N	26.33 E
Edirne, state, Tur.	34	B9	41.20 N	26.40 E
Edison, Ga., U.S.	134	F14	31.33 N	84.44 W
Edison National Historic Site, hist., N.J., U.S.	194		40.47 N	74.14 W
Edison Park, ngh., Il., U.S.	196		42.01 N	87.49 W
Edisto, stm., S.C., U.S.	132	D5	32.32 N	80.25 W
Edisto, North Fork, stm., S.C., U.S.	132	C4	33.15 N	80.53 W
Edisto Island, i., S.C., U.S.	132	D5	32.35 N	80.20 W
Edith, Mount, mtn., Mt., U.S.	146	D15	46.26 N	111.11 W
Edith Cavell, Mount, mtn., Ab., Can.	144	D12	52.40 N	118.03 W
Edithvale, Austl.	192b		38.02 S	145.07 E
Edjeleh, Alg.	84	D6	27.38 N	9.51 E
Edmond, Ok., U.S.	138	F11	35.39 N	97.28 W
Edmonds, Wa., U.S.	146	C4	47.48 N	122.22 W
Edmondson Heights, Md., U.S.	202b		39.18 N	76.43 W
Edmonston, Md., U.S.	202c		38.57 N	76.56 W
Edmonton, Austl.	98	A5	17.01 S	145.45 E
Edmonton, Ab., Can.	144	C17	53.33 N	113.28 W
Edmonton, Ky., U.S.	130	G12	36.58 N	85.36 W
Edmonton, ngh., Eng., U.K.	178		51.37 N	0.04 W
Edmore, Mi., U.S.	126	E4	43.24 N	85.02 W
Edmore, N.D., U.S.	142	F15	48.25 N	98.29 W
Edmundston, N.B., Can.	122	C8	47.22 N	68.19 W
Edna, Ks., U.S.	130	G2	37.04 N	95.21 W
Edna, Pa., U.S.	197b		40.19 N	79.39 W
Edna, Tx., U.S.	136	E11	28.58 N	96.38 W
Edogawa, ngh., Japan	186		35.42 N	139.52 E
Edolo, Italy	30	D7	46.10 N	10.19 E
Edremit, Tur.	34	D10	39.35 N	27.00 E
Edremit Körfezi, b., Tur.	34	D9	39.30 N	26.45 E
Edrovo, Russia	26	C16	57.54 N	33.40 E
Edsall Park, Va., U.S.	202c		38.48 N	77.11 W
Edsbro, Swe.	16	H16	59.53 N	18.29 E
Edsbruk, Swe.	16	I14	58.01 N	16.28 E
Edsbyn, Swe.	16	F13	61.22 N	15.48 E
Edson, Ab., Can.	144	C14	53.35 N	116.26 W
Edson Butte, mtn., Or., U.S.	146	H2	42.52 N	124.20 W
Eduardo Castex, Arg.	172	G5	35.55 S	64.17 W
Eduni, Mount, mtn., N.T., Can.	110	C5	64.15 N	128.04 W
Edward, stm., Austl.	98	J4	35.29 S	144.52 E
Edward, Lake, l., Afr.	86	E5	0.23 S	29.35 E
Edwardes Park, p.o.i., Austl.	192b		37.43 S	145.00 E
Edward Island, i., On., Can.	128	C10	48.23 N	88.37 W
Edwards, Ms., U.S.	134	E8	32.20 N	90.36 W
Edwards, N.Y., U.S.	126	D14	44.19 N	75.14 W
Edwards, stm., Il., U.S.	130	C7	41.08 N	90.58 W
Edwards Air Force Base, mil., Ca., U.S.	148	I8	34.54 N	117.52 W
Edwards Airport, arpt., N.Y., U.S.	194		40.45 N	73.03 W
Edwards Butte, mtn., Or., U.S.	146	E3	45.23 N	123.41 W
Edwards Gardens, p.o.i., On., Can.	193b		43.44 N	79.22 W
Edwards Plateau, plat., Tx., U.S.	136	D7	30.45 N	100.47 W
Edwards Run, stm., N.J., U.S.	203		39.48 N	75.12 W
Edwardsville, Il., U.S.	130	F8	38.48 N	89.57 W
Edward VII Peninsula, pen., Ant.	103	C25	77.40 S	154.59 W
Eek, Ak., U.S.	109	D7	60.12 N	162.14 W
Eeklo, Bel.	20	C12	51.11 N	3.34 E
Eel, stm., Ca., U.S.	148	C2	40.37 N	124.19 W
Eel, stm., In., U.S.	130	E10	39.06 N	86.57 W
Eel, stm., In., U.S.	130	C12	40.45 N	86.22 W
Eel, Middle Fork, stm., Ca., U.S.	148	D3	39.42 N	123.20 W
Eel, North Fork, stm., Ca., U.S.	148	C2	39.57 N	123.26 W
Eel, South Fork, stm., Ca., U.S.	148	C2	40.22 N	123.55 W
Eems (Ems), stm., Eur.	20	A16	53.19 N	7.03 E
Eesti see Estonia, ctry., Eur.	12	G12	59.00 N	26.00 E
Éfaté, i., Vanuatu	101d	k17	17.40 S	168.25 E
Eferding, Aus.	30	B10	48.18 N	14.01 E
Efes (Ephesus), hist., Tur.	34	F10	37.54 N	27.20 E
Effigy Mounds National Monument, p.o.i., Ia., U.S.	130	A6	43.06 N	91.13 W
Effingham, Eng., U.K.	178		51.16 N	0.24 W
Effingham, Il., U.S.	130	E9	39.06 N	88.32 W
Effingham, Ks., U.S.	130	E2	39.31 N	95.24 W
Efimovskij, Russia	26	A17	59.30 N	34.40 E
Eflâni, Tur.	34	B15	41.26 N	32.57 E
Eforie Nord, Rom.	36	E15	44.01 N	28.38 E
Eforie Sud, Rom.	36	F15	44.00 N	28.37 E
Efremov, Russia	26	G20	53.09 N	38.07 E
Eg, stm., Mong.	50	F9	49.23 N	103.38 E
Ega, stm., Spain	28	B9	42.19 N	1.55 W
Egadi, Isole, is., Italy	32	G5	37.58 N	12.16 E
Egaña, Arg.	172	H8	36.58 S	59.07 W
Egan Range, mts., Nv., U.S.	150	D2	39.00 N	115.00 W
Eganville, On., Can.	126	C12	45.31 N	77.05 W
Egbe, Nig.	191a		6.33 N	3.17 E
Ege Denizi see Aegean Sea, s.	34	E7	38.30 N	25.00 E
Egedesminde (Aasiaat), Grnld.	108	D15	68.42 N	52.48 W
Egegik, Ak., U.S.	109	E8	58.12 N	157.22 W
Eger see Cheb, Czech Rep.	24	F8	50.04 N	12.22 E
Eger, Hung.	36	B7	47.53 N	20.23 E
Eger see Ohře, stm., Eur.	24	F9	50.31 N	14.08 E
Egerpohl, Ger.	181		51.07 N	7.27 E
Egersund, Nor.	16	I4	58.27 N	6.00 E
Egerton, Eng., U.K.	180		53.38 N	2.26 W
Egeskov, hist., Den.	16	L8	55.11 N	10.30 E
Egg Creek, stm., N.D., U.S.	142	F12	48.21 N	100.47 W
Eggenburg, Aus.	24	H11	48.38 N	15.48 E
Eggenfelden, Ger.	24	H8	48.24 N	12.45 E
Eggerscheid, Ger.	181		51.19 N	6.53 E
Egg Harbor City, N.J., U.S.	124	E11	39.31 N	74.38 W
Egg Lagoon, Austl.	98	L5	39.38 S	143.59 E
Eggum, Nor.	14	D4	68.18 N	13.41 E
Egilsstaðir, Ice.	12a	k32	65.15 N	14.22 W
Égletons, Fr.	22	D7	45.23 N	2.02 E
Eglin Air Force Base, mil., Fl., U.S.	134	G12	30.29 N	86.30 W
Eglinton Island, i., N.T., Can.	109	A16	75.48 N	118.30 W
Égly, Fr.	179		48.35 N	2.13 E
Egmont, Cape, c., N.Z.	102	D5	39.17 S	173.45 E
Egmont, Mount see Taranaki, Mount, vol., N.Z.	102	D6	39.17 S	174.03 E
Egmont Bay, b., P.E., Can.	122	D12	46.35 N	64.12 W
Egmont National Park, p.o.i., N.Z.	102	D5	39.15 S	174.05 E
Egorevsk, Russia	26	E22	55.22 N	39.02 E
Egorlyk, stm., Russia	42	C9	46.32 N	41.50 E
Egorlykskaja, Russia	40	H12	46.33 N	40.39 E
Egota, ngh., Japan	186		35.43 N	139.40 E
Egremont, Ab., Can.	144	B17	54.02 N	113.07 W
Eğridir, Tur.	34	F13	37.52 N	30.49 E
Eğridir Gölü, l., Tur.	34	E13	38.02 N	30.53 E
Egtved, Den.	16	L7	55.37 N	9.18 E
Éguas, stm., Braz.	170	G3	13.25 S	44.14 W
Egvekinot, Russia	50	C25	66.17 N	179.11 W
Egypt, ctry., Afr.	82	B5	27.00 N	30.00 E
Egyptian Museum, bldg., Egypt	191c		30.03 N	31.14 E
Eha-Amufu, Nig.	84	H6	6.37 N	7.45 E
Ehegnadzor see Yeghegnador, Arm.	42	F17	39.45 N	45.21 E
Ehime, state, Japan	56	F5	33.40 N	132.50 E
Ehingen, Ger.	24	H5	48.16 N	9.43 E
Ehingen, ngh., Ger.	181		51.22 N	6.42 E
Ehrenberg, Az., U.S.	150	J2	33.38 N	114.30 W
Ehrhardt, S.C., U.S.	132	C4	33.05 N	81.00 W
Ehringhausen, Ger.	181		51.11 N	7.33 E
Ehringhausen, ngh., Ger.	181		51.09 N	7.11 E
Ehwa Women's University, educ., Kor., S.	189b		37.34 N	126.56 E
Ei, Japan	56	H3	31.12 N	130.30 E
Eibar, Spain	28	A8	43.11 N	2.27 W
Eibiswald, Aus.	30	D12	46.41 N	15.14 E
Eich-Berg, hill, Ger.	182a		52.39 N	13.50 E
Eiche, Ger.	182a		52.34 N	13.36 E
Eiche, Ger.	182a		52.25 N	12.58 E
Eichenbrandt, Ger.	182a		52.38 N	13.51 E
Eichlinghofen, ngh., Ger.	181		51.29 N	7.24 E
Eichstädt, Ger.	182a		52.42 N	13.07 E
Eichstätt, Ger.	24	H7	48.53 N	11.11 E
Eicken, ngh., Ger.	181		51.13 N	6.26 E
Eickerend, Ger.	181		51.13 N	6.34 E
Eickerkopf, hill, Ger.	181		51.21 N	7.42 E
Eide, Nor.	16	E5	62.54 N	7.25 E
Eidfjord, Nor.	16	G5	60.27 N	7.04 E
Eidslandet, Nor.	16	G3	60.43 N	5.48 E
Eidsvåg, Nor.	16	E6	62.46 N	8.03 E
Eidsvold, Austl.	98	E8	25.22 S	151.07 E
Eidsvoll, Nor.	16	G9	60.19 N	11.14 E
Eifel, mts., Ger.	24	F2	50.13 N	6.42 E
Eiffel, Tour, hist., Fr.	179		48.51 N	2.18 E
Eifgenbach, stm., Ger.	181		51.05 N	7.09 E
Eigen, ngh., Ger.	181		51.33 N	6.57 E
Eigerøya, i., Nor.	16	I3	58.26 N	5.57 E
Eigg, i., Scot., U.K.	10	E6	56.53 N	6.10 W
Eight Degree Channel, strt., Asia	62	G3	8.00 N	73.00 E
Eight Mile Creek, stm., On., Can.	202a		43.14 N	79.11 W
Eights Coast, cst., Ant.	103	C31	73.28 S	92.48 W
Eighty Four, Pa., U.S.	197b		40.11 N	80.08 W
Eighty Mile Beach, cst., Austl.	96	C4	19.45 S	121.00 E
Eikedalsvatnet, l., Nor.	16	E5	62.33 N	8.09 E
Eikeren, l., Nor.	16	H7	59.42 N	9.49 E
Eildon, Austl.	98	K5	37.14 S	145.55 E
Eildon, Lake, res., Austl.	98	K5	37.09 S	145.52 E
Eilenburg, Ger.	24	E8	51.27 N	12.37 E
Eiler Rasmussen, Kap, c., Grnld.	108	A21	82.35 N	21.20 W
Eina, Nor.	16	G8	60.38 N	10.36 E
Einasleigh, Austl.	98	B5	18.30 S	144.05 E
Einasleigh, stm., Austl.	98	A4	17.30 S	142.17 E
Einbeck, Ger.	24	E5	51.49 N	9.52 E
Eindhoven, Neth.	20	C14	51.26 N	5.28 E
Einme, Mya.	64	D2	16.53 N	95.12 E
Einsiedeln, Switz.	24	I4	47.08 N	8.44 E
Eirauli, India	190c		19.10 N	72.59 E
Éire see Ireland, ctry., Eur.	6	E7	53.00 N	8.00 W
Eirunepé, Braz.	164	E4	6.38 S	69.52 W
Eisack see Isarco, stm., Italy	30	D8	46.21 N	11.17 E
Eiseb, stm., Afr.	90	B4	20.33 S	20.59 E
Eisenach, Ger.	26	E6	50.59 N	10.18 E
Eisenberg, Ger.	24	F7	50.58 N	11.53 E
Eisenerz, Aus.	30	C11	47.33 N	14.53 E
Eisenhower Center, bldg., Ks., U.S.	138	C11	38.54 N	97.12 W
Eisenhower Memorial Park, p.o.i., N.Y., U.S.	194		40.44 N	73.34 W
Eisenhüttenstadt, Ger.	24	D10	52.09 N	14.37 E
Eisenstadt, Aus.	30	C13	47.50 N	16.31 E
Eisfeld, Ger.	24	F6	50.25 N	10.54 E
Eišiškės, Lith.	26	F7	54.10 N	25.02 E
Eislingen, Ger.	24	H5	48.41 N	9.42 E
Eitorf, Ger.	24	F3	50.46 N	7.27 E
Eivissa (Iviza), Spain	28	F12	38.54 N	1.25 E
Eivissa (Ibiza), i., Spain	28	F12	39.00 N	1.25 E
Eja, stm., Russia	40	H11	46.39 N	38.35 E
Ejby, Den.	16	L7	55.26 N	9.57 E
Ejea de los Caballeros, Spain	28	B9	42.07 N	1.08 W
Ejeda, Madag.	88	E7	24.20 S	44.31 E
Ejército Rebelde, Presa, res., Cuba	204b		23.01 N	82.20 W
Ejido, Ven.	168	C6	8.33 N	71.13 W
Ejido Jaboncillos, Mex.	154	A7	28.57 N	102.47 W
Ejigbo, Nig.	191a		6.33 N	3.18 E
Ejin Horo Qi, China	58	B3	39.27 N	109.40 E
Ejin Qi, China	52	C5	41.51 N	100.55 E
Ejsk, Russia	40	H11	46.42 N	38.16 E
Ejskij liman, b., Russia	38	G17	46.42 N	38.25 E
Ejura, Ghana	84	H4	7.22 N	1.22 W
Ejutla de Crespo, Mex.	154	G10	16.33 N	96.44 W
Ekalaka, Mt., U.S.	140	B8	45.53 N	104.33 W
Ekāli, Grc.	185c		38.07 N	23.50 E
Ekaterinburg, Russia	48	C10	56.50 N	60.36 E
Ekaterinino, Russia	26	E16	55.48 N	33.57 E
Ekaterinodar see Krasnodar, Russia	40	I11	45.02 N	38.59 E
Ekaterinoslav see Dnipropetrovs'k, Ukr.	38	E14	48.28 N	34.57 E
Ekaterinoslavka, Russia	50	F14	50.22 N	129.06 E
Ekaterinovka, Russia	38	F17	47.32 N	38.23 E
Ekaterinovka, Russia	38	G17	46.41 N	38.45 E
Ekaterinovka, ngh., Russia	183b		55.46 N	37.23 E
Ekateriny, proliv, strt., Russia	54	B17	44.30 N	146.45 E
Ekenäs see Tammisaari, Fin.	18	H10	59.58 N	23.26 E
Ekenässjön, Swe.	16	J13	57.30 N	15.01 E
Ekibastuz, Kaz.	48	D13	51.43 N	75.19 E
Ekimčan, Russia	50	F15	53.04 N	132.56 E
Ekimoviči, Russia	26	F16	54.07 N	33.18 E
Eko see Lagos, Nig.	84	H5	6.27 N	3.24 E
Ekoln, l., Swe.	16	H15	59.45 N	17.37 E
Ekonda, Russia	50	C10	65.45 N	105.20 E
Eksāra, India	190b		22.38 N	88.17 E
Eksjö, Swe.	16	J12	57.40 N	14.58 E
Ekwan, stm., On., Can.	110	E14	53.12 N	82.13 W
Ela, Mya.	64	C3	19.37 N	96.14 E
El Aaiún (Laayoune), W. Sah.	84	D2	27.09 N	13.11 W
El-Abbâsîya, ngh., Egypt	191c		30.04 N	31.17 E
Elabuga, Russia	40	D17	55.46 N	52.05 E
El 'Açâba, plat., Maur.	84	F2	16.00 N	12.00 W
El Affroun, Alg.	28	H13	36.28 N	2.37 E
El Agreb, Alg.	84	C6	30.49 N	5.41 E
El Aguacate, Ven.	204c		10.28 N	66.59 W
El Agustino, Peru	204d		12.03 S	76.59 W
El Agustino, Cerro, hill, Peru	204d		12.04 S	77.00 W
El Ahijadero, Cerro, mtn., Mex.	136	E1	29.42 N	106.17 W
Elaine, Ar., U.S.	134	C8	34.18 N	90.51 W
El-'Aiyât, Egypt	76	I2	29.36 N	31.15 E
El-Alamein, Egypt	82	A5	30.49 N	28.57 E
El Álamo, Mex.	136	H8	26.29 N	99.46 W
El Álamo, Mex.	136	G7	27.31 N	100.50 W
El Álamo, Mex.	148	L9	31.36 N	116.03 W
El Álamo, stm., Mex.	136	G2	27.32 N	105.25 W
El Almirez, Cerro, mtn., Mex.	136	G2	27.22 N	105.57 W
El Alto, Arg.	172	D5	28.18 S	65.22 W
Elam, Pa., U.S.	203		39.51 N	75.32 W
El Amparo de Apure, Ven.	168	D6	7.06 N	70.45 W
Elan', Russia	40	F13	50.57 N	43.44 E
Elan, stm., Rom.	36	C15	46.04 N	28.05 E
Élancourt, Fr.	179		48.47 N	1.58 E
Elancy, Russia	50	F10	52.47 N	106.23 E
Elandsfontein, S. Afr.	191d		26.10 S	28.12 E
Elandsvlei, S. Afr.	90	H4	32.18 S	19.33 E
El Ángel, Ec.	168	G2	0.37 N	77.56 W
Elan'-Koleno, Russia	40	F12	51.08 N	41.14 E
Elanora Heights, Austl.	192a		33.42 S	151.17 E
El Arco, Mex.	154	A2	28.00 N	113.25 W
El-Arish, Egypt	76	G4	31.08 N	33.50 E
El Arrayán, Chile	204e		33.21 S	70.28 W
El Asnam see Ech Cheliff, Alg.	84	B5	36.10 N	1.20 E
Elassóna, Grc.	34	D5	39.53 N	22.11 E
Elat, Isr.	76	I5	29.33 N	34.57 E
Elat, Gulf of see Aqaba, Gulf of, b.	76	J5	29.05 N	34.44 E
Elath see Elat, Isr.	76	I5	29.33 N	34.57 E
El Ávila, Cerro, mtn., Ven.	204c		10.33 N	66.52 W
El Ávila, Parque Nacional, p.o.i., Ven.	168	B8	10.33 N	66.40 W
Elazığ, Tur.	42	F8	38.40 N	39.14 E
Elazığ, state, Tur.	42	F8	38.35 N	39.30 E
El-Azîzîya, Egypt	191c		29.52 N	31.15 E
Elba, Al., U.S.	134	F12	31.24 N	86.04 W
Elba, Isola d', i., Italy	30	H7	42.46 N	10.17 E
El-Badâri, Egypt	76	K2	26.59 N	31.25 E
El-Badrashein, Egypt	191c		29.51 N	31.16 E
El-Bahnasa, Egypt	76	J1	28.31 N	30.39 E
El-Bahr el-Ahmar, state, Egypt	191c		29.58 N	31.21 E
El-Ballâs, Egypt	74	G3	26.01 N	32.46 E
El-Balyana, Egypt	74	G2	26.13 N	32.00 E
El'ban, Russia	50	F16	50.05 N	136.31 E
El Banco, Col.	168	C4	9.00 N	73.58 W
El-Barâgîl, Egypt	191c		30.04 N	31.09 E
El Barco de Ávila, Spain	28	D5	40.21 N	5.31 W
El Barco de Valdeorras see O Barco de Valdeorras, Spain	28	B4	42.25 N	6.59 W
El Barreal, Mex.	150	L9	31.16 N	107.08 W
El Barreal, l., Mex.	150	L10	31.12 N	106.41 W
El-Barsha, Egypt	76	K1	27.43 N	30.54 E
Elbasan, Alb.	32	C14	41.06 N	20.05 E
Elbasani see Elbasan, Alb.	32	C14	41.06 N	20.05 E
El-Basâtîn, ngh., Egypt	191c		29.59 N	31.16 E
El Baúl, Ven.	168	C7	8.53 N	68.19 W
El Baúl, Cerro, mtn., Mex.	154	G11	16.36 N	94.13 W
Elbe (Labe), stm., Eur.	24	C7	53.53 N	9.01 E
Elbe-Havel-Kanal, can., Ger.	24	D8	52.24 N	12.25 E
Elberfeld, ngh., Ger.	181		51.16 N	7.08 E
El Bermejo, Cerro, mtn., Mex.	136	G4	27.21 N	103.06 W
Elbert, Co., U.S.	138	B4	39.12 N	104.31 W
Elbert, Mount, mtn., Co., U.S.	138	B2	39.07 N	106.27 W
Elberta, Mi., U.S.	126	D3	44.36 N	86.13 W
Elberton, Ga., U.S.	132	B3	34.06 N	82.51 W
Elbe-Seitenkanal, can., Ger.	20	B19	53.22 N	10.30 E
Elbeuf, Fr.	20	E10	49.17 N	1.01 E
Elbeyli, Tur.	76	B8	36.40 N	37.28 E
El Beyyadh, Alg.	84	C5	33.40 N	1.00 E
Elbing see Elbląg, Pol.	24	B15	54.10 N	19.24 E
Elbistan, Tur.	42	F7	38.12 N	37.11 E
Elbląg, Pol.	24	B15	54.10 N	19.24 E
El Bluff, Nic.	156	G6	12.01 N	83.41 W
El Bonillo, Spain	28	F8	38.56 N	2.32 W
El Bosque, Chile	204e		33.34 S	70.41 W
El Boulaida, Alg.	84	B5	36.28 N	2.49 E
Elbow, Sk., Can.	142	C7	51.07 N	106.35 W
Elbow, stm., Ab., Can.	144	E16	51.02 N	114.02 W
Elbow Lake, Mn., U.S.	128	E3	45.59 N	95.58 W
El'brus, gora (Elbrus, Mount), mtn., Russia	42	D10	43.21 N	42.26 E
Elbrus, Mount see El'brus, gora, mtn., Russia	42	D10	43.21 N	42.26 E
El'brusskij, Russia	42	D10	43.34 N	42.07 E
El-Burg, Egypt	76	G1	31.35 N	30.59 E
El-Burgâya, Egypt	76	J1	28.09 N	30.44 E
Elburz Mountains see Alborz, Reshteh-ye Kūhhā-ye, mts., Iran	74	B13	36.00 N	53.00 E
El Caburé, Arg.	172	B6	26.01 S	62.22 W
El Cadillal, Embalse, res., Arg.	172	C5	26.34 S	65.13 W
El Cajon, Ca., U.S.	148	K9	32.47 N	116.56 W
El Calafate, Arg.	166	J2	50.20 S	72.16 W
El Callao, Ven.	168	D11	7.21 N	61.48 W
El Calvario, Col.	168	E5	4.21 N	73.43 W
El Calvario, Ven.	168	C8	9.00 N	66.58 W
El Calvario, ngh., Cuba	204b		23.05 N	82.20 W
El Campamento, P.R.	158a	b3	18.22 N	66.28 W
El Campamento, ngh., Spain	184a		40.24 N	3.46 W
El Campo, Tx., U.S.	136	E11	29.11 N	96.16 W
El Capitan, mtn., Mt., U.S.	146	D12	46.01 N	114.23 W
El Caracol Depósito de Evaporación Solar, sci., Mex.	204a		19.35 N	99.00 W
El Caribe, Ven.	204c		10.37 N	66.50 W
El Carmen, Arg.	172	B5	24.23 S	65.16 W
El Carmen, Chile	204e		33.21 S	70.43 W
El Carmen, Col.	168	C5	8.30 N	73.27 W
El Carmen, Ven.	204c		10.24 N	67.01 W
El Carmen, Ven.	204c		10.24 N	66.50 W
El Carmen, stm., Mex.	120	F9	30.20 N	106.35 W
El Carmen, Canal, can., Chile	204e		33.18 S	70.41 W
El Carmen de Bolívar, Col.	168	C4	9.42 N	75.06 W
El Carricito, Mex.	154	A7	28.24 N	103.24 W
El Carril, Arg.	172	B5	25.06 S	65.27 W
El Cedrito, Mex.	154	A8	29.11 N	101.59 W
El Centinela, Mex.	148	K10	32.35 N	115.40 W
El Centro, Ca., U.S.	148	K10	32.47 N	115.33 W
El Cerrito, Col.	168	F3	3.42 N	76.19 W
El Cerro Del Aripo, mtn., Trin.	159f	s12	10.43 N	61.15 W
Elche see Elx, Spain	28	F10	38.15 N	0.42 W
Elche de la Sierra, Spain	28	F8	38.27 N	2.03 W
El Chile, Montaña, mtn., Nic.	156	E4	14.22 N	86.51 W
Elcho, Wi., U.S.	128	F9	45.24 N	89.12 W
Elcho Island, i., Austl.	96	B7	11.56 S	135.45 E
El Chorrillo, Arg.	172	F4	33.18 S	66.16 W
El Cocuy, Col.	168	D5	6.25 N	72.27 W
El Cojo, Ven.	204c		10.36 N	66.53 W
El Cojo, Quebrada, stm., Ven.	204c		10.37 N	66.53 W
El Colorado, Arg.	172	C8	26.18 S	59.22 W
El Cóndor, Cerro, vol., Arg.	172	C3	26.38 S	68.22 W
El Corazón, Ec.	168	H2	1.12 S	79.06 W
El Corozo, Ven.	204c		10.35 N	66.58 W
El Corpus, Hond.	156	F4	13.16 N	87.03 W
El Corte de Madera Creek, stm., Ca., U.S.	200		37.19 N	122.20 W
El Cortijo, Chile	204e		33.22 S	70.42 W
El Coto, P.R.	158a	b2	18.27 N	66.44 W
El Coyote, Laguna, l., Mex.	136	G4	27.14 N	103.17 W
El Cozón, Mex.	154	F6	31.14 N	112.31 W
El Cuy, Arg.	166	G3	39.55 S	68.20 W
El'cy, Russia	26	D16	56.40 N	33.50 E
Elda, Spain	28	F10	38.29 N	0.47 W
El-Deir, Egypt	74	H3	25.20 N	32.35 E
Elder Island, i., N.Y., U.S.	194		40.38 N	73.23 W
Elder Mills, On., Can.	193b		43.49 N	79.38 W
El Desemboque, Mex.	120	G6	29.32 N	112.24 W
El Desemboque, Mex.	120	F6	30.32 N	112.58 W
El'dikan, Russia	50	D16	60.46 N	135.09 E
El-Dilingât, Egypt	76	H1	30.49 N	30.31 E
El Diviso, Col.	168	G2	1.22 N	78.13 W
El Djazaïr (Alger), Alg.	84	B5	36.46 N	3.02 E
El Djazaïr see Algeria, ctry., Afr.	84	D5	28.00 N	3.00 E
El Djelfa, Alg.	84	C5	34.41 N	3.14 E
Eldon, Ia., U.S.	130	D5	40.55 N	92.12 W
Eldon, Mo., U.S.	130	F5	38.21 N	92.35 W
El-Doqqi, Egypt	191c		30.04 N	31.15 E
Eldora, Ia., U.S.	130	B4	42.21 N	93.06 W
Eldora, Pa., U.S.	197b		40.10 N	79.53 W
Eldorado, Arg.	172	C10	26.24 S	54.38 W
Eldorado, Braz.	172	B13	24.32 S	48.06 W
El Dorado, Ar., U.S.	134	D6	33.12 N	92.40 W
Eldorado, Il., U.S.	130	G9	37.48 N	88.26 W
El Dorado, Ks., U.S.	138	D12	37.48 N	96.51 W
Eldorado, Ok., U.S.	138	G9	34.28 N	99.39 W
Eldorado, Tx., U.S.	136	D7	30.51 N	100.36 W
El Dorado, Ven.	168	D11	6.44 N	61.36 W
Eldoradopark, S. Afr.	191d		26.18 S	27.53 E
El Dorado Park, p.o.i., Ca., U.S.	198		33.49 N	118.05 W
Eldorado Peak, mtn., Wa., U.S.	146	B5	48.32 N	121.08 W
El Dorado Springs, Mo., U.S.	130	G4	37.52 N	94.01 W
Eldoret, Kenya	86	D7	0.31 N	35.17 E
Eldred, Pa., U.S.	124	C7	41.57 N	78.23 W
Eldridge, Ia., U.S.	130	C7	41.39 N	90.35 W
Eldridges Hill, N.J., U.S.	203		39.40 N	75.18 W
Eleanor, W.V., U.S.	124	F4	38.31 N	81.56 W
Elec, Russia	26	H21	52.37 N	38.30 E
Electra, Tx., U.S.	138	G10	34.02 N	98.54 W
Electric City, Wa., U.S.	146	C7	47.55 N	119.01 W
Elefantes (Olifants), stm., Afr.	90	D10	24.06 S	32.38 E
Elefsína, Grc.	34	E6	38.02 N	23.32 E
Elefsína, Grc.	185c		38.02 N	23.32 E
Elefsís Airport, arpt., Grc.	185c		38.04 N	23.34 E
Eleftheroúpoli, Grc.	34	C7	40.55 N	24.15 E
El Eglab, des., Alg.	84	D3	26.25 N	5.00 W
Eleja, Lat.	26	D6	56.25 N	23.40 E
Elektrostal', Russia	26	E21	55.46 N	38.27 E
Elena, Blg.	36	G12	42.56 N	25.52 E
El Encantado, Ven.	204c		10.27 N	66.47 W
El Encanto, Col.	168	H5	1.41 S	73.13 W
El Encanto, Guat.	156	D3	17.17 N	89.34 W
Elenskij, Russia	26	G18	53.29 N	35.22 E
Elepete, Nig.	191a		6.41 N	3.28 E
Elephanta Caves, cv., India	190c		18.58 N	72.56 E
Elephanta Island (Ghārāpuri), i., India	190c		18.57 N	72.55 E
Elephant Butte Lake State Park, p.o.i., N.M., U.S.	150	J9	33.11 N	107.14 W
Elephant Butte Reservoir, res., N.M., U.S.	150	J9	33.17 N	107.09 W
Elephant Mountain, mtn., Me., U.S.	122	F6	44.46 N	70.46 W
Elesbão Veloso, Braz.	170	D4	6.13 S	42.08 W
El Estor, Guat.	156	E3	15.31 N	89.21 W
Eleuthera, i., Bah.	152	B9	25.10 N	76.13 W
Eleva, Wi., U.S.	128	G7	44.34 N	91.27 W
Eleven Point, stm., U.S.	130	H6	36.08 N	91.05 W
Elevsínos, Kólpos, b., Grc.	185c		38.02 N	23.34 E
El Fahs, Tun.	32	H3	36.22 N	9.54 E
El Faro, P.R.	158a	c2	18.00 N	66.47 W
El-Fashn, Egypt	76	J1	28.49 N	30.54 E
El-Fayoum, Egypt	76	I1	29.19 N	30.50 E
El Ferrol del Caudillo see Ferrol, Spain	28	A2	43.29 N	8.13 W
Elfgen, Ger.	181		51.05 N	6.32 E
El-Fiqrîya, Egypt	76	K1	27.56 N	30.49 E
Elfrida, Az., U.S.	150	L7	31.41 N	109.41 W
Elfros, Sk., Can.	142	C10	51.43 N	103.52 W
El Fud, Eth.	82	F8	7.20 N	42.50 E
El Fuerte, Mex.	154	B4	26.24 N	108.37 W
Elgåhogna, mtn., Nor.	16	E10	62.08 N	12.05 E
El Galpón, Arg.	172	B5	25.23 S	64.38 W
El-Gamâlîya, ngh., Egypt	191c		30.03 N	31.16 E
El Gavilán, Cerro, mtn., Mex.	136	H2	26.03 N	105.46 W
Elgin, Scot., U.K.	10	D9	57.38 N	3.18 W
Elgin, Il., U.S.	130	B9	42.02 N	88.16 W
Elgin, Ia., U.S.	130	B6	42.57 N	91.37 W
Elgin, Mn., U.S.	128	G6	44.07 N	92.14 W
Elgin, Ne., U.S.	140	F14	41.58 N	98.05 W
Elgin, N.D., U.S.	140	A11	46.24 N	101.51 W
Elgin, Ok., U.S.	138	G10	34.46 N	98.17 W
Elgin, Or., U.S.	146	E9	45.34 N	117.55 W
Elgin, Tx., U.S.	136	D10	30.20 N	97.22 W
El-Gindîya, Egypt	76	J1	28.34 N	30.50 E
El-Gîza (Giza), Egypt	76	H1	30.01 N	31.12 E
El-Gîza (Giza), Egypt	191c		30.01 N	31.13 E
El-Gîza, state, Egypt	191c		30.00 N	31.10 E
El Goléa see El Menia, Alg.	84	C5	30.32 N	2.53 E
El Goloso, ngh., Spain	184a		40.33 N	3.42 W
Elgon, Mount, mtn., Afr.	86	D6	1.08 N	34.33 E
Elgoras, gora, mtn., Russia	14	D22	68.06 N	31.30 E
Elgpiggen, mtn., Nor.	16	E9	62.09 N	11.22 E
El Grara, Alg.	84	C5	32.47 N	4.30 E
El Grove see O Grove, Spain	28	B2	42.29 N	8.51 W
El Guaje, Mex.	154	A7	28.05 N	103.17 W
El Guamo, Col.	168	B4	10.02 N	74.59 W
El Guanábano, Ven.	204c		10.24 N	67.01 W
El Guapo, Ven.	168	B9	10.09 N	65.57 W
El Guarapo, Ven.	204c		10.36 N	66.58 W
El Guayabo de Abajo, Mex.	154	C5	26.00 N	107.25 W
El Hachero, Cerro, mtn., Mex.	136	H2	26.16 N	105.19 W
El Hammâmi, reg., Maur.	84	E2	23.03 N	11.30 W
El-Hamûl, Egypt	76	G2	31.18 N	31.09 E
El Hank, clf., Afr.	84	E3	24.23 N	6.35 W
El Hatillo, Ven.	204c		10.26 N	66.49 W
El Hatillo, Quebrada, stm., Ven.	204c		10.27 N	66.47 W
El-Hawâmdîya, Egypt	76	I2	29.54 N	31.15 E
El-Hawâmdîya, Egypt	191c		29.54 N	31.15 E
El Hierro, i., Spain	84	D1	27.45 N	18.00 W
El-Hilmîya, ngh., Egypt	191c		30.07 N	31.19 E
Elhovka, Russia	40	E17	53.55 N	50.15 E
Elhovo, Blg.	36	G13	42.10 N	26.34 E
El Huecú, Arg.	172	H2	37.37 S	70.35 W
El Huisache, Mex.	154	D8	22.54 N	100.24 W
Eliase, Indon.	60	G9	8.19 S	130.45 E
Eliasville, Tx., U.S.	136	B9	32.57 N	98.46 W
Elida, N.M., U.S.	138	H5	33.56 N	103.39 W
Elila, stm., D.R.C.	86	E5	2.44 S	25.52 E
Elim, S. Afr.	90	I4	34.35 S	19.45 E
Elim, Ak., U.S.	109	D7	64.37 N	162.15 W
El-Imâm, ngh., Egypt	191c		30.01 N	31.16 E
Elin Pelin, Blg.	36	G10	42.40 N	23.36 E
Élisabethville see Lubumbashi, D.R.C.	86	G5	11.41 S	27.28 E
Élisabethville, Fr.	179		48.58 N	1.51 E
Elisenvaara, Russia	18	F16	61.23 N	29.45 E
Eliseu Martins, Braz.	170	E4	8.13 S	43.42 W
El-Iskandarîya (Alexandria), Egypt	82	A6	31.11 N	29.54 E
Elista, Russia	40	H14	46.19 N	44.15 E
Elizabeth, Austl.	98	J2	34.43 S	138.39 E
Elizabeth, Co., U.S.	138	B4	39.21 N	104.35 W
Elizabeth, Il., U.S.	130	B7	42.18 N	90.13 W
Elizabeth, La., U.S.	134	G6	30.52 N	92.48 W
Elizabeth, N.J., U.S.	124	D11	40.40 N	74.12 W
Elizabeth, W.V., U.S.	124	E4	39.03 N	81.24 W
Elizabeth, stm., N.J., U.S.	194		40.38 N	74.12 W

Name Page Map Ref. Latitude Longitude

Elizabeth, Lake, res., Ca., U.S. 200 37.33 N 121.58 W
Elizabeth, West Branch, stm., N.J., U.S. 194 40.42 N 74.14 W
Elizabeth City, N.C., U.S. 124 H9 36.18 N 76.13 W
Elizabeth Lake, l., Mi., U.S. 199 42.38 N 83.23 W
Elizabeth Lake Estates, Mi., U.S. 199 42.38 N 83.22 W
Elizabeth Park, p.o.i., Mi., U.S. 199 42.07 N 83.11 W
Elizabethton, Tn., U.S. 124 H3 36.20 N 82.13 W
Elizabethtown, Il., U.S. 130 G9 37.26 N 88.18 W
Elizabethtown, Ky., U.S. 130 G12 37.41 N 85.51 W
Elizabethtown, N.Y., U.S. 126 D16 44.13 N 73.35 W
Elizabethtown, N.C., U.S. 132 B7 34.37 N 78.36 W
Elizabethtown, Pa., U.S. 124 D9 40.09 N 76.36 W
Eliza Howell Park, p.o.i., Mi., U.S. 199 42.24 N 83.16 W
Elizarovo, Russia 40 B14 58.32 N 44.49 E
Elizavetovka, Russia 38 G17 46.39 N 38.53 E
Elizavety, mys, c., Russia 50 F17 54.23 N 142.41 E
Elizovo, Russia 50 F20 53.09 N 158.23 E
El-Jadida, Mor. 84 C3 33.14 N 8.30 W
El Jaralito, Mex. 154 B6 26.07 N 104.10 W
El Jebel, Co., U.S. 138 B1 39.23 N 107.04 W
Elk, Pol. 24 C18 53.49 N 22.22 E
Elk, stm., Ab., Can. 144 D14 52.56 N 115.43 W
Elk, stm., B.C., Can. 144 F16 49.10 N 115.14 W
Ełk, stm., Pol. 24 C18 53.30 N 22.47 E
Elk, stm., U.S. 134 C11 34.46 N 87.16 W
Elk, stm., Co., U.S. 150 C10 40.28 N 106.57 W
Elk, stm., Ks., U.S. 138 D12 37.14 N 95.42 W
Elk, stm., Mn., U.S. 128 F4 45.17 N 93.35 W
Elk, stm., Mo., U.S. 130 H3 36.39 N 94.46 W
Elk, stm., W.V., U.S. 124 F4 38.21 N 81.38 W
Elk, stm., Wi., U.S. 128 F8 45.42 N 90.36 W
Elkader, Ia., U.S. 130 B6 42.51 N 91.24 W
El-Karnak (Karnak), Egypt 74 H3 25.42 N 32.40 E
Elk City, Ok., U.S. 138 F9 35.25 N 99.24 W
Elk City Lake, res., Ks., U.S. 138 D12 37.15 N 95.48 W
Elk Creek, Ca., U.S. 148 D3 39.35 N 122.32 W
Elk Creek, stm., Ok., U.S. 138 F9 34.48 N 99.09 W
Elk Creek, stm., S.D., U.S. 140 C10 44.15 N 102.22 W
El Kef, Tun. 84 B6 36.11 N 8.43 E
El-Kelaa-Srarhna, Mor. 84 C3 31.57 N 7.17 W
Ēl Kerē, Eth. 82 F8 5.51 N 42.05 E
Elk Grove, Ca., U.S. 148 E4 38.24 N 121.22 W
Elk Grove Village, Il., U.S. 196 42.00 N 87.58 W
El-Khânka, Egypt 76 H2 30.13 N 31.21 E
El-Kharaqânîya, Egypt 191c 30.10 N 31.10 E
El-Khârga, Egypt 82 B6 25.26 N 30.32 E
Elkhart, In., U.S. 130 C12 41.40 N 85.57 W
Elkhart, Ks., U.S. 138 D7 37.00 N 101.53 W
Elkhart, Tx., U.S. 136 C12 31.37 N 95.34 W
Elkhart Lake, Wi., U.S. 126 E2 43.50 N 88.00 W
Elkhead Creek, stm., Co., U.S. 150 C9 40.31 N 107.26 W
Elkhead Mountains, mts., Co., U.S. 150 C9 40.51 N 107.23 W
El Khnâchîch, clf., Mali 84 E4 21.50 N 3.45 W
Elkhorn, Mb., Can. 142 D12 49.58 N 101.14 W
Elk Horn, Ia., U.S. 130 C2 41.35 N 95.03 W
Elkhorn, Wi., U.S. 130 B9 42.40 N 88.33 W
Elkhorn, stm., Ne., U.S. 118 F17 41.07 N 96.19 W
Elkhorn City, Ky., U.S. 124 G3 37.18 N 82.20 W
Elkhorn Mountain, mtn., B.C., Can. 144 G5 49.48 N 125.50 W
Elkhovo see Elhovo, Blg. 36 G13 42.10 N 26.34 E
El-Khusûs, Egypt 191c 30.09 N 31.19 E
Elkin, N.C., U.S. 124 H5 36.14 N 80.50 W
Elkins, W.V., U.S. 124 F6 38.55 N 79.51 W
Elk Island, i., Mb., Can. 142 D17 50.45 N 96.32 W
Elk Island National Park, p.o.i., Ab., Can. 144 C18 53.35 N 112.54 W
Elkland, Pa., U.S. 124 C8 41.59 N 77.17 W
Elk Mountain, Wy., U.S. 150 B10 41.42 N 106.25 W
Elk Mountain, mtn., Wy., U.S. 150 B10 41.38 N 106.32 W
Elko, B.C., Can. 144 G15 49.18 N 115.07 W
Elko, Nv., U.S. 148 C10 40.50 N 115.45 W
Elk Peak, mtn., Mt., U.S. 146 D16 46.27 N 110.46 W
Elk Point, Ab., Can. 144 C20 53.53 N 110.53 W
Elk Point, S.D., U.S. 130 B1 42.41 N 96.40 W
Elk Rapids, Mi., U.S. 126 D4 44.53 N 85.24 W
Elkridge, Md., U.S. 202b 39.12 N 76.42 W
Elk River, Id., U.S. 146 D10 46.46 N 116.11 W
Elk River, Mn., U.S. 128 F5 45.18 N 93.35 W
Elkton, Ky., U.S. 130 H10 36.48 N 87.09 W
Elkton, Md., U.S. 124 E10 39.36 N 75.50 W
Elkton, Mi., U.S. 126 E6 43.49 N 83.10 W
Elkton, S.D., U.S. 128 G2 44.14 N 96.28 W
Elkton, Va., U.S. 124 F7 38.24 N 78.37 W
El-Kunaîyisa, Egypt 191c 29.59 N 31.11 E
El-Kuntilla, Egypt 76 H5 30.00 N 34.41 E
Elkville, Il., U.S. 130 G8 37.54 N 89.13 W
Ellás see Greece, ctry., Eur. 6 H13 39.00 N 22.00 E
Ellaville, Ga., U.S. 132 D1 32.14 N 84.18 W
Ellé, stm., Fr. 20 F5 47.48 N 3.31 W
Ellef Ringnes Island, i., Nu., Can. 108 B5 78.40 N 102.35 W
Ellen, Mount, mtn., Ut., U.S. 150 E6 38.07 N 110.49 W
Ellendale, Mn., U.S. 128 H5 43.52 N 93.18 W
Ellendale, N.D., U.S. 140 A14 46.00 N 98.31 W
Ellensburg, Wa., U.S. 146 C6 46.59 N 120.32 W
Ellenton, Ga., U.S. 132 E2 31.10 N 83.35 W
Eller, ngh., Ger. 181 51.12 N 6.51 E
Ellerbe, N.C., U.S. 132 A6 35.04 N 79.45 W
Ellesmere, Lake, l., N.Z. 102 F5 43.48 S 172.25 E
Ellesmere Island, i., Nu., Can. 108 B9 81.00 N 80.00 W
Ellesmere Park, Eng., U.K. 180 53.29 N 2.20 W
Ellesmere Port and Neston, mun., Eng., U.K. 180 53.17 N 2.55 W
Ellettsville, In., U.S. 130 E11 39.13 N 86.37 W
Ellice, stm., Nu., Can. 110 B10 68.03 N 103.59 W
Ellice Islands see Tuvalu, ctry., Oc. 92 D8 8.00 S 178.00 E
Ellichpur see Achalpur, India 70 H6 21.18 N 77.30 E
Ellicott Creek Park, p.o.i., N.Y., U.S. 202a 43.01 N 78.50 W
Ellicottville, N.Y., U.S. 124 B7 42.16 N 78.41 W
Ellijay, Ga., U.S. 132 B1 34.41 N 84.28 W
El Limoncito, Ven. 204c 10.29 N 66.47 W
El Limón de Teachi, Mex. 154 C5 24.43 N 107.08 W
Ellinghorst, ngh., Ger. 181 51.34 N 6.57 E
Ellington, Mo., U.S. 130 G7 37.14 N 90.58 W
Ellinikó, Grc. 185c 37.53 N 23.44 E
Elliniko International Airport, arpt., Grc. 185c 37.54 N 23.44 E
Ellinwood, Ks., U.S. 138 C10 38.21 N 98.34 W
Elliot, S. Afr. 90 G8 31.19 S 27.51 E
Elliot, Mount, mtn., Austl. 98 B6 19.29 S 146.58 E
Elliot Lake, On., Can. 126 B7 46.23 N 82.38 W
Elliot Lake, l., Mb., Can. 142 B18 52.55 N 95.20 W
Elliott, Ia., U.S. 130 C2 41.08 N 95.11 W
Elliott, Ms., U.S. 134 D9 33.39 N 89.41 W
Elliott Key, i., Fl., U.S. 132 K5 25.26 N 80.11 W
Ellis, Ks., U.S. 138 C9 38.56 N 99.33 W
Ellis Island, i., N.J., U.S. 194 40.42 N 74.02 W
Ellisras, S. Afr. 90 C8 23.39 S 27.45 E
Elliston, Austl. 96 F6 33.38 S 134.54 E
Elliston, Mt., U.S. 146 D14 46.33 N 112.26 W
Ellisville, Ms., U.S. 134 F9 31.36 N 89.11 W
Ellon, Scot., U.K. 10 D10 57.22 N 2.04 W
Ellora, India 70 H5 20.01 N 75.11 E
Ellora Caves, hist., India 69 A2 20.01 N 75.16 E
Ellore see Elūru, India 69 C5 16.42 N 81.06 E
Elloree, S.C., U.S. 132 C5 33.31 N 80.34 W
Ellös, Swe. 16 I9 58.10 N 11.29 E
Ellsworth, Ks., U.S. 138 C10 38.44 N 98.13 W
Ellsworth, Me., U.S. 122 F8 44.32 N 68.25 W
Ellsworth, Mi., U.S. 126 C4 45.10 N 85.14 W
Ellsworth, Mn., U.S. 128 H3 43.30 N 96.00 W
Ellsworth, Wi., U.S. 128 G6 44.43 N 92.29 W
Ellsworth Air Force Base, mil., S.D., U.S. 140 C9 44.08 N 103.05 W
Ellsworth Land, reg., Ant. 103 C32 75.30 S 80.00 W
Ellsworth Mountains, mts., Ant. 103 C32 79.00 S 85.00 W
El Lucero, Mex. 136 I4 25.53 N 103.25 W
Ellwangen, Ger. 24 H6 48.57 N 10.08 E
Ellwood City, Pa., U.S. 124 D5 40.51 N 80.17 W
Elm, stm., U.S. 140 B14 45.36 N 98.16 W
Elm, stm., Il., U.S. 130 F9 38.23 N 88.14 W
Elm, stm., N.D., U.S. 142 G16 47.16 N 96.50 W
Elma, Ia., U.S. 128 H6 43.14 N 92.26 W
Elma, Wa., U.S. 146 D3 47.00 N 123.24 W
El-Maâdi, ngh., Egypt 191c 29.58 N 31.15 E
Elmadağ, Tur. 42 F5 39.54 N 33.14 E
Elmadağ, mtn., Tur. 34 D16 39.49 N 33.00 E
El-Mahalla el-Kubra, Egypt 76 H2 30.58 N 31.10 E
El-Maimûn, Egypt 76 I2 29.14 N 31.11 E
Elmalı, Tur. 34 G12 36.43 N 29.55 E
Elmalı Bendi, dam., Tur. 185b 41.04 N 29.06 E
El-Manâwât, Egypt 191c 29.55 N 31.14 E
El Maneadero, Mex. 120 F4 31.41 N 116.35 W
El-Manshâh, Egypt 74 G2 26.28 N 31.48 E
El-Mansûra, Egypt 76 G2 31.02 N 31.23 E
El Manteco, Ven. 168 D10 7.24 N 62.29 W
El-Manzala, Egypt 76 G2 31.08 N 31.56 E
El-Marâghâ, Egypt 74 G2 26.41 N 31.36 E
El-Marg, ngh., Egypt 191c 30.09 N 31.20 E
El-Masara, ngh., Egypt 191c 29.54 N 31.17 E
Elmas Burnu, c., Tur. 185b 41.13 N 29.13 E
El Masnou, Spain 184d 41.29 N 2.19 E
El-Matarîya, Egypt 76 G3 31.10 N 32.01 E
El-Matarîya, ngh., Egypt 191c 30.07 N 31.19 E
Elmbridge, mun., Eng., U.K. 178 51.22 N 0.23 W
Elm Brook, stm., Ma., U.S. 201 42.29 N 71.16 W
Elm City, N.C., U.S. 124 I8 35.48 N 77.51 W
Elm Creek, Mb., Can. 142 E16 49.40 N 97.59 W
Elm Creek, Ne., U.S. 140 G13 40.42 N 99.23 W
Elm Creek, stm., Mn., U.S. 128 H4 43.45 N 94.11 W
Elm Creek, stm., S.D., U.S. 140 C10 44.20 N 102.42 W
Elm Creek, stm., Tx., U.S. 136 F7 28.54 N 100.12 W
Elm Creek, stm., Tx., U.S. 136 B8 32.40 N 99.41 W
Elm Creek, stm., Tx., U.S. 138 H10 33.12 N 98.50 W
El Médano, Mex. 154 C3 24.32 N 111.30 W
El Menia, Alg. 84 C5 30.32 N 2.53 E
Elmer, N.J., U.S. 124 E10 39.35 N 75.10 W
Elmhurst, Il., U.S. 130 C9 41.53 N 87.56 W
Elmhurst, ngh., N.Y., U.S. 194 40.44 N 73.53 W
El Mijao, Ven. 204c 10.23 N 66.48 W
El Minao, P.R. 158a b3 18.21 N 66.04 W
El-Minya (Minya), Egypt 76 J1 28.05 N 30.45 E
Elmira, On., Can. 126 E9 43.35 N 80.33 W
Elmira, P.E., Can. 122 D14 46.26 N 62.04 W
Elmira, N.Y., U.S. 124 B9 42.05 N 76.48 W
El Mirage Lake, l., Ca., U.S. 148 I8 34.38 N 117.35 W
Elmo, Mt., U.S. 146 C12 47.50 N 114.18 W
El Molinillo, Spain 28 E6 39.28 N 4.13 W
Elmont, N.Y., U.S. 194 40.42 N 73.42 W
El Monte Airport, arpt., Ca., U.S. 198 34.06 N 118.02 W
El Moral, Mex. 136 F7 28.51 N 100.39 W
Elmore, Austl. 98 K5 36.30 S 144.37 E
Elmore, Mn., U.S. 128 H4 43.30 N 94.05 W
Elmore, Oh., U.S. 124 C2 41.28 N 83.18 W
Elmore City, Ok., U.S. 138 G11 34.37 N 97.23 W
El Morro, hist., P.R. 158a b3 18.28 N 66.07 W
El Morro National Monument, p.o.i., N.M., U.S. 150 H8 35.05 N 108.22 W
Elm Point, c., N.Y., U.S. 194 40.49 N 73.46 W
El Mreyyé, reg., Maur. 84 F3 19.12 N 7.43 W
Elmsdale, N.S., Can. 122 F13 44.58 N 63.29 W
Elmshorn, Ger. 24 C5 53.45 N 9.39 E
Elm Springs, Ar., U.S. 130 H3 36.12 N 94.14 W
Elmsta, Swe. 16 H16 59.57 N 18.49 E
El Mulato, Mex. 136 E3 29.22 N 104.10 W
El-Mutî'a, Egypt 76 K2 27.08 N 31.17 E
Elmvale, On., Can. 126 D10 44.34 N 79.51 W
Elmwood, Il., U.S. 128 K8 40.46 N 89.57 W
Elmwood, Md., U.S. 202b 39.21 N 76.32 W
Elmwood, Ma., U.S. 201 42.00 N 70.57 W
Elmwood, Ne., U.S. 128 K2 40.50 N 96.17 W
Elmwood, Wi., U.S. 128 G6 44.46 N 92.08 W
Elmwood, ngh., Pa., U.S. 203 39.56 N 75.14 W
Elmwood Park, N.J., U.S. 194 40.54 N 74.07 W
Elmwood Park, p.o.i., Pa., U.S. 203 40.08 N 75.21 W
El-Narrânîya, Egypt 191c 29.58 N 31.10 E
El-Nasser, Egypt 74 H3 24.31 N 32.57 E
Elne, Fr. 22 G8 42.36 N 2.58 E
El Negralejo, Spain 184a 40.24 N 3.31 W
El Negrito, Hond. 156 E4 15.18 N 87.42 W
El Nevado, Cerro see Nevado, Cerro, mtn., Arg. 172 G3 35.34 S 68.28 W
El Nihuil, Arg. 172 G3 34.54 S 68.45 W
El'nja, Russia 26 F16 54.34 N 33.11 E
El Nopal, Cerro, mtn., Mex. 154 A5 28.15 N 107.36 W
Elnora, Ab., Can. 144 D17 51.59 N 113.12 W
Elnora, In., U.S. 130 F10 38.52 N 87.05 W
El Oasis, Ven. 204c 10.35 N 66.59 W
El-Obeid see Al-Ubayyid, Sudan 82 E6 13.11 N 30.13 E
Eloguj, stm., Russia 48 B15 63.12 N 87.46 E
Eloise, Fl., U.S. 132 H4 28.00 N 81.44 W
Elora, On., Can. 126 E9 43.41 N 80.25 W
Elora, Tn., U.S. 134 B12 35.00 N 86.21 W
Elorn, stm., Fr. 20 F4 48.26 N 4.17 W
Elortondo, Arg. 172 F7 33.42 S 61.37 W
Elorza, Ven. 168 D7 7.03 N 69.31 W
El Otate, Cerro, mtn., Mex. 136 F1 28.26 N 106.06 W
Èloten, Turkmen. 72 B9 37.17 N 62.22 E
El Otro Lado, Ven. 204c 10.24 N 66.49 W
Eloy, Az., U.S. 150 K5 32.45 N 111.33 W
Eloy Alfaro, Ec. 168 I2 2.10 S 79.49 W
El Pacayal, Mex. 154 H12 15.37 N 92.01 W
El Palmar, Ven. 168 D10 7.59 N 61.53 W
El Palmar, Ven. 204c 10.38 N 66.52 W
El Palmar de los Sepúlveda, Mex. 154 C5 25.43 N 107.55 W
El Palmito, Mex. 136 I8 25.54 N 99.18 W
El Palomar, Arg. 206 34.36 S 58.36 W
El Palomar, Base Aérea Militar, mil., Arg. 206 34.37 S 58.37 W
El Palqui, Chile 172 E2 30.45 S 70.56 W
El Pando, Cerro, mtn., Mex. 136 D2 30.15 N 105.19 W
El Pantanoso, Arroyo, stm., Arg. 206 34.47 S 58.40 W
El Pao, Ven. 168 C7 9.38 N 68.07 W
El Pao, Ven. 168 D10 8.00 N 62.39 W
El Papiol, Spain 184d 41.26 N 2.01 E
El Pardo, ngh., Spain 184a 40.31 N 3.47 W
El Pardo, Embalse de, res., Spain 184a 40.33 N 3.48 W
El Pardo, Monte de, hills, Spain 184a 40.33 N 3.48 W
El Paso, Il., U.S. 130 D8 40.44 N 89.00 W
El Paso, Tx., U.S. 136 C1 31.47 N 106.27 W
El Paso de Robles see Paso Robles, Ca., U.S. 148 H5 35.38 N 120.41 W
El Paso Peaks, mtn., Ca., U.S. 148 H8 35.28 N 117.43 W
El Paují, Ven. 204c 10.26 N 66.49 W
El Pedregal, ngh., Ven. 204c 10.30 N 66.51 W
El Peñuelo, Mex. 154 C8 24.34 N 100.46 W
El Peral, Chile 204e 33.35 S 70.34 W
El Perú, Ven. 168 D11 7.17 N 61.48 W
Elphinstone, Mb., Can. 142 D13 50.32 N 100.19 W
El Pilar, Ven. 168 B10 10.32 N 63.09 W
El Pinar, Parque Nacional, p.o.i., Ven. 204c 10.29 N 66.56 W
El Piñón, Col. 168 B4 10.23 N 74.48 W
El Pintado, Arg. 172 B7 24.38 S 61.26 W
El Piojo, Arroyo, stm., Arg. 206 34.50 S 58.45 W
El Piquete, Arg. 172 B5 24.13 S 64.39 W
El Pital, Cerro, mtn., N.A. 156 E3 14.23 N 89.08 W
El Planchón, Volcán (Planchón, Cerro del), vol., S.A. 172 G2 35.13 S 70.34 W
El Plantío, ngh., Spain 184a 40.28 N 3.49 W
El Plomo, Mex. 150 L4 31.14 N 112.04 W
El Polvorín, P.R. 158a b3 18.25 N 66.16 W
El Porcal, Spain 184a 40.18 N 3.32 W
El Portal, Ca., U.S. 148 F6 37.40 N 119.46 W
El Porvenir, Mex. 120 F10 31.14 N 105.52 W
El Porvenir, Mex. 136 G3 27.32 N 104.56 W
El Porvenir, Mex. 148 K9 32.04 N 116.37 W
El Porvenir, Pan. 156 H8 9.33 N 78.58 W
El Potrero, Mex. 136 H7 26.23 N 100.27 W
El Potro, Cerro (Potro, Cerro del), mtn., S.A. 172 D3 28.24 S 69.39 W
El Prat de Llobregat, Spain 28 C13 41.20 N 2.05 E
El Progreso, Hond. 156 E4 15.23 N 87.49 W
El Puerto de Santa María, Spain 28 H4 36.36 N 6.13 W
El Puesto, Arg. 172 C4 27.56 S 67.38 W
El-Qâhira (Cairo), Egypt 76 H2 30.03 N 31.14 E
El-Qâhira (Cairo), Egypt 191c 30.03 N 31.15 E
El-Qâhira, state, Egypt 191c 30.02 N 31.17 E
El Qala, Alg. 32 H2 36.53 N 8.26 E
El-Qalag, Egypt 191c 30.11 N 31.21 E
El-Qalyûbîya, state, Egypt 191c 30.10 N 31.15 E
El-Qantara el-Sharqîya, Egypt 76 H3 30.51 N 32.19 E
El-Qasr, Egypt 82 B5 25.42 N 28.55 E
El Quebrachal, Arg. 172 B5 25.16 S 64.02 W
El Quelite, Mex. 154 D5 23.32 N 106.28 W
Elquera Bushland, p.o.i., Austl. 192a 33.42 S 151.04 E
Elqui, stm., Chile 172 D2 29.53 S 71.16 W
El-Quseima, Egypt 76 H5 30.40 N 34.22 E
El-Qûsîya, Egypt 76 K1 27.26 N 30.49 E
El Rama, Nic. 156 F5 12.10 N 84.12 W
El Rastro, Ven. 168 C8 9.03 N 67.27 W
El Real de Santa María, Pan. 156 I9 8.07 N 77.43 W
El Recreo, ngh., Ven. 204c 10.30 N 66.53 W
El Remolino, Mex. 136 F6 28.43 N 101.03 W
El Reno, Ok., U.S. 138 F10 35.31 N 97.57 W
El-Ridîsîya Bahri, Egypt 74 H3 24.56 N 32.53 E
El Rio, Ca., U.S. 148 I6 34.13 N 119.10 W
El Rito, N.M., U.S. 138 E2 36.20 N 106.11 W
El Rito, stm., N.M., U.S. 138 E2 36.11 N 106.13 W
El Roble, Mesa, mtn., Mex. 120 F5 31.30 N 115.31 W
Elrose, Sk., Can. 142 C6 51.13 N 108.01 W
Elroy, Wi., U.S. 128 H8 43.44 N 90.15 W
Elsa, Yk., Can. 110 C3 63.54 N 135.27 W
Elsa, Tx., U.S. 136 H9 26.17 N 97.59 W
Elsa, stm., Italy 30 G8 43.43 N 10.52 E
El-Saff, Egypt 76 I2 29.34 N 31.16 E
El-Sa'îd (Upper Egypt), hist. reg., Egypt 74 G2 27.09 N 31.02 E
El Salado, Chile 172 C2 26.24 S 70.19 W
El Salado, Parque Nacional, p.o.i., Ec. 168 I1 2.12 S 80.00 W
El Salto, Mex. 154 D6 23.46 N 105.21 W
El Salvador, Chile 172 C3 26.17 S 69.47 W
El Salvador, ctry., N.A. 156 F3 13.50 N 88.55 W
El Samán de Apure, Ven. 168 D7 7.53 N 68.41 W
Elšanka, Russia 40 F15 51.49 N 46.23 E
El Sásabe, stm., Mex. 150 L5 30.40 N 112.01 W
Elsass see Alsace, hist. reg., Fr. 20 F16 48.30 N 7.30 E
El Sauz, Mex. 154 A5 29.02 N 106.16 W
El Sauzal, Mex. 120 F4 31.54 N 116.41 W
Elsberry, Mo., U.S. 130 E7 39.09 N 90.47 W
Elsburg, S. Afr. 191d 26.15 S 28.12 E
El Seibo, Dom. Rep. 156 C13 18.45 N 69.02 W
Elsen Nur, l., China 52 D3 35.13 N 92.08 E
Elsie, Mi., U.S. 130 A13 43.05 N 84.22 W
El-Simbillawein, Egypt 76 H2 30.53 N 31.27 E
Elsinore see Helsingør, Den. 16 K10 56.02 N 12.36 E
Elsinore, Ut., U.S. 150 E4 38.40 N 112.08 W
Elsinore, Lake, l., Ca., U.S. 148 J8 33.39 N 117.20 W
El Sitio, Ven. 204c 10.28 N 66.46 W
El'sk, Bela. 38 B8 51.48 N 29.10 E
El Socorro, Ven. 168 C9 9.00 N 65.45 W
El Soliseño, Mex. 136 I10 26.01 N 97.48 W
El Sombrero, Ven. 168 C8 9.23 N 66.58 W
Elspark, S. Afr. 191d 26.16 S 28.14 E
Elsterwerda, Ger. 24 E9 51.27 N 13.31 E
Elstree Aerodrome, arpt., Eng., U.K. 178 51.39 N 0.19 W
El Sueco, Mex. 120 G9 29.53 N 106.23 W
El-Suweis (Suez), Egypt 76 I3 29.58 N 32.33 E
El Tajín, hist., Mex. 154 E10 20.27 N 97.23 W
El Tala, Arg. 172 C5 26.06 S 65.16 W
El-Tâlbîya, Egypt 191c 30.00 N 31.11 E
El Tambo, Col. 168 G3 1.24 N 77.22 W
El Tanque, Mex. 136 H8 26.27 N 99.37 W
El Tarf, Alg. 32 H2 36.46 N 8.19 E
El Tecuán, Mex. 154 C5 25.29 N 107.00 W
Eltham, ngh., Eng., U.K. 178 51.27 N 0.04 E
El-Thamad, Egypt 76 I5 29.40 N 34.18 E
Eltham Palace, bldg., Eng., U.K. 178 51.27 N 0.03 E
El Tigre, Ven. 168 C9 8.53 N 64.14 W
Eltmann, Ger. 24 G6 49.58 N 10.39 E
El Toco, Chile 166 D3 22.04 S 69.35 W
El Tocuyo, Ven. 168 C7 9.47 N 69.47 W
El'ton, Russia 40 G15 49.07 N 46.50 E
Elton, Eng., U.K. 180 53.16 N 2.49 W
Elton, La., U.S. 134 G6 30.28 N 92.41 W
El'ton, ozero, l., Russia 40 G15 49.08 N 46.41 E
El Toreo, p.o.i., Mex. 204a 19.27 N 99.13 W
El Toro, mtn., P.R. 158a b4 18.16 N 65.49 W
El Tránsito, Chile 172 D2 28.50 S 70.17 W
El Trébol, Arg. 172 F7 32.11 S 61.43 W
El Triunfo, Mex. 154 D3 23.47 N 110.08 W
El Tule, Mex. 136 G1 27.03 N 106.16 W
El Tunal, Arg. 172 B5 25.15 S 64.22 W
El Tuparro, Parque Nacional, p.o.i., Col. 168 E7 5.15 N 68.31 W
El-Tûr, Egypt 76 J4 28.14 N 33.37 E
El Turbio, Arg. 166 J2 51.41 S 72.08 W
El-Uqsor (Luxor), Egypt 74 H3 25.42 N 32.38 E
Elura see Ellora, India 70 H5 20.01 N 75.11 E
Elūru, India 69 C5 16.42 N 81.06 E
Elva, Est. 26 B9 58.13 N 26.25 E
El Valle, Pan. 156 H7 8.36 N 80.08 W
El Valle, ngh., Ven. 204c 10.27 N 66.55 W
Elvas, Port. 28 F3 38.53 N 7.10 W
El Vendrell, Spain 28 C12 41.13 N 1.32 E
Elverlingsen, Ger. 181 51.17 N 7.42 E
Elverum, Nor. 16 G9 60.53 N 11.33 E
El Viejo, Nic. 156 F4 12.39 N 87.10 W
El Vigía, Ven. 168 C6 8.38 N 71.38 W
El Vínculo, Ven. 158g p20 12.03 N 69.56 W
Elvira, Arg. 172 G8 35.14 S 59.28 W
El Volcán, Chile 172 F2 33.47 S 70.13 W
El Wad, Alg. 84 C6 33.21 N 6.52 E
El Wak, Kenya 86 D8 2.49 N 40.56 E
El-Wâsta, Egypt 76 I2 29.20 N 31.12 E
Elwell, Lake, res., Mt., U.S. 146 B15 48.21 N 111.18 W
Elwood, Austl. 192b 37.53 S 144.59 E
Elwood, In., U.S. 130 D12 40.16 N 85.49 W
Elwood, Ks., U.S. 130 E3 39.45 N 94.52 W
Elwood, Ne., U.S. 140 G13 40.35 N 99.52 W
Elwood Park, Pa., U.S. 197b 40.10 N 80.17 W
Elwyn, Pa., U.S. 203 39.54 N 75.24 W
Elx, Spain 28 F10 38.15 N 0.42 W
Ely, Eng., U.K. 10 I13 52.24 N 0.16 E
Ely, Mn., U.S. 128 D7 47.54 N 91.52 W
Ely, Nv., U.S. 150 D2 39.14 N 114.52 W
El Yagual, Ven. 168 D7 7.30 N 68.25 W
Elyria, Oh., U.S. 124 C3 41.22 N 82.05 W
Elyria Airport, arpt., Oh., U.S. 197a 41.20 N 82.06 W
Elysian Park, p.o.i., Ca., U.S. 198 34.05 N 118.14 W
El Yunque, mtn., P.R. 158a b4 18.19 N 65.48 W
Elywood Park, p.o.i., Oh., U.S. 197a 41.23 N 82.06 W
El-Zamâlik, ngh., Egypt 191c 30.04 N 31.13 E
El Zamural, Ven. 204c 10.27 N 67.00 W
El-Zarqa, Egypt 76 G2 31.13 N 31.38 E
El-Zaytûn, ngh., Egypt 191c 30.06 N 31.19 E
El Zig-Zag, Ven. 204c 10.33 N 66.58 W
Émaé, i., Vanuatu 101d k17 17.04 S 168.22 E
Emajõgi, stm., Est. 26 B9 58.27 N 27.14 E
Emam Khomeyni Mosque, rel., Iran 185d 35.40 N 51.25 E
Emāmshahr, Iran 74 B6 36.25 N 54.59 E
Emån, stm., Swe. 16 J14 57.07 N 16.30 E
Émancé, Fr. 179 48.35 N 1.44 E
Emba, Kaz. 48 E9 48.49 N 58.09 E
Emba, stm., Kaz. 48 E9 46.43 N 53.08 E
Embarras, stm., Ab., Can. 144 C14 53.27 N 116.37 W
Embarras, stm., Il., U.S. 130 F10 38.38 N 87.37 W
Embarras, North Fork, stm., Il., U.S. 130 E10 38.54 N 87.59 W
Embarrass, Wi., U.S. 128 G10 44.39 N 88.42 W
Embarrass, stm., Mn., U.S. 128 D6 47.23 N 92.24 W
Embarrass, stm., Wi., U.S. 128 G10 44.23 N 88.44 W
Embid, Spain 28 C9 40.58 N 1.42 W
Embira see Envira, stm., Braz. 164 E3 6.41 S 69.47 W
Emborcação, Represa da, res., Braz. 170 J2 18.26 S 47.50 W
Embreeville, Pa., U.S. 203 39.56 N 75.44 W
Embreeville, Tn., U.S. 124 H3 36.10 N 82.27 W
Embrun, On., Can. 126 C14 45.16 N 75.16 W
Embrun, Fr. 22 E12 44.34 N 6.29 E
Embu, Kenya 86 E7 0.32 S 37.27 E
Embu, mun., Braz. 205b 23.40 S 46.50 W
Embu-Guaçu, mun., Braz. 205b 23.48 S 46.48 W
Embu-mirim, stm., Braz. 205b 23.39 S 46.51 W
Emca, Russia 12 E19 63.04 N 40.20 E
Emca, stm., Russia 12 E19 63.31 N 41.52 E
Emden, Ger. 24 C3 53.22 N 7.12 E
Emden, Il., U.S. 128 K9 40.17 N 89.28 W
Emel'janovka, Russia 18 D17 63.55 N 30.55 E
Emelle, Al., U.S. 134 E10 32.43 N 88.18 W
Emerado, N.D., U.S. 142 G16 47.55 N 97.23 W
Émerainville, Fr. 179 48.49 N 2.37 E
Emerald, Austl. 98 D7 23.31 S 148.09 E
Emerson, Mb., Can. 142 E16 49.00 N 97.12 W
Emerson, Ar., U.S. 134 D5 33.05 N 93.11 W
Emerson, Ga., U.S. 134 C14 34.08 N 84.45 W
Emerson, Ia., U.S. 130 C2 41.00 N 95.25 W
Emerson, Ne., U.S. 128 I2 42.16 N 96.43 W
Emerson, N.J., U.S. 194 40.58 N 74.01 W
Emery, S.D., U.S. 140 D15 43.36 N 97.37 W
Emery, Ut., U.S. 150 E5 38.55 N 111.14 W
Emet, Tur. 34 D12 39.20 N 29.15 E
Emgayet, Libya 82 B2 29.04 N 12.58 E
Emiliano Mitre, Canal, strt., Arg. 206 34.36 S 58.18 W
Emiliano Zapata, Mex. 154 G13 17.44 N 91.46 W
Emilia-Romagna, state, Italy 30 F8 44.30 N 11.00 E
Emin, China 52 B1 46.31 N 83.37 E
Emine, nos, c., Blg. 36 G14 42.43 N 27.53 E
Eminence, Ky., U.S. 130 F12 38.22 N 85.10 W
Eminence, Mo., U.S. 130 G6 37.09 N 91.21 W
Emirdağ, Tur. 34 D14 39.01 N 31.09 E
Emir Dağları, mts., Tur. 34 E14 38.51 N 31.12 E
Emita, Austl. 99a m13 40.00 S 147.54 E
Emlembe, mtn., Afr. 90 D10 25.52 S 30.59 E
Emlenton, Pa., U.S. 126 G10 41.10 N 79.41 W
Emmaboda, Swe. 16 K13 56.37 N 15.32 E
Emmaste, Est. 26 B5 58.43 N 22.33 E
Emmaus, Pa., U.S. 124 D10 40.32 N 75.29 W
Emmaville, Austl. 98 G8 29.26 S 151.36 E
Emmen, stm., Switz. 22 B13 47.13 N 7.34 E
Emmen, Neth. 14 B15 52.46 N 6.54 E
Emmendingen, Ger. 24 H3 48.07 N 7.51 E
Emmerich, Ger. 24 E2 51.50 N 6.14 E
Emmet, Austl. 98 E5 24.39 S 144.28 E
Emmet, Ar., U.S. 134 D5 33.43 N 93.28 W
Emmetsburg, Ia., U.S. 130 A3 43.06 N 94.40 W
Emmett, Id., U.S. 146 G10 43.52 N 116.30 W
Emmiganūru, India 69 D3 15.46 N 77.28 E
Emmitsburg, Md., U.S. 124 E8 39.42 N 77.19 W
Emmonak, Ak., U.S. 109 D7 62.46 N 164.30 W
Emo, On., Can. 128 C5 48.38 N 93.50 W
Emőd, Hung. 36 B7 47.56 N 20.49 E
Emory, Tx., U.S. 136 B12 32.53 N 95.45 W
Emory, stm., Tn., U.S. 130 H13 35.57 N 84.31 W
Emory Peak, mtn., Tx., U.S. 136 E4 29.13 N 103.18 W
Empalme, Mex. 154 A3 27.58 N 110.49 W
Empangeni, S. Afr. 90 F10 28.44 S 31.54 E
Empedrado, Arg. 172 C8 27.57 S 58.48 W
Emperor Jimmu, Tomb of, hist., Japan 188 34.29 N 135.47 E
Emperor Nintoku, Tomb of, hist., Japan 188 34.34 N 135.29 E
Emperor Seamounts, unds. 174 E19 42.00 N 170.00 E
Emperor Tenchi, Tomb of, hist., Japan 188 34.59 N 135.48 E
Empire, La., U.S. 134 H9 29.23 N 89.36 W
Empire, Nv., U.S. 148 C6 40.34 N 119.20 W
Empoli, Italy 30 G7 43.43 N 10.57 E
Emporia, Ks., U.S. 130 F1 38.24 N 96.10 W
Emporia, Va., U.S. 124 H8 36.41 N 77.32 W
Emporium, Pa., U.S. 124 C7 41.30 N 78.14 W
Empress, Ab., Can. 142 D4 50.56 N 109.59 W
Empty Quarter see Ar-Rub' al-Khālī, des., Asia 72 E6 20.00 N 51.00 E
Ems (Eems), stm., Eur. 20 A16 53.19 N 7.03 E
Emscher, stm., Ger. 181 51.34 N 6.42 E
Emscherbruch, reg., Ger. 181 51.34 N 7.09 E
Emsdetten, Ger. 24 D3 52.10 N 7.32 E
Emst, ngh., Ger. 181 51.21 N 7.30 E
Emsworth Dam, dam., Pa., U.S. 197b 40.30 N 80.05 W
Emu, China 54 C8 43.44 N 128.09 E
Emukae, Japan 56 F2 33.21 N 129.40 E
Emu Park, Austl. 98 D8 23.15 S 150.49 E
Emu Plains, Austl. 192a 33.45 S 150.41 E
Emuren, Nig. 191a 6.40 N 3.31 E
En see Inn, stm., Eur. 30 B10 48.34 N 13.28 E
Ēna, Russia 14 E22 67.35 N 31.09 E
Ēna, stm., Russia 14 E21 67.36 N 31.11 E
Enånger, Swe. 16 F15 61.32 N 17.02 E
Enard Bay, b., Scot., U.K. 10 C7 58.09 N 5.23 W
Enarotali, Indon. 60 F10 3.56 S 136.23 E
Enašimskij Polkan, gora, mtn., Russia 48 C16 59.50 N 92.52 E
Enbek, Kaz. 48 E13 48.53 N 77.12 E
Encampment, Wy., U.S. 150 B10 41.12 N 106.47 W
Encampment, stm., U.S. 150 B10 41.18 N 106.43 W
Encantado, Braz. 172 D11 29.15 S 51.53 W
Encantado, ngh., Braz. 205a 22.54 S 43.18 W
Encarnação, ngh., Port. 184c 38.47 N 9.06 W
Encarnación, Para. 172 C9 27.20 S 55.52 W
Enchi, Ghana 84 H4 5.48 N 2.49 W
Enchilayas, Mex. 120 F6 30.53 N 112.49 W
Encinal, Tx., U.S. 136 F8 28.02 N 99.21 W
Encinitas, Ca., U.S. 148 J8 33.02 N 117.17 W
Encino, N.M., U.S. 138 G3 34.38 N 105.29 W
Encino, Tx., U.S. 136 H9 26.56 N 98.07 W
Encino, ngh., Ca., U.S. 198 34.09 N 118.30 W
Encino Reservoir, res., Ca., U.S. 198 34.05 N 118.31 W
Encontrados, Ven. 168 C5 9.03 N 72.13 W
Encounter Bay, b., Austl. 98 J2 35.35 S 138.44 E
Encruzilhada, Braz. 170 H5 15.31 S 40.54 W
Encruzilhada do Sul, Braz. 172 E11 30.32 S 52.31 W
Encs, Hung. 36 A8 48.20 N 21.08 E
Endako, B.C., Can. 144 B5 54.05 N 125.02 W
Endako, stm., B.C., Can. 144 B5 54.03 N 124.54 W
Ende, Indon. 60 G7 8.50 S 121.39 E
Endeavor, Wi., U.S. 128 H9 43.42 N 89.28 W
Endeavour, Sk., Can. 142 B11 52.09 N 102.40 W
Endeavour Strait, strt., Austl. 96 B8 10.50 S 142.04 E
Endelave, i., Den. 16 L8 55.45 N 10.18 E
Enderby, B.C., Can. 144 F11 50.32 N 119.09 W
Enderby Land, reg., Ant. 103 B10 68.04 S 52.52 E
Enderlin, N.D., U.S. 140 A15 46.37 N 97.36 W
Endicott, N.Y., U.S. 124 B9 42.06 N 76.03 W
Endicott, Wa., U.S. 146 D9 46.57 N 117.48 W
Endicott Mountains, mts., Ak., U.S. 109 C9 67.50 N 152.00 W
Endō, Japan 186 35.23 N 139.27 E
Endongin, Russia 50 F11 53.27 N 113.00 E
Ene, stm., Peru 164 F3 11.09 S 74.14 W
Enewetak, at., Marsh. Is. 94 B7 11.38 N 162.16 E
Enez, Tur. 34 C9 40.44 N 26.03 E
Enfida, Tun. 32 H4 36.07 N 10.23 E
Enfield, Austl. 192a 33.53 S 151.06 E
Enfield, N.H., U.S. 122 G4 43.38 N 72.08 W
Enfield, N.C., U.S. 124 H8 36.10 N 77.40 W
Engan, Nor. 16 D6 63.09 N 8.32 E
Engaño, Cabo, c., Dom. Rep. 156 C13 18.37 N 68.19 W
Engcobo, S. Afr. 90 G9 31.40 S 27.59 E
Engelberg, Switz. 30 D5 46.49 N 8.24 E
Engelhard, N.C., U.S. 132 A10 35.30 N 75.59 W
Engeløya, i., Nor. 14 D5 67.56 N 15.08 E
Engel's, Russia 40 F15 51.28 N 46.07 E
Engen, B.C., Can. 144 B6 54.01 N 124.18 W
Engenheiro Navarro, Braz. 170 I3 17.16 S 43.54 W
Engenho, Ilha do, i., Braz. 205a 22.50 S 43.07 W
Engenho de Dentro, ngh., Braz. 205a 22.54 S 43.18 W
Engenho do Mato, Braz. 205a 22.52 S 43.01 W
Engenho Nôvo, ngh., Braz. 205a 22.55 S 43.17 W
Engeren, l., Nor. 16 F10 61.35 N 12.02 E
Enggano, Pulau, i., Indon. 66 F2 5.24 S 102.16 E
Enghershatu, mtn., Erit. 82 D7 16.40 N 38.20 E
Enghien-les-Bains, Fr. 179 48.58 N 2.19 E
Enghien-Moisselles, Aéroport d', arpt., Fr. 179 49.02 N 2.21 E
England, Ar., U.S. 134 C6 34.32 N 91.58 W
England, state, U.K. 10 I12 52.30 N 1.30 W
Englefield, Cape, c., Nu., Can. 110 B13 69.50 N 85.33 W
Englefield Green, Eng., U.K. 178 51.26 N 0.35 W
Englehart, On., Can. 114 C11 47.49 N 79.51 W
Englewood, B.C., Can. 144 F3 50.32 N 126.53 W
Englewood, Co., U.S. 138 B4 39.39 N 104.58 W
Englewood, Fl., U.S. 132 J3 26.57 N 82.21 W
Englewood, Ks., U.S. 138 D8 37.02 N 99.58 W
Englewood, Tn., U.S. 132 A1 35.26 N 84.29 W
Englewood, ngh., Il., U.S. 196 41.47 N 87.39 W
Englewood Cliffs, N.J., U.S. 194 40.53 N 73.57 W
English, In., U.S. 130 F11 38.20 N 86.27 W
English, stm., On., Can. 128 A4 50.11 N 95.03 W
English, stm., Ia., U.S. 130 C6 41.28 N 91.29 W
English Bāzār see Ingrāj Bāzār, India 70 F12 24.59 N 88.08 E
English Channel, strt., Eur. 20 D7 50.13 N 2.20 W
English Coast, cst., Ant. 103 C33 73.45 S 73.00 W
Engozero, Russia 18 B20 65.48 N 33.55 E
Engozero, ozero, l., Russia 18 B20 65.45 N 33.35 E
Engure, Lat. 26 C6 57.10 N 23.13 E
Engures ezers, l., Lat. 26 C6 57.16 N 23.06 E
Enid, Ok., U.S. 138 E11 36.23 N 97.52 W
Enid Lake, res., Ms., U.S. 134 C9 34.09 N 89.50 W
Enisej, stm., Russia 50 C6 71.53 N 82.20 E
Enisejsk, Russia 48 C16 58.26 N 92.10 E
Enisejskij krjaž, mts., Russia 48 C16 59.00 N 93.00 E
Enisejskij zaliv, b., Russia 50 B5 72.30 N 80.00 E
Eniwetok see Enewetak, at., Marsh. Is. 94 B7 11.38 N 162.16 E
eNjesuthi, mtn., Afr. 88 F4 29.09 S 29.23 E

Name	Page	Map Ref.	Latitude	Longitude
Enka, N.C., U.S.	132	A3	35.33 N	82.39 W
Enkhuizen, Neth.	20	B14	52.42 N	5.17 E
Enköping, Swe.	16	H15	59.38 N	17.04 E
Enmedio, Mex.	136	E4	29.04 N	103.29 W
Enmedio, Cerro de, mtn., Mex.	154	F8	19.48 N	100.36 W
Enna, Italy	32	G8	37.34 N	14.16 E
Ennadai Lake, l., Nu., Can.	110	C11	61.00 N	101.15 W
Ennedi, plat., Chad	82	D4	17.15 N	22.00 E
Ennell, Lough, l., Ire.	10	H5	53.28 N	7.24 W
Ennepe, stm., Ger.	181		51.22 N	7.27 E
Ennepestausee, res., Ger.	181		51.14 N	7.25 E
Ennery, Fr.	179		49.05 N	2.06 E
Enngonia, Austl.	98	G5	29.19 S	145.50 E
Ennis, Ire.	10	I3	52.51 N	8.59 W
Ennis, Mt., U.S.	146	E15	45.20 N	111.44 W
Ennis, Tx., U.S.	136	B11	32.20 N	96.37 W
Enniscorthy, Ire.	10	I6	52.29 N	6.34 W
Enniskillen, N. Ire., U.K.	10	G5	54.20 N	7.38 W
Ennis Lake, l., Mt., U.S.	146	E15	45.26 N	111.41 W
Ennistimon, Ire.	10	I3	52.57 N	9.17 W
Enns, Aus.	30	B11	48.13 N	14.28 E
Enns, stm., Aus.	30	B11	48.14 N	14.31 E
Eno, Fin.	18	E17	62.48 N	30.09 E
Enochs, Tx., U.S.	138	H6	33.51 N	102.45 W
Enon, Oh., U.S.	124	E2	39.52 N	83.56 W
Enontekiö, Fin.	14	D14	68.23 N	23.36 E
Enoree, stm., S.C., U.S.	132	B4	34.26 N	81.25 W
Enosburg Falls, Vt., U.S.	122	F4	44.54 N	72.48 W
Enotaevka, Russia	40	H15	47.14 N	47.01 E
Enozero, ozero, l., Russia	14	D28	68.06 N	37.55 E
Enping, China	58	J5	22.10 N	112.17 E
Enrekang, Indon.	66	E11	3.34 S	119.46 E
Enrique Urien, Arg.	172	C7	27.33 S	60.31 W
Enriquillo, Dom. Rep.	156	D12	17.53 N	71.15 W
Enriquillo, Lago, l., Dom. Rep.	156	C12	18.27 N	71.39 W
Enschede, Neth.	20	B15	52.13 N	6.54 E
Ensenada, Arg.	172	G9	34.51 S	57.54 W
Ensenada, Mex.	120	F4	31.52 N	116.36 W
Ensenada, P.R.	158a	c2	17.58 N	66.56 W
Ensenada, state, Arg.	206		34.50 S	58.00 W
Enshi, China	58	F3	30.14 N	109.27 E
Enshū-nada, s., Japan	56	E10	34.27 N	137.38 E
Entebbe, Ug.	86	D6	0.04 N	32.28 E
Enterprise, N.T., Can.	110	C7	60.33 N	116.08 W
Enterprise, Al., U.S.	134	F13	31.18 N	85.51 W
Enterprise, Ca., U.S.	148	D4	40.34 N	122.21 W
Enterprise, Ks., U.S.	138	C11	38.54 N	97.05 W
Enterprise, Ms., U.S.	134	E10	32.10 N	88.49 W
Enterprise, Or., U.S.	146	E9	45.25 N	117.16 W
Enterprise, Ut., U.S.	150	F3	37.34 N	113.42 W
Entiat, stm., Wa., U.S.	146	B6	47.39 N	120.12 W
Entinas, Punta, c., Spain	28	H8	36.41 N	2.46 W
Entraygues, Fr.	22	E8	44.39 N	2.34 E
Entrepeñas, Embalse de, res., Spain	28	D8	40.31 N	2.44 W
Entre Rios, Bol.	166	D4	21.31 S	64.09 W
Entre Rios, Braz.	170	G7	11.57 S	38.03 W
Entre-Rios see Malema, Moz.	88	C6	14.56 S	37.24 E
Entre Ríos, state, Arg.	172	E8	32.00 S	59.00 W
Entre Rios de Minas, Braz.	170	K3	20.40 S	44.03 W
Entrevaux, Fr.	22	F12	43.57 N	6.49 E
Entroncamento, Port.	28	E2	39.27 N	8.28 W
Entwistle, Ab., Can.	144	C16	53.35 N	114.59 W
Enugu, Nig.	84	H6	6.27 N	7.27 E
Enumclaw, Wa., U.S.	146	C5	47.12 N	121.58 W
Enurmino, Russia	50	C26	66.55 N	171.47 W
Envalira, Port d', p., And.	22	G7	42.33 N	1.48 E
Envigado, Col.	168	D4	6.10 N	75.34 W
Envira, stm., Braz.	164	E3	6.41 S	69.47 W
Enyamba, D.R.C.	86	E5	3.30 S	24.50 E
Enyang, China	58	F2	31.47 N	106.37 E
Enyellé, Congo	86	D3	2.50 N	18.01 E
Enz, stm., Ger.	20	E18	49.00 N	9.09 E
Eo, stm., Spain	28	A3	43.31 N	7.02 W
Eolia, Mo., U.S.	130	E6	39.13 N	91.01 W
Eolie, Isole (Lipari, Isole), is., Italy	32	F8	38.30 N	14.50 E
Epanomí, Grc.	34	C5	40.26 N	22.56 E
Épars, Bois de l', p.o.i., Fr.	179		48.45 N	1.45 E
Epecuén, Lago, l., Arg.	172	H6	37.07 S	62.53 W
Epena, Congo	86	D3	1.21 N	17.27 E
Épernay, Fr.	20	E12	49.02 N	3.57 E
Épervier, Colline à l', hill, Qc., Can.	122	A4	48.58 N	73.02 W
Epes, Al., U.S.	134	E10	32.41 N	88.07 W
Ephesus see Efes, hist., Tur.	34	F10	37.54 N	27.20 E
Ephraim, Ut., U.S.	150	D5	39.21 N	111.35 W
Ephrata, Pa., U.S.	124	D9	40.10 N	76.11 W
Ephrata, Wa., U.S.	146	C7	47.18 N	119.32 W
Épi, i., Vanuatu	101d	k17	16.42 S	168.15 E
Épiais-lès-Louvres, Fr.	179		49.02 N	2.33 E
Epidavros, hist., Grc.	34	F6	37.35 N	23.02 E
Epifan', Russia	26	G21	53.49 N	38.33 E
Épila, Spain	28	C9	41.36 N	1.17 W
Épinal, Fr.	20	F15	48.11 N	6.26 E
Épinay-sous-Sénart, Fr.	179		48.42 N	2.31 E
Épinay-sur-Orge, Fr.	179		48.40 N	2.20 E
Épinay-sur-Seine, Fr.	179		48.57 N	2.19 E
Epirus see Ípeiros, hist. reg., Grc.	34	D3	39.40 N	20.50 E
Episkopí, Cyp.	76	D3	34.40 N	32.54 E
Épône, Fr.	179		48.57 N	1.49 E
Eppendorf, ngh., Ger.	181		51.27 N	7.11 E
Eppenhausen, ngh., Ger.	181		51.21 N	7.31 E
Epping, Austl.	192a		33.46 S	151.05 E
Epping Forest, mun., Eng., U.K.	178		51.43 N	0.10 E
Epping Green, Eng., U.K.	178		51.45 N	0.07 W
Epping Green, Eng., U.K.	178		51.44 N	0.05 E
Epping Upland, Eng., U.K.	178		51.43 N	0.06 E
Epsom, Eng., U.K.	10	J12	51.20 N	0.16 W
Epsom and Ewell, mun., Eng., U.K.	178		51.20 N	0.16 W
Epsom Downs Race Course, p.o.i., Eng., U.K.	178		51.19 N	0.15 W
Epukiro, Nmb.	90	B4	21.41 S	19.06 E
Epukiro, stm., Nmb.	90	B4	20.50 S	20.55 E
Eqlīd, Iran	74	E13	30.53 N	52.41 E
Equality, Il., U.S.	130	G9	37.44 N	88.20 W
Equatorial Guinea, ctry., Afr.	84	I6	2.00 N	9.00 E
Era, stm., Italy	30	G7	43.40 N	10.37 E
Erac Creek, stm., Austl.	98	F5	26.51 S	145.45 E
Éragny, Fr.	179		49.01 N	2.06 E
Erahtur, Russia	40	D12	54.43 N	41.09 E
Erangal, ngh., India	190c		19.10 N	72.47 E
Erap, Pap. N. Gui.	101a	b4	6.35 S	146.46 E
Erath, La., U.S.	134	H6	29.57 N	92.02 W
Erave, Pap. N. Gui.	101a	b3	6.46 S	143.50 E
Erawan National Park, p.o.i., Thai.	64	E4	14.25 N	99.05 E
Erbaa, Tur.	42	E7	40.39 N	36.34 E
Erbach, Ger.	24	G5	49.39 N	8.59 E
Erbogačon, Russia	48	B19	61.16 N	108.00 E
Ercevo, Russia	12	F18	60.47 N	40.05 E
Erciyes Dağı, vol., Tur.	8	H16	38.32 N	35.28 E
Ercolano, Italy	32	D8	40.48 N	14.20 E
Érd, Hung.	36	B5	47.24 N	18.53 E
Erdao, stm., China	54	C8	42.37 N	127.12 E
Erdaobaihe, China	54	C8	42.22 N	128.06 E
Erdaohezi, China	54	B8	45.07 N	129.36 E
Erdek, Tur.	34	C10	40.24 N	27.48 E
Erdemli, Tur.	42	G6	36.37 N	34.18 E
Erdenheim, Pa., U.S.	203		40.05 N	75.12 W
Erding, Ger.	24	H7	48.18 N	11.54 E
Erebato, stm., Ven.	168	E9	5.54 N	64.16 W
Erebus, Mount, mtn., Ant.	103	C21	77.32 S	167.08 E
Erechim, Braz.	172	C11	27.38 S	52.17 W
Ereğli, Tur.	34	B14	41.16 N	31.25 E
Ereğli, Tur.	42	G5	37.30 N	34.03 E
Eregun, Nig.	191a		6.36 N	3.22 E
Erei, Monti, mts., Italy	32	G8	37.27 N	14.19 E
Erenhot, China	52	C7	43.39 N	111.59 E
Erenköy, ngh., Tur.	185b		40.58 N	29.04 E
Erepecuru, Lago do, l., Braz.	164	D6	1.19 S	56.35 W
Eresma, stm., Spain	28	C6	41.26 N	4.44 W
Eresós, Grc.	34	D8	39.10 N	25.55 E
Erevan see Yerevan, Arm.	42	E11	40.11 N	44.30 E
Erfoud, Mor.	84	C4	31.26 N	4.14 W
Erft, stm., Ger.	24	E2	51.13 N	6.43 E
Erfurt, Ger.	24	F7	50.58 N	11.01 E
Ergač, Russia	40	C20	57.30 N	56.38 E
Ergani, Tur.	42	F8	38.16 N	39.46 E
Ergene, stm., Tur.	34	B10	41.02 N	26.21 E
Ergeni, hills, Russia	40	H14	47.00 N	44.00 E
Ergeninskij, Russia	40	H14	47.06 N	44.28 E
Erges (Erjas), stm., Eur.	28	E4	39.40 N	7.00 W
Ērgļi, Lat.	26	D8	56.53 N	25.39 E
Ergun (Argun'), stm., Asia	46	D16	53.18 N	121.26 E
Ergun Youqi, China	52	A9	50.14 N	120.10 E
Ergun Zuoqi, China	50	F13	50.46 N	121.32 E
Er Hai, l., China	52	F5	25.48 N	100.11 E
Erholungsgebiet Wienerberg, p.o.i., Aus.	182b		48.10 N	16.21 E
Erhulai, China	54	D6	41.22 N	125.07 E
Eria, stm., Spain	28	B5	42.03 N	5.44 W
Eriboll, Loch, b., Scot., U.K.	10	C8	58.29 N	4.41 W
Erice, Italy	32	F6	38.02 N	12.35 E
Ericeira, Port.	28	F1	38.58 N	9.24 W
Erichsen Lake, l., Nu., Can.	110	A14	70.38 N	80.21 W
Ericht, Loch, l., Scot., U.K.	10	E8	56.48 N	4.24 W
Erick, Ok., U.S.	138	F9	35.13 N	99.52 W
Erickson, B.C., Can.	144	G14	49.05 N	116.28 W
Erickson, Mb., Can.	142	D14	50.30 N	99.55 W
Ericson, Ne., U.S.	140	F14	41.46 N	98.40 W
Erie, Co., U.S.	138	A3	40.03 N	105.03 W
Erie, Il., U.S.	130	C7	41.39 N	90.04 W
Erie, Ks., U.S.	130	G2	37.34 N	95.14 W
Erie, Pa., U.S.	124	B5	42.07 N	80.03 W
Erie, Lake, l., N.A.	124	B4	42.15 N	81.00 W
Erie Basin, b., N.Y., U.S.	194		40.40 N	74.01 W
Erie Beach, On., Can.	202a		42.53 N	78.57 W
Erie Canal see New York State Barge Canal, can., N.Y., U.S.	126	E12	43.05 N	78.43 W
Erie County Fairgrounds, p.o.i., N.Y., U.S.	202a		42.45 N	78.49 W
Eriksdale, Mb., Can.	142	D15	50.52 N	98.06 W
Erimo-misaki, c., Japan	54	D15	41.55 N	143.14 E
Erin, On., Can.	126	E9	43.46 N	80.03 W
Erin, Tn., U.S.	130	H10	36.18 N	87.41 W
Erindale, On., Can.	193b		43.32 N	79.39 W
Eriskay, i., Scot., U.K.	10	D5	57.04 N	7.17 W
Erith, ngh., Eng., U.K.	178		51.29 N	0.10 E
Eritrea, ctry., Afr.	82	D7	15.20 N	39.00 E
Erivan see Yerevan, Arm.	42	E11	40.11 N	44.30 E
Erjas (Erges), stm., Eur.	28	E4	39.40 N	7.00 W
Erkelenz, Ger.	24	E2	51.05 N	6.19 E
Erken, l., Swe.	16	H16	59.51 N	18.34 E
Erkner, Ger.	24	D9	52.24 N	13.44 E
Erkner, Forst, for., Ger.	182a		52.22 N	13.47 E
Erlangen, Ger.	24	G7	49.36 N	11.01 E
Erldunda, Austl.	96	E6	25.13 S	133.11 E
Erle, ngh., Ger.	181		51.33 N	7.05 E
Erling, Lake, res., Ar., U.S.	134	D5	33.05 N	93.32 W
Ermak, Kaz.	48	D13	52.02 N	76.56 E
Ermakovskaja, Russia	40	G12	48.03 N	41.18 E
Ermakovskoe, Russia	48	D16	53.16 N	92.23 E
Ermelindo Matarazo, ngh., Braz.	205b		23.29 S	46.29 W
Ermelo, S. Afr.	90	E10	26.31 S	29.59 E
Ermenek, Tur.	42	G5	36.37 N	32.55 E
Ermenek, stm., Tur.	76	B3	36.35 N	33.23 E
Ermentau, Kaz.	48	D12	51.37 N	73.07 E
Ermica, Russia	12	C25	66.59 N	52.19 E
Ermidas, Port.	28	G2	38.00 N	8.24 W
Ermil Post, Sudan	86	B5	13.36 N	27.35 E
Ermineskin Indian Reserve, ind. res., Ab., Can.	144	D17	52.51 N	113.29 W
Ermington, Austl.	192a		33.48 S	151.04 E
Ermolaevo, Russia	40	E19	52.45 N	55.47 E
Ermolino, Russia	26	E19	55.12 N	36.35 E
Ermoúpoli, Grc.	34	F7	37.26 N	24.56 E
Erne, Lower Lough, l., N. Ire., U.K.	10	G4	54.27 N	7.45 W
Erne, Upper Lough, l., Eur.	10	G5	54.14 N	7.32 W
Ernée, Fr.	20	F8	48.17 N	0.55 W
Ernst Thälmann, Pioneerpark, p.o.i., Ger.	182a		52.28 N	13.33 E
Ernst-Thälmann-Stadion, p.o.i., Ger.	182a		52.23 N	13.05 E
Erode, India	69	F3	11.20 N	77.43 E
Erofej Pavlovič, Russia	50	F13	53.57 N	121.56 E
Eromanga, Austl.	98	F4	26.40 S	143.16 E
Erongo, state, Nmb.	90	C2	22.12 S	14.45 E
Erongo, mtn., Nmb.	90	B2	21.37 S	15.34 E
Eropol, Russia	50	C22	65.16 N	168.42 E
Erota, Erit.	82	D7	16.11 N	37.54 E
Er-Rachidia, Mor.	84	C4	31.57 N	4.26 W
Errego, Moz.	88	D6	16.00 S	37.14 E
Errigal Mountain, mtn., Ire.	10	F4	55.02 N	8.07 W
Errinundra National Park, p.o.i., Austl.	98	K7	37.18 S	148.51 E
Erris Head, c., Ire.	10	G2	54.18 N	10.00 W
Errol Heights, Or., U.S.	146	E4	45.28 N	122.34 W
Erromango, i., Vanuatu	101d	l17	18.45 S	169.05 E
Erseka, Alb.	32	D14	40.20 N	20.41 E
Erši, Russia	26	F17	54.23 N	34.11 E
Eršiči, Russia	26	G15	53.40 N	32.45 E
Erskine, Mn., U.S.	128	D2	47.38 N	95.57 W
Erskine, Lake, l., N.J., U.S.	194		41.06 N	74.15 W
Erskine Park, Austl.	192a		33.49 S	150.47 E
Eršov, Russia	40	F16	51.20 N	48.15 E
Erstein, Fr.	20	F16	48.25 N	7.40 E
Ertai, China	52	B3	46.03 N	90.08 E
Ertil', Russia	40	F12	51.51 N	40.49 E
Ertis see Irtysh, stm., Asia	48	C11	61.05 N	68.47 E
Ertix see Irtysh, stm., Asia	48	C11	61.05 N	68.47 E
Ertoma, Russia	12	E22	63.32 N	47.48 E
Ertra see Eritrea, ctry., Afr.	82	D7	15.20 N	39.00 E
Ertuğrul, Tur.	34	D10	39.34 N	27.42 E
Ertvågøya, i., Nor.	16	D6	63.12 N	8.22 E
Erudina, Austl.	98	H2	31.29 S	139.22 E
Erunkan, Nig.	191a		6.37 N	3.24 E
Eruslan, stm., Russia	40	F15	50.21 N	46.25 E
Erva, Ponta da, c., Port.	184c		38.50 N	8.58 W
Erval, Braz.	172	F11	32.02 S	53.24 W
Erve, stm., Fr.	20	G8	47.50 N	0.19 W
Ervy-le-Châtel, Fr.	20	F12	48.02 N	3.54 E
Erwin, N.C., U.S.	132	A7	35.20 N	78.40 W
Erwin, Tn., U.S.	124	H3	36.08 N	82.24 W
Erwood, Sk., Can.	142	B11	52.50 N	102.12 W
Erykly, Russia	40	D17	55.10 N	51.24 E
Erýmanthos, mtn., Grc.	34	F4	37.59 N	21.51 E
Erythrés, Grc.	34	E6	38.13 N	23.19 E
Eryuan, China	52	F4	26.06 N	99.56 E
Erzgebirge see Ore Mountains, mts., Eur.	24	F9	50.37 N	12.53 E
Erzhan, China	54	B8	43.57 N	128.44 E
Erzin, Russia	48	D17	50.15 N	95.08 E
Erzincan, Tur.	42	F8	39.43 N	39.30 E
Erzincan, state, Tur.	42	F8	39.40 N	39.30 E
Erzurum, Tur.	42	F9	39.54 N	41.17 E
Erzurum, state, Tur.	42	E9	40.00 N	41.30 E
Èsa, stm., Bela.	26	F11	54.53 N	28.41 E
Esa'ala, Pap. N. Gui.	101a	b5	9.44 S	150.48 E
Esashi, Japan	54	D14	41.51 N	140.09 E
Esbjerg, Den.	16	L6	55.28 N	8.27 E
Esbly, Fr.	179		48.54 N	2.49 E
Esbo see Espoo, Fin.	18	G11	60.13 N	24.39 E
Esborn, Ger.	181		51.23 N	7.20 E
Esca, stm., Spain	28	B10	42.36 N	1.00 W
Escada, Braz.	170	E8	8.22 S	35.14 W
Escalante, Ut., U.S.	150	F5	37.46 N	111.35 W
Escalante, stm., Ut., U.S.	150	F6	37.16 N	110.52 W
Escalante, stm., Ven.	168	C5	9.11 N	71.45 W
Escalante Desert, des., Ut., U.S.	150	F3	37.50 N	113.30 W
Escalón, Mex.	154	B6	26.45 N	104.19 W
Escalon, Ca., U.S.	148	F5	37.47 N	120.59 W
Escalona, Spain	28	D6	40.09 N	4.24 W
Escambia, stm., Fl., U.S.	134	G11	30.32 N	87.11 W
Escanaba, Mi., U.S.	126	C2	45.44 N	87.03 W
Escanaba, stm., Mi., U.S.	126	B2	45.47 N	87.04 W
Escandón, Puerto, p., Spain	28	D10	40.15 N	1.00 W
Escárcega, Mex.	156	C2	18.37 N	90.44 W
Escarpada Point, c., Phil.	68	A4	18.30 N	122.13 E
Escarpment, N.Y., U.S.	202a		43.10 N	79.00 W
Escatawpa, stm., U.S.	134	G10	30.20 N	88.33 W
Escaut see Schelde, stm., Eur.	20	C13	51.21 N	4.15 E
Esch-sur-Alzette, Lux.	20	E15	49.30 N	5.58 E
Eschwege, Ger.	20	C18	51.11 N	10.03 E
Eschweiler, Ger.	20	D15	50.49 N	6.16 E
Esclaves, Côte des see Slave Coast, cst., Afr.	84	H5	6.21 N	3.00 E
Escobar, state, Arg.	206		34.23 S	58.46 W
Escobar, Arroyo, stm., Arg.	206		34.21 S	58.44 W
Escobedo, Mex.	136	G6	27.13 N	101.21 W
Escobedo, Mex.	154	A7	29.04 N	102.21 W
Escocesa, Bahía, b., Dom. Rep.	156	C13	19.25 N	69.45 W
Escondido, Ca., U.S.	148	J8	33.07 N	117.04 W
Escondido, stm., Mex.	136	F7	28.40 N	100.29 W
Escondido, stm., Nic.	156	F5	12.04 N	83.44 W
Escorial see San Lorenzo de El Escorial, Spain	28	D6	40.35 N	4.08 W
Escuadrón 020001, ngh., Mex.	204a		19.22 N	99.06 W
Escuinapa de Hidalgo, Mex.	154	D5	22.50 N	105.48 W
Escuintla, Guat.	156	E2	14.18 N	90.46 W
Escuintla, Mex.	154	H12	15.18 N	92.40 W
Escuminac, Point, c., N.B., Can.	122	C12	47.04 N	64.49 W
Eséka, Cam.	86	D2	3.39 N	10.47 E
Eşen, Tur.	34	G12	36.27 N	29.16 E
Eşen (Köca), stm., Tur.	34	G12	36.17 N	29.16 E
Esenler, ngh., Tur.	185b		41.02 N	28.51 E
Esenoviči, Russia	26	C17	57.17 N	34.14 E
Ésera, stm., Spain	28	B11	42.06 N	0.14 E
Eşfahān, Iran	74	D12	32.39 N	51.39 E
Eşfahān, state, Iran	74	D13	33.00 N	52.00 E
Esgueva, stm., Spain	28	C6	41.40 N	4.43 W
Eshkāshem, Afg.	72	B11	36.42 N	71.33 E
Eshowe, S. Afr.	90	F10	28.53 S	31.27 E
Esh-Sham see Dimashq, Syria	76	E7	33.30 N	36.18 E
Esigodini, Zimb.	90	B9	20.17 S	28.55 E
Esil', Kaz.	48	D11	51.57 N	66.24 E
Esil see Ishim, stm., Asia	48	C12	57.42 N	71.11 E
Esino, stm., Italy	30	G10	43.38 N	13.22 E
Esk, Austl.	98	F9	27.15 S	152.24 E
Esk, stm., U.K.	10	F9	54.58 N	3.02 W
Ěškar-Ola, Russia	40	C15	56.38 N	47.52 E
Eskdale, W.V., U.S.	124	F4	38.04 N	81.26 W
Es'ki, Russia	26	C19	57.56 N	36.22 E
Eski Dzhumaya see Tărgovište, Blg.	36	F13	43.15 N	26.34 E
Eskifjördur, Ice.	12a	k33	65.03 N	13.57 W
Eskilstrup, Den.	24	B7	54.51 N	11.53 E
Eskilstuna, Swe.	16	H14	59.22 N	16.30 E
Eskimo Lakes, l., N.T., Can.	110	B4	69.11 N	132.37 W
Eskimo Point see Arviat, Nu., Can.	110	C12	61.07 N	94.06 W
Eskipazar, Tur.	34	C15	40.57 N	32.31 E
Eskişehir, Tur.	34	D13	39.46 N	30.30 E
Eskişehir, state, Tur.	34	D14	39.35 N	31.10 E
Eskridge, Ks., U.S.	130	F1	38.51 N	96.06 W
Esla, stm., Spain	28	C5	41.29 N	6.03 W
Eslāmābād, Iran	74	C10	34.06 N	46.31 E
Eslāmshahr, Iran	74	C12	35.33 N	51.14 E
Eslöv, Swe.	16	L11	55.50 N	13.18 E
Eşme, Tur.	34	E11	38.23 N	28.58 E
Esmeralda, Austl.	98	B4	18.52 S	142.35 E
Esmeralda, Cuba	156	B8	21.51 N	78.06 W
Esmeralda, Isla, i., Chile	166	I1	48.57 S	75.25 W
Esmeraldas, Ec.	168	G2	0.56 N	79.39 W
Esmeraldas, state, Ec.	168	G2	0.40 N	79.30 W
Esmeraldas, stm., Ec.	168	G2	0.57 N	79.38 W
Esmond, N.D., U.S.	142	F14	48.02 N	99.45 W
Esnagami Lake, l., On., Can.	128	A11	50.19 N	86.50 W
Espada, Punta, c., Col.	168	A6	12.05 N	71.07 W
Espalion, Fr.	22	E8	44.31 N	2.46 E
España see Spain, ctry., Eur.	28	E7	40.00 N	4.00 W
Espanola, On., Can.	126	B8	46.15 N	81.46 W
Espanola, N.M., U.S.	138	F2	35.59 N	106.04 W
Espejo, Spain	28	G6	37.41 N	4.33 W
Espeland, Nor.	16	G3	60.21 N	5.27 E
Espelkamp, Ger.	24	D4	52.22 N	8.37 E
Espera, Arroyo, mth., Arg.	206		34.24 S	58.36 W
Espera Feliz, Braz.	170	K5	20.38 S	41.54 W
Esperança, Braz.	164	D4	4.24 S	69.52 W
Esperança, Braz.	170	D8	7.01 S	35.51 W
Esperance, Austl.	96	F4	33.51 S	121.53 E
Esperantina, Braz.	170	B4	3.54 S	42.14 W
Esperantinópolis, Braz.	170	C3	4.53 S	44.53 W
Esperanza, Arg.	172	E7	31.26 S	60.55 W
Esperanza, Mex.	154	B4	27.36 N	109.55 W
Esperanza, P.R.	158a	b5	18.06 N	65.28 W
Esperanza, sci., Ant.	103	B35	63.24 S	56.59 W
Esperanza Inlet, b., B.C., Can.	144	G3	49.50 N	126.56 W
Esperito, Arroyo, mth., Arg.	206		34.23 S	58.36 W
Espevær, Nor.	16	H3	59.36 N	5.10 E
Espichel, Cabo, c., Port.	28	F1	38.25 N	9.12 W
Espinal, Col.	168	E4	4.08 N	74.52 W
Espinazo, Mex.	136	H6	26.16 N	101.06 W
Espingarda, stm., Braz.	170	E2	10.03 S	47.13 W
Espinhaço, Serra do, mts., Braz.	170	J4	17.25 S	43.39 W
Espinho, Port.	28	D2	41.00 N	8.37 W
Espinillo, Arg.	172	B8	24.58 S	58.33 W
Espino, Ven.	168	C9	8.32 N	66.00 W
Espinosa, Braz.	170	H4	14.56 S	42.48 W
Espírito Santo see Vila Velha, Braz.	170	K5	20.20 S	40.17 W
Espírito Santo, state, Braz.	170	J5	19.30 S	40.30 W
Espiritu Santo, i., Vanuatu	101d	j16	15.15 S	166.50 E
Espíritu Santo, Isla del, i., Mex.	154	C3	24.29 N	110.20 W
Espita, Mex.	156	B3	21.01 N	88.18 W
Esplanada, Braz.	170	F7	11.47 S	37.57 W
Espoo (Esbo), Fin.	18	G11	60.13 N	24.39 E
Es Port de Pollença, Spain	28	E14	39.54 N	3.04 E
Esposende, Port.	28	C2	41.32 N	8.46 W
Esposizione Universale di Roma, p.o.i., Italy	185a		41.50 N	12.28 E
Espugues de Llobregat, Spain	184d		41.22 N	2.05 E
Espumoso, Braz.	172	D11	28.43 S	52.51 W
Espungabera, Moz.	90	B11	20.26 S	32.46 E
Esquatzel Coulee, stm., Wa., U.S.	146	D7	46.16 N	119.07 W
Esquel, Arg.	166	H2	42.53 S	71.18 W
Esquimalt, B.C., Can.	144	H7	48.25 N	123.24 W
Esquina, Arg.	172	D8	30.01 S	59.31 W
Esquiú, Arg.	172	D5	29.22 S	65.18 W
Essandsjøen, l., Nor.	16	D9	63.04 N	12.00 E
Essaouira, Mor.	84	C3	31.30 N	9.45 W
Essarts, Fr.	179		48.30 N	1.46 E
Essej, Russia	50	C9	68.28 N	102.08 E
Essen, Ger.	24	E3	51.28 N	7.00 E
Essen, Ger.	181		51.28 N	7.01 E
Essenberg, ngh., Ger.	181		51.26 N	6.42 E
Essendon, Eng., U.K.	178		51.46 N	0.09 W
Essendon, Mount, mtn., Austl.	96	D3	24.57 S	120.27 E
Essen-Mülheim, Flughafen, arpt., Ger.	181		51.24 N	6.58 E
Essentuki, Russia	42	C10	44.02 N	42.51 E
Essequibo, stm., Guy.	164	C6	7.03 N	58.26 W
Es Sers, Tun.	32	H3	36.04 N	9.02 E
Essex, On., Can.	126	F7	42.10 N	82.48 W
Essex, Ia., U.S.	130	D2	40.50 N	95.18 W
Essex, Md., U.S.	124	E9	39.18 N	76.28 W
Essex, Mt., U.S.	146	B13	48.16 N	113.36 W
Essex, stm., Ma., U.S.	201		42.39 N	70.46 W
Essex Bay, b., Ma., U.S.	201		42.39 N	70.44 W
Essex Fells, N.J., U.S.	194		40.49 N	74.17 W
Essex Junction, Vt., U.S.	122	F3	44.29 N	73.06 W
Essex Skypark, arpt., Md., U.S.	202b		39.18 N	76.28 W
Essexville, Mi., U.S.	126	E6	43.36 N	83.49 W
Essington, Pa., U.S.	203		39.52 N	75.18 W
Essling, ngh., Aus.	182b		48.13 N	16.32 E
Esslingen am Neckar, Ger.	24	H5	48.45 N	9.16 E
Essojla, Russia	18	F20	61.50 N	33.09 E
Essonne, state, Fr.	20	F11	48.36 N	2.20 E
Essvik, Swe.	16	E15	62.18 N	17.24 E
Est, Baie de l', b., Qc., Can.	122	B2	48.24 N	75.02 W
Est, Gare, trans., Fr.	179		48.53 N	2.22 E
Est, Île de l', i., Qc., Can.	122	C15	47.36 N	61.27 W
Est, Pointe de l', c., Qc., Can.	122	A15	49.08 N	61.41 W
Estacada, Or., U.S.	146	E4	45.17 N	122.19 W
Estaca de Bares, Punta da, c., Spain	28	A3	43.47 N	7.40 W
Estaca de Bares, Punta de la see Estaca de Bares, Punta da, c., Spain	28	A3	43.47 N	7.40 W
Estacado, Llano, pl., U.S.	138	H6	33.30 N	102.40 W
Estación Adolfo Rodriguez Sáa see Santa Rosa del Conlara, Arg.	172	F5	32.20 S	65.11 W
Estación Colonia Alvear Norte see General Alvear, Arg.	172	G4	34.58 S	67.41 W
Estación Conchos, Mex.	136	G2	27.59 N	105.17 W
Estación Foguista J. F. Juárez see El Galpón, Arg.	172	B5	25.23 S	64.38 W
Estación Gobernador Vera see Vera, Arg.	172	D7	29.28 S	60.13 W
Estación J. J. Castelli see Castelli, Arg.	172	B7	25.57 S	60.37 W
Estación J. M. Lencinas see Las Catitas, Arg.	172	F3	33.17 S	68.03 W
Estación Justino Solari see Mariano I. Loza, Arg.	172	D8	29.22 S	58.12 W
Estación Manuel F. Mantilla see Pedro R. Fernández, Arg.	172	D8	28.44 S	58.40 W
Estación San Antonio de La Paz see San Antonio, Arg.	172	D5	28.56 S	65.06 W
Estación Vela see María Ignacia, Arg.	172	H8	37.24 S	59.31 W
Estado, Parque do, p.o.i., Braz.	205b		23.39 S	46.37 W
Estados, Isla de los, i., Arg.	166	J4	54.48 S	64.32 W
Eşţahbān, Iran	74	F13	29.08 N	54.04 E
Estância, Braz.	170	F7	11.16 S	37.26 W
Estancia, N.M., U.S.	138	G2	34.45 N	106.03 W
Estanislao del Campo, Arg.	172	B7	25.04 S	60.06 W
Estarreja, Port.	28	D2	40.45 N	8.33 W
Estats, Pic d' (Estats, Pique d'), mtn., Eur.	28	B12	42.40 N	1.24 E
Estats, Pico de see Estats, Pic d', mtn., Eur.	28	B12	42.40 N	1.24 E
Estats, Pico de see Estats, Pique d', mtn., Eur.	28	B12	42.40 N	1.24 E
Estats, Pique d' (Estats, Pic d'), mtn., Eur.	28	B12	42.40 N	1.24 E
Estcourt, S. Afr.	90	F9	29.00 S	29.52 E
Este, Italy	30	E8	45.13 N	11.38 E
Este, stm., Ger.	20	A18	53.33 N	9.48 E
Este, Parque Nacional del, p.o.i., Ven.	204c		10.30 N	66.50 W
Este, Punta, c., P.R.	158a	b5	18.08 N	65.16 W
Esteban Echeverría, state, Arg.	206		34.51 S	58.32 W
Esteio, Braz.	172	D12	29.51 S	51.10 W
Estelí, Nic.	156	F4	13.05 N	86.21 W
Estella, Spain	28	B8	42.40 N	2.00 W
Estelline, S.D., U.S.	128	G2	44.34 N	96.54 W
Estelline, Tx., U.S.	138	G8	34.32 N	100.26 W
Estepa, Spain	28	G6	37.17 N	4.52 W
Estepona, Spain	28	H5	36.26 N	5.08 W
Esterhazy, Sk., Can.	142	D11	50.39 N	102.05 W
Estes Park, Co., U.S.	140	G7	40.22 N	105.31 W
Este Sudeste, Cayos del, is., Col.	156	F7	12.26 N	81.28 W
Estevan, Sk., Can.	142	E10	49.08 N	103.00 W
Estevan Point, B.C., Can.	144	G4	49.23 N	126.32 W
Estherville, Ia., U.S.	128	H4	43.24 N	94.49 W
Estill, S.C., U.S.	132	D4	32.45 N	81.14 W
Estissac, Fr.	20	F12	48.16 N	3.48 E
Estiva, stm., Braz.	170	G3	12.23 S	45.05 W
Estiva, Ribeirão da, stm., Braz.	205b		23.44 S	46.23 W
Estling, Lake, l., N.J., U.S.	194		40.53 N	74.30 W
Eston, Sk., Can.	142	C5	51.10 N	108.46 W
Estonia, ctry., Eur.	12	G12	59.00 N	26.00 E
Estrela, Braz.	172	D11	29.29 S	51.57 W
Estrela, mtn., Port.	28	D3	40.19 N	7.37 W
Estrela, stm., Braz.	205a		22.43 S	43.13 W
Estrela, Serra da, mts., Port.	28	D3	40.20 N	7.38 W
Estrela do Norte, Braz.	170	G1	13.47 S	49.03 W
Estrela do Sul, Braz.	170	J2	18.45 S	47.42 W
Estremadura, hist. reg., Port.	28	E1	39.15 N	9.10 W
Estremoz, Port.	28	F3	38.51 N	7.35 W
Estrondo, Serra do, plat., Braz.	170	E1	9.00 S	48.45 W
Estuary, Sk., Can.	142	D4	50.56 N	109.48 W
Eszék see Osijek, Cro.	30	E15	45.33 N	18.42 E
Esztergom, Hung.	36	B5	47.47 N	18.45 E
Étables, Fr.	20	F6	48.37 N	2.50 W
Etadunna, Austl.	98	G2	28.43 S	138.38 E
Etah, Grnld.	108	B11	78.19 N	72.38 W
Etah, India	70	E7	27.33 N	78.39 E
Étain, Fr.	20	E14	49.12 N	5.38 E
Étampes, Fr.	20	F11	48.26 N	2.10 E
Etamunbanie, Lake, l., Austl.	98	F2	26.15 S	139.44 E
Étaples, Fr.	20	D10	50.31 N	1.38 E
Etāwah, India	70	E7	26.46 N	79.01 E
Etchemin, stm., Qc., Can.	122	D5	46.46 N	71.14 W
Etchojoa, Mex.	154	B4	26.54 N	109.38 W
Ethan, S.D., U.S.	140	D14	43.32 N	97.59 W
Ethel, Ms., U.S.	134	D9	33.07 N	89.27 W
Ethel, Mount, mtn., Co., U.S.	150	C10	40.39 N	106.41 W
Ethelbert, Mb., Can.	142	C13	51.31 N	100.22 W
Ethel Creek, Austl.	96	D4	22.52 S	120.09 E
Etherow, stm., Eng., U.K.	180		53.24 N	2.03 W
Ethiopia, ctry., Afr.	82	F7	9.00 N	39.00 E
Ethiopian Plateau, plat., Eth.	82	E7	10.00 N	38.10 E
Ethridge, Mt., U.S.	146	B14	48.33 N	112.07 W
Ethridge, Tn., U.S.	134	B11	35.19 N	87.18 W
Etigo-heiya, pl., Japan	56	B12	37.45 N	139.00 E
Etili, Tur.	34	C9	39.59 N	26.54 E
Étiolles, Fr.	179		48.38 N	2.29 E
Etive, Loch, l., Scot., U.K.	10	E7	56.29 N	5.09 W
Etjo, mtn., Nmb.	90	B3	21.09 S	16.30 E
E. T. Joshua Airport, arpt., St. Vin.	159e	o11	13.09 N	61.13 W
Etna, Ca., U.S.	148	B3	41.27 N	122.52 W
Etna, Wy., U.S.	146	G16	43.01 N	111.00 W
Etna, stm., Nor.	16	F7	60.49 N	10.04 E
Etna, Monte, vol., Italy	32	G8	37.45 N	15.00 E
Etne, Nor.	16	H3	59.40 N	5.56 E
Etobicoke, ngh., On., Can.	126	E10	43.38 N	79.33 W
Etolin Island, i., Ak., U.S.	109	E13	56.08 N	132.22 W
Etolin Strait, strt., Ak., U.S.	109	D6	60.19 N	165.15 W
Etomami, stm., Sk., Can.	142	B11	52.48 N	102.22 W
Eton, Austl.	98	C7	21.16 S	148.58 E
Eton College, educ., Eng., U.K.	178		51.30 N	0.36 W
Etorofu-tō see Iturup, ostrov, i., Russia	52	C14	44.51 N	147.26 E
Etosha Pan, pl., Nmb.	88	D2	18.45 S	16.15 E
Etoumbi, Congo	86	D2	0.00 N	14.56 E
Etowah, Tn., U.S.	134	B14	35.19 N	84.31 W
Etowah, stm., Ga., U.S.	134	C14	34.15 N	85.11 W
Étretat, Fr.	20	E9	49.42 N	0.12 E
Etsch see Adige, stm., Italy	30	E8	45.10 N	12.20 E
Ettelbruck, Lux.	20	E15	49.50 N	6.05 E
Et Tîdra, i., Maur.	84	F1	19.44 N	16.24 W
Ettlingen, Ger.	24	H4	48.57 N	8.23 E
Etzikom Coulee, stm., Ab., Can.	142	E2	49.23 N	111.18 W
Etzná, hist., Mex.	156	C2	19.35 N	90.15 W
Eu, Fr.	20	D10	50.03 N	1.25 E
Eua, i., Tonga	94	F9	21.22 S	174.56 W
Eua Iki, i., Tonga	100e	n15	21.07 S	174.58 W
Euboea see Évvoia, i., Grc.	34	E6	38.34 N	23.50 E
Euboea, Gulf of see Vóreios Evvoïkós, b., Grc.	34	E6	38.45 N	23.08 E
Euchiniko, stm., B.C., Can.	144	C6	53.14 N	123.30 W
Eucla, Austl.	96	F5	31.41 S	128.53 E
Euclid, Oh., U.S.	124	C4	41.35 N	81.31 W
Euclid Creek, stm., Oh., U.S.	197a		41.35 N	81.35 W
Euclid Creek Reservation, p.o.i., Oh., U.S.	197a		41.33 N	81.32 W
Euclides da Cunha, Braz.	170	F6	10.30 S	39.00 W
Eucumbene, Lake, res., Austl.	98	K7	36.06 S	148.44 E
Eudora, Ar., U.S.	134	D7	33.07 N	91.15 W
Eudora, Ks., U.S.	130	F2	38.56 N	95.05 W
Eudunda, Austl.	98	J2	34.10 S	139.04 E
Eufaula, Al., U.S.	134	F13	31.53 N	85.09 W
Eufaula, Ok., U.S.	134	B3	35.16 N	95.35 W
Eufaula Lake, res., Ok., U.S.	134	B3	35.17 N	95.31 W
Eugene, Or., U.S.	146	F3	44.03 N	123.04 W
Eugenia, Punta, c., Mex.	154	B1	27.50 N	115.04 W
Eugenio Bustos, Arg.	172	F3	33.48 S	69.06 W
Eugmo, i., Fin.	18	D9	63.49 N	22.45 E
Eugowra, Austl.	98	I7	33.26 S	148.22 E
Eulo, Austl.	98	G5	28.09 S	145.02 E
Eume, stm., Spain	28	A2	43.24 N	8.10 W
Eumemmerring Creek, stm., Austl.	192b		38.03 S	145.10 E
Eumungerie, Austl.	98	H7	31.57 S	148.37 E
Eunápolis, Braz.	170	I6	16.22 S	39.34 W
Eungella National Park, p.o.i., Austl.	98	C7	21.00 S	148.30 E
Eunice, La., U.S.	134	G6	30.29 N	92.25 W
Eunice, N.M., U.S.	136	B4	32.26 N	103.09 W
Eupen, Bel.	24	F2	50.37 N	6.01 E
Euphrates (Al-Furāt), stm., Asia	72	C6	30.59 N	47.26 E
Eupora, Ms., U.S.	134	D9	33.32 N	89.16 W
Eure, state, Fr.	20	E10	49.10 N	1.00 E
Eure, stm., Fr.	20	E10	49.17 N	1.02 E
Eure-et-Loir, state, Fr.	20	F10	48.30 N	1.30 E
Eureka, Can.	108	A8	79.59 N	85.57 W
Eureka, Ca., U.S.	148	C1	40.47 N	124.09 W
Eureka, Il., U.S.	128	K9	40.43 N	89.15 W
Eureka, Ks., U.S.	138	D12	37.49 N	96.17 W
Eureka, Mt., U.S.	146	B11	48.53 N	115.02 W
Eureka, Nv., U.S.	148	D10	39.33 N	115.59 W

Name	Page	Map Ref.	Latitude	Longitude
Eureka, S.C., U.S.	132	B4	34.43 N	81.11 W
Eureka, S.D., U.S.	140	B13	45.46 N	99.37 W
Eureka, Ut., U.S.	150	C4	39.58 N	112.09 W
Eureka Springs, Ar., U.S.	130	H4	36.23 N	93.44 W
Eurinilla Creek, stm., Austl.	98	H3	30.56 S	140.01 E
Euroa, Austl.	98	K5	36.45 S	145.34 E
Euro Disney, Parc, p.o.i., Fr.	179		48.51 N	2.47 E
Europa, Île, i., Reu.	88	E7	22.19 S	40.20 E
Europa, Picos de, mts., Spain	28	A6	43.12 N	4.48 W
Europa Island see Europa, Île, i., Reu.	88	E7	22.19 S	40.20 E
Europa Point, c., Gib.	28	H5	36.07 N	5.20 W
Europe, cont.	4	C13	50.00 N	28.00 E
Euskal Herriko, state, Spain	28	A8	43.00 N	2.30 W
Euskirchen, Ger.	24	F2	50.39 N	6.48 E
Eustace, Tx., U.S.	136	B12	32.19 N	96.00 W
Eustis, Fl., U.S.	132	H4	28.51 N	81.41 W
Eustis, Ne., U.S.	140	G12	40.40 N	100.02 W
Eustis, Lake, l., Fl., U.S.	132	H4	28.50 N	81.44 W
Euston, Austl.	98	J4	34.35 S	142.44 E
Euston Station, trans., Eng., U.K.	178		51.32 N	0.08 W
Eutaw, Al., U.S.	134	E11	32.50 N	87.53 W
Eutin, Ger.	24	B6	54.08 N	10.37 E
Eutsuk Lake, l., B.C., Can.	144	C4	53.19 N	126.43 W
Eva, Al., U.S.	134	C12	34.20 N	86.46 W
Evadale, Tx., U.S.	136	D13	30.21 N	94.04 W
Eva Downs, Austl.	96	C6	17.59 S	134.51 E
Evandale, Austl.	99a	n13	41.34 S	147.14 E
Evans, Co., U.S.	140	G8	40.22 N	104.41 W
Evans, Lac, l., Qc., Can.	110	E15	50.55 N	77.00 W
Evans, Mount, mtn., Co., U.S.	138	B3	39.35 N	105.38 W
Evansburg, Ab., Can.	144	C15	53.36 N	115.01 W
Evansburg, Pa., U.S.	203		40.11 N	75.26 W
Evans City, Pa., U.S.	124	D5	40.45 N	80.03 W
Evans Creek, stm., Or., U.S.	146	H3	42.26 N	123.10 W
Evansdale, Ia., U.S.	128	I6	42.28 N	92.16 W
Evans Head, c., Austl.	98	G9	29.07 S	153.26 E
Evans Strait, strt., Nu., Can.	110	C14	63.15 N	82.00 W
Evanston, Il., U.S.	130	B10	42.02 N	87.40 W
Evanston, Pa., U.S.	197b		40.16 N	79.41 W
Evanston, Wy., U.S.	150	B6	41.17 N	110.58 W
Evansville, Il., U.S.	130	F8	38.05 N	89.56 W
Evansville, In., U.S.	130	F10	37.58 N	87.32 W
Evansville, Mn., U.S.	128	E3	45.59 N	95.40 W
Evansville, Wi., U.S.	130	B8	42.46 N	89.17 W
Evansville, Wy., U.S.	140	E6	42.49 N	106.15 W
Evant, Tx., U.S.	136	C9	31.28 N	98.09 W
Eva Perón see La Plata, Arg.	172	G8	34.55 S	57.57 W
Evart, Mi., U.S.	126	E4	43.54 N	85.15 W
Evaz, Iran	74	G14	27.46 N	53.59 E
Eve, Fr.	179		49.05 N	2.42 E
Evecquemont, Fr.	179		49.02 N	1.57 E
Eveking, Ger.	181		51.14 N	7.44 E
Eveleth, Mn., U.S.	128	D6	47.27 N	92.32 W
Evening Shade, Ar., U.S.	130	H6	36.04 N	91.37 W
Evenkamp, Ger.	181		51.40 N	7.39 E
Evensk, Russia	50	D20	61.57 N	159.14 E
Everard, Lake, l., Austl.	96	F6	31.24 S	135.06 E
Everard, Mount, mtn., B.C., Can.	144	E5	51.05 N	125.45 W
Everest, Ks., U.S.	130	E2	39.40 N	95.25 W
Everest, Mount (Qomolangma Feng), mtn., Asia	70	D11	27.59 N	86.56 E
Everett, N.J., U.S.	194		40.21 N	74.09 W
Everett, Pa., U.S.	124	E7	40.00 N	78.22 W
Everett, Wa., U.S.	146	C4	47.58 N	122.11 W
Everett, Mount, mtn., Ma., U.S.	124	B12	42.06 N	73.27 W
Everglades, The, sw., Fl., U.S.	132	K4	26.00 N	80.40 W
Everglades City, Fl., U.S.	132	K4	25.50 N	81.23 W
Everglades National Park, p.o.i., Fl., U.S.	132	K5	25.27 N	80.53 W
Evergreen, Al., U.S.	134	F12	31.25 N	86.57 W
Evergreen, Ca., U.S.	148	H5	35.54 N	120.26 W
Evergreen, Mt., U.S.	146	B12	48.12 N	114.16 W
Evergreen Plaza, shp. cen., Il., U.S.	196		41.43 N	87.41 W
Evermann, Cerro, vol., Mex.	154	F3	18.48 N	110.59 W
Eversael, Ger.	181		51.33 N	6.39 E
Everton, ngh., Eng., U.K.	180		53.25 N	2.58 W
Everton Football Ground, p.o.i., Eng., U.K.	180		53.26 N	2.58 W
Evesham, Sk., Can.	142	B4	52.23 N	109.49 W
Evesham, Eng., U.K.	10	I11	52.05 N	1.57 W
Évian-les-Bains, Fr.	22	C12	46.24 N	6.35 E
Evijärvi, Fin.	8	D10	63.22 N	23.27 E
Eving, ngh., Ger.	181		51.33 N	7.29 E
Evingsen, Ger.	181		51.18 N	7.44 E
Evje, Nor.	16	I5	58.36 N	7.51 E
Evlah see Yevlax, Azer.	42	E12	40.36 N	47.08 E
Evlaševo, Russia	40	E15	53.06 N	46.49 E
Évora, Port.	28	F3	38.33 N	7.54 W
Évora, state, Port.	28	F3	38.35 N	7.45 W
Evoron, ozero, l., Russia	50	F16	51.28 N	136.30 E
Evpatorija see Yevpatoriia, Ukr.	38	H12	45.12 N	33.22 E
Évreux, Fr.	22	E10	49.01 N	1.09 E
Évron, Fr.	20	F8	48.09 N	0.23 W
Evros see Maritsa, stm., Eur.	34	C9	40.44 N	26.02 E
Évros see Maritsa, stm., Eur.	34	C9	40.44 N	26.02 E
Evrótas, stm., Grc.	34	F5	36.48 N	22.41 E
Évry, Fr.	20	F11	48.38 N	2.26 E
Évry-les-Châteaux, Fr.	179		48.39 N	2.38 E
E. V. Spence Reservoir, res., Tx., U.S.	136	C7	31.55 N	100.34 W
Évvoia, i., Grc.	34	E6	38.34 N	23.50 E
Évzonos, mtn., Grc.	185c		37.57 N	23.49 E
Ewa, Hi., U.S.	100a	b3	21.20 N	158.02 W
Ewan, N.J., U.S.	203		39.42 N	75.11 W
Ewan Lake, l., N.J., U.S.	203		39.42 N	75.11 W
Ewansville, N.J., U.S.	203		39.59 N	74.44 W
Ewe, Loch, b., Scot., U.K.	10	D7	57.48 N	5.38 W
Ewell, Eng., U.K.	178		51.21 N	0.15 W
Ewen, Mi., U.S.	128	E9	46.32 N	89.16 W
Ewenkiku Zizhiqi, China	50	G12	49.06 N	119.43 E
Ewing, Ne., U.S.	140	E14	42.15 N	98.21 W
Ewing, Va., U.S.	124	H2	36.38 N	83.25 W
Ewingsville, Pa., U.S.	197b		40.24 N	80.06 W
Ewo, Congo	86	E2	0.53 S	14.48 E
Ewu, Nig.	191a		6.33 N	3.19 E
Exaltación, Bol.	166	B3	13.15 S	65.17 W
Excelsior Mountain, mtn., Ca., U.S.	148	E6	38.02 N	119.18 W
Excelsior Park, p.o.i., Austl.	192a		33.45 S	151.01 E
Excelsior Springs, Mo., U.S.	130	E3	39.20 N	94.13 W
Exchange Station, trans., Eng., U.K.	180		53.25 N	2.59 W
Exe, stm., Eng., U.K.	10	K9	50.41 N	3.29 W
Exeter, On., Can.	126	E8	43.20 N	81.28 W
Exeter, Eng., U.K.	10	K9	50.43 N	3.31 W
Exeter, Ca., U.S.	148	G6	36.17 N	119.08 W
Exeter, Ne., U.S.	140	G15	40.38 N	97.26 W
Exeter, N.H., U.S.	122	G6	42.59 N	70.57 W
Exeter Sound, strt., Nu., Can.	108	D13	66.14 N	62.00 W
Exhibition Park, p.o.i., On., Can.	193b		43.38 N	79.25 W
Exhibition Stadium, p.o.i., On., Can.	193b		43.38 N	79.25 W
Exira, Ia., U.S.	130	C3	41.35 N	94.52 W
Exmoor, plat., Eng., U.K.	10	J9	51.08 N	3.44 W
Exmoor National Park, p.o.i., Eng., U.K.	10	J9	51.08 N	3.38 W
Exmore, Va., U.S.	124	G10	37.31 N	75.49 W
Exmouth, Austl.	96	D2	21.56 S	114.07 E
Exmouth, Eng., U.K.	10	K9	50.37 N	3.24 W
Exmouth Gulf, b., Austl.	96	D2	22.00 S	114.20 E
Expedition Range, mts., Austl.	98	E7	24.30 S	149.05 E
Experiment, Ga., U.S.	132	C1	33.17 N	84.17 W
Expo Memorial Park, p.o.i., Japan	188		34.48 N	135.32 E
Exposition Park, p.o.i., Ca., U.S.	198		34.01 N	118.17 W
Exshaw, Ab., Can.	144	E15	51.03 N	115.15 W
Extremadura, state, Spain	28	E4	39.15 N	6.15 W
Exu, Braz.	170	D6	7.31 S	39.43 W
Exuma Cays, is., Bah.	152	C9	24.15 N	76.30 W
Exuma Sound, strt., Bah.	152	C9	24.11 N	76.00 W
Eyasi, Lake, l., Tan.	86	E6	3.40 S	35.05 E
Eydehamn, Nor.	16	I6	58.31 N	8.53 E
Eyebrow, Sk., Can.	142	D7	50.48 N	106.08 W
Eyehill Creek, stm., Can.	142	B4	52.39 N	109.39 W
Eyemouth, Scot., U.K.	10	F10	55.52 N	2.06 W
Eye Peninsula, pen., Scot., U.K.	10	C6	58.13 N	6.13 W
Eyhorne Street, Eng., U.K.	178		51.16 N	0.38 E
Eyjafjörður, b., Ice.	12a	j30	65.54 N	18.15 W
Eyl, Som.	86	C9	7.58 N	49.49 E
Eyl, val., Som.	86	C9	7.57 N	49.50 E
Eylar Mountain, mtn., Ca., U.S.	148	F4	37.28 N	121.33 W
Eymoutiers, Fr.	22	D7	45.44 N	1.44 E
Eynsford, Eng., U.K.	178		51.22 N	0.13 E
Eyota, Mn., U.S.	128	H6	43.59 N	92.13 W
Eyrarbakki, Ice.	12a	l29	63.52 N	21.10 W
Eyre, Austl.	96	F5	32.15 S	126.18 E
Eyre Creek, stm., Austl.	96	F2	26.24 S	139.03 E
Eyre North, Lake, l., Austl.	96	E7	28.33 S	137.14 E
Eyre Peninsula, pen., Austl.	96	F7	33.14 S	135.48 E
Eyre South, Lake, l., Austl.	96	E7	29.17 S	137.25 E
Eysturoy, i., Far. Is.	12b	n34	62.12 N	6.54 W
Eyüp, ngh., Tur.	185b		41.03 N	28.55 E
Eyvānekey, Iran	74	C13	35.20 N	52.03 E
Eyzaguirre, Canal, can., Chile	204e		33.36 S	70.41 W
Ézanville, Fr.	179		49.02 N	2.22 E
Ezbekîya, ngh., Egypt	191c		30.03 N	31.15 E
Ezeiza, Aeropuerto Internacional de, arpt., Arg.	206		34.49 S	58.32 W
Ezequiel Ramos Mexía, Embalse, res., Arg.	166	G3	39.27 S	69.00 W
Ezere, Lat.	26	D5	56.23 N	22.20 E
Ezerėlis, Lith.	26	F6	54.52 N	23.36 E
Ezine, Tur.	34	D9	39.47 N	26.20 E
Ezjaryšča, Bela.	26	E12	55.50 N	29.59 E
F				
Faaborg, Den.	16	L8	55.06 N	10.15 E
Faaone, Fr. Poly.	100h	v22	17.39 S	149.18 W
Fabens, Tx., U.S.	136	C1	31.30 N	106.09 W
Fåberg, Nor.	16	F8	61.10 N	10.22 E
Faber Lake, l., N.T., Can.	110	C7	63.56 N	117.15 W
Fabreville, ngh., Qc., Can.	193a		45.34 N	73.50 W
Fabriano, Italy	30	G9	43.20 N	12.53 E
Facatativá, Col.	168	E4	4.48 N	74.21 W
Fachi, Niger	84	F7	18.06 N	11.34 E
Facpi Point, c., Guam	100c	j9	13.20 N	144.38 E
Factoryville, Pa., U.S.	124	C10	41.33 N	75.46 W
Fada, Chad	82	D4	17.12 N	21.34 E
Fada-Ngourma, Burkina	84	G5	12.03 N	0.21 E
Faddeevskij, ostrov, i., Russia	50	A18	75.27 N	144.19 E
Faddeja, zaliv, b., Russia	50	A10	76.40 N	107.20 E
Fadian Point, c., Guam	100c	j10	13.26 N	144.49 E
Fadiffolu Atoll, at., Mald.	62a	h12	5.25 N	73.30 E
Faenza, Italy	30	F8	44.17 N	11.52 E
Faeroe Islands see Færøerne, is., Far. Is.	8	C7	62.00 N	7.00 W
Færøerne see Faroe Islands, dep., Eur.	12b	n34	62.00 N	7.00 W
Færøerne (Faroe Islands), is., Far. Is.	8	C7	62.00 N	7.00 W
Faete, Monte, mtn., Italy	185a		41.45 N	12.44 E
Fafa, Mali	84	F5	15.20 N	0.45 E
Fafe, Port.	28	C2	41.27 N	8.09 W
Făgăraș, Rom.	36	D11	45.50 N	24.59 E
Făgărașului, Munții, mts., Rom.	36	D11	45.30 N	24.52 E
Fagernes, Nor.	16	F7	60.59 N	9.15 E
Fagersta, Swe.	16	G13	60.00 N	15.48 E
Făget, Rom.	36	D9	45.51 N	22.10 E
Faguibine, Lac, l., Mali	84	F4	16.48 N	3.49 W
Fagurhólsmýri, Ice.	12a	l31	63.52 N	16.39 W
Fahrlander See, l., Ger.	182a		52.27 N	13.01 E
Fairbairn Park, p.o.i., Austl.	192b		37.47 S	144.55 E
Fairbank, Ia., U.S.	130	B5	42.38 N	92.02 W
Fairbanks, Ak., U.S.	109	D10	64.50 N	147.42 W
Fairbanks, La., U.S.	134	E6	32.36 N	92.03 W
Fair Bluff, N.C., U.S.	132	B6	34.18 N	79.01 W
Fairborn, Oh., U.S.	124	E1	39.48 N	84.01 W
Fairburn, Ga., U.S.	134	D14	33.34 N	84.34 W
Fairbury, Il., U.S.	128	K10	40.44 N	88.30 W
Fairbury, Ne., U.S.	138	A11	40.08 N	97.11 W
Fairchance, Pa., U.S.	124	E6	39.49 N	79.45 W
Fairchild, Wi., U.S.	128	G8	44.35 N	90.57 W
Fairchild Air Force Base, mil., Wa., U.S.	146	C9	47.38 N	117.39 W
Fairfax, Al., U.S.	134	E13	32.47 N	85.11 W
Fairfax, De., U.S.	203		39.47 N	75.32 W
Fairfax, Mn., U.S.	128	G4	44.31 N	94.42 W
Fairfax, Mo., U.S.	130	D2	40.20 N	95.23 W
Fairfax, Ok., U.S.	138	E12	36.34 N	96.40 W
Fairfax, S.C., U.S.	132	D4	32.57 N	81.14 W
Fairfax, S.D., U.S.	140	D14	43.00 N	98.51 W
Fairfax, Vt., U.S.	126	D16	44.39 N	73.00 W
Fairfax, Va., U.S.	124	F8	38.50 N	77.18 W
Fairfax Forest, Va., U.S.	202c		38.52 N	77.15 W
Fairfax Park, Va., U.S.	202c		38.47 N	77.14 W
Fairfax Station, Va., U.S.	202c		38.48 N	77.19 W
Fairfield, Al., U.S.	134	D12	33.29 N	86.57 W
Fairfield, Ca., U.S.	148	E3	38.15 N	122.02 W
Fairfield, Id., U.S.	146	G12	43.21 N	114.47 W
Fairfield, Il., U.S.	130	F9	38.22 N	88.21 W
Fairfield, Ia., U.S.	130	C6	41.00 N	91.57 W
Fairfield, Me., U.S.	122	F7	44.35 N	69.36 W
Fairfield, Mt., U.S.	146	C15	47.37 N	111.59 W
Fairfield, Ne., U.S.	140	G14	40.25 N	98.05 W
Fairfield, N.J., U.S.	194		40.53 N	74.16 W
Fairfield, Oh., U.S.	124	E1	39.20 N	84.33 W
Fairfield, Tx., U.S.	136	C11	31.42 N	96.10 W
Fairfield University, educ., Ct., U.S.	194		41.09 N	73.15 W
Fairgrove, Mi., U.S.	126	E6	43.31 N	83.32 W
Fairhaven, Ma., U.S.	124	C15	41.38 N	70.54 W
Fair Haven, N.Y., U.S.	126	E13	43.18 N	76.42 W
Fair Haven, Vt., U.S.	126	E16	43.35 N	73.16 W
Fair Haven, Va., U.S.	202c		38.47 N	77.05 W
Fairhaven Bay, l., Ma., U.S.	201		42.26 N	71.21 W
Fair Head, c., N. Ire., U.K.	10	F6	55.13 N	6.09 W
Fairhope, Al., U.S.	134	G11	30.31 N	87.53 W
Fair Isle, i., Scot., U.K.	10	B11	59.31 N	1.38 W
Fairknoll, Md., U.S.	202c		39.05 N	76.59 W
Fairland, In., U.S.	130	E12	39.35 N	85.51 W
Fairland, Md., U.S.	202c		39.05 N	76.58 W
Fairland, Ok., U.S.	130	H3	36.44 N	94.50 W
Fairlane Town Center, shp. cen., Mi., U.S.	199		42.19 N	83.13 W
Fairlee, Va., U.S.	202c		38.52 N	77.16 W
Fairleigh Dickinson University (Florham-Madison), educ., N.J., U.S.	194		40.46 N	74.26 W
Fairleigh Dickinson University, educ., N.J., U.S.	194		40.50 N	74.07 W
Fairleigh Dickinson University (Teaneck), educ., N.J., U.S.	194		40.53 N	74.02 W
Fairlie, N.Z.	102	G4	44.06 S	170.48 E
Fairmont, Mn., U.S.	128	H4	43.39 N	94.27 W
Fairmont, Ne., U.S.	140	G15	40.38 N	97.35 W
Fairmont, N.C., U.S.	132	B6	34.29 N	79.07 W
Fairmont, Pa., U.S.	197b		40.19 N	79.43 W
Fairmont, W.V., U.S.	124	E5	39.28 N	80.07 W
Fairmont Hot Springs, B.C., Can.	144	F14	50.19 N	115.52 W
Fairmont Terrace, Ca., U.S.	200		37.43 N	122.07 W
Fairmount, Ga., U.S.	134	C14	34.26 N	84.42 W
Fairmount, Il., U.S.	130	D10	40.02 N	87.50 W
Fairmount, In., U.S.	130	D12	40.25 N	85.38 W
Fairmount, N.D., U.S.	128	E2	46.02 N	96.37 W
Fairmount Park, p.o.i., Pa., U.S.	203		40.00 N	75.12 W
Fair Ness, c., Nu., Can.	110	C16	63.24 N	72.01 W
Fair Oaks, Ca., U.S.	148	E4	38.38 N	121.16 W
Fairoaks, Pa., U.S.	197b		40.34 N	80.13 W
Fairoaks Airport, arpt., Eng., U.K.	178		51.21 N	0.32 W
Fair Plain, Mi., U.S.	130	B11	42.05 N	86.27 W
Fairplains, N.C., U.S.	124	H4	36.11 N	81.09 W
Fairplay, Co., U.S.	138	B3	39.13 N	106.00 W
Fairport, On., Can.	193b		43.49 N	79.05 W
Fairport Beach, On., Can.	193b		43.48 N	79.06 W
Fairseat, Eng., U.K.	178		51.20 N	0.20 E
Fairview, Ga., U.S.	134	C13	34.56 N	85.19 W
Fairview, Il., U.S.	130	D7	40.38 N	90.09 W
Fairview, Ks., U.S.	130	E2	39.49 N	95.44 W
Fairview, Mi., U.S.	126	D5	44.43 N	84.03 W
Fairview, Mt., U.S.	142	G9	47.51 N	104.03 W
Fairview, N.J., U.S.	194		40.51 N	73.58 W
Fairview, Ok., U.S.	138	E10	36.15 N	98.29 W
Fairview, Tn., U.S.	130	I10	35.58 N	87.07 W
Fairview, Ut., U.S.	150	D5	39.37 N	111.26 W
Fairview Mall, shp. cen., On., Can.	193b		43.47 N	79.21 W
Fairview Park, In., U.S.	130	E10	39.40 N	87.24 W
Fairview Peak, mtn., Nv., U.S.	148	D7	39.12 N	118.09 W
Fairview Peak, mtn., Or., U.S.	146	G4	43.35 N	122.39 W
Fairview Pointe Claire Centre, shp. cen., Qc., Can.	193a		45.28 N	73.50 W
Fairview Village, Pa., U.S.	203		40.10 N	75.23 W
Fairville, Pa., U.S.	203		39.51 N	75.38 W
Fairweather, Mount see Fairweather Mountain, mtn., N.A.	109	E12	58.54 N	137.32 W
Fairweather Mountain, mtn., N.A.	109	E12	58.54 N	137.32 W
Fairy Stone State Park, p.o.i., Va., U.S.	124	H5	36.48 N	80.06 W
Faisalabad (Lyallpur), Pak.	70	C4	31.25 N	73.05 E
Faison, N.C., U.S.	132	A7	35.06 N	78.08 W
Faistós, hist., Grc.	34	H7	35.02 N	24.53 E
Faith, S.D., U.S.	140	B10	45.00 N	102.01 W
Faiyum see El-Fayoum, Egypt	76	I1	29.19 N	30.50 E
Faizābād, India	70	E9	26.47 N	82.08 E
Fajansovyj, Russia	26	F17	54.03 N	34.22 E
Fajardo, P.R.	158a	b4	18.19 N	65.39 W
Fajou, Îlet à, i., Guad.	159c	h5	16.21 N	61.35 W
Fajr, Bi'r, well, Sau. Ar.	76	J8	28.50 N	37.52 E
Fajr, Wādī, stm., Sau. Ar.	74	E6	30.17 N	38.18 E
Fajr, Wādī, stm., Sau. Ar.	76	J8	29.10 N	38.09 E
Fakel, Russia	40	C18	57.39 N	53.05 E
Fakse, Den.	16	L10	55.15 N	12.07 E
Fakse Bugt, b., Den.	16	L10	55.10 N	12.15 E
Faku, China	52	C9	42.30 N	123.24 E
Falaba, S.L.	84	H2	9.51 N	11.19 W
Falaise, Fr.	20	F8	48.53 N	0.12 W
Fālākāta, India	70	E12	26.30 N	89.12 E
Falam, Mya.	64	A1	22.53 N	93.41 E
Falāvarjān, Iran	74	D12	32.31 N	51.29 E
Fălciu, Rom.	36	C15	46.18 N	28.08 E
Falcognana di Sotto, ngh., Italy	185a		41.45 N	12.33 E
Falcón, state, Ven.	168	B7	11.01 N	69.30 W
Falcon, Cape, c., Or., U.S.	146	E2	45.46 N	123.59 W
Falcón, Presa (Falcon Reservoir), res., N.A.	136	H8	26.37 N	99.11 W
Falconara Marittima, Italy	30	G10	43.37 N	13.24 E
Falconcrest, Pa., U.S.	203		39.58 N	75.33 W
Falcon Heights, Or., U.S.	148	A4	42.08 N	121.47 W
Falcon Reservoir (Falcón, Presa), res., N.A.	136	H8	26.37 N	99.11 W
Falelatai, Samoa	101c	g11	13.54 S	172.00 W
Falémé, stm., Afr.	84	G2	14.45 N	12.14 W
Faleshty see Fălești, Mol.	38	F6	47.34 N	27.43 E
Fălești, Mol.	38	F6	47.34 N	27.43 E
Falfurrias, Tx., U.S.	136	G9	27.13 N	98.08 W
Fáliro, Órmos, b., Grc.	185c		37.56 N	23.40 E
Falkefjellet, mtn., Nor.	14	B20	70.15 N	29.45 E
Falkenberg, Ger.	24	E9	51.34 N	13.14 E
Falkenberg, Swe.	16	K10	56.54 N	12.29 E
Falkenberg, ngh., Ger.	182a		52.34 N	13.33 E
Falkenhagener See, l., Ger.	182a		52.34 N	13.08 E
Falkenrehde, Ger.	182a		52.30 N	12.56 E
Falkensee, Ger.	24	D9	52.34 N	13.04 E
Falkenstein, Ger.	24	F8	50.28 N	12.22 E
Falkirk, Scot., U.K.	10	E9	56.00 N	3.46 W
Falkland, B.C., Can.	144	F11	50.29 N	119.34 W
Falkland Islands, dep., S.A.	166	J4	51.45 S	59.00 W
Falkland Islands, is., Falk. Is.	4	J9	51.41 S	59.08 W
Falkland Sound, strt., Falk. Is.	166	J5	51.44 S	59.24 W
Falköping, Swe.	16	I11	58.10 N	13.32 E
Falkville, Al., U.S.	134	C12	34.22 N	86.54 W
Fall, stm., Ks., U.S.	138	D13	37.24 N	95.40 W
Fallbrook, Ca., U.S.	148	J8	33.22 N	117.14 W
Fallbrook Square, shp. cen., Ca., U.S.	198		34.12 N	118.38 W
Fall Creek, Wi., U.S.	128	G7	44.45 N	91.16 W
Fall Creek Falls State Park, p.o.i., Tn., U.S.	134	B13	35.38 N	85.21 W
Fallen Jerusalem, i., Br. Vir. Is.	158b	e9	18.25 N	64.27 W
Fallentimber Creek, stm., Ab., Can.	144	E16	51.46 N	114.38 W
Falling, stm., Va., U.S.	124	G7	37.00 N	78.55 W
Fallon, Mt., U.S.	140	A7	46.50 N	105.07 W
Fallon, Nv., U.S.	148	D7	39.29 N	118.46 W
Fall River, Ks., U.S.	130	G1	37.36 N	96.01 W
Fall River, Ma., U.S.	124	C14	41.41 N	71.10 W
Fall River, Wi., U.S.	128	H9	43.22 N	89.02 W
Fall River Lake, res., Ks., U.S.	130	G1	37.42 N	96.08 W
Fall River Mills, Ca., U.S.	148	C4	41.00 N	121.26 W
Falls City, Ne., U.S.	130	D2	40.03 N	95.36 W
Falls City, Or., U.S.	146	F3	44.51 N	123.26 W
Falls Creek, Pa., U.S.	124	C7	41.08 N	78.47 W
Falls Lake, res., N.C., U.S.	124	I7	36.01 N	78.42 W
Falls Pond, l., Ma., U.S.	201		41.58 N	71.20 W
Falls Run, stm., Md., U.S.	202b		39.22 N	76.52 W
Falmouth, Jam.	158d	i13	18.28 N	77.39 W
Falmouth, Eng., U.K.	10	K7	50.09 N	5.03 W
Falmouth, Ky., U.S.	124	F1	38.40 N	84.20 W
Falmouth, Me., U.S.	122	G6	43.43 N	70.14 W
Falmouth, Ma., U.S.	124	C15	41.33 N	70.37 W
Falmouth, Va., U.S.	124	F8	38.19 N	77.28 W
Falmouth Bay, b., Eng., U.K.	10	K8	50.05 N	5.01 W
False Bay, b., S. Afr.	90	I4	34.12 S	18.40 E
False Divi Point, c., India	69	D5	15.43 N	80.49 E
False Pass, Ak., U.S.	109	F7	54.52 N	163.24 W
Falset, Spain	28	C11	41.08 N	0.49 E
Falso, Cabo, c., Dom. Rep.	156	D12	17.46 N	71.40 W
Falster, i., Den.	24	B8	54.48 N	11.58 E
Falsterbo, Swe.	16	L10	55.23 N	12.50 E
Fălticeni, Rom.	36	B13	47.27 N	26.19 E
Falun, Swe.	16	G13	60.36 N	15.38 E
Famagusta see Gazimağusa, N. Cyp.	76	C4	35.06 N	33.57 E
Famaillá, Arg.	172	C5	27.03 S	65.24 W
Famatina, Arg.	172	D4	28.55 S	67.30 W
Famatina, Sierra de, mts., Arg.	172	D4	28.46 S	67.50 W
Famenne, reg., Bel.	20	D14	50.10 N	5.15 E
Family Lake, l., Mb., Can.	142	B18	51.53 N	95.27 W
Fanado, stm., Braz.	170	I4	17.06 S	42.37 W
Fanchang, China	58	F8	31.05 N	118.11 E
Fanch'eng see Xiangfan, China	58	F4	32.01 N	112.08 E
Fanchon, Pointe, c., Haiti	156	C10	18.26 N	74.29 W
Fancy, St. Vin.	159e	o11	13.22 N	61.10 W
Fancy Creek, stm., Ks., U.S.	138	B12	39.28 N	96.45 W
Faneromenis Monastery, rel., Grc.	185c		37.59 N	23.26 E
Fang, Thai.	64	C4	19.55 N	99.12 E
Fangak, Sudan	82	F6	9.04 N	30.51 E
Fangcheng, China	58	E5	33.15 N	112.59 E
Fangcheng, China	58	K3	21.46 N	108.21 E
Fängersee, l., Ger.	182a		52.35 N	13.50 E
Fango, stm., Fr.	22	G14	42.25 N	8.39 E
Fangxian, China	58	E4	32.02 N	110.44 E
Fangzheng, China	52	B10	45.49 N	128.50 E
Fanhões, Port.	184c		38.53 N	9.09 W
Fanipal', Bela.	26	G10	53.45 N	27.20 E
Fanjiatun, China	54	C6	43.42 N	125.04 E
Fannaråki, mtn., Nor.	16	F5	61.31 N	7.55 E
Fannich, Loch, l., Scot., U.K.	10	D7	57.38 N	5.00 W
Fanning Island see Tabuaeran, at., Kir.	94	C11	3.51 N	159.18 W
Fanny, Mount, mtn., Or., U.S.	146	E9	45.20 N	117.41 W
Fanny Bay, B.C., Can.	144	G6	49.30 N	124.49 W
Fano, Italy	30	G10	43.50 N	13.01 E
Fanø, i., Den.	16	L6	55.25 N	8.25 E
Fan Si Pan, mtn., Viet.	64	A6	22.15 N	103.46 E
Fantasy Island, p.o.i., N.Y., U.S.	202a		43.02 N	78.58 W
Fanwood, N.J., U.S.	194		40.38 N	74.23 W
Faraday, sci., Ant.	103	B34	65.15 S	64.15 W
Faradje, D.R.C.	86	D5	3.43 N	29.44 E
Faradofay see Tôlañaro, Madag.	88	F8	25.02 S	47.00 E
Farafangana, Madag.	88	E8	22.49 S	47.49 E
Farāh, Afg.	72	C9	32.21 N	62.04 E
Farāh, stm., Afg.	72	C9	31.26 N	61.26 E
Farahābād, Iran	185d		35.42 N	51.30 E
Farallón, Paso del, strt., Arg.	206		34.41 S	57.57 W
Farallon de Pajaros, i., N. Mar. Is.	94	A5	20.32 N	144.54 E
Farallon Islands, is., Ca., U.S.	148	F2	37.43 N	123.07 W
Faranah, Gui.	84	G2	10.02 N	10.45 W
Farasān, Jazā'ir, is., Sau. Ar.	72	F5	16.48 N	41.54 E
Farbovane, Ukr.	38	C10	50.09 N	31.51 E
Farcău, Vârful, mtn., Rom.	36	B11	47.56 N	24.27 E
Farcy, Fr.	179		48.31 N	2.37 E
Fardes, stm., Spain	28	G7	37.35 N	2.59 W
Fareara, Pointe, c., Fr. Poly.	100h	w23	17.52 S	149.09 W
Fareham, Eng., U.K.	10	K11	50.50 N	1.11 W
Farewell, Ak., U.S.	109	D9	62.31 N	153.54 W
Farewell, Cape, c., N.Z.	102	E5	40.30 S	172.41 E
Färgelanda, Swe.	16	I9	58.33 N	11.59 E
Fargo, N.D., U.S.	128	E2	46.52 N	96.47 W
Far Hills, N.J., U.S.	194		40.41 N	74.38 W
Faria, stm., Braz.	205a		22.53 S	43.15 W
Faribault, Mn., U.S.	128	G5	44.17 N	93.16 W
Faribault, Lac, l., Qc., Can.	110	D16	59.00 N	72.00 W
Farīdābad, India	70	D6	28.23 N	77.17 E
Farīdkot, India	70	C5	30.39 N	74.46 E
Farīdpur, Bngl.	70	G12	23.36 N	89.51 E
Farīdpur, India	70	D7	28.12 N	79.32 E
Färila, Swe.	16	F13	61.48 N	15.51 E
Farilhões, is., Port.	28	E1	39.27 N	9.32 W
Farim, Gui.-B.	84	G2	12.29 N	15.13 W
Farina, Il., U.S.	130	F9	38.49 N	88.47 W
Farington, Eng., U.K.	180		53.43 N	2.42 W
Farinha, stm., Braz.	170	D2	6.50 S	47.30 W
Fariske, Tur.	76	B3	36.37 N	32.37 E
Fâriskur, Egypt	76	G2	31.19 N	31.43 E
Farit, Amba, mtn., Eth.	82	E7	10.56 N	38.58 E
Färjestaden, Swe.	16	K14	56.39 N	16.29 E
Farleigh, Eng., U.K.	178		51.19 N	0.02 W
Farley, Ia., U.S.	130	B7	42.26 N	91.00 W
Farley Green, Eng., U.K.	178		51.12 N	0.29 W
Farmahīn, Iran	74	C11	34.30 N	49.41 E
Farmer City, Il., U.S.	130	D9	40.14 N	88.37 W
Farmersburg, In., U.S.	130	E10	39.14 N	87.22 W
Farmersville, Il., U.S.	130	E8	39.26 N	89.39 W
Farmersville, Tx., U.S.	134	D2	33.10 N	96.21 W
Farmerville, La., U.S.	134	E6	32.46 N	92.24 W
Farmingdale, N.Y., U.S.	194		40.43 N	73.26 W
Farmington, Il., U.S.	130	D7	40.41 N	90.00 W
Farmington, Ia., U.S.	128	K7	40.38 N	91.43 W
Farmington, Me., U.S.	122	F6	44.40 N	70.09 W
Farmington, Mn., U.S.	128	G5	44.38 N	93.08 W
Farmington, Mo., U.S.	130	G7	37.47 N	90.25 W
Farmington, Mt., U.S.	146	C14	47.54 N	112.11 W
Farmington, N.H., U.S.	122	G5	43.23 N	71.03 W
Farmington, N.M., U.S.	150	G8	36.44 N	108.12 W
Farmington, Ut., U.S.	150	C5	40.59 N	111.53 W
Farmington Hills, Mi., U.S.	199		42.28 N	83.23 W
Far Mountain, mtn., B.C., Can.	144	D5	52.46 N	125.17 W
Farm Pond, l., Ma., U.S.	201		42.17 N	71.26 W
Farm Pond, l., Ma., U.S.	201		42.14 N	71.21 W
Farmville, N.C., U.S.	132	A8	35.35 N	77.35 W
Farmville, Va., U.S.	124	G7	37.17 N	78.23 W
Farnam, Ne., U.S.	140	G12	40.42 N	100.12 W
Farnborough, Eng., U.K.	10	J12	51.17 N	0.46 W
Farnborough, ngh., Eng., U.K.	178		51.21 N	0.04 E
Farncombe, Eng., U.K.	178		51.12 N	0.36 W
Farne Islands, is., Eng., U.K.	10	F11	55.38 N	1.38 W
Farnham, Qc., Can.	126	C16	45.17 N	72.58 W
Farnham, Mount, mtn., B.C., Can.	144	F14	50.28 N	116.27 W
Farnham Common, Eng., U.K.	178		51.33 N	0.37 W
Farnham Royal, Eng., U.K.	178		51.32 N	0.37 W
Farningham, Eng., U.K.	178		51.23 N	0.13 E
Farnworth, Eng., U.K.	180		53.23 N	2.44 W
Faro, Braz.	164	D6	2.10 S	56.44 W
Faro, Yk., Can.	110	C4	62.12 N	133.12 W
Faro, Port.	28	H3	37.01 N	7.55 W
Faro, state, Port.	28	G2	37.15 N	8.00 W
Faroe Islands, dep., Eur.	12b	n34	62.00 N	7.00 W
Faroe Islands see Færøerne, is., Far. Is.	8	C7	62.00 N	7.00 W
Fårön, i., Swe.	16	J17	57.56 N	19.08 E
Fårösund, Swe.	16	J17	57.51 N	19.03 E
Farquhar, Atoll de, i., Sey.	89b	I12	10.10 S	51.10 E
Farquhar, Cape, c., Austl.	96	D2	23.38 S	113.38 E
Farragut, Ia., U.S.	130	D2	40.43 N	95.28 W
Farragut State Recreation Area, p.o.i., Id., U.S.	146	C10	47.55 N	116.35 W
Farrar, stm., Scot., U.K.	10	D8	57.25 N	4.39 W
Farrar Pond, l., Ma., U.S.	201		42.25 N	71.21 W
Farrars Creek, stm., Austl.	98	E3	25.18 S	140.48 E
Farrāshband, Iran	74	F13	28.51 N	52.05 E
Farrell, Pa., U.S.	124	C5	41.12 N	80.30 W
Farrer Park, p.o.i., Sing.	189c		1.19 N	103.51 E
Farrington Lake, l., N.J., U.S.	194		40.26 N	74.28 W
Farrington Lake Heights, N.J., U.S.	194		40.26 N	74.27 W
Farris, b., Nor.	16	H7	59.05 N	10.00 E
Far Rockaway, ngh., N.Y., U.S.	194		40.36 N	73.45 W
Farrukhābād, India	70	E7	27.23 N	79.34 E
Farrukhnagar, India	190a		28.43 N	77.23 E
Fārs, state, Iran	74	F13	29.00 N	53.00 E
Fársala, Grc.	34	D5	39.17 N	22.23 E
Fārsī, Jazīreh-ye, i., Iran	74	F12	27.58 N	50.07 E
Farsø, Den.	16	K7	56.47 N	9.21 E
Farsund, Nor.	16	I4	58.05 N	6.47 E
Fartak, Ra's, c., Yemen	72	F7	15.38 N	52.11 E
Farvel, Kap, c., Grnld.	108	F17	59.45 N	43.59 W
Farwell, Mi., U.S.	126	E5	43.50 N	84.51 W
Farwell, Tx., U.S.	138	G6	34.23 N	103.00 W
Fasā, Iran	74	F13	28.56 N	53.38 E
Fasano, Italy	32	D11	40.50 N	17.21 E
Fastiv, Ukr.	38	C8	50.04 N	29.55 E
Fastnet Rock, r., Ire.	10	J3	51.23 N	9.35 W
Fatehābād, India	70	D5	29.30 N	75.27 E
Fatehjang, Pak.	70	B4	33.33 N	72.38 E
Fatehpur, India	70	F8	25.55 N	80.48 E
Fatehpur, India	70	E5	27.59 N	74.57 E
Fatehpur, Pak.	70	C3	31.08 N	71.12 E
Fatehpur Sīkri, India	70	E6	27.06 N	77.40 E
Fathom Five National Marine Park, p.o.i., On., Can.	126	C8	45.16 N	81.40 W
Fatick, Sen.	84	G1	14.19 N	16.24 W
Fátima, Port.	28	E2	39.37 N	8.38 W
Fatshan see Foshan, China	58	J5	23.02 N	113.06 E
Fat Tong Point, c., China	189d		22.16 N	114.15 E
Fatu Hiva, i., Fr. Poly.	94	E13	10.28 S	138.38 W
Fatumu, Tonga	100e	n14	21.12 S	175.06 W
Fatundu, D.R.C.	86	E3	4.08 S	17.14 E
Fatwā, India	70	F10	25.30 N	85.18 E
Fauabu, Sol. Is.	101b	e9	8.34 S	160.43 E
Faubert, Île des, i., Qc., Can.	193a		45.19 N	73.52 W
Faucilles, Monts, mts., Fr.	20	F15	48.08 N	6.25 E
Faucon-de-Barcelonnette, Fr.	22	E12	44.24 N	6.40 E
Faulkton, S.D., U.S.	140	B13	45.02 N	99.07 W
Faulquemont, Fr.	24	G2	49.02 N	6.36 E
Fauquier, B.C., Can.	144	G12	49.51 N	118.04 W
Făurei, Rom.	36	D14	45.05 N	27.18 E
Fauresmith, S. Afr.	90	F7	29.41 S	25.18 E
Fauro Island, i., Sol. Is.	101b	d6	6.55 S	156.04 E
Fauske, Nor.	14	E6	67.16 N	15.23 E
Faust, Ab., Can.	144	A15	55.18 N	115.38 W
Fåvang, Nor.	16	F8	61.27 N	10.11 E
Favara, Italy	32	G7	37.19 N	13.39 E
Favières, Fr.	179		48.46 N	2.47 E
Favignana, Isola, i., Italy	32	G6	37.56 N	12.19 E
Favoriten, ngh., Aus.	182b		48.11 N	16.23 E
Favrieux, Fr.	179		48.57 N	1.39 E
Fawcett, Ab., Can.	144	B16	54.32 N	114.06 W
Fawcett Lake, l., Ab., Can.	144	A17	55.16 N	113.35 W
Fawkham Green, Eng., U.K.	178		51.22 N	0.17 E
Fawkner, Austl.	192b		37.43 S	144.58 E
Fawkner Park, p.o.i., Austl.	192b		37.50 S	144.59 E
Fawn, stm., On., Can.	110	E13	55.21 N	88.20 W
Fawn, stm., U.S.	130	C12	41.49 N	85.40 W
Fawnie Nose, mtn., B.C., Can.	144	C5	53.16 N	125.08 W
Fawnie Range, mts., B.C., Can.	144	C5	53.14 N	125.00 W
Fawsett Farms, Md., U.S.	202c		38.59 N	77.14 W
Faxaflói, b., Ice.	12a	k28	64.25 N	23.00 W
Faxinal, Braz.	172	A12	23.59 S	51.19 W
Faxinal do Soturno, Braz.	172	D11	29.35 S	53.25 W
Faya-Largeau, Chad	82	D3	17.56 N	19.07 E
Fayd, Sau. Ar.	72	D5	27.16 N	42.23 E
Fayerweather Island, i., Ct., U.S.	194		41.08 N	73.13 W

Name	Page	Map Ref.	Latitude	Longitude
Fayette, Al., U.S.	134	D11	33.41 N	87.49 W
Fayette, Ia., U.S.	130	B6	42.50 N	91.48 W
Fayette, Ms., U.S.	134	F7	31.42 N	91.03 W
Fayette, Mo., U.S.	130	E5	39.08 N	92.41 W
Fayette, Oh., U.S.	124	C1	41.40 N	84.19 W
Fayetteville, Ar., U.S.	130	H3	36.04 N	94.09 W
Fayetteville, Ga., U.S.	134	D14	33.27 N	84.27 W
Fayetteville, N.C., U.S.	132	A7	35.03 N	78.52 W
Fayetteville, Tn., U.S.	134	B12	35.09 N	86.34 W
Fayetteville, W.V., U.S.	124	F4	38.03 N	81.06 W
Fâyid, Egypt	76	H3	30.18 N	32.18 E
Faylakah, i., Kuw.	74	F11	29.26 N	48.20 E
Fayyum see El-Fayoum, Egypt	76	I1	29.19 N	30.50 E
Fāzilka, India	70	C5	30.24 N	74.01 E
Fāzilpur, Pak.	70	D3	29.17 N	70.27 E
Fazzān, hist. reg., Libya	82	B2	26.00 N	14.00 E
Fdérik, Maur.	84	E2	22.41 N	12.42 W
Feale, stm., Ire.	10	I3	52.28 N	9.37 W
Feani, mtn., Fr. Poly.	100g	s18	9.46 S	139.04 W
Fear, Cape, c., N.C., U.S.	132	C8	33.57 N	77.55 W
Fearnhead, Eng., U.K.	180		53.25 N	2.33 W
Feather, stm., Ca., U.S.	148	D4	38.53 N	121.36 W
Feather, Middle Fork, stm., Ca., U.S.	148	D5	39.32 N	121.25 W
Feather, North Fork, stm., Ca., U.S.	148	D4	39.33 N	121.27 W
Feather, North Fork, East Branch, stm., Ca., U.S.	148	C5	40.01 N	121.13 W
Feather, South Fork, stm., Ca., U.S.	148	D4	39.32 N	121.25 W
Featherbed Top, mtn., Eng., U.K.	180		53.26 N	1.52 W
Featherly Regional Park, p.o.i., Ca., U.S.	198		33.52 N	117.42 W
Fécamp, Fr.	20	E9	49.45 N	0.22 E
Fedala see Mohammedia, Mor.	84	C3	33.41 N	7.23 W
Federación, Arg.	172	E8	31.00 S	57.55 W
Federal, Arg.	172	E8	30.56 S	58.47 W
Federal, Pa., U.S.	197b		40.23 N	80.09 W
Federally Administered Tribal Areas, state, Pak.	70	B2	32.42 N	69.54 E
Federal Republic of Germany see Germany, ctry., Eur.	6	E11	51.00 N	10.00 E
Federalsburg, Md., U.S.	124	F10	38.41 N	75.46 W
Fedje, Nor.	16	G2	60.46 N	4.43 E
Fedorivka, Ukr.	38	D14	49.22 N	35.07 E
Fedorivka, Ukr.	38	F15	47.32 N	36.32 E
Fëdorovka, Russia	38	F17	47.20 N	38.23 E
Fëdorovka, Russia	40	E19	53.10 N	55.11 E
Fedoseevka, Russia	40	H13	46.52 N	44.00 E
Fedoseevskaja, Russia	12	E19	62.06 N	40.38 E
Fedovo, Russia	18	E26	62.23 N	39.50 E
Fehérgyarmat, Hung.	36	A9	47.59 N	22.31 E
Fehér-Körös see Crişul Alb, stm., Eur.	36	C8	46.42 N	21.16 E
Fehmarn, i., Ger.	24	B7	54.28 N	11.08 E
Fehmarnbelt, strt., Eur.	24	B7	54.35 N	11.15 E
Feia, Lagoa, b., Braz.	170	L5	22.00 S	41.20 W
Feigumfossen, wtfl., Nor.	16	F5	61.23 N	7.26 E
Fei Huang, stm., China	58	E8	34.15 N	120.17 E
Feijó, Braz.	164	E3	8.11 S	70.24 W
Feiketu, China	54	B7	45.44 N	127.09 E
Feira de Santana, Braz.	170	G6	12.15 S	38.57 W
Feixi, China	58	F7	31.42 N	117.09 E
Feixian, China	58	D7	35.15 N	117.58 E
Fejér, state, Hung.	36	B5	47.10 N	18.35 E
Feke, Tur.	76	A6	37.49 N	35.55 E
Fekete-Körös see Crişul Negru, stm., Eur.	36	C8	46.42 N	21.16 E
Fekete-víz, stm., Eur.	30	E15	45.51 N	18.51 E
Felanitx, Spain	28	E14	39.28 N	3.08 E
Felda, Fl., U.S.	132	J4	26.33 N	81.26 W
Feldbach, Aus.	30	D12	46.57 N	15.53 E
Feldberg, mtn., Ger.	24	I4	47.52 N	8.00 E
Felderbach, stm., Ger.	181		51.22 N	7.08 E
Feldhausen, ngh., Ger.	181		51.37 N	6.59 E
Feldkirch, Aus.	30	C6	47.14 N	9.36 E
Feldmark, Ger.	181		51.41 N	6.38 E
Feliciano, P.R.	158a	b1	18.28 N	67.08 W
Feliciano, Arroyo, stm., Arg.	172	E8	31.05 S	59.54 W
Felipe Carrillo Puerto, Mex.	156	C4	19.34 N	88.01 W
Felix, Cape, c., Nu., Can.	110	B11	69.53 N	97.56 W
Felixlândia, Braz.	170	J3	18.46 S	44.52 W
Felixstowe, Eng., U.K.	10	I14	51.57 N	1.20 E
Felixton, S. Afr.	90	F10	28.50 S	31.53 E
Félix U. Gómez, Mex.	120	G7	29.49 N	111.30 W
Felletin, Fr.	22	D8	45.52 N	2.09 E
Fellingsbro, Swe.	16	H13	59.26 N	15.36 E
Fellows Creek, stm., Mi., U.S.	199		42.17 N	83.26 W
Fellowship, N.J., U.S.	203		39.55 N	74.58 W
Fellsmere, Fl., U.S.	132	I5	27.46 N	80.36 W
Fellwick, Pa., U.S.	203		40.08 N	75.11 W
Feltham, ngh., Eng., U.K.	178		51.27 N	0.24 W
Felt Lake, l., Ca., U.S.	200		37.23 N	122.11 W
Feltre, Italy	30	E8	46.01 N	11.53 E
Femer Bælt see Fehmarnbelt, strt., Eur.	24	B7	54.35 N	11.15 E
Femunden, l., Nor.	16	E8	62.08 N	11.51 E
Femundsenden, Nor.	16	F10	61.55 N	11.55 E
Femundsmarka Nasjonalpark, p.o.i., Nor.	16	E9	62.20 N	12.07 E
Fen, stm., China	58	B4	35.27 N	110.34 E
Fena Valley Reservoir, res., Guam	100c	j9	13.21 N	144.42 E
Fenelon Falls, On., Can.	126	D11	44.32 N	78.43 W
Fener, ngh., Tur.	185b		41.02 N	28.56 E
Fenerbahce Stadium, p.o.i., Tur.	185b		40.59 N	29.02 E
Fener Burnu, c., Tur.	42	E8	41.05 N	39.25 E
Fénérive see Fenoarivo Atsinanana, Madag.	88	D8	17.23 S	49.24 E
Fener Tepesi, hill, Tur.	185b		41.09 N	28.47 E
Fengcheng, China	52	C9	40.27 N	124.04 E
Fengcheng, China	58	G6	28.10 N	115.45 E
Fengdu, China	58	G2	29.57 N	107.47 E
Fengfeng, China	58	C6	36.28 N	114.13 E
Fenggang, China	58	G2	28.01 N	107.45 E
Fenghuang, China	58	H3	27.58 N	109.19 E
Fengjiabao, China	58	C1	36.12 N	104.53 E
Fengjie, China	58	F3	31.02 N	109.32 E
Fengning, China	54	A7	41.13 N	116.36 E
Fengqing, China	52	G4	24.39 N	99.53 E
Fengqiu, China	58	D6	35.02 N	114.24 E
Fengshan, China	58	K4	22.01 N	109.59 E
Fengtai, China	58	E7	32.42 N	116.42 E
Fengtai, China	58	B7	39.50 N	116.16 E
Fengtien see Shenyang, China	52	C9	41.48 N	123.24 E
Fengxi, China	58	F3	31.48 N	109.50 E
Fengxian, China	58	E2	33.57 N	106.39 E
Fengxian, China	58	D7	34.42 N	116.35 E
Fengxiang, China	58	D2	34.29 N	107.29 E
Fengyang, China	58	E7	32.51 N	117.33 E
Fengyüan, Tai.	58	I9	24.15 N	120.43 E
Fengzhen, China	58	A5	40.26 N	113.08 E
Fenholloway, stm., Fl., U.S.	132	F2	29.58 N	83.47 W
Feni, Bngl.	70	G13	23.00 N	91.24 E
Fenino, Russia	183b		55.44 N	37.57 E
Feniscowles, Eng., U.K.	180		53.43 N	2.32 W
Fennimore, Wi., U.S.	130	B7	42.59 N	90.39 W
Fennville, Mi., U.S.	130	B11	42.35 N	86.05 W
Feno, Capo di, c., Fr.	22	H14	41.57 N	8.36 E
Fenoarivo Atsinanana, Madag.	88	D8	17.23 S	49.24 E
Fensfjorden, b., Nor.	16	G2	60.49 N	5.01 E
Fenshui, stm., China	58	G8	29.48 N	119.39 E
Fenton, Mi., U.S.	124	B2	42.48 N	83.42 W
Fentress, Tx., U.S.	136	E10	29.45 N	97.46 W
Fenway Park, p.o.i., Ma., U.S.	201		42.21 N	71.06 W
Fenwick, W.V., U.S.	124	F5	38.13 N	80.35 W
Fenyang, China	58	C4	37.15 N	111.47 E
Fenyi, China	58	H6	27.48 N	114.40 E
Feodosiia, Ukr.	38	H14	45.02 N	35.22 E
Feodosiis'ka zatoka, b., Ukr.	38	I14	45.02 N	35.34 E
Fer, Cap de, c., Alg.	84	B6	37.05 N	7.10 E
Feragen, l., Nor.	16	E9	62.31 N	11.54 E
Ferbitz, Ger.	182a		52.30 N	13.01 E
Ferch, Ger.	182a		52.19 N	12.56 E
Fercher Berge, hill, Ger.	182a		52.19 N	12.57 E
Ferdig, Mt., U.S.	146	B15	48.45 N	111.46 W
Ferdinand, In., U.S.	130	F11	38.13 N	86.52 W
Ferdows, Iran	76	C8	34.00 N	58.09 E
Fère-Champenoise, Fr.	20	F13	48.45 N	3.59 E
Feren, l., Nor.	16	D9	63.34 N	11.51 E
Ferencváros, ngh., Hung.	182c		47.28 N	19.06 E
Ferentino, Italy	30	I10	41.42 N	13.15 E
Fergana, Uzb.	48	F12	40.23 N	71.47 E
Fergana Mountains see Ferganskij hrebet, mts., Kyrg.	48	F12	41.00 N	74.00 E
Ferganskij hrebet, mts., Kyrg.	48	F12	41.00 N	74.00 E
Fergus, On., Can.	126	E9	43.42 N	80.22 W
Fergus Falls, Mn., U.S.	118	E2	46.17 N	96.04 W
Ferguson, B.C., Can.	144	F13	50.41 N	117.29 W
Ferguson, Ky., U.S.	130	G13	37.03 N	84.36 W
Ferguson, Mo., U.S.	130	F7	38.45 N	90.18 W
Ferguson, Pa., U.S.	203		40.07 N	74.54 W
Fergusson Island, i., Pap. N. Gui.	101a	b5	9.31 S	150.38 E
Ferihegyi Airport, arpt., Hung.	182c		47.26 N	19.15 E
Ferkessédougou, C. Iv.	84	H4	9.36 N	5.12 W
Ferland, On., Can.	128	A10	50.18 N	88.25 W
Ferlo, reg., Sen.	84	F2	15.07 N	14.00 W
Ferme-Neuve, Qc., Can.	126	B14	46.42 N	75.27 W
Fermiers, Île aux, i., Qc., Can.	193a		45.40 N	73.27 W
Fermo, Italy	30	G10	43.09 N	13.42 E
Fermont, Qc., Can.	110	E17	52.46 N	67.04 W
Fermoselle, Spain	28	C4	41.18 N	6.23 W
Fermoy, Ire.	10	I4	52.07 N	8.17 W
Fernández, Arg.	172	C6	27.56 S	63.53 W
Fernandina, Isla, i., Ec.	164a	i11	0.25 S	91.29 W
Fernandina Beach, Fl., U.S.	132	F4	30.39 N	81.27 W
Fernando de la Mora, Para.	172	B9	25.17 S	57.36 W
Fernando de Noronha, Ilha, i., Braz.	162	F11	3.51 S	32.25 W
Fernandópolis, Braz.	166	D6	20.16 S	50.15 W
Fernando Póo see Bioko, i., Eq. Gui.	84	I6	3.30 N	8.40 E
Fernán-Núñez, Spain	28	G6	37.40 N	4.43 W
Ferndale, S. Afr.	191d		26.05 S	27.59 E
Ferndale, Ca., U.S.	148	C1	40.34 N	124.15 W
Ferndale, Wa., U.S.	146	B4	48.50 N	122.35 W
Fernie, B.C., Can.	144	G15	49.29 N	115.03 W
Fernilee, Eng., U.K.	180		53.18 N	1.58 W
Fernilee Reservoir, res., Eng., U.K.	180		53.17 N	1.59 W
Fernley, Nv., U.S.	148	D6	39.36 N	119.14 W
Ferno, Italy	184b		45.37 N	8.45 E
Fern Park, Fl., U.S.	132	H4	28.38 N	81.21 W
Fern Ridge Lake, res., Or., U.S.	146	F3	44.05 N	123.16 W
Fernwood, Id., U.S.	146	C10	47.06 N	116.23 W
Fernwood, Pa., U.S.	203		39.57 N	75.15 W
Ferny Creek, Austl.	192b		37.53 S	145.21 E
Ferokh, India	69	F2	11.10 N	75.50 E
Ferozepore see Fīrozpur, India	70	C5	30.55 N	74.37 E
Ferrandina, Italy	32	D10	40.29 N	16.26 E
Ferrara, Italy	30	F8	44.50 N	11.36 E
Ferrato, Capo, c., Italy	32	E3	39.18 N	9.37 E
Ferraz de Vasconcelos, mun., Braz.	205b		23.33 S	46.21 W
Ferré, Cap, c., Mart.	159c	I7	14.27 N	60.49 W
Ferreira do Alentejo, Port.	28	F2	38.03 N	8.07 W
Ferreira Gomes, Braz.	164	C7	0.47 N	51.07 W
Ferrell, N.J., U.S.	203		39.41 N	75.12 W
Ferreñafe, Peru	164	E2	6.37 S	79.47 W
Ferret, Cap, c., Fr.	22	E4	44.36 N	1.15 W
Ferriday, La., U.S.	134	F7	31.37 N	91.33 W
Ferrières, Fr.	20	F11	48.05 N	2.47 E
Ferris, Tx., U.S.	136	B11	32.32 N	96.39 W
Ferro see El Hierro, i., Spain	84	D1	27.45 N	18.00 W
Ferrol, Spain	28	A2	43.29 N	8.13 W
Ferron, Ut., U.S.	150	D5	39.05 N	111.08 W
Ferron Creek, stm., Ut., U.S.	150	D5	39.09 N	110.54 W
Ferry, Pointe, c., Guad.	159c	h5	16.19 N	61.47 W
Ferry Point Park, p.o.i., N.Y., U.S.	194		40.49 N	73.50 W
Ferrysburg, Mi., U.S.	130	A11	43.04 N	86.12 W
Ferry Village, N.Y., U.S.	202a		43.58 N	78.57 W
Fertile, Mn., U.S.	128	D2	47.31 N	96.16 W
Ferto-tavi Nemzeti Park, p.o.i., Hung.	36	B3	47.37 N	16.53 E
Ferzikovo, Russia	26	F19	54.30 N	36.45 E
Fès, Mor.	84	C3	34.02 N	5.00 W
Feshi, D.R.C.	86	F3	6.06 S	18.08 E
Fessenden, N.D., U.S.	142	G14	47.38 N	99.37 W
Festus, Mo., U.S.	130	F7	38.13 N	90.24 W
Festvåg, Nor.	14	E5	67.25 N	14.46 E
Feteşti, Rom.	36	E14	44.22 N	27.50 E
Fethiye, Tur.	34	G12	36.37 N	29.07 E
Fethiye Körfezi, b., Tur.	34	G11	36.40 N	29.00 E
Fetisovo, Kaz.	48	F8	42.45 N	52.39 E
Fetlar, i., Scot., U.K.	10a	n19	60.35 N	0.51 W
Fetsund, Nor.	16	H9	59.55 N	11.09 E
Feucherolles, Fr.	179		48.52 N	1.58 E
Feucht, Ger.	24	G7	49.22 N	11.12 E
Feuchtwangen, Ger.	24	G6	49.10 N	10.19 E
Feuilles, stm., Qc., Can.	110	D16	58.39 N	70.24 W
Feuilles, Baie aux, b., Qc., Can.	110	D16	58.55 N	69.20 W
Feurs, Fr.	22	D10	45.44 N	4.13 E
Fevik, Nor.	16	I6	58.23 N	8.42 E
Fevzipaşa, Tur.	76	A7	37.05 N	36.41 E
Feyzābād, Afg.	70	B11	37.07 N	70.34 E
Fez see Fès, Mor.	84	C3	34.02 N	5.00 W
Fezzan see Fazzān, hist. reg., Libya	82	B2	26.00 N	14.00 E
Ffestiniog, Wales, U.K.	10	I9	52.58 N	3.56 W
F. Gilbert Hills State Forest, p.o.i., Ma., U.S.	201		42.03 N	71.17 W
Fiambalá, Arg.	172	C4	27.41 S	67.38 W
Fianarantsoa, Madag.	88	E8	21.25 S	47.07 E
Fianga, Chad	82	F3	9.55 N	15.08 E
Fichē, Eth.	82	F7	9.48 N	38.44 E
Fichtelberg, mtn., Ger.	24	F8	50.26 N	12.57 E
Fichtelgebirge, mts., Eur.	24	F7	50.01 N	11.55 E
Fichtenau, Ger.	182a		52.27 N	13.42 E
Ficksburg, S. Afr.	90	F8	28.52 S	27.53 E
Fidalgo, stm., Braz.	170	E4	7.27 S	42.32 W
Fiddlers Hamlet, Eng., U.K.	178		51.41 N	0.08 E
Fiddyment Creek, stm., Il., U.S.	196		41.36 N	88.03 W
Fidenza, Italy	30	F7	44.52 N	10.04 E
Field, B.C., Can.	144	E14	51.24 N	116.29 W
Fieldale, Va., U.S.	124	H6	36.42 N	79.56 W
Field Museum, bldg., Il., U.S.	196		41.53 N	87.37 W
Fieldsboro, N.J., U.S.	203		40.08 N	74.43 W
Fieldstone, N.J., U.S.	194		40.44 N	74.33 W
Fier, Alb.	32	D13	40.44 N	19.34 E
Fier, Porţile de see Iron Gate, val., Eur.	36	E9	44.41 N	22.31 E
Fiéra Campionaria, p.o.i., Italy	184b		45.28 N	9.09 E
Fieri see Fier, Alb.	32	D13	40.44 N	19.34 E
Fierras, mtn., Swe.	14	F6	66.32 N	15.55 E
Fiery Creek, stm., Austl.	98	B2	18.22 S	139.52 E
Fierzës, Liqeni i, res., Alb.	32	B14	42.10 N	20.16 E
Fife Lake, Sk., Can.	142	E8	49.12 N	105.44 W
Fife Lake, Mi., U.S.	126	D4	44.34 N	85.20 W
Fife Lake, l., Sk., Can.	142	E8	49.13 N	105.51 W
Fife Ness, c., Scot., U.K.	10	E10	56.17 N	2.36 W
Fifield, Wi., U.S.	128	F8	45.52 N	90.25 W
Fifteenmile Creek, stm., Or., U.S.	146	E5	45.36 N	121.07 W
Fifteenmile Creek, stm., Wy., U.S.	140	C4	44.00 N	107.59 W
Fifth Cataract see Khāmis, Ash-Shallāl al-, wtfl., Sudan	82	D6	18.22 N	33.46 E
Figeac, Fr.	22	E7	44.36 N	2.01 E
Figeholm, Swe.	16	J14	57.22 N	16.33 E
Fighting Island, i., On., Can.	199		42.13 N	83.07 W
Figtree, Zimb.	88	E4	20.21 S	28.18 E
Figueira, Braz.	205a		22.42 S	43.27 W
Figueira da Foz, Port.	28	D2	40.09 N	8.50 W
Figueras see Figueres, Spain	28	B13	42.16 N	2.58 E
Figueres, Spain	28	B13	42.16 N	2.58 E
Figuig, Mor.	84	C4	32.07 N	1.13 W
Fiji, ctry., Oc.	92	E8	18.00 S	178.00 E
Fiji Islands, is., Fiji	94	E8	18.00 S	178.00 E
Filabusi, Zimb.	90	B9	20.32 S	29.16 E
Filadélfia, Braz.	170	D2	7.20 S	47.29 W
Filadelfia, Italy	32	F10	38.48 N	16.18 E
Fil'akovo, Slvk.	24	H15	48.16 N	19.50 E
Filatova Gora, Russia	26	C11	57.40 N	28.10 E
Filchner Ice Shelf, ice, Ant.	103	C1	79.00 S	40.00 W
Filey, Eng., U.K.	10	G12	54.12 N	0.17 W
Fili, ngh., Russia	183b		55.45 N	37.31 E
Filiaşi, Rom.	36	E10	44.33 N	23.32 E
Filiatrá, Grc.	34	F4	37.10 N	21.35 E
Filicudi, Isola, i., Italy	32	F8	38.34 N	14.34 E
Filingué, Niger	84	G5	14.21 N	3.19 E
Filipino Cemetery and Memorial, misc. cult., Phil.	187f		14.31 N	121.02 E
Filippoi, hist., Grc.	34	B7	41.00 N	24.16 E
Filipstad, Swe.	16	H12	59.43 N	14.09 E
Fillefjell, mts., Nor.	16	F5	61.08 N	7.46 E
Fillmore, Sk., Can.	142	E10	49.52 N	103.25 W
Fillmore, Ca., U.S.	148	I7	34.24 N	118.54 W
Fillmore, Ut., U.S.	150	D4	38.58 N	112.19 W
Fils, stm., Ger.	20	F18	48.42 N	9.25 E
Filtu, Eth.	82	F8	5.06 N	40.40 E
Fimi, stm., D.R.C.	86	E3	3.01 S	16.56 E
Finale Emilia, Italy	30	F8	44.50 N	11.17 E
Finale Ligure, Italy	30	F5	44.10 N	8.20 E
Finca El Rey, Parque Nacional, p.o.i., Arg.	172	B5	25.00 S	64.40 W
Finchley, ngh., Eng., U.K.	178		51.36 N	0.10 W
Finderne, N.J., U.S.	194		40.34 N	74.35 W
Findhorn, stm., Scot., U.K.	10	D8	57.38 N	3.38 W
Findlay, Il., U.S.	130	E9	39.31 N	88.45 W
Findlay, Oh., U.S.	124	C2	41.02 N	83.38 W
Findlay, Mount, mtn., B.C., Can.	144	F14	50.04 N	116.28 W
Fine Arts, Museum of, bldg., Ma., U.S.	201		42.20 N	71.06 W
Fingal, N.D., U.S.	142	H16	46.46 N	97.47 W
Fingoè, Moz.	88	D5	15.11 S	31.52 E
Finike, Tur.	34	G13	36.20 N	30.08 E
Finike Körfezi, b., Tur.	34	G13	36.17 N	30.16 E
Finistère, state, Fr.	20	F5	48.20 N	4.00 W
Finisterre, Mex.	136	H4	25.59 N	103.15 W
Finisterre, Cabo de see Fisterra, Cabo de, c., Spain	28	B1	42.53 N	9.16 W
Finke, Austl.	96	E6	25.35 S	134.34 E
Finke, Mount, hill, Austl.	96	F6	30.55 S	134.02 E
Finkenkrug, Ger.	182a		52.34 N	13.03 E
Finland, ctry., Eur.	12	C12	64.00 N	26.00 E
Finland, Gulf of, b., Eur.	18	H10	60.00 N	27.00 E
Finland Station, trans., Russia	183a		59.57 N	30.22 E
Finlay, stm., B.C., Can.	110	D5	56.00 N	123.56 W
Finley, Austl.	98	J5	35.38 S	145.34 E
Finley, N.D., U.S.	142	G16	47.29 N	97.49 W
Finley Creek, stm., Mo., U.S.	130	G5	36.57 N	93.21 W
Finleyville Airport, arpt., Pa., U.S.	197b		40.15 N	80.01 W
Finmoore, B.C., Can.	144	C7	53.58 N	123.36 W
Finnegan, Ab., Can.	144	E18	51.08 N	112.03 W
Finneidfjord, Nor.	14	F4	66.11 N	13.49 E
Finnis, Cape, c., Austl.	96	F6	33.38 S	134.51 E
Finnkneet, mtn., Nor.	16	B10	65.45 N	12.48 E
Finnmark, state, Nor.	12	B11	70.00 N	25.00 E
Finnmarksvidda, plat., Nor.	14	C14	69.10 N	23.50 E
Finnøy, i., Nor.	16	H3	59.10 N	5.50 E
Finnskogen, for., Swe.	16	G10	60.40 N	12.40 E
Finnsnes, Nor.	14	C9	69.14 N	18.00 E
Finnvollheia, mtn., Nor.	16	C8	64.07 N	10.53 E
Finocchio, ngh., Italy	185a		41.53 N	12.41 E
Fins, Oman	72	E8	22.55 N	59.12 E
Finsbury, S. Afr.	191d		26.13 S	27.39 E
Finschhafen, Pap. N. Gui.	101a	b4	6.33 S	147.50 E
Finse, Nor.	16	G5	60.36 N	7.30 E
Finskij zaliv see Finland, Gulf of, b., Eur.	18	H10	60.00 N	27.00 E
Finspång, Swe.	16	I13	58.42 N	15.46 E
Finsterwalde, Ger.	24	E9	51.37 N	13.42 E
Fiora, stm., Italy	30	H8	42.19 N	11.34 E
Fiordland National Park, p.o.i., N.Z.	102	G2	45.30 S	167.20 E
Fiorenzuola d'Arda, Italy	30	F6	44.55 N	9.54 E
Fiorito, ngh., Arg.	206		34.42 S	58.27 W
Firat see Euphrates, stm., Asia	72	C6	30.59 N	47.26 E
Firebaugh, Ca., U.S.	148	G5	36.51 N	120.27 W
Fire Island Inlet, b., N.Y., U.S.	194		40.38 N	73.16 W
Fire Island National Seashore, p.o.i., N.Y., U.S.	124	D12	40.39 N	73.06 W
Fire Island Pines, N.Y., U.S.	194		40.40 N	73.04 W
Fire Islands, is., N.Y., U.S.	194		40.40 N	73.11 W
Firenze (Florence), Italy	30	G8	43.46 N	11.13 E
Firenzuola, Italy	30	F8	44.07 N	11.23 E
Firesteel Creek, stm., S.D., U.S.	140	D14	43.42 N	97.58 W
Firgrove, Eng., U.K.	180		53.37 N	2.08 W
Firmat, Arg.	172	F7	33.26 S	61.30 W
Firminy, Fr.	22	D10	45.23 N	4.17 E
Firovo, Russia	26	C16	57.29 N	33.43 E
Fīrozābād, India	70	E7	27.09 N	78.23 E
Fīrozpur, India	70	C5	30.55 N	74.37 E
Fīrozpur Jhirka, India	70	E6	27.48 N	76.57 E
Firsanovka, Russia	183b		55.57 N	37.15 E
First Broad, stm., N.C., U.S.	132	A4	35.11 N	81.37 W
First Cataract, wtfl., Egypt	82	C6	24.07 N	32.53 E
First Cliff, clf., Ma., U.S.	201		42.12 N	70.43 W
First Herring Brook, stm., Ma., U.S.	201		42.11 N	70.45 W
First Watchung Mountain, mtn., N.J., U.S.	194		40.55 N	74.10 W
Firth, Ne., U.S.	128	K2	40.32 N	96.36 W
Firth, stm., N.A.	109	C11	69.32 N	139.23 W
Fīrūzābād, Iran	74	F13	28.50 N	52.34 E
Fīrūz Kūh, Iran	74	C13	35.46 N	52.45 E
Fischeln, ngh., Ger.	181		51.18 N	6.35 E
Fish, stm., Nmb.	90	E3	28.05 S	17.10 E
Fish, stm., Al., U.S.	134	G11	30.21 N	87.51 W
Fish, stm., Me., U.S.	122	D8	47.15 N	68.35 W
Fish Brook, stm., Ma., U.S.	201		42.42 N	71.13 W
Fish Brook, stm., Ma., U.S.	201		42.38 N	70.58 W
Fish Canyon, val., Ca., U.S.	198		34.11 N	117.55 W
Fish Creek, stm., Mt., U.S.	140	A3	46.17 N	109.13 W
Fisheating Creek, stm., Fl., U.S.	132	J4	26.58 N	81.06 W
Fisher, Ar., U.S.	134	B7	35.29 N	90.58 W
Fisher, Il., U.S.	130	D9	40.18 N	88.21 W
Fisher, La., U.S.	136	C14	31.29 N	93.27 W
Fisher, stm., Mb., Can.	142	C16	51.33 N	97.11 W
Fisher, stm., Mt., U.S.	146	B11	48.22 N	115.19 W
Fisher Bay, b., Mb., Can.	142	C17	51.37 N	97.13 W
Fisher Bay, b., Mi., U.S.	199		42.36 N	82.39 W
Fisher Branch, Mb., Can.	142	C16	51.04 N	97.37 W
Fisher Channel, strt., B.C., Can.	144	D3	52.06 N	127.53 W
Fisher Heights, Pa., U.S.	197b		40.10 N	79.54 W
Fisherman's Wharf, hist., Ca., U.S.	200		37.48 N	122.25 W
Fisher Peak, mtn., Va., U.S.	124	H5	36.33 N	80.50 W
Fisher River Indian Reserve, ind. res., Mb., Can.	142	C16	51.26 N	97.20 W
Fishers Island, i., N.Y., U.S.	124	C14	41.16 N	71.59 W
Fishers Peak, mtn., Co., U.S.	138	D4	37.06 N	104.28 W
Fisher Strait, strt., Nu., Can.	110	C14	63.15 N	80.30 W
Fisherville, On., Can.	193b		43.47 N	79.28 W
Fishguard, Wales, U.K.	10	J8	51.59 N	4.58 W
Fishhausen see Primorsk, Russia	26	F2	54.44 N	20.00 E
Fishing Creek, Md., U.S.	124	F9	38.19 N	76.13 W
Fishing Creek, stm., Ky., U.S.	132	B4	37.06 N	84.43 W
Fishing Creek, stm., N.C., U.S.	124	H8	35.56 N	77.31 W
Fishing Lake, l., Mb., Can.	142	B18	52.07 N	95.25 W
Fishing Lake, l., Sk., Can.	142	C10	51.50 N	103.32 W
Fishmoor Reservoir, res., Eng., U.K.	180		53.44 N	2.28 W
Fishpool, Eng., U.K.	180		53.35 N	2.17 W
Fisk, Mo., U.S.	130	H7	36.47 N	90.12 W
Fiskárdo, Grc.	34	E3	38.26 N	20.34 E
Fiskebøl, Nor.	14	D5	68.25 N	14.49 E
Fismes, Fr.	20	E12	49.18 N	3.41 E
Fišt, gora, mtn., Russia	42	C8	43.58 N	39.54 E
Fisterra, Cabo de, c., Spain	28	B1	42.53 N	9.16 W
Fitchburg, Ma., U.S.	124	B14	42.34 N	71.48 W
Fitjar, Nor.	16	H3	59.56 N	5.20 E
Fito, Mount, vol., Samoa	101c	g12	13.56 S	171.43 W
Fitri, Lac, l., Chad	82	E3	12.50 N	17.27 E
Fitzgerald, Ga., U.S.	132	E2	31.43 N	83.15 W
Fitz Henry, Pa., U.S.	197b		40.10 N	79.45 W
Fitz Hugh Sound, strt., B.C., Can.	144	E3	51.40 N	127.57 W
Fitz Roy, Arg.	166	I3	47.02 S	67.14 W
Fitzroy, Austl.	192b		37.48 S	144.59 E
Fitzroy, stm., Austl.	96	C4	17.32 S	123.34 E
Fitzroy, stm., Austl.	98	D7	23.31 S	150.48 E
Fitz Roy, Monte (Chaltel, Cerro), mtn., S.A.	166	I2	49.17 S	73.05 W
Fitzroy Crossing, Austl.	96	C5	18.11 S	125.34 E
Fitzwilliam Island, i., On., Can.	126	C8	45.28 N	81.45 W
Fiuggi, Italy	30	I10	41.48 N	13.13 E
Fiume see Rijeka, Cro.	30	E11	45.20 N	14.27 E
Fiumicino, Italy	30	I9	41.46 N	12.13 E
Five Corners, Ma., U.S.	201		42.01 N	71.07 W
Five Cowrie Creek, mth., Nig.	191a		6.27 N	3.27 E
Five Dock, Austl.	192a		33.52 S	151.08 E
Five Forks, Va., U.S.	202c		38.47 N	77.16 W
Five Islands, N.S., Can.	122	E12	45.24 N	64.02 W
Five Islands Harbour, b., Antig.	159b	f4	17.05 N	61.53 W
Fivemile Creek, stm., Ct., U.S.	194		41.03 N	73.27 W
Fivemile Creek, stm., Wy., U.S.	140	D4	43.14 N	108.10 W
Five Points, N.M., U.S.	138	F2	35.03 N	106.39 W
Five Points, Pa., U.S.	203		39.50 N	75.42 W
Fivizzano, Italy	30	F7	44.14 N	10.07 E
Fizi, D.R.C.	86	E5	4.18 S	28.56 E
Fjærlandsfjorden, b., Nor.	16	F4	61.17 N	6.44 E
Fjällåsen, Swe.	14	E11	67.29 N	20.04 E
Fjällsjöälven, stm., Swe.	16	D14	63.29 N	16.50 E
Fjellværøya, i., Nor.	16	D7	63.38 N	9.05 E
Fjerritslev, Den.	16	J7	57.05 N	9.16 E
Fjugesta, Swe.	16	H12	59.10 N	14.51 E
Flag Creek, stm., Il., U.S.	196		41.43 N	87.55 W
Flagler, Co., U.S.	138	B5	39.17 N	103.04 W
Flagler Beach, Fl., U.S.	132	G4	29.29 N	81.09 W
Flagstaff, S. Afr.	90	G9	31.03 S	29.30 E
Flagstaff, Az., U.S.	150	H5	35.11 N	111.39 W
Flagstaff Lake, res., Me., U.S.	122	E6	45.10 N	70.15 W
Flagtown, N.J., U.S.	194		40.31 N	74.41 W
Flakensee, l., Ger.	182a		52.25 N	13.46 E
Flakstadøya, i., Nor.	14	D4	68.03 N	13.20 E
Flåm, Nor.	16	G5	60.51 N	7.07 E
Flamands, Anse des, Guad.	159a	b2	17.55 N	62.51 W
Flambeau, stm., Wi., U.S.	128	F8	45.17 N	91.13 W
Flambeau, South Fork, stm., Wi., U.S.	128	F8	45.38 N	90.47 W
Flamborough, On., Can.	126	E9	43.20 N	79.53 W
Flamborough Head, c., Eng., U.K.	10	G12	54.07 N	0.05 W
Fläming, reg., Ger.	24	E8	52.00 N	12.44 E
Flaming Gorge National Recreation Area, p.o.i., U.S.	150	B7	41.08 N	109.33 W
Flaming Gorge Reservoir, res., U.S.	150	B7	41.13 N	109.35 W
Flanagan, Il., U.S.	130	D9	40.52 N	88.51 W
Flanagan Passage, strt., V.I.U.S.	158b	e8	18.18 N	64.39 W
Flanders, On., Can.	128	C6	48.43 N	92.04 W
Flanders, N.J., U.S.	194		40.50 N	74.41 W
Flanders Airport, arpt., N.J., U.S.	194		40.50 N	74.41 W
Flandorf, Aus.	182b		48.21 N	16.23 E
Flandreau, S.D., U.S.	128	G2	44.02 N	96.35 W
Flåren, l., Swe.	16	K12	57.02 N	14.06 E
Flash, The, l., Eng., U.K.	180		53.29 N	2.33 W
Flasher, N.D., U.S.	140	A11	46.26 N	101.16 W
Flåsjön, l., Swe.	16	C13	64.06 N	15.51 E
Flat, Ak., U.S.	109	D8	62.27 N	158.01 W
Flat, Tx., U.S.	136	C10	31.18 N	97.38 W
Flat, stm., N.T., Can.	110	C5	61.31 N	125.21 W
Flat, stm., Mi., U.S.	126	E4	42.55 N	85.20 W
Flatbush, ngh., N.Y., U.S.	194		40.39 N	73.56 W
Flat Creek, stm., Mo., U.S.	138	E15	36.49 N	93.39 W
Flat Creek, stm., Mt., U.S.	146	C16	47.42 N	109.50 W
Flat Creek, stm., N.J., U.S.	194		40.27 N	74.10 W
Flatey, Ice.	12a	k28	65.22 N	22.55 W
Flateyri, Ice.	12a	j28	66.03 N	23.31 W
Flathead (Flathead, North Fork), stm., N.A.	144	H16	48.28 N	114.04 W
Flathead, stm., Mt., U.S.	146	C12	47.22 N	114.47 W
Flathead, Middle Fork, stm., Mt., U.S.	146	B13	48.28 N	114.03 W
Flathead, North Fork (Flathead), stm., N.A.	144	H16	48.28 N	114.04 W
Flathead, South Fork, stm., Mt., U.S.	146	B13	48.23 N	114.05 W
Flathead Indian Reservation, ind. res., Mt., U.S.	146	C12	47.30 N	114.25 W
Flathead Lake, l., Mt., U.S.	146	C12	47.52 N	114.08 W
Flat Lake, l., Ab., Can.	144	B17	54.39 N	112.55 W
Flat Lick, Ky., U.S.	124	H2	36.49 N	83.46 W
Flatonia, Tx., U.S.	136	E10	29.41 N	97.06 W
Flatow, Ger.	182a		52.44 N	12.57 E
Flatow see Złotów, Pol.	24	C13	53.21 N	17.02 E
Flat River, P.E., Can.	122	D14	46.01 N	62.52 W
Flat River, Mo., U.S.	130	G7	37.51 N	90.31 W
Flat Rock, Al., U.S.	134	C13	34.45 N	85.42 W
Flat Rock, Il., U.S.	130	F10	38.54 N	87.40 W
Flatruet, hills, Swe.	16	E10	62.45 N	12.50 E
Flattery, Cape, c., Austl.	96	B9	14.57 S	145.20 E
Flattery, Cape, c., Wa., U.S.	146	B2	48.23 N	124.43 W
Flatts, Ber.	158e	k15	32.19 N	64.44 W
Flatwillow Creek, stm., Mt., U.S.	142	H5	46.55 N	107.56 W
Flatwood, U.S.	134	E11	32.09 N	87.21 W
Flaugherty Run, stm., Pa., U.S.	197b		40.33 N	80.13 W
Flaunden, Eng., U.K.	178		51.42 N	0.32 W
Flåvatn, l., Nor.	16	H6	59.18 N	8.48 E
Flaxcombe, Sk., Can.	142	C4	51.29 N	109.35 W
Flax Pond, l., Ma., U.S.	201		42.29 N	70.57 W
Flax Pond, l., N.Y., U.S.	194		40.58 N	73.08 W
Flaxton, N.D., U.S.	142	F11	48.53 N	102.23 W
Flaxville, Mt., U.S.	142	F8	48.48 N	105.10 W
Fleetwing Estates, Pa., U.S.	203		40.07 N	74.51 W
Fleetwood, Eng., U.K.	10	H10	53.55 N	3.01 W
Fleetwood, Pa., U.S.	124	D10	40.27 N	75.49 W
Flehe, ngh., Ger.	181		51.12 N	6.47 E
Fleischman Village, Md., U.S.	202c		38.51 N	76.57 W
Flekkefjord, Nor.	16	I4	58.17 N	6.40 E
Flekkerøy, i., Nor.	16	I5	58.04 N	7.59 E
Fleming, Co., U.S.	140	G10	40.40 N	102.50 W
Fleming Creek, stm., Mi., U.S.	199		42.16 N	83.40 W
Fleming-Neon, Ky., U.S.	124	G3	37.11 N	82.42 W
Flemingsburg, Ky., U.S.	124	F2	38.25 N	83.44 W
Flemington Racecourse, p.o.i., Austl.	192b		37.47 S	144.55 E
Flen, Swe.	16	H14	59.04 N	16.35 E
Flensborg Fjord, b., Eur.	24	B6	54.50 N	9.50 E
Flensburg, Ger.	24	B5	54.46 N	9.25 E
Flensburger Förde see Flensborg Fjord, b., Eur.	24	B6	54.50 N	9.50 E
Flers, Fr.	20	F8	48.45 N	0.34 W
Flesberg, Nor.	16	H7	59.51 N	9.27 E
Fletcher, N.C., U.S.	132	A3	35.25 N	82.31 W
Fletcher, Ok., U.S.	138	G10	34.49 N	98.15 W
Fletcher Moss Museum, bldg., Eng., U.K.	180		53.25 N	2.14 W
Fletcher Pond, l., Mi., U.S.	126	D5	44.58 N	83.52 W
Fletchers Creek, stm., On., Can.	193b		43.38 N	79.42 W
Fleurance, Fr.	22	F6	43.50 N	0.40 E
Fleury-Mérogis, Fr.	179		48.38 N	2.22 E
Fleuth, stm., Ger.	181		51.32 N	6.26 E
Flexanville, Fr.	179		48.51 N	1.44 E
Fley, ngh., Ger.	181		51.23 N	7.30 E
Flierich, Ger.	181		51.35 N	7.48 E
Flight Locks, sci., On., Can.	202a		43.08 N	79.12 W
Flinders, stm., Austl.	98	A3	17.36 S	140.36 E
Flinders Bay, b., Austl.	96	F3	34.23 S	115.19 E
Flinders Island, i., Austl.	99a	m14	40.00 S	148.00 E
Flinders Ranges National Park, p.o.i., Austl.	98	H2	31.22 S	138.40 E
Flinders Reefs, rf., Austl.	98	A7	17.37 S	148.31 E
Flinders Street Station, trans., Austl.	192b		37.49 S	144.58 E
Flin Flon, Mb., Can.	110	E10	54.46 N	101.53 W
Flingern, ngh., Ger.	181		51.14 N	6.49 E
Flins-sur-Seine, Fr.	179		48.58 N	1.52 E
Flint, Wales, U.K.	10	H9	53.14 N	3.07 W
Flint, Mi., U.S.	130	A14	43.00 N	83.41 W
Flint, i., Kir.	94	E11	11.25 S	151.47 W
Flint, stm., U.S.	134	C12	34.30 N	86.31 W
Flint, stm., Ga., U.S.	134	G14	30.46 N	84.47 W
Flint, stm., Mi., U.S.	126	E6	43.20 N	84.03 W
Flint Castle, hist., Wales, U.K.	180		53.16 N	3.07 W
Flint Creek, stm., Al., U.S.	134	C11	34.34 N	86.55 W
Flint Creek, stm., Mt., U.S.	146	D13	46.39 N	113.08 W
Flint Creek Range, mts., Mt., U.S.	146	D13	46.20 N	113.05 W
Flint Hills, hills, Ks., U.S.	138	D12	37.43 N	96.36 W
Flint Lake, l., Nu., Can.	110	B16	69.14 N	74.20 W
Flinton, Austl.	98	F7	27.53 S	149.33 E
Flint Peak, mtn., Ca., U.S.	198		34.10 N	118.12 W
Flint Pond, l., Ma., U.S.	201		42.40 N	71.26 W

Name	Page	Map Ref.	Latitude	Longitude
Flintshire, mun., Wales, U.K.	180		53.15 N	3.10 W
Flints Pond, l., Ma., U.S.	201		42.26 N	71.19 W
Flintville, Tn., U.S.	134	B12	35.03 N	86.25 W
Flippin, Ar., U.S.	130	H5	36.17 N	92.35 W
Flisa, Nor.	16	G10	60.37 N	12.01 E
Flisa, stm., Nor.	16	G10	60.34 N	12.01 E
Fliseggi, mtn., Nor.	16	H5	59.50 N	7.48 E
Flix, Pantà de, res., Spain	28	C11	41.15 N	0.27 E
Floby, Swe.	16	I11	58.08 N	13.19 E
Floda, Swe.	16	J10	57.48 N	12.21 E
Flomaton, Al., U.S.	134	F11	31.00 N	87.16 W
Flomot, Tx., U.S.	138	G8	34.14 N	100.59 W
Floodwood, Mn., U.S.	128	E6	46.55 N	92.55 W
Flora, Il., U.S.	130	F9	38.39 N	88.29 W
Flora, In., U.S.	130	D11	40.32 N	86.31 W
Flora, Ms., U.S.	134	E8	32.32 N	90.19 W
Florac, Fr.	22	E9	44.19 N	3.36 E
Florala, Al., U.S.	134	F12	31.00 N	86.19 W
Floral City, Fl., U.S.	132	H3	28.44 N	82.18 W
Floral Park, Mt., U.S.	146	E14	45.59 N	112.30 W
Flora Vista, N.M., U.S.	150	G8	36.47 N	108.05 W
Flore, Piton, mtn., St. Luc.	159c	m7	13.58 N	60.57 W
Florence see Firenze, Italy	30	G8	43.46 N	11.13 E
Florence, Al., U.S.	134	C11	34.47 N	87.40 W
Florence, Az., U.S.	150	J5	33.02 N	111.23 W
Florence, Co., U.S.	138	C3	38.23 N	105.06 W
Florence, Ks., U.S.	138	C12	38.14 N	96.55 W
Florence, N.J., U.S.	203		40.07 N	74.49 W
Florence, Or., U.S.	146	G2	43.58 N	124.05 W
Florence, S.C., U.S.	132	B6	34.10 N	79.47 W
Florence, Tx., U.S.	136	D10	30.50 N	97.47 W
Florence, Wi., U.S.	126	C1	45.55 N	88.14 W
Florencia, Col.	168	G4	1.36 N	75.36 W
Florencio Varela, state, Arg.	206		34.52 S	58.15 W
Florentia, S. Afr.	191d		26.16 S	28.08 E
Florentino Ameghino, Embalse, res., Arg.	166	H3	43.53 S	66.25 W
Florenville, Bel.	20	E14	49.41 N	5.18 E
Flores, Braz.	170	D7	7.51 S	37.59 W
Flores, ngh., Arg.	206		34.38 S	58.28 W
Flores, i., Indon.	60	G7	8.37 S	120.55 E
Flores, Laut (Flores Sea), s., Indon.	60	G6	8.00 S	120.00 E
Flores, Selat, strt., Indon.	60	G7	8.13 S	123.02 E
Flores de Goiás, Braz.	170	H2	14.33 S	47.04 W
Flores Island, i., B.C., Can.	144	G4	49.20 N	126.10 W
Flores Sea see Flores, Laut, s., Indon.	60	G6	8.00 S	120.00 E
Floresta, Braz.	170	E6	8.36 S	38.34 W
Floresta, ngh., Arg.	206		34.38 S	58.29 W
Floresta Azul, Braz.	170	H6	14.54 S	39.44 W
Florestal de Monsanto, Parque, p.o.i., Port.	184c		38.43 N	9.11 W
Florești, Mol.	38	F7	47.53 N	28.18 E
Floresville, Tx., U.S.	136	E9	29.08 N	98.09 W
Floriano, Braz.	170	D4	6.47 S	43.01 W
Floriano Peixoto, Braz.	164	E4	9.02 S	67.24 W
Florianópolis, Braz.	172	C13	27.35 S	48.32 W
Florida, Col.	168	F3	3.21 N	76.15 W
Florida, Cuba	156	B8	21.31 N	78.13 W
Florida, P.R.	158a	b2	18.22 N	66.34 W
Florida, P.R.	158a	b4	18.14 N	65.47 W
Florida, S. Afr.	191d		26.11 S	27.55 E
Florida, Ur.	172	G9	34.06 S	56.12 W
Florida, ngh., Arg.	206		34.31 S	58.30 W
Florida, state, U.S.	112	F11	28.00 N	82.00 W
Florida, stm., Co., U.S.	150	F9	37.03 N	107.52 W
Florida, Estrecho de la see Florida, Straits of, strt., N.A.	112	G11	24.58 N	79.45 W
Florida, Straits of, strt., N.A.	112	G11	24.58 N	79.45 W
Florida Bay, b., Fl., U.S.	132	L5	24.57 N	80.48 W
Floridablanca, Col.	168	D5	6.59 N	73.05 W
Florida Caverns State Park, p.o.i., Fl., U.S.	134	G13	30.50 N	85.18 W
Florida City, Fl., U.S.	132	K5	25.27 N	80.29 W
Florida Islands, is., Sol. Is.	101b	e9	8.53 S	160.08 E
Florida Keys, is., Fl., U.S.	116	H12	24.47 N	81.06 W
Florida Lake, res., S. Afr.	191d		26.11 S	27.54 E
Floridia, Italy	32	G9	37.05 N	15.09 E
Florido, stm., Mex.	154	B6	27.43 N	105.10 W
Floridsdorf, ngh., Aus.	182b		48.16 N	16.24 E
Floridsdorfer Brücke, trans., Aus.	182b		48.14 N	16.23 E
Florien, La., U.S.	136	C14	31.26 N	93.27 W
Flórina, Grc.	34	C4	40.47 N	21.24 E
Florissant, Mo., U.S.	130	F7	38.47 N	90.20 W
Florissant Fossil Beds National Monument, p.o.i., Co., U.S.	138	B3	38.54 N	105.16 W
Florø, Nor.	16	F3	61.35 N	5.01 E
Flotantes, Jardines, p.o.i., Mex.	204a		19.16 N	99.06 W
Flöthbach, stm., Ger.	181		51.17 N	6.26 E
Flotte, Cap de, c., N. Cal.	101d	m16	21.09 S	167.23 E
Flourtown, Pa., U.S.	203		40.06 N	75.12 W
Flovær, is., Nor.	16	B9	65.52 N	11.51 E
Flower Hill, N.Y., U.S.	194		40.48 N	73.40 W
Flowery Branch, Ga., U.S.	132	B2	34.11 N	83.55 W
Floyd, N.M., U.S.	138	G5	34.12 N	103.34 W
Floyd, Va., U.S.	124	H5	36.54 N	80.19 W
Floyd, stm., Ia., U.S.	128	I2	42.29 N	96.24 W
Floydada, Tx., U.S.	138	G7	33.59 N	101.20 W
Floyds Fork, stm., Ky., U.S.	130	F12	37.59 N	85.40 W
Flumendosa, stm., Italy	32	E3	39.26 N	9.37 E
Fluminimaggiore, Italy	32	E2	39.26 N	8.30 E
Flüren, Ger.	181		51.41 N	6.33 E
Flushing see Vlissingen, Neth.	20	C12	51.27 N	3.35 E
Flushing, Mi., U.S.	130	A14	43.03 N	83.50 W
Flushing, ngh., N.Y., U.S.	194		40.45 N	73.49 W
Flushing Airport, arpt., N.Y., U.S.	194		40.47 N	73.50 W
Flushing Bay, b., N.Y., U.S.	194		40.47 N	73.51 W
Flushing Meadow-Corona Park, p.o.i., N.Y., U.S.	194		40.45 N	73.51 W
Fluvanna, Tx., U.S.	136	B6	32.53 N	101.09 W
Fluvià, stm., Spain	28	B13	42.10 N	3.02 E
Fly, stm.	94	D5	8.14 S	142.09 E
Fly Creek, stm., Mt., U.S.	140	B5	45.59 N	107.59 W
Foam Lake, Sk., Can.	142	C10	51.38 N	103.31 W
Fobbing, Eng., U.K.	178		51.32 N	0.29 E
Foča, Bos.	36	F5	43.30 N	18.46 E
Foça, Tur.	34	E9	38.39 N	26.46 E
Focene, ngh., Italy	185a		41.48 N	12.14 E
Focșani, Rom.	36	D14	45.42 N	27.11 E
Foding Shan, mtn., China	58	H3	27.20 N	108.03 E
Foeni, Rom.	36	D7	45.30 N	20.53 E
Fogang, China	58	J5	23.52 N	113.31 E
Foggaret ez Zoua, Alg.	84	D5	27.23 N	2.52 E
Foggia, Italy	32	C9	41.27 N	15.32 E
Foglia, stm., Italy	30	G9	43.55 N	12.55 E
Fogo, i., C.V.	85a	k10	14.53 N	24.22 W
Fogo Island, i., Nf., Can.	111a	j23	49.38 N	54.10 W
Fogueteiro, Port.	184c		38.37 N	9.07 W
Foguista J. F. Juárez see El Galpón, Arg.	172	B5	25.23 S	64.38 W
Föhr, i., Ger.	24	B4	54.43 N	8.30 E
Fóia, mtn., Port.	28	G2	37.19 N	8.36 W
Foix, Fr.	22	G7	42.58 N	1.36 E
Foix, hist. reg., Fr.	22	F7	43.00 N	1.40 E
Fojnica, Bos.	36	F4	43.58 N	17.54 E
Fokino, Russia	26	G17	53.26 N	34.25 E
Fokku, Nig.	84	G5	11.40 N	4.31 E
Folda, b., Nor.	12	C6	67.36 N	14.50 E
Foldafjorden, b., Nor.	16	C8	64.42 N	11.00 E
Foldereid, Nor.	16	C9	64.58 N	12.08 E
Folégandros, i., Grc.	34	G7	36.38 N	24.54 E
Foley, Al., U.S.	134	G11	30.24 N	87.41 W
Foley, Mn., U.S.	128	F5	45.40 N	93.54 W
Foleyet, On., Can.	114	B9	48.14 N	82.26 W
Foley Island, i., Nu., Can.	110	B15	68.32 N	75.06 W
Folgefonni, ice, Nor.	16	H4	60.01 N	6.21 E
Foligno, Italy	30	H9	42.58 N	12.41 E
Folkestone, Eng., U.K.	10	J14	51.05 N	1.10 E
Folkston, Ga., U.S.	132	F3	30.50 N	82.00 W
Folkwangmuseum, bldg., Ger.	181		51.27 N	7.00 E
Follafoss, Nor.	16	C9	63.59 N	11.06 E
Follainville-Dennemont, Fr.	179		49.01 N	1.43 E
Folldal, Nor.	16	E8	62.08 N	10.03 E
Folle Anse, Pointe de, c., Guad.	159c	i6	15.56 N	61.19 W
Follebu, Nor.	16	F8	61.13 N	10.16 E
Follett, Tx., U.S.	138	E8	36.26 N	100.08 W
Föllinge, Swe.	16	D12	63.40 N	14.37 E
Follonica, Italy	30	H7	42.55 N	10.45 E
Follonica, Golfo di, b., Italy	30	H7	42.53 N	10.40 E
Folly Branch, stm., Md., U.S.	202b		38.56 N	76.49 W
Folsom, Ca., U.S.	148	E4	38.40 N	121.10 W
Folsom, Pa., U.S.	203		39.53 N	75.19 W
Folsom Lake, res., Ca., U.S.	148	E4	38.42 N	121.06 W
Fomboni, Com.	88	C7	12.16 S	43.43 E
Fomin, Russia	48	E6	46.57 N	43.39 E
Fominiči, Russia	26	F17	54.07 N	34.41 E
Fominskaja, Russia	12	F23	61.17 N	48.42 E
Fominskoe, Russia	26	A22	58.58 N	39.06 E
Fominskoe, Russia	40	B12	59.42 N	42.04 E
Fonda, Ia., U.S.	130	B3	42.34 N	94.50 W
Fonda, N.Y., U.S.	124	B11	42.57 N	74.22 W
Fond-du-Lac, Sk., Can.	110	D9	59.19 N	107.10 W
Fond du Lac, Wi., U.S.	128	H10	43.46 N	88.26 W
Fond du Lac, stm., Sk., Can.	110	D9	59.16 N	106.00 W
Fond du Lac Indian Reservation, ind. res., Mn., U.S.	128	E6	46.45 N	92.37 W
Fondi, Italy	32	C7	41.21 N	13.25 E
Fongen, mtn., Nor.	16	D9	63.10 N	11.36 E
Fonni, Italy	32	D3	40.07 N	9.14 E
Fonsagrada see A Fonsagrada, Spain	28	A3	43.07 N	7.03 W
Fonseca, Col.	168	B5	10.53 N	72.50 W
Fonseca, Golfo de, b., N.A.	156	F4	13.10 N	87.40 W
Fontainebleau, Fr.	20	F11	48.24 N	2.42 E
Fontainebleau, S. Afr.	191d		26.07 S	27.59 E
Fontana, Arg.	172	C8	27.22 S	59.05 W
Fontana, Ca., U.S.	148	I8	34.06 N	117.26 W
Fontana Lake, res., N.C., U.S.	132	A2	35.25 N	83.37 W
Fontanelas, Port.	184c		38.51 N	9.26 W
Fontanelle, Ia., U.S.	128	J4	41.17 N	94.33 W
Fontas, stm., Can.	110	D6	58.17 N	121.44 W
Fonte, Braz.	205b		23.25 S	46.21 W
Fonte Boa, Braz.	168	I8	2.31 S	66.01 W
Fontenay-aux-Roses, Fr.	179		48.47 N	2.17 E
Fontenay-en-Parisis, Fr.	179		49.03 N	2.27 E
Fontenay-le-Comte, Fr.	22	C5	46.28 N	0.48 W
Fontenay-le-Fleury, Fr.	179		48.49 N	2.03 E
Fontenay-lès-Briis, Fr.	179		48.37 N	2.09 E
Fontenay-le-Vicomte, Fr.	179		48.33 N	2.24 E
Fontenay-Saint-Père, Fr.	179		49.02 N	1.45 E
Fontenay-sous-Bois, Fr.	179		48.51 N	2.29 E
Fontenelle, Qc., Can.	122	B12	48.52 N	64.33 W
Fontenelle Creek, stm., Wy., U.S.	146	H16	42.05 N	110.08 W
Fontenelle Reservoir, res., Wy., U.S.	146	H16	42.04 N	110.07 W
Font Hill Manor, Md., U.S.	202b		39.17 N	76.52 W
Fontur, c., Ice.	12a	j32	66.22 N	14.35 W
Fonyód, Hung.	36	C4	46.44 N	17.34 E
Foochow see Fuzhou, China	58	H8	26.06 N	119.17 E
Foot Creek, stm., S.D., U.S.	140	B14	45.24 N	98.29 W
Foothills, Ab., Can.	144	C14	53.04 N	116.47 W
Footville, Wi., U.S.	130	B8	42.40 N	89.12 W
Foping, China	58	E3	33.21 N	108.00 E
Fora, Ponta de, c., Braz.	205a		22.57 S	43.07 W
Foraker, Mount, mtn., Ak., U.S.	109	D9	62.56 N	151.26 W
Forari, Vanuatu	101d	k17	17.39 S	168.31 E
Forbach, Fr.	20	E15	49.11 N	6.53 E
Forbach, Ger.	24	H4	48.40 N	8.21 E
Forbes, Austl.	98	I7	33.23 S	148.00 E
Forbes, Mount, mtn., Ab., Can.	144	E14	51.52 N	116.56 W
Forbesganj, India	76	E11	26.18 N	87.16 E
Forcados, Nig.	84	H6	5.21 N	5.25 E
Forcalquier, Fr.	22	F11	43.57 N	5.46 E
Forchheim, Ger.	24	G7	49.43 N	11.04 E
Ford, Ks., U.S.	138	D9	37.38 N	99.45 W
Ford, stm., Mi., U.S.	126	B2	45.40 N	87.09 W
Ford City, Ca., U.S.	148	H6	35.09 N	119.27 W
Ford City, Pa., U.S.	124	D6	40.45 N	79.31 W
Ford City, shp. cen., Il., U.S.	196		41.46 N	87.44 W
Ford Dam, dam., Mi., U.S.	199		42.13 N	83.33 W
Ford Dry Lake, l., Ca., U.S.	150	J2	33.37 N	114.58 W
Førde, Nor.	16	F3	61.27 N	5.52 E
Førde, Nor.	16	H3	59.36 N	5.29 E
Førdefjorden, b., Nor.	16	F3	61.29 N	5.10 E
Fordham University, educ., N.Y., U.S.	194		40.51 N	73.53 W
Ford Lake, l., Mi., U.S.	199		42.13 N	83.36 W
Ford Mansion, hist., N.J., U.S.	194		40.48 N	74.28 W
Ford Motor Company (River Rouge Plant), sci., Mi., U.S.	199		42.18 N	83.10 W
Ford Museum, bldg., Mi., U.S.	199		42.18 N	83.14 W
Ford Ranges, mts., Ant.	103	C26	77.00 S	145.00 W
Fords, N.J., U.S.	194		40.31 N	74.18 W
Fords Bridge, Austl.	98	G5	29.45 S	145.26 E
Fordsburg, ngh., S. Afr.	191d		26.13 S	28.02 E
Fordsville, Ky., U.S.	130	G11	37.38 N	86.43 W
Fordville, N.D., U.S.	142	F16	48.13 N	97.47 W
Fordyce, Ar., U.S.	134	D6	33.48 N	92.25 W
Forécariah, Gui.	84	H2	9.25 N	13.05 W
Forel, Mont, mtn., Grnld.	108	D18	66.58 N	36.48 W
Foreman, Ar., U.S.	134	D4	33.43 N	94.23 W
Foremost, Ab., Can.	142	E2	49.28 N	111.26 W
Forepaugh Airport, arpt., Oh., U.S.	197a		41.21 N	81.30 W
Forest, On., Can.	126	E8	43.05 N	81.59 W
Forest, Ms., U.S.	134	E9	32.21 N	89.28 W
Forest, Middle Branch, stm., N.D., U.S.	142	F16	48.12 N	97.48 W
Forest Academy Park, p.o.i., Russia	183a		59.59 N	30.21 E
Forest Acres, S.C., U.S.	132	B5	33.59 N	80.58 W
Forestburg, Ab., Can.	144	D18	52.34 N	112.02 W
Forest City, Ia., U.S.	128	H5	43.15 N	93.38 W
Forest City, N.C., U.S.	132	A4	35.19 N	81.51 W
Forest City, Pa., U.S.	124	C10	41.39 N	75.27 W
Forest Gate, ngh., Eng., U.K.	178		51.33 N	0.02 E
Forest Grove, B.C., Can.	144	E9	51.46 N	121.06 W
Forest Grove, Pa., U.S.	197b		40.18 N	75.04 W
Forest Heights, Md., U.S.	202c		38.49 N	77.00 W
Forest Hill, Austl.	192b		37.50 S	145.11 E
Foresthill, Ca., U.S.	148	D5	39.01 N	120.49 W
Forest Hill, ngh., On., Can.	193b		43.42 N	79.24 W
Forest Hill Park, p.o.i., Oh., U.S.	197a		41.31 N	81.35 W
Forest Hill Parkway, p.o.i., Oh., U.S.	197a		41.33 N	81.36 W
Forest Hills, Pa., U.S.	197b		40.25 N	79.51 W
Forest Hills, ngh., N.Y., U.S.	194		40.42 N	73.51 W
Forest Home, Al., U.S.	134	F12	31.52 N	86.50 W
Forestier Peninsula, pen., Austl.	99a	o14	42.57 S	147.55 E
Forest Knolls, Md., U.S.	202c		39.02 N	77.01 W
Forest Lake, Mn., U.S.	128	F5	45.16 N	92.59 W
Forest Lake, l., Il., U.S.	196		42.13 N	88.03 W
Forest Lake, l., Ma., U.S.	201		42.43 N	71.15 W
Forest Lawn Memorial Park, misc. cult., Ca., U.S.	198		34.09 N	118.19 W
Forest Manor, Md., U.S.	202c		38.50 N	76.53 W
Forest Park, Ga., U.S.	132	C1	33.38 N	84.22 W
Forest Park, Il., U.S.	196		41.52 N	87.48 W
Forest Park, ngh., Md., U.S.	202b		39.19 N	76.41 W
Forest Park, p.o.i., N.Y., U.S.	194		40.42 N	73.51 W
Forest River, Il., U.S.	196		42.05 N	87.54 W
Forest View, Il., U.S.	196		41.49 N	87.47 W
Forestville, Austl.	192a		33.46 S	151.13 E
Forestville, Qc., Can.	122	B7	48.44 N	69.05 W
Forestville, Md., U.S.	202c		38.50 N	76.52 W
Forestville, Wi., U.S.	126	D2	44.41 N	87.28 W
Forestville Mystery Cave State Park, p.o.i., Mn., U.S.	128	H6	43.39 N	92.14 W
Forfar, Scot., U.K.	10	E10	56.38 N	2.54 W
Forfry, Fr.	179		49.03 N	2.51 E
Forgan, Ok., U.S.	138	E8	36.54 N	100.32 W
Forge Acres, Md., U.S.	202b		39.25 N	76.27 W
Forge Heights, Md., U.S.	202b		39.25 N	76.25 W
Forges-les-Bains, Fr.	179		48.38 N	2.06 E
Forges-les-Eaux, Fr.	20	E10	49.36 N	1.32 E
Forget, Pointe, c., Qc., Can.	193a		45.27 N	73.58 W
Forggensee, l., Ger.	30	C7	47.36 N	10.44 E
Forillon, Parc national de, p.o.i., Qc., Can.	122	B12	48.52 N	64.17 W
Forked Deer, stm., Tn., U.S.	130	I8	35.55 N	89.35 W
Forked Deer, Middle Fork, stm., Tn., U.S.	134	B9	36.00 N	89.12 W
Forked Deer, North Fork, stm., Tn., U.S.	134	A9	36.00 N	89.26 W
Forks, Wa., U.S.	146	C2	47.57 N	124.23 W
Forleti, Arroyo, stm., Arg.	206		34.35 S	58.41 W
Forlì, Italy	30	F9	44.13 N	12.02 E
Forman, N.D., U.S.	140	A15	46.06 N	97.38 W
Formazza, Italy	30	D5	46.22 N	8.25 E
Formby Hills, hills, Eng., U.K.	180		53.34 N	3.06 W
Formby Point, c., Eng., U.K.	10	H9	53.33 N	3.06 W
Formentera, i., Spain	28	F12	38.42 N	1.28 E
Formentor, Cap de, c., Spain	28	E14	39.57 N	3.12 E
Formia, Italy	32	C7	41.15 N	13.36 E
Formiga, Braz.	170	K3	20.27 S	45.25 W
Formiga, stm., Braz.	170	F1	11.15 S	48.27 W
Formosa, Arg.	172	C8	26.09 S	58.11 W
Formosa, Braz.	170	H2	15.32 S	47.20 W
Formosa, state, Arg.	166	D4	25.00 S	60.00 W
Formosa see Taiwan, ctry., Asia	52	G9	23.30 N	121.00 E
Formosa see Taiwan, i., Tai.	46	G16	23.26 N	121.00 E
Formosa, Serra, plat., Braz.	164	F6	12.00 S	55.00 W
Formosa Strait see Taiwan Strait, strt., Asia	58	I8	24.00 N	119.00 E
Formoso, stm., Braz.	170	G3	13.26 S	44.14 W
Fornæs, c., Den.	16	K9	56.25 N	10.57 E
Forncelle, Italy	30	G8	43.55 N	11.05 E
Forney, Tx., U.S.	136	B11	32.45 N	96.28 W
Fornosovo, Russia	26	A13	59.34 N	30.34 E
Fornovo di Taro, Italy	30	F7	44.41 N	10.06 E
Forolhogna, mtn., Nor.	16	E8	62.39 N	10.45 E
Foro Romano, hist., Italy	185a		41.54 N	12.29 E
Føroyar see Faroe Islands, dep., Eur.	12b	n34	62.00 N	7.00 W
Forres, Scot., U.K.	10	D9	57.36 N	3.38 W
Forrest, Austl.	96	F5	30.50 S	128.06 E
Forrest, Il., U.S.	130	D9	40.44 N	88.24 W
Forrestal Research Center, sci., N.J., U.S.	194		40.21 N	74.37 W
Forrest City, Ar., U.S.	134	B8	35.00 N	90.47 W
Forreston, Il., U.S.	128	I9	42.07 N	89.34 W
Forsan, Tx., U.S.	136	B6	32.07 N	101.22 W
Forsayth, Austl.	98	B4	18.35 S	143.36 E
Forsby, Fin.	18	G12	60.30 N	25.56 E
Forserum, Swe.	16	J12	57.42 N	14.29 E
Forshaga, Swe.	16	H11	59.31 N	13.28 E
Forsnäs, Swe.	14	F9	66.13 N	18.37 E
Forssa, Fin.	18	G10	60.48 N	23.40 E
Forst, Ger.	24	E10	51.44 N	14.37 E
Forster, Austl.	98	I9	32.11 S	152.31 E
Forstwald, ngh., Ger.	181		51.18 N	6.30 E
Forsyth, Ga., U.S.	132	C2	33.02 N	83.56 W
Forsyth, Mo., U.S.	130	H4	36.41 N	93.07 W
Forsyth, Mt., U.S.	140	A6	46.16 N	106.41 W
Forsyth Range, mts., Austl.	98	D4	22.45 S	143.15 E
Fort, ngh., India	190c		18.56 N	72.50 E
Fort Abbās, Pak.	70	D4	29.11 N	72.51 E
Fort Adams, Ms., U.S.	134	F7	31.05 N	91.32 W
Fort Albany, On., Can.	110	E14	52.12 N	81.40 W
Fort Alexander Indian Reserve, ind. res., Mb., Can.	142	D17	50.36 N	96.16 W
Fortaleza, Braz.	170	B6	3.43 S	38.29 W
Fortaleza do Ituxi, Braz.	164	E4	7.28 S	66.19 W
Fortaleza dos Nogueiras, Braz.	170	D2	6.58 S	46.08 W
Fort Amherst National Historic Park, p.o.i., P.E., Can.	122	D13	46.12 N	63.09 W
Fort Anne National Historic Park, p.o.i., N.S., Can.	122	F11	44.44 N	65.26 W
Fort Apache Indian Reservation, ind. res., Az., U.S.	150	J6	34.01 N	110.28 W
Fort-Archambault see Sarh, Chad	82	F3	9.09 N	18.23 E
Fort Assiniboine, Ab., Can.	144	B16	54.19 N	114.46 W
Fort Atkinson, Wi., U.S.	130	B9	42.55 N	88.50 W
Fort Augustus, Scot., U.K.	10	D8	57.08 N	4.41 W
Fort Baker, mil., Ca., U.S.	200		37.50 N	122.29 W
Fort Battleford National Historic Park, p.o.i., Sk., Can.	142	B5	52.42 N	108.15 W
Fort Bayard see Zhanjiang, China	58	K4	21.12 N	110.22 E
Fort Beaufort, S. Afr.	90	H8	32.46 S	26.37 E
Fort Beauséjour National Historic Park, p.o.i., N.B., Can.	122	E12	45.51 N	64.18 W
Fort Belknap Agency, Mt., U.S.	142	F5	48.28 N	108.45 W
Fort Belknap Indian Reservation, ind. res., Mt., U.S.	142	F5	48.16 N	108.38 W
Fort Belvoir, mil., Va., U.S.	124	F8	38.42 N	77.09 W
Fort Benjamin Harrison, mil., In., U.S.	130	E11	39.52 N	86.00 W
Fort Benning, mil., Ga., U.S.	134	E14	32.22 N	84.50 W
Fort Benton, Mt., U.S.	146	C16	47.49 N	110.40 W
Fort Berthold Indian Reservation, ind. res., N.D., U.S.	142	G11	47.40 N	102.25 W
Fort Bidwell, Ca., U.S.	148	B5	41.51 N	120.09 W
Fort Bliss, mil., U.S.	136	B1	32.15 N	106.00 W
Fort Bowie National Historic Site, p.o.i., Az., U.S.	150	K7	32.09 N	109.24 W
Fort Bragg, Ca., U.S.	148	D2	39.26 N	123.47 W
Fort Bragg, mil., N.C., U.S.	132	A6	35.06 N	79.09 W
Fort Branch, In., U.S.	130	F10	38.15 N	87.35 W
Fort Bridger, Wy., U.S.	150	B6	41.19 N	110.23 W
Fort Calhoun, Ne., U.S.	130	C1	41.26 N	96.01 W
Fort Campbell, mil., U.S.	130	H10	36.36 N	87.35 W
Fort Carson, mil., Co., U.S.	138	C4	38.41 N	104.46 W
Fort Chambly National Historic Park, p.o.i., Qc., Can.	126	C16	45.27 N	73.17 W
Fort Chipewyan, Ab., Can.	110	D8	58.43 N	111.09 W
Fort Clatsop National Memorial, p.o.i., Or., U.S.	146	D3	46.08 N	123.53 W
Fort Cobb, Ok., U.S.	138	F10	35.05 N	98.26 W
Fort Cobb Reservoir, res., Ok., U.S.	138	F10	35.12 N	98.29 W
Fort Collins, Co., U.S.	140	G7	40.34 N	105.05 W
Fort Constantine, Austl.	98	C3	20.28 S	140.37 E
Fort-Coulonge, Qc., Can.	126	C13	45.50 N	76.44 W
Fort Covington, N.Y., U.S.	126	C15	44.59 N	74.29 W
Fort-Dauphin see Tôlañaro, Madag.	88	F8	25.02 S	47.00 E
Fort Davis, Al., U.S.	134	E13	32.14 N	85.43 W
Fort Davis, Tx., U.S.	136	D4	30.35 N	103.53 W
Fort Davis National Historic Site, p.o.i., Tx., U.S.	136	D4	30.34 N	103.54 W
Fort Defiance, Az., U.S.	150	H7	35.44 N	109.04 W
Fort-de-France, Mart.	159c	k6	14.36 N	61.04 W
Fort-de-France, Baie de, b., Mart.	159c	k6	14.34 N	61.04 W
Fort-de-France-Lamentin, Aérodrome de, arpt., Mart.	159c	k7	14.35 N	61.00 W
Fort Deposit, Al., U.S.	134	F12	31.59 N	86.34 W
Fort Detrick, mil., Md., U.S.	124	E8	39.27 N	77.26 W
Fort Dix, mil., N.J., U.S.	124	E11	40.00 N	74.33 W
Fort Dodge, Ia., U.S.	130	B3	42.29 N	94.10 W
Fort Donelson National Battlefield, p.o.i., Tn., U.S.	130	H10	36.26 N	87.49 W
Fort Duchesne, Ut., U.S.	150	C7	40.18 N	109.52 W
Fort Dupont Park, p.o.i., D.C., U.S.	202c		38.53 N	76.57 W
Forte dei Marmi, Italy	30	G7	43.57 N	10.10 E
Forte de Magoito, Port.	184c		38.52 N	9.27 W
Fort Edward, N.Y., U.S.	126	E16	43.16 N	73.34 W
Fort Erie, On., Can.	126	F11	42.54 N	78.55 W
Fort Erie Race Track, p.o.i., On., Can.	202a		42.55 N	78.56 W
Fortescue, stm., Austl.	96	D3	21.00 S	116.05 E
Fort Eustis, mil., Va., U.S.	124	G9	37.07 N	76.35 W
Fortezza, Italy	30	D8	46.47 N	11.36 E
Fort Fairfield, Me., U.S.	122	D9	46.46 N	67.49 W
Fort Foote Village, Md., U.S.	202c		38.46 N	77.01 W
Fort-Foureau see Kousséri, Cam.	86	B2	12.04 N	15.01 E
Fort Frances, On., Can.	128	C5	48.37 N	93.23 W
Fort Franklin see Déline, N.T., Can.	110	B6	65.11 N	123.30 W
Fort Fraser, B.C., Can.	144	B6	54.03 N	124.35 W
Fort Frederica National Monument, p.o.i., Ga., U.S.	132	E4	31.12 N	81.26 W
Fort Gaines, Ga., U.S.	134	F13	31.36 N	85.02 W
Fort Garland, Co., U.S.	138	D3	37.25 N	105.26 W
Fort Gay, W.V., U.S.	124	F3	38.07 N	82.36 W
Fort George, hist., On., Can.	202a		43.15 N	79.04 W
Fort George G. Meade, mil., Md., U.S.	124	E9	39.03 N	76.45 W
Fort Gibson, Ok., U.S.	130	I2	35.48 N	95.15 W
Fort Good Hope, N.T., Can.	110	B5	66.15 N	128.36 W
Fort Gordon, mil., Ga., U.S.	132	C3	33.22 N	82.11 W
Fort-Gouraud see Fdérik, Maur.	84	E2	22.41 N	12.42 W
Forth, stm., Scot., U.K.	10	E8	56.01 N	3.33 W
Forth, Firth of, b., Scot., U.K.	10	E10	56.07 N	2.57 W
Fort Hall, Id., U.S.	146	G14	43.01 N	112.26 W
Fort Hall Indian Reservation, ind. res., Id., U.S.	146	G14	43.10 N	112.10 W
Fort Hamilton, mil., N.Y., U.S.	194		40.37 N	74.02 W
Fort Hill see Chitipa, Mwi.	88	B5	9.42 S	33.16 E
Fort Hill, mil., Va., U.S.	124	F8	38.05 N	77.18 W
Fort Hood, mil., Tx., U.S.	136	C10	31.08 N	97.46 W
Fort Huachuca, mil., Az., U.S.	150	L6	31.33 N	110.20 W
Fortine, Mt., U.S.	146	B12	48.46 N	114.53 W
Fortín Uno, Arg.	172	I5	38.51 S	65.16 W
Fort Irwin, mil., Ca., U.S.	148	H9	35.20 N	116.40 W
Fort Jackson, mil., S.C., U.S.	132	B5	34.02 N	80.49 W
Fort Jeudy, Point of, c., Gren.	159e	r10	12.00 N	61.42 W
Fort Johnston see Mangochi, Mwi.	88	C6	14.27 S	35.15 E
Fort Jones, Ca., U.S.	148	B3	41.36 N	122.50 W
Fort Kent, Me., U.S.	122	C8	47.15 N	68.35 W
Fort Klamath, Or., U.S.	146	H4	42.43 N	121.59 W
Fort Knox, mil., Ky., U.S.	130	G12	37.54 N	85.53 W
Fort-Lamy see N'Djamena, Chad	82	E3	12.07 N	15.02 E
Fort Laramie, Wy., U.S.	140	E8	42.12 N	104.30 W
Fort Laramie National Historic Site, p.o.i., Wy., U.S.	140	E8	42.12 N	104.34 W
Fort Larned National Historic Site, p.o.i., Ks., U.S.	138	C9	38.10 N	99.12 W
Fort Lauderdale, Fl., U.S.	132	J5	26.06 N	80.08 W
Fort Leavenworth, mil., Ks., U.S.	130	E2	39.21 N	94.56 W
Fort Lee, mil., Va., U.S.	124	G8	37.14 N	77.20 W
Fort Lennox National Historic Park, p.o.i., Qc., Can.	126	C16	45.06 N	73.16 W
Fort Leonard Wood, mil., Mo., U.S.	130	G5	37.45 N	92.07 W
Fort Lewis, mil., Wa., U.S.	146	D4	46.56 N	122.41 W
Fort Liard, N.T., Can.	110	C6	60.13 N	123.26 W
Fort-Liberté, Haiti	156	C12	19.39 N	71.50 W
Fort Lincoln State Park, p.o.i., N.D., U.S.	140	A11	46.45 N	100.52 W
Fort Loramie, Oh., U.S.	124	D1	40.20 N	84.22 W
Fort Loudoun Lake, res., Tn., U.S.	134	B15	35.45 N	84.11 W
Fort Lupton, Co., U.S.	138	A4	40.05 N	104.48 W
Fort Lyon Canal, can., Co., U.S.	138	C5	38.11 N	102.31 W
Fort MacKay, Ab., Can.	110	D8	57.11 N	111.37 W
Fort Macleod, Ab., Can.	144	G17	49.42 N	113.24 W
Fort Madison, Ia., U.S.	130	D6	40.37 N	91.18 W
Fort Malden National Historic Park, p.o.i., On., Can.	199		42.06 N	83.07 W
Fort Matanzas National Monument, p.o.i., Fl., U.S.	132	G4	29.40 N	81.18 W
Fort McClellan, mil., Al., U.S.	134	D13	33.43 N	85.47 W
Fort McDermitt Indian Reservation, ind. res., U.S.	148	B8	42.00 N	117.34 W
Fort McDowell Indian Reservation, ind. res., Az., U.S.	150	J5	33.38 N	111.41 W
Fort McMurray, Ab., Can.	110	D8	56.44 N	111.24 W
Fort McNair, mil., D.C., U.S.	202c		38.52 N	77.04 W
Fort McPherson, N.T., Can.	110	B4	67.24 N	134.51 W
Fort Meade, Fl., U.S.	132	I4	27.45 N	81.48 W
Fort Mill, S.C., U.S.	132	A5	35.00 N	80.56 W
Fort Mitchell, Al., U.S.	134	E13	32.21 N	85.01 W
Fort Mojave Indian Reservation, ind. res., Az., U.S.	150	I2	34.55 N	114.35 W
Fort Monmouth, mil., N.J., U.S.	124	D11	40.19 N	74.02 W
Fort Morgan, Co., U.S.	138	A5	40.15 N	103.48 W
Fort Myer, mil., Va., U.S.	202c		38.53 N	77.05 W
Fort Myers, Fl., U.S.	132	J4	26.38 N	81.52 W
Fort Myers Beach, Fl., U.S.	132	J4	26.27 N	81.56 W
Fort Necessity National Battlefield, p.o.i., Pa., U.S.	124	E6	39.47 N	79.39 W
Fort Neck, pen., N.Y., U.S.	194		40.39 N	73.28 W
Fort Nelson, B.C., Can.	110	D6	58.48 N	122.41 W
Fort Nelson, stm., B.C., Can.	110	D6	59.31 N	124.02 W
Fort Niagara Beach, N.Y., U.S.	202a		43.16 N	79.03 W
Fort Niagara State Park, p.o.i., N.Y., U.S.	202a		43.16 N	79.03 W
Fort Nonsense, hist., N.J., U.S.	194		40.48 N	74.29 W
Fort Norman see Tulita, N.T., Can.	110	C5	64.54 N	125.33 W
Fort Ogden, Fl., U.S.	132	I4	27.05 N	81.57 W
Fortore, stm., Italy	32	C9	41.55 N	15.17 E
Fort Payne, Al., U.S.	134	C13	34.26 N	85.43 W
Fort Peck, Mt., U.S.	142	F7	48.00 N	106.27 W
Fort Peck Dam, dam., Mt., U.S.	142	G7	48.00 N	106.25 W
Fort Peck Indian Reservation, ind. res., Mt., U.S.	142	F8	48.22 N	105.40 W
Fort Peck Lake, res., Mt., U.S.	142	G7	47.45 N	106.44 W
Fort Pierce, Fl., U.S.	132	I5	27.26 N	80.19 W
Fort Pierre, S.D., U.S.	140	C12	44.21 N	100.22 W
Fort Pitt Tunnels, trans., Pa., U.S.	197b		40.25 N	80.00 W
Fort Plain, N.Y., U.S.	124	B11	42.55 N	74.37 W
Fort Point National Historic Site, hist., Ca., U.S.	200		37.48 N	122.28 W
Fort Polk, mil., La., U.S.	134	F5	31.04 N	93.09 W
Fort Portal, Ug.	86	D6	0.40 N	30.17 E
Fort Providence, N.T., Can.	110	C7	61.20 N	117.35 W
Fort Pulaski National Monument, p.o.i., Ga., U.S.	132	E5	32.00 N	80.54 W
Fort Qu'Appelle, Sk., Can.	142	D10	50.46 N	103.48 W
Fort Raleigh National Historic Site, p.o.i., N.C., U.S.	124	I10	35.54 N	75.40 W
Fort Randall Dam, dam., S.D., U.S.	140	D14	43.03 N	98.33 W
Fort Recovery, Oh., U.S.	124	D1	40.24 N	84.46 W
Fort Resolution, N.T., Can.	110	C8	61.10 N	113.38 W
Fortress Mountain, mtn., Wy., U.S.	146	F17	44.20 N	109.47 W
Fort Riley, mil., Ks., U.S.	138	B12	39.08 N	96.46 W
Fort Rixon, Zimb.	90	B9	20.00 S	29.15 E
Fort Robinson State Park, p.o.i., Ne., U.S.	140	E9	42.41 N	103.30 W
Fort Rodd Hill National Historic Park, p.o.i., B.C., Can.	144	H7	48.26 N	123.28 W
Fortrose, Scot., U.K.	10	D8	57.35 N	4.07 W
Fort Rosebery see Mansa, Zam.	88	C4	11.12 S	28.53 E
Fort Rucker, mil., Al., U.S.	134	F13	31.20 N	85.42 W
Fort Saint James, B.C., Can.	144	B6	54.27 N	124.15 W
Fort Saint John, B.C., Can.	110	D6	56.16 N	120.54 W
Fort Salonga, N.Y., U.S.	194		40.55 N	73.18 W
Fort Sam Houston, mil., Tx., U.S.	136	E9	29.27 N	98.27 W
Fort Saskatchewan, Ab., Can.	144	C17	53.42 N	113.14 W
Fort Scott, Ks., U.S.	130	G3	37.49 N	94.42 W
Fort-Ševčenko, Kaz.	48	F7	44.30 N	50.15 E
Fort Severn, On., Can.	110	D13	55.59 N	87.37 W
Fort Sill, mil., Ok., U.S.	138	G10	34.40 N	98.25 W
Fort Simpson, N.T., Can.	110	C6	61.50 N	121.22 W
Fort Sisseton State Park, p.o.i., S.D., U.S.	140	B15	45.39 N	97.32 W
Fort Smith, N.T., Can.	110	C8	60.00 N	111.54 W
Fort Smith, Ar., U.S.	134	B4	35.23 N	94.25 W
Fort Steele, B.C., Can.	144	G15	49.36 N	115.38 W
Fort Stewart, mil., Ga., U.S.	132	D4	31.58 N	81.38 W

Name	Page	Map Ref.	Latitude	Longitude
Fort Stockton, Tx., U.S.	136	D5	30.53 N	102.52 W
Fort Sumner, N.M., U.S.	138	G4	34.29 N	104.14 W
Fort Sumter National Monument, p.o.i., S.C., U.S.	132	D6	32.44 N	79.51 W
Fort Supply, Ok., U.S.	138	E9	36.34 N	99.34 W
Fort Thomas, Az., U.S.	150	J7	33.03 N	110.00 W
Fort Thompson, S.D., U.S.	140	C13	44.03 N	99.24 W
Fort Tilden, mil., N.Y., U.S.	194		40.33 N	73.53 W
Fort Totten, N.D., U.S.	142	G14	47.58 N	98.59 W
Fort Totten Park, p.o.i., D.C., U.S.	202c		38.57 N	77.00 W
Fort Towson, Ok., U.S.	134	D3	34.01 N	95.16 W
Fortuna, Arg.	172	G5	35.07 S	65.23 W
Fortuna, C.R.	156	G5	10.28 N	84.36 W
Fortuna, Ca., U.S.	148	C1	40.35 N	124.08 W
Fortuna Ledge see Marshall, Ak., U.S.	109	D7	61.53 N	162.05 W
Fortune Bay, b., Nf., Can.	111a	j22	47.25 N	55.25 W
Fortune Ditch, can., Oh., U.S.	197a		41.20 N	82.03 W
Fortuneswell, Eng., U.K.	10	K10	50.34 N	2.27 W
Fort Union National Monument, p.o.i., N.M., U.S.	138	F3	35.55 N	105.03 W
Fort Union Trading Post National Historic Site, p.o.i., U.S.	142	G9	48.00 N	104.03 W
Fort Valley, Ga., U.S.	132	D2	32.33 N	83.52 W
Fort Vermilion, Ab., Can.	110	D7	58.22 N	116.02 W
Fort Victoria, hist., Ber.	158e	k16	32.23 N	64.40 W
Fortville, In., U.S.	130	E12	39.55 N	85.50 W
Fort Walton Beach, Fl., U.S.	134	G12	30.24 N	86.37 W
Fort Washakie, Wy., U.S.	140	E4	43.00 N	108.52 W
Fort Washington State Park, p.o.i., Pa., U.S.	203		40.07 N	75.14 W
Fort Wayne, In., U.S.	130	C12	41.04 N	85.07 W
Fort Wayne Military Museum, bldg., Mi., U.S.	199		42.18 N	83.06 W
Fort Wellington National Historic Park, p.o.i., On., Can.	126	D14	44.44 N	75.31 W
Fort White, Fl., U.S.	132	G3	29.55 N	82.42 W
Fort William, Scot., U.K.	10	E7	56.49 N	5.06 W
Fort Worth, Tx., U.S.	136	B10	32.43 N	97.19 W
Fort Yates, N.D., U.S.	140	A12	46.04 N	100.38 W
Fort Yukon, Ak., U.S.	109	C10	66.34 N	145.14 W
Fort Yuma Indian Reservation, ind. res., Ca., U.S.	150	K2	32.48 N	114.34 W
Forum, p.o.i., Qc., Can.	193a		45.29 N	73.35 W
Forūr, Jazīreh-ye, i., Iran	74	G14	26.17 N	54.30 E
Fosen, pen., Nor.	16	D8	63.45 N	10.25 E
Fosforescente, Bahía, b., P.R.	158a	c1	17.58 N	67.00 W
Foshan, China	58	J5	23.02 N	113.06 E
Fosheim Peninsula, pen., Nu., Can.	108	B9	79.56 N	84.57 W
Fosnavåg, Nor.	16	E3	62.20 N	5.38 E
Foso, Ghana	84	H4	5.41 N	1.16 W
Fossa Eugeniana, can., Ger.	181		51.33 N	6.36 E
Fossano, Italy	30	F4	44.33 N	7.43 E
Fosse-Martin, Fr.	179		49.05 N	2.54 E
Fosses, Fr.	179		49.06 N	2.29 E
Fossil, Or., U.S.	146	F6	44.59 N	120.12 W
Fossil Butte National Monument, p.o.i., Wy., U.S.	146	I16	41.50 N	110.40 W
Fossil Lake, l., Or., U.S.	146	G6	43.18 N	120.15 W
Fossombrone, Italy	30	G9	43.41 N	12.48 E
Fosston, Mn., U.S.	128	D3	47.34 N	95.45 W
Foster, Austl.	98	L6	38.39 S	146.11 E
Foster Bugt, strt., Grnld.	108	C21	73.15 N	21.30 W
Foster Creek, stm., S.D., U.S.	140	C14	44.33 N	98.12 W
Fosters, Al., U.S.	134	D11	33.05 N	87.41 W
Fosters Pond, l., Ma., U.S.	201		42.37 N	71.08 W
Foster Street, Eng., U.K.	178		51.46 N	0.09 E
Fostoria, Oh., U.S.	124	C2	41.09 N	83.24 W
Fót, Hung.	182c		47.37 N	19.12 E
Fóti-Somlyó, hill, Hung.	182c		47.38 N	19.13 E
Fougamou, Gabon	86	E2	1.12 S	10.34 E
Fougères, Fr.	20	F7	48.21 N	1.12 W
Fouju, Fr.	179		48.35 N	2.47 E
Fouke, Ar., U.S.	134	D5	33.15 N	93.53 W
Foula, i., Scot., U.K.	10	A10	60.08 N	2.05 W
Foulamôri, Gui.	84	G2	12.09 N	13.50 W
Fouling see Fuling, China	58	G2	29.42 N	107.23 E
Foulwind, Cape, c., N.Z.	102	E4	41.45 S	171.28 E
Foumban, Cam.	86	C2	5.43 N	10.54 E
Foum-el-Hassan, Mor.	84	D3	28.59 N	8.55 W
Foum-Zguid, Mor.	84	C3	30.05 N	6.51 W
Foundiougne, Sen.	84	G1	14.06 N	16.28 W
Fountain, Co., U.S.	138	C4	38.41 N	104.41 W
Fountain, Fl., U.S.	134	G13	30.30 N	85.24 W
Fountain City, Wi., U.S.	128	G7	44.07 N	91.42 W
Fountain Creek, stm., Co., U.S.	138	C4	38.15 N	104.35 W
Fountain Green, Ut., U.S.	150	D5	39.37 N	111.38 W
Fountain Inn, S.C., U.S.	132	B3	34.42 N	82.12 W
Fountain Peak, mtn., Ca., U.S.	148	I10	34.57 N	115.32 W
Fountain Place, La., U.S.	134	G7	30.30 N	91.09 W
Fourche LaFave, stm., Ar., U.S.	134	C6	34.58 N	92.35 W
Fourche Maline, stm., Ok., U.S.	134	C3	34.55 N	94.46 W
Fourchu, N.S., Can.	122	E16	45.43 N	60.15 W
Four Corners, Or., U.S.	146	F4	44.55 N	122.58 W
Four Elms, Eng., U.K.	178		51.13 N	0.06 E
Four Hole Swamp, stm., S.C., U.S.	132	C5	33.02 N	80.24 W
Fouriesburg, S. Afr.	90	F9	28.37 S	28.12 E
Fourmies, Fr.	20	D13	50.01 N	4.03 E
Four Mile Creek, stm., On., Can.	202a		43.15 N	79.08 W
Fourmile Creek, stm., N.Y., U.S.	202a		43.17 N	79.00 W
Four Mile Creek State Park, p.o.i., N.Y., U.S.	202a		43.16 N	79.00 W
Fourmile Draw, stm., N.M., U.S.	136	B3	32.40 N	104.18 W
Four Mile Run, stm., Va., U.S.	202c		38.50 N	77.02 W
Four Mountains, Islands of, is., Ak., U.S.	109a	g24	52.56 N	169.59 W
Fourneau, Pointe à, c., Qc., Can.	193a		45.22 N	73.51 W
Fournier, Mont, mtn., Qc., Can.	122	C6	47.06 N	70.09 W
Foúrnoi, i., Grc.	34	F9	37.34 N	26.29 E
Four Oaks, N.C., U.S.	132	A7	35.26 N	78.25 W
Fourqueux, Fr.	179		48.53 N	2.04 E
Fours, Fr.	20	H12	46.49 N	3.43 E
Fourth Cataract see Rābi', Ash-Shallāl ar-, wtfl., Sudan	82	D6	18.43 N	32.03 E
Fourth Cliff, clf., Ma., U.S.	201		42.09 N	70.42 W
Four Towns, Mi., U.S.	199		42.37 N	83.25 W
Fous, Pointe des, c., Dom.	159c	j6	15.12 N	61.20 W
Fouta Djalon, reg., Gui.	84	G2	11.30 N	12.30 W
Foux, Cap à, c., Haiti	156	C11	19.41 N	73.26 W
Foveaux Strait, strt., N.Z.	102	H2	46.35 S	168.00 E
Fowler, Ca., U.S.	148	G6	36.38 N	119.40 W
Fowler, Co., U.S.	138	C4	38.07 N	104.01 W
Fowler, In., U.S.	130	D10	40.37 N	87.19 W
Fowler, Mi., U.S.	130	A13	43.00 N	84.44 W
Fowler Creek, stm., Mi., U.S.	199		42.17 N	83.30 W
Fowlers Bay, Austl.	96	F6	31.58 S	132.25 E
Fowlerton, Tx., U.S.	136	F9	28.28 N	98.48 W
Fowlerville, Mi., U.S.	124	B1	42.39 N	84.04 W
Fowman, Iran	74	B11	37.13 N	49.19 E
Fox, stm., U.S.	130	D5	40.16 N	91.29 W
Fox, stm., U.S.	130	B9	41.20 N	88.49 W
Fox, stm., Wi., U.S.	128	H10	44.31 N	88.00 W
Foxboro Raceway, p.o.i., Ma., U.S.	201		42.06 N	71.16 W
Foxboro Stadium, p.o.i., Ma., U.S.	201		42.05 N	71.16 W
Fox Brook, stm., N.J., U.S.	194		41.03 N	74.13 W
Fox Chapel, Pa., U.S.	197b		40.30 N	79.55 W
Fox Chase, ngh., Pa., U.S.	203		40.04 N	75.05 W
Fox Chase Manor, Pa., U.S.	203		40.05 N	75.06 W
Fox Creek, Ab., Can.	144	B14	54.23 N	116.50 W
Foxe Basin, b., Nu., Can.	110	B15	68.25 N	77.00 W
Foxe Channel, strt., Nu., Can.	110	C15	64.30 N	80.00 W
Foxen, l., Swe.	16	H9	59.23 N	11.52 E
Foxe Peninsula, pen., Nu., Can.	110	C15	65.00 N	76.00 W
Foxford, Ire.	10	H3	53.59 N	9.06 W
Foxhall, Md., U.S.	202c		39.04 N	77.03 W
Fox Hills, Md., U.S.	202c		39.02 N	77.11 W
Fox Hollow Lake, l., N.J., U.S.	194		41.02 N	74.40 W
Fox Islands, is., Ak., U.S.	109a	g25	54.00 N	168.00 W
Fox Lake, Il., U.S.	130	B9	42.24 N	88.10 W
Fox Lake, Wi., U.S.	128	H10	43.34 N	88.53 W
Foxpark, Wy., U.S.	150	B10	41.05 N	106.10 W
Fox Point, c., N.Y., U.S.	194		40.54 N	73.35 W
Foxvale, Ma., U.S.	201		42.02 N	71.14 W
Fox Valley, Austl.	192a		33.45 S	151.06 E
Fox Valley, Sk., Can.	142	D4	50.28 N	109.28 W
Foxwist Green, Eng., U.K.	180		53.12 N	2.34 W
Foxworth, Ms., U.S.	134	F9	31.14 N	89.52 W
Foyle, stm., Eur.	10	G5	55.03 N	7.14 W
Foyle, Lough, b., Eur.	10	F5	55.06 N	7.08 W
Foynes, Ire.	10	I3	52.37 N	9.07 W
Foz do Areia, Represa de, res., Braz.	172	B12	26.00 S	51.35 W
Foz do Cunene, Ang.	88	D1	17.13 S	11.45 E
Foz do Iguaçu, Braz.	172	B10	25.33 S	54.35 W
Foz do Jordão, Braz.	164	E3	9.23 S	71.56 W
Foz Giraldo, Port.	28	E3	39.59 N	7.43 W
Fraction Run, stm., Il., U.S.	196		41.34 N	88.04 W
Fraga, Arg.	172	F5	33.30 S	65.47 W
Fraga, Spain	28	C11	41.31 N	0.21 E
Fragrant Hills Park, p.o.i., China	189a		39.59 N	116.11 E
Fragua, Sierra de la, mts., Mex.	136	H5	26.47 N	102.24 W
Fraile Muerto, Ur.	172	F10	32.30 S	54.31 W
Framingham, Ma., U.S.	124	B14	42.16 N	71.25 W
Framingham State College, educ., Ma., U.S.	201		42.18 N	71.26 W
Frampol, Pol.	24	F18	50.40 N	22.40 E
França, Braz.	170	F5	11.34 S	40.35 W
Franca, Braz.	170	K2	20.32 S	47.23 W
Francavilla al Mare, Italy	30	H11	42.25 N	14.17 E
Francavilla Fontana, Italy	32	D11	40.32 N	17.35 E
France, ctry., Fr.	6	F9	46.00 N	2.00 E
Frances, stm., Yk., Can.	110	C5	60.16 N	129.09 W
Frances Lake, l., Yk., Can.	110	C4	61.25 N	129.22 W
Francés Viejo, Cabo, c., Dom. Rep.	156	C13	19.39 N	69.55 W
Francesville, In., U.S.	130	C11	40.58 N	86.52 W
Franceville, Gabon	86	E2	1.38 S	13.34 E
Franche-Comté, hist. reg., Fr.	22	B12	47.00 N	6.00 E
Francia, Ur.	172	F9	32.32 S	56.37 W
Francia, Estación de, trans., Spain	184d		41.23 N	2.11 E
Francis, Sk., Can.	142	D10	50.06 N	103.52 W
Francis Case, Lake, res., S.D., U.S.	140	D14	43.15 N	98.57 W
Francisco Beltrão, Braz.	172	C11	26.04 S	53.03 W
Francisco I. Madero, Mex.	136	I4	25.45 N	103.20 W
Francisco I. Madero, Mex.	154	C6	24.32 N	104.19 W
Francisco I. Madero, Presa, res., Mex.	136	F2	28.07 N	105.41 W
Francisco Murguía, Mex.	154	C7	24.00 N	103.01 W
Francisco Sá, Braz.	170	I4	16.27 S	43.29 W
Francisco Zarco, Mex.	148	K9	32.05 N	116.33 W
Francis E. Warren Air Force Base, mil., Wy., U.S.	140	F7	41.09 N	104.52 W
Francistown, Bots.	90	B8	21.09 S	27.30 E
Francofonte, Italy	32	G8	37.14 N	14.53 E
François Lake, B.C., Can.	144	B5	54.04 N	125.44 W
Francois Lake, l., B.C., Can.	144	C5	54.02 N	125.43 W
Franconia Notch State Park, p.o.i., N.H., U.S.	122	F5	44.06 N	71.43 W
Franconville, Fr.	179		48.59 N	2.14 E
Francs Peak, mtn., Wy., U.S.	140	C3	43.58 N	109.20 W
Frank, Pa., U.S.	197b		40.16 N	79.48 W
Frank and Poet Drain, can., Mi., U.S.	199		42.06 N	83.12 W
Frankby, Eng., U.K.	180		53.22 N	3.08 W
Frankel City, Tx., U.S.	136	B5	32.23 N	102.47 W
Franken, hist. reg., Ger.	24	G6	50.00 N	10.00 E
Frankenberg, Ger.	24	F9	50.54 N	13.03 E
Frankenberg, Ger.	24	E4	51.03 N	8.48 E
Frankenmuth, Mi., U.S.	126	E6	43.19 N	83.44 W
Frankfield, Jam.	158d	i13	18.08 N	77.22 W
Frankford, On., Can.	126	D12	44.11 N	77.36 W
Frankford, Mo., U.S.	130	E6	39.28 N	91.19 W
Frankford, ngh., Pa., U.S.	203		40.01 N	75.05 W
Frankford Arsenal, mil., Pa., U.S.	203		40.00 N	75.04 W
Frankfort, S. Afr.	90	E9	27.16 S	28.30 E
Frankfort, In., U.S.	130	D11	40.16 N	86.30 W
Frankfort, Ks., U.S.	138	B12	39.42 N	96.25 W
Frankfort, Ky., U.S.	130	F13	38.12 N	84.50 W
Frankfort, Mi., U.S.	126	D3	44.38 N	86.13 W
Frankfort, N.Y., U.S.	124	A10	43.02 N	75.04 W
Frankfort, Oh., U.S.	124	E2	39.24 N	83.10 W
Frankfort, S.D., U.S.	140	C14	44.52 N	98.18 W
Frankfurt, Ger.	24	D10	52.20 N	14.32 E
Frankfurt am Main, Ger.	24	F4	50.07 N	8.40 E
Frank G. Bonelli Regional County Park, p.o.i., Ca., U.S.	198		34.05 N	117.49 W
Franklin, S. Afr.	90	G9	30.19 S	29.27 E
Franklin, Az., U.S.	150	K7	32.40 N	109.04 W
Franklin, Ga., U.S.	134	D13	33.17 N	85.06 W
Franklin, Id., U.S.	146	H15	42.01 N	111.48 W
Franklin, Il., U.S.	130	E7	39.37 N	90.03 W
Franklin, In., U.S.	130	E11	39.28 N	86.03 W
Franklin, Ky., U.S.	130	H11	36.43 N	86.34 W
Franklin, La., U.S.	134	H7	29.47 N	91.30 W
Franklin, Me., U.S.	122	F8	44.35 N	68.13 W
Franklin, Ma., U.S.	124	B14	42.05 N	71.23 W
Franklin, Mi., U.S.	199		42.31 N	83.18 W
Franklin, Ne., U.S.	138	A10	40.05 N	98.56 W
Franklin, N.H., U.S.	122	G5	43.26 N	71.39 W
Franklin, N.J., U.S.	124	C11	41.07 N	74.35 W
Franklin, N.C., U.S.	132	A2	35.10 N	83.22 W
Franklin, Oh., U.S.	124	E1	39.33 N	84.18 W
Franklin, Pa., U.S.	124	C6	41.23 N	79.49 W
Franklin, Tn., U.S.	130	I11	35.54 N	86.52 W
Franklin, Tx., U.S.	136	C11	31.01 N	96.29 W
Franklin, Va., U.S.	126	H9	36.40 N	76.55 W
Franklin, W.V., U.S.	124	F6	38.38 N	79.20 W
Franklin, Wi., U.S.	130	B10	42.51 N	87.59 W
Franklin Bay, b., N.T., Can.	110	B5	69.45 N	126.00 W
Franklin Canyon Reservoir, res., Ca., U.S.	198		34.06 N	118.25 W
Franklin Delano Roosevelt National Historic Site, p.o.i., N.Y., U.S.	124	C12	41.46 N	73.56 W
Franklin Delano Roosevelt Park, p.o.i., Pa., U.S.	203		39.54 N	75.11 W
Franklin D. Roosevelt Lake, res., Wa., U.S.	112	B4	48.20 N	118.10 W
Franklin Farms, Pa., U.S.	197b		40.10 N	80.16 W
Franklin Gordon Wild Rivers National Park, p.o.i., Austl.	99a	o12	42.22 S	145.46 E
Franklin Grove, Il., U.S.	130	C8	41.50 N	89.18 W
Franklin Institute, bldg., Pa., U.S.	203		39.57 N	75.11 W
Franklin Lake, l., Nu., Can.	110	B12	66.56 N	96.08 W
Franklin Lake, l., Nv., U.S.	148	C10	40.28 N	115.19 W
Franklin Lake, l., N.J., U.S.	194		40.59 N	74.13 W
Franklin Lakes, N.J., U.S.	194		41.01 N	74.12 W
Franklin Mountains, mts., N.T., Can.	110	B5	62.58 N	123.42 W
Franklin Park, Md., U.S.	202c		39.03 N	77.06 W
Franklin Park, N.J., U.S.	194		40.26 N	74.32 W
Franklin Park, Va., U.S.	202c		38.55 N	77.09 W
Franklin Park, p.o.i., Ma., U.S.	201		42.18 N	71.06 W
Franklin Pond, l., N.J., U.S.	194		41.06 N	74.35 W
Franklin Ridge, mtn., Ca., U.S.	200		38.00 N	122.10 W
Franklin Roosevelt Park, ngh., S. Afr.	191d		26.09 S	27.59 E
Franklin State Forest, p.o.i., Ma., U.S.	201		42.04 N	71.26 W
Franklin Strait, strt., Nu., Can.	110	A11	72.00 N	96.00 W
Franklinton, La., U.S.	134	G8	30.50 N	90.09 W
Franklinton, N.C., U.S.	124	H7	36.06 N	78.27 W
Franklinville, N.Y., U.S.	124	B7	42.20 N	78.27 W
Frankston, Tx., U.S.	136	B12	32.03 N	95.30 W
Frankton, In., U.S.	130	D12	40.13 N	85.46 W
Frankville, Al., U.S.	134	F10	31.38 N	88.08 W
Frånö, Swe.	16	E15	62.54 N	17.50 E
Fransfontein, Nmb.	90	B2	20.12 S	15.01 E
Fränsta, Swe.	16	E14	62.30 N	16.09 E
Frantsa-Iosifa, Zemlja, is., Russia	46	B9	81.00 N	55.00 E
Franzensburg, hist., Aus.	182b		48.04 N	16.22 E
Franzensfeste see Fortezza, Italy	30	D8	46.47 N	11.36 E
Franz Josef Land see Frantsa-Iosifa, Zemlja, is., Russia	46	B9	81.00 N	55.00 E
Franz-Josefs-Bahnhof, trans., Aus.	182b		48.13 N	16.21 E
Frascati, Italy	30	I9	41.48 N	12.40 E
Fraser, B.C., Can.	144	G13	49.37 N	116.58 W
Fraser, Co., U.S.	138	B3	39.56 N	105.49 W
Fraser, Mi., U.S.	199		42.32 N	82.56 W
Fraser, stm., B.C., Can.	144	F9	49.06 N	123.11 W
Fraser, stm., Co., U.S.	138	A3	40.06 N	105.58 W
Fraser, Mount, mtn., Austl.	96	E3	25.39 S	118.23 E
Fraserburg, S. Afr.	90	G5	31.55 S	21.30 E
Fraserburgh, Scot., U.K.	10	D11	57.41 N	2.00 W
Fraser Island, i., Austl.	98	E9	25.15 S	153.10 E
Fraser Lake, B.C., Can.	144	B6	54.03 N	124.51 W
Fraser Lake, l., B.C., Can.	144	B6	54.05 N	124.41 W
Fraser Plateau, plat., B.C., Can.	144	D7	52.00 N	123.00 W
Fraser Range, Austl.	96	F4	32.02 S	122.48 E
Frattócchie, Italy	185a		41.46 N	12.37 E
Frauenfeld, Switz.	30	C5	47.33 N	8.54 E
Fray Bentos, Ur.	172	F8	33.08 S	58.17 W
Fray Jorge, Parque Nacional, p.o.i., Chile	172	E2	30.40 S	71.40 W
Fray Marcos, Ur.	172	G10	34.11 S	55.43 W
Frazee, Mn., U.S.	118	E3	46.43 N	95.42 W
Frazer, Mt., U.S.	142	F7	48.03 N	106.03 W
Frechilla, Spain	28	B6	42.08 N	4.50 W
Freckleton, Eng., U.K.	180		53.45 N	2.52 W
Fredensborg, Den.	16	L10	55.58 N	12.24 E
Frederic, Wi., U.S.	128	F6	45.39 N	92.28 W
Frederica, De., U.S.	124	E10	39.00 N	75.27 W
Fredericia, Den.	16	L7	55.35 N	9.46 E
Frederick, Md., U.S.	124	E8	39.24 N	77.23 W
Frederick, Ok., U.S.	138	G9	34.23 N	99.00 W
Frederick, S.D., U.S.	140	B14	45.49 N	98.29 W
Frederick Hills, hills, Austl.	96	B7	12.42 S	135.57 E
Frederick Reef, rf., Austl.	96	C10	20.58 S	154.23 E
Fredericksburg, Ia., U.S.	130	B5	42.57 N	92.12 W
Fredericksburg, Tx., U.S.	136	D9	30.16 N	98.51 W
Fredericksburg, Va., U.S.	124	F8	38.17 N	77.27 W
Fredericktown, Mo., U.S.	130	G7	37.33 N	90.17 W
Fredericktown, Oh., U.S.	124	D3	40.29 N	82.33 W
Frederico Westphalen, Braz.	172	C11	27.20 S	53.24 W
Fredericton, N.B., Can.	122	E10	45.57 N	66.38 W
Fredericton Junction, N.B., Can.	122	E10	45.39 N	66.37 W
Frederik Hendrik-eiland see Yos Sudarso, Pulau, i., Indon.	60	G10	7.50 S	138.30 E
Frederiksborg, state, Den.	16	L10	55.56 N	12.18 E
Frederiksdal, Grnld.	108	E17	59.59 N	44.38 W
Frederikshåb (Paamiut), Grnld.	108	E15	62.00 N	49.41 W
Frederikshavn, Den.	16	J8	57.26 N	10.32 E
Frederikssund, Den.	16	L9	55.49 N	12.04 E
Frederiksted, V.I.U.S.	158c	h10	17.43 N	64.52 W
Frederiksværk, Den.	16	K9	55.58 N	12.01 E
Fredonia, Az., U.S.	150	G4	36.03 N	112.08 W
Fredonia, Ks., U.S.	130	G2	37.32 N	95.49 W
Fredonia, N.Y., U.S.	124	B6	42.26 N	79.19 W
Fredonia, N.D., U.S.	140	A13	46.18 N	99.06 W
Fredrika, Swe.	16	C16	64.04 N	18.24 E
Fredriksberg, Swe.	16	G12	60.08 N	14.23 E
Fredrikstad, Nor.	16	H8	59.12 N	10.56 E
Fredvang, Nor.	14	D3	68.05 N	13.07 E
Freeburg, Il., U.S.	130	F8	38.24 N	89.54 W
Freeburg, Mo., U.S.	130	F6	38.18 N	91.55 W
Freeland, Mi., U.S.	126	E5	43.31 N	84.07 W
Freeland, Pa., U.S.	124	C9	41.01 N	75.55 W
Freel Peak, mtn., Ca., U.S.	148	E6	38.52 N	119.54 W
Freels, Cape, c., Nf., Can.	111a	j23	46.37 N	53.34 W
Freels, Cape, c., Nf., Can.	111a	j23	49.15 N	53.28 W
Freeman, S.D., U.S.	140	D15	43.21 N	97.25 W
Freeman, stm., Ab., Can.	144	B15	54.18 N	114.46 W
Freeport, Bah.	132	J7	26.30 N	78.39 W
Freeport, N.S., Can.	122	F10	44.16 N	66.19 W
Freeport, Fl., U.S.	134	G12	30.29 N	86.08 W
Freeport, Il., U.S.	130	B8	42.17 N	89.37 W
Freeport, Me., U.S.	122	G6	43.51 N	70.06 W
Freeport, N.Y., U.S.	126	H16	40.39 N	73.35 W
Freeport, Pa., U.S.	124	D6	40.40 N	79.41 W
Freeport, Tx., U.S.	136	F12	28.57 N	95.21 W
Freer, Tx., U.S.	136	G9	27.52 N	98.37 W
Free State, state, S. Afr.	90	F8	28.30 S	27.00 E
Freetown, Antig.	159b	f4	17.03 N	61.42 W
Freetown, S.L.	84	H2	8.29 N	13.12 W
Freezeout Lake, l., Mt., U.S.	146	C14	47.39 N	112.03 W
Fregenal de la Sierra, Spain	28	F4	38.10 N	6.39 W
Frei, Nor.	16	D5	63.02 N	7.49 E
Freiberg, Ger.	24	F9	50.54 N	13.20 E
Freiburg see Fribourg, Switz.	30	D4	46.47 N	7.08 E
Freiburg im Breisgau, Ger.	24	I3	47.59 N	7.50 E
Freie Universität, educ., Ger.	182a		52.26 N	13.16 E
Freirina, Chile	172	D2	28.30 S	71.06 W
Freisenbruch, ngh., Ger.	181		51.27 N	7.06 E
Freising, Ger.	24	H7	48.24 N	11.44 E
Freistadt, Aus.	30	B11	48.30 N	14.30 E
Freital, Ger.	24	F9	51.00 N	13.39 E
Freixial, Port.	184c		38.54 N	9.09 W
Fréjus, Fr.	22	F12	43.26 N	6.44 E
Frémainville, Fr.	179		49.04 N	1.52 E
Fremantle, Austl.	96	F3	32.03 S	115.45 E
Fremont, Ca., U.S.	148	F4	37.33 N	121.59 W
Fremont, In., U.S.	124	C1	41.44 N	84.55 W
Fremont, Ia., U.S.	130	C5	41.12 N	92.26 W
Fremont, Mi., U.S.	126	E4	43.28 N	85.56 W
Fremont, Ne., U.S.	130	C1	41.26 N	96.29 W
Fremont, N.C., U.S.	132	A8	35.32 N	77.58 W
Fremont, Oh., U.S.	124	C2	41.20 N	83.07 W
Fremont, Wi., U.S.	128	G10	44.15 N	88.52 W
Fremont, stm., Ut., U.S.	150	E6	38.24 N	110.42 W
Fremont Canyon, val., Ca., U.S.	198		33.48 N	117.42 W
Fremont Island, i., Ut., U.S.	150	B4	41.10 N	112.20 W
Fremont Lake, res., Wy., U.S.	146	H16	42.57 N	109.48 W
French, stm., On., Can.	126	B9	45.56 N	80.53 W
French Broad, stm., U.S.	124	I3	35.46 N	82.43 W
Frenchburg, Ky., U.S.	124	G2	37.56 N	83.38 W
Frenchcap Cay, i., V.I.U.S.	158b	f7	18.14 N	64.51 W
French Creek, stm., U.S.	124	C6	41.23 N	79.49 W
French Creek, stm., Oh., U.S.	197a		41.27 N	82.07 W
French Creek, stm., S.D., U.S.	140	D9	43.38 N	102.55 W
French Creek, South Branch, stm., Pa., U.S.	203		40.10 N	75.42 W
French Guiana, dep., S.A.	164	C7	4.00 N	53.00 W
French Island, i., Austl.	98	L5	38.21 S	145.21 E
French Lick, In., U.S.	130	F11	38.32 N	86.37 W
Frenchman (Frenchman Creek), stm., N.A.	142	E5	48.30 N	107.15 W
Frenchman Bay, b., Me., U.S.	122	F8	44.25 N	68.12 W
Frenchman Creek (Frenchman), stm., N.A.	142	E5	48.30 N	107.15 W
Frenchman Creek, stm., U.S.	140	G11	40.13 N	100.50 W
Frenchman's Bay, b., On., Can.	193b		43.49 N	79.05 W
Frenchmans Cap, mtn., Austl.	99a	o12	42.16 S	145.50 E
Frenchman's Creek, stm., On., Can.	202a		42.56 N	78.56 W
Frenchmans Creek, stm., Ca., U.S.	200		37.29 N	122.27 W
French Polynesia, dep., Oc.	174	K24	15.00 S	140.00 W
Frenchs Forest, Austl.	192a		33.45 S	151.14 E
French Somaliland see Djibouti, ctry., Afr.	82	E8	11.30 N	43.00 E
French Stream, stm., Ma., U.S.	201		42.07 N	70.53 W
Freneuse, Fr.	179		49.03 N	1.36 E
Frenštát pod Radhoštěm, Czech Rep.	24	G14	49.33 N	18.14 E
Frentani, Monti dei, mts., Italy	30	I11	41.54 N	14.37 E
Frépillon, Fr.	179		49.03 N	2.12 E
Fresco, C. Iv.	84	H3	5.05 N	5.34 W
Fresco, stm., Braz.	164	E7	6.39 S	52.00 W
Freshfield, Eng., U.K.	180		53.34 N	3.04 W
Freshfield, Mount, mtn., Can.	144	E14	51.44 N	116.57 W
Fresh Meadows, ngh., N.Y., U.S.	194		40.44 N	73.48 W
Fresh Pond, l., Ma., U.S.	201		42.23 N	71.09 W
Fresh Pond, l., N.Y., U.S.	194		40.55 N	73.18 W
Fresnes, Fr.	179		48.45 N	2.19 E
Fresnes-sur-Marne, Fr.	179		48.56 N	2.45 E
Fresnillo, Mex.	154	D7	23.09 N	102.51 W
Fresno, Col.	168	E4	5.09 N	75.01 W
Fresno, Ca., U.S.	148	G6	36.45 N	119.46 W
Fresno, stm., Ca., U.S.	148	F6	37.00 N	120.30 W
Fresno Reservoir, res., Mt., U.S.	146	B16	48.37 N	109.58 W
Fresvikbreen, ice, Nor.	16	F4	61.02 N	6.45 E
Freu, Cap des, c., Spain	28	E14	39.44 N	3.27 E
Freudenberg, Ger.	182a		52.42 N	13.49 E
Freudenstadt, Ger.	24	H4	48.28 N	8.24 E
Frewena, Austl.	96	C7	19.25 S	135.23 E
Frewsburg, N.Y., U.S.	124	B6	42.03 N	79.11 W
Freycinet National Park, p.o.i., Austl.	99a	o14	42.13 S	148.18 E
Freycinet Peninsula, pen., Austl.	99a	o14	42.13 S	148.18 E
Freyre, Arg.	172	E6	31.10 S	62.06 W
Fria, Gui.	84	G2	10.20 N	13.34 W
Fria, Cape, c., Nmb.	88	D1	18.29 S	12.02 E
Friant, Ca., U.S.	148	G6	36.59 N	119.42 W
Friars Point, Ms., U.S.	134	C8	34.22 N	90.38 W
Frías, Arg.	172	D5	28.38 S	65.07 W
Fribourg (Freiburg), Switz.	30	D4	46.47 N	7.08 E
Frick Park, p.o.i., Pa., U.S.	197b		40.26 N	79.54 W
Friday Harbor, Wa., U.S.	146	B3	48.31 N	123.01 W
Fridley, Mn., U.S.	128	F5	45.05 N	93.15 W
Fridtjof Nansen, Mount, mtn., Ant.	103	D25	85.21 S	167.32 W
Friedberg, Aus.	30	C12	47.27 N	16.02 E
Friedberg, Ger.	24	H7	48.21 N	10.59 E
Friedberg, Ger.	24	F4	50.20 N	8.45 E
Friedenau, ngh., Ger.	182a		52.28 N	13.20 E
Friedland, Ger.	24	C9	53.39 N	13.33 E
Friedrich-Ebert-Brücke, trans., Ger.	181		51.28 N	6.43 E
Friedrich Krupp-Aktiengesellschaft, sci., Ger.	181		51.28 N	7.00 E
Friedrichsfeld, Ger.	181		51.38 N	6.39 E
Friedrichsfelde, ngh., Ger.	182a		52.31 N	13.31 E
Friedrichshafen, Ger.	24	I5	47.39 N	9.28 E
Friedrichshagen, ngh., Ger.	182a		52.27 N	13.38 E
Friedrichshain, ngh., Ger.	182a		52.31 N	13.25 E
Friedrichshof, Ger.	182a		52.19 N	13.46 E
Friedrichstadt, Ger.	24	B4	54.22 N	9.05 E
Friedrichstrasse, Bahnhof, trans., Ger.	182a		52.31 N	13.24 E
Frielas, Port.	184c		38.49 N	9.09 W
Friemersheim, ngh., Ger.	181		51.23 N	6.42 E
Friend, Ne., U.S.	140	G15	40.39 N	97.17 W
Friends Colony, ngh., India	190a		28.34 N	77.16 E
Friendship, N.Y., U.S.	124	B7	42.12 N	78.08 W
Friendship, Tn., U.S.	130	I8	35.54 N	89.14 W
Friendship, Wi., U.S.	128	G9	43.58 N	89.48 W
Friendship Creek, stm., N.J., U.S.	203		39.55 N	74.43 W
Friern Barnet, ngh., Eng., U.K.	178		51.37 N	0.10 W
Fries, Va., U.S.	124	H4	36.43 N	80.59 W
Friesach, Aus.	30	D11	46.56 N	14.23 E
Friesische Inseln see Frisian Islands, is., Eur.	20	A14	53.34 N	6.11 E
Fries Mills, N.J., U.S.	203		39.39 N	75.03 W
Friitala, Fin.	18	F8	61.25 N	21.52 E
Frillendorf, ngh., Ger.	181		51.28 N	7.05 E
Frindsbury, Eng., U.K.	178		51.24 N	0.30 E
Frinsted, Eng., U.K.	178		51.17 N	0.43 E
Frintrop, ngh., Ger.	181		51.29 N	6.55 E
Frio, stm., Tx., U.S.	136	F9	28.29 N	98.11 W
Frio, Cabo, c., Braz.	170	L5	22.53 S	42.00 W
Frio Draw, stm., U.S.	138	G6	34.49 N	102.18 W
Friona, Tx., U.S.	138	G6	34.38 N	102.43 W
Frisco, Tx., U.S.	136	A11	33.09 N	96.49 W
Frisco City, Al., U.S.	134	F11	31.25 N	87.24 W
Frisco Creek, stm., U.S.	138	E7	36.34 N	101.23 W
Frisian Islands, is., Eur.	20	A14	53.26 N	5.50 E
Fristad, Swe.	16	J10	57.49 N	12.59 E
Fritch, Tx., U.S.	138	F7	35.38 N	101.36 W
Fritsla, Swe.	16	J10	57.32 N	12.46 E
Fritzlar, Ger.	24	E5	51.08 N	9.17 E
Friuli, hist. reg., Italy	30	E9	46.00 N	13.00 E
Friuli-Venezia Giulia, state, Italy	30	D10	46.15 N	13.00 E
Frjazino, Russia	26	E21	55.56 N	38.03 E
Frjazino, Russia	183b		55.58 N	38.04 E
Frobisher, Sk., Can.	142	E11	49.12 N	102.26 W
Frobisher Bay, b., Nu., Can.	110	C17	62.30 N	66.00 W
Frobisher Lake, l., Sk., Can.	110	D9	56.21 N	108.16 W
Frodsham, Eng., U.K.	180		53.18 N	2.44 W
Frohavet, strt., Nor.	16	D7	63.52 N	9.26 E
Frohlinde, ngh., Ger.	181		51.32 N	7.21 E
Frohnau, ngh., Ger.	182a		52.38 N	13.18 E
Frohnhausen, Ger.	181		51.29 N	7.48 E
Frohnhausen, ngh., Ger.	181		51.27 N	6.58 E
Froid, Mt., U.S.	142	F9	48.21 N	104.30 W
Frolovo, Russia	40	G13	49.47 N	43.39 E
Froman Run, stm., Pa., U.S.	197b		40.12 N	80.00 W
Fromberg, Mt., U.S.	140	B4	45.23 N	108.55 W
Frombork, Pol.	24	B15	54.22 N	19.43 E
Frome, Eng., U.K.	10	J10	51.14 N	2.19 W
Frome, stm., Austl.	98	G2	29.42 S	138.45 E
Frome, Lake, l., Austl.	98	H2	30.41 S	139.47 E
Frome Downs, Austl.	98	H2	31.13 S	139.45 E
Frömern, Ger.	181		51.30 N	7.44 E
Frönsberg, Ger.	181		51.21 N	7.46 E
Fronteiras, Braz.	170	D5	7.05 S	40.37 W
Frontenac, Ks., U.S.	130	G3	37.27 N	94.41 W
Frontera, Mex.	154	B8	26.56 N	101.27 W
Frontera, Mex.	154	F12	18.32 N	92.38 W
Frontier, Sk., Can.	142	E5	49.12 N	108.34 W
Frontier, Wy., U.S.	146	I16	41.49 N	110.32 W
Frontino, Col.	164	B2	6.46 N	76.08 W
Frontino, Páramo, mtn., Col.	168	D3	6.26 N	76.06 W
Frontón, Isla, i., Peru	204d		12.07 S	77.11 W
Front Range, mts., Co., U.S.	118	H13	39.34 N	105.48 W
Front Royal, Va., U.S.	124	F7	38.55 N	78.11 W
Frosinone, Italy	32	C7	41.38 N	13.20 E
Frösön, Swe.	16	D12	63.11 N	14.36 E
Frost, Tx., U.S.	136	B11	32.04 N	96.48 W
Frostburg, Md., U.S.	124	E7	39.39 N	78.55 W
Frostisen, mtn., Nor.	14	D8	68.12 N	17.12 E
Frostproof, Fl., U.S.	132	I4	27.44 N	81.31 W
Frövi, Swe.	16	H13	59.28 N	15.23 E
Frøya, i., Nor.	16	D6	63.43 N	8.42 E
Frøya, i., Nor.	16	F2	61.47 N	4.51 E
Frøyfjorden, strt., Nor.	16	D6	63.39 N	8.38 E
Frøyningsfjellet, mtn., Nor.	16	B11	65.00 N	13.03 E
Frøysjøen, b., Nor.	16	F2	61.48 N	5.05 E
Fruges, Fr.	20	D11	50.31 N	2.08 E
Fruita, Co., U.S.	150	D8	39.09 N	108.43 W
Fruitdale, Al., U.S.	134	F10	31.20 N	88.24 W
Fruitdale, Or., U.S.	146	H3	42.24 N	123.19 W
Fruithurst, Al., U.S.	134	D13	33.43 N	85.26 W
Fruitland, Id., U.S.	146	F10	44.00 N	116.54 W
Fruitland, Md., U.S.	124	F10	38.19 N	75.36 W
Fruitport, Mi., U.S.	130	A11	43.08 N	86.09 W
Fruitvale, B.C., Can.	144	G13	49.06 N	117.32 W
Fruitvale, Wa., U.S.	146	D6	46.36 N	120.32 W
Fruitville, Fl., U.S.	132	I3	27.19 N	82.27 W
Frumușita, Rom.	36	D14	45.40 N	28.04 E
Frunze see Biškek, Kyrg.	48	F12	42.52 N	74.34 E
Frunze, Ukr.	38	G13	46.15 N	35.52 E
Frunzivka, Ukr.	38	F8	47.20 N	29.45 E
Frutal, Braz.	170	J1	20.01 S	48.56 W
Frutigen, Switz.	30	D4	46.34 N	7.38 E
Frýdek-Místek, Czech Rep.	24	G14	49.41 N	18.21 E
Frýdlant, Czech Rep.	24	F11	50.55 N	15.04 E
Frye, Pa., U.S.	197b		40.11 N	79.56 W
Fryeburg, Me., U.S.	122	G6	44.00 N	70.58 W
Fryerning, Eng., U.K.	178		51.41 N	0.22 E
Fryingpan, stm., Co., U.S.	138	B2	39.22 N	107.02 W
Fu, stm., China	58	F7	28.45 N	116.20 E
Fu, stm., China	58	G6	29.51 N	115.26 E
Fu, stm., China	58	F2	31.03 N	105.17 E
Fua'amotu, Tonga	100e	o14	21.15 S	175.08 W
Fua'amotu International Airport, arpt., Tonga	100e	n14	21.14 S	175.08 W
Fu'an, China	58	H8	27.08 N	119.41 E
Fuchs-Berg, hill, Ger.	182a		52.27 N	13.51 E
Fuchū, Japan	56	E6	34.34 N	133.14 E
Fuchun, stm., China	58	G8	30.06 N	120.10 E
Fucino, Conca del, bas., Italy	30	H10	42.01 N	13.31 E
Fudan University, educ., China	187b		31.17 N	121.29 E
Fuding, China	58	H9	27.21 N	120.13 E
Fuego, Volcán de, vol., Guat.	156	E2	14.29 N	90.53 W

Name	Page	Map Ref.	Latitude	Longitude
Fuelbeckestausee, res., Ger.	181		51.15 N	7.40 E
Fuencaliente, Spain	28	F6	38.24 N	4.18 W
Fuencarral, ngh., Spain	184a		40.30 N	3.41 W
Fuengirola, Spain	28	H6	36.32 N	4.38 W
Fuenlabrada, Spain	184a		40.17 N	3.48 W
Fuensalida, Spain	28	D6	40.02 N	4.12 W
Fuensanta, Embalse de la, res., Spain	28	F8	38.23 N	2.13 W
Fuente, Mex.	136	F7	28.40 N	100.32 W
Fuente de Cantos, Spain	28	F4	38.15 N	6.18 W
Fuente de Oro, Col.	168	F5	3.27 N	73.36 W
Fuente Obejuna, Spain	28	F5	38.15 N	5.26 W
Fuentesaúco, Spain	28	C5	41.13 N	5.29 W
Fuentes de Ebro, Spain	28	C10	41.30 N	0.37 W
Fuerte, stm., Mex.	154	B4	25.51 N	109.25 W
Fuerte Olimpo, Para.	166	D5	21.04 S	57.52 W
Fuerteventura, i., Spain	84	D2	28.20 N	14.00 W
Fuerza, Castillo de la, hist., Cuba	204b		23.09 N	82.21 W
Fuga Island, i., Phil.	68	A3	18.52 N	121.22 E
Fugloy, i., Far. Is.	12b	m34	62.20 N	6.17 W
Fugløya, i., Nor.	14	E4	67.04 N	13.48 E
Fugløya, i., Nor.	14	B11	70.16 N	20.15 E
Fugou, China	58	D6	34.03 N	114.23 E
Fuhai, China	52	B2	47.07 N	87.24 E
Fuhlenbrock, ngh., Ger.	181		51.32 N	6.54 E
Fuhse, stm., Ger.	20	B18	52.38 N	9.59 E
Fuji, Japan	56	D11	35.08 N	138.39 E
Fuji, stm., Japan	56	D11	35.07 N	138.39 E
Fuji, Mount see Fuji-san, vol., Japan	56	D11	35.22 N	138.44 E
Fujian, state, China	58	I8	26.00 N	118.00 E
Fujieda, Japan	56	E11	34.52 N	138.15 E
Fujikubo, Japan	186		35.50 N	139.32 E
Fujin, China	52	B11	47.15 N	132.01 E
Fujinomiya, Japan	56	D11	35.12 N	138.38 E
Fuji-san (Fuji, Mount), vol., Japan	56	D11	35.22 N	138.44 E
Fujisawa, Japan	56	D12	35.20 N	139.29 E
Fujiyama see Fuji-san, vol., Japan	56	D11	35.22 N	138.44 E
Fuji-yoshida, Japan	56	D11	35.29 N	138.48 E
Fukagawa, Japan	54	C14	43.43 N	142.03 E
Fukagawa, ngh., Japan	186		35.40 N	139.48 E
Fukami, Japan	186		35.28 N	139.28 E
Fukang, China	52	C2	44.09 N	87.58 E
Fuka Shan, mtn., China	52	B9	47.56 N	120.56 E
Fukave, i., Tonga	100e	n14	21.05 S	175.02 W
Fukaya, Japan	56	C12	36.11 N	139.17 E
Fukiai, ngh., Japan	188		34.42 N	135.12 E
Fukien see Fujian, state, China	58	I8	26.00 N	118.00 E
Fukuchiyama, Japan	56	D8	35.18 N	135.07 E
Fukue, Japan	56	G1	32.41 N	128.50 E
Fukuei Chiao, c., Tai.	58	I9	25.18 N	121.32 E
Fukue-jima, i., Japan	56	G1	32.40 N	128.45 E
Fukui, Japan	56	C9	36.04 N	136.13 E
Fukui, Japan	188		34.51 N	135.34 E
Fukui, state, Japan	56	D9	36.00 N	136.15 E
Fukuoka, Japan	56	F3	33.34 N	130.24 E
Fukuoka, state, Japan	56	F3	33.45 N	130.30 E
Fukuroi, Japan	56	E10	34.44 N	137.55 E
Fukushima, Japan	56	B13	37.45 N	140.28 E
Fukushima, state, Japan	56	B13	37.08 N	140.00 E
Fukushima, ngh., Japan	188		34.42 N	135.29 E
Fukusumi, Japan	188		34.37 N	135.56 E
Fukutani, ngh., Japan	188		34.43 N	135.02 E
Fukuyama, Japan	56	E6	34.29 N	133.22 E
Fūlādī, Kūh-e, mtn., Afg.	72	C10	34.38 N	67.32 E
Fūlād Mahalleh, Iran	74	B13	36.03 N	53.45 E
Fulaga, i., Fiji	101e	q20	19.09 S	178.35 W
Fulaga Passage, strt., Fiji	101e	q20	18.52 S	178.48 W
Fulda, Ger.	24	F5	50.33 N	9.41 E
Fulda, Mn., U.S.	128	H3	43.52 N	95.35 W
Fulda, stm., Ger.	24	E5	51.25 N	9.39 E
Fulerum, ngh., Ger.	181		51.26 N	6.57 E
Fulham, ngh., Eng., U.K.	178		51.29 N	0.12 W
Fuling, China	58	G2	29.42 N	107.23 E
Fullarton, stm., Austl.	98	C3	20.17 S	141.09 E
Fullerton, Ca., U.S.	148	J8	33.52 N	117.55 W
Fullerton, Md., U.S.	202b		39.22 N	76.31 W
Fullerton, Ne., U.S.	140	F14	41.22 N	97.58 W
Fullerton Municipal Airport, arpt., Ca., U.S.	198		33.52 N	117.59 W
Fullerton Point, c., Antig.	159b	f4	17.06 N	61.53 W
Fulmer, Eng., U.K.	178		51.33 N	0.34 W
Fulong, China	58	J2	22.59 N	107.40 E
Fulpmes, Aus.	24	I7	47.10 N	11.21 E
Fulton, Al., U.S.	134	F11	31.47 N	87.43 W
Fulton, Ar., U.S.	134	D5	33.37 N	93.49 W
Fulton, Il., U.S.	130	C7	41.51 N	90.09 W
Fulton, Ks., U.S.	130	F3	38.00 N	94.41 W
Fulton, Ky., U.S.	130	H9	36.30 N	88.52 W
Fulton, Ms., U.S.	134	C10	34.14 N	88.24 W
Fulton, Mo., U.S.	130	F5	38.51 N	91.56 W
Fulton, N.Y., U.S.	126	E13	43.19 N	76.25 W
Fulton, Tx., U.S.	136	F10	28.04 N	97.02 W
Fulton, stm., B.C., Can.	144	B4	54.48 N	126.09 W
Fultondale, Al., U.S.	134	D12	33.36 N	86.47 W
Fuluälven, stm., Swe.	16	F11	61.18 N	13.04 E
Fulufjället, mtn., Swe.	16	F10	61.33 N	12.43 E
Fulufjället (Fulufjellet), mts., Eur.	16	F10	61.31 N	12.44 E
Fulufjellet (Fulufjället), mts., Eur.	16	F10	61.31 N	12.44 E
Fumay, Fr.	20	D13	49.59 N	4.42 E
Fumel, Fr.	22	E6	44.29 N	0.56 E
Funa, stm., D.R.C.	191b		4.23 S	15.19 E
Funabashi, Japan	56	D12	35.42 N	139.58 E
Funafuti, Tuvalu	92	D8	8.29 S	179.11 E
Funafuti, i., Tuvalu	92	D8	8.29 S	179.11 E
Funan see Fushun, China	52	C9	41.51 N	123.54 E
Funan, China	58	E6	32.37 N	115.34 E
Funasaka, Japan	188		34.48 N	135.17 E
Funäsdalen, Swe.	16	E10	62.33 N	12.32 E
Funchal, Port.	84	C1	32.38 N	16.53 W
Fundación, Col.	168	B4	10.31 N	74.11 W
Fundão, Port.	28	D3	40.08 N	7.29 W
Fundão, Ilha do, i., Braz.	205a		22.51 S	43.14 W
Funde, India	190c		18.54 N	72.58 E
Fundo, Arroio, stm., Braz.	205a		22.58 S	43.22 W
Fundy, Bay of, b., Can.	122	F10	45.00 N	66.00 W
Fundy National Park, p.o.i., N.B., Can.	122	E11	45.38 N	65.00 W
Fünfkirchen see Pécs, Hung.	36	C5	46.04 N	18.13 E
Funhalouro, Moz.	90	C12	23.05 S	34.23 E
Funing, China	58	E8	33.46 N	119.48 E
Funing, China	64	A7	23.33 N	105.37 E
Funiu Shan, mts., China	58	E5	33.40 N	112.30 E
Funkturm, bldg., Ger.	182a		52.31 N	13.16 E
Funne, stm., Ger.	181		51.42 N	7.36 E
Funnel Creek, stm., Austl.	96	D9	22.19 S	148.56 E
Funnel Hill, hill, India	190c		18.54 N	73.07 E
Funsi, Ghana	84	G4	10.16 N	1.57 W
Funtua, Nig.	84	G6	11.30 N	7.18 E
Fuping, China	58	D3	34.45 N	109.08 E
Fuqing, China	58	I8	25.43 N	119.22 E
Fuquay-Varina, N.C., U.S.	132	A7	35.35 N	78.47 W
Fur, i., Den.	16	K7	56.48 N	9.00 E
Furancungo, Moz.	88	C5	14.53 S	33.36 E
Furculeşti, Rom.	36	F12	43.52 N	25.08 E
Fūrg, Iran	74	F14	28.18 N	55.13 E
Furmanov, Russia	40	C12	57.15 N	41.06 E
Furmanovo, Kaz.	40	G16	49.40 N	49.28 E
Furnace Brook, stm., Ma., U.S.	201		42.06 N	70.43 W
Furnace Creek, stm., Md., U.S.	202b		39.11 N	76.35 W
Furnace Pond, l., Ma., U.S.	201		42.03 N	70.49 W
Furnas, Represa de, res., Braz.	170	K2	21.12 S	45.56 W
Furneaux Group, is., Austl.	99a	m13	40.10 S	148.05 E
Furnes see Veurne, Bel.	20	C11	51.04 N	2.40 E
Furqlus, Syria	76	D8	34.34 N	37.05 E
Fürstenberg see Fürstenberg / Havel, Ger.	24	C9	53.11 N	13.08 E
Fürstenberg / Havel, Ger.	24	C9	53.11 N	13.08 E
Fürstenfeld, Aus.	30	C13	47.02 N	16.07 E
Fürstenfeldbruck, Ger.	24	H7	48.10 N	11.15 E
Fürstenwalde, Ger.	24	D9	52.21 N	14.04 E
Fürth, Ger.	24	G6	49.28 N	10.59 E
Furth im Wald, Ger.	24	G8	49.18 N	12.50 E
Furubō-san, hill, Japan	188		34.53 N	135.19 E
Furudal, Swe.	16	F13	61.10 N	15.09 E
Furukawa, Japan	56	C10	36.14 N	137.11 E
Furukawa, Japan	56	A13	38.34 N	140.58 E
Furusund, Swe.	16	H16	59.40 N	18.55 E
Furuyakami, Japan	186		35.55 N	139.32 E
Fürwiggestausee, res., Ger.	181		51.09 N	7.41 E
Fury and Hecla Strait, strt., Nu., Can.	110	B14	69.56 N	84.00 W
Fusagasugá, Col.	168	E4	4.20 N	74.22 W
Fusan see Pusan, Kor., S.	54	G8	35.06 N	129.02 E
Fuse see Higashiōsaka, Japan	56	E8	34.39 N	135.35 E
Fuse, Japan	186		35.53 N	140.00 E
Fushan, China	58	D4	35.59 N	111.50 E
Fushan, China	58	C9	37.29 N	121.16 E
Fushimi, ngh., Japan	188		34.55 N	135.46 E
Fushun, China	52	C9	41.51 N	123.54 E
Fushun, China	58	G1	29.11 N	104.59 E
Fusilier, Sk., Can.	142	C4	51.51 N	109.46 W
Fusong, China	52	C10	42.19 N	127.16 E
Füssen, Ger.	24	I6	47.34 N	10.42 E
Fuste, Picacho del, mtn., Mex.	136	G5	27.35 N	102.43 W
Fusui, China	58	J2	22.37 N	107.54 E
Futamata see Tenryū, Japan	56	E10	34.52 N	137.49 E
Futamatagawa, ngh., Japan	186		35.28 N	139.33 E
Futang, China	58	I5	24.23 N	112.07 E
Futatabi-yama, mtn., Japan	188		34.43 N	135.11 E
Futatsubashi, ngh., Japan	186		35.28 N	139.30 E
Fu Tau Fan Chau, i., China	189d		22.21 N	114.22 E
Futrikelv, Nor.	14	C9	69.46 N	19.02 E
Futtsu-misaki, c., Japan	186		35.19 N	139.46 E
Futun, stm., China	58	H7	26.48 N	117.47 E
Futuna, Île, i., Wal./F.	94	E9	14.18 S	178.08 W
Futuyu, China	58	B6	39.19 N	114.46 E
Fuwa, Egypt	76	G1	31.12 N	30.33 E
Fuxian see Wafangdian, China	58	B9	39.37 N	122.00 E
Fuxian Hu, l., China	52	G5	24.29 N	102.53 E
Fuxin, China	52	C9	42.08 N	121.44 E
Fuxing Dao, i., China	187b		31.17 N	121.23 E
Fuyang, China	58	E6	32.54 N	115.49 E
Fuyang, stm., China	58	C6	38.11 N	116.04 E
Fuyu, China	52	B9	47.48 N	124.28 E
Fuyu, China	52	B9	45.10 N	124.49 E
Fuyuan, China	52	F5	25.39 N	104.12 E
Fuyuan, China	52	B11	48.21 N	134.17 E
Fuzhou, China	58	H8	26.06 N	119.17 E
Fuzhou, China	58	G7	28.01 N	116.20 E
Füzuli, Azer.	42	F12	39.35 N	47.09 E
Fylde, mun., Eng., U.K.	180		53.46 N	2.53 W
Fylí, Grc.	185c		38.06 N	23.40 E
Fylí, hist., Grc.	34	E6	38.06 N	23.40 E
Fyn, state, Den.	16	L8	55.20 N	10.25 E
Fyn, i., Den.	16	L8	55.20 N	10.30 E
Fyne, Loch, b., Scot., U.K.	10	E7	56.00 N	5.24 W
Fyresdal, Nor.	16	H6	59.11 N	8.06 E
Fyresvatnet, l., Nor.	16	H5	59.05 N	8.10 E

G

Name	Page	Map Ref.	Latitude	Longitude
Gaaden, Aus.	182b		48.03 N	16.12 E
Gaalkacyo, Som.	86	C9	6.46 N	47.26 E
Gabare, Blg.	36	F10	43.18 N	23.55 E
Gabarus, N.S., Can.	122	E16	45.50 N	60.09 W
Gabarus Bay, b., N.S., Can.	122	E16	45.51 N	60.07 W
Gabas, stm., Fr.	22	F5	43.46 N	0.42 W
Gabbs, Nv., U.S.	148	E8	38.52 N	117.55 W
Gabela, Ang.	88	C1	10.51 S	14.21 E
Gaberones see Gaborone, Bots.	90	D7	24.40 S	25.56 E
Gabès, Tun.	84	C7	33.53 N	10.05 E
Gabès, Golfe de, b., Tun.	84	C7	34.13 N	10.30 E
Gabiarra, Braz.	170	I6	16.15 S	39.41 W
Gabii, hist., Italy	185a		41.54 N	12.43 E
Gąbin, Pol.	24	D15	52.24 N	19.43 E
Gable Mountain, mtn., B.C., Can.	144	B9	54.30 N	121.40 W
Gablonz see Jablonec nad Nisou, Czech Rep.	24	F11	50.43 N	15.10 E
Gabon, ctry., Afr.	84	J7	1.00 S	11.45 E
Gaborone, Bots.	90	D7	24.40 S	25.56 E
Gabras, Sudan	82	E5	10.17 N	26.14 E
Gabriel Strait, strt., Nu., Can.	110	C17	61.45 N	65.30 W
Gabriel y Galán, Embalse de, res., Spain	28	D4	40.15 N	6.07 W
Gabrovo, Blg.	36	G12	42.51 N	25.19 E
Gacé, Fr.	20	F9	48.47 N	0.17 E
Gachetá, Col.	168	E5	4.49 N	73.38 W
Gachsārān, Iran	74	E12	30.12 N	50.47 E
Gackle, N.D., U.S.	140	A13	46.37 N	99.08 W
Gacko, Bos.	36	F5	43.10 N	18.32 E
Gädäbäy, Azer.	42	E11	40.34 N	45.49 E
Gadag, India	69	D2	15.25 N	75.37 E
Gādarwāra, India	70	G7	22.55 N	78.47 E
Gäddede, Swe.	16	C12	64.29 N	14.09 E
Gade, stm., Eng., U.K.	178		51.38 N	0.28 W
Gado Bravo, Ilha do, i., Braz.	170	F4	10.54 S	42.51 W
Gádor, Spain	28	H8	36.56 N	2.28 W
Gadra, Pak.	70	F3	25.40 N	70.37 E
Gadsden, Al., U.S.	134	C12	34.00 N	86.00 W
Gadsden, Az., U.S.	150	K2	32.33 N	114.46 W
Gadwāl, India	69	C3	16.14 N	77.48 E
Gael Hamke Bugt, b., Grnld.	108	C22	74.00 N	20.30 W
Găeşti, Rom.	36	E12	44.43 N	25.19 E
Gaeta, Italy	32	C7	41.12 N	13.34 E
Gaeta, Golfo di, b., Italy	32	C7	41.06 N	13.30 E
Gaferut, i., Micron.	94	C5	9.12 N	145.23 E
Gaffney, S.C., U.S.	132	A4	35.04 N	81.39 W
Gafour, Tun.	32	H3	36.19 N	9.19 E
Gafsa, Tun.	84	C6	34.24 N	8.48 E
Gag, Pulau, i., Indon.	60	F8	0.27 S	129.52 E
Gagarin, Russia	26	E17	55.32 N	34.58 E
Gage, Ok., U.S.	138	E9	36.18 N	99.45 W
Gagere, stm., Nig.	84	G6	13.20 N	6.22 E
Gages Lake, Il., U.S.	196		42.21 N	87.59 W
Gages Lake, l., Il., U.S.	196		42.21 N	88.00 W
Gagetown, N.B., Can.	122	E10	45.46 N	66.09 W
Gagetown, Canadian Forces Base, mil., N.B., Can.	122	E10	45.43 N	66.15 W
Gaggenau, Ger.	24	H4	48.48 N	8.19 E
Gagino, Russia	40	D14	55.14 N	45.02 E
Gagliano del Capo, Italy	32	E12	39.50 N	18.22 E
Gagnoa, C. Iv.	84	H3	6.07 N	5.56 W
Gagnon, Lac, l., Qc., Can.	126	B14	46.07 N	75.07 W
Gagny, Fr.	179		48.53 N	2.32 E
Gagra, Geor.	42	D9	43.20 N	40.15 E
Gaibandha, Bngl.	70	F12	25.19 N	89.32 E
Gaigalava, Lat.	26	D10	56.43 N	27.03 E
Gail, Tx., U.S.	136	B6	32.46 N	101.27 W
Gail, stm., Aus.	30	D10	46.36 N	13.53 E
Gaillac, Fr.	22	F7	43.54 N	1.55 E
Gaillimh see Galway, Ire.	10	H3	53.16 N	9.03 W
Gaillon, Fr.	179		49.02 N	1.54 E
Gailtaler Alpen, mts., Aus.	30	D10	46.41 N	13.11 E
Gaimán, Arg.	166	H3	43.17 S	65.29 W
Gainesboro, Tn., U.S.	130	H12	36.21 N	85.39 W
Gainesville, Fl., U.S.	132	G3	29.39 N	82.18 W
Gainesville, Ga., U.S.	132	B2	34.18 N	83.49 W
Gainesville, Mo., U.S.	130	H5	36.36 N	92.26 W
Gainesville, Tx., U.S.	138	H11	33.37 N	97.08 W
Gainsborough, Sk., Can.	142	E12	49.10 N	101.25 W
Gainsborough, Eng., U.K.	10	H12	53.23 N	0.46 W
Gainsborough Creek, stm., Can.	142	E12	49.10 N	101.02 W
Gairdner, Lake, l., Austl.	96	F7	31.33 S	135.56 E
Gairloch, Scot., U.K.	10	D7	57.42 N	5.40 W
Gairloch, Loch, b., Scot., U.K.	10	D6	57.43 N	5.45 W
Gaithersburg, Md., U.S.	124	E8	39.08 N	77.11 W
Gaixian, China	58	A10	40.23 N	122.22 E
Gaizina Kalns, hill, Lat.	26	D8	56.52 N	25.56 E
Gajā, India	190b		22.52 N	88.10 E
Gajendragarh, India	69	D2	15.43 N	75.58 E
Gajly, gora, hill, Turkmen.	42	E15	40.02 N	53.17 E
Gajny, Russia	48	B8	60.18 N	54.18 E
Gajuapara, stm., Braz.	170	C2	4.17 S	47.25 W
Gajutino, Russia	26	B21	58.42 N	38.32 E
Gakarosa, mtn., S. Afr.	90	E6	27.54 S	23.33 E
Gakona, Ak., U.S.	109	D10	62.18 N	145.18 W
Gakugsa, Russia	18	F23	61.33 N	36.27 E
Galahad, Ab., Can.	144	D19	52.30 N	111.55 W
Galâla el Baharîya, Gebel el-, mts., Egypt	76	I3	29.20 N	32.00 E
Galâla el-Qiblîya, Gebel el-, mts., Egypt	76	J3	28.42 N	32.22 E
Galamares, Port.	184c		38.48 N	9.25 W
Galán, Cerro, mtn., Arg.	172	C4	25.56 S	66.54 W
Galana, stm., Kenya	86	E7	3.09 S	40.08 E
Galanta, Slvk.	24	H13	48.11 N	17.43 E
Galapagos Islands see Colón, Archipiélago de, is., Ec.	164a	h12	0.42 N	91.30 W
Galaroza, Spain	28	G4	37.55 N	6.42 W
Galashiels, Scot., U.K.	10	F10	55.37 N	2.50 W
Galata, ngh., Tur.	185b		41.01 N	28.58 E
Galata Köprüsü, trans., Tur.	185b		41.00 N	28.57 E
Galata Tower, bldg., Tur.	185b		41.01 N	28.58 E
Galați, Rom.	36	D14	45.26 N	28.02 E
Galați, state, Rom.	36	D14	45.45 N	27.45 E
Galatia, Il., U.S.	130	G9	37.50 N	88.36 W
Galatina, Italy	32	D12	40.10 N	18.10 E
Galátsion, Grc.	185c		38.01 N	23.45 E
Galatz see Galați, Rom.	36	D14	45.26 N	28.02 E
Galax, Va., U.S.	124	H5	36.39 N	80.56 W
Galaxídi, Grc.	34	E5	38.22 N	22.22 E
Galdhøpiggen, mtn., Nor.	16	F6	61.37 N	8.17 E
Gale, Lac, l., Qc., Can.	126	B13	46.45 N	76.50 W
Galeana, Mex.	130	F9	30.07 N	107.38 W
Galeana, Mex.	154	C8	24.49 N	100.04 W
Galeh Dār, Iran	74	G13	27.38 N	52.42 E
Galela, Indon.	60	E8	1.49 N	127.50 E
Galena, Ak., U.S.	109	D8	64.44 N	156.57 W
Galena, Il., U.S.	130	B7	42.24 N	90.25 W
Galena, Ks., U.S.	130	G3	37.05 N	94.38 W
Galena, Mo., U.S.	130	H4	36.48 N	93.28 W
Galena Park, Tx., U.S.	136	E12	29.43 N	95.13 W
Galeota Point, c., Trin.	159f	s13	10.08 N	60.59 W
Galera, Punta, c., Chile	166	G2	39.58 S	73.40 W
Galera, Punta, c., Ec.	168	G1	0.49 N	80.03 W
Galera, Punta de sa, c., Spain	28	E12	39.07 N	1.32 E
Galera Point, c., Trin.	159f	s13	10.49 N	60.54 W
Galeras, Volcán, vol., Col.	168	G3	1.13 N	77.22 W
Galeria, hist., Italy	185a		42.02 N	12.18 E
Galeria, Fosso la, stm., Italy	185a		41.48 N	12.21 E
Galesburg, Il., U.S.	130	D7	40.56 N	90.22 W
Gales Point, c., Ma., U.S.	201		42.33 N	70.47 W
Galesville, Wi., U.S.	128	G7	44.04 N	91.20 W
Galeton, Pa., U.S.	124	C8	41.44 N	77.39 W
Galheiros, Braz.	170	G2	13.18 S	46.25 W
Gali, Geor.	42	D9	42.37 N	41.44 E
Gali, Torrente de, stm., Spain	184d		41.28 N	2.00 E
Galiano Island, i., B.C., Can.	144	H7	48.56 N	123.29 W
Galič, Russia	40	B13	58.22 N	42.21 E
Galicia, state, Spain	28	B2	42.45 N	8.00 W
Galicia, hist. reg., Eur.	24	G18	49.33 N	22.36 E
Galičica Nacionalni Park, p.o.i., Mac.	34	C3	40.59 N	20.52 E
Galicja see Galicia, hist. reg., Eur.	24	G18	49.33 N	22.36 E
Galičskaja vozvyšennost', hills, Russia	12	G20	58.25 N	42.20 E
Galičskoe, ozero, l., Russia	12	G20	58.24 N	42.18 E
Galilee, Lake, l., Austl.	98	D5	22.21 S	145.48 E
Galilee, Sea of see Kinneret, Yam, l., Isr.	76	F6	32.48 N	35.35 E
Galiléia, Braz.	170	J5	19.00 S	41.32 W
Galina Point, c., Jam.	158d	i14	18.24 N	76.53 W
Galindo Creek, stm., Ca., U.S.	200		37.58 N	122.02 W
Galion, Oh., U.S.	124	D3	40.43 N	82.47 W
Galion, Baie du, b., Mart.	159c	k7	14.42 N	60.54 W
Galisteo Creek, stm., N.M., U.S.	138	F3	35.31 N	106.22 W
Galite, Canal de la, strt., Tun.	32	G2	37.20 N	9.00 E
Galiuro Mountains, mts., Az., U.S.	150	K6	32.40 N	110.20 W
Galkhausen, Ger.	181		51.05 N	6.58 E
Gallarate, Italy	30	E5	45.40 N	8.47 E
Gallatin, Mo., U.S.	130	E3	39.54 N	93.57 W
Gallatin, Pa., U.S.	197b		40.12 N	79.53 W
Gallatin, Tn., U.S.	130	H11	36.23 N	86.26 W
Gallatin, stm., U.S.	146	E15	45.56 N	111.30 W
Gallatin Range, mts., Mt., U.S.	146	E15	45.15 N	111.05 W
Galle, Sri L.	69	H5	6.02 N	80.13 E
Gállego, stm., Spain	28	C10	41.39 N	0.50 W
Gallegos, stm., Arg.	166	J3	51.35 S	68.59 W
Galleyend, Eng., U.K.	178		51.42 N	0.29 E
Galleywood, Eng., U.K.	178		51.42 N	0.28 E
Galliano, La., U.S.	134	H8	29.26 N	90.18 W
Gallicano nel Lazio, Italy	185a		41.52 N	12.49 E
Gallinas, stm., N.M., U.S.	138	F4	35.09 N	104.55 W
Gallinas, Punta, c., Col.	168	A6	12.27 N	71.39 W
Gallinas Creek, stm., Ca., U.S.	200		38.01 N	122.30 W
Gallinas Peak, mtn., N.M., U.S.	138	G3	34.13 N	105.45 W
Gallipoli, Italy	32	D11	40.03 N	17.59 E
Gallipoli see Gelibolu, Tur.	34	C9	40.25 N	26.41 E
Gallipoli Peninsula see Gelibolu Yarımadası, pen., Tur.	34	C9	40.20 N	26.30 E
Gallipolis, Oh., U.S.	124	F3	38.48 N	82.11 W
Gällivare, Swe.	14	E11	67.08 N	20.40 E
Gällö, Swe.	16	E13	62.55 N	15.14 E
Gallo, Capo, c., Italy	32	F7	38.13 N	13.19 E
Gallo Arroyo, stm., N.M., U.S.	138	G3	33.51 N	104.46 W
Galloo Island, i., N.Y., U.S.	126	E13	43.54 N	76.25 W
Galloupes Point, c., Ma., U.S.	201		42.28 N	70.53 W
Galloway, hist. reg., Scot., U.K.	10	G8	54.56 N	4.18 W
Galloway, Mull of, c., Scot., U.K.	10	G8	54.38 N	4.52 W
Galloway Creek, stm., Md., U.S.	202b		39.18 N	76.23 W
Galloway Creek, stm., Mi., U.S.	199		42.39 N	83.12 W
Gallius, Fr.	179		48.48 N	1.48 E
Gallup, N.M., U.S.	150	H8	35.31 N	108.44 W
Gallur, Spain	28	C9	41.53 N	1.18 W
Gallura, reg., Italy	32	C3	41.01 N	9.12 E
Gally, Ru de, stm., Fr.	179		48.53 N	1.53 E
Galoa Harbour, b., Fiji	101e	q19	19.04 S	178.12 E
Galoppatóio, p.o.i., Italy	185a		41.49 N	12.35 E
Galt, Ca., U.S.	148	E4	38.15 N	121.18 W
Galtat Zemmour, W. Sah.	84	D2	25.15 N	12.20 W
Galty Mountains, mts., Ire.	10	I4	52.22 N	8.08 W
Galva, Il., U.S.	130	C7	41.09 N	90.02 W
Galva, Ia., U.S.	128	I3	42.30 N	95.25 W
Galva, Ks., U.S.	128	C11	38.22 N	97.32 W
Galvarino, Chile	172	I1	38.25 S	72.47 W
Galveston, In., U.S.	130	D11	40.34 N	86.11 W
Galveston, Tx., U.S.	136	E13	29.17 N	94.47 W
Galveston Bay, b., Tx., U.S.	136	E13	29.36 N	94.57 W
Galveston Island, i., Tx., U.S.	136	E13	29.13 N	94.55 W
Gálvez, Arg.	172	F7	32.02 S	61.13 W
Galvin, Austl.	192b		37.51 S	144.49 E
Galway (Gaillimh), Ire.	10	H3	53.16 N	9.03 W
Galway, state, Ire.	10	H4	53.20 N	9.00 W
Galway Bay, b., Ire.	10	H3	53.10 N	9.15 W
Gam (Jin), stm., Asia	64	A7	21.54 N	105.11 E
Gama, Isla, i., Arg.	166	H4	40.29 S	62.12 W
Gamagōri, Japan	56	E10	34.49 N	137.14 E
Gamaliel, Ky., U.S.	130	H12	36.38 N	85.47 W
Gamarra, Col.	168	C5	8.20 N	73.43 W
Gamay, Phil.	68	D5	12.24 N	125.17 E
Gamba, China	70	D12	28.17 N	88.31 E
Gambaga, Ghana	84	G4	10.32 N	0.26 W
Gambais, Fr.	179		48.46 N	1.40 E
Gambaiseuil, Fr.	179		48.45 N	1.44 E
Gambēla, Eth.	82	F6	8.14 N	34.35 E
Gambell, Ak., U.S.	109	D5	63.46 N	171.44 W
Gambia (Gambie), stm., Afr.	84	G1	13.28 N	16.34 W
Gambia, The, ctry., Afr.	84	G1	13.30 N	15.30 W
Gambie (Gambia), stm., Afr.	84	G2	13.28 N	16.34 W
Gambier, Îles, is., Fr. Poly.	94	F13	21.18 S	136.19 W
Gamboa, Pan.	168	C2	9.06 N	79.41 W
Gamboli, Pak.	70	D2	29.51 N	68.26 E
Gamboma, Congo	86	E3	1.53 S	15.51 E
Gamboula, C.A.R.	86	D2	4.07 N	15.09 E
Game Creek, stm., N.J., U.S.	203		39.41 N	75.28 W
Gamensee, l., Ger.	182a		52.40 N	13.51 E
Gamka, stm., S. Afr.	90	H5	33.17 S	21.38 E
Gamlakarleby see Kokkola, Fin.	18	D10	63.50 N	23.08 E
Gamla Uppsala, Swe.	16	H15	59.54 N	17.37 E
Gamleby, Swe.	16	J14	57.54 N	16.23 E
Gammelstad, rel., Swe.	14	G12	65.38 N	22.01 E
Gammon, stm., Can.	142	C18	51.15 N	95.37 W
Gammon Ranges National Park, p.o.i., Austl.	98	H2	30.29 S	139.12 E
Gamō, Japan	186		35.52 N	139.48 E
Gamoep, S. Afr.	90	F4	29.54 S	18.25 E
Ga-Mogara, stm., S. Afr.	90	E6	27.07 S	22.56 E
Gamova, mys, c., Russia	54	C9	42.33 N	131.12 E
Gampoko, Congo	191b		4.16 S	15.10 E
Gampola, Sri L.	69	H5	7.09 N	80.34 E
Gampoui, Congo	191b		4.08 S	15.22 E
Gan, stm., China	52	B10	49.11 N	125.09 E
Gan, stm., China	58	G6	29.18 N	116.03 E
Ganado, Az., U.S.	150	H7	35.42 N	109.32 W
Ganado, Tx., U.S.	136	E11	29.02 N	96.31 W
Gananoque, On., Can.	126	D13	44.19 N	76.10 W
Ganāveh, Iran	74	F12	29.34 N	50.31 E
Gäncä, Azer.	42	E12	40.41 N	46.20 E
Gand see Gent, Bel.	20	C12	51.03 N	3.43 E
Ganda, Ang.	88	C1	13.01 S	14.38 E
Gandadiwata, Bulu, mtn., Indon.	66	E11	2.42 S	119.27 E
Gandajika, D.R.C.	86	F4	6.43 S	23.56 E
Gandak (Nārāyani), stm., Asia	70	E10	25.38 N	85.10 E
Gándara, Spain	28	A2	43.30 N	8.10 W
Gander, Nf., Can.	111a	j23	48.57 N	54.34 W
Ganderkesee, Ger.	24	C4	53.02 N	8.32 E
Gandesa, Spain	28	C11	41.03 N	0.25 E
Găndeşti, Mol.	38	F7	47.53 N	28.22 E
Gandevi, India	70	H4	20.48 N	73.00 E
Gāndhīnagar, India	70	G4	23.12 N	72.39 E
Gandhi Reservoir see Gāndhi Sāgar, res., India	70	F5	24.27 N	75.28 E
Gāndhi Sāgar, res., India	70	F5	24.27 N	75.28 E
Gandía, Spain	28	F10	38.57 N	0.11 W
Gandu, Braz.	170	G6	13.43 S	39.28 W
Ganga see Ganges, stm., Asia	70	G13	21.58 N	90.56 E
Gangādharpur, India	190b		22.36 N	88.11 E
Gangalingolo, Congo	191b		4.20 S	15.09 E
Gan Gan, Arg.	166	H3	42.31 S	68.16 W
Gangānagar, India	70	D4	29.55 N	73.51 E
Gangāpur, India	69	B2	19.40 N	75.04 E
Gangāpur, India	70	E6	26.29 N	76.43 E
Gangāpur, India	70	F5	25.12 N	74.16 E
Gangārāmpur, India	70	F12	25.24 N	88.31 E
Gangaw, Mya.	64	A2	22.10 N	94.08 E
Gangāwati, India	69	D3	15.26 N	76.32 E
Gangdhār, India	70	G5	23.58 N	75.38 E
Gangdisê Shan, mts., China	70	D11	31.00 N	82.00 E
Ganges, B.C., Can.	144	H7	48.51 N	123.30 W
Ganges, Fr.	22	F9	43.56 N	3.42 E
Ganges (Ganga) (Padma), stm., Asia	70	G13	21.58 N	90.56 E
Ganges, Mouths of the, mth., Asia	70	H12	22.00 N	89.00 E
Ganghu, China	70	B11	32.05 N	86.45 E
Gangi, Italy	32	G8	37.49 N	14.13 E
Gangmar Co, l., China	70	B10	33.39 N	84.18 E
Gangneung see Kangnŭng, Kor., S.	54	F8	37.45 N	128.54 E
Gangoa, China	52	D5	37.17 N	100.14 E
Gangotri, India	70	C7	30.59 N	78.59 E
Gangotri, India	70	C7	31.00 N	78.20 E
Gangou, China	58	A8	40.31 N	119.16 E
Gangoumen, China	54	D2	41.40 N	116.35 E
Gang Ranch, B.C., Can.	144	E8	51.31 N	122.18 W
Gangtok, India	70	E12	27.18 N	88.38 E
Gangu, China	58	D1	34.45 N	105.20 E
Gangweon see Kangwŏn-do, state, Kor., S.	56	B1	37.36 N	128.21 E
Ganjuškino, Kaz.	40	H16	46.36 N	49.16 E
Ganlan Shan, mtn., China	70	C12	29.54 N	90.02 E
Gannan, China	52	B9	47.56 N	123.29 E
Gannat, Fr.	22	C9	46.06 N	3.11 E
Gannett Peak, mtn., Wy., U.S.	140	D3	43.11 N	109.39 W
Gannvalley, S.D., U.S.	140	C14	44.02 N	99.00 W
Ganquan, China	58	C3	36.17 N	109.21 E
Gansbaai, S. Afr.	90	I4	34.33 S	19.22 E
Gansu, state, China	52	D5	37.00 N	103.00 E
Ganta, Lib.	84	H3	7.13 N	8.58 W
Gantang, China	58	J3	22.58 N	109.00 E
Gantang, China	58	H8	26.55 N	119.37 E
Gantt, Al., U.S.	134	F12	31.24 N	86.29 W
Gantung, Indon.	66	E6	2.58 S	108.09 E
Ganxi, China	58	G3	29.02 N	109.32 E
Ganyanchi, China	58	C1	36.39 N	105.17 E
Ganyesa, S. Afr.	90	E7	26.35 S	24.10 E
Ganzê, China	52	E4	31.37 N	100.01 E
Ganzhou, China	58	I6	25.52 N	114.54 E
Gao, Mali	84	F4	16.16 N	0.02 W
Gao'an, China	58	G6	28.25 N	115.22 E
Gaobaita, China	189a		39.53 N	116.30 E
Gaobeidian, China	189a		39.54 N	116.33 E
Gaochun, China	58	F8	31.19 N	118.52 E
Gaodianzi, China	58	F4	30.37 N	110.00 E
Gaohebu, China	58	F7	30.42 N	116.49 E
Gaojiabu, China	58	B4	38.31 N	110.19 E
Gaojian, China	52	F9	29.03 N	121.14 E
Gaojiazhai, China	187b		31.23 N	121.33 E
Gaojiazhen, China	58	F2	30.04 N	107.52 E
Gaolan, China	52	D5	36.17 N	103.57 E
Gaolan Dao, i., China	58	K5	21.55 N	113.15 E
Gaolong, China	58	H5	26.56 N	113.45 E
Gaona, Arg.	172	B5	25.12 S	64.05 W
Gaoping, China	58	D5	35.47 N	112.55 E
Gaoqiao, China	58	G2	28.06 N	106.36 E
Gaotan, China	58	E3	32.23 N	108.17 E
Gaotang, China	58	C7	36.52 N	116.13 E
Gaoua, Burkina	84	G4	10.19 N	3.11 W
Gaoual, Gui.	84	G2	11.45 N	13.12 W
Gaoxian, China	52	F5	28.20 N	104.38 E
Gaoyi, China	58	C6	37.36 N	114.35 E
Gaoyou, China	58	E8	32.46 N	119.25 E
Gaoyou Hu, l., China	58	E8	32.50 N	119.20 E
Gaozhangjia, China	58	C2	36.07 N	107.15 E
Gaozhou, China	58	K4	21.55 N	110.50 E
Gap, Fr.	22	E12	44.34 N	6.04 E
Gapālnagar, India	190b		22.49 N	88.08 E
Gar, China	70	B8	32.16 N	79.59 E
Gar, stm., China	70	C8	32.29 N	79.40 E
Gara, Lough, l., Ire.	10	H4	53.55 N	8.26 W
Garachiné, Pan.	156	H8	8.04 N	78.22 W
Garagumskij kanal (Kara-Kum Canal), can., Turkmen.	72	B9	37.34 N	65.40 E
Garagumskij kanal imeni Prezidenta Turkmenistana S.A. Nijazova see Garagumskij ka, can., Turkmen.	72	B9	37.34 N	65.40 E
Garagumy (Kara-Kum), des., Turkmen.	72	A8	39.00 N	60.00 E
Garah, Austl.	98	G7	29.04 S	149.38 E
Garaina, Pap. N. Gui.	101a	b4	7.51 S	147.07 E
Garānberia, India	190b		22.24 N	88.34 E
Garancières, Fr.	179		48.49 N	1.46 E
Garanhuns, Braz.	170	E7	8.54 S	36.29 W
Garara, Pap. N. Gui.	101a	b4	8.37 S	148.17 E
Garbagna, Italy	184b		45.23 N	8.39 E
Garbagnate Milanese, Italy	184b		45.35 N	9.05 E
Garbatella, ngh., Italy	185a		41.52 N	12.29 E
Garber, Ok., U.S.	138	E11	36.26 N	97.35 W
Garberville, Ca., U.S.	148	C2	40.06 N	123.46 W
Gârbovu, Rom.	36	E10	44.44 N	23.22 E
Garça, Braz.	170	L1	22.13 S	49.39 W
Garcevo, Russia	26	H15	52.45 N	32.59 E
Garches, Fr.	179		48.51 N	2.11 E
Garcia, Mex.	120	G8	29.58 N	108.21 W
García, Laguna, l., Arg.	206		34.58 S	58.09 W
García de Sola, Embalse de, res., Spain	28	E5	39.15 N	5.05 W
Gard, state, Fr.	22	F10	44.00 N	4.00 E
Gard, stm., Fr.	22	F10	43.51 N	4.37 E
Garda, Italy	30	E7	45.34 N	10.42 E
Garda, Lago di, l., Italy	30	E7	45.40 N	10.41 E
Garde, Lac la, l., Qc., Can.	126	B11	46.46 N	78.14 W
Gardelegen, Ger.	24	D7	52.31 N	11.23 E
Garden, stm., On., Can.	126	B6	46.31 N	84.08 W
Garden City, Ga., U.S.	132	D4	32.06 N	81.09 W
Garden City, Ks., U.S.	138	C8	37.58 N	100.51 W
Garden City, Mo., U.S.	130	F3	38.33 N	94.11 W
Garden City, Tx., U.S.	136	C6	31.51 N	101.28 W
Garden City, ngh., Egypt	191c		30.02 N	31.14 E
Garden City see Qasr al-Dubārā, ngh., Egypt	191c		30.02 N	31.14 E
Garden City Park, N.Y., U.S.	194		40.44 N	73.39 W
Garden City Raceway, p.o.i., On., Can.	202a		43.09 N	79.11 W
Gardendale, Al., U.S.	134	D12	33.39 N	86.48 W
Garden Gate Village, Ca., U.S.	200		37.20 N	122.02 W
Garden Grove, Ca., U.S.	148	J7	33.45 N	117.56 W
Garden Grove, Ia., U.S.	130	D4	40.50 N	93.36 W
Garden Island, i., Mi., U.S.	126	C4	45.47 N	85.29 W
Garden Peninsula, pen., Mi., U.S.	126	C3	45.47 N	86.30 W
Garden Plain, Ks., U.S.	138	D11	37.39 N	97.41 W
Garden Reach, India	70	G12	22.33 N	88.17 E

Name	Page	Map Ref.	Latitude	Longitude
Garden State Arts Center, bldg., N.J., U.S.	194		40.24 N	74.11 W
Garden State Park Race Track, p.o.i., N.J., U.S.	203		39.55 N	75.02 W
Garden State Plaza, shp. cen., N.J., U.S.	194		40.55 N	74.05 W
Gardenton, Mb., Can.	142	E17	49.04 N	96.39 W
Gárdevárri, hill, Nor.	14	B15	70.37 N	24.58 E
Gardey, Arg.	172	H8	37.17 S	59.21 W
Gardeyz, Afg.	72	C10	33.36 N	69.13 E
Gardfjället, mtn., Swe.	16	B13	65.25 N	15.41 E
Gardiner, Me., U.S.	122	F7	44.13 N	69.46 W
Gardiner, Mt., U.S.	146	E16	45.01 N	110.42 W
Gardiner, Or., U.S.	146	G2	43.44 N	124.05 W
Gardiner Dam, dam., Sk., Can.	142	C6	51.17 N	106.51 W
Gardiners Bay, b., N.Y., U.S.	124	C13	41.08 N	72.10 W
Gardiners Creek, stm., Austl.	192b		37.50 S	145.02 E
Gardner, Ks., U.S.	130	F3	38.49 N	94.55 W
Gardner, Ma., U.S.	124	B13	42.34 N	71.59 W
Gardner Canal, b., B.C., Can.	144	C2	53.27 N	128.17 W
Gardnerville, Nv., U.S.	148	E6	38.56 N	119.43 W
Gareloi Island, i., Ak., U.S.	109a	g23	51.47 N	178.48 W
Garenfeld, ngh., Ger.	181		51.24 N	7.31 E
Gares see Puente la Reina, Spain	28	B9	42.40 N	1.49 W
Gare Simon, Congo	191b		4.15 S	15.11 E
Garessio, Italy	30	F5	44.12 N	8.01 E
Garet, Mont, vol., Vanuatu	101d	j16	14.16 S	167.30 E
Garfield, Ks., U.S.	138	C9	38.04 N	99.14 W
Garfield, N.M., U.S.	150	K9	32.44 N	107.16 W
Garfield, Wa., U.S.	146	C9	47.00 N	117.08 W
Garfield Mountain, mtn., Mt., U.S.	146	F14	44.31 N	112.37 W
Garfield Park, De., U.S.	203		39.42 N	75.33 W
Garfield Park, p.o.i., Il., U.S.	196		41.53 N	87.43 W
Garfield Park, p.o.i., Oh., U.S.	197a		41.26 N	81.36 W
Garfield Peak, mtn., Wy., U.S.	140	E5	42.47 N	107.18 W
Gargaliánoi, Grc.	34	F4	37.04 N	21.39 E
Gargano, Promontorio del, mts., Italy	30	I12	41.50 N	16.00 E
Gargano, Testa del, c., Italy	30	I13	41.49 N	16.12 E
Gargantua, Cape, c., On., Can.	114	C8	47.35 N	85.01 W
Gargenville, Fr.	179		49.00 N	1.49 E
Garges-lès-Gonesse, Fr.	179		48.58 N	2.25 E
Gargnäs, Swe.	16	B15	65.19 N	17.56 E
Gargždai, Lith.	26	E4	55.42 N	21.24 E
Garhākota, India	70	G7	23.47 N	79.11 E
Garhi Jasaya, India	190a		28.46 N	77.16 E
Garhi Katiya, India	190a		28.45 N	77.16 E
Garibaldi, Braz.	172	D12	29.15 S	51.32 W
Garibaldi, B.C., Can.	144	G7	49.58 N	123.09 W
Garibaldi, Or., U.S.	146	E3	45.33 N	123.55 W
Garibaldi, Mount, vol., B.C., Can.	144	G8	49.51 N	122.59 W
Garibaldi Provincial Park, p.o.i., B.C., Can.	144	G8	49.55 N	122.46 W
Gariep Dam, res., S. Afr.	90	G7	30.40 S	25.40 E
Garies, S. Afr.	90	G4	30.32 S	17.59 E
Garigliano, stm., Italy	32	C7	41.09 N	13.50 E
Gariglione, Monte, mtn., Italy	32	E10	39.09 N	16.41 E
Garín, Arroyo, stm., Arg.	206		34.23 S	58.43 W
Garin Regional Park, p.o.i., Ca., U.S.	200		37.38 N	122.03 W
Garipçe Burnu, c., Tur.	185b		41.13 N	29.07 E
Garissa, Kenya	86	E7	0.26 S	39.38 E
Gariya, India	190b		22.28 N	88.23 E
Gārji, India	190b		22.51 N	88.19 E
Garkida, Nig.	84	G7	10.24 N	12.36 E
Garland, Al., U.S.	134	F12	31.33 N	86.49 W
Garland, Md., U.S.	202b		39.11 N	76.39 W
Garland, Tx., U.S.	136	B11	32.54 N	96.38 W
Garland, Ut., U.S.	150	B4	41.45 N	112.09 W
Garland Park, p.o.i., On., Can.	193b		43.44 N	79.35 W
Garlasco, Italy	30	E5	45.12 N	8.55 E
Garliava, Lith.	26	F6	54.49 N	23.52 E
Garlin, Fr.	22	F5	43.34 N	0.15 W
Garm, Taj.	72	B11	39.01 N	70.22 E
Garmī, Iran	74	A10	39.01 N	48.03 E
Garmisch-Partenkirchen, Ger.	24	I7	47.29 N	11.05 E
Garmo, Qullai see Kommunizma, pik, mtn., Taj.	72	B11	38.57 N	72.01 E
Garmsār, Iran	74	C13	35.14 N	52.19 E
Garnavillo, Ia., U.S.	130	B6	42.52 N	91.14 W
Garne, Fr.	179		48.41 N	1.58 E
Garner, Ia., U.S.	130	A4	43.06 N	93.36 W
Garner, N.C., U.S.	124	I7	35.42 N	78.36 W
Garnet Range, mts., Mt., U.S.	146	D13	46.49 N	113.23 W
Garnett, Ks., U.S.	130	F2	38.16 N	95.14 W
Garnpung Lake, l., Austl.	98	I4	33.30 S	143.12 E
Garnvik, Nor.	14	A19	71.03 N	28.14 E
Garona (Garonne), stm., Eur.	22	E5	45.01 N	0.35 W
Garonne (Garona), stm., Eur.	22	E5	45.01 N	0.35 W
Garoowe, Som.	86	C9	8.24 N	48.28 E
Garoua, Cam.	86	C2	9.18 N	13.23 E
Garoua Boulaï, Cam.	86	C2	5.54 N	14.33 E
Garpenberg, Swe.	16	G14	60.19 N	16.12 E
Garqu Yan, China	52	E3	33.53 N	92.18 E
Garqu Yan, China	70	A14	34.29 N	92.35 E
Garraf, Costa de, cst., Spain	184d		41.16 N	2.02 E
Garrel, Ger.	24	D3	52.57 N	8.02 E
Garret Mountain Reservation, p.o.i., N.J., U.S.	194		40.54 N	74.11 W
Garretson, S.D., U.S.	128	H2	43.42 N	96.30 W
Garrett, In., U.S.	130	C12	41.20 N	85.06 W
Garrett, Ky., U.S.	124	G3	37.28 N	82.49 W
Garrett Park Estates, Md., U.S.	202c		39.02 N	77.06 W
Garrison, Mt., U.S.	146	D14	46.31 N	112.48 W
Garrison, N.D., U.S.	142	G12	47.39 N	101.25 W
Garrison, Tx., U.S.	136	C13	31.49 N	94.29 W
Garrison Dam, dam., N.D., U.S.	142	G12	47.22 N	101.25 W
Garrovillas, Spain	28	E4	39.43 N	6.33 W
Garry, stm., Scot., U.K.	10	E8	56.43 N	3.46 W
Garry Bay, b., Nu., Can.	110	B13	68.55 N	85.05 W
Garry Lake, l., Nu., Can.	110	B10	66.00 N	100.00 W
Garsen, Kenya	86	E7	2.15 S	40.04 E
Garsjøen, l., Nor.	14	C19	69.55 N	28.56 E
Garson, On., Can.	126	B9	46.33 N	80.51 W
Garston, Eng., U.K.	178		51.41 N	0.23 W
Garston, ngh., Eng., U.K.	180		53.21 N	2.53 W
Garswood, Eng., U.K.	180		53.29 N	2.40 W
Gartenstadt, ngh., Ger.	181		51.30 N	7.26 E
Gartrop-Bühl, Ger.	181		51.40 N	6.49 E
Garut, Indon.	66	G5	7.12 S	107.53 E
Garvey Reservoir, res., Ca., U.S.	198		34.13 N	118.07 W
Garwin, Ia., U.S.	130	B5	42.05 N	92.40 W
Garwolin, Pol.	24	E17	51.54 N	21.37 E
Garwood, N.J., U.S.	194		40.39 N	74.19 W
Garwood, Tx., U.S.	136	E11	29.27 N	96.24 W
Gary, In., U.S.	130	C10	41.35 N	87.20 W
Gary, S.D., U.S.	128	G2	44.47 N	96.27 W
Gary, Tx., U.S.	136	B13	32.07 N	94.22 W
Gary, W.V., U.S.	124	G4	37.20 N	81.39 W
Garyarsa, China	70	C8	31.43 N	80.19 E
Gary Harbor, b., In., U.S.	196		41.38 N	87.20 W
Gary Municipal Airport, arpt., In., U.S.	196		41.37 N	87.25 W
Garza, Arg.	172	D6	28.09 S	63.32 W
Garza Ayala, Mex.	136	H7	26.29 N	100.02 W
Garzón, Col.	168	F4	2.12 N	75.37 W
Garzón, Ur.	172	G10	34.37 S	54.32 W
Gas, Fr.	179		48.34 N	1.40 E
Gasan-Kuli, Turkmen.	72	B7	37.27 N	54.00 E
Gas City, In., U.S.	130	D12	40.29 N	85.36 W
Gascogne (Gascony), hist. reg., Fr.	22	F5	43.36 N	0.22 E
Gascogne, Golfe de see Biscay, Bay of, b., Eur.	8	G8	44.00 N	4.00 W
Gasconade, stm., Mo., U.S.	130	F6	38.40 N	91.32 W
Gasconade, Osage Fork, stm., Mo., U.S.	130	G5	37.44 N	92.26 W
Gascony see Gascogne, hist. reg., Fr.	22	F5	43.36 N	0.22 E
Gascoyne, stm., Austl.	96	D2	24.52 S	113.38 E
Gascoyne Junction, Austl.	96	D3	25.03 S	115.12 E
Gashaka, Nig.	84	H7	7.22 N	11.28 E
Gashua, Nig.	84	G7	12.52 N	11.02 E
Gasline, On., Can.	202a		42.53 N	79.11 W
Gaspar, Braz.	172	C13	26.55 S	48.54 W
Gaspard Creek, stm., B.C., Can.	144	E8	51.34 N	122.17 W
Gasparilla Island, i., Fl., U.S.	132	J3	26.46 N	82.16 W
Gaspé, Qc., Can.	122	B12	48.49 N	64.28 W
Gaspé, Baie de, b., Qc., Can.	122	B12	48.46 N	64.17 W
Gaspé, Cap, c., Qc., Can.	122	B12	48.45 N	64.10 W
Gaspe Peninsula see Gaspésie, Péninsule de la, pen., Qc., Can.	122	B11	48.30 N	65.00 W
Gaspereau Lake, l., N.S., Can.	122	F12	44.58 N	64.33 W
Gaspésie, Parc Provincial de la, p.o.i., Qc., Can.	122	A10	48.55 N	66.01 W
Gaspésie, Péninsule de la (Gaspe Peninsula), pen., Qc., Can.	122	B11	48.30 N	65.00 W
Gas-san, mtn., Japan	56	A12	38.32 N	140.01 E
Gassaway, W.V., U.S.	124	F5	38.40 N	80.48 W
Gasskatjåhkkå, mtn., Nor.	14	E7	67.38 N	16.10 E
Gastein see Badgastein, Aus.	30	C10	47.07 N	13.08 E
Gasteiz (Vitoria), Spain	28	B8	42.51 N	2.40 W
Gaston, Lake, res., U.S.	124	H7	36.30 N	77.56 W
Gastonia, N.C., U.S.	132	A4	35.15 N	81.11 W
Gastonville, Pa., U.S.	197b		40.15 N	79.59 W
Gastoúni, Grc.	34	F4	37.51 N	21.15 E
Gastre, Arg.	166	H3	42.16 S	69.13 W
Gåsværet, is., Nor.	16	A9	66.03 N	12.01 E
Gata, Cabo de, c., Spain	28	H8	36.43 N	2.11 W
Gata, Sierra de, mts., Spain	28	D4	40.16 N	6.43 W
Gătaia, Rom.	36	D8	45.26 N	21.26 E
Gátas, Akrotírion, c., Cyp.	76	D4	34.34 N	33.02 E
Gatčina, Russia	26	A13	59.33 N	30.07 E
Gate, Ok., U.S.	138	E8	36.51 N	100.03 W
Gateacre, ngh., Eng., U.K.	180		53.23 N	2.51 W
Gate City, Va., U.S.	124	H3	36.38 N	82.35 W
Gatehouse of Fleet, Scot., U.K.	10	G8	54.53 N	4.12 W
Gateshead, Eng., U.K.	10	G11	54.57 N	1.38 W
Gateshead Island, i., Nu., Can.	110	A11	70.35 N	100.27 W
Gates Mills, Oh., U.S.	197a		41.31 N	81.24 W
Gatesville, N.C., U.S.	124	H9	36.24 N	76.44 W
Gatesville, Tx., U.S.	136	C10	31.25 N	97.44 W
Gateway, Co., U.S.	150	E8	38.41 N	108.59 W
Gateway National Recreation Area, p.o.i., U.S.	194		40.34 N	74.06 W
Gateway of India, hist., India	190c		18.55 N	72.50 E
Gateway Stadium, p.o.i., Oh., U.S.	197a		41.30 N	81.41 W
Gathurst, Eng., U.K.	180		53.34 N	2.42 W
Gatineau, Qc., Can.	126	C14	45.29 N	75.38 W
Gatineau, stm., Qc., Can.	114	D13	45.27 N	75.41 W
Gatineau, Parc de la, p.o.i., Qc., Can.	126	C13	45.30 N	76.05 W
Gatley, Eng., U.K.	180		53.23 N	2.14 W
Gatlinburg, Tn., U.S.	124	I2	35.42 N	83.30 W
Gato, Arroyo del, stm., Arg.	206		34.55 S	58.37 W
Gato, Arroyo del, stm., Arg.	206		34.51 S	57.56 W
Gato Negro, Ven.	204c		10.33 N	66.57 W
Gatow, Flugplatz, arpt., Ger.	182a		52.28 N	13.08 E
Gattinara, Italy	30	E5	45.36 N	8.21 E
Gatton, Austl.	98	F9	27.33 S	152.17 E
Gatún, Lago, res., Pan.	156	H7	9.12 N	79.55 W
Gatun Lake see Gatún, Lago, res., Pan.	156	H7	9.12 N	79.55 W
Gatvand, Iran	74	D11	32.15 N	48.49 E
Gau, i., Fiji	101e	q19	17.59 S	179.16 E
Gauer Lake, l., Mb., Can.	110	E11	57.00 N	97.50 W
Gauguin, Musée, bldg., Fr. Poly.	100h	v22	17.45 S	149.23 W
Gauhāti see Guwāhāti, India	70	E13	26.11 N	91.44 E
Gauja (Koiva), stm., Eur.	26	C7	57.09 N	24.16 E
Gaujiena, Lat.	26	C9	57.30 N	26.27 E
Gaukler Point, c., Mi., U.S.	199		42.27 N	82.52 W
Gaula, stm., Nor.	16	D8	63.19 N	10.16 E
Gauldalen, val., Nor.	16	E8	62.57 N	10.42 E
Gauley, stm., W.V., U.S.	124	F4	38.09 N	81.12 W
Gauley Bridge, W.V., U.S.	124	F4	38.09 N	81.12 W
Gaurela, India	70	G8	22.45 N	81.54 E
Gauribidanūr, India	69	E3	13.37 N	77.31 E
Gausdal, val., Nor.	16	F7	61.18 N	9.52 E
Gause, Tx., U.S.	136	D11	30.47 N	96.43 W
Gaustatoppen, mtn., Nor.	16	H6	59.50 N	8.35 E
Gäutan, l., Swe.	16	B13	65.39 N	15.25 E
Gauteng, state, S. Afr.	90	D9	26.00 S	28.15 E
Gavà, Spain	28	C12	41.19 N	2.01 E
Gāvanpāda, India	190c		18.57 N	73.01 E
Gavāter, Khalīj-e see Gwātar Bay, b., Asia	72	E9	25.05 N	61.36 E
Gávdos, i., Grc.	34	I7	34.50 N	24.06 E
Gávea, ngh., Braz.	205a		22.58 S	43.14 W
Gávea, Hipódromo da, p.o.i., Braz.	205a		22.58 S	43.13 W
Gávea, Pedra da, mtn., Braz.	205a		23.00 S	43.17 W
Gavia, Arroyo de la, stm., Spain	184a		40.21 N	3.40 W
Gavião, stm., Braz.	170	H5	14.06 S	41.01 W
Gavilán, Ven.	204c		10.24 N	66.51 W
Gavins Point Dam, dam., U.S.	140	E15	42.48 N	97.40 W
Gāv Khūnī, Bātlāq-e, sw., Iran	74	D13	32.10 N	52.50 E
Gävle, Swe.	16	G15	60.40 N	17.10 E
Gävleborg, state, Swe.	16	F14	61.30 N	16.15 E
Gävlebukten, b., Swe.	16	G15	60.41 N	17.24 E
Gavlefjorden, b., Nor.	14	C6	68.53 N	15.23 E
Gavorrano, Italy	30	H7	42.55 N	10.54 E
Gavrilov-Jam, Russia	40	C11	57.17 N	39.51 E
Gavry, Russia	26	D10	56.55 N	27.51 E
Gawachab, Nmb.	90	E3	27.03 S	17.52 E
Gāwān, India	70	F10	24.36 N	85.55 E
Gāwīlgarh Hills, hills, India	70	H6	21.25 N	77.15 E
Gawler, Austl.	98	J2	34.36 S	138.44 E
Gawler Ranges, mts., Austl.	96	F7	32.20 S	135.24 E
Gawsworth, Eng., U.K.	180		53.13 N	2.10 W
Gawthorpe Hall, hist., Eng., U.K.	180		53.48 N	2.18 W
Gaya, India	70	F10	24.47 N	85.00 E
Gaya, Niger	84	G5	11.53 N	3.27 E
Gaya, Nig.	84	G6	11.51 N	9.00 E
Gaylord, Mi., U.S.	126	C5	45.01 N	84.40 W
Gaylord, Mn., U.S.	128	G4	44.33 N	94.13 W
Gayndah, Austl.	98	E8	25.37 S	151.36 E
Gays Mills, Wi., U.S.	128	H8	43.18 N	90.50 W
Gayton, Eng., U.K.	180		53.19 N	3.06 W
Gaza see Ghazzah, Gaza	76	G5	31.30 N	34.28 E
Gaza, state, Moz.	90	C11	23.30 S	32.45 E
Gazandzhyk see Gazandzyk, Turkmen.	72	B8	39.14 N	55.31 E
Gazandzyk, Turkmen.	72	B8	39.14 N	55.31 E
Gazaoua, Niger	84	G6	13.31 N	7.54 E
Gaza Strip, dep., Asia	76	G5	31.25 N	34.23 E
Gazelle Peninsula, pen., Pap. N. Gui.	101a	a5	4.32 S	151.54 E
Gazeran, Fr.	179		48.38 N	1.46 E
Gazeran, Bois de, p.o.i., Fr.	179		48.40 N	1.45 E
Gaziantep, Tur.	42	G7	37.04 N	37.23 E
Gaziantep, state, Tur.	42	G7	37.00 N	37.20 E
Gazimağusa (Famagusta), N. Cyp.	76	C4	35.06 N	33.57 E
Gazimağusa Körfezi, b., N. Cyp.	76	C5	35.14 N	34.02 E
Gazipaşa, Tur.	34	G15	36.17 N	32.18 E
Gazira Sporting Club, p.o.i., Egypt	191c		30.04 N	31.13 E
Gazivoda Jezero, res., Yugo.	36	G7	42.55 N	20.41 E
Gbanga, Lib.	84	H3	7.00 N	9.28 W
Gbogbo, Nig.	191a		6.36 N	3.31 E
Gboko, Nig.	84	H6	7.19 N	8.59 E
Gcoverega, Bots.	88	D3	19.08 S	24.15 E
Gdańsk (Danzig), Pol.	24	B14	54.21 N	18.38 E
Gdansk, Gulf of, b., Eur.	8	D12	54.40 N	19.15 E
Gdańska, Zatoka see Gdansk, Gulf of, b., Eur.	8	D12	54.40 N	19.15 E
Gdan'skij zaliv see Gdansk, Gulf of, b., Eur.	8	D12	54.40 N	19.15 E
Gdov, Russia	26	B10	58.45 N	27.49 E
Gdynia, Pol.	24	B14	54.31 N	18.31 E
Gearhart Mountain, mtn., Or., U.S.	148	A5	42.30 N	120.53 W
Geary, N.B., Can.	122	E10	45.46 N	66.29 W
Geary, Ok., U.S.	138	F10	35.38 N	98.19 W
Geauga Lake Park, p.o.i., Oh., U.S.	197a		41.21 N	81.23 W
Gebe, Pulau, i., Indon.	60	E8	0.03 S	129.23 E
Gebiz, Tur.	34	F13	37.06 N	30.56 E
Gebze, Tur.	34	C12	40.48 N	29.25 E
Geçitkale, N. Cyp.	76	C4	35.15 N	33.45 E
Geddes, Mi., U.S.	199		42.16 N	83.40 W
Geddes, S.D., U.S.	140	D14	43.15 N	98.41 W
Gediz, Tur.	34	D12	39.02 N	29.25 E
Gediz (Hermus), stm., Tur.	34	E10	38.35 N	26.47 E
Gedongdalem, Indon.	66	F4	5.02 S	105.24 E
Gedser, Den.	24	B7	54.34 N	11.56 E
Geduld, S. Afr.	191d		26.15 S	28.25 E
Gee Cross, Eng., U.K.	180		53.26 N	2.04 W
Geel, Bel.	20	C13	51.09 N	4.59 E
Geelong, Austl.	98	L5	38.08 S	144.21 E
Geelvink Channel, strt., Austl.	96	E2	28.30 S	114.10 E
Geesthacht, Ger.	24	C6	53.26 N	10.22 E
Geeveston, Austl.	99a	o13	43.10 S	146.55 E
Gefle see Gävle, Swe.	16	G15	60.40 N	17.10 E
Gehackte Berge, hills, Ger.	182a		52.41 N	13.30 E
Ge Hu, l., China	58	F8	31.36 N	119.51 E
Geiger, Al., U.S.	134	E10	32.52 N	88.18 W
Geikie, stm., Sk., Can.	110	D9	57.45 N	103.52 W
Geilo, Nor.	16	G6	60.32 N	8.14 E
Geiranger, Nor.	16	E5	62.05 N	7.13 E
Geisecke, Ger.	181		51.27 N	7.37 E
Geisenfeld, Ger.	24	H7	48.41 N	11.36 E
Geislingen an der Steige, Ger.	24	H5	48.37 N	9.49 E
Geistenbeck, ngh., Ger.	181		51.09 N	6.27 E
Geistown, Pa., U.S.	124	D7	40.17 N	78.51 W
Geist Reservoir, res., Pa., U.S.	203		39.57 N	75.24 W
Geita, Tan.	86	E6	2.51 S	32.10 E
Geithus, Nor.	16	H7	59.54 N	9.56 E
Geittinden, mtn., Nor.	16	B11	65.47 N	13.46 E
Gejah, India	190a		28.31 N	77.23 E
Gejiu, China	52	G5	23.22 N	103.09 E
Gela, Italy	32	G8	37.04 N	14.15 E
Gela, stm., Italy	32	G8	37.03 N	14.15 E
Gela, Golfo di, b., Italy	32	H7	37.03 N	14.10 E
Geladandong, mtn., China	52	E3	33.27 N	91.06 E
Gelādī, Eth.	82	F9	6.58 N	46.24 E
Gelan, China	58	F2	30.02 N	107.06 E
Gelang, Tanjong, c., Malay.	64	K6	3.58 N	103.26 E
Gelasa, Selat, strt., Indon.	66	E5	2.55 S	107.13 E
Geldern, Ger.	20	C15	51.31 N	6.19 E
Geleen, Neth.	20	D14	50.58 N	5.49 E
Gelembe, Tur.	34	D10	39.10 N	27.50 E
Gelendost, Tur.	34	E14	38.07 N	30.59 E
Gelendžik, Russia	40	I11	44.33 N	38.05 E
Gelgaudiškis, Lith.	26	E6	55.05 N	23.00 E
Gelib see Jilib, Som.	86	D8	0.30 N	42.46 E
Gelibolu, Tur.	34	C9	40.25 N	26.41 E
Gelibolu Yarımadası (Gallipoli Peninsula), pen., Tur.	34	C9	40.20 N	26.30 E
Gellep-Stratum, ngh., Ger.	181		51.20 N	6.41 E
Gellibrand, Point, c., Austl.	192b		37.52 S	144.54 E
Gellibrand River, Austl.	98	L4	38.32 S	143.32 E
Gelnhausen, Ger.	20	D18	50.12 N	9.11 E
Gelsenkirchen, Ger.	24	E2	51.30 N	7.06 E
Gelsenkirchen-Horst, Galopprennbahn, p.o.i., Ger.	181		51.32 N	7.02 E
Gemas, Malay.	64	K6	2.35 N	102.36 E
Gembrook, Austl.	98	K5	37.57 S	145.32 E
Gemena, D.R.C.	86	D3	3.14 N	19.46 E
Gemerek, Tur.	42	F7	39.10 N	36.04 E
Gemert, Neth.	24	E1	51.33 N	5.41 E
Gemla, Swe.	16	K12	56.52 N	14.39 E
Gemlik, Tur.	34	C12	40.25 N	29.09 E
Gemlik Körfezi, b., Tur.	34	C11	40.25 N	28.55 E
Gemona del Friuli, Italy	30	D10	46.16 N	13.08 E
Gemsa, Egypt	76	K4	27.38 N	33.35 E
Gemsbok National Park, p.o.i., Bots.	90	D5	25.15 S	21.10 E
Gemünden, Ger.	24	F5	50.03 N	9.41 E
Gen, stm., China	52	A9	50.14 N	119.21 E
Genaibashi, Japan	186		35.21 N	140.04 E
Genalē (Jubba), stm., Afr.	86	C8	0.14 S	42.39 E
Gencek, Tur.	76	A2	37.27 N	31.34 E
Gending, Indon.	66	G8	7.48 S	113.18 E
General Acha, Arg.	172	H5	37.23 S	64.36 W
General Alvear, Arg.	172	H8	36.00 S	60.01 W
General Alvear, Arg.	172	G4	34.58 S	67.41 W
General Arenales, Arg.	172	G7	34.17 S	61.18 W
General Belgrano, Arg.	172	G8	35.46 S	58.29 W
General Bernardo O'Higgins, sci., Ant.	103	B35	63.19 S	57.54 W
General Bravo, Mex.	154	C9	25.47 N	99.10 W
General Cabrera, Arg.	172	F6	32.48 S	63.52 W
General Campos, Arg.	172	E8	31.31 S	58.24 W
General Carneiro, Braz.	166	C6	15.42 S	52.45 W
General Carrera, Lago, l., S.A.	166	I2	46.26 S	71.39 W
General Conesa, Arg.	166	H4	40.06 S	64.26 W
General Conesa, Arg.	172	H9	36.30 S	57.19 W
General Daniel Cerri, Arg.	172	I6	38.41 S	62.23 W
General del Sur, Cementerio, misc. cult., Ven.	204c		10.28 N	66.55 W
General Elizardo Aquino, Para.	172	B9	24.27 S	56.52 W
General Elizardo Aquino, Para.	172	C9	26.56 S	56.13 W
General Enrique Martínez, Ur.	172	F10	33.13 S	53.54 W
General Escobedo, Mex.	136	I7	25.49 N	100.20 W
General Escobedo, Mex.	154	C6	25.29 N	105.14 W
General Eugenio A. Garay, Para.	166	D4	20.30 S	62.10 W
General Eugenio Garay, Para.	172	B9	25.58 S	56.07 W
General Galarza, Arg.	172	F8	32.43 S	59.23 W
General Güemes, Arg.	172	B5	24.39 S	65.02 W
General Guido, Arg.	172	H8	36.39 S	57.48 W
General José de San Martín, Arg.	172	C8	26.32 S	59.20 W
General Juan José Ríos, Mex.	154	C4	25.45 N	108.49 W
General Juan Madariaga, Arg.	172	H9	37.00 S	57.08 W
General La Madrid, Arg.	172	H7	37.14 S	61.17 W
General Las Heras, state, Arg.	206		34.56 S	58.51 W
General Lavalle, Arg.	172	H9	36.25 S	56.57 W
General Levalle, Arg.	172	G5	34.00 S	63.54 W
General Manuel Belgrano, Cerro, mtn., Arg.	172	D4	29.01 S	67.49 W
General Motors Corporation (Pontiac Division), sci., Mi., U.S.	199		42.49 N	83.17 W
General Motors Proving Grounds, sci., Mi., U.S.	199		42.35 N	83.41 W
General Motors Technical Center, sci., Mi., U.S.	199		42.31 N	83.02 W
General'nyj, stm., Russia	183a		60.00 N	30.32 E
General Pacheco, Arg.	206		34.28 S	58.38 W
General Pico, Arg.	172	G6	35.39 S	63.45 W
General Pinedo, Arg.	172	C7	27.19 S	61.16 W
General Pinto, Arg.	172	G7	34.45 S	61.53 W
General Pizarro, Arg.	172	B6	24.12 S	64.00 W
General Ramírez, Arg.	172	F7	32.10 S	60.13 W
General Roca, Arg.	166	G3	39.01 S	67.35 W
General San Martín, Arg.	172	G8	34.33 S	58.32 W
General San Martín, Arg.	172	H5	37.58 S	63.36 W
General San Martín, state, Arg.	206		34.34 S	58.34 W
General Santos, Phil.	68	G5	6.07 N	125.10 E
General Sarmiento, state, Arg.	206		34.32 S	58.43 W
General Terán, Mex.	154	C9	25.15 N	99.40 W
General Toševo, Blg.	36	F14	43.42 N	28.01 E
General Toshevo see General Toševo, Blg.	36	F14	43.42 N	28.01 E
General Treviño, Mex.	136	H8	26.13 N	99.28 W
General Trias, Mex.	136	F1	28.20 N	106.22 W
General Viamonte, Arg.	172	G7	34.59 S	61.02 W
General Villegas, Arg.	172	G6	35.02 S	63.01 W
General Warren Village, Pa., U.S.	203		40.02 N	75.32 W
General Zuazua, Mex.	136	I7	25.53 N	100.06 W
Genesee, Id., U.S.	146	D9	46.33 N	116.59 W
Genesee, stm., U.S.	126	F12	43.15 N	77.36 W
Geneseo, Il., U.S.	130	C7	41.27 N	90.08 W
Geneseo, Ks., U.S.	138	C10	38.30 N	98.09 W
Geneseo, N.Y., U.S.	124	B8	42.47 N	77.48 W
Geneva see Genève, Switz.	30	D3	46.12 N	6.08 E
Geneva, Al., U.S.	134	F13	31.01 N	85.51 W
Geneva, Il., U.S.	128	J10	41.52 N	88.17 W
Geneva, In., U.S.	130	D13	40.35 N	84.56 W
Geneva, Ne., U.S.	140	G15	40.31 N	97.36 W
Geneva, N.Y., U.S.	124	B8	42.52 N	76.59 W
Geneva, Oh., U.S.	124	C4	41.48 N	80.56 W
Geneva, Lake, l., Eur.	30	D3	46.24 N	6.22 E
Genève (Geneva), Switz.	30	D3	46.12 N	6.08 E
Genève, Lac de see Geneva, Lake, l., Eur.	30	D3	46.24 N	6.22 E
Genf see Genève, Switz.	30	D3	46.12 N	6.08 E
Genghis Khan, Wall of, hist., Asia	50	G11	49.52 N	118.07 E
Gengma, China	52	G4	23.35 N	99.07 E
Génicourt, Fr.	179		49.05 N	2.04 E
Genil, stm., Spain	28	G5	37.41 N	5.19 W
Genk, Bel.	20	C14	50.58 N	5.30 E
Genkai-nada, s., Japan	56	F2	34.00 N	130.00 E
Gennargentu, Monti del, mts., Italy	32	E3	40.01 N	9.19 E
Gennebreck, Ger.	181		51.19 N	7.12 E
Gennevilliers, Fr.	179		48.56 N	2.18 E
Genoa, Austl.	98	K7	37.28 S	149.34 E
Genoa see Genova, Italy	30	F5	44.25 N	8.57 E
Genoa, Il., U.S.	130	B9	42.05 N	88.41 W
Genoa, Ne., U.S.	140	F15	41.26 N	97.43 W
Genoa, Oh., U.S.	124	C2	41.31 N	83.22 W
Genoa, Wi., U.S.	128	H7	43.34 N	91.12 W
Genova (Genoa), Italy	30	F5	44.25 N	8.57 E
Genova, Golfo di, b., Italy	30	G5	44.10 N	8.55 E
Genrietty, ostrov, i., Russia	50	A20	76.58 N	156.38 E
Gensan see Wŏnsan, Kor., N.	54	E7	39.09 N	127.26 E
Gens de Terre, stm., Qc., Can.	126	A13	46.53 N	76.07 W
Genshagen, Ger.	182a		52.19 N	13.19 E
Genshagener Heide, for., Ger.	182a		52.20 N	13.18 E
Genshiryoku-kenkyūsho, sci., Japan	56	C13	36.27 N	140.36 E
Gent (Ghent), Bel.	20	C12	51.03 N	3.43 E
Genteng, Gili, i., Indon.	66	G8	7.11 S	113.54 E
Genthin, Ger.	24	D8	52.24 N	12.09 E
Gentilly, Fr.	179		48.49 N	2.21 E
Gentio do Ouro, Braz.	170	F4	11.25 S	42.30 W
Gentry, Ar., U.S.	130	H3	36.16 N	94.30 W
Genyem, Indon.	101a	a3	2.44 S	140.09 E
Genzano di Roma, Italy	30	I9	41.42 N	12.41 E
Geographe Bay, b., Austl.	96	F3	33.35 S	115.15 E
Geographical Society Ø, i., Grnld.	108	C21	72.57 N	23.15 W
Geok-Tepe, Turkmen.	72	B8	38.09 N	57.57 E
George, S. Afr.	90	H6	33.57 S	22.27 E
George, Ia., U.S.	128	H2	43.20 N	96.00 W
George, stm., Qc., Can.	110	D17	58.45 N	66.08 W
George, Cape, c., N.S., Can.	122	E15	45.52 N	61.55 W
George, Lake, l., Austl.	96	D4	22.36 S	123.40 E
George, Lake, l., Austl.	98	J7	35.05 S	149.25 E
George, Lake, l., N.A.	126	B5	46.31 N	84.10 W
George, Lake, l., Ug.	86	E6	0.02 N	30.12 E
George, Lake, l., Fl., U.S.	132	G4	29.17 N	81.36 W
George, Lake, res., N.Y., U.S.	126	E16	43.34 N	73.35 W
George H. Crosby Manitou State Park, p.o.i., Mn., U.S.	128	D7	47.29 N	91.10 W
George Mason University, educ., Va., U.S.	202c		38.50 N	77.17 W
Georges Island, i., Ma., U.S.	201		42.19 N	70.56 W
Georges River Bridge, trans., Austl.	192a		34.00 S	151.07 E
Georges Run, stm., Pa., U.S.	197b		40.23 N	80.06 W
Georgetown, Austl.	98	B4	18.17 S	143.32 E
George Town, Austl.	99a	n13	41.06 S	146.48 E
Georgetown, On., Can.	126	E9	43.39 N	79.55 W
Georgetown, P.E., Can.	122	D14	46.11 N	62.32 W
George Town, Cay. Is.	156	C7	19.17 N	81.22 W
Georgetown, Gam.	84	G2	13.32 N	14.45 W
Georgetown, Guy.	164	B6	6.48 N	58.08 W
George Town (Penang), Malay.	64	J5	5.25 N	100.18 E
Georgetown, St. Vin.	159e	o11	13.17 N	61.07 W
Georgetown, Co., U.S.	138	B3	39.43 N	105.40 W
Georgetown, De., U.S.	124	F10	38.41 N	75.23 W
Georgetown, Fl., U.S.	132	G4	29.23 N	81.38 W
Georgetown, Ga., U.S.	134	F13	31.53 N	85.06 W
Georgetown, Id., U.S.	146	H15	42.29 N	111.22 W
Georgetown, Il., U.S.	130	E10	39.58 N	87.38 W
Georgetown, Ky., U.S.	124	F1	38.12 N	84.34 W
Georgetown, Ms., U.S.	134	F8	31.52 N	90.10 W
Georgetown, N.J., U.S.	203		40.04 N	74.39 W
Georgetown, Oh., U.S.	124	F2	38.50 N	83.52 W
Georgetown, S.C., U.S.	132	C6	33.22 N	79.17 W
Georgetown, Tx., U.S.	136	D10	30.37 N	97.40 W
Georgetown, ngh., D.C., U.S.	202c		38.54 N	77.03 W
Georgetown Lake, res., Mt., U.S.	146	D13	46.10 N	113.17 W
Georgetown Rowley State Forest, p.o.i., Ma., U.S.	201		42.42 N	70.58 W
Georgetown University, educ., D.C., U.S.	202c		38.54 N	77.04 W
George V Coast, cst., Ant.	103	B19	68.42 S	147.04 E
George Washington Birthplace National Monument, p.o.i., Va., U.S.	124	F9	38.11 N	76.56 W
George Washington Bridge, trans., U.S.	194		40.51 N	73.57 W
George Washington Carver National Monument, p.o.i., Mo., U.S.	130	H3	37.00 N	94.21 W
George West, Tx., U.S.	136	F9	28.19 N	98.07 W
Georgia, ctry., Asia	42	D11	42.00 N	44.00 E
Georgia, state, U.S.	116	D11	32.50 N	83.15 W
Georgia, Strait of, strt., N.A.	144	G7	49.20 N	124.00 W
Georgiana, Al., U.S.	134	F12	31.38 N	86.44 W
Georgian Bay, b., On., Can.	126	C9	45.15 N	80.50 W
Georgian Bay Islands National Park, p.o.i., On., Can.	126	D9	44.54 N	79.52 W
Georgievka, Kaz.	48	E14	49.19 N	81.34 E
Georgievsk, Russia	42	C10	44.09 N	43.29 E
Georgievskoe, Russia	18	H23	59.44 N	36.51 E
Georgina, stm., Austl.	98	D2	24.36 S	139.28 E
Georgiu-Dež see Liski, Russia	40	F11	50.58 N	39.30 E
Georg von Neumayer, sci., Ant.	103	B3	70.37 S	8.21 W
Gera, Ger.	24	F7	50.52 N	12.04 E
Geral, Serra, mts., Braz.	172	C12	26.30 S	50.30 W
Geral, Serra, clf., Braz.	170	F3	11.15 S	46.30 W
Gerald, Mo., U.S.	130	F6	38.24 N	91.20 W
Geral de Goiás, Serra, clf., Braz.	170	G2	13.00 S	46.15 W
Geraldine, Mt., U.S.	146	C16	47.35 N	110.15 W
Geraldton, Austl.	96	E2	28.46 S	114.37 E
Geraldton, On., Can.	128	B11	49.40 N	86.59 W
Gerard, Lake, l., N.J., U.S.	194		41.06 N	74.33 W
Gérardmer, Fr.	20	F15	48.04 N	6.52 E
Gerber, Ca., U.S.	148	C3	40.04 N	122.09 W
Gerber Reservoir, res., Or., U.S.	148	A4	42.12 N	121.06 W
Gerdine, Mount, mtn., Ak., U.S.	109	D9	61.35 N	152.26 W
Gerdview, S. Afr.	191d		26.10 S	28.11 E
Gerede, Tur.	34	C15	40.48 N	32.11 E
Gereja Cathedral, rel., Indon.	187e		6.10 S	106.49 E
Gerenzano, Italy	184b		45.38 N	9.00 E
Gereshk, Afg.	72	C9	31.49 N	64.33 E
Gérgal, Spain	28	G8	37.07 N	2.33 W
Gerik, Malay.	64	J5	5.25 N	101.08 E
Gering, Ne., U.S.	140	F9	41.49 N	103.39 W
Geriş, Tur.	76	B2	36.57 N	31.43 E
Gerlachovský štít, mtn., Slvk.	24	G16	49.10 N	20.09 E
Gerli, ngh., Arg.	206		34.41 S	58.23 W
German Democratic Republic see Germany, ctry., Eur.	6	E11	51.00 N	10.00 E
Germania Land, reg., Grnld.	108	B21	77.10 N	20.00 W
Germantown, Il., U.S.	130	F8	38.33 N	89.32 W
Germantown, Tn., U.S.	134	B9	35.05 N	89.48 W
Germantown, Wi., U.S.	130	A9	43.13 N	88.06 W
Germantown, ngh., Pa., U.S.	203		40.03 N	75.11 W
Germany, ctry., Eur.	6	E11	51.00 N	10.00 E
Germany, Federal Republic of see Germany, ctry., Eur.	6	E11	51.00 N	10.00 E

Name	Page	Map Ref.	Latitude	Longitude
Germany Flats, pl., N.J., U.S.	194		41.05 N	74.39 W
Germencik, Tur.	34	F10	37.52 N	27.37 E
Germfask, Mi., U.S.	126	B4	46.15 N	85.56 W
Germiston, S. Afr.	90	E9	26.13 S	28.11 E
Germiston, state, S. Afr.	191d		26.15 S	28.10 E
Germiston South, S. Afr.	191d		26.15 S	28.10 E
Gernika, Spain	28	A8	43.19 N	2.41 W
Gero, Japan	56	D10	35.48 N	137.14 E
Geroliménas, Grc.	34	G5	36.29 N	22.23 E
Gerolzhofen, Ger.	24	G6	49.54 N	10.21 E
Gerona see Girona, Spain	28	B13	41.59 N	2.49 E
Geronimo, Ok., U.S.	138	G10	34.29 N	98.22 W
Gerrards Cross, Eng., U.K.	178		51.35 N	0.34 W
Gerresheim, ngh., Ger.	181		51.14 N	6.52 E
Gers, state, Fr.	22	F6	43.40 N	0.30 E
Gers, stm., Fr.	22	F6	44.08 N	0.38 E
Gerthe, ngh., Ger.	181		51.31 N	7.17 E
Gêrzê, China	70	B10	32.25 N	84.12 E
Geseke, Ger.	24	E4	51.38 N	8.31 E
Geser, Indon.	60	F9	3.53 S	130.55 E
Gesoa, Pap. N. Gui.	101a	b3	8.25 S	143.39 E
Geta, Fin.	18	G6	60.22 N	19.52 E
Getafe, Spain	28	D7	40.18 N	3.43 W
Getafe, Aeropuerto, arpt., Spain	184a		40.18 N	3.43 W
Gethaoli, India	190c		19.08 N	73.01 E
Getinge, Swe.	16	K10	56.48 N	12.45 E
Gettysburg, Pa., U.S.	124	E8	39.50 N	77.13 W
Gettysburg, S.D., U.S.	140	C13	45.00 N	99.56 W
Gettysburg National Military Park, p.o.i., Pa., U.S.	124	E8	39.49 N	77.14 W
Getúlio Vargas, Braz.	172	C11	27.53 S	52.15 W
Geumpang, Indon.	64	J2	4.50 N	96.08 E
Gevaş, Tur.	42	F10	38.18 N	43.07 E
Gevgelija, Mac.	34	B5	41.08 N	22.30 E
Geweke, ngh., Ger.	181		51.22 N	7.25 E
Gex, Fr.	22	C12	46.19 N	6.02 E
Geyikli, Tur.	34	D9	39.48 N	26.12 E
Geyser, Mt., U.S.	146	C16	47.15 N	110.29 W
Geyserville, Ca., U.S.	148	E3	38.42 N	122.54 W
Geyve, Tur.	34	C13	40.32 N	30.18 E
Gezīret Muhammad, Egypt	191c		30.07 N	31.12 E
Ghaapplato, plat., S. Afr.	90	E7	27.29 S	24.19 E
Ghadāmis, Libya	82	B1	30.12 N	9.33 E
Ghafe, India	190c		19.05 N	73.07 E
Ghagghar, stm., India	70	D5	29.30 N	74.51 E
Ghāghra, stm., Asia	70	E9	25.44 N	84.48 E
Ghakhar, Pak.	70	B4	32.18 N	74.09 E
Ghana, ctry., Afr.	84	H4	8.00 N	1.00 W
Ghansoli, India	190c		19.08 N	72.59 E
Ghanzi, Bots.	90	B5	21.42 S	21.39 E
Ghanzi, state, Bots.	90	C6	22.00 S	23.00 E
Gharandal, hist., Jord.	76	H6	30.05 N	35.12 E
Ghārāpuri, India	190c		18.54 N	72.56 E
Gharaunda, India	70	D6	29.32 N	76.58 E
Ghardaïa, Alg.	84	C5	32.32 N	3.40 E
Ghardimaou, Tun.	32	H2	36.26 N	8.26 E
Gharrāf, Shaṭṭ al-, stm., Iraq	74	E10	32.30 N	45.48 E
Gharroli, ngh., India	190a		28.37 N	77.20 E
Gharyān, Libya	82	A2	32.10 N	13.01 E
Ghāt, Libya	82	C2	24.55 N	10.11 E
Ghatampur, India	190b		22.54 N	88.10 E
Ghatere, Mount, mtn., Sol. Is.	101b	d8	7.49 S	158.54 E
Ghātkopar, ngh., India	190c		19.05 N	72.54 E
Ghātprabha, stm., India	69	C2	16.21 N	75.49 E
Ghātsīla, India	70	G11	22.35 N	86.28 E
Ghawdex (Gozo), i., Malta	32	H8	36.03 N	14.15 E
Ghazāl, Baḥr al-, stm., Sudan	82	F6	9.27 N	30.20 E
Ghāziābād, India	70	D6	28.40 N	77.18 E
Ghāzīpur, India	70	F9	25.35 N	83.35 E
Ghazipur, India	190b		22.36 N	88.34 E
Ghāzīpur, ngh., India	190a		28.38 N	77.19 E
Ghazīr, Leb.	76	D6	34.01 N	35.40 E
Ghazlūna, Pak.	70	C1	31.27 N	67.54 E
Ghaznī, Afg.	72	C10	33.33 N	68.25 E
Ghaznī, state, Afg.	70	B1	33.26 N	67.58 E
Ghaznī, stm., Afg.	70	B2	32.32 N	67.55 E
Ghazni Khel, Pak.	70	B3	32.33 N	70.44 E
Ghazzah (Gaza), Gaza	76	G5	31.30 N	34.28 E
Ghazzah, Leb.	76	E6	33.40 N	35.49 E
Ghazzah, Wādī see Besor, Naḥal, stm., Asia	76	G5	31.27 N	34.22 E
Gheā, stm., India	190b		22.52 N	88.19 E
Ghennes Heights, Pa., U.S.	197b		40.09 N	79.56 W
Ghent see Gent, Bel.	20	C12	51.03 N	3.43 E
Gheora, ngh., India	190a		28.42 N	77.01 E
Gheorgheni, Rom.	36	C12	46.43 N	25.36 E
Gherla, Rom.	36	C11	47.01 N	23.53 E
Gheroo, Gezîret, i., Egypt	76	G1	31.22 N	30.06 E
Ghesar, India	190c		19.09 N	73.05 E
Ghilarza, Italy	32	D2	40.07 N	8.49 E
Ghīnah, Wādī al-, stm., Sau. Ar.	76	H9	30.26 N	38.14 E
Ghisonaccia, Fr.	22	H15	42.00 N	9.24 E
Ghizo see Gizo Island, i., Sol. Is.	101b	e7	8.04 S	156.48 E
Ghizunabeana Islands, is., Sol. Is.	101b	d8	7.31 S	158.42 E
Ghogha, India	70	H4	21.36 N	72.00 E
Ghonda, ngh., India	190a		28.41 N	77.16 E
Ghondi, ngh., India	190a		28.42 N	77.16 E
Ghoshpur, India	190b		22.23 N	88.29 E
Ghotki, Pak.	70	E2	27.59 N	69.17 E
Ghubaysh, Sudan	82	E5	12.08 N	27.21 E
Ghudāf, Wādī al-, stm., Iraq	74	D8	32.56 N	43.31 E
Ghunthur, Syria	76	D8	34.23 N	37.09 E
Ghurab, Gebel, hill, Egypt	76	J2	28.58 N	31.16 E
Ghūriān, Afg.	72	C9	34.20 N	61.29 E
Ghushuri, India	190b		22.37 N	88.22 E
Giang, Viet.	64	E8	15.41 N	107.46 E
Giang see Gianh, stm., Viet.	64	C7	17.42 N	106.26 E
Gianh, stm., Viet.	64	C7	17.42 N	106.26 E
Giannitsá, Grc.	34	C5	40.47 N	22.25 E
Giannutri, Isola di, i., Italy	30	H8	42.15 N	11.06 E
Giant Mountain, mtn., N.Y., U.S.	126	D16	44.10 N	73.44 W
Giant's Castle, mtn., S. Afr.	90	F9	29.21 S	29.27 E
Giant's Castle Game Reserve, ind. res., S. Afr.	90	F9	29.16 S	29.30 E
Giant's Causeway, misc. cult., N. Ire., U.K.	10	F6	55.14 N	6.30 W
Giants Stadium, p.o.i., N.J., U.S.	194		40.49 N	74.05 W
Gia Rai, Viet.	64	H7	9.13 N	105.27 E
Giarre, Italy	32	G9	37.43 N	15.11 E
Gibara, Cuba	156	B9	21.06 N	76.08 W
Gibbon, Mn., U.S.	128	G4	44.32 N	94.31 W
Gibbon, Ne., U.S.	140	G14	40.45 N	98.49 W
Gibbons, Ab., Can.	144	C17	53.50 N	113.20 W
Gibbonsville, Id., U.S.	146	E13	45.33 N	113.56 W
Gibb River, Austl.	96	C5	16.24 S	126.23 E
Gibbsboro, N.J., U.S.	203		39.50 N	74.58 W
Gibeon, Nmb.	90	D3	25.07 S	17.45 E
Gibostad, Nor.	14	C8	69.21 N	18.03 E
Gibraleón, Spain	28	G3	37.23 N	6.58 W
Gibraltar, Gib.	28	H5	36.08 N	5.20 W
Gibraltar, dep., Eur.	84	B3	36.08 N	5.21 W
Gibraltar, Estrecho de see Gibraltar, Strait of, strt.	84	B3	35.57 N	5.36 W
Gibraltar, Strait of, strt.	84	B3	35.57 N	5.36 W
Gibraltar Point, c., On., Can.	193b		43.36 N	79.23 W
Gibraltar Point, c., Eng., U.K.	10	H13	53.06 N	0.19 E
Gibsland, La., U.S.	134	E5	32.33 N	93.03 W
Gibson, Austl.	96	F4	33.39 S	121.49 E
Gibson, Ga., U.S.	132	C3	33.14 N	82.35 W
Gibson, Lake, res., On., Can.	202a		43.06 N	79.14 W
Gibson City, Il., U.S.	130	D9	40.27 N	88.21 W
Gibson Desert, des., Austl.	96	D4	24.30 S	126.00 E
Gibsons, B.C., Can.	144	G7	49.24 N	123.30 W
Giddalūr, India	69	D4	15.21 N	78.55 E
Giddings, Tx., U.S.	136	D11	30.10 N	96.56 W
Gideälven, stm., Swe.	16	D16	63.20 N	19.07 E
Gidea Park, ngh., Eng., U.K.	178		51.35 N	0.12 E
Gideåvallen, Swe.	16	D16	63.29 N	18.58 E
Gideon, Mo., U.S.	130	H8	36.27 N	89.55 W
Gidgi, Lake, l., Austl.	96	E5	29.03 S	126.02 E
Giedraičiai, Lith.	26	E8	55.04 N	25.15 E
Gielsdorf, Ger.	182a		52.36 N	13.52 E
Gien, Fr.	20	G11	47.40 N	2.38 E
Gierath, Ger.	181		51.07 N	6.33 E
Giesenkirchen, ngh., Ger.	181		51.09 N	6.30 E
Giessen, Ger.	24	F4	50.35 N	8.40 E
Giessen see Grosse Aue, stm., Ger.	20	B17	52.37 N	9.10 E
Gifatīn, Gezîra, is., Egypt	76	K4	27.13 N	33.56 E
Gifford, Fl., U.S.	132	I5	27.40 N	80.24 W
Gifford, stm., Nu., Can.	110	A14	70.19 N	83.01 W
Gifford Creek, Austl.	96	D3	24.02 S	116.12 E
Gifgâfa, Bîr, well, Egypt	76	H4	30.27 N	33.11 E
Gifhorn, Ger.	24	D6	52.28 N	10.32 E
Gif-sur-Yvette, Fr.	179		48.42 N	2.08 E
Gifu, Japan	56	D9	35.25 N	136.45 E
Gifu, state, Japan	56	D10	35.45 N	137.00 E
Gigant, Russia	40	H12	46.30 N	41.20 E
Giganta, Sierra de la, mts., Mex.	154	C3	25.21 N	111.16 W
Gigen, Blg.	36	F11	43.42 N	24.29 E
Gigena see Alcira, Arg.	172	F5	32.46 S	64.20 W
Gigha Island, i., Scot., U.K.	10	F7	55.40 N	5.45 W
Giglio, Isola del, i., Italy	30	H7	42.21 N	10.54 E
Gihu see Gifu, Japan	56	D9	35.25 N	136.45 E
Gijón, Spain	28	A5	43.32 N	5.40 W
Gila, stm., U.S.	150	K2	32.43 N	114.33 W
Gila, Middle Fork, stm., N.M., U.S.	150	J8	33.13 N	108.15 W
Gila Bend, Az., U.S.	150	K4	32.56 N	112.43 W
Gila Bend Indian Reservation, ind. res., Az., U.S.	150	J4	33.00 N	112.45 W
Gila Bend Mountains, mts., Az., U.S.	150	J3	33.12 N	113.00 W
Gila Cliff Dwellings National Monument, p.o.i., N.M., U.S.	150	J8	33.02 N	108.16 W
Gila Mountains, mts., Az., U.S.	150	J7	33.07 N	109.49 W
Gīlān, state, Iran	74	B11	37.15 N	49.30 E
Gīlān-e Gharb, Iran	74	C9	34.08 N	45.55 E
Gila River Indian Reservation, ind. res., Az., U.S.	150	J4	33.12 N	112.00 W
Gilbert, La., U.S.	134	E7	32.02 N	91.39 W
Gilbert, stm., Austl.	96	C8	16.34 S	141.15 E
Gilbert, Mount, mtn., B.C., Can.	144	F6	50.53 N	124.16 W
Gilbert Airport, arpt., Oh., U.S.	197a		41.22 N	81.58 W
Gilbert Islands see Kiribati, ctry., Oc.	92	D9	5.00 S	170.00 W
Gilbert Islands, is., Kir.	94	C8	0.30 S	174.00 E
Gilbert Lake, l., Mi., U.S.	199		42.34 N	83.17 W
Gilbertown, Al., U.S.	134	F10	31.52 N	88.19 W
Gilbert Peak, mtn., Wa., U.S.	146	D5	46.29 N	121.24 W
Gilbert Plains, Mb., Can.	142	C13	51.08 N	100.29 W
Gilbert River, Austl.	98	B4	18.11 S	142.52 E
Gilbués, Braz.	170	E3	9.50 S	45.20 W
Gildford, Mt., U.S.	146	B16	48.34 N	110.18 W
Gilford Island, i., B.C., Can.	144	F4	50.44 N	126.20 W
Gilgandra, Austl.	98	H7	31.43 S	148.39 E
Gilgil, Kenya	86	E7	0.29 S	36.18 E
Gil Gil Creek, stm., Austl.	98	G8	29.09 S	148.50 E
Gilgit, Pak.	62	A3	35.53 N	74.21 E
Gilgo Island, i., N.Y., U.S.	194		40.38 N	73.25 W
Gilgo State Park, p.o.i., N.Y., U.S.	194		40.38 N	73.22 W
Gilirang, Indon.	66	E12	3.54 S	120.09 E
Gil Island, i., B.C., Can.	144	C1	53.10 N	129.08 W
Giljuj, stm., Russia	50	F14	53.58 N	127.27 E
Gillam, Mb., Can.	110	D12	56.21 N	94.43 W
Gilleleje, Den.	16	K10	56.06 N	12.18 E
Gillen, Lake, l., Austl.	96	E5	26.13 S	124.39 E
Gillespie, Il., U.S.	130	E8	39.07 N	89.48 W
Gillett, Ar., U.S.	134	C7	34.07 N	91.23 W
Gillett, Wi., U.S.	126	D1	44.53 N	88.17 W
Gillette, N.J., U.S.	194		40.41 N	74.28 W
Gillette, Wy., U.S.	140	C7	44.17 N	105.30 W
Gillian, Lake, l., Nu., Can.	110	B16	69.33 N	75.26 W
Gillies Hill, N.J., U.S.	194		40.51 N	74.28 W
Gillingham, Eng., U.K.	10	J13	51.22 N	0.33 E
Gillingham, mun., Eng., U.K.	178		51.22 N	0.35 E
Gills Rock, Wi., U.S.	126	C3	45.16 N	86.59 W
Gilman, Il., U.S.	130	D10	40.45 N	87.58 W
Gilman, Ia., U.S.	130	C5	41.52 N	92.47 W
Gilman, Wi., U.S.	128	F8	45.10 N	90.48 W
Gilman Lake, N.J., U.S.	203		39.41 N	75.11 W
Gilmer, Il., U.S.	196		42.14 N	88.02 W
Gilmer, Tx., U.S.	136	B13	32.44 N	94.56 W
Gilmore City, Ia., U.S.	130	B3	42.43 N	94.26 W
Gilroy, Ca., U.S.	148	F4	37.00 N	121.34 W
Gilston Park, p.o.i., Eng., U.K.	178		51.48 N	0.04 E
Giltner, Ne., U.S.	140	G14	40.46 N	98.08 W
Giluwe, Mount, mtn., Pap. N. Gui.	101a	b3	6.02 S	143.50 E
Gimån, stm., Swe.	16	E14	62.28 N	16.20 E
Gīmbī, Eth.	82	F7	9.10 N	35.50 E
Gimcheon see Kimch'ŏn, Kor., S.	54	F8	36.07 N	128.07 E
Gimie, Mount, vol., St. Luc.	159c	m6	13.52 N	61.01 W
Gimli, Mb., Can.	112	D16	50.38 N	96.59 W
Gimo, Swe.	18	G5	60.10 N	18.11 E
Gimolskoe, ozero, l., Russia	18	D19	63.00 N	32.19 E
Gimoly, Russia	18	E19	62.57 N	32.31 E
Gimone, stm., Fr.	22	F6	44.00 N	1.07 E
Gimpu, Indon.	66	D12	1.37 S	120.01 E
Gimsafjorden, strt., Nor.	16	B9	65.20 N	11.55 E
Ginderich, Ger.	181		51.39 N	6.32 E
Gineina, Râs el-, mtn., Egypt	76	I4	29.01 N	33.58 E
Ginger Hill, Pa., U.S.	197b		40.12 N	80.00 W
Ginger Island, i., Br. Vir. Is.	158b	e9	18.23 N	64.28 W
Gingin, Austl.	96	F3	31.21 S	115.54 E
Gin Gin, Austl.	98	E8	24.59 S	151.57 E
Gingko Petrified Forest State Park, p.o.i., Wa., U.S.	146	C6	46.59 N	120.01 W
Gingoog, Phil.	68	F5	8.48 N	125.06 E
Gīnīr, Eth.	82	F8	7.09 N	40.46 E
Ginkakuji Temple, rel., Japan	188		35.03 N	135.47 E
Ginosa, Italy	32	D10	40.35 N	16.46 E
Ginza, ngh., Japan	186		35.40 N	139.47 E
Ginzo de Limia see Xinzo de Limia, Spain	28	B3	42.03 N	7.42 W
Gioia, Golfo di, b., Italy	32	F9	38.28 N	15.50 E
Gioia del Colle, Italy	32	D10	40.48 N	16.55 E
Gioia Tauro, Italy	32	F9	38.26 N	15.54 E
Giong Rieng, Viet.	64	H7	9.56 N	105.18 E
Gipuzkoako, co., Spain	28	A8	43.10 N	2.10 W
Girafi, Wadi (Paran, Naḥal), stm.	76	I5	30.24 N	35.09 E
Giralia, Austl.	96	D2	22.41 S	114.21 E
Giraltovce, Slvk.	24	G17	49.08 N	21.32 E
Girard, Il., U.S.	130	E8	39.26 N	89.46 W
Girard, Ks., U.S.	130	G3	37.30 N	94.50 W
Girard, Oh., U.S.	124	C5	41.09 N	80.43 W
Girard, Pa., U.S.	124	C5	41.59 N	80.19 W
Girard, Tx., U.S.	138	H8	33.22 N	100.40 W
Girardot, Col.	168	E4	4.18 N	74.47 W
Girardville, Qc., Can.	122	A4	49.00 N	72.33 W
Giraud, Pointe, c., Dom.	159c	j6	15.19 N	61.15 W
Girei, Russia	40	I12	45.26 N	40.40 E
Giresun, Tur.	42	E8	40.54 N	38.24 E
Giresun, state, Tur.	42	E8	40.30 N	38.30 E
Girga, Egypt	74	G2	26.20 N	31.53 E
Girgarre, Austl.	98	K5	36.25 S	144.58 E
Girgaum, ngh., India	190c		18.57 N	72.48 E
Girīḍīh, India	70	F11	24.11 N	86.18 E
Girilambone, Austl.	98	H6	31.15 S	146.54 E
Girna, stm., India	70	H5	21.08 N	75.19 E
Gir National Park, p.o.i., India	70	H3	21.00 N	70.50 E
Girne (Kyrenia), N. Cyp.	76	C4	35.19 N	33.20 E
Giromagny, Fr.	22	I2	47.44 N	6.49 E
Girón, Ec.	164	D2	3.09 S	79.09 W
Girona, Spain	28	B13	41.59 N	2.49 E
Girona, co., Spain	28	B13	42.00 N	2.40 E
Gironde, state, Fr.	22	E5	44.45 N	0.35 W
Gironde, est., Fr.	22	D5	45.20 N	0.45 W
Girou, stm., Fr.	22	F7	43.46 N	1.19 E
Gir Range, mts., India	70	H3	21.18 N	71.00 E
Girtys Run, stm., Pa., U.S.	197b		40.28 N	79.58 W
Giru, Austl.	98	B6	19.30 S	147.06 E
Giruá, Braz.	172	D10	28.02 S	54.21 W
Girvan, Scot., U.K.	10	F8	55.14 N	4.51 W
Girvas, Russia	18	E20	62.28 N	33.39 E
Girwa see Kamālī, stm., Asia	70	D8	28.12 N	81.02 E
Gisborne, N.Z.	102	D8	38.39 S	178.00 E
Giscome, B.C., Can.	144	B8	54.04 N	122.21 W
Gislaved, Swe.	16	J11	57.18 N	13.32 E
Gisors, Fr.	20	E10	49.16 N	1.47 E
Gitarama, Rw.	86	E5	2.03 S	29.43 E
Gitega, Bdi.	86	E5	3.21 S	29.54 E
Gitnadoix River Recreation Area, p.o.i., B.C., Can.	144	B2	54.10 N	129.08 W
Giulianova, Italy	30	H10	42.45 N	13.57 E
Giulie, Alpi see Julian Alps, mts., Eur.	30	D10	46.00 N	14.00 E
Giurgiu, Rom.	36	F12	43.54 N	25.58 E
Giurgiu, state, Rom.	36	E13	44.10 N	26.00 E
Giuvala, Pasul, p., Rom.	36	D12	45.27 N	25.16 E
Give, Den.	16	L7	55.51 N	9.15 E
Givet, Fr.	20	D13	50.08 N	4.49 E
Givors, Fr.	20	D10	45.35 N	4.46 E
Giyon, Eth.	82	F7	8.31 N	37.58 E
Giza see El-Gîza, Egypt	76	H1	30.01 N	31.12 E
Giza see El-Gîza, Egypt	191c		30.01 N	31.13 E
Gîza, Turat el-, can., Egypt	191c		29.50 N	31.16 E
Gižduvan, Uzb.	48	F10	40.06 N	64.40 E
Gižiga, Russia	50	D21	62.03 N	160.30 E
Gižiginskaja guba, b., Russia	50	D20	61.30 N	158.00 E
Gizo, Sol. Is.	101b	e7	8.06 S	156.49 E
Gizo Island, i., Sol. Is.	101b	e7	8.04 S	156.48 E
Giżycko, Pol.	24	B17	54.02 N	21.46 E
Gjandža see Gäncä, Azer.	42	E12	40.41 N	46.20 E
Gjerdøya, i., Nor.	14	F3	66.37 N	13.01 E
Gjesvær, Nor.	14	A16	71.05 N	25.19 E
Gjevilvasskamman, mtn., Nor.	16	E7	62.45 N	9.19 E
Gjevilvatnet, l., Nor.	16	E7	62.41 N	9.25 E
Gjevsjøen, l., Eur.	16	C11	64.03 N	13.03 E
Gjevtele, mtn., Nor.	16	E9	62.53 N	11.54 E
Gjirokastër, Alb.	32	D14	40.04 N	20.09 E
Gjirokastra see Gjirokastër, Alb.	32	D14	40.04 N	20.09 E
Gjoa Haven, Nu., Can.	110	B11	68.38 N	95.54 W
Gjøvik, Nor.	16	G8	60.48 N	10.41 E
Gjuesevo, Blg.	36	G9	42.14 N	22.28 E
Gjuhëzës, Kepi i, c., Alb.	32	D13	40.25 N	19.18 E
Gjumri, Arm.	42	E10	40.47 N	43.50 E
Glace Bay, N.S., Can.	122	D17	46.12 N	59.57 W
Glacier, B.C., Can.	144	E13	51.16 N	117.31 W
Glacier Bay, b., Ak., U.S.	109	E12	58.40 N	136.00 W
Glacier Hills, N.J., U.S.	194		40.51 N	74.28 W
Glacier National Park, p.o.i., B.C., Can.	144	E13	51.15 N	117.35 W
Glacier National Park, p.o.i., Mt., U.S.	146	B12	48.35 N	113.40 W
Glacier Peak, vol., Wa., U.S.	146	B5	48.07 N	121.07 W
Glacier Strait, strt., Nu., Can.	108	B10	76.12 N	79.15 W
Glad', Russia	26	A15	59.07 N	32.06 E
Gladbach see Mönchengladbach, Ger.	24	E2	51.11 N	6.25 E
Gladbrook, Ia., U.S.	130	B5	42.10 N	92.42 W
Gladden, Pa., U.S.	197b		40.21 N	80.11 W
Gladden Heights, Pa., U.S.	197b		40.22 N	80.15 W
Glade Creek, stm., Wa., U.S.	146	D7	45.53 N	119.41 W
Glade Spring, Va., U.S.	124	H4	36.47 N	81.46 W
Gladesville, Austl.	192a		33.50 S	151.08 E
Gladewater, Tx., U.S.	136	B12	32.32 N	94.56 W
Gladstad, Nor.	16	B9	65.41 N	11.56 E
Gladstone, Austl.	98	D8	23.51 S	151.15 E
Gladstone, Mb., Can.	142	D14	50.13 N	98.57 W
Gladstone, Mi., U.S.	126	C2	45.50 N	87.00 W
Gladstone, Mo., U.S.	130	E3	39.12 N	94.33 W
Gladstone Brook, stm., N.J., U.S.	194		40.43 N	74.40 W
Gladwin, Mi., U.S.	126	D5	43.58 N	84.29 W
Gladwyne, Pa., U.S.	203		40.02 N	75.17 W
Glafsfjorden, l., Swe.	16	H10	59.34 N	12.37 E
Glåma, stm., Nor.	16	G9	59.10 N	10.57 E
Glamoč, Bos.	36	E3	44.03 N	16.50 E
Glamsbjerg, Den.	16	L8	55.16 N	10.07 E
Glan, Phil.	68	H5	5.48 N	125.11 E
Glan, l., Swe.	16	I13	58.37 N	15.58 E
Glan, stm., Aus.	30	D11	46.36 N	14.25 E
Glan, stm., Ger.	20	E16	49.46 N	7.42 E
Glan-y-Don, Wales, U.K.	180		53.19 N	3.15 W
Glaris see Glarus, Switz.	30	C6	47.02 N	9.04 E
Glarner Alpen, mts., Switz.	30	D6	46.50 N	9.04 E
Glarus, Switz.	30	C6	47.02 N	9.04 E
Glarus Alps see Glarner Alpen, mts., Switz.	30	D6	46.50 N	9.04 E
Glasco, Ks., U.S.	138	B11	39.21 N	97.50 W
Glasgow, Scot., U.K.	10	F8	55.53 N	4.15 W
Glasgow, Ky., U.S.	130	G12	37.00 N	85.54 W
Glasgow, Mo., U.S.	130	E5	39.13 N	92.50 W
Glasgow, Mt., U.S.	142	F7	48.11 N	106.38 W
Glasgow, Va., U.S.	124	G6	37.38 N	79.27 W
Glashütte, ngh., Ger.	181		51.13 N	6.52 E
Glas Maol, mtn., Scot., U.K.	10	E9	56.52 N	3.22 W
Glass, Loch, l., Scot., U.K.	10	D8	57.42 N	4.29 W
Glassboro, N.J., U.S.	124	E10	39.41 N	75.06 W
Glassboro State College, educ., N.J., U.S.	203		39.42 N	75.07 W
Glassmanor, Md., U.S.	202c		38.49 N	76.59 W
Glass Mountains, mts., Tx., U.S.	136	D4	30.23 N	103.14 W
Glastonbury, Eng., U.K.	10	J10	51.09 N	2.43 W
Glatz see Kłodzko, Pol.	24	F12	50.26 N	16.39 E
Glauchau, Ger.	24	F8	50.49 N	12.33 E
Glava, Swe.	16	H10	59.33 N	12.35 E
Glaze Brook, stm., Eng., U.K.	180		53.25 N	2.27 W
Glazebury, Eng., U.K.	180		53.28 N	2.30 W
Glaževo, Russia	26	A14	59.40 N	32.05 E
Glazov, Russia	40	B18	58.08 N	52.39 E
Glazunovka, Russia	26	H19	52.29 N	36.19 E
Gleason, Tn., U.S.	130	H9	36.13 N	88.36 W
Glehn, Ger.	181		51.10 N	6.35 E
Gleichen, Ab., Can.	144	F17	50.52 N	113.03 W
Gleinalpe, mts., Aus.	30	C12	47.15 N	15.03 E
Gleisdorf, Aus.	30	C12	47.06 N	15.43 E
Gleiwitz see Gliwice, Pol.	24	F14	50.17 N	18.40 E
Glen Acres, Pa., U.S.	203		39.58 N	75.34 W
Glen Alpine, N.C., U.S.	132	A4	35.43 N	81.46 W
Glenarchy, On., Can.	193b		43.29 N	79.46 W
Glen Arm, Md., U.S.	202b		39.27 N	76.30 W
Glen Ashton Farms, Pa., U.S.	203		40.06 N	74.55 W
Glenavon, Sk., Can.	142	D10	50.11 N	103.10 W
Glenboro, Mb., Can.	142	E14	49.33 N	99.16 W
Glenburn, N.D., U.S.	142	F12	48.30 N	101.13 W
Glen Burnie, Md., U.S.	124	E9	39.09 N	76.37 W
Glen Canyon, val., U.S.	150	F6	37.10 N	110.50 W
Glen Canyon Dam, dam., Az., U.S.	150	G5	36.56 N	111.27 W
Glen Canyon National Recreation Area, p.o.i., U.S.	150	F6	37.15 N	110.57 W
Glencoe, Austl.	98	K3	37.41 S	140.36 E
Glencoe, On., Can.	126	F8	42.44 N	81.42 W
Glencoe, S. Afr.	90	F9	28.11 S	30.06 E
Glencoe, Al., U.S.	134	D13	33.57 N	85.57 W
Glencoe, Il., U.S.	196		42.08 N	87.45 W
Glencoe, Mn., U.S.	128	G4	44.46 N	94.09 W
Glen Cove, N.Y., U.S.	124	D12	40.51 N	73.38 W
Glendale, Az., U.S.	150	J4	33.32 N	112.11 W
Glendale, Ca., U.S.	148	I7	34.08 N	118.13 W
Glendale, Ms., U.S.	134	F9	31.21 N	89.18 W
Glendale, Or., U.S.	146	H3	42.44 N	123.25 W
Glendale, Ut., U.S.	150	F4	37.19 N	112.35 W
Glendale, Wi., U.S.	130	A10	43.08 N	87.56 W
Glendale Heights, Il., U.S.	196		41.54 N	88.04 W
Glendale Heights, Md., U.S.	202c		38.59 N	76.49 W
Glendive, Mt., U.S.	142	G9	47.06 N	104.42 W
Glendo, Wy., U.S.	140	E7	42.29 N	105.01 W
Glendon, Ab., Can.	144	B19	54.15 N	111.08 W
Glendora, N.J., U.S.	203		39.50 N	75.04 W
Glendo Reservoir, res., Wy., U.S.	140	E8	42.31 N	104.57 W
Glendo State Park, p.o.i., Wy., U.S.	140	E8	42.33 N	104.58 W
Glen Echo, Md., U.S.	202c		38.58 N	77.08 W
Glen Echo Amusement Park, p.o.i., Md., U.S.	202c		38.58 N	77.08 W
Glen Echo Heights, Md., U.S.	202c		38.58 N	77.08 W
Gleneden Beach, Or., U.S.	146	F2	44.52 N	124.02 W
Glen Elder, Ks., U.S.	138	B10	39.29 N	98.17 W
Glenelg, stm., Austl.	98	K3	38.03 S	140.59 E
Glen Ellyn, Il., U.S.	196		41.52 N	88.04 W
Glen Ellyn Countryside, Il., U.S.	196		41.55 N	88.04 W
Glenfield, Austl.	192a		33.58 S	150.54 E
Glenfield, Pa., U.S.	197b		40.31 N	80.08 W
Glen Flora, Tx., U.S.	136	E11	29.21 N	96.12 W
Glengarriff, Ire.	10	J3	51.45 N	9.33 W
Glengyle, Austl.	98	E2	24.54 S	139.37 E
Glenhaven, Austl.	192a		33.42 S	151.00 E
Glen Head, N.Y., U.S.	194		40.50 N	73.37 W
Glenhuntly, Austl.	192b		37.54 S	145.03 E
Glen Innes, Austl.	98	G8	29.44 S	151.44 E
Glen Island, i., N.Y., U.S.	194		40.53 N	73.47 W
Glen Mills, Pa., U.S.	203		39.55 N	75.30 W
Glenmora, La., U.S.	134	G6	30.58 N	92.35 W
Glenmore, Md., U.S.	202b		39.11 N	76.36 W
Glenmorgan, Austl.	98	F7	27.15 S	149.41 E
Glennallen, Ak., U.S.	109	D10	62.05 N	145.32 W
Glenn Dale, Md., U.S.	202c		38.59 N	76.49 W
Glenns Ferry, Id., U.S.	146	H11	42.57 N	115.17 W
Glennville, Ga., U.S.	132	E4	31.56 N	81.55 W
Glen Oak, Il., U.S.	196		41.53 N	88.02 W
Glenolden, Pa., U.S.	203		39.54 N	75.17 W
Glenoma, Wa., U.S.	146	D4	46.30 N	122.09 W
Glenormiston, Austl.	96	D7	22.55 S	138.51 E
Glenreagh, Austl.	98	G9	30.03 S	152.59 E
Glen Riddle, Pa., U.S.	203		39.54 N	75.26 W
Glenridge, Ma., U.S.	201		42.14 N	71.19 W
Glen Ridge, N.J., U.S.	194		40.48 N	74.12 W
Glen Robertson, On., Can.	126	C15	45.21 N	74.29 W
Glen Rock, N.J., U.S.	194		40.57 N	74.08 W
Glen Rock, Pa., U.S.	124	E9	39.47 N	76.43 W
Glenrock, Wy., U.S.	140	E7	42.51 N	105.52 W
Glen Rose, Tx., U.S.	136	B10	32.14 N	97.45 W
Glenrothes, Scot., U.K.	10	E9	56.12 N	3.10 W
Glenroy, Austl.	96	D2	21.46 S	114.49 E
Glenroy, Austl.	192b		37.42 S	144.55 E
Glens Falls, N.Y., U.S.	126	E16	43.18 N	73.38 W
Glenshaw, Pa., U.S.	197b		40.31 N	79.58 W
Glen Stewart Park, p.o.i., On., Can.	193b		43.41 N	79.18 W
Glenties, Ire.	10	G4	54.47 N	8.17 W
Glen Ullin, N.D., U.S.	140	A11	46.48 N	101.49 W
Glenview Countryside, Il., U.S.	196		42.04 N	87.50 W
Glenville, Mn., U.S.	128	H5	43.34 N	93.16 W
Glenville, N.Y., U.S.	194		41.04 N	73.50 W
Glenville, W.V., U.S.	124	F5	38.56 N	80.50 W
Glenvista, S. Afr.	191d		26.17 S	28.13 E
Glen Waverley, Austl.	192b		37.53 S	145.10 E
Glen Wild Lake, l., N.J., U.S.	194		41.02 N	74.20 W
Glenwood, Ab., Can.	144	G17	49.22 N	113.30 W
Glenwood, Al., U.S.	134	F12	31.39 N	86.10 W
Glenwood, Ar., U.S.	134	C5	34.19 N	93.32 W
Glenwood, Ga., U.S.	132	D3	32.10 N	82.40 W
Glenwood, Il., U.S.	196		41.32 N	87.36 W
Glenwood, Ia., U.S.	130	C2	41.02 N	95.44 W
Glenwood, Mn., U.S.	128	F3	45.39 N	95.23 W
Glenwood, N.M., U.S.	150	J8	33.18 N	108.53 W
Glenwood, Ut., U.S.	150	E5	38.46 N	111.59 W
Glenwood, Va., U.S.	124	H6	36.35 N	79.21 W
Glenwood City, Wi., U.S.	128	F6	45.03 N	92.10 W
Glenwood Landing, N.Y., U.S.	194		40.50 N	73.39 W
Glenwood Park, Md., U.S.	202c		38.58 N	76.50 W
Glenwood Springs, Co., U.S.	138	B1	39.33 N	107.19 W
Glenwoodville see Glenwood, Ab., Can.	144	G17	49.22 N	113.30 W
Glidden, Ia., U.S.	130	B3	42.03 N	94.43 W
Glidden, Wi., U.S.	128	E8	46.08 N	90.34 W
Glide, Or., U.S.	146	G3	43.17 N	123.06 W
Gliener Berg, hill, Ger.	182a		52.42 N	13.00 E
Glimåkra, Swe.	16	K12	56.17 N	14.08 E
Glina, Cro.	30	E13	45.20 N	16.05 E
Glindowsee, l., Ger.	182a		52.21 N	12.56 E
Glinka, Russia	26	F15	54.39 N	32.52 E
Glittertinden, mtn., Nor.	16	F6	61.39 N	8.33 E
Gliwice, Pol.	24	F14	50.17 N	18.40 E
Gljadjanskoe, Russia	48	D10	54.54 N	65.06 E
G. L. Martin State Airport, arpt., Md., U.S.	202b		39.20 N	76.25 W
Globe, Az., U.S.	150	J6	33.23 N	110.47 W
Glodeanu-Siliştea, Rom.	36	E13	44.50 N	26.46 E
Glodeni, Mol.	38	F6	47.46 N	27.32 E
Glodok, ngh., Indon.	187e		6.08 S	106.48 E
Glogau see Głogów, Pol.	24	E11	51.39 N	16.05 E
Gloggnitz, Aus.	24	I11	47.40 N	15.55 E
Głogów, Pol.	24	E11	51.39 N	16.05 E
Głogówek, Pol.	24	F13	50.21 N	17.51 E
Głogów Małopolski, Pol.	24	F17	50.10 N	21.58 E
Glomfjord, Nor.	14	F4	66.49 N	13.56 E
Glommersträsk, Swe.	16	B17	65.15 N	19.36 E
Glorieta, N.M., U.S.	138	F3	35.34 N	105.49 W
Glorieuses. Îles, is., Reu.	88	C8	11.30 S	47.20 E
Glorioso Islands see Glorieuses. Îles, is., Reu.	88	C8	11.30 S	47.20 E
Glörstausee, res., Ger.	181		51.14 N	7.29 E
Gloster, Ms., U.S.	134	F7	31.11 N	91.01 W
Glotovka, Russia	40	E15	53.57 N	46.42 E
Glotovo, Russia	12	E23	63.30 N	49.24 E
Gloucester, Austl.	98	H9	32.01 S	151.57 E
Gloucester, Eng., U.K.	10	J10	51.53 N	2.14 W
Gloucester, Ma., U.S.	124	B15	42.37 N	70.39 W
Gloucester, Va., U.S.	124	G9	37.24 N	76.31 W
Gloucester City, N.J., U.S.	203		39.53 N	75.07 W
Gloucester Fisherman, hist., Ma., U.S.	201		42.36 N	70.40 W
Gloucester Island, i., Austl.	98	B7	20.01 S	148.27 E
Glouster, Oh., U.S.	124	E3	39.29 N	82.04 W
Glover, stm., Ok., U.S.	134	C4	34.01 N	94.56 W
Glover-Archbold Park, p.o.i., D.C., U.S.	202c		38.55 N	77.05 W
Gloversville, N.Y., U.S.	124	A11	43.03 N	74.20 W
Glowno, Pol.	24	E15	51.58 N	19.44 E
Głubczyce, Pol.	24	F13	50.11 N	17.50 E
Glubokij, Russia	40	H13	47.00 N	42.46 E
Glubokij, Russia	40	G12	48.31 N	40.19 E
Glubokij, mys, c., Russia	18	C24	64.20 N	37.20 E
Glubokoe see Hlybokae, Bela.	26	E10	55.08 N	27.42 E
Glubokoe, Kaz.	48	D14	50.07 N	82.18 E
Głucholazy, Pol.	24	F13	50.19 N	17.23 E
Glückauf-Kampfbahn, p.o.i., Ger.	181		51.32 N	7.05 E
Glücksburg, Ger.	24	B5	54.50 N	9.33 E
Glückstadt, Ger.	24	C5	53.47 N	9.25 E
Glucomanka, gora, mtn., Russia	54	B11	45.10 N	135.48 E
Gluhovo, Russia	183b		55.46 N	37.16 E
Gluškovo, Russia	38	B13	51.21 N	34.37 E
Glyfáda, Grc.	185c		37.52 N	23.45 E
Glyndon, Mn., U.S.	128	E2	46.52 N	96.35 W
Glyngøre, Den.	16	K6	56.45 N	8.52 E
Gmelinka, Russia	40	F15	50.22 N	46.54 E
Gmünd, Aus.	30	D10	46.54 N	13.32 E
Gmünd, Aus.	30	B12	48.46 N	14.58 E
Gmund am Tegernsee, Ger.	30	C8	47.45 N	11.44 E
Gmunden, Aus.	30	C10	47.55 N	13.47 E
Gnalta, Austl.	98	H4	31.03 S	142.20 E
Gnaraloo, Austl.	96	D2	23.47 S	113.31 E
Gnarp, Swe.	16	E15	62.03 N	17.16 E
Gnesen see Gniezno, Pol.	24	D13	52.31 N	17.36 E
Gnesta, Swe.	16	H15	59.02 N	17.19 E
Gnezdovo, Russia	26	F14	54.46 N	31.51 E
Gniew, Pol.	24	C14	53.51 N	18.49 E
Gniewkowo, Pol.	24	D14	52.54 N	18.25 E
Gniezno, Pol.	24	D13	52.31 N	17.36 E
Gnilec, Russia	26	H19	52.21 N	36.00 E
Gnjilane, Yugo.	36	G8	42.28 N	21.29 E
Gnoien, Ger.	24	C8	53.57 N	12.43 E
Gnosjö, Swe.	16	J11	57.22 N	13.44 E
Gnowangerup, Austl.	96	F3	33.56 S	118.00 E
Gō, stm., Japan	56	E5	35.01 N	132.13 E
Goa, Phil.	68	D4	13.41 N	123.29 E
Goa, state, India	69	D2	15.20 N	74.00 E
Goalen Head, c., Austl.	98	K8	36.32 S	150.02 E
Goālpāra, India	70	E13	26.10 N	90.37 E
Goaso, Ghana	84	H4	6.47 N	2.30 W
Goat Island, i., Antig.	159b	e4	17.42 N	61.50 W
Goat Island, i., N.Y., U.S.	202a		43.05 N	79.04 W
Goat Mountain, mtn., Mt., U.S.	146	C13	47.21 N	113.21 W
Goat Point, c., Antig.	159b	e4	17.43 N	61.51 W
Goba, Eth.	82	F7	7.00 N	39.58 E
Gobabis, Nmb.	90	C4	22.26 S	18.57 E
Göbel, Tur.	34	D11	40.00 N	28.09 E
Gobernador Gregores, Arg.	166	I2	48.46 S	70.15 W
Gobernador Ingeniero Valentín Virasoro, Arg.	172	D9	28.03 S	56.01 W
Gobernador Juan E. Martínez, Arg.	172	D8	28.53 S	58.56 W
Gobernador Monteverde, Arg.	206		34.48 S	58.16 W
Gobernador Vera see Vera, Arg.	172	D7	29.28 S	60.13 W
Gobi, des., Asia	58	A4	41.05 N	111.48 E
Gobi Desert, des., Asia	52	C6	43.00 N	105.00 E
Gobindapur, India	190b		22.23 N	88.25 E
Gobindpur, India	190b		22.55 N	88.12 E
Gobles, Mi., U.S.	130	B12	42.21 N	85.52 W
Gobō, Japan	56	F8	33.53 N	135.10 E
Gobza, stm., Russia	26	E14	55.16 N	31.31 E
Goce Delčev, Blg.	36	H10	41.34 N	23.45 E
Goch, Ger.	24	E2	51.41 N	6.09 E
Gochas, Nmb.	90	D4	24.52 S	18.47 E
Go Cong, Viet.	187c		10.50 N	106.50 E

Name | Page | Map Ref. | Latitude | Longitude

Godafoss, wtfl., Ice. 12a k31 65.40 N 17.32 W
Godāvari, stm., India 69 C5 16.58 N 81.46 E
Godāvari, Mouths of the, mth., India 69 C6 16.17 N 81.52 E
Godbout, Qc., Can. 122 A9 49.19 N 67.37 W
Goddard Space Flight Center, bldg., Md., U.S. 202c 39.00 N 76.52 W
Goderich, On., Can. 126 E8 43.44 N 81.42 W
Godfrey, Il., U.S. 130 F7 38.56 N 90.11 W
Godhavn (Qeqertarsuaq), Grnld. 108 D15 69.15 N 53.33 W
Godhra, India 70 G4 22.45 N 73.36 E
Gōdo, Japan 186 35.51 N 139.44 E
Gödöllő, Hung. 36 B6 47.35 N 19.21 E
Gödöllő, Hung. 182c 47.36 N 19.22 E
Gödöllői Dombság, hills, Hung. 182c 47.37 N 19.16 E
Godoy Cruz, Arg. 172 F3 32.55 S 68.50 W
Gods, stm., Mb., Can. 110 D12 56.22 N 92.51 W
Gods Lake, Mb., Can. 110 E12 54.39 N 94.08 W
Gods Lake, l., Mb., Can. 110 E12 54.42 N 94.14 W
Gods Mercy, Bay of, b., Nu., Can. 110 C13 63.30 N 86.10 W
Godthåb (Nuuk), Grnld. 108 E15 64.11 N 51.44 W
Godwin Austen see K2, mtn., Asia 62 A4 35.53 N 76.30 E
Goeie Hoop, Kaap die see Good Hope, Cape of, c., S. Afr. 90 I4 34.20 S 18.28 E
Goéland, Lac au, l., Qc., Can. 114 B12 49.47 N 76.48 W
Goes, Neth. 20 C12 51.30 N 3.52 E
Goff, Ks., U.S. 130 E2 39.40 N 95.56 W
Goff Creek, stm., Ok., U.S. 138 E7 36.43 N 101.28 W
Goffle Brook, stm., N.J., U.S. 194 40.56 N 74.08 W
Goff's Oak, Eng., U.K. 178 51.43 N 0.05 W
Goffstown, N.H., U.S. 122 G5 43.01 N 71.35 W
Gogebic, Lake, res., Mi., U.S. 128 E9 46.29 N 89.33 W
Göggingen, Ger. 24 H6 48.20 N 10.52 E
Gogland, ostrov, i., Russia 18 H14 60.05 N 26.58 E
Gogoi, Moz. 90 B11 20.15 S 33.05 E
Gogrial, Sudan 82 F5 8.31 N 28.06 E
Gohad, India 70 E7 26.25 N 78.26 E
Gohpur, India 70 E14 26.52 N 93.38 E
Gohr, Ger. 181 51.06 N 6.43 E
Goiana, Braz. 170 D8 7.33 S 34.59 W
Goiandira, Braz. 170 J1 18.08 S 48.06 W
Goianésia, Braz. 170 H1 15.18 S 49.08 W
Goiânia, Braz. 170 I1 16.40 S 49.16 W
Goianinha, Braz. 170 D8 6.16 S 35.12 W
Goiás, Braz. 166 C6 15.55 S 50.07 W
Goiás, state, Braz. 166 C7 16.00 S 50.00 W
Goiatuba, Braz. 170 J1 18.00 S 49.21 W
Goichran, India 70 C7 31.03 N 78.07 E
Goio-Erê, Braz. 172 B11 24.10 S 53.01 W
Gôio-Erê, stm., Braz. 172 B11 24.12 S 53.18 W
Góis, Port. 28 D2 40.09 N 8.06 W
Goito, Italy 30 E7 45.16 N 10.39 E
Gojō, Japan 56 E8 34.20 N 135.42 E
Gojra, Pak. 70 C4 31.08 N 72.41 E
Gök, stm., Tur. 42 E6 41.23 N 35.07 E
Gokāk, India 69 C2 16.08 N 74.49 E
Gokase, stm., Japan 56 G4 32.34 N 131.41 E
Gökçeada, i., Tur. 34 C8 40.10 N 25.50 E
Gokōmutsumi, Japan 186 35.48 N 139.59 E
Gökova Körfezi (Kerme, Gulf of), b., Tur. 34 G10 36.53 N 27.50 E
Göksu, stm., Tur. 42 G5 36.19 N 34.03 E
Göksu, stm., Tur. 76 A6 37.43 N 35.49 E
Göksu, stm., Tur. 185b 41.06 N 29.03 E
Göktepe, Tur. 34 F11 37.15 N 28.36 E
Göktürk, ngh., Tur. 185b 41.11 N 28.53 E
Gokwe, Zimb. 88 D4 18.06 S 28.55 E
Gol, Nor. 16 G6 60.42 N 8.56 E
Golabāri, India 190b 22.36 N 88.20 E
Golāghāt, India 62 C7 26.30 N 93.58 E
Gola Gokarannāth, India 70 D8 28.05 N 80.28 E
Gołańcz, Pol. 24 D13 52.56 N 17.17 E
Gölbaşı, Tur. 34 D15 39.48 N 32.50 E
Gölbaşı, Tur. 76 A8 37.47 N 37.39 E
Golborne, Eng., U.K. 180 53.29 N 2.36 W
Golconda, hist., India 69 C4 17.27 N 78.23 E
Golcar, Eng., U.K. 180 53.39 N 1.51 W
Golconda, Il., U.S. 130 G9 37.21 N 88.29 W
Golconda, Nv., U.S. 148 C8 40.57 N 117.29 W
Gölcük, Tur. 34 C12 40.44 N 29.49 E
Gölcük, Tur. 34 D10 39.18 N 27.59 E
Goldap, Pol. 24 B18 54.18 N 22.17 E
Gold Beach, Or., U.S. 148 A1 42.24 N 124.24 W
Goldbergtunnel, trans., Ger. 181 51.21 N 7.28 E
Goldboro, N.S., Can. 122 E15 45.12 N 61.40 W
Gold Bridge, B.C., Can. 144 F8 50.50 N 122.49 W
Gold Coast see Southport, Austl. 98 F9 27.57 S 153.24 E
Gold Coast, cst., Ghana 84 I4 5.19 N 0.35 W
Gold Creek, stm., B.C., Can. 144 G15 49.04 N 115.12 W
Golden, B.C., Can. 144 E13 51.18 N 116.57 W
Golden, Co., U.S. 138 B3 39.45 N 105.12 W
Golden, Il., U.S. 130 D7 40.06 N 91.00 W
Golden Bay, b., N.Z. 102 E5 40.40 S 172.50 E
Golden Brook, stm., N.H., U.S. 201 42.44 N 71.19 W
Golden City, Mo., U.S. 130 G3 37.23 N 94.05 W
Goldendale, Wa., U.S. 146 E6 45.49 N 120.49 W
Golden Ears Provincial Park, p.o.i., B.C., Can. 144 G8 49.30 N 122.25 W
Golden Gate Bridge, trans., Ca., U.S. 200 37.49 N 122.28 W
Golden Gate Fields Race Track, p.o.i., Ca., U.S. 200 37.53 N 122.19 W
Golden Gate Highlands National Park, p.o.i., S. Afr. 90 F9 28.30 S 28.40 E
Golden Gate National Recreation Area, p.o.i., Ca., U.S. 200 37.49 N 122.31 W
Golden Gate Park, p.o.i., Ca., U.S. 200 37.46 N 122.28 W
Golden Green, Eng., U.K. 178 51.12 N 0.21 E
Golden Hinde, mtn., B.C., Can. 144 G5 49.40 N 125.45 W
Golden Horn see Haliç, b., Tur. 185b 41.02 N 28.58 E
Golden Lake, l., On., Can. 126 C12 45.34 N 77.21 W
Golden Meadow, La., U.S. 134 H8 29.22 N 90.15 W
Golden Prairie, Sk., Can. 142 D4 50.14 N 109.38 W
Golden Ring Mall, shp. cen., Md., U.S. 202b 39.20 N 76.29 W
Golden Spike National Historic Site, p.o.i., Ut., U.S. 150 B4 41.38 N 112.35 W
Golders Green, ngh., Eng., U.K. 178 51.35 N 0.12 W
Goldfield, Ia., U.S. 130 B4 42.44 N 93.55 W
Goldfield, Nv., U.S. 148 F8 37.42 N 117.13 W
Gold Mountain, mtn., Nv., U.S. 148 F8 37.15 N 117.18 W
Goldonna, La., U.S. 134 E6 32.01 N 92.54 W
Gold River, B.C., Can. 144 G4 49.41 N 126.08 W
Gold Rock, On., Can. 128 B6 49.26 N 92.42 W
Goldsboro, N.C., U.S. 132 A7 35.23 N 77.59 W
Goldsmith, Tx., U.S. 136 B5 31.58 N 102.36 W
Goldston, N.C., U.S. 132 A6 35.35 N 79.19 W
Goldsworthy, Austl. 96 D3 20.21 S 119.30 E
Goldthwaite, Tx., U.S. 136 C9 31.26 N 98.34 W
Golela, S. Afr. 90 E10 27.20 S 31.52 E
Goleniów, Pol. 24 C10 53.33 N 14.50 E
Golestan Palace, bldg., Iran 185d 35.41 N 51.25 E
Goleta, Ca., U.S. 148 I6 34.26 N 119.50 W
Golevo, Russia 183b 55.48 N 37.19 E
Golf, Il., U.S. 196 42.03 N 87.48 W
Golfito, C.R. 156 H6 8.37 N 83.09 W
Golf Manor, N.J., U.S. 203 39.42 N 75.28 W
Golf Mill, shp. cen., Il., U.S. 196 42.03 N 87.50 W
Golfo Aranci, Italy 32 C3 41.00 N 9.38 E
Golfo de Santa Clara, Mex. 120 F5 31.41 N 114.29 W
Golfside, Mi., U.S. 199 42.15 N 83.41 W
Golfview Hills, Il., U.S. 196 41.47 N 87.56 W
Gölhisar, Tur. 34 F12 37.09 N 29.31 E
Goliad, Tx., U.S. 136 F10 28.40 N 97.23 W
Golicyno, Russia 26 E19 55.36 N 37.00 E
Golicyno, Russia 40 E13 55.37 N 44.07 E
Golina, Pol. 24 D14 52.14 N 18.05 E
Golin Baixing, China 54 B4 44.53 N 121.49 E
Goljama Kamčija, stm., Blg. 36 F14 43.03 N 27.26 E
Goljam Perelik, mtn., Blg. 36 H11 41.36 N 24.34 E
Goljanovo, ngh., Russia 183b 55.49 N 37.48 E
Gölköy, Tur. 42 E7 40.42 N 37.38 E
Gollnow see Goleniów, Pol. 24 C10 53.33 N 14.50 E
Golm, Ger. 182a 52.24 N 12.58 E
Gölmarmara, Tur. 34 E10 38.42 N 27.55 E
Golmud, China 52 D3 36.24 N 94.53 E
Golmud, stm., China 62 A7 36.35 N 95.11 E
Golo, stm., Fr. 22 G15 42.31 N 9.31 E
Golodnaja Guba, ozero, l., Russia 12 C24 67.52 N 52.48 E
Golovčino, Russia 38 C14 50.32 N 35.47 E
Golovin, Ak., U.S. 109 D7 64.33 N 163.02 W
Golovskoe, Russia 48 C18 55.31 N 105.33 E
Golpāyegān, Iran 74 D12 33.27 N 50.17 E
Gölpazarı, Tur. 34 C13 40.18 N 30.18 E
Golspie, Scot., U.K. 10 D9 57.58 N 3.58 W
Golub-Dobrzyń, Pol. 24 C14 53.07 N 19.02 E
Golva, N.D., U.S. 140 A8 46.44 N 103.59 W
Golynki, Russia 26 F14 54.51 N 31.22 E
Golyšmanovo, Russia 48 C11 56.23 N 68.22 E
Golzheim, ngh., Ger. 181 51.15 N 6.46 E
Goma, D.R.C. 86 E5 1.41 S 29.13 E
Gomang Co, l., China 70 C12 31.12 N 89.11 E
Gomas, Sierra de, mts., Mex. 136 H7 26.21 N 100.29 W
Gomati, stm., India 70 E8 25.31 N 83.09 E
Goma Tsétsé, Congo 191b 4.14 S 15.08 E
Gombe, Nig. 84 G7 10.17 N 11.10 E
Gombi, Nig. 84 G7 10.10 N 12.44 E
Gomel' see Homel', state, Bela. 40 E6 52.30 N 30.00 E
Gometz-la-Ville, Fr. 179 48.40 N 2.08 E
Gometz-le-Châtel, Fr. 179 48.41 N 2.08 E
Gómez Farías, Mex. 154 A5 29.17 N 107.42 W
Gómez Palacio, Mex. 154 C7 25.34 N 103.29 W
Gómez Plata, Col. 168 D4 6.40 N 75.12 W
Gomīshān, Iran 74 B14 37.04 N 54.04 E
Gommécourt, Fr. 179 49.05 N 1.36 E
Gomo Co, l., China 70 B10 33.39 N 85.48 E
Gomogomo, Indon. 101a b1 6.40 S 134.43 E
Gomoh, India 70 G10 23.52 N 86.10 E
Gomorovići, Russia 18 G21 60.53 N 34.46 E
Gompa, India 70 A6 35.02 N 77.20 E
Gomshall, Eng., U.K. 178 51.13 N 0.27 W
Gonābād, Iran 72 C8 34.21 N 58.41 E
Gonaïves, Haiti 156 C11 19.26 N 72.41 W
Gonam, Russia 50 E15 57.21 N 131.13 E
Gonam, stm., Russia 50 E14 57.18 N 131.14 E
Gonarezhou National Park, p.o.i., Zimb. 90 B10 21.30 S 32.00 E
Gonâve, Golfe de la, b., Haiti 156 C11 19.00 N 73.30 W
Gonâve, Île de la, i., Haiti 156 C11 18.51 N 73.03 W
Gonbad-e Qābūs, Iran 74 B14 37.16 N 55.09 E
Gonçalves Dias, Braz. 170 C3 4.57 S 44.14 W
Gončarovka, Russia 38 C18 50.32 N 39.30 E
Gonda, India 70 E8 27.07 N 81.57 E
Gondal, India 70 G3 21.57 N 70.48 E
Gondar see Gonder, Eth. 82 E7 12.36 N 37.27 E
Gondarbal, India 70 A5 34.13 N 74.47 E
Gonder, Eth. 82 E7 12.36 N 37.27 E
Gondia, India 70 H8 21.27 N 80.11 E
Gönen, Tur. 34 C10 40.06 N 27.39 E
Gong, stm., China 58 I6 25.57 N 115.27 E
Gong'an, China 58 F5 30.03 N 112.13 E
Gongcheng, China 58 I4 24.49 N 110.48 E
Gongchenqiao, China 58 F8 30.20 N 120.08 E
Gongdian, China 58 G7 28.06 N 116.56 E
Gonggar, China 70 D13 29.15 N 90.48 E
Gongga Shan, mtn., China 46 G14 29.35 N 101.51 E
Gonghe, China 52 D5 36.15 N 100.37 E
Gongliu, China 48 F14 43.28 N 82.13 E
Gongola, stm., Nig. 84 G7 9.29 N 12.02 E
Gongpengzi, China 54 B6 45.09 N 125.39 E
Gongshiya, China 70 C10 31.25 N 84.37 E
Gongxi, China 58 H6 27.37 N 115.51 E
Gongxian, China 58 D5 34.48 N 113.02 E
Gongyemiao, China 54 C4 43.36 N 121.01 E
Gongzhuling, China 54 C9 43.30 N 124.49 E
Goñi, Ur. 172 F9 33.31 S 56.26 W
Goniądz, Pol. 24 C18 53.29 N 22.45 E
Gonjo, China 52 E4 30.43 N 98.19 E
Gōnoura, Japan 56 F2 33.44 N 129.41 E
Gonzaga, Phil. 68 A4 18.15 N 121.59 E
Gonzales, Ca., U.S. 148 G4 36.30 N 121.24 W
Gonzales, La., U.S. 134 G8 30.14 N 90.55 W
Gonzales, Tx., U.S. 136 E10 29.30 N 97.27 W
González, Mex. 154 D9 22.50 N 98.25 W
González Moreno, Arg. 172 G6 35.33 S 63.21 W
González Ortega, Mex. 150 K1 32.38 N 115.26 W
Goochland, Va., U.S. 124 G8 37.40 N 77.53 W
Good Easter, Eng., U.K. 178 51.47 N 0.21 E
Goodenough Island, i., Pap. N. Gui. 101a b5 9.20 S 150.15 E
Gooderham, On., Can. 126 D11 44.53 N 78.22 W
Goodeve, Sk., Can. 142 C10 51.04 N 103.10 W
Goodfellow Air Force Base, mil., Tx., U.S. 136 C7 31.26 N 100.25 W
Good Hope, Cape of (Goeie Hoop, Kaap die), c., S. Afr. 90 I4 34.20 S 18.28 E
Good Hope Mountain, mtn., B.C., Can. 144 E6 51.09 N 124.10 W
Goodhouse, S. Afr. 90 F4 28.54 S 18.14 E
Goodhue, Mn., U.S. 128 G6 44.23 N 92.38 W
Gooding, Id., U.S. 146 H12 42.56 N 114.42 W
Goodland, Fl., U.S. 132 K4 25.55 N 81.39 W
Goodland, In., U.S. 128 K11 40.45 N 87.17 W
Goodland, Ks., U.S. 138 B7 39.20 N 101.43 W
Goodlands, Mb., Can. 142 E13 49.04 N 100.33 W
Goodman, Ms., U.S. 134 D8 32.58 N 89.54 W
Goodman, Wi., U.S. 126 C1 45.38 N 88.23 W
Goodnews Bay, Ak., U.S. 109 E7 59.07 N 161.35 W
Goodnight, Co., U.S. 138 C4 38.14 N 104.43 W
Goodooga, Austl. 98 G6 29.07 S 147.27 E
Goodrich, N.D., U.S. 142 G13 47.27 N 100.08 W
Goodrich, Tx., U.S. 136 D13 30.36 N 94.57 W
Good Spirit Lake, l., Sk., Can. 142 C11 51.32 N 102.40 W
Good Spirit Lake Provincial Park, p.o.i., Sk., Can. 142 C10 51.32 N 102.43 W
Good Thunder, Mn., U.S. 128 H5 44.00 N 94.04 W
Goodview, Mn., U.S. 128 G7 44.04 N 91.41 W
Goodwater, Al., U.S. 134 D12 33.03 N 86.03 W
Goodwell, Ok., U.S. 138 E7 36.35 N 101.38 W
Goodwives, stm., Ct., U.S. 194 41.04 N 73.28 W
Goodyear, Az., U.S. 150 J4 33.26 N 112.21 W
Goole, Eng., U.K. 10 H12 53.42 N 0.52 W
Goolgowi, Austl. 98 I5 33.58 S 145.42 E
Goomburra, Austl. 98 G9 28.03 S 152.07 E
Goonda, Moz. 90 A11 19.50 S 33.59 E
Goondiwindi, Austl. 98 G8 28.32 S 150.18 E
Goongarrie, Austl. 96 F4 30.02 S 121.10 E
Goonyella, Austl. 98 C6 21.47 S 147.57 E
Goose, stm., Ab., Can. 144 B14 54.57 N 117.11 W
Goose, stm., N.D., U.S. 142 G16 47.27 N 96.52 W
Goose Bay, b., Mi., U.S. 199 42.35 N 82.41 W
Gooseberry Creek, stm., Wy., U.S. 140 C4 43.54 N 108.03 W
Goose Creek, S.C., U.S. 132 C6 32.59 N 80.02 W
Goose Creek, stm., U.S. 146 H13 42.26 N 113.53 W
Goose Creek, stm., Ne., U.S. 140 E12 42.00 N 100.02 W
Goose Island, i., B.C., Can. 144 E2 51.57 N 128.26 W
Goose Lake, l., Sk., Can. 142 C6 51.45 N 107.23 W
Goose Lake, l., U.S. 148 B5 41.57 N 120.25 W
Goostrey, Eng., U.K. 180 53.13 N 2.20 W
Gooty, India 69 D3 15.07 N 77.37 E
Gopālganj, Bngl. 70 G12 23.00 N 89.50 E
Gopālganj, India 70 E10 26.27 N 84.26 E
Gopālnagar, India 190b 22.50 N 88.14 E
Gopālpur, India 190b 22.38 N 88.27 E
Gopichettipālaiyam, India 69 F3 11.27 N 77.40 E
Gopinagar, India 190b 22.50 N 88.07 E
Göppingen, Ger. 24 H5 48.42 N 9.39 E
Goqên, China 52 F4 29.08 N 97.13 E
Go Quao, Viet. 64 H7 9.45 N 105.19 E
Góra, Pol. 24 E12 51.40 N 16.32 E
Góra Kalwaria, Pol. 24 E17 51.59 N 21.13 E
Gorakhpur, India 70 E9 26.45 N 83.22 E
Goras, India 70 F6 25.32 N 76.57 E
Goražde, Bos. 36 F5 43.40 N 18.58 E
Gorčuha, Russia 40 C13 57.42 N 43.41 E
Gorda, Punta, c., Cuba 156 A6 22.23 N 82.09 W
Gorda, Punta, c., Nic. 156 E6 14.19 N 83.12 W
Gorda, Punta, c., Ca., U.S. 148 C1 40.15 N 124.20 W
Gordeevka, Russia 26 H14 52.58 N 31.58 E
Gördes, Tur. 34 E11 38.54 N 28.18 E
Gordion, hist., Tur. 34 D15 39.41 N 32.01 E
Gordo, Al., U.S. 134 D11 33.19 N 87.54 W
Gordon, Ga., U.S. 132 D2 32.53 N 83.19 W
Gordon, Ne., U.S. 140 E10 42.48 N 102.12 W
Gordon, Wi., U.S. 128 E7 46.14 N 91.47 W
Gordon, Lake, res., Austl. 99a o13 42.42 S 146.12 E
Gordon Creek, stm., Ne., U.S. 140 E11 42.48 N 100.39 W
Gordon Downs, Austl. 96 C5 18.44 S 128.35 E
Gordon Horne Peak, mtn., B.C., Can. 144 E12 51.46 N 118.50 W
Gordon Indian Reserve, ind. res., Sk., Can. 142 C9 51.16 N 104.16 W
Gordon Lakes, N.J., U.S. 194 41.03 N 74.22 W
Gordonsville, Va., U.S. 124 F7 38.07 N 78.10 W
Gordonvale, Austl. 98 A5 17.05 S 145.47 E
Gore, Austl. 98 G8 28.18 S 151.29 E
Gore, N.S., Can. 122 E13 45.07 N 63.42 W
Goré, Chad 82 F3 7.54 N 16.38 E
Gorē, Eth. 82 F7 8.08 N 35.32 E
Gore, N.Z. 102 H3 46.05 S 168.57 E
Gore Bay, On., Can. 126 C7 45.54 N 82.27 W
Goreda, Indon. 60 F9 3.39 S 134.59 E
Goree, Tx., U.S. 138 H9 33.29 N 99.30 W
Gore Hill, Austl. 192a 33.49 S 151.11 E
Goreloe, Russia 40 E12 52.57 N 41.28 E
Gorelovo, ngh., Russia 183a 59.47 N 30.08 E
Gorelovo Airport, arpt., Russia 183a 59.47 N 30.05 E
Gorelyj, stm., Russia 183a 59.58 N 30.28 E
Gore Mountain, mtn., Vt., U.S. 122 F5 44.55 N 71.48 W
Gorenki, Russia 183b 55.48 N 37.55 E
Gore Point, c., Austl. 98 A2 17.38 S 139.55 E
Gore Range, mts., Co., U.S. 140 H6 39.53 N 106.27 W
Goretovka, stm., Russia 183b 55.56 N 37.20 E
Goreville, Il., U.S. 130 G8 37.33 N 88.58 W
Gorey, Ire. 10 I6 52.40 N 6.18 W
Gorgān, Iran 74 B14 36.50 N 54.25 E
Gorgān, stm., Iran 74 B14 36.59 N 54.00 E
Gorgona, Isla, i., Col. 168 F2 2.57 N 78.11 W
Gorgona, Isola di, i., Italy 30 G6 43.26 N 9.54 E
Gorgota, Rom. 36 E13 44.45 N 26.05 E
Gorgova, Rom. 36 D16 45.10 N 29.09 E
Gorham, Me., U.S. 122 G6 43.41 N 70.26 W
Gorham, N.H., U.S. 122 F5 44.22 N 71.10 W
Gorhambury House, hist., Eng., U.K. 178 51.47 N 0.24 W
Gori, Geor. 42 D11 41.58 N 44.06 E
Goria, India 190b 22.24 N 88.29 E
Gorica see Gorizia, Italy 30 E10 45.57 N 13.37 E
Goricy, Russia 26 C19 57.09 N 36.43 E
Gorinchem, Neth. 20 C14 51.49 N 5.00 E
Goris, Arm. 42 F12 39.30 N 46.20 E
Gorizia (Gorica), Italy 30 E10 45.57 N 13.37 E
Gorj, state, Rom. 36 E10 45.00 N 23.20 E
Gorjačegorsk, Russia 50 E6 55.24 N 88.53 E
Gorjačij Ključ, Russia 42 C8 44.37 N 39.07 E
Gor'kaja Balka, Russia 40 H12 46.06 N 40.41 E
Gorkhā, Nepal 70 E10 28.00 N 84.37 E
Gorki see Horki, Bela. 26 F13 54.16 N 30.58 E
Gorki see Nižnij Novgorod, Russia 12 H21 56.18 N 44.00 E
Gorki see Nizjnij Novgorod, Russia 40 C14 56.18 N 44.00 E
Gorki, Russia 48 A11 65.04 N 65.17 E
Gorki, Russia 183b 55.57 N 37.55 E
Gor'kij see Nižnij Novgorod, Russia 12 H21 56.18 N 44.00 E
Gor'kij see Nizjnij Novgorod, Russia 40 C14 56.18 N 44.00 E
Gorki Vtorye, Russia 183b 55.44 N 37.11 E
Gorkiy Reservoir see Gor'kovskoe vodohranilišče, res., Russia 40 C13 57.01 N 43.09 E
Gor'kovskoe vodohranilišče (Gorkiy Reservoir), res., Russia 40 C13 57.01 N 43.09 E
Gorky Park, p.o.i., Russia 183b 55.44 N 37.36 E
Gorla Maggiore, Italy 184b 45.40 N 8.53 E
Gorla Minore, Italy 184b 45.39 N 8.54 E
Gorlice, Pol. 24 G17 49.39 N 21.09 E
Görlitz, Ger. 24 E10 51.09 N 14.59 E
Gorman, Tx., U.S. 136 B9 32.12 N 98.40 W
Gorna Dzhumaya see Blagoevgrad, Blg. 36 G10 42.01 N 23.06 E
Gorna Orjahovica, Blg. 36 F12 43.07 N 25.42 E
Gornjak, Russia 48 D14 51.00 N 81.28 E
Gornji Milanovac, Yugo. 36 E7 44.01 N 20.26 E
Gornji Vakuf, Bos. 36 F4 43.56 N 17.34 E
Gorno-Altajsk, Russia 48 D15 51.58 N 85.51 E
Gorno-Altay see Altaj, state, Russia 48 D15 51.00 N 86.00 E
Gornovodnoe, Russia 54 C11 43.42 N 134.44 E
Gornozavodsk, Russia 40 B21 58.22 N 58.19 E
Gornozavodsk, Russia 52 B13 46.32 N 141.51 E
Gornye Ključi, Russia 54 B10 45.11 N 133.30 E
Gornyj, Russia 40 F16 51.46 N 48.31 E
Gornyj, Russia 54 B11 44.57 N 133.59 E
Gornyj Balyklej, Russia 40 G14 49.33 N 45.04 E
Gorodec, Russia 26 B12 58.32 N 29.48 E
Gorodec, Russia 40 C13 56.38 N 43.28 E
Gorodišče see Haradzišča, Bela. 26 G9 53.19 N 26.01 E
Gorodišče, Russia 26 A15 59.37 N 32.08 E
Gorodišče, Russia 40 E14 53.16 N 45.41 E
Gorodn'a, stm., Russia 183b 55.38 N 37.48 E
Gorodno, Russia 26 C12 57.32 N 29.35 E
Gorohove, Russia 26 D13 56.30 N 30.27 E
Goroka, Pap. N. Gui. 101a b4 6.05 S 145.24 E
Gorong, Pulau, i., Indon. 60 F9 3.59 S 131.24 E
Gorongosa, stm., Moz. 90 B12 20.36 S 34.40 E
Gorongosa, Serra da, mtn., Moz. 88 D5 18.24 S 34.02 E
Gorontalo, Indon. 60 E7 0.32 N 123.04 E
Górowo Iławeckie, Pol. 24 B16 54.17 N 20.30 E
Gorple Reservoirs, res., Eng., U.K. 180 53.47 N 2.06 W
Gorron, Fr. 20 F8 48.25 N 0.49 W
Goršečnoe, Russia 40 F10 51.31 N 38.02 E
Gorsedd, Wales, U.K. 180 53.17 N 3.16 W
Gorskaja, Russia 183a 60.03 N 29.59 E
Gorškovo, Russia 26 F20 54.26 N 37.59 E
Gort, Ire. 10 H4 53.04 N 8.49 W
Gorton, ngh., Eng., U.K. 180 53.27 N 2.10 W
Goru, Vârful, mtn., Rom. 36 D13 45.48 N 26.25 E
Görükle, Tur. 34 C11 40.14 N 28.47 E
Gorutuba, stm., Braz. 170 H4 14.57 S 43.33 W
Goryn' see Haryn', stm., Eur. 40 F5 52.08 N 27.17 E
Goryn' see Horyn', stm., Eur. 40 F5 52.08 N 27.17 E
Görz see Gorizia, Italy 30 E10 45.57 N 13.37 E
Górzno, Pol. 24 C15 53.12 N 19.38 E
Gorzów Śląski, Pol. 24 E14 51.02 N 18.24 E
Gorzów Wielkopolski (Landsberg), Pol. 24 D11 52.44 N 15.14 E
Goschen Strait, strt., Pap. N. Gui. 101a c5 10.09 S 150.56 E
Gosen, Ger. 182a 52.24 N 13.43 E
Gosen, Japan 56 B12 37.44 N 139.11 E
Gosford, Austl. 98 I8 33.25 S 151.20 E
Gosforth Park, p.o.i., S. Afr. 191d 26.14 S 28.10 E
Gosforth Park Race Course, p.o.i., S. Afr. 191d 26.14 S 28.08 E
Goshen, N.S., Can. 122 E15 45.22 N 61.59 W
Goshen, Ca., U.S. 148 G6 36.21 N 119.25 W
Goshen, In., U.S. 130 C12 41.35 N 85.49 W
Goshen, N.Y., U.S. 124 C11 41.24 N 74.20 W
Goshute Indian Reservation, ind. res., U.S. 150 D2 39.53 N 114.08 W
Goshute Lake, l., Nv., U.S. 150 C2 40.07 N 114.41 W
Goshute Valley, val., Nv., U.S. 150 C2 40.40 N 114.30 W
Goslar, Ger. 24 E6 51.54 N 10.26 E
Gosnells, Austl. 96 F3 32.03 S 115.59 E
Gospić, Cro. 30 F12 44.32 N 15.22 E
Gosport, In., U.S. 130 E11 39.20 N 86.40 W
Gossa, i., Nor. 16 E4 62.49 N 6.53 E
Gosse, ngh., Ger. 181 51.08 N 7.01 E
Gosser Hill, Pa., U.S. 197b 40.37 N 79.37 W
Gossinga, Sudan 82 F5 8.38 N 25.58 E
Gostagaevskaja, Russia 38 I16 45.01 N 37.30 E
Gostiščevo, Russia 38 C15 50.46 N 36.39 E
Gostivar, Mac. 34 B3 41.47 N 20.55 E
Gostynin, Pol. 24 D15 52.25 N 19.28 E
Göta, stm., Swe. 16 I10 57.41 N 11.52 E
Göta Kanal, can., Swe. 16 I12 58.50 N 13.59 E
Got Creek, stm., N.Y., U.S. 202a 43.03 N 78.42 W
Gotebo, Ok., U.S. 138 F10 35.04 N 98.52 W
Göteborg (Gothenburg), Swe. 16 J9 57.43 N 11.58 E
Gotemba, Japan 56 D11 35.18 N 138.56 E
Götene, Swe. 16 I11 58.31 N 13.31 E
Gotești, Mol. 38 G7 46.08 N 28.10 E
Gotha, Ger. 24 F6 50.57 N 10.42 E
Gothem, Swe. 16 J16 57.35 N 18.45 E
Gothenburg see Göteborg, Swe. 16 J9 57.43 N 11.58 E
Gothenburg, Ne., U.S. 140 G12 40.55 N 100.09 W
Gothèye, Niger 84 G5 13.51 N 1.33 E
Gotland, state, Swe. 12 G8 57.30 N 18.30 E
Gotland, i., Swe. 16 J16 57.30 N 18.33 E
Gotō-rettō, is., Japan 56 F1 32.50 N 129.00 E
Gotska Sandön, i., Swe. 16 I16 58.22 N 19.15 E
Gōtsu, Japan 56 D5 34.59 N 132.13 E
Götterswickerhamm, Ger. 181 51.35 N 6.40 E
Gottesbrücke, Ger. 182a 52.25 N 13.49 E
Göttin, Ger. 182a 52.27 N 12.54 E
Göttingen, Ger. 24 E5 51.32 N 9.56 E
Göttinsee, l., Ger. 182a 52.28 N 12.54 E
Gottwaldov see Zlín, Czech Rep. 24 G13 49.13 N 17.40 E
Götzendorf, Aus. 182b 48.01 N 16.35 E
Götzis, Aus. 24 I5 47.19 N 9.38 E
Goubangzi, China 54 D4 41.21 N 121.46 E
Goubone, Chad 82 C3 20.43 N 17.08 E
Gouda, Neth. 20 B13 52.00 N 4.42 E
Goudge, Arg. 172 G3 34.40 S 68.10 W
Goudiri, Sen. 84 G2 14.11 N 12.43 W
Goudoumaria, Niger 84 G7 13.43 N 11.11 E
Gouet, stm., Fr. 20 F6 48.32 N 2.44 W
Gough Island, i., St. Hel. 80 K5 40.20 S 10.00 W
Gough Lake, l., Ab., Can. 144 D18 52.02 N 112.28 W
Gouin, Réservoir, res., Qc., Can. 122 B1 48.37 N 74.55 W
Goulais, stm., On., Can. 126 B6 46.54 N 83.55 W
Goulburn, Austl. 98 J7 34.45 S 149.42 E
Goulburn Islands, is., Austl. 96 B6 11.33 S 133.26 E
Goulburn River National Park, p.o.i., Austl. 98 I7 32.20 S 150.14 E
Gould, Ar., U.S. 134 D7 33.59 N 91.33 W
Gould City, Mi., U.S. 126 B4 46.05 N 85.42 W
Goulds, Fl., U.S. 132 K5 25.33 N 80.22 W
Goumbou, Mali 84 G3 14.59 N 7.27 W
Gouménissa, Grc. 34 C5 40.55 N 22.27 E
Goundam, Mali 84 F4 16.25 N 3.39 W
Goundi, Chad 82 F3 9.22 N 17.22 E
Goupillières, Fr. 179 48.53 N 1.46 E
Gouraya, Alg. 28 H12 36.34 N 1.55 E
Gourbeyre, Guad. 159c h5 15.59 N 61.42 W
Gourdhead Run, stm., Pa., U.S. 197b 40.33 N 79.57 W
Gourdon, Fr. 22 E7 44.44 N 1.22 E
Gouré, Niger 84 G7 13.59 N 10.16 E
Gourin, Fr. 20 F5 48.08 N 3.36 W
Gourma-Rharous, Mali 84 F4 16.51 N 1.55 W
Gournay-en-Bray, Fr. 20 E10 49.28 N 1.43 E
Gournay-sur-Marne, Fr. 179 48.52 N 2.34 E
Gouro, Chad 82 D3 19.33 N 19.33 E
Goussonville, Fr. 179 48.55 N 1.46 E
Gouveia, Braz. 170 J4 18.27 S 43.45 W
Gouveia, Port. 184c 38.50 N 9.26 W
Gouverneur, N.Y., U.S. 126 D14 44.20 N 75.28 W
Gouyave, Gren. 159e q10 12.09 N 61.43 W
Govan, Sk., Can. 142 C9 51.18 N 105.00 W
Go Vap, Viet. 187c 10.49 N 106.41 E
Gove, Ks., U.S. 138 C8 38.58 N 100.28 W
Govea, stm., Cuba 204b 22.56 N 82.30 W
Govena, mys, c., Russia 50 E22 59.48 N 166.05 E
Govenlock, Sk., Can. 142 E4 49.11 N 109.50 W
Governador, Ilha do, i., Braz. 205a 22.48 S 43.12 W
Governador Valadares, Braz. 170 J5 18.52 S 41.58 W
Government House, bldg., Norf. I. 100i y25 29.03 S 167.57 E
Governor Dodge State Park, p.o.i., Wi., U.S. 130 A7 43.00 N 90.07 W
Governor Generoso, Phil. 68 G6 6.38 N 126.04 E
Governor Printz Park, p.o.i., Pa., U.S. 203 39.52 N 75.18 W
Governor's Harbour, Bah. 132 K9 25.11 N 76.14 W
Governors Island, i., N.Y., U.S. 194 40.41 N 74.01 W
Govind Ballabh Pant Reservoir see Govind Ballabh Pant Sāgar, res., India 70 F9 24.05 N 82.50 E
Govind Ballabh Pant Sāgar, res., India 70 F9 24.05 N 82.50 E
Govind Reservoir see Govind Sāgar, res., India 70 C6 31.25 N 76.28 E
Govind Sāgar, res., India 70 C6 31.25 N 76.28 E
Gowanda, N.Y., U.S. 124 B7 42.27 N 78.55 W
Gowan Range, mts., Austl. 98 E5 25.00 S 145.00 E
Gower, Mo., U.S. 130 E3 39.36 N 94.35 W
Gowmal, Afg. 70 B2 32.31 N 68.51 E
Gowmal (Gumal), stm., Asia 70 B2 31.36 N 70.48 E
Gowrie, Ia., U.S. 130 B3 42.16 N 94.17 W
Goya, Arg. 172 D8 29.08 S 59.15 W
Goyania see Goiânia, Braz. 170 I1 16.40 S 49.16 W
Goyave, Guad. 159c h5 16.07 N 61.34 W
Goyaves, Grande Rivière à, stm., Guad. 159c h5 16.18 N 61.36 W
Goyaves, Îlets à, is., Guad. 159c h5 16.10 N 61.48 W
Göyçay, Azer. 42 E12 40.38 N 47.44 E
Goyer, Île, i., Qc., Can. 193a 45.29 N 73.17 W
Göynük, Tur. 34 C13 40.24 N 30.47 E
Göynük, stm., Tur. 34 C13 40.19 N 30.05 E
Goyt, stm., Eng., U.K. 180 53.24 N 2.09 W
Göytäpä, Azer. 42 F13 39.07 N 48.36 E
Goz Beïda, Chad 82 E4 12.13 N 21.25 E
Gozdnica, Pol. 24 E11 51.25 N 15.06 E
Gozha Co, l., China 62 A5 34.58 N 80.58 E
Gözne, Tur. 76 A5 36.59 N 34.34 E
Gozo see Għawdex, i., Malta 32 H8 36.03 N 14.15 E
Göz Tepe, hill, Tur. 185b 41.06 N 29.06 E
Graaff-Reinet, S. Afr. 90 H7 32.15 S 24.32 E
Grabo, C. Iv. 84 I3 4.55 N 7.30 W
Grabow, Ger. 24 C7 53.17 N 11.33 E
Grabowiec, Pol. 24 F19 50.49 N 23.33 E
Grabów nad Prosną, Pol. 24 E14 51.30 N 18.08 E
Gračac, Cro. 30 F12 44.17 N 15.49 E
Gračanica, Bos. 36 E5 44.41 N 18.18 E
Gračanica, Manastir, rel., Yugo. 36 G8 42.36 N 21.09 E
Grace, Id., U.S. 146 H15 42.35 N 111.43 W
Gracefield, Qc., Can. 126 B13 46.05 N 76.03 W
Graceville, Fl., U.S. 134 G13 30.57 N 85.31 W
Graceville, Mn., U.S. 128 F2 45.34 N 96.26 W
Gračevka, Russia 40 I13 45.12 N 42.24 E
Gracia, ngh., Spain 184d 41.23 N 2.09 E
Gracias a Dios, Cabo, c., N.A. 156 E6 14.59 N 83.09 W
Gradačac, Bos. 36 E5 44.52 N 18.25 E
Gradaús, Braz. 164 E7 7.43 S 51.09 W
Grado, Italy 30 E10 45.40 N 13.23 E
Grado, Spain 28 A4 43.23 N 6.03 W
Grad Sofija, state, Blg. 36 G10 42.40 N 23.20 E
Grady, Ar., U.S. 134 C7 34.05 N 91.42 W
Grady, N.M., U.S. 138 G5 34.49 N 103.19 W
Gradyville, Pa., U.S. 203 39.57 N 75.28 W
Grænlandshav see Greenland Sea, s. 106 B22 77.00 N 1.00 W
Grænlandssund see Denmark Strait, strt. 106 C20 67.00 N 25.00 W
Graettinger, Ia., U.S. 128 H4 43.14 N 94.45 W
Grafenau, Ger. 24 H9 48.52 N 13.25 E
Grafenberg, ngh., Ger. 181 51.14 N 6.50 E
Gräfenhainichen, Ger. 24 E8 51.43 N 12.27 E
Grafing bei München, Ger. 24 H7 48.02 N 11.57 E
Gråfjell, mtn., Nor. 16 G7 60.16 N 9.29 E
Graford, Tx., U.S. 136 B9 32.55 N 98.14 W
Gräfrath, ngh., Ger. 181 51.13 N 7.04 E
Grafton, Austl. 98 G9 29.41 S 152.56 E
Grafton, Il., U.S. 130 F7 38.58 N 90.26 W
Grafton, N.D., U.S. 142 F16 48.25 N 97.25 W
Grafton, W.V., U.S. 124 E5 39.20 N 80.01 W
Grafton, Wi., U.S. 126 E2 43.19 N 87.56 W
Grafton, Cape, c., Austl. 98 A5 16.52 S 145.55 E
Grafty Green, Eng., U.K. 178 51.12 N 0.41 E
Graham, Ca., U.S. 198 34.15 N 118.31 W
Graham, N.C., U.S. 124 H6 36.04 N 79.24 W
Graham, Tx., U.S. 136 A9 33.06 N 98.34 W
Graham, Mount, mtn., Az., U.S. 150 K7 32.42 N 109.52 W
Graham Creek, stm., In., U.S. 130 F12 38.48 N 85.39 W
Graham Hill County Park, p.o.i., N.Y., U.S. 194 41.07 N 73.48 W
Graham Island, i., B.C., Can. 110 E4 53.47 N 132.33 W
Graham Island, i., Nu., Can. 108 B7 77.25 N 90.30 W
Graham Lake, res., Me., U.S. 122 F8 44.40 N 68.23 W
Graham Land, reg., Ant. 103 B34 66.08 S 64.30 W
Graham Memorial Park, p.o.i., Md., U.S. 202b 39.25 N 76.30 W
Graham Moore, Cape, c., Nu., Can. 110 A15 72.54 N 76.09 W
Grahamstad see Grahamstown, S. Afr. 90 H8 33.18 S 26.31 E
Grahamstown, S. Afr. 90 H8 33.18 S 26.31 E

Name	Page	Map Ref.	Latitude	Longitude
Graian Alps see Grayiske alper, mts., Eur.	30	E4	45.30 N	7.10 E
Graie, Alpi see Grayiske alper, mts., Eur.	30	E4	45.30 N	7.10 E
Grain Coast, cst., Lib.	84	I3	5.00 N	9.00 W
Grainfield, Ks., U.S.	138	B8	39.06 N	100.27 W
Grajagan, Indon.	66	H9	8.35 S	114.13 E
Grajaú, Braz.	170	C2	5.47 S	46.07 W
Grajaú, stm., Braz.	170	B3	3.40 S	44.49 W
Grajewo, Pol.	24	C18	53.39 N	22.28 E
Grajvoron, Russia	38	C14	50.29 N	35.40 E
Gram, Den.	16	L7	55.17 N	9.04 E
Gramacho, Braz.	205a		22.44 S	43.18 W
Gramada, Blg.	36	F9	43.50 N	22.39 E
Gramat, Fr.	22	E7	44.46 N	1.43 E
Gramatneusiedl, Aus.	182b		48.02 N	16.29 E
Grambling, La., U.S.	134	E6	32.32 N	92.42 W
Gramilla, Arg.	172	C5	27.18 S	64.37 W
Grammichele, Italy	32	G8	37.13 N	14.38 E
Grampian Mountains, mts., Scot., U.K.	10	E9	56.55 N	4.00 W
Grampians National Park, p.o.i., Austl.	98	K3	37.20 S	142.30 E
Gramsh, Alb.	32	D14	40.53 N	20.12 E
Gramshi see Gramsh, Alb.	32	D14	40.53 N	20.12 E
Gran see Esztergom, Hung.	36	B5	47.47 N	18.45 E
Gran, Nor.	16	G8	60.21 N	10.34 E
Granada, Col.	168	F5	3.31 N	73.42 W
Granada, Nic.	156	G5	11.55 N	85.57 W
Granada, Spain	28	G7	37.10 N	3.35 W
Granada, Co., U.S.	138	C6	38.04 N	102.18 W
Granada, Mn., U.S.	128	H4	43.41 N	94.20 W
Granada, co., Spain	28	G7	37.15 N	3.15 W
Granada Hills, ngh., Ca., U.S.	198		34.16 N	118.31 W
Granadella see La Granadella, Spain	28	C11	41.21 N	0.39 E
Granado, Peru	204d		12.04 S	76.57 W
Gran Altiplanicie Central, plat., Arg.	166	I2	48.55 S	69.08 W
Granard, Ire.	10	H5	53.46 N	7.29 W
Granbury, Tx., U.S.	136	B10	32.26 N	97.47 W
Granbury, Lake, res., Tx., U.S.	136	B10	32.25 N	97.45 W
Granby, Qc., Can.	122	E4	45.24 N	72.43 W
Granby, Co., U.S.	138	A3	40.05 N	105.57 W
Granby, Mo., U.S.	130	H3	36.55 N	94.15 W
Granby, stm., B.C., Can.	144	G12	49.01 N	118.26 W
Granby, Lake, res., Co., U.S.	138	A2	40.09 N	105.50 W
Gran Canaria, i., Spain	84	D1	27.51 N	15.37 W
Gran Chaco, reg., S.A.	166	D5	23.00 S	60.00 W
Grand, stm., On., Can.	126	E9	42.51 N	79.34 W
Grand, stm., U.S.	130	E4	39.22 N	93.06 W
Grand, stm., Mi., U.S.	130	A11	43.03 N	86.13 W
Grand, stm., Oh., U.S.	124	C4	41.45 N	81.16 W
Grand, stm., S.D., U.S.	140	B12	45.34 N	100.28 W
Grand, stm., Wi., U.S.	128	H9	43.44 N	89.15 W
Grand, East Fork, stm., U.S.	130	D3	40.11 N	94.22 W
Grand, Lac, l., Qc., Can.	126	A12	47.10 N	77.21 W
Grand, North Fork, stm., U.S.	140	B10	45.45 N	102.14 W
Grand, South Fork, stm., S.D., U.S.	140	B9	45.45 N	102.14 W
Grandas, Spain	28	A4	43.13 N	6.52 W
Grand Bahama, i., Bah.	132	J7	26.38 N	78.25 W
Grand Ballon, mtn., Fr.	20	G16	47.55 N	7.08 E
Grand Bank, Nf., Can.	111a	j22	47.05 N	55.45 W
Grand-Bassam, C. Iv.	84	H4	5.13 N	3.45 W
Grand Bay, N.B., Can.	122	E10	45.18 N	66.11 W
Grand Bay, Al., U.S.	134	G10	30.28 N	88.20 W
Grand Beach, Mb., Can.	142	D17	50.33 N	96.37 W
Grand Bend, On., Can.	126	E8	43.16 N	81.47 W
Grand Blanc, Mi., U.S.	124	B2	42.55 N	83.37 W
Grand-Bourg, Guad.	159c	i6	15.53 N	61.19 W
Grand Caille Point, c., St. Luc.	159c	m6	13.52 N	61.04 W
Grand Calumet, stm., U.S.	196		41.38 N	87.34 W
Grand Calumet, Île du, i., Qc., Can.	126	C13	45.44 N	76.41 W
Grand Canal see Da Yunhe, can., China	58	E8	32.10 N	119.33 E
Grand Canal, can., Ire.	10	H6	53.20 N	6.14 W
Grand Cane, La., U.S.	136	B14	32.05 N	93.49 W
Grand Canyon, Az., U.S.	150	G4	36.02 N	112.09 W
Grand Canyon, val., Az., U.S.	150	G4	36.21 N	112.30 W
Grand Canyon National Park, p.o.i., Az., U.S.	150	G4	36.19 N	112.53 W
Grand Case, Guad.	159a	a1	18.06 N	63.03 W
Grand Cayman, i., Cay. Is.	156	C7	19.20 N	81.15 W
Grand Central Terminal, trans., N.Y., U.S.	194		40.45 N	73.59 W
Grand Cess, Lib.	84	I3	4.34 N	8.12 W
Grandchamp, Fr.	179		48.43 N	1.37 E
Grand Chenier, La., U.S.	134	H6	29.45 N	92.58 W
Grand Coulee, Wa., U.S.	146	C8	47.56 N	118.59 W
Grand Coulee Dam, dam., Wa., U.S.	146	C8	47.56 N	119.00 W
Grand Cul de Sac, Guad.	159a	b2	17.54 N	62.48 W
Grand Cul-de-Sac Marin, b., Guad.	159c	h5	16.20 N	61.35 W
Grande, stm., Arg.	172	A5	23.37 S	65.27 W
Grande, stm., Arg.	172	G3	36.52 S	69.45 W
Grande, stm., Bol.	166	C4	15.49 S	64.46 W
Grande, stm., Braz.	166	C7	20.07 S	51.00 W
Grande, stm., Braz.	170	F4	11.05 S	43.09 W
Grande, stm., Braz.	205a		22.55 S	43.25 W
Grande, stm., Braz.	205b		23.45 S	46.22 W
Grande, stm., S.A.	166	J3	53.46 S	67.40 W
Grande, stm., Ven.	168	C11	8.47 N	60.38 W
Grande, Arroyo, stm., Arg.	206		34.45 S	58.08 W
Grande, Arroyo, stm., Ur.	172	F9	33.08 S	57.08 W
Grande, Bahía, b., Arg.	166	J3	51.15 S	68.30 W
Grande, Boca, mth., Ven.	168	C11	8.38 N	60.30 W
Grande, Cerro, mtn., Mex.	136	G2	27.54 N	105.07 W
Grande, Cerro, mtn., Mex.	136	D1	30.14 N	106.13 W
Grande, Cerro, mtn., Mex.	154	E7	21.45 N	103.05 W
Grande, Cerro, mtn., Mex.	154	A5	28.46 N	107.32 W
Grande, Cuchilla, mts., Ur.	172	F10	33.25 S	55.06 W
Grande, Ilha, i., Braz.	170	L4	23.09 S	44.14 W
Grande, Ilha, i., Braz.	172	A11	23.44 S	53.47 W
Grande, Naviglio, can., Italy	184b		45.35 N	8.42 E
Grande, Ponta, c., Braz.	170	I6	16.21 S	39.01 W
Grande, Rio (Bravo) (Rio Grande), stm., N.A.	120	H13	25.56 N	97.08 W
Grande, Serra, mts., Braz.	170	D5	6.00 S	40.52 W
Grande, Sierra, mts., Mex.	136	E2	29.40 N	105.02 W
Grande-Anse, N.B., Can.	122	C11	47.48 N	65.11 W
Grande-Anse, Qc., Can.	122	C4	47.05 N	72.55 W
Grande Anse, La, b., Qc., Can.	193a		45.23 N	73.53 W
Grande Anse Bay, b., Gren.	159e	q10	12.02 N	61.45 W
Grande Baie, La, b., Qc., Can.	193a		45.29 N	74.00 W
Grande Cache, Ab., Can.	144	C11	53.55 N	119.07 W
Grande Cayemite, i., Haiti	156	C11	18.37 N	73.45 W
Grande Chartreuse, Couvent de la, rel., Fr.	22	D11	45.22 N	5.50 E
Grande Comore see Njazidja, i., Com.	88	C7	11.35 S	43.20 E
Grande de Añasco, stm., P.R.	158a	b1	18.16 N	67.11 W
Grande de Arecibo, stm., P.R.	158a	b2	18.28 N	66.42 W
Grande de Loíza, stm., P.R.	158a	b3	18.26 N	65.52 W
Grande de Manacapuru, Lago, l., Braz.	168	I11	3.04 S	61.25 W
Grande de Manatí, stm., P.R.	158a	b3	18.29 N	66.32 W
Grande de Matagalpa, stm., Nic.	156	F6	12.54 N	83.31 W
Grande de Santiago, stm., Mex.	154	E6	21.37 N	105.27 W
Grande do Gurupá, Ilha, i., Braz.	164	D7	1.00 S	51.30 W
Grande-Entrée, Qc., Can.	122	C15	47.33 N	61.33 W
Grande Île de Criques, i., D.R.C.	191b		4.20 S	15.25 E
Grande Pointe, c., Guad.	159a	b2	17.53 N	62.50 W
Grande Prairie, Ab., Can.	144	A12	55.10 N	118.47 W
Grand Erg de Bilma, des., Niger	84	F7	18.30 N	14.00 E
Grand Erg Occidental, des., Alg.	84	C5	30.56 N	1.35 E
Grand Erg Oriental, des., Alg.	84	C6	30.30 N	7.00 E
Grande-Rivière, Qc., Can.	122	B12	48.24 N	64.28 W
Grande Rivière, La, stm., Qc., Can.	110	E15	53.49 N	78.57 W
Grande Ronde, stm., U.S.	146	E9	46.04 N	116.59 W
Grandes, Salinas, pl., Arg.	172	A4	23.43 S	65.56 W
Grandes, Salinas, pl., Arg.	172	D5	30.06 S	65.13 W
Grandes Antillas, Islas see Greater Antilles, is., N.A.	106	H15	20.00 N	74.00 W
Grande Sauldre, stm., Fr.	20	G11	47.22 N	1.54 E
Grand-Étang, N.S., Can.	122	D15	46.35 N	61.01 W
Grande-Terre, i., Guad.	159c	h6	16.18 N	61.22 W
Grande Vigie, Pointe de la, c., Guad.	159c	g6	16.30 N	61.27 W
Grand Falls, N.B., Can.	122	C9	47.02 N	67.44 W
Grandfalls, Tx., U.S.	136	C5	31.19 N	102.50 W
Grandfather Mountain, mtn., N.C., U.S.	124	H4	36.07 N	81.48 W
Grandfield, Ok., U.S.	136	G10	34.13 N	98.41 W
Grand Forks, B.C., Can.	144	G12	49.02 N	118.26 W
Grand Forks, N.D., U.S.	128	D1	47.55 N	97.03 W
Grand Forks Air Force Base, mil., N.D., U.S.	142	G16	47.57 N	97.25 W
Grand Haven, Mi., U.S.	130	A11	43.03 N	86.12 W
Grand Hers, stm., Fr.	28	A12	43.18 N	1.32 E
Grandin, Lac, l., N.T., Can.	110	C7	63.59 N	119.00 W
Grandioznyj, pik, mtn., Russia	48	D17	53.50 N	96.11 E
Grand Island, Ne., U.S.	140	G10	40.55 N	98.21 W
Grand Island, i., Mi., U.S.	126	B3	46.30 N	86.40 W
Grand Isle, La., U.S.	134	H9	29.13 N	89.59 W
Grand Junction, Co., U.S.	150	D8	39.04 N	108.33 W
Grand Junction, Ia., U.S.	130	B3	42.01 N	94.14 W
Grand Junction, Tn., U.S.	134	B9	35.03 N	89.11 W
Grand Lake, Co., U.S.	138	A3	40.15 N	105.51 W
Grand Lake, l., N.B., Can.	122	D11	45.53 N	66.03 W
Grand Lake, l., N.A.	122	E9	45.41 N	67.48 W
Grand Lake, l., La., U.S.	134	H5	29.52 N	92.44 W
Grand Lake, l., Mi., U.S.	126	C6	45.17 N	83.29 W
Grand Lake, res., Oh., U.S.	124	D1	40.31 N	84.30 W
Grand Ledge, Mi., U.S.	124	B1	42.45 N	84.44 W
Grand Lieu, Lac de (Grand-Lieu, Lac de), l., Fr.	20	G6	47.06 N	1.40 W
Grand-Lieu, Lac de (Grand Lieu, Lac de), l., Fr.	20	G6	47.06 N	1.40 W
Grand Manan, N.B., Can.	122	F10	44.42 N	66.48 W
Grand Manan Channel, strt., N.A.	122	F9	44.44 N	66.59 W
Grand Manan Island, i., N.B., Can.	122	F10	44.42 N	66.48 W
Grand Marais, Mi., U.S.	126	B4	46.39 N	86.00 W
Grand Marais, Mn., U.S.	128	D8	47.45 N	90.20 W
Grand Meadow, Mn., U.S.	128	H6	43.42 N	92.34 W
Grand-Mère, Qc., Can.	126	B17	46.37 N	72.41 W
Grand Mesa, mtn., Co., U.S.	150	E8	39.00 N	108.00 W
Grândola, Port.	28	F2	38.10 N	8.33 W
Grand Pabos, stm., Qc., Can.	122	B11	48.19 N	64.41 W
Grand Palace, bldg., Thai.	187a		13.45 N	100.30 E
Grand Portage, Mn., U.S.	128	D9	47.56 N	89.42 W
Grand Portage Indian Reservation, ind. res., Mn., U.S.	128	D8	47.57 N	89.46 W
Grand Portage National Monument, p.o.i., Mn., U.S.	128	C9	48.02 N	89.36 W
Grand Prairie, Tx., U.S.	136	B11	32.44 N	96.59 W
Grand Pré National Historic Park, p.o.i., N.S., Can.	122	E12	45.08 N	64.18 W
Grand Prix Airport, arpt., Mi., U.S.	199		42.33 N	83.11 W
Grand Rapids, Mb., Can.	142	A14	53.11 N	99.16 W
Grand Rapids, Mi., U.S.	130	B12	42.57 N	85.39 W
Grand Rapids, Mn., U.S.	128	D5	47.14 N	93.31 W
Grand Rhône, stm., Fr.	22	F10	43.20 N	4.50 E
Grand' Rivière, Mart.	159c	k6	14.51 N	61.10 W
Grand Roy, Gren.	159e	q10	12.07 N	61.44 W
Grand Ruisseau, Le, stm., Qc., Can.	193a		45.39 N	73.12 W
Grand Saline, Tx., U.S.	136	B12	32.40 N	95.42 W
Grand Sault see Grand Falls, N.B., Can.	122	C9	47.02 N	67.44 W
Grands-Jardins, Parc de conservation des, ind. res., Qc., Can.	122	C6	47.41 N	70.51 W
Grand Staircase--Escalante National Monument, p.o.i., Ut., U.S.	150	F5	37.30 N	111.30 W
Grand Teton, mtn., Wy., U.S.	146	G16	43.44 N	110.48 W
Grand Teton National Park, p.o.i., Wy., U.S.	146	F16	43.55 N	110.46 W
Grand Tower, Il., U.S.	130	G8	37.37 N	89.29 W
Grand Traverse Bay, b., Mi., U.S.	126	C4	45.02 N	85.30 W
Grand Traverse Bay, East Arm, b., Mi., U.S.	126	D4	44.51 N	85.27 W
Grand Traverse Bay, West Arm, b., Mi., U.S.	126	D4	44.51 N	85.35 W
Grand Turk, T./C. Is.	156	B12	21.27 N	71.08 W
Grand Union Canal, can., Eng., U.K.	178		51.30 N	0.02 W
Grandview, Mb., Can.	142	C13	51.10 N	100.42 W
Grandview, Mo., U.S.	130	F3	38.53 N	94.32 W
Grandview, Pa., U.S.	197b		40.10 N	79.52 W
Grandview, Tx., U.S.	136	B10	32.15 N	97.11 W
Grandview, Wa., U.S.	146	D6	46.15 N	119.54 W
Grand View, Wi., U.S.	128	E7	46.22 N	91.06 W
Grand View-on-Hudson, N.Y., U.S.	194		41.44 N	73.55 W
Grand Wash Cliffs, clf., Az., U.S.	150	H3	35.40 N	113.54 W
Grañén, Spain	28	C10	41.56 N	0.21 W
Graneros, Chile	172	G2	34.03 S	70.42 W
Granfjället, mtn., Swe.	16	F10	61.15 N	12.57 E
Grangärde, Swe.	16	G12	60.16 N	14.59 E
Grange, Eng., U.K.	180		53.23 N	3.09 W
Grange, Bois de la, p.o.i., Fr.	179		48.45 N	2.30 E
Grange Hill, Eng., U.K.	178		51.37 N	0.05 E
Granger, Tx., U.S.	136	D10	30.43 N	97.26 W
Granger, Wa., U.S.	146	D6	46.20 N	120.11 W
Granger, Wy., U.S.	150	B6	41.36 N	109.58 W
Granger Draw, stm., Tx., U.S.	136	D7	30.20 N	100.56 W
Granger Lake, res., Tx., U.S.	136	D10	30.42 N	97.22 W
Granges see Grenchen, Switz.	30	C4	47.11 N	7.23 E
Grängesberg, Swe.	16	G13	60.04 N	15.00 E
Grangeville, Id., U.S.	146	E10	45.55 N	116.07 W
Gran Guardia, Arg.	172	B8	25.51 S	58.54 W
Granite, Md., U.S.	202b		39.21 N	76.51 W
Granite, Ok., U.S.	138	G9	34.57 N	99.22 W
Granite City, Il., U.S.	130	F7	38.42 N	90.08 W
Granite Falls, Mn., U.S.	128	G3	44.48 N	95.33 W
Granite Falls, N.C., U.S.	124	I4	35.48 N	81.26 W
Granite Falls, Wa., U.S.	146	B5	48.04 N	121.58 W
Granite Mountains, mts., Wy., U.S.	140	E5	42.39 N	107.33 W
Granite Pass, p., Wy., U.S.	140	C5	44.38 N	107.31 W
Granite Peak, Austl.	96	E4	25.38 S	121.21 E
Granite Peak, mtn., Mt., U.S.	146	E17	45.10 N	109.48 W
Granite Peak, mtn., Mt., U.S.	146	E14	45.34 N	112.02 W
Granite Peak, mtn., Nv., U.S.	148	C6	40.48 N	119.25 W
Granite Peak, mtn., Nv., U.S.	148	B8	41.40 N	117.35 W
Granite Range, mts., Nv., U.S.	148	B6	41.04 N	119.27 W
Graniteville, S.C., U.S.	132	C4	33.33 N	81.48 W
Graniteville, Vt., U.S.	122	F4	44.09 N	72.29 W
Granitola, Capo, c., Italy	32	G6	37.34 N	12.41 E
Granja, Braz.	170	B5	3.06 S	40.50 W
Granja, Port.	184c		38.51 N	9.06 W
Granki, Russia	26	F14	54.51 N	31.26 E
Gran Laguna Salada, l., Arg.	166	H3	44.24 S	67.23 W
Gränna, Swe.	16	J12	58.00 N	14.27 E
Granollers, Spain	28	C13	41.37 N	2.17 E
Granön, Swe.	16	C17	64.14 N	19.18 E
Gran Paradiso, mtn., Italy	30	E4	45.32 N	7.16 E
Gran Paradiso, Parco Nazionale del, p.o.i., Italy	30	E4	45.34 N	7.18 E
Gran Rio, stm., Sur.	164	C6	4.01 N	55.29 W
Gran Sasso d'Italia, mts., Italy	30	H10	42.27 N	13.42 E
Gransee, Ger.	24	C9	53.00 N	13.09 E
Grant, Fl., U.S.	132	I5	27.55 N	80.31 W
Grant, Mi., U.S.	126	E4	43.20 N	85.48 W
Grant, Ne., U.S.	140	G11	40.50 N	101.43 W
Grant, stm., Wi., U.S.	128	I8	42.39 N	90.44 W
Grant, Mount, mtn., Nv., U.S.	148	E7	38.34 N	118.48 W
Grant City, Mo., U.S.	130	D3	40.29 N	94.25 W
Grantham, Eng., U.K.	10	I12	52.55 N	0.39 W
Grant-Kohrs Ranch National Historic Site, p.o.i., Mt., U.S.	146	D14	46.25 N	112.40 W
Grantley Adams International Airport, arpt., Barb.	159d	n9	13.04 N	59.29 W
Grant Mills, R.I., U.S.	201		41.57 N	71.26 W
Grantown-on-Spey, Scot., U.K.	10	D9	57.19 N	3.37 W
Grant Park, Il., U.S.	130	C10	41.14 N	87.38 W
Grant Park, p.o.i., Il., U.S.	196		41.52 N	87.37 W
Grant Point, c., Nu., Can.	110	B11	68.22 N	98.37 W
Grant Range, mts., Nv., U.S.	148	E10	38.23 N	115.27 W
Grants, N.M., U.S.	150	H9	35.09 N	107.50 W
Grantsburg, Wi., U.S.	128	F6	45.46 N	92.40 W
Grants Pass, Or., U.S.	148	A2	42.26 N	123.19 W
Grant-Suttie Bay, b., Nu., Can.	110	B15	69.47 N	77.15 W
Grantsville, Ut., U.S.	150	C4	40.36 N	112.27 W
Grantsville, W.V., U.S.	124	F4	38.55 N	81.05 W
Grantville, Ga., U.S.	134	D14	33.14 N	84.50 W
Granum, Ab., Can.	144	G17	49.51 N	113.31 W
Granville, Austl.	192a		33.50 S	151.01 E
Granville, Fr.	20	F7	48.50 N	1.35 W
Granville, Il., U.S.	128	J9	41.15 N	89.13 W
Granville, N.Y., U.S.	126	E16	43.24 N	73.15 W
Granville, N.D., U.S.	142	F13	48.16 N	100.50 W
Granville, Oh., U.S.	124	D3	40.03 N	82.31 W
Granville, W.V., U.S.	124	E5	39.38 N	79.59 W
Granville Lake, l., Mb., Can.	110	D10	56.16 N	100.29 W
Granvin, Nor.	16	G4	60.32 N	6.44 E
Grão Mogol, Braz.	170	I4	16.34 S	42.54 W
Grape Creek, stm., Co., U.S.	138	C3	38.26 N	105.16 W
Grape Island, i., Ma., U.S.	201		42.16 N	70.55 W
Grapeland, Tx., U.S.	136	C12	31.29 N	95.28 W
Grapevine Lake, res., Tx., U.S.	136	B10	32.59 N	97.06 W
Grapevine Peak, mtn., Nv., U.S.	148	G8	36.57 N	117.08 W
Grappenhall, Eng., U.K.	180		53.22 N	2.32 W
Gras, Lac de, l., N.T., Can.	110	C8	64.30 N	110.30 W
Graskop, S. Afr.	90	D10	24.55 S	30.50 E
Grasmere Lake, l., N.Y., U.S.	194		40.36 N	74.05 W
Gräsö, i., Swe.	16	G16	60.24 N	18.25 E
Grasonville, Md., U.S.	124	F9	38.57 N	76.12 W
Grass, stm., N.Y., U.S.	126	D15	44.59 N	74.43 W
Grass, North Branch, stm., N.Y., U.S.	126	D14	44.25 N	75.05 W
Grass, South Branch, stm., N.Y., U.S.	126	D15	44.25 N	75.06 W
Grass Creek, Wy., U.S.	140	D4	43.56 N	108.38 W
Grass Creek, stm., Wy., U.S.	140	D4	43.51 N	108.22 W
Grasscroft, Eng., U.K.	180		53.32 N	2.02 W
Grasse, Fr.	22	F12	43.40 N	6.55 E
Grassendale, ngh., Eng., U.K.	180		53.21 N	2.54 W
Grassflat, Pa., U.S.	124	D7	40.59 N	78.07 W
Grass Hassock Channel, strt., N.Y., U.S.	194		40.36 N	73.48 W
Grasshopper Creek, stm., Mt., U.S.	146	E13	45.06 N	112.47 W
Grass Island, i., N.Y., U.S.	194		40.39 N	73.18 W
Grasslands National Park, p.o.i., Sk., Can.	142	E6	49.04 N	106.57 W
Grass Range, Mt., U.S.	142	G5	47.03 N	108.49 W
Grass Valley, Ca., U.S.	148	D4	39.13 N	121.03 W
Grass Valley, Or., U.S.	146	E6	45.21 N	120.46 W
Grassy, Austl.	99a	n12	40.02 S	144.03 E
Grassy Bay, b., N.Y., U.S.	194		40.38 N	73.48 W
Grassy Brook, stm., On., Can.	202a		43.03 N	79.07 W
Grassy Hill, mtn., China	189d		22.25 N	114.09 E
Grassy Island, i., Ct., U.S.	194		41.04 N	73.23 W
Grassy Island Lake, l., Ab., Can.	142	C3	51.52 N	110.21 W
Grassy Lake, Ab., Can.	144	G19	49.49 N	111.43 W
Grassy Plains, B.C., Can.	144	C5	53.57 N	125.53 W
Grassy Sprain Reservoir, res., N.Y., U.S.	194		40.58 N	73.51 W
Gråsten, Den.	16	M7	54.55 N	9.36 E
Grästorp, Swe.	16	I10	58.20 N	12.41 E
Graterford, Pa., U.S.	203		40.13 N	75.27 W
Graterford State Correctional Institution, bldg., Pa., U.S.	203		40.14 N	75.26 W
Gratztown, Pa., U.S.	197b		40.14 N	79.47 W
Graudenz see Grudziądz, Pol.	24	C14	53.29 N	18.44 E
Graulhet, Fr.	22	F7	43.46 N	2.00 E
Gravatá, stm., Braz.	170	I4	16.53 S	42.10 W
Grave Creek, stm., Or., U.S.	146	H3	42.39 N	123.35 W
Gravelbourg, Sk., Can.	142	E7	49.52 N	106.34 W
Gravelines, Fr.	20	D11	50.58 N	2.08 E
Gravelly Bay, b., On., Can.	202a		42.52 N	79.15 W
Gravelly Brook, stm., N.J., U.S.	194		40.25 N	74.13 W
Gravelly Pond, l., Ma., U.S.	201		42.36 N	70.48 W
Gravelotte, S. Afr.	90	C10	23.54 S	30.31 E
Gravenhage, 's- see 's-Gravenhage, Neth.	20	B13	52.05 N	4.17 E
Gravenhurst, On., Can.	126	D10	44.55 N	79.22 W
Grave Peak, mtn., Id., U.S.	146	D12	46.24 N	114.44 W
Graves, The, is., Ma., U.S.	201		42.22 N	70.52 W
Gravesend, Austl.	98	G8	29.35 S	150.20 E
Gravesend, Eng., U.K.	10	J13	51.26 N	0.23 E
Gravesend Bay, b., N.Y., U.S.	194		40.36 N	74.01 W
Gravesham, mun., Eng., U.K.	178		51.25 N	0.24 E
Gravette, Ar., U.S.	130	H3	36.25 N	94.27 W
Gravina in Puglia, Italy	32	D10	40.49 N	16.25 E
Gray, Fr.	20	G14	47.26 N	5.35 E
Gray, Ga., U.S.	132	D2	33.00 N	83.31 W
Gray, Ky., U.S.	124	H1	36.56 N	84.00 W
Grayback Mountain, mtn., Or., U.S.	148	A2	42.07 N	123.18 W
Grayiske alper, mts., Eur.	30	E4	45.30 N	7.10 E
Grayling, Mi., U.S.	126	D5	44.39 N	84.42 W
Graylyn Crest, De., U.S.	203		39.48 N	75.31 W
Grays, Eng., U.K.	10	J13	51.28 N	0.19 E
Grays, stm., Wa., U.S.	146	D3	46.18 N	123.40 W
Grays Harbor, b., Wa., U.S.	146	D2	46.56 N	124.03 W
Grays Lake, l., Il., U.S.	196		42.21 N	88.03 W
Grays Lake, sw., Id., U.S.	146	G15	43.04 N	111.26 W
Grays Lake Outlet, stm., Id., U.S.	146	G15	43.28 N	111.43 W
Grayson, Sk., Can.	142	D11	50.42 N	102.37 W
Grayson, Al., U.S.	134	C11	34.17 N	87.20 W
Grayson, Ky., U.S.	124	F3	38.19 N	82.57 W
Grayson, La., U.S.	134	E6	32.02 N	92.06 W
Grays Peak, mtn., Co., U.S.	138	B3	39.37 N	105.45 W
Grays Point, Austl.	192a		34.04 S	151.05 E
Graysville, Tn., U.S.	134	B13	35.26 N	85.05 W
Grayville, Il., U.S.	130	F9	38.15 N	88.00 W
Graz, Aus.	30	C12	47.04 N	15.26 E
Grazalema, Spain	28	H5	36.46 N	5.22 W
Graždanka, ngh., Russia	183a		60.00 N	30.24 E
Gr'azeva, stm., Russia	183b		55.51 N	37.08 E
Gr'aznovo, ngh., Russia	183b		55.57 N	37.34 E
Grdelica, Yugo.	36	G9	42.54 N	22.03 E
Greasby, Eng., U.K.	180		53.23 N	3.07 W
Great, stm., Gren.	159e	q10	12.08 N	61.36 W
Great Alfold see Alföld, pl., Hung.	36	C7	47.00 N	20.00 E
Great Altcar, Eng., U.K.	180		53.33 N	3.01 W
Great America, p.o.i., Ca., U.S.	200		37.24 N	121.59 W
Great Amwell, Eng., U.K.	178		51.48 N	0.01 W
Great Artesian Basin, bas., Austl.	98	E3	25.00 S	143.00 E
Great Australian Bight, b., Austl.	96	F5	35.00 S	130.00 E
Great Barrier Island, i., N.Z.	102	C6	36.10 S	175.25 E
Great Barrier Reef, rf., Austl.	96	C9	18.00 S	146.50 E
Great Barrier Reef Marine Park, p.o.i., Austl.	98	C8	21.00 S	151.00 E
Great Barrington, Ma., U.S.	124	B12	42.11 N	73.21 W
Great Barrow, Eng., U.K.	180		53.12 N	2.48 W
Great Basin, bas., U.S.	112	C4	40.00 N	117.00 W
Great Basin National Park, p.o.i., Nv., U.S.	150	E2	38.55 N	114.14 W
Great Bear, stm., N.T., Can.	110	B6	64.54 N	125.36 W
Great Bear Lake, l., N.T., Can.	110	B6	66.00 N	120.00 W
Great Beaver Lake, l., B.C., Can.	144	B7	54.25 N	123.43 W
Great Belt see Storebælt, strt., Den.	16	L8	55.30 N	11.00 E
Great Bend, Ks., U.S.	138	C10	38.21 N	98.45 W
Great Bitter Lake see Murrat el-Kubra, Buheirat, l., Egypt	74	E3	30.20 N	32.23 E
Great Bookham, Eng., U.K.	178		51.16 N	0.22 W
Great Braxted, Eng., U.K.	178		51.48 N	0.42 E
Great Brewster Island, i., Ma., U.S.	201		42.20 N	70.53 W
Great Britain, i., U.K.	8	E9	54.00 N	2.00 W
Great Brook, stm., N.J., U.S.	194		40.42 N	74.31 W
Great Buddha, rel., Japan	186		35.19 N	139.32 E
Great Budworth, Eng., U.K.	180		53.18 N	2.30 W
Great Burstead, Eng., U.K.	178		51.36 N	0.25 E
Great Camanoe, i., Br. Vir. Is.	158b	e8	18.29 N	64.32 W
Great Captain Island, i., Ct., U.S.	194		40.59 N	73.38 W
Great Central, B.C., Can.	144	G6	49.19 N	124.59 W
Great Central Lake, l., B.C., Can.	144	G5	49.26 N	125.08 W
Great Channel, strt., Asia	62	G7	6.25 N	94.20 E
Great Chazy, stm., N.Y., U.S.	126	D16	44.56 N	73.23 W
Great Coharie Creek, stm., N.C., U.S.	132	A7	34.49 N	78.22 W
Great Cove, b., N.Y., U.S.	194		40.43 N	73.14 W
Great Crosby, Eng., U.K.	180		53.29 N	3.01 W
Great Dismal Swamp, sw., U.S.	124	H9	36.28 N	76.27 W
Great Ditch, can., N.J., U.S.	194		40.24 N	74.31 W
Great Divide Basin, bas., Wy., U.S.	140	F4	42.00 N	108.10 W
Great Dividing Range, mts., Austl.	96	C8	25.00 S	147.00 E
Great Driffield, Eng., U.K.	10	H12	54.00 N	0.26 W
Great Duck Island, i., On., Can.	126	C6	45.40 N	82.57 W
Greater Antilles, is., N.A.	106	H15	20.00 N	74.00 W
Greater Khingan Range see Da Hinggan Ling, mts., China	52	B9	49.00 N	122.00 E
Greater London, co., Eng., U.K.	178		51.30 N	0.10 W
Greater London, hist. reg., Eng., U.K.	178		51.30 N	0.10 W
Greater Manchester, co., Eng., U.K.	180		53.30 N	2.20 W
Greater Manchester, hist. reg., Eng., U.K.	180		53.30 N	2.20 W
Greater Sunda Islands, is., Asia	60	F4	2.00 S	110.00 E
Great Exuma, i., Bah.	152	C9	23.32 N	75.50 W
Great Falls, Mb., Can.	142	D18	50.27 N	96.01 W
Great Falls, Mt., U.S.	146	C15	47.29 N	111.16 W
Great Falls, S.C., U.S.	132	B5	34.34 N	80.54 W
Great Falls, wtfl., U.S.	202c		39.00 N	77.16 W
Great Falls Park, p.o.i., Va., U.S.	202c		39.00 N	77.15 W
Great Gaddesden, Eng., U.K.	178		51.47 N	0.30 W
Great Grimsby see Grimsby, Eng., U.K.	10	H12	53.34 N	0.04 W
Great Hameldon, hill, Eng., U.K.	180		53.45 N	2.19 W
Great Himalayan National Park, p.o.i., India	70	C6	31.57 N	77.05 E
Greathouse Peak, mtn., Mt., U.S.	146	D17	46.46 N	109.21 W
Great Inagua, i., Bah.	156	B11	21.05 N	73.18 W
Great Indian Desert (Thar Desert), des., Asia	70	E3	27.00 N	71.00 E
Great Island, i., N.Y., U.S.	194		41.05 N	73.44 W
Great Island, i., N.Y., U.S.	194		40.38 N	73.30 W
Great Karroo (Groot Karroo), plat., S. Afr.	90	H6	32.46 S	22.31 E
Great Kills, ngh., N.Y., U.S.	194		40.33 N	74.10 W
Great Kills Harbor, b., N.Y., U.S.	194		40.32 N	74.08 W
Great Kills Park, p.o.i., N.Y., U.S.	194		40.33 N	74.08 W
Great La Cloche Island, i., On., Can.	126	B8	46.01 N	81.52 W
Great Lake, res., Austl.	99a	n13	41.51 S	146.44 E
Great Lakes Naval Training Center, mil., Il., U.S.	130	B10	42.18 N	87.50 W
Great Lakes Steel Works, sci., Mi., U.S.	199		42.15 N	83.08 W
Great Malvern, Eng., U.K.	10	I10	52.07 N	2.19 W
Great Marton, Eng., U.K.	180		53.48 N	3.02 W
Great Meadows National Wildlife Refuge, ind. res., Ma., U.S.	201		42.29 N	71.20 W
Great Miami, stm., U.S.	130	E13	39.06 N	84.49 W
Great Misery Island, i., Ma., U.S.	201		42.33 N	70.48 W
Great Namaqualand (Groot Namaland), hist. reg., Nmb.	90	D3	25.00 S	17.00 E
Great Neck, N.Y., U.S.	194		40.48 N	73.43 W
Great Neck, pen., Ma., U.S.	201		42.42 N	70.48 W
Great Neck, pen., N.Y., U.S.	194		40.50 N	73.45 W
Great Neck Estates, N.Y., U.S.	194		40.47 N	73.44 W
Great Nicobar, i., India	62	G7	7.00 N	93.50 E
Great Notch Reservoir, res., N.J., U.S.	194		40.53 N	74.12 W
Great Ouse, stm., Eng., U.K.	10	I12	52.47 N	0.22 E
Great Oxney Green, Eng., U.K.	178		51.44 N	0.25 E
Great Palm Island, i., Austl.	98	B6	18.43 S	146.37 E
Great Parndon, Eng., U.K.	178		51.45 N	0.05 E
Great Patchogue Lake, l., N.Y., U.S.	194		40.46 N	73.01 W
Great Pee Dee, stm., S.C., U.S.	132	C6	33.17 N	79.16 W
Great Piece Meadows, sw., N.J., U.S.	194		40.54 N	74.19 W
Great Plain of the Koukdjuak, pl., Nu., Can.	110	B16	66.00 N	73.00 W
Great Plains, pl., N.A.	112	C7	42.00 N	100.00 W
Great Point, c., Ma., U.S.	124	C15	41.23 N	70.02 W
Great Pubnico Lake, l., N.S., Can.	122	G11	43.42 N	65.40 W
Great River, N.Y., U.S.	194		40.45 N	73.10 W
Great Ruaha, stm., Tan.	86	F7	7.55 S	37.48 E
Great Sacandaga Lake, res., N.Y., U.S.	126	E15	43.06 N	74.12 W
Great Sale Cay, i., Bah.	132	I7	27.00 N	78.12 W
Great Salt Lake, l., Ut., U.S.	150	B4	41.10 N	112.30 W
Great Salt Lake Desert, des., Ut., U.S.	150	C3	40.40 N	113.30 W
Great Salt Plains Lake, res., Ok., U.S.	138	E10	36.44 N	98.12 W
Great Sand Dunes National Monument, p.o.i., Co., U.S.	138	D3	37.45 N	105.32 W
Great Sand Hills, hills, Sk., Can.	142	D4	50.35 N	109.05 W
Great Sandy Desert, des., Austl.	96	D4	21.30 S	125.00 E
Great Sandy National Park, p.o.i., Austl.	98	E9	24.48 S	153.12 E
Great Scarcies, stm., Afr.	84	H2	8.53 N	13.09 W
Great Sea Reef, rf., Fiji	101e	p19	16.15 S	179.00 E
Great Sitkin Island, i., Ak., U.S.	109a	g23	52.03 N	176.07 W
Great Slave Lake, l., N.T., Can.	110	C8	61.30 N	114.00 W
Great Smoky Mountains, mts., U.S.	132	A2	35.35 N	83.32 W
Great Smoky Mountains National Park, p.o.i., U.S.	132	A2	35.39 N	83.30 W
Great Sound, b., Ber.	158e	k15	32.17 N	64.51 W
Great Sutton, Eng., U.K.	180		53.17 N	2.56 W
Great Swamp, sw., N.J., U.S.	194		40.43 N	74.28 W
Great Swamp National Wildlife Refuge, ind. res., N.J., U.S.	194		40.43 N	74.28 W
Great Tenasserim, stm., Mya.	64	F4	12.24 N	98.36 E
Great Tobago, i., Br. Vir. Is.	158b	e7	18.27 N	64.49 W
Great Totham, Eng., U.K.	178		51.47 N	0.43 E
Great Victoria Desert, des., Austl.	96	E5	28.30 S	127.45 E
Great Wall see Chang Cheng, hist., China	52	D6	40.00 N	112.30 E
Great Waltham, Eng., U.K.	178		51.48 N	0.28 E

Name	Page	Map Ref.	Latitude	Longitude
Great Warley, Eng., U.K.	178		51.35 N	0.17 E
Great Western Forum, p.o.i., Ca., U.S.	198		33.57 N	118.20 W
Great Yarmouth, Eng., U.K.	10	I14	52.37 N	1.43 E
Great Zab (Az-Zāb al-Kabīr) (Büyükzap), stm., Asia	74	B9	36.00 N	43.21 E
Grebbestad, Swe.	16	I9	58.40 N	11.17 E
Grebnevo, Russia	183b		55.58 N	38.05 E
Gréboun, mtn., Niger	84	F6	20.00 N	8.35 E
Grecco, Ur.	172	F9	32.47 S	57.03 W
Greco, ngh., Italy	184b		45.30 N	9.13 E
Greco Island, i., Ca., U.S.	200		37.31 N	122.11 W
Gredos, Sierra de, mts., Spain	28	D5	40.19 N	4.51 W
Greece, N.Y., U.S.	126	E12	43.11 N	77.40 W
Greece, ctry., Eur.	6	H13	39.00 N	22.00 E
Greeley, Co., U.S.	140	G8	40.25 N	104.41 W
Greeley, Ks., U.S.	130	F2	38.20 N	95.10 W
Greeley, Ne., U.S.	140	F14	41.33 N	98.31 W
Greeleyville, S.C., U.S.	132	C6	33.34 N	79.59 W
Greely Fiord, b., Nu., Can.	108	A9	80.30 N	81.40 W
Green, stm., N.B., Can.	122	C8	47.18 N	68.08 W
Green, stm., U.S.	112	C6	38.11 N	109.53 W
Green, stm., Il., U.S.	130	C8	41.45 N	89.11 W
Green, stm., Ky., U.S.	130	G10	37.54 N	87.30 W
Green, stm., N.D., U.S.	146	G17	46.51 N	102.35 W
Green, stm., Wa., U.S.	146	D4	46.22 N	122.34 W
Green, stm., Wa., U.S.	146	C5	47.30 N	122.18 W
Green Acres, De., U.S.	203		39.47 N	75.29 W
Green Acres, shp. cen., N.Y., U.S.	194		40.40 N	73.43 W
Green Bay, Wi., U.S.	126	D1	44.31 N	88.01 W
Green Bay, b., U.S.	126	D2	44.58 N	87.34 W
Greenbelt, Md., U.S.	202c		39.00 N	76.52 W
Greenbelt Park, p.o.i., Md., U.S.	202c		38.59 N	76.54 W
Greenbooth Reservoir, res., Eng., U.K.	180		53.38 N	2.13 W
Greenbrier, Ar., U.S.	134	B6	35.14 N	92.23 W
Green Brier, Tn., U.S.	130	H11	36.25 N	86.48 W
Greenbrier, stm., W.V., U.S.	124	F6	37.38 N	80.53 W
Green Brook, N.J., U.S.	194		40.36 N	74.27 W
Green Brook, stm., N.J., U.S.	194		40.33 N	74.32 W
Greenburg, La., U.S.	134	G8	30.49 N	90.40 W
Greenbush, Mn., U.S.	128	C2	48.41 N	96.09 W
Green Cape, c., Austl.	98	K8	37.15 S	150.02 E
Greencastle, In., U.S.	130	E11	39.38 N	86.51 W
Greencastle, Pa., U.S.	124	E8	39.47 N	77.43 W
Green City, Mo., U.S.	130	D5	40.16 N	92.57 W
Green Cove Springs, Fl., U.S.	132	G4	29.59 N	81.41 W
Green Creek, stm., Pa., U.S.	203		39.53 N	75.28 W
Greendale, Austl.	192a		33.55 S	150.39 E
Greendale, In., U.S.	130	E13	39.06 N	84.51 W
Greene, Ia., U.S.	130	B5	42.53 N	92.47 W
Greene, N.Y., U.S.	124	B10	42.20 N	75.46 W
Greeneville, Tn., U.S.	124	H3	36.09 N	82.49 W
Greenfield, Eng., U.K.	180		53.32 N	2.01 W
Greenfield, Ca., U.S.	124	B13	36.19 N	121.14 W
Greenfield, Il., U.S.	130	E7	39.20 N	90.12 W
Greenfield, Ia., U.S.	130	C3	41.18 N	94.27 W
Greenfield, Ma., U.S.	122	H4	42.35 N	72.36 W
Greenfield, Mo., U.S.	130	G4	37.24 N	93.50 W
Greenfield, Oh., U.S.	124	E2	39.20 N	83.23 W
Greenfield, Ok., U.S.	138	F10	35.43 N	98.22 W
Greenfield, Tn., U.S.	130	H9	36.09 N	88.48 W
Greenfield-Park, Qc., Can.	193a		45.29 N	73.29 W
Greenfields Village, N.J., U.S.	203		75.10 N	39.49 W
Greenfield Village, hist., Mi., U.S.	199		42.18 N	83.14 W
Greenford, ngh., Eng., U.K.	178		51.32 N	0.21 W
Green Forest, Ar., U.S.	130	H4	36.19 N	93.26 W
Green Harbor, stm., Ma., U.S.	201		42.05 N	70.39 W
Green Hill, Pa., U.S.	203		39.59 N	75.36 W
Greenhill, ngh., Eng., U.K.	178		51.35 N	0.20 W
Greenhills, S. Afr.	191d		26.10 S	27.40 E
Greenhithe, Eng., U.K.	178		51.27 N	0.17 E
Greenhorn Creek, stm., Co., U.S.	138	C4	38.08 N	104.38 W
Green Hut Park, N.J., U.S.	194		40.50 N	74.39 W
Green Island, i., Gren.	159e	q10	12.13 N	61.35 W
Green Island Bay, b., Phil.	68	E2	10.14 N	119.21 E
Green Islands, is., Pap. N. Gui.	94	D6	4.30 S	154.10 E
Green Knoll, N.J., U.S.	194		40.36 N	74.36 W
Green Lake, Wi., U.S.	128	H10	43.50 N	88.57 W
Green Lake, l., B.C., Can.	144	E9	51.24 N	121.15 W
Green Lake, l., Mi., U.S.	199		42.36 N	83.25 W
Green Lake, l., N.Y., U.S.	202a		42.45 N	78.45 W
Green Lake, l., Wi., U.S.	128	H9	43.48 N	88.59 W
Greenland, Ar., U.S.	130	I3	35.59 N	94.10 W
Greenland, Mi., U.S.	128	E9	46.46 N	89.06 W
Greenland, dep., N.A.	108	C17	70.00 N	40.00 W
Greenland see Grønland, i., Grnld.	106	B18	70.00 N	40.00 W
Greenland Basin, unds.	176	A14	73.30 N	5.00 W
Greenland Sea, s.	106	B22	77.00 N	1.00 W
Greenlawn, N.Y., U.S.	194		40.52 N	73.21 W
Greenlawn Park, Pa., U.S.	203		40.07 N	74.51 W
Greenleaf, Ks., U.S.	138	B11	39.43 N	96.59 W
Green Lookout Mountain, mtn., Wa., U.S.	146	E4	45.51 N	122.06 W
Green Meadows, Md., U.S.	202c		38.58 N	76.57 W
Greenmount, Eng., U.K.	180		53.37 N	2.20 W
Green Mountains, mts., N.A.	122	F4	43.45 N	72.45 W
Green Oak Lake, l., Mi., U.S.	199		42.27 N	83.43 W
Green Oaks, Il., U.S.	196		42.18 N	87.55 W
Greenock, Scot., U.K.	10	F8	55.56 N	4.45 W
Greenock, Pa., U.S.	197b		40.19 N	79.48 W
Greenore Point, c., Ire.	10	I6	52.14 N	6.19 W
Greenough, stm., Austl.	96	E3	28.51 S	114.38 E
Green Peter Lake, res., Or., U.S.	146	F4	44.28 N	122.30 W
Green Point, c., N.Y., U.S.	194		40.43 N	73.06 W
Green Pond, Al., U.S.	134	D11	33.13 N	87.07 W
Green Pond, N.J., U.S.	194		41.01 N	74.29 W
Green Pond, l., N.J., U.S.	194		41.00 N	74.30 W
Green Pond Brook, stm., N.J., U.S.	194		40.53 N	74.34 W
Greenport, N.Y., U.S.	124	C13	41.06 N	72.21 W
Green Ridge, Pa., U.S.	203		39.51 N	75.25 W
Green River, Pap. N. Gui.	101a	a3	3.54 S	141.10 E
Green River, Ut., U.S.	150	D7	38.59 N	110.08 W
Green River, Wy., U.S.	150	B7	41.31 N	109.28 W
Green River Lake, res., Ky., U.S.	130	G12	37.14 N	85.18 W
Greensboro, Al., U.S.	134	E11	32.42 N	87.35 W
Greensboro, Fl., U.S.	134	G14	30.33 N	84.43 W
Greensboro, Ga., U.S.	132	C2	33.34 N	83.11 W
Greensboro, N.C., U.S.	124	H6	36.04 N	79.47 W
Greensborough, Austl.	192b		37.42 S	145.06 E
Greensburg, In., U.S.	130	E12	39.19 N	85.28 W
Greensburg, Ks., U.S.	138	D9	37.36 N	99.17 W
Greensburg, Ky., U.S.	130	G12	37.15 N	85.29 W
Greensburg, Pa., U.S.	124	D6	40.18 N	79.32 W
Greens Farms, Ct., U.S.	194		41.07 N	73.19 W
Greenside, ngh., S. Afr.	191d		26.09 S	28.01 E
Greens Peak, mtn., Az., U.S.	150	I7	34.07 N	109.35 W
Green Springs, Oh., U.S.	124	C2	41.15 N	83.02 W
Greenstead, Eng., U.K.	178		51.42 N	0.14 E
Green Street, Eng., U.K.	178		51.40 N	0.16 W
Green Street Green, ngh., Eng., U.K.	178		51.21 N	0.04 E
Green Swamp, sw., N.C., U.S.	132	B7	34.07 N	78.20 W
Greentown, In., U.S.	130	D12	40.28 N	85.57 W
Green Tree, Pa., U.S.	197b		40.24 N	80.02 W
Greenup, Il., U.S.	130	E9	39.14 N	88.09 W
Greenup, Ky., U.S.	124	F3	38.34 N	82.51 W
Greenvale, Austl.	98	B5	18.58 S	145.00 E
Greenvale, N.Y., U.S.	194		40.49 N	73.38 W
Green Valley, Az., U.S.	150	L6	31.49 N	111.00 W
Green Valley, Il., U.S.	130	D8	40.24 N	89.37 W
Greenview, Il., U.S.	130	D8	40.04 N	89.44 W
Green Village, N.J., U.S.	194		40.44 N	74.27 W
Greenville, Lib.	84	H3	5.01 N	9.02 W
Greenville, Al., U.S.	134	F12	31.49 N	86.37 W
Greenville, Ca., U.S.	148	C5	40.09 N	120.56 W
Greenville, Fl., U.S.	132	F2	30.29 N	83.37 W
Greenville, Ga., U.S.	134	D14	33.01 N	84.42 W
Greenville, Il., U.S.	130	F8	38.53 N	89.24 W
Greenville, Ky., U.S.	130	G10	37.12 N	87.10 W
Greenville, Me., U.S.	122	E7	45.26 N	69.34 W
Greenville, Mi., U.S.	130	A12	43.10 N	85.15 W
Greenville, Ms., U.S.	134	D7	33.24 N	91.03 W
Greenville, Mo., U.S.	130	G7	37.07 N	90.26 W
Greenville, N.Y., U.S.	194		40.59 N	73.49 W
Greenville, N.C., U.S.	132	A8	35.36 N	77.22 W
Greenville, Oh., U.S.	124	D1	40.05 N	84.37 W
Greenville, Pa., U.S.	124	C5	41.24 N	80.23 W
Greenville, S.C., U.S.	132	B3	34.51 N	82.23 W
Greenville, Tx., U.S.	136	A11	33.08 N	96.06 W
Greenville Place, De., U.S.	203		39.46 N	75.36 W
Greenwater Lake, l., On., Can.	128	C8	48.34 N	90.25 W
Greenwater Lake Provincial Park, p.o.i., Sk., Can.	142	B10	52.31 N	103.27 W
Greenwich, Austl.	192a		33.50 S	151.11 E
Greenwich, Ct., U.S.	124	C12	41.01 N	73.37 W
Greenwich, N.Y., U.S.	126	E16	43.05 N	73.29 W
Greenwich, Oh., U.S.	124	C3	41.01 N	82.31 W
Greenwich Cove, b., Ct., U.S.	194		41.01 N	73.35 W
Greenwich Creek, stm., Ct., U.S.	194		41.02 N	73.37 W
Greenwich Observatory, sci., Eng., U.K.	178		51.28 N	0.00 W
Greenwich Point, c., Ct., U.S.	194		41.00 N	73.34 W
Greenwich Village, hist., N.Y., U.S.	194		40.44 N	74.00 W
Greenwood, B.C., Can.	144	G12	49.05 N	118.41 W
Greenwood, Ar., U.S.	134	B4	35.12 N	94.15 W
Greenwood, In., U.S.	130	E11	39.36 N	86.06 W
Greenwood, Ma., U.S.	201		42.29 N	71.04 W
Greenwood, Ms., U.S.	134	D8	33.31 N	90.10 W
Greenwood, Ne., U.S.	130	D1	40.57 N	96.26 W
Greenwood, S.C., U.S.	132	B3	34.11 N	82.09 W
Greenwood, Wi., U.S.	128	G8	44.46 N	90.35 W
Greenwood, Lake, res., S.C., U.S.	132	B4	34.14 N	82.01 W
Greenwood Cemetery, misc. cult., N.Y., U.S.	194		40.39 N	73.59 W
Greenwood Lake, l., Ma., U.S.	201		42.00 N	71.17 W
Greenwood Race Track, p.o.i., On., Can.	193b		43.40 N	79.19 W
Greer, S.C., U.S.	132	B3	34.56 N	82.13 W
Greers Ferry Lake, res., Ar., U.S.	134	B6	35.32 N	92.07 W
Grées, Alpes see Grayiske alper, mts., Eur.	30	E4	45.30 N	7.10 E
Greeson, Lake, res., Ar., U.S.	134	C5	34.12 N	93.43 W
Greetland, Eng., U.K.	180		53.41 N	1.52 W
Greffiers, Fr.	179		48.37 N	1.51 E
Grefrath, Ger.	181		51.10 N	6.38 E
Gregg, Pa., U.S.	197b		40.24 N	80.10 W
Gregório, stm., Braz.	164	E3	6.49 S	70.39 W
Gregory, Mi., U.S.	124	B1	42.27 N	84.05 W
Gregory, S.D., U.S.	140	D13	43.13 N	99.25 W
Gregory, Tx., U.S.	136	G10	27.55 N	97.17 W
Gregory, stm., Austl.	96	C7	17.53 S	139.16 E
Gregory, Lake, l., Austl.	96	E3	25.35 S	119.53 E
Gregory, Lake, l., Austl.	96	D5	20.14 S	127.25 E
Gregory, Lake, l., Austl.	98	G2	28.55 S	139.00 E
Gregory Range, mts., Austl.	98	B4	19.00 S	143.05 E
Grégy-sur-Yerre, Fr.	179		48.40 N	2.37 E
Greifenhagen see Gryfino, Pol.	24	C10	53.13 N	14.28 E
Greifenstein, Aus.	182b		48.21 N	16.15 E
Greiffenburg, hist., Ger.	181		51.20 N	6.38 E
Greifswald, Ger.	24	B9	54.05 N	13.23 E
Greifswalder Bodden, b., Ger.	24	B9	54.15 N	13.35 E
Grein, Aus.	30	B11	48.14 N	14.51 E
Greiz, Ger.	24	F8	50.39 N	12.12 E
Gremiha, Russia	14	D30	68.03 N	39.27 E
Gremjače, Russia	38	B17	51.29 N	39.01 E
Gremjačinsk, Russia	40	B20	58.34 N	57.50 E
Grenaa, Den.	16	K8	56.24 N	10.52 E
Grenada, Ms., U.S.	134	D9	33.46 N	89.48 W
Grenada, ctry., N.A.	159e	q10	12.07 N	61.40 W
Grenada Lake, res., Ms., U.S.	134	C9	33.50 N	89.40 W
Grenadier Pond, l., On., Can.	193b		43.38 N	79.28 W
Grenadines, is., N.A.	159e	p11	12.40 N	61.15 W
Grenchen, Switz.	30	C4	47.11 N	7.23 E
Grenen, c., Den.	16	J8	57.44 N	10.39 E
Grenfell, Austl.	98	I7	33.54 S	148.09 E
Grenfell, Sk., Can.	142	D11	50.25 N	102.56 W
Grenloch, N.J., U.S.	203		39.47 N	75.03 W
Grenoble, Fr.	22	D11	45.10 N	5.42 E
Grenola, Ks., U.S.	138	D12	37.20 N	96.27 W
Grenora, N.D., U.S.	140	F10	48.37 N	103.56 W
Grense Jakobselv, Nor.	14	C21	69.46 N	30.50 E
Grenville, Gren.	159e	q10	12.07 N	61.37 W
Grenville, Cape, c., Austl.	94	E5	11.58 S	143.13 E
Grenville Bay, b., Gren.	159e	q10	12.05 N	61.36 W
Grenz-Berge, hill, Ger.	182a		52.27 N	13.44 E
Gréoux-les-Bains, Fr.	22	F11	43.45 N	5.52 E
Gresham, Or., U.S.	146	E4	45.29 N	122.25 W
Gresham Park, Ga., U.S.	132	C1	33.41 N	84.18 W
Gresik, Indon.	66	E3	2.18 S	103.56 E
Gresik, Indon.	66	G8	7.09 S	112.38 E
Gressåmoen Nasjonalpark, p.o.i., Nor.	16	C11	64.15 N	13.08 E
Gressey, Fr.	179		48.50 N	1.37 E
Gressoney-Saint-Jean, Italy	30	E4	45.48 N	7.48 E
Gressy, Fr.	179		48.58 N	2.41 E
Gresten, Aus.	24	I11	47.59 N	15.00 E
Gretna, Mb., Can.	142	E16	49.01 N	97.33 W
Gretna, La., U.S.	134	H8	29.54 N	90.03 W
Gretna, Va., U.S.	124	H6	36.57 N	79.21 W
Gretna Green, Scot., U.K.	10	F9	54.59 N	3.02 W
Grevel, ngh., Ger.	181		51.34 N	7.33 E
Greven, Ger.	24	D3	52.05 N	7.37 E
Grevená, Grc.	34	C4	40.04 N	21.25 E
Grevenbroich, Ger.	24	E2	51.05 N	6.35 E
Grevesmühlen, Ger.	24	C7	53.51 N	11.11 E
Greville Bay, b., N.S., Can.	122	E12	45.21 N	64.37 W
Greybull, Wy., U.S.	140	C4	44.29 N	108.03 W
Greybull, stm., Wy., U.S.	140	C4	44.28 N	108.03 W
Grey Eagle, Mn., U.S.	128	F4	45.49 N	94.44 W
Grey Islands, is., Nf., Can.	111a	i22	50.50 N	55.37 W
Greylock, Mount, mtn., Ma., U.S.	124	B12	42.38 N	73.10 W
Greymouth, N.Z.	102	F4	42.27 S	171.12 E
Grey Range, mts., Austl.	98	F4	27.00 S	143.35 E
Greys, stm., Wy., U.S.	146	H16	43.10 N	111.00 W
Greystanes, Austl.	192a		33.49 S	150.55 E
Greytown, S. Afr.	90	F10	29.04 S	30.35 E
Gribanovskij, Russia	40	F12	51.27 N	41.57 E
Gribbel Island, i., B.C., Can.	144	C1	53.25 N	129.00 W
Gribingui, stm., C.A.R.	86	C3	8.33 N	19.04 E
Gridino, Russia	18	B21	65.54 N	34.38 E
Gridley, Ca., U.S.	148	D4	39.21 N	121.41 W
Gridley, Il., U.S.	130	D9	40.44 N	88.52 W
Griebnitz-see, l., Ger.	182a		52.24 N	13.06 E
Griekwastad, S. Afr.	90	F6	28.50 S	23.15 E
Griesbach im Rottal, Ger.	24	H9	48.28 N	13.11 E
Griesheim, Ger.	24	G4	49.52 N	8.34 E
Griffin, Sk., Can.	142	E10	49.39 N	103.25 W
Griffin, Ga., U.S.	132	C1	33.15 N	84.15 W
Griffin, Lake, l., Fl., U.S.	132	H4	28.52 N	81.50 W
Griffiss Air Force Base, mil., N.Y., U.S.	126	E14	43.14 N	75.26 W
Griffith, Austl.	98	J5	34.17 S	146.02 E
Griffith Airport, arpt., In., U.S.	196		41.31 N	87.23 W
Griffith Park, p.o.i., Ca., U.S.	198		34.09 N	118.17 W
Grifton, N.C., U.S.	132	A8	35.22 N	77.26 W
Griggs Drain, can., Mi., U.S.	199		42.11 N	83.26 W
Griggstown, N.J., U.S.	194		40.26 N	74.36 W
Griggsville, Il., U.S.	130	E7	39.42 N	90.43 W
Grignols, Fr.	22	E5	44.23 N	0.02 W
Grignon, Fr.	179		48.51 N	1.57 E
Grigny, Fr.	179		48.40 N	2.24 E
Grigoriopol, Mol.	38	F8	47.08 N	29.18 E
Grijalva, stm., N.A.	154	G12	17.04 N	93.27 W
Grim, Cape, c., Austl.	99a	n12	40.39 S	144.42 E
Grimari, C.A.R.	86	C3	5.44 N	20.02 E
Grimeford Village, Eng., U.K.	180		53.36 N	2.34 W
Grimlinghausen, Ger.	181		51.10 N	6.44 E
Grimma, Ger.	24	E8	51.14 N	12.43 E
Grimmen, Ger.	24	B9	54.06 N	13.02 E
Grimsargh, Eng., U.K.	180		53.48 N	2.38 W
Grimsby, On., Can.	126	E10	43.11 N	79.33 W
Grimsby, Eng., U.K.	10	H12	53.34 N	0.04 W
Grimsel Pass, p., Switz.	30	D5	46.33 N	8.20 E
Grimsey, i., Ice.	12a	j30	66.32 N	18.00 W
Grimshaw, Ab., Can.	110	D7	56.11 N	117.37 W
Grímsstaðir, Ice.	12a	k31	65.38 N	16.08 W
Grimstad, Nor.	16	I6	58.20 N	8.36 E
Grímsvötn, vol., Ice.	12a	k31	64.24 N	17.22 W
Grindavík, Ice.	12a	l28	63.50 N	22.26 W
Grindelwald, Switz.	30	D5	46.37 N	8.01 E
Grindsted, Den.	16	L6	55.45 N	8.56 E
Grindstone Provincial Recreation Park, p.o.i., Mb., Can.	142	C16	51.08 N	96.53 W
Grinëvo, Russia	26	H16	52.33 N	33.04 E
Grinnell, Ia., U.S.	130	C5	41.44 N	92.43 W
Grinnell, Lake, l., N.J., U.S.	194		41.06 N	74.38 W
Grinnell Peninsula, pen., Nu., Can.	108	B7	76.40 N	95.00 W
Grintavec, mtn., Slvn.	30	D11	46.21 N	14.32 E
Grinzing, ngh., Aus.	182b		48.15 N	16.21 E
Gripsholm Slott, hist., Swe.	16	H14	59.15 N	17.13 E
Griqualand East, hist. reg., S. Afr.	90	G9	30.21 S	29.03 E
Griqualand West, hist. reg., S. Afr.	90	F6	28.20 S	23.30 E
Grisee see Gresik, Indon.	66	G8	7.09 S	112.38 E
Grise Fiord, Nu., Can.	108	B9	76.25 N	82.54 W
Gris-Nez, Cap, c., Fr.	20	D10	50.52 N	1.35 E
Grisslehamn, Swe.	16	G16	60.06 N	18.48 E
Griswold, Mb., Can.	142	E13	49.47 N	100.25 W
Griswold, Ia., U.S.	130	C2	41.13 N	95.10 W
Griswold Creek, stm., Oh., U.S.	197a		41.27 N	81.23 W
Grisy-Suisnes, Fr.	179		48.41 N	2.40 E
Grivenskaja, Russia	38	H17	45.38 N	38.09 E
Grizzly Bear Mountain, mtn., N.T., Can.	110	B6	65.22 N	121.00 W
Grizzly Bear's Head and Lead Man Indian Reserve, ind. res., Sk., Can.	142	B5	52.33 N	108.16 W
Grizzly Creek, stm., Ca., U.S.	200		37.52 N	122.06 W
Grizzly Island, i., Ca., U.S.	200		38.08 N	121.58 W
Grizzly Mountain, mtn., Id., U.S.	146	C10	47.43 N	116.06 W
Grizzly Mountain, mtn., Or., U.S.	146	F6	44.26 N	120.57 W
Grizzly Mountain, mtn., Wa., U.S.	146	B8	48.25 N	118.30 W
Grizzly Slough, stm., Ca., U.S.	200		38.06 N	121.53 W
Grjadcy, Russia	26	D14	56.23 N	31.56 E
Grjady, Russia	18	I18	58.57 N	31.59 E
Grjazi, Russia	40	E11	52.29 N	39.57 E
Grjazovec, Russia	40	B12	58.53 N	40.15 E
Grmeč, mts., Bos.	36	E3	44.42 N	16.18 E
Groaíras, Braz.	170	B5	3.53 S	40.23 W
Grobblershoop, S. Afr.	90	F5	28.55 S	20.59 E
Gröben, Ger.	182a		52.17 N	13.10 E
Gröbener See, l., Ger.	182a		52.17 N	13.11 E
Grobiņa, Lat.	26	D4	56.32 N	21.10 E
Groblersdal, S. Afr.	90	D9	25.10 S	29.24 E
Grodków, Pol.	24	F13	50.41 N	17.23 E
Grodno see Hrodna, Bela.	26	G6	53.40 N	23.50 E
Grodno see Hrodna, state, Bela.	26	G8	53.30 N	25.00 E
Grodzisk Mazowiecki, Pol.	24	D16	52.06 N	20.37 E
Grodzisk Wielkopolski, Pol.	24	D12	52.14 N	16.22 E
Groen, stm., S. Afr.	90	G6	30.39 S	23.16 E
Groesbeck, Tx., U.S.	136	C11	31.30 N	96.32 W
Grofa, hora, mtn., Ukr.	38	E2	48.37 N	23.56 E
Grogol, Kali, stm., Indon.	187e		6.10 S	106.47 E
Grogol-hilir, ngh., Indon.	187e		6.13 S	106.47 E
Groix, Fr.	20	G5	47.37 N	3.26 W
Groix, Île de, i., Fr.	20	G5	47.37 N	3.27 W
Grójec, Pol.	24	E16	51.52 N	20.52 E
Grokgak, Indon.	66	H9	8.11 S	114.46 E
Grombalia, Tun.	32	H4	36.36 N	10.30 E
Gromoslavka, Russia	40	G13	48.11 N	43.36 E
Gronau, Ger.	24	D3	52.12 N	7.00 E
Grong, Nor.	16	C10	64.28 N	12.17 E
Groningen, Neth.	20	A15	53.12 N	6.33 E
Groningen, Sur.	164	B6	5.47 N	55.28 W
Grønland see Greenland, dep., N.A.	108	C17	70.00 N	40.00 W
Grønland, i., Grnld.	106	B18	70.00 N	40.00 W
Grønlandshavet see Greenland Sea, s.	106	B22	77.00 N	1.00 W
Gronlid, Sk., Can.	142	A9	53.05 N	104.26 W
Groom, Tx., U.S.	138	F7	35.12 N	101.06 W
Groom Lake, l., Nv., U.S.	148	F10	37.16 N	115.48 W
Groot, stm., S. Afr.	90	H7	33.44 S	24.37 E
Groot-Berg, stm., S. Afr.	90	H4	32.46 S	18.07 E
Groot-Brakrivier, S. Afr.	90	I6	34.02 S	22.16 E
Grootdraaidam, res., S. Afr.	90	E9	26.54 S	29.24 E
Groote Eylandt, i., Austl.	96	B7	13.59 S	136.37 E
Grootfontein, Nmb.	88	D2	19.34 S	18.05 E
Grootgeluk, S. Afr.	90	C8	23.40 S	27.30 E
Groot Karasberge, mts., Nmb.	90	E4	27.21 S	18.42 E
Groot Karroo see Great Karroo, plat., S. Afr.	90	H6	32.46 S	22.31 E
Groot-Kei, stm., S. Afr.	90	H9	32.40 S	28.21 E
Groot Laagte, stm., Afr.	90	B5	20.53 S	21.22 E
Grootlaagte see Groot Laagte, stm., Afr.	90	B5	20.53 S	21.22 E
Groot-Marico, S. Afr.	90	D8	25.37 S	26.26 E
Groot Namaland see Great Namaqualand, hist. reg., Nmb.	90	D3	25.00 S	17.00 E
Groot-Swartberge, mts., S. Afr.	90	H6	33.22 S	22.20 E
Groot-Vis, stm., S. Afr.	90	H8	33.29 S	27.05 E
Grootvloer, pl., S. Afr.	90	F5	30.00 S	20.40 E
Gropeni, Rom.	36	D14	45.03 N	27.53 E
Gros Bois, Parc de, p.o.i., Fr.	179		48.44 N	2.32 E
Gros Islet, St. Luc.	159c	I7	14.05 N	60.56 W
Groslay, Fr.	179		48.59 N	2.21 E
Gros-Morne, Mart.	159c	k6	14.41 N	61.00 W
Gros Morne, mtn., Nf., Can.	111a	j22	49.36 N	57.48 W
Gros Piton, vol., St. Luc.	159c	m6	13.49 N	61.04 W
Grosrouvre, Fr.	179		48.47 N	1.46 E
Grossa, Ponta, c., Braz.	205a		22.47 S	43.11 W
Gross Ache (Tiroler Ache), stm., Eur.	30	C9	47.51 N	12.31 E
Grosse Aue, stm., Ger.	20	B17	52.37 N	9.10 E
Grosse Herrenwiese, sw., Ger.	182a		52.17 N	13.20 E
Grosse Île, La, i., Qc., Can.	122	C15	47.37 N	61.31 W
Grossenbaum, ngh., Ger.	181		51.22 N	6.47 E
Grossenhain, Ger.	24	E9	51.17 N	13.32 E
Grosse Pointe, Mi., U.S.	124	B3	42.23 N	82.54 W
Grosse Pointe, c., Guad.	159c	h6	16.00 N	61.16 W
Grosser Arber, mtn., Ger.	24	G9	49.07 N	13.07 E
Grosser Beerberg, mtn., Ger.	24	F6	50.37 N	10.44 E
Grosser Plessower See, l., Ger.	182a		52.23 N	12.54 E
Grosser Priel, mtn., Aus.	30	C11	47.43 N	14.04 E
Grosser Ravens-Berg, hill, Ger.	182a		52.21 N	13.04 E
Grosser Seddiner See, l., Ger.	182a		52.17 N	13.02 E
Grosser Wannsee, l., Ger.	182a		52.26 N	13.11 E
Grosser Zern-see, l., Ger.	182a		52.24 N	12.56 E
Grosseto, Italy	30	H8	42.45 N	11.06 E
Grosse Tulln, stm., Aus.	30	B12	48.20 N	16.04 E
Gross-Gerau, Ger.	24	G4	49.55 N	8.29 E
Gross Glienicke, Ger.	182a		52.28 N	13.07 E
Gross Glienicker See, l., Ger.	182a		52.28 N	13.06 E
Grossglockner, mtn., Aus.	30	C9	47.04 N	12.42 E
Grossjedlersdorf, ngh., Aus.	182b		48.17 N	16.25 E
Gross Kienitz, Ger.	182a		52.19 N	13.28 E
Gross-Machnow, Ger.	182a		52.16 N	13.28 E
Grossos, Braz.	170	C7	4.59 S	37.09 W
Gross-Schulzendorf, Ger.	182a		52.16 N	13.21 E
Grossvenediger, mtn., Aus.	30	C9	47.06 N	12.21 E
Grosswardein see Oradea, Rom.	36	B8	47.03 N	21.55 E
Gross Ziethen, Ger.	182a		52.44 N	13.01 E
Gross Ziethen, Ger.	182a		52.24 N	13.27 E
Gros Ventre, stm., Wy., U.S.	146	G16	43.33 N	110.48 W
Groton, N.Y., U.S.	126	F13	42.35 N	76.21 W
Groton, S.D., U.S.	140	B14	45.27 N	98.06 W
Grøtøya, i., Nor.	14	B9	70.10 N	18.51 E
Grøtsundet, b., Nor.	14	C10	69.48 N	19.28 E
Grottaglie, Italy	32	D11	40.32 N	17.25 E
Grottammare, Italy	30	G11	42.59 N	13.51 E
Grottoes, Va., U.S.	124	F7	38.15 N	78.48 W
Grouard Mission, Ab., Can.	110	D7	55.32 N	116.09 W
Groundhog, stm., On., Can.	114	B9	49.43 N	81.58 W
Grouse Creek, stm., Ks., U.S.	138	D12	36.59 N	96.55 W
Grouse Creek, stm., Ut., U.S.	150	B3	41.22 N	113.55 W
Grouse Creek Mountain, mtn., Id., U.S.	146	F13	44.22 N	113.54 W
Grov, Nor.	14	D8	68.41 N	17.06 E
Grove, Ok., U.S.	130	H3	36.35 N	94.46 W
Grove, Pa., U.S.	203		40.01 N	75.38 W
Grove City, Mn., U.S.	128	F4	45.08 N	94.41 W
Grove City, Oh., U.S.	124	E2	39.52 N	83.05 W
Grove City, Pa., U.S.	124	C5	41.09 N	80.04 W
Grove Hill, Al., U.S.	134	F11	31.42 N	87.46 W
Groveland, Fl., U.S.	132	H4	28.34 N	81.52 W
Grove Mountains, mts., Ant.	103	C12	72.53 S	74.53 E
Grove Park, ngh., Eng., U.K.	178		51.26 N	0.01 E
Grover City, Ca., U.S.	148	H5	35.09 N	120.38 W
Grover Cleveland Birthplace, hist., N.J., U.S.	194		40.50 N	74.16 W
Grover Cleveland Park, p.o.i., N.Y., U.S.	202a		42.57 N	78.49 W
Grovers Mills, N.J., U.S.	194		40.19 N	74.37 W
Groves, Tx., U.S.	136	E14	29.57 N	93.54 W
Groveton, N.H., U.S.	122	F5	44.35 N	71.30 W
Groveton, Pa., U.S.	197b		40.30 N	80.06 W
Groveton, Tx., U.S.	136	C12	31.02 N	95.07 W
Groveton, Va., U.S.	202c		38.46 N	77.05 W
Grovetown, Ga., U.S.	132	C3	33.26 N	82.11 W
Growa Point, c., Lib.	84	I3	4.21 N	7.36 W
Growler Peak, mtn., Az., U.S.	150	K3	32.24 N	113.07 W
Growler Wash, stm., Az., U.S.	150	K3	32.36 N	113.30 W
Groznyj, Russia	42	D11	43.18 N	45.40 E
Grube, Ger.	182a		52.26 N	12.57 E
Grubišno Polje, Cro.	30	E14	45.42 N	17.10 E
Grudziądz, Pol.	24	C14	53.29 N	18.44 E
Gruetli-Laager, Tn., U.S.	134	B13	35.22 N	85.39 W
Grugapark, p.o.i., Ger.	181		51.26 N	7.00 E
Gruia, Rom.	36	E9	44.16 N	22.41 E
Grulla, Tx., U.S.	136	H9	26.15 N	98.38 W
Grumman-Bethpage Airport, arpt., N.Y., U.S.	194		40.45 N	73.29 W
Grumman Corporation, sci., N.Y., U.S.	194		40.45 N	73.30 W
Grumme, ngh., Ger.	181		51.30 N	7.14 E
Grumo Appula, Italy	32	D10	41.00 N	16.42 E
Grums, Swe.	16	H11	59.21 N	13.06 E
Grünau, Nmb.	90	E4	27.44 S	18.22 E
Grünau, ngh., Ger.	182a		52.25 N	13.34 E
Grünau im Almtal, Aus.	24	I9	47.51 N	13.57 E
Grünberg see Zielona Góra, Pol.	24	E11	51.56 N	15.30 E
Grundy, Va., U.S.	124	G3	37.15 N	82.06 W
Grundy Center, Ia., U.S.	130	B5	42.21 N	92.46 W
Grundy Lake Provincial Park, p.o.i., On., Can.	126	C9	45.56 N	80.32 W
Grünefeld, Ger.	182a		52.41 N	12.58 E
Grünewald, Ger.	181		51.13 N	7.37 E
Grunewald, ngh., Ger.	182a		52.30 N	13.17 E
Grunewald, Berliner Forst, for., Ger.	182a		52.28 N	13.13 E
Grunewald, Jagdschloss, hist., Ger.	182a		52.28 N	13.16 E
Grüntal, Ger.	182a		52.45 N	13.44 E
Grunthal, Mb., Can.	142	E17	49.25 N	96.52 W
Grušino, Russia	40	B13	59.27 N	44.07 E
Gruver, Tx., U.S.	138	E7	36.15 N	101.24 W
Gruzdžiai, Lith.	26	D6	56.06 N	23.14 E
Gruzija see Georgia, ctry., Asia	42	D11	42.00 N	44.00 E
Gruznovka, Russia	50	E10	55.09 N	105.12 E
Grybów, Pol.	24	G16	49.37 N	20.57 E
Gryfice, Pol.	24	C11	53.55 N	15.12 E
Gryfino, Pol.	24	C10	53.13 N	14.28 E
Grythyttan, Swe.	16	H12	59.42 N	14.32 E
Grytøya, i., Nor.	14	D7	68.55 N	16.27 E
Grytviken, S. Geor.	166	J9	54.17 S	36.31 W
Gstaad, Switz.	30	D4	46.27 N	7.16 E
Guacanayabo, Golfo de, b., Cuba	156	B9	20.28 N	77.30 W
Guacara, Ven.	168	B7	10.14 N	67.53 W
Guacarí, Col.	168	F3	3.46 N	76.20 W
Gu Achi, Az., U.S.	150	K4	32.19 N	112.02 W
Guachiría, stm., Col.	168	E6	5.26 N	70.35 W
Guachochi, Mex.	154	B5	26.51 N	107.04 W
Guadajoz, stm., Spain	28	G6	37.49 N	4.50 W
Guadalajara, Mex.	154	E7	20.40 N	103.20 W
Guadalajara, Spain	28	D7	40.38 N	3.10 W
Guadalajara, co., Spain	28	D8	40.50 N	2.30 W
Guadalcanal, Spain	28	F5	38.06 N	5.49 W
Guadalcanal, state, Sol. Is.	101b	f9	9.50 S	160.00 E
Guadalcanal, i., Sol. Is.	101b	e9	9.32 S	160.12 E
Guadalén, stm., Spain	28	F7	38.05 N	3.32 W
Guadalén, Embalse de, res., Spain	28	F7	38.11 N	3.28 W
Guadalentín, stm., Spain	28	G9	37.59 N	1.04 W
Guadalete, stm., Spain	28	H4	36.35 N	6.13 W
Guadalhorce, stm., Spain	28	G6	36.40 N	4.27 W
Guadalimar, stm., Spain	28	F7	37.59 N	3.44 W
Guadalmena, stm., Spain	28	F8	38.18 N	2.56 W
Guadalmez, stm., Spain	28	F6	38.45 N	5.03 W
Guadalope, stm., Spain	28	D10	41.15 N	0.03 W
Guadalquivir, stm., Spain	28	H4	36.47 N	6.24 W
Guadalquivir, Marismas del, sw., Spain	28	G4	37.03 N	6.18 W
Guadalupe, Col.	168	F4	2.02 N	75.45 W
Guadalupe, Mex.	136	F7	28.08 N	100.38 W
Guadalupe, Mex.	154	D7	22.43 N	102.30 W
Guadalupe, Mex.	154	C8	25.41 N	100.15 W
Guadalupe, Ca., U.S.	148	I5	34.58 N	120.33 W
Guadalupe, ngh., Braz.	205a		22.50 S	43.23 W
Guadalupe, stm., Mex.	148	L9	32.05 N	116.53 W
Guadalupe, stm., Ca., U.S.	200		37.25 N	121.58 W
Guadalupe, stm., Tx., U.S.	136	E10	28.27 N	96.49 W
Guadalupe, Basílica de, rel., Mex.	204a		19.29 N	99.07 W
Guadalupe, Isla, i., Mex.	120	G3	29.02 N	118.21 W
Guadalupe, Presa de, res., Mex.	204a		19.37 N	99.16 W
Guadalupe, Sierra de, mts., Mex.	204a		19.35 N	99.08 W
Guadalupe, Sierra de, mts., Spain	28	E5	39.29 N	5.28 W
Guadalupe Bravos, Mex.	120	F10	31.19 N	105.58 W
Guadalupe del Norte, can., Mex.	204a		19.34 N	99.01 W
Guadalupe Mountains, mts., U.S.	136	B3	32.07 N	104.54 W
Guadalupe Mountains National Park, p.o.i., Tx., U.S.	136	C3	31.55 N	104.55 W
Guadalupe Peak, mtn., Tx., U.S.	136	C3	31.50 N	104.52 W
Guadalupe Slough, stm., Ca., U.S.	200		37.27 N	122.02 W
Guadalupe Victoria, Mex.	136	G6	27.46 N	101.03 W
Guadalupe Victoria, Mex.	150	K1	32.19 N	115.04 W
Guadalupe Victoria, Mex.	154	C6	24.26 N	104.07 W
Guadalupita, N.M., U.S.	138	E3	36.08 N	105.15 W
Guadarrama, Puerto de, p., Spain	28	D6	40.42 N	4.08 W
Guadarrama, Sierra de, mts., Spain	28	D6	40.50 N	4.00 W
Guadazaón, stm., Spain	28	E9	39.44 N	1.38 W
Guadeloupe, dep., N.A.	152a	h15	16.15 N	61.35 W
Guadeloupe, Passage de la see Guadeloupe Passage, strt., N.A.	152a	h15	16.45 N	61.30 W
Guadeloupe Channel see Dominica Passage, strt., N.A.	159c	i5	15.45 N	61.30 W
Guadeloupe Passage, strt., N.A.	152a	h15	16.45 N	61.30 W
Guadiana, stm., Eur.	28	G3	37.10 N	7.23 W
Guadiana Menor, stm., Spain	28	G7	37.56 N	3.13 W
Guadiaro, stm., Spain	28	H5	36.17 N	5.16 W
Guadiato, stm., Spain	28	F5	37.48 N	5.03 W
Guadiela, stm., Spain	28	D8	40.22 N	2.49 W
Guadix, Spain	28	G7	37.18 N	3.08 W
Guafo, Isla, i., Chile	166	H1	43.36 S	74.43 W
Guaianases, ngh., Braz.	205b		23.33 S	46.25 W
Guaíba, Braz.	172	E12	30.06 S	51.19 W
Guaíba, est., Braz.	172	E12	30.18 S	51.08 W
Guaicaipuro, state, Ven.	204c		10.25 N	66.57 W
Guaimaca, Hond.	156	E4	14.31 N	86.54 W
Guainía, state, Col.	168	F7	2.30 N	69.00 W
Guainía, stm., S.A.	168	F8	1.59 N	67.07 W
Guaió, stm., Braz.	205b		23.31 S	46.19 W
Guaiquinima, Cerro, mtn., Ven.	168	E10	5.49 N	63.41 W
Guaíra, Braz.	170	K1	20.19 S	48.18 W
Guaíra, Braz.	172	B10	24.05 S	54.14 W
Guairá, state, Para.	172	B9	25.45 S	56.30 W
Guairá, Salto del (Sete Quedas, Salto das), wtfl., S.A.	172	B10	24.02 S	54.14 W

Name	Page	Map Ref.	Latitude	Longitude
Guaire, stm., Ven.	204c		10.25 N	66.46 W
Guáitara, stm., Col.	168	G3	1.33 N	77.26 W
Guaitecas, Islas, is., Chile	166	H2	43.57 S	73.50 W
Guajaba, Cayo, i., Cuba	156	B9	21.50 N	77.30 W
Guajará-Açu, Braz.	170	A1	1.38 S	48.07 W
Guajará-Mirim, Braz.	166	B3	10.47 S	65.22 W
Guajataca, stm., P.R.	158a	b2	18.29 N	66.57 W
Guajataca, Lago de, res., P.R.	158a	b2	18.23 N	66.55 W
Guaje, Laguna del, l., Mex.	154	A7	28.00 N	103.13 W
Gualaca, Pan.	156	H6	8.31 N	82.18 W
Gualaceo, Ec.	168	I2	2.53 S	78.46 W
Gualala, Ca., U.S.	148	E2	38.45 N	123.31 W
Gualaquiza, Ec.	164	D2	3.22 S	78.35 W
Gualdo Tadino, Italy	30	G9	43.13 N	12.46 E
Gualeguay, Arg.	172	F8	33.09 S	59.20 W
Gualeguay, stm., Arg.	172	F8	33.19 S	59.38 W
Gualeguaychú, Arg.	172	F8	33.01 S	58.31 W
Gualicho, Salina del, pl., Arg.	166	H4	40.24 S	65.15 W
Guam, dep., Oc.	100c	j10	13.28 N	144.47 E
Guamá, stm., Braz.	170	A1	1.27 S	48.18 W
Guamal, Col.	168	F5	3.52 N	73.44 W
Guamal, Col.	168	C4	9.10 N	74.13 W
Guamal, Quebrada, stm., Ven.	204c		10.31 N	66.59 W
Guaminí, Arg.	172	H6	37.01 S	62.24 W
Guam International Airport, arpt., Guam	100c	j10	13.29 N	144.48 E
Guamo, Col.	168	E4	4.02 N	74.58 W
Guamote, Ec.	168	H2	1.56 S	78.42 W
Guamúchil, Mex.	154	C4	25.27 N	108.05 W
Guamués, stm., Col.	168	G3	0.33 N	76.32 W
Gua Musang, Malay.	64	J5	4.51 N	101.58 E
Guanábana, P.R.	158a	b1	18.00 N	67.07 W
Guanabara, Baía de, b., Braz.	205a		22.50 S	43.10 W
Guanabara, Palácio, bldg., Braz.	205a		22.56 S	43.11 W
Guanacaste, Cordillera de, mts., C.R.	156	G5	10.45 N	85.05 W
Guanaceví, Mex.	154	C6	25.56 N	105.56 W
Guanahacabibes, Golfo de, b., Cuba	156	A5	22.08 N	84.35 W
Guana Island, i., Br. Vir. Is.	158b	e8	18.29 N	64.34 W
Guanaja, Hond.	156	D5	16.27 N	85.53 W
Guanaja, Isla de, i., Hond.	156	D5	16.28 N	85.53 W
Guanajibo, stm., P.R.	158a	b1	18.10 N	67.10 W
Guanajibo, Punta, c., P.R.	158a	b1	18.10 N	67.10 W
Guanajuato, Mex.	154	E8	21.01 N	101.16 W
Guanajuato, state, Mex.	154	E8	21.00 N	101.00 W
Guanambi, Braz.	170	H4	14.13 S	42.47 W
Guanaparo, Caño, stm., Ven.	168	C7	8.11 N	68.36 W
Guañape, Islas, is., Peru	164	E2	8.33 S	78.57 W
Guanare, Ven.	168	C7	9.02 N	69.46 W
Guanare, stm., Ven.	168	C7	8.13 N	67.45 W
Guanarito, Ven.	168	C7	8.43 N	69.12 W
Guanay, Cerro, mtn., Ven.	168	D8	5.51 N	66.18 W
Guanay, Cerro, hill, Peru	204d		12.07 S	77.13 W
Guandacol, Arg.	172	D3	29.30 S	68.32 W
Guandu, China	58	I5	24.17 N	113.53 E
Guane, Cuba	156	A5	22.12 N	84.05 W
Guang'an, China	58	F2	30.27 N	106.37 E
Guang'anmen Station, trans., China	189a		39.53 N	116.20 E
Guangchang, China	58	H7	26.50 N	116.19 E
Guangde, China	58	F8	30.52 N	119.25 E
Guangdong, state, China	58	J6	23.00 N	113.00 E
Guangfeng, China	58	G8	28.25 N	118.11 E
Guangfu, China	187b		31.21 N	121.19 E
Guanghua see Laohekou, China	58	E4	32.25 N	111.36 E
Guangji, China	58	G6	29.51 N	115.33 E
Guangling, China	58	B6	39.45 N	114.16 E
Guangming Ding, mtn., China	58	F7	30.07 N	118.09 E
Guangnan, China	52	G5	24.10 N	105.06 E
Guangxi, state, China	52	G6	24.00 N	109.00 E
Guangyuan, China	58	E1	32.24 N	105.49 E
Guangze, China	58	H7	27.33 N	117.20 E
Guangzhou (Canton), China	58	J5	23.08 N	113.16 E
Guanhães, Braz.	170	J4	18.45 S	42.53 W
Guánica, P.R.	158a	c2	18.00 N	66.54 W
Guánica, Laguna de, l., P.R.	158a	b2	18.00 N	66.54 W
Guanipa, stm., Ven.	168	C10	9.55 N	62.26 W
Guano, Ec.	168	H2	1.35 S	78.38 W
Guano Creek, stm., Or., U.S.	146	H7	42.12 N	119.31 W
Guanta, Ven.	168	B9	10.13 N	64.36 W
Guantánamo, Cuba	156	B10	20.08 N	75.12 W
Guantao, China	58	C6	36.31 N	115.17 E
Guanting Shuiku, res., China	58	A6	40.17 N	115.35 E
Guanxian, China	52	E5	31.00 N	103.36 E
Guanxian, China	58	C6	36.28 N	115.26 E
Guanyun, China	58	D8	34.17 N	119.15 E
Guapí, Col.	168	F3	2.36 N	77.54 W
Guapiara, Braz.	172	B13	24.11 S	48.33 W
Guápiles, C.R.	156	G6	10.12 N	83.47 W
Guapo Bay, b., Trin.	159f	s12	10.12 N	61.38 W
Guaporé, Braz.	172	D11	28.50 S	51.53 W
Guaporé (Iténez), stm., S.A.	166	B4	11.54 S	65.00 W
Guaqui, Bol.	166	C3	16.35 S	68.51 W
Guará, stm., Braz.	170	G3	12.59 S	44.49 W
Guara, Sierra de, mts., Spain	28	B10	42.16 N	0.15 W
Guarabira, Braz.	170	D8	6.51 S	35.29 W
Guaracarumbo, Ven.	204c		10.34 N	66.59 W
Guaraci, Braz.	170	K1	20.29 S	48.56 W
Guaraciaba do Norte, Braz.	170	C5	4.10 S	40.46 W
Guaraciana, Braz.	170	I4	17.03 S	43.39 W
Guaraí, stm., Braz.	205a		22.42 S	43.02 W
Guaranda, Ec.	168	H2	1.36 S	78.59 W
Guaraniaçu, Braz.	172	B11	25.05 S	52.57 W
Guarani de Goiás, Braz.	170	G2	13.57 S	46.30 W
Guarapari, Braz.	170	K5	20.39 S	40.30 W
Guarapuava, Braz.	172	B12	25.22 S	51.29 W
Guaraqueçaba, Braz.	172	B13	25.17 S	48.19 W
Guarará, stm., Braz.	205b		23.39 S	46.30 W
Guararé, Pan.	156	I7	7.49 N	80.17 W
Guaratiba, Morro de, mtn., Braz.	205a		23.04 S	43.33 W
Guaratinga, Braz.	170	I6	16.34 S	39.40 W
Guaratinguetá, Braz.	170	L3	22.48 S	45.11 W
Guaratuba, Braz.	172	B13	25.53 S	48.35 W
Guarda, Port.	28	D3	40.32 N	7.15 W
Guarda, state, Port.	28	D3	40.40 N	7.15 W
Guardafui, Cape see Gwardafuy, Gees, c., Som.	86	B10	11.49 N	51.16 E
Guardia Escolta, Arg.	172	D6	29.01 S	62.05 W
Guardiagrele, Italy	30	H11	42.11 N	14.12 E
Guardia Mitre, Arg.	166	H4	40.26 S	63.41 W
Guardo, Spain	28	B6	42.47 N	4.50 W
Guareim see Cuareim, stm., S.A.	172	E9	30.11 S	57.36 W
Guareim see Quaraí, stm., S.A.	172	E9	30.11 S	57.36 W
Guareña, Spain	28	F4	38.50 N	6.06 W
Guareña, stm., Spain	28	C5	41.29 N	5.22 W
Guarenas, Ven.	168	B8	10.27 N	66.37 W
Guarenas, stm., Ven.	204c		10.30 N	66.45 W
Guarico, Ven.	168	C7	9.32 N	69.46 W
Guárico, state, Ven.	168	C8	8.40 N	66.35 W
Guárico, stm., Ven.	168	C8	7.54 N	67.22 W
Guárico, Embalse del, l., Ven.	168	C8	9.03 N	67.20 W
Guariquito, stm., Ven.	168	C8	7.39 N	66.19 W
Guarulhos, Braz.	170	L2	23.28 S	46.31 W
Guarulhos, mun., Braz.	205b		23.26 S	46.29 W
Guasare, stm., Ven.	168	B5	11.02 N	72.01 W
Guasave, Mex.	154	C4	25.34 N	108.27 W
Guasdualito, Ven.	168	D6	7.15 N	70.44 W
Guasipati, Ven.	168	D11	7.28 N	61.53 W
Guastalla, Italy	30	F7	44.55 N	10.39 E
Guatemala, Guat.	156	E2	14.37 N	90.32 W
Guatemala, ctry., N.A.	152	D6	15.30 N	90.15 W
Guatemala Basin, unds.	174	H29	11.00 N	95.00 W
Guateque, Col.	168	E5	5.00 N	73.28 W
Guatimozín, Arg.	172	F6	33.28 S	62.26 W
Guatopo, Parque Nacional, p.o.i., Ven.	168	C8	10.03 N	66.32 W
Guatraché, Arg.	172	H6	37.40 S	63.32 W
Guatuaro Point, c., Trin.	159f	s13	10.20 N	60.59 W
Guaviare, state, Col.	168	G5	2.00 N	72.00 W
Guaviare, stm., Col.	168	E7	4.04 N	67.43 W
Guaxindiba, stm., Braz.	205a		22.44 S	43.02 W
Guaxupé, Braz.	170	K2	21.18 S	46.42 W
Guayabal, Cuba	156	B9	20.41 N	77.36 W
Guayabal, Ven.	168	D8	8.00 N	67.24 W
Guayabal, Lago, res., P.R.	158a	b2	18.06 N	66.30 W
Guayabero, stm., Col.	168	F5	2.35 N	72.46 W
Guayacán, Chile	172	D2	29.58 S	71.20 W
Guayaguayare, Trin.	159f	s12	10.08 N	61.02 W
Guayama, P.R.	158a	c3	17.58 N	66.07 W
Guayana see Ciudad Guayana, Ven.	168	C10	8.21 N	62.39 W
Guayana see Guyana, ctry., S.A.	164	C6	5.00 N	59.00 W
Guayana, Macizo de see Guiana Highlands, mts., S.A.	164	C5	3.26 N	58.02 W
Guayaneco, Archipiélago, is., Chile	166	I1	47.45 S	75.10 W
Guayanés, Punta, c., P.R.	158a	b4	18.04 N	65.48 W
Guayanilla, P.R.	158a	b2	18.01 N	66.47 W
Guayanilla, Bahía de, b., P.R.	158a	c2	18.00 N	66.46 W
Guayape, stm., Hond.	156	E4	14.27 N	85.59 W
Guayapo, stm., Ven.	168	E8	4.32 N	67.37 W
Guayaquil, Ec.	168	I1	2.11 S	79.54 W
Guayaquil, Golfo de, b., S.A.	164	D1	2.57 S	80.36 W
Guayaramerín, Bol.	166	B3	10.49 S	65.24 W
Guayas, state, Ec.	168	H1	1.55 S	80.21 W
Guayas, stm., Ec.	168	I2	2.41 S	79.56 W
Guaycora, Mex.	154	A4	28.50 N	109.21 W
Guaymallén, Arg.	172	F3	32.53 S	68.47 W
Guaymas, Mex.	154	B3	27.54 N	110.54 W
Guaynabo, P.R.	158a	b3	18.21 N	66.04 W
Guayquiraró, stm., Arg.	172	E8	30.18 S	59.25 W
Guayuriba, stm., Col.	168	F5	3.53 N	73.06 W
Guazapares, Mex.	154	B4	27.22 N	108.15 W
Guazárachi, Mex.	154	B5	26.58 N	106.43 W
Guazunamby, Arroyo, stm., Arg.	206		34.24 S	58.38 W
Guba, D.R.C.	86	G5	10.38 S	26.26 E
Guba, Eth.	82	E7	11.15 N	35.16 E
Gubaha, Russia	48	C9	58.51 N	57.33 E
Gûbâl, Madîq (Jubal, Strait of), strt., Egypt	76	K4	27.40 N	33.55 E
Gubany, Russia	26	D13	56.36 N	30.41 E
Gubavica, wtfl., Cro.	30	G13	43.27 N	16.52 E
Gubbi, India	69	E3	13.19 N	76.56 E
Gubbio, Italy	30	G9	43.21 N	12.34 E
Guben, Ger.	24	E10	51.57 N	14.42 E
Guben see Gubin, Pol.	24	E10	51.57 N	14.43 E
Gubin, Pol.	24	E10	51.57 N	14.43 E
Gubkin, Russia	40	F10	51.16 N	37.32 E
Gucheng, China	58	E4	32.18 N	111.35 E
Gūdalūr, India	69	G3	9.36 N	77.11 E
Gúdar, Sierra de, mts., Spain	28	D10	40.27 N	0.42 W
Gudauta, Geor.	42	D9	43.06 N	40.37 E
Gudbrandsdalen, val., Nor.	16	F7	61.29 N	10.00 E
Gudermes, Russia	42	D12	43.21 N	46.05 E
Gudhjem, Den.	16	L12	55.12 N	14.58 E
Gudivāda, India	69	C5	16.25 N	81.00 E
Gudiyāttam, India	69	E4	12.56 N	78.52 E
Güdül, Tur.	34	C15	40.13 N	32.15 E
Gūdūr, India	69	D4	14.08 N	79.51 E
Gudvangen, Nor.	16	G4	60.52 N	6.50 E
Guebwiller, Fr.	20	G16	47.54 N	7.11 E
Gué-de-Longroi, Fr.	179		48.30 N	1.43 E
Guéhenno, Calvaire de, rel., Fr.	20	G6	47.54 N	2.39 W
Guéherville, Fr.	179		48.32 N	1.53 E
Güejar, stm., Col.	168	F5	2.54 N	73.13 W
Guékédou, Gui.	84	H2	8.33 N	10.07 W
Guélengdeng, Chad	82	E3	10.54 N	15.32 E
Guelma, Alg.	84	B6	36.28 N	7.26 E
Guelmime, Mor.	84	D2	28.56 N	10.05 W
Guelph, On., Can.	126	E9	43.33 N	80.15 W
Guéné, Benin	84	G5	11.43 N	3.12 E
Guer, Fr.	20	G6	47.54 N	2.07 W
Guéra, Massif de, mtn., Chad	82	E3	11.55 N	18.12 E
Guérande, Fr.	20	G6	47.19 N	2.25 W
Guercif, Mor.	84	C4	34.14 N	3.20 W
Guerdjoumane, Djebel, mtn., Alg.	28	H13	36.24 N	2.49 E
Güere, stm., Ven.	168	C9	9.49 N	65.07 W
Guéréda, Chad	82	E4	14.30 N	22.05 E
Guéret, Fr.	22	C7	46.10 N	1.52 E
Guerla Mandata Shan, mtn., China	70	C8	30.27 N	81.23 E
Guermantes, Fr.	179		48.51 N	2.42 E
Guernes, Fr.	179		49.01 N	1.38 E
Guernesey see Guernsey, dep., Eur.	6	F8	49.28 N	2.35 W
Guerneville, Ca., U.S.	148	E3	38.28 N	122.59 W
Guernica see Gernika, Spain	28	A8	43.19 N	2.41 W
Guernica y Luno see Gernika, Spain	28	A8	43.19 N	2.41 W
Guernsey, Wy., U.S.	140	E8	42.16 N	104.44 W
Guernsey, dep., Eur.	6	F8	49.28 N	2.35 W
Guernsey, i., Guern.	20	E6	49.31 N	2.27 W
Guernsey Reservoir, res., Wy., U.S.	140	E8	42.19 N	104.49 W
Guernsey State Park, p.o.i., Wy., U.S.	140	E7	42.20 N	104.50 W
Guerrero, Mex.	136	F7	28.18 N	100.23 W
Guerrero, Mex.	154	A5	28.33 N	107.30 W
Guerrero, state, Mex.	154	G9	17.40 N	100.00 W
Guerrero Negro, Mex.	154	B1	27.58 N	114.02 W
Guerville, Fr.	179		48.57 N	1.44 E
Guesle, stm., Fr.	179		48.36 N	1.40 E
Gueydan, La., U.S.	134	G6	30.01 N	92.30 W
Guga, Russia	50	F16	52.42 N	137.32 E
Gugē, mtn., Eth.	82	F7	6.10 N	37.24 E
Gugging, Aus.	182b		48.19 N	16.15 E
Guguan, i., N. Mar. Is.	94	B5	17.18 N	145.50 E
Gui, stm., China	58	I4	23.28 N	111.18 E
Guiana Basin, unds.	176	G9	11.00 N	52.00 W
Guiana Highlands, mts., S.A.	164	C5	3.26 N	58.02 W
Guiana Island, i., Antig.	159b	f4	17.07 N	61.44 W
Güicán, Col.	168	D5	6.28 N	72.25 W
Guichi, China	58	F7	30.38 N	117.28 E
Guichón, Ur.	172	F9	32.21 S	57.12 W
Guide, China	52	D5	36.01 N	101.26 E
Guide Rock, Ne., U.S.	140	G14	40.04 N	98.20 W
Guidimouni, Niger	84	G6	13.43 N	9.31 E
Guiding, China	58	H2	26.34 N	107.13 E
Guier, Lac de, l., Sen.	84	F1	16.12 N	15.50 W
Guijalo, Phil.	68	D4	13.44 N	123.51 E
Guijuelo, Spain	28	D5	40.33 N	5.40 W
Guilarte, Monte, mtn., P.R.	158a	b2	18.09 N	66.46 W
Guildford, Austl.	192a		33.51 S	150.59 E
Guildford, Eng., U.K.	10	J12	51.14 N	0.34 W
Guildford, mun., Eng., U.K.	178		51.16 N	0.32 W
Guildford Cathedral, rel., Eng., U.K.	178		51.14 N	0.35 W
Guildhall, Vt., U.S.	122	F5	44.34 N	71.34 W
Guilford, Me., U.S.	122	E7	45.10 N	69.23 W
Guilin, China	58	I4	25.17 N	110.17 E
Guillaume-Delisle, Lac, l., Qc., Can.	110	D15	56.15 N	76.17 W
Guillaumes, Fr.	22	E12	44.05 N	6.51 E
Guillermo E. Hudson, Arg.	206		34.47 S	58.10 W
Guillestre, Fr.	22	E12	44.39 N	6.38 E
Guilvinec, Fr.	20	G4	47.47 N	4.17 W
Guimarães, Braz.	170	B3	2.08 S	44.36 W
Guimaras Island, i., Phil.	68	E4	10.35 N	122.37 E
Guimba, Phil.	68	C3	15.39 N	120.45 E
Guin, Al., U.S.	134	D11	33.58 N	87.55 W
Guinan, China	52	D5	35.35 N	100.39 E
Guinayang, Phil.	187f		14.42 N	121.08 E
Guinayangan, Phil.	68	D4	13.53 N	122.27 E
Guindulman, Phil.	68	F5	9.46 N	124.29 E
Guiné, Golfo da see Guinea, Gulf of, b., Afr.	84	I6	2.00 N	2.30 E
Guinea, ctry., Afr.	84	G2	11.00 N	10.00 W
Guinea, Golfo de see Guinea, Gulf of, b., Afr.	84	I6	2.00 N	2.30 E
Guinea, Gulf of, b., Afr.	84	I6	2.00 N	2.30 E
Guinea Basin, unds.	176	H13	0.30 N	5.00 W
Guinea-Bissau, ctry., Afr.	84	G1	12.00 N	15.00 W
Guinea Ecuatorial see Equatorial Guinea, ctry., Afr.	84	I6	2.00 N	9.00 E
Guiné-Bissau see Guinea-Bissau, ctry., Afr.	84	G1	12.00 N	15.00 W
Guinée see Guinea, ctry., Afr.	84	G2	11.00 N	10.00 W
Guinée, Golfe de see Guinea, Gulf of, b., Afr.	84	I6	2.00 N	2.30 E
Güines, Cuba	156	A7	22.50 N	82.01 W
Guingamp, Fr.	20	F5	48.33 N	3.09 W
Güinope, Hond.	156	F4	13.50 N	86.50 W
Guiperreux, Fr.	179		48.40 N	1.42 E
Guiperreux, Étang de, l., Fr.	179		48.40 N	1.43 E
Guiping, China	58	J4	23.23 N	110.04 E
Guipúzcoa see Gipuzkoako, co., Spain	28	A8	43.10 N	2.10 W
Guir, Hammada du, des., Afr.	84	C4	30.45 N	3.15 W
Guiratinga, Braz.	166	C6	16.21 S	53.45 W
Güiria, Ven.	168	B10	10.35 N	62.17 W
Guisan Bourg, Fr. Gu.	164	C7	4.24 N	51.55 W
Guitiriz, Spain	28	A3	43.11 N	7.54 W
Guitrancourt, Fr.	179		49.01 N	1.47 E
Guitry, C. Iv.	84	H3	5.31 N	5.14 W
Guiuan, Phil.	68	E5	11.02 N	125.43 E
Guixian, China	58	J3	23.06 N	109.38 E
Guiyang, China	58	I5	25.44 N	112.43 E
Guiyang, China	58	H2	26.34 N	106.42 E
Güiza, stm., Col.	168	G2	1.21 N	78.35 W
Guizhou, state, China	52	F6	27.00 N	107.00 E
Gujarāt, state, India	62	D3	22.00 N	72.00 E
Gūjar Khān, Pak.	70	B4	33.15 N	73.17 E
Gujiazhai, China	187b		31.22 N	121.28 E
Gujrānwāla, Pak.	70	B4	32.09 N	74.10 E
Gujrāt, Pak.	70	B4	32.34 N	74.04 E
Gukou, China	58	H8	26.25 N	118.38 E
Gukovo, Russia	38	E18	48.03 N	39.57 E
Gul, Tanjong, c., Sing.	189c		1.17 N	103.39 E
Gulargambone, Austl.	98	H7	31.20 S	148.28 E
Gulbarga, India	69	C3	17.20 N	76.50 E
Gulbene, Lat.	26	C9	57.10 N	26.45 E
Guldasteh, Iran	185d		35.36 N	51.16 E
Güldüzü, Tur.	76	B8	36.50 N	37.06 E
Guledagudda, India	69	C2	16.02 N	75.46 E
Gülek Boğazı, p., Tur.	76	A5	37.18 N	34.46 E
Gulf Hammock, Fl., U.S.	132	G3	29.15 N	82.43 W
Gulf Islands National Seashore, p.o.i., U.S.	134	G10	30.14 N	88.42 W
Gulfport, Ms., U.S.	134	G9	30.22 N	89.05 W
Gulf Shores, Al., U.S.	134	G11	30.15 N	87.40 W
Gulf State Park, p.o.i., Al., U.S.	134	G11	30.16 N	87.40 W
Gulgong, Austl.	98	I7	32.21 S	149.32 E
Gulian, China	50	F13	52.56 N	122.19 E
Gulistan, Uzb.	48	F11	40.30 N	68.46 E
Guliya Shan, mtn., China	52	B9	49.48 N	122.25 E
Gulja see Yining, China	48	F14	43.54 N	81.18 E
Guljanci, Blg.	36	F11	43.38 N	24.41 E
Gulkana, Ak., U.S.	109	D10	62.16 N	145.24 W
Gull, stm., On., Can.	128	B9	49.49 N	89.05 W
Gullfoss, wtfl., Ice.	12a	k29	64.24 N	20.07 W
Gull Island, i., Mi., U.S.	199		42.32 N	82.41 W
Gull Lake, Sk., Can.	142	D5	50.08 N	108.27 W
Gull Lake, l., Ab., Can.	144	D16	52.33 N	114.02 W
Gull Lake, l., Mn., U.S.	128	E4	46.28 N	94.20 W
Gullspång, Swe.	16	H12	58.59 N	14.07 E
Güllük, Tur.	34	F10	37.14 N	27.36 E
Güllük Körfezi, b., Tur.	34	F10	37.12 N	27.20 E
Gülnar, Tur.	42	G5	36.20 N	33.25 E
Gulph Mills, Pa., U.S.	203		40.04 N	75.21 W
Gülpınar, Tur.	34	D9	39.32 N	26.07 E
Gul'šad, Kaz.	48	E12	46.37 N	74.21 E
Gulsvik, Nor.	16	G7	60.24 N	9.36 E
Gulu, China	70	D12	28.05 N	89.18 E
Gulu, Ug.	86	D6	2.47 N	32.18 E
Guluogongba, China	70	C8	34.20 N	84.59 E
Gumaca, Phil.	68	D4	13.55 N	122.06 E
Gumal (Gowmal), stm., Asia	70	B2	31.36 N	70.48 E
Gumbalie, Austl.	98	G5	29.59 S	145.23 E
Gumbinnen see Gusev, Russia	26	F5	54.35 N	22.12 E
Gumdag, Turkmen.	72	B7	39.12 N	54.35 E
Gumel, Nig.	84	G6	12.36 N	9.24 E
Gumla, India	70	G10	23.02 N	84.33 E
Gumma, state, Japan	56	C11	36.30 N	139.00 E
Gummersbach, Ger.	24	E3	51.01 N	7.33 E
Gumpas Pond, l., N.H., U.S.	201		42.44 N	71.22 W
Gumpas Pond Brook, stm., U.S.	201		42.42 N	71.21 W
Gumpoldskirchen, Aus.	182b		48.03 N	16.17 E
Gum Swamp Creek, stm., Ga., U.S.	132	D2	32.08 N	82.55 W
Gümüşçay, Tur.	34	C10	40.16 N	27.17 E
Gümüşhane, Tur.	42	E8	40.28 N	39.27 E
Gümüşhane, state, Tur.	42	E8	40.15 N	39.30 E
Gümüşköy, ngh., Tur.	185b		41.14 N	28.58 E
Gümüşsu, Tur.	34	E12	38.12 N	30.01 E
Guna, India	70	F6	24.38 N	77.18 E
Gunbar South, Austl.	98	J5	34.02 S	145.23 E
Gun Creek, stm., N.Y., U.S.	202a		43.03 N	78.55 W
Gunda, Russia	50	F11	52.47 N	111.44 E
Gundagai, Austl.	98	J7	35.04 S	148.06 E
Gundji, D.R.C.	86	D4	2.04 N	21.27 E
Gundlupet, India	69	F3	11.48 N	76.41 E
Gündoğdu, Tur.	34	C10	40.16 N	27.08 E
Gündoğmuş, Tur.	34	G14	36.48 N	31.59 E
Güney, Tur.	34	E12	38.09 N	29.04 E
Güngören, ngh., Tur.	185b		41.01 N	28.53 E
Gungu, D.R.C.	86	F3	5.42 S	19.18 E
Gunmi, Nig.	84	G6	12.08 N	5.06 E
Gunnar, Sk., Can.	110	D9	59.22 N	108.53 W
Gunnariyn, Mong.	52	B5	45.36 N	102.00 E
Gunnarn, Swe.	16	B15	65.00 N	17.40 E
Gunnarsbyn, Swe.	14	F12	66.04 N	21.49 E
Gunnbjørn Fjeld, mtn., Grnld.	108	D19	68.53 N	30.00 W
Gunnebo, Swe.	16	J14	57.43 N	16.32 E
Gunnedah, Austl.	98	H8	30.58 S	150.15 E
Gunning Island, i., N.J., U.S.	194		40.22 N	73.59 W
Gunnison, Co., U.S.	138	C2	38.32 N	106.55 W
Gunnison, Ut., U.S.	150	D5	39.09 N	111.49 W
Gunnison, stm., Co., U.S.	150	E8	39.03 N	108.34 W
Gunnison, Lake Fork, stm., Co., U.S.	150	E9	38.26 N	107.24 W
Gunnison, North Fork, stm., Co., U.S.	150	E9	38.47 N	107.50 W
Gunong Mulu National Park, p.o.i., Malay.	66	A9	4.10 N	114.55 E
Gun Point, c., Gren.	159e	p11	12.31 N	61.26 W
Gunpowder Creek, stm., Austl.	98	B2	19.14 S	139.59 E
Gunpowder Falls State Park, p.o.i., Md., U.S.	124	E9	39.36 N	76.41 W
Gunsan see Kunsan, Kor., S.	54	F7	35.58 N	126.43 E
Guntakal, India	69	D3	15.10 N	77.22 E
Guntersville, Al., U.S.	134	C12	34.21 N	86.17 W
Guntersville Dam, dam., Al., U.S.	134	C12	34.26 N	86.23 W
Guntersville Lake, res., Al., U.S.	134	C12	34.31 N	86.08 W
Guntung, Indon.	66	C2	1.38 N	101.34 E
Guntūr, India	69	C5	16.18 N	80.26 E
Gunungkencana, Indon.	66	G4	6.34 S	106.04 E
Gunungmegang, Indon.	66	E3	3.27 S	103.50 E
Gunungsahilan, Indon.	66	C2	0.01 N	101.11 E
Gunungsitoli, Indon.	64	L3	1.15 N	97.36 E
Gunungtua, Indon.	66	C1	1.31 N	99.37 E
Gunupur, India	69	B6	19.04 N	83.49 E
Günz, stm., Ger.	30	B7	48.27 N	10.16 E
Günzburg, Ger.	24	H6	48.27 N	10.17 E
Gunzenhausen, Ger.	24	G6	49.07 N	10.45 E
Guo, stm., China	58	E6	32.57 N	117.12 E
Guoyang, China	58	E7	33.30 N	116.12 E
Guoyangzhen, China	58	B5	38.52 N	112.45 E
Gupis, Pak.	62	A3	36.13 N	73.25 E
Gura, Russia	40	C17	57.18 N	51.25 E
Gurabo, P.R.	158a	b4	18.15 N	65.57 W
Gura Galbehei, Mol.	38	G7	46.41 N	28.42 E
Gurahonț, Rom.	36	C9	46.15 N	22.21 E
Gura Humorului, Rom.	36	B12	47.33 N	25.54 E
Gurais, India	70	A5	34.39 N	74.47 E
Gurban Obo, China	52	C7	43.13 N	112.21 E
Gurdāspur, India	70	B5	32.05 N	75.26 E
Gurdon, Ar., U.S.	134	D5	33.55 N	93.09 W
Güre, Tur.	34	E12	38.39 N	29.08 E
Gurev see Atyrau, Kaz.	48	E8	47.07 N	51.55 E
Gurevsk, Russia	26	F3	54.46 N	20.36 E
Gurevsk, Russia	48	D15	54.16 N	85.54 E
Gurghiului, Munții, mts., Rom.	36	C12	46.41 N	25.12 E
Gurgueia, stm., Braz.	170	D4	6.50 S	43.23 W
Gurha, India	70	F3	25.11 N	71.40 E
Guri, Embalse de, res., Ven.	168	D10	7.30 N	62.50 W
Gurk, stm., Aus.	30	D11	46.36 N	14.31 E
Gurlevo, Russia	26	A11	59.28 N	28.53 E
Gurnet Point, c., Ma., U.S.	201		42.01 N	70.34 W
Gürpınar, Tur.	42	F10	38.18 N	43.22 E
Gurskoe, Russia	50	F16	50.18 N	138.06 E
Gurskøya, i., Nor.	16	E3	62.15 N	5.41 E
Gürsu, Tur.	34	C12	40.12 N	29.11 E
Gürün, Tur.	42	F7	38.43 N	37.17 E
Gurupá, Braz.	164	D7	1.25 S	51.38 W
Gurupi, Braz.	170	F1	11.43 S	49.02 W
Gurupi, stm., Braz.	164	D8	1.15 S	46.08 W
Guru Sikhar, mtn., India	70	F4	24.39 N	72.46 E
Gurvan Sayhan uul, mts., Mong.	52	C5	43.37 N	103.46 E
Gusau, Nig.	84	G6	12.09 N	6.40 E
Gusev, Russia	26	F5	54.35 N	22.12 E
Gusevo, Russia	26	D16	56.05 N	33.20 E
Gušgy, Turkmen.	72	B9	35.16 N	62.20 E
Gushan, China	58	B10	39.53 N	123.35 E
Gu Shan, mtn., China	58	H8	26.05 N	119.22 E
Gushi, China	58	E6	32.10 N	115.40 E
Gus'-Hrustal'nyj, Russia	40	D12	55.36 N	40.40 E
Gusino, Russia	26	F14	54.43 N	31.19 E
Gusinoozersk, Russia	50	F10	51.16 N	106.30 E
Gus'-Hrustal'nyy see Gus'-Hrustal'nyj, Russia	40	D12	55.36 N	40.40 E
Gusong, China	58	G1	28.18 N	105.13 E
Guspini, Italy	32	E2	39.32 N	8.37 E
Güssing, Aus.	30	C13	47.03 N	16.19 E
Gustav Holm, Kap, c., Grnld.	108	D19	67.00 N	34.00 W
Gustavia, Guad.	159a	b2	17.54 N	62.51 W
Gustavo A. Madero, ngh., Mex.	204a		19.29 N	99.07 W
Gustavus, Ak., U.S.	109	E12	58.25 N	135.44 W
Gustia, India	190b		22.59 N	88.26 E
Gustine, Ca., U.S.	148	F5	37.14 N	120.59 W
Gustine, Tx., U.S.	136	C9	31.49 N	98.22 W
Güstrow, Ger.	24	C8	53.47 N	12.10 E
Gusum, Swe.	16	I14	58.16 N	16.30 E
Güterfelde, Ger.	182a		52.22 N	13.12 E
Gütersloh, Ger.	24	E4	51.54 N	8.23 E
Guthrie, Ky., U.S.	130	H10	36.38 N	87.10 W
Guthrie, Ok., U.S.	138	F11	35.52 N	97.25 W
Guthrie, Tx., U.S.	138	H8	33.36 N	100.19 W
Guthrie Center, Ia., U.S.	138	C3	41.40 N	94.29 W
Gutian, China	58	H8	26.35 N	118.46 E
Gutiérrez Zamora, Mex.	154	E10	20.27 N	97.05 W
Guton, gora, mtn., Russia	42	E12	41.51 N	46.45 E
Guttenberg, Ia., U.S.	130	B6	42.47 N	91.05 W
Guttenberg, N.J., U.S.	194		40.47 N	74.00 W
Gutuevskij, ostrov, i., Russia	183a		59.54 N	30.14 E
Gutulia Nasjonalpark, p.o.i., Nor.	16	E9	62.02 N	12.12 E
Güvem, Tur.	34	C15	40.35 N	32.39 E
Guwāhāti, India	70	E13	26.11 N	91.44 E
Guxian, China	58	E5	32.25 N	113.37 E
Guyana, ctry., S.A.	164	C6	5.00 N	59.00 W
Guyancourt, Fr.	179		48.46 N	2.04 E
Guyancourt, Aéroport de, arpt., Fr.	179		48.45 N	2.05 E
Guyane see French Guiana, dep., S.A.	164	C7	4.00 N	53.00 W
Guyang, China	58	A4	41.02 N	110.03 E
Guye, China	58	B8	39.43 N	118.25 E
Guy Fawkes River National Park, p.o.i., Austl.	98	H9	30.02 S	152.18 E
Guymon, Ok., U.S.	138	E7	36.41 N	101.28 W
Guyonne, Ruisseau la, stm., Fr.	179		48.49 N	1.52 E
Guyot, Mount, mtn., U.S.	124	I2	35.42 N	83.15 W
Guyra, Austl.	98	H8	30.13 S	151.39 E
Guysborough, N.S., Can.	122	E15	45.22 N	61.31 W
Guyton, Ga., U.S.	132	D4	32.19 N	81.23 W
Guyuan, China	58	D2	35.59 N	106.17 E
Guzar, Uzb.	48	G11	38.36 N	66.15 E
Güzelsu, Tur.	76	B2	36.54 N	31.52 E
Güzelyurt, N. Cyp.	76	C3	35.11 N	33.00 E
Güzelyurt Körfezi, b., N. Cyp.	76	C3	35.14 N	32.50 E
Guzhang, China	58	G3	28.31 N	109.57 E
Guzhen, China	58	E7	33.18 N	117.18 E
Guzmán, Mex.	120	F9	31.13 N	107.27 W
Guzmán, Mex.	154	F7	19.41 N	103.28 W
Guzmán, Laguna de, l., Mex.	150	L9	31.16 N	107.27 W
Gvardejsk, Russia	26	F4	54.39 N	21.05 E
Gvarv, Nor.	16	H7	59.23 N	9.10 E
Gvozdena Vrata see Iron Gate, val., Eur.	36	E9	44.41 N	22.31 E
Gwa, Mya.	64	D2	17.35 N	94.35 E
Gwaai, Zimb.	88	D4	19.17 S	27.41 E
Gwabegar, Austl.	98	H7	30.36 S	148.58 E
Gwādar, Pak.	62	C1	25.07 N	62.19 E
Gwāl Haidarzai, Pak.	70	C2	30.43 N	68.50 E
Gwalia, Austl.	96	E4	28.55 S	121.20 E
Gwalior (Lashkar), India	70	E7	26.12 N	78.09 E
Gwanda, Zimb.	88	E4	20.57 S	28.59 E
Gwane, D.R.C.	86	D5	4.43 N	25.49 E
Gwangju see Kwangju, Kor., S.	54	G7	35.08 N	126.54 E
Gwardafuy, Gees, c., Som.	86	B10	11.49 N	51.16 E
Gwātar Bay, b., Asia	72	E9	25.05 N	61.36 E
Gwayi, stm., Zimb.	88	D4	17.59 S	26.55 E
Gwda, stm., Pol.	24	C12	53.03 N	16.44 E
Gweebarra Bay, b., Ire.	10	G4	54.52 N	8.26 W
Gweedore, Ire.	10	F4	55.03 N	8.14 W
Gweru, Zimb.	88	D4	19.27 S	29.49 E
Gweta, Bots.	88	E4	20.11 S	25.15 E
Gwinhurst, De., U.S.	203		39.47 N	75.29 W
Gwinn, Mi., U.S.	126	B2	46.17 N	87.25 W
Gwinner, N.D., U.S.	140	A15	46.12 N	97.38 W
Gwydir, stm., Austl.	98	G7	29.35 S	148.41 E
Gwynedd, Pa., U.S.	203		40.12 N	75.15 W
Gwynedd Square, Pa., U.S.	203		40.13 N	75.18 W
Gwynedd Valley, Pa., U.S.	203		40.11 N	75.15 W
Gwynns Falls, stm., Md., U.S.	202b		39.16 N	76.37 W
Gwynns Falls Park, p.o.i., Md., U.S.	202b		39.18 N	76.41 W
Gyál, Hung.	182c		47.23 N	19.14 E
Gyáli-patak, stm., Hung.	182c		47.24 N	19.07 E
Gyangtse see Gyangzê, China	52	F2	28.55 N	89.33 E
Gyangzê, China	52	F2	28.55 N	89.33 E
Gyaring Co, l., China	70	C12	31.04 N	88.23 E
Gyaring Hu, l., China	52	E4	34.54 N	97.14 E
Gyáros, i., Grc.	34	F7	37.37 N	24.43 E
Gyda, Russia	50	B4	70.52 N	78.24 E
Gydanskaja guba, b., Russia	50	B4	71.20 N	76.30 E
Gydanskij poluostrov, pen., Russia	50	B4	70.50 N	79.00 E
Gyeongbog Palace, bldg., Kor., S.	189b		37.36 N	126.57 E
Gyeongju see Kyŏngju, Kor., S.	54	G8	35.50 N	129.13 E
Gyirong, China	70	D10	28.28 N	85.21 E
Gyirong, China	70	D10	28.57 N	85.13 E
Gyldenløves Fjord, b., Grnld.	108	E17	64.11 N	40.58 W
Gymea Bay, Austl.	192a		34.02 S	151.05 E
Gym Peak, mtn., N.M., U.S.	150	K9	32.04 N	107.35 W
Gympie, Austl.	98	F9	26.11 S	152.40 E
Gyobingauk, Mya.	64	C2	18.13 N	95.38 E
Gyoma, Hung.	36	C7	46.55 N	20.49 E
Gyöngyös, Hung.	36	B6	47.47 N	19.55 E
Győr (Raab), Hung.	36	B4	47.40 N	17.38 E
Győr-Moson-Sopron, state, Hung.	36	B4	47.35 N	17.15 E
Gypsum, Co., U.S.	138	B2	39.39 N	106.56 W
Gypsum, Ks., U.S.	138	C11	38.42 N	97.25 W
Gypsum Creek, stm., U.S.	150	F7	37.08 N	109.51 W
Gypsum Creek, stm., Ks., U.S.	138	C11	38.52 N	97.23 W
Gypsumville, Mb., Can.	142	C15	51.46 N	98.37 W
Gýtheio, Grc.	34	G5	36.45 N	22.33 E
Gyula, Hung.	36	C8	46.38 N	21.20 E
Gyulafehérvár see Alba Iulia, Rom.	36	C10	46.04 N	23.34 E
Gyzylarbat, Turkmen.	72	B8	38.58 N	56.16 E
Gžat', stm., Russia	26	E17	55.48 N	34.42 E
Gzhatsk see Gagarin, Russia	26	E17	55.32 N	34.58 E

H

Name	Page	Map Ref.	Latitude	Longitude
Haag, Aus.	24	H10	48.06 N	14.33 E
Haag in Oberbayern, Ger.	24	H8	48.09 N	12.10 E
Haaksbergen, Neth.	24	D2	52.09 N	6.44 E
Haapajärvi, Fin.	18	D12	63.45 N	25.20 E
Haapajärvi, l., Fin.	18	D13	63.34 N	26.56 E
Haapamäki, Fin.	18	E11	62.14 N	24.27 E
Haapavesi, Fin.	18	C12	64.07 N	25.21 E
Haapiti, Fr. Poly.	100h	v20	17.33 S	149.51 W
Haapsalu, Est.	26	B6	58.56 N	23.33 E
Haar, Ger.	24	H7	48.06 N	11.43 E
Haar, ngh., Ger.	181		51.26 N	7.13 E
Ha'Arava ('Arabah, Wādī al-), val., Asia	76	H6	30.34 N	35.12 E
Ha'Arava (Jayb, Wādī al-), stm., Asia	76	H6	30.59 N	35.24 E
Haarby, Den.	16	L8	55.12 N	10.07 E
Haarlem, Neth.	20	B13	52.23 N	4.38 E
Haarzopf, ngh., Ger.	181		51.25 N	6.58 E
Haast, N.Z.	102	F3	43.52 S	169.01 E

Name Page Map Ref. Latitude Longitude

Haava, Canal, strt., Fr. Poly. 100g s18 9.52 S 139.04 W
Habana, Bahía de la, b., Cuba 204b 23.08 N 82.20 W
Habaqila, China 52 C6 42.01 N 105.59 E
Habariha, Russia 12 D24 65.51 N 52.15 E
Habarovsk, Russia 50 G16 48.25 N 135.08 E
Habary, Russia 48 D13 53.37 N 79.35 E
Ḥabashīyah, Jabal, mts., Yemen 72 F7 16.40 N 49.40 E
Habbān, Yemen 72 G6 14.19 N 47.03 E
Ḥabbānīyah, Buḥayrat al-, res., Iraq 74 D8 33.17 N 43.29 E
Haberfield, Austl. 192a 33.53 S 151.08 E
Habermehl Peak, mtn., Ant. 103 C6 71.49 S 6.38 E
Habiganj, Bngl. 70 F13 24.22 N 91.24 E
Habinghorst, Ger. 181 51.35 N 7.18 E
Habo, Swe. 16 J12 57.54 N 14.04 E
Haboe, Russia 183a 59.53 N 30.46 E
Habomai Islands see Malaja Kuril'skaja Grjada, is., Russia 54 C17 43.38 N 146.24 E
Habomai-shotō see Malaja Kuril'skaja Grjada, is., Russia 54 C17 43.38 N 146.24 E
Habu, Japan 188 34.27 N 135.24 E
Habur see Khābūr, Nahr al-, stm., Asia 74 C7 35.08 N 40.26 E
Habutaki, Japan 188 34.25 N 135.26 E
Hache, Lac la, l., B.C., Can. 144 E9 51.50 N 121.34 W
Hachijō, Japan 188 34.37 N 135.48 E
Hachijō-jima, i., Japan 56 F12 33.05 N 139.48 E
Hachiman, Japan 56 D9 35.45 N 136.57 E
Hachiman see Ōmi-hachiman, Japan 56 D8 35.08 N 136.06 E
Hachinohe, Japan 54 D14 40.30 N 141.29 E
Hachiōji, Japan 56 D12 35.39 N 139.20 E
Hack, Mount, mtn., Austl. 98 H2 30.46 S 138.48 E
Hackås, Swe. 16 E12 62.56 N 14.30 E
Hackberry, Az., U.S. 150 H3 35.23 N 113.43 W
Hackberry, La., U.S. 134 H5 29.59 N 93.21 W
Hackberry Creek, stm., Ks., U.S. 138 C8 38.48 N 100.03 W
Hackensack, stm., U.S. 194 40.43 N 74.06 W
Hackett, Ar., U.S. 134 B4 35.10 N 94.24 W
Hackett, Pa., U.S. 197b 40.15 N 80.01 W
Hacketts, Eng., U.K. 178 51.45 N 0.05 W
Hackettstown, N.J., U.S. 124 D11 40.51 N 74.49 W
Hacking, stm., Austl. 192a 34.04 S 151.06 E
Hacking, Port, b., Austl. 192a 34.05 S 151.09 E
Hackleburg, Al., U.S. 134 C11 34.16 N 87.49 W
Hackney, ngh., Eng., U.K. 178 51.33 N 0.03 W
Håckren, l., Swe. 16 D11 63.12 N 13.22 E
Hadāli, Pak. 70 B4 32.17 N 72.11 E
Hadārba, Ra's see Ḥadāribah, Ra's al-, c., Sudan 82 C7 22.03 N 36.52 E
Ḥadāribah, Ra's al-, c., Sudan 82 C7 22.03 N 36.52 E
HaDarom, state, Isr. 76 H5 30.40 N 34.50 E
Ḥadd, Ra's al-, c., Oman 72 E8 22.32 N 59.48 E
Haddam, Ks., U.S. 138 B11 39.51 N 97.18 W
Haddington, Scot., U.K. 10 F10 55.57 N 2.46 W
Haddock, Ga., U.S. 132 C2 33.01 N 83.25 W
Haddon Downs, Austl. 98 F3 26.21 S 140.50 E
Haddon Hills, N.J., U.S. 203 39.54 N 75.03 W
Hadejia, Nig. 84 G7 12.27 N 10.03 E
Hadejia, stm., Nig. 84 G6 12.50 N 10.51 E
Haden, Austl. 98 F8 27.13 S 151.53 E
Ḥadera, Isr. 76 F5 32.26 N 34.55 E
Hadersdorf, ngh., Aus. 182b 48.13 N 16.14 E
Hadersfeld, Aus. 182b 48.20 N 16.15 E
Haderslev, Den. 16 L7 55.15 N 9.30 E
Hadfield, Austl. 192b 37.42 S 144.56 E
Hadfield, Eng., U.K. 180 53.28 N 1.58 W
Hadiach, Ukr. 38 C12 50.22 N 34.00 E
Hadībū, Yemen 72 G7 12.38 N 54.01 E
Hadım, Tur. 34 F15 36.59 N 32.28 E
Ḥadīthah, Iraq 74 C8 34.02 N 42.21 E
Hadleigh, Eng., U.K. 178 51.33 N 0.37 E
Hadleigh Castle, hist., Eng., U.K. 178 51.33 N 0.36 E
Hadley Bay, b., Nu., Can. 110 A9 72.28 N 108.11 W
Hadlock, Wa., U.S. 146 B4 48.01 N 122.45 W
Ḥadraj, Wādī, stm., Asia 76 H8 30.30 N 38.11 E
Ḥaḍramawt, reg., Yemen 72 F6 15.00 N 50.00 E
Hadrian's Wall, misc. cult., Eng., U.K. 10 F10 54.59 N 2.26 W
Hadseløya, i., Nor. 14 D5 68.32 N 14.48 E
Hadsten, Den. 16 K8 56.19 N 10.02 E
Hadsund, Den. 16 K7 56.43 N 10.07 E
Hadyai see Hat Yai, Thai. 64 I5 7.00 N 100.28 E
Hadyžensk, Russia 42 C8 44.26 N 39.33 E
Hadzilavičy, Bela. 26 G13 53.04 N 30.15 E
Haeju, Kor., N. 54 E6 38.02 N 125.42 E
Haemgon-ni, ngh., Kor., S. 189b 37.35 N 126.49 E
Haena, Hi., U.S. 100a a2 22.13 N 159.34 W
Haenam, Kor., S. 54 G7 34.34 N 126.36 E
Haenertsburg, S. Afr. 90 G10 23.55 S 29.56 E
Haffner Bjerg, mtn., Grnld. 108 B13 76.26 N 62.18 W
Hafford, Sk., Can. 142 B6 52.44 N 107.21 W
Haffouz, Tun. 32 I3 35.37 N 9.40 E
Hafirat al-'Ayda, Sau. Ar. 74 G6 26.26 N 39.12 E
Hafit, Jabal, mtn., Oman 74 H14 24.03 N 55.46 E
Hāfizābād, Pak. 70 B4 32.04 N 73.41 E
Hāflong, India 70 F14 25.10 N 93.02 E
Hafnarfjörður, Ice. 12a k28 64.03 N 21.57 W
Haft Gel, Iran 74 E11 31.26 N 49.32 E
Hagan, Ga., U.S. 132 D3 32.08 N 81.56 W
Hagari, stm., India 69 D3 15.44 N 76.55 E
Hagåtña, Guam 100c j9 13.28 N 144.44 E
Hagemeister Island, i., Ak., U.S. 109 E7 58.38 N 160.55 W
Hagen, Ger. 24 E3 51.22 N 7.28 E
Hagenbrunn, Aus. 182b 48.20 N 16.25 E
Hagenow, Ger. 24 C7 53.25 N 11.11 E
Hagensborg, B.C., Can. 144 D4 52.22 N 126.32 W
Hägere Selam, Eth. 86 C7 6.29 N 38.32 E
Hagerman, Id., U.S. 146 H12 42.49 N 114.53 W
Hagerman, N.M., U.S. 136 A3 33.06 N 104.19 W
Hagerman Corners, On., Can. 193b 43.50 N 79.18 W
Hagerstown, In., U.S. 130 E12 39.54 N 85.08 W
Hagerstown, Md., U.S. 124 E8 39.38 N 77.43 W
Hagersville, On., Can. 126 F9 42.57 N 80.02 W
Hagetmau, Fr. 22 F5 43.39 N 0.34 W
Hagfors, Swe. 16 G11 60.01 N 13.42 E
Haggetts Pond, l., Ma., U.S. 201 42.39 N 71.12 W
Haggin, Mount, mtn., Mt., U.S. 146 D13 46.05 N 113.05 W
Hagi, Japan 56 E4 34.24 N 131.24 E
Ha Giang, Viet. 64 A7 22.50 N 104.59 E
Hagitani, Japan 188 34.54 N 135.35 E
Hagley Museum, bldg., De., U.S. 203 39.46 N 75.35 W
Hagondange, Fr. 20 E15 49.15 N 6.10 E
Hags Head, c., Ire. 10 I3 52.56 N 9.28 W
Hague, Sk., Can. 142 B7 52.30 N 106.23 W
Hague, N.D., U.S. 140 A13 46.01 N 99.59 W
Hague, Cap de la, c., Fr. 20 E7 49.43 N 1.55 W
Hague, The see 's-Gravenhage, Neth. 20 B13 52.05 N 4.17 E
Haguenau, Fr. 20 F16 48.49 N 7.47 E
Hagues Peak, mtn., Co., U.S. 140 G7 40.29 N 105.38 W
Hāhipur, India 190b 22.47 N 88.10 E
Hahira, Ga., U.S. 132 F2 30.57 N 83.21 W
Hahnenberg, Ger. 181 51.12 N 7.24 E
Hahnerberg, ngh., Ger. 181 51.13 N 7.09 E
Hahntown, Pa., U.S. 197b 40.19 N 79.44 W
Hai, stm., China 54 E2 38.58 N 117.42 E
Hai'an, China 58 E9 32.32 N 120.26 E
Haibatpur, India 190a 28.37 N 77.26 E
Haibei, China 52 B10 47.39 N 126.52 E
Haicheng, China 58 A10 40.50 N 122.45 E
Haichow Bay see Haizhou Wan, b., China 58 D8 35.11 N 119.35 E
Haichur, stm., Ukr. 38 F15 47.57 N 36.10 E
Haidargarh, India 70 E8 26.36 N 81.21 E
Haidarpur, ngh., India 190a 28.43 N 77.09 E
Hai Duong, Viet. 64 B8 20.56 N 106.19 E
Haifa see Hefa, Isr. 76 F5 32.48 N 35.00 E
Haifa see Hefa, state, Isr. 76 F5 32.35 N 35.00 E
Haifa, Bay of see Ḥefa, Mifraz, b., Isr. 76 F5 32.52 N 35.03 E
Haifeng, China 58 J6 22.58 N 115.20 E
Haifuzhen, China 58 E10 31.59 N 121.40 E
Haig, Austl. 96 F5 31.01 S 126.05 E
Haig, Mount, mtn., Can. 144 G16 49.17 N 114.29 W
Haigh, Eng., U.K. 180 53.35 N 2.36 W
Haigler, Ne., U.S. 138 A7 40.01 N 101.55 W
Haijima, Japan 186 35.42 N 139.21 E
Haikang, China 58 K3 20.55 N 110.05 E
Haikou, China 58 K4 20.03 N 110.21 E
Haikou, China 58 G9 28.18 N 120.04 E
Hā'il, Sau. Ar. 72 D5 27.31 N 41.42 E
Hailākāndi, India 70 F14 24.41 N 92.34 E
Hailar, China 52 B8 49.11 N 119.43 E
Hailar, stm., China 52 B8 49.29 N 117.51 E
Hailey, Eng., U.K. 178 51.46 N 0.01 W
Hailey, Id., U.S. 146 G12 43.31 N 114.19 W
Haileybury, On., Can. 114 C11 47.26 N 79.37 W
Haileyville, Ok., U.S. 134 C3 34.51 N 95.35 W
Hailin, China 52 C10 44.32 N 129.23 E
Hailing Dao, i., China 58 K4 21.37 N 111.55 E
Hailun, China 52 B10 47.27 N 126.58 E
Hailuoto, Fin. 18 B11 65.00 N 24.42 E
Hailuoto, i., Fin. 18 B11 65.02 N 24.42 E
Haiman Tepesi, hill, Tur. 185b 41.12 N 29.15 E
Haimen, China 58 J7 23.11 N 116.37 E
Haimen, China 58 G9 28.41 N 121.26 E
Hainan, state, China 58 L3 19.00 N 109.30 E
Hainan Dao (Hainan Island), i., China 58 L4 19.00 N 109.30 E
Hainan Island see Hainan Dao, i., China 58 L4 19.00 N 109.30 E
Hainan Strait see Qiongzhou Haixia, strt., China 58 K3 20.10 N 110.15 E
Hainault, ngh., Eng., U.K. 178 51.36 N 0.06 E
Haines, Ak., U.S. 109 E12 59.14 N 135.26 W
Haines, Or., U.S. 146 F8 44.54 N 117.55 W
Haines City, Fl., U.S. 132 H4 28.06 N 81.37 W
Haines Junction, Yk., Can. 110 C3 60.45 N 137.28 W
Hainesville, Il., U.S. 196 42.21 N 88.04 W
Hainfeld, Aus. 24 H11 48.01 N 15.45 E
Haining, China 58 F9 30.31 N 120.41 E
Hai Ninh, Viet. 64 B8 21.32 N 107.55 E
Hai Phong, Viet. 64 B8 20.51 N 106.40 E
Haiphong see Hai Phong, Viet. 64 B8 20.51 N 106.40 E
Haiši, Geor. 42 D10 42.57 N 42.12 E
Haisyn, Ukr. 38 E8 48.48 N 29.23 E
Haïti see Haiti, ctry., N.A. 156 C11 19.00 N 72.25 W
Haiti, ctry., N.A. 156 C11 19.00 N 72.25 W
Haïti see Hispaniola, i., N.A. 152 D10 19.00 N 71.00 W
Haitou, China 58 L3 19.30 N 108.57 E
Haituan, China 52 D4 38.45 N 96.45 E
Haivoron, Ukr. 38 E8 48.20 N 29.53 E
Haiwee Reservoir, res., Ca., U.S. 148 G8 36.10 N 117.57 W
Haiyuan, China 58 C1 36.33 N 105.38 E
Haizhou, China 58 D8 34.34 N 119.07 E
Haizhou Wan, b., China 58 D8 35.11 N 119.35 E
Hajdú-Bihar, state, Hung. 36 B8 47.25 N 21.30 E
Hajdúböszörmény, Hung. 36 B8 47.40 N 21.31 E
Hajdúnánás, Hung. 36 B8 47.50 N 21.26 E
Hajdúszoboszló, Hung. 36 B8 47.26 N 21.24 E
Hajiki-saki, c., Japan 56 A11 38.19 N 138.31 E
Hājīpur, India 70 F10 25.41 N 85.12 E
Hajipur, India 190b 22.57 N 88.19 E
Hajnówka, Pol. 24 D19 52.43 N 23.35 E
Hakai Recreation Area, p.o.i., B.C., Can. 144 E2 51.42 N 128.01 W
Hakasija, state, Russia 48 D16 53.00 N 90.00 E
Hakha, Mya. 64 A1 22.39 N 93.35 E
Hakkâri, Tur. 42 G10 37.33 N 43.45 E
Hakkâri, state, Tur. 42 G10 37.20 N 43.45 E
Hakkas, Swe. 14 F12 66.55 N 21.34 E
Hakken-san, mtn., Japan 56 E8 34.09 N 135.54 E
Hako-dake, mtn., Japan 54 B15 44.40 N 142.25 E
Hakodate, Japan 54 D14 41.45 N 140.43 E
Hakone-yama, vol., Japan 56 D12 35.14 N 139.02 E
Haktanır, Tur. 76 B9 36.51 N 38.50 E
Hakui, Japan 56 C9 36.53 N 136.47 E
Haku-san, vol., Japan 56 C9 36.09 N 136.46 E
Haku-san-kokuritsu-kōen, p.o.i., Japan 56 C9 36.12 N 136.47 E
Hal see Halle, Bel. 20 D13 50.44 N 4.15 E
Hāla, Pak. 70 F2 25.48 N 68.25 E
Halab (Aleppo), Syria 76 B8 36.12 N 37.09 E
Ḥalab, state, Syria 76 B8 36.00 N 37.30 E
Halabjah, Iraq 74 C10 35.09 N 46.03 E
Halachó, Mex. 156 B2 20.31 N 90.05 W
Halahai, China 54 B6 44.40 N 125.07 E
Ḥalā'ib, Sudan 82 C7 22.13 N 36.38 E
Halas-patak, stm., Hung. 182c 47.24 N 19.20 E
Halaula, Hi., U.S. 100a c6 20.13 N 155.45 W
Hålaveden, hills, Swe. 16 I12 58.06 N 14.45 E
Halawa, Cape, c., Hi., U.S. 100a b5 21.09 N 156.42 W
Halbach, ngh., Ger. 181 51.12 N 7.12 E
Halberstadt, Ger. 24 E7 51.53 N 11.03 E
Halbrite, Sk., Can. 142 E10 49.28 N 103.33 W
Halcon, Mount, mtn., Phil. 68 D3 13.16 N 121.00 E
Halden, Nor. 16 H9 59.08 N 11.23 E
Halden, ngh., Ger. 181 51.23 N 7.31 E
Haldensleben, Ger. 24 D7 52.17 N 11.24 E
Haldimand, On., Can. 126 F10 42.56 N 79.50 W
Haldwāni, India 70 D7 29.13 N 79.31 E
Hale, Eng., U.K. 180 53.20 N 2.48 W
Hale, Mo., U.S. 130 E4 39.36 N 93.20 W
Haleakala Crater, crat., Hi., U.S. 100a c5 20.43 N 156.13 W
Haleakala National Park, p.o.i., Hi., U.S. 100a c5 20.44 N 156.13 W
Halebarns, Eng., U.K. 180 53.22 N 2.19 W
Hale Center, Tx., U.S. 138 G7 34.04 N 101.50 W
Hale Creek, stm., Ca., U.S. 200 37.23 N 122.06 W
Haledon, N.J., U.S. 194 40.56 N 74.11 W
Haledon Reservoir, res., N.J., U.S. 194 40.59 N 74.12 W
Hale Head, c., Eng., U.K. 180 53.19 N 2.48 W
Halenkov, Czech Rep. 24 G14 49.18 N 18.08 E
Hale Street, Eng., U.K. 178 51.13 N 0.24 E
Halewood, Eng., U.K. 180 53.22 N 2.49 W
Haleyville, Al., U.S. 134 C11 34.13 N 87.37 W
Half Day, Il., U.S. 196 42.12 N 87.56 W
Halfeti, Tur. 76 A8 37.15 N 37.53 E
Half Hollow Hills, N.Y., U.S. 194 40.48 N 73.21 W
Halfmoon Bay, B.C., Can. 144 G6 49.31 N 123.54 W
Halfmoon Bay, b., Austl. 192b 37.58 S 145.00 E
Half Moon Bay, b., Ca., U.S. 200 37.29 N 122.28 W
Half Moon Bay Airport, arpt., Ca., U.S. 200 37.31 N 122.30 W
Half Moon Bay State Beach, p.o.i., Ca., U.S. 200 37.29 N 122.27 W
Halfway, Md., U.S. 124 E8 39.37 N 77.45 W
Halfway, Or., U.S. 146 F9 44.51 N 117.06 W
Haliburton, On., Can. 126 C11 45.02 N 78.31 W
Halibut Point, c., Ma., U.S. 201 42.42 N 70.38 W
Haliç (Golden Horn), b., Tur. 185b 41.02 N 28.58 E
Halicarnassus, hist., Tur. 34 F10 37.03 N 27.23 E
Halifax, Austl. 98 B6 18.35 S 146.17 E
Halifax, N.S., Can. 122 F13 44.38 N 63.35 W
Halifax, Eng., U.K. 10 H11 53.44 N 1.52 W
Halifax, N.C., U.S. 124 H8 36.19 N 77.35 W
Halifax, Va., U.S. 124 H7 36.45 N 78.55 W
Halifax, Canadian Forces Base, mil., N.S., Can. 122 F13 44.43 N 63.38 W
Halifax Bay, b., Austl. 98 B6 18.50 S 146.30 E
Halifax Citadel National Historic Park, p.o.i., N.S., Can. 122 F13 44.36 N 63.39 W
Halifax Harbour, b., N.S., Can. 122 F13 44.35 N 63.31 W
Halim Perdanakusuma International Airport, arpt., Indon. 187e 6.16 S 106.54 E
Halimun, Gunung, mtn., Indon. 66 G5 6.42 S 106.26 E
Halingen, Ger. 181 51.27 N 7.44 E
Haliyāl, India 69 D2 15.19 N 74.45 E
Haljala, Est. 26 A9 59.25 N 26.15 E
Haljasavėj, Russia 48 B13 63.22 N 78.20 E
Halkalı, ngh., Tur. 185b 41.02 N 28.47 E
Halkapınar, Tur. 76 A5 37.25 N 34.13 E
Hálkavárri, mtn., Nor. 14 B16 69.56 N 25.24 E
Halkett, Cape, c., Ak., U.S. 109 B9 70.48 N 152.14 W
Halkyn, Wales, U.K. 180 53.14 N 3.11 W
Halkyn Mountain, mtn., Wales, U.K. 180 53.14 N 3.13 W
Halladale, stm., Scot., U.K. 10 C9 58.33 N 3.54 W
Hallam, Austl. 192b 38.01 S 145.06 E
Hallam Peak, mtn., B.C., Can. 144 D12 52.11 N 118.46 W
Halland, state, Swe. 16 J10 56.45 N 13.00 E
Hallandale, Fl., U.S. 132 K5 25.58 N 80.08 W
Hallāniyah, Juzur al- (Kuria Muria Islands), is., Oman 72 F8 17.32 N 55.56 E
Halla-san, mtn., Kor., S. 54 H7 33.22 N 126.32 E
Hall Basin, b., N.A. 108 A13 81.30 N 63.30 W
Hällbymagasinet, l., Swe. 16 C14 63.56 N 17.13 E
Halle, Bel. 20 D13 50.44 N 4.15 E
Halle, Ger. 24 E7 51.29 N 11.58 E
Hällefors, Swe. 16 H12 59.46 N 14.32 E
Hälleforsnäs, Swe. 16 H14 59.09 N 16.29 E
Hallein, Aus. 30 C10 47.41 N 13.06 E
Hällekis, Swe. 16 I11 58.37 N 13.25 E
Hallen, Swe. 18 D11 63.10 N 14.04 E
Hallettsville, Tx., U.S. 136 E11 29.26 N 96.56 W
Halley, sci., Ant. 103 C2 75.36 S 26.46 W
Halliday, N.D., U.S. 142 G11 47.20 N 102.20 W
Halligen, is., Ger. 24 B4 54.35 N 8.35 E
Halling, Eng., U.K. 178 51.21 N 0.27 E
Hallingdalen, val., Nor. 16 G6 60.34 N 9.09 E
Hallingdalselvi, stm., Nor. 16 G6 60.25 N 9.29 E
Hallingsåfallet, wtfl., Swe. 16 C12 64.21 N 14.23 E
Hallingskarvet, mts., Nor. 16 G5 60.37 N 7.51 E
Hall in Tirol, Aus. 30 C8 47.17 N 11.30 E
Hall Islands, is., Micron. 94 C6 8.34 N 151.59 E
Halliste, stm., Est. 26 B8 58.30 N 25.03 E
Hall-i'-th'-Wood, p.o.i., Eng., U.K. 180 53.36 N 2.26 W
Hall Lake, l., Nu., Can. 110 B14 68.41 N 82.17 W
Hall Land, reg., Grnld. 108 A14 81.11 N 58.39 W
Hall Mountain, mtn., Wa., U.S. 146 B9 48.49 N 117.15 W
Hällnäs, Swe. 16 C17 64.18 N 19.37 E
Hallock, Mn., U.S. 128 C2 48.46 N 96.57 W
Hallowell, Me., U.S. 122 F7 44.17 N 69.47 W
Hall Peninsula, pen., Nu., Can. 110 C17 63.30 N 66.00 W
Halls, Tn., U.S. 130 I8 35.52 N 89.23 W
Hallsberg, Swe. 16 H13 59.04 N 15.07 E
Halls Brook, stm., Ma., U.S. 201 42.00 N 70.43 W
Halls Creek, Austl. 96 C5 18.14 S 127.39 E
Halls Creek, stm., Ut., U.S. 150 F6 37.27 N 110.44 W
Halls Gap, Austl. 98 K4 37.07 S 142.31 E
Hallstahammar, Swe. 16 H13 59.37 N 16.13 E
Hallstavik, Swe. 16 G16 60.03 N 18.35 E
Hallstead, Pa., U.S. 124 C10 41.57 N 75.44 W
Hallsville, Mo., U.S. 130 E5 39.07 N 92.13 W
Hallsville, Tx., U.S. 136 B13 32.30 N 94.34 W
Halmahera, i., Indon. 60 E8 1.00 N 128.00 E
Halmahera, Laut (Halmahera Sea), s., Indon. 60 F8 1.00 S 129.00 E
Halmahera Sea see Halmahera, Laut, s., Indon. 60 F8 1.00 S 129.00 E
Hal'mer-Ju, Russia 48 A10 67.57 N 64.45 E
Halmstad, Swe. 16 K10 56.39 N 12.53 E
Halopeniči, Bela. 26 F11 54.31 N 28.57 E
Haloučyn, Bela. 26 F12 54.04 N 29.55 E
Halpine Village, Md., U.S. 202c 39.04 N 77.07 W
Hals, Den. 16 K8 56.59 N 10.19 E
Halsafjorden, b., Nor. 16 D6 63.03 N 8.11 E
Halsall, Eng., U.K. 180 53.35 N 2.57 W
Hal'šany, Bela. 26 F8 54.15 N 26.00 E
Halsey, Ne., U.S. 140 F12 41.54 N 100.16 W
Halsey, Or., U.S. 146 F3 44.23 N 123.06 W
Hälsingborg see Helsingborg, Swe. 16 K10 56.02 N 12.42 E
Hälsingland, hist. reg., Swe. 16 F14 61.30 N 17.00 E
Halstad, Mn., U.S. 128 D2 47.20 N 96.49 W
Halstead, Eng., U.K. 178 51.20 N 0.08 E
Halstead, Ks., U.S. 138 D11 38.00 N 97.30 W
Halstow Marshes, sw., Eng., U.K. 178 51.29 N 0.33 E
Haltern, Ger. 24 E3 51.44 N 7.10 E
Haltiatunturi, mtn., Eur. 14 C12 69.18 N 21.16 E
Haltom City, Tx., U.S. 136 B10 32.47 N 97.16 W
Halton, Eng., U.K. 180 53.20 N 2.42 W
Halton, mun., Eng., U.K. 180 53.20 N 2.44 W
Halton, mun., Eng., U.K. 180 53.20 N 2.44 W
Halton Hills see Georgetown, On., Can. 126 E9 43.39 N 79.55 W
Halūzonī, Wādī el-, val., Egypt 191c 30.05 N 31.24 E
Halvorson, Mount, mtn., B.C., Can. 144 C10 53.15 N 120.33 W
Halych, Ukr. 38 D3 49.07 N 24.43 E
Halys see Kızılırmak, stm., Tur. 42 F7 41.43 N 35.57 E
Ham, ngh., Eng., U.K. 178 51.26 N 0.19 W
Ham, stm., Nmb. 90 F4 28.32 S 19.33 E
Hamada, Japan 56 E4 34.53 N 132.04 E
Hamadān, Iran 74 C11 34.47 N 48.30 E
Hamadān, state, Iran 74 C11 35.00 N 48.40 E
Hamāh, Syria 76 C7 35.08 N 36.44 E
Ḥamāh, state, Syria 76 C8 35.10 N 37.00 E
Hamamatsu, Japan 56 E10 34.43 N 137.42 E
Haman, Kor., S. 56 D1 35.15 N 128.24 E
Hamana-ko, l., Japan 56 E10 34.43 N 137.34 E
Hamano, Japan 186 35.33 N 140.08 E
Hamar, Nor. 16 G8 60.47 N 11.05 E
Ha Marakabei, Leso. 90 F9 29.32 S 28.09 E
Hamar-Daban, hrebet, mts., Russia 50 F9 51.22 N 103.40 E
Hamarøya, i., Nor. 14 D6 68.05 N 15.25 E
Hamāta, Gebel, mtn., Egypt 74 H4 24.12 N 35.00 E
Hambaek-san, mtn., Kor., S. 56 B1 37.09 N 128.55 E
Hambantota, Sri L. 69 H5 6.07 N 81.07 E
Hamber Provincial Park, p.o.i., B.C., Can. 144 D12 52.21 N 117.50 W
Hamborn, ngh., Ger. 181 51.29 N 6.46 E
Hamburg, Ger. 24 C6 53.33 N 9.59 E
Hamburg, Ar., U.S. 134 D7 33.13 N 91.48 W
Hamburg, Ia., U.S. 130 D2 40.36 N 95.39 W
Hamburg, N.J., U.S. 124 C11 41.09 N 74.34 W
Hamburg, N.Y., U.S. 124 B7 42.43 N 78.49 W
Hamburg, Pa., U.S. 124 D9 40.33 N 75.59 W
Hamburg, state, Ger. 24 C6 53.35 N 10.00 E
Hamburg Airport, arpt., N.Y., U.S. 202a 42.42 N 78.55 W
Hamburg Mountains, mts., N.J., U.S. 194 41.08 N 74.32 W
Hamburgsund, Swe. 16 I9 58.33 N 11.16 E
Hamḍ, Wādī al-, stm., Sau. Ar. 74 H5 25.54 N 36.38 E
Hamden, Ct., U.S. 124 C13 41.24 N 72.53 W
Hamden, Oh., U.S. 124 E3 39.09 N 82.31 W
Häme, state, Fin. 18 F11 61.30 N 24.30 E
Häme, reg., Fin. 18 F12 61.45 N 25.10 E
Hämeenkangas, for., Fin. 18 F9 61.44 N 22.36 E
Hämeenkylä, Fin. 18 G11 60.15 N 24.49 E
Hämeenlinna (Tavastehus), Fin. 18 G11 60.58 N 24.30 E
HaMelaḥ, Yam see Dead Sea, l., Asia 76 G6 31.30 N 35.30 E
Hamelin, Austl. 96 E2 26.24 S 114.09 E
Hameln, Ger. 24 D5 52.06 N 9.22 E
HaMerkaz, state, Isr. 76 F5 32.05 N 34.55 E
Hamersley Range, mts., Austl. 96 D3 22.24 S 117.33 E
Hamgyŏng-sanjulgi, mts., Kor., N. 54 D8 41.00 N 128.30 E
Ham House, hist., Eng., U.K. 178 51.27 N 0.19 W
Hamhŭng, Kor., N. 54 E7 39.54 N 127.32 E
Hami, China 52 C3 42.50 N 93.30 E
Hamilton, Austl. 98 K4 37.44 S 142.01 E
Hamilton, Ber. 158e k15 32.17 N 64.47 W
Hamilton, On., Can. 126 E10 43.15 N 79.51 W
Hamilton, N.Z. 102 C6 37.47 S 175.17 E
Hamilton, Scot., U.K. 10 F8 55.46 N 4.02 W
Hamilton, Al., U.S. 134 C11 34.08 N 87.59 W
Hamilton, Ga., U.S. 134 E14 32.45 N 84.52 W
Hamilton, Il., U.S. 130 D6 40.23 N 91.20 W
Hamilton, Ks., U.S. 130 G1 37.58 N 96.09 W
Hamilton, Mi., U.S. 130 B12 42.40 N 86.00 W
Hamilton, Mo., U.S. 130 E3 39.44 N 94.00 W
Hamilton, Mt., U.S. 146 D12 46.14 N 114.09 W
Hamilton, N.Y., U.S. 124 B10 42.49 N 75.33 W
Hamilton, N.C., U.S. 124 I8 35.56 N 77.12 W
Hamilton, Oh., U.S. 124 E1 39.23 N 84.33 W
Hamilton, Tx., U.S. 136 C9 31.41 N 98.07 W
Hamilton, ngh., Md., U.S. 202b 39.21 N 76.33 W
Hamilton, stm., Austl. 98 D3 23.42 S 139.45 E
Hamilton, Lake, res., Ar., U.S. 134 C5 34.26 N 93.05 W
Hamilton, Mount, mtn., Ca., U.S. 148 F4 37.21 N 121.38 W
Hamilton, Mount, mtn., Nv., U.S. 148 D10 39.14 N 115.32 W
Hamilton Air Force Base, mil., Ca., U.S. 200 38.03 N 122.31 W
Hamilton City, Ca., U.S. 148 D3 39.44 N 122.00 W
Hamilton Creek Indian Reserve, ind. res., B.C., Can. 144 G10 50.04 N 120.32 W
Hamilton Dome, Wy., U.S. 140 D4 43.46 N 108.36 W
Hamilton Hotel, Austl. 98 D3 22.46 S 140.36 E
Hamilton Mountain, mtn., N.Y., U.S. 126 E15 43.25 N 74.22 W
Hamilton Square, N.J., U.S. 203 40.13 N 74.39 W
Hamina, Fin. 18 G14 60.33 N 27.19 E
Hamiota, Mb., Can. 142 D13 50.11 N 100.36 W
Hāmir, Wādī, stm., Asia 74 E7 31.38 N 42.12 E
Hamīrpur, India 70 F7 25.56 N 80.07 E
Hamlet, N.C., U.S. 132 B6 34.53 N 79.42 W
Hamley Bridge, Austl. 98 J2 34.21 S 138.40 E
Hamlin, Tx., U.S. 136 B7 32.53 N 100.07 W
Hamlin, W.V., U.S. 124 F3 38.16 N 82.06 W
Hamlin Lake, l., Mi., U.S. 126 D3 44.02 N 86.27 W
Hamlin Valley Wash, stm., U.S. 150 E2 38.53 N 114.00 W
Hamm, Ger. 24 E3 51.40 N 7.49 E
Hamm, ngh., Ger. 181 51.12 N 6.44 E
Hamm, ngh., Ger. 181 51.23 N 7.03 E
Hammålsfjellet, mtn., Nor. 16 E9 62.27 N 11.17 E
Ḥammām at-Turkumān, Syria 76 B9 36.32 N 39.03 E
Hammamet, Tun. 84 B7 36.24 N 10.37 E
Hammamet, Golfe de, b., Tun. 84 B7 36.05 N 10.40 E
Hammam Lif, Tun. 32 H4 36.44 N 10.20 E
Hammār, Hawr al-, l., Iraq 74 E10 30.47 N 47.10 E
Hammarstrand, Swe. 16 D14 63.06 N 16.21 E
Hammarvik, Nor. 16 D6 63.42 N 8.47 E
Hamme, stm., Ger. 20 A17 53.10 N 8.44 E
Hammel, Den. 16 K7 56.15 N 9.52 E
Hammelburg, Ger. 24 F5 50.07 N 9.53 E
Hammerdal, Swe. 16 D13 63.35 N 15.21 E
Hammerfest, Nor. 14 B14 70.40 N 23.42 E
Hämmern, Ger. 181 51.08 N 7.21 E
Hammershus, hist., Den. 16 L12 55.16 N 14.45 E
Hammersmith, ngh., Eng., U.K. 178 51.30 N 0.14 W
Hammon, Ok., U.S. 138 F9 35.38 N 99.22 W
Hammond, In., U.S. 130 C10 41.34 N 87.30 W
Hammond, La., U.S. 134 G8 30.30 N 90.27 W
Hammond, Wi., U.S. 128 G6 44.58 N 92.25 W
Hammond Island, i., Ca., U.S. 200 38.06 N 121.57 W
Hammond Pond Park, p.o.i., Ma., U.S. 201 42.19 N 71.11 W
Hammondsport, N.Y., U.S. 126 F12 42.24 N 77.12 W
Hammondville, Austl. 192a 33.57 S 150.57 E
Hamningberg, Nor. 14 B21 70.32 N 30.26 E
Hamorton, Pa., U.S. 203 39.52 N 75.39 W
Hamoyet see Hamoyet, Jabal, mtn., Afr. 82 D7 17.33 N 38.02 E
Hamoyet, Jabal, mtn., Afr. 82 D7 17.33 N 38.02 E
Hampden, Me., U.S. 122 F8 44.44 N 68.50 W
Hampden, N.D., U.S. 142 F15 48.32 N 98.39 W
Hampden Sydney, Va., U.S. 124 G7 37.14 N 78.28 W
Hampi, India 69 D3 15.23 N 76.36 E
Hampshire, Il., U.S. 128 I10 42.05 N 88.31 W
Hampshire Heights, Pa., U.S. 197b 40.20 N 79.33 W
Hampstead, Qc., Can. 193a 45.29 N 73.38 W
Hampstead, N.C., U.S. 132 B8 34.23 N 77.43 W
Hampstead, ngh., Eng., U.K. 178 51.33 N 0.11 W
Hampstead Heath, p.o.i., Eng., U.K. 178 51.34 N 0.10 W
Hampton, Austl. 192b 37.56 S 145.00 E
Hampton, N.B., Can. 122 E11 45.32 N 65.50 W
Hampton, Ar., U.S. 134 D6 33.32 N 92.28 W
Hampton, Fl., U.S. 132 G3 29.51 N 82.08 W
Hampton, Ga., U.S. 132 C1 33.23 N 84.16 W
Hampton, Ia., U.S. 130 B4 42.44 N 93.12 W
Hampton, Ne., U.S. 140 G15 40.52 N 97.52 W
Hampton, N.H., U.S. 122 H6 42.56 N 70.50 W
Hampton, S.C., U.S. 132 D4 32.52 N 81.06 W
Hampton, Tn., U.S. 124 H3 36.17 N 82.11 W
Hampton, Va., U.S. 124 G9 37.01 N 76.20 W
Hampton, ngh., Eng., U.K. 178 51.25 N 0.22 W
Hampton Bays, N.Y., U.S. 124 D13 40.52 N 72.31 W
Hampton Butte, mtn., Or., U.S. 146 G6 43.46 N 120.17 W
Hampton National Historic Site, hist., Md., U.S. 202b 39.25 N 76.35 W
Hampton Park, Austl. 192b 38.02 S 145.15 E
Hampton Tableland, plat., Austl. 96 F5 31.57 S 126.41 E
Hamra, Swe. 16 F13 61.39 N 14.59 E
Hamrā', Al-Hamādah al-, des., Libya 82 B2 30.00 N 12.00 E
Hamra, As Saquia al, stm., W. Sah. 84 D2 27.12 N 13.23 W
Hamra, Gebel el-, mtn., Egypt 76 I5 29.39 N 34.47 E
Hamsara, stm., Russia 48 D16 52.42 N 95.48 E
Hams Fork, stm., Wy., U.S. 140 F2 41.35 N 109.58 W
Ham Tan, Viet. 64 G8 10.40 N 107.46 E
Hāmūn, Daryācheh-ye, l., Iran 72 C9 30.43 N 61.06 E
Han, stm., China 58 I7 23.41 N 116.38 E
Han, stm., China 58 F5 30.33 N 114.17 E
Han, Nong, l., Thai. 64 D7 17.12 N 104.11 E
Hana, Hi., U.S. 100a c6 20.45 N 155.59 W
Hanahan, S.C., U.S. 132 D5 32.54 N 80.01 W
Ḥanak, Sau. Ar. 74 H5 25.33 N 37.00 E
Hanamaki, Japan 54 E14 39.23 N 141.07 E
Hanamenu, Baie, b., Fr. Poly. 100g r18 9.45 S 139.08 W
Hananui see Anglem, Mount, mtn., N.Z. 102 H2 46.44 S 167.56 E
Hanapepe, Hi., U.S. 100a b2 21.54 N 159.35 W
Hanateio, Fr. Poly. 100g s18 9.59 S 139.06 W
Hanatetena, Fr. Poly. 100g s18 9.57 S 139.04 W
Hanau am Main, Ger. 24 F4 50.08 N 8.55 E
Hanaui, Fr. Poly. 100g r18 9.45 S 139.05 W
Hanawa, Japan 186 35.13 N 139.53 E
Hanbury, stm., N.T., Can. 110 C9 63.37 N 104.33 W
Hancavičy, Bela. 26 H9 52.45 N 26.26 E
Hâncești, Mol. 38 G7 46.49 N 28.36 E
Hanceville, B.C., Can. 144 E7 51.55 N 123.03 W
Hanceville, Al., U.S. 134 C12 34.04 N 86.45 W
Hancheng, China 52 D7 35.29 N 110.25 E
Hancheng, China 58 D4 35.28 N 110.25 E
Hanches, Fr. 179 48.36 N 1.39 E
Hanchō, Japan 188 34.49 N 135.27 E
Han-ch'ŏn, stm., Kor., S. 189b 37.33 N 127.02 E
Hancock, Md., U.S. 124 E7 39.41 N 78.10 W
Hancock, Mi., U.S. 128 D10 47.07 N 88.36 W
Hancock, Mn., U.S. 128 F3 45.29 N 95.48 W
Hancock, N.Y., U.S. 124 C10 41.57 N 75.17 W
Hancock, Wi., U.S. 128 G9 44.08 N 89.31 W
Hancock, Lake, l., Fl., U.S. 132 I3 27.58 N 81.50 W
Handa, Japan 56 E9 34.53 N 136.55 E
Handan, China 58 C6 36.36 N 114.27 E
Handforth, Eng., U.K. 180 53.21 N 2.13 W
Handlová, Slvk. 24 H14 48.43 N 18.45 E
Handöl, Swe. 16 D10 63.15 N 12.26 E
Handsworth, Sk., Can. 142 E10 49.50 N 102.58 W
Handyga, Russia 50 D16 62.39 N 135.32 E
HaNegev (Negev Desert), reg., Isr. 76 H5 30.30 N 34.55 E
Hanford, Ca., U.S. 148 G6 36.19 N 119.38 W
Han-gang Bridge, trans., Kor., S. 189b 37.32 N 126.56 E
Hanga Roa, Chile 100l e29 27.08 S 109.25 W
Hangayn nuruu, mts., Mong. 52 B4 47.32 N 98.41 E
Hangchow see Hangzhou, China 58 F9 30.15 N 120.10 E
Hangchow Bay see Hangzhou Wan, b., China 58 F9 30.14 N 120.46 E
Hanggin Houqi, China 58 A2 40.57 N 107.14 E
Hanggin Qi, China 58 B3 39.55 N 108.52 E
Hang Hau Town, China 189d 22.19 N 114.16 E
Hanging Gardens, p.o.i., India 190c 18.58 N 72.48 E
Hanging Rock State Park, p.o.i., N.C., U.S. 124 H5 36.25 N 80.15 W
Hanging Woman Creek, stm., U.S. 140 C6 45.18 N 106.31 W
Hangman Creek, stm., U.S. 146 C9 47.38 N 117.26 W
Hangö see Hanko, Fin. 18 H10 59.49 N 22.58 E
Hangokurt, Russia 48 B10 61.59 N 64.16 E
Hangu, China 58 B7 39.15 N 117.47 E
Hangu, Pak. 70 B3 33.32 N 71.04 E
Hanguang, China 58 I5 24.16 N 113.08 E
Hangzhou, China 58 F9 30.15 N 120.10 E
Hangzhou Wan, b., China 58 F9 30.14 N 120.46 E
Hanhimaa, Fin. 14 E16 67.56 N 25.03 E
Hani, Russia 50 E13 57.04 N 120.56 E
Hani, Tur. 42 F9 38.24 N 40.23 E
Hanino, Russia 26 F19 54.12 N 36.36 E
Ḥanīsh, is., Yemen 72 G5 13.49 N 42.47 E
Hanish Islands see Ḥanīsh, is., Yemen 72 G5 13.49 N 42.47 E
Hanjalipan, Indon. 66 E8 2.13 S 112.45 E
Hanjiang, China 58 I8 25.30 N 119.06 E
Hanka, ozero see Khanka, Lake, l., Asia 54 B10 45.11 N 132.25 E
Hankasalmi, Fin. 18 E13 62.18 N 26.30 E
Hankinson, N.D., U.S. 128 E2 46.04 N 96.54 W
Hanko (Hangö), Fin. 18 H10 59.49 N 22.58 E

Name	Page	Map Ref.	Latitude	Longitude
Hankow see Wuhan, China	58	F6	30.34 N	114.16 E
Hanks Pond, l., N.J., U.S.	194		41.05 N	74.26 W
Hānle, India	70	B7	32.47 N	78.59 E
Hanley, Sk., Can.	142	C7	51.36 N	106.26 W
Hanmer, On., Can.	126	B8	46.39 N	80.55 W
Hanmiao, China	54	B4	44.33 N	119.59 E
Hanna, Ab., Can.	144	E19	51.39 N	111.56 W
Hanna, Ok., U.S.	134	B3	35.11 N	95.53 W
Hanna, Wy., U.S.	150	B10	41.52 N	106.34 W
Hanna City, Il., U.S.	130	D8	40.41 N	89.47 W
Hannaford, N.D., U.S.	142	G15	47.18 N	98.10 W
Hannah, N.D., U.S.	142	F15	48.58 N	98.42 W
Hannah Bay, b., On., Can.	110	E14	51.14 N	79.51 W
Hannam Bridge, trans., Kor., S.	189b		37.32 N	127.00 E
Hannibal, Mo., U.S.	130	E6	39.42 N	91.22 W
Hanningfield Reservoir, res., Eng., U.K.	178		51.39 N	0.31 E
Hannover, Ger.	24	D5	52.23 N	9.44 E
Hanö, i., Swe.	16	L12	56.00 N	14.50 E
Hanöbukten, b., Swe.	16	L12	55.45 N	14.30 E
Hanoi see Ha Noi, Viet.	64	B7	21.01 N	105.50 E
Ha Noi, Viet.	64	B7	21.01 N	105.50 E
Hanover, On., Can.	126	D8	44.08 N	81.01 W
Hanover see Hannover, Ger.	24	D5	52.23 N	9.44 E
Hanover, S. Afr.	90	G7	31.04 S	24.26 E
Hanover, Il., U.S.	130	B7	42.15 N	90.16 W
Hanover, In., U.S.	130	F12	38.43 N	85.28 W
Hanover, Ks., U.S.	138	B12	39.53 N	96.52 W
Hanover, N.H., U.S.	122	G4	43.42 N	72.17 W
Hanover, N.M., U.S.	150	K8	32.49 N	108.05 W
Hanover, Pa., U.S.	124	E9	39.48 N	76.59 W
Hanover, Va., U.S.	124	G8	37.45 N	77.22 W
Hanover, Isla, i., Chile	166	J2	50.57 S	74.45 W
Hanover Airport, arpt., N.J., U.S.	194		40.50 N	74.21 W
Hanover Center, Ma., U.S.	201		42.07 N	70.50 W
Hansard, B.C., Can.	144	B9	54.05 N	121.52 W
Hansdiha, India	70	F11	24.35 N	87.05 E
Hansen Dam, dam., Ca., U.S.	198		34.16 N	118.23 W
Hānsi, India	70	D5	29.06 N	75.57 E
Hansi, India	70	B6	32.26 N	77.49 E
Hansia, India	190b		22.48 N	88.24 E
Hanska, Mn., U.S.	128	G4	44.08 N	94.29 W
Hans Lollik Island, i., V.I.U.S.	158b	e7	18.24 N	64.54 W
Hansnes, Nor.	14	B10	69.57 N	19.34 E
Hanstholm, Den.	16	J6	57.07 N	8.38 E
Hantajskoe, ozero, l., Russia	50	C6	68.21 N	91.01 E
Hantau, Kaz.	48	F12	44.13 N	73.47 E
Hantsport, N.S., Can.	122	E12	45.04 N	64.11 W
Hantu, Pulau, i., Sing.	189c		1.14 N	103.45 E
Hanty-Mansijsk, Russia	48	B11	60.59 N	69.01 E
Hantzsch, stm., Nu., Can.	110	B16	67.32 N	72.29 W
Hanumāngarh, India	62	C3	29.35 N	74.19 E
Hanumangarh, India	70	D5	29.34 N	74.19 E
Hanušovice, Czech Rep.	24	F12	50.04 N	16.55 E
Hanuy, stm., Mong.	52	B5	49.20 N	102.21 E
Hanwood, Austl.	98	J6	34.21 S	146.02 E
Hanworth, ngh., Eng., U.K.	178		51.26 N	0.23 W
Hanyin, China	58	E3	32.42 N	108.54 E
Hanzhong, China	58	E2	33.04 N	107.02 E
Hanzhuang, China	58	D7	34.35 N	117.22 E
Haojiadian, China	58	F5	31.47 N	113.44 E
Hāora, India	70	G12	22.35 N	88.20 E
Hāora Bridge, trans., India	190b		22.35 N	88.21 E
Hāora Railroad Station, trans., India	190b		22.35 N	88.21 E
Haoxue, China	58	F5	30.05 N	112.20 E
Haparanda, Swe.	14	G14	65.50 N	24.06 E
Hapatoni, Baie, b., Fr. Poly.	100g	s18	9.57 S	139.07 W
Hapčeranga, Russia	50	G11	49.41 N	112.22 E
Happy, Tx., U.S.	138	G7	34.45 N	101.52 W
Happy Camp, Ca., U.S.	148	B2	41.42 N	123.27 W
Happy Jack, Az., U.S.	150	I5	34.45 N	111.11 W
Happy Valley-Goose Bay, Nf., Can.	110	E18	53.20 N	60.25 W
Happy Valley Race Course, p.o.i., China	189d		22.16 N	114.10 E
Hapsford, Eng., U.K.	180		53.16 N	2.48 W
Hapton, Eng., U.K.	180		53.47 N	2.19 W
Hāpur, India	70	D6	28.44 N	77.46 E
Ḩaql, Sau. Ar.	74	F4	29.18 N	34.57 E
Hara, Japan	186		35.50 N	139.46 E
Haraa, stm., Mong.	50	G10	49.37 N	105.49 E
Harabali, Russia	40	H15	47.23 N	47.15 E
Ḩaraḑ, Sau. Ar.	72	E6	24.08 N	49.02 E
Haradok, Bela.	26	E13	55.27 N	29.58 E
Harads, Swe.	14	F11	66.05 N	20.59 E
Haradzec, Bela.	26	H7	52.12 N	24.40 E
Haradzec, Bela.	26	H13	52.58 N	30.20 E
Haradzec, Bela.	26	G13	53.32 N	30.02 E
Haradzeja, Bela.	26	G9	53.18 N	26.32 E
Haradzišča, Bela.	26	G9	53.19 N	26.01 E
Harajuku, Japan	186		35.54 N	139.21 E
Haramachi, Japan	56	B13	37.38 N	140.58 E
Haramachida, Japan	186		35.33 N	139.27 E
Harampur, Russia	48	B13	64.15 N	78.06 E
Haranor, Russia	52	A8	50.06 N	116.40 E
Harany, Bela.	26	E12	55.25 N	29.02 E
Harar see Hārer, Eth.	82	F8	9.18 N	42.07 E
Harare, Zimb.	88	D5	17.50 S	31.03 E
Harāt, India	190b		22.53 N	88.11 E
Harazé Mangueigne, Chad	82	E4	9.57 N	20.53 E
Harbala, Russia	50	D13	64.07 N	120.17 E
Harbāti, India	190b		22.55 N	88.33 E
Harbavičy, Bela.	26	G13	53.49 N	30.41 E
Harbin, China	52	B10	45.44 N	126.38 E
Harbiye, Tur.	76	B7	36.09 N	36.09 E
Harboør, Den.	16	K6	56.37 N	8.12 E
Harbor, Or., U.S.	148	A1	42.05 N	124.15 W
Harbor Beach, Mi., U.S.	126	E7	43.50 N	82.39 W
Harbor City, ngh., Ca., U.S.	198		33.48 N	118.17 W
Harbor Isle, N.Y., U.S.	194		40.36 N	73.40 W
Harbor Springs, Mi., U.S.	126	C4	45.25 N	84.59 W
Harbor Tunnel, trans., Md., U.S.	202b		39.15 N	76.34 W
Harbour Breton, Nf., Can.	111a	j22	47.30 N	55.48 W
Harbourville, N.S., Can.	122	E12	45.08 N	64.48 W
Harcuvar Mountains, mts., Az., U.S.	150	J3	34.00 N	113.30 W
Harda, India	70	G6	22.20 N	77.05 E
Hardangerfjorden, b., Nor.	16	H3	60.10 N	6.00 E
Hardangerjøkulen, ice, Nor.	16	G5	60.33 N	7.26 E
Hardangervidda, plat., Nor.	16	G6	60.20 N	7.30 E
Hardangervidda Nasjonalpark, p.o.i., Nor.	16	G5	60.08 N	7.27 E
Hardap, state, Nmb.	90	D3	24.15 S	17.00 E
Hardeeville, S.C., U.S.	132	D4	32.17 N	81.04 W
Hardenberg, Neth.	24	D2	52.34 N	6.37 E
Harderwijk, Neth.	20	B14	52.21 N	5.37 E
Hardesty, Ok., U.S.	138	E7	36.36 N	101.11 W
Hardin, Il., U.S.	130	E7	39.09 N	90.37 W
Hardin, Mt., U.S.	140	B5	45.43 N	107.36 W
Harding, S. Afr.	90	G9	30.34 S	29.56 E
Harding, Ma., U.S.	201		42.12 N	71.27 W
Harding, Lake, res., U.S.	134	E13	32.40 N	85.06 W
Hardinsburg, Ky., U.S.	130	G11	37.45 N	86.27 W
Hardisty, Ab., Can.	144	D19	52.40 N	111.18 W
Hardisty Lake, l., N.T., Can.	110	C7	64.32 N	117.44 W
Hardoi, India	70	E8	27.23 N	80.08 E
Hardricourt, Fr.	179		49.01 N	1.54 E
Hardscrabble Wash, stm., Az., U.S.	150	I7	34.38 N	109.27 W
Hardt, Ger.	181		51.07 N	6.58 E
Hardtner, Ks., U.S.	138	D10	37.00 N	98.37 W
Hardwār see Haridwār, India	70	D7	29.56 N	78.07 E
Hardwick, Ga., U.S.	132	C2	33.02 N	83.13 W
Hardwick, Vt., U.S.	122	F4	44.30 N	72.22 W
Hardwood, La., U.S.	134	G7	30.49 N	91.23 W
Hardwood Ridge, mtn., Pa., U.S.	124	C10	41.15 N	75.22 W
Hardy, Ar., U.S.	130	H6	36.19 N	91.28 W
Hardy, Ne., U.S.	140	G15	40.00 N	97.56 W
Hardy Bay, b., N.T., Can.	109	B16	75.03 N	115.24 W
Hardys Pond, l., Ma., U.S.	201		42.25 N	71.15 W
Hare Bay, b., Nf., Can.	111a	i22	51.16 N	55.51 W
Harefield, ngh., Eng., U.K.	178		51.36 N	0.29 W
Hareid, Nor.	16	E4	62.22 N	6.01 E
Hareidlandet, i., Nor.	16	E3	62.21 N	5.57 E
Hare Indian, stm., N.T., Can.	110	B5	66.17 N	128.38 W
Hareøen, i., Grnld.	108	C14	70.25 N	54.53 W
Hārer, Eth.	82	F8	9.18 N	42.07 E
Harewood Park, Md., U.S.	202b		39.23 N	76.22 W
Harford Heights, Pa., U.S.	197b		40.22 N	79.46 W
Hargeville, Fr.	179		48.53 N	1.45 E
Hargeysa, Som.	86	C8	9.33 N	44.04 E
Harghita, state, Rom.	36	C12	46.35 N	25.30 E
Harghita, Munții, mts., Rom.	36	C12	46.17 N	25.39 E
Har Hu, l., China	52	D4	38.15 N	97.40 E
Hari, stm., Indon.	66	D3	1.04 S	104.12 E
Harīb, Yemen	72	G6	14.57 N	45.30 E
Haridwār, India	70	D7	29.56 N	78.07 E
Harigabessho, Japan	188		34.37 N	135.58 E
Harihar, India	69	D2	14.30 N	75.48 E
Harik, Russia	48	D18	54.14 N	101.39 E
Hārim, Syria	76	B7	36.12 N	36.31 E
Harim, Jabal al-, mtn., Oman	74	H15	25.58 N	56.14 E
Haripāl, India	190b		22.49 N	88.07 E
Haripur, India	190b		22.56 N	88.14 E
Harīpur, Pak.	70	B4	34.01 N	72.54 E
Harīrūd (Tedžen), stm., Asia	72	C9	37.23 N	60.30 E
Harischandra Range, mts., India	69	B1	19.21 N	73.59 E
Hārithān, Syria	76	B8	36.16 N	37.05 E
Haritonovo, Russia	12	F22	61.24 N	47.29 E
Harjavalta, Fin.	18	F9	61.18 N	22.08 E
Harkaway, Austl.	192b		38.00 S	145.21 E
Harkers Island, N.C., U.S.	132	B9	34.41 N	76.33 W
Harker Village, N.J., U.S.	203		39.51 N	75.09 W
Harkortsee, l., Ger.	181		51.24 N	7.25 E
Har'kov see Kharkiv, Ukr.	38	C15	49.59 N	36.14 E
Harlan, Ia., U.S.	130	C2	41.39 N	95.19 W
Harlan, Ky., U.S.	124	H2	36.50 N	83.19 W
Harlan County Lake, res., Ne., U.S.	138	A9	40.04 N	99.13 W
Hârlău, Rom.	36	B13	47.26 N	26.54 E
Harlem, Fl., U.S.	132	J5	26.44 N	80.53 W
Harlem, Ga., U.S.	132	C3	33.24 N	82.18 W
Harlem, Mt., U.S.	142	F5	48.31 N	108.46 W
Harlem, ngh., N.Y., U.S.	194		40.49 N	73.56 W
Harlem River, strt., N.Y., U.S.	194		40.48 N	73.54 W
Harlesden, ngh., Eng., U.K.	178		51.32 N	0.15 W
Harleton, Tx., U.S.	136	B13	32.41 N	94.35 W
Harlingen, Neth.	20	A14	53.10 N	5.26 E
Harlingen, Tx., U.S.	136	H10	26.11 N	97.41 W
Harlington, ngh., Eng., U.K.	178		51.29 N	0.26 W
Harlovka, Russia	14	D28	68.46 N	37.16 E
Harlovka, stm., Russia	14	D28	68.46 N	37.18 E
Harlow, Eng., U.K.	10	J13	51.46 N	0.07 E
Harlow, mun., Eng., U.K.	178		51.44 N	0.07 E
Harlowton, Mt., U.S.	146	D17	46.26 N	109.50 W
Harlpur, India	190b		22.42 N	88.10 E
Harlu, Russia	18	F17	61.48 N	30.56 E
Harman, W.V., U.S.	124	F6	38.54 N	79.32 W
Harmancık, Tur.	34	D12	39.40 N	29.09 E
Harmånger, Swe.	16	F15	61.56 N	17.13 E
Harmanli, Blg.	36	H12	41.55 N	25.55 E
Harmar Heights, Pa., U.S.	197b		40.33 N	79.49 W
Harmarville, Pa., U.S.	197b		40.32 N	79.51 W
Hármashatár-hegy, mtn., Hung.	182c		47.33 N	19.00 E
Harmonville, Pa., U.S.	203		40.06 N	75.17 W
Harmony, In., U.S.	130	E10	39.31 N	87.03 W
Harmony, Mn., U.S.	128	H6	43.33 N	92.01 W
Harmony Brook, stm., N.J., U.S.	194		40.48 N	74.34 W
Harmony Hills, De., U.S.	203		39.42 N	75.41 W
Harmonyville, Pa., U.S.	203		40.11 N	75.43 W
Harnai, India	69	C1	17.47 N	73.07 E
Harnātānr, India	70	E10	27.18 N	84.01 E
Harney Basin, bas., Or., U.S.	146	G7	43.15 N	119.00 W
Harney Lake, l., Or., U.S.	146	G7	43.14 N	119.07 W
Harney Peak, mtn., S.D., U.S.	140	D9	43.51 N	103.31 W
Härnösand, Swe.	16	E15	62.38 N	17.56 E
Har nuur, l., Mong.	52	B3	48.06 N	93.12 E
Haro, Spain	28	B8	42.35 N	2.51 W
Haro, Cabo, c., Mex.	154	B3	27.50 N	110.53 W
Harola, India	190a		28.36 N	77.19 E
Harold Hill, ngh., Eng., U.K.	178		51.36 N	0.13 E
Harold Parker State Forest, p.o.i., Ma., U.S.	201		42.37 N	71.05 W
Harold Wood, ngh., Eng., U.K.	178		51.36 N	0.14 E
Harovsk, Russia	12	F18	59.59 N	40.12 E
Harøya, i., Nor.	16	E4	62.44 N	6.27 E
Harøyfjorden, strt., Nor.	16	E4	62.43 N	6.35 E
Harpanahalli, India	69	D3	14.46 N	75.59 E
Harpen, ngh., Ger.	181		51.29 N	7.16 E
Harper, Lib.	84	I3	4.22 N	7.43 W
Harper, Ks., U.S.	138	D10	37.17 N	98.01 W
Harper, Tx., U.S.	136	D8	30.17 N	99.14 W
Harper, Mount, mtn., Ak., U.S.	109	D11	64.14 N	143.50 W
Harper Lake, l., Ca., U.S.	148	H8	35.02 N	117.17 W
Harpers Ferry National Historical Park, p.o.i., U.S.	124	E8	39.13 N	77.45 W
Harpurhey, ngh., Eng., U.K.	180		53.31 N	2.13 W
Harpur Hill, Eng., U.K.	180		53.14 N	1.54 W
Harqin Qi, China	52	C8	41.56 N	118.42 E
Harquahala Mountain, mtn., Az., U.S.	150	J3	33.49 N	113.21 W
Harrai, India	70	G7	22.36 N	79.13 E
Harran, Tur.	76	B10	36.51 N	39.01 E
Harrell, Ar., U.S.	134	D6	33.31 N	92.24 W
Harricana, stm., Can.	110	E15	51.09 N	79.47 W
Harriman, Tn., U.S.	130	I13	35.56 N	84.32 W
Harriman State Park, p.o.i., N.Y., U.S.	124	C11	41.14 N	74.10 W
Harrington, De., U.S.	124	F10	38.55 N	75.34 W
Harrington, Me., U.S.	122	F9	44.37 N	67.48 W
Harrington, Wa., U.S.	146	C8	47.28 N	118.14 W
Harrington Creek, stm., Ca., U.S.	200		37.19 N	122.18 W
Harrington Drain, can., Mi., U.S.	199		42.36 N	82.54 W
Harrington Park, N.J., U.S.	194		40.59 N	73.58 W
Harrington Sound, b., Ber.	158e	k15	32.20 N	64.43 W
Harris, Sk., Can.	142	C6	51.44 N	107.35 W
Harris, Monts.	159a	d3	16.44 N	62.10 W
Harris, Mn., U.S.	128	F5	45.35 N	92.58 W
Harris, reg., Scot., U.K.	10	D6	57.55 N	6.50 W
Harris, Lake, l., Fl., U.S.	132	H4	28.46 N	81.49 W
Harris, Sound of, strt., Scot., U.K.	10	D5	57.45 N	7.10 W
Harris Brook, stm., Ma., U.S.	201		42.44 N	71.13 W
Harrisburg, Ar., U.S.	134	B8	35.33 N	90.43 W
Harrisburg, Il., U.S.	130	G9	37.43 N	88.32 W
Harrisburg, Ne., U.S.	140	F9	41.33 N	103.44 W
Harrisburg, Or., U.S.	146	F3	44.16 N	123.10 W
Harrisburg, Pa., U.S.	124	D8	40.16 N	76.53 W
Harris Creek, stm., Austl.	192a		33.57 S	150.57 E
Harrisfield, Austl.	192b		37.57 S	145.11 E
Harrismith, S. Afr.	90	F9	28.16 S	29.07 E
Harrison, Ar., U.S.	130	H4	36.14 N	93.06 W
Harrison, Id., U.S.	146	C10	47.27 N	116.46 W
Harrison, Mi., U.S.	126	D5	44.01 N	84.47 W
Harrison, Ne., U.S.	140	E9	42.39 N	103.52 W
Harrison, N.J., U.S.	194		40.44 N	74.09 W
Harrison Bay, b., Ak., U.S.	109	B9	70.30 N	151.30 W
Harrisonburg, La., U.S.	134	F7	31.46 N	91.49 W
Harrisonburg, Va., U.S.	124	F7	38.26 N	78.51 W
Harrison City, Pa., U.S.	197b		40.21 N	79.39 W
Harrison Islands, is., Nu., Can.	110	B13	69.13 N	90.30 W
Harrison Lake, l., B.C., Can.	144	G9	49.33 N	121.52 W
Harrisons Brook, stm., N.J., U.S.	194		40.38 N	74.34 W
Harrisonville, Md., U.S.	202b		39.23 N	77.50 W
Harrisonville, Mo., U.S.	130	F3	38.39 N	94.20 W
Harrisonville, N.J., U.S.	203		39.41 N	75.15 W
Harris Park, Austl.	192a		33.49 S	151.01 E
Harris Pond, l., N.H., U.S.	201		42.45 N	71.16 W
Harriston, On., Can.	126	E9	43.54 N	80.51 W
Harriston, Ms., U.S.	134	F7	31.43 N	91.01 W
Harrisville, Mi., U.S.	126	D6	44.39 N	83.17 W
Harrisville, N.Y., U.S.	126	D14	44.08 N	75.19 W
Harrisville, W.V., U.S.	124	E4	39.12 N	81.03 W
Harrodsburg, Ky., U.S.	130	G13	37.45 N	84.50 W
Harrogate, Eng., U.K.	10	H11	53.59 N	1.32 W
Harrold, Tx., U.S.	138	G9	34.05 N	99.01 W
Harrop Lake, l., Mb., Can.	142	B18	52.38 N	95.58 W
Harrow, On., Can.	126	F7	42.02 N	82.54 W
Harrow on the Hill, ngh., Eng., U.K.	178		51.34 N	0.20 W
Harrow School, educ., Eng., U.K.	178		51.34 N	0.20 W
Harrowsmith, On., Can.	126	D13	44.24 N	76.39 W
Harry S. Truman Reservoir, res., Mo., U.S.	130	F4	38.11 N	93.35 W
Har Sai Shan, mtn., China	52	D4	35.26 N	97.36 E
Harsens Island, i., Mi., U.S.	199		42.35 N	82.38 W
Harsīn, Iran	74	C10	34.16 N	47.34 E
Hârșova, Rom.	36	E14	44.41 N	27.57 E
Harsprånget, Swe.	14	F10	66.52 N	19.50 E
Harstad, Nor.	14	D7	68.47 N	16.34 E
Harstena, Swe.	16	I15	58.15 N	17.01 E
Harsūd, India	70	G6	22.05 N	76.43 E
Harsvik, Nor.	16	C7	64.02 N	9.58 E
Hart, Mi., U.S.	126	E3	43.41 N	86.21 W
Hart, Tx., U.S.	138	G6	34.23 N	102.07 W
Hart, stm., Yk., Can.	110	B3	65.51 N	136.23 W
Hartbees, stm., S. Afr.	90	F5	28.45 S	20.32 E
Hartberg, Aus.	30	C12	47.16 N	15.58 E
Hårteigen, hill, Nor.	16	G5	60.13 N	7.02 E
Hartford, Eng., U.K.	180		53.15 N	2.33 W
Hartford, Al., U.S.	134	F13	31.06 N	85.41 W
Hartford, Ar., U.S.	134	C4	35.01 N	94.22 W
Hartford, Ct., U.S.	124	C13	41.46 N	72.40 W
Hartford, Ks., U.S.	130	F2	38.18 N	95.57 W
Hartford, Ky., U.S.	130	G11	37.27 N	86.54 W
Hartford, Mi., U.S.	130	B11	42.12 N	86.09 W
Hartford, N.J., U.S.	203		39.58 N	74.53 W
Hartford, S.D., U.S.	128	H2	43.37 N	96.57 W
Hartford, Wi., U.S.	128	H10	43.19 N	88.22 W
Hartford City, In., U.S.	130	D12	40.26 N	85.21 W
Hartington, Ne., U.S.	140	E15	42.37 N	97.15 W
Hart Island, i., N.Y., U.S.	194		40.51 N	73.46 W
Hart Lake, res., Or., U.S.	148	A6	42.24 N	119.51 W
Hartland, N.B., Can.	122	D9	46.18 N	67.32 W
Hartland, Me., U.S.	122	F7	44.53 N	69.26 W
Hartland Point, c., Eng., U.K.	10	J8	51.01 N	4.31 W
Hartlepool, Eng., U.K.	10	G11	54.42 N	1.12 W
Hartley, Eng., U.K.	178		51.23 N	0.19 E
Hartley, Ia., U.S.	128	H3	43.10 N	95.28 W
Hartley, Tx., U.S.	138	F6	35.53 N	102.23 W
Hartley Bay, B.C., Can.	144	C1	53.24 N	129.16 W
Hartlip, Eng., U.K.	178		51.21 N	0.39 E
Hart Mountain, mtn., Mb., Can.	142	B12	52.29 N	101.25 W
Hartney, Mb., Can.	142	E13	49.28 N	100.31 W
Hartola, Fin.	18	F13	61.34 N	26.01 E
Harts, stm., S. Afr.	90	E7	28.24 S	24.16 E
Hartselle, Al., U.S.	132	C12	34.26 N	86.56 W
Hartshorne, Ok., U.S.	134	C3	34.50 N	95.33 W
Hartsville, Pa., U.S.	203		40.14 N	75.05 W
Hartsville, S.C., U.S.	132	B5	34.22 N	80.04 W
Hartsville, Tn., U.S.	130	H11	36.23 N	86.09 W
Hartville, Mo., U.S.	130	G5	37.15 N	92.30 W
Hartwell, Ga., U.S.	132	B3	34.21 N	82.55 W
Hartwell Lake, res., U.S.	132	B2	34.27 N	82.51 W
Hartwick Pines State Park, p.o.i., Mi., U.S.	126	D5	44.47 N	84.41 W
Hartz Mountains National Park, p.o.i., Austl.	99a	o13	43.12 S	146.40 E
Haruki, Japan	188		34.29 N	135.23 E
Hārūnābād, Pak.	70	D4	29.36 N	73.07 E
Haruniye, Tur.	76	A7	37.16 N	36.27 E
Harūr, India	69	E4	12.02 N	78.29 E
Har-Us, Mong.	52	B3	48.58 N	92.02 E
Har-Us nuur, l., Mong.	52	B3	48.00 N	92.10 E
Ḩarūt, stm., Afg.	72	C9	31.29 N	61.16 E
Harvard, Il., U.S.	130	B9	42.25 N	88.36 W
Harvard, Ne., U.S.	140	G14	40.36 N	98.05 W
Harvard University, educ., Ma., U.S.	201		42.22 N	71.07 W
Harvel, Eng., U.K.	178		51.21 N	0.22 E
Harvey, N.B., Can.	122	E12	45.44 N	64.45 W
Harvey, Il., U.S.	130	C10	41.36 N	87.38 W
Harvey, N.D., U.S.	142	G14	47.45 N	99.55 W
Harwich, Eng., U.K.	10	J14	51.56 N	1.16 E
Harwick, Pa., U.S.	197b		40.34 N	79.48 W
Harwood, Eng., U.K.	180		53.35 N	2.23 W
Harwood Heights, Il., U.S.	196		41.58 N	87.48 W
Harwood Park, Md., U.S.	202b		39.12 N	76.44 W
Haryāna, state, India	70	D6	29.20 N	76.20 E
Haryn' (Horyn'), stm., Eur.	40	F5	52.08 N	27.17 E
Harz, mts., Ger.	24	E6	51.45 N	10.30 E
Hasalbag, China	62	A4	37.51 N	76.43 E
Ḩasanābād, Iran	185d		35.44 N	51.19 E
Ḩasanābād-e Khāleșeh, Iran	185d		35.37 N	51.12 E
Hasan Dağı, vol., Tur.	42	F6	38.08 N	34.12 E
Hasankale see Pasinler, Tur.	42	E9	39.59 N	41.41 E
Hasavjurt, Russia	42	D12	43.15 N	46.35 E
Hasbrouck Heights, N.J., U.S.	194		40.51 N	74.04 W
Hasdo, stm., India	70	G9	21.43 N	82.44 E
Hase, Japan	188		34.32 N	135.54 E
Hase, stm., Ger.	24	D3	52.41 N	7.18 E
Hase, stm., Japan	188		34.34 N	135.38 E
Haselhorst, ngh., Ger.	182a		52.33 N	13.15 E
Hasenkamp, Arg.	172	E8	31.30 S	59.51 W
Ḩashā', Jabal al-, mtn., Yemen	72	G5	13.45 N	44.30 E
Hashima, Japan	56	D9	35.19 N	136.42 E
Hashimoto, Japan	56	E8	34.19 N	135.37 E
Hashimoto, Japan	188		34.26 N	135.23 E
Hasht Sāl, ngh., India	190a		28.38 N	77.03 E
Hāsilpur, Pak.	70	D4	29.42 N	72.33 E
Haskayne, Eng., U.K.	180		53.34 N	2.58 W
Haskell, Ok., U.S.	130	I2	35.49 N	95.40 W
Haskell, Tx., U.S.	136	A8	33.09 N	99.44 W
Haskell Pond, l., Ma., U.S.	201		42.37 N	70.44 W
Hasketh Bank, Eng., U.K.	180		53.43 N	2.51 W
Haskovo, Blg.	36	H12	41.56 N	25.33 E
Haskovo, state, Blg.	36	G12	42.00 N	25.30 E
Hasköy, ngh., Tur.	185b		41.02 N	28.58 E
Hasle, Den.	16	L12	55.11 N	14.42 E
Haslemere, Eng., U.K.	10	J12	51.05 N	0.42 W
Haslev, Den.	16	L9	55.20 N	11.57 E
Haslingden Grane, Eng., U.K.	180		53.42 N	2.21 W
Hasnācha, India	190b		22.26 N	88.09 E
Haspe, ngh., Ger.	181		51.21 N	7.26 E
Hasperos Canyon, val., N.M., U.S.	138	H3	33.53 N	105.18 W
Hasper-Stausee, res., Ger.	181		51.18 N	7.25 E
Haspra, Ukr.	38	I13	44.27 N	34.08 E
Ḩașș, Jabal al-, hill, Syria	76	C8	35.52 N	37.22 E
Hassa, Tur.	76	B7	36.49 N	36.34 E
Hassan, India	69	E3	12.59 N	76.06 E
Hassayampa, stm., Az., U.S.	150	J4	33.19 N	112.42 W
Hassel, Ger.	181		51.39 N	7.30 E
Hassel, ngh., Ger.	181		51.36 N	7.03 E
Hasselbeck-Schwarzbach, Ger.	181		51.16 N	6.53 E
Hassels, ngh., Ger.	181		51.10 N	6.53 E
Hassel Sound, strt., Nu., Can.	108	B6	78.23 N	98.44 W
Hasselt, Bel.	20	D14	50.56 N	5.20 E
Hassfurt, Ger.	24	F6	50.02 N	10.30 E
Hassi Bel Guebbour, Alg.	84	D6	28.41 N	6.30 E
Hassi Messaoud, Alg.	84	C6	31.41 N	6.04 E
Hässleholm, Swe.	16	K11	56.09 N	13.45 E
Hasten, ngh., Ger.	181		51.12 N	7.09 E
Hästen, ngh., Ger.	181		51.09 N	7.06 E
Hastings, Barb.	159d	n8	13.04 N	59.34 W
Hastings, On., Can.	126	D11	44.18 N	77.57 W
Hastings, N.Z.	102	D7	39.38 S	176.50 E
Hastings, Eng., U.K.	10	K13	50.51 N	0.34 E
Hastings, Fl., U.S.	132	G4	29.43 N	81.30 W
Hastings, Il., U.S.	196		41.41 N	87.58 W
Hastings, Mi., U.S.	130	B12	42.38 N	85.16 W
Hastings, Mn., U.S.	128	G6	44.44 N	92.50 W
Hastings, Ne., U.S.	140	G14	40.34 N	98.23 W
Hastings-on-Hudson, N.Y., U.S.	194		40.59 N	73.52 W
Hastingwood, Eng., U.K.	178		51.45 N	0.09 E
Hasty, Co., U.S.	138	C5	38.06 N	102.57 W
Hašuri, Geor.	42	E10	41.59 N	43.35 E
Hasvik, Nor.	14	B13	70.29 N	22.09 E
Haswell, Co., U.S.	138	C5	38.27 N	103.09 W
Hatanga, Russia	50	B9	71.58 N	102.30 E
Hatanga, stm., Russia	50	B9	72.45 N	105.16 E
Hatangskij zaliv, b., Russia	50	B10	73.34 N	109.44 E
Hatay (Antioch), Tur.	42	G7	36.12 N	36.10 E
Hatay, state, Tur.	42	G7	36.30 N	36.15 E
Hatch, N.M., U.S.	150	K9	32.40 N	107.09 W
Hatch, Ut., U.S.	150	F4	37.39 N	112.26 W
Hat Chao Mai National Park, p.o.i., Thai.	64	I4	7.14 N	99.32 E
Hatchet Creek, stm., Al., U.S.	134	D12	32.51 N	86.26 W
Hatchet Lake, N.S., Can.	122	F13	44.34 N	63.38 W
Hatchie, stm., U.S.	134	B9	35.32 N	89.53 W
Hatchlands, hist., Eng., U.K.	178		51.15 N	0.28 W
Hatchmere, Eng., U.K.	180		53.15 N	2.40 W
Hatch Wash, stm., Ut., U.S.	150	E7	38.23 N	109.32 W
Hat Creek, stm., U.S.	140	D9	43.15 N	103.35 W
Hat Creek, stm., Ca., U.S.	148	C4	40.59 N	121.33 W
Hațeg, Rom.	36	D9	45.36 N	22.57 E
Hatfield, Austl.	98	I4	33.52 S	143.45 E
Hatfield, Ar., U.S.	134	C4	34.29 N	94.22 W
Hatfield, Ma., U.S.	124	B13	42.22 N	72.35 W
Hatfield Aerodrome, arpt., Eng., U.K.	178		51.46 N	0.16 W
Hatfield House, hist., Eng., U.K.	178		51.46 N	0.13 W
Hatfield Swamp, sw., N.J., U.S.	194		40.50 N	74.20 W
Hatgal, Mong.	48	D18	50.25 N	100.08 E
Hāthras, India	70	E7	27.36 N	78.03 E
Ha Tien, Viet.	64	G7	10.22 N	104.29 E
Hatillo, P.R.	158a	a2	18.29 N	66.49 W
Ha Tinh, Viet.	64	C7	18.20 N	105.54 E
Hatinoe see Hachinohe, Japan	54	D14	40.30 N	141.29 E
Hatiozi see Hachiōji, Japan	56	D12	35.39 N	139.20 E
Hatip, Tur.	34	F15	37.46 N	32.24 E
Hātisāla, India	190b		22.33 N	88.32 E
Hato, Bocht van, b., Neth. Ant.	158g	p21	12.13 N	68.58 W
Hato Mayor del Rey, Dom. Rep.	156	C13	18.46 N	69.15 W
Hato Rey, P.R.	158a	b3	18.25 N	66.03 W
Ḩatoųnja, Bela.	26	G13	53.17 N	30.32 E
Hāt Pīplia, India	70	G6	22.46 N	76.18 E
Hatsutomi, Japan	186		35.46 N	140.01 E
Hatta, India	70	F7	24.07 N	79.36 E
Hatteras, N.C., U.S.	132	A10	35.13 N	75.41 W
Hatteras, Cape, c., N.C., U.S.	132	A10	35.13 N	75.31 W
Hatteras Island, i., N.C., U.S.	132	A10	35.24 N	75.29 W
Hattfjelldal, Nor.	16	B11	65.35 N	13.59 E
Hattiesburg, Ms., U.S.	134	F9	31.19 N	89.17 W
Hatton, Eng., U.K.	180		53.20 N	2.36 W
Hatton, Al., U.S.	134	C11	34.34 N	87.24 W
Hatton, N.D., U.S.	142	G16	47.37 N	97.26 W
Hatton, ngh., Eng., U.K.	178		51.28 N	0.25 W
Hattori, Japan	188		34.52 N	135.36 E
Hattori, Japan	188		34.46 N	135.27 E
Hatunsaray, Tur.	76	A3	37.34 N	32.22 E
Hatvan, Hung.	36	B6	47.40 N	19.41 E
Hat Yai, Thai.	64	I5	7.00 N	100.28 E
Ḩatyničy, Bela.	26	H9	52.37 N	26.18 E
Hatyrka, Russia	50	D24	62.03 N	175.16 E
Hatzfeld, ngh., Ger.	181		51.17 N	7.11 E
Haubstadt, In., U.S.	130	F10	38.12 N	87.34 W
Hāudullāpur, India	190b		22.25 N	88.33 E
Hauge, Nor.	16	I4	58.19 N	6.17 E
Haugesund, Nor.	16	H3	59.25 N	5.18 E
Haughton Green, Eng., U.K.	180		53.27 N	2.06 W
Haugsdorf, Aus.	24	H11	48.41 N	16.04 E
Hauja, stm., Bela.	26	F8	53.49 N	25.35 E
Haukeligrend, Nor.	16	H5	59.45 N	7.31 E
Haukipudas, Fin.	18	B12	65.11 N	25.21 E
Haukivesi, l., Fin.	18	E14	62.06 N	28.28 E
Haukivuori, Fin.	18	E14	62.00 N	27.17 E
Hauldres, Ru des, stm., Fr.	179		48.37 N	2.28 E
Haunts Creek, strt., N.Y., U.S.	194		40.37 N	73.31 W
Hauraki Gulf, b., N.Z.	102	C6	36.35 S	175.04 E
Hausa, Nig.	191a		6.37 N	3.21 E
Hausach, Ger.	24	H4	48.17 N	8.09 E
Haussee, l., Ger.	182a		52.38 N	13.41 E
Haut, Isle au, i., Me., U.S.	122	F8	44.03 N	68.38 W
Haut Atlas, mts., Mor.	84	C3	31.47 N	6.04 W
Haut-Bout, Fr.	179		48.32 N	1.55 E
Haute-Corse, state, Fr.	22	G15	42.30 N	9.00 E
Haute-Garonne, state, Fr.	22	F7	43.25 N	1.30 E
Haute-Loire, state, Fr.	22	D9	45.05 N	3.50 E
Haute-Marne, state, Fr.	20	F14	48.05 N	5.10 E
Hautes-Alpes, state, Fr.	22	E12	44.40 N	6.30 E
Haute-Saône, state, Fr.	20	G14	47.40 N	6.10 E
Haute-Savoie, state, Fr.	22	C12	46.00 N	6.20 E
Hautes Fagnes (Hohes Venn), mts., Eur.	20	D15	50.30 N	6.05 E
Hautes-Pyrénées, state, Fr.	22	F6	43.00 N	0.10 E
Haute-Vienne, state, Fr.	22	D7	45.50 N	1.15 E
Haute-Volta see Burkina Faso, ctry., Afr.	84	G4	13.00 N	1.30 W
Haut-Folin, mtn., Fr.	20	H13	47.00 N	4.02 E
Haut-Rhin, state, Fr.	20	G16	47.53 N	7.13 E
Hauts-de-Seine, state, Fr.	179		48.50 N	2.11 E
Haut Sheila, N.B., Can.	122	C11	47.28 N	64.57 W
Hauts Plateaux, reg., Afr.	84	C5	34.00 N	0.00 W
Hauula, Hi., U.S.	100a	b4	21.36 N	157.55 W
Hauwâret el-Maqta', Egypt	76	I1	29.15 N	30.53 E
Hauz Rāni, ngh., India	190a		28.32 N	77.13 E
Havana see La Habana, Cuba	156	A6	23.06 N	82.26 W
Havana, Ar., U.S.	134	B5	35.06 N	93.31 W
Havana, Fl., U.S.	134	G14	30.37 N	84.24 W
Havana, Il., U.S.	130	D7	40.17 N	90.03 W
Havana, N.D., U.S.	140	B15	45.56 N	97.37 W
Havannah, Canal de la, strt., N. Cal.	101d	n16	22.21 S	167.00 E
Havant, Eng., U.K.	10	K12	50.51 N	0.59 W
Havast, Uzb.	48	F11	40.13 N	68.49 E
Havasu, Lake, res., U.S.	150	I2	34.28 N	114.22 W
Havasu Creek, stm., Az., U.S.	150	H4	36.18 N	112.45 W
Havasupai Indian Reservation, ind. res., Az., U.S.	150	G4	36.08 N	112.38 W
Havdrup, Den.	16	L10	55.32 N	12.07 E
Havel, stm., Ger.	24	D8	52.52 N	12.00 E
Havelberg, Ger.	24	D8	52.49 N	12.04 E
Havelberg, hill, Ger.	182a		52.28 N	13.12 E
Haveli, Pak.	70	C4	30.26 N	73.42 E
Havel-Kanal, can., Ger.	182a		52.36 N	13.12 E
Havelland, reg., Ger.	24	D8	52.36 N	12.30 E
Havelländischer Grosser Hauptkanal, can., Ger.	182a		52.37 N	13.03 E
Havelock, On., Can.	126	D12	44.25 N	77.52 W
Havelock, N.C., U.S.	132	B9	34.53 N	76.54 W
Haven, Ks., U.S.	138	D11	37.53 N	97.46 W
Haverford, Pa., U.S.	203		40.00 N	75.17 W
Haverford College, educ., Pa., U.S.	203		40.00 N	75.18 W
Haverfordwest, Wales, U.K.	10	J7	51.48 N	4.58 W
Haverhill, Eng., U.K.	10	I13	52.05 N	0.26 E
Haverhill, Ma., U.S.	124	B14	42.46 N	71.05 W
Haverhill Airport, arpt., Ma., U.S.	201		42.48 N	71.04 W
Haverhill-Riverside Airport, arpt., Ma., U.S.	201		42.46 N	71.02 W
Hāveri, India	69	D2	14.46 N	75.24 E
Havering-atte-Bower, ngh., Eng., U.K.	178		51.37 N	0.11 E
Havering's Grove, Eng., U.K.	178		51.38 N	0.23 E
Havern, l., Swe.	16	E13	62.17 N	15.07 E
Haverö, Swe.	16	E13	62.24 N	15.05 E
Haviland, Ks., U.S.	138	D9	37.37 N	99.06 W
Haviland Brook, stm., Ct., U.S.	194		41.07 N	73.33 W
Ḩavīq, Iran	74	A11	38.09 N	48.52 E
Havířov, Czech Rep.	24	G14	49.46 N	18.28 E
Havlíčkův Brod, Czech Rep.	24	G11	49.36 N	15.34 E
Havøysund, Nor.	14	A16	70.59 N	24.39 E
Havran, Tur.	34	D10	39.32 N	27.05 E
Havre see Le Havre, Fr.	20	E8	49.29 N	0.08 E
Havre, Mt., U.S.	146	B17	48.32 N	109.40 W
Havre-Aubert, Qc., Can.	122	C15	47.14 N	61.51 W
Havre Aubert, Île du, i., Qc., Can.	122	C14	47.14 N	61.57 W
Havre de Grace, Md., U.S.	124	E9	39.32 N	76.05 W
Havre North, Mt., U.S.	146	B17	48.34 N	109.41 W
Havsa, Tur.	34	B9	41.33 N	26.49 E
Haw, stm., N.C., U.S.	132	A7	35.27 N	78.50 W
Hawaii, state, U.S.	100a	b5	20.00 N	157.45 W
Hawaii, i., Hi., U.S.	100a	c6	19.29 N	155.30 W
Hawaiian Gardens, Ca., U.S.	198		33.49 N	118.04 W
Hawaiian Islands, is., Hi., U.S.	174	G22	24.00 N	167.00 W
Hawaiian Ridge, unds.	174	G21	24.48 N	167.02 W
Hawaii Volcanoes National Park, p.o.i., Hi., U.S.	100a	d6	19.23 N	155.17 W
Hawara, Pyramid of see Hauwâret el-Maqta', Egypt	76	I1	29.15 N	30.53 E
Hawarden, Sk., Can.	142	C7	51.25 N	106.36 W
Hawarden, Ia., U.S.	130	A1	42.59 N	96.29 W
Hawashîya, Wadi, stm., Egypt	76	J3	28.34 N	32.55 E
Hawea, Lake, l., N.Z.	102	G3	44.30 S	169.17 E
Hawera, N.Z.	102	D6	39.35 S	174.17 E
Hawesville, Ky., U.S.	130	G11	37.53 N	86.45 W
Hawi, Hi., U.S.	100a	c6	20.14 N	155.49 W
Hawick, Scot., U.K.	10	F10	55.25 N	2.47 W
Hawk Creek, stm., Mn., U.S.	128	F3	44.44 N	95.25 W
Hawke, Cape, c., Austl.	98	I9	32.13 S	152.33 E
Hawke Bay, b., N.Z.	102	D7	39.20 S	177.30 E
Hawker, Austl.	98	H2	31.53 S	138.25 E
Hawkes, Mount, mtn., Ant.	103	D36	83.56 S	55.44 W

Name Page Map Ref. Latitude Longitude
Hawkes Brook, stm., Ma., U.S. 201 42.45 N 71.08 W
Hawkesbury, On., Can. 126 C15 45.36 N 74.36 W
Hawkesbury Island, i., B.C., Can. 144 C1 53.38 N 129.00 W
Hawkes Pond, l., Ma., U.S. 201 42.30 N 71.02 W
Hawkeye, Ia., U.S. 130 B6 42.56 N 91.57 W
Hawkins, Tx., U.S. 136 B12 32.36 N 95.12 W
Hawkins, Wi., U.S. 128 F8 45.30 N 90.43 W
Hawkinsville, Ga., U.S. 132 D2 32.17 N 83.28 W
Hawk Junction, On., Can. 114 B8 48.05 N 84.34 W
Hawk Lake, On., Can. 128 B4 49.48 N 93.59 W
Haw Knob, mtn., U.S. 132 A1 35.19 N 84.02 W
Hawksbill, mtn., Va., U.S. 124 F7 38.33 N 78.23 W
Hawksbill Creek, b., Bah. 132 J7 26.40 N 78.43 W
Hawkwell, Eng., U.K. 178 51.36 N 0.40 E
Hawkwood, Austl. 98 E8 25.46 S 150.48 E
Hawley, Eng., U.K. 178 51.25 N 0.14 E
Hawley, Mn., U.S. 128 E2 46.52 N 96.19 W
Hawley, Pa., U.S. 124 C10 41.29 N 75.10 W
Hawn State Park, p.o.i., Mo., U.S. 130 G7 37.50 N 90.15 W
Haworth, N.J., U.S. 194 40.57 N 73.59 W
Haw Par Villa, bldg., Sing. 189c 1.16 N 103.47 E
Hawrān, Wādī, stm., Iraq 74 D7 33.58 N 42.34 E
Hawthorn, Austl. 192b 37.49 S 145.02 E
Hawthorne, Fl., U.S. 132 G3 29.35 N 82.05 W
Hawthorne, Nv., U.S. 148 E7 38.31 N 118.36 W
Hawthorne Lake, l., N.J., U.S. 194 41.03 N 74.35 W
Hawthorne Municipal Airport, arpt., Ca., U.S. 198 33.55 N 118.20 W
Hawthorne Race Course, p.o.i., Il., U.S. 196 41.50 N 87.45 W
Hawthorn Woods, Il., U.S. 196 42.13 N 88.03 W
Hawwâret 'Adlan, Egypt 76 I1 29.12 N 30.57 E
Hawza, W. Sah. 84 D2 27.07 N 10.55 W
Haxtun, Co., U.S. 140 G10 40.38 N 102.37 W
Hay, Austl. 98 J5 34.30 S 144.50 E
Hay, stm., Austl. 96 D7 25.14 S 138.00 E
Hay, stm., Can. 110 D7 60.51 N 115.43 W
Hay, stm., Wi., U.S. 128 F7 44.59 N 91.50 W
Hay, Cape, c., N.T., Can. 109 B17 74.25 N 113.00 W
Hay, South Fork, stm., Wi., U.S. 128 F6 45.03 N 91.56 W
Hayang, Kor., S. 56 D1 35.53 N 128.48 E
Hayange, Fr. 20 E14 49.20 N 6.01 E
HaYarden see Jordan, stm., Asia 76 F6 31.45 N 35.33 E
Hayastan see Armenia, ctry., Asia 42 E11 40.00 N 45.00 E
Haybān, Jabal, mtn., Sudan 82 E6 11.15 N 30.31 E
Haydarlı, Tur. 34 E13 38.16 N 30.23 E
Hayden, Az., U.S. 150 J6 33.01 N 110.47 W
Hayden, Co., U.S. 150 C9 40.30 N 107.14 W
Hayden Peak, mtn., Id., U.S. 146 H10 42.59 N 116.39 W
Haydenville, Oh., U.S. 124 E3 39.29 N 82.19 W
Haydock Park Race Course, p.o.i., Eng., U.K. 180 53.29 N 2.37 W
Hayes, La., U.S. 134 G6 30.06 N 92.55 W
Hayes, ngh., Eng., U.K. 178 51.23 N 0.01 E
Hayes, ngh., Eng., U.K. 178 51.31 N 0.25 W
Hayes, stm., Mb., Can. 110 D12 57.02 N 92.13 W
Hayes, stm., Nu., Can. 110 B11 67.08 N 95.18 W
Hayes, Mount, mtn., Ak., U.S. 109 D10 63.37 N 146.43 W
Hayes Center, Ne., U.S. 140 G11 40.30 N 101.01 W
Hayesville, N.C., U.S. 132 A2 35.02 N 83.49 W
Hayesville, Or., U.S. 146 F4 44.59 N 122.58 W
Hayfield, Eng., U.K. 180 53.23 N 1.57 W
Hayfield, Mn., U.S. 128 H6 43.53 N 92.51 W
Hayford Peak, mtn., Nv., U.S. 148 G10 36.40 N 115.11 W
Hayfork, Ca., U.S. 148 C2 40.34 N 123.10 W
Hayfork Bally, mtn., Ca., U.S. 148 C2 40.39 N 123.13 W
Hayfork Creek, stm., Ca., U.S. 148 C2 40.37 N 123.27 W
Hay Lakes, Ab., Can. 144 C17 53.11 N 113.02 W
Haymakers Run, stm., Pa., U.S. 197b 40.25 N 79.43 W
Haymana, Tur. 34 D15 39.26 N 32.30 E
Haynes, Ar., U.S. 134 C8 34.53 N 90.47 W
Haynes Creek, stm., N.J., U.S. 203 39.53 N 74.50 W
Haynesville, La., U.S. 134 E5 32.57 N 93.08 W
Hayneville, Al., U.S. 134 E12 32.11 N 86.34 W
Hay Point, c., Austl. 98 C7 21.17 S 149.16 E
Hayrabolu, Tur. 34 B10 41.11 N 27.07 E
Hay River, N.T., Can. 110 C7 60.49 N 115.48 W
Hays, Ab., Can. 144 F19 50.06 N 111.47 W
Hays, Ks., U.S. 138 C9 38.52 N 99.18 W
Hays, Mt., U.S. 142 F5 47.59 N 108.40 W
Hays, ngh., Pa., U.S. 197b 40.23 N 79.56 W
Hays Mill Creek, stm., N.J., U.S. 203 39.44 N 74.50 W
Hay Springs, Ne., U.S. 140 E10 42.41 N 102.41 W
Haystack Mountain, mtn., Nv., U.S. 148 B10 41.39 N 115.38 W
Haysville, Ks., U.S. 138 D11 37.33 N 97.20 W
Haysville, Pa., U.S. 197b 40.32 N 80.09 W
Hayti, Mo., U.S. 130 H8 36.13 N 89.44 W
Hayti, S.D., U.S. 140 C15 44.39 N 97.12 W
Hayward, Ca., U.S. 148 F3 37.40 N 122.04 W
Hayward, Wi., U.S. 128 E7 46.00 N 91.29 W
Hayward Brook, stm., Ma., U.S. 201 42.22 N 71.20 W
Hayward Municipal Airport, arpt., Ca., U.S. 200 37.40 N 122.08 W
Haywards Heath, Eng., U.K. 10 J13 51.00 N 0.06 W
Haywood, Mb., Can. 142 E15 49.40 N 98.10 W
HaẒafon, state, Isr. 76 F6 32.50 N 35.20 E
Hazard, Ky., U.S. 124 G2 37.14 N 83.12 W
Hazārībāg, India 70 G10 23.59 N 85.22 E
Ḥazawzā', Sabkhat, l., Sau. Ar. 76 H9 30.48 N 38.10 E
Hazebrouck, Fr. 20 D11 50.43 N 2.32 E
Hazel, stm., Va., U.S. 124 F7 38.33 N 77.51 W
Hazel Crest, Il., U.S. 196 41.34 N 87.41 W
Hazel Green, Wi., U.S. 128 I8 42.31 N 90.26 W
Hazel Kirk, Pa., U.S. 197b 40.11 N 79.57 W
Hazel Park Raceway, p.o.i., Mi., U.S. 199 42.29 N 83.05 W
Hazelton, B.C., Can. 144 A3 55.14 N 127.41 W
Hazelton, Id., U.S. 146 H12 42.36 N 114.08 W
Hazelton, N.D., U.S. 140 A12 46.28 N 100.17 W
Hazelton Mountains, mts., B.C., Can. 144 B3 54.18 N 127.16 W
Hazelton Peak, mtn., Wy., U.S. 140 C5 44.06 N 107.03 W
Hazelwood, N.C., U.S. 132 A2 35.28 N 83.00 W
Hazelwood, ngh., Pa., U.S. 197b 40.25 N 79.56 W
Hazen, Ar., U.S. 134 C7 34.47 N 91.34 W
Hazen, N.D., U.S. 142 G12 47.17 N 101.37 W
Hazen, Lake, l., Nu., Can. 108 A11 81.48 N 70.39 W
Hazlehurst, Ga., U.S. 132 E3 31.52 N 82.35 W
Hazlehurst, Ms., U.S. 134 F8 31.52 N 90.23 W
Hazlet, Sk., Can. 142 D5 50.25 N 108.36 W
Hazleton, Ia., U.S. 130 B6 42.37 N 91.54 W
Hazleton, Pa., U.S. 124 D9 40.57 N 75.58 W
Hazlett, Lake, l., Austl. 96 D5 21.31 S 128.36 E
Ḥazor HaGelilit, Isr. 76 E6 32.59 N 35.32 E
He, stm., China 58 I4 23.26 N 111.29 E
He, stm., China 58 H6 27.01 N 114.51 E
Headland, Al., U.S. 134 F13 31.20 N 85.21 W
Headley, Eng., U.K. 178 51.17 N 0.16 W
Headley, Mount, mtn., Mt., U.S. 146 C11 47.44 N 115.15 W
Head of the Harbor, N.Y., U.S. 194 40.54 N 73.10 W
Heald Green, Eng., U.K. 180 53.22 N 2.14 W
Heald Moor, for., Eng., U.K. 180 53.44 N 2.10 W
Healdsburg, Ca., U.S. 148 E3 38.36 N 122.51 W
Healdton, Ok., U.S. 138 G11 34.13 N 97.29 W
Healesville, Austl. 98 K5 37.39 S 145.31 E
Healy, Ks., U.S. 138 C8 38.36 N 100.37 W
Heard Island, i., Austl. 174 O10 53.06 S 73.30 E
Heard Pond, l., Ma., U.S. 201 42.21 N 71.22 W
Hearne, Tx., U.S. 136 D11 30.52 N 96.36 W
Hearst, On., Can. 114 B9 49.41 N 83.42 W
Hearst, stm., N.D., U.S. 142 H12 46.46 N 100.50 W
Heart Lake, l., Ab., Can. 144 A19 55.02 N 111.30 W
Heart Lake, l., On., Can. 193b 43.44 N 79.48 W
Heart Lake Indian Reserve, ind. res., Ab., Can. 144 A19 55.04 N 111.32 W
Heart Pond, l., Ma., U.S. 201 42.34 N 71.23 W
Heath, Pointe, c., Qc., Can. 122 A15 49.05 N 61.42 W
Heathcote, Austl. 98 K5 36.54 S 144.41 E
Heathcote, Austl. 192a 34.05 S 151.01 E
Heathcote Brook, stm., N.J., U.S. 194 40.23 N 74.37 W
Heatherton, Austl. 192b 37.58 S 145.06 E
Heathmont, Austl. 192b 37.49 S 145.15 E
Heath Springs, S.C., U.S. 132 B5 34.35 N 80.40 W
Heathsville, Va., U.S. 124 G9 37.54 N 76.28 W
Heatley, Eng., U.K. 180 53.24 N 2.27 W
Heaton Hall, hist., Eng., U.K. 180 53.32 N 2.15 W
Heaton Moor, Eng., U.K. 180 53.25 N 2.11 W
Heaton Park, p.o.i., Eng., U.K. 180 53.32 N 2.15 W
Heaven, Temple of, rel., China 189a 39.53 N 116.25 E
Heavener, Ok., U.S. 134 C4 34.53 N 94.36 W
Heaverham, Eng., U.K. 178 51.18 N 0.15 E
Heaviley, Eng., U.K. 180 53.24 N 2.09 W
Hebao Dao, i., China 58 K5 21.52 N 113.09 E
Hebbronville, Tx., U.S. 136 G9 27.18 N 98.40 W
Hebbville, Md., U.S. 202b 39.20 N 77.46 W
Hebden Water, stm., Eng., U.K. 180 53.44 N 2.00 W
Hebei, state, China 52 D8 38.00 N 116.00 E
Hebel, Austl. 98 G6 28.58 S 147.47 E
Heber, Az., U.S. 150 I6 34.25 N 110.35 W
Heber City, Ut., U.S. 150 C5 40.31 N 111.25 W
Heber Springs, Ar., U.S. 134 B6 35.29 N 92.01 W
Hebgen Lake, res., Mt., U.S. 146 F15 44.47 N 111.15 W
Hebi, China 58 D6 35.58 N 114.08 E
Hebrides, is., Scot., U.K. 10 E5 57.00 N 6.30 W
Hebrides, Sea of the, s., Scot., U.K. 10 D5 57.00 N 7.00 W
Hebron, Nf., Can. 108 F13 58.12 N 62.38 W
Hebron, Il., U.S. 130 B9 42.27 N 88.26 W
Hebron, In., U.S. 130 C10 41.18 N 87.11 W
Hebron, Md., U.S. 124 F10 38.25 N 75.41 W
Hebron, Ne., U.S. 138 A11 40.09 N 97.35 W
Hebron, N.D., U.S. 142 H11 46.54 N 102.02 W
Hebron see Al-Khalīl, W.B. 76 G6 31.32 N 35.06 E
Heby, Swe. 16 H14 59.56 N 16.51 E
Hecate Strait, strt., B.C., Can. 110 E4 53.00 N 131.00 W
Hecelchakán, Mex. 156 B2 20.10 N 90.08 W
Hechi, China 58 I3 24.42 N 108.02 E
Hechiceros, Mex. 136 F4 28.33 N 103.38 W
Hechingen, Ger. 24 H4 48.21 N 8.57 E
Hechuan, China 58 G2 29.59 N 106.15 E
Hecla, Mb., Can. 142 C17 51.07 N 96.40 W
Hecla, S.D., U.S. 140 B14 45.53 N 98.09 W
Hecla, Cape, c., Nu., Can. 108 A13 82.53 N 64.40 W
Hecla Island, i., Mb., Can. 142 D17 51.06 N 96.42 W
Hecla Provincial Park, p.o.i., Mb., Can. 142 C17 51.09 N 96.39 W
Hectanooga, N.S., Can. 122 F10 44.06 N 66.02 W
Hector, Mn., U.S. 128 G4 44.44 N 94.43 W
Hedal, Nor. 16 G7 60.37 N 9.42 E
Heddalsvatnet, l., Nor. 16 H6 59.30 N 9.18 E
Hedding, N.J., U.S. 203 40.06 N 74.44 W
Hede, Swe. 16 E11 62.25 N 13.29 E
Hedemora, Swe. 16 G13 60.16 N 15.59 E
Hedenäset, Swe. 14 F14 66.13 N 23.41 E
Hedensted, Den. 16 L7 55.46 N 9.42 E
Hedesunda, Swe. 16 G14 60.24 N 16.59 E
Hedesundafjärdarna, l., Swe. 16 G14 60.20 N 17.00 E
He Devil, mtn., Id., U.S. 146 E10 45.21 N 116.33 W
Hedgerley, Eng., U.K. 178 51.35 N 0.36 W
Hedley, B.C., Can. 144 G10 49.21 N 120.05 W
Hedley, Tx., U.S. 138 G8 34.52 N 100.38 W
Hedmark, state, Nor. 16 F9 61.30 N 11.45 E
Hedmarken, reg., Nor. 16 F9 60.50 N 11.15 E
Hedostrov, ostrov, i., Russia 18 C23 64.03 N 36.46 E
Hedrick, Ia., U.S. 130 C5 41.10 N 92.18 W
Hedutne, India 190c 19.10 N 73.06 E
Heerdt, ngh., Ger. 181 51.13 N 6.43 E
Heerenveen, Neth. 20 B14 52.57 N 5.55 E
Heerlen, Neth. 20 D15 50.53 N 5.58 E
Ḥefa (Haifa), Isr. 76 F5 32.48 N 35.00 E
Ḥefa, state, Isr. 76 F5 32.35 N 35.00 E
Ḥefa, Mifraz (Haifa, Bay of), b., Isr. 76 F5 32.52 N 35.03 E
Hefei, China 58 F7 31.51 N 117.16 E
Heffron Park, p.o.i., Austl. 192a 33.57 S 151.15 E
Heflin, Al., U.S. 134 D13 33.38 N 85.35 W
Hegang, China 54 B11 47.19 N 130.16 E
Hegewisch, ngh., Il., U.S. 196 41.40 N 87.33 W
Hegra, Nor. 16 D9 63.28 N 11.07 E
Hegura-jima, i., Japan 56 B9 37.50 N 136.55 E
Heguri, Japan 188 34.38 N 135.42 E
Heho, Mya. 64 B3 20.43 N 96.49 E
Hei, stm., China 58 A7 40.41 N 116.26 E
Heichengzhen, China 58 C1 36.17 N 106.09 E
Heidberg, hill, Ger. 181 51.15 N 7.21 E
Heide, Ger. 24 B5 54.11 N 9.05 E
Heide, ngh., Ger. 181 51.26 N 7.01 E
Heide, ngh., Ger. 181 51.31 N 6.52 E
Heidelberg, Ger. 24 G4 49.24 N 8.41 E
Heidelberg, S. Afr. 90 E9 26.30 S 28.21 E
Heidelberg, Ms., U.S. 134 F10 31.53 N 88.59 W
Heidelberg, Pa., U.S. 197b 40.23 N 80.05 W
Heidelberg, state, S. Afr. 191d 26.19 S 28.16 E
Heidenheim, Ger. 24 G6 49.01 N 10.44 E
Heidenreichstein, Aus. 24 H11 48.52 N 15.07 E
Heider Ditch, can., Oh., U.S. 197a 41.31 N 82.01 W
Heidhausen, ngh., Ger. 181 51.23 N 7.01 E
Heidhof, ngh., Ger. 181 51.11 N 7.11 E
Heihe, China 52 A10 50.14 N 127.29 E
Heijō see P'yŏngyang, Kor., N. 54 E6 39.01 N 125.44 E
Heikkilä, Fin. 18 A16 66.00 N 29.33 E
Heil, Ger. 181 51.38 N 7.35 E
Heilbad Heiligenstadt, Ger. 24 E6 51.22 N 10.08 E
Heilbron, S. Afr. 90 E8 27.17 S 27.58 E
Heilbronn, Ger. 24 G5 49.08 N 9.12 E
Heilenbecker-Stausee, res., Ger. 181 51.15 N 7.22 E
Heilhornet, mtn., Nor. 16 B10 65.04 N 12.09 E
Heiligenblut, Aus. 30 C9 47.02 N 12.50 E
Heiligenhafen, Ger. 24 B6 54.22 N 10.58 E
Heiligensee, ngh., Ger. 182a 52.36 N 13.13 E
Hei Ling Chau, i., China 189d 22.15 N 114.02 E
Heilong (Amur), stm., Asia 50 F14 52.56 N 141.10 E
Heilongguan, China 58 C4 36.19 N 111.11 E
Heilongjiang, state, China 54 B8 45.05 N 130.18 E
Heilongjiang see Amur, stm., Asia 50 F16 52.56 N 141.10 E
Heilongjiang see Heilong, stm., Asia 50 F16 52.56 N 141.10 E
Heilungkiang see Heilongjiang, state, China 54 B8 45.05 N 130.18 E
Heimaey, i., Ice. 12a l29 63.26 N 20.17 W
Heimdal, Nor. 16 D8 63.21 N 10.22 E
Heinävesi, Fin. 18 E15 62.26 N 28.35 E
Heinersdorf, Ger. 182a 52.23 N 13.20 E
Heinersdorf, ngh., Ger. 182a 52.34 N 13.27 E
Heinola, Fin. 18 F13 61.12 N 26.02 E
Heishan, China 54 D4 41.41 N 122.07 E
Heishanguan, China 58 B5 38.33 N 113.41 E
Heishuisi, China 58 C3 36.05 N 108.47 E
Heisingen, ngh., Ger. 181 51.25 N 7.04 E
Heisler, Ab., Can. 144 D18 52.41 N 112.13 W
Heissen, ngh., Ger. 181 51.26 N 6.56 E
Hejaz see Al-Ḥijāz, reg., Sau. Ar. 72 D4 24.30 N 38.30 E
Hejian, China 58 B7 38.25 N 116.04 E
Hejiang, China 58 G1 28.48 N 105.50 E
Hejin, China 58 D4 35.35 N 110.41 E
Hejing, China 52 C2 42.18 N 86.18 E
Hekimhan, Tur. 42 F8 38.49 N 37.58 E
Hekla, vol., Ice. 12a k30 64.00 N 19.39 W
Hekou, China 52 G5 22.35 N 103.57 E
Hekou, China 58 G3 28.22 N 108.14 E
Hekou, China 58 G4 29.57 N 111.04 E
Hel, Pol. 24 B14 54.37 N 18.48 E
Helagsfjället, mtn., Swe. 16 E10 62.55 N 12.27 E
Helan Mountains see Helan Shan, mts., China 58 B1 38.40 N 105.57 E
Helan Shan, mts., China 58 B1 38.40 N 105.57 E
Helbra, Ger. 24 E7 51.33 N 11.29 E
Helder see Den Helder, Neth. 20 B13 52.57 N 4.46 E
Helder, Den see Den Helder, Neth. 20 B13 52.57 N 4.46 E
Helechos, Cañada de los, stm., Mex. 204a 19.22 N 99.12 W
Helen, Mount, hill, Austl. 98 C3 21.34 S 141.13 E
Helena, Ar., U.S. 134 C8 34.32 N 90.35 W
Helena, Mt., U.S. 146 D14 46.35 N 112.02 W
Helena, Ok., U.S. 138 E10 36.32 N 98.16 W
Helenental, val., Aus. 182b 48.01 N 16.11 E
Helensburgh, Scot., U.K. 10 E8 56.00 N 4.44 W
Helenwood, Tn., U.S. 130 H13 36.25 N 84.32 W
Helga å, stm., Swe. 16 K12 55.51 N 14.14 E
Helgoland, i., Ger. 24 B3 54.11 N 7.52 E
Helgoländer Bucht, b., Ger. 24 C4 54.02 N 8.29 E
Helgøya, i., Nor. 14 B10 70.08 N 19.27 E
Heli, China 52 B11 47.03 N 130.17 E
Helicoide, shp. cen., Ven. 204c 10.29 N 66.55 W
Heliópolis, Braz. 205a 22.45 S 43.25 W
Heliopolis see Misr el-Gedīda, ngh., Egypt 191c 30.06 N 31.20 E
Heliopolis Aerodrome, arpt., Egypt 191c 30.04 N 31.19 E
Heliopolis Racing Club, p.o.i., Egypt 191c 30.06 N 31.19 E
Helixi, China 58 F8 30.39 N 118.59 E
Heljul'ja, Russia 18 F17 61.44 N 30.41 E
Hell, Nor. 16 D8 63.27 N 10.53 E
Helleh, stm., Iran 74 F12 29.09 N 50.39 E
Hellersen, Ger. 181 51.12 N 7.39 E
Hellesylt, Nor. 16 E4 62.04 N 6.53 E
Hell Gate, strt., N.Y., U.S. 194 40.47 N 73.56 W
Helligvær, is., Nor. 14 E4 67.24 N 13.55 E
Hellín, Spain 28 F9 38.30 N 1.41 W
Hell Point, c., N.S., Can. 122 F12 44.15 N 64.15 W
Hells Canyon, val., U.S. 146 E10 45.17 N 116.40 W
Hells Canyon National Recreation Area, p.o.i., Or., U.S. 146 E10 45.37 N 116.45 W
Hellsee, l., Ger. 182a 52.45 N 13.35 E
Hells Gate, val., B.C., Can. 144 G9 49.47 N 121.27 W
Hell-Ville see Andoany, Madag. 88 C8 13.23 S 48.15 E
Helmand, stm., Asia 62 B1 31.19 N 61.29 E
Helmcken Falls, wtfl., B.C., Can. 144 E10 51.57 N 120.12 W
Helmeringhausen, Nmb. 90 D3 25.54 S 16.57 E
Helmetta, N.J., U.S. 194 40.22 N 74.25 W
Helmetta Pond, l., N.J., U.S. 194 40.23 N 74.26 W
Hel'miaziv, Ukr. 38 D10 49.49 N 31.50 E
Helmond, Neth. 20 C14 51.29 N 5.40 E
Helmsdale, Scot., U.K. 10 C9 58.07 N 3.39 W
Helmsdale, stm., Scot., U.K. 10 C8 58.06 N 3.39 W
Helmshore, Eng., U.K. 180 53.41 N 2.20 W
Helmstedt, Ger. 24 D6 52.13 N 11.00 E
Helong, China 54 C10 42.31 N 128.58 E
Helper, Ut., U.S. 150 D6 39.41 N 110.51 W
Helsby Hill, hill, Eng., U.K. 180 53.16 N 2.46 W
Helsingborg, Swe. 16 K10 56.02 N 12.42 E
Helsingfors see Helsinki, Fin. 18 G12 60.09 N 24.57 E
Helsingør, Den. 16 K10 56.02 N 12.36 E
Helsinki (Helsingfors), Fin. 18 G12 60.09 N 24.57 E
Helska, Mierzeja, pen., Pol. 24 B14 54.42 N 18.38 E
Helston, Eng., U.K. 10 K7 50.05 N 5.15 W
Helvecia, Arg. 172 E7 31.06 S 60.05 W
Helvetia see Switzerland, ctry., Eur. 30 D5 47.00 N 8.00 E
Helwan, Egypt 76 I2 29.51 N 31.20 E
Helwan, Egypt 191c 29.51 N 31.20 E
Helwan Observatory, sci., Egypt 76 I2 29.52 N 31.21 E
Helwan Observatory, sci., Egypt 191c 29.52 N 31.21 E
Hemau, Ger. 24 G7 49.03 N 11.47 E
Hemāvati, stm., India 69 E2 12.31 N 76.26 E
Hemel Hempstead, Eng., U.K. 10 J12 51.45 N 0.28 W
Hemet, Ca., U.S. 148 J9 33.44 N 116.58 W
Hemford, N.S., Can. 122 F12 44.30 N 64.47 W
Hemingford, Ne., U.S. 140 E9 42.19 N 103.04 W
Hemingway, S.C., U.S. 132 C6 33.45 N 79.26 W
Hemmerden, Ger. 181 51.07 N 6.36 E
Hemnesberget, Nor. 14 F4 66.13 N 13.36 E
Hemphill, Tx., U.S. 136 C14 31.20 N 93.50 W
Hempstead, Tx., U.S. 136 D11 30.05 N 96.04 W
Hempstead Harbor, b., N.Y., U.S. 194 40.50 N 73.39 W
Hempstead Lake, l., N.Y., U.S. 194 40.41 N 73.38 W
Hempstead Lake State Park, p.o.i., N.Y., U.S. 194 40.41 N 73.38 W
Hemse, Swe. 16 J16 57.14 N 18.22 E
Hemsedal, Nor. 16 G6 60.51 N 8.34 E
Hemsedal, val., Nor. 16 G6 60.48 N 8.43 E
Hemsön, i., Swe. 16 E16 62.43 N 18.05 E
Hen, Nor. 16 G8 60.12 N 10.15 E
Henan, China 52 E5 34.35 N 101.34 E
Henan, state, China 58 E6 34.00 N 114.00 E
Henbury, Austl. 96 D6 24.32 S 133.14 E
Henbury, Eng., U.K. 180 53.15 N 2.11 W
Hendek, Tur. 34 C13 40.48 N 30.45 E
Henderson, Arg. 172 H7 36.18 S 61.43 W
Henderson, Ky., U.S. 130 G10 37.49 N 87.35 W
Henderson, Mn., U.S. 128 G5 44.31 N 93.54 W
Henderson, Ne., U.S. 140 G15 40.46 N 97.48 W
Henderson, Nv., U.S. 150 G1 36.02 N 114.58 W
Henderson, N.C., U.S. 124 H7 36.19 N 78.23 W
Henderson, Tn., U.S. 134 B10 35.26 N 88.38 W
Henderson, Tx., U.S. 136 B13 32.08 N 94.48 W
Henderson Creek, stm., Il., U.S. 130 C7 40.52 N 91.01 W
Hendersonville, N.C., U.S. 132 A3 35.18 N 82.27 W
Hendersonville, Tn., U.S. 130 H11 36.17 N 86.37 W
Hendījān, Iran 74 E11 30.13 N 49.43 E
Hendon, ngh., Eng., U.K. 178 51.35 N 0.14 W
Hendorābī, Jazīreh-ye, i., Iran 74 G13 26.40 N 53.37 E
Hendricks, Mn., U.S. 128 G2 44.30 N 96.25 W
Hendricks, W.V., U.S. 124 E6 39.04 N 79.38 W
Hendrik Verwoerddam see Gariep Dam, res., S. Afr. 90 G7 30.40 S 25.40 E
Henefer, Ut., U.S. 150 B5 41.01 N 111.28 W
Hengām, Jazīreh-ye, i., Iran 74 G14 26.39 N 55.53 E
Henganofi, Pap. N. Gui. 101a b4 6.14 S 145.35 E
Hengchow see Hengyang, China 58 H5 26.54 N 112.36 E
Hengdaozi, China 54 C7 43.18 N 127.18 E
Hengelo, Neth. 20 B15 52.15 N 6.47 E
Hengfeng, China 58 G7 28.25 N 117.33 E
Henggouzi, China 54 C6 43.12 N 124.46 E
Henglu, China 54 D7 41.25 N 126.00 E
Hengsen, Ger. 181 51.29 N 7.38 E
Hengshan, China 58 H5 27.15 N 112.51 E
Hengshan, China 58 C3 37.56 N 109.17 E
Heng Shan, mtn., China 58 H5 27.16 N 112.35 E
Heng Shan, mts., China 58 B6 39.30 N 113.45 E
Hengshui, China 58 C6 37.43 N 115.41 E
Hengsteysee, res., Ger. 181 51.25 N 7.28 E
Hengxian, China 58 J3 22.40 N 109.12 E
Hengyang, China 58 H5 26.54 N 112.36 E
Heniches'k, Ukr. 38 G13 46.10 N 34.48 E
Hénin-Beaumont, Fr. 20 D11 50.25 N 2.56 E
Henlopen, Cape, c., De., U.S. 124 F10 38.47 N 75.05 W
Hennan, l., Swe. 16 E13 62.06 N 15.46 E
Hennebont, Fr. 20 G5 47.48 N 3.16 W
Hennef, Ger. 24 F3 50.46 N 7.16 E
Hennepin, Il., U.S. 130 C8 41.15 N 89.20 W
Hennepin, Point, c., Mi., U.S. 199 42.12 N 83.09 W
Hennersdorf, Aus. 182b 48.07 N 16.22 E
Hennessey, Ok., U.S. 138 E11 36.06 N 97.53 W
Henniker, N.H., U.S. 122 G5 43.11 N 71.49 W
Henning, Mn., U.S. 128 E3 46.19 N 95.27 W
Henning, Tn., U.S. 134 B9 35.40 N 89.34 W
Henrichenburg, Ger. 181 51.35 N 7.19 E
Henrietta, N.Y., U.S. 124 A8 43.03 N 77.37 W
Henrietta, Tx., U.S. 138 H10 33.49 N 98.12 W
Henrietta Island see Genrietty, ostrov, i., Russia 50 A20 76.58 N 156.38 E
Henrietta Maria, Cape, c., On., Can. 110 D14 55.08 N 82.19 W
Henri Pittier, Parque Nacional, p.o.i., Ven. 168 B8 10.25 N 67.43 W
Henry, Il., U.S. 130 C8 41.06 N 89.21 W
Henry, S.D., U.S. 140 C15 44.51 N 97.27 W
Henry, Cape, c., Va., U.S. 124 H10 36.55 N 76.01 W
Henry, Mount, mtn., Mt., U.S. 146 B11 48.53 N 115.31 W
Henry, Mount, hill, Austl. 192a 33.50 S 150.38 E
Henryetta, Ok., U.S. 134 B2 35.27 N 95.59 W
Henry Horton State Park, p.o.i., Tn., U.S. 134 B12 35.35 N 86.42 W
Henry Kater, Cape, c., Nu., Can. 110 B17 69.10 N 66.45 W
Henry Mountains, mts., Ut., U.S. 150 F6 38.00 N 110.50 W
Henrys Fork, stm., U.S. 150 B7 40.58 N 109.34 W
Henrys Fork, stm., Id., U.S. 146 F15 43.45 N 111.56 W
Henry W. Coe State Park, p.o.i., Ca., U.S. 148 F4 37.12 N 121.27 W
Hensall, On., Can. 126 E8 43.28 N 81.29 W
Henshaw, Lake, res., Ca., U.S. 148 J9 33.14 N 116.44 W
Hensley, Ar., U.S. 134 C6 34.30 N 92.12 W
Henslow, Cape, c., Sol. Is. 101b e9 9.56 S 160.38 E
Henson Creek, stm., Md., U.S. 202b 38.46 N 77.00 W
Hentiesbaai, Nmb. 90 C2 22.06 S 14.16 E
Hentiyn nuruu, mts., Mong. 50 G10 48.30 N 108.30 E
Henty, Austl. 98 J6 35.31 S 147.02 E
Henzada, Mya. 64 D2 17.38 N 95.28 E
Hepburn, Sk., Can. 142 B7 52.31 N 106.43 W
Hephzibah, Ga., U.S. 132 C3 33.18 N 82.07 W
Heping, China 58 K5 22.00 N 112.59 E
Heping, China 58 H7 27.10 N 117.18 E
Heppenheim, Ger. 24 G4 49.38 N 8.38 E
Heppner, Or., U.S. 146 E7 45.21 N 119.32 W
Heptonstall, Eng., U.K. 180 53.45 N 2.01 W
Heptonstall Moor, stm., Eng., U.K. 180 53.46 N 2.05 W
Hepu, China 58 K3 21.40 N 109.11 E
Hequ, China 58 B4 39.26 N 111.10 E
Héraðsflói, b., Ice. 12a k32 65.43 N 14.13 W
Herāt, Afg. 72 C9 34.20 N 62.11 E
Hérault, state, Fr. 22 F9 43.40 N 3.30 E
Hérault, stm., Fr. 22 F9 43.17 N 3.26 E
Herbert, Sk., Can. 142 D6 50.26 N 107.12 W
Herbertabad, India 62 F7 11.43 N 92.36 E
Herbert Hoover National Historic Site, p.o.i., Ia., U.S. 130 C6 41.37 N 91.21 W
Herberton, Austl. 98 A5 17.24 S 145.23 E
Herbertsdale, S. Afr. 90 H5 34.00 S 21.45 E
Herborn, Ger. 24 F4 50.40 N 8.18 E
Herbringhauser-Stausee, res., Ger. 181 51.14 N 7.16 E
Herceg-Novi, Yugo. 36 G5 42.27 N 18.32 E
Herculaneum, Mo., U.S. 130 F7 38.16 N 90.23 W
Hércules, Mex. 154 A7 28.03 N 103.53 W
Hercules, Ca., U.S. 200 38.01 N 122.17 W
Herðubreið, vol., Ice. 12a k31 65.12 N 16.19 W
Heredia, C.R. 156 G6 9.59 N 84.07 W
Hereford, Eng., U.K. 10 I10 52.03 N 2.43 W
Hereford, Az., U.S. 150 L6 31.26 N 110.05 W
Hereford, Tx., U.S. 138 G6 34.49 N 102.24 W
Hereke, Tur. 34 C12 40.48 N 29.40 E
Herencia, Spain 28 E7 39.22 N 3.21 W
Herford, Ger. 24 D4 52.06 N 8.40 E
Herington, Ks., U.S. 138 C11 38.40 N 96.56 W
Herisau, Switz. 30 C6 47.23 N 9.16 E
Herkimer, N.Y., U.S. 126 E15 43.02 N 74.58 W
Herlen see Kerulen, stm., Asia 52 B7 48.45 N 117.02 E
Herleshausen, Ger. 24 E6 51.00 N 10.09 E
Herlong, Ca., U.S. 148 C5 40.08 N 120.08 W
Hermagor, Aus. 30 D10 46.37 N 13.22 E
Herman, Mn., U.S. 128 F2 45.47 N 96.09 W
Herman, Ne., U.S. 130 C1 41.40 N 96.12 W
Herman, Lake, l., Ca., U.S. 200 38.05 N 122.09 W
Hermanas, Mex. 136 G6 27.13 N 101.13 W
Hermanavičy, Bela. 26 E10 55.25 N 27.44 E
Herman Eksteen Park, p.o.i., S. Afr. 191d 26.10 S 28.02 E
Hermann, Mo., U.S. 130 F6 38.42 N 91.26 W
Hermanns-Denkmal, hist., Ger. 24 E4 51.55 N 8.50 E
Hermannskogel, mtn., Aus. 182b 48.16 N 16.18 E
Hermannstadt see Sibiu, Rom. 36 D11 45.47 N 24.09 E
Hermansverk, Nor. 16 F4 61.10 N 6.54 E
Hermansville, Mi., U.S. 126 C2 45.42 N 87.36 W
Hermanus, S. Afr. 90 I4 34.24 S 19.16 E
Hermanville, Ms., U.S. 134 F8 31.57 N 90.50 W
Hermeray, Fr. 179 48.38 N 1.41 E
Hermidale, Austl. 98 H6 31.32 S 146.43 E
Hermiston, Or., U.S. 146 E7 45.50 N 119.17 W
Hermitage, Ar., U.S. 134 D6 33.28 N 92.10 W
Hermitage, Mo., U.S. 130 G4 37.56 N 93.19 W
Hermitage Park, Md., U.S. 202c 39.05 N 77.04 W
Hermit Islands, is., Pap. N. Gui. 101a a4 1.30 S 145.05 E
Hermleigh, Tx., U.S. 136 B7 32.38 N 100.46 W
Hermon, Mount (Shaykh, Jabal ash-), mtn., Asia 76 E6 33.25 N 35.51 E
Hermosa Beach, Ca., U.S. 198 33.51 N 118.23 W
Hermosillo, Mex. 150 K1 32.30 N 114.59 W
Hermosillo, Mex. 154 A3 29.05 N 110.58 W
Hermoso, Cerro, mtn., Ec. 168 H2 1.13 S 78.17 W
Hermus see Gediz, stm., Tur. 34 E10 38.35 N 26.47 E
Hermyingyi, Mya. 64 E4 14.15 N 98.21 E
Hernád (Hornád), stm., Eur. 24 H17 47.59 N 21.02 E
Hernals, ngh., Aus. 182b 48.13 N 16.20 E
Hernandarias, Arg. 172 E8 31.13 S 59.58 W
Hernandarias, Para. 172 B10 25.21 S 54.39 W
Hernando, Arg. 172 F6 32.26 S 63.43 W
Hernando, Fl., U.S. 132 H3 28.54 N 82.22 W
Hernando, Ms., U.S. 134 C9 34.50 N 89.59 W
Herndon, Ks., U.S. 138 B8 39.54 N 100.46 W
Herndon, Pa., U.S. 124 D9 40.42 N 76.50 W
Herne, Ger. 20 C16 51.32 N 7.13 E
Herne Bay, Eng., U.K. 10 J14 51.21 N 1.07 E
Herning, Den. 16 K6 56.08 N 8.59 E
Hernwood Heights, Md., U.S. 202b 39.22 N 77.50 W
Heroica Zitácuaro, Mex. 154 F8 19.26 N 100.21 W
Herongate, Eng., U.K. 178 51.36 N 0.21 E
Heron Island, i., Austl. 98 D8 23.26 S 151.55 E
Heron Lake, Mn., U.S. 128 H3 43.47 N 95.19 W
Hérons, Île aux, i., Qc., Can. 193a 45.25 N 73.35 W
Heronsgate, Eng., U.K. 178 51.38 N 0.31 W
Hérouville, Fr. 179 49.06 N 2.08 E
Hérouville-Saint-Clair, Fr. 20 E8 49.11 N 0.20 W
Herøyholmen, Nor. 16 A10 65.59 N 12.18 E
Herpuči, Russia 50 F16 53.00 N 138.53 E
Herradura, Arg. 172 C8 26.29 S 58.18 W
Herreid, S.D., U.S. 140 B12 45.50 N 100.04 W
Herrera, Arg. 172 D6 28.26 S 63.04 W
Herrera del Duque, Spain 28 E6 39.10 N 5.03 W
Herrera de Pisuerga, Spain 28 B6 42.36 N 4.19 W
Herrick, Austl. 99a n13 41.06 S 147.52 E
Herrick Creek, stm., B.C., Can. 144 B9 54.15 N 121.28 W
Herricks, N.Y., U.S. 194 40.45 N 73.40 W
Herrin, Il., U.S. 130 G8 37.48 N 89.01 W
Herring Brook, stm., Ma., U.S. 201 42.10 N 70.44 W
Herring Cove, N.S., Can. 122 F13 44.34 N 63.34 W
Herring Run, stm., Md., U.S. 202b 39.18 N 76.31 W
Herring Run Park, p.o.i., Md., U.S. 202b 39.19 N 76.33 W
Herrs Island, i., Pa., U.S. 197b 40.28 N 79.58 W
Hers, stm., Fr. 22 F8 43.12 N 1.44 E
Hersbruck, Ger. 24 G7 49.30 N 11.25 E
Herschel, Sk., Can. 142 C5 51.38 N 108.21 W
Herschel, S. Afr. 90 G8 30.36 S 27.11 E
Herschel Island, i., Yk., Can. 109 C12 69.35 N 139.05 W
Herscher, Il., U.S. 130 C9 41.02 N 88.06 W
Hersham, Eng., U.K. 178 51.22 N 0.23 W
Hershey, Ne., U.S. 140 F11 41.09 N 101.00 W
Hershey, Pa., U.S. 124 D9 40.17 N 76.39 W
Herstal, Bel. 20 D14 50.40 N 5.38 E
Hertford, Eng., U.K. 10 J12 51.48 N 0.05 W
Hertford, N.C., U.S. 124 H9 36.11 N 76.28 W
Hertingfordbury, Eng., U.K. 178 51.48 N 0.06 W
Hertogenbosch, 's- see 's-Hertogenbosch, Neth. 20 C14 51.41 N 5.19 E
Hertsa, Ukr. 38 E5 48.09 N 26.16 E
Hertsmere, mun., Eng., U.K. 178 51.41 N 0.17 W
Hertzogville, S. Afr. 90 F7 28.07 S 25.31 E
Herval d'Oeste, Braz. 172 C12 27.11 S 51.29 W
Hervás, Spain 28 D5 40.16 N 5.51 W
Hervest, Ger. 181 51.40 N 7.01 E
Hervey Bay, b., Austl. 98 E9 25.00 S 153.00 E
Hervey-Jonction, Qc., Can. 122 D4 46.51 N 72.28 W
Herzberg, Ger. 24 E9 51.41 N 13.14 E
Herzberg am Harz, Ger. 24 E6 51.38 N 10.19 E
Hesarak, Iran 185d 35.47 N 51.19 E
Hesdin, Fr. 20 D11 50.22 N 2.02 E
Heshan, China 58 J3 23.42 N 108.55 E
Heshui, China 58 J4 22.18 N 111.52 E
Heshun, China 58 C5 37.19 N 113.35 E
Hesketh Bank, Eng., U.K. 180 53.42 N 2.51 W
Hesketh Out Marsh, sw., Eng., U.K. 180 53.43 N 2.55 W
Heskin Green, Eng., U.K. 180 53.38 N 2.42 W
Hesperia, Mi., U.S. 126 E3 43.33 N 86.02 W
Hesperus Mountain, mtn., Co., U.S. 150 F8 37.27 N 108.05 W
Hess, stm., Yk., Can. 110 C4 63.34 N 133.57 W
Hesselø, i., Den. 16 K9 56.11 N 11.43 E
Hessen, state, Ger. 24 F5 50.30 N 9.15 E
Hesston, Ks., U.S. 138 C11 38.08 N 97.25 W
Hestkjølen, mtn., Nor. 16 C12 64.19 N 14.02 E
Hestmona, mtn., Nor. 14 F3 66.32 N 12.48 E
Heston, ngh., Eng., U.K. 178 51.29 N 0.22 W
Het, stm., Laos 64 B6 20.49 N 104.00 E
Heta, stm., Russia 50 B8 71.54 N 102.06 E

Name	Page	Map Ref.	Latitude	Longitude
Hetai, China	58	J5	23.28 N	112.18 E
Hetang, China	58	H8	26.40 N	119.09 E
Hetaundā, Nepal	70	E10	27.25 N	85.01 E
Hetch Hetchy Aqueduct, aq., Ca., U.S.	148	F4	37.28 N	122.19 W
Hetian, China	58	I7	25.39 N	116.25 E
Hetögeln, l., Swe.	16	C12	64.24 N	14.18 E
Hetolambina, Russia	14	F24	66.18 N	33.15 E
Hettinger, N.D., U.S.	140	B10	46.00 N	102.38 W
Hettstedt, Ger.	24	E7	51.38 N	11.30 E
Hetzendorf, ngh., Aus.	182b		48.10 N	16.18 E
Heung (Huang), stm., Asia	64	D5	17.48 N	101.33 E
Heuvelton, N.Y., U.S.	126	D14	44.37 N	75.24 W
Heven, Ger.	181		51.26 N	7.17 E
Heves, Hung.	36	B7	47.35 N	20.17 E
Heves, state, Hung.	36	A7	47.50 N	20.15 E
Hewanorra International Airport, arpt., St. Luc.	159c	m7	13.43 N	60.57 W
Hewlett, N.Y., U.S.	194		40.38 N	73.41 W
Hewlett Bay Park, N.Y., U.S.	194		40.38 N	73.42 W
Hewlett Harbor, N.Y., U.S.	194		40.38 N	73.41 W
Hewlett Neck, N.Y., U.S.	194		40.37 N	73.42 W
Hewlett Point, c., N.Y., U.S.	194		40.50 N	73.45 W
Hewu, China	58	H5	26.41 N	113.40 E
Hexham, Eng., U.K.	10	F11	54.58 N	2.06 W
Hexian, China	58	I4	24.18 N	111.39 E
Hexigten Qi, China	54	C2	43.14 N	117.31 E
Hextable, Eng., U.K.	178		51.25 N	0.11 E
Heyang, China	58	D3	35.14 N	110.07 E
Heybeli, ngh., Tur.	185b		40.53 N	29.05 E
Heybeli Ada, i., Tur.	185b		40.53 N	29.05 E
Heybridge, Eng., U.K.	178		51.40 N	0.22 E
Heybridge, Eng., U.K.	178		51.44 N	0.41 E
Heyburn, Id., U.S.	146	H13	42.34 N	113.45 W
Heysham, Eng., U.K.	10	G10	54.01 N	2.54 W
Heyuan, China	58	J6	23.43 N	114.41 E
Heywood, Austl.	98	L3	38.07 S	141.38 E
Heyworth, Il., U.S.	130	D9	40.18 N	88.58 W
Heze, China	58	D6	35.14 N	115.26 E
Hezheng, China	52	D5	35.27 N	103.16 E
Hialeah, Fl., U.S.	132	K5	25.50 N	80.16 W
Hian, Ghana	84	G4	10.41 N	2.27 W
Hiaohexi, China	58	F6	31.20 N	114.04 E
Hiawassee, Ga., U.S.	132	B2	34.57 N	83.45 W
Hiawatha, Ks., U.S.	130	E2	39.51 N	95.32 W
Hiawatha, Ut., U.S.	150	D6	39.28 N	111.00 W
Hibbard, Qc., Can.	122	C2	47.52 N	74.02 W
Hibbing, Mn., U.S.	128	D5	47.25 N	92.56 W
Hibbs, Point, c., Austl.	99a	o12	42.37 S	145.15 E
Hibernia, N.J., U.S.	194		40.57 N	74.30 W
Hibiny, Russia	14	E24	67.41 N	33.12 E
Hickman, Ky., U.S.	130	H8	36.34 N	89.11 W
Hickman, Ne., U.S.	128	K2	40.38 N	96.39 W
Hickman, Pa., U.S.	197b		40.23 N	80.09 W
Hickory, Ms., U.S.	134	E9	32.19 N	89.01 W
Hickory, N.C., U.S.	124	I4	35.44 N	81.21 W
Hickory Creek, stm., Il., U.S.	196		41.30 N	88.06 W
Hickory Flat, Ms., U.S.	134	C9	34.37 N	89.11 W
Hickory Run State Park, p.o.i., Pa., U.S.	124	C10	41.02 N	75.41 W
Hicks, Point, c., Austl.	98	K7	37.47 S	149.16 E
Hicksville, Oh., U.S.	124	C1	41.17 N	84.45 W
Hico, Tx., U.S.	136	C9	31.57 N	98.02 W
Hida see Hita, Japan	56	F3	33.18 N	130.56 E
Hidalgo, Mex.	116	H3	24.14 N	99.26 W
Hidalgo, Mex.	154	B8	25.58 N	100.26 W
Hidalgo, Mex.	154	B9	27.47 N	99.52 W
Hidalgo, Mex.	154	C9	24.09 N	104.35 W
Hidalgo, state, Mex.	154	E9	20.30 N	99.00 W
Hidalgo del Parral, Mex.	154	B6	26.56 N	105.40 W
Hida-sammyaku, mts., Japan	56	C10	36.25 N	137.40 E
Hiddinghausen, Ger.	181		51.22 N	7.17 E
Hidra, i., Nor.	16	I4	58.13 N	6.35 E
Hidrolândia, Braz.	170	I1	16.58 S	49.14 W
Hieflau, Aus.	30	C11	47.36 N	14.44 E
Hien, Viet.	64	E8	15.54 N	107.34 E
Hienghène, N. Cal.	101d	m15	20.41 S	164.55 E
Hierapolis see Pamukkale, hist., Tur.	34	F12	37.58 N	29.19 E
Hiesfeld, Ger.	181		51.33 N	6.46 E
Hietzing, ngh., Aus.	182b		48.11 N	16.18 E
Higashi, ngh., Japan	188		34.41 N	135.31 E
Higashibetsuin, Japan	188		34.56 N	135.34 E
Higashihiroshima, Japan	56	E5	34.25 N	132.43 E
Higashiichiki, Japan	56	H3	31.40 N	130.20 E
Higashikurume, Japan	186		35.45 N	139.32 E
Higashimonzen, Japan	186		35.56 N	139.40 E
Higashinada, ngh., Japan	188		34.43 N	135.16 E
Higashinakano, Japan	186		35.38 N	139.25 E
Higashinari, ngh., Japan	188		34.40 N	135.33 E
Higashine, Japan	56	A13	38.26 N	140.24 E
Higashinose, Japan	188		34.55 N	135.30 E
Higashiōizumi, ngh., Japan	186		35.45 N	139.36 E
Higashiōsaka, Japan	56	E8	34.39 N	135.35 E
Higashisumiyoshi, ngh., Japan	188		34.37 N	135.32 E
Higashiura, Japan	188		34.33 N	135.00 E
Higashiyama, ngh., Japan	188		35.00 N	135.48 E
Higashiyamato, Japan	186		35.44 N	139.26 E
Higashiyodogawa, ngh., Japan	188		34.44 N	135.31 E
Higasi Sina Kai see East China Sea, s., Asia	52	F9	30.00 N	126.00 E
Higbee, Mo., U.S.	130	E5	39.18 N	92.30 W
Higgins, Tx., U.S.	138	E8	36.07 N	100.02 W
Higgins Lake, l., Mi., U.S.	126	D5	44.29 N	84.44 W
Higginsville, Austl.	96	F4	31.44 S	121.43 E
Higginsville, Mo., U.S.	130	E4	39.04 N	93.43 W
Higham Upshire, Eng., U.K.	178		51.26 N	0.28 E
High Bar Indian Reserve, ind. res., B.C., Can.	144	E8	51.06 N	121.59 W
High Beach, Eng., U.K.	178		51.39 N	0.02 E
Highbury, Austl.	96	C8	16.25 S	143.09 E
Highcliff, Pa., U.S.	197b		40.32 N	80.03 W
Higher Ballam, Eng., U.K.	180		53.46 N	2.59 W
Higher Broughton, ngh., Eng., U.K.	180		53.30 N	2.15 W
Higher Hogshead, hill, Eng., U.K.	180		53.42 N	2.09 W
Higher Penwortham, Eng., U.K.	180		53.45 N	2.44 W
Higher Walton, Eng., U.K.	180		53.22 N	2.37 W
Higher Whitley, Eng., U.K.	180		53.19 N	2.35 W
Highett, Austl.	192b		37.57 S	145.03 E
High Halstow, Eng., U.K.	178		51.27 N	0.34 E
High Hill, hill, N.Y., U.S.	194		40.49 N	73.25 W
High Island, i., China	189d		22.22 N	114.21 E
High Island, i., Mi., U.S.	126	C4	45.43 N	85.40 W
High Island Creek, stm., Mn., U.S.	128	G4	44.34 N	93.54 W
High Island Reservoir, res., China	189d		22.23 N	114.21 E
Highland, Il., U.S.	130	F8	38.44 N	89.40 W
Highland, In., U.S.	130	C10	41.33 N	87.27 W
Highland, Ks., U.S.	130	E2	39.49 N	95.16 W
Highland, Mi., U.S.	199		42.38 N	83.37 W
Highland, Pa., U.S.	197b		40.33 N	80.04 W
Highland Creek, stm., On., Can.	193b		43.46 N	79.08 W
Highland Hills, Il., U.S.	196		41.52 N	88.01 W
Highland Home, Al., U.S.	134	F12	31.57 N	86.18 W
Highland Lake, Il., U.S.	196		42.21 N	88.04 W
Highland Lake, Ma., U.S.	201		42.41 N	72.37 W
Highland Lake, l., Il., U.S.	196		42.22 N	88.04 W
Highland Lake, l., N.J., U.S.	194		41.10 N	74.28 W
Highland-on-the-Lake, N.Y., U.S.	202a		42.42 N	79.59 W
Highland Park, Il., U.S.	130	B10	42.10 N	87.46 W
Highland Park, Md., U.S.	202c		38.54 N	76.54 W
Highland Park, ngh., Ca., U.S.	198		34.07 N	118.13 W
Highland Park, p.o.i., Ma., U.S.	201		42.30 N	70.55 W
Highland Park, p.o.i., Pa., U.S.	197b		40.29 N	79.55 W
Highland Peak, mtn., Ca., U.S.	148	E6	38.33 N	119.45 W
Highlands, N.J., U.S.	124	D12	40.24 N	73.59 W
Highlands, N.C., U.S.	132	A2	35.03 N	83.12 W
Highlands, Tx., U.S.	136	E12	29.48 N	95.03 W
Highlands North, ngh., S. Afr.	191d		26.09 S	28.05 E
Highlandtown, ngh., Md., U.S.	202b		39.17 N	76.33 W
High Laver, Eng., U.K.	178		51.45 N	0.13 E
High Legh, Eng., U.K.	180		53.21 N	2.27 W
High Level, Ab., Can.	110	D7	58.31 N	117.08 W
Highmore, S.D., U.S.	140	C13	44.31 N	99.26 W
High Ongar, Eng., U.K.	178		51.43 N	0.16 E
High Park, p.o.i., On., Can.	193b		43.39 N	79.28 W
High Peak, mun., Eng., U.K.	180		53.23 N	1.55 W
High Peak, mtn., Phil.	68	C3	15.29 N	120.07 E
High Point, N.C., U.S.	124	I5	35.57 N	80.00 W
High Point, mtn., N.J., U.S.	124	C11	41.19 N	74.40 W
High Point, mtn., Wy., U.S.	150	B9	41.37 N	107.47 W
High Point State Park, p.o.i., N.J., U.S.	124	C11	41.18 N	74.41 W
High River, Ab., Can.	144	F17	50.34 N	113.52 W
High Rock, Bah.	132	J7	26.37 N	78.17 W
High Rock, mtn., Md., U.S.	124	E6	39.33 N	79.06 W
Highrock Lake, l., Mb., Can.	110	D10	55.45 N	100.30 W
Highrock Lake, l., Sk., Can.	110	D9	57.04 N	105.29 W
High Rock Lake, res., N.C., U.S.	132	A5	35.37 N	80.17 W
High Springs, Fl., U.S.	132	G3	29.49 N	82.35 W
High Tatra Mountains see Tatry, mts., Eur.	24	G15	49.11 N	20.08 E
Hightstown, N.J., U.S.	124	D11	40.16 N	74.31 W
High Willhays, mtn., Eng., U.K.	10	K9	50.40 N	4.00 W
Highwood, Mt., U.S.	146	C16	47.34 N	110.47 W
Highwood, stm., Ab., Can.	144	F17	50.49 N	113.46 W
Highwood Baldy, mtn., Mt., U.S.	146	C16	47.27 N	110.37 W
Highwood Creek, stm., Mt., U.S.	146	C16	47.40 N	111.00 W
Highwood Mountains, mts., Mt., U.S.	146	C16	47.25 N	110.30 W
High Wycombe, Eng., U.K.	10	J12	51.37 N	0.45 W
Higuera de Abuya, Mex.	154	C5	24.15 N	107.05 W
Higuera de Zaragoza, Mex.	154	B4	25.57 N	109.17 W
Higueras, Mex.	136	I8	25.58 N	100.01 W
Higüero, Punta, c., P.R.	158a	b1	18.22 N	67.15 W
Higüey, Dom. Rep.	156	C13	18.37 N	68.42 W
Hiidenportin kansallispuisto, p.o.i., Fin.	18	D15	63.50 N	28.59 E
Hiitola, Russia	18	F16	61.14 N	29.43 E
Hiiumaa, i., Est.	26	B5	58.55 N	22.38 E
Híjar, Spain	28	C10	41.11 N	0.27 W
Hikari, Japan	56	F4	33.57 N	131.56 E
Hikarigaoka, Japan	186		35.50 N	139.58 E
Hikawa Shrine, rel., Japan	186		35.54 N	139.38 E
Hikiura, Japan	188		34.33 N	134.58 E
Hikone, Japan	56	D9	35.15 N	136.15 E
Hikurangi, mtn., N.Z.	102	C8	37.55 S	178.04 E
Hilbert, Wi., U.S.	126	D1	44.08 N	88.09 W
Hilbre Islands, is., Eng., U.K.	180		53.23 N	3.13 W
Hilbre Point, c., Eng., U.K.	180		53.23 N	3.12 W
Hilda, Ab., Can.	142	D3	50.28 N	110.03 W
Hildburghausen, Ger.	24	F6	50.25 N	10.44 E
Hildenborough, Eng., U.K.	178		51.13 N	0.15 E
Hildesheim, Ger.	24	D5	52.09 N	9.57 E
Hildreth, Ne., U.S.	138	A9	40.20 N	99.02 W
Hilgen, Ger.	181		51.06 N	7.09 E
Hiliotaluwa, Indon.	64	L3	0.42 N	97.52 E
Hilla see Al-Ḥillah, Iraq	74	D9	32.28 N	44.26 E
Hillaby, Mount, mtn., Barb.	159d	n8	13.12 N	59.35 W
Hill Air Force Base, mil., Ut., U.S.	150	B3	41.03 N	113.12 W
Hillandale, Md., U.S.	202c		39.01 N	76.58 W
Hillandale Heights, Md., U.S.	202c		39.01 N	76.59 W
Hill Bank, Belize	156	D3	17.35 N	88.42 W
Hill City, Ks., U.S.	138	B9	39.21 N	99.50 W
Hill City, Mn., U.S.	128	D5	46.59 N	93.35 W
Hill City, S.D., U.S.	140	D9	43.55 N	103.34 W
Hill Creek, stm., Ut., U.S.	150	D7	39.55 N	109.39 W
Hillcrest Heights, Md., U.S.	202c		38.49 N	76.57 W
Hillcrest Mines, Ab., Can.	144	G16	49.34 N	114.22 W
Hillcrest Park, Ca., U.S.	200		38.07 N	122.16 W
Hillerød, Den.	16	L10	55.56 N	12.18 E
Hilli, Bngl.	70	F12	25.16 N	89.00 E
Hilliard, Fl., U.S.	132	F4	30.41 N	81.54 W
Hill Island Lake, l., N.T., Can.	110	C9	60.29 N	109.50 W
Hillister, Tx., U.S.	136	D13	30.39 N	94.23 W
Hillman, Mi., U.S.	126	C6	45.03 N	83.54 W
Hills, Mn., U.S.	128	H2	43.31 N	96.21 W
Hillsboro, Il., U.S.	130	E8	39.08 N	89.29 W
Hillsboro, Ks., U.S.	138	C11	38.21 N	97.12 W
Hillsboro, Mo., U.S.	130	F7	38.14 N	90.33 W
Hillsboro, N.M., U.S.	150	K9	32.55 N	107.33 W
Hillsboro, N.D., U.S.	128	D1	47.24 N	97.03 W
Hillsboro, Oh., U.S.	124	E2	39.11 N	83.36 W
Hillsboro, Or., U.S.	146	E3	45.31 N	122.58 W
Hillsboro, Tx., U.S.	136	B10	32.00 N	97.07 W
Hillsboro, Wi., U.S.	128	H8	43.38 N	90.20 W
Hillsboro Canal, can., Fl., U.S.	132	J5	26.19 N	80.05 W
Hillsborough, N.B., Can.	122	E12	45.55 N	64.39 W
Hillsborough, Gren.	159e	q11	12.28 N	61.27 W
Hillsborough, N.C., U.S.	124	H6	36.04 N	79.06 W
Hillsborough, stm., Fl., U.S.	132	H3	27.56 N	82.27 W
Hillsborough, Cape, c., Austl.	98	C7	20.55 S	149.01 E
Hillsborough Bay, b., P.E., Can.	122	D13	46.10 N	63.05 W
Hillsdale, Mi., U.S.	130	C13	41.55 N	84.37 W
Hillsdale, N.J., U.S.	194		41.00 N	74.02 W
Hillsdale, shp. cen., Ca., U.S.	200		37.32 N	122.18 W
Hillsdale Lake, l., Ks., U.S.	130	F3	38.40 N	94.55 W
Hillside, Il., U.S.	196		41.52 N	87.54 W
Hillside, N.J., U.S.	194		40.42 N	74.13 W
Hillside, ngh., N.Y., U.S.	194		40.42 N	73.47 W
Hillside Heights, De., U.S.	203		39.41 N	75.41 W
Hillston, Austl.	98	I5	33.29 S	145.32 E
Hillsville, Va., U.S.	124	H5	36.45 N	80.44 W
Hillswick, Scot., U.K.	10a	n18	60.29 N	1.29 W
Hilltop Center, shp. cen., Ca., U.S.	200		37.59 N	122.19 W
Hillview Reservoir, res., N.Y., U.S.	194		40.55 N	73.52 W
Hillwood, Va., U.S.	202c		38.52 N	77.10 W
Hilo, Hi., U.S.	100a	d6	19.42 N	155.04 W
Hilo Bay, b., Hi., U.S.	100a	d6	19.46 N	155.04 W
Hilok, Russia	50	F11	51.21 N	110.27 E
Hilok, stm., Russia	50	F10	51.18 N	106.58 E
Hilovo, Russia	26	C12	57.46 N	29.23 E
Hilton, N.Y., U.S.	126	E12	43.17 N	77.47 W
Hilton Head Island, i., S.C., U.S.	132	D5	32.12 N	80.45 W
Hiltrop, ngh., Ger.	181		51.30 N	7.15 E
Hilvan, Tur.	76	A9	37.34 N	38.57 E
Hilversum, Neth.	20	B14	52.13 N	5.11 E
Hima, Ky., U.S.	124	G2	37.07 N	83.46 W
Himāchal Pradesh, state, India	70	B6	32.00 N	77.00 E
Himalayas, mts., Asia	46	F11	29.00 N	83.00 E
Himalayas, mts., Asia	46	G12	28.00 N	84.00 E
Himalaya Shan see Himalayas, mts., Asia	46	G12	28.00 N	84.00 E
Himanka, Fin.	18	C10	64.02 N	23.38 E
Himarë, Alb.	32	D13	40.07 N	19.44 E
Himatnagar, India	70	G4	23.34 N	72.58 E
Himeji, Japan	56	E7	34.49 N	134.42 E
Himi, Japan	56	C9	36.51 N	136.59 E
Himki, Russia	26	E20	55.53 N	37.26 E
Himki, Russia	183b		55.54 N	37.26 E
Himki-Hovrino, ngh., Russia	183b		55.51 N	37.30 E
Himkinskoe vodohranilišče, res., Russia	183b		55.51 N	37.28 E
Himmelbjerget, hill, Den.	16	K7	56.06 N	9.42 E
Himmelgeist, ngh., Ger.	181		51.10 N	6.49 E
Himmerland, pen., Den.	16	K7	56.51 N	9.30 E
Ḥimṣ (Homs), Syria	76	D7	34.44 N	36.43 E
Ḥimṣ, state, Syria	74	C6	34.15 N	38.00 E
Ḥīnah, Syria	76	E6	33.21 N	35.56 E
Hinchinbrook Island, i., Austl.	98	B6	18.23 S	146.17 E
Hinchinbrook Island, i., Ak., U.S.	109	D10	60.22 N	146.28 W
Hinchinbrook Island National Park, p.o.i., Austl.	98	B6	18.22 S	146.15 E
Hinckley, Il., U.S.	130	C9	41.46 N	88.37 W
Hinckley, Mn., U.S.	128	E5	46.00 N	92.56 W
Hinckley, Ut., U.S.	150	D4	39.19 N	112.40 W
Hindan, stm., India	190a		28.30 N	77.27 E
Hindang, Phil.	68	E5	10.26 N	124.44 E
Hindås, Swe.	16	J10	57.39 N	12.23 E
Hindaun, India	70	E6	26.43 N	77.01 E
Hindenburg see Zabrze, Pol.	24	F14	50.18 N	18.46 E
Hindley Green, Eng., U.K.	180		53.31 N	2.32 W
Hindman, Ky., U.S.	124	G3	37.20 N	82.59 W
Hindmarsh, Lake, l., Austl.	98	J3	36.03 S	141.55 E
Hindu Kush, mts., Asia	72	B11	36.00 N	71.30 E
Hindupur, India	69	E3	13.49 N	77.29 E
Hi-Nella, N.J., U.S.	203		39.50 N	75.01 W
Hines, Or., U.S.	146	G7	43.33 N	119.05 W
Hinesville, Ga., U.S.	132	E4	31.49 N	81.30 W
Hinganghāt, India	70	H7	20.33 N	78.50 E
Hingham, Ma., U.S.	124	B15	42.14 N	70.53 W
Hingham Harbor, b., Ma., U.S.	201		42.15 N	70.53 W
Hingol, stm., Pak.	62	C2	25.22 N	65.30 E
Hingoli, India	69	B3	19.43 N	77.08 E
Hinigaran, Phil.	68	E4	10.17 N	122.51 E
Hınıs, Tur.	42	F9	39.20 N	41.44 E
Hinlopenstretet, strt., Nor.	108	A29	79.19 N	20.16 E
Hinnerjoki, Fin.	18	G9	60.59 N	21.58 E
Hinnøya, i., Nor.	14	D6	68.32 N	15.58 E
Hino, stm., Japan	56	D6	35.27 N	133.22 E
Hinojosa del Duque, Spain	28	F5	38.30 N	5.09 W
Hinokage, Japan	56	G4	32.38 N	131.23 E
Hinsdale, Mt., U.S.	142	F6	48.23 N	107.05 W
Hinsdale, N.H., U.S.	124	B13	42.46 N	72.28 W
Hinsel, ngh., Ger.	181		51.26 N	7.05 E
Hinterrhein, stm., Switz.	30	D6	46.49 N	9.24 E
Hintersdorf, Aus.	182b		48.18 N	16.13 E
Hinton, Ab., Can.	144	C13	53.24 N	117.33 W
Hinton, Ok., U.S.	138	F10	35.27 N	98.21 W
Hinton, W.V., U.S.	124	G5	37.40 N	80.53 W
Hípico, Club, p.o.i., Chile	204e		33.28 S	70.41 W
Hipólito, Mex.	154	C8	25.40 N	101.26 W
Hipólito Yrigoyen, Arg.	172	F4	32.56 S	66.19 W
Hirado, Japan	56	F2	33.22 N	129.33 E
Hirado-shima, i., Japan	56	F2	33.20 N	129.30 E
Hirakata, Japan	186		35.56 N	139.33 E
Hirakawa, Japan	188		34.52 N	135.47 E
Hīrākud, India	70	H9	21.29 N	83.52 E
Hīrākud Reservoir, res., India	70	H10	21.35 N	83.48 E
Hiram, Me., U.S.	122	G6	43.52 N	70.48 W
Hirano, ngh., Japan	188		34.36 N	135.34 E
Hiraoka see Higashiōsaka, Japan	56	E8	34.39 N	135.35 E
Hirāpur, India	70	F7	24.21 N	79.13 E
Hirara, Japan	52	G10	24.47 N	125.17 E
Hirata, Japan	56	D5	35.26 N	132.49 E
Hiratsuka, Japan	56	D12	35.19 N	139.21 E
Hirhafok, Alg.	84	E6	23.38 N	5.45 E
Hiriyūr, India	69	E3	13.57 N	76.36 E
Hīrmand, stm., Asia	70	A1	34.22 N	67.54 E
Hirnyk, Ukr.	38	E16	48.03 N	37.22 E
Hirnyk, Ukr.	38	C3	50.20 N	24.12 E
Hirnyts'ke, Ukr.	38	F13	47.42 N	34.08 E
Hirooka, Japan	186		35.15 N	140.04 E
Hirosaki, Japan	54	D14	40.35 N	140.28 E
Hiroshima, Japan	56	E5	34.23 N	132.28 E
Hiroshima, state, Japan	56	E5	34.30 N	133.00 E
Hirosima see Hiroshima, Japan	56	E5	34.23 N	132.28 E
Hirota, Japan	188		34.45 N	135.21 E
Hirovo, Russia	26	B16	58.56 N	33.24 E
Hirschberg see Jelenia Góra, Pol.	24	F11	50.54 N	15.43 E
Hirschfelde, Ger.	182a		52.38 N	13.48 E
Hirschstetten, ngh., Aus.	182b		48.14 N	16.29 E
Hirshfeld Brook, stm., N.J., U.S.	194		40.57 N	74.02 W
Hirs'ke, Ukr.	38	E17	48.46 N	38.30 E
Hirs'kyi Tikych, stm., Ukr.	38	D9	48.47 N	30.52 E
Hirson, Fr.	20	E13	49.55 N	4.05 E
Hirtshals, Den.	16	J7	57.35 N	9.58 E
Hirvosti, Russia	183a		59.57 N	30.37 E
Hisābpur, India	190b		22.51 N	88.32 E
Hisai, Japan	188		34.25 N	135.28 E
Hisār, India	70	D5	29.09 N	75.43 E
Hisarönü, Tur.	34	B14	41.33 N	32.01 E
Hislaviči, Russia	26	F15	54.11 N	32.09 E
Ḥismā, pl., Sau. Ar.	76	J5	28.11 N	34.52 E
Hispaniola, i., N.A.	152	D10	19.00 N	71.00 W
Histjakovo see Torez, Ukr.	38	E17	48.01 N	38.37 E
Hisua, India	70	F10	24.49 N	85.24 E
Hisyah, Syria	76	D7	34.24 N	36.46 E
Hīt, Iraq	74	D8	33.38 N	42.49 E
Hita, Japan	56	F3	33.18 N	130.56 E
Hitachi, Japan	56	C13	36.36 N	140.39 E
Hitachi-ōta, Japan	56	C13	36.32 N	140.31 E
Hitati see Hitachi, Japan	56	C13	36.36 N	140.39 E
Hitchcock, Tx., U.S.	136	E12	29.20 N	95.00 W
Hitchins, Ky., U.S.	124	F3	38.16 N	82.55 W
Hither Green, ngh., Eng., U.K.	178		51.27 N	0.01 W
Hitiaa, Fr. Poly.	100h	v22	17.36 S	149.18 W
Hitokura, Japan	188		34.55 N	135.25 E
Hitotsubashi University, educ., Japan	186		35.42 N	139.27 E
Hitoyoshi, Japan	56	G3	32.12 N	130.46 E
Hitra, i., Nor.	16	D6	63.33 N	8.45 E
Hittarp, Swe.	16	K10	56.05 N	12.39 E
Hitze-Berge, hill, Ger.	182a		52.35 N	13.07 E
Hiu, i., Vanuatu	101d	i16	13.08 S	166.33 E
Hiuchiga-take, vol., Japan	56	C12	36.57 N	139.17 E
Hiuchi-nada, s., Japan	56	E6	34.05 N	133.20 E
Hiva, Uzb.	48	F10	41.24 N	60.22 E
Hiva Oa, i., Fr. Poly.	100g	s19	9.45 S	139.00 W
Hiwannee, Ms., U.S.	134	F10	31.48 N	88.41 W
Hiwasa, Japan	56	F7	33.44 N	134.32 E
Hiwassee, stm., U.S.	134	B14	35.19 N	84.48 W
Hiwassee Lake, res., N.C., U.S.	132	A1	35.06 N	84.07 W
Hixon, B.C., Can.	144	C8	53.26 N	122.36 W
Hixson, Tn., U.S.	134	B13	35.08 N	85.14 W
Hiyoshi, ngh., Japan	186		35.33 N	139.39 E
Hjälmaren, l., Swe.	16	H13	59.15 N	15.45 E
Hjelm, i., Den.	16	K8	56.07 N	10.48 E
Hjelmeland, Nor.	16	H4	59.14 N	6.11 E
Hjelmsøya, i., Nor.	14	A15	71.03 N	24.42 E
Hjerkinn, Nor.	16	E7	62.15 N	9.31 E
Hjerttinden, mtn., Nor.	14	C9	68.59 N	18.11 E
Hjo, Swe.	16	I12	58.18 N	14.16 E
Hjørring, Den.	16	J7	57.28 N	9.59 E
Hkakabo Razi, mtn., Mya.	62	C8	28.17 N	97.45 E
Hkok (Kok), stm., Asia	64	B4	20.14 N	100.08 E
Hladkivka, Ukr.	38	G11	46.23 N	32.36 E
Hlaingbwe, Mya.	64	D3	17.06 N	97.49 E
Hlathikulu, Swaz.	90	E10	26.59 S	31.24 E
Hlebnikovo, Russia	183b		55.58 N	37.31 E
Hlegu, Mya.	64	D3	17.05 N	96.13 E
Hlinsko, Czech Rep.	24	G11	49.45 N	15.55 E
Hlobane, S. Afr.	90	E10	27.42 S	31.00 E
Hlobyne, Ukr.	38	D12	49.22 N	33.17 E
Hlohovec, Slvk.	24	H13	48.25 N	17.48 E
Hlotse, Leso.	90	F9	28.57 S	28.00 E
Hlučín, Czech Rep.	24	G14	49.54 N	18.10 E
Hluhluwe, S. Afr.	90	F11	28.03 S	32.17 E
Hluhluwe Game Reserve, ind. res., S. Afr.	90	F10	28.05 S	32.04 E
Hlukhiv, Ukr.	38	B12	51.40 N	33.54 E
Hluša, Bela.	26	G11	53.04 N	28.51 E
Hlusk, Bela.	26	H11	52.53 N	28.41 E
Hluškavičy, Bela.	38	B6	51.34 N	27.46 E
Hlyboka, Ukr.	38	E4	48.05 N	25.56 E
Hlybokae, Bela.	26	E10	55.08 N	27.42 E
Hlyniany, Ukr.	38	D3	49.49 N	24.31 E
Hmawbi, Mya.	64	D2	17.06 N	96.00 E
Hmelita, Russia	26	E16	55.24 N	33.53 E
Hmel'nickij see Khmel'nyts'kyi, Ukr.	38	D5	49.25 N	27.00 E
Hmost', stm., Russia	26	E15	54.46 N	32.34 E
H. Neely Henry Lake, res., Al., U.S.	134	D12	33.52 N	86.03 W
Hnivan', Ukr.	38	D7	49.06 N	28.20 E
Hnyla Lypa, stm., Ukr.	38	D3	49.07 N	24.45 E
Hnylyi Tikych, stm., Ukr.	38	D9	48.47 N	30.54 E
Hnylyi Yelanets', stm., Ukr.	38	F10	47.19 N	31.43 E
Ho, Ghana	84	H5	6.35 N	0.27 E
Hoa Binh, Viet.	64	B7	20.49 N	105.20 E
Hoare Bay, b., Nu., Can.	108	D13	65.22 N	63.08 W
Hoa Thoi, Viet.	187c		10.44 N	106.35 E
Hoback, stm., Wy., U.S.	146	G16	43.19 N	110.44 W
Hobart, Austl.	99a	o13	42.52 S	147.18 E
Hobart, Ok., U.S.	138	F9	35.01 N	99.05 W
Hobbs, N.M., U.S.	136	B4	32.42 N	103.08 W
Hobbs Coast, cst., Ant.	103	C28	75.30 S	131.55 W
Hobe Sound, Fl., U.S.	132	I5	27.03 N	80.07 W
Hobgood, N.C., U.S.	124	H8	36.02 N	77.24 W
Hobq Shamo, des., China	58	A2	40.30 N	107.55 E
Hobro, Den.	16	K7	56.38 N	9.48 E
Hobson, Mt., U.S.	146	C17	47.00 N	109.53 W
Hobson Lake, l., B.C., Can.	144	D10	52.30 N	120.20 W
Hobsons Bay, b., Austl.	192b		37.51 S	144.56 E
Hoburgen, c., Swe.	16	K15	56.54 N	18.08 E
Hobyo, Som.	86	C9	5.20 N	48.31 E
Hocalar, Tur.	34	E12	38.34 N	29.58 E
Hochalmspitze, mtn., Aus.	30	C10	47.01 N	13.19 E
Hochfeld, Nmb.	90	B3	21.29 S	17.51 E
Hochfeld, ngh., Ger.	181		51.25 N	6.46 E
Hochgolling, mtn., Aus.	30	C10	47.16 N	13.45 E
Hochheide, ngh., Ger.	181		51.27 N	6.41 E
Ho Chi Minh City see Thanh Pho Ho Chi Minh, Viet.	64	G8	10.45 N	106.40 E
Hochkönig, mtn., Aus.	30	C10	47.25 N	13.04 E
Hochlar, Ger.	181		51.36 N	7.10 E
Hochschwab, mtn., Aus.	30	C12	47.37 N	15.09 E
Höchstadt an der Aisch, Ger.	24	G6	49.42 N	10.47 E
Höchsten, ngh., Ger.	181		51.27 N	7.29 E
Hochstetter Forland, pen.	108	B21	75.30 N	19.45 W
Ho Chung, China	189d		22.22 N	114.14 E
Hocimsk, Bela.	26	G15	53.26 N	32.35 E
Hockenheim, Ger.	24	G4	49.19 N	8.33 E
Hockessin, De., U.S.	203		39.47 N	75.41 W
Hocking, stm., Oh., U.S.	130	E15	39.35 N	82.35 W
Hocking Hills State Park, p.o.i., Oh., U.S.	124	E3	39.30 N	82.32 W
Hockomock Swamp, sw., Ma., U.S.	201		41.59 N	71.05 W
Hōd, reg., Maur.	84	F3	16.10 N	8.40 W
Hodal, India	70	E6	27.54 N	77.22 E
Hodasy, Bela.	26	G14	53.56 N	31.28 E
Hoddlesden, Eng., U.K.	180		53.42 N	2.26 W
Hodeida see Al-Ḥudaydah, Yemen	72	G5	14.48 N	42.57 E
Hodge, La., U.S.	134	E6	32.16 N	92.43 W
Hodgenville, Ky., U.S.	130	G12	37.34 N	85.44 W
Hodges Brook, stm., Ma., U.S.	201		41.58 N	71.14 W
Hodgeville, Sk., Can.	142	D7	50.06 N	106.56 W
Hodgkins, Il., U.S.	196		41.46 N	87.51 W
Hodgson, Mb., Can.	142	C16	51.12 N	97.33 W
Hódmezővásárhely, Hung.	36	C7	46.25 N	20.20 E
Hodna, Chott el, l., Alg.	84	B6	35.25 N	4.45 E
Hodogaya, ngh., Japan	186		35.27 N	139.36 E
Hodogaya Baseball Ground, p.o.i., Japan	186		35.27 N	139.35 E
Hodonín, Czech Rep.	24	H13	48.50 N	17.08 E
Hodžanor'jah, gora, mtn., Uzb.	48	G11	38.40 N	67.57 E
Hodžejli, Uzb.	48	F9	42.48 N	59.25 E
Hœdic, Île de, i., Fr.	20	G6	47.20 N	2.52 W
Hoehne, Co., U.S.	138	D4	37.16 N	104.22 W
Hoei see Huy, Bel.	20	D14	50.31 N	5.14 E
Hoek van Holland, Neth.	20	C12	51.58 N	4.08 E
Hoeningen, Ger.	181		51.05 N	6.41 E
Hoerstgen, Ger.	181		51.30 N	6.27 E
Hoeryŏng-ŭp, Kor., N.	54	C8	42.26 N	129.46 E
Hoeyang-ŭp, Kor., N.	54	E7	38.42 N	127.36 E
Hof, Ger.	24	F7	50.18 N	11.55 E
Hof, Ice.	12a	k32	64.33 N	14.37 W
Hōf, Gebel, hills, Egypt	191c		29.55 N	31.21 E
Hōf, Wādī, val., Egypt	191c		29.53 N	31.18 E
Hofburg, bldg., Aus.	182b		48.12 N	16.22 E
Höfðakaupstaður, Ice.	12a	k29	65.49 N	20.17 W
Hoffman, Mn., U.S.	128	F3	45.49 N	95.48 W
Hoffman Island, i., N.Y., U.S.	194		40.35 N	74.03 W
Hoffman Station, N.Y., U.S.	202a		43.04 N	78.50 W
Hoffnung, Ger.	181		51.07 N	7.13 E
Hofgeismar, Ger.	24	E5	51.29 N	9.23 E
Hofheim am Taunus, Ger.	24	F4	50.05 N	8.26 E
Hofheim in Unterfranken, Ger.	24	F6	50.07 N	10.31 E
Höflein an der Donau, Aus.	182b		48.21 N	16.17 E
Hofmeyr, S. Afr.	90	G7	31.38 S	25.48 E
Höfn, Ice.	12a	k32	64.17 N	15.09 W
Hofors, Swe.	16	G14	60.32 N	16.17 E
Hofsjökull, ice, Ice.	12a	k30	64.50 N	18.54 W
Hofstede, ngh., Ger.	181		51.30 N	7.12 E
Hofstra University, educ., N.Y., U.S.	194		40.43 N	73.36 W
Hōfu, Japan	56	E4	34.02 N	131.34 E
Hofuf see Al-Hufūf, Sau. Ar.	72	D6	25.22 N	49.34 E
Höganäs, Swe.	16	K10	56.12 N	12.33 E
Hogan Lake, l., On., Can.	126	C11	45.52 N	78.30 W
Hogansville, Ga., U.S.	134	D14	33.10 N	84.54 W
Hogback Mountain, mtn., Mt., U.S.	146	F14	44.54 N	112.07 W
Hogback Mountain, mtn., Ne., U.S.	140	F9	41.40 N	103.44 W
Hogback Mountain, mtn., S.C., U.S.	132	A3	35.10 N	82.17 W
Hogeland, Mt., U.S.	142	F5	48.51 N	108.39 W
Hoggar see Ahaggar, mts., Alg.	84	E6	23.00 N	6.30 E
Høg-Gia, mtn., Nor.	16	E8	62.24 N	10.04 E
Hoghton, Eng., U.K.	180		53.44 N	2.35 W
Hoghton Tower, hist., Eng., U.K.	180		53.44 N	2.34 W
Hog Island, i., Ma., U.S.	201		42.40 N	70.46 W
Hog Island, i., Mi., U.S.	126	C4	45.48 N	85.22 W
Högkullen, hill, Swe.	16	I11	58.35 N	13.23 E
Högsby, Swe.	16	J13	57.09 N	16.02 E
Høgtinden, mtn., Nor.	14	F5	66.58 N	14.34 E
Høgtuva, mtn., Nor.	14	F4	66.26 N	13.42 E
Hoh, stm., Wa., U.S.	146	C2	47.44 N	124.26 W
Hohe Acht, mtn., Ger.	24	F2	50.23 N	7.00 E
Hohenau an der March, Aus.	24	H12	48.36 N	16.54 E
Hohenbudberg, ngh., Ger.	181		51.23 N	6.40 E
Hohenheide, Ger.	181		51.29 N	7.47 E
Hohenlimburg, Schloss, hist., Ger.	181		51.21 N	7.34 E
Hohensalza see Inowrocław, Pol.	24	D14	52.48 N	18.15 E
Hohenschönhausen, ngh., Ger.	182a		52.33 N	13.30 E
Hohenwald, Tn., U.S.	134	B11	35.33 N	87.33 W
Hohenzollernkanal, can., Ger.	182a		52.32 N	13.20 E
Hoher Dachstein, mtn., Aus.	30	C10	47.28 N	13.35 E
Hoherlehme, Ger.	182a		52.19 N	13.37 E
Hohes Venn (Hautes Fagnes), mts., Eur.	20	D15	50.30 N	6.05 E
Hohe Tauern, mts., Aus.	30	C9	47.05 N	12.55 E
Hohhot, China	58	A4	40.48 N	111.38 E
Hohoe, Ghana	84	H5	7.08 N	0.28 E
Hōhoku, Japan	56	E3	34.17 N	130.57 E
Ho-Ho-Kus, N.J., U.S.	194		40.59 N	74.06 W
Hohokus Brook, stm., N.J., U.S.	194		40.57 N	74.06 W
Hoholeve, Ukr.	38	D12	49.55 N	33.48 E
Hohol'skij, Russia	40	F11	51.34 N	38.45 E
Höhscheid, ngh., Ger.	181		51.09 N	7.04 E
Hohultslätt, Swe.	16	K13	56.58 N	15.39 E
Hoh Xil Hu, l., China	52	D3	35.35 N	91.06 E
Hoh Xil Shan, mts., China	52	D2	35.33 N	90.37 E
Hoi An, Viet.	64	E9	15.53 N	108.20 E
Hoihong see Haikang, China	58	K3	20.55 N	110.05 E
Hoihow see Haikou, China	58	K4	20.03 N	110.21 E
Hoima, Ug.	86	D6	1.26 N	31.21 E
Hoisington, Ks., U.S.	138	C10	38.31 N	98.46 W
Hoisten, Ger.	181		51.08 N	6.42 E
Hoi Xuan, Viet.	64	B7	20.22 N	105.06 E
Hojāi, India	70	E14	26.00 N	92.51 E
Højer, Den.	16	M6	54.58 N	8.43 E
Hojniki, Bela.	38	B8	51.53 N	29.59 E
Hōjō, Japan	56	F5	33.57 N	132.47 E
Hokah, Mn., U.S.	128	H7	43.45 N	91.23 W
Hokang see Hegang, China	52	B11	47.19 N	130.16 E
Hökensås, hills, Swe.	16	I12	58.11 N	14.08 E
Hokes Bluff, Al., U.S.	134	D13	33.58 N	85.52 W
Hokitika, N.Z.	102	F4	42.44 S	170.57 E
Hokkaidō, i., Japan	54	C16	44.00 N	143.00 E
Hokksund, Nor.	16	H7	59.45 N	9.53 E
Hokōji, Japan	188		34.52 N	135.07 E
Hok So Wan, China	189d		22.13 N	114.14 E
Hol, Nor.	16	G6	60.37 N	8.18 E
Holalkere, India	69	D3	14.02 N	76.11 E
Hola Prystan', Ukr.	38	G11	46.31 N	32.31 E
Holbæk, Den.	16	L9	55.43 N	11.43 E
Holberg, B.C., Can.	144	F2	50.40 N	128.01 W
Holborn, ngh., Eng., U.K.	178		51.31 N	0.07 W
Holbrook, Austl.	98	J6	35.43 S	147.18 E
Holbrook, Az., U.S.	150	I6	34.54 N	110.10 W
Holbrook, Il., U.S.	196		41.32 N	87.38 W
Holbrook, Md., U.S.	202b		39.24 N	76.51 W
Holbrook, Ne., U.S.	138	A8	40.18 N	100.00 W
Holden, Ab., Can.	144	C18	53.14 N	112.13 W
Holden, Mo., U.S.	130	F4	38.43 N	93.59 W
Holden, Ut., U.S.	150	D4	39.06 N	112.16 W
Holden, W.V., U.S.	132	G3	37.49 N	82.04 W
Holden Village, Wa., U.S.	146	B6	48.12 N	120.46 W
Holdenville, Ok., U.S.	134	B2	35.05 N	96.24 W
Holder, Fl., U.S.	132	H3	28.58 N	82.25 W
Holderness, pen., Eng., U.K.	10	H12	53.47 N	0.10 W
Holdfast, Sk., Can.	142	D8	50.58 N	105.25 W
Holdingford, Mn., U.S.	128	F4	45.44 N	94.28 W
Holdrege, Ne., U.S.	140	G13	40.26 N	99.22 W
Hold With Hope, reg., Grnld.	108	C22	73.36 N	21.37 W
Hole in the Mountain Peak, mtn., Nv., U.S.	148	C10	40.55 N	115.08 W
Hølen, Nor.	16	H8	59.32 N	10.44 E
Hole Narsipur, India	69	E3	12.47 N	76.15 E
Holešov, Czech Rep.	24	G13	49.19 N	17.34 E

Name	Page	Map Ref.	Latitude	Longitude
Holetown, Barb.	159d	n8	13.10 N	59.37 W
Holgate, Oh., U.S.	124	C1	41.14 N	84.07 W
Holguín, Cuba	156	B9	20.53 N	76.15 W
Holíč, Slvk.	24	H13	48.48 N	17.09 E
Holiday Lake Amusement Park, p.o.i., N.J., U.S.	203		40.02 N	74.56 W
Holitna, stm., Ak., U.S.	109	D8	61.40 N	157.10 W
Höljes, Swe.	16	G10	60.54 N	12.36 E
Hollabrunn, Aus.	30	B13	48.33 N	16.05 E
Holland, Mb., Can.	142	E15	49.36 N	98.52 W
Holland, Mi., U.S.	130	B11	42.46 N	86.06 W
Holland, Pa., U.S.	203		40.10 N	74.59 W
Holland, Tx., U.S.	136	D10	30.52 N	97.24 W
Holland, hist. reg., Neth.	20	B13	52.05 N	4.34 E
Holland see Netherlands, ctry., Eur.	20	B15	52.15 N	5.30 E
Hollandale, Ms., U.S.	134	D8	33.10 N	90.51 W
Hollande, Étangs de, l., Fr.	179		48.44 N	1.48 E
Hollandia see Jayapura, Indon.	60	F11	2.32 S	140.42 E
Hollandsbird Island, i., Nmb.	90	D2	24.39 S	14.31 E
Holland Tunnel, trans., U.S.	194		40.44 N	74.02 W
Höllensteinberg, mtn., Aus.	182b		48.06 N	16.11 E
Holley, N.Y., U.S.	126	E11	43.13 N	78.01 W
Holliday, Tx., U.S.	138	H10	33.49 N	98.41 W
Holliday Creek, stm., Tx., U.S.	138	H10	33.55 N	98.28 W
Holliday Park, p.o.i., Mi., U.S.	199		42.21 N	83.24 W
Hollingbourne, Eng., U.K.	178		51.16 N	0.38 E
Hollingworth, Eng., U.K.	180		53.28 N	1.59 W
Hollingworth Lake, l., Eng., U.K.	180		53.38 N	2.06 W
Hollins, Eng., U.K.	180		53.34 N	2.17 W
Hollins, Va., U.S.	124	G6	37.20 N	79.56 W
Hollins Green, Eng., U.K.	180		53.25 N	2.27 W
Hollinswood, Va., U.S.	202c		38.55 N	77.13 W
Hollis, Ok., U.S.	138	G9	34.40 N	99.55 W
Hollis, ngh., N.Y., U.S.	194		40.43 N	73.46 W
Hollister, Ca., U.S.	148	G4	36.50 N	121.24 W
Holloman Air Force Base, mil., N.M., U.S.	136	B1	32.51 N	106.05 W
Holloway Terrace, De., U.S.	203		39.42 N	75.32 W
Hollow Rock, Tn., U.S.	130	H9	36.03 N	88.14 W
Holly, Co., U.S.	138	C6	38.03 N	102.07 W
Holly, Mount, hill, N.J., U.S.	203		40.00 N	74.47 W
Holly Brook, N.J., U.S.	203		39.59 N	74.48 W
Holly Grove, Ar., U.S.	134	C7	34.35 N	91.11 W
Holly Hill, Fl., U.S.	132	G4	29.14 N	81.02 W
Holly Hill, S.C., U.S.	132	C5	33.19 N	80.24 W
Holly Park, Va., U.S.	202c		38.50 N	77.17 W
Holly Pond, l., Ct., U.S.	194		41.03 N	73.30 W
Holly River State Park, p.o.i., W.V., U.S.	124	F5	38.40 N	80.21 W
Holly Run, stm., N.J., U.S.	203		39.47 N	75.03 W
Holly Springs, Ms., U.S.	134	C9	34.45 N	89.27 W
Hollywood, Fl., U.S.	132	J5	26.00 N	80.08 W
Hollywood, Pa., U.S.	203		40.05 N	75.06 W
Hollywood, Mount, mtn., Ca., U.S.	198		34.08 N	118.18 W
Hollywood Bowl, p.o.i., Ca., U.S.	198		34.07 N	118.20 W
Hollywood Park Race Track, p.o.i., Ca., U.S.	198		33.57 N	118.20 W
Hollywood Reservoir, res., Ca., U.S.	198		34.07 N	118.20 W
Holm, Russia	26	C14	57.08 N	31.11 E
Holman, N.T., Can.	110	A7	70.43 N	117.42 W
Hólmavík, Ice.	12a	k28	65.43 N	21.43 W
Holme, Eng., U.K.	180		53.33 N	1.50 W
Holmec, Russia	26	D16	56.20 N	33.21 E
Holme Chapel, Eng., U.K.	180		53.45 N	2.11 W
Holmen, Nor.	16	G8	60.40 N	10.22 E
Holmen, Wi., U.S.	128	H7	43.57 N	91.15 W
Holmes, Pa., U.S.	203		39.54 N	75.19 W
Holmes, Mount, mtn., Wy., U.S.	146	F16	44.49 N	110.51 W
Holmesburg, ngh., Pa., U.S.	203		40.02 N	75.03 W
Holmes Creek, stm., U.S.	134	G13	30.29 N	85.51 W
Holmesglen, Austl.	192b		37.53 S	145.06 E
Holmes Run, stm., Va., U.S.	202c		38.48 N	77.07 W
Holmes Run Acres, Va., U.S.	202c		38.51 N	77.13 W
Holmestrand, Nor.	16	H8	59.29 N	10.18 E
Holmeswood, Eng., U.K.	180		53.39 N	2.52 W
Holmia, Guy.	168	E12	4.58 N	59.34 W
Holm Land, pen., Grnld.	102	A22	80.22 N	18.00 W
Holm Ø, i., Grnld.	108	C14	74.30 N	57.00 W
Holmogorskaja, Russia	12	E19	63.49 N	40.39 E
Holmogory, Russia	12	D19	64.13 N	41.38 E
Holmön, i., Swe.	16	D18	63.47 N	20.53 E
Holmsbu, Nor.	16	H8	59.33 N	10.26 E
Holmsjön, l., Swe.	16	E13	62.25 N	15.19 E
Holmsjön, l., Swe.	16	E14	62.40 N	16.34 E
Holmsk, Russia	50	G17	47.02 N	142.03 E
Holmskij, Russia	38	I17	44.50 N	38.23 E
Holmsland Klit, sand, Den.	16	K5	56.00 N	8.08 E
Holmsund, Swe.	16	D18	63.42 N	20.22 E
Holm-Žirkovskij, Russia	26	E16	55.30 N	33.30 E
Holoby, Ukr.	38	B4	51.05 N	25.01 E
Holod, Rom.	36	C9	46.47 N	22.08 E
Holohit, Punta, c., Mex.	156	B3	21.34 N	88.12 W
Holohory, mts., Ukr.	38	D3	49.43 N	24.33 E
Holon, Isr.	76	F5	32.00 N	34.46 E
Holoog, Nmb.	90	E4	27.27 S	17.57 E
Holovanivs'k, Ukr.	38	E9	48.23 N	30.28 E
Holovne, Ukr.	38	B2	51.21 N	24.04 E
Holroyd, Austl.	192a		33.50 S	150.58 E
Holstebro, Den.	16	K6	56.21 N	8.37 E
Holstein, Ia., U.S.	130	B2	42.29 N	95.32 W
Holsteinsborg (Sisimiut), Grnld.	108	D15	66.55 N	53.40 W
Holsterhausen, Ger.	181		51.41 N	6.57 E
Holston, stm., Tn., U.S.	124	H2	35.57 N	83.51 W
Holston, North Fork, stm., U.S.	124	H3	36.33 N	82.37 W
Holston High Knob, mtn., Tn., U.S.	124	H3	36.27 N	82.05 W
Holsworthy, Eng., U.K.	10	K8	50.49 N	4.21 W
Holt, Al., U.S.	134	D11	33.14 N	87.26 W
Holt, Fl., U.S.	134	G12	30.42 N	86.44 W
Holt, Mi., U.S.	124	B1	42.38 N	84.30 W
Holt Creek, stm., Ne., U.S.	140	E14	42.28 N	98.50 W
Holten, ngh., Ger.	181		51.31 N	6.48 E
Holter Lake, res., Mt., U.S.	146	D14	46.55 N	111.57 W
Holthausen, Ger.	181		51.23 N	7.13 E
Holthausen, Ger.	181		51.12 N	7.01 E
Holthausen, ngh., Ger.	181		51.34 N	7.26 E
Holton, Ks., U.S.	130	E2	39.27 N	95.44 W
Holts Summit, Mo., U.S.	130	F5	38.39 N	92.07 W
Holtville, Ca., U.S.	148	K10	32.48 N	115.22 W
Holubivka, Ukr.	38	E14	48.52 N	35.20 E
Holy Cross, Ak., U.S.	109	D8	62.12 N	159.47 W
Holy Cross Mountain, mtn., B.C., Can.	144	C10	53.47 N	120.47 W
Holyhead, Wales, U.K.	10	H8	53.18 N	4.38 W
Holy Island, i., Eng., U.K.	10	F11	55.40 N	1.47 W
Holy Island, i., Ma., U.S.	201		42.43 N	70.50 W
Holyoke, Co., U.S.	140	G10	40.35 N	102.18 W
Holyoke, Ma., U.S.	124	B13	42.11 N	72.37 W
Holyrood, Ks., U.S.	138	C10	38.35 N	98.24 W
Holýšov, Czech Rep.	24	G9	49.35 N	13.06 E
Holywell Green, Eng., U.K.	180		53.41 N	1.52 W
Holzbüttgen, Ger.	181		51.12 N	6.37 E
Holzkirchen, Ger.	24	I7	47.52 N	11.42 E
Holzminden, Ger.	24	E5	51.49 N	9.27 E
Hom, stm., Nmb.	90	F4	28.50 S	18.37 E
Homa Bay, Kenya	86	E6	0.31 S	34.27 E
Homalin, Mya.	62	D7	24.51 N	94.56 E
Homathko, stm., B.C., Can.	144	E6	50.54 N	124.48 W
Homathko Icefield, ice, B.C., Can.	144	E6	51.05 N	124.30 W
Homāyūnshahr see Khomeynīshahr, Iran	74	D12	32.41 N	51.32 E
Homberg, Ger.	24	E5	51.02 N	9.24 E
Homberg, Ger.	181		51.18 N	6.56 E
Hombori Tondo, mtn., Mali	84	F4	15.16 N	1.40 W
Hombre Muerto, Salar del, pl., Arg.	172	B4	25.21 S	67.04 W
Hombruch, ngh., Ger.	181		51.29 N	7.26 E
Homburg, Ger.	24	G3	49.18 N	7.21 E
Homburg see Bad Homburg vor der Höhe, Ger.	24	F4	50.14 N	8.36 E
Home Bay, b., Nu., Can.	110	B17	68.45 N	67.10 W
Homebush Bay, b., Austl.	192a		33.50 S	151.05 E
Home Creek, stm., Tx., U.S.	136	C8	31.28 N	99.13 W
Homedale, Id., U.S.	146	G10	43.37 N	116.56 W
Home Hill, Austl.	98	B6	19.39 S	147.24 E
Homel', Bela.	26	H13	52.25 N	30.59 E
Homel', state, Bela.	40	E6	52.30 N	30.00 E
Homeland Park, S.C., U.S.	132	B3	34.26 N	82.39 W
Home Park, The, p.o.i., Eng., U.K.	178		51.28 N	0.36 W
Homer, Ak., U.S.	109	E9	59.39 N	151.30 W
Homer, Ga., U.S.	132	B2	34.20 N	83.29 W
Homer, La., U.S.	134	E5	32.47 N	93.04 W
Homer, Ne., U.S.	130	B1	42.18 N	96.29 W
Homer, N.Y., U.S.	124	B9	42.38 N	76.10 W
Homer City, Pa., U.S.	124	D6	40.31 N	79.09 W
Homer, hill, Ger.	181		51.11 N	7.39 E
Homerville, Ga., U.S.	132	E3	31.02 N	82.45 W
Homer Wash, stm., Ca., U.S.	150	I2	34.14 N	115.05 W
Homer Youngs Peak, mtn., Mt., U.S.	146	E13	45.19 N	113.41 W
Homestead, Austl.	98	C5	20.22 S	145.39 E
Homestead, Fl., U.S.	132	K5	25.28 N	80.28 W
Homestead, Pa., U.S.	197b		40.24 N	79.54 W
Homestead National Monument of America, p.o.i., Ne., U.S.	138	A11	40.15 N	96.48 W
Homestead Valley, Ca., U.S.	200		37.54 N	122.32 W
Hometown, Il., U.S.	196		41.44 N	87.43 W
Hometown, Al., U.S.	134	D12	33.28 N	86.48 W
Homewood, ngh., Pa., U.S.	197b		40.27 N	79.54 W
Homewood Acres, Il., U.S.	196		41.34 N	87.43 W
Homino, stm., Spain	22	G2	42.45 N	3.25 W
Hominy, Ok., U.S.	134	A2	36.24 N	96.23 W
Hominy Creek, stm., Ok., U.S.	138	E12	36.20 N	96.00 W
Hommarsåk, Nor.	16	I3	58.58 N	5.42 E
Hommelstø, Nor.	16	B10	65.24 N	12.33 E
Hommura, Japan	56	E12	34.22 N	139.16 E
Homnābād, India	69	C3	17.46 N	77.06 E
Homochitto, stm., Ms., U.S.	134	F7	31.12 N	91.31 W
Homoine, Moz.	90	C12	23.52 S	35.09 E
Homosassa, Fl., U.S.	132	H3	28.46 N	82.36 W
Homs see Al-Khums, Libya	82	A2	32.39 N	14.16 E
Homs see Ḥimş, Syria	76	D7	34.44 N	36.43 E
Homutovka, Russia	38	B13	51.55 N	34.32 E
Homutovo, Russia	26	H20	52.51 N	37.27 E
Honaker, Va., U.S.	124	H4	37.00 N	81.58 W
Honan see Henan, state, China	58	E6	34.00 N	114.00 E
Honāvar, India	69	D2	14.16 N	74.26 E
Honaz, Tur.	34	F12	37.45 N	29.17 E
Hon Chong, Viet.	64	G7	10.09 N	104.36 E
Honda, Col.	168	E4	5.12 N	74.44 W
Honda, Bahía, b., Col.	168	A6	12.21 N	71.47 W
Honda Bay, b., Phil.	68	F2	9.53 N	118.49 E
Hondeklipbaai, S. Afr.	90	G3	30.20 S	17.18 E
Hon Dien, Nui, mtn., Viet.	64	G9	11.33 N	108.38 E
Hondo, Ab., Can.	144	A16	55.04 N	114.02 W
Hondo, Japan	56	G3	32.27 N	130.11 E
Hondo, N.M., U.S.	138	H3	33.24 N	105.17 W
Hondo, Tx., U.S.	136	E8	29.20 N	99.08 W
Hondo, stm., Mex.	204a		19.26 N	99.15 W
Hondo, stm., N.A.	156	C3	18.29 N	88.18 W
Hondo, Rio, stm., Ca., U.S.	198		33.55 N	118.10 W
Hondo Creek, stm., Tx., U.S.	136	E8	28.55 N	99.10 W
Hondoji Temple, rel., Japan	186		35.51 N	139.56 E
Hondsrug, mts., Neth.	20	B15	52.55 N	6.50 E
Honduras, ctry., N.A.	152	E7	15.00 N	86.30 W
Honduras, Cabo de, c., Hond.	156	D5	16.01 N	86.00 W
Honduras, Golfo de see Honduras, Gulf of, b., N.A.	156	D3	16.04 N	87.57 W
Honduras, Gulf of, b., N.A.	156	D3	16.04 N	87.57 W
Honea Path, S.C., U.S.	132	B3	34.27 N	82.23 W
Hønefoss, Nor.	16	G8	60.10 N	10.15 E
Honesdale, Pa., U.S.	124	C10	41.34 N	75.15 W
Honey Creek, stm., Ia., U.S.	130	B4	42.08 N	93.03 W
Honey Creek, stm., Mo., U.S.	128	K5	39.53 N	93.34 W
Honeydew, S. Afr.	191d		26.05 S	27.55 E
Honeygo Run, stm., Md., U.S.	202b		39.22 N	76.25 W
Honey Grove, Tx., U.S.	134	D3	33.35 N	95.55 W
Honey Lake, l., Ca., U.S.	134	C5	40.16 N	120.19 W
Honeymoon Bay, B.C., Can.	144	H6	48.48 N	124.10 W
Honeyville, Ut., U.S.	150	B4	41.38 N	112.05 W
Honfleur, Fr.	20	E9	49.24 N	0.14 E
Høng, Den.	16	L9	55.31 N	11.17 E
Hong, stm., China	58	J2	22.34 N	115.32 E
Hong, Song see Red, stm., Asia	62	D9	20.18 N	106.32 E
Hon Gai, Viet.	64	B8	21.02 N	107.03 E
Hong Hu, l., China	58	F5	29.52 N	113.23 E
Hongik University, educ., Kor., S.	189b		37.33 N	126.56 E
Hongjiang, China	58	H4	27.04 N	109.58 E
Hong Kong see Xianggang, China	58	J6	22.15 N	114.10 E
Hong Kong see Xianggang, state, China	52	G7	22.15 N	114.10 E
Hong Kong, i., China	189d		22.15 N	114.11 E
Hong Kong, University of, educ., China	189d		22.17 N	114.08 E
Hongkou Park, p.o.i., China	187b		31.16 N	121.28 E
Hongliuyuan, China	48	F17	41.01 N	95.24 E
Hong Ngu, Viet.	64	G7	10.48 N	105.21 E
Hongō, ngh., Japan	186		35.42 N	139.47 E
Hongor, Mong.	52	B7	45.48 N	112.56 E
Hongqi, China	54	B7	44.22 N	126.32 E
Hongqiao, China	187b		31.12 N	121.22 E
Hongshanzi, China	54	C2	42.34 N	117.14 E
Hongshi, China	54	C7	42.58 N	127.04 E
Hongshui, stm., China	58	J3	23.47 N	109.31 E
Hongtong, China	58	C4	36.17 N	111.40 E
Hongtu Zhang, mtn., China	58	J6	23.46 N	115.56 E
Honguedo, Détroit d', strt., Qc., Can.	122	A12	49.04 N	63.44 W
Hongyōtoku, Japan	186		35.41 N	139.55 E
Hongze, China	58	E8	33.17 N	118.50 E
Hongze Hu, l., China	58	E8	33.16 N	118.34 E
Honiara, Sol. Is.	101b	e8	9.26 S	159.57 E
Honiton, Eng., U.K.	10	K9	50.48 N	3.11 W
Honjō, Japan	54	E13	39.23 N	140.03 E
Honkamäki, hill, Fin.	18	D14	62.58 N	27.04 E
Honker Bay, b., Ca., U.S.	200		38.04 N	121.56 W
Honkorab, Râs, c., Egypt	74	H4	24.33 N	35.09 E
Hönne, stm., Ger.	181		51.28 N	7.46 E
Honningsvåg, Nor.	14	B17	70.58 N	26.00 E
Honokaa, Hi., U.S.	100a	c6	20.04 N	155.28 W
Honolulu, Hi., U.S.	100a	b4	21.19 N	157.51 W
Honomu, Hi., U.S.	100a	d6	19.53 N	155.07 W
Hon Quan, Viet.	64	G8	11.38 N	106.36 E
Honshū, i., Japan	54	G13	36.00 N	138.00 E
Höntrop, ngh., Ger.	181		51.27 N	7.08 E
Honuapo Bay, b., Hi., U.S.	100a	d6	19.04 N	155.32 W
Honuu, Russia	50	C17	66.28 N	143.10 E
Hoo, Eng., U.K.	178		51.25 N	0.34 E
Hood, stm., Nu., Can.	110	B9	67.22 N	108.54 W
Hood, Mount, vol., Or., U.S.	146	E5	45.22 N	121.41 W
Hood Canal, b., Wa., U.S.	146	C4	47.38 N	122.52 W
Hoodoo Peak, mtn., Wa., U.S.	146	B6	48.15 N	120.19 W
Hood Point, c., Austl.	96	F3	34.23 S	119.34 E
Hood Pond, l., Ma., U.S.	201		42.40 N	70.57 W
Hood River, Or., U.S.	146	E5	45.42 N	121.30 W
Hoodsport, Wa., U.S.	146	C3	47.24 N	123.09 W
Hoods Range, mts., Austl.	98	G5	28.35 S	144.30 E
Hoogeveen, Neth.	20	B15	52.43 N	6.29 E
Hoogeveense Vaart, can., Neth.	20	B15	52.41 N	6.11 E
Hooiberg, hill, Aruba	158g	o20	12.31 N	69.59 W
Hook, ngh., Eng., U.K.	178		51.22 N	0.18 W
Hooker, Ok., U.S.	138	E7	36.51 N	101.12 W
Hooker Creek, Austl.	96	C6	18.18 S	130.37 E
Hook Head, c., Ire.	10	I6	52.07 N	6.55 W
Hookina, Austl.	98	H2	31.46 S	138.20 E
Hook Island, i., Austl.	98	C7	20.08 S	148.55 E
Hook Mountain State Park, p.o.i., N.Y., U.S.	194		41.09 N	73.55 W
Hook Point, c., Austl.	98	E9	25.47 S	153.04 E
Hooks, Tx., U.S.	134	D4	33.28 N	94.16 W
Hoolehua, Hi., U.S.	100a	b4	21.10 N	157.04 W
Hoonah, Ak., U.S.	109	E12	58.07 N	135.26 W
Hoopa, Ca., U.S.	148	B2	41.03 N	123.39 W
Hoopa Valley Indian Reservation, ind. res., Ca., U.S.	148	B2	41.06 N	123.39 W
Hooper, Ne., U.S.	130	C1	41.35 N	96.33 W
Hooper Bay, Ak., U.S.	109	D6	61.31 N	166.06 W
Hoopes Reservoir, res., De., U.S.	203		39.47 N	75.37 W
Hoopeston, Il., U.S.	130	D10	40.27 N	87.39 W
Hoople, N.D., U.S.	142	F16	48.31 N	97.38 W
Hoopstad, S. Afr.	90	E7	27.50 S	25.54 E
Hoopstick Brook, stm., N.J., U.S.	194		40.39 N	74.41 W
Höör, Swe.	16	L11	55.56 N	13.32 E
Hoorn, Neth.	20	B14	52.38 N	5.03 E
Hoosick Falls, N.Y., U.S.	122	H3	42.54 N	73.20 W
Hooton, Eng., U.K.	180		53.18 N	2.57 W
Hoot Owl Estates, N.J., U.S.	203		39.53 N	74.50 W
Hoover Dam, dam., U.S.	150	G2	36.02 N	114.43 W
Hooversville, Pa., U.S.	126	H11	40.08 N	78.54 W
Hopatcong, N.J., U.S.	124	D11	40.56 N	74.37 W
Hopatcong State Park, p.o.i., N.J., U.S.	194		40.55 N	74.40 W
Hop Brook, stm., N.J., U.S.	194		40.19 N	74.08 W
Hope, B.C., Can.	144	G9	49.22 N	121.25 W
Hope, Ar., U.S.	134	D5	33.40 N	93.35 W
Hope, In., U.S.	130	E12	39.18 N	85.46 W
Hope, N.D., U.S.	142	G16	47.19 N	97.43 W
Hope, Ben, mtn., Scot., U.K.	10	C8	58.24 N	4.37 W
Hope, Point, c., Ak., U.S.	109	C6	68.20 N	166.49 W
Hopedale, Il., U.S.	130	D8	40.24 N	89.24 W
Hopedale, La., U.S.	134	H9	29.49 N	89.39 W
Hopefield, S. Afr.	90	H4	33.04 S	18.21 E
Hopeh see Hebei, state, China	52	D8	38.00 N	116.00 E
Hope Island, i., B.C., Can.	144	F3	50.55 N	127.54 W
Hopelawn, N.J., U.S.	194		40.31 N	74.17 W
Hopelchén, Mex.	156	C3	19.46 N	89.51 W
Hope Mills, N.C., U.S.	132	B7	34.58 N	78.56 W
Hopër, stm., Russia	40	F13	49.36 N	42.18 E
Hopes Advance, Cap, c., Qc., Can.	110	C17	61.04 N	69.34 W
Hopetoun, Austl.	96	F4	33.56 S	120.07 E
Hopetoun, Austl.	98	J4	35.44 S	142.21 E
Hopetown, S. Afr.	90	F6	29.35 S	24.03 E
Hope Valley, R.I., U.S.	124	C14	41.30 N	71.43 W
Hopewell, Va., U.S.	124	G8	37.18 N	77.17 W
Hopewell Culture National Historic Park, p.o.i., Oh., U.S.	124	E2	39.23 N	83.00 W
Hopewell Islands, is., Nu., Can.	110	D14	58.21 N	78.04 W
Hopi see Hebi, China	58	D6	35.58 N	114.08 E
Hopi Buttes, mtn., Az., U.S.	150	H6	35.20 N	110.15 W
Hopi Indian Reservation, ind. res., Az., U.S.	150	H6	35.45 N	110.35 W
Hopkins, Mo., U.S.	130	D3	40.32 N	94.49 W
Hopkins, stm., Austl.	98	K4	38.24 S	142.30 E
Hopkins Creek, stm., N.Y., U.S.	202a		43.17 N	78.46 W
Hopkinsville, Ky., U.S.	130	H10	36.51 N	87.29 W
Hopkinton, Ia., U.S.	130	B6	42.20 N	91.14 W
Hopland, Ca., U.S.	148	E2	38.58 N	123.06 W
Hopólite Bouchard, Arg.	172	G6	34.43 S	63.29 W
Hoppegarten, Ger.	182a		52.31 N	13.40 E
Hoppenrade, Ger.	182a		52.32 N	12.56 E
Hoppo see Hepu, China	58	K3	21.40 N	109.11 E
Hopsfjorden, b., Nor.	14	B18	70.46 N	28.04 E
Ho Pui, China	189d		22.25 N	114.03 E
Hopwood, Mount, hill, Austl.	98	C5	21.49 S	144.26 E
Hoquiam, Wa., U.S.	146	C3	46.58 N	123.52 W
Hor, Russia	50	G16	47.52 N	134.57 E
Hor, stm., Russia	50	G16	47.48 N	134.41 E
Horatio, Ar., U.S.	134	D4	33.56 N	94.21 W
Horatio Gardens, Il., U.S.	196		42.10 N	87.57 W
Horažďovice, Czech Rep.	24	G9	49.19 N	13.42 E
Hörby, Swe.	16	L11	55.51 N	13.38 E
Hordaland, state, Nor.	16	G4	60.15 N	6.30 E
Hörde, ngh., Ger.	181		51.29 N	7.30 E
Horezu, Rom.	36	D10	45.08 N	24.01 E
Horgen, Switz.	22	B14	47.15 N	8.35 E
Horhany, mts., Ukr.	38	E3	48.28 N	24.08 E
Hořice, Czech Rep.	24	F11	50.22 N	15.38 E
Horicon, Wi., U.S.	128	H10	43.26 N	88.37 W
Horigane, Japan	186		35.50 N	139.27 E
Horinger, China	58	A4	40.22 N	111.48 E
Horinouchi, ngh., Japan	186		35.41 N	139.40 E
Horinsk, Russia	50	F10	52.09 N	109.46 E
Horizontina, Braz.	172	C10	27.37 S	54.17 W
Horki, Bela.	26	F13	54.16 N	30.58 E
Horlick Mountains, mts., Ant.	103	D29	85.23 S	120.59 W
Horlivka, Ukr.	38	E17	48.19 N	38.03 E
Horlovo, Russia	26	E21	55.19 N	38.48 E
Hormigueros, P.R.	158a	b1	18.09 N	67.07 W
Hormoz, Jazīreh-ye, i., Iran	74	G15	27.04 N	56.28 E
Hormozgān, state, Iran	74	G15	27.36 N	56.27 E
Hormuz, Strait of, strt., Asia	72	D8	26.34 N	56.15 E
Horn, Aus.	30	B12	48.40 N	15.40 E
Horn, Nor.	16	B10	65.35 N	12.17 E
Horn, c., Ice.	12a	j28	66.28 N	22.28 W
Horn, stm., N.T., Can.	110	C7	61.31 N	117.58 W
Horn, Cape see Hornos, Cabo de, c., Chile	166	K3	55.58 S	67.16 W
Hornad (Hernád), stm., Eur.	24	H17	47.59 N	21.02 E
Hornaday, stm., Can.	110	B6	69.20 N	123.50 W
Hornafjörđur, b., Ice.	12a	k32	64.17 N	15.16 W
Hornavan, l., Swe.	14	F8	66.10 N	17.46 E
Hornbeak, Tn., U.S.	130	H8	36.19 N	89.17 W
Hornbeck, La., U.S.	134	F5	31.19 N	93.24 W
Hornbrook, Ca., U.S.	148	B3	41.54 N	122.32 W
Hornby, On., Can.	193b		43.34 N	79.50 W
Hornby Bay, b., N.T., Can.	110	B7	66.35 N	117.50 W
Horncastle, Eng., U.K.	10	H12	53.12 N	0.06 W
Hornchurch, ngh., Eng., U.K.	178		51.34 N	0.12 E
Horndal, Swe.	16	G14	60.17 N	16.24 E
Horndon on the Hill, Eng., U.K.	178		51.31 N	0.25 E
Hornebach, stm., Ger.	181		51.39 N	7.38 E
Horneburg, Ger.	181		51.38 N	7.18 E
Hörnefors, Swe.	16	D17	63.37 N	19.56 E
Hornell, N.Y., U.S.	124	B8	42.19 N	77.38 W
Hornepayne, On., Can.	114	B8	49.12 N	84.46 W
Horn Hill, Eng., U.K.	178		51.37 N	0.32 W
Hornindalsvatnet, l., Nor.	16	F4	61.56 N	6.22 E
Horn Island, i., Ms., U.S.	134	G10	30.14 N	88.43 W
Horn Lake, Ms., U.S.	134	C8	34.58 N	90.01 W
Hornos, Cabo de (Horn, Cape), c., Chile	166	K3	55.58 S	67.16 W
Hornos, Islas de, is., Ur.	206		34.25 S	57.55 W
Hornostaïvka, Ukr.	38	F12	47.00 N	33.44 E
Horn Plateau, plat., N.T., Can.	110	C6	62.07 N	120.16 W
Horn Pond, l., Ma., U.S.	201		42.28 N	71.09 W
Hornsea, Eng., U.K.	10	H12	53.54 N	0.11 W
Hornsey, ngh., Eng., U.K.	178		51.35 N	0.07 W
Hornslet, Den.	16	K8	56.18 N	10.19 E
Horodenka, Ukr.	38	E4	48.40 N	25.30 E
Horodkivka, Ukr.	38	E7	48.23 N	28.41 E
Horodne, Ukr.	38	H7	45.53 N	28.51 E
Horodnia, Ukr.	38	B10	51.53 N	31.36 E
Horodnytsia, Ukr.	38	C6	50.48 N	27.22 E
Horodok, Ukr.	38	D5	49.09 N	26.34 E
Horodok, Ukr.	38	D2	49.46 N	23.38 E
Horodyshche, Ukr.	38	D18	49.03 N	39.40 E
Horodyshche, Ukr.	38	D10	49.17 N	31.27 E
Horog, Taj.	72	B11	37.29 N	71.33 E
Horokhiv, Ukr.	38	C3	50.30 N	24.45 E
Horol', Russia	54	B10	44.25 N	132.04 E
Horošovo, ngh., Russia	183b		55.47 N	37.28 E
Hořovice, Czech Rep.	24	G9	49.50 N	13.53 E
Horqin Youyi Qianqi, China	52	B9	46.04 N	122.03 E
Horqin Youyi Zhongqi, China	54	B4	45.09 N	121.24 E
Horqin Zuoyi Houqi, China	52	C9	42.57 N	122.20 E
Horqin Zuoyi Zhongqi, China	52	C9	44.07 N	123.19 E
Horqueta, Para.	166	D5	23.20 S	57.03 W
Horrem, Ger.	181		51.06 N	6.48 E
Horseback Knob, hill, Oh., U.S.	124	E2	39.14 N	83.06 W
Horse Cave, Ky., U.S.	130	G12	37.10 N	85.54 W
Horse Creek, Wy., U.S.	140	F7	41.24 N	105.12 W
Horse Creek, stm., U.S.	140	F8	41.56 N	103.58 W
Horse Creek, stm., Co., U.S.	138	C5	38.05 N	103.19 W
Horse Creek, stm., Fl., U.S.	132	I4	27.06 N	81.58 W
Horse Creek, stm., Mo., U.S.	130	G3	37.45 N	93.52 W
Horsefly, B.C., Can.	144	D9	52.20 N	121.25 W
Horsefly Lake, l., B.C., Can.	144	D10	52.25 N	121.00 W
Horsehead Creek, stm., S.D., U.S.	140	D9	43.18 N	103.25 W
Horsehead Lake, l., N.D., U.S.	142	G13	47.01 N	99.47 W
Horseheads, N.Y., U.S.	124	B9	42.11 N	76.49 W
Horse Islands, is., Nf., Can.	111a	i22	50.13 N	55.45 W
Horsell, Eng., U.K.	178		51.19 N	0.34 W
Horseneck Brook, stm., Ct., U.S.	194		41.01 N	73.38 W
Horsens, Den.	16	L7	55.52 N	9.52 E
Horseshoe Bend, Ar., U.S.	130	H6	36.14 N	91.42 W
Horseshoe Bend, Id., U.S.	146	G10	43.55 N	116.11 W
Horseshoe Bend National Military Park, p.o.i., Al., U.S.	134	D13	33.00 N	85.46 W
Horseshoe Cove, b., N.J., U.S.	194		40.27 N	74.00 W
Horseshoe Creek, stm., Wy., U.S.	140	E7	42.27 N	104.58 W
Horseshoe Falls, wtfl., N.A.	202a		43.05 N	79.04 W
Horseshoe Lake, l., Mb., Can.	142	B18	52.12 N	95.50 W
Horseshoe Lake, l., Mi., U.S.	199		42.24 N	83.45 W
Horseshoe Lake, l., N.J., U.S.	194		40.52 N	74.38 W
Horsham, Austl.	98	K4	36.42 S	142.11 E
Horsham, Eng., U.K.	10	J12	51.04 N	0.20 W
Hørsholm, Den.	16	L10	55.52 N	12.29 E
Horsley, Austl.	192a		33.51 S	150.51 E
Horšovský Týn, Czech Rep.	24	G8	49.31 N	12.56 E
Horst, ngh., Ger.	181		51.32 N	7.02 E
Horstmar, Ger.	181		51.36 N	7.33 E
Horsunlu, Tur.	34	F11	37.55 N	28.36 E
Horta, ngh., Spain	184d		41.26 N	2.00 E
Hortaleza, ngh., Spain	184a		40.28 N	3.39 W
Hortavær, is., Nor.	16	B9	65.12 N	11.26 E
Horten, Nor.	16	H8	59.24 N	10.28 E
Hortobágy, reg., Hung.	36	B8	47.34 N	21.12 E
Hortobágyi Nemzeti Park, p.o.i., Hung.	36	B8	47.30 N	21.05 E
Horton, Eng., U.K.	178		51.28 N	0.32 W
Horton, Ks., U.S.	130	E2	39.39 N	95.31 W
Horton, stm., N.T., Can.	110	B6	70.01 N	126.53 W
Horton Kirby, Eng., U.K.	178		51.23 N	0.15 E
Horton Lake, l., N.T., Can.	110	B6	67.28 N	122.27 W
Hortonville, Wi., U.S.	128	G10	44.19 N	88.38 W
Hory, Bela.	26	F14	54.16 N	31.13 E
Horyn' (Haryn'), stm., Eur.	40	F5	52.08 N	27.17 E
Hōryūji Temple, rel., Japan	188		34.36 N	135.44 E
Hosa'ina, Eth.	82	F7	7.37 N	37.56 E
Hösbach, Ger.	24	F5	49.59 N	9.11 E
Hosedahard, Russia	48	A9	67.02 N	59.23 E
Hosei University, educ., Japan	186		35.42 N	139.44 E
Hoševtovo, Russia	40	H15	47.02 N	47.50 E
Hoseynābād, Iran	74	C10	35.33 N	47.08 E
Hoseynīyeh-ye Khodā-Dād, Iran	74	D11	32.41 N	48.13 E
Hosford, Fl., U.S.	134	G14	30.23 N	84.47 W
Hošgort, Russia	50	C2	65.28 N	65.41 E
Hoshāb, Pak.	62	C1	26.01 N	63.54 E
Hoshangābād, India	70	G6	22.45 N	77.43 E
Hoshcha, Ukr.	38	C5	50.36 N	26.40 E
Hoshiārpur, India	70	C5	31.31 N	75.54 E
Hoshiarpur, India	190a		28.35 N	77.22 E
Hosh Isa, Egypt	76	H1	30.54 N	30.17 E
Hoskins, Pap. N. Gui.	101a	b5	5.27 S	150.24 E
Hosmer, B.C., Can.	144	G15	49.35 N	114.58 W
Hosmer, S.D., U.S.	140	B13	45.34 N	99.28 W
Hospers, Ia., U.S.	130	A2	43.04 N	95.54 W
Hospet, India	69	D3	15.16 N	76.23 E
Hospital de Órbigo, Spain	28	B5	42.28 N	5.53 W
Hospitalet see L'Hospitalet de Llobregat, Spain	28	C13	41.21 N	2.06 E
Hossa, Fin.	18	B16	65.25 N	29.34 E
Hossegor, Fr.	22	F4	43.40 N	1.25 W
Hosston, La., U.S.	136	B14	32.53 N	93.53 W
Hosta Butte, mtn., N.M., U.S.	150	H8	35.35 N	108.12 W
Hoste, Isla, i., Chile	166	K3	55.05 S	69.15 W
Hostigrām, India	190b		22.26 N	88.31 E
Hosūr, India	69	E3	12.43 N	77.49 E
Hot, Thai.	64	C4	18.04 N	98.34 E
Hota, Japan	186		35.08 N	139.51 E
Hotagen, Swe.	16	C12	63.58 N	14.11 E
Hotagen, l., Swe.	16	D11	63.52 N	14.27 E
Hotagsfjällen, mts., Swe.	16	C12	64.20 N	14.29 E
Hotaka-dake, mtn., Japan	56	C10	36.18 N	137.39 E
Hotamış, Tur.	76	A4	37.36 N	33.21 E
Hotan, stm., China	62	A5	40.29 N	80.55 E
Hotarele, Rom.	36	E13	44.10 N	26.23 E
Hotazel, S. Afr.	90	E6	27.14 S	22.58 E
Hotchkiss, Co., U.S.	150	E9	38.47 N	107.43 W
Hot Creek Range, mts., Nv., U.S.	148	E9	38.30 N	116.25 W
Hotevilla, Az., U.S.	150	H6	35.55 N	110.40 W
Hotilovo, Russia	26	C17	57.43 N	34.04 E
Hoting, Swe.	16	C14	64.06 N	16.09 E
Hot'kovo, Russia	26	G18	53.45 N	35.14 E
Hot'kovo, Russia	26	D21	56.15 N	38.00 E
Hot'kovo, Russia	26	H18	52.56 N	35.23 E
Hot Springs, Ar., U.S.	134	C5	34.30 N	93.03 W
Hot Springs, Mt., U.S.	146	C12	47.37 N	114.40 W
Hot Springs see Truth or Consequences, N.M., U.S.	150	J9	33.08 N	107.15 W
Hot Springs, N.C., U.S.	124	I3	35.53 N	82.50 W
Hot Springs, S.D., U.S.	140	D9	43.26 N	103.28 W
Hot Springs, Va., U.S.	124	F6	37.59 N	79.49 W
Hot Springs National Park see Hot Springs, Ar., U.S.	134	C5	34.30 N	93.03 W
Hot Springs Peak, mtn., Ca., U.S.	148	C5	40.22 N	120.07 W
Hot Springs Peak, mtn., Nv., U.S.	148	B8	41.22 N	117.26 W
Hot Springs State Park, p.o.i., Wy., U.S.	140	D4	43.40 N	108.10 W
Hot Sulphur Springs, Co., U.S.	138	A2	40.04 N	106.06 W
Hottah Lake, l., N.T., Can.	110	B7	65.04 N	118.29 W
Hottentotsbaai, b., Nmb.	90	E2	26.05 S	14.58 E
Hotynec, Russia	26	G18	53.07 N	35.24 E
Houaïlou, N. Cal.	101d	m15	21.17 S	165.36 E
Houamuang, Laos	64	B6	20.08 N	103.37 E
Houat, Île de, i., Fr.	20	G6	47.23 N	2.57 W
Houdan, Fr.	20	F10	48.47 N	1.36 E
Houeillès, Fr.	22	E6	44.12 N	0.02 E
Hougang, Sing.	189c		1.22 N	103.54 E
Hough Green, Eng., U.K.	180		53.23 N	2.47 W
Houghton, Mi., U.S.	128	D10	47.06 N	88.36 W
Houghton, N.Y., U.S.	124	B7	42.25 N	78.10 W
Houghton Estate, ngh., S. Afr.	191d		26.10 S	28.04 E
Houghton Green, Eng., U.K.	180		53.25 N	2.34 W
Houghton Lake, Mi., U.S.	126	D5	44.18 N	84.45 W
Houghton Lake, l., Sk., Can.	142	B8	52.23 N	105.08 W
Houghton Lake, l., Mi., U.S.	126	D4	44.20 N	84.45 W
Houilles, Fr.	179		48.56 N	2.11 E
Houlka, Ms., U.S.	134	C10	34.02 N	89.01 W
Houlton, Me., U.S.	122	D9	46.07 N	67.50 W
Houma, China	58	D4	35.36 N	111.20 E
Houma, Tonga	100e	n13	21.09 S	175.19 W
Houma, La., U.S.	134	H8	29.35 N	90.42 W
Hound Creek, stm., Mt., U.S.	146	C15	47.12 N	111.23 W
Houndé, Burkina	84	G4	11.29 N	3.31 W
Hourn, Loch, b., Scot., U.K.	10	D7	57.08 N	5.36 W
Hourtin, Étang d', l., Fr.	22	D4	45.09 N	1.07 W
Housatonic, Ma., U.S.	124	B12	42.15 N	73.22 W
House, N.M., U.S.	138	G5	34.38 N	103.54 W
House of Seven Gables, hist., Ma., U.S.	201		42.32 N	70.53 W
Houston, B.C., Can.	144	B4	54.24 N	126.39 W
Houston, Mn., U.S.	128	H7	43.45 N	91.34 W
Houston, Ms., U.S.	134	D10	33.53 N	88.59 W
Houston, Mo., U.S.	130	G6	37.19 N	91.57 W
Houston, Tx., U.S.	136	E12	29.45 N	95.21 W
Houston, stm., La., U.S.	134	G5	30.15 N	93.12 W
Houston, Lake, res., Tx., U.S.	136	E12	29.58 N	95.08 W
Hout, stm., S. Afr.	90	C9	23.04 S	29.33 E
Houtman Abrolhos, is., Austl.	96	E2	28.43 S	113.48 E
Houtskär, i., Fin.	18	G8	60.12 N	21.22 E
Houtzdale, Pa., U.S.	124	D7	40.49 N	78.22 W
Houx, Fr.	179		48.34 N	1.37 E
Houxinqiu, China	54	C5	42.33 N	122.43 E
Hova, Swe.	16	I12	58.52 N	14.13 E
Hovd, Mong.	52	B3	47.59 N	91.38 E
Hovd, Mong.	52	C5	44.39 N	102.23 E
Hovd, stm., Mong.	48	E16	48.04 N	92.13 E
Hovden, Nor.	16	H5	59.34 N	7.21 E
Hovden, i., Nor.	16	F2	61.41 N	4.52 E
Hove, Eng., U.K.	10	K12	50.49 N	0.09 W
Hoven, S.D., U.S.	140	B13	45.14 N	99.46 W
Hovenweep National Monument, p.o.i., U.S.	150	F7	37.23 N	109.00 W
Hoverla, hora, mtn., Ukr.	38	E3	48.09 N	24.26 E
Hovgaard Ø, i., Grnld.	108	A22	79.53 N	18.40 W
Hovmantorp, Swe.	16	K12	56.47 N	15.08 E
Hövsgöl, Mong.	52	C6	43.36 N	109.38 E
Hövsgöl nuur, l., Mong.	48	D18	51.00 N	100.30 E
Hovu-Aksy, Russia	48	D16	51.07 N	93.40 E
Hövüün, Mong.	52	C5	43.08 N	102.04 E

Name	Page	Map Ref.	Latitude	Longitude
Howa, Ouadi see Howar, Wādī, val., Afr.	82	D5	17.28 N	27.06 E
Howar, Wādī, val., Afr.	82	D5	17.28 N	27.06 E
Howard, Austl.	98	E9	25.19 S	152.33 E
Howard, Ks., U.S.	138	D12	37.28 N	96.15 W
Howard, Pa., U.S.	124	D8	41.00 N	77.39 W
Howard, S.D., U.S.	140	C15	44.00 N	97.32 W
Howard, Wi., U.S.	126	D1	44.32 N	88.03 W
Howard Beach, ngh., N.Y., U.S.	194		40.40 N	73.51 W
Howard City, Mi., U.S.	126	E4	43.23 N	85.27 W
Howard Draw, stm., Tx., U.S.	136	D6	30.08 N	101.34 W
Howard Heights, Md., U.S.	202b		39.17 N	76.50 W
Howard Lake, Mn., U.S.	128	F4	45.03 N	94.04 W
Howard Prairie Lake, res., Or., U.S.	148	A3	42.14 N	122.24 W
Howard University, educ., D.C., U.S.	202c		38.55 N	77.01 W
Howe, In., U.S.	130	C12	41.43 N	85.25 W
Howe, Tx., U.S.	134	D2	33.30 N	96.36 W
Howe, Cape, c., Austl.	98	K7	37.30 S	149.58 E
Howe Green, Eng., U.K.	178		51.42 N	0.32 E
Howe Island, i., On., Can.	126	D13	44.17 N	76.15 W
Howell, Mi., U.S.	124	B2	42.36 N	83.55 W
Howell Airport, arpt., Il., U.S.	196		41.39 N	87.45 W
Howells, Ne., U.S.	140	F15	41.43 N	97.00 W
Howells Pond, l., N.J., U.S.	194		41.03 N	74.42 W
Howe Sound, strt., B.C., Can.	144	G7	49.22 N	123.18 W
Howick, S. Afr.	90	F10	29.29 S	30.13 E
Howitt, Mount, mtn., Austl.	98	K6	37.10 S	146.39 E
Howland, Me., U.S.	122	E8	45.15 N	68.39 W
Howland Island, i., Oc.	94	C9	0.48 N	176.38 W
Howrah see Hāora, India	70	G12	22.35 N	88.20 E
Howse Peak, mtn., Can.	144	E14	51.49 N	116.41 W
Howser, B.C., Can.	144	F13	50.18 N	116.58 W
Howson Peak, mtn., B.C., Can.	144	B3	54.25 N	127.44 W
Hoxie, Ar., U.S.	130	H6	36.03 N	90.59 W
Hoxie, Ks., U.S.	138	B8	39.21 N	100.26 W
Höxter, Ger.	24	E5	51.46 N	9.22 E
Hoxtolgay, China	52	B2	46.31 N	85.59 E
Hoxton Park, Austl.	192a		33.55 S	150.51 E
Hoxton Park Aerodrome, arpt., Austl.	192a		33.54 S	150.50 E
Hoy, i., Scot., U.K.	10	C9	58.51 N	3.20 W
Høyanger, Nor.	16	F4	61.13 N	6.04 E
Hoyerswerda, Ger.	24	E10	51.26 N	14.14 E
Høylandet, Nor.	16	C10	64.37 N	12.19 E
Hoyleton, Il., U.S.	130	F8	38.27 N	89.15 W
Hoyos, Spain	28	D4	40.10 N	6.42 W
Höytiäinen, l., Fin.	16	E12	62.51 N	29.43 E
Hoyt Lakes, Mn., U.S.	128	D6	47.31 N	92.08 W
Hpru-so, Mya.	64	C3	19.25 N	97.08 E
Hradec Králové, Czech Rep.	24	F11	50.12 N	15.49 E
Hradyz'k, Ukr.	38	D12	49.13 N	33.07 E
Hradzjanka, Bela.	26	G11	53.32 N	28.44 E
Hrandziči, Bela.	26	G6	53.43 N	23.49 E
Hranice, Czech Rep.	24	G13	49.33 N	17.45 E
Hranitne, Ukr.	38	F16	47.27 N	37.52 E
Hraniv, Ukr.	38	E8	48.52 N	29.34 E
Hrapun', Bela.	38	B6	51.42 N	27.29 E
Hrazdan, Arm.	42	E11	40.29 N	44.45 E
Hrebinka, Ukr.	38	C11	50.07 N	32.26 E
Hrebinky, Ukr.	38	D9	49.57 N	30.12 E
Hrèsk, Bela.	26	G10	53.10 N	27.29 E
Hriňová, Slvk.	24	H15	48.35 N	19.31 E
Hristoforovo, Russia	12	F22	60.54 N	47.14 E
Hrodna, Bela.	26	G6	53.40 N	23.50 E
Hrodna, state, Bela.	26	G8	53.30 N	25.00 E
Hroma, stm., Russia	50	B17	71.36 N	144.25 E
Hromivka, Ukr.	38	G13	46.18 N	34.05 E
Hromokliia, stm., Ukr.	38	F11	47.21 N	32.14 E
Hron, stm., Slvk.	24	H14	47.48 N	18.45 E
Hronov, Czech Rep.	24	F12	50.28 N	16.10 E
Hrubieszów, Pol.	24	F19	50.48 N	23.56 E
Hrubý Jeseník, mts., Czech Rep.	24	F13	50.04 N	17.16 E
Hrun', Ukr.	38	C13	50.13 N	34.36 E
Hrustal'nyj, Russia	54	B11	44.24 N	135.06 E
Hrvatska see Croatia, ctry., Eur.	30	E13	45.10 N	15.30 E
Hryhorivka, Ukr.	38	B11	51.02 N	32.51 E
Hryhorivka, Ukr.	38	G12	46.17 N	33.44 E
Hryhorivka, Ukr.	38	C9	50.04 N	30.37 E
Hrymailiv, Ukr.	38	D5	49.19 N	26.01 E
Hryniava, Ukr.	38	E3	47.59 N	24.49 E
Hryshkivtsi, Ukr.	38	D7	49.56 N	28.36 E
Hrytsiv, Ukr.	38	C6	49.58 N	27.12 E
Hsichih, Tai.	187d		25.04 N	121.39 E
Hsientung, Tai.	187d		25.09 N	121.44 E
Hsi-hseng, Mya.	64	B3	20.09 N	97.15 E
Hsilo, Tai.	58	J9	23.48 N	120.27 E
Hsim, stm., Mya.	64	B4	20.47 N	98.30 E
Hsinchu, Tai.	58	I9	24.48 N	120.58 E
Hsinhailien see Lianyungang, China	58	D8	34.36 N	119.10 E
Hsinpeit'ou, ngh., Tai.	187d		25.09 N	121.30 E
Hsintien, Tai.	58	I9	24.56 N	121.32 E
Hsintien, stm., Tai.	187d		25.02 N	121.29 E
Hsipaw, Mya.	64	A3	22.36 N	97.18 E
Hsüeh Shan, mtn., Tai.	58	I9	24.23 N	121.13 E
Hsuphāng, Mya.	64	B4	20.17 N	98.42 E
Hua'an, China	58	I7	25.01 N	117.33 E
Huab, stm., Nmb.	90	B2	20.14 S	14.13 E
Huacao, China	187b		31.14 N	121.19 E
Huacaraje, Bol.	166	B4	13.33 S	63.45 W
Huachipa, Peru	204d		12.00 S	76.56 W
Huacho, Peru	164	F2	11.08 S	77.36 W
Huachuca City, Az., U.S.	150	L6	31.38 N	110.19 W
Huaco, Arg.	172	E3	30.08 S	68.31 W
Huadian, China	52	C10	42.58 N	126.44 E
Huading Shan, mtn., China	58	G9	29.15 N	121.05 E
Hua Hin, Thai.	64	F4	12.34 N	99.56 E
Huai, stm., China	58	E7	32.58 N	118.17 E
Huai, stm., China	58	C6	37.30 N	115.00 E
Huai'an, China	58	E8	33.30 N	119.08 E
Huai'an, China	58	A6	40.40 N	114.24 E
Huaibin, China	58	E6	32.26 N	115.24 E
Huaicheng see Huai'an, China	58	E8	33.30 N	119.08 E
Huaide see Gongzhuling, China	52	C9	43.30 N	124.49 E
Huaidezhen, China	54	C6	43.52 N	124.45 E
Huaiji, China	58	I5	24.00 N	112.20 E
Huailai, China	58	A6	40.23 N	115.33 E
Huainan, China	58	E7	32.39 N	117.00 E
Huairou, China	58	A7	40.18 N	116.37 E
Huaiyang, China	58	E6	33.44 N	114.53 E
Huai Yot, Thai.	64	I4	7.15 N	99.33 E
Huaiyuan, China	58	E7	32.57 N	117.11 E
Huaiyu Shan, mts., China	58	G7	28.50 N	117.50 E
Huajiang, China	58	I4	25.50 N	110.21 E
Huajuapan de León, Mex.	154	G10	17.48 N	97.45 W
Hualahuises, Mex.	154	C9	24.53 N	99.40 W
Hualalai, vol., Hi., U.S.	100a	d6	19.42 N	155.52 W
Hualañé, Chile	172	G2	34.57 S	71.50 W
Hualapai Indian Reservation, ind. res., Az., U.S.	150	H3	35.38 N	113.30 W
Hualapai Mountains, mts., Az., U.S.	150	I3	34.48 N	113.50 W
Hualapai Peak, mtn., Az., U.S.	150	H3	35.04 N	113.54 W
Hualfín, Arg.	172	C4	27.14 S	66.50 W
Hualien, Tai.	58	J9	23.58 N	121.35 E
Huallaga, stm., Peru	164	E2	5.05 S	75.36 W
Huallamarca, Museo, bldg., Peru	204d		12.05 S	77.02 W
Huallanca, Peru	164	E2	8.49 S	77.51 W
Hualong, China	52	D5	36.03 N	102.19 E
Huambo, Ang.	88	C2	12.45 S	15.44 E
Huamei Shan, mtn., China	58	I5	25.28 N	113.58 E
Huan, stm., China	58	F6	30.40 N	114.20 E
Huanan, China	52	B11	46.13 N	130.32 E
Huancabamba, Peru	164	E2	5.14 S	79.26 W
Huancabamba, Peru	164	F2	10.22 S	75.32 W
Huancané, Peru	164	G4	15.11 S	69.45 W
Huancavelica, Peru	164	F2	12.47 S	75.00 W
Huancayo, Peru	164	F2	12.05 S	75.12 W
Huanchaca, Serranía de, mts., S.A.	166	B4	14.30 S	60.39 W
Huang (Heung), stm., Asia	64	D5	17.48 N	101.33 E
Huang (Yellow), stm., China	52	D8	37.48 N	118.53 E
Huang, stm., Tai.	187d		25.14 N	121.37 E
Huangchuan, China	58	E6	32.07 N	115.02 E
Huangduqiao, China	58	G9	29.18 N	120.55 E
Huanggai Hu, l., China	58	G5	29.42 N	113.30 E
Huanggang, China	58	F6	30.27 N	114.52 E
Huangganglian, mtn., China	54	C2	43.32 N	117.35 E
Huanggang Shan, mtn., China	58	H7	27.50 N	117.45 E
Huang Hai see Yellow Sea, s., Asia	54	G5	36.00 N	123.00 E
Huangho see Huang, stm., China	52	D8	37.48 N	118.53 E
Huanghua, China	58	B7	38.22 N	117.21 E
Huangjinbu, China	58	G7	28.27 N	116.47 E
Huangling, China	58	D3	35.36 N	109.14 E
Huanglong, China	58	D3	35.29 N	109.49 E
Huangnihe, China	54	C7	43.32 N	127.59 E
Huangpi, China	58	F6	30.52 N	114.22 E
Huangqi, China	58	H8	26.20 N	119.54 E
Huangshahe, China	58	H4	26.03 N	110.58 E
Huangshan, China	58	G8	29.45 N	118.18 E
Huangshan see Guangming Ding, mtn., China	58	F7	30.07 N	118.09 E
Huangshanguan, China	58	C8	37.31 N	120.16 E
Huangshi, China	58	G4	29.01 N	111.07 E
Huangshi, China	58	F6	30.12 N	115.05 E
Huangtang Hu, l., China	58	G6	30.00 N	114.12 E
Huangtugang, China	58	F6	31.24 N	115.05 E
Huangtuliangzi, China	58	A8	41.12 N	118.45 E
Huangtuling, China	58	H5	27.18 N	113.30 E
Huanguelén, Arg.	172	H7	37.04 S	61.57 W
Huangxian, China	58	C9	37.38 N	120.32 E
Huangyan, China	58	G9	28.39 N	121.15 E
Huangyuan, China	52	D5	36.40 N	101.15 E
Huangzhong, China	52	D5	36.31 N	101.39 E
Huangzhu, China	58	L4	19.27 N	110.25 E
Huanjiang, China	58	I3	24.49 N	108.15 E
Huanren, China	52	C10	41.13 N	125.19 E
Huanta, Peru	164	F3	12.56 S	74.15 W
Huánuco, Peru	164	E2	9.55 S	76.14 W
Huanuni, Bol.	166	C3	18.16 S	66.49 W
Huanxian, China	58	C2	36.46 N	107.10 E
Huaqiao, China	58	H4	27.28 N	110.02 E
Huara, Chile	166	C3	19.59 S	69.47 W
Huaral, Peru	164	F2	11.30 S	77.12 W
Huaraz, Peru	164	E2	9.31 S	77.32 W
Huariaca, Peru	164	F2	10.26 S	76.07 W
Huarmey, Peru	164	F2	10.03 S	78.09 W
Huarocondo, Peru	164	F3	13.25 S	72.13 W
Huarong, China	58	G5	29.30 N	112.34 E
Huasaga, stm., S.A.	168	I3	2.44 S	76.55 W
Hua Sai, Thai.	64	H5	8.02 N	100.18 E
Huascarán, Nevado, mtn., Peru	164	E2	9.07 S	77.37 W
Huasco, Chile	172	D2	28.28 S	71.15 W
Huasco, stm., Chile	172	D2	28.27 S	71.13 W
Huatabampo, Mex.	154	B4	26.49 N	109.38 W
Huating, China	58	D2	35.09 N	106.38 E
Huatong, China	58	J2	23.00 N	106.40 E
Huatong, China	58	A9	40.02 N	121.55 E
Huauchinango, Mex.	154	E9	20.11 N	98.03 W
Huautla, Mex.	152	C5	21.02 N	98.17 W
Huautla, Mex.	154	F10	18.08 N	96.50 W
Huaxian, China	58	J5	23.22 N	113.12 E
Huaxian, China	58	D6	35.34 N	114.30 E
Huaxian, China	58	D3	34.29 N	109.45 E
Huaynamota, stm., Mex.	154	E6	21.57 N	104.31 W
Huayna Potosí, Nevado, mtn., Bol.	166	C3	16.16 S	68.11 W
Huazamota, Mex.	154	D6	22.29 N	104.31 W
Huazhou, China	58	K4	21.38 N	110.36 E
Hubbard, Ia., U.S.	130	B4	42.18 N	93.17 W
Hubbard, Tx., U.S.	136	C11	31.50 N	96.48 W
Hubbard Creek, stm., Tx., U.S.	136	B8	32.53 N	98.52 W
Hubbard Creek Reservoir, l., Tx., U.S.	136	B8	32.47 N	99.00 W
Hubbard Lake, l., Mi., U.S.	126	D6	44.48 N	83.32 W
Hubbards, N.S., Can.	122	F12	44.38 N	64.04 W
Hubbell, Mi., U.S.	128	D10	47.09 N	88.25 W
Hubbell Trading Post National Historic Site, p.o.i., Az., U.S.	150	H7	35.43 N	109.33 W
Hubbelrath, ngh., Ger.	181		51.16 N	6.55 E
Hubei, state, China	58	F5	31.00 N	112.00 E
Huberdeau, Qc., Can.	126	C15	45.59 N	74.36 W
Hubli-Dhārwār, India	69	D2	15.20 N	75.08 E
Hubuleng, China	58	A4	41.16 N	111.07 E
Hubynykha, Ukr.	38	E14	48.47 N	35.14 E
Huchow see Huzhou, China	58	F9	30.51 N	120.05 E
Huckarde, ngh., Ger.	181		51.32 N	7.24 E
Hucking, Eng., U.K.	178		51.18 N	0.39 E
Huckingen, ngh., Ger.	181		51.22 N	6.43 E
Huckleberry Island, i., N.Y., U.S.	194		40.53 N	73.45 W
Huckleberry Mountain, mtn., Or., U.S.	146	G4	43.51 N	122.19 W
Hucknall, Eng., U.K.	10	H11	53.02 N	1.12 W
Huddart Park, p.o.i., Ca., U.S.	200		37.26 N	122.19 W
Hudderfield Narrow Canal, can., Eng., U.K.	180		53.29 N	2.06 W
Huddersfield, Eng., U.K.	10	H11	53.38 N	1.47 W
Huddinge, Swe.	16	H15	59.14 N	17.58 E
Huddle Park Municipal Golf Course, p.o.i., S. Afr.	191d		26.09 S	28.07 E
Huder, China	52	A9	50.00 N	121.38 E
Hudgens Creek, stm., Ar., U.S.	134	D7	33.37 N	91.59 W
Hudiksvall, Swe.	16	F15	61.44 N	17.07 E
Hudson, Fl., U.S.	132	H3	28.21 N	82.41 W
Hudson, Ia., U.S.	130	B5	42.24 N	92.27 W
Hudson, Mi., U.S.	124	C1	41.51 N	84.21 W
Hudson, N.Y., U.S.	126	F16	42.15 N	73.46 W
Hudson, N.C., U.S.	124	I4	35.50 N	81.29 W
Hudson, Oh., U.S.	124	C4	41.13 N	81.25 W
Hudson, S.D., U.S.	128	H2	43.07 N	96.27 W
Hudson, Wi., U.S.	128	G6	44.58 N	92.44 W
Hudson, Wy., U.S.	140	E4	42.54 N	108.34 W
Hudson, co., N.J., U.S.	194		40.44 N	74.02 W
Hudson, stm., U.S.	126	G16	40.41 N	74.02 W
Hudson, stm., Ga., U.S.	132	B2	34.14 N	83.10 W
Hudson, Baie d' see Hudson Bay, b., Can.	110	C13	60.00 N	86.00 W
Hudson, Détroit d' see Hudson Strait, strt., Can.	110	C16	62.30 N	72.00 W
Hudson Bay, Sk., Can.	142	B11	52.51 N	102.23 W
Hudson Bay, b., Can.	110	C13	60.00 N	86.00 W
Hudson Falls, N.Y., U.S.	126	E16	43.18 N	73.35 W
Hudson Hope see Hudson's Hope, B.C., Can.	110	D6	56.01 N	121.55 W
Hudson's Hope, B.C., Can.	110	D6	56.01 N	121.55 W
Hudson Strait, strt., Can.	116	C16	62.30 N	72.00 W
Hudžand, Taj.	72	A10	40.16 N	69.38 E
Hue, Viet.	64	D8	16.28 N	107.34 E
Huebra, stm., Spain	28	D4	41.02 N	6.48 W
Huechuraba, Chile	204e		33.21 S	70.40 W
Huedin, Rom.	36	C10	46.52 N	23.02 E
Huehuetenango, Guat.	156	E2	15.20 N	91.26 W
Huejotitán, Mex.	136	G1	27.03 N	106.10 W
Huejutla de Reyes, Mex.	154	E9	21.10 N	98.30 W
Huelgoat, Fr.	20	F5	48.22 N	3.45 W
Huelma, Spain	28	G7	37.39 N	3.27 W
Huelva, Spain	28	G4	37.16 N	6.57 W
Huelva, co., Spain	28	G4	37.30 N	6.55 W
Huelva, stm., Spain	28	G4	37.26 N	6.00 W
Huentelauquén, Chile	172	E2	31.34 S	71.32 W
Huércal-Overa, Spain	28	G8	37.23 N	1.57 W
Huerfano, stm., Co., U.S.	138	C4	38.14 N	104.15 W
Huerfano Mountain, mtn., N.M., U.S.	150	G9	36.26 N	107.51 W
Huerlumada, China	70	B13	32.49 N	89.59 E
Huerva, stm., Spain	28	C9	41.39 N	0.51 W
Huesca, Spain	28	B10	42.08 N	0.24 W
Huesca, co., Spain	28	B10	42.05 N	0.10 W
Huéscar, Spain	28	G8	37.48 N	2.32 W
Huetamo de Núñez, Mex.	154	F8	18.35 N	100.53 W
Huete, Spain	28	D8	40.08 N	2.41 W
Hueytown, Al., U.S.	134	D11	33.25 N	87.03 W
Hufrat an-Nahās, Sudan	82	F4	9.44 N	24.18 E
Huftarøy, i., Nor.	16	G3	60.02 N	5.15 E
Hügel, Villa, bldg., Ger.	181		51.25 N	7.01 E
Hugh Butler Lake, res., Ne., U.S.	140	G12	40.22 N	100.42 W
Hughenden, Austl.	98	C5	20.50 S	144.13 E
Hughes, Ak., U.S.	109	C9	66.02 N	154.14 W
Hughes, Ar., U.S.	134	C8	34.56 N	90.28 W
Hughes, stm., Mb., Can.	124	E4	56.45 N	100.01 W
Hughes Airport, arpt., Ca., U.S.	198		33.58 N	118.25 W
Hughes Springs, Tx., U.S.	136	B13	33.00 N	94.37 W
Hughesville, Pa., U.S.	124	C9	41.14 N	76.43 W
Hugh Keenleyside Dam, dam., B.C., Can.	144	G12	49.20 N	117.49 W
Hughson, Ca., U.S.	148	F5	37.36 N	120.51 W
Hugh Town, Eng., U.K.	10	L6	49.54 N	6.18 W
Hugli, stm., India	70	H12	21.36 N	87.59 E
Hugo, Co., U.S.	138	B5	39.08 N	103.27 W
Hugo, Ok., U.S.	134	C3	34.01 N	95.31 W
Hugo Lake, res., Ok., U.S.	134	C3	34.03 N	95.24 W
Hugoton, Ks., U.S.	138	D7	37.10 N	101.20 W
Huguenot Lake, l., N.Y., U.S.	194		40.56 N	73.47 W
Huhar, stm., China	54	B4	43.54 N	120.44 E
Huhehot see Hohhot, China	58	A4	40.48 N	111.38 E
Huiarau Range, mts., N.Z.	102	D7	38.40 S	177.04 E
Huib-Hoch Plateau, plat., Nmb.	90	E3	27.05 S	16.34 E
Huichang, China	58	I6	25.34 N	115.47 E
Huichapan, Mex.	154	E9	20.21 N	99.40 W
Huicheng see Huilai, China	58	J7	23.02 N	116.17 E
Hŭich'ŏn, Kor., N.	54	D7	40.10 N	126.16 E
Huiji, stm., China	58	D6	33.52 N	115.37 E
Huila, state, Col.	168	F4	2.30 N	75.45 W
Huila, Nevado del, vol., Col.	168	F3	2.59 N	75.58 W
Huilai, China	58	J7	23.02 N	116.17 E
Huili, China	52	F5	26.40 N	102.14 E
Huillapima, Arg.	172	D4	28.43 S	65.58 W
Huimin, China	58	C7	37.29 N	117.31 E
Huinan, China	52	C10	42.40 N	126.02 E
Huinca Renancó, Arg.	172	G5	34.50 S	64.22 W
Hüinghausen, Ger.	181		51.11 N	7.48 E
Huining, China	58	D1	35.42 N	105.03 E
Huisachal, Mex.	136	H6	26.47 N	101.07 W
Huishui, China	58	H2	26.07 N	106.24 E
Huisne, stm., Fr.	20	F9	48.00 N	0.11 E
Huitong, China	58	H3	26.54 N	109.31 E
Huitzo, Mex.	154	G10	17.16 N	96.51 W
Huitzuco de los Figueroa, Mex.	154	F9	18.18 N	99.21 W
Huixian, China	58	E2	33.45 N	106.16 E
Huixian, China	58	D5	35.32 N	113.54 E
Huixtla, Mex.	154	H12	15.08 N	92.27 W
Huiyang see Huizhou, China	58	J6	23.05 N	114.24 E
Huize, China	52	F5	26.24 N	103.17 E
Huizhou, China	58	J6	23.05 N	114.24 E
Hujiazhuang, China	187b		31.21 N	121.25 E
Hŭksan-chedo, is., Kor., S.	54	G6	34.30 N	125.20 E
Hukui see Fukui, Japan	56	C9	36.04 N	136.13 E
Hukuntsi, Bots.	90	D5	24.00 S	21.46 E
Hukuoka see Fukuoka, Japan	56	F3	33.34 N	130.24 E
Hukusima see Fukushima, Japan	56	B13	37.45 N	140.28 E
Hukuyama see Fukuyama, Japan	56	E6	34.29 N	133.22 E
Hulan, China	52	B7	45.58 N	126.36 E
Hulan Ergi, China	52	B9	47.11 N	123.38 E
Hulbert, Mi., U.S.	126	B4	46.21 N	85.09 W
Hulbert, Ok., U.S.	130	I2	35.55 N	95.08 W
Huldrefossen, wtfl., Nor.	16	F3	61.28 N	5.58 E
Hulett, Wy., U.S.	140	C8	44.40 N	104.36 W
Hulga, stm., Russia	44	B10	64.20 N	61.01 E
Huliaipole, Ukr.	38	F15	47.39 N	36.14 E
Hulin, China	52	B11	45.46 N	132.59 E
Hulín, Czech Rep.	24	G13	49.19 N	17.27 E
Hulin, stm., China	54	B4	45.00 N	122.22 E
Huliu, stm., China	58	A6	40.13 N	114.37 E
Hull, Qc., Can.	126	C14	45.26 N	75.43 W
Hull, Il., U.S.	130	E6	39.42 N	91.12 W
Hull, Ia., U.S.	128	H2	43.11 N	96.08 W
Hull, Tx., U.S.	136	D13	30.08 N	94.38 W
Hull Bay, b., Ma., U.S.	201		42.18 N	70.53 W
Hullo, Est.	26	A6	58.59 N	23.17 E
Hulløya, i., Nor.	14	D7	68.04 N	16.16 E
Hulmeville, Pa., U.S.	203		40.08 N	74.55 W
Hüls, Ger.	181		51.40 N	7.08 E
Hülser Berg, ngh., Ger.	181		51.24 N	6.31 E
Hülser Berg, hill, Ger.	181		51.23 N	6.33 E
Hultsfred, Swe.	16	J13	57.30 N	15.51 E
Hulun see Hailar, China	52	B8	49.11 N	119.43 E
Hulun Nur, l., China	52	B8	49.01 N	117.32 E
Huma, China	50	F14	51.42 N	126.39 E
Huma, Tonga	100e	o15	21.19 S	174.57 E
Huma, stm., China	50	F14	51.37 N	126.41 E
Humacao, P.R.	158a	b4	18.06 N	65.49 W
Humahuaca, Arg.	166	D3	23.12 S	65.21 W
Humaitá, Braz.	164	E5	7.29 S	63.01 W
Humaitá, Para.	172	C8	27.04 S	58.31 W
Humansdorp, S. Afr.	90	I7	34.01 S	24.46 E
Humansville, Mo., U.S.	130	G4	37.47 N	93.34 W
Humara, Jabal al-, hill, Sudan	82	D6	16.16 N	30.59 E
Humarock, Ma., U.S.	201		42.08 N	70.41 W
Humayun's Tomb, hist., India	190a		28.36 N	77.15 E
Humbe, Ang.	88	D1	16.38 S	14.54 E
Humber, stm., Eng., U.K.	10	H12	53.39 N	0.10 W
Humber Bay, b., On., Can.	193b		43.38 N	79.29 W
Humberto de Campos, Braz.	170	B4	2.37 S	43.27 W
Humber Valley Park, p.o.i., On., Can.	193b		43.39 N	79.30 W
Humbird, Wi., U.S.	128	G8	44.31 N	90.53 W
Humboldt, Sk., Can.	142	B8	52.11 N	105.06 W
Humboldt, Az., U.S.	150	I4	34.30 N	112.14 W
Humboldt, Il., U.S.	130	E9	39.35 N	88.19 W
Humboldt, Ia., U.S.	130	B3	42.43 N	94.12 W
Humboldt, Ks., U.S.	130	G2	37.48 N	95.26 W
Humboldt, Ne., U.S.	130	D2	40.10 N	95.56 W
Humboldt, S.D., U.S.	140	D15	43.38 N	97.04 W
Humboldt, Tn., U.S.	134	B10	35.49 N	88.54 W
Humboldt, mtn., N. Cal.	101d	m16	21.53 S	166.25 E
Humboldt, stm., Nv., U.S.	148	C7	40.00 N	118.32 W
Humboldt, North Fork, stm., Nv., U.S.	148	B10	40.55 N	115.33 W
Humboldt, Planetario, bldg., Ven.	204c		10.30 N	66.50 W
Humboldt, South Fork, stm., Nv., U.S.	148	C10	40.44 N	115.56 W
Humboldt Bay, b., Ca., U.S.	148	C1	40.49 N	124.08 W
Humboldt Gletscher, ice, Grnld.	108	B13	79.30 N	63.00 W
Humboldt Lake, l., Nv., U.S.	148	D7	39.58 N	118.38 W
Humboldt Park, p.o.i., Il., U.S.	196		41.54 N	87.42 W
Humboldt Redwoods State Park, p.o.i., Ca., U.S.	148	C1	40.19 N	124.00 W
Hume, Ca., U.S.	148	G7	36.48 N	118.53 W
Hume, Lake, res., Austl.	98	J6	36.08 S	147.02 E
Humeburn, Austl.	98	F5	27.23 S	145.13 E
Hu Men, est., China	58	J5	22.54 N	113.32 E
Humenné, Slvk.	24	H17	48.56 N	21.55 E
Húmera, Spain	184a		40.26 N	3.47 W
Humeston, Ia., U.S.	130	D4	40.51 N	93.29 W
Hummi, ozero, l., Russia	50	F16	50.19 N	137.19 E
Humphrey, Ar., U.S.	134	C7	34.26 N	91.42 W
Humphrey, Ne., U.S.	140	F15	41.41 N	97.29 W
Humphreys, Mount, mtn., Ca., U.S.	148	F7	37.17 N	118.40 W
Humphreys Peak, mtn., Az., U.S.	150	H5	35.20 N	111.40 W
Humpolec, Czech Rep.	24	G11	49.32 N	15.21 E
Humppila, Fin.	16	G10	60.56 N	23.20 E
Humptulips, stm., Wa., U.S.	146	C3	47.01 N	124.02 W
Humpty Doo, Austl.	96	B6	12.35 S	131.20 E
Hūn, Libya	82	B3	29.07 N	15.56 E
Hun, stm., China	52	C9	41.00 N	122.26 E
Hun, stm., China	54	D6	40.51 N	125.42 E
Hunabasi see Funabashi, Japan	56	D12	35.42 N	139.58 E
Húnaflói, b., Ice.	12a	j29	65.50 N	20.50 W
Hunan, state, China	58	H4	28.00 N	111.00 E
Hunchun, China	52	C11	42.52 N	130.21 E
Huncoat, Eng., U.K.	180		53.46 N	2.20 W
Hundested, Den.	16	L9	55.57 N	11.51 E
Hundorp, Nor.	16	F7	61.33 N	9.54 E
Hundred, W.V., U.S.	124	E5	39.40 N	80.28 W
Hundred End, Eng., U.K.	180		53.42 N	2.53 W
Hunedoara, Rom.	36	D9	45.45 N	22.55 E
Hunedoara, state, Rom.	36	C9	45.45 N	23.00 E
Hünfeld, Ger.	24	F5	50.40 N	9.45 E
Hungary, ctry., Eur.	36	B6	47.00 N	20.00 E
Hŭngdŏki-dong, Kor., N.	54	E7	39.50 N	127.38 E
Hungerford, Austl.	98	G5	28.59 S	144.24 E
Hungerford, Tx., U.S.	136	E11	29.24 N	96.05 W
Hung Long, Viet.	187c		10.40 N	106.39 E
Hŭngnam see Hŭngdŏki-dong, Kor., N.	54	E7	39.50 N	127.38 E
Hungry Horse, Mt., U.S.	146	B12	48.22 N	114.02 W
Hungry Horse Dam, dam., Mt., U.S.	146	B13	48.14 N	114.04 W
Hungry Horse Reservoir, res., Mt., U.S.	146	B12	48.15 N	113.50 W
Hung Yen, Viet.	64	B8	20.39 N	106.04 E
Huningue, Fr.	24	I3	47.36 N	7.35 E
Hunjiang, China	52	C10	41.57 N	126.28 E
Hunker, Pa., U.S.	197b		40.12 N	79.38 W
Hunlen Falls, wtfl., B.C., Can.	144	D5	52.15 N	125.46 W
Hunnebostrand, Swe.	16	I9	58.27 N	11.18 E
Hunsberge, mts., Nmb.	90	E3	27.45 S	17.12 E
Hunsrück, mts., Ger.	24	G3	49.45 N	7.08 E
Hunstanton, Eng., U.K.	10	I13	52.56 N	0.29 E
Hunsūr, India	69	E3	12.17 N	76.17 E
Hunswinkel, Ger.	181		51.05 N	7.48 E
Hunte, stm., Ger.	24	D4	53.13 N	8.28 E
Hunter, N.D., U.S.	128	D1	47.11 N	97.13 W
Hunter, stm., Austl.	98	I8	32.46 S	151.43 E
Hunter Island, i., Austl.	99a	n12	40.32 S	144.45 E
Hunter Island, i., B.C., Can.	144	D2	51.54 N	128.02 W
Hunter Island, i., N.Y., U.S.	194		40.53 N	73.47 W
Hunter Mountain, mtn., N.Y., U.S.	124	B11	42.10 N	74.14 W
Hunter River, P.E., Can.	122	D13	46.21 N	63.21 W
Hunters, Wa., U.S.	146	B8	48.07 N	118.12 W
Hunters Bay, b., Mya.	64	C1	19.55 N	93.22 E
Hunters Hill, Austl.	192a		33.50 S	151.09 E
Hunters Point, c., Ca., U.S.	200		37.43 N	122.22 W
Hunter Wash, stm., N.M., U.S.	150	G8	36.17 N	108.33 W
Huntingburg, In., U.S.	130	F11	38.18 N	86.57 W
Huntingdon, Qc., Can.	126	C15	45.05 N	74.10 W
Huntingdon, Eng., U.K.	10	I12	52.19 N	0.11 W
Huntingdon, Pa., U.S.	124	D7	40.29 N	78.00 W
Huntingdon, Tn., U.S.	134	I9	36.00 N	88.25 W
Huntingdon Valley, Pa., U.S.	203		40.07 N	75.03 W
Huntingdon Valley Creek, stm., Pa., U.S.	203		40.07 N	75.04 W
Hunting Island State Park, p.o.i., S.C., U.S.	132	D5	32.20 N	80.30 W
Hunting Ridge, Va., U.S.	202c		38.55 N	77.12 W
Huntington, In., U.S.	130	D12	40.52 N	85.28 W
Huntington, Or., U.S.	146	F9	44.21 N	117.15 W
Huntington, Tx., U.S.	136	C13	31.16 N	94.34 W
Huntington, Ut., U.S.	150	D5	39.19 N	110.57 W
Huntington, Va., U.S.	202c		38.48 N	77.15 W
Huntington, W.V., U.S.	124	F3	38.24 N	82.26 W
Huntington Bay, N.Y., U.S.	194		40.53 N	73.24 W
Huntington Bay, b., N.Y., U.S.	194		40.55 N	73.25 W
Huntington Beach, Ca., U.S.	148	J7	33.39 N	117.59 W
Huntington Beach, N.Y., U.S.	194		40.54 N	73.23 W
Huntington Creek, stm., Nv., U.S.	150	C1	40.37 N	115.43 W
Huntington Creek, stm., Ut., U.S.	150	D6	39.10 N	110.54 W
Huntington Harbor, b., N.Y., U.S.	194		40.54 N	73.26 W
Huntington Library, sci., Ca., U.S.	198		34.08 N	118.07 W
Huntington Park, p.o.i., Oh., U.S.	197a		41.29 N	81.56 W
Huntington Woods, Mi., U.S.	199		42.28 N	83.10 W
Hunting Valley, Oh., U.S.	197a		41.31 N	81.23 W
Huntland, Tn., U.S.	134	B12	35.03 N	86.16 W
Huntley, Mt., U.S.	140	B4	45.53 N	108.19 W
Huntly, N.Z.	102	C6	37.33 S	175.08 E
Huntly, Scot., U.K.	10	D10	57.26 N	2.48 W
Hunt Mountain, mtn., Wy., U.S.	140	C5	44.44 N	107.45 W
Hunton, Eng., U.K.	178		51.13 N	0.28 E
Hunt's Cross, ngh., Eng., U.K.	180		53.21 N	2.51 W
Huntsville, On., Can.	126	C10	45.19 N	79.12 W
Huntsville, Al., U.S.	134	C12	34.43 N	86.35 W
Huntsville, Ar., U.S.	130	H4	36.05 N	93.44 W
Huntsville, Mo., U.S.	130	E5	39.26 N	92.33 W
Huntsville, Tn., U.S.	130	H13	36.24 N	84.29 W
Huntsville, Tx., U.S.	136	D12	30.43 N	95.32 W
Huntsville, Ut., U.S.	150	B5	41.16 N	111.46 W
Hünxerwald, p.o.i., Ger.	181		51.40 N	6.50 E
Hunyuan, China	58	B5	39.41 N	113.40 E
Huoergeluo, China	52	B9	45.33 N	120.55 E
Huong Hoa, Viet.	64	D8	16.38 N	106.46 E
Huong Khe, Viet.	64	C7	18.11 N	105.42 E
Huon Gulf, b., Pap. N. Gui.	101a	b4	7.10 S	147.25 E
Huon Peninsula, pen., Pap. N. Gui.	101a	b4	6.25 S	147.25 E
Huonville, Austl.	99a	o13	43.01 S	147.02 E
Huoqiu, China	58	E7	32.20 N	116.16 E
Huoshan, China	58	F7	31.24 N	116.20 E
Huo Shan, mtn., China	58	F7	31.06 N	116.12 E
Huoxian, China	58	C4	36.37 N	111.40 E
Huraymilā, Sau. Ar.	74	H10	25.07 N	46.08 E
Hurd, Cape, c., On., Can.	126	C8	45.13 N	81.41 W
Hurdiyo, Som.	86	B10	10.34 N	51.08 E
Hurdsfield, Eng., U.K.	180		53.16 N	2.06 W
Hüren Tovon uul, mtn., Mong.	52	C4	44.45 N	95.09 E
Hurepoix, reg., Fr.	179		48.37 N	2.07 E
Hure Qi, China	52	C9	42.43 N	121.47 E
Hurffville, N.J., U.S.	203		39.46 N	75.07 W
Hurghada, Egypt	76	K4	27.14 N	33.50 E
Hurley, Ms., U.S.	134	G10	30.39 N	88.29 W
Hurley, N.M., U.S.	150	K8	32.41 N	108.07 W
Hurley, S.D., U.S.	140	D15	43.17 N	97.04 W
Hurley, Wi., U.S.	128	E8	46.26 N	90.10 W
Hurlock, Md., U.S.	124	F10	38.37 N	75.51 W
Huron, Ca., U.S.	148	G5	36.12 N	120.05 W
Huron, Oh., U.S.	124	C3	41.23 N	82.32 W
Huron, S.D., U.S.	140	C14	44.21 N	98.12 W
Huron, stm., Mi., U.S.	124	B2	42.02 N	83.11 W
Huron, Lake, l., N.A.	126	D7	44.30 N	82.15 W
Huron Mountains, hills, Mi., U.S.	126	B2	46.48 N	87.55 W
Hurricane, Ut., U.S.	150	F3	37.10 N	113.17 W
Hurricane Cliffs, clf., U.S.	150	F3	37.15 N	113.10 W
Hurricane Creek, stm., Ar., U.S.	134	C6	34.06 N	92.24 W
Hurricane Creek, stm., Ga., U.S.	132	E3	31.15 N	82.08 W
Hurricane Lake, l., N.D., U.S.	142	F14	48.25 N	99.30 W
Hurricane Wash, stm., Az., U.S.	150	G3	37.00 N	113.23 W
Hurstbridge, Austl.	98	K5	37.38 S	145.11 E
Hurst Green, Eng., U.K.	178		51.15 N	0.01 E
Hurstwood Reservoir, res., Eng., U.K.	180		53.47 N	2.10 W
Hurt, Va., U.S.	124	G6	37.05 N	79.18 W
Hurtado, stm., Chile	172	E2	30.35 S	71.10 W
Hurtsboro, Al., U.S.	134	E13	32.14 N	85.25 W
Hurum, pen., Nor.	16	H8	59.39 N	10.29 E
Hurunui, stm., N.Z.	102	F4	42.54 S	173.16 E
Hurup, Den.	16	K6	56.45 N	8.25 E
Hurzuf, Ukr.	38	I13	44.33 N	34.17 E
Husainīwāla, India	70	C5	30.59 N	74.32 E
Husainpur, Bngl.	70	F13	24.25 N	90.40 E
Húsavík, Far. Is.	12b	n34	61.49 N	6.40 W
Húsavík, Ice.	12a	j31	66.02 N	17.19 W
Huse see Higashiōsaka, Japan	56	E8	34.39 N	135.35 E
Husen, ngh., Ger.	181		51.33 N	7.36 E
Hushan, China	54	B9	45.35 N	130.35 E
Hushitai, China	54	C5	41.56 N	123.30 E
Huși, Rom.	36	C15	46.40 N	28.04 E
Husiatyn, Ukr.	38	D5	49.05 N	26.11 E
Huskvarna, Swe.	16	J12	57.47 N	14.18 E
Huslia, Ak., U.S.	109	C8	65.39 N	156.21 W
Husnes, Nor.	16	H3	59.52 N	5.44 E
Husnesfjorden, strt., Nor.	16	H3	59.51 N	5.37 E
Hussar, Ab., Can.	144	E18	51.01 N	112.39 W
Hustadvika, strt., Nor.	16	E4	63.02 N	7.04 E
Hustisford, Wi., U.S.	128	H10	43.20 N	88.35 W
Husum, Ger.	24	B4	54.28 N	9.03 E
Husum, Swe.	16	D17	63.20 N	19.10 E
Hutag, Mong.	52	B5	49.23 N	102.39 E
Hutag-Uul, Mong.	52	C7	43.23 N	110.13 E
Hutanopan, Indon.	66	C1	0.39 N	99.42 E
Hutayim, Harrat, lav., Sau. Ar.	74	G6	26.14 N	40.10 E
Hutchinson, S. Afr.	90	G6	31.29 S	23.11 E
Hutchinson, Ks., U.S.	138	C11	38.03 N	97.55 W
Hutchinson, Mn., U.S.	128	G4	44.53 N	94.22 W
Hutchinson, stm., N.Y., U.S.	194		40.52 N	73.50 W
Hutchinson Island, i., Fl., U.S.	132	I5	27.21 N	80.15 W
Hutch Mountain, mtn., Az., U.S.	150	I5	34.47 N	111.22 W
Huti, Ukr.	38	C14	50.08 N	35.19 E
Hutsonville, Il., U.S.	130	E10	39.05 N	87.39 W
Hütteldorf, ngh., Aus.	182b		48.12 N	16.16 E
Hüttenheim, ngh., Ger.	181		51.22 N	6.43 E
Huttig, Ar., U.S.	134	D6	33.02 N	92.11 W
Hutto, Tx., U.S.	136	D10	30.32 N	97.32 W
Hutton, Eng., U.K.	178		51.38 N	0.22 E
Hutton, Eng., U.K.	180		53.44 N	2.46 W
Hutton, Mount, mtn., Austl.	98	E7	25.51 S	148.20 E
Huttrop, ngh., Ger.	181		51.27 N	7.03 E
Hutuo, stm., China	58	B5	38.11 N	116.03 E
Huwei, Tai.	58	J9	23.42 N	120.26 E
Huxford, Al., U.S.	134	F11	31.12 N	87.28 W

Name	Page	Map Ref.	Latitude	Longitude
Huxi, China	58	H6	26.10 N	114.42 E
Huxian, China	58	D3	34.10 N	108.33 E
Huxley, Ab., Can.	144	E17	51.56 N	113.14 W
Huy, Bel.	20	D14	50.31 N	5.14 E
Huyton-with-Roby, Eng., U.K.	180		53.25 N	2.52 W
Hüyük, Tur.	34	F14	37.57 N	31.35 E
Hūzgān, Iran	74	E11	31.27 N	48.04 E
Huzhen, China	58	G9	28.48 N	120.15 E
Huzhou, China	58	F9	30.51 N	120.05 E
Huzisawa see Fujisawa, Japan	56	D12	35.20 N	139.29 E
Hvaler, is., Nor.	16	H8	59.02 N	10.58 E
Hvalovo, Russia	18	H19	59.56 N	32.45 E
Hvalynsk, Russia	40	E16	52.29 N	48.05 E
Hvannadalshnúkur, mtn., Ice.	12a	k31	64.01 N	16.41 W
Hvar, Cro.	30	G13	43.10 N	16.26 E
Hvar, Otok, i., Cro.	30	G13	43.09 N	16.45 E
Hvardiis'ke, Ukr.	38	H13	45.07 N	34.01 E
Hvardiis'ke, Ukr.	38	E14	48.43 N	35.18 E
Hvardiis'ke, Ukr.	38	D5	49.20 N	26.42 E
Hvarski Kanal, strt., Cro.	30	G13	43.15 N	16.37 E
Hvastoviči, Russia	26	G18	53.27 N	35.06 E
Hvatovka, Russia	40	E15	52.21 N	46.33 E
Hveragerði, Ice.	12a	k29	64.00 N	21.12 W
Hvide Sande, Den.	16	K5	56.01 N	8.07 E
Hvittingfoss, Nor.	16	H7	59.29 N	10.00 E
Hvojnaja, Russia	26	B17	58.54 N	34.30 E
Hvolsvöllur, Ice.	12a	l29	63.45 N	20.15 W
Hwainan see Huainan, China	58	E7	32.39 N	117.00 E
Hwaining see Anqing, China	58	F7	30.30 N	117.02 E
Hwange, Zimb.	88	D4	18.22 S	26.30 E
Hwang-hae see Yellow Sea, s., Asia	54	F5	36.00 N	123.00 E
Hwangju-ŭp, Kor., N.	54	E6	38.40 N	125.47 E
Hwangshih see Huangshi, China	58	F6	30.12 N	115.05 E
Hyakuri-kichi, Kōkū-jieitai-, mil., Japan	56	C13	36.11 N	140.25 E
Hyannis, Ma., U.S.	124	C15	41.39 N	70.16 W
Hyannis, Ne., U.S.	140	F11	41.59 N	101.45 W
Hyargas nuur, l., Mong.	52	B3	49.12 N	93.24 E
Hyattville, Wy., U.S.	140	C5	44.14 N	107.38 W
Hyco, stm., U.S.	124	H7	36.41 N	78.43 W
Hyco Lake, res., N.C., U.S.	124	H6	36.30 N	79.04 W
Hyden, Austl.	96	F3	32.26 S	118.52 E
Hyden, Ky., U.S.	124	G2	37.08 N	83.23 W
Hyde Park, Guy.	164	B6	6.30 N	58.16 W
Hyde Park, N.Y., U.S.	124	C12	41.47 N	73.56 W
Hyde Park, Vt., U.S.	122	F4	44.35 N	72.36 W
Hyde Park, ngh., Il., U.S.	196		41.48 N	87.36 W
Hyde Park, ngh., Ma., U.S.	201		42.15 N	71.08 W
Hyde Park, p.o.i., Austl.	192a		33.53 S	151.13 E
Hyde Park, p.o.i., Eng., U.K.	178		51.30 N	0.10 W
Hyde Park, p.o.i., N.Y., U.S.	202a		43.06 N	79.01 W
Hyderābād, India	69	C4	17.23 N	78.29 E
Hyderābād, Pak.	70	F2	25.22 N	68.21 E
Hydra see Ýdra, i., Grc.	34	F6	37.20 N	23.29 E
Hydraulic, B.C., Can.	144	D9	52.36 N	121.42 W
Hydro, Ok., U.S.	138	F10	35.33 N	98.34 W
Hydrographers Passage, strt., Austl.	98	C7	20.45 S	150.15 E
Hyères, Fr.	22	F12	43.07 N	6.07 E
Hyères, Îles d', is., Fr.	22	G12	43.00 N	6.17 E
Hyesan, Kor., N.	54	D8	41.23 N	128.10 E
Hyland, stm., Can.	110	C5	59.51 N	128.11 W
Hylestad, Nor.	16	H5	59.05 N	7.32 E
Hyltebruk, Swe.	16	K11	57.00 N	13.17 E
Hymera, In., U.S.	130	E10	39.11 N	87.17 W
Hyndburn, mun., Eng., U.K.	180		53.45 N	2.23 W
Hyndman, Pa., U.S.	124	E7	39.49 N	78.42 W
Hyndman Peak, mtn., Id., U.S.	146	G12	43.45 N	114.08 W
Hyōgo, state, Japan	56	D7	35.00 N	135.00 E
Hyōgo, ngh., Japan	188		34.39 N	135.10 E
Hyŏn-ni, Kor., S.	56	B1	37.58 N	128.20 E
Hyrum, Ut., U.S.	150	B5	41.38 N	111.51 W
Hyrynsalmi, Fin.	18	C15	64.40 N	28.31 E
Hysham, Mt., U.S.	140	A5	46.18 N	107.14 W
Hysvær, is., Nor.	16	B9	65.45 N	11.46 E
Hythe, Ab., Can.	144	A11	55.19 N	119.34 W
Hythe, Eng., U.K.	10	J13	51.04 N	1.04 E
Hythe End, Eng., U.K.	178		51.27 N	0.32 W
Hyūga, Japan	56	G4	32.25 N	131.38 E
Hyūga-nada, s., Japan	56	G4	32.00 N	131.35 E
Hyvinge see Hyvinkää, Fin.	18	G11	60.38 N	24.52 E
Hyvinkää (Hyvinge), Fin.	18	G11	60.38 N	24.52 E
I				
Iacanga, Braz.	170	K1	21.53 S	49.01 W
Iaciara, Braz.	170	H2	14.08 S	46.42 W
Iaco (Yaco), stm., S.A.	164	E4	9.01 S	68.35 W
Iaçu, Braz.	170	G5	12.45 S	40.12 W
Iaeger, W.V., U.S.	124	G4	37.27 N	81.48 W
Ialomița, state, Rom.	36	E14	44.40 N	27.20 E
Ialomița, stm., Rom.	36	E13	44.42 N	27.51 E
Ialomiței, Balta, sw., Rom.	36	E14	44.30 N	28.00 E
Ialpug, stm., Eur.	36	C15	45.41 N	28.35 E
Iamonia, Lake, l., Fl., U.S.	134	G14	30.38 N	84.14 W
Iano, Monte, mtn., Italy	185a		41.46 N	12.44 E
Iapó, stm., Braz.	172	B12	24.30 S	50.24 W
Iapu, Braz.	170	J4	19.26 S	42.13 W
Iargara, Mol.	38	G7	46.26 N	28.27 E
Iași, Rom.	36	B14	47.10 N	27.35 E
Iași, state, Rom.	36	B14	47.15 N	27.15 E
Iatt, Lake, res., La., U.S.	134	F6	31.35 N	92.39 W
Iauaretê, Braz.	168	G7	0.35 N	69.12 W
Iazu, Rom.	36	E14	44.43 N	27.25 E
Ib, stm., India	70	G10	21.32 N	83.50 E
Iba, Phil.	68	C2	15.20 N	119.58 E
Ibadan, Nig.	84	H5	7.23 N	3.54 E
Ibagué, Col.	168	E4	4.26 N	75.15 W
Ibaiti, Braz.	172	A12	23.50 S	50.11 W
Iban, Pegunungan see Iran Mountains, mts., Asia	66	B9	2.05 N	114.55 E
Ibănești, Rom.	36	A13	48.04 N	26.22 E
Ibapah Peak, mtn., Ut., U.S.	150	D3	39.50 N	113.55 W
Ibar, stm., Yugo.	36	F7	43.43 N	20.45 E
Ibaraki, state, Japan	56	C13	36.30 N	140.30 E
Ibarra, Ec.	168	G2	0.21 N	78.07 W
Ibarreta, Arg.	172	B8	25.13 S	59.52 W
Ibb, Yemen	72	G5	13.57 N	44.10 E
Ibbenbüren, Ger.	24	D3	52.16 N	7.43 E
Ibembo, D.R.C.	86	D4	2.38 N	23.36 E
Iberá, Esteros del, sw., Arg.	172	D8	28.03 S	57.10 W
Iberia, Mo., U.S.	130	F5	38.05 N	92.17 W
Iberian Mountains see Ibérico, Sistema, mts., Spain	28	C8	40.59 N	1.56 W
Iberian Peninsula, pen., Eur.	8	G7	40.00 N	5.00 W
Ibérica, Península see Iberian Peninsula, pen., Eur.	8	G7	40.00 N	5.00 W
Ibérico, Sistema (Iberian Mountains), mts., Spain	28	C8	40.59 N	1.56 W
Ibese, Nig.	191a		6.33 N	3.29 E
Ibi, Nig.	84	H6	8.11 N	9.44 E
Ibiá, Braz.	170	J2	19.28 S	46.31 W
Ibiapina, Braz.	170	B5	3.55 S	40.54 W
Ibicaraí, Braz.	170	H6	14.51 S	39.37 W
Ibicuí, Braz.	170	H5	14.50 S	39.58 W
Ibicuí, stm., Braz.	172	D9	29.25 S	56.46 W
Ibipira, Braz.	170	D3	6.31 S	44.38 W
Ibiquera, Braz.	170	G5	12.38 S	40.56 W
Ibiraçu, Braz.	170	J5	19.49 S	40.21 W
Ibirama, Braz.	172	C13	27.03 S	49.30 W
Ibirapuã, Braz.	170	I5	17.40 S	40.07 W
Ibirapuera, ngh., Braz.	205b		23.37 S	46.40 W
Ibirapuera, Parque, p.o.i., Braz.	205b		23.35 S	46.39 W
Ibirapuitã, stm., Braz.	172	D9	29.21 S	55.57 W
Ibirataia, Braz.	170	H6	14.04 S	39.37 W
Ibirubá, Braz.	172	D11	28.38 S	53.06 W
Ibitiara, Braz.	170	G4	12.39 S	42.13 W
Ibitinga, Braz.	170	K1	21.46 S	48.48 W
Ibiza see Eivissa, Spain	28	F12	38.54 N	1.25 E
Ibiza see Eivissa, i., Spain	28	F12	39.00 N	1.25 E
Iblei, Monti, mts., Italy	32	H8	37.10 N	14.50 E
Ibn Hāni', Ra's, c., Syria	76	C6	35.34 N	35.46 E
Ibonma, Indon.	60	F9	3.27 S	133.31 E
Ibor, stm., Spain	28	E5	39.47 N	5.32 W
Ibotirama, Braz.	170	G4	12.10 S	43.12 W
Iboundji, Mont, mtn., Gabon	86	E2	1.08 S	11.48 E
Ibresi, Russia	40	D15	55.17 N	47.03 E
İbriktepe, Tur.	34	B9	40.59 N	26.28 E
Ibshawāi, Egypt	76	I1	29.21 N	30.40 E
Ibusuki, Japan	56	H3	31.15 N	130.38 E
Ica, Peru	164	F2	14.03 S	75.44 W
Iča, stm., Lat.	26	D10	56.51 N	26.58 E
Içá (Putumayo), stm., S.A.	164	D4	3.06 S	67.56 W
Icabarú, stm., Ven.	168	E10	4.45 N	62.14 W
Icacos Point, c., Trin.	159f	s12	10.03 N	61.56 W
Içamaquã, stm., Braz.	172	D10	28.34 S	56.00 W
Icamole, Mex.	136	I7	25.55 N	100.43 W
Içana, Braz.	168	G8	0.21 N	67.19 W
Içana (Isana), stm., S.A.	168	G7	0.25 N	67.19 W
Icaño, Arg.	172	D5	28.54 S	65.19 W
Icaño, Arg.	172	D6	28.41 S	62.54 W
Icatu, Braz.	170	B3	2.46 S	44.04 W
Iceberg Pass, p., Co., U.S.	140	G7	40.25 N	105.44 W
İçel (Mersin), Tur.	42	G6	36.48 N	34.37 E
İçel, state, Tur.	42	G5	36.45 N	34.00 E
Iceland, ctry., Eur.	12a	k30	65.00 N	18.00 W
Iceland see Ísland, i., Ice.	8	B5	65.00 N	18.00 W
Iceland Basin, unds.	176	C11	59.00 N	23.00 W
Icém, Braz.	170	K1	20.19 S	49.12 W
Ice Mountain, mtn., B.C., Can.	144	B9	54.25 N	121.08 W
Ichaikaronji, India	69	C2	16.40 N	74.27 E
Ichawaynochaway Creek, stm., Ga., U.S.	134	F14	31.10 N	84.28 W
Ichchāpuram, India	69	B7	19.06 N	84.41 E
Ichikawa, Japan	56	D12	35.44 N	139.55 E
Ichinomiya, Japan	56	G4	32.57 N	131.07 E
Ichinomiya, Japan	56	D9	35.18 N	136.48 E
Ichinomoto, Japan	188		34.37 N	135.50 E
Ichinose, Japan	188		34.53 N	135.10 E
Ichkeul, Lac, l., Tun.	32	G3	37.10 N	9.40 E
Ichnia, Ukr.	38	C11	50.51 N	32.24 E
Icicle Creek, stm., Wa., U.S.	146	C6	47.34 N	120.39 W
Ičinskaja Sopka, vulkan, vol., Russia	50	E20	55.42 N	157.34 E
Ickenham, ngh., Eng., U.K.	178		51.34 N	0.27 W
Ickern, Ger.	181		51.36 N	7.21 E
Icó, Braz.	170	D6	6.24 S	38.51 W
Icy Cape, c., Ak., U.S.	109	B7	70.20 N	161.52 W
Ida, Mi., U.S.	124	C2	41.54 N	83.34 W
Ida, Mount see Ídi Óros, mtn., Grc.	34	H7	35.18 N	24.43 E
Ida, Mount, mtn., Jam.	158d	j13	17.58 N	77.43 W
Idabel, Ok., U.S.	134	D4	33.53 N	94.49 W
Ida Grove, Ia., U.S.	130	B2	42.20 N	95.28 W
Idah, Nig.	84	H6	7.06 N	6.44 E
Idaho, state, U.S.	146	G12	45.00 N	115.00 W
Idaho City, Id., U.S.	146	G11	43.49 N	115.50 W
Idaho Falls, Id., U.S.	146	G14	43.30 N	112.02 W
Idaho National Engineering Laboratory, sci., Id., U.S.	146	G14	43.40 N	112.45 W
Idaho Springs, Co., U.S.	138	B3	39.44 N	105.30 W
Idalou, Tx., U.S.	138	H7	33.39 N	101.40 W
Idanha-a-Nova, Port.	28	E3	39.55 N	7.13 W
Idāppādi, India	69	F3	11.34 N	77.51 E
Idar, India	70	G4	23.50 N	73.01 E
Idar-Oberstein, Ger.	24	G3	49.42 N	7.19 E
Iddo, ngh., Nig.	191a		6.28 N	3.23 E
Idel', Russia	18	C21	64.08 N	34.14 E
Idelès, Alg.	84	E6	23.50 N	5.57 E
Idi, Indon.	64	J3	4.57 N	97.46 E
Idi Amin Dada, Lac see Edward, Lake, l., Afr.	86	E5	0.23 S	29.35 E
Idice, stm., Italy	30	F8	44.35 N	11.52 E
Idimu, Nig.	191a		6.35 N	3.17 E
Idiofa, D.R.C.	86	F3	5.01 S	19.35 E
Ídi Óros, mtn., Grc.	34	H7	35.18 N	24.43 E
Idkerberget, Swe.	16	G13	60.23 N	15.13 E
Idku, Bahra el-, l., Egypt	76	G1	31.16 N	30.17 E
Idle Hill, Eng., U.K.	178		51.15 N	0.08 E
Idlib, Syria	76	C7	35.56 N	36.38 E
Idlib, state, Syria	76	C7	35.50 N	36.40 E
Ídolo, Isla del, i., Mex.	154	E10	21.25 N	97.27 W
Idomogu, Nig.	191a		6.43 N	3.30 E
Idoukâl-en-Taghès, mtn., Niger	84	F6	17.43 N	8.45 E
Idre, Swe.	16	F10	61.51 N	12.43 E
Idria see Idrija, Slvn.	30	D11	46.00 N	14.01 E
Idrica, Russia	26	D11	56.19 N	28.53 E
Idrija, Slvn.	30	D11	46.00 N	14.01 E
Idrijca, stm., Slvn.	30	D10	46.09 N	13.45 E
Idro, Lago d', l., Italy	30	E7	45.46 N	10.30 E
Idroscalo, l., Italy	184b		45.28 N	9.18 E
Idutywa, S. Afr.	90	H9	32.06 S	28.17 E
Idylwood, Va., U.S.	202c		38.54 N	77.12 W
Iecava, Lat.	26	D7	56.36 N	24.09 E
Iecava, stm., Lat.	26	D7	56.41 N	23.42 E
Ieper, Bel.	20	D11	50.51 N	2.52 E
Ierápetra, Grc.	34	H8	35.01 N	25.44 E
Ierissós, Grc.	34	C6	40.24 N	23.52 E
Ierzu, Italy	32	E3	39.47 N	9.32 E
Iesi see Jesi, Italy	30	G10	43.31 N	13.14 E
Iesolo, Italy	30	E9	45.32 N	12.38 E
Ifakara, Tan.	86	F7	8.09 S	36.41 E
Ifako, Nig.	191a		6.39 N	3.20 E
Ifanadiana, Madag.	88	E8	21.18 S	47.38 E
Ife, Nig.	84	H5	7.28 N	4.33 E
Iferouâne, Niger	84	F6	19.04 N	8.24 E
Iferten see Yverdon-les-Bains, Switz.	30	D3	46.47 N	6.38 E
Ifjord, Nor.	14	B18	70.29 N	27.06 E
Ifôghas, Adrar des, mts., Afr.	84	F5	20.00 N	2.00 E
Igal, Hung.	36	C4	46.30 N	17.56 E
Igan, Malay.	66	B7	2.49 N	111.43 E
Igan, stm., Malay.	66	B7	2.50 N	111.39 E
Iganga, Ug.	86	D6	0.37 N	33.28 E
Iganmu, ngh., Nig.	191a		6.29 N	3.22 E
Igaporã, Braz.	170	G4	13.46 S	42.43 W
Igara, Braz.	170	F5	10.24 S	40.07 W
Igara Paraná, stm., Col.	168	H5	2.08 S	71.44 W
Igarapé-Açu, Braz.	164	D8	1.07 S	47.36 W
Igarapé-Miri, Braz.	170	B1	1.59 S	48.57 W
Igarka, Russia	48	A15	67.28 N	86.37 E
Igatpuri, India	69	B1	19.41 N	73.33 E
Igaun, Nig.	191a		6.42 N	3.23 E
Igbobi, Nig.	191a		6.32 N	3.22 E
Igboho, Nig.	84	H5	8.50 N	3.45 E
Igbologun, Nig.	191a		6.25 N	3.20 E
Iğdır, Tur.	34	B16	41.14 N	33.07 E
Iğdır, Tur.	42	F11	39.55 N	44.03 E
Iğdır, state, Tur.	42	F10	39.55 N	44.00 E
Iggesund, Swe.	16	F15	61.38 N	17.04 E
Igharghar, Oued, stm., Alg.	84	D6	28.07 N	6.11 E
Ightham, Eng., U.K.	178		51.17 N	0.17 E
Ightham Mote, hist., Eng., U.K.	178		51.15 N	0.16 E
Igiugig, Ak., U.S.	109	E8	59.20 N	155.55 W
Iglau see Jihlava, Czech Rep.	24	G11	49.23 N	15.35 E
Iglesias, Italy	32	E2	39.19 N	8.31 E
Iglesias, Cerro las, mtn., Mex.	154	B5	26.16 N	106.38 W
Iglesiente, reg., Italy	32	E2	39.18 N	8.40 E
Iglino, Russia	40	D20	54.49 N	56.25 E
Igloolik, Nu., Can.	110	B14	69.22 N	81.48 W
'Igma, Gebel el-, mts., Egypt	76	I4	29.07 N	33.57 E
Ignacio, Co., U.S.	150	F9	37.08 N	107.37 W
Ignalina, Lith.	26	E9	55.21 N	26.10 E
Ignatei, Mol.	38	F7	47.41 N	28.40 E
Ignatovka, Russia	40	E15	53.56 N	47.38 E
Ignatovo, Russia	18	G24	60.47 N	37.48 E
İğneada, Tur.	34	B10	41.53 N	27.59 E
İğneada Burnu, c., Tur.	34	B11	41.54 N	28.02 E
Igny, Fr.	179		48.45 N	2.14 E
Igoumenitsa, Grc.	34	D3	39.30 N	20.16 E
Igra, Russia	40	C18	57.32 N	53.03 E
Igreja, Morro da, mtn., Braz.	172	D13	28.08 S	49.30 W
Igreja Nova, Braz.	170	F7	10.07 S	36.38 W
Iguaçu (Iguazú), stm., S.A.	172	B10	25.35 S	54.35 W
Iguaçu, Cataratas do see Iguassu Falls, wtfl., S.A.	172	B10	25.41 S	54.26 W
Iguaçu, Parque Nacional do, p.o.i., Braz.	172	B11	25.25 S	53.52 W
Iguaçu, Saltos do see Iguassu Falls, wtfl., S.A.	172	B10	25.41 S	54.26 W
Iguaí, Braz.	170	H5	14.44 S	40.05 W
Iguala, Mex.	154	F9	18.21 N	99.32 W
Igualada, Spain	28	C12	41.34 N	1.39 E
Iguana, stm., Ven.	168	C9	7.53 N	65.38 W
Iguape, Braz.	172	B14	24.42 S	47.33 W
Iguape, stm., Braz.	172	B13	24.39 S	47.23 W
Iguará, stm., Braz.	170	B4	3.28 S	43.55 W
Iguassu Falls, wtfl., S.A.	172	B10	25.41 S	54.26 W
Iguatemi, stm., Braz.	172	A10	23.42 S	54.30 W
Iguatu, Braz.	170	D6	6.22 S	39.18 W
Iguazú (Iguaçu), stm., S.A.	172	B10	25.35 S	54.35 W
Iguazú, Cataratas del see Iguassu Falls, wtfl., S.A.	172	B10	25.41 S	54.26 W
Iguazú, Parque Nacional, p.o.i., S.A.	172	B10	25.40 S	54.17 W
Iguéla, Gabon	86	E1	1.56 S	9.19 E
Iguéla, Lagune, b., Gabon	86	E1	1.58 S	9.29 E
Iguîdi, 'Erg, sand, Afr.	84	D3	27.53 N	4.45 W
Igžej, Russia	48	D18	54.01 N	103.08 E
Iharaña, Madag.	88	C9	13.21 S	50.00 E
Iheya-shima, i., Japan	55a	I18	27.03 N	127.58 E
Ihnâsiya el-Madina, Egypt	76	I1	29.04 N	30.56 E
Ihosy, Madag.	88	E8	22.23 S	46.07 E
Ih Tal, China	54	C5	43.13 N	122.14 E
Ihtiman, Blg.	36	G10	42.25 N	23.49 E
Iida, Japan	56	D10	35.31 N	137.50 E
Iijärvi, l., Fin.	14	C18	69.27 N	27.51 E
Iijoki, stm., Fin.	18	B12	65.19 N	25.19 E
Iisaku, Est.	26	A10	59.06 N	27.19 E
Iisalmi, Fin.	18	E14	63.32 N	27.17 E
Iisvesi, Fin.	18	E14	62.39 N	27.02 E
Iittala, Fin.	18	F11	61.04 N	24.10 E
Iivaara, hill, Fin.	18	B16	65.48 N	29.40 E
Iiyama, Japan	56	C11	36.51 N	138.22 E
Iizuka, Japan	56	F3	33.38 N	130.41 E
Ijâfene, des., Maur.	84	E3	22.04 N	7.42 W
Ijaiye, Nig.	191a		6.40 N	3.18 E
Ijebu-Ode, Nig.	84	H5	6.48 N	3.55 E
Ijesa-Tedo, Nig.	191a		6.30 N	3.19 E
IJmuiden, Neth.	20	B13	52.27 N	4.36 E
IJssel, stm., Neth.	20	B15	52.35 N	5.50 E
IJsselmeer, l., Neth.	20	B14	52.45 N	5.25 E
Ijuí, Braz.	172	D11	28.23 S	53.55 W
Ijuí, stm., Braz.	172	D10	27.58 S	55.20 W
Iju Junction, Nig.	191a		6.40 N	3.19 E
Iju Water Works, sci., Nig.	191a		6.40 N	3.20 E
IJzer, stm., Eur.	20	C11	51.09 N	2.44 E
Ik, stm., Russia	40	D18	55.40 N	53.27 E
Ika, Russia	48	C19	59.19 N	106.23 E
Ikaalinen, Fin.	18	F10	61.45 N	23.04 E
Ikali, D.R.C.	86	E4	1.59 S	21.01 E
Ikamba, D.R.C.	191b		4.22 S	15.16 E
Ikaría, i., Grc.	34	F9	37.36 N	26.05 E
Ikast, Den.	16	K7	56.08 N	9.10 E
Ikatskij hrebet, mts., Russia	50	F11	54.00 N	111.00 E
Ikeda, Japan	56	E6	34.00 N	133.47 E
Ikej, Russia	48	D17	54.11 N	100.04 E
Ikeja, Nig.	84	H5	6.35 N	3.20 E
Ikela, D.R.C.	86	E4	1.11 S	23.16 E
Ikerre, Nig.	84	H6	7.30 N	5.14 E
Ikeura, Japan	188		34.30 N	135.25 E
Iki, i., Japan	56	F2	33.47 N	129.43 E
İkizce, Tur.	34	D15	39.35 N	32.40 E
Ikom, Nig.	84	H6	5.58 N	8.42 E
Ikoma-sanchi, mts., Japan	188		34.40 N	135.40 E
Ikoma-yama, mtn., Japan	188		34.40 N	135.40 E
Ikorec, stm., Russia	38	B18	50.58 N	39.45 E
Ikot-Ekpene, Nig.	84	H6	5.11 N	7.42 E
Ikoyi, ngh., Nig.	191a		6.27 N	3.26 E
Ikoyi Island, i., Nig.	191a		6.27 N	3.26 E
Ikoyi Prison, bldg., Nig.	191a		6.25 N	3.25 E
Ikša, Russia	26	D20	56.10 N	37.30 E
Iksa, stm., Russia	18	E26	62.34 N	39.49 E
Ikuata, Nig.	191a		6.25 N	3.22 E
Ikungu, Tan.	86	F6	1.33 S	33.40 E
Ikuno, Japan	56	D7	35.10 N	134.48 E
Ikuno, ngh., Japan	188		34.39 N	135.34 E
Ikurangi, hill, Cook Is.	100j	a26	21.13 S	159.45 W
Ikusu, stm., D.R.C.	191b		4.24 S	15.14 E
Ikuta, Japan	186		35.36 N	139.32 E
Ikva, stm., Ukr.	38	C4	50.33 N	25.23 E
Ila, Nig.	84	H6	8.01 N	4.55 E
Ilagan, Phil.	68	B3	17.08 N	121.53 E
Ilaiyānkudi, India	69	G4	9.37 N	78.38 E
Īlām, Iran	74	D10	33.38 N	46.25 E
Ilām, Nepal	70	E11	26.55 N	87.56 E
Īlām, state, Iran	74	D10	33.15 N	46.45 E
Ilam see Sri Lanka, ctry., Asia	69	G5	7.00 N	81.00 E
Ilan, Tai.	58	I9	24.46 N	121.45 E
Ilanskij, Russia	48	C17	56.14 N	96.06 E
Ilara, Nig.	191a		6.42 N	3.27 E
Ilaro, Nig.	84	H5	6.52 N	3.00 E
Iława, Pol.	16	C15	53.35 N	19.33 E
Ilbenge, Russia	50	D13	62.44 N	124.25 E
Ilchester, Md., U.S.	202b		39.15 N	76.45 W
Île-à-la-Crosse, Sk., Can.	110	D9	55.26 N	107.55 W
Ilebo, D.R.C.	86	E4	4.19 S	20.36 E
Île-de-France, hist. reg., Fr.	20	E11	49.00 N	2.20 E
Île de France, i., Grnld.	108	B22	77.47 N	17.53 W
Île-du-Prince-Édouard see Prince Edward Island, state, Can.	122	D13	46.20 N	63.20 W
Ilek, stm., Asia	40	E18	51.29 N	53.19 E
Ileksa, stm., Russia	18	D23	62.28 N	36.55 E
Ilesha, Nig.	84	H5	7.38 N	4.45 E
Îles Loyauté, state, N. Cal.	101d	m16	21.00 S	167.00 E
Île Tintamarre, i., Anguilla	159a	a2	18.06 N	62.59 W
Ilevskij Pogost, Russia	12	F20	60.40 N	43.47 E
Ileza, Russia	12	F20	60.41 N	43.50 E
Ilford, Mb., Can.	110	D11	56.04 N	95.36 W
Ilford, ngh., Eng., U.K.	178		51.33 N	0.05 E
Ilfracombe, Austl.	98	D5	23.29 S	144.30 E
Ilfracombe, Eng., U.K.	10	J8	51.12 N	4.07 W
Ilhabela, Braz.	170	L3	23.45 S	45.19 W
Ilha de Moçambique, Moz.	88	D7	15.02 S	40.41 E
Ilha Grande, Baía da, b., Braz.	170	L3	23.09 S	44.30 W
Ilha Solteira, Represa de, res., Braz.	166	D6	20.20 S	51.19 W
Ílhavo, Port.	28	D2	40.36 N	8.40 W
Ilhea Point, c., Nmb.	90	C2	23.24 S	14.26 E
Ilhéos see Ilhéus, Braz.	170	H6	14.47 S	39.02 W
Ilhéus, Braz.	170	H6	14.47 S	39.02 W
Ilia, Rom.	36	D9	45.56 N	22.40 E
Iliamna, Ak., U.S.	109	E8	59.45 N	154.51 W
Iliamna Lake, l., Ak., U.S.	109	D9	59.36 N	154.48 W
Il'ič, Kaz.	48	F11	40.50 N	68.31 E
Ilıca, Tur.	34	D10	39.53 N	27.46 E
Ilicínea, Braz.	170	K3	20.55 S	45.49 W
Iliff, Co., U.S.	140	G9	40.45 N	103.04 W
Iliff, Lake, l., N.J., U.S.	194		41.02 N	74.43 W
Iligan, Phil.	68	F5	8.14 N	124.15 E
Iligan Bay, b., Phil.	68	F5	8.25 N	124.05 E
Iliniza, vol., Ec.	168	H2	0.39 S	78.43 W
Ilion, N.Y., U.S.	124	A10	43.01 N	75.02 W
Ilio Point, c., Hi., U.S.	100a	b4	21.13 N	157.15 W
Ilioúpolis, Grc.	185c		37.56 N	23.45 E
Ilir, Russia	48	C18	55.13 N	100.41 E
Ilirska Bistrica, Slvn.	30	E11	45.34 N	14.15 E
Ilisós, stm., Grc.	185c		37.57 N	23.41 E
Ilizi, Alg.	84	D6	26.28 N	8.28 E
Il'ja, Bela.	26	F10	54.25 N	27.18 E
Iljino, Russia	26	E14	55.56 N	31.40 E
Iljinskij, Russia	18	F19	61.01 N	32.42 E
Iljinskij, Russia	40	B19	58.34 N	55.41 E
Il'jinskij, Russia	50	G17	47.59 N	142.12 E
Iljinskij, Russia	183b		55.37 N	38.06 E
Iljinskoe, Russia	26	G18	53.14 N	35.26 E
Iljinskoe, Russia	26	C21	57.19 N	38.30 E
Iljinskoe, Russia	26	D20	56.57 N	37.09 E
Iljinskoe, Russia	183b		55.46 N	37.15 E
Iljinsko-Podomskoe, Russia	12	F23	61.07 N	47.58 E
Il'jiny gory, hills, Russia	26	D17	56.34 N	34.12 E
Il'ka, Russia	50	F10	51.43 N	108.30 E
Ilkal, India	69	D3	15.57 N	76.06 E
Ilkley, Eng., U.K.	10	H11	53.55 N	1.49 W
Ill, stm., Aus.	22	B15	47.18 N	9.34 E
Illampu, Nevado, mtn., Bol.	166	C9	15.50 S	68.34 W
Illana Bay, b., Phil.	68	G4	7.25 N	123.45 E
Illapel, Chile	172	E2	31.38 S	71.09 W
Ille-et-Vilaine, state, Fr.	20	F7	48.10 N	1.30 W
Illéla, Niger	84	G6	14.27 N	5.15 E
Iller, stm., Ger.	24	I6	48.22 N	9.59 E
Illertissen, Ger.	24	H6	48.13 N	10.06 E
Illescas, Mex.	154	D7	23.13 N	102.06 W
Illescas, Spain	28	D7	40.06 N	3.50 W
Illichivs'k, Ukr.	38	G9	46.18 N	30.39 E
Illimani, Nevado, mtn., Bol.	166	C3	16.50 S	67.54 W
Illingworth, Eng., U.K.	180		53.45 N	1.54 W
Illinois, state, U.S.	130	D8	40.00 N	89.00 W
Illinois, stm., U.S.	134	B3	35.30 N	95.06 W
Illinois, stm., Co., U.S.	140	G6	40.44 N	106.18 W
Illinois, stm., Il., U.S.	130	E7	38.57 N	90.25 W
Illinois, stm., Or., U.S.	146	H3	42.33 N	124.03 W
Illinois and Michigan Canal, can., Il., U.S.	196		41.32 N	88.05 W
Illinois at Chicago, University of, educ., Il., U.S.	196		41.52 N	87.39 W
Illinois Institute of Technology, educ., Il., U.S.	196		41.50 N	87.38 W
Illinois Peak, mtn., U.S.	146	C11	47.02 N	115.04 W
Illintsi, Ukr.	38	D8	49.06 N	29.13 E
Illiopolis, Il., U.S.	130	E8	39.51 N	89.14 W
Illovo, S. Afr.	191d		26.08 S	28.03 E
Ilmajoki, Fin.	18	E9	62.44 N	22.35 E
Il'men', ozero, l., Russia	26	B14	58.17 N	31.20 E
Ilo, Peru	164	G3	17.38 S	71.19 W
Iloilo, Phil.	68	E4	10.42 N	122.33 E
Ilomantsi, Fin.	18	E17	62.40 N	30.56 E
Ilorin, Nig.	84	H5	8.29 N	4.32 E
Ilovais'k, Ukr.	38	F17	47.55 N	38.11 E
Ilovatka, Russia	40	F14	50.30 N	45.52 E
Ilovka, Russia	38	C17	50.42 N	38.39 E
Ilovlja, Russia	40	G14	49.18 N	43.59 E
Ilovlja, stm., Russia	40	G14	49.13 N	43.54 E
Iłowa, Pol.	24	E11	51.30 N	15.11 E
Il'pyrskij, Russia	50	D21	59.59 N	164.17 E
Ilsan-ni, Kor., S.	189b		37.41 N	126.46 E
Il'skij, Russia	40	I11	44.50 N	38.34 E
Ilūkste, Lat.	26	E9	55.57 N	26.20 E
Ilulissat see Jakobshavn, Grnld.	108	D15	69.13 N	51.06 W
Ilverich, Ger.	181		51.17 N	6.42 E
Ilwaki, Indon.	60	G8	7.55 S	126.24 E
Ilwŏl-san, mtn., Kor., S.	56	C2	36.50 N	129.06 E
Ilz, stm., Ger.	30	B10	48.34 N	13.28 E
Iłża, Pol.	26	E17	51.10 N	21.14 E
Imabari, Japan	56	E5	34.03 N	133.00 E
Imadomi, Japan	186		35.28 N	140.06 E
Imaichi, Japan	56	C12	36.43 N	139.41 E
Imajuku, Japan	186		35.58 N	139.21 E
Imajuku, ngh., Japan	186		35.29 N	139.32 E
Imaki, Japan	188		34.24 N	135.46 E
Imambara, rel., India	190b		22.54 N	88.25 E
Imandra, Russia	14	E24	67.49 N	33.13 E
Imandra, ozero, l., Russia	14	E22	67.33 N	33.00 E
Imari, Japan	56	F2	33.16 N	129.52 E
Imaruí, Braz.	172	D13	28.20 S	48.48 W
Imaruí, Lagoa do, l., Braz.	172	D13	28.21 S	48.52 W
Imatra, Fin.	18	F15	61.10 N	28.46 E
Imavere, Est.	26	B8	58.44 N	25.46 E
Imbâba, ngh., Egypt	191c		30.04 N	31.13 E
Imbabura, state, Ec.	168	G2	0.22 N	78.25 W
Imbituba, Braz.	172	D13	28.13 S	48.40 W
Imbituva, Braz.	172	B12	25.14 S	50.36 W
Imboaçu, Canal, can., Braz.	205a		22.48 S	43.04 W
Imeni Babuškina, Russia	40	B13	59.44 N	43.07 E
Imeni Cjurupy, Russia	26	E21	55.30 N	38.39 E
Imeni Karla Libknehta, Russia	38	B14	51.37 N	35.29 E
Imeni Kirova, Kaz.	48	E13	46.27 N	77.11 E
Imeni Kirova, Russia	50	E14	59.44 N	128.10 E
Imeni Poliny Osipenko, Russia	50	F16	52.25 N	136.29 E
Imeni Stepana Razina, Russia	40	D14	54.53 N	44.18 E
Imeni Željabova, Russia	26	A19	58.57 N	36.35 E
Īmī, Eth.	82	F8	6.27 N	42.11 E
Imías, Cuba	156	B10	20.04 N	74.39 W
Imilac, Chile	172	B3	24.13 S	68.51 W
İmişli, Azer.	42	F12	39.52 N	48.03 E
Imlay, Nv., U.S.	148	C7	40.39 N	118.09 W
Imlay City, Mi., U.S.	130	A14	43.01 N	83.05 W
Immenstadt, Ger.	24	I6	47.33 N	10.13 E
Immigrath, Ger.	181		51.06 N	6.57 E
Immokalee, Fl., U.S.	132	J4	26.25 N	81.25 W
Imnaha, stm., Or., U.S.	146	E10	45.49 N	116.46 W
Imola, Italy	30	F8	44.21 N	11.42 E
Imonda, Pap. N. Gui.	101a	a3	3.19 S	141.10 E
Imore, Nig.	191a		6.26 N	3.17 E
Imoro, Nig.	191a		6.43 N	3.30 E
Im Ostholz, ngh., Ger.	181		51.26 N	7.12 E
Imotski, Cro.	30	G14	43.26 N	17.13 E
Impasugong, Phil.	68	F5	8.18 N	125.00 E
Imperatriz, Braz.	170	C2	5.31 S	47.28 W
Imperia, Italy	30	G5	43.53 N	8.02 E
Imperial, Sk., Can.	142	C8	51.20 N	105.25 W
Imperial, Ca., U.S.	148	K10	32.51 N	115.34 W
Imperial, Ne., U.S.	140	G11	40.31 N	101.38 W
Imperial, Tx., U.S.	136	C5	31.16 N	102.41 W
Imperial Beach, Ca., U.S.	148	K8	32.35 N	117.06 W
Imperial Dam, dam., U.S.	150	K2	32.55 N	114.30 W
Imperial de Aragón, Canal, can., Spain	28	C10	42.01 N	1.32 W
Imperial Mills, Ab., Can.	144	B19	54.59 N	111.44 W
Imperial Palace, bldg., Japan	186		35.41 N	139.45 E
Imperial Valley, val., Ca., U.S.	120	E5	32.50 N	115.30 W
Impfondo, Congo	86	D3	1.37 N	18.03 E
Imphāl, India	62	D7	24.47 N	93.56 E
Impilahti, Russia	18	F18	61.40 N	31.08 E
İmralı Adası, i., Tur.	34	C11	40.32 N	28.32 E
Imroz, Tur.	34	C8	40.11 N	25.54 E
Imst, Aus.	30	C7	47.13 N	10.43 E
Imuris, Mex.	120	F7	30.46 N	110.51 W
Imute, Nig.	191a		6.42 N	3.29 E
Imwŏn-ni, Kor., S.	56	B2	37.14 N	129.19 E
In, Nor.	16	G3	60.25 N	5.28 E
Ina, Japan	56	D10	35.50 N	137.57 E
Ina, Japan	186		35.59 N	139.38 E
Ina, Il., U.S.	130	F9	38.09 N	88.54 W
Inaba, Japan	188		34.26 N	135.27 E
Inada, Japan	188		34.54 N	135.08 E
Inage, Japan	186		35.38 N	140.05 E
Inajá, Braz.	170	E7	8.54 S	37.49 W
Inakona, Sol. Is.	101b	e8	9.49 S	160.02 E
I-n-Amenas, Alg.	84	D6	28.02 N	9.34 E
Inamuragasaki Point, hist., Japan	186		35.18 N	139.32 E
Inanda, S. Afr.	191d		26.07 S	28.03 E
Iñapari, Peru	164	F4	10.56 S	69.35 W
Inarajan, Guam	100c	j9	13.16 N	144.44 E
Inari, Fin.	14	D17	68.54 N	26.59 E
Inarigda, Russia	48	B19	63.12 N	107.40 E
Inarijärvi, l., Fin.	14	C18	69.00 N	28.00 E
Inarijoki see Anárjohka, stm., Eur.	14	D16	69.26 N	25.49 E
Inawashiro-ko, l., Japan	56	B12	37.30 N	140.03 E
In Belbel, Alg.	84	D5	27.53 N	1.09 E
Inca, Spain	28	E13	39.43 N	2.55 E
Inca de Oro, Chile	172	C3	26.44 S	69.54 W
Incaguasi, Chile	172	D2	29.12 S	71.00 W
Incahuasi, Cerro de, mtn., S.A.	172	C3	27.02 S	68.18 W
Incahuasi, Nevado de see Incahuasi, Cerro de, mtn., S.A.	172	C3	27.02 S	68.18 W
Ince, Eng., U.K.	180		53.17 N	2.49 W
Ince Blundell, Eng., U.K.	180		53.31 N	3.02 W
İnce Burun, c., Tur.	34	C10	42.05 N	34.58 E
Ince-in-Makerfield, Eng., U.K.	180		53.32 N	2.37 W
İncekum Burnu, c., Tur.	42	G5	36.16 N	33.58 E
İncesu, Tur.	42	F6	38.37 N	35.10 E
Inchelium, Wa., U.S.	146	B8	48.17 N	118.11 W
Inch'ŏn, Kor., S.	54	F7	37.28 N	126.38 E
Inchwagh Lake, l., Mi., U.S.	199		42.27 N	83.41 W
İncirliova, Tur.	34	F10	37.50 N	27.43 E
Incline Village, Nv., U.S.	148	D5	39.15 N	119.57 W
Incomati (Komati), stm., Afr.	90	E10	25.44 S	32.41 E
Incudine, Monte, mtn., Fr.	22	H15	41.51 N	9.12 E
Incy, Russia	14	G31	65.56 N	40.42 E
Indaal, Loch, b., Scot., U.K.	10	F6	55.45 N	6.21 W
Indaiá, stm., Braz.	170	J3	18.27 S	45.22 W
Indalsälven, stm., Swe.	16	E14	62.32 N	17.26 E
Indé, Mex.	136	I2	25.54 N	105.13 W
Indefatigable see Santa Cruz, Isla, i., Ec.	164a	i11	0.38 S	90.23 W
Independence, Ca., U.S.	148	G7	36.48 N	118.11 W
Independence, Ia., U.S.	130	B6	42.28 N	91.53 W
Independence, Ks., U.S.	138	G2	37.13 N	95.42 W
Independence, Ky., U.S.	130	F13	38.56 N	84.32 W
Independence, La., U.S.	134	G8	30.38 N	90.30 W
Independence, Mo., U.S.	130	E3	39.04 N	94.24 W
Independence, Oh., U.S.	197a		41.23 N	81.38 W
Independence, Or., U.S.	146	F3	44.51 N	123.10 W
Independence, Va., U.S.	124	H4	36.37 N	81.09 W
Independence, Wi., U.S.	128	G7	44.20 N	91.25 W
Independence, stm., N.Y., U.S.	126	E14	43.44 N	75.24 W
Independence Creek, stm., Tx., U.S.	136	D6	30.26 N	101.43 W
Independence Fjord, b., Grnld.	108	A20	81.59 N	24.05 W
Independence Hall, hist., Pa., U.S.	203		39.57 N	75.09 W
Independence Mountains, mts., Nv., U.S.	148	B9	41.17 N	116.00 W
Independencia, Bol.	166	C3	17.07 S	66.53 W
Independência, Braz.	170	C5	5.23 S	40.19 W
Independencia, Chile	204e		33.23 S	70.40 W
Independencia, Peru	204d		11.59 S	77.02 W
Independența, Rom.	36	F15	43.59 N	28.04 E
Inder, ozero, l., Kaz.	40	G17	48.27 N	51.54 E
Inderborskij, Kaz.	42	E8	48.32 N	51.42 E
In der Bredde, Ger.	181		51.20 N	7.23 E
Indi, India	69	C2	17.10 N	75.57 E

Name	Page	Map Ref.	Latitude	Longitude
India, ctry., Asia	62	D4	20.00 N	77.00 E
India Brook, stm., N.J., U.S.	194		40.47 N	74.37 W
India Gate, hist., India	190a		28.37 N	77.18 E
Indialantic, Fl., U.S.	132	H5	28.05 N	80.34 W
Indian, stm., Ma., U.S.	201		42.47 N	70.58 W
Indian, stm., Mi., U.S.	126	B3	45.58 N	86.14 W
Indian, stm., N.Y., U.S.	126	D14	44.24 N	75.39 W
Indiana, Pa., U.S.	124	D6	40.35 N	79.08 W
Indiana, state, U.S.	130	D11	40.00 N	86.15 W
Indiana Dunes National Lakeshore, p.o.i., In., U.S.	130	C10	41.41 N	86.58 W
Indiana Harbor, b., In., U.S.	196		41.40 N	87.27 W
Indiana Harbor Canal, can., In., U.S.	196		41.40 N	87.27 W
Indianapolis, In., U.S.	130	E11	39.46 N	86.08 W
Indian Bayou, stm., Ar., U.S.	134	C7	34.13 N	91.51 W
Indian Brook, N.S., Can.	122	D16	46.23 N	60.31 W
Indian Church, Belize	156	D3	17.45 N	88.39 W
Indian Creek, Il., U.S.	196		42.14 N	87.59 W
Indian Creek, stm., Il., U.S.	128	J10	41.25 N	88.45 W
Indian Creek, stm., Il., U.S.	130	E7	39.55 N	90.32 W
Indian Creek, stm., Il., U.S.	196		42.11 N	87.55 W
Indian Creek, stm., Md., U.S.	202c		38.59 N	76.55 W
Indian Creek, stm., Mo., U.S.	130	H3	36.32 N	94.29 W
Indian Creek, stm., N.M., U.S.	150	H8	36.11 N	108.23 W
Indian Creek, stm., N.Y., U.S.	194		40.43 N	73.06 W
Indian Creek, stm., Oh., U.S.	197a		41.17 N	81.31 W
Indian Creek, stm., S.D., U.S.	140	C9	44.39 N	103.19 W
Indian Creek, stm., Tn., U.S.	134	B11	35.22 N	88.08 W
Indian Grave Mountain, hill, Ga., U.S.	132	C1	32.59 N	84.21 W
Indian Head, Sk., Can.	142	D10	50.32 N	103.40 W
Indian Head, stm., Ma., U.S.	201		42.04 N	70.52 W
Indian Head Park, Il., U.S.	196		41.47 N	87.54 W
Indian Head Pond, l., Ma., U.S.	201		42.03 N	70.51 W
Indian Lake, N.Y., U.S.	126	E15	43.47 N	74.15 W
Indian Lake, l., On., Can.	126	A7	47.07 N	82.09 W
Indian Lake, l., Mi., U.S.	126	B3	45.59 N	86.20 W
Indian Lake, l., N.J., U.S.	194		40.53 N	74.29 W
Indian Mills Brook, stm., N.J., U.S.	203		39.47 N	74.44 W
Indian Mills Lake, l., N.J., U.S.	203		39.48 N	74.44 W
Indian Ocean, oc.	174	K10	10.00 S	70.00 E
Indianola, Ia., U.S.	130	C4	41.21 N	93.33 W
Indianola, Ms., U.S.	134	D8	33.27 N	90.39 W
Indianola, Ne., U.S.	138	A8	40.14 N	100.24 W
Indianola, Pa., U.S.	197b		40.34 N	79.51 W
Indianópolis, Braz.	170	J1	19.03 S	47.56 W
Indianópolis, ngh., Braz.	205b		23.36 S	46.38 W
Indian Peak, mtn., Ut., U.S.	150	E3	38.16 N	113.53 W
Indian Peak, mtn., Wy., U.S.	146	F17	44.47 N	109.51 W
Indian Queen Estates, Md., U.S.	202c		38.46 N	77.02 W
Indian River, Mi., U.S.	126	C5	45.23 N	84.37 W
Indian Rock, mtn., Wa., U.S.	146	E6	45.59 N	120.49 W
Indian Springs, Nv., U.S.	148	G10	36.34 N	115.41 W
Indian Springs, Va., U.S.	202c		38.49 N	77.10 W
Indiantown, Fl., U.S.	132	I5	27.01 N	80.28 W
Indian Town Point, c., Antig.	159b	f4	17.05 N	61.41 W
Indiera Alta, P.R.	158a	b2	18.09 N	66.53 W
Indiga, Russia	12	C23	67.41 N	48.58 E
Indigirka, stm., Russia	50	C18	70.48 N	148.53 E
Indija, Yugo.	36	D7	45.03 N	20.05 E
Indin, Mya.	70	H14	20.21 N	92.40 E
Indio, Ca., U.S.	148	J9	33.43 N	116.13 W
Indira Gandhi Canal, can., India	70	E4	31.07 N	74.56 E
Indira Gandhi International Airport, arpt., India	190a		28.35 N	77.07 E
Indispensable Strait, strt., Sol. Is.	101b	e9	8.53 S	160.23 E
Indochina, reg., Asia	64	D7	16.00 N	107.00 E
Indonesia, ctry., Asia	44	J16	5.00 S	120.00 E
Indonesia, University of, educ., Indon.	187e		6.12 S	106.51 E
Indonesia in Miniature, p.o.i., Indon.	187e		6.08 S	106.49 E
Indore, India	70	G5	22.42 N	75.51 E
Indragiri, stm., Indon.	66	D3	0.22 S	103.26 E
Indramayu, Indon.	66	G6	6.20 S	108.19 E
Indrāvati, stm., India	69	B6	18.43 N	80.17 E
Indravati Tiger Reserve, p.o.i., India	69	B5	19.05 N	80.34 E
Indre, state, Fr.	22	C7	46.45 N	1.30 E
Indre, stm., Fr.	20	G10	47.16 N	0.19 E
Indre-et-Loire, state, Fr.	20	G9	47.15 N	0.45 E
Indura, Bela.	26	G6	53.27 N	23.52 E
Indus, stm., Asia	62	D2	24.59 N	68.16 E
Industry, Il., U.S.	130	D7	40.19 N	90.36 W
Industry, Tx., U.S.	136	D11	29.58 N	96.30 W
İnebolu, Tur.	42	E5	41.58 N	33.45 E
İnece, Tur.	34	B10	41.41 N	27.06 E
İnecik, Tur.	34	C10	40.56 N	27.16 E
In Ecker, Alg.	84	E6	24.01 N	5.04 E
İnegöl, Tur.	34	C12	40.05 N	29.31 E
Ineu, Rom.	36	C8	46.26 N	21.50 E
Inez, Ky., U.S.	124	G3	37.51 N	82.32 W
Inez, Tx., U.S.	136	F11	28.54 N	96.47 W
Inez, Lake, l., N.J., U.S.	194		41.01 N	74.17 W
Inferior, Laguna, b., Mex.	154	G11	16.17 N	94.40 W
Infiernillo, Canal del, strt., Mex.	120	G6	29.07 N	112.12 W
Infiernillo, Presa del, res., Mex.	154	F7	18.37 N	101.46 W
Infiesto, Spain	28	A5	43.21 N	5.22 W
Ing, stm., Thai.	64	C5	20.11 N	100.27 E
Ingá, Braz.	170	D8	7.17 S	35.36 W
Ingabu, Mya.	64	D2	17.49 N	95.16 E
Ingal, Niger	84	F6	16.47 N	6.55 E
Ingall Point, c., On., Can.	128	B10	49.38 N	88.45 W
Ingarö, i., Swe.	16	H16	59.16 N	18.28 E
Ingatestone Hall, hist., Eng., U.K.	178		51.39 N	0.23 E
Ingelheim, Ger.	24	G4	49.58 N	8.04 E
Ingelstad, Swe.	16	K12	56.43 N	14.56 E
Ingende, D.R.C.	86	E3	0.12 S	18.58 E
Ingeniería, Universidad Nacional de, educ., Peru	204d		12.02 S	77.02 W
Ingeniero Budge, ngh., Arg.	206		34.43 S	58.28 W
Ingeniero Jacobacci, Arg.	166	H3	41.19 S	69.33 W
Ingeniero Luiggi, Arg.	172	G5	35.23 S	64.28 W
Ingeniero White, Arg.	172	I6	38.47 S	62.16 W
Ingersoll, On., Can.	126	E9	43.02 N	80.52 W
Ingham, Austl.	98	B6	18.39 S	146.09 E
Inglefield Land, reg., Grnld.	108	B12	78.40 N	70.00 W
Ingleside, Austl.	192a		33.41 S	151.13 E
Ingleside, Tx., U.S.	136	G10	27.52 N	97.12 W
Ingleside, ngh., Ca., U.S.	200		37.43 N	122.28 W
Inglewood, Austl.	98	G8	28.25 S	151.04 E
Inglewood, Austl.	98	K4	36.34 S	143.51 E
Inglewood, Ca., U.S.	148	J7	33.57 N	118.20 W
Inglis, Mb., Can.	142	D12	50.57 N	101.15 W
Ingolf Fjord, b., Grnld.	108	A22	80.36 N	18.50 W
Ingolstadt, Ger.	24	H7	48.45 N	11.25 E
Ingomar, Pa., U.S.	197b		40.35 N	80.05 W
Ingonish, N.S., Can.	122	D16	46.41 N	60.23 W
Ingøya, i., Nor.	14	A14	71.03 N	24.03 E
Ingrāj Bāzār, India	70	F12	24.59 N	88.08 E
Ingram, Pa., U.S.	197b		40.26 N	80.04 W
Ingram, Tx., U.S.	136	D8	30.04 N	99.13 W
Ingrave, Eng., U.K.	178		51.36 N	0.21 E
Ingrid Christensen Coast, cst., Ant.	103	B12	70.00 S	76.49 E
In Guezzam, Alg.	84	F6	19.27 N	5.47 E
Inguri, stm., Geor.	42	D10	42.23 N	41.33 E
Ingušetija, state, Russia	42	D11	43.15 N	45.00 E
Ingushetia see Ingušetija, state, Russia	42	D11	43.15 N	45.00 E
Ingwiller, Fr.	24	H3	48.51 N	7.28 E
Inhaca, Ilha da, i., Moz.	90	E11	26.00 S	32.57 E
Inhafenga, Moz.	90	B11	20.35 S	33.53 E
Inhambane, Moz.	90	C12	23.52 S	35.23 E
Inhambane, state, Moz.	90	C12	23.00 S	34.30 E
Inhambane, Baía de, b., Moz.	90	C12	23.48 S	35.27 E
Inhambupe, Braz.	170	F6	11.49 S	38.20 W
Inhaminga, Moz.	88	D5	18.25 S	35.01 E
Inhapim, Braz.	170	J4	19.32 S	42.06 W
Inharrime, Moz.	90	D12	24.29 S	35.01 E
Inhassoro, Moz.	90	B12	21.31 S	35.10 E
Inhaúma, Braz.	170	J3	19.30 S	44.21 W
Inhaúma, ngh., Braz.	205a		22.52 S	43.17 W
Inhomirim, stm., Braz.	205a		22.41 S	43.13 W
Inhul, stm., Ukr.	38	F11	46.59 N	31.58 E
Inhulets', Ukr.	38	F12	47.43 N	33.14 E
Inhulets', stm., Ukr.	38	G11	46.41 N	32.49 E
Inhulo-Kam'ianka, Ukr.	38	E11	48.15 N	32.31 E
Inhuma, Braz.	170	D5	6.40 S	41.42 W
Inhumas, Braz.	170	I1	16.21 S	49.29 W
Iniesta, Spain	28	E9	39.26 N	1.45 W
Inimutaba, Braz.	170	J3	18.44 S	44.23 W
Inírida, stm., Col.	168	F7	3.54 N	67.51 W
Inis see Ennis, Ire.	10	I3	52.51 N	8.59 W
Inis Córthaidh see Enniscorthy, Ire.	10	I6	52.29 N	6.34 W
Inishbofin, i., Ire.	10	H2	53.37 N	10.12 W
Inishmore, i., Ire.	10	H3	53.08 N	9.46 W
Inishowen, pen., Ire.	10	F5	55.12 N	7.20 W
Inishturk, i., Ire.	10	H2	53.42 N	10.06 W
Inja, Russia	50	E17	59.23 N	144.46 E
Inja, stm., Russia	50	D18	59.21 N	144.55 E
Inje, Kor., S.	56	A1	38.04 N	128.10 E
Injune, Austl.	98	E7	25.51 S	148.34 E
Inkeroinen, Fin.	18	G13	60.42 N	26.50 E
Inkom, Id., U.S.	146	H14	42.49 N	112.16 W
Inkster, N.D., U.S.	142	F16	48.09 N	97.39 W
Inland Lake, l., Mb., Can.	142	B14	52.17 N	99.42 W
Inland Sea see Seto-naikai, s., Japan	56	E5	34.21 N	133.36 E
Inle Lake, l., Mya.	64	B3	20.32 N	96.55 E
Inman, Ks., U.S.	138	C11	38.14 N	97.48 W
Inman, S.C., U.S.	132	A3	35.02 N	82.04 W
Inman Mills, S.C., U.S.	132	A3	35.03 N	82.05 W
Inn, stm., Eur.	30	B10	48.34 N	13.28 E
Innamincka, Austl.	98	F3	27.45 S	140.43 E
Innbygda, Nor.	16	F10	61.19 N	12.16 E
Inndyr, Nor.	14	E4	67.02 N	14.01 E
Inner Channel, strt., Belize	156	D3	16.34 N	88.17 W
Innerfolda, b., Nor.	16	C9	64.56 N	12.00 E
Inner Harbor, b., N.Y., U.S.	194		40.52 N	73.28 W
Inner Hebrides, is., Scot., U.K.	10	E6	56.35 N	6.27 W
Inner Mongolia see Nei Monggol, state, China	52	C7	43.00 N	115.00 E
Inner Sister Island, i., Austl.	98	L6	39.41 S	147.55 E
Inner Sound, strt., Scot., U.K.	10	D7	57.25 N	5.56 W
Innerste, stm., Ger.	20	B19	52.15 N	9.50 E
Innhavet, Nor.	14	E6	67.58 N	15.57 E
Innisfail, Austl.	98	A6	17.33 S	146.01 E
Innisfail, Ab., Can.	144	D17	52.01 N	113.57 W
Innisfree, Ab., Can.	144	C19	53.22 N	111.31 W
Innokentevka, Russia	56	G16	49.40 N	136.54 E
Innoko, stm., Ak., U.S.	109	D8	62.11 N	159.43 W
Innolovo, Russia	183a		59.47 N	29.59 E
Innoshima, Japan	56	E6	34.17 N	133.10 E
Innsbruck, Aus.	30	C8	47.16 N	11.24 E
Innviertel, reg., Aus.	30	B10	48.13 N	13.18 E
Ino, Japan	56	F6	33.32 N	133.25 E
Inokashira Park, p.o.i., Japan	186		35.42 N	139.34 E
Inola, Ok., U.S.	130	H2	36.09 N	95.30 W
Inongo, D.R.C.	86	E3	1.55 S	18.17 E
Inoni, Congo	86	E3	3.04 S	15.39 E
İnönü, Tur.	34	D13	39.48 N	30.08 E
Inoue, Japan	188		34.48 N	135.03 E
Inowrocław, Pol.	24	D14	52.48 N	18.15 E
Inrath, ngh., Ger.	181		51.21 N	6.32 E
In Salah, Alg.	84	D5	27.11 N	2.29 E
Insar, Russia	40	E14	53.51 N	44.22 E
Insch, Scot., U.K.	10	D10	57.20 N	2.37 W
Inscription, Cape, c., Austl.	96	E2	25.31 S	112.57 E
Inscription Point, c., Austl.	192a		34.00 S	151.13 E
Insjön, Swe.	16	G13	60.40 N	15.05 E
Inspiration, Az., U.S.	150	J5	33.25 N	110.59 W
Insterburg see Černjahovsk, Russia	26	F4	54.38 N	21.49 E
Instow, Sk., Can.	142	E5	49.44 N	108.17 W
Inta, Russia	48	A10	66.01 N	60.08 E
Intendente Alvear, Arg.	172	G6	35.14 S	63.35 W
Intepe, Tur.	34	D9	40.00 N	26.18 E
Interlagos, ngh., Braz.	205b		23.42 S	46.42 W
Interlaken, Switz.	30	D4	46.41 N	7.50 E
Interlândia, Braz.	170	I1	16.12 S	49.01 W
Internacional (Guarulhos), Aeroporto, arpt., Braz.	205b		23.29 S	46.28 W
International Falls, Mn., U.S.	128	C5	48.36 N	93.24 W
International Peace Garden, misc. cult., N.A.	142	E14	49.00 N	100.04 W
International Trade Fair, p.o.i., Iran	185d		35.47 N	51.24 E
Interstate State Park, p.o.i., U.S.	128	F6	45.23 N	92.40 W
Inthanon, Doi, mtn., Thai.	64	C4	18.35 N	98.29 E
Intiyaco, Arg.	172	D7	28.40 S	60.04 W
Intracoastal Waterway, U.S.	116	G4	26.04 N	97.12 W
Intracoastal Waterway, U.S.	132	L4	24.33 N	81.46 W
Intu, Indon.	66	D9	0.15 S	115.21 E
Intutu, Peru	164	D3	3.34 S	74.42 W
Inubō-saki, c., Japan	56	D13	35.42 N	140.52 E
Inukjuak, Qc., Can.	110	D15	58.28 N	78.06 W
Inuvik, N.T., Can.	110	B4	68.19 N	133.38 W
In'va, stm., Russia	40	B19	58.55 N	54.31 E
Inveraray, Scot., U.K.	10	E7	56.14 N	5.04 W
Inverbervie, Scot., U.K.	10	E10	56.50 N	2.17 W
Invercargill, N.Z.	102	H3	46.24 S	168.22 E
Inverell, Austl.	98	G8	29.46 S	151.06 E
Invergordon, Scot., U.K.	10	D8	57.41 N	4.10 W
Inverloch, Austl.	98	L5	38.38 S	145.43 E
Invermay, Sk., Can.	142	C10	51.48 N	103.10 W
Invermere, B.C., Can.	144	F14	50.29 N	116.02 W
Inverness, N.S., Can.	122	D15	46.14 N	61.18 W
Inverness, Scot., U.K.	10	D8	57.28 N	4.14 W
Inverness, Ca., U.S.	148	E3	38.06 N	122.51 W
Inverness, Fl., U.S.	132	H3	28.50 N	82.19 W
Inverness, Ms., U.S.	134	D8	33.21 N	90.35 W
Inverurie, Scot., U.K.	10	D10	57.17 N	2.23 W
Inverway, Austl.	96	C5	17.50 S	129.38 E
Investigator Strait, strt., Austl.	96	G7	35.25 S	137.10 E
Inwood, Mb., Can.	142	D16	50.30 N	97.30 W
Inwood, Ia., U.S.	128	H2	43.18 N	96.26 W
Inwood, N.Y., U.S.	194		40.37 N	73.44 W
Inwood Hill Park, p.o.i., N.Y., U.S.	194		40.52 N	73.56 W
Inyangani, mtn., Zimb.	88	D5	18.17 S	32.50 E
Inyan Kara Mountain, mtn., Wy., U.S.	140	C8	44.13 N	104.21 W
Inyathi, Zimb.	88	D4	19.40 S	28.47 E
Inyo, Mount, mtn., Ca., U.S.	148	G8	36.44 N	117.59 W
Inyokern, Ca., U.S.	148	H8	35.39 N	117.47 W
Inyo Mountains, mts., Ca., U.S.	148	G8	36.48 N	118.00 W
Inyonga, Tan.	86	F6	6.43 S	32.03 E
Inza, Russia	40	E15	53.50 N	46.22 E
Inzana Lake, l., B.C., Can.	144	B6	54.58 N	124.40 W
Inžavino, Russia	40	E13	52.19 N	42.29 E
Inzer, Russia	40	D20	54.12 N	57.33 E
Inzer, stm., Russia	40	D20	54.29 N	56.27 E
Inzersdorf, ngh., Aus.	182b		48.09 N	16.21 E
Ioánnina, Grc.	34	D3	39.39 N	20.51 E
Iokanga, stm., Russia	14	E30	68.00 N	39.38 E
Iola, Ks., U.S.	130	G2	37.55 N	95.23 W
Iola, Wi., U.S.	128	G9	44.30 N	89.07 W
Ioma, Pap. N. Gui.	101a	b4	8.20 S	147.50 E
Iona, Ang.	88	D1	16.49 S	12.19 E
Iona, N.S., Can.	122	D16	45.58 N	60.49 W
Iona, Id., U.S.	146	G15	43.31 N	111.55 W
Iona, i., Scot., U.K.	10	E6	56.19 N	6.24 W
Iona College, educ., N.Y., U.S.	194		40.56 N	73.47 W
Ione, Ca., U.S.	148	E5	38.21 N	120.55 W
Ione, Or., U.S.	146	E7	45.30 N	119.49 W
Ione, Wa., U.S.	146	B9	48.42 N	117.27 W
Iongo, Ang.	88	B2	9.12 S	17.44 E
Ionia, Mi., U.S.	130	A12	42.59 N	85.04 W
Ionian Islands see Iónioi Nísoi, is., Grc.	34	D2	38.30 N	20.30 E
Ionian Sea, s., Eur.	8	H12	39.00 N	19.00 E
Ionio, Mar see Ionian Sea, s., Eur.	8	H12	39.00 N	19.00 E
Iónioi Nísoi, state, Grc.	34	E3	38.15 N	20.30 E
Iónioi Nísoi (Ionian Islands), is., Grc.	34	D2	38.30 N	20.30 E
Iónion Pélagos see Ionian Sea, s., Eur.	8	H12	39.00 N	19.00 E
Iony, ostrov, i., Russia	50	E17	56.24 N	143.22 E
Iori, stm., Asia	42	E11	41.02 N	46.27 E
Iorskoe ploskogore, plat., Geor.	42	E12	41.20 N	46.00 E
Íos, Grc.	34	G8	36.43 N	25.18 E
Íos, i., Grc.	34	G8	36.43 N	25.20 E
Ioscoe, Lake, l., N.J., U.S.	194		41.02 N	74.19 W
Iosegun, stm., Ab., Can.	144	B14	54.44 N	117.10 W
Iosegun Lake see Fox Creek, Ab., Can.	144	B14	54.23 N	116.50 W
Iota, La., U.S.	134	G6	30.19 N	92.29 W
Iowa, La., U.S.	134	G5	30.13 N	93.00 W
Iowa, state, U.S.	128	I5	42.15 N	93.15 W
Iowa, stm., Ia., U.S.	130	C6	41.09 N	91.00 W
Iowa, South Fork, stm., Ia., U.S.	128	I5	42.17 N	93.05 W
Iowa City, Ia., U.S.	130	C6	41.39 N	91.31 W
Iowa Falls, Ia., U.S.	130	B4	42.31 N	93.15 W
Iowa Park, Tx., U.S.	138	H10	33.57 N	98.39 W
Ipa, stm., Bela.	26	H12	52.05 N	29.10 E
Ipameri, Braz.	170	I1	17.43 S	48.09 W
Ipanema, stm., Braz.	170	E7	9.52 S	37.14 W
Ipanguaçu, Braz.	170	C7	5.30 S	36.52 W
Ipatinga, Braz.	170	J4	19.28 S	42.33 W
Ipatovo, Russia	40	I13	45.42 N	42.54 E
Ipaumirim, Braz.	170	D6	6.47 S	38.43 W
Ipava, Il., U.S.	130	D7	40.20 N	90.19 W
Ípeiros, state, Grc.	34	D3	39.30 N	20.30 E
Ípeiros, hist. reg., Grc.	34	D3	39.40 N	20.50 E
Ipel' (Ipoly), stm., Eur.	24	I14	47.48 N	18.52 E
Ipiales, Col.	168	G3	0.50 N	77.38 W
Ipiaú, Braz.	170	H6	14.08 S	39.44 W
Ipirá, Braz.	170	G6	12.09 S	39.44 W
Ipiranga, Braz.	172	B12	25.00 S	50.35 W
Ipiranga, Braz.	205a		22.43 S	43.12 W
Ipiranga, ngh., Braz.	205b		23.36 S	46.35 W
Ipiranga, stm., Braz.	205a		22.48 S	43.44 W
Ipiranga, Canal, can., Braz.	205a		22.46 S	43.37 W
Ipiranga, Museu do, bldg., Braz.	205b		23.35 S	46.36 W
Ipixuna, Braz.	170	C3	4.22 S	44.34 W
Ipoh, Malay.	64	J5	4.35 N	101.04 E
Ipojuca, stm., Braz.	170	E7	8.24 S	34.57 W
Ipoly (Ipel'), stm., Eur.	24	I14	47.48 N	18.52 E
Iporá, Braz.	166	C6	16.26 S	51.07 W
Iporã, Braz.	172	A11	23.59 S	53.37 W
Ipota, Vanuatu	101d	I17	18.54 S	169.19 E
Ippodromo, p.o.i., Italy	185a		41.49 N	12.26 E
Ippodromo, p.o.i., Italy	185a		41.57 N	12.29 E
Ippodromo, p.o.i., Italy	185a		41.49 N	12.34 E
Ippy, C.A.R.	86	C4	6.15 N	21.11 E
İpsala, Tur.	34	C9	40.55 N	26.23 E
Ipswich, Austl.	98	F9	27.37 S	152.46 E
Ipswich, Eng., U.K.	10	I14	52.03 N	1.09 E
Ipswich, Ma., U.S.	124	B15	42.41 N	70.50 W
Ipswich, S.D., U.S.	140	B13	45.26 N	99.01 W
Ipu, Braz.	170	C5	4.20 S	40.42 W
Ipubi, Braz.	170	D5	7.39 S	40.07 W
Ipuc' (Iput'), stm., Eur.	26	H14	52.25 N	31.04 E
Ipueiras, Braz.	170	C5	4.33 S	40.43 W
Ipuh, Indon.	66	E2	3.00 S	101.28 E
Ipupiara, Braz.	170	F4	11.49 S	42.37 W
Iput' (Ipuc'), stm., Eur.	26	H14	52.25 N	31.04 E
Iqaluit, Nu., Can.	106	C17	63.44 N	68.28 W
Iqfahs, Egypt	76	J1	28.46 N	30.48 E
Iquique, Chile	166	D2	20.13 S	70.08 W
Iquitos, Peru	164	D3	3.46 S	73.14 W
Ira, Tx., U.S.	136	B7	32.35 N	101.00 W
Iraan, Tx., U.S.	136	D6	30.54 N	101.54 W
Iracema, Braz.	170	C6	5.48 S	38.18 W
Iracoubo, Fr. Gu.	164	B7	5.29 N	53.13 W
Irajá, ngh., Braz.	205a		22.51 S	43.19 W
Irajá, stm., Braz.	205a		22.49 S	43.17 W
Irákleia, i., Grc.	34	G8	36.50 N	25.27 E
Irákleio, Grc.	34	H8	35.19 N	25.07 E
Irákleion, Grc.	185c		38.04 N	23.46 E
Iran, ctry., Asia	72	C7	32.00 N	53.00 E
Īrān see Iran, ctry., Asia	72	C7	32.00 N	53.00 E
Iran, Pegunungan, mts., Asia	94	C2	2.05 N	114.55 E
Iran Mountains, mts., Asia	66	B9	2.05 N	114.55 E
Īrānshahr, Iran	72	D9	27.12 N	60.41 E
Irapa, Ven.	168	B10	10.33 N	62.33 W
Irapuato, Mex.	154	E8	20.41 N	101.21 W
Iraq, ctry., Asia	74	D9	33.00 N	44.00 E
Irará, Braz.	170	F6	12.02 S	38.45 W
Irati, Braz.	172	B12	25.27 S	50.39 W
Irati, stm., Eur.	28	B9	42.45 N	1.23 W
Irauçuba, Braz.	170	B6	3.45 S	39.47 W
Irazú, Volcán, vol., C.R.	156	G6	9.58 N	83.53 W
Irbejskoe, Russia	48	C17	55.38 N	95.27 E
Irbeni väin (Irbes jūras šaurums), strt., Eur.	26	C5	57.48 N	22.05 E
Irbenskij proliv see Irbeni väin, strt., Eur.	26	C5	57.48 N	22.05 E
Irbenskij proliv see Irbes jūras šaurums, strt., Eur.	26	C5	57.48 N	22.05 E
Irbes jūras šaurums (Irbeni väin), strt., Eur.	26	C5	57.48 N	22.05 E
Irbid, Jord.	76	F6	32.33 N	35.51 E
Irbid, state, Jord.	76	F6	32.30 N	35.45 E
Irbil, Iraq	74	B8	36.11 N	44.01 E
Irbil, state, Iraq	74	B9	36.10 N	44.00 E
Irbit, Russia	48	C10	57.40 N	63.04 E
Irby, Eng., U.K.	180		53.21 N	3.07 W
Irdning, Aus.	30	C11	47.30 N	14.06 E
Irdyn', Ukr.	38	D10	49.22 N	31.43 E
Ire, Mount, mtn., Sol. Is.	101b	e9	9.10 S	161.05 E
Irebu, D.R.C.	86	E3	0.38 S	17.45 E
Irecê, Braz.	170	F5	11.19 S	41.51 W
Iregua, stm., Spain	28	B8	42.28 N	2.24 W
Ireland, ctry., Eur.	6	E7	53.00 N	8.00 W
Ireland, i., Eur.	8	E7	53.20 N	8.00 W
Ireland Brook, stm., N.J., U.S.	194		40.25 N	74.29 W
Iren', stm., Russia	40	C20	57.27 N	56.56 E
Irene, S.D., U.S.	140	D15	43.04 N	97.09 W
Ireng (Maú), stm., S.A.	168	F12	3.34 N	59.51 W
Iresick Brook, stm., N.J., U.S.	194		40.24 N	74.22 W
Ireton, Ia., U.S.	130	B1	42.58 N	96.19 W
Irgiz, Kaz.	48	E10	48.38 N	61.15 E
Iri, Kor., S.	54	G7	35.56 N	126.57 E
Irian see New Guinea, i.	101a	b3	5.00 S	140.00 E
Iriba, Chad	84	E4	15.07 N	22.15 E
Iriga, Phil.	68	D4	13.25 N	123.25 E
Irîgui, reg., Afr.	84	F3	16.43 N	5.30 W
Iriklinskij, Russia	48	D9	51.40 N	58.38 E
Iringa, Tan.	86	F7	7.46 S	35.41 E
Irinjālakuda, India	69	F3	10.20 N	76.13 E
Iriomote-jima, i., Japan	52	G9	24.20 N	123.50 E
Iriri, stm., Braz.	164	D7	3.48 S	52.36 W
Iriri, stm., Braz.	205a		22.41 S	43.05 W
Irish, Mount, mtn., Nv., U.S.	148	F10	37.38 N	115.24 W
Irish Sea, s., Eur.	10	H7	53.30 N	5.20 W
Irishtown, Austl.	99a	n12	40.54 S	145.08 E
Irituia, Braz.	170	A2	1.45 S	47.25 W
Iriyamazu, Japan	186		35.16 N	139.39 E
Irkineeva, stm., Russia	48	C17	58.29 N	96.49 E
Irklieevskaja, Russia	40	I11	45.50 N	39.39 E
Irkliiv, Ukr.	38	D11	49.32 N	32.20 E
Irkutsk, Russia	48	D18	52.17 N	104.17 E
Irma, Ab., Can.	144	D19	52.55 N	111.14 W
Irminger Basin, unds.	176	B10	61.01 N	35.27 W
Irnijärvi, l., Fin.	18	B16	65.36 N	29.05 E
Iroise, b., Fr.	20	F4	48.13 N	4.54 W
Iron Belt, Wi., U.S.	128	E8	46.24 N	90.19 W
Iron Bottom Sound, strt., Sol. Is.	101b	e8	9.16 S	160.04 E
Iron Bridge, On., Can.	126	B6	46.16 N	83.13 W
Iron City, Tn., U.S.	134	B11	35.01 N	87.34 W
Iron Cove, b., Austl.	192a		33.52 S	151.10 E
Iron Creek, stm., Ab., Can.	144	D19	52.42 N	111.13 W
Irondale, Al., U.S.	134	D12	33.32 N	86.42 W
Irondale, Mo., U.S.	130	G7	37.49 N	90.40 W
Irondequoit, N.Y., U.S.	126	E12	43.12 N	77.33 W
Iron Gate, val., Eur.	36	E9	44.41 N	22.31 E
Ironia, N.J., U.S.	194		40.49 N	74.37 W
Iron Knob, Austl.	96	F7	32.43 S	137.08 E
Iron Mountain, Mi., U.S.	126	C1	45.48 N	88.03 W
Iron Mountain, mtn., Az., U.S.	150	J5	33.27 N	111.10 W
Iron Mountain, mtn., Ca., U.S.	198		34.17 N	117.43 W
Iron Mountains, mts., U.S.	124	H4	36.30 N	81.52 W
Iron Range, Austl.	96	B8	12.39 S	143.22 E
Iron River, Mi., U.S.	128	E10	46.05 N	88.38 W
Iron River, Wi., U.S.	128	E7	46.33 N	91.24 W
Ironton, Mn., U.S.	128	E4	46.27 N	94.00 W
Ironton, Mo., U.S.	130	G7	37.35 N	90.37 W
Ironton, Oh., U.S.	124	F3	38.32 N	82.40 W
Ironwood, Mi., U.S.	128	E8	46.27 N	90.09 W
Ironworks Creek, stm., Pa., U.S.	203		40.10 N	74.59 W
Iroquois, On., Can.	126	D14	44.50 N	75.19 W
Iroquois, S.D., U.S.	140	C15	44.22 N	97.51 W
Iroquois, stm., U.S.	130	C10	41.04 N	87.48 W
Iroquois Falls, On., Can.	114	B10	48.46 N	80.40 W
Irō-zaki, c., Japan	56	E11	34.36 N	138.50 E
Irpin', Ukr.	38	C11	50.31 N	30.15 E
Irpin', stm., Ukr.	38	C8	50.46 N	30.28 E
Irrawaddy see Ayeyarwady, stm., Mya.	62	E8	15.50 N	95.04 E
Irrawaddy, Mouths of the see Ayeyarwady, Mouths of the, mth., Mya.	64	E2	15.39 N	94.44 E
Irricana, Ab., Can.	144	E17	51.18 N	113.37 W
Irrigon, Or., U.S.	146	E7	45.53 N	119.29 W
Irsha, stm., Ukr.	38	C7	50.46 N	29.30 E
Irshava, Ukr.	38	E2	48.19 N	23.03 E
Irsina, Italy	32	D10	40.45 N	16.15 E
Irtyš, Russia	48	D12	54.29 N	74.22 E
Irtyš see Irtysh, stm., Asia	48	C11	61.05 N	68.47 E
Irtysh (Ertix) (Irtyš), stm., Asia	48	C11	61.05 N	68.47 E
Irtyshsk see Irtyšsk, Kaz.	48	D12	53.19 N	75.27 E
Irtyšsk, Kaz.	48	D12	53.19 N	75.27 E
Iruma Air Base, mil., Japan	186		35.50 N	139.24 E
Irún, Spain	28	A9	43.21 N	1.47 W
Iruña see Pamplona, Spain	28	B9	42.48 N	1.39 W
Irurzun, Spain	28	B9	42.55 N	1.49 W
Irú Tepuy, mtn., Ven.	168	E11	5.23 N	61.02 W
Irvine, Ab., Can.	142	E3	49.57 N	110.16 W
Irvine, Scot., U.K.	10	F8	55.36 N	4.40 W
Irvine, Ky., U.S.	124	G2	37.41 N	83.58 W
Irvine Park, p.o.i., Ca., U.S.	198		33.48 N	117.45 W
Irvines Landing, B.C., Can.	144	G6	49.38 N	124.02 W
Irvinestown, N. Ire., U.K.	10	G5	54.28 N	7.37 W
Irving, Tx., U.S.	136	B11	32.48 N	96.56 W
Irving Park, ngh., Il., U.S.	196		41.57 N	87.43 W
Irvington, Ky., U.S.	130	G11	37.53 N	86.16 W
Irvington, ngh., Md., U.S.	202b		39.17 N	76.41 W
Irwin, Pa., U.S.	197b		40.19 N	79.42 W
Irwindale, Ca., U.S.	198		34.06 N	117.56 W
Isa, Nig.	84	G6	13.11 N	6.24 E
Isaac, stm., Austl.	98	D7	22.52 S	149.19 E
Isaac Lake, l., B.C., Can.	144	C10	53.12 N	120.56 W
Isaba, Spain	28	B10	42.52 N	0.55 W
Isabel, S.D., U.S.	140	B11	45.23 N	101.25 W
Isabel, state, Sol. Is.	101b	d8	7.42 S	159.26 E
Isabela, Phil.	68	G3	6.43 N	121.57 E
Isabela, P.R.	158a	a1	18.30 N	67.01 W
Isabela, Cabo, c., Dom. Rep.	156	C12	19.55 N	71.01 W
Isabela, Isla, i., Ec.	164a	i11	0.30 S	91.06 W
Isabelia, Cordillera, mts., Nic.	156	F5	13.29 N	85.31 W
Isabella, stm., Mn., U.S.	128	D7	47.47 N	91.46 W
Isabella Indian Reservation, ind. res., Mi., U.S.	126	E4	43.41 N	84.48 W
Isábena, stm., Spain	28	B11	42.11 N	0.20 E
Isaccea, Rom.	36	D15	45.16 N	28.27 E
Isachsen, Nu., Can.	108	B5	78.47 N	103.30 W
Isachsen, Cape, c., Nu., Can.	108	B4	79.18 N	105.27 W
Ísafjarðardjúp, b., Ice.	12a	j28	66.10 N	23.00 W
Ísafjörður, Ice.	12a	j28	66.02 N	23.07 W
Isagatedo, Nig.	191a		6.32 N	3.20 E
Isahaya, Japan	56	G3	32.50 N	130.03 E
Isak, Indon.	64	J3	4.25 N	96.54 E
Isaka, Tan.	86	E6	3.54 S	32.55 E
Īsa Khel, Pak.	70	B3	32.41 N	71.16 E
Isakly, Russia	40	D17	54.07 N	51.31 E
Isakovo, Russia	26	E17	55.11 N	34.39 E
Isakovo, Russia	183b		55.59 N	37.23 E
Işalniţa, Rom.	36	E10	44.24 N	23.44 E
Isana (Içana), stm., S.A.	168	G7	0.25 N	67.19 W
Isando, S. Afr.	191d		26.09 S	28.12 E
Isanga, D.R.C.	86	E4	1.25 S	22.21 E
Isangel, Vanuatu	101d	I17	19.31 S	169.16 E
Isanti, Mn., U.S.	128	F5	45.29 N	93.14 W
Isar, stm., Eur.	24	I7	48.48 N	12.58 E
Isarco (Eisack), stm., Italy	30	D8	46.21 N	11.17 E
Isarog, Mount, vol., Phil.	68	D4	13.39 N	123.23 E
Isasi, Nig.	191a		6.40 N	3.23 E
İscehisar, Tur.	34	E13	38.53 N	30.44 E
Iščerskaja, Russia	42	D11	43.42 N	45.07 E
Ischia, Italy	32	D7	40.44 N	13.57 E
Ischia, Isola d', i., Italy	32	D7	40.43 N	13.54 E
Ischl see Bad Ischl, Aus.	30	C10	47.42 N	13.37 E
Iscuandé, stm., Col.	168	F3	2.34 N	78.02 W
Ise, Japan	56	E9	34.29 N	136.42 E
Ise, stm., Ger.	20	B19	52.29 N	10.33 E
Isefjord, b., Den.	16	L9	55.52 N	11.49 E
Isen, stm., Ger.	30	B9	48.15 N	12.40 E
Iseo, Lago d', l., Italy	30	E6	45.44 N	10.04 E
Isère, state, Fr.	22	D11	45.10 N	5.50 E
Isère, stm., Fr.	22	D11	44.59 N	4.51 E
Iseri, Nig.	191a		6.39 N	3.23 E
Iseri-Oke, Nig.	191a		6.38 N	3.23 E
Iseri-Osun, Nig.	191a		6.31 N	3.17 E
Iserlohn, Ger.	24	E3	51.22 N	7.41 E
Isernia, Italy	32	C8	41.36 N	14.13 E
Isesaki, Japan	56	C12	36.19 N	139.12 E
Ise-shima-kokuritsu-kōen, p.o.i., Japan	56	E9	34.23 N	136.48 E
Iset', stm., Russia	8	D22	56.35 N	66.17 E
Ise-wan, b., Japan	56	E9	34.43 N	136.43 E
Iseyin, Nig.	84	H5	7.58 N	3.35 E
Isezaki see Isesaki, Japan	56	C12	36.19 N	139.12 E
Isfahan see Eşfahān, Iran	74	D12	32.39 N	51.39 E
Isfara, Taj.	72	A11	40.07 N	70.39 E
Isfjellet, mtn., Nor.	14	C11	69.26 N	20.50 E
Isheri-Olofin, Nig.	191a		6.35 N	3.17 E
Isherton, Guy.	168	F12	2.19 N	59.22 W
Ishi, stm., Japan	188		34.35 N	135.38 E
Ishigaki, Japan	52	G9	24.21 N	124.09 E
Ishikari, stm., Japan	54	C14	43.15 N	141.22 E
Ishikari-wan, b., Japan	54	C14	43.25 N	141.00 E
Ishikawa, state, Japan	56	C9	36.45 N	136.45 E
Ishikiri, Japan	188		34.41 N	135.39 E
Ishim (Išim), stm., Asia	48	C12	57.42 N	71.11 E
Ishinomaki, Japan	56	A14	38.25 N	141.18 E
Ishinomaki-wan, b., Japan	56	A14	38.18 N	141.18 E
Ishioka, Japan	56	C13	36.11 N	140.16 E
Ishiyama, Japan	188		34.58 N	135.55 E
Ishizuchi-san, mtn., Japan	56	F6	33.45 N	133.07 E
Ishpeming, Mi., U.S.	126	B2	46.29 N	87.39 W
Ishuizu, stm., Japan	188		34.33 N	135.27 E
Ishurdi, Bngl.	70	F12	24.07 N	89.04 E
Isidro Casanova, Arg.	206		34.42 S	58.35 W
Isigny-sur-Mer, Fr.	20	E7	49.19 N	1.06 W
Işıklı, Tur.	34	E12	38.19 N	29.51 E
Işıklı Burnu, c., Tur.	185b		41.14 N	29.15 E
Isil'kul', Russia	48	C12	54.54 N	71.15 E
Išim, Russia	48	C11	56.07 N	69.30 E
Išim see Ishim, stm., Asia	48	C12	57.42 N	71.11 E
Išimbaj, Russia	40	E20	53.26 N	56.02 E
Išimskaja ravnina, pl., Asia	48	C11	55.00 N	70.00 E
Isiolo, Kenya	86	D7	0.21 N	37.34 E
Isipingo, ngh., S. Afr.	90	G10	29.58 S	30.56 E
Isiro, D.R.C.	86	D5	2.45 N	27.37 E
Isis, Austl.	98	E9	25.13 S	152.26 E
Isisford, Austl.	98	E5	24.15 S	144.26 E
Isjangulovo, Russia	40	E20	52.10 N	56.37 E
Iskăr, stm., Blg.	36	F11	43.44 N	24.26 E
Iskăr, Jazovir, res., Blg.	36	G10	42.28 N	23.35 E
Iskele, N. Cyp.	76	C4	35.17 N	33.52 E
İskenderun, Tur.	42	G7	36.35 N	36.10 E
İskenderun Körfezi (Alexandretta, Gulf of), b., Tur.	42	G6	36.30 N	35.40 E
Iskininskij, Kaz.	40	H18	47.13 N	52.41 E
Iskitim, Russia	48	D14	54.38 N	83.17 E
Iškoras, mtn., Nor.	14	C16	69.15 N	25.18 E
Iskut, stm., B.C., Can.	110	D4	56.45 N	131.45 W
Isla, Mex.	154	G11	18.00 N	95.29 W
Isla, Salar de la, pl., Chile	172	B3	25.49 S	68.53 W
Islač, stm., Bela.	26	G9	53.55 N	26.13 E
Islâhiye, Tur.	42	G7	37.01 N	36.38 E
Islāmābād, Pak.	70	B4	33.38 N	73.04 E
Islāmkot, Pak.	70	F3	24.41 N	70.10 E
Islāmpur, India	69	C2	17.02 N	74.14 E
Islāmpur, India	70	F10	25.08 N	85.12 E
Islāmpur, India	70	E12	26.15 N	88.11 E
Isla Mujeres, Mex.	156	B4	21.12 N	86.43 W
Island, Ky., U.S.	130	G10	37.26 N	87.08 W
Ísland see Iceland, ctry., Eur.	12a	k30	65.00 N	18.00 W
Ísland (Iceland), i., Ice.	8	B5	65.00 N	18.00 W
Island, stm., Eng., U.K.	180		53.44 N	2.51 W
Island Creek, Ma., U.S.	201		42.00 N	70.43 W
Island Falls, Me., U.S.	122	E8	46.00 N	68.17 W
Island Harbour, Anguilla	159a	a1	18.15 N	63.00 W
Island Lake, Mb., Can.	110	E12	53.58 N	94.44 W
Island Lake, Mi., U.S.	199		42.31 N	83.44 W
Island Lake, l., Mb., Can.	110	E12	53.47 N	94.25 W
Island Park, Id., U.S.	146	F15	44.26 N	111.24 W
Island Park, N.Y., U.S.	194		40.36 N	73.39 W
Island Park Reservoir, res., Id., U.S.	146	F15	44.23 N	111.32 W
Island Pond, Vt., U.S.	122	F5	44.48 N	71.53 W

Name	Page	Map Ref.	Latitude	Longitude
Islands, Bay of, b., Nf., Can.	111a	j22	49.10 N	58.15 W
Íslandshaf see Norwegian Sea, s., Eur.	176	A14	70.00 N	2.00 E
Isla Patrulla, Ur.	172	F10	32.59 S	54.35 W
Isla Vista, Ca., U.S.	148	I6	34.24 N	119.52 W
Islay, i., Scot., U.K.	10	F6	55.48 N	6.17 W
Isle, Mn., U.S.	128	E5	46.08 N	93.28 W
Isle, stm., Fr.	22	E5	44.55 N	0.15 W
Isle-Adam, Forêt de l', p.o.i., Fr.	179		49.05 N	2.15 E
Isle of Hope, Ga., U.S.	132	E4	31.58 N	81.04 W
Isle of Man, dep., Eur.	10	G8	54.15 N	4.30 W
Isle of Wight, Va., U.S.	124	H9	36.54 N	76.42 W
Isle Royale National Park, p.o.i., Mi., U.S.	128	C10	47.58 N	88.54 W
Islesboro Island, i., Me., U.S.	122	F8	44.18 N	68.54 W
Isleta, N.M., U.S.	138	G2	34.54 N	106.40 W
Isleta Indian Reservation, ind. res., N.M., U.S.	138	G2	34.55 N	106.45 W
Isleton, Ca., U.S.	148	E4	38.09 N	121.36 W
Isleworth, ngh., Eng., U.K.	178		51.28 N	0.20 W
Islington, ngh., On., Can.	193b		43.39 N	79.32 W
Islip, N.Y., U.S.	194		40.43 N	73.12 W
Islip Terrace, N.Y., U.S.	194		40.44 N	73.11 W
Islón, Chile	172	D2	29.53 S	71.10 W
Ismailia, Egypt	76	H3	30.35 N	32.15 E
Ismailia, Turat el-, can., Egypt	191c		30.04 N	31.16 E
Ismā'īliyah, ngh., Egypt	191c		30.03 N	31.14 E
Isna, Egypt	74	H3	25.17 N	32.33 E
Isny, Ger.	24	I6	47.41 N	10.02 E
Isogo, ngh., Japan	186		35.23 N	139.37 E
Isojoki, Fin.	18	E8	62.07 N	21.58 E
Isoka, Zam.	88	C5	10.08 S	32.38 E
Isokyrö, Fin.	18	D9	63.00 N	22.19 E
Isola, Ms., U.S.	134	D8	33.15 N	90.35 W
Isola del Liri, Italy	30	I10	41.40 N	13.34 E
Isola di Capo Rizzuto, Italy	32	F11	38.58 N	17.06 E
Isolo, Nig.	191a		6.32 N	3.19 E
Isonzo, stm., Eur.	30	E10	45.43 N	13.33 E
Iso-Syöte, hill, Fin.	18	B14	65.37 N	27.35 E
Isparta, Tur.	34	F13	37.46 N	30.33 E
Isparta, state, Tur.	34	F13	38.00 N	31.00 E
Isperih, Blg.	36	F13	43.43 N	26.50 E
Ispica, Italy	32	H8	36.47 N	14.55 E
İspir, Tur.	42	E9	40.29 N	41.00 E
Israel, ctry., Asia	76	G5	31.30 N	34.45 E
Israel, stm., N.H., U.S.	122	F5	44.29 N	71.36 W
Isrā'īl see Israel, ctry., Asia	76	G5	31.30 N	34.45 E
Issa, Russia	40	E14	53.51 N	44.50 E
Issa, stm., Russia	26	D11	56.58 N	28.48 E
Issano, Guy.	168	E12	5.48 N	59.23 W
Isser, Oued, stm., Alg.	28	H14	36.50 N	3.39 E
Issia, C. Iv.	84	H3	6.24 N	6.32 W
Issoire, Fr.	22	D9	45.33 N	3.15 E
Issou, Fr.	179		48.59 N	1.48 E
Issoudun, Fr.	20	H10	46.57 N	2.00 E
Issuna, Tan.	86	F6	5.20 S	34.46 E
Issyk-Kul', Kyrg.	48	F13	42.27 N	76.11 E
Issyk-Kul, Lake see Issyk-Kul', ozero, l., Kyrg.	48	F13	42.25 N	77.15 E
Issyk-Kul', ozero, l., Kyrg.	48	F13	42.25 N	77.15 E
Īstādeh-ye Moqor, Āb-e, l., Afg.	72	C10	32.29 N	67.54 E
Istana Presidential Palace, bldg., Indon.	187e		6.10 S	106.49 E
İstanbul, Tur.	34	B12	41.01 N	28.59 E
İstanbul, Tur.	185b		41.01 N	28.58 E
İstanbul, state, Tur.	34	B11	41.10 N	28.45 E
Istanbul (Ataturk) International Airport, arpt., Tur.	185b		40.58 N	28.49 E
Istanbul University, educ., Tur.	185b		41.00 N	28.58 E
Istead Rise, Eng., U.K.	178		51.24 N	0.22 E
Isteren, l., Nor.	16	F9	61.58 N	11.47 E
Istiaía, Grc.	34	E6	38.57 N	23.09 E
İstinye, ngh., Tur.	185b		41.06 N	29.03 E
Istiqlal Mosque, rel., Indon.	187e		6.10 S	106.50 E
Istmina, Col.	168	E3	5.09 N	76.41 W
Isto, Mount, mtn., Ak., U.S.	109	C11	69.12 N	143.48 W
Istobnoe, Russia	38	B17	51.16 N	38.39 E
Istok, Yugo.	36	G7	42.47 N	20.29 E
Istra, Russia	26	E19	55.54 N	36.50 E
Istra see Istria, pen., Eur.	30	E10	45.16 N	13.56 E
Istria, pen., Eur.	30	E10	45.16 N	13.56 E
Isunba, Nig.	191a		6.27 N	3.17 E
Itá, Para.	172	B9	25.30 S	57.21 W
Itabaiana, Braz.	170	D8	7.20 S	35.20 W
Itabaiana, Braz.	170	F7	10.41 S	37.26 W
Itabaianinha, Braz.	170	F7	11.16 S	37.47 W
Itabapoana, Braz.	170	K5	21.18 S	40.58 W
Itabashi, ngh., Japan	186		35.45 N	139.43 E
Itaberá, Braz.	170	L1	23.51 S	49.08 W
Itaberaba, Braz.	170	G5	12.31 S	40.17 W
Itaberaí, Braz.	166	C7	16.01 S	49.47 W
Itabi, Braz.	170	F7	10.07 S	37.06 W
Itabira, Braz.	170	J4	19.38 S	43.13 W
Itaboraí, mun., Braz.	205a		22.43 S	43.00 W
Itabuna, Braz.	170	H6	14.47 S	39.16 W
Itacajá, Braz.	170	E2	8.19 S	47.45 W
Itacambiruçu, stm., Braz.	170	I4	16.43 S	42.36 W
Itacaré, Braz.	170	H6	14.18 S	39.00 W
Itacoatiara, Braz.	164	D6	3.07 S	58.25 W
Itacoatiara, Ponta de, c., Braz.	205a		22.59 S	43.02 W
Itacurubí del Rosario, Para.	172	B9	24.32 S	56.51 W
Itaeté, Braz.	170	G5	12.59 S	40.58 W
Itaguaçu, Braz.	170	J5	19.48 S	40.51 W
Itaguajé, Braz.	166	D6	22.36 S	51.59 W
Itaguara, Braz.	170	K3	20.23 S	44.29 W
Itaguari, stm., Braz.	170	H3	14.16 S	44.25 W
Itaguatins, Braz.	170	C2	5.46 S	47.29 W
Itagüí, Col.	168	D4	6.09 N	75.37 W
Itaí, Braz.	172	A13	23.25 S	49.05 W
Itá Ibaté, Arg.	172	C9	27.26 S	57.21 W
Itaiçaba, Braz.	170	C7	4.40 S	37.51 W
Itaim, stm., Braz.	170	D5	7.01 S	42.00 W
Itainópolis, Braz.	170	D5	7.24 S	41.31 W
Itaiópolis, Braz.	172	C12	26.21 S	49.59 W
Itaipu, Braz.	205a		22.44 S	43.26 W
Itaipu, Lagoa de, b., Braz.	205a		22.58 S	43.02 W
Itaipu, Ponta de, c., Braz.	205a		22.59 S	43.03 W
Itaipu, Represa de see Itaipu Reservoir, res., S.A.	172	B10	24.55 S	54.25 W
Itaipu Reservoir, res., S.A.	172	B10	24.55 S	54.25 W
Itäisen Suomenlahden kansallispuisto, p.o.i., Fin.	18	G14	60.15 N	27.00 E
Itaituba, Braz.	164	D6	4.14 S	55.59 W
Itajaí, Braz.	172	C13	26.54 S	48.39 W
Itajaí do Sul, stm., Braz.	172	C13	27.12 S	49.38 W
Itajubá, Braz.	170	L3	22.25 S	45.27 W
Itaju do Colônia, Braz.	170	H6	15.11 S	39.45 W
Itajuípe, Braz.	170	H6	14.40 S	39.17 W
Itaki, Nig.	191a		6.43 N	3.17 E
Itala Game Reserve, ind. res., S. Afr.	90	E10	27.31 S	31.19 E
Italia see Italy, ctry., Eur.	6	G11	43.00 N	13.00 E
Itálica, hist., Spain	28	G4	37.26 N	6.03 W
Italy, Tx., U.S.	136	B11	32.09 N	96.53 W
Italy, ctry., Eur.	6	G11	43.00 N	13.00 E
Itamaraju, Braz.	170	I6	17.02 S	39.32 W
Itamarandiba, Braz.	170	I4	17.51 S	42.51 W
Itamarandiba, stm., Braz.	170	I4	17.18 S	42.48 W
Itamari, Braz.	170	G6	13.47 S	39.36 W
Itamataré, Braz.	170	B2	2.16 S	46.22 W
Itambacuri, Braz.	170	I5	18.02 S	41.39 W
Itambé, Braz.	170	H5	15.14 S	40.36 W
Itämeri see Baltic Sea, s., Eur.	8	D12	57.00 N	19.00 E
Itami, Japan	56	E8	34.47 N	135.24 E
Itami, Camp, mil., Japan	188		34.47 N	135.24 E
Itampolo, Madag.	88	E7	24.41 S	43.57 E
Itānagar, India	70	E14	27.09 N	93.33 E
Itanhaém, Braz.	172	B14	24.10 S	46.47 W
Itanhém, Braz.	170	I5	17.09 S	40.20 W
Itaobim, Braz.	170	I5	16.33 S	41.29 W
Itaocaia, Braz.	205a		22.58 S	43.01 W
Itapaci, Braz.	166	C7	14.57 S	49.34 W
Itapagipe, Braz.	170	J1	19.54 S	49.22 W
Itapajé, Braz.	170	B6	3.41 S	39.34 W
Itaparica, Ilha de, i., Braz.	170	G6	13.00 S	38.42 W
Itaparica, Represa de, res., Braz.	170	E6	8.50 S	38.40 W
Itapebi, Braz.	170	H6	15.57 S	39.31 W
Itapecerica, Braz.	170	K3	20.28 S	45.07 W
Itapecerica da Serra, mun., Braz.	205b		23.44 S	46.52 W
Itapecuru-Mirim, Braz.	170	B3	3.24 S	44.20 W
Itapemirim, Braz.	170	K5	21.00 S	40.48 W
Itapera, Braz.	170	B4	2.32 S	43.47 W
Itaperuna, Braz.	170	K5	21.12 S	41.53 W
Itapetim, Braz.	170	D7	7.22 S	37.11 W
Itapetinga, Braz.	170	H5	15.15 S	40.16 W
Itapetininga, Braz.	170	L1	23.35 S	48.02 W
Itapetininga, stm., Braz.	172	A14	23.36 S	48.28 W
Itapeva, Braz.	170	L1	23.58 S	48.52 W
Itapevi, mun., Braz.	205b		23.31 S	46.55 W
Itapicuru, Braz.	170	F6	11.18 S	38.13 W
Itapicuru, stm., Braz.	170	B3	2.50 S	44.11 W
Itapicuru, stm., Braz.	170	F6	11.44 S	37.30 W
Itapipoca, Braz.	170	B6	3.30 S	39.35 W
Itapiranga, Braz.	164	D6	2.44 S	58.00 W
Itapiranga, Braz.	172	C11	27.08 S	53.47 W
Itapiraputã, Braz.	166	C6	15.52 S	50.36 W
Itapitanga, Braz.	170	H6	14.26 S	39.34 W
Itapiúna, Braz.	170	C6	4.33 S	38.57 W
Itápolis, Braz.	170	K1	21.32 S	48.48 W
Itaporã de Goiás, Braz.	170	D1	8.00 S	48.39 W
Itaporanga, Braz.	170	D6	7.18 S	38.10 W
Itaporanga, Braz.	170	L1	23.42 S	49.28 W
Itaporanga d'Ajuda, Braz.	170	F7	11.00 S	37.17 W
Itapúa, state, Para.	172	C10	26.50 S	55.50 W
Itaquaquecetuba, mun., Braz.	205b		23.28 S	46.20 W
Itaquara, Braz.	170	G6	13.26 S	39.57 W
Itaquari, Braz.	170	K5	20.19 S	40.22 W
Itaquaxiara, Braz.	205b		23.47 S	46.51 W
Itaquaxiara, Ribeirão, stm., Braz.	205b		23.44 S	46.47 W
Itaquera, Ribeirão, stm., Braz.	205b		23.28 S	46.26 W
Itaqui, Braz.	172	D9	29.07 S	56.32 W
Itaquyry, Para.	172	B10	24.58 S	55.09 W
Itarantim, Braz.	170	H5	15.39 S	40.03 W
Itararé, Braz.	172	B13	24.06 S	49.21 W
Itararé, stm., Braz.	172	A13	23.42 S	49.37 W
Itārsi, India	70	G6	22.36 N	77.46 E
Itarumã, Braz.	166	C6	18.42 S	51.25 W
Itasca, Il., U.S.	196		41.58 N	88.00 W
Itasca, Tx., U.S.	136	B10	32.10 N	97.08 W
Itasca, Lake, l., Mn., U.S.	128	D3	47.12 N	95.13 W
Itasca State Park, p.o.i., Mn., U.S.	128	D3	47.18 N	95.18 W
Itata, stm., Chile	172	H1	36.23 S	72.52 W
Itatí, Arg.	172	C8	27.16 S	58.14 W
Itatinga, Braz.	170	L1	23.06 S	48.37 W
Itatira, Braz.	170	C6	4.30 S	39.37 W
Itatolo, Congo	191b		4.09 S	15.15 E
Itatupã, Braz.	164	D7	0.37 S	51.12 W
Itaú, Braz.	170	C7	5.50 S	37.59 W
Itaueira, Braz.	170	D4	7.36 S	43.02 W
Itaueira, stm., Braz.	170	D4	6.40 S	42.55 W
Itaúna, Braz.	170	K3	20.04 S	44.34 W
Itaúna, Morro do, hill, Braz.	205a		22.46 S	43.02 W
Itbayat Island, i., Phil.	58	K9	20.46 N	121.50 E
Itéa, Grc.	34	E5	38.26 N	22.25 E
Itenes see Guaporé, stm., S.A.	166	B4	11.54 S	65.00 W
Itenes see Iténez, stm., S.A.	166	B4	11.54 S	65.00 W
Iténez (Guaporé), stm., S.A.	166	B4	11.54 S	65.00 W
Ithaca, Mi., U.S.	126	E5	43.17 N	84.36 W
Ithaca, N.Y., U.S.	124	B9	42.26 N	76.29 W
Ithaca see Itháki, i., Grc.	34	E3	38.25 N	20.40 E
Itháki, Grc.	34	E3	38.22 N	20.42 E
Itháki, i., Grc.	34	E3	38.25 N	20.40 E
Ithan Creek, stm., Pa., U.S.	203		40.00 N	75.21 W
Itikawa see Ichikawa, Japan	56	D12	35.44 N	139.55 E
Itimbiri, stm., D.R.C.	86	D4	2.02 N	22.44 E
Itinga, Braz.	170	I5	16.36 S	41.46 W
Itinga, stm., Braz.	170	I5	16.35 S	41.45 W
Itinomiya see Ichinomiya, Japan	56	D9	35.18 N	136.48 E
Itiquira, stm., Braz.	166	C5	17.18 S	56.43 W
Itirapina, Braz.	170	L2	22.15 S	47.49 W
Itire, Nig.	191a		6.31 N	3.21 E
Itiruçu, Braz.	170	G5	13.31 S	40.08 W
Itiúba, Braz.	170	F6	10.41 S	39.51 W
Itla el-Bâsha, hill, Egypt	76	K3	27.31 N	32.20 E
Itō, Japan	56	E12	34.58 N	139.06 E
Itoigawa, Japan	56	B10	37.02 N	137.51 E
Itoko, D.R.C.	86	E4	0.57 S	21.43 E
Iton, stm., Fr.	20	F9	49.09 N	1.11 E
Itororó, Braz.	170	H5	15.07 S	40.05 W
Itsuki, Japan	56	G3	32.24 N	130.50 E
Itsuwa, Japan	56	G3	32.31 N	130.11 E
Itta Bena, Ms., U.S.	134	D8	33.30 N	90.19 W
Itter, stm., Ger.	181		51.09 N	6.52 E
Itteville, Fr.	179		48.31 N	2.21 E
Ittiri, Italy	32	D2	40.36 N	8.34 E
Ittoqqortoormiit see Scoresbysund, Grnld.	108	C21	70.29 N	21.58 W
Itu, Braz.	170	L2	23.16 S	47.17 W
Itu, stm., Braz.	172	D10	29.24 S	55.51 W
Ituaçu, Braz.	170	G5	13.49 S	41.18 W
Ituango, Col.	168	D4	7.05 N	75.43 W
Ituberá, Braz.	170	G6	13.44 S	39.08 W
Itueta, Braz.	170	J5	19.24 S	41.10 W
Ituí, stm., Braz.	164	E3	4.38 S	70.15 W
Ituim, stm., Braz.	172	D12	28.38 S	51.23 W
Ituiutaba, Braz.	170	J1	18.58 S	49.27 W
Itula, D.R.C.	86	E5	3.25 S	27.52 E
Itumbiara, Braz.	170	J1	18.24 S	49.12 W
Ituna, Sk., Can.	142	C10	51.10 N	103.30 W
Itupiranga, Braz.	164	E8	5.11 S	49.21 W
Ituporanga, Braz.	172	C13	27.23 S	49.36 W
Iturama, Braz.	166	C6	19.44 S	50.11 W
Iturbe, Para.	172	B9	26.01 S	56.30 W
Iturbide, Mex.	156	C3	19.38 N	89.35 W
Iturup, ostrov, i., Russia	52	C14	44.51 N	147.26 E
Ituverava, Braz.	170	K2	20.20 S	47.47 W
Ituxi, stm., Braz.	164	E4	7.17 S	64.50 W
Ituzaingó, Arg.	172	C9	27.36 S	56.40 W
Ītyop'iya see Ethiopia, ctry., Afr.	82	F7	9.00 N	39.00 E
Itzehoe, Ger.	24	C5	53.55 N	9.32 E
Iu̯e, Bela.	26	G8	53.55 N	25.46 E
Iuka, Ms., U.S.	134	C10	34.48 N	88.10 W
Iul'tin, Russia	50	C25	67.43 N	178.50 W
Iúna, Braz.	170	K5	20.20 S	41.31 W
Iva, S.C., U.S.	132	B3	34.18 N	82.39 W
Ivacèvičy, Bela.	26	H8	52.42 N	25.21 E
Ivačovo, Russia	18	G23	60.32 N	36.21 E
Ivaí, stm., Braz.	166	D6	23.18 S	53.43 W
Ivaiporã, Braz.	172	B12	24.14 S	51.40 W
Ivajlovgrad, Blg.	36	H13	41.32 N	26.08 E
Ivalo, Fin.	14	D18	68.39 N	27.31 E
Ivalojoki, stm., Fin.	14	D18	68.46 N	27.36 E
Ivanava, Bela.	26	H8	52.09 N	25.32 E
Ivančice, Czech Rep.	24	G12	49.06 N	16.22 E
Ivane-Puste, Ukr.	38	E5	48.38 N	26.11 E
Ivangorod, Russia	26	A11	59.24 N	28.10 E
Ivangrad, Yugo.	36	G6	42.51 N	19.52 E
Ivanhoe, Austl.	98	I5	32.55 S	144.19 E
Ivanhoe, Austl.	192b		37.46 S	145.03 E
Ivanhoe, Ca., U.S.	148	G6	36.23 N	119.12 W
Ivanhoe, Il., U.S.	196		42.17 N	88.02 W
Ivanhoe, Mn., U.S.	118	G2	44.27 N	96.15 W
Ivanhoe, Va., U.S.	124	H4	36.50 N	80.59 W
Ivanić Grad, Cro.	30	E13	45.42 N	16.24 E
Ivanišči, Russia	26	D18	56.35 N	35.13 E
Ivaniv, Ukr.	38	D7	49.29 N	28.22 E
Ivanivka, Ukr.	38	G13	46.42 N	34.33 E
Ivanivka, Ukr.	38	G9	46.58 N	30.28 E
Ivanjica, Yugo.	36	F7	43.35 N	20.14 E
Ivankov, Ukr.	38	C8	50.56 N	29.54 E
Ivan'kovo, Russia	26	F20	54.44 N	37.57 E
Ivan'kovskoe vodohranilišče, res., Russia	26	D19	56.37 N	36.30 E
Ivano-Frankivs'k, Ukr.	38	E3	48.55 N	24.43 E
Ivano-Frankivs'k, co., Ukr.	38	E3	48.45 N	24.30 E
Ivano-Frankove, Ukr.	38	D2	49.55 N	23.44 E
Ivanopil', Ukr.	38	D7	49.51 N	28.13 E
Ivanovka, Russia	50	F14	50.21 N	127.59 E
Ivanovka, Russia	54	B10	43.57 N	132.28 E
Ivanovo, Russia	40	C12	57.00 N	40.58 E
Ivanovo-Voznesensk see Ivanovo, Russia	40	C12	57.00 N	40.58 E
Ivanovskaja, Russia	38	H17	45.15 N	38.28 E
Ivanovskaja oblast', co., Russia	40	C13	57.00 N	41.00 E
Ivanovskoe, Russia	26	A11	59.16 N	28.50 E
Ivanovskoe, Russia	38	B13	51.36 N	34.56 E
Ivanovskoe, Russia	183a		59.46 N	30.47 E
Ivanovy Ludy, ostrova, is., Russia	18	B22	65.45 N	34.52 E
Ivanpah Lake, l., Ca., U.S.	148	H10	35.34 N	115.24 W
Ivanteevka, Russia	40	E16	52.15 N	49.05 E
Ivanteevka, Russia	183b		55.58 N	37.55 E
Ivanteevo, Russia	26	C16	57.47 N	33.07 E
Ivanychi, Ukr.	38	C3	50.38 N	24.21 E
Ivanytsia, Ukr.	38	C11	50.47 N	32.37 E
Ivdel', Russia	48	B9	60.41 N	60.27 E
Ive see Iu̯e, Bela.	26	G8	53.55 N	25.46 E
Iver, Eng., U.K.	178		51.31 N	0.30 W
Iver Heath, Eng., U.K.	178		51.32 N	0.31 W
Iverny, Fr.	179		49.00 N	2.47 E
Ivigtut, Grnld.	108	E16	61.12 N	48.10 W
Ivindo, stm., Gabon	86	D2	0.09 S	12.09 E
Ivinheima, stm., Braz.	166	D6	23.14 S	53.41 W
Iviza see Eivissa, Spain	28	F12	38.54 N	1.25 E
Ivjanec, Bela.	26	G9	53.53 N	26.44 E
Ivnja, Russia	38	B15	51.03 N	36.08 E
Ivnytsia, Ukr.	38	C8	50.09 N	29.02 E
Ivohibe, Madag.	88	E8	22.29 S	46.53 E
Ivory Coast see Cote d'Ivoire, ctry., Afr.	84	H3	8.00 N	5.00 W
Ivory Coast, cst., C. Iv.	84	I3	5.04 N	5.15 W
Ivösjön, l., Swe.	16	K12	56.06 N	14.27 E
Ivot, Russia	26	G17	53.40 N	34.12 E
Ivot, Ukr.	38	A12	51.59 N	33.29 E
Ivotka, stm., Ukr.	38	A12	51.58 N	33.20 E
Ivrea, Italy	30	E4	45.28 N	7.53 E
İvrindi, Tur.	34	D10	39.33 N	27.28 E
Ivujivik, Qc., Can.	110	C15	62.23 N	77.54 W
Ivy Hatch, Eng., U.K.	178		51.16 N	0.16 E
Ivyland, Pa., U.S.	203		40.12 N	75.04 W
Iwafune, Japan	188		34.44 N	135.54 E
Iwaki, Japan	56	B13	37.03 N	140.55 E
Iwaki-san, vol., Japan	54	D14	40.39 N	140.18 E
Iwakuni, Japan	56	E5	34.10 N	132.14 E
Iwami, Japan	56	D7	35.35 N	134.20 E
Iwanuma, Japan	56	A13	38.06 N	140.52 E
Iwaoka, ngh., Japan	188		34.44 N	134.58 E
Iwase, Japan	186		35.17 N	139.52 E
Iwata, Japan	56	E10	34.42 N	137.51 E
Iwate, state, Japan	56	A14	38.51 N	141.15 E
Iwate-san, vol., Japan	54	E14	39.51 N	141.00 E
Iwaya see Awaji, Japan	56	E8	34.35 N	135.00 E
Iwaya, Japan	188		34.35 N	135.02 E
Iwayama, Japan	188		34.52 N	135.52 E
Iwazono, Japan	188		34.45 N	135.19 E
'Iweibid, Gebel, mtn., Egypt	76	H3	30.06 N	32.09 E
Iwo, Nig.	84	H5	7.37 N	4.11 E
Ixiamas, Bol.	166	B3	13.45 S	68.09 W
Ixmiquilpan, Mex.	154	E9	20.28 N	99.12 W
Ixopo, S. Afr.	90	G10	30.08 S	29.59 E
Ixtapa, Mex.	154	G8	17.39 N	101.36 W
Ixtepec, Mex.	154	G11	16.32 N	95.05 W
Ixtlán de Juárez, Mex.	154	G10	17.20 N	96.29 W
Ixtlán del Río, Mex.	154	E6	21.02 N	104.22 W
Iyo, Japan	56	F5	33.45 N	132.42 E
Iyo-mishima, Japan	56	F6	33.58 N	133.33 E
Iyo-nada, s., Japan	56	F5	33.40 N	132.20 E
Iž, stm., Russia	40	C18	55.57 N	52.40 E
Izabal, Lago de, l., Guat.	156	E3	15.30 N	89.10 W
Īzad Khvāst, Iran	74	E13	31.30 N	52.07 E
Izamal, Mex.	156	B3	20.56 N	89.01 W
Izapa, hist., Mex.	154	H12	14.55 N	92.10 W
Izberbaš, Russia	42	D12	42.33 N	47.52 E
Izbica, Pol.	24	F19	50.52 N	23.09 E
Izbica, Pol.	24	B13	54.40 N	17.28 E
Izdëškovo, Russia	26	E16	55.08 N	33.37 E
Izegem, Bel.	20	D12	50.55 N	3.12 E
Īzeh, Iran	74	E11	31.49 N	49.52 E
Iževsk, Russia	40	C18	56.50 N	53.11 E
Iziaslav, Ukr.	38	C5	50.06 N	26.49 E
Izium, Ukr.	38	D16	49.12 N	37.16 E
Ižma, stm., Russia	48	B8	65.19 N	52.55 E
Izmaïl, Ukr.	38	H7	45.21 N	28.50 E
Izmajlovo, ngh., Russia	183b		55.48 N	37.46 E
Izmajlovo Park, p.o.i., Russia	183b		55.46 N	37.47 E
Izmalkovo, Russia	26	H21	52.41 N	37.58 E
İzmir (Smyrna), Tur.	34	E10	38.26 N	27.09 E
İzmir, state, Tur.	34	E10	38.30 N	27.15 E
İzmir Körfezi, b., Tur.	34	E9	38.33 N	26.39 E
İzmit (Kocaeli), Tur.	34	C12	40.47 N	29.57 E
İzmit Körfezi, b., Tur.	34	C12	40.45 N	29.35 E
Iznájar, Embalse de, res., Spain	28	G6	37.16 N	4.20 W
Iznalloz, Spain	28	G7	37.23 N	3.31 W
İznik, Tur.	34	C12	40.25 N	29.43 E
İznik Gölü, l., Tur.	34	C12	40.26 N	29.30 E
Iznoski, Russia	26	E18	54.59 N	35.18 E
Izoplit, Russia	26	D19	56.38 N	36.12 E
Ižora, stm., Russia	183a		59.48 N	30.36 E
Izozog, Bañados del, sw., Bol.	166	C4	18.48 S	62.10 W
Izra53, Syria	76	F7	32.51 N	36.15 E
Izsák, Hung.	36	C6	46.48 N	19.20 E
Iztacalco, ngh., Mex.	204a		19.23 N	99.07 W
Iztaccíhuatl, Volcán, vol., Mex.	154	F9	19.09 N	98.37 W
Iztaccíhuatl y Popocatéptl, Parques Nacionales, p.o.i., Mex.	154	F9	19.10 N	98.38 W
Iztapalapa, ngh., Mex.	204a		19.21 N	99.06 W
Izucar de Matamoros, Mex.	154	F9	18.35 N	98.27 W
Izu-hantō, pen., Japan	56	E11	34.52 N	138.56 E
Izuhara, Japan	56	E2	34.12 N	129.17 E
Izu Islands see Izu-shotō, is., Japan	56	F13	32.00 N	140.00 E
Izumi, Japan	56	G3	32.03 N	130.21 E
Izumi, Japan	56	A13	38.20 N	140.53 E
Izumi, Japan	56	E8	34.29 N	135.26 E
Izumi, ngh., Japan	186		35.25 N	139.30 E
Izumo, Japan	56	D5	35.22 N	132.46 E
Izu-shotō (Izu Islands), is., Japan	56	F13	32.00 N	140.00 E
Izu Trench, unds.	174	G17	31.00 N	142.00 E
Izuwara, Japan	188		34.53 N	135.32 E
Izvestij CIK, ostrova, is., Russia	50	A5	75.55 N	82.30 E
Izvorul Muntelui, Lacul, l., Rom.	36	B12	47.00 N	26.00 E
J				
Jääsjärvi, l., Fin.	18	F13	61.35 N	26.07 E
Jabal, Bahr al- (Mountain Nile), stm., Sudan	82	F6	9.30 N	30.30 E
Jabal al-Awliyā', Sudan	82	D6	15.11 N	32.31 E
Jabal Lubnān, state, Leb.	76	D6	33.50 N	35.40 E
Jabalón, stm., Spain	28	F7	38.53 N	4.04 W
Jabalpur, India	70	G7	23.10 N	79.56 E
Jabālyah, Gaza	76	G5	31.31 N	34.29 E
Jabbūl, Sabkhat al-, l., Syria	76	C8	36.03 N	37.39 E
Jabiru, Austl.	96	B6	12.40 S	132.53 E
Jablah, Syria	76	C6	35.21 N	35.56 E
Jablanac, Cro.	30	F11	44.42 N	14.53 E
Jablanica, Bos.	36	F4	43.39 N	17.45 E
Jablanica, stm., Yugo.	36	G8	43.07 N	21.56 E
Jablaničko jezero, res., Bos.	36	F4	43.41 N	17.48 E
Jablines, Fr.	179		48.55 N	2.46 E
Jablonec nad Nisou, Czech Rep.	24	F11	50.43 N	15.10 E
Jablonica, Slvk.	24	H13	48.37 N	17.25 E
Jabłonka, Pol.	24	G15	49.28 N	19.42 E
Jablonovyj hrebet, mts., Russia	50	F11	53.30 N	115.00 E
Jabłonowo Pomorskie, Pol.	24	C15	53.22 N	19.07 E
Jablunkov, Czech Rep.	24	G14	49.34 N	18.45 E
Jaboncillos Creek, stm., Tx., U.S.	136	G10	27.23 N	97.44 W
Jabonga, Phil.	68	F5	9.18 N	125.33 E
Jaboticabal, Braz.	170	K1	21.15 S	48.19 W
Jabung, Tanjung, c., Indon.	64	D4	1.01 S	104.21 E
Jaca, Spain	28	B10	42.34 N	0.33 W
Jacala, Mex.	154	E9	21.01 N	99.11 W
Jacana, Austl.	192b		37.42 S	144.55 E
Jacaraci, Braz.	170	H4	14.51 S	42.26 W
Jacaré, stm., Braz.	170	F5	10.06 S	42.13 W
Jacaré, stm., Braz.	170	G5	13.50 S	40.42 W
Jacareí, Braz.	170	L2	23.18 S	45.57 W
Jacarezinho, Braz.	166	D7	23.09 S	49.58 W
Jáchal, stm., Arg.	172	E3	31.15 S	67.41 W
Jaciara, Braz.	166	C5	15.56 S	54.56 W
Jacinto, Braz.	170	I5	16.10 S	40.16 W
Jacinto Aráuz, Arg.	172	I6	38.05 S	63.26 W
Jacinto City, Tx., U.S.	136	E12	29.46 N	95.14 W
Jacinto Machado, Braz.	172	D13	29.00 S	49.46 W
Jack Creek, stm., Or., U.S.	146	G5	42.59 N	121.32 W
Jackfish Lake, l., Sk., Can.	142	A5	53.05 N	108.25 W
Jackhead Harbour, Mb., Can.	142	C16	51.51 N	97.16 W
Jackman, Me., U.S.	122	E6	45.37 N	70.15 W
Jack Mountain, mtn., Mt., U.S.	146	D14	46.21 N	112.18 W
Jack Mountain, mtn., Wa., U.S.	146	B6	48.47 N	120.58 W
Jackpot, Nv., U.S.	146	I12	41.59 N	114.41 W
Jacksboro, Tn., U.S.	124	H1	36.19 N	84.10 W
Jacksboro, Tx., U.S.	138	H10	33.13 N	98.09 W
Jacks Fork, stm., Mo., U.S.	130	G6	37.11 N	91.16 W
Jacks Island, i., Pa., U.S.	197b		40.37 N	79.43 W
Jackson, Al., U.S.	134	F11	31.30 N	87.53 W
Jackson, Ca., U.S.	148	E5	38.21 N	120.46 W
Jackson, Ga., U.S.	132	C1	33.17 N	83.57 W
Jackson, Ky., U.S.	124	G2	37.33 N	83.24 W
Jackson, La., U.S.	134	G7	30.49 N	91.13 W
Jackson, Mi., U.S.	124	B1	42.15 N	84.24 W
Jackson, Mn., U.S.	128	H4	43.37 N	94.59 W
Jackson, Ms., U.S.	134	E8	32.17 N	90.11 W
Jackson, Mo., U.S.	130	G8	37.22 N	89.40 W
Jackson, N.C., U.S.	124	H8	36.23 N	77.25 W
Jackson, Oh., U.S.	124	E3	39.02 N	82.38 W
Jackson, S.C., U.S.	132	C4	33.19 N	81.47 W
Jackson, Tn., U.S.	134	B10	35.37 N	88.49 W
Jackson, Wy., U.S.	146	G16	43.29 N	110.45 W
Jackson, stm., Va., U.S.	124	G6	37.47 N	79.46 W
Jackson, Lake, l., Fl., U.S.	134	G14	30.31 N	84.19 W
Jackson, Mount, mtn., Ant.	103	C34	71.23 S	63.21 W
Jackson, Mount, mtn., Austl.	96	F3	30.15 S	119.16 E
Jackson Brook, stm., N.J., U.S.	194		40.53 N	74.34 W
Jackson Creek, stm., Can.	142	E12	49.17 N	100.55 W
Jackson Heights, ngh., N.Y., U.S.	194		40.45 N	73.53 W
Jackson Lake, l., Wy., U.S.	146	G16	43.55 N	110.40 W
Jackson Lake, res., Ga., U.S.	132	C2	33.22 N	83.52 W
Jackson Mountain, mtn., Me., U.S.	122	F6	44.46 N	70.31 W
Jackson Park, p.o.i., On., Can.	199		42.17 N	83.01 W
Jackson Park, p.o.i., Il., U.S.	196		41.47 N	87.35 W
Jacksonville, Al., U.S.	134	D13	33.48 N	85.45 W
Jacksonville, Ar., U.S.	134	C6	34.52 N	92.07 W
Jacksonville, Fl., U.S.	132	F4	30.19 N	81.41 W
Jacksonville, Il., U.S.	130	E7	39.43 N	90.13 W
Jacksonville, N.J., U.S.	203		40.03 N	74.46 W
Jacksonville, N.C., U.S.	132	B8	34.45 N	77.26 W
Jacksonville, Or., U.S.	148	A2	42.19 N	122.57 W
Jacksonville, Tx., U.S.	136	C12	31.57 N	95.16 W
Jacksonville Beach, Fl., U.S.	132	F4	30.17 N	81.23 W
Jacksonville Naval Air Station, mil., Fl., U.S.	132	F4	30.14 N	81.41 W
Jacks Run, stm., Pa., U.S.	197b		40.13 N	79.35 W
Jacktown Acres, Pa., U.S.	197b		40.19 N	79.45 W
Jacmel, Haiti	156	C11	18.14 N	72.31 W
Jaco, Mex.	154	B6	27.50 N	104.00 W
Jacob, Morne, mtn., Mart.	159c	k6	14.46 N	61.06 W
Jacobābād, Pak.	70	D2	28.16 N	68.25 E
Jacobina, Braz.	170	F5	11.11 S	40.31 W
Jacob Riis Park, p.o.i., N.Y., U.S.	194		40.34 N	73.52 W
Jacobsdal, S. Afr.	90	F7	29.07 S	24.46 E
Jacques-Cartier, Qc., Can.	193a		45.31 N	73.29 W
Jacques-Cartier, Mont, mtn., Qc., Can.	122	A11	48.59 N	65.56 W
Jacques-Cartier, Parc de conservation de la, ind. res., Qc., Can.	122	C5	47.20 N	71.21 W
Jacques-Cartier, Pont, trans., Qc., Can.	193a		45.31 N	73.32 W
Jacquet River, N.B., Can.	122	C11	47.55 N	66.01 W
Jacu, stm., Braz.	170	D8	6.10 S	35.05 W
Jacu, Rio do, stm., Braz.	205b		23.29 S	46.27 W
Jacuí, stm., Braz.	172	D11	30.01 S	51.14 W
Jacuípe, stm., Braz.	170	F5	12.30 S	39.05 W
Jacumba, Ca., U.S.	148	K9	32.36 N	116.11 W
Jacundá, Braz.	164	D8	4.30 S	49.25 W
Jacupiranga, Braz.	172	B13	24.41 S	48.00 W
Jacuriaí, stm., Braz.	170	F6	10.57 S	39.35 W
Jada, Nig.	84	H7	8.45 N	12.09 E
Jade Buddha, Temple of the, rel., China	187b		31.14 N	121.26 E
Jadebusen, b., Ger.	24	C4	53.30 N	8.10 E
Jade Run, stm., N.J., U.S.	203		39.56 N	74.45 W
Jadīdah, Iraq	74	D8	33.57 N	42.27 E
J.A.D. Jensens Nunatakker, mtn., Grnld.	108	E16	62.49 N	48.53 W
Jadotville see Likasi, D.R.C.	86	J6	10.58 S	26.43 E
Jadransko more see Adriatic Sea, s., Eur.	8	G11	42.30 N	16.00 E
Jadransko morje see Adriatic Sea, s., Eur.	8	G11	42.30 N	16.00 E
Jadraque, Spain	28	D8	40.55 N	2.55 W
Jadrin, Russia	40	D15	55.55 N	46.12 E
Jādū, Libya	82	A2	31.57 N	12.03 E
Jaén, Peru	164	E2	5.42 S	78.47 W
Jaén, Spain	28	G7	37.46 N	3.47 W
Jaén, co., Spain	28	G7	38.00 N	3.30 W
Jæren, reg., Nor.	16	I3	58.43 N	5.37 E
Jāfarābād, India	70	H3	20.52 N	71.22 E
Ja'farābād, Iran	74	C12	35.43 N	50.42 E
Jāfarpur, ngh., India	190a		28.40 N	77.01 E
Jaffa, Cape, c., Austl.	98	K2	36.57 S	139.40 E
Jaffna, Sri L.	69	G4	9.39 N	80.01 E
Jaffna Lagoon, b., Sri L.	69	G5	9.33 N	80.16 E
Jaffrey, N.H., U.S.	124	B13	42.48 N	72.01 W
Jafr, Qā' al-, depr., Jord.	76	H7	30.17 N	36.20 E
Jägala, stm., Est.	26	A8	59.28 N	25.09 E
Jagalūr, India	69	D3	14.31 N	76.21 E
Jāgan, Pak.	70	D2	28.03 N	68.35 E
Jagannāthganj Ghāt, Bngl.	70	F12	24.44 N	89.49 E
Jagannāthpūr, India	190b		22.43 N	88.19 E
Jagatnagar, India	190b		22.47 N	88.13 E
Jagatpur, ngh., India	190a		28.44 N	77.14 E
Jagatsingpur, India	70	H11	20.16 N	86.10 E
Jagdalpur, India	69	B6	19.05 N	82.02 E
Jageljurta, gora, hill, Russia	14	E28	67.33 N	38.02 E
Jägerndorf see Krnov, Czech Rep.	24	F13	50.05 N	17.42 E
Jagersfontein, S. Afr.	90	F7	29.46 S	25.26 E
Jaggayyapeta, India	69	C5	16.53 N	80.05 E
Jagny-sous-Bois, Fr.	179		49.05 N	2.27 E
Jagodnoe, Russia	50	D18	62.32 N	149.36 E
Jagraon, India	70	C5	30.46 N	75.28 E
Jagst, stm., Ger.	24	G5	49.14 N	9.11 E
Jagtiāl, India	69	B4	18.47 N	78.55 E
Jaguaquara, Braz.	170	G6	13.31 S	39.58 W
Jaguarão, Braz.	172	F11	32.34 S	53.23 W
Jaguarão (Yaguarón), stm., S.A.	172	F11	32.42 S	53.06 W
Jaguarari, Braz.	170	F5	10.16 S	40.12 W
Jaguaretama, Braz.	170	C6	5.37 S	38.46 W
Jaguari, Braz.	172	D10	29.29 S	54.41 W
Jaguariaíva, Braz.	172	B13	24.15 S	49.42 W
Jaguaribara, Braz.	170	C6	5.40 S	38.37 W
Jaguaribe, Braz.	170	C6	5.53 S	38.37 W
Jaguaribe, stm., Braz.	170	C7	4.25 S	37.45 W
Jaguaripe, Braz.	170	G6	13.08 S	38.52 W
Jaguaruna, Braz.	172	D13	28.37 S	49.01 W
Jagüey Grande, Cuba	156	A7	22.31 N	81.07 W
Jāgulia, India	190b		22.44 N	88.32 E
Jahānābād, India	70	F10	25.13 N	84.59 E
Jahangirpur, ngh., India	190a		28.44 N	77.13 E
Jahrom, Iran	74	F13	28.29 N	53.33 E
Jahroma, Russia	26	D20	56.17 N	37.30 E
Jaicós, Braz.	170	D5	7.21 S	41.08 W
Jailolo, Indon.	60	E8	1.04 N	127.28 E
Jaimanitas, stm., Cuba	204b		23.05 N	82.29 W
Jainti, India	70	E12	26.41 N	89.32 E
Jaintiāpur, Bngl.	70	F14	25.08 N	92.07 E
Jaipur, India	70	E5	26.54 N	75.48 E
Jaipur Hāt, Bngl.	70	F12	25.06 N	89.01 E
Jais, India	70	E8	26.15 N	81.33 E
Jaisalmer, India	70	E3	26.54 N	70.54 E
Jaito, India	70	C5	30.26 N	74.53 E
Jaja, Russia	48	C15	56.11 N	86.26 E
Jājapur, India	70	H11	20.51 N	86.20 E
Jājarm, Iran	74	B15	36.56 N	56.24 E
Jajce, Bos.	36	E4	44.20 N	17.16 E
Jajjha, Pak.	70	D3	28.45 N	70.34 E
Jajsan, Kaz.	40	F20	50.51 N	56.12 E
Jakarta, Indon.	66	G5	6.10 S	106.50 E
Jakarta, Indon.	187e		6.10 S	106.48 E
Jakarta, Teluk, b., Indon.	66	F5	6.03 S	106.48 E
Jakarta Kota Station, trans., Indon.	187e		6.08 S	106.49 E
Jakau̯levičy, Bela.	26	F13	54.20 N	30.31 E
Jake Creek Mountain, mtn., Nv., U.S.	148	B9	41.13 N	116.54 W
Jākhal, India	70	D5	29.48 N	75.48 E
Jakhāu, India	70	G2	23.13 N	68.43 E
Jakkonen, Russia	14	F20	66.33 N	29.52 E
Jakobshavn (Ilulissat), Grnld.	108	D15	69.13 N	51.06 W
Jakobstad see Pietarsaari, Fin.	18	D9	63.40 N	22.42 E

Name	Page	Map Ref.	Latitude	Longitude
Jakovlevka, Russia	54	B10	44.25 N	133.28 E
Jakovlevo, Russia	40	F10	50.51 N	36.26 E
Jakša, Russia	48	B9	61.48 N	56.49 E
Jakšur-Bodja, Russia	40	C18	57.11 N	53.10 E
Jakunvara, Russia	18	E18	62.42 N	31.41 E
Jakupica, mts., Mac.	34	B4	41.43 N	21.26 E
Jakutija, state, Russia	50	D14	67.00 N	125.00 E
Jakutsk, Russia	50	D14	62.02 N	129.42 E
Jal, N.M., U.S.	136	B4	32.06 N	103.11 W
Jalaid Qi, China	52	B9	46.43 N	122.54 E
Jalājil, Sau. Ar.	74	H9	25.41 N	45.28 E
Jalālābād, Afg.	72	C11	34.26 N	70.26 E
Jalālpur, India	70	E9	26.18 N	82.44 E
Jalan Besar Stadium, p.o.i., Sing.	189c		1.18 N	103.52 E
Jalandhar, India	70	C5	31.19 N	75.34 E
Jalan Kayu, Sing.	189c		1.24 N	103.52 E
Jalapa, Guat.	156	E3	14.38 N	89.59 W
Jalapa see Xalapa, Mex.	154	F10	19.31 N	96.54 W
Jalasjärvi, Fin.	18	E9	62.29 N	22.45 E
Jālaun, India	70	E7	26.09 N	79.21 E
Jales, Braz.	166	D6	20.15 S	50.32 W
Jalesar, India	70	E7	27.28 N	78.18 E
Jaleshwar, India	70	H11	21.48 N	87.14 E
Jālgaon, India	70	H5	21.01 N	75.34 E
Jālgaon, India	70	H6	21.03 N	76.32 E
Jal'gelevo, Russia	183a		59.44 N	29.57 E
Jalguba, Russia	18	F21	61.52 N	34.33 E
Jalingo, Nig.	84	H7	8.53 N	11.21 E
Jalisco, state, Mex.	154	E6	20.20 N	103.40 W
Jalizava, Bela.	26	G11	53.23 N	29.00 E
Jallas see Xallas, stm., Spain	28	B2	42.54 N	9.07 W
Jālna, India	69	B2	19.50 N	75.53 E
Jalón, stm., Spain	28	C8	41.46 N	1.03 W
Jālor, India	70	F4	25.21 N	72.37 E
Jalostotitlán, Mex.	154	E7	21.10 N	102.27 W
Jalpa, Mex.	154	E7	21.37 N	102.59 W
Jalpāiguri, India	70	E12	26.30 N	88.42 E
Jalpan, Mex.	154	E9	21.10 N	99.17 W
Jalpan de Serra see Jalpan, Mex.	154	E9	21.10 N	99.17 W
Jalta see Yalta, Ukr.	38	I13	44.30 N	34.10 E
Jaltepec, stm., Mex.	154	G11	17.26 N	94.58 W
Jaluit, at., Marsh. Is.	94	C7	5.58 N	169.43 E
Jalūlā', Iraq	74	C9	34.11 N	45.12 E
Jalutorovsk, Russia	48	C11	56.39 N	66.17 E
Jamaame, Som.	86	E8	0.00 N	42.42 E
Jāmāibāti, India	190b		22.51 N	88.08 E
Jamaica, ngh., N.Y., U.S.	194		40.42 N	73.47 W
Jamaica, ctry., N.A.	156	D8	18.15 N	77.30 W
Jamaica, i., Jam.	106	H15	18.15 N	77.30 W
Jamaica Channel, strt., N.A.	156	C10	18.00 N	75.30 W
Jamaica Plain, ngh., Ma., U.S.	201		42.19 N	71.06 W
Jamaica Pond, l., Ma., U.S.	201		42.19 N	71.07 W
Jamal, poluostrov, pen., Russia	50	B2	70.00 N	70.00 E
Jam-Alin', hrebet, mts., Russia	50	F15	53.00 N	134.36 E
Jamālpur, Bngl.	70	F12	24.55 N	89.56 E
Jamālpur, India	70	F11	25.18 N	86.29 E
Jamanota, hill, Aruba	158g	p20	12.29 N	69.57 W
Jamantau, gora, mtn., Russia	40	D21	54.15 N	58.06 E
Jamanxim, stm., Braz.	164	E6	4.44 S	56.26 W
Jamari, stm., Braz.	164	E5	8.26 S	63.29 W
Jamarovka, Russia	50	F11	50.34 N	110.25 E
Jamašurma, Russia	40	D16	55.59 N	49.33 E
Jambelí, Canal de, strt., Ec.	168	I1	2.49 S	79.51 W
Jambi, Indon.	66	D3	1.36 S	103.36 E
Jambi, state, Indon.	66	D3	1.30 S	103.00 E
Jambin, Austl.	98	E8	24.11 S	150.21 E
Jamboaye, stm., Indon.	64	J3	5.07 N	97.39 E
Jambol, Blg.	36	G13	42.29 N	26.30 E
Jambongan, Pulau, i., Malay.	68	G1	6.40 N	117.27 E
Jambuair, Tanjung, c., Indon.	64	J3	5.14 N	97.29 E
Jambusar, India	70	G4	22.03 N	72.48 E
James, stm., Ab., Can.	144	E16	51.54 N	114.33 W
James, stm., U.S.	118	F17	42.51 N	97.18 W
James, stm., Mo., U.S.	130	H4	36.44 N	93.30 W
James, stm., Va., U.S.	124	G8	36.56 N	76.25 W
James, Isla, i., Chile	166	H2	44.57 S	74.07 W
James, Lake, res., N.C., U.S.	124	I4	35.45 N	81.53 W
James Bay, b., Can.	110	E14	53.30 N	80.30 W
James City, N.C., U.S.	132	A9	35.05 N	77.02 W
James Craik, Arg.	172	F6	32.09 S	63.28 W
James Gardens, p.o.i., On., Can.	193b		43.40 N	79.31 W
James Island, S.C., U.S.	132	D6	32.43 N	79.56 W
Jameson Raid Memorial, hist., S. Afr.	191d		26.11 S	27.49 E
James Point, c., Bah.	132	K9	25.20 N	76.21 W
Jamesport, Mo., U.S.	130	E4	39.58 N	93.48 W
James Ross, Cape, c., N.T., Can.	109	B17	74.40 N	114.25 W
James Ross Island, i., Ant.	103	B35	64.15 S	57.44 W
James Ross Strait, strt., Nu., Can.	110	A11	69.40 N	95.30 W
James Smith Indian Reserve, ind. res., Sk., Can.	142	A9	53.08 N	104.52 W
Jamestown, Austl.	98	I2	33.12 S	138.35 E
Jamestown, S. Afr.	90	G8	31.07 S	26.48 E
Jamestown, Ca., U.S.	148	F5	37.56 N	120.25 W
Jamestown, Ks., U.S.	138	B11	39.35 N	97.52 W
Jamestown, Ky., U.S.	130	H12	36.59 N	85.03 W
Jamestown, N.Y., U.S.	124	B6	42.06 N	79.14 W
Jamestown, N.C., U.S.	124	I6	35.59 N	79.56 W
Jamestown, N.D., U.S.	142	H15	46.54 N	98.42 W
Jamestown, Oh., U.S.	124	E2	39.39 N	83.45 W
Jamestown, Tn., U.S.	130	H13	36.24 N	84.55 W
Jamestown, misc. cult., Va., U.S.	124	G9	37.12 N	76.46 W
Jamestown Reservoir, res., N.D., U.S.	142	G15	46.58 N	98.43 W
Jamison Town, Austl.	192a		33.46 S	150.41 E
Jam-Ižora, Russia	183a		59.42 N	30.36 E
Jām Jodhpur, India	70	G3	21.53 N	70.02 E
Jamkhandi, India	69	C2	16.30 N	75.17 E
Jamm, Russia	26	B11	58.25 N	28.06 E
Jammalamadugu, India	69	D4	14.50 N	78.23 E
Jammerbugten, b., Den.	16	J6	57.18 N	9.22 E
Jammu, India	70	B5	32.42 N	74.50 E
Jammu and Kashmir, state, India	72	C12	34.00 N	76.00 E
Jammu and Kashmir see Kashmir, hist. reg., Asia	62	B4	34.00 N	76.00 E
Jammu and Kashmir (Kashmir), hist. reg., Asia	62	B4	34.00 N	76.00 E
Jammu and Kashmir see Jammu and Kashmīr, hist. reg., Asia	62	B4	34.00 N	76.00 E
Jamnagar (Navanagar), India	70	G3	22.28 N	70.03 E
Jamor, stm., Port.	184c		38.42 N	9.15 W
Jampang-kulon, Indon.	66	G5	7.15 S	106.37 E
Jāmpur, India	190b		22.56 N	88.12 E
Jāmpur, Pak.	70	D3	29.38 N	70.35 E
Jämsä, Fin.	18	F12	61.52 N	25.12 E
Jämsänkoski, Fin.	18	F12	61.55 N	25.11 E
Jamshedpur, India	70	G10	22.48 N	86.11 E
Jamsk, Russia	50	E19	59.35 N	154.09 E
Jämtland, state, Swe.	16	D12	63.00 N	14.40 E
Jamūi, India	70	F11	24.55 N	86.13 E
Jamuna, stm., India	190b		22.57 N	88.35 E
Jamundí, Col.	168	F3	3.15 N	76.32 W
Jana, stm., Russia	50	C16	71.31 N	136.38 E
Janāi, India	190b		22.43 N	88.16 E
Janas, Port.	184c		38.49 N	9.26 W
Janaúba, Braz.	170	H4	15.48 S	43.19 W
Janaucu, Ilha, i., Braz.	164	C7	0.30 N	50.10 W
Janaul, Russia	40	C19	56.16 N	54.56 E
Janavičy, Bela.	26	E13	55.17 N	30.42 E
Jand, Pak.	70	B4	33.26 N	72.01 E
Jandaia, Braz.	166	C6	17.06 S	50.07 W
Jandaíra, Braz.	170	F7	11.34 S	37.42 W
Jandaq, Iran	74	C14	34.03 N	54.24 E
Jandiāla, India	70	C5	31.35 N	75.02 E
Jandira, mun., Braz.	205b		23.32 S	46.54 W
Jandowae, Austl.	98	F8	26.47 S	151.06 E
Jándula, stm., Spain	28	F7	38.03 N	4.05 W
Jándula, Embalse de, res., Spain	28	F6	38.15 N	3.55 W
Janeiro, stm., Braz.	170	F2	11.51 S	45.09 W
Janesville, Ca., U.S.	148	C5	40.17 N	120.31 W
Janesville, Mn., U.S.	128	G5	44.07 N	93.42 W
Janesville, Wi., U.S.	130	B9	42.40 N	88.59 W
Jangamo, Moz.	90	D12	24.07 S	35.19 E
Jangeru, Indon.	66	E10	2.22 S	116.29 E
Jangijul', Uzb.	48	F11	41.09 N	69.06 E
Jangīpur, India	70	F11	24.27 N	88.03 E
Jangoon, India	69	C4	17.43 N	79.10 E
Janikowo, Pol.	24	D14	52.44 N	18.08 E
Janīn, W.B.	76	F6	32.27 N	35.18 E
Janino, Russia	183a		59.56 N	30.36 E
Janisjarvi, ozero, l., Russia	18	E17	61.59 N	30.57 E
Janiskoski, Russia	14	D19	68.56 N	28.47 E
Janiuay, Phil.	68	E4	10.56 N	122.30 E
Janja, Bos.	36	E6	44.40 N	19.15 E
Jankan, hrebet, mts., Russia	50	E12	55.45 N	118.00 E
Jan Kempdorp, S. Afr.	90	E7	27.54 S	24.51 E
Janlohong, Indon.	66	B10	2.15 N	117.03 E
Jan Mayen, i., Nor.	106	B22	71.02 N	8.19 W
Jannali, Austl.	192a		34.01 S	151.04 E
Jannali Park, p.o.i., Austl.	192a		34.01 S	151.03 E
Janos, Mex.	120	F8	30.53 N	108.11 W
Jánoshalma, Hung.	36	C6	46.17 N	19.19 E
Jánosháza, Hung.	36	B4	47.07 N	17.10 E
János-hegy, mtn., Hung.	182c		47.31 N	18.58 E
Janowiec Wielkopolski, Pol.	24	D13	52.44 N	17.31 E
Janów Lubelski, Pol.	24	F18	50.42 N	22.24 E
Jansen, Sk., Can.	142	C9	51.48 N	104.42 W
Jansenville, S. Afr.	90	H7	32.57 S	24.40 E
Janskij, Russia	50	C15	68.35 N	134.45 E
Janskij zaliv, b., Russia	50	B16	71.50 N	136.00 E
Jantarnyj, Russia	26	F2	54.52 N	19.57 E
Jantra, stm., Blg.	36	F12	43.39 N	25.33 E
Januária, Braz.	170	H3	15.28 S	44.22 W
Januário Cicco, Braz.	170	D8	6.09 S	35.35 W
Jan Van Riebeeck Park, p.o.i., S. Afr.	191d		26.10 S	27.59 E
Janville-sur-Juine, Fr.	179		48.31 N	2.16 E
Janvry, Fr.	179		48.39 N	2.09 E
Jaora, India	70	G5	23.38 N	75.07 E
Japan, ctry., Asia	52	D12	36.00 N	138.00 E
Japan, Sea of (East Sea), s., Asia	52	C11	40.00 N	135.00 E
Japan Basin, unds.	174	E16	39.51 N	132.10 E
Japan Trench, unds.	174	F17	37.00 N	143.00 E
Japaratinga, Braz.	170	E8	9.05 S	35.15 W
Japaratuba, Braz.	170	F7	10.35 S	36.56 W
Japi, Braz.	170	D8	6.27 S	35.56 W
Japonskoe more see Japan, Sea of, s., Asia	52	C11	40.00 N	135.00 E
Japtiksalja, Russia	50	C3	69.22 N	72.31 E
Japurá, Braz.	168	H8	1.50 S	66.32 W
Japurá (Caquetá), stm., S.A.	164	D5	3.08 S	64.46 W
Jaqué, Pan.	168	D2	7.31 N	78.10 W
Jaqueri-mirim, stm., Braz.	205b		23.31 S	46.51 W
Jar, Russia	40	B18	58.14 N	52.06 E
Jār, Jabal, mtn., Sau. Ar.	74	H6	24.34 N	38.18 E
Jarābulus, Syria	76	B9	36.49 N	38.01 E
Jaraguá, Braz.	170	H1	15.45 S	49.20 W
Jaraguá, ngh., Braz.	205b		23.27 S	46.44 W
Jaraguá, Pico do, mtn., Braz.	205b		23.26 S	46.46 W
Jaraguá do Sul, Braz.	172	C13	26.29 S	49.04 W
Jaraicejo, Spain	28	E5	39.40 N	5.49 W
Jaraíz de la Vera, Spain	28	D5	40.04 N	5.45 W
Jarales, N.M., U.S.	138	G2	34.37 N	106.45 W
Jarama, stm., Spain	28	D7	40.02 N	3.39 W
Jarama, Canal del, can., Spain	184a		40.18 N	3.32 W
Jaramānah, Syria	76	E7	33.29 N	36.21 E
Jaramillo, Arg.	166	I3	47.11 S	67.09 W
Jaransk, Russia	40	C15	57.18 N	47.53 E
Jarānwāla, Pak.	70	C4	31.19 N	73.25 E
Jarash, Jord.	76	F6	32.16 N	35.54 E
Jarash, hist., Jord.	76	F6	32.17 N	35.53 E
Jarbidge, stm., U.S.	148	B10	42.19 N	115.38 W
Järbo, Swe.	16	G14	60.42 N	16.36 E
Jarcevo, Russia	26	E15	55.03 N	32.42 E
Jardim, Braz.	166	D5	21.28 S	56.08 W
Jardim, Braz.	170	D6	7.35 S	39.16 W
Jardim América, ngh., Braz.	205b		23.34 S	46.41 W
Jardim de Piranhas, Braz.	170	D7	6.22 S	37.20 W
Jardim Paulista, ngh., Braz.	205b		23.35 S	46.40 W
Jardín América, Arg.	172	C10	27.02 S	55.14 W
Jardines de la Reina, Archipiélago de los, is., Cuba	156	B8	20.50 N	78.55 W
Jardinópolis, Braz.	170	K2	21.01 S	47.49 W
Jarenga, Russia	12	E23	62.42 N	49.30 E
Jarensk, Russia	12	E23	62.09 N	49.02 E
Jargalang, China	54	C5	43.05 N	122.54 E
Jargalant, Mong.	52	B4	45.44 N	97.06 E
Jari, stm., Braz.	164	C7	1.09 S	51.53 W
Jāria Jhānjail, Bngl.	70	F13	25.00 N	90.40 E
Jaridih, India	70	G11	23.37 N	86.03 E
Jarīr, Wādī al-, stm., Sau. Ar.	74	H8	25.28 N	42.20 E
Jarkand see Shache, China	48	G13	38.24 N	77.14 E
Jarkino, Russia	48	C17	59.07 N	99.24 E
Järna, Swe.	16	H15	59.05 N	17.33 E
Jarnac, Fr.	22	D5	45.40 N	0.10 W
Jarnema, Russia	18	E26	62.57 N	39.24 E
Jarocin, Pol.	24	D13	51.58 N	17.30 E
Jarohta, Russia	48	C17	58.57 N	98.57 E
Jaroměř, Czech Rep.	24	F11	50.21 N	15.55 E
Jaroslaviči, Russia	18	G21	60.29 N	34.31 E
Jaroslavl', Russia	40	C11	57.37 N	39.51 E
Jaroslavl' Station, trans., Russia	183b		55.47 N	37.39 E
Jaroslavskaja oblast', co., Russia	40	B12	57.45 N	39.00 E
Jarosław, Pol.	24	F18	50.01 N	22.40 E
Järpen, Swe.	16	D11	63.21 N	13.26 E
Jarratt, Va., U.S.	124	H8	36.48 N	77.28 W
Jarreau, La., U.S.	134	G7	30.38 N	91.28 W
Jarry, Parc, p.o.i., Qc., Can.	193a		45.32 N	73.38 W
Jar-Sale, Russia	48	A12	66.50 N	70.52 E
Jartai Yanchi, l., China	58	B1	39.43 N	105.37 E
Jaru, stm., Braz.	164	F5	10.05 S	61.59 W
Jarud Qi, China	52	C9	44.33 N	120.54 E
Järva-Jaani, Est.	26	A8	59.02 N	25.53 E
Järvakandi, Est.	26	B7	58.47 N	24.49 E
Järvelä, Fin.	18	G12	60.51 N	25.15 E
Järvenpää, Fin.	18	G12	60.29 N	25.05 E
Jarvie, Ab., Can.	144	B17	54.26 N	113.59 W
Jarvis, On., Can.	126	F9	42.53 N	80.04 W
Jarvisburg, N.C., U.S.	124	H10	36.12 N	75.52 W
Jarvis Island, i., Oc.	94	D10	0.22 S	160.01 W
Järvsö, Swe.	16	F14	61.43 N	16.10 E
Jasai, India	190c		18.56 N	73.01 E
Jašalta, Russia	40	H13	46.20 N	42.16 E
Jasdan, India	70	G3	22.00 N	71.08 E
Jasel'da, stm., Bela.	26	H8	52.07 N	26.26 E
Jasenevo, ngh., Russia	183b		55.36 N	37.33 E
Jasenki, Russia	38	B17	51.32 N	38.12 E
Jasenskaja, Russia	38	G17	46.21 N	38.16 E
Jashpurnagar, India	62	D5	22.53 N	84.09 E
Jasień, Pol.	24	E11	51.46 N	15.01 E
Jasikan, Ghana	84	H5	7.24 N	0.28 E
Jāsk, Iran	72	D8	25.39 N	57.46 E
Jaskhar, India	190c		18.54 N	72.59 E
Jaskino, Russia	183b		55.40 N	37.16 E
Jaškul', Russia	48	E7	46.10 N	45.20 E
Jasło, Pol.	24	G17	49.45 N	21.28 E
Jasnogorsk, Russia	26	F20	54.28 N	37.42 E
Jasnyj, Russia	50	F14	53.17 N	127.59 E
Jason Islands, is., Falk. Is.	166	J4	51.08 S	60.53 W
Jasonville, In., U.S.	130	E10	39.09 N	87.12 W
Jasper, Ab., Can.	144	D12	52.52 N	118.04 W
Jasper, Al., U.S.	134	D11	33.49 N	87.16 W
Jasper, Ar., U.S.	130	I4	36.00 N	93.11 W
Jasper, Fl., U.S.	132	F3	30.31 N	82.56 W
Jasper, Ga., U.S.	132	B1	34.27 N	84.25 W
Jasper, In., U.S.	130	F11	38.23 N	86.56 W
Jasper, Mn., U.S.	128	H2	43.51 N	96.23 W
Jasper, Mo., U.S.	130	G3	37.20 N	94.18 W
Jasper, Tn., U.S.	132	B13	35.04 N	85.37 W
Jasper, Tx., U.S.	136	D13	30.53 N	94.00 W
Jasper Lake, l., Ab., Can.	144	C13	53.04 N	118.02 W
Jasper National Park, p.o.i., Ab., Can.	144	D13	52.53 N	118.03 W
Jasra, India	70	F8	25.18 N	81.48 E
Jassy see Iaşi, Rom.	36	B14	47.10 N	27.35 E
Jastarnia, Pol.	24	B14	54.42 N	18.39 E
Jastrebovka, Russia	38	B16	51.27 N	37.32 E
Jastrowie, Pol.	24	C12	53.25 N	16.48 E
Jászapáti, Hung.	36	B7	47.30 N	20.09 E
Jászberény, Hung.	36	B6	47.30 N	19.54 E
Jász-Nagykun-Szolnok, state, Hung.	36	B7	47.12 N	20.11 E
Jataí, Braz.	166	C6	17.52 S	51.44 W
Jatapu, stm., Braz.	164	D6	2.29 S	58.14 W
Jatate, stm., Mex.	154	G13	16.43 N	91.31 W
Jati, Braz.	170	D6	7.41 S	39.01 W
Jāti, Pak.	70	F2	24.21 N	68.16 E
Jatinegara, ngh., Indon.	187e		6.13 S	106.52 E
Játiva see Xàtiva, Spain	28	F10	38.59 N	0.31 W
Jatni, India	70	H10	20.09 N	85.42 E
Jatniel, S. Afr.	191d		26.07 S	28.19 E
Jaú, Braz.	170	L1	22.18 S	48.33 W
Jaú, stm., Braz.	168	I10	1.53 S	61.22 W
Jaú, Parque Nacional do, p.o.i., Braz.	168	I10	2.30 S	63.00 W
Jauaperi, stm., Braz.	168	H11	1.28 S	61.33 W
Jauá Sarisariñama, Parque Nacional, p.o.i., Ven.	168	E9	4.36 N	64.06 W
Jauer see Jawor, Pol.	24	E12	51.03 N	16.12 E
Jauja, Peru	164	F2	11.47 S	75.29 W
Jauli, India	190a		28.44 N	77.21 E
Jaunguibene, Lat.	26	C9	57.04 N	26.36 E
Jaunjelgava, Lat.	26	D7	56.36 N	25.04 E
Jaunpiebalga, Lat.	26	C9	57.09 N	26.02 E
Jaunpils, Lat.	26	D6	56.42 N	23.00 E
Jaunpur, India	70	F9	25.44 N	82.41 E
Jauza, stm., Russia	183b		55.45 N	37.38 E
Java, S.D., U.S.	140	B13	45.30 N	99.54 W
Java see Jawa, i., Indon.	66	H6	7.29 S	109.59 E
Javādi Hills, hills, India	69	E4	12.35 N	78.50 E
Javalambre, mtn., Spain	28	D9	40.06 N	1.03 W
Javari see Yavarí, stm., S.A.	164	D3	4.21 S	70.02 W
Javas, Russia	40	D13	54.25 N	42.50 E
Java Sea see Jawa, Laut, s., Indon.	66	F6	5.00 S	110.00 E
Java Trench, unds.	174	J13	10.27 S	109.54 E
Jávea see Xàbia, Spain	28	F11	38.47 N	0.10 E
Javor, mts., Bos.	36	E5	44.06 N	18.54 E
Javorie, mtn., Slvk.	24	H15	48.25 N	19.16 E
Javorník, Czech Rep.	24	F13	50.23 N	16.59 E
Javorová skála, mtn., Czech Rep.	24	G10	49.31 N	14.30 E
Jävr, stm., Russia	14	D20	68.08 N	30.06 E
Jävre, Swe.	14	G12	65.09 N	21.30 E
Jävsjön see Gjevsjøen, l., Eur.	16	C11	64.03 N	13.03 E
Jawa (Java), i., Indon.	66	H6	7.29 S	109.59 E
Jawa, Laut (Java Sea), s., Indon.	66	F6	5.00 S	110.00 E
Jawa Barat, state, Indon.	66	G5	7.00 S	107.00 E
Jawa Tengah, state, Indon.	66	G7	7.30 S	110.00 E
Jawa Timur, state, Indon.	66	G8	8.00 S	113.00 E
Jawhar, Som.	86	D9	2.47 N	45.30 E
Jawi, Indon.	66	D6	0.48 S	109.15 E
Jawor, Pol.	24	E12	51.03 N	16.12 E
Jaworzno, Pol.	24	F15	50.11 N	19.14 E
Jay, Fl., U.S.	134	G11	30.57 N	87.09 W
Jay, Ok., U.S.	130	H3	36.25 N	94.46 W
Jaya, Puncak (Jaya Peak), mtn., Indon.	60	F10	4.05 S	137.11 E
Jaya Peak see Jaya, Puncak, mtn., Indon.	60	F10	4.05 S	137.11 E
Jayapura, Indon.	60	F11	2.32 S	140.42 E
Jayb, Wādī al- (Ha'Arava), stm., Asia	76	H6	30.59 N	35.24 E
Jay Cooke State Park, p.o.i., Mn., U.S.	128	E6	46.41 N	92.23 W
Jaynes, Az., U.S.	150	K5	32.15 N	111.00 W
Jay Peak, mtn., Vt., U.S.	122	F4	44.55 N	72.32 W
Jaypur, India	69	B6	18.51 N	82.34 E
Jayrūd, Syria	76	E7	33.49 N	36.44 E
Jayton, Tx., U.S.	138	H8	33.14 N	100.34 W
Jayuya, P.R.	158a	b2	18.13 N	66.36 W
Jažel'bicy, Russia	26	B15	58.02 N	32.57 E
Jazevec, Russia	12	D22	65.41 N	46.30 E
Jažma, Russia	12	C21	66.55 N	44.31 E
Jazykovo, Russia	40	D15	54.17 N	47.22 E
Jazzīn, Leb.	76	E6	33.32 N	35.35 E
J.B. Thomas, Lake, res., Tx., U.S.	136	B6	32.35 N	101.10 W
Jeanerette, La., U.S.	134	H7	29.54 N	91.40 W
Jeannette Island see Žannetty, ostrov, i., Russia	50	A20	76.43 N	158.00 E
Jebba, Nig.	84	H5	9.07 N	4.49 E
Jebel, Rom.	36	D8	45.33 N	21.14 E
Jebus, Indon.	66	D4	1.44 S	105.27 E
Jedburgh, Scot., U.K.	10	F10	55.28 N	2.33 W
Jeddah see Jiddah, Sau. Ar.	72	E4	21.30 N	39.11 E
Jeddito Wash, stm., Az., U.S.	150	H6	35.23 N	110.44 W
Jedlesee, ngh., Aus.	182b		48.16 N	16.23 E
Jędrzejów, Pol.	24	F16	50.38 N	20.18 E
Jedwabne, Pol.	24	C18	53.17 N	22.18 E
Jeesiöjoki, stm., Fin.	14	E17	67.24 N	26.35 E
Jeffara (Al-Jifārah), pl., Afr.	82	A2	32.30 N	11.45 E
Jeffers, Mn., U.S.	128	G3	44.04 N	95.10 W
Jefferson, Ga., U.S.	132	B2	34.07 N	83.34 W
Jefferson, Ia., U.S.	130	C3	42.00 N	94.22 W
Jefferson, N.J., U.S.	203		39.45 N	75.13 W
Jefferson, N.C., U.S.	124	H4	36.24 N	81.28 W
Jefferson, Oh., U.S.	124	C5	41.44 N	80.46 W
Jefferson, Or., U.S.	146	F3	44.43 N	123.00 W
Jefferson, Pa., U.S.	197b		40.18 N	80.03 W
Jefferson, S.C., U.S.	132	B5	34.39 N	80.23 W
Jefferson, S.D., U.S.	130	B1	42.36 N	96.33 W
Jefferson, Tx., U.S.	136	B13	32.45 N	94.20 W
Jefferson, Wi., U.S.	130	A9	43.00 N	88.48 W
Jefferson, stm., Mt., U.S.	146	E14	45.56 N	111.30 W
Jefferson, Mount, mtn., U.S.	146	F15	44.34 N	111.30 W
Jefferson, Mount, mtn., Nv., U.S.	148	E9	38.46 N	116.55 W
Jefferson, Mount, vol., Or., U.S.	146	F5	44.40 N	121.47 W
Jefferson City, Mo., U.S.	130	F5	38.34 N	92.11 W
Jefferson City, Tn., U.S.	124	H2	36.07 N	83.29 W
Jefferson Farms, De., U.S.	203		39.40 N	75.34 W
Jefferson Manor, Va., U.S.	202c		38.47 N	77.04 W
Jefferson Park, ngh., Il., U.S.	196		41.59 N	87.46 W
Jeffersontown, Ky., U.S.	130	F12	38.12 N	85.35 W
Jefferson Village, Va., U.S.	202c		38.52 N	77.10 W
Jeffersonville, Ga., U.S.	132	D2	32.40 N	83.20 W
Jeffersonville, In., U.S.	130	F12	38.16 N	85.44 W
Jeffrey City, Wy., U.S.	140	E5	42.29 N	107.47 W
Jeffries Creek, stm., S.C., U.S.	132	B6	34.05 N	79.32 W
Jega, Nig.	84	G5	12.13 N	4.23 E
Jeju see Cheju, Kor., S.	54	H7	33.30 N	126.31 E
Jejur, India	190b		22.53 N	88.08 E
Jēkabpils, Lat.	26	D8	56.30 N	25.52 E
Jekyll Island, i., Ga., U.S.	132	E4	31.04 N	81.25 W
Jekyll Island State Park, p.o.i., Ga., U.S.	132	E4	31.02 N	81.25 W
Jelai, stm., Indon.	66	E7	3.00 S	110.43 E
Jelenia Góra, Pol.	24	F11	50.54 N	15.43 E
Jelgava, Lat.	26	D6	56.38 N	23.43 E
Jelgavkrasti, Lat.	26	C7	57.28 N	24.26 E
Jellico, Tn., U.S.	124	H1	36.35 N	84.07 W
Jellicoe, On., Can.	128	B11	49.41 N	87.31 W
Jelling, Den.	16	L7	55.45 N	9.26 E
Jelm Mountain, mtn., Wy., U.S.	140	F7	41.06 N	105.58 W
Jeløya, i., Nor.	16	H8	59.27 N	10.38 E
Jelšava, Slvk.	24	H16	48.38 N	20.13 E
Jemaja, Pulau, i., Indon.	66	B4	2.55 N	105.45 E
Jember, Indon.	66	H8	8.10 S	113.41 E
Jemez, stm., N.M., U.S.	138	F2	35.22 N	106.30 W
Jemez Canyon Reservoir, res., N.M., U.S.	138	F1	35.28 N	106.39 W
Jemez Indian Reservation, ind. res., N.M., U.S.	138	F2	35.36 N	106.47 W
Jemez Springs, N.M., U.S.	138	F2	35.46 N	106.42 W
Jemnice, Czech Rep.	24	H11	49.00 N	15.35 E
Jempang, Kenohan, l., Indon.	66	D9	0.26 S	116.12 E
Jena, Ger.	24	F7	50.56 N	11.35 E
Jena, La., U.S.	134	F6	31.40 N	92.08 W
Jenbach, Aus.	24	I7	47.24 N	11.46 E
Jendouba, Tun.	32	H2	36.29 N	8.46 E
Jeneponto, Indon.	66	F11	5.41 S	119.44 E
Jenkins, Ky., U.S.	114	H9	37.09 N	82.38 W
Jenkins, Mount, mtn., Austl.	96	E5	25.36 S	129.41 E
Jenkinsville, S.C., U.S.	132	B4	34.14 N	81.19 W
Jenks, Ok., U.S.	130	H2	36.01 N	95.59 W
Jennersdorf, Aus.	30	D13	46.56 N	16.08 E
Jennifer Branch, stm., Md., U.S.	202b		39.25 N	76.30 W
Jennings, Fl., U.S.	132	F2	30.36 N	83.05 W
Jennings, La., U.S.	134	G6	30.12 N	92.39 W
Jensen, Ut., U.S.	150	C7	40.22 N	109.21 W
Jensen Beach, Fl., U.S.	132	I5	27.13 N	80.13 W
Jens Munk Island, i., Nu., Can.	110	B14	69.40 N	80.04 W
Jens Munks Ø, i., Grnld.	108	E17	64.39 N	40.30 W
Jenu, Indon.	66	D6	0.36 S	109.51 E
Jeonju see Chŏnju, Kor., S.	54	G7	35.49 N	127.09 E
Jepara, Indon.	66	G7	6.35 S	110.40 E
Jeparit, Austl.	98	K4	36.08 S	141.58 E
Jeppo see Jepua, Fin.	18	D9	63.24 N	22.38 E
Jeptha Knob, hill, Ky., U.S.	130	F12	38.11 N	85.07 W
Jepua, Fin.	18	D9	63.24 N	22.38 E
Jequié, Braz.	170	G5	13.52 S	40.04 W
Jequitaí, Braz.	170	I3	17.14 S	44.26 W
Jequitinhonha, Braz.	170	I5	16.27 S	41.00 W
Jequitinhonha, stm., Braz.	170	I5	15.51 S	38.53 W
Jerada, Mor.	84	C4	34.19 N	2.10 W
Jerba, Île de, i., Tun.	84	C7	33.48 N	10.54 E
Jerécuaro, Mex.	154	E8	20.08 N	100.30 W
Jérémie, Haiti	156	C10	18.39 N	74.07 W
Jeremoabo, Braz.	170	F6	10.06 S	38.19 W
Jerevan see Yerevan, Arm.	42	E11	40.11 N	44.30 E
Jerez de García Salinas, Mex.	154	D7	22.38 N	102.59 W
Jerez de la Frontera, Spain	28	H4	36.41 N	6.08 W
Jerez de los Caballeros, Spain	28	F4	38.18 N	6.46 W
Jericho, Austl.	98	D6	23.35 S	146.07 E
Jericho see Arīḥā, Gaza	76	G6	31.51 N	35.27 E
Jericho, N.J., U.S.	203		39.48 N	75.09 W
Jericó, Braz.	170	D7	6.33 S	37.48 W
Jericoacoara, Ponta de, c., Braz.	170	B5	2.48 S	40.29 W
Jerid, Chott, l., Tun.	84	C6	33.42 N	8.26 E
Jerilderie, Austl.	98	J5	35.21 S	145.43 E
Jerimoth Hill, hill, R.I., U.S.	124	C14	41.52 N	71.46 W
Jermuk, Arm.	48	G7	39.51 N	45.41 E
Jeroaquara, Braz.	166	C6	15.23 S	50.25 W
Jerome, Az., U.S.	150	I4	34.43 N	112.07 W
Jerome, Id., U.S.	146	H12	42.43 N	114.30 W
Jerónimos, Mosteiro dos, rel., Port.	184c		38.42 N	9.12 W
Jersey, dep., Eur.	10	L10	49.15 N	2.10 W
Jersey, i., Jersey	20	E6	49.12 N	2.08 W
Jersey City, N.J., U.S.	124	D11	40.44 N	74.03 W
Jersey City State College, educ., N.J., U.S.	194		40.43 N	74.05 W
Jersey Mountain, mtn., Id., U.S.	146	E11	45.29 N	115.34 W
Jersey Shore, Pa., U.S.	126	G12	41.12 N	77.15 W
Jerseyville, Il., U.S.	130	E7	39.06 N	90.19 W
Jerte, stm., Spain	28	D5	39.57 N	6.17 W
Jerumenha, Braz.	170	D4	7.05 S	43.30 W
Jerusalem see Yerushalayim, Isr.	76	G6	31.46 N	35.13 E
Jervis, Cape, c., Austl.	98	J1	35.37 S	138.05 E
Jervis Bay, b., Austl.	98	J8	35.04 S	150.43 E
Jervis Bay Territory, co., Austl.	98	J8	35.05 S	150.44 E
Jervis Inlet, b., B.C., Can.	144	F7	49.46 N	124.10 W
Jesenice, Czech Rep.	24	F9	50.05 N	13.28 E
Jeseník, Czech Rep.	24	F13	50.13 N	17.12 E
Jesi (Iesi), Italy	30	G10	43.31 N	13.14 E
Jesselton see Kota Kinabalu, Malay.	68	G1	5.57 N	116.04 E
Jessen, Ger.	24	E9	51.46 N	12.57 E
Jessheim, Nor.	16	G9	60.08 N	11.11 E
Jessore, Bngl.	70	G12	23.09 N	89.12 E
Jessup Park, p.o.i., Ca., U.S.	198		34.15 N	118.24 W
Jesup, Ga., U.S.	132	E4	31.35 N	81.53 W
Jesup, Ia., U.S.	130	B5	42.28 N	92.03 W
Jesús Carranza, Mex.	154	G11	17.23 N	95.02 W
Jesús María, Arg.	172	E5	30.58 S	64.05 W
Jesús María, Mex.	154	C5	25.05 N	107.27 W
Jesús María, Peru	204d		12.04 S	77.04 W
Jesús Menéndez, Cuba	156	B9	21.09 N	76.28 W
Jet, Ok., U.S.	138	E10	36.40 N	98.11 W
Jetmore, Ks., U.S.	138	C9	38.05 N	99.52 W
Jet Propulsion Laboratory, sci., Ca., U.S.	198		34.12 N	118.11 W
Jetpur, India	70	H3	21.43 N	70.38 E
Jeune Landing, B.C., Can.	144	F3	50.26 N	127.29 W
Jever, Ger.	24	C3	53.34 N	7.53 E
Jevíčko, Czech Rep.	24	G12	49.37 N	16.43 E
Jevišovka, stm., Czech Rep.	30	B12	48.49 N	16.28 E
Jevnaker, Nor.	16	G8	60.14 N	10.24 E
Jewel Cave National Monument, p.o.i., S.D., U.S.	140	D8	43.44 N	103.51 W
Jewell, Ia., U.S.	130	B4	42.18 N	93.38 W
Jewell, Ks., U.S.	138	B10	39.40 N	98.09 W
Jewell Ridge, Va., U.S.	124	G4	37.11 N	81.47 W
Jewett, Il., U.S.	130	E9	39.11 N	88.15 W
Jewett, Tx., U.S.	136	C11	31.21 N	96.08 W
Jewett City, Ct., U.S.	124	C13	41.36 N	71.58 W
Jewettville, N.Y., U.S.	202a		42.43 N	78.52 W
Jey, ngh., Iran	185d		35.41 N	51.21 E
Jezercës, maja e, mtn., Alb.	32	B13	42.26 N	19.49 E
Jeziorany, Pol.	24	B16	53.58 N	20.46 E
Jhābua, India	70	G5	22.44 N	74.35 E
Jha Jha, India	70	F11	24.46 N	86.22 E
Jhālakāti, Bngl.	70	G13	22.38 N	90.12 E
Jhālāwār, India	70	F6	24.35 N	76.10 E
Jhālod, India	70	G5	23.05 N	74.09 E
Jhang Sadar, Pak.	70	C4	31.16 N	72.19 E
Jhānsi, India	70	F7	25.26 N	78.34 E
Jhārgrām, India	70	G11	22.27 N	86.59 E
Jharia, India	70	G11	23.45 N	86.25 E
Jhārsuguda, India	70	H10	21.51 N	84.01 E
Jhelum, Pak.	70	B4	32.56 N	73.43 E
Jhelum, stm., Asia	70	C4	31.12 N	72.08 E
Jhenkāri, India	190b		22.46 N	88.18 E
Jhil Kuranga, ngh., India	190a		28.40 N	77.17 E
Jhinkpāni, India	70	G10	22.24 N	85.46 E
Jhok Rind, Pak.	70	C3	31.27 N	70.26 E
Jhunjhunūn, India	70	D5	28.08 N	75.24 E
Jiaban, China	58	I2	25.08 N	107.07 E
Jiaban, China	58	I2	25.38 N	107.07 E
Jiacha, China	70	D14	29.07 N	92.38 E
Jiading, China	58	F9	31.23 N	121.13 E
Jiāganj, India	70	F12	24.14 N	88.16 E
Jiahe, China	58	I5	25.43 N	112.05 E
Jiali, China	52	E3	30.44 N	93.20 E
Jialing see Guangyuan, China	58	E1	32.24 N	105.49 E
Jialing, stm., China	58	G2	29.34 N	106.34 E
Jialu, stm., China	58	E5	33.37 N	114.37 E
Jiamusi, China	52	B11	46.48 N	130.22 E
Ji'an, China	52	C10	41.05 N	126.09 E
Ji'an, China	58	H6	27.06 N	114.58 E
Jian, stm., China	58	H8	26.39 N	118.10 E
Jianchang, China	58	B10	39.56 N	122.34 E
Jianchang, China	58	A8	40.48 N	119.47 E
Jianchaxi, China	58	G2	28.09 N	107.59 E
Jianchuan, China	52	F4	26.34 N	99.53 E
Jiande, China	58	G8	29.28 N	119.15 E
Jiang'an, China	58	G1	28.44 N	105.03 E
Jiangcheng, China	52	G5	22.42 N	101.49 E
Jiangdu, China	58	E8	32.25 N	119.34 E
Jiange, China	58	E1	32.06 N	105.27 E
Jianghua, China	58	I4	24.56 N	111.41 E
Jiangjin, China	58	G2	29.16 N	106.15 E
Jiangkou, China	58	J4	23.34 N	110.11 E
Jiangkou, China	58	H3	27.40 N	108.48 E
Jiangkou, China	58	F4	30.26 N	111.42 E
Jiangkou, China	58	E2	33.43 N	107.01 E
Jiangkou, China	58	G4	29.40 N	110.25 E
Jiangle, China	58	H7	26.42 N	117.28 E
Jiangling, China	58	F5	30.19 N	112.11 E
Jiangmen, China	58	J5	22.34 N	113.04 E
Jiangmifeng, China	54	B7	43.57 N	126.44 E
Jiangshan, China	58	G8	28.44 N	118.37 E
Jiangsu, state, China	58	E8	33.00 N	120.00 E
Jiangtun, China	58	J5	23.43 N	112.37 E
Jiangwan Airport, arpt., China	187b		31.20 N	121.30 E
Jiangxi, China	64	A5	22.49 N	101.50 E
Jiangxi, state, China	58	H6	28.00 N	116.00 E
Jiangya, China	58	G4	29.17 N	110.39 E
Jiangyin, China	58	F9	31.53 N	120.15 E
Jiangyou, China	58	F1	31.46 N	104.43 E
Jiangzhasiji, China	70	C12	30.25 N	88.56 E
Jiangzhong, China	70	D14	29.07 N	93.24 E
Jianhe, China	58	H3	26.27 N	108.33 E
Jianli, China	58	G5	29.49 N	112.53 E
Jianning, China	58	H7	26.50 N	116.49 E
Jian'ou, China	58	H8	27.02 N	118.19 E
Jianping, China	52	C8	41.23 N	119.38 E
Jianshi, China	58	F3	30.35 N	109.43 E
Jianshui, China	52	G5	23.37 N	102.49 E
Jianyang, China	52	E5	30.24 N	104.32 E
Jianyang, China	58	H8	27.20 N	118.06 E
Jiaocheng, China	58	C4	37.32 N	112.08 E
Jiaohe, China	52	C10	43.43 N	127.20 E
Jiaolai, stm., China	54	C4	43.40 N	123.11 E
Jiaonan, China	58	D8	35.50 N	119.58 E
Jiaotong University, educ., China	187b		31.12 N	121.25 E
Jiaoxian, China	58	C8	36.17 N	119.59 E

K

Name	Page	Map Ref.	Latitude	Longitude
Kamensk-Šahtinskij, Russia	40	G12	48.18 N	40.16 E
Kamensk-Ural'skij, Russia	48	C10	56.25 N	61.55 E
Kamenz, Ger.	24	E10	51.16 N	14.05 E
Kāmet, mtn., Asia	70	C7	30.54 N	79.37 E
Kamiah, Id., U.S.	146	D10	46.13 N	116.02 W
Kamiak Butte, mtn., Wa., U.S.	146	D10	46.49 N	116.56 W
Kamiakotani, Japan	188		34.56 N	135.23 E
Kam'iane, Ukr.	38	F14	47.53 N	35.25 E
Kam'iane, Ukr.	38	B6	51.31 N	27.36 E
Kam'ianets'-Podil's'kyi, Ukr.	38	E5	48.40 N	26.36 E
Kam'ianka, Ukr.	38	D11	49.02 N	32.06 E
Kam'ianka, Ukr.	38	D18	49.38 N	39.22 E
Kam'ianka, stm., Ukr.	38	F12	47.39 N	34.00 E
Kam'ianka-Buz'ka, Ukr.	38	C3	50.06 N	24.21 E
Kam'ianka-Dniprovs'ka, Ukr.	38	F13	47.28 N	34.25 E
Kam'ians'ke, Ukr.	38	H8	45.49 N	29.15 E
Kam'ianyi Brid, Ukr.	38	C6	50.24 N	27.49 E
Kamiasō, Japan	186		35.35 N	139.30 E
Kamień Krajeński, Pol.	24	C13	53.32 N	17.31 E
Kamienna, stm., Pol.	24	F17	51.05 N	21.48 E
Kamienna Góra, Pol.	24	F12	50.46 N	16.02 E
Kamień Pomorski, Pol.	24	B10	53.58 N	14.46 E
Kamieńsk, Pol.	24	E15	51.11 N	19.32 E
Kamieskroon, S. Afr.	90	G3	30.09 S	17.56 E
Kamigyō, ngh., Japan	188		35.02 N	135.45 E
Kamiishihara, Japan	186		35.39 N	139.32 E
Kamiiso, Japan	54	D14	41.49 N	140.39 E
Kamikitazawa, ngh., Japan	186		35.40 N	139.38 E
Kamikume, Japan	188		34.55 N	135.03 E
Kamilukuak Lake, l., Can.	110	C10	62.18 N	101.41 W
Kamimaki, Japan	188		34.34 N	135.43 E
Kamimizo, Japan	186		35.33 N	139.22 E
Kamina, D.R.C.	86	F4	8.44 S	25.00 E
Kaminak Lake, l., Nu., Can.	110	C12	62.09 N	95.06 W
Kamin'-Kashyrs'kyi, Ukr.	38	B3	51.37 N	24.58 E
Kamino-shima, i., Japan	56	E2	34.35 N	129.25 E
Kaminoyama, Japan	56	A13	38.09 N	140.17 E
Kaminuriak Lake, l., Nu., Can.	110	C12	62.59 N	95.35 W
Kamioka, Japan	56	C10	36.19 N	137.18 E
Kamiotawa, Japan	188		34.54 N	135.31 E
Kamioyamada, Japan	186		35.35 N	139.24 E
Kamishinden, Japan	188		34.49 N	135.30 E
Kamitakino, Japan	188		34.57 N	134.59 E
Kamitomi, Japan	186		35.49 N	139.31 E
Kamitsuruma, Japan	186		35.31 N	139.25 E
Kamitsushima, Japan	56	E2	34.38 N	129.28 E
Kamiyugi, Japan	186		35.37 N	139.23 E
Kamjanec, Bela.	26	H6	52.24 N	23.49 E
Kamkhat Muḩaywir, hill, Jord.	76	G7	31.08 N	36.30 E
Kamloops, B.C., Can.	144	F10	50.40 N	120.20 W
Kamloops Indian Reserve, ind. res., B.C., Can.	144	F10	50.42 N	120.17 W
Kammuri-yama, mtn., Japan	56	E5	34.28 N	132.05 E
Kamnik, Slvn.	30	D11	46.13 N	14.37 E
Kamo, Arm.	42	E11	40.21 N	45.08 E
Kamo, Japan	56	B12	37.39 N	139.03 E
Kamo, Japan	188		34.55 N	135.13 E
Kamo, stm., Japan	188		34.56 N	135.44 E
Kamoa Mountains, mts., Guy.	164	C6	1.37 N	59.00 W
Kamojima, Japan	56	E7	34.04 N	134.22 E
Kāmoke, Pak.	70	B5	31.58 N	74.13 E
Kamoshida, ngh., Japan	186		35.34 N	139.30 E
Kamp, stm., Aus.	30	B12	48.22 N	15.48 E
Kāmpa, India	190b		22.56 N	88.28 E
Kampala, Ug.	86	D6	0.19 N	32.34 E
Kampar, Malay.	64	J5	4.18 N	101.09 E
Kampar, stm., Indon.	66	C3	0.13 N	102.41 E
Kamparkalns, hill, Lat.	26	C5	57.09 N	22.31 E
Kampar Kanan, stm., Indon.	66	C2	0.16 N	101.41 E
Kampen, Neth.	20	B14	52.33 N	5.54 E
Kampfe, Lake, l., N.J., U.S.	194		41.02 N	74.21 W
Kamphaeng, Khao, mtn., Thai.	64	E4	14.37 N	99.18 E
Kamphaeng Phet, Thai.	64	D4	16.28 N	99.32 E
Kampinoski Park Narodowy, p.o.i., Pol.	24	D16	52.20 N	20.35 E
Kamp'o, Kor., S.	56	D2	35.47 N	129.29 E
Kâmpóng Cham, Camb.	64	G7	12.00 N	105.27 E
Kâmpóng Chhnăng, Camb.	64	F7	12.14 N	104.39 E
Kâmpóng Kântuŏt, Camb.	64	G7	11.25 N	104.48 E
Kâmpóng Saôm, Camb.	64	G6	10.37 N	103.30 E
Kâmpóng Saôm, Chhâk, b., Camb.	64	G6	10.50 N	103.32 E
Kampong Tebing Runtoh, Malay.	189c		1.26 N	103.40 E
Kâmpóng Thum, Camb.	64	F7	12.41 N	104.53 E
Kâmpóng Trâlach, Camb.	64	G7	11.56 N	104.42 E
Kampong Ulu, Mya.	64	G4	10.04 N	98.31 E
Kâmpôt, Camb.	64	G7	10.37 N	104.11 E
Kampsville, Il., U.S.	130	E7	39.17 N	90.37 W
Kamptee see Kāmthi, India	70	H7	21.13 N	79.12 E
Kampti, Burkina	84	G4	10.08 N	3.27 W
Kampuchea see Cambodia, ctry., Asia	64	F7	13.00 N	105.00 E
Kâmpŭchéa see Cambodia, ctry., Asia	64	F7	13.00 N	105.00 E
Kampungbaru, Indon.	66	D3	1.04 S	102.58 E
Kampung Lanas, Malay.	66	A10	5.20 N	116.30 E
Kampung Litang, Malay.	66	A11	5.20 N	118.29 E
Kampung Merutai Besar, Malay.	66	A11	4.23 N	117.47 E
Kamrau, Teluk, b., Indon.	60	F9	3.32 S	133.37 E
Kamsack, Sk., Can.	142	C12	51.34 N	101.54 W
Kamskoe vodohranilišče, res., Russia	46	C9	58.52 N	56.15 E
Kamsuuma, Som.	86	D8	0.11 N	42.46 E
Kāmthi, India	70	H7	21.13 N	79.12 E
Kam Tin, China	189d		22.27 N	114.03 E
Kamuela, Hi., U.S.	100a	d6	20.01 N	155.39 W
Kamui-misaki, c., Japan	54	C14	43.19 N	140.20 E
Kámuk, Cerro, mtn., C.R.	156	H6	9.17 N	83.01 W
Kamundan, stm., Indon.	60	F9	2.17 S	132.38 E
Kamyšev, Russia	40	H13	46.39 N	42.39 E
Kamyševatskaja, Russia	40	H10	46.24 N	37.56 E
Kamyshna, stm., Eur.	38	D18	48.55 N	39.55 E
Kamyšin, Russia	40	F14	50.06 N	45.23 E
Kamyšlov, Russia	48	C10	56.51 N	62.42 E
Kamyšnaja see Kamyshna, stm., Eur.	38	D18	48.55 N	39.55 E
Kamyzjak, Russia	40	H16	46.06 N	48.04 E
Kan, Iran	74	C12	35.43 N	51.15 E
Kan, stm., Russia	48	C17	56.30 N	93.47 E
Kanaaupscow, stm., Qc., Can.	110	E15	53.40 N	76.44 W
Kanab, Ut., U.S.	150	F4	37.03 N	112.31 W
Kanab Creek, stm., U.S.	150	G4	36.23 N	112.38 W
Kanab Plateau, plat., U.S.	150	G4	36.35 N	112.45 W
Kanaga Island, i., Ak., U.S.	109a	g23	51.44 N	177.18 W
Kanagawa, state, Japan	56	D12	35.30 N	139.15 E
Kanagawa, ngh., Japan	186		35.28 N	139.38 E
Kanai, Japan	186		35.35 N	139.28 E
Kanakapura, India	69	E3	12.32 N	77.25 E
Kanākir, Syria	76	E7	33.15 N	36.05 E
Kanamachi, ngh., Japan	186		35.46 N	139.53 E
Kanamori, Japan	186		35.32 N	139.28 E
Kanan, Japan	188		34.29 N	135.38 E
Kananaskis, stm., Ab., Can.	144	F15	51.05 N	115.03 W
Kananga (Luluabourg), D.R.C.	86	F4	5.54 S	22.25 E
Kananggar, Indon.	66	I12	10.03 S	120.20 E
Kanangra-Boyd National Park, p.o.i., Austl.	98	I7	33.58 S	150.01 E
Kanaoka, Japan	188		34.33 N	135.32 E
Kanarraville, Ut., U.S.	150	F3	37.31 N	113.13 W
Kanaš, Russia	40	D15	55.30 N	47.28 E
Kanaudi, India	70	G8	23.41 N	81.23 E
Kanava, Russia	40	H14	47.12 N	45.23 E
Kanawha, Ia., U.S.	130	B4	42.56 N	93.47 W
Kanawha, stm., W.V., U.S.	124	F4	38.49 N	82.08 W
Kanaya, Japan	186		35.10 N	139.50 E
Kanazawa, Japan	56	C9	36.34 N	136.39 E
Kanazawa, ngh., Japan	186		35.20 N	139.38 E
Kanbauk, Mya.	64	E3	14.34 N	98.02 E
Kanchanaburi, Thai.	64	F4	14.01 N	99.32 E
Kanchanadit, Thai.	64	H4	9.09 N	99.28 E
Kanchanjanggā (Kānchenjunga), mtn., Asia	70	E12	27.41 N	88.09 E
Kānchenjunga (Kanchanjanggā), mtn., Asia	70	E12	27.41 N	88.09 E
Kānchipuram, India	69	E4	12.50 N	79.42 E
Kanchow see Ganzhou, China	58	I6	25.52 N	114.54 E
Kańczuga, Pol.	24	F18	49.59 N	22.24 E
Kanda, Japan	56	F3	33.46 N	130.59 E
Kanda, ngh., Japan	186		35.42 N	139.46 E
Kandahār see Qandahār, Afg.	72	C10	31.36 N	65.42 E
Kandahar see Qandahār, Afg.	72	C10	31.36 N	65.42 E
Kandahar, Sk., Can.	142	C9	51.45 N	104.21 W
Kandāhu, Pak.	70	E2	27.33 N	69.24 E
Kandalakša, Russia	14	E23	67.09 N	32.24 E
Kandalakšskaja guba, b., Russia	14	F24	66.55 N	32.45 E
Kandale, D.R.C.	86	F3	6.01 S	19.24 E
Kandang, Indon.	64	K3	3.03 N	97.19 E
Kandangan, Indon.	66	E9	2.47 S	115.15 E
Kandanghaur, Indon.	66	G6	6.20 S	108.06 E
Kandava, Lat.	26	C5	57.04 N	22.49 E
Kandé, Togo	84	H5	9.57 N	1.03 E
Kandhkot, Pak.	70	D2	28.14 N	69.11 E
Kandi, Benin	84	G5	11.08 N	2.56 E
Kandi, India	70	G12	23.57 N	88.02 E
Kandi, Tanjung, c., Indon.	60	E7	1.17 N	121.27 E
Kandilli, ngh., Tur.	185b		41.04 N	29.03 E
Kandıra, Tur.	34	B13	41.04 N	30.09 E
Kandivli, ngh., India	190c		19.12 N	72.51 E
Kandla, India	70	G3	23.00 N	70.13 E
Kandos, Austl.	98	I7	32.51 S	149.58 E
Kandreho, Madag.	88	D8	17.29 S	46.05 E
Kandrian, Pap. N. Gui.	101a	b4	6.12 S	149.32 E
Kandy, Sri L.	69	H5	7.17 N	80.37 E
Kane, Il., U.S.	130	E7	39.10 N	90.20 W
Kane, Pa., U.S.	124	C7	41.39 N	78.48 W
Kane Basin, b., N.A.	108	B12	79.30 N	69.00 W
Kaneda, Japan	186		35.28 N	139.22 E
Kanem, state, Chad	82	E3	15.00 N	16.00 E
Kaneohe, Hi., U.S.	100a	b4	21.25 N	157.48 W
Kaneohe Bay, b., Hi., U.S.	100a	b4	21.28 N	157.49 W
Kanëvka, Russia	14	E30	67.08 N	39.38 E
Kanevskaja, Russia	40	H11	46.05 N	38.57 E
Kang, Bots.	90	C6	23.40 S	22.46 E
Kangaba, Mali	84	G3	11.56 N	8.26 W
Kangal, Tur.	42	F7	39.13 N	37.26 E
Kangalassy, Russia	50	D15	62.14 N	129.50 E
Kangâmiut, Grnld.	110	D15	65.50 N	53.20 W
Kangān, Iran	74	G13	27.50 N	52.04 E
Kānganheri, ngh., India	190a		28.33 N	76.59 E
Kangar, Malay.	64	I5	6.26 N	100.12 E
Kangaroo Ground, Austl.	192b		37.41 S	145.13 E
Kangaroo Island, i., Austl.	96	G7	35.50 S	137.05 E
Kangasala, Fin.	18	F11	61.28 N	24.04 E
Kangasniemi, Fin.	18	E13	61.59 N	26.37 E
Kangāvar, Iran	74	C10	34.30 N	47.57 E
Kangbao, China	52	C7	41.50 N	114.36 E
Kangding, China	62	C9	30.04 N	102.01 E
Kangean, Kepulauan (Kangean Islands), is., Indon.	66	G9	6.55 S	115.30 E
Kangean, Pulau, i., Indon.	66	G9	6.54 S	115.20 E
Kangean Islands see Kangean, Kepulauan, is., Indon.	66	G9	6.55 S	115.30 E
Kangeeak Point, c., Nu., Can.	110	B18	67.58 N	64.42 W
Kangerlussuaq, b., Grnld.	108	D19	68.25 N	32.36 W
Kangersuatsiaq see Prøven, Grnld.	108	C14	72.23 N	55.32 W
Kanger Valley National Park, p.o.i., India	69	B6	19.01 N	82.04 E
Kanggup'o, Kor., N.	54	D7	41.06 N	127.31 E
Kanggye, Kor., N.	54	D7	40.58 N	126.35 E
Kanghwa-do, i., Kor., S.	54	F7	37.40 N	126.27 E
Kangiqsualujjuaq, Qc., Can.	110	D17	58.41 N	65.59 W
Kangiqsujuaq, Qc., Can.	110	C16	61.34 N	71.57 W
Kangirsuk, Qc., Can.	110	C17	60.01 N	70.00 W
Kangmar, China	52	F2	28.33 N	89.43 E
Kangnam, ngh., Kor., S.	189b		37.30 N	127.01 E
Kangnichumike, China	70	B8	33.10 N	80.59 E
Kangnŭng, Kor., S.	54	F8	37.45 N	128.54 E
Kango, Gabon	86	D2	0.11 N	10.05 E
Kangping, China	52	C9	42.44 N	123.20 E
Kangpu, China	52	F4	27.43 N	99.02 E
Kangrinboqê Feng, mtn., China	70	C8	31.04 N	81.18 E
Kangshan, Tai.	58	J9	22.47 N	120.16 E
Kangsŏ, Kor., N.	54	E6	38.58 N	125.26 E
Kangto, mtn., Asia	70	D14	27.52 N	92.30 E
Kangwŏn-do, state, Kor., S.	56	B1	37.36 N	128.21 E
Kangyidaung, Mya.	64	D2	16.55 N	94.53 E
Kanha National Park, p.o.i., India	70	G8	22.09 N	80.37 E
Kanhar, stm., India	70	F9	24.28 N	83.08 E
Kanheri Caves, cv., India	190c		19.13 N	72.52 E
Kanhsien see Ganzhou, China	58	I6	25.52 N	114.54 E
Kani, Mya.	64	A2	22.26 N	94.50 E
Kaniama, D.R.C.	86	F4	7.33 S	24.09 E
Kanibadam, Taj.	72	A11	40.17 N	70.26 E
Kaniet Islands, is., Pap. N. Gui.	101a	a4	0.53 S	145.30 E
Kanigiri, India	69	D4	15.23 N	79.30 E
Kanihāula, ngh., India	190a		28.44 N	77.01 E
Kanin, poluostrov, pen., Russia	12	C21	68.00 N	45.00 E
Kaningo, Kenya	86	E7	0.47 S	38.32 E
Kanin-Kamen', mts., Russia	12	B21	68.18 N	45.00 E
Kanin Nos, Russia	12	B20	68.39 N	43.16 E
Kanin Nos, mys, c., Russia	12	B20	68.39 N	43.17 E
Kaniv, Ukr.	38	D10	49.45 N	31.27 E
Kaniva, Austl.	98	K3	36.22 S	141.14 E
Kanivs'ke vodoskhovyshche, res., Ukr.	38	D10	50.00 N	31.20 E
Kanjiža, Yugo.	36	C7	46.03 N	20.04 E
Kānjur, ngh., India	190c		19.08 N	72.56 E
Kanjutino, Russia	26	E16	55.32 N	33.15 E
Kankaanpää, Fin.	18	F9	61.48 N	22.25 E
Kankakee, Il., U.S.	130	C10	41.06 N	87.51 W
Kankakee, stm., U.S.	130	C10	41.23 N	88.13 W
Kankan, Gui.	84	G3	10.23 N	9.18 W
Kankar, ngh., India	190a		28.46 N	77.06 E
Kānker, India	70	H8	20.16 N	81.30 E
Kankō see Hamhŭng, Kor., N.	54	E7	39.54 N	127.32 E
Kankunskij, Russia	50	E14	57.37 N	126.01 E
Kanlıavşar, Tur.	76	A9	37.13 N	38.16 E
Kanlıca, ngh., Tur.	185b		41.06 N	29.04 E
Kanmaw Kyun, i., Mya.	64	G4	11.40 N	98.28 E
Kannabi-san, hill, Japan	188		34.48 N	135.44 E
Kannack, Viet.	64	E9	14.06 N	108.38 E
Kannad, India	70	H5	20.14 N	75.06 E
Kannapolis, N.C., U.S.	132	A5	35.29 N	80.37 W
Kannauj, India	70	E7	27.03 N	79.54 E
Kanniyākumari, India	69	G3	8.05 N	77.32 E
Kannod, India	70	G6	22.39 N	76.44 E
Kannonkoski, Fin.	18	D12	62.58 N	25.16 E
Kannon-zaki, c., Japan	186		35.15 N	139.45 E
Kannur see Cannanore, India	69	F2	11.51 N	75.22 E
Kannus, Fin.	18	D10	63.53 N	23.54 E
Kano, Nig.	84	G6	12.00 N	8.30 E
Kanokovo, Russia	42	C9	44.51 N	41.19 E
Kanonerskij, ostrov, i., Russia	183a		59.54 N	30.13 E
Kanonji, Japan	56	E6	34.07 N	133.39 E
Kanopolis, Ks., U.S.	138	C10	38.42 N	98.09 W
Kanopolis Lake, res., Ks., U.S.	138	C11	38.38 N	98.00 W
Kanorado, Ks., U.S.	138	B6	39.19 N	102.02 W
Kanosh, Ut., U.S.	150	E4	38.48 N	112.26 W
Kanouse Brook, stm., N.J., U.S.	194		41.02 N	74.26 W
Kanouse Mountain, mtn., N.J., U.S.	194		41.04 N	74.25 W
Kanowit, Malay.	66	B8	2.06 N	112.08 E
Kanoya, Japan	56	H3	31.23 N	130.51 E
Kanō-zan, hill, Japan	186		35.15 N	139.57 E
Kanozero, ozero, l., Russia	14	E25	67.02 N	34.07 E
Kanpetlet, Mya.	64	B1	21.12 N	94.02 E
Kanpoli, India	190c		19.04 N	73.09 E
Kānpur (Cawnpore), India	70	E7	26.27 N	80.19 E
Kansai International Airport, arpt., Japan	188		34.26 N	135.15 E
Kānsāripāra, India	190b		22.56 N	88.14 E
Kansas, Il., U.S.	130	E10	39.32 N	87.56 W
Kansas, state, U.S.	138	C10	38.45 N	98.15 W
Kansas, stm., Ks., U.S.	138	B13	39.07 N	94.36 W
Kansas City, Ks., U.S.	130	E3	39.06 N	94.38 W
Kansas City, Mo., U.S.	130	E3	39.06 N	94.33 W
Kansei Gakuin University, educ., Japan	188		34.46 N	135.21 E
Kansei University, educ., Japan	188		34.46 N	135.31 E
Kanshi, China	58	I7	24.54 N	116.53 E
Kansk, Russia	48	C17	56.12 N	95.43 E
Kansŏng, Kor., S.	56	A1	38.22 N	128.29 E
Kansu see Gansu, state, China	52	D5	37.00 N	103.00 E
Kantalvi, India	190c		18.54 N	73.03 E
Kantang, Thai.	64	I4	7.24 N	99.31 E
Kantchari, Burkina	84	G5	12.29 N	1.30 E
Kantemirovka, Russia	38	D18	49.42 N	39.51 E
Kānth, India	70	D7	29.06 N	78.37 E
Kantharalak, Thai.	64	E7	14.38 N	104.39 E
Kantishna, stm., Ak., U.S.	109	D9	64.46 N	149.58 W
Kantō-heiya, pl., Japan	56	D12	36.00 N	139.30 E
Kanton, i., Kir.	94	D9	2.48 S	171.40 W
Kantō-sanchi, mts., Japan	56	D11	35.50 N	138.50 E
Kantu-long, Mya.	64	C3	19.58 N	97.36 E
Kantunilkín, Mex.	156	B4	21.06 N	87.29 W
Kanturk, Ire.	10	I3	52.11 N	8.54 W
Kanuku Mountains, mts., Guy.	168	F12	3.12 N	59.30 W
Kanuma, Japan	56	C12	36.33 N	139.45 E
Kanus, Nmb.	90	E4	27.52 S	18.38 E
Kanye, Bots.	90	D7	24.59 S	25.19 E
Kanyutkwin, Mya.	64	C3	18.20 N	96.29 E
Kanzaki, stm., Japan	188		34.42 N	135.25 E
Kanzanavolok, Russia	18	E23	62.18 N	36.59 E
Kaohiung see Kaohsiung, Tai.	58	J8	22.38 N	120.17 E
Kaohsiung, Tai.	58	J8	22.38 N	120.17 E
Kaohsiunghsien, Tai.	58	J9	22.38 N	120.21 E
Kaoka Bay, b., Sol. Is.	101b	e9	9.41 S	160.40 E
Kaoko Veld, plat., Nmb.	88	D1	20.00 S	14.00 E
Kaolack, Sen.	84	G1	14.08 N	16.04 W
Kaolin, Pa., U.S.	203		39.48 N	75.43 W
Kaolinovo, Blg.	36	F14	43.37 N	27.07 E
Kaolun see Kowloon, China	189d		22.18 N	114.10 E
Kaoma, Zam.	88	C3	14.47 S	24.48 E
Kaouar, reg., Niger	84	F7	18.52 N	12.52 E
Kapaa, Hi., U.S.	100a	a2	22.04 N	159.19 W
Kapadvanj, India	70	G4	23.00 N	73.03 E
Kapahiang, Indon.	66	E3	3.38 S	102.33 E
Kapan, Arm.	42	F12	39.12 N	46.24 E
Kapanga, D.R.C.	86	F4	8.23 S	22.34 E
Kapaonik, mts., Yugo.	36	F7	43.20 N	20.50 E
Kapatkevičy, Bela.	26	H11	52.18 N	28.48 E
Kapčagaj, Kaz.	48	F13	43.52 N	77.04 E
Kapčagajskoe vodohranilišče, res., Kaz.	48	F13	43.48 N	77.42 E
Kapcèvičy, Bela.	26	H11	52.13 N	28.19 E
Kapchagay Reservoir see Kapčagajskoe vodohranilišče, res., Kaz.	48	F13	43.48 N	77.42 E
Kapellen, Ger.	181		51.08 N	6.38 E
Kapellerfeld, Aus.	182b		48.19 N	16.30 E
Kapfenberg, Aus.	30	C12	47.27 N	15.17 E
Kapıdağ Yarımadası, pen., Tur.	34	C10	40.28 N	27.50 E
Kapikotongwa, stm., On., Can.	128	A11	50.33 N	87.40 W
Kapingamarangi, at., Micron.	94	C6	1.04 N	154.46 E
Kapiri Mposhi, Zam.	88	C4	13.57 S	28.40 E
Kapisigdlit, Grnld.	108	E16	64.26 N	50.16 W
Kapiskau, stm., On., Can.	110	E14	52.46 N	81.59 W
Kapit, Malay.	66	C8	2.00 N	112.55 E
Kapitanivka, Ukr.	38	E10	48.54 N	31.43 E
Kaplan, La., U.S.	134	G6	29.59 N	92.16 W
Kaplice, Czech Rep.	24	H10	48.44 N	14.29 E
Kapoe, Thai.	64	H4	9.35 N	98.32 E
Kapoeta, Sudan	82	G6	4.47 N	33.35 E
Kapona, D.R.C.	86	F5	7.12 S	29.08 E
Kaporskoe, Russia	183a		59.45 N	29.58 E
Kapos, stm., Hung.	36	C5	46.44 N	18.28 E
Kaposvár, Hung.	36	C4	46.21 N	17.47 E
Kaposvar Creek, stm., Sk., Can.	142	D12	50.31 N	101.56 W
Kapotn'a, ngh., Russia	183b		55.38 N	37.48 E
Kapp, Nor.	16	G8	60.42 N	10.53 E
Kappeln, Ger.	24	B5	54.39 N	9.55 E
Kappelshamn, Swe.	16	J16	57.51 N	18.47 E
Kaprun, Aus.	24	I8	47.15 N	12.45 E
Kaptai, Bngl.	70	G14	22.28 N	92.11 E
Kaptai Lake see Karnaphuli Reservoir, res., Bngl.	70	G14	22.37 N	92.12 E
Kapuas, stm., Indon.	66	D6	0.09 S	109.08 E
Kapuas, stm., Indon.	66	E9	3.01 S	114.22 E
Kapuas Hulu, Pegunungan see Upper Kapuas Mountains, mts., Asia	66	C8	1.15 N	113.30 E
Kapuas Hulu, Pergunungan see Upper Kapuas Mountains, mts., Asia	66	C8	1.15 N	113.30 E
Kapunda, Austl.	98	J2	34.20 S	138.54 E
Kapūrthala, India	70	C5	31.22 N	75.23 E
Kapuskasing, On., Can.	114	B9	49.25 N	82.25 W
Kapuskasing, stm., On., Can.	114	B9	49.37 N	82.15 W
Kapustin Jar, Russia	40	G14	48.35 N	45.44 E
Kapustnoe, Russia	14	E25	67.19 N	34.13 E
Kapustyne, Ukr.	38	E10	48.56 N	31.12 E
Kapuvár, Hung.	36	B4	47.35 N	17.01 E
Kapyl', Bela.	26	G10	53.08 N	27.06 E
Kapyrevščina, Russia	26	E15	55.15 N	32.52 E
Kara, Russia	50	C1	69.14 N	64.59 E
Kara, stm., Russia	50	C2	69.07 N	64.44 E
Kara-Balta, Kyrg.	48	F12	42.47 N	73.50 E
Karabanovo, Russia	26	D21	56.19 N	38.42 E
Karabaš, Russia	48	C9	55.29 N	60.13 E
Karabiğa, Tur.	34	C10	40.25 N	27.18 E
Kara-Bogaz-Gol, zaliv, b., Turkmen.	72	A7	41.14 N	53.24 E
Kara-Bogaz-Gol Gulf see Kara-Bogaz-Gol, zaliv, b., Turkmen.	72	A7	41.14 N	53.24 E
Karabük, Tur.	34	B15	41.12 N	32.39 E
Karabula, Russia	48	C17	58.07 N	97.20 E
Karaburun, Tur.	34	E9	38.38 N	26.30 E
Karabutak, Kaz.	48	D10	49.57 N	60.07 E
Karacabey, Tur.	34	C11	40.11 N	28.21 E
Karačaevo-Čerkesija, state, Russia	42	D9	44.00 N	42.00 E
Karačaevsk, Russia	42	D9	43.46 N	41.55 E
Karacaköy, Tur.	34	B11	41.23 N	28.25 E
Karacasu, Tur.	34	F11	37.43 N	28.36 E
Karaçay, Tur.	76	B6	36.08 N	36.03 E
Karačev, Russia	26	G17	53.07 N	34.59 E
Karachay see Karačaevo-Čerkesija, state, Russia	42	D9	44.00 N	42.00 E
Karachay-Cherkessia see Karačaevo-Čerkesija, state, Russia	42	D9	44.00 N	42.00 E
Karāchi, Pak.	62	D2	24.53 N	67.01 E
Karād, India	69	C2	17.16 N	74.11 E
Kara Deniz see Black Sea, s.	42	D5	43.00 N	35.00 E
Karaftit, Russia	50	F11	54.12 N	111.54 E
Karagaj, Russia	40	B19	58.16 N	54.55 E
Karaganda, Kaz.	48	E12	49.52 N	73.09 E
Karagayly see Karkaralinsk, Kaz.	48	E13	49.24 N	75.29 E
Karagel', Turkmen.	72	B7	39.23 N	53.12 E
Karagie, vpadina, depr., Kaz.	42	D14	43.20 N	51.29 E
Karaginskij, ostrov, i., Russia	50	E21	58.50 N	164.00 E
Karaginskij zaliv, b., Russia	50	E21	58.50 N	164.00 E
Kara Gölü, l., Tur.	34	G12	36.39 N	29.39 E
Karagoš, gora, mtn., Russia	48	D15	51.44 N	89.24 E
Karahallı, Tur.	34	E12	38.20 N	29.32 E
Karaidel', Russia	40	D20	55.50 N	56.53 E
Karaidel'skij, Russia	40	D20	55.47 N	57.03 E
Kāraikāl, India	69	F4	10.56 N	79.49 E
Kāraikkudi, India	69	F4	10.03 N	78.46 E
Karaisalı, Tur.	76	A6	37.15 N	35.03 E
Karaitivu, i., Sri L.	69	G4	8.27 N	79.47 E
Karaj, Iran	74	C12	35.49 N	50.58 E
Karaj, stm., Iran	185d		35.35 N	51.11 E
Kara-Kala, Turkmen.	72	B8	38.25 N	56.17 E
Karakaralong, Pulau, is., Indon.	60	E8	4.33 N	125.38 E
Karakax, stm., China	70	A7	35.21 N	78.46 E
Karakaya Barajı, res., Tur.	42	F8	38.28 N	38.30 E
Karakelong, Pulau, i., Indon.	68	H6	4.17 N	126.30 E
Karakojyn, ozero, l., Kaz.	48	E11	46.09 N	68.36 E
Karakol, Kyrg.	48	F13	42.29 N	78.23 E
Karakoram Pass, p., Asia	70	A6	35.30 N	77.47 E
Karakoram Range, mts., Asia	62	A4	35.30 N	77.00 E
Karakorum Shan see Karakoram Range, mts., Asia	62	A4	35.30 N	77.00 E
Karakorum Shankou see Karakoram Pass, p., Asia	70	A6	35.30 N	77.47 E
Karakul', Uzb.	48	G10	39.31 N	63.54 E
Kara-Kum see Garagumy, des., Turkmen.	48	A8	39.00 N	60.00 E
Kara-Kum Canal see Garagumskij kanal, can., Turkmen.	72	B9	37.34 N	65.40 E
Karakumy see Garagumy, des., Turkmen.	72	A8	39.00 N	60.00 E
Karakuni, Japan	188		34.28 N	135.28 E
Karala, ngh., India	190a		28.44 N	77.02 E
Karalundi, Austl.	96	E3	26.08 S	118.41 E
Karam, Russia	48	C19	55.09 N	107.35 E
Karama, stm., Indon.	66	E11	2.18 S	119.07 E
Karamai see Karamay, China	52	B1	45.35 N	84.51 E
Karaman, Tur.	42	G5	37.10 N	33.13 E
Karaman, state, Tur.	42	G5	37.00 N	33.00 E
Karamanlı, Tur.	34	F12	37.22 N	29.49 E
Karamay, China	52	B1	45.35 N	84.51 E
Karambu, Indon.	66	E10	3.54 S	116.04 E
Karamea Bight, b., N.Z.	102	E4	41.30 S	171.40 E
Karamürsel, Tur.	34	C12	40.42 N	29.36 E
Karamyševo, Russia	26	C11	57.45 N	28.45 E
Karamyševo, Russia	48	C18	57.33 N	100.56 E
Karamzino, Russia	26	D17	56.00 N	34.33 E
Karang, Tanjung, c., Indon.	66	D11	0.39 S	119.44 E
Karangagung, Indon.	66	E4	2.22 S	104.27 E
Karangasem, Indon.	66	H9	8.27 S	115.36 E
Karangnunggal, Indon.	66	G6	7.37 S	108.06 E
Karanja, India	70	H6	20.28 N	77.29 E
Karanjia, India	70	H10	21.47 N	85.58 E
Karaoba, Kaz.	42	B17	47.06 N	56.19 E
Karapınar, Tur.	42	G5	37.43 N	33.33 E
Karapyshi, Ukr.	38	D9	49.38 N	30.47 E
Karaš, Russia	26	D22	56.54 N	39.24 E
Karas, state, Nmb.	90	E4	26.55 S	18.45 E
Karaşar, Tur.	34	C14	40.20 N	31.59 E
Karasay, China	62	A5	36.46 N	83.48 E
Karasburg, Nmb.	90	F4	28.01 S	18.45 E
Kara Sea see Karskoe more, s., Russia	46	B10	76.00 N	80.00 E
Karasengir, mys, c., Turkmen.	42	E15	40.42 N	52.50 E
Karašica see Fekete-víz, stm., Eur.	30	E15	45.51 N	18.51 E
Kárášjohka, stm., Nor.	14	C15	69.26 N	25.48 E
Karasjok, Nor.	14	C16	69.27 N	25.31 E
Karasu, Kaz.	48	D11	52.39 N	65.28 E
Karasu, Tur.	34	B13	41.05 N	30.41 E
Karasu, stm., Tur.	42	F9	39.43 N	40.16 E
Karasuk, Russia	48	D13	53.43 N	78.02 E
Karatal, Kaz.	48	E15	47.37 N	85.09 E
Karatal, stm., Kaz.	48	E13	46.28 N	77.07 E
Karataş, Tur.	76	B6	36.34 N	35.23 E
Karataş Burun, c., Tur.	76	B6	36.34 N	35.22 E
Karatau, Kaz.	48	F11	43.10 N	70.28 E
Karatau, hrebet, mts., Kaz.	48	F11	43.35 N	68.52 E
Karatau Range see Karatau, hrebet, mts., Kaz.	48	F11	43.35 N	68.52 E
Karatjaure, l., Swe.	14	F9	66.43 N	18.37 E
Karatobe, Kaz.	48	E8	49.41 N	53.30 E
Karaton, Kaz.	48	E8	46.25 N	53.31 E
Karatsu, Japan	56	F2	33.26 N	129.58 E
Karaul, Kaz.	48	E13	48.57 N	79.16 E
Karaul, Russia	50	B5	70.05 N	83.11 E
Karauli, India	70	E6	26.31 N	77.03 E
Karauzek, Russia	40	H16	47.15 N	48.25 E
Karavanke, mts., Eur.	8	F11	46.28 N	14.15 E
Karave, India	190c		19.01 N	73.01 E
Karawa, D.R.C.	86	D4	3.20 N	20.17 E
Karawang, Indon.	66	G5	6.18 S	107.17 E
Karawang, Tanjung, c., Indon.	66	F5	5.55 S	107.01 E
Karawanken, mts., Eur.	30	D11	46.28 N	14.15 E
Karažal, Kaz.	48	E12	48.01 N	70.49 E
Karažanbas, Kaz.	40	I17	45.15 N	51.17 E
Karbalā', Iraq	74	D9	32.36 N	44.01 E
Karbalā', state, Iraq	74	D9	32.30 N	43.45 E
Karbeyaz, Tur.	76	C7	35.59 N	36.16 E
Kårböle, Swe.	16	F13	61.59 N	15.18 E
Karcag, Hung.	36	B7	47.18 N	20.55 E
Karczew, Pol.	24	D17	52.04 N	21.15 E
Kardámaina, Grc.	34	G10	36.46 N	27.07 E
Kardámyla, Grc.	34	E9	38.32 N	26.06 E
Kardeljevo, Cro.	30	G14	43.04 N	17.26 E
Kárditsa, Grc.	34	D4	39.22 N	21.55 E
Kärdla, Est.	26	A5	58.59 N	22.45 E
Kardymovo, Russia	26	F15	54.53 N	32.26 E
Kărdžali, Blg.	36	H12	41.38 N	25.22 E
Karea, India	190b		22.42 N	88.33 E
Karelia see Karelija, state, Russia	12	D15	64.00 N	32.30 E
Karelia, hist. reg., Eur.	18	E18	63.00 N	32.00 E
Karèličy, Bela.	26	G9	53.34 N	26.07 E
Karelija, state, Russia	12	D15	64.00 N	32.30 E
Karel'skij Gorodok, Russia	26	B19	58.04 N	36.30 E
Karema, Tan.	86	F6	6.48 S	30.26 E
Karen, India	62	F7	12.52 N	92.52 E
Karepole, Russia	12	D20	65.32 N	43.39 E
Karera, India	190a		28.41 N	77.23 E
Karesuando, Swe.	14	D13	68.25 N	22.30 E
Kärevere, Est.	26	B9	58.26 N	26.29 E
Kargali, Russia	40	D17	55.10 N	50.55 E
Kargalinskaja, Russia	42	D12	43.44 N	46.28 E
Karganaj, Russia	50	C24	65.19 N	175.11 E
Kargasok, Russia	48	C14	59.04 N	80.49 E
Kargat, Russia	48	C14	55.11 N	80.17 E
Kargil, India	70	A6	34.35 N	76.05 E
Karginskij, stm., Russia	183a		59.50 N	30.01 E
Kargopol', Russia	18	F25	61.30 N	38.57 E
Karhijärvi, l., Fin.	18	F9	61.34 N	22.29 E
Karhula, Fin.	18	G13	60.30 N	26.56 E
Karhutunturi, hill, Fin.	14	E20	67.11 N	29.07 E
Kariba, Zimb.	88	D4	16.31 S	28.48 E
Kariba, Lake, res., Afr.	88	D4	17.00 S	28.00 E
Karibib, Nmb.	90	B2	21.56 S	15.51 E
Kariega, stm., S. Afr.	90	H6	33.02 S	23.28 E
Karigasniemi, Fin.	14	C16	69.24 N	25.49 E
Karimata, Kepulauan, is., Indon.	66	D6	1.25 S	109.05 E
Karimata, Pulau, i., Indon.	66	D6	1.36 S	108.55 E
Karimata, Selat, strt., Indon.	66	E6	2.05 S	108.40 E
Karīmganj, India	70	F14	24.50 N	92.23 E
Karīmnagar, India	69	B4	18.26 N	79.09 E
Karimunjawa, Kepulauan, is., Indon.	66	F7	5.50 S	110.25 E
Karimunjawa, Pulau, i., Indon.	66	F7	5.51 S	110.27 E
Karin, Som.	86	B9	10.59 N	49.12 E
Karis see Karjaa, Fin.	18	G10	60.04 N	23.38 E
Karisimbi, Volcan, vol., Afr.	86	E5	1.30 S	29.27 E
Káristos, Grc.	34	E7	38.01 N	24.25 E
Kariya, Japan	56	D10	34.59 N	136.59 E
Kariye Museum, rel., Tur.	185b		41.01 N	28.55 E
Karjaa, Fin.	18	G10	60.04 N	23.38 E
Kārkal, India	69	E2	13.11 N	74.59 E
Karkaralinsk, Kaz.	48	E13	49.24 N	75.29 E
Karkar Dūmān, ngh., India	190a		28.39 N	77.18 E
Karkar Island, i., Pap. N. Gui.	101a	a4	4.40 S	146.00 E
Karkas, Kūh-e, mts., Iran	74	D12	33.27 N	51.48 E
Karkheh, stm., Iran	74	D10	31.41 N	47.47 E
Karkinit Gulf see Karkinits'ka zatoka, b., Ukr.	38	H11	45.55 N	33.00 E
Karkinits'ka zatoka, b., Ukr.	38	H11	45.55 N	33.00 E
Karkkila, Fin.	18	G11	60.32 N	24.12 E
Karkku, Fin.	18	F9	61.25 N	23.00 E
Karkonoski Park Narodowy, p.o.i., Pol.	24	F11	50.45 N	15.35 E
Karkūk, Iraq	74	C9	35.28 N	44.23 E
Kärla, Est.	26	B5	58.20 N	22.14 E
Karleby see Kokkola, Fin.	18	D10	63.50 N	23.08 E
Karlholmsbruk, Swe.	16	G15	60.31 N	17.36 E
Karlik Shan, mtn., China	52	C3	43.05 N	94.19 E
Karlino, Pol.	24	B11	54.02 N	15.52 E
Karlivka, Ukr.	38	D14	49.28 N	35.09 E
Karl-Marx-Stadt see Chemnitz, Ger.	24	F8	50.49 N	12.55 E
Karlobag, Cro.	30	F12	44.31 N	15.04 E
Karlovac, Cro.	30	E12	45.29 N	15.32 E
Karlovo, Blg.	36	G11	42.38 N	24.48 E
Karlovy Vary, Czech Rep.	24	F8	50.13 N	12.52 E
Karlsborg, Swe.	14	G14	65.48 N	23.17 E
Karlsborg, Swe.	16	I12	58.31 N	14.31 E
Karlsburg see Alba Iulia, Rom.	36	C10	46.04 N	23.34 E
Karlshamn, Swe.	16	K12	56.09 N	14.51 E
Karlshorst, ngh., Ger.	182a		52.29 N	13.32 E

Name	Page	Map Ref.	Latitude	Longitude
Karlshorst, Trabrennbahn, p.o.i., Ger.	182a		52.29 N	13.31 E
Karlskoga, Swe.	16	H12	59.20 N	14.32 E
Karlskrona, Swe.	16	K13	56.10 N	15.35 E
Karlsöarna, is., Swe.	16	J15	57.17 N	17.58 E
Karlsøya, i., Nor.	14	B11	70.00 N	19.56 E
Karlsøyvær, is., Nor.	14	E5	67.34 N	14.42 E
Karlsruhe, Ger.	24	G4	49.00 N	8.22 E
Karlstad, Swe.	16	H11	59.22 N	13.30 E
Karlstad, Mn., U.S.	128	C2	48.33 N	96.32 W
Karlstadt, Ger.	24	G5	49.57 N	9.46 E
Karluk, Ak., U.S.	109	E9	57.34 N	154.28 W
Karma, Bela.	26	G13	53.07 N	30.48 E
Karma, Bela.	26	H14	52.19 N	31.26 E
Karma, Niger	84	G5	13.43 N	1.45 E
Karmah see Karmah an Nuzul, Sudan	82	D6	19.40 N	30.26 E
Karmah an Nuzul, Sudan	82	D6	19.40 N	30.26 E
Karmāla, India	69	B2	18.24 N	75.11 E
Karmanovka, Kaz.	40	G17	49.24 N	50.20 E
Karmanovo, Russia	26	E17	55.50 N	34.51 E
Karmøy, i., Nor.	16	H3	59.15 N	5.15 E
Karnack, Tx., U.S.	136	B13	32.40 N	94.10 W
Karnak see El-Karnak, Egypt	74	H3	25.42 N	32.40 E
Karnak, Il., U.S.	130	G9	37.17 N	88.58 W
Karnāl, India	70	D6	29.41 N	76.59 E
Karnāla Fort, hist., India	190c		18.53 N	73.07 E
Karnāli, stm., Asia	70	D8	28.17 N	81.02 E
Karnāli, stm., Nepal	70	D8	28.44 N	81.15 E
Karnap, ngh., Ger.	181		51.31 N	7.01 E
Karnaphuli Reservoir, res., Bngl.	70	G14	22.37 N	92.12 E
Karnātaka, state, India	62	F4	14.00 N	76.00 E
Karnaukhivka, Ukr.	38	E13	48.27 N	34.45 E
Karnes City, Tx., U.S.	136	F10	28.53 N	97.54 W
Karnische Alpen see Carnic Alps, mts., Eur.	30	D10	46.35 N	13.02 E
Karnobat, Blg.	36	G13	42.39 N	26.59 E
Kärnten, state, Aus.	30	D10	46.50 N	13.50 E
Karoli, India	70	G7	22.55 N	79.03 E
Karolinenhof, ngh., Ger.	182a		52.23 N	13.38 E
Karonga, Mwi.	88	B5	9.54 S	33.55 E
Karonie, Austl.	96	F4	30.57 S	122.31 E
Karoo National Park, p.o.i., S. Afr.	90	H6	32.17 S	24.30 E
Karoonda, Austl.	98	J2	35.05 S	139.53 E
Karor, Pak.	70	C3	31.13 N	70.57 E
Karosa, Indon.	66	D11	1.48 S	119.20 E
Karow, ngh., Ger.	182a		52.37 N	13.29 E
Kärpänkylä, Fin.	18	B16	65.54 N	29.54 E
Kárpathos, Grc.	34	H10	35.30 N	27.12 E
Kárpathos, i., Grc.	34	H10	35.40 N	27.09 E
Karpats'kyi Pryrodnyi Natsional'nyi Park, p.o.i., Ukr.	38	E3	48.25 N	24.30 E
Karpaty see Carpathian Mountains, mts., Eur.	8	F13	48.00 N	24.00 E
Karpenísi, Grc.	34	E4	38.55 N	21.39 E
Karpogory, Russia	12	D21	64.00 N	44.23 E
Karpovo, Russia	18	G23	60.01 N	36.44 E
Karpuzlu, Tur.	34	F10	37.33 N	27.49 E
Karratha, Austl.	96	D3	20.43 S	116.47 E
Karrats Fjord, b., Grnld.	108	C14	71.20 N	54.00 W
Kars, Tur.	42	E10	40.35 N	43.04 E
Kars, state, Tur.	42	E10	40.35 N	43.00 E
Karsakpaj, Kaz.	48	E11	47.49 N	66.44 E
Kärsämäki, Fin.	18	D12	63.58 N	25.44 E
Karsantı, Tur.	76	A6	37.33 N	35.23 E
Kårsatjåkka, mtn., Swe.	14	E9	67.40 N	18.21 E
Kārsava, Lat.	26	D10	56.47 N	27.41 E
Karši, Uzb.	48	G11	38.51 N	65.47 E
Karsin, Pol.	24	C13	53.54 N	17.55 E
Karskoe more (Kara Sea), s., Russia	46	B10	76.00 N	80.00 E
Karstula, Fin.	18	E11	62.52 N	24.48 E
Karsun, Russia	40	D15	54.11 N	46.59 E
Kartala, vol., Com.	88	C7	11.45 S	43.22 E
Kartaly, Russia	48	D10	53.03 N	60.38 E
Kartārpur, India	70	C5	31.26 N	75.29 E
Karthaus, Pa., U.S.	124	C7	41.07 N	78.06 W
Karttula, Fin.	18	E13	62.53 N	26.57 E
Kartuzy, Pol.	24	B14	54.19 N	18.12 E
Käru, Est.	26	B8	58.50 N	25.10 E
Karufa, Indon.	60	F9	3.50 S	133.26 E
Karumba, Austl.	98	A3	17.27 S	140.50 E
Kārūn, stm., Iran	74	D11	30.25 N	48.09 E
Karungi, Swe.	14	F14	66.03 N	23.57 E
Karunjie, Austl.	96	C5	16.16 S	127.11 E
Karup, Den.	16	K7	56.18 N	9.10 E
Karūr, India	69	F4	10.57 N	78.05 E
Karvala, Russia	183a		59.41 N	30.09 E
Kårvik, Nor.	14	C9	69.52 N	18.55 E
Karviná, Czech Rep.	24	G14	49.51 N	18.31 E
Kārwār, India	69	D1	14.48 N	74.07 E
Karyés, Grc.	34	C7	40.16 N	24.17 E
Karymskoe, Russia	50	F11	51.37 N	114.20 E
Karynžaryk, peski, sand, Kaz.	42	D16	42.35 N	54.00 E
Kas, Sudan	82	E4	12.30 N	24.17 E
Kaş, Tur.	34	G12	36.11 N	29.40 E
Kasadi, stm., India	190c		19.01 N	73.03 E
Kasagi-sanchi, mts., Japan	188		34.37 N	135.56 E
Kasahata, Japan	186		35.54 N	139.25 E
Kasai, ngh., Japan	186		35.39 N	139.53 E
Kasai (Cassai), stm., Afr.	86	E3	3.01 S	16.56 E
Kasaji, D.R.C.	86	G4	10.22 S	23.27 E
Kasama, Japan	56	C13	36.22 N	140.15 E
Kasama, Zam.	88	C5	10.12 S	31.10 E
Kasane, Bots.	88	D3	17.49 S	25.08 E
Kasanga, Tan.	86	F6	8.28 S	31.09 E
Kasangulu, D.R.C.	86	E3	4.34 S	15.10 E
Kasaoka, Japan	56	E6	34.30 N	133.30 E
Kasar, Ras see Kasr, Ra's, c., Afr.	82	D7	18.01 N	38.34 E
Kāsaragod, India	69	E2	12.29 N	74.59 E
Kasari, stm., Est.	26	B7	58.46 N	23.45 E
Kasba, India	70	F11	25.50 N	87.32 E
Kasba Lake, l., Can.	110	C10	60.18 N	102.07 W
Kaschau see Košice, Slvk.	24	H17	48.43 N	21.16 E
Kascjukoŭka, Bela.	26	H13	52.31 N	30.56 E
Kascjukovičy, Bela.	26	G14	53.20 N	32.03 E
Kåseberga, Swe.	16	L11	55.23 N	14.03 E
Kaseda, Japan	56	H3	31.24 N	130.19 E
Kasempa, Zam.	88	C4	13.27 S	25.50 E
Kasenga, D.R.C.	86	G5	10.21 S	28.36 E
Kasenye, D.R.C.	86	D6	1.23 N	30.25 E
Kasese, D.R.C.	86	E5	1.38 S	27.07 E
Kasese, Ug.	86	D6	0.10 N	30.05 E
Kasetsart University, educ., Thai.	187a		13.51 N	100.34 E
Kaset Sombun, Thai.	64	D5	16.16 N	101.56 E
Kāsganj, India	70	E7	27.48 N	78.38 E
Kashabowie Lake, l., On., Can.	128	C8	48.41 N	90.24 W
Kāshān, Iran	74	D12	33.59 N	51.26 E
Kashgar see Kashit, China	48	G13	39.27 N	75.59 E
Kashihara, Japan	56	E8	34.30 N	135.47 E
Kashima, Japan	56	F3	33.07 N	130.06 E
Kashima-nada, s., Japan	56	C13	36.15 N	140.45 E
Kashing see Jiaxing, China	58	F9	30.45 N	120.44 E
Kashio, ngh., Japan	186		35.25 N	139.33 E
Kāshīpur, India	70	D7	29.12 N	78.57 E
Kashit, China	48	G13	39.27 N	75.59 E
Kashiwazaki, Japan	56	B11	37.22 N	138.33 E
Kashiwazaki, Japan	186		35.56 N	139.42 E
Kāshmar, Iran	72	B8	35.13 N	58.27 E
Kashmir (Jammu and Kashmīr), hist. reg., Asia	62	A3	34.00 N	76.00 E
Kashmor, Pak.	70	D2	28.25 N	69.35 E
Kashperivka, Ukr.	38	D8	49.26 N	29.41 E
Kasia, India	70	E9	26.44 N	83.55 E
Kasilovo, Russia	38	C14	50.38 N	35.37 E
Kasimbar, Indon.	66	D12	0.08 S	120.01 E
Kasimov, Russia	40	D12	54.56 N	41.23 E
Kāsimpur, India	190b		22.46 N	88.31 E
Kašin, Russia	26	C20	57.21 N	37.36 E
Kāsināthpur, India	190b		22.35 N	88.31 E
Kāsipur, India	190b		22.25 N	88.10 E
Kašira, Russia	26	F21	54.51 N	38.10 E
Kasiruta, Pulau, i., Indon.	60	E8	0.25 S	127.12 E
Kaskabulak, Kaz.	48	E13	49.33 N	79.53 E
Kaškarancy, Russia	14	F26	66.21 N	36.01 E
Kaskaskia, stm., Il., U.S.	130	F8	37.58 N	89.57 W
Kasker, Swe.	14	G9	65.51 N	18.00 E
Kaskinen, Fin.	18	E8	62.23 N	21.13 E
Kaskö see Kaskinen, Fin.	18	E8	62.23 N	21.13 E
Kaslo, B.C., Can.	144	G14	49.54 N	116.55 W
Kasnja, Russia	26	E17	55.24 N	34.20 E
Kasnja, stm., Russia	26	E17	55.48 N	34.25 E
Kasongo, D.R.C.	86	E5	4.27 S	26.40 E
Kasongo-Lunda, D.R.C.	86	F3	6.28 S	16.50 E
Kásos, i., Grc.	34	H9	35.22 N	26.53 E
Kasota, Mn., U.S.	128	G5	44.17 N	93.58 W
Kaspijsk, Russia	42	D12	42.52 N	47.38 E
Kaspijskij, Russia	40	I15	45.23 N	47.21 E
Kaspijskoe more see Caspian Sea, s.	48	F7	41.18 N	50.59 E
Kaspiyskiy, Russia	42	C12	45.23 N	47.21 E
Kasplja, Russia	26	F14	54.59 N	31.38 E
Kasplja, stm., Eur.	26	E13	55.24 N	30.43 E
Kasr, Ra's, c., Afr.	82	D7	18.01 N	38.34 E
Kassa see Košice, Slvk.	24	H17	48.43 N	21.16 E
Kassab, Syria	76	C6	35.55 N	35.58 E
Kassalā, Sudan	82	D7	15.26 N	36.22 E
Kassándra, pen., Grc.	34	C6	40.06 N	23.22 E
Kassandra, Gulf of see Kassándras, Kólpos, b., Grc.	34	C6	40.06 N	23.30 E
Kassándras, Kólpos, b., Grc.	34	C6	40.06 N	23.30 E
Kassel, Ger.	24	E5	51.19 N	9.28 E
Kasserine, Tun.	84	B6	35.09 N	8.49 E
Kasslerfeld, ngh., Ger.	181		51.26 N	6.45 E
Kasson, Mn., U.S.	128	G6	44.01 N	92.45 W
Kastamonu, Tur.	42	E5	41.23 N	33.46 E
Kastamonu, state, Tur.	42	E5	41.40 N	33.45 E
Kastaniés, Grc.	34	B9	41.38 N	26.28 E
Kastelholm, Fin.	18	G7	60.14 N	20.04 E
Kastélli, Grc.	34	H6	35.30 N	23.37 E
Kastellorizo see Megisti, i., Grc.	34	G12	36.08 N	29.36 E
Kastl, Ger.	24	G7	49.21 N	11.42 E
Kastoría, Grc.	34	C4	40.31 N	21.16 E
Kastorias, Límni, l., Grc.	34	C4	40.30 N	21.18 E
Kastornoe, Russia	40	F11	51.48 N	38.07 E
Kastrakíou, Techniti Límni, res., Grc.	34	E4	38.49 N	21.20 E
Kasugai, Japan	56	D9	35.14 N	136.58 E
Kasuga Shrine, rel., Japan	188		34.41 N	135.51 E
Kasulu, Tan.	86	E6	4.34 S	30.05 E
Kasumi, Japan	56	D7	35.38 N	134.38 E
Kasumiga-ura, l., Japan	56	C13	36.02 N	140.23 E
Kasungan, Indon.	66	E8	1.59 S	113.24 E
Kasūr, Pak.	70	C5	31.07 N	74.27 E
Kaszuby, hist. reg., Pol.	24	B13	54.17 N	17.55 E
Kataba, Zam.	88	D4	16.05 S	25.05 E
Katagum, Nig.	84	G7	12.17 N	10.21 E
Katahdin, Mount, mtn., Me., U.S.	122	E7	45.55 N	68.55 W
Katai, India	190c		19.10 N	73.05 E
Katako-Kombe, D.R.C.	86	E4	3.24 S	24.24 E
Katakura, Japan	188		34.29 N	135.31 E
Katanga, hist. reg., D.R.C.	86	F4	10.00 S	26.00 E
Katanga, stm., Russia	48	C18	60.08 N	102.14 E
Katangi, India	70	G7	23.27 N	79.49 E
Katangli, Russia	50	F17	51.42 N	143.14 E
Katanning, Austl.	96	F3	33.41 S	117.33 E
Katano, Japan	188		34.47 N	135.40 E
Kataoka, Japan	188		35.03 N	135.58 E
Katase, Japan	186		35.19 N	139.29 E
Katašin, Russia	26	H15	52.36 N	32.10 E
Katav-Ivanovsk, Russia	40	D20	54.44 N	58.11 E
Katayama, Japan	186		35.46 N	139.34 E
Katchall Island, i., India	62	G7	7.55 N	93.23 E
Katepwa Beach, Sk., Can.	142	D10	50.42 N	103.38 W
Katerini, Grc.	34	C5	40.16 N	22.30 E
Katernberg, ngh., Ger.	181		51.29 N	7.04 E
Katernberg, ngh., Ger.	181		51.16 N	7.06 E
Katerynopil', Ukr.	38	E9	48.56 N	30.59 E
Kates Needle, mtn., N.A.	109	E13	57.03 N	132.03 W
Katete, Zam.	88	C5	14.04 S	32.03 E
Katha, Mya.	62	D8	24.09 N	96.20 E
Katherīna, Gebel, mtn., Egypt	76	J4	28.31 N	33.57 E
Katherine, Austl.	96	B6	14.29 S	132.16 E
Katherine, stm., Austl.	96	B6	14.39 S	131.42 E
Katherine Creek, stm., Austl.	98	D4	23.47 S	143.44 E
Kāthiāwār Peninsula, pen., India	70	G3	22.00 N	71.00 E
Kathla, India	70	C6	31.59 N	76.47 E
Kāthmāṇḍau (Kathmandu), Nepal	70	E10	27.42 N	85.18 E
Kathmandu see Kāthmāṇḍau, Nepal	70	E10	27.42 N	85.18 E
Kathor, India	70	H4	21.17 N	72.57 E
Kathua, India	70	B5	32.22 N	75.31 E
Kati, Mali	84	G3	12.44 N	8.04 W
Katibas, stm., Malay.	66	C8	2.01 N	112.33 E
Katihār, India	70	F11	25.32 N	87.33 E
Katimik Lake, l., Mb., Can.	142	B14	52.54 N	99.22 W
Katiola, C. Iv.	84	H4	8.08 N	5.06 W
Katipunan, Phil.	68	F4	8.30 N	123.17 E
Ka Tiriti o te Moana see Southern Alps, mts., N.Z.	102	F4	43.30 S	170.30 E
Kātlang, Pak.	70	A4	34.22 N	72.04 E
Katlehong, S. Afr.	191d		26.19 S	28.09 E
Katmai, Mount, vol., Ak., U.S.	109	E8	58.17 N	154.56 W
Kātmāndu see Kāthmāṇḍau, Nepal	70	E10	27.42 N	85.18 E
Katni see Murwāra, India	70	G8	23.50 N	80.23 E
Káto Achaïa, Grc.	34	E4	38.08 N	21.32 E
Kātol, India	70	H7	21.16 N	78.35 E
Katompi, D.R.C.	86	F5	6.07 S	26.13 E
Katon-Karagaj, Kaz.	48	E15	49.10 N	85.36 E
Katoomba, Austl.	98	I8	33.42 S	150.17 E
Katowice, Pol.	24	F14	50.16 N	19.00 E
Katrineholm, Swe.	16	I14	58.59 N	16.11 E
Katsina, Nig.	84	G6	12.59 N	7.36 E
Katsina Ala, stm., Afr.	84	F1	7.48 N	8.52 E
Katsura, ngh., Japan	188		34.59 N	135.42 E
Katsura, stm., Japan	188		34.53 N	135.42 E
Katsushika, ngh., Japan	186		35.43 N	139.51 E
Katsuta, Japan	56	C13	36.23 N	140.31 E
Katsuura, Japan	56	D13	35.09 N	140.19 E
Katsuyama, Japan	56	D6	35.05 N	133.41 E
Katsuyama, Japan	56	C9	36.03 N	136.30 E
Kattakurgan, Uzb.	48	G11	39.55 N	66.16 E
Kattavía, Grc.	34	H10	35.57 N	27.45 E
Kattegat, strt., Eur.	16	K8	57.00 N	11.00 E
Kattegatt see Kattegat, strt., Eur.	16	K8	57.00 N	11.00 E
Katterat, Nor.	14	D8	68.24 N	17.59 E
Katternberg, ngh., Ger.	181		51.09 N	7.02 E
Katthammarsvik, Swe.	16	J16	57.26 N	18.50 E
Kattowitz see Katowice, Pol.	24	F14	50.16 N	19.00 E
Katul, Jabal, mtn., Sudan	82	E5	14.16 N	29.23 E
Katun', stm., Russia	48	D15	52.25 N	85.00 E
Katunino, Russia	40	B14	58.01 N	45.36 E
Kātwa, India	70	G11	23.38 N	88.08 E
Katwijk aan Zee, Neth.	20	B13	52.12 N	4.24 E
Katy Hill, mtn., Monts.	159a	d3	16.45 N	62.11 W
Katyn, Russia	26	F14	54.47 N	31.44 E
Kąty Wrocławskie, Pol.	24	E12	51.01 N	16.47 E
Katzenbuckel, mtn., Ger.	24	G5	49.28 N	9.02 E
Kauai, i., Hi., U.S.	100a	b2	22.00 N	159.30 W
Kauai Channel, strt., Hi., U.S.	100a	b3	21.45 N	158.50 W
Kau Desert, des., Hi., U.S.	100a	d6	19.19 N	155.22 W
Kaufbeuren, Ger.	24	I6	47.53 N	10.37 E
Kaufman, Tx., U.S.	136	B11	32.35 N	96.20 W
Kauhajoki, Fin.	18	E9	62.26 N	22.13 E
Kauhanevan-Pohjankankaan kansallispuisto, p.o.i., Fin.	18	E9	62.08 N	22.25 E
Kauhava, Fin.	18	D10	63.05 N	23.02 E
Kauiki Head, c., Hi., U.S.	100a	c6	20.45 N	155.59 W
Kaujuitoq see Resolute, Nu., Can.	108	C7	74.41 N	94.53 W
Kaukauna, Wi., U.S.	126	D1	44.15 N	88.16 W
Kaukau Veld, plat., Afr.	88	D3	19.30 S	20.30 E
Kaukonen, Fin.	14	E15	67.28 N	24.55 E
Kaula, i., Hi., U.S.	100a	b1	21.39 N	160.32 W
Kaulakahi Channel, strt., Hi., U.S.	100a	b2	21.59 N	159.57 W
Kauliranta, Fin.	14	F14	66.27 N	23.42 E
Kaulsdorf, ngh., Ger.	182a		52.31 N	13.33 E
Kaulsdorf-Süd, ngh., Ger.	182a		52.29 N	13.34 E
Kaumalapau, Hi., U.S.	100a	c4	20.47 N	156.59 W
Kaunakakai, Hi., U.S.	100a	b4	21.05 N	157.01 W
Kaunas, Lith.	26	F6	54.54 N	23.53 E
Kaupanger, Nor.	16	F5	61.11 N	7.13 E
Kaura-Namoda, Nig.	84	G6	12.35 N	6.34 E
Kausa, India	190c		19.10 N	73.02 E
Kau Sai Chau, i., China	189d		22.22 N	114.18 E
Kausala, Fin.	18	G13	60.53 N	26.22 E
Kaustinen, Fin.	18	D10	63.32 N	23.41 E
Kautokeino, Nor.	14	C10	69.00 N	23.02 E
Kauttua, Fin.	18	F9	61.06 N	22.08 E
Kau-ye Kyun, i., Mya.	64	G4	10.59 N	98.31 E
Kavača, Russia	50	D23	60.15 N	169.54 E
Kavacık, Tur.	34	D11	39.40 N	28.30 E
Kavadarci, Mac.	34	B5	41.26 N	22.00 E
Kavaja see Kavajë, Alb.	32	C13	41.12 N	19.33 E
Kavajë, Alb.	32	C13	41.12 N	19.33 E
Kavaklıdere, Tur.	34	F11	37.26 N	28.21 E
Kavála, Grc.	34	C7	40.56 N	24.24 E
Kavalerovo, Russia	54	B11	44.15 N	135.02 E
Kāvali, India	69	D4	14.54 N	79.59 E
Kavaratti, India	62	F3	10.33 N	72.38 E
Kavaratti Island, i., India	62	F3	10.33 N	72.38 E
Kavarna, Blg.	36	F15	43.26 N	28.21 E
Kavarskas, Lith.	26	E7	55.25 N	24.54 E
Kāveri (Cauvery), stm., India	69	E3	11.08 N	79.50 E
Kāveri Falls, wtfl., India	69	E3	12.15 N	77.07 E
Kavieng, Pap. N. Gui.	101a	a5	2.34 S	150.47 E
Kavīr, Dasht-e, des., Iran	74	C14	34.40 N	54.30 E
Kävlinge, Swe.	16	L11	55.47 N	13.06 E
Kaw, Ok., U.S.	138	E12	36.45 N	96.51 W
Kawa, Mya.	64	D3	17.05 N	96.28 E
Kawagama Lake, l., On., Can.	126	C10	45.18 N	78.45 W
Kawagoe, Japan	56	D12	35.54 N	139.29 E
Kawaguchi, Japan	56	D12	35.47 N	139.43 E
Kawai, Japan	188		34.35 N	135.45 E
Kawaihae Bay, b., Hi., U.S.	100a	d6	20.02 N	155.51 W
Kawaihoa, c., Hi., U.S.	100a	b1	21.47 N	160.12 W
Kawaikini, mtn., Hi., U.S.	100a	a2	22.04 N	159.30 W
Kawakubo, Japan	188		34.54 N	135.38 E
Kawamata, Japan	56	B13	37.39 N	140.36 E
Kawambwa, Zam.	88	B4	9.48 S	29.04 E
Kawanishi, Japan	188		34.35 N	135.47 E
Kawanoe, Japan	56	E6	34.00 N	133.34 E
Kawara, Japan	188		34.59 N	135.18 E
Kawarai, Japan	186		35.25 N	140.05 E
Kawardha, India	70	H8	22.01 N	81.15 E
Kawasaki, Japan	56	D12	35.32 N	139.41 E
Kawasaki, Japan	186		35.30 N	139.42 E
Kawasaki-kō, b., Japan	186		35.30 N	139.47 E
Kawasaki Stadium, p.o.i., Japan	186		35.32 N	139.43 E
Kawashima, ngh., Japan	186		35.28 N	139.35 E
Kawatana, Japan	56	F2	33.04 N	129.52 E
Kawawa, ngh., Japan	186		35.31 N	139.33 E
Kawbein, Mya.	64	D3	16.33 N	97.52 E
Kawdut, Mya.	64	E3	15.30 N	97.47 E
Kaweenakumik Lake, l., Mb., Can.	142	B14	52.52 N	99.30 W
Kawhia Harbour, b., N.Z.	102	D6	38.05 S	174.50 E
Kawich Peak, mtn., Nv., U.S.	148	F9	37.58 N	116.27 W
Kawich Range, mts., Nv., U.S.	148	F9	37.51 N	116.23 W
Kawinda, Indon.	66	H11	8.07 S	118.04 E
Kawit, Phil.	187f		14.27 N	120.54 E
Kawkareik, Mya.	64	D4	16.33 N	98.14 E
Kaw Lake, res., Ok., U.S.	138	E12	36.48 N	96.55 W
Kawludo, Mya.	64	C3	18.29 N	97.19 E
Kawm Bira, Egypt	191c		30.05 N	31.08 E
Kawm Ishfīn, Egypt	191c		30.11 N	31.15 E
Kawnipi Lake, l., On., Can.	128	C7	48.25 N	91.17 W
Kawthaung, Mya.	64	H4	9.59 N	98.33 E
Kax, stm., China	48	F14	43.37 N	81.47 E
Kaxgar, stm., China	48	G13	39.25 N	76.25 E
Kaya, Burkina	84	G4	13.05 N	1.05 W
Kayaapu, Indon.	66	F3	5.29 S	102.20 E
Kayah, state, Mya.	64	C3	19.15 N	97.30 E
Kayak Island, i., Ak., U.S.	109	E11	59.54 N	144.27 W
Kāyalpattinam, India	69	G4	8.33 N	78.06 E
Kayan, Mya.	64	D3	16.54 N	96.34 E
Kayan, stm., Indon.	66	B10	2.55 N	117.34 E
Kayang-san, hill, Kor., S.	189b		37.33 N	126.43 E
Kāyankulam, India	69	G3	9.10 N	76.30 E
Kaycee, Wy., U.S.	140	D6	43.42 N	106.40 W
Kayenta, Az., U.S.	150	G6	36.41 N	110.14 W
Kayes, Mali	84	G2	14.27 N	11.26 W
Kay Gardens, N.J., U.S.	203		39.45 N	75.25 W
Kayin, state, Mya.	64	D3	17.30 N	97.45 E
Kayış Dağı, mtn., Tur.	185b		40.59 N	29.10 E
Kaymaz, Tur.	34	D14	39.31 N	31.11 E
Kaypak, Tur.	76	A7	37.08 N	36.27 E
Kayseri, Tur.	42	F6	38.44 N	35.29 E
Kayseri, state, Tur.	42	F7	38.30 N	35.55 E
Kaysville, Ut., U.S.	150	B5	41.03 N	111.56 W
Kayuadi, Pulau, i., Indon.	66	G12	6.48 S	120.47 E
Kayuagung, Indon.	66	E4	3.22 S	104.50 E
Kayumas, Indon.	66	G9	7.55 S	114.08 E
Kazače, Russia	50	B16	70.44 N	136.12 E
Kazačinskoe, Russia	48	C19	56.16 N	107.36 E
Kazačinskoe, Russia	50	E7	57.49 N	93.19 E
Kazahskij melkosopočnik (Kazakh Hills), hills, Kaz.	48	D12	49.00 N	72.00 E
Kazahskij zaliv, b., Kaz.	42	D15	42.38 N	52.23 E
Kazahstan see Kazakhstan, ctry., Asia	48	E10	47.00 N	76.00 E
Kazakh Hills see Kazahskij melkosopočnik, hills, Kaz.	48	D12	49.00 N	72.00 E
Kazakhstan, ctry., Asia	48	E10	47.00 N	76.00 E
Kazaki, Russia	26	H21	52.37 N	38.16 E
Kazalinsk, Kaz.	48	E10	45.45 N	62.05 E
Kazan', Russia	40	D16	55.50 N	49.04 E
Kazan, Russia	46	D8	55.50 N	49.04 E
Kazan, stm., Can.	110	C11	64.10 N	95.22 W
Kazancı, Tur.	76	B3	36.30 N	32.52 E
Kazanka, Ukr.	38	F11	47.50 N	32.50 E
Kazanlăk, Blg.	36	G12	42.37 N	25.24 E
Kazanlı, Tur.	76	B5	36.50 N	34.44 E
Kazanovka, Russia	26	G21	53.46 N	38.34 E
Kazan-rettō, is., Japan	46	G18	25.00 N	141.00 E
Kazanskoe, Russia	48	C11	55.38 N	69.13 E
Kazan' Station, trans., Russia	183b		55.46 N	37.40 E
Kazantyp, mys, c., Ukr.	38	H14	45.28 N	35.51 E
Kazarman, Kyrg.	72	A11	41.24 N	74.01 E
Kazbek, gora, vol.	42	D11	42.42 N	44.31 E
Kaz Dağı, mtn., Tur.	34	D9	39.42 N	26.50 E
Kazenyi Torets', stm., Ukr.	38	E16	48.38 N	37.32 E
Kāzerūn, Iran	74	F12	29.36 N	51.39 E
Kazimierza Wielka, Pol.	24	F16	50.16 N	20.29 E
Kazimierz Dolny, Pol.	24	E18	51.19 N	22.00 E
Kazincbarcika, Hung.	36	A7	48.15 N	20.39 E
Kazinka, Russia	38	C16	50.14 N	37.51 E
Kazinka, Russia	40	E11	52.32 N	39.45 E
Kāzipāra, India	190b		22.43 N	88.31 E
Kaziranga National Park, p.o.i., India	70	E14	26.45 N	93.23 E
Kaz'jany, Bela.	26	E9	55.18 N	26.52 E
Kazlouščyna, Bela.	26	G8	53.19 N	25.16 E
Kazlų Rūda, Lith.	26	F6	54.44 N	23.30 E
Kaztalovka, Kaz.	48	E7	49.46 N	48.41 E
Kazula, Moz.	88	D5	15.23 S	33.37 E
Kazvin see Qazvīn, Iran	74	B11	36.16 N	49.58 E
Kazym, Russia	48	B11	63.41 N	66.45 E
Kazym, stm., Russia	48	B11	63.52 N	65.53 E
Kazyr, stm., Russia	48	D16	53.50 N	93.07 E
Kbal Dâmrei, Camb.	64	E7	14.06 N	105.20 E
Kcynia, Pol.	24	C13	52.59 N	17.29 E
Kdyně, Czech Rep.	24	G9	49.23 N	13.02 E
Kéa, Grc.	34	F7	37.37 N	24.21 E
Kéa, i., Grc.	34	F7	37.38 N	24.20 E
Keaau, Hi., U.S.	100a	d6	19.38 N	155.02 W
Keahole Point, c., Hi., U.S.	100a	d5	19.44 N	156.03 W
Kealaikahiki, Lae o, c., Hi., U.S.	100a	c5	20.32 N	156.42 W
Kealaikahiki Channel, strt., Hi., U.S.	100a	c5	20.40 N	156.45 W
Kealakekua Bay, b., Hi., U.S.	100a	d5	19.28 N	155.56 W
Keams Canyon, Az., U.S.	150	H6	35.48 N	110.12 W
Keanapapa Point, c., Hi., U.S.	100a	c4	20.53 N	157.03 W
Kean College of New Jersey, educ., N.J., U.S.	194		40.41 N	74.14 W
Kearney, Mo., U.S.	130	E3	39.22 N	94.21 W
Kearney, Ne., U.S.	130	G13	40.41 N	99.04 W
Kearns, Ut., U.S.	150	C4	40.38 N	112.00 W
Kearny, Az., U.S.	150	J6	33.06 N	110.53 W
Kearsley, Eng., U.K.	180		53.32 N	2.23 W
Keasbey, N.J., U.S.	194		40.31 N	74.19 W
Keb', stm., Russia	26	C11	57.44 N	28.28 E
Kebajoran, ngh., Indon.	187e		6.13 S	106.46 E
Keban Barajı, res., Tur.	42	F8	38.55 N	38.55 E
Keban Reservoir see Keban Barajı, res., Tur.	42	F8	38.55 N	38.55 E
Kébémer, Sen.	84	F1	15.22 N	16.27 W
Kebnekaise, mtn., Swe.	14	D9	67.55 N	18.35 E
K'ebrī Dehar, Eth.	82	F8	6.44 N	44.16 E
Kecel, Hung.	30	D16	46.31 N	19.15 E
Kech, stm., Pak.	62	C1	25.59 N	62.43 E
Kechika, stm., B.C., Can.	110	D5	59.37 N	127.07 W
Keçiborlu, Tur.	34	F13	37.59 N	30.17 E
Kecskemét, Hung.	36	C6	46.54 N	19.42 E
Kedah, state, Malay.	64	J5	6.00 N	100.40 E
Kėdainiai, Lith.	26	E6	55.17 N	23.59 E
Kedgwick, N.B., Can.	122	C9	47.38 N	67.22 W
Kedgwick, stm., Can.	122	C9	47.39 N	67.29 W
Kediri, Indon.	66	G8	7.49 S	112.01 E
Kedon, Russia	50	D20	64.08 N	159.14 E
Kédougou, Sen.	84	G2	12.33 N	12.10 W
Kedrozero, Russia	18	E21	62.21 N	34.30 E
Kędzierzyn-Koźle, Pol.	24	F14	50.20 N	18.12 E
Keefers, B.C., Can.	144	F9	50.02 N	121.33 W
Keele, stm., N.T., Can.	110	C5	64.24 N	124.50 W
Keele Peak, mtn., Yk., Can.	110	C4	63.26 N	130.19 W
Keeling Islands see Cocos Islands, dep., Oc.	174	K12	12.10 S	96.55 E
Keelung see Chilung, Tai.	58	I9	25.07 N	121.43 E
Keene, Ky., U.S.	130	G13	37.56 N	84.37 W
Keene, N.H., U.S.	124	B13	42.55 N	72.17 W
Keene, Tx., U.S.	136	B10	32.24 N	97.19 W
Keenesburg, Co., U.S.	138	A4	40.06 N	104.31 W
Keeney Knob, mtn., W.V., U.S.	124	G5	37.47 N	80.42 W
Keeneyville, Il., U.S.	196		41.59 N	88.07 W
Keer-Weer, Cape, c., Austl.	96	B8	13.51 S	141.28 E
Keeseville, N.Y., U.S.	126	D16	44.30 N	73.28 W
Keesler Air Force Base, mil., Ms., U.S.	134	G10	30.26 N	88.55 W
Keetmanshoop, Nmb.	90	E3	26.35 S	18.08 E
Keewatin, On., Can.	128	B4	49.44 N	94.38 W
Keewatin, Mn., U.S.	128	D5	47.23 N	93.04 W
Kefaloniá, i., Grc.	34	E3	38.13 N	20.34 E
Kefamenanu, Indon.	60	G7	9.25 S	124.28 E
Kefar Naḥum (Capernaum), hist., Isr.	76	F6	32.53 N	35.34 E
Kefar Sava, Isr.	76	F5	32.11 N	34.54 E
Keffi, Nig.	84	H6	8.50 N	7.52 E
Keflavík, Ice.	12a	k28	64.01 N	22.34 W
Kega, Russia	18	B23	65.08 N	43.53 E
Ke Ga, Mui, c., Viet.	64	G8	10.41 N	107.59 E
Ke Ga, Mui, c., Viet.	64	F9	12.53 N	109.26 E
Kegalla, Sri L.	69	H5	7.14 N	80.21 E
Kegonzhake, China	70	B11	33.00 N	87.53 E
Keg River, Ab., Can.	110	D7	57.44 N	117.39 W
Kegums, Lat.	26	D7	56.44 N	24.44 E
Kehiwin Indian Reserve, ind. res., Ab., Can.	144	B19	54.05 N	110.50 W
Kehra, Est.	26	A8	59.20 N	25.20 E
Ke-hsi Mānsām, Mya.	64	B3	21.56 N	97.51 E
Kehychivka, Ukr.	38	D14	49.17 N	35.46 E
Keighley, Eng., U.K.	10	H10	53.52 N	1.54 W
Keijō see Sŏul, Kor., S.	54	F7	37.33 N	127.00 E
Keila, Est.	26	A7	59.18 N	24.25 E
Keimoes, S. Afr.	90	F5	28.42 S	20.58 E
Keio University, educ., Japan	186		35.38 N	139.45 E
Keiser, Ar., U.S.	134	B8	35.40 N	90.05 W
Keitele, Fin.	18	D13	63.10 N	26.20 E
Keitele, l., Fin.	18	E13	62.57 N	25.59 E
Keith, Austl.	98	K3	36.05 S	140.20 E
Keith, Scot., U.K.	10	D10	57.32 N	2.57 W
Keith Arm, b., N.T., Can.	110	B6	65.20 N	122.15 W
Keithley Creek, B.C., Can.	144	D9	52.45 N	121.25 W
Keithsburg, Il., U.S.	128	J8	41.06 N	90.56 W
Keiyasi, Fiji	101e	p18	17.54 S	177.45 E
Keizer, Or., U.S.	146	F3	44.59 N	123.00 W
Kejimkujik National Park, p.o.i., N.S., Can.	122	F11	44.21 N	65.18 W
Kejvy, mts., Russia	14	E28	67.40 N	37.30 E
Kekaha, Hi., U.S.	100a	b2	21.58 N	159.42 W
Kékes, mtn., Hung.	36	B7	47.51 N	20.01 E
Kekri, India	70	F5	25.57 N	75.09 E
K'elafo, Eth.	82	F8	5.36 N	44.18 E
Kelai, stm., Indon.	66	C10	2.09 N	117.30 E
Kelan, China	58	B4	38.43 N	111.32 E
Kelani, stm., Sri L.	69	H5	6.58 N	79.52 E
Kelantan, state, Malay.	64	J6	5.20 N	102.00 E
Kelantan, stm., Malay.	64	J6	6.11 N	102.14 E
Kelapa, Indon.	66	D4	1.52 S	105.39 E
Kelbia, Sebkhet, l., Tun.	32	I4	35.51 N	10.16 E
Kélékélé, Congo	191b		4.20 S	15.08 E
Kelenföld, ngh., Hung.	182c		47.28 N	19.03 E
Keles, Tur.	34	D12	39.54 N	29.15 E
Keleti-főcsatorna, can., Hung.	24	I17	48.01 N	21.20 E
Keleti Pályaudvar, trans., Hung.	182c		47.30 N	19.06 E
Kelheim, Ger.	24	H7	48.55 N	11.52 E
Kelibia, Tun.	32	H5	36.51 N	11.06 E
Kéllé, Congo	86	E2	0.03 S	14.29 E
Keller, Wa., U.S.	146	B8	48.05 N	118.40 W
Kellerberrin, Austl.	96	F3	31.38 S	117.42 E
Keller Lake, l., N.T., Can.	110	C6	63.56 N	121.33 W
Kellett, Cape, c., N.T., Can.	109	B14	71.58 N	125.59 W
Kelleys Island, i., Oh., U.S.	124	C3	41.36 N	82.41 W
Kelliher, Sk., Can.	118	B14	51.15 N	103.44 W
Kellogg, Id., U.S.	146	C10	47.31 N	116.07 W
Kellogg, Ia., U.S.	130	C5	41.43 N	92.54 W
Kellogg, Mn., U.S.	128	G6	44.18 N	91.59 W
Kellojärvi, l., Fin.	18	C15	64.13 N	29.00 E
Kelloselkä, Fin.	14	F19	66.56 N	28.52 E
Kells, Ire.	10	H6	53.44 N	6.52 W
Kelly Air Force Base, mil., Tx., U.S.	136	E9	29.24 N	98.35 W
Kelly Run, stm., Pa., U.S.	197b		40.15 N	79.55 W
Kelly Run, stm., Pa., U.S.	197b		40.13 N	79.45 W
Kellyville, Austl.	192a		33.43 S	150.57 E
Kellyville, Ok., U.S.	134	B2	35.57 N	96.13 W
Kelmė, Lith.	26	E5	55.37 N	22.54 E
Kel'mentsi, Ukr.	40	G5	48.28 N	26.50 E
Kelmentsi, Ukr.	42	A2	48.28 N	26.50 E
Kélo, Chad	82	F3	9.18 N	15.48 E
Kelolokan, Indon.	66	C10	1.09 N	117.52 E
Kelottijärvi, Fin.	14	D13	68.32 N	21.59 E
Kelowna, B.C., Can.	144	G11	49.53 N	119.29 W
Kelsey Bay, B.C., Can.	144	F5	50.23 N	125.58 W
Kelseyville, Ca., U.S.	148	D3	38.58 N	122.51 W
Kelso, Scot., U.K.	10	F10	55.35 N	2.26 W
Kelso, Wa., U.S.	146	D4	46.08 N	122.54 W
Keluang, Malay.	64	K6	2.01 N	103.19 E
Keluang, Tanjung, c., Indon.	66	E7	3.02 S	110.37 E
Kelujärvi, Fin.	14	E18	67.27 N	27.02 E
Kelvedon Hatch, Eng., U.K.	178		51.40 N	0.16 E
Kelvington, Sk., Can.	142	B10	52.10 N	103.30 W
Kelvin Island, i., On., Can.	128	B10	49.51 N	88.39 W
Kelzenberg, Ger.	181		51.07 N	6.30 E
Kem', Russia	18	C21	64.56 N	34.35 E
Kem', stm., Russia	18	C21	64.57 N	34.41 E
Kema, stm., Russia	18	G24	60.25 N	37.24 E
Kémah, Congo	191b		4.11 S	15.13 E
Kemah, Tur.	42	F8	39.36 N	39.02 E
Kemah, Tx., U.S.	136	E12	29.32 N	95.01 W
Kemano, B.C., Can.	144	C2	53.31 N	127.57 W
Kemayoran Airport, arpt., Indon.	187e		6.09 S	106.51 E
Kembé, C.A.R.	86	D4	4.38 N	21.56 E
Kemena, stm., Malay.	66	B8	3.10 N	113.03 E
Kemer, Tur.	34	G12	36.38 N	29.21 E
Kemer, Tur.	34	F13	37.21 N	30.03 E
Kemer, Tur.	34	G13	36.35 N	30.33 E
Kemer, stm., Tur.	185b		41.04 N	29.07 E
Kemer Barajı, res., Tur.	34	F11	37.31 N	28.34 E
Kemerburgaz, ngh., Tur.	185b		41.09 N	28.54 E
Kemerhisar, Tur.	76	A5	37.48 N	34.36 E
Kemerovo, Russia	48	C15	55.23 N	86.03 E
Kemi, Fin.	18	B11	65.45 N	24.33 E
Kemie, Fin.	18	E17	62.14 N	30.20 E
Kemijärvi, Fin.	14	F18	66.43 N	27.23 E
Kemijärvi, l., Fin.	14	F18	66.36 N	27.24 E
Kemijoki, stm., Fin.	14	F16	65.46 N	24.29 E
Kemiö see Kimito, Fin.	18	G9	60.10 N	22.44 E
Kemlja, Russia	40	D14	54.41 N	45.14 E
Kemmerer, Wy., U.S.	146	I16	41.48 N	110.32 W
Kemminghausen, ngh., Ger.	181		51.34 N	7.29 E
Kemmuna (Comino), i., Malta	32	H8	36.00 N	14.20 E
Kemnader See, l., Ger.	181		51.25 N	7.15 E
Kemnath, Ger.	24	G7	49.52 N	11.54 E
Kemp, Tx., U.S.	136	B11	32.26 N	96.13 W
Kemp, Lake, res., Tx., U.S.	138	H9	33.45 N	99.13 W
Kempele, Fin.	18	C12	64.55 N	25.31 E
Kempener Land, reg., Ger.	181		51.19 N	6.29 E
Kemper see Quimper, Fr.	20	F5	48.00 N	4.06 W
Kemp Mill, Md., U.S.	202c		39.02 N	77.01 W
Kempner, Tx., U.S.	136	C9	31.05 N	98.00 W
Kemps Bay, Bah.	152	C9	24.00 N	77.32 W
Kemps Creek, stm., Austl.	192a		33.51 S	150.46 E
Kempsey, Austl.	98	H9	31.05 S	152.50 E
Kempt, Lac, l., Qc., Can.	110	F16	47.24 N	74.14 W
Kempten, Ger.	24	I6	47.43 N	10.18 E
Kempton Park, state, S. Afr.	191d		26.06 S	28.14 E
Kempton Park Race Course, p.o.i., Eng., U.K.	178		51.25 N	0.23 W
Kemptville, On., Can.	126	C14	45.01 N	75.38 W
Kemsing, Eng., U.K.	178		51.18 N	0.14 E
Kemujan, Pulau, i., Indon.	66	F7	5.48 S	110.28 E
Kemul, Kong, mtn., Indon.	66	C10	1.52 N	116.13 E
Ken, stm., India	70	F8	25.46 N	80.31 E
Ken, Loch, l., Scot., U.K.	10	F8	55.01 N	4.05 W
Kena, stm., Russia	18	E25	62.05 N	39.01 E

Name	Page	Map Ref.	Latitude	Longitude
Kenai, Ak., U.S.	109	D9	60.33 N	151.13 W
Kenai Mountains, mts., Ak., U.S.	109	E9	60.00 N	150.00 W
Kenai Peninsula, pen., Ak., U.S.	109	E9	60.10 N	150.00 W
Kenansville, Fl., U.S.	132	I5	27.52 N	80.58 W
Kenansville, N.C., U.S.	132	B7	34.57 N	77.57 W
Kenaston, Sk., Can.	142	C7	51.30 N	106.16 W
Kenberma, Ma., U.S.	201		42.17 N	70.52 W
Kenbridge, Va., U.S.	124	H7	36.57 N	78.07 W
Kendai, India	70	G9	22.44 N	82.36 E
Kendal, Sk., Can.	142	D10	50.14 N	103.35 W
Kendal, Indon.	66	G7	6.55 S	110.09 E
Kendal, Eng., U.K.	10	G10	54.19 N	2.44 W
Kendall, Austl.	98	H9	31.38 S	152.43 E
Kendall, Fl., U.S.	132	K5	25.39 N	80.19 W
Kendall, Wi., U.S.	128	H8	43.47 N	90.22 W
Kendall, Cape, c., Nu., Can.	110	C13	63.36 N	87.09 W
Kendallville, In., U.S.	130	C12	41.26 N	85.15 W
Kendari, Indon.	60	F7	3.56 S	122.35 E
Kendawangan, Indon.	66	E7	2.30 S	110.12 E
Kendirli-Kajasanskoe plato, plat., Kaz.	42	D15	42.25 N	53.00 E
Kendrāparha, India	70	H11	20.30 N	86.25 E
Kendrew, S. Afr.	90	H7	32.32 S	24.29 E
Kendrick, Fl., U.S.	132	G3	29.14 N	82.10 W
Kendrick, Id., U.S.	146	D10	46.36 N	116.39 W
Kendua, India	190b		22.34 N	88.10 E
Kendujhargarh, India	70	H10	21.37 N	85.36 E
Kenedy, Tx., U.S.	136	F10	28.48 N	97.50 W
Kenema, S.L.	84	H2	7.52 N	11.11 W
Kenesaw, Ne., U.S.	140	G14	40.37 N	98.39 W
Kenga, Russia	48	C14	57.27 N	81.00 E
Kenge, D.R.C.	86	E3	4.51 S	16.55 E
Kĕng Hkam, Mya.	64	B4	21.01 N	98.29 E
Keng Hkam, Mya.	64	B3	21.26 N	97.03 E
Kĕng Tung, Mya.	64	B4	21.17 N	99.36 E
Kengun-chūtonchi, Rikujō-jieitai-, mil., Japan	56	G3	32.46 N	130.45 E
Kenhardt, S. Afr.	90	F5	29.19 S	21.09 E
Kéniéba, Mali	84	G2	12.49 N	11.15 W
Kenilworth, Il., U.S.	196		42.05 N	87.43 W
Kenilworth, N.J., U.S.	194		40.40 N	74.17 W
Kenilworth, Ut., U.S.	150	D6	39.43 N	110.49 W
Keningau, Malay.	66	A10	5.20 N	116.09 E
Kénitra, Mor.	84	C3	34.16 N	6.34 W
Kenley, ngh., Eng., U.K.	178		51.19 N	0.06 W
Kenly, N.C., U.S.	132	A7	35.35 N	78.07 W
Kenmare, Ire.	10	J3	51.53 N	9.35 W
Kenmare, N.D., U.S.	142	F11	48.41 N	102.04 W
Kenmare River, stm., Ire.	10	J2	51.53 N	9.33 W
Kenmawr, Pa., U.S.	197b		40.28 N	80.06 W
Kennard, Tx., U.S.	136	C12	31.21 N	95.11 W
Kennebec, S.D., U.S.	140	D13	43.54 N	99.51 W
Kennebec, stm., Me., U.S.	122	F7	43.45 N	69.46 W
Kennebecasis Bay, b., N.B., Can.	122	E11	45.25 N	66.01 W
Kennebunk, Me., U.S.	122	G6	43.23 N	70.32 W
Kennedy, Al., U.S.	134	D11	33.35 N	87.59 W
Kennedy, Cape see Canaveral, Cape, c., Fl., U.S.	132	H5	28.27 N	80.32 W
Kennedy, Mount, mtn., B.C., Can.	144	F5	50.49 N	125.33 W
Kennedy, Mount, mtn., Yk., Can.	110	C3	60.30 N	139.00 W
Kennedy Channel, strt., Can.	108	A12	80.45 N	66.29 W
Kennedy Lake, l., B.C., Can.	144	G5	49.03 N	125.33 W
Kennedy Peak, mtn., Mya.	62	D7	23.19 N	93.45 E
Kenner, La., U.S.	134	G8	29.59 N	90.15 W
Kennet, stm., Eng., U.K.	10	J11	51.27 N	0.57 W
Kennetcook, N.S., Can.	122	E13	45.10 N	63.43 W
Kennett, Mo., U.S.	130	H7	36.14 N	90.02 W
Kennewick, Wa., U.S.	146	D7	46.12 N	119.06 W
Kenney Dam, dam., B.C., Can.	144	C6	53.37 N	124.58 W
Kennywood Park, p.o.i., Pa., U.S.	197b		40.23 N	79.52 W
Kenogami, stm., On., Can.	110	E13	51.05 N	84.30 W
Kénogami, Lac, res., Qc., Can.	122	B5	48.20 N	71.23 W
Keno Hill, Yk., Can.	110	C3	63.54 N	135.17 W
Kenora, On., Can.	128	B4	49.46 N	94.29 W
Kenosha, Wi., U.S.	130	B10	42.35 N	87.49 W
Kenova, W.V., U.S.	124	F3	38.23 N	82.35 W
Kenoza Lake, l., Ma., U.S.	201		42.47 N	71.03 W
Kenozero, ozero, l., Russia	18	E25	62.03 N	38.14 E
Kensal, N.D., U.S.	142	G15	47.17 N	98.45 W
Kensett, Ar., U.S.	134	B7	35.14 N	91.40 W
Kensico Lake, l., N.Y., U.S.	194		41.07 N	73.45 W
Kensington, Austl.	192a		33.55 S	151.14 E
Kensington, P.E., Can.	122	D13	46.26 N	63.38 W
Kensington, Ks., U.S.	138	B9	39.45 N	99.01 W
Kensington, Md., U.S.	202c		39.01 N	77.04 W
Kensington, ngh., S. Afr.	191d		26.12 S	28.06 E
Kensington, ngh., N.Y., U.S.	194		40.39 N	73.58 W
Kensington, ngh., Pa., U.S.	203		39.58 N	75.08 W
Kensington and Chelsea, ngh., Eng., U.K.	178		51.29 N	0.11 W
Kensington Estates, Md., U.S.	202c		39.02 N	77.05 W
Kensington Metropolitan Park, p.o.i., Mi., U.S.	199		42.32 N	83.39 W
Kensington Park, Fl., U.S.	132	I3	27.21 N	82.31 W
Kent, Oh., U.S.	124	C4	41.08 N	81.21 W
Kent, Wa., U.S.	146	C4	47.23 N	122.12 W
Kentau, Kaz.	48	F11	43.30 N	68.30 E
Kentfield, Ca., U.S.	200		37.57 N	122.33 W
Kent Group, is., Austl.	98	L6	39.27 S	147.19 E
Kenthurst, Austl.	192a		33.40 S	151.00 E
Kentland, In., U.S.	130	D10	40.45 N	87.26 W
Kentland, Md., U.S.	202c		38.55 N	76.53 W
Kenton, Mi., U.S.	128	E10	46.30 N	88.52 W
Kenton, Oh., U.S.	124	D2	40.38 N	83.36 W
Kenton, Tn., U.S.	130	H8	36.12 N	89.00 W
Kent Park, Ma., U.S.	201		42.06 N	70.41 W
Kent Park, p.o.i., S. Afr.	191d		26.08 S	28.04 E
Kent Peninsula, pen., Nu., Can.	110	B9	68.30 N	107.00 W
Kentrikí Makedonía, state, Grc.	34	C6	40.30 N	23.00 E
Kentucky, state, U.S.	130	G12	37.30 N	85.15 W
Kentucky, stm., Ky., U.S.	130	F13	38.40 N	85.11 W
Kentucky, Middle Fork, stm., Ky., U.S.	124	G2	37.34 N	83.40 W
Kentucky, North Fork, stm., Ky., U.S.	124	G2	37.35 N	83.40 W
Kentucky, South Fork, stm., Ky., U.S.	124	G2	37.34 N	83.42 W
Kentucky Lake, res., U.S.	130	H9	36.41 N	88.03 W
Kent Village, Md., U.S.	202c		38.55 N	76.53 W
Kentville, N.S., Can.	122	E12	45.04 N	64.29 W
Kentwood, La., U.S.	134	G8	30.56 N	90.30 W
Kent Woodlands, Ca., U.S.	200		37.57 N	122.34 W
Kenvil, N.J., U.S.	194		40.52 N	74.37 W
Kenwood, Md., U.S.	202b		39.21 N	76.31 W
Kenwood, ngh., Il., U.S.	196		41.49 N	87.36 W
Kenwood, hist., Eng., U.K.	178		51.34 N	0.10 W
Kenya, ctry., Afr.	82	G7	1.00 N	38.00 E
Kenya, Mount see Kirinyaga, mtn., Kenya	86	E7	0.09 S	37.18 E
Kenyon, Eng., U.K.	180		53.27 N	2.34 W
Kenyon, Mn., U.S.	128	G6	44.16 N	93.00 W
Ken-zaki, c., Japan	186		35.08 N	139.41 E
Keokea, Hi., U.S.	100a	c5	20.42 N	156.21 W
Keokuk, Ia., U.S.	130	D6	40.23 N	91.23 W
Keoladeo National Park, p.o.i., India	70	E6	27.10 N	77.20 E
Keon Park, Austl.	192b		37.42 S	145.01 E
Keo Nua, Deo, p., Asia	64	C7	18.23 N	105.09 E
Keosauqua, Ia., U.S.	130	D5	40.44 N	91.57 W
Keota, Ia., U.S.	130	C6	41.22 N	91.56 W
Keota, Ok., U.S.	134	B4	35.14 N	94.55 W
Keowee, Lake, res., S.C., U.S.	132	B2	34.45 N	82.55 W
Kepa, Russia	18	B19	65.09 N	32.07 E
Kepa, stm., Russia	18	C19	64.48 N	32.19 E
Kepi, Indon.	60	G10	6.32 S	139.19 E
Kępice, Pol.	24	B12	54.14 N	16.53 E
Kepina, Russia	12	D19	65.23 N	41.51 E
Kępno, Pol.	24	E13	51.16 N	18.00 E
Kepo, Indon.	66	E5	2.56 S	106.32 E
Keppel Bay, b., Austl.	98	D8	23.23 S	150.54 E
Keppel Harbour, b., Sing.	189c		1.16 N	103.50 E
Kepsut, Tur.	34	D11	39.41 N	28.08 E
Kerala, state, India	69	F3	10.00 N	76.30 E
Keramadoo, mtn., Palau	100b	f8	7.31 N	134.32 E
Keramian, Pulau, i., Indon.	66	F9	5.04 S	114.36 E
Kerandin, Indon.	66	D4	0.12 S	104.43 E
Kerang, Austl.	98	J4	35.44 S	143.55 E
Keratéa, Grc.	34	F6	37.48 N	23.58 E
Keratsinion, Grc.	185c		37.58 N	23.37 E
Kerava, Fin.	18	G12	60.24 N	25.07 E
Keravat, Pap. N. Gui.	101a	a5	4.17 S	152.01 E
Kerbela see Karbalā', Iraq	74	D9	32.36 N	44.01 E
Kerby, Or., U.S.	148	A2	42.12 N	123.37 W
Kerč' see Kerch, Ukr.	38	H15	45.21 N	36.27 E
Kerčenskij proliv see Kerch Strait, strt., Eur.	38	I15	45.22 N	36.40 E
Kerch, Ukr.	38	H15	45.21 N	36.27 E
Kerchens'ka protoka see Kerch Strait, strt., Eur.	38	I15	45.22 N	36.40 E
Kerchens'kyi pivostriv, pen., Ukr.	38	H15	45.15 N	36.00 E
Kerch Strait, strt., Eur.	38	I15	45.22 N	36.40 E
Kerec, mys, c., Russia	18	B26	65.20 N	39.43 E
Kerema, Pap. N. Gui.	101a	b4	7.59 S	145.47 E
Keremeos, B.C., Can.	144	G11	49.12 N	119.49 W
Kerempe Burnu, c., Tur.	34	A16	42.00 N	33.20 E
Keren, Erit.	82	D7	15.46 N	38.27 E
Kerend, Iran	74	C10	34.15 N	46.13 E
Kerens, Tx., U.S.	136	B11	32.08 N	96.13 W
Kerepes, Hung.	182c		47.34 N	19.18 E
Keret', Russia	14	F24	66.15 N	33.32 E
Keret', ozero, l., Russia	18	B19	65.53 N	32.59 E
Kerewan, Gam.	84	G1	13.28 N	16.05 W
Kerga, Russia	12	E21	62.38 N	46.00 E
Kerguelen, Archipel de, is., Afr.	2	J17	49.15 S	69.10 E
Kerguélen, Îles de, is., Afr.	80	K12	49.15 S	69.10 E
Kerguelen Plateau, unds.	174	O10	55.00 S	75.00 E
Keri, Grc.	34	F3	37.40 N	20.48 E
Kericho, Kenya	86	E7	0.22 S	35.15 E
Kerimäki, Fin.	18	F16	61.55 N	29.17 E
Kerinci, Gunung, vol., Indon.	66	D2	1.41 S	101.16 E
Keritang, Indon.	66	D3	0.51 S	102.39 E
Kerka, stm., Hung.	30	D13	46.27 N	16.38 E
Kerkenna, Îles, is., Tun.	84	C7	34.44 N	11.12 E
Kerkhoven, Mn., U.S.	128	F3	45.11 N	95.19 W
Kerkiči, Turkmen.	72	B10	37.49 N	65.12 E
Kerkrade, Neth.	24	F2	50.52 N	6.04 E
Kérkyra (Corfu), Grc.	34	D2	39.37 N	19.55 E
Kérkyra (Corfu), i., Grc.	34	D2	39.40 N	19.45 E
Kermadec Islands, is., N.Z.	94	F9	29.16 S	177.55 W
Kermadec Ridge, unds.	174	M20	30.30 S	178.30 W
Kermadec Trench, unds.	174	M21	30.01 S	176.26 W
Kermajärvi, l., Fin.	18	E15	62.28 N	28.40 E
Kermān, Iran	72	C8	30.17 N	57.03 E
Kerman, Ca., U.S.	148	G5	36.43 N	120.03 W
Kermān, state, Iran	74	E14	30.14 N	56.05 E
Kermānshāh (Bākhtarān), Iran	74	C10	34.18 N	47.03 E
Kermānshāh, state, Iran	74	C10	34.30 N	47.00 E
Kermānshāhān see Kermānshāh, state, Iran	74	C10	34.30 N	47.00 E
Kerme, Gulf of see Gökova Körfezi, b., Tur.	34	G10	36.53 N	27.50 E
Kermit, Tx., U.S.	136	C4	31.51 N	103.05 W
Kern, stm., Ca., U.S.	148	H7	35.13 N	119.15 W
Kern, South Fork, stm., Ca., U.S.	148	H7	35.39 N	118.27 W
Kernersville, N.C., U.S.	124	H5	36.06 N	80.04 W
Kernville, Ca., U.S.	148	H7	35.46 N	118.26 W
Kérouané, Gui.	84	H3	9.16 N	9.01 W
Kerridge, Eng., U.K.	180		53.17 N	2.06 W
Kerridge Hill, hill, Eng., U.K.	180		53.17 N	2.06 W
Kerrobert, Sk., Can.	142	C4	51.55 N	109.08 W
Kerruish Park, p.o.i., Oh., U.S.	197a		41.26 N	81.34 W
Kerrville, Tx., U.S.	136	D8	30.02 N	99.07 W
Kerry, state, Ire.	10	I3	52.12 N	9.58 W
Kerry Head, c., Ire.	10	I2	52.24 N	9.56 W
Kershaw, S.C., U.S.	132	B5	34.33 N	80.35 W
Kersley, B.C., Can.	144	D8	52.48 N	122.25 W
Kerspestausee, res., Ger.	181		51.08 N	7.30 E
Kertamulia, Indon.	66	D6	0.23 S	109.07 E
Kerteminde, Den.	16	L8	55.26 N	10.39 E
Kertih, Malay.	64	J6	4.30 N	103.26 E
Kerulen, stm., Asia	52	B7	48.45 N	117.02 E
Kerzaz, Alg.	84	D4	29.32 N	1.31 W
Kerzendorf, Ger.	182a		52.16 N	13.17 E
Ke Sach, Viet.	64	H8	9.46 N	105.58 E
Kesagami Lake, l., On., Can.	114	A10	50.23 N	80.15 W
Kesälahti, Fin.	18	F16	61.53 N	29.49 E
Keşan, Tur.	34	C9	40.52 N	26.38 E
Kesbern, Ger.	181		51.20 N	7.42 E
Kesennuma, Japan	54	E14	38.54 N	141.34 E
Keshan, China	52	B10	48.01 N	125.52 E
Keshena, Wi., U.S.	128	G10	44.52 N	88.38 W
Keshod, India	70	H3	21.18 N	70.14 E
Keskin, Tur.	42	F5	39.41 N	33.37 E
Keski-Suomi, state, Fin.	18	E12	62.30 N	25.30 E
Keskozero, Russia	18	F20	61.23 N	33.14 E
Kes'ma, Russia	26	B20	58.27 N	37.04 E
Kesova Gora, Russia	26	C20	57.35 N	37.18 E
Kessebüren, Ger.	181		51.31 N	7.43 E
Kestell, S. Afr.	90	F9	28.17 S	28.37 E
Kesten'ga, Russia	18	B18	65.54 N	31.49 E
Kestilä, Fin.	18	C13	64.20 N	26.18 E
Keston, ngh., Eng., U.K.	178		51.22 N	0.02 E
Keswick, Eng., U.K.	10	G9	54.36 N	3.08 W
Keszthely, Hung.	36	C4	46.46 N	17.15 E
Ket', stm., Russia	48	C14	58.54 N	81.32 E
Keta, Ghana	84	H5	5.55 N	0.59 E
Keta, ozero, l., Russia	50	C6	68.43 N	90.00 E
Ketam, Pulau, i., Sing.	189c		1.24 N	103.57 E
Ketapang, Indon.	66	D6	1.52 S	109.58 E
Ketapang, Indon.	66	F4	5.44 S	105.46 E
Ketapang, Indon.	66	G8	6.54 S	113.17 E
Ketaun, Indon.	66	E2	3.22 S	101.48 E
Ketčenery, Russia	40	H14	47.17 N	44.35 E
Ketchikan, Ak., U.S.	109	E13	55.20 N	131.35 W
Ketchum, Id., U.S.	146	G12	43.41 N	114.23 W
Kete-Krachi, Ghana	84	H4	7.47 N	0.03 W
Ketoj, ostrov, i., Russia	50	G19	47.20 N	152.28 E
Kętrzyn, Pol.	24	B17	54.04 N	21.23 E
Kettering, Eng., U.K.	10	I12	52.23 N	0.44 W
Kettering, Md., U.S.	202c		38.53 N	76.49 W
Kettering, Oh., U.S.	124	E1	39.41 N	84.10 W
Kettle, stm., N.A.	144	H12	48.40 N	118.05 W
Kettle, stm., Mn., U.S.	128	E6	45.51 N	92.43 W
Kettle Creek, stm., Pa., U.S.	126	G12	41.17 N	77.50 W
Kettle Falls, Wa., U.S.	146	B8	48.36 N	118.03 W
Kettleshulme, Eng., U.K.	180		53.19 N	2.01 W
Kęty, Pol.	24	G15	49.53 N	19.12 E
Keudepasi, Indon.	64	J2	4.18 N	95.56 E
Keudeteunom, Indon.	64	J2	4.27 N	95.48 E
Keuka Lake, l., N.Y., U.S.	124	B8	42.27 N	77.10 W
Keukenhof, misc. cult., Neth.	20	B13	52.16 N	4.33 E
Keul', Russia	48	C18	58.25 N	102.49 E
Keuruusselkä, l., Fin.	18	E11	62.10 N	24.40 E
Keuruu, Fin.	18	E11	62.15 N	24.43 E
Kevdo-Mel'sitovo, Russia	40	E13	53.09 N	43.53 E
Kevelaer, Ger.	24	E2	51.35 N	6.14 E
Kevin, Mt., U.S.	146	B14	48.44 N	111.57 W
Kevon luonnonpuisto, ind. res., Fin.	14	C17	69.35 N	26.43 E
Kew, T./C. Is.	156	A12	21.56 N	72.00 W
Kewanee, Il., U.S.	130	C7	41.14 N	89.55 W
Kewanna, In., U.S.	130	D11	41.00 N	86.24 W
Kewaunee, Wi., U.S.	126	D2	44.27 N	87.30 W
Keweenaw Bay, b., Mi., U.S.	128	E10	46.57 N	88.19 W
Keweenaw Peninsula, pen., Mi., U.S.	128	D11	47.12 N	88.25 W
Keweenaw Point, c., Mi., U.S.	128	D11	47.27 N	87.50 W
Kew Gardens, p.o.i., On., Can.	193b		43.40 N	79.18 W
Kew Gardens, p.o.i., Eng., U.K.	178		51.28 N	0.18 W
Key, Lough, l., Ire.	10	G4	54.00 N	8.15 W
Keyangkeer Shan, mtn., China	70	C11	31.20 N	87.25 E
Keya Paha, stm., U.S.	140	D13	42.54 N	99.00 W
Keyes, Ok., U.S.	138	E6	36.48 N	102.15 W
Keyhole Reservoir, res., Wy., U.S.	140	C8	44.21 N	104.51 W
Keyhole State Park, p.o.i., Wy., U.S.	140	C7	44.22 N	104.49 W
Key Largo, Fl., U.S.	132	K5	25.06 N	80.25 W
Key Largo, i., Fl., U.S.	132	K5	25.11 N	80.21 W
Keyport, N.J., U.S.	194		40.25 N	74.12 W
Keyport Harbor, b., N.J., U.S.	194		40.26 N	74.12 W
Keysborough, Austl.	192b		38.00 S	145.10 E
Keyser, W.V., U.S.	124	E7	39.26 N	78.59 W
Keystone, Ia., U.S.	130	B5	42.00 N	92.11 W
Keystone, S.D., U.S.	140	D9	43.53 N	103.25 W
Keystone, W.V., U.S.	124	G4	37.23 N	81.25 W
Keystone Lake, res., Ok., U.S.	134	A2	36.16 N	96.25 W
Keystone Peak, mtn., Az., U.S.	150	L5	31.53 N	111.13 W
Keysville, Va., U.S.	124	G7	37.01 N	78.29 W
Keytesville, Mo., U.S.	130	E5	39.25 N	92.56 W
Key West, Fl., U.S.	132	L4	24.33 N	81.47 W
Key West Naval Air Station, mil., Fl., U.S.	132	L4	24.34 N	81.41 W
Kez, Russia	32	C8	57.54 N	53.44 E
Kezi, Zimb.	88	E4	20.56 S	28.28 E
Kežma, Russia	48	C18	58.59 N	101.09 E
Kežmarok, Slvk.	24	G16	49.07 N	20.25 E
Kgalagadi, state, Bots.	90	D5	25.00 S	22.00 E
Kgatleng, state, Bots.	90	D8	24.28 S	26.05 E
Khabīr, Kūh-e, mtn., Iran	74	F15	28.48 N	56.26 E
Khābūr, Nahr al-, stm., Asia	74	C7	35.08 N	40.26 E
Khādar, India	190a		28.33 N	77.22 E
Khadaungnge Taung, mtn., Mya.	64	C2	18.57 N	94.37 E
Khadki, India	69	B1	18.34 N	73.52 E
Khadra, Alg.	28	H11	36.14 N	0.32 E
Khadzhybeis'kyi lyman, l., Ukr.	38	G9	46.39 N	30.33 E
Khagaria, India	70	F11	25.30 N	86.27 E
Khāgrāmuri, India	190b		22.26 N	88.14 E
Khairāgarh, India	70	H8	21.25 N	80.59 E
Khairna, India	190c		19.06 N	73.01 E
Khairpur, Pak.	70	E2	27.31 N	68.45 E
Khairpur, Pak.	70	D4	29.34 N	72.14 E
Khairwāra, India	70	F4	23.59 N	73.35 E
Khajrāho, India	70	F8	24.50 N	79.58 E
Khajuri, ngh., India	190a		28.43 N	77.16 E
Khakassia see Hakasija, state, Russia	48	D16	53.00 N	90.00 E
Kha Khaeng, stm., Thai.	64	E4	14.55 N	99.07 E
Khakhea, Bots.	90	D6	24.44 S	23.31 E
Khalatse, India	70	A6	34.19 N	76.52 E
Khālidī, Khirbat al-, hist., Jord.	76	I6	29.39 N	35.14 E
Khalīya, Gebel, mtn., Egypt	76	I3	29.55 N	32.09 E
Khalkhāl, Iran	74	B11	37.37 N	48.32 E
Khālsar, India	70	A6	34.31 N	77.40 E
Khalturyne, Ukr.	38	D14	49.31 N	35.17 E
Khalūf, Oman	72	E8	20.28 N	58.03 E
Khambhāliya, India	70	G2	22.13 N	69.38 E
Khambhāt, India	70	G4	22.18 N	72.37 E
Khambhāt, Gulf of, b., India	70	H3	20.56 N	72.26 E
Khāmgaon, India	70	H6	20.41 N	76.34 E
Khāmis, Ash-Shallāl al- (Fifth Cataract), wtfl., Sudan	82	D6	18.22 N	33.46 E
Khamīs Mushayt, Sau. Ar.	72	F5	18.18 N	42.44 E
Khamkeut, Laos	64	C7	18.14 N	104.39 E
Khammam, India	69	C5	17.14 N	80.09 E
Khan, stm., Laos	64	C6	19.53 N	102.08 E
Khan, stm., Nmb.	90	C2	22.41 S	14.54 E
Khānābād, Afg.	72	B10	36.41 N	69.07 E
Khān Abū Shāmāt, Syria	76	E7	33.41 N	36.53 E
Khān al-Baghdādī, Iraq	74	D8	33.51 N	42.33 E
Khānaqīn, Iraq	74	C9	34.20 N	45.23 E
Khancoban, Austl.	98	K7	36.13 S	148.07 E
Khandela, India	70	E5	27.36 N	75.30 E
Khandwa, India	70	H6	21.49 N	76.20 E
Khāneh Khvodī, Iran	74	B15	36.00 N	56.00 E
Khānewāl, Pak.	70	C3	30.18 N	71.55 E
Khāngarh, Pak.	70	D3	28.21 N	71.42 E
Khāngarh, Pak.	70	D3	29.54 N	71.09 E
Khangchendzonga National Park, p.o.i., India	70	E12	27.50 N	88.14 E
Khangkhai, Laos	64	C6	19.27 N	103.14 E
Khania, Gulf of see Chanión, Kólpos, b., Grc.	34	H6	35.34 N	23.57 E
Khanka, Lake, l., Asia	54	B10	45.11 N	132.25 E
Khanna, India	70	C6	30.42 N	76.11 E
Khānpur, India	190b		22.40 N	88.16 E
Khānpur, Pak.	70	D3	28.38 N	70.39 E
Khānpur, ngh., India	190a		28.34 N	77.01 E
Khānpur, ngh., India	190a		28.31 N	77.14 E
Khān Shaykhūn, Syria	76	C7	35.26 N	36.39 E
Khansiir, Raas, c., Som.	86	B9	10.51 N	45.48 E
Khān Yūnus, Gaza	76	G5	31.20 N	34.17 E
Khao Laem Reservoir, res., Thai.	64	E4	14.55 N	98.32 E
Khao Saming, Thai.	64	F6	12.21 N	102.23 E
Khao Sok National Park, p.o.i., Thai.	64	H4	8.52 N	98.35 E
Khao Yoi, Thai.	64	F4	13.12 N	99.49 E
Khapalu, Pak.	70	A6	35.09 N	76.20 E
Kharagpur, India	70	G11	22.20 N	87.20 E
Khārān, Pak.	62	C2	28.36 N	65.26 E
Kharānoq, Iran	74	D14	32.20 N	54.39 E
Khāravli, hill, India	190c		18.54 N	72.55 E
Kharāyij, Sabkhat al-, l., Syria	76	C8	35.40 N	37.21 E
Khārghar, India	190c		19.03 N	73.04 E
Kharg Island see Khārk, Jazīreh-ye, i., Iran	74	F12	29.15 N	50.19 E
Khargon, India	70	H5	21.49 N	75.36 E
Khāriān Cantonment, Pak.	70	B4	32.48 N	73.53 E
Khariār Road, India	70	H9	20.54 N	82.31 E
Khārk, Jazīreh-ye (Kharg Island), i., Iran	74	F12	29.15 N	50.19 E
Kharkiv, Ukr.	38	C15	49.59 N	36.14 E
Kharkiv, co., Ukr.	38	D15	49.30 N	36.30 E
Kharmān, Kūh-e, mtn., Iran	74	F13	29.13 N	53.35 E
Kharri, India	190b		22.55 N	88.14 E
Khartoum see Al-Kharṭūm, Sudan	82	D6	15.34 N	32.31 E
Khartoum North see Al-Kharṭām Bahrī, Sudan	82	D6	15.38 N	32.32 E
Khartsyz'k, Ukr.	38	E17	48.02 N	38.09 E
Khāsbāti, India	190b		22.55 N	88.25 E
Khasebake, Bots.	90	B7	20.40 S	24.23 E
Khāsh, Afg.	72	C9	31.28 N	62.44 E
Khāsh, Iran	72	D9	28.13 N	61.12 E
Khashm al-Qirbah, Sudan	82	D7	14.57 N	35.54 E
Khashshab, Turat el-, can., Egypt	191c		29.53 N	31.17 E
Khatauli, India	70	D6	29.16 N	77.43 E
Khatt, Oued al, stm., W. Sah.	84	D2	26.55 N	13.02 W
Khāvda, India	70	G2	23.50 N	69.43 E
Khawsa, Mya.	64	E3	15.00 N	97.47 E
Khayāla, ngh., India	190a		28.40 N	77.06 E
Khaybar, Kowtal-e see Khyber Pass, p., Asia	70	A3	34.05 N	71.07 E
Khayerpur, India	190b		22.35 N	88.33 E
Khayra Bil, l., India	190b		22.52 N	88.29 E
Khayung, stm., Thai.	64	E7	15.07 N	104.41 E
Khazar, Daryā-ye see Caspian Sea, s.	48	F7	41.18 N	50.59 E
Kheardaha, India	190b		22.29 N	88.28 E
Khe Bo, Viet.	64	C7	19.09 N	104.40 E
Khed, India	69	C1	17.43 N	73.23 E
Khefapur, India	190a		28.30 N	77.05 E
Kheil, Katîb el-, sand, Egypt	76	H3	30.33 N	32.31 E
Khejurdaha, India	190b		22.59 N	88.10 E
Khemis el Khechna, Alg.	28	H14	36.38 N	3.19 E
Khemis Melyana, Alg.	28	H13	36.15 N	2.13 E
Khemmarat, Thai.	64	D7	16.01 N	105.13 E
Khenchla, Alg.	84	B6	35.28 N	7.10 E
Khenifra, Mor.	84	C3	32.57 N	5.41 W
Khenyen, India	190b		22.59 N	88.19 E
Khera, ngh., India	190a		28.46 N	77.08 E
Khersān, stm., Iran	74	E12	31.33 N	50.21 E
Kherson, Ukr.	38	G11	46.38 N	32.35 E
Kherson, co., Ukr.	38	G12	46.45 N	33.30 E
Khersones, mys, c., Ukr.	38	I12	44.33 N	33.26 E
Khetia, India	70	H5	21.40 N	74.36 E
Khewāri, Pak.	70	E2	26.37 N	68.54 E
Khichripur, ngh., India	190a		28.37 N	77.19 E
Khilkāpur, India	190b		22.46 N	88.29 E
Khíos, Grc.	72	B2	38.22 N	26.08 E
Khipro, Pak.	70	F2	25.49 N	69.21 E
Khiri Mat, Thai.	64	D4	16.49 N	99.47 E
Khisfīn, Golan	76	F6	32.51 N	35.49 E
Khlong Khlung, Thai.	64	D4	16.12 N	99.42 E
Khlong Thom, Thai.	64	I4	7.55 N	99.08 E
Khlong Yai, Thai.	64	G6	11.46 N	102.53 E
Khlung, Thai.	64	F6	12.27 N	102.13 E
Khmel'nyts'kyi, Ukr.	38	D5	49.25 N	27.00 E
Khmel'nyts'kyi, co., Ukr.	38	D6	49.30 N	27.00 E
Khmel'ove, Ukr.	38	E10	48.34 N	31.24 E
Khmil'nyk, Ukr.	38	D7	49.34 N	27.58 E
Khoai, Hon, i., Viet.	64	H7	8.26 N	104.50 E
Khodoriv, Ukr.	38	D3	49.24 N	24.19 E
Khok Kloi, Thai.	64	H4	8.16 N	98.18 E
Khok Pho, Thai.	64	I5	6.43 N	101.05 E
Khok Samrong, Thai.	64	E5	15.03 N	100.43 E
Kholm, Afg.	72	B10	36.41 N	67.41 E
Kholmy, Ukr.	38	B11	51.52 N	32.35 E
Khomām, Iran	74	B11	37.22 N	49.38 E
Khomas, state, Nmb.	90	C3	22.30 S	17.00 E
Khomas Hochland, plat., Nmb.	90	C3	22.27 S	16.20 E
Khomeyn, Iran	74	D11	33.36 N	50.08 E
Khomeynīshahr, Iran	74	D12	32.41 N	51.32 E
Khomodimo, Bots.	90	C6	22.46 S	23.53 E
Khomutets', Ukr.	38	C12	50.06 N	33.44 E
Khondmāl Hills, hills, India	70	H10	20.20 N	84.00 E
Khong see Nu, stm., Asia	62	C8	16.33 N	97.39 E
Khong see Salween, stm., Asia	62	C8	16.33 N	97.39 E
Khong see Mekong, stm., Asia	64	G7	10.33 N	105.26 E
Khoni, India	190c		19.10 N	73.07 E
Khon Kaen, Thai.	64	D6	16.26 N	102.50 E
Khorāsān, state, Iran	74	C15	34.32 N	56.33 E
Khordha, India	70	H10	20.10 N	85.37 E
Khorel, India	190b		22.42 N	88.19 E
Khorixas, Nmb.	90	B2	20.21 S	14.58 E
Khorog see Horog, Taj.	72	B11	37.29 N	71.33 E
Khorol, Ukr.	38	D12	49.47 N	33.17 E
Khorol, stm., Ukr.	38	D12	49.28 N	33.47 E
Khorostkiv, Ukr.	38	D4	49.12 N	25.55 E
Khorramābād, Iran	74	D11	33.28 N	48.21 E
Khorram Daraq, Iran	74	B11	36.26 N	48.36 E
Khorramshahr, Iran	74	E11	30.25 N	48.11 E
Khoru, India	190b		22.51 N	88.31 E
Khoteshiv, Ukr.	38	B3	51.42 N	24.47 E
Khotin', Ukr.	38	B13	51.07 N	34.46 E
Khotyn, Ukr.	38	E5	48.30 N	26.30 E
Khouribga, Mor.	84	C3	32.52 N	6.54 W
Khowai, India	70	F13	24.05 N	91.38 E
Khowst, Afg.	72	C10	33.20 N	69.55 E
Khrisokhoús, Kólpos, b., Cyp.	76	C3	35.06 N	32.25 E
Khrystynivka, Ukr.	38	E8	48.48 N	29.59 E
Khuff, Sau. Ar.	74	H9	24.54 N	44.42 E
Khuis, Bots.	90	E5	26.39 S	21.49 E
Khuīyāla, India	70	E3	27.14 N	70.30 E
Khu Khan, Thai.	64	E7	14.42 N	104.12 E
Khukhra, Ukr.	38	C13	50.12 N	34.49 E
Khulna, Bngl.	70	G12	22.48 N	89.34 E
Khulna, state, Bngl.	70	G12	22.45 N	89.30 E
Khŭm Bathéay, Camb.	64	G7	11.53 N	104.55 E
Khumbur Kholē Ghar, mtn., Afg.	70	B2	32.49 N	68.47 E
Khun Tan, Doi, mtn., Thai.	64	C4	18.30 N	99.20 E
Khunti, India	70	G10	23.04 N	85.17 E
Khurai, India	70	F7	24.02 N	78.20 E
Khuralji Khās, ngh., India	190a		28.39 N	77.17 E
Khurasan see Khorāsān, state, Iran	74	C15	34.32 N	56.33 E
Khurigāchi, India	190b		22.49 N	88.20 E
Khurja, India	70	D6	28.15 N	77.51 E
Khurr, Wādī al-, stm., Iraq	74	E8	31.54 N	44.29 E
Khurramshahr see Khorramshahr, Iran	74	E11	30.25 N	48.11 E
Khushāb, Pak.	70	B4	32.18 N	72.21 E
Khushk Khurd, ngh., India	190a		28.46 N	77.10 E
Khust, Ukr.	38	E2	48.10 N	23.18 E
Khuzdār, Pak.	62	C2	27.48 N	66.37 E
Khūzestān, state, Iran	74	E11	31.00 N	49.00 E
Khvor, Iran	74	D14	33.46 N	55.04 E
Khvormūj, Iran	74	F12	28.38 N	51.21 E
Khvoy, Iran	74	A9	38.32 N	44.57 E
Khwae Noi (Kwai), stm., Thai.	64	E4	14.00 N	99.31 E
Khyber Pass, p., Asia	70	A3	34.05 N	71.07 E
Khynchesht see Hâncești, Mol.	38	G7	46.49 N	28.36 E
Khyriv, Ukr.	38	D1	49.31 N	22.48 E
Kia, Sol. Is.	101b	d8	7.33 S	158.26 E
Kiama, Austl.	98	J8	34.41 S	150.51 E
Kiama, D.R.C.	86	F3	7.11 S	17.38 E
Kiamba, Phil.	68	H5	5.59 N	124.37 E
Kiambi, D.R.C.	86	F5	7.18 S	28.00 E
Kiamichi, stm., Ok., U.S.	134	C3	33.56 N	95.14 W
Kiamusze see Jiamusi, China	52	B11	46.48 N	130.22 E
Kian see Ji'an, China	58	H6	27.06 N	114.58 E
Kiana, Ak., U.S.	109	C7	66.59 N	160.27 W
Kiangarow, Mount, mtn., Austl.	98	F8	26.50 S	151.31 E
Kiangsi see Jiangxi, state, China	58	H6	28.00 N	116.00 E
Kiangsu see Jiangsu, state, China	58	E8	33.00 N	120.00 E
Kiaohsien see Jiaoxian, China	58	C8	36.17 N	119.59 E
Kibæk, Den.	16	K6	56.02 N	8.51 E
Kibangou, Congo	86	E2	3.29 S	12.19 E
Kibanseke, D.R.C.	191b		4.26 S	15.23 E
Kibar, India	70	B7	32.19 N	78.00 E
Kibaya, Tan.	86	F7	5.18 S	36.33 E
Kibler Park, S. Afr.	191d		26.18 S	28.00 E
Kibombo, D.R.C.	86	E5	3.54 S	25.55 E
Kibondo, Tan.	86	E6	3.35 S	30.42 E
Kibouendé, Congo	191b		4.17 S	15.09 E
Kibouendé, Congo	191b		4.19 S	15.11 E
Kibouendé I, Congo	191b		4.11 S	15.09 E
Kibouendé II, Congo	191b		4.12 S	15.09 E
Kibre Mengist, Eth.	82	F7	5.52 N	39.00 E
Kıbrıs see Cyprus, ctry., Asia	76	C4	35.00 N	33.00 E
Kıbrıs see Cyprus, i., Asia	46	F7	35.00 N	33.00 E
Kıbrısçık, Tur.	34	C14	40.25 N	31.51 E
Kibuye, Rw.	86	E5	2.02 S	29.24 E
Kičevo, Mac.	34	B3	41.31 N	20.57 E
Kichijōji, Japan	186		35.42 N	139.35 E
Kıcık Qafqaz daqları see Lesser Caucasus, mts., Asia	42	E11	41.00 N	44.35 E
Kickapoo, stm., Wi., U.S.	128	H8	43.04 N	90.52 W
Kickapoo Creek, stm., Il., U.S.	128	K10	40.07 N	89.26 W
Kickapoo Creek, stm., Tx., U.S.	136	C8	31.30 N	99.57 W
Kickapoo Creek, stm., Tx., U.S.	136	B12	32.15 N	95.28 W
Kickapoo Indian Reservation, ind. res., Ks., U.S.	130	E2	39.40 N	95.40 W
Kicking Horse Pass, p., Can.	144	E14	51.27 N	116.20 W
Kičmengskij Gorodok, Russia	12	F21	60.00 N	45.49 E
Kidal, Mali	84	F5	18.26 N	1.24 E
Kidapawan, Phil.	68	G5	7.02 N	125.00 E
Kidatu, Tan.	86	F7	7.40 S	36.58 E
Kidbrooke, ngh., Eng., U.K.	178		51.28 N	0.02 E
Kidderminster, Eng., U.K.	10	I10	52.23 N	2.15 W
Kidderpore, ngh., India	190b		22.31 N	88.19 E
Kidderpore Docks, trans., India	190b		22.33 N	88.19 E
Kidira, Sen.	84	G2	14.27 N	12.13 W
Kidnappers, Cape, c., N.Z.	102	D7	39.38 S	177.04 E
Kidston, Austl.	98	B5	18.51 S	144.11 E
Kiefersfelden, Ger.	24	I8	47.37 N	12.11 E
Kiekebusch, Ger.	182a		52.21 N	13.33 E
Kiel, Ger.	24	B6	54.19 N	10.07 E
Kiel, Wi., U.S.	128	H10	43.54 N	88.01 W
Kiel Bay see Kieler Bucht, b., Ger.	24	B6	54.35 N	10.35 E
Kiel Canal see Nord-Ostsee-Kanal, can., Ger.	24	B5	53.54 N	9.09 E
Kielce, Pol.	24	F16	50.52 N	20.37 E
Kieler Bucht, b., Ger.	24	B6	54.35 N	10.35 E
Kienberg, Ger.	182a		52.40 N	12.54 E
Kiepanjaure, l., Swe.	14	D11	68.31 N	20.11 E
Kierling, Aus.	182b		48.19 N	16.17 E
Kierspe-Bahnhof, Ger.	181		51.08 N	7.37 E
Kiester, Mn., U.S.	128	H5	43.32 N	93.42 W
Kieta, Pap. N. Gui.	101b	d6	6.13 S	155.37 E
Kietrz, Pol.	24	F13	50.05 N	18.01 E
Kiev see Kyïv, Ukr.	38	C9	50.26 N	30.30 E
Kievka, Kaz.	48	D12	50.16 N	71.34 E
Kievka, Russia	40	H13	46.04 N	42.55 E
Kiev Reservoir see Kyïvs'ke vodoskhovyshche, res., Ukr.	38	C9	50.51 N	30.31 E
Kievskoe, Russia	38	H16	45.02 N	37.52 E
Kievskoe vodohranilišče see Kyïvs'ke vodoskhovyshche, res., Ukr.	38	C9	50.51 N	30.31 E
Kiev Station, trans., Russia	183b		55.45 N	37.34 E
Kiffa, Maur.	84	F2	16.36 N	11.24 W
Kifisiá, Grc.	34	E6	38.03 N	23.47 E
Kifisós, stm., Grc.	34	E6	38.26 N	23.15 E
Kifisós, stm., Grc.	185c		37.57 N	23.40 E
Kifrī, Iraq	74	C9	34.42 N	44.58 E
Kigač, stm., Eur.	42	B13	46.28 N	49.10 E
Kigali, Rw.	86	E6	1.56 S	30.03 E
Kigoma, Tan.	86	E5	4.52 S	29.37 E
Kihčik, Russia	50	F20	53.24 N	156.03 E

Name	Page	Map Ref.	Latitude	Longitude
Kihei, Hi., U.S.	100a	c5	20.47 N	156.27 W
Kihniö, Fin.	18	E10	62.12 N	23.11 E
Kihnu, i., Est.	26	B6	58.07 N	23.59 E
Kiholo Bay, b., Hi., U.S.	100a	d5	19.52 N	155.56 W
Kii-hantō, pen., Japan	56	F8	33.54 N	135.39 E
Kiik, Kaz.	48	E12	47.30 N	72.54 E
Kiiminginjoki, stm., Fin.	18	B12	65.11 N	25.20 E
Kii-nagashima, Japan	56	E9	34.11 N	136.20 E
Kiirun see Chilung, Tai.	58	I9	25.07 N	121.43 E
Kii-sanchi, mts., Japan	56	E8	34.07 N	135.47 E
Kii-suidō, strt., Japan	56	F7	33.54 N	134.54 E
Kijasovo, Russia	40	C18	56.20 N	53.07 E
Kijma, Kaz.	48	D11	51.35 N	67.33 E
Kikai-shima, i., Japan	55a	k20	28.19 N	129.59 E
Kikenka, stm., Russia	183a		59.52 N	30.04 E
Kikerino, Russia	26	A12	59.27 N	29.37 E
Kikimi, D.R.C.	191b		4.26 S	15.25 E
Kikinda, Yugo.	36	D7	45.49 N	20.28 E
Kikládes (Cyclades), is., Grc.	34	F7	37.30 N	25.00 E
Kikori, Pap. N. Gui.	101a	b3	7.23 S	144.14 E
Kikori, stm., Pap. N. Gui.	101a	b3	7.22 S	144.14 E
Kikuchi, Japan	56	G3	32.58 N	130.49 E
Kikuna, Japan	186		35.10 N	139.40 E
Kikvidze, Russia	40	F13	50.44 N	43.04 E
Kikwit, D.R.C.	86	F3	5.02 S	18.49 E
Kil, Nor.	16	I7	58.54 N	9.19 E
Kil, Swe.	16	H11	59.31 N	13.19 E
Kilafors, Swe.	16	F14	61.14 N	16.34 E
Kīlakkarai, India	69	G4	9.14 N	78.47 E
Kilambé, Cerro, mtn., Nic.	156	F5	13.34 N	85.42 W
Kilauea, Hi., U.S.	100a	a2	22.12 N	159.24 W
Kilauea Crater, crat., Hi., U.S.	100a	d6	19.25 N	155.17 W
Kilauea Point, c., Hi., U.S.	100a	a2	22.13 N	159.24 W
Kilbasan, Tur.	76	A4	37.19 N	33.12 E
Kilbrannan Sound, strt., Scot., U.K.	10	F7	55.40 N	5.25 W
Kilbuck Mountains, mts., Ak., U.S.	109	D8	60.50 N	159.45 W
Kilbuck Run, stm., Pa., U.S.	197b		40.31 N	80.08 W
Kilchu-ŭp, Kor., N.	54	D8	40.58 N	129.20 E
Kilcoy, Austl.	98	F9	26.57 S	152.33 E
Kildare, Ire.	10	H6	53.09 N	6.54 W
Kildare, state, Ire.	10	H6	53.15 N	6.45 W
Kildare, Cape, c., P.E., Can.	122	D13	46.53 N	63.59 W
Kildeer, Il., U.S.	196		42.10 N	88.03 W
Kil'din, ostrov, i., Russia	14	C25	69.20 N	34.09 E
Kil'dinstroj, Russia	14	C24	68.48 N	33.09 E
Kildonan, B.C., Can.	144	G6	49.00 N	124.59 W
Kildurk, Austl.	96	C5	16.26 S	129.39 E
Kilembe, D.R.C.	86	F3	5.40 S	19.55 E
Kilgore, Tx., U.S.	136	B13	32.23 N	94.52 W
Kilian Island, i., Nu., Can.	109	B18	73.34 N	107.46 W
Kilibo, Benin	84	H5	8.34 N	2.36 E
Kılıç, Tur.	34	C12	40.38 N	29.23 E
Kiliia, Ukr.	38	H8	45.27 N	29.16 E
Kilikollūr, India	69	G3	8.54 N	76.37 E
Kilimanjaro, mtn., Tan.	86	E7	3.04 S	37.22 E
Kilimli, Tur.	34	B14	41.28 N	31.50 E
Kilindoni, Tan.	86	F7	7.54 S	39.40 E
Kilingi-Nõmme, Est.	26	B7	58.09 N	24.58 E
Kilis, Tur.	42	G7	36.43 N	37.07 E
Kiliys'ke hyrlo see Chilia, Bratul, stm., Eur.	36	D16	45.23 N	29.35 E
Kilkare Woods, Ca., U.S.	200		37.38 N	121.55 W
Kilkee, Ire.	10	I3	52.40 N	9.38 W
Kilkenny, Ire.	10	I5	52.39 N	7.14 W
Kilkenny, state, Ire.	10	I5	52.40 N	7.20 W
Kilkieran Bay, b., Ire.	10	H3	53.15 N	9.45 W
Kilkis, Grc.	34	C5	40.59 N	22.52 E
Killala, Ire.	10	G3	54.12 N	9.13 W
Killala Bay, b., Ire.	10	G3	54.15 N	9.10 W
Killaloe, Ire.	10	I4	52.49 N	8.26 W
Killaloe Station, On., Can.	126	C12	45.32 N	77.25 W
Killam, Ab., Can.	144	D19	52.48 N	111.51 W
Killara, Austl.	192a		33.46 S	151.09 E
Killarney, Austl.	98	G9	28.20 S	152.17 E
Killarney, Mb., Can.	142	E14	49.11 N	99.41 W
Killarney, On., Can.	126	C8	45.57 N	81.30 W
Killarney, Ire.	10	I3	52.03 N	9.30 W
Killarney, Lake, l., Bah.	158f	m18	25.02 N	77.25 W
Killarney Heights, Austl.	192a		33.46 S	151.13 E
Killarney Provincial Park, p.o.i., On., Can.	126	B8	46.05 N	81.23 W
Killbuck, Oh., U.S.	124	D4	40.29 N	81.58 W
Killdeer, N.D., U.S.	142	G11	47.21 N	102.45 W
Killeen, Tx., U.S.	136	C10	31.07 N	97.43 W
Killen, Al., U.S.	134	C11	34.51 N	87.32 W
Killington Peak, mtn., Vt., U.S.	122	G4	43.36 N	72.49 W
Killinig Island, i., Can.	108	E13	60.24 N	64.40 W
Killinkoski, Fin.	18	E10	62.23 N	23.52 E
Killpecker Creek, stm., Wy., U.S.	150	B7	41.35 N	109.14 W
Kill Van Kull, strt., U.S.	194		40.39 N	74.05 W
Killybegs, Ire.	10	G4	54.38 N	8.27 W
Kilmallock, Ire.	10	I4	52.24 N	8.33 W
Kilmarnock, Scot., U.K.	10	F8	55.36 N	4.29 W
Kilmarnock, Va., U.S.	124	G9	37.42 N	76.22 W
Kil'mez', Russia	40	C17	57.00 N	51.20 E
Kil'mez', stm., Russia	40	C17	56.57 N	50.28 E
Kilmichael, Ms., U.S.	134	D9	33.26 N	89.34 W
Kilmore, Austl.	98	K5	37.17 S	144.56 E
Kilo, Indon.	66	H11	8.20 S	118.24 E
Kilokri, ngh., India	190a		28.35 N	77.16 E
Kilombero, stm., Tan.	86	F7	8.31 S	37.22 E
Kilomines, D.R.C.	86	D5	1.47 N	30.14 E
Kilosa, Tan.	86	F7	6.50 S	36.59 E
Kilpisjärvi, Fin.	14	C11	69.03 N	20.49 E
Kil'pjavr, Russia	14	C23	69.06 N	32.25 E
Kilrush, Ire.	10	I3	52.38 N	9.28 W
Kilsyth, Austl.	192b		37.48 S	145.19 E
Kiltān Island, i., India	62	F3	11.29 N	73.00 E
Kilwa, D.R.C.	86	F5	9.17 S	28.20 E
Kilwa Kivinje, Tan.	86	F7	8.47 S	39.20 E
Kilwa Masoko, Tan.	86	F7	8.55 S	39.30 E
Kilyos, ngh., Tur.	185b		41.15 N	29.02 E
Kim, Co., U.S.	138	D5	37.14 N	103.21 W
Kimaam, Indon.	60	G10	7.59 S	138.55 E
Kimba, Austl.	96	F7	33.07 S	136.25 E
Kimball, Mn., U.S.	128	F4	45.19 N	94.18 W
Kimball, Ne., U.S.	140	F9	41.14 N	103.40 W
Kimball, S.D., U.S.	140	D13	43.44 N	98.57 W
Kimball, Mount, mtn., Ak., U.S.	109	D11	63.14 N	144.39 W
Kimbe Bay, b., Pap. N. Gui.	101a	b5	5.15 S	150.31 E
Kimberley, B.C., Can.	144	G15	49.41 N	115.58 W
Kimberley, S. Afr.	90	F7	28.44 S	24.45 E
Kimberley Downs, Austl.	96	C4	17.25 S	124.20 E
Kimberley Plateau, plat., Austl.	96	C5	17.00 S	127.00 E
Kimberling City, Mo., U.S.	130	H4	36.38 N	93.25 W
Kimberly, Id., U.S.	146	H12	42.32 N	114.21 W
Kimberly, Wi., U.S.	128	G10	44.16 N	88.19 W
Kimbwala, D.R.C.	191b		4.22 S	15.12 E
Kimch'aek, Kor., N.	54	D8	40.40 N	129.12 E
Kimch'ŏn, Kor., S.	54	F8	36.07 N	128.07 E
Kimhae, Kor., S.	56	D1	35.14 N	128.52 E
Kimito, Fin.	18	G9	60.10 N	22.44 E
Kimito, i., Fin.	18	G9	60.07 N	22.40 E
Kimi-tōge, hill, Japan	188		34.43 N	135.06 E
Kim Kim, stm., Malay.	189c		1.26 N	103.58 E
Kim-me-ni-oli Wash, stm., N.M., U.S.	150	H8	36.07 N	108.11 W
Kimmirut, Nu., Can.	110	C17	62.51 N	69.52 W
Kímolos, i., Grc.	34	G7	36.48 N	24.34 E
Kimovaara, Russia	18	D17	63.38 N	31.00 E
Kimovsk, Russia	26	F21	53.57 N	38.32 E
Kim Plan, Pa., U.S.	197b		40.20 N	79.44 W
Kimp'o, Kor., S.	189b		37.37 N	126.43 E
Kimp'o International Airport, arpt., Kor., S.	189b		37.33 N	126.48 E
Kimpombo, Congo	191b		4.17 S	15.10 E
Kimpō-zan, mtn., Japan	56	D11	35.53 N	138.38 E
Kimry, Russia	26	D20	56.52 N	37.21 E
Kimsquit, B.C., Can.	144	D4	52.48 N	126.56 W
Kimu, stm., Japan	186		35.56 N	139.57 E
Kimuenza, D.R.C.	191b		4.27 S	15.17 E
Kinabalu, Gunong, mtn., Malay.	68	G1	6.05 N	116.33 E
Kinabalu National Park, p.o.i., Malay.	68	H1	6.05 N	116.33 E
Kinabatangan, stm., Malay.	68	H1	5.46 N	118.20 E
Kınalı, ngh., Tur.	185b		40.55 N	29.03 E
Kınalı Ada, i., Tur.	185b		40.55 N	29.03 E
Kinaūni, India	190a		28.39 N	77.23 E
Kinbasket Lake, res., B.C., Can.	144	E13	51.57 N	118.03 W
Kincaid, Sk., Can.	142	E6	49.40 N	107.00 W
Kincardine, On., Can.	126	D8	44.10 N	81.37 W
Kinchafoonee Creek, stm., Ga., U.S.	134	F14	31.36 N	84.08 W
Kinchara, India	190b		22.53 N	88.32 E
Kinchega National Park, p.o.i., Austl.	98	I4	32.33 S	142.19 E
Kincheloe Air Force Base, mil., Mi., U.S.	126	B5	46.15 N	84.28 W
Kinda, D.R.C.	86	F4	9.19 S	25.03 E
Kindamba, Congo	86	E2	3.44 S	14.31 E
Kindberg, Aus.	24	I11	47.30 N	15.26 E
Kinde, Mi., U.S.	126	E7	43.56 N	82.59 W
Kinder, La., U.S.	134	G6	30.28 N	92.51 W
Kinder Reservoir, res., Eng., U.K.	180		53.23 N	1.55 W
Kinder Scout, mtn., Eng., U.K.	20	A7	53.23 N	1.52 W
Kindersley, Sk., Can.	142	C4	51.29 N	109.09 W
Kindia, Gui.	84	G2	10.04 N	12.51 W
Kindley Field, arpt., Ber.	158e	k16	32.22 N	64.41 W
Kindred, N.D., U.S.	128	E1	46.39 N	97.01 W
Kindu, D.R.C.	86	E5	2.56 S	25.55 E
Kinel', Russia	40	E17	53.13 N	50.38 E
Kinelahta, Russia	18	F19	61.25 N	32.31 E
Kineo, Mount, mtn., Me., U.S.	122	E7	45.43 N	69.40 W
Kinešma, Russia	40	C12	57.26 N	42.07 E
King, N.C., U.S.	124	H5	36.16 N	80.21 W
King, Mount, mtn., Austl.	98	E6	25.10 S	147.31 E
Kingabwa, ngh., D.R.C.	191b		4.19 S	15.20 E
King and Queen Court House, Va., U.S.	124	G9	37.40 N	76.52 W
Kingaroy, Austl.	98	F8	26.32 S	151.50 E
King City, On., Can.	126	E10	43.55 N	79.31 W
King City, Ca., U.S.	148	G4	36.11 N	121.07 W
King City, Mo., U.S.	130	D3	40.03 N	94.31 W
Kingfield, Me., U.S.	122	F6	44.57 N	70.09 W
Kingfisher, Ok., U.S.	138	F11	35.51 N	97.55 W
King George, Va., U.S.	124	F8	38.15 N	77.11 W
King George, Mount, mtn., B.C., Can.	144	F15	50.35 N	115.24 W
King George Islands, is., Nu., Can.	110	D14	57.20 N	78.25 W
King George's Dock, trans., India	190b		22.32 N	88.18 E
King George Sound, strt., Austl.	96	G3	35.03 S	117.57 E
King George's Reservoir, res., Eng., U.K.	178		51.39 N	0.01 W
King George VI Reservoir, res., Eng., U.K.	178		51.27 N	0.32 W
King Hill, Id., U.S.	146	G11	43.00 N	115.11 W
Kingisepp, Russia	26	A11	59.22 N	28.36 E
King Island, i., Austl.	99a	m12	39.50 S	144.00 E
King Island, i., B.C., Can.	144	D3	52.12 N	127.42 W
King Lear Peak, mtn., Nv., U.S.	148	B7	41.12 N	118.34 W
King Leopold Ranges, mts., Austl.	96	C4	17.30 S	125.45 E
Kingman, Az., U.S.	150	H2	35.11 N	114.03 W
Kingman, Ks., U.S.	138	D10	37.38 N	98.06 W
Kingman Reef, rf., Oc.	94	C10	6.24 N	162.22 W
Kingman Mountain, mtn., Or., U.S.	146	H3	42.42 N	123.14 W
King Mountain, mtn., Or., U.S.	146	G8	43.49 N	118.52 W
King of Prussia Plaza, shp. cen., Pa., U.S.	203		40.05 N	75.25 W
Kingombe, D.R.C.	86	E5	3.52 S	26.32 E
Kingoonya, Austl.	96	F7	30.54 S	135.19 E
King Peak, mtn., Ca., U.S.	148	C1	40.10 N	124.08 W
Kingri, Pak.	70	C2	30.26 N	69.48 E
Kings, Ms., U.S.	134	E8	32.24 N	90.51 W
Kings, stm., Ar., U.S.	130	H4	36.35 N	93.37 W
Kings, stm., Ca., U.S.	148	G6	36.03 N	119.49 W
Kings, stm., Nv., U.S.	148	B7	41.31 N	118.08 W
Kings, North Fork, stm., Ca., U.S.	148	F7	36.52 N	119.07 W
Kings Beach, Ca., U.S.	148	D5	39.14 N	120.01 W
Kingsbridge, Eng., U.K.	10	K9	50.17 N	3.46 W
Kingsburg, Ca., U.S.	148	G6	36.30 N	119.33 W
Kingsbury, ngh., Eng., U.K.	178		51.35 N	0.17 W
Kings Canyon National Park, p.o.i., Ca., U.S.	148	G7	36.56 N	118.34 W
Kingscote, Austl.	96	G7	35.39 S	137.37 E
King's Cross Station, trans., Eng., U.K.	178		51.32 N	0.07 W
Kingsdown, Eng., U.K.	178		51.21 N	0.17 E
Kingsford, Austl.	192a		33.56 S	151.14 E
Kingsford, Mi., U.S.	126	C1	45.47 N	88.04 W
Kingsgate, B.C., Can.	144	G14	49.00 N	116.11 W
Kingsgrove, Austl.	192a		33.57 S	151.06 E
Kingshill, V.I.U.S.	158c	h10	17.43 N	64.47 W
Kingsland, Ar., U.S.	134	D6	33.51 N	92.17 W
Kingsland, Ga., U.S.	132	F4	30.47 N	81.41 W
Kingsland, Tx., U.S.	136	D9	30.39 N	98.26 W
Kingsley, S. Afr.	90	E10	27.56 S	30.32 E
Kingsley, Eng., U.K.	180		53.16 N	2.40 W
Kingsley, Ia., U.S.	130	B2	42.35 N	95.58 W
Kingsley, Mi., U.S.	126	D4	44.34 N	85.31 W
Kingsley Dam, dam., Ne., U.S.	140	F11	41.11 N	101.39 W
King's Lynn, Eng., U.K.	10	I13	52.45 N	0.24 E
Kings Manor, Pa., U.S.	203		40.05 N	75.21 W
Kings Mountain, N.C., U.S.	132	A4	35.14 N	81.20 W
Kings Mountain National Military Park, p.o.i., S.C., U.S.	132	A4	35.07 N	81.33 W
King Solomon's Mines see Mikhrot Timna', hist., Isr.	76	I5	29.45 N	34.56 E
King Sound, strt., Austl.	96	C4	17.00 S	123.30 E
Kings Park, Va., U.S.	202c		38.48 N	77.14 W
Kings Peak, mtn., Ut., U.S.	150	C6	40.46 N	110.22 W
Kings Plaza, shp. cen., N.Y., U.S.	194		40.37 N	73.55 W
Kingsport, Tn., U.S.	124	H3	36.33 N	82.34 W
King Sterndale, Eng., U.K.	180		53.15 N	1.52 W
Kingston, N.S., Can.	122	E11	44.59 N	64.57 W
Kingston, On., Can.	126	D13	44.14 N	76.30 W
Kingston, Jam.	158d	i14	18.00 N	76.48 W
Kingston, N.Z.	102	G3	45.20 S	168.42 E
Kingston, Norf. I.	100i	y25	29.03 S	167.58 E
Kingston, Ga., U.S.	134	C14	34.14 N	84.56 W
Kingston, Ma., U.S.	124	B15	41.59 N	70.43 W
Kingston, Mo., U.S.	130	E3	39.38 N	94.02 W
Kingston, N.J., U.S.	194		40.22 N	74.36 W
Kingston, N.Y., U.S.	124	C11	41.55 N	74.00 W
Kingston, Oh., U.S.	124	E3	39.27 N	82.55 W
Kingston, Ok., U.S.	134	C2	34.00 N	96.42 W
Kingston, Pa., U.S.	124	C10	41.15 N	75.53 W
Kingston, Tn., U.S.	130	I13	35.52 N	84.31 W
Kingston Bay, b., Ma., U.S.	201		42.00 N	70.42 W
Kingston Southeast, Austl.	98	K2	36.50 S	139.51 E
Kingston upon Hull, Eng., U.K.	10	H12	53.45 N	0.19 W
Kingston upon Thames, Eng., U.K.	10	J12	51.25 N	0.19 W
Kingstown see Dún Laoghaire, Ire.	10	H6	53.17 N	6.08 W
Kingstown, St. Vin.	159e	o11	13.09 N	61.13 W
Kingstree, S.C., U.S.	132	C6	33.40 N	79.49 W
Kingsville, Austl.	192b		37.49 S	144.52 E
Kingsville, On., Can.	126	G7	42.01 N	82.43 W
Kingsville, Md., U.S.	202b		39.26 N	76.25 W
Kingsville, Tx., U.S.	136	G10	27.30 N	97.51 W
Kingsville Naval Air Station, mil., Tx., U.S.	136	G10	27.31 N	97.47 W
Kingswood, Austl.	192a		33.46 S	150.43 E
Kingswood, Eng., U.K.	178		51.17 N	0.13 W
Kingswood Park, Pa., U.S.	203		40.07 N	74.51 W
Kingtechen see Jingdezhen, China	58	G7	29.17 N	117.12 E
Kingussie, Scot., U.K.	10	D8	57.04 N	4.03 W
King William, Va., U.S.	124	G8	37.40 N	77.01 W
King William Island, i., Nu., Can.	110	B11	69.00 N	97.30 W
King William's Town, S. Afr.	90	H8	32.51 S	27.22 E
Kinhwa see Jinhua, China	58	G8	29.06 N	119.39 E
Kınık, Tur.	34	D10	39.05 N	27.23 E
Kinira, stm., S. Afr.	90	G9	30.48 S	29.03 E
Kinistino, Sk., Can.	142	B9	52.56 N	105.01 W
Kinkala, Congo	86	E2	4.22 S	14.45 E
Kinker Creek, stm., Ca., U.S.	200		38.02 N	121.52 W
Kinkora, N.J., U.S.	203		40.07 N	74.45 W
Kinlochleven, Scot., U.K.	10	E8	56.42 N	4.57 W
Kinmundy, Il., U.S.	130	F9	38.46 N	88.50 W
Kinn, Nor.	16	F2	61.33 N	4.45 E
Kinna, Swe.	16	J10	57.30 N	12.40 E
Kinnaird Head, c., Scot., U.K.	10	D10	57.42 N	2.00 W
Kinnarodden, c., Nor.	14	A18	71.07 N	27.38 E
Kinneret, Yam (Galilee, Sea of), l., Isr.	76	F6	32.48 N	35.35 E
Kinnula, Fin.	18	D11	63.21 N	24.56 E
Kino, stm., Japan	56	E8	34.13 N	135.08 E
Kinosaki, Japan	56	D7	35.37 N	134.49 E
Kinpoku-san, mtn., Japan	56	A11	38.05 N	138.20 E
Kinrola, Austl.	98	D7	23.45 S	148.48 E
Kinross, Scot., U.K.	10	E9	56.12 N	3.25 W
Kinsale, Ire.	10	J4	51.42 N	8.30 W
Kinsale, Monts.	159a	d3	16.41 N	62.12 W
Kinsale, Old Head of, c., Ire.	10	J4	51.37 N	8.32 W
Kinsarvik, Nor.	16	G4	60.22 N	6.44 E
Kinshasa (Léopoldville), D.R.C.	86	E3	4.20 S	15.17 E
Kinshasa (Léopoldville), D.R.C.	191b		4.18 S	15.18 E
Kinshasa (Ndolo) Airport, arpt., D.R.C.	191b		4.20 S	15.19 E
Kinshasa (Ndjili) Airport, arpt., D.R.C.	191b		4.23 S	15.27 E
Kinshasa-Est, ngh., D.R.C.	191b		4.18 S	15.18 E
Kinshasa-Ouest, ngh., D.R.C.	191b		4.20 S	15.15 E
Kins'ka, stm., Ukr.	38	F14	47.30 N	35.04 E
Kinsley, Ks., U.S.	138	D9	37.55 N	99.24 W
Kinsman, Oh., U.S.	124	C5	41.26 N	80.35 W
Kinston, Al., U.S.	134	F12	31.12 N	86.10 W
Kinston, N.C., U.S.	132	A8	35.15 N	77.34 W
Kintambo, Rapides de, wtfl., Afr.	191b		4.19 S	15.15 E
Kintampo, Ghana	84	H4	8.03 N	1.43 W
Kintap, Indon.	66	E9	3.56 S	115.04 E
Kintari, Mont, hill, Congo	191b		4.08 S	15.23 E
Kintélé, Congo	191b		4.09 S	15.21 E
Kintsana, Congo	191b		4.19 S	15.10 E
Kintyre, pen., Scot., U.K.	10	F7	55.32 N	5.35 W
Kintyre, Mull of, c., Scot., U.K.	10	F7	55.18 N	5.48 W
Kinuseo Falls, wtfl., B.C., Can.	144	B9	54.47 N	121.11 W
Kinuso, Ab., Can.	144	A15	55.20 N	115.26 W
Kinyangiri, Tan.	86	E6	4.26 S	34.36 E
Kinyeti, mtn., Sudan	82	G6	3.57 N	32.54 E
Kinzia, D.R.C.	86	E3	3.36 S	18.26 E
Kinzig, stm., Ger.	20	D18	50.07 N	8.54 E
Kinzua, Or., U.S.	146	E7	44.59 N	120.03 W
Kinzua Creek, stm., Pa., U.S.	124	C7	41.46 N	78.51 W
Kinzua Dam, dam., Pa., U.S.	124	C6	41.50 N	79.01 W
Kioshkokwi Lake, l., On., Can.	126	B11	46.04 N	78.53 W
Kiowa, Co., U.S.	138	B4	39.20 N	104.27 W
Kiowa, Ks., U.S.	138	D10	37.01 N	98.29 W
Kiowa, Ok., U.S.	134	C3	34.44 N	95.54 W
Kiowa Creek, stm., Ok., U.S.	138	E8	36.46 N	99.55 W
Kiowa Creek, stm., Co., U.S.	138	A4	39.38 N	104.27 W
Kipawa, stm., Qc., Can.	126	B11	47.02 N	79.23 W
Kipawa, Lac, res., Qc., Can.	126	A10	46.53 N	78.59 W
Kipembawe, Tan.	86	F6	7.38 S	33.21 E
Kipengere Range, mts., Tan.	86	F6	9.22 S	34.25 E
Kipili, Tan.	86	F6	7.26 S	30.36 E
Kipini, Kenya	86	E8	2.30 S	40.31 E
Kipling, Sk., Can.	142	D11	50.06 N	102.37 W
Kipnuk, Ak., U.S.	109	E7	59.56 N	164.03 W
Kipushi, D.R.C.	86	G5	11.45 S	27.14 E
Kirakira, Sol. Is.	101b	f9	10.27 S	161.55 E
Kirandul, India	69	B5	18.45 N	81.16 E
Kirané, Mali	84	F2	15.24 N	10.14 W
Kiraụ, Bela.	38	B8	51.29 N	29.25 E
Kiraụsk, Bela.	26	G12	53.16 N	29.29 E
Kiraz, Tur.	34	E11	38.14 N	28.12 E
Kirazlı, Tur.	34	C9	40.02 N	26.41 E
Kırbaçbayırı, mtn., Tur.	185b		40.56 N	29.10 E
Kırbaşı, Tur.	34	C14	40.00 N	31.51 E
Kirbla, Est.	26	B6	58.44 N	23.57 E
Kirbyville, Tx., U.S.	136	D14	30.39 N	93.53 W
Kırcasalih, Tur.	34	B9	41.23 N	26.49 E
Kirchberg, Ger.	24	G5	49.13 N	9.57 E
Kirch-Berg, hill, Ger.	182a		52.27 N	13.02 E
Kirchderne, ngh., Ger.	181		51.33 N	7.30 E
Kirchdorf an der Krems, Aus.	24	I10	47.56 N	14.07 E
Kirchende, Ger.	181		51.25 N	7.26 E
Kirchheimbolanden, Ger.	24	G4	49.40 N	8.01 E
Kirchheim unter Teck, Ger.	20	F18	48.39 N	9.27 E
Kirchhellen Heide, for., Ger.	181		51.36 N	6.53 E
Kirchhofen, Ger.	182a		52.22 N	13.53 E
Kirchhörde, ngh., Ger.	181		51.27 N	7.27 E
Kirchlinde, ngh., Ger.	181		51.32 N	7.22 E
Kirchmöser, Ger.	24	D8	52.22 N	12.25 E
Kirchschlag in der Buckligen Welt, Aus.	24	I12	47.30 N	16.15 E
Kirdâsa, Egypt	191c		30.02 N	31.07 E
Kireç, Tur.	34	D11	39.33 N	28.22 E
Kireevsk, Russia	26	G20	53.55 N	37.56 E
Kirejkovo, Russia	26	G18	53.39 N	35.49 E
Kirenga, stm., Russia	48	C19	57.45 N	108.06 E
Kirensk, Russia	48	C19	57.48 N	108.10 E
Kirghizia see Kyrgyzstan, ctry., Asia	48	F12	41.30 N	75.00 E
Kirgizija see Kyrgyzstan, ctry., Asia	48	F12	41.30 N	75.00 E
Kirgiz-Mijaki, Russia	40	E19	53.38 N	54.48 E
Kirgiz Range, mts., Asia	48	F12	42.28 N	73.50 E
Kirgizskij hrebet see Kirgiz Range, mts., Asia	48	F12	42.28 N	73.50 E
Kiri, D.R.C.	86	E3	1.27 S	19.00 E
Kiribati, ctry., Oc.	92	D9	5.00 S	170.00 W
Kiribati see Gilbert Islands, is., Kir.	94	C8	0.30 S	174.00 E
Kırıkhan, Tur.	42	G7	36.30 N	36.22 E
Kirikiri Prisons, bldg., Nig.	191a		6.27 N	3.19 E
Kırıkkale, Tur.	42	F5	39.51 N	33.31 E
Kırıkkale, state, Tur.	42	F5	40.00 N	33.45 E
Kirillov, Russia	18	H25	59.51 N	38.21 E
Kirillovka, Russia	183b		55.57 N	37.20 E
Kirillovo, Russia	40	C14	57.06 N	45.24 E
Kirillovskoe, Russia	18	G16	60.28 N	29.16 E
Kirin see Jilin, China	52	C10	43.50 N	126.32 E
Kirin see Jilin, state, China	52	C10	44.00 N	126.00 E
Kirinyaga (Kenya, Mount), mtn., Kenya	86	E7	0.09 S	37.18 E
Kirishima-Yaku-kokuritsu-kōen, p.o.i., Japan	56	H3	31.03 N	130.18 E
Kirishima-yama, vol., Japan	56	H3	31.55 N	130.51 E
Kiriši, Russia	26	A15	59.27 N	32.01 E
Kiritimati (Christmas Island), at., Kir.	94	C11	1.48 N	157.19 W
Kiriwina Islands (Trobriand Islands), is., Pap. N. Gui.	101a	b5	8.35 S	151.05 E
Kirizume-tōge, hill, Japan	188		34.56 N	135.16 E
Kirja, Russia	40	D15	55.04 N	46.51 E
Kirjanovskaja Kontora, Russia	48	C18	58.18 N	104.20 E
Kırka, Tur.	34	D13	39.17 N	30.31 E
Kırkağaç, Tur.	34	D10	39.06 N	27.40 E
Kirkby Lonsdale, Eng., U.K.	10	G10	54.12 N	2.36 W
Kirkcaldy, Scot., U.K.	10	E9	56.07 N	3.10 W
Kirkcudbright, Scot., U.K.	10	G8	54.50 N	4.03 W
Kirkdale, ngh., Eng., U.K.	180		53.26 N	2.59 W
Kirkee see Khadki, India	69	B1	18.34 N	73.52 E
Kirkenær, Nor.	16	G10	60.27 N	12.03 E
Kirkenes, Nor.	14	C21	69.43 N	30.01 E
Kirkjubæjarklaustur, Ice.	12a	I30	63.47 N	18.05 W
Kirkkonummi, Fin.	18	G11	60.08 N	24.25 E
Kirkland, Qc., Can.	193a		45.27 N	73.52 W
Kirkland, Il., U.S.	130	B9	42.05 N	88.50 W
Kirkland, Tx., U.S.	138	G8	34.23 N	100.03 W
Kirkland, Wa., U.S.	146	C4	47.40 N	122.12 W
Kirkland Creek, stm., Az., U.S.	150	I4	34.32 N	113.00 W
Kirkland Lake, On., Can.	114	B10	48.09 N	80.01 W
Kırklareli, Tur.	34	B10	41.44 N	27.13 E
Kırklareli, state, Tur.	34	B10	41.40 N	27.30 E
Kirklees, mun., Eng., U.K.	180		53.36 N	1.52 W
Kirklees, mun., Eng., U.K.	180		53.36 N	1.52 W
Kirkleyditch, Eng., U.K.	180		53.18 N	2.12 W
Kirklin, In., U.S.	130	D11	40.11 N	86.21 W
Kirkpatrick, Mount, mtn., Ant.	103	D21	84.20 S	166.19 E
Kirkpatrick Lake, l., Ab., Can.	144	E19	51.52 N	111.18 W
Kirksville, Mo., U.S.	130	D5	40.11 N	92.34 W
Kirkūk see Karkūk, Iraq	74	C9	35.28 N	44.23 E
Kirkwall, Scot., U.K.	10	B9	58.59 N	2.58 W
Kirkwood, S. Afr.	90	H7	33.24 S	25.26 E
Kirkwood, Il., U.S.	130	D7	40.52 N	90.44 W
Kirkwood, Mo., U.S.	130	F7	38.34 N	90.24 W
Kirkwood, N.J., U.S.	203		39.50 N	75.01 W
Kirmir, stm., Tur.	34	C15	40.00 N	31.41 E
Kirn, Ger.	24	G3	49.47 N	7.27 E
Kirov, Russia	26	F17	54.04 N	34.18 E
Kirov, Russia	40	B16	58.35 N	49.40 E
Kirova, zaliv see Qızılağac körfäzi, b., Azer.	42	F13	39.09 N	49.03 E
Kirovabad see Gäncä, Azer.	42	E12	40.41 N	46.20 E
Kirovakan see Vanadzor, Arm.	42	E11	40.48 N	44.29 E
Kirov Bay see Qızılağac körfäzi, b., Azer.	42	F13	39.09 N	49.03 E
Kirove, Ukr.	38	F14	47.40 N	35.41 E
Kirove, Ukr.	38	E16	48.24 N	37.56 E
Kirovo-Čepeck, Russia	40	B17	58.32 N	50.02 E
Kirovohrad, Ukr.	38	E11	48.30 N	32.15 E
Kirovohrad, co., Ukr.	38	E11	48.30 N	32.00 E
Kirovsk, Russia	14	E24	67.36 N	33.40 E
Kirovsk, Russia	18	H18	59.52 N	31.01 E
Kirovsk, Russia	183a		59.52 N	31.00 E
Kirovsk, Turkmen.	72	B9	37.41 N	60.23 E
Kirovs'k, Ukr.	38	E17	48.38 N	38.39 E
Kirovskaja oblast', co., Russia	40	B17	58.17 N	49.01 E
Kirovs'ke, Ukr.	38	H14	45.12 N	35.11 E
Kirovs'ke, Ukr.	38	E17	48.08 N	38.22 E
Kirovskie ostrova, is., Russia	183a		59.58 N	30.15 E
Kirovskij, Kaz.	48	F13	44.54 N	78.13 E
Kirovskij, Russia	40	I16	45.51 N	48.07 E
Kirovskij, Russia	50	F20	54.15 N	155.49 E
Kirovskij, Russia	54	B10	45.05 N	133.30 E
Kirov Stadium, p.o.i., Russia	183a		59.58 N	30.14 E
Kirpičnyj Zavod, Russia	183a		60.01 N	30.48 E
Kirriemuir, Scot., U.K.	10	E9	56.40 N	3.00 W
Kirs, Russia	48	C8	59.21 N	52.14 E
Kirsanov, Russia	40	E13	52.39 N	42.44 E
Kırşehir, Tur.	42	F6	39.09 N	34.10 E
Kırşehir, state, Tur.	42	F6	39.20 N	34.10 E
Kīrthar Range, mts., Pak.	62	C2	27.00 N	67.10 E
Kirtland, N.M., U.S.	150	G8	36.44 N	108.22 W
Kirtland Air Force Base, mil., N.M., U.S.	138	G2	35.02 N	106.37 W
Kiruna, Swe.	14	E11	67.51 N	20.16 E
Kirundu, D.R.C.	86	E5	0.43 S	25.31 E
Kirwan Heights, Pa., U.S.	197b		40.22 N	80.06 W
Kirwin, Ks., U.S.	138	B9	39.41 N	99.06 W
Kirwin Reservoir, res., Ks., U.S.	138	B9	39.39 N	99.10 W
Kiryū, Japan	56	C12	36.24 N	139.20 E
Kiržač, Russia	26	D21	56.09 N	38.52 E
Kisa, Swe.	16	J13	58.00 N	15.38 E
Kisaichi, Japan	188		34.46 N	135.42 E
Kisangani (Stanleyville), D.R.C.	86	D5	0.31 N	25.11 E
Kisar, Pulau, i., Indon.	60	G8	8.05 S	127.10 E
Kisaran, Indon.	66	B1	2.59 N	99.37 E
Kisarazu, Japan	56	D12	35.22 N	139.56 E
Kisbér, Hung.	36	B5	47.30 N	18.01 E
Kisbey, Sk., Can.	142	E11	49.39 N	102.41 W
Kiselëvsk, Russia	48	D15	53.59 N	86.38 E
Kisen-yama, hill, Japan	188		34.54 N	135.51 E
Kīsh, Jazīreh-ye, i., Iran	74	G13	26.32 N	53.56 E
Kishanganj, India	70	E11	26.06 N	87.57 E
Kishangarh, India	70	E3	27.52 N	70.34 E
Kishangarh, ngh., India	190a		28.31 N	77.08 E
Kishangarh Bās, India	70	E5	26.35 N	74.51 E
Kishi, Nig.	84	H5	9.05 N	3.51 E
Kishinev see Chişinău, Mol.	38	F7	47.01 N	28.50 E
Kishiwada, Japan	56	E8	34.27 N	135.23 E
Kishorganj, Bngl.	70	F13	24.25 N	90.46 E
Kishtwār, India	70	B5	33.19 N	75.45 E
Kishwaukee, stm., Il., U.S.	128	I9	42.10 N	89.07 W
Kisii, Kenya	86	E6	0.39 S	34.45 E
Kisiju, Tan.	86	F7	7.24 S	39.20 E
Kısıklı, ngh., Tur.	185b		41.01 N	29.03 E
Kısırkaya, ngh., Tur.	185b		41.14 N	28.58 E
Kısırmandıra, ngh., Tur.	185b		41.14 N	28.49 E
Kisiwada see Kishiwada, Japan	56	E8	34.27 N	135.23 E
Kiska Island, i., Ak., U.S.	109a	g22	51.59 N	177.31 E
Kiskatinaw, stm., B.C., Can.	144	A10	55.10 N	120.13 W
Kiska Volcano, vol., Ak., U.S.	109a	g22	52.07 N	177.36 E
Kis-Kevély, hill, Hung.	182c		47.38 N	18.59 E
Kiskimere, Pa., U.S.	197b		40.37 N	79.35 W
Kiskörei-viztároló, res., Hung.	36	B7	47.35 N	20.40 E
Kiskőrös, Hung.	36	C6	46.37 N	19.17 E
Kiskunfélegyháza, Hung.	36	C6	46.43 N	19.50 E
Kiskunhalas, Hung.	36	C6	46.25 N	19.29 E
Kiskunmajsa, Hung.	36	C6	46.29 N	19.44 E
Kiskunsági Nemzeti Park, p.o.i., Hung.	36	C6	46.40 N	19.25 E
Kislovodsk, Russia	42	D10	43.55 N	42.44 E
Kismaayo, Som.	86	E8	0.21 S	42.32 E
Kismet, N.Y., U.S.	194		40.38 N	73.12 W
Kisnema, Russia	18	G24	60.20 N	37.39 E
Kiso, Japan	186		35.34 N	139.26 E
Kiso, stm., Japan	56	D9	35.04 N	136.44 E
Kiso-sammyaku, mts., Japan	56	D10	35.43 N	137.50 E
Kispest, ngh., Hung.	182c		47.27 N	19.08 E
Kissena Park, p.o.i., N.Y., U.S.	194		40.45 N	73.49 W
Kissidougou, Gui.	84	H2	9.11 N	10.06 W
Kissimmee, Fl., U.S.	132	H4	28.17 N	81.24 W
Kissimmee, stm., Fl., U.S.	132	I4	27.08 N	80.52 W
Kissimmee, Lake, l., Fl., U.S.	132	I4	27.55 N	81.16 W
Kississing Lake, l., Mb., Can.	110	D10	55.10 N	101.20 W
Kissū, Jabal, mtn., Sudan	82	C5	21.35 N	25.09 E
Kistarcsa, Hung.	182c		47.33 N	19.16 E
Kistefjell, mtn., Nor.	14	D10	68.36 N	19.37 E
Kisújszállás, Hung.	36	B7	47.12 N	20.46 E
Kisuki, Japan	56	D5	35.17 N	132.54 E
Kisumu, Kenya	86	E6	0.05 S	34.45 E
Kisvárda, Hung.	36	A9	48.13 N	22.05 E
Kita, Mali	84	G3	13.02 N	9.29 W
Kita, ngh., Japan	186		35.45 N	139.44 E
Kita, ngh., Japan	188		35.03 N	135.45 E
Kita, ngh., Japan	188		34.45 N	135.08 E
Kita, ngh., Japan	188		34.42 N	135.30 E
Kitaa see Vestgrønland, state, Grnld.	108	D16	65.01 N	45.04 W
Kitaibaraki, Japan	56	C13	36.48 N	140.45 E
Kitain Temple, rel., Japan	186		35.54 N	139.30 E
Kitairiso, Japan	186		35.50 N	139.26 E
Kitakami, stm., Japan	54	E14	38.24 N	141.19 E
Kitakata, Japan	56	B12	37.39 N	139.52 E
Kitakyūshū, Japan	56	F3	33.53 N	130.50 E
Kitale, Kenya	86	D7	1.01 N	35.00 E
Kitamachi, ngh., Japan	186		35.46 N	139.39 E
Kitamba, ngh., D.R.C.	191b		4.19 S	15.14 E
Kitami, Japan	54	C15	43.48 N	143.54 E
Kitangiri, Lake, l., Tan.	86	E6	4.03 S	34.19 E
Kitano, Japan	186		35.47 N	139.26 E
Kitanoshinden, Japan	186		35.48 N	139.26 E
Kitatajima, Japan	186		35.56 N	139.30 E
Kitatawara, Japan	188		34.44 N	135.42 E
Kit Carson, Co., U.S.	138	C6	38.45 N	102.47 W
Kitchener, On., Can.	126	E9	43.27 N	80.28 W
Kitee, Fin.	18	E17	62.06 N	30.09 E
Kitega see Gitega, Bdi.	86	E5	3.21 S	29.54 E
Kitgum, Ug.	86	D6	3.17 N	32.52 E
Kithārah, Khirbat, hist., Jord.	76	I6	29.33 N	35.08 E
Kitimat, B.C., Can.	144	B2	54.00 N	128.41 W
Kitimat, stm., B.C., Can.	144	B2	54.05 N	128.39 W
Kitimat Ranges, mts., B.C., Can.	144	C2	53.06 N	128.06 W
Kitinen, stm., Fin.	14	E17	67.08 N	27.29 E
Kitíou, Akrotírion, c., Cyp.	76	D4	34.49 N	33.36 E
Kitlope, stm., B.C., Can.	144	C3	53.09 N	127.46 W
Kitlope Lake, l., B.C., Can.	144	C2	53.07 N	127.47 W
Kitridge Point, c., Barb.	159d	n9	13.09 N	59.25 W
Kit's Coty House, bldg., Eng., U.K.	178		51.19 N	0.30 E
Kitsman', Ukr.	38	E4	48.26 N	25.46 E
Kitsuki, Japan	56	F4	33.24 N	131.37 E
Kittanning, Pa., U.S.	124	D6	40.49 N	79.30 W
Kitt Green, Eng., U.K.	180		53.33 N	2.41 W
Kittilä, Fin.	14	E15	67.39 N	24.54 E
Kittitas, Wa., U.S.	146	D6	46.58 N	120.25 W
Kitt Peak National Observatory, sci., Az., U.S.	150	K5	31.58 N	111.36 W
Kitui, Kenya	86	E7	1.21 S	38.00 E
Kitunda, Tan.	86	F6	6.47 S	33.11 E
Kitwanga, B.C., Can.	144	A2	55.06 N	128.03 W
Kitwangar Indian Reserve, ind. res., B.C., Can.	144	A2	55.06 N	128.04 W
Kitwe, Zam.	88	C4	12.49 S	28.13 E
Kityang see Jieyang, China	58	J7	23.33 N	116.20 E
Kitzbühel, Aus.	30	C9	47.27 N	12.23 E

Name	Page	Map Ref.	Latitude	Longitude
Kitzingen, Ger.	24	G6	49.44 N	10.10 E
Kiukiang see Jiujiang, China	58	G6	29.43 N	115.58 E
Kiukiu, c., Fr. Poly.	100g	s18	9.46 S	139.09 W
Kiunga, Kenya	86	E8	1.44 S	41.28 E
Kiunga, Pap. N. Gui.	101a	b3	6.09 S	141.14 E
Kiuruvesi, Fin.	18	D13	63.38 N	26.37 E
Kivalina, Ak., U.S.	109	C7	67.44 N	164.32 W
Kiveriči, Russia	26	C19	57.21 N	36.35 E
Kivertsi, Ukr.	38	C4	50.50 N	25.28 E
Kivijärvi, Fin.	18	D12	63.04 N	25.05 E
Kivijärvi, l., Fin.	18	D11	63.10 N	25.09 E
Kivik, Swe.	16	L12	55.40 N	14.14 E
Kiviõli, Est.	26	A9	59.21 N	26.59 E
Kivshyvata, Ukr.	38	D9	49.29 N	30.38 E
Kivu, Lake, l., Afr.	86	E5	2.02 S	28.54 E
Kıyıköy, Tur.	34	B11	41.38 N	28.05 E
Kiyiu Lake, l., Sk., Can.	142	C5	51.36 N	108.53 W
Kiyl, stm., Kaz.	40	G19	49.27 N	54.52 E
Kiyotani, Japan	188		34.52 N	134.59 E
Kizëma, Russia	12	F21	61.06 N	44.52 E
Kızılcabölük, Tur.	34	F11	37.37 N	29.00 E
Kızılcahamam, Tur.	34	C15	40.28 N	32.39 E
Kızıldağ Milli Parkı, p.o.i., Tur.	34	E14	37.58 N	31.28 E
Kızılhisar, Tur.	34	F12	37.32 N	29.17 E
Kızılırmak (Halys), stm., Tur.	42	F7	41.43 N	35.57 E
Kızılören, Tur.	34	F15	37.53 N	32.06 E
Kiziltašskij liman, b., Russia	42	C7	45.08 N	37.02 E
Kızıltepe, Tur.	42	G9	37.11 N	40.36 E
Kızıltoprak, ngh., Tur.	185b		40.58 N	29.03 E
Kızılyaka, Tur.	76	A3	37.08 N	32.54 E
Kizimkazi, Tan.	86	F7	6.26 S	39.28 E
Kızkalesi, hist., Tur.	76	B4	36.28 N	34.04 E
Kızkulesi, trans., Tur.	185b		41.01 N	29.00 E
Kizljar, Russia	42	D12	43.50 N	46.42 E
Kizljarskij zaliv, b., Russia	42	C12	44.30 N	46.55 E
Kizuki, Japan	186		35.34 N	139.40 E
Kizuri, Japan	188		34.39 N	135.34 E
Kizyl-Atrek, Turkmen.	72	B7	37.35 N	54.47 E
Kizyl-Su, Turkmen.	72	B7	39.46 N	53.00 E
Kjahta, Russia	50	F10	50.21 N	106.26 E
Kjanda, Russia	18	C25	64.17 N	38.04 E
Kjellerup, Den.	16	K7	56.17 N	9.26 E
Kjøllefjord, Nor.	14	A18	70.56 N	27.21 E
Kjøpsvik, Nor.	14	D7	68.05 N	16.21 E
Kjumetundra, gora, mtn., Russia	14	E22	67.27 N	31.33 E
Kjungej-Ala-Too, hrebet, mts., Asia	48	F13	42.50 N	77.00 E
Kjusjur, Russia	50	B14	70.37 N	127.18 E
Kjustendil, Blg.	36	G9	42.17 N	22.41 E
Klabat, Gunung, vol., Indon.	60	E8	1.28 N	125.02 E
Kladanj, Bos.	36	E5	44.13 N	18.41 E
Kladno, Czech Rep.	24	F10	50.08 N	14.05 E
Kladovo, Yugo.	36	E9	44.36 N	22.36 E
Klaeng, Thai.	64	F5	12.47 N	101.38 E
Klagan, Malay.	68	G1	5.58 N	117.23 E
Klagenfurt, Aus.	30	D11	46.37 N	14.18 E
Klahoose Indian Reserve, ind. res., B.C., Can.	144	F6	50.31 N	124.19 W
Klaipėda (Memel), Lith.	26	E3	55.43 N	21.08 E
Klakah, Indon.	66	G8	7.59 S	113.15 E
Klaksvík, Far. Is.	12b	m34	62.13 N	6.34 W
Klamath, Ca., U.S.	148	B1	41.32 N	124.03 W
Klamath, stm., U.S.	148	B2	41.32 N	124.05 W
Klamath Falls, Or., U.S.	148	A4	42.13 N	121.47 W
Klamath Marsh, sw., Or., U.S.	146	H5	42.54 N	121.44 W
Klamath Mountains, mts., U.S.	118	G4	41.31 N	123.14 W
Klamono, Indon.	60	F9	1.07 S	131.28 E
Klang, Malay.	64	K5	3.02 N	101.27 E
Klangenan, Indon.	66	G6	6.42 S	108.30 E
Klangenang, Indon.	66	G6	6.46 S	108.27 E
Klangpi, Mya.	70	G14	23.00 N	93.19 E
Klarälven (Trysilelva), stm., Eur.	16	F9	59.19 N	13.28 E
Klatovy, Czech Rep.	24	G9	49.23 N	13.17 E
Klausenburg see Cluj-Napoca, Rom.	36	C10	46.46 N	23.36 E
Klawer, S. Afr.	90	G4	31.44 S	18.39 E
Kleck, Bela.	26	G9	53.03 N	26.38 E
Klecko, Pol.	24	D13	52.36 N	17.29 E
Kleczew, Pol.	24	D14	52.22 N	18.11 E
Kledering, ngh., Aus.	182b		48.08 N	16.26 E
Kleef, Ger.	181		51.11 N	6.56 E
Kleena Kleene, B.C., Can.	144	E6	51.56 N	124.50 W
Klein-Biesbokspruit, stm., S. Afr.	191d		26.16 S	28.29 E
Klein Bonaire, i., Neth. Ant.	158g	p23	12.08 N	68.18 W
Kleinburg, On., Can.	193b		43.50 N	79.38 W
Klein Curaçao, i., Neth. Ant.	158g	q22	11.59 N	68.38 W
Kleine Emscher, stm., Ger.	181		51.31 N	6.43 E
Kleineichen, Ger.	181		51.08 N	7.21 E
Kleinenbroich, Ger.	181		51.12 N	6.35 E
Kleiner Ravens-Berg, hill, Ger.	182a		52.22 N	13.04 E
Kleiner Wannsee, l., Ger.	182a		52.25 N	13.10 E
Kleiner Zernsee, l., Ger.	182a		52.26 N	12.55 E
Kleinhammer, Ger.	181		51.14 N	7.46 E
Klein-Jukskei, stm., S. Afr.	191d		26.08 S	27.56 E
Klein Karroo see Little Karroo, plat., S. Afr.	90	H5	33.45 S	21.30 E
Klein Kienitz, Ger.	182a		52.18 N	13.29 E
Klein Namaland see Little Namaqualand, hist. reg., S. Afr.	90	F3	29.00 S	17.00 E
Kleinschönebeck, Ger.	182a		52.29 N	13.43 E
Klein Ziethen, Ger.	182a		52.23 N	13.27 E
Klein Ziethener-Berge, hill, Ger.	182a		52.22 N	13.26 E
Klekovača, mtn., Bos.	36	E3	44.26 N	16.31 E
Klemme, Ia., U.S.	130	A4	43.00 N	93.36 W
Klemtu, B.C., Can.	144	D2	52.36 N	128.31 W
Klerksdorp, S. Afr.	90	E8	26.51 S	26.39 E
Klesiv, Ukr.	38	B5	51.18 N	26.54 E
Klet', mtn., Czech Rep.	24	H10	48.52 N	14.17 E
Kletnja, Russia	26	G16	53.23 N	33.13 E
Kletskij, Russia	40	G13	49.18 N	43.03 E
Klevan', Ukr.	38	C4	50.44 N	26.01 E
Kleve, Ger.	24	E2	51.47 N	6.08 E
Kley, ngh., Ger.	181		51.30 N	7.22 E
Kličau, Bela.	26	G12	53.29 N	29.20 E
Klickitat, Wa., U.S.	146	E5	45.49 N	121.09 W
Klickitat, stm., Wa., U.S.	146	E5	45.41 N	121.17 W
Kliedbruch, reg., Ger.	181		51.22 N	6.33 E
Klimavičy, Bela.	26	G14	53.36 N	31.57 E
Klimino, Russia	48	C17	58.38 N	98.41 E
Klimovo, Russia	26	H15	52.23 N	32.11 E
Klimovsk, Russia	26	E20	55.21 N	37.32 E
Klimov Zavod, Russia	26	F17	54.49 N	34.56 E
Klimpfjäll, Swe.	16	B12	65.03 N	14.54 E
Klin, Russia	26	D19	56.20 N	36.42 E
Klinaklini, stm., B.C., Can.	144	E5	51.04 N	125.35 W
Klincovka, Russia	40	F16	51.40 N	49.10 E
Klincy, Russia	26	H15	52.45 N	32.14 E
Kline Ditch, can., Oh., U.S.	197a		41.28 N	82.04 W
Kling, Phil.	68	H5	5.57 N	124.41 E
Klingenthal, Ger.	24	F8	50.21 N	12.27 E
Klínovec, mtn., Czech Rep.	24	F8	50.24 N	12.58 E
Klintehamn, Swe.	16	J16	57.23 N	18.11 E
Klip, stm., S. Afr.	90	E9	27.03 S	29.04 E
Klip, stm., S. Afr.	191d		26.19 S	27.53 E
Klipdale, S. Afr.	90	I4	34.18 S	19.57 E
Klippan, Swe.	16	K11	56.07 N	13.09 E
Klippfjället, mtn., Swe.	16	B13	65.18 N	15.41 E
Klipplaat, S. Afr.	90	H7	33.01 S	24.20 E
Klippoortje, S. Afr.	191d		26.13 S	28.10 E
Klipriviersberg, mts., S. Afr.	191d		26.17 S	28.02 E
Kliptown, S. Afr.	191d		26.17 S	27.53 E
Klishkivtsi, Ukr.	38	E5	48.25 N	26.17 E
Klisura, Blg.	36	G11	42.42 N	24.27 E
Klitmøller, Den.	16	J6	57.02 N	8.31 E
Kljascicy, Bela.	26	E11	55.53 N	28.36 E
Kljas'ma, Russia	183b		55.59 N	37.50 E
Kljaz'ma, Russia	183b		55.58 N	37.27 E
Kljazma, stm., Russia	26	E21	55.48 N	38.50 E
Kljaz'ma, stm., Russia	40	C12	56.10 N	42.58 E
Kljaz'minskoe vodohranilišče, res., Russia	183b		55.59 N	37.35 E
Ključ, Bos.	36	E3	44.32 N	16.46 E
Ključevaja, Russia	12	D19	65.16 N	41.35 E
Ključevskaja Sopka, vulkan, vol., Russia	50	E21	56.04 N	160.38 E
Ključi, Russia	50	E21	56.18 N	160.50 E
Ključovka, Russia	40	F19	51.24 N	55.49 E
Kljukvenka, Russia	48	C15	58.32 N	85.51 E
Klobbicke, Ger.	182a		52.46 N	13.48 E
Kłobuck, Pol.	24	F14	50.54 N	18.56 E
Klobuticy, Russia	26	B12	58.34 N	29.35 E
Kłodawa, Pol.	24	D14	52.15 N	18.54 E
Kłodzko, Pol.	24	F12	50.26 N	16.39 E
Kløfta, Nor.	16	G9	60.04 N	11.09 E
Klomnice, Pol.	24	F15	50.55 N	19.22 E
Klondike, hist. reg., Yk., Can.	110	C3	63.58 N	138.50 W
Klooga, Est.	26	A7	59.19 N	24.16 E
Klosterhardt, ngh., Ger.	181		51.31 N	6.53 E
Klosterneuburg, Aus.	30	B13	48.18 N	16.20 E
Kloten, Switz.	30	C5	47.26 N	8.34 E
Klotz, Lac, l., Qc., Can.	110	C16	60.30 N	73.43 W
Klötze, Ger.	24	D7	52.37 N	11.10 E
Kluane, stm., Yk., Can.	109	D12	61.52 N	139.42 W
Kluane Lake, l., Yk., Can.	110	C3	61.15 N	138.46 W
Kluang, Indon.	66	E3	2.39 S	103.54 E
Kluczbork, Pol.	24	F14	50.58 N	18.13 E
Klungkung, Indon.	66	H9	8.32 S	115.24 E
Knaddah, Syria	76	C7	35.46 N	36.12 E
Knaphill, Eng., U.K.	178		51.19 N	0.37 W
Knapp, Wi., U.S.	128	G6	44.57 N	92.04 W
Knäred, Swe.	16	K11	56.30 N	13.20 E
Knauertown, Pa., U.S.	203		40.10 N	75.44 W
Kneehills Creek, stm., Ab., Can.	144	E17	51.29 N	112.50 W
Knee Lake, l., Mb., Can.	110	D12	55.06 N	94.36 W
Knees, The, mtn., Co., U.S.	150	F8	37.13 N	108.48 W
Knevicy, Russia	26	C15	57.55 N	32.09 E
Kneža, Blg.	36	F11	43.30 N	24.05 E
Knić, Yugo.	36	F7	43.56 N	20.44 E
Knickerbocker, Tx., U.S.	136	C7	31.20 N	100.38 W
Knife, stm., N.D., U.S.	142	G12	47.19 N	101.22 W
Knife River Indian Villages National Historic Site, p.o.i., N.D., U.S.	142	G12	47.21 N	101.23 W
Knight Inlet, b., B.C., Can.	144	F4	50.42 N	125.43 W
Knighton, Wales, U.K.	10	I9	52.20 N	3.03 W
Knights Landing, Ca., U.S.	148	E4	38.47 N	121.42 W
Knightstown, In., U.S.	130	E12	39.47 N	85.31 W
Knin, Cro.	30	F13	44.02 N	16.11 E
Knippa, Tx., U.S.	136	E8	29.18 N	99.38 W
Knittelfeld, Aus.	30	C11	47.12 N	14.49 E
Knivskjelodden, c., Nor.	14	A16	71.09 N	25.34 E
Knivsta, Swe.	16	H15	59.43 N	17.48 E
Knjaževac, Yugo.	36	F9	43.34 N	22.15 E
Knjažji Gory, Russia	26	D18	56.04 N	35.13 E
Knob Noster, Mo., U.S.	130	F4	38.46 N	93.33 W
Knockholt, Eng., U.K.	178		51.18 N	0.06 E
Knockholt Pound, Eng., U.K.	178		51.19 N	0.08 E
Knokke-Heist, Bel.	20	C12	51.21 N	3.17 E
Knole, hist., Eng., U.K.	178		51.16 N	0.12 E
Knolls Green, Eng., U.K.	180		53.19 N	2.18 W
Knollwood, Il., U.S.	196		42.17 N	87.53 W
Knollwood, Md., U.S.	202c		39.02 N	76.58 W
Knosós, hist., Grc.	34	H8	35.16 N	25.12 E
Knott's Berry Farm, p.o.i., Ca., U.S.	198		33.50 N	118.00 W
Knotty Ash, ngh., Eng., U.K.	180		53.25 N	2.54 W
Knotty Green, Eng., U.K.	178		51.37 N	0.39 W
Knowland State Arboretum and Park, p.o.i., Ca., U.S.	200		37.45 N	122.09 W
Knowltonwood, Pa., U.S.	203		39.53 N	75.24 W
Knowsley, Eng., U.K.	180		53.27 N	2.51 W
Knowsley, mun., Eng., U.K.	180		53.27 N	2.50 W
Knowsley, mun., Eng., U.K.	180		53.27 N	2.50 W
Knowsley Hall, bldg., Eng., U.K.	180		53.26 N	2.50 W
Knowsley Park, p.o.i., Eng., U.K.	180		53.27 N	2.49 W
Knox, In., U.S.	130	C11	41.17 N	86.36 W
Knox, Pa., U.S.	124	C6	41.14 N	79.32 W
Knox, Cape, c., B.C., Can.	110	E4	54.10 N	133.03 W
Knox City, Tx., U.S.	138	H9	33.24 N	99.49 W
Knox Coast, cst., Ant.	103	B15	66.55 S	103.52 E
Knoxfield, Austl.	192b		37.53 S	145.15 E
Knoxville, Ga., U.S.	132	D2	32.43 N	84.00 W
Knoxville, Il., U.S.	130	D7	40.54 N	90.17 W
Knoxville, Ia., U.S.	130	C4	41.19 N	93.06 W
Knoxville, Tn., U.S.	124	I2	35.58 N	83.55 W
Knuckles, mtn., Sri L.	69	H5	7.24 N	80.48 E
Knud Rasmussen Land, reg., Grnld.	108	A14	80.00 N	48.00 W
Knutsholstinden, mtn., Nor.	16	F6	61.26 N	8.34 E
Knysna, S. Afr.	90	I6	34.02 S	23.04 E
Knyszyn, Pol.	24	C18	53.19 N	22.55 E
Koala Sanctuary, ind. res., Austl.	192a		33.40 S	151.10 E
Kob', Russia	48	C18	55.26 N	101.21 E
Koba, Indon.	66	E5	2.30 S	106.23 E
Kőbánya, ngh., Hung.	182c		47.29 N	19.10 E
Kobar Sink, depr., Eth.	82	E8	13.35 N	40.50 E
Kobayashi, Japan	56	H3	31.56 N	130.59 E
Kōbe, Japan	56	E8	34.41 N	135.10 E
Kōbe, Japan	188		34.41 N	135.10 E
Kōbe-kō, b., Japan	188		34.40 N	135.12 E
Kobeliaky, Ukr.	38	D13	49.08 N	34.12 E
København (Copenhagen), Den.	16	L10	55.40 N	12.33 E
København, state, Den.	16	L10	55.45 N	12.25 E
Kōbe University, educ., Japan	188		34.43 N	135.14 E
Kobjaj, Russia	50	D14	63.34 N	126.29 E
Koblenz, Ger.	24	F3	50.21 N	7.35 E
K'obo, Eth.	82	E7	12.14 N	39.36 E
Kobona, Russia	18	G18	60.01 N	31.36 E
Koboža, Russia	26	B18	58.48 N	35.02 E
Koboža, stm., Russia	26	A18	58.52 N	36.17 E
Kobrinskoe, Russia	26	A13	59.25 N	30.07 E
Kobroor, Pulau, i., Indon.	60	G10	6.12 S	134.32 E
Kobryn, Bela.	26	H7	52.13 N	24.20 E
Kobuk, Ak., U.S.	109	C8	66.54 N	156.51 W
Kobuk, stm., Ak., U.S.	109	C8	66.33 N	161.32 W
Kobuleti, Geor.	42	E9	41.49 N	41.47 E
Kobylin, Pol.	24	E13	51.43 N	17.13 E
Kobyzhcha, Ukr.	38	C10	50.50 N	31.30 E
Köca see Eşen, stm., Tur.	34	G12	36.17 N	29.16 E
Kocaali, Tur.	34	B13	41.03 N	30.51 E
Kocaaliler, Tur.	76	A1	37.19 N	30.44 E
Kocaavşar, stm., Tur.	34	D10	40.09 N	27.56 E
Kocaeli see İzmit, Tur.	34	C12	40.47 N	29.57 E
Kocaeli, state, Tur.	34	C12	40.55 N	29.55 E
Kočani, Mac.	34	B5	41.55 N	22.25 E
Koçarlı, Tur.	34	F10	37.45 N	27.42 E
Kocasinan, ngh., Tur.	185b		41.01 N	28.50 E
Kočečum, stm., Russia	50	C8	64.16 N	100.11 E
Kočenga, stm., Russia	50	E9	55.54 N	104.06 E
Kočetovka, Russia	40	E12	52.58 N	40.29 E
Kočevje, Slvn.	30	E11	45.38 N	14.52 E
Kočevo, Russia	48	C8	59.36 N	54.18 E
Kŏch'ang, Kor., S.	54	G7	35.41 N	127.55 E
Koch Bihār, India	70	E12	26.19 N	89.27 E
Kocher, stm., Ger.	24	G5	49.13 N	9.12 E
Kocheriv, Ukr.	38	C8	50.21 N	29.21 E
Kochi (Cochin), India	69	G3	9.56 N	76.15 E
Kōchi, Japan	56	F6	33.33 N	133.32 E
Kōchi, state, Japan	56	F6	33.40 N	133.30 E
Koch Island, i., Nu., Can.	110	B15	69.38 N	78.15 W
Koch Peak, mtn., Mt., U.S.	146	E15	45.02 N	111.28 W
Kock, Pol.	24	E18	51.38 N	22.28 E
Kockoma, Russia	18	C21	64.01 N	34.13 E
Kocksoord, S. Afr.	191d		26.13 S	27.39 E
Kočubej, Russia	42	C12	44.23 N	46.33 E
Kodaikānal, India	69	F3	10.13 N	77.29 E
Kodar, hrebet, mts., Russia	50	E12	57.15 N	118.10 E
Kodāri, Nepal	70	E10	27.56 N	85.56 E
Kodarma, India	70	F10	24.27 N	85.36 E
Kodera, ngh., Japan	188		34.41 N	135.04 E
Kodiak, Ak., U.S.	109	E9	57.48 N	152.22 W
Kodiak Island, i., Ak., U.S.	109	E9	57.30 N	153.30 W
Kodina, stm., Russia	18	D27	63.37 N	39.03 E
Kodinār, India	70	H3	20.47 N	70.41 E
Kodino, Russia	18	D26	63.43 N	39.37 E
Kodok, Sudan	82	F6	9.53 N	32.05 E
Kodra, Ukr.	38	C8	50.35 N	29.33 E
Kodyma, Ukr.	38	E8	48.05 N	29.08 E
Kodyma, stm., Ukr.	38	F9	47.59 N	30.48 E
Koës, Nmb.	90	D4	25.56 S	19.07 E
Kofa Mountains, mts., Az., U.S.	150	J3	33.22 N	113.56 W
Koffiefontein, S. Afr.	90	F7	29.24 S	25.00 E
Kofiau, Pulau, i., Indon.	60	F8	1.11 S	129.49 E
Kofirnihon see Ordžonikidzeabad, Taj.	72	B10	38.32 N	69.01 E
Köflach, Aus.	30	C12	47.04 N	15.05 E
Koforidua, Ghana	84	H4	6.04 N	0.16 W
Kōfu, Japan	56	D11	35.39 N	138.34 E
Koga, Japan	56	C12	36.11 N	139.42 E
Kogaluc, stm., Qc., Can.	110	D15	59.43 N	77.36 W
Kogaluc, Baie, b., Qc., Can.	110	D15	59.20 N	77.53 W
Kogan, Austl.	98	F8	27.03 S	150.46 E
Kogane, Japan	186		35.50 N	139.56 E
Kogarah, Austl.	192a		33.58 S	151.08 E
Kogarah Bay, b., Austl.	192a		33.59 S	151.07 E
Kógchi, Ákra, c., Grc.	185c		37.53 N	23.27 E
Køge, Den.	16	L10	55.27 N	12.11 E
Køge Bugt, b., Den.	16	L10	55.30 N	12.20 E
Kogon, stm., Gui.	84	G2	11.02 N	14.40 W
Kohala Mountains, mts., Hi., U.S.	100a	c6	20.05 N	155.45 W
Kohanava, Bela.	26	F12	54.28 N	30.01 E
Kohāt, Pak.	70	B3	33.35 N	71.26 E
Kohatk Wash, stm., Az., U.S.	150	K4	32.37 N	111.55 W
Kohila, Est.	26	A7	59.10 N	24.45 E
Kohīma, India	62	C7	25.39 N	94.05 E
Kohkīlūyeh va Boyer Aḥmadī, state, Iran	74	E12	30.40 N	50.40 E
Kohlberg, hill, Ger.	181		51.18 N	7.46 E
Kohler, Wi., U.S.	126	E2	43.44 N	87.44 W
Kōhoku, ngh., Japan	186		35.31 N	139.38 E
Kohtla-Järve, Est.	26	A10	59.23 N	27.15 E
Kohu see Kōfu, Japan	56	D11	35.39 N	138.34 E
Kohyl'nyk (Cogâlnic), stm., Eur.	36	C15	45.49 N	29.38 E
Koide, Japan	56	B11	37.13 N	138.57 E
Koigi, Est.	26	B8	58.50 N	25.45 E
Koihoa, India	62	G7	8.11 N	93.29 E
Koil-Aligarh see Alīgarh, India	70	E6	27.53 N	78.04 E
Koindu, S.L.	84	H2	8.27 N	10.20 W
Koiter, res., Fin.	18	D17	62.58 N	30.45 E
Koiva (Gauja), stm., Eur.	26	C7	57.09 N	24.16 E
Koivusuon luonnonpuisto, ind. res., Fin.	18	E18	62.58 N	31.05 E
Kojda, Russia	12	C20	66.22 N	42.29 E
Kōje-do, i., Kor., S.	54	G8	34.52 N	128.37 E
Kojetín, Czech Rep.	24	G13	49.21 N	17.18 E
Kojgorodok, Russia	48	B8	60.25 N	50.58 E
Kojonup, Austl.	96	F3	33.50 S	117.09 E
Kok (Hkok), stm., Asia	64	B4	20.14 N	100.08 E
Kokalaat, Kaz.	48	E10	49.48 N	64.13 E
Kokand, Uzb.	48	F12	40.31 N	70.55 E
Kokanee Glacier Provincial Park, p.o.i., B.C., Can.	144	G13	49.47 N	117.10 W
Kōkar, i., Fin.	18	H7	59.55 N	20.53 E
Kokas, Indon.	60	F9	2.43 S	132.24 E
Kokava nad Rimavicou, Slvk.	24	H15	48.33 N	19.49 E
Kokčetav, Kaz.	48	D12	53.17 N	69.23 E
Kokee State Park, p.o.i., Hi., U.S.	100a	a2	22.08 N	159.38 W
Kokemäenjoki, stm., Fin.	18	F8	61.32 N	21.42 E
Kokemäki, Fin.	18	F9	61.14 N	22.22 E
Kokenau, Indon.	60	F10	4.41 S	136.25 E
Ko Kha, Thai.	64	C4	18.11 N	99.24 E
Kokhav HaYarden, hist., Isr.	76	F6	32.36 N	35.31 E
Kokinu, Japan	186		35.59 N	139.59 E
Kokiu see Gejiu, China	52	G5	23.22 N	103.09 E
Kokkilai Lagoon, b., Sri L.	69	G5	9.01 N	80.54 E
Kokkola (Gamlakarleby), Fin.	18	D10	63.50 N	23.08 E
Koknese, Lat.	26	D8	56.39 N	25.29 E
Kokoda, Pap. N. Gui.	101a	b4	8.52 S	147.44 E
Kokomo, In., U.S.	130	D11	40.29 N	86.08 W
Kokomo, Ms., U.S.	134	F8	31.11 N	90.00 W
Kokong, Bots.	90	D6	24.21 S	23.03 E
Koko Nor see Qinghai Hu, l., China	52	D5	36.48 N	100.06 E
Kokopo, Pap. N. Gui.	101a	a5	4.19 S	152.13 E
Kokorevka, Russia	26	H17	52.34 N	34.17 E
Kokoškino, Russia	183b		55.38 N	37.11 E
Kokovka, Russia	18	E26	62.17 N	39.30 E
Kokpekti, Kaz.	48	E14	48.45 N	82.23 E
Koksan-ŭp, Kor., N.	54	E7	38.46 N	126.40 E
Kökshetaū see Kokčetav, Kaz.	48	D12	53.17 N	69.23 E
Koksoak, stm., Qc., Can.	110	D17	58.31 N	68.10 W
Kokstad, S. Afr.	90	G9	30.32 S	29.25 E
Kokubu, Japan	56	H3	31.43 N	130.46 E
Kokubunji, Japan	186		35.42 N	139.29 E
Kokubunji Temple, rel., Japan	186		35.44 N	139.55 E
Kol, stm., Iran	74	F14	27.00 N	55.45 E
Kola, Russia	14	D23	68.53 N	33.00 E
Kola, stm., Russia	14	D24	68.52 N	33.00 E
Kolachel, India	69	G3	8.10 N	77.16 E
Kolaka, Indon.	60	F7	4.04 S	121.36 E
Kolangār, Afg.	70	A2	34.00 N	69.00 E
Kola Peninsula see Kol'skij poluostrov, pen., Russia	12	C17	67.17 N	36.20 E
Kolār, India	69	E4	13.08 N	78.08 E
Kolāras, India	70	F6	25.12 N	77.35 E
Kolār Gold Fields, India	69	E4	12.56 N	78.16 E
Kolari, Fin.	14	E14	67.21 N	23.51 E
Kolarovgrad see Šumen, Blg.	36	F13	43.16 N	26.56 E
Kolárovo, Slvk.	24	I13	47.54 N	18.01 E
Kolåsen, Swe.	16	D10	63.45 N	12.58 E
Kolašin, Yugo.	36	G6	42.49 N	19.31 E
Kolatsel'ga, Russia	18	F19	61.40 N	32.14 E
Kolāyat, India	70	E4	27.52 N	72.55 E
Kolbäck, Swe.	16	H14	59.34 N	16.14 E
Kolberg see Kołobrzeg, Pol.	24	B11	54.10 N	15.34 E
Kolbio, Kenya	86	E8	1.08 S	41.13 E
Kolbotn, Nor.	16	H8	59.49 N	10.49 E
Kolbuszowa, Pol.	24	F17	50.15 N	21.47 E
Kol'čugino, Russia	26	D22	56.18 N	39.22 E
Kolda, Sen.	84	G2	12.53 N	14.57 W
Kolding, Den.	16	L7	55.29 N	9.27 E
Kole, D.R.C.	86	D5	2.07 N	25.20 E
Kole, D.R.C.	86	E4	3.28 S	22.26 E
Kolea, Alg.	28	H13	36.38 N	2.45 E
Kole Kalyan, ngh., India	190c		19.06 N	72.51 E
Kolenté see Great Scarcies, stm., Afr.	84	H2	8.53 N	13.09 W
Koležma, Russia	18	C22	64.13 N	35.52 E
Kolga, Est.	26	A8	59.31 N	25.43 E
Kolguev, ostrov, i., Russia	48	A7	69.05 N	49.15 E
Kolhāpur, India	69	C4	16.06 N	78.19 E
Kolhāpur, India	69	C2	16.42 N	74.13 E
Kolho, Fin.	18	E11	62.07 N	24.30 E
Koli, Russia	26	A17	59.30 N	34.29 E
Koli, hill, Fin.	18	D16	63.07 N	29.41 E
Koliadivka, Ukr.	38	D18	49.05 N	39.12 E
Koliba see Corubal, stm., Afr.	84	G2	11.56 N	15.02 W
Koliganek, Ak., U.S.	109	E8	59.48 N	157.25 W
Kolima, l., Fin.	18	D12	63.18 N	25.45 E
Kolín, Czech Rep.	24	F11	50.01 N	15.12 E
Kolin kansallispuisto, p.o.i., Fin.	18	D16	63.09 N	29.43 E
Kolisne, Ukr.	38	G8	46.02 N	29.56 E
Koljubakino, Russia	26	E19	55.39 N	36.32 E
Kolka, Lat.	26	C5	57.45 N	22.35 E
Kolkač, Russia	18	H25	59.42 N	38.52 E
Kolkasrags, c., Lat.	26	C5	57.45 N	22.35 E
Kolky, Ukr.	38	B4	51.07 N	25.41 E
Kolky, Ukr.	38	B5	51.35 N	26.38 E
Kollam see Quilon, India	69	G3	8.52 N	76.35 E
Kollegāl, India	69	E3	12.09 N	77.06 E
Kolleru Lake, l., India	69	C5	16.34 N	81.09 E
Kolmården, hills, Swe.	16	I14	58.40 N	16.40 E
Kolmogorovo, Russia	48	C16	59.15 N	91.17 E
Köln (Cologne), Ger.	24	E2	50.55 N	6.57 E
Kolno, Pol.	24	C17	53.24 N	21.55 E
Koło, Pol.	24	D14	52.11 N	18.38 E
Koloa, Hi., U.S.	100a	b2	21.54 N	159.27 W
Kołobrzeg, Pol.	24	B11	54.10 N	15.34 E
Kolodnja, Russia	26	F15	54.48 N	32.10 E
Kologriv, Russia	40	B14	58.49 N	44.18 E
Kolojar, Russia	40	E15	52.34 N	46.55 E
Kolokani, Mali	84	G3	13.34 N	8.02 W
Kolom'agi, ngh., Russia	183a		60.00 N	30.17 E
Kolomak, Ukr.	38	D14	49.50 N	35.18 E
Kolombangara Island, i., Sol. Is.	101b	d7	8.00 S	157.05 E
Kolomea see Kolomyia, Ukr.	38	E4	48.32 N	25.02 E
Kolomenskoe, ngh., Russia	183b		55.40 N	37.41 E
Kolomjagi Airport, arpt., Russia	183a		60.01 N	30.17 E
Kolomna, Russia	26	E21	55.04 N	38.49 E
Kolomyia, Ukr.	38	E4	48.32 N	25.02 E
Kolonga, Tonga	100e	n14	21.08 S	175.04 W
Kolonia, Micron.	100d	m11	6.57 N	158.12 E
Kolonie Stolp, Ger.	182a		52.28 N	13.46 E
Kolonodale, Indon.	60	F7	2.01 S	121.20 E
Kolora, India	190b		22.55 N	88.22 E
Kolosib, India	70	F14	24.14 N	92.42 E
Kolosovka, Russia	48	C12	56.27 N	73.37 E
Kolovai, Tonga	100e	n13	21.06 S	175.20 W
Koloveden kansallispuisto, p.o.i., Fin.	18	E14	62.13 N	27.51 E
Kolozero, ozero, l., Russia	14	D23	68.16 N	33.14 E
Kolozsvár see Cluj-Napoca, Rom.	36	C10	46.46 N	23.36 E
Kolp', stm., Russia	18	H23	59.19 N	36.50 E
Kolpa see Kupa, stm., Eur.	30	E12	45.28 N	16.22 E
Kolpaševo, Russia	48	C14	58.19 N	82.56 E
Kolpino, Russia	26	A13	59.45 N	30.36 E
Kolpny, Russia	26	H19	52.13 N	37.01 E
Kol'skij poluostrov (Kola Peninsula), pen., Russia	12	C17	67.17 N	36.20 E
Kol'skij zaliv, b., Russia	14	C24	69.12 N	33.30 E
Koltuši, Russia	183a		59.56 N	30.40 E
Kolubara, stm., Yugo.	30	F17	44.40 N	20.14 E
Koluszki, Pol.	24	E15	51.44 N	19.49 E
Koluton, Kaz.	48	D11	51.44 N	69.24 E
Kolvereid, Nor.	16	C9	64.51 N	11.36 E
Kolvica, Russia	14	E24	67.04 N	33.00 E
Kolvickoe, ozero, l., Russia	14	E24	67.04 N	33.29 E
Kolwezi, D.R.C.	86	G5	10.43 S	25.28 E
Kolyma, stm., Russia	50	C20	69.37 N	161.18 E
Kolyma Plain see Kolymskaja nizmennost', pl., Russia	50	C19	68.30 N	154.00 E
Kolymskaja, Russia	50	C20	68.44 N	158.44 E
Kolymskaja nizmennost' (Kolyma Plain), pl., Russia	50	C19	68.30 N	154.00 E
Kolyšlej, Russia	40	E14	52.41 N	44.31 E
Kom see Qom, Iran	74	C12	34.38 N	50.53 E
Kom, mtn., Blg.	36	F10	43.10 N	23.03 E
Koma, Mya.	64	E4	15.38 N	98.11 E
Komadugu Gana, stm., Nig.	84	G7	13.03 N	12.24 E
Komagane, Japan	56	D10	35.43 N	137.56 E
Komagfjord, Nor.	14	B14	70.15 N	23.25 E
Komagome, ngh., Japan	186		35.44 N	139.45 E
Komandorskie ostrova, is., Russia	46	D20	55.00 N	167.00 E
Komandorski Islands see Komandorskie ostrova, is., Russia	46	D20	55.00 N	167.00 E
Komandorski Islands see Komandorskije Kamčatka, is., Russia	174	D19	55.00 N	167.00 E
Komandorskije Kamčatka, is., Russia	174	D19	55.00 N	167.00 E
Komandorski Village, Ca., U.S.	200		37.43 N	121.54 W
Komariči, Russia	26	H17	52.24 N	34.47 E
Komarivka, Ukr.	38	B11	51.14 N	32.08 E
Komárno, Slvk.	24	I14	47.45 N	18.08 E
Komarno, Ukr.	38	D2	49.38 N	23.41 E
Komarnyky, Ukr.	38	E2	48.59 N	23.04 E
Komárom, Hung.	36	B5	47.44 N	18.07 E
Komárom-Esztergom, state, Hung.	36	B5	47.40 N	18.15 E
Komarovo, Russia	26	B16	58.39 N	33.26 E
Komati (Incomati), stm., Afr.	90	E10	25.44 S	32.41 E
Komatipoort, S. Afr.	90	D10	25.25 S	31.55 E
Komatsu, Japan	56	C9	36.24 N	136.27 E
Komatsushima, Japan	56	E7	34.00 N	134.35 E
Komdhārā, India	190b		22.53 N	88.14 E
Kome Island, i., Ug.	86	E6	0.05 S	32.45 E
Komenoi, Japan	186		35.55 N	140.01 E
Komering, stm., Indon.	66	F4	3.00 S	104.50 E
Komfane, Indon.	60	G9	5.38 S	134.43 E
Komga, S. Afr.	90	H8	32.34 S	27.56 E
Komi, state, Russia	48	B8	64.00 N	54.00 E
Kominato see Amatsu-kominato, Japan	56	D13	35.07 N	140.09 E
Kominternivs'ke, Ukr.	38	G9	46.49 N	30.56 E
Komissarovo, Russia	54	B9	44.58 N	131.46 E
Komissarovskij, Russia	40	H13	47.29 N	42.59 E
Komló, Hung.	36	C5	46.13 N	18.14 E
Kommunarka, Russia	183b		55.34 N	37.29 E
Kommunarsk see Alchevs'k, Ukr.	38	E17	48.29 N	38.47 E
Kommunary, Russia	18	G16	60.53 N	29.47 E
Kommunizma, pik, mtn., Taj.	72	B11	38.57 N	72.01 E
Komodo, Indon.	66	H11	8.35 S	119.29 E
Komodo, Pulau, i., Indon.	66	H11	8.33 S	119.28 E
Komodo National Park, p.o.i., Indon.	66	H11	8.37 S	119.35 E
Komoé, stm., Afr.	84	H4	5.12 N	3.43 W
Kom Ombo, Egypt	74	H3	24.28 N	32.56 E
Komoran, Pulau, i., Indon.	60	G10	8.18 S	138.45 E
Komorn see Komárno, Slvk.	24	I14	47.45 N	18.08 E
Komoro, Japan	56	C11	36.19 N	138.26 E
Komotiní, Grc.	34	B8	41.07 N	25.25 E
Kompaniïvka, Ukr.	38	E11	48.15 N	32.12 E
Kompasberg, mtn., S. Afr.	90	G7	31.45 S	24.32 E
Komrat see Comrat, Mol.	38	G7	46.18 N	28.39 E
Komsomolec, Kaz.	48	D10	53.46 N	62.02 E
Komsomolec, zaliv, b., Kaz.	48	E8	45.30 N	52.45 E
Komsomol'sk, Russia	40	C12	57.01 N	40.23 E
Komsomol'sk, Russia	48	C15	57.24 N	86.00 E
Komsomol's'ke, Ukr.	38	F17	47.40 N	38.04 E
Komsomol's'ke, Ukr.	38	D7	49.43 N	28.40 E
Komsomol's'ke, Ukr.	38	D15	49.35 N	36.33 E
Komsomol'skij, Kaz.	48	A10	47.19 N	53.40 E
Komsomol'skij, Russia	40	D14	54.26 N	45.51 E
Komsomol'skij, Russia	40	I14	45.20 N	46.02 E
Komsomol'sk-na-Amure, Russia	50	F16	50.33 N	137.00 E
Komsomol'skoj Pravdy, ostrova, is., Russia	50	A10	77.20 N	107.40 E
Kömürcüpınar, ngh., Tur.	185b		41.15 N	28.51 E
Komyshnia, Ukr.	38	C12	50.12 N	33.41 E
Komyshuvakha, Ukr.	38	F14	47.43 N	35.31 E
Kona, India	190b		22.37 N	88.18 E
Kona Coast State Park, p.o.i., Hi., U.S.	100a	d6	19.46 N	156.02 W
Konakovo, Russia	26	D19	56.42 N	36.46 E
Konakpınar, Tur.	34	D10	39.26 N	27.53 E
Konan see Hŭngdŏki-dong, Kor., N.	54	E7	39.50 N	127.38 E
Kōnan, ngh., Japan	186		35.22 N	139.35 E
Konar, stm., Asia	70	A3	34.36 N	70.53 E
Konārak, India	70	I11	19.54 N	86.07 E
Konawa, Ok., U.S.	134	C2	34.57 N	96.45 W
Končanskoe-Suvorovskoe, Russia	26	B17	58.39 N	34.04 E
Konch, India	70	F7	25.59 N	79.09 E
Konda, stm., Russia	48	B10	60.42 N	69.39 E
Kondagaon, India	69	B5	19.36 N	81.40 E
Kondega, Russia	18	G20	60.13 N	33.30 E
Kondiaronk, Lac, l., Qc., Can.	126	B13	46.57 N	76.48 W
Kondinin, Austl.	96	F3	32.30 S	118.16 E
Kondli, ngh., India	190a		28.37 N	77.19 E
Kondoa, Tan.	86	E7	4.52 S	35.47 E
Kondol', Russia	40	E14	52.49 N	45.02 E
Kondopoga, Russia	18	E21	62.12 N	34.17 E
Kondostrov, ostrov, i., Russia	18	C23	64.13 N	36.38 E
Kondratevo, Russia	18	G15	60.38 N	28.08 E
Kondrovo, Russia	26	F18	54.48 N	35.56 E
Kondukūr, India	69	D4	15.12 N	79.54 E
Kondūz, Afg.	72	B10	36.44 N	68.51 E
Koné, N. Cal.	101d	m15	21.04 S	164.52 E
Konëvo, Russia	18	E26	62.06 N	39.16 E
Kong, stm., Asia	64	F8	13.32 N	105.57 E
Kŏng, Kaôh, i., Camb.	64	G6	11.20 N	103.00 E
Kongcheng, China	58	F7	31.02 N	117.05 E
Kong Christian IX Land, reg., Grnld.	108	D18	68.00 N	36.00 W
Kong Christian X Land, reg., Grnld.	108	C19	73.50 N	28.30 W
Kong Frederik VIII Land, reg., Grnld.	108	B19	78.00 N	24.00 W
Kong Frederik VI Kyst, cst., Grnld.	108	E17	63.15 N	42.15 W
Konginkangas, Fin.	18	E12	62.46 N	25.48 E
Kongjiawopeng, China	54	B5	43.58 N	122.41 E
Kongju, Kor., S.	54	F7	36.27 N	127.07 E
Kongmoon see Jiangmen, China	58	J5	22.34 N	113.04 E
Kongolo, D.R.C.	86	F5	5.23 S	27.01 E
Kongor, Sudan	82	F6	7.09 N	31.20 E
Kongō-sanchi, mts., Japan	188		34.27 N	135.41 E
Kong Oscar Fjord, strt., Grnld.	108	C21	72.22 N	24.00 W
Kongsberg, Nor.	16	H7	59.39 N	9.38 E
Kongsfjord, Nor.	14	B20	70.43 N	29.17 E
Kongsmoen, Nor.	16	C10	64.53 N	12.24 E
Kongsvinger, Nor.	16	G10	60.11 N	12.00 E
Kongsvoll, Nor.	16	E7	62.18 N	9.37 E
Kongur Shan, mtn., China	48	G13	38.37 N	75.20 E
Kong Wilhelms Land, reg., Grnld.	108	B21	75.45 N	22.45 W
Konice, Czech Rep.	24	G12	49.35 N	16.54 E
Koniecpol, Pol.	24	F15	50.47 N	19.41 E

Name	Page	Map Ref.	Latitude	Longitude
Königgrätz see Hradec Králové, Czech Rep.	24	F11	50.12 N	15.49 E
Königsberg see Chojna, Pol.	24	D10	52.57 N	14.25 E
Königsberg see Kaliningrad, Russia	26	F3	54.42 N	20.30 E
Königsborn, Ger.	181		51.33 N	7.41 E
Königsbrunn, Aus.	182b		48.21 N	16.25 E
Königshardt, ngh., Ger.	181		51.33 N	6.51 E
Königslutter, Ger.	20	B19	52.15 N	10.49 E
Königstetten, Aus.	182b		48.18 N	16.09 E
Königswinter, Ger.	24	F3	50.40 N	7.12 E
Konin, Pol.	24	D14	52.13 N	18.15 E
Konispol, Alb.	32	E14	39.39 N	20.09 E
Konispoli see Konispol, Alb.	32	E14	39.39 N	20.09 E
Kónitsa, Grc.	34	C3	40.03 N	20.45 E
Konjic, Bos.	36	F4	43.39 N	17.57 E
Könkämäälven (Könkämäeno), stm., Eur.	14	D12	68.28 N	22.15 E
Könkämäeno (Könkämäälven), stm., Eur.	14	D12	68.28 N	22.15 E
Konkiep, stm., Nmb.	90	E3	28.03 S	17.19 E
Konkouré, stm., Gui.	84	G2	9.56 N	13.41 W
Konkudera, Russia	50	E11	57.33 N	112.30 E
Konkug University, educ., Kor., S.	189b		37.32 N	127.05 E
Konna, Mali	84	G4	14.57 N	3.53 W
Konnevesi, l., Fin.	18	E13	62.37 N	26.37 E
Konnur, India	69	C2	16.13 N	74.45 E
Konohana, ngh., Japan	188		34.41 N	135.26 E
Kōnoike, Japan	188		34.42 N	135.37 E
Konoša, Russia	12	F18	60.58 N	40.15 E
Kōnosu, Japan	56	C12	36.03 N	139.31 E
Konotop, Ukr.	38	B12	51.14 N	33.12 E
Konradshöhe, ngh., Ger.	182a		52.35 N	13.14 E
Końskie, Pol.	24	E16	51.11 N	20.25 E
Konstantinovka, Russia	40	C17	56.41 N	50.53 E
Konstantinovka see Kostiantynivka, Ukr.	38	E16	48.31 N	37.43 E
Konstantinovka, ngh., Russia	183a		59.47 N	30.08 E
Konstantinovsk, Russia	40	H12	47.34 N	41.06 E
Konstantinovskie Porogi, Russia	18	G24	60.34 N	37.04 E
Konstantinovskij, Russia	26	C22	57.49 N	39.36 E
Konstantinovskoe, Russia	40	I13	45.18 N	42.37 E
Konstantynów Łódzki, Pol.	24	E15	51.45 N	19.20 E
Konstanz, Ger.	24	I5	47.39 N	9.10 E
Kontagora, Nig.	84	G5	10.24 N	5.26 E
Kontcha, Cam.	86	C2	7.57 N	12.14 E
Kontha, Mya.	64	C3	19.29 N	96.02 E
Kontiolahti, Fin.	18	E16	62.47 N	29.51 E
Kontiomäki, Fin.	18	C15	64.21 N	28.05 E
Kontseba, Ukr.	38	E8	48.06 N	29.56 E
Kon Tum, Viet.	64	E8	14.20 N	108.00 E
Kontum, Plateau du, plat., Viet.	64	F9	13.55 N	108.05 E
Konya, Tur.	34	F15	37.52 N	32.31 E
Konya, state, Tur.	42	F5	38.00 N	33.00 E
Konyr, Kaz.	40	F18	50.24 N	53.24 E
Konyševka, Russia	38	B14	51.50 N	35.17 E
Konz, Ger.	24	G2	49.41 N	6.34 E
Konza, Kenya	86	E7	1.44 S	37.06 E
Konžakovskij Kamen', gora, mtn., Russia	48	C9	59.38 N	59.08 E
Koocanusa, Lake, res., N.A.	146	B11	48.58 N	115.10 W
Kookynie, Austl.	96	E4	29.20 S	121.29 E
Koolamarra, Austl.	98	C3	20.08 S	140.10 E
Koolatah, Austl.	96	C8	15.53 S	142.27 E
Koolau Range, mts., Hi., U.S.	100a	b4	21.26 N	157.53 W
Kooloonong, Austl.	98	J4	34.53 S	143.09 E
Koondrook, Austl.	98	J4	35.39 S	144.07 E
Koonga, Est.	26	B7	58.35 N	24.12 E
Koontz Lake, In., U.S.	130	C11	41.24 N	86.28 W
Koorawatha, Austl.	98	J7	34.02 S	148.33 E
Koosa, Est.	26	B9	58.32 N	27.05 E
Koosharem, Ut., U.S.	150	E4	38.30 N	111.53 W
Kooskia, Id., U.S.	146	D11	46.08 N	115.58 W
Kootenai (Kootenay), stm., N.A.	144	G14	49.18 N	117.39 W
Kootenay (Kootenai), stm., N.A.	144	G14	49.18 N	117.39 W
Kootenay Indian Reserve, ind. res., B.C., Can.	144	G15	49.37 N	115.45 W
Kootenay Lake, l., B.C., Can.	144	G14	49.35 N	116.50 W
Kootenay National Park, p.o.i., B.C., Can.	144	E14	51.00 N	116.00 W
Kopāganj, India	70	E9	26.01 N	83.34 E
Kopaihorod, Ukr.	38	E6	48.51 N	27.48 E
Kopanovka, Russia	40	H15	47.26 N	46.48 E
Kopanskaja, Russia	38	G17	46.16 N	38.28 E
Kopargaon, India	69	B2	19.52 N	74.28 E
Koparkhairna, India	190c		19.06 N	72.59 E
Koparpāda, India	190c		19.02 N	73.04 E
Kópasker, Ice.	12a	j31	66.20 N	16.24 W
Kópavogur, Ice.	12a	k29	64.05 N	21.52 W
Kopejsk, Russia	48	C10	55.06 N	61.37 E
Köpenick, Schloss, bldg., Ger.	182a		52.27 N	13.34 E
Koper, Slvn.	30	E10	45.32 N	13.43 E
Kopervik, Nor.	16	H3	59.17 N	5.18 E
Kopetdag, hrebet see Kopet Mountains, mts., Asia	72	B8	37.50 N	58.00 E
Kopet Mountains, mts., Asia	72	B8	37.50 N	58.00 E
Kopevo, Russia	48	D15	55.00 N	89.48 E
Köping, Swe.	16	H13	59.30 N	15.59 E
Koplik, Alb.	32	B13	42.13 N	19.25 E
Köpmanholmen, Swe.	16	D16	63.10 N	18.34 E
Kopore, Russia	26	A12	59.43 N	28.59 E
Koporskaja guba, b., Russia	26	A11	59.50 N	28.55 E
Koppal, India	69	D3	15.20 N	76.09 E
Koppang, Nor.	16	F9	61.34 N	11.03 E
Koppány, stm., Hung.	36	C5	46.35 N	18.26 E
Kopparberg, Swe.	16	H12	59.53 N	15.00 E
Koppeh Dāgh see Kopet Mountains, mts., Asia	72	B8	37.50 N	58.00 E
Kopperå, Nor.	16	D9	63.24 N	11.51 E
Koppies, S. Afr.	90	E8	27.12 S	27.35 E
Koppom, Swe.	16	H10	59.43 N	12.11 E
Kopri, India	190c		19.11 N	72.58 E
Koprivnica, Cro.	30	D13	46.09 N	16.50 E
Köprü, stm., Tur.	34	F13	36.50 N	31.10 E
Köprülü Kanyon Milli Parkı, p.o.i., Tur.	34	F13	37.13 N	31.11 E
Köprüören, Tur.	34	D12	39.30 N	29.47 E
Kopychyntsi, Ukr.	38	D4	49.05 N	25.56 E
Kopylovo, Russia	12	F21	60.35 N	45.04 E
Kopys', Bela.	26	F13	54.19 N	30.17 E
Kor, stm., Iran	74	F13	29.31 N	53.26 E
Korab (Korabit, Maja e), mtn., Eur.	36	H7	41.47 N	20.34 E
Korabit, Maja e (Korab), mtn., Eur.	36	H7	41.47 N	20.34 E
Korablino, Russia	40	E12	53.55 N	40.02 E
Koralpe, mts., Aus.	30	D12	46.47 N	14.56 E
Korāput, India	69	B6	18.48 N	82.43 E
Korarou, Lac, l., Mali	84	F4	15.15 N	3.16 W
Korat see Nakhon Ratchasima, Thai.	64	E6	14.58 N	102.05 E
Koratla, India	69	B4	18.49 N	78.42 E
Korba, India	70	G9	22.21 N	82.41 E
Korba, Tun.	32	H4	36.35 N	10.52 E
Korbach, Ger.	24	E4	51.16 N	8.52 E
Korbeniči, Russia	18	G21	60.14 N	34.37 E
Korbol, Chad	82	F3	9.59 N	17.43 E
Korça see Korçë, Alb.	32	D14	40.37 N	20.47 E
Korçë, Alb.	32	D14	40.37 N	20.47 E
Korčula, Cro.	30	H14	42.57 N	17.07 E
Korčula, Otok, i., Cro.	30	H13	42.57 N	16.50 E
Korčulanski Kanal, strt., Cro.	30	G13	43.03 N	16.40 E
Kordestān, state, Iran	74	C10	35.30 N	47.00 E
Kordestān see Kurdistan, hist. reg., Asia	8	H17	37.00 N	45.00 E
Kordestān see Kurdistān, hist. reg., Asia	72	B5	37.00 N	45.00 E
Kord Kūy, Iran	74	B14	36.48 N	54.07 E
Korea, National Museum of, bldg., Kor., S.	189b		37.35 N	126.58 E
Korea, North, ctry., Asia	54	D7	40.00 N	127.00 E
Korea, South, ctry., Asia	54	G8	36.30 N	128.00 E
Korea Bay, b., Asia	54	E5	39.00 N	124.00 E
Korea Strait, strt., Asia	56	F1	34.00 N	129.00 E
Korea University, educ., Kor., S.	189b		37.36 N	127.02 E
Korekozevo, Russia	26	F19	54.20 N	36.11 E
Korelakša, Russia	18	B19	65.31 N	32.24 E
Korenëvo, Russia	40	F9	51.23 N	34.54 E
Korenëvo, Russia	183b		55.40 N	38.00 E
Korenovsk, Russia	40	I11	45.27 N	39.26 E
Korets', Ukr.	38	C6	50.37 N	27.09 E
Korets', Ukr.	38	C5	50.35 N	27.01 E
Korf, Russia	50	D22	60.21 N	165.56 E
Kõrgessaare, Est.	26	A5	58.59 N	22.31 E
Korhogo, C. Iv.	84	H3	9.27 N	5.38 W
Kōri, Japan	188		34.47 N	135.39 E
Korientzé, Mali	84	F4	15.23 N	3.46 W
Korim, Indon.	60	F10	0.55 S	136.04 E
Korinthiakós Kólpos (Corinth, Gulf of), b., Grc.	34	E5	38.12 N	22.35 E
Kórinthos, Grc.	34	F5	37.56 N	22.57 E
Kőris-hegy, mtn., Hung.	36	B4	47.18 N	17.45 E
Koritsa see Korçë, Alb.	32	D14	40.37 N	20.47 E
Koriukivka, Ukr.	38	B11	51.45 N	32.15 E
Kōriyama, Japan	56	B13	37.24 N	140.23 E
Korjakskaja Sopka, vulkan, vol., Russia	50	F20	53.20 N	158.43 E
Korjakskoe nagor'e, mts., Russia	50	D22	62.30 N	172.00 E
Korjažma, Russia	12	F22	61.18 N	47.08 E
Korkino, Russia	48	D10	54.53 N	61.21 E
Korkino, Russia	48	D19	54.22 N	105.12 E
Korkinskoe, ozero, l., Russia	183a		59.55 N	30.44 E
Korkuteli, Tur.	34	F13	37.04 N	30.12 E
Korla, China	52	C2	41.44 N	86.09 E
Korliki, Russia	48	B14	61.31 N	82.22 E
Korma see Karma, Bela.	26	H14	52.19 N	31.26 E
Körmend, Hung.	36	C3	47.01 N	16.36 E
Kornat, Otok, i., Cro.	30	G12	43.50 N	15.16 E
Kornati, Nacionalni Park, p.o.i., Cro.	30	G12	43.50 N	15.20 E
Körnebach, stm., Ger.	181		51.35 N	7.38 E
Korner, Mt., U.S.	146	A14	48.59 N	112.15 W
Kornetspruit see Makhaleng, stm., Afr.	90	G8	30.02 S	27.27 E
Korneuburg, Aus.	30	B13	48.20 N	16.20 E
Kornëvo, Russia	183a		60.03 N	30.45 E
Kórnik, Pol.	24	D13	52.17 N	17.04 E
Kornsjø, Nor.	16	I9	58.57 N	11.40 E
Kornyn, Ukr.	38	C8	50.05 N	29.32 E
Koro, i., Fiji	101e	p19	17.16 S	179.24 E
Koroča, Russia	40	F10	50.48 N	37.11 E
Köroğlu Tepesi, mtn., Tur.	34	C14	40.31 N	31.53 E
Korogwe, Tan.	86	F7	5.08 S	38.28 E
Koroit, Austl.	98	L4	38.17 S	142.21 E
Koroleve, Ukr.	24	H19	48.09 N	23.08 E
Korolëvščina, Russia	26	E14	55.48 N	31.46 E
Koromba, mtn., Fiji	101e	p18	17.53 S	177.34 E
Koromere see East Cape, c., N.Z.	102	C8	37.41 S	178.33 E
Koromiri, i., Cook Is.	100j	b27	21.15 S	159.43 W
Koromo see Toyota, Japan	56	D10	35.05 N	137.09 E
Koronadal, Phil.	68	G5	6.29 N	124.50 E
Koróni, Grc.	34	G4	36.48 N	21.56 E
Korónia, Límni, l., Grc.	34	C6	40.41 N	23.07 E
Koronowo, Pol.	24	C13	53.18 N	17.56 E
Korop, Ukr.	38	B11	51.34 N	32.56 E
Korópi, Grc.	34	F6	37.54 N	23.52 E
Korópi, Grc.	185c		37.54 N	23.53 E
Koror, Palau	100b	g8	7.20 N	134.30 E
Koror see Oreor, i., Palau	100b	g8	7.20 N	134.29 E
Kororoit Creek, stm., Austl.	192b		37.52 S	144.52 E
Körös, stm., Hung.	36	C7	46.43 N	20.11 E
Koro Sea, s., Fiji	94	E9	18.00 S	179.50 E
Korosten', Ukr.	38	C7	50.57 N	28.38 E
Korostyshiv, Ukr.	38	C7	50.19 N	29.04 E
Koroteckaja, Russia	18	G25	60.18 N	38.40 E
Korotojak, Russia	38	C18	50.59 N	39.11 E
Koro Toro, Chad	82	D3	16.04 N	18.30 E
Korotovo, Russia	26	B20	58.57 N	37.27 E
Korotyš, Russia	26	H20	52.22 N	37.26 E
Korovino, Russia	38	B15	51.24 N	36.45 E
Korovin Volcano, vol., Ak., U.S.	109a	g24	52.22 N	174.10 W
Korovou, Fiji	101e	p19	17.48 S	178.33 E
Korovyntsi, Ukr.	38	C12	50.48 N	33.45 E
Koroyanitu, mtn., Fiji	101e	p18	17.40 S	177.35 E
Korožečna, stm., Russia	26	C21	57.31 N	38.17 E
Korpilahti, Fin.	18	E12	62.01 N	25.31 E
Korpilombolo, Swe.	14	F14	66.51 N	23.04 E
Korpo see Korppoo, Fin.	18	G8	60.10 N	21.34 E
Korppoo, Fin.	18	G8	60.10 N	21.34 E
Korsakov, Russia	50	G17	46.37 N	142.47 E
Korsakovo, Russia	26	G20	53.15 N	37.21 E
Korselbränna, Swe.	16	C13	64.27 N	15.36 E
Korševo, Russia	38	B19	51.11 N	40.07 E
Korsnäs, Fin.	18	E8	62.47 N	21.11 E
Korsnäs, Swe.	16	G13	60.35 N	15.43 E
Korso, Fin.	18	G12	60.21 N	25.06 E
Korsør, Den.	16	L9	55.20 N	11.08 E
Korsträsk, Swe.	14	G11	65.40 N	20.52 E
Koršunovo, Russia	48	C20	58.36 N	110.09 E
Korsun'-Shevchenkivs'kyi, Ukr.	38	D10	49.24 N	31.16 E
Korsze, Pol.	24	B17	54.10 N	21.08 E
Kortelisy, Ukr.	38	B3	51.29 N	24.25 E
Kortrijk, Bel.	20	D12	50.50 N	3.16 E
Korucam, Cape see Koruçam Burnu, c., N. Cyp.	76	C3	35.22 N	32.56 E
Koruçam Burnu, c., N. Cyp.	76	C3	35.22 N	32.56 E
Korucu, Tur.	34	D10	39.28 N	27.22 E
Korumburra, Austl.	98	L5	38.26 S	145.49 E
Korvatunturi, mtn., Fin.	14	D20	68.04 N	29.19 E
Koryak Mountains see Korjakskoe nagor'e, mts., Russia	50	D22	62.30 N	172.00 E
Korydallós, Grc.	185c		37.59 N	23.39 E
Koryŏng, Kor., S.	56	D1	35.43 N	128.16 E
Kos, Grc.	34	G10	36.53 N	27.17 E
Kos (Cos), i., Grc.	34	G10	36.50 N	27.10 E
Kosa, Russia	48	C8	59.56 N	54.59 E
Kosa, Russia	50	F10	54.46 N	108.50 E
Kosa Arabats'ka strilka, spit, Ukr.	38	H14	45.46 N	34.56 E
Kosachivka, Ukr.	38	B9	51.11 N	30.36 E
Kosai, Japan	56	E10	34.42 N	137.33 E
Kosaja Gora, Russia	26	F20	54.07 N	37.33 E
Kosava, Bela.	26	H8	52.45 N	25.09 E
Kosčagyl, Kaz.	48	E8	46.51 N	53.48 E
Kościan, Pol.	24	D12	52.05 N	16.39 E
Kościerzyna, Pol.	24	B14	54.07 N	17.59 E
Kosciusko, Ms., U.S.	134	D9	33.03 N	89.35 W
Kosciuszko, Mount, mtn., Austl.	98	K7	36.26 S	148.15 E
Kosciuszko National Park, p.o.i., Austl.	98	K6	36.03 S	148.16 E
Kose, Est.	26	A8	59.11 N	25.10 E
Kose, Japan	188		34.25 N	135.46 E
Košehabl', Russia	42	C9	44.53 N	40.31 E
Koshien Stadium, p.o.i., Japan	188		34.42 N	135.22 E
Koshigoe, Japan	186		35.18 N	139.30 E
Koshikijima-rettō, is., Japan	56	H2	31.45 N	129.49 E
Koshkonong, Mo., U.S.	130	H6	36.35 N	91.38 W
Koshkonong, Lake, l., Wi., U.S.	130	B9	42.51 N	88.56 W
Kōshoku, Japan	56	C11	36.31 N	138.08 E
Koshu see Kwangju, Kor., S.	54	G7	35.08 N	126.54 E
Košice, Slvk.	24	H17	48.43 N	21.16 E
Kosigi, India	69	D3	15.51 N	77.13 E
Kosi Kalan, India	70	E6	27.47 N	77.26 E
Kosimeer, l., S. Afr.	90	E11	26.55 S	32.51 E
Kosino, ngh., Russia	183b		55.43 N	37.52 E
Kosiv, Ukr.	38	E4	48.19 N	25.05 E
Kosju, Russia	48	A9	65.38 N	59.02 E
Kösk, Tur.	34	F11	37.51 N	28.03 E
Koškar, Kaz.	40	H18	47.30 N	53.27 E
Koski, Fin.	18	G10	60.39 N	23.08 E
Koskol', Kaz.	48	E11	49.32 N	67.04 E
Koskolovo, Russia	18	H15	59.40 N	28.27 E
Koskullskulle, Swe.	14	E11	67.11 N	20.44 E
Koslan, Russia	12	E23	63.28 N	48.40 E
Köslin see Koszalin, Pol.	24	B12	54.11 N	16.12 E
Kosogor, Russia	40	C15	57.07 N	47.34 E
Kosŏng, Kor., N.	56	E1	34.58 N	128.18 E
Kosŏng-ŭp, Kor., N.	54	E8	38.40 N	128.19 E
Kosovo-Metohija, co., Yugo.	36	G7	42.35 N	21.00 E
Kosovska Mitrovica, Yugo.	36	G7	42.53 N	20.52 E
Kosrae, i., Micron.	94	C7	5.19 N	162.59 E
Kösreli, Tur.	76	A6	37.12 N	35.58 E
Kosse, Tx., U.S.	136	C11	31.17 N	96.38 W
Kossou, Lac de, res., C. Iv.	84	H3	7.15 N	5.41 W
Kosta, Swe.	16	K13	56.50 N	15.24 E
Kostajnica, Cro.	30	E13	45.14 N	16.31 E
Kostenec, Blg.	36	G10	42.16 N	23.49 E
Koster, S. Afr.	90	D8	25.52 S	26.53 E
Kostiantynivka, Ukr.	38	F10	47.49 N	31.09 E
Kostiantynivka, Ukr.	38	E16	48.31 N	37.43 E
Kostiantynivka, Ukr.	38	D14	49.56 N	35.07 E
Kostino, Russia	40	E17	52.11 N	51.19 E
Kostino, Russia	183b		55.55 N	37.51 E
Kost'kovo, Russia	18	G20	60.02 N	33.16 E
Kostomukša, Russia	18	C17	64.38 N	30.42 E
Kostonjärvi, l., Fin.	18	B14	65.47 N	28.27 E
Kostopil', Ukr.	38	C5	50.52 N	26.27 E
Kostroma, Russia	40	C12	57.46 N	40.57 E
Kostroma, stm., Russia	40	B12	57.47 N	40.55 E
Kostromskaja oblast', co., Russia	40	B14	58.30 N	44.00 E
Kostrzyn, Pol.	24	D10	52.35 N	14.39 E
Kosugaya, ngh., Japan	186		35.22 N	139.33 E
Kosum Phisai, Thai.	64	D6	16.14 N	103.03 E
Koszalin, Pol.	24	B12	54.11 N	16.12 E
Kőszeg, Hung.	36	B3	47.23 N	16.32 E
Koszyce, Pol.	24	F16	50.10 N	20.34 E
Kota, India	70	G9	22.18 N	82.02 E
Kota, India	70	F5	25.10 N	75.50 E
Kotaagung, Indon.	66	F4	5.29 S	104.36 E
Kotabaharu, Indon.	66	D7	0.48 S	111.32 E
Kotabangun, Indon.	66	D10	0.16 S	116.34 E
Kotabaru see Jayapura, Indon.	60	F11	2.32 S	140.42 E
Kotabaru, Indon.	66	D2	1.08 S	101.43 E
Kotabaru, Indon.	66	E10	3.14 S	116.14 E
Kota Belud, Malay.	68	G1	6.29 N	116.32 E
Kota Bharu, Malay.	64	I6	6.08 N	102.15 E
Kotabumi, Indon.	66	F4	4.49 S	104.52 E
Kotadabok, Indon.	66	D4	0.32 S	104.31 E
Kot Addu, Pak.	70	C3	30.28 N	70.58 E
Kota Kinabalu, Malay.	68	G1	5.57 N	116.04 E
Kota Kota see Nkhotakota, Mwi.	88	C5	12.54 S	34.16 E
Kotala, Fin.	14	E19	67.01 N	29.02 E
Kotamobagu, Indon.	62	E7	0.43 N	124.18 E
Kotapinang, Indon.	66	C1	1.54 N	100.04 E
Kotatengah, Indon.	66	C2	1.05 N	100.32 E
Kota Tinggi, Malay.	64	L6	1.44 N	103.54 E
Kotawaringin, Indon.	66	E7	2.29 S	111.26 E
Kotcho Lake, l., B.C., Can.	110	D6	59.05 N	121.10 W
Kot Chutta, Pak.	70	D3	29.52 N	70.38 E
Kotel, Blg.	36	G13	42.53 N	26.27 E
Kotel'nič, Russia	40	B16	58.18 N	48.19 E
Kotel'nikovo, Russia	40	H13	47.37 N	43.08 E
Kotel'nyj, ostrov, i., Russia	50	A16	75.45 N	138.44 E
Kotelnyj, ostrov, i., Russia	50	B3	73.14 N	70.33 E
Kotel'va, Ukr.	38	C13	50.03 N	34.46 E
Köthen, Ger.	24	E7	51.45 N	11.58 E
Koti see Kōchi, Japan	56	F6	33.33 N	133.32 E
Kotido, Ug.	86	D6	3.00 N	34.06 E
Kotikovo, Russia	50	G17	49.08 N	144.14 E
Kotivka, Ukr.	38	D13	49.08 N	34.56 E
Kotka, Fin.	18	G13	60.27 N	26.56 E
Kot Kapūra, India	70	C5	30.32 N	74.51 E
Kotkino, Russia	12	C24	67.02 N	51.03 E
Kotlas, Russia	12	F22	61.15 N	46.39 E
Kotli, Pak.	70	B4	33.29 N	73.52 E
Kotlik, Ak., U.S.	109	D7	63.02 N	163.33 W
Kotly, Russia	26	A11	59.35 N	28.42 E
Kōtō, ngh., Japan	186		35.41 N	139.48 E
Kôtomo, Île, i., N. Cal.	101d	n16	22.39 S	167.31 E
Kotor, Yugo.	36	G5	42.25 N	18.46 E
Kotoriba, Cro.	30	D13	46.21 N	16.50 E
Kotor Varoš, Bos.	36	E4	44.37 N	17.21 E
Kotovo, Russia	40	F14	50.18 N	44.48 E
Kotovsk, Russia	40	E12	52.35 N	41.31 E
Kotovs'k, Ukr.	38	F8	47.44 N	29.32 E
Kot Pūtli, India	70	E6	27.43 N	76.12 E
Kotra, India	70	F4	24.22 N	73.11 E
Kotra, India	190b		22.46 N	88.34 E
Kotri, Pak.	70	F2	25.21 N	68.16 E
Kotrung see Uttarpara-Kotrung, India	190b		22.40 N	88.21 E
Kottagūdem, India	69	C5	17.32 N	80.38 E
Kottayam, India	69	G3	9.35 N	76.31 E
Kotte see Sri Jayawardenepura, Sri L.	69	H4	6.53 N	79.54 E
Kotto, stm., C.A.R.	86	C4	4.13 N	22.02 E
Kottūru, India	69	D3	14.49 N	76.13 E
Kotuj, stm., Russia	50	B9	71.54 N	102.06 E
Kotzebue, Ak., U.S.	109	C7	66.53 N	162.35 W
Kotzebue Sound, strt., Ak., U.S.	109	C7	66.20 N	163.00 W
Kötzting, Ger.	24	G8	49.10 N	12.51 E
Kouaoua, N. Cal.	101d	m15	21.24 S	165.49 E
Koubansaki, Congo	191b		4.22 S	15.09 E
Koŭbča, Bela.	26	G12	53.39 N	29.14 E
Kouchibouguac National Park, p.o.i., N.B., Can.	122	D11	46.50 N	65.00 W
Koudougou, Burkina	84	G4	12.15 N	2.22 W
Kouga, stm., S. Afr.	90	H7	33.40 S	24.23 E
Kougaberge, mts., S. Afr.	90	H6	33.40 S	23.50 E
Koukdjuak, stm., Nu., Can.	110	B16	66.43 N	72.58 W
Kouki, C.A.R.	86	C3	7.09 N	17.18 E
Koúklia, Cyp.	76	D3	34.42 N	32.34 E
Koulamoutou, Gabon	86	E2	1.08 S	12.29 E
Koulikoro, Mali	84	G3	12.51 N	7.33 W
Koumac, N. Cal.	101d	m15	20.33 S	164.17 E
Koumala, Austl.	98	C7	21.33 S	149.14 E
Koumbia, Gui.	84	G2	11.48 N	13.30 W
Koumi, Japan	56	C11	36.05 N	138.28 E
Koumpentoum, Sen.	84	G2	13.58 N	14.33 W
Koumra, Chad	82	F3	8.54 N	17.33 E
Koundâra, Gui.	84	G2	12.28 N	13.17 W
Koungheul, Sen.	84	G1	13.58 N	14.48 W
Kounradskij, Kaz.	48	E12	46.57 N	74.58 E
Kountze, Tx., U.S.	136	D13	30.22 N	94.19 W
Kourou, Fr. Gu.	164	B7	5.09 N	52.38 W
Kouroussa, Gui.	84	G3	10.39 N	9.52 W
Kousséri, Cam.	86	B2	12.04 N	15.01 E
Koussi, Emi, mtn., Chad	82	D3	19.50 N	18.30 E
Koutiala, Mali	84	G3	12.23 N	5.28 W
Kouts, In., U.S.	130	C10	41.19 N	87.00 W
Kouvola, Fin.	18	G13	60.52 N	26.41 E
Kova, Russia	48	C18	58.17 N	100.21 E
Kovada Milli Parkı, p.o.i., Tur.	34	F13	37.36 N	30.50 E
Kovalivka, Ukr.	38	F10	47.16 N	31.44 E
Kovarzino, Russia	18	G25	60.08 N	38.34 E
Kovda, Russia	14	F23	66.41 N	32.49 E
Kovdor, Russia	14	E21	67.33 N	30.29 E
Kovdozero, ozero, res., Russia	14	F21	66.47 N	32.00 E
Kovel', Ukr.	38	B3	51.13 N	24.41 E
Kovilpatti, India	69	G3	9.10 N	77.52 E
Kovin, Yugo.	36	E7	44.44 N	20.59 E
Kovno see Kaunas, Lith.	26	F6	54.54 N	23.53 E
Kovrov, Russia	40	C12	56.22 N	41.19 E
Kovūr, India	69	D5	14.28 N	79.59 E
Kovylkino, Russia	40	D13	54.02 N	43.55 E
Kovža, Russia	18	F26	61.08 N	38.58 E
Kovžinskij Zavod, Russia	18	G23	60.25 N	37.05 E
Kovžskoe, ozero, l., Russia	18	G24	60.51 N	37.19 E
Kowal, Pol.	24	D15	52.31 N	19.09 E
Kowalewo Pomorskie, Pol.	24	C14	53.09 N	18.54 E
Kowangge, Indon.	66	H11	8.16 S	118.32 E
Kowel see Kovel', Ukr.	38	B3	51.13 N	24.41 E
Kowie see Port Alfred, S. Afr.	90	H8	33.35 S	26.53 E
Kowloon see Jiulong, China	58	J5	22.18 N	114.10 E
Kowloon see Jiulong, China	189d		22.18 N	114.10 E
Kowloon City, China	189d		22.19 N	114.11 E
Kowloon Peak, mtn., China	189d		22.21 N	114.13 E
Kowŏn-ŭp, Kor., N.	54	E7	39.26 N	127.14 E
Kowt-e 'Ashrow, Afg.	72	C10	34.26 N	68.49 E
Koxtag, China	62	A4	37.21 N	78.00 E
Koyama, ngh., Japan	186		35.37 N	139.43 E
Koyambattur see Coimbatore, India	69	F3	10.59 N	76.58 E
Köyceğiz, Tur.	34	G11	36.58 N	28.41 E
Köyceğiz Gölü, l., Tur.	34	G11	36.55 N	28.40 E
Koyna Reservoir, res., India	69	C1	17.36 N	73.45 E
Koyuk, Ak., U.S.	109	D7	64.56 N	161.08 W
Koyukuk, Ak., U.S.	109	D8	64.53 N	157.43 W
Koyukuk, stm., Ak., U.S.	109	C8	64.56 N	157.29 W
Koža, Russia	40	C16	57.47 N	48.55 E
Koža, stm., Russia	18	D25	63.37 N	38.42 E
Kozacha Lopan', Ukr.	38	D15	50.19 N	36.10 E
Kozachi Laheri, Ukr.	38	G11	46.42 N	32.58 E
Kō-zaki, c., Japan	56	E2	34.05 N	129.13 E
Kozan, Tur.	42	G6	37.26 N	35.49 E
Kozáni, Grc.	34	C4	40.18 N	21.48 E
Kožany, Russia	26	H14	52.48 N	31.44 E
Kozara, mts., Bos.	36	E4	44.58 N	17.00 E
Kozats'ke, Ukr.	38	B12	51.17 N	33.30 E
Kozdinga, Russia	12	E22	63.43 N	47.32 E
Kozelets', Ukr.	38	C10	50.54 N	31.07 E
Kozel'shchyna, Ukr.	38	D12	49.13 N	33.51 E
Kozel'sk, Russia	26	F18	54.02 N	35.47 E
Koževnikovo, Russia	48	C14	56.15 N	83.58 E
Kozhanka, Ukr.	38	D8	49.57 N	29.48 E
Kozhikode (Calicut), India	69	F2	11.15 N	75.47 E
Koziatyn, Ukr.	38	D7	49.43 N	28.50 E
Koziegłowy, Pol.	24	F15	50.36 N	19.08 E
Kozienice, Pol.	24	E17	51.35 N	21.33 E
Kozino, Russia	183b		55.54 N	37.11 E
Kozlov Bereg, Russia	26	D10	58.57 N	27.44 E
Kozlovo, Russia	26	D19	56.30 N	36.15 E
Kozlovo, Russia	26	C18	57.34 N	35.28 E
Kozlu, Tur.	34	B14	41.26 N	31.46 E
Koźmin, Pol.	24	E13	51.49 N	17.27 E
Koz'mino, Russia	12	F22	61.56 N	48.19 E
Koz'modemjansk, Russia	40	C15	56.20 N	46.34 E
Koz'mogorodskoe, Russia	12	D21	65.31 N	44.54 E
Kozova, Ukr.	38	D4	49.25 N	25.09 E
Kožozero, ozero, l., Russia	18	D23	63.06 N	38.10 E
Kožposëlok, Russia	18	D25	63.10 N	38.05 E
Kożuchów, Pol.	24	E11	51.44 N	15.35 E
Kožuhovo, Russia	183b		55.43 N	37.54 E
Kozuka, Japan	186		35.09 N	139.57 E
Kozukue, ngh., Japan	186		35.30 N	139.36 E
Kōzu-shima, i., Japan	56	E12	34.13 N	139.10 E
Kozuya, Japan	188		34.52 N	135.45 E
Kozyn, Ukr.	38	C9	50.14 N	30.39 E
Kpalimé, Togo	84	H5	6.54 N	0.38 E
Kra, Isthmus of, isth., Asia	64	H4	10.02 N	98.51 E
Kraai, stm., S. Afr.	90	G8	30.40 S	26.45 E
Krabi, Thai.	64	H4	8.03 N	98.54 E
Krâchéh, Camb.	64	F8	12.29 N	106.02 E
Kraeva, Russia	54	B9	44.54 N	131.08 E
Kragan, Indon.	66	G7	6.40 S	111.35 E
Kragerø, Nor.	16	I7	58.52 N	9.24 E
Kragujevac, Yugo.	36	F7	44.01 N	20.55 E
Krahenhöhe, ngh., Ger.	181		51.10 N	7.06 E
Krainburg see Kranj, Slvn.	30	D11	46.15 N	14.21 E
Krajenka, Pol.	24	C13	53.18 N	17.00 E
Krajnovka, Russia	42	C12	43.57 N	47.23 E
Krakatoa see Rakata, Pulau, i., Indon.	66	G4	6.10 S	105.26 E
Krâkôr, Camb.	64	F7	12.32 N	104.12 E
Krakovets', Ukr.	38	D2	49.57 N	23.07 E
Kraków, Pol.	24	F15	50.03 N	19.57 E
Kralendijk, Neth. Ant.	158g	p23	12.09 N	68.16 W
Kraljevica, Cro.	30	E11	45.16 N	14.34 E
Kraljevo, Yugo.	36	F7	43.43 N	20.41 E
Kralovice, Czech Rep.	24	G9	49.59 N	13.29 E
Kralupy nad Vltavou, Czech Rep.	24	F10	50.14 N	14.18 E
Kramators'k, Ukr.	38	E16	48.43 N	37.32 E
Kramfors, Swe.	16	E15	62.56 N	17.47 E
Krampnitz, Ger.	182a		52.28 N	13.04 E
Krampnitzsee, l., Ger.	182a		52.27 N	13.03 E
Krångede, Swe.	16	D14	63.08 N	16.05 E
Kranídi, Grc.	34	F6	37.22 N	23.09 E
Kranj (Krainburg), Slvn.	30	D11	46.15 N	14.21 E
Kranji, Sing.	189c		1.26 N	103.45 E
Kranji, stm., Sing.	189c		1.26 N	103.45 E
Kranji Reservoir, res., Sing.	189c		1.26 N	103.45 E
Kranji War Memorial, hist., Sing.	189c		1.26 N	103.45 E
Kranskop, S. Afr.	90	F10	28.58 S	30.50 E
Krapina, Cro.	30	D12	46.10 N	15.53 E
Krapivna, Russia	26	G18	53.37 N	35.30 E
Krapkowice, Pol.	24	F13	50.29 N	17.57 E
Krasavino, Russia	12	F22	60.57 N	46.28 E
Krasavka, Russia	40	F13	51.10 N	43.24 E
Krasieo, stm., Thai.	64	E4	14.49 N	100.04 E
Krasivaja Meča, stm., Russia	26	G21	53.21 N	38.03 E
Kraskino, Russia	54	C9	42.43 N	130.46 E
Kraskovo, Russia	183b		55.39 N	37.59 E
Krāslava, Lat.	26	E10	55.53 N	27.10 E
Krasna, stm., Ukr.	38	D17	49.01 N	38.16 E
Krasnae, Bela.	26	F10	54.14 N	27.05 E
Krasnaja Gora, Russia	18	G22	60.15 N	35.39 E
Krasnaja Gora, Russia	26	G14	53.00 N	31.35 E
Krasnaja Gorbatka, Russia	40	D12	55.52 N	41.45 E
Krasnaja Jaruga, Russia	38	C14	50.47 N	35.39 E
Krasnaja Slabada, Bela.	26	H10	52.51 N	27.10 E
Krasnaja Zarja, Russia	26	H20	52.47 N	37.41 E
Krasnaluki, Bela.	26	F11	54.37 N	28.50 E
Krasna Poliana, Ukr.	38	F16	47.33 N	37.04 E
Krasnapolle, Bela.	26	G14	53.20 N	31.24 E
Krasneno, Russia	50	D23	64.38 N	174.49 E
Kraśnik, Pol.	24	F18	50.55 N	22.13 E
Kraśnik Fabryczny, Pol.	24	F18	50.55 N	22.13 E
Krasni Okny, Ukr.	38	F8	47.32 N	29.27 E
Krasnoarmejsk, Russia	26	D21	56.08 N	38.08 E
Krasnoarmejsk, Russia	40	F14	51.01 N	45.41 E
Krasnoarmejskaja, Russia	40	I11	45.21 N	38.12 E
Krasnoarmejskij, Russia	40	H13	47.00 N	42.12 E
Krasnoarmejskij, Russia	50	C23	69.32 N	172.01 E
Krasnoarmejskoe, Russia	40	E17	52.43 N	50.00 E
Krasnoarmiis'k, Ukr.	38	E16	48.17 N	37.09 E
Krasnoborsk, Russia	12	F21	61.30 N	46.06 E
Krasnobród, Pol.	24	F19	50.32 N	23.12 E
Krasnodar, Russia	40	I11	45.02 N	38.59 E
Krasnodarskij kraj, co., Russia	42	C8	45.30 N	39.00 E
Krasnodon, Ukr.	38	E18	48.16 N	39.45 E
Krasnoe, Russia	26	G16	53.06 N	33.55 E
Krasnoe, Russia	38	C17	50.20 N	38.49 E
Krasnoe, Russia	38	C17	50.56 N	38.40 E
Krasnoe, Russia	40	H11	46.43 N	39.33 E
Krasnoe, Russia	40	B15	59.15 N	47.45 E
Krasnoe, Russia	40	E11	52.51 N	38.47 E
Krasnoe, ozero, l., Russia	50	D23	64.30 N	174.24 E
Krasnoe Selo, Russia	26	A12	59.44 N	30.06 E
Krasnoe Selo, ngh., Russia	183a		59.44 N	30.05 E
Krasnoe Znamja, Russia	26	C18	57.26 N	35.13 E
Krasnofarfornyj, Russia	26	A14	59.08 N	31.51 E
Krasnogorodskoe, Russia	26	D11	56.50 N	28.16 E
Krasnogorsk, Russia	26	E20	55.48 N	37.19 E
Krasnogorsk, Russia	50	G17	48.24 N	142.06 E
Krasnogorskij, Russia	40	C16	56.09 N	48.19 E
Krasnogorskij Rog, mys, c., Russia	18	C25	64.50 N	38.21 E
Krasnogvardejskoe, Russia	38	C17	50.38 N	38.23 E
Krasnohorivka, Ukr.	38	F16	47.59 N	37.30 E
Krasnohrad, Ukr.	38	D14	49.22 N	35.27 E
Krasnohvardiis'ke, Ukr.	38	H13	45.30 N	34.18 E
Krasnoil's'k, Ukr.	38	E4	48.01 N	25.36 E
Krasnojarovo, Russia	50	F14	51.28 N	128.26 E
Krasnojarsk, Russia	48	C16	56.00 N	92.53 E
Krasnojarskoe vodohranilišče, res., Russia	48	D16	55.00 N	92.00 E
Krasnoje Selo, ngh., Russia	183a		59.44 N	30.05 E
Krasnokamsk, Russia	40	B19	58.04 N	55.52 E
Krasnokuts'k, Ukr.	38	C14	50.03 N	35.08 E
Krasnolese, Russia	26	F5	54.24 N	22.23 E
Krasnolesnyj, Russia	40	F11	51.52 N	39.35 E
Krasnomajskij, Russia	26	C17	57.36 N	34.23 E
Krasnoostrovskij, Russia	18	G15	60.17 N	28.38 E
Krasnopavlivka, Ukr.	38	D15	49.08 N	36.19 E
Krasnoperekops'k, Ukr.	38	H12	45.57 N	33.47 E
Krasnopillia, Ukr.	38	C14	50.46 N	35.16 E
Krasnorečenskij, Russia	54	B11	44.41 N	135.14 E
Krasnoščele, Russia	14	E28	67.21 N	37.01 E
Krasnosel'kup, Russia	48	A14	65.42 N	82.27 E
Krasnosielc, Pol.	24	C17	53.02 N	21.10 E
Krasnosil's'ke, Ukr.	38	H11	45.14 N	32.40 E
Krasnoslobodsk, Russia	40	G14	48.42 N	44.34 E
Krasnoturjinsk, Russia	48	C10	59.46 N	60.11 E
Krasnoufimsk, Russia	40	C20	56.37 N	57.46 E
Krasnoural'sk, Russia	48	C10	58.20 N	60.03 E
Krasnousol'skij, Russia	40	E20	53.53 N	56.29 E
Krasnovišersk, Russia	48	B9	60.23 N	57.05 E
Krasnovka, Russia	38	E19	48.46 N	40.07 E
Krasnovodsk see Turkmenbaši, Turkmen.	72	B7	40.00 N	52.57 E
Krasnovodskaja kosa, spit, Turkmen.	42	F15	39.53 N	52.55 E
Krasnovodskij poluostrov, pen., Turkmen.	72	A7	40.24 N	53.13 E
Krasnovodskij zaliv, b., Turkmen.	42	F15	39.50 N	53.15 E
Krasnozavodsk, Russia	26	D21	56.26 N	38.14 E
Krasnozërskoe, Russia	48	D14	53.59 N	79.14 E
Krasnoznamensk, Russia	26	F5	54.57 N	22.29 E
Krasnoznamenskoe, Kaz.	48	D11	51.02 N	69.28 E
Krasnye Baki, Russia	40	C14	57.07 N	45.09 E
Krasnye Barrikady, Russia	40	H15	46.13 N	47.53 E
Krasnye Gory, Russia	26	B12	58.56 N	29.37 E
Krasnyi Kut, Ukr.	38	E17	48.12 N	38.48 E
Krasnyi Luch, Ukr.	38	E17	48.08 N	38.55 E
Krasnyi Lyman, Ukr.	38	D17	48.59 N	37.49 E
Krasnyj, Russia	26	F14	54.33 N	31.26 E
Krasnyj Bor, Russia	183a		59.41 N	30.41 E
Krasnyj Čikoj, Russia	50	F10	50.19 N	108.44 E

Name	Page	Map Ref.	Latitude	Longitude
Krasnyj Gorodok, Russia	26	C16	57.11 N	33.44 E
Krasnyj Guljaj, Russia	40	D16	54.00 N	48.22 E
Krasnyj Holm, Russia	26	B20	58.03 N	37.07 E
Krasnyj Holm, Russia	40	F19	51.35 N	54.10 E
Krasnyj Huduk, Russia	40	H15	46.18 N	46.57 E
Krasnyj Jar, Russia	40	H16	46.32 N	48.21 E
Krasnyj Jar, Russia	40	F14	50.42 N	44.44 E
Krasnyj Jar, Russia	48	C12	55.14 N	72.55 E
Krasnyj Jar, Russia	48	C14	57.08 N	84.30 E
Krasnyj Kl'ič, Russia	40	D20	55.26 N	56.12 E
Krasnyj Kut, Russia	40	F15	50.57 N	46.58 E
Krasnyj Liman, Russia	38	B18	51.32 N	39.52 E
Krasnyj Log, Russia	38	B18	51.23 N	39.45 E
Krasnyj Luč, Russia	26	C13	57.02 N	30.03 E
Krasnyj Manyč, Russia	40	I14	45.30 N	44.42 E
Krasnyj Oktjabr', Russia	26	D21	56.07 N	38.53 E
Krasnyj Rog, Russia	26	H16	52.57 N	33.45 E
Krasnyj Stroitel', ngh., Russia	183b		55.35 N	37.37 E
Krasnyj Sulin, Russia	40	H12	47.52 N	40.03 E
Krasnyj Tkač, Russia	26	E22	55.28 N	39.05 E
Krasnystaw, Pol.	24	E19	50.58 N	23.11 E
Krasuha, Russia	26	C16	57.23 N	33.16 E
Krasyliv, Ukr.	38	D6	49.39 N	26.58 E
Kraszna see Crasna, stm., Eur.	24	I18	48.03 N	22.20 E
Kratovo, Mac.	34	A5	42.05 N	22.11 E
Krâvanh, Chuŏr Phnum, mts., Camb.	64	F6	12.00 N	103.15 E
Kray, ngh., Ger.	181		51.28 N	7.05 E
Kražiai, Lith.	26	E5	55.36 N	22.40 E
Krbava, reg., Cro.	30	F12	44.40 N	15.35 E
Krebs, Ok., U.S.	134	C3	34.55 N	95.43 W
Krečetovo, Russia	18	G25	60.57 N	38.27 E
Krečevicy, Russia	26	B14	58.37 N	31.23 E
Krefeld, Ger.	24	E2	51.20 N	6.34 E
Kremastón, Technití Límni, res., Grc.	34	E4	38.54 N	21.30 E
Kremenchug see Kremenchuk, Ukr.	38	D12	49.04 N	33.25 E
Kremenchug Reservoir see Kremenchuts'ke vodoskhovyshche, res., Ukr.	38	D11	49.20 N	32.30 E
Kremenchuk, Ukr.	38	D12	49.04 N	33.25 E
Kremenchuts'ke vodoskhovyshche, res., Ukr.	38	D11	49.20 N	32.30 E
Kremenčug see Kremenchuk, Ukr.	38	D12	49.04 N	33.25 E
Kremenčugskoe vodohranilišče see Kremenchuts'ke vodoskhovyshche, res., Ukr.	38	D11	49.20 N	32.30 E
Kremenets', Ukr.	38	C4	50.06 N	25.44 E
Kremenskoe, Russia	26	E18	55.06 N	35.57 E
Kremenskoj, Russia	40	H12	47.49 N	41.09 E
Kreminna, Ukr.	38	D17	49.02 N	38.13 E
Kremlin, bldg., Russia	183b		55.45 N	37.37 E
Kremmling, Co., U.S.	138	A2	40.03 N	106.23 W
Krems, stm., Aus.	30	B12	48.23 N	15.42 E
Krems an der Donau, Aus.	30	B12	48.24 N	15.36 E
Krepoljin, Yugo.	36	E8	44.15 N	21.36 E
Kress, Tx., U.S.	138	G7	34.21 N	101.45 W
Kressey Lake, l., N.J., U.S.	203		39.44 N	75.07 W
Kresta, zaliv, b., Russia	50	C25	65.50 N	179.09 W
Krestcy, Russia	26	B15	58.14 N	32.31 E
Krestcy, Russia	26	B22	58.22 N	38.59 E
Krest-Maër, Russia	50	C17	67.38 N	144.47 E
Kretinga, Lith.	26	E4	55.53 N	21.14 E
Kreuzberg, Ger.	181		51.09 N	7.27 E
Kreuzberg, ngh., Ger.	182a		52.30 N	13.23 E
Kreuznach see Bad Kreuznach, Ger.	24	G3	49.51 N	7.52 E
Krèva, Bela.	26	F9	54.19 N	26.17 E
Kribi, Cam.	86	D1	2.55 N	9.54 E
Kričov see Kryčaŭ, Bela.	26	G14	53.42 N	31.43 E
Křimice, Czech Rep.	24	G9	49.45 N	13.18 E
Krimnicksee, l., Ger.	182a		52.18 N	13.39 E
Krishna, stm., India	69	C5	15.50 N	80.52 E
Krishna, Mouths of the, mth., India	69	D5	15.38 N	80.57 E
Krishnagiri, India	69	E4	12.31 N	78.13 E
Krishnamāti, India	190b		22.40 N	88.32 E
Krishnanagar, India	70	G12	23.24 N	88.30 E
Krishnapur, India	190b		22.36 N	88.26 E
Krishnarāja Sāgara, res., India	69	E3	12.28 N	76.28 E
Krishnarājpet, India	69	E3	12.39 N	76.29 E
Kristdala, Swe.	16	J14	57.23 N	16.12 E
Kristiania see Oslo, Nor.	16	H8	59.55 N	10.45 E
Kristianopel, Swe.	16	K14	56.14 N	16.01 E
Kristiansand, Nor.	16	I6	58.10 N	8.00 E
Kristianstad, Swe.	16	K12	56.01 N	14.09 E
Kristiansund, Nor.	16	D5	63.06 N	7.46 E
Kristiinankaupunki (Kristinestad), Fin.	18	E8	62.16 N	21.21 E
Kristineberg, Swe.	16	B16	65.03 N	18.38 E
Kristinehamn, Swe.	16	H11	59.20 N	14.07 E
Kristinestad see Kristiinankaupunki, Fin.	18	E8	62.16 N	21.21 E
Kríti, state, Grc.	34	H7	35.29 N	25.01 E
Kríti (Crete), i., Grc.	34	H7	35.12 N	25.00 E
Kritikón Pélagos (Crete, Sea of), s., Grc.	34	H8	35.54 N	25.01 E
Kritzendorf, Aus.	182b		48.20 N	16.18 E
Krivaja, stm., Bos.	36	E5	44.26 N	18.09 E
Kriva Palanka, Mac.	34	A5	42.12 N	22.20 E
Krivcy, Russia	18	F23	61.48 N	36.57 E
Kriviči see Kryvičy, Bela.	26	F10	54.43 N	27.17 E
Krivodol, Blg.	36	F10	43.23 N	23.28 E
Krivoj Rog see Kryvyi Rih, Ukr.	38	F12	47.53 N	33.21 E
Krivonosovo, Russia	38	D18	49.55 N	39.16 E
Krivošeino, Russia	48	C14	57.20 N	83.57 E
Križevci, Cro.	30	D13	46.04 N	16.34 E
Krjučkovo, Russia	26	C18	57.03 N	35.34 E
Krjukovo, Russia	26	E20	55.58 N	37.10 E
Krjukovo, Russia	50	C20	66.30 N	159.32 E
Krk, Otok, i., Cro.	30	E11	45.05 N	14.35 E
Krn, mtn., Slvn.	30	D10	46.16 N	13.40 E
Krnov, Czech Rep.	24	F13	50.05 N	17.42 E
Krobia, Pol.	24	E12	51.47 N	16.59 E
Krøderen, l., Nor.	16	G7	60.15 N	9.38 E
Krokek, Swe.	16	I14	58.40 N	16.21 E
Krokodil, stm., S. Afr.	90	D8	24.11 S	26.52 E
Krokom, Swe.	16	D12	63.20 N	14.26 E
Krokowa, Pol.	24	B14	54.47 N	18.11 E
Krolevets', Ukr.	38	B12	51.33 N	33.23 E
Krom, stm., S. Afr.	90	G4	31.03 S	18.58 E
Kroměříž, Czech Rep.	24	G13	49.17 N	17.23 E
Kromy, Russia	26	H18	52.41 N	35.45 E
Kronach, Ger.	24	F7	50.14 N	11.20 E
Krone, Ger.	181		51.27 N	7.20 E
Krŏng Kaôh Kŏng, Camb.	64	G6	11.37 N	102.59 E
Krŏng Kêb, Camb.	64	G7	10.29 N	104.18 E
Kronoberg, state, Swe.	16	K12	56.40 N	14.40 E
Kronoby see Kruunupyy, Fin.	18	D9	63.42 N	23.00 E
Kronockaja Sopka, vulkan, vol., Russia	50	F21	54.44 N	160.31 E
Kronockij zaliv, b., Russia	50	F21	54.12 N	160.36 E
Kronoki, Russia	50	F21	54.36 N	161.10 E
Kronprins Christian Land, reg., Grnld.	108	A22	80.57 N	18.36 W
Kronstadt see Braşov, Rom.	36	D12	45.39 N	25.37 E
Kronštadt, Russia	26	A12	59.59 N	29.47 E
Kroonstad, S. Afr.	90	E8	27.40 S	27.14 E
Kropotkin, Russia	40	I12	45.26 N	40.34 E
Kropotkin, Russia	50	E12	58.30 N	115.17 E
Krościenko nad Dunajcem, Pol.	24	G16	49.27 N	20.26 E
Kroshna, Ukr.	38	C7	50.17 N	28.41 E
Krośniewice, Pol.	24	D15	52.15 N	19.10 E
Krosno, Pol.	24	G17	49.41 N	21.45 E
Krosno Odrzańskie, Pol.	24	D11	52.03 N	15.06 E
Krossinsee, l., Ger.	182a		52.22 N	13.41 E
Krotoszyn, Pol.	24	E13	51.42 N	17.26 E
Krotz Springs, La., U.S.	134	G7	30.32 N	91.45 W
Kroya, Indon.	66	G6	7.37 S	109.14 E
Krško, Slvn.	30	E12	45.58 N	15.29 E
Krudenburg, Ger.	181		51.39 N	6.45 E
Kruger National Park, p.o.i., S. Afr.	90	C10	24.00 S	31.40 E
Krugersdorp, S. Afr.	90	E8	26.05 S	27.47 E
Krugersdorp, state, S. Afr.	191d		26.05 S	27.35 E
Krugersdorp Race Course, p.o.i., S. Afr.	191d		26.08 S	27.45 E
Krugersdorp West, S. Afr.	191d		26.06 S	27.45 E
Krugloe, Russia	38	G18	47.00 N	39.14 E
Kruhlae, Bela.	26	F12	54.14 N	29.48 E
Krui, Indon.	66	F3	5.13 S	103.55 E
Kruis, Kaap see Cross, Cape, c., Nmb.	90	B1	21.46 S	13.57 E
Kruisfontein, S. Afr.	90	H7	34.00 S	24.41 E
Kruja see Krujë, Alb.	32	C13	41.30 N	19.46 E
Krujë, Alb.	32	C13	41.30 N	19.46 E
Krukut, Kali, stm., Indon.	187e		6.12 S	106.48 E
Kruleyščyna, Bela.	26	E10	55.01 N	27.47 E
Krumbach, Ger.	24	H6	48.14 N	10.22 E
Krumme Lanke, l., Ger.	182a		52.27 N	13.14 E
Krummendammer Heide, for., Ger.	182a		52.28 N	13.39 E
Krummensee, Ger.	182a		52.36 N	13.42 E
Krumovgrad, Blg.	36	H12	41.27 N	25.40 E
Krung Thep (Bangkok), Thai.	64	F5	13.45 N	100.31 E
Krung Thep (Bangkok), Thai.	187a		13.45 N	100.31 E
Krung Thep Mahanakhon, state, Thai.	187a		13.47 N	100.43 E
Krung Thon Bridge, trans., Thai.	187a		13.47 N	100.30 E
Krupec, Russia	40	F9	51.37 N	34.20 E
Krüpelsee, l., Ger.	182a		52.18 N	13.42 E
Krupki, Bela.	26	F12	54.19 N	29.08 E
Kruså, Den.	16	M7	54.51 N	9.24 E
Kruščičko jezero, res., Cro.	30	F12	44.39 N	15.18 E
Kruševac, Yugo.	36	F8	43.34 N	21.19 E
Kruševo, Mac.	34	B4	41.22 N	21.14 E
Krušinovka, Bela.	26	G12	53.12 N	29.49 E
Krušné hory see Ore Mountains, mts., Eur.	24	F9	50.37 N	12.53 E
Kruszwica, Pol.	24	D14	52.40 N	18.18 E
Krutcy, Russia	26	C12	57.10 N	29.23 E
Krutinka, Russia	48	C12	56.00 N	71.32 E
Krutoe, Russia	26	H20	52.25 N	37.28 E
Krutoj Log, Russia	40	C20	57.52 N	58.12 E
Kruunupyy, Fin.	18	D9	63.42 N	23.00 E
Kruzenšterna, proliv, strt., Russia	50	G19	48.26 N	153.44 E
Kruzof Island, i., Ak., U.S.	109	E12	57.10 N	135.40 W
Krýa Vrýsi, Grc.	34	C5	40.41 N	22.19 E
Kryčaŭ, Bela.	26	G14	53.42 N	31.43 E
Krydor, Sk., Can.	142	B6	52.47 N	107.04 W
Krylatskoe, ngh., Russia	183b		55.45 N	37.26 E
Krylbo, Swe.	16	G14	60.07 N	16.13 E
Krym, Respublika, state, Ukr.	42	C5	45.00 N	34.00 E
Krymsk, Russia	40	I10	44.55 N	37.58 E
Kryms'ki hory, mts., Ukr.	38	I13	44.45 N	34.25 E
Kryms'kyi pivostriv (Crimean Peninsula), pen., Ukr.	38	H12	45.00 N	34.00 E
Krynica, Pol.	24	G16	49.25 N	20.57 E
Krynychky, Ukr.	38	E13	48.22 N	34.27 E
Krynychne, Ukr.	38	H7	45.32 N	28.40 E
Kryve Ozero, Ukr.	38	F9	47.57 N	30.20 E
Kryvičy, Bela.	26	F10	54.43 N	27.17 E
Kryvošyn, Bela.	26	H9	52.52 N	26.08 E
Kryvyi Rih, Ukr.	38	F12	47.53 N	33.21 E
Kryzhopil', Ukr.	38	E7	48.22 N	28.52 E
Krzepice, Pol.	24	F14	50.58 N	18.46 E
Krzeszowice, Pol.	24	F15	50.08 N	19.37 E
Krzna, stm., Pol.	24	D19	52.07 N	23.32 E
Krzywiń, Pol.	24	D12	51.58 N	16.49 E
Krzyż, Pol.	24	D11	52.53 N	15.58 E
Ksaverivka, Ukr.	38	C9	50.03 N	30.13 E
Kšen', stm., Russia	26	H20	52.13 N	37.46 E
Ksenevka, Russia	50	F12	53.34 N	118.44 E
Ksenskij, Russia	40	F10	51.51 N	37.43 E
Książ Wielkopolski, Pol.	24	D13	52.05 N	17.14 E
Kstovo, Russia	40	C14	56.10 N	44.09 E
Kuah, Malay.	64	I4	6.18 N	99.51 E
Kuai, stm., China	58	E7	33.10 N	117.25 E
Kuala, Indon.	66	B4	2.56 N	105.48 E
Kualacenako, Indon.	66	D3	0.29 S	102.40 E
Kuala Kangsar, Malay.	64	J5	4.46 N	100.56 E
Kualakapuas, Indon.	66	E9	3.02 S	114.24 E
Kualakerian, Indon.	66	C8	0.48 N	113.18 E
Kuala Krai, Malay.	64	J6	5.31 N	102.12 E
Kuala Kubu Baharu, Malay.	64	K5	3.33 N	101.38 E
Kualakurun, Indon.	66	D8	1.05 S	113.52 E
Kualalangsa, Indon.	64	J4	4.32 N	98.01 E
Kuala Lipis, Malay.	64	J6	4.10 N	102.03 E
Kuala Lumpur, Malay.	64	K5	3.10 N	101.42 E
Kualamanjual, Indon.	66	D8	1.24 S	112.00 E
Kuala Nerang, Malay.	64	I5	6.15 N	100.36 E
Kualapesaguan, Indon.	66	E6	2.02 S	110.07 E
Kuala Pilah, Malay.	64	K6	2.44 N	102.15 E
Kuala Rompin, Malay.	64	K6	2.47 N	103.30 E
Kuala Sepetang, Malay.	64	J5	4.50 N	100.37 E
Kuala Sibuti, Malay.	66	A8	4.02 N	113.46 E
Kualasimpang, Indon.	64	J3	4.17 N	98.03 E
Kuala Terengganu, Malay.	64	J6	5.19 N	103.08 E
Kualu, stm., Indon.	66	B1	2.42 N	99.57 E
Kuamut, Malay.	66	A10	5.13 N	117.28 E
Kuamut, stm., Malay.	66	A10	5.13 N	117.29 E
Kuancheng, China	58	A8	40.37 N	118.31 E
Kuandian, China	52	C9	40.43 N	124.47 E
Kuan Shan, mtn., Tai.	58	J9	23.14 N	120.54 E
Kuantan, Malay.	64	K6	3.49 N	103.20 E
Kuban (Kuban'), stm., Russia	38	H16	45.09 N	37.42 E
Kuban', stm., Russia	42	C7	45.20 N	37.24 E
Kubenskoe, Russia	40	B11	59.26 N	39.40 E
Kubenskoe, ozero, l., Russia	40	B11	59.39 N	39.28 E
Kubokawa, Japan	56	F6	33.12 N	133.08 E
Kubovo, Russia	18	E24	61.58 N	37.14 E
Kubrat, Blg.	36	F13	43.48 N	26.31 E
Kubumesaai, Indon.	66	C9	1.25 N	115.07 E
Kučema, Russia	12	D20	65.36 N	42.30 E
Kučerla, Russia	40	I13	45.22 N	43.40 E
Kučevo, Yugo.	36	E8	44.28 N	21.43 E
Kuchaibuni, India	70	G11	22.16 N	86.10 E
Kuchāman, India	70	E5	27.09 N	74.52 E
Kuchinarai, Thai.	64	D7	16.32 N	104.03 E
Kuching, Malay.	66	C7	1.33 N	110.19 E
Kuchino-shima, i., Japan	55a	k20	29.57 N	129.55 E
Küchnay Darweyshān, Afg.	72	C9	30.59 N	64.10 E
Kuchurhan, stm., Eur.	36	B16	46.32 N	29.58 E
Kučino, Russia	183b		55.45 N	37.58 E
Kučintundra, gora, hill, Russia	14	C22	69.03 N	31.06 E
Kuçova see Kuçovë, Alb.	32	D13	40.47 N	19.55 E
Kuçovë, Alb.	32	D13	40.47 N	19.55 E
Küçükbakkal, ngh., Tur.	185b		40.58 N	29.06 E
Küçükçekmece, ngh., Tur.	185b		40.59 N	28.46 E
Küçükçekmece Gölü, l., Tur.	185b		41.00 N	28.46 E
Küçükköy, ngh., Tur.	185b		41.04 N	28.54 E
Küçükkuyu, Tur.	34	D9	39.33 N	26.34 E
Kūd, India	70	B5	33.04 N	75.17 E
Kudamatsu, Japan	56	F4	33.59 N	131.52 E
Kudap, Indon.	66	C3	1.16 N	102.25 E
Kudat, Malay.	68	G1	6.52 N	116.46 E
Kudeevskij, Russia	40	D20	54.52 N	56.44 E
Kudever', Russia	26	D12	56.46 N	29.24 E
Kudirkos Naumiestis, Lith.	26	F5	54.44 N	22.52 E
Kudremukh, mtn., India	69	E2	13.08 N	75.16 E
Kudrovo, Russia	183a		59.54 N	30.31 E
Kudus, Indon.	66	G7	6.48 S	110.50 E
Kudymkar, Russia	48	C8	59.01 N	54.38 E
Kueda, Russia	40	C19	56.26 N	55.36 E
Kuee Ruins, hist., Hi., U.S.	100a	d6	19.21 N	155.23 W
Kufstein, Aus.	30	C9	47.35 N	12.10 E
Kuganavdlok, Russia	18	E23	62.13 N	36.52 E
Kugluktuk, Nu., Can.	110	B8	67.47 N	115.10 W
Kugmallit Bay, b., N.T., Can.	109	C13	69.33 N	133.25 W
Kugoeja, stm., Russia	40	H11	46.34 N	39.37 E
Kūhdasht, Iran	74	D10	33.31 N	47.35 E
Kuhësi see Kukës, Alb.	32	B14	42.05 N	20.26 E
Kuhmo, Fin.	18	C16	64.07 N	29.31 E
Kuhmoinen, Fin.	18	F11	61.34 N	25.11 E
Kuhn Ø, i., Grnld.	108	C22	74.53 N	20.15 W
Kūhpāyeh, Iran	74	D13	32.43 N	52.26 E
Kuial'nyts'kyi lyman, l., Ukr.	38	G9	46.38 N	30.43 E
Kuibysheve, Ukr.	38	I12	44.38 N	33.52 E
Kuibysheve, Ukr.	38	F15	47.21 N	36.39 E
Kuibyshevka, Ukr.	38	F10	47.38 N	31.42 E
Kuiseb, stm., S. Afr.	90	C2	22.57 S	14.29 E
Kuitan, China	58	J7	23.04 N	115.59 E
Kuito, Ang.	88	C2	12.22 S	16.55 E
Kuiu Island, i., Ak., U.S.	109	E13	56.45 N	134.10 W
Kuivaniemi, Fin.	18	B11	65.34 N	25.07 E
Kuivastu, Est.	26	B6	58.34 N	23.21 E
Kuja, Russia	12	C25	67.46 N	53.10 E
Kuja, Russia	18	B27	65.05 N	40.06 E
Kuja, stm., Russia	18	B27	65.05 N	40.05 E
Kujang-ŭp, Kor., N.	54	E7	39.52 N	126.01 E
Kujawsko-Pomorskie, state, Pol.	24	C14	53.00 N	18.30 E
Kujawy, reg., Pol.	24	D14	52.45 N	18.41 E
Kujbyšev see Samara, Russia	40	E16	53.11 N	50.06 E
Kujbyšev, Russia	48	C13	55.27 N	78.18 E
Kujbyševo, Russia	38	F17	47.48 N	38.54 E
Kujbyševskij, Kaz.	48	D11	53.16 N	66.55 E
Kujbyševskij Zaton, Russia	40	D16	55.09 N	49.09 E
Kujbyševskoe vodohranilišče, res., Russia	40	D16	54.30 N	48.30 E
Kujgan, Kaz.	48	E12	45.24 N	74.09 E
Kuji, stm., Japan	56	C13	36.28 N	140.37 E
Kujirai, Japan	186		35.56 N	139.27 E
Kujten-Uul see Tavan-Bogdo-Ula, gora, mtn., Asia	48	E15	49.08 N	87.48 E
Kujū-san, vol., Japan	56	F4	33.05 N	131.15 E
Kukalaya, stm., Nic.	156	F5	13.39 N	83.37 W
Kukan, Russia	50	G15	49.11 N	133.28 E
Kukawa, Nig.	84	G7	12.55 N	13.34 E
Kukës, Alb.	32	B14	42.05 N	20.26 E
Kukkola, Fin.	18	B10	65.58 N	24.01 E
Kukmor, Russia	40	C17	56.10 N	50.54 E
Kukoboj, Russia	26	B22	58.42 N	39.54 E
Kukol', Russia	42	A15	59.50 N	32.36 E
Kukshi, India	70	G5	22.12 N	74.45 E
Kukuj, Russia	26	A15	59.21 N	32.34 E
Kukukus Lake, l., On., Can.	128	B7	49.47 N	91.41 W
Kukup, Malay.	64	L6	1.19 N	103.27 E
Kukurtli, Turkmen.	72	B8	39.59 N	58.39 E
Kukuštan, Russia	40	C20	57.39 N	56.29 E
Kula, Blg.	36	F9	43.53 N	22.32 E
Kula, Tur.	34	E11	38.32 N	28.39 E
Kula, Yugo.	36	D6	45.36 N	19.32 E
Kulāchi, Pak.	70	C3	31.55 N	70.27 E
Kulagino, Russia	26	H15	52.56 N	32.24 E
Kula Gulf, strt., Sol. Is.	101b	e7	8.02 S	157.16 E
Kulai, Malay.	64	L6	1.39 N	103.36 E
Kula Kangri, mtn., Bhu.	70	E13	28.03 N	90.22 E
Kulakši, Russia	42	B16	47.10 N	55.24 E
Kulandy, Kaz.	48	E9	46.06 N	59.31 E
Kular, Russia	50	B15	70.41 N	134.11 E
Kulaura, Bngl.	70	F13	24.32 N	92.03 E
Kulautuva, Lith.	26	F6	54.56 N	24.04 E
Kuldīga, Lat.	26	D4	56.58 N	21.59 E
Kuldja see Yining, China	48	F14	43.54 N	81.18 E
Kul'dur, Russia	50	G15	49.12 N	131.38 E
Kule, Bots.	90	C5	23.00 S	20.09 E
Kulebaki, Russia	40	D13	55.24 N	42.32 E
Kulen Vakuf, Bos.	36	E3	44.33 N	16.05 E
Kulgera, Austl.	96	E6	25.50 S	133.19 E
Kulgunino, Russia	40	E20	53.34 N	56.55 E
Kulim, Malay.	64	J5	5.22 N	100.33 E
Kuljab, Taj.	72	B10	37.54 N	69.47 E
Kulju, Fin.	18	F10	61.23 N	23.46 E
Kulkyne Creek, stm., Austl.	98	H5	30.36 S	144.03 E
Küllenhahn, ngh., Ger.	181		51.14 N	7.08 E
Kullamaa, Est.	26	B6	58.53 N	24.05 E
Kullu, India	70	B6	31.57 N	77.06 E
Kulm, N.D., U.S.	140	A14	46.17 N	98.56 W
Kulmbach, Ger.	24	F7	50.06 N	11.26 E
Kuloj, Russia	12	F20	61.01 N	42.29 E
Kuloj, Russia	12	D20	64.59 N	43.30 E
Kuloj, stm., Russia	12	D20	66.01 N	43.22 E
Kulotino, Russia	26	B16	58.27 N	33.22 E
Kulpsville, Pa., U.S.	203		40.15 N	75.20 W
Kul'sary, Kaz.	48	E8	46.58 N	54.02 E
Kültepe, hist., Tur.	42	F6	38.44 N	35.34 E
Kulti, India	70	G11	23.44 N	86.51 E
Kultsjön, l., Swe.	16	B13	65.00 N	15.14 E
Kultuk, Russia	48	D18	51.43 N	103.41 E
Kulu, Tur.	34	D16	39.06 N	33.05 E
Kulunda, Russia	48	D13	52.33 N	78.55 E
Kulundinskaja ravnina, pl., Asia	48	D13	53.00 N	79.00 E
Kulundinskoe, ozero, l., Russia	48	D13	53.00 N	79.36 E
Kuluqi, China	52	A9	50.25 N	124.06 E
Kulwin, Austl.	98	J4	35.01 S	142.38 E
Kulykiv, Ukr.	38	D3	49.56 N	24.03 E
Kulykivka, Ukr.	38	B10	51.22 N	31.38 E
Kum see Qom, Iran	74	C12	34.38 N	50.53 E
Kum, stm., Tur.	34	E10	38.39 N	27.31 E
Kuma, stm., Japan	56	G3	32.29 N	130.36 E
Kuma, stm., Russia	42	C11	44.56 N	46.27 E
Kumagaya, Japan	56	C12	36.08 N	139.23 E
Kumai, Indon.	66	E7	2.44 S	111.43 E
Kumai, Indon.	66	E8	3.22 S	112.32 E
Kumai, Teluk, b., Indon.	66	E7	3.00 S	111.43 E
Kumajri see Gjumri, Arm.	42	E10	40.47 N	43.50 E
Kumamoto, Japan	56	G3	32.48 N	130.43 E
Kumamoto, state, Japan	56	G3	32.45 N	130.50 E
Kumano, Japan	56	F9	33.54 N	136.07 E
Kumano, stm., Japan	56	F8	33.43 N	136.00 E
Kumano-nada, s., Japan	56	F9	33.47 N	136.20 E
Kumanovo, Mac.	34	A4	42.08 N	21.42 E
Kumara, Russia	50	F14	51.34 N	126.43 E
Kumārghāt, India	70	F14	24.04 N	92.04 E
Kumasi, Ghana	84	H4	6.41 N	1.37 W
Kumatori, Japan	188		34.24 N	135.22 E
Kumba, Cam.	86	D1	4.37 N	9.26 E
Kumbakonam, India	69	F4	10.57 N	79.22 E
Kumbarilla, Austl.	98	F8	27.19 S	150.52 E
Kumbe, Indon.	60	G11	8.20 S	140.13 E
Kumbo, Cam.	86	C2	6.12 N	10.40 E
Kumdanlı, Tur.	34	E13	38.20 N	30.58 E
Kume-jima, i., Japan	55a	I18	26.20 N	126.47 E
Kumeny, Russia	40	B16	58.07 N	49.56 E
Kŭm-gang, stm., Kor., S.	54	F7	35.59 N	126.42 E
Kuminskij, Russia	48	C11	58.49 N	65.57 E
Kumiyama, Japan	188		34.53 N	135.45 E
Kumizawa, ngh., Japan	186		35.23 N	139.31 E
Kumla, Swe.	16	H13	59.07 N	15.09 E
Kumlinge, i., Fin.	18	G7	60.16 N	20.47 E
Kumluca, Tur.	34	G13	36.21 N	30.12 E
Kumluca, Tur.	34	B15	41.27 N	32.28 E
Kummavuopio, Swe.	14	D11	68.54 N	20.51 E
Kumo, Nig.	84	H7	10.00 N	11.12 E
Kumon Range, mts., Mya.	62	C8	26.08 N	97.09 E
Kumora, Russia	50	E11	55.56 N	111.18 E
Kumphawapi, Thai.	64	D6	17.06 N	103.01 E
Kumputunuri, mtn., Fin.	14	E16	67.43 N	25.29 E
Kumskoj, Russia	40	I15	44.59 N	46.03 E
Kumta, India	69	D2	14.25 N	74.24 E
Kumu, D.R.C.	86	D5	3.03 N	25.09 E
Kumuh, Russia	42	D12	42.11 N	47.05 E
Kumukahi, Cape, c., Hi., U.S.	149a	o16	19.31 N	154.49 W
Kumul see Hami, China	52	C3	42.50 N	93.30 E
Kümüx, China	52	C2	42.13 N	88.13 E
Kŭmya-ŭp, Kor., N.	54	E7	39.32 N	127.14 E
Kumzār, Oman	74	G15	26.20 N	56.25 E
Kuna, Id., U.S.	146	G10	43.29 N	116.24 W
Kunar see Konar, stm., Asia	70	A3	34.36 N	70.53 E
Kunashiri-tō see Kunašir, ostrov, i., Russia	54	C17	44.10 N	146.00 E
Kunašir, ostrov (Kunashiri-tō), i., Russia	54	C17	44.10 N	146.00 E
Kunaširskij proliv see Nemuro Strait, strt., Asia	54	C16	44.00 N	145.20 E
Kuncëvo, ngh., Russia	183b		55.44 N	37.26 E
Kunchhā, Nepal	70	D10	28.07 N	84.20 E
Kunda, Est.	26	A9	59.29 N	26.31 E
Kunda Hills, hills, India	69	F3	11.10 N	76.30 E
Kundam, India	70	G8	23.13 N	80.21 E
Kundāpura, India	69	E2	13.37 N	74.41 E
Kundar, stm., Asia	70	C2	31.36 N	68.53 E
Kunderu, stm., India	69	D4	14.38 N	78.41 E
Kundiān, Pak.	70	B3	32.27 N	71.29 E
Kundiawa, Pap. N. Gui.	101a	b3	6.00 S	144.59 E
Kundla, India	70	H3	21.20 N	71.18 E
Kundur, Pulau, i., Indon.	66	C3	0.45 N	103.26 E
Kunene, state, Nmb.	90	B2	20.34 S	14.37 E
Kunene (Cunene), stm., Afr.	88	D1	17.15 S	11.45 E
Kunersdorf, Forst, for., Ger.	182a		52.17 N	12.59 E
Kunes, Nor.	14	B17	70.21 N	26.28 E
Kungälv, Swe.	16	J9	57.52 N	11.59 E
Kunggyü Yumco, l., China	70	C9	30.37 N	82.08 E
Kunghit Island, i., B.C., Can.	110	E4	52.06 N	131.04 W
Kung-pei-tien, Tai.	187d		25.06 N	121.38 E
Kungrad, Uzb.	48	F9	43.03 N	58.50 E
Kungsbacka, Swe.	16	J9	57.28 N	12.04 E
Kungshamn, Swe.	16	I9	58.21 N	11.15 E
Kungsör, Swe.	16	H14	59.25 N	16.07 E
Kungur, Russia	40	C20	57.26 N	56.57 E
Kunhegyes, Hung.	36	B7	47.22 N	20.38 E
Kunhing, Mya.	64	B4	21.17 N	98.25 E
Kun'ie, Ukr.	38	D16	49.22 N	37.14 E
Kuningan, Indon.	66	G6	6.58 S	108.28 E
Kunisaki, Japan	56	F4	33.33 N	131.43 E
Kunisaki-hantō, pen., Japan	56	F4	33.30 N	131.40 E
Kunitachi, Japan	186		35.41 N	139.26 E
Kunja, Russia	26	D13	56.17 N	30.59 E
Kunja, stm., Russia	26	D13	57.09 N	31.10 E
Kunkuri, India	70	G9	22.43 N	83.57 E
Kunlong, Mya.	62	D8	23.23 N	98.39 E
Kunlun Mountains see Kunlun Shan, mts., China	62	A5	36.30 N	88.00 E
Kunlun Shan, mts., China	62	A5	36.30 N	88.00 E
Kunming, China	52	F5	25.02 N	102.42 E
Kunming Hu, l., China	189a		39.59 N	116.15 E
Kunnamkulam, India	69	F2	10.38 N	76.04 E
Kunost', Russia	18	G24	60.00 N	37.37 E
Kunovice, Czech Rep.	24	G13	49.02 N	17.28 E
Kunsan, Kor., S.	54	F7	35.58 N	126.43 E
Kunshan, China	58	F9	31.23 N	120.57 E
Kunting, China	58	G9	29.48 N	121.56 E
Kununurra, Austl.	96	C5	15.46 S	128.44 E
Kunwi, Kor., S.	56	C1	36.15 N	128.34 E
Kunya, Nig.	84	G6	12.13 N	8.32 E
Künzelsau, Ger.	24	G5	49.16 N	9.41 E
Kuolajarvi, Russia	14	E20	66.58 N	29.11 E
Kuopio, Fin.	18	E14	62.53 N	27.42 E
Kuopio, state, Fin.	18	D14	63.00 N	27.30 E
Kuorboaivi, mtn., Fin.	14	C18	69.40 N	27.43 E
Kuorpukas, gora, hill, Russia	14	C21	69.19 N	30.26 E
Kuortane, Fin.	18	E10	62.48 N	23.30 E
Kupa, stm., Eur.	30	E12	45.28 N	16.22 E
Kup'abal, Kor., S.	189b		37.37 N	126.54 E
Kupang, Indon.	60	H7	10.11 S	123.34 E
Kupanskoe, Russia	26	D21	56.49 N	38.38 E
Kupavna, Russia	183b		55.45 N	38.08 E
Kupferberg, Ger.	181		51.09 N	7.27 E
Kupferdreh, ngh., Ger.	181		51.23 N	7.05 E
Kupiano, Pap. N. Gui.	101a	c4	10.05 S	148.11 E
Kup'ians'k, Ukr.	38	D16	49.42 N	37.38 E
Kup'ians'k-Vuzlovyi, Ukr.	38	D16	49.39 N	37.40 E
Kupino, Russia	48	D13	54.21 N	77.16 E
Kupiškis, Lith.	26	E7	55.50 N	24.58 E
Küplü, Tur.	34	B9	41.08 N	26.22 E
Kupper Airport, arpt., N.J., U.S.	194		40.31 N	74.36 W
Kupreanof Island, i., Ak., U.S.	109	E13	56.45 N	133.31 W
Kupychiv, Ukr.	38	B3	50.59 N	24.42 E
Kuqa, China	48	F14	41.43 N	82.54 E
Kuqa, China	48	F14	41.11 N	83.28 E
Kür (Kura), stm., Asia	42	F13	39.16 N	49.25 E
Kura (Kür), stm., Asia	42	E11	39.16 N	49.25 E
Kura, stm., Russia	42	C11	44.04 N	44.55 E
Kuragino, Russia	48	D16	53.53 N	92.41 E
Kurakaki, Japan	188		34.59 N	135.28 E
Kurakhivka, Ukr.	38	E16	48.01 N	37.22 E
Kurakhove, Ukr.	38	F16	47.58 N	37.17 E
Kuramā', Ḩarrat, lav., Sau. Ar.	74	H7	24.30 N	40.15 E
Kuramo Waters, b., Nig.	191a		6.26 N	3.26 E
Kuranami, Japan	186		35.27 N	140.00 E
Kuranec, Bela.	26	F9	54.33 N	26.57 E
Kurar, ngh., India	190c		19.11 N	72.52 E
Kurashiki, Japan	56	E6	34.36 N	133.46 E
Kurasiki see Kurashiki, Japan	56	E6	34.36 N	133.46 E
Kurauli, India	70	E7	27.23 N	78.59 E
Kuraymah, Sudan	82	D6	18.33 N	31.51 E
Kurayoshi, Japan	56	D6	35.26 N	133.49 E
Kurba, Russia	26	C22	57.33 N	39.30 E
Kurbağalı, stm., Tur.	185b		40.59 N	29.02 E
Kurčatov, Russia	40	F9	51.39 N	35.36 E
Kurčum, Kaz.	48	E14	48.35 N	83.33 E
Kürdämir, Azer.	42	E13	40.20 N	48.09 E
Kür dili, spit, Azer.	42	F13	39.03 N	49.11 E
Kurdistan see Kordestān, state, Iran	74	C10	35.30 N	47.00 E
Kurdistan, hist. reg., Asia	8	H17	37.00 N	45.00 E
Kurdistān, hist. reg., Asia	72	B5	37.00 N	45.00 E
Kurdufān, hist. reg., Sudan	82	E6	13.00 N	30.00 E
Kurduvādi, India	69	B2	18.05 N	75.25 E
Kure, Japan	56	E5	34.14 N	132.34 E
Küre Dağları, mts., Tur.	8	G15	41.45 N	34.00 E
Kurejka, stm., Russia	50	C7	66.28 N	87.14 E
Kurenalus see Pudasjärvi, Fin.	18	B13	65.21 N	26.59 E
Kuresaare, Est.	26	B5	58.15 N	22.30 E
Kurgal'džinskij, Kaz.	48	D12	50.35 N	70.01 E
Kurgan, Russia	48	C11	55.27 N	65.20 E
Kurgan-Tjube, Taj.	72	B10	37.50 N	68.46 E
Kurgolovo, Russia	26	A10	59.46 N	28.06 E
Kuria, i., Kir.	94	C8	0.12 N	173.24 E
Kuriachivka, Ukr.	38	D17	49.38 N	38.41 E
Kuriachivka, Ukr.	38	D18	49.22 N	39.37 E
Kuria Muria Islands see Ḩallānīyah, Juzur al-, is., Oman	72	F8	17.32 N	55.56 E
Kuridala, Austl.	98	C3	21.17 S	140.30 E
Kurīgrām, Bngl.	70	F12	25.48 N	89.38 E
Kurihama, Japan	186		35.13 N	139.43 E
Kurikka, Fin.	18	E9	62.36 N	22.24 E
Kuril Islands see Kuril'skie ostrova, is., Russia	46	E19	47.14 N	152.17 E
Kuril'sk, Russia	52	B14	45.13 N	147.53 E
Kuril'skie ostrova (Kuril Islands), is., Russia	46	E19	47.14 N	152.17 E
Kuril Strait see Pervyj Kuril'skij proliv, strt., Russia	50	F20	50.50 N	156.36 E
Kuril Trench, unds.	174	E18	47.00 N	155.00 E
Kuřim, Czech Rep.	24	G12	49.17 N	16.32 E
Kurin', Ukr.	38	B11	51.09 N	32.45 E
Kurinjippadi, India	69	F4	11.33 N	79.36 E
Kurinskaja kosa see Kür dili, spit, Azer.	42	F13	39.03 N	49.11 E
Kurinskaya, Cape see Kür dili, spit, Azer.	42	F13	39.03 N	49.11 E
Kurinwás, stm., Nic.	156	F5	12.48 N	83.41 W
Kurjanovskaja, Russia	12	F19	60.18 N	41.32 E
Kurkiëki, Russia	18	F16	61.18 N	29.54 E
Kurkino, Russia	26	G21	53.25 N	38.39 E
Kurkino, ngh., Russia	183b		55.53 N	37.23 E
Kurkliai, Lith.	26	E8	55.24 N	25.04 E
Kurl, ngh., Ger.	181		51.35 N	7.35 E
Kurla, ngh., India	190c		19.05 N	72.53 E
Kurleja, Russia	50	F12	52.11 N	119.07 E
Kurmuk, Sudan	82	E6	10.33 N	34.17 E
Kurnell, Austl.	192a		34.01 S	151.13 E
Kurnell Peninsula, pen., Austl.	192a		34.02 S	15.11 E
Kurnool, India	69	D3	15.49 N	78.02 E
Kurobe, Japan	56	C10	36.51 N	137.25 E
Kuropatkino, Russia	40	H14	46.30 N	45.19 E
Kurort Schmalkalden, Ger.	24	F6	50.43 N	10.27 E
Kurosu, Japan	186		35.51 N	139.23 E
Kurovskoe, Russia	26	E21	55.35 N	38.56 E
Kurow, N.Z.	102	G4	44.45 S	170.28 E
Kuroya, Japan	186		35.55 N	139.44 E
Kursavka, Russia	42	C10	44.27 N	42.30 E
Kuršėnai, Lith.	26	D6	55.59 N	22.55 E
Kurseong, India	70	E12	26.53 N	88.17 E
Kuršių marios see Courland Lagoon, b., Eur.	26	E3	55.00 N	21.00 E
Kuršiu nerija (Kuršskaja kosa), spit, Eur.	26	E3	55.16 N	20.57 E
Kursk, Russia	40	F9	51.44 N	36.11 E
Kurskaja, Russia	42	C11	44.02 N	44.27 E
Kurskaja oblast', co., Russia	40	F10	51.40 N	36.00 E
Kursk Station, trans., Russia	183b		55.46 N	37.40 E
Kurššskaja kosa (Kuršiu nerija), spit, Eur.	26	E3	55.16 N	20.57 E
Kurššskij zaliv see Courland Lagoon, b., Eur.	26	E3	55.00 N	21.00 E
Kursu, Fin.	14	F19	66.47 N	28.07 E
Kuršumlija, Yugo.	36	F8	43.08 N	21.18 E
Kurşunlu, Tur.	34	C16	40.50 N	33.16 E
Kurtalan, Tur.	42	F9	37.57 N	41.42 E
Kūrtī, Sudan	82	D6	18.07 N	31.35 E
Kurtistown, Hi., U.S.	100a	d6	19.36 N	155.03 W
Kurtoğlu Burnu, c., Tur.	34	G11	36.39 N	28.50 E
Kuru, Fin.	18	F10	61.52 N	23.43 E
Kurucaşile, Tur.	34	B15	41.50 N	32.43 E
Kuruçeşme, ngh., Tur.	185b		41.03 N	29.02 E
Kuruktag, mts., China	52	C2	41.14 N	90.03 E
Kurum, Pap. N. Gui.	101a	a4	4.44 S	145.55 E
Kuruman, S. Afr.	90	E6	27.27 S	23.26 E
Kuruman, stm., S. Afr.	90	E5	26.56 S	20.39 E
Kurumanheuwels, mts., S. Afr.	90	E6	27.35 S	23.26 E
Kurume, Japan	56	F3	33.18 N	130.30 E
Kurumkan, Russia	50	F11	54.19 N	110.18 E
Kurunegala, Sri L.	69	H5	7.28 N	80.22 E
Kuruqi, China	52	B9	48.58 N	123.50 E
Kuryk, Kaz.	42	D14	43.11 N	51.40 E
Kuryongp'o, Kor., S.	56	C2	35.58 N	129.31 E

Name	Page	Map Ref.	Latitude	Longitude
Kurzeme see Courland, hist. reg., Lat.	26	C5	56.50 N	22.30 E
Kusabe, Japan	188		34.31 N	135.29 E
Kuşadası, Tur.	34	F10	37.50 N	27.15 E
Kuşadası Körfezi, b., Tur.	34	F9	37.50 N	27.08 E
Kušalino, Russia	26	C18	57.07 N	36.04 E
Kusan-ni, Kor., S.	56	B1	37.43 N	128.48 E
Kusan-ni, Kor., S.	189b		37.29 N	126.45 E
Kusawa Lake, l., Yk., Can.	109	D12	60.20 N	136.22 W
Kuščevskaja, Russia	40	H11	46.33 N	39.37 E
Kusel, Ger.	24	G3	49.32 N	7.24 E
Kuş Gölü, l., Tur.	34	C10	40.10 N	28.01 E
Kuş Gölü Milli Parkı, p.o.i., Tur.	34	C10	40.15 N	27.55 E
Kushālgarh, India	70	G5	23.11 N	74.27 E
Kusheriki, Nig.	84	G6	10.32 N	6.26 E
Kushihiki, Japan	186		35.55 N	139.36 E
Kushikino, Japan	56	H3	31.45 N	130.18 E
Kushima, Japan	56	H4	31.27 N	131.10 E
Kushimoto, Japan	56	F8	33.29 N	135.46 E
Kushira, Japan	188		34.28 N	135.43 E
Kushiro, Japan	54	C16	42.58 N	144.23 E
Kushnytsia, Ukr.	38	E2	48.27 N	23.14 E
Kushtia, Bngl.	70	G12	23.54 N	89.07 E
Kushuhum, Ukr.	38	F14	47.42 N	35.12 E
Kushui, China	52	C3	42.09 N	94.21 E
Kusiro see Kushiro, Japan	54	C16	42.58 N	144.23 E
Kusiyāra, stm., Bngl.	70	F13	24.41 N	91.22 E
Kuskokwim, stm., Ak., U.S.	109	D7	60.15 N	162.29 W
Kuskokwim Bay, b., Ak., U.S.	109	E7	59.31 N	162.52 W
Kuskokwim Mountains, mts., Ak., U.S.	109	D8	62.24 N	157.07 W
Kuskovo, ngh., Russia	183b		55.44 N	37.49 E
Kuškušara, Russia	18	C27	64.56 N	40.21 E
Kušmā, Nepal	70	D9	28.12 N	83.41 E
Kušmurun, Kaz.	48	D10	52.26 N	64.37 E
Kušmurun, ozero, l., Kaz.	48	D10	52.40 N	64.48 E
Kušnarenkovo, Russia	40	D19	55.06 N	55.20 E
Kusria, India	190b		22.58 N	88.14 E
Küssnacht am Rigi, Switz.	24	I4	47.05 N	8.27 E
Kustanaj, Kaz.	48	D10	53.12 N	63.37 E
Küstenkanal, can., Ger.	20	B16	52.57 N	7.18 E
Kūstī, Sudan	82	E6	13.10 N	32.40 E
Küstrin see Kostrzyn, Pol.	24	D10	52.35 N	14.39 E
Kusu, Japan	56	F4	33.16 N	131.09 E
Kušum, stm., Kaz.	40	F17	49.14 N	50.24 E
Kusumba, India	190b		22.27 N	88.24 E
Kusung, Kor., S.	56	C1	36.17 N	128.55 E
Kušva, Russia	40	B21	58.17 N	59.45 E
Kut, Ko, i., Thai.	64	G6	11.40 N	102.35 E
Kutabaru, Indon.	66	D3	0.44 S	102.56 E
Kutabuloh, Indon.	64	K3	3.27 N	97.03 E
Kutacane, Indon.	64	K3	3.30 N	97.48 E
Kütahya, Tur.	34	D13	39.25 N	29.58 E
Kütahya, state, Tur.	34	D12	39.20 N	29.30 E
Kutaisi, Geor.	42	D10	42.15 N	42.41 E
Kūt al-Imāra see Al-Kūt, Iraq	74	D9	32.30 N	45.49 E
Kutanibong, Indon.	64	K3	3.54 N	96.21 E
Kutaradja see Banda Aceh, Indon.	64	J2	5.33 N	95.19 E
Kutch, Gulf of see Kachchh, Gulf of, b., India	70	G2	22.36 N	69.29 E
Kutch, Rann of (Kachchh, Rann of), reg., Asia	70	F2	24.15 N	70.46 E
Kuteinykove, Ukr.	38	F17	47.48 N	38.17 E
Kutima, Russia	48	C19	57.10 N	108.17 E
Kutina, Cro.	30	E13	45.28 N	16.46 E
Kutiyāna, India	70	H3	21.38 N	69.59 E
Kutná Hora, Czech Rep.	24	G11	49.57 N	15.16 E
Kutno, Pol.	24	D15	52.14 N	19.22 E
Kutse Game Reserve, ind. res., Bots.	90	C7	23.30 S	24.05 E
Kutsjerla, Russia	42	C10	45.22 N	43.40 E
Kuttura, Fin.	14	D17	68.26 N	26.32 E
Kuttusoja, Fin.	14	E19	67.46 N	28.47 E
Kuttuzi, Russia	183a		59.45 N	30.04 E
Kutu, D.R.C.	86	E3	2.42 S	18.08 E
Kutubdia Island, i., Bngl.	70	H13	21.49 N	91.51 E
Kutum, Sudan	82	E4	14.11 N	24.39 E
Kúty, Slvk.	24	H13	48.40 N	17.03 E
Kuty, Ukr.	38	E4	48.16 N	25.11 E
Kutztown, Pa., U.S.	124	D10	40.30 N	75.46 W
Kuujjuaq, Qc., Can.	110	D17	58.06 N	68.25 W
Kuuli-Majak, Turkmen.	72	A7	40.15 N	52.44 E
Kuusamo, Fin.	18	B15	65.58 N	29.10 E
Kuusankoski, Fin.	18	G13	60.54 N	26.36 E
Kuvango, Ang.	88	C2	14.27 S	16.17 E
Kuvšinovo, Russia	26	C17	57.01 N	34.11 E
Kuwabara, Japan	188		34.53 N	135.15 E
Kuwait see Al-Kuwayt, Kuw.	74	F11	29.19 N	47.59 E
Kuwait, ctry., Asia	74	F10	29.30 N	47.45 E
Kuwait Bay see Kuwayt, Jūn al-, b., Kuw.	74	F10	29.30 N	48.00 E
Kuwana, Japan	56	D9	35.04 N	136.42 E
Kuwayt, Jūn al- (Kuwait Bay), b., Kuw.	74	F10	29.30 N	48.00 E
Kuybyshev Reservoir see Kujbyševskoe vodohranilišče, res., Russia	40	D16	54.30 N	48.30 E
Kuye, stm., China	58	B4	38.21 N	110.44 E
Kuyucak, Tur.	34	F11	37.54 N	28.28 E
Kuzaranda, Russia	18	E22	62.22 N	35.31 E
Kuze, ngh., Japan	188		34.57 N	135.43 E
Kuzema, Russia	18	B21	65.21 N	34.16 E
Kuzemyn, Ukr.	38	C13	50.08 N	34.39 E
Kužener, Russia	40	C16	56.46 N	48.56 E
Kuženkino, Russia	26	C16	57.43 N	33.58 E
Kuzey Kıbrıs see Cyprus, North, ctry., Asia	76	C4	35.15 N	33.40 E
Kuz'minči, Russia	26	F16	54.15 N	33.41 E
Kuz'minka, stm., Russia	183a		59.48 N	30.31 E
Kuz'minki, ngh., Russia	183b		55.42 N	37.48 E
Kuz'movka, Russia	48	B16	62.20 N	92.06 E
Kuzneck, Russia	40	E15	53.06 N	46.35 E
Kuzneckij Alatau, mts., Russia	48	D15	54.45 N	88.00 E
Kuznečnoe, Russia	18	F16	61.08 N	29.50 E
Kuznecova, Russia	52	B12	46.15 N	138.04 E
Kuznecovka, Russia	26	D11	56.18 N	28.34 E
Kuznetsovs'k, Ukr.	38	B4	51.22 N	25.52 E
Kuzomen', Russia	12	D20	64.16 N	42.52 E
Kuzomen', Russia	14	F27	66.16 N	36.53 E
Kuzovatovo, Russia	40	E15	53.32 N	47.40 E
Kuzucubelen, Tur.	76	B5	36.51 N	34.26 E
Kuzuha, Japan	188		34.52 N	135.41 E
Kuzuryū, stm., Japan	56	C9	36.13 N	136.08 E
Kvænangen, b., Nor.	14	B11	70.05 N	21.13 E
Kvænangsbotn, Nor.	14	C13	69.44 N	22.04 E
Kvaløya, i., Nor.	14	C9	69.40 N	18.30 E
Kvaløya, i., Nor.	14	B14	70.37 N	23.52 E
Kvaløya, i., Nor.	16	B8	65.01 N	11.07 E
Kvam, Nor.	16	F7	61.40 N	9.43 E
Kvanndal, Nor.	16	G4	60.28 N	6.37 E
Kvarnbergsvattnet, l., Swe.	16	C10	64.35 N	13.56 E
Kvarner, b., Cro.	30	F11	44.48 N	14.11 E
Kvarnerić, b., Cro.	30	F11	44.45 N	14.35 E
Kvenær, Nor.	16	D6	63.31 N	8.23 E
Kverkfjöll, vol., Ice.	12a	k31	64.43 N	16.38 W
Kvichak Bay, b., Ak., U.S.	109	E8	58.35 N	157.39 W
Kvien, l., Swe.	16	G11	60.24 N	13.48 E
Kvigtinden, mtn., Nor.	16	B11	65.13 N	13.47 E
Kvikkjokk, Swe.	14	F8	66.57 N	17.43 E
Kvilegga, mtn., Nor.	16	E4	62.06 N	6.42 E
Kvina, stm., Nor.	16	I4	58.16 N	6.54 E
Kvissleby, Swe.	16	E15	62.17 N	17.22 E
Kvitseid, Nor.	16	H6	59.23 N	8.30 E
Kwa, stm., D.R.C.	86	E3	3.10 S	16.11 E
Kwahae-ri, ngh., Kor., S.	189b		37.33 N	126.50 E
Kwai see Khwae Noi, stm., Thai.	64	E4	14.00 N	99.31 E
Kwajalein, at., Marsh. Is.	94	C7	9.06 N	167.20 E
Kwakoegron, Sur.	164	B6	5.15 N	55.20 W
Kwambilo, stm., D.R.C.	191b		4.26 S	15.20 E
Kwamisa, mtn., Ghana	84	H4	7.08 N	1.53 W
Kwamouth, D.R.C.	86	E3	3.11 S	16.13 E
Kwanak-san, mtn., Kor., S.	189b		37.27 N	126.58 E
Kwando (Cuando), stm., Afr.	88	D3	18.29 S	23.36 E
Kwangchow see Guangzhou, China	58	J5	23.08 N	113.16 E
Kwangju, Kor., S.	54	G7	35.08 N	126.54 E
Kwango (Cuango), stm., Afr.	86	E3	3.12 S	17.23 E
Kwangsi Chuang see Guangxi, state, China	52	G6	24.00 N	109.00 E
Kwangtung see Guangdong, state, China	58	J6	23.00 N	113.00 E
Kwanmo-bong, mtn., Kor., N.	54	D8	41.42 N	129.13 E
Kwansan-ni, Kor., S.	189b		37.43 N	126.51 E
Kwanto Plain see Kantō-heiya, pl., Japan	56	D12	36.00 N	139.30 E
Kwa-Thema, S. Afr.	191d		26.18 S	28.23 E
KwaZulu-Natal, state, S. Afr.	90	F10	28.40 S	30.40 E
Kweichow see Guizhou, state, China	52	F6	27.00 N	107.00 E
Kweihwa see Hohhot, China	58	A4	40.48 N	111.38 E
Kweilin see Guilin, China	58	I4	25.17 N	110.17 E
Kweiyang see Guiyang, China	58	H2	26.34 N	106.42 E
Kwekwe, Zimb.	88	D4	18.56 S	29.48 E
Kweneng, state, Bots.	90	C7	24.00 S	24.00 E
Kwenge (Caengo), stm., Afr.	88	B2	4.50 S	18.44 E
Kwethluk, Ak., U.S.	109	D7	60.48 N	161.26 W
Kwidzyn, Pol.	24	C14	53.44 N	18.56 E
Kwigillingok, Ak., U.S.	109	E7	59.52 N	163.07 W
Kwikila, Pap. N. Gui.	101a	b4	9.52 S	147.44 E
Kwilu (Cuilo), stm., Afr.	86	E3	3.22 S	17.22 E
Kwun Tong, China	189d		22.19 N	114.12 E
Kyabra, Austl.	98	F4	26.18 S	143.08 E
Kyabra Creek, stm., Austl.	98	E4	25.35 S	142.46 E
Kyabram, Austl.	98	K5	36.18 S	145.03 E
Kyaikkami, Mya.	64	D3	16.04 N	97.34 E
Kyaiklat, Mya.	64	D2	16.26 N	95.43 E
Kyaikto, Mya.	64	D3	17.17 N	97.01 E
Kya-in, Mya.	64	D4	16.02 N	98.08 E
Kyaka, Tan.	86	E6	1.15 S	31.25 E
Kyalite, Austl.	98	J4	34.57 S	143.29 E
Kyaløysletta, Nor.	14	C9	69.42 N	18.53 E
Kyancutta, Austl.	96	F7	33.08 S	135.33 E
Ky Anh, Viet.	64	C8	18.04 N	106.17 E
Kyat-aw, Mya.	64	F4	12.26 N	98.20 E
Kyaukhnyat, Mya.	64	C3	18.15 N	97.31 E
Kyaukkyi, Mya.	64	C3	18.20 N	96.46 E
Kyaukmyaung, Mya.	64	A3	22.32 N	97.02 E
Kyaukpa, Mya.	64	F4	13.05 N	98.59 E
Kyaukpyu, Mya.	64	C1	19.25 N	93.33 E
Kyaukpyu, Mya.	64	C1	19.05 N	93.51 E
Kyaukse, Mya.	64	B2	21.36 N	96.08 E
Kyauktaw, Mya.	70	H14	20.49 N	92.59 E
Kyaunggon, Mya.	64	D2	17.05 N	95.10 E
Kybartai, Lith.	26	F5	54.38 N	22.45 E
Kyebang-san, mtn., Kor., S.	54	F8	37.43 N	128.29 E
Kyeikdon, Mya.	64	E4	16.00 N	98.25 E
Kyeintali, Mya.	64	C2	18.00 N	94.29 E
Kyidaunggan, Mya.	64	C3	19.52 N	96.12 E
Kyindwe, Mya.	64	B1	20.56 N	93.51 E
Kyiv (Kiev), Ukr.	38	C9	50.26 N	30.30 E
Kyïv, co., Ukr.	38	C9	50.15 N	30.30 E
Kyïvs'ke vodoskhovyshche, res., Ukr.	38	C9	50.51 N	30.31 E
Kyjov, Czech Rep.	24	G13	49.00 N	17.08 E
Kykotsmovi Village, Az., U.S.	150	H6	35.52 N	110.37 W
Kyle, Sk., Can.	142	D5	50.50 N	108.02 W
Kyle, S.D., U.S.	140	D10	43.25 N	102.10 W
Kyle, Tx., U.S.	136	E10	29.59 N	97.52 W
Kyle, Lake, res., Zimb.	90	B10	20.12 S	31.22 E
Kyle of Lochalsh, Scot., U.K.	10	D7	57.17 N	5.43 W
Kyllini, Grc.	34	F4	37.55 N	21.08 E
Kyllini, mtn., Grc.	34	F5	37.57 N	22.23 E
Kými, Grc.	34	E7	38.37 N	24.06 E
Kymi, state, Fin.	18	F14	61.00 N	28.00 E
Kyn, Russia	40	C21	57.47 N	58.30 E
Kyneton, Austl.	98	K5	37.15 S	144.27 E
Kynšperk nad Ohří, Czech Rep.	24	F8	50.07 N	12.32 E
Kynuna, Austl.	98	C3	21.33 S	141.56 E
Kyoga, Lake, l., Ug.	86	D6	1.30 N	33.00 E
Kyōga-misaki, c., Japan	56	D8	35.46 N	135.13 E
Kyogle, Austl.	98	G9	28.37 S	153.00 E
Kyoha-ri, Kor., S.	189b		37.46 N	126.46 E
Kyohyŏn-ni, Kor., S.	189b		37.43 N	126.58 E
Kyŏmip'o see Songnim, Kor., N.	54	E6	38.44 N	125.38 E
Kyondo, Mya.	64	D4	16.35 N	98.02 E
Kyŏnggi-man, b., Asia	54	F6	37.25 N	125.58 E
Kyŏngju, Kor., S.	54	G8	35.50 N	129.13 E
Kyŏngsan, Kor., S.	56	D1	35.49 N	128.44 E
Kyŏngsang-bukto, state, Kor., S.	56	C1	36.19 N	128.46 E
Kyŏngsang-namdo, state, Kor., S.	56	D1	35.27 N	128.47 E
Kyŏngsŏng see Sŏul, Kor., S.	54	F7	37.33 N	127.00 E
Kyŏngsŏng-ŭp, Kor., N.	54	D8	41.34 N	129.36 E
Kyonkadun, Mya.	64	D2	16.04 N	95.38 E
Kyonmange, Mya.	64	D2	16.30 N	95.50 E
Kyonpyaw, Mya.	64	D2	17.17 N	95.12 E
Kyōto, Japan	56	D8	34.59 N	135.45 E
Kyōto, Japan	188		35.00 N	135.45 E
Kyōto, state, Japan	56	D8	35.05 N	135.45 E
Kyōto-bonchi, mts., Japan	188		35.03 N	135.45 E
Kyōto Race Track, p.o.i., Japan	188		34.54 N	135.44 E
Kyōto University, educ., Japan	188		35.02 N	135.46 E
Kyparissia, Grc.	34	F4	37.14 N	21.39 E
Kyparissiakós Kólpos, b., Grc.	34	F4	37.23 N	21.33 E
Kyra, Russia	50	G11	49.34 N	111.58 E
Kyren, Russia	48	D18	51.39 N	102.08 E
Kyrenia see Girne, N. Cyp.	76	C4	35.19 N	33.20 E
Kyrgyzstan, ctry., Asia	48	F12	41.30 N	75.00 E
Kyritz, Ger.	24	D8	52.56 N	12.23 E
Kyrkheden, Swe.	16	G11	60.10 N	13.30 E
Kyrksæterøra, Nor.	16	D7	63.17 N	9.05 E
Kyrkslätt see Kirkkonummi, Fin.	18	G11	60.08 N	24.25 E
Kyrö, Fin.	18	G9	60.42 N	22.44 E
Kyrönjoki, stm., Fin.	18	D8	63.11 N	21.56 E
Kyrösjärvi, l., Fin.	18	F9	61.44 N	23.11 E
Kyröskoski, Fin.	18	F10	61.39 N	23.10 E
Kyrykivka, Ukr.	38	C14	50.22 N	35.07 E
Kyshen'ky, Ukr.	38	E13	48.53 N	34.08 E
Kyshyn, Ukr.	38	B6	51.08 N	27.41 E
Ky Son, Viet.	64	C7	19.23 N	104.08 E
Kyštym, Russia	48	C10	55.42 N	60.32 E
Kyte, stm., Il., U.S.	128	J9	41.59 N	89.19 W
Kýthira, Grc.	34	G5	36.09 N	22.58 E
Kýthira, i., Grc.	34	G5	36.17 N	22.57 E
Kýthnos, i., Grc.	34	F7	37.24 N	24.26 E
Kyūhōji, Japan	188		34.38 N	135.35 E
Kyunchaung, Mya.	64	E4	15.32 N	98.13 E
Kyundon, Mya.	64	B2	20.32 N	95.49 E
Kyunghee University, educ., Kor., S.	189b		37.37 N	127.04 E
Kyungyi, i., Mya.	64	E3	15.04 N	97.44 E
Kyuquot, B.C., Can.	144	F3	50.02 N	127.23 W
Kyuquot Sound, strt., B.C., Can.	144	G3	50.02 N	127.15 W
Kyūshū, i., Japan	56	G2	33.00 N	131.00 E
Kyushu-Palau Ridge, unds.	174	H16	20.00 N	136.00 E
Kyūshū-sanchi, mts., Japan	56	G4	32.35 N	131.17 E
Kywebwe, Mya.	64	C3	18.41 N	96.24 E
Kywong, Austl.	98	J6	34.59 S	146.44 E
Kyyjärvi, Fin.	18	D11	63.01 N	24.34 E
Kyyvesi, l., Fin.	18	E13	61.58 N	27.07 E
Kyzan, Kaz.	40	I18	44.48 N	52.49 E
Kyzyl, Russia	48	D16	51.42 N	94.23 E
Kyzylbair, Turkmen.	72	B8	38.13 N	55.39 E
Kyzyl-Kija, Kyrg.	48	F12	40.15 N	72.07 E
Kyzyl-Kommuna, Kaz.	48	E11	48.45 N	67.30 E
Kyzylkum, des., Asia	48	F10	42.00 N	64.00 E
Kyzyloba, Kaz.	40	G17	49.37 N	50.37 E
Kyzyltu, Kaz.	48	E13	47.41 N	75.41 E
Kyzyluj, Kaz.	48	E11	48.08 N	65.27 E
Kyzylžar, Kaz.	48	E12	48.17 N	69.38 E
Kzyl-Orda, Kaz.	48	F11	44.51 N	65.30 E
Kzyltu, Kaz.	48	D12	53.38 N	72.18 E
L				
Laa an der Thaya, Aus.	30	B13	48.42 N	16.23 E
Laab im Walde, Aus.	182b		48.09 N	16.11 E
Laaerberg, hill, Aus.	182b		48.09 N	16.24 E
La Aguja, Cabo de, c., Col.	168	B4	11.18 N	74.11 W
Laakajärvi, l., Fin.	18	D14	63.50 N	27.56 E
La Albuera, Spain	28	F4	38.42 N	6.49 W
La Albufera see L'Albufera, l., Spain	28	E10	39.20 N	0.22 W
La Alcarria, reg., Spain	28	D8	40.45 N	2.45 W
La Aldehuela, Spain	184a		40.18 N	3.36 W
La Algaba, Spain	28	G4	37.27 N	6.00 W
La Almarcha, Spain	28	E8	39.41 N	2.22 W
La Almunia de Doña Godina, Spain	28	C9	41.28 N	1.22 W
Läänemeri see Baltic Sea, s., Eur.	8	D12	57.00 N	19.00 E
La Antigua, Salina, pl., Arg.	172	D4	29.49 S	66.09 W
Laar, ngh., Ger.	181		51.28 N	6.43 E
La Araucanía, state, Chile	172	I1	38.09 S	72.31 W
Laas Caanood see Laascaanood, Som.	86	C9	8.28 N	47.21 E
Laascaanood, Som.	86	C9	8.28 N	47.21 E
La Ascensión, hill, Mex.	154	C8	24.19 N	99.54 W
La Asunción, Ven.	168	B10	11.01 N	63.51 W
La Atravesada, Loma, hill, Mex.	120	F6	29.57 N	112.12 W
Laau Point, c., Hi., U.S.	100a	b4	21.06 N	157.18 W
La Aurora, Chile	204e		33.36 S	70.38 W
Laayoune see El Aaiún, W. Sah.	84	D2	27.09 N	13.11 W
La Azufrosa, Mex.	136	F7	28.14 N	100.50 W
Laba, stm., Russia	42	C9	45.11 N	39.41 E
La Babia, Mex.	154	A7	28.34 N	102.04 W
Labadieville, La., U.S.	134	H8	29.49 N	90.57 W
La Baie, Qc., Can.	122	B6	48.20 N	70.52 W
La Banda, Arg.	172	C5	27.44 S	64.14 W
La Bandera, Cerro, mtn., Mex.	154	C6	24.35 N	105.07 W
La Bañeza, Spain	28	B5	42.17 N	5.52 W
La Barca, Mex.	154	E7	20.16 N	102.33 W
La Barceloneta, ngh., Spain	184d		41.22 N	2.11 E
La Barge, Wy., U.S.	146	H16	42.15 N	110.12 W
La Barge Creek, stm., Wy., U.S.	146	H16	42.09 N	110.11 W
Labasa, Fiji	101e	p19	16.26 S	179.24 E
La Bâte, Fr.	179		48.35 N	2.01 E
La Baule-Escoublac, Fr.	20	G6	47.17 N	2.23 W
L'Abbé, Fr.	179		48.34 N	1.50 E
Labé, Gui.	84	G2	11.19 N	12.17 W
Labe (Elbe), stm., Eur.	24	C7	53.53 N	9.01 E
Labelle, Qc., Can.	126	B15	46.17 N	74.43 W
La Belle, Fl., U.S.	132	J4	26.45 N	81.26 W
La Belle, Mo., U.S.	130	D6	40.07 N	91.54 W
Labengke, Pulau, i., Indon.	60	F7	3.27 S	122.25 E
Laberge, Lake, l., Yk., Can.	110	C4	61.16 N	135.13 W
Labette Creek, stm., Ks., U.S.	130	G2	37.03 N	95.05 W
Labi, Bru.	66	A9	4.24 N	114.27 E
Labian, Tanjong, c., Malay.	66	A11	5.18 N	119.14 E
La Biche, stm., Ab., Can.	144	B18	55.00 N	112.44 W
Labin, Cro.	30	E11	45.05 N	14.07 E
Labinsk, Russia	42	C9	44.37 N	40.43 E
Labis, Malay.	64	K6	2.23 N	103.01 E
La Bisbal d'Empordà, Spain	28	C13	41.57 N	3.01 E
Łabiszyn, Pol.	24	D13	52.57 N	17.55 E
Labkovičy, Bela.	26	G14	53.50 N	31.45 E
Lablâbah, Wādī el-, val., Egypt	191c		30.02 N	31.19 E
La Blanca, Chile	204e		33.31 S	70.41 W
La Blanca Grande, Laguna, l., Arg.	172	I5	38.26 S	63.55 W
Labná, hist., Mex.	156	B3	20.15 N	89.31 W
Laboe, Ger.	24	B6	54.24 N	10.13 E
La Boissière, Fr.	179		48.46 N	1.59 E
La Boissière-Ecole, Fr.	179		48.41 N	1.39 E
Laborde, Arg.	172	F6	33.09 S	62.52 W
La Borde, Fr.	179		48.32 N	2.50 E
Laborec, stm., Slvk.	24	G17	48.36 N	22.00 E
Laborie, St. Luc.	159c	m7	13.45 N	60.59 W
La Bostonnais, Qc., Can.	122	C4	47.31 N	72.42 W
Laboulaye, Arg.	172	G6	34.07 S	63.23 W
La Boyera, Ven.	204c		10.25 N	66.50 W
La Boyera, Ven.	204c		10.25 N	66.57 W
Labrador, reg., Nf., Can.	106	D16	54.00 N	62.00 W
Labrador Basin, unds.	176	C9	53.00 N	48.00 W
Labrador City, Nf., Can.	110	E17	52.56 N	66.54 W
Labrador Sea, s., N.A.	106	D17	57.00 N	53.00 W
Lábrea, Braz.	164	E5	7.16 S	64.47 W
La Brea, Trin.	159f	s12	10.13 N	61.36 W
Labrit, Fr.	22	E5	44.06 N	0.33 W
La Broquerie, Mb., Can.	142	E17	49.29 N	96.27 W
Labuan, Malay.	66	A9	5.17 N	115.15 E
Labuan, state, Malay.	66	A9	5.21 N	115.13 E
Labuan, Pulau, i., Malay.	66	A9	5.19 N	115.13 E
Labuchongshan, mts., China	70	C10	30.14 N	84.43 E
La Bufadora, Mex.	148	L9	31.43 N	116.42 W
Labuhan, Indon.	66	G4	6.23 S	105.50 E
Labuhanbajo, Indon.	66	H11	8.29 S	119.53 E
Labuhanbatu, Indon.	66	B2	2.14 N	100.13 E
Labuhanbilik, Indon.	66	B2	2.31 N	100.10 E
Labuhanmarege, Indon.	66	G12	7.08 S	120.38 E
Labuhanpandan, Indon.	66	H10	8.23 S	116.43 E
Labuhanruku, Indon.	66	B1	3.12 N	99.33 E
Labuk, stm., Malay.	68	H1	5.53 N	117.29 E
Labuk, Telukan, b., Malay.	68	G1	6.07 N	117.46 E
Labu Kananga, Indon.	66	H10	8.08 S	117.47 E
Labutta, Mya.	64	D2	16.09 N	94.43 E
Labytnangi, Russia	48	A11	66.39 N	66.25 E
Laç, Alb.	32	C13	41.38 N	19.43 E
Lača, ozero, l., Russia	18	F25	61.20 N	38.48 E
Lac-à-Beauce, Qc., Can.	122	C4	47.19 N	72.46 W
La Cadena, Mex.	136	I3	25.53 N	104.11 W
L'Acadie, Qc., Can.	193a		45.19 N	73.21 W
L'Acadie, stm., Qc., Can.	122	E3	45.29 N	73.16 W
La Calera, Chile	172	F2	32.46 S	71.11 W
La Calera, Peru	204d		12.12 S	76.54 W
La Campana, Spain	28	G5	37.34 N	5.26 W
La Canada Flintridge, Ca., U.S.	148	I7	34.11 N	118.11 W
La Canada Verde Creek, stm., Ca., U.S.	198		33.52 N	118.02 W
Lacanau, Fr.	22	D4	44.58 N	1.05 W
Lacanau, Étang de, l., Fr.	22	E4	44.58 N	1.07 W
La Candelaria, Arg.	172	C5	26.06 S	65.06 W
La Candelaria, Mex.	136	C1	31.00 N	106.32 W
La Cañiza see A Cañiza, Spain	28	B2	42.13 N	8.16 W
Lacantum, stm., Mex.	156	D2	16.33 N	90.40 W
La Capelle-en-Thiérache, Fr.	20	D12	49.58 N	3.54 E
La Carlota, Arg.	172	F6	33.25 S	63.17 W
La Carlota, Phil.	68	E4	10.25 N	122.55 E
La Carolina, Spain	28	F7	38.16 N	3.36 W
Lacaune, Fr.	22	F8	43.43 N	2.42 E
Lac-Bouchette, Qc., Can.	122	B4	48.15 N	72.11 W
Laccadive, Minicoy and Amīndīvi Islands see Lakshadweep, state, India	62	F3	10.00 N	73.00 E
Laccadive Islands see Lakshadweep, is., India	62	F3	10.00 N	73.00 E
Lac Courte Oreilles Indian Reservation, ind. res., Wi., U.S.	128	F7	45.49 N	91.22 W
Lac du Flambeau, Wi., U.S.	128	F8	45.58 N	89.52 W
Lac du Flambeau Indian Reservation, ind. res., Wi., U.S.	128	E9	45.59 N	89.51 W
Lac-Édouard, Qc., Can.	122	C4	47.39 N	72.16 W
La Ceiba, Hond.	156	E4	15.46 N	86.47 W
La Ceiba, Ven.	168	C6	9.28 N	71.03 W
La Celle-les-Bordes, Fr.	179		48.38 N	1.57 E
La Celle-Saint-Cloud, Fr.	179		48.51 N	2.08 E
La Center, Ky., U.S.	130	G9	37.04 N	88.58 W
Lacepede Bay, b., Austl.	98	K2	36.51 S	139.45 E
Lac-Etchemin, Qc., Can.	122	D6	46.24 N	70.30 W
Lacey, Wa., U.S.	146	C4	47.02 N	122.48 W
Lacey Creek, stm., Il., U.S.	196		41.50 N	88.03 W
Lac-Frontière, Qc., Can.	122	D6	46.41 N	70.00 W
La Chaise-Dieu, Fr.	22	D9	45.19 N	3.42 E
La Chapelle-d'Angillon, Fr.	20	G11	47.22 N	2.26 E
La Chapelle-Gauthier, Fr.	179		48.33 N	2.54 E
La Charité-sur-Loire, Fr.	20	G12	47.10 N	3.00 E
La Châtaigneraie, Fr.	22	C5	46.39 N	0.44 W
La Châtre, Fr.	20	H11	46.34 N	1.59 E
La Chaux-de-Fonds, Switz.	30	C3	47.06 N	6.49 E
Lach Dennis, Eng., U.K.	180		53.15 N	2.26 W
Lachenaie, Qc., Can.	193a		45.42 N	73.34 W
Lachhmangarh Sīkar, India	70	E5	27.49 N	74.58 E
Lachine, Qc., Can.	126	C16	45.26 N	73.40 W
Lachine, Canal de, can., Qc., Can.	193a		45.26 N	73.40 W
Lachine, Rapides de, wtfl., Qc., Can.	193a		45.25 N	73.36 W
La Chira, Punta, c., Peru	204d		12.13 S	77.03 W
La Chivera, Ven.	204c		10.37 N	66.54 W
Lachkaltsap Indian Reserve, ind. res., B.C., Can.	144	A1	55.02 N	129.32 W
Lachlan, stm., Austl.	98	J5	34.20 S	143.53 E
La Chorrera, Col.	168	H5	1.12 S	72.54 W
La Chorrera, Pan.	156	H8	8.52 N	79.46 W
Lachute, Qc., Can.	126	C15	45.39 N	74.20 W
Laçi see Laç, Alb.	32	C13	41.38 N	19.43 E
La Ciénaga, Arg.	172	C4	27.29 S	67.00 W
La Cinta Creek, stm., N.M., U.S.	138	F4	35.24 N	104.06 W
La Ciotat, Fr.	22	F11	43.10 N	5.35 E
La Cisterna, Chile	204e		33.33 S	70.41 W
La Citadelle, hist., Haiti	156	C11	19.35 N	72.14 W
La Ciudad, Mex.	154	D6	23.42 N	105.43 W
Lackawanna, N.Y., U.S.	124	B7	42.49 N	78.50 W
Lackawanna, Lake, l., N.J., U.S.	194		40.57 N	74.42 W
Lackland Air Force Base, mil., Tx., U.S.	136	E9	29.27 N	98.37 W
Lackoe, Russia	26	B21	58.04 N	38.08 E
Lac La Biche, Ab., Can.	144	B18	54.45 N	111.58 W
Lac la Hache, B.C., Can.	144	E9	51.49 N	121.28 W
Laclede, Id., U.S.	146	B10	48.09 N	116.45 W
Laclede, Mo., U.S.	130	E4	39.47 N	93.09 W
La Clotilde, Arg.	172	C7	27.06 S	60.36 W
Lac-Mégantic, Qc., Can.	122	E6	45.34 N	70.52 W
Lac-Nominingue, Qc., Can.	126	B14	46.23 N	75.01 W
La Cocha, Arg.	172	C5	27.45 S	65.35 W
La Colmena, Mex.	204a		19.36 N	99.18 W
La Colorada, Mex.	154	A3	28.47 N	110.35 W
La Columna see Bolívar, Pico, mtn., Ven.	168	C6	8.32 N	71.00 W
La Coma, Mex.	154	C9	24.28 N	98.18 W
Lacombe, Ab., Can.	144	D17	52.28 N	113.45 W
Lacombe, La., U.S.	134	G9	30.18 N	89.56 W
Lacon, Il., U.S.	130	D8	41.01 N	89.24 W
Lacona, Ia., U.S.	130	C4	41.11 N	93.24 W
La Concepción, Pan.	156	H6	8.31 N	82.36 W
La Concepción, Ven.	168	B5	10.38 N	71.50 W
Laconi, Italy	32	E2	39.50 N	9.03 E
Laconia, N.H., U.S.	122	G5	43.31 N	71.28 W
Laconia, Gulf of see Lakonikós Kólpos, b., Grc.	34	G5	36.40 N	22.38 E
La Conner, Wa., U.S.	146	B4	48.23 N	122.30 W
La Consulta, Arg.	172	F3	33.43 S	69.07 W
Lacoochee, Fl., U.S.	132	H3	28.28 N	82.09 W
La Coruña see A Coruña, Spain	28	A2	43.21 N	8.24 W
La Coruña see A Coruña, co., Spain	28	A2	43.10 N	8.30 W
La Coste, Tx., U.S.	136	E9	29.19 N	98.49 W
La Courneuve, Fr.	179		48.56 N	2.23 E
La Courtine, Fr.	22	D8	45.42 N	2.16 E
Lac qui Parle, stm., Mn., U.S.	128	G2	45.04 N	95.56 W
Lac qui Parle, West Branch, stm., Mn., U.S.	128	G2	44.55 N	96.02 W
Lacre Punt, c., Neth. Ant.	158g	p23	12.01 N	68.14 W
La Crescent, Mn., U.S.	128	H7	43.49 N	91.18 W
La-Croche, Qc., Can.	122	C4	47.36 N	72.44 W
La Crosse, In., U.S.	130	C11	41.18 N	86.53 W
La Crosse, Ks., U.S.	138	C9	38.32 N	99.17 W
La Crosse, Va., U.S.	124	H7	36.41 N	78.05 W
Lacrosse, Wa., U.S.	146	D9	46.47 N	117.53 W
La Crosse, Wi., U.S.	128	H7	43.47 N	91.14 W
La Crosse, stm., Wi., U.S.	128	H7	43.49 N	91.16 W
La Cruz, Arg.	172	D9	29.09 S	56.38 W
La Cruz, Col.	168	G3	1.35 N	76.58 W
La Cruz, C.R.	152	E7	11.03 N	85.38 W
La Cruz, Mex.	136	F7	28.33 N	100.48 W
La Cruz, Mex.	136	G2	27.52 N	105.13 W
La Cruz, Ur.	172	F9	33.58 S	56.14 W
La Cruz, Cerro, mtn., Mex.	154	G8	17.55 N	101.31 W
La Cruz de Río Grande, Nic.	156	F5	13.05 N	84.09 W
Lacs, Rivière des see Des Lacs, stm., N.A.	142	F11	48.17 N	101.25 W
Lac Seul, On., Can.	128	A6	50.19 N	92.17 W
Lac Seul Indian Reserve, ind. res., On., Can.	128	A6	50.15 N	92.10 W
La Cuesta, P.R.	158a	b2	18.25 N	66.49 W
La Cumbre, Arg.	172	E5	30.59 S	64.29 W
La Cumbre, Ven.	204c		10.32 N	66.57 W
Lac Vieux Desert Indian Reservation, ind. res., Mi., U.S.	128	E9	46.20 N	89.10 W
La Cygne, Ks., U.S.	130	F3	38.20 N	94.45 W
Ladainha, Braz.	170	I5	17.39 S	41.44 W
Ladākh, hist. reg., Pak.	70	A7	34.49 N	79.48 E
Ladākh Range, mts., Asia	62	B4	34.00 N	78.00 E
Ladan, Ukr.	38	C11	50.31 N	32.35 E
Ladd, Il., U.S.	128	J9	41.22 N	89.12 W
Ladder Creek, stm., Ks., U.S.	138	C7	38.48 N	100.52 W
Laddingford, Eng., U.K.	178		51.12 N	0.25 E
Laddonia, Mo., U.S.	130	E6	39.15 N	91.38 W
Ladeburg, Ger.	182a		52.42 N	13.35 E
La Défense, bldg., Fr.	179		48.53 N	2.15 E
La Dehesa, Chile	204e		33.22 S	70.33 W
Ladera Heights, Ca., U.S.	198		33.59 N	118.22 W
La Désirade, i., Guad.	159c	h6	16.19 N	61.03 W
Ládi, Grc.	34	B9	41.27 N	26.17 E
La Digue, i., Sey.	89b	j13	4.21 S	55.50 E
Ladismith, S. Afr.	90	H5	33.29 S	21.15 E
Ladispoli, Italy	30	I9	41.57 N	12.04 E
Lādīz, Iran	72	D9	28.54 N	61.17 E
Ladner, B.C., Can.	144	G7	49.05 N	123.04 W
Lādnūn, India	70	E5	27.38 N	74.23 E
Ladoga, In., U.S.	130	E11	39.54 N	86.48 W
Ladoga, Lake see Ladožskoe ozero, l., Russia	18	G18	61.00 N	31.30 E
La Dolorita, Ven.	204c		10.29 N	66.47 W
Ladonia, Tx., U.S.	134	D2	33.26 N	95.56 W
La Dorada, Col.	168	E4	5.27 N	74.41 W
La Doré, Qc., Can.	122	B4	48.43 N	72.39 W
La Dormida, Arg.	172	F4	33.21 S	67.55 W
Lado Sarāi, ngh., India	190a		28.32 N	77.12 E
Ladožskoe Ozero, Russia	18	G18	60.08 N	31.01 E
Ladožskoe ozero (Ladoga, Lake), l., Russia	18	G18	61.00 N	31.30 E
Ladožskoe ozero (Lake Ladoga), l., Russia	183a		59.57 N	31.04 E
Lādpur, ngh., India	190a		28.44 N	76.59 E
Laduškin, Russia	26	F3	54.34 N	20.14 E
Ladva, Russia	18	F21	61.21 N	34.38 E
Ladva-Vetka, Russia	18	F21	61.22 N	34.27 E
Lady, Fr.	179		48.35 N	2.54 E
Lady Ann Strait, strt., Nu., Can.	108	B10	75.40 N	79.50 W
Lady Barron, Austl.	99a	n14	40.12 S	148.14 E
Ladybrand, S. Afr.	90	F8	29.11 S	27.27 E
Lady Elliot Island, i., Austl.	98	E9	24.05 S	152.41 E
Lady Grey, S. Afr.	90	G8	30.42 S	27.13 E
Ladysmith, B.C., Can.	144	H7	48.58 N	123.47 W
Ladysmith, S. Afr.	90	F9	28.33 S	29.46 E
Ladysmith, Wi., U.S.	128	F7	45.27 N	91.06 W
Ladyzhyn, Ukr.	38	E8	48.40 N	29.16 E
Lae, Pap. N. Gui.	101a	b4	6.43 S	146.59 E
Laem, Khao, mtn., Thai.	64	E5	14.27 N	101.30 E
Laem Ngop, Thai.	64	F6	12.10 N	102.25 E
La Encantada, Mex.	154	C8	25.17 N	101.04 W
Laer, ngh., Ger.	181		51.28 N	7.16 E
Lærdalsøyri, Nor.	16	F5	61.06 N	7.29 E
La Escondida, Mex.	136	H8	26.16 N	99.46 W
La Esmeralda, Mex.	154	B7	27.17 N	103.39 W
La Esmeralda, Ven.	168	F9	3.11 N	65.33 W
Læsø, i., Den.	16	J9	57.16 N	11.01 E
La Esperanza, Cuba	156	A6	22.46 N	83.44 W
La Esperanza, Hond.	156	E3	14.18 N	88.10 W
La Esperanza, Mex.	136	H4	26.46 N	104.00 W
La Esperanza, Mex.	136	I3	25.52 N	104.49 W
La Esperanza, Mex.	150	K2	32.06 N	114.47 W
La Esperanza, P.R.	158a	b3	18.22 N	66.06 W
La Estación, ngh., Spain	184a		40.27 N	3.48 W
La Estrada see A Estrada, Spain	28	B2	42.41 N	8.29 W
La Estrella, Ven.	204c		10.25 N	66.48 W
La Estrella, Cerro, mtn., Mex.	204a		19.20 N	99.05 W
Lafa, China	54	C7	43.50 N	127.21 E
La Falda, Arg.	172	E5	31.06 S	64.28 W
La Farge, Wi., U.S.	128	H8	43.34 N	90.38 W
Lafayette, Al., U.S.	134	E13	32.53 N	85.24 W
Lafayette, Ca., U.S.	148	F3	37.53 N	122.06 W
Lafayette, Co., U.S.	138	A3	39.59 N	105.05 W
Lafayette, Ga., U.S.	134	C13	34.42 N	85.17 W
Lafayette, In., U.S.	130	D11	40.24 N	86.52 W
Lafayette, La., U.S.	134	G6	30.13 N	92.01 W
Lafayette, Mn., U.S.	128	G4	44.26 N	94.23 W
Lafayette, Tn., U.S.	130	H11	36.30 N	86.01 W
Lafayette, Mount, mtn., N.H., U.S.	122	F5	44.10 N	71.38 W
Lafayette Hill, Pa., U.S.	203		40.05 N	75.15 W
Lafayette Reservoir, res., Ca., U.S.	200		37.53 N	122.08 W
Lafayette Water Tunnel, trans., Ca., U.S.	200		37.54 N	122.12 W
La Fe, Cuba	156	B6	21.44 N	82.45 W
La Feria, Tx., U.S.	136	H10	26.09 N	97.49 W
Laferrere, Arg.	206		34.45 S	58.35 W
La Ferté-Bernard, Fr.	20	F9	48.11 N	0.39 E
La Ferté-Macé, Fr.	20	F8	48.35 N	0.21 W
La Ferté-Saint-Aubin, Fr.	20	G10	47.42 N	1.56 E
Lafia, Nig.	84	H6	8.29 N	8.31 E

Name	Page	Map Ref.	Latitude	Longitude
Lafiagi, Nig.	84	H6	8.50 N	5.24 E
Laflèche, Qc., Can.	193a		45.30 N	73.28 W
Lafleche, Sk., Can.	142	E7	49.41 N	106.35 W
La Flèche, Fr.	20	G8	47.41 N	0.04 W
La Floresta, Spain	184d		41.27 N	2.04 E
La Florida, Chile	204e		33.33 S	70.34 W
La Florida, Guat.	156	D2	16.33 N	90.27 W
La Florida, Spain	184d		41.31 N	2.12 E
La Foa, N. Cal.	101d	m15	21.43 S	165.49 E
La Follette, Tn., U.S.	124	H1	36.22 N	84.07 W
La Fontaine, In., U.S.	130	D12	40.40 N	85.43 W
Lafontaine, Parc, p.o.i., Qc., Can.	193a		45.32 N	73.34 W
Lafourche, Bayou, stm., La., U.S.	134	H8	29.04 N	90.13 W
La Fragua, Arg.	172	C5	26.06 S	64.19 W
La Francia, Arg.	172	E6	31.24 S	62.38 W
La Fregeneda, Spain	28	C4	40.59 N	6.50 W
La Frette-sur-Seine, Fr.	179		48.58 N	2.11 E
La Fría, Ven.	168	C5	8.12 N	72.14 W
La Fuente de San Esteban, Spain	28	D4	40.48 N	6.15 W
La Galite, i., Tun.	84	B6	37.32 N	8.56 E
La Gallareta, Arg.	172	D7	29.34 S	60.22 W
La Gallega, Spain	28	C7	41.54 N	3.16 W
Lagan, Swe.	16	K11	56.55 N	13.59 E
Lagan, stm., Swe.	16	K11	56.32 N	12.56 E
Lagan, stm., N. Ire., U.K.	10	G6	54.36 N	5.55 W
Lagangzong, China	70	D13	28.05 N	91.04 E
La Garenne-Colombes, Fr.	179		48.55 N	2.15 E
Lagarto, Braz.	170	F7	10.55 S	37.41 W
Lagarto Creek, stm., Tx., U.S.	136	F9	28.09 N	97.54 W
Lagawe, Phil.	68	B3	16.49 N	121.05 E
Lage, China	70	D10	29.26 N	85.56 E
Lage see Laxe, Spain	28	A1	43.13 N	9.00 W
Lågen, stm., Nor.	16	H7	59.02 N	10.03 E
Lågen, stm., Nor.	16	F8	61.09 N	10.24 E
Lages, Braz.	172	C12	27.48 S	50.17 W
Laghmān, state, Afg.	70	A3	34.34 N	70.12 E
Laghouat, Alg.	84	C5	33.50 N	2.51 E
La Giustiniana, ngh., Italy	185a		41.59 N	12.24 E
Lagkadás, Grc.	34	C5	40.45 N	23.04 E
Lagkádia, Grc.	34	F5	37.41 N	22.02 E
La Gloria, Col.	168	C5	8.37 N	73.47 W
Lagny-le-Sec, Fr.	179		49.05 N	2.45 E
Lago, Mount, mtn., Wa., U.S.	146	B6	48.49 N	120.32 W
Lagoa da Prata, Braz.	170	K3	20.02 S	45.33 W
Lagoa Formosa, Braz.	170	J2	18.47 S	46.24 W
Lagoa Vermelha, Braz.	172	D12	28.13 S	51.32 W
Lago da Pedra, Braz.	170	C3	4.19 S	45.10 W
Lago Kolonie, Aruba	158g	p20	12.26 N	69.52 W
Lagolândia, Braz.	170	H1	15.37 S	49.02 W
Lagolovo, Russia	183a		59.42 N	30.00 E
La Gomera, i., Spain	84	D1	28.06 N	17.11 W
Lagonegro, Italy	32	D9	40.07 N	15.45 E
Lagonoy Gulf, b., Phil.	68	D4	13.35 N	123.45 E
Lago Posadas, Arg.	166	I2	47.30 S	71.38 W
Lagos, Nig.	84	H5	6.27 N	3.24 E
Lagos, Nig.	191a		6.27 N	3.24 E
Lagos, Port.	28	G2	37.06 N	8.40 W
Lagos (Ikeja) Airport, arpt., Nig.	191a		6.35 N	3.20 E
Lagos, University of, educ., Nig.	191a		6.32 N	3.24 E
Lagos de Moreno, Mex.	154	E8	21.21 N	101.53 W
Lagos Harbour, b., Nig.	191a		6.26 N	3.24 E
Lagos Island, i., Nig.	191a		6.27 N	3.26 E
Lagos Lagoon, b., Nig.	191a		6.30 N	3.26 E
Lagos Terminus, trans., Nig.	191a		6.28 N	3.23 E
La Gouèra, W. Sah.	84	E1	20.50 N	17.04 W
La Goulette, Tun.	32	H4	36.49 N	10.18 E
Lago Viedma, Arg.	166	I2	49.48 S	72.05 W
La Granadella, Spain	28	C11	41.21 N	0.39 E
La Grande, Or., U.S.	146	E8	45.19 N	118.04 W
La Grande Deux, Réservoir, res., Qc., Can.	110	E15	53.40 N	76.55 W
La Grande Quatre, Réservoir, res., Qc., Can.	110	E16	54.00 N	73.15 W
La98Grange, Austl.	96	C4	18.42 S	121.50 E
La Grange, Ga., U.S.	134	D13	33.02 N	85.01 W
Lagrange, In., U.S.	130	C12	41.38 N	85.23 W
La Grange, Ky., U.S.	130	F12	38.24 N	85.22 W
La Grange, Mo., U.S.	130	D6	40.02 N	91.29 W
La Grange, N.C., U.S.	132	A8	35.18 N	77.47 W
La Grange, Tx., U.S.	136	E11	29.54 N	96.52 W
Lagrange, Wy., U.S.	140	F8	41.37 N	104.10 W
Lagrange Bay, b., Austl.	96	C4	18.38 S	121.42 E
La Grange Highlands, Il., U.S.	196		41.50 N	87.51 W
La Grange Park, Il., U.S.	196		41.50 N	87.51 W
La Granja, Chile	204e		33.32 S	70.39 W
La Gran Sabana, pl., Ven.	168	E10	5.20 N	62.03 W
La Grita, Ven.	156	H12	8.07 N	72.00 W
La Grue Bayou, stm., Ar., U.S.	134	C7	34.11 N	91.11 W
La Guadeloupe, Qc., Can.	122	E6	45.57 N	70.55 W
La Guajira, state, Col.	156	G11	11.30 N	72.30 W
La Guajira, Península de, pen., S.A.	168	A6	12.00 N	71.40 W
La Guardia, Arg.	172	D5	29.33 S	65.27 W
La Guardia, Bol.	166	C4	17.54 S	63.20 W
La Guardia see A Guardia, Spain	28	C2	41.54 N	8.52 W
Laguardia, Spain	28	B8	42.33 N	2.34 W
La Gudiña see A Gudiña, Spain	28	B3	42.04 N	7.08 W
La Guêpière, Fr.	179		48.35 N	1.50 E
La Guerche-sur-l'Aubois, Fr.	20	G11	46.57 N	2.57 E
Laguiole, Fr.	22	E8	44.41 N	2.51 E
Laguna, Braz.	172	D13	28.28 S	48.46 W
Laguna, N.M., U.S.	150	H9	35.02 N	107.27 W
Laguna, Arroyo de la, stm., Ca., U.S.	200		37.35 N	121.53 W
Laguna, Ilha da, i., Braz.	164	D7	1.40 S	51.00 W
Laguna Beach, Ca., U.S.	148	J8	33.32 N	117.46 W
Laguna Creek, stm., Az., U.S.	150	G7	36.53 N	109.43 W
Laguna Dam, dam., U.S.	150	K2	32.50 N	114.31 W
Laguna de Jaco, Mex.	136	G4	27.51 N	103.55 W
Laguna Indian Reservation, ind. res., N.M., U.S.	150	I9	35.04 N	107.21 W
Laguna Larga, Arg.	172	E6	31.46 S	63.48 W
Laguna Limpia, Arg.	172	C8	26.29 S	59.41 W
Laguna Paiva, Arg.	172	E7	31.17 S	60.39 W
Lagunas, Peru	164	E2	5.12 S	75.39 W
Lagunas de Chacagua, Parque Nacional, p.o.i., Mex.	154	H9	16.00 N	97.00 W
Lagunillas, Bol.	166	C4	19.38 S	63.43 W
Laha, China	52	B9	48.12 N	124.37 E
La Habana (Havana), Cuba	156	A6	23.06 N	82.26 W
La Habana (Havana), Cuba	204b		23.08 N	82.22 W
La Habana, Universidad de, educ., Cuba	204b		23.08 N	82.22 W
La Habra Heights, Ca., U.S.	198		33.57 N	117.57 W
Lahad Datu, Malay.	66	A11	5.01 N	118.19 E
Lahad Datu, Telukan, b., Malay.	66	A11	4.51 N	118.24 E
Lahaina, Hi., U.S.	100a	c5	20.52 N	156.40 W
Laham, Indon.	66	C9	0.17 N	115.23 E
La Harpe, Il., U.S.	128	K7	40.34 N	90.57 W
La Harpe, Ks., U.S.	130	G2	37.55 N	95.17 W
Lahat, Indon.	66	E3	3.48 S	103.32 E
La Hauteville, Fr.	179		48.42 N	1.37 E
LaHave, stm., N.S., Can.	122	F12	44.16 N	64.21 W
La Häy-les-Rosas, Fr.	179		48.47 N	2.21 E
Lahdenpohja, Russia	18	F17	61.31 N	30.11 E
Lahemaa rahvus, p.o.i., Est.	18	H13	59.32 N	25.53 E
Lahewa, Indon.	64	L3	1.23 N	97.09 E
Lahfān, Bi'r, well, Egypt	76	G4	31.01 N	33.52 E
Lahi, Ava, strt., Tonga	100e	n14	21.02 S	175.09 W
La Higuera, Chile	172	D2	29.30 S	71.13 W
Lahij, Yemen	72	G5	13.01 N	44.53 E
Lāhījān, Iran	74	B12	37.12 N	50.00 E
Lahišyn, Bela.	26	H9	52.20 N	25.59 E
Lahn, stm., Ger.	20	D17	50.18 N	7.35 E
Lahnstein, Ger.	24	F3	50.18 N	7.36 E
Lahojsk, Bela.	26	F10	54.11 N	27.53 E
Laholm, Swe.	16	K10	56.31 N	13.03 E
Laholmsbukten, b., Swe.	16	K10	56.35 N	12.50 E
La Honda Creek, stm., Ca., U.S.	200		37.18 N	122.16 W
Lahontan Reservoir, res., Nv., U.S.	148	D6	39.23 N	119.10 W
Lahore, Pak.	70	C5	31.35 N	74.19 E
La Horqueta, Col.	168	F5	3.05 N	72.50 W
La Horqueta, Arroyo, stm., Arg.	206		34.41 S	58.51 W
La Houssaye-en-Brie, Fr.	179		48.45 N	2.53 E
Lahr, Ger.	24	H3	48.20 N	7.51 E
Lahri, Pak.	70	D2	29.10 N	68.12 E
Lāhrūd, Iran	74	A10	38.30 N	47.49 E
Lahta, ngh., Russia	183a		60.00 N	30.09 E
Lahti, Fin.	18	F12	60.59 N	25.39 E
Lahtinskij Razliv, ozero, l., Russia	183a		60.00 N	30.11 E
La Huacana, Mex.	154	F8	18.58 N	101.49 W
La Huerta, N.M., U.S.	136	B3	32.28 N	104.12 W
La Hunière, Fr.	179		48.36 N	1.52 E
Lahva, Bela.	26	H10	52.12 N	27.06 E
Laï, Chad	82	F3	9.23 N	16.18 E
Laiagam, Pap. N. Gui.	101a	b3	5.29 S	143.30 E
Laibach see Ljubljana, Slvn.	30	D11	46.03 N	14.31 E
Laibin, China	58	J3	23.41 N	109.13 E
Lai Chau, Viet.	64	A6	22.03 N	103.09 E
Laichow Bay see Laizhou Wan, b., China	58	C8	37.20 N	119.18 E
Laifeng, China	58	G3	29.31 N	109.15 E
L'Aigle, Fr.	20	F9	48.45 N	0.38 E
L'Aigle Creek, stm., Ar., U.S.	134	D6	33.11 N	92.08 W
Laignes, Fr.	20	G13	47.51 N	4.22 E
Laihia, Fin.	18	E8	62.58 N	22.00 E
Lai-hka, Mya.	64	B3	21.16 N	97.40 E
Laimbélé, Mont, mtn., Vanuatu	101d	k16	16.20 S	167.31 E
Lainate, Italy	184b		45.34 N	9.02 E
Laingsburg, S. Afr.	90	H5	33.11 S	20.51 E
Laingsburg, Mi., U.S.	124	B1	42.53 N	84.21 W
Lainioälven, stm., Swe.	14	E13	67.22 N	22.40 E
Lainsitz (Lužnice), stm., Eur.	30	B11	48.45 N	14.52 E
Lainville, Fr.	179		49.04 N	1.49 E
Lainz, ngh., Aus.	182b		48.11 N	16.17 E
Lainzer Tiergarten, p.o.i., Aus.	182b		48.10 N	16.14 E
Laird Hill, Tx., U.S.	136	B13	32.21 N	94.54 W
Lairg, Scot., U.K.	10	C8	58.01 N	4.24 W
Lairiri, Pic, mtn., Vanuatu	101d	j16	15.27 S	166.48 E
Lais, Indon.	66	C12	0.47 N	120.26 E
Lais, Indon.	66	E3	3.31 S	102.02 E
Lais, Phil.	68	G5	6.19 N	125.38 E
Laisälven, stm., Swe.	14	F6	65.37 N	17.27 E
Laisamis, Kenya	86	D7	1.36 N	37.48 E
Laisvall, Swe.	14	F8	66.04 N	17.11 E
Laitila, Fin.	18	G8	60.52 N	21.42 E
Laiwu, China	58	C7	36.11 N	117.39 E
Laixi, China	58	C9	36.51 N	120.29 E
Laiyang, China	58	C9	36.58 N	120.42 E
Laizhou Bay see Laizhou Wan, b., China	58	C8	37.20 N	119.18 E
Laizhou Wan (Laichow Bay), b., China	58	C8	37.20 N	119.18 E
Laja, stm., Chile	172	H2	37.16 S	72.43 W
Laja, stm., Russia	18	C27	64.32 N	40.15 E
Laja, Laguna de la, l., Chile	172	H2	37.21 S	71.18 W
Laja, Salto del, wtfl., Chile	172	H2	37.23 S	71.25 W
La Jara, Co., U.S.	138	D3	37.17 N	105.57 W
La Jara, reg., Spain	28	E5	39.41 N	5.05 W
La Jara Canyon, val., N.M., U.S.	150	G9	36.45 N	107.22 W
La Jara Creek, stm., Co., U.S.	138	D2	37.22 N	105.45 W
La Jarita, Mex.	136	F4	28.03 N	103.20 W
Lajas, P.R.	158a	b1	18.04 N	67.03 W
Laje, Braz.	170	G6	13.09 S	39.25 W
Laje, Ilha da, i., Braz.	205a		22.57 S	43.09 W
Laje, Ponta da, c., Port.	184c		38.40 N	9.19 W
Laje, Ribeira de, stm., Port.	184c		38.41 N	9.19 W
Lajeado, Braz.	172	D11	29.24 S	51.57 W
Lajeado Velho, ngh., Braz.	205b		23.32 S	46.23 W
Lajedo, Braz.	170	E7	8.40 S	36.19 W
Lajes, Braz.	170	C7	5.41 S	36.14 W
Lajinha, Braz.	170	K5	20.09 S	41.37 W
Laji Shan, mts., China	52	D5	36.13 N	102.15 E
Lajkovo, Russia	183b		55.42 N	37.13 E
Lajord, Sk., Can.	142	D9	50.14 N	104.09 W
Lajosmizse, Hung.	36	B6	47.01 N	19.33 E
La Joya, Mex.	150	K3	32.09 N	113.56 W
Lajta (Leitha), stm., Eur.	24	I12	47.53 N	17.18 E
La Junta, Co., U.S.	138	D5	37.59 N	103.32 W
Lakaband, Pak.	70	C2	31.00 N	69.32 E
Lakar Kūh, mtn., Iran	72	C8	31.02 N	57.06 E
Lakatoro, Vanuatu	101d	k16	16.07 S	167.26 E
Lakaträsk, Swe.	14	F12	66.16 N	21.09 E
Lake, Ms., U.S.	134	E9	32.20 N	89.19 W
Lake Accotink Park, p.o.i., Va., U.S.	202c		38.48 N	77.14 W
Lake Alfred, Fl., U.S.	132	H4	28.05 N	81.44 W
Lake Andes, S.D., U.S.	140	D14	43.09 N	98.32 W
Lake Angelus, Mi., U.S.	199		42.42 N	83.19 W
Lake Arthur, La., U.S.	134	G6	30.04 N	92.40 W
Lake Arthur, N.M., U.S.	136	A3	32.59 N	104.21 W
Lakeba, i., Fiji	101e	q20	18.13 S	178.47 W
Lakeba Passage, strt., Fiji	101e	q20	18.00 S	178.46 W
Lake Barcroft, Va., U.S.	202c		38.51 N	77.09 W
Lake Benton, Mn., U.S.	128	G2	44.15 N	96.17 W
Lake Brownwood, Tx., U.S.	136	C8	31.48 N	99.01 W
Lake Butler, Fl., U.S.	132	G3	30.01 N	82.20 W
Lake Cargelligo, Austl.	98	I6	33.18 S	146.22 E
Lake Charles, La., U.S.	134	G5	30.13 N	93.13 W
Lake Chelan National Recreation Area, p.o.i., Wa., U.S.	146	B6	48.20 N	120.40 W
Lake City, Ar., U.S.	134	B8	35.49 N	90.26 W
Lake City, Co., U.S.	138	C1	38.01 N	107.19 W
Lake City, Fl., U.S.	132	F3	30.11 N	82.37 W
Lake City, Ia., U.S.	130	B3	42.15 N	94.43 W
Lake City, Mi., U.S.	126	D4	44.20 N	85.13 W
Lake City, Mn., U.S.	128	G6	44.27 N	92.16 W
Lake City, Pa., U.S.	124	B5	42.00 N	80.21 W
Lake City, S.C., U.S.	132	C6	33.52 N	79.45 W
Lake City, Tn., U.S.	124	H1	36.13 N	84.09 W
Lake Corpus Christi State Park, p.o.i., Tx., U.S.	136	F10	28.05 N	97.52 W
Lake Cowichan, B.C., Can.	144	H6	48.50 N	124.03 W
Lake Creek, stm., Tx., U.S.	136	D12	30.15 N	95.29 W
Lake Crystal, Mn., U.S.	128	G4	44.06 N	94.13 W
Lake Dallas, Tx., U.S.	136	A10	33.07 N	97.01 W
Lake Delton, Wi., U.S.	128	H9	43.35 N	89.47 W
Lake District National Park, p.o.i., Eng., U.K.	10	G9	54.27 N	3.02 W
Lake Elsinore, Ca., U.S.	148	J8	33.40 N	117.19 W
Lake Fairfax County Park, p.o.i., Va., U.S.	202c		38.58 N	77.19 W
Lakefield, On., Can.	126	D11	44.25 N	78.15 W
Lakefield, S. Afr.	191d		26.11 S	28.18 E
Lakefield, Mn., U.S.	128	H3	43.40 N	95.10 W
Lake Forest, Il., U.S.	130	B10	42.15 N	87.49 W
Lake Forest, N.J., U.S.	194		40.58 N	74.36 W
Lake Fork, stm., Ut., U.S.	150	C6	40.13 N	110.07 W
Lake Fork Reservoir, res., Tx., U.S.	136	B12	32.50 N	95.35 W
Lake Geneva, Wi., U.S.	130	B9	42.35 N	88.26 W
Lake George, N.Y., U.S.	126	E16	43.25 N	73.43 W
Lake Grace, Austl.	96	F3	33.05 S	118.28 E
Lake Grinnell, N.J., U.S.	194		41.06 N	74.38 W
Lake Grove, N.Y., U.S.	194		40.51 N	73.06 W
Lake Harbor, Fl., U.S.	132	J5	26.42 N	80.49 W
Lake Harbour see Kimmirut, Nu., Can.	110	C17	62.51 N	69.52 W
Lake Havasu City, Az., U.S.	150	I2	34.28 N	114.20 W
Lake Havasu State Park, p.o.i., Az., U.S.	150	I2	34.23 N	114.13 W
Lake Helen, Fl., U.S.	132	H4	28.59 N	81.14 W
Lakehurst, N.J., U.S.	124	D11	40.00 N	74.19 W
Lake Intervale, N.J., U.S.	194		40.53 N	74.25 W
Lake Isabella, Ca., U.S.	148	H7	35.38 N	118.27 W
Lake Jackson, Tx., U.S.	136	E12	29.02 N	95.26 W
Lake King, Austl.	96	F3	33.05 S	119.41 E
Lakeland, Fl., U.S.	132	H3	28.03 N	81.57 W
Lakeland, Ga., U.S.	132	E2	31.02 N	83.04 W
Lake Linden, Mi., U.S.	128	D10	47.11 N	88.24 W
Lake Lookover, N.J., U.S.	194		41.09 N	74.24 W
Lake Louise, Ab., Can.	144	E14	51.26 N	116.12 W
Lakemba, Austl.	192a		33.55 S	151.05 E
Lake Mead National Recreation Area, p.o.i., U.S.	150	G2	36.00 N	114.30 W
Lake Meredith National Recreation Area, p.o.i., Tx., U.S.	138	F7	35.40 N	101.40 W
Lake Mills, Ia., U.S.	128	H5	43.25 N	93.32 W
Lake Mills, Wi., U.S.	130	A9	43.04 N	88.54 W
Lake Minchumina, Ak., U.S.	109	D9	63.53 N	152.20 W
Lake Mohawk see Sparta, N.J., U.S.	124	C11	41.01 N	74.38 W
Lakemont, Pa., U.S.	124	D7	40.27 N	78.23 W
Lake Murray State Park, p.o.i., Ok., U.S.	138	H11	34.01 N	97.00 W
Lake Nash, Austl.	96	D7	20.58 S	137.55 E
Lake Norden, S.D., U.S.	140	C15	44.34 N	97.13 W
Lake Normandy Estates, Md., U.S.	202c		39.03 N	77.11 W
Lake Odessa, Mi., U.S.	130	B12	42.47 N	85.08 W
Lake of the Ozarks State Park, p.o.i., Mo., U.S.	130	F5	38.06 N	92.36 W
Lake Oswego, Or., U.S.	146	E4	45.25 N	122.42 W
Lake Ozark, Mo., U.S.	130	F5	38.13 N	92.37 W
Lake Park, Fl., U.S.	132	J5	26.47 N	80.03 W
Lake Park, Ia., U.S.	128	H3	43.27 N	95.19 W
Lake Park, Mn., U.S.	128	E2	46.52 N	96.04 W
Lake Placid, Fl., U.S.	132	I4	27.17 N	81.21 W
Lake Placid, N.Y., U.S.	126	D15	44.17 N	73.59 W
Lake Pleasant, N.Y., U.S.	126	E15	43.28 N	74.24 W
Lakeport, Ca., U.S.	148	D3	39.02 N	122.54 W
Lakeport, Mi., U.S.	126	E7	43.06 N	82.29 W
Lake Preston, S.D., U.S.	140	C15	44.21 N	97.22 W
Lake Providence, La., U.S.	134	E7	32.48 N	91.10 W
Lake Ridge, N.J., U.S.	194		40.24 N	74.15 W
Lake Ronkonkoma, N.Y., U.S.	194		40.50 N	73.07 W
Lakes Entrance, Austl.	98	K7	37.53 S	147.59 E
Lake Shawnee, N.J., U.S.	194		40.59 N	74.36 W
Lakeshore, Ms., U.S.	134	G9	30.14 N	89.26 W
Lakeside, S. Afr.	191d		26.06 S	28.09 E
Lakeside, Ca., U.S.	148	K9	32.51 N	116.55 W
Lakeside, Mt., U.S.	146	B12	48.00 N	114.13 W
Lakeside, Or., U.S.	146	G2	43.34 N	124.10 W
Lakeside, shp. cen., Mi., U.S.	199		42.37 N	83.00 W
Lake Stevens, Wa., U.S.	146	B4	48.00 N	122.03 W
Lake Stockholm, N.J., U.S.	194		41.04 N	74.31 W
Lake Success, N.Y., U.S.	194		40.46 N	73.43 W
Lake Swannanoa, N.J., U.S.	194		41.01 N	74.31 W
Lake Tahoe-Nevada State Park, p.o.i., Nv., U.S.	148	D6	39.13 N	119.55 W
Lake Telemark, N.J., U.S.	194		40.57 N	74.30 W
Lake Temescal Regional Park, p.o.i., Ca., U.S.	200		37.51 N	122.14 W
Laketown, Ut., U.S.	146	I15	41.50 N	111.20 W
Lake View, Ar., U.S.	134	C8	34.24 N	90.49 W
Lake View, Ia., U.S.	130	B2	42.18 N	95.03 W
Lakeview, Mi., U.S.	126	E4	43.26 N	85.16 W
Lakeview, Mi., U.S.	130	B12	42.17 N	85.12 W
Lakeview, Oh., U.S.	124	D2	40.28 N	83.55 W
Lakeview, Or., U.S.	148	A5	42.11 N	120.20 W
Lake View, S.C., U.S.	132	B6	34.20 N	79.10 W
Lakeview, Tx., U.S.	138	G8	34.40 N	100.42 W
Lakeview, ngh., Il., U.S.	196		41.57 N	87.39 W
Lakeview Mountain, mtn., B.C., Can.	144	G10	49.03 N	120.09 W
Lakeview Park, p.o.i., Pa., U.S.	203		40.12 N	75.32 W
Lake Village, Ar., U.S.	134	D7	33.19 N	91.17 W
Lakeville, Mn., U.S.	128	G5	44.39 N	93.15 W
Lake Wales, Fl., U.S.	132	I4	27.54 N	81.35 W
Lake Wilson, Mn., U.S.	128	G3	43.59 N	95.56 W
Lakewood, Co., U.S.	138	B3	39.43 N	105.07 W
Lakewood, N.J., U.S.	124	D11	40.06 N	74.13 W
Lakewood, Oh., U.S.	124	C4	41.29 N	81.48 W
Lakewood, Wa., U.S.	146	C4	47.10 N	122.31 W
Lakewood, Wi., U.S.	126	C1	45.17 N	88.30 W
Lakewood Center, shp. cen., Ca., U.S.	198		33.51 N	118.09 W
Lakewood Park, N.D., U.S.	142	F15	48.04 N	98.53 W
Lakewood Park, p.o.i., Oh., U.S.	197a		41.29 N	81.47 W
Lake Worth, Fl., U.S.	132	J5	26.36 N	80.03 W
Lakhdaria, Alg.	28	H14	36.34 N	3.35 E
Lākheri, India	70	F6	25.39 N	76.11 E
Lakhīmpur, India	70	D8	27.56 N	80.46 E
Lakhipur, India	70	F14	24.48 N	93.01 E
Lakhnādon, India	70	G7	22.35 N	79.37 E
Lakin, Ks., U.S.	138	D7	37.56 N	101.14 W
Lakinsk, Russia	40	C11	56.01 N	39.57 E
Lakonikós Kólpos (Laconia, Gulf of), b., Grc.	34	G5	36.40 N	22.38 E
Lakota, N.D., U.S.	142	F15	48.02 N	98.21 W
Laksefjorden, b., Nor.	14	B17	70.49 N	26.54 E
Lakselv, Nor.	14	B15	70.03 N	24.55 E
Lakshadweep, state, India	62	F3	10.00 N	73.00 E
Lakshadweep, is., India	62	F3	10.00 N	73.00 E
Lakshadweep Sea, s., Asia	62	G3	7.00 N	76.00 E
Lākshām, Bngl.	70	G13	23.14 N	91.08 E
Lakshmanpur, India	190b		22.38 N	88.16 E
Lakshmeshwar, India	69	D2	15.07 N	75.28 E
Lakshmi Narayan Temple, rel., India	190a		28.38 N	77.12 E
La Laja, Chile	172	H1	37.18 S	72.40 W
La Lajilla, Mex.	154	B9	26.47 N	99.37 W
Lāla Mūsa, Pak.	70	B4	32.41 N	73.57 E
Lâlapaşa, Tur.	34	B9	41.50 N	26.44 E
Lalara, Gabon	86	D2	0.20 N	11.25 E
L'Albufera, l., Spain	28	E10	39.20 N	0.22 W
Laleham, Austl.	98	D7	23.55 S	148.46 E
Laleham, Eng., U.K.	178		51.25 N	0.30 W
La Leona, Mex.	136	I6	25.52 N	101.05 W
La Leonesa, Arg.	172	C8	27.02 S	58.42 W
Lālganj, India	70	F10	25.51 N	85.10 E
Lalībela, Eth.	82	E7	12.00 N	39.02 E
La Libertad, Guat.	156	D2	16.47 N	90.07 W
La Ligua, Chile	172	F2	32.27 S	71.15 W
La Lima, Hond.	156	E3	15.25 N	87.55 W
Lalín, Spain	28	B2	42.40 N	8.06 W
Lalin, stm., China	54	B7	45.29 N	125.41 E
Lalindi, Indon.	66	I12	10.12 S	120.11 E
La Línea de la Concepción, Spain	28	H5	36.10 N	5.20 W
Lalitpur, India	70	F7	24.41 N	78.25 E
Lalitpur, Nepal	70	E10	27.40 N	85.19 E
La Llagosta, Spain	184d		41.31 N	2.12 E
Lalla Khedidja, Tamgout de, mtn., Alg.	28	H15	36.27 N	4.12 E
Lālmanir Hāt, Bngl.	70	F12	25.54 N	89.27 E
La Loche, Sk., Can.	110	D9	56.29 N	109.25 W
La Lora, plat., Spain	28	B7	42.45 N	4.00 W
Lalor Park, Austl.	192a		33.45 S	150.56 E
La Loupe, Fr.	20	F10	48.28 N	1.00 E
La Louvière, Bel.	20	D13	50.28 N	4.12 E
L'Alpe-d'Huez, Fr.	22	D12	45.06 N	6.04 E
Lālpur, India	70	G2	22.11 N	69.57 E
Lal'sk, Russia	12	F22	60.45 N	47.37 E
Lālsot, India	70	E6	26.34 N	76.20 E
La Luz, Mex.	136	I10	25.49 N	97.29 W
La Luz, Mex.	154	C10	24.12 N	97.52 W
La Luz, N.M., U.S.	136	A2	32.59 N	105.56 W
Lama, ozero, l., Russia	50	C7	69.31 N	90.26 E
La Macarena, Parque Nacional, p.o.i., Col.	168	F5	2.44 N	73.48 W
La Macarena, Serranía de, mts., Col.	168	F5	2.45 N	73.55 W
La Maddalena, Italy	32	C3	41.13 N	9.24 E
La Madrid, Arg.	172	C5	27.38 S	65.15 W
Lamadrid, Mex.	136	G6	27.05 N	101.50 W
Lamag, Malay.	66	A10	5.27 N	117.48 E
La Magdalena, Mex.	136	H1	26.52 N	106.19 W
La Magdalena, Río de, stm., Mex.	204a		19.21 N	99.11 W
La Majada, Ven.	204c		10.27 N	67.01 W
Lama-Kara, Togo	84	H5	9.32 N	1.12 E
La Malbaie, Qc., Can.	122	C6	47.39 N	70.09 W
La Malmaison, hist., Fr.	179		48.52 N	2.10 E
Lamaload Reservoir, res., Eng., U.K.	180		53.16 N	2.02 W
La Mancha, reg., Spain	28	E8	39.21 N	2.28 W
La Manche see English Channel, strt., Eur.	20	D7	50.13 N	2.20 W
Lamandau, stm., Indon.	66	E7	2.43 S	111.32 E
Lamap, Vanuatu	101d	k16	16.26 S	167.48 E
Lamar, Co., U.S.	138	C6	38.05 N	102.37 W
Lamar, Mo., U.S.	130	G3	37.29 N	94.16 W
Lamar, S.C., U.S.	132	B5	34.10 N	80.03 W
Lamar, stm., Wy., U.S.	146	F16	44.56 N	110.24 W
La Marañosa, Spain	184a		40.17 N	3.35 W
Lamarche, Fr.	20	F14	48.03 N	5.45 E
La Mariposa, Embalse, res., Ven.	204c		10.24 N	66.56 W
La Marmora, Punta, mtn., Italy	32	D3	39.59 N	9.20 E
La Maroma, Mex.	136	F7	28.34 N	100.45 W
Lamarque, Arg.	166	G3	39.23 S	65.41 W
La Marque, Tx., U.S.	136	E12	29.22 N	94.58 W
La Marsa, Tun.	32	H4	36.53 N	10.20 E
La Martre, Qc., Can.	122	A10	49.11 N	66.10 W
Lamas, Peru	164	E2	6.25 S	76.35 W
Lamastre, Fr.	22	E10	44.58 N	4.33 E
La Matanza see Matanza, state, Arg.	206		34.46 S	58.37 W
Lama Temple, rel., China	189a		39.56 N	116.25 E
Lamballe, Fr.	20	F6	48.28 N	2.31 W
Lambaréné, Gabon	86	E1	0.42 S	10.13 E
Lambari, stm., Braz.	170	J3	19.30 S	45.00 W
Lambayeque, Peru	164	E2	6.41 S	79.53 W
Lambay Island, i., Ire.	10	H7	53.29 N	6.01 W
Lambe, Nig.	191a		6.42 N	3.21 E
Lambert, Ms., U.S.	134	C8	34.12 N	90.17 W
Lambert, Mt., U.S.	142	G9	47.40 N	104.35 W
Lambert, Cape, c., Pap. N. Gui.	101a	a5	4.12 S	151.32 E
Lambert Glacier, ice, Ant.	103	C11	71.00 S	70.00 E
Lambert Land, reg., Grnld.	108	B21	79.15 N	20.30 W
Lamberton, Mn., U.S.	128	G3	44.13 N	95.16 W
Lambertsbaai see Lambert's Bay, S. Afr.	90	H4	32.05 S	18.18 E
Lambert's Bay, S. Afr.	90	H4	32.05 S	18.18 E
Lambeth, On., Can.	126	F8	42.54 N	81.18 W
Lambourne End, Eng., U.K.	178		51.38 N	0.08 E
Lambrate, ngh., Italy	184b		45.29 N	9.15 E
Lambro, Parco, p.o.i., Italy	184b		45.30 N	9.15 E
Lambs Terrace, N.J., U.S.	203		39.46 N	75.02 W
Lambton, S. Afr.	191d		26.15 S	28.10 E
Lambton, Cape, c., N.T., Can.	110	A6	71.05 N	123.10 W
Lame Deer, Mt., U.S.	140	B6	45.38 N	106.40 W
La Media Luna, Arrecifes de, rf., Hond.	156	E6	15.13 N	82.36 W
La Méditerranée see Mediterranean Sea, s.	80	C7	35.00 N	20.00 E
Lamego, Port.	28	C3	41.05 N	7.49 W
Lameirão, Morro do, hill, Braz.	205a		22.54 S	43.31 W
La Mendieta, Arg.	172	B5	24.19 S	64.58 W
Lamentin, Guad.	159c	h5	16.16 N	61.38 W
Lamèque, N.B., Can.	122	C12	47.48 N	64.39 W
Lamèque, Île, i., N.B., Can.	122	C12	47.49 N	64.35 W
La Merced, Arg.	172	B5	24.58 S	65.29 W
La Merced, Arg.	172	D5	28.09 S	65.38 W
Lameroo, Austl.	98	J3	35.19 S	140.30 E
La Mesa, Ca., U.S.	148	K8	32.46 N	117.02 W
La Mesa, N.M., U.S.	150	K10	32.07 N	106.42 W
Lamesa, Tx., U.S.	136	B6	32.44 N	101.57 W
La Mesa Dam, dam., Phil.	187f		14.43 N	121.04 E
Lamía, Grc.	34	E5	38.53 N	22.26 E
Lamine, stm., Mo., U.S.	130	F4	38.58 N	92.50 W
Lamington National Park, p.o.i., Austl.	98	G9	28.14 S	153.10 E
La Mirada Creek, stm., Ca., U.S.	198		33.53 N	118.01 W
La Misión, Mex.	148	K9	32.05 N	116.51 W
Lamitan, Phil.	68	G4	6.40 N	122.07 E
Lamlam, Mount, hill, Guam	100c	j9	13.20 N	144.40 E
Lamma Island, i., China	189d		22.12 N	114.07 E
Lammeulo, Indon.	64	J2	5.14 N	95.55 E
Lammhult, Swe.	16	J12	57.09 N	14.35 E
Lammi, Fin.	18	F12	61.05 N	25.01 E
Lamming Mills, B.C., Can.	144	C10	53.21 N	120.19 W
La Moille, Il., U.S.	130	C8	41.31 N	89.16 W
Lamoille, Nv., U.S.	148	C10	40.43 N	115.28 W
Lamoille, stm., Vt., U.S.	122	F3	44.36 N	73.13 W
La Moine, stm., Il., U.S.	130	D7	39.58 N	90.30 W
La Moine, East Fork, stm., Il., U.S.	128	K8	40.23 N	90.56 W
La Molina, Peru	204d		12.05 S	76.57 W
Lamon Bay, b., Phil.	68	C4	14.28 N	122.01 E
Lamone, stm., Italy	30	F9	44.31 N	12.15 E
Lamongan, Indon.	66	G8	7.07 S	112.25 E
Lamoni, Ia., U.S.	130	D3	40.37 N	93.56 W
Lamont, Ab., Can.	144	C18	53.45 N	112.46 W
Lamont, Ca., U.S.	148	H6	35.15 N	118.55 W
Lamont, Ia., U.S.	128	I7	42.35 N	91.38 W
Lamont, Ok., U.S.	138	E11	36.41 N	97.33 W
La Monte, Mo., U.S.	130	F4	38.46 N	93.25 W
La Mosquitia, hist. reg., Hond.	152	D8	15.00 N	83.45 W
La Mothe, Lac, l., Qc., Can.	122	B5	48.46 N	71.10 W
La Mothe-Achard, Fr.	20	H7	46.37 N	1.40 W
Lamotrek, at., Micron.	94	C5	7.20 N	146.20 E
La Mott, Pa., U.S.	203		40.04 N	75.08 W
Lamotte-Beuvron, Fr.	20	G10	47.36 N	2.02 E
La Moure, N.D., U.S.	140	A14	46.20 N	98.16 W
La Moustique, stm., Guad.	159c	h5	16.10 N	61.34 W
Lampang, Thai.	64	C4	18.16 N	99.28 E
Lampasas, Tx., U.S.	136	C9	31.03 N	98.10 W
Lampasas, stm., Tx., U.S.	136	C9	30.58 N	97.24 W
Lampazos de Naranjo, Mex.	154	B8	27.01 N	100.31 W
Lampedusa, Isola di, i., Italy	32	I6	35.31 N	12.35 E
Lampertheim, Ger.	24	G4	49.36 N	8.28 E
Lampeter, Wales, U.K.	10	I8	52.07 N	4.05 W
Lamphun, Thai.	64	C4	18.35 N	99.01 E
Lampinsaari, Fin.	18	C11	64.24 N	25.09 E
Lampione, Isola di, i., Italy	32	I6	35.34 N	12.19 E
Lampman, Sk., Can.	142	E11	49.22 N	102.44 W
Lampung, state, Indon.	66	F4	5.00 S	105.00 E
Lamskoe, Russia	26	H21	52.57 N	38.03 E
Lamu, Kenya	86	E8	2.16 S	40.53 E
Lāmu, Mya.	64	C2	19.14 N	94.10 E
La Muerte, Cerro, mtn., C.R.	156	H6	9.33 N	83.45 W
Lam Uk Wei, China	189d		22.26 N	114.22 E
La Mure, Fr.	22	E11	44.54 N	5.46 E
Lan', stm., Bela.	26	H10	52.08 N	27.17 E
Lan, Loi, mtn., Mya.	64	C3	19.40 N	97.55 E
Lana, Italy	30	D8	46.36 N	11.09 E
Lanai, i., Hi., U.S.	100a	c4	20.50 N	156.55 W
Lanai City, Hi., U.S.	100a	c5	20.49 N	156.55 W
Lanaihale, mtn., Hi., U.S.	100a	c5	20.49 N	156.52 W
Lanalhue, Lago, l., Chile	172	H1	37.55 S	73.17 W
Lanao, Lake see Sultan Alonto, Lake, l., Phil.	68	G5	7.53 N	124.15 E
Lanark, On., Can.	126	C13	45.01 N	76.21 W
Lanark, Scot., U.K.	10	F9	55.40 N	3.47 W
Lanark, Il., U.S.	130	B8	42.06 N	89.50 W
La Nava de Ricomalillo, Spain	28	E5	39.39 N	4.59 W
Lanbi Kyun, i., Mya.	64	G4	10.50 N	98.15 E
Lancang, China	64	A4	23.00 N	100.02 E
Lancang see Mekong, stm., Asia	64	G7	10.33 N	105.26 E
Lancashire, De., U.S.	203		39.49 N	75.29 W
Lancaster, On., Can.	126	C15	45.08 N	74.29 W
Lancaster, Eng., U.K.	10	G10	54.02 N	2.50 W
Lancaster, Ca., U.S.	148	I7	34.41 N	118.08 W
Lancaster, Ky., U.S.	130	G13	37.37 N	84.35 W
Lancaster, Mn., U.S.	128	C2	48.49 N	96.49 W
Lancaster, Mo., U.S.	130	D5	40.31 N	92.31 W
Lancaster, N.H., U.S.	122	F5	44.29 N	71.34 W
Lancaster, Oh., U.S.	124	E3	39.42 N	82.36 W
Lancaster, Pa., U.S.	124	D9	40.02 N	76.18 W
Lancaster, S.C., U.S.	132	B5	34.43 N	80.46 W
Lancaster, Tx., U.S.	136	B11	32.36 N	96.45 W
Lancaster, Va., U.S.	124	G9	37.45 N	76.28 W
Lancaster, Wi., U.S.	130	B7	42.50 N	90.42 W
Lancaster Canal, can., Eng., U.K.	180		53.46 N	2.43 W
Lancaster Sound, strt., Nu., Can.	108	C8	74.13 N	84.00 W
Lancaster Village, De., U.S.	203		39.45 N	75.35 W
Lance Creek, Wy., U.S.	140	D8	43.01 N	104.39 W
Lance Creek, stm., Wy., U.S.	140	D8	43.13 N	104.37 W
Lancelin, Austl.	96	F2	31.01 S	115.19 E
Lanchow see Lanzhou, China	52	D5	36.04 N	103.42 E
Lanchyn, Ukr.	38	E3	48.34 N	24.46 E
Lanciano, Italy	30	H11	42.14 N	14.23 E
Lanco, Chile	166	G2	39.26 S	72.46 W
Lancun, China	58	C9	36.24 N	120.11 E
Łańcut, Pol.	24	F18	50.04 N	22.14 E
Land, reg., Nor.	16	G7	60.48 N	9.52 E
Lândana, Ang.	88	B1	5.12 S	12.08 E
Landau an der Isar, Ger.	24	H8	48.39 N	12.41 E
Landau in der Pfalz, Ger.	24	G4	49.11 N	8.07 E
Landeck, Aus.	30	C7	47.08 N	10.34 E
Landegode, i., Nor.	14	E5	67.24 N	14.19 E
Landegodefjorden, strt., Nor.	14	E4	67.23 N	14.28 E
Lander, Wy., U.S.	140	E4	42.50 N	108.44 W
Landerneau, Fr.	20	F4	48.27 N	4.15 W
Landes, state, Fr.	22	F5	44.20 N	1.00 W
Landes, reg., Fr.	22	E5	44.10 N	0.51 W
Landeshut see Kamienna Góra, Pol.	24	F12	50.46 N	16.02 E
Landete, Spain	28	E9	39.54 N	1.21 W
Landham Brook, stm., Ma., U.S.	201		42.22 N	71.25 W
Landhausen, Ger.	181		51.24 N	7.45 E
Landis, Sk., Can.	142	B5	52.12 N	108.28 W
Landis, N.C., U.S.	132	A5	35.32 N	80.37 W
Lando, S.C., U.S.	132	B4	34.46 N	81.01 W
Land O'Lakes, Wi., U.S.	128	E9	46.09 N	89.13 W
Landösjön, l., Swe.	16	D11	63.35 N	14.03 E
Landover Estates, Md., U.S.	202c		38.56 N	76.54 W
Landover Hills, Md., U.S.	202c		38.57 N	76.53 W
Landover Mall, shp. cen., Md., U.S.	202c		38.55 N	76.51 W

Name	Page	Map Ref.	Latitude	Longitude
Landreth Draw, stm., Tx., U.S.	136	C5	31.15 N	102.28 W
Landri Sales, Braz.	170	D3	7.16 S	43.55 W
Landrum, S.C., U.S.	132	A3	35.10 N	82.11 W
Landsberg see Gorzów Wielkopolski, Pol.	24	D11	52.44 N	15.14 E
Landsberg am Lech, Ger.	30	B7	48.03 N	10.53 E
Landsberg an der Warthe see Gorzów Wielkopolski, Pol.	24	D11	52.44 N	15.14 E
Landsborough, Austl.	98	F9	26.49 S	152.58 E
Landsborough Creek, stm., Austl.	98	D5	22.28 S	144.34 E
Landsbro, Swe.	16	J12	57.23 N	14.55 E
Land's End, c., Eng., U.K.	10	K7	50.03 N	5.44 W
Landshut, Ger.	24	H8	48.32 N	12.08 E
Landskrona, Swe.	16	L10	55.52 N	12.50 E
Landsman Creek, stm., Co., U.S.	138	B6	39.36 N	102.12 W
Landweg, Ger.	181		51.29 N	7.37 E
Landwehrbach, stm., Ger.	181		51.26 N	6.26 E
Lane, mth., Fr.	20	G9	47.16 N	0.19 E
Lane Cove, Austl.	192a		33.49 S	151.10 E
Lane Cove, stm., Austl.	192a		33.48 S	151.09 E
Lane Cove River Park, p.o.i., Austl.	192a		33.47 S	151.09 E
La Negra, Chile	172	A2	23.46 S	70.19 W
Lanesboro, Mn., U.S.	128	H6	43.43 N	91.59 W
Lanett, Al., U.S.	134	E13	32.52 N	85.11 W
Lanezi Lake, l., B.C., Can.	144	C10	53.03 N	120.56 W
Lang, Sk., Can.	142	E9	49.55 N	104.23 W
La'nga Co, l., China	70	C8	30.42 N	81.13 E
Langa-Langa, D.R.C.	86	E3	3.54 S	15.56 E
Långan, stm., Swe.	16	D12	63.18 N	14.44 E
Langao, China	58	E3	32.11 N	109.00 E
Langarūd, Iran	74	B12	37.11 N	50.08 E
Långban, Swe.	16	H12	59.51 N	14.16 E
Langbank, Sk., Can.	142	D11	50.03 N	102.18 W
Lang Bay, B.C., Can.	144	G6	49.47 N	124.21 W
Langdale, Al., U.S.	134	E13	32.49 N	85.10 W
Langdon, N.D., U.S.	142	F15	48.45 N	98.22 W
Langdon Hills, Eng., U.K.	178		51.34 N	0.25 E
Langeac, Fr.	22	D9	45.06 N	3.30 E
Langeais, Fr.	20	G9	47.19 N	0.24 E
Langeberg, mts., S. Afr.	90	H5	33.58 S	20.26 E
Langeland, i., Den.	16	M8	55.00 N	10.50 E
Langelandsbælt, strt., Den.	16	L9	54.52 N	10.52 E
Langelmävesi, l., Fin.	18	F11	61.32 N	24.22 E
Langenbielau see Bielawa, Pol.	24	F12	50.40 N	16.37 E
Langenbochum, Ger.	181		51.37 N	7.07 E
Langenburg, Sk., Can.	142	D12	50.51 N	101.41 W
Langendreer, ngh., Ger.	181		51.28 N	7.19 E
Langenhagen, Ger.	24	D5	52.26 N	9.44 E
Langenhorst, Ger.	181		51.22 N	7.02 E
Langensalza see Bad Langensalza, Ger.	24	E6	51.06 N	10.39 E
Langenthal, Switz.	30	C4	47.13 N	7.47 E
Langeoog, i., Ger.	24	C3	53.44 N	7.32 E
Langerfeld, ngh., Ger.	181		51.16 N	7.15 E
Langer See, l., Ger.	182a		52.25 N	13.38 E
Langesund, Nor.	16	I7	59.00 N	9.45 E
Langesundsfjorden, b., Nor.	16	I7	59.00 N	9.47 E
Langfang, China	58	B7	39.30 N	116.41 E
Långfjället, mts., Swe.	16	E10	62.05 N	12.28 E
Langfjorden, b., Nor.	16	E5	62.45 N	7.55 E
Langford, Eng., U.K.	178		51.45 N	0.40 E
Langford, S.D., U.S.	140	B15	45.35 N	97.49 W
Langgam, Indon.	66	C2	0.14 N	101.43 E
Langgapayung, Indon.	66	C1	1.43 N	99.56 E
Langham, Sk., Can.	142	B6	52.22 N	106.57 W
Langhe, hist. reg., Italy	30	F4	44.30 N	8.00 E
Langho, Eng., U.K.	180		53.48 N	2.27 W
Langholm, Scot., U.K.	10	F10	55.09 N	3.00 W
Langhorne Acres, Va., U.S.	202c		38.51 N	77.16 W
Langhorne Gardens, Pa., U.S.	203		40.11 N	74.53 W
Langhorne Manor, Pa., U.S.	203		40.10 N	74.55 W
Langhorne Terrace, Pa., U.S.	203		40.10 N	74.57 W
Langjökull, ice, Ice.	12a	k29	64.42 N	20.12 W
Lang Ka, Doi, mtn., Thai.	64	C4	19.00 N	99.24 E
Langkawi, Pulau, i., Malay.	64	I4	6.23 N	99.50 E
Langley, B.C., Can.	144	G8	49.06 N	122.39 W
Langley, Eng., U.K.	178		51.14 N	0.35 E
Langley, Eng., U.K.	178		51.30 N	0.33 W
Langley, Eng., U.K.	180		53.15 N	2.05 W
Langley, Ok., U.S.	134	A3	36.27 N	95.03 W
Langley Air Force Base, mil., Va., U.S.	124	G9	37.05 N	76.22 W
Langley Forest, Va., U.S.	202c		38.57 N	77.10 W
Langley Hill, hill, Ca., U.S.	200		37.20 N	122.14 W
Langley Park, Md., U.S.	202c		38.59 N	76.58 W
Langlo, stm., Austl.	98	E5	26.26 S	146.05 E
Langlois, Or., U.S.	146	H2	42.54 N	124.26 W
Langmazong, China	70	C12	30.52 N	89.58 E
Lang Mo, Viet.	64	D8	17.15 N	106.27 E
Långnäs, Fin.	18	G7	60.06 N	20.15 E
Langnau im Emmental, Switz.	30	D4	46.56 N	7.47 E
Langogne, Fr.	22	E9	44.43 N	3.50 E
Langon, Fr.	22	E5	44.33 N	0.14 W
Langøya, i., Nor.	14	D5	68.44 N	14.50 E
Langping, China	58	F4	30.36 N	110.19 E
Langqên see Sutlej, stm., Asia	70	C8	29.20 N	71.02 E
Langreo, Spain	28	A5	43.18 N	5.41 W
Langres, Fr.	20	G14	47.51 N	5.19 E
Langres, Plateau de, plat., Fr.	20	G14	47.41 N	5.03 E
Langruth, Mb., Can.	142	D15	50.22 N	98.40 W
Langruzong, China	70	C13	31.50 N	91.26 E
Langsa, Indon.	64	J3	4.28 N	97.58 E
Langsa, Teluk, b., Indon.	64	J4	4.33 N	98.01 E
Langschede, Ger.	181		51.29 N	7.43 E
Långsele, Swe.	16	D14	63.11 N	17.04 E
Langshan, China	58	A2	41.03 N	107.27 E
Långshyttan, Swe.	16	G14	60.27 N	16.02 E
Lang Son, Viet.	64	B8	21.51 N	106.44 E
Langstaff, On., Can.	193b		43.50 N	79.25 W
Langst-Kierst, Ger.	181		51.18 N	6.43 E
Langstrand, Nor.	14	B13	70.41 N	23.11 E
Lang Suan, Thai.	64	H4	9.56 N	99.04 E
Langting, India	70	F14	25.30 N	93.05 E
Languedoc, hist. reg., Fr.	22	F8	44.00 N	4.00 E
L'Anguille, stm., Ar., U.S.	134	B8	34.43 N	90.40 W
Langundu, Tanjung, c., Indon.	66	H11	8.49 S	118.55 E
Langxi, China	58	F8	31.07 N	119.10 E
Langzhong, China	58	F1	31.34 N	105.58 E
Lanham, Md., U.S.	202c		38.58 N	76.51 W
Lanigan, Sk., Can.	142	C8	51.52 N	105.02 W
Lanigan Creek, stm., Sk., Can.	142	C9	51.50 N	105.15 W
Lanín, Volcán, vol., S.A.	166	G2	39.38 S	71.30 W
Lanivtsi, Ukr.	38	D5	49.51 N	26.04 E
Länkäran, Azer.	42	F13	38.45 N	48.51 E
Länkipohja, Fin.	18	F11	61.44 N	24.48 E
Lank-Latum, Ger.	181		51.18 N	6.41 E
Lankwitz, ngh., Ger.	182a		52.26 N	13.21 E
Lanling, China	54	B7	45.15 N	126.12 E
Lanna, Ukr.	38	D14	49.21 N	35.16 E
Lannemezan, Fr.	22	F6	43.07 N	0.23 E
Lannilis, Fr.	20	F4	48.34 N	4.31 W
Lannion, Fr.	20	F5	48.44 N	3.27 W
Lannion, Baie de, b., Fr.	20	F5	48.44 N	3.42 W
L'Annonciation, Qc., Can.	126	B15	46.24 N	74.51 W
Lanping, China	52	F4	26.29 N	99.23 E
Lansdowne, Austl.	192a		33.54 S	150.59 E
Lansdowne, India	70	D7	29.49 N	78.41 E
Lansdowne, Md., U.S.	202b		39.14 N	76.39 W
Lansdowne, Pa., U.S.	203		39.56 N	75.16 W
Lansdowne House, On., Can.	110	E13	52.14 N	87.53 W
L'Anse, Mi., U.S.	126	B1	46.44 N	88.26 W
L' Anse Indian Reservation, ind. res., Mi., U.S.	126	B1	46.48 N	88.22 W
Lansford, N.D., U.S.	142	F12	48.37 N	101.22 W
Lanshan, China	58	I4	25.18 N	111.52 E
Lansing, Ia., U.S.	128	H7	43.21 N	91.13 W
Lansing, Mi., U.S.	126	F5	42.44 N	84.33 W
Lansing, ngh., On., Can.	193b		43.45 N	79.25 W
Lansing Municipal Airport, arpt., Il., U.S.	196		41.32 N	87.32 W
Lansjärv, Swe.	14	F13	66.38 N	22.13 E
Lanstrop, ngh., Ger.	181		51.34 N	7.34 E
Lantana, Fl., U.S.	132	J5	26.35 N	80.04 W
Lantau Island, i., China	58	J5	22.17 N	113.59 E
Lanta Yai, Ko, i., Thai.	64	I4	7.34 N	99.03 E
Lantian, China	58	D3	34.02 N	109.11 E
Lantianchang, China	189a		39.58 N	116.17 E
La Nurra, reg., Italy	32	D2	40.43 N	8.17 E
Lanús, state, Arg.	206		34.42 S	58.28 W
Lanusei, Italy	32	E3	39.53 N	9.32 E
Lanxi, China	58	G8	29.12 N	119.28 E
Lan Yü, i., Tai.	58	J9	22.03 N	121.32 E
Lanzarote, i., Spain	84	D2	29.00 N	13.40 W
Lanzendorf, Aus.	182b		48.06 N	16.26 E
Lanzhou, China	52	D5	36.04 N	103.42 E
Lanzo Torinese, Italy	30	E4	45.16 N	7.28 E
Lao see Laos, ctry., Asia	64	C6	18.00 N	105.00 E
Lao, stm., Italy	32	E9	39.46 N	15.47 E
Lao, stm., Thai.	64	C4	19.55 N	99.54 E
Laoag, Phil.	68	A3	18.11 N	120.35 E
Laoang, Phil.	68	D5	12.35 N	125.01 E
Lao Bao, Viet.	64	D8	16.36 N	106.37 E
Lao Cai, Viet.	64	A6	22.30 N	103.58 E
Laodao, stm., China	58	G5	28.15 N	112.59 E
Laofu, China	54	C3	42.13 N	118.17 E
Laoha, stm., China	54	C9	43.25 N	120.45 E
Laoheishan, China	54	C9	43.44 N	130.52 E
Laohekou, China	58	E4	32.25 N	111.36 E
Laohokow see Laohekou, China	58	E4	32.25 N	111.36 E
Laohumiao, China	189a		39.58 N	116.20 E
Laois, state, Ire.	10	I5	53.00 N	7.24 W
Lao Ling, mtn., China	54	C9	43.27 N	130.11 E
Laon, Fr.	20	E12	49.34 N	3.38 E
Laona, Wi., U.S.	128	F10	45.33 N	88.40 W
La Orchila, Isla, i., Ven.	168	B8	11.48 N	66.09 W
La Oroya, Peru	164	F2	11.30 S	75.55 W
Laos, ctry., Asia	64	C6	18.00 N	105.00 E
Laoshan Wan, b., China	58	C9	36.24 N	120.45 E
Lapa, Braz.	172	B13	25.45 S	49.43 W
Lapa, ngh., Braz.	205a		22.55 S	43.11 W
Lapa, ngh., Braz.	205b		23.32 S	46.42 W
Lapacičy, Bela.	26	G13	53.34 N	30.53 E
Lapai, Nig.	84	H6	9.06 N	6.45 E
Lapalisse, Fr.	22	C9	46.15 N	3.38 E
La Palma, Col.	168	E4	5.22 N	74.25 W
La Palma, Pan.	156	H8	8.24 N	78.09 W
La Palma, Pan.	156	I7	7.41 N	80.10 W
La Palma, Ca., U.S.	198		33.50 N	118.02 W
La Palma, i., Spain	84	D1	28.40 N	17.52 W
La Palma de Cervelló, Spain	184d		41.25 N	1.58 E
La Palma del Condado, Spain	28	G4	37.23 N	6.33 W
La Paloma, Ur.	172	G10	34.40 S	54.10 W
La Pampa, state, Arg.	166	G3	37.00 S	66.00 W
Lapão, Braz.	170	F5	11.23 S	41.49 W
La Paragua, Ven.	168	D10	6.50 N	63.18 W
La Pasión, stm., Guat.	156	D2	16.29 N	90.31 W
La Paya, Parque Nacional, p.o.i., Col.	168	G4	0.09 N	74.55 W
La Paz, Arg.	172	E8	30.43 S	59.37 W
La Paz, Arg.	172	F4	33.27 S	67.33 W
La Paz, Bol.	166	C3	16.30 S	68.09 W
La Paz, Col.	168	B5	10.24 N	73.09 W
La Paz, Hond.	156	E4	14.18 N	87.41 W
La Paz, Mex.	154	D8	23.41 N	100.43 W
La Paz, Mex.	154	C3	24.10 N	110.18 W
La Paz, Ur.	172	G9	34.46 S	56.13 W
La Paz, Bahía de, b., Mex.	154	C3	24.16 N	110.28 W
La Paz Centro, Nic.	156	F4	12.20 N	86.40 W
La Pedrera, Col.	168	H7	1.18 S	69.43 W
Lapeer, Mi., U.S.	130	A14	43.02 N	83.18 W
La Perla, Mex.	154	A6	28.18 N	104.33 W
La Perla, Peru	204d		12.05 S	77.08 W
La Perouse, Bahía, b., Chile	100l	e30	27.05 S	109.17 W
La Perouse Strait, strt., Asia	52	B13	45.45 N	142.00 E
Laperuza, proliv see La Perouse Strait, strt., Asia	52	B13	45.45 N	142.00 E
La Pesca, Mex.	154	D10	23.47 N	97.46 W
La Piedad de Cabadas, Mex.	154	E7	20.20 N	102.01 W
La Pine, Or., U.S.	146	G5	43.39 N	121.30 W
Lapinjärvi, Fin.	18	G13	60.38 N	26.13 E
Lapinlahti, Fin.	18	D14	63.21 N	27.25 E
La Pintana, Chile	204e		33.37 S	70.38 W
La Place, La., U.S.	134	G8	30.03 N	90.28 W
Lap Lae, Thai.	64	D4	17.36 N	100.00 E
La Plaine, Dom.	159c	j6	15.19 N	61.15 W
Lapland, hist. reg., Eur.	14	E15	67.50 N	26.36 E
La Plata, Arg.	172	G8	34.55 S	57.57 W
La Plata, Col.	168	F4	2.23 N	75.53 W
La Plata, Md., U.S.	124	F9	38.31 N	76.58 W
La Plata, Mo., U.S.	130	D5	40.01 N	92.28 W
La Plata, state, Arg.	206		34.55 S	58.04 W
La Plata, stm., U.S.	150	G8	36.44 N	108.15 W
La Plata, Universidad Nacional de, educ., Arg.	206		35.55 S	57.57 W
La Plata Peak, mtn., Co., U.S.	138	B2	39.02 N	106.28 W
La Playa, ngh., Cuba	204b		23.06 N	82.27 W
La Pobla de Segur, Spain	28	B12	42.14 N	0.58 E
La Pocatière, Qc., Can.	122	C6	47.21 N	70.01 W
Lapominka, Russia	18	C27	64.47 N	40.27 E
Laporte, Co., U.S.	140	G7	40.37 N	105.08 W
La Porte, In., U.S.	130	C11	41.36 N	86.42 W
La Porte, Oh., U.S.	197a		41.19 N	82.05 W
Laporte, Pa., U.S.	124	C9	41.25 N	76.29 W
La Porte City, Ia., U.S.	130	B5	42.18 N	92.10 W
Laposo, Bulu, mtn., Indon.	66	F11	4.29 S	119.47 E
La Potherie, Lac, l., Qc., Can.	110	D16	58.50 N	72.24 W
La Poveda, Spain	184a		40.19 N	3.29 W
La Poza Grande, Mex.	154	C2	25.47 N	112.05 W
Lappajärvi, Fin.	18	D10	63.13 N	23.37 E
Lappajärvi, l., Fin.	18	D10	63.08 N	23.40 E
Lappeenranta (Villmanstrand), Fin.	18	F15	61.03 N	28.12 E
Lappfjärd see Lapväärtti, Fin.	18	E8	62.15 N	21.30 E
Lappi, Fin.	18	F8	61.05 N	21.50 E
Lappi, state, Fin.	14	E17	66.00 N	27.00 E
Lappträsk see Lapinjärvi, Fin.	18	G13	60.38 N	26.13 E
La Prele Creek, stm., Wy., U.S.	140	E7	42.51 N	105.29 W
Laprida, Arg.	172	D5	28.22 S	64.31 W
Laprida, Arg.	172	H7	37.32 S	60.49 W
La Providencia, Mex.	136	H2	26.41 N	105.55 W
La Pryor, Tx., U.S.	136	F8	28.56 N	99.50 W
Lâpseki, Tur.	34	C9	40.21 N	26.41 E
Lapta, N. Cyp.	76	C4	35.20 N	33.11 E
Laptev Sea see Laptevyh, more, s., Russia	48	B4	76.00 N	126.00 E
Laptevyh, more, s., Russia	48	B4	76.00 N	126.00 E
Lapua, Fin.	18	E10	62.58 N	23.06 E
Lapuanjoki, stm., Fin.	18	E10	63.33 N	22.29 E
La Puebla de Montalbán, Spain	28	E6	39.52 N	4.21 W
Lapuente, Ur.	172	E10	31.37 S	54.53 W
La Puerta, Arg.	172	D5	28.10 S	65.48 W
La Puerta de Cabrera, Mex.	136	H2	26.03 N	105.14 W
Lapu-Lapu, Phil.	68	E4	10.18 N	123.57 E
La Punta, Peru	204d		12.05 S	77.11 W
La Purísima, Chile	204e		33.34 S	70.39 W
La Purísima, Mex.	154	B2	26.09 N	112.03 W
Lăpuş, Rom.	36	B11	47.30 N	24.01 E
La Push, Wa., U.S.	146	C2	47.54 N	124.38 W
Lapväärtti, Fin.	18	E8	62.15 N	21.30 E
Lapwai, Id., U.S.	146	D10	46.27 N	116.47 W
Łapy, Pol.	24	C18	52.59 N	22.53 E
La Queue-en-Brie, Fr.	179		48.47 N	2.35 E
La Queue-lès-Yvelines, Fr.	179		48.48 N	1.46 E
La Quiaca, Arg.	166	D3	22.06 S	65.35 W
L'Àquila, Italy	30	H10	42.21 N	13.23 E
Lār, Iran	74	G14	27.40 N	54.19 E
Lara, state, Ven.	168	B7	10.10 N	69.50 W
Laracha, Spain	28	A2	43.14 N	8.36 W
Larache, Mor.	84	B3	35.11 N	6.09 W
Laragne-Montéglin, Fr.	22	E11	44.18 N	5.48 E
Lārak, Jazīreh-ye, i., Iran	74	G15	26.52 N	56.22 E
Laramie, Wy., U.S.	140	F7	41.19 N	105.35 W
Laramie, stm., U.S.	140	E8	42.14 N	104.37 W
Laramie Mountains, mts., Wy., U.S.	140	F7	41.54 N	105.30 W
Laramie Peak, mtn., Wy., U.S.	140	E7	42.17 N	105.27 W
Laranjal, Braz.	170	K4	21.21 S	42.28 W
Laranjeiras, Braz.	170	F7	10.48 S	37.10 W
Laranjeiras, ngh., Braz.	205a		22.56 S	43.11 W
Laranjeiras do Sul, Braz.	172	B11	25.24 S	52.24 W
Larantuka, Indon.	60	G7	8.19 S	122.58 E
Larap, Phil.	68	C4	14.16 N	122.37 E
Larat, Indon.	60	G9	7.08 S	131.43 E
Larat, Pulau, i., Indon.	60	G9	7.07 S	131.49 E
Larb Creek, stm., Mt., U.S.	142	F6	48.25 N	107.16 W
Lärbro, Swe.	16	J16	57.47 N	18.48 E
Larche, Col de see Larche Pass, p., Eur.	30	F3	44.25 N	6.52 E
Larche Pass, p., Eur.	30	F3	44.25 N	6.52 E
Larchmont Harbor, b., N.Y., U.S.	194		40.55 N	73.45 W
Larchwood, Ia., U.S.	128	H2	43.27 N	96.26 W
Larde, Moz.	88	D6	16.28 S	39.43 E
Lardeau, B.C., Can.	144	F13	50.08 N	116.58 W
L'Ardoise, N.S., Can.	122	E16	45.37 N	60.45 W
Lardy, Fr.	179		48.31 N	2.16 E
Laredo, Spain	28	A7	43.24 N	3.25 W
Laredo, Tx., U.S.	136	G8	27.30 N	99.30 W
Laredo Sound, strt., B.C., Can.	144	D2	52.32 N	128.53 W
La Reforma, Mex.	154	C4	25.06 N	108.05 W
La Reina, Chile	204e		33.27 S	70.33 W
La Réole, Fr.	22	E5	44.35 N	0.02 W
Lares, P.R.	158a	b2	18.17 N	66.52 W
Larga, Mol.	38	E5	48.22 N	26.50 E
Larga, Laguna, l., Tx., U.S.	136	G10	27.30 N	97.25 W
Largo, Fl., U.S.	132	I3	27.55 N	82.47 W
Largo, Cañon, val., N.M., U.S.	150	G9	36.23 N	107.28 W
Largo, Cayo, i., Cuba	156	B7	21.38 N	81.28 W
Largo Creek, stm., N.M., U.S.	150	I8	34.29 N	108.57 W
Largs, Scot., U.K.	10	F8	55.47 N	4.52 W
Lariang, Indon.	66	D11	1.27 S	119.17 E
Lariang, stm., Indon.	66	D11	1.25 S	119.17 E
Larimore, N.D., U.S.	142	G16	47.54 N	97.37 W
Larino, Italy	30	I11	41.48 N	14.53 E
Lario see Como, Lago di, l., Italy	30	D6	46.01 N	9.15 E
La Rioja, Arg.	172	D4	29.24 S	66.50 W
La Rioja, state, Arg.	172	D4	30.00 S	67.30 W
La Rioja, state, Spain	28	B8	42.15 N	2.30 W
Lárisa, Grc.	34	D5	39.38 N	22.25 E
Larisa Station, trans., Grc.	185c		37.59 N	23.43 E
Larissa see Lárisa, Grc.	34	D5	39.38 N	22.25 E
Laristan see Hormozgān, state, Iran	74	G15	27.36 N	56.27 E
Larjak, Russia	48	B14	61.06 N	80.15 E
Larjan, Russia	26	A16	59.30 N	33.46 E
Lārkāna, Pak.	62	C2	27.33 N	68.12 E
Larnaca see Larnaka, Cyp.	76	D4	34.55 N	33.38 E
Larnaka (Larnaca), Cyp.	76	D4	34.55 N	33.38 E
Lárnakos, Kólpos, b., Cyp.	76	D4	34.55 N	33.45 E
Larne, N. Ire., U.K.	10	G7	54.51 N	5.49 W
Larned, Ks., U.S.	128	C9	38.10 N	99.05 W
La Robla, Spain	28	B5	42.48 N	5.36 W
La Roca de la Sierra, Spain	28	E4	39.07 N	6.41 W
La Rochefoucauld, Fr.	22	D6	45.44 N	0.23 E
La Rochelle, Fr.	22	C4	46.09 N	1.09 W
La Roche-sur-Yon, Fr.	22	C4	46.40 N	1.26 W
La Rochette, Fr.	179		48.30 N	2.40 E
La Roda, Spain	28	E8	39.12 N	2.09 W
La Romaine, Qc., Can.	111a	i21	50.13 N	60.39 W
La Romana, Dom. Rep.	156	C13	18.25 N	68.58 W
La Ronge, Sk., Can.	110	D10	55.06 N	105.16 W
Laroquebrou, Fr.	22	D8	44.58 N	2.11 E
Larose, La., U.S.	134	H8	29.33 N	90.22 W
Larose, Pointe, c., Mart.	159c	k7	14.39 N	60.53 W
La Route, Fr.	179		48.48 N	2.47 E
Larrimah, Austl.	96	C6	15.34 S	133.13 E
Larroque, Arg.	172	F8	33.01 S	59.00 W
Larrys River, N.S., Can.	122	E15	45.13 N	61.23 W
Larsen Air Park, arpt., Mi., U.S.	199		42.11 N	83.33 W
Larsen Ice Shelf, ice, Ant.	103	B34	68.23 S	62.18 W
La Rubia, Arg.	172	E7	30.08 S	61.47 W
La Rue, Oh., U.S.	124	D2	40.34 N	83.23 W
La Rumorosa, Mex.	148	K9	32.31 N	116.04 W
Laruns, Fr.	22	G5	42.59 N	0.25 W
Larvik, Nor.	16	H8	59.03 N	10.01 E
Larzac, Causse du, plat., Fr.	22	F9	43.50 N	3.25 E
La Sabana, Arg.	172	C7	27.55 S	59.59 W
La Sabanilla, Mex.	154	C8	25.08 N	101.44 W
Las Adjuntas, Ven.	204c		10.26 N	67.01 W
La Sal, Ut., U.S.	150	E7	38.18 N	109.15 W
La Salle, Co., U.S.	140	G8	40.21 N	104.42 W
La Salle, Il., U.S.	130	C8	41.20 N	89.05 W
La Salle, stm., Mb., Can.	142	E16	49.45 N	97.08 W
Lasalle, Parc, p.o.i., Qc., Can.	193a		45.26 N	73.40 W
La Salle College, educ., Pa., U.S.	203		40.02 N	75.09 W
La Sal Mountains, mts., Ut., U.S.	150	E7	38.30 N	109.10 W
Lasan, Indon.	66	C9	1.12 N	115.13 E
Las Animas, Co., U.S.	138	C5	38.04 N	103.13 W
La Santa, Cerro, mtn., P.R.	158a	b3	18.07 N	66.03 W
Las Arenas, P.R.	158a	b1	18.01 N	67.08 W
La Sarre, Qc., Can.	114	B11	48.47 N	79.11 W
Las Arrias, Arg.	172	E6	30.22 S	63.35 W
La Sauceda, Mex.	136	F7	28.26 N	100.38 W
Las Auras, Mex.	136	H8	26.23 N	99.17 W
Las Ballenas, Canal de, strt., Mex.	120	G6	29.13 N	113.31 W
Las Bonitas, Ven.	168	D9	7.51 N	65.40 W
Las Breñas, Arg.	172	C7	27.05 S	61.05 W
Las Cabezas de San Juan, Spain	28	G5	36.59 N	5.55 W
Las Cabras, Chile	172	G2	34.14 S	71.24 W
Lascano, Ur.	172	F10	33.40 S	54.12 W
Las Casitas, mtn., Mex.	154	D4	23.32 N	109.59 W
Las Catitas, Arg.	172	F3	33.17 S	68.03 W
Las Catonas, Arroyo, stm., Arg.	206		34.37 S	58.43 W
Lascaux, Grotte de, cv., Fr.	22	E6	45.02 N	1.09 E
Las Cejas, Arg.	172	C5	26.52 S	64.43 W
Las Choapas, Mex.	154	G11	17.54 N	94.05 W
Las Chorreras, Mex.	154	A6	28.50 N	105.18 W
Las Condes, Chile	204e		33.22 S	70.31 W
Lascone, Monte, hill, Italy	185a		41.59 N	12.23 E
Las Cruces, N.M., U.S.	150	K10	32.18 N	106.46 W
Las Cuatas, Mex.	136	D2	30.03 N	105.55 W
Las Cuevas, Mex.	154	A8	29.38 N	101.19 W
Las Cumaraguas, Ven.	158g	p20	12.05 N	69.53 W
Las Delicias, Mex.	154	H13	15.59 N	91.53 W
La Selle, Morne, mtn., Haiti	156	C11	18.22 N	71.59 W
La Serena, Chile	172	D2	29.53 S	71.15 W
La Serena, reg., Spain	28	F5	38.45 N	5.30 W
La Seu d'Urgell, Spain	28	B12	42.21 N	1.27 E
La Seyne, Fr.	22	F11	43.06 N	5.52 E
Las Flores, Arg.	172	G8	36.01 S	59.06 W
Las Flores, P.R.	158a	b3	18.02 N	66.21 W
Las Flores, Ven.	204c		10.34 N	66.56 W
Las Flores, Arroyo, stm., Arg.	172	H7	35.35 S	59.01 W
Las Flores, Cerro, mtn., Mex.	154	G11	16.43 N	95.30 W
Las Flores Canyon, val., Ca., U.S.	198		34.03 N	118.38 W
Las Garcitas, Arg.	172	C8	26.36 S	59.48 W
Las Guayabas, Mex.	154	C10	23.59 N	97.47 W
Las Harquetas, Arroyo, stm., Arg.	206		34.29 S	58.38 W
Lashburn, Sk., Can.	142	A4	53.08 N	109.36 W
Lāsh-e Joveyn, Afg.	72	C9	31.42 N	61.35 E
Las Heras, Arg.	166	I3	46.31 S	68.55 W
Las Heras, Arg.	172	F3	32.51 S	68.49 W
Lashio, Mya.	64	A3	22.56 N	97.44 E
Lashkar see Gwalior, India	70	E7	26.12 N	78.09 E
Lashkar Gāh, Afg.	72	C9	31.34 N	64.21 E
Las Hormigas, Mex.	154	C9	25.30 N	98.44 W
Lasia, Pulau, i., Indon.	64	K3	2.10 N	96.37 E
Las Iglesias, Mex.	136	G6	27.35 N	101.21 W
La Silla de Caracas, mtn., Ven.	204c		10.33 N	66.51 W
Łasin, Pol.	24	C15	53.32 N	19.05 E
La Sirena, Ven.	158g	p20	11.59 N	69.59 W
Läsjerd, Iran	74	C13	35.20 N	53.04 E
Łask, Pol.	24	E15	51.36 N	19.07 E
Łaskarzew, Pol.	24	E17	51.48 N	21.37 E
Las Lajas, Arg.	172	I2	38.30 S	70.21 W
Las Lajas, Pan.	156	H7	8.15 N	81.52 W
Las Lajitas, Arg.	172	B5	24.43 S	64.12 W
Las Lomitas, Arg.	172	B7	24.42 S	60.35 W
Lašma, Russia	40	D12	54.56 N	41.08 E
Las Malvinas, Arg.	172	G3	34.52 S	68.14 W
Las Mareas, P.R.	158a	c3	17.56 N	66.09 W
Las Margaritas, Mex.	154	G13	16.19 N	91.57 W
Las Marianas, Arg.	172	G8	35.03 S	59.31 W
Las Marías, P.R.	158a	b1	18.15 N	67.00 W
Las Mayas, Ven.	204c		10.26 N	66.56 W
Las Mercedes, Ven.	168	C8	9.05 N	66.24 W
Las Minas, Ven.	204c		10.27 N	66.52 W
Las Minas, Cerro, mtn., Hond.	156	E3	14.33 N	88.39 W
Las Minillas, Cerro, mtn., Chile	204e		33.31 S	70.29 W
Las Moras Creek, stm., Tx., U.S.	136	E7	29.00 N	100.38 W
Las Nieves, Mex.	154	B6	26.24 N	105.22 W
Las Nopaleras, Cerro, mtn., Mex.	154	C7	25.08 N	103.14 W
La Solana, Spain	28	F7	38.56 N	3.13 W
Las Ortegas, Arroyo, stm., Arg.	206		34.45 S	58.32 W
Las Ovejas, Arg.	172	H2	37.01 S	70.45 W
Las Palmas, Arg.	172	C8	27.06 S	58.38 W
Las Palmas, P.R.	158a	b3	17.59 N	66.01 W
Las Palmas de Gran Canaria, Spain	84	D1	28.07 N	15.26 W
Las Palomas, Mex.	120	F9	31.44 N	107.37 W
Las Perdices, Canal, can., Chile	204e		33.31 S	70.33 W
La Spezia, Italy	30	F6	44.07 N	9.49 E
Las Piedras, P.R.	158a	b4	18.11 N	65.52 W
Las Piedras, Ur.	172	G9	34.43 S	56.13 W
Las Piedras, stm., Peru	164	F3	12.31 S	69.13 W
Las Piñas, Phil.	187f		14.29 N	120.59 E
Las Piñas, P.R.	158a	b4	18.15 N	65.54 W
Las Plumas, Arg.	166	H3	43.43 S	67.14 W
Lasqueti Island, i., B.C., Can.	144	G6	49.29 N	124.17 W
Las Raíces Creek, stm., Tx., U.S.	136	F8	28.09 N	99.02 W
Las Rejas, Chile	204e		33.28 S	70.44 W
Las Rosas, Arg.	172	F7	32.29 S	61.34 W
Las Rosas, Chile	204e		33.35 S	70.37 W
Las Rosas, Mex.	154	G12	16.22 N	92.21 W
Las Rosas de Madrid, Spain	184a		40.29 N	3.52 W
Las Sales, Canal, can., Mex.	204a		19.26 N	99.03 W
Lassance, Braz.	170	I3	17.54 S	44.34 W
Lassen Peak, vol., Ca., U.S.	148	C4	40.29 N	121.31 W
Lassen Volcanic National Park, p.o.i., Ca., U.S.	148	C4	40.29 N	121.26 W
L'Assomption, stm., Qc., Can.	126	B16	45.43 N	73.29 W
Lassy, Fr.	179		49.06 N	2.27 E
Las Tablas, Pan.	156	I7	7.46 N	80.17 W
Las Tinajas, Arg.	172	C6	27.28 S	62.54 W
Last Mountain, mtn., Sk., Can.	142	C9	51.07 N	104.54 W
Last Mountain Lake, l., Sk., Can.	142	C8	51.06 N	105.15 W
Las Tórtolas, Cerro (Tórtolas, Cerro de las), mtn., S.A.	172	D2	29.56 S	69.53 W
Las Toscas, Arg.	172	D8	28.21 S	59.16 W
Lastoursville, Gabon	86	E2	0.47 S	12.41 E
Lastovo, Otok, i., Cro.	30	H13	42.45 N	16.53 E
Lastovski Kanal, strt., Cro.	30	H13	42.50 N	16.59 E
Las Trampas Creek, stm., Ca., U.S.	200		37.53 N	122.03 W
Las Trampas Peak, mtn., Ca., U.S.	200		37.50 N	122.03 W
Las Trampas Regional Park, p.o.i., Ca., U.S.	200		37.50 N	122.03 W
Las Trampas Ridge, mtn., Ca., U.S.	200		37.49 N	122.02 W
Las Tunas, Cuba	156	B9	20.58 N	76.57 W
Las Tunas, Arroyo, stm., Arg.	206		34.27 S	58.41 W
Las Tunas, Punta, c., P.R.	158a	a2	18.29 N	66.38 W
Las Tunas Beach, p.o.i., Ca., U.S.	198		34.02 N	118.36 W
Las Tunas Grandes, Laguna, l., Arg.	172	H6	35.58 S	62.25 W
La Suze-sur-Sarthe, Fr.	20	G8	47.53 N	0.02 E
Las Varas, Mex.	120	G8	29.28 N	108.01 W
Las Varas, Mex.	154	E6	21.10 N	105.09 W
Las Varillas, Arg.	172	E6	31.52 S	62.42 W
Las Vegas, P.R.	158a	b1	18.11 N	67.01 W
Las Vegas, Nv., U.S.	148	G10	36.10 N	115.07 W
Las Vegas, N.M., U.S.	138	F3	35.36 N	105.13 W
Las Vegas, Ven.	168	C7	9.32 N	68.37 W
Latacunga, Ec.	168	H2	0.55 S	78.36 W
La Tagua, Col.	168	H4	0.03 S	74.38 W
Latakia see Al-Lādhiqīyah, Syria	76	C6	35.31 N	35.47 E
Latambar, Pak.	70	B3	33.07 N	70.51 E
Lata Mountain, vol., Am. Sam.	101c	h13	14.14 S	169.27 W
Lätäseno, stm., Fin.	14	D13	68.28 N	22.16 E
Låtefoss, wtfl., Nor.	16	H4	59.57 N	6.35 E
Latehar, India	70	G10	23.44 N	84.30 E
Lately Common, Eng., U.K.	180		53.29 N	2.30 W
Laterrière, Qc., Can.	122	B5	48.19 N	71.07 W
La Teste-de-Buch, Fr.	22	E4	44.37 N	1.08 W
Lāthi, India	70	H3	21.44 N	71.23 E
Lathrop, Mo., U.S.	130	E3	39.32 N	94.19 W
Lathrup Village, Mi., U.S.	199		42.29 N	83.14 W
La Tiama, Ven.	204c		10.26 N	66.46 W
Latimer, Eng., U.K.	178		51.41 N	0.33 W
Latimer, Ia., U.S.	128	I5	42.45 N	93.22 W
Latina, Italy	32	C6	41.29 N	12.50 E
Latisana, Italy	30	E10	45.47 N	13.00 E
Latium see Lazio, state, Italy	32	B6	42.00 N	12.30 E
Latjuga, Russia	12	D23	64.17 N	48.46 E
Latnaja, Russia	38	B17	51.39 N	38.54 E
La Toma, Arg.	172	F5	33.03 S	65.37 W
Latorica see Latorytsia, stm., Eur.	24	H18	48.30 N	21.54 E
Latornell, stm., Ab., Can.	144	B12	54.57 N	118.00 W
La Torrecilla, mtn., P.R.	158a	b3	18.12 N	66.20 W
La Tortuga, Isla, i., Ven.	168	B9	10.56 N	65.20 W
Latorytsia, stm., Eur.	24	H18	48.30 N	21.54 E
Latouche Treville, Cape, c., Austl.	96	C4	18.28 S	121.49 E
La Tour-d'Auvergne, Fr.	22	D8	45.32 N	2.41 E
La Tour-du-Pin, Fr.	22	D11	45.34 N	5.26 E
La Tourette Park, p.o.i., N.Y., U.S.	194		40.35 N	74.08 W
Latowicz, Pol.	24	D17	52.01 N	21.47 E
Lat Phrao, Khlong, can., Thai.	187a		13.48 N	100.35 E
La Trimouille, Fr.	22	C7	46.28 N	1.02 E
La Trinidad, Nic.	156	F4	12.56 N	86.12 W
La Trinidad, Phil.	68	B3	16.28 N	120.35 E
La Trinidad, Ven.	204c		10.27 N	66.52 W
La Trinidad de Orichuna, Ven.	168	D7	7.07 N	69.45 W
La Trinité, Mart.	159c	k7	14.44 N	60.58 W
Latrobe, Austl.	99a	n13	41.14 S	146.23 E
Latrobe, Pa., U.S.	124	D6	40.18 N	79.22 W
Latrobe University, educ., Austl.	192b		37.43 S	145.03 E
Latta, S.C., U.S.	132	B6	34.20 N	79.26 W
Lattingtown, N.Y., U.S.	194		40.54 N	73.36 W
La Tuilerie, Fr.	179		48.34 N	2.08 E
La Tuque, Qc., Can.	122	C4	47.25 N	72.46 W
Lātūr, India	69	B3	18.24 N	76.35 E
Latvia, ctry., Eur.	26	D7	57.00 N	25.00 E
Latvija see Latvia, ctry., Eur.	26	D7	57.00 N	25.00 E
Lau, Nig.	84	H7	9.11 N	11.17 E
Lauchhammer, Ger.	24	E9	51.30 N	13.47 E
Lauderdale, Ms., U.S.	134	E10	32.31 N	88.30 W
Lauenburg, Ger.	24	C6	53.22 N	10.33 E
Lauenburg see Lębork, Pol.	24	B13	54.32 N	17.45 E
Lauf an der Pegnitz, Ger.	24	G7	49.30 N	11.16 E
Laufersfort, Schloss, hist., Ger.	181		51.25 N	6.37 E
Lauge Koch Kyst, cst., Grnld.	108	B13	76.28 N	61.45 W
Laughery Creek, stm., In., U.S.	130	F13	39.01 N	84.53 W
Laughlin, Nv., U.S.	150	H2	35.10 N	114.34 W
Laughlin Air Force Base, mil., Tx., U.S.	136	E7	29.22 N	100.47 W
Laughlin Peak, mtn., N.M., U.S.	138	E4	36.38 N	104.12 W
Lau Group, is., Fiji	94	E9	18.20 S	178.30 W
Lauhanvuoren kansallispuisto, p.o.i., Fin.	18	E9	62.08 N	22.09 E
Lauis see Lugano, Switz.	30	D5	46.00 N	8.57 E
Laukaa, Fin.	18	E12	62.25 N	25.57 E
Laukøya, i., Nor.	14	B11	70.07 N	20.50 E
Laukuva, Lith.	26	E5	55.37 N	22.14 E
Laun, Thai.	64	G4	10.10 N	98.42 E
Launceston, Austl.	99a	n13	41.25 S	147.08 E
Launceston, Eng., U.K.	10	K8	50.38 N	4.21 W
Launglon, Mya.	64	F3	13.57 N	98.06 E
La Unión, Chile	166	H2	40.18 S	73.04 W
La Unión, Col.	168	G3	1.36 N	77.08 W
La Unión, El Sal.	156	F4	13.20 N	87.51 W
La Unión, Mex.	154	G8	17.58 N	101.49 W
La Unión, Spain	28	G10	37.37 N	0.52 W
La Unión, N.M., U.S.	136	C1	31.57 N	106.39 W
La Unión, Ven.	168	C8	8.13 N	67.46 W
La Unión, Ven.	204c		10.25 N	66.48 W

Name	Page	Map Ref.	Latitude	Longitude
Laupendahl, ngh., Ger.	181		51.21 N	6.56 E
Laupheim, Ger.	24	H5	48.13 N	9.53 E
Laura, Austl.	96	C8	15.32 S	144.26 E
La Urbana, Ven.	168	D8	7.08 N	66.56 W
Laurel, De., U.S.	124	F10	38.33 N	75.34 W
Laurel, Fl., U.S.	132	I3	27.07 N	82.27 W
Laurel, In., U.S.	130	E12	39.29 N	85.11 W
Laurel, Md., U.S.	124	E9	39.06 N	76.50 W
Laurel, Ms., U.S.	134	F9	31.41 N	89.07 W
Laurel, Mt., U.S.	140	B4	45.40 N	108.46 W
Laurel, Ne., U.S.	140	E15	42.26 N	97.05 W
Laurel, Mount, hill, N.J., U.S.	203		39.56 N	74.53 W
Laurel Bay, S.C., U.S.	132	D5	32.27 N	80.47 W
Laureldale, Pa., U.S.	124	D10	40.23 N	75.55 W
Laureles, Ur.	172	E10	31.21 S	55.51 W
Laurel Gardens, Pa., U.S.	197b		40.31 N	80.01 W
Laurel Hill, N.C., U.S.	132	B6	34.48 N	79.32 W
Laurel Hollow, N.Y., U.S.	194		40.52 N	73.28 W
Laurel Reservoir, res., Ct., U.S.	194		41.10 N	73.33 W
Laurel Ridge State Park, p.o.i., Pa., U.S.	124	E6	39.58 N	79.23 W
Laurel River Lake, res., Ky., U.S.	124	G1	36.56 N	84.12 W
Laurel Springs, N.J., U.S.	203		39.49 N	75.00 W
Laurelville, Oh., U.S.	130	E15	39.28 N	82.44 W
Laurence Harbor, N.J., U.S.	194		40.27 N	74.14 W
Laurencekirk, Scot., U.K.	10	E10	56.50 N	2.28 W
Laurens, Ia., U.S.	130	B3	42.50 N	94.51 W
Laurens, S.C., U.S.	132	B3	34.30 N	82.00 W
Laurentides, Les, plat., Qc., Can.	110	F16	48.00 N	71.00 W
Lauria Inferiore, Italy	32	D9	40.03 N	15.49 E
Lau Ridge, unds.	174	L21	21.00 S	178.30 W
Laurier, Mb., Can.	142	D14	50.53 N	99.33 W
Laurier-Station, Qc., Can.	122	D5	46.32 N	71.38 W
Laurinburg, N.C., U.S.	132	B6	34.46 N	79.27 W
Lauritsala, Fin.	18	F15	61.04 N	28.16 E
Laurium, Mi., U.S.	128	D10	47.14 N	88.26 W
Lauro, Monte, mtn., Italy	32	G8	37.07 N	14.49 E
Lausanne, Switz.	30	D3	46.31 N	6.37 E
Lausitzer Neisse (Nysa Łużycka), stm., Eur.	24	E10	52.04 N	14.45 E
Laut, Pulau, i., Indon.	66	A5	4.43 N	107.59 E
Laut, Pulau, i., Indon.	66	E10	3.40 S	116.10 E
Laut, Selat, strt., Indon.	66	E9	3.25 S	116.03 E
Lauta, Ger.	24	E9	51.27 N	14.04 E
Lautaro, Chile	172	I1	38.31 S	72.25 W
Lauterbach, Ger.	24	F5	50.38 N	9.23 E
Lauter Sachsen, Ger.	24	F8	50.33 N	12.44 E
Laut Kecil, Kepulauan, is., Indon.	66	F9	4.48 S	115.43 E
Lautoka, Fiji	101e	p18	17.37 S	177.27 E
Lauttakylä, Fin.	18	F9	61.10 N	22.41 E
Lauvsnes, Nor.	16	C8	64.29 N	10.55 E
Lauzerte, Fr.	22	E7	44.15 N	1.08 E
Lava (Łyna), stm., Eur.	24	B16	54.37 N	21.13 E
Lava Beds National Monument, p.o.i., Ca., U.S.	148	B4	41.44 N	121.31 W
Lavaca, stm., Tx., U.S.	136	E11	28.49 N	96.34 W
Lavaca Bay, b., Tx., U.S.	136	F11	28.37 N	96.35 W
Lava Hot Springs, Id., U.S.	146	H15	42.38 N	112.01 W
Lavaisse, Arg.	172	F5	33.49 S	65.24 W
Laval, Qc., Can.	126	C16	45.33 N	73.44 W
Laval, Fr.	20	F8	48.04 N	0.46 W
Laval-des-Rapides, ngh., Qc., Can.	193a		45.33 N	73.42 W
La Vall d'Uixó, Spain	28	E10	39.49 N	0.14 W
Lavalle, Arg.	172	D5	28.11 S	65.06 W
Lavalle, Arg.	172	D8	29.01 S	59.10 W
La Valley, Co., U.S.	138	D3	37.06 N	105.20 W
Laval-Ouest, ngh., Qc., Can.	193a		45.33 N	73.52 W
Lāvān, Jazīreh-ye, i., Iran	74	G13	26.48 N	53.14 E
Lavant, stm., Aus.	30	D11	46.38 N	14.57 E
Lavapié, Punta, c., Chile	172	H1	37.09 S	73.34 W
Lávara, Grc.	34	B9	41.16 N	26.22 E
Lavassaare, Est.	26	B7	58.31 N	24.22 E
La Vecilla de Curueño, Spain	28	B5	42.51 N	5.24 W
La Vega, Dom. Rep.	156	C12	19.13 N	70.30 W
La Vega, ngh., Ven.	204c		10.28 N	66.57 W
Lavela, Russia	12	E21	63.37 N	45.32 E
La Vela, Cabo de, c., Col.	168	A5	12.13 N	72.09 W
La Vela de Coro, Ven.	168	B7	11.27 N	69.34 W
Lavelanet, Fr.	22	G7	42.56 N	1.50 E
Lavello, Italy	32	C9	41.03 N	15.48 E
La Venada, Mex.	136	I10	25.48 N	97.33 W
La Venta, hist., Mex.	154	F11	18.08 N	94.03 W
La Ventura, Mex.	154	C8	24.38 N	100.53 W
La Vera, reg., Spain	28	D5	40.09 N	5.42 W
La Verde, Arg.	172	C8	27.06 S	59.24 W
La Vergne, Tn., U.S.	130	H11	36.00 N	86.34 W
La Verne, Ca., U.S.	198		34.06 N	117.46 W
Laverne, Ok., U.S.	138	E9	36.42 N	99.53 W
La Vernia, Tx., U.S.	136	E9	29.21 N	98.07 W
Laverock, Pa., U.S.	203		40.05 N	75.11 W
La Verrière, Fr.	179		48.45 N	1.57 E
Laverton, Austl.	96	E4	28.37 S	122.24 E
La Veta, Co., U.S.	138	D4	37.30 N	105.00 W
Lavia, Fin.	18	F9	61.35 N	22.35 E
Lavic Lake, l., Ca., U.S.	148	I9	34.40 N	116.21 W
La Victoria, Peru	204d		12.04 S	77.02 W
Lavieille, Lake, l., On., Can.	126	C11	45.52 N	78.14 W
Lavik, Nor.	16	F3	61.06 N	5.30 E
La Vila Joiosa, Spain	28	F10	38.30 N	0.14 W
La Ville-du-Bois, Fr.	179		48.40 N	2.16 E
La Villeneuve-Saint-Martin, Fr.	179		49.04 N	1.58 E
Lavillette, N.B., Can.	122	C11	47.16 N	65.17 W
La Viña, Arg.	172	B5	25.27 S	65.34 W
Lavina, Mt., U.S.	140	A4	46.17 N	108.56 W
La Vista, Ne., U.S.	130	C1	41.10 N	96.02 W
Lavnatundra, gora, hill, Russia	14	D20	68.27 N	30.04 E
Lavonia, Ga., U.S.	132	B2	34.26 N	83.06 W
La Voulte-sur-Rhône, Fr.	22	E10	44.48 N	4.46 E
Lavoutte, Anse, b., St. Luc.	159c	I7	14.04 N	60.55 W
Lavradia, Port.	184c		38.40 N	9.03 W
Lavras, Braz.	170	K3	21.13 S	45.00 W
Lavras, stm., Braz.	205a		23.00 S	43.33 W
Lavras do Sul, Braz.	172	E11	30.49 S	53.54 W
Lávrio, Grc.	34	F7	37.44 N	24.03 E
Lavumisa, Swaz.	90	E10	27.18 S	31.53 E
Lávvoaivi, hill, Nor.	14	D14	68.53 N	23.38 E
Lawang, Indon.	66	G8	7.49 S	112.42 E
Lawas, Malay.	66	A9	4.51 N	115.24 E
Lawatu, Indon.	66	E12	2.53 S	120.17 E
Lawdar, Yemen	72	G6	13.52 N	45.52 E
Lawers, Ben, mtn., Scot., U.K.	10	E8	56.34 N	4.13 W
Lawgi, Austl.	98	E8	24.35 S	150.38 E
Lawit, Gunong, mtn., Malay.	64	J6	5.25 N	102.35 E
Lawksawk, Mya.	64	B3	21.03 N	96.55 E
Lawler, Ia., U.S.	130	A5	43.04 N	92.08 W
Lawlor, Mount, mtn., Ca., U.S.	198		34.16 N	118.06 W
Lawn, Tx., U.S.	136	B8	32.08 N	99.44 W
Lawndale, N.C., U.S.	132	A4	35.25 N	81.33 W
Lawndale, ngh., Il., U.S.	196		41.51 N	87.43 W
Lawndale, ngh., Pa., U.S.	203		40.03 N	75.05 W
Lawn Hill, Austl.	96	C7	18.35 S	138.36 E
Lawn Hill Creek, stm., Austl.	96	C7	18.05 S	139.07 E
Lawnside, N.J., U.S.	203		39.51 N	75.01 W
Lawqah, Sau. Ar.	74	F8	29.49 N	42.45 E
Lawra, Ghana	84	G4	10.38 N	2.53 W
Lawrence, In., U.S.	130	E12	39.50 N	86.00 W
Lawrence, Ks., U.S.	130	F2	38.59 N	95.13 W
Lawrence, Ma., U.S.	124	B14	42.42 N	71.09 W
Lawrence, Ne., U.S.	138	A10	40.17 N	98.15 W
Lawrence, N.Y., U.S.	194		40.36 N	73.43 W
Lawrence, Pa., U.S.	197b		40.18 N	80.09 W
Lawrence Brook, stm., N.J., U.S.	194		40.29 N	74.24 W
Lawrenceburg, In., U.S.	130	E13	39.05 N	84.51 W
Lawrenceburg, Ky., U.S.	130	F13	38.02 N	84.53 W
Lawrenceburg, Tn., U.S.	134	B11	35.14 N	87.20 W
Lawrence Fork, stm., Ne., U.S.	140	F9	41.36 N	103.14 W
Lawrence Institute of Technology, educ., Mi., U.S.	199		42.28 N	83.15 W
Lawrence Marsh, sw., N.Y., U.S.	194		40.36 N	73.42 W
Lawrence Municipal Airport, arpt., Ma., U.S.	201		42.43 N	71.07 W
Lawrenceville, Il., U.S.	130	F10	38.43 N	87.41 W
Lawrenceville, N.J., U.S.	124	D11	40.17 N	74.43 W
Lawrenceville, Va., U.S.	124	H8	36.45 N	77.50 W
Lawrenceville, ngh., Pa., U.S.	197b		40.28 N	79.57 W
Lawson, Mo., U.S.	130	E3	39.26 N	94.12 W
Lawtey, Fl., U.S.	132	F3	30.01 N	82.04 W
Lawton, Mi., U.S.	130	B12	42.09 N	85.51 W
Lawton, N.D., U.S.	142	F15	48.17 N	98.22 W
Lawton, Ok., U.S.	138	G10	34.37 N	98.23 W
Lawton, ngh., Cuba	204b		23.06 N	82.21 W
Lawu, Gunung, vol., Indon.	66	G7	7.37 S	111.11 E
Lawyer Creek, stm., Id., U.S.	146	D10	46.13 N	116.01 W
Lawz, Jabal al-, mtn., Sau. Ar.	74	F4	28.40 N	35.18 E
Laxå, Swe.	16	I12	58.59 N	14.37 E
Laxe, Spain	28	A1	43.13 N	9.00 W
Laxenburg, Aus.	182b		48.04 N	16.21 E
Laxenburger Park, p.o.i., Aus.	182b		48.04 N	16.22 E
Lay Lake, res., Al., U.S.	134	D12	33.03 N	86.30 W
Layon, stm., Fr.	20	G8	47.23 N	0.50 W
Layou, St. Vin.	159e	o11	13.12 N	61.15 W
Layou, stm., Dom.	159c	j6	15.23 N	61.25 W
Layton, Ut., U.S.	150	B4	41.04 N	111.57 W
Laytons Lake, l., N.J., U.S.	203		39.42 N	75.26 W
Laytonville, Ca., U.S.	148	D2	39.41 N	123.28 W
La Zarca, Mex.	154	C6	25.50 N	104.44 W
Lazarev, Russia	50	F17	52.12 N	141.30 E
Lázaro Cárdenas, Mex.	120	F4	30.32 N	115.55 W
Lázaro Cárdenas, Mex.	154	G7	17.57 N	102.12 W
Lázaro Cárdenas, Presa, res., Mex.	154	C6	25.35 N	105.01 W
Lazdijai, Lith.	26	F6	54.13 N	23.31 E
Lazio, state, Italy	32	B6	42.00 N	12.30 E
Lazirky, Ukr.	38	C11	50.05 N	32.39 E
Lazo, Russia	54	C10	43.22 N	133.53 E
La Zorra, Quebrada, stm., Ven.	204c		10.36 N	67.03 W
Lazurne, Ukr.	38	G11	46.05 N	32.31 E
Lazzate, Italy	184b		45.40 N	9.05 E
Lea, stm., Eng., U.K.	10	J12	51.30 N	0.00 W
Léach, Camb.	64	F6	12.21 N	103.46 E
Leach Pond, l., Ma., U.S.	201		42.04 N	71.09 W
Leachville, Ar., U.S.	130	I7	35.56 N	90.15 W
Lead, S.D., U.S.	140	C9	44.21 N	103.45 W
Leadbetter Point, c., Wa., U.S.	146	D2	46.38 N	124.03 W
Leaden Roding, Eng., U.K.	178		51.48 N	0.19 E
Leader, Sk., Can.	142	D4	50.53 N	109.31 W
Lead Hill, hill, Mo., U.S.	130	H4	36.49 N	93.06 W
Leadore, Id., U.S.	146	F13	44.41 N	113.22 W
Leadville, Co., U.S.	138	B2	39.15 N	106.17 W
Leaf, stm., Mn., U.S.	128	E3	46.29 N	94.54 W
Leaf, stm., Ms., U.S.	134	F10	31.00 N	88.45 W
Leaf Lake, l., Sk., Can.	142	A11	53.02 N	102.07 W
Leaghur, Lake, l., Austl.	98	I4	33.37 S	143.04 E
League City, Tx., U.S.	136	E12	29.30 N	95.05 W
Leakesville, Ms., U.S.	134	F10	31.09 N	88.33 W
Leakey, Tx., U.S.	136	E8	29.43 N	99.45 W
Leakin Park, p.o.i., Md., U.S.	202b		39.18 N	76.42 W
Leak Run, stm., Pa., U.S.	197b		40.27 N	79.47 W
Leaksville, N.C., U.S.	124	H6	36.29 N	79.53 W
Lealman, Fl., U.S.	132	I3	27.50 N	82.40 W
Leamington, On., Can.	126	F7	42.02 N	82.35 W
Leamington see Royal Leamington Spa, Eng., U.K.	10	I11	52.17 N	1.31 W
Leamington Spa see Royal Leamington Spa, Eng., U.K.	10	I11	52.17 N	1.31 W
Le'an, China	58	H6	27.25 N	115.49 E
Leandro, Braz.	170	C3	5.59 S	44.55 W
Leandro N. Alem, Arg.	172	C10	27.36 S	55.19 W
Leane, Lough, l., Ire.	10	I3	52.03 N	9.33 W
Learmonth, Austl.	96	D2	22.14 S	114.05 E
Leary, Ga., U.S.	134	F14	31.28 N	84.30 W
Leaside, mun., On., Can.	193b		43.42 N	79.22 W
Leask, Sk., Can.	142	A7	53.00 N	106.46 W
Leatherman Peak, mtn., Id., U.S.	146	F13	44.05 N	113.44 W
Lea Town, Eng., U.K.	180		53.46 N	2.48 W
Leavenworth, Ks., U.S.	130	E2	39.18 N	94.55 W
Leavenworth, Wa., U.S.	146	C6	47.36 N	120.40 W
Leavesden Aerodrome, arpt., Eng., U.K.	178		51.42 N	0.27 W
Leawood, Ks., U.S.	130	F3	38.58 N	94.37 W
Łeba, Pol.	24	B13	54.45 N	17.32 E
Łeba, stm., Pol.	24	B13	54.42 N	17.25 E
Lebak, Phil.	68	G5	6.30 N	124.02 E
Lebam, Wa., U.S.	146	D3	46.33 N	123.33 W
Lebanon, In., U.S.	130	D11	40.02 N	86.28 W
Lebanon, Ks., U.S.	138	B10	39.48 N	98.33 W
Lebanon, Ky., U.S.	130	G12	37.34 N	85.15 W
Lebanon, Mo., U.S.	130	G5	37.41 N	92.40 W
Lebanon, N.H., U.S.	122	G4	43.38 N	72.14 W
Lebanon, Oh., U.S.	124	E1	39.25 N	84.12 W
Lebanon, Or., U.S.	146	F3	44.32 N	122.54 W
Lebanon, Pa., U.S.	124	D9	40.20 N	76.25 W
Lebanon, S.D., U.S.	140	B13	45.03 N	99.46 W
Lebanon, Tn., U.S.	130	H11	36.12 N	86.17 W
Lebanon, Va., U.S.	124	H3	36.54 N	82.04 W
Lebanon, ctry., Asia	76	E6	34.00 N	36.00 E
Lebanon Junction, Ky., U.S.	130	G12	37.50 N	85.43 W
Lebec, Ca., U.S.	148	I7	34.50 N	118.51 W
Lebedevka, Kaz.	40	F18	50.12 N	54.07 E
Lebedino, Russia	40	D16	55.13 N	49.51 E
Lebedjan', Russia	40	E11	53.00 N	39.08 E
Lebedyn, Ukr.	38	C13	50.34 N	34.28 E
Lebedyn, Ukr.	38	E10	48.57 N	31.31 E
Lebesby, Nor.	14	B18	70.33 N	27.02 E
Le Bic, Qc., Can.	122	B8	48.22 N	68.43 W
Lebjaže, Kaz.	48	D13	51.28 N	77.46 E
Lebjaže, Russia	40	C16	57.24 N	49.31 E
Lebjaž'ja, stm., Russia	14	E29	67.04 N	38.33 E
Le Blanc, Fr.	20	H10	46.37 N	1.03 E
Le Blanc-Mesnil, Fr.	179		48.56 N	2.28 E
Leblon, ngh., Braz.	205a		22.59 S	43.13 W
Lebo, D.R.C.	86	D4	4.29 N	23.58 E
Lebo, Ks., U.S.	130	F2	38.25 N	95.51 W
Le Bois-Dieu, Fr.	179		48.39 N	1.43 E
Lebombo Mountains, hills, Afr.	90	E11	25.15 S	32.00 E
Lebongtandai, Indon.	66	E2	3.02 S	101.55 E
Lębork, Pol.	24	B13	54.32 N	17.45 E
Le Boulay, Fr.	179		48.47 N	1.40 E
Le Bourget, Fr.	179		48.56 N	2.26 E
Lebrija, Spain	28	H4	36.55 N	6.04 W
Lebrija, stm., Col.	168	D5	8.08 N	73.47 W
Łebsko, Jezioro, l., Pol.	24	B13	54.43 N	17.24 E
Lebu, Chile	172	H1	37.37 S	73.39 W
Le Buisson de Massoury, sw., Fr.	179		48.30 N	2.43 E
Le Carbet, Mart.	159c	k6	14.42 N	61.10 W
Lecce, Italy	32	D12	40.21 N	18.10 E
Lecco, Italy	30	E6	45.51 N	9.23 E
Le Center, Mn., U.S.	128	G5	44.23 N	93.44 W
Lech, stm., Eur.	24	I6	48.44 N	10.56 E
Lechainá, Grc.	34	F4	37.56 N	21.16 E
Le Champ-Renault, Fr.	179		49.06 N	2.31 E
Lechang, China	58	I5	25.08 N	113.20 E
Le Château-d'Oléron, Fr.	22	D4	45.52 N	1.12 W
Le Chêne-Rogneux, Fr.	179		48.46 N	1.46 E
Le Chesnay, Fr.	179		48.50 N	2.07 E
Le Chesne, Fr.	20	E13	49.30 N	4.45 E
Le Cheylard, Fr.	22	E10	44.54 N	4.25 E
Lechiguanas, Islas de las, is., Arg.	172	F8	33.26 S	59.42 W
Lechtaler Alpen, mts., Aus.	30	C7	47.18 N	10.40 E
Lechuga, Arroyo, stm., Cuba	204b		23.01 N	82.16 W
Lechuguilla, Cerro, mtn., Mex.	154	D6	22.19 N	104.15 W
Lecinone, Monte, mtn., Italy	185a		41.59 N	12.48 E
Le Claire, Ia., U.S.	130	C7	41.35 N	90.20 W
Lecompte, La., U.S.	134	F6	31.05 N	92.23 W
Le Coudray-Montceaux, Fr.	179		48.34 N	2.31 E
Le Creusot, Fr.	20	H13	46.48 N	4.25 E
Le Croisic, Fr.	20	G6	47.18 N	2.31 W
Łęczna, Pol.	24	E18	51.17 N	22.55 E
Łęczyca, Pol.	24	D15	52.04 N	19.12 E
Leda, stm., Ger.	20	A16	53.12 N	7.25 E
Lederach, Pa., U.S.	203		40.16 N	75.24 W
Ledesma, Spain	28	C4	41.05 N	6.00 W
Ledgewood, N.J., U.S.	194		40.52 N	74.39 W
Le Diamant, Mart.	159c	l6	14.28 N	61.01 W
Ledjanaja, gora, mtn., Russia	50	D23	61.53 N	171.09 E
Ledkovo, Russia	12	C24	67.14 N	50.42 E
Ledmozero, Russia	18	C19	64.16 N	32.03 E
Ledo, India	62	C8	27.17 N	95.44 E
Ledo, Indon.	66	C6	1.01 N	109.35 E
Ledong, China	58	L3	18.43 N	109.10 E
Le Donjon, Fr.	22	C9	46.21 N	3.47 E
Le Dorat, Fr.	22	C7	46.13 N	1.05 E
Ledsham, Eng., U.K.	180		53.16 N	2.58 W
Ledu, China	52	D5	36.28 N	102.23 E
Leduc, Ab., Can.	144	C17	53.15 N	113.32 W
Ledyczek, Pol.	24	C12	53.32 N	16.56 E
Lee, Ma., U.S.	124	B12	42.18 N	73.15 W
Lee, stm., Ire.	10	J3	51.54 N	8.24 W
Lee Boulevard Heights, Va., U.S.	202c		38.52 N	77.09 W
Leechburg, Pa., U.S.	124	D6	40.37 N	79.36 W
Leechburg Airport, arpt., Pa., U.S.	197b		40.37 N	79.34 W
Leech Lake, l., Sk., Can.	142	C11	51.04 N	102.30 W
Leech Lake, l., Mn., U.S.	128	D4	47.09 N	94.23 W
Leech Lake Indian Reservation, ind. res., Mn., U.S.	128	D4	47.20 N	94.13 W
Leedey, Ok., U.S.	138	F9	35.52 N	99.20 W
Leedom Estates, De., U.S.	203		39.41 N	75.35 W
Leeds, Eng., U.K.	10	H11	53.50 N	1.35 W
Leeds, Al., U.S.	134	D12	33.32 N	86.32 W
Leeds, N.D., U.S.	142	F14	48.17 N	99.26 W
Leeds and Liverpool Canal, can., Eng., U.K.	180		53.25 N	2.59 W
Leek, Eng., U.K.	10	H10	53.06 N	2.01 W
Leelanau, Lake, l., Mi., U.S.	126	D4	44.56 N	85.42 W
Leelanau Peninsula, pen., Mi., U.S.	126	C4	45.04 N	85.37 W
Leer, Ger.	24	C3	53.14 N	7.27 E
Lees, Eng., U.K.	180		53.32 N	2.04 W
Leesburg, Fl., U.S.	132	H4	28.48 N	81.53 W
Leesburg, Ga., U.S.	132	E1	31.43 N	84.09 W
Leesburg, Va., U.S.	124	E8	39.06 N	77.34 W
Lees Summit, Mo., U.S.	130	F3	38.54 N	94.22 W
Leesville, La., U.S.	134	F5	31.08 N	93.16 W
Leesville, S.C., U.S.	132	C4	33.55 N	81.30 W
Leesville, Tx., U.S.	136	E10	29.24 N	97.44 W
Leesville Lake, res., Oh., U.S.	124	D4	40.29 N	81.10 W
Leesville Lake, res., Va., U.S.	124	H6	37.04 N	79.24 W
Leeton, Austl.	98	J6	34.33 S	146.24 E
Leeu-Gamka, S. Afr.	90	H6	32.46 S	21.58 E
Leeupan, pl., S. Afr.	191d		26.14 S	28.19 E
Leeuwarden, Neth.	20	A14	53.12 N	5.47 E
Leeuwin, Cape, c., Austl.	96	F2	34.22 S	115.08 E
Lee Vining, Ca., U.S.	148	F6	37.57 N	119.07 W
Leeward, Îles see Leeward Islands, is., N.A.	152a	h15	17.00 N	63.00 W
Leeward Islands, is., N.A.	152a	h15	17.00 N	63.00 W
Lefèvre, Pointe, c., N. Cal.	101d	m16	20.55 S	167.01 E
Lefferts Lake, l., N.J., U.S.	194		40.25 N	74.14 W
Lefkáda, Grc.	34	E3	38.49 N	20.42 E
Lefkáda, i., Grc.	34	E3	38.42 N	20.39 E
Léfka Óri, mts., Grc.	34	H7	35.18 N	24.01 E
Lefke, N. Cyp.	76	C3	35.07 N	32.52 E
Lefkímmi, Grc.	34	D2	39.25 N	20.04 E
Lefkoşa see Nicosia, N. Cyp.	74	C3	35.10 N	33.22 E
Lefkosia see Nicosia, Cyp.	76	C4	35.10 N	33.22 E
Lefors, Tx., U.S.	138	F8	35.26 N	100.47 W
Le François, Mart.	159c	k7	14.36 N	60.54 W
Lefroy, Lake, l., Austl.	96	F4	31.15 S	121.40 E
Lega Hida, Eth.	82	F8	7.56 N	41.04 E
Legal, Ab., Can.	144	C17	53.56 N	113.36 W
Leganés, Spain	28	D7	40.19 N	3.45 W
Legaspi, Phil.	68	D4	13.07 N	123.44 E
Leggett, Ca., U.S.	148	D2	39.51 N	123.42 W
Leghorn see Livorno, Italy	30	G7	43.33 N	10.19 E
Legion, Zimb.	90	B9	21.20 S	28.31 E
Legion of Honor, Palace of the, bldg., Ca., U.S.	200		37.47 N	122.30 W
Legionowo, Pol.	24	D16	52.24 N	20.55 E
Legnago, Italy	30	E8	45.11 N	11.17 E
Legnano, Italy	30	E5	45.36 N	8.55 E
Legnica, Pol.	24	E12	51.12 N	16.09 E
Le Gosier, Guad.	159c	h6	16.12 N	61.28 W
Le Grand, Ca., U.S.	148	F5	37.13 N	120.13 W
Le Grau-du-Roi, Fr.	22	F10	43.32 N	4.08 E
Le Guelta, Alg.	28	H11	36.21 N	0.49 E
Leguer, stm., Fr.	20	F5	48.44 N	3.31 W
Legume, Austl.	98	G9	28.24 S	152.18 E
Leh, India	70	A6	34.09 N	77.35 E
Le Havre, Fr.	20	E8	49.29 N	0.08 E
Lehčevo, Blg.	36	F10	43.32 N	23.32 E
Lehi, Ut., U.S.	150	C5	40.24 N	111.50 W
Lehigh, Ia., U.S.	130	B3	42.21 N	94.03 W
Lehigh, Ok., U.S.	134	C2	34.28 N	96.13 W
Lehigh Acres, Fl., U.S.	132	J4	26.36 N	81.38 W
Lehighton, Pa., U.S.	124	D10	40.49 N	75.42 W
Lehnitzsee, l., Ger.	182a		52.45 N	13.16 E
Lehr, N.D., U.S.	140	A13	46.16 N	99.22 W
Lehrte, Ger.	24	D5	52.22 N	9.58 E
Lehta, Russia	12	F23	60.49 N	48.27 E
Lehta, Russia	18	C20	64.25 N	33.59 E
Lehtimäki, Fin.	18	E10	62.47 N	23.55 E
Lehtse, Est.	26	A8	59.14 N	25.47 E
Lehua, i., Hi., U.S.	100a	a1	22.01 N	160.05 W
Lehututu, Bots.	90	C5	23.57 S	21.50 E
Lei, stm., China	58	H5	26.54 N	112.39 E
Leiah, Pak.	70	C3	30.57 N	70.56 E
Leião, Port.	184c		38.44 N	9.18 W
Leibnitz, Aus.	30	D12	46.47 N	15.31 E
Leicester, Eng., U.K.	10	I11	52.38 N	1.07 W
Leichhardt, Austl.	192a		33.53 S	151.07 E
Leichhardt, stm., Austl.	98	A2	17.35 S	139.47 E
Leichhardt Falls, wtfl., Austl.	98	B2	18.13 S	139.52 E
Leichhardt Range, mts., Austl.	98	C6	20.53 S	147.30 E
Leiden (Leyden), Neth.	20	B13	52.09 N	4.30 E
Leigh, Eng., U.K.	178		51.12 N	0.13 E
Leigh Canal, can., Eng., U.K.	180		53.28 N	2.21 W
Leigh Creek South, Austl.	98	H2	30.27 S	138.25 E
Leighton, Al., U.S.	134	C11	34.42 N	87.31 W
Leighton Buzzard, Eng., U.K.	10	J12	51.55 N	0.39 W
Leikanger, Nor.	16	F4	61.11 N	6.50 E
Leikanger, Nor.	16	E3	62.08 N	5.16 E
Leiktho, Mya.	64	C3	19.13 N	96.35 E
Leinan, Sk., Can.	142	D6	50.30 N	107.46 W
Leinavatn, l., Nor.	14	D10	68.27 N	19.48 E
Leine, stm., Ger.	24	D5	52.43 N	9.35 E
Leinster, hist. reg., Ire.	10	I6	53.05 N	7.00 W
Leinster, Mount, mtn., Ire.	10	I6	52.37 N	6.44 W
Leipalingis, Lith.	26	F6	54.05 N	23.51 E
Leipsic, Oh., U.S.	124	C2	41.05 N	83.59 W
Leipsoí, i., Grc.	34	F9	37.18 N	26.46 E
Leipzig, Ger.	24	E8	51.20 N	12.23 E
Leira, Nor.	16	A11	66.05 N	13.03 E
Leira, Nor.	16	G7	60.57 N	9.20 E
Leiria, Port.	28	E2	39.44 N	8.47 W
Leiria, state, Port.	28	E2	39.45 N	8.45 W
Leirvik, Nor.	16	H3	59.47 N	5.29 E
Leisi, Est.	26	B5	58.34 N	22.40 E
Leisler, Mount, mtn., Austl.	96	D6	23.28 S	129.17 E
Leitariegos, Puerto de, p., Spain	28	A4	43.00 N	6.25 W
Leitchfield, Ky., U.S.	130	G11	37.29 N	86.17 W
Leitha (Lajta), stm., Eur.	24	I12	47.53 N	17.18 E
Leithe, ngh., Ger.	181		51.29 N	7.06 E
Leitrim, Ire.	10	H4	54.00 N	8.04 W
Leitrim, state, Ire.	10	H5	54.00 N	8.00 W
Leivádia, Grc.	34	E5	38.26 N	22.55 E
Leixi, China	58	H5	27.09 N	112.51 E
Leiyang, China	58	H5	26.24 N	112.51 E
Lei Yue Mun, strt., China	189d		22.16 N	114.14 E
Leizhou Bandao, pen., China	58	K4	20.47 N	110.05 E
Lejasciems, Lat.	26	C9	57.15 N	26.33 E
Leka, i., Nor.	16	B9	65.05 N	11.37 E
Lekafjorden, strt., Nor.	16	C9	65.04 N	11.44 E
Lekeitio, Spain	28	A8	43.21 N	2.29 W
Leknes, Nor.	14	D4	68.09 N	13.36 E
Le Kremlin-Bicêtre, Fr.	179		48.49 N	2.21 E
Leksand, Swe.	16	G12	60.43 N	15.01 E
Leksdalsvatnet, l., Nor.	16	D9	63.52 N	11.37 E
Lekšmozero, ozero, l., Russia	18	F25	61.43 N	38.06 E
Leksozero, ozero, l., Russia	18	D17	63.46 N	30.58 E
Leksvik, Nor.	16	D8	63.40 N	10.37 E
Le Lamentin, Mart.	159c	k6	14.37 N	61.00 W
Leland, Il., U.S.	130	C9	41.36 N	88.47 W
Leland, Mi., U.S.	126	C4	45.01 N	85.45 W
Leland, Ms., U.S.	134	D8	33.24 N	90.54 W
Lelång, l., Swe.	16	H10	59.09 N	12.07 E
Lel'čycy, Bela.	38	B7	51.46 N	28.20 E
Leleiwi Point, c., Hi., U.S.	100a	d7	19.44 N	155.00 W
Leleque, Arg.	166	H2	42.22 S	71.05 W
Leles, Indon.	66	G5	7.07 S	107.53 E
Lelewau, Indon.	66	E12	3.04 S	121.04 E
Leli Shan, mtn., China	70	B8	33.26 N	81.42 E
Le Locle, Switz.	30	C3	47.03 N	6.45 E
Le Lorrain, Mart.	159c	k6	14.49 N	61.04 W
Lelystad, Neth.	20	B14	52.30 N	5.28 E
Lema, Nig.	84	G5	12.57 N	4.14 E
Le Maire, Estrecho de, strt., Arg.	166	J4	54.49 S	64.59 W
Léman, Lac see Geneva, Lake, l., Eur.	30	D3	46.24 N	6.22 E
Le Mans, Fr.	20	G9	48.00 N	0.12 E
Le Marin, Mart.	159c	l7	14.28 N	60.52 W
Le Mars, Ia., U.S.	130	B1	42.47 N	96.09 W
Lema Shilindi, Eth.	82	G8	4.55 N	42.06 E
Lemay, Mo., U.S.	130	F7	38.31 N	90.16 W
Lemba-Gaba, D.R.C.	191b		4.27 S	15.18 E
Lembak, Indon.	66	C10	0.53 N	117.31 E
Lemberg, Sk., Can.	142	D10	50.43 N	103.11 W
Lemberg see L'viv, Ukr.	38	D2	49.50 N	24.02 E
Lemberg, mtn., Ger.	24	H4	48.09 N	8.45 E
Lemdiyya, Alg.	28	H13	36.11 N	2.51 E
Leme, Braz.	170	L2	22.11 S	47.22 W
Leme, Morro do, hill, Braz.	205a		22.58 S	43.10 W
Le Mée-sur-Seine, Fr.	179		48.32 N	2.38 E
Le Mesle, Fr.	179		48.43 N	1.41 E
Le Mesnil-Amelot, Fr.	179		49.01 N	2.36 E
Le Mesnil-Aubry, Fr.	179		49.03 N	2.24 E
Le Mesnil-le-Roi, Fr.	179		48.56 N	2.08 E
Le Mesnil-Saint-Denis, Fr.	179		48.45 N	1.58 E
Lemesós (Limassol), Cyp.	76	D4	34.41 N	33.02 E
Lemgo, Ger.	20	B17	52.01 N	8.54 E
Lemhi, stm., Id., U.S.	146	F13	45.11 N	113.53 W
Lemhi Pass, p., U.S.	146	F13	44.58 N	113.27 W
Lemhi Range, mts., Id., U.S.	146	F13	44.33 N	113.36 W
Lemieux Islands, is., Nu., Can.	108	E13	64.01 N	64.30 W
Lemin, China	58	K3	21.09 N	109.45 E
Leming, Tx., U.S.	136	E9	29.03 N	98.28 W
Lemitar, N.M., U.S.	138	G2	34.09 N	106.54 W
Lemland, i., Fin.	18	H6	60.03 N	20.09 E
Lemmatsi, Est.	26	B9	58.19 N	26.37 E
Lemmenjoen kansallispuisto, p.o.i., Fin.	14	D16	68.39 N	26.00 E
Lemmenjoki, stm., Fin.	14	D17	68.50 N	26.25 E
Lemmon, S.D., U.S.	140	B10	45.56 N	102.09 W
Lemmon, Mount, mtn., Az., U.S.	150	K6	32.26 N	110.47 W
Lemnos see Límnos, i., Grc.	34	D8	39.55 N	25.17 E
Lemoncove, Ca., U.S.	148	G7	36.23 N	119.01 W
Lemon Creek, stm., N.Y., U.S.	194		40.31 N	74.12 W
Lemon Heights, Ca., U.S.	198		33.46 N	117.48 W
Lemont, Pa., U.S.	126	H12	40.47 N	77.49 W
Le Mont-Dore, N. Cal.	101d	n16	22.16 S	166.33 E
Lemoore, Ca., U.S.	148	G6	36.18 N	119.45 W
Lemoore Naval Air Station, mil., Ca., U.S.	148	G5	36.19 N	119.55 W
Lemoro, Indon.	66	D12	1.28 S	121.05 E
Le Moule, Guad.	159c	h6	16.20 N	61.21 W
Le Moutier, Fr.	179		48.50 N	1.42 E
LeMoyne, Qc., Can.	193a		45.31 N	73.29 W
Lempa, stm., N.A.	156	F3	13.14 N	88.49 W
Lempäälä, Fin.	18	F10	61.19 N	23.45 E
Lempe, Indon.	66	D12	1.41 S	120.15 E
Lemro, stm., Mya.	64	B1	20.19 N	93.17 E
Lemukutan, Pulau, i., Indon.	66	C6	0.45 N	108.43 E
Le Murge, hills, Italy	32	C10	40.52 N	16.42 E
Lemutan, Indon.	66	B9	3.04 N	115.48 E
Le Muy, Fr.	22	F12	43.28 N	6.33 E
Lemvig, Den.	16	K6	56.32 N	8.18 E
Lemyethna, Mya.	64	D2	17.36 N	95.09 E
Len, stm., Eng., U.K.	178		51.16 N	0.31 E
Lena, Il., U.S.	130	B8	42.22 N	89.49 W
Lena, Wi., U.S.	126	D1	44.57 N	88.02 W
Lena, stm., Russia	50	B14	72.25 N	126.40 E
Lenape, Pa., U.S.	203		39.55 N	75.38 W
Lenart, Slvn.	30	D12	46.34 N	15.49 E
Lenasia, S. Afr.	191d		26.17 S	27.50 E
Lencloître, Fr.	20	H9	46.49 N	0.19 E
Lençóis, Braz.	170	G5	12.33 S	41.23 W
Lençóis Maranhenses, Parque Nacional dos, p.o.i., Braz.	170	B4	2.25 S	43.12 W
Lendery, Russia	18	D18	63.26 N	31.14 E
Lendinara, Italy	30	E8	45.05 N	11.36 E
Lengelscheid, Ger.	181		51.08 N	7.40 E
Lenger, Kaz.	48	F12	42.11 N	69.53 E
Lenggor, stm., Malay.	64	K6	2.27 N	103.37 E
Lenghu, China	52	D3	38.49 N	93.26 E
Lenglingen, l., Nor.	16	C11	64.15 N	13.42 E
Lengshuikeng, China	58	H7	27.55 N	117.08 E
Lengshuitan, China	58	H4	26.27 N	111.35 E
Lengua de Vaca, Punta, c., Chile	172	E2	30.14 S	71.38 W
Lenhovda, Swe.	16	J13	57.00 N	15.15 E
Lenina, gora, hill, Russia	183b		55.42 N	37.31 E
Lenina, pik see Lenin Peak, mtn., Asia	72	B11	39.20 N	72.55 E
Leninabad see Hudžand, Taj.	72	A10	40.16 N	69.38 E
Leninakan see Gjumri, Arm.	42	E10	40.47 N	43.50 E
Lenin Central Stadium, p.o.i., Russia	183b		55.43 N	37.33 E
Lenine, Ukr.	38	H14	45.18 N	35.47 E
Leningrad see Sankt-Peterburg, Russia	18	H17	59.56 N	30.15 E
Leningradskaja, Russia	38	G18	46.18 N	39.23 E
Leningradskaja oblast', state, Russia	183a		59.55 N	30.35 E
Leningradskaja oblast', co., Russia	12	G15	60.00 N	32.00 E
Lenino, ngh., Russia	183b		55.37 N	37.41 E
Leninogor see Leninogorsk, Kaz.	48	D14	50.21 N	83.30 E
Leninogorsk, Kaz.	48	D14	50.21 N	83.30 E
Leninogorsk, Russia	40	D18	54.34 N	52.28 E
Lenin Peak, mtn., Asia	72	B11	39.20 N	72.55 E
Leninsk, Kaz.	48	E10	45.39 N	63.18 E
Leninsk, Russia	40	G14	48.42 N	45.12 E
Leninsk, Uzb.	48	F12	40.39 N	72.14 E
Lenins'ke, Ukr.	38	H14	45.15 N	35.54 E
Lenins'ke, Ukr.	38	B12	51.27 N	33.14 E
Leninskij, Russia	26	F20	54.18 N	37.27 E
Leninsk-Kuzneckij, Russia	48	D15	54.41 N	86.11 E
Leninskoe, Russia	40	B15	58.18 N	47.04 E
Leninskoe, Russia	50	G15	47.59 N	132.37 E
Leninváros see Tiszaújváros, Hung.	36	B7	47.55 N	21.02 E
Len'ki, Russia	48	D14	52.57 N	80.24 E
Lenkoran' see Länkäran, Azer.	42	F13	38.45 N	48.51 E
Lenni, Pa., U.S.	203		39.54 N	75.27 W
Lennonville, Austl.	96	E3	27.58 S	117.51 E
Lennox, S.D., U.S.	128	H2	43.21 N	96.54 W
Lennox, Isla, i., Chile	166	K3	55.17 S	66.49 W
Lennoxville, Qc., Can.	122	E5	45.21 N	71.49 W
Lenoir, N.C., U.S.	124	I4	35.55 N	81.32 W
Lenoir City, Tn., U.S.	124	I1	35.47 N	84.16 W
Lenora, Czech Rep.	24	H9	48.55 N	13.48 E
Lenore Lake, l., Sk., Can.	142	B9	52.30 N	104.57 W
Lenox, Ga., U.S.	132	E2	31.16 N	83.27 W
Lenox, Ia., U.S.	130	D3	40.53 N	94.32 W
Lenox, Ma., U.S.	124	B12	42.21 N	73.16 W
Lenox, Tn., U.S.	130	H8	36.05 N	89.29 W
Lens, Fr.	20	D11	50.25 N	2.49 E
Lensk, Russia	48	B20	60.43 N	114.56 E
Lentate sul Seveso, Italy	184b		45.41 N	9.07 E
Lenti, Hung.	36	C3	46.37 N	16.33 E
Lentini, Italy	32	G9	37.16 N	15.00 E
Lentua, l., Fin.	18	C16	64.14 N	29.36 E
Lentvaris, Lith.	26	F8	54.38 N	25.03 E
Lenya, Mya.	64	G4	11.27 N	98.59 E
Lenya, stm., Mya.	64	G4	11.43 N	98.49 E
Lenz, S. Afr.	191d		26.19 S	27.49 E
Léo, Burkina	84	G4	11.05 N	2.05 W
Leoben, Aus.	30	C12	47.22 N	15.05 E
Léogâne, Haiti	156	C11	18.31 N	72.38 W
Leola, Ar., U.S.	134	C6	34.10 N	92.35 W
Leola, S.D., U.S.	140	B14	45.43 N	98.56 W
Leominster, Eng., U.K.	10	I10	52.13 N	2.44 W
Leominster, Ma., U.S.	124	B14	42.31 N	71.45 W
Léon, Fr.	22	F4	43.52 N	1.18 W
León, Mex.	154	E8	21.07 N	101.41 W
León, Nic.	156	F4	12.25 N	86.52 W
León, Spain	28	B5	42.36 N	5.34 W
Leon, Ia., U.S.	130	D4	40.44 N	93.44 W
Leon, Ks., U.S.	138	D12	37.41 N	96.46 W
León, co., Spain	28	B5	42.35 N	6.00 W
Leon, stm., Tx., U.S.	136	C10	30.58 N	97.24 W
Leon, Arroyo, stm., Ca., U.S.	200		37.28 N	122.25 W
León, Montes de, mts., Spain	28	B4	42.30 N	6.18 W
Leona, stm., Tx., U.S.	136	F8	28.45 N	99.11 W
Leonard, Tx., U.S.	134	D2	33.23 N	96.14 W
Leonardo, N.J., U.S.	194		40.25 N	74.03 W

Name	Page	Map Ref.	Latitude	Longitude
Leonardtown, Md., U.S.	124	F9	38.17 N	76.37 W
Leonardville, Nmb.	90	C4	23.29 S	18.47 E
Leonardville, Ks., U.S.	138	B12	39.21 N	96.51 W
Leonberg, Ger.	24	H4	48.47 N	9.01 E
Leondale, S. Afr.	191d		26.18 S	28.12 E
León de los Aldamas see León, Mex.	154	E8	21.07 N	101.41 W
Leones, Arg.	172	F6	32.40 S	62.17 W
Leonforte, Italy	32	G8	37.38 N	14.23 E
Leongatha, Austl.	98	L5	38.28 S	145.56 E
Leonia, N.J., U.S.	194		40.51 N	73.59 W
Leonídio, Grc.	34	F5	37.10 N	22.52 E
Leoniha, Russia	18	H25	59.37 N	38.52 E
Leonora, Austl.	96	E4	28.53 S	121.20 E
Leontárion, Grc.	185c		37.59 N	23.51 E
Leontevo, Russia	26	B19	58.57 N	36.34 E
Leonville, La., U.S.	134	G6	30.28 N	91.58 W
Leopard, Pa., U.S.	203		40.01 N	75.27 W
Leopold and Astrid Coast, cst., Ant.	103	B13	67.55 S	85.41 E
Leopoldau, ngh., Aus.	182b		48.16 N	16.27 E
Léopold II, Lac see Mai-Ndombe, Lac, l., D.R.C.	86	E3	2.25 S	18.17 E
Leopoldina, Braz.	170	K4	21.31 S	42.38 W
Leopoldo de Bulhões, Braz.	170	I1	16.37 S	48.45 W
Leopoldsdorf, Aus.	182b		48.06 N	16.24 E
Leopoldstadt, ngh., Aus.	182b		48.13 N	16.23 E
Léopoldville see Kinshasa, D.R.C.	86	E3	4.20 S	15.17 E
Leoti, Ks., U.S.	138	C7	38.28 N	101.21 W
Leova, Mol.	38	G7	46.28 N	28.16 E
Leovo see Leova, Mol.	38	G7	46.28 N	28.16 E
Le Palais, Fr.	20	G5	47.20 N	3.09 W
Lepanto see Náfpaktos, Grc.	34	E4	38.23 N	21.48 E
Lepanto, Ar., U.S.	134	B8	35.36 N	90.19 W
Lepar, Pulau, i., Indon.	66	E5	2.57 S	106.50 E
Le Pâté, Fr.	179		48.32 N	2.18 E
Lepe, Spain	28	G3	37.15 N	7.12 W
Le Pecq, Fr.	179		48.54 N	2.07 E
Lepel', Bela.	26	F11	54.53 N	28.42 E
Le Perray-en-Yuelines, Fr.	179		48.42 N	1.51 E
Le Perreux-sur-Marne, Fr.	179		48.51 N	2.30 E
Le Petit-Clamart, bldg., Fr.	179		48.47 N	2.14 E
Lephephe, Bots.	90	C7	23.22 S	25.50 E
Le Pin, Fr.	179		48.55 N	2.38 E
L'Épine, Fr.	179		48.32 N	2.21 E
Leping, China	58	G7	28.57 N	117.05 E
Lepini, Monti, mts., Italy	32	C7	41.35 N	13.00 E
L'Épiphanie, Qc., Can.	126	C16	45.50 N	73.28 W
Le Plessis-aux-Bois, Fr.	179		49.00 N	2.46 E
Le Plessis-Bouchard, Fr.	179		49.00 N	2.14 E
Le Plessis-Pâté, Fr.	179		48.37 N	2.20 E
Le Plessis-Trévise, Fr.	179		48.49 N	2.34 E
Le Pontel, Fr.	179		48.49 N	1.53 E
Lepontine, Alpi see Lepontine Alps, mts., Eur.	30	D6	46.25 N	8.40 E
Lepontine Alps, mts., Eur.	30	D6	46.25 N	8.40 E
Le Port-Marly, Fr.	179		48.53 N	2.06 E
Leppävirta, Fin.	18	E14	62.28 N	27.46 E
Leppington, Austl.	192a		33.58 S	150.49 E
Lepreau, Point, c., N.B., Can.	122	E10	45.04 N	66.27 W
Le Prêcheur, Mart.	159c	k6	14.48 N	61.13 W
Le Pré-Saint-Gervais, Fr.	179		48.53 N	2.25 E
Lepsi see Lepsy, Kaz.	48	E13	46.13 N	78.56 E
Lepsy, Kaz.	48	E13	46.13 N	78.56 E
Le Puy, Fr.	22	D9	45.03 N	3.53 E
Lequeitio see Lekeitio, Spain	28	A8	43.21 N	2.29 W
Le Raincy, Fr.	179		48.54 N	2.31 E
Lercara Friddi, Italy	32	G7	37.45 N	13.36 E
Lerche, ngh., Ger.	181		51.37 N	7.43 E
Lerdo, Mex.	154	C7	25.32 N	103.31 W
Lerici, Italy	30	F6	44.05 N	9.54 E
Lérida, Col.	168	G6	0.01 N	71.01 W
Lérida see Lleida, Spain	28	C11	41.37 N	0.37 E
Lerma, Spain	28	C7	42.00 N	3.45 W
Lerma, stm., Mex.	154	E8	20.12 N	102.41 W
Le Robert, Mart.	159c	k7	14.41 N	60.56 W
Léros, i., Grc.	185c		37.59 N	23.32 E
Leroux Wash, stm., Az., U.S.	150	H6	34.54 N	110.12 W
Le Roy, Il., U.S.	130	D9	40.20 N	88.45 W
Le Roy, Ks., U.S.	130	F2	38.05 N	95.38 W
Le Roy, Mn., U.S.	128	H6	43.30 N	92.29 W
Le Roy, N.Y., U.S.	124	B7	42.58 N	77.58 W
Lerum, Swe.	16	J10	57.46 N	12.16 E
Lerwick, Scot., U.K.	10	A11	60.09 N	1.09 W
Les Abymes, Guad.	159c	h5	16.16 N	61.30 W
Le Saint-Esprit, Mart.	159c	k7	14.33 N	60.55 W
Les Aix-d'Angillon, Fr.	20	G11	47.11 N	2.33 E
Les Alluets-le-Roi, Fr.	179		48.55 N	1.55 E
Les Andelys, Fr.	20	E10	49.14 N	1.25 E
Les Anses-d'Arlets, Mart.	159c	l6	14.29 N	61.05 W
Les Bordes, Fr.	179		48.39 N	1.58 E
Les Borges Blanques, Spain	28	C11	41.31 N	0.52 E
Lesbos see Lésvos, i., Grc.	34	D9	39.10 N	26.20 E
Les Bréviaires, Fr.	179		48.42 N	1.49 E
Les Cayes, Haiti	156	C11	18.12 N	73.45 W
Les Chaises, Fr.	179		48.39 N	1.42 E
Lesches, Fr.	179		48.54 N	2.47 E
Les Clayes-sous-Bois, Fr.	179		48.49 N	1.59 E
Les Essarts-le-Roi, Fr.	179		48.43 N	1.54 E
Les Fonts, Spain	184d		41.32 N	2.02 E
Les Galleries d'Anjou Tétreaultville, shp. cen., Qc., Can.	193a		45.35 N	73.34 W
Les Gâtines, Fr.	179		48.48 N	1.58 E
Les Granges-le-Roi, Fr.	179		48.30 N	2.01 E
Les Grésillons, Fr.	179		48.56 N	2.01 E
Lesh see Lezhë, Alb.	32	C13	41.47 N	19.39 E
Leshan, China	52	F5	29.34 N	103.45 E
Les Herbiers, Fr.	20	H7	46.52 N	1.01 W
Lésigny, Fr.	179		48.45 N	2.37 E
Lesina, Lago di, b., Italy	30	I12	41.53 N	15.26 E
Lesja, Nor.	16	E6	62.07 N	8.51 E
Lesjaskog, Nor.	16	E6	62.14 N	8.21 E
Lesjöfors, Swe.	16	H12	59.59 N	14.11 E
Lesken, Russia	42	D10	43.16 N	43.49 E
Lesko, Pol.	24	G18	49.28 N	22.21 E
Leskovac, Yugo.	36	F8	43.00 N	21.57 E
Leskov Island, i., S. Geor.	103	A1	56.40 S	28.09 W
Les'ky, Ukr.	38	D11	49.20 N	32.13 E
Les Laurentides see Laurentides, Les, plat., Qc., Can.	110	F16	48.00 N	71.00 W
Leslie, Ar., U.S.	130	I5	35.49 N	92.34 W
Leslie, Ga., U.S.	132	E1	31.57 N	84.04 W
Leslie, Mi., U.S.	124	B1	42.26 N	84.25 W
Leslie, W.V., U.S.	124	F5	37.58 N	80.46 W
Les Lilas, Fr.	179		48.53 N	2.25 E
Les Loges, Fr.	179		48.34 N	2.03 E
Les Loges-en-Josas, Fr.	179		48.46 N	2.09 E
Lesmo, Italy	184b		45.39 N	9.18 E
Les Molières, Fr.	179		48.40 N	2.04 E
Les Mureaux, Fr.	179		49.00 N	1.55 E
Leśna, Pol.	24	E11	51.01 N	15.16 E
Lesneven, Fr.	20	F4	48.34 N	4.19 W
Lešnica, Yugo.	36	E6	44.39 N	19.19 E
Lesnoe, Russia	26	B18	58.17 N	35.32 E
Lesnoj, Russia	48	C11	56.55 N	67.15 E
Lesnoj, ngh., Russia	183a		60.00 N	30.19 E
Lesnoj Gorodok, Russia	183b		55.39 N	37.13 E
Lesnye Poljany, Russia	40	B18	59.00 N	52.25 E
Lesnye Poljany, Russia	183b		55.57 N	37.53 E
Lesogorsk, Russia	50	G17	49.25 N	142.07 E
Lesogorskij, Russia	18	F15	61.03 N	28.55 E
Lesosibirsk, Russia	50	E7	58.14 N	92.28 E
Lesotho, ctry., Afr.	90	F9	29.30 S	28.30 E
Lesozavodsk, Russia	54	B10	45.28 N	133.23 E
Lesozavodskij, Russia	14	F23	66.42 N	32.43 E
Les Pavillons-sous-Bois, Fr.	179		48.55 N	2.30 E
Les Ruelles, Fr.	179		48.40 N	1.37 E
Les Sables-d'Olonne, Fr.	20	H7	46.30 N	1.47 W
Les Saintes, is., Guad.	159c	i5	15.52 N	61.37 W
Lessay, Fr.	20	E7	49.13 N	1.32 W
Lesse, stm., Bel.	20	D14	50.14 N	4.54 E
Lessebo, Swe.	16	K13	56.45 N	15.16 E
Lesser Antilles, is.	106	H16	15.00 N	61.00 W
Lesser Caucasus, mts., Asia	42	E11	41.00 N	44.35 E
Lesser Khingan Range see Xiao Hinggan Ling, mts., China	52	B10	48.45 N	127.00 E
Lesser Slave, stm., Ab., Can.	144	A16	55.09 N	114.03 W
Lesser Slave Lake, l., Ab., Can.	110	D8	55.28 N	115.10 W
Lesser Sunda Islands see Tenggara, Nusa, is., Indon.	60	G6	9.00 S	120.00 E
Lester, Pa., U.S.	203		39.52 N	75.17 W
L'Esterre, Gren.	159e	q10	12.28 N	61.28 W
Lestijärvi, Fin.	18	D11	63.32 N	24.38 E
Lestijoki, stm., Fin.	18	D10	64.04 N	23.38 E
Lestock, Sk., Can.	142	C9	51.20 N	104.01 W
Les Trois-Îlets, Mart.	159c	k6	14.31 N	61.01 W
Le Sueur, Mn., U.S.	128	G5	44.28 N	93.54 W
Le Sueur, stm., Mn., U.S.	128	G5	44.07 N	94.03 W
Lesueur, Mount, hill, Austl.	96	F2	30.10 S	115.11 E
Lešukonskoe, Russia	12	D21	64.52 N	45.41 E
Les Ulis, Fr.	179		48.41 N	2.11 E
Lésvos (Lesbos), i., Grc.	34	D9	39.10 N	26.20 E
Leszno, Pol.	24	E12	51.50 N	16.34 E
Letaba, stm., S. Afr.	90	C10	23.58 S	31.49 E
L'Étang-la-Ville, Fr.	179		48.52 N	2.05 E
Letcher, S.D., U.S.	140	D14	43.53 N	98.08 W
Letchmore Heath, Eng., U.K.	178		51.40 N	0.20 W
Letchworth State Park, p.o.i., N.Y., U.S.	124	B8	42.42 N	77.56 W
Letea, Ostrovul, i., Rom.	36	D16	45.20 N	29.20 E
Le Temple, Fr.	179		49.00 N	1.58 E
Letenye, Hung.	36	C3	46.25 N	16.43 E
Le Tertre-Saint-Denis, Fr.	179		48.56 N	1.36 E
Lethbridge, Austl.	192a		33.44 S	150.48 E
Lethbridge, Ab., Can.	144	G18	49.41 N	112.48 W
Lethem, Guy.	168	F12	3.23 N	59.47 W
Le Thillay, Fr.	179		49.00 N	2.28 E
Le Thillot, Fr.	22	B12	47.52 N	6.45 E
Leti, Kepulauan, is., Indon.	60	G8	8.13 S	127.50 E
Leticia, Col.	164	D4	4.09 S	69.55 W
Letlhakane, Bots.	90	B7	21.24 S	25.35 E
Letlhakeng, Bots.	90	D7	24.06 S	25.00 E
Letneozerskij, Russia	18	D27	63.22 N	40.20 E
Letnerečenskij, Russia	18	C21	64.17 N	34.23 E
Letnij bereg, cst., Russia	18	C25	64.46 N	38.28 E
Letnij Navolok, Russia	18	B24	65.08 N	37.03 E
Letnjaja, stm., Russia	18	B24	65.08 N	34.38 E
Letnjaja Zolotica, Russia	18	B23	64.57 N	36.49 E
Letovo, Russia	183b		55.34 N	37.24 E
Letpadan, Mya.	64	D2	17.47 N	95.45 E
Le Tremblay-sur-Mauldre, Fr.	179		48.47 N	1.53 E
Le Tréport, Fr.	20	D10	50.03 N	1.22 E
Letsôk-aw Kyun, i., Mya.	64	G4	11.37 N	98.15 E
Letterkenny, Ire.	10	G5	54.57 N	7.44 W
Letung, Indon.	66	B4	2.51 N	105.42 E
Letychiv, Ukr.	36	D6	49.23 N	27.37 E
Leu, Rom.	36	E11	44.11 N	24.00 E
Léua, Ang.	88	C3	11.39 S	20.27 E
Leucas see Lefkáda, i., Grc.	34	E3	38.42 N	20.39 E
Leucate, Étang de, l., Fr.	22	G9	42.51 N	3.00 E
Leudeville, Fr.	179		48.34 N	2.20 E
Leuk, Switz.	30	D4	46.19 N	7.38 E
Leumeah, Austl.	192a		34.03 S	150.50 E
Leuser, Gunung, mtn., Indon.	64	K3	3.45 N	97.11 E
Leutkirch, Ger.	24	I6	47.49 N	10.01 E
Leuven, Bel.	20	D13	50.53 N	4.42 E
Leuville-sur-Orge, Fr.	179		48.37 N	2.16 E
Levack, On., Can.	126	B8	46.38 N	81.22 W
Le Val-d'Albian, Fr.	179		48.45 N	2.11 E
Levallois-Perret, Fr.	179		48.54 N	2.18 E
Le Val-Saint-Germain, Fr.	179		48.34 N	2.04 E
Levan, Ut., U.S.	150	D5	39.33 N	111.51 W
Levanger, Nor.	16	D9	63.45 N	11.18 E
Levante, Riviera di, cst., Italy	30	F6	44.14 N	9.25 E
Levanzo, Isola di, i., Italy	32	F6	38.00 N	12.20 E
Le Vauclin, Mart.	159c	k7	14.33 N	60.51 W
Leveaux Mountain, hill, Mn., U.S.	128	D8	47.37 N	90.47 W
Level Green, Pa., U.S.	197b		40.24 N	79.43 W
Levelland, Tx., U.S.	138	H6	33.35 N	102.22 W
Leven, Loch, l., Scot., U.K.	10	E9	56.12 N	3.22 W
Leven Point, c., S. Afr.	90	E11	27.55 S	32.35 E
Levenshulme, ngh., Eng., U.K.	180		53.27 N	2.10 W
Leveque, Cape, c., Austl.	96	C4	16.25 S	122.55 E
Levering, Mi., U.S.	126	C5	45.38 N	84.46 W
Leverkusen, Ger.	24	E3	51.03 N	6.59 E
Lever Park, p.o.i., Eng., U.K.	180		53.37 N	2.34 W
Le Vésinet, Fr.	179		48.54 N	2.08 E
Levice, Slvk.	24	H14	48.12 N	18.36 E
Le Vigan, Fr.	22	E9	43.59 N	3.35 E
Levin, N.Z.	102	E6	40.35 S	175.18 E
Levino, Russia	18	G24	60.29 N	37.28 E
Lévis, Qc., Can.	122	D5	46.48 N	71.10 W
Levisa Fork, stm., U.S.	124	G3	38.06 N	82.36 W
Lévis-Saint Nom, Fr.	179		48.43 N	1.58 E
Levítha, i., Grc.	34	F9	37.00 N	26.28 E
Levittown, P.R.	158a	b3	18.27 N	66.14 W
Levittown see Willingboro, N.J., U.S.	124	D11	40.02 N	74.53 W
Levittown, N.Y., U.S.	124	D12	40.43 N	73.30 W
Levittown, Pa., U.S.	124	D11	40.08 N	74.50 W
Levittown Discount World, shp. cen., Pa., U.S.	203		40.09 N	74.49 W
Levkosia see Nicosia, Cyp.	76	C4	35.10 N	33.22 E
Levoča, Slvk.	24	H16	49.01 N	20.35 E
Levroux, Fr.	20	H10	46.59 N	1.37 E
Levski, Blg.	36	F12	43.21 N	25.09 E
Lev Tolstoj, Russia	40	E11	53.12 N	39.27 E
Levuka, Fiji	101e	p19	17.41 S	178.50 E
Lévuo, stm., Lith.	26	E7	56.03 N	24.21 E
Lewapaku, Indon.	66	H11	9.47 S	119.41 E
Lewe, Mya.	64	C3	19.38 N	96.07 E
Lewellen, Ne., U.S.	140	F10	41.19 N	102.08 W
Lewer, stm., Nmb.	90	D3	25.32 S	17.43 E
Lewes, De., U.S.	124	F10	38.46 N	75.08 W
Lewin Brzeski, Pol.	24	F13	50.45 N	17.37 E
Lewis, Ia., U.S.	128	J3	41.18 N	95.06 W
Lewis, Ks., U.S.	138	D9	37.56 N	99.15 W
Lewis, stm., Wa., U.S.	146	E4	45.51 N	122.47 W
Lewis, Butt of, c., Scot., U.K.	10	C6	58.31 N	6.16 W
Lewis, East Fork, stm., Wa., U.S.	146	E4	45.52 N	122.43 W
Lewis, Isle of, i., Scot., U.K.	10	C6	58.08 N	6.44 W
Lewis, Mount, mtn., Nv., U.S.	148	C9	40.24 N	116.51 W
Lewis and Clark Caverns State Park, p.o.i., Mt., U.S.	146	E15	45.49 N	111.13 W
Lewis and Clark Lake, res., U.S.	140	E15	42.51 N	97.50 W
Lewis and Clark Range, mts., Mt., U.S.	146	C13	47.27 N	113.04 W
Lewisburg, Ky., U.S.	130	H10	36.59 N	86.56 W
Lewisburg, Pa., U.S.	124	D9	40.57 N	76.53 W
Lewisburg, Tn., U.S.	134	B12	35.27 N	86.47 W
Lewisdale, Md., U.S.	202c		38.58 N	76.58 W
Lewis Gut, b., Ct., U.S.	194		41.09 N	73.09 W
Lewisham, S. Afr.	191d		26.07 S	27.49 E
Lewisham Location, S. Afr.	191d		26.10 S	27.47 E
Lewis-Lockport Airport, arpt., Il., U.S.	196		41.36 N	88.05 W
Lewisport, Ky., U.S.	130	G11	37.56 N	86.54 W
Lewis Range, mts., N.A.	146	B13	48.45 N	113.40 W
Lewis Run, Pa., U.S.	124	C7	41.52 N	78.40 W
Lewis Run, stm., Pa., U.S.	197b		40.17 N	79.55 W
Lewis Smith Lake, res., Al., U.S.	134	C11	33.59 N	87.08 W
Lewiston, Ca., U.S.	148	C3	40.43 N	122.48 W
Lewiston, Id., U.S.	146	D10	46.24 N	117.00 W
Lewiston, Me., U.S.	122	F6	44.06 N	70.12 W
Lewiston, Mi., U.S.	126	D5	44.53 N	84.18 W
Lewiston, Mn., U.S.	128	H7	43.58 N	91.52 W
Lewiston, N.Y., U.S.	126	E11	43.10 N	79.01 W
Lewiston, Ut., U.S.	146	I15	41.59 N	111.51 W
Lewiston Orchards, Id., U.S.	146	D10	46.23 N	116.59 W
Lewistown, Il., U.S.	130	D7	40.23 N	90.09 W
Lewistown, Mo., U.S.	130	D6	40.05 N	91.48 W
Lewistown, Mt., U.S.	146	C17	47.03 N	109.26 W
Lewistown, Pa., U.S.	124	D8	40.35 N	77.33 W
Lewisville, N.B., Can.	122	D12	46.06 N	64.45 W
Lewisville, Ar., U.S.	134	D5	33.21 N	93.35 W
Lewisville, Tx., U.S.	136	A10	33.03 N	96.59 W
Lewisville Lake, res., Tx., U.S.	138	H11	33.08 N	97.00 W
Lewvan, Sk., Can.	142	D9	50.00 N	104.05 W
Lexa, Ar., U.S.	134	C8	34.35 N	90.44 W
Lexington, Ga., U.S.	132	C2	33.52 N	83.06 W
Lexington, Il., U.S.	130	D9	40.38 N	88.46 W
Lexington, Ky., U.S.	124	F1	38.02 N	84.30 W
Lexington, Ma., U.S.	124	B14	42.26 N	71.13 W
Lexington, Mi., U.S.	126	E7	43.16 N	82.31 W
Lexington, Ms., U.S.	134	D8	33.07 N	90.03 W
Lexington, Mo., U.S.	130	E4	39.10 N	93.52 W
Lexington, Ne., U.S.	140	G13	40.47 N	99.44 W
Lexington, N.C., U.S.	124	I5	35.49 N	80.15 W
Lexington, Ok., U.S.	138	F11	35.01 N	97.20 W
Lexington, Or., U.S.	146	E7	45.26 N	119.40 W
Lexington, S.C., U.S.	132	C4	33.58 N	81.14 W
Lexington, Tn., U.S.	134	B10	35.39 N	88.23 W
Lexington, Tx., U.S.	136	D10	30.25 N	97.01 W
Lexington, Va., U.S.	124	G6	37.46 N	79.27 W
Lexington Park, Md., U.S.	124	F9	38.15 N	76.27 W
Leybourne, Eng., U.K.	178		51.18 N	0.25 E
Leyden see Leiden, Neth.	20	B13	52.09 N	4.30 E
Leye, China	58	I2	24.48 N	106.34 E
Leyond, stm., Mb., Can.	142	C17	51.39 N	96.28 W
Leyre, stm., Fr.	22	E5	44.39 N	1.01 W
Leyte, i., Phil.	68	E5	10.50 N	124.50 E
Leyte Gulf, b., Phil.	68	E5	10.50 N	125.25 E
Leyton, ngh., Eng., U.K.	178		51.33 N	0.01 W
Leżajsk, Pol.	24	F18	50.15 N	22.25 E
Lézarde, stm., Mart.	159c	k6	14.35 N	61.01 W
Lezhë, Alb.	32	C13	41.47 N	19.39 E
Lezhi, China	58	F1	30.16 N	105.01 E
Lëzna, Bela.	26	E13	55.02 N	30.48 E
L'gov, Russia	40	F9	51.39 N	35.16 E
Lhasa, China	52	F3	29.38 N	91.07 E
Lhasa, stm., China	70	C13	29.20 N	90.45 E
L'Hautil, Fr.	179		49.00 N	2.01 E
Lhazê, China	70	D11	29.10 N	87.41 E
Lhokkruet, Indon.	64	J2	4.52 N	95.24 E
Lhoknga, Indon.	64	J2	5.28 N	95.14 E
Lhokseumawe, Indon.	64	J3	5.11 N	97.08 E
Lhoksukon, Indon.	64	J3	5.02 N	97.19 E
Lhorong, China	52	E4	30.47 N	95.51 E
L'Hospitalet de Llobregat, Spain	28	C13	41.21 N	2.06 E
Lhozhag, China	70	D13	28.22 N	90.50 E
Lhuntsi Dzong, Bhu.	70	E13	27.39 N	91.09 E
Lhünzê, China	52	F3	28.24 N	92.36 E
Li, Thai.	64	D4	17.48 N	98.57 E
Li, stm., China	58	G4	29.12 N	112.10 E
Li, stm., Thai.	64	D4	18.25 N	98.42 E
Liadova, stm., Ukr.	38	E6	48.29 N	27.36 E
Liamuiga, Mount, vol., St. K./N.	159a	c2	17.22 N	62.48 W
Lian, stm., China	58	H5	27.48 N	112.51 E
Lian, stm., China	58	I5	24.02 N	113.18 E
Liancheng, China	58	I7	25.42 N	116.45 E
Lianga, Phil.	68	F6	8.37 N	126.05 E
Liangbao, China	58	D4	34.31 N	110.50 E
Liangbingtai, China	54	C8	43.12 N	128.47 E
Liangbuaya, Indon.	66	C10	0.05 N	116.46 E
Liangdang, China	58	E2	33.55 N	106.15 E
Liangheguan, China	58	E3	33.04 N	109.07 E
Lianghekou, China	58	G3	29.14 N	108.46 E
Liangjiang, China	58	J3	23.25 N	108.22 E
Liangmentou, China	58	G9	28.58 N	121.12 E
Liangpa, China	58	I2	24.11 N	106.14 E
Liangping, China	58	F2	30.39 N	107.46 E
Liangshui, stm., China	189a		39.49 N	116.40 E
Liangyuan, China	58	E7	31.59 N	117.33 E
Liangzhou see Wuwei, China	52	D5	37.55 N	102.37 E
Liangzi Hu, l., China	58	F6	30.16 N	114.34 E
Lianhuapao, China	54	B8	45.32 N	129.48 E
Lianhua Shan, mts., China	58	J6	23.37 N	115.46 E
Lianjiang, China	58	K4	21.36 N	110.17 E
Liannan, China	58	I5	24.42 N	112.17 E
Lianozovo, ngh., Russia	183b		55.54 N	37.35 E
Lianshui, China	58	E8	33.46 N	119.15 E
Lianxian, China	58	I5	24.46 N	112.21 E
Lianyuan, China	58	H4	27.43 N	111.18 E
Lianyungang, China	58	D8	34.36 N	119.10 E
Lianyun Shan, mtn., China	58	G5	28.32 N	113.50 E
Lianzhou see Hepu, China	58	K3	21.40 N	109.11 E
Liao, stm., China	52	C9	40.40 N	122.09 E
Liaocheng, China	58	C7	36.26 N	115.59 E
Liaodong Bandao (Liaotung Peninsula), pen., China	58	B10	39.55 N	122.18 E
Liaodong Wan (Liaotung, Gulf of), b., China	58	A9	40.30 N	121.30 E
Liaoning, state, China	52	C9	41.00 N	123.00 E
Liaotung, Gulf of see Liaodong Wan, b., China	58	A9	40.30 N	121.30 E
Liaotung Peninsula see Liaodong Bandao, pen., China	58	B10	39.55 N	122.18 E
Liaoyang, China	52	C9	41.16 N	123.10 E
Liaoyuan, China	52	C10	42.54 N	125.08 E
Liaozhong, China	54	D5	41.30 N	122.44 E
Liapádes, Grc.	34	D2	39.40 N	19.44 E
Liard, stm., Can.	110	C6	61.50 N	121.18 W
Liard River, B.C., Can.	110	D5	59.25 N	126.05 W
Liashchivka, Ukr.	38	D11	49.32 N	32.41 E
Liat, Pulau, i., Indon.	66	E5	2.53 S	107.05 E
Libagon, Phil.	68	E5	10.18 N	125.03 E
Líbano, Col.	168	E4	4.55 N	75.03 W
Libau see Liepāja, Lat.	26	D3	56.31 N	21.01 E
Libby, Mt., U.S.	146	B11	48.23 N	115.32 W
Libby Dam, dam., Mt., U.S.	146	B11	48.24 N	115.20 W
Libenge, D.R.C.	86	D3	3.39 N	18.38 E
Liberal, Ks., U.S.	138	D8	37.02 N	100.55 W
Liberal, Mo., U.S.	130	G3	37.33 N	94.31 W
Liberdade, ngh., Braz.	205b		23.35 S	46.37 W
Liberec, Czech Rep.	24	F11	50.46 N	15.03 E
Liberia, C.R.	156	G5	10.37 N	85.26 W
Liberia, ctry., Afr.	84	H3	6.30 N	9.30 W
Liberta, Antig.	159b	f4	17.01 N	61.47 W
Libertad, Ven.	168	C7	9.23 N	68.44 W
Libertad, Ven.	168	C7	8.21 N	69.38 W
Libertador, Arg.	172	E8	30.12 S	59.23 W
Libertador, state, Ven.	204c		10.27 N	66.57 W
Libertador General Bernardo O'Higgins, state, Chile	172	G2	34.31 S	71.13 W
Liberty, In., U.S.	130	E13	39.37 N	84.54 W
Liberty, Ky., U.S.	130	G13	37.19 N	84.56 W
Liberty, Ms., U.S.	134	F8	31.09 N	90.48 W
Liberty, Mo., U.S.	130	E3	39.14 N	94.25 W
Liberty, N.Y., U.S.	124	C11	41.48 N	74.44 W
Liberty, N.C., U.S.	124	I6	35.51 N	79.34 W
Liberty, Pa., U.S.	197b		40.20 N	79.51 W
Liberty, S.C., U.S.	132	B3	34.47 N	82.41 W
Liberty, Tx., U.S.	136	D13	30.03 N	94.47 W
Liberty Acres, Ca., U.S.	198		34.04 N	118.12 W
Liberty Center, Oh., U.S.	126	G5	41.26 N	84.00 W
Liberty Corner, N.J., U.S.	194		40.39 N	74.34 W
Liberty Hill, Tx., U.S.	136	D10	30.39 N	97.55 W
Liberty Island, i., N.J., U.S.	194		40.41 N	74.03 W
Liberty Manor, Md., U.S.	202b		39.21 N	76.47 W
Liberty Tree Mall, shp. cen., Ma., U.S.	201		42.33 N	70.57 W
Liberty Tunnel, trans., Pa., U.S.	197b		40.26 N	80.01 W
Libertyville, Il., U.S.	130	B10	42.18 N	87.55 W
Lībiyā see Libya, ctry., Afr.	82	B3	27.00 N	17.00 E
Lībīyah, Aṣ-Ṣaḥrā' al- see Libyan Desert, des., Afr.	82	C5	24.00 N	25.00 E
Libo, China	58	I2	25.28 N	107.53 E
Libobo, Tanjung, c., Indon.	60	F8	0.54 S	128.25 E
Libode, S. Afr.	90	G9	31.32 S	29.01 E
Libourne, Fr.	22	E5	44.55 N	0.14 W
Librazhd, Alb.	32	C14	41.11 N	20.18 E
Libres, Mex.	154	F10	19.28 N	97.41 W
Libreville, Gabon	86	D1	0.24 N	9.28 E
Libro Point, c., Phil.	68	E2	11.24 N	119.29 E
Libu, China	58	J4	23.39 N	111.32 E
Liburung, Indon.	66	F12	4.59 S	120.06 E
Libya, ctry., Afr.	82	B3	27.00 N	17.00 E
Libyan Desert, des., Afr.	82	C5	24.00 N	25.00 E
Libyan Plateau, plat., Afr.	82	A4	30.41 N	25.54 E
Licancábur, Volcán, vol., S.A.	166	D3	22.50 S	67.50 W
Licantén, Chile	172	G1	34.59 S	72.06 W
Licata, Italy	32	G7	37.06 N	13.56 E
Lice, Tur.	42	F9	38.27 N	40.39 E
Lich, Ger.	24	F4	50.31 N	8.49 E
Licheng, China	58	C5	36.29 N	113.21 E
Licheng see Liyang, China	58	F8	31.26 N	119.29 E
Lichfield, Eng., U.K.	10	I11	52.41 N	1.48 W
Lichinga, Moz.	88	C6	13.16 S	35.14 E
Lichitișeni, Rom.	36	C14	46.23 N	27.17 E
Lichtenau, Ger.	24	E5	51.11 N	9.43 E
Lichtenberg, ngh., Ger.	182a		52.31 N	13.29 E
Lichtenburg, S. Afr.	90	E7	26.09 S	26.10 E
Lichtendorf, Ger.	181		51.28 N	7.37 E
Lichtenfels, Ger.	24	F7	50.09 N	11.04 E
Lichtenplatz, ngh., Ger.	181		51.15 N	7.12 E
Lichtenrade, ngh., Ger.	182a		52.23 N	13.25 E
Lichterfelde, ngh., Ger.	182a		52.26 N	13.19 E
Lichuan, China	58	H7	27.17 N	116.54 E
Lichuan, China	58	F3	30.16 N	108.45 E
Lickershamn, Swe.	16	J16	57.49 N	18.32 E
Licking, Mo., U.S.	130	G6	37.30 N	91.51 W
Licking, stm., Ky., U.S.	124	F1	39.05 N	84.30 W
Licking, North Fork, stm., Ky., U.S.	130	F14	38.34 N	84.12 W
Licking, South Fork, stm., Ky., U.S.	124	F1	38.40 N	84.20 W
Ličko Polje, val., Cro.	30	F12	44.35 N	15.25 E
Lick Run, stm., Pa., U.S.	197b		40.17 N	79.57 W
Lid', Russia	18	H22	59.38 N	35.03 E
Lida, Bela.	26	G8	53.53 N	25.18 E
Lidan, stm., Swe.	16	I11	58.30 N	13.10 E
Lidcombe, Austl.	192a		33.52 S	151.03 E
Liddon Gulf, b., N.T., Can.	109	B17	75.03 N	113.00 W
Liden, Swe.	16	E14	62.42 N	16.48 E
Lidgerwood, N.D., U.S.	128	E1	46.04 N	97.09 W
Lídice, Pan.	156	H8	8.44 N	79.54 W
Lidingö, Swe.	16	H16	59.22 N	18.08 E
Lidköping, Swe.	16	I11	58.29 N	13.10 E
Lido Beach, N.Y., U.S.	194		40.35 N	73.38 W
Lido di Ostia, Italy	30	I9	41.44 N	12.16 E
Lidzbark, Pol.	24	C15	53.16 N	19.50 E
Lidzbark Warmiński, Pol.	24	B16	54.07 N	20.35 E
Liebenbergsvlei, stm., S. Afr.	90	E9	27.19 S	28.31 E
Liebig, Mount, mtn., Austl.	96	D6	23.18 S	131.22 E
Liechtenstein, ctry., Eur.	30	C6	47.09 N	9.35 E
Liedberg, Ger.	181		51.10 N	6.32 E
Liège (Luik), Bel.	20	D14	50.38 N	5.34 E
Liegnitz see Legnica, Pol.	24	E12	51.12 N	16.09 E
Lieksa, Fin.	18	D17	63.20 N	30.02 E
Lielais Liepu kalns, hill, Lat.	26	D10	56.14 N	27.35 E
Lielupe, stm., Lat.	26	D6	57.00 N	23.56 E
Lielvārde, Lat.	26	D7	56.43 N	24.51 E
Lienz, Aus.	30	D9	46.49 N	12.46 E
Liepāja, Lat.	26	D3	56.31 N	21.01 E
Liepājas ezers, l., Lat.	26	D4	56.29 N	21.03 E
Liepna, Lat.	26	C10	57.25 N	27.26 E
Liepnitzsee, l., Ger.	182a		52.45 N	13.30 E
Lier, Bel.	20	C13	51.08 N	4.34 E
Lierbyen, Nor.	16	H8	59.47 N	10.15 E
Lierenfeld, ngh., Ger.	181		51.13 N	6.51 E
Lierre see Lier, Bel.	20	C13	51.08 N	4.34 E
Lieser, stm., Ger.	20	D15	49.54 N	7.00 E
Liesing, ngh., Aus.	182b		48.08 N	16.17 E
Liesing, stm., Aus.	182b		48.08 N	16.28 E
Liesjärven kansallispuisto, p.o.i., Fin.	18	G10	60.40 N	23.54 E
Liestal, Switz.	30	C4	47.28 N	7.44 E
Liești, Rom.	36	D14	45.38 N	27.32 E
Lietuva see Lithuania, ctry., Eur.	26	E7	56.00 N	24.00 E
Lieusaint, Fr.	179		48.38 N	2.33 E
Lieutel, stm., Fr.	179		48.49 N	1.52 E
Lieutenant Robert J. Palenscar Memorial Airport, arpt., N.J., U.S.	203		39.51 N	75.03 W
Liévin, Fr.	20	D11	50.25 N	2.46 E
Lièvre, stm., Qc., Can.	114	C13	45.31 N	75.25 W
Lièvres, Île aux, i., Qc., Can.	122	C7	47.52 N	69.42 W
Liezen, Aus.	30	C11	47.34 N	14.14 E
Liffey, stm., Ire.	10	H6	53.20 N	6.14 W
Lifford, Ire.	10	G5	54.50 N	7.28 W
Lifou, i., N. Cal.	101d	m16	20.43 S	167.14 E
Lifoula, Congo	191b		4.06 S	15.25 E
Liftwood, De., U.S.	203		39.47 N	75.31 W
Ligačovo, Russia	183b		55.56 N	37.15 E
Ligao, Phil.	68	D4	13.14 N	123.33 E
Līgatne, Lat.	26	C7	57.11 N	24.59 E
Lighthouse Beach, cst., Nig.	191a		6.24 N	3.22 E
Lighthouse Point, Fl., U.S.	132	J5	26.16 N	80.05 W
Lighthouse Point, c., Fl., U.S.	134	H14	29.54 N	84.21 W
Lighthouse Point, c., Mi., U.S.	126	C4	45.11 N	85.32 W
Lightning Creek, stm., Sk., Can.	142	E12	49.10 N	101.43 W
Lightning Creek, stm., Wy., U.S.	140	D7	43.18 N	104.21 W
Lightning Ridge, Austl.	98	G6	29.31 S	148.00 E
Lignières, Fr.	20	H11	46.45 N	2.11 E
Lignite, N.D., U.S.	142	F11	48.52 N	102.33 W
Ligny-en-Barrois, Fr.	20	F14	48.41 N	5.19 E
Ligonha, stm., Moz.	88	D6	16.53 S	39.08 E
Ligonier, In., U.S.	130	C12	41.27 N	85.33 W
Ligonier, Pa., U.S.	126	H10	40.14 N	79.14 W
Ligovo, Russia	18	G18	60.12 N	31.47 E
Ligovo, ngh., Russia	183a		59.50 N	30.12 E
Ligovskij kanal, can., Russia	183a		59.47 N	30.10 E
Ligui, Mex.	154	C3	25.43 N	111.16 W
Ligure, Mar see Ligurian Sea, s., Eur.	30	G5	43.30 N	9.00 E
Liguria, state, Italy	30	F6	44.30 N	9.00 E
Ligurian Sea, s., Eur.	30	G5	43.30 N	9.00 E
Ligurienne, Mer see Ligurian Sea, s., Eur.	30	G5	43.30 N	9.00 E
Lihačova, mys, c., Russia	54	C10	42.44 N	132.51 E
Lihir Island, i., Pap. N. Gui.	101a	a5	3.09 S	152.35 E
Lihoborka, stm., Russia	183b		55.50 N	37.38 E
Lihoslavl', Russia	26	C18	57.07 N	35.28 E
Lihou Reefs and Cays, rf., Austl.	98	A8	17.25 S	151.40 E
Lihue, Hi., U.S.	100a	b2	21.58 N	159.22 W
Lihuel Calel, Parque Nacional, p.o.i., Arg.	172	H5	37.58 S	65.32 W
Lihula, Est.	26	B6	58.41 N	23.50 E
Liivi laht see Riga, Gulf of, b., Eur.	26	C6	57.30 N	23.35 E
Lijiang, China	52	F5	26.52 N	100.14 E
Lik, stm., Laos	64	C6	18.22 N	102.34 E
Likasi (Jadotville), D.R.C.	86	J6	10.58 S	26.43 E
Likati, D.R.C.	86	D4	3.22 N	23.52 E
Likely, B.C., Can.	144	D9	52.36 N	121.31 W
Likėnai, Lith.	26	D7	56.10 N	24.37 E
Likenäs, Swe.	16	G10	60.40 N	12.58 E
Liki, Indon.	66	D2	1.36 S	101.09 E
Likino-Dulevo, Russia	26	E21	55.41 N	38.57 E
Liknes, Nor.	16	I4	58.19 N	6.59 E
Likova, stm., Russia	183b		55.34 N	37.21 E
Lilbourn, Mo., U.S.	130	H8	36.35 N	89.37 W
L'Île-Cadieux, Qc., Can.	193a		45.25 N	74.01 W
L'Île-Rousse, Fr.	22	G14	42.37 N	8.56 E
Lilibeo, Capo see Boeo, Capo, c., Italy	32	G6	37.48 N	12.26 E
Lilienfeld, Aus.	30	B12	48.01 N	15.36 E
Liling, China	58	H5	27.40 N	113.29 E
Lilla Edet, Swe.	16	I10	58.07 N	12.08 E
Lilla Luleälven, stm., Swe.	14	F11	66.26 N	20.39 E
Lillby, Fin.	18	D10	63.28 N	23.00 E
Lille, Fr.	20	D12	50.38 N	3.07 E
Lillebælt, strt., Den.	16	L7	55.20 N	9.45 E
Lillebonne, Fr.	20	E9	49.31 N	0.32 E
Lillehammer, Nor.	16	F8	61.07 N	10.28 E
Lillers, Fr.	20	D11	50.34 N	2.29 E
Lillesand, Nor.	16	I6	58.15 N	8.24 E
Lillestrøm, Nor.	16	H9	59.57 N	11.03 E
Lillhärdal, Swe.	16	F11	61.51 N	14.03 E
Lillington, N.C., U.S.	132	A7	35.23 N	78.48 W
Lillinonah, Lake, res., Ct., U.S.	124	C12	41.28 N	73.20 W
Lilli Pilli, Austl.	192a		34.04 S	151.07 E
Lilljorm, l., Swe.	16	C12	64.42 N	14.01 E
Lillooet, B.C., Can.	144	F9	50.42 N	121.56 W
Lillooet, stm., B.C., Can.	144	G8	49.44 N	122.07 W
Lillooet Lake, l., B.C., Can.	144	F8	50.13 N	122.29 W
Lilongwe, Mwi.	88	C5	13.59 S	33.44 E
Lilo Viejo, Arg.	172	C6	26.56 S	62.57 W
Liloy, Phil.	68	F4	8.06 N	122.40 E
Liluāh, India	190b		22.35 N	88.23 E
Lily, Ky., U.S.	124	G1	37.01 N	84.04 W
Lily Cache Creek, stm., Il., U.S.	196		41.41 N	88.07 W
Lilydale, Austl.	99a	n13	41.15 S	147.12 E
Lilyfield, Austl.	192a		33.52 S	151.10 E
Lilyvale, S. Afr.	191d		26.06 S	28.25 E
Lim, stm., Eur.	30	G16	43.44 N	19.12 E
Lima, Para.	172	A9	23.50 S	56.31 W
Lima, Peru	164	F2	12.04 S	77.02 W
Lima, Peru	204d		12.03 S	77.03 W
Lima, Swe.	16	G11	60.55 N	13.23 E
Lima, Mt., U.S.	146	F14	44.38 N	112.35 W
Lima, N.Y., U.S.	124	B8	42.53 N	77.37 W
Lima, Oh., U.S.	124	D1	40.44 N	84.07 W
Lima, Pa., U.S.	203		39.55 N	75.26 W
Lima (Limia), stm., Eur.	28	C2	41.42 N	8.42 W
Lima, Punta, c., P.R.	158a	b4	18.11 N	65.41 W
Limanowa, Pol.	24	G16	49.43 N	20.24 E
Limão, ngh., Braz.	205b		23.30 S	46.40 W
Lima Reservoir, res., Mt., U.S.	146	F14	44.38 N	112.17 W
Limarí, stm., Chile	172	E2	30.43 S	71.42 W
Limas, Indon.	66	C4	0.11 N	104.32 E
Limassol see Lemesós, Cyp.	76	D4	34.41 N	33.02 E
Limavady, N. Ire., U.K.	10	F6	55.03 N	6.56 W
Limay, stm., Arg.	166	G3	38.59 S	68.00 W
Limay Mahuida, Arg.	172	H4	37.12 S	66.42 W

Name	Page	Map Ref.	Latitude	Longitude
Limbang, Malay.	66	A9	4.45 N	115.00 E
Limbang, stm., Malay.	66	A9	4.51 N	115.00 E
Limbara, Monte, mtn., Italy	32	D3	40.51 N	9.10 E
Limbaži, Lat.	26	C7	57.30 N	24.43 E
Limbdi, India	70	G3	22.33 N	71.48 E
Limbe, Cam.	86	D1	4.01 N	9.12 E
Limbé, Haiti	156	C11	19.42 N	72.24 W
Limbrick, Eng., U.K.	180		53.38 N	2.36 W
Limbujan see Pio V. Corpuz, Phil.	68	E5	11.53 N	124.03 E
Limburg an der Lahn, Ger.	24	F4	50.23 N	8.04 E
Lim Chu Kang, Sing.	189c		1.26 N	103.43 E
Limefield, Eng., U.K.	180		53.37 N	2.18 W
Limeira, Braz.	170	L2	22.33 S	47.23 W
Limekiln Canyon, val., Ca., U.S.	198		34.18 N	118.33 W
Limerick, Sk., Can.	142	E7	49.39 N	106.16 W
Limerick (Luimneach), Ire.	10	I4	52.40 N	8.38 W
Limerick, Pa., U.S.	203		40.14 N	75.32 W
Limerick, state, Ire.	10	I4	52.30 N	8.45 W
Lime Springs, Ia., U.S.	128	H6	43.26 N	92.16 W
Limestone, Me., U.S.	122	D9	46.54 N	67.49 W
Limestone, Lake, res., Tx., U.S.	136	C11	31.24 N	96.20 W
Limestone Canyon, val., Ca., U.S.	198		33.45 N	117.41 W
Lime Street Station, trans., Eng., U.K.	180		53.25 N	2.59 W
Limfjorden, l., Den.	16	K6	56.54 N	8.58 E
Limia (Lima), stm., Eur.	28	C2	41.42 N	8.42 W
Limingen, l., Nor.	16	C11	64.47 N	13.36 E
Liminka, Fin.	18	C12	64.48 N	25.26 E
Limit Brook, stm., U.S.	201		42.42 N	71.25 W
Limmared, Swe.	16	J11	57.32 N	13.21 E
Limmen Bight, b., Austl.	96	B7	14.45 S	135.40 E
Límnos, i., Grc.	34	D8	39.55 N	25.17 E
Limoeiro, Braz.	170	D8	7.52 S	35.27 W
Limoeiro do Norte, Braz.	170	C6	5.08 S	38.05 W
Limoges, Fr.	22	D7	45.49 N	1.15 E
Limoges-Fourches, Fr.	179		48.38 N	2.40 E
Limogne, Fr.	22	E7	44.24 N	1.46 E
Limón, Hond.	156	E5	15.50 N	85.30 W
Limon, Co., U.S.	138	B5	39.15 N	103.41 W
Limone Piemonte, Italy	30	F4	44.11 N	7.34 E
Limousin, Plateau du, plat., Fr.	22	D7	45.42 N	1.25 E
Limoux, Fr.	22	F8	43.04 N	2.12 E
Limpopo, stm., Afr.	90	D11	25.12 S	33.31 E
Limu, China	58	I4	25.02 N	110.51 E
Linaälven, stm., Swe.	14	F12	66.48 N	22.10 E
Līnah, Sau. Ar.	74	F8	28.43 N	43.47 E
Linahamari, Russia	14	C22	69.39 N	31.22 E
Lin'an, China	58	F8	30.13 N	119.42 E
Linapacan Island, i., Phil.	68	E2	11.27 N	119.49 E
Linares, Chile	172	G2	35.50 S	71.35 W
Linares, Mex.	154	C9	24.51 N	99.33 W
Linares, Spain	28	F7	38.05 N	3.37 W
Linariá, Grc.	34	E7	38.51 N	24.32 E
Linas, Fr.	179		48.38 N	2.16 E
Linas-Montlhéry, Domaine Militaire de, mil., Fr.	179		48.37 N	2.13 E
Lince, Peru	204d		12.06 S	77.03 W
Linch, Wy., U.S.	140	D6	43.36 N	106.11 W
Lincheng, China	58	C6	37.26 N	114.28 E
Lincoln, Arg.	172	G7	34.51 S	61.31 W
Lincoln, Eng., U.K.	10	H12	53.13 N	0.32 W
Lincoln, Ar., U.S.	130	I3	35.57 N	94.25 W
Lincoln, Ca., U.S.	148	E4	38.53 N	121.17 W
Lincoln, Il., U.S.	130	D8	40.08 N	89.21 W
Lincoln, Ks., U.S.	138	B10	39.02 N	98.08 W
Lincoln, Me., U.S.	122	E8	45.22 N	68.30 W
Lincoln, Mi., U.S.	126	D6	44.41 N	83.24 W
Lincoln, Mo., U.S.	130	F4	38.23 N	93.20 W
Lincoln, Mt., U.S.	146	D14	46.57 N	112.40 W
Lincoln, Ne., U.S.	128	K2	40.48 N	96.41 W
Lincoln, N.H., U.S.	122	F5	44.02 N	71.40 W
Lincoln, Pa., U.S.	197b		40.18 N	79.51 W
Lincoln, Mount, mtn., Co., U.S.	138	B2	39.21 N	106.07 W
Lincoln Boyhood National Memorial, p.o.i., In., U.S.	130	F11	38.08 N	86.58 W
Lincoln Center, bldg., N.Y., U.S.	194		40.46 N	73.59 W
Lincoln City, Or., U.S.	146	F2	44.57 N	124.00 W
Lincoln Creek, stm., Ne., U.S.	140	F15	40.54 N	97.06 W
Lincoln Estates, Il., U.S.	196		41.31 N	87.49 W
Lincoln Hav see Lincoln Sea, s., N.A.	108	A14	83.00 N	56.00 W
Lincoln Heights, Pa., U.S.	197b		40.19 N	79.37 W
Lincolnia Heights, Va., U.S.	202c		38.50 N	77.09 W
Lincoln Memorial, hist., D.C., U.S.	202c		38.53 N	77.03 W
Lincoln Park, Co., U.S.	138	C3	38.25 N	105.12 W
Lincoln Park, Ga., U.S.	132	D1	32.51 N	84.19 W
Lincoln Park, Mi., U.S.	124	B2	42.14 N	83.10 W
Lincoln Park, N.J., U.S.	194		40.55 N	74.18 W
Lincoln Park, p.o.i., Ca., U.S.	200		37.46 N	122.30 W
Lincoln Park, p.o.i., Il., U.S.	196		41.56 N	87.38 W
Lincoln Park Airport, arpt., N.J., U.S.	194		40.57 N	74.19 W
Lincoln Place, ngh., Pa., U.S.	197b		40.22 N	79.55 W
Lincoln Sea, s., N.A.	108	A14	83.00 N	56.00 W
Lincoln's New Salem State Park, p.o.i., Il., U.S.	130	D8	39.58 N	89.52 W
Lincolnton, Ga., U.S.	132	C3	33.47 N	82.28 W
Lincolnton, N.C., U.S.	132	A4	35.28 N	81.15 W
Lincoln Tunnel, trans., U.S.	194		40.46 N	74.01 W
Lincoln Village, Ca., U.S.	148	F4	38.00 N	121.19 W
Lincolnwood, Il., U.S.	196		42.00 N	87.43 W
Lincolnwood Hills, Il., U.S.	196		41.31 N	87.54 W
Linconia, Pa., U.S.	203		40.08 N	74.59 W
Lind, Wa., U.S.	146	C8	46.58 N	118.36 W
Linda-a-Velha, Port.	184c		38.43 N	9.14 W
Lindale, Ga., U.S.	134	C13	34.11 N	85.10 W
Lindale, Tx., U.S.	136	B12	32.31 N	95.24 W
Lindau, Ger.	24	I5	47.33 N	9.42 E
Lind Coulee, stm., Wa., U.S.	146	C8	47.04 N	119.00 W
Linde, stm., Russia	50	C13	64.57 N	124.36 E
Linden, Guy.	164	B6	6.04 N	58.16 W
Linden, Al., U.S.	134	E11	32.18 N	87.47 W
Linden, In., U.S.	130	D11	40.11 N	86.53 W
Linden, Mi., U.S.	124	B2	42.49 N	83.46 W
Linden, Pa., U.S.	197b		40.14 N	80.08 W
Linden, Tn., U.S.	134	B11	35.36 N	87.50 W
Linden, Tx., U.S.	136	A13	33.00 N	94.22 W
Linden, ngh., S. Afr.	191d		26.08 S	28.00 E
Linden Airport, arpt., N.J., U.S.	194		40.37 N	74.15 W
Linden-Dahlhausen, ngh., Ger.	181		51.26 N	7.09 E
Lindenhorst, ngh., Ger.	181		51.33 N	7.27 E
Lindenhurst, Pa., U.S.	203		40.14 N	74.54 W
Linderhausen, Ger.	181		51.18 N	7.17 E
Linderödsåsen, hills, Swe.	16	K11	55.50 N	13.52 E
Lindesberg, Swe.	16	H13	59.35 N	15.12 E
Lindesnes, c., Nor.	16	J4	58.00 N	7.02 E
Lindfield, Austl.	192a		33.47 S	151.10 E
Lindi, Tan.	86	F7	9.59 S	39.42 E
Lindi, stm., D.R.C.	86	D5	0.33 N	25.04 E
Lindley, S. Afr.	90	E8	27.53 S	27.55 E
Lindome, Swe.	16	J9	57.34 N	12.04 E
Lindon, Co., U.S.	138	B5	39.43 N	103.24 W
Lindos, Grc.	34	G11	36.05 N	28.04 E
Líndos, hist., Grc.	34	G10	36.05 N	28.03 E
Lindozero, Russia	18	E20	62.27 N	33.13 E
Lind Point, c., V.I.U.S.	158b	e7	18.20 N	64.48 W
Lindsay, On., Can.	126	D11	44.20 N	78.44 W
Lindsay, Ca., U.S.	148	G6	36.12 N	119.05 W
Lindsay, Ne., U.S.	140	F15	41.40 N	97.40 W
Lindsay, Ok., U.S.	138	G11	34.49 N	97.36 W
Lindsborg, Ks., U.S.	138	C11	38.34 N	97.40 W
Lindy Lake, N.J., U.S.	194		41.05 N	74.22 W
Line Creek, stm., Ms., U.S.	134	D10	33.34 N	88.42 W
Line Islands, is., Oc.	94	C11	0.05 N	157.00 W
Linesøya, i., Nor.	16	C7	64.01 N	9.54 E
Linesville, Pa., U.S.	124	C5	41.38 N	80.25 W
Lineville, Al., U.S.	134	D13	33.18 N	85.45 W
Lineville, Ia., U.S.	130	D4	40.34 N	93.32 W
Linëvo, Russia	40	F14	50.52 N	44.49 E
Linfen, China	58	C4	36.05 N	111.31 E
Linford, Eng., U.K.	178		51.29 N	0.25 E
Linganamakki Reservoir, res., India	69	D2	14.04 N	74.54 E
Lingao, China	58	L3	19.54 N	109.40 E
Lingayen, Phil.	68	B3	16.01 N	120.14 E
Lingayen Gulf, b., Phil.	68	B3	16.15 N	120.14 E
Lingbi, China	58	E7	33.32 N	117.33 E
Lingbo, Swe.	16	F14	61.02 N	16.41 E
Lingchuan, China	58	D5	35.46 N	113.26 E
Lingchuan, China	58	I4	25.23 N	110.18 E
Lingen, Ger.	24	D3	52.31 N	7.19 E
Lingesestausee, res., Ger.	181		51.06 N	7.32 E
Lingfengwei, China	58	I6	24.43 N	115.38 E
Lingga, Kepulauan, is., Indon.	66	C4	0.05 S	104.35 E
Lingga, Pulau, i., Indon.	66	D4	0.12 S	104.35 E
Lingle, Wy., U.S.	140	E8	42.06 N	104.20 W
Lingling see Yongzhou, China	58	H4	26.13 N	111.37 E
Lingma, China	58	J2	23.23 N	107.54 E
Lingomo II, D.R.C.	86	D4	0.42 N	22.01 E
Lingqiu, China	58	B6	39.26 N	114.13 E
Lingshan, China	58	J3	22.25 N	109.17 E
Lingshi, China	58	C4	36.54 N	111.43 E
Lingshui, China	58	L4	18.29 N	110.02 E
Linguère, Sen.	84	F2	15.22 N	15.07 W
Lingwala, D.R.C.	191b		4.22 S	15.17 E
Lingwu, China	58	B2	38.06 N	106.20 E
Lingxian, China	58	H5	26.29 N	113.45 E
Lingyuan, China	58	A8	41.15 N	119.16 E
Linh, Ngoc, mtn., Viet.	64	E9	15.04 N	107.59 E
Linhai, China	58	G9	28.51 N	121.07 E
Linhares, Braz.	170	J5	19.23 S	40.04 W
Linhe, China	58	A2	40.48 N	107.30 E
Linhigh, Md., U.S.	202b		39.21 N	76.31 W
Linhó, Port.	184c		38.46 N	9.23 W
Linjiang, China	54	D7	41.48 N	126.55 E
Linköping, Swe.	16	I13	58.24 N	15.36 E
Linkou, China	52	B11	45.18 N	130.16 E
Linksfield, ngh., S. Afr.	191d		26.10 S	28.06 E
Linksmakalnis, Lith.	26	F6	54.44 N	23.55 E
Linkuva, Lith.	26	D6	56.05 N	23.59 E
Linli, China	58	G4	29.18 N	111.37 E
Linmeyer, S. Afr.	191d		26.16 S	28.04 E
Linn, Ks., U.S.	138	B11	39.40 N	97.05 W
Linn, Mo., U.S.	130	F6	38.29 N	91.51 W
Linn, ngh., Ger.	181		51.20 N	6.38 E
Linnansaaren kansallispuisto, p.o.i., Fin.	18	E15	62.05 N	28.28 E
Linndale, Oh., U.S.	197a		41.27 N	81.46 W
Linnhe, Loch, b., Scot., U.K.	10	E7	56.39 N	5.21 W
Linosa, Isola di, i., Italy	32	I6	35.52 N	12.51 E
Linqi, China	58	D5	35.48 N	113.53 E
Linqing, China	58	C6	36.50 N	115.41 E
Linqu, China	58	C8	36.30 N	118.31 E
Linquan, China	58	E6	33.03 N	115.15 E
Linru, China	58	D5	34.09 N	112.50 E
Lins, Braz.	170	K1	21.40 S	49.45 W
Linstead, Jam.	158d	i13	18.08 N	77.02 W
Lintan, China	52	E5	34.36 N	103.42 E
Linthal, Switz.	30	D6	46.53 N	8.59 E
Linthicum Heights, Md., U.S.	202b		39.12 N	76.39 W
Linthwaite, Eng., U.K.	180		53.37 N	1.51 W
Linton, Eng., U.K.	178		51.13 N	0.31 E
Linton, In., U.S.	130	E10	39.01 N	87.10 W
Linton, N.D., U.S.	140	A12	46.16 N	100.14 W
Lintong, China	58	D3	34.19 N	109.05 E
Linton Park, p.o.i., Eng., U.K.	178		51.13 N	0.31 E
Linum, Ger.	182a		52.46 N	12.53 E
Linville, N.C., U.S.	124	H4	36.04 N	81.52 W
Linwood, Pa., U.S.	203		39.49 N	75.24 W
Linwu, China	58	I5	25.16 N	112.20 E
Linxi, China	52	C8	43.36 N	118.02 E
Linxi, China	54	C3	43.36 N	118.02 E
Linxia, China	52	D5	35.36 N	103.12 E
Linxian, China	58	C5	36.03 N	114.00 E
Linxian, China	58	C4	37.46 N	110.57 E
Linyi, China	58	D8	35.04 N	118.22 E
Linyi, China	58	D4	35.12 N	110.59 E
Linyi, China	58	C7	37.10 N	116.51 E
Linz, Aus.	30	B11	48.17 N	14.18 E
Lio Matoh, Malay.	66	B9	3.11 N	115.17 E
Lion, Golfe du, b., Fr.	22	G10	43.00 N	4.00 E
Lion, Gulf of see Lion, Golfe du, b., Fr.	22	G10	43.00 N	4.00 E
Lionel Town, Jam.	158d	j13	17.48 N	77.15 W
Lion Rock, hill, China	189d		22.22 N	114.11 E
Lion Rock Tunnel, trans., China	189d		22.21 N	114.09 E
Liouesso, Congo	86	D3	1.02 N	15.41 E
Lipa, Phil.	68	D3	13.56 N	121.09 E
Lipan, Tx., U.S.	136	B9	32.31 N	98.03 W
Lipany, Slvk.	24	G16	49.09 N	20.57 E
Lipari, Italy	32	F8	38.28 N	14.57 E
Lipari, Isola, i., Italy	32	F9	38.29 N	14.56 E
Lipari, Isole see Eolie, Isole, is., Italy	32	F8	38.30 N	14.50 E
Lipatkain, Indon.	66	D2	0.01 S	101.12 E
Lipcani, Mol.	38	E5	48.16 N	26.48 E
Lipeck, Russia	40	E11	52.36 N	39.37 E
Lipeck see Lipeckaja oblast', co., Russia	40	E11	52.30 N	39.00 E
Lipeckaja oblast', co., Russia	40	E11	52.30 N	39.00 E
Liperi, Fin.	18	E16	62.31 N	29.23 E
Lipetsk see Lipeckaja oblast', co., Russia	40	E11	52.30 N	39.00 E
Lípez, Cerro, mtn., Bol.	166	D3	21.55 S	66.53 W
Lipiany, Pol.	24	C10	53.00 N	14.57 E
Lipicy, Russia	26	G20	53.21 N	37.16 E
Lipin Bor, Russia	18	G24	60.15 N	38.12 E
Liping, China	58	H3	26.16 N	108.59 E
Lipka, stm., Russia	183b		55.45 N	37.11 E
Lipkany see Lipcani, Mol.	38	E5	48.16 N	26.48 E
Lipki, Russia	26	G20	53.55 N	37.42 E
Lipliave, Ukr.	38	D10	49.47 N	31.33 E
Lipník nad Bečvou, Czech Rep.	24	G13	49.31 N	17.34 E
Lipniški, Bela.	26	F8	54.00 N	25.36 E
Lipno, Pol.	24	D15	52.50 N	19.10 E
Lipno, údolní nádrž, res., Czech Rep.	24	H10	48.43 N	14.04 E
Lipoa Point, c., Hi., U.S.	100a	b5	21.01 N	156.38 W
Lipova, Rom.	36	C8	46.05 N	21.42 E
Lipovcy, Russia	54	B9	44.12 N	131.43 E
Lipovka, Russia	38	C18	50.52 N	40.02 E
Lippe, stm., Ger.	24	E2	51.38 N	6.36 E
Lippehne see Lipiany, Pol.	24	C10	53.00 N	14.57 E
Lippstadt, Ger.	24	E4	51.39 N	8.19 E
Lipscomb, Tx., U.S.	138	E8	36.13 N	100.16 W
Lipsko, Pol.	24	E17	51.09 N	21.39 E
Lipton, Sk., Can.	142	D10	50.55 N	103.51 W
Liptovská Teplička, Slvk.	24	G15	48.59 N	20.06 E
Liptovský Mikuláš, Slvk.	24	G15	49.04 N	19.37 E
Liptrap, Cape, c., Austl.	98	L5	38.54 S	145.55 E
Lipu, China	58	I4	24.25 N	110.29 E
Lira, Ug.	86	D6	2.15 N	32.54 E
Lira, Ven.	204c		10.26 N	66.46 W
Liri, stm., Italy	32	C7	41.24 N	13.51 E
Liria see Llíria, Spain	28	E10	39.37 N	0.36 W
Liro, Vanuatu	101d	k17	16.28 S	168.14 E
Lisala, D.R.C.	86	D4	2.08 N	21.31 E
Lisboa (Lisbon), Port.	28	F1	38.42 N	9.08 W
Lisboa (Lisbon), Port.	184c		38.43 N	9.08 W
Lisboa, state, Port.	28	E1	38.48 N	9.16 W
Lisboa, state, Port.	184c		38.48 N	9.16 W
Lisbon see Lisboa, Port.	28	F1	38.42 N	9.08 W
Lisbon, N.H., U.S.	122	F5	44.12 N	71.54 W
Lisbon, N.D., U.S.	140	A15	46.26 N	97.41 W
Lisbon, Oh., U.S.	124	D5	40.46 N	80.45 W
Lisbon Falls, Me., U.S.	122	F6	44.00 N	70.03 W
Lisburn, N. Ire., U.K.	10	G6	54.31 N	6.03 W
Lisburne, Cape, c., Ak., U.S.	109	C6	68.52 N	166.14 W
Liscannor Bay, b., Ire.	10	I3	52.55 N	9.25 W
Liscia, stm., Italy	32	C3	41.11 N	9.18 E
Lishchynivka, Ukr.	38	D13	49.16 N	34.13 E
Lishe, China	58	G9	29.48 N	121.28 E
Lishi, China	58	C4	37.30 N	111.08 E
Lishu, China	52	C9	43.20 N	124.34 E
Lishui, China	58	G8	28.26 N	119.54 E
Lishuzhen, China	54	B9	45.04 N	130.41 E
Lisičansk see Lysychans'k, Ukr.	38	E17	48.54 N	38.26 E
Lisicy, Russia	26	D19	56.47 N	36.21 E
Lisieux, Sk., Can.	142	E7	49.16 N	105.59 W
Lisieux, Fr.	20	E9	49.08 N	0.14 E
Lisij Nos, Russia	183a		60.01 N	30.00 E
Lisivshchyna, Ukr.	38	C7	50.47 N	28.35 E
Lisjön, l., Swe.	16	G12	60.07 N	14.16 E
Liski, Russia	40	F11	50.58 N	39.30 E
L'Isle-Jourdain, Fr.	22	C6	46.14 N	0.41 E
Lisman, Al., U.S.	134	E10	32.10 N	88.17 W
Lismore, Austl.	98	G9	28.48 S	153.16 E
Lismore, N.S., Can.	122	E14	45.42 N	62.16 W
Lismore, Ire.	10	I5	52.08 N	7.56 W
Lismore Island, i., Scot., U.K.	10	E7	56.29 N	5.33 W
Lišov, Czech Rep.	24	G10	49.00 N	14.36 E
Lisses, Fr.	179		48.36 N	2.26 E
Lissy, Fr.	179		48.38 N	2.42 E
Lista, pen., Nor.	16	I4	58.07 N	6.40 E
Listafjorden, b., Nor.	16	I4	58.11 N	6.37 E
Lister, stm., Ger.	181		51.05 N	7.45 E
Lištica, Bos.	36	F4	43.23 N	17.36 E
Listowel, On., Can.	126	E9	43.44 N	80.56 W
Listowel, Ire.	10	I3	52.27 N	9.29 W
Lit, Swe.	16	D12	63.19 N	14.49 E
Litang, China	52	F5	29.59 N	100.15 E
Litang, China	58	J3	23.12 N	109.08 E
Litchfield, Il., U.S.	130	E8	39.10 N	89.39 W
Litchfield, Mi., U.S.	124	B1	42.02 N	84.45 W
Litchfield, Mn., U.S.	128	F4	45.07 N	94.31 W
Litchfield, Ne., U.S.	140	F13	41.09 N	99.09 W
Litchfield Park, Az., U.S.	150	J4	33.29 N	112.21 W
Litchville, N.D., U.S.	140	A14	46.39 N	98.11 W
Lithgow, Austl.	98	I8	33.29 S	150.08 E
Líthino, Ákra, c., Grc.	34	I7	34.55 N	24.44 E
Lithonia, Ga., U.S.	134	D14	33.42 N	84.06 W
Lithuania, ctry., Eur.	26	E7	56.00 N	24.00 E
Litija, Slvn.	30	D11	46.03 N	14.50 E
Lititz, Pa., U.S.	124	D9	40.09 N	76.18 W
Litóchoro, Grc.	34	C5	40.06 N	22.30 E
Litoměřice, Czech Rep.	24	F10	50.32 N	14.07 E
Litomyšl, Czech Rep.	24	G12	49.52 N	16.19 E
Litovel, Czech Rep.	24	G13	49.42 N	17.05 E
Litovko, Russia	50	G16	49.14 N	135.10 E
Little, stm., On., Can.	199		42.20 N	82.56 W
Little, stm., U.S.	134	B8	31.34 N	92.15 W
Little, stm., U.S.	134	D5	33.36 N	93.50 W
Little, stm., Al., U.S.	134	F11	31.18 N	87.46 W
Little, stm., Al., U.S.	134	C13	34.14 N	85.40 W
Little, stm., Ga., U.S.	132	E2	30.51 N	83.21 W
Little, stm., Ga., U.S.	132	C3	33.41 N	82.15 W
Little, stm., Ga., U.S.	132	C2	33.13 N	83.24 W
Little, stm., Ky., U.S.	130	H10	36.51 N	87.58 W
Little, stm., Ma., U.S.	201		42.46 N	70.51 W
Little, stm., Ma., U.S.	201		42.37 N	70.42 W
Little, stm., N.C., U.S.	132	A7	35.40 N	78.16 W
Little, stm., N.C., U.S.	132	A7	35.15 N	78.42 W
Little, stm., Ok., U.S.	138	F11	35.00 N	96.21 W
Little, stm., S.C., U.S.	132	B3	33.50 N	82.21 W
Little, stm., S.C., U.S.	132	B4	34.11 N	81.45 W
Little, stm., S.C., U.S.	132	B4	34.10 N	81.11 W
Little, stm., Tn., U.S.	134	B15	35.39 N	83.43 W
Little, stm., Tx., U.S.	136	D11	30.50 N	96.40 W
Little, stm., Va., U.S.	124	G5	37.04 N	80.35 W
Little, Mountain Fork, stm., U.S.	134	C4	33.56 N	94.34 W
Little Abaco, i., Bah.	132	J8	26.54 N	77.43 W
Little Amwell, Eng., U.K.	178		51.47 N	0.02 W
Little Andaman, i., India	62	F7	10.45 N	92.30 E
Little Arkansas, stm., Ks., U.S.	138	C11	37.43 N	97.22 W
Little Baddow, Eng., U.K.	178		51.44 N	0.35 E
Little Bay, b., N.Y., U.S.	194		40.48 N	73.47 W
Little Bear, stm., Ut., U.S.	150	B5	41.44 N	111.55 W
Little Bear Creek, stm., U.S.	138	D6	37.43 N	101.43 W
Little Bear Creek Reservoir, res., Al., U.S.	134	C11	34.26 N	87.57 W
Little Beaver Creek, stm., U.S.	138	B7	39.49 N	101.03 W
Little Beaver Creek, stm., U.S.	140	A8	46.17 N	103.56 W
Little Belt see Lillebælt, strt., Den.	16	L7	55.20 N	9.45 E
Little Belt Mountains, mts., Mt., U.S.	146	D16	46.45 N	110.35 W
Little Berkhamsted, Eng., U.K.	178		51.45 N	0.08 W
Little Bighorn, stm., U.S.	140	B5	45.44 N	107.34 W
Little Bighorn Battlefield National Monument, p.o.i., Mt., U.S.	140	B5	45.32 N	107.20 W
Little Bitter Lake see Murrat el-Sughra, Buheirat, l., Egypt	76	H3	30.13 N	32.33 E
Little Bitterroot, stm., Mt., U.S.	146	C12	47.29 N	114.20 W
Little Black, stm., U.S.	130	H7	36.25 N	90.45 W
Little Black Bear Indian Reserve, ind. res., Sk., Can.	142	C10	51.00 N	103.23 W
Little Blackfoot, stm., Mt., U.S.	146	D14	46.31 N	112.47 W
Little Black Mountain, mts., U.S.	124	H3	36.55 N	83.00 W
Little Blue, stm., U.S.	140	G16	40.15 N	98.00 W
Little Bow, stm., Ab., Can.	144	F17	49.53 N	112.28 W
Little Buffalo, stm., Can.	110	C8	61.00 N	113.46 W
Little Bullhead, Mb., Can.	142	C17	51.40 N	96.49 W
Little Burstead, Eng., U.K.	178		51.36 N	0.24 E
Little Calumet, stm., U.S.	196		41.39 N	87.34 W
Little Carpathians see Malé Karpaty, mts., Slvk.	24	H13	48.30 N	17.20 E
Little Cayman, i., Cay. Is.	156	C7	19.42 N	80.01 W
Little Chalfont, Eng., U.K.	178		51.40 N	0.34 W
Little Chartiers Creek, stm., Pa., U.S.	197b		40.17 N	80.08 W
Little Chute, Wi., U.S.	126	D1	44.16 N	88.18 W
Little Colorado, stm., Az., U.S.	150	H5	36.11 N	111.48 W
Little Cottonwood, stm., Mn., U.S.	128	G4	44.15 N	94.20 W
Little Creek, stm., N.J., U.S.	203		39.56 N	74.48 W
Little Current, On., Can.	126	C8	45.58 N	81.55 W
Little Current, stm., On., Can.	128	A12	50.36 N	86.43 W
Little Cypress Bayou, stm., Tx., U.S.	136	B13	32.42 N	94.05 W
Little Deep Creek, stm., N.D., U.S.	142	F12	48.34 N	100.52 W
Little Deer Creek, stm., Pa., U.S.	197b		40.33 N	79.50 W
Little Deschutes, stm., Or., U.S.	146	G5	43.51 N	121.27 W
Little Desert, des., Austl.	98	K3	36.35 S	141.20 E
Little Desert National Park, p.o.i., Austl.	98	K3	36.34 S	141.28 E
Little Don, stm., On., Can.	193b		43.42 N	79.20 W
Little Dry Creek, stm., Mt., U.S.	142	G7	47.20 N	106.22 W
Little Ease Run, stm., N.J., U.S.	203		39.39 N	75.04 W
Little Eau Pleine, stm., Wi., U.S.	128	G9	44.40 N	89.40 W
Little End, Eng., U.K.	178		51.41 N	0.14 E
Little Etobicoke Creek, stm., On., Can.	193b		43.37 N	79.34 W
Little Falls, Mn., U.S.	128	E4	45.58 N	94.21 W
Little Falls, N.J., U.S.	194		40.52 N	74.12 W
Little Falls, N.Y., U.S.	126	E15	43.02 N	74.51 W
Little Ferry, N.J., U.S.	194		40.51 N	74.02 W
Littlefield, Tx., U.S.	138	H6	33.55 N	102.20 W
Littlefork, Mn., U.S.	128	C5	48.22 N	93.33 W
Little Fork, stm., Mn., U.S.	128	C5	48.31 N	93.35 W
Little Fort, B.C., Can.	144	E10	51.24 N	120.13 W
Little Hulton, Eng., U.K.	180		53.32 N	2.25 W
Little Humboldt, stm., Nv., U.S.	148	B8	41.01 N	117.42 W
Little Humboldt, North Fork, stm., Nv., U.S.	148	B8	41.25 N	117.10 W
Little Humboldt, South Fork, stm., Nv., U.S.	148	B9	41.24 N	117.09 W
Little Hurricane Creek, stm., Ga., U.S.	132	E3	31.14 N	82.08 W
Little Inagua, i., Bah.	156	B11	21.30 N	73.00 W
Little Island Pond, l., N.H., U.S.	201		42.43 N	71.17 W
Little Juniata, stm., Pa., U.S.	126	H11	40.33 N	78.03 W
Little Kanawha, stm., W.V., U.S.	124	E4	39.15 N	81.34 W
Little Kanawha, West Fork, stm., W.V., U.S.	124	F5	38.57 N	81.16 W
Little Karroo (Klein Karroo), plat., S. Afr.	90	H5	33.45 S	21.30 E
Little Lake, l., La., U.S.	134	H8	29.30 N	90.10 W
Little Laramie, stm., Wy., U.S.	140	F7	41.28 N	105.44 W
Little Laver, Eng., U.K.	178		51.46 N	0.14 E
Little Leigh, Eng., U.K.	180		53.17 N	2.35 W
Little Lever, Eng., U.K.	180		53.34 N	2.22 W
Little London, Jam.	158d	i12	18.13 N	78.10 W
Little Lost, stm., Id., U.S.	146	F13	43.45 N	112.59 W
Little Manistee, stm., Mi., U.S.	126	D3	44.15 N	86.18 W
Little Manitou Lake, l., Sk., Can.	142	C8	51.43 N	105.30 W
Little Medicine Bow, stm., Wy., U.S.	140	E6	41.58 N	106.17 W
Little Mexico, Tx., U.S.	136	D5	30.57 N	102.52 W
Little Missouri, stm., U.S.	118	D14	47.36 N	102.16 W
Little Missouri, stm., Ar., U.S.	134	D5	33.48 N	92.53 W
Little Muddy, stm., Il., U.S.	130	F8	37.49 N	89.11 W
Little Muddy, stm., N.D., U.S.	142	F10	48.07 N	103.36 W
Little Mulberry Creek, stm., Al., U.S.	134	E12	32.26 N	86.51 W
Little Nahant, Ma., U.S.	201		42.25 N	70.56 W
Little Namaqualand (Klein Namaland), hist. reg., S. Afr.	90	F3	29.00 S	17.00 E
Little Neck, Ma., U.S.	201		42.42 N	70.48 W
Little Neck, ngh., N.Y., U.S.	194		40.46 N	73.44 W
Little Neck Bay, b., N.Y., U.S.	194		40.47 N	73.46 W
Little Nemaha, stm., Ne., U.S.	128	K2	40.18 N	95.39 W
Little Neshaminy Creek, stm., Pa., U.S.	203		40.15 N	75.02 W
Little Nicobar, i., India	62	G7	7.20 N	93.40 E
Little Ohoopee, stm., Ga., U.S.	132	D3	32.27 N	82.25 W
Little Osage, stm., U.S.	130	G3	38.01 N	94.14 W
Little Ouse, stm., Eng., U.K.	10	I13	52.29 N	0.21 E
Little Patuxent, stm., Md., U.S.	202b		39.11 N	76.52 W
Little Pee Dee, stm., S.C., U.S.	132	B6	33.42 N	79.11 W
Little Pic, stm., On., Can.	128	C12	48.48 N	86.37 W
Little Pine and Lucky Man Indian Reserve, ind. res., Sk., Can.	142	B4	52.56 N	109.05 W
Little Pine Creek, stm., Pa., U.S.	197b		40.31 N	79.57 W
Little Platte, stm., Mo., U.S.	138	B14	39.23 N	94.41 W
Little Plum Creek, stm., Pa., U.S.	197b		40.30 N	79.51 W
Little Popo Agie River, stm., Wy., U.S.	140	E4	42.54 N	108.35 W
Little Porcupine Creek, stm., Mt., U.S.	142	H7	46.17 N	106.33 W
Little Powder, stm., U.S.	140	B7	45.27 N	105.20 W
Little Pucketa Creek, stm., Pa., U.S.	197b		40.33 N	79.45 W
Little Quill Lake, l., Sk., Can.	142	C10	51.55 N	104.05 W
Little Rann of Kachchh, reg., India	70	G3	23.25 N	71.15 E
Little Red, stm., Ar., U.S.	134	B7	35.10 N	91.25 W
Little Red, Middle Fork, stm., Ar., U.S.	134	B6	35.35 N	92.09 W
Little Red Deer, stm., Ab., Can.	144	E16	52.03 N	114.08 W
Little River, N.Z.	102	F5	43.46 S	172.46 E
Little River, Ks., U.S.	138	C10	38.24 N	98.01 W
Little Rock, Ar., U.S.	134	C6	34.44 N	92.17 W
Little Rock, stm., U.S.	128	H2	43.15 N	96.15 W
Little Rock Air Force Base, mil., Ar., U.S.	134	C6	34.54 N	92.07 W
Little Rocky Mountains, mts., Mt., U.S.	142	G5	48.00 N	108.33 W
Little Sable Point, c., Mi., U.S.	126	E3	43.38 N	86.32 W
Little Sac, stm., Mo., U.S.	130	G4	37.39 N	93.45 W
Little Saint Bernard Pass, p., Eur.	30	E3	45.41 N	6.51 E
Little Salkehatchie, stm., S.C., U.S.	132	C5	32.48 N	80.52 W
Little Salmon, stm., Id., U.S.	146	E10	45.25 N	116.19 W
Little Salt Lake, l., Ut., U.S.	150	F4	37.55 N	112.53 W
Little Sandy, stm., Ky., U.S.	124	F3	38.34 N	82.51 W
Little Sandy, East Fork, stm., Ky., U.S.	124	F3	38.29 N	82.50 W
Little Sandy Creek, stm., Wy., U.S.	140	E3	42.06 N	109.27 W
Little Saskatchewan, stm., Mb., Can.	142	E13	49.52 N	100.08 W
Little Sewickley Creek, stm., Pa., U.S.	197b		40.33 N	80.12 W
Little Sewickley Creek, stm., Pa., U.S.	197b		40.15 N	79.45 W
Little Silver, N.J., U.S.	194		40.20 N	74.02 W
Little Sioux, stm., U.S.	128	J2	41.48 N	96.06 W
Little Sioux, West Fork, stm., Ia., U.S.	130	B2	42.04 N	96.01 W
Little Sitkin Island, i., Ak., U.S.	109a	g22	51.57 N	178.32 E
Little Smoky, stm., Ab., Can.	110	E7	55.39 N	117.38 W
Little Snake, stm., U.S.	150	C8	40.27 N	108.26 W
Little Sound, b., Ber.	158e	k15	32.15 N	64.51 W
Little Southwest Miramichi, stm., N.B., Can.	122	D10	46.56 N	65.49 W
Little Stanney, Eng., U.K.	180		53.15 N	2.53 W
Littlestown, Pa., U.S.	124	E8	39.44 N	77.05 W
Little Sugarloaf, hill, Austl.	192b		37.41 S	145.19 E
Little Sutton, Eng., U.K.	180		53.17 N	2.57 W
Little Tallapoosa, stm., U.S.	134	D13	33.19 N	85.34 W
Little Tennessee, stm., U.S.	132	A1	35.47 N	84.15 W
Little Thurrock, Eng., U.K.	178		51.28 N	0.21 E
Little Timber Creek, stm., N.J., U.S.	203		39.53 N	75.08 W
Little Tinicum Island, i., Pa., U.S.	203		39.51 N	75.17 W
Little Tobago, i., Br. Vir. Is.	158b	e7	18.26 N	64.50 W
Little Tobago, i., Trin.	159f	r13	11.18 N	60.30 W
Littleton, Eng., U.K.	178		51.24 N	0.28 W
Littleton, Co., U.S.	138	B3	39.37 N	105.01 W
Littleton, N.H., U.S.	122	F5	44.18 N	71.46 W
Littleton, N.C., U.S.	124	H8	36.25 N	77.54 W
Littleton, W.V., U.S.	124	E5	39.41 N	80.30 W
Little Traverse Bay, b., Mi., U.S.	126	C4	45.23 N	85.04 W
Little Turtle, stm., On., Can.	128	C6	48.47 N	92.39 W
Little Valley, N.Y., U.S.	124	B7	42.14 N	78.47 W
Little Vienna Estates, Va., U.S.	202c		38.54 N	77.18 W
Little Wabash, stm., Il., U.S.	130	F9	37.53 N	88.05 W
Little Waltham, Eng., U.K.	178		51.47 N	0.29 E
Little Warley, Eng., U.K.	178		51.35 N	0.19 E
Little Washita, stm., Ok., U.S.	138	G10	34.58 N	97.52 W
Little White, stm., S.D., U.S.	140	D12	43.43 N	100.40 W
Little White Mountain, mtn., B.C., Can.	144	G11	49.42 N	119.20 W
Little Wichita, stm., Tx., U.S.	138	H10	33.53 N	97.58 W
Little Wichita, East Fork, stm., Tx., U.S.	138	H10	33.52 N	98.05 W
Little Wind, stm., Wy., U.S.	140	D4	42.57 N	108.29 W
Little Wind, North Fork, stm., Wy., U.S.	140	D3	43.00 N	108.52 W
Little Wind, South Fork, stm., Wy., U.S.	140	E3	42.59 N	108.49 W
Little Wolf, stm., Wi., U.S.	128	G10	44.22 N	88.48 W
Little Wood, stm., Id., U.S.	146	G12	42.56 N	114.22 W
Little Zab (Az-Zāb as-Saghīr) (Zāb-e Kūchek), stm., Asia	74	C9	35.14 N	43.25 E
Littoria see Latina, Italy	32	C6	41.29 N	12.50 E
Litvínov, Czech Rep.	24	F9	50.35 N	13.36 E
Litvinovo, Russia	18	H25	59.34 N	38.01 E
Lityn, Ukr.	38	D7	49.19 N	28.05 E
Litzmannstadt see Łódź, Pol.	24	E15	51.47 N	19.30 E
Liu, stm., China	54	C6	42.39 N	126.02 E
Liu, stm., China	54	C5	41.52 N	122.51 E
Liu, stm., China	58	I3	23.48 N	109.32 E
Liuaniua see Ontong Java, at., Sol. Is.	94	D7	5.19 S	159.16 E
Liuba, China	58	E2	33.40 N	106.59 E
Liubar, Ukr.	38	D6	49.55 N	27.45 E
Liubashivka, Ukr.	38	F9	47.49 N	30.15 E
Liubech, Ukr.	38	B9	51.42 N	30.39 E
Liubeshiv, Ukr.	38	B4	51.46 N	25.31 E
Liubliana see Ljubljana, Slvn.	30	D11	46.03 N	14.31 E
Liuboml', Ukr.	38	B2	51.13 N	24.02 E
Liubotyn, Ukr.	38	D14	49.56 N	35.57 E
Liubymivka, Ukr.	38	G12	46.49 N	33.32 E
Liuchen, China	58	J4	23.09 N	110.27 E
Liucheng, China	58	I3	24.39 N	109.14 E
Liuchow see Liuzhou, China	58	I3	24.18 N	109.22 E
Liucura, Chile	172	I2	38.39 S	71.05 W
Liudaogou, China	54	D7	41.33 N	127.14 E
Liufang, China	58	H7	27.55 N	116.24 E
Liufentzu, Tai.	187d		24.57 N	121.35 E
Liuhe, China	52	C10	42.14 N	125.43 E
Liuheng Dao, i., China	58	G10	29.43 N	122.08 E
Liujia, China	58	I2	24.51 N	107.21 E

Name	Page	Map Ref.	Latitude	Longitude
Liujiazhai, China	187b		31.21 N	121.27 E
Liujiazi, China	58	A9	41.01 N	120.17 E
Liulicun, China	189a		39.56 N	116.28 E
Liupan Shan, mts., China	58	D2	35.35 N	106.10 E
Liushui, China	54	B6	44.18 N	124.08 E
Liushuquan, China	48	F16	39.20 N	118.05 E
Liuten'ka, Ukr.	38	C13	50.12 N	34.02 E
Liuxi, stm., China	58	J5	23.22 N	112.53 E
Liuyang, China	58	G5	28.07 N	113.37 E
Liuyang, stm., China	58	G5	28.13 N	112.58 E
Liuzhai, China	58	I2	25.15 N	107.24 E
Liuzhou, China	58	I3	24.18 N	109.22 E
Livada, Rom.	36	B10	47.52 N	23.07 E
Livadija, Russia	54	C10	42.51 N	132.38 E
Līvāni, Lat.	26	D9	56.22 N	26.11 E
Livanjsko Polje, val., Bos.	36	E3	43.55 N	16.45 E
Lively, On., Can.	126	B8	46.25 N	81.09 W
Lively Island, i., Falk. Is.	166	J5	52.02 S	58.30 W
Livengood, Ak., U.S.	109	C10	65.32 N	148.33 W
Livenka, Russia	38	C17	50.27 N	38.17 E
Livenza, stm., Italy	30	E9	45.35 N	12.51 E
Live Oak, Ca., U.S.	148	D4	39.16 N	121.39 W
Live Oak, Fl., U.S.	132	F2	30.17 N	82.59 W
Live Oak Creek, stm., Tx., U.S.	136	D6	30.39 N	101.42 W
Liverdy-en-Brie, Fr.	179		48.42 N	2.47 E
Liveringa, Austl.	96	C4	18.02 S	124.09 E
Livermore, Ca., U.S.	148	F4	37.40 N	121.46 W
Livermore, Ia., U.S.	130	B3	42.52 N	94.11 W
Livermore, Ky., U.S.	130	G10	37.29 N	87.08 W
Livermore, Mount, mtn., Tx., U.S.	136	D3	30.38 N	104.10 W
Livermore Falls, Me., U.S.	122	F6	44.28 N	70.11 W
Liverpool, N.S., Can.	122	F12	44.02 N	64.43 W
Liverpool, Eng., U.K.	10	H10	53.24 N	2.57 W
Liverpool, Eng., U.K.	180		53.25 N	2.55 W
Liverpool, Pa., U.S.	124	D8	40.34 N	76.59 W
Liverpool, mun., Eng., U.K.	180		53.25 N	2.55 W
Liverpool, mun., Eng., U.K.	180		53.25 N	2.55 W
Liverpool, Cape, c., Nu., Can.	108	C10	73.38 N	78.06 W
Liverpool, University of, educ., Eng., U.K.	180		53.24 N	2.58 W
Liverpool Airport, arpt., Eng., U.K.	180		53.21 N	2.52 W
Liverpool Bay, b., N.T., Can.	110	A5	69.46 N	130.04 W
Liverpool Bay, b., N.S., Can.	122	G12	44.02 N	64.37 W
Liverpool Bay, b., Eng., U.K.	10	H9	53.26 N	3.19 W
Liverpool Football Ground, p.o.i., Eng., U.K.	180		53.26 N	2.57 W
Liverpool Range, mts., Austl.	98	H8	31.51 S	150.18 E
Livigno, Italy	30	D7	46.30 N	10.06 E
Livilliers, Fr.	179		49.06 N	2.06 E
Livingston, Guat.	156	E3	15.49 N	88.45 W
Livingston, Al., U.S.	134	E10	32.35 N	88.12 W
Livingston, Ca., U.S.	148	F5	37.23 N	120.43 W
Livingston, Il., U.S.	130	F8	38.58 N	89.45 W
Livingston, Ky., U.S.	124	G1	37.17 N	84.13 W
Livingston, La., U.S.	134	G8	30.29 N	90.44 W
Livingston, Mt., U.S.	146	E16	45.40 N	110.33 W
Livingston, Tn., U.S.	130	H12	36.23 N	85.19 W
Livingston, Tx., U.S.	136	D13	30.42 N	94.56 W
Livingston, Wi., U.S.	130	B7	42.54 N	90.25 W
Livingston, Lake, res., Tx., U.S.	136	D12	30.43 N	95.07 W
Livingstone, Zam.	88	D4	17.52 S	25.51 E
Livingstone, Chutes de see Livingstone Falls, wtfl., Afr.	86	F2	4.50 S	14.28 E
Livingstone Falls, wtfl., Afr.	86	F2	4.50 S	14.28 E
Livingstone Mountains, mts., N.Z.	102	G3	45.08 S	168.05 E
Livingstonia, Mwi.	88	C5	10.36 S	34.06 E
Livingston Mall, shp. cen., N.J., U.S.	194		40.47 N	74.21 W
Livingston Manor, N.Y., U.S.	124	C11	41.54 N	74.49 W
Livno, Bos.	36	F4	43.49 N	17.00 E
Livny, Russia	26	H20	52.25 N	37.36 E
Livø, i., Den.	16	K7	56.52 N	9.05 E
Livojoki, stm., Fin.	18	B14	65.23 N	26.47 E
Livonia, La., U.S.	134	G7	30.32 N	91.32 W
Livonia, Mi., U.S.	124	B2	42.23 N	83.21 W
Livonia, N.Y., U.S.	124	B8	42.49 N	77.39 W
Livonia Mall, shp. cen., Mi., U.S.	199		42.26 N	83.20 W
Livorno (Leghorn), Italy	30	G7	43.33 N	10.19 E
Livramento see Santana do Livramento, Braz.	172	E10	30.52 S	55.30 W
Livramento do Brumado, Braz.	170	G5	13.39 S	41.50 W
Livry-Gargan, Fr.	179		48.56 N	2.33 E
Livry-sur-Seine, Fr.	179		48.31 N	2.41 E
Liwa, Indon.	66	F3	5.03 S	104.04 E
Liwale, Tan.	86	F7	9.45 S	37.55 E
Liwonde, Mwi.	88	D5	14.59 S	35.15 E
Lixi, China	58	G6	29.15 N	114.47 E
Lixian, China	58	G4	29.30 N	111.37 E
Lixian, China	58	D1	34.08 N	105.06 E
Lixian see Black, stm., Asia	64	A6	21.14 N	105.21 E
Lixin, China	58	H7	26.52 N	116.42 E
Lixin, China	58	E7	33.07 N	116.11 E
Lixoúri, Grc.	34	E3	38.11 N	20.25 E
Liyang, China	58	F8	31.26 N	119.29 E
Lizarda, Braz.	170	E2	9.36 S	46.41 W
Lizard Head Peak, mtn., Wy., U.S.	132	E3	42.47 N	109.11 W
Lizard Point, c., Eng., U.K.	10	L7	49.57 N	5.12 W
Lizard Point Indian Reserve, ind. res., Mb., Can.	142	D12	50.40 N	100.57 W
Lizarra see Estella, Spain	28	B8	42.40 N	2.00 W
Liznovka, Russia	38	C18	50.07 N	39.29 E
Ližmozero, ozero, l., Russia	18	E21	62.37 N	34.05 E
Ljadiny, Russia	18	F25	61.33 N	38.20 E
Ljady, Bela.	26	F14	54.35 N	31.11 E
Ljady, Russia	26	B11	58.38 N	28.47 E
Ljahavičy, Bela.	26	G9	53.00 N	26.18 E
Ljahoviči see Ljahavičy, Bela.	26	G9	53.00 N	26.18 E
Ljahovskie ostrova, is., Russia	50	B17	73.30 N	141.00 E
Ljamca, Russia	18	C23	64.26 N	37.05 E
Ljamen'ga, Russia	18	G21	59.51 N	44.32 E
Ljangasovo, Russia	40	B16	58.30 N	49.30 E
Ljapičev, Russia	40	G13	48.29 N	43.33 E
Ljaskavičy, Bela.	26	H11	52.07 N	28.09 E
Ljaskelja, Russia	18	F18	61.45 N	31.00 E
Ljasnaja, Bela.	26	G8	52.59 N	25.46 E
Ljasnaja, stm., Bela.	26	H6	52.10 N	23.30 E
Ljavozero, ozero, l., Russia	14	D27	68.15 N	36.19 E
Ljuban', Bela.	26	H12	52.37 N	29.08 E
Ljuban', Bela.	26	H10	52.47 N	28.00 E
Ljuban', Russia	26	A14	59.21 N	31.15 E
Ljubča, Bela.	26	G8	53.45 N	26.03 E
Ljubercy, Russia	26	E20	55.41 N	37.53 E
Ljubercy, Russia	183b		55.41 N	37.53 E
Ljubimec, Blg.	36	H13	41.51 N	26.05 E
Ljubimovka, Russia	38	B14	51.30 N	35.38 E
Ljubinje, Bos.	36	G5	42.57 N	18.05 E
Ljubljana, Slvn.	30	D11	46.03 N	14.31 E
Ljubnica, Russia	26	C15	57.57 N	32.46 E
Ljubohna, Russia	26	G17	53.30 N	34.24 E
Ljubostan', Russia	38	B14	51.18 N	35.43 E
Ljubovija, Yugo.	36	E6	44.11 N	19.22 E
Ljubuški, Bos.	36	F4	43.12 N	17.33 E
Ljubytino, Russia	26	B16	58.48 N	33.23 E
Ljudinovo, Russia	26	G17	53.51 N	34.28 E
Ljudkovo, Russia	26	F17	54.35 N	34.44 E
Ljugarn, Swe.	16	J16	57.19 N	18.43 E
Ljungan, stm., Swe.	16	E14	62.18 N	17.24 E
Ljungaverk, Swe.	16	E14	62.29 N	16.03 E
Ljungby, Swe.	16	K11	56.50 N	13.56 E
Ljungbyholm, Swe.	16	K14	56.37 N	16.11 E
Ljungdalen, Swe.	16	E10	62.51 N	12.47 E
Ljungsbro, Swe.	16	I13	58.32 N	15.33 E
Ljungskile, Swe.	16	I9	58.13 N	11.56 E
Ljusdal, Swe.	16	F14	61.49 N	16.06 E
Ljusina, Bela.	26	H9	52.37 N	26.30 E
Ljusnan, stm., Swe.	16	F13	61.09 N	17.09 E
Ljusne, Swe.	16	F15	61.12 N	17.07 E
Ljusterö, i., Swe.	16	H16	59.31 N	18.37 E
Ljuta, stm., Russia	26	B11	58.34 N	28.40 E
Llançà, Spain	28	B14	42.22 N	3.09 E
Llancanelo, Laguna, l., Arg.	172	G3	35.34 S	69.08 W
Llandeilo, Wales, U.K.	10	J8	51.53 N	4.00 W
Llandilo, Austl.	192a		33.43 S	150.45 E
Llandovery, Wales, U.K.	10	I9	51.59 N	3.48 W
Llandrindod Wells, Wales, U.K.	10	I9	52.14 N	3.22 W
Llandudno, Wales, U.K.	10	H9	53.19 N	3.50 W
Llanelli, Wales, U.K.	10	J8	51.41 N	4.09 W
Llanes, Spain	28	A6	43.25 N	4.45 W
Llangefni, Wales, U.K.	10	H8	53.15 N	4.19 W
Llangollen, Wales, U.K.	10	H9	52.58 N	3.11 W
Llanidloes, Wales, U.K.	10	I9	52.27 N	3.32 W
Llano, Tx., U.S.	136	D9	30.45 N	98.40 W
Llano, stm., Tx., U.S.	136	D8	30.38 N	98.25 W
Llano Colorado, Mex.	148	L9	31.43 N	115.58 W
Llanos, pl., S.A.	168	D7	5.00 N	70.00 W
Llanquihue, Lago, l., Chile	166	H2	41.08 S	72.48 W
Llansá see Llançà, Spain	28	B14	42.22 N	3.09 E
Llavallol, ngh., Arg.	206		34.48 S	58.28 W
Lleida, Spain	28	C11	41.37 N	0.37 E
Lleida, co., Spain	28	B12	42.00 N	1.10 E
Llentrisca, Cap, c., Spain	28	F12	38.51 N	1.15 E
Llera de Canales, Mex.	154	D9	23.19 N	99.01 W
Llerena, Spain	28	F4	38.14 N	6.00 W
Lleulleu, Lago, l., Chile	172	I1	38.10 S	73.19 W
Llico, Chile	172	G1	34.44 S	72.04 W
Llíria, Spain	28	E10	39.37 N	0.36 W
Llivia, Spain	28	B12	42.28 N	1.57 E
Llobregat, Delta del, del., Spain	184d		41.17 N	2.08 E
Llorente, Phil.	68	E5	11.24 N	125.32 E
Lloyd Harbor, b., N.Y., U.S.	194		40.55 N	73.27 W
Lloydminster, Sk., Can.	110	E9	53.16 N	110.01 W
Lloyd Neck, pen., N.Y., U.S.	194		40.56 N	73.28 W
Llucena, Spain	28	D10	40.08 N	0.16 W
Lluchmayor see Llucmajor, Spain	28	E13	39.28 N	2.53 E
Llucmajor, Spain	28	E13	39.28 N	2.53 E
Llullaillaco, Cerro (Llullaillaco, Volcán), vol., S.A.	166	D3	24.43 S	68.33 W
Llullaillaco, Volcán, vol., S.A.	172	B3	24.43 S	68.33 W
Lo (Panlong), stm., Asia	64	A7	21.17 N	105.26 E
Loa, Ut., U.S.	150	E5	38.24 N	111.38 W
Loa, stm., Chile	166	D3	21.25 S	70.03 W
Loa, stm., Congo	191b		4.20 S	15.11 E
Loami, Il., U.S.	136	E8	39.40 N	89.51 W
Loanda see Luanda, Ang.	88	B1	8.49 S	13.14 E
Loanda, Braz.	166	D6	23.00 S	53.11 W
Loange (Luangue), stm., Afr.	86	F3	4.17 S	20.02 E
Loantaka Brook, stm., N.J., U.S.	194		40.43 N	74.28 W
Lo Aranguiz, Chile	204e		33.23 S	70.40 W
Lobamba, Swaz.	90	E10	26.27 S	31.12 E
Loban, Russia	12	D21	65.42 N	45.23 E
Lobanovo, Russia	26	G21	53.04 N	38.14 E
Lo Barnechea, Chile	204e		33.21 S	70.31 W
Lobatse, Bots.	90	D7	25.13 S	25.40 E
Löbau, Ger.	24	E10	51.05 N	14.39 E
Lobau, pl., Aus.	182b		48.10 N	16.32 E
Lobaye, stm., C.A.R.	86	D3	3.40 N	18.34 E
Lobbs Run, stm., Pa., U.S.	197b		40.15 N	79.55 W
Lobelville, Tn., U.S.	134	B11	35.46 N	87.46 W
Lo Benitez, Chile	204e		33.34 S	70.42 W
Lobería, Arg.	172	I8	38.09 S	58.46 W
Lo Bernales, Chile	204e		33.34 S	70.34 W
Łobez, Pol.	24	C11	53.38 N	15.37 E
Lobito, Ang.	86	G2	12.21 S	13.33 E
Lobitos Creek, stm., Ca., U.S.	200		37.22 N	122.24 W
Lobnja, Russia	26	D20	56.00 N	37.29 E
Lobos, Arg.	172	G8	35.11 S	59.05 W
Lobos, Cay, i., Bah.	156	A9	22.23 N	77.28 W
Lobos, Isla, i., Mex.	154	B3	27.20 N	110.35 W
Lo Boza, Chile	204e		33.23 S	70.46 W
Lobskoe, Russia	18	E22	62.44 N	35.16 E
Lobva, Russia	48	C10	59.11 N	60.29 E
Łobżenica, Pol.	24	C13	53.16 N	17.15 E
Locarno, Switz.	30	D5	46.10 N	8.47 E
Lo Castillo, Aeropuerto, arpt., Chile	204e		33.23 S	70.36 W
Lochboisdale, Scot., U.K.	10	D5	57.09 N	7.18 W
Lochearn, Md., U.S.	202b		39.21 N	76.43 W
Loches, Fr.	20	G10	47.07 N	0.59 E
Loch Garman see Wexford, Ire.	10	I6	52.19 N	6.27 W
Lochgilphead, Scot., U.K.	10	E7	56.02 N	5.26 W
Lochinver, Scot., U.K.	10	C7	58.08 N	5.14 W
Lochmaddy, Scot., U.K.	10	D5	57.35 N	7.09 W
Loch Raven Dam, dam., Md., U.S.	202b		39.26 N	76.33 W
Lochsa, stm., Id., U.S.	146	D12	46.08 N	115.36 W
Loch Sport, Austl.	98	K6	38.03 S	147.34 E
Lochy, Loch, l., Scot., U.K.	10	D8	56.56 N	4.57 W
Lock, Austl.	96	F7	33.34 S	135.45 E
Lockeport, N.S., Can.	122	G11	43.42 N	65.08 W
Lockerbie, Scot., U.K.	10	F9	55.07 N	3.22 W
Lockesburg, Ar., U.S.	134	D4	33.58 N	94.10 W
Lockhart, Austl.	98	J6	35.13 S	146.43 E
Lockhart, Tx., U.S.	136	E10	29.53 N	97.40 W
Lock Haven, Pa., U.S.	124	C8	41.07 N	77.26 W
Lockheed Aircraft Corporation, sci., Ca., U.S.	198		34.12 N	118.22 W
Lockheed Aircraft Corporation, sci., Ca., U.S.	200		37.25 N	122.02 W
Lockney, Tx., U.S.	138	G7	34.07 N	101.26 W
Löcknitz, Ger.	24	C10	53.26 N	14.12 E
Löcknitz, stm., Ger.	182a		52.25 N	13.49 E
Lockport, Mb., Can.	142	D17	50.05 N	96.56 W
Lockport, Il., U.S.	130	C9	41.35 N	88.02 W
Lockport, La., U.S.	134	H8	29.38 N	90.32 W
Lockport, N.Y., U.S.	126	E11	43.09 N	78.41 W
Lockport Lock, trans., Il., U.S.	196		41.35 N	88.04 W
Lockview, Pa., U.S.	197b		40.10 N	79.55 W
Lockwood, Mo., U.S.	130	G4	37.23 N	93.57 W
Locminé, Fr.	20	G6	47.52 N	2.49 W
Loc Ninh, Viet.	64	G8	11.53 N	106.37 E
Locri, Italy	32	F10	38.14 N	16.16 E
Locumba, Peru	164	G3	17.36 S	70.46 W
Locust Creek, stm., U.S.	130	D4	39.40 N	93.17 W
Locust Fork, stm., Al., U.S.	134	D11	33.33 N	87.11 W
Locust Grove, N.Y., U.S.	194		40.48 N	73.30 W
Locust Grove, Ok., U.S.	130	H2	36.12 N	95.10 W
Locust Point, c., N.Y., U.S.	194		40.49 N	73.48 W
Lod (Lydda), Isr.	76	G5	31.58 N	34.54 E
Lodal Creek, stm., Pa., U.S.	203		40.14 N	75.27 W
Lodalskåpa, mtn., Nor.	16	F5	61.47 N	7.10 E
Loddon, stm., Austl.	98	K4	35.20 S	143.34 E
Lodejnoe Pole, Russia	18	G20	60.43 N	33.34 E
Lodève, Fr.	22	F9	43.42 N	3.18 E
Lodge Creek, stm., N.A.	142	F4	48.36 N	109.13 W
Lodge Grass, Mt., U.S.	140	B5	45.19 N	107.22 W
Lodgepole, Ab., Can.	144	C15	53.06 N	115.19 W
Lodgepole, Ne., U.S.	140	F10	41.09 N	102.38 W
Lodgepole Creek, stm., U.S.	140	F10	40.57 N	102.23 W
Lodhrān, Pak.	70	D3	29.32 N	71.38 E
Lodi, Italy	30	E6	45.19 N	9.30 E
Lodi, Ca., U.S.	148	E4	38.07 N	121.15 W
Lodi, Wi., U.S.	128	H9	43.18 N	89.31 W
Løding, Nor.	14	E5	67.18 N	14.43 E
Lødingen, Nor.	14	D6	68.24 N	15.59 E
Lodi Park, p.o.i., India	190a		28.36 N	77.13 E
Lodja, D.R.C.	86	E4	3.26 S	23.26 E
Lodosa, Spain	28	B8	42.25 N	2.04 W
Lodsch see Łódź, Pol.	24	E15	51.47 N	19.30 E
Lodwar, Kenya	86	D7	3.08 N	35.38 E
Łódź, Pol.	24	E15	51.47 N	19.30 E
Łódzkie, state, Pol.	24	E15	51.30 N	19.30 E
Loei, Thai.	64	D5	17.27 N	101.31 E
Loei, stm., Thai.	64	D5	17.51 N	101.36 E
Loen, Nor.	16	F4	61.52 N	6.52 E
Loeriesfontein, S. Afr.	90	G4	30.56 S	19.26 E
Lo Espejo, Chile	204e		33.32 S	70.43 W
Lo Espejo, Canal, can., Chile	204e		33.32 S	70.43 W
Loeŭ, Bela.	38	B9	51.56 N	30.48 E
Lofer, Aus.	30	C9	47.34 N	12.41 E
Lofoten, is., Nor.	14	D4	68.08 N	14.09 E
Lofoten Basin, unds.	176	A14	70.00 N	4.00 E
Lofotodden, c., Nor.	14	E3	67.49 N	12.48 E
Lofsdalen, Swe.	16	E11	62.07 N	13.13 E
Lofthus, Nor.	16	G4	60.20 N	6.40 E
Loftus, Austl.	192a		34.03 S	151.03 E
Lofty, Mount, mtn., Austl.	192b		37.43 S	145.17 E
Log, Russia	40	G13	49.29 N	43.51 E
Loga, Niger	84	G5	13.36 N	3.14 E
Logan, Ia., U.S.	130	C2	41.38 N	95.47 W
Logan, Ks., U.S.	138	B9	39.39 N	99.34 W
Logan, N.M., U.S.	138	F5	35.22 N	103.25 W
Logan, Oh., U.S.	124	E3	39.31 N	82.25 W
Logan, Ut., U.S.	150	B5	41.44 N	111.50 W
Logan, W.V., U.S.	124	G4	37.50 N	81.59 W
Logan, ngh., Pa., U.S.	203		40.02 N	75.09 W
Logan, stm., Ut., U.S.	150	A5	41.44 N	111.54 W
Logan, Mount, mtn., Yk., Can.	110	C2	60.34 N	140.24 W
Logan, Mount, mtn., Wa., U.S.	146	B6	48.32 N	120.57 W
Logan Creek, stm., Mo., U.S.	130	G7	37.08 N	90.46 W
Logan Creek, stm., Ne., U.S.	140	E15	41.37 N	96.29 W
Logandale, Nv., U.S.	150	G2	36.35 N	114.29 W
Logan International Airport, arpt., Ma., U.S.	201		42.22 N	71.00 W
Logan Island, i., On., Can.	128	A10	50.07 N	88.27 W
Logan Martin Lake, res., Al., U.S.	134	D12	33.34 N	86.13 W
Logan Mountains, mts., Yk., Can.	110	C5	61.45 N	128.38 W
Logan Pass, p., Mt., U.S.	146	B13	48.42 N	113.44 W
Logansport, In., U.S.	130	D11	40.44 N	86.21 W
Logansport, La., U.S.	136	C14	31.58 N	93.59 W
Logan Square, ngh., Il., U.S.	196		41.56 N	87.42 W
Loganville, Ga., U.S.	132	C2	33.50 N	83.54 W
Lögdeälven, stm., Swe.	16	C16	63.33 N	19.26 E
Lognes, Fr.	179		48.50 N	2.38 E
Lognes-Émerainville, Aérodrome de, arpt., Fr.	179		48.49 N	2.37 E
Løgnin, b., Nor.	16	C9	64.24 N	11.19 E
Logone, stm., Afr.	82	F3	12.15 N	15.02 E
Logoualé, C. Iv.	84	H3	7.07 N	7.33 W
Logroño, Spain	28	B8	42.28 N	2.26 W
Logrosán, Spain	28	E5	39.20 N	5.29 W
Løgstør, Den.	16	K7	56.57 N	9.15 E
Logudoro, reg., Italy	32	D2	40.35 N	8.40 E
Løgumkloster, Den.	16	L6	55.03 N	8.57 E
Loh, i., Vanuatu	101d	i16	13.21 S	166.38 E
Lohārdaga, India	70	G10	23.25 N	84.41 E
Lohāru, India	70	D5	28.25 N	75.48 E
Lohausen, ngh., Ger.	181		51.16 N	6.44 E
Lohauserholz, ngh., Ger.	181		51.39 N	7.48 E
Lohberg, Ger.	181		51.35 N	6.46 E
Löhdorf, ngh., Ger.	181		51.09 N	7.01 E
Lo Hermida, Chile	204e		33.29 S	70.33 W
Lohheide, ngh., Ger.	181		51.30 N	6.40 E
Lohiniva, Fin.	14	E15	67.08 N	24.57 E
Lohino, Russia	183b		55.42 N	37.19 E
Lohja, Fin.	18	G11	60.14 N	24.04 E
Lohjanjärvi, l., Fin.	18	G10	60.13 N	23.55 E
Löhme, Ger.	182a		52.37 N	13.40 E
Lohmühle, Ger.	181		51.31 N	6.40 E
Löhne, Ger.	20	B17	52.11 N	8.40 E
Lohne, Ger.	24	D4	52.39 N	8.14 E
Lohnen, Ger.	181		51.36 N	6.39 E
Lohr am Main, Ger.	20	D18	49.59 N	9.34 E
Lohrville, Ia., U.S.	130	B3	42.16 N	94.32 W
Loi (Nanlei), stm., Asia	64	B4	21.18 N	100.43 E
Loi, Phou, mtn., Laos	64	B6	20.16 N	103.12 E
Loi-kaw, Mya.	64	C3	19.40 N	97.12 E
Loimaa, Fin.	18	G9	60.51 N	23.03 E
Loimijoki, stm., Fin.	18	G10	61.12 N	22.37 E
Loi Mwe, Mya.	64	B4	21.10 N	99.45 E
Loing, stm., Fr.	20	F11	48.23 N	2.48 E
Loing, Canal du, can., Fr.	20	F11	48.17 N	2.41 E
Loir, stm., Fr.	20	G8	47.33 N	0.31 W
Loire, state, Fr.	22	D10	45.30 N	4.00 E
Loire, stm., Fr.	22	B4	47.17 N	2.00 W
Loire, Canal latéral à la, can., Fr.	22	B8	47.37 N	2.44 E
Loire-Atlantique, state, Fr.	20	G7	47.20 N	1.35 W
Loiret, state, Fr.	20	F11	47.55 N	2.20 E
Loir-et-Cher, state, Fr.	20	G10	47.30 N	1.30 E
Loisdale, Va., U.S.	202c		38.46 N	77.11 W
Loíza Aldea, P.R.	158a	b4	18.26 N	65.53 W
Loja, Ec.	164	D2	3.59 S	79.11 W
Loja, Spain	28	G6	37.10 N	4.08 W
Lojga, Russia	12	F21	61.04 N	44.36 E
Lojmola, Russia	18	F18	61.58 N	31.43 E
Lokachi, Ukr.	38	C3	50.44 N	24.39 E
Lokandu, D.R.C.	86	E5	2.31 S	25.46 E
Lokan Reservoir see Lokan tekojärvi, res., Fin.	14	E18	67.55 N	27.40 E
Lokan tekojärvi, res., Fin.	14	E18	67.55 N	27.40 E
Lökbatan, Azer.	42	E13	40.20 N	49.43 E
Løken, Nor.	16	H9	59.47 N	11.28 E
Lokeren, Bel.	20	C13	51.06 N	4.00 E
Loket, Czech Rep.	24	F8	50.10 N	12.45 E
Lokhvytsia, Ukr.	38	C12	50.22 N	33.16 E
Lokichar, Kenya	86	D7	2.22 N	35.39 E
Lokichokio, Kenya	86	D6	4.12 N	34.20 E
Lokitaung, Kenya	86	D7	4.15 N	35.45 E
Lokka, Fin.	14	E18	67.49 N	27.43 E
Løkken, Den.	16	J7	57.22 N	9.43 E
Løkken, Nor.	16	D7	63.07 N	9.42 E
Loknja, Russia	26	D13	56.49 N	30.08 E
Lokoja, Nig.	84	H6	7.48 N	6.43 E
Lokolama, D.R.C.	86	E3	2.33 S	19.52 E
Lokomotiv Central Stadium, p.o.i., Russia	183b		55.48 N	37.45 E
Lokosovo, Russia	50	D3	61.09 N	74.44 E
Lokot', Russia	26	H17	52.34 N	34.35 E
Lokoua, stm., Congo	191b		4.06 S	15.16 E
Loksa, Est.	26	A8	59.34 N	25.44 E
Loks Land, i., Nu., Can.	108	E13	62.26 N	64.38 W
Lola, Gui.	84	H3	7.48 N	8.31 W
Lola, Mount, mtn., Ca., U.S.	148	D5	39.26 N	120.22 W
Loleta, Ca., U.S.	148	C1	40.38 N	124.13 W
Loliondo, Tan.	86	E7	2.00 S	35.40 E
Lolita, Tx., U.S.	136	F11	28.50 N	96.32 W
Lolland, i., Den.	16	M9	54.46 N	11.16 E
Lolo, Mt., U.S.	146	D12	46.45 N	114.06 W
Lolo Creek, stm., Id., U.S.	146	D11	46.28 N	116.15 W
Lolo Creek, stm., Mt., U.S.	146	D12	46.44 N	114.03 W
Lolodorf, Cam.	86	D2	3.14 N	10.43 E
Lolo Pass, p., U.S.	146	D12	46.37 N	114.35 W
Lolowai, Vanuatu	101d	j16	15.17 S	167.59 E
Loltong, Vanuatu	101d	j17	15.33 S	168.08 E
Lolvavana, Passage, strt., Vanuatu	101d	j16	15.25 S	168.08 E
Lolworth Range, mts., Austl.	98	C5	20.20 S	145.15 E
Lom, Blg.	36	F10	43.49 N	23.15 E
Lom, Nor.	16	F6	61.51 N	8.33 E
Lom, Russia	26	C22	57.52 N	39.09 E
Lom, stm., Afr.	82	F2	5.19 N	13.24 E
Lom, stm., Blg.	36	F9	43.50 N	23.14 E
Loma Blanca, Chile	204e		33.30 S	70.47 W
Loma Blanca, Mex.	136	C1	31.38 N	106.21 W
Lomaloma, Fiji	101e	p20	17.17 S	178.59 W
Lomami, stm., D.R.C.	86	D4	0.46 N	24.17 E
Loma Ridge, mtn., Ca., U.S.	198		33.45 N	117.43 W
Lomas Chapultepec, ngh., Mex.	204a		19.26 N	99.13 W
Lomas de Monreal, Mex.	150	L5	31.17 N	110.55 W
Lomas de Zamora, Arg.	172	G8	34.46 S	58.24 W
Lomas de Zamora, state, Arg.	206		34.45 S	58.24 W
Lomax, Il., U.S.	130	D6	40.40 N	91.03 W
Łomazy, Pol.	24	E19	51.55 N	23.10 E
Lombardia, state, Italy	30	E6	45.30 N	9.30 E
Lombardy see Lombardia, state, Italy	30	E6	45.30 N	9.30 E
Lombardy East, S. Afr.	191d		26.07 S	28.08 E
Lomblen, Pulau, i., Indon.	60	G7	8.25 S	123.30 E
Lombo do Tejo, Mouchão do, i., Port.	184c		38.52 N	9.00 W
Lombok, Indon.	66	H10	8.30 S	116.40 E
Lombok, i., Indon.	66	H10	8.45 S	116.30 E
Lombok, Selat, strt., Indon.	66	H9	8.30 S	115.50 E
Lombovka, stm., Russia	14	E30	67.43 N	40.28 E
Lombovskij zaliv, b., Russia	14	E31	67.46 N	40.27 E
Lomé, Togo	84	H5	6.07 N	1.13 E
Lomela, D.R.C.	86	E4	2.16 S	23.16 E
Lomela, stm., D.R.C.	86	E4	0.17 S	20.45 E
Lometa, Tx., U.S.	136	C9	31.12 N	98.23 W
Lomié, Cam.	86	D2	3.08 N	13.37 E
Lomira, Wi., U.S.	128	H10	43.34 N	88.26 W
Lom Kao, Thai.	64	D5	16.53 N	101.13 E
Lommel, Bel.	20	C14	51.13 N	5.19 E
Lomnice nad Popelkou, Czech Rep.	24	F11	50.32 N	15.22 E
Lomond, Ab., Can.	144	F18	50.21 N	112.38 W
Lomond, Loch, l., N.S., Can.	122	E16	45.45 N	60.36 W
Lomond, Loch, l., On., Can.	128	C9	48.15 N	89.19 W
Lomond, Loch, l., Scot., U.K.	10	E8	56.05 N	4.36 W
Lomond, Loch, l., Il., U.S.	196		42.17 N	88.01 W
Lomonosov, Russia	26	A12	59.54 N	29.47 E
Lomonosov, Russia	183a		59.55 N	29.46 E
Lomonosovka, Kaz.	48	D11	52.47 N	66.27 E
Lomonosov Moscow State University, educ., Russia	183b		55.43 N	37.32 E
Lomovoe, Russia	12	D19	64.01 N	40.40 E
Lompobatang, Gunung, mtn., Indon.	66	F11	5.20 S	119.55 E
Lompoc, Ca., U.S.	148	I5	34.38 N	120.27 W
Lom Sak, Thai.	64	D5	16.45 N	101.12 E
Lomseggi, mtn., Nor.	16	F6	61.49 N	8.21 E
Łomża, Pol.	24	C18	53.10 N	22.04 E
Lonaconing, Md., U.S.	124	E7	39.33 N	78.58 W
Lonāvale, India	69	B1	18.44 N	73.24 E
Loncoche, Chile	166	G2	39.21 S	72.37 W
Loncopué, Arg.	172	I2	38.04 S	70.36 W
London, On., Can.	126	F8	42.58 N	81.14 W
London, Eng., U.K.	10	J12	51.30 N	0.10 W
London, Eng., U.K.	178		51.30 N	0.10 W
London, Ar., U.S.	134	B5	35.19 N	93.15 W
London, Ky., U.S.	124	G1	37.07 N	84.05 W
London, Oh., U.S.	124	E2	39.53 N	83.26 W
London, Tx., U.S.	136	D8	30.40 N	99.34 W
London Colney, Eng., U.K.	178		51.43 N	0.18 W
Londonderry, N.S., Can.	122	E13	45.28 N	63.36 W
Londonderry (Derry), N. Ire., U.K.	10	F6	54.59 N	7.20 W
Londonderry, Cape, c., Austl.	96	B5	13.45 S	126.56 E
Londonderry, Isla, i., Chile	166	K2	55.02 S	70.34 W
London Zoo, p.o.i., Eng., U.K.	178		51.32 N	0.09 W
Londres, Arg.	172	C4	27.42 S	67.08 W
Londrina, Braz.	166	D6	23.18 S	51.09 W
Lone Grove, Ok., U.S.	138	G11	34.10 N	97.15 W
Lonely Lake, l., Mb., Can.	142	C14	51.09 N	99.05 W
Lonelyville, N.Y., U.S.	194		40.39 N	73.11 W
Lone Mountain, mtn., Nv., U.S.	148	E8	38.01 N	117.29 W
Lone Oak, Ky., U.S.	130	G9	37.02 N	88.39 W
Lone Oak, Tx., U.S.	136	A12	33.00 N	95.56 W
Lone Pine, Ca., U.S.	148	G7	36.37 N	118.03 W
Lone Rock, Wi., U.S.	130	A7	43.10 N	90.12 W
Lone Star, Tx., U.S.	136	B13	32.55 N	94.42 W
Lone Tree, Ia., U.S.	130	C6	41.29 N	91.25 W
Lone Tree Creek, stm., U.S.	140	G8	40.25 N	104.35 W
Lone Wolf, Ok., U.S.	138	G9	34.59 N	99.14 W
Long, Thai.	64	C4	18.05 N	99.50 E
Long, stm., China	58	I3	24.32 N	109.15 E
Long, Loch, b., Scot., U.K.	10	E8	56.02 N	4.53 W
Longa, Ang.	88	C2	14.36 S	18.29 E
Longá, stm., Braz.	170	B5	3.09 S	41.55 W
Longa, proliv, strt., Russia	50	B24	70.16 N	177.53 E
Long Akah, Malay.	66	B9	3.19 N	114.47 E
Long'an, China	58	I3	25.03 N	109.00 E
Longana, Vanuatu	101d	j17	15.18 S	167.59 E
Longarone, Italy	30	D9	46.16 N	12.17 E
Long Arroyo, stm., N.M., U.S.	138	H4	33.03 N	104.16 W
Longasy, Russia	18	E21	61.59 N	35.06 E
Longaví, Chile	172	G2	35.57 S	71.41 W
Longbangun, Indon.	66	C9	0.37 N	115.13 E
Long Bay, b., Austl.	192a		33.58 S	151.16 E
Long Bay, b., U.S.	132	C7	33.35 N	78.45 W
Long Beach, Ca., U.S.	148	J7	33.46 N	118.11 W
Long Beach, Ms., U.S.	134	G9	30.21 N	89.09 W
Long Beach, N.Y., U.S.	124	D12	40.35 N	73.39 W
Long Beach, Wa., U.S.	146	D2	46.21 N	124.02 W
Long Beach, cst., N.J., U.S.	124	E11	39.38 N	74.10 W
Long Beach Breakwater, trans., Ca., U.S.	198		33.43 N	118.09 W
Long Beach Middle Harbor, b., Ca., U.S.	198		33.45 N	118.13 W
Long Beach Municipal Airport, arpt., Ca., U.S.	198		33.49 N	118.09 W
Long Beach Naval Station, mil., Ca., U.S.	198		33.45 N	118.14 W
Longbeleh, Indon.	66	C10	0.16 N	116.10 E
Longboat Key, Fl., U.S.	132	I3	27.26 N	82.40 W
Long Branch, N.J., U.S.	124	D12	40.18 N	73.59 W
Long Branch, mun., On., Can.	193b		43.35 N	79.32 W
Long Branch Lake, res., Mo., U.S.	130	E5	39.49 N	92.31 W
Long Cane Creek, stm., S.C., U.S.	132	B3	33.57 N	82.24 W
Long Cay, i., Bah.	156	A10	22.35 N	74.21 W
Longchamp, Hippodrome de, p.o.i., Fr.	179		48.51 N	2.14 E
Longchang, China	58	G1	29.21 N	105.17 E
Longchêne, Fr.	179		48.38 N	2.00 E
Longchuan, China	58	I6	24.06 N	115.15 E
Long Creek, Or., U.S.	146	F7	44.42 N	119.06 W
Long Creek, stm., N.A.	142	E10	49.06 N	102.59 W
Longde, China	58	D2	35.40 N	106.09 E
Longdendale, val., Eng., U.K.	180		53.29 N	1.56 W
Long Ditton, Eng., U.K.	178		51.23 N	0.20 W
Long Eaton, Eng., U.K.	10	I11	52.53 N	1.16 W
Longfellow National Historic Site, hist., Ma., U.S.	201		42.23 N	71.08 W
Longfield, Eng., U.K.	178		51.24 N	0.18 E
Longford, Austl.	98	L6	38.09 S	147.05 E
Longford, Ire.	10	H5	53.43 N	7.48 W
Longford, Md., U.S.	202b		39.25 N	76.39 W
Longford, state, Ire.	10	H5	53.40 N	7.40 W
Longford Park, p.o.i., Eng., U.K.	180		53.27 N	2.17 W
Longgungtur, Indon.	66	C8	0.11 N	112.10 E
Long Harbour, b., China	189d		22.27 N	114.20 E
Longhorn Cavern State Park, p.o.i., Tx., U.S.	136	D9	30.20 N	98.30 W
Long Hu, l., China	58	F6	29.58 N	116.10 E
Longhua, China	58	A7	41.17 N	117.43 E
Longhua Airport, arpt., China	187b		31.10 N	121.26 E
Longhua Pagoda, rel., China	187b		31.11 N	121.26 E
Longhui, China	58	H4	27.08 N	110.59 E
Longiram, Indon.	66	C9	0.01 S	115.38 E
Long Island, i., Antig.	159b	f4	17.09 N	61.45 W
Long Island, i., Austl.	98	D7	22.09 S	149.54 E
Long Island, i., Bah.	152	C10	23.15 N	75.07 W
Long Island, i., Nu., Can.	110	E14	54.52 N	79.20 W
Long Island, i., N.S., Can.	122	F10	44.19 N	66.16 W
Long Island see Arop Island, i., Pap. N. Gui.	101a	b4	5.20 S	147.05 E
Long Island, i., Ma., U.S.	201		42.19 N	70.58 W
Long Island, i., N.Y., U.S.	124	D12	40.47 N	73.16 W
Long Island City, ngh., N.Y., U.S.	194		40.45 N	73.56 W
Long Island Sound, strt., U.S.	124	C12	41.05 N	72.58 W
Long Island University, educ., N.Y., U.S.	194		40.41 N	73.59 W
Long Island University (C.W. Post Center), educ., N.Y., U.S.	194		40.49 N	73.36 W
Longitudinal, Valle, val., Chile	172	H1	36.00 S	72.00 W
Longjiang, China	52	B9	47.20 N	123.11 E
Longjohn Slough, stm., Il., U.S.	196		41.43 N	87.53 W
Longka, China	70	B7	33.08 N	79.50 E
Long Ke, China	189d		22.23 N	114.22 E
Longkou, China	58	C9	37.38 N	120.20 E
Longlac, On., Can.	128	B12	49.48 N	86.31 W
Long Lake, N.Y., U.S.	128	E15	43.58 N	74.25 W
Long Lake, l., On., Can.	110	F13	44.40 N	76.45 W
Long Lake, l., On., Can.	128	B12	49.30 N	86.50 W
Long Lake, l., Mi., U.S.	126	C6	45.12 N	83.28 W
Long Lake, l., Mi., U.S.	199		42.36 N	83.28 W
Long Lake, l., Mi., U.S.	199		42.37 N	83.44 W
Long Lake, l., N.Y., U.S.	126	D15	44.04 N	74.20 W
Long Lake, l., N.D., U.S.	140	A12	46.43 N	100.06 W
Long Lake, res., Wa., U.S.	146	C9	47.53 N	117.40 W
Long Lake Creek, stm., N.D., U.S.	140	A13	46.40 N	100.15 W
Long Lake Shores, Mi., U.S.	199		42.35 N	83.19 W
Long Lama, Malay.	66	B9	3.45 N	114.23 E
Longleaf, La., U.S.	134	F6	31.00 N	92.33 W
Long Leaf Park, N.C., U.S.	132	B8	34.14 N	77.50 W
Longli, China	58	H2	26.27 N	106.58 E
Longlin, China	52	G6	24.50 N	105.31 E

Name Page Map Ref. Latitude Longitude

Longling, China 52 G4 24.35 N 98.41 E
Longmeadow, Ma., U.S. 124 B13 42.02 N 72.34 W
Longming, China 64 A8 22.58 N 107.11 E
Long Moc, Viet. 64 C7 18.51 N 105.01 E
Longmont, Co., U.S. 138 A3 40.10 N 105.06 W
Long Mountain, mtn., Mo., U.S. 130 H5 36.41 N 92.21 W
Longnan, China 58 I6 24.53 N 114.47 E
Longnawan, Indon. 66 C9 1.47 N 114.52 E
Long Neck, pen., Ct., U.S. 194 41.03 N 73.29 W
Long Neck Point, c., Ct., U.S. 194 41.02 N 73.29 W
Longperrier, Fr. 179 49.03 N 2.40 E
Long Pine, Ne., U.S. 140 E13 42.32 N 99.42 W
Long Point, Austl. 192a 34.01 S 150.54 E
Long Point, c., Bah. 158f n18 25.01 N 77.20 W
Long Point, c., N.S., Can. 122 D16 46.51 N 60.19 W
Long Point, c., Ca., U.S. 198 33.44 N 118.23 W
Long Point, c., V.I.U.S. 158b e7 18.19 N 64.52 W
Long Point, pen., Mb., Can. 142 A15 53.00 N 98.45 W
Long Point, pen., On., Can. 126 F9 42.33 N 80.13 W
Long Point Bay, b., On., Can. 126 F9 42.40 N 80.14 W
Long Pond, l., U.S. 201 42.41 N 71.21 W
Longpont, Fr. 179 48.38 N 2.17 E
Long Prairie, Mn., U.S. 128 F4 45.58 N 94.52 W
Long Prairie, stm., Mn., U.S. 128 F4 46.19 N 94.37 W
Longquan, China 58 G8 28.02 N 119.06 E
Long Range Mountains, mts., Nf., Can. 111a j22 49.00 N 57.39 W
Longreach, Austl. 98 D5 23.26 S 144.14 E
Long Reach, b., N.B., Can. 122 E10 45.27 N 66.07 W
Long Reef Point, c., Austl. 192a 33.45 S 151.19 E
Long Run, stm., Il., U.S. 196 41.37 N 88.03 W
Long Run, stm., Pa., U.S. 197b 40.20 N 79.48 W
Long-Sault, On., Can. 126 C15 45.02 N 74.50 W
Longsegah, Indon. 66 B10 2.14 N 116.44 E
Longshan, China 58 G3 29.28 N 109.20 E
Longsheng, China 58 I3 25.47 N 110.00 E
Longs Peak, mtn., Co., U.S. 138 A3 40.15 N 105.37 W
Longtan, China 58 G3 28.19 N 109.00 E
Longtanhu Park, p.o.i., China 189a 39.53 N 116.26 E
Long Teru, Malay. 66 B9 3.52 N 114.15 E
Long Thanh, Viet. 64 G8 10.47 N 106.57 E
Longton, Eng., U.K. 180 53.43 N 2.48 W
Longton, Ks., U.S. 130 G1 37.22 N 96.04 W
Longtown, Eng., U.K. 10 F10 55.00 N 2.58 W
Long Truong, Viet. 187c 10.49 N 106.49 E
Longué, Fr. 20 G8 47.23 N 0.06 W
Longuesse, Fr. 179 49.04 N 1.56 E
Longueuil, Qc., Can. 126 C16 45.32 N 73.29 W
Longueville, Austl. 192a 33.50 S 151.10 E
Longuyon, Fr. 20 E14 49.26 N 5.36 E
Longview, Ab., Can. 144 F16 50.32 N 114.14 W
Long View, N.C., U.S. 124 I4 35.43 N 81.23 W
Longview, Tx., U.S. 136 B13 32.30 N 94.44 W
Longview, Wa., U.S. 146 D4 46.07 N 122.56 W
Longvilliers, Fr. 179 48.35 N 2.00 E
Longwai, Indon. 66 C10 0.46 N 116.33 E
Longwood Gardens, p.o.i., Pa., U.S. 203 39.52 N 75.40 W
Longwood Lake, N.J., U.S. 194 40.59 N 74.52 W
Longworth, B.C., Can. 144 C9 53.54 N 121.28 W
Longwy, Fr. 20 E14 49.31 N 5.46 E
Longxi, China 52 E5 34.56 N 104.41 E
Longxian, China 58 D2 34.49 N 106.57 E
Long Xuyen, Viet. 64 G7 10.22 N 105.25 E
Longyan, China 58 I7 25.05 N 117.01 E
Longyearbyen, Nor. 108 B28 78.13 N 15.41 E
Longyou, China 58 G8 29.02 N 119.10 E
Longzhen, China 52 B10 48.41 N 126.42 E
Longzhou, China 58 J2 22.20 N 106.51 E
Loni, India 190a 28.45 N 77.17 E
Lonigo, Italy 30 E8 45.23 N 11.23 E
Löningen, Ger. 24 D3 52.44 N 7.46 E
Lonja, stm., Cro. 30 E13 45.21 N 16.42 E
Lonoke, Ar., U.S. 134 C7 34.47 N 91.54 W
Lonquimay, Volcán, vol., Chile 172 I2 38.22 S 71.35 W
Lönsboda, Swe. 16 K12 56.23 N 14.19 E
Lonsdale, Mn., U.S. 128 G5 44.28 N 93.26 W
Lons-le-Saunier, Fr. 22 C11 46.40 N 5.32 E
Lontra, stm., Braz. 170 D1 6.29 S 48.38 W
Loo, Russia 42 D8 43.42 N 39.35 E
Loogootee, In., U.S. 130 F11 38.40 N 86.54 W
Lookeba, Ok., U.S. 138 F10 35.21 N 98.22 W
Looking Glass, stm., Mi., U.S. 126 F5 42.52 N 84.53 W
Lookout, Cape, c., N.C., U.S. 132 B9 34.35 N 76.32 W
Lookout, Cape, c., Or., U.S. 146 E2 45.20 N 124.00 W
Lookout Mountain, mtn., Or., U.S. 146 F6 44.20 N 120.22 W
Lookout Mountain, mts., U.S. 134 C13 34.33 N 85.33 W
Lookout Pass, p., U.S. 146 C11 47.27 N 115.42 W
Lookout Ridge, mts., Ak., U.S. 109 C8 69.07 N 158.36 W
Loolmalassin, vol., Tan. 86 E7 3.03 S 35.49 E
Loomis, Ne., U.S. 140 G13 40.28 N 99.30 W
Loomis, Wa., U.S. 146 B7 48.49 N 119.38 W
Loon Creek, stm., Id., U.S. 146 F12 44.48 N 114.48 W
Loongana, Austl. 96 F5 30.57 S 127.02 E
Loon Lake, l., Mi., U.S. 199 42.41 N 83.22 W
Loop, Tx., U.S. 136 B5 32.55 N 102.25 W
Loop, ngh., Il., U.S. 196 41.53 N 87.38 W
Loop Head, c., Ire. 10 I2 52.33 N 9.55 W
Loose, Eng., U.K. 178 51.14 N 0.31 E
Lop, China 54 A5 37.04 N 80.10 E
Lop, stm., Viet. 64 F8 13.16 N 107.22 E
Lopandino, Russia 26 H17 52.28 N 34.49 E
Lopatina, gora, mtn., Russia 50 F17 50.52 N 143.10 E
Lopatino, Russia 40 E14 52.37 N 45.47 E
Lopatka, mys, c., Russia 50 F20 50.53 N 156.40 E
Lopatovo, Russia 26 D12 56.08 N 29.10 E
Lopatyn, Ukr. 38 C3 50.13 N 24.50 E
Lop Buri, Thai. 64 E5 14.48 N 100.37 E
Lopévi, i., Vanuatu 101d k17 16.30 S 168.20 E
López, Mex. 154 B6 26.59 N 105.01 W
Lopez, Cap, c., Gabon 86 E1 0.37 S 8.42 E
Lop Nur, l., China 52 C3 40.29 N 90.15 E
Loppa, i., Nor. 14 B12 70.21 N 21.25 E
Loppi, Fin. 18 G11 60.43 N 24.25 E
Lo Prado, Chile 204e 33.26 S 70.45 W
Lopšen'ga, Russia 18 C24 64.58 N 37.41 E
Loptjuga, Russia 12 E22 63.15 N 47.54 E
Lopuhovka, Russia 40 F14 51.59 N 44.41 E
Łopuszno, Pol. 24 F16 50.57 N 20.15 E
Lora, stm., Ven. 168 C5 9.23 N 72.30 W
Lora, Hāmūn-i-, l., Asia 62 C1 29.17 N 64.46 E
Lora del Río, Spain 28 G5 37.39 N 5.31 W
Lorain, Oh., U.S. 124 C3 41.27 N 82.10 W
Lorain County Regional Airport, arpt., Oh., U.S. 197a 41.20 N 82.11 W
Loraine, Tx., U.S. 136 B7 32.24 N 100.42 W
Loralai, Pak. 70 C2 30.21 N 68.36 E
Lorca, Spain 28 G9 37.40 N 1.41 W
Lord Howe Island, i., Austl. 94 G6 31.33 S 159.05 E
Lord Howe Rise, unds. 174 L19 32.00 S 162.00 E
Lord Mayor Bay, b., Nu., Can. 110 B12 69.44 N 92.00 W
Lordsburg, N.M., U.S. 150 K8 32.21 N 108.42 W
Lord's Cricket Ground, p.o.i., Eng., U.K. 178 51.32 N 0.10 W
Loreauville, La., U.S. 134 G7 30.03 N 91.44 W
Loreley, misc. cult., Ger. 24 F3 50.08 N 7.45 E
Lorena, Braz. 170 L3 22.44 S 45.07 W
Lorengau, Pap. N. Gui. 101a a4 2.01 S 147.15 E
Lorenzo, Tx., U.S. 138 H7 33.40 N 101.32 W
Lorenzo Geyres, Ur. 172 F9 32.06 S 57.56 W
Lorestān, state, Iran 74 D11 33.30 N 48.30 E
Loreto, Arg. 172 C9 27.46 S 57.16 W
Loreto, Mex. 154 D8 22.16 N 101.58 W
Loreto, Mex. 154 B3 26.01 N 111.21 W
Loreto, state, Peru 168 H4 1.53 S 73.50 W
Lorette, Mb., Can. 142 E17 49.44 N 96.51 W
Loretto, Ky., U.S. 130 G12 37.38 N 85.24 W
Loretto, Tn., U.S. 134 B11 35.04 N 87.26 W
Lorica, Col. 168 C4 9.13 N 75.49 W
Lorient, Fr. 20 G5 47.44 N 3.22 W
L'Orignal, On., Can. 126 C15 45.36 N 74.41 W
Lorimer Park, p.o.i., Pa., U.S. 203 40.06 N 75.05 W
Lorimor, Ia., U.S. 130 C3 41.07 N 94.02 W
Lőrinci, Hung. 36 B6 47.43 N 19.41 E
Loring, Mt., U.S. 142 F6 48.47 N 107.51 W
Loring, Aeródromo de, arpt., Spain 184a 40.22 N 3.47 W
Loriol-sur-Drôme, Fr. 22 E10 44.44 N 4.48 E
Loris, S.C., U.S. 132 B7 34.03 N 78.53 W
Lorman, Ms., U.S. 134 F7 31.49 N 91.03 W
L'Orme, Fr. 179 48.39 N 1.41 E
Lorn, Firth of, b., Scot., U.K. 10 E6 56.18 N 5.43 W
Lorne, Austl. 98 L5 38.32 S 143.58 E
Lorne, N.B., Can. 122 C10 47.52 N 66.07 W
Lörrach, Ger. 24 I3 47.37 N 7.39 E
Lorraine, hist. reg., Fr. 20 F14 49.00 N 6.00 E
Los, Swe. 16 F13 61.44 N 15.10 E
Los, Îles de, is., Gui. 84 H2 9.30 N 13.48 W
Losada, stm., Col. 168 F4 2.13 N 73.51 W
Los Aguacates, Ven. 204c 10.35 N 66.48 W
Los Alamitos, Ca., U.S. 198 33.48 N 118.04 W
Los Alamitos Armed Forces Reserve Center, mil., Ca., U.S. 198 33.47 N 118.03 W
Los Alamitos Race Course, p.o.i., Ca., U.S. 198 33.48 N 118.03 W
Los Alamos, Ca., U.S. 148 I5 34.44 N 120.17 W
Los Alamos, N.M., U.S. 138 F2 35.53 N 106.18 W
Los Aldamas, Mex. 154 B9 26.02 N 99.12 W
Los Andes, Chile 172 F2 32.50 S 70.35 W
Los Angeles, Chile 172 H1 37.26 S 72.19 W
Los Angeles, Ca., U.S. 148 I7 34.03 N 118.14 W
Los Angeles, Ca., U.S. 198 34.03 N 118.14 W
Los Angeles Aqueduct, aq., Ca., U.S. 148 H7 35.21 N 118.02 W
Los Angeles Coliseum and Sports Arena, p.o.i., Ca., U.S. 198 34.01 N 118.17 W
Los Angeles Convention Center, bldg., Ca., U.S. 198 34.03 N 118.17 W
Los Angeles County Fairgrounds, p.o.i., Ca., U.S. 198 34.05 N 117.46 W
Los Angeles County Museum of Art, bldg., Ca., U.S. 198 34.05 N 118.22 W
Los Angeles Harbor, b., Ca., U.S. 198 33.42 N 118.16 W
Los Antiguos, Arg. 166 I2 46.33 S 71.35 W
Los Banos, Ca., U.S. 148 F5 37.03 N 120.50 W
Los Berros, Arg. 172 E3 31.56 S 68.39 W
Los Blancos, Arg. 166 D4 23.35 S 62.37 W
Los Bolones, Cerro, mtn., Mex. 154 G12 16.39 N 92.34 W
Los Cerrillos, Arg. 172 E5 31.58 S 65.26 W
Los Cerrillos, Aeropuerto, arpt., Chile 204e 33.30 S 70.43 W
Los Cerritos Center, shp. cen., Ca., U.S. 198 33.52 N 118.05 W
Los Coconos, Cerro, mtn., Mex. 136 H2 26.21 N 105.58 W
Los Conquistadores, Arg. 172 E8 30.35 S 58.28 W
Los Cuatro Álamos, Chile 204e 33.32 S 70.44 W
Los Dos Caminos, Ven. 204c 10.31 N 66.50 W
Loseley House, hist., Eng., U.K. 178 51.13 N 0.36 W
Losevo, Russia 38 C18 50.40 N 40.02 E
Los Frentones, Arg. 172 C7 26.24 S 61.24 W
Los Fresnos, Tx., U.S. 136 H10 26.04 N 97.28 W
Los Garza, Mex. 136 H8 26.23 N 99.46 W
Los Gatos, Ca., U.S. 148 F4 37.12 N 121.59 W
Los Hermanos, Islas, is., Ven. 168 B9 11.45 N 64.25 W
Los Herreras, Mex. 136 I8 25.53 N 99.24 W
Loshkarivka, Ukr. 38 F13 47.58 N 34.09 E
Losi, Nig. 191a 6.40 N 3.31 E
Łosice, Pol. 24 D18 52.12 N 22.42 E
Los Idolos, Parque Arqueológico de, hist., Col. 168 G3 1.55 N 76.10 W
Losinga, stm., Russia 14 E28 67.04 N 37.51 E
Lošinj, Otok, i., Cro. 30 F11 44.36 N 14.24 E
Losinoborskaja, Russia 48 C15 58.27 N 89.28 E
Los Jazmines, Presa, res., Mex. 204a 19.25 N 99.16 W
Los Juncos, stm., Mex. 136 D1 30.44 N 106.25 W
Los Juríes, Arg. 172 D6 28.28 S 62.06 W
Los Lagos, Chile 166 G2 39.51 S 72.47 W
Los Llanos, P.R. 158a b3 18.02 N 66.24 W
Los López, Mex. 136 H8 26.14 N 99.06 W
Los Lunas, N.M., U.S. 138 G2 34.48 N 106.44 W
Los'mino, Russia 26 E17 55.04 N 34.24 E
Los Mochis, Mex. 154 C4 25.47 N 108.59 W
Los Molinos, Ca., U.S. 148 C3 40.01 N 122.05 W
Los Naranjos, Ven. 204c 10.27 N 66.48 W
Lošnica, Bela. 26 F11 54.17 N 28.45 E
Los Nietos, Ca., U.S. 198 33.58 N 118.04 W
Los Nogales, Mex. 136 H8 26.14 N 99.42 W
Losolava, Vanuatu 101d j16 14.11 S 167.34 E
Los Olmos Creek, stm., Tx., U.S. 136 G9 27.16 N 97.46 W
Los Olmos Creek, stm., Tx., U.S. 136 H9 26.22 N 98.48 W
Los Padillas, N.M., U.S. 138 G2 34.58 N 106.41 W
Los Palacios, Arg. 172 D3 29.20 S 68.12 W
Los Palacios, Cuba 156 A6 22.35 N 83.14 W
Los Palacios y Villafranca, Spain 28 G4 37.10 N 5.55 W
Los Perros, Arroyo, stm., Arg. 206 34.37 S 58.46 W
Los Picachos, Parque Nacional, p.o.i., Col. 168 F4 2.57 N 74.34 W
Los Pinos, ngh., Cuba 204b 23.04 N 82.23 W
Los Pinos, stm., Co., U.S. 150 F9 36.48 N 107.36 W
Los Polvorines, Arg. 206 34.30 S 58.41 W
Los Quillayes, Chile 204e 33.34 S 70.37 W
Los Quirquinchos, Arg. 172 F7 33.22 S 61.44 W
Los Rábanos, P.R. 158a b2 18.11 N 66.50 W
Los Remedios, stm., Mex. 204a 19.31 N 99.05 W
Los Reyes la Paz, Mex. 204a 19.21 N 98.58 W
Los Ríos, state, Ec. 168 H2 1.30 S 79.25 W
Los Rodríguez, Mex. 154 B8 27.11 N 101.21 W
Los Roques, Islas, is., Ven. 168 B8 11.50 N 66.45 W
Los Sauces, Chile 172 H1 37.57 S 72.50 W
Lössel, Ger. 181 51.21 N 7.39 E
Lossiemouth, Scot., U.K. 10 D9 57.43 N 3.17 W
Lossnen, l., Swe. 16 E10 62.26 N 12.48 E
Lost, stm., U.S. 148 A4 41.56 N 121.30 W
Lost, stm., In., U.S. 130 F11 38.32 N 86.49 W
Lost, stm., Mn., U.S. 128 D3 47.49 N 96.03 W
Lost, stm., W.V., U.S. 124 E7 39.04 N 78.35 W
Los Taques, Ven. 168 B6 11.50 N 70.15 W
Lost Creek, stm., Al., U.S. 134 D11 33.38 N 87.14 W
Lost Creek, stm., Ar., U.S. 134 C6 34.09 N 92.29 W
Lost Creek, stm., Ut., U.S. 150 B5 41.04 N 111.32 W
Lost Creek, stm., Wy., U.S. 140 E4 42.00 N 108.11 W
Lost Draw, stm., Tx., U.S. 138 H6 32.58 N 102.01 W
Los Telares, Arg. 172 D6 28.59 S 63.26 W
Los Teques, Ven. 168 B8 10.20 N 67.02 W
Los Testigos, Islas, is., Ven. 168 B10 11.22 N 63.06 W
Lost Hills, Ca., U.S. 148 H6 35.37 N 119.40 W
Lostine, stm., Or., U.S. 146 E9 45.33 N 117.29 W
Lost Nation, Ia., U.S. 130 C7 41.58 N 90.48 W
Lostock, stm., Eng., U.K. 180 53.40 N 2.48 W
Lostock Gralam, Eng., U.K. 180 53.16 N 2.28 W
Los Trancos Creek, stm., Ca., U.S. 200 37.25 N 122.12 W
Los Trancos Woods, Ca., U.S. 200 37.21 N 122.12 W
Lost River Range, mts., Id., U.S. 146 G13 44.10 N 113.35 W
Lost Trail Pass, p., U.S. 146 E13 45.41 N 113.57 W
Losuia, Pap. N. Gui. 101a b5 8.32 S 151.03 E
Los Vidrios, Mex. 120 F6 31.59 N 113.25 W
Los Vilos, Chile 172 E2 31.53 S 71.29 W
Los Yébenes, Spain 28 E7 39.34 N 3.51 W
Losynivka, Ukr. 38 C10 50.50 N 31.55 E
Lot, state, Fr. 22 E7 44.35 N 1.40 E
Lot, stm., Fr. 22 E7 44.18 N 0.19 E
Lota, Chile 172 H1 37.05 S 73.09 W
Lotak, Indon. 66 D9 0.08 S 115.48 E
Løten, Nor. 16 G9 60.48 N 11.21 E
Lot-et-Garonne, state, Fr. 22 E6 44.20 N 0.20 E
Lothair, S. Afr. 90 E10 26.23 S 30.26 E
Lothringen see Lorraine, hist. reg., Fr. 20 F14 49.00 N 6.00 E
Loto, D.R.C. 86 E4 2.51 S 22.23 E
Lotošino, Russia 26 D18 56.13 N 35.38 E
Lotrului, Munții, mts., Rom. 36 D11 45.26 N 24.03 E
Lotsane, stm., Bots. 90 C8 22.41 S 28.10 E
Lott, Tx., U.S. 136 C10 31.12 N 97.02 W
Lotta (Lutto), stm., Eur. 14 D19 68.40 N 30.15 E
Löttringhausen, ngh., Ger. 181 51.27 N 7.27 E
Lotts Creek, stm., Ga., U.S. 132 D4 32.08 N 81.47 W
Lottsford Branch, stm., Md., U.S. 202c 38.55 N 76.49 W
Lotuke, Jabal, mtn., Sudan 82 G6 4.07 N 33.48 E
Lotung, Tai. 58 I9 24.41 N 121.46 E
Louang Namtha, Laos 64 B5 20.56 N 101.24 E
Louangphrabang, Laos 64 C6 19.52 N 102.07 E
Loubomo, Congo 86 E2 4.11 S 12.40 E
Loudéac, Fr. 20 F6 48.10 N 2.45 W
Louden Cove, b., N.Y., U.S. 194 41.05 N 73.43 W
Loudon, Tn., U.S. 132 A1 35.44 N 84.20 W
Loudonville, Oh., U.S. 124 D3 40.38 N 82.14 W
Loudun, Fr. 20 G9 47.00 N 0.04 E
Loué, Fr. 20 F8 48.00 N 0.08 W
Loue, stm., Fr. 20 H14 47.01 N 5.26 E
Louga, Sen. 84 F1 15.37 N 16.13 W
Louge, Arg. 172 H7 36.57 S 61.40 W
Louge, stm., Fr. 22 F6 43.27 N 1.19 E
Loughborough, Eng., U.K. 10 I11 52.46 N 1.13 W
Loughrea, Ire. 10 H4 53.12 N 8.34 W
Loughton, Eng., U.K. 178 51.39 N 0.03 E
Louhans, Fr. 20 H14 46.37 N 5.13 E
Louhi, Russia 18 A20 66.04 N 33.02 E
Louin, Ms., U.S. 134 E9 32.04 N 89.15 W
Louisa, Ky., U.S. 124 F3 38.06 N 82.36 W
Louisa, Va., U.S. 124 F8 38.01 N 78.00 W
Louisbourg, N.S., Can. 122 E16 45.56 N 59.58 W
Louisbourg National Historic Site, p.o.i., N.S., Can. 122 E17 45.56 N 59.57 W
Louis Bull Indian Reserve, ind. res., Ab., Can. 144 D17 52.53 N 113.35 W
Louisburg, Ks., U.S. 130 F3 38.37 N 94.40 W
Louisburg, N.C., U.S. 124 H7 36.05 N 78.17 W
Louisdale, N.S., Can. 122 E15 45.37 N 61.03 W
Louise, Ms., U.S. 134 D8 32.58 N 90.35 W
Louise, Tx., U.S. 136 E11 29.06 N 96.25 W
Louiseville, Qc., Can. 126 B17 46.15 N 72.56 W
Louisiade Archipelago, is., Pap. N. Gui. 96 B10 11.00 S 153.00 E
Louisiana, Mo., U.S. 130 E6 39.27 N 91.03 W
Louisiana, state, U.S. 116 E6 31.15 N 92.15 W
Lou Island, i., Pap. N. Gui. 101a a4 2.23 S 147.20 E
Louis Trichardt, S. Afr. 90 C9 23.02 S 29.54 E
Louisville, Al., U.S. 134 F13 31.47 N 85.33 W
Louisville, Ga., U.S. 132 C3 32.59 N 82.24 W
Louisville, Il., U.S. 130 F9 38.46 N 88.30 W
Louisville, Ky., U.S. 130 F12 38.14 N 85.45 W
Louisville, Ms., U.S. 134 D9 33.07 N 89.03 W
Louisville, Ne., U.S. 130 D2 41.00 N 96.09 W
Louisville, Oh., U.S. 124 D4 40.49 N 81.16 W
Louisville Ridge, unds. 174 M22 35.27 S 170.20 W
Louis-XIV, Pointe, c., Qc., Can. 110 E14 54.37 N 79.44 W
Loukanga, Congo 191b 4.20 S 15.09 E
Loukoua, stm., Congo 191b 4.09 S 15.08 E
Loulé, Port. 28 G2 37.08 N 8.02 W
Loum, Cam. 86 D1 4.42 N 9.44 E
Loumou, Congo 191b 4.08 S 15.09 E
Lount Lake, l., On., Can. 128 A4 50.10 N 94.20 W
Louny, Czech Rep. 24 F9 50.21 N 13.47 E
Loup, stm., Ne., U.S. 140 F14 41.24 N 97.17 W
Loup City, Ne., U.S. 140 F14 41.16 N 98.57 W
Loups Marins, Lacs des, l., Qc., Can. 110 D16 56.27 N 73.53 W
Lourdes, Fr. 22 F5 43.06 N 0.03 W
Lourel de Baixo, Port. 184c 38.49 N 9.22 W
Lourenço Marques see Maputo, Moz. 90 D11 25.58 S 32.34 E
Loures, Port. 28 F1 38.50 N 9.10 W
Loures, stm., Port. 184c 38.50 N 9.08 W
Lourinhã, Port. 28 E1 39.14 N 9.17 W
Lourosa, Port. 28 D2 40.19 N 7.56 W
Lousã, Port. 28 D2 40.06 N 8.15 W
Lousa, Port. 184c 38.53 N 9.12 W
Louse Creek, stm., N.D., U.S. 140 A11 46.21 N 100.56 W
Lou Shan, mtn., China 54 B8 45.14 N 128.59 E
Loutézou, Île de, i., Congo 191b 4.22 S 15.10 E
Louth, Austl. 98 H5 30.32 S 145.06 E
Louth, Ire. 10 H6 53.57 N 6.33 W
Louth, Eng., U.K. 10 H13 53.22 N 0.00 W
Louth, state, Ire. 10 H6 53.55 N 6.30 W
Loutrá Aidipsoú, Grc. 34 E6 38.51 N 23.03 E
Loutre, stm., Mo., U.S. 130 F6 38.42 N 91.24 W
Loutre, Bayou de, stm., U.S. 134 E6 32.40 N 92.08 W
Loutrópyrgos, Grc. 185c 38.02 N 23.28 E
Louvain see Leuven, Bel. 20 D13 50.53 N 4.42 E
Louveciennes, Fr. 179 48.52 N 2.07 E
Louviers, Fr. 20 E10 49.13 N 1.10 E
Louviers, Co., U.S. 138 B4 39.30 N 105.00 W
Louvre, bldg., Fr. 179 48.52 N 2.20 E
Louwsburg, S. Afr. 90 E10 27.40 S 31.09 E
Lövånger, Swe. 16 C19 64.22 N 21.18 E
Lovat', stm., Russia 26 D13 58.12 N 31.27 E
Loveč, Blg. 36 F11 43.08 N 24.43 E
Loveč, state, Blg. 36 F11 43.20 N 25.00 E
Love Clough, Eng., U.K. 180 53.44 N 2.17 W
Lovedale, Pa., U.S. 197b 40.17 N 79.52 W
Lovelady, Tx., U.S. 136 C12 31.07 N 95.27 W
Loveland, Co., U.S. 140 G7 40.24 N 105.05 W
Lovell, Wy., U.S. 140 C4 44.50 N 108.23 W
Lovell Island, i., Ma., U.S. 201 42.20 N 70.56 W
Lovell Village, St. Vin. 159e p11 12.53 N 61.11 W
Lovelock, Nv., U.S. 148 C7 40.11 N 118.28 W
Lovely, Ky., U.S. 124 G3 37.49 N 82.24 W
Lovere, Italy 30 E6 45.48 N 10.03 E
Loves Green, Eng., U.K. 178 51.43 N 0.24 E
Loves Park, Il., U.S. 130 B8 42.19 N 89.02 W
Loviisa, Fin. 18 G13 60.27 N 26.13 E
Lovilia, Ia., U.S. 130 C5 41.08 N 92.54 W
Loving, N.M., U.S. 136 B3 32.17 N 104.05 W
Loving, Tx., U.S. 138 H10 33.15 N 98.30 W
Lovingston, Va., U.S. 124 G7 37.45 N 78.52 W
Lovington, Il., U.S. 130 E9 39.42 N 88.38 W
Lovington, N.M., U.S. 136 B4 32.56 N 103.21 W
Lovisa see Loviisa, Fin. 18 G13 60.27 N 26.13 E
Lovosice, Czech Rep. 24 F9 50.31 N 14.03 E
Lovozero, Russia 14 D25 68.00 N 35.01 E
Lovozero, Russia 18 B17 64.59 N 29.50 E
Lovozero, ozero, l., Russia 14 E26 67.54 N 35.12 E
Løvsøya, i., Nor. 16 E4 62.37 N 6.12 E
Lövstabruk, Swe. 16 G15 60.24 N 17.53 E
Lövstabukten, b., Swe. 16 G15 60.35 N 17.45 E
Lóvua, Ang. 88 B3 7.21 S 20.16 E
Low, Qc., Can. 126 C14 45.48 N 75.57 W
Low, Cape, c., Nu., Can. 110 C13 63.07 N 85.18 W
Lowa, D.R.C. 86 E5 1.24 S 25.50 E
Lowa, stm., D.R.C. 86 E5 1.24 S 25.52 E
Lowber, Pa., U.S. 197b 40.15 N 79.46 W
Lowden, Ia., U.S. 130 C7 41.51 N 90.55 W
Lowder Brook, stm., Ma., U.S. 201 43.14 N 71.11 W
Lowell, Ar., U.S. 130 H3 36.15 N 94.07 W
Lowell, In., U.S. 130 C10 41.17 N 87.25 W
Lowell, Ma., U.S. 124 B14 42.38 N 71.19 W
Lowell, Mi., U.S. 130 B12 42.56 N 85.20 W
Lowell, Or., U.S. 146 G4 43.55 N 122.46 W
Lowell, Lake, res., Id., U.S. 146 G10 43.33 N 116.40 W
Lowell, University of, educ., Ma., U.S. 201 42.39 N 71.20 W
Lowell-Dracut State Forest, p.o.i., Ma., U.S. 201 42.40 N 71.22 W
Löwen, stm., Nmb. 90 E3 27.11 S 17.40 E
Löwenberg, Ger. 24 D9 52.53 N 13.09 E
Löwenbruch, Ger. 182a 52.18 N 13.19 E
Lowe Pond, l., Ma., U.S. 201 42.41 N 70.59 W
Lower Aetna Lake, l., N.J., U.S. 203 39.51 N 74.48 W
Lower Arrow Lake, res., B.C., Can. 144 G12 49.40 N 118.08 W
Lower Austria see Niederösterreich, state, Aus. 30 B13 48.20 N 15.50 E
Lower Bershire Valley, N.J., U.S. 194 40.54 N 74.37 W
Lower Broughton, ngh., Eng., U.K. 180 53.29 N 2.15 W
Lower Brule Indian Reservation, ind. res., S.D., U.S. 140 C13 44.05 N 99.54 W
Lower California see Baja California, pen., Mex. 152 B2 27.53 N 113.27 W
Lower Darwen, Eng., U.K. 180 53.43 N 2.28 W
Lower Egypt see Misr el-Bahrī, hist. reg., Egypt 76 G1 31.01 N 31.02 E
Lower Eltham Park, p.o.i., Austl. 192b 37.45 S 145.09 E
Lower Fort Garry National Historic Park, p.o.i., Mb., Can. 142 D16 50.09 N 96.55 W
Lower Glenelg National Park, p.o.i., Austl. 98 L3 38.03 S 141.20 E
Lower Halstow, Eng., U.K. 178 51.22 N 0.40 E
Lower Higham, Eng., U.K. 178 51.26 N 0.28 E
Lower Hope, The, mth., Eng., U.K. 178 51.28 N 0.28 E
Lower Huron Metropolitan Park, p.o.i., Mi., U.S. 199 42.12 N 83.25 W
Lower Hutt, N.Z. 102 E6 41.12 S 174.55 E
Lower Keechi Creek, stm., Tx., U.S. 136 C12 31.08 N 95.45 W
Lower Klamath Lake, l., Ca., U.S. 148 B4 41.57 N 121.38 W
Lower Lake, l., U.S. 148 B5 41.15 N 120.02 W
Lower Manitou Lake, l., On., Can. 128 B5 49.15 N 93.00 W
Lower Montville, N.J., U.S. 194 40.54 N 74.22 W
Lower Mystic Lake, l., Ma., U.S. 201 42.26 N 71.09 W
Lower Nazeing, Eng., U.K. 178 51.44 N 0.01 E
Lower Peirce Reservoir, res., Sing. 189c 1.22 N 103.49 E
Lower Peover, Eng., U.K. 180 53.16 N 2.23 W
Lower Place, Eng., U.K. 180 53.36 N 2.09 W
Lower Plenty, Austl. 192b 37.44 S 145.06 E
Lower Post, B.C., Can. 110 D5 59.56 N 128.28 W
Lower Red Lake, l., Mn., U.S. 128 D4 47.56 N 95.00 W
Lower River Rouge, stm., Mi., U.S. 199 42.18 N 83.14 W
Lower Rouge Parkway, p.o.i., Mi., U.S. 199 42.18 N 83.20 W
Lower Saxony see Niedersachsen, state, Ger. 24 D5 52.40 N 9.00 E
Lower Seletar Reservoir, res., Sing. 189c 1.24 N 103.51 E
Lower Stoke, Eng., U.K. 178 51.27 N 0.38 E
Lower Trajan's Wall, misc. cult., Eur. 36 D15 45.40 N 28.30 E
Lower Van Norman Lake, res., Ca., U.S. 198 34.17 N 118.29 W
Lower West End Point, c., Anguilla 159a a1 18.10 N 63.10 W
Lower West Pubnico, N.S., Can. 122 G11 43.37 N 65.48 W
Lower Whitley, Eng., U.K. 180 53.18 N 2.35 W
Lower Woods Harbour, N.S., Can. 122 G11 43.31 N 65.44 W
Lowestoft, Eng., U.K. 10 I14 52.28 N 1.44 E
Lowgar, state, Afg. 70 A2 33.50 N 69.00 E
Łowicz, Pol. 24 D15 52.06 N 19.56 E
Lowmoor, Va., U.S. 124 G6 37.47 N 79.52 W
Lowrah, Hāmūn-e see Lora, Hāmūn-i-, l., Asia 62 C1 29.17 N 64.46 E
Lowries Run, stm., Pa., U.S. 197b 40.30 N 80.05 W
Low Rocky Point, c., Austl. 99a o12 42.58 S 145.29 E
Lowry City, Mo., U.S. 130 F4 38.08 N 93.43 W
Low Tatra Mountains see Nízke Tatry, mts., Slvk. 24 H16 48.54 N 19.40 E
Lowton, Eng., U.K. 180 53.28 N 2.35 W
Lowton Common, Eng., U.K. 180 53.29 N 2.33 W
Lowville, N.Y., U.S. 126 E14 43.47 N 75.29 W
Loxley, Al., U.S. 134 G11 30.37 N 87.45 W
Loxton, Austl. 98 J3 34.27 S 140.34 E
Loxton, S. Afr. 90 G6 31.28 S 22.20 E
Loyal, Wi., U.S. 128 G8 44.43 N 90.29 W
Loyal, Loch, l., Scot., U.K. 10 C8 58.23 N 4.21 W
Loyalsock Creek, stm., Pa., U.S. 126 G13 41.14 N 76.56 W
Loyalton, Ca., U.S. 148 D5 39.40 N 120.14 W
Loyalty Islands see Loyauté, Îles, is., N. Cal. 101d m17 21.00 S 167.00 E
Loyang, Sing. 189c 1.22 N 103.58 E
Loyauté, Îles (Loyalty Islands), is., N. Cal. 101d m17 21.00 S 167.00 E
Loyola College, educ., Md., U.S. 202b 39.21 N 76.37 W
Loyola Marymount University, educ., Ca., U.S. 198 33.58 N 118.25 W
Loyola University, educ., Il., U.S. 196 42.00 N 87.39 W
Loyoro, Ug. 86 D6 3.20 N 34.15 E
Lozère, state, Fr. 22 E9 44.30 N 3.30 E
Loznica, Yugo. 36 E6 44.31 N 19.14 E
Lozno-Oleksandrivka, Ukr. 38 D17 49.50 N 38.44 E
L'Ozone, ngh., D.R.C. 191b 4.21 S 15.14 E
Lozova, Ukr. 38 E15 48.53 N 36.19 E
Lozove, Ukr. 36 D6 49.17 N 27.17 E
Lozoyuela, Spain 28 D7 40.56 N 3.36 W
Lualaba, stm., Afr. 86 E5 0.22 N 25.21 E
Luama, stm., D.R.C. 86 E5 4.45 S 26.52 E
Lu'an, China 58 F7 31.44 N 116.29 E
Luan, stm., China 54 E3 39.23 N 119.16 E
Luancheng, China 58 J3 22.47 N 108.53 E
Luanda, Ang. 88 B1 8.49 S 13.14 E
Luando, stm., Ang. 88 C2 10.21 S 16.26 E
Luang, Khao (Maw Taung), mtn., Asia 64 G4 11.39 N 99.35 E
Luang, Khao, mtn., Thai. 64 H4 8.31 N 99.44 E
Luang, Thale, l., Thai. 64 I5 7.29 N 100.15 E
Luang Chiang Dao, Doi, mtn., Thai. 64 C4 19.23 N 98.54 E
Luanginga, stm., Afr. 88 C3 15.11 S 22.55 E
Luang Phrabang, Thiu Khao see Luang Prabang Range, mts., Asia 64 C5 18.30 N 101.15 E
Luang Prabang see Louangphrabang, Laos 64 C6 19.52 N 102.07 E
Luang Prabang Range, mts., Asia 64 C5 18.30 N 101.15 E
Luangue (Loange), stm., Afr. 86 F3 4.17 S 20.02 E
Luanguinga, stm., Afr. 86 G4 15.11 S 22.55 E
Luangwa, Zam. 86 G6 15.36 S 30.25 E
Luangwa, stm., Afr. 88 C5 15.37 S 30.25 E
Luanhaizi, China 70 A14 34.27 N 93.12 E
Luanping, China 58 A7 40.57 N 117.20 E
Luanshya, Zam. 88 C4 13.07 S 28.24 E
Luan Toro, Arg. 172 H5 36.12 S 65.05 W
Luanxian, China 58 B8 39.45 N 118.44 E
Luapula, stm., Afr. 86 G5 9.23 S 28.31 E
Luar, Danau, l., Indon. 66 C8 0.55 N 112.15 E
Luarca, Spain 28 A4 43.32 N 6.32 W
Luau, Ang. 86 G4 10.42 S 22.13 E
Luba, Eq. Gui. 84 I6 3.27 N 8.33 E
Lubaantun, hist., Belize 156 D3 16.17 N 88.58 W
Lubaczów, Pol. 24 F19 50.09 N 23.07 E
Lubalo, Ang. 88 B2 9.09 S 19.16 E
Lubań, Pol. 24 E11 51.07 N 15.17 E
Lubāna, Lat. 26 D9 56.54 N 26.41 E
Lubang, Phil. 68 D3 13.51 N 120.06 E
Lubang Islands, is., Phil. 68 D3 13.45 N 120.17 E
Lubango, Ang. 88 C1 14.54 S 13.29 E
Lubāns, l., Lat. 26 D9 56.46 N 26.53 E
Lübars, ngh., Ger. 182a 52.37 N 13.22 E
Lubartów, Pol. 24 E18 51.28 N 22.36 E
Lubawa, Pol. 24 C15 53.30 N 19.45 E
Lubaynī, Bahr el-, can., Egypt 191c 29.56 N 31.11 E
Lübben, Ger. 24 E9 51.56 N 13.53 E
Lübbenau, Ger. 24 E9 51.51 N 13.57 E
Lubber Brook, stm., Ma., U.S. 201 42.33 N 71.09 W
Lubbers Run, stm., N.J., U.S. 194 40.56 N 74.43 W
Lubbock, Tx., U.S. 138 H7 33.35 N 101.50 W
Lubbub Creek, stm., Al., U.S. 134 D11 33.04 N 88.10 W
Lubec, Me., U.S. 122 F9 44.51 N 66.59 W
Lübeck, Ger. 24 C6 53.52 N 10.40 E
Lubefu, D.R.C. 86 E4 4.43 S 24.25 E
Lubefu, stm., D.R.C. 86 E4 4.10 S 22.59 E
Lubelska, Wyżyna, plat., Pol. 24 E18 51.00 N 23.00 E
Lubelskie, state, Pol. 24 E18 51.15 N 22.45 E
Lüben see Lubin, Pol. 24 E12 51.24 N 16.12 E
Lubiana see Ljubljana, Slvn. 30 D11 46.03 N 14.31 E
Lubień Kujawski, Pol. 24 D15 52.24 N 19.09 E
Lubilash, stm., D.R.C. 86 F4 6.02 S 23.44 E
Lubin, Pol. 24 E12 51.24 N 16.12 E
Lubja, stm., Russia 183a 59.58 N 30.30 E
Lubjany, Russia 40 D17 56.01 N 51.24 E
Lublin, Pol. 24 E18 51.14 N 22.34 E
Lubliniec, Pol. 24 F14 50.40 N 18.41 E
L'ublino, ngh., Russia 183b 55.41 N 37.44 E
Lubnān see Lebanon, ctry., Asia 76 E6 34.00 N 36.00 E
Lubny, Ukr. 38 C11 50.01 N 33.00 E
Lubomierz, Pol. 24 F11 51.00 N 15.27 E
Luboń, Pol. 24 D12 52.20 N 16.53 E
Lubraniec, Pol. 24 D14 52.31 N 18.52 E
Lubsko, Pol. 24 E10 51.47 N 14.58 E

Name	Page	Map Ref.	Latitude	Longitude
Lübtheen, Ger.	24	C7	53.18 N	11.05 E
Lubu, China	58	J5	23.10 N	112.16 E
Lubuagan, Phil.	68	B3	17.21 N	121.10 E
Lubudi, D.R.C.	86	G5	9.57 S	25.58 E
Lubudi, stm., D.R.C.	84	B4	9.13 S	25.37 E
Lubukambacang, Indon.	66	D2	0.37 S	101.24 E
Lubukbatang, Indon.	66	F4	4.03 S	104.12 E
Lubukbertubung, Indon.	66	C3	0.02 N	102.06 E
Lubuklinggau, Indon.	66	E3	3.17 S	102.51 E
Lubukpakam, Indon.	66	B1	3.33 N	98.52 E
Lubuksikaping, Indon.	66	C1	0.07 N	100.10 E
Lubumbashi (Élisabethville), D.R.C.	86	G5	11.41 S	27.28 E
Lubuskie, state, Pol.	24	D11	52.15 N	15.15 E
Lubutu, D.R.C.	86	E5	0.44 S	26.35 E
Lübz, Ger.	24	C7	53.27 N	12.02 E
Lucan, On., Can.	126	E8	43.11 N	81.23 W
Lucanas, Peru	164	F3	14.36 S	74.14 W
Lucania see Basilicata, state, Italy	32	D10	40.30 N	16.10 E
Lucania, hist. reg., Italy	32	D10	40.30 N	16.00 E
Lucania, Mount, mtn., Yk., Can.	110	C3	61.01 N	140.28 W
Lucapa, Ang.	88	B3	8.25 S	20.44 E
Lucas, Ia., U.S.	130	C4	41.01 N	93.26 W
Lucas, Ks., U.S.	138	B10	39.03 N	98.30 W
Lucas Heights, Austl.	192a		34.02 S	150.58 E
Lucas Valley, Ca., U.S.	200		38.03 N	122.35 W
Lucasville, Oh., U.S.	124	F3	38.52 N	82.59 W
Lucban, Phil.	68	C3	14.06 N	121.32 E
Lucca, Italy	30	G7	43.51 N	10.29 E
Lucea, Jam.	158d	i12	18.26 N	78.10 W
Luce Bay, b., Scot., U.K.	10	G8	54.44 N	4.48 W
Lucedale, Ms., U.S.	134	G10	30.58 N	88.33 W
Lucena, Phil.	68	D3	13.56 N	121.36 E
Lucena, Spain	28	G6	37.24 N	4.28 W
Lucena del Cid see Llucena, Spain	28	D10	40.08 N	0.16 W
Luc-en-Diois, Fr.	22	E11	44.36 N	5.26 E
Lučenec, Slvk.	24	H15	48.19 N	19.40 E
Lucera, Italy	32	C9	41.30 N	15.19 E
Lucerne see Luzern, Switz.	30	C5	47.03 N	8.18 E
Lucerne, Ca., U.S.	148	D3	39.05 N	122.47 W
Lucerne, Lake of see Vierwaldstätter See, l., Switz.	30	D5	46.59 N	8.20 E
Lucerne Lake, l., Ca., U.S.	148	I9	34.31 N	116.57 W
Lucero, Lake, l., N.M., U.S.	136	B1	32.42 N	106.26 W
Luchena, stm., Spain	28	G8	37.44 N	1.50 W
Lucheng, China	58	I1	24.20 N	105.59 E
Luchou see Luzhou, China	58	G1	28.53 N	105.26 E
Luchou, Tai.	187d		25.05 N	121.28 E
Luchow see Luzhou, China	58	G1	28.53 N	105.26 E
Lüchow, Ger.	24	C7	52.58 N	11.09 E
Luchuan, China	58	J4	22.20 N	110.15 E
Lucinda, Austl.	98	B6	18.32 S	146.19 E
Lucindale, Austl.	98	K3	36.58 S	140.21 E
Lucira, Ang.	88	C1	13.52 S	12.31 E
Luck see Luts'k, Ukr.	38	C4	50.44 N	25.19 E
Luck, Wi., U.S.	128	F6	45.34 N	92.28 W
Luckau, Ger.	24	E9	51.51 N	13.42 E
Luckenwalde, Ger.	24	D9	52.05 N	13.10 E
Luckhoff, S. Afr.	90	F7	29.44 S	24.45 E
Luckiamute, stm., Or., U.S.	146	F3	44.45 N	123.09 W
Luck Lake, l., Sk., Can.	142	C6	51.05 N	107.07 W
Lucknow, On., Can.	126	E8	43.57 N	81.30 W
Lucknow, India	70	E8	26.51 N	80.55 E
Lucky Lake, Sk., Can.	142	D6	50.59 N	107.07 W
Lucky Peak Lake, res., Id., U.S.	146	G11	43.33 N	116.00 W
Luçon, Fr.	22	C4	46.27 N	1.09 W
Lucon, Pa., U.S.	203		40.14 N	75.25 W
Lučosa, stm., Bela.	26	E13	55.10 N	30.11 E
Lucusse, Ang.	88	C3	12.31 S	20.48 E
Lucy Creek, Austl.	96	D7	22.25 S	136.17 E
Lučyn, Bela.	26	G12	53.01 N	30.01 E
Lüda see Dalian, China	58	B9	38.53 N	121.34 E
Luda Kamčija, stm., Blg.	36	G14	43.02 N	27.26 E
Ludao, China	54	C8	43.51 N	129.19 E
Ludbreg, Cro.	30	D13	46.15 N	16.36 E
Luddenden, Eng., U.K.	180		53.44 N	1.56 W
Luddenham, Austl.	192a		33.53 S	150.41 E
Luddesdown, Eng., U.K.	178		51.22 N	0.24 E
Lüdenscheid, Ger.	24	E3	51.13 N	7.37 E
Lüderitz, Nmb.	90	E2	26.39 S	15.09 E
Ludhiāna, India	70	C5	30.54 N	75.50 E
Ludian, China	52	F5	27.12 N	103.35 E
Ludington, Mi., U.S.	126	E3	43.57 N	86.26 W
Ludlow, Eng., U.K.	10	I10	52.22 N	2.43 W
Ludlow, Ma., U.S.	124	B13	42.09 N	72.28 W
Ludlow, Vt., U.S.	122	G4	43.23 N	72.42 W
Ludogorie, reg., Blg.	36	F13	43.46 N	26.56 E
Ludoni, Russia	26	B12	58.12 N	29.20 E
Ludowici, Ga., U.S.	132	E4	31.42 N	81.44 W
Luduș, Rom.	36	C11	46.28 N	24.06 E
Ludvika, Swe.	16	G13	60.08 N	15.11 E
Ludwigsburg, Ger.	24	H5	48.53 N	9.11 E
Ludwigsfelde, Ger.	24	D9	52.17 N	13.16 E
Ludwigsfelder-Heide, for., Ger.	182a		52.18 N	13.14 E
Ludwigshafen am Rhein, Ger.	24	G4	49.28 N	8.26 E
Ludwigslust, Ger.	24	C7	53.19 N	11.30 E
Ludwigsort see Laduškin, Russia	26	F3	54.34 N	20.14 E
Ludza, Lat.	26	D10	56.32 N	27.44 E
Luebo, D.R.C.	86	F4	5.20 S	21.24 E
Lueders, Tx., U.S.	136	B8	32.46 N	99.38 W
Luena, Ang.	88	C3	11.47 S	19.54 E
Luena, D.R.C.	86	F5	9.27 S	25.47 E
Luena, stm., Ang.	88	C3	12.30 S	22.34 E
Luepa, Ven.	168	E11	5.43 N	61.31 W
Lueyang, China	58	E2	33.19 N	106.09 E
Lufeng, China	58	J6	22.56 N	115.37 E
Lufico, Ang.	88	B1	6.23 S	13.29 E
Lufira, stm., D.R.C.	86	F5	8.21 S	26.26 E
Lufkin, Tx., U.S.	136	C13	31.20 N	94.43 W
Luga, Russia	26	B12	58.44 N	29.51 E
Luga, stm., Russia	26	A11	59.40 N	28.18 E
Lugano, Switz.	30	D5	46.00 N	8.57 E
Lugano, Lago di, l., Eur.	30	E5	46.00 N	9.00 E
Lugansk see Luhans'k, Ukr.	38	E18	48.33 N	39.20 E
Luganville, Vanuatu	101d	j16	15.30 S	167.10 E
Lugards Falls, wtfl., Kenya	86	E7	3.01 S	38.42 E
Lugarno, Austl.	192a		33.59 S	151.03 E
Lugela, Moz.	88	D6	16.25 S	36.43 E
Lugenda, stm., Moz.	88	C6	11.25 S	38.29 E
Luggarus see Locarno, Switz.	30	D5	46.10 N	8.47 E
Luginino, Russia	26	C18	57.42 N	35.18 E
Lugnaquillia Mountain, mtn., Ire.	10	I6	52.58 N	6.27 W
Lugo, Italy	30	F8	44.25 N	11.54 E
Lugo, Spain	28	A3	43.00 N	7.33 W
Lugo, co., Spain	28	B3	43.00 N	7.25 W
Lugoj, Rom.	36	D8	45.41 N	21.54 E
Lugos see Lugoj, Rom.	36	D8	45.41 N	21.54 E
Lugovoj, Kaz.	48	F12	42.56 N	72.45 E
Lugovskij, Russia	50	E11	58.03 N	112.53 E
Luhanka, Fin.	18	F12	61.47 N	25.40 E
Luhans'k, Ukr.	38	E18	48.33 N	39.20 E
Luhans'k, co., Ukr.	38	D18	49.00 N	39.00 E
Luhe, China	58	E8	32.20 N	118.50 E
Luhe, stm., Ger.	20	A18	53.23 N	10.12 E
Luhovicy, Russia	26	F21	54.58 N	39.03 E
Luhyny, Ukr.	38	B7	51.04 N	28.22 E
Luiana, Ang.	88	D3	17.22 S	23.02 E
Luido, Moz.	90	B12	21.30 S	34.40 E
Luik see Liège, Bel.	20	D14	50.38 N	5.34 E
Luimneach see Limerick, Ire.	10	I4	52.40 N	8.38 W
Luino, Italy	30	D5	46.00 N	8.44 E
Luipaardsvlei, S. Afr.	191d		26.16 S	27.42 E
Luiro, stm., Fin.	14	E18	67.10 N	27.29 E
Luís Correia, Braz.	170	B5	2.53 S	41.40 W
Luisen-Berg, hill, Ger.	182a		52.27 N	13.07 E
Luis Guillón, Arg.	206		34.48 S	58.27 W
Luishia, D.R.C.	86	G5	11.10 S	27.02 E
Luis L. León, Presa, res., Mex.	136	F2	28.55 N	105.17 W
Luis Muñoz Marín, Aeropuerto Internacional, arpt., P.R.	158a	b3	18.26 N	66.00 W
Luis Peña, Cayo de, i., P.R.	158a	b5	18.18 N	65.19 W
Luitpold Coast, cst., Ant.	103	C1	77.52 S	32.36 W
Luiza, D.R.C.	86	F4	7.11 S	22.24 E
Luján, Arg.	172	F4	32.22 S	65.55 W
Luján, stm., Arg.	206		34.26 S	58.32 W
Luján de Cuyo, Arg.	172	F3	33.02 S	68.52 W
Lujia, China	187b		31.22 N	121.18 E
Lujiang, China	58	F7	31.14 N	117.17 E
Lukachukai Creek, stm., Az., U.S.	150	G7	36.38 N	109.36 W
Lukang, Tai.	58	I9	24.02 N	120.25 E
Luke Air Force Base, mil., Az., U.S.	150	J4	33.32 N	112.22 W
Lukenie, stm., D.R.C.	86	E3	2.44 S	18.09 E
Lukens, Mount, mtn., Ca., U.S.	198		34.16 N	118.14 W
Lukeville, Az., U.S.	150	L4	31.53 N	112.48 W
Luki, Bela.	26	G9	53.29 N	26.15 E
Lukiv, Ukr.	38	B3	51.13 N	24.19 E
Lukojanov, Russia	40	D14	55.01 N	44.28 E
Lukolela, D.R.C.	86	F4	5.22 S	24.31 E
Lukolela, D.R.C.	86	E3	1.03 S	17.11 E
Lukovit, Blg.	36	F11	43.12 N	24.10 E
Łuków, Pol.	24	E18	51.56 N	22.22 E
Lukuga, stm., D.R.C.	86	F5	5.39 S	26.54 E
Lukula, D.R.C.	86	F2	5.22 S	12.57 E
Lukulu, Zam.	88	C3	14.24 S	23.16 E
Lukunga, stm., D.R.C.	191b		4.25 S	15.14 E
Lula, Ms., U.S.	134	C8	34.27 N	90.28 W
Lulaka, stm., D.R.C.	86	E4	0.52 S	20.10 E
Luleå, Swe.	14	G13	65.35 N	22.10 E
Luleälven, stm., Swe.	14	G12	65.45 N	21.44 E
Lüleburgaz, Tur.	34	B10	41.25 N	27.21 E
Lules, Arg.	172	C5	26.56 S	65.21 W
Luliang, China	52	G5	25.02 N	103.38 E
Lüliang Shan, mts., China	58	C4	37.25 N	111.20 E
Luliao, Tai.	187d		25.07 N	121.39 E
Luling, Tx., U.S.	136	E10	29.40 N	97.38 W
Lullingstone Castle, hist., Eng., U.K.	178		51.21 N	0.12 E
Lulonga, D.R.C.	86	D3	0.37 N	18.22 E
Lulonga, stm., D.R.C.	86	D3	0.37 N	18.21 E
Lulua, stm., D.R.C.	86	F4	5.02 S	21.06 E
Luluabourg see Kananga, D.R.C.	86	F4	5.54 S	22.25 E
Lumajang, Indon.	66	H8	8.07 S	113.13 E
Lumajangdong Co, l., China	70	B8	34.00 N	81.38 E
Lumaku, Gunong, mtn., Malay.	66	A9	4.52 N	115.38 E
Lumaling, China	70	D14	29.51 N	92.36 E
Lumana, D.R.C.	86	E5	3.46 S	26.23 E
Lumb, Eng., U.K.	180		53.42 N	1.58 W
Lumbala Kaquengue, Ang.	88	C3	12.39 S	22.34 E
Lumbala N'guimbo, Ang.	88	C3	14.06 S	21.26 E
Lumber, stm., U.S.	132	B6	34.12 N	79.10 W
Lumber City, Ga., U.S.	132	E3	31.55 N	82.40 W
Lumberport, W.V., U.S.	124	E5	39.22 N	80.20 W
Lumberton, Ms., U.S.	134	G9	31.00 N	89.29 W
Lumberton, N.J., U.S.	203		39.57 N	74.48 W
Lumberton, N.C., U.S.	132	B7	34.37 N	79.00 W
Lumberton, Tx., U.S.	136	D13	30.14 N	94.12 W
Lumbis, Indon.	66	A10	4.15 N	116.18 E
Lumbo, Moz.	88	D7	15.03 S	40.39 E
Lumbovka, Russia	14	E31	67.42 N	40.33 E
Lumbrales, Spain	28	D4	40.56 N	6.41 W
Lumby, B.C., Can.	144	F12	50.14 N	118.59 W
Lumding, India	70	F14	25.45 N	93.10 E
Lumphăt, Camb.	64	F8	13.30 N	106.58 E
Lumphini Park, p.o.i., Thai.	187a		13.44 N	100.33 E
Lumpkin, Ga., U.S.	134	E14	32.03 N	84.47 W
Lumsden, Sk., Can.	142	D9	50.38 N	104.51 W
Lumu, Indon.	66	E11	2.12 S	119.09 E
Lumut, Malay.	64	J5	4.13 N	100.38 E
Lumut, Tanjung, c., Indon.	66	E4	3.50 S	105.57 E
Lün, Mong.	52	B6	47.52 N	105.15 E
Lunada Bay, b., Ca., U.S.	198		33.46 N	118.25 W
Luna Pier, Mi., U.S.	124	C2	41.47 N	83.26 W
Lūnāvāda, India	70	G4	23.07 N	73.36 E
Lund, B.C., Can.	144	G6	49.57 N	124.42 W
Lund, Swe.	16	L11	55.42 N	13.11 E
Lund, Nv., U.S.	148	E10	38.51 N	115.00 W
Lundar, Mb., Can.	142	D15	50.41 N	98.01 W
Lundazi, Zam.	88	C5	12.18 S	33.08 E
Lunde, Nor.	16	H7	59.17 N	9.06 E
Lundevatn, l., Nor.	16	I4	58.21 N	6.36 E
Lundy, i., Eng., U.K.	10	J8	51.10 N	4.40 W
Lune, stm., Eng., U.K.	10	G10	54.02 N	2.50 W
Lüneburg, Ger.	24	C6	53.15 N	10.24 E
Lüneburger Heide, reg., Ger.	24	D6	53.08 N	10.04 E
Lunel, Fr.	22	F10	43.40 N	4.08 E
Lünen, Ger.	24	E3	51.36 N	7.31 E
Lunenburg, N.S., Can.	122	F12	44.22 N	64.19 W
Lunenburg, Va., U.S.	124	H7	36.57 N	78.16 W
Lünern, Ger.	181		51.33 N	7.46 E
Lunéville, Fr.	20	F15	48.35 N	6.29 E
Lunge'nake, China	70	C10	31.45 N	85.55 E
Lunggar, China	70	C9	31.04 N	83.56 E
Lunghezza, ngh., Italy	185a		41.55 N	12.40 E
Lunglei, India	70	G14	22.53 N	92.44 E
Lungtsin see Longzhou, China	58	J2	22.20 N	106.51 E
Lunguè-Bungo (Lungwebungu), stm., Afr.	88	C3	14.19 S	23.12 E
Lungwebungu (Lunguè-Bungo), stm., Afr.	88	C3	14.19 S	23.12 E
Lūni, India	70	E4	26.00 N	73.00 E
Lūni, stm., India	70	F3	24.36 N	71.16 E
Lunin, Bela.	26	H9	52.18 N	26.34 E
Luninec, Bela.	26	H9	52.14 N	26.49 E
Lunino, Russia	40	E14	53.35 N	45.13 E
Lūnkaransar, India	70	D4	28.29 N	73.45 E
Lunna, Bela.	26	G7	53.27 N	24.16 E
Lunndörrsfjällen, mtn., Swe.	16	D11	63.00 N	13.00 E
Lunt, Eng., U.K.	180		53.31 N	2.59 W
Luntai, China	48	F14	41.46 N	84.10 E
Lunyuk, Indon.	66	H10	8.57 S	117.14 E
Luo, stm., China	58	D4	34.40 N	110.07 E
Luo, stm., China	58	D4	34.49 N	113.02 E
Luobei, China	52	B11	47.34 N	130.50 E
Luobu, China	58	I3	24.31 N	109.43 E
Luobumiao, China	58	A2	40.19 N	107.29 E
Luocheng, China	58	I3	24.47 N	108.53 E
Luochuan, China	58	D3	35.44 N	109.25 E
Luoding, China	58	J4	22.46 N	111.33 E
Luofu, D.R.C.	86	E5	0.08 S	29.13 E
Luohe, China	58	E6	33.34 N	114.02 E
Luoji, China	58	E7	32.05 N	117.13 E
Luojiatun, China	58	A8	40.10 N	118.33 E
Luonan, China	58	D4	34.05 N	110.03 E
Luoning, China	58	D4	34.25 N	111.42 E
Luoqi, China	58	G2	29.46 N	106.57 E
Luoqiao, China	58	H8	26.28 N	119.01 E
Luosto, hill, Fin.	14	E17	67.09 N	26.52 E
Luotian, China	58	F6	30.46 N	115.23 E
Luowenba, China	58	F2	31.48 N	107.51 E
Luoxiao Shan, mts., China	58	H6	26.00 N	114.00 E
Luoyang, China	58	D5	34.41 N	112.26 E
Luoyuan, China	58	H8	26.29 N	119.35 E
Luoyukou, China	58	B4	38.26 N	110.52 E
Luozi, D.R.C.	86	F2	4.56 S	14.08 E
Lupanshui, China	52	F5	26.37 N	104.47 E
Lupar, stm., Malay.	66	C7	1.20 N	111.19 E
Łupawa, Pol.	24	B13	54.25 N	17.26 E
Lupeni, Rom.	36	D10	45.21 N	23.13 E
Lupire, Ang.	88	C2	14.38 S	19.34 E
Lupon, Phil.	68	G6	6.54 N	125.59 E
Luputa, D.R.C.	86	F4	7.10 S	23.43 E
Luqiao, China	58	G9	28.34 N	121.23 E
Luqiao, China	58	E7	32.33 N	117.13 E
Luqu, China	52	E5	34.38 N	102.13 E
Luque, Spain	28	G6	37.32 N	4.15 W
Luquillo, P.R.	158a	b4	18.22 N	65.42 W
Luquillo, Sierra de, mts., P.R.	158a	b4	18.17 N	65.47 W
Luray, Va., U.S.	124	F7	38.38 N	78.27 W
Lure, Fr.	20	G15	47.41 N	6.29 E
Luremo, Ang.	88	B2	8.31 S	17.49 E
Lurgan, N. Ire., U.K.	10	G6	54.27 N	6.20 W
Luribay, Bol.	166	C3	17.05 S	67.38 W
Lurigancho, Peru	204d		12.02 S	77.01 W
Lurín, Peru	164	F2	12.17 S	76.52 W
Lúrio, Moz.	88	C7	13.31 S	40.30 E
Lúrio, stm., Moz.	88	C6	13.30 S	40.31 E
Lurnea, Austl.	192a		33.56 S	150.54 E
Lurøy, i., Nor.	14	F3	66.25 N	12.51 E
Lürrip, ngh., Ger.	181		51.12 N	6.28 E
Lusaka, Zam.	88	D4	15.24 S	28.17 E
Lusambo, D.R.C.	86	E4	4.57 S	23.29 E
Lusanga, D.R.C.	86	E3	4.49 S	18.45 E
Lusangi, D.R.C.	86	E5	4.37 S	27.07 E
Luscar, Ab., Can.	144	C13	53.04 N	117.24 W
Luseland, Sk., Can.	142	B4	52.05 N	109.24 W
Lush, Mount, mtn., Austl.	96	C5	17.02 S	127.30 E
Lushan, China	58	E5	33.44 N	112.53 E
Lu Shan, mtn., China	58	G6	29.31 N	115.58 E
Lushi, China	58	D4	34.05 N	111.02 E
Lushnja see Lushnjë, Alb.	32	D13	40.56 N	19.43 E
Lushnjë, Alb.	32	D13	40.56 N	19.43 E
Lushoto, Tan.	86	E7	4.47 S	38.17 E
Lüshun (Port Arthur), China	58	B9	38.48 N	121.15 E
Lusikisiki, S. Afr.	90	G9	31.22 S	29.34 E
Lusk, Wy., U.S.	140	E8	42.45 N	104.27 W
Lussac-les-Châteaux, Fr.	22	C6	46.24 N	0.44 E
Luster, Nor.	16	F5	61.25 N	7.25 E
Lustrafjorden, b., Nor.	16	F5	61.20 N	7.22 E
Lusutfu see Maputo, stm., Afr.	90	E11	26.10 S	32.41 E
Lūt, Dasht-e, des., Iran	72	C8	32.00 N	58.00 E
Lü Tao, i., Tai.	58	J9	22.40 N	121.29 E
Lutcher, La., U.S.	134	G8	30.02 N	90.41 W
Lute, Md., U.S.	202c		39.04 N	77.03 W
Lutembo, Ang.	88	C3	13.28 S	21.22 E
Lutesville, Mo., U.S.	130	G7	37.17 N	89.59 W
Lutexu, stm., D.R.C.	191b		4.24 S	15.12 E
Lütgendortmund, ngh., Ger.	181		51.30 N	7.21 E
Luther, Mi., U.S.	126	D4	44.02 N	85.40 W
Luther, Ok., U.S.	138	F11	35.40 N	97.11 W
Luther Lake, res., On., Can.	126	E9	43.56 N	80.25 W
Lutherstadt Eisleben, Ger.	24	E7	51.31 N	11.33 E
Lutherstadt Wittenberg, Ger.	24	E8	51.52 N	12.38 E
Lutherville-Timonium, Md., U.S.	202b		39.25 N	76.37 W
Luti, Sol. Is.	101b	d7	7.14 S	156.59 E
Luton, Eng., U.K.	10	J12	51.52 N	0.25 W
Luton, Eng., U.K.	178		51.22 N	0.32 E
Lutong, Malay.	66	A8	4.28 N	113.59 E
Łutselk'e, N.T., Can.	110	C8	62.22 N	110.55 W
Luts'k, Ukr.	38	C4	50.44 N	25.19 E
Lutto (Lotta), stm., Eur.	14	D19	68.40 N	30.15 E
Luttrell, Tn., U.S.	134	A15	36.11 N	83.44 W
Lüttringhausen, ngh., Ger.	181		51.13 N	7.14 E
Lutuhyne, Ukr.	38	E18	48.24 N	39.13 E
Lutz, Fl., U.S.	132	H3	28.09 N	82.27 W
Lutz Hill, Md., U.S.	202b		39.20 N	76.32 W
Lützow, Ger.	24	C7	53.39 N	11.11 E
Lutzow-Holm Bay, b., Ant.	103	B8	69.10 S	37.30 E
Lutzville, S. Afr.	90	G4	31.32 S	18.23 E
Luuq, Som.	86	D8	3.47 N	42.32 E
Luusalma, Russia	18	B18	65.03 N	31.34 E
Luusua, Fin.	14	F18	66.28 N	27.18 E
Luverne, Al., U.S.	134	F12	31.42 N	86.15 W
Lu Verne, Ia., U.S.	128	I4	42.54 N	94.04 W
Luverne, Mn., U.S.	128	H2	43.39 N	96.12 W
Luvozero, Russia	18	C17	64.26 N	30.42 E
Luvua, stm., D.R.C.	86	F5	6.45 S	26.57 E
Luvuvhu, stm., S. Afr.	90	C10	22.24 S	31.18 E
Luwegu, stm., Tan.	86	F7	8.31 S	37.23 E
Luwingu, Zam.	88	C4	10.15 S	29.55 E
Luwuk, Indon.	60	F7	0.56 S	122.47 E
Luxapallila Creek, stm., U.S.	134	D11	33.28 N	88.26 W
Luxembourg, Lux.	20	E14	49.36 N	6.07 E
Luxembourg, ctry., Eur.	20	E15	49.45 N	6.05 E
Luxembourg, Jardin du, p.o.i., Fr.	179		48.51 N	2.19 E
Luxemburg, Wi., U.S.	126	D2	44.32 N	87.42 W
Luxemburg see Luxembourg, ctry., Eur.	20	E15	49.45 N	6.05 E
Luxeuil-les-Bains, Fr.	20	G15	47.48 N	6.22 E
Luxi, China	52	G5	24.31 N	103.46 E
Luxi, China	52	G4	24.21 N	98.22 E
Luxi Dao, i., China	58	G9	27.59 N	121.11 E
Luxmanor, Md., U.S.	202c		39.02 N	77.07 W
Luxor see El-Uqsor, Egypt	74	H3	25.42 N	32.38 E
Luxora, Ar., U.S.	134	B9	35.45 N	89.55 W
Lu Xun Museum, bldg., China	187b		31.16 N	121.28 E
Lu Xun Park, p.o.i., China	187b		31.16 N	121.28 E
Luy, stm., Fr.	22	F5	43.39 N	1.08 W
Luyanó, stm., Cuba	204b		23.07 N	82.21 W
Luyuan, China	189a		39.54 N	116.27 E
Luz, Braz.	170	J3	19.47 S	45.39 W
Luz, Braz.	205a		22.48 S	43.05 W
Luz, ngh., Port.	184c		38.46 N	9.10 W
Luz, Estação da, trans., Braz.	205b		23.32 S	46.38 W
Luz, Ponta da, c., Braz.	205a		22.47 S	43.05 W
Luza, Russia	12	F22	60.37 N	47.16 E
Luza, Russia	18	E24	62.40 N	37.05 E
Luža, Russia	26	A14	59.58 N	31.56 E
Luzern (Lucerne), Switz.	30	C5	47.03 N	8.18 E
Luzhai, China	58	I3	24.33 N	109.48 E
Luzhai, China	187b		31.20 N	121.22 E
Luzhou, China	58	G1	28.53 N	105.26 E
Luziânia, Braz.	170	I2	16.15 S	47.54 W
Lužická Nisa see Lausitzer Neisse, stm., Eur.	24	E10	52.04 N	14.45 E
Lužická Nisa see Nysa Łużycka, stm., Eur.	24	E10	52.04 N	14.45 E
Luzilândia, Braz.	170	B4	3.28 S	42.22 W
Lužki, Bela.	26	E10	55.21 N	27.52 E
Lužnice, stm., Eur.	24	G10	49.13 N	14.23 E
Lužniki, ngh., Russia	183b		55.43 N	37.33 E
Luzon, i., Phil.	68	B3	16.00 N	121.00 E
Luzon Strait, strt., Asia	46	G16	20.30 N	121.00 E
Lužskaja guba, b., Russia	26	A11	59.45 N	28.20 E
Luzy, Fr.	20	H12	46.48 N	3.58 E
L'va, stm., Eur.	38	B6	52.00 N	27.30 E
L'va Tolstogo, Russia	26	F19	54.36 N	36.02 E
L'viv, Ukr.	38	D2	49.50 N	24.02 E
L'viv, co., Ukr.	38	D2	49.30 N	24.00 E
L'vov see L'viv, Ukr.	38	D2	49.50 N	24.02 E
L'vovskij, Russia	26	E20	55.19 N	37.31 E
Lwów see L'viv, Ukr.	38	D2	49.50 N	24.02 E
Lwówek, Pol.	24	D12	52.27 N	16.10 E
Lwówek Śląski, Pol.	24	E11	51.07 N	15.35 E
Lyallpur see Faisalabad, Pak.	70	C4	31.25 N	73.05 E
Lychkove, Ukr.	38	D14	49.05 N	35.12 E
Lyck see Ełk, Pol.	24	C18	53.49 N	22.22 E
Lyckeby, Swe.	16	K13	56.12 N	15.39 E
Lyčkovo, Russia	26	C15	57.55 N	32.23 E
Lycksele, Swe.	16	C16	64.35 N	18.41 E
Lycoming Creek, stm., Pa., U.S.	126	G12	41.13 N	77.01 W
Lydd, Eng., U.K.	10	K13	50.57 N	0.55 E
Lydda see Lod, Isr.	76	G5	31.58 N	34.54 E
Lydenburg, S. Afr.	90	D10	25.07 S	30.27 E
Lydenburgh County Park, p.o.i., N.Y., U.S.	194		40.50 N	73.14 W
Lydgate, Eng., U.K.	180		53.44 N	2.07 W
Lydia Mills, S.C., U.S.	132	B4	34.26 N	81.54 W
Lydiate, Eng., U.K.	180		53.32 N	2.57 W
Lye Green, Eng., U.K.	178		51.43 N	0.35 W
Lyell, Mount, mtn., Can.	144	E13	51.57 N	117.06 W
Lyerly, Ga., U.S.	134	C13	34.24 N	85.24 W
Lyford, Tx., U.S.	136	H10	26.24 N	97.46 W
Lygna, stm., Nor.	16	I5	58.08 N	7.03 E
Lygnern, l., Swe.	16	J10	57.29 N	12.20 E
Lyhivka, Ukr.	38	D15	49.09 N	36.03 E
Lykens, Pa., U.S.	124	D9	40.33 N	76.42 W
Lykhivka, Ukr.	38	E12	48.41 N	33.55 E
Lykošino, Russia	26	B16	58.06 N	33.43 E
Lyle, Mn., U.S.	128	H6	43.30 N	92.56 W
Lyl'jok, stm., Russia	14	E30	67.56 N	39.17 E
Lyman, Ukr.	38	H8	45.41 N	29.47 E
Lyman, Ukr.	38	D15	49.35 N	36.28 E
Lyman, Ne., U.S.	140	F8	41.54 N	104.02 W
Lyman, S.C., U.S.	132	B3	34.57 N	82.07 W
Lyman, Wy., U.S.	150	B6	41.20 N	110.19 W
Lymans'ke, Ukr.	38	G9	46.36 N	30.00 E
Lymany, Ukr.	38	G10	46.43 N	31.58 E
Lyme Bay, b., Eng., U.K.	10	K9	50.37 N	2.52 W
Lyme Hall, hist., Eng., U.K.	180		53.20 N	2.03 W
Lyme Park, p.o.i., Eng., U.K.	180		53.21 N	2.04 W
Lymm, Eng., U.K.	180		53.23 N	2.29 W
Lymyshivka, Ukr.	38	A10	52.04 N	31.38 E
Łyna (Lava), stm., Eur.	24	B16	54.37 N	21.13 E
Lynbrook, N.Y., U.S.	194		40.39 N	73.41 W
Lynch, Ne., U.S.	140	E14	42.49 N	98.27 W
Lynch, ngh., Arg.	206		34.36 S	58.31 W
Lynch, Lac, l., Qc., Can.	126	B12	46.24 N	77.05 W
Lynchburg, Oh., U.S.	124	E2	39.14 N	83.47 W
Lynchburg, S.C., U.S.	132	B5	34.03 N	80.04 W
Lynchburg, Tn., U.S.	134	B12	35.16 N	86.22 W
Lynchburg, Va., U.S.	124	G6	37.24 N	79.09 W
Lynd, stm., Austl.	98	A4	16.27 S	143.18 E
Lynden, Wa., U.S.	146	B4	48.56 N	122.26 W
Lyndhurst, Austl.	98	B5	19.13 S	144.22 E
Lyndhurst, Austl.	192b		38.03 S	145.15 E
Lyndhurst, N.J., U.S.	194		40.48 N	74.07 W
Lyndon, Ks., U.S.	130	F2	38.36 N	95.41 W
Lyndon, Ky., U.S.	130	F12	38.15 N	85.36 W
Lyndon, stm., Austl.	96	D2	23.29 S	114.08 E
Lyndon B. Johnson, Lake, res., Tx., U.S.	136	D9	30.33 N	98.22 W
Lyndon B. Johnson National Historical Site, p.o.i., Tx., U.S.	136	D9	30.15 N	98.38 W
Lyndon B. Johnson Space Center, sci., Tx., U.S.	136	E12	29.34 N	95.05 W
Lyne, Eng., U.K.	178		51.23 N	0.33 W
Lyngdal, Nor.	16	I4	58.08 N	7.05 E
Lyngen, b., Nor.	14	C11	69.54 N	20.29 E
Lyngør, Nor.	16	I7	58.37 N	9.06 E
Lyngseidet, Nor.	14	C11	69.34 N	20.13 E
Lynn, Al., U.S.	134	C11	34.02 N	87.32 W
Lynn, In., U.S.	130	D13	40.03 N	84.55 W
Lynn, Ma., U.S.	124	B14	42.28 N	70.57 W
Lynndyl, Ut., U.S.	150	D4	39.31 N	112.22 W
Lynne Acres, Md., U.S.	202b		39.21 N	76.45 W
Lynn Harbor, b., Ma., U.S.	201		42.27 N	70.57 W
Lynn Haven, Fl., U.S.	134	G13	30.14 N	85.38 W
Lynn Lake, Mb., Can.	110	D10	56.50 N	101.00 W
Lynnville, Ia., U.S.	130	C5	41.34 N	92.47 W
Lynn Woods, p.o.i., Ma., U.S.	201		42.29 N	70.59 W
Lynovytsia, Ukr.	38	C11	50.28 N	32.22 E
Lynton, Eng., U.K.	10	J9	51.14 N	3.50 W
Lyntupy, Bela.	26	E9	55.03 N	26.19 E
Lynwood, Il., U.S.	196		41.32 N	87.32 W
Lynx Lake, l., N.T., Can.	110	C9	62.25 N	106.21 W
Lyon, Fr.	22	D10	45.45 N	4.49 E
Lyon, stm., Scot., U.K.	10	E8	56.37 N	4.00 W
Lyon, Gare, trans., Fr.	179		48.51 N	2.23 E
Lyon Inlet, b., Nu., Can.	110	B14	66.32 N	83.53 W
Lyon Mountain, N.Y., U.S.	126	D15	44.44 N	73.54 W
Lyon Mountain, mtn., N.Y., U.S.	126	D16	44.41 N	73.53 W
Lyonnais, hist. reg., Fr.	22	D10	45.44 N	4.40 E
Lyonnais, Monts du, mts., Fr.	22	D10	45.40 N	4.30 E
Lyons, Co., U.S.	138	A3	40.13 N	105.15 W
Lyons, In., U.S.	130	F10	38.59 N	87.05 W
Lyons, Ks., U.S.	138	C10	38.20 N	98.12 W
Lyons, Mi., U.S.	126	F5	42.58 N	84.56 W
Lyons, Ne., U.S.	130	C1	41.56 N	96.29 W
Lyons, N.Y., U.S.	126	E13	43.03 N	76.59 W
Lyons, stm., Austl.	96	D3	25.01 S	115.10 E
Lyons Creek, stm., On., Can.	202a		43.03 N	79.04 W
Lyons Run, stm., Pa., U.S.	197b		40.25 N	79.43 W
Lyonsville, N.J., U.S.	194		40.57 N	74.25 W
Lypets'ke, Ukr.	38	F8	47.46 N	29.41 E
Lypova Dolyna, Ukr.	38	C12	50.34 N	33.48 E
Lypovets', Ukr.	38	D7	49.14 N	29.03 E
Lyptsi, Ukr.	38	C15	50.11 N	36.24 E
Lys, stm., Italy	30	E4	45.35 N	7.47 E
Lysa Hora, Ukr.	38	E10	48.10 N	31.06 E
Lysá pod Makytou, Slvk.	24	G14	49.11 N	18.13 E
Lysefjorden, b., Nor.	16	I4	58.59 N	6.14 E
Lysekil, Swe.	16	I9	58.16 N	11.27 E
Lysets', Ukr.	38	E3	48.52 N	24.36 E
Lyshnivka, Ukr.	38	B4	51.28 N	25.25 E
Lysianka, Ukr.	38	D9	49.14 N	30.49 E
Łysica, mtn., Pol.	24	F16	50.54 N	20.55 E
Lysina, mtn., Czech Rep.	24	F8	50.02 N	12.37 E
Lyskovo, Russia	40	D14	56.01 N	45.02 E
Lysogorka, Russia	38	F18	47.41 N	39.11 E
Lysterfield, Austl.	192b		37.56 S	145.18 E
Lysterfield, hill, Austl.	192b		37.56 S	145.16 E
Lysterfield Reservoir, res., Austl.	192b		37.58 S	145.18 E
Lys'va, Russia	40	B20	58.06 N	57.48 E
Lysychans'k, Ukr.	38	E17	48.54 N	38.26 E
Lysye Gory, Russia	40	F14	51.32 N	44.49 E
Lytham Saint Anne's, Eng., U.K.	10	H9	53.44 N	2.58 W
Lytle, Tx., U.S.	136	E9	29.13 N	98.47 W
Lytton, B.C., Can.	144	F9	50.14 N	121.34 W
Lytvynivka, Ukr.	38	D18	49.18 N	39.27 E

M

Name	Page	Map Ref.	Latitude	Longitude
Ma, stm., Asia	64	B7	19.46 N	105.52 E
Maalaea Bay, b., Hi., U.S.	100a	c5	20.47 N	156.29 W
Ma'ān, Jord.	76	H6	30.12 N	35.44 E
Ma'ān, state, Jord.	76	H7	30.20 N	36.30 E
Maaninka, Fin.	18	D14	63.09 N	27.19 E
Ma'anshan, China	58	F8	31.42 N	118.30 E
Maardu, Est.	26	A8	59.27 N	25.03 E
Maarianhamina (Mariehamn), Fin.	18	G6	60.06 N	19.56 E
Ma'arrat an-Nu'mān, Syria	76	C7	35.38 N	36.40 E
Ma'arrat Mişrīn, Syria	76	B7	36.01 N	36.41 E
Maas (Meuse), stm., Eur.	20	F14	51.49 N	5.00 E
Maasin, Phil.	68	E5	10.08 N	124.51 E
Maastricht, Neth.	20	D14	50.51 N	5.42 E
Maave, Moz.	90	B12	21.05 S	34.49 E
Mabalane, Moz.	90	C11	23.46 S	32.38 E
Mabank, Tx., U.S.	136	B11	32.22 N	96.05 W
Mabaruma, Guy.	168	C12	8.11 N	59.47 W
Mabashi, Japan	186		35.49 N	139.55 E
Mabau, Indon.	66	E7	2.16 S	111.52 E
Mabeleapodi, Bots.	90	B6	20.56 S	22.32 E
Mabel Lake, l., B.C., Can.	144	F12	50.35 N	118.44 W
Maben, Ms., U.S.	134	D9	33.33 N	89.05 W
Mablethorpe, Eng., U.K.	10	H13	53.20 N	0.15 E
Mableton, Ga., U.S.	134	D14	33.49 N	84.34 W
Mabote, Moz.	90	C12	22.02 S	34.08 E
Mabou, N.S., Can.	122	D15	46.04 N	61.22 W
Mabrak, Jabal, mtn., Jord.	76	H6	30.13 N	35.29 E
Mabton, Wa., U.S.	146	D6	46.12 N	119.59 W
Mabuasehube Game Reserve, ind. res., Bots.	90	D6	25.10 S	22.10 E
Mača, Russia	50	E12	59.53 N	117.33 E
Maca, Ven.	204c		10.28 N	66.48 W
Maca, Cerro, vol., Chile	166	H2	45.06 S	73.12 W
Macachín, Arg.	172	H6	37.08 S	63.41 W
Macaco, Morro do, hill, Braz.	205a		22.56 S	43.07 W
Macaé, Braz.	170	L5	22.23 S	41.47 W
Macaíba, Braz.	170	C8	5.51 S	35.21 W
Macajuba, Braz.	170	G5	12.10 S	40.22 W
Macalister, B.C., Can.	144	D8	52.27 N	122.24 W
Macalister, stm., Austl.	98	K6	38.02 S	146.58 E
Macalister, Mount, mtn., Austl.	98	J7	34.27 S	149.45 E
MacAlpine Lake, l., Nu., Can.	110	B10	66.37 N	102.51 W
Macan, Kepulauan, is., Indon.	66	G12	6.39 S	121.00 E
Macão, Port.	28	E2	39.33 N	8.00 W
Macao see Macau, dep., Asia	58	J5	22.10 N	113.33 E
Macapá, Braz.	164	C7	0.02 N	51.03 W
Macará, Ec.	164	D2	4.22 S	79.56 W
Macarani, Braz.	170	H5	15.32 S	40.25 W
Macarao, Ven.	204c		10.26 N	67.02 W
Macarao, stm., Ven.	204c		10.26 N	67.01 W
Macareo, Caño, stm., Ven.	168	C11	9.47 N	61.34 W
MacArthur, Phil.	68	E5	10.50 N	125.00 E
MacArthur, Il., U.S.	196		41.39 N	87.44 W
Macas, Ec.	168	I2	2.19 S	78.07 W
Macau, Braz.	170	C7	5.07 S	36.38 W
Macau, Macao	58	J5	22.12 N	113.32 E
Macau, dep., Asia	58	J5	22.10 N	113.33 E
Macaúbas, Braz.	170	G4	13.01 S	42.40 W
Macaya, Pic, mtn., Haiti	156	C11	18.25 N	74.00 W
Maccarese, ngh., Italy	185a		41.53 N	12.13 E
Maccarese, Bonifica di, reg., Italy	185a		41.51 N	12.13 E
MacClenny, Fl., U.S.	132	F3	30.16 N	82.07 W
Macclesfield, Eng., U.K.	10	H10	53.15 N	2.08 W
Macclesfield, mun., Eng., U.K.	180		53.17 N	2.15 W
Macclesfield Canal, can., Eng., U.K.	180		53.24 N	2.03 W
Macclesfield Forest, for., Eng., U.K.	180		53.15 N	2.03 W
Macculloch, Cape, c., Nu., Can.	110	A16	72.29 N	75.09 W
Macdhui, Ben, mtn., Afr.	90	G9	30.39 S	27.58 E
Macdiarmid, On., Can.	128	B10	49.26 N	88.08 W
MacDill Air Force Base, mil., Fl., U.S.	132	I3	27.51 N	82.29 W
Macdonald, Lake, l., Austl.	96	D5	23.30 S	129.00 E
MacDonald Pass, p., Mt., U.S.	146	D14	46.34 N	112.18 W
Macdonald Range, mts., B.C., Can.	144	G16	49.12 N	114.46 W
MacDonnell Ranges, mts., Austl.	96	D6	23.52 S	133.14 E
Macduff, Scot., U.K.	10	D10	57.40 N	2.30 W
Macdui, Ben, mtn., Scot., U.K.	10	D9	57.05 N	3.39 W
Maceday Lake, l., Mi., U.S.	199		42.42 N	83.26 W

Name	Page	Map Ref.	Latitude	Longitude
Macedonia, hist. reg., Eur.	34	C4	41.00 N	23.00 E
Macedonia, ctry., Eur.	34	B4	41.50 N	22.00 E
Maceió, Braz.	170	E8	9.40 S	35.43 W
Maceira, Port.	184c		38.52 N	9.19 W
Macenta, Gui.	84	H3	8.32 N	9.28 W
Maceo, Col.	168	D4	6.32 N	74.48 W
Macerata, Italy	30	G10	43.18 N	13.26 E
MacFarlane, stm., Sk., Can.	110	D9	59.18 N	108.02 W
Macgillycuddy's Reeks, mts., Ire.	10	J3	52.00 N	9.46 W
MacGregor, Mb., Can.	142	D15	49.57 N	98.49 W
Machachi, Ec.	168	H2	0.30 S	78.33 W
Machada, Mata Nacional da, p.o.i., Port.	184c		38.36 N	9.02 W
Machado, Braz.	170	K3	21.40 S	45.55 W
Machado, stm., Braz.	164	F5	8.01 S	62.53 W
Machagai, Arg.	172	C7	26.55 S	60.02 W
Machaila, Moz.	90	C11	22.15 S	32.55 E
Machakos, Kenya	86	E7	1.31 S	37.16 E
Machala, Ec.	164	D2	3.15 S	79.57 W
Machalí, Chile	172	G2	34.15 S	70.40 W
Machalilla, Parque Nacional, p.o.i., Ec.	168	H1	1.30 S	80.45 W
Machaneng, Bots.	90	C8	23.10 S	27.30 E
Machanga, Moz.	90	B12	20.58 S	34.59 E
Machaquilá, stm., Guat.	156	D3	16.12 N	90.00 W
Machattie, Lake, l., Austl.	98	E2	24.50 S	139.48 E
Machaze, Moz.	90	B11	20.49 S	33.25 E
Macheke, Zimb.	88	D5	18.08 S	31.50 E
Machekhy, Ukr.	38	D13	49.31 N	34.26 E
Macheng, China	58	F6	31.10 N	115.01 E
Macherio, Italy	184b		45.38 N	9.16 E
Mācherla, India	69	C4	16.28 N	79.26 E
Machery, Fr.	179		48.36 N	2.05 E
Machias, Me., U.S.	122	F9	44.42 N	67.27 W
Machias, stm., Me., U.S.	122	F9	44.40 N	67.21 W
Machilīpatnam (Bandar), India	69	C5	16.11 N	81.08 E
Machiques, Ven.	168	B5	10.03 N	72.31 W
Machkund, res., India	69	B6	18.26 N	82.35 E
Macho, Arroyo del, stm., N.M., U.S.	138	H4	33.36 N	104.28 W
Machupicchu, hist., Peru	164	F3	13.07 S	72.34 W
Machu Picchu see Machupicchu, hist., Peru	164	F3	13.07 S	72.34 W
Maciá, Arg.	172	F8	32.10 S	59.23 W
Macia, Moz.	90	D11	25.03 S	33.11 E
Măcin, Rom.	36	D15	45.15 N	28.10 E
Macina see Massina, reg., Mali	84	G4	14.37 N	4.38 W
Macintyre, stm., Austl.	98	G7	28.38 N	149.41 E
Mackay, Austl.	98	C7	21.09 S	149.11 E
Mackay, Id., U.S.	146	G13	43.54 N	113.37 W
Mackay, Lake, l., Austl.	96	D5	22.26 S	128.48 E
MacKay Lake, l., N.T., Can.	110	C8	63.54 N	110.22 W
Mackenzie, stm., Austl.	98	D7	23.37 S	149.45 E
Mackenzie, stm., N.T., Can.	110	B4	68.40 N	134.12 W
Mackenzie Bay, b., Can.	109	C12	69.00 N	136.30 W
Mackenzie King Island, i., Can.	108	B3	77.45 N	112.00 W
Mackenzie Mountains, mts., Can.	110	C4	64.00 N	130.00 W
Mackinac, Straits of, strt., Mi., U.S.	126	C5	45.49 N	84.42 W
Mackinac Bridge, trans., Mi., U.S.	126	C5	45.48 N	84.44 W
Mackinac Island, Mi., U.S.	126	C5	45.50 N	84.36 W
Mackinac Island, i., Mi., U.S.	114	D8	45.51 N	84.37 W
Mackinac Island State Park, p.o.i., Mi., U.S.	126	C5	45.51 N	84.37 W
Mackinaw, Il., U.S.	130	D8	40.32 N	89.21 W
Mackinaw, stm., Il., U.S.	130	D9	40.32 N	89.43 W
Mackinaw City, Mi., U.S.	126	C5	45.46 N	84.43 W
Mackinnon Road, Kenya	86	E7	3.43 S	39.02 E
Macklin, Sk., Can.	142	B4	52.20 N	109.56 W
Macksville, Austl.	98	H9	30.43 S	152.54 E
Macksville, Ks., U.S.	138	C9	38.57 N	98.58 W
Maclean, Austl.	98	G9	29.28 S	153.12 E
Maclear, S. Afr.	90	G9	31.03 S	28.20 E
Macleay, stm., Austl.	98	H9	30.52 S	153.01 E
Macleod, Austl.	192b		37.43 S	145.04 E
Macleod, Lake, l., Austl.	96	D2	24.04 S	113.41 E
Maclovio Herrera, Mex.	154	A6	29.05 N	105.08 W
Macmillan, stm., Yk., Can.	110	C4	62.51 N	135.52 W
Macomb, Il., U.S.	130	D7	40.27 N	90.40 W
Macomb Mall, shp. cen., Mi., U.S.	199		42.32 N	82.55 W
Macomer, Italy	32	D2	40.15 N	8.46 E
Macomia, Moz.	88	C6	12.15 S	40.06 E
Mâcon, Fr.	22	C10	46.18 N	4.49 E
Macon, Ga., U.S.	132	D2	32.50 N	83.36 W
Macon, Il., U.S.	130	E9	39.42 N	89.00 W
Macon, Ms., U.S.	134	D10	33.06 N	88.33 W
Macon, Mo., U.S.	130	E5	39.43 N	92.28 W
Macon, Bayou, stm., U.S.	134	E7	31.54 N	91.32 W
Macondo, Ang.	88	C3	12.33 S	23.46 E
Mâconnais, Monts du, mts., Fr.	22	C10	46.25 N	4.46 E
Macorís, Cabo, c., Dom. Rep.	156	C12	19.46 N	70.27 W
Macouba, Pointe de, c., Mart.	159c	k6	14.53 N	61.09 W
Macoupin Creek, stm., Il., U.S.	130	E8	39.11 N	90.35 W
Macovane, Moz.	90	B12	21.29 S	35.03 E
Macquarie, stm., Austl.	98	H6	30.08 S	147.23 E
Macquarie, stm., Austl.	99a	n13	41.44 S	147.08 E
Macquarie, Lake, l., Austl.	98	I8	33.05 S	151.34 E
Macquarie Fields, Austl.	192a		33.59 S	150.53 E
Macquarie Harbour, b., Austl.	99a	o12	42.19 S	145.23 E
Macquarie Island, i., Austl.	103	A20	54.30 S	158.56 E
Macquarie Marshes, sw., Austl.	98	H6	30.40 S	147.35 E
Macquarie Ridge, unds.	174	O18	56.53 S	158.27 E
Macquarie University, educ., Austl.	192a		33.46 S	151.06 E
MacRitchie Reservoir, res., Sing.	189c		1.21 N	103.50 E
Mac. Robertson Land, reg., Ant.	103	C10	70.15 S	65.04 E
Macroom, Ire.	10	J3	51.54 N	8.57 W
MacTier, On., Can.	126	C10	45.08 N	79.45 W
Macucuau, stm., Braz.	168	H11	0.37 S	61.23 W
Macugnaga, Italy	30	E4	45.58 N	7.57 E
Macujer, Col.	168	G5	0.23 N	72.55 W
Macul, Chile	204e		33.30 S	70.34 W
Macumba, stm., Austl.	96	E7	27.52 S	137.21 E
Macuro, Ven.	168	B10	10.39 N	61.56 W
Macusani, Peru	164	F3	14.03 S	70.25 W
Macuspana, Mex.	154	G12	17.45 N	92.35 W
Macuto, Ven.	204c		10.37 N	66.53 W
Mad, stm., On., Can.	126	D9	44.23 N	79.53 W
Mad, stm., Ca., U.S.	148	C2	40.56 N	124.08 W
Mad, stm., Oh., U.S.	130	E13	39.45 N	84.11 W
Mad, stm., Vt., U.S.	122	F4	44.17 N	72.42 W
Mādabā, Jord.	76	G6	31.43 N	35.47 E
Madagascar, ctry., Afr.	88	D8	19.00 S	46.00 E
Madagascar, i., Madag.	4	H16	20.00 S	47.00 E
Madagascar Basin, unds.	174	L8	27.00 S	52.59 E
Madagascar Plateau, unds.	174	M7	30.00 S	45.00 E
Madagasikara see Madagascar, ctry., Afr.	88	D8	19.00 S	46.00 E
Madā'in Şāliḩ, Sau. Ar.	72	D4	26.48 N	37.54 E
Madama, Niger	84	E7	21.57 N	13.38 E
Madame, Isle, i., N.S., Can.	122	E16	45.33 N	61.02 W
Madan, Blg.	36	H11	41.30 N	24.56 E
Madanapalle, India	69	E4	13.33 N	78.30 E
Madang, Pap. N. Gui.	101a	b4	5.16 S	145.45 E
Madanpur, India	190b		22.40 N	88.32 E
Madanpur Dabās, ngh., India	190a		28.43 N	77.02 E
Madaoua, Niger	84	G6	14.04 N	5.57 E
Mādārīpur, Bngl.	70	G13	23.09 N	90.11 E
Mādārīpur, India	190b		22.54 N	88.27 E
Madawaska, Me., U.S.	122	C8	47.21 N	68.21 W
Madawaska, stm., On., Can.	126	C13	45.27 N	76.20 W
Madawaska Highlands, plat., On., Can.	126	C11	45.15 N	77.35 W
Madaya, Mya.	64	A3	22.12 N	96.06 E
Maddalena, Colle della see Larche Pass, p., Eur.	30	F3	44.25 N	6.52 E
Maddalena, Isola, i., Italy	32	C3	41.14 N	9.24 E
Maddaloni, Italy	32	C8	41.02 N	14.23 E
Maddela, Phil.	68	B3	16.21 N	121.41 E
Maddock, N.D., U.S.	142	G14	47.57 N	99.31 W
Madeira, i., Port.	84	C1	32.44 N	17.00 W
Madeira, stm., S.A.	164	E5	3.21 S	58.44 W
Madeira, Arquipélago da (Madeira Islands), is., Port.	84	C1	32.40 N	16.45 W
Madeira Islands see Madeira, Arquipélago da, is., Port.	84	C1	32.40 N	16.45 W
Mädelegabel, mtn., Eur.	24	I6	47.18 N	10.18 E
Madeleine, Îles de la, is., Qc., Can.	122	C15	47.30 N	61.45 W
Madeleine, Pointe, c., Qc., Can.	193a		45.27 N	73.57 W
Madeleine-Centre, Qc., Can.	122	A11	49.13 N	65.23 W
Madelia, Mn., U.S.	128	G4	44.03 N	94.25 W
Madeline Island, i., Wi., U.S.	128	E8	46.47 N	90.40 W
Maden, Tur.	42	F8	38.23 N	39.40 E
Madera, Mex.	154	A4	29.11 N	108.09 W
Madera, Ca., U.S.	148	G5	36.58 N	120.03 W
Madera see Madeira, stm., S.A.	164	E5	3.21 S	58.44 W
Madetkoski, Fin.	14	E17	67.54 N	26.45 E
Madgaon, India	69	D1	15.16 N	73.57 E
Madh, ngh., India	190c		19.08 N	72.47 E
Madhepura, India	70	F11	25.55 N	86.47 E
Madhubani, India	70	E10	26.21 N	86.04 E
Madhudaha, India	190b		22.31 N	88.25 E
Madhugiri, India	69	E3	13.39 N	77.12 E
Madhupur, India	70	F11	24.16 N	86.39 E
Madhyamgrām, India	190b		22.42 N	88.27 E
Madhya Pradesh, state, India	62	D4	23.00 N	79.00 E
Madibogo, S. Afr.	90	E7	26.25 S	25.11 E
Madida, China	54	C9	42.56 N	130.45 E
Madidi, stm., Bol.	166	B3	12.31 S	66.58 W
Madill, Ok., U.S.	134	C2	34.05 N	96.46 W
Madimba, D.R.C.	86	E3	4.58 S	15.09 E
Madīnat ash-Sha'b, Yemen	72	G5	12.47 N	44.52 E
Madīnat ath Thawrah, Syria	76	C9	35.51 N	38.41 E
Madingo-Kayes, Congo	86	E2	4.25 S	11.41 E
Madingou, Congo	86	E2	4.09 S	13.33 E
Madirovalo, Madag.	88	D8	16.25 S	46.30 E
Madison, Al., U.S.	134	C12	34.42 N	86.44 W
Madison, Fl., U.S.	132	F2	30.27 N	83.24 W
Madison, Ga., U.S.	132	C2	33.35 N	83.28 W
Madison, In., U.S.	130	F12	38.44 N	85.23 W
Madison, Ks., U.S.	130	F1	38.08 N	96.08 W
Madison, Me., U.S.	122	F7	44.48 N	69.53 W
Madison, Mn., U.S.	128	F2	45.00 N	96.11 W
Madison, Mo., U.S.	130	E5	39.28 N	92.12 W
Madison, Ne., U.S.	140	F15	41.49 N	97.27 W
Madison, N.C., U.S.	124	H5	36.23 N	79.57 W
Madison, Oh., U.S.	130	C4	41.46 N	81.03 W
Madison, Pa., U.S.	197b		40.15 N	79.41 W
Madison, S.D., U.S.	140	C15	44.00 N	97.06 W
Madison, Va., U.S.	124	F7	38.22 N	78.15 W
Madison, W.V., U.S.	124	F4	38.03 N	81.49 W
Madison, Wi., U.S.	128	H9	43.04 N	89.22 W
Madison, stm., U.S.	146	E15	45.56 N	111.30 W
Madison, West Fork, stm., Mt., U.S.	146	F15	44.53 N	111.34 W
Madison Heights, Va., U.S.	124	G6	37.25 N	79.07 W
Madison Park, N.J., U.S.	194		40.26 N	74.19 W
Madison Range, mts., Mt., U.S.	146	E15	45.12 N	111.30 W
Madison Square Garden, p.o.i., N.Y., U.S.	194		40.45 N	74.00 W
Madisonville, Ky., U.S.	130	G10	37.19 N	87.29 W
Madisonville, La., U.S.	134	G8	30.24 N	90.09 W
Madisonville, Tn., U.S.	132	A1	35.31 N	84.22 W
Madisonville, Tx., U.S.	136	D12	30.56 N	95.55 W
Madiun, Indon.	66	G7	7.37 S	111.31 E
Madiyi, China	58	G4	28.14 N	110.30 E
Madoc, On., Can.	126	D12	44.30 N	77.28 W
Mado Gashi, Kenya	86	D7	0.43 N	39.10 E
Madoi, China	52	E4	34.54 N	98.11 E
Madon, stm., Fr.	20	F15	48.36 N	6.06 E
Madona, Lat.	26	D9	56.51 N	26.13 E
Madonie, mts., Italy	32	G7	37.52 N	13.58 E
Madonna di Campiglio, Italy	30	D7	46.13 N	10.49 E
Madora, Bela.	26	G13	53.09 N	30.11 E
Madrakah, Ra's al-, c., Oman	72	F8	19.00 N	57.50 E
Madras see Chennai, India	69	E5	13.05 N	80.15 E
Madras, Or., U.S.	146	F5	44.37 N	121.07 W
Madras see Tamil Nādu, state, India	69	F4	11.00 N	78.15 E
Madre, Laguna, b., Mex.	154	C10	25.00 N	97.40 W
Madre, Laguna, b., Tx., U.S.	136	H10	26.58 N	97.25 W
Madre, Sierra see Madre de Chiapas, Sierra, mts., N.A.	154	G12	16.01 N	93.08 W
Madre, Sierra, mts., Phil.	68	B4	16.20 N	122.00 E
Madre de Chiapas, Sierra, mts., N.A.	154	G12	16.01 N	93.08 W
Madre de Dios, stm., S.A.	166	B3	10.23 S	65.23 W
Madre de Dios, Isla, i., Chile	166	J1	50.15 S	75.04 W
Madre del Sur, Sierra, mts., Mex.	154	G9	17.00 N	100.00 W
Madre Occidental, Sierra, mts., Mex.	152	B3	25.00 N	105.00 W
Madre Oriental, Sierra, mts., Mex.	154	F9	21.26 N	99.50 W
Madrid, Spain	28	D7	40.24 N	3.41 W
Madrid, Spain	184a		40.24 N	3.41 W
Madrid, Al., U.S.	134	F13	31.02 N	85.23 W
Madrid, Ia., U.S.	134	C4	41.52 N	93.49 W
Madrid, Ne., U.S.	140	G11	40.51 N	101.32 W
Madrid, state, Spain	28	D7	40.30 N	3.40 W
Madridejos, Spain	28	E7	39.28 N	3.32 W
Madrillon, Va., U.S.	202c		38.55 N	77.14 W
Madroñera, Spain	28	E5	39.26 N	5.46 W
Madura, Austl.	96	F5	31.54 S	126.59 E
Madura see Madurai, India	69	G4	9.54 N	78.07 E
Madura, i., Indon.	66	G8	7.00 S	113.20 E
Madura, Selat, strt., Indon.	66	G8	7.25 S	113.25 E
Madurai, India	69	G4	9.54 N	78.07 E
Madurāntakam, India	69	E4	12.30 N	79.53 E
Madureira, Serra de, mts., Braz.	205a		22.49 S	43.31 W
Maduru, stm., Sri L.	69	H5	7.51 N	81.30 E
Mãe, Ilha da, i., Braz.	205a		22.59 S	43.04 W
Maebaru, Japan	56	F3	33.33 N	130.12 E
Maebashi, Japan	56	C11	36.22 N	139.04 E
Maeda, Japan	188		34.55 N	135.08 E
Mae Hong Son, Thai.	64	C3	19.15 N	97.56 E
Mae Klong, stm., Thai.	64	E4	14.07 N	99.28 E
Maelstrom see Moskenstraumen, strt., Nor.	14	E3	67.47 N	12.47 E
Maeno, ngh., Japan	186		35.46 N	139.42 E
Mae Ping Mae Hat Mae Kor National Park, p.o.i., Thai.	64	D4	17.35 N	98.45 E
Mae Ramat, Thai.	64	D4	16.58 N	98.31 E
Mae Rim, Thai.	64	C4	18.54 N	98.57 E
Mae Sariang, Thai.	64	C3	18.09 N	97.56 E
Maeser, Ut., U.S.	150	C7	40.28 N	109.35 W
Mae Sot, Thai.	64	D4	16.42 N	98.34 E
Maestra, Sierra, mts., Cuba	156	B9	20.05 N	76.24 W
Maestu, Spain	28	B8	42.44 N	2.25 W
Mae Tha, Thai.	64	C4	18.28 N	99.08 E
Maevatanana, Madag.	88	D8	16.56 S	46.50 E
Maéwo, i., Vanuatu	101d	j17	15.10 S	168.10 E
Mafeking, Mb., Can.	142	B12	52.41 N	101.06 W
Mafeking see Mafikeng, S. Afr.	90	D7	25.53 S	25.39 E
Mafeteng, Leso.	90	F8	29.49 S	27.15 E
Maffliers, Fr.	179		49.05 N	2.19 E
Maffra, Austl.	98	K6	37.58 S	146.58 E
Mafia Island, i., Tan.	86	F8	7.50 S	39.50 E
Mafikeng, S. Afr.	90	D7	25.53 S	25.39 E
Mafra, Braz.	172	C13	26.08 S	49.48 W
Mafra, Port.	28	F1	38.56 N	9.19 W
Magadan, Russia	50	E19	59.34 N	150.50 E
Magadi, Kenya	86	E7	1.56 S	36.18 E
Magaguadavic Lake, l., N.B., Can.	122	E9	45.43 N	67.12 W
Magalhães Bastos, ngh., Braz.	205a		22.53 S	43.23 W
Magalhães de Almeida, Braz.	170	B4	3.24 S	42.12 W
Magallanes see Punta Arenas, Chile	166	J2	53.09 S	70.55 W
Magallanes, Phil.	68	D4	12.49 N	123.50 E
Magallanes, Estrecho de see Magellan, Strait of, strt., S.A.	166	J2	54.00 S	71.00 W
Magangué, Col.	168	C4	9.17 N	74.47 W
Mağara, Tur.	76	B4	36.43 N	33.52 E
Magaria, Niger	84	G6	12.59 N	8.54 E
Magat, stm., Phil.	68	B3	17.02 N	121.49 E
Magazine Mountain, mtn., Ar., U.S.	134	B5	35.10 N	93.38 W
Magboro, Nig.	191a		6.43 N	3.24 E
Magdagači, Russia	50	F14	53.26 N	125.49 E
Magdalena, Arg.	172	G9	35.04 S	57.30 W
Magdalena, Bol.	166	B4	13.20 S	64.08 W
Magdalena, Mex.	154	E7	20.54 N	103.57 W
Magdalena, Peru	204d		12.06 S	77.05 W
Magdalena, N.M., U.S.	150	I9	34.07 N	107.14 W
Magdalena, state, Col.	156	H10	10.00 N	74.00 W
Magdalena, stm., Col.	168	B4	11.06 N	74.50 W
Magdalena, stm., Mex.	120	F6	30.42 N	112.08 W
Magdalena, Bahía, b., Mex.	154	C2	24.35 N	112.00 W
Magdalena, Isla, i., Chile	166	H2	44.40 S	73.10 W
Magdalena, Punta, c., Col.	168	F3	3.56 N	77.21 W
Magdalena Contreras, ngh., Mex.	204a		19.18 N	99.17 W
Magdalena de Kino, Mex.	120	F7	30.37 N	110.57 W
Magdalen Laver, Eng., U.K.	178		51.45 N	0.11 E
Magdeburg, Ger.	24	D7	52.07 N	11.37 E
Magé, mun., Braz.	205a		22.41 S	43.07 W
Magee, Ms., U.S.	134	F9	31.52 N	89.44 W
Magelang, Indon.	66	G7	7.28 S	110.13 E
Magellan, Strait of, strt., S.A.	166	J2	54.00 S	71.00 W
Magenta, Italy	30	E5	45.28 N	8.52 E
Mageroya, i., Nor.	14	A16	71.02 N	25.41 E
Magetan, Indon.	66	G7	7.39 S	111.19 E
Maggiorasca, Monte, mtn., Italy	30	F6	44.33 N	9.29 E
Maggiore, stm., Italy	185a		41.54 N	12.16 E
Maggiore, Lago, l., Eur.	30	D5	45.55 N	8.35 E
Maghāgha, Egypt	76	J1	28.39 N	30.50 E
Maghama, Maur.	84	F2	15.30 N	12.50 W
Magholpur, ngh., India	190a		28.42 N	77.06 E
Magic Reservoir, res., Id., U.S.	146	G12	43.16 N	114.22 W
Magill Heights, Pa., U.S.	197b		40.37 N	79.52 W
Māgina, mtn., Spain	28	G7	37.43 N	3.28 W
Maginu, Japan	186		35.35 N	139.36 E
Maglaj, Bos.	36	E5	44.33 N	18.05 E
Magliana, ngh., Italy	185a		41.50 N	12.25 E
Magliana, Fosso, stm., Italy	185a		41.49 N	12.25 E
Maglić, mtn., Bos.	36	F5	43.16 N	18.44 E
Maglie, Italy	32	D12	40.06 N	18.17 E
Maglód, Hung.	182c		47.27 N	19.21 E
M'aglovo, Russia	183a		59.53 N	30.41 E
Magnago, Italy	184b		45.35 N	8.48 E
Magnanville, Fr.	179		48.58 N	1.41 E
Magnesia see Manisa, Tur.	34	E10	38.36 N	27.25 E
Magnet, Mb., Can.	142	C14	51.19 N	99.30 W
Magnetawan, stm., On., Can.	126	C10	45.45 N	80.38 W
Magnetic Island, i., Austl.	98	B6	19.08 S	146.50 E
Magnetity, Russia	14	D23	68.42 N	33.05 E
Magnitogorsk, Russia	48	D9	53.25 N	59.05 E
Magnolia, Ar., U.S.	134	D5	33.15 N	93.14 W
Magnolia, Ma., U.S.	201		42.35 N	70.43 W
Magnolia, Ms., U.S.	134	F8	31.09 N	90.27 W
Magnolia, N.J., U.S.	203		39.51 N	75.02 W
Magnor, Nor.	16	H10	59.57 N	12.13 E
Magny-le-Hongre, Fr.	179		48.52 N	2.49 E
Magny-les-Hameaux, Fr.	179		48.44 N	2.04 E
Mago, Russia	50	F17	53.15 N	140.13 E
Mago, i., Fiji	101e	p20	17.27 S	179.09 W
Magog, Qc., Can.	122	E4	45.16 N	72.08 W
Magoito, Port.	184c		38.52 N	9.26 W
Magome, ngh., Japan	186		35.35 N	139.43 E
Magoúla, Grc.	185c		38.04 N	23.32 E
Magozal, Mex.	154	E10	21.33 N	97.58 W
Magpie, Qc., Can.	110	E17	50.19 N	64.29 W
Magra, stm., Italy	30	F6	44.05 N	9.57 E
Magrath, Ab., Can.	144	G18	49.25 N	112.52 W
Magro, stm., Spain	28	E9	39.11 N	0.24 W
Magruder Mountain, mtn., Nv., U.S.	148	F8	37.25 N	117.33 W
Magu, stm., Braz.	170	B4	2.56 S	41.50 W
Maguan, China	64	A7	23.01 N	104.23 E
Maguanying, China	189a		39.52 N	116.17 E
Maguari, Cabo, c., Braz.	164	D8	0.18 S	48.22 W
Magude, Moz.	90	D11	25.01 S	32.39 E
Magumeri, Nig.	84	G7	12.04 N	12.48 E
Māgura, Bngl.	70	G12	23.28 N	89.25 E
Maguse Lake, l., Nu., Can.	110	C12	61.38 N	95.11 W
Maguzhan, China	70	C11	31.14 N	87.59 E
Magway, Mya.	64	B2	20.30 N	94.30 E
Magway, state, Mya.	64	B2	20.30 N	94.30 E
Magwood Park, p.o.i., On., Can.	193b		43.39 N	79.30 W
Magyarország see Hungary, ctry., Eur.	36	B6	47.00 N	20.00 E
Mahābād, Iran	74	B9	36.45 N	45.43 E
Mahābaleshwar, India	69	C1	17.55 N	73.39 E
Mahabe, Madag.	88	D8	17.05 S	45.19 E
Mahābhārat Lek, mts., Nepal	70	E10	28.07 N	82.25 E
Mahabharat Range see Mahābhārat Lek, mts., Nepal	70	E10	28.07 N	82.25 E
Mahabo, Madag.	88	E7	20.23 S	44.40 E
Mahačkala, Russia	42	D12	42.58 N	47.29 E
Mahād, India	69	B1	18.06 N	73.27 E
Mahādeo Hills, hills, India	70	G7	22.20 N	78.35 E
Mahādeo Range, mts., India	69	C2	17.39 N	74.13 E
Mahagi, D.R.C.	86	D6	2.18 N	31.01 E
Mahajamba, stm., Madag.	88	D8	15.31 S	47.08 E
Mahājan, India	70	D4	28.48 N	73.52 E
Mahajanga, Madag.	88	D8	15.43 S	46.18 E
Mahākālī (Sārda), stm., Asia	70	D8	27.23 N	81.19 E
Mahakam, stm., Indon.	66	D9	0.35 S	117.16 E
Mahalapye, Bots.	88	E4	23.06 S	26.50 E
Mahalla el-Kubra see El-Mahalla el-Kubra, Egypt	76	H2	30.58 N	31.10 E
Maḩallāt, Iran	74	D12	33.52 N	50.34 E
Maham, India	70	D6	28.58 N	76.18 E
Mahānadi, stm., India	70	H8	20.19 N	86.47 E
Mahanoro, Madag.	88	D8	19.54 S	48.48 E
Mahanoy City, Pa., U.S.	124	D9	40.48 N	76.08 W
Mahao, China	54	C7	43.09 N	127.59 E
Mahape, India	190c		19.07 N	73.01 E
Maharagama, Sri L.	69	H4	7.03 N	80.01 E
Mahārājganj, India	70	E10	26.07 N	84.29 E
Mahārājpur, India	70	F7	25.01 N	79.44 E
Mahārājpur, India	190a		28.39 N	77.20 E
Mahārāshtra, state, India	62	E4	19.00 N	76.00 E
Mahārlū, Daryācheh-ye, l., Iran	74	F13	29.25 N	52.50 E
Mahāsamund, India	70	H9	21.06 N	82.06 E
Maha Sarakham, Thai.	64	D6	16.11 N	103.18 E
Maha Sawat, Khlong, can., Thai.	187a		13.47 N	100.28 E
Mahates, Col.	168	B4	10.14 N	75.12 W
Mahaut, Dom.	159c	j6	15.21 N	61.23 W
Mahaweli, stm., Sri L.	69	H5	8.26 N	81.13 E
Mahaxai, Laos	64	D7	17.24 N	105.12 E
Mahbūbābād, India	69	C4	17.35 N	80.00 E
Mahbūbnagar, India	69	C4	16.44 N	77.59 E
Mahd adh-Dhahab, Sau. Ar.	72	E5	23.30 N	40.52 E
Mahdalynivka, Ukr.	38	E13	48.55 N	34.56 E
Mahdia, Guy.	168	E12	5.15 N	59.08 W
Mahe, India	69	F2	11.42 N	75.32 E
Mahé, i., Sey.	89b	j13	4.40 S	55.28 E
Mahébourg, Mrts.	89a	i10	20.24 S	57.42 E
Mahendra Giri, mtn., India	69	B7	18.58 N	84.21 E
Mahendranagar, Nepal	70	D7	28.57 N	80.10 E
Mahenge, Tan.	86	F7	8.40 S	36.47 E
Maheriv, Ukr.	38	C2	50.07 N	23.43 E
Mahesāna, India	70	G4	23.36 N	72.23 E
Mahesgādi, India	190b		22.39 N	88.33 E
Maheshtala, India	190b		22.30 N	88.15 E
Maheshwar, India	70	G5	22.11 N	75.35 E
Mahi, stm., India	70	G4	22.13 N	72.45 E
Mahia Peninsula, pen., N.Z.	102	D7	39.10 S	177.53 E
Mahiāri, India	190b		22.35 N	88.14 E
Māhikpur, India	190b		22.32 N	88.14 E
Mahilëu, Bela.	26	G13	53.55 N	30.20 E
Mahilëu, state, Bela.	26	G13	53.45 N	30.30 E
Māhīm, ngh., India	190c		19.03 N	72.49 E
Māhīm, stm., India	190c		19.03 N	72.51 E
Māhīm Bay, b., India	190c		19.02 N	72.50 E
Mahina, Fr. Poly.	100h	u21	17.30 S	149.29 W
Mahishdānga, India	190b		22.54 N	88.11 E
Mahlabatini, S. Afr.	90	F10	28.14 S	31.28 E
Mahlsdorf, ngh., Ger.	182a		52.31 N	13.37 E
Mahlsdorf-Süd, ngh., Ger.	182a		52.29 N	13.36 E
Mahmūdābād, India	70	E8	27.18 N	81.07 E
Maḩmūdābād, Iran	74	B12	36.37 N	52.16 E
Mahmudiye, Tur.	34	D14	39.29 N	30.59 E
Mahmūdpur, India	190a		28.46 N	77.22 E
Mahmudpur, India	190b		22.41 N	88.09 E
Mahmutbey, ngh., Tur.	185b		41.03 N	28.49 E
Mahmutşevketpaşa, ngh., Tur.	185b		41.09 N	29.11 E
Mahnomen, Mn., U.S.	128	D2	47.18 N	95.58 W
Mahoba, India	70	F7	25.17 N	79.52 E
Mahogany Mountain, mtn., Or., U.S.	146	G9	43.14 N	117.16 W
Mahogany Tree, Anguilla	159a	a1	18.13 N	63.03 W
Mahomet, Il., U.S.	130	D9	40.11 N	88.24 W
Mahón see Maó, Spain	28	E15	39.53 N	4.15 E
Mahone Bay, N.S., Can.	122	F12	44.27 N	64.22 W
Mahone Bay, b., N.S., Can.	122	F12	44.30 N	64.15 W
Mahood Falls, B.C., Can.	144	E10	51.51 N	120.39 W
Mahood Lake, l., B.C., Can.	144	E10	51.55 N	120.24 W
Mahora, Spain	28	E9	39.13 N	1.44 W
Mahoras Brook, stm., N.J., U.S.	194		40.25 N	74.08 W
Mahrāt, Jabal, plat., Yemen	72	F7	17.05 N	51.30 E
Mahrauli, ngh., India	190a		28.31 N	77.11 E
Mahrauni, India	70	F7	24.34 N	78.43 E
Māhul, ngh., India	190c		19.01 N	72.53 E
Mahuva, India	70	H3	21.05 N	71.46 E
Mahwah, N.J., U.S.	194		41.06 N	74.09 W
Mahwah, stm., U.S.	194		41.06 N	74.10 W
Mai, Île de, i., Qc., Can.	193a		45.36 N	73.50 W
Maia, Port.	28	C2	41.14 N	8.36 W
Maiaky, Ukr.	38	G9	46.24 N	30.16 E
Maicao, Col.	168	B5	11.22 N	72.14 W
Maîche, Fr.	20	G15	47.15 N	6.47 E
Maichen, China	58	K3	20.20 N	109.59 E
Maicuru, stm., Braz.	164	D7	2.11 S	54.17 W
Maidan, p.o.i., India	190b		22.33 N	88.21 E
Maiden, N.C., U.S.	132	A4	35.34 N	81.12 W
Maidenhead, Eng., U.K.	10	J12	51.31 N	0.44 W
Maidstone, Austl.	192b		37.47 S	144.52 E
Maidstone, Sk., Can.	142	A4	53.05 N	109.17 W
Maidstone, Eng., U.K.	10	J13	51.16 N	0.31 E
Maidstone, mun., Eng., U.K.	178		51.17 N	0.35 E
Maiduguri, Nig.	84	G7	11.50 N	13.09 E
Maignelay, Fr.	20	E11	49.33 N	2.31 E
Mai Gudo, mtn., Eth.	82	F7	7.29 N	37.12 E
Maihar, India	70	F8	24.15 N	80.46 E
Maijoma, Mex.	136	F3	28.55 N	104.21 W
Maikala Range, mts., India	70	G8	22.30 N	81.30 E
Maikoor, Pulau, i., Indon.	60	G9	6.13 S	134.17 E
Maikop see Majkop, Russia	42	C8	44.36 N	40.06 E
Mailāni, India	70	D8	28.17 N	80.20 E
Main, stm., Ger.	24	F4	49.59 N	8.17 E
Main, stm., N. Ire., U.K.	10	G6	54.43 N	6.18 W
Maināguri, India	70	E12	26.34 N	88.49 E
Mainburg, Ger.	24	H7	48.38 N	11.46 E
Main Channel, strt., On., Can.	126	C8	45.22 N	81.41 W
Maincourt-sur-Yvette, Fr.	179		48.43 N	1.58 E
Main Creek, stm., N.Y., U.S.	194		40.34 N	74.11 W
Maincy, Fr.	179		48.33 N	2.42 E
Mai-Ndombe, Lac, l., D.R.C.	86	E3	2.25 S	18.17 E
Main-Donau-Kanal, can., Ger.	24	G7	49.02 N	11.34 E
Maine, hist. reg., Fr.	20	F8	48.14 N	0.05 W
Maine, state, U.S.	122	E7	45.15 N	69.15 W
Maine, stm., Ire.	10	I3	52.09 N	9.45 W
Maine, Gulf of, b., N.A.	122	G8	43.00 N	68.00 W
Maine-et-Loire, state, Fr.	20	G8	47.25 N	0.30 W
Maïné-Soroa, Niger	84	G7	13.13 N	12.01 E
Mainguerin, Fr.	179		48.32 N	1.51 E
Mainhardt, Ger.	24	G5	49.04 N	9.33 E
Mainland, Pa., U.S.	203		40.15 N	75.22 W
Mainland, i., Scot., U.K.	10	B9	59.04 N	3.07 W
Mainland, i., Scot., U.K.	10a	n18	60.16 N	1.16 W
Mainpuri, India	70	E7	27.13 N	79.01 E
Maintenon, Fr.	20	F10	48.35 N	1.35 E
Maintirano, Madag.	88	D7	18.02 S	44.01 E
Mainz, Ger.	24	G4	50.00 N	8.16 E
Maio, i., C.V.	85a	k10	15.11 N	23.10 W
Maipo, stm., Chile	172	F2	33.37 S	71.37 W
Maipo, Volcán, vol., S.A.	172	G3	34.10 S	69.50 W
Maipú, Arg.	172	F3	32.58 S	68.47 W
Maipú, Arg.	172	H8	36.51 S	57.54 W
Maipú, ngh., Chile	172	F2	33.30 S	70.44 W
Maiqihamiao, China	54	C4	43.22 N	120.46 E
Maiquetía, Ven.	168	B8	10.35 N	66.57 W
Maira see Mera, stm., Eur.	30	D6	46.12 N	9.26 E
Maira, stm., Italy	30	F3	44.50 N	7.38 E
Mairābāri, India	70	E14	26.27 N	92.25 E
Mairi, Braz.	170	F5	11.42 S	40.08 W
Mairiporã, mun., Braz.	205b		23.24 S	46.37 W
Maišiagala, Lith.	26	F8	54.52 N	25.04 E
Maiskhāl Island, i., Bngl.	70	H13	21.36 N	91.56 E
Maisonneuve, Parc, p.o.i., Qc., Can.	193a		45.33 N	73.34 W
Maisons-Alfort, Fr.	179		48.48 N	2.26 E
Maisons-Laffitte, Château de, hist., Fr.	179		48.57 N	2.09 E
Maitani, Japan	188		34.49 N	135.22 E
Maitembge, Bots.	88	E4	20.05 S	27.08 E
Maitland, Austl.	96	F7	34.22 S	137.39 E
Maitland, Austl.	98	I8	32.44 S	151.33 E
Maitland, N.S., Can.	122	E13	45.18 N	63.31 W
Maitland, stm., On., Can.	126	E8	43.45 N	81.43 W
Maitri, sci., Ant.	103	C6	70.46 S	12.00 E
Maíz, Islas del, is., Nic.	156	F6	12.15 N	83.00 W
Maizhokunggar, China	52	F3	29.50 N	91.43 E
Maizuru, Japan	56	D8	35.28 N	135.24 E
Maja, stm., Russia	50	E15	60.24 N	134.33 E
Majačnyj, Russia	40	E19	52.40 N	55.41 E
Majadahonda, Spain	184a		40.29 N	3.52 W
Majagual, Col.	168	C4	8.32 N	74.38 W
Majari, stm., Braz.	168	F11	3.26 N	60.59 W
Majavatn, Nor.	16	B11	65.10 N	13.22 E
Majene, Indon.	66	E11	3.32 S	118.57 E
Majevica, mts., Bos.	36	E5	44.36 N	18.44 E
Majī, Eth.	82	F7	6.10 N	35.35 E
Majia, stm., China	58	C7	38.07 N	117.49 E
Majiang, China	58	J4	23.44 N	111.05 E
Majiang, China	58	H2	26.28 N	107.28 E
Majiangzong, China	70	C12	30.28 N	90.03 E
Majidun Creek, stm., Nig.	191a		6.38 N	3.28 E
Majja, Russia	50	D15	61.43 N	130.16 E
Majkain, Kaz.	48	D13	51.27 N	75.49 E
Majkop, Russia	42	C8	44.36 N	40.06 E
Majnan, India	190b		22.59 N	88.09 E
Majŏn-ni, Kor., S.	189b		37.36 N	126.41 E
Major, Puig, mtn., Spain	28	E13	39.48 N	2.47 E
Majorca see Mallorca, i., Spain	28	E13	39.30 N	3.00 E
Majseevičy, Bela.	26	G11	53.13 N	28.17 E
Majskij, Russia	38	F19	47.41 N	40.06 E
Majskij, Russia	42	D11	43.38 N	44.04 E
Majskij, Russia	50	F14	52.16 N	129.32 E
Majskoe, Kaz.	48	D13	50.54 N	78.14 E
Majuro, at., Marsh. Is.	94	C8	7.05 N	171.09 E
Maka, Sen.	84	G2	13.40 N	14.17 W
Makabana, Congo	86	E2	3.26 S	12.38 E
Makah Indian Reservation, ind. res., Wa., U.S.	146	B1	48.18 N	124.36 W
Makahuena Point, c., Hi., U.S.	100a	b2	21.52 N	159.27 W
Makala, D.R.C.	191b		4.25 S	15.17 E
Makale, Indon.	66	E11	3.06 S	119.51 E
Makallé, Arg.	172	C8	27.11 S	59.18 W
Makālu, mtn., Asia	70	E11	27.54 N	87.06 E
Makanapur, India	190a		28.38 N	77.21 E
Makanči, Kaz.	48	E14	46.46 N	82.00 E
Makapuu Head, c., Hi., U.S.	100a	b4	21.18 N	157.39 W
Makarakomburu, Mount, mtn., Sol. Is.	101b	e8	9.43 S	160.02 E
Makarev, Russia	40	C13	57.52 N	43.46 E
Makari, Cam.	86	B2	12.35 N	14.27 E
Makar-Ib, Russia	12	E23	63.37 N	49.28 E
Makariv, Ukr.	38	C8	50.27 N	29.49 E
Makarov, Russia	50	G17	48.37 N	142.46 E
Makarska, Cro.	30	G14	43.17 N	17.01 E
Makasar see Ujungpandang, Indon.	66	F11	5.08 S	119.24 E
Makasar, Selat (Makassar Strait), strt., Indon.	66	D11	2.00 S	117.30 E
Makassar Strait see Makasar, Selat, strt., Indon.	66	D11	2.00 S	117.30 E
Makat, Kaz.	48	E8	47.39 N	53.21 E
Makati, Phil.	187f		14.34 N	121.02 E
Makawao, Hi., U.S.	100a	c5	20.51 N	156.18 W
Makedonija see Macedonia, hist. reg., Eur.	34	C4	41.00 N	23.00 E
Makedonija see Macedonia, ctry., Eur.	34	B4	41.50 N	22.00 E

Name	Page	Map Ref.	Latitude	Longitude
Makeevka see Makiïvka, Ukr.	38	E16	48.02 N	37.58 E
Makeni, S.L.	84	H2	8.53 N	12.03 W
Makgadikgadi, pl., Bots.	88	E4	20.16 S	25.42 E
Makgadikgadi Pans Game Reserve, ind. res., Bots.	90	B7	20.30 S	24.45 E
Makhaleng, stm., Afr.	90	G8	30.02 S	27.27 E
Mākhālpur, India	190b		22.56 N	88.10 E
Makham, Thai.	64	F5	12.42 N	102.10 E
Maki, Indon.	60	F9	3.11 S	134.12 E
Maki, Japan	56	B11	37.45 N	138.53 E
Maki, Japan	188		34.52 N	135.04 E
Makiïvka, Ukr.	38	E16	48.02 N	37.58 E
Makiïvka, Ukr.	38	C10	50.40 N	31.50 E
Makindu, Kenya	86	E7	2.15 S	37.49 E
M'akino, Russia	183b		55.48 N	37.22 E
Makinsk, Kaz.	48	D11	52.38 N	70.24 E
Makira, state, Sol. Is.	101b	f10	10.33 S	162.16 E
Makira Harbour, b., Sol. Is.	101b	f9	10.23 S	161.25 E
Makkah (Mecca), Sau. Ar.	72	E4	21.26 N	39.50 E
Makkovik, Nf., Can.	110	D19	55.05 N	59.11 W
Makó, Hung.	36	C7	46.13 N	20.30 E
Makogai, i., Fiji	101e	p19	17.27 S	178.58 E
Makok-ni, Kor., S.	189b		37.43 N	126.38 E
Makokou, Gabon	86	D2	0.34 N	12.51 E
Makona see Moa, stm., Afr.	84	H2	6.59 N	11.33 W
Makongolosi, Tan.	86	F6	8.24 S	33.09 E
Makoshika State Park, p.o.i., Mt., U.S.	142	G9	47.03 N	104.41 W
Makoshyne, Ukr.	38	B11	51.27 N	32.20 E
Makoua, Congo	86	E3	0.00 N	15.38 E
Makov, Slvk.	24	G14	49.23 N	18.28 E
Maków Mazowiecki, Pol.	24	D16	52.51 N	21.05 E
Maków Podhalański, Pol.	24	G15	49.44 N	19.39 E
Makrai, India	70	G6	22.02 N	77.09 E
Makrāna, India	70	E5	27.02 N	74.42 E
Makrān Coast, cst., Asia	72	D9	25.12 N	60.50 E
Makrany, Bela.	38	B3	51.50 N	24.15 E
Maksatiha, Russia	26	C18	57.48 N	35.53 E
Maksimkin Jar, Russia	48	C15	58.40 N	86.48 E
Maksymovychi, Ukr.	38	B8	51.13 N	29.37 E
Maktar, Tun.	32	I3	35.51 N	9.12 E
Mākū, Iran	74	A9	39.17 N	44.31 E
Makuhari, Japan	186		35.39 N	140.03 E
Makumbi, D.R.C.	86	F4	5.51 S	20.41 E
Makung, Tai.	58	J8	23.33 N	119.34 E
Makurazaki, Japan	56	H3	31.15 N	130.17 E
Makurdi, Nig.	84	H6	7.43 N	8.31 E
Makushin Volcano, vol., Ak., U.S.	109	F6	53.53 N	166.50 W
Makušino, Russia	48	C11	55.12 N	67.14 E
Makwassie, S. Afr.	90	E8	27.19 S	26.00 E
Māl, India	70	E12	26.52 N	88.45 E
Mala see Mallow, Ire.	10	I4	52.08 N	8.39 W
Mala, Peru	164	F2	12.39 S	76.37 W
Malå, Swe.	16	B16	65.11 N	18.45 E
Mala, Punta, c., Pan.	156	I8	7.28 N	80.00 W
Malabang, Phil.	68	G5	7.38 N	124.03 E
Malabar, Austl.	192a		33.58 S	151.15 E
Malabar Coast, cst., India	69	F2	11.00 N	75.00 E
Malabar Hill, hill, India	190c		18.57 N	72.48 E
Malabar Point, c., India	190c		18.57 N	72.47 E
Mala Bilozirka, Ukr.	38	F13	47.14 N	34.55 E
Malabo, Eq. Gui.	84	I6	3.44 N	8.46 E
Malacacheta, Braz.	170	I4	17.50 S	42.05 W
Malacañang Palace, bldg., Phil.	187f		14.36 N	120.59 E
Malacatepec, Volcán, vol., Mex.	204a		19.10 N	99.16 W
Malacca see Melaka, Malay.	64	K6	2.12 N	102.15 E
Malacca, Strait of, strt., Asia	64	K5	2.30 N	101.20 E
Malacky, Slvk.	24	H13	48.25 N	17.01 E
Malād, ngh., India	190c		19.11 N	72.51 E
Malad, stm., U.S.	146	H14	42.14 N	112.18 W
Malad City, Id., U.S.	146	H14	42.12 N	112.15 W
Malad Creek, stm., India	190c		19.08 N	72.48 E
Mala Divytsia, Ukr.	38	C11	50.41 N	32.10 E
Maladzečna, Bela.	26	F9	54.19 N	26.51 E
Malafede, stm., Italy	185a		41.47 N	12.24 E
Málaga, Col.	168	D5	6.42 N	72.44 W
Málaga, Spain	28	H6	36.43 N	4.25 W
Malaga, N.M., U.S.	136	B3	32.13 N	104.04 W
Málaga, co., Spain	28	H6	36.50 N	4.40 W
Malagarasi, Tan.	86	F6	5.05 S	30.48 E
Malagash, N.S., Can.	122	E13	45.46 N	63.22 W
Malagasy Republic see Madagascar, ctry., Afr.	88	D8	19.00 S	46.00 E
Malagón, Spain	28	E7	39.10 N	3.51 W
Malagón, stm., Spain	28	G3	37.35 N	7.29 W
Malahovka, Russia	183b		55.39 N	38.00 E
Mălăiești, Mol.	38	G8	46.58 N	29.33 E
Malaimbandy, Madag.	88	E8	20.17 S	45.36 E
Malaita, state, Sol. Is.	101b	d9	7.49 S	161.52 E
Malaita, i., Sol. Is.	101b	e9	9.00 S	161.00 E
Malaja Bykovka, Russia	40	F15	51.53 N	47.43 E
Malaja Kuril'skaja Grjada (Habomai-shotō), is., Russia	54	C17	43.38 N	146.24 E
Malaja Neva, mth., Russia	183a		59.57 N	30.15 E
Malaja Ochta, ngh., Russia	183a		59.56 N	30.24 E
Malaja Višera, Russia	26	B15	58.51 N	32.14 E
Malaka see Melaka, Malay.	64	K6	2.12 N	102.15 E
Malaka, Selat see Malacca, Strait of, strt., Asia	64	K5	2.30 N	101.20 E
Malaka, Sempitan, strt., Indon.	64	J2	5.42 N	95.24 E
Malakāl, Sudan	82	F6	9.31 N	31.39 E
Malakal, i., Palau	100b	g7	7.19 N	134.27 E
Malākand, Pak.	70	A3	34.34 N	71.56 E
Mala Kapela, mts., Cro.	30	F12	44.50 N	15.30 E
Malakoff, Fr.	179		48.49 N	2.19 E
Malakoff, Tx., U.S.	136	B12	32.11 N	96.01 W
Malakpur, ngh., India	190a		28.42 N	77.12 E
Malakula, i., Vanuatu	101d	k16	16.15 S	167.30 E
Malala, Pap. N. Gui.	101a	b4	5.16 S	147.09 E
Malamala, Indon.	66	E12	3.25 S	120.53 E
Malambo, Col.	168	B4	10.46 N	74.46 W
Malån, stm., Swe.	16	B16	65.00 N	19.45 E
Mālancha, India	190b		22.55 N	88.26 E
Malang, Indon.	66	H8	7.58 S	112.37 E
Malangen, b., Nor.	14	C8	69.25 N	18.25 E
Malanggwā, Nepal	70	E10	26.51 N	85.33 E
Malangka, Tanjung, c., Indon.	66	C12	1.19 N	120.49 E
Malanje, Ang.	88	B2	9.31 S	16.19 E
Malanville, Benin	84	G5	11.52 N	3.23 E
Malanzán, Arg.	172	E4	30.48 S	66.37 W
Mala Panew, stm., Pol.	24	F14	50.43 N	17.52 E
Malapardis Brook, stm., N.J., U.S.	194		40.49 N	74.25 W
Mälaren, l., Swe.	16	H15	59.30 N	17.12 E
Malargüe, Arg.	172	G3	35.28 S	69.35 W
Malartic, Qc., Can.	114	B11	48.08 N	78.07 W
Malaryta, Bela.	38	B2	51.47 N	24.04 E
Malaspina, Arg.	166	H3	44.56 S	66.54 W
Malaspina Glacier, ice, Ak., U.S.	109	E11	59.50 N	140.30 W
Malaspina Strait, strt., B.C., Can.	144	G6	49.44 N	124.20 W
Malassis, Fr.	179		48.38 N	2.03 E
Malāṭīyah, Egypt	76	J1	28.42 N	30.51 E
Mala Tokmachivka, Ukr.	38	F14	47.32 N	35.53 E
Malatya, Tur.	42	F8	38.20 N	38.18 E
Malatya, state, Tur.	42	F7	38.30 N	38.10 E
Malau, Vanuatu	101d	j16	15.10 S	166.48 E
Malaut, India	70	C5	30.13 N	74.29 E
Malavalli, India	69	E3	12.22 N	77.03 E
Mala Vyska, Ukr.	38	E10	48.39 N	31.38 E
Malawali, Pulau, i., Malay.	68	G1	7.03 N	117.18 E
Malawi, ctry., Afr.	88	C5	13.30 S	34.00 E
Malaŵi see Malawi, ctry., Afr.	88	C5	13.30 S	34.00 E
Malaŵi, Lake see Nyasa, Lake, l., Afr.	88	C5	12.00 S	34.30 E
Malaya see Semenanjung Malaysia, hist. reg., Malay.	64	K6	4.00 N	102.00 E
Malayagiri, mtn., India	70	H10	21.23 N	85.16 E
Mala Yanysil', Ukr.	38	F16	47.22 N	37.20 E
Malaybalay, Phil.	68	F5	8.09 N	125.07 E
Malāyer, Iran	74	C11	34.17 N	48.49 E
Malay Peninsula, pen., Asia	64	I5	6.00 N	101.00 E
Malay Reef, rf., Austl.	98	B7	18.01 S	149.09 E
Malaysia, ctry., Asia	64	J6	2.30 N	112.30 E
Malazgirt, Tur.	42	F10	39.08 N	42.33 E
Malbaie, La, b., Qc., Can.	122	B12	48.34 N	64.14 W
Malbon, Austl.	98	C3	21.04 S	140.18 E
Malbooma, Austl.	96	F6	30.40 S	134.11 E
Malbork, Pol.	24	B15	54.01 N	19.02 E
Malbrán, Arg.	172	D6	29.21 S	62.26 W
Mal'cevo, Russia	183b		55.56 N	37.57 E
Mal'čevskaja, Russia	40	G12	49.03 N	40.22 E
Malchin, Ger.	24	C8	53.43 N	12.46 E
Malchow, Ger.	24	C8	53.28 N	12.25 E
Malchow, ngh., Ger.	182a		52.35 N	13.29 E
Malcolm, Austl.	96	E4	28.55 S	121.30 E
Malcolm Island, i., B.C., Can.	144	F4	50.38 N	126.57 W
Malcom, Ia., U.S.	130	C5	41.42 N	92.33 W
Malcompeth see Mahābaleshwar, India	69	C1	17.55 N	73.39 E
Malczyce, Pol.	24	E12	51.12 N	16.31 E
Malden, Mo., U.S.	130	H7	36.33 N	89.58 W
Malden, i., Kir.	94	D11	4.03 S	154.59 W
Malden, stm., Ma., U.S.	201		42.24 N	71.05 W
Maldive Islands, is., Mald.	46	I11	5.00 N	73.00 E
Mal di Ventre, Isola di, i., Italy	32	D2	39.58 N	8.17 E
Maldives, ctry., Asia	44	I11	3.15 N	73.00 E
Maldon, mun., Eng., U.K.	178		51.43 N	0.40 E
Maldonado, Ur.	172	G10	34.55 S	54.56 W
Malè, Italy	30	D7	46.21 N	10.54 E
Male', Mald.	62a	i12	4.09 N	73.29 E
Male, Mya.	64	A2	23.02 N	95.58 E
Maléas, Ákra, c., Grc.	34	G6	36.26 N	23.12 E
Male' Atoll, at., Mald.	62a	i12	4.25 N	73.30 E
Mālegaon, India	70	H5	20.33 N	74.32 E
Malé Karpaty (Little Carpathians), mts., Slvk.	24	H13	48.30 N	17.20 E
Malek Kandī, Iran	74	B10	37.09 N	46.06 E
Malema, Moz.	88	C6	14.56 S	37.24 E
Malen'ga, Russia	18	D23	63.51 N	36.27 E
Malente, Ger.	24	B6	54.10 N	10.33 E
Male Polissia, reg., Ukr.	38	C3	50.08 N	24.36 E
Māler Kotla, India	70	C5	30.31 N	75.52 E
Malesherbes, Fr.	20	F11	48.17 N	2.25 E
Malgomaj, l., Swe.	16	C13	64.43 N	16.14 E
Malhanskij hrebet, mts., Russia	50	F10	50.24 N	108.06 E
Malha Wells see Al Māliḥah, Sudan	82	D5	15.07 N	26.10 E
Malheur, stm., Or., U.S.	146	F9	44.03 N	116.58 W
Malheur, North Fork, stm., Or., U.S.	146	F8	43.45 N	118.04 W
Malheur, South Fork, stm., Or., U.S.	146	G8	43.33 N	118.10 W
Malheur Lake, l., Or., U.S.	146	G8	43.20 N	118.45 W
Mali, Gui.	84	G2	12.04 N	12.17 W
Mali, ctry., Afr.	84	F4	17.00 N	4.00 W
Mali, stm., Mya.	62	C8	25.42 N	97.30 E
Malianjingzi, China	52	C4	41.33 N	95.17 E
Malien, stm., Tai.	187d		25.11 N	121.41 E
Malienkang, Tai.	187d		25.10 N	121.39 E
Maligne, stm., Ab., Can.	144	D13	52.55 N	118.02 W
Maligne Lake, l., Ab., Can.	144	D13	52.40 N	117.34 W
Maliïvka, Ukr.	38	F11	47.29 N	32.44 E
Malik, Sudan	82	F6	6.03 N	31.36 E
Malik, Wādī al-, val., Sudan	82	D5	18.02 N	30.58 E
Mali Kyun, i., Mya.	64	F4	13.06 N	98.16 E
Malili, Indon.	66	E12	2.41 S	121.03 E
Målilla, Swe.	16	J13	57.23 N	15.49 E
Malin, Or., U.S.	148	A4	42.00 N	121.24 W
Malinaltepec, Mex.	154	G9	17.05 N	98.39 W
Malinau, Indon.	66	B10	3.34 N	116.38 E
Malindi, Kenya	86	E8	3.12 S	40.06 E
Malines see Mechelen, Bel.	20	C13	51.02 N	4.28 E
Malingping, Indon.	66	G4	6.47 S	106.00 E
Malin Head, c., Ire.	10	F5	55.22 N	7.23 W
Malino, Indon.	66	F11	5.16 S	119.51 E
Malino, Russia	183b		55.58 N	37.13 E
Malino, Bukit, mtn., Indon.	66	C12	0.42 N	120.50 E
Malinoa, i., Tonga	100e	n14	21.00 S	175.09 W
Malipāra, India	190b		22.57 N	88.14 E
Mali Rajinac, mtn., Cro.	30	F12	44.48 N	15.00 E
Malita, Phil.	68	G5	6.24 N	125.36 E
Ma Liu Shui, China	189d		22.25 N	114.12 E
Maliwun, Mya.	64	G4	10.14 N	98.36 E
Malizhen, China	64	A7	23.08 N	104.42 E
Maljamar, N.M., U.S.	136	B4	32.51 N	103.46 W
Malka, Russia	50	F20	53.19 N	157.28 E
Malkāpur, India	70	H6	20.53 N	76.12 E
Malkara, Tur.	34	C9	40.52 N	26.55 E
Malko Tărnovo, Blg.	34	A10	41.59 N	27.31 E
Malko Tărnovo, Blg.	36	G14	41.59 N	27.31 E
Mallāh, Syria	76	F7	32.30 N	36.51 E
Mallaig, Ab., Can.	144	B19	54.12 N	111.22 W
Mallaig, Scot., U.K.	10	E7	57.00 N	5.49 W
Mallala, Austl.	98	J2	34.26 S	138.30 E
Mallan luonnonpuisto, ind. res., Fin.	14	C11	69.04 N	20.40 E
Mallard Reservoir, res., Ca., U.S.	200		38.01 N	122.03 W
Mallawi, Egypt	76	K1	27.44 N	30.50 E
Mallersdorf-Pfaffenberg, Ger.	24	H8	48.46 N	12.16 E
Mallery Lake, l., Nu., Can.	110	C11	63.55 N	98.25 W
Mallet, Braz.	172	B12	25.53 S	50.49 W
Malligasta, Arg.	172	D4	29.11 S	67.26 W
Mall in Columbia, The, shp. cen., Md., U.S.	202b		39.13 N	76.52 W
Mallorca (Majorca), i., Spain	28	E13	39.30 N	3.00 E
Mallow, Ire.	10	I4	52.08 N	8.39 W
Malm, Nor.	16	C9	64.04 N	11.13 E
Malmbäck, Swe.	16	J12	57.35 N	14.28 E
Malmberget, Swe.	14	E11	67.10 N	20.40 E
Malmédy, Bel.	24	F2	50.25 N	6.01 E
Malmesbury, S. Afr.	90	H4	33.27 S	18.43 E
Malmö, Swe.	16	L11	55.35 N	13.01 E
Malmok, c., Neth. Ant.	158g	p23	12.18 N	68.23 W
Malmön, Swe.	16	I9	58.20 N	11.19 E
Malmslätt, Swe.	16	I13	58.25 N	15.32 E
Malmstrom Air Force Base, mil., Mt., U.S.	146	C15	47.30 N	111.10 W
Malmyž, Russia	40	C17	56.31 N	50.41 E
Malnoue, Fr.	179		48.50 N	2.36 E
Malo, i., Vanuatu	101d	j16	15.41 S	167.09 E
Maloarhangel'sk, Russia	26	H19	52.24 N	36.29 E
Maloelap, at., Marsh. Is.	94	C8	8.45 N	171.03 E
Maloe Skuratovo, Russia	26	G19	53.32 N	37.00 E
Malojaroslavec, Russia	26	E19	55.00 N	36.27 E
Malojaz, Russia	40	D21	55.10 N	58.10 E
Malokaterynivka, Ukr.	38	F14	47.38 N	35.16 E
Malolos, Guam	100c	j10	13.17 N	144.45 E
Malolos, Phil.	68	C3	14.50 N	120.48 E
Malomykhailivka, Ukr.	38	E15	48.05 N	36.24 E
Malonabatovskij, Russia	40	G13	48.57 N	43.40 E
Malone, Fl., U.S.	134	G13	30.57 N	85.09 W
Malone, N.Y., U.S.	126	D15	44.51 N	74.16 W
Malonga, D.R.C.	86	G4	10.25 S	23.09 E
Małopolska, reg., Pol.	24	G17	50.09 N	21.46 E
Małopolskie, state, Pol.	24	G16	49.45 N	20.15 E
Malošujka, Russia	18	D24	63.44 N	37.24 E
Malotkavičy, Bela.	26	H8	52.07 N	25.56 E
Malott, Wa., U.S.	146	B7	48.16 N	119.42 W
Małowice, Pol.	24	E11	51.34 N	15.27 E
Måløy, Nor.	16	F3	61.56 N	5.07 E
Malozemel'skaja Tundra, reg., Russia	12	C24	68.16 N	52.41 E
Malpartida de Plasencia, Spain	28	E4	39.59 N	6.02 W
Malpas, Austl.	98	J3	34.43 S	140.37 E
Malpe, India	69	E2	13.22 N	74.42 E
Malpelo, Isla de, i., Col.	162	E6	3.59 N	81.35 W
Malpeque Bay, b., P.E., Can.	122	D13	46.30 N	63.47 W
Malprabha, stm., India	69	D2	16.11 N	76.03 E
Mālpura, India	70	E5	26.17 N	75.23 E
Malše, stm., Eur.	30	B11	48.58 N	14.28 E
Målselva, stm., Nor.	14	C9	69.14 N	18.29 E
Målsnes, Nor.	14	C9	69.19 N	18.33 E
Malta, Braz.	170	D7	6.54 S	37.31 W
Malta, Lat.	26	D10	56.20 N	27.09 E
Malta, Mt., U.S.	142	F6	48.21 N	107.52 W
Malta, Oh., U.S.	124	E4	39.38 N	81.51 W
Malta, ctry., Eur.	32	I8	35.50 N	14.35 E
Malta, i., Malta	32	I8	35.53 N	14.27 E
Malta, stm., Lat.	26	D10	56.43 N	26.52 E
Malta, Canale di see Malta Channel, strt., Eur.	32	H8	36.22 N	14.38 E
Malta Channel, strt., Eur.	32	H8	36.22 N	14.38 E
Maltahöhe, Nmb.	90	D3	24.50 S	16.59 E
Maltepe, ngh., Tur.	185b		40.55 N	29.08 E
Malton, Eng., U.K.	10	G12	54.08 N	0.48 W
Malton, ngh., On., Can.	193b		43.42 N	79.38 W
Maltsch see Malše, stm., Eur.	30	B11	48.58 N	14.28 E
Malugou, China	54	C8	43.38 N	128.24 E
Maluku (Moluccas), is., Indon.	60	F8	2.00 S	128.00 E
Maluku, Laut (Molucca Sea), s., Indon.	60	F8	0.00 N	125.00 E
Ma'lūlā, Syria	76	E7	33.50 N	36.33 E
Malu Mare, Rom.	36	E10	44.15 N	23.51 E
Malumfashi, Nig.	84	G6	11.47 N	7.37 E
Malunda, Indon.	66	E11	3.00 S	118.51 E
Malung, Swe.	16	G11	60.41 N	13.42 E
Malvaglia, Italy	184b		45.31 N	8.47 E
Mālvan, India	69	C1	16.03 N	73.28 E
Malveira, Port.	184c		38.45 N	9.27 W
Malvern, Austl.	192b		37.52 S	145.02 E
Malvern see Great Malvern, Eng., U.K.	10	I10	52.07 N	2.19 W
Malvern, Ar., U.S.	134	C6	34.22 N	92.48 W
Malvern, Ia., U.S.	128	K3	41.00 N	95.35 W
Malvern, Oh., U.S.	124	D4	40.41 N	81.11 W
Malvern, Pa., U.S.	203		40.02 N	75.31 W
Malvern, ngh., S. Afr.	191d		26.12 S	28.06 E
Malverne, N.Y., U.S.	194		40.40 N	73.40 W
Malvérnia, Moz.	90	C10	22.07 S	31.38 E
Malvinas Sur, Arg.	172	D8	29.37 S	59.03 W
Malý Dunaj, stm., Slvk.	24	H13	47.54 N	18.01 E
Malye Porogi, Russia	183a		59.47 N	30.42 E
Malyj, ostrov, i., Russia	18	G15	60.01 N	28.01 E
Malyja Haradzjačy, Bela.	26	H11	52.33 N	28.20 E
Malyj Anjuj, stm., Russia	50	C21	68.30 N	160.55 E
Malyj Enisej, stm., Russia	50	F8	51.43 N	94.28 E
Malyj Kavkaz see Lesser Caucasus, mts., Asia	42	E11	41.00 N	44.35 E
Malyj Tajmyr, ostrov, i., Russia	50	A10	78.08 N	107.12 E
Malyj Tjuters, ostrov, i., Russia	18	H13	59.49 N	26.56 E
Malyj Uzen', stm., Eur.	40	G16	48.57 N	49.37 E
Malyj Žužmuj, ostrov, i., Russia	18	C22	64.37 N	35.40 E
Malyn, Ukr.	38	C8	50.46 N	29.14 E
Malynivka, Ukr.	38	D15	49.48 N	36.44 E
Malyševo, Russia	26	C18	57.50 N	35.38 E
Mama, Russia	50	E11	58.18 N	112.53 E
Mamadyš, Russia	40	D17	55.42 N	51.23 E
Mamaia, Rom.	36	E15	44.15 N	28.37 E
Mamakan, Russia	50	E11	57.47 N	114.01 E
Mamanguape, Braz.	170	D8	6.50 S	35.07 W
Mamaroneck, stm., N.Y., U.S.	194		40.57 N	73.44 W
Mamaroneck Harbor, b., N.Y., U.S.	194		40.56 N	73.43 W
Mamasa, Indon.	66	E11	2.57 S	119.22 E
Mamasa, stm., Indon.	66	E11	3.31 S	119.43 E
Mambaí, Braz.	170	H2	14.28 S	46.07 W
Mambajao, Phil.	68	F5	9.14 N	124.42 E
Mambasa, D.R.C.	86	D5	1.21 N	29.03 E
Mamberamo, stm., Indon.	60	F10	1.34 S	137.52 E
Mamburao, Phil.	68	D3	13.14 N	120.34 E
Mamehaktebo, Indon.	66	C9	0.11 N	115.29 E
Mameigwess Lake, l., On., Can.	128	B6	49.34 N	91.49 W
Ma-Me-O Beach, Ab., Can.	144	C17	52.58 N	113.57 W
Mamera, Ven.	204c		10.27 N	66.59 W
Mamera, Quebrada, stm., Ven.	204c		10.27 N	66.59 W
Mamers, Fr.	20	F9	48.20 N	0.22 E
Mamfe, Cam.	86	C1	5.46 N	9.17 E
Mamie, N.C., U.S.	124	H10	36.07 N	75.50 W
Mamljutka, Kaz.	48	D11	54.56 N	68.32 E
Mammoth, Az., U.S.	150	K6	32.43 N	110.38 W
Mammoth Cave National Park, p.o.i., Ky., U.S.	130	G11	37.11 N	86.07 W
Mammoth Lakes, Ca., U.S.	148	F7	37.38 N	118.58 W
Mammoth Spring, Ar., U.S.	130	H6	36.29 N	91.32 W
Mamonovo, Russia	26	F2	54.27 N	19.56 E
Mamonovo, Russia	183b		55.36 N	37.49 E
Mamonovo, Russia	183b		55.41 N	37.19 E
Mamont, Pa., U.S.	197b		40.29 N	79.36 W
Mamoré, stm., S.A.	166	B3	10.24 S	65.23 W
Mamou, Gui.	84	G2	10.22 N	12.04 W
Mamou, La., U.S.	134	G6	30.37 N	92.25 W
Mampikony, Madag.	88	D8	16.06 S	47.38 E
Mamraš, Russia	42	E13	41.44 N	48.19 E
Mamry, Jezioro, l., Pol.	24	B17	54.07 N	21.43 E
Mamuju, Indon.	66	E11	2.41 S	118.54 E
Mamuno, Bots.	90	C5	22.16 S	20.01 E
Mamykovo, Russia	40	D17	54.38 N	50.34 E
Man, C. Iv.	84	H3	7.24 N	7.33 W
Man, India	70	B7	33.51 N	78.32 E
Man, W.V., U.S.	124	G4	37.44 N	81.52 W
Mana, Hi., U.S.	100a	a2	22.01 N	159.46 W
Måna, stm., Nor.	16	H6	59.52 N	8.01 E
Manabí, state, Ec.	168	H2	0.30 S	79.59 W
Manacacías, stm., Col.	168	F5	4.22 N	72.03 W
Manacapuru, Braz.	168	I11	3.17 S	60.36 W
Manacapuru, stm., Braz.	168	I11	3.10 S	60.40 W
Manacor, Spain	28	E14	39.33 N	3.12 E
Manado, Indon.	60	E7	1.29 N	124.50 E
Manaenki, Russia	26	G19	53.42 N	36.27 E
Managua, Nic.	156	F4	12.08 N	86.16 W
Managua, Aeropuerto, arpt., Cuba	204b		23.00 N	82.17 W
Managua, Lago de, l., Nic.	156	F4	12.20 N	86.20 W
Manakara, Madag.	88	E8	22.08 S	48.00 E
Manakau, mtn., N.Z.	102	F5	42.14 S	173.37 E
Manākhah, Yemen	72	G5	15.06 N	43.43 E
Manalapan Brook, stm., N.J., U.S.	194		40.24 N	74.23 W
Manāli, India	70	B6	32.16 N	77.09 E
Manama see Al-Manāmah, Bahr.	74	G12	26.13 N	50.35 E
Manamansalo, i., Fin.	18	C13	64.21 N	27.04 E
Manam Island, i., Pap. N. Gui.	101a	a4	4.04 S	145.02 E
Mánamo, Caño, stm., Ven.	168	C10	9.54 N	62.15 W
Mananara Avaratra, Madag.	88	D8	16.10 S	49.45 E
Mananjary, Madag.	88	E8	21.13 S	48.20 E
Manankoro, Mali	84	G3	10.28 N	7.26 W
Manantenina, Madag.	88	E8	24.17 S	47.19 E
Manãos see Manaus, Braz.	168	I11	3.06 S	60.01 W
Manapiare, stm., Ven.	168	E8	5.01 N	66.16 W
Manapire, stm., Ven.	168	C8	7.41 N	66.06 W
Manappārai, India	69	F4	10.36 N	78.25 E
Manār, stm., India	69	B3	18.39 N	77.43 E
Manas, China	52	C2	44.18 N	86.13 E
Manās, stm., Asia	70	E13	26.11 N	90.44 E
Manasarowar Lake see Mapam Yumco, l., China	70	C8	30.40 N	81.29 E
Manas Hu, l., China	52	B2	45.43 N	85.54 E
Manāslu, mtn., Nepal	70	D10	28.33 N	84.33 E
Manasquan, N.J., U.S.	124	D11	40.09 N	74.02 W
Manassa, Co., U.S.	138	D3	37.10 N	105.56 W
Manassas, Va., U.S.	124	F8	38.45 N	77.28 W
Manassas National Battlefield Park, p.o.i., Va., U.S.	124	F8	38.50 N	77.32 W
Mănăstirea, Rom.	36	E13	44.13 N	26.54 E
Manatee, stm., Fl., U.S.	132	I3	27.30 N	82.34 W
Manatí, Col.	168	B4	10.27 N	74.58 W
Manatí, P.R.	158a	b3	18.26 N	66.29 W
Manatuto, Indon.	60	G8	8.30 S	126.00 E
Manaul, Phil.	68	D3	12.27 N	121.24 E
Manaung, Mya.	64	C1	18.49 N	93.39 E
Manaus, Braz.	168	I11	3.06 S	60.01 W
Manavgat, Tur.	34	G14	36.47 N	31.26 E
Manawa, Wi., U.S.	128	G10	44.27 N	88.55 W
Mānāwāla, Pak.	70	C4	31.35 N	73.40 E
Manāwar, India	70	G5	22.13 N	75.05 E
Manawoka, Pulau, i., Indon.	60	F9	4.06 S	131.18 E
Manayunk, ngh., Pa., U.S.	203		40.01 N	75.13 W
Manban, China	64	A6	23.05 N	103.10 E
Manbij, Syria	76	B8	36.31 N	37.57 E
Mancelona, Mi., U.S.	126	D4	44.53 N	85.04 W
Mancenille, Baie de see Manzanillo Bay, b., N.A.	156	C12	19.45 N	71.46 W
Mancha Real, Spain	28	G7	37.47 N	3.36 W
Manche, state, Fr.	20	E7	49.00 N	1.10 W
Mancheng, China	58	B6	38.55 N	115.19 E
Mancherāl, India	69	B4	18.51 N	79.26 E
Manchester, Eng., U.K.	10	H10	53.27 N	2.14 W
Manchester, Eng., U.K.	180		53.28 N	2.15 W
Manchester, Ct., U.S.	124	C13	41.47 N	72.31 W
Manchester, Ga., U.S.	134	E14	32.51 N	84.36 W
Manchester, Ia., U.S.	130	B6	42.29 N	91.27 W
Manchester, Ky., U.S.	124	G2	37.08 N	83.46 W
Manchester, Mi., U.S.	124	B1	42.08 N	84.02 W
Manchester, N.H., U.S.	122	H5	42.59 N	71.27 W
Manchester, Oh., U.S.	124	F2	38.41 N	83.36 W
Manchester, Tn., U.S.	134	B12	35.28 N	86.05 W
Manchester, Vt., U.S.	122	G3	43.10 N	73.04 W
Manchester, mun., Eng., U.K.	180		53.27 N	2.13 W
Manchester, mun., Eng., U.K.	180		53.27 N	2.13 W
Manchester City Football Ground, p.o.i., Eng., U.K.	180		53.27 N	2.14 W
Manchester Docks, trans., Eng., U.K.	180		53.28 N	2.17 W
Manchester International Airport, arpt., Eng., U.K.	180		53.21 N	2.15 W
Manchester Race Course, p.o.i., Eng., U.K.	180		53.30 N	2.16 W
Manchester Ship Canal, can., Eng., U.K.	180		53.19 N	2.57 W
Manchester United Football Ground, p.o.i., Eng., U.K.	180		53.28 N	2.18 W
Manchioneal, Jam.	158d	i14	18.01 N	76.17 W
Manchuria see Dong San Shen, hist. reg., China	52	B10	47.00 N	125.00 E
Manciano, Italy	30	H8	42.35 N	11.30 E
Máncora, Peru	164	D1	4.06 S	81.03 W
Mancos, Co., U.S.	150	F8	37.20 N	108.17 W
Mancos, stm., U.S.	150	F8	36.58 N	108.58 W
Mand, stm., India	70	G9	21.41 N	83.15 E
Mand, stm., Iran	74	F12	28.09 N	51.16 E
Manda, Tan.	86	G6	10.28 S	34.35 E
Manda, Jabal, mtn., Sudan	82	F4	8.39 N	24.27 E
Mandabe, Madag.	88	E7	21.02 S	44.55 E
Mandaguari, Braz.	172	A12	23.32 S	51.40 W
Mandai Orchid Gardens, p.o.i., Sing.	189c		1.24 N	103.47 E
Manda Island, i., Kenya	86	E8	2.15 S	40.57 E
Mandal, Mong.	52	B6	48.22 N	106.44 E
Mandal, Nor.	16	J5	58.02 N	7.27 E
Mandala, Puncak, mtn., Indon.	60	F10	4.43 S	140.18 E
Mandalay, Mya.	64	A2	21.58 N	96.05 E
Mandalay, state, Mya.	64	B2	21.00 N	96.00 E
Mandale Station, trans., India	190c		19.03 N	72.56 E
Mandalī, Iraq	74	D9	33.45 N	45.32 E
Mandalkia, India	190b		22.43 N	88.08 E
Mandaluyong, Phil.	187f		14.35 N	121.02 E
Mandan, N.D., U.S.	140	A11	46.49 N	100.53 W
Mandāoli, ngh., India	190a		28.38 N	77.18 E
Mandaon, Phil.	60	C7	12.14 N	123.16 E
Mandar, Teluk, b., Indon.	66	E11	3.36 S	119.17 E
Mandara, Monts (Mandara Mountains), mts., Afr.	82	F2	10.45 N	13.40 E
Mandara Mountains (Mandara, Monts), mts., Afr.	82	E2	10.45 N	13.40 E
Mandas, Italy	32	E3	39.38 N	9.08 E
Mandaue, Phil.	68	E4	10.20 N	123.55 E
Mandeb, Bab el, strt.	82	E8	12.44 N	43.20 E
Mandera, Kenya	86	D8	3.55 N	41.51 E
Manderson, Wy., U.S.	140	C5	44.16 N	107.57 W
Mandeville, Jam.	158d	i13	18.02 N	77.30 W
Mandeville, La., U.S.	134	G8	30.21 N	90.03 W
Mandi, India	70	C6	31.42 N	76.56 E
Mandiangin, Indon.	66	E3	2.01 S	102.59 E
Mandi Bahāuddīn, Pak.	70	B4	32.34 N	73.29 E
Mandi Būrewāla, Pak.	70	C4	30.09 N	72.40 E
Mandi Dabwāli, India	70	D5	29.57 N	74.42 E
Mandimba, Moz.	88	C6	14.21 S	35.39 E
Mandioli, Pulau, i., Indon.	60	F8	0.44 S	127.14 E
Mandioré, Lagoa, l., S.A.	166	C5	18.08 S	57.33 W
Mandioré, Laguna see Mandioré, Lagoa, l., S.A.	166	C5	18.08 S	57.33 W
Mandla, India	70	G8	22.35 N	80.22 E
Mandlakazi, Moz.	90	D11	24.42 S	33.52 E
Mandø, i., Den.	16	L6	55.16 N	8.33 E
Mandora, Austl.	96	C4	19.44 S	120.51 E
Mándra, Grc.	185c		38.04 N	23.30 E
Māndrā, India	190b		22.55 N	88.07 E
Mandra, Pak.	70	B4	33.21 N	73.14 E
Mandres-les-Roses, Fr.	179		48.42 N	2.33 E
Mandriola, ngh., Italy	185a		41.45 N	12.30 E
Mandritsara, Madag.	88	D8	15.50 S	48.49 E
Mandsaur, India	70	F5	24.03 N	75.04 E
Māndu, India	70	G5	22.21 N	75.28 E
Mandun, China	64	A4	22.18 N	100.04 E
Manduria, Italy	32	D11	40.23 N	17.37 E
Māndvi, India	70	H4	21.15 N	73.18 E
Māndvi, India	70	G2	22.50 N	69.21 E
Mandvi, ngh., India	190c		18.57 N	72.50 E
Mandya, India	69	E3	12.31 N	76.53 E
Manendragarh, India	70	G9	23.12 N	82.12 E
Manevychi, Ukr.	38	B4	51.17 N	25.31 E
Manfalūt, Egypt	76	K1	27.19 N	30.58 E
Manfredonia, Italy	30	I12	41.38 N	15.54 E
Manfredonia, Golfo di, b., Italy	32	C10	41.35 N	16.05 E
Manga, Braz.	170	H3	14.44 S	43.55 W
Manga, reg., Niger	84	F7	14.20 N	12.30 E
Mangabeiras, Chapada das, hills, Braz.	170	E2	9.54 S	46.31 W
Mangagoy, Phil.	68	F6	8.10 N	126.22 E
Mangai, D.R.C.	86	E3	4.02 S	19.32 E
Mangaia, i., Cook Is.	94	F11	21.54 S	157.54 W
Mangalagiri, India	69	C5	16.25 N	80.33 E
Mangaldai, India	70	E14	26.25 N	92.00 E
Mangalia, Rom.	36	F15	43.49 N	28.34 E
Mangalore, India	69	E2	12.52 N	74.50 E
Mangalvedha, India	69	C2	17.30 N	75.26 E
Manganês, stm., Braz.	170	F1	10.21 S	48.27 W
Manganji, Japan	186		35.40 N	139.26 E
Mangawān, India	70	F8	24.39 N	81.33 E
Mangbwalu, D.R.C.	86	D6	2.00 N	30.01 E
Mangchang, China	58	I2	25.08 N	107.31 E
Mange, China	70	B9	32.23 N	83.47 E
Mangela, Mount see Nanggala Hill, mtn., Sol. Is.	101b	e7	8.16 S	157.43 E
Manggar, Indon.	66	E6	2.52 S	108.15 E
Mangham, La., U.S.	134	E7	32.19 N	91.46 W
Mangin Range, mts., Mya.	62	C8	24.20 N	95.42 E
Mangistau, state, Kaz.	42	C15	44.13 N	52.46 E
Mangistau, gory, mts., Kaz.	42	D15	44.05 N	52.15 E
Mangkalihat, Tanjung, c., Indon.	66	C11	1.01 N	118.59 E
Mangkutana, Indon.	66	E12	2.23 S	120.47 E
Manglares, Cabo, c., Col.	168	G2	1.36 N	79.02 W
Mangla Reservoir, res., Pak.	70	B4	33.10 N	73.40 E
Mangnai, China	48	G16	37.50 N	91.45 E
Mangochi, Mwi.	88	C6	14.27 S	35.15 E
Mangoky, stm., Madag.	88	E7	21.20 S	43.32 E
Mangole, Pulau, i., Indon.	60	F8	1.51 S	125.51 E
Mangrol, India	70	H2	21.07 N	70.06 E
Mangrove Cay, i., Bah.	116	H14	24.16 N	77.31 W
Mangrūl Pīr, India	70	H6	20.18 N	77.20 E
Mangsang, Indon.	66	E4	2.12 S	104.02 E
Mangshi see Luxi, China	52	G4	24.21 N	98.22 E
Mangu, stm., D.R.C.	191b		4.24 S	15.24 E
Mangueira, Lagoa, b., Braz.	172	F11	33.06 S	52.48 W
Mangueirinha, Braz.	172	B11	25.56 S	52.11 W
Mangui, China	50	F13	52.03 N	122.04 E
Mangum, Ok., U.S.	138	G9	34.52 N	99.29 W
Mangya, China	52	D3	37.40 N	90.50 E
Mangyšlak, Kaz.	42	D14	43.39 N	51.15 E
Mangyšlak, plato, plat., Kaz.	42	D15	43.22 N	52.30 E
Manhasset, N.Y., U.S.	194		40.47 N	73.42 W
Manhasset Bay, b., N.Y., U.S.	194		40.50 N	73.43 W
Manhasset Hills, N.Y., U.S.	194		40.46 N	73.41 W
Manhasset Neck, pen., N.Y., U.S.	194		40.50 N	73.42 W
Manhattan, Ks., U.S.	138	B11	39.11 N	96.34 W
Manhattan, Mt., U.S.	146	E15	45.51 N	111.20 W
Manhattan, ngh., N.Y., U.S.	194		40.47 N	73.58 W
Manhattan Beach State Park, p.o.i., Ca., U.S.	198		33.54 N	118.25 W
Manhattan Bridge, trans., N.Y., U.S.	194		40.42 N	73.59 W
Manhattan College, educ., N.Y., U.S.	194		40.53 N	73.54 W
Manhiça, Moz.	90	D11	25.24 S	32.48 E
Mān Hpāng, Mya.	64	A4	22.40 N	98.33 E
Manhuaçu, Braz.	170	K4	20.15 S	42.02 W
Manhuaçu, stm., Braz.	170	J5	19.30 S	41.06 W
Manhumirim, Braz.	170	K4	20.21 S	41.57 W
Maní, P.R.	158a	b1	18.15 N	67.10 W
Maniago, Italy	30	D9	46.10 N	12.42 E
Manianga, Congo	191b		4.10 S	15.19 E
Manica, Moz.	88	D5	18.55 S	32.52 E
Manica, state, Moz.	90	B11	20.43 S	33.09 E
Manicaland, state, Zimb.	90	B11	20.15 S	32.30 E
Manic Deux, Réservoir, res., Qc., Can.	122	A8	49.23 N	68.09 W
Manicoré, Braz.	164	E5	5.49 S	61.16 W
Manicouagan, stm., Qc., Can.	110	E17	49.10 N	68.09 W
Manicouagan, Réservoir, res., Qc., Can.	110	E17	51.22 N	68.44 W
Maniganggo, China	52	E4	31.55 N	99.10 E

Name	Page	Map Ref.	Latitude	Longitude
Manignan, C. Iv.	84	G3	10.00 N	7.50 W
Manigotagan, Mb., Can.	142	C17	51.06 N	96.16 W
Manigotagan, stm., Can.	142	C17	51.09 N	96.36 W
Manihiki, at., Cook Is.	94	E10	10.24 S	161.01 W
Manitsoq see Sukkertoppen, Grnld.	108	D15	65.25 N	52.56 W
Mānikganj, Bngl.	70	G13	23.51 N	90.01 E
Mānikpur, India	70	F8	25.04 N	81.04 E
Manila, Phil.	68	C3	14.35 N	120.59 E
Manila, Phil.	187f		14.35 N	121.00 E
Manila, Ar., U.S.	130	I7	35.52 N	90.10 W
Manila, Ut., U.S.	150	C7	40.59 N	109.43 W
Manila Bay, b., Phil.	68	C3	14.30 N	120.45 E
Manila Cathedral, rel., Phil.	187f		14.35 N	120.59 E
Manilla, Austl.	98	H8	30.45 S	150.43 E
Manilla, Ia., U.S.	128	J3	41.53 N	95.14 W
Manily, Russia	50	D22	62.27 N	165.33 E
Manimbaya, Tanjung, c., Indon.	66	D11	0.00 N	119.37 E
Maningrida, Austl.	96	B6	12.03 S	134.13 E
Maninjau, Danau, l., Indon.	66	D1	0.20 S	100.11 E
Manino, Russia	26	G17	53.58 N	34.21 E
Manipa, Selat, strt., Indon.	60	F8	3.20 S	127.23 E
Manipur, state, India	62	C7	25.00 N	94.00 E
Manipur, stm., Asia	64	A1	22.50 N	93.54 E
Manique de Baixo, Port.	184c		38.44 N	9.22 W
Manisa, Tur.	34	E10	38.36 N	27.25 E
Manisa, state, Tur.	34	E11	38.50 N	28.10 E
Manistee, Mi., U.S.	126	D3	44.14 N	86.18 W
Manistee, stm., Mi., U.S.	126	D3	44.14 N	86.19 W
Manistique, Mi., U.S.	126	C3	45.57 N	86.14 W
Manistique, stm., Mi., U.S.	126	B3	45.57 N	86.12 W
Manistique, West Branch, stm., Mi., U.S.	126	B3	46.01 N	86.08 W
Manistique Lake, l., Mi., U.S.	126	B4	46.13 N	85.46 W
Manito, Il., U.S.	128	K9	40.25 N	89.46 W
Manitoba, state, Can.	110	D11	54.00 N	97.00 W
Manitoba, Lake, l., Mb., Can.	142	D15	50.47 N	98.43 W
Manitou, Mb., Can.	142	E15	49.14 N	98.32 W
Manitou, stm., On., Can.	128	B5	48.50 N	93.21 W
Manitou, Lake, l., On., Can.	126	C7	45.47 N	82.02 W
Manitou Beach, Sk., Can.	142	C8	51.42 N	105.26 W
Manitou Lake, l., On., Can.	126	B10	46.01 N	79.00 W
Manitou Lake, l., Sk., Can.	142	B4	52.45 N	109.45 W
Manitoulin Island, i., On., Can.	126	C7	45.47 N	82.20 W
Manitou Springs, Co., U.S.	138	C3	38.51 N	104.54 W
Manitowaning, On., Can.	126	C8	45.44 N	81.48 W
Manitowish Waters, Wi., U.S.	128	E9	46.07 N	89.51 W
Manitowoc, Wi., U.S.	126	D2	44.05 N	87.39 W
Manitowoc, stm., Wi., U.S.	126	D1	44.05 N	87.38 W
Maniwaki, Qc., Can.	126	B13	46.22 N	75.58 W
Manizales, Col.	168	E4	5.04 N	75.30 W
Manja, Madag.	88	F7	21.26 S	44.19 E
Manjakandriana, Madag.	88	D8	18.54 S	47.46 E
Manjeri, India	69	F3	11.07 N	76.07 E
Mānjra, stm., India	69	B3	18.49 N	77.52 E
Manjuk, gora, hill, Russia	14	E30	67.18 N	39.24 E
Mankanza, D.R.C.	86	D3	1.33 N	19.04 E
Man Kat, Mya.	64	A3	22.05 N	98.01 E
Mankato, Ks., U.S.	138	B10	39.47 N	98.12 W
Mankato, Mn., U.S.	128	G4	44.09 N	94.01 W
Mankayane, Swaz.	90	E10	26.41 S	31.04 E
Mankera, Pak.	70	C3	31.23 N	71.26 E
Mankinholes, Eng., U.K.	180		53.42 N	2.03 W
Man'kivka, Ukr.	38	E9	48.58 N	30.20 E
Mankota, Sk., Can.	142	E6	49.26 N	107.05 W
Mānkundu, India	190b		22.50 N	88.22 E
Manley, Eng., U.K.	180		53.14 N	2.45 W
Manley Hot Springs, Ak., U.S.	109	D9	64.58 N	150.37 W
Manleys Corner, Ma., U.S.	201		42.03 N	71.04 W
Manlleu, Spain	28	B13	42.00 N	2.17 E
Manly, Ia., U.S.	128	H5	43.17 N	93.12 W
Manly Warringah War Memorial Park, p.o.i., Austl.	192a		33.46 S	151.15 E
Manmād, India	70	H5	20.14 N	74.26 E
Manna, Indon.	66	F3	4.27 S	102.54 E
Mannahill, Austl.	98	I3	32.26 S	139.59 E
Mannar, Sri L.	69	G4	8.58 N	79.54 E
Mannar, Gulf of, b., Asia	69	G4	8.30 N	79.00 E
Mannārgudi, India	69	F4	10.39 N	79.27 E
Mannar Island, i., Sri L.	69	G4	9.03 N	79.50 E
Mann Creek, stm., Mi., U.S.	199		42.32 N	83.44 W
Mannford, Ok., U.S.	134	A2	36.08 N	96.21 W
Mannheim, Ger.	24	G4	49.29 N	8.28 E
Manni, China	70	A11	34.48 N	87.15 E
Manning, Ia., U.S.	128	C2	41.54 N	95.04 W
Manning, N.D., U.S.	142	G11	47.13 N	102.46 W
Manning, S.C., U.S.	132	C5	33.41 N	80.12 W
Manning Provincial Park, p.o.i., B.C., Can.	144	G10	49.08 N	120.54 W
Manning Strait, strt., Sol. Is.	101b	d7	7.24 S	158.00 E
Mannswörth, ngh., Aus.	182b		48.09 N	16.31 E
Mannu, Riu, stm., Italy	32	D2	40.50 N	8.23 E
Mannum, Austl.	98	J2	34.55 S	139.18 E
Mannville, Ab., Can.	144	C19	53.20 N	111.10 W
Manoel Ribas, Braz.	172	B12	24.31 S	51.39 W
Manoharpur, India	70	G10	22.22 N	85.12 E
Manokwari, Indon.	60	F9	0.51 S	134.04 E
Manombo Atsimo, Madag.	88	E7	22.57 S	43.28 E
Manono, D.R.C.	86	F5	7.18 S	27.25 E
Manor, Sk., Can.	142	E11	49.36 N	102.04 W
Manor, Tx., U.S.	136	D10	30.20 N	97.33 W
Manorhaven, N.Y., U.S.	194		40.50 N	73.42 W
Manori, ngh., India	190c		19.12 N	72.47 E
Manori Creek, b., India	190c		19.12 N	72.48 E
Manori Point, c., India	190c		19.11 N	72.47 E
Manoron, Mya.	64	G4	11.35 N	99.00 E
Manosque, Fr.	22	F11	43.50 N	5.46 E
Manouane, Qc., Can.	122	C2	47.13 N	74.23 W
Manouane, Lac, l., Qc., Can.	122	C2	47.34 N	74.07 W
Manouane, Lac, res., Qc., Can.	110	E16	50.42 N	70.45 W
Manown, Pa., U.S.	197b		40.13 N	79.54 W
Manpaka, Congo	191b		4.18 S	15.12 E
Manp'o, Kor., N.	54	D7	41.09 N	126.18 E
Man Point, c., St. Vin.	159e	o11	13.02 N	61.12 W
Mānpur, India	70	H8	20.22 N	80.44 E
Manquehue, Cerro, mtn., Chile	204e		33.21 S	70.36 W
Manra, at., Kir.	94	D9	4.27 S	171.15 W
Manresa, Spain	28	C12	41.43 N	1.49 E
Manresa Island, i., Ct., U.S.	194		41.04 N	73.25 W
Mānsa, India	70	C5	29.59 N	75.23 E
Mansa, Zam.	88	C4	11.12 S	28.53 E
Mansafis, Egypt	76	J1	28.00 N	30.49 E
Mānsehra, Pak.	70	A4	34.20 N	73.11 E
Mansel Island, i., Nu., Can.	110	C14	62.00 N	79.50 W
Mansfield, Austl.	98	K6	37.03 S	146.05 E
Mansfield, Eng., U.K.	10	H11	53.09 N	1.12 W
Mansfield, Ar., U.S.	134	B4	35.04 N	94.14 W
Mansfield, Ga., U.S.	132	C2	33.31 N	83.43 W
Mansfield, Il., U.S.	130	D9	40.12 N	88.30 W
Mansfield, La., U.S.	136	B14	32.02 N	93.42 W
Mansfield, Mo., U.S.	130	G5	37.05 N	92.34 W
Mansfield, N.J., U.S.	203		40.05 N	74.43 W
Mansfield, Oh., U.S.	124	D3	40.45 N	82.31 W
Mansfield, Pa., U.S.	124	C8	41.48 N	77.04 W
Mansfield, Tx., U.S.	136	B10	32.34 N	97.08 W
Mansfield, Mount, mtn., Vt., U.S.	122	F4	44.33 N	72.49 W
Mansfield Municipal Airport, arpt., Ma., U.S.	201		42.00 N	71.12 W
Mansieville Location, S. Afr.	191d		26.05 S	27.45 E
Mānsinhapur, India	190b		22.39 N	88.09 E
Mansion, St. K./N.	159a	c2	17.22 N	62.45 W
Mansle, Fr.	22	D6	45.53 N	0.11 E
Mansôa, Gui.-B.	84	G1	12.04 N	15.19 W
Manson, Ia., U.S.	130	B3	42.31 N	94.32 W
Manson, Wa., U.S.	146	C6	47.53 N	120.09 W
Mansucum, Pan.	156	H9	9.02 N	77.49 W
Mansura see El-Mansûra, Egypt	76	G2	31.02 N	31.23 E
Mansura, La., U.S.	134	F6	31.03 N	92.03 W
Mansûrîya, Turat el-, can., Egypt	191c		30.04 N	31.06 E
Manta, Ec.	168	H1	0.57 S	80.42 W
Manta, Bahía de, b., Ec.	168	H1	0.45 S	80.34 W
Mantagao, stm., Mb., Can.	142	C16	52.09 N	97.55 W
Mantalingajan, Mount, mtn., Phil.	68	F1	8.48 N	117.40 E
Mantanani Besar, Pulau, i., Malay.	68	G1	6.42 N	116.21 E
Manteca, Ca., U.S.	148	F4	37.48 N	121.12 W
Mantecal, Ven.	168	D7	7.34 N	69.09 W
Mantena, Braz.	170	J5	18.45 S	40.58 W
Manteno, Il., U.S.	130	C10	41.15 N	87.49 W
Manteo, N.C., U.S.	124	I10	35.54 N	75.40 W
Mantes-Chérence, Aérodrome de, arpt., Fr.	179		49.05 N	1.41 E
Mantes-la-Jolie, Fr.	20	F10	48.59 N	1.42 E
Mantes-la-Ville, Fr.	179		48.58 N	1.42 E
Manti, Ut., U.S.	150	D5	39.15 N	111.38 W
Mantilla, ngh., Cuba	204b		23.04 N	82.20 W
Mantiqueira, Serra da, mts., Braz.	170	L3	22.14 S	44.52 W
Manton, Mi., U.S.	126	D4	44.24 N	85.23 W
Mantorville, Mn., U.S.	128	G6	44.03 N	92.46 W
Mantos Blancos, Chile	172	A2	23.26 S	70.02 W
Mántova, Italy	30	E7	45.09 N	10.47 E
Mantsinsaari, ostrov, i., Russia	18	F18	61.21 N	31.36 E
Mänttä, Fin.	18	E11	62.01 N	24.38 E
Mantua, Cuba	156	A5	22.17 N	84.17 W
Mantua see Mántova, Italy	30	E7	45.09 N	10.47 E
Mantua, Oh., U.S.	124	C4	41.15 N	81.14 W
Mantua, Va., U.S.	202c		38.51 N	77.15 W
Mantua Creek, stm., N.J., U.S.	203		39.51 N	75.14 W
Mantua Creek, Chestnut Branch, stm., N.J., U.S.	203		39.47 N	75.10 W
Mantua Creek, Porch Branch, stm., N.J., U.S.	203		39.46 N	75.07 W
Mantua Hills, Va., U.S.	202c		38.51 N	77.16 W
Mantua Terrace, N.J., U.S.	203		39.48 N	75.10 W
Manturovo, Russia	38	B16	51.27 N	37.07 E
Manturovo, Russia	40	B14	58.19 N	44.46 E
Mäntyharju, Fin.	18	F13	61.24 N	26.53 E
Mäntyluoto, Fin.	18	F8	61.35 N	21.30 E
Manu, Peru	164	F3	12.16 S	70.56 W
Manuae, at., Cook Is.	94	E11	19.21 S	158.56 W
Manuae, at., Fr. Poly.	94	E11	16.30 S	154.40 W
Manua Islands, is., Am. Sam.	101c	h13	14.13 S	169.35 W
Manuel, Mex.	154	D9	22.44 N	98.19 W
Manuel Alves, stm., Braz.	170	F2	11.17 S	48.27 W
Manuel Alves Grande, stm., Braz.	170	D2	7.26 S	47.35 W
Manuel Benavides, Mex.	154	A6	29.04 N	103.54 W
Manuel F. Mantilla see Pedro R. Fernández, Arg.	172	D8	28.44 S	58.40 W
Manuel Urbano, Braz.	164	E4	8.51 S	69.18 W
Manuguru, India	69	B5	18.00 N	80.43 E
Manui, Pulau, i., Indon.	60	F7	3.35 S	123.08 E
Manukau, N.Z.	102	C6	37.02 S	174.54 E
Manukau Harbour, b., N.Z.	102	C6	37.01 S	174.44 E
Manursing Island, i., N.Y., U.S.	194		40.58 N	73.40 W
Manursing Island Park, p.o.i., N.Y., U.S.	194		40.58 N	73.40 W
Manus Island, i., Pap. N. Gui.	101a	a4	2.05 S	147.00 E
Manvel, N.D., U.S.	128	C1	48.05 N	97.10 W
Mānwat, India	69	B3	19.18 N	76.30 E
Many, La., U.S.	136	C14	31.33 N	93.29 W
Manyal Shīḥah, Egypt	191c		29.57 N	31.14 E
Manyara, Lake, l., Tan.	86	E7	3.35 S	35.50 E
Manyberries, Ab., Can.	142	E3	49.23 N	110.44 W
Manyč, stm., Russia	8	F17	47.14 N	40.15 E
Manyč-Gudilo, ozero, l., Russia	40	H13	46.24 N	42.38 E
Many Island Lake, l., Can.	142	D3	50.08 N	110.02 W
Manyoni, Tan.	86	F6	5.44 S	34.50 E
Many Peaks, Austl.	98	E8	24.32 S	151.23 E
Manza, D.R.C.	86	F5	7.54 S	26.44 E
Mānzai, Pak.	70	C2	30.06 N	68.53 E
Manzala, Bahra el-, l., Egypt	76	G3	31.16 N	32.02 E
Manzanares, Spain	28	E7	38.59 N	3.22 W
Manzanares, stm., Spain	28	D7	40.18 N	3.31 W
Manzanares, Canal del, can., Spain	184a		40.23 N	3.41 W
Manzanilla Point, c., Trin.	159f	s13	10.31 N	61.00 W
Manzanillo, Cuba	156	B9	20.20 N	77.07 W
Manzanillo, Mex.	154	F6	19.02 N	104.19 W
Manzanillo, Bahía de see Manzanillo Bay, b., N.A.	156	C12	19.45 N	71.46 W
Manzanillo, Punta, c., Pan.	156	H8	9.38 N	79.32 W
Manzanillo Bay, b., N.A.	156	C12	19.45 N	71.46 W
Manzanilloso, Cerro, mtn., Mex.	136	F1	28.17 N	106.03 W
Manzano, N.M., U.S.	138	G2	34.38 N	106.20 W
Manzanola, Co., U.S.	138	C5	38.06 N	103.51 W
Manzano Peak, mtn., N.M., U.S.	138	G2	34.35 N	106.26 W
Manzheliia, Ukr.	38	D12	49.19 N	33.38 E
Manzhouli, China	52	B8	49.34 N	117.27 E
Manzini, Swaz.	90	E10	26.30 S	31.25 E
Mao, Chad	82	E3	14.07 N	15.18 E
Mao, Dom. Rep.	156	C12	19.33 N	71.04 W
Maó, Spain	28	E15	39.53 N	4.15 E
Maoba, China	58	F3	30.02 N	108.59 E
Maocifan, China	58	F5	31.40 N	112.53 E
Maoke, Pegunungan, mts., Indon.	101a	a2	4.00 S	138.00 E
Maolin, China	54	C5	43.57 N	123.24 E
Maoming, China	58	K4	21.41 N	110.51 E
Ma On Shan, mtn., China	189d		22.25 N	114.15 E
Ma On Shan Tsuen, China	189d		22.24 N	114.14 E
Maoping, China	58	F4	30.24 N	110.30 E
Mapaga, Indon.	66	D11	0.09 S	119.49 E
Mapam Yumco, l., China	70	C8	30.40 N	81.29 E
Mapan, Indon.	66	E7	2.21 S	111.10 E
Mapane, Indon.	66	D12	1.25 S	120.38 E
Mapari, stm., Braz.	168	I8	1.49 S	66.49 W
Mapastepec, Mex.	154	H12	15.26 N	92.54 W
Mapi, Indon.	60	G10	7.05 S	139.23 E
Mapida, Indon.	66	D11	0.38 S	119.49 E
Mapimí, Mex.	154	C6	25.49 N	103.51 W
Mapimí, Bolsón de, des., Mex.	154	B6	26.30 N	104.00 W
Mapimí, Bufa de, mtn., Mex.	136	I4	25.47 N	103.48 W
Mapinhane, Moz.	90	C12	22.15 S	35.08 E
Mapire, Ven.	168	D9	7.45 N	64.42 W
Mapiri, Bol.	166	C3	15.15 S	68.10 W
Mapixari, Ilha, i., Braz.	168	I9	2.11 S	65.08 W
Maple, ngh., On., Can.	193b		43.51 N	79.31 W
Maple, stm., U.S.	140	A14	45.47 N	98.33 W
Maple, stm., Ia., U.S.	130	B2	42.00 N	95.59 W
Maple, stm., Mi., U.S.	130	A13	42.59 N	84.56 W
Maple, stm., Mn., U.S.	128	H5	44.04 N	94.01 W
Maple, stm., N.D., U.S.	142	H16	46.56 N	96.55 W
Maple Airfield, arpt., On., Can.	193b		43.51 N	79.32 W
Maple Creek, Sk., Can.	142	E4	49.54 N	109.29 W
Maple Creek, stm., Ne., U.S.	140	F16	41.33 N	96.33 W
Maple Cross, Eng., U.K.	178		51.37 N	0.30 W
Maple Glen, Pa., U.S.	203		40.11 N	75.11 W
Maple Lake, Mn., U.S.	128	F4	45.13 N	94.00 W
Maple Leaf Gardens, p.o.i., On., Can.	193b		43.40 N	79.23 W
Maple Meadow Brook, stm., Ma., U.S.	201		42.33 N	71.09 W
Maple Mount, Ky., U.S.	130	G10	37.42 N	87.26 W
Maple Ridge, B.C., Can.	144	G8	49.12 N	122.34 W
Maple Shade, N.J., U.S.	203		39.57 N	74.59 W
Maplesville, Al., U.S.	134	E12	32.47 N	86.52 W
Mapleton, Ia., U.S.	130	B2	42.10 N	95.47 W
Mapleton, Mn., U.S.	128	H5	43.55 N	93.57 W
Mapleton, Or., U.S.	146	F3	44.01 N	123.52 W
Mapleton, Ut., U.S.	150	C5	40.07 N	111.34 W
Maplewood, N.J., U.S.	194		40.43 N	74.14 W
Maplewood Terrace, Pa., U.S.	197b		40.17 N	79.32 W
Mapocho, stm., Chile	204e		33.25 S	70.47 W
Mapocho, Estación, trans., Chile	204e		33.26 S	70.40 W
Map'odaegyo Bridge, trans., Kor., S.	189b		37.32 N	126.56 E
Mapuera, stm., Braz.	164	C6	1.05 S	57.02 W
Mapulanguene, Moz.	90	D11	24.28 S	32.03 E
Maputo, Moz.	90	D11	25.58 S	32.34 E
Maputo, state, Moz.	90	D11	26.00 S	32.25 E
Maputo, stm., Afr.	90	E11	26.10 S	32.41 E
Maputo, Baía de, b., Moz.	90	D11	26.05 S	32.46 E
Maqên Gangri, mtn., China	52	E4	34.55 N	99.18 E
Maqna, Sau. Ar.	74	F4	28.24 N	34.44 E
Maquan, stm., China	70	C9	29.32 N	84.07 E
Maqueda, Spain	28	D6	40.04 N	4.22 W
Maquela do Zombo, Ang.	88	B2	6.02 S	15.06 E
Maquereau, Pointe au, c., Qc., Can.	122	B12	48.12 N	64.47 W
Maquiaú, stm., Braz.	168	G10	1.28 N	63.24 W
Maquinchao, Arg.	166	H3	41.14 S	68.41 W
Maquoketa, Ia., U.S.	130	B7	42.03 N	90.39 W
Maquoketa, stm., Ia., U.S.	130	B7	42.11 N	90.18 W
Maquoketa, North Fork, stm., Ia., U.S.	130	B7	42.04 N	90.39 W
Mår, l., Nor.	16	G6	60.07 N	8.13 E
Mar, Laguna, b., Cuba	204b		23.05 N	82.30 W
Mar, Serra do, mts., Braz.	166	E7	23.30 S	45.30 W
Mara, stm., Afr.	86	E7	1.31 S	33.58 E
Maraã, Braz.	168	H9	1.49 S	65.23 W
Maraa, Fr. Poly.	100h	v21	17.44 S	149.34 W
Marabá, Braz.	170	C1	5.20 S	49.05 W
Marabahan, Indon.	66	E9	3.00 S	114.45 E
Maraboon, Lake, res., Austl.	98	D6	23.41 S	148.04 E
Maracá, Ilha de, i., Braz.	164	C7	2.05 N	50.25 W
Maracá, Ilha de, i., Braz.	168	F11	3.26 N	61.39 W
Maracaçumé, stm., Braz.	170	A3	1.27 S	45.41 W
Maracaibo, Ven.	168	B6	10.40 N	71.37 W
Maracaibo, Lago de, l., Ven.	168	C6	9.43 N	71.49 W
Maracaju, Braz.	166	D5	21.37 S	55.09 W
Maracaju, Serra de, hills, S.A.	166	D5	21.31 S	55.37 W
Maracanã, Braz.	164	D8	0.46 S	47.27 W
Maracanã, ngh., Braz.	205a		22.54 S	43.14 W
Maracanã, Estádio do, p.o.i., Braz.	205a		22.55 S	43.14 W
Maracanaú, Braz.	170	B6	3.52 S	38.38 W
Maracás, Braz.	170	G5	13.26 S	40.25 W
Maracay, Ven.	168	B8	10.15 N	67.36 W
Marādah, Libya	82	B3	29.12 N	19.12 E
Maradi, Niger	84	G6	13.29 N	7.06 E
Marāghah, Sabkhat al-, l., Syria	76	C8	35.39 N	37.40 E
Marāgheh, Iran	74	B10	37.22 N	46.14 E
Maragogipe, Braz.	170	G6	12.46 S	38.55 W
Maragoji, Braz.	170	E8	9.00 S	35.13 W
Marahuaca, Cerro, mtn., Ven.	168	F9	3.34 N	65.27 W
Maraial, Braz.	170	E8	8.47 S	35.50 W
Maraisburg see Roodepoort-Maraisburg, S. Afr.	191d		26.11 S	27.56 E
Marais des Cygnes, stm., U.S.	130	F3	38.01 N	94.14 W
Marajó, Baía de, b., Braz.	164	D8	1.00 S	48.30 W
Marajó, Ilha de, i., Braz.	164	D8	1.00 S	49.30 W
Maralal, Kenya	86	D7	1.05 N	36.41 E
Maralaleng, Bots.	90	D6	25.45 S	22.43 E
Marali, C.A.R.	86	C3	6.01 N	18.24 E
Maralinga, Austl.	96	F6	30.10 S	131.35 E
Maramasike, i., Sol. Is.	101b	e9	9.32 S	161.27 E
Marambio, sci., Ant.	103	B35	64.14 S	56.43 W
Marampa, S.L.	84	H2	8.40 N	12.27 W
Maramsilli Reservoir, res., India	70	H8	20.31 N	81.40 E
Maramureș, state, Rom.	36	B10	47.40 N	24.00 E
Maran, Malay.	64	K6	3.34 N	102.45 E
Marana, Az., U.S.	150	K5	32.29 N	111.12 W
Marand, Iran	74	A9	38.25 N	45.46 E
Marang, Malay.	64	J6	5.12 N	103.12 E
Marang, Mya.	64	G4	10.28 N	98.47 E
Marangá, stm., Braz.	205a		22.51 S	43.23 W
Marangani, Peru	164	F3	14.19 S	71.13 W
Marangas, Phil.	68	F1	8.40 N	117.37 E
Maranguape, Braz.	170	B6	3.53 S	38.40 W
Maranhão, state, Braz.	164	D9	5.00 S	45.00 W
Maranhão, stm., Braz.	170	H1	13.58 S	48.20 W
Marano, Italy	184b		45.38 N	8.38 E
Marano, Laguna di, b., Italy	30	E10	45.44 N	13.10 E
Maranoa, stm., Austl.	98	F7	27.43 S	148.44 E
Marañón, stm., Peru	164	D2	4.28 S	73.29 W
Marans, Fr.	22	C5	46.18 N	0.59 W
Maraoli, ngh., India	190c		19.03 N	72.54 E
Marapendi, Lagoa de, b., Braz.	205a		23.01 S	43.24 W
Marapicu, Morro do, mtn., Braz.	205a		22.50 S	43.36 W
Maraş see Kahramanmaraş, Tur.	42	G7	37.35 N	36.56 E
Maraş, state, Tur.	74	B5	38.00 N	37.05 E
Marasany, Russia	40	C19	57.26 N	54.27 E
Marasende, Pulau, i., Indon.	66	F10	5.07 S	118.08 E
Mărășești, Rom.	36	D14	45.52 N	27.14 E
Maratasã, stm., Braz.	170	C4	4.12 S	42.14 W
Maratea, Italy	32	E9	39.59 N	15.45 E
Marathon, Austl.	98	C4	20.50 S	143.34 E
Marathon, On., Can.	128	C12	48.43 N	86.22 W
Marathon, N.Y., U.S.	124	B9	42.26 N	76.02 W
Marathon, Tx., U.S.	136	D4	30.12 N	103.14 W
Marathon, Wi., U.S.	128	G9	44.55 N	89.50 W
Marathónas, Grc.	34	E6	38.09 N	23.57 E
Maratua, Pulau, i., Indon.	66	B11	2.15 N	118.34 E
Maraú, Braz.	170	H6	14.03 S	39.00 W
Marau, Braz.	172	D11	28.24 S	52.18 W
Marauiá, stm., Braz.	168	H9	0.25 S	65.11 W
Maravari, Sol. Is.	101b	d7	7.51 S	156.42 E
Maravilha, Braz.	172	C11	26.45 S	53.09 W
Maravillas, Mex.	154	B6	27.22 N	104.29 W
Maravillas Creek, stm., Tx., U.S.	136	E4	29.33 N	102.46 W
Marav Lake, l., Pak.	70	D2	29.04 N	69.18 E
Maravovo, Sol. Is.	101b	e8	9.18 S	159.36 E
Marawi, Phil.	68	F5	8.01 N	124.16 E
Marawwah, i., U.A.E.	74	H13	24.17 N	53.14 E
Marayes, Arg.	172	E4	31.27 S	67.20 W
Marayong, Austl.	192a		33.45 S	150.54 E
Marbella, Spain	28	H6	36.30 N	4.52 W
Marble, Mn., U.S.	128	D5	47.19 N	93.17 W
Marble, N.C., U.S.	132	A2	35.10 N	83.55 W
Marble Bar, Austl.	96	D3	21.10 S	119.44 E
Marble Canyon, val., Az., U.S.	150	G5	36.30 N	111.50 W
Marble Falls, Tx., U.S.	136	D9	30.34 N	98.16 W
Marble Hall, S. Afr.	90	D9	24.57 S	29.13 E
Marblehead, Oh., U.S.	124	C3	41.32 N	82.43 W
Marblehead Neck, pen., Ma., U.S.	201		42.29 N	70.51 W
Marble Hill, Mo., U.S.	130	G8	37.18 N	89.58 W
Marblemount, Wa., U.S.	146	B5	48.32 N	121.27 W
Marble Rock, Ia., U.S.	128	I6	42.57 N	92.52 W
Marburg, Ger.	24	F4	50.48 N	8.46 E
Marburg, S. Afr.	90	G10	30.44 S	30.22 E
Marburg an der Drau see Maribor, Slvn.	30	D12	46.33 N	15.38 E
Marca, Ponta da, c., Ang.	88	D1	16.30 S	11.42 E
Marcal, stm., Hung.	36	B4	47.40 N	17.37 E
Marcali, Hung.	36	C4	46.35 N	17.24 E
Marcallo con Casone, Italy	184b		45.29 N	8.52 E
Marcelin, Sk., Can.	142	B7	52.55 N	106.47 W
Marceline, Mo., U.S.	130	E5	39.43 N	92.57 W
Marcelino Ramos, Braz.	172	C11	27.28 S	51.55 W
Marcella, N.J., U.S.	194		40.59 N	74.28 W
March, Eng., U.K.	10	I12	52.33 N	0.04 E
March (Morava), stm., Eur.	24	H12	48.10 N	16.59 E
March Air Force Base, mil., Ca., U.S.	148	J8	33.54 N	117.15 W
Marchais, Fr.	179		48.31 N	2.03 E
Marche, state, Italy	30	G10	43.30 N	13.15 E
Marche, hist. reg., Fr.	22	C7	46.05 N	2.10 E
Marche-en-Famenne, Bel.	20	D14	50.13 N	5.19 E
Marchegg, Aus.	30	B13	48.16 N	16.55 E
Marchémoret, Fr.	179		49.03 N	2.46 E
Marchena, Spain	28	G5	37.19 N	5.24 W
Marchena, Isla, i., Ec.	164a	h11	0.21 N	90.29 W
Marches see Marche, state, Italy	30	G10	43.30 N	13.15 E
Marchfeld, reg., Aus.	182b		48.17 N	16.31 E
Mar Chiquita, Laguna, b., Arg.	172	H9	37.38 S	57.23 W
Mar Chiquita, Laguna, l., Arg.	172	E6	30.42 S	62.36 W
Marchykhyna Buda, Ukr.	38	A13	51.57 N	34.03 E
Marcigny, Fr.	22	C10	46.17 N	4.02 E
Marcilly, Fr.	179		49.02 N	2.53 E
Marco, Braz.	170	B5	3.08 S	40.09 W
Marcola, Or., U.S.	146	F4	44.10 N	122.51 W
Marco Polo Bridge, trans., China	189a		39.52 N	116.12 E
Marcos Juárez, Arg.	172	F6	32.42 S	62.06 W
Marcos Paz, state, Arg.	206		34.49 S	58.49 W
Marcoussis, Fr.	179		48.39 N	2.14 E
Marcq, Fr.	179		48.52 N	1.49 E
Mărculești, Mol.	38	B14	47.52 N	28.14 E
Marcus, Ia., U.S.	130	B2	42.49 N	95.48 W
Marcus Baker, Mount, mtn., Ak., U.S.	109	D10	61.26 N	147.45 W
Marcus Hook Creek, stm., Pa., U.S.	203		39.49 N	75.25 W
Marcus Island see Minami-Tori-shima, i., Japan	46	G19	24.18 N	153.58 E
Marcy, Mount, mtn., N.Y., U.S.	126	D16	44.07 N	73.56 W
Mardalsfoss, wtfl., Nor.	16	E6	62.28 N	8.11 E
Mardān, Pak.	70	A4	34.11 N	72.02 E
Mardarivka, Ukr.	38	F8	47.31 N	29.45 E
Mar de Cães, Vala de, can., Port.	184c		38.51 N	8.59 W
Mar del Plata, Arg.	172	H9	37.59 S	57.33 W
Mardin, Tur.	42	G9	37.18 N	40.44 E
Mardin, state, Tur.	42	G9	37.25 N	41.00 E
Mar Dyke, stm., Eng., U.K.	178		51.29 N	0.14 E
Maré, i., N. Cal.	101d	m17	21.30 S	167.58 E
Mare a Brăilei, Insula, i., Rom.	36	D15	45.00 N	28.00 E
Marea de Portillo, Cuba	156	C9	19.55 N	77.11 W
Marechal Cândido Rondon, Braz.	172	B10	24.33 S	54.03 W
Marechal Deodoro, Braz.	170	E8	9.43 S	35.54 W
Maree, Loch, l., Scot., U.K.	10	D7	57.42 N	5.30 W
Mareeba, Austl.	98	A5	16.59 S	145.24 E
Mareil-en-France, Fr.	179		49.04 N	2.26 E
Mareil-le-Guyon, Fr.	179		48.47 N	1.51 E
Mareil-Marly, Fr.	179		48.53 N	2.05 E
Mare Island Strait, strt., Ca., U.S.	200		38.06 N	122.17 W
Marek, Indon.	66	F12	4.49 S	120.20 E
Maremma, reg., Italy	30	H8	42.27 N	11.26 E
Marengo, Il., U.S.	130	B9	42.14 N	88.36 W
Marengo, In., U.S.	130	F11	38.22 N	86.20 W
Marengo, Ia., U.S.	130	C5	41.47 N	92.03 W
Marenisco, Mi., U.S.	128	E9	46.22 N	89.41 W
Marennes, Fr.	22	D4	45.48 N	1.06 W
Marettimo, Isola, i., Italy	32	G5	37.58 N	12.03 E
Mareuil-lès-Meaux, Fr.	179		48.56 N	2.52 E
Marevo, Russia	26	C14	57.18 N	32.04 E
Marfa, Tx., U.S.	136	D3	30.18 N	104.01 W
Margai Caka, l., China	62	A6	35.00 N	87.00 E
Margaree, N.S., Can.	122	D15	46.24 N	61.03 W
Margaree Harbour, N.S., Can.	122	D15	46.26 N	61.07 W
Margaret, stm., Austl.	96	C5	18.10 S	125.37 E
Margaret Bay, B.C., Can.	144	E3	51.19 N	127.28 W
Margarethenhöhe, ngh., Ger.	181		51.26 N	6.58 E
Margaret River, Austl.	96	F2	33.57 S	115.04 E
Margaret Roding, Eng., U.K.	178		51.47 N	0.19 E
Margaretting, Eng., U.K.	178		51.41 N	0.25 E
Margaretville, N.Y., U.S.	124	B11	42.09 N	74.38 W
Margarita, Isla de, i., Ven.	168	B9	11.00 N	64.00 W
Margate, S. Afr.	90	G10	30.54 S	30.19 E
Margate, Eng., U.K.	10	J14	51.23 N	1.24 E
Margate, Fl., U.S.	132	J5	26.14 N	80.12 W
Margate City, N.J., U.S.	124	E11	39.19 N	74.29 W
Margecany, Slvk.	24	H16	48.53 N	21.01 E
Margelan see Margilan, Uzb.	48	F12	40.28 N	71.43 E
Margherita see Jamaame, Som.	86	E8	0.00 N	42.42 E
Margherita di Savoia, Italy	32	C10	41.22 N	16.06 E
Margherita Peak, mtn., Afr.	86	D5	0.22 N	29.51 E
Marghita, Rom.	36	B9	47.20 N	22.21 E
Margilan, Uzb.	48	F12	40.28 N	71.43 E
Margit Híd, trans., Hung.	182c		47.31 N	19.02 E
Margit-sziget, i., Hung.	182c		47.32 N	19.03 E
Margonin, Pol.	24	D13	52.58 N	17.05 E
Margosatubig, Phil.	68	G4	7.33 N	123.09 E
Mārgow, Dasht-e, des., Afg.	72	C9	30.45 N	63.10 E
Marguerite, Pic see Margherita Peak, mtn., Afr.	86	D5	0.22 N	29.51 E
Marha, Russia	50	D13	60.36 N	123.19 E
Marha, stm., Russia	50	C12	63.26 N	118.52 E
Marhanets', Ukr.	38	F13	47.38 N	34.38 E
Mari, Pap. N. Gui.	101a	b3	9.11 S	141.42 E
Maria, Îles, is., Fr. Poly.	94	F11	21.44 S	154.37 W
Mariabrunn, ngh., Aus.	182b		48.12 N	16.14 E
María Cleofas, Isla, i., Mex.	154	E5	21.18 N	106.14 W
María Elena, Chile	166	D3	22.19 S	69.39 W
Mariager, Den.	16	K8	56.38 N	9.59 E
María Grande, Arg.	172	E8	31.39 S	59.53 W
María Ignacia, Arg.	172	H8	37.24 S	59.31 W
Maria Island, i., Austl.	96	B7	14.52 S	135.44 E
Maria Island National Park, p.o.i., Austl.	99a	o14	42.37 S	148.04 E
Mariakani, Kenya	86	E7	3.50 S	39.28 E
María La Baja, Col.	168	B4	9.59 N	75.18 W
Maria Lanzendorf, Aus.	182b		48.06 N	16.25 E
María Madre, Isla, i., Mex.	154	E5	21.37 N	106.35 W
María Magdalena, Isla, i., Mex.	154	E5	21.27 N	106.25 W
Mariana, Braz.	170	K4	20.22 S	43.25 W
Mariana Isalnds, is., Oc.	94	B5	15.59 N	145.43 E
Mariana Ridge, unds.	174	H17	17.00 N	146.00 E
Mariana Trench, unds.	174	H17	15.01 N	147.29 E
Mar'ianivka, Ukr.	38	C3	50.28 N	24.48 E
Marian Lake, l., N.T., Can.	110	C7	62.59 N	116.13 W
Marianna, Ar., U.S.	134	C8	34.46 N	90.45 W
Marianna, Fl., U.S.	134	G13	30.46 N	85.14 W
Mariannelund, Swe.	16	J13	57.37 N	15.37 E
Mariano I. Loza, Arg.	172	D8	29.22 S	58.12 W
Mariano J. Haedo, Arg.	206		34.38 S	58.36 W
Mariánské Lázně, Czech Rep.	24	G8	49.58 N	12.42 E
Marias, stm., Mt., U.S.	146	B16	47.56 N	110.30 W
Marias, Dry Fork, stm., Mt., U.S.	146	B14	48.22 N	111.44 W
Marias Pass, p., Mt., U.S.	146	B13	48.19 N	113.20 W
María Teresa, Arg.	172	G6	34.01 S	61.54 W
Maria Theresiopel see Subotica, Yugo.	36	C6	46.05 N	19.40 E
Mariato, Punta, c., Pan.	156	I7	7.13 N	80.53 W
Mariazell, Aus.	30	C12	47.46 N	15.18 E
Maribo, Den.	16	M9	54.46 N	11.30 E
Maribojoc Bay, b., Phil.	68	F4	9.43 N	123.50 E
Maribor, Slvn.	30	D12	46.33 N	15.38 E
Maribyrnong, Austl.	192b		37.46 S	144.54 E
Marica, Russia	38	B14	51.45 N	35.16 E
Maricá, mun., Braz.	205a		22.57 S	42.59 W
Marica see Maritsa, stm., Eur.	34	A8	40.44 N	26.02 E
Maricao, P.R.	158a	b2	18.11 N	66.58 W
Maricha Bil, l., India	190b		22.55 N	88.31 E
Marico, stm., Afr.	90	D8	24.11 S	26.52 E
Maricopa, Az., U.S.	150	J4	33.03 N	112.02 W
Maricopa, Ca., U.S.	148	H6	35.03 N	119.24 W
Maricopa Indian Reservation, ind. res., Az., U.S.	150	K4	33.00 N	112.05 W
Maricunga, Salar de, pl., Chile	172	C3	26.55 S	69.05 W
Marié, stm., Braz.	168	H8	0.25 S	66.24 W
Marie Byrd Land, reg., Ant.	103	C29	80.00 S	120.00 W
Mariec, Russia	40	C16	56.31 N	49.50 E
Marie Curtis Park, p.o.i., On., Can.	193b		43.35 N	79.33 W
Mariefred, Swe.	16	H15	59.15 N	17.14 E
Marie-Galante, i., Guad.	159c	i6	15.56 N	61.16 W
Mariehamn see Maarianhamina, Fin.	18	G6	60.06 N	19.56 E
Mari El see Marij El, state, Russia	40	C15	56.30 N	48.00 E
Marienbad see Mariánské Lázně, Czech Rep.	24	G8	49.58 N	12.42 E
Marien-Berg, hill, Ger.	182a		52.22 N	13.32 E
Marienburg see Malbork, Pol.	24	B15	54.01 N	19.02 E
Mariendorf, ngh., Ger.	182a		52.26 N	13.23 E
Mariental, Nmb.	90	D4	24.37 S	17.57 E
Marienville, Pa., U.S.	124	C6	41.28 N	79.07 W
Marienwerder see Kwidzyn, Pol.	24	C14	53.44 N	18.56 E
Maries, stm., Mo., U.S.	130	F5	38.30 N	92.00 W
Mariestad, Swe.	16	I11	58.42 N	13.51 E
Marieta, stm., Ven.	168	E8	4.59 N	66.22 W
Marietta, Ga., U.S.	134	D14	33.57 N	84.32 W
Marietta, Mn., U.S.	128	G2	44.59 N	96.26 W
Marietta, Oh., U.S.	124	E4	39.24 N	81.27 W
Marietta, Ok., U.S.	138	H11	33.55 N	97.07 W
Marieville, Qc., Can.	126	C16	45.25 N	73.10 W
Marignane, Fr.	22	F11	43.24 N	5.12 E
Marigot, Dom.	159c	i6	15.31 N	61.18 W
Marigot, Guad.	159a	a1	18.04 N	63.04 W
Mariinsk, Russia	48	C15	56.12 N	87.44 E
Mariinski Theatre, bldg., Russia	183a		59.55 N	30.18 E
Mariinskoe, Russia	50	F17	51.43 N	140.11 E
Marijampolė, Lith.	26	F6	54.33 N	23.21 E
Marij El, state, Russia	40	C15	56.30 N	48.00 E
Marikina, Phil.	187f		14.38 N	121.06 E
Marikina, stm., Phil.	187f		14.33 N	121.04 E
Marília, Braz.	166	D7	22.12 S	49.56 W

Name	Page	Map Ref.	Latitude	Longitude
Marimba, Ang.	88	B2	8.21 S	16.58 E
Marín, Mex.	136	I7	25.52 N	100.03 W
Marín, Spain	28	B2	42.23 N	8.42 W
Marina, ngh., Ca., U.S.	200		37.47 N	122.27 W
Marina del Rey, Ca., U.S.	198		33.50 N	118.25 W
Marina del Rey, b., Ca., U.S.	198		33.58 N	118.27 W
Marina di Gioiosa Ionica, Italy	32	F10	38.18 N	16.20 E
Marina di Ravenna, Italy	30	F9	44.29 N	12.16 E
Marina Fall, wtfl., Guy.	168	E12	5.21 N	59.28 W
Mar"ina Horka, Bela.	26	G11	53.30 N	28.10 E
Marin City, Ca., U.S.	200		37.52 N	122.21 W
Marinduque, i., Phil.	68	D3	13.24 N	121.58 E
Marine City, Mi., U.S.	124	B3	42.43 N	82.29 W
Marine Museum, bldg., Ca., U.S.	198		33.43 N	118.17 W
Marine Park, p.o.i., Ma., U.S.	201		42.20 N	71.01 W
Marine Parkway Bridge, trans., N.Y., U.S.	194		40.34 N	73.53 W
Marinette, Wi., U.S.	126	C2	45.05 N	87.37 W
Maringá, Braz.	166	D6	23.25 S	51.55 W
Maringouin, La., U.S.	134	G7	30.29 N	91.31 W
Marinha Grande, Port.	28	E1	39.44 N	8.55 W
Marinho, stm., Braz.	205a		23.00 S	43.27 W
Mar'inka, Ukr.	38	F16	47.55 N	37.33 E
Marin Mall, shp. cen., Ca., U.S.	200		37.56 N	122.31 W
Marino, Vanuatu	101d	j16	14.59 S	168.07 E
Marin Peninsula, pen., Ca., U.S.	200		37.51 N	122.31 W
Marinskij Posad, Russia	40	C15	56.06 N	47.43 E
Marintu, Indon.	66	C6	0.20 N	110.01 E
Mario, Monte, hill, Italy	185a		41.55 N	12.27 E
Marion, Al., U.S.	134	E11	32.37 N	87.19 W
Marion, Ar., U.S.	134	B8	35.12 N	90.11 W
Marion, Il., U.S.	130	G9	37.43 N	88.56 W
Marion, In., U.S.	130	D12	40.33 N	85.39 W
Marion, Ia., U.S.	130	B6	42.01 N	91.36 W
Marion, Ks., U.S.	138	C12	38.21 N	97.00 W
Marion, Ky., U.S.	130	G9	37.20 N	88.04 W
Marion, La., U.S.	134	E6	32.54 N	92.14 W
Marion, Mi., U.S.	126	D4	44.06 N	85.08 W
Marion, Ms., U.S.	134	E10	32.25 N	88.39 W
Marion, N.C., U.S.	124	I4	35.41 N	82.00 W
Marion, N.D., U.S.	140	A14	46.36 N	98.19 W
Marion, Oh., U.S.	124	D2	40.35 N	83.07 W
Marion, S.C., U.S.	132	B6	34.10 N	79.23 W
Marion, S.D., U.S.	140	D15	43.25 N	97.15 W
Marion, Va., U.S.	124	H4	36.50 N	81.31 W
Marion, Wi., U.S.	128	G10	44.40 N	88.53 W
Marion, Lake, res., S.C., U.S.	132	C5	33.32 N	80.28 W
Marion Bay, b., Austl.	99a	o14	42.48 S	147.55 E
Marion County Lake, res., Ks., U.S.	138	C11	38.24 N	97.08 W
Marion Downs, Austl.	98	D2	23.22 S	139.39 E
Marion Junction, Al., U.S.	134	E11	32.26 N	87.14 W
Marion Reef, rf., Austl.	98	B9	19.10 S	152.17 E
Marionville, Mo., U.S.	130	G4	37.00 N	93.38 W
Mariópolis, Braz.	172	C11	26.21 S	52.21 W
Maripa, Ven.	168	D9	7.26 N	65.07 W
Mariposa, Ca., U.S.	148	F5	37.29 N	119.58 W
Mariquita, Col.	168	E4	5.11 N	74.54 W
Mariscala, Ur.	172	F10	34.02 S	54.46 W
Mariscal Estigarribia, Para.	166	D4	22.01 S	60.36 W
Marisco, Ponta do, c., Braz.	205a		23.01 S	43.17 W
Marissa, Il., U.S.	130	F8	38.14 N	89.45 W
Maritime Alps, mts., Eur.	30	F4	44.15 N	7.10 E
Maritime Atlas see Atlas Tellien, mts., Alg.	80	C6	36.00 N	3.00 E
Maritimes, Alpes see Maritime Alps, mts., Eur.	30	F4	44.15 N	7.10 E
Maritsa (Évros) (Evros) (Marica) (Meriç), stm., Eur.	34	C9	40.44 N	26.02 E
Marittime, Alpi see Maritime Alps, mts., Eur.	30	F4	44.15 N	7.10 E
Mari-Turek, Russia	40	C16	56.47 N	49.37 E
Maritzburg see Pietermaritzburg, S. Afr.	90	F10	29.36 S	30.23 E
Mariupol', Ukr.	38	F16	47.06 N	37.34 E
Mariusa, Caño, stm., Ven.	168	C11	9.34 N	61.12 W
Mariusa, Isla, i., Ven.	159f	t12	9.45 N	61.18 W
Marīvān, Iran	74	C10	35.31 N	46.10 E
Mariveles, Phil.	68	C3	14.26 N	120.29 E
Mariyampole see Marijampolė, Lith.	26	F6	54.33 N	23.21 E
Märjamaa, Est.	26	B7	58.54 N	24.26 E
Marjanovka, Russia	48	D12	54.57 N	72.38 E
Marjino, Russia	183a		59.50 N	29.56 E
Marjino, Russia	183a		59.54 N	31.00 E
Marjino, Russia	183b		55.52 N	37.18 E
Marjinsko, Russia	26	B11	58.49 N	28.32 E
Marka, Som.	86	D8	1.42 N	44.45 E
Mark Acres, Pa., U.S.	197b		40.21 N	79.42 W
Markakol', ozero, l., Kaz.	48	E15	48.45 N	85.48 E
Märkāpur, India	69	D4	15.47 N	79.15 E
Markaryd, Swe.	16	K11	56.28 N	13.35 E
Markazī, state, Iran	74	C12	34.30 N	49.45 E
Markdale, On., Can.	126	D9	44.18 N	80.39 W
Marked Tree, Ar., U.S.	134	B8	35.32 N	90.25 W
Markesan, Wi., U.S.	128	H10	43.42 N	88.59 W
Market Harborough, Eng., U.K.	10	I12	52.28 N	0.55 W
Market Shop, St. K./N.	159a	c2	17.07 N	62.34 W
Markham, On., Can.	126	E10	43.52 N	79.16 W
Markham, Il., U.S.	196		41.35 N	87.41 W
Markham, Tx., U.S.	136	F11	28.57 N	96.04 W
Markham Bay, b., Nu., Can.	110	C16	63.30 N	71.48 W
Markit, China	48	G13	38.54 N	77.38 E
Markivka, Ukr.	38	D18	49.31 N	39.34 E
Markle, In., U.S.	130	D12	40.49 N	85.20 W
Markle, Pa., U.S.	197b		40.34 N	79.39 W
Markleeville, Ca., U.S.	148	E6	38.41 N	119.47 W
Markley Canyon, val., Ca., U.S.	200		38.00 N	121.50 W
Markópoulo, Grc.	185c		37.54 N	23.54 E
Markovo, Russia	50	D23	64.40 N	170.26 E
Marks, Russia	40	F15	51.42 N	46.44 E
Marks, Ms., U.S.	134	C8	34.15 N	90.16 W
Marksville, La., U.S.	134	F6	31.07 N	92.05 W
Marktheidenfeld, Ger.	24	G5	49.50 N	9.36 E
Marktoberdorf, Ger.	24	I6	47.46 N	10.37 E
Marktredwitz, Ger.	24	G8	50.00 N	12.05 E
Mark Twain Lake, res., Mo., U.S.	130	E6	39.30 N	91.44 W
Markvue Manor, Pa., U.S.	197b		40.20 N	79.46 W
Marl, Ger.	20	C16	51.38 N	7.05 E
Marlboro, Ab., Can.	144	C14	53.33 N	116.46 W
Marlboro, N.Y., U.S.	124	C11	41.36 N	73.58 W
Marlboro, Pa., U.S.	203		39.54 N	75.42 W
Marlborough, Austl.	98	D7	22.49 S	149.53 E
Marlborough, Guy.	164	B6	7.29 N	58.37 W
Marlborough, Ma., U.S.	124	B14	42.21 N	71.32 W
Marle, Fr.	20	E12	49.44 N	3.46 E
Marles-en-Brie, Fr.	179		48.44 N	2.53 E
Marlette, Mi., U.S.	126	E6	43.19 N	83.04 W
Marley, Il., U.S.	196		41.33 N	87.55 W
Marley Creek, stm., Il., U.S.	196		41.31 N	87.52 W
Marley Neck, pen., Md., U.S.	202b		39.12 N	76.33 W
Marlin, Tx., U.S.	136	C11	31.17 N	96.52 W
Marlinton, W.V., U.S.	124	F5	38.13 N	80.06 W
Marl-Loemühle, Flughafen, arpt., Ger.	181		51.39 N	7.10 E
Marlow, Ok., U.S.	138	G11	34.38 N	97.57 W
Marlpit Hill, Eng., U.K.	178		51.13 N	0.04 E
Marlton Heights, N.J., U.S.	203		39.40 N	75.21 W
Marly, Forêt de, p.o.i., Fr.	179		48.52 N	2.03 E
Marly-la-Ville, Fr.	179		49.05 N	2.30 E
Marma, Swe.	16	F14	61.16 N	16.53 E
Marmaduke, Ar., U.S.	130	H7	36.10 N	90.23 W
Marmande, Fr.	22	E6	44.30 N	0.10 E
Marmara, Sea of see Marmara Denizi, s., Tur.	34	C10	40.40 N	28.15 E
Marmara Adası, i., Tur.	34	C10	40.39 N	27.37 E
Marmara Denizi (Marmara, Sea of), s., Tur.	34	C10	40.40 N	28.15 E
Marmara Ereğlisi, Tur.	34	C10	40.58 N	27.57 E
Marmara Gölü, l., Tur.	34	E10	38.37 N	28.01 E
Marmaris, Tur.	34	G11	36.48 N	28.17 E
Marmarītā, Syria	76	D7	34.47 N	36.15 E
Marmarth, N.D., U.S.	140	A8	46.17 N	103.55 W
Marmaton, stm., U.S.	130	G3	37.59 N	94.19 W
Marmelos, Braz.	164	E5	6.08 S	61.51 W
Marmelos, stm., Braz.	164	E5	6.05 S	61.45 W
Marmet, W.V., U.S.	124	F4	38.13 N	81.34 W
Marmion Lake, l., On., Can.	128	C7	48.54 N	91.30 W
Marmolada, mtn., Italy	30	D8	46.26 N	11.51 E
Marmora, On., Can.	126	D12	44.28 N	77.40 W
Marnate, Italy	184b		45.38 N	8.54 E
Marnay, Fr.	20	G14	47.17 N	5.46 E
Marne, Ger.	24	C4	53.57 N	9.00 E
Marne, Mi., U.S.	130	A12	43.02 N	85.48 W
Marne, state, Fr.	20	E13	48.55 N	4.10 E
Marne à la Saône, Canal de la, can., Fr.	20	F14	48.43 N	4.36 E
Marne au Rhin, Canal de la, can., Fr.	24	H3	48.35 N	7.46 E
Maroa, Il., U.S.	130	D8	40.02 N	88.56 W
Maroa, Ven.	168	F8	2.43 N	67.33 W
Maroantsetra, Madag.	88	D8	15.26 S	49.44 E
Marobi Raghza, Pak.	70	B2	32.36 N	69.52 E
Marol, ngh., India	190c		19.07 N	72.53 E
Marolles-en-Brie, Fr.	179		48.44 N	2.33 E
Marolles-en-Hurepoix, Fr.	179		48.34 N	2.18 E
Maromandia, Madag.	88	C8	14.12 S	48.05 E
Maromme, Fr.	20	E10	49.28 N	1.02 E
Maromokotro, mtn., Madag.	88	C8	14.01 S	48.58 E
Marondera, Zimb.	88	D5	18.10 S	31.31 E
Maroni (Marowijne), stm., S.A.	164	C7	5.34 N	54.00 W
Maroondah Aqueduct, aq., Austl.	192b		37.42 S	145.01 E
Maros, Indon.	66	F11	5.00 S	119.34 E
Maros (Mureș), stm., Eur.	36	C7	46.15 N	20.11 E
Marosvásárhely see Târgu Mureș, Rom.	36	C11	46.32 N	24.34 E
Maroua, Cam.	86	B2	10.36 N	14.19 E
Maroubra, Austl.	192a		33.57 S	151.16 E
Marovoay, Madag.	88	D8	16.06 S	46.38 E
Marowijne (Maroni), stm., S.A.	164	C7	5.34 N	54.00 W
Marquand, Mo., U.S.	130	G7	37.25 N	90.09 W
Marquard, S. Afr.	90	F8	28.40 S	27.26 E
Marquesas Islands see Marquises, Îles, is., Fr. Poly.	94	D12	8.58 S	139.30 W
Marquesas Keys, is., Fl., U.S.	132	L3	24.34 N	82.08 W
Marquette, Ks., U.S.	138	C11	38.33 N	97.49 W
Marquette, Mi., U.S.	126	B2	46.32 N	87.23 W
Marquette Park, p.o.i., Il., U.S.	196		41.46 N	87.42 W
Márquez, Peru	204d		11.57 S	77.08 W
Marquis, Gren.	159e	q10	12.05 N	61.37 W
Marquis, Cape, c., St. Luc.	159c	l7	14.03 N	60.53 W
Marquises, Îles, is., Fr. Poly.	94	D12	8.58 S	139.30 W
Marracuene, Moz.	90	D11	25.44 S	32.40 E
Marradi, Italy	30	F8	44.04 N	11.36 E
Marrah, Jabal, vol., Sudan	82	E4	13.02 N	24.20 E
Marrah, Jabal, mts., Sudan	82	E4	13.45 N	24.30 E
Marrakech, Mor.	84	C3	31.38 N	8.00 W
Marrakesh see Marrakech, Mor.	84	C3	31.38 N	8.00 W
Marrawah, Austl.	99a	n12	40.56 S	144.41 E
Marree, Austl.	96	E7	29.39 S	138.04 E
Marrero, La., U.S.	134	H8	29.53 N	90.06 W
Marrickville, Austl.	192a		33.55 S	151.09 E
Marromeu, Moz.	88	D6	18.15 S	35.51 E
Marrupa, Moz.	88	C6	13.11 S	37.29 E
Mars, Pa., U.S.	124	D6	40.41 N	80.00 W
Mars, stm., Qc., Can.	122	C5	48.20 N	70.53 W
Marsá al-Burayqah, Libya	82	A3	30.23 N	19.35 E
Marsabit, Kenya	86	D7	2.20 N	37.59 E
Marsala, Italy	32	G6	37.48 N	12.26 E
Marsange, stm., Fr.	179		48.43 N	2.45 E
Marsangue, stm., Fr.	179		48.40 N	2.47 E
Marscheid, ngh., Ger.	181		51.14 N	7.14 E
Marsciano, Italy	30	H9	42.55 N	12.19 E
Marsden, Austl.	98	I5	33.45 S	147.31 E
Marsden, Eng., U.K.	180		53.36 N	1.56 W
Marsden Park, Austl.	192a		33.42 S	150.50 E
Marseille, Fr.	22	F11	43.18 N	5.23 E
Marseille-en-Beauvaisis, Fr.	20	E11	49.34 N	1.57 E
Marseilles, Il., U.S.	130	C9	41.19 N	88.41 W
Marsfield, Austl.	192a		33.47 S	151.07 E
Marsfjället, mtn., Swe.	16	B13	65.05 N	15.28 E
Marshall, Lib.	84	H2	6.10 N	10.22 W
Marshall, Ak., U.S.	109	D7	61.53 N	162.05 W
Marshall, Ar., U.S.	130	I5	35.54 N	92.38 W
Marshall, Il., U.S.	130	E10	39.23 N	87.41 W
Marshall, Mi., U.S.	124	B1	42.16 N	84.57 W
Marshall, Mn., U.S.	128	G3	44.27 N	95.47 W
Marshall, Mo., U.S.	130	E4	39.07 N	93.11 W
Marshall, N.C., U.S.	124	I3	35.48 N	82.40 W
Marshall, Tx., U.S.	136	B13	32.32 N	94.22 W
Marshall, Va., U.S.	124	F8	38.51 N	77.51 W
Marshall, stm., Austl.	96	D7	22.58 S	136.42 E
Marshallberg, N.C., U.S.	132	B9	34.43 N	76.30 W
Marshall Canyon Regional Park, p.o.i., Ca., U.S.	198		34.09 N	117.43 W
Marshall Islands, ctry., Oc.	92	B7	11.00 N	168.00 E
Marshall Islands, is., Marsh. Is.	94	B7	9.00 N	168.00 E
Marshallton, Pa., U.S.	203		39.57 N	75.41 W
Marshalltown, Ia., U.S.	130	B5	42.02 N	92.54 W
Marshallville, Ga., U.S.	132	D2	32.27 N	83.56 W
Marshbank Metropolitan Park, p.o.i., Mi., U.S.	199		42.36 N	83.23 W
Marsh Creek, stm., Ca., U.S.	200		37.53 N	121.49 W
Marsh Creek, stm., Mi., U.S.	199		42.06 N	83.13 W
Marsh Creek, stm., Pa., U.S.	203		40.03 N	75.43 W
Marshes Creek, stm., N.J., U.S.	194		40.36 N	74.13 W
Marshfield, Mo., U.S.	130	G5	37.20 N	92.54 W
Marshfield, Wi., U.S.	128	G8	44.40 N	90.10 W
Marshfield Airport, arpt., Ma., U.S.	201		42.06 N	70.40 W
Marshfield Center, Ma., U.S.	201		42.07 N	70.43 W
Marsh Harbour, Bah.	132	J8	26.31 N	77.03 W
Mars Hill, Me., U.S.	122	D9	46.30 N	67.51 W
Mars Hill, N.C., U.S.	124	I3	35.49 N	82.33 W
Marsh Island, i., La., U.S.	134	H7	29.35 N	91.53 W
Marsh Peak, mtn., Ut., U.S.	150	C7	40.43 N	109.50 W
Marshside, Eng., U.K.	180		53.40 N	2.58 W
Marshville, N.C., U.S.	132	A5	34.59 N	80.22 W
Marshyhope Creek, stm., U.S.	124	F10	38.31 N	75.45 W
Marsing, Id., U.S.	146	G10	43.31 N	116.49 W
Märsta, Swe.	16	H15	59.37 N	17.51 E
Marstal, Den.	16	M8	54.51 N	10.30 E
Marston, Eng., U.K.	180		53.16 N	2.30 W
Marstrand, Swe.	16	J9	57.53 N	11.36 E
Mart, Tx., U.S.	136	C11	31.32 N	96.49 W
Marta, stm., Italy	30	H8	42.14 N	11.41 E
Martaban, Gulf of, b., Mya.	64	D3	16.46 N	97.00 E
Martapura, Indon.	66	E9	3.24 S	114.50 E
Martapura, Indon.	66	F4	4.18 S	104.20 E
Martel, Fr.	22	E7	44.56 N	1.37 E
Marten, ngh., Ger.	181		51.31 N	7.23 E
Marten Lake, l., On., Can.	126	B10	46.41 N	79.40 W
Marte R. Gómez, Presa, res., Mex.	136	H9	26.08 N	98.58 W
Marthaguy Creek, stm., Austl.	98	H6	30.16 S	147.34 E
Marthall, Eng., U.K.	180		53.17 N	2.18 W
Martha's Vineyard, i., Ma., U.S.	124	C15	41.24 N	70.37 W
Martí, Cuba	156	B9	21.09 N	77.26 W
Martigny, Switz.	30	D4	46.06 N	7.04 E
Martigues, Fr.	22	F11	43.24 N	5.03 E
Martin, Slvk.	24	G14	49.04 N	18.55 E
Martin, Ky., U.S.	124	G3	37.33 N	82.46 W
Martin, Mi., U.S.	130	B12	42.32 N	85.37 W
Martin, N.D., U.S.	142	G13	47.49 N	100.07 W
Martin, S.D., U.S.	140	D11	43.10 N	101.44 W
Martin, Tn., U.S.	130	H9	36.20 N	88.51 W
Martín, stm., Spain	28	C10	41.17 N	0.18 W
Martín, Arroyo, stm., Arg.	206		34.51 S	58.04 W
Martina Franca, Italy	32	D11	40.42 N	17.19 E
Martindale, Tx., U.S.	136	E10	29.50 N	97.50 W
Martindale Pond, l., On., Can.	202a		43.11 N	79.16 W
Mărtinești, Rom.	36	D14	45.30 N	27.25 E
Martinez, Ca., U.S.	148	E3	38.01 N	122.07 W
Martinez, Ga., U.S.	132	C3	33.30 N	82.04 W
Martínez de la Torre, Mex.	154	E10	20.04 N	97.02 W
Martinho Campos, Braz.	170	J3	19.19 S	45.14 W
Martini Creek, stm., Ca., U.S.	200		37.33 N	122.31 W
Martinique, dep., N.A.	159c	k6	14.40 N	61.00 W
Martinique Channel see Martinique Passage, strt., N.A.	159c	k6	15.10 N	61.15 W
Martinique Passage, strt., N.A.	159c	k6	15.10 N	61.15 W
Martin Lake, res., Al., U.S.	134	E12	32.48 N	85.54 W
Martin Lake, res., Tx., U.S.	136	B13	32.14 N	94.34 W
Martin Marietta Corporation, sci., Md., U.S.	202b		39.20 N	76.26 W
Martinniemi, Fin.	18	B12	65.13 N	25.18 E
Martinópole, Braz.	170	B5	3.15 S	40.41 W
Martín Pérez, stm., Cuba	204b		23.07 N	82.20 W
Martin Run, stm., Oh., U.S.	197a		41.27 N	82.12 W
Martinsberg, Aus.	30	B12	48.22 N	15.09 E
Martins Brook, stm., Ma., U.S.	201		42.34 N	71.06 W
Martinsburg, W.V., U.S.	124	E7	39.27 N	77.57 W
Martinscroft, Eng., U.K.	180		53.24 N	2.31 W
Martins Ferry, Oh., U.S.	124	D5	40.06 N	80.43 W
Martins Pond, l., Ma., U.S.	201		42.36 N	71.08 W
Martinsville, Il., U.S.	130	E10	39.20 N	87.53 W
Martinsville, In., U.S.	130	E11	39.25 N	86.25 W
Martinsville, N.J., U.S.	194		40.36 N	74.34 W
Martinsville, Va., U.S.	124	H6	36.40 N	79.52 W
Martin Vaz, Ilhas, is., Braz.	162	H12	20.30 S	28.51 W
Martisovo, Russia	26	D14	56.34 N	31.55 E
Marton, Eng., U.K.	180		53.12 N	2.13 W
Martorell, Spain	184d		41.28 N	1.56 E
Martorelles de Baix, Spain	184d		41.32 N	2.14 E
Martos, Spain	28	G7	37.43 N	3.58 W
Martova, Ukr.	38	D15	49.57 N	36.56 E
Martre, Lac la, l., N.T., Can.	110	C7	63.15 N	117.55 W
Martti, Fin.	14	E19	67.28 N	28.22 E
Martuk, Kaz.	40	F20	50.45 N	56.30 E
Martynivka, Ukr.	38	D10	49.37 N	31.16 E
Martynovych, Ukr.	38	B8	51.16 N	29.37 E
Martyrs Shrine, rel., Tai.	187d		25.05 N	121.32 E
Marudi, Malay.	66	A9	4.11 N	114.19 E
Marudu, Telukan, b., Malay.	68	G1	6.45 N	116.55 E
Marugame, Japan	56	E6	34.16 N	133.47 E
Maruim, Braz.	170	F7	10.43 S	37.04 W
Marula, Zimb.	90	B9	20.28 S	28.04 E
Maruoka, Japan	56	C9	36.09 N	136.16 E
Marusino, Russia	183b		55.42 N	37.59 E
Marutea, at., Fr. Poly.	94	E12	17.00 S	143.10 W
Marv Dasht, Iran	74	F13	29.51 N	52.48 E
Marve, ngh., India	190c		19.12 N	72.49 E
Marvejols, Fr.	22	E9	44.33 N	3.18 E
Marvell, Ar., U.S.	134	C8	34.33 N	90.56 W
Marvila, ngh., Port.	184c		38.44 N	9.06 W
Marvine, Mount, mtn., Ut., U.S.	150	E5	38.40 N	111.39 W
Mar Vista, ngh., Ca., U.S.	198		34.00 N	118.27 W
Mārwār, India	70	F4	25.43 N	73.36 E
Marwitz, Ger.	182a		52.41 N	13.09 E
Marwitzer Heide, for., Ger.	182a		52.40 N	13.06 E
Marxloh, ngh., Ger.	181		51.31 N	6.46 E
Mary, Turkmen.	72	B9	37.34 N	61.49 E
Mary, stm., Austl.	98	E9	25.29 S	152.50 E
Maryborough, Austl.	98	E9	25.32 S	152.42 E
Maryborough, Austl.	98	K4	37.03 S	143.44 E
Marydale, S. Afr.	90	F5	29.23 S	22.05 E
Maryfield, Sk., Can.	142	E12	49.50 N	101.32 W
Mary Kathleen, Austl.	98	C2	20.46 S	139.58 E
Maryland, state, U.S.	124	E8	39.00 N	76.45 W
Maryland, University of (Baltimore County Campus), educ., Md., U.S.	202b		39.15 N	76.43 W
Maryland, University of, educ., Md., U.S.	202c		38.59 N	76.57 W
Maryland Gardens Park, p.o.i., On., Can.	193b		43.47 N	79.32 W
Maryland Historical Society, bldg., Md., U.S.	202b		39.18 N	76.37 W
Maryland Park, Md., U.S.	202c		38.53 N	76.54 W
Marylebone, Eng., U.K.	180		53.34 N	2.38 W
Maryneal, Tx., U.S.	136	B7	32.14 N	100.27 W
Marynivka, Ukr.	38	F9	47.46 N	30.53 E
Maryport, Eng., U.K.	10	G9	54.43 N	3.29 W
Marys, stm., Nv., U.S.	148	B10	41.04 N	115.16 W
Marys Creek, stm., Id., U.S.	148	A9	42.20 N	115.46 W
Marys Peak, mtn., Or., U.S.	146	F3	44.30 N	123.33 W
Marysvale, Ut., U.S.	150	E4	38.27 N	112.13 W
Marysville, B.C., Can.	144	G14	49.38 N	115.56 W
Marysville, N.B., Can.	122	D10	45.58 N	66.34 W
Marysville, Ca., U.S.	148	D4	39.08 N	121.35 W
Marysville, Ks., U.S.	128	L2	39.50 N	96.38 W
Marysville, Mi., U.S.	124	B3	42.54 N	82.28 W
Marysville, Oh., U.S.	124	D2	40.13 N	83.21 W
Marysville, Pa., U.S.	126	H13	40.20 N	76.56 W
Marysville, Wa., U.S.	146	B4	48.03 N	122.10 W
Maryvale, ngh., On., Can.	193b		43.46 N	79.18 W
Maryville, Mo., U.S.	130	D3	40.20 N	94.52 W
Maryville, Tn., U.S.	124	I2	35.45 N	83.58 W
Marzagão, Braz.	170	I1	17.59 S	48.38 W
Marzahn, ngh., Ger.	182a		52.33 N	13.33 E
Marzo, Punta, c., Col.	168	D3	6.50 N	77.42 W
Masada see Meẓada, Ḥorvot, hist., Isr.	76	G6	31.19 N	35.21 E
Más Afuera, Isla see Alejandro Selkirk, Isla, i., Chile	162	I6	33.45 S	80.46 W
Masai Mara Game Reserve, ind. res., Kenya	86	E7	1.15 S	35.15 E
Masai Steppe, plat., Tan.	86	E7	4.45 S	37.00 E
Masaka, Ug.	86	E6	0.20 S	31.44 E
Masaki, Japan	186		35.13 N	140.02 E
Masalembu Besar, Pulau, i., Indon.	66	F9	5.33 S	114.25 E
Masallı, Azer.	42	F13	39.02 N	48.41 E
Masamba, Indon.	66	E12	2.33 S	120.19 E
Masan, Kor., S.	54	G8	35.12 N	128.34 E
Masasi, Tan.	86	G7	10.44 S	38.48 E
Masatepe, Nic.	156	G4	11.54 N	86.08 W
Más a Tierra, Isla see Róbinson Crusoe, Isla, i., Chile	162	I7	33.38 S	78.52 W
Masaya, Nic.	156	G4	11.58 N	86.05 W
Masbate, Phil.	68	D4	12.21 N	123.38 E
Masbate, i., Phil.	68	E4	12.15 N	123.30 E
Mascareignes, Îles see Mascarene Islands, is., Afr.	89a	i10	21.00 S	57.00 E
Mascarene Basin, unds.	174	K8	15.00 S	56.00 E
Mascarene Islands, is., Afr.	89a	i10	21.00 S	57.00 E
Mascarene Plateau, unds.	174	J8	10.00 S	59.55 E
Mascasín, Arg.	172	E4	31.22 S	66.59 W
Mascot, Austl.	192a		33.56 S	151.12 E
Mascot, Tn., U.S.	124	H2	36.03 N	83.44 W
Mascota, Mex.	154	E6	20.31 N	104.47 W
Mascoutah, Il., U.S.	130	F8	38.29 N	89.47 W
Mascuppic Lake, l., Ma., U.S.	201		42.41 N	71.23 W
Masefield, Sk., Can.	142	E6	49.08 N	107.49 W
Masel'gskaja, Russia	18	D21	63.10 N	34.17 E
Maseru, Leso.	90	F8	29.18 S	27.29 E
Mashābih, i., Sau. Ar.	74	H5	25.37 N	36.30 E
Mashan, China	58	J3	23.50 N	108.16 E
Mashava, Zimb.	88	D5	20.03 S	30.29 E
Mashbury, Eng., U.K.	178		51.47 N	0.24 E
Masheve, Ukr.	38	A11	52.05 N	32.47 E
Mashhad, Iran	72	B8	36.17 N	59.35 E
Mashi, China	58	G6	29.03 N	114.21 E
Mashi see Cuando, stm., Afr.	88	D3	18.29 S	23.36 E
Mashi see Kwando, stm., Afr.	88	D3	18.29 S	23.36 E
Mashiko, Japan	56	C13	36.28 N	140.06 E
Mashivka, Ukr.	38	D13	49.26 N	34.52 E
Mashra' ar Raqq, Sudan	82	F5	8.25 N	29.15 E
Masīlah, Wādī al-, stm., Yemen	72	F6	15.09 N	51.07 E
Masi-Manimba, D.R.C.	86	E3	4.46 S	17.57 E
Masin, Indon.	60	G10	6.15 S	139.19 E
Masina, India	190b		22.55 N	88.32 E
Masindi, Ug.	86	D6	1.40 N	31.42 E
Masira, Gulf of see Maṣīrah, Khalīj, b., Oman	72	F8	20.10 N	58.15 E
Maṣīrah, i., Oman	72	E8	20.26 N	58.47 E
Maṣīrah, Khalīj, b., Oman	72	F8	20.10 N	58.15 E
Masisea, Peru	164	E3	8.36 S	74.20 W
Masjed-e Soleymān, Iran	74	E11	31.57 N	49.17 E
Mask, Lough, l., Ire.	10	H3	53.35 N	9.22 W
Maskanah, Syria	76	B8	36.01 N	38.04 E
Masku, Fin.	18	G9	60.34 N	22.06 E
Maskwa, stm., Mb., Can.	142	D18	50.33 N	96.08 W
Masljanino, Russia	48	D14	54.19 N	84.13 E
Maslova, Russia	183a		59.57 N	30.48 E
Maslovka, Russia	38	B18	51.33 N	39.15 E
Maslozero, ozero, l., Russia	18	D19	63.29 N	32.58 E
Masoala, Cap see Masoala, Tanjona, c., Madag.	88	D9	15.57 S	50.12 E
Masoala, Tanjona, c., Madag.	88	D9	15.57 S	50.12 E
Mason, Mi., U.S.	130	B13	42.34 N	84.26 W
Mason, Oh., U.S.	124	E1	39.21 N	84.18 W
Mason, Tn., U.S.	134	B9	35.24 N	89.32 W
Mason, Tx., U.S.	136	D8	30.44 N	99.14 W
Mason, W.V., U.S.	124	E3	39.00 N	82.01 W
Mason City, Il., U.S.	130	D8	40.11 N	89.41 W
Mason City, Ia., U.S.	130	A4	43.09 N	93.12 W
Mason City, Ne., U.S.	140	F13	41.13 N	99.18 W
Masonicus Brook, stm., N.J., U.S.	194		41.06 N	74.09 W
Masons Creek, stm., N.J., U.S.	203		39.59 N	74.51 W
Masonville, N.J., U.S.	203		39.59 N	74.52 W
Måsøy, i., Nor.	14	A15	71.01 N	24.59 E
Maspeth, ngh., N.Y., U.S.	194		40.43 N	73.55 W
Masqat (Muscat), Oman	72	E8	23.35 N	58.32 E
Massa, Italy	30	F7	44.02 N	10.08 E
Massachusetts, state, U.S.	124	B13	42.15 N	71.50 W
Massachusetts (Boston), University of, educ., Ma., U.S.	201		42.19 N	71.03 W
Massachusetts Bay, b., Ma., U.S.	124	B15	42.20 N	70.50 W
Massachusetts Correctional Institution, bldg., Ma., U.S.	201		42.07 N	71.18 W
Massachusetts Institute of Technology, educ., Ma., U.S.	201		42.21 N	71.06 W
Massaciuccoli, Lago di, l., Italy	30	G7	43.50 N	10.19 E
Massacre Lake, l., Nv., U.S.	148	B6	41.39 N	119.35 W
Massafra, Italy	32	D11	40.35 N	17.07 E
Massaguet, Chad	82	E3	12.28 N	15.26 E
Massa Marittima, Italy	30	G7	43.02 N	10.53 E
Massangena, Moz.	90	B11	21.32 S	32.56 E
Massapequa Park, N.Y., U.S.	194		40.40 N	73.27 W
Massapequa Reserve County Park, p.o.i., N.Y., U.S.	194		40.42 N	73.27 W
Massapoag Brook, stm., Ma., U.S.	201		42.09 N	71.09 W
Massapoag Lake, l., Ma., U.S.	201		42.06 N	71.11 W
Massawa (Mitsiwa), Erit.	82	D7	15.37 N	39.25 E
Massé, Ruisseau, stm., Qc., Can.	193a		45.28 N	73.17 W
Massena, Ia., U.S.	130	C3	41.15 N	94.46 W
Massena, N.Y., U.S.	126	D15	44.55 N	74.53 W
Massenya, Chad	82	E3	11.24 N	16.09 E
Masset, B.C., Can.	110	E4	54.01 N	132.07 W
Masseube, Fr.	22	F6	43.26 N	0.35 E
Massey, On., Can.	126	B7	46.12 N	82.04 W
Massey Sound, strt., Nu., Can.	108	B7	78.22 N	94.01 W
Massiac, Fr.	22	D9	45.15 N	3.12 E
Massiaru, Est.	26	B7	58.00 N	24.35 E
Massillon, Oh., U.S.	124	D4	40.47 N	81.31 W
Massina, D.R.C.	191b		4.22 S	15.22 E
Massina, Mali	84	G3	13.58 N	5.21 W
Massina, reg., Mali	84	G4	14.37 N	4.38 W
Massinga, Moz.	90	C12	23.19 S	35.23 E
Massingir, Moz.	90	C11	23.55 S	32.12 E
Massive, Mount, mtn., Co., U.S.	138	B2	39.12 N	106.28 W
Masson Island, i., Ant.	103	B14	66.08 S	96.34 E
Massow see Maszewo, Pol.	24	C11	53.29 N	15.02 E
Massy, Fr.	179		48.44 N	2.17 E
Mastābah, Sau. Ar.	72	E4	20.51 N	39.27 E
Maštağa, Azer.	42	E14	40.32 N	49.58 E
Masterson, Tx., U.S.	138	F6	35.38 N	101.58 W
Masterton, N.Z.	102	E6	40.57 S	175.39 E
Mastic Point, Bah.	132	K8	25.04 N	77.58 W
Mastok, Bela.	26	F13	53.59 N	30.28 E
Mastung, Pak.	62	C2	29.47 N	66.51 E
Masty, Bela.	26	G7	53.24 N	24.32 E
Masuda, Japan	56	E4	34.40 N	131.51 E
Māsūleh, Iran	74	B11	37.09 N	48.58 E
Masulipatam see Machilipatnam, India	69	C5	16.11 N	81.08 E
Masurai, Gunung, mtn., Indon.	66	E2	2.30 S	101.51 E
Masuria see Mazury, reg., Pol.	24	C16	53.45 N	21.00 E
Masvingo, Zimb.	88	E5	20.03 S	30.49 E
Masvingo, state, Zimb.	90	B10	21.04 S	30.57 E
Maṣyāf, Syria	76	C7	35.04 N	36.20 E
Maszewo, Pol.	24	C11	53.29 N	15.02 E
Mat, stm., Alb.	32	C14	41.39 N	19.34 E
Mata Amarilla, Arg.	166	I2	49.36 S	71.12 W
Mataba, Mount, mtn., Phil.	187f		14.42 N	121.10 E
Matabeleland North, state, Zimb.	90	A9	19.50 S	28.15 E
Matabeleland South, state, Zimb.	90	B9	21.36 S	29.03 E
Matabuena, Spain	28	C7	41.06 N	3.47 W
Matachel, stm., Spain	28	F5	38.49 N	6.16 W
Matacuni, stm., Ven.	168	F9	2.55 N	65.16 W
Mata de Plátano, Quebrada, stm., Ven.	204c		10.35 N	66.46 W
Matadero Creek, stm., Ca., U.S.	200		37.26 N	122.08 W
Mata de São João, Braz.	170	G6	12.31 S	38.17 W
Matadi, D.R.C.	86	F2	5.48 S	13.28 E
Matador, Tx., U.S.	138	G8	34.01 N	100.49 W
Matagalpa, Nic.	156	F5	12.59 N	85.44 W
Matagami, Qc., Can.	114	B12	49.45 N	77.38 W
Matagorda, Tx., U.S.	136	F12	28.41 N	95.57 W
Matagorda Island, i., Tx., U.S.	136	F11	28.14 N	96.37 W
Matagorda Peninsula, pen., Tx., U.S.	136	F11	28.32 N	96.07 W
Mata Grande, Braz.	170	E7	9.07 S	37.44 W
Matahiae, Pointe, c., Fr. Poly.	100h	w22	17.49 S	149.17 W
Matāi, Egypt	76	J1	28.24 N	30.46 E
Mataiea, Fr. Poly.	100h	w22	17.45 S	149.22 W
Mataiva, at., Fr. Poly.	94	E12	14.53 S	148.40 W
Mataj, Kaz.	48	E13	45.54 N	78.42 E
Matak, Pulau, i., Indon.	66	B5	3.18 N	106.16 E
Matakana, Austl.	98	I5	32.59 S	145.53 E
Matala, Ang.	88	C1	14.44 S	15.02 E
Matale, Sri L.	69	H5	7.28 N	80.37 E
Matam, Sen.	84	F2	15.40 N	13.16 W
Matamoros, Mex.	154	C10	25.53 N	97.30 W
Matamoros, Mex.	154	C7	25.32 N	103.13 W
Matan, Indon.	66	D6	1.53 S	110.00 E
Matandu, stm., Tan.	86	F7	8.42 S	39.21 E
Matane, Qc., Can.	122	B9	48.50 N	67.31 W
Matang, China	58	G5	29.16 N	113.04 E
Matanni, Pak.	70	B3	33.47 N	71.32 E
Matanza, state, Arg.	206		34.46 S	58.37 W
Matanza, Aeródromo, arpt., Arg.	206		34.44 S	58.30 W
Matanzas, Cuba	156	A7	23.03 N	81.34 W
Matanzas, Mex.	154	E8	21.39 N	101.38 W
Matapan, Cape see Taínaro, Ákra, c., Grc.	34	G5	36.24 N	22.29 E
Matape, stm., Mex.	154	A3	28.19 N	110.34 W
Matapédia, Qc., Can.	122	C9	47.58 N	66.56 W
Matapédia, Lac, l., Qc., Can.	122	B9	48.32 N	67.33 W
Mataquito, stm., Chile	172	G2	34.57 S	72.11 W
Matara, Sri L.	69	I5	5.56 N	80.33 E
Mataram, Indon.	66	H9	8.35 S	116.06 E
Mataranka, Austl.	96	B6	14.56 S	133.06 E
Mataró, Spain	28	C13	41.32 N	2.26 E
Matarraña, stm., Spain	28	C11	41.14 N	0.22 E
Matas, mtn., Spain	184d		41.30 N	2.16 E
Matasiri, Pulau, i., Indon.	66	F9	4.47 S	115.48 E
Mätäsvaara, Fin.	18	D16	63.26 N	29.31 E
Matatepai, c., Fr. Poly.	100g	r18	9.42 S	139.02 W
Matatiele, S. Afr.	90	G9	30.20 S	28.49 E
Mātātīla Dam, dam., India	72	D12	25.06 N	78.22 E
Matatula, Cape, c., Am. Sam.	101c	h12	14.15 S	170.34 W
Matā'utu, Wal./F.	92	E9	13.16 S	176.08 W
Mataval, Baie de, b., Fr. Poly.	100h	v21	17.30 S	149.31 W
Matavera, Cook Is.	100j	a27	21.13 S	159.44 W
Mataveri, Chile	100l	e29	27.10 S	109.27 E

Name	Page	Map Ref.	Latitude	Longitude
Mataveri, Aeropuerto, arpt., Chile	100l	f29	27.10 S	109.25 W
Mataveri Airstrip see Mataveri, Aeropuerto, arpt., Chile	100l	f29	27.10 S	109.25 W
Matchaponix Brook, stm., N.J., U.S.	194		40.23 N	74.23 W
Matching, Eng., U.K.	178		51.47 N	0.13 E
Matching Green, Eng., U.K.	178		51.47 N	0.14 E
Matching Tye, Eng., U.K.	178		51.47 N	0.12 E
Mataeu see Clutha, stm., N.Z.	102	G3	46.19 S	169.49 E
Matehuala, Mex.	154	D8	23.40 N	100.38 W
Mateke Hills, hills, Zimb.	90	B10	21.51 S	30.54 E
Matera, Italy	32	D10	40.40 N	16.36 E
Matese, Monti del, mts., Italy	32	C8	41.27 N	14.22 E
Mátészalka, Hung.	36	B9	47.57 N	22.20 E
Matete, stm., D.R.C.	191b		4.24 S	15.20 E
Mateur, Tun.	32	G3	37.02 N	9.40 E
Matewan, W.V., U.S.	124	G3	37.38 N	82.13 W
Matfors, Swe.	16	E14	62.21 N	17.02 E
Matha, Fr.	22	D5	45.52 N	0.19 W
Mather, Mb., Can.	142	E14	49.06 N	99.08 W
Mather, Pa., U.S.	124	E5	39.55 N	80.04 W
Matheson, On., Can.	114	B10	48.32 N	80.28 W
Matheson Island, Mb., Can.	142	C17	51.44 N	96.55 W
Mathews, Va., U.S.	124	G9	37.26 N	76.19 W
Mathis, Tx., U.S.	136	F10	28.05 N	97.48 W
Māthle, India	190b		22.35 N	88.14 E
Mathura (Muttra), India	70	E6	27.30 N	77.41 E
Mathura Bīl, l., India	190b		22.56 N	88.29 E
Mathurai see Madurai, India	69	G4	9.54 N	78.07 E
Matiacoali, Burkina	84	G5	12.21 N	1.01 E
Matiāri, Pak.	70	F2	25.36 N	68.27 E
Matias Barbosa, Braz.	170	K4	21.52 S	43.19 W
Matías Romero, Mex.	154	G11	16.53 N	95.02 W
Matícora, stm., Ven.	168	B6	11.01 N	71.09 W
Matinecock, N.Y., U.S.	194		40.53 N	73.38 W
Matinha, Braz.	170	B3	3.06 S	45.01 W
Matinicock Point, c., N.Y., U.S.	194		40.54 N	73.38 W
Matinicus Island, i., Me., U.S.	122	G8	43.51 N	68.53 W
Matipó, Braz.	170	K4	20.20 S	42.23 W
Matiyure, stm., Ven.	168	D7	7.46 N	68.14 W
Matkasel'kja, Russia	18	F17	61.58 N	30.33 E
Mātli, Pak.	70	F2	25.02 N	68.39 E
Mato, stm., Ven.	168	D9	7.10 N	65.06 W
Mato, Cerro, mtn., Ven.	168	D9	7.15 N	65.15 W
Matobe, Indon.	66	E2	2.46 S	100.11 E
Mato Grosso, state, Braz.	164	F6	12.00 S	57.00 W
Mato Grosso, Planalto do, plat., Braz.	166	B5	14.58 S	53.36 W
Mato Grosso, Plateau of see Mato Grosso, Planalto do, plat., Braz.	166	B5	14.58 S	53.36 W
Mato Grosso do Sul, state, Braz.	166	C6	20.00 S	55.00 W
Matola Rio, Moz.	90	D11	25.57 S	32.26 E
Matopos, Zimb.	90	B9	20.23 S	28.31 E
Matosinhos, Port.	28	C2	41.10 N	8.41 W
Matoso, Ponta do, c., Braz.	205a		22.50 S	43.11 W
Matouying, China	58	B8	39.18 N	118.47 E
Mato Verde, Braz.	170	H4	15.23 S	42.52 W
Matozinhos, Braz.	170	J3	19.33 S	44.05 W
Mátra, mts., Hung.	36	B6	47.53 N	19.56 E
Matrah, Oman	72	E8	23.37 N	58.31 E
Matraville, Austl.	192a		33.54 S	151.18 E
Matrei in Osttirol, Aus.	30	D9	47.00 N	12.32 E
Matsubushi, Japan	186		35.55 N	139.49 E
Matsudo, Japan	56	D12	35.46 N	139.54 E
Matsudo Race Track, p.o.i., Japan	186		35.48 N	139.55 E
Matsue, Japan	56	D6	35.28 N	133.04 E
Matsugasaki, Japan	186		35.53 N	139.58 E
Matsumoto, Japan	56	C10	36.13 N	137.58 E
Matsuōji, Japan	186		35.08 N	140.01 E
Matsuo-san, mtn., Japan	188		34.38 N	135.44 E
Matsusaka, Japan	56	E9	34.34 N	136.32 E
Matsu Tao, i., Tai.	58	H8	26.09 N	119.56 E
Matsutō, Japan	56	C9	36.31 N	136.34 E
Matsuura, Japan	56	F2	33.18 N	129.36 E
Matsuyama, Japan	56	F5	33.50 N	132.46 E
Mattagami, stm., On., Can.	110	F14	51.20 N	80.26 W
Mattamuskeet, Lake, l., N.C., U.S.	132	A9	35.30 N	76.11 W
Mattapan, ngh., Ma., U.S.	201		42.16 N	71.06 W
Mattaponi, stm., Va., U.S.	124	G8	37.30 N	76.47 W
Mattawa, On., Can.	126	B11	46.18 N	78.41 W
Mattawa, Wa., U.S.	146	D7	46.43 N	119.56 W
Mattawa, stm., On., Can.	126	B11	46.18 N	78.41 W
Mattawamkeag, Me., U.S.	122	E8	45.30 N	68.21 W
Mattawamkeag, stm., Me., U.S.	122	E8	45.31 N	68.22 W
Matterhorn, mtn., Eur.	30	D4	45.59 N	7.43 E
Matterhorn, mtn., Nv., U.S.	148	B10	41.49 N	115.23 W
Mattersburg, Aus.	24	I12	47.44 N	16.23 E
Matthews Mountain, hill, Mo., U.S.	130	G7	37.29 N	90.21 W
Matthews Ridge, Guy.	168	D11	7.29 N	60.11 W
Matthew Town, Bah.	156	B11	21.00 N	73.41 W
Matthias Church, rel., Hung.	182c		47.30 N	19.02 E
Mattice, On., Can.	114	B9	49.37 N	83.16 W
Mattighofen, Aus.	30	B10	48.05 N	13.09 E
Mattoon, Il., U.S.	130	E9	39.28 N	88.22 W
Mattoon, Wi., U.S.	128	F9	45.02 N	89.02 W
Mattox Draw, stm., Ks., U.S.	138	C7	38.06 N	101.08 W
Mattydale, N.Y., U.S.	126	E13	43.06 N	76.07 W
Matu, Malay.	66	B7	2.42 N	111.29 E
Matua, Indon.	66	E7	3.00 S	110.45 E
Matudo see Matsudo, Japan	56	D12	35.46 N	139.54 E
Matue see Matsue, Japan	56	D6	35.28 N	133.04 E
Matuku, i., Fiji	101e	q19	19.10 S	179.46 E
Matumoto see Matsumoto, Japan	56	C10	36.13 N	137.58 E
Maturín, Ven.	168	C10	9.43 N	63.11 W
Maturino, Russia	26	A20	59.06 N	37.55 E
Matutina, Braz.	170	J2	19.13 S	45.58 W
Matuzaka see Matsusaka, Japan	56	E9	34.34 N	136.32 E
Matveev Kurgan, Russia	40	H11	47.34 N	38.51 E
Matveevo, Russia	40	C20	57.47 N	57.50 E
Matxitxako, Cabo, c., Spain	28	A8	43.27 N	2.45 W
Mátyásföld, ngh., Hung.	182c		47.31 N	19.13 E
Matysiv, Ukr.	38	D10	49.02 N	31.33 E
Maú (Ireng), stm., S.A.	168	F12	3.34 N	59.51 W
Maúa, Moz.	88	C6	13.51 S	37.09 E
Mauá, mun., Braz.	205b		23.40 S	46.27 W
Mau Aimma, India	70	F8	25.41 N	81.56 E
Maubeuge, Fr.	20	D12	50.17 N	3.58 E
Mauchamps, Fr.	179		48.32 N	2.12 E
Maud, Ok., U.S.	134	B2	35.08 N	96.46 W
Maud, Tx., U.S.	134	D4	33.20 N	94.20 W
Maudaha, India	70	F7	25.41 N	80.07 E
Maude, Austl.	98	J5	34.28 S	144.17 E
Maudétour-en-Vexin, Fr.	179		49.06 N	1.47 E
Mauer, ngh., Aus.	182b		48.09 N	16.16 E
Mauerbach, Aus.	182b		48.15 N	16.10 E
Mauerbach, stm., Aus.	182b		48.12 N	16.14 E
Maués, Braz.	164	D6	3.22 S	57.42 W
Maués, stm., Braz.	164	D6	3.43 S	57.36 W
Maués-Açu see Maués, stm., Braz.	164	D6	3.43 S	57.36 W
Mauganj, India	70	F8	24.39 N	81.53 E
Mauga Silisili, mtn., Samoa	101c	g11	13.35 S	172.27 W
Maui, i., Hi., U.S.	100a	c5	20.45 N	156.15 W
Mauk, Indon.	66	F5	6.03 S	106.30 E
Mauldin, S.C., U.S.	132	B3	34.47 N	82.18 W
Mauldre, stm., Fr.	179		48.58 N	1.49 E
Maule, state, Chile	172	G2	35.30 S	71.18 W
Maule, stm., Chile	172	G1	35.18 S	72.24 W
Maule, Laguna del, l., Chile	172	G2	36.04 S	70.30 W
Mauléon, Fr.	20	H8	46.55 N	0.44 W
Mauléon-Licharre, Fr.	22	F5	43.14 N	0.53 W
Maulette, Fr.	179		48.48 N	1.37 E
Maulvi Bāzār, Bngl.	70	F13	24.29 N	91.47 E
Maumee, Oh., U.S.	130	C14	41.34 N	83.38 W
Maumee, stm., U.S.	130	C13	41.41 N	83.27 W
Maumelle, Lake, res., Ar., U.S.	134	C6	34.53 N	92.35 W
Maumere, Indon.	60	G7	8.37 S	122.12 E
Maun, Bots.	88	D3	19.59 S	23.25 E
Maunabo, P.R.	158a	b4	18.00 N	65.54 W
Mauna Kea, vol., Hi., U.S.	100a	d6	19.50 N	155.28 W
Maunaloa, Hi., U.S.	100a	b4	21.07 N	157.13 W
Mauna Loa, vol., Hi., U.S.	100a	d6	19.29 N	155.36 W
Maunath Bhanjan, India	70	F9	25.56 N	83.33 E
Maungaroa, mtn., Cook Is.	100j	a26	21.13 S	159.48 W
Maungdaw, Mya.	70	H14	20.43 N	92.23 E
Maungmagan, Mya.	64	E3	14.09 N	98.06 E
Maunoir, Lac, l., N.T., Can.	110	B6	67.30 N	125.00 W
Maupihaa, at., Fr. Poly.	94	E11	16.49 S	153.55 W
Maupin, Or., U.S.	146	E5	45.10 N	121.05 W
Mau Rānīpur, India	70	F7	25.15 N	79.08 E
Maurecourt, Fr.	179		49.00 N	2.04 E
Mauregard, Fr.	179		49.02 N	2.35 E
Maurepas, Fr.	179		48.45 N	1.55 E
Maurepas, Lake, l., La., U.S.	134	G8	30.15 N	90.30 W
Maures, mts., Fr.	22	F12	43.16 N	6.23 E
Mauriac, Fr.	22	D8	45.12 N	2.20 E
Maurice, Lake, l., Austl.	96	E6	29.28 S	130.58 E
Mauricie, Parc national de la, p.o.i., Qc., Can.	114	C14	46.45 N	73.00 W
Maurino, Canal, can., Chile	204e		33.34 S	70.32 W
Mauritania, ctry., Afr.	84	F2	20.00 N	12.00 W
Mauritanie see Mauritania, ctry., Afr.	84	F2	20.00 N	12.00 W
Mauriti, Braz.	170	D6	7.23 S	38.46 W
Mauritius, ctry., Afr.	89a	h10	20.17 S	57.33 E
Mauritius, i., Mrts.	80	I11	20.17 S	57.33 E
Mauron, Fr.	20	F6	48.05 N	2.18 W
Maurs, Fr.	22	E8	44.43 N	2.11 E
Maury, stm., Va., U.S.	124	G6	37.37 N	79.27 W
Mauston, Wi., U.S.	128	H8	43.47 N	90.04 W
Mausund, Nor.	16	D6	63.52 N	8.39 E
Mautau, c., Fr. Poly.	100g	r19	9.42 S	138.59 W
Mautau, Pointe see Mautau, c., Fr. Poly.	100g	r19	9.42 S	138.59 W
Mauterndorf, Aus.	30	C10	47.07 N	13.40 E
Mauthausen, Aus.	30	B11	48.14 N	14.31 E
Mauthen, Aus.	30	D9	46.40 N	12.59 E
Mauvais Coulee, stm., N.D., U.S.	142	F14	48.21 N	99.07 W
Mava, Pap. N. Gui.	101a	b3	6.47 S	141.26 E
Mavaca, stm., Ven.	168	F9	2.31 N	65.09 W
Mavasjaure, l., Swe.	14	F7	66.53 N	16.21 E
Māvelikara, India	69	G3	9.11 N	76.32 E
Maverick, Az., U.S.	150	J7	33.43 N	109.32 W
Mavinga, Ang.	88	D3	15.47 S	20.21 E
Mavrovo Nacionalni Park, p.o.i., Mac.	34	B3	41.40 N	20.46 E
Mavuradonha Mountains, mts., Zimb.	88	D5	16.30 S	31.20 E
Ma Wan, i., China	189d		22.21 N	114.03 E
Mawangkanli Shan, mtn., China	70	A8	34.20 N	80.33 E
Mawchi, Mya.	64	C3	18.49 N	97.09 E
Mawdesley, Eng., U.K.	180		53.38 N	2.46 W
Mawi, India	190a		28.39 N	77.25 E
Mawkhi, Mya.	64	D4	16.17 N	98.53 E
Mawlaik, Mya.	62	D7	23.37 N	94.24 E
Mawlamyaing see Mawlamyine, Mya.	64	D3	16.30 N	97.38 E
Mawlamyine, Mya.	64	D3	16.30 N	97.38 E
Mawqaq, Sau. Ar.	74	G7	27.25 N	41.08 E
Mawson, sci., Ant.	103	B11	67.40 S	63.42 E
Maw Taung (Luang, Khao), mtn., Asia	64	G4	11.39 N	99.35 E
Max, N.D., U.S.	142	G12	47.49 N	101.17 W
Maxaranguape, Braz.	170	C8	5.31 S	35.16 W
Maxcanú, Mex.	156	B3	20.35 N	89.59 W
Maxixe, Moz.	90	C12	23.51 S	35.20 E
Maxon Creek, stm., Tx., U.S.	136	E5	29.53 N	102.23 W
Maxton, N.C., U.S.	132	B6	34.44 N	79.21 W
Maxville, On., Can.	126	C15	45.17 N	74.51 W
Maxwell, Ca., U.S.	148	D3	39.16 N	122.11 W
Maxwell, Ia., U.S.	128	J5	41.53 N	93.23 W
Maxwell, Ne., U.S.	130	F12	41.04 N	100.31 W
Maxwell, N.M., U.S.	138	E4	36.32 N	104.33 W
Maxwell Air Force Base, mil., Al., U.S.	134	E12	32.23 N	86.21 W
May, Tx., U.S.	136	B9	31.58 N	98.55 W
May, Cape, pen., N.J., U.S.	124	F11	38.58 N	74.54 W
May, Isle of, i., Scot., U.K.	10	E10	56.11 N	2.33 W
May, Mount, mtn., Ab., Can.	144	B11	54.02 N	119.58 W
Maya, Montañas see Maya Mountains, mts., N.A.	156	D3	16.36 N	89.04 W
Maya, Pulau, i., Indon.	66	D6	1.10 S	109.35 E
Mayaguana, i., Bah.	156	A11	22.23 N	72.57 W
Mayaguana Passage, strt., Bah.	156	A11	22.32 N	73.15 W
Mayagüez, P.R.	158a	b1	18.12 N	67.08 W
Mayagüez, Aeropuerto, arpt., P.R.	158a	b1	18.15 N	67.09 W
Mayagüez, Bahía de, b., P.R.	158a	b1	18.12 N	67.10 W
Mayala, Congo	191b		4.21 S	15.09 E
Mayama, Congo	86	E2	3.51 S	14.53 E
Mayamey, Iran	74	B14	36.24 N	55.38 E
Maya Mountains, mts., N.A.	156	D3	16.36 N	89.04 W
Mayang, China	58	H3	27.41 N	109.35 E
Māyāpur, India	190b		22.27 N	88.08 E
Mayarí, Cuba	156	B10	20.39 N	75.40 W
Mayaro Bay, b., Trin.	159l	s13	10.16 N	60.59 W
Maybole, Scot., U.K.	10	F8	55.21 N	4.41 W
Maydena, Austl.	99a	o13	42.55 S	146.30 E
Maydh, Som.	86	B9	10.59 N	47.07 E
Maydī, Yemen	72	F5	16.19 N	42.48 E
Mayen, Ger.	24	F3	50.19 N	7.13 E
Mayenne, Fr.	20	F8	48.18 N	0.36 W
Mayenne, state, Fr.	20	F8	48.05 N	0.40 W
Mayenne, stm., Fr.	20	F8	47.29 N	0.31 W
Mayer, Az., U.S.	150	I4	34.24 N	112.14 W
Mayersville, Ms., U.S.	134	E7	32.54 N	91.03 W
Mayerthorpe, Ab., Can.	144	C15	53.54 N	115.02 W
Mayfair, ngh., S. Afr.	191d		26.12 S	28.01 E
Mayfair, ngh., Pa., U.S.	203		40.02 N	75.03 W
Mayfield, Ky., U.S.	130	H9	36.44 N	88.38 W
Mayfield, Oh., U.S.	197a		41.33 N	81.26 W
Mayfield, Ut., U.S.	150	D5	39.06 N	111.42 W
Mayfield Creek, stm., Ky., U.S.	130	H9	36.56 N	89.05 W
Mayfield Lake, res., Wa., U.S.	146	D4	46.31 N	122.33 W
Mayflower, Ar., U.S.	134	C6	34.57 N	92.25 W
Mayford, Eng., U.K.	178		51.18 N	0.34 W
Māyir, Syria	76	B8	36.28 N	37.11 E
Maykain see Majkain, Kaz.	48	D13	51.27 N	75.49 E
Maymont, Sk., Can.	142	B6	52.34 N	107.40 W
Maymyo, Mya.	64	A3	22.02 N	96.28 E
Maynard, Ia., U.S.	130	B6	42.46 N	91.52 W
Maynardville, Tn., U.S.	124	H2	36.14 N	83.47 W
Mayne, stm., Austl.	98	D3	23.32 S	141.15 E
Maynooth, Ire.	10	H6	53.23 N	6.34 W
Mayo, Yk., Can.	110	C3	63.36 N	135.51 W
Mayo, Fl., U.S.	132	F2	30.03 N	83.10 W
Mayo, state, Ire.	10	H3	53.54 N	9.15 W
Mayo, stm., Arg.	166	I3	45.46 S	69.43 W
Mayo, stm., Col.	168	G3	1.40 N	77.19 W
Mayo, stm., Mex.	154	B4	26.43 N	109.47 W
Mayodan, N.C., U.S.	124	H5	36.24 N	79.58 W
Mayo Ndaga, Nig.	84	H7	6.54 N	11.25 E
Mayon Volcano, vol., Phil.	68	D4	13.15 N	123.41 E
Mayor Buratovich, Arg.	166	G4	39.16 S	62.37 W
Mayo Reservoir, res., N.C., U.S.	124	H7	36.29 N	78.53 W
Mayor Island, i., N.Z.	102	C7	37.17 S	176.14 E
Mayotte, dep., Afr.	86	G9	12.50 S	45.10 E
Mayoyoque, Col.	168	G4	0.41 N	75.21 W
May Pen, Jam.	158d	j13	17.58 N	77.14 W
Mayport Naval Station, mil., Fl., U.S.	132	F4	30.22 N	81.24 W
Mayrán, Desierto de, des., Mex.	136	I5	25.51 N	102.22 W
Mayreau, i., St. Vin.	159e	p11	12.38 N	61.23 W
Mayrhofen, Aus.	24	I7	47.10 N	11.51 E
Maysān, state, Iraq	74	E10	32.00 N	47.00 E
Mays Landing, N.J., U.S.	124	E11	39.26 N	74.43 W
Maysville, Ky., U.S.	124	F2	38.38 N	83.45 W
Maysville, Mo., U.S.	130	E3	39.53 N	94.21 W
Maysville, N.C., U.S.	132	B8	34.54 N	77.13 W
Maysville, Ok., U.S.	138	G11	34.48 N	97.24 W
Mayumba, Gabon	86	E2	3.22 S	10.40 E
Māyūram, India	69	F4	11.05 N	79.39 E
Mayville, Mi., U.S.	126	E6	43.20 N	83.21 W
Mayville, N.Y., U.S.	124	B6	42.15 N	79.29 W
Mayville, N.D., U.S.	142	G16	47.29 N	97.19 W
Mayville, Wi., U.S.	128	H10	43.29 N	88.32 W
Maywood, Ca., U.S.	198		33.59 N	118.11 W
Maywood, Ne., U.S.	140	G12	40.38 N	100.37 W
Maywood, N.J., U.S.	194		40.54 N	74.03 W
Maywood Race Track, p.o.i., Il., U.S.	196		41.44 N	87.50 W
Mayyit, Al-Bahr al- see Dead Sea, l., Asia	76	G6	31.30 N	35.30 E
Maza, Arg.	172	H6	36.48 S	63.20 W
Mazabuka, Zam.	88	D4	15.51 S	27.45 E
Mazagan see El-Jadida, Mor.	84	C3	33.14 N	8.30 W
Mazagão, Braz.	164	D7	0.07 S	51.17 W
Mazagaon, ngh., India	190c		18.57 N	72.50 E
Mazamet, Fr.	22	F8	43.29 N	2.22 E
Mazán, stm., Peru	168	I4	2.49 S	74.12 W
Māzandarān, state, Iran	74	B13	36.30 N	53.30 E
Mazara, Val di, reg., Italy	32	G7	37.50 N	13.00 E
Mazara del Vallo, Italy	32	G6	37.39 N	12.35 E
Mazār-e Sharīf, Afg.	72	B10	36.42 N	67.06 E
Mazarrón, Golfo de, b., Spain	28	G9	37.30 N	1.18 W
Mazaruni, stm., Guy.	168	D11	6.16 N	60.07 W
Mazatenango, Guat.	156	E2	14.31 N	91.30 W
Mazatlán, Mex.	154	D5	23.13 N	106.25 W
Mazatzal Mountains, mts., Az., U.S.	150	J5	33.55 N	111.27 W
Mazatzal Peak, mtn., Az., U.S.	150	I5	34.03 N	111.28 W
Mažeikiai, Lith.	26	D5	56.18 N	22.21 E
Mazenod, Sk., Can.	142	E7	49.52 N	106.15 W
Mazhūr, Khubb al-, sand, Sau. Ar.	74	G8	27.45 N	43.55 E
Mazilovo, ngh., Russia	183b		55.44 N	37.26 E
Mazīnān, Iran	74	B15	36.19 N	56.48 E
Mazinga, mtn., Neth. Ant.	159a	c2	17.29 N	62.57 W
Mazirbe, Lat.	26	C5	57.40 N	22.19 E
Mazoe see Mazowe, stm., Afr.	88	D5	16.32 S	33.25 E
Mazomanie, Wi., U.S.	130	A8	43.10 N	89.47 W
Mazon, Il., U.S.	130	C9	41.14 N	88.25 W
Mazowe, stm., Afr.	88	D5	16.32 S	33.25 E
Mazowieckie, state, Pol.	24	D16	52.15 N	21.00 E
Mazsalaca, Lat.	26	C8	57.52 N	25.03 E
Mazunga, Zimb.	88	E4	21.43 S	29.52 E
Mazury (Masuria), reg., Pol.	24	C16	53.45 N	21.00 E
Mazyr, Bela.	38	A8	52.02 N	29.15 E
Mbabane, Swaz.	90	E10	26.20 S	31.09 E
Mbabo, Tchabal, mtn., Cam.	86	C2	7.16 N	12.09 E
M'bahiakro, C. Iv.	84	H4	7.27 N	4.21 W
Mbaïki, C.A.R.	86	D3	3.52 N	17.59 E
Mbaké, Sen.	84	G1	14.48 N	15.55 W
Mbala, Zam.	86	F6	8.51 S	31.21 E
Mbalabala, Zimb.	90	B9	20.26 S	29.02 E
Mbale, Ug.	86	D6	1.04 N	34.10 E
Mbalmayo, Cam.	86	D2	3.31 N	11.30 E
Mbalouro, stm., Congo	191b		4.09 S	15.21 E
Mbalourou, Congo	191b		4.09 S	15.21 E
Mbamba Bay, Tan.	86	G7	11.18 S	34.47 E
Mbamou, Pointe, c., Congo	191b		4.16 S	15.19 E
Mbandaka (Coquilhatville), D.R.C.	86	D3	0.01 N	18.14 E
Mbanga, Cam.	86	D1	4.29 N	9.34 E
Mbanika Island, i., Sol. Is.	101b	e8	9.05 S	159.12 E
M'banza Congo, Ang.	86	B1	6.16 S	14.15 E
Mbanza-Ngungu, D.R.C.	86	F3	5.14 S	14.52 E
Mbarara, Ug.	86	E6	0.36 S	30.38 E
Mbashe, stm., S. Afr.	90	H9	32.14 S	28.52 E
Mbava Island, i., Sol. Is.	101b	d7	7.49 S	156.32 E
Mbé, Cam.	86	C2	7.47 N	13.33 E
Mbembesi, Zimb.	90	A9	19.59 S	28.55 E
Mberengwa, Zimb.	90	B10	20.30 S	29.54 E
Mbeya, Tan.	86	F6	8.54 S	33.30 E
Mbigou, Gabon	86	E2	1.53 S	11.55 E
Mbinda, Congo	86	E2	2.07 S	12.53 E
Mbinga, Tan.	86	G7	10.55 S	35.01 E
Mbini, Eq. Gui.	84	I6	1.34 N	9.36 E
Mbini, stm., Afr.	84	I6	1.34 N	9.37 E
Mboi, D.R.C.	86	F4	6.55 S	21.52 E
Mboki, C.A.R.	86	C5	5.19 N	25.58 E
Mbola, Sol. Is.	101b	e9	9.37 S	160.38 E
Mbomou (Bomu), stm., Afr.	82	G4	4.08 N	22.29 E
Mborokua, i., Sol. Is.	101b	e8	9.02 S	158.45 E
Mborong, Indon.	66	H12	8.47 S	120.36 E
Mbouda, Cam.	86	C2	5.37 N	10.15 E
Mbour, Sen.	84	G1	14.25 N	16.57 W
Mbout, Maur.	84	F2	16.02 N	12.35 W
Mbuji-Mayi (Bakwanga), D.R.C.	86	F4	6.07 S	23.39 E
Mbuluzi, stm., Swaz.	90	E10	26.07 S	31.52 E
Mburucuyá, Arg.	172	D8	28.02 S	58.13 W
Mbwemkuru, stm., Tan.	86	F7	9.29 S	39.39 E
McAdam, N.B., Can.	122	E9	45.35 N	67.19 W
McAdoo, Pa., U.S.	124	D9	40.54 N	75.59 W
McAlester, Ok., U.S.	134	C3	34.55 N	95.46 W
McAllen, Tx., U.S.	136	H9	26.12 N	98.13 W
McArthur, Oh., U.S.	124	E3	39.14 N	82.27 W
McArthur, stm., Austl.	96	C7	15.48 S	136.40 E
McArthur River, Austl.	96	C7	16.38 S	135.50 E
McAuley, Mb., Can.	142	D12	50.17 N	101.23 W
McBain, Mi., U.S.	126	D4	44.11 N	85.12 W
McBee, S.C., U.S.	132	B5	34.28 N	80.15 W
McBeth Fjord, b., Nu., Can.	110	B17	69.35 N	68.16 W
McBride, B.C., Can.	144	C10	53.18 N	120.10 W
McCall, Id., U.S.	146	F10	44.54 N	116.05 W
McCall Creek, Ms., U.S.	134	F8	31.30 N	90.40 W
McCamey, Tx., U.S.	136	C5	31.08 N	102.13 W
McCammon, Id., U.S.	146	H14	42.38 N	112.13 W
McCandless, Pa., U.S.	197b		40.34 N	80.02 W
McCarteney Creek, stm., Wa., U.S.	146	C7	47.15 N	120.05 W
McCarthy, Ak., U.S.	109	D11	61.26 N	142.55 W
McCauley Island, i., B.C., Can.	110	E4	53.40 N	130.15 W
McChord Air Force Base, mil., Wa., U.S.	146	C4	47.08 N	122.29 W
McClarens Run, stm., Pa., U.S.	197b		40.27 N	80.12 W
McCleary, Wa., U.S.	146	C3	47.03 N	123.15 W
McClees Creek, stm., N.J., U.S.	194		40.22 N	74.03 W
McClellan Creek, stm., Tx., U.S.	138	F8	35.22 N	100.33 W
McClellanville, S.C., U.S.	132	C6	33.05 N	79.27 W
McClintock, Mount, mtn., Ant.	103	D21	80.13 S	157.26 E
McCloud, Ca., U.S.	148	B3	41.14 N	122.08 W
McCloud, stm., Ca., U.S.	148	B3	40.46 N	122.18 W
McClure, Il., U.S.	130	G8	37.18 N	89.25 W
McClure, Pa., U.S.	124	D8	40.42 N	77.20 W
Mcclusky, N.D., U.S.	142	G13	47.28 N	100.26 W
McColl, S.C., U.S.	132	B6	34.40 N	79.32 W
McComas, W.V., U.S.	124	G4	37.20 N	81.16 W
McComb, Ms., U.S.	134	F8	31.14 N	90.27 W
McConaughy, Lake, res., Ne., U.S.	140	F11	41.15 N	101.50 W
McConnell Air Force Base, mil., Ks., U.S.	138	D11	37.38 N	97.15 W
McConnellsburg, Pa., U.S.	124	E7	39.55 N	78.00 W
McConnells Mill, Pa., U.S.	197b		40.15 N	80.15 W
McConnelsville, Oh., U.S.	124	E4	39.39 N	81.50 W
McCook, Il., U.S.	196		41.48 N	87.50 W
McCook, Ne., U.S.	138	A8	40.12 N	100.37 W
McCormick, S.C., U.S.	132	C3	33.54 N	82.17 W
McCormick Place, bldg., Il., U.S.	196		41.51 N	87.37 W
McCoy Creek, stm., Or., U.S.	146	G8	43.03 N	118.49 W
McCreary, Mb., Can.	142	D14	50.46 N	99.29 W
McCrory, Ar., U.S.	134	B7	35.15 N	91.12 W
McCullough, Pa., U.S.	197b		40.22 N	79.38 W
McCullough Mountain, mtn., Nv., U.S.	148	H10	35.36 N	115.11 W
McCune, Ks., U.S.	130	G2	37.21 N	95.01 W
McCurtain, Ok., U.S.	134	B4	35.09 N	94.58 W
McDade, Tx., U.S.	136	D10	30.16 N	97.14 W
McDavid, Fl., U.S.	134	G11	30.51 N	87.19 W
McDermitt, Nv., U.S.	148	B8	41.59 N	117.43 W
McDermott, Oh., U.S.	124	F2	38.50 N	83.05 W
McDonald, Ks., U.S.	138	B7	39.46 N	101.21 W
McDonald, Lake, l., Mt., U.S.	146	B12	48.35 N	113.55 W
McDonald Park, p.o.i., Ca., U.S.	200		37.18 N	122.17 W
McDonogh, Md., U.S.	202b		39.24 N	76.46 W
McDonough, Ga., U.S.	132	C1	33.26 N	84.08 W
McDougal, Mount, mtn., Wy., U.S.	146	H16	42.54 N	110.36 W
McDowell Peak, mtn., Az., U.S.	150	J5	33.40 N	111.50 W
McElmo Creek, stm., U.S.	150	F8	37.13 N	109.12 W
Mc Ennen Airport, arpt., Mi., U.S.	199		42.12 N	83.37 W
Mcensk, Russia	26	G19	53.16 N	36.35 E
McEwen, Tn., U.S.	130	H10	36.06 N	87.38 W
McFadden, Wy., U.S.	150	B10	41.39 N	106.07 W
McFarland, Ca., U.S.	148	H6	35.41 N	119.13 W
McFarland, Wi., U.S.	128	H9	43.00 N	89.17 W
McGehee, Ar., U.S.	134	D7	33.37 N	91.23 W
McGill, Nv., U.S.	150	D2	39.24 N	114.48 W
McGill, Université, educ., Qc., Can.	193a		45.30 N	73.35 W
McGillivray, Lac, l., Qc., Can.	126	B12	46.04 N	77.06 W
McGinnis Slough Wildlife Refuge, ind. res., Il., U.S.	196		41.39 N	87.52 W
McGrath, Ak., U.S.	109	D8	62.58 N	155.38 W
McGraw, N.Y., U.S.	124	B9	42.36 N	76.05 W
McGregor, Ia., U.S.	130	A6	43.01 N	91.10 W
McGregor, Tx., U.S.	136	C10	31.25 N	97.24 W
McGregor, stm., B.C., Can.	144	B9	54.10 N	122.01 W
McGregor Lake, l., Ab., Can.	144	F18	50.31 N	112.53 W
McGregor Range, mts., Austl.	98	F4	26.40 S	142.45 E
McGuire, Mount, mtn., Id., U.S.	146	E12	45.10 N	114.36 W
McHenry, Il., U.S.	130	B9	42.20 N	88.16 W
McHenry, Ms., U.S.	134	G9	30.42 N	89.09 W
Mchinji, Mwi.	88	C5	13.41 S	32.55 E
McIntosh, Al., U.S.	134	F10	31.15 N	88.01 W
McIntosh, Mn., U.S.	128	D3	47.37 N	95.53 W
McIntosh, S.D., U.S.	140	B11	45.54 N	101.20 W
McIntyre Bay, b., On., Can.	128	B10	49.27 N	88.40 W
McKay Creek, stm., Or., U.S.	146	E8	45.40 N	118.50 W
McKeand, stm., Nu., Can.	110	C17	65.25 N	68.06 W
McKee, Ky., U.S.	124	G2	37.25 N	84.00 W
McKee Creek, stm., Il., U.S.	130	E7	39.46 N	90.36 W
McKeesport, Pa., U.S.	124	D6	40.20 N	79.51 W
McKenzie, Al., U.S.	134	F12	31.32 N	86.43 W
McKenzie, Tn., U.S.	130	H9	36.08 N	88.31 W
McKenzie, stm., Or., U.S.	146	F4	44.07 N	123.05 W
McKenzie Bridge, Or., U.S.	146	F4	44.10 N	122.11 W
McKenzie Island, On., Can.	118	B19	51.04 N	93.49 W
McKinlay, Austl.	98	C3	21.16 S	141.17 E
McKinlay, stm., Austl.	98	C3	20.28 S	141.14 E
McKinley, Mount, mtn., Ak., U.S.	109	D9	63.04 N	151.00 W
McKinley Airport, arpt., Mi., U.S.	199		42.33 N	82.58 W
McKinley Park, p.o.i., Pa., U.S.	197b		40.25 N	80.00 W
McKinleyville, Ca., U.S.	148	C1	40.57 N	124.05 W
McKinney, Tx., U.S.	134	D2	33.12 N	96.36 W
McKittrick Summit, mtn., Ca., U.S.	148	H6	35.18 N	119.46 W
McKnight Village, Pa., U.S.	197b		40.31 N	80.00 W
McLain, Ms., U.S.	134	F10	31.06 N	88.49 W
McLaughlin, S.D., U.S.	140	B12	45.48 N	100.48 W
McLaughlin Run, stm., Pa., U.S.	197b		40.22 N	80.07 W
McLaurin, Ms., U.S.	134	F9	31.10 N	89.13 W
McLean, Sk., Can.	142	D9	50.30 N	104.04 W
McLean, Il., U.S.	130	D8	40.18 N	89.10 W
McLean, Tx., U.S.	138	F8	35.14 N	100.35 W
McLean Hamlet, Va., U.S.	202c		38.56 N	77.13 W
McLean Mountain, mtn., Me., U.S.	122	C8	47.07 N	68.50 W
McLeansboro, Il., U.S.	130	F9	38.05 N	88.32 W
McLennan, Ab., Can.	110	D7	55.40 N	116.51 W
McLeod, stm., Ab., Can.	144	C15	54.09 N	115.42 W
McLeod Bay, b., N.T., Can.	110	C8	62.52 N	109.58 W
McLeod Lake, B.C., Can.	144	B7	54.59 N	123.02 W
M'Clintock Channel, strt., Nu., Can.	110	A10	72.00 N	102.00 W
McLoughlin, Mount, mtn., Or., U.S.	148	A3	42.27 N	122.19 W
McLouth, Ks., U.S.	130	E2	39.11 N	95.12 W
McLure, B.C., Can.	144	E10	51.03 N	120.15 W
M'Clure Strait, strt., N.T., Can.	109	B16	74.31 N	116.53 W
McMahon, Sk., Can.	142	D6	50.05 N	107.32 W
McMichael Art Collection, bldg., On., Can.	193b		43.50 N	79.37 W
McMinnville, Or., U.S.	146	E3	45.12 N	123.11 W
McMinnville, Tn., U.S.	134	B13	35.41 N	85.47 W
McMurdo, sci., Ant.	103	C22	77.50 S	166.25 E
McMurdo Sound, strt., Ant.	103	C22	77.28 S	164.22 E
McNary, Az., U.S.	150	I7	34.04 N	109.51 W
McNeil, Ar., U.S.	134	D5	33.21 N	93.12 W
McNeill, Ms., U.S.	134	G9	30.41 N	89.39 W
McPhail, stm., Mb., Can.	142	B17	52.44 N	96.28 W
McPhee Reservoir, res., Co., U.S.	150	F8	37.32 N	108.32 W
McPherson, Ks., U.S.	138	C11	38.22 N	97.39 W
McQueeney, Tx., U.S.	136	E9	29.35 N	98.02 W
McRae, Ar., U.S.	134	B7	35.07 N	91.49 W
McRae, Ga., U.S.	132	D3	32.04 N	82.54 W
McRoberts, Ky., U.S.	130	G15	37.12 N	82.40 W
McVeigh, Ky., U.S.	124	G3	37.32 N	82.15 W
McVickers Brook, stm., N.J., U.S.	194		40.45 N	74.38 W
McVille, N.D., U.S.	142	G15	47.45 N	98.10 W
McWilliams, Al., U.S.	134	F11	31.49 N	87.05 W
Mdandu, Tan.	86	F6	9.08 S	34.42 E
Mdantsane, S. Afr.	90	H8	32.55 S	27.42 E
M'drak, Viet.	64	F9	12.41 N	108.47 E
Meacham, Sk., Can.	142	B8	52.06 N	105.46 W
Mead, Ne., U.S.	130	C1	41.13 N	96.29 W
Mead, Lake, res., U.S.	150	G2	36.07 N	114.26 W
Meade, Ks., U.S.	138	D8	37.17 N	100.20 W
Meade, stm., Ak., U.S.	109	B8	70.54 N	156.00 W
Meaden Peak, mtn., Co., U.S.	150	C9	40.46 N	107.03 W
Meade Peak, mtn., Id., U.S.	146	H15	42.30 N	111.15 W
Meadow, Tx., U.S.	138	H6	33.20 N	102.12 W
Meadow, Ut., U.S.	150	E4	38.53 N	112.24 W
Meadowbank Park, p.o.i., Austl.	192a		33.49 S	151.06 E
Meadow Brook, stm., Ma., U.S.	201		42.03 N	70.58 W
Meadow Brook, stm., Pa., U.S.	203		40.07 N	75.04 W
Meadow Creek, stm., Id., U.S.	146	E11	46.03 N	115.18 W
Meadow Island, i., N.Y., U.S.	194		40.36 N	73.33 W
Meadow Lake, Sk., Can.	110	E9	54.08 N	108.26 W
Meadow Lake, l., N.Y., U.S.	194		40.44 N	73.50 W
Meadowlands Race Track, p.o.i., N.J., U.S.	194		40.49 N	74.05 W
Meadowlark Airport, arpt., Ca., U.S.	198		33.43 N	118.02 W
Meadowood, De., U.S.	203		39.43 N	75.47 W
Meadowood, Md., U.S.	202c		39.04 N	77.00 W
Meadows, Island of, i., N.Y., U.S.	194		40.34 N	74.12 W
Meadows Race Track, The, p.o.i., Pa., U.S.	197b		40.13 N	80.12 W
Meadowvale, ngh., On., Can.	193b		43.37 N	79.43 W
Meadow Valley Wash, stm., Nv., U.S.	150	G2	36.39 N	114.34 W
Meadowview, Va., U.S.	124	H3	36.46 N	81.51 W
Meadville, Ms., U.S.	134	F8	31.28 N	90.54 W
Meadville, Mo., U.S.	130	E4	39.47 N	93.18 W
Meadville, Pa., U.S.	124	C5	41.38 N	80.08 W
Meaford, On., Can.	126	D9	44.35 N	80.35 W
Meaghers Grant, N.S., Can.	122	F13	44.55 N	63.14 W
Mealhada, Port.	28	D2	40.22 N	8.26 W
Meandarra, Austl.	98	F7	27.20 S	149.52 E
Meander River, Ab., Can.	110	D7	59.01 N	117.39 W
Mearim, stm., Braz.	170	B3	3.17 S	44.47 W
Meath, state, Ire.	10	H6	53.35 N	6.40 W
Meath, hist. reg., Ire.	10	H6	53.44 N	6.50 W
Meaux, Fr.	20	F11	48.57 N	2.53 E
Meaux-Esbly, Aérodrome de, arpt., Fr.	179		48.55 N	2.50 E
Mebisere, Nig.	191a		6.42 N	3.31 E
Mebonden, Nor.	16	D8	63.13 N	11.02 E
Mecaya, stm., Col.	168	G4	0.29 N	75.10 W
Mecca see Makkah, Sau. Ar.	72	E4	21.26 N	39.50 E
Mečetka, Russia	40	F11	50.54 N	40.04 E
Mechanicsburg, Oh., U.S.	124	D2	40.04 N	83.33 W
Mechanicsville, Ia., U.S.	130	C6	41.54 N	91.14 W
Mechanicsville, Va., U.S.	124	G8	37.35 N	77.22 W
Mechanicville, N.Y., U.S.	124	B12	42.54 N	73.41 W
Mechebylove, Ukr.	38	D15	49.04 N	36.42 E
Mechelen (Malines), Bel.	20	C13	51.02 N	4.28 E
Mechita, Arg.	172	G7	35.04 S	60.24 W
Mecidiye, Tur.	34	C9	40.37 N	26.32 E
Meckinghoven, Ger.	181		51.37 N	7.19 E
Mecklenburg, hist. reg., Ger.	24	C7	53.39 N	11.27 E
Mecklenburger Bucht, b., Ger.	24	B7	54.20 N	11.40 E
Mecklenburg-Vorpommern, state, Ger.	24	C8	53.45 N	12.30 E
Mecsek, mts., Hung.	36	C5	46.12 N	18.16 E
Mecubúri, Moz.	88	C6	14.49 S	38.42 E

Name	Page	Map Ref.	Latitude	Longitude
Mecula, Moz.	88	C6	12.05 S	37.38 E
Meda, Port.	28	D3	40.58 N	7.16 W
Medak, India	69	B4	18.03 N	78.17 E
Médan, Fr.	179		48.57 N	2.00 E
Medan, Indon.	66	B1	3.35 N	98.40 E
Médanos, Arg.	172	I6	38.49 S	62.40 W
Medanosa, Punta, c., Arg.	166	I3	48.06 S	65.55 W
Medaryville, In., U.S.	130	C11	41.05 N	86.52 W
Mede, Italy	30	E5	45.06 N	8.44 E
Medeiros Neto, Braz.	170	I5	17.21 S	40.13 W
Medellín, Col.	168	D4	6.15 N	75.35 W
Médenine, Tun.	84	C6	33.19 N	10.30 E
Medenychi, Ukr.	38	D2	49.25 N	23.45 E
Mederdra, Maur.	84	F1	16.53 N	15.40 W
Medevi, Swe.	16	I12	58.40 N	14.57 E
Medford, Ok., U.S.	138	E11	36.48 N	97.42 W
Medford, Or., U.S.	148	A3	42.19 N	122.52 W
Medford, Wi., U.S.	128	F8	45.08 N	90.20 W
Medford Farms, N.J., U.S.	203		39.52 N	74.45 W
Medford Lakes, N.J., U.S.	203		39.51 N	74.48 W
Medgidia, Rom.	36	E15	44.16 N	28.15 E
Medgyes see Mediaș, Rom.	36	C11	46.09 N	24.21 E
Mediapolis, Ia., U.S.	130	C6	41.00 N	91.09 W
Mediaș, Rom.	36	C11	46.09 N	24.21 E
Medical Lake, Wa., U.S.	146	C9	47.36 N	117.42 W
Medicine Bow, Wy., U.S.	150	B10	41.54 N	106.13 W
Medicine Bow, stm., Wy., U.S.	150	A10	42.03 N	106.50 W
Medicine Bow Mountains, mts., U.S.	140	G6	41.10 N	106.10 W
Medicine Bow Peak, mtn., Wy., U.S.	150	B10	41.21 N	106.19 W
Medicine Creek, stm., Mo., U.S.	130	D4	39.42 N	93.24 W
Medicine Creek, stm., Ne., U.S.	140	G12	40.16 N	100.08 W
Medicine Creek, stm., S.D., U.S.	140	D12	44.06 N	99.42 W
Medicine Hat, Ab., Can.	142	D3	50.02 N	110.41 W
Medicine Knoll Creek, stm., S.D., U.S.	140	C13	44.17 N	100.04 W
Medicine Lake, Mt., U.S.	142	F9	48.30 N	104.30 W
Medicine Lodge, Ks., U.S.	138	D10	37.16 N	98.34 W
Medicine Lodge, stm., U.S.	138	D10	36.49 N	98.20 W
Medicine Rocks State Park, p.o.i., Mt., U.S.	140	A8	46.01 N	104.35 W
Medina, Braz.	170	I5	16.14 S	41.28 W
Medina see Al-Madīnah, Sau. Ar.	72	E4	24.27 N	39.36 E
Medina, N.Y., U.S.	126	E11	43.12 N	78.22 W
Medina, N.D., U.S.	142	H14	46.53 N	99.17 W
Medina, Oh., U.S.	124	C4	41.07 N	81.51 W
Medina, Tx., U.S.	136	E8	29.48 N	99.15 W
Medina, stm., Tx., U.S.	136	E9	29.12 N	98.15 W
Medinaceli, Spain	28	C8	41.10 N	2.26 W
Medina del Campo, Spain	28	C6	41.18 N	4.55 W
Medina de Rioseco, Spain	28	C5	41.52 N	5.02 W
Medinah, Il., U.S.	196		41.59 N	88.01 W
Medina Lake, res., Tx., U.S.	136	E9	29.35 N	98.58 W
Medina-Sidonia, Spain	28	H5	36.27 N	5.55 W
Medinat al-Faiyum see El-Fayoum, Egypt	76	I1	29.19 N	30.50 E
Medininkai, Lith.	26	F8	54.32 N	25.42 E
Medinīpur, India	70	G11	22.26 N	87.20 E
Medio, Punta, c., Chile	172	C2	27.07 S	70.55 W
Medio Creek, stm., Tx., U.S.	136	F10	28.18 N	97.18 W
Mediterranean Sea, s.	80	C7	35.00 N	20.00 E
Méditerranée, Mer see Mediterranean Sea, s.	80	C7	35.00 N	20.00 E
Mediterraneo, Mar see Mediterranean Sea, s.	80	C7	35.00 N	20.00 E
Mediterráneo, Mar see Mediterranean Sea, s.	80	C7	35.00 N	20.00 E
Mediterrània, Mar see Mediterranean Sea, s.	80	C7	35.00 N	20.00 E
Medje, D.R.C.	86	D5	2.23 N	27.18 E
Medjerda, Monts de la see Medjerda Mountains, mts., Afr.	32	H2	36.33 N	8.20 E
Medjerda, Oued, stm., Afr.	32	H3	37.05 N	10.13 E
Medjerda Mountains, mts., Afr.	32	H2	36.33 N	8.20 E
Medjez el Bab, Tun.	32	H3	36.38 N	9.36 E
Medkovec, Blg.	36	F10	43.37 N	23.10 E
Mednoe, Russia	26	D18	56.55 N	35.28 E
Mednogorsk, Russia	48	D9	51.24 N	57.35 E
Médoc, reg., Fr.	22	D5	45.20 N	1.00 W
Medora, In., U.S.	130	F11	38.49 N	86.10 W
Medora, N.D., U.S.	142	H10	46.54 N	103.32 W
Médouneu, Gabon	86	D2	0.59 N	10.55 E
Meductic, N.B., Can.	122	E9	45.59 N	67.29 W
Medveďa, Yugo.	36	G8	42.50 N	21.34 E
Medvedevskoe, Russia	26	B18	58.57 N	35.56 E
Medvedica, stm., Russia	26	C19	57.04 N	37.31 E
Medvedica, stm., Russia	40	G13	49.35 N	42.39 E
Medvedickij, Russia	40	F14	50.47 N	44.43 E
Medvedkovo, ngh., Russia	183b		55.53 N	37.38 E
Medvedok, Russia	40	C17	57.23 N	50.02 E
Medvėgalis, hill, Lith.	26	E5	55.38 N	22.45 E
Medvenka, Russia	38	B15	51.24 N	36.07 E
Medvěnka, stm., Russia	183b		55.44 N	37.12 E
Medvežegorsk, Russia	18	E21	62.54 N	34.28 E
Medvežij ostrova, is., Russia	50	B21	70.46 N	161.22 E
Medvežji Ozëra, Russia	183b		55.52 N	37.59 E
Medvežji ozera, l., Russia	183b		55.52 N	38.00 E
Medvyn, Ukr.	38	D9	49.23 N	30.47 E
Medway, mun., Eng., U.K.	178		51.24 N	0.31 E
Medway, stm., N.S., Can.	122	F12	44.07 N	64.38 W
Medway Towns, mun., Eng., U.K.	178		51.24 N	0.31 E
Medyn', Russia	26	F18	54.57 N	35.52 E
Medzhybizh, Ukr.	38	D6	49.26 N	27.25 E
Medzilaborce, Slvk.	24	G17	49.16 N	21.54 E
Meeberrie, Austl.	96	E3	26.58 S	115.58 E
Meekatharra, Austl.	96	E3	26.35 S	118.29 E
Meeker, Co., U.S.	150	C9	40.02 N	107.55 W
Meeks Bay, Ca., U.S.	148	D5	39.01 N	120.06 W
Meeladeen, Som.	86	B9	10.23 N	49.49 E
Meeman-Shelby Forest State Park, p.o.i., Tn., U.S.	134	B8	35.19 N	90.03 W
Meerane, Ger.	24	F8	50.51 N	12.28 E
Meerbeck, Ger.	181		51.28 N	6.39 E
Meersburg, Ger.	24	I5	47.41 N	9.17 E
Meerut, India	70	D6	28.59 N	77.41 E
Meeteetse, Wy., U.S.	140	C4	44.08 N	108.53 W
Mēga, Eth.	82	G7	4.08 N	38.16 E
Mega, Pulau, i., Indon.	66	E2	3.28 S	100.39 E
Megáli Préspa, Límni see Prespa, Lake, l., Eur.	32	D14	40.54 N	21.02 E
Megálo Chorió, Grc.	34	G10	36.27 N	27.21 E
Megalópoli, Grc.	34	F5	37.24 N	22.08 E
Mégantic, Lac, l., Qc., Can.	122	E5	45.32 N	70.53 W
Mégara, Grc.	34	E6	37.59 N	23.20 E
Megargel, Tx., U.S.	138	H10	33.27 N	98.55 W
Mégaron, Kólpos, b., Grc.	185c		37.56 N	23.20 E
Megasini, mtn., India	70	H11	21.38 N	86.21 E
Meghālaya, state, India	70	F13	25.30 N	91.15 E
Meghna, stm., Bngl.	70	G13	22.49 N	90.42 E
Megion, Russia	48	B13	61.02 N	76.07 E
Megisti, i., Grc.	34	G12	36.08 N	29.36 E
Megra, Russia	12	C19	66.09 N	41.37 E
Megra, Russia	18	G24	60.09 N	37.14 E
Meguro, ngh., Japan	186		35.38 N	139.42 E
Meguro, stm., Japan	186		35.37 N	139.45 E
Mehadia, Rom.	36	E9	44.55 N	22.20 E
Mehakit, Indon.	66	E9	2.49 S	115.58 E
Mehamn, Nor.	14	A18	71.01 N	27.52 E
Mehanom, mys, c., Ukr.	38	I14	44.48 N	35.04 E
Mehar, Pak.	62	C2	27.11 N	67.49 E
Meharry, Mount, mtn., Austl.	96	D3	22.59 S	118.35 E
Mehedinți, state, Rom.	36	E10	44.30 N	22.50 E
Mehekar, India	70	H6	20.10 N	76.31 E
Meherrin, stm., U.S.	124	H7	36.25 N	76.56 W
Mehidpur, India	70	G5	23.27 N	75.39 E
Mehikoorma, Est.	26	B10	58.14 N	27.27 E
Mehndāwal, India	70	E9	26.58 N	83.06 E
Mehpālpur, ngh., India	190a		28.33 N	77.08 E
Mehrābād, Iran	74	B10	36.53 N	47.55 E
Mehrābād, ngh., Iran	185d		35.40 N	51.20 E
Mehrabad International Airport, arpt., Iran	185d		35.41 N	51.19 E
Mehram Nagar, ngh., India	190a		28.34 N	77.07 E
Mehrān, Iran	74	D10	33.07 N	46.10 E
Mehrān, stm., Iran	74	G14	26.49 N	55.33 E
Mehren'ga, Russia	12	F19	61.44 N	40.57 E
Mehrenga, stm., Russia	12	E19	63.15 N	41.23 E
Mehrīz, Iran	74	E14	31.35 N	54.28 E
Mehrow, Ger.	182a		52.34 N	13.37 E
Mehrum, Ger.	181		51.35 N	6.37 E
Mè-hsa-tè, Mya.	64	C3	19.32 N	97.39 E
Mehtarlām, Afg.	72	C11	34.39 N	70.13 E
Mehun-sur-Yèvre, Fr.	20	G11	47.08 N	2.12 E
Mei, stm., China	58	I7	24.24 N	116.34 E
Mei, stm., China	58	H7	25.58 N	115.26 E
Meia Meia, Tan.	86	F7	5.48 S	35.47 E
Meia Ponte, stm., Braz.	170	I1	17.34 S	49.25 W
Meichuan, China	58	F6	30.08 N	115.35 E
Meide, Ger.	181		51.11 N	6.55 E
Meiderich, ngh., Ger.	181		51.28 N	6.46 E
Meidling, ngh., Aus.	182b		48.11 N	16.20 E
Meierkaisong, China	70	C10	30.54 N	84.31 E
Meiersberg, Ger.	181		51.17 N	6.57 E
Meiganga, Cam.	86	C2	6.34 N	14.06 E
Meighen Island, i., Nu., Can.	108	A5	79.55 N	99.30 W
Meigs, Ga., U.S.	132	E1	31.04 N	84.05 W
Meigs Field, arpt., Il., U.S.	196		41.51 N	87.36 W
Meihekou, China	52	C10	42.31 N	125.40 E
Meiji Shrine, rel., Japan	186		35.41 N	139.42 E
Meikeng, China	58	J6	23.58 N	114.03 E
Meiktila, Mya.	64	B2	20.51 N	95.52 E
Meiners Oaks, Ca., U.S.	148	I6	34.27 N	119.16 W
Meiningen, Ger.	24	F6	50.34 N	10.25 E
Meio, Ilha do, i., Braz.	205a		23.02 S	43.17 W
Meishan, China	52	E5	30.03 N	103.50 E
Meissen, Ger.	24	E9	51.10 N	13.28 E
Meiss Lake, l., Ca., U.S.	148	B3	41.51 N	122.03 W
Meitan, China	58	H2	27.46 N	107.42 E
Meixian see Meizhou, China	58	I7	24.20 N	116.07 E
Meizhai, China	58	I3	25.30 N	108.50 E
Meizhou, China	58	I7	24.20 N	116.07 E
Mejillones, Chile	166	D2	23.06 S	70.26 W
Mejillones, Península, pen., Chile	172	A2	23.19 S	70.42 W
Mejnypil'gyno, Russia	50	D24	62.34 N	177.02 E
Mejorada del Campo, Spain	184a		40.24 N	3.29 W
Mékambo, Gabon	86	D2	1.00 N	13.57 E
Mek'elē, Eth.	82	E7	13.29 N	39.28 E
Mékhé, Sen.	84	F1	15.06 N	16.37 W
Mekhtar, Pak.	70	C2	30.28 N	69.22 E
Meknès, Mor.	84	C3	33.54 N	5.33 W
Mekong (Khong) (Lancang) (Mékôngk), stm., Asia	64	G7	10.33 N	105.26 E
Mekongga, Gunung, mtn., Indon.	60	F7	3.38 S	121.15 E
Mékôngk see Mekong, stm., Asia	64	G7	10.33 N	105.26 E
Mekoryuk, Ak., U.S.	109	D6	60.23 N	166.12 W
Melado, stm., Chile	172	H2	35.42 S	71.04 W
Melaka, Malay.	64	K6	2.12 N	102.15 E
Melaka, state, Malay.	64	K6	2.15 N	102.15 E
Melaka, Selat see Malacca, Strait of, strt., Asia	64	K5	2.30 N	101.20 E
Melalap, Malay.	66	A10	5.14 N	115.59 E
Melanesia, is., Oc.	94	D7	5.00 S	164.00 E
Mélanésie see Melanesia, is., Oc.	94	D7	5.00 S	164.00 E
Melawi, stm., Indon.	66	D8	0.05 N	111.29 E
Melayu, stm., Malay.	189c		1.27 N	103.42 E
Melbourne, Austl.	98	K5	37.48 S	144.57 E
Melbourne, Austl.	192b		37.49 S	144.58 E
Melbourne, Ar., U.S.	130	H6	36.03 N	91.55 W
Melbourne, Fl., U.S.	132	H5	28.05 N	80.36 W
Melbourne, Ia., U.S.	128	J5	41.56 N	93.06 W
Melbourne, University of, educ., Austl.	192b		37.48 S	144.58 E
Melbourne Island, i., Nu., Can.	110	B10	68.30 N	104.45 W
Melbu, Nor.	14	D5	68.30 N	14.48 E
Melcher, Ia., U.S.	130	C4	41.13 N	93.14 W
Melchor, Isla, i., Chile	166	I2	45.08 S	73.57 W
Melchor Múzquiz, Mex.	154	A8	27.52 N	101.31 W
Melchor Ocampo, Mex.	136	H8	26.03 N	99.33 W
Meldorf, Ger.	24	B4	54.05 N	9.05 E
Meldrum Bay, On., Can.	126	C6	45.55 N	83.07 W
Meldrum Creek, B.C., Can.	144	D8	52.06 N	122.22 W
Mele, India	190b		22.49 N	88.09 E
Mélé, Baie, b., Vanuatu	101d	k17	17.44 S	168.15 E
Melekeok, Palau	100b	g8	7.28 N	134.37 E
Melekess see Dimitrovgrad, Russia	40	D16	54.13 N	49.36 E
Melenki, Russia	40	D12	55.20 N	41.38 E
Meleuz, Russia	40	E19	52.57 N	55.55 E
Mélèzes, stm., Qc., Can.	110	D16	57.40 N	69.29 W
Melfa, stm., Italy	32	C7	41.30 N	13.35 E
Melfi, Chad	82	E3	11.03 N	17.56 E
Melfi, Italy	32	C9	40.59 N	15.39 E
Melfjorden, b., Nor.	14	F4	66.33 N	13.26 E
Melfort, Sk., Can.	142	B9	52.52 N	104.36 W
Melgar, Col.	168	E4	4.12 N	74.39 W
Mel'guny, Russia	40	E12	52.09 N	40.52 E
Melhus, Nor.	16	D8	63.17 N	10.16 E
Meliane, Oued, stm., Tun.	32	H4	36.46 N	10.17 E
Meliau, Indon.	66	D7	0.08 S	110.16 E
Meliau, Gunong, mtn., Malay.	68	H1	5.50 N	117.14 E
Melide, Spain	28	B3	42.54 N	8.00 W
Meligalás, Grc.	34	F4	37.13 N	21.58 E
Melihovo, Russia	38	C15	50.42 N	36.47 E
Melilla, Sp. N. Afr.	84	B4	35.17 N	2.56 W
Melimoyu, Cerro, vol., Chile	166	H2	44.05 S	72.52 W
Melincué, Arg.	172	F7	33.37 S	61.27 W
Melissia, Grc.	185c		38.03 N	23.50 E
Melita, Mb., Can.	142	E12	49.16 N	100.58 W
Melito di Porto Salvo, Italy	32	G9	37.55 N	15.47 E
Melitopol', Ukr.	38	G14	46.50 N	35.21 E
Melívoia, Grc.	34	D5	39.45 N	22.48 E
Melk, Aus.	30	B12	48.13 N	15.20 E
Mellakoski, Fin.	14	F15	66.23 N	24.26 E
Mellansel, Swe.	16	D16	63.25 N	18.19 E
Melle, Fr.	22	C5	46.13 N	0.08 W
Mellègue, Oued, stm., Afr.	32	I2	36.05 N	8.32 E
Mellen, Wi., U.S.	128	E8	46.19 N	90.39 W
Mellerud, Swe.	16	I10	58.42 N	12.28 E
Mellette, S.D., U.S.	140	B14	45.09 N	98.29 W
Mellid see Melide, Spain	28	B3	42.54 N	8.00 W
Melling, Eng., U.K.	180		53.30 N	2.56 W
Mellish Reef, at., Austl.	96	C11	17.25 S	155.50 E
Mellit, Sudan	82	E5	14.08 N	25.33 E
Mellone, Monte, hill, Italy	185a		41.50 N	12.43 E
Mellor, Eng., U.K.	180		53.46 N	2.32 W
Mellor Brook, Eng., U.K.	180		53.47 N	2.33 W
Melmoth, S. Afr.	90	F10	28.37 S	31.24 E
Mělník, Czech Rep.	24	F10	50.20 N	14.29 E
Mel'nikovo, Russia	18	G16	60.54 N	29.43 E
Mel'nytsia-Podil's'ka, Ukr.	38	E5	48.36 N	26.10 E
Melo, Ur.	172	F10	32.21 S	54.10 W
Melolo, Indon.	66	H12	9.56 S	120.39 E
Melos see Mílos, i., Grc.	34	G7	36.40 N	24.22 E
Melrhir, Chott, l., Alg.	84	C6	34.18 N	6.17 E
Melrose, Austl.	96	E4	27.55 S	121.18 E
Melrose, Austl.	98	I6	32.41 S	146.57 E
Melrose, Scot., U.K.	10	F10	55.36 N	2.44 W
Melrose, Mn., U.S.	128	F4	45.40 N	94.49 W
Melrose, N.M., U.S.	138	G5	34.25 N	103.37 W
Melrose, Wi., U.S.	128	G8	44.07 N	90.59 W
Melrose, ngh., N.Y., U.S.	194		40.49 N	73.55 W
Melrose Park, Pa., U.S.	203		40.04 N	75.08 W
Melstone, Mt., U.S.	140	A5	46.35 N	107.52 W
Melsungen, Ger.	24	E5	51.08 N	9.32 E
Meltaus, Fin.	14	F16	66.54 N	25.20 E
Meltham, Eng., U.K.	180		53.36 N	1.51 W
Melton Mowbray, Eng., U.K.	10	I12	52.46 N	0.53 W
Meltosjärvi, Fin.	14	F15	66.32 N	24.39 E
Melúa, Col.	168	F5	3.55 N	72.50 W
Melun, Fr.	20	F11	48.32 N	2.39 E
Melun, Mya.	64	B1	20.14 N	93.24 E
Melūr, India	69	F4	10.02 N	78.21 E
Melvern, Ks., U.S.	130	F2	38.30 N	95.38 W
Melvern Lake, res., Ks., U.S.	130	F1	38.29 N	95.49 W
Melville, Sk., Can.	142	D11	50.55 N	102.48 W
Melville, La., U.S.	134	G7	30.41 N	91.44 W
Melville, N.Y., U.S.	194		40.47 N	73.24 W
Melville, ngh., S. Afr.	191d		26.11 S	28.00 E
Melville, Cape, c., Austl.	96	B9	14.11 S	144.30 E
Melville Bugt, b., Grnld.	108	B21	75.46 N	61.57 W
Melville Hall Airport, arpt., Dom.	159c	i6	15.32 N	61.18 W
Melville Hills, hills, Can.	110	B7	69.17 N	122.34 W
Melville Island, i., Austl.	96	B6	11.40 S	131.00 E
Melville Island, i., Can.	109	A17	75.15 N	109.59 W
Melville Peninsula, pen., Nu., Can.	110	B14	68.00 N	84.00 W
Melvin, Il., U.S.	128	K10	40.34 N	88.14 W
Melvin, Ky., U.S.	124	G3	37.21 N	82.42 W
Melvin, Tx., U.S.	136	C8	31.11 N	99.34 W
Melvin, Lough, l., Eur.	10	G4	54.26 N	8.10 W
Melvindale, Mi., U.S.	199		42.16 N	83.10 W
Melyana, Alg.	28	H13	36.17 N	2.12 E
Mélykút, Hung.	36	C6	46.13 N	19.22 E
Memala, Indon.	66	D8	1.45 S	112.36 E
Mêmar Co, l., China	66	A9	34.13 N	82.16 E
Memba, Moz.	88	C7	14.11 S	40.31 E
Membalong, Indon.	66	E5	3.09 S	107.38 E
Memboro, Indon.	66	H11	9.23 S	119.32 E
Memel see Klaipėda, Lith.	26	E3	55.43 N	21.08 E
Memel, S. Afr.	90	E9	27.40 S	29.34 E
Mēmele (Nemunėlis), stm., Eur.	26	D7	56.24 N	24.10 E
Memewin, Lac, l., Qc., Can.	126	B11	46.28 N	78.40 W
Memmingen, Ger.	24	I6	47.59 N	10.11 E
Memo, stm., Ven.	168	C8	9.15 N	66.40 W
Memorial Bridge, trans., Thai.	187a		13.44 N	100.30 E
Memorial Stadium, p.o.i., Md., U.S.	202b		39.20 N	76.36 W
Mémót, Camb.	64	G8	11.49 N	106.10 E
Mempawah, Indon.	66	C6	0.19 N	108.57 E
Memphis, Fl., U.S.	132	I3	27.32 N	82.34 W
Memphis, Mi., U.S.	124	B3	42.53 N	82.46 W
Memphis, Mo., U.S.	130	D5	40.27 N	92.10 W
Memphis, Tn., U.S.	134	B9	35.08 N	90.02 W
Memphis, Tx., U.S.	138	G8	34.43 N	100.32 W
Memphis Naval Air Station, mil., Tn., U.S.	134	B9	35.21 N	89.52 W
Memphrémagog, Lac (Memphremagog, Lake), l., N.A.	122	E4	45.02 N	72.15 W
Memphremagog, Lake (Memphrémagog, Lac), l., N.A.	122	E4	45.02 N	72.15 W
Memramcook, N.B., Can.	122	D12	45.58 N	64.34 W
Mena, Ukr.	38	B11	51.31 N	32.13 E
Mena, Ar., U.S.	134	C4	34.35 N	94.15 W
Menado see Manado, Indon.	60	E7	1.29 N	124.50 E
Menahga, Mn., U.S.	128	E3	46.45 N	95.06 W
Menai, Austl.	192a		34.01 S	151.01 E
Menai Strait, strt., Wales, U.K.	10	H8	53.10 N	4.14 W
Ménaka, Mali	84	F5	15.55 N	2.23 E
Menan, Id., U.S.	146	G15	43.43 N	111.58 W
Menard, Tx., U.S.	136	D8	30.54 N	99.46 W
Menasha, Wi., U.S.	128	G10	44.12 N	88.26 W
Menate, Indon.	66	D8	0.14 S	113.01 E
Menchykury, Ukr.	38	F13	47.04 N	34.47 E
Mend, China	54	C5	43.38 N	123.07 E
Mendanau, Pulau, i., Indon.	66	E5	2.51 S	107.26 E
Mendawai, Indon.	66	E8	2.59 S	113.16 E
Mendawai, stm., Indon.	66	E8	3.13 S	113.19 E
Mende, Fr.	22	E9	44.30 N	3.30 E
Mendebo, mts., Eth.	82	F7	6.54 N	39.47 E
Mendeleevsk, Russia	40	D18	55.53 N	52.18 E
Menden, Ger.	20	C16	51.26 N	7.47 E
Menden, ngh., Ger.	181		51.24 N	6.54 E
Mendenhall, Ms., U.S.	134	F9	31.57 N	89.52 W
Mendenhall, Pa., U.S.	203		39.51 N	75.38 W
Méndez, Mex.	154	C9	25.06 N	98.35 W
Mendī, Eth.	82	F7	9.47 N	35.06 E
Mendi, Pap. N. Gui.	101a	b3	6.10 S	143.40 E
Mendip Hills, hills, Eng., U.K.	10	J10	51.15 N	2.40 W
Mendocino, Ca., U.S.	148	D2	39.18 N	123.47 W
Mendocino, Cape, c., Ca., U.S.	148	C1	40.25 N	124.23 W
Mendocino Fracture Zone, unds.	174	E24	40.00 N	145.00 W
Mendon, Il., U.S.	130	D6	40.05 N	91.17 W
Mendon, Pa., U.S.	197b		40.11 N	79.41 W
Mendota, Ca., U.S.	148	G5	36.45 N	120.22 W
Mendota, Il., U.S.	130	C8	41.33 N	89.06 W
Mendoza, Arg.	172	F3	32.53 S	68.49 W
Mendoza, Peru	164	E2	6.20 S	77.24 W
Mendoza, state, Arg.	172	G4	34.30 S	68.30 W
Mendoza, stm., Arg.	172	F3	32.30 S	68.17 W
Mendung, Indon.	66	C3	0.30 N	103.10 E
Mene de Mauroa, Ven.	168	B6	10.41 N	71.00 W
Mene Grande, Ven.	168	C6	9.50 N	70.55 W
Menemen, Tur.	34	E9	38.36 N	27.04 E
Menen, Bel.	20	D12	50.47 N	3.07 E
MenesJärvi, Fin.	14	D17	68.43 N	26.24 E
Menfi, Italy	32	G6	37.36 N	12.58 E
Mengban, China	64	A5	23.08 N	100.18 E
Mengcheng, China	58	E7	33.16 N	116.32 E
Mengede, ngh., Ger.	181		51.34 N	7.23 E
Mengellang, Palau	100b	f8	7.41 N	134.38 E
Mengen, Tur.	34	C14	40.56 N	32.04 E
Menggala, Indon.	66	F4	4.29 S	105.14 E
Menggudai, China	58	B3	38.10 N	108.15 E
Menghai, China	52	G5	21.58 N	100.26 E
Menghun, China	64	B5	21.44 N	100.23 E
Mengjiawan, China	58	B3	38.37 N	109.41 E
Mengjiazhai, China	187b		31.18 N	121.19 E
Mengjin, China	58	D5	34.50 N	112.26 E
Mengla, China	64	B5	21.27 N	101.18 E
Menglian, China	64	A4	22.21 N	99.34 E
Menglinghausen, ngh., Ger.	181		51.28 N	7.25 E
Mengwang, China	64	A5	22.23 N	100.30 E
Mengxian, China	58	D5	34.54 N	112.47 E
Mengyin, China	58	D7	35.42 N	117.55 E
Mengzhe, China	64	A5	22.00 N	100.16 E
Mengzi, China	52	G5	23.22 N	103.24 E
Menihek Lakes, l., Nf., Can.	110	E17	54.00 N	66.35 W
Menin see Menen, Bel.	20	D12	50.47 N	3.07 E
Menindee, Austl.	98	I4	32.23 S	142.25 E
Meningie, Austl.	98	J2	35.42 S	139.19 E
Menjuša, Russia	26	B13	58.23 N	30.42 E
Menlo Park, Ca., U.S.	148	F3	37.27 N	122.11 W
Menlo Park Mall, shp. cen., N.J., U.S.	194		40.32 N	74.20 W
Menlo Park Terrace, N.J., U.S.	194		40.32 N	74.20 W
Mennecy, Fr.	179		48.34 N	2.26 E
Menno, S.D., U.S.	140	D15	43.14 N	97.34 W
Meno, Ok., U.S.	138	E10	36.23 N	98.10 W
Menominee, Mi., U.S.	126	C2	45.07 N	87.36 W
Menominee, stm., U.S.	126	C2	45.05 N	87.35 W
Menominee Indian Reservation, ind. res., Wi., U.S.	128	F10	44.58 N	88.43 W
Menomonee Falls, Wi., U.S.	130	A9	43.10 N	88.05 W
Menomonie, Wi., U.S.	128	G7	44.52 N	91.55 W
Menongue, Ang.	88	C2	14.39 S	17.41 E
Menor, Mar, b., Spain	28	G10	37.43 N	0.48 W
Menorca (Minorca), i., Spain	28	D15	40.00 N	4.00 E
Mentasta Lake, Ak., U.S.	109	D11	62.54 N	143.43 W
Mentawai, Kepulauan, is., Indon.	60	F2	2.00 S	99.30 E
Mentawai, Selat, strt., Indon.	60	F3	1.45 S	100.00 E
Menteng, ngh., Indon.	187e		6.12 S	106.50 E
Menton, Fr.	22	F13	43.47 N	7.29 E
Mentone, Austl.	192b		37.59 S	145.05 E
Mentone see Menton, Fr.	22	F13	43.47 N	7.29 E
Mentone, Tx., U.S.	136	C4	31.42 N	103.36 W
Mentor, Oh., U.S.	124	C4	41.39 N	81.20 W
Mentzdam see Darlington Dam, res., S. Afr.	90	H7	33.10 S	25.09 E
Menucourt, Fr.	179		49.02 N	1.59 E
Menyapa, Gunung, mtn., Indon.	66	C9	1.05 N	116.05 E
Menyuan, China	52	D5	37.21 N	101.39 E
Menzel Bourguiba, Tun.	32	G3	37.09 N	9.47 E
Menzel Bou Zelfa, Tun.	32	H4	36.41 N	10.36 E
Menzelerheide, Ger.	181		51.37 N	6.31 E
Menzelinsk, Russia	40	D18	55.42 N	53.06 E
Menzel Temime, Tun.	32	H5	36.47 N	10.59 E
Menzies, Austl.	96	E4	29.41 S	121.01 E
Menzies, Mount, mtn., Ant.	103	C10	73.30 S	61.50 E
Meobbaai, b., Nmb.	90	D2	24.25 S	14.34 E
Meola Āgri, India	190a		28.42 N	77.23 E
Meopham, Eng., U.K.	178		51.22 N	0.22 E
Meopham Station, Eng., U.K.	178		51.23 N	0.21 E
Meoqui, Mex.	154	A6	28.16 N	105.29 W
Meota, Sk., Can.	142	A5	53.02 N	108.27 W
Meppel, Neth.	20	B15	52.41 N	6.11 E
Meppen, Ger.	24	D3	52.42 N	7.18 E
Meqerghane, Sebkha, pl., Alg.	84	D5	26.19 N	1.20 E
Mequinenza, Embalse de, res., Spain	28	C10	41.19 N	0.06 E
Mequon, Wi., U.S.	130	A10	43.13 N	87.58 W
Mera, stm., Eur.	30	D6	46.12 N	9.26 E
Merah, Indon.	66	C10	0.37 N	116.49 E
Meråker, Nor.	16	D9	63.26 N	11.45 E
Meramec, stm., Mo., U.S.	130	F7	38.23 N	90.20 W
Meramec State Park, p.o.i., Mo., U.S.	130	F6	38.13 N	91.04 W
Meran see Merano, Italy	30	D8	46.40 N	11.09 E
Meran, Nig.	191a		6.38 N	3.16 E
Meranggau, Indon.	66	D7	0.12 S	110.15 E
Merangin, stm., Indon.	66	E2	2.09 S	102.47 E
Merano (Meran), Italy	30	D8	46.40 N	11.09 E
Meratus, Pegunungan, mts., Indon.	66	E9	2.45 S	115.40 E
Merauke, Indon.	60	G11	8.29 S	140.24 E
Merbau, Indon.	66	C3	1.06 N	102.32 E
Merbein, Austl.	98	J4	34.10 S	142.03 E
Merca see Marka, Som.	86	D8	1.42 N	44.45 E
Mercaderes, Col.	168	G3	1.48 N	77.10 W
Mercāra, India	69	E2	12.25 N	75.44 E
Merced, Ca., U.S.	148	F5	37.18 N	120.28 W
Merced, stm., Ca., U.S.	148	F5	37.21 N	120.58 W
Merced, Lake, l., Ca., U.S.	200		37.43 N	122.29 W
Merced, South Fork, stm., Ca., U.S.	148	F6	37.39 N	119.53 W
Mercedario, Cerro, mtn., Arg.	172	E2	31.58 S	70.07 W
Mercedes, Arg.	172	D8	29.11 S	58.03 W
Mercedes, Arg.	172	G8	34.39 S	59.26 W
Mercedes, Arg.	172	E3	30.06 S	68.41 W
Mercedes, Tx., U.S.	136	H10	26.08 N	97.54 W
Mercedes, Ur.	172	F8	33.15 S	58.01 W
Mercer, Mo., U.S.	130	D4	40.30 N	93.32 W
Mercer, Pa., U.S.	124	C5	41.13 N	80.14 W
Mercer, Wi., U.S.	128	E8	46.09 N	90.03 W
Mercersburg, Pa., U.S.	124	E7	39.49 N	77.54 W
Mercês, Port.	184c		38.47 N	9.19 W
Merchants Bay, b., Nu., Can.	108	D13	67.10 N	62.50 W
Merchantville, N.J., U.S.	203		39.56 N	75.04 W
Mercier (Saint-Philomène), Qc., Can.	193a		45.19 N	73.45 W
Mercier, Pont, trans., Qc., Can.	193a		45.25 N	73.39 W
Mercoal, Ab., Can.	144	C13	53.09 N	117.05 W
Mercury, Nv., U.S.	148	G10	36.39 N	115.59 W
Mercury Islands, is., N.Z.	102	C6	36.35 S	175.55 E
Mercy, Cape, c., Nu., Can.	108	E13	64.54 N	63.34 W
Mercy Bay, b., N.T., Can.	109	B16	74.07 N	118.55 W
Merdeka Bridge, trans., Sing.	189c		1.18 N	103.53 E
Méré, Fr.	179		48.47 N	1.49 E
Mere, Eng., U.K.	180		53.20 N	2.25 W
Mere, The, l., Eng., U.K.	180		53.20 N	2.24 W
Mere Brow, Eng., U.K.	180		53.40 N	2.53 W
Mereclough, Eng., U.K.	180		53.46 N	2.11 W
Meredale, S. Afr.	191d		26.17 S	27.59 E
Meredith, N.H., U.S.	122	G5	43.39 N	71.30 W
Meredith, Cape, c., Falk. Is.	166	J4	52.15 S	60.38 W
Meredith, Lake, res., Tx., U.S.	138	F7	35.36 N	101.42 W
Meredosia, Il., U.S.	130	E7	39.49 N	90.33 W
Mereeg, Som.	86	D9	3.46 N	47.18 E
Merefa, Ukr.	38	D15	49.50 N	36.04 E
Méré Lava, i., Vanuatu	101d	j17	14.25 S	168.03 E
Mereni, Mol.	38	G8	46.58 N	29.04 E
Merenkurkku (Norra Kvarken), strt., Eur.	18	D7	63.27 N	20.42 E
Merevari, stm., Ven.	168	E9	4.28 N	63.55 W
Mereworth, Eng., U.K.	178		51.15 N	0.23 E
Merëža, Russia	26	A19	59.01 N	36.24 E
Mergui, Mya.	64	F4	12.26 N	98.36 E
Mergui Archipelago, is., Mya.	64	G3	12.00 N	98.00 E
Meria, India	190b		22.59 N	88.20 E
Meribah, Austl.	98	J3	34.42 S	140.50 E
Meriç, Tur.	34	B9	41.12 N	26.25 E
Meriç see Maritsa, stm., Eur.	34	C9	40.44 N	26.02 E
Mérida, Mex.	150	K1	32.34 N	114.59 W
Mérida, Mex.	156	B3	20.58 N	89.37 W
Mérida, Spain	28	F4	38.55 N	6.20 W
Mérida, Ven.	168	C6	8.36 N	71.08 W
Mérida, state, Ven.	168	C6	8.30 N	71.10 W
Mérida, Cordillera de, mts., Ven.	168	C6	8.40 N	71.00 W
Meriden, N.J., U.S.	194		40.57 N	74.28 W
Meridian, Ga., U.S.	132	E4	31.27 N	81.22 W
Meridian, Id., U.S.	146	G10	43.36 N	116.21 W
Meridian, Ms., U.S.	134	E10	32.22 N	88.42 W
Meridian, Tx., U.S.	136	C10	31.55 N	97.39 W
Meridian Naval Air Station, mil., Ms., U.S.	134	E10	32.33 N	88.34 W
Meridianville, Al., U.S.	134	C12	34.50 N	86.35 W
Mériel, Fr.	179		49.05 N	2.12 E
Mérignac, Fr.	22	E5	44.51 N	0.38 W
Merigold, Ms., U.S.	134	D8	33.50 N	90.43 W
Merikarvia, Fin.	18	F8	61.51 N	21.30 E
Merimbula, Austl.	98	K7	36.53 S	149.54 E
Merín, Laguna (Mirim, Lagoa), b., S.A.	172	F11	32.45 S	52.50 W
Merinda, Austl.	98	B7	20.01 S	148.10 E
Meringur, Austl.	98	J3	34.22 S	141.09 E
Merino, Co., U.S.	140	G9	40.29 N	103.21 W
Merinos, Ur.	172	F9	32.23 S	56.54 W
Merion Station, Pa., U.S.	203		39.59 N	75.15 W
Meriwether Farms, Pa., U.S.	203		39.58 N	75.34 W
Merizo, Guam	100c	j9	13.15 N	144.40 E
Merkel, Tx., U.S.	136	B7	32.28 N	100.01 W
Merkendorf, Ger.	24	G6	49.12 N	10.42 E
Merkinė, Lith.	26	F7	54.09 N	24.11 E
Merkourovoúni, mtn., Grc.	185c		37.54 N	23.48 E
Merkulavičy, Bela.	26	H13	52.59 N	30.35 E
Merkys, stm., Lith.	26	F8	54.14 N	24.33 E
Merlimau, Pulau, i., Sing.	189c		1.17 N	103.42 E
Merlin, On., Can.	126	F7	42.14 N	82.14 W
Merlin, Or., U.S.	146	H3	42.31 N	123.24 W
Merlo, Arg.	172	F5	32.20 S	65.00 W
Merlo, state, Arg.	206		34.40 S	58.45 W
Merlo, Aeródromo, arpt., Arg.	206		34.41 S	58.45 W
Merlynston, Austl.	192b		37.43 S	144.58 E
Merna, Ne., U.S.	140	F13	41.29 N	99.45 W
Meron, Har (Meron, Mount), mtn., Isr.	76	E6	32.59 N	35.25 E
Meron, Mount see Meron, Har, mtn., Isr.	76	E6	32.59 N	35.25 E
Merouane, Chott, l., Alg.	84	C6	34.04 N	6.00 E
Merredin, Austl.	96	F3	31.29 S	118.16 E
Merrick, N.Y., U.S.	194		40.39 N	73.33 W
Merrick, mtn., Scot., U.K.	10	F8	55.08 N	4.29 W
Merrick Bay, b., N.Y., U.S.	194		40.38 N	73.33 W
Merrickville, On., Can.	126	D14	44.55 N	75.50 W
Merrifield, Va., U.S.	202c		38.52 N	77.13 W
Merrill, Ia., U.S.	130	B1	42.43 N	96.14 W
Merrill, Mi., U.S.	126	E5	43.24 N	84.19 W
Merrill, Or., U.S.	148	A4	42.02 N	121.35 W
Merrill, Wi., U.S.	128	F9	45.10 N	89.40 W
Merrillan, Wi., U.S.	128	G8	44.27 N	90.49 W
Merrill C. Meigs Field, arpt., Il., U.S.	196		41.52 N	87.37 W
Merrillville, In., U.S.	130	C10	41.28 N	87.18 W
Merrimack, stm., U.S.	122	H5	42.49 N	70.48 W
Merrimack College, educ., Ma., U.S.	201		42.40 N	71.08 W
Merrimac Terrace, Ma., U.S.	201		42.49 N	71.00 W
Merriman, Ne., U.S.	140	E11	42.55 N	101.41 W
Merrionette Park, Il., U.S.	196		41.41 N	87.42 W
Merritt, B.C., Can.	144	F10	50.06 N	120.46 W
Merritt, Lake, res., Ca., U.S.	200		37.48 N	122.16 W
Merritt Island, Fl., U.S.	132	H5	28.21 N	80.42 W
Merritt Reservoir, res., Ne., U.S.	140	E11	42.37 N	100.53 W
Merriwa, Austl.	98	I8	32.08 S	150.21 E
Mer Rouge, La., U.S.	134	E7	32.46 N	91.48 W
Merrygoen, Austl.	98	H7	31.50 S	149.14 E
Merrylands, Austl.	192a		33.50 S	150.59 E
Merrymount Park, p.o.i., Ma., U.S.	201		42.16 N	71.01 W
Merryville, La., U.S.	136	D14	30.45 N	93.32 W
Mersa Matruh, Egypt	82	A5	31.20 N	27.13 E
Mersa Matruh, state, Egypt	191c		29.55 N	31.09 E
Merscheid, ngh., Ger.	181		51.10 N	7.01 E
Mersea Island, i., Eng., U.K.	10	J14	51.47 N	0.56 E
Merseburg, Ger.	24	E7	51.21 N	11.59 E
Mersey, stm., Austl.	99a	n13	41.10 S	146.22 E
Mersey, stm., N.S., Can.	122	F12	44.02 N	64.43 W
Merseyside, co., Eng., U.K.	180		53.25 N	2.50 W
Merseyside, hist. reg., Eng., U.K.	180		53.25 N	2.50 W

Name	Page	Map Ref.	Latitude	Longitude
Mersey Tunnel, trans., Eng., U.K.	180		53.24 N	3.00 W
Mersin see İçel, Tur.	42	G6	36.48 N	34.37 E
Mersing, Malay.	64	K6	2.25 N	103.50 E
Mērsrags, Lat.	26	C6	57.21 N	23.05 E
Merstham, Eng., U.K.	178		51.16 N	0.09 W
Merta, India	70	E5	26.39 N	74.02 E
Merta Road, India	70	E4	26.43 N	73.55 E
Merthyr Tydfil, Wales, U.K.	10	J9	51.45 N	3.22 W
Merti, Kenya	86	D7	1.02 N	38.39 E
Mértola, Port.	28	G3	37.38 N	7.40 W
Mertvyj Kultuk, sor, l., Kaz.	42	C15	45.25 N	54.00 E
Mertz Glacier Tongue, ice, Ant.	103	B19	67.31 S	144.57 E
Mertzon, Tx., U.S.	136	C7	31.16 N	100.49 W
Méru, Fr.	20	E11	49.14 N	2.08 E
Meru, Kenya	86	D7	0.03 N	37.39 E
Meruoca, Braz.	170	B5	3.28 S	40.28 W
Merweville, S. Afr.	90	H5	32.39 S	21.30 E
Merwin, Lake, res., Wa., U.S.	146	E4	45.58 N	122.29 W
Mëry, Bela.	26	E10	55.37 N	27.38 E
Méry-sur-Oise, Fr.	179		49.04 N	2.11 E
Merzifon, Tur.	42	E6	40.52 N	35.27 E
Merzig, Ger.	24	G2	49.26 N	6.38 E
Mesa, Az., U.S.	150	J5	33.25 N	111.49 W
Mesa, stm., Spain	28	C9	41.13 N	1.48 W
Mesabi Range, hills, Mn., U.S.	128	D6	47.30 N	92.50 W
Mesagne, Italy	32	D11	40.33 N	17.48 E
Mesa Mountain, mtn., Co., U.S.	138	D2	37.55 N	106.38 W
Mesáras, Órmos, b., Grc.	34	H7	34.53 N	24.19 E
Mesa Verde National Park, p.o.i., Co., U.S.	150	F8	37.14 N	108.26 W
Mescalero, N.M., U.S.	138	H3	33.10 N	105.46 W
Mescalero Apache Indian Reservation, ind. res., N.M., U.S.	138	H3	33.12 N	105.40 W
Meščerino, Russia	26	G20	53.36 N	37.23 E
Meščerskij, ngh., Russia	183b		55.40 N	37.25 E
Meschede, Ger.	24	E4	51.20 N	8.17 E
Mescit Tepe, mtn., Tur.	48	F6	40.22 N	41.11 E
Meščovsk, Russia	26	F18	54.18 N	35.17 E
Meščura, Russia	12	E24	63.20 N	50.55 E
Mèsè Atet, Mya.	64	C3	18.38 N	97.39 E
Mesero, Italy	184b		45.30 N	8.51 E
Mesewa see Massawa, Erit.	82	D7	15.37 N	39.25 E
Mesgarābād, Iran	185d		35.37 N	51.31 E
Mesgouez, Lac, l., Qc., Can.	110	E16	51.25 N	75.06 W
Meshed see Mashhad, Iran	72	B8	36.17 N	59.35 E
Meshgīn Shahr, Iran	74	A10	38.24 N	47.40 E
Mesick, Mi., U.S.	126	D4	44.23 N	85.42 W
Mesilla, N.M., U.S.	150	K10	32.15 N	106.45 W
Mesjagutovo, Russia	40	D20	55.31 N	58.15 E
Meškuičiai, Lith.	26	D6	56.04 N	23.28 E
Meskum, Indon.	66	C3	1.34 N	102.01 E
Mesógeia, hist. reg., Grc.	185c		37.56 N	23.53 E
Mesogéios Thálassa see Mediterranean Sea, s.	80	C7	35.00 N	20.00 E
Mesolóngi, Grc.	34	E4	38.22 N	21.15 E
Mesopotamia, hist. reg., Asia	74	D9	34.00 N	44.00 E
Mesquita, Braz.	170	J4	19.13 S	42.35 W
Mesquite, Nv., U.S.	150	G2	36.48 N	114.03 W
Mesquite, Tx., U.S.	136	B11	32.46 N	96.36 W
Messalo, stm., Moz.	88	C6	11.40 S	40.25 E
Messina, Italy	32	F9	38.11 N	15.33 E
Messina, S. Afr.	90	C9	22.22 S	30.01 E
Messina, Gulf of see Messiniakós Kólpos, b., Grc.	34	G5	36.48 N	22.07 E
Messina, Stretto di, strt., Italy	32	F9	38.08 N	15.35 E
Messíni, Grc.	34	F4	37.03 N	22.00 E
Messíni, hist., Grc.	34	F4	37.12 N	21.52 E
Messiniakós Kólpos, b., Grc.	34	G5	36.48 N	22.07 E
Messix Peak, mtn., Ut., U.S.	150	B4	41.29 N	112.31 W
Messkirch, Ger.	24	H5	47.59 N	9.06 E
Messojaha, stm., Russia	50	C4	67.54 N	77.28 E
Messy, Fr.	179		48.58 N	2.42 E
Mestá, Grc.	34	E8	38.15 N	25.53 E
Mesta (Néstos), stm., Eur.	34	B6	40.51 N	24.48 E
Mestghanem, Alg.	84	B4	35.56 N	0.05 E
Mestre, ngh., Italy	30	E9	45.29 N	12.13 E
Mesuji, stm., Indon.	66	E4	4.08 S	105.48 E
Meta, state, Col.	168	F5	3.30 N	73.00 W
Meta, stm., S.A.	168	D7	6.10 N	67.28 W
Métabetchouan, Qc., Can.	122	B5	48.26 N	71.52 W
Métabetchouane, stm., Qc., Can.	122	B4	48.25 N	71.58 W
Metagācha, India	190b		22.38 N	88.31 E
Meta Incognita Peninsula, pen., Nu., Can.	110	C17	62.45 N	68.30 W
Metairie, La., U.S.	134	H8	29.58 N	90.09 W
Metaline Falls, Wa., U.S.	146	B9	48.51 N	117.21 W
Metallifere, Colline, mts., Italy	30	G7	43.12 N	10.57 E
Metallostroj, Russia	183a		59.47 N	30.33 E
Metamora, Il., U.S.	130	D8	40.47 N	89.21 W
Metán, Arg.	172	B5	25.30 S	64.57 W
Metangula, Moz.	88	C5	12.41 S	34.49 E
Metapán, El Sal.	156	E3	14.19 N	89.26 W
Metaponto, hist., Italy	32	D10	40.23 N	16.50 E
Metapontum see Metaponto, hist., Italy	32	D10	40.23 N	16.50 E
Metauro, stm., Italy	30	G9	43.50 N	13.03 E
Meteghan, N.S., Can.	122	F10	44.12 N	66.07 W
Metéora, rel., Grc.	34	D4	39.46 N	21.36 E
Meteor Crater, crat., Az., U.S.	150	H6	35.10 N	110.56 W
Metharaw, Mya.	64	D4	16.11 N	98.07 E
Methler, Ger.	181		51.35 N	7.37 E
Methow, Wa., U.S.	146	B7	48.07 N	120.00 W
Methow, stm., Wa., U.S.	146	B6	48.02 N	119.53 W
Methven, N.Z.	102	F4	43.38 S	171.37 E
Metica, stm., Col.	168	F5	4.09 N	72.55 W
Metiskow, Ab., Can.	142	B3	52.24 N	110.37 W
Metković, Cro.	30	G14	43.03 N	17.39 E
Metlakatla, Ak., U.S.	109	E13	55.06 N	131.34 W
Metlatonoc, Mex.	154	G9	17.10 N	98.21 W
Metlika, Slvn.	30	E12	45.38 N	15.18 E
Meto, Bayou, stm., Ar., U.S.	134	C7	34.04 N	91.26 W
Metolius, stm., Or., U.S.	146	F5	44.35 N	121.16 W
Metropolis, Il., U.S.	130	G9	37.09 N	88.44 W
Metropolitan, Mi., U.S.	126	C2	45.59 N	87.51 W
Metropolitan Beach, p.o.i., Mi., U.S.	199		42.35 N	82.48 W
Metropolitan Museum of Art, bldg., N.Y., U.S.	194		40.47 N	73.58 W
Métsovo, Grc.	34	D4	39.46 N	21.10 E
Mettawa, Il., U.S.	196		42.14 N	87.56 W
Metter, Ga., U.S.	132	D3	32.23 N	82.03 W
Mettetal Airport, arpt., Mi., U.S.	199		42.21 N	83.27 W
Mettuppālaiyam, India	69	F3	11.18 N	76.56 E
Mettūr, India	69	F3	11.47 N	77.48 E
Metz, Fr.	20	E15	49.07 N	6.09 E
Metzingen, Ger.	24	H5	48.32 N	9.17 E
Metzkausen, Ger.	181		51.16 N	6.57 E
Meu, stm., Fr.	20	F7	48.00 N	1.45 W
Meudon, Fr.	179		48.48 N	2.14 E
Meudon, Bois de, p.o.i., Fr.	179		48.47 N	2.12 E
Meul, stm., S. Afr.	90	F9	27.56 S	28.51 E
Meulaboh, Indon.	64	J2	4.08 N	96.07 E
Meureudu, Indon.	64	J3	5.14 N	96.15 E
Meurthe, stm., Fr.	20	F15	48.46 N	6.08 E
Meurthe-et-Moselle, state, Fr.	20	F15	48.35 N	6.10 E
Meuse, state, Fr.	20	E14	49.00 N	5.30 E
Meuse (Maas), stm., Eur.	20	F14	51.49 N	5.00 E
Meuselwitz, Ger.	24	E8	51.02 N	12.18 E
Mexia, Tx., U.S.	136	C11	31.40 N	96.29 W
Mexiana, Ilha, i., Braz.	164	C8	0.02 S	49.35 W
Mexicali, Mex.	120	E5	32.38 N	115.29 W
Mexican Hat, Ut., U.S.	150	F7	37.11 N	109.52 W
México see Ciudad de México, Mex.	154	F9	19.24 N	99.09 W
Mexico, Me., U.S.	122	F6	44.33 N	70.32 W
Mexico, Mo., U.S.	130	E6	39.10 N	91.53 W
Mexico, N.Y., U.S.	126	E13	43.27 N	76.13 W
México, state, Mex.	154	F9	19.20 N	99.45 W
Mexico, ctry., N.A.	152	C4	23.00 N	102.00 W
México see Mexico, ctry., N.A.	152	C4	23.00 N	102.00 W
México, Golfo de see Mexico, Gulf of, b., N.A.	152	B6	25.00 N	90.00 W
Mexico, Gulf of, b., N.A.	152	B6	25.00 N	90.00 W
Mexico Basin, unds.	176	F5	25.05 N	91.53 W
Mexico Bay, b., N.Y., U.S.	126	E13	43.32 N	76.17 W
Mexico Beach, Fl., U.S.	134	H13	29.56 N	85.23 W
Mexico City see Ciudad de México, Mex.	154	F9	19.24 N	99.09 W
Mey, Castle of, hist., Scot., U.K.	10	C9	58.38 N	3.13 W
Meycauayan, Phil.	68	C3	14.44 N	120.57 E
Meydān-e Gel, pl., Iran	74	F14	29.04 N	54.50 E
Meydān Khvolah, Afg.	70	B2	33.36 N	69.51 E
Meyersdale, Pa., U.S.	124	E6	39.48 N	79.01 W
Meymaneh, Afg.	72	B9	35.55 N	64.48 E
Meymeh, Iran	74	D12	33.26 N	51.09 E
Meymeh (Tīb), stm., Asia	74	D10	32.01 N	47.14 E
Meyronne, Sk., Can.	142	E7	49.40 N	106.49 W
Meyungs, Palau	100b	g7	7.21 N	134.27 E
Méža (M'oža), stm., Eur.	26	E14	55.43 N	31.30 E
Meža, stm., Slvn.	30	D11	46.33 N	15.02 E
Meẓada, Ḥorvot (Masada), hist., Isr.	76	G6	31.19 N	35.21 E
Mezcala, Mex.	154	G9	17.55 N	99.36 W
Mezcalapa, stm., Mex.	154	G12	17.57 N	92.54 W
Mezdra, Blg.	36	F10	43.08 N	23.43 E
Meždurečensk, Russia	48	D15	53.40 N	88.06 E
Meždurečenskij, Russia	48	C10	59.35 N	65.54 E
Mèze, Fr.	22	F9	43.25 N	3.35 E
Mézel, Fr.	22	F12	43.59 N	6.11 E
Mezen', Russia	12	D21	65.50 N	44.14 E
Mezen', stm., Russia	12	D23	65.52 N	44.08 E
Mézenc, Mont, mtn., Fr.	22	E10	44.55 N	4.11 E
Mezenskaja guba, b., Russia	12	C20	66.40 N	43.45 E
Mezhyrich, Ukr.	38	C13	50.41 N	34.29 E
Mežica, Slvn.	30	D11	46.31 N	14.50 E
Mézières-sur-Seine, Fr.	179		48.58 N	1.48 E
Mézin, Fr.	22	E6	44.03 N	0.16 E
Mezőberény, Hung.	36	C8	46.49 N	21.01 E
Mezőcsát, Hung.	36	B7	47.49 N	20.54 E
Mezőkovácsháza, Hung.	36	C7	46.24 N	20.54 E
Mezőkövesd, Hung.	36	B7	47.48 N	20.34 E
Mezőtúr, Hung.	36	B7	47.00 N	20.37 E
Mezquital, Mex.	154	D6	23.29 N	104.22 W
Mezquital, stm., Mex.	154	D6	22.49 N	104.54 W
Mézy, Fr.	179		49.00 N	1.53 E
Mezzomerico, Italy	184b		45.37 N	8.36 E
Mfangano Island, i., Kenya	86	E6	0.28 S	34.01 E
Mgači, Russia	50	F17	51.04 N	142.15 E
Mgeta, Tan.	86	F7	8.17 S	36.06 E
Mglin, Russia	26	G15	53.03 N	32.50 E
M'Goun, Irhil, mtn., Mor.	84	C3	31.31 N	6.25 W
M'hai, B'nom, mtn., Viet.	64	G8	11.21 N	107.50 E
Mhasvād, India	69	C2	17.37 N	74.47 E
Mhow, India	70	G5	22.33 N	75.45 E
Mi, stm., China	58	H5	27.09 N	112.51 E
Mi, stm., China	58	C8	37.07 N	119.09 E
Mia, Oued, stm., Alg.	84	D5	30.47 N	4.54 E
Mia-dong, ngh., Kor., S.	189b		37.37 N	127.01 E
Miahuatlán de Porfirio Díaz, Mex.	154	G10	16.19 N	96.36 W
Miajadas, Spain	28	E5	39.09 N	5.54 W
Miamèrè, C.A.R.	86	C4	8.52 N	19.50 E
Miami, Mb., Can.	142	E15	49.20 N	98.10 W
Miami, Az., U.S.	150	J6	33.23 N	110.52 W
Miami, Fl., U.S.	132	K5	25.47 N	80.13 W
Miami, Ok., U.S.	130	H3	36.52 N	94.52 W
Miami, Tx., U.S.	138	F8	35.41 N	100.38 W
Miami Beach, Fl., U.S.	132	K5	25.47 N	80.07 W
Miami Canal, can., Fl., U.S.	132	J5	25.47 N	80.14 W
Miamisburg, Oh., U.S.	124	E1	39.38 N	84.16 W
Miami Springs, Fl., U.S.	132	K5	25.49 N	80.17 W
Miān Channūn, Pak.	70	C4	30.26 N	72.20 E
Mianchi, China	58	D4	34.45 N	111.45 E
Miāndoāb, Iran	74	B10	36.57 N	46.06 E
Miandrivazo, Madag.	88	D8	19.32 S	45.27 E
Mianduhe, China	52	B9	49.05 N	121.02 E
Miāneh, Iran	74	B10	37.25 N	47.42 E
Miang, Phu, mtn., Thai.	64	D5	17.43 N	101.01 E
Miangas, Pulau, i., Indon.	68	H6	5.33 N	126.35 E
Mianning, China	52	F5	28.39 N	102.09 E
Mianus, East Branch, stm., U.S.	194		41.06 N	73.35 W
Mianus Reservoir, res., U.S.	194		41.08 N	73.37 W
Miānwāli, Pak.	70	B3	32.34 N	71.32 E
Mianxian, China	58	E2	33.09 N	106.50 E
Mianyang, China	58	F1	31.28 N	104.43 E
Mianzhu, China	52	E5	31.26 N	104.09 E
Miaodao Qundao, is., China	58	B9	38.07 N	120.49 E
Miaoli, Tai.	58	I9	24.33 N	120.48 E
Miao Ling, mts., China	58	I2	26.15 N	107.26 E
Miass, Russia	48	C10	54.59 N	60.06 E
Miass, stm., Russia	48	C10	56.05 N	64.30 E
Miastko, Pol.	24	B12	54.00 N	16.58 E
Mica, S. Afr.	90	D10	24.07 S	30.48 E
Mica Mountain, mtn., Az., U.S.	150	K6	32.13 N	110.33 W
Micang Shan, mts., China	58	E2	32.41 N	107.07 E
Micanopy, Fl., U.S.	132	G3	29.30 N	82.16 W
Miccosukee, Lake, res., Fl., U.S.	132	F2	30.33 N	83.58 W
Miccosukee Indian Reservation, ind. res., Fl., U.S.	132	J5	26.10 N	80.50 W
Michalovce, Slvk.	24	H17	48.45 N	21.55 E
Michaud, Point, c., N.S., Can.	122	E16	45.34 N	60.41 W
Micheal Peak, mtn., B.C., Can.	144	C4	53.32 N	126.26 W
Michel, B.C., Can.	144	G16	49.40 N	114.46 W
Michelson, Mount, mtn., Ak., U.S.	109	C11	69.19 N	144.17 W
Miches, Dom. Rep.	156	C13	18.59 N	69.03 W
Michigamme, stm., Mi., U.S.	126	B2	46.04 N	88.13 W
Michigan, N.D., U.S.	142	F15	48.01 N	98.07 W
Michigan, state, U.S.	114	E8	44.00 N	85.00 W
Michigan, stm., Co., U.S.	140	G6	40.52 N	106.20 W
Michigan, Lake, l., U.S.	126	E2	44.00 N	87.00 W
Michigan, University of, educ., Mi., U.S.	199		42.17 N	83.44 W
Michigan Center, Mi., U.S.	126	F5	42.13 N	84.19 W
Michigan City, In., U.S.	130	C11	41.42 N	86.53 W
Michigan Stadium, p.o.i., Mi., U.S.	199		42.16 N	83.45 W
Michigan State Fair Grounds, p.o.i., Mi., U.S.	199		42.27 N	83.07 W
Michillinda, Ca., U.S.	198		34.07 N	118.05 W
Michipicoten Island, i., On., Can.	114	C7	47.45 N	85.45 W
Michoacán, state, Mex.	154	F8	19.10 N	101.50 W
Michów, Pol.	24	E18	51.31 N	22.19 E
Mickleham, Eng., U.K.	178		51.16 N	0.19 W
Mickleton, N.J., U.S.	203		39.47 N	75.14 W
Mickle Trafford, Eng., U.K.	180		53.13 N	2.50 W
Micoud, St. Luc.	159c	m7	13.49 N	60.53 W
Micronesia, is., Oc.	94	C6	11.00 N	159.00 E
Micronesia, Federated States of, ctry., Oc.	92	C6	5.00 N	152.00 E
Mičurinsk, Russia	40	E12	52.53 N	40.28 E
Midai, Pulau, i., Indon.	66	B5	3.00 N	107.47 E
Midale, Sk., Can.	142	E10	49.23 N	103.25 W
Mid-Atlantic Ridge, unds.	176	F9	50.00 S	9.00 W
Midbar Yehuda see Wilderness of Judaea, des., Asia	76	G6	31.30 N	35.18 E
Middelburg, Neth.	20	C12	51.30 N	3.37 E
Middelburg, S. Afr.	90	D9	25.46 S	29.28 E
Middelburg, S. Afr.	90	G7	31.29 S	25.00 E
Middelfart, Den.	16	L7	55.30 N	9.45 E
Middle, stm., B.C., Can.	144	A5	54.51 N	125.07 W
Middle, stm., Ia., U.S.	130	C3	41.29 N	93.24 W
Middle, stm., Mn., U.S.	128	C1	48.22 N	97.05 W
Middle Alkali Lake, l., Ca., U.S.	148	B5	41.31 N	120.06 W
Middle America Trench, unds.	174	H29	14.43 N	95.01 W
Middle Andaman, i., India	62	F7	12.30 N	92.50 E
Middle Bay, b., N.Y., U.S.	194		40.37 N	73.36 W
Middleboro, Ma., U.S.	124	C15	41.53 N	70.55 W
Middle Bosque, stm., Tx., U.S.	136	C10	31.29 N	97.15 W
Middlebourne, W.V., U.S.	124	E5	39.29 N	80.53 W
Middle Breakwater, trans., Ca., U.S.	198		33.43 N	118.13 W
Middlebro, Mb., Can.	128	B3	49.00 N	95.25 W
Middle Brook, stm., N.J., U.S.	194		40.39 N	74.41 W
Middle Brook, stm., N.J., U.S.	194		40.33 N	74.33 W
Middle Brook, East Branch, stm., N.J., U.S.	194		40.35 N	74.33 W
Middle Brook, West Branch, stm., N.J., U.S.	194		40.35 N	74.33 W
Middleburg, N.Y., U.S.	124	B11	42.36 N	74.19 W
Middleburg, Pa., U.S.	124	D8	40.46 N	77.02 W
Middlebury, Vt., U.S.	126	E16	44.01 N	73.10 W
Middlebush, N.J., U.S.	194		40.29 N	74.32 W
Middle Caicos, i., T./C. Is.	156	B12	21.47 N	71.47 W
Middle Channel, mth., Mi., U.S.	199		42.33 N	82.42 W
Middle Concho, stm., Tx., U.S.	136	C7	31.27 N	100.25 W
Middle Fabius, stm., Mo., U.S.	130	D5	39.58 N	91.35 W
Middlefield, Oh., U.S.	124	C4	41.27 N	81.04 W
Middlegate, Norf. I.	100i	y25	29.02 S	167.57 E
Middle Ground, i., India	190c		18.55 N	72.51 E
Middle Harbour, b., Austl.	192a		33.48 S	151.14 E
Middle Head, c., Austl.	192a		33.50 S	151.16 E
Middle Loup, stm., Ne., U.S.	140	F14	41.16 N	98.24 W
Middlemount, Austl.	98	D7	22.49 S	148.37 E
Middle Musquodoboit, N.S., Can.	122	E13	45.03 N	63.09 W
Middle Nodaway, stm., Ia., U.S.	130	C3	40.54 N	95.00 W
Middle Pease, stm., Tx., U.S.	138	G8	34.14 N	100.07 W
Middle Point, Oh., U.S.	124	D1	40.50 N	84.23 W
Middleport, Oh., U.S.	124	E3	39.01 N	82.03 W
Middle Raccoon, stm., Ia., U.S.	128	J4	41.34 N	94.12 W
Middle Reservoir, res., Ma., U.S.	201		42.27 N	71.07 W
Middle River Neck, pen., Md., U.S.	202b		39.22 N	76.23 W
Middle River Rouge, stm., Mi., U.S.	199		42.20 N	83.15 W
Middle Rouge Parkway, p.o.i., Mi., U.S.	199		42.21 N	83.21 W
Middle Run, stm., De., U.S.	203		39.41 N	75.43 W
Middlesboro, Ky., U.S.	124	H2	36.36 N	83.43 W
Middlesbrough, Eng., U.K.	10	G11	54.34 N	1.13 W
Middlesex, Belize	156	D3	17.02 N	88.31 W
Middlesex, N.J., U.S.	194		40.34 N	74.29 W
Middlesex, N.C., U.S.	124	I7	35.47 N	78.12 W
Middlesex Fells Reservation, p.o.i., Ma., U.S.	201		42.27 N	71.07 W
Middlesex Reservoir, res., N.J., U.S.	194		40.37 N	74.19 W
Middle Stewiacke, N.S., Can.	122	E13	45.12 N	63.07 W
Middleton, Austl.	98	D3	22.21 S	141.33 E
Middleton, N.S., Can.	122	F11	44.56 N	65.04 W
Middleton, Mi., U.S.	126	E5	43.11 N	84.42 W
Middleton, Tn., U.S.	134	B10	35.04 N	88.53 W
Middleton, Wi., U.S.	130	A8	43.05 N	89.29 W
Middleton Island, i., Ak., U.S.	109	E10	59.26 N	146.19 W
Middleton Pond, l., Ma., U.S.	201		42.36 N	71.02 W
Middleton Reef, at., Austl.	96	E11	29.22 S	159.09 E
Middletown, Ca., U.S.	148	E3	38.44 N	122.36 W
Middletown, Ct., U.S.	124	C13	41.33 N	72.38 W
Middletown, De., U.S.	124	E10	39.26 N	75.43 W
Middletown, Il., U.S.	128	K9	40.05 N	89.35 W
Middletown, In., U.S.	130	D12	40.02 N	85.32 W
Middletown, Ky., U.S.	130	F12	38.15 N	85.32 W
Middletown, Md., U.S.	124	E8	39.26 N	77.32 W
Middletown, N.Y., U.S.	124	C11	41.27 N	74.25 W
Middletown, Oh., U.S.	124	E1	39.30 N	84.23 W
Middletown, Pa., U.S.	124	D9	40.11 N	76.44 W
Middletown, R.I., U.S.	124	C14	41.32 N	71.17 W
Middletown, Va., U.S.	124	E7	39.01 N	78.16 W
Middleville, Mi., U.S.	130	B12	42.42 N	85.27 W
Middleville, N.Y., U.S.	194		43.08 N	74.58 W
Middle Yegua Creek, stm., Tx., U.S.	136	D11	30.18 N	96.44 W
Middle Yuba, stm., Ca., U.S.	148	D5	39.22 N	121.08 W
Midge Hall, Eng., U.K.	180		53.42 N	2.45 W
Midgic, N.B., Can.	122	E12	45.59 N	64.17 W
Midgley, Eng., U.K.	180		53.44 N	1.58 W
Midhordland, reg., Nor.	16	G3	60.10 N	5.15 E
Midi, Canal du, can., Fr.	22	F7	43.36 N	1.24 E
Midi de Bigorre, Pic du, mtn., Fr.	22	G6	42.56 N	0.08 E
Mid-Indian Basin, unds.	174	J10	10.00 S	80.00 E
Mid-Indian Ridge, unds.	174	L10	12.00 S	66.00 E
Midland, On., Can.	126	D10	44.44 N	79.52 W
Midland, Ca., U.S.	150	J2	33.52 N	114.48 W
Midland, Mi., U.S.	126	E5	43.36 N	84.13 W
Midland, N.C., U.S.	132	A5	35.13 N	80.29 W
Midland, S.D., U.S.	140	C11	44.03 N	101.10 W
Midland, Tx., U.S.	136	C5	31.59 N	102.04 W
Midland Beach, ngh., N.Y., U.S.	194		40.34 N	74.05 W
Midland Park, N.J., U.S.	194		40.59 N	74.08 W
Midlands, state, Zimb.	90	B10	20.40 S	30.01 E
Midleton, Ire.	10	J4	51.55 N	8.10 W
Midlothian, Tx., U.S.	136	B11	32.29 N	97.00 W
Midlothian Creek, stm., Il., U.S.	196		41.39 N	87.40 W
Midnapore, Ab., Can.	144	F16	50.55 N	114.05 W
Midnapore see Medinīpur, India	70	G11	22.26 N	87.20 E
Midongy Atsimo, Madag.	88	E8	23.35 S	47.01 E
Midori, ngh., Japan	186		35.32 N	139.34 E
Midori, stm., Japan	56	G3	32.41 N	130.38 E
Mid-Pacific Mountains, unds.	174	G19	20.00 N	170.00 E
Midsayap, Phil.	68	G5	7.11 N	124.32 E
Midshipman Point, c., Ca., U.S.	200		38.07 N	122.27 W
Midvale, De., U.S.	203		39.39 N	75.37 W
Midvale, Id., U.S.	146	F10	44.28 N	116.43 W
Midville, Ga., U.S.	132	D3	32.49 N	82.14 W
Midway, B.C., Can.	144	G12	49.00 N	118.47 W
Midway, Al., U.S.	134	E13	32.04 N	85.31 W
Midway, Ky., U.S.	130	F13	38.08 N	84.41 W
Midway, Tx., U.S.	136	C12	31.01 N	95.44 W
Midway, Ut., U.S.	150	C5	40.31 N	111.28 W
Midway City, Ca., U.S.	198		33.45 N	118.00 W
Midway Islands, dep., Oc.	44	G22	28.13 N	177.22 W
Midway Mall, shp. cen., Oh., U.S.	197a		41.24 N	82.07 W
Midway Park, N.C., U.S.	132	B8	34.44 N	77.22 W
Midwest, Wy., U.S.	140	D6	43.24 N	106.17 W
Midwest City, Ok., U.S.	138	F11	35.28 N	97.23 W
Midyan, reg., Sau. Ar.	74	G4	27.45 N	36.11 E
Midyat, Tur.	42	G9	37.25 N	41.23 E
Midžor (Midžur), mtn., Eur.	36	F9	43.23 N	22.42 E
Midžur (Midžor), mtn., Eur.	36	F9	43.23 N	22.42 E
Mie, Japan	56	G4	32.58 N	131.35 E
Mie, state, Japan	56	E9	34.30 N	136.30 E
Miechów, Pol.	24	F16	50.22 N	20.02 E
Międzybórz, Pol.	24	E13	51.24 N	17.39 E
Międzychód, Pol.	24	D11	52.36 N	15.54 E
Międzylesie, Pol.	24	F12	50.09 N	16.42 E
Międzyrzec Podlaski, Pol.	24	D18	51.59 N	22.46 E
Międzyrzecz, Pol.	24	D11	52.26 N	15.35 E
Międzyzdroje, Pol.	24	C10	53.55 N	14.27 E
Miélan, Fr.	22	F6	43.26 N	0.18 E
Mielec, Pol.	24	F17	50.17 N	21.27 E
Mielno, Pol.	24	B11	54.15 N	16.02 E
Mien, l., Swe.	16	K12	56.25 N	14.51 E
Mient'ienhuo Shan, mtn., Tai.	187d		25.11 N	121.30 E
Mier, Mex.	154	B9	26.25 N	99.09 W
Miercurea-Ciuc, Rom.	36	C12	46.22 N	25.48 E
Mieres, Spain	28	A5	43.15 N	5.45 W
Mieroszów, Pol.	24	F12	50.40 N	16.11 E
Miersdorf, Ger.	182a		52.20 N	13.37 E
Miersig, Rom.	36	C8	46.53 N	21.51 E
Mier y Noriega, Mex.	154	D8	23.24 N	100.07 W
Miesbach, Ger.	24	I7	47.47 N	11.49 E
Mī'ēso, Eth.	82	F8	9.14 N	40.45 E
Mieszkowice, Pol.	24	D10	52.46 N	14.29 E
Mifflinburg, Pa., U.S.	126	H12	40.54 N	77.03 W
Miguel Alemán, Presa, res., Mex.	154	F10	18.13 N	96.32 W
Miguel Alves, Braz.	170	C4	4.10 S	42.54 W
Miguel Auza, Mex.	154	C7	24.17 N	103.23 W
Miguel Calmon, Braz.	170	F5	11.26 S	40.36 W
Miguel Couto, Braz.	205a		22.43 S	43.27 W
Migueles, Arroyo de los, stm., Spain	184a		40.20 N	3.32 W
Miguel Hidalgo, Presa, res., Mex.	154	B4	26.32 N	108.34 W
Miguelópolis, Braz.	170	K1	20.12 S	48.03 W
Miguel Riglos, Arg.	172	H6	36.51 S	63.42 W
Migyaunglaung, Mya.	64	E3	14.38 N	98.07 E
Mihăești, Rom.	36	D12	45.06 N	25.00 E
Mihai Viteazu, Rom.	36	E15	44.39 N	28.41 E
Mihajlov, Russia	40	D11	54.14 N	39.02 E
Mihajlovka, Russia	38	D18	49.53 N	39.38 E
Mihajlovka, Russia	40	F13	50.04 N	43.14 E
Mihajlovka, Russia	48	D14	51.49 N	79.43 E
Mihajlovka, Russia	48	E7	47.37 N	46.52 E
Mihajlovka, Russia	50	E11	55.29 N	114.09 E
Mihajlovka, Russia	54	C10	43.55 N	132.00 E
Mihajlovka, Russia	183a		59.43 N	30.01 E
Mihajlovka, Russia	183a		60.04 N	30.14 E
Mihajlovo-Aleksandrovskij, Russia	38	D19	49.12 N	40.15 E
Mihajlovska, Kaz.	40	F19	50.17 N	55.23 E
Mihajlovskaja, Russia	40	F12	50.57 N	41.53 E
Mihajlovskij, Russia	12	F20	60.03 N	43.28 E
Mihajlovskoe, Russia	26	B20	58.22 N	37.39 E
Mihajlovskoe, Russia	183b		55.35 N	37.35 E
Mihalgazi, Tur.	34	C13	40.01 N	30.34 E
Mihalıççık, Tur.	34	D14	39.51 N	31.29 E
Mihanavičy, Bela.	26	G10	53.45 N	27.40 E
Mihara, Japan	56	E6	34.23 N	133.04 E
Mihara-yama, vol., Japan	56	E12	34.43 N	139.24 E
Mihel'sonovskij, Russia	183b		55.42 N	37.54 E
Mihnevo, Russia	26	E20	55.07 N	37.58 E
Mihninskaja, Russia	12	F21	60.25 N	46.14 E
Mijaly, Kaz.	40	G18	48.53 N	53.47 E
Mijares see Millars, stm., Spain	28	D10	39.55 N	0.02 W
Mijiang, China	54	C9	42.59 N	130.09 E
Mikame, Japan	56	F5	33.22 N	132.26 E
Mikasa, Japan	54	C14	43.14 N	141.52 E
Mikaševičy, Bela.	26	H10	52.13 N	27.29 E
Mikatou, Congo	191b		4.16 S	15.08 E
Mikhailo-Kotsiubyns'ke, Ukr.	38	B10	51.26 N	31.04 E
Mikhrot Timna'(King Solomon's Mines), hist., Isr.	76	I5	29.45 N	34.56 E
Mikindani, Tan.	86	G8	10.17 S	40.06 E
Mikkaichi, Japan	188		34.26 N	135.35 E
Mikkeli (Sankt Michel), Fin.	18	F14	61.41 N	27.16 E
Mikkeli, state, Fin.	18	F14	62.00 N	27.30 E
Mikkelsberget, mtn., Nor.	16	G9	60.26 N	11.50 E
Mikołajki, Pol.	24	C17	53.48 N	21.34 E
Mikołów, Pol.	24	F14	50.09 N	19.02 E
Mikre, Blg.	36	F11	43.02 N	24.31 E
Mikrí Préspa, Límni, l., Eur.	32	D15	40.46 N	21.06 E
Mikšino, Russia	26	C18	57.14 N	35.42 E
Mikstat, Pol.	24	E14	51.32 N	17.59 E
Mikulino, Russia	26	E14	55.03 N	31.05 E
Mikulkin, mys, c., Russia	12	C22	67.49 N	46.38 E
Mikulov, Czech Rep.	24	H12	48.48 N	16.38 E
Mikumi, Tan.	86	F7	7.30 S	37.01 E
Mikun', Russia	12	E23	62.21 N	50.05 E
Mikuni, Japan	56	C9	36.13 N	136.09 E
Mikura-jima, i., Japan	56	F12	33.52 N	139.36 E
Milaca, Mn., U.S.	128	F5	45.45 N	93.39 W
Miladummadulu Atoll, at., Mald.	62a	h12	6.15 N	73.15 E
Milagres, Braz.	170	D6	7.17 S	38.57 W
Milagro, Arg.	172	E5	31.00 S	65.59 W
Milagro, Ec.	168	I2	2.07 S	79.35 W
Milagros, Phil.	68	D4	12.13 N	123.30 E
Milan see Milano, Italy	30	E6	45.28 N	9.11 E
Milan, Ga., U.S.	132	D2	32.01 N	83.03 W
Milan, In., U.S.	130	E12	39.07 N	85.07 W
Milan, Mi., U.S.	124	B2	42.05 N	83.41 W
Milan, Mn., U.S.	128	F3	45.06 N	95.53 W
Milan, Mo., U.S.	130	D4	40.12 N	93.07 W
Milan, N.M., U.S.	150	H9	35.10 N	107.55 W
Milan, Tn., U.S.	130	I9	35.55 N	88.46 W
Milan Federal Correctional Institution, bldg., Mi., U.S.	199		42.06 N	83.40 W
Milang, Austl.	98	J2	35.24 S	138.57 E
Milange, Moz.	88	D6	16.05 S	35.46 E
Milano (Milan), Italy	30	E6	45.28 N	9.11 E
Milano (Milan), Italy	184b		45.28 N	9.12 E
Milano, Tx., U.S.	136	D11	30.42 N	96.52 W
Milâs, Tur.	34	F10	37.18 N	27.46 E
Milašavičy, Bela.	38	B6	51.39 N	27.56 E
Milaslavičy, Bela.	26	G15	53.41 N	32.15 E
Milavidy, Bela.	26	H8	52.55 N	25.44 E
Milazzo, Italy	32	F9	38.13 N	15.14 E
Milazzo, Golfo di, b., Italy	32	F9	38.15 N	15.20 E
Milbank, S.D., U.S.	128	F2	45.13 N	96.38 W
Milbanke Sound, strt., B.C., Can.	144	D2	52.18 N	128.33 W
Milburn, Ok., U.S.	134	C2	34.13 N	96.33 W
Milburn Creek, stm., N.Y., U.S.	194		40.38 N	73.36 W
Milden, Sk., Can.	142	C6	51.30 N	107.31 W
Mildmay, On., Can.	126	D8	44.02 N	81.07 W
Mildred, Pa., U.S.	124	C9	41.28 N	76.22 W
Mildura, Austl.	98	J4	34.11 S	142.10 E
Mile, China	52	G5	24.26 N	103.26 E
Miles, Austl.	98	F8	26.39 S	150.10 E
Miles, Tx., U.S.	136	C7	31.35 N	100.10 W
Miles, stm., Ma., U.S.	201		42.40 N	70.51 W
Miles City, Mt., U.S.	140	A7	46.24 N	105.50 W
Milestone, Sk., Can.	142	E9	49.59 N	104.31 W
Milesville, Pa., U.S.	197b		40.12 N	79.52 W
Milet, hist., Tur.	34	F10	37.28 N	27.15 E
Miletto, Monte, mtn., Italy	32	C8	41.27 N	14.22 E
Milevsko, Czech Rep.	24	G10	49.27 N	14.22 E
Milford, De., U.S.	124	F10	38.54 N	75.25 W
Milford, Il., U.S.	130	D10	40.37 N	87.41 W
Milford, In., U.S.	130	C12	41.24 N	85.50 W
Milford, Ia., U.S.	128	H3	43.19 N	95.09 W
Milford, Me., U.S.	122	F8	44.56 N	68.38 W
Milford, Md., U.S.	202b		39.21 N	76.44 W
Milford, Ma., U.S.	124	B14	42.08 N	71.31 W
Milford, Mi., U.S.	124	B2	42.35 N	83.35 W
Milford, N.H., U.S.	124	B14	42.50 N	71.39 W
Milford, Pa., U.S.	124	C11	41.19 N	74.48 W
Milford, Ut., U.S.	150	E4	38.23 N	113.00 W
Milford Brook, stm., N.J., U.S.	194		40.19 N	74.17 W
Milford Center, Oh., U.S.	124	D2	40.10 N	83.26 W
Milford Cross Roads, De., U.S.	203		39.43 N	75.44 W
Milford Haven, Wales, U.K.	10	J7	51.43 N	5.02 W
Milford Lake, res., Ks., U.S.	138	B11	39.15 N	97.00 W
Milford Ridge, Md., U.S.	202b		39.21 N	76.45 W
Milford Sound, strt., N.Z.	102	G2	44.31 S	167.48 E
Milford Station, N.S., Can.	122	E13	45.03 N	63.26 W
Milh, Bahr al-, res., Iraq	74	D8	32.46 N	43.35 E
Mili, at., Marsh. Is.	94	C8	6.03 N	171.54 E
Milian, stm., Malay.	66	A10	5.14 N	117.29 E
Milicz, Pol.	24	E13	51.31 N	17.17 E
Milíes, Grc.	34	D6	39.20 N	23.09 E
Miljatino, Russia	26	F17	54.29 N	34.20 E
Milk, stm., N.A.	118	C12	48.03 N	106.19 W
Milk, North Fork (North Milk), stm., N.A.	146	B13	49.08 N	112.23 W
Milk Creek, stm., Co., U.S.	150	C9	40.23 N	107.45 W
Mil'kovo, Russia	50	F20	54.41 N	158.38 E
Milk River, Ab., Can.	144	G18	49.09 N	112.04 W
Milk River Ridge Reservoir, res., Ab., Can.	144	G18	49.22 N	112.35 W
Mill, stm., Ct., U.S.	194		41.08 N	73.16 W
Mill, stm., Ma., U.S.	201		42.38 N	70.41 W
Mill, stm., Ma., U.S.	201		42.12 N	70.57 W
Mill, stm., Ma., U.S.	201		42.08 N	71.21 W
Mill, stm., Ma., U.S.	201		42.44 N	70.52 W
Mill, stm., N.Y., U.S.	194		40.38 N	73.39 W
Millard, Ne., U.S.	130	C1	41.12 N	96.07 W
Millars, stm., Spain	28	D10	39.55 N	0.02 W
Millau, Fr.	22	E9	44.05 N	3.04 E
Millboro, Va., U.S.	124	F6	37.58 N	79.35 W
Millbourne, Pa., U.S.	203		39.58 N	75.15 W
Millbrook, On., Can.	126	D11	44.08 N	78.26 W
Millbrook, Ma., U.S.	201		42.03 N	70.41 W
Millbrook, N.J., U.S.	194		40.52 N	74.33 W
Millbrook, N.Y., U.S.	124	C12	41.47 N	73.41 W
Mill Brook, stm., Ma., U.S.	201		42.31 N	71.18 W
Mill Brook, stm., N.J., U.S.	194		40.53 N	74.32 W
Mill Brook, stm., N.J., U.S.	194		40.29 N	74.23 W
Mill Brook, stm., N.J., U.S.	194		40.25 N	74.06 W
Millburn, N.J., U.S.	194		40.44 N	74.18 W
Mill City, Or., U.S.	146	F4	44.45 N	122.27 W
Millcreek, Pa., U.S.	124	B5	42.04 N	80.08 W
Millcreek, Ut., U.S.	150	C5	40.27 N	111.54 W
Mill Creek, W.V., U.S.	124	F5	38.43 N	79.58 W
Mill Creek, stm., Austl.	192a		33.59 S	151.01 E
Mill Creek, stm., De., U.S.	203		39.42 N	75.39 W
Mill Creek, stm., In., U.S.	130	E11	39.29 N	86.56 W
Mill Creek, stm., Ia., U.S.	128	I3	42.46 N	95.32 W
Mill Creek, stm., Ks., U.S.	138	B11	39.55 N	96.56 W
Mill Creek, stm., N.J., U.S.	194		40.48 N	74.03 W

Name Page Map Ref. Latitude Longitude

Mill Creek, stm., N.J., U.S. 203 40.02 N 74.55 W
Mill Creek, stm., Oh., U.S. 197a 41.25 N 81.38 W
Mill Creek, stm., Pa., U.S. 203 40.08 N 74.52 W
Mill Creek, stm., Pa., U.S. 203 40.03 N 75.16 W
Milledgeville, Ga., U.S. 132 C2 33.04 N 83.13 W
Milledgeville, Il., U.S. 130 C8 41.57 N 89.46 W
Mille Lacs, Lac des, l., On., Can. 128 B8 48.50 N 90.30 W
Mille Lacs Kathio State Park, p.o.i., Mn., U.S. 128 E5 46.08 N 93.43 W
Mille Lacs Lake, l., Mn., U.S. 128 E5 46.15 N 93.40 W
Millemont, Fr. 179 48.49 N 1.45 E
Millen, Ga., U.S. 132 D4 32.48 N 81.56 W
Miller, Mo., U.S. 130 G4 37.13 N 93.50 W
Miller, S.D., U.S. 140 C14 44.31 N 98.59 W
Miller Creek, stm., Ca., U.S. 200 38.02 N 122.30 W
Miller Mountain, mtn., Nv., U.S. 148 E7 38.03 N 118.11 W
Millerovo, Russia 40 G12 48.56 N 40.24 E
Miller Peak, mtn., Az., U.S. 150 L6 31.24 N 110.19 W
Millersburg, Ky., U.S. 124 F1 38.18 N 84.09 W
Millersburg, Mi., U.S. 126 C5 45.20 N 84.03 W
Millersburg, Oh., U.S. 124 D4 40.33 N 81.54 W
Millersburg, Pa., U.S. 124 D9 40.32 N 76.57 W
Millers Creek, stm., Tx., U.S. 138 H9 33.27 N 99.14 W
Millers Ferry, Al., U.S. 134 E11 32.06 N 87.22 W
Millers Island, Md., U.S. 202b 39.14 N 76.24 W
Millers Pond, l., N.Y., U.S. 194 40.51 N 73.12 W
Millersport, Oh., U.S. 126 I7 39.53 N 82.32 W
Millers Run, stm., Pa., U.S. 197b 40.22 N 80.07 W
Millerton, N.Y., U.S. 124 C12 41.57 N 73.30 W
Millerton Lake, res., Ca., U.S. 148 F6 37.01 N 119.41 W
Millet, Ab., Can. 144 C17 53.05 N 113.29 W
Millett, Tx., U.S. 136 F8 28.35 N 99.12 W
Millevaches, Plateau de, plat., Fr. 22 D8 45.39 N 2.07 E
Mill Green, Eng., U.K. 178 51.41 N 0.22 E
Mill Hall, Pa., U.S. 124 C8 41.06 N 77.29 W
Mill Hill, ngh., Eng., U.K. 178 51.37 N 0.13 W
Mill Hill, hill, Eng., U.K. 180 53.25 N 1.54 W
Millicent, Austl. 98 K3 37.35 S 140.20 E
Milligan, Fl., U.S. 134 G12 30.45 N 86.38 W
Milligan, Ne., U.S. 140 G15 40.30 N 97.24 W
Milligan Gulch, stm., N.M., U.S. 150 J9 33.36 N 107.01 W
Milligantown, Pa., U.S. 197b 40.33 N 79.41 W
Milliken, On., Can. 193b 43.49 N 79.18 W
Millington, Mi., U.S. 126 E6 43.16 N 83.31 W
Millington, Tn., U.S. 134 B9 35.20 N 89.54 W
Millinocket, Me., U.S. 122 E8 45.39 N 68.42 W
Mill Island, i., Ant. 103 B15 65.30 S 100.40 E
Mill Island, i., Nu., Can. 110 C15 64.00 N 78.00 W
Millmerran, Austl. 98 F8 27.52 S 151.16 E
Mill Neck, N.Y., U.S. 194 40.52 N 73.34 W
Mill Neck, pen., N.Y., U.S. 194 40.53 N 73.33 W
Mill Neck Creek, b., N.Y., U.S. 194 40.54 N 73.33 W
Mill Pond, l., N.Y., U.S. 194 40.53 N 73.22 W
Millport, Al., U.S. 134 D10 33.33 N 88.04 W
Mill Run Acres, Va., U.S. 202c 38.58 N 77.17 W
Millry, Al., U.S. 134 F10 31.38 N 88.18 W
Mills, Wy., U.S. 140 E6 42.50 N 106.21 W
Mills Creek, stm., Austl. 98 D4 22.24 S 143.05 E
Mills Creek, stm., Ca., U.S. 200 37.27 N 122.25 W
Mills Lake, l., N.T., Can. 110 C7 61.30 N 118.10 W
Millstatt, Aus. 30 D10 46.48 N 13.34 E
Millstone, N.J., U.S. 194 40.29 N 74.35 W
Millstone, stm., N.J., U.S. 194 40.33 N 74.34 W
Millstream, Austl. 96 D3 21.37 S 117.04 E
Milltown, In., U.S. 130 F11 38.20 N 86.16 W
Milltown, Mt., U.S. 146 D13 46.52 N 113.52 W
Milltown, Wi., U.S. 128 F6 45.31 N 92.30 W
Milltown Malbay, Ire. 10 I3 52.52 N 9.24 W
Millvale, Pa., U.S. 197b 40.28 N 79.58 W
Mill Valley, Ca., U.S. 148 F3 37.54 N 122.32 W
Millville, N.J., U.S. 124 E10 39.23 N 75.02 W
Millville Lake, N.H., U.S. 201 42.48 N 71.13 W
Millville Lake, l., N.H., U.S. 201 42.48 N 71.13 W
Millwood, Md., U.S. 202c 38.53 N 76.53 W
Millwood, Va., U.S. 124 E7 39.04 N 78.02 W
Millwood Lake, res., Ar., U.S. 134 D4 33.45 N 94.00 W
Milmont Park, Pa., U.S. 203 39.53 N 75.20 W
Milne Land, i., Grnld. 108 C20 70.41 N 26.45 W
Milnor, N.D., U.S. 140 A15 46.15 N 97.27 W
Milo, Ab., Can. 144 F18 50.34 N 112.52 W
Milo, Ia., U.S. 128 J5 41.17 N 93.26 W
Milon-la-Chapelle, Fr. 179 48.44 N 2.03 E
Milos, Grc. 34 G7 36.44 N 24.26 E
Milos, i., Grc. 34 G7 36.40 N 24.22 E
Miłosław, Pol. 24 D13 52.12 N 17.29 E
Milove, Ukr. 38 D19 49.23 N 40.08 E
Milpa Alta, ngh., Mex. 204a 19.11 N 99.01 W
Milparinka, Austl. 98 G3 29.45 S 141.56 E
Milroy, In., U.S. 130 E12 39.29 N 85.28 W
Milroy, Pa., U.S. 124 D8 40.42 N 77.35 W
Milspe, Ger. 181 51.18 N 7.21 E
Miltenberg, Ger. 24 G5 49.41 N 9.15 E
Milton, On., Can. 126 E10 43.30 N 79.52 W
Milton, N.Z. 102 H4 46.06 S 169.58 E
Milton, Fl., U.S. 134 G11 30.38 N 87.02 W
Milton, Ia., U.S. 130 D5 40.40 N 92.09 W
Milton, N.J., U.S. 194 41.02 N 74.32 W
Milton, N.D., U.S. 142 F15 48.37 N 98.02 W
Milton, Pa., U.S. 126 G13 41.01 N 76.50 W
Milton, Vt., U.S. 126 D16 44.38 N 73.06 W
Milton, Wi., U.S. 130 B9 42.46 N 88.56 W
Milton-Freewater, Or., U.S. 146 E8 45.55 N 118.23 W
Milton Harbor, b., N.Y., U.S. 194 40.57 N 73.42 W
Milton Keynes, Eng., U.K. 10 I12 52.01 N 0.45 W
Milton Point, c., N.Y., U.S. 194 40.57 N 73.42 W
Miltonvale, Ks., U.S. 138 B11 39.20 N 97.25 W
Miltou, Chad 82 E3 10.13 N 17.26 E
Miluo, stm., China 58 G5 28.50 N 113.03 E
Miluvatka, Ukr. 38 D17 49.20 N 38.11 E
Milverton, On., Can. 126 E8 43.34 N 80.55 W
Milwaukee, Wi., U.S. 128 H11 43.02 N 87.55 W
Milwaukee, stm., Wi., U.S. 128 H11 43.02 N 87.54 W
Milwaukie, Or., U.S. 146 E4 45.26 N 122.35 W
Milybulak, Kaz. 48 E13 48.57 N 75.13 E
Mimbres, stm., N.M., U.S. 150 K9 32.14 N 107.36 W
Mimbres Mountains, mts., N.M., U.S. 150 K9 32.45 N 107.45 W
Mimi, stm., Japan 56 G4 32.20 N 131.37 E
Mimico, ngh., On., Can. 193b 43.37 N 79.30 W
Mimico Creek, stm., On., Can. 193b 43.37 N 79.29 W
Mimizan-les-Bains, Fr. 22 E4 44.11 N 1.13 W
Mimoň, Czech Rep. 24 F10 50.39 N 14.44 E
Mimoso, Braz. 170 H1 15.04 S 48.08 W
Mimoso do Sul, Braz. 170 K5 21.03 S 41.21 W
Mims, Fl., U.S. 132 H5 28.40 N 80.50 W
Min, stm., China 52 F5 28.46 N 104.37 E
Min, stm., China 58 I8 26.04 N 119.32 E
Mina, Mex. 136 H7 26.01 N 100.31 W
Mina, Nv., U.S. 148 E7 38.23 N 118.05 W
Minā' al-Aḥmadī, Kuw. 74 F11 28.51 N 48.15 E
Mīnāb, Iran 72 D8 27.07 N 57.04 E
Minahasa, pen., Indon. 60 E7 1.00 N 124.35 E
Minakuchi, Japan 56 E9 34.57 N 136.10 E
Minam, stm., Or., U.S. 146 E9 45.37 N 117.43 W
Minamata, Japan 56 G3 32.11 N 130.25 E
Minami, ngh., Japan 186 35.24 N 139.36 E
Minami, ngh., Japan 188 34.58 N 135.45 E
Minami, ngh., Japan 188 34.40 N 135.31 E
Minami-Alps-kokuritsu-kōen, p.o.i., Japan 56 D11 35.40 N 138.13 E
Minamisenju, ngh., Japan 186 35.44 N 139.48 E
Minami-Tori-shima, i., Japan 46 G19 24.18 N 153.58 E
Minas, Cuba 156 B9 21.29 N 77.36 W
Minas, Indon. 66 C2 0.50 N 101.28 E
Minas, Ur. 172 G10 34.22 S 55.14 W
Minas Basin, b., N.S., Can. 122 E12 45.20 N 64.00 W
Minas Channel, strt., N.S., Can. 122 E12 45.15 N 64.45 W
Minas de Barroterán, Mex. 154 B8 27.39 N 101.19 W
Minas de Corrales, Ur. 172 E10 31.34 S 55.28 W
Minas de Matahambre, Cuba 156 A5 22.35 N 83.57 W
Minas de Oro, Hond. 156 E4 14.45 N 87.19 W
Minas de Riotinto, Spain 28 G4 37.42 N 6.35 W
Minas Gerais, state, Braz. 166 C8 18.00 S 44.00 W
Minas Novas, Braz. 170 I4 17.15 S 42.36 W
Minatare, Ne., U.S. 140 F9 41.47 N 103.29 W
Minatitlán, Mex. 154 F11 17.59 N 94.32 W
Minato, Japan 186 35.13 N 139.52 E
Minato, ngh., Japan 186 35.39 N 139.45 E
Minato, ngh., Japan 188 34.39 N 135.26 E
Minato, stm., Japan 186 35.13 N 139.52 E
Minbu, Mya. 64 B2 20.10 N 94.52 E
Minbya, Mya. 64 B1 20.21 N 93.16 E
Minbyin, Mya. 64 C1 19.17 N 93.32 E
Mincio, stm., Italy 30 E7 45.04 N 10.58 E
Minco, Ok., U.S. 138 F11 35.19 N 97.56 W
Minčol, mtn., Slvk. 24 G17 49.15 N 20.59 E
Mindanao, i., Phil. 68 G5 8.00 N 125.00 E
Mindanao, stm., Phil. 68 G5 7.15 N 124.13 E
Mindanao Sea see Bohol Sea, s., Phil. 68 F5 9.10 N 124.25 E
Mindego Creek, stm., Ca., U.S. 200 37.18 N 122.15 W
Mindego Hill, hill, Ca., U.S. 200 37.18 N 122.13 W
Mindelheim, Ger. 24 H6 48.02 N 10.29 E
Mindelo, C.V. 85a k10 16.52 N 24.59 W
Mindemoya, On., Can. 126 C7 45.43 N 82.09 W
Minden, On., Can. 126 D11 44.55 N 78.43 W
Minden, Ger. 24 D4 52.17 N 8.55 E
Minden, La., U.S. 134 E5 32.36 N 93.17 W
Minden, Ne., U.S. 140 G14 40.29 N 98.56 W
Minden, Nv., U.S. 148 E6 38.57 N 119.45 W
Minden, W.V., U.S. 124 G4 37.58 N 81.07 W
Minden City, Mi., U.S. 126 E7 43.40 N 82.46 W
Mindenmines, Mo., U.S. 130 G3 37.28 N 94.35 W
Minderoo, Austl. 96 D3 21.59 S 115.03 E
Mindon, Mya. 64 C2 19.20 N 94.44 E
Mindoro, i., Phil. 68 D3 12.50 N 121.05 E
Mindoro Strait, strt., Phil. 68 D3 12.20 N 120.40 E
Mine, Japan 56 E4 34.09 N 131.13 E
Minear Lake, l., Il., U.S. 196 42.17 N 87.57 W
Minebank Run, stm., Md., U.S. 202b 39.25 N 76.32 W
Mine Brook, stm., Ma., U.S. 201 42.08 N 71.26 W
Mine Brook, stm., Ma., U.S. 201 42.09 N 71.15 W
Mine Brook, stm., N.J., U.S. 194 40.41 N 74.38 W
Mine Centre, On., Can. 128 C6 48.45 N 92.36 W
Minehead, Eng., U.K. 10 J9 51.12 N 3.28 W
Mineiros, Braz. 166 C6 17.34 S 52.34 W
Mineola, Tx., U.S. 136 B12 32.40 N 95.29 W
Mineral, Wa., U.S. 146 D4 46.42 N 122.10 W
Mineral de Cucharas, Mex. 154 D6 22.52 N 105.19 W
Mineral'nye Vody, Russia 42 C10 44.12 N 43.07 E
Mineral Point, Wi., U.S. 130 B7 42.51 N 90.10 W
Mineral Springs, Ar., U.S. 134 D5 33.52 N 93.55 W
Mineral Wells, Tx., U.S. 136 B9 32.47 N 98.06 W
Minersville, Pa., U.S. 126 H13 40.41 N 76.17 W
Minersville, Ut., U.S. 150 E4 38.12 N 112.55 W
Mine Run, stm., Pa., U.S. 203 40.15 N 75.28 W
Minerva, Oh., U.S. 124 D4 40.43 N 81.05 W
Minervino Murge, Italy 32 C9 41.05 N 16.04 E
Mineville, N.Y., U.S. 126 D16 44.05 N 73.31 W
Minfeng, China 62 A5 37.03 N 82.39 E
Minga, D.R.C. 86 G5 11.26 S 27.41 E
Mingäçevir, Azer. 42 E12 40.45 N 47.02 E
Mingäçevir su anbarı (Mingechaur Reservoir), res., Azer. 42 E12 40.54 N 46.48 E
Mingāora, Pak. 62 B3 34.48 N 72.20 E
Mingary, Austl. 98 I3 32.08 S 140.43 E
Mingečaur see Mingäçevir, Azer. 42 E12 40.45 N 47.02 E
Mingečaurskoe vodohranilišče see Mingäçevir su anbarı, res., Azer. 42 E12 40.54 N 46.48 E
Mingechaur Reservoir see Mingäçevir su anbarı, res., Azer. 42 E12 40.54 N 46.48 E
Mingela, Austl. 98 B6 19.51 S 146.37 E
Mingenew, Austl. 96 E3 29.11 S 115.26 E
Mingin, Mya. 64 A2 22.52 N 94.38 E
Mingir, Mol. 38 G7 46.40 N 28.19 E
Minglanilla, Spain 28 E9 39.32 N 1.36 W
Mingo Creek, stm., Pa., U.S. 197b 40.13 N 79.57 W
Mingo Creek, stm., Pa., U.S. 203 40.10 N 75.32 W
Mingo Junction, Oh., U.S. 124 D5 40.19 N 80.36 W
Mingo Lake, l., Nu., Can. 110 C16 64.35 N 72.10 W
Mingorría, Spain 28 D6 40.45 N 4.40 W
Mingrel'skaja, Russia 38 I17 45.00 N 38.20 E
Mingshui, China 52 B10 47.10 N 125.54 E
Mingulay, i., Scot., U.K. 10 E5 56.49 N 7.38 W
Ming Village, shp. cen., Sing. 189c 1.18 N 103.45 E
Mingyuegou, China 54 C8 43.07 N 128.54 E
Minhang, China 58 F9 31.00 N 121.25 E
Minh Hai, Viet. 64 H7 9.00 N 105.10 E
Minhla, Mya. 64 B2 19.57 N 95.01 E
Minhla, Mya. 64 C2 17.57 N 95.42 E
Minho, hist. reg., Port. 28 C2 41.40 N 8.30 W
Minho (Miño), stm., Eur. 28 B2 41.54 N 8.47 W
Minićevo, Yugo. 36 F9 43.41 N 22.18 E
Minicoy Island, i., India 62 G3 8.16 N 73.03 E
Minier, Il., U.S. 130 D8 40.25 N 89.18 W
Minigwal, Lake, l., Austl. 96 E4 29.35 S 123.12 E
Minija, stm., Lith. 26 E4 55.21 N 21.15 E
Minilya, Austl. 96 D2 23.51 S 113.58 E
Minilya, stm., Austl. 96 D2 24.00 S 114.55 E
Miniota, Mb., Can. 142 D12 50.08 N 101.02 W
Ministro Rivadavia, Arg. 206 34.51 S 58.22 W
Minitonas, Mb., Can. 142 B12 52.05 N 101.02 W
Min-Kuš, Kyrg. 48 F12 41.40 N 74.28 E
Minle, China 52 D5 38.27 N 100.56 E
Minna, Nig. 84 H6 9.37 N 6.33 E
Minneapolis, Ks., U.S. 138 B11 39.07 N 97.42 W
Minneapolis, Mn., U.S. 128 G5 44.58 N 93.15 W
Minnechaduza Creek, stm., U.S. 140 E12 42.53 N 100.29 W
Minnedosa, Mb., Can. 142 D14 50.14 N 99.48 W
Minnehaha, Wa., U.S. 146 E4 45.39 N 122.37 W
Minneola, Ks., U.S. 138 D8 37.26 N 100.00 W
Minneosa Creek, stm., U.S. 138 F6 35.30 N 102.46 W
Minneota, Mn., U.S. 128 G2 44.33 N 96.00 W
Minnesota, state, U.S. 128 E4 46.00 N 94.15 W
Minnesota, stm., Mn., U.S. 128 G5 44.53 N 93.10 W
Minnesota Lake, Mn., U.S. 128 H5 43.50 N 93.50 W
Minnewanka, Lake, res., Ab., Can. 144 E15 51.15 N 115.20 W
Minnewaukan, N.D., U.S. 142 F14 48.03 N 99.14 W
Minnitaki Lake, l., On., Can. 128 B6 49.58 N 92.00 W
Mino, Japan 56 D9 35.32 N 136.55 E
Miño (Minho), stm., Eur. 28 B2 41.54 N 8.47 W
Minō, stm., Japan 188 34.47 N 134.57 E
Minocqua, Wi., U.S. 128 F9 45.53 N 89.40 W
Mino-Mikawa-kōgen, plat., Japan 56 D10 35.11 N 137.23 E
Minong, Wi., U.S. 128 E7 46.05 N 91.49 W
Minonk, Il., U.S. 130 D8 40.53 N 89.01 W
Minorca see Menorca, i., Spain 28 D15 40.00 N 4.00 E
Minoshō, Japan 188 34.39 N 135.49 E
Minot, Ma., U.S. 201 42.14 N 70.45 W
Minot, N.D., U.S. 142 F12 48.13 N 101.17 W
Minot Air Force Base, mil., N.D., U.S. 142 F12 48.26 N 101.21 W
Minqin, China 52 D5 38.41 N 103.10 E
Minqing, China 58 H8 26.11 N 118.52 E
Minquadale, De., U.S. 203 39.42 N 75.34 W
Minquan, China 58 D6 34.38 N 115.08 E
Minquiers, Plateau des, is., Jersey 20 F6 48.58 N 2.04 W
Min Shan, mts., China 52 E5 33.46 N 103.31 E
Minshât el-Bakkâri, Egypt 191c 30.01 N 31.08 E
Minshât Muhammad ʿAlī, Egypt 76 I1 29.10 N 30.38 E
Minsk, Bela. 26 G10 53.54 N 27.33 E
Minsk, state, Bela. 26 G10 53.45 N 27.45 E
Minskae uzvyšša, plat., Bela. 26 F10 53.59 N 27.16 E
Mińsk Mazowiecki, Pol. 24 D17 52.10 N 21.34 E
Minster, Oh., U.S. 124 D1 40.23 N 84.22 W
Minta, Cam. 86 D2 4.34 N 12.46 E
Mintard, Ger. 181 51.22 N 6.54 E
Minto, Austl. 192a 34.01 S 150.51 E
Minto, Mb., Can. 142 E13 49.23 N 100.00 W
Minto, N.B., Can. 122 D10 46.05 N 66.05 W
Minto, Yk., Can. 110 C3 62.35 N 136.49 W
Minto, N.D., U.S. 128 C1 48.17 N 97.21 W
Minto, Lac, l., Qc., Can. 110 D16 57.12 N 74.57 W
Minto Inlet, b., N.T., Can. 110 A7 71.20 N 117.00 W
Minton, Sk., Can. 142 E9 49.10 N 104.36 W
Minturn, Co., U.S. 138 B2 39.35 N 106.27 W
Minûf, Egypt 76 H1 30.27 N 30.55 E
Minulovo, Russia 183a 60.03 N 30.45 E
Minumadai-yōsui, can., Japan 186 35.50 N 139.42 E
Minusinsk, Russia 48 D16 53.42 N 91.41 E
Minvoul, Gabon 86 D2 2.09 N 12.08 E
Minxian, China 52 E5 34.26 N 104.01 E
Minya see El-Minya, Egypt 76 J1 28.05 N 30.45 E
Minya el-Qamh, Egypt 76 H2 30.31 N 31.21 E
Minya Konka see Gongga Shan, mtn., China 46 G14 29.35 N 101.51 E
Minyat el-Sîrig, ngh., Egypt 191c 30.05 N 31.15 E
Mio, Mi., U.S. 126 D5 44.39 N 84.07 W
Miquan, China 48 F15 44.03 N 87.32 E
Miquon, Pa., U.S. 203 40.04 N 75.16 W
Mir, Bela. 26 G9 53.27 N 26.28 E
Mira, Port. 28 D2 40.25 N 8.43 W
Mira, stm., N.S., Can. 122 E16 46.04 N 59.48 W
Mira, stm., Col. 168 G2 1.36 N 79.02 W
Mira, stm., Port. 28 G2 37.40 N 8.43 W
Mīrābād, Afg. 72 C9 30.24 N 61.50 E
Mira Bay, b., N.S., Can. 122 D17 46.02 N 59.56 W
Mirabel, Qc., Can. 193a 45.40 N 74.00 W
Mirabella, Gulf of see Mirampéllou, Kólpos, b., Grc. 34 H8 35.13 N 25.56 E
Mirabello, Ippodromo, p.o.i., Italy 184b 45.36 N 9.17 E
Miracema do Tocantins, Braz. 170 E1 9.32 S 48.24 W
Mirador, Braz. 170 D3 6.22 S 44.22 W
Mirador, Cerro, mtn., Peru 204d 11.57 S 77.02 W
Miradouro, Braz. 170 K4 20.53 S 42.20 W
Miraflores, Arg. 172 D4 28.35 S 65.54 W
Miraflores, Col. 168 G5 1.24 N 72.17 W
Miraflores, Col. 168 E5 5.13 N 73.12 W
Miraflores, Peru 204d 12.07 S 77.02 W
Miraflores, Palacio, bldg., Ven. 204c 10.31 N 66.55 W
Mīrah, Wādī al-, stm., Asia 74 D7 32.37 N 41.49 E
Miraj, India 69 C2 16.49 N 74.38 E
Miramar, Arg. 172 E6 30.55 S 62.39 W
Miramar, Arg. 172 I9 38.15 S 57.51 W
Miramar, Moz. 90 C12 23.47 S 35.32 E
Miramar, ngh., Cuba 204b 23.07 N 82.25 W
Miramare, Castello di, hist., Italy 30 E10 45.42 N 13.43 E
Miramas, Fr. 22 F10 43.35 N 5.00 E
Mirambeau, Fr. 22 D5 45.23 N 0.34 W
Miramichi Bay, b., N.B., Can. 122 C11 47.08 N 65.08 W
Mirampéllou, Kólpos, b., Grc. 34 H8 35.13 N 25.56 E
Mīram Shāh, Pak. 70 B2 33.00 N 70.05 E
Mīrān, Pak. 70 C3 31.23 N 70.43 E
Miranda, Austl. 192a 34.02 S 151.06 E
Miranda, Braz. 166 D5 20.14 S 56.23 W
Miranda, Col. 168 F3 3.15 N 76.14 W
Miranda, Ca., U.S. 148 C2 40.13 N 123.48 W
Miranda, state, Ven. 168 B8 10.15 N 66.25 W
Miranda, stm., Braz. 166 D5 19.24 S 57.19 W
Miranda, Aerodromo, arpt., Ven. 204c 10.29 N 66.50 W
Miranda de Ebro, Spain 28 B7 42.41 N 2.56 W
Miranda do Douro, Port. 28 C4 41.29 N 6.16 W
Mirande, Fr. 22 F6 43.31 N 0.25 E
Mirandela, Port. 28 C3 41.29 N 7.11 W
Mirando City, Tx., U.S. 136 G8 27.26 N 99.00 W
Mirandola, Italy 30 F8 44.53 N 11.03 E
Mira Táglio, Italy 30 E9 45.26 N 12.07 E
Miravalles, Volcán, vol., C.R. 156 G5 10.45 N 85.10 W
Miravete, Puerto de, p., Spain 28 E5 39.42 N 5.44 W
Mirbāṭ, Oman 72 F7 16.59 N 54.42 E
Mirecourt, Fr. 20 F15 48.18 N 6.08 E
Miri, Malay. 66 A9 4.22 N 113.59 E
Miria, Niger 84 G6 13.43 N 9.09 E
Miriam Vale, Austl. 98 E8 24.20 S 151.34 E
Mirim, Lagoa (Merín, Laguna), b., S.A. 172 F11 32.45 S 52.50 W
Mirimichi, Lake, l., Ma., U.S. 201 42.02 N 71.18 W
Miriñay, stm., Arg. 172 D9 30.10 S 57.37 W
Mirinzal, Braz. 170 A3 2.03 S 44.47 W
Miritiparaná, stm., Col. 168 H6 1.11 S 70.02 W
Miriyama, Pap. N. Gui. 101a a3 3.57 S 141.43 E
Mirke, ngh., Ger. 181 51.16 N 7.09 E
Mirna, stm., Cro. 30 E10 45.18 N 13.36 E
Mirnoe Ozero, Russia 48 C13 57.45 N 78.56 E
Mirnyj, Russia 40 E17 53.30 N 50.18 E
Mirnyj, Russia 50 D11 62.31 N 113.58 E
Mirnyy, sci., Ant. 103 B14 66.33 S 92.59 E
Mironeasa, Rom. 36 B14 46.58 N 27.25 E
Miroslav, Czech Rep. 24 H12 48.56 N 16.18 E
Mirosławiec, Pol. 24 C12 53.20 N 16.05 E
Mirove, Ukr. 38 F13 47.45 N 34.44 E
Mirow, Ger. 24 C8 53.16 N 12.49 E
Mirpur, Bngl. 70 G13 23.47 N 90.21 E
Mirpur, Pak. 70 B4 33.08 N 73.44 E
Mirpur Batoro, Pak. 70 F2 24.43 N 68.15 E
Mirpur Khās, Pak. 70 F2 25.31 N 69.00 E
Mirror, Ab., Can. 144 D17 52.27 N 113.07 W
Mirror Lake, l., Ma., U.S. 201 42.05 N 71.20 W
Mirror Lake, l., N.J., U.S. 194 40.29 N 74.22 W
Miryang, Kor., S. 54 G8 35.29 N 128.45 E
Miry Run, stm., N.J., U.S. 203 40.15 N 74.49 W
Mirzāpur, India 70 F9 25.08 N 82.34 E
Mirzāpur, India 190b 22.50 N 88.24 E
Misailovo, Russia 183b 55.34 N 37.49 E
Misaki see Miura, Japan 56 D12 35.08 N 139.37 E
Misantla, Mex. 154 F10 19.56 N 96.50 W
Misasa, Japan 56 D6 35.24 N 133.54 E
Misato, Japan 186 35.50 N 139.53 E
Misawa, Japan 54 D14 40.41 N 141.24 E
Misbourne, stm., Eng., U.K. 178 51.34 N 0.29 W
Miscou Centre, N.B., Can. 122 C12 47.56 N 64.33 W
Miscou Island, i., N.B., Can. 122 C12 47.56 N 64.31 W
Miscou Point, c., N.B., Can. 122 B12 48.00 N 64.32 W
Misdrov see Międzyzdroje, Pol. 24 C10 53.55 N 14.27 E
Misenheimer, N.C., U.S. 132 A5 35.29 N 80.17 W
Misericórdia, Serra da, mtn., Braz. 205a 22.51 S 43.17 W
Mish'āb, Ra's al-, c., Sau. Ar. 74 F11 28.12 N 48.36 E
Mishan, China 52 B11 45.32 N 131.52 E
Mishawaka, In., U.S. 130 C11 41.39 N 86.09 W
Mishawum Lake, l., Ma., U.S. 201 42.30 N 71.08 W
Mishe-Mokwa, Lake, l., N.J., U.S. 203 39.52 N 74.48 W
Mishicot, Wi., U.S. 126 D2 44.14 N 87.38 W
Mi-shima, i., Japan 56 E4 34.46 N 131.09 E
Misima Island, i., Pap. N. Gui. 96 B10 10.41 S 152.44 E
Misinto, Italy 184b 45.40 N 9.05 E
Misiones, state, Arg. 172 C10 27.00 S 55.00 W
Misiones, state, Para. 172 C9 27.00 S 57.00 W
Misión Santa Rosa, Para. 166 D4 21.46 S 61.43 W
Misión San Vicente, Mex. 120 F4 31.20 N 116.15 W
Miškino, Russia 183a 59.42 N 30.45 E
Miskitos, Cayos, is., Nic. 156 E6 14.23 N 82.46 W
Miskolc, Hung. 36 A7 48.06 N 20.46 E
Mislinja, stm., Slvn. 30 D12 46.34 N 15.01 E
Mislivna, mtn., Czech Rep. 24 H10 48.40 N 14.44 E
Mišnëvo, Russia 26 G19 53.58 N 36.21 E
Misool, Pulau, i., Indon. 60 F9 1.52 S 130.10 E
Miṣr see Egypt, ctry., Afr. 82 B5 27.00 N 30.00 E
Miṣrātah, Libya 82 A3 32.22 N 15.05 E
Misr el-Bahrî (Lower Egypt), hist. reg., Egypt 76 G1 31.04 N 31.05 E
Misr el-Gedîda (Heliopolis), ngh., Egypt 191c 30.06 N 31.20 E
Misrikh, India 70 E8 27.25 N 80.32 E
Missinaibi, stm., On., Can. 114 A9 50.44 N 81.30 W
Missinaibi Lake, l., On., Can. 114 B9 48.21 N 83.42 W
Missinaibi Lake Provincial Park, p.o.i., On., Can. 114 B8 48.25 N 83.35 W
Mission, B.C., Can. 144 G8 49.08 N 122.17 W
Mission, S.D., U.S. 140 D12 43.17 N 100.37 W
Mission, Tx., U.S. 136 H9 26.13 N 98.19 W
Mission, ngh., Ca., U.S. 200 37.45 N 122.25 W
Mission Beach, Austl. 98 A6 17.52 S 146.06 E
Mission Creek, stm., Ca., U.S. 200 37.32 N 121.55 W
Mission Hills, ngh., Ca., U.S. 198 34.16 N 118.27 W
Mission Mountain, hill, Ok., U.S. 130 H3 36.02 N 94.35 W
Mission Peak, mtn., Ca., U.S. 200 37.31 N 121.53 W
Mission Range, mts., Mt., U.S. 146 C13 47.29 N 113.58 W
Mission Viejo, Ca., U.S. 148 J8 33.35 N 117.39 W
Miss Irene Point, c., St. Vin. 159e p10 12.35 N 61.27 W
Missisa Lake, l., On., Can. 110 E14 52.18 N 85.12 W
Mississagi, stm., On., Can. 126 B6 46.10 N 83.00 W
Mississagi Provincial Park, p.o.i., On., Can. 126 B7 46.35 N 82.43 W
Mississauga, On., Can. 126 E10 43.35 N 79.36 W
Mississinewa, stm., U.S. 130 D12 40.45 N 86.01 W
Mississippi, state, U.S. 134 D9 32.50 N 89.30 W
Mississippi, stm., On., Can. 126 C13 45.26 N 76.18 W
Mississippi, stm., U.S. 112 E9 28.59 N 89.08 W
Mississippi Choctaw Indian Reservation, ind. res., Ms., U.S. 134 E9 32.47 N 89.15 W
Mississippi Lake, l., On., Can. 126 C13 45.04 N 76.10 W
Mississippi River Delta, del., La., U.S. 116 F8 29.10 N 89.15 W
Mississippi Sound, strt., U.S. 134 G10 30.15 N 88.40 W
Mississippi State, Ms., U.S. 134 D10 33.26 N 88.47 W
Missoula, Mt., U.S. 146 D12 46.51 N 114.00 W
Missouri, state, U.S. 120 F5 38.30 N 93.30 W
Missouri, stm., U.S. 112 D9 38.48 N 90.07 W
Missouri, Coteau du, hills, U.S. 140 A13 46.00 N 99.30 W
Missouri Buttes, mtn., Wy., U.S. 140 C8 44.37 N 104.47 W
Missouri City, Tx., U.S. 136 E12 29.37 N 95.32 W
Missouri Valley, Ia., U.S. 130 C2 41.33 N 95.53 W
Mistake Creek, stm., Austl. 98 D6 21.38 S 146.50 E
Mistassibi, stm., Qc., Can. 114 A14 50.06 N 72.15 W
Mistassini, Qc., Can. 122 B4 48.53 N 72.12 W
Mistassini, stm., Qc., Can. 122 B4 49.09 N 72.36 W
Mistassini, Lac, l., Qc., Can. 110 E16 51.00 N 73.37 W
Mistatim, Sk., Can. 142 B10 52.52 N 103.22 W
Mistawasis Indian Reserve, ind. res., Sk., Can. 142 A6 53.06 N 106.48 W
Mistelbach an der Zaya, Aus. 30 B13 48.34 N 16.35 E
Misterbianco, Italy 32 G9 37.30 N 15.00 E
Misti, Volcán, vol., Peru 164 G3 16.18 S 71.24 W
Mistissini, Qc., Can. 114 A14 50.25 N 73.50 W
Mistky, Ukr. 38 D17 49.20 N 38.29 E
Mistretta, Italy 32 G8 37.56 N 14.22 E
Misumi, Japan 56 G3 32.36 N 130.27 E
Misumi, Japan 56 E4 34.46 N 131.58 E
Mišutino, Russia 26 A19 59.30 N 36.01 E
Mita, Punta de, c., Mex. 154 E6 20.47 N 105.32 W
Mitau see Jelgava, Lat. 26 D6 56.38 N 23.43 E
Mitcham, Austl. 192b 37.49 S 145.12 E
Mitcham, ngh., Eng., U.K. 178 51.24 N 0.10 W
Mitchell, Austl. 98 F6 26.29 S 147.57 E
Mitchell, On., Can. 126 E8 43.28 N 81.12 W
Mitchell, In., U.S. 130 F11 38.43 N 86.28 W
Mitchell, Ne., U.S. 140 F9 41.56 N 103.48 W
Mitchell, Or., U.S. 146 F6 44.34 N 120.09 W
Mitchell, S.D., U.S. 140 D14 43.42 N 98.01 W
Mitchell, stm., Austl. 96 C8 15.12 S 141.35 E
Mitchell, stm., Austl. 98 K6 37.53 S 147.40 E
Mitchell, Lake, res., Al., U.S. 134 E12 32.48 N 86.27 W
Mitchell, Mount, mtn., N.C., U.S. 124 I3 35.46 N 82.16 W
Mitchell Field, arpt., Il., U.S. 196 41.55 N 88.15 W
Mitchell Lake, l., B.C., Can. 144 D10 52.53 N 120.36 W
Mitchellville, Ia., U.S. 128 J5 41.40 N 93.21 W
Mitchelstown, Ire. 10 I4 52.16 N 8.16 W
Mitchinamecus, stm., Qc., Can. 122 C2 47.03 N 75.06 W
Mitchinamecus, Réservoir, res., Qc., Can. 122 C1 47.21 N 75.07 W
Mīt Ghamr, Egypt 76 H2 30.43 N 31.16 E
Mīt Halfah, Egypt 191c 30.10 N 31.14 E
Mithapur, India 70 G2 22.25 N 69.01 E
Mithi, Pak. 70 F2 24.44 N 69.48 E
Míthymna, Grc. 34 D9 39.22 N 26.10 E
Mitiaro, i., Cook Is. 94 E11 19.48 S 157.43 W
Mitidja, Plaine de la, pl., Alg. 28 H14 36.45 N 3.00 E
Mitino, Russia 18 G23 60.34 N 36.48 E
Mitino, ngh., Russia 183b 55.51 N 37.21 E
Mitis, Lac, l., Qc., Can. 122 B9 48.17 N 67.45 W
Mitiškovo, Russia 26 F16 54.40 N 33.31 E
Mitla, hist., Mex. 154 G10 16.55 N 96.17 W
Mito, Japan 56 C13 36.22 N 140.28 E
Mito, Japan 186 35.10 N 139.37 E
Mitrofanovka, Russia 38 C18 49.58 N 39.42 E
Mīt Ruhayna, Egypt 191c 29.51 N 31.15 E
Mitry-le-Neuf, Fr. 179 48.57 N 2.36 E
Mitry-Mory, Fr. 179 48.59 N 2.37 E
Mitsio, Nosy, i., Madag. 88 C8 12.54 S 48.36 E
Mitsiwa see Massawa, Erit. 82 D7 15.37 N 39.25 E
Mitsubori, Japan 186 35.56 N 139.56 E
Mitsuike Park, p.o.i., Japan 186 35.31 N 139.39 E
Mitsukaidō, Japan 56 C13 36.01 N 139.59 E
Mitsuke, Japan 56 B11 37.31 N 138.55 E
Mitsushima, Japan 56 E2 34.16 N 129.19 E
Mitsuzaku, Japan 186 35.25 N 140.00 E
Mitsuzawa Park Race Track, p.o.i., Japan 186 35.27 N 139.36 E
Mittainville, Fr. 179 48.40 N 1.39 E
Mittån, stm., Swe. 16 E10 62.27 N 13.12 E
Mitte, ngh., Ger. 182a 52.31 N 13.24 E
Mittellandkanal, can., Ger. 24 D5 52.14 N 11.42 E
Mittenwald, Ger. 24 I7 47.27 N 11.15 E
Mittersill, Aus. 30 C9 47.16 N 12.28 E
Mittweida, Ger. 24 E9 50.59 N 12.59 E
Mitú, Col. 168 G6 1.08 N 70.03 W
Mitumba, Monts, mts., D.R.C. 86 F5 6.00 S 29.00 E
Mitwaba, D.R.C. 86 F5 8.36 S 27.20 E
Mitzic, Gabon 86 D2 0.46 N 11.33 E
Miura, Japan 56 D12 35.08 N 139.37 E
Mius, stm., Eur. 38 E17 47.16 N 38.48 E
Miwa, Japan 188 34.31 N 135.51 E
Mixcoac, ngh., Mex. 204a 19.23 N 99.12 W
Mixcoac, Presa de, res., Mex. 204a 19.22 N 99.14 W
Mixian, China 58 D5 34.31 N 113.22 E
Miya, stm., Japan 56 E9 34.31 N 136.42 E
Miyafarkin see Silvan, Tur. 42 F9 38.09 N 41.00 E
Miyagi, state, Japan 56 A13 38.29 N 140.52 E
Miyāh, Wadi el-, stm., Egypt 74 H4 24.51 N 32.52 E
Miyahara, Japan 186 35.56 N 139.37 E
Miyajima, Japan 56 E5 34.17 N 132.19 E
Miyake, Japan 188 34.35 N 135.47 E
Miyake-jima, i., Japan 56 E12 34.05 N 139.32 E
Miyako, Japan 54 E14 39.38 N 141.57 E
Miyakojima, ngh., Japan 188 34.43 N 135.33 E
Miyako-jima, i., Japan 52 G10 24.47 N 125.20 E
Miyakonojō, Japan 56 H4 31.43 N 131.04 E
Miyama, Japan 56 E9 34.06 N 136.13 E
Miyāni, India 70 H2 21.49 N 69.22 E
Miyanojō, Japan 56 H3 31.54 N 130.27 E
Miyazaki, Japan 56 H4 31.54 N 131.25 E
Miyazaki, state, Japan 56 G4 32.15 N 131.25 E
Miyazu, Japan 56 D8 35.32 N 135.11 E
Miyoshi, Japan 56 E5 34.48 N 132.50 E
Miyoshi, Japan 186 35.50 N 139.31 E
Miyun, China 58 A7 40.22 N 116.50 E
Miyun Shuiku, res., China 58 A7 40.29 N 116.56 E
Mīzan Teferī, Eth. 82 F7 6.56 N 35.28 E
Mizdah, Libya 82 A2 31.26 N 12.59 E
Mize, Ms., U.S. 134 F9 31.51 N 89.33 W
Mizen Head, c., Ire. 10 J3 51.27 N 9.48 W
Mizen Head, c., Ire. 10 I6 52.52 N 6.04 W
Miževičy, Bela. 26 G8 52.58 N 25.05 E
Mizhhir'ia, Ukr. 38 E2 48.32 N 23.30 E
Mizhi, China 58 C4 37.45 N 110.10 E
Mizil, Rom. 36 E13 44.59 N 26.27 E
Mizoch, Ukr. 38 C5 50.23 N 26.11 E
Mizonokuchi, Japan 186 35.36 N 139.37 E
Mizonuma, Japan 186 35.48 N 139.36 E
Mizoram, state, India 70 G14 23.30 N 93.00 E
Mizpah Creek, stm., Mt., U.S. 140 A7 46.16 N 105.17 W
Mizpě Ramon, Isr. 76 H5 30.36 N 34.49 E
Mizque, Bol. 166 C3 17.56 S 65.19 W
Mizue, ngh., Japan 186 35.41 N 139.54 E
Mizukaidō see Mitsukaidō, Japan 56 C13 36.01 N 139.59 E
Mizuko, Japan 186 35.50 N 139.34 E
Mizusawa, Japan 54 E14 39.08 N 141.08 E
Mizutori, Japan 188 34.47 N 135.45 E
Mjadzel, Bela. 26 F9 54.53 N 26.57 E
Mjagostrov, ostrov, i., Russia 18 C23 64.21 N 35.55 E
Mjagozero, Russia 18 G21 60.21 N 34.49 E
Mjakiševo, Russia 26 D11 56.34 N 28.54 E
Mjakit, Russia 50 D19 61.24 N 152.03 E
Mjaksa, Russia 26 B21 58.53 N 38.11 E
Mjällom, Swe. 16 E16 62.59 N 18.25 E

Name	Page	Map Ref.	Latitude	Longitude
Mjandozero, ozero, l., Russia	18	C24	64.43 N	37.30 E
Mjatlevo, Russia	26	F18	54.53 N	35.41 E
Mjölby, Swe.	16	I13	58.19 N	15.08 E
Mjörn, l., Swe.	16	J10	57.54 N	12.25 E
Mjøsa, l., Nor.	16	G8	60.40 N	11.00 E
Mkalama, Tan.	86	E6	4.07 S	34.38 E
Mkhondvo, stm., Afr.	90	E10	26.40 S	31.26 E
Mkokotoni, Tan.	86	F7	5.52 S	39.16 E
Mkomazi, stm., S. Afr.	90	G10	30.11 S	30.48 E
Mkulwe, Tan.	86	F6	8.33 S	32.19 E
Mkushi, Zam.	88	C4	13.39 S	29.18 E
Mkuze, S. Afr.	90	E10	27.35 S	32.00 E
Mkuze, stm., S. Afr.	90	E11	27.53 S	32.29 E
Mkuze Game Reserve, ind. res., S. Afr.	90	E11	27.40 S	32.15 E
Mladá Boleslav, Czech Rep.	24	F11	50.25 N	14.54 E
Mladenovac, Yugo.	36	E7	44.26 N	20.45 E
Mlanje Peak see Sapitwa, mtn., Mwi.	88	D6	15.57 S	35.36 E
Mlava, stm., Yugo.	36	E8	44.45 N	21.13 E
Mława, Pol.	24	C16	53.07 N	20.22 E
Mlembe see Emlembe, mtn., Afr.	90	D10	25.52 S	30.59 E
Mljet, Otok, i., Cro.	30	H14	42.45 N	17.30 E
Mljet Nacionalni Park, p.o.i., Cro.	30	H14	42.47 N	17.25 E
Mljetski Kanal, strt., Cro.	30	H14	42.48 N	17.35 E
Mlyniv, Ukr.	38	C4	50.30 N	25.37 E
Mmabatho, S. Afr.	90	D7	25.51 S	25.38 E
Mmadinare, Bots.	90	B8	21.57 S	27.46 E
Mnene, Zimb.	90	B9	20.37 S	30.03 E
Mnevniki, ngh., Russia	183b		55.45 N	37.28 E
Mníšek pod Brdy, Czech Rep.	24	G10	49.52 N	14.16 E
Moa, stm., Afr.	84	H2	6.59 N	11.33 W
Moab, Ut., U.S.	150	E7	38.34 N	109.33 W
Moala, i., Fiji	101e	r18	18.36 S	179.53 E
Moama, Austl.	98	K5	36.06 S	144.46 E
Moamba, Moz.	90	D11	25.36 S	32.14 E
Moanda, Gabon	86	E2	1.33 S	13.13 E
Moar Lake, l., Can.	142	C18	51.57 N	95.10 W
Moate, Ire.	10	H5	53.23 N	7.42 W
Moatize, Moz.	88	D5	16.08 S	33.43 E
Moaulanui, Puu, crat., Hi., U.S.	100a	c5	20.34 N	156.34 W
Moba, D.R.C.	86	F5	7.03 S	29.43 E
Moba, Nig.	191a		6.27 N	3.28 E
Mobara, Japan	56	D13	35.25 N	140.18 E
Mobaye, C.A.R.	86	D4	4.19 N	21.11 E
Mobberley, Eng., U.K.	180		53.19 N	2.20 W
Mobeetie, Tx., U.S.	138	F8	35.31 N	100.26 W
Moberly, Mo., U.S.	130	E5	39.25 N	92.26 W
Mobile, Al., U.S.	134	G10	30.41 N	88.02 W
Mobile, Az., U.S.	150	J4	33.03 N	112.16 W
Mobile, stm., Al., U.S.	134	F11	30.38 N	87.55 W
Mobile Bay, b., Al., U.S.	134	G11	30.33 N	87.59 W
Mobridge, S.D., U.S.	140	B12	45.32 N	100.25 W
Mobutu Sese Seko, Lac see Albert, Lake, l., Afr.	86	D6	1.40 N	31.00 E
Moca, Dom. Rep.	156	C12	19.23 N	70.31 W
Moca, P.R.	158a	b1	18.24 N	67.07 W
Mocajuba, Braz.	170	B1	2.34 S	49.29 W
Moçambique see Mozambique, ctry., Afr.	88	D5	18.15 S	35.00 E
Moçambique, Canal de see Mozambique Channel, strt., Afr.	88	D7	19.00 S	41.00 E
Moçâmedes see Namibe, Ang.	88	D1	15.11 S	12.09 E
Mo Cay, Viet.	64	G8	10.07 N	106.20 E
Moc Chau, Viet.	64	B7	20.51 N	104.37 E
Mocha see Al-Mukhā, Yemen	72	G5	13.18 N	43.15 E
Mochudi, Bots.	90	D8	24.23 S	26.08 E
Möckeln, l., Swe.	16	K11	56.40 N	14.10 E
Mockfjärd, Swe.	16	G12	60.29 N	14.58 E
Mocksville, N.C., U.S.	124	I5	35.53 N	80.33 W
Moclips, Wa., U.S.	146	C2	47.13 N	124.12 W
Môco, Morro de, mtn., Ang.	88	C2	12.28 S	15.10 E
Mocoa, Col.	168	G3	1.08 N	76.37 W
Mococa, Braz.	170	K2	21.27 S	47.00 W
Mocodoene, Moz.	90	C12	23.39 S	35.09 E
Mocoretá, Arg.	172	E8	30.37 S	57.58 W
Moctezuma, Mex.	120	G8	29.48 N	109.42 W
Moctezuma, stm., Mex.	120	G8	29.08 N	109.40 W
Moctezuma, stm., Mex.	154	E9	21.58 N	98.34 W
Mocuba, Moz.	88	D6	16.50 S	36.59 E
Mocubela, Moz.	88	D6	16.53 S	37.48 E
Mocubúri see Mecubúri, Moz.	88	C6	14.49 S	38.42 E
Močurica, stm., Blg.	36	G13	42.30 N	26.31 E
Modane, Fr.	22	D12	45.12 N	6.40 E
Modāsa, India	70	G4	23.27 N	73.17 E
Modder, stm., S. Afr.	90	F7	29.02 S	24.37 E
Modderbee, S. Afr.	191d		26.10 S	28.24 E
Modder East, S. Afr.	191d		26.11 S	28.26 E
Modderfontein, S. Afr.	191d		26.06 S	28.09 E
Modderfontein, stm., S. Afr.	191d		26.13 S	28.10 E
Model City, N.Y., U.S.	202a		43.11 N	78.59 W
Módena, Italy	30	F7	44.39 N	10.55 E
Modern Art, Museum of, bldg., N.Y., U.S.	194		40.46 N	73.58 W
Modeste, Mount, mtn., B.C., Can.	144	H6	48.37 N	124.06 W
Modesto, Ca., U.S.	148	F4	37.38 N	120.59 W
Modica, Italy	32	H8	36.52 N	14.46 E
Modjeska, Ca., U.S.	198		33.43 N	117.37 W
Mödling, Aus.	30	B13	48.04 N	16.17 E
Mödling, stm., Aus.	182b		48.04 N	16.22 E
Modot, Mong.	52	B6	47.43 N	109.02 E
Modowi, Indon.	60	F9	4.06 S	134.39 E
Modra, Slvk.	24	H13	48.19 N	17.18 E
Modriča, Bos.	36	E5	44.57 N	18.18 E
Mo Duc, Viet.	64	E9	14.57 N	108.52 E
Moe, Austl.	98	L6	38.11 S	146.15 E
Moeda, Braz.	170	K3	20.20 S	44.03 W
Moei (Thaungyin), stm., Asia	64	D3	17.49 N	97.41 E
Moelv, Nor.	16	G8	60.56 N	10.42 E
Moema, Braz.	170	J3	19.47 S	45.23 W
Moengo, Sur.	164	B7	5.37 N	54.24 W
Moen-jo-Daro, hist., Pak.	62	C2	27.18 N	68.10 E
Moenkopi, Az., U.S.	150	G5	36.05 N	111.13 W
Moenkopi Wash, stm., Az., U.S.	150	G6	35.53 N	111.26 W
Moeris, Lake see Qārūn, Birket, l., Egypt	76	I1	29.28 N	30.38 E
Moero, Lac see Mweru, Lake, l., Afr.	86	F5	9.00 S	28.45 E
Moersbach, stm., Ger.	181		51.33 N	6.36 E
Moeskroen see Mouscron, Bel.	20	D12	50.44 N	3.13 E
Moffat, Scot., U.K.	10	F9	55.19 N	3.26 W
Moffit, N.D., U.S.	140	A12	46.40 N	100.17 W
Mofoluku, Nig.	191a		6.33 N	3.20 E
Moga, India	70	C5	30.48 N	75.10 E
Mogadiscio see Muqdisho, Som.	86	D9	2.02 N	45.20 E
Mogadishu see Muqdisho, Som.	86	D9	2.02 N	45.20 E
Mogador see Essaouira, Mor.	84	C3	31.30 N	9.45 W
Mogadouro, Port.	28	C4	41.20 N	6.38 W
Mogalakwena, stm., S. Afr.	90	C9	22.28 S	28.55 E
Mogami, stm., Japan	56	A13	38.54 N	139.49 E
Mogapinyana, Bots.	90	C8	22.19 S	27.27 E
Mogaung, Mya.	62	C8	25.18 N	96.56 E
Mogdy, Russia	50	F15	50.34 N	133.46 E
Mogees, Pa., U.S.	203		40.06 N	75.19 W
Mogent, stm., Spain	184d		41.33 N	2.15 E
Mogi, Serra do, mts., Braz.	205b		23.47 S	46.20 W
Mogielnica, Pol.	24	E16	51.42 N	20.43 E
Mogilëv see Mahilëu, Bela.	26	G13	53.55 N	30.20 E
Mogilëv see Mahilëu, state, Bela.	26	G13	53.45 N	30.30 E
Mogilno, Pol.	24	D13	52.39 N	17.58 E
Mogincual, Moz.	88	D7	15.35 S	40.25 E
Mogoča, Russia	50	F12	53.44 N	119.44 E
Mogoča, stm., Russia	26	B19	58.00 N	36.26 E
Mogočin, Russia	48	C14	57.43 N	83.33 E
Mogogh, Sudan	82	F6	8.26 N	31.19 E
Mogojtuj, Russia	50	F12	51.16 N	114.54 E
Mogok, Mya.	64	A3	22.56 N	96.30 E
Mogollon Mountains, mts., N.M., U.S.	150	J8	33.25 N	108.40 W
Mogollon Rim, clf., Az., U.S.	150	I6	34.25 N	110.50 W
Mogor, Afg.	70	B1	32.51 N	67.51 E
Mogotes, Col.	168	D5	6.28 N	72.59 W
Mogotón, mtn., N.A.	156	F4	13.45 N	86.23 W
Moguer, Spain	28	G4	37.16 N	6.50 W
Mogyoród, Hung.	182c		47.36 N	19.15 E
Mogyoródi-patak, stm., Hung.	182c		47.36 N	19.05 E
Mogzon, Russia	50	F11	51.44 N	111.57 E
Mohács, Hung.	36	C5	46.00 N	18.40 E
Mohall, N.D., U.S.	142	F12	48.46 N	101.30 W
Mohammed, Râs, c., Egypt	76	K5	27.43 N	34.14 E
Mohammedia, Mor.	84	C3	33.41 N	7.23 W
Mohana, India	70	F6	25.54 N	77.46 E
Mohania, India	70	F9	25.09 N	83.38 E
Mohanpur, India	190a		28.44 N	77.10 E
Mohawk, Mi., U.S.	128	D10	47.18 N	88.23 W
Mohawk, stm., N.Y., U.S.	124	B11	42.46 N	73.41 W
Mohawk, Lake, l., N.J., U.S.	194		41.02 N	74.41 W
Mohawk Mountain, mtn., Ct., U.S.	124	C12	41.49 N	73.17 W
Mohe, China	50	F13	53.28 N	122.20 E
Moheda, Swe.	16	K12	56.59 N	14.34 E
Mohéli see Mwali, i., Com.	88	C7	12.17 S	43.41 E
Mohelnice, Czech Rep.	24	G12	49.46 N	16.55 E
Mohican, stm., Oh., U.S.	124	D3	40.21 N	82.08 W
Mohican, Cape, c., Ak., U.S.	109	D6	60.11 N	167.24 W
Mohili, ngh., India	190c		19.06 N	72.53 E
Mohlakeng, S. Afr.	191d		26.13 S	27.42 E
Möhne, stm., Ger.	20	C17	51.27 N	7.57 E
Mohnyin, Mya.	62	D8	24.46 N	96.22 E
Mohokare (Caledon), stm., Afr.	90	F8	30.30 S	26.04 E
Mohrin see Moryń, Pol.	24	D10	52.51 N	14.23 E
Mohyla-Bel'mak, hora, hill, Ukr.	38	F15	47.20 N	36.35 E
Mohyliv, Ukr.	38	E13	48.51 N	34.30 E
Mohyliv-Podil's'kyi, Ukr.	38	E6	48.27 N	27.46 E
Moi, Nor.	16	I4	58.28 N	6.32 E
Moindou, N. Cal.	101d	m15	21.41 S	165.39 E
Moinești, Rom.	36	C13	46.28 N	26.29 E
Moira, stm., On., Can.	122	D12	44.08 N	77.22 W
Moiraba, Braz.	170	B1	2.27 S	49.25 W
Mo i Rana, Nor.	14	F5	66.19 N	14.10 E
Mõisaküla, Est.	26	B8	58.05 N	25.12 E
Moiseevka, Russia	48	C13	58.04 N	76.16 E
Moisenay, Fr.	179		48.34 N	2.44 E
Moisés Ville, Arg.	172	E7	30.43 S	61.28 W
Moisie, Qc., Can.	110	E17	50.13 N	66.09 W
Moisie, stm., Qc., Can.	110	E17	50.15 N	66.04 W
Moison Creek, stm., On., Can.	199		42.18 N	82.40 W
Moissac, Fr.	22	E7	44.06 N	1.05 E
Moïssala, Chad	82	F3	8.20 N	17.45 E
Moisselles, Fr.	179		49.03 N	2.20 E
Moisson, Fr.	179		49.05 N	1.40 E
Moisson, Forêt de, p.o.i., Fr.	179		49.03 N	1.39 E
Moissy-Cramayel, Fr.	179		48.38 N	2.36 E
Moitaco, Ven.	168	C9	7.59 N	64.20 W
Mojácar, Spain	28	G9	37.08 N	1.51 W
Mojana, Brazo, stm., Col.	156	H10	9.02 N	74.46 W
Mojave, Ca., U.S.	148	H7	35.03 N	118.10 W
Mojave, stm., Ca., U.S.	148	H9	35.06 N	116.03 W
Mojave Desert, des., Ca., U.S.	120	D4	35.00 N	117.00 W
Mojero, stm., Russia	50	C9	68.44 N	103.38 E
Mojiguaçu, stm., Braz.	170	K2	20.53 S	48.10 W
Mojikit Lake, res., On., Can.	128	A10	50.36 N	88.10 W
Moji-Mirim, Braz.	170	L2	22.26 S	46.57 W
Mojo, Eth.	82	F7	8.35 N	39.07 E
Moju, Braz.	170	A1	1.53 S	48.46 W
Moju, stm., Braz.	164	D8	1.39 S	48.26 W
Mojynkum, peski, des., Kaz.	48	F12	44.20 N	71.00 E
Mōka, Japan	56	C12	36.26 N	140.01 E
Mokāma, India	70	F10	25.23 N	85.55 E
Mokapu Peninsula, pen., Hi., U.S.	100a	b4	21.27 N	157.45 W
Mokau, stm., N.Z.	102	D6	38.42 S	174.36 E
Mok-Dong Stadium, p.o.i., Kor., S.	189b		37.32 N	126.53 E
Mokelumne, stm., Ca., U.S.	148	E5	38.13 N	121.30 W
Mokhotlong, Leso.	90	F9	29.19 S	29.00 E
Moklakan, Russia	50	F12	54.56 N	118.56 E
Moknine, Tun.	84	B7	35.38 N	10.54 E
Mokochu, Khao, mtn., Thai.	64	D4	15.56 N	99.06 E
Mokokchūng, India	62	C7	26.19 N	94.32 E
Mokolo, Cam.	86	B2	10.44 N	13.48 E
Mokolo, stm., S. Afr.	90	C8	23.14 S	27.43 E
Mokou, Congo	191b		4.13 S	15.13 E
Mokpalin, Mya.	64	D3	17.26 N	96.53 E
Mokp'o, Kor., S.	54	G7	34.47 N	126.23 E
Mokraja Bujgola, stm., Russia	42	C10	44.47 N	44.21 E
Mokraja Ol'hovka, Russia	40	F14	50.28 N	44.59 E
Mokrān, Savāhel-e see Makrān Coast, cst., Asia	72	D9	25.12 N	60.50 E
Mokri Yaly, stm., Ukr.	38	F15	48.03 N	36.44 E
Mokša, stm., Russia	40	D13	54.44 N	41.52 E
Mokvyn, Ukr.	38	C5	50.57 N	26.50 E
Mokwa, Nig.	84	H5	9.17 N	5.03 E
Mol, Bel.	20	C14	51.11 N	5.06 E
Mola di Bari, Italy	32	C11	41.03 N	17.05 E
Molalla, Or., U.S.	146	E4	45.08 N	122.34 W
Moláoi, Grc.	34	G5	36.48 N	22.51 E
Molar, Cerro de la, mtn., Mex.	136	H2	26.30 N	105.24 W
Molara, Isola, i., Italy	32	D3	40.52 N	9.43 E
Molat, Otok, i., Cro.	30	F11	44.14 N	14.48 E
Moldary, Kaz.	48	D13	50.47 N	78.28 E
Moldau see Vltava, stm., Czech Rep.	24	F10	50.20 N	14.28 E
Moldavia, hist. reg., Rom.	36	C13	46.23 N	27.12 E
Moldavia see Moldova, ctry., Eur.	38	F7	47.00 N	29.00 E
Moldavija see Moldova, ctry., Eur.	38	F7	47.00 N	29.00 E
Molde, Nor.	16	E5	62.44 N	7.10 E
Moldefjorden, b., Nor.	16	E4	62.43 N	7.04 E
Moldova, ctry., Eur.	38	F7	47.00 N	29.00 E
Moldova, stm., Rom.	36	B13	46.52 N	26.57 E
Moldova Nouă, Rom.	36	E8	44.46 N	21.40 E
Moldoveanu, Vârful, mtn., Rom.	36	D11	45.35 N	24.44 E
Môle, Cap du, c., Haiti	156	C11	19.49 N	73.24 W
Mole Creek, Austl.	99a	n13	41.33 S	146.23 E
Molega Lake, l., N.S., Can.	122	F12	44.22 N	64.53 W
Molegbe, D.R.C.	86	D4	4.13 N	20.53 E
Molène, Île de, i., Fr.	20	F3	48.23 N	4.57 W
Molepolole, Bots.	90	D7	24.24 S	25.31 E
Molėtai, Lith.	26	E8	55.14 N	25.25 E
Mole Valley, mun., Eng., U.K.	178		51.16 N	0.18 W
Molfetta, Italy	32	C10	41.11 N	16.35 E
Molina, Chile	172	G2	35.06 S	71.16 W
Molina de Aragón, Spain	28	D9	40.50 N	1.52 W
Molina de Segura, Spain	28	F9	38.03 N	1.12 W
Moline, Il., U.S.	130	C7	41.30 N	90.30 W
Moline, Ks., U.S.	138	D12	37.21 N	96.18 W
Molinière Point, c., Gren.	159e	q10	12.05 N	61.45 W
Molino, Fl., U.S.	134	G11	30.43 N	87.18 W
Molino de Rosas, ngh., Mex.	204a		19.22 N	99.13 W
Molino de Valdo de Piedras, Mex.	136	E3	29.50 N	104.40 W
Molinos, Arg.	172	B4	25.26 S	66.18 W
Molise, state, Italy	32	C8	41.35 N	14.30 E
Molkom, Swe.	16	H11	59.36 N	13.43 E
Möll, stm., Aus.	30	D10	46.49 N	13.22 E
Mölle, Swe.	16	K10	56.17 N	12.29 E
Möllen, Ger.	181		51.35 N	6.42 E
Mollendo, Peru	164	G3	17.00 S	72.01 W
Möllensee, l., Ger.	182a		52.26 N	13.51 E
Möllersdorf, Aus.	182b		48.02 N	16.18 E
Molles, Ur.	172	F9	33.03 S	56.28 W
Mollet del Vallès, Spain	184d		41.33 N	2.13 E
Mollington, Eng., U.K.	180		53.13 N	2.55 W
Mölln, Ger.	24	C6	53.37 N	10.41 E
Mollösund, Swe.	16	I9	58.04 N	11.29 E
Molly Ann Brook, stm., N.J., U.S.	194		40.55 N	74.11 W
Mölndal, Swe.	16	J9	57.41 N	11.55 E
Mölnlycke, Swe.	16	J10	57.39 N	12.07 E
Molochans'k, Ukr.	38	F14	47.12 N	35.35 E
Molochna, stm., Ukr.	38	F14	46.26 N	35.24 E
Molochnyi lyman, b., Ukr.	38	G13	46.30 N	35.20 E
Moločnoe, Russia	26	A22	59.17 N	39.41 E
Molodečno see Maladzečna, Bela.	26	F9	54.19 N	26.51 E
Molodežnaja, sci., Ant.	103	B9	67.35 S	46.35 E
Molodogvardejskoe, Kaz.	48	D11	54.02 N	70.45 E
Molodoj Tud, Russia	26	D16	56.26 N	33.36 E
Mologa, stm., Russia	26	B19	58.51 N	37.07 E
Molokai, i., Hi., U.S.	100a	b5	21.07 N	157.00 W
Molokai Fracture Zone, unds.	174	G24	23.00 N	148.00 W
Molokovo, Russia	26	B19	58.10 N	36.45 E
Moloma, stm., Russia	40	B16	58.49 N	48.37 E
Molong, Austl.	98	I7	33.05 S	148.51 E
Molopo, stm., Afr.	90	E5	28.30 S	20.12 E
Molotov see Perm', Russia	40	C20	58.00 N	56.15 E
Molotovsk see Severodvinsk, Russia	18	C26	64.34 N	39.50 E
Moloundou, Cam.	86	D3	2.02 N	15.13 E
Molsheim, Fr.	20	F16	48.32 N	7.30 E
Molson Lake, l., Mb., Can.	110	E11	54.12 N	96.45 W
Molteno, S. Afr.	90	G8	31.22 S	26.21 E
Molu, Pulau, i., Indon.	60	G9	6.45 S	131.33 E
Moluccas see Maluku, is., Indon.	60	F8	2.00 S	128.00 E
Molucca Sea see Maluku, Laut, s., Indon.	60	F8	0.00 N	125.00 E
Molvoticy, Russia	26	C15	57.25 N	32.20 E
Molžaninovo, ngh., Russia	183b		55.56 N	37.22 E
Moma, Moz.	88	D6	16.50 S	39.08 E
Moma, stm., Russia	50	C17	66.25 N	143.10 E
Mombaça, Braz.	170	C6	5.45 S	39.38 W
Mombaça, Corrego, stm., Braz.	205b		23.46 S	46.47 W
Mombasa, Kenya	86	E7	4.03 S	39.40 E
Mombetsu, Japan	54	B15	44.21 N	143.21 E
Mombuey, Spain	28	B4	42.02 N	6.19 W
Momčilgrad, Blg.	36	H12	41.31 N	25.25 E
Momence, Il., U.S.	130	C10	41.09 N	87.39 W
Momi, Fiji	101e	p18	17.55 S	177.16 E
Momotombo, Volcán, vol., Nic.	156	F4	12.26 N	86.33 W
Momozaka, Japan	188		34.51 N	135.02 E
Mompono, D.R.C.	86	D4	0.06 N	21.38 E
Mompós, Col.	168	C4	9.12 N	74.24 W
Momskij hrebet, mts., Russia	50	C18	66.00 N	146.00 E
Mon, Mya.	64	C3	18.31 N	96.38 E
Mon, state, Mya.	64	E3	17.30 N	97.00 E
Møn, i., Den.	16	L10	55.00 N	12.19 E
Mona, Ut., U.S.	150	D5	39.49 N	111.51 W
Mona, Canal de la see Mona Passage, strt., N.A.	152	D11	18.30 N	67.45 W
Mona, Isla de, i., P.R.	152a	h14	18.05 N	67.54 W
Mona, Punta, c., C.R.	156	H6	9.36 N	82.38 W
Monaca, Pa., U.S.	124	D5	40.40 N	80.16 W
Monach Islands, is., Scot., U.K.	10	D5	57.31 N	7.38 W
Monaco, Mon.	22	F13	43.44 N	7.24 E
Monaco, ctry., Eur.	22	F13	43.45 N	7.25 E
Monadhliath Mountains, mts., Scot., U.K.	10	D8	57.13 N	4.21 W
Monadnock Mountain, mtn., N.H., U.S.	124	B13	42.52 N	72.07 W
Monagas, state, Ven.	168	C10	9.20 N	63.00 W
Monaghan, Ire.	10	G6	54.15 N	6.58 W
Monaghan, state, Ire.	10	G6	54.10 N	7.00 W
Monahans, Tx., U.S.	136	C5	31.35 N	102.53 W
Monahans Draw, stm., Tx., U.S.	136	C5	31.54 N	101.46 W
Monahans Sandhills State Park, p.o.i., Tx., U.S.	136	C5	31.38 N	102.50 W
Monakino, Russia	54	C10	43.24 N	133.27 E
Monango, N.D., U.S.	140	A14	46.09 N	98.35 W
Mona Passage, strt., N.A.	152	D11	18.30 N	67.45 W
Monapo, Moz.	88	C7	14.55 S	40.16 E
Mona Quimbundo, Ang.	88	B2	9.53 S	19.59 E
Monarch, S.C., U.S.	132	B4	34.42 N	81.34 W
Monarch Mountain, mtn., B.C., Can.	144	E5	51.54 N	125.53 W
Monarch Pass, p., Co., U.S.	138	C2	38.30 N	106.20 W
Monashee Mountains, mts., B.C., Can.	118	B6	50.30 N	118.30 W
Monashee Provincial Park, p.o.i., B.C., Can.	144	F12	50.27 N	118.14 W
Monash University, educ., Austl.	192b		37.55 S	145.08 E
Monas National Monument, p.o.i., Indon.	187e		6.10 S	106.49 E
Monastir see Bitola, Mac.	34	B4	41.01 N	21.20 E
Monastir, Tun.	84	B7	35.47 N	10.50 E
Monastyrščina, Russia	26	F14	54.20 N	31.50 E
Monastyrskoe, ozero, l., Russia	18	E24	62.51 N	37.07 E
Monastyryshche, Ukr.	38	D9	48.59 N	29.50 E
Monastyrys'ka, Ukr.	38	D4	49.05 N	25.10 E
Monbulk, Austl.	192b		37.52 S	145.25 E
Monbulk Creek, stm., Austl.	192b		37.54 S	145.15 E
Moncalieri, Italy	30	F4	45.00 N	7.41 E
Moncalvo, Italy	30	E5	45.03 N	8.13 E
Monção, Braz.	170	B3	3.29 S	45.15 W
Monção, Port.	28	B2	42.04 N	8.29 W
Mončegorsk, Russia	14	E23	67.55 N	32.49 E
Mončeozero, ozero, l., Russia	14	D23	68.00 N	32.48 E
Mönchengladbach, Ger.	24	E2	51.11 N	6.25 E
Mönchengladbach Flughafen, arpt., Ger.	181		51.14 N	6.29 E
Monchique, Port.	28	G2	37.19 N	8.33 W
Moncks Corner, S.C., U.S.	132	C5	33.11 N	80.00 W
Monclova, Mex.	154	B8	26.53 N	101.24 W
Moncton, N.B., Can.	122	D12	46.05 N	64.47 W
Monday, stm., Para.	172	B10	25.36 S	54.35 W
Mondego, stm., Port.	28	D3	40.08 N	8.45 W
Mondego, Cabo, c., Port.	28	D1	40.11 N	8.54 W
Mondeor, S. Afr.	191d		26.17 S	28.00 E
Mondjamboli, D.R.C.	86	D4	2.28 N	22.05 E
Mondo, Chad	82	E3	13.46 N	15.31 E
Mondoñedo, Spain	28	A3	43.25 N	7.21 W
Mondoubleau, Fr.	20	F9	47.59 N	0.54 E
Mondovi, Wi., U.S.	128	G7	44.34 N	91.39 W
Mondovì, Italy	30	F4	44.23 N	7.49 E
Mondragone, Italy	32	C7	41.07 N	13.53 E
Monds Island, i., N.J., U.S.	203		39.50 N	75.19 W
Mondy, Russia	48	D18	51.41 N	100.57 E
Monemvasía, Grc.	34	G6	36.41 N	23.01 E
Monero, N.M., U.S.	138	E2	36.53 N	106.52 W
Monessen, Pa., U.S.	124	D6	40.08 N	79.52 W
Monesterio, Spain	28	F4	38.05 N	6.16 W
Monett, Mo., U.S.	130	H4	36.55 N	93.55 W
Monette, Ar., U.S.	130	I7	35.53 N	90.20 W
Monfalcone, Italy	30	E10	45.48 N	13.31 E
Monferrato, hist. reg., Italy	30	F5	44.55 N	8.05 E
Monforte, Port.	28	E3	39.03 N	7.26 W
Monforte de Lemos, Spain	28	B3	42.31 N	7.30 W
Monga, D.R.C.	86	D4	4.12 N	22.49 E
Mongaguá, Braz.	172	B14	24.05 S	46.36 W
Mongalla, Sudan	82	F6	5.10 N	31.46 E
Mongat, Spain	184d		41.28 N	2.17 E
Mongaup, stm., N.Y., U.S.	124	C11	41.25 N	74.45 W
Mongbyŏn-ni, Kor., S.	189b		37.40 N	126.44 E
Monge, mtn., Port.	184c		38.46 N	9.26 W
Mongers Lake, l., Austl.	96	E3	29.27 S	116.44 E
Monggon Qulu, China	52	B8	48.36 N	119.49 E
Möng Hai, Mya.	64	B4	20.46 N	99.49 E
Möng Hpāyak, Mya.	64	B4	20.52 N	99.54 E
Möng Hsat, Mya.	64	B4	20.30 N	99.13 E
Monghyr see Munger, India	70	F11	25.22 N	86.28 E
Mongibello see Etna, Monte, vol., Italy	32	G8	37.45 N	15.00 E
Möng Küng, Mya.	64	B3	21.36 N	97.32 E
Möng Ma, Mya.	64	B4	21.37 N	99.54 E
Möng Mit, Mya.	64	A3	23.06 N	96.40 E
Möng Nai, Mya.	64	B3	20.31 N	97.52 E
Möng Nawng, Mya.	64	B4	21.38 N	98.07 E
Mongo, Chad	82	E3	12.11 N	18.42 E
Mongol Altayn nuruu, mts., Asia	52	B3	46.30 N	93.00 E
Mongol Ard Uls see Mongolia, ctry., Asia	44	E14	46.00 N	105.00 E
Mongolia, ctry., Asia	44	E14	46.00 N	105.00 E
Mongonu, Nig.	84	G7	12.40 N	13.36 E
Mongororo, Chad	82	E4	12.01 N	22.28 E
Möng Pai, Mya.	64	C3	19.44 N	97.05 E
Möng Pan, Mya.	64	B4	20.19 N	98.22 E
Möng Pawn, Mya.	64	B3	20.49 N	97.28 E
Möng Ping, Mya.	64	A4	22.22 N	99.02 E
Mong Tung Hang, China	189d		22.20 N	114.02 E
Mongu, Zam.	88	D3	15.16 S	23.08 E
Möng Yai, Mya.	64	A4	22.26 N	98.02 E
Möng Yawng, Mya.	64	B5	21.11 N	100.22 E
Monheim, Ger.	24	H6	48.50 N	10.51 E
Monico, Wi., U.S.	128	F9	45.35 N	89.10 W
Monida Pass, p., U.S.	146	F14	44.33 N	112.17 W
Monino, Russia	26	E21	55.50 N	38.10 E
Moniquirá, Col.	168	E5	5.52 N	73.34 W
Möniste, Est.	26	C9	57.36 N	26.34 E
Monistrol-sur-Loire, Fr.	22	D10	45.17 N	4.09 E
Monitor Range, mts., Nv., U.S.	148	D9	38.46 N	116.34 W
Monitor Valley, val., Nv., U.S.	148	E9	39.00 N	116.40 W
Monk, Pointe, c., Qc., Can.	193a		45.29 N	73.57 W
Monken Hadley, ngh., Eng., U.K.	178		51.40 N	0.11 W
Mońki, Pol.	24	C18	53.23 N	22.48 E
Monkira, Austl.	98	E3	24.49 S	140.33 E
Monkman Provincial Park, p.o.i., B.C., Can.	144	B9	54.36 N	121.11 W
Monkoto, D.R.C.	86	E4	1.37 S	20.40 E
Monks Heath, Eng., U.K.	180		53.16 N	2.14 W
Monmouth, Wales, U.K.	10	J10	51.49 N	2.43 W
Monmouth, Il., U.S.	130	D7	40.54 N	90.38 W
Monmouth, Or., U.S.	146	F3	44.50 N	123.13 W
Monmouth Beach, N.J., U.S.	194		40.19 N	73.58 W
Monmouth Hills, N.J., U.S.	194		40.24 N	74.00 W
Monmouth Mountain, mtn., B.C., Can.	144	E7	51.00 N	123.47 W
Mono, stm., Afr.	84	H5	6.16 N	1.48 E
Mono, Caño, stm., Col.	168	E7	4.32 N	67.52 W
Mono Island, i., Sol. Is.	101b	d6	7.21 S	155.33 E
Mono Lake, l., Ca., U.S.	148	F7	38.00 N	119.00 W
Monon, In., U.S.	130	D11	40.51 N	86.52 W
Monona, Ia., U.S.	128	H7	43.02 N	91.22 W
Monona, Wi., U.S.	130	A8	43.03 N	89.19 W
Monongahela, stm., U.S.	124	E6	40.26 N	80.00 W
Monongahela Brook, stm., N.J., U.S.	203		39.47 N	75.09 W
Monopoli, Italy	32	D11	40.57 N	17.17 E
Monor, Hung.	36	B6	47.20 N	19.26 E
Mono Road Station, On., Can.	193b		43.51 N	79.51 W
Monponsett Pond, l., Ma., U.S.	201		42.01 N	70.51 W
Monreal, Spain	28	B9	42.42 N	1.29 W
Monreal del Campo, Spain	28	D9	40.47 N	1.21 W
Monreale, Italy	32	F7	38.05 N	13.17 E
Monroe, Ga., U.S.	132	C2	33.47 N	83.42 W
Monroe, Ia., U.S.	130	C4	41.31 N	93.05 W
Monroe, La., U.S.	134	E6	32.30 N	92.06 W
Monroe, Mi., U.S.	124	C2	41.54 N	83.24 W
Monroe, N.J., U.S.	194		41.06 N	74.38 W
Monroe, N.Y., U.S.	124	C11	41.19 N	74.11 W
Monroe, N.C., U.S.	132	B5	34.59 N	80.32 W
Monroe, Or., U.S.	146	F3	44.18 N	123.17 W
Monroe, Ut., U.S.	150	E4	38.37 N	112.07 W
Monroe, Va., U.S.	124	G6	37.29 N	79.07 W
Monroe, Wa., U.S.	146	C4	47.51 N	121.58 W
Monroe, Wi., U.S.	130	B8	42.36 N	89.38 W
Monroe City, In., U.S.	130	F10	38.36 N	87.21 W
Monroe City, Mo., U.S.	130	E6	39.38 N	91.44 W
Monroe Lake, res., In., U.S.	130	E11	39.04 N	86.25 W
Monroeville, Al., U.S.	134	F11	31.31 N	87.19 W
Monroeville, In., U.S.	124	D1	40.58 N	84.52 W
Monroeville, Oh., U.S.	124	C3	41.14 N	82.42 W
Monroeville, Pa., U.S.	124	D6	40.25 N	79.45 W
Monroeville Mall, shp. cen., Pa., U.S.	197b		40.26 N	79.48 W
Monrovia, Lib.	84	H2	6.19 N	10.47 W
Monrovia Mountain Park, p.o.i., Ca., U.S.	198		34.10 N	118.10 W
Monrovia Peak, mtn., Ca., U.S.	198		34.13 N	117.58 W
Mons, Bel.	20	D12	50.27 N	3.56 E
Monschau, Ger.	24	F2	50.33 N	6.14 E
Monsefú, Peru	164	E2	6.51 S	79.51 W
Monselice, Italy	30	E8	45.14 N	11.44 E
Monsenhor Hipólito, Braz.	170	D5	6.59 S	41.07 W
Monsenhor Tabosa, Braz.	170	C5	4.47 S	40.04 W
Monson, Me., U.S.	122	E7	45.17 N	69.30 W
Mönsterås, Swe.	16	J14	57.02 N	16.26 E
Montabaur, Ger.	24	F3	50.26 N	7.50 E
Montagne, Neth. Ant.	158g	p23	12.12 N	68.16 W
Montagu, S. Afr.	90	H5	33.45 S	20.06 E
Montague, P.E., Can.	122	D14	46.09 N	62.39 W
Montague, Ca., U.S.	148	B3	41.44 N	122.30 W
Montague, Mi., U.S.	126	E3	43.24 N	86.21 W
Montague, Tx., U.S.	138	H11	33.38 N	97.42 W
Montague, Isla, i., Mex.	120	F5	31.43 N	114.43 W
Montague Island, i., Ak., U.S.	109	E10	60.09 N	147.17 W
Montagu Island, i., S. Geor.	103	A2	58.25 S	26.20 W
Montaigu, Fr.	20	H7	46.59 N	1.19 W
Montainville, Fr.	179		48.53 N	1.52 E
Montalbán, Spain	28	D10	40.50 N	0.48 W
Montalbancito, Ven.	204c		10.28 N	66.59 W
Montalbano Ionico, Italy	32	D10	40.17 N	16.33 E
Montalcino, Italy	30	G8	43.03 N	11.29 E
Montalegre, Port.	28	C3	41.49 N	7.47 W
Montalet-le-Bois, Fr.	179		49.03 N	1.50 E
Montalto, mtn., Italy	32	F9	38.10 N	15.55 E
Montalto di Castro, Italy	30	H8	42.21 N	11.35 E
Montana, Blg.	36	F10	43.24 N	23.14 E
Montana, state, Blg.	36	F10	43.30 N	23.30 E
Montana, state, U.S.	118	D11	47.00 N	110.00 W
Montaña de Covadonga, Parque Nacional de la, p.o.i., Spain	28	A5	43.14 N	4.58 W
Montana Indian Reserve, ind. res., Ab., Can.	144	D17	52.43 N	113.27 W
Montánchez, Spain	28	E4	39.13 N	6.09 W
Montanha, Braz.	170	J5	18.07 S	40.21 W
Montara Beach, p.o.i., Ca., U.S.	200		37.33 N	122.31 W
Montara Mountain, mts., Ca., U.S.	200		37.32 N	122.27 W
Montargil, Port.	28	E2	39.05 N	8.10 W
Montargis, Fr.	20	G11	48.00 N	2.44 E
Montauban, Fr.	22	E7	44.01 N	1.21 E
Montauk, N.Y., U.S.	124	C14	41.02 N	71.57 W
Montauk Point, c., N.Y., U.S.	124	C14	41.04 N	71.51 W
Montauk State Park, p.o.i., Mo., U.S.	130	G6	37.27 N	91.40 W
Monta Vista, Ca., U.S.	200		37.19 N	122.03 W
Montbard, Fr.	20	G13	47.37 N	4.20 E
Montbéliard, Fr.	20	G15	47.31 N	6.46 E
Mont Belvieu, Tx., U.S.	136	E13	29.51 N	94.53 W
Montblanc, Spain	28	C12	41.22 N	1.09 E
Montblanch see Montblanc, Spain	28	C12	41.22 N	1.09 E
Montbrison, Fr.	22	D9	45.37 N	4.03 E
Montbron, Fr.	22	D6	45.40 N	0.30 E
Montcada i Reixas, Spain	184d		41.29 N	2.11 E
Montceau-les-Mines, Fr.	20	H13	46.40 N	4.21 E
Montchanin, De., U.S.	203		39.47 N	75.35 W
Montchauvet, Fr.	179		48.54 N	1.38 E
Montclair, Ca., U.S.	148	I8	34.05 N	117.40 W
Montclair State College, educ., N.J., U.S.	194		40.51 N	74.12 W
Mont Clare, Pa., U.S.	203		40.08 N	75.30 W
Mont-de-Marsan, Fr.	22	F5	43.53 N	0.30 W
Montdidier, Fr.	20	E11	49.38 N	2.34 E
Monte, Castel del, hist., Italy	32	C10	41.05 N	16.16 E
Monte, Laguna del, l., Arg.	172	H6	37.00 S	62.28 W
Monteagle, Tn., U.S.	134	B13	35.14 N	85.50 W
Monteagudo, Bol.	166	C4	19.49 S	63.59 W
Monte Albán, hist., Mex.	154	G10	17.02 N	96.45 W
Monte Alegre, Braz.	164	D7	2.00 S	54.04 W
Monte Alegre, Braz.	170	D8	6.04 S	35.20 W
Monte Alegre de Goiás, Braz.	170	G2	13.08 S	46.58 W
Monte Alegre de Minas, Braz.	170	J1	18.49 S	48.49 W
Monte Alegre de Sergipe, Braz.	170	F7	10.01 S	37.32 W
Monte Alegre do Piauí, Braz.	170	E3	9.46 S	45.17 W
Monte Azul, Braz.	170	H4	15.09 S	42.52 W
Montebello, Qc., Can.	126	C14	45.39 N	74.56 W
Montebello, P.R.	158a	b2	18.22 N	66.30 W
Monte Compatri, Italy	185a		41.48 N	12.44 E
Montecarlo, Arg.	172	C10	26.34 S	54.45 W
Monte Carmelo, Braz.	170	J2	18.43 S	47.29 W
Monte Caseros, Arg.	172	E9	30.15 S	57.38 W
Montecassino, Abbazia di, rel., Italy	32	C7	41.29 N	13.48 E
Montecatini Terme, Italy	30	G7	43.53 N	10.47 E
Monte Chingolo, ngh., Arg.	206		34.45 S	58.20 W
Montecito, Ca., U.S.	148	I6	34.26 N	119.37 W
Monte Comán, Arg.	172	G4	34.35 S	67.52 W
Monte Creek, B.C., Can.	144	F11	50.39 N	119.57 W
Monte Cristi, Dom. Rep.	156	C12	19.51 N	71.38 W
Monte Cristo, Bol.	166	B4	14.43 S	61.14 W
Montecristo, Isola di, i., Italy	30	H7	42.20 N	10.19 E
Monte do Carmo, Braz.	170	F1	10.45 S	48.07 W
Monte Escobedo, Mex.	154	D7	22.17 N	103.32 W
Monte Estoril, Port.	184c		38.42 N	9.24 W

Name	Page	Map Ref.	Latitude	Longitude
Montefalco, Italy	30	H9	42.53 N	12.39 E
Montefiascone, Italy	30	H8	42.33 N	12.01 E
Montefrío, Spain	28	G6	37.19 N	4.01 W
Montego Bay, Jam.	158d	i12	18.27 N	77.54 W
Monte Grande, Chile	172	E2	30.06 S	70.31 W
Montegut, La., U.S.	134	H8	29.28 N	90.32 W
Monteiro, Braz.	170	D7	7.53 S	37.07 W
Montejicar, Spain	28	G7	37.34 N	3.30 W
Montejinni, Austl.	96	C6	16.36 S	131.47 E
Montelavar, Port.	184c		38.51 N	9.20 W
Montelíbano, Col.	168	C4	8.05 N	75.29 W
Montélimar, Fr.	22	E10	44.33 N	4.44 E
Monte Lindo, stm., Para.	172	A9	23.53 S	57.17 W
Montellano, Spain	28	H5	37.00 N	5.34 W
Montello, Nv., U.S.	150	B2	41.14 N	114.14 W
Montello, Wi., U.S.	128	H9	43.47 N	89.19 W
Monte Maíz, Arg.	172	F6	33.12 S	62.36 W
Montemayor, Meseta de, plat., Arg.	166	H3	44.20 S	66.10 W
Montemor, Port.	184c		38.49 N	9.12 W
Montemor, mtn., Port.	184c		38.49 N	9.12 W
Montemorelos, Mex.	154	C9	25.11 N	99.49 W
Montemor-o-Novo, Port.	28	F2	38.38 N	8.12 W
Montemor-o-Velho, Port.	28	D2	40.10 N	8.40 W
Montemuro, mtn., Port.	28	C2	40.58 N	7.56 W
Montenegro, Braz.	172	D12	29.42 S	51.30 W
Montenegro see Crna Gora, state, Yugo.	36	G6	42.30 N	19.18 E
Monte Pascoal, Parque Nacional de, p.o.i., Braz.	170	I6	16.54 S	39.24 W
Monte Patria, Chile	172	E2	30.41 S	70.56 W
Monte Porzio Catone, Italy	185a		41.49 N	12.43 E
Montepuez, Moz.	88	C6	13.07 S	38.59 E
Montepulciano, Italy	30	G8	43.05 N	11.46 E
Monte Quemado, Arg.	172	B6	25.47 S	62.49 W
Monterado, Indon.	66	C6	0.45 N	109.07 E
Montereau-Faut-Yonne, Fr.	20	F11	48.23 N	2.57 E
Montereau-sur-le-Jard, Fr.	179		48.35 N	2.40 E
Monterey, Ca., U.S.	148	G3	36.35 N	121.53 W
Monterey, Tn., U.S.	130	H12	36.08 N	85.16 W
Monterey, Va., U.S.	124	F6	38.23 N	79.35 W
Monterey Bay, b., Ca., U.S.	148	G3	36.48 N	121.54 W
Montería, Col.	168	C3	8.45 N	75.52 W
Montero, Bol.	164	G5	17.20 S	63.15 W
Monteros, Arg.	172	C5	27.10 S	65.30 W
Monterotondo, Italy	30	H9	42.03 N	12.36 E
Monterrey, Mex.	154	C8	25.40 N	100.18 W
Monterrico, Hipódromo de, p.o.i., Peru	204d		12.06 S	76.59 W
Montes Altos, Braz.	170	C2	5.50 S	47.04 W
Montesano, Wa., U.S.	146	C3	46.58 N	123.35 W
Monte San Savino, Italy	30	G8	43.19 N	11.42 E
Monte Sant'Angelo, Italy	30	I12	41.42 N	15.56 E
Monte Santo, Braz.	170	F6	10.25 S	39.19 W
Monte Santu, Capo di, c., Italy	32	D3	40.04 N	9.43 E
Montes Claros, Braz.	170	I4	16.43 S	43.51 W
Montesilvano Marina, Italy	30	H11	42.31 N	14.08 E
Montespaccato, ngh., Italy	185a		41.54 N	12.23 E
Montevallo, Al., U.S.	134	D12	33.05 N	86.51 W
Montevarchi, Italy	30	G8	43.31 N	11.34 E
Monteverde Nuovo, ngh., Italy	185a		41.51 N	12.27 E
Montevideo, Mn., U.S.	128	G3	44.56 N	95.43 W
Montevideo, Ur.	172	G9	34.54 S	56.11 W
Monte Vista, Co., U.S.	138	D2	37.34 N	106.08 W
Montévrain, Fr.	179		48.53 N	2.45 E
Montezuma, Ga., U.S.	132	D1	32.17 N	84.02 W
Montezuma, In., U.S.	130	E10	39.46 N	87.21 W
Montezuma, Ia., U.S.	130	C5	41.35 N	92.31 W
Montezuma, Ks., U.S.	138	D8	37.35 N	100.26 W
Montezuma Castle National Monument, p.o.i., Az., U.S.	150	I4	34.38 N	110.49 W
Montezuma Creek, stm., Ut., U.S.	150	F7	37.15 N	109.18 W
Montezuma Hills, hills, Ca., U.S.	200		38.07 N	121.51 W
Montfermeil, Fr.	179		48.54 N	2.34 E
Montfort, Wi., U.S.	130	B7	42.58 N	90.25 W
Montgé, Fr.	179		49.02 N	2.45 E
Montgenèvre, Col de, p., Fr.	22	D12	44.56 N	6.43 E
Montgeron, Fr.	179		48.42 N	2.27 E
Montgeroult, Fr.	179		49.05 N	2.00 E
Montgomery see Sāhīwāl, Pak.	70	C4	30.40 N	73.06 E
Montgomery, Al., U.S.	134	E12	32.23 N	86.18 W
Montgomery, La., U.S.	134	F6	31.40 N	92.53 W
Montgomery, Mn., U.S.	128	G5	44.26 N	93.34 W
Montgomery, Pa., U.S.	124	C8	41.09 N	76.53 W
Montgomery, Tx., U.S.	136	D12	30.23 N	95.42 W
Montgomery, W.V., U.S.	124	F4	38.10 N	81.19 W
Montgomery City, Mo., U.S.	130	F6	38.58 N	91.30 W
Montgomery Knolls, Md., U.S.	202b		39.14 N	76.48 W
Montgomery Mall, shp. cen., Md., U.S.	202c		39.01 N	77.09 W
Montgomery Square, Md., U.S.	202c		39.04 N	77.09 W
Montgomeryville, Pa., U.S.	203		40.15 N	75.15 W
Montgomeryville Airport, arpt., Pa., U.S.	203		40.15 N	75.14 W
Montguyon, Fr.	22	D5	45.13 N	0.11 W
Monthey, Switz.	30	D3	46.15 N	6.56 E
Monthyon, Fr.	179		49.00 N	2.50 E
Monticello, Ar., U.S.	134	D7	33.38 N	91.47 W
Monticello, Fl., U.S.	132	F2	30.32 N	83.52 W
Monticello, Ga., U.S.	132	C2	33.18 N	83.41 W
Monticello, Il., U.S.	130	D9	40.00 N	88.34 W
Monticello, In., U.S.	130	D11	40.44 N	86.45 W
Monticello, Ia., U.S.	130	B6	42.14 N	91.11 W
Monticello, Ky., U.S.	130	H13	36.49 N	84.51 W
Monticello, Mn., U.S.	128	F5	45.18 N	93.47 W
Monticello, Ms., U.S.	134	F8	31.33 N	90.06 W
Monticello, Mo., U.S.	130	D6	40.07 N	91.42 W
Monticello, N.Y., U.S.	124	C11	41.39 N	74.41 W
Monticello, Ut., U.S.	150	F7	37.52 N	109.20 W
Monticello, Wi., U.S.	130	B8	42.44 N	89.35 W
Monticello, hist., Va., U.S.	124	G7	38.00 N	78.30 W
Monticello Woods, Va., U.S.	202c		38.47 N	77.10 W
Montiel, Campo de, pl., Spain	28	F8	38.46 N	2.44 W
Montignac, Fr.	22	D7	45.04 N	1.10 E
Montigny-le-Bretonneux, Fr.	179		48.46 N	2.02 E
Montigny-le-Roi, Fr.	20	G14	48.00 N	5.30 E
Montigny-lès-Cormeilles, Fr.	179		48.59 N	2.12 E
Montigny-lès-Metz, Fr.	20	E15	49.06 N	6.09 E
Montigny-sur-Aube, Fr.	20	F13	47.57 N	4.46 E
Montijo, Pan.	156	I7	7.59 N	81.03 W
Montijo, Port.	28	F2	38.42 N	8.57 W
Montijo, Spain	28	F4	38.55 N	6.37 W
Montijo, Aeroporto, arpt., Port.	184c		38.42 N	9.02 W
Montijo, Golfo de, b., Pan.	156	I7	7.40 N	81.07 W
Montilla, Spain	28	G6	37.35 N	4.38 W
Montivilliers, Fr.	20	E9	49.32 N	0.11 E
Montjay-la-Tour, Fr.	179		48.55 N	2.40 E
Mont-Joli, Qc., Can.	122	B8	48.37 N	68.07 W
Montjuich, Faro de, trans., Spain	184d		41.21 N	2.11 E
Montjuich, Parque de, p.o.i., Spain	184d		41.21 N	2.09 E
Mont-Laurier, Qc., Can.	126	B14	46.32 N	75.30 W
Montlhéry, Tour de, p.o.i., Fr.	179		48.38 N	2.16 E
Montlignon, Fr.	179		49.01 N	2.17 E
Montlouet, Fr.	179		48.31 N	1.43 E
Mont-Louis, Fr.	22	G8	42.30 N	2.07 E
Montluçon, Fr.	22	C8	46.20 N	2.36 E
Montmagny, Qc., Can.	122	D6	46.58 N	70.33 W
Montmagny, Fr.	179		48.58 N	2.21 E
Montmartre, ngh., Fr.	179		48.53 N	2.21 E
Montmédy, Fr.	20	E14	49.31 N	5.22 E
Montmeló, Spain	184d		41.33 N	2.15 E
Montmirail, Fr.	20	F12	48.52 N	3.31 E
Montmorency, Austl.	192b		37.43 S	145.07 E
Montmorency, Fr.	179		49.00 N	2.20 E
Montmorency, stm., Qc., Can.	122	C5	46.52 N	71.07 W
Montmorency, Forêt de, p.o.i., Fr.	179		49.02 N	2.16 E
Montmorillon, Fr.	22	C6	46.26 N	0.52 E
Monto, Austl.	98	E8	24.52 S	151.07 E
Montone, stm., Italy	30	G8	44.23 N	12.12 E
Mont-Orford, Parc de récréation du, p.o.i., Qc., Can.	122	E4	45.21 N	72.11 W
Montoro, Spain	28	F6	38.00 N	4.22 W
Montour Falls, N.Y., U.S.	124	B9	42.21 N	76.50 W
Montour Run, stm., Pa., U.S.	197b		40.31 N	80.08 W
Montour Run, stm., Pa., U.S.	197b		40.36 N	79.57 W
Montoursville, Pa., U.S.	124	C9	41.15 N	76.55 W
Mont Park, Austl.	192b		37.43 S	145.04 E
Montparnasse, Gare, trans., Fr.	179		48.51 N	2.19 E
Montpelier, Jam.	158d	i13	18.22 N	77.55 W
Montpelier, Id., U.S.	146	H15	42.19 N	111.18 W
Montpelier, In., U.S.	130	D12	40.32 N	85.16 W
Montpelier, Md., U.S.	202c		39.04 N	76.51 W
Montpelier, Ms., U.S.	134	D10	33.43 N	88.56 W
Montpelier, Oh., U.S.	124	C1	41.34 N	84.35 W
Montpelier, Vt., U.S.	122	F4	44.15 N	72.34 W
Montpellier, Fr.	22	F9	43.36 N	3.52 E
Mont-Pichet, Fr.	179		48.53 N	2.54 E
Montréal-Ménesterol, Fr.	22	D6	45.00 N	0.09 E
Montréal, Qc., Can.	126	C16	45.29 N	73.33 W
Montréal, Qc., Can.	193a		45.31 N	73.34 W
Montreal, Wi., U.S.	128	E8	46.25 N	90.14 W
Montreal, stm., On., Can.	126	A10	47.06 N	79.28 W
Montreal, stm., U.S.	128	E8	46.33 N	90.24 W
Montréal, Base des Forces Canadiennes, mil., Qc., Can.	193a		45.31 N	73.25 W
Montréal, Université de, educ., Qc., Can.	193a		45.30 N	73.37 W
Montreal Lake, l., Sk., Can.	110	E9	54.20 N	105.40 W
Montréal-Ouest, Qc., Can.	193a		45.27 N	73.39 W
Montreal Water Works Aqueduct, aq., Qc., Can.	193a		45.26 N	73.36 W
Montreuil, Fr.	179		48.52 N	2.26 E
Montreuil-sur-Mer, Fr.	20	D10	50.27 N	1.46 E
Montreux, Switz.	30	D3	46.26 N	6.54 E
Montrose, Austl.	192b		37.49 S	145.21 E
Montrose, Scot., U.K.	10	E10	56.42 N	2.28 W
Montrose, Co., U.S.	150	E9	38.28 N	107.52 W
Montrose, Ia., U.S.	130	D6	40.31 N	91.25 W
Montrose, Mi., U.S.	126	E6	43.10 N	83.53 W
Montrose, Pa., U.S.	124	C10	41.50 N	75.52 W
Montrose, S.D., U.S.	140	D15	43.42 N	97.11 W
Montrose Harbor, b., Il., U.S.	196		41.58 N	87.38 W
Montrose Hill, Pa., U.S.	197b		40.30 N	79.51 W
Montross, Va., U.S.	124	F9	38.05 N	76.49 W
Montrouge, Fr.	179		48.49 N	2.19 E
Mont Royal, Parc, p.o.i., Qc., Can.	193a		45.31 N	73.35 W
Mont Royal Tunnel, trans., Qc., Can.	193a		45.31 N	73.38 W
Montry, Fr.	179		48.53 N	2.50 E
Monts, Pointe des, c., Qc., Can.	122	A9	49.19 N	67.22 W
Mont-Sainte-Anne, Parc du, p.o.i., Qc., Can.	122	C5	47.08 N	70.55 W
Mont-Saint-Michel, Qc., Can.	126	B14	46.47 N	75.20 W
Mont-Saint-Michel, Baie du, b., Fr.	20	F7	48.41 N	1.34 W
Mont-Saint-Michel, Le, rel., Fr.	20	F7	48.36 N	1.30 W
Montserrat, dep., N.A.	159a	d3	16.45 N	62.12 W
Montserrat, Monasterio de see Montserrat, Monestir de, rel., Spain	28	C12	41.36 N	1.49 E
Montserrat, Monestir de, rel., Spain	28	C12	41.36 N	1.49 E
Montsoult, Fr.	179		49.04 N	2.19 E
Mont-Tremblant, Parc de récréation du, p.o.i., Qc., Can.	126	B15	46.30 N	74.10 W
Montuenga, Spain	28	C6	41.02 N	4.37 W
Montvale, N.J., U.S.	194		41.02 N	74.01 W
Montville, N.J., U.S.	194		40.54 N	74.23 W
Montville Airpark, arpt., N.J., U.S.	194		40.56 N	74.20 W
Monument, S. Afr.	191d		26.06 S	27.43 E
Monument, Or., U.S.	146	F7	44.49 N	119.25 W
Monument Draw, stm., U.S.	136	B5	32.27 N	102.20 W
Monument Draw, stm., Tx., U.S.	136	D5	30.51 N	102.33 W
Monument Peak, mtn., Co., U.S.	150	D9	39.43 N	107.55 W
Monument Peak, mtn., Id., U.S.	146	H12	42.07 N	114.14 W
Monument Valley, val., U.S.	150	F6	37.05 N	110.20 W
Monviso, mtn., Italy	30	F4	44.40 N	7.07 E
Monyo, Mya.	64	C2	17.58 N	95.30 E
Monywa, Mya.	64	A2	22.06 N	95.08 E
Monza, Italy	30	E6	45.35 N	9.16 E
Monze, Zam.	88	D4	16.16 S	27.29 E
Monzen, Japan	56	B9	37.17 N	136.45 E
Monzón, Spain	28	C11	41.54 N	0.11 E
Moóca, ngh., Braz.	205b		23.33 S	46.35 W
Moóca, Ribeirão da, stm., Braz.	205b		23.36 S	46.35 W
Moody, Tx., U.S.	136	C10	31.18 N	97.21 W
Moody Air Force Base, mil., Ga., U.S.	132	F2	30.59 N	83.11 W
Moody Wood Dale Airport, arpt., Il., U.S.	196		41.59 N	87.58 W
Mooi, stm., S. Afr.	90	F10	28.46 S	30.34 E
Moolawatana, Austl.	98	G2	29.54 S	139.42 E
Moon, Mountains of the see Ruwenzori, mts., Afr.	86	D6	0.20 N	29.53 E
Moonachie, N.J., U.S.	194		40.50 N	74.02 W
Moonbeam, On., Can.	114	B9	49.21 N	82.09 W
Moon Crest, Pa., U.S.	197b		40.32 N	80.11 W
Moonee Valley Racecourse, p.o.i., Austl.	192b		37.46 S	144.56 E
Moonie, Austl.	98	F8	27.44 S	150.21 E
Moonie, stm., Austl.	98	G7	29.19 S	148.43 E
Moon Island, i., Ma., U.S.	201		42.18 N	71.00 W
Moora, Austl.	96	F3	30.38 S	116.00 E
Moorabbin Airport, arpt., Austl.	192b		37.59 S	145.09 E
Mooraberree, Austl.	98	E3	25.14 S	140.59 E
Moorbad Lobenstein, Ger.	24	F7	50.26 N	11.39 E
Moorcroft, Wy., U.S.	140	C8	44.15 N	104.56 W
Moore, Eng., U.K.	180		53.21 N	2.38 W
Moore, Id., U.S.	146	G13	43.44 N	113.24 W
Moore, Mt., U.S.	146	D17	46.58 N	109.43 W
Moore, Ok., U.S.	138	F11	35.21 N	97.28 W
Moore, Tx., U.S.	136	E8	29.03 N	99.01 W
Moore, Lake, l., Austl.	96	E3	29.43 S	117.31 E
Moorea, i., Fr. Poly.	100h	v20	17.32 S	149.50 W
Moorebank, Austl.	192a		33.56 S	150.56 E
Moorefield, W.V., U.S.	124	E7	39.03 N	78.58 W
Moore Haven, Fl., U.S.	132	J4	26.49 N	81.05 W
Moore Lake, l., Mi., U.S.	199		42.37 N	83.36 W
Mooreland, Ok., U.S.	138	E9	36.26 N	99.12 W
Moore Point, c., On., Can.	193b		43.48 N	79.03 W
Moore Reservoir, res., U.S.	122	F4	44.20 N	71.52 W
Moores Creek National Battlefield, p.o.i., N.C., U.S.	132	B7	34.24 N	78.08 W
Moore's Island, i., Bah.	132	J8	26.18 N	77.33 W
Moorestown Mall, shp. cen., N.J., U.S.	203		39.56 N	74.58 W
Mooresville, In., U.S.	130	E11	39.36 N	86.22 W
Mooresville, N.C., U.S.	132	A5	35.35 N	80.48 W
Mooreville, Mi., U.S.	199		42.06 N	83.44 W
Moorhead, Mn., U.S.	128	E2	46.53 N	96.45 W
Moorhead, Ms., U.S.	134	D8	33.27 N	90.30 W
Mooringsport, La., U.S.	136	B14	32.41 N	93.57 W
Moornanyah Lake, l., Austl.	98	I4	33.00 S	143.55 E
Mooroolbark, Austl.	192b		37.47 S	145.19 E
Moorreesburg, S. Afr.	90	H4	33.08 S	18.39 E
Moorside, Eng., U.K.	180		53.34 N	2.04 W
Moosbrunn, Aus.	182b		48.01 N	16.28 E
Moosburg an der Isar, Ger.	24	H7	48.28 N	11.56 E
Moose, stm., Me., U.S.	122	E6	45.41 N	69.45 W
Moosehead Lake, l., Me., U.S.	122	E7	45.37 N	69.39 W
Moose Heights, B.C., Can.	144	C8	53.05 N	122.30 W
Moose Hill, hill, Ma., U.S.	201		42.07 N	71.13 W
Moose Island, i., Mb., Can.	142	C16	51.38 N	97.08 W
Moose Jaw, Sk., Can.	142	D8	50.23 N	105.32 W
Moose Jaw, stm., Sk., Can.	142	D8	50.34 N	105.16 W
Moose Lake, Mn., U.S.	128	E6	46.27 N	92.45 W
Moose Lake, l., Ab., Can.	144	B19	54.15 N	110.55 W
Mooselookmeguntic Lake, l., Me., U.S.	122	F6	44.53 N	70.48 W
Moose Mountain, mtn., Sk., Can.	142	E11	49.45 N	102.37 W
Moose Mountain Creek, stm., Sk., Can.	142	E11	49.12 N	102.12 W
Moose Mountain Provincial Park, p.o.i., Sk., Can.	142	E11	49.48 N	102.25 W
Moose Pass, Ak., U.S.	109	D10	60.30 N	149.23 W
Moosomin, Sk., Can.	142	D12	50.08 N	101.40 W
Moosomin Indian Reserve, ind. res., Sk., Can.	142	A5	53.06 N	108.13 W
Moosonee, On., Can.	110	E14	51.16 N	80.39 W
Mootwingee National Park, p.o.i., Austl.	98	H4	31.03 S	142.29 E
Mopane, S. Afr.	90	C9	22.36 S	29.51 E
Mopeia, Moz.	88	D6	17.58 S	35.43 E
Mopipi, Bots.	90	B7	21.07 S	24.55 E
Moppo see Mokp'o, Kor., S.	54	G7	34.47 N	126.23 E
Mopti, Mali	84	G4	14.29 N	4.11 W
Moquegua, Peru	164	G3	17.12 S	70.57 W
Mór, Hung.	36	B5	47.22 N	18.12 E
Mòr, Glen, val., Scot., U.K.	10	E8	57.08 N	4.38 W
Mora, Cam.	86	B2	11.02 N	14.08 E
Mora, India	190c		18.54 N	72.56 E
Mora, Port.	28	F2	38.56 N	8.09 W
Mora, Swe.	16	F12	61.00 N	14.34 E
Mora, Mn., U.S.	128	F5	45.52 N	93.17 W
Mora, N.M., U.S.	138	F3	35.58 N	105.21 W
Mora, stm., N.M., U.S.	138	E3	35.44 N	104.23 W
Mora, Arroyo, stm., N.M., U.S.	138	G4	34.01 N	104.19 W
Morač, stm., Bela.	26	H10	52.34 N	27.35 E
Morača, Manastir, rel., Yugo.	36	G6	42.44 N	19.20 E
Morādābād, India	70	D7	28.50 N	78.46 E
Morada Nova, Braz.	170	C6	5.07 S	38.23 W
Morada Nova de Minas, Braz.	170	J3	18.36 S	45.21 W
Mora de Rubielos, Spain	28	D10	40.15 N	0.45 W
Morąg, Pol.	24	C15	53.55 N	19.56 E
Morainvilliers, Fr.	179		48.56 N	1.56 E
Moral de Calatrava, Spain	28	F7	38.50 N	3.35 W
Moraleda, Canal, strt., Chile	166	H2	44.30 S	73.30 W
Morales, Laguna de, b., Mex.	154	D10	23.42 N	97.45 W
Moramanga, Madag.	88	D8	18.57 S	48.13 E
Moran, Ks., U.S.	130	G2	37.54 N	95.10 W
Moran, Mi., U.S.	126	B5	45.59 N	84.50 W
Moran, Tx., U.S.	136	B8	32.32 N	99.10 W
Moranbah, Austl.	98	D6	22.00 S	148.02 E
Morangis, Fr.	179		48.42 N	2.20 E
Morant Bay, Jam.	158d	j14	17.53 N	76.25 W
Morant Cays, is., Jam.	156	D10	17.24 N	75.59 W
Morant Point, c., Jam.	158d	j14	17.54 N	76.11 W
Morar, Loch, l., Scot., U.K.	10	E7	56.57 N	5.43 W
Moratalla, Spain	28	F9	38.11 N	1.53 W
Moratuwa, Sri L.	69	H4	6.47 N	79.52 E
Morava, hist. reg., Czech Rep.	24	G13	49.30 N	17.00 E
Morava (March), stm., Eur.	24	H12	48.10 N	16.59 E
Morāveh Tappeh, Iran	74	B14	37.54 N	55.57 E
Moravia, Ia., U.S.	130	D5	40.53 N	92.49 W
Moravia, N.Y., U.S.	124	B9	42.42 N	76.24 W
Moravská Ostrava see Ostrava, Czech Rep.	24	G14	49.50 N	18.17 E
Moravská Třebová, Czech Rep.	24	G12	49.45 N	16.39 E
Moravské Budějovice, Czech Rep.	24	G11	49.02 N	15.48 E
Moravský Krumlov, Czech Rep.	24	G12	49.03 N	16.18 E
Morawa, Austl.	96	E3	29.12 S	116.00 E
Morawhanna, Guy.	168	C12	8.17 N	59.44 W
Moray Firth, b., Scot., U.K.	10	D9	58.01 N	3.04 W
Morbi, India	70	G3	22.49 N	70.50 E
Morbihan, state, Fr.	20	G6	47.55 N	2.50 W
Morbras, stm., Fr.	179		48.47 N	2.29 E
Morcenx, Fr.	22	E5	44.01 N	0.54 W
Morden, Mb., Can.	142	E15	49.11 N	98.05 W
Morden, ngh., Eng., U.K.	178		51.24 N	0.12 W
Mordovia see Mordovija, state, Russia	40	D14	54.30 N	44.00 E
Mordovija, state, Russia	40	D14	54.30 N	44.00 E
Mordovo, Russia	48	D6	52.05 N	40.45 E
Mordves, Russia	26	F21	54.34 N	38.13 E
Mordvinia see Mordovija, state, Russia	40	D14	54.30 N	44.00 E
Mordy, Pol.	24	D18	52.12 N	22.30 E
More, Ben, mtn., Scot., U.K.	10	E8	56.22 N	4.35 W
More, Ben, mtn., Scot., U.K.	10	E7	56.25 N	6.01 W
More Assynt, Ben, mtn., Scot., U.K.	10	C8	58.08 N	4.53 W
Moreau, stm., S.D., U.S.	140	B12	45.19 N	100.19 W
Moreau, North Fork, stm., S.D., U.S.	140	B9	45.08 N	102.50 W
Moreau, South Fork, stm., S.D., U.S.	140	B9	45.08 N	102.50 W
Moreau Peak, mtn., S.D., U.S.	140	B9	45.21 N	103.43 W
Moreauville, La., U.S.	134	F7	31.01 N	91.58 W
Morec, Russia	40	F14	51.01 N	44.02 E
Morecambe, Eng., U.K.	10	G9	54.03 N	2.52 W
Morecambe Bay, b., Eng., U.K.	10	G9	54.06 N	2.59 W
Moree, Austl.	98	G7	29.28 S	149.51 E
Morehead, Ky., U.S.	124	F2	38.10 N	83.26 W
Morehead City, N.C., U.S.	132	B9	34.43 N	76.44 W
Morehouse, Mo., U.S.	130	H8	36.51 N	89.41 W
Moreland, Austl.	192b		37.45 S	144.58 E
Moreland, Ga., U.S.	134	D14	33.17 N	84.46 W
Moreland, Ky., U.S.	130	G13	37.30 N	84.49 W
Moreland Hills, Oh., U.S.	197a		41.27 N	81.29 W
Morelia, Mex.	154	F8	19.42 N	101.11 W
Morell, P.E., Can.	122	D14	46.25 N	62.41 W
Morella, Austl.	98	D4	22.58 S	143.51 E
Morella, Spain	28	D10	40.37 N	0.06 W
Morelos, Mex.	136	F7	28.25 N	100.52 W
Morelos, Mex.	136	I2	25.44 N	105.14 W
Morelos, Mex.	154	B5	26.42 N	107.40 W
Morelos, state, Mex.	154	F9	18.45 N	99.00 W
Morena, India	70	E6	26.26 N	78.02 E
Morena, Sierra, mtn., Ca., U.S.	200		37.25 N	122.18 W
Morena, Sierra, mts., Spain	28	F5	38.00 N	5.00 W
Morenci, Az., U.S.	150	J7	33.04 N	109.21 W
Morenci, Mi., U.S.	124	C1	41.43 N	84.13 W
Moreni, Rom.	36	D12	44.59 N	25.38 E
Moreno, state, Arg.	206		34.36 S	58.48 W
Moreno, Bahía, b., Chile	172	A2	23.36 S	70.29 W
Møre og Romsdal, state, Nor.	16	E5	62.40 N	7.50 E
Moresby Island, i., B.C., Can.	110	E4	52.50 N	131.55 W
Moreton, Austl.	96	B8	12.26 S	142.37 E
Moreton, Eng., U.K.	178		51.44 N	0.14 E
Moreton Island, i., Austl.	98	F9	27.10 S	153.24 E
Moreuil, Fr.	20	E11	49.46 N	2.29 E
Morey Peak, mtn., Nv., U.S.	148	E9	38.38 N	116.16 W
Morez, Fr.	20	H14	46.30 N	6.01 E
Morgan, Austl.	98	I2	34.01 S	139.40 E
Morgan, Ga., U.S.	134	F14	31.32 N	84.35 W
Morgan, Mn., U.S.	128	G3	44.24 N	94.56 W
Morgan, Mt., U.S.	142	F6	48.59 N	107.50 W
Morgan, Pa., U.S.	197b		40.22 N	80.08 W
Morgan, Tx., U.S.	136	B10	32.00 N	97.37 W
Morgan, Ut., U.S.	150	B5	41.03 N	111.40 W
Morgan City, Al., U.S.	134	C12	34.27 N	86.34 W
Morgan City, La., U.S.	134	H7	29.42 N	91.12 W
Morgan Creek, stm., Tx., U.S.	136	B6	32.19 N	100.55 W
Morganfield, Ky., U.S.	130	G10	37.41 N	87.54 W
Morgan Hill, Ca., U.S.	148	F4	37.06 N	121.38 W
Morganito, Ven.	168	E8	5.05 N	67.44 W
Morgan Park, ngh., Il., U.S.	196		41.42 N	87.40 W
Morgan State College, educ., Md., U.S.	202b		39.21 N	76.35 W
Morganton, N.C., U.S.	124	I4	35.44 N	81.41 W
Morgantown, In., U.S.	130	E11	39.22 N	86.15 W
Morgantown, Ky., U.S.	130	G11	37.13 N	86.41 W
Morgantown, Ms., U.S.	134	F7	31.34 N	91.20 W
Morgantown, Ms., U.S.	134	F8	31.18 N	89.54 W
Morgantown, W.V., U.S.	124	E6	39.37 N	79.57 W
Morganza, La., U.S.	134	G7	30.44 N	91.35 W
Morgenzon, S. Afr.	90	E9	26.44 S	29.37 E
Morghāb (Murgab), stm., Asia	72	B9	38.37 N	61.09 E
Morguilla, Punta, c., Chile	166	G2	37.43 S	73.39 W
Mori, Japan	188		34.32 N	135.00 E
Moriah, Mount, mtn., Nv., U.S.	150	D2	39.17 N	114.12 W
Moriarty, N.M., U.S.	138	G2	35.00 N	106.03 W
Morice, stm., B.C., Can.	144	B4	54.24 N	126.44 W
Morice Lake, l., B.C., Can.	144	B3	54.00 N	127.37 W
Morichal Largo, stm., Ven.	168	C10	9.26 N	62.24 W
Moricsala rezervāts, ind. res., Lat.	26	C5	57.17 N	22.11 E
Morija, Leso.	90	F8	29.37 S	27.30 E
Moriki, Nig.	84	G6	12.52 N	6.30 E
Moringen, Ger.	24	E5	51.42 N	9.52 E
Morino, Russia	26	C13	57.53 N	30.21 E
Morinville, Ab., Can.	144	C17	53.48 N	113.40 W
Morioka, Japan	54	E14	39.42 N	141.08 E
Morīri, Tso, l., India	70	B6	32.54 N	78.20 E
Morisset, Austl.	98	I8	33.06 S	151.28 E
Moriston, stm., Scot., U.K.	10	D8	57.12 N	4.36 W
Morivione, ngh., Italy	184b		45.26 N	9.12 E
Morivs'k, Ukr.	38	B9	51.05 N	30.53 E
Morjakovskij Zaton, Russia	48	C14	56.41 N	84.39 E
Morjärv, Swe.	14	F13	66.03 N	22.42 E
Morki, Russia	40	C16	56.25 N	49.00 E
Morkill, stm., B.C., Can.	144	C10	53.36 N	120.41 W
Morkiny Gory, Russia	26	C19	57.32 N	36.18 E
Mörkö, i., Swe.	16	I15	58.59 N	17.40 E
Morkoka, stm., Russia	50	D11	65.10 N	115.50 E
Morlaix, Fr.	20	F5	48.34 N	3.50 W
Morley, Mi., U.S.	126	E4	43.28 N	85.26 W
Morley Green, Eng., U.K.	180		53.20 N	2.16 W
Mörlunda, Swe.	16	J13	57.18 N	15.52 E
Mormal', Bela.	26	H12	52.45 N	29.52 E
Mormanno, Italy	32	E10	39.53 N	16.00 E
Mormon Lake, l., Az., U.S.	150	I5	34.57 N	111.27 W
Mormon Peak, mtn., Nv., U.S.	150	G2	36.57 N	114.27 W
Mormon Reservoir, res., Id., U.S.	146	G12	43.15 N	114.49 W
Mormugao, India	69	D1	15.24 N	73.48 E
Morna, India	190a		28.35 N	77.22 E
Morne-à-l'Eau, Guad.	159c	h6	16.20 N	61.26 W
Morne du Vitet, hill, Guad.	159a	b2	17.54 N	62.48 W
Morne Trois Pitons National Park, p.o.i., Dom.	159c	j6	15.19 N	61.18 W
Morney, Austl.	98	E3	25.22 S	141.28 E
Morningside, Md., U.S.	202c		38.50 N	76.53 W
Morningside Park, p.o.i., On., Can.	193b		43.47 N	79.12 W
Morning Sun, Ia., U.S.	130	C6	41.05 N	91.14 W
Mornington, Austl.	98	L5	38.13 S	145.02 E
Mornington, Isla, i., Chile	166	I1	49.45 S	75.23 W
Mornington Island, i., Austl.	96	C7	16.33 S	139.24 E
Mornou, Hadjer, mtn., Chad	82	D4	17.16 N	23.10 E
Moro, Or., U.S.	146	E6	45.28 N	120.44 W
Morobe, Pap. N. Gui.	101a	b4	7.48 S	147.39 E
Morocco, In., U.S.	130	D10	40.56 N	87.26 W
Morocco, ctry., Afr.	84	C4	32.00 N	5.00 W
Moro Creek, stm., Ar., U.S.	134	D6	33.17 N	92.21 W
Morogoro, Tan.	86	F7	6.49 S	37.40 E
Moro Gulf, b., Phil.	68	G4	6.51 N	123.00 E
Moroka, S. Afr.	191d		26.16 S	27.52 E
Morokweng, S. Afr.	90	E6	26.07 S	23.46 E
Moroleón, Mex.	154	E8	20.07 N	101.11 W
Morombe, Madag.	88	E7	21.44 S	43.21 E
Morón, Arg.	172	G8	34.38 S	58.36 W
Morón, Cuba	156	A8	22.06 N	78.37 W
Mörön, Mong.	52	B5	49.38 N	100.09 E
Morón, Ven.	168	B7	10.29 N	68.11 W
Morón, state, Arg.	206		34.37 S	58.37 W
Morón, Aeródromo, arpt., Arg.	206		34.41 S	58.38 W
Morón, Arroyo, stm., Arg.	206		34.33 S	58.37 W
Morona, stm., S.A.	168	I3	4.45 S	77.04 W
Morona Santiago, state, Ec.	168	I3	2.31 S	77.50 W
Morondava, Madag.	88	E7	20.17 S	44.16 E
Morón de Almazán, Spain	28	C8	41.24 N	2.23 W
Morón de la Frontera, Spain	28	G5	37.07 N	5.26 W
Morongo Indian Reservation, ind. res., Ca., U.S.	148	J9	33.58 N	116.48 W
Moroni, Com.	88	C7	11.42 S	43.14 E
Moroni, Ut., U.S.	150	D5	39.31 N	111.35 W
Moron Us, stm., China	52	E3	34.40 N	94.55 E
Moros, stm., Spain	28	D6	41.03 N	4.15 W
Morošečnoe, Russia	50	E20	56.22 N	156.13 E
Morotai, i., Indon.	60	E8	2.20 N	128.25 E
Moroto, Ug.	86	D6	2.31 N	34.39 E
Moroto, mtn., Ug.	86	D6	2.32 N	34.46 E
Morovis, P.R.	158a	b3	18.20 N	66.24 W
Morozovka, Russia	38	C18	50.08 N	39.39 E
Morozovsk, Russia	40	G12	48.21 N	41.50 E
Morpeth, Eng., U.K.	10	F11	55.10 N	1.41 W
Morra, Monte, mtn., Italy	185a		42.02 N	12.50 E
Morral, Arroyo del, stm., Spain	184d		41.29 N	2.03 E
Morrill, Ne., U.S.	140	F9	41.57 N	103.57 W
Morrilton, Ar., U.S.	134	B6	35.09 N	92.44 W
Morrin, Ab., Can.	144	E18	51.39 N	112.45 W
Morrinhos, Braz.	170	B5	3.14 S	40.07 W
Morrinhos, Braz.	170	I1	17.43 S	49.06 W
Morrinsville, N.Z.	102	C6	37.39 S	175.31 E
Morris, Mb., Can.	142	E16	49.21 N	97.22 W
Morris, Il., U.S.	130	C9	41.21 N	88.25 W
Morris, Mn., U.S.	128	F3	45.35 N	95.55 W
Morris, Ok., U.S.	134	B3	35.37 N	95.51 W
Morris, stm., Mb., Can.	142	E16	49.21 N	97.21 W
Morrisburg, On., Can.	126	D14	44.54 N	75.10 W
Morris Dam, dam., Ca., U.S.	198		34.11 N	117.53 W
Morris Jesup, Kap, c., Grnld.	108	A19	83.35 N	33.47 W
Morris Lake, l., N.J., U.S.	194		41.03 N	74.37 W
Morrison, Arg.	172	F6	32.36 S	62.50 W
Morrison, Il., U.S.	130	C8	41.48 N	89.57 W
Morrison Creek, stm., On., Can.	193b		43.28 N	79.39 W
Morrisonville, Il., U.S.	130	E8	39.24 N	89.27 W
Morris Park, p.o.i., Pa., U.S.	203		39.59 N	75.15 W
Morristown, Az., U.S.	150	J4	33.52 N	112.39 W
Morristown, In., U.S.	130	E12	39.40 N	85.42 W
Morristown, Mn., U.S.	128	G5	44.14 N	93.26 W
Morristown, S.D., U.S.	140	B11	45.55 N	101.45 W
Morristown, Tn., U.S.	124	H2	36.13 N	83.17 W
Morristown Airport, arpt., N.J., U.S.	194		40.48 N	74.25 W
Morrisville, N.Y., U.S.	124	B10	42.53 N	75.38 W
Morrisville, Pa., U.S.	126	H15	40.12 N	74.47 W
Morro, Ec.	168	I1	2.39 S	80.19 W
Morro, Castillo del (Morro Castle), hist., Cuba	204b		23.09 N	82.21 W
Morro, Punta, c., Mex.	156	C2	19.39 N	90.40 W
Morro Agudo, Braz.	205a		22.45 S	43.29 W
Morro Bay, Ca., U.S.	148	H5	35.22 N	120.50 W
Morro do Chapéu, Braz.	170	F5	11.33 S	41.09 W
Morros, Braz.	170	B3	2.52 S	44.03 W
Morrosquillo, Golfo de, b., Col.	168	C4	9.35 N	75.40 W
Morrow, La., U.S.	134	G6	30.49 N	92.05 W
Morrow Island, i., Ca., U.S.	200		38.07 N	122.05 W
Morrow Mountain State Park, p.o.i., N.C., U.S.	132	A5	35.23 N	80.05 W
Mörrum, Swe.	16	K12	56.10 N	14.45 E
Morrumbala, Moz.	88	D6	17.21 S	35.34 E
Morrumbene, Moz.	90	C12	23.39 S	35.21 E
Mors, i., Den.	16	K6	56.50 N	8.45 E
Morsang-sur-Orge, Fr.	179		48.40 N	2.21 E
Moršansk, Russia	40	E12	53.25 N	41.48 E
Morščihino, Russia	183b		55.56 N	37.20 E
Morse, Sk., Can.	142	D6	50.25 N	107.03 W
Morse, La., U.S.	134	G6	30.07 N	92.30 W
Morse, Tx., U.S.	138	E7	36.03 N	101.28 W
Mörsenbroich, ngh., Ger.	181		51.15 N	6.48 E
Morses Pond, l., Ma., U.S.	201		42.18 N	71.19 W
Morsi, India	70	H6	21.20 N	78.01 E
Mörsil, Swe.	16	D11	63.19 N	13.40 E
Morskaja Masel'ga, Russia	18	D21	63.06 N	34.54 E
Mörskom see Myrskylä, Fin.	18	G12	60.39 N	25.50 E
Morson, On., Can.	128	B4	49.07 N	94.18 W
Morstein, Pa., U.S.	203		40.01 N	75.35 W
Mort, India	190a		28.43 N	77.25 E
Morta, India	190a		28.44 N	77.27 E
Mortagne-au-Perche, Fr.	20	F9	48.31 N	0.33 E
Mortagne-sur-Sèvre, Fr.	20	G8	47.00 N	0.57 W
Mortain, Fr.	20	F8	48.39 N	0.56 W
Mortara, Italy	30	E5	45.15 N	8.44 E
Morteau, Fr.	20	G15	47.03 N	6.35 E
Morteros, Arg.	172	E6	30.42 S	62.00 W
Mortes, stm., Braz.	166	B6	11.43 S	50.42 W
Mortlach, Sk., Can.	142	D7	50.28 N	106.03 W
Mortlake, Austl.	98	L4	38.04 S	142.48 E
Mortlake, Austl.	192a		33.51 S	151.07 E
Mortlake, ngh., Eng., U.K.	178		51.28 N	0.16 W
Mortlock Islands, is., Micron.	94	C6	5.27 N	153.40 E
Morton, Il., U.S.	130	D8	40.36 N	89.27 W
Morton, Mn., U.S.	128	G4	44.33 N	94.59 W

Name	Page	Map Ref.	Latitude	Longitude
Morton, Ms., U.S.	134	E9	32.21 N	89.39 W
Morton, Pa., U.S.	203		39.55 N	75.20 W
Morton, Tx., U.S.	138	H6	33.43 N	102.45 W
Morton, Wa., U.S.	146	D4	46.32 N	122.16 W
Morton, Mount, hill, Austl.	192b		37.56 S	145.20 E
Morton Arboretum, p.o.i., Il., U.S.	196		41.49 N	88.04 W
Morton National Park, p.o.i., Austl.	98	J7	34.57 S	150.11 E
Mortons Gap, Ky., U.S.	130	G10	37.14 N	87.28 W
Mortorness del Vallès, Spain	184d		41.33 N	2.16 E
Morua, Vanuatu	101d	k17	16.54 S	168.32 E
Morumbi, ngh., Braz.	205b		23.36 S	46.42 E
Morumbi, Estádio do, p.o.i., Braz.	205b		23.37 S	46.43 W
Moruya, Austl.	98	J7	35.55 S	150.04 E
Morvan, mts., Fr.	20	G13	47.05 N	4.00 E
Morvant, Trin.	159f	s12	10.39 N	61.28 W
Morven, Austl.	98	F6	26.23 S	147.03 E
Morven, Ga., U.S.	132	F2	30.56 N	83.29 W
Morven, N.C., U.S.	132	B5	34.50 N	80.00 W
Morven, mtn., Scot., U.K.	10	C9	58.14 N	3.42 W
Morwell, Austl.	98	L6	38.14 S	146.24 E
Moryń, Pol.	28	D10	52.51 N	14.23 E
Morzine, Fr.	22	C12	46.10 N	6.42 E
Moržovec, ostrov, i., Russia	12	C20	66.44 N	42.35 E
Moša, stm., Russia	40	D17	62.24 N	39.48 E
Mosal'sk, Russia	26	F17	54.29 N	34.57 E
Mosbach, Ger.	24	G5	49.21 N	9.08 E
Mosby, Nor.	16	I5	58.12 N	7.55 E
Mosby Woods, Va., U.S.	202c		38.52 N	77.18 W
Moscavide, Port.	184c		38.47 N	9.06 W
Moščnyj, ostrov, i., Russia	18	H14	60.00 N	27.50 E
Moscos Islands, is., Mya.	64	E3	14.19 N	97.45 E
Moscow see Moskva, Russia	26	E20	55.44 N	37.38 E
Moscow, Id., U.S.	146	D10	46.43 N	117.00 W
Moscow see Moskva, stm., Russia	26	E20	55.04 N	38.51 E
Moscow Air Terminal, arpt., Russia	183b		55.48 N	37.32 E
Moscow Circus, p.o.i., Russia	183b		55.43 N	37.33 E
Moscow Station, trans., Russia	183a		59.56 N	30.22 E
Moscow Victory Park, p.o.i., Russia	183a		59.52 N	30.20 E
Moscow Zoo, p.o.i., Russia	183b		55.46 N	37.34 E
Mosel (Moselle), stm., Eur.	24	G2	50.22 N	7.36 E
Moselebe, stm., Bots.	90	D7	25.01 S	23.12 E
Moselle, Ms., U.S.	134	F9	31.30 N	89.16 W
Moselle, state, Fr.	20	F15	49.00 N	6.30 E
Moselle (Mosel), stm., Eur.	24	G2	50.22 N	7.36 E
Moselotte, stm., Fr.	20	F15	48.00 N	6.37 E
Mošenskoe, Russia	26	B17	58.31 N	34.35 E
Mosers River, N.S., Can.	122	F14	44.59 N	62.16 W
Moses Lake, Wa., U.S.	146	C7	47.07 N	119.16 W
Moses Lake, res., Wa., U.S.	146	C7	47.06 N	119.19 W
Moses Point, Ak., U.S.	109	D7	64.42 N	162.03 W
Moses Power Plant, dam., N.Y., U.S.	202a		43.09 N	79.02 W
Mosetse, Bots.	90	B8	20.38 S	26.33 E
Moshaweng, stm., S. Afr.	90	E6	26.43 S	22.28 E
Mosheim, Tn., U.S.	124	H3	36.11 N	82.57 W
Moshi, Tan.	86	E7	3.20 S	37.20 E
Moshny, Ukr.	38	D10	49.31 N	31.44 E
Mosinee, Wi., U.S.	128	G9	44.47 N	89.42 W
Mosjøen, Nor.	16	B11	65.51 N	13.11 E
Moskalvo, Russia	50	F17	53.33 N	142.29 E
Moskenesøya, i., Nor.	14	E4	67.59 N	13.06 E
Moskenstraumen, strt., Nor.	14	E3	67.47 N	12.47 E
Moskháton, Grc.	185c		37.57 N	23.41 E
Moskosel, Swe.	14	G10	65.52 N	19.28 E
Moskovskaja oblast', state, Russia	183b		55.85 N	37.40 E
Moskovskaja oblast', co., Russia	40	C10	55.30 N	37.30 E
Moskovskaja Slav'anka, Russia	183a		59.45 N	30.30 E
Moskovskaja vozvyšennost', plat., Russia	26	D20	56.05 N	37.08 E
Moskva (Moscow), Russia	26	E20	55.44 N	37.38 E
Moskva (Moscow), Russia	183b		55.45 N	37.35 E
Moskva, stm., Russia	26	E20	55.04 N	38.51 E
Moskva, Gorod, mun., Russia	183b		55.45 N	37.35 E
Moskvy, kanal imeni, can., Russia	26	D20	56.44 N	37.06 E
Mosomane, Bots.	90	C8	24.01 S	26.19 E
Mosoni-Duna, stm., Hung.	30	C14	47.53 N	17.19 E
Mosonmagyaróvár, Hung.	36	B4	47.51 N	17.16 E
Mosopa, Bots.	90	D7	24.46 S	25.24 E
Mospyne, Ukr.	38	F17	47.52 N	38.03 E
Mosqueiro, Braz.	164	D8	1.10 S	48.27 W
Mosquera, Col.	168	F2	2.29 N	78.26 W
Mosquero, N.M., U.S.	138	F5	35.46 N	103.57 W
Mosquito, Punta, c., Pan.	156	H9	9.07 N	77.53 W
Mosquito Brook, stm., Ma., U.S.	201		42.40 N	71.02 W
Mosquito Coast see Mosquitos, Costa de, hist. reg., Nic.	156	F6	13.00 N	83.45 W
Mosquito Creek, stm., Ia., U.S.	130	C2	41.10 N	95.50 W
Mosquito Creek Lake, res., Oh., U.S.	124	C5	41.22 N	80.45 W
Mosquito Creek State Park, p.o.i., Oh., U.S.	124	C5	41.19 N	80.45 W
Mosquitos, Costa de, hist. reg., Nic.	156	F6	13.00 N	83.45 W
Mosquitos, Golfo de los, b., Pan.	156	H7	9.00 N	81.15 W
Moss, Nor.	16	H8	59.25 N	10.41 E
Mossaka, Congo	86	E3	1.09 S	16.50 E
Mossbank, Sk., Can.	142	E7	49.56 N	105.59 W
Moss Bank, Eng., U.K.	180		53.29 N	2.44 W
Moss Bank Park, p.o.i., Eng., U.K.	180		53.36 N	2.28 W
Moss Beach, Ca., U.S.	200		37.32 N	122.31 W
Mossburn, N.Z.	102	G3	45.39 S	168.14 E
Mosselbaai (Mossel Bay), S. Afr.	90	I6	34.10 S	22.07 E
Mossel Bay see Mosselbaai, S. Afr.	90	I6	34.10 S	22.07 E
Mossgiel, Austl.	98	I5	33.15 S	144.34 E
Mossleigh, Ab., Can.	144	F17	50.43 N	113.20 W
Mossley, Eng., U.K.	180		53.32 N	2.02 W
Mossley Hill, ngh., Eng., U.K.	180		53.23 N	2.55 W
Mossman, Austl.	96	C9	16.28 S	145.23 E
Mossmans Brook, stm., N.J., U.S.	194		41.03 N	74.27 W
Moss Moor, for., Eng., U.K.	180		53.37 N	2.00 W
Moss Mountain, mtn., Ar., U.S.	134	C6	34.50 N	92.40 W
Mossø, l., Den.	16	K7	56.02 N	9.46 E
Mossoró, Braz.	170	C7	5.11 S	37.20 W
Moss Point, Ms., U.S.	134	G10	30.24 N	88.32 W
Moss Point, c., Oh., U.S.	197a		41.37 N	81.32 W
Moss Side, Eng., U.K.	180		53.46 N	2.57 W
Moss Vale, Austl.	98	J8	34.33 S	150.22 E
Mossy, stm., Mb., Can.	142	C13	51.41 N	99.52 W
Most, Czech Rep.	24	F9	50.30 N	13.38 E
Mostar, Bos.	36	F4	43.20 N	17.48 E
Mostardas, Braz.	172	E12	31.06 S	50.57 W
Møsting, Kap, c., Grnld.	108	E17	64.00 N	41.00 W
Mostiștea, stm., Rom.	36	E13	44.07 N	26.52 E
Móstoles, Spain	184a		40.19 N	3.51 W
Mostovaja, Russia	26	D16	56.12 N	33.07 E
Mostove, Ukr.	38	F9	47.24 N	30.59 E
Mostyn, Malay.	66	A11	4.35 N	118.12 E
Mostys'ka, Ukr.	38	D2	49.47 N	23.08 E
Mosul see Al-Mawṣil, Iraq	74	B8	36.20 N	43.07 E
Møsvatnet, l., Nor.	16	H5	59.52 N	8.05 E
Mot'a, Eth.	82	E7	11.04 N	37.53 E
Mota, i., Vanuatu	101d	i16	13.49 S	167.42 E
Mota del Cuervo, Spain	28	E8	39.30 N	2.51 W
Mota del Marqués, Spain	28	C5	41.38 N	5.10 W
Motagua, stm., N.A.	156	E3	15.43 N	88.13 W
Motal', Bela.	26	H8	52.18 N	25.36 E
Motala, Swe.	16	I12	58.32 N	15.03 E
Mota Lava, i., Vanuatu	101d	i16	13.40 S	167.40 E
Motane, i., Fr. Poly.	100g	s19	9.58 S	138.49 W
Motaze, Moz.	90	D11	24.47 S	32.51 E
Mote Park, p.o.i., Eng., U.K.	178		51.17 N	0.34 E
Moteve, Cap, c., Fr. Poly.	100g	s18	9.57 S	139.02 W
Mother Brook, can., Ma., U.S.	201		42.15 N	71.10 W
Motherwell, Scot., U.K.	10	F9	55.48 N	3.59 W
Motihāri, India	70	E10	26.39 N	84.54 E
Motilla del Palancar, Spain	28	E9	39.33 N	1.54 W
Motloutse, stm., Bots.	90	B9	22.13 S	29.00 E
Motopu, Fr. Poly.	100g	s18	9.55 S	139.03 W
Motor Island, i., N.Y., U.S.	202a		42.58 N	78.56 W
Motovskij zaliv, b., Russia	14	C23	69.33 N	32.30 E
Motozintla de Mendoza, Mex.	154	H12	15.22 N	92.14 W
Motril, Spain	28	H7	36.44 N	3.31 W
Motru, Rom.	36	E10	44.50 N	23.00 E
Mott, N.D., U.S.	140	A10	46.22 N	102.19 W
Mottingham, ngh., Eng., U.K.	178		51.26 N	0.03 E
Mottram in Longdendale, Eng., U.K.	180		53.27 N	2.01 W
Motts Creek, stm., N.Y., U.S.	194		40.38 N	73.45 W
Motu, stm., N.Z.	102	C7	37.51 S	177.35 E
Motueka, N.Z.	102	E5	41.06 S	173.00 E
Motul de Felipe Carrillo Puerto, Mex.	156	B3	21.06 N	89.16 W
Motutapu, i., Cook Is.	100j	a27	21.14 S	159.43 W
Motutoa, i., Cook Is.	100j	a26	21.11 S	159.48 W
Motygino, Russia	48	C17	58.11 N	94.39 E
Motyklejka, Russia	50	E18	59.25 N	148.42 E
Motyzhyn, Ukr.	38	C8	50.22 N	29.56 E
Mouaskar, Alg.	84	B5	35.23 N	0.07 E
Mouchoir Passage, strt., N.A.	156	B12	21.10 N	71.00 W
Moudjéria, Maur.	84	F2	17.53 N	12.20 W
Moúdros, Grc.	34	D8	39.53 N	25.16 E
Mouhoun see Volta Noire, stm., Afr.	84	H4	8.40 N	0.59 W
Mouhoun see Black Volta, stm., Afr.	84	H4	8.40 N	0.59 W
Mouila, Gabon	86	E2	1.52 S	11.00 E
Moulamein, Austl.	98	J5	35.05 S	144.02 E
Mould Bay, N.T., Can.	109	A16	76.14 N	119.20 W
Mouldsworth, Eng., U.K.	180		53.14 N	2.44 W
Moule à Chique, Cap, c., St. Luc.	159c	m7	13.43 N	60.57 W
Moulin, Île du, i., Qc., Can.	193a		45.41 N	73.32 W
Moulins, Fr.	22	C9	46.33 N	3.19 E
Moulmein see Mawlamyine, Mya.	64	D3	16.30 N	97.38 E
Moulmeingyun, Mya.	64	D2	16.23 N	95.16 E
Moulouya, Oued, stm., Mor.	84	C4	35.08 N	2.21 W
Moulton, Al., U.S.	134	C11	34.29 N	87.17 W
Moulton, Ia., U.S.	130	D5	40.41 N	92.40 W
Moulton, Tx., U.S.	136	E10	29.34 N	97.09 W
Moultrie, Ga., U.S.	132	E2	31.10 N	83.46 W
Moultrie, Lake, res., S.C., U.S.	132	C5	33.18 N	80.03 W
Mouly, N. Cal.	101d	m16	20.43 S	166.25 E
Mounana, Gabon	86	E2	1.18 S	13.13 E
Mound Bayou, Ms., U.S.	134	D8	33.53 N	90.43 W
Mound City, Il., U.S.	130	G8	37.05 N	89.09 W
Mound City, Ks., U.S.	130	F3	38.08 N	94.49 W
Mound City, Mo., U.S.	130	D2	40.08 N	95.14 W
Mound City, S.D., U.S.	140	B12	45.43 N	100.04 W
Moundou, Chad	82	F3	8.34 N	16.05 E
Moundridge, Ks., U.S.	128	C11	38.12 N	97.31 W
Mounds, Ok., U.S.	134	B2	35.52 N	96.03 W
Moundsville, W.V., U.S.	124	E5	39.54 N	80.44 W
Moundville, Al., U.S.	134	E11	32.59 N	87.37 W
Moungali, ngh., Congo	191b		4.15 S	15.17 E
Moung Roessei, Camb.	64	F6	12.46 N	103.27 E
Mounlapamôk, Laos	64	E7	14.19 N	105.51 E
Mountain, Wi., U.S.	126	C1	45.10 N	88.29 W
Mountain, stm., N.T., Can.	110	C5	65.41 N	128.50 W
Mountainair, N.M., U.S.	138	G2	34.31 N	106.14 W
Mountainaire, Az., U.S.	150	H5	35.05 N	111.39 W
Mountain Brook, Al., U.S.	134	D12	33.30 N	86.45 W
Mountain City, Ga., U.S.	132	B2	34.55 N	83.22 W
Mountain City, Nv., U.S.	148	B10	41.49 N	115.56 W
Mountain City, Tn., U.S.	124	H4	36.29 N	81.49 W
Mountain Creek, Al., U.S.	134	E12	32.43 N	86.29 W
Mountain Grove, Mo., U.S.	130	G5	37.08 N	92.16 W
Mountain Home, Ar., U.S.	130	H5	36.20 N	92.23 W
Mountain Home, Id., U.S.	146	G11	43.08 N	115.41 W
Mountain Home Air Force Base, mil., Id., U.S.	146	G11	43.03 N	115.52 W
Mountain Iron, Mn., U.S.	128	D6	47.31 N	92.37 W
Mountain Lake, Mn., U.S.	128	H3	43.56 N	94.55 W
Mountain Lake, l., N.J., U.S.	194		40.53 N	74.27 W
Mountain Nile (Jabal, Bahr al-), stm., Sudan	82	F6	9.30 N	30.30 E
Mountain Park, Ab., Can.	144	D13	52.55 N	117.14 W
Mountain Pine, Ar., U.S.	134	C5	34.34 N	93.10 W
Mountain Spring Lakes, N.J., U.S.	194		41.02 N	74.23 W
Mountain Valley Lake, l., Pa., U.S.	197b		40.18 N	79.35 W
Mountain View, Ar., U.S.	130	I5	35.52 N	92.06 W
Mountain View, Ca., U.S.	148	F3	37.23 N	122.04 W
Mountain View, Mo., U.S.	130	G6	36.59 N	91.42 W
Mountain View, Ok., U.S.	138	F10	35.06 N	98.44 W
Mountain View, Wy., U.S.	140	E6	42.52 N	106.23 W
Mountain View, Wy., U.S.	150	B6	41.16 N	110.18 W
Mountain Village, Ak., U.S.	109	D7	62.05 N	163.44 W
Mountain Zebra National Park, p.o.i., S. Afr.	90	H7	32.16 S	25.29 E
Mount Airy, N.C., U.S.	124	H5	36.29 N	80.36 W
Mount Airy, ngh., Pa., U.S.	203		40.04 N	75.12 W
Mount Alida, S. Afr.	90	F10	29.11 S	30.20 E
Mount Angel, Or., U.S.	146	E4	45.04 N	122.47 W
Mount Ann Park, p.o.i., Ma., U.S.	201		42.37 N	70.44 W
Mount Aspiring National Park, p.o.i., N.Z.	102	G3	44.04 S	169.20 E
Mount Assiniboine Provincial Park, p.o.i., B.C., Can.	144	E15	50.54 N	115.40 W
Mount Athos see Ágio Óros, state, Grc.	34	C7	40.15 N	24.15 E
Mount Augustus, Austl.	96	D3	24.20 S	116.55 E
Mount Ayliff, S. Afr.	90	G9	30.48 S	29.21 E
Mount Ayr, Ia., U.S.	130	D3	40.43 N	94.14 W
Mount Baldy, Ca., U.S.	198		34.14 N	117.40 W
Mount Barker, Austl.	96	F3	34.37 S	117.40 E
Mount Barker, Austl.	98	J2	35.03 S	138.50 E
Mount Berry, Ga., U.S.	134	C13	34.17 N	85.11 W
Mount Blue State Park, p.o.i., Me., U.S.	122	F6	44.43 N	70.22 W
Mount Brydges, On., Can.	126	F8	42.54 N	81.28 W
Mount Buffalo National Park, p.o.i., Austl.	98	K6	36.45 S	146.45 E
Mount Calm, Tx., U.S.	136	C11	31.45 N	96.53 W
Mount Carleton Provincial Park, p.o.i., N.B., Can.	122	C10	47.23 N	66.50 W
Mount Carmel, Il., U.S.	130	F10	38.24 N	87.46 W
Mount Carmel, Pa., U.S.	124	D9	40.47 N	76.25 W
Mount Carroll, Il., U.S.	130	B8	42.05 N	89.58 W
Mount Charles, On., Can.	193b		43.41 N	79.40 W
Mount Clare, W.V., U.S.	124	E5	39.12 N	80.20 W
Mount Clemens, Mi., U.S.	124	B3	42.35 N	82.53 W
Mount Colah, Austl.	192a		33.41 S	151.07 E
Mount Cook National Park, p.o.i., N.Z.	102	F4	43.35 S	170.15 E
Mount Currie Indian Reserve, ind. res., B.C., Can.	144	F8	50.19 N	122.42 W
Mount Dandenong, Austl.	192b		37.50 S	145.22 E
Mount Dennis, ngh., On., Can.	193b		43.42 N	79.30 W
Mount Diablo Creek, stm., Ca., U.S.	200		38.02 N	122.02 W
Mount Dora, Fl., U.S.	132	H4	28.48 N	81.38 W
Mount Druitt, Austl.	192a		33.46 S	150.49 E
Mount Eba, Austl.	96	F7	30.11 S	135.39 E
Mount Enterprise, Tx., U.S.	136	C13	31.54 N	94.42 W
Mount Ephraim, N.J., U.S.	203		39.52 N	75.05 W
Mount Evelyn, Austl.	192b		37.47 S	145.23 E
Mount Fern, N.J., U.S.	194		40.52 N	74.34 W
Mount Field National Park, p.o.i., Austl.	99a	o13	42.40 S	146.35 E
Mount Forest, On., Can.	126	D9	43.59 N	80.43 W
Mount Frere, S. Afr.	90	G9	30.53 S	29.00 E
Mount Gambier, Austl.	98	K3	37.49 S	140.46 E
Mount Garnet, Austl.	98	A5	17.42 S	145.05 E
Mount Gay, W.V., U.S.	124	G3	37.50 N	82.00 W
Mount Gilead, N.C., U.S.	132	A6	35.12 N	80.00 W
Mount Greenwood, ngh., Il., U.S.	196		41.42 N	87.43 W
Mount Hagen, Pap. N. Gui.	101a	b3	5.51 S	144.14 E
Mount Hebron, Md., U.S.	202b		39.18 N	76.50 W
Mount Holly, N.C., U.S.	132	A4	35.17 N	81.01 W
Mount Holly Springs, Pa., U.S.	126	H12	40.06 N	77.10 W
Mount Hope, Austl.	96	F7	34.06 S	135.21 E
Mount Hope, Ks., U.S.	138	D11	37.52 N	97.39 W
Mount Hope, N.J., U.S.	194		40.56 N	74.33 W
Mount Hope, W.V., U.S.	124	G4	37.53 N	81.10 W
Mount Hope Lake, l., N.J., U.S.	194		40.56 N	74.32 W
Mount Horeb, Wi., U.S.	130	B8	43.00 N	89.43 W
Mount Howitt, Austl.	98	F4	26.31 S	142.16 E
Mount Hunter Rivulet, stm., Austl.	192a		34.02 S	150.40 E
Mount Ida, Ar., U.S.	134	C5	34.33 N	93.38 W
Mount Isa, Austl.	98	C2	20.44 S	139.29 E
Mount Jackson, Va., U.S.	124	F7	38.44 N	78.38 W
Mount Jewett, Pa., U.S.	124	C7	41.43 N	78.38 W
Mount Juliet, Tn., U.S.	130	H11	36.12 N	86.31 W
Mount Kaputar National Park, p.o.i., Austl.	98	H8	30.16 S	150.10 E
Mount Laurel, N.J., U.S.	203		39.56 N	74.54 W
Mount Lebanon, Pa., U.S.	124	D6	40.22 N	80.01 W
Mount Lofty Ranges, mts., Austl.	98	J2	33.56 S	138.48 E
Mount Magnet, Austl.	96	E3	28.04 S	117.51 E
Mount Manara, Austl.	98	I4	32.29 S	143.56 E
Mount Margaret, Austl.	98	F4	26.54 S	143.21 E
Mountmellick, Ire.	10	H5	53.07 N	7.20 W
Mount Misery Point, c., N.Y., U.S.	194		40.58 N	73.05 W
Mount Monger, Austl.	96	F4	31.04 S	121.58 E
Mount Morgan, Austl.	96	D8	23.39 S	150.23 E
Mount Morris, Il., U.S.	128	I9	42.03 N	89.25 W
Mount Morris, Mi., U.S.	130	A14	43.07 N	83.41 W
Mount Morris, N.Y., U.S.	124	B8	42.43 N	77.52 W
Mount Nebo, Pa., U.S.	197b		40.33 N	80.06 W
Mountnessing, Eng., U.K.	178		51.39 N	0.21 E
Mount Olive, Il., U.S.	130	E8	39.04 N	89.43 W
Mount Olive, Ms., U.S.	134	F9	31.45 N	89.39 W
Mount Olive, N.C., U.S.	132	A7	35.11 N	78.04 W
Mount Oliver, Pa., U.S.	197b		40.28 N	79.59 W
Mount Olivet, Ky., U.S.	124	F1	38.31 N	84.02 W
Mount Orab, Oh., U.S.	124	E2	39.01 N	83.54 W
Mount Perry, Austl.	98	E8	25.09 S	151.38 E
Mount Pleasant, On., Can.	126	E9	43.04 N	80.18 W
Mount Pleasant, Ia., U.S.	130	C6	40.57 N	91.32 W
Mount Pleasant, Mi., U.S.	126	E5	43.35 N	84.46 W
Mount Pleasant, N.C., U.S.	132	A5	35.23 N	80.26 W
Mount Pleasant, Pa., U.S.	124	D6	40.08 N	79.32 W
Mount Pleasant, S.C., U.S.	132	D6	32.47 N	79.52 W
Mount Pleasant, Tn., U.S.	134	B11	35.32 N	87.12 W
Mount Pleasant, Tx., U.S.	134	D4	33.09 N	94.58 W
Mount Pleasant, Ut., U.S.	150	D5	39.32 N	111.27 W
Mount Pleasant Park, p.o.i., Md., U.S.	202b		39.22 N	76.35 W
Mount Pritchard, Austl.	192a		33.54 S	150.54 E
Mount Pulaski, Il., U.S.	130	D8	40.00 N	89.16 W
Mount Rainier, Md., U.S.	202c		38.56 N	76.57 W
Mount Rainier National Park, p.o.i., Wa., U.S.	146	D5	46.52 N	121.43 W
Mount Revelstoke National Park, p.o.i., B.C., Can.	144	E12	51.06 N	118.03 W
Mount Riddock, Austl.	96	D6	23.01 S	134.39 E
Mount Robson Provincial Park, p.o.i., B.C., Can.	144	C11	52.58 N	118.50 W
Mount Royal, N.J., U.S.	203		39.49 N	75.13 W
Mount Rushmore National Memorial, p.o.i., S.D., U.S.	140	D9	43.53 N	103.26 W
Mount Saint Helens National Volcanic Monument, p.o.i., Wa., U.S.	146	D4	46.12 N	122.11 W
Mount Sarah, Austl.	96	E7	26.57 S	135.22 E
Mount's Bay, b., Eng., U.K.	10	L7	50.03 N	5.25 W
Mount Selinda, Zimb.	90	B11	20.25 S	32.43 E
Mount Seymour Provincial Park, p.o.i., B.C., Can.	144	G8	49.22 N	122.55 W
Mount Shasta, Ca., U.S.	148	B3	41.19 N	122.18 W
Mount Sinai, N.Y., U.S.	194		40.57 N	73.02 W
Mount Sinai Harbor, b., N.Y., U.S.	194		40.57 N	73.02 W
Mount Somers, N.Z.	102	F4	43.43 S	171.24 E
Mount Spokane State Park, p.o.i., Wa., U.S.	146	B9	47.58 N	117.13 W
Mount Sterling, Il., U.S.	130	E7	39.58 N	90.45 W
Mount Sterling, Ky., U.S.	124	F2	38.03 N	83.57 W
Mount Sterling, Oh., U.S.	124	E2	39.42 N	83.15 W
Mount Stewart, P.E., Can.	122	D14	46.21 N	62.53 W
Mount Surprise, Austl.	98	B5	18.09 S	144.19 E
Mount Uniacke, N.S., Can.	122	F13	44.54 N	63.51 W
Mount Union, Pa., U.S.	124	D8	40.23 N	77.52 W
Mount Vernon, Austl.	96	D3	24.13 S	118.14 E
Mount Vernon, Al., U.S.	134	F10	31.05 N	88.00 W
Mount Vernon, Ga., U.S.	132	D3	32.11 N	82.35 W
Mount Vernon, Il., U.S.	130	F8	38.18 N	88.54 W
Mount Vernon, In., U.S.	130	G10	37.55 N	87.53 W
Mount Vernon, Ia., U.S.	130	C6	41.55 N	91.24 W
Mount Vernon, Ky., U.S.	124	G1	37.20 N	84.21 W
Mount Vernon, Mo., U.S.	130	G4	37.06 N	93.49 W
Mount Vernon, Oh., U.S.	124	D3	40.23 N	82.28 W
Mount Vernon, Or., U.S.	146	F7	44.24 N	119.05 W
Mount Vernon, Pa., U.S.	197b		40.17 N	79.48 W
Mount Vernon, S.D., U.S.	140	D14	43.42 N	98.15 W
Mount Vernon, Tx., U.S.	134	D3	33.11 N	95.13 W
Mount Vernon, Wa., U.S.	146	B4	48.24 N	122.19 W
Mount Vernon, hist., Va., U.S.	124	F8	38.47 N	77.06 W
Mount Victory, Oh., U.S.	124	D2	40.32 N	83.31 W
Mount Washington, Md., U.S.	202b		39.23 N	76.41 W
Mount Washington, ngh., Md., U.S.	202b		39.22 N	76.40 W
Mount Waverley, Austl.	192b		37.53 S	145.08 E
Mount William National Park, p.o.i., Austl.	99a	n13	40.56 S	148.15 E
Mount Willoughby, Austl.	96	E6	27.59 S	134.08 E
Mount Wolf, Pa., U.S.	126	H13	40.04 N	76.42 W
Moura, Austl.	98	E8	24.37 S	149.59 E
Moura, Braz.	168	H11	1.29 S	61.37 W
Moura, Port.	28	F3	38.08 N	7.27 W
Mourdi, Dépression du, depr., Chad	82	D4	18.10 N	23.00 E
Mourdiah, Mali	84	G3	14.28 N	7.28 W
Mourne Mountains, mts., N. Ire., U.K.	10	G6	54.10 N	6.04 W
Mouscron, Bel.	20	D12	50.44 N	3.13 E
Moussa 'Ali, mtn., Afr.	86	B8	12.28 N	42.24 E
Mousseaux-sur-Seine, Fr.	179		49.03 N	1.39 E
Moussoro, Chad	82	E3	13.37 N	16.29 E
Moussy-le-Neuf, Fr.	179		49.04 N	2.36 E
Moussy-le-Vieux, Fr.	179		49.03 N	2.38 E
Moustique, Morne, mtn., Guad.	159c	h5	16.07 N	61.42 W
Moutier, Switz.	30	C4	47.17 N	7.22 E
Moûtiers, Fr.	22	D12	45.28 N	6.31 E
Moutong, Indon.	60	E7	0.28 N	121.13 E
Mouzáki, Grc.	34	D4	39.26 N	21.40 E
Movenda, D.R.C.	86	D4	2.56 N	21.26 E
Moville, Ire.	10	F5	55.11 N	7.01 W
Moville, Ia., U.S.	130	B1	42.28 N	96.04 W
Moweaqua, Il., U.S.	130	E8	39.37 N	89.00 W
Mowry Slough, stm., Ca., U.S.	200		37.29 N	122.03 W
Moxotó, stm., Braz.	170	E7	9.19 S	38.14 W
Moy, stm., Ire.	10	H3	54.08 N	9.08 W
Moyahua, Mex.	154	E7	21.16 N	103.10 W
Moyale, Kenya	86	D7	3.32 N	39.02 E
Moyamba, S.L.	84	H2	8.09 N	12.25 W
Moyen Atlas, mts., Mor.	84	C4	33.30 N	5.00 W
Moyeuvre-Grande, Fr.	20	E14	49.15 N	6.03 E
Moyie, B.C., Can.	144	G15	49.16 N	115.48 W
Moyie, stm., N.A.	144	H14	48.42 N	116.11 W
Moyie Springs, Id., U.S.	146	B10	48.43 N	116.11 W
Moylan, Pa., U.S.	203		39.54 N	75.23 W
Moyo, Pulau, i., Indon.	66	H10	8.15 S	117.34 E
Moyobamba, Peru	164	E2	6.04 S	76.56 W
Moyu, China	62	A4	37.16 N	79.44 E
M'oža (Mëža), stm., Eur.	26	E14	55.43 N	31.30 E
Možaevka, Russia	38	E18	48.44 N	39.45 E
Možajsk, Russia	26	E18	55.30 N	36.01 E
Možajskij, ngh., Russia	183a		59.43 N	30.07 E
Mozambique, ctry., Afr.	88	D5	18.15 S	35.00 E
Mozambique, Canal du see Mozambique Channel, strt., Afr.	88	D7	19.00 S	41.00 E
Mozambique Channel, strt., Afr.	88	D7	19.00 S	41.00 E
Mozambique Plateau, unds.	174	M6	32.00 S	35.00 E
Mozarlândia, Braz.	166	B6	14.47 S	50.35 W
Mozdok, Russia	42	D11	43.44 N	44.38 E
Možga, Russia	40	C17	56.26 N	52.12 E
Mozhabong Lake, l., On., Can.	126	B7	46.57 N	82.04 W
Mozolevo, Russia	26	A16	59.17 N	33.47 E
Mozu, Japan	188		34.34 N	135.29 E
Mozuli, Russia	26	D11	56.36 N	28.11 E
Mozzate, Italy	184b		45.41 N	8.57 E
Mpala, D.R.C.	86	F5	6.44 S	29.31 E
Mpanda, Tan.	86	F6	6.20 S	31.03 E
Mphoengs, Zimb.	90	B8	21.10 S	27.51 E
Mpika, Zam.	86	C5	11.52 S	31.24 E
Mpila, ngh., Congo	191b		4.14 S	15.18 E
Mpoka, D.R.C.	86	E3	1.26 S	17.02 E
Mporokoso, Zam.	86	B5	9.23 S	30.06 E
Mpui, Tan.	86	F6	8.21 S	31.50 E
Mpulungu, Zam.	86	B5	8.46 S	31.07 E
Mpumalanga, state, S. Afr.	90	E9	26.00 S	30.30 E
Mpwapwa, Tan.	86	F7	6.19 S	36.25 E
Mqanduli, S. Afr.	90	G9	31.48 S	28.44 E
Mrągowo, Pol.	26	G4	53.52 N	21.18 E
Mrakovo, Russia	40	E20	52.43 N	56.37 E
Mrkonjić Grad, Bos.	36	E3	44.25 N	17.05 E
Mrocza, Pol.	24	C13	53.14 N	17.36 E
M'Saken, Tun.	32	I4	35.44 N	10.35 E
Mscislau, Bela.	26	F14	54.01 N	31.44 E
Msciž, Bela.	26	F11	54.34 N	28.10 E
Mšinskaja, Russia	26	A12	59.01 N	29.57 E
Msta, Russia	26	C17	57.55 N	34.28 E
Msta, stm., Russia	26	B15	58.28 N	31.27 E
Mszana Dolna, Pol.	24	G16	49.40 N	20.05 E
Mszczonów, Pol.	24	E16	51.58 N	20.31 E
Mtama, Tan.	86	G7	10.20 S	39.22 E
Mtamvuna, stm., S. Afr.	90	G9	31.04 S	30.11 E
Mtubatuba, S. Afr.	90	F11	28.24 S	32.09 E
Mtwara, Tan.	86	G8	10.21 S	40.15 E
Mu, N. Cal.	101d	m16	21.03 S	167.24 E
Mu, stm., Mya.	64	A2	22.20 N	95.30 E
Mu, Cerro, mtn., S.A.	168	C5	9.27 N	73.10 W
Mu'a, Tonga	100e	n14	21.11 S	175.07 W
Mualang, Indon.	66	C7	0.41 N	111.18 E
Muaná, Braz.	170	A1	1.31 S	49.13 W
Muanda, D.R.C.	86	F2	5.57 S	12.22 E
Muang Bèng, Laos	64	B5	20.21 N	101.41 E
Muang Hay, Laos	64	B5	21.03 N	101.48 E
Muang Hinboun, Laos	64	D7	17.37 N	104.36 E
Muang Hôngsa, Laos	64	C5	19.42 N	101.20 E
Muang Houn, Laos	64	B5	20.09 N	101.27 E
Muang Hounxianghoung, Laos	64	B6	21.37 N	102.18 E
Muang Huang, Laos	64	C6	18.45 N	103.42 E
Muang Khammouan, Laos	64	D7	17.24 N	104.49 E
Muang Khao, Laos	64	C6	19.45 N	103.25 E
Muang Khi, Laos	64	C5	18.27 N	101.45 E
Muang Không, Laos	64	F7	14.07 N	105.51 E
Muang Khôngxédôn, Laos	64	E7	15.34 N	105.49 E
Muang La, Laos	64	B6	20.52 N	102.07 E
Muang Liap, Laos	64	C5	18.29 N	101.40 E
Muang Long, Laos	64	B5	20.56 N	100.46 E
Muang Meung, Laos	64	B5	20.43 N	100.28 E
Muang Ngoy, Laos	64	B6	20.42 N	102.40 E
Muang Nong, Laos	64	D8	16.24 N	106.25 E
Muang Ou Nua, Laos	64	A5	22.18 N	101.47 E
Muang Ou Tai, Laos	64	A5	22.07 N	101.47 E
Muang Pakbèng, Laos	64	C5	19.54 N	101.08 E
Muang Pak-Lay, Laos	64	C5	18.13 N	101.24 E
Muang Paktha, Laos	64	B5	20.05 N	100.36 E
Muang Pakxan, Laos	64	C6	18.24 N	103.39 E
Muang Peun, Laos	64	B6	20.13 N	103.52 E
Muang Phalan, Laos	64	D7	16.39 N	105.33 E
Muang Phiang, Laos	64	C5	19.06 N	101.32 E
Muang Phônthong, Laos	64	E7	15.05 N	105.39 E
Muang Phoun, Laos	64	C6	19.07 N	102.43 E
Muang Sam Sip, Thai.	64	E7	15.31 N	104.44 E
Muang Sing, Laos	64	B5	21.10 N	101.09 E
Muang Soum, Laos	64	C6	18.46 N	102.31 E
Muang Souvannakhili, Laos	64	E7	15.22 N	105.49 E
Muang Souy, Laos	64	C6	19.31 N	102.54 E
Muang Sung, Laos	64	B6	20.18 N	102.27 E
Muang Thadua, Laos	64	C5	19.25 N	101.50 E
Muang Thatèng, Laos	64	E8	15.25 N	106.22 E
Muang Thathôm, Laos	64	C6	19.00 N	103.36 E
Muang Va, Laos	64	B6	21.53 N	102.19 E
Muang Vangviang, Laos	64	C6	18.55 N	102.26 E
Muang Vapi, Laos	64	E7	15.40 N	105.55 E
Muang Xaignabouri, Laos	64	C5	19.16 N	101.42 E
Muang Xamtong, Laos	64	C6	19.51 N	103.50 E
Muang Xay, Laos	64	B5	20.41 N	101.59 E
Muang Xépôn, Laos	64	D8	16.42 N	106.12 E
Muang Xon, Laos	64	B6	20.27 N	103.19 E
Muang Yo, Laos	64	B5	21.30 N	101.51 E
Muang You, Laos	64	C6	19.51 N	102.54 E
Muar, Malay.	64	L6	2.02 N	102.34 E
Muar, stm., Malay.	64	K6	2.02 N	102.33 E
Muara, Bru.	66	A9	5.01 N	115.03 E
Muaraaman, Indon.	66	E3	3.07 S	102.11 E
Muaraancalung, Indon.	66	C10	0.24 N	116.35 E
Muarabeliti, Indon.	66	E3	3.15 S	103.02 E
Muarabenangin, Indon.	66	D9	0.58 S	115.20 E
Muarabinuangeun, Indon.	66	G5	6.49 S	105.52 E
Muarabungo, Indon.	66	D2	1.29 S	102.06 E
Muaradua, Indon.	66	F4	4.32 S	104.04 E
Muaraenim, Indon.	66	E3	3.39 S	103.47 E
Muaragusung, Indon.	66	C10	1.28 N	117.12 E
Muarajuloi, Indon.	66	D8	0.12 S	114.04 E
Muarakaman, Indon.	66	D10	0.09 S	116.44 E
Muarakelingi, Indon.	66	E3	3.03 S	103.13 E
Muarakumpe, Indon.	66	D4	1.24 S	104.01 E
Muaralabuh, Indon.	66	D2	1.28 S	101.02 E
Muaralakitan, Indon.	66	E3	2.52 S	103.17 E
Muaralasan, Indon.	66	C10	1.41 N	117.06 E
Muaralembu, Indon.	66	D2	0.23 S	101.21 E
Muaramawai, Indon.	66	C10	0.29 N	116.54 E
Muarapangean, Indon.	66	B10	2.40 N	116.44 E
Muarapantai, Indon.	66	D2	0.45 S	101.43 E
Muarapayang, Indon.	66	D9	1.15 S	115.56 E
Muararupit, Indon.	66	E3	2.44 S	102.54 E
Muarasabak, Indon.	66	D3	1.08 S	103.49 E
Muarasiberut, Indon.	66	D1	1.36 S	99.11 E
Muarasipongi, Indon.	66	C1	0.37 N	99.51 E
Muaratebo, Indon.	66	D3	1.28 S	102.27 E
Muarateladang, Indon.	66	E4	2.53 S	103.59 E
Muaratembesi, Indon.	66	D3	1.42 S	103.07 E
Muaratewe, Indon.	66	D9	0.56 S	114.52 E
Muaratuhup, Indon.	66	D9	0.39 S	114.48 E
Muaratunan, Indon.	66	D10	1.24 S	116.38 E
Muarawahau, Indon.	66	C10	1.02 N	116.50 E
Muāri, Rās, c., Pak.	62	D2	24.49 N	66.40 E
Mubārakpur, India	70	E9	26.04 N	83.17 E
Mubārakpur Dabās, ngh., India	190a		28.43 N	77.03 E
Mubende, Ug.	86	D6	0.34 N	31.23 E
Mubi, Nig.	84	G7	10.16 N	13.15 E
Mubur, Pulau, i., Indon.	66	B5	3.20 N	106.12 E
Mucaitá, stm., Braz.	170	D4	6.59 S	42.39 W
Mucajaí, stm., Braz.	168	F11	2.23 N	60.49 W
Mucha, Tai.	187d		24.59 N	121.34 E
Much Hoole, Eng., U.K.	180		53.42 N	2.48 W
Muchinga Escarpment, clf., Zam.	88	C4	14.30 S	29.38 E
Muchinga Mountains, mts., Zam.	88	C5	11.40 S	31.44 E
Mucifal, Port.	184c		38.48 N	9.26 W
Muckadilla, Austl.	98	F7	26.35 S	148.21 E
Muckalee Creek, stm., Ga., U.S.	134	F14	31.36 N	84.08 W
Mučkas, Russia	12	D23	64.01 N	48.28 E
Muckendorf an der Donau, Aus.	182b		48.20 N	16.09 E
Mucking, Eng., U.K.	178		51.30 N	0.26 E
Mucojo, Moz.	86	C7	12.04 S	40.26 E
Muconda, Ang.	88	C3	10.36 S	21.19 E
Mucuchies, Ven.	168	C6	8.45 N	70.54 W
Mucujê, Braz.	170	G5	13.00 S	41.23 W
Muçum, Braz.	172	D11	29.09 S	51.53 W
Mucun, China	58	H6	26.44 N	114.00 E
Mucur, Tur.	42	F6	39.04 N	34.23 E
Mucuri, Braz.	170	J6	18.05 S	39.34 W
Mucuri, stm., Braz.	170	J6	18.05 S	39.33 W
Mud, stm., Ky., U.S.	130	G11	37.12 N	86.53 W
Mud, stm., W.V., U.S.	114	H10	38.24 N	82.17 W
Muda, stm., Malay.	64	J5	5.34 N	100.20 E
Mudan, stm., China	52	B10	46.18 N	129.32 E
Mudanjiang, China	52	C10	44.35 N	129.36 E
Mudanya, Tur.	34	C11	40.22 N	28.53 E
Mud Creek, stm., Ia., U.S.	128	H2	43.15 N	96.15 W
Mud Creek, stm., Ne., U.S.	140	F13	41.01 N	98.53 W
Mud Creek, stm., Ok., U.S.	138	G11	33.54 N	97.28 W
Mud Creek, stm., S.D., U.S.	140	B14	45.10 N	98.23 W
Mud Creek, stm., Tx., U.S.	136	C12	31.47 N	94.58 W
Muddus Nationalpark, p.o.i., Swe.	14	F11	67.00 N	20.16 E
Muddværet, is., Nor.	16	B9	65.34 N	11.43 E
Muddy, stm., Nv., U.S.	150	G2	36.27 N	114.20 W

Name	Page	Map Ref.	Latitude	Longitude
Muddy Boggy Creek, stm., Ok., U.S.	134	C3	34.02 N	95.47 W
Muddy Branch, stm., Md., U.S.	202c		39.03 N	77.18 W
Muddy Brook, stm., Ct., U.S.	194		41.07 N	73.20 W
Muddy Creek, stm., U.S.	194		41.03 N	74.02 W
Muddy Creek, stm., Mo., U.S.	130	F4	38.50 N	93.03 W
Muddy Creek, stm., Mt., U.S.	146	B15	47.56 N	111.46 W
Muddy Creek, stm., Ut., U.S.	150	E6	38.23 N	110.42 W
Muddy Creek, stm., Wy., U.S.	140	E8	42.33 N	104.58 W
Muddy Creek, stm., Wy., U.S.	140	E6	41.59 N	106.07 W
Muddy Creek, stm., Wy., U.S.	140	D4	43.17 N	108.11 W
Muddy Creek, stm., Wy., U.S.	150	B6	41.33 N	110.17 W
Muddy Creek, stm., Wy., U.S.	150	B9	41.02 N	107.39 W
Muddy Gut, b., Md., U.S.	202b		39.17 N	76.26 W
Muddy Peak, mtn., Nv., U.S.	150	G2	36.18 N	114.42 W
Mudgee, Austl.	98	I7	32.36 S	149.35 E
Mudhol, India	69	C2	16.20 N	75.16 E
Mudjuga, Russia	18	D26	63.46 N	39.17 E
Mud'jugskij, ostrov, i., Russia	18	C27	64.55 N	40.15 E
Mud Lake, l., Id., U.S.	146	G14	43.53 N	112.23 W
Mud Lake, l., Nv., U.S.	148	F8	37.52 N	117.04 W
Mud Lake Reservoir, res., S.D., U.S.	140	B14	45.47 N	98.13 W
Mudon, Mya.	64	D3	16.15 N	97.44 E
Mudongzhen, China	58	G2	29.34 N	106.51 E
Mudurnu, Tur.	34	C14	40.28 N	31.13 E
Mudurnu, stm., Tur.	34	C13	40.49 N	30.34 E
Mueda, Moz.	88	C6	11.40 S	39.33 E
Muelle de los Bueyes, Nic.	156	G5	12.04 N	84.32 W
Muenster, Tx., U.S.	138	H11	33.39 N	97.22 W
Muerto, Mar, l., Mex.	154	G11	16.08 N	94.08 W
Muezerskij, Russia	18	D19	63.57 N	31.59 E
Mufulira, Zam.	88	C4	12.33 S	28.14 E
Mufu Shan, mtn., China	58	G5	29.02 N	113.54 E
Mufu Shan, mts., China	58	G6	29.00 N	114.00 E
Müggelberge, hill, Ger.	182a		52.25 N	13.39 E
Müggelheim, ngh., Ger.	182a		52.25 N	13.40 E
Muggio, Italy	184b		45.36 N	9.14 E
Mughal Sarāi, India	70	F9	25.16 N	83.07 E
Mugi, Japan	56	F7	33.40 N	134.25 E
Mu Gia, Deo, p., Asia	64	D7	17.40 N	105.45 E
Muğla, Tur.	34	F11	37.13 N	28.22 E
Muğla, state, Tur.	34	F11	37.10 N	28.30 E
Mugodzjary, gory, hills, Kaz.	48	E9	49.00 N	58.40 E
Muhammad Qawl, Sudan	82	C7	20.55 N	37.08 E
Muhanovo, Russia	26	D21	56.31 N	38.20 E
Muhavec, stm., Bela.	26	H7	52.04 N	23.39 E
Muhen, Russia	50	G16	48.12 N	136.07 E
Muhino, Russia	50	F14	52.16 N	127.14 E
Muḥīt, Maṣrif el-, can., Egypt	191c		30.07 N	31.06 E
Mühlacker, Ger.	24	H4	48.56 N	8.50 E
Mühldorf am Inn, Ger.	24	H8	48.14 N	12.31 E
Mühlenbecker See, l., Ger.	182a		52.41 N	13.24 E
Mühlen-Berg, hill, Ger.	182a		52.23 N	13.15 E
Mühlenfliess, stm., Ger.	182a		52.26 N	13.41 E
Mühlenrahmede, Ger.	181		51.16 N	7.40 E
Mühlhausen, Ger.	24	E6	51.12 N	10.28 E
Mühlhausen, Ger.	181		51.33 N	7.44 E
Muhlig-Hofmann Mountains, mts., Ant.	103	C5	72.10 S	4.52 E
Mühlleiten, Aus.	182b		48.10 N	16.34 E
Mühlviertel, reg., Aus.	30	B11	48.25 N	14.10 E
Muhola, Fin.	18	D11	63.19 N	25.03 E
Muhos, Fin.	18	C12	64.49 N	25.59 E
Muḥradah, Syria	76	C7	35.15 N	36.35 E
Muhtolovo, Russia	40	D13	55.27 N	43.12 E
Muhu, i., Est.	26	B6	58.36 N	23.13 E
Muhu väin, strt., Est.	26	B6	58.44 N	23.18 E
Muié, Ang.	88	C3	14.20 S	20.37 E
Mui Hopohoponga Point, c., Tonga	100e	n14	21.08 S	175.02 W
Muineachán see Monaghan, Ire.	10	G6	54.15 N	6.58 W
Muine Bheag, Ire.	10	I6	52.42 N	6.56 W
Muir Beach, Ca., U.S.	200		37.52 N	122.35 W
Muirkirk, Md., U.S.	202c		39.03 N	76.53 W
Muir Woods, Ca., U.S.	200		37.53 N	122.34 W
Muisne, Ec.	168	G1	0.36 N	80.01 W
Muite, Moz.	88	C6	14.02 S	39.00 E
Mui Wo, China	189d		22.16 N	113.59 E
Muja, Russia	50	E12	56.24 N	115.38 E
Mujāhidpur, ngh., India	190a		28.34 N	77.13 E
Mujnak, Uzb.	48	F9	43.46 N	59.01 E
Mukacheve, Ukr.	40	G3	48.26 N	22.44 E
Mukah, Malay.	66	B8	2.53 N	112.06 E
Mukalla see Al-Mukallā, Yemen	72	G6	14.32 N	49.07 E
Mukandpur, ngh., India	190a		28.44 N	77.11 E
Mukandwara, India	70	F6	24.49 N	76.00 E
Mukatsjeve, Ukr.	36	A9	48.26 N	22.44 E
Mukāwir, hist., Jord.	76	G6	31.34 N	35.38 E
Mukdahan, Thai.	64	D7	16.32 N	104.43 E
Mukden see Shenyang, China	52	C9	41.48 N	123.24 E
Mukeriān, India	70	C5	31.56 N	75.37 E
Mukharram al-Fawqānī, Syria	76	D8	34.49 N	37.04 E
Mukho, Kor., S.	56	B2	37.32 N	129.06 E
Mukilteo, Wa., U.S.	146	C4	47.56 N	122.18 W
Mukinbudin, Austl.	96	F3	30.54 S	118.12 E
Mukomuko, Indon.	66	E2	2.35 S	101.07 E
Mukry, Turkmen.	72	B10	37.35 N	65.43 E
Muktsar, India	70	C5	30.28 N	74.30 E
Mukur, Kaz.	40	G19	48.03 N	54.30 E
Mukwonago, Wi., U.S.	130	B9	42.52 N	88.19 W
Mūl, India	69	A4	20.04 N	79.40 E
Mula, China	52	F5	29.39 N	100.38 E
Mula, Spain	28	F9	38.02 N	1.30 W
Mula, stm., India	69	B1	18.34 N	74.20 E
Mula, stm., India	69	B2	19.31 N	74.49 E
Mulaku Atoll, at., Mald.	62a	i12	3.00 N	73.30 E
Mulaly, Kaz.	48	E13	45.26 N	78.18 E
Mulan, China	52	B10	45.56 N	128.02 E
Muland, ngh., India	190c		19.10 N	72.57 E
Mulas, Punta, c., P.R.	158a	b5	18.09 N	65.26 W
Mulas, Punta de, c., Cuba	156	B10	21.01 N	75.35 W
Mulatos, Mex.	154	A4	28.38 N	108.51 W
Mulayit Taung, mtn., Mya.	64	D4	16.11 N	98.32 E
Mulbāgal, India	69	E4	13.10 N	78.23 E
Mulberry, Ar., U.S.	134	B4	35.30 N	94.03 W
Mulberry, Fl., U.S.	132	I4	27.54 N	81.58 W
Mulberry, In., U.S.	130	D11	40.20 N	86.39 W
Mulberry, stm., Ar., U.S.	134	B5	35.27 N	94.02 W
Mulberry Creek, stm., Al., U.S.	134	E12	32.27 N	86.52 W
Mulberry Creek, stm., Tx., U.S.	138	G8	34.37 N	100.54 W
Mulberry Fork, stm., Al., U.S.	134	D12	33.33 N	87.11 W
Mulberry Mountain, mtn., Ar., U.S.	130	I5	35.52 N	92.59 W
Mulchatna, stm., Ak., U.S.	109	D8	59.39 N	157.08 W
Mulchén, Chile	172	H1	37.43 S	72.14 W
Mulde, stm., Ger.	24	E8	51.52 N	12.14 E
Muldersdrif se Loop, stm., S. Afr.	191d		26.06 S	27.51 E
Muldoon, Tx., U.S.	136	E10	29.49 N	97.04 W
Muldraugh, Ky., U.S.	130	G12	37.56 N	85.59 W
Muldrow, Ok., U.S.	134	B4	35.25 N	94.36 W
Mule Creek, stm., Ks., U.S.	138	D9	37.05 N	99.00 W
Mulegé, Mex.	154	B2	26.52 N	111.59 W
Muleshoe, Tx., U.S.	138	G6	34.13 N	102.43 W
Mulevala, Moz.	88	D6	16.26 S	37.35 E
Mulgoa Creek, stm., Austl.	192a		33.46 S	150.39 E
Mulgowie, Austl.	98	F9	27.43 S	152.22 E
Mulgrave, Austl.	192b		37.56 S	145.12 E
Mulgrave, N.S., Can.	122	E15	45.37 N	61.25 W
Mulhacén, mtn., Spain	28	G7	37.03 N	3.19 W
Mulhall, Ok., U.S.	138	E11	36.03 N	97.24 W
Mülheimer Ruhrtalbrüke, trans., Ger.	181		51.23 N	6.54 E
Mulhouse, Fr.	20	G16	47.44 N	7.20 E
Muling, China	54	B9	44.56 N	130.31 E
Muling, China	54	B9	44.30 N	130.15 E
Muling, stm., China	54	B9	45.24 N	131.33 E
Mulinu'u, Cape, c., Samoa	101a	g11	13.30 S	172.48 W
Mülki, India	69	E2	13.05 N	74.47 E
Mull, Island of, i., Scot., U.K.	10	E6	56.27 N	6.00 W
Mull, Sound of, strt., Scot., U.K.	10	E7	56.32 N	5.50 W
Mullan, Id., U.S.	118	D8	47.27 N	115.48 W
Mullen, Ne., U.S.	140	E11	42.01 N	101.02 W
Mullengudgery, Austl.	98	H6	31.41 S	147.26 E
Muller, Pegunungan, mts., Indon.	66	C8	0.40 N	113.50 E
Mullet Peninsula, pen., Ire.	10	G2	54.14 N	10.01 W
Mullet Pond Bay, Neth. Ant.	159a	a1	18.03 N	63.07 W
Mullett Lake, l., Mi., U.S.	126	C5	45.30 N	84.30 W
Mullewa, Austl.	96	E3	28.32 S	115.31 E
Müllheim, Ger.	24	I3	47.48 N	7.37 E
Mullica, Alquatka Branch, stm., N.J., U.S.	203		39.47 N	74.48 W
Mullica, Sleeper Branch, stm., N.J., U.S.	203		39.39 N	74.40 W
Mulligan, stm., Austl.	96	D7	25.00 S	138.34 E
Mullin, Tx., U.S.	136	C9	31.33 N	98.39 W
Mullingar, Ire.	10	H5	53.31 N	7.20 W
Mullins, S.C., U.S.	132	B6	34.12 N	79.15 W
Mullinville, Ks., U.S.	138	D9	37.35 N	99.28 W
Mullovka, Russia	40	D16	54.12 N	49.22 E
Mullsjö, Swe.	16	J11	57.55 N	13.52 E
Mullumbimby, Austl.	98	G9	28.33 S	153.30 E
Mullum Mullum Creek, stm., Austl.	192b		37.44 S	145.10 E
Mulobezi, Zam.	88	D4	16.50 S	25.07 E
Mulongo, D.R.C.	86	F5	7.49 S	26.59 E
Mulshi Lake, res., India	69	B1	18.32 N	73.28 E
Multai, India	70	H7	21.46 N	78.16 E
Multān, Pak.	70	C3	30.11 N	71.27 E
Multé, Mex.	156	D2	17.41 N	91.24 W
Multia, Fin.	18	E11	62.24 N	24.48 E
Mulu, Gunong, mtn., Malay.	66	A9	4.04 N	114.56 E
Mulumbe, Monts, mts., D.R.C.	86	F5	8.41 S	27.28 E
Mulvane, Ks., U.S.	138	D11	37.28 N	97.14 W
Mumbai (Bombay), India	69	B1	18.57 N	72.50 E
Mumbai (Bombay), India	190c		18.58 N	72.50 E
Mumbai University, educ., India	190c		18.56 N	72.50 E
Mumbra, India	190c		19.11 N	73.01 E
Mumbwa, Zam.	88	D4	14.59 S	27.04 E
Mumen, China	58	E2	32.08 N	106.28 E
Mumeng, Pap. N. Gui.	101a	b4	6.59 S	146.36 E
Mumford, Tx., U.S.	136	D11	30.43 N	96.34 W
Mumra, Russia	40	I15	45.46 N	47.39 E
Mun, stm., Thai.	64	E7	15.18 N	105.30 E
Muna, Mex.	156	B3	20.29 N	89.43 W
Muna, stm., Russia	50	C13	67.53 N	123.04 E
Muna, Pulau, i., Indon.	60	F7	4.52 S	122.27 E
Munābāo, India	70	F3	25.44 N	70.16 E
Muna el-Amir, Egypt	191c		29.54 N	31.15 E
Munajly, Kaz.	40	H19	46.46 N	54.32 E
Munbong-ni, Kor., S.	189b		37.43 N	126.49 E
Muncar, Indon.	66	H9	8.26 S	114.20 E
Münchberg, Ger.	24	F7	50.11 N	11.47 E
Münchehofe, Ger.	182a		52.30 N	13.40 E
München (Munich), Ger.	24	H7	48.07 N	11.34 E
Münchendorf, Aus.	182b		48.02 N	16.23 E
Munchique, Cerro, mtn., Col.	168	F3	2.32 N	76.57 W
Munchique, Parque Nacional, p.o.i., Col.	168	F3	2.30 N	77.10 W
Muncie, In., U.S.	130	D12	40.11 N	85.22 W
Muncy, Pa., U.S.	124	C9	41.12 N	76.47 W
Mundare, Ab., Can.	144	C18	53.35 N	112.20 W
Munday, Tx., U.S.	138	H9	33.26 N	99.37 W
Mundelein, Il., U.S.	130	B9	42.16 N	87.57 W
Mündelheim, ngh., Ger.	181		51.21 N	6.41 E
Münden, Ger.	24	E5	51.24 N	9.39 E
Mündka, ngh., India	190a		28.41 N	77.02 E
Mundo, stm., Spain	28	F8	38.18 N	1.40 W
Mundon Hill, Eng., U.K.	178		51.41 N	0.42 E
Mundo Novo, Braz.	170	F5	11.54 S	40.26 W
Mundra, India	70	G2	22.52 N	69.51 E
Mundrabilla, Austl.	96	F5	31.51 S	127.52 E
Mundubbera, Austl.	98	E8	25.35 S	151.18 E
Munford, Tn., U.S.	134	B9	35.26 N	89.48 W
Munfordville, Ky., U.S.	130	G12	37.16 N	85.53 W
Mungallala, Austl.	98	F6	26.27 S	147.31 E
Mungallala Creek, stm., Austl.	98	F6	28.53 S	147.04 E
Mungana, Austl.	96	C8	17.05 S	144.23 E
Mungar Junction, Austl.	98	E9	25.36 S	152.35 E
Mungbere, D.R.C.	86	D5	2.37 N	28.30 E
Mungeli, India	70	G8	22.04 N	81.41 E
Munger, India	70	F11	25.22 N	86.28 E
Mungeranie, Austl.	98	F2	28.00 S	138.36 E
Mungindi, Austl.	98	G7	28.58 S	148.58 E
Mungo, Ang.	88	C2	11.48 S	16.16 E
Mungo National Park, p.o.i., Austl.	98	I4	33.44 S	143.02 E
Munhango, Ang.	88	C2	12.09 S	18.32 E
Munich see München, Ger.	24	H7	48.07 N	11.34 E
Municipal Stadium, p.o.i., Tai.	187d		25.03 N	121.33 E
Muniesa, Spain	28	C10	41.01 N	0.48 W
Munim, stm., Braz.	170	B3	2.48 S	44.04 W
Munirka, ngh., India	190a		28.34 N	77.10 E
Munising, Mi., U.S.	126	B3	46.24 N	86.38 W
Muniz Freire, Braz.	170	K5	20.28 S	41.25 W
Munkács see Mukatsjeve, Ukr.	36	A9	48.26 N	22.44 E
Munkács see Mukacheve, Ukr.	40	G3	48.26 N	22.44 E
Munkedal, Swe.	16	I9	58.28 N	11.40 E
Munkfors, Swe.	16	H11	59.50 N	13.32 E
Munksund, Swe.	14	G12	65.17 N	21.30 E
Munku-Sardyk, gora, mtn., Asia	48	D17	51.45 N	100.32 E
Munozero, Russia	12	C16	67.03 N	34.11 E
Munozero, ozero, l., Russia	14	E25	67.01 N	34.43 E
Munpal-li, Kor., S.	189b		37.45 N	126.43 E
Munro, ngh., Arg.	206		34.32 S	58.31 W
Munsey Park, N.Y., U.S.	194		40.48 N	73.41 W
Munsfjället, mtn., Swe.	16	C12	64.18 N	14.30 E
Münsingen, Ger.	24	H5	48.24 N	9.29 E
Munson, Ab., Can.	144	E18	51.34 N	112.44 W
Munsons Corners, N.Y., U.S.	124	B9	42.34 N	76.12 W
Munster, Fr.	24	H3	48.02 N	7.08 E
Münster, Ger.	24	D3	51.57 N	7.37 E
Munster, Ger.	24	C6	52.59 N	10.05 E
Munster, hist. reg., Ire.	10	I4	52.17 N	8.55 W
Münsterkirche, rel., Ger.	181		51.27 N	7.01 E
Munte, Indon.	66	C11	0.28 N	119.54 E
Muntele Mare, Vârful, mtn., Rom.	36	C10	46.29 N	23.14 E
Muntok, Indon.	66	E4	2.03 S	105.09 E
Munuscong Lake, l., N.A.	126	B5	46.12 N	84.13 W
Muodoslompolo, Swe.	14	E14	67.56 N	23.27 E
Muojärvi, l., Fin.	18	B16	65.55 N	29.38 E
Muong Het, Laos	64	B6	20.49 N	104.00 E
Muong Hinh, Viet.	64	C7	19.48 N	105.03 E
Muong Khoua, Laos	64	B6	21.05 N	102.30 E
Muong Saiapoun, Laos	64	C5	18.23 N	101.31 E
Muong Te, Viet.	64	A6	22.28 N	102.37 E
Muonio, Fin.	14	E14	67.58 N	23.39 E
Muonioälven (Muonionjoki), stm., Eur.	14	D13	67.10 N	23.35 E
Muonionjoki (Muonioälven), stm., Eur.	14	D13	67.10 N	23.35 E
Muping, China	58	C9	37.23 N	121.36 E
Muqaṭṭa', Sudan	82	E7	14.39 N	35.51 E
Muqayshit, i., U.A.E.	74	H13	24.10 N	53.45 E
Muqdisho (Mogadiscio), Som.	86	D9	2.02 N	45.20 E
Muqui, Braz.	170	K5	20.57 S	41.20 W
Mur (Mura), stm., Eur.	30	D12	46.17 N	16.53 E
Mura (Mur), stm., Eur.	30	D12	46.17 N	16.53 E
Muradiye, Tur.	34	E10	38.37 N	27.08 E
Muradiye, Tur.	42	F10	38.58 N	43.49 E
Murafa, stm., Ukr.	38	E7	48.13 N	28.14 E
Murai Reservoir, res., Sing.	189c		1.24 N	103.41 E
Murajá, Braz.	164	D8	0.47 S	47.56 W
Murakami, Japan	56	A12	38.13 N	139.28 E
Murana, Indon.	60	F9	3.33 S	133.49 E
Muraši, Russia	40	B16	59.23 N	48.58 E
Muraški, Russia	183b		55.59 N	37.45 E
Murat, Fr.	22	D8	45.07 N	2.52 E
Murat, stm., Tur.	42	F9	38.40 N	39.52 E
Murat Dağı, mtn., Tur.	34	E12	38.58 N	29.11 E
Muratlı, Tur.	34	B10	41.10 N	27.30 E
Muratpur, India	190b		22.59 N	88.27 E
Murau, Aus.	30	C11	47.06 N	14.09 E
Muravera, Italy	32	E3	39.25 N	9.34 E
Muravëvo, Russia	26	D17	56.13 N	34.09 E
Murayama, Japan	56	A13	38.27 N	140.22 E
Murayama-chosuichi, res., Japan	186		35.45 N	139.25 E
Murça, Port.	28	C3	41.24 N	7.27 W
Mürcheh Khvort, Iran	74	D12	33.06 N	51.30 E
Murchison, Austl.	98	K5	36.37 S	145.14 E
Murchison, Tx., U.S.	136	B12	32.17 N	95.45 W
Murchison, stm., Austl.	96	E2	27.42 S	114.08 E
Murchison, Mount, mtn., Austl.	96	E3	26.46 S	116.25 E
Murchison, Mount, mtn., N.Z.	102	F4	43.01 S	171.22 E
Murchison Falls see Kabalega Falls, wtfl., Ug.	86	D6	2.16 N	31.41 E
Murcia, Spain	28	G9	37.58 N	1.07 W
Murcia, state, Spain	28	G9	38.00 N	1.30 W
Mur-de-Barrez, Fr.	22	E8	44.51 N	2.39 E
Murder Creek, stm., Al., U.S.	134	F11	31.04 N	87.06 W
Murdo, S.D., U.S.	140	D12	43.52 N	100.41 W
Mureaux, Aérodrome des, arpt., Fr.	179		49.00 N	1.57 E
Mureck, Aus.	30	D12	46.42 N	15.45 E
Mürefte, Tur.	34	C10	40.42 N	27.17 E
Mureș, state, Rom.	36	C11	46.35 N	24.40 E
Mureș (Maros), stm., Eur.	36	C7	46.15 N	20.11 E
Muret, Fr.	22	F7	43.27 N	1.19 E
Murewa, Zimb.	88	D5	17.40 S	31.47 E
Murfreesboro, Ar., U.S.	134	C5	34.03 N	93.41 W
Murfreesboro, N.C., U.S.	124	H8	36.26 N	77.05 W
Murfreesboro, Tn., U.S.	130	I11	35.50 N	86.23 W
Murgab, Taj.	72	B11	38.09 N	73.58 E
Murgab (Morghāb), stm., Asia	72	B9	38.37 N	61.09 E
Murgeni, Rom.	36	C14	46.12 N	28.01 E
Murgha Kibzai, Pak.	70	C2	30.44 N	69.25 E
Murgon, Austl.	98	F8	26.14 S	151.56 E
Muri, Cook Is.	100j	a27	21.14 S	159.43 W
Muria, Gunung, mtn., Indon.	66	G7	6.36 S	110.53 E
Muriaé, Braz.	170	K4	21.08 S	42.23 W
Muriaé, stm., Braz.	170	K5	21.43 S	41.21 W
Murias de Paredes, Spain	28	B4	42.51 N	6.11 W
Muribeca, Braz.	170	F7	10.23 S	36.53 W
Muribeca dos Guararapes, Braz.	170	E8	8.10 S	35.01 W
Murici, Braz.	170	E8	9.19 S	35.56 W
Muricizal, stm., Braz.	170	D1	6.39 S	48.40 W
Murīdke, Pak.	70	C5	31.47 N	74.15 E
Muriege, Ang.	88	C3	9.54 S	21.13 E
Murih, Pulau, i., Indon.	66	C6	1.54 N	108.38 E
Murino, Russia	183a		60.03 N	30.27 E
Murinskij, stm., Russia	183a		60.01 N	30.28 E
Muriqui, stm., Braz.	205a		22.52 S	43.02 W
Mūrītānīyā see Mauritania, ctry., Afr.	84	F2	20.00 N	12.00 W
Müritz, l., Ger.	24	C8	53.25 N	12.43 E
Murjek, Swe.	14	F11	66.28 N	20.54 E
Murmansk, Russia	14	D24	68.58 N	33.05 E
Murmanskaja oblast', co., Russia	12	C16	68.00 N	35.00 E
Murmanskij bereg, cst., Russia	14	C26	68.45 N	37.15 E
Murmaši, Russia	14	D23	68.49 N	32.49 E
Murmino, Russia	40	D12	54.36 N	40.02 E
Murnau, Ger.	24	I7	47.40 N	11.11 E
Muro Lucano, Italy	32	D9	40.45 N	15.29 E
Murom, Russia	40	D12	55.34 N	42.02 E
Muromcevo, Russia	48	C13	56.22 N	75.13 E
Muroran, Japan	54	C14	42.19 N	140.59 E
Muros, Spain	28	B1	42.46 N	9.03 W
Muros e Noia, Ría de, est., Spain	28	B1	42.45 N	9.00 W
Muros y Noya, Ría de see Muros e Noia, Ría de, est., Spain	28	B1	42.45 N	9.00 W
Muroto, Japan	56	F7	33.17 N	134.09 E
Muroto-zaki, c., Japan	56	F7	33.15 N	134.11 E
Murovani Kurylivtsi, Ukr.	38	E6	48.43 N	27.32 E
Murowana Goślina, Pol.	24	D13	52.34 N	17.03 E
Murphy, Id., U.S.	146	G10	43.13 N	116.33 W
Murphy, N.C., U.S.	132	A1	35.05 N	84.02 W
Murphy Lake, l., B.C., Can.	144	D9	52.03 N	121.14 W
Murphys, Ca., U.S.	148	E5	38.09 N	120.26 W
Murphysboro, Il., U.S.	130	G8	37.45 N	89.20 W
Murr, stm., Ger.	20	F18	48.56 N	9.15 E
Murra Murra, Austl.	98	G6	28.16 S	146.48 E
Murrat el-Kubra, Buheirat (Great Bitter Lake), l., Egypt	74	E3	30.20 N	32.23 E
Murrat el-Sughra, Buheirat (Little Bitter Lake), l., Egypt	76	H3	30.13 N	32.33 E
Murray, Ia., U.S.	130	C3	41.02 N	93.57 W
Murray, Ky., U.S.	130	H9	36.36 N	88.19 W
Murray, Ut., U.S.	150	C5	40.38 N	111.53 W
Murray, stm., Austl.	98	J2	35.22 S	139.20 E
Murray, stm., B.C., Can.	144	B9	54.54 N	121.07 W
Murray, Lake, l., Pap. N. Gui.	101a	b3	7.00 S	141.30 E
Murray, Lake, res., S.C., U.S.	132	B4	34.04 N	81.23 W
Murray Bridge, Austl.	98	J2	35.07 S	139.15 E
Murray Downs, Austl.	96	D6	21.03 S	134.41 E
Murray Fracture Zone, unds.	174	F24	32.59 N	134.53 W
Murray Harbour, P.E., Can.	122	E14	45.59 N	62.31 W
Murray Head, c., P.E., Can.	122	D14	46.00 N	62.28 W
Murray Maxwell Bay, b., Nu., Can.	110	A14	70.00 N	80.00 W
Murray River, P.E., Can.	122	D14	46.00 N	62.36 W
Murraysburg, S. Afr.	90	G6	31.57 S	23.45 E
Murrayville, Il., U.S.	130	E7	39.35 N	90.15 W
Murree, Pak.	70	B4	33.55 N	73.24 E
Murrhardt, Ger.	24	H5	48.58 N	9.34 E
Murri, stm., Col.	168	D3	6.32 N	76.50 W
Murrumbidgee, stm., Austl.	98	J4	34.41 S	143.07 E
Murrumburrah, Austl.	98	J7	34.33 S	148.21 E
Murrupula, Moz.	88	D6	15.24 S	38.45 E
Murrurundi, Austl.	98	H8	31.45 S	150.50 E
Murry Hill, Pa., U.S.	197b		40.17 N	80.09 W
Murrysville, Pa., U.S.	197b		40.25 N	79.41 W
Mursala, Pulau, i., Indon.	64	L4	1.38 N	98.32 E
Murshidābād, India	70	F12	24.11 N	88.16 E
Mürşitpınar, Tur.	76	B9	36.55 N	38.22 E
Murska Sobota, Slvn.	30	D13	46.39 N	16.09 E
Murtajāpur, India	70	H6	20.44 N	77.21 E
Murtal, Port.	184c		38.42 N	9.22 W
Murtee, Austl.	98	H4	31.35 S	143.30 E
Murter, Otok, i., Cro.	30	G12	43.48 N	15.37 E
Murtle Lake, l., B.C., Can.	144	D11	52.08 N	119.38 W
Murtoa, Austl.	98	K4	36.36 S	142.27 E
Murtosa, Port.	28	D2	40.44 N	8.37 W
Muru, Capu di, c., Fr.	22	H14	41.45 N	8.39 E
Murud, India	69	B1	18.19 N	72.59 E
Murud, Gunong, mtn., Malay.	66	B9	3.52 N	115.30 E
Murukta, Russia	50	C9	67.46 N	102.02 E
Murung, stm., Indon.	66	C9	0.11 S	114.04 E
Murupara, N.Z.	102	D7	38.27 S	176.42 E
Mururoa, at., Fr. Poly.	94	F13	21.52 S	138.55 W
Murvaul Creek, stm., Tx., U.S.	136	B13	32.05 N	94.13 W
Murwāra (Katni), India	70	G8	23.50 N	80.23 E
Murwillumbah, Austl.	98	G9	28.20 S	153.24 E
Mürz, stm., Aus.	30	C12	47.25 N	15.17 E
Murzuq, Libya	82	B2	25.55 N	13.55 E
Murzūq, Idhān, des., Libya	82	C2	24.30 N	13.00 E
Mürzzuschlag, Aus.	30	C12	47.35 N	15.41 E
Muş, Tur.	42	F9	38.43 N	41.28 E
Muş, state, Tur.	42	F9	39.00 N	42.00 E
Mūša (Mūsa), stm., Eur.	26	D6	56.24 N	24.10 E
Mūsa (Mūša), stm., Eur.	26	D6	56.24 N	24.10 E
Mūsa, Gebel (Sinai, Mount), mtn., Egypt	76	J5	28.32 N	33.59 E
Musa Āli Terara see Moussa 'Ali, mtn., Afr.	86	B8	12.28 N	42.24 E
Musadi, D.R.C.	86	E4	2.30 S	22.47 E
Musā'id, Libya	82	A4	31.34 N	25.03 E
Mūsa Khel Bāzār, Pak.	70	C2	30.51 N	69.49 E
Musala, mtn., Blg.	36	G10	42.11 N	23.34 E
Musandam, pen., Oman	74	G15	26.18 N	56.24 E
Musan-ŭp, Kor., N.	54	C8	42.13 N	129.13 E
Musar, India	190b		22.54 N	88.14 E
Musashimurayama, Japan	186		35.45 N	139.23 E
Musashino-daichi, plat., Japan	186		35.45 N	139.35 E
Musay'īd, Qatar	74	H12	24.59 N	51.32 E
Muscat see Masqaṭ, Oman	72	E8	23.35 N	58.32 E
Muscat and Oman see Oman, ctry., Asia	72	F8	22.00 N	58.00 E
Muscatatuck, stm., In., U.S.	130	F12	38.46 N	86.09 W
Muscatatuck, Vernon Fork, stm., In., U.S.	130	E12	38.45 N	85.54 W
Muscatine, Ia., U.S.	130	C6	41.25 N	91.02 W
Muscle Shoals, Al., U.S.	134	C11	34.44 N	87.40 W
Muscow, Mount, mtn., B.C., Can.	144	C3	53.17 N	127.09 W
Muscoda, Wi., U.S.	130	A7	43.11 N	90.25 W
Musconetcong Lake, l., N.J., U.S.	194		40.54 N	74.42 W
Muscongus Bay, b., Me., U.S.	122	G7	43.55 N	69.20 W
Muscowpetung Indian Reserve, ind. res., Sk., Can.	142	D9	50.45 N	104.15 W
Musgrave, Austl.	96	B8	14.47 S	143.30 E
Mus-Haja, gora, mtn., Russia	50	D17	62.35 N	140.50 E
Mushie, D.R.C.	86	E3	3.00 S	16.56 E
Mushin, Nig.	84	H5	6.31 N	3.21 E
Mūsi, stm., India	69	C4	16.41 N	79.41 E
Musi, stm., Indon.	66	E3	2.21 S	104.54 E
Musicians Seamounts, unds.	174	F22	31.00 N	162.00 W
Muskeg, stm., Ab., Can.	144	C12	54.01 N	119.03 W
Muskeg Lake Indian Reserve, ind. res., Sk., Can.	142	B6	52.58 N	106.57 W
Muskegon, Mi., U.S.	130	A11	43.13 N	86.14 W
Muskegon, stm., Mi., U.S.	126	E4	43.13 N	86.19 W
Muskingum, stm., Oh., U.S.	124	E4	39.24 N	81.27 W
Muskingum Brook, stm., N.J., U.S.	203		39.48 N	74.44 W
Muskö, i., Swe.	16	I16	59.00 N	18.06 E
Muskoday Indian Reserve, ind. res., Sk., Can.	142	A8	53.06 N	105.30 W
Muskogee, Ok., U.S.	130	I2	35.44 N	95.22 W
Muskoka, Lake, l., On., Can.	126	C10	45.01 N	79.25 W
Muskowekwan Indian Reserve, ind. res., Sk., Can.	142	C10	51.19 N	104.06 W
Muskrat Creek, stm., Wy., U.S.	140	E5	43.09 N	108.12 W
Muskrat Lake, l., On., Can.	126	C12	45.40 N	76.54 W
Musocco, ngh., Italy	184b		45.30 N	9.08 E
Musoma, Tan.	86	E6	1.30 S	33.48 E
Musone, stm., Italy	30	G10	43.28 N	13.38 E
Musquapsink Brook, stm., N.J., U.S.	194		40.59 N	74.01 W
Musquaro, Lac, l., Qc., Can.	111a	i21	50.30 N	60.56 W
Musquash Brook, stm., N.H., U.S.	201		42.42 N	71.26 W
Musquashcut Pond, l., Ma., U.S.	201		42.13 N	70.46 W
Musquodoboit Harbour, N.S., Can.	122	F13	44.47 N	63.08 W
Mussau Island, i., Pap. N. Gui.	101a	a4	1.26 S	149.36 E
Musselshell, stm., Mt., U.S.	142	G6	47.26 N	107.54 W
Mussende, Ang.	88	C2	10.30 S	16.01 E
Mussidan, Fr.	22	D6	45.02 N	0.22 E
Mussomeli, Italy	32	G7	37.35 N	13.45 E
Mussuma, Ang.	88	C3	14.12 S	21.53 E
Mustafakemalpaşa, Tur.	34	C11	40.02 N	28.25 E
Mustafa Kemal Paşa, stm., Tur.	34	D11	40.08 N	28.33 E
Mustahīl, Eth.	82	F8	5.15 N	44.45 E
Mustajõe, Est.	26	C9	57.59 N	26.58 E
Mustāng, Nepal	70	D9	29.10 N	83.58 E
Mustang Draw, stm., Tx., U.S.	136	B6	32.12 N	101.36 W
Mustang Island, i., Tx., U.S.	136	G11	27.52 N	96.07 W
Musters, Lago, l., Arg.	166	I3	45.27 S	69.13 W
Mustinka, stm., Mn., U.S.	128	F2	45.46 N	96.37 W
Mustique, i., St. Vin.	159e	p11	12.53 N	61.11 W
Mustjala, Est.	26	B5	58.27 N	22.14 E
Mustla, Est.	26	B8	58.14 N	25.52 E
Musturud, Egypt	191c		30.08 N	31.17 E
Mustvee, Est.	26	B9	58.51 N	26.56 E
Musu-dan, c., Kor., N.	54	D8	40.51 N	129.42 E
Muswellbrook, Austl.	98	I8	32.16 S	150.53 E
Muszyna, Pol.	24	G16	49.21 N	20.54 E
Mût, Egypt	82	B5	25.29 N	28.58 E
Mut, Tur.	42	G5	36.38 N	33.27 E
Mutá, Ponta do, c., Braz.	170	G6	13.53 S	38.56 W
Mu'tah, Jord.	76	G6	31.06 N	35.42 E
Mutanda, Moz.	90	B11	20.58 S	33.35 E
Mutankiang see Mudanjiang, China	52	C10	44.35 N	129.36 E
Mutare, Zimb.	88	D5	18.58 S	32.39 E
Mutis, Gunung, mtn., Indon.	60	G7	9.34 S	124.14 E
Mutlu (Rezovska), stm., Eur.	36	G14	41.59 N	28.01 E
Mutoko, Zimb.	88	D5	17.24 S	32.12 E
Mutoraj, Russia	48	B17	61.20 N	100.30 E
Mutsamudu, Com.	88	C7	12.08 S	44.25 E
Mutshatsha, D.R.C.	86	G4	10.38 S	24.27 E
Mutsu, Japan	54	D14	41.17 N	141.10 E
Mutsuai, Japan	186		35.08 N	139.38 E
Mutsuura, ngh., Japan	186		35.19 N	139.37 E
Mutsu-wan, b., Japan	54	D14	41.05 N	140.55 E
Muttaburra, Austl.	98	D5	22.33 S	144.32 E
Mutton Bay, Qc., Can.	111a	i22	50.46 N	59.01 W
Muttontown, N.Y., U.S.	194		40.49 N	73.33 W
Muttra see Mathura, India	70	E6	27.30 N	77.41 E
Mutual, Pa., U.S.	197b		40.14 N	79.30 W
Mutuípe, Braz.	170	G6	13.13 S	39.31 W
Mutum, Braz.	170	J5	19.48 S	41.26 W
Mutusjärvi, l., Fin.	14	C17	68.59 N	26.48 E
Muurola, Fin.	14	F16	66.22 N	25.23 E
Mu Us Shamo (Ordos Desert), des., China	58	B3	38.45 N	109.10 E
Müvattupula, India	69	F3	9.58 N	76.34 E
Muxaluando, Ang.	88	B1	8.07 S	14.17 E
Muxima, Ang.	88	B1	9.31 S	13.56 E
Muyinga, Bdi.	86	E6	2.52 S	30.19 E
Muyumba, D.R.C.	86	F5	7.13 S	27.02 E
Muzaffarābād, Pak.	70	A4	34.21 N	73.27 E
Muzaffargarh, Pak.	70	C3	30.03 N	71.11 E
Muzaffarnagar, India	70	D6	29.28 N	77.42 E
Muzaffarpur, India	70	E10	26.07 N	85.22 E
Muzat, stm., China	52	C2	41.31 N	85.45 E
Muži, Russia	48	A10	65.24 N	64.41 E
Muzillac, Fr.	20	G6	47.33 N	2.29 W
Muztag, mtn., China	52	D2	36.25 N	87.25 E
Muztag, mtn., China	62	A5	36.03 N	80.07 E
Mvolo, Sudan	82	F6	6.03 N	29.55 E
Mvoti, stm., S. Afr.	90	F10	29.22 S	31.18 E
Mvuma, Zimb.	88	D5	19.17 S	30.32 E
Mwadui, Tan.	86	E6	3.30 S	33.33 E
Mwali, i., Com.	88	C7	12.17 S	43.41 E
Mwanza, Tan.	86	E6	2.31 S	32.54 E
Mweelrea, mtn., Ire.	10	H3	53.38 N	9.50 W
Mweka, D.R.C.	86	E4	4.51 S	21.34 E
Mwene-Ditu, D.R.C.	86	F4	7.03 S	23.26 E
Mwenezi, Zimb.	88	E5	21.28 S	30.37 E
Mwenezi, stm., Afr.	90	B10	22.38 S	31.44 E
Mwenga, D.R.C.	86	E5	3.01 S	28.24 E
Mweru, Lake, l., Afr.	86	F5	9.00 S	28.45 E
Mweru Wantipa, Lake, l., Zam.	88	B4	8.45 S	29.40 E
Mwilitau Islands, is., Pap. N. Gui.	101a	a4	2.50 S	146.20 E
Mwinilunga, Zam.	88	C3	11.44 S	24.27 E
Myaing, Mya.	64	B2	21.36 N	94.51 E
Myājlār, India	70	E3	26.15 N	70.23 E
Myakka, stm., Fl., U.S.	132	I3	27.00 N	82.15 W
Myakka River State Park, p.o.i., Fl., U.S.	132	I3	27.15 N	82.17 W
Myall Lakes National Park, p.o.i., Austl.	98	I9	32.28 S	152.22 E
Myanaung, Mya.	64	C2	18.17 N	95.19 E
Myanmar (Burma), ctry., Asia	62	D8	22.00 N	98.00 E
Myaungmya, Mya.	64	D2	16.34 N	94.54 E
Myawadi, Mya.	64	D4	16.41 N	98.29 E
Mycenae see Mykines, hist., Grc.	34	F5	37.44 N	22.45 E
Myckelgensjö, Swe.	16	D15	63.34 N	17.36 E
Myebon, Mya.	64	B1	20.03 N	93.22 E
Myingyan, Mya.	64	B2	21.27 N	95.23 E
Myinmoletkat Taung, mtn., Mya.	64	F4	13.28 N	98.48 E
Myitkyinā, Mya.	62	C8	25.23 N	97.24 E
Myitnge, stm., Mya.	64	B3	21.52 N	95.52 E
Myitta, Mya.	64	E4	14.09 N	98.30 E
Myittha, Mya.	64	B3	21.24 N	96.08 E
Myittha, stm., Mya.	64	A2	22.01 N	94.10 E
Myjava, Slvk.	24	H13	48.46 N	17.34 E
Mykhailivka, Ukr.	38	D15	49.19 N	36.28 E
Mykhailivka, Ukr.	38	F14	47.16 N	35.13 E
Mykil's'ke-na-Dnipri, Ukr.	38	E14	48.10 N	35.10 E
Mykines, i., Far. Is.	12b	m34	62.06 N	7.36 W

Name	Page	Map Ref.	Latitude	Longitude
Mykines, hist., Grc.	34	F5	37.44 N	22.45 E
Mykolaïv, Ukr.	38	G11	46.57 N	31.59 E
Mykolaïv, Ukr.	38	D2	49.31 N	23.58 E
Mykolaïv, co., Ukr.	38	F11	47.15 N	31.45 E
Mykolaïvka, Ukr.	38	I12	44.58 N	33.37 E
Mykolaïvka, Ukr.	38	F13	47.06 N	34.14 E
Mykolaïvka, Ukr.	38	G8	46.23 N	29.24 E
Mykolaïvka, Ukr.	38	F9	47.33 N	30.25 E
Mykolaïvka, Ukr.	38	E16	48.51 N	37.46 E
Mykolaïvka, Ukr.	38	B13	51.04 N	34.02 E
Mykolaïvka, Ukr.	38	F12	47.38 N	33.13 E
Mýkonos, Grc.	34	F8	37.26 N	25.20 E
Mýkonos, i., Grc.	34	F8	37.27 N	25.21 E
Mykulyntsi, Ukr.	38	D4	49.24 N	25.38 E
Myla, Russia	12	D24	65.25 N	50.49 E
Myllendonk, Schloss, hist., Ger.	181		51.13 N	6.29 E
Myllykoski, Fin.	18	G13	60.47 N	26.48 E
Myllymäki, Fin.	18	E11	62.31 N	24.18 E
Mymensingh (Nasirābād), Bngl.	70	F13	24.44 N	90.24 E
Mynämäki, Fin.	18	G8	60.40 N	22.00 E
Mynaral, Kaz.	48	E12	45.24 N	73.40 E
Mynfontein, S. Afr.	90	G6	30.54 S	23.56 E
Myo-gyi, Mya.	64	B3	21.26 N	96.20 E
Myohaung, Mya.	64	B1	20.35 N	93.11 E
Myohyang-san, mtn., Kor., N.	54	D7	40.00 N	126.20 E
Myojin-dake, mtn., Japan	188		34.57 N	135.36 E
Myōken-zan, mtn., Japan	188		34.56 N	135.28 E
Myōken-zan, hill, Japan	188		34.30 N	134.57 E
Myōkō-san, vol., Japan	56	C11	36.52 N	138.07 E
Myŏnmong-ni, ngh., Kor., S.	189b		37.35 N	127.05 E
Myra, hist., Tur.	34	G12	36.15 N	29.54 E
Mýrdalsjökull, ice, Ice.	12a	I30	63.40 N	19.05 W
Myre, Nor.	14	D5	68.55 N	15.05 E
Myrhorod, Ukr.	38	D12	49.57 N	33.36 E
Mýrina, Grc.	34	D7	39.53 N	25.04 E
Myrivs'ke, Ukr.	38	E12	48.05 N	33.24 E
Myrnam, Ab., Can.	144	C19	53.40 N	111.13 W
Myrnyi, Ukr.	38	C7	50.56 N	28.33 E
Myronivka, Ukr.	38	D9	49.39 N	30.59 E
Myropil', Ukr.	38	C6	50.06 N	27.41 E
Myropillia, Ukr.	38	B14	51.01 N	35.15 E
Myrskylä, Fin.	18	G12	60.39 N	25.50 E
Myrtle Beach, S.C., U.S.	132	C7	33.42 N	78.52 W
Myrtle Beach State Park, p.o.i., S.C., U.S.	132	C7	33.37 N	78.58 W
Myrtle Creek, Or., U.S.	146	G3	43.02 N	123.16 W
Myrtle Grove, Fl., U.S.	134	G11	30.26 N	87.18 W
Myrtle Point, Or., U.S.	146	G2	43.03 N	124.07 W
Myrtletowne, Ca., U.S.	148	C1	40.47 N	124.04 W
Myrtóön Pélagos, s., Grc.	34	G6	36.58 N	23.43 E
Mysen, Nor.	16	H9	59.33 N	11.20 E
Myshuryn Rih, Ukr.	38	E12	48.50 N	33.57 E
Myškino, Russia	26	C21	57.47 N	38.27 E
Myślenice, Pol.	24	G15	49.50 N	19.57 E
Myślibórz, Pol.	24	D10	52.55 N	14.51 E
Mysłowice, Pol.	24	F15	50.15 N	19.07 E
Mysore, India	69	E3	12.18 N	76.38 E
Mysore see Karnātaka, state, India	62	F4	14.00 N	76.00 E
Mystic, Ct., U.S.	124	C14	41.21 N	71.58 W
Mystic, Ia., U.S.	130	D5	40.46 N	92.56 W
Mystic, stm., Ma., U.S.	201		42.23 N	71.03 W
Mystrás, hist., Grc.	34	F5	37.04 N	22.21 E
Mys Vhodnoj, Russia	50	B6	73.51 N	86.40 E
Myszków, Pol.	24	F15	50.35 N	19.21 E
Myszyniec, Pol.	24	C17	53.22 N	21.20 E
Myt, Russia	40	C13	56.47 N	42.19 E
My Tho, Viet.	64	G8	10.21 N	106.22 E
Mytholm, Eng., U.K.	180		53.44 N	2.01 W
Mytholmroyd, Eng., U.K.	180		53.44 N	1.59 W
Mytilíni, Grc.	34	D9	39.06 N	26.33 E
Mytišči, Russia	26	E20	55.55 N	37.46 E
Mytišino, Russia	26	F16	54.48 N	34.01 E
Myton, Ut., U.S.	150	C6	40.12 N	110.03 W
Mývatn, I., Ice.	12a	k31	65.37 N	16.56 W
Myzove, Ukr.	38	B3	51.22 N	24.31 E
Mzimba, Mwi.	88	C5	11.53 S	33.33 E
Mzimvubu, stm., S. Afr.	90	G9	31.37 S	29.33 E
Mzintlava, stm., S. Afr.	90	G9	31.10 S	29.17 E
Mzuzu, Mwi.	88	C5	11.23 S	33.57 E

N

Name	Page	Map Ref.	Latitude	Longitude
Na (Tengtiao), stm., Asia	64	A6	22.19 N	103.07 E
Naab, stm., Ger.	24	G7	49.01 N	12.02 E
Naachtpunkt Brook, stm., N.J., U.S.	194		40.54 N	74.15 W
Naalehu, Hi., U.S.	100a	d6	19.03 N	155.35 W
Naaman Creek, stm., U.S.	203		39.48 N	75.27 W
Naaman Creek, South Branch, stm., De., U.S.	203		39.49 N	75.27 W
Naamans Garden, De., U.S.	203		39.49 N	75.31 W
Naantali, Fin.	18	G8	60.29 N	22.04 E
Naarn, stm., Aus.	30	B11	48.10 N	14.44 E
Naas, Ire.	10	H6	53.12 N	6.40 W
Näätämö, Fin.	14	C19	69.39 N	29.04 E
Nababeep, S. Afr.	90	F3	29.36 S	17.46 E
Nabābpur, India	190b		22.42 N	88.12 E
Nabadwīp see Navadwip, India	70	G12	23.25 N	88.22 E
Nabari, Japan	56	E9	34.37 N	136.05 E
Nabas, Phil.	68	E4	11.49 N	122.05 E
Nabberu, Lake, I., Austl.	96	E4	25.36 S	120.30 E
Nabburg, Ger.	24	G8	49.27 N	12.10 E
Naberežnoe, Russia	183b		55.57 N	37.58 E
Naberežnye Čelny, Russia	40	D18	55.42 N	52.19 E
Nabeul, Tun.	84	B7	36.26 N	10.46 E
Nābha, India	70	C6	30.22 N	76.09 E
Nab Hill, hill, Eng., U.K.	180		53.47 N	1.57 W
Nabire, Indon.	60	F10	3.21 S	135.29 E
Nabī Shu'ayb, Jabal an-, mtn., Yemen	72	F5	15.17 N	43.59 E
Nabnasset Pond, I., Ma., U.S.	201		42.37 N	71.26 W
Nabogame, Mex.	154	B5	26.13 N	106.56 W
Naboomspruit, S. Afr.	90	D9	24.31 S	28.43 E
Nabouwalu, Fiji	101e	p19	16.59 S	178.42 E
Nabq, Egypt	76	J5	28.05 N	34.25 E
Nabua, Phil.	68	D4	13.22 N	123.22 E
Nabula, China	70	C8	31.52 N	80.08 E
Nābulus, W.B.	76	F6	32.13 N	35.16 E
Nacala, Moz.	88	C7	14.33 S	40.40 E
Nacala-a-Velha, Moz.	88	C7	14.32 S	40.37 E
Naches, stm., Wa., U.S.	146	D6	46.37 N	120.30 W
Nachi-katsuura, Japan	56	F8	33.33 N	135.53 E
Nachingwea, Tan.	86	G7	10.22 S	38.45 E
Nāchna, India	70	E3	27.29 N	71.43 E
Náchod, Czech Rep.	24	F12	50.24 N	16.10 E
Nachrodt-Wiblingwerde, Ger.	181		51.19 N	7.37 E
Nächstebreck, ngh., Ger.	181		51.18 N	7.14 E
Nachuge, India	62	F7	10.44 N	92.22 E
Nachvak Fiord, b., Nf., Can.	108	F13	59.07 N	63.19 W
Nacimiento, Chile	172	H1	37.29 S	72.40 W
Nacimiento, stm., Ca., U.S.	148	H4	35.50 N	120.45 W
Nacimiento, Lake, res., Ca., U.S.	148	H5	35.45 N	121.00 W
Nacka, Swe.	16	H16	59.19 N	18.09 E
Naco, Mex.	120	F8	31.22 N	109.58 W
Naco, Az., U.S.	150	L7	31.20 N	109.56 W
Nacogdoches, Tx., U.S.	136	C13	31.35 N	94.39 W
Nácori Chico, Mex.	120	G8	29.39 N	109.00 W
Nacozari de García, Mex.	120	F8	30.24 N	109.39 W
Nacula, i., Fiji	101e	p18	16.53 S	177.25 E
Ñacunday, Para.	172	B10	26.00 S	54.45 W
Nada, ngh., Japan	188		34.44 N	135.14 E
Nadābhānga, India	190b		22.24 N	88.14 E
Nadarivatu, Fiji	101e	p18	17.34 S	177.58 E
Nadela, Spain	28	B3	42.58 N	7.29 W
Nadi, Fiji	101e	p18	17.48 S	177.25 E
Nadiād, India	70	G4	22.41 N	72.52 E
Nadi Bay, b., Fiji	101e	p18	17.44 S	177.25 E
Nadir, V.I.U.S.	158b	e7	18.19 N	64.52 W
Nădlac, Rom.	36	C7	46.10 N	20.45 E
Nadporože, Russia	18	G21	60.28 N	34.18 E
Naduri, Fiji	101e	p19	16.27 S	179.09 E
Nadvirna, Ukr.	38	E3	48.37 N	24.35 E
Nadvoicy, Russia	18	D21	63.51 N	34.16 E
Nadym, Russia	48	A12	65.34 N	72.38 E
Nadym, stm., Russia	48	A12	66.13 N	72.00 E
Naenwa, India	70	F5	25.46 N	75.51 E
Nærbø, Nor.	16	I3	58.40 N	5.39 E
Næstved, Den.	16	L9	55.14 N	11.46 E
Nafada, Nig.	84	G7	11.04 N	11.19 E
Nafarros, Port.	184c		38.49 N	9.25 W
Näfels, Switz.	30	C5	47.05 N	9.03 E
Nafī, Sau. Ar.	72	D5	24.57 N	43.42 E
Náfpaktos, Grc.	34	E4	38.23 N	21.48 E
Náfplio, Grc.	34	F5	37.34 N	22.48 E
Nafūsah, Jabal, hills, Libya	82	A2	31.50 N	12.00 E
Naga, Phil.	68	D4	13.37 N	123.10 E
Nagahama, Japan	56	F5	33.36 N	132.29 E
Nagahama, Japan	56	D9	35.23 N	136.16 E
Naga Hills, mts., Asia	62	C7	26.00 N	95.00 E
Nagai, Japan	56	A12	38.06 N	140.02 E
Nagai, Japan	186		35.12 N	139.37 E
Nagai Island, i., Ak., U.S.	109	F7	55.11 N	159.55 W
Nagai Park, p.o.i., Japan	188		34.36 N	135.31 E
Nāgāland, state, India	62	C7	26.00 N	95.00 E
Nagano, Japan	56	C11	36.38 N	138.11 E
Nagano, state, Japan	56	C10	36.00 N	138.00 E
Nagao, Japan	188		34.50 N	135.43 E
Nagaoka, Japan	56	B11	37.27 N	138.51 E
Nagaon, India	70	E14	26.21 N	92.41 E
Nāgappattinam, India	69	F4	10.45 N	79.50 E
Nagara, Japan	188		34.26 N	135.44 E
Nagara, stm., Japan	56	D9	35.06 N	136.41 E
Nagarhole Tiger Reserve, ind. res., India	69	E3	12.05 N	76.00 E
Nāgārjuna Sāgar, res., India	69	C4	16.33 N	79.14 E
Nagarote, Nic.	156	F4	12.16 N	86.34 W
Nagar Pārkar, Pak.	70	F3	24.22 N	70.45 E
Nagasaki, Japan	56	G2	32.44 N	129.52 E
Nagasaki, state, Japan	56	G2	33.00 N	129.45 E
Nagasawa, Japan	186		35.12 N	139.41 E
Nagasu see Usa, Japan	56	F4	33.33 N	131.22 E
Nagata, ngh., Japan	188		34.40 N	135.09 E
Nagataki, Japan	188		34.23 N	135.20 E
Nagatino, ngh., Russia	183b		55.41 N	37.41 E
Nagato, Japan	56	E4	34.21 N	131.11 E
Nagatsuda, ngh., Japan	186		35.32 N	139.30 E
Nāgaur, India	70	E4	27.12 N	73.44 E
Nāgāvali, stm., India	69	B6	18.13 N	83.56 E
Nagda, India	70	G5	23.27 N	75.25 E
Nāgercoil, India	69	G3	8.10 N	77.26 E
Nag Hammâdi, Egypt	74	G2	26.02 N	32.14 E
Nagīna, India	70	D7	29.26 N	78.26 E
Nagla, India	190a		28.31 N	77.22 E
Nagłowice, Pol.	24	F15	50.40 N	20.06 E
Nago, Japan	55a	I19	26.34 N	127.59 E
Nagog Pond, I., Ma., U.S.	201		42.31 N	71.26 W
Nagold, Ger.	24	H4	48.32 N	8.43 E
Nagold, stm., Ger.	20	F17	48.52 N	8.41 E
Nagore, Russia	26	D21	56.55 N	38.17 E
Nagornyj, Russia	50	E13	55.57 N	124.55 E
Nagornyj, Russia	183a		59.43 N	30.16 E
Nagorsk, Russia	40	B17	59.18 N	50.46 E
Nagoya, Japan	56	D9	35.10 N	136.55 E
Nāgpur, India	70	H7	21.09 N	79.05 E
Nagqu, China	52	E3	31.30 N	92.04 E
Nag's Head, c., St. K./N.	159a	c2	17.13 N	62.39 W
Nagu, i., Fin.	18	G8	60.10 N	21.47 E
Nagua, Dom. Rep.	156	C13	19.22 N	69.50 W
Naguabo, P.R.	158a	b4	18.12 N	65.44 W
Naguna, Île see Nguna, Île, i., Vanuatu	101d	k17	17.26 S	168.20 E
Nagyatád, Hung.	36	C4	46.13 N	17.23 E
Nagybajom, Hung.	36	C4	46.23 N	17.32 E
Nagybánya see Baia Mare, Rom.	36	B10	47.39 N	23.35 E
Nagyecsed, Hung.	36	B9	47.51 N	22.25 E
Nagykálló, Hung.	36	B8	47.53 N	21.51 E
Nagykanizsa, Hung.	36	C4	46.27 N	16.59 E
Nagykáta, Hung.	36	B6	47.24 N	19.44 E
Nagy-Kevély, hill, Hung.	182c		47.37 N	18.59 E
Nagykőrös, Hung.	36	B7	47.01 N	19.46 E
Nagy-Milic (Veľký Milič), mtn., Eur.	24	H17	48.35 N	21.28 E
Nagytarcsa, Hung.	182c		47.32 N	19.17 E
Nagytétény, ngh., Hung.	182c		47.24 N	18.58 E
Nagyvarad see Oradea, Rom.	36	B8	47.03 N	21.55 E
Naha, Japan	55a	I18	26.12 N	127.41 E
Nahabinka, stm., Russia	183b		55.51 N	37.12 E
Nahabino, Russia	183b		55.51 N	37.11 E
Nahabuan, Indon.	66	C9	0.49 N	114.05 E
Nāhan, India	70	C6	30.32 N	77.16 E
Nahang (Nihing), stm., Asia	62	C1	25.58 N	62.44 E
Nahanni Butte, N.T., Can.	110	C6	61.01 N	123.20 W
Nahant Beach, cst., Ma., U.S.	201		42.27 N	70.56 W
Nahariyya, Isr.	76	E6	33.00 N	35.06 E
Naharpur, ngh., India	190a		28.42 N	77.07 E
Nahāvand, Iran	74	C11	34.11 N	48.22 E
Nahe, China	52	B9	48.29 N	124.52 E
Nahe, stm., Ger.	24	G3	49.58 N	7.53 E
Nahičevan' see Naxçıvan, Azer.	42	F11	39.12 N	45.24 E
Nahirne, Ukr.	38	H7	45.25 N	28.27 E
Nahma, Mi., U.S.	126	C3	45.50 N	86.40 W
Nahmer, ngh., Ger.	181		51.20 N	7.35 E
Nahmer, stm., Ger.	181		51.21 N	7.35 E
Nahodka, Russia	48	A13	67.43 N	77.35 E
Nahodka, Russia	50	C12	42.48 N	132.52 E
Nahoe, Fr. Poly.	100g	r19	9.44 S	138.55 W
Nahoi, Cap, c., Vanuatu	101d	j16	14.38 S	166.36 E
Nahr al-Urdunn see Jordan, stm., Asia	76	F6	31.45 N	35.33 E
Nahuel Huapi, Arg.	166	H2	41.04 S	71.08 W
Nahuel Huapi, Lago, I., Arg.	166	H2	40.58 S	71.30 W
Nahuel Niyeu, Arg.	166	H3	40.30 S	66.33 W
Nahunta, Ga., U.S.	132	E4	31.12 N	81.58 W
Nâhya, Egypt	191c		30.03 N	31.07 E
Naica, Mex.	154	B6	27.51 N	105.29 W
Naicam, Sk., Can.	142	B9	52.25 N	104.29 W
Naiguatá, Pico, mtn., Ven.	204c		10.33 N	66.46 W
Naila, Ger.	24	F7	50.19 N	11.41 E
Naimakka, Swe.	14	D12	68.40 N	21.30 E
Naiman Qi, China	52	C9	42.53 N	120.42 E
Nā'īn, Iran	74	D13	32.52 N	53.05 E
Naini Tāl, India	70	D7	29.23 N	79.26 E
Nainpur, India	70	G8	22.25 N	80.08 E
Nairai, i., Fiji	101e	p19	17.49 S	179.24 E
Nairn, Scot., U.K.	10	D9	57.35 N	3.53 W
Nairn, La., U.S.	134	H9	29.25 N	89.38 W
Nairobi, Kenya	86	E7	1.16 S	36.48 E
Nairobi Airport, arpt., N.J., U.S.	194		41.08 N	74.21 W
Naissaar, i., Est.	26	A7	59.33 N	24.31 E
Naitauba, i., Fiji	101e	p20	17.01 S	179.16 W
Naivasha, Kenya	86	E7	0.44 S	36.26 E
Naizishan, China	54	C7	43.38 N	127.26 E
Najac, Fr.	22	E8	44.13 N	1.59 E
Najafābād, Iran	74	D12	32.38 N	51.21 E
Najafgarh, ngh., India	190a		28.37 N	76.59 E
Najafgarh Drain, can., India	190a		28.43 N	77.14 E
Najasa, stm., Cuba	156	B9	20.42 N	77.58 W
Najd (Nejd), hist. reg., Sau. Ar.	72	D5	26.07 N	44.39 E
Najībābād, India	70	D7	29.36 N	78.20 E
Najin, Kor., N.	54	C9	42.15 N	130.18 E
Najio, Japan	188		34.50 N	135.18 E
Najstenjarvi, Russia	18	E19	62.15 N	32.40 E
Naka, Japan	188		35.49 N	140.03 E
Naka, Japan	188		34.50 N	135.48 E
Naka, Japan	188		34.42 N	135.45 E
Naka, Japan	188		34.50 N	135.56 E
Naka, ngh., Japan	186		35.27 N	139.39 E
Naka, stm., Japan	56	C13	36.20 N	140.35 E
Naka, stm., Japan	186		35.39 N	139.51 E
Nakadōri-shima, i., Japan	56	G2	32.57 N	129.04 E
Nakagami, Japan	186		35.49 N	139.21 E
Nakagawa, ngh., Japan	186		35.33 N	139.35 E
Nakagyō, ngh., Japan	186		35.01 N	135.45 E
Nakajima, Japan	186		35.26 N	139.56 E
Nakajima, Japan	186		35.18 N	139.58 E
Nakajō, Japan	56	A12	38.02 N	139.24 E
Nakama, Japan	56	F3	33.48 N	130.43 E
Nakambé see Volta Blanche, stm., Afr.	84	G4	8.56 N	1.09 W
Nakambé see White Volta, stm., Afr.	84	G4	8.56 N	1.09 W
Nakaminato, Japan	56	C13	36.20 N	140.36 E
Nakamura, Japan	56	G5	32.59 N	132.56 E
Nakanbe see Volta Blanche, stm., Afr.	84	G4	8.56 N	1.09 W
Nakanbe see White Volta, stm., Afr.	84	G4	8.56 N	1.09 W
Nakano, Japan	56	C11	36.44 N	138.22 E
Nakano, Japan	186		35.20 N	139.54 E
Nakano, Japan	188		34.58 N	135.58 E
Nakano, ngh., Japan	186		35.42 N	139.42 E
Nakanobu, ngh., Japan	186		35.36 N	139.43 E
Nakano-shima, i., Japan	55a	k19	29.49 N	129.52 E
Nakaōzō, ngh., Japan	188		34.51 N	135.11 E
Nakasongola, Ug.	86	D6	1.19 N	32.28 E
Nakatō, Japan	186		35.45 N	139.24 E
Nakatomi, Japan	186		35.49 N	139.30 E
Nakatsu, Japan	56	F4	33.35 N	131.11 E
Nakatsu, Japan	186		35.30 N	139.20 E
Nakatsugawa, Japan	56	D10	35.29 N	137.30 E
Nakauchigami, Japan	188		34.56 N	135.10 E
Nakayama, ngh., Japan	186		35.31 N	139.33 E
Nakazuma, Japan	186		35.58 N	139.35 E
Nakéty, N. Cal.	101d	m16	21.32 S	166.02 E
Nakhl, Egypt	76	I4	29.54 N	33.44 E
Nakhola, India	70	E14	26.06 N	92.12 E
Nakhon Nayok, Thai.	64	E5	14.12 N	101.13 E
Nakhon Pathom, Thai.	64	F5	13.49 N	100.04 E
Nakhon Phanom, Thai.	64	D7	17.24 N	104.47 E
Nakhon Ratchasima, Thai.	64	E6	14.58 N	102.05 E
Nakhon Sawan, Thai.	64	E4	15.41 N	100.06 E
Nakhon Si Thammarat, Thai.	64	H5	8.26 N	99.58 E
Nakhon Thai, Thai.	64	D5	17.06 N	100.50 E
Nakhtarana, India	70	G2	23.20 N	69.15 E
Nakina, On., Can.	128	A12	50.10 N	86.42 W
Nakkaş, stm., Tur.	185b		41.00 N	28.45 E
Nakło nad Notecią, Pol.	24	C13	53.08 N	17.35 E
Naknek, Ak., U.S.	109	E8	58.44 N	157.02 W
Nakodar, India	70	C5	31.07 N	75.28 E
Nakonde, Zam.	88	B5	9.21 S	32.42 E
Nakskov, Den.	16	M9	54.50 N	11.07 E
Näkten, I., Swe.	16	E12	62.52 N	14.38 E
Naktong-gang, stm., Kor., S.	56	C1	35.03 N	128.53 E
Nakuru, Kenya	86	E7	0.17 S	36.04 E
Nakusp, B.C., Can.	144	F13	50.14 N	117.48 W
Nālanda, India	70	F10	25.07 N	85.24 E
Nalayh, Mong.	52	B6	47.45 N	107.17 E
Nalázi, Moz.	90	D11	24.02 S	33.19 E
Nalbāri, India	70	E13	26.26 N	91.24 E
Nal'čik, Russia	42	D10	43.29 N	43.36 E
Naldsjön, I., Swe.	16	D12	63.23 N	14.17 E
Nałęczów, Pol.	24	E18	51.18 N	22.08 E
Nalgonda, India	69	C4	17.03 N	79.16 E
Naliang, China	58	K2	21.42 N	107.51 E
Nālikul, India	190b		22.49 N	88.11 E
Nallamala Hills, mts., India	69	D4	15.43 N	78.52 E
Nallıhan, Tur.	34	C14	40.11 N	31.21 E
Nalón, stm., Spain	28	A5	43.29 N	6.06 W
Nalong, China	58	J2	23.34 N	106.03 E
Nālūt, Libya	82	A2	31.52 N	10.59 E
Nam (Nan'a), stm., Asia	64	B4	21.33 N	98.37 E
Namaacha, Moz.	90	D10	25.59 S	32.01 E
Namacurra, Moz.	88	D6	17.30 S	37.01 E
Namadgi National Park, p.o.i., Austl.	98	J7	35.45 S	148.57 E
Namak, Daryācheh-ye, I., Iran	74	C12	34.30 N	51.50 E
Namak, Kavīr-e, des., Iran	72	C8	34.46 N	57.45 E
Namakan Lake, I., N.A.	128	C6	48.27 N	92.35 W
Nāmakkal, India	69	F4	11.13 N	78.10 E
Namamugi, ngh., Japan	186		35.29 N	139.41 E
Namanga, Kenya	86	E7	2.32 S	36.48 E
Namangan, Uzb.	48	F12	41.00 N	71.40 E
Namanyere, Tan.	86	F6	7.30 S	31.02 E
Namapa, Moz.	88	C6	13.42 S	39.48 E
Namarrói, Moz.	88	D6	15.56 S	36.54 E
Namatanai, Pap. N. Gui.	101a	a5	3.39 S	152.28 E
Nambe Indian Reservation, ind. res., N.M., U.S.	138	F3	35.52 N	105.57 W
Nambour, Austl.	98	F9	26.38 S	152.57 E
Nambucca Heads, Austl.	98	H9	30.38 S	153.00 E
Nam Can, Viet.	64	H7	8.45 N	104.59 E
Namch'ang, Kor., S.	56	D2	35.26 N	129.17 E
Nam Co, I., China	52	E3	30.41 N	90.32 E
Namdalen, val., Nor.	16	C10	64.38 N	12.35 E
Nam Dinh, Viet.	64	B7	20.25 N	106.10 E
Nämdö, i., Swe.	16	H16	59.11 N	18.42 E
Nam Du, Quan Dao, is., Viet.	64	H7	9.42 N	104.22 E
Nameh, Indon.	66	B10	2.33 N	116.21 E
Namekagon, stm., Wi., U.S.	128	E7	46.04 N	92.00 W
Namen see Namur, Bel.	20	D13	50.28 N	4.52 E
Namerikawa, Japan	56	C10	36.45 N	137.20 E
Nametil, Moz.	88	D6	15.44 S	39.21 E
Nam-gang, stm., Kor., N.	54	E7	39.01 N	125.52 E
Namhae-do, i., Kor., S.	54	G8	34.48 N	127.57 E
Namhan-gang, stm., Kor., S.	54	F7	37.30 N	127.18 E
Namhkam, Mya.	62	D8	23.49 N	97.40 E
Namhsan, Mya.	64	A3	22.58 N	97.10 E
Namib Desert, des., Nmb.	88	E1	23.00 S	15.00 E
Namibe, Ang.	88	D1	15.11 S	12.09 E
Namibia, ctry., Afr.	88	E2	22.00 S	17.00 E
Namib Naukluft Park, ind. res., Nmb.	90	D2	24.40 S	15.16 E
Namie, Japan	56	B14	37.29 N	141.00 E
Namies, S. Afr.	90	F4	29.16 S	19.13 E
Namīn, Iran	74	A11	38.23 N	48.28 E
Namji-ri, Kor., S.	56	D1	35.23 N	128.29 E
Nam Kwo Chau, i., China	189d		22.15 N	114.21 E
Namlan, Mya.	64	A3	22.15 N	97.24 E
Namlea, Indon.	60	F8	3.16 S	127.06 E
Namling, China	70	D12	29.40 N	89.04 E
Nam Nao National Park, p.o.i., Thai.	64	D5	16.45 N	101.37 E
Nam Ngum Reservoir, res., Laos	64	C6	18.33 N	102.37 E
Namnoi, Khao, mtn., Mya.	64	G4	10.36 N	98.38 E
Namo, Indon.	66	D11	1.26 S	119.59 E
Namoi, stm., Austl.	98	H7	30.00 S	148.04 E
Namoya, D.R.C.	86	E5	4.01 S	27.33 E
Nampa, Id., U.S.	146	G10	43.34 N	116.33 W
Nampala, Mali	84	F3	15.16 N	5.32 W
Nam Pat, Thai.	64	D5	17.44 N	100.31 E
Nampawng, Mya.	64	A3	22.45 N	97.51 E
Nam Phan (Cochin China), hist. reg., Viet.	64	G8	11.00 N	107.00 E
Nam Phong, Thai.	64	D6	16.44 N	102.48 E
Namp'o, Kor., N.	54	E6	38.45 N	125.23 E
Namp'ot'ae-san, mtn., Kor., N.	54	D8	41.43 N	128.26 E
Nampula, Moz.	88	D6	15.06 S	39.15 E
Namsang, Mya.	64	B3	20.53 N	97.43 E
Namsan Park, p.o.i., Kor., S.	189b		37.34 N	126.59 E
Namsen, stm., Nor.	16	C10	64.28 N	11.41 E
Namsos, Nor.	16	C9	64.28 N	11.31 E
Namsskogan, Nor.	16	C11	64.56 N	13.10 E
Nam Tok, Thai.	64	E4	14.14 N	99.04 E
Nam Tok Mae Surin National Park, p.o.i., Thai.	64	C4	19.10 N	98.02 E
Namtu, Mya.	64	A3	23.03 N	97.23 E
Namu, B.C., Can.	144	E3	51.49 N	127.51 W
Namuka-I-Lau, i., Fiji	101e	q20	18.51 S	178.38 W
Namúli, Serra, mts., Moz.	88	D6	15.15 S	37.08 E
Namur (Namen), Bel.	20	D13	50.28 N	4.52 E
Namutoni, Nmb.	88	D2	18.49 S	16.56 E
Namwala, Zam.	88	D4	15.45 S	26.26 E
Namwŏn, Kor., S.	54	G7	35.25 N	127.22 E
Namysłów, Pol.	24	E13	51.04 N	17.43 E
Nan, Thai.	64	C5	18.46 N	100.46 E
Nan, stm., Thai.	64	C5	15.42 N	100.09 E
Nan'a (Nam), stm., Asia	64	B4	21.33 N	98.37 E
Nanaimo, B.C., Can.	144	G6	49.09 N	123.56 W
Nānākheri, ngh., India	190a		28.31 N	76.59 E
Nanam, Kor., N.	54	D8	41.42 N	129.42 E
Nan'an, China	58	I8	24.57 N	118.23 E
Nanango, Austl.	98	F8	26.41 S	152.00 E
Nanao, Japan	56	B9	37.02 N	136.58 E
Nanao-wan, b., Japan	56	B10	37.09 N	136.54 E
Nanas Channel, strt., Asia	189c		1.25 N	103.58 E
Nanatsu-jima, is., Japan	56	B9	37.36 N	136.53 E
Nanbu, China	58	F1	31.20 N	106.03 E
Nancefield, S. Afr.	191d		26.17 S	27.53 E
Nancha, China	52	B10	47.07 N	129.16 E
Nanchang, China	58	G6	28.41 N	115.53 E
Nancheng, China	58	H7	27.34 N	116.39 E
Nancheng see Hanzhong, China	58	E2	33.02 N	107.02 E
Nanchong, China	58	F2	30.47 N	106.04 E
Nanchuan, China	58	G2	29.10 N	107.05 E
Nancowry Island, i., India	62	G7	7.59 N	93.32 E
Nancy, Fr.	20	F15	48.41 N	6.10 E
Nanda Devi, mtn., India	70	C8	30.23 N	79.59 E
Nāndāha, India	190b		22.50 N	88.17 E
Nandaime, Nic.	156	G4	11.46 N	86.04 W
Nandan, Japan	56	E7	34.15 N	134.42 E
Nānded, India	69	B3	19.09 N	77.18 E
Nāndgaon, India	70	H5	20.18 N	74.38 E
Nāndgaon, India	190c		18.58 N	73.08 E
Nandi Drug, mtn., India	69	E3	13.25 N	77.42 E
Nandikotkūr, India	69	D4	15.51 N	78.16 E
Nandu, China	58	F8	31.26 N	119.18 E
Nandu, stm., China	58	L4	20.01 N	110.23 E
Nāndūra, India	70	H6	20.49 N	76.28 E
Nandurbār, India	70	H5	21.22 N	74.15 E
Nandy, Fr.	179		48.35 N	2.34 E
Nandyāl, India	69	D4	15.28 N	78.28 E
Nanfen, China	54	D5	41.05 N	123.45 E
Nanfeng, China	58	H7	27.12 N	116.32 E
Nangabadau, Indon.	66	C7	1.01 N	111.54 E
Nanga-Eboko, Cam.	86	D2	4.40 N	12.22 E
Nangakelawit, Indon.	66	C8	0.23 N	112.26 E
Nangalangki, Indon.	66	D7	1.14 S	111.39 E
Nangal Dewat, ngh., India	190a		28.33 N	77.06 E
Nangamau, Indon.	66	D7	0.06 S	111.54 E
Nangamuntatai, Indon.	66	D8	0.19 S	112.21 E
Nangaobat, Indon.	66	C8	0.56 N	113.12 E
Nanga Parbat, mtn., Pak.	62	A3	35.15 N	74.36 E
Nangapinoh, Indon.	66	D7	0.20 S	111.43 E
Nangaraun, Indon.	66	C8	0.37 N	113.09 E
Nangarhār, state, Afg.	70	A3	34.12 N	70.18 E
Nangatayap, Indon.	66	D7	1.32 S	110.33 E
Nanggala Hill, mtn., Sol. Is.	101b	e7	8.16 S	157.43 E
Nangi, India	190b		22.31 N	88.13 E
Nangin, Mya.	64	G4	10.30 N	98.30 E
Nangka, stm., Phil.	187f		14.41 N	121.06 E
Nangloi, ngh., India	190a		28.41 N	77.05 E
Nāngloi, ngh., India	190a		28.40 N	77.02 E
Nangloi Jat, ngh., India	190a		28.41 N	77.04 E
Nangnim-ŭp, Kor., N.	54	D7	40.59 N	127.06 E
Nangō, Japan	56	H4	31.32 N	131.23 E
Nangong, China	58	C6	37.20 N	115.22 E
Nang Rong, Thai.	64	E6	14.38 N	102.48 E
Nanguan, China	58	C5	37.00 N	112.32 E
Nanhai see Foshan, China	58	J5	23.02 N	113.06 E
Nan Hai see South China Sea, s., Asia	46	I15	10.00 N	113.00 E
Nanhe, China	58	C6	37.00 N	114.40 E
Nanhua, China	52	F5	25.14 N	101.10 E
Nan Hulsan Hu, I., China	52	D4	36.43 N	95.49 E
Nanhutou, China	54	C8	44.34 N	128.56 E
Nanika Lake, I., B.C., Can.	144	C3	53.45 N	127.40 W
Naniwa, ngh., Japan	188		34.39 N	135.30 E
Nanjangūd, India	69	E3	12.06 N	76.40 E
Nanjiang, China	58	E9	32.43 N	120.50 E
Nanjiang, China	58	E2	32.33 N	107.30 E
Nanjing, China	58	I7	24.30 N	117.22 E
Nanjing (Nanking), China	58	E8	32.02 N	118.47 E
Nankang, China	58	I6	25.42 N	114.44 E
Nankang, ngh., Tai.	187d		25.03 N	121.36 E
Nanking see Nanjing, China	58	E8	32.02 N	118.47 E
Nankoku, Japan	56	F6	33.34 N	133.39 E
Nankye, Mya.	64	E4	14.19 N	98.10 E
Nanle, China	58	C6	36.04 N	115.11 E
Nanlei (Loi), stm., Asia	64	B4	21.18 N	100.43 E
Nanling, China	58	F8	30.55 N	118.20 E
Nan Ling, mts., China	58	I5	25.00 N	112.00 E
Nanliu, stm., China	58	J3	21.39 N	109.05 E
Nanlou Shan, mtn., China	54	C7	43.27 N	126.42 E
Nan Madol, i., Micron.	100d	m12	6.51 N	158.21 E
Nannerch, Wales, U.K.	180		53.13 N	3.15 W
Nannine, Austl.	96	E3	26.52 S	118.22 E
Nanning, China	58	J3	22.48 N	108.19 E
Nanniwan, China	58	C3	36.19 N	109.38 E
Nannup, Austl.	96	F3	33.58 S	115.45 E
Na Noi, Thai.	64	C5	18.18 N	100.42 E
Nānole, ngh., India	190c		19.01 N	72.55 E
Nanortalik, Grnld.	108	E16	60.07 N	45.13 W
Nanoshi, India	190c		18.56 N	73.05 E
Nanpan, stm., China	52	G5	24.57 N	106.08 E
Nānpāra, India	70	E8	27.52 N	81.30 E
Nanpiao, China	58	A9	41.09 N	120.39 E
Nanping, China	52	E5	33.07 N	104.20 E
Nanping, China	58	K2	21.49 N	107.30 E
Nanping, China	58	H8	26.38 N	118.10 E
Nanpu Bridge, trans., China	187b		31.12 N	121.30 E
Nansa, stm., Spain	28	A6	43.22 N	4.28 W
Nansei, Japan	56	E9	34.21 N	136.41 E
Nansei-shotō (Ryukyu Islands), is., Japan	52	F10	25.44 N	126.57 E
Nansen Sound, strt., Nu., Can.	108	A7	81.00 N	90.35 W
Nanshan Island, i., Asia	60	C6	10.43 N	115.49 E
Nansunzhai, China	187b		31.21 N	121.27 E
Nant, Fr.	22	E9	44.01 N	3.18 E
Nantais, Lac, I., Qc., Can.	110	C16	60.59 N	74.00 W
Nantai-zan, vol., Japan	56	C12	36.45 N	139.29 E
Nantasket Beach, Ma., U.S.	201		42.16 N	70.52 W
Nanterre, Fr.	20	F11	48.51 N	2.12 E
Nantes, Fr.	20	G7	47.13 N	1.32 W
Nantes à Brest, Canal de, can., Fr.	20	F5	48.14 N	3.36 W
Nanteuil-lès-Meaux, Fr.	179		48.56 N	2.54 E
Nanticoke, Pa., U.S.	124	C9	41.12 N	76.00 W
Nanticoke, stm., U.S.	124	F10	38.21 N	75.51 W
Nantmeal Village, Pa., U.S.	203		40.08 N	75.42 W
Nanto, Japan	56	E9	34.15 N	136.27 E
Nanton, Ab., Can.	144	F17	50.21 N	113.46 W
Nantong, China	58	E9	32.01 N	120.50 E
Nant'ou, Tai.	58	J9	23.55 N	120.40 E
Nantouillet, Fr.	179		49.00 N	2.42 E
Nantua, Fr.	22	C11	46.09 N	5.35 E
Nantucket, Ma., U.S.	124	C15	41.16 N	70.06 W
Nantucket Island, i., Ma., U.S.	124	C15	41.16 N	70.03 W
Nantucket Sound, strt., Ma., U.S.	124	C15	41.30 N	70.15 W
Nantulo, Moz.	88	C6	12.17 S	39.04 E
Nanty Glo, Pa., U.S.	126	H11	40.27 N	78.49 W
Nanu, Pap. N. Gui.	101a	b3	8.55 S	142.45 E
Nanuet Mall, shp. ctr., N.Y., U.S.	194		41.06 N	74.01 W
Nanuku Passage, strt., Fiji	101e	p20	16.45 S	179.15 W
Nanumea, at., Tuvalu	94	D8	5.41 S	176.08 E
Nanuque, Braz.	170	I5	17.49 S	40.20 W
Nanusa, Kepulauan, is., Indon.	60	E8	4.42 N	127.06 E
Nanxi, China	58	G1	28.50 N	104.58 E
Nanxian, China	58	G5	29.20 N	112.19 E
Nanxiang, China	58	F9	31.17 N	121.17 E
Nanxiong, China	58	I6	25.06 N	114.19 E
Nanyang, China	58	E5	33.00 N	112.32 E
Nanyang Hu, I., China	58	D7	35.12 N	116.38 E
Nanyang Technological University, educ., Sing.	189c		1.21 N	103.41 E
Nanyi Hu, I., China	58	F8	31.06 N	118.53 E
Nan-yō, Japan	56	A13	38.03 N	140.10 E
Nanyuan Airport, arpt., China	189a		39.47 N	116.23 E
Nanyuki, Kenya	86	D7	0.01 N	37.05 E
Nanzamu, China	54	C6	41.58 N	124.25 E
Nanzhang, China	58	F4	31.48 N	111.42 E
Nanzhao, China	58	E5	33.29 N	112.26 E
Nao, Cabo de la see Nau, Cap de la, c., Spain	28	F11	38.43 N	0.13 E
Naoābād, India	190b		22.28 N	88.27 E
Naococane, Lac, I., Qc., Can.	110	E16	52.52 N	70.40 W
Naogaon, Bngl.	70	F12	24.48 N	88.56 E
Naokot, Pak.	70	F2	24.50 N	69.26 E
Não-Me-Toque, Braz.	172	D11	28.27 S	52.48 W
Naong, Bukit, mtn., Malay.	66	B8	2.40 N	112.52 E
Naopukuria, India	190b		22.55 N	88.16 E
Náousa, Grc.	34	C5	40.36 N	22.03 E
Naozhou Dao, i., China	58	K4	20.55 N	110.35 E
Napa, Ca., U.S.	148	E3	38.17 N	122.16 W
Napa, stm., Ca., U.S.	148	E3	38.04 N	122.14 W
Napajedla, Czech Rep.	24	G13	49.10 N	17.30 E
Napaku, Indon.	66	B9	2.30 N	115.55 E
Napalkovo, Russia	50	C3	70.03 N	73.49 E
Napanee, On., Can.	126	D12	44.14 N	76.57 W
Napassoq, Grnld.	108	D15	65.03 N	52.24 W
Napé, Laos	64	C7	18.18 N	105.06 E
Naperville, Il., U.S.	130	C9	41.46 N	88.08 W
Napido, Indon.	60	F10	0.39 S	135.24 E
Napier, N.Z.	102	D7	39.29 S	176.53 E
Napier, Mount, hill, Austl.	96	C5	17.32 S	129.10 E
Napier Mountains, mts., Ant.	103	B10	66.30 S	53.40 E
Napinka, Mb., Can.	142	E13	49.19 N	100.49 W
Naples see Napoli, Italy	32	D8	40.51 N	14.16 E
Naples, Fl., U.S.	132	J4	26.08 N	81.47 W
Naples, Id., U.S.	146	B10	48.34 N	116.23 W
Naples, N.Y., U.S.	124	B8	42.36 N	77.24 W
Naples, Tx., U.S.	134	D4	33.11 N	94.41 W
Napo, China	64	A7	23.16 N	105.54 E
Napo, state, Ec.	168	H3	0.30 S	77.00 W
Napo, stm., S.A.	164	D3	3.28 S	72.38 W
Napoleon, N.D., U.S.	140	A13	46.30 N	99.45 W
Napoleon, Oh., U.S.	124	C1	41.22 N	84.07 W
Napoleonville, La., U.S.	134	H7	29.56 N	91.01 W
Napoli (Naples), Italy	32	D8	40.51 N	14.16 E
Napoli, Golfo di, b., Italy	32	D7	40.42 N	14.14 E
Nappamerrie, Austl.	98	F3	27.36 S	141.07 E
Nappanee, In., U.S.	130	C12	41.26 N	85.58 W

Name	Page	Map Ref.	Latitude	Longitude
Napu, Indon.	66	H11	9.24 S	119.48 E
Naqâda, Egypt	74	H3	25.54 N	32.43 E
Naqadeh, Iran	74	B9	36.57 N	45.23 E
Nar, stm., Eng., U.K.	10	I13	52.44 N	0.23 E
Nara, Japan	56	E8	34.40 N	135.50 E
Nara, Mali	84	F3	15.10 N	7.17 W
Nara, state, Japan	56	E8	34.30 N	135.50 E
Nāra, stm., Pak.	70	F2	24.03 N	69.05 E
Nara, stm., Russia	26	E20	54.52 N	37.24 E
Nara-bonchi, bas., Japan	188		34.38 N	135.50 E
Narač, Bela.	26	F9	54.55 N	26.44 E
Narač, stm., Bela.	26	F9	54.26 N	26.39 E
Narač, vozero, l., Bela.	26	F9	54.51 N	26.46 E
Naracoorte, Austl.	98	K3	36.57 S	140.43 E
Naradhan, Austl.	98	I6	33.37 S	146.19 E
Naraina, ngh., India	190a		28.37 N	77.08 E
Naraini, India	70	F8	25.10 N	80.28 E
Naramata, B.C., Can.	144	G11	49.35 N	119.35 W
Naranjal, Ec.	168	I2	2.42 S	79.37 W
Naranjal, Ven.	204c		10.28 N	67.02 W
Naranjito, P.R.	158a	b3	18.18 N	66.14 W
Narao, Japan	56	G2	32.49 N	129.03 E
Nara Park, p.o.i., Japan	188		34.41 N	135.52 E
Narasannapeta, India	69	B7	18.24 N	84.03 E
Narasapur, India	69	C5	16.26 N	81.42 E
Narasaraopet, India	69	C4	16.14 N	80.03 E
Narasun, Russia	52	A7	50.06 N	112.59 E
Narat, China	48	F14	43.21 N	83.58 E
Narathiwat, Thai.	64	I5	6.25 N	101.49 E
Naraụ (Narew), stm., Eur.	24	D17	52.31 N	21.05 E
Nara Visa, N.M., U.S.	138	F5	35.36 N	103.06 W
Nara Women's University, educ., Japan	188		34.42 N	135.49 E
Nārāyanganj, Bngl.	70	G13	23.36 N	90.29 E
Nārāyani (Gandak), stm., Asia	70	E10	25.38 N	85.10 E
Nārāyanpāra, India	190b		22.54 N	88.19 E
Nārāyanpet, India	69	C3	16.44 N	77.29 E
Nārāyanpur, India	190b		22.29 N	88.34 E
Narberth, Pa., U.S.	203		40.00 N	75.15 W
Narbonne, Fr.	22	F8	43.11 N	2.59 E
Narborough see Fernandina, Isla, i., Ec.	164a	i11	0.25 S	91.29 W
Narcea, stm., Spain	28	A4	43.28 N	6.06 W
Narcondam Island, i., India	64	F2	13.25 N	94.17 E
Narcosli Creek, stm., B.C., Can.	144	D8	52.49 N	122.27 W
Nardò, Italy	32	D11	40.10 N	18.01 E
Nare, stm., Col.	168	D4	6.12 N	74.34 W
Nares Stræde see Nares Strait, strt., N.A.	108	B11	80.30 N	68.00 W
Nares Strait, strt., N.A.	108	B11	80.30 N	68.00 W
Narew (Naraụ), stm., Eur.	24	D17	52.31 N	21.05 E
Nargund, India	69	D2	15.43 N	75.23 E
Narhan, India	190c		19.08 N	73.07 E
Nariai, Japan	188		34.53 N	135.38 E
Narimba, Her Majesty's Air Station (Royal Australi, mil., Austl.	192a		33.43 S	150.53 E
Nariño, state, Col.	168	G3	1.30 N	78.00 W
Narita, Japan	56	D13	35.47 N	140.19 E
Nariva Swamp, sw., Trin.	159f	s12	10.25 N	61.04 W
Nar'jan-Mar, Russia	12	C25	67.37 N	52.59 E
Narkatiāganj, India	70	E10	27.06 N	84.27 E
Narlı, Tur.	76	A8	37.24 N	37.10 E
Narmada, stm., India	70	G4	21.40 N	72.44 E
Narmak, ngh., Iran	185d		35.43 N	51.29 E
Narman, Tur.	42	E10	40.18 N	41.58 E
Nārnaul, India	70	D6	28.02 N	76.06 E
Narni, Italy	30	H9	42.31 N	12.30 E
Narodnaja, gora, mtn., Russia	48	B10	65.04 N	60.09 E
Narodnaya, Mount see Narodnaja, gora, mtn., Russia	48	B10	65.04 N	60.09 E
Narodychi, Ukr.	38	B7	51.11 N	29.03 E
Naro-Fominsk, Russia	26	E19	55.22 N	36.44 E
Narok, Kenya	86	E7	1.05 S	35.51 E
Narol, Pol.	24	F19	50.22 N	23.21 E
Narón see Gándara, Spain	28	A2	43.30 N	8.10 W
Narooma, Austl.	98	K8	36.13 S	150.07 E
Naroulja, Bela.	38	B8	51.47 N	29.31 E
Narovčat, Russia	40	E13	53.52 N	43.41 E
Nārowāl, Pak.	70	B5	32.05 N	74.52 E
Närpes see Närpiö, Fin.	18	E8	62.27 N	21.18 E
Närpiö, Fin.	18	E8	62.27 N	21.18 E
Narrabeen Lagoon, b., Austl.	192a		33.43 S	151.17 E
Narrabri, Austl.	98	H7	30.20 S	149.47 E
Narran, stm., Austl.	98	G6	29.51 S	147.20 E
Narrandera, Austl.	98	J6	34.45 S	146.33 E
Narraway, stm., Can.	144	B11	54.43 N	119.55 W
Narraweena, Austl.	192a		33.45 S	151.16 E
Narre Warren, Austl.	192b		38.02 S	145.19 E
Narre Warren North, Austl.	192b		37.59 S	145.19 E
Narrogin, Austl.	96	F3	32.56 S	117.10 E
Narromine, Austl.	98	I7	32.14 S	148.14 E
Narrows, The, strt., St. K./N.	159a	c2	17.12 N	62.37 W
Narrows, The, strt., N.Y., U.S.	194		40.37 N	74.03 W
Narsaq see Narssaq, Grnld.	108	E16	60.55 N	46.02 W
Narsimhapur, India	70	G7	22.56 N	79.12 E
Narsinghgarh, India	70	G6	23.42 N	77.05 E
Narsīpatnam, India	69	C6	17.39 N	82.38 E
Narssaq, Grnld.	108	E16	60.55 N	46.02 W
Naru, Japan	56	G1	32.49 N	128.56 E
Naruko, Japan	56	A13	38.44 N	140.43 E
Naruo, Japan	188		34.43 N	135.23 E
Naruto, Japan	56	E7	34.10 N	134.36 E
Narva, Est.	26	A11	59.22 N	28.12 E
Narva, Russia	48	C16	55.25 N	93.39 E
Narva, stm., Eur.	26	A11	59.28 N	28.02 E
Narva-Jõesuu, Est.	26	A10	59.26 N	28.03 E
Narva laht see Narvskij zaliv, b., Eur.	18	H14	59.30 N	27.40 E
Narvik, Nor.	14	D8	68.26 N	17.25 E
Narvskij zaliv, b., Eur.	18	H14	59.30 N	27.40 E
Narvskoe vodohranilišče, l., Eur.	18	H15	59.16 N	28.11 E
Narwāna, India	70	D6	29.36 N	76.06 E
Narwietooma, Austl.	96	D6	23.11 S	132.38 E
Narym, Russia	48	C14	58.55 N	81.35 E
Naryn, Kyrg.	48	F13	41.26 N	75.59 E
Naryn (Syr-Darja), stm., Asia	72	A11	46.06 N	60.47 E
Naryn-Huduk, Russia	40	I15	45.26 N	46.32 E
Narynkol, Kaz.	48	F13	42.43 N	80.12 E
Naryškino, Russia	26	H18	52.57 N	35.43 E
Nås, Swe.	16	G12	60.27 N	14.29 E
Näsåker, Swe.	16	D14	63.26 N	16.54 E
Na San, Thai.	64	H4	8.47 N	99.22 E
Năsăud, Rom.	36	B11	47.18 N	24.26 E
Nasawa, Vanuatu	101d	j17	15.13 S	168.09 E
Nasbinals, Fr.	22	E9	44.40 N	3.03 E
Nasca, Peru	164	F2	14.50 S	74.57 W
Naschel, Arg.	172	F5	32.54 S	65.22 W
Nase see Naze, Japan	55a	k19	28.21 N	129.29 E
Nash, Tx., U.S.	134	D4	33.27 N	94.08 W
Nāshik, India	70	H4	20.00 N	73.47 E
Nashoba Brook, stm., Ma., U.S.	201		42.28 N	71.24 W
Nashua, Ia., U.S.	130	B5	42.57 N	92.33 W
Nashua, Mt., U.S.	142	F7	48.07 N	106.21 W
Nashua, N.H., U.S.	124	B14	42.46 N	71.28 W
Nashville, On., Can.	193b		43.50 N	79.40 W
Nashville, Ar., U.S.	134	D5	33.56 N	93.51 W
Nashville, Ga., U.S.	132	E2	31.12 N	83.14 W
Nashville, Il., U.S.	130	F8	38.20 N	89.23 W
Nashville, In., U.S.	130	E11	39.11 N	86.14 W
Nashville, Mi., U.S.	130	B12	42.35 N	85.05 W
Nashville, N.C., U.S.	124	I8	35.57 N	77.58 W
Nashville, Tn., U.S.	130	H11	36.09 N	86.47 W
Nashwaak, stm., N.B., Can.	122	D10	45.57 N	66.37 W
Nashwaaksis, N.B., Can.	122	D10	45.59 N	66.39 W
Nashwauk, Mn., U.S.	128	D5	47.22 N	93.10 W
Našice, Cro.	30	E15	45.29 N	18.04 E
Nasielsk, Pol.	24	D16	52.35 N	20.48 E
Näsijärvi, l., Fin.	18	F10	61.36 N	23.44 E
Nāşir, Sudan	82	F6	8.36 N	33.04 E
Nāşir, Buhayrat see Nasser, Lake, res., Afr.	82	C6	22.40 N	32.00 E
Nâsir, Buheirat see Nasser, Lake, res., Afr.	82	C6	22.40 N	32.00 E
Nasirābād see Mymensingh, Bngl.	70	F13	24.44 N	90.24 E
Nasīrābād, India	70	E5	26.18 N	74.44 E
Nasīrābād, Pak.	70	D2	28.22 N	68.24 E
Naslat el-Sammân, Egypt	191c		29.59 N	31.08 E
Nasr, Egypt	76	H1	30.36 N	30.23 E
Nasrābād, Iran	74	C12	34.05 N	51.23 E
Nasrānī, Jabal an-, mtn., Syria	76	D8	34.06 N	37.24 E
Nass, stm., B.C., Can.	144	E5	54.58 N	129.40 W
Nassarawa, Nig.	84	H6	8.30 N	7.42 E
Nassau, Bah.	132	K8	25.04 N	77.19 W
Nassau, N.Y., U.S.	124	B12	42.30 N	73.36 W
Nassau Coliseum, p.o.i., N.Y., U.S.	194		40.43 N	73.36 W
Nassau International Airport, arpt., Bah.	158f	m18	25.02 N	77.28 W
Nassau Island, i., Cook Is.	94	E10	11.34 S	165.24 W
Nassau Shores, N.Y., U.S.	194		40.39 N	73.26 W
Nassawadox, Va., U.S.	124	G10	37.28 N	75.51 W
Nasser, Lake (Nâsir, Buheirat), res., Afr.	82	C6	22.40 N	32.00 E
Nassereith, Aus.	24	I6	47.19 N	10.50 E
Nässjö, Swe.	16	J12	57.39 N	14.42 E
Nastapoka Islands, is., Nu., Can.	110	D15	56.56 N	76.42 W
Nastashka, Ukr.	38	D9	49.39 N	30.19 E
Nastauli, India	190a		28.43 N	77.22 E
Nasu, Japan	56	B13	37.01 N	140.06 E
Nasu-dake, vol., Japan	56	B12	37.07 N	139.58 E
Nasukoin Mountain, mtn., Mt., U.S.	146	B12	48.48 N	114.35 W
Nasva, Russia	26	D13	56.34 N	30.08 E
Nata, Bots.	88	E4	20.12 S	26.11 E
Natá, Pan.	156	H7	8.20 N	80.31 W
Nata, stm., Afr.	90	B8	20.09 S	27.43 E
Natagaima, Col.	168	F4	3.37 N	75.05 W
Nātāgarh, India	190b		22.42 N	88.25 E
Natal, Braz.	170	C8	5.47 S	35.13 W
Natal, B.C., Can.	144	G16	49.43 N	114.51 W
Natal, Indon.	66	C1	0.33 N	99.07 E
Natal see KwaZulu-Natal, state, S. Afr.	90	F10	28.40 S	30.40 E
Natalevka, Russia	38	F17	47.10 N	38.28 E
Natalia, Tx., U.S.	136	E9	29.11 N	98.51 W
Natalkuz Lake, res., B.C., Can.	144	C5	53.25 N	125.10 W
Natalspruit, stm., S. Afr.	191d		26.19 S	28.10 E
Natanes Plateau, plat., Az., U.S.	150	J6	33.36 N	110.28 W
Natash, Wadi, stm., Egypt	74	H4	24.27 N	33.16 E
Natashquan, stm., Can.	111a	i21	50.11 N	61.35 W
Natchez, Ms., U.S.	134	F7	31.33 N	91.23 W
Natchez Trace Parkway, p.o.i., U.S.	134	E9	32.00 N	91.00 W
Natchez Trace State Park, p.o.i., Tn., U.S.	134	B10	35.46 N	88.16 W
Natchitoches, La., U.S.	134	F5	31.45 N	93.05 W
Natco Lake, l., N.J., U.S.	194		40.26 N	74.09 W
Natewa Bay, b., Fiji	101e	p19	16.35 S	179.40 E
Na Thawi, Thai.	64	I5	6.44 N	100.41 E
Nāthdwāra, India	70	F4	24.55 N	73.49 E
Nathia Gali, Pak.	70	A4	34.02 N	73.22 E
Natick Laboratories, mil., Ma., U.S.	201		42.17 N	71.22 W
Natimuk, Austl.	98	K3	36.45 S	141.55 E
Nation, stm., B.C., Can.	144	A7	55.15 N	123.43 W
National Agricultural Research Center, sci., Md., U.S.	202c		39.02 N	76.52 W
National Airport, arpt., Mi., U.S.	199		42.19 N	83.25 W
National Arboretum, p.o.i., D.C., U.S.	202c		38.54 N	76.58 W
National Assembly, bldg., Thai.	187a		13.46 N	100.31 E
National City, Ca., U.S.	148	K8	32.40 N	117.05 W
National Gallery, bldg., Eng., U.K.	178		51.31 N	0.08 W
National Institute of Health, bldg., Md., U.S.	202c		39.00 N	77.06 W
National Maritime Museum, bldg., Eng., U.K.	178		51.29 N	0.00 W
National Museum, bldg., Indon.	187e		6.11 S	106.49 E
National Museum, bldg., Thai.	187a		13.46 N	100.30 E
National Park, N.J., U.S.	203		39.51 N	75.10 W
National Taiwan Normal University, educ., Tai.	187d		25.02 N	121.31 E
National Taiwan University, educ., Tai.	187d		25.01 N	121.32 E
National Zoological Park, p.o.i., D.C., U.S.	202c		38.56 N	77.03 W
Natitingou, Benin	84	G5	10.19 N	1.21 E
Native Bay, b., Nu., Can.	110	C14	63.52 N	82.30 W
Natividade, Braz.	170	F2	11.42 S	47.47 W
Natividad, ngh., Mex.	204a		19.14 N	99.05 W
Nativitas, Church of the, rel., W.B.	76	G5	31.43 N	35.12 E
Natkyizin, Mya.	64	E3	14.55 N	97.56 E
Natoma, Ks., U.S.	138	B9	39.11 N	99.00 W
Natong, China	64	A8	23.05 N	107.46 E
Nator, Bngl.	70	F12	24.24 N	88.59 E
Natori, Japan	56	A13	38.08 N	140.51 E
Natorp, Ger.	181		51.30 N	7.38 E
Natron, Lake, l., Afr.	86	E7	2.25 S	36.00 E
Natrūn, Wadi el-, val., Egypt	76	H1	30.15 N	30.24 E
Nättarö, i., Swe.	16	I16	58.52 N	18.07 E
Nattaset, mtn., Fin.	14	D18	68.12 N	27.20 E
Nattaung, mtn., Mya.	64	C3	18.48 N	97.02 E
Nattavaara, Swe.	14	F12	66.45 N	21.03 E
Nattwerder, Ger.	182a		52.26 N	12.56 E
Natuna Besar, i., Indon.	66	A6	4.00 N	108.15 E
Natuna Besar, Kepulauan, is., Indon.	66	A6	4.40 N	108.00 E
Natuna Selatan, Kepulauan, is., Indon.	66	B6	2.45 N	109.00 E
Natural Bridge, misc. cult., Va., U.S.	124	G6	37.38 N	79.33 W
Natural Bridges National Monument, p.o.i., Ut., U.S.	150	F6	37.36 N	109.59 W
Natural Bridge State Resort Park, p.o.i., Ky., U.S.	124	G1	37.47 N	83.42 W
Naturaliste, Cape, c., Austl.	96	F2	33.32 S	115.01 E
Naturita, Co., U.S.	150	E8	38.13 N	108.33 W
Naturita Creek, stm., Co., U.S.	150	E8	38.13 N	108.32 W
Naturno, Italy	30	D7	46.39 N	10.59 E
Naturns see Naturno, Italy	30	D7	46.39 N	10.59 E
Nau, Cap de la, c., Spain	28	F11	38.43 N	0.13 E
Naucalpan de Juárez, Mex.	204a		19.28 N	99.14 W
Naucelle, Fr.	22	E8	44.12 N	2.20 E
Nauchnyi, Ukr.	38	I13	44.44 N	34.01 E
Naucratis, hist., Egypt	76	H1	30.54 N	30.36 E
Naude, India	190c		19.03 N	73.06 E
Nauen, Ger.	24	D8	52.36 N	12.52 E
Nauener Luch, sw., Ger.	182a		52.37 N	12.55 E
Nauener Stadtforst, p.o.i., Ger.	182a		52.38 N	12.58 E
Naugatuck, Ct., U.S.	124	C12	41.29 N	73.03 W
Naughton, On., Can.	126	B8	46.24 N	81.10 W
Naujamiestis, Lith.	26	E6	55.41 N	24.06 E
Naujan, Lake, l., Phil.	68	D3	13.10 N	121.21 E
Naujoji Akmenė, Lith.	26	D5	56.19 N	22.55 E
Naulavaara, hill, Fin.	18	D15	63.46 N	28.23 E
Naumburg, Ger.	24	E7	51.09 N	11.47 E
Naumovščina, Russia	26	B11	58.27 N	28.21 E
Naunglon, Mya.	64	D3	16.44 N	97.38 E
Naungpale, Mya.	64	C3	19.33 N	97.08 E
Naupada, ngh., India	190c		19.04 N	72.50 E
Nauplia see Náfplio, Grc.	34	F5	37.34 N	22.48 E
Nā'ūr, Jord.	76	G6	31.54 N	35.51 E
Nauraushaun Brook, stm., N.Y., U.S.	194		41.03 N	73.59 W
Nauru, ctry., Oc.	100f	p17	0.32 S	166.55 E
Nauru, i., Nauru	94	D7	0.32 S	166.55 E
Nauru International Airport, arpt., Nauru	100f	q17	0.32 S	166.54 E
Nauru Local Government Council see Domaneab, bldg., Nauru	100f	q16	0.31 S	166.55 E
Nauški, Russia	50	F10	50.28 N	106.08 E
Nausori, Fiji	101e	p19	18.02 S	178.32 E
Naustdal, Nor.	16	F3	61.31 N	5.43 E
Nauta, Peru	164	D3	4.31 S	73.33 W
Nautanwa, India	70	E9	27.25 N	83.25 E
Nautla, Mex.	154	E10	20.12 N	96.47 W
Nautsi, Russia	14	D20	68.59 N	29.01 E
Nauvoo, Il., U.S.	130	D6	40.32 N	91.22 W
Nava, Mex.	154	A8	28.25 N	100.46 W
Nava, Arroyo de la, stm., Spain	184a		40.31 N	3.46 W
Nava del Rey, Spain	28	C5	41.19 N	5.05 W
Navadwip, India	70	G12	23.25 N	88.22 E
Navael'nja, Bela.	26	G8	53.27 N	25.35 E
Navahermosa, Spain	28	E6	39.38 N	4.27 W
Navahrudak, Bela.	26	G8	53.35 N	25.49 E
Navajo, N.M., U.S.	150	H7	35.55 N	109.01 W
Navajo, stm., U.S.	150	D7	37.01 N	107.09 W
Navajo Creek, stm., Az., U.S.	150	G6	37.00 N	111.24 W
Navajo Hopi Joint Use Area, ind. res., Az., U.S.	150	G6	36.20 N	110.13 W
Navajo Indian Reservation, ind. res., U.S.	150	G7	36.38 N	109.45 W
Navajo Mountain, mtn., Ut., U.S.	150	F6	37.02 N	110.52 W
Navajo National Monument, p.o.i., Az., U.S.	150	G6	36.43 N	110.29 W
Navajo Reservoir, res., U.S.	150	G9	36.58 N	107.26 W
Naval, Phil.	60	C7	11.34 N	124.24 E
Navalmoral de la Mata, Spain	28	E5	39.53 N	5.33 W
Navalvillar de Pela, Spain	28	E5	39.06 N	5.28 W
Navan, Ire.	10	H6	53.39 N	6.41 W
Navanagar see Jamnagar, India	70	G3	22.28 N	70.03 E
Navapolack, Bela.	26	E11	55.32 N	28.35 E
Navāpur, India	70	H4	21.09 N	73.47 E
Navarin, mys, c., Russia	50	D24	62.16 N	179.05 E
Navarino, Isla, i., Chile	166	K3	55.04 S	67.49 W
Navarra, state, Spain	28	B9	42.40 N	1.30 W
Navarre, Oh., U.S.	124	D4	40.43 N	81.30 W
Navarro, Arg.	172	G8	35.00 S	59.16 W
Navarro, stm., Ca., U.S.	148	D2	39.11 N	123.45 W
Navarro Mills Lake, res., Tx., U.S.	136	C11	31.56 N	96.44 W
Navasëlki, Bela.	26	H7	52.02 N	24.21 E
Navasëlki, Bela.	26	H11	52.23 N	28.34 E
Navasota, Tx., U.S.	136	D11	30.22 N	96.05 W
Navasota, stm., Tx., U.S.	136	D11	30.19 N	96.09 W
Navassa, N.C., U.S.	132	B8	34.16 N	77.55 W
Navassa Island, i., N.A.	156	C10	18.24 N	75.00 W
Naver, stm., Scot., U.K.	10	C8	58.30 N	4.13 W
Navesink, N.J., U.S.	194		40.23 N	74.02 W
Navesink River, b., N.J., U.S.	194		40.23 N	73.58 W
Navesnoe, Russia	26	H20	52.17 N	37.56 E
Navesti, stm., Est.	26	B8	58.29 N	24.54 E
Navestock, Eng., U.K.	178		51.39 N	0.13 E
Navestock Side, Eng., U.K.	178		51.39 N	0.16 E
Navia, Arg.	172	G4	34.47 S	66.35 W
Navia, Spain	28	A4	43.32 N	6.42 W
Navia, stm., Spain	28	A4	43.33 N	6.43 W
Navidad, Chile	172	F2	33.56 S	71.50 W
Navidad, stm., Tx., U.S.	136	E11	28.41 N	96.34 W
Navio, Riacho do, stm., Braz.	170	E6	8.38 S	38.34 W
Naviti, i., Fiji	101e	p18	17.07 S	177.15 E
Navlja, Russia	26	H17	52.49 N	34.30 E
Navlja, stm., Russia	26	H17	52.42 N	34.03 E
Nāvodari, Rom.	36	E15	44.19 N	28.36 E
Navoi, Uzb.	48	F11	40.07 N	65.22 E
Navojoa, Mex.	154	B4	27.04 N	109.26 W
Navolato, Mex.	154	C5	24.45 N	107.42 W
Navotas, Phil.	187f		14.39 N	120.57 E
Navsāri, India	70	H4	20.57 N	72.56 E
Navua, Fiji	101e	q19	18.14 S	178.10 E
Navy Island, i., On., Can.	202a		43.04 N	79.01 W
Navy Pier, trans., Il., U.S.	196		41.53 N	87.36 W
Nawa see Naha, Japan	55a	I18	26.12 N	127.41 E
Nawābganj, Bngl.	70	F12	24.35 N	88.17 E
Nawābganj, India	70	E8	26.56 N	81.12 E
Nawābshāh, Pak.	70	E2	26.14 N	68.24 E
Nawāda, India	70	F10	24.52 N	85.32 E
Nāwah, Afg.	70	B1	32.19 N	67.53 E
Nawa Kot, Pak.	70	D3	28.20 N	71.22 E
Nawalapitiya, Sri L.	69	H5	7.02 N	80.32 E
Nawalgarh, India	70	E5	27.50 N	75.16 E
Nawāpāra, India	70	H8	20.57 N	81.53 E
Naxçıvan, Azer.	42	F11	39.12 N	45.25 E
Naxçıvan Muxtar Respublikası, state, Azer.	42	F11	39.20 N	45.30 E
Naxi, China	58	G1	28.46 N	105.22 E
Náxos, Grc.	34	F8	37.06 N	25.23 E
Náxos, i., Grc.	34	F8	37.03 N	25.31 E
Nayābās, India	190a		28.35 N	77.19 E
Nayāgarh, India	70	H10	20.08 N	85.06 E
Nayarit, state, Mex.	154	E6	22.00 N	105.00 W
Nayau, i., Fiji	101e	p20	17.58 S	179.03 W
Nāy Band, Iran	74	G13	27.23 N	52.38 E
Nāy Band, Kūh-e, mtn., Iran	72	C8	32.26 N	57.22 E
Naylor, Mo., U.S.	130	H7	36.34 N	90.36 W
Nayong Pilipino, bldg., Phil.	187f		14.31 N	121.00 E
Nayoro, Japan	54	B15	44.21 N	142.28 E
Nayyāl, Wādī, stm., Sau. Ar.	74	F6	28.36 N	39.03 E
Nazaré, Braz.	170	D2	6.23 S	47.40 W
Nazaré, Port.	28	E1	39.35 N	9.03 W
Nazaré da Mata, Braz.	170	D8	7.44 S	35.14 W
Nazaré do Piauí, Braz.	170	D4	6.59 S	42.40 W
Nazareth see Naẓerat, Isr.	76	F6	32.41 N	35.18 E
Nazareth, Pa., U.S.	124	D10	40.44 N	75.18 W
Nazareth, Vanuatu	101d	j17	15.28 S	168.09 E
Nazarevo, Russia	183b		55.59 N	37.16 E
Nazarovo, Russia	48	C16	56.00 N	90.22 E
Nazas, Mex.	154	C6	25.14 N	104.08 W
Nazas, stm., Mex.	154	C6	25.34 N	105.02 W
Nazca Ridge, unds.	176	K5	22.00 S	82.00 W
Naze, Japan	55a	k19	28.21 N	129.29 E
Naze, The see Lindesnes, c., Nor.	16	J4	58.00 N	7.02 E
Nazeing, Eng., U.K.	178		51.44 N	0.03 E
Naẓerat (Nazareth), Isr.	76	F6	32.41 N	35.18 E
Naẓerat 'Illit, Isr.	76	F6	32.42 N	35.18 E
Nazija, Russia	26	A14	59.50 N	31.35 E
Nazilli, Tur.	34	F11	37.54 N	28.19 E
Nazimiha, Russia	183b		55.59 N	38.08 E
Nazimovo, Russia	48	C16	59.30 N	90.55 E
Nazina, Russia	48	B13	60.09 N	78.52 E
Nāzir Hāt, Bngl.	70	G13	22.37 N	91.47 E
Nazko, stm., B.C., Can.	144	D7	53.07 N	123.33 W
Nazlet el-'Amûdein, Egypt	76	J1	28.14 N	30.42 E
Nazlet Khalîfa, Egypt	191c		30.01 N	31.10 E
Nazran', Russia	42	D11	43.12 N	44.46 E
Nazrēt, Eth.	82	F7	8.32 N	39.16 E
Nazwá, Oman	72	E8	22.56 N	57.31 E
Nazyvaevsk, Russia	48	C12	55.34 N	71.20 E
N. B. C. Studios, sci., Ca., U.S.	198		34.09 N	118.20 W
N'dalatando, Ang.	88	B1	9.18 S	14.53 E
Ndali, Benin	84	H5	9.51 N	2.43 E
Ndélé, C.A.R.	86	C4	8.24 N	20.38 E
Ndendé, Gabon	86	E2	2.23 S	11.23 E
N'Djamena (Fort-Lamy), Chad	82	E3	12.07 N	15.02 E
Ndjili, ngh., D.R.C.	191b		4.20 S	15.22 E
Ndjili, stm., D.R.C.	191b		4.19 S	15.24 E
Ndjili, Grande Île de la, i., D.R.C.	191b		4.19 S	15.24 E
Ndjolé, Gabon	86	E2	0.07 S	10.44 E
Ndogo, Lagune, l., Gabon	86	E2	2.31 S	9.47 E
Ndola, Zam.	88	C4	12.57 S	28.38 E
Ndolo, ngh., D.R.C.	191b		4.19 S	15.19 E
Nduindui, Vanuatu	101d	j16	15.23 S	167.46 E
Ndumu Game Reserve, ind. res., S. Afr.	90	E11	26.53 S	32.15 E
Ne, Japan	186		35.47 N	140.03 E
Nea, stm., Eur.	16	D9	63.15 N	10.59 E
Neabul Creek, stm., Austl.	98	F6	27.45 S	147.31 E
Néa Chalkidón, Grc.	185c		38.02 N	23.43 E
Néa Erythraía, Grc.	185c		38.05 N	23.49 E
Néa Filadélfeia, Grc.	185c		38.02 N	23.44 E
Neagh, Lough, l., N. Ire., U.K.	10	G6	54.37 N	6.23 W
Neagră, Marea see Black Sea, s.	42	D5	43.00 N	35.00 E
Neah Bay, Wa., U.S.	146	B2	48.21 N	124.37 W
Néa Ionía, Grc.	185c		38.02 N	23.45 E
Neale, Lake, l., Austl.	96	D6	24.22 S	130.03 E
Néa Liósia, Grc.	185c		38.02 N	23.42 E
Neamț, state, Rom.	36	B13	47.00 N	26.30 E
Nean see Nea, stm., Eur.	16	D9	63.15 N	10.59 E
Neandertal, Naturschutzgebiet, p.o.i., Ger.	181		51.15 N	7.00 E
Néa Páfos (Paphos), Cyp.	76	D3	34.46 N	32.25 E
Néa Pentéli, Grc.	185c		38.04 N	23.52 E
Néa Péramos, Grc.	185c		38.00 N	23.26 E
Neápoli, Grc.	34	G6	36.30 N	23.04 E
Neápoli, Grc.	34	H8	35.15 N	25.37 E
Near Islands, is., Ak., U.S.	109a	g21	52.36 N	173.02 E
Near North Side, ngh., Il., U.S.	196		41.54 N	87.38 W
Néa Smýrni, Grc.	185c		37.57 N	23.43 E
Neath, Wales, U.K.	10	J9	51.39 N	3.48 W
Neauphle-le-Vieux, Fr.	179		48.49 N	1.52 E
Nebine Creek, stm., Austl.	98	G6	29.21 S	146.45 E
Nebitdag, Turkmen.	72	B7	39.30 N	54.22 E
Neblina, Cerro de la see Neblina, Pico da, mtn., S.A.	168	G9	0.49 N	65.59 W
Neblina, Pico da, mtn., S.A.	168	G9	0.49 N	65.59 W
Nebo, Il., U.S.	130	E7	39.26 N	90.46 W
Nebo, Mount, mtn., Ut., U.S.	150	D5	39.49 N	111.46 W
Nebolči, Russia	26	A16	59.06 N	33.22 E
Nebraska, state, U.S.	118	G16	41.30 N	100.00 W
Nebraska City, Ne., U.S.	130	D2	40.40 N	95.51 W
Nebrodi, Monti, mts., Italy	32	G8	37.54 N	14.35 E
Necedah, Wi., U.S.	128	G8	44.01 N	90.04 W
Nechaiane, Ukr.	38	G10	46.56 N	31.33 E
Nechako, stm., B.C., Can.	144	C7	53.54 N	122.43 W
Nechako Plateau, plat., B.C., Can.	144	B6	54.00 N	124.30 W
Nechako Range, mts., B.C., Can.	144	C6	53.20 N	124.37 W
Nechako Reservoir, res., B.C., Can.	144	C5	53.33 N	124.52 W
Neche, N.D., U.S.	142	F16	48.59 N	97.33 W
Neches, Tx., U.S.	136	C12	31.52 N	95.30 W
Neches, stm., Tx., U.S.	136	D13	29.58 N	93.52 W
Nechí, Col.	168	C4	8.06 N	74.48 W
Nechí, stm., Col.	168	D4	8.05 N	74.46 W
Nechranice, vodní nádrž, res., Czech Rep.	24	F9	50.21 N	13.22 E
Neckar, stm., Ger.	24	G5	49.30 N	8.26 E
Neckarsulm, Ger.	24	G5	49.10 N	9.13 E
Neck Creek, stm., N.Y., U.S.	194		40.36 N	74.12 W
Necker, Md., U.S.	202b		39.23 N	76.29 W
Necker Island, i., Br. Vir. Is.	158b	d9	18.32 N	64.21 W
Necochea, Arg.	172	I8	38.33 S	58.44 W
Nedalssjön, l., Swe.	16	E10	62.55 N	12.11 E
Nedanchychi, Ukr.	38	B9	51.30 N	30.37 E
Ned Brown Preserve, p.o.i., Il., U.S.	196		42.02 N	88.01 W
Nederland, Tx., U.S.	136	E13	29.57 N	93.59 W
Nederland see Netherlands, ctry., Eur.	20	B15	52.15 N	5.30 E
Nederlandse Antillen see Netherlands Antilles, dep., N.A.	158g	p22	12.15 N	68.45 W
Nedlitz, ngh., Ger.	182a		52.26 N	13.03 E
Nêdong, China	52	F3	29.12 N	91.46 E
Nedre Soppero, Swe.	14	E13	68.00 N	21.45 E
Nedryhailiv, Ukr.	38	C12	50.50 N	33.53 E
Nedstrand, Nor.	16	H3	59.21 N	5.51 E
Neebish Island, i., Mi., U.S.	126	B5	46.16 N	84.09 W
Needhams Point, c., Barb.	159d	n8	13.05 N	59.36 W
Needle Mountain, mtn., Wy., U.S.	146	F17	44.05 N	109.37 W
Needles, Ca., U.S.	150	I2	34.50 N	114.36 W
Needville, Tx., U.S.	136	E12	29.23 N	95.50 W
Neegro, Qooriga, b., Som.	86	C10	7.57 N	49.54 E
Ñeembucú, state, Para.	172	C8	27.00 S	58.00 W
Neenah, Wi., U.S.	128	G10	44.10 N	88.27 W
Neepawa, Mb., Can.	142	D14	50.14 N	99.28 W
Neersen, Ger.	181		51.15 N	6.29 E
Nee Soon, Sing.	189c		1.24 N	103.49 E
Nefedevo, Russia	183b		55.54 N	37.10 E
Nefëdovo, Russia	48	C12	58.50 N	72.35 E
Nefta, Tun.	84	C6	33.52 N	7.53 E
Neftçala, Azer.	42	F13	39.23 N	49.15 E
Neftejugansk, Russia	48	B12	61.05 N	72.35 E
Neftekumsk, Russia	42	C11	44.44 N	44.46 E
Nefza, Tun.	32	H3	36.58 N	9.04 E
Negage, Ang.	88	B2	7.45 S	15.16 E
Négala, Mali	84	G3	12.52 N	8.27 W
Negapatam see Nāgappattinam, India	69	F4	10.45 N	79.50 E
Negara, Indon.	66	E9	2.38 S	115.06 E
Negara, Indon.	66	H9	8.21 S	114.37 E
Negara, stm., Indon.	66	E9	2.57 S	114.46 E
Negaunee, Mi., U.S.	126	B2	46.29 N	87.35 W
Negēlē, Eth.	82	F7	5.19 N	39.34 E
Negeribatin, Indon.	66	F4	4.34 S	104.30 E
Negeri Sembilan, state, Malay.	64	K6	2.45 N	102.10 E
Negev Desert see HaNegev, reg., Isr.	76	H5	30.30 N	34.55 E
Negishi, Japan	186		35.51 N	139.23 E
Negombo, Sri L.	69	H4	7.13 N	79.51 E
Negotin, Yugo.	36	E9	44.13 N	22.33 E
Negra, Laguna, l., Ur.	172	G11	34.03 S	53.40 W
Negra, Punta, c., Belize	156	D3	16.14 N	88.34 W
Negrais, Port.	184c		38.53 N	9.17 W
Negras, Lomas, hill, Peru	204d		11.55 S	77.06 W
Negreira, Spain	28	B2	42.54 N	8.43 W
Nègres, Pointe des, c., Mart.	159c	k6	14.36 N	61.06 W
Negrești, Rom.	36	C14	46.51 N	27.26 E
Negrești-Oaș, Rom.	36	B10	47.52 N	23.25 E
Negritos, Peru	164	D1	4.39 S	81.17 W
Negro, stm., Arg.	166	H4	41.02 S	62.47 W
Negro, stm., Braz.	172	C13	26.01 S	50.29 W
Negro, stm., Col.	168	E4	5.46 N	74.29 W
Negro, stm., Para.	172	B9	24.23 S	57.10 W
Negro, stm., S.A.	168	I11	3.08 S	59.55 W
Negro, stm., S.A.	172	F9	33.25 S	58.27 W
Negro, Cerro, mtn., Arg.	166	H3	44.09 S	69.30 W
Negros, i., Phil.	68	F4	10.00 N	123.00 E
Negru Vodă, Rom.	36	F15	43.49 N	28.13 E
Neguac, N.B., Can.	122	C11	47.15 N	65.05 W
Nehaevskij, Russia	40	F12	50.24 N	41.45 E
Nehalem, stm., Or., U.S.	146	E3	45.39 N	123.56 W
Neharèlae, Bela.	26	G9	53.35 N	27.03 E
Nehawka, Ne., U.S.	130	D1	40.49 N	95.59 W
Nehbandān, Iran	72	C8	31.32 N	60.02 E
Nehe see Nahe, China	52	B9	48.29 N	124.52 E
Nehonsey Brook, stm., N.J., U.S.	203		39.49 N	75.18 W
Néhoué, Baie de, b., N. Cal.	101d	m14	20.20 S	164.06 E
Nehru Planetarium, bldg., India	190c		18.59 N	72.49 E
Neiba, Dom. Rep.	156	C12	18.28 N	71.25 W
Neidpath, Sk., Can.	142	D6	50.13 N	107.15 W
Neiges, Piton des, mtn., Reu.	89a	i10	21.05 S	55.29 E
Neihart, Mt., U.S.	146	D16	46.55 N	110.43 W
Neihu, Tai.	187d		25.05 N	121.34 E
Neijiang, China	58	G1	29.35 N	105.03 E
Neikiang see Neijiang, China	58	G1	29.35 N	105.03 E
Neilburg, Sk., Can.	142	B4	52.50 N	109.38 W
Neillsville, Wi., U.S.	128	G8	44.33 N	90.35 W
Neimen, Ger.	181		51.29 N	7.48 E
Nei Monggol, state, China	52	C7	43.00 N	115.00 E
Nei Mongol see Nei Monggol, state, China	52	C7	43.00 N	115.00 E
Neiqiu, China	58	C6	37.17 N	114.30 E
Neira, Col.	168	E4	5.08 N	75.30 W
Neishuishan, Tai.	187d		25.09 N	121.43 E
Neisse see Nysa, Pol.	24	F13	50.28 N	17.21 E
Neisse see Nysa Łużycka, stm., Eur.	24	E10	52.04 N	14.45 E
Neisse see Lausitzer Neisse, stm., Eur.	24	E10	52.04 N	14.45 E
Neiva, Col.	168	F4	2.55 N	75.16 W
Neixiang, China	58	E4	33.12 N	111.57 E
Neixpa, stm., Mex.	154	F7	18.04 N	102.47 W
Neja, Russia	40	B13	58.17 N	43.49 E
Nejanilini Lake, l., Mb., Can.	110	D11	59.33 N	97.46 W
Nejapa de Madero, Mex.	154	G11	16.37 N	95.57 W
Nejd see Najd, hist. reg., Sau. Ar.	72	D5	26.07 N	44.39 E
Nejdek, Czech Rep.	24	F8	50.18 N	12.46 E
Nek'emtē, Eth.	82	F7	9.02 N	36.29 E
Nekhâb, hist., Egypt	74	H3	25.10 N	32.48 E
Nekhvoroshcha, Ukr.	38	D13	49.09 N	34.41 E
Nekoosa, Wi., U.S.	128	G9	44.18 N	89.53 W
Nekrasovka, Russia	183b		55.41 N	37.56 E
Neksø, Den.	16	L13	55.03 N	15.07 E
Nela Park, p.o.i., Oh., U.S.	197a		41.33 N	81.33 W
Nelichu, mtn., Sudan	82	F6	6.08 N	34.25 E
Nelidovo, Russia	26	D15	56.13 N	32.47 E
Neligh, Ne., U.S.	140	E14	42.08 N	98.02 W
Neljaty, Russia	50	E12	56.29 N	115.42 E
Nel'kan, Russia	50	E16	57.40 N	136.09 E
Nellikuppam, India	69	F4	11.46 N	79.40 E
Nellis Air Force Base, mil., Nv., U.S.	150	G1	36.20 N	115.01 W
Nellis Weapons Range, mil., Nv., U.S.	148	F9	37.15 N	116.20 W
Nellore, India	69	D4	14.26 N	79.58 E
Nel'ma, Russia	50	G16	47.39 N	139.09 E
Nelson, B.C., Can.	144	G13	49.28 N	117.17 W
Nelson, N.Z.	102	E5	41.17 S	173.15 E

Name	Page	Map Ref.	Latitude	Longitude
Nelson, Ne., U.S.	138	A10	40.12 N	98.04 W
Nelson, stm., Mb., Can.	110	D12	57.08 N	92.20 W
Nelson, Cape, c., Austl.	98	L3	38.25 S	141.32 E
Nelson, Estrecho, strt., Chile	166	J2	51.36 S	74.59 W
Nelson Lakes National Park, p.o.i., N.Z.	102	E5	41.55 S	172.44 E
Nelson Reservoir, res., Mt., U.S.	142	F6	48.29 N	107.34 W
Nelson's Dockyard, hist., Antig.	159b	f4	17.00 N	61.45 W
Nelsonville, Oh., U.S.	124	E3	39.27 N	82.13 W
Nelspoort, S. Afr.	90	H6	32.06 S	23.00 E
Nelspruit, S. Afr.	90	D10	25.28 S	30.59 E
Néma, Maur.	84	F3	16.37 N	7.15 W
Nemadji, stm., U.S.	128	E6	46.41 N	92.01 W
Nemaha, Ne., U.S.	130	D2	40.20 N	95.40 W
Neman, Russia	26	E4	55.01 N	22.02 E
Neman (Nëman) (Nemunas), stm., Eur.	26	E4	55.20 N	21.15 E
Nëman (Neman) (Nemunas), stm., Eur.	26	G7	55.20 N	21.15 E
Nematābād, ngh., Iran	185d		35.38 N	51.21 E
Nembe, Nig.	84	I6	4.35 N	6.26 E
Nembrala, Indon.	96	B4	10.55 S	122.49 E
Nemčinovka, Russia	183b		55.43 N	37.23 E
Nemenčinė, Lith.	26	F8	54.51 N	25.30 E
Nemeriči, Russia	26	G16	53.51 N	33.59 E
Nemi, Lago di, l., Italy	185a		41.43 N	12.42 E
Nemira Mare, Vârful, mtn., Rom.	36	C13	46.15 N	26.19 E
Nemours, Fr.	20	F11	48.16 N	2.41 E
Nemovychi, Ukr.	38	B5	51.15 N	26.37 E
Nemunas (Neman) (Nëman), stm., Eur.	26	E4	55.20 N	21.15 E
Nemunėlis (Mēmele), stm., Eur.	26	D7	56.24 N	24.10 E
Nemuro, Japan	54	C16	43.19 N	145.35 E
Nemuro-kaikyō see Nemuro Strait, strt., Asia	54	C16	44.00 N	145.20 E
Nemuro Strait, strt., Asia	54	C16	44.00 N	145.20 E
Nemyriv, Ukr.	38	D8	48.58 N	28.50 E
Nemyriv, Ukr.	38	C2	50.06 N	23.26 E
Nemzeti Museum, bldg., Hung.	182c		47.29 N	19.05 E
Nen, stm., China	52	B9	45.25 N	124.39 E
Nenagh, Ire.	10	I4	52.51 N	8.11 W
Nenana, Ak., U.S.	109	D10	64.32 N	149.05 W
Nenana, stm., Ak., U.S.	109	D10	64.34 N	149.06 W
Nenaševo, Russia	26	F20	54.35 N	37.28 E
Nendo, i., Sol. Is.	94	E7	10.45 S	165.54 E
Nene, stm., Eng., U.K.	10	I13	52.48 N	0.12 E
Neneckij avtonomnyj okrug, mun., Russia	12	C23	67.13 N	49.27 E
Nenets see Neneckij avtonomnyj okrug, mun., Russia	12	C23	67.13 N	49.27 E
Nenetsia see Neneckij avtonomnyj okrug, mun., Russia	12	C23	67.13 N	49.27 E
Nenggiri, stm., Malay.	64	J5	4.53 N	101.48 E
Nenneper Fleuth, stm., Ger.	181		51.32 N	6.26 E
Nenoksa, Russia	18	C26	64.37 N	39.10 E
Neodesha, Ks., U.S.	130	G2	37.25 N	95.40 W
Neoga, Il., U.S.	130	E9	39.19 N	88.27 W
Néo Karlovási, Grc.	34	F9	37.48 N	26.42 E
Neola, Ia., U.S.	130	C2	41.27 N	95.38 W
Neola, Ut., U.S.	150	C6	40.26 N	110.01 W
Néon Fáliron, Grc.	185c		37.57 N	23.40 E
Néon Psikhikón, Grc.	185c		38.00 N	23.47 E
Neopit, Wi., U.S.	128	G10	44.58 N	88.49 W
Neópolis, Braz.	170	F7	10.19 S	36.35 W
Neosho, Mo., U.S.	130	H3	36.52 N	94.22 W
Neosho, stm., U.S.	130	H2	35.47 N	95.17 W
Nepa, stm., Russia	48	C19	59.15 N	108.11 E
Nepal, ctry., Asia	70	E10	28.00 N	84.00 E
Nepāl see Nepal, ctry., Asia	70	E10	28.00 N	84.00 E
Nepālganj, Nepal	70	D8	28.03 N	81.37 E
Nepa Nagar, India	70	H6	21.26 N	76.23 E
Nepean Island, i., Norf. I.	100i	y25	29.04 S	167.57 E
Nepeña, Peru	164	E2	9.09 S	78.22 W
Nepewassi Lake, l., On., Can.	126	B9	46.19 N	80.40 W
Nephi, Ut., U.S.	150	D5	39.42 N	111.50 W
Nephin, mtn., Ire.	10	G3	54.01 N	9.22 W
Nepisiguit, stm., N.B., Can.	122	C10	47.39 N	65.36 W
Nepisiguit Bay, b., N.B., Can.	122	C11	47.46 N	65.32 W
Népliget, p.o.i., Hung.	182c		47.29 N	19.07 E
Nepomuk, Czech Rep.	24	G9	49.29 N	13.36 E
Neponset, stm., Ma., U.S.	201		42.17 N	71.02 W
Neponset Reservoir, res., Ma., U.S.	201		42.05 N	71.15 W
Neponset River Reservation, p.o.i., Ma., U.S.	201		42.13 N	71.08 W
Neprjadva, stm., Russia	26	G21	53.40 N	38.39 E
Nép-sziget, i., Hung.	182c		47.34 N	19.05 E
Neptune, N.J., U.S.	124	D11	40.12 N	74.01 W
Neptune Beach, Fl., U.S.	132	F4	30.19 N	81.24 W
Nera, stm., Italy	30	H9	42.26 N	12.24 E
Nérac, Fr.	22	E6	44.08 N	0.20 E
Neráki, Grc.	185c		38.01 N	23.27 E
Nerča, stm., Russia	50	F12	51.56 N	116.38 E
Nerčinsk, Russia	50	F12	51.58 N	116.35 E
Nerčinskij Zavod, Russia	50	F12	51.18 N	119.36 E
Nerehta, Russia	40	C12	57.27 N	40.34 E
Nereta, Lat.	26	D8	56.12 N	25.19 E
Neretva, stm., Eur.	30	G15	43.01 N	17.26 E
Nerima, ngh., Japan	186		35.44 N	139.39 E
Neriquinha, Ang.	88	D3	16.00 S	21.43 E
Neris (Vilija), stm., Eur.	26	F6	54.53 N	23.52 E
Nerja, Spain	28	H7	36.45 N	3.51 W
Nerjungri, Russia	50	E13	56.40 N	124.39 E
Nerl', Russia	26	C20	57.03 N	37.58 E
Nerl', stm., Russia	26	D22	56.48 N	39.15 E
Nerl' (Nerl'), stm., Russia	26	C20	57.07 N	37.38 E
Nerl' (Nerl'), stm., Russia	26	C20	57.07 N	37.38 E
Neroj, Russia	48	D17	54.28 N	97.49 E
Nerópolis, Braz.	170	I1	16.24 S	49.13 W
Nerul, India	190c		19.02 N	73.01 E
Nerussa, stm., Russia	26	H16	52.32 N	33.48 E
Nerva, Spain	28	G4	37.42 N	6.32 W
Nerviano, Italy	184b		45.33 N	8.58 E
Nerville-la-Forêt, Fr.	179		49.05 N	2.17 E
Nes, Neth.	24	C1	53.26 N	5.45 E
Nes, Nor.	16	C10	64.34 N	12.32 E
Nes, Nor.	16	G7	60.33 N	9.57 E
Nes', Russia	12	C21	66.37 N	44.36 E
Nes, Har, mtn., Isr.	76	H5	30.22 N	34.37 E
Nesbyen, Nor.	16	G7	60.34 N	9.06 E
Neščarda, vozero, l., Bela.	26	E12	55.53 N	29.04 E
Nescochague Creek, stm., N.J., U.S.	203		39.39 N	74.41 W
Nescochague Creek, Great Swamp Branch, stm., N.J., U.S.	203		39.41 N	74.43 W
Nesconset, N.Y., U.S.	194		40.51 N	73.09 W
Nesebăr, Blg.	36	G14	42.40 N	27.42 E
Neshaminy Hills, Pa., U.S.	203		40.10 N	74.57 W
Neshaminy Mall, shp. cen., Pa., U.S.	203		40.08 N	74.57 W
Neshaminy State Park, p.o.i., Pa., U.S.	203		40.05 N	74.55 W
Neshaminy Woods, Pa., U.S.	203		40.10 N	74.57 W
Nesjøen, l., Nor.	16	E9	62.59 N	12.00 E
Neskaupstaður, Ice.	12a	k32	65.09 N	13.42 W
Nesna, Nor.	14	F3	66.11 N	13.02 E
Nesøya, i., Nor.	14	F3	66.35 N	12.38 E
Nespelem, Wa., U.S.	146	B7	48.09 N	118.58 W
Ness, Eng., U.K.	180		53.17 N	3.03 W
Ness, Loch, l., Scot., U.K.	10	D8	57.16 N	4.29 W
Ness City, Ks., U.S.	138	C9	38.27 N	99.54 W
Nesselrode, Mount, mtn., N.A.	109	E13	58.58 N	134.18 W
Nesselwang, Ger.	24	I6	47.36 N	10.29 E
Nesterkovo, Russia	26	A13	59.09 N	30.32 E
Nesterov, Russia	26	F5	54.38 N	22.34 E
Nestoïta, Ukr.	38	F8	47.46 N	29.21 E
Néstos (Mesta), stm., Eur.	34	B6	40.51 N	24.48 E
Nesttun, Nor.	16	G3	60.18 N	5.21 E
Nestucca, stm., Or., U.S.	146	E3	45.09 N	123.58 W
Netanya, Isr.	76	F5	32.20 N	34.51 E
Nete, stm., Bel.	20	C13	51.04 N	4.25 E
Nether Alderley, Eng., U.K.	180		53.17 N	2.14 W
Netherdale, Austl.	98	C7	21.07 S	148.30 E
Netherlands, ctry., Eur.	20	B15	52.15 N	5.30 E
Netherlands Antilles, dep., N.A.	158g	p22	12.15 N	68.45 W
Netherlands Guiana see Suriname, ctry., S.A.	164	C6	4.00 N	56.00 W
Netherton, Eng., U.K.	180		53.30 N	2.58 W
Neto, stm., Italy	32	E10	39.12 N	17.09 E
Netolice, Czech Rep.	24	G10	49.03 N	14.11 E
Netoma, stm., Russia	18	E24	62.13 N	37.27 E
Netrakona, Bngl.	70	F13	24.52 N	90.43 E
Nette, ngh., Ger.	181		51.33 N	7.25 E
Nettilling Fiord, b., Nu., Can.	110	B17	65.56 N	68.06 W
Nettilling Lake, l., Nu., Can.	110	B17	66.30 N	70.40 W
Nett Lake, l., Mn., U.S.	128	C5	48.07 N	93.05 W
Nettleden, Eng., U.K.	178		51.47 N	0.32 W
Nettlestead, Eng., U.K.	178		51.15 N	0.25 E
Nettlestead Green, Eng., U.K.	178		51.14 N	0.25 E
Nettleton, Ms., U.S.	134	C10	34.05 N	88.37 W
Nettuno, Italy	32	C6	41.27 N	12.39 E
Neubrandenburg, Ger.	24	C9	53.33 N	13.15 E
Neuburg an der Donau, Ger.	24	H7	48.44 N	11.11 E
Neuchâtel, Switz.	30	D3	46.59 N	6.54 E
Neuchâtel, Lac de, l., Switz.	30	D3	46.52 N	6.47 E
Neudamm see Dębno, Pol.	24	D10	52.44 N	14.42 E
Neudorf, Sk., Can.	142	D11	50.43 N	102.59 W
Neudorf, ngh., Ger.	181		51.25 N	6.47 E
Neuemühle, Ger.	182a		52.18 N	13.39 E
Neuenburg see Neuchâtel, Switz.	30	D3	46.59 N	6.54 E
Neuenhagen, Ger.	24	D9	52.31 N	13.39 E
Neuenhof, ngh., Ger.	181		51.10 N	7.13 E
Neuenhoven, Ger.	181		51.08 N	6.31 E
Neue Niers, stm., Ger.	181		51.16 N	6.26 E
Neuenkamp, ngh., Ger.	181		51.26 N	6.44 E
Neuerburg, Ger.	24	F2	49.59 N	6.18 E
Neu-Erlaa, ngh., Aus.	182b		48.08 N	16.19 E
Neues Palais, hist., Ger.	182a		52.24 N	13.01 E
Neu Fahrland, Ger.	182a		52.26 N	13.03 E
Neuf-Brisach, Fr.	24	H3	48.00 N	7.31 E
Neufchâteau, Bel.	20	E14	49.50 N	5.25 E
Neufchâteau, Fr.	20	F14	48.21 N	5.41 E
Neufchâtel-en-Bray, Fr.	20	E10	49.43 N	1.26 E
Neufmontiers-lès-Meaux, Fr.	179		48.58 N	2.50 E
Neu-Hartmannsdorf, Ger.	182a		52.22 N	13.51 E
Neuilly-sur-Marne, Fr.	179		48.51 N	2.32 E
Neu-Isenburg, Ger.	24	F4	50.03 N	8.41 E
Neukagran, ngh., Aus.	182b		48.14 N	16.27 E
Neukirchen, Ger.	181		51.07 N	6.41 E
Neulangerwisch, Ger.	182a		52.19 N	13.04 E
Neuman Creek, stm., N.Y., U.S.	202a		42.42 N	78.48 W
Neumarkt see Târgu Mureş, Rom.	36	C11	46.32 N	24.34 E
Neumarkt in der Oberpfalz, Ger.	24	G7	49.16 N	11.27 E
Neumarkt-Sankt Veit, Ger.	24	H8	48.21 N	12.29 E
Neumünster, Ger.	24	B6	54.04 N	9.59 E
Neun, stm., Laos	64	C6	19.42 N	104.02 E
Neunkirchen, Aus.	30	C13	47.43 N	16.05 E
Neunkirchen, Ger.	20	E16	49.20 N	7.10 E
Neuquén, Arg.	166	G3	38.57 S	68.04 W
Neuquén, state, Arg.	166	G2	39.00 S	70.00 W
Neuquén, stm., Arg.	166	G3	38.59 S	68.00 W
Neurara, Chile	172	B3	24.10 S	68.29 W
Neureisenberg, Aus.	182b		48.01 N	16.30 E
Neurode see Nowa Ruda, Pol.	24	F12	50.35 N	16.30 E
Neuruppin, Ger.	24	D8	52.55 N	12.48 E
Neusalz see Nowa Sól, Pol.	24	E11	51.47 N	15.42 E
Neusatz see Novi Sad, Yugo.	36	D6	45.14 N	19.49 E
Neuse, stm., N.C., U.S.	116	C14	35.08 N	76.30 W
Neuseddin, Ger.	182a		52.18 N	12.59 E
Neusiedl am See, Aus.	30	C13	47.56 N	16.50 E
Neusiedler See, l., Eur.	30	C13	47.50 N	16.45 E
Neusohl see Banská Bystrica, Slvk.	24	H15	48.44 N	19.09 E
Neuss, Ger.	24	E2	51.12 N	6.41 E
Neusserweyhe, Ger.	181		51.13 N	6.39 E
Neustadt, Ger.	24	F7	50.44 N	11.44 E
Neustadt an der Aisch, Ger.	24	G6	49.34 N	10.37 E
Neustadt an der Waldnaab, Ger.	24	G8	49.44 N	12.10 E
Neustadt an der Weinstrasse, Ger.	24	G4	49.20 N	8.08 E
Neustadt bei Coburg, Ger.	24	F6	50.19 N	11.06 E
Neustadt in Holstein, Ger.	24	B6	54.06 N	10.49 E
Neustettin see Szczecinek, Pol.	24	C12	53.42 N	16.42 E
Neustift am Walde, ngh., Aus.	182b		48.15 N	16.18 E
Neustrelitz, Ger.	24	C9	53.22 N	13.04 E
Neu Töplitz, Ger.	182a		52.27 N	12.54 E
Neutral Hills, hills, Ab., Can.	142	B3	52.10 N	110.50 W
Neu-Ulm, Ger.	24	H6	48.23 N	10.00 E
Neuvic, Fr.	22	D8	45.23 N	2.16 E
Neuville-sur-Oise, Fr.	179		49.01 N	2.04 E
Neuville-sur-Saône, Fr.	22	D10	45.51 N	4.50 E
Neuwaldegg, ngh., Aus.	182b		48.14 N	16.17 E
Neuwarp see Nowe Warpno, Pol.	24	C10	53.43 N	14.17 E
Neuwerk, ngh., Ger.	181		51.13 N	6.28 E
Neuwied, Ger.	24	F3	50.25 N	7.28 E
Neva, stm., Russia	26	A13	59.49 N	30.58 E
Nevada, Ia., U.S.	130	B4	42.01 N	93.27 W
Nevada, Mo., U.S.	130	G3	37.50 N	94.20 W
Nevada, state, U.S.	112	D4	39.00 N	117.00 W
Nevada, Sierra, mts., Spain	28	G7	37.05 N	3.10 W
Nevada, Sierra, mts., Ca., U.S.	148	F5	38.00 N	119.15 W
Nevada City, Ca., U.S.	148	D4	39.16 N	121.00 W
Nevada Creek, stm., Mt., U.S.	146	D14	46.53 N	113.02 W
Nevado, Cerro, mtn., Arg.	172	G3	35.34 S	68.28 W
Nevado, Cerro, mtn., Col.	168	E4	3.59 N	74.04 W
Nevado de Colima, Parque Nacional del, p.o.i., Mex.	154	F7	19.31 N	103.36 W
Nevado de Toluca, Parque Nacional, p.o.i., Mex.	154	F8	19.10 N	99.44 W
Nevali, India	190c		19.01 N	73.07 E
Neve, Serra da, mts., Ang.	88	C1	13.52 S	13.26 E
Nevel', Russia	26	D12	56.01 N	29.56 E
Nevel'sk, Russia	50	G17	46.39 N	141.52 E
Nevel'skogo, proliv, strt., Russia	50	F17	52.05 N	141.35 E
Nevendon, Eng., U.K.	178		51.36 N	0.30 E
Never, Russia	50	F13	53.58 N	124.09 E
Nevers, Fr.	20	G12	46.59 N	3.08 E
Nevertire, Austl.	98	H6	31.50 S	147.42 E
Nevesinje, Bos.	36	F5	43.15 N	18.06 E
Nevėžis, stm., Lith.	26	E6	54.55 N	23.46 E
Neville Island, Pa., U.S.	197b		40.31 N	80.08 W
Neville Island, i., Pa., U.S.	197b		40.31 N	80.08 W
Nevinnomyssk, Russia	42	C9	44.37 N	41.55 E
Nevis, i., St. K./N.	159a	c2	17.10 N	62.34 W
Nevis, Ben, mtn., Scot., U.K.	10	E7	56.48 N	5.01 W
Nevis, Loch, b., Scot., U.K.	10	D7	57.01 N	5.43 W
Nevis Peak, vol., St. K./N.	159a	c2	17.09 N	62.35 W
Nevjansk, Russia	48	C10	57.29 N	60.13 E
Nevlunghavn, Nor.	16	I7	58.58 N	9.52 E
Nevşehir, Tur.	42	F6	38.37 N	34.43 E
Nevşehir, state, Tur.	42	F6	38.50 N	34.40 E
Nevskoe, Russia	26	B13	58.07 N	30.28 E
New, stm., Belize	156	D3	18.20 N	88.22 W
New, stm., Guy.	164	C6	3.21 N	57.34 W
New, stm., Eng., U.K.	178		51.40 N	0.01 W
New, stm., U.S.	124	F4	38.09 N	81.11 W
New, stm., U.S.	148	K10	33.06 N	115.40 W
New, stm., Az., U.S.	150	J4	33.31 N	112.18 W
New, stm., Fl., U.S.	132	F3	29.55 N	82.24 W
New, stm., Fl., U.S.	134	G14	29.50 N	84.39 W
New, stm., N.C., U.S.	132	B8	34.32 N	77.20 W
New, stm., S.C., U.S.	132	D4	32.08 N	80.50 W
New, stm., Tn., U.S.	130	H13	36.25 N	84.38 W
Newabāgam, India	190b		22.48 N	88.24 E
New Addington, ngh., Eng., U.K.	178		51.21 N	0.01 W
Newala, Tan.	86	G7	10.56 S	39.16 E
New Albany, In., U.S.	130	F12	38.17 N	85.49 W
New Albany, Ms., U.S.	134	C9	34.29 N	89.00 W
New Albin, Ia., U.S.	128	H7	43.29 N	91.17 W
New Alexandria, Va., U.S.	202c		38.47 N	77.03 W
New Amsterdam, Guy.	164	B6	6.14 N	57.30 W
New Angledool, Austl.	98	G6	29.07 S	147.57 E
Newark, Ar., U.S.	134	B7	35.42 N	91.26 W
Newark, De., U.S.	124	E10	39.40 N	75.45 W
Newark, N.J., U.S.	124	D11	40.43 N	74.09 W
Newark, N.Y., U.S.	124	A8	43.02 N	77.05 W
Newark, Oh., U.S.	124	D3	40.03 N	82.24 W
Newark Bay, b., U.S.	194		40.39 N	74.09 W
Newark Bay Bridge, trans., N.J., U.S.	194		40.42 N	74.07 W
Newark Lake, l., Nv., U.S.	148	D10	39.40 N	115.43 W
Newark-on-Trent, Eng., U.K.	10	H12	53.05 N	0.49 W
Newark Slough, stm., Ca., U.S.	200		37.31 N	122.05 W
Newark Valley, N.Y., U.S.	124	B9	42.13 N	76.11 W
New Athens, Il., U.S.	130	F8	38.19 N	89.52 W
New Augusta, Ms., U.S.	134	F9	31.12 N	89.02 W
Newaygo, Mi., U.S.	126	E4	43.25 N	85.48 W
New Baden, Il., U.S.	130	F8	38.32 N	89.41 W
New Baltimore, Mi., U.S.	124	B3	42.40 N	82.43 W
New Bedford, Ma., U.S.	124	C15	41.38 N	70.56 W
Newberg, Or., U.S.	146	E4	45.18 N	122.57 W
New Berlin, Il., U.S.	130	E8	39.43 N	89.54 W
New Berlin, N.Y., U.S.	124	B10	42.38 N	75.19 W
New Berlin, Wi., U.S.	130	B9	42.58 N	88.06 W
Newbern, Al., U.S.	134	E11	32.35 N	87.31 W
New Bern, N.C., U.S.	132	A8	35.06 N	77.03 W
Newbern, Tn., U.S.	130	H8	36.06 N	89.15 W
Newberry, Fl., U.S.	132	G3	29.38 N	82.36 W
Newberry, Mi., U.S.	126	B4	46.21 N	85.28 W
Newberry, S.C., U.S.	132	B4	34.16 N	81.36 W
Newberry National Volcanic Monument, p.o.i., Or., U.S.	146	G5	43.45 N	121.15 W
Newbery, Aeroparque, arpt., Arg.	206		34.35 S	58.24 W
New Bethlehem, Pa., U.S.	124	D6	40.59 N	79.19 W
New Bloomfield, Pa., U.S.	124	H12	40.25 N	77.10 W
Newbold Island, i., N.J., U.S.	203		40.08 N	74.45 W
New Boston, Il., U.S.	130	C7	41.10 N	90.59 W
New Boston, Oh., U.S.	124	F3	38.45 N	82.56 W
New Boston, Tx., U.S.	134	D4	33.27 N	94.25 W
New Braunfels, Tx., U.S.	136	E9	29.42 N	98.07 W
New Brighton, Eng., U.K.	180		53.26 N	3.03 W
New Brighton, ngh., N.Y., U.S.	194		40.38 N	74.06 W
New Britain, Ct., U.S.	124	C13	41.40 N	72.45 W
New Britain, i., Pap. N. Gui.	101a	b5	6.00 S	150.00 E
New Brockton, Al., U.S.	134	F12	31.22 N	85.55 W
Newbrook, Ab., Can.	144	B17	54.19 N	112.56 W
New Brooklyn County Park, p.o.i., N.J., U.S.	203		39.43 N	74.57 W
New Brunswick, N.J., U.S.	124	D11	40.29 N	74.26 W
New Brunswick, state, Can.	122	D10	46.30 N	66.15 W
New Buffalo, Mi., U.S.	130	C11	41.47 N	86.44 W
New Bullards Bar Reservoir, res., Ca., U.S.	148	D4	39.25 N	121.08 W
Newburg, Mo., U.S.	130	G6	37.55 N	91.54 W
Newburgh, On., Can.	126	D12	44.19 N	76.53 W
Newburgh, Eng., U.K.	180		53.35 N	2.47 W
Newburgh, In., U.S.	130	G10	37.56 N	87.24 W
Newburgh, N.Y., U.S.	124	C11	41.30 N	74.01 W
Newburgh Heights, Oh., U.S.	197a		41.27 N	81.39 W
Newbury, Eng., U.K.	10	J11	51.24 N	1.19 W
Newburyport, Ma., U.S.	124	B15	42.48 N	70.51 W
New Caledonia, dep., Oc.	92	F7	21.30 S	165.30 E
New Caledonia see Nouvelle-Calédonie, i., N. Cal.	101d	m15	21.32 S	165.42 E
New Caledonia Basin, unds.	174	L19	30.09 S	165.11 E
New Canada, ngh., S. Afr.	191d		26.13 S	27.57 E
New Carlisle, Qc., Can.	122	B11	48.00 N	65.20 W
New Carlisle, Oh., U.S.	124	E1	39.56 N	84.01 W
New Carrollton, Md., U.S.	202c		38.58 N	76.52 W
New Cassel, N.Y., U.S.	194		40.45 N	73.34 W
New Castile see Castilla-La Nueva, hist. reg., Spain	84	B4	39.59 N	3.45 W
New Castille see Castilla la Nueva, hist. reg., Spain	28	E7	40.00 N	3.40 W
Newcastle, Austl.	98	I8	32.55 S	151.45 E
Newcastle, N.B., Can.	122	C11	47.00 N	65.34 W
New Castle see Clarington, On., Can.	126	E11	43.54 N	78.35 W
Newcastle, St. K./N.	159a	c2	17.12 N	62.34 W
Newcastle, S. Afr.	90	E9	27.45 S	29.55 E
Newcastle, N. Ire., U.K.	10	G7	54.12 N	5.53 W
Newcastle, Ca., U.S.	148	E4	38.52 N	121.08 W
New Castle, Co., U.S.	138	B1	39.35 N	107.32 W
New Castle, De., U.S.	124	E10	39.39 N	75.33 W
New Castle, In., U.S.	130	E12	39.55 N	85.22 W
New Castle, Ky., U.S.	130	F12	38.25 N	85.09 W
Newcastle, Ne., U.S.	128	I2	42.39 N	96.51 W
Newcastle, Ok., U.S.	128	F11	35.15 N	97.36 W
New Castle, Pa., U.S.	124	D5	40.59 N	80.21 W
Newcastle, Tx., U.S.	136	A9	33.12 N	98.43 W
New Castle, Va., U.S.	124	G5	37.30 N	80.06 W
Newcastle, Wy., U.S.	140	D8	43.51 N	104.13 W
Newcastle Bay, b., Austl.	96	B8	10.52 S	142.38 E
Newcastle Mine, Ab., Can.	144	E18	51.26 N	112.45 W
Newcastle-under-Lyme, Eng., U.K.	10	I10	53.00 N	2.13 W
Newcastle upon Tyne, Eng., U.K.	10	G10	54.58 N	1.40 W
Newcastle Waters, Austl.	96	C6	17.22 S	133.24 E
Newcastle West, Ire.	10	I3	52.27 N	9.03 W
New City, N.Y., U.S.	124	C11	41.08 N	74.00 W
Newclare, ngh., S. Afr.	191d		26.11 S	27.58 E
Newcomerstown, Oh., U.S.	124	D4	40.16 N	81.36 W
New Concord, Oh., U.S.	124	D4	39.59 N	81.43 W
New Croton Aqueduct, aq., N.Y., U.S.	194		41.11 N	73.49 W
New Cumberland, W.V., U.S.	124	D5	40.29 N	80.35 W
New Dayton, Ab., Can.	144	G18	49.25 N	112.22 W
Newdegate, Austl.	96	F3	33.05 S	119.01 E
New Delhi, India	70	D6	28.36 N	77.12 E
New Delhi, India	190a		28.36 N	77.12 E
New Delhi Railroad Station, trans., India	190a		28.39 N	77.13 E
New Denver, B.C., Can.	144	F13	49.59 N	117.22 W
New Edinburg, Ar., U.S.	134	D6	33.44 N	92.13 W
New Effington, S.D., U.S.	128	F2	45.51 N	96.55 W
New Egypt, N.J., U.S.	124	D11	40.04 N	74.32 W
Newell, Ia., U.S.	130	B2	42.36 N	95.00 W
Newell, S.D., U.S.	140	C9	44.42 N	103.24 W
Newell, W.V., U.S.	124	D5	40.36 N	80.34 W
Newell, Lake, l., Ab., Can.	144	F19	50.25 N	111.56 W
New Ellenton, S.C., U.S.	132	C4	33.25 N	81.41 W
Newellton, La., U.S.	134	E7	32.04 N	91.14 W
New Eltham, ngh., Eng., U.K.	178		51.26 N	0.04 E
New England, N.D., U.S.	140	A10	46.32 N	102.52 W
New England National Park, p.o.i., Austl.	98	H9	30.29 S	152.26 E
New England Range, mts., Austl.	98	G8	29.51 S	151.44 E
Newenham, Cape, c., Ak., U.S.	109	E7	58.39 N	162.10 W
New Falconwood, N.Y., U.S.	202a		42.59 N	78.58 W
Newfane, N.Y., U.S.	126	E11	43.16 N	78.41 W
Newfane, Vt., U.S.	124	A13	42.58 N	72.38 W
New Ferry, Eng., U.K.	180		53.22 N	2.59 W
Newfield Pond, l., Ma., U.S.	201		42.38 N	71.22 W
New Florence, Mo., U.S.	130	F6	38.55 N	91.27 W
New Florence, Pa., U.S.	124	D6	40.22 N	79.04 W
New Fork, stm., Wy., U.S.	140	E3	42.34 N	109.56 W
Newfound Gap, p., U.S.	124	I2	35.35 N	83.26 W
Newfoundland, N.J., U.S.	194		40.44 N	74.29 W
Newfoundland, state, Can.	110	E19	48.16 N	59.28 W
Newfoundland, i., Nf., Can.	106	E17	48.30 N	56.00 W
Newfoundland Basin, unds.	176	D9	45.00 N	40.00 W
New Franklin, Mo., U.S.	130	E5	39.00 N	92.44 W
New Freedom, Pa., U.S.	124	E9	39.44 N	76.42 W
New Galloway, Scot., U.K.	10	F8	55.04 N	4.09 W
New Garden, Pa., U.S.	203		39.49 N	75.45 W
Newgate, B.C., Can.	144	G15	49.00 N	115.08 W
Newgate Street, Eng., U.K.	178		51.44 N	0.07 W
New Georgia, i., Sol. Is.	101b	e7	8.09 S	157.25 E
New Georgia Group, is., Sol. Is.	101b	d7	8.30 S	157.20 E
New Georgia Sound, strt., Sol. Is.	101b	d8	8.00 S	158.10 E
New Germany, N.S., Can.	122	F12	44.32 N	64.42 W
New Glarus, Wi., U.S.	130	B8	42.48 N	89.38 W
New Glasgow, N.S., Can.	122	E14	45.35 N	62.37 W
New Guinea, i.	101a	b3	5.00 S	140.00 E
Newgulf, Tx., U.S.	136	E12	29.16 N	95.54 W
Newhalem, Wa., U.S.	146	B5	48.40 N	121.15 W
New Hamburg, On., Can.	126	E9	43.23 N	80.42 W
New Hampshire, state, U.S.	122	G5	43.35 N	71.40 W
New Hampton, Ia., U.S.	130	A5	43.03 N	92.19 W
New Hanover, S. Afr.	90	F10	29.21 S	30.30 E
New Hanover, i., Pap. N. Gui.	101a	a4	2.30 S	150.15 E
New Harmony, In., U.S.	130	F10	38.07 N	87.56 W
New Hartford, Ia., U.S.	128	I6	42.34 N	92.37 W
Newhaven, Eng., U.K.	10	K13	50.48 N	0.03 E
New Haven, Ct., U.S.	124	C13	41.18 N	72.55 W
New Haven, Il., U.S.	130	G9	37.54 N	88.07 W
New Haven, In., U.S.	130	C12	41.03 N	85.02 W
New Haven, Ky., U.S.	130	G12	37.39 N	85.35 W
New Haven, Mo., U.S.	130	F6	38.36 N	91.13 W
New Haven, W.V., U.S.	124	F3	38.58 N	81.58 W
New Hazelton, B.C., Can.	144	A3	55.15 N	127.35 W
New Hebrides see Vanuatu, ctry., Oc.	92	E7	16.00 S	167.00 E
New Hebrides, is., Vanuatu	94	E7	16.00 S	167.00 E
New Hebrides Trench, unds.	174	L20	22.30 S	170.00 E
Newhebron, Ms., U.S.	134	F9	31.44 N	89.58 W
New Hempstead, N.Y., U.S.	194		41.08 N	74.03 W
New Hey, Eng., U.K.	180		53.36 N	2.06 W
New Hogan Lake, res., Ca., U.S.	148	E5	38.09 N	120.48 W
New Holland, Oh., U.S.	124	E2	39.32 N	83.15 W
New Holland, Pa., U.S.	124	D9	40.06 N	76.05 W
New Holstein, Wi., U.S.	126	E1	43.57 N	88.04 W
New Hope, Al., U.S.	134	C12	34.31 N	86.25 W
New Hudson, Mi., U.S.	199		42.30 N	83.36 W
New Hyde Park, N.Y., U.S.	194		40.44 N	73.41 W
New Hythe, Eng., U.K.	178		51.19 N	0.27 E
New Iberia, La., U.S.	134	G7	30.00 N	91.49 W
Newington, Eng., U.K.	178		51.21 N	0.40 E
New Ireland, i., Pap. N. Gui.	101a	a5	3.20 S	152.00 E
New Jersey, state, U.S.	124	D11	40.15 N	74.30 W
New Jersey Institute of Technology, educ., N.J., U.S.	194		40.45 N	74.11 W
New Johnsonville, Tn., U.S.	130	I10	36.01 N	87.58 W
New Kensington, Pa., U.S.	124	D6	40.33 N	79.45 W
New Kent, Va., U.S.	124	G9	37.31 N	76.58 W
Newkirk, Ok., U.S.	128	E11	36.52 N	97.03 W
Newkirk Estates, De., U.S.	203		39.42 N	75.36 W
New Kowloon see Xinjiulong, China	58	J6	22.20 N	114.09 E
New Kowloon see Xinjiulong, China	189d		22.20 N	114.10 E
New Lagos, ngh., Nig.	191a		6.30 N	3.22 E
New Lake, l., N.C., U.S.	132	A9	35.38 N	76.20 W
Newlands, Austl.	98	C6	21.11 S	147.54 E
Newlands, ngh., S. Afr.	191d		26.11 S	27.58 E
New Lane, Eng., U.K.	180		53.37 N	2.52 W
New Leipzig, N.D., U.S.	140	A11	46.22 N	101.58 W
New Lexington, Oh., U.S.	124	E3	39.42 N	82.12 W
New Lisbon, Wi., U.S.	128	H8	43.52 N	90.09 W
New Liskeard, On., Can.	114	C11	47.31 N	79.39 W
New Llano, La., U.S.	134	F5	31.06 N	93.16 W
New London, Ct., U.S.	124	C13	41.21 N	72.07 W
New London, Ia., U.S.	130	D6	40.55 N	91.23 W
New London, Mn., U.S.	128	F3	45.18 N	94.56 W
New London, Mo., U.S.	130	E6	39.35 N	91.23 W
New London, N.H., U.S.	122	G5	43.24 N	72.00 W
New London, Oh., U.S.	124	C3	41.04 N	82.23 W
New London, Tx., U.S.	136	B13	32.15 N	94.56 W
New London, Wi., U.S.	128	G10	44.23 N	88.43 W
New Longton, Eng., U.K.	180		53.44 N	2.45 W
Newlonsburg, Pa., U.S.	197b		40.25 N	79.40 W
New Madrid, Mo., U.S.	130	H8	36.35 N	89.32 W
Newman, Austl.	96	D3	23.20 S	119.44 E
Newman, Ca., U.S.	148	F4	37.18 N	121.01 W
Newman, Il., U.S.	130	E10	39.47 N	87.59 W
Newman Grove, Ne., U.S.	140	F15	41.44 N	97.46 W
Newmarket, On., Can.	126	D10	44.03 N	79.27 W
Newmarket, Ire.	10	I4	52.14 N	9.00 W
Newmarket, S. Afr.	191d		26.17 S	28.08 E
Newmarket, Eng., U.K.	10	I13	52.14 N	0.24 E
New Market, Al., U.S.	134	C12	34.54 N	86.25 W
New Market, Ia., U.S.	130	D3	40.43 N	94.53 W
Newmarket, N.H., U.S.	122	G5	43.05 N	70.56 W
New Market, N.J., U.S.	194		40.34 N	74.27 W
New Market, Va., U.S.	124	F7	38.38 N	78.40 W
Newmarket Race Course, p.o.i., S. Afr.	191d		26.17 S	28.08 E
New Martinsville, W.V., U.S.	124	E5	39.38 N	80.51 W
New Meadows, Id., U.S.	146	F10	44.58 N	116.17 W
New Mexico, state, U.S.	120	D10	34.30 N	106.00 W
New Milford, Ct., U.S.	124	C12	41.35 N	73.24 W
New Milford, N.J., U.S.	194		40.56 N	74.01 W
New Milford, Pa., U.S.	124	C10	41.53 N	75.42 W
New Millpond, l., N.Y., U.S.	194		40.50 N	73.13 W
Newnan, Ga., U.S.	134	D14	33.22 N	84.48 W
Newnans Lake, l., Fl., U.S.	132	G3	29.39 N	82.13 W
New Norcia, Austl.	96	F3	30.58 S	116.12 E
New Norfolk, Austl.	99a	o13	42.46 S	147.03 E
New Norway, Ab., Can.	144	D18	52.53 N	112.58 W
New Orleans, La., U.S.	134	G9	29.57 N	90.04 W
New Orleans Naval Air Station, mil., La., U.S.	134	H8	29.51 N	90.01 W
New Paltz, N.Y., U.S.	124	C11	41.45 N	74.05 W
New Paris, Oh., U.S.	130	E13	39.51 N	84.47 W
New Philadelphia, Oh., U.S.	124	D4	40.30 N	81.27 W
New Pine Creek, Or., U.S.	148	A5	42.00 N	120.17 W
New Plymouth, N.Z.	102	D5	39.04 S	174.05 E
New Plymouth, Id., U.S.	146	G10	43.58 N	116.49 W
Newport, Austl.	192a		33.40 S	151.19 E
Newport, Austl.	192b		37.51 S	144.53 E
Newport, Qc., Can.	122	B12	48.16 N	64.45 W
Newport, Eng., U.K.	10	K11	50.42 N	1.18 W
Newport, Wales, U.K.	10	J10	51.35 N	3.00 W
Newport, Ar., U.S.	134	B7	35.36 N	91.16 W
Newport, In., U.S.	130	E10	39.53 N	87.25 W
Newport, Ky., U.S.	124	E1	39.05 N	84.29 W
Newport, Me., U.S.	122	F7	44.50 N	69.16 W
Newport, N.H., U.S.	122	G4	43.21 N	72.10 W
Newport, N.C., U.S.	132	B9	34.46 N	76.52 W
Newport, Or., U.S.	146	F2	44.38 N	124.02 W
Newport, Pa., U.S.	124	D8	40.28 N	77.08 W
Newport, R.I., U.S.	124	C14	41.29 N	71.18 W
Newport, Tn., U.S.	124	I2	35.58 N	83.11 W
Newport, Vt., U.S.	122	F4	44.55 N	72.13 W
Newport, Wa., U.S.	146	B9	48.11 N	117.07 W
Newport Beach, Ca., U.S.	148	J7	33.36 N	117.55 W
Newport News, Va., U.S.	124	G9	36.58 N	76.25 W
New Port Richey, Fl., U.S.	132	H3	28.14 N	82.42 W
Newportville, Pa., U.S.	203		40.09 N	74.53 W
Newportville Terrace, Pa., U.S.	203		40.07 N	74.54 W
New Prague, Mn., U.S.	128	G5	44.32 N	93.35 W
New Providence, i., Bah.	132	L8	25.02 N	77.24 W
Newquay, Eng., U.K.	10	K7	50.24 N	5.05 W
New Redruth, S. Afr.	191d		26.16 S	28.07 E
New Richland, Mn., U.S.	128	H5	43.53 N	93.29 W
New Richmond, Qc., Can.	122	B10	48.10 N	65.53 W
New Richmond, Oh., U.S.	124	F1	38.56 N	84.16 W
New Richmond, Wi., U.S.	128	F6	45.07 N	92.32 W
New River, St. K./N.	159a	c2	17.08 N	62.33 W
New Road, N.S., Can.	122	F13	44.44 N	63.28 W
New Roads, La., U.S.	134	G7	30.41 N	91.26 W
New Rochelle, N.Y., U.S.	124	D12	40.54 N	73.48 W
New Rockford, N.D., U.S.	142	G14	47.40 N	99.08 W
New Ross, N.S., Can.	122	F12	44.44 N	64.26 W
New Ross, Ire.	10	I6	52.23 N	6.56 W
Newry, N. Ire., U.K.	10	G6	54.09 N	6.21 W
Newry, S.C., U.S.	132	B3	34.42 N	82.55 W
New Salem, N.D., U.S.	140	A11	46.50 N	101.25 W
New Sarum see Salisbury, Eng., U.K.	10	J11	51.05 N	1.48 W
Newsham Park, p.o.i., Eng., U.K.	180		53.25 N	2.56 W
New Sharon, Ia., U.S.	130	C5	41.28 N	92.38 W
New Siberian Islands see Novosibirskie ostrova, is., Russia	50	A18	75.00 N	142.00 E
New Smyrna Beach, Fl., U.S.	132	G5	29.01 N	80.55 W
New South Wales, state, Austl.	98	I6	33.00 S	146.00 E
New South Wales, University of, educ., Austl.	192a		33.55 S	151.14 E
New South Wales Lawn Tennis Association Courts, p.o.i., Austl.	192a		33.53 S	151.14 E
New Square, N.Y., U.S.	194		41.08 N	74.02 W
New Stuyahok, Ak., U.S.	109	E8	59.29 N	157.20 W
New Tazewell, Tn., U.S.	132	H2	36.27 N	83.36 W
New Tecumseth, On., Can.	126	D10	44.08 N	79.51 W
Newton, Eng., U.K.	180		53.16 N	2.43 W
Newton, Ga., U.S.	134	F14	31.18 N	84.21 W

Name	Page	Map Ref.	Latitude	Longitude
Newton, Il., U.S.	130	F9	38.59 N	88.09 W
Newton, Ia., U.S.	130	C4	41.41 N	93.02 W
Newton, Ks., U.S.	138	C11	38.02 N	97.20 W
Newton, Ma., U.S.	124	B14	42.20 N	71.12 W
Newton, Ms., U.S.	134	E9	32.19 N	89.10 W
Newton, N.J., U.S.	124	C11	41.03 N	74.44 W
Newton, N.C., U.S.	124	I4	35.40 N	81.13 W
Newton, Tx., U.S.	136	D14	30.50 N	93.45 W
Newton Abbot, Eng., U.K.	20	D5	50.32 N	3.37 W
Newton Brook, ngh., On., Can.	193b		43.48 N	79.24 W
Newton Center, Ma., U.S.	201		42.20 N	71.12 W
Newton Falls, N.Y., U.S.	126	D15	44.12 N	74.58 W
Newton Highlands, Ma., U.S.	201		42.19 N	71.13 W
Newton Lower Falls, Ma., U.S.	201		42.19 N	71.23 W
Newton Stewart, Scot., U.K.	10	G8	54.57 N	4.29 W
Newton Upper Falls, Ma., U.S.	201		42.19 N	71.13 W
Newtonville, Ma., U.S.	201		42.21 N	71.13 W
New Toronto, ngh., On., Can.	193b		43.36 N	79.30 W
Newtown, Eng., U.K.	180		53.21 N	2.00 W
Newtown, Wales, U.K.	10	I9	52.31 N	3.18 W
New Town, N.D., U.S.	142	F11	47.58 N	102.29 W
Newtown, ngh., Austl.	192a		33.54 S	151.11 E
Newtownabbey, N. Ire., U.K.	10	G6	54.40 N	5.56 W
Newtownards, N. Ire., U.K.	10	G7	54.35 N	5.42 W
Newtown Creek, stm., N.Y., U.S.	194		40.44 N	73.58 W
Newtown Creek, stm., Pa., U.S.	203		40.13 N	74.56 W
New Ulm, Mn., U.S.	128	G4	44.18 N	94.27 W
New Ulm, Tx., U.S.	136	E11	29.53 N	96.29 W
New Utrecht, ngh., N.Y., U.S.	194		40.36 N	73.59 W
New Vernon, N.J., U.S.	194		40.45 N	74.30 W
New Vienna, Oh., U.S.	124	E2	39.19 N	83.42 W
Newville, Pa., U.S.	124	D8	40.10 N	77.23 W
New Washington, Oh., U.S.	124	D3	40.57 N	82.50 W
New Waterford, N.S., Can.	122	D16	46.15 N	60.05 W
New Waverly, Tx., U.S.	136	D12	30.32 N	95.29 W
New Westminster, B.C., Can.	144	G8	49.12 N	122.54 W
New Whiteland, In., U.S.	130	E11	39.33 N	86.06 W
New Wilmington, Pa., U.S.	124	C5	41.07 N	80.19 W
New Woodbine Racetrack, p.o.i., On., Can.	193b		43.43 N	79.36 W
New York, N.Y., U.S.	124	D12	40.43 N	74.00 W
New York, N.Y., U.S.	194		40.43 N	74.01 W
New York, co., N.Y., U.S.	194		40.47 N	73.58 W
New York, state, U.S.	114	E13	43.00 N	75.00 W
New York, City College of, educ., N.Y., U.S.	194		40.49 N	73.57 W
New York, Polytechnic Institute of, educ., N.Y., U.S.	194		40.42 N	73.59 W
New York, State University of (Stony Brook), educ., N.Y., U.S.	194		40.55 N	73.08 W
New York, State University of (Buffalo), educ., N.Y., U.S.	202a		42.57 N	78.49 W
New York, State University of, College at Buffalo, educ., N.Y., U.S.	202a		42.56 N	78.53 W
New York at Buffalo, State University of, educ., N.Y., U.S.	202a		42.56 N	78.49 W
New York Mills, Mn., U.S.	128	E3	46.30 N	95.23 W
New York State Barge Canal, can., N.Y., U.S.	126	E12	43.05 N	78.43 W
New York Stock Exchange, bldg., N.Y., U.S.	194		40.42 N	74.01 W
New Zealand, ctry., Oc.	102	D4	41.00 S	174.00 E
Neye, Ger.	181		51.07 N	7.22 E
Neyestausee, res., Ger.	181		51.08 N	7.24 E
Neyrīz, Iran	74	F14	29.12 N	54.19 E
Neyshābūr, Iran	72	B8	36.11 N	58.52 E
Neyveli, India	69	F4	11.36 N	79.26 E
Neyyāttinkara, India	69	G3	8.25 N	77.05 E
Nezahualcóyotl, Presa, res., Mex.	154	G12	17.10 N	93.40 W
Nezavertailovca, Mol.	38	G8	46.36 N	29.56 E
Neznanka, stm., Russia	183b		55.34 N	37.21 E
Nezperce, Id., U.S.	146	D10	46.14 N	116.14 W
Nez Perce Indian Reservation, ind. res., Id., U.S.	146	D10	46.20 N	116.30 W
Nez Perce National Historical Park, p.o.i., Id., U.S.	146	E10	45.50 N	116.15 W
Nezpique, Bayou, stm., La., U.S.	134	G6	30.12 N	92.35 W
Ngabang, Indon.	66	C6	0.22 N	109.58 E
Ngabé, Congo	86	E3	3.13 S	16.09 E
Ngadirojo, Indon.	66	H7	8.12 S	111.19 E
Ngaliema, Baie de, b., D.R.C.	191b		4.19 S	15.16 E
Ngamaba, Congo	191b		4.14 S	15.16 E
Ngamba, ngh., Congo	191b		4.15 S	15.18 E
Ngambé, Cam.	86	D2	4.14 N	10.37 E
Ngami, Lake, l., Bots.	90	B6	20.28 S	22.46 E
Ngamiland, state, Bots.	90	B6	20.43 S	22.15 E
Ngamouéri, Congo	191b		4.14 S	15.14 E
Ngangala, Sudan	82	G6	4.42 N	31.55 E
Ngangla Ringco, l., China	70	C9	31.33 N	83.00 E
Nganglong Kangri, mtn., China	70	B8	32.49 N	81.03 E
Nganglong Kangri, mts., China	70	B9	32.00 N	83.00 E
Ngangzê Co, l., China	70	C11	31.00 N	87.04 E
Nganjuk, Indon.	66	G7	7.35 S	111.54 E
Ngao, Thai.	64	C5	18.45 N	99.58 E
Ngaoui, Mont, mtn., Afr.	82	F3	6.40 N	14.57 E
Ngaoundéré, Cam.	86	C2	7.19 N	13.35 E
Ngapali, Mya.	64	C2	18.25 N	94.20 E
Ngape, Mya.	64	B2	20.00 N	94.38 E
Ngaputaw, Mya.	64	D2	16.32 N	94.42 E
Ngara, Tan.	86	E6	2.28 S	30.38 E
Ngaruroro, stm., N.Z.	102	D7	39.34 S	176.55 E
Ngat, stm., Thai.	64	C4	19.07 N	98.59 E
Ngatangiia, Cook Is.	100j	a27	21.14 S	159.43 W
Ngatangiia Harbour, b., Cook Is.	100j	a27	21.13 S	159.42 W
Ngathainggyaung, Mya.	64	D2	17.24 N	95.05 E
Ngau Tau Kok see Kwun Tong, China	189d		22.19 N	114.12 E
Ngawi, Indon.	66	G7	7.24 S	111.25 E
Ngay Nua, Laos	64	B5	21.50 N	101.54 E
Ngcheangel, is., Palau	60	D9	8.03 N	134.42 E
Ngchesar, Palau	100b	g8	7.28 N	134.36 E
Ngeaur, i., Palau	60	D9	6.54 N	134.08 E
Ngereklmadel, Palau	100b	g7	7.29 N	134.29 E
Ngerkeai, Palau	100b	g8	7.25 N	134.30 E
Ngerkeel see Ngerkeai, Palau	100b	g8	7.25 N	134.30 E
Ngermechau, Palau	100b	f8	7.35 N	134.38 E
Ngermetengel, Palau	100b	f7	7.31 N	134.30 E
Ngeruktabel, i., Palau	100b	h7	7.14 N	134.24 E
Ngetbong, Palau	100b	f8	7.36 N	134.35 E
Ngetkib, Palau	100b	g7	7.22 N	134.31 E
Nggatokae Island, i., Sol. Is.	101b	e8	8.46 S	158.11 E
Nggela Pile, i., Sol. Is.	101b	e9	9.07 S	160.19 E
Nggela Sule, i., Sol. Is.	101b	e8	9.02 S	160.12 E
Nghia Dan, Viet.	64	C7	19.18 N	105.26 E
Nghia Hanh, Viet.	64	E9	15.03 N	108.47 E
Ngiap, stm., Laos	64	C6	18.24 N	103.36 E
Ngidinga, D.R.C.	86	F3	5.37 S	15.17 E
Ng'iro, mtn., Kenya	86	D7	2.10 N	36.49 E
Ngiro, Ewaso, stm., Kenya	86	D7	2.07 S	36.02 E
Ngo, Congo	86	E3	2.29 S	15.45 E
Ngoko, stm., Afr.	86	D3	1.39 N	16.03 E
Ngom, stm., China	62	B8	31.08 N	97.10 E
Ngomahuru, Zimb.	90	B10	20.24 S	30.42 E
Ngombe, D.R.C.	191b		4.24 S	15.11 E
Ngomeni, Ras, c., Kenya	86	E8	2.58 S	40.14 E
Ngong, Kenya	86	E7	1.22 S	36.39 E
Ngoring Hu, l., China	52	E4	34.53 N	97.41 E
Ngorongoro Crater, crat., Tan.	86	E7	3.10 S	35.35 E
Ngorongoro Crater Conservation Area, p.o.i., Tan.	86	E6	3.00 S	35.30 E
Ngounié, stm., Gabon	86	E2	0.37 S	10.17 E
Ngouri, Chad	82	E3	13.37 N	15.21 E
Ngudiabaka, stm., D.R.C.	191b		4.25 S	15.11 E
Nguigmi, Niger	84	G7	14.15 N	13.06 E
Ngulu, at., Micron.	94	C4	8.27 N	137.29 E
Ngum, stm., Laos	64	C6	18.08 N	103.05 E
Nguna, Île, i., Vanuatu	101d	k17	17.26 S	168.20 E
Ngunju, Tanjung, c., Indon.	66	I12	10.18 S	120.26 E
Nguru, Nig.	84	G7	12.52 N	10.27 E
Nha Be, Viet.	187c		10.42 N	106.44 E
Nha Be, stm., Viet.	187c		10.39 N	106.44 E
Nhacoongo, Moz.	90	D12	24.18 S	35.15 E
Nhamundá, stm., Braz.	164	D6	1.57 S	56.58 W
Nha Nam, Viet.	64	B8	21.26 N	106.06 E
Nha Trang, Viet.	64	F9	12.16 N	109.11 E
Nhill, Austl.	98	K3	36.20 S	141.39 E
Nhoma, stm., Afr.	88	D2	19.23 S	22.11 E
Nhon Trach, Viet.	187c		10.43 N	106.51 E
Nhulunbuy, Austl.	96	B7	12.11 S	136.46 E
Niafounké, Mali	84	F4	15.58 N	3.58 W
Niagara, Wi., U.S.	126	C1	45.46 N	88.00 W
Niagara County Historical Center, bldg., N.Y., U.S.	202a		43.10 N	78.43 W
Niagara Falls, On., Can.	126	E10	43.05 N	79.01 W
Niagara Falls, On., Can.	202a		43.06 N	79.04 W
Niagara Falls, N.Y., U.S.	124	A6	43.05 N	79.05 W
Niagara Falls, N.Y., U.S.	202a		43.05 N	79.03 W
Niagara Falls Airport, arpt., On., Can.	202a		43.02 N	79.08 W
Niagara Falls International Airport, arpt., N.Y., U.S.	202a		43.06 N	78.56 W
Niagara-on-the-Lake, On., Can.	126	E10	43.14 N	79.04 W
Niagara University, educ., N.Y., U.S.	202a		43.08 N	79.02 W
Niagassola, Gui.	84	G3	12.18 N	9.07 W
Niah, Malay.	66	B8	3.51 N	113.43 E
Niakaramandougou, C. Iv.	84	H4	8.39 N	5.17 W
Niamey, Niger	84	G5	13.31 N	2.07 E
Niangara, D.R.C.	86	D5	3.42 N	27.53 E
Niangay, Lac, l., Mali	84	F4	15.50 N	3.00 W
Niangoloko, Burkina	84	G4	10.17 N	4.55 W
Niangua, stm., Mo., U.S.	130	G5	38.02 N	92.49 W
Nia-Nia, D.R.C.	86	D5	1.25 N	27.37 E
Niantic, Il., U.S.	130	E8	39.51 N	89.10 W
Nianyushan, China	58	G7	29.11 N	117.04 E
Nianzishan, China	52	B9	47.30 N	122.53 E
Niari, stm., Congo	86	E2	3.56 S	12.12 E
Nias, Pulau, i., Indon.	64	L3	1.05 N	97.35 E
Niassa, Lago see Nyasa, Lake, l., Afr.	88	C5	12.00 S	34.30 E
Niatupo, Pan.	156	H8	9.24 N	78.29 W
Nibe, Den.	16	J7	56.58 N	9.38 E
Nibra, India	190b		22.36 N	88.16 E
Nīca, Lat.	26	D4	56.18 N	21.07 E
Nicaea see İznik, Tur.	34	C12	40.25 N	29.43 E
Nicaragua, ctry., N.A.	156	F5	13.00 N	85.00 W
Nicaragua, Lago de, l., Nic.	156	G5	11.38 N	85.26 W
Nicaragua, Lake see Nicaragua, Lago de, l., Nic.	156	G5	11.38 N	85.26 W
Nicastro, Italy	32	F10	38.59 N	16.20 E
Nice, Fr.	22	F13	43.43 N	7.15 E
Niceville, Fl., U.S.	134	G12	30.31 N	86.29 W
Nichinan, Japan	56	H4	31.35 N	131.22 E
Nicholas Channel (San Nicolás, Canal de), strt., N.A.	152	C8	23.20 N	80.21 W
Nicholasville, Ky., U.S.	130	G13	37.53 N	84.34 W
Nicholls, Ga., U.S.	132	E3	31.31 N	82.38 W
Nicholl's Town, Bah.	132	K7	25.09 N	78.00 W
Nichols, Ca., U.S.	200		38.02 N	121.59 W
Nichols Brook, stm., Ma., U.S.	201		42.37 N	70.59 W
Nicholson, Ms., U.S.	134	G9	30.28 N	89.42 W
Nicholson, Pa., U.S.	124	C10	41.37 N	75.47 W
Nichols Run, stm., Va., U.S.	202b		39.03 N	77.18 W
Nickel Centre, On., Can.	126	B8	46.36 N	80.50 W
Nickerson, Ks., U.S.	138	C10	38.09 N	98.04 W
Nicobar Islands, is., India	62	G7	8.00 N	93.30 E
Nicola, B.C., Can.	144	F10	50.09 N	120.40 W
Nicola, stm., B.C., Can.	144	F9	50.25 N	121.19 W
Nicolae Bălcescu, Rom.	36	B13	47.34 N	26.52 E
Nicola Lake, l., B.C., Can.	144	F10	50.10 N	120.30 W
Nicola Mameet Indian Reserve, ind. res., B.C., Can.	144	F10	50.12 N	120.51 W
Nicolet, Qc., Can.	122	D4	46.13 N	72.37 W
Nicolet, Lake, l., Mi., U.S.	126	B5	46.21 N	84.11 W
Nicolet Sud-Ouest, stm., Qc., Can.	122	E5	46.13 N	72.36 W
Nicoll Bay, b., N.Y., U.S.	194		40.43 N	73.07 W
Nicollet, Mn., U.S.	128	G4	44.16 N	94.11 W
Nicoll Point, c., N.Y., U.S.	194		40.42 N	73.09 W
Nicomedia see İzmit, Tur.	34	C11	40.47 N	29.57 E
Nicosia (Lefkosia) (Levkosía), Cyp.	76	C4	35.10 N	33.22 E
Nicosia, N. Cyp.	74	C3	35.10 N	33.22 E
Nicosia, Italy	32	G8	37.45 N	14.24 E
Nicotera, Italy	32	F9	38.34 N	15.57 E
Nicoya, C.R.	156	G5	10.08 N	85.27 W
Nicoya, Golfo de, b., C.R.	156	H5	9.47 N	84.48 W
Nicoya, Peninsula de, pen., C.R.	156	H5	10.00 N	85.25 W
Nicheroy see Niterói, Braz.	170	L4	22.53 S	43.06 W
Nida, Lith.	26	E3	55.18 N	21.00 E
Nida, stm., Pol.	24	F16	50.17 N	20.51 E
Nidadavole, India	69	C5	16.54 N	81.40 E
Nidd, stm., Eng., U.K.	10	G11	54.00 N	1.13 W
Nidda, stm., Ger.	20	D17	50.06 N	8.33 E
Nidelva, stm., Nor.	16	I6	58.25 N	8.43 E
Nidzica, Pol.	24	C16	53.21 N	20.26 E
Niebüll, Ger.	24	B4	54.47 N	8.50 E
Niederbonsfeld, Ger.	181		51.23 N	7.08 E
Niederbronn-les-Bains, Fr.	24	H3	48.57 N	7.38 E
Niederdonk, Ger.	181		51.14 N	6.41 E
Niederelfringhausen, Ger.	181		51.21 N	7.10 E
Niedere Tauern, mts., Aus.	30	C11	47.18 N	14.00 E
Nieder-Kassel, ngh., Ger.	181		51.14 N	6.45 E
Nieder-Neuendorf, Ger.	182a		52.37 N	13.12 E
Niedersachsen, state, Ger.	24	D5	52.40 N	9.00 E
Niederschöneweide, ngh., Ger.	182a		52.27 N	13.31 E
Niekerkshoop, S. Afr.	90	F6	29.19 S	22.50 E
Niellé, C. Iv.	84	G3	10.12 N	5.38 W
Niemba, D.R.C.	86	F5	5.57 S	28.24 E
Niemeyer, ngh., Braz.	205a		23.00 S	43.15 W
Niemisel, Swe.	14	F13	66.00 N	22.00 E
Niemodlin, Pol.	24	F13	50.39 N	17.37 E
Nienburg, Ger.	24	D5	52.38 N	9.13 E
Niepkuhlen, stm., Ger.	181		51.29 N	6.31 E
Niepołomice, Pol.	24	F16	50.02 N	20.12 E
Niers, stm., Eur.	20	C15	51.42 N	5.57 E
Nierst, Ger.	181		51.19 N	6.43 E
Niesky, Ger.	24	E10	51.17 N	14.49 E
Nieszawa, Pol.	24	D14	52.49 N	18.53 E
Nieu-Bethesda, S. Afr.	90	G7	31.50 S	24.33 E
Nieuport see Nieuwpoort, Bel.	20	C11	51.08 N	2.45 E
Nieuw Amsterdam, Sur.	164	B6	5.52 N	55.04 W
Nieuw Nickerie, Sur.	164	B6	5.56 N	56.59 W
Nieuwoudtville, S. Afr.	90	G4	31.22 S	19.06 E
Nieuwpoort, Bel.	20	C11	51.08 N	2.45 E
Nieuwpoort, Neth. Ant.	158g	p22	12.03 N	68.49 W
Nievería, Peru	204d		11.59 S	76.55 W
Nièvre, state, Fr.	20	G12	47.05 N	3.30 E
Nifisha, Egypt	76	H3	30.33 N	32.14 E
Niğde, Tur.	42	G6	37.59 N	34.44 E
Niğde, state, Tur.	42	F6	38.00 N	34.45 E
Nigei Island, i., B.C., Can.	144	F3	50.52 N	127.42 W
Nigel, S. Afr.	90	E9	26.25 S	28.28 E
Niger, ctry., Afr.	82	D1	16.00 N	8.00 E
Niger, stm., Afr.	84	H6	4.17 N	6.04 E
Niger Delta, del., Nig.	84	I6	4.37 N	7.05 E
Nigeria, ctry., Afr.	82	E1	10.00 N	8.00 E
Nigerian Museum, bldg., Nig.	191a		6.20 N	3.24 E
Nightcaps, N.Z.	102	G3	45.58 S	168.02 E
Nighthawk, Wa., U.S.	146	B7	48.58 N	119.38 W
Nigríta, Grc.	34	C6	40.55 N	23.30 E
Niheidât el-Sûd, Gebel el-, mtn., Egypt	76	J3	28.01 N	32.21 E
Nihing (Nahang), stm., Asia	62	C1	25.58 N	62.44 E
Nihommatsu, Japan	56	B13	37.35 N	140.26 E
Nihon see Japan, ctry., Asia	52	D12	36.00 N	138.00 E
Nihonbashi, ngh., Japan	186		35.41 N	139.47 E
Nihon-kai see Japan, Sea of, s., Asia	52	C11	40.00 N	135.00 E
Nihon University, educ., Japan	186		35.42 N	139.45 E
Nihuil, Embalse del, res., Arg.	172	G3	35.05 S	68.45 W
Niigata, Japan	56	B11	37.55 N	139.04 E
Niigata, state, Japan	56	B11	37.23 N	138.54 E
Niihama, Japan	56	F6	33.57 N	133.16 E
Niihau, i., Hi., U.S.	100a	b1	21.55 N	160.10 W
Nii-jima, i., Japan	56	E12	34.22 N	139.16 E
Niimi, Japan	56	D6	34.59 N	133.28 E
Niinisalo, Fin.	18	F9	61.51 N	22.26 E
Niitsu, Japan	56	B12	37.47 N	139.07 E
Níjar, Spain	28	H8	36.58 N	2.12 W
Nijiaqiao, China	187b		31.14 N	121.21 E
Nijil, Jord.	76	H6	30.31 N	35.32 E
Nijmegen, Neth.	20	C14	51.50 N	5.50 E
Nijo Castle, hist., Japan	188		35.01 N	135.45 E
Nijvel see Nivelles, Bel.	20	D13	50.36 N	4.20 E
Níkaia, Grc.	185c		37.58 N	23.39 E
Nikel', Russia	14	C21	69.24 N	30.15 E
Nikiforovo, Russia	183b		55.50 N	38.05 E
Nikitovka, Russia	38	C17	50.22 N	38.25 E
Nikkaluokta Kapell, rel., Swe.	14	E9	67.51 N	19.01 E
Nikki, Benin	84	G5	9.56 N	3.12 E
Nikkō, Japan	56	C12	36.45 N	139.37 E
Nikkō-kokuritsu-kōen, p.o.i., Japan	56	B12	36.49 N	139.33 E
Nikolaev see Mykolaïv, Ukr.	38	G11	46.57 N	31.59 E
Nikolaevka, Russia	40	H15	46.19 N	47.43 E
Nikolaevka, Russia	40	H11	47.18 N	38.49 E
Nikolaevo, Russia	26	B12	58.16 N	29.27 E
Nikolaevsk, Russia	40	G14	50.01 N	45.27 E
Nikolaevsk-na-Amure, Russia	50	F17	53.08 N	140.44 E
Nikolassee, ngh., Ger.	182a		52.26 N	13.12 E
Nikolo-Berëzovka, Russia	40	C19	56.05 N	54.17 E
Nikolo-Hovanskoe, Russia	183b		55.36 N	37.27 E
Nikol'sk, Russia	40	E14	53.42 N	46.05 E
Nikol'sk, Russia	40	B14	59.31 N	45.26 E
Nikolski, Ak., U.S.	109	F6	52.56 N	168.52 W
Nikol'skij, Russia	18	G21	60.57 N	34.00 E
Nikol'skij Toržok, Russia	18	H25	59.53 N	38.46 E
Nikol'skoe, Russia	26	E18	55.26 N	35.04 E
Nikol'skoe, Russia	26	H19	52.39 N	36.04 E
Nikol'skoe, Russia	40	B14	59.23 N	44.36 E
Nikol'skoe, Russia	40	E19	52.01 N	55.42 E
Nikol'skoe, Russia	40	F12	50.34 N	41.09 E
Nikol'skoe, Russia	50	E22	55.11 N	165.58 E
Nikol'skoe, Russia	183a		59.41 N	30.47 E
Nikol'skoe, Russia	183b		55.46 N	37.54 E
Nikol'skoe-Urjupino, Russia	183b		55.48 N	37.13 E
Nikonova Gora, Russia	18	G23	60.21 N	36.06 E
Nikopol, Blg.	36	F11	43.42 N	24.53 E
Nikopol', Ukr.	38	F13	47.34 N	34.24 E
Niksar, Tur.	42	E7	40.35 N	36.57 E
Nīkshahr, Iran	72	D9	26.12 N	60.12 E
Nikšić, Yugo.	36	G5	42.46 N	18.55 E
Nikulino, Russia	26	E16	55.16 N	33.50 E
Nikulino, ngh., Russia	183b		55.40 N	37.28 E
Nikumaroro, at., Kir.	94	D9	4.40 S	174.32 W
Nikunau, i., Kir.	94	D8	1.21 S	176.27 E
Nîl, Bahr el- see Nile, stm., Afr.	82	B6	30.10 N	31.07 E
Nîl, Nahr an- see Nile, stm., Afr.	82	B6	30.10 N	31.07 E
Nila, Pulau, i., Indon.	60	G9	6.44 S	129.31 E
Nilakka, l., Fin.	18	D13	63.08 N	26.33 E
Niland, Ca., U.S.	148	J10	33.14 N	115.30 W
Nile (Nîl, Bahr el-) (Nîl, Nahr an-), stm., Afr.	82	B6	30.10 N	31.07 E
Nile (Bahr el-Nîl), stm., Afr.	191c		30.10 N	31.06 E
Nile Delta, del., Egypt	76	H1	30.56 N	31.03 E
Niles, Il., U.S.	130	B10	42.01 N	87.47 W
Niles, Mi., U.S.	130	C11	41.49 N	86.15 W
Niles, Oh., U.S.	124	C5	41.10 N	80.44 W
Niles Canyon, val., Ca., U.S.	200		37.36 N	121.56 W
Niles Pond, l., Ma., U.S.	201		42.35 N	70.40 W
Nilgani, India	190b		22.46 N	88.26 E
Nilgaut, Lac, l., Qc., Can.	126	B12	46.35 N	77.14 W
Nīlgiri, India	70	H11	21.28 N	86.46 E
Nilivaara, Swe.	14	E12	67.13 N	21.38 E
Nilka, China	48	F14	43.47 N	82.29 E
Nilópolis, mun., Braz.	205a		22.49 S	43.26 W
Nilsiä, Fin.	18	D15	63.12 N	28.06 E
Nilüfer, stm., Tur.	34	C11	40.19 N	28.27 E
Nīlwāl, ngh., India	190a		28.40 N	76.59 E
Nīmach, India	70	F5	24.28 N	74.52 E
Nimba, Mont see Nimba, Mount, mtn., Afr.	84	H3	7.37 N	8.25 W
Nimba, Mount, mtn., Afr.	84	H3	7.37 N	8.25 W
Nimbāhera, India	70	F5	24.36 N	74.40 E
Nimen'ga, stm., Russia	18	D24	63.49 N	37.37 E
Nimen'ga, guba, b., Russia	18	D24	63.51 N	37.25 E
Nîmes, Fr.	22	F10	43.50 N	4.21 E
Nimmitabel, Austl.	98	K7	36.31 S	149.16 E
Nimpkish Lake, l., B.C., Can.	144	F3	50.25 N	126.59 W
Nimrod Lake, res., Ar., U.S.	134	C5	34.57 N	93.14 W
Nimta, India	190b		22.40 N	88.25 E
Nimule, Sudan	82	G6	3.36 N	32.02 E
Niña Bonita, Presa, res., Cuba	204b		23.02 N	82.29 W
Nīnawā, state, Iraq	74	C8	36.00 N	42.30 E
Nīnawá (Nineveh), hist., Iraq	74	B8	36.25 N	43.10 E
Ninda, Ang.	88	C3	14.48 S	21.22 E
Nindigully, Austl.	98	G7	28.21 S	148.49 E
Nine Ashes, Eng., U.K.	178		51.42 N	0.18 E
Nine Degree Channel, strt., India	62	G3	9.00 N	73.00 E
Nine Mile Creek, stm., Ut., U.S.	150	D6	39.50 N	109.52 W
Ninemile Island, i., Pa., U.S.	197b		40.29 N	79.52 W
Ninepin Group, is., China	189d		22.16 N	114.21 E
Nineteen Hundred Five Memorial Cemetery, misc. cult., Russia	183a		59.51 N	30.27 E
Ninette, Mb., Can.	142	E14	49.24 N	99.38 W
Ninetyeast Ridge, unds.	174	K11	4.00 S	90.00 E
Ninety Mile Beach, cst., Austl.	98	L6	38.13 S	147.23 E
Ninety Six, S.C., U.S.	132	B3	34.10 N	82.01 W
Nineveh see Nīnawá, hist., Iraq	74	B8	36.25 N	43.10 E
Ninfas, Punta, c., Arg.	166	H4	42.57 S	64.20 W
Ninga, Mb., Can.	142	E14	49.13 N	99.52 W
Ningaloo, Austl.	96	D2	22.41 S	113.41 E
Ning'an, China	54	B8	44.20 N	129.27 E
Ningbo, China	58	G9	29.52 N	121.32 E
Ningcheng, China	52	C8	41.33 N	119.20 E
Ningde, China	58	H8	26.43 N	119.33 E
Ningdu, China	58	H6	26.31 N	115.58 E
Ningguo, China	58	F8	30.37 N	118.58 E
Ninghai, China	58	G9	29.17 N	121.24 E
Ninghua, China	58	H7	26.15 N	116.39 E
Ningi, Nig.	84	G6	11.04 N	9.33 E
Ningjing Shan, mts., China	52	F4	28.34 N	98.55 E
Ningming, China	58	J2	22.07 N	107.05 E
Ningnan, China	52	F5	27.11 N	102.39 E
Ningqiang, China	58	E2	32.49 N	106.13 E
Ningshan, China	58	E3	33.19 N	108.18 E
Ningsia Hui see Ningxia, state, China	52	D6	37.00 N	106.00 E
Ningsia Hui Autonomous Region see Ningxia, state, China	52	D6	37.00 N	106.00 E
Ningwu, China	58	B5	39.03 N	112.11 E
Ningxia, state, China	52	D6	37.00 N	106.00 E
Ningxian, China	58	D2	35.30 N	107.54 E
Ningxiang, China	58	G5	28.15 N	112.33 E
Ningyuan, China	58	I4	25.37 N	111.46 E
Ninh Binh, Viet.	64	B7	20.15 N	105.59 E
Ninh Hoa, Viet.	64	F9	12.28 N	109.08 E
Ninhue, Chile	172	H1	36.24 S	72.24 W
Ninigo Group, is., Pap. N. Gui.	101a	a3	1.15 S	144.15 E
Ninnescah, stm., Ks., U.S.	138	D11	37.20 N	97.10 W
Ninnescah, North Fork, stm., Ks., U.S.	138	D10	37.34 N	97.42 W
Ninnescah, South Fork, stm., Ks., U.S.	138	D10	37.34 N	97.42 W
Ninohe, Japan	54	D14	40.16 N	141.18 E
Ninoy Aquino International Airport, arpt., Phil.	187f		14.31 N	121.01 E
Niny, Russia	42	C10	44.29 N	43.56 E
Nioaque, Braz.	166	D5	21.08 S	55.49 W
Niobrara, Ne., U.S.	140	E14	42.45 N	98.03 W
Niobrara, stm., U.S.	140	E14	42.46 N	98.03 W
Nioghalvfjerdsfjorden, ice, Grnld.	108	B22	79.30 N	21.30 W
Nioki, D.R.C.	86	E3	2.39 S	17.42 E
Niono, Mali	84	G3	14.15 N	5.58 W
Nioro, Mali	84	F3	15.13 N	9.35 W
Niort, Fr.	22	C5	46.19 N	0.27 W
Niota, Tn., U.S.	134	B14	35.31 N	84.33 W
Nipan, Austl.	98	E8	24.47 S	150.01 E
Nipāni, India	69	C2	16.24 N	74.22 E
Nipawin, Sk., Can.	110	E10	53.22 N	104.00 W
Nipe, Bahía de, b., Cuba	156	B10	20.47 N	75.42 W
Nipigon, On., Can.	128	B10	49.00 N	88.15 W
Nipigon, stm., On., Can.	128	B10	49.00 N	88.15 W
Nipigon, Lake, res., On., Can.	128	B10	49.40 N	88.33 W
Nipigon Bay, b., On., Can.	128	C10	48.53 N	87.56 W
Nipissing, Lake, l., On., Can.	126	B10	46.15 N	79.41 W
Nipomo, Ca., U.S.	148	H5	35.02 N	120.28 W
Nippenicket, Lake, l., Ma., U.S.	201		41.58 N	71.03 W
Niquelândia, Braz.	170	H1	14.27 S	48.27 W
Niquero, Cuba	156	B9	20.02 N	77.34 W
Niquivil, Arg.	172	E3	30.25 S	68.41 W
Nīr, Iran	74	A10	38.02 N	47.59 E
Nīra, stm., India	69	B2	17.58 N	75.08 E
Nirasaki, Japan	56	D11	35.42 N	138.27 E
Nirgua, Ven.	168	B7	10.09 N	68.33 W
Nirmal, India	69	B4	19.05 N	78.21 E
Nirmāli, India	70	E11	26.18 N	86.34 E
Niš, Yugo.	36	F8	43.19 N	21.54 E
Nisa, Port.	28	E3	39.30 N	7.38 W
Nişāb, Sau. Ar.	74	F9	29.11 N	44.43 E
Nişāb, Yemen	72	G6	14.30 N	46.29 E
Nišava, stm., Eur.	36	F9	43.22 N	21.46 E
Niscemi, Italy	32	G8	37.09 N	14.23 E
Nischintāpur, India	190b		22.26 N	88.22 E
Nish see Niš, Yugo.	36	F8	43.19 N	21.54 E
Nishan, China	70	B10	33.35 N	85.30 E
Nishapur see Neyshābūr, Iran	72	B8	36.11 N	58.52 E
Nishi, ngh., Japan	186		35.27 N	139.38 E
Nishi, ngh., Japan	188		34.41 N	135.30 E
Nishiarai, ngh., Japan	186		35.47 N	139.47 E
Nishibetsuin, Japan	188		34.58 N	135.31 E
Nishikiori, Japan	188		34.29 N	135.34 E
Nishikyō, ngh., Japan	188		34.59 N	135.40 E
Nishimori, ngh., Japan	188		34.45 N	135.01 E
Nishinari, ngh., Japan	188		34.38 N	135.28 E
Nishio, Japan	56	E10	34.52 N	137.03 E
Nishitoda, ngh., Japan	188		34.43 N	135.00 E
Nishiwaki, Japan	56	E7	34.58 N	134.58 E
Nishiyodogawa, ngh., Japan	188		34.42 N	135.27 E
Nisling, stm., Yk., Can.	110	C3	62.30 N	139.27 W
Nisporeni, Mol.	38	F7	47.04 N	28.11 E
Nisqually, stm., Wa., U.S.	146	D4	47.05 N	122.41 W
Nissan, stm., Swe.	16	K11	56.41 N	12.52 E
Nissequogue, N.Y., U.S.	194		40.54 N	73.12 W
Nissequogue, stm., N.Y., U.S.	194		40.54 N	73.13 W
Nissequogue, Northeast Branch, stm., N.Y., U.S.	194		40.50 N	73.13 W
Nissequogue River State Park, p.o.i., N.Y., U.S.	194		40.51 N	73.13 W
Nisser, l., Nor.	16	H6	59.10 N	8.29 E
Nissum Bredning, b., Den.	16	K6	56.38 N	8.22 E
Nissum Fjord, b., Den.	16	K5	56.21 N	8.11 E
Nisswa, Mn., U.S.	128	E4	46.30 N	94.17 W
Nistru see Dniester, stm., Eur.	24	G19	46.19 N	30.16 E
Nísyros, i., Grc.	34	G10	36.35 N	27.08 E
Nitalas, India	190c		19.06 N	73.08 E
Nītaure, Lat.	26	C8	57.10 N	25.10 E
Niterói, Braz.	170	L4	22.53 S	43.06 W
Niterói, mun., Braz.	205a		22.56 S	43.04 W
Nith, stm., On., Can.	126	E9	43.11 N	80.22 W
Nith, stm., Scot., U.K.	10	F9	54.58 N	3.34 W
Nithāri, India	190a		28.35 N	77.21 E
Nithāri, ngh., India	190a		28.42 N	77.03 E
Nithi River, B.C., Can.	144	B5	54.01 N	125.01 W
Nitinat Lake, l., B.C., Can.	144	H6	48.45 N	124.45 W
Nitra, Slvk.	24	H14	48.18 N	18.05 E
Nitra, stm., Slvk.	24	H14	47.47 N	18.08 E
Nitro, W.V., U.S.	124	F4	38.24 N	81.50 W
Nittedal, Nor.	16	G8	60.04 N	10.53 E
Niu Aunfo Point, c., Tonga	100e	n13	21.04 S	175.20 W
Niue, dep., Oc.	92	E10	19.02 S	169.52 W
Niuke, China	70	C9	30.41 N	82.03 E
Niulakita, i., Tuvalu	94	E8	10.45 S	179.30 E
Niut, Gunung, mtn., Indon.	66	C6	1.00 N	109.55 E
Niutao, i., Tuvalu	94	D8	6.06 S	177.18 E
Niutoushan, China	54	B7	45.09 N	126.45 E
Niutou Shan, i., China	58	G9	29.07 N	121.56 E
Niuzhuang, China	58	A10	40.56 N	122.32 E
Niva, stm., Russia	14	E23	67.07 N	32.25 E
Nivala, Fin.	18	D11	63.56 N	24.58 E
Nive, stm., Austl.	98	E6	25.59 S	146.25 E
Nive, stm., Fr.	22	F4	43.29 N	1.28 W
Nivelles, Bel.	20	D13	50.36 N	4.20 E
Nivernais, hist. reg., Fr.	20	H12	47.00 N	3.30 E
Niverville, Mb., Can.	142	E16	49.36 N	97.03 W
Nivnoe, Russia	26	G15	53.11 N	32.35 E
Nivskij, Russia	14	E23	67.15 N	32.26 E
Nixa, Mo., U.S.	130	G4	37.02 N	93.17 W
Nixon, Nv., U.S.	148	D6	39.50 N	119.21 W
Nixon, Tx., U.S.	136	E10	29.16 N	97.45 W
Niyodo, stm., Japan	56	F6	33.28 N	133.28 E
Niža, Russia	12	C20	66.17 N	43.16 E
Nizāmābād, India	69	B4	18.40 N	78.05 E
Nizām Sāgar, res., India	69	B3	18.08 N	77.57 E
Nižegorodskaja oblast', co., Russia	40	C14	56.30 N	45.00 E
Nizhyn, Ukr.	38	B10	51.02 N	31.53 E
Nizino, Russia	183a		59.50 N	29.53 E
Nizip, Tur.	42	G7	37.01 N	37.48 E
Nizjnij Novgorod (Gorki), Russia	40	C14	56.18 N	44.00 E
Nízke Tatry, mts., Slvk.	24	H16	48.54 N	19.40 E
Nízke Tatry, Narodny Park, p.o.i., Slvk.	24	H15	48.56 N	19.34 E
Nižmozero, Russia	18	C24	64.25 N	37.56 E
Nižneangarsk, Russia	50	E10	55.47 N	109.34 E
Nižnebakanskij, Russia	38	I16	44.51 N	37.51 E
Nižnedevick, Russia	38	B17	51.33 N	38.21 E
Nižnee Kujto, ozero, l., Russia	18	C18	64.58 N	31.38 E
Nižnee Kumozero, ozero, l., Russia	18	B20	65.29 N	33.11 E
Nižnee Zolotica, Russia	14	G31	65.41 N	40.11 E
Nižneilimsk, Russia	48	C18	57.10 N	103.23 E
Nižnekamsk, Russia	40	D17	55.32 N	51.57 E
Nižnekamskoe vodohranilišče, res., Russia	40	C18	55.50 N	53.00 E
Nižne-Nagol'naja, Russia	38	E19	49.00 N	39.58 E
Nižnetambovskoe, Russia	50	F16	50.55 N	138.12 E
Nižneudinsk, Russia	48	D17	54.53 N	99.01 E
Nižnevartovsk, Russia	48	B13	60.55 N	76.33 E
Nižnie Ostrovcy, Russia	183b		55.35 N	38.01 E
Nižnie Sergi, Russia	40	C21	56.39 N	59.17 E
Nižnij Baskunčak, Russia	40	G15	48.13 N	46.49 E
Nižnij Casučej, Russia	50	F12	50.31 N	115.08 E
Nižnij Čir, Russia	40	G13	48.22 N	43.04 E
Nižnij Kuranah, Russia	50	E14	58.50 N	125.37 E
Nižnij Novgorod (Gorki), Russia	12	H21	56.18 N	44.00 E
Nižnij Ol'šan, Russia	40	F11	50.45 N	38.55 E
Nižnij Paramonov, Russia	40	H12	47.57 N	41.57 E
Nižnij Pjandž, Taj.	72	B10	37.10 N	68.31 E
Nižnij Tagil, Russia	40	B21	57.55 N	59.58 E
Nižnij Vjalozërskij, Russia	14	F26	66.44 N	35.11 E
Nižnjaja Grajvoronka, Russia	38	B16	51.47 N	37.45 E
Nižnjaja Irga, Russia	40	C20	56.51 N	57.26 E
Nižnjaja Karelina, Russia	48	C19	57.58 N	107.48 E
Nižnjaja Peša, Russia	12	C22	66.44 N	47.38 E
Nižnjaja Pojma, Russia	48	C17	56.09 N	97.12 E
Nižnjaja Tavda, Russia	48	C11	57.40 N	66.09 E
Nižnjaja Tunguska, stm., Russia	48	B16	65.46 N	87.54 E
Nizza Monferrato, Italy	30	F5	44.46 N	8.19 E
Nizzana, Isr.	76	H5	30.53 N	34.26 E
Njandoma, Russia	12	F19	61.40 N	40.13 E
Njasviž, Bela.	26	G9	53.13 N	26.41 E
Njazidja, i., Com.	88	C7	11.35 S	43.20 E
Njesuthi, mtn., Afr.	90	F9	29.09 S	29.23 E
Njinjo, Tan.	86	F7	8.46 S	38.48 E
Njombe, Tan.	88	B5	9.19 S	34.45 E
Njombe, stm., Tan.	86	F7	6.56 S	35.06 E
Njuhča, Russia	12	E22	63.26 N	46.27 E
Njuhča, Russia	18	D23	63.54 N	36.16 E
Njuja, Russia	50	D12	60.32 N	116.14 E
Njuja, stm., Russia	48	B20	60.32 N	116.17 E
Njuk, ozero, l., Russia	18	C17	64.27 N	31.45 E
Njuksenica, Russia	12	F21	60.24 N	44.09 E
Njunis, mtn., Nor.	14	D10	68.45 N	19.31 E
Njurba, Russia	50	D12	63.17 N	118.20 E
Njurunda, Swe.	16	E15	62.15 N	17.23 E
Njuvčim, Russia	48	B8	61.22 N	50.36 E
Nkambe, Cam.	86	C2	6.34 N	10.41 E

Name	Page	Map Ref.	Latitude	Longitude
Nkawkaw, Ghana	84	H4	6.33 N	0.46 W
Nkayi, Zimb.	88	D4	19.00 S	28.53 E
Nkhata Bay, Mwi.	88	C5	11.36 S	34.17 E
Nkhotakota, Mwi.	88	C5	12.54 S	34.16 E
Nkomi, Lagune, l., Gabon	86	E1	1.37 S	9.17 E
Nkongsamba, Cam.	86	D2	4.57 N	9.56 E
Nkwalini, S. Afr.	90	F10	28.43 S	31.31 E
Nmai, stm., Mya.	62	C8	25.42 N	97.30 E
Noābād, India	190b		22.34 N	88.31 E
Noākhāli, Bngl.	70	G13	22.49 N	91.06 E
Noak Hill, ngh., Eng., U.K.	178		51.37 N	0.14 E
Noatak, Ak., U.S.	109	C7	67.34 N	162.59 W
Noatak, stm., Ak., U.S.	109	C8	67.00 N	162.30 W
Nobeoka, Japan	56	G4	32.34 N	131.40 E
Nobidome, Japan	186		35.48 N	139.35 E
Nobidome-yōsui, aq., Japan	186		35.44 N	139.27 E
Noble, Il., U.S.	130	F9	38.41 N	88.13 W
Noble, Ok., U.S.	138	F11	35.08 N	97.23 W
Noble Park, Austl.	192b		37.58 S	145.10 E
Noblestown, Pa., U.S.	197b		40.24 N	80.12 W
Noblesville, In., U.S.	130	D12	40.02 N	86.00 W
Noboribetsu, Japan	54	C14	42.27 N	141.11 E
Noborito, Japan	186		35.37 N	139.34 E
Nobres, Braz.	166	B5	14.44 S	56.20 W
Nocatee, Fl., U.S.	132	I4	27.09 N	81.52 W
Noccundra, Austl.	98	F4	27.49 S	142.36 E
Noce, stm., Italy	30	D8	46.09 N	11.04 E
Nocera Inferiore, Italy	32	D8	40.44 N	14.38 E
Nockatunga, Austl.	98	F4	27.43 S	142.43 E
Nocona, Tx., U.S.	138	H11	33.47 N	97.43 W
Nocupétaro, Mex.	154	F8	18.49 N	101.04 W
Nodaway, stm., U.S.	130	D2	39.53 N	94.56 W
Nodera, Japan	188		34.45 N	134.56 E
Noel, Mo., U.S.	130	H3	36.32 N	94.28 W
Noetinger, Arg.	172	F6	32.21 S	62.18 W
Nogales, Mex.	120	F7	31.18 N	110.56 W
Nogales, Az., U.S.	150	L5	31.21 N	110.56 W
Nogaro, Fr.	22	F5	43.46 N	0.02 W
Nogent-le-Rotrou, Fr.	20	F9	48.19 N	0.49 E
Nogent-sur-Marne, Fr.	179		48.50 N	2.29 E
Nogent-sur-Seine, Fr.	20	F12	48.29 N	3.30 E
Noginsk, Russia	26	E21	55.51 N	38.27 E
Nogisaki, Japan	186		35.57 N	139.58 E
Nogliki, Russia	50	F17	51.48 N	143.08 E
Nogoa, stm., Austl.	98	E6	23.33 S	148.32 E
Nogoyá, Arg.	172	F8	32.24 S	59.48 W
Nógrád, state, Hung.	36	B6	48.00 N	19.35 E
Noguera Pallaresa, stm., Spain	28	B11	41.54 N	0.53 E
Noguera Ribagorçana, stm., Spain	28	B11	41.41 N	0.42 E
Nohar, India	70	D5	29.09 N	74.45 E
Nohta, India	70	G7	23.40 N	79.35 E
Noia, Spain	28	B2	42.47 N	8.53 W
Noir, Causse, plat., Fr.	22	E9	44.10 N	3.15 E
Noir, Isla, i., Chile	166	J2	54.29 S	73.01 W
Noire, stm., Qc., Can.	126	B13	45.54 N	76.56 W
Noire, Montagne, mts., Fr.	22	F8	43.25 N	2.20 E
Noirmoutier, Île de, i., Fr.	20	H6	47.00 N	2.15 W
Noirmoutier-en-l'Île, Fr.	20	H6	46.59 N	2.14 W
Noiseau, Fr.	179		48.47 N	2.33 E
Noisiel, Fr.	179		48.51 N	2.37 E
Noisy-le-Grand, Fr.	179		48.51 N	2.33 E
Noisy-le-Roi, Fr.	179		48.51 N	2.04 E
Noisy-le-Sec, Fr.	179		48.53 N	2.28 E
Nojima-zaki, c., Japan	56	E12	34.56 N	139.53 E
Nokaneng, Bots.	88	D3	19.40 S	22.12 E
Nōke, Japan	188		34.26 N	135.29 E
Nokha Mandi, India	70	E4	27.33 N	73.28 E
Nokia, Fin.	18	F10	61.29 N	23.30 E
Nokilalaki, Bulu, mtn., Indon.	66	D12	1.18 S	120.13 E
Nok Kundi, Pak.	62	C1	28.47 N	62.40 E
Nokogiri-yama, hill, Japan	186		35.09 N	139.51 E
Nokomis, Sk., Can.	142	C8	51.31 N	105.00 W
Nokomis, Fl., U.S.	132	I3	27.07 N	82.27 W
Nokomis, Il., U.S.	130	E8	39.18 N	89.17 W
Nokou, Chad	82	E2	14.34 N	14.46 E
Nokpan-ni, ngh., Kor., S.	189b		37.36 N	126.56 E
Nokuku, Vanuatu	101d	j16	14.53 S	166.35 E
Nola, C.A.R.	86	D3	3.31 N	16.03 E
Nola, Italy	32	D8	40.55 N	14.30 E
Nolan, stm., Tx., U.S.	136	B10	32.05 N	97.28 W
Nolichucky, stm., U.S.	124	H2	36.06 N	83.14 W
Nolin, stm., Ky., U.S.	130	G11	37.12 N	86.15 W
Nolin Lake, res., Ky., U.S.	130	G11	37.20 N	86.10 W
Nolinsk, Russia	40	C16	57.33 N	49.56 E
Nólsoy, i., Far. Is.	12b	n34	61.59 N	6.38 W
Nomad, Pap. N. Gui.	101a	b3	6.18 S	142.12 E
Nomahegan Brook, stm., N.J., U.S.	194		40.41 N	74.18 W
Nombre de Dios, Mex.	154	D6	23.50 N	104.13 W
Nombre de Dios, Pan.	156	H8	9.35 N	79.28 W
Nome, Ak., U.S.	109	D6	64.30 N	165.24 W
Nomozaki, Japan	56	G2	32.34 N	129.45 E
Nomtsas, Nmb.	90	D3	24.25 S	16.51 E
Nonacho Lake, l., N.T., Can.	110	C8	61.42 N	109.40 W
Nonburg, Russia	12	D24	65.31 N	50.51 E
Nondalton, Ak., U.S.	109	D8	60.00 N	154.49 W
Nong'an, China	52	C10	44.25 N	125.10 E
Nong Bua Lamphu, Thai.	64	D6	17.13 N	102.26 E
Nong Han, Thai.	64	D6	17.22 N	103.06 E
Nong Hèt, Laos	64	C7	19.30 N	103.58 E
Nong Khai, Thai.	64	D6	17.52 N	102.44 E
Nongoma, S. Afr.	90	E10	27.57 S	31.39 E
Nongpoh, India	70	F13	25.55 N	91.50 E
Nongstoin, India	70	F13	25.31 N	91.16 E
Nonoaí, Braz.	172	C11	27.21 S	52.46 W
Nonoava, Mex.	154	B5	27.29 N	106.43 W
Nono de Julho, Túnel, trans., Braz.	205b		23.34 S	46.39 W
Nonogasta, Arg.	172	D4	29.18 S	67.30 W
Nonouti, at., Kir.	94	D8	0.38 S	174.25 E
Nonsuch Bay, b., Antig.	159b	f4	17.04 N	61.41 W
Non Sung, Thai.	64	E6	15.11 N	102.16 E
Nonthaburi, Thai.	64	F5	13.51 N	100.31 E
Nonthaburi, state, Thai.	187a		13.52 N	100.27 E
Nontron, Fr.	22	D6	45.32 N	0.40 E
Nooksack, Wa., U.S.	146	B4	48.55 N	122.19 W
Nooksack, stm., Wa., U.S.	146	B4	48.46 N	122.41 W
Noonan, N.D., U.S.	142	F10	48.53 N	103.01 W
Noon Hill, hill, Ma., U.S.	201		42.09 N	71.19 W
Noonkanbah, Austl.	96	C4	18.29 S	124.50 E
Noordoewer, Nmb.	90	F3	28.45 S	17.37 E
Noordoostpolder, reg., Neth.	20	B14	52.42 N	5.45 E
Noordpunt, c., Neth. Ant.	158g	p21	12.22 N	69.08 W
Noordwijk aan Zee, Neth.	20	B13	52.13 N	4.25 E
Noord Zee see North Sea, s., Eur.	8	D9	56.00 N	3.00 E
Noormarkku, Fin.	18	F8	61.35 N	21.53 E
Noorvik, Ak., U.S.	109	C7	66.52 N	160.59 W
Nootka Island, i., B.C., Can.	144	G4	49.44 N	126.45 W
Nootka Sound, strt., B.C., Can.	144	G4	49.33 N	126.38 W
Nopiming Provincial Park, p.o.i., Mb., Can.	142	D18	50.49 N	95.49 W
No Point, Point, c., Ct., U.S.	194		41.09 N	73.08 W
Nóqui, Ang.	88	B1	5.54 S	13.22 E
Nora, Swe.	16	H12	59.31 N	15.02 E
Norah, is., Erit.	82	D7	16.02 N	40.03 E
Nora Islands see Norah, is., Erit.	82	D7	16.02 N	40.03 E
Noralee, B.C., Can.	144	B4	53.59 N	126.26 W
Nora Springs, Ia., U.S.	130	A5	43.08 N	93.00 W
Norberg, Swe.	16	G13	60.04 N	15.56 E
Norborne, Mo., U.S.	130	E4	39.18 N	93.40 W
Norcatur, Ks., U.S.	138	B8	39.50 N	100.11 W
Norcia, Italy	30	H10	42.48 N	13.04 E
Norcross, Ga., U.S.	134	D14	33.56 N	84.12 W
Nord, Grnld.	108	A22	81.43 N	17.48 W
Nord, state, Fr.	20	D12	50.20 N	3.40 E
Nord, state, N. Cal.	101d	m15	20.49 S	164.54 E
Nord, Canal du, can., Fr.	20	E11	50.15 N	3.06 E
Nord, Gare, trans., Fr.	179		48.53 N	2.21 E
Nordaustlandet, i., Nor.	108	B29	79.42 N	22.51 E
Nordbögge, Ger.	181		51.37 N	7.44 E
Nordborg, Den.	16	L7	55.03 N	9.45 E
Nordegg, Ab., Can.	144	D14	52.28 N	116.04 W
Nordegg, stm., Ab., Can.	144	D15	52.53 N	115.19 W
Norden, Ger.	24	C3	53.35 N	7.12 E
Norden, Eng., U.K.	180		53.38 N	2.13 W
Nordenham, Ger.	24	C4	53.29 N	8.29 E
Nordenšel'da, arhipelag, is., Russia	50	A8	76.45 N	95.59 E
Nordenskjold Archipelago see Nordenšel'da, arhipelag, is., Russia	50	A8	76.45 N	95.59 E
Norderney, i., Ger.	24	C3	53.43 N	7.11 E
Norderstedt, Ger.	24	C6	53.43 N	9.59 E
Nordfjord, b., Nor.	16	F3	61.54 N	5.12 E
Nordfjord, reg., Nor.	16	F3	61.52 N	5.30 E
Nordfjordeid, Nor.	16	F3	61.54 N	6.00 E
Nordfold, Nor.	14	E5	67.45 N	15.10 E
Nordfolda, b., Nor.	14	E6	67.46 N	15.22 E
Nordfriesische Inseln see North Frisian Islands, is., Eur.	16	L6	55.12 N	8.12 E
Nordfrisiske Øer see North Frisian Islands, is., Eur.	16	L6	55.12 N	8.12 E
Nordgrønland (Avanersuaq), state, Grnld.	108	B14	79.56 N	49.59 W
Nordhausen, Ger.	24	E6	51.29 N	10.47 E
Nordheim, Tx., U.S.	136	F10	28.55 N	97.35 W
Nordhelle, hill, Ger.	181		51.09 N	7.46 E
Nordhordland, reg., Nor.	16	G3	60.41 N	5.13 E
Nordhorn, Ger.	24	D2	52.26 N	7.04 E
Nordic Park, Il., U.S.	196		41.57 N	88.02 W
Nordingrå, Swe.	16	E16	62.56 N	18.18 E
Nordjylland, state, Den.	16	K7	57.00 N	9.50 E
Nordkanal, can., Ger.	181		51.10 N	6.42 E
Nordkapp (North Cape), c., Nor.	14	A16	71.09 N	25.46 E
Nordkinnhalvøya, pen., Nor.	14	B18	70.57 N	27.44 E
Nordkjosbotn, Nor.	14	C10	69.13 N	19.30 E
Nordland, state, Nor.	12	C6	67.00 N	14.40 E
Nördlingen, Ger.	24	H6	48.51 N	10.29 E
Nordmaling, Swe.	16	D17	63.35 N	19.30 E
Nordman, Id., U.S.	146	B9	48.38 N	116.56 W
Nordmela, Nor.	14	C6	69.08 N	15.41 E
Nordmøre, reg., Nor.	16	D6	63.04 N	8.22 E
Nordostrundingen, c., Grnld.	108	A23	81.36 N	12.09 W
Nord-Ostsee-Kanal (Kiel Canal), can., Ger.	24	B5	53.54 N	9.09 E
Nordøyane, is., Nor.	16	E4	62.40 N	6.15 E
Nordrhein-Westfalen, state, Ger.	24	E4	51.30 N	7.30 E
Nordsee see North Sea, s., Eur.	8	D9	56.00 N	3.00 E
Nordsjøen see North Sea, s., Eur.	8	D9	56.00 N	3.00 E
Nord-Statland, Nor.	16	C9	64.30 N	11.07 E
Nordstrand, i., Ger.	24	B4	54.30 N	8.53 E
Nord-Trøndelag, state, Nor.	16	C10	64.25 N	12.00 E
Nordvik, Russia	50	B11	74.01 N	111.29 E
Nore, stm., Ire.	10	I5	52.25 N	6.57 W
Norefjell, mts., Nor.	16	G7	60.18 N	9.25 E
Norf, Ger.	181		51.09 N	6.43 E
Norf, stm., Ger.	181		51.11 N	6.44 E
Norfolk, Ma., U.S.	201		42.07 N	71.19 W
Norfolk, Ne., U.S.	140	E15	42.01 N	97.24 W
Norfolk, Va., U.S.	124	H9	36.50 N	76.16 W
Norfolk Island, dep., Norf. I.	100i	x25	29.02 S	167.57 E
Norfolk Island, i., Norf. I.	94	F7	29.02 S	167.57 E
Norfolk Island Aerodrome, arpt., Norf. I.	100i	y24	29.03 S	167.56 E
Norfolk Island National Park, p.o.i., Norf. I.	100i	y25	29.00 S	167.56 E
Norfolk Naval Air Station, mil., Va., U.S.	124	H9	36.57 N	76.18 W
Norfolk Ridge, unds.	174	L19	29.00 S	168.00 E
Norfork Lake, res., U.S.	130	H5	36.20 N	92.14 W
Norge see Norway, ctry., Eur.	12	E4	62.00 N	10.00 E
Nori, Russia	50	C3	66.12 N	72.19 E
Norikura-dake, vol., Japan	56	C10	36.06 N	137.33 E
Noril'sk, Russia	50	C6	69.19 N	88.13 E
Norkvaløya, i., Nor.	14	B9	70.11 N	19.10 E
Norley, Eng., U.K.	180		53.15 N	2.39 W
Norlina, N.C., U.S.	124	H7	36.26 N	78.11 W
Normal, Il., U.S.	130	D9	40.30 N	88.58 W
Norman, Ar., U.S.	134	C5	34.27 N	93.41 W
Norman, Ok., U.S.	138	F11	35.13 N	97.26 W
Norman, stm., Austl.	98	B3	17.28 S	140.50 E
Norman, Lake, res., N.C., U.S.	132	A4	35.29 N	80.58 W
Normanby Island, i., Pap. N. Gui.	101a	c5	10.05 S	151.05 E
Norman Creek, b., Md., U.S.	202b		39.18 N	76.25 W
Normandes, Îles see Channel Islands, is., Eur.	10	L10	49.20 N	2.20 W
Normandie, hist. reg., Fr.	20	E9	49.00 N	0.05 W
Normandie, Collines de, hills, Fr.	20	F8	48.42 N	0.27 W
Normandin, Qc., Can.	122	B4	48.50 N	72.32 W
Normandy see Normandie, hist. reg., Fr.	20	E9	49.00 N	0.05 W
Normandy, Hills of see Normandie, Collines de, hills, Fr.	20	F8	48.42 N	0.27 W
Normandy Heights, Md., U.S.	202b		39.17 N	76.48 W
Normangee, Tx., U.S.	136	C11	31.01 N	96.07 W
Normanhurst, Austl.	192a		33.43 S	151.06 E
Norman Island, i., Br. Vir. Is.	158b	e8	18.19 N	64.36 W
Norman Park, Ga., U.S.	132	E2	31.15 N	83.40 W
Normanton, Austl.	98	A3	17.40 S	141.05 E
Norman Wells, N.T., Can.	110	B5	65.16 N	126.41 W
Nor Marsh, sw., Eng., U.K.	178		51.24 N	0.38 E
Norogachi, Mex.	154	B5	27.15 N	107.07 W
Noroton, stm., Ct., U.S.	194		41.03 N	73.31 W
Noroton Point, c., Ct., U.S.	194		41.03 N	73.26 W
Norphlet, Ar., U.S.	134	D6	33.19 N	92.39 W
Norquay, Sk., Can.	142	C11	51.52 N	102.06 W
Ñorquinco, Arg.	166	H2	41.51 S	70.54 W
Norra Dellen, l., Swe.	16	F14	61.54 N	16.41 E
Norrahammar, Swe.	16	J12	57.42 N	14.08 E
Norra Kvarken (Merenkurkku), strt., Eur.	18	D7	63.27 N	20.42 E
Norra Storfjället, mtn., Swe.	16	B13	65.52 N	15.17 E
Norra Ulvön, i., Swe.	16	E16	62.59 N	18.38 E
Norrbotten, state, Swe.	14	E11	66.00 N	20.00 E
Nørresundby, Den.	16	J7	57.03 N	9.55 E
Norrfjärden, Swe.	14	G12	65.26 N	21.30 E
Norridgewock, Me., U.S.	122	F7	44.42 N	69.47 W
Norris, Tn., U.S.	124	H1	36.11 N	84.05 W
Norris City, Il., U.S.	130	G9	37.58 N	88.19 W
Norris Dam State Park, p.o.i., Tn., U.S.	124	H2	36.15 N	83.55 W
Norris Lake, res., Tn., U.S.	124	H1	36.16 N	84.01 W
Norristown, Pa., U.S.	124	D10	40.06 N	75.20 W
Norrköping, Swe.	16	I14	58.35 N	16.11 E
Norroway Brook, stm., Ma., U.S.	201		42.11 N	71.03 W
Norrsundet, Swe.	16	G15	60.55 N	17.09 E
Norrtälje, Swe.	16	H16	59.46 N	18.43 E
Norseman, Austl.	96	F4	32.11 S	121.47 E
Norsjö, Swe.	16	C17	64.55 N	19.29 E
Norsjø, l., Nor.	16	H6	59.18 N	9.20 E
Norsk, Russia	50	F15	52.20 N	129.54 E
Norskehavet see Norwegian Sea, s., Eur.	176	A14	70.00 N	2.00 E
Norske Øer, is., Grnld.	108	B22	79.07 N	17.40 W
Norsup, Vanuatu	101d	k16	16.05 S	167.23 E
Norte, Cabo, c., Braz.	164	C8	1.38 N	49.56 W
Norte, Cabo, c., Chile	100l	e29	27.03 S	109.23 W
Norte, Canal, strt., Arg.	206		34.37 S	58.15 W
Norte, Cayo, i., P.R.	158a	b5	18.20 N	65.15 W
Norte, Estación del, trans., Spain	184a		40.25 N	3.43 W
Norte, Estación del, trans., Spain	184d		41.24 N	2.02 E
Norte, Punta, c., Arg.	166	H4	42.05 S	63.46 W
Norte, Serra do, plat., Braz.	164	F6	11.20 S	59.00 W
Norte de Santander, state, Col.	168	C5	8.00 N	73.00 W
Nortelândia, Braz.	166	B5	14.25 S	56.48 W
North, S.C., U.S.	132	C4	33.36 N	81.06 W
North, stm., Al., U.S.	134	D11	33.15 N	87.30 W
North, stm., Ia., U.S.	130	C3	41.31 N	93.27 W
North, stm., Ma., U.S.	201		42.10 N	70.43 W
North, stm., Mo., U.S.	130	E6	39.51 N	91.26 W
North, stm., Wa., U.S.	146	D3	46.42 N	123.53 W
North, Cape, c., N.S., Can.	122	C16	47.02 N	60.24 W
North Adams, Ma., U.S.	124	B12	42.42 N	73.06 W
North Adams, Mi., U.S.	124	C1	41.58 N	84.32 W
North Albanian Alps, mts., Eur.	32	B13	42.27 N	19.47 E
North Albany, Or., U.S.	146	F3	44.39 N	123.06 W
Northallerton, Eng., U.K.	10	G11	54.20 N	1.26 W
Northam, Austl.	96	F3	31.39 S	116.40 E
Northam, S. Afr.	90	D8	25.03 S	27.11 E
North America, cont.	4	C5	45.00 N	100.00 W
North American Basin, unds.	176	E7	30.00 N	60.00 W
North Amityville, N.Y., U.S.	194		40.41 N	73.25 W
Northampton, Austl.	96	E2	28.21 S	114.38 E
Northampton, Eng., U.K.	10	I12	52.14 N	0.54 W
Northampton, Md., U.S.	202c		38.52 N	76.49 W
Northampton, Ma., U.S.	124	B13	42.19 N	72.38 W
Northampton, Pa., U.S.	124	D10	40.41 N	75.29 W
North Andaman, i., India	62	F7	13.15 N	92.55 E
North Anna, stm., Va., U.S.	124	G8	37.48 N	77.24 W
North Anson, Me., U.S.	122	F7	44.51 N	69.54 W
North Arlington, N.J., U.S.	194		40.47 N	74.08 W
North Atlanta, Ga., U.S.	132	C1	33.51 N	84.20 W
North Attleboro National Fish Hatchery, p.o.i., Ma., U.S.	201		42.00 N	71.17 W
North Auburn, Austl.	192a		33.50 S	151.02 E
North Augusta, S.C., U.S.	132	C4	33.30 N	81.57 W
North Aulatsivik Island, i., Nf., Can.	108	F13	59.45 N	64.04 W
North Australian Basin, unds.	174	K14	14.30 S	116.30 E
Northaw, Eng., U.K.	178		51.42 N	0.09 W
North Babylon, N.Y., U.S.	194		40.42 N	73.19 W
North Baltimore, Oh., U.S.	124	C2	41.10 N	83.39 W
North Balwyn, Austl.	192b		37.48 S	145.05 E
North Battleford, Sk., Can.	142	B5	52.46 N	108.16 W
North Bay, On., Can.	126	B10	46.18 N	79.26 W
North Bay Shore, N.Y., U.S.	194		40.45 N	73.16 W
North Beach, ngh., Ca., U.S.	200		37.48 N	122.25 W
North Bellmore, N.Y., U.S.	194		40.41 N	73.32 W
North Bend, B.C., Can.	144	G9	49.52 N	121.27 W
North Bend, Ne., U.S.	128	J2	41.27 N	96.46 W
North Bend, Or., U.S.	146	G2	43.24 N	124.13 W
North Benfleet, Eng., U.K.	178		51.35 N	0.32 E
North Bennington, Vt., U.S.	124	B12	42.54 N	73.13 W
North Bergen, N.J., U.S.	194		40.47 N	74.02 W
North Berwick, Scot., U.K.	10	E10	56.03 N	2.44 W
North Berwick, Me., U.S.	122	G6	43.18 N	70.43 W
North Blinman, Austl.	98	H2	31.06 S	138.41 E
North Boggy Creek, stm., Ok., U.S.	134	C2	34.22 N	96.03 W
North Borneo see Sabah, state, Malay.	68	H1	5.04 N	117.28 E
North Bosque, stm., Tx., U.S.	136	C10	31.34 N	97.13 W
North Bourke, Austl.	98	H5	30.02 S	145.56 E
North Box Hill, Austl.	192b		37.48 S	145.07 E
North Braddock, Pa., U.S.	197b		40.23 N	79.50 W
North Branch, Mi., U.S.	126	E6	43.13 N	83.11 W
North Branch, Mn., U.S.	128	F6	45.30 N	92.58 W
Northbridge, Austl.	192a		33.49 S	151.13 E
Northbrook, Pa., U.S.	203		39.55 N	75.41 W
North Caicos, i., T./C. Is.	156	B12	21.56 N	71.59 W
North Caldwell, N.J., U.S.	194		40.51 N	74.16 W
North Canadian, stm., Ok., U.S.	138	F12	35.17 N	95.31 W
North Canton, Ga., U.S.	134	C14	34.15 N	84.29 W
North Canton, Oh., U.S.	124	D4	40.52 N	81.21 W
North Cape, c., P.E., Can.	122	C13	47.02 N	64.00 W
North Cape, c., N.Z.	102	B5	34.25 S	173.02 E
North Cape see Nordkapp, c., Nor.	14	A16	71.09 N	25.46 E
North Caribou Lake, l., On., Can.	110	E12	52.50 N	90.40 W
North Carolina, state, U.S.	116	C13	35.30 N	80.00 W
North Cascades National Park, p.o.i., Wa., U.S.	146	B5	48.30 N	121.00 W
North Chagrin Reservation, p.o.i., Oh., U.S.	197a		41.34 N	81.26 W
North Channel, strt., On., Can.	126	B7	46.02 N	82.50 W
North Channel, strt., U.K.	10	G7	55.10 N	5.40 W
North Channel, stm., N.Y., U.S.	194		40.36 N	73.53 W
North Channel, mth., Mi., U.S.	199		42.38 N	82.40 W
North Charleston, S.C., U.S.	132	D5	32.52 N	79.59 W
North Chicago, Il., U.S.	130	B10	42.19 N	87.50 W
North Chungcheong see Ch'ungch'ŏng-bukto, state, Kor., S.	56	B1	37.00 N	128.20 E
Northchurch, Eng., U.K.	178		51.46 N	0.36 W
Northcliff, ngh., S. Afr.	191d		26.09 S	27.58 E
Northcliffe, Austl.	96	F3	34.38 S	116.07 E
North Cohasset, Ma., U.S.	201		42.15 N	70.50 W
North College Hill, Oh., U.S.	130	E13	39.13 N	84.33 W
North Collins, N.Y., U.S.	126	F11	42.36 N	78.56 W
North Commerce Lake, l., Mi., U.S.	199		42.35 N	83.30 W
North Concho, stm., Tx., U.S.	136	C7	31.27 N	100.25 W
North Conway, N.H., U.S.	122	F5	44.03 N	71.07 W
Northcote, Austl.	192b		37.46 S	145.00 E
North Cray, ngh., Eng., U.K.	178		51.26 N	0.08 E
North Creek, N.Y., U.S.	126	E15	43.42 N	73.59 W
North Creek, stm., Il., U.S.	196		41.33 N	87.37 W
North Crossett, Ar., U.S.	134	D7	33.09 N	91.56 W
North Crosswicks, N.J., U.S.	203		40.10 N	74.39 W
North Croton Creek, stm., Tx., U.S.	138	H8	33.24 N	100.00 W
North Cyprus see Cyprus, North, ctry., Asia	76	C4	35.15 N	33.40 E
North Dakota, state, U.S.	142	G13	47.30 N	100.15 W
North Dorset Downs, hills, Eng., U.K.	10	K10	50.48 N	2.24 W
North Downs, hills, Eng., U.K.	10	J13	51.20 N	0.10 E
North Eagle Butte, S.D., U.S.	140	B11	45.00 N	101.16 W
North East, Md., U.S.	124	E10	39.36 N	75.55 W
North East, Pa., U.S.	124	B6	42.12 N	79.50 W
North-East, state, Bots.	90	B8	21.00 S	27.30 E
Northeast Cape, Ak., U.S.	109	D6	63.18 N	168.42 W
Northeast Cape Fear, stm., N.C., U.S.	132	B8	34.14 N	77.57 W
Northeast Creek, stm., Md., U.S.	202b		39.18 N	76.29 W
Northeastern University, educ., Ma., U.S.	201		42.20 N	71.05 W
North East Land see Nordaustlandet, i., Nor.	108	B29	79.42 N	22.51 E
North East Point, c., Bah.	156	A11	22.44 N	73.51 W
North East Point, c., Bah.	156	B11	21.19 N	73.01 W
Northeast Providence Channel, strt., Bah.	132	K8	25.40 N	77.09 W
Northeim, Ger.	24	E6	51.42 N	10.00 E
North English, Ia., U.S.	130	C5	41.30 N	92.04 W
Northern see HaZafon, state, Isr.	76	F6	32.50 N	35.20 E
Northern Cape, state, S. Afr.	90	G5	29.00 S	21.00 E
Northern Cheyenne Indian Reservation, ind. res., Mt., U.S.	140	B6	45.31 N	106.45 W
Northern Circārs, hills, India	69	B6	18.00 N	83.15 E
Northern Cook Islands, is., Cook Is.	94	E10	10.00 S	161.00 W
Northern Division, state, Fiji	101e	p20	16.17 S	179.22 W
Northern Donets, stm., Eur.	40	G10	47.35 N	40.54 E
Northern Dvina see Severnaja Dvina, stm., Russia	12	D20	64.40 N	39.51 E
Northern Indian Lake, l., Mb., Can.	110	D11	57.21 N	97.18 W
Northern Ireland, state, U.K.	10	G6	54.40 N	6.45 W
Northern Light Lake, l., On., Can.	128	C8	48.14 N	90.31 W
Northern Mariana Islands, dep., Oc.	92	B6	16.00 N	149.00 E
Northern Province, state, S. Afr.	90	C9	23.30 S	29.30 E
Northern Range, mts., Trin.	159f	s12	10.44 N	61.15 W
Northern Sporades see Vóreioi Sporades, is., Grc.	34	D6	39.15 N	23.55 E
Northern Territory, state, Austl.	96	D6	20.00 S	134.00 E
Northern Transvaal see Northern Province, state, S. Afr.	90	C9	23.30 S	29.30 E
North Esk, stm., Scot., U.K.	10	E10	56.45 N	2.26 W
North Essendon, Austl.	192b		37.45 S	144.54 E
Northey Island, i., Eng., U.K.	178		51.44 N	0.43 E
North Fabius, stm., U.S.	130	D6	39.53 N	91.27 W
North Fair Oaks, Ca., U.S.	200		37.28 N	122.12 W
Northfield, Il., U.S.	196		42.05 N	87.46 W
Northfield, Ma., U.S.	124	B13	42.41 N	72.27 W
Northfield, Mn., U.S.	128	G5	44.27 N	93.09 W
Northfield, Vt., U.S.	122	F4	44.09 N	72.39 W
Northfield Airport, arpt., Oh., U.S.	197a		41.17 N	81.31 W
Northfield Center, Oh., U.S.	197a		41.19 N	81.32 W
Northfield Park Race Track, p.o.i., Oh., U.S.	197a		41.21 N	81.31 W
Northfield Village, Oh., U.S.	197a		41.21 N	81.31 W
Northfield Woods, Il., U.S.	196		42.05 N	87.52 W
North Fiji Basin, unds.	174	K20	16.00 S	174.00 E
North Fitzroy, Austl.	192b		37.47 S	144.59 E
North Flinders Range, mts., Austl.	98	H2	31.00 S	139.00 E
North Fond du Lac, Wi., U.S.	128	H10	43.48 N	88.28 W
North Foreland, c., Eng., U.K.	10	J14	51.23 N	1.25 E
North Fork, Ca., U.S.	148	F6	37.13 N	119.30 W
North Fork, stm., U.S.	130	H5	36.12 N	92.17 W
North Fort Myers, Fl., U.S.	132	J4	26.40 N	81.52 W
North Freedom, Wi., U.S.	128	H8	43.27 N	89.52 W
North Frisian Islands, is., Eur.	16	L6	55.12 N	8.12 E
Northgate, shp. cen., Ca., U.S.	200		38.00 N	122.33 W
North Glen Ellyn, Il., U.S.	196		41.54 N	88.04 W
Northglenn, Co., U.S.	138	B4	39.53 N	104.58 W
North Grand Island Bridge, trans., N.Y., U.S.	202a		43.04 N	78.59 W
North Great River, N.Y., U.S.	194		40.44 N	73.10 W
North Gulfport, Ms., U.S.	134	G9	30.24 N	89.05 W
North Gyeongsang see Kyŏngsang-bukto, state, Kor., S.	56	C1	36.19 N	128.46 E
North Haledon, N.J., U.S.	194		40.57 N	74.11 W
North Hanover, Ma., U.S.	201		42.08 N	70.52 W
North Harbor, b., Phil.	187f		14.36 N	120.57 E
North Harbour, b., Austl.	192a		33.49 S	151.17 E
North Head, c., Austl.	192a		33.49 S	151.18 E
North Henik Lake, l., Nu., Can.	110	C11	61.45 N	97.40 W
North Hero, Vt., U.S.	126	D16	44.49 N	73.17 W
North Highlands, Ca., U.S.	148	E4	38.40 N	121.22 W
North Hills, De., U.S.	203		39.46 N	75.30 W
North Hills, Il., U.S.	196		42.18 N	88.01 W
North Hills, N.Y., U.S.	194		40.47 N	73.41 W
North Hollywood, ngh., Ca., U.S.	198		34.10 N	118.23 W
North Holmwood, Eng., U.K.	178		51.13 N	0.20 W
North Horr, Kenya	86	D7	3.19 N	37.04 E
North Irwin, Pa., U.S.	197b		40.20 N	79.43 W
North Island, i., N.Z.	102	C5	39.00 S	176.00 E
North Judson, In., U.S.	130	C11	41.12 N	86.45 W
North Kent Island, i., Nu., Can.	108	B7	76.40 N	90.08 W
North Kingsville, Oh., U.S.	124	C5	41.54 N	80.42 W
North Knife Lake, l., Mb., Can.	110	D11	58.05 N	97.05 W
North Korea see Korea, North, ctry., Asia	54	D7	40.00 N	127.00 E
North Lake, l., N.Y., U.S.	194		41.09 N	73.41 W
North Lakhimpur, India	62	C7	27.14 N	94.06 E
Northland, shp. cen., Mi., U.S.	199		42.27 N	83.13 W
North Laramie, stm., Wy., U.S.	140	E7	42.07 N	104.55 W
North Las Vegas, Nv., U.S.	150	G1	36.12 N	115.06 W
North La Veta Pass, p., Co., U.S.	138	D3	37.36 N	105.13 W
North Liberty, In., U.S.	130	C11	41.32 N	86.25 W
North Lindenhurst, N.Y., U.S.	194		40.42 N	73.22 W
North Line Island, i., N.Y., U.S.	194		40.38 N	73.29 W
North Little Rock, Ar., U.S.	134	C6	34.45 N	92.16 W
North Llano, stm., Tx., U.S.	136	D8	30.29 N	99.45 W
North Logan, Ut., U.S.	146	I15	41.46 N	111.48 W
North Loon Mountain, mtn., Id., U.S.	146	E11	45.07 N	115.52 W
North Loup, Ne., U.S.	140	F14	41.29 N	98.46 W
North Loup, stm., Ne., U.S.	140	F14	41.16 N	98.24 W
North Magnetic Pole, misc. cult.	108	B4	77.19 N	101.49 W
North Mamm Peak, mtn., Co., U.S.	150	D9	39.23 N	107.52 W
North Manchester, In., U.S.	130	D12	40.59 N	85.46 W
North Manitou Island, i., Mi., U.S.	126	C3	45.06 N	86.01 W
North Mankato, Mn., U.S.	128	G4	44.10 N	94.02 W
North Manly, Austl.	192a		33.46 S	151.16 E
North Marshfield, Ma., U.S.	201		42.08 N	70.46 W
North Massapequa, N.Y., U.S.	194		40.42 N	73.27 W
Northmead, Austl.	192a		33.47 S	151.00 E
Northmead, S. Afr.	191d		26.10 S	28.20 E
North Merrick, N.Y., U.S.	194		40.41 N	73.33 W
North Miami, Fl., U.S.	132	K5	25.53 N	80.09 W
North Miami Beach, Fl., U.S.	132	K5	25.55 N	80.08 W
North Milk (Milk, North Fork), stm., N.A.	146	B13	49.08 N	112.23 W
North Moreau Creek, stm., Mo., U.S.	130	F5	38.29 N	92.18 W
North Muskegon, Mi., U.S.	126	E3	43.15 N	86.15 W
North Myrtle Beach, S.C., U.S.	132	C7	33.48 N	78.42 W
North Narrabeen, Austl.	192a		33.42 S	151.18 E
North New Hyde Park, N.Y., U.S.	194		40.44 N	73.41 W
North New River Canal, can., Fl., U.S.	132	J5	26.06 N	80.07 W
North Newton, Ks., U.S.	138	C11	38.04 N	97.21 W
North Ockendon, ngh., Eng., U.K.	178		51.32 N	0.18 E
North Ogden, Ut., U.S.	150	B5	41.19 N	111.57 W
Northolt Aerodrome, arpt., Eng., U.K.	178		51.33 N	0.23 W
Northome, Mn., U.S.	128	D4	47.51 N	94.16 W
Northop, Wales, U.K.	180		53.12 N	3.08 W
North Ore Creek, stm., Mi., U.S.	199		42.43 N	83.47 W
North Ossetia see Severnaja Osetija, state, Russia	42	D11	43.00 N	44.15 E
Northowram, Eng., U.K.	180		53.44 N	1.50 W
North Palisade, mtn., Ca., U.S.	148	F7	37.06 N	118.31 W
North Palm Beach, Fl., U.S.	132	J5	26.49 N	80.03 W
North Park, Il., U.S.	130	B8	42.20 N	89.03 W
North Park, ngh., Il., U.S.	196		41.59 N	87.43 W
North Park, p.o.i., Pa., U.S.	197b		40.36 N	80.00 W
North Park Lake, l., Pa., U.S.	197b		40.36 N	80.00 W
North Parramatta, Austl.	192a		33.48 S	151.00 E
North Patchogue, N.Y., U.S.	194		40.47 N	73.00 W
North Peak, mtn., Ca., U.S.	200		37.33 N	122.28 W
North Pease, stm., Tx., U.S.	138	G8	34.15 N	100.07 W
North Pelham, N.H., U.S.	201		42.46 N	71.21 W
North Pelham, N.Y., U.S.	194		40.55 N	73.48 W
North Peninsula, pen., On., Can.	128	A10	50.10 N	88.20 W
North Philadelphia, ngh., Pa., U.S.	203		39.58 N	75.09 W
North Philadelphia Airport, arpt., Pa., U.S.	203		40.05 N	75.01 W
North Piney Creek, stm., Wy., U.S.	146	H16	42.31 N	110.05 W
North Plains, pl., N.M., U.S.	150	I8	34.30 N	108.15 W
North Platte, Ne., U.S.	140	F12	41.08 N	100.46 W
North Platte, stm., U.S.	140	F11	41.07 N	100.42 W
North Plympton, Ma., U.S.	201		41.59 N	70.48 W
North Point, China	189d		22.17 N	114.12 E
North Point, c., Barb.	159d	n8	13.19 N	59.36 W
North Point, c., Md., U.S.	202b		39.12 N	76.27 W
North Point, c., Mi., U.S.	126	C6	45.02 N	83.16 W
North Pole, misc. cult.	106	A1	90.00 N	0.00 W
Northport, Al., U.S.	134	D11	33.13 N	87.34 W
Northport, Mi., U.S.	126	C4	45.07 N	85.36 W
Northport, Wa., U.S.	146	B9	48.54 N	117.46 W
North Portal, Sk., Can.	142	E11	49.00 N	102.32 W
Northport Bay, b., N.Y., U.S.	194		40.55 N	73.23 W
Northport Harbor, b., N.Y., U.S.	194		40.53 N	73.22 W
North Powder, Or., U.S.	146	E8	45.00 N	117.56 W
North Raccoon, stm., Ia., U.S.	130	C3	41.32 N	93.58 W

Name Page Map Ref. Latitude Longitude

North Ram, stm., Ab., Can. 144 D14 52.14 N 115.39 W
North Randall, Oh., U.S. 197a 41.27 N 81.32 W
North Reservoir, res., Ma., U.S. 201 42.28 N 71.07 W
North Rhine-Westphalia see Nordrhein-Westfalen, state, Ger. 24 E4 51.30 N 7.30 E
North Richland Hills, Tx., U.S. 136 B10 32.49 N 97.14 W
North Richmond, Ca., U.S. 200 37.57 N 122.22 W
Northridge, ngh., Ca., U.S. 198 34.14 N 118.33 W
Northridge Fashion Center, shp. cen., Ca., U.S. 198 34.13 N 118.33 W
North Rim, Az., U.S. 150 G4 36.11 N 112.02 W
North Riverside, Il., U.S. 196 41.50 N 87.49 W
North Riverside Park Mall, shp. cen., Il., U.S. 196 41.51 N 87.49 W
North Rocks, Austl. 192a 33.46 S 151.02 E
North Ronaldsay, i., Scot., U.K. 10 B10 59.22 N 2.26 W
North Rustico, P.E., Can. 122 D13 46.26 N 63.20 W
North Ryde, Austl. 192a 33.48 S 151.07 E
North Salt Lake, Ut., U.S. 150 C5 40.50 N 111.54 W
North Santiam, stm., Or., U.S. 146 F4 44.41 N 123.00 W
North Saskatchewan, stm., Can. 110 E9 53.14 N 105.04 W
North Saugeen, stm., On., Can. 126 D8 44.18 N 81.15 W
North Sea, s., Eur. 8 D9 56.00 N 3.00 E
North Sentinel Island, i., India 62 F7 11.33 N 92.15 E
North Shoal Lake, l., Mb., Can. 142 D16 50.29 N 97.40 W
Northshore, shp. cen., Ma., U.S. 201 42.32 N 70.57 W
North Shore Channel, can., Il., U.S. 196 42.05 N 87.41 W
North Shore City, N.Z. 102 C6 36.47 S 174.46 E
North Shoshone Peak, mtn., Nv., U.S. 148 D8 39.09 N 117.29 W
North Siberian Lowland see Severo-Sibirskaja nizmennost', pl., Russia 50 B6 73.00 N 100.00 E
North Sioux City, S.D., U.S. 130 B1 42.31 N 96.29 W
North Skunk, stm., Ia., U.S. 130 C5 41.14 N 92.01 W
North Solitary Island, i., Austl. 98 G9 29.55 S 153.23 E
North Solomons, state, Pap. N. Gui. 101b c7 6.03 S 156.22 E
North Sound, strt., Antig. 159b f4 17.08 N 61.44 W
North Sound, strt., Scot., U.K. 10 B10 59.18 N 2.46 W
North Spicer Island, i., Nu., Can. 110 B15 68.30 N 78.52 W
North Springfield, Va., U.S. 202c 38.48 N 77.12 W
North Stamford Reservoir, res., Ct., U.S. 194 41.08 N 73.32 W
North Star, De., U.S. 203 39.46 N 75.43 W
North Sterling Reservoir, res., Co., U.S. 140 G9 40.46 N 103.17 W
North Stradbroke Island, i., Austl. 98 F9 27.32 S 153.27 E
North Sudbury, Ma., U.S. 201 42.24 N 71.24 W
North Sulphur, stm., Tx., U.S. 134 D3 33.23 N 95.21 W
North Sumatra see Sumatera Utara, state, Indon. 64 K4 2.24 N 99.53 E
North Sunday Creek, stm., Mt., U.S. 140 A6 46.26 N 105.53 W
North Sydney, Austl. 192a 33.50 S 151.13 E
North Sydney, N.S., Can. 122 D16 46.13 N 60.16 W
North Taranaki Bight, b., N.Z. 102 D6 38.45 S 174.22 E
North Tarrytown, N.Y., U.S. 194 41.05 N 73.51 W
North Tea Lake, l., On., Can. 126 C10 45.56 N 79.03 W
North Terre Haute, In., U.S. 130 E10 39.31 N 87.22 W
North Tewksbury, Ma., U.S. 201 42.38 N 71.14 W
North Thompson, stm., B.C., Can. 144 E11 50.41 N 120.20 W
North Toe, stm., N.C., U.S. 124 H3 35.56 N 82.11 W
North Troy, Vt., U.S. 122 E4 44.59 N 72.24 W
North Tule Draw, stm., Tx., U.S. 138 G7 34.29 N 101.35 W
North Tunica, Ms., U.S. 134 C8 34.42 N 90.23 W
North Turramurra, Austl. 192a 33.43 S 151.09 E
North Uist, i., Scot., U.K. 10 D5 57.36 N 7.26 W
Northumberland Isles, is., Austl. 98 C7 21.39 S 149.53 E
Northumberland National Park, p.o.i., Eng., U.K. 10 F10 55.18 N 2.12 W
Northumberland Strait, strt., Can. 122 D12 46.00 N 63.30 W
North Umpqua, stm., Or., U.S. 146 G4 43.16 N 123.26 W
Northvale, N.J., U.S. 194 41.00 N 73.56 W
North Valley Hills, hills, Pa., U.S. 203 40.02 N 75.40 W
North Valley Stream, N.Y., U.S. 194 40.41 N 73.42 W
North Vancouver, B.C., Can. 144 G7 49.18 N 123.04 W
North Vandergrift, Pa., U.S. 197b 40.36 N 79.34 W
North Vernon, In., U.S. 130 E12 39.00 N 85.37 W
North Versailles, Pa., U.S. 197b 40.22 N 79.48 W
North Vietnam see Vietnam, ctry., Asia 64 E9 16.00 N 108.00 E
Northville, N.Y., U.S. 126 E15 43.13 N 74.10 W
Northville Downs, p.o.i., Mi., U.S. 199 42.26 N 83.29 W
North Wantagh, N.Y., U.S. 194 40.41 N 73.30 W
North Washington, Pa., U.S. 197b 40.32 N 79.36 W
Northway, Ak., U.S. 109 D11 62.58 N 141.55 W
North-West, state, S. Afr. 90 E7 26.30 S 25.00 E
North West Bluff, c., Monts. 159a d3 16.48 N 62.12 W
North West Cape, c., Austl. 96 D2 21.48 S 114.09 E
Northwestern University, educ., Il., U.S. 196 42.04 N 87.40 W
Northwestern University (Chicago Campus), educ., Il., U.S. 196 41.54 N 87.37 W
North-West Frontier, state, Pak. 70 A4 34.26 N 72.31 E
Northwest Harbor, b., Md., U.S. 202b 39.16 N 76.35 W
Northwest Highlands, mts., Scot., U.K. 10 D8 57.30 N 5.00 W
Northwest Miramichi, stm., N.B., Can. 122 C10 46.58 N 65.34 W
Northwest Pacific Basin, unds. 174 F18 40.00 N 155.00 E
Northwest Providence Channel, strt., Bah. 132 J7 26.10 N 78.20 W
Northwest Territories, state, Can. 110 C6 65.00 N 120.00 W
North Weymouth, Ma., U.S. 201 42.15 N 70.57 W
North Wichita, stm., Tx., U.S. 138 H9 33.43 N 99.30 W
North Wilkesboro, N.C., U.S. 124 H4 36.10 N 81.08 W
North Willow Creek, stm., Mt., U.S. 142 H5 46.50 N 107.53 W
North Wilmington, Ma., U.S. 201 42.34 N 71.09 W
North Windham, Me., U.S. 122 G6 43.50 N 70.26 W
Northwood, Ia., U.S. 128 H5 43.26 N 93.13 W
Northwood, N.D., U.S. 142 G16 47.43 N 97.34 W
Northwood, ngh., Eng., U.K. 178 51.37 N 0.25 W
North Woodslee, On., Can. 199 42.13 N 82.43 W
Northwood Village, Md., U.S. 202c 39.02 N 77.01 W
North Yamhill, stm., Or., U.S. 146 E3 45.13 N 123.08 W
North York, ngh., On., Can. 126 E10 43.46 N 79.25 W
North York Moors National Park, p.o.i., Eng., U.K. 10 G12 54.22 N 0.58 W
North Yuba, stm., Ca., U.S. 148 D5 39.22 N 121.08 W
North Zulch, Tx., U.S. 136 D11 30.54 N 96.06 W
Norton, N.B., Can. 122 E11 45.38 N 65.42 W
Norton, Eng., U.K. 180 53.20 N 2.40 W
Norton, Ks., U.S. 138 B9 39.50 N 99.53 W
Norton, Va., U.S. 124 H3 36.56 N 82.38 W
Norton Basin, b., N.Y., U.S. 194 40.36 N 73.47 W
Norton Creek, stm., Mi., U.S. 199 42.34 N 83.34 W
Norton Heath, Eng., U.K. 178 51.43 N 0.19 E
Norton Reservoir, res., Ma., U.S. 201 41.59 N 71.12 W
Norton Shores, Mi., U.S. 130 A11 43.09 N 86.15 W
Norton Sound, strt., Ak., U.S. 109 D6 63.50 N 164.00 W
Nortonville, On., Can. 193b 43.43 N 79.44 W
Nortonville, Ks., U.S. 130 E2 39.25 N 95.20 W
Nortorf, Ger. 24 B5 54.10 N 9.51 E
Norumbega Reservoir, res., Ma., U.S. 201 42.20 N 71.18 W
Norvegia, Cape, c., Ant. 103 C3 71.25 S 12.18 W
Norvin Green State Forest, p.o.i., N.J., U.S. 194 41.03 N 74.20 W
Norwalk, Ct., U.S. 126 C12 41.07 N 73.25 W
Norwalk, Ia., U.S. 130 C4 41.28 N 93.40 W
Norwalk, Oh., U.S. 124 C3 41.14 N 82.36 W
Norwalk Harbor, b., Ct., U.S. 194 41.06 N 73.24 W
Norwalk Islands, is., Ct., U.S. 194 41.03 N 73.23 W
Norway, Ia., U.S. 130 C6 41.54 N 91.55 W
Norway, Me., U.S. 122 F6 44.13 N 70.31 W
Norway, Mi., U.S. 126 C2 45.47 N 87.57 W
Norway, ctry., Eur. 12 E4 62.00 N 10.00 E
Norway Bay, b., Nu., Can. 110 A10 71.05 N 104.30 W
Norway House, Mb., Can. 110 E11 53.58 N 97.48 W
Norwegian Basin, unds. 176 B13 68.00 N 2.00 W
Norwegian Sea, s., Eur. 176 A14 70.00 N 2.00 E
Norwell, Ma., U.S. 201 42.09 N 70.47 W
Norwich, On., Can. 126 E9 42.58 N 80.35 W
Norwich, Eng., U.K. 10 I14 52.37 N 1.17 E
Norwich, Ct., U.S. 124 C13 41.31 N 72.05 W
Norwich, Ks., U.S. 138 D11 37.27 N 97.50 W
Norwich, N.Y., U.S. 124 B10 42.32 N 75.31 W
Norwin Heights, Pa., U.S. 197b 40.20 N 79.44 W
Norwood, On., Can. 126 D11 44.23 N 77.59 W
Norwood, Co., U.S. 150 E8 38.08 N 108.17 W
Norwood, Ma., U.S. 124 B14 42.11 N 71.12 W
Norwood, Mn., U.S. 128 G5 44.46 N 93.55 W
Norwood, N.J., U.S. 194 40.59 N 73.57 W
Norwood, N.Y., U.S. 126 D14 44.44 N 74.59 W
Norwood, N.C., U.S. 132 A5 35.13 N 80.07 W
Norwood, Oh., U.S. 124 E1 39.09 N 84.26 W
Norwood, Pa., U.S. 203 39.53 N 75.17 W
Norwood, ngh., S. Afr. 191d 26.10 S 28.04 E
Norwood Memorial Airport, arpt., Ma., U.S. 201 42.11 N 71.10 W
Norwood Park, ngh., Il., U.S. 196 41.59 N 87.48 W
Norwood Pond, l., Ma., U.S. 201 42.35 N 70.52 W
Nosate, Italy 184b 45.33 N 8.43 E
Nosbonsing, Lake, l., On., Can. 126 B10 46.12 N 79.13 W
Nose, ngh., Japan 188 34.49 N 135.09 E
Nose Creek, stm., Ab., Can. 144 B11 54.52 N 119.38 W
Noshaq see Nowshāk, mtn., Asia 62 A3 36.26 N 71.50 E
Noshiro, Japan 54 D13 40.12 N 140.01 E
Nosivka, Ukr. 38 C10 50.56 N 31.35 E
Nosop (Nossob), stm., Afr. 90 D5 26.53 S 20.41 E
Nosovaja, Russia 26 B26 68.15 N 54.30 E
Nosovo, Russia 26 C10 57.06 N 27.48 E
Nosovščina, Russia 18 E24 62.56 N 37.03 E
Nosratābād, Iran 72 D8 29.54 N 59.59 E
Nossa Senhora das Dores, Braz. 170 F7 10.28 S 37.12 W
Nossa Senhora do Ó, ngh., Braz. 205b 23.30 S 46.41 W
Nossebro, Swe. 16 I10 58.11 N 12.45 E
Nossob (Nosop), stm., Afr. 90 D5 26.53 S 20.41 E
Nosy-Varika, Madag. 88 E8 20.35 S 48.31 E
Nota, stm., Eur. 14 D20 68.09 N 30.15 E
Notasulga, Al., U.S. 134 E13 32.33 N 85.40 W
Notch Cliff, Md., U.S. 202b 39.27 N 76.31 W
Notch Hill, B.C., Can. 144 F11 50.50 N 119.27 W
Notch Peak, mtn., Ut., U.S. 150 D3 39.08 N 113.24 W
Noteć, stm., Pol. 24 D11 52.44 N 15.24 E
Nótio Aigaío, state, Grc. 34 G9 37.00 N 25.30 E
Noto, Italy 32 H9 36.53 N 15.04 E
Noto, Japan 56 B10 37.18 N 137.08 E
Noto, Golfo di, b., Italy 32 H9 36.50 N 15.12 E
Notodden, Nor. 16 H7 59.33 N 9.15 E
Noto-hantō, pen., Japan 56 B10 37.20 N 137.00 E
Notozero, ozero, l., Russia 14 F22 66.28 N 32.05 E
Notre-Dame, N.B., Can. 122 D12 46.18 N 64.42 W
Notre-Dame, rel., Fr. 179 48.51 N 2.21 E
Notre-Dame, Bois, p.o.i., Fr. 179 48.45 N 2.35 E
Notre-Dame, Monts, mts., Qc., Can. 122 B10 48.10 N 68.00 W
Notre-Dame, Ruisseau, stm., Qc., Can. 193a 45.41 N 73.26 W
Notre Dame Bay, b., Nf., Can. 111a j22 49.45 N 55.15 W
Notre Dame de Lourdes, Mb., Can. 142 E15 49.31 N 98.33 W
Notre-Dame-des-Victoires, ngh., Qc., Can. 193a 45.35 N 73.34 W
Notre-Dame-du-Haut, rel., Fr. 20 G15 47.43 N 6.37 E
Notre-Dame-du-Laus, Qc., Can. 126 B14 46.05 N 75.35 W
Notrees, Tx., U.S. 136 C5 31.55 N 102.45 W
Nottawasaga, stm., On., Can. 126 D10 44.31 N 80.00 W
Nottawasaga Bay, b., On., Can. 126 D9 44.35 N 80.15 W
Nottaway, stm., Qc., Can. 110 E15 51.20 N 78.56 W
Nøtterøy, i., Nor. 16 H8 59.12 N 10.24 E
Nottingham, Eng., U.K. 10 I11 52.57 N 1.06 W
Nottingham, Pa., U.S. 203 40.07 N 74.58 W
Nottingham Island, i., Nu., Can. 110 C15 63.20 N 77.55 W
Nottingham Park, Il., U.S. 196 41.46 N 87.48 W
Notting Hill, Austl. 192b 37.54 S 145.08 E
Nottoway, Va., U.S. 124 G7 37.08 N 78.05 W
Nottoway, stm., Va., U.S. 124 G8 36.32 N 76.55 W
Notukeu Creek, stm., Sk., Can. 142 E6 49.55 N 106.29 W
Notwane, stm., Afr. 90 D8 23.45 S 26.57 E
Nouâdhibou, Maur. 84 E1 20.55 N 17.02 W
Nouâdhibou, Râs, c., Afr. 84 E1 20.46 N 17.03 W
Nouakchott, Maur. 84 F1 18.06 N 15.58 W
Nouâmghâr, Maur. 84 F1 19.22 N 16.30 W
Noŭka, Bela. 26 E13 55.26 N 30.23 E
Nouméa, N. Cal. 101d n16 22.17 S 166.26 E
Nounsley, Eng., U.K. 178 51.46 N 0.36 E
Noupoort, S. Afr. 90 G7 31.11 S 24.57 E
Nourunen, gora, mtn., Russia 18 A17 66.07 N 30.13 E
Nouveau-Québec, Cratère du, crat., Qc., Can. 110 C16 61.17 N 73.40 W
Nouvelle, Qc., Can. 122 B10 48.07 N 66.18 W
Nouvelle, stm., Qc., Can. 122 B10 48.05 N 66.15 W
Nouvelle-Calédonie (New Caledonia), i., N. Cal. 101d m15 21.32 S 165.42 E
Nouvelle-Écosse see Nova Scotia, state, Can. 110 G18 45.00 N 63.00 W
Nouvelle-France, Cap de, c., Qc., Can. 110 C16 62.27 N 73.42 W
Nouvelles-Hébrides see Vanuatu, ctry., Oc. 92 E7 16.00 S 167.00 E
Nova Andradina, Braz. 166 D6 22.14 S 53.20 W
Nova Astrakhan', Ukr. 38 D17 49.07 N 38.36 E
Nová Baňa, Slvk. 24 H14 48.25 N 18.39 E
Nova Bila, Ukr. 38 D18 49.46 N 39.11 E
Nova Borova, Ukr. 38 C7 50.42 N 28.39 E
Nová Bystřice, Czech Rep. 24 G11 49.01 N 15.06 E
Nova Cachoeirinha, ngh., Braz. 205b 23.28 S 46.40 W
Nova Caipemba, Ang. 88 B1 7.26 S 14.37 E
Nova Era, Braz. 170 J4 19.46 S 43.00 W
Nova Freixo see Cuamba, Moz. 88 C6 14.47 S 36.32 E
Nova Friburgo, Braz. 170 L4 22.16 S 42.31 W
Nova Goa see Panaji, India 69 D1 15.29 N 73.49 E
Nova Gorica, Slvn. 30 D10 45.58 N 13.39 E
Nova Gradiška, Cro. 30 E14 45.15 N 17.22 E
Nova Granada, Braz. 170 K1 20.29 S 49.19 W
Nova Iguaçu, Braz. 170 L4 22.44 S 43.27 W
Nova Iguaçu, mun., Braz. 205a 22.45 S 43.29 W
Nova Ivanivka, Ukr. 38 H8 45.55 N 29.05 E
Novaja, Russia 183b 55.48 N 38.03 E
Novaja, ngh., Russia 183a 60.02 N 30.28 E
Novaja Kalitva, Russia 38 C18 50.05 N 40.01 E
Novaja Kazanka, Kaz. 48 E7 48.56 N 49.36 E
Novaja Ladoga, Russia 18 G19 60.04 N 32.14 E
Novaja Maluksa, Russia 26 A14 59.39 N 31.21 E
Novaja Ropša, Russia 183a 59.45 N 29.53 E
Novaja Sibir', ostrov, i., Russia 50 B19 75.00 N 149.00 E
Novaja Zemlja, is., Russia 46 B9 74.00 N 57.00 E
Nova Kakhovka, Ukr. 38 G12 46.45 N 33.25 E
Nováky, Slvk. 24 H14 48.43 N 18.33 E
Nova Lamego, Gui.-B. 84 G2 12.16 N 14.13 W
Novaliches Reservoir, res., Phil. 187f 14.43 N 121.05 E
Nova Lima, Braz. 170 K4 19.59 S 43.50 W
Nova Lisboa see Huambo, Ang. 88 C2 12.45 S 15.44 E
Novalukoml', Bela. 26 F12 54.38 N 29.11 E
Nova Maiachka, Ukr. 38 G12 46.36 N 33.14 E
Nova Mambone, Moz. 90 B12 20.59 S 35.00 E
Nova Milanese, Italy 184b 45.35 N 9.12 E
Nova Odesa, Ukr. 38 F10 47.18 N 31.47 E
Nova Olinda, Braz. 170 D6 7.06 S 39.40 W
Nova Olinda do Norte, Braz. 164 D6 3.53 S 59.04 W
Nová Paka, Czech Rep. 24 F11 50.29 N 15.31 E
Nova Ponte, Braz. 170 J2 19.08 S 47.40 W
Nova Praha, Ukr. 38 E11 48.33 N 32.54 E
Nova Prata, Braz. 172 D12 28.47 S 51.36 W
Novara, Italy 30 E5 45.27 N 8.37 E
Nova Roma, Braz. 170 G2 13.46 S 46.52 W
Nova Russas, Braz. 170 C5 4.42 S 40.34 W
Nova Scotia, state, Can. 110 G18 45.00 N 63.00 W
Nova Sloboda, Ukr. 38 B13 51.22 N 34.07 E
Nova Soure, Braz. 170 F6 11.14 S 38.29 W
Novate Milanese, Italy 184b 45.32 N 9.08 E
Novato, Ca., U.S. 148 E3 38.06 N 122.33 W
Novato Creek, stm., Ca., U.S. 200 38.06 N 122.29 W
Nova Ushytsia, Ukr. 38 E6 48.50 N 27.17 E
Nova Varoš, Yugo. 36 F6 43.27 N 19.48 E
Nova Venécia, Braz. 170 J5 18.42 S 40.23 W
Nova Viçosa, Braz. 170 I6 17.53 S 39.22 W
Nova Vida, Braz. 164 F5 10.11 S 62.47 W
Nova Vodolaha, Ukr. 38 D14 49.42 N 35.52 E
Novaya Zemlya see Novaja Zemlja, is., Russia 46 B9 74.00 N 57.00 E
Nova Zagora, Blg. 36 G13 42.30 N 26.01 E
Nova Zburivka, Ukr. 38 G11 46.27 N 32.26 E
Nové Hrady, Czech Rep. 24 H10 48.47 N 14.46 E
Novelda, Spain 28 F10 38.23 N 0.46 W
Nové Město, Czech Rep. 24 F12 50.21 N 16.09 E
Nové Mesto nad Váhom, Slvk. 24 H13 48.45 N 17.50 E
Nové Město na Moravě, Czech Rep. 24 G12 49.33 N 16.03 E
Nové Zámky, Slvk. 24 I14 47.59 N 18.10 E
Novgorod, Russia 26 B14 58.31 N 31.18 E
Novgorodskaja oblast, co., Russia 12 G15 58.15 N 33.00 E
Novgorodskaja oblast', co., Russia 26 B15 58.15 N 33.00 E
Novhorodka, Ukr. 38 E11 48.21 N 32.39 E
Novhorod-Sivers'kyi, Ukr. 38 A11 51.59 N 33.16 E
Novhorods'ke, Ukr. 38 E16 48.19 N 37.51 E
Novi Basy, Ukr. 38 C13 50.51 N 34.54 E
Novi Bečej, Yugo. 36 D7 45.36 N 20.09 E
Novi Beograd, Yugo. 36 E7 44.47 N 20.23 E
Novi Bilokorovychi, Ukr. 38 B7 51.06 N 28.04 E
Novice, Tx., U.S. 136 C8 31.58 N 99.37 W
Novigrad, Cro. 30 F12 44.11 N 15.33 E
Novigrad, Cro. 30 E10 45.18 N 13.33 E
Novikovo, Russia 50 G17 46.21 N 143.21 E
Novi Ligure, Italy 30 F5 44.46 N 8.47 E
Novi Lyon Drain, can., Mi., U.S. 199 42.30 N 83.38 W
Novinger, Mo., U.S. 130 D5 40.13 N 92.42 W
Novinka, Russia 18 G20 60.08 N 33.34 E
Novi Pazar, Blg. 36 F14 43.20 N 27.11 E
Novi Pazar, Yugo. 36 F7 43.08 N 20.30 E
Novi Sad, Yugo. 36 D6 45.14 N 19.49 E
Novi Sanzhary, Ukr. 38 D13 49.20 N 34.19 E
Novi Vinodolski, Cro. 30 E11 45.08 N 14.48 E
Novka see Noŭka, Bela. 26 E13 55.26 N 30.23 E
Novo, Lago, l., Braz. 164 C7 1.27 N 50.42 W
Novoaidar, Ukr. 38 E18 48.57 N 39.01 E
Novo Airão, Braz. 168 I11 1.56 S 61.22 W
Novoaleksandrovo, Russia 183b 55.59 N 37.33 E
Novoaleksandrovsk, Russia 40 I12 45.29 N 41.12 E
Novoalekseevka, Kaz. 40 F19 50.08 N 55.39 E
Novoaltajsk, Russia 48 D14 53.24 N 83.56 E
Novoanninskij, Russia 40 F13 50.32 N 42.41 E
Novoarchangel'skoje, ngh., Russia 183b 55.55 N 37.33 E
Novoarhangel'skoe, ngh., Russia 183b 55.55 N 37.33 E
Novo Aripuanã, Braz. 164 E5 5.07 S 60.21 W
Novoarkhanhel's'k, Ukr. 38 E9 48.39 N 30.48 E
Novoazovs'k, Ukr. 38 F17 47.07 N 38.04 E
Novobatajsk, Russia 38 G18 46.53 N 39.47 E
Novobelaja, Russia 38 D18 49.49 N 39.18 E
Novobogatinskoe, Kaz. 40 H17 47.21 N 51.10 E
Novobohdanivka, Ukr. 38 F14 47.09 N 35.19 E
Novobratcevskij, ngh., Russia 183b 55.51 N 37.23 E
Novočerkassk, Russia 40 H11 47.25 N 40.06 E
Novocimljanskaja, Russia 40 G13 47.59 N 42.16 E
Novo Cruzeiro, Braz. 170 I5 17.29 S 41.52 W
Novodanylivka, Ukr. 38 G13 46.38 N 34.59 E
Novoderevjankov-Skaja, Russia 38 G17 46.19 N 38.44 E
Novodubovoe, Russia 40 E11 52.18 N 39.12 E
Novodugino, Russia 26 E17 55.37 N 34.17 E
Novodvinsk, Russia 18 C27 64.25 N 40.48 E
Novodžerelievskaja, Russia 38 H17 45.46 N 38.40 E
Novoe, Russia 48 C11 58.53 N 68.40 E
Novoe Kovalëvo, Russia 183a 59.59 N 30.34 E
Novoe Mašozero, Russia 18 C20 64.24 N 33.25 E
Novoenisejsk, Russia 48 C16 58.18 N 92.24 E
Novoe Zareče, Russia 26 C17 57.42 N 34.22 E
Novogireevo, ngh., Russia 183b 55.45 N 37.49 E
Novo Hamburgo, Braz. 172 D12 29.42 S 51.08 W
Novo Horizonte, Braz. 170 K1 21.27 S 49.13 W
Novohovrino, ngh., Russia 183b 55.52 N 37.30 E
Novohrad-Volyns'kyi, Ukr. 38 C6 50.35 N 27.37 E
Novohrodivka, Ukr. 38 E16 48.13 N 37.20 E
Novohryhorivka, Ukr. 38 G13 46.24 N 34.58 E
Novohupalivka, Ukr. 38 E14 48.01 N 35.25 E
Novoiljinskij, Russia 40 C19 57.54 N 55.28 E
Novoivanivka, Ukr. 38 D12 49.44 N 33.29 E
Novoivanovskoe, Russia 183b 55.43 N 37.22 E
Novoizborsk, Russia 26 C10 57.50 N 27.59 E
Novojamskoe, Russia 26 H17 52.13 N 34.27 E
Novokačalinsk, Russia 54 B10 45.06 N 132.02 E
Novokaširsk, Russia 26 F21 54.51 N 38.15 E
Novokazalinsk, Kaz. 48 F10 45.51 N 62.07 E
Novokrasne, Ukr. 38 E10 48.01 N 31.21 E
Novokubansk, Russia 40 I12 45.06 N 41.03 E
Novokujbyševsk, Russia 40 E16 53.05 N 49.55 E
Novokuzneck, Russia 48 D15 53.44 N 87.07 E
Novolazarevskaja, sci., Ant. 103 C6 70.45 S 11.49 E
Novoleuškovskaja, Russia 40 H11 45.59 N 39.59 E
Novomelovoe, Russia 38 B17 51.22 N 38.12 E
Novo Mesto, Slvn. 30 E12 45.48 N 15.10 E
Novominskaja, Russia 38 G17 46.18 N 38.57 E
Novomoskovsk (Stalinogorsk), Russia 26 F21 54.05 N 38.12 E
Novomoskovs'k, Ukr. 38 E14 48.37 N 35.12 E
Novomykhailivka, Ukr. 38 F16 47.51 N 37.29 E
Novomykolaïvka, Ukr. 38 G11 46.13 N 32.45 E
Novomykolaïvka, Ukr. 38 F14 47.58 N 35.54 E
Novomyrhorod, Ukr. 38 E10 48.46 N 31.38 E
Novonikolaevsk see Novosibirsk, Russia 48 C14 55.01 N 82.52 E
Novonikolaevskij, Russia 40 F13 50.58 N 42.22 E
Novonikol'skoe, Russia 26 A16 59.24 N 33.13 E
Novonikol'skoe, Russia 183b 55.50 N 37.15 E
Novooleksandrivka, Ukr. 38 E18 48.16 N 39.38 E
Novooleksiïvka, Ukr. 38 G13 46.13 N 34.39 E
Novo Oriente, Braz. 170 C5 5.32 S 40.46 W
Novopavlovskaja, Russia 40 D10 43.57 N 43.38 E
Novopetrovskoe, Russia 26 E19 55.58 N 36.28 E
Novopodrezkovo, ngh., Russia 183b 55.57 N 37.21 E
Novopokrovka, Ukr. 38 E13 48.03 N 34.37 E
Novopokrovskaja, Russia 40 I12 45.57 N 40.41 E
Novopskov, Ukr. 38 D18 49.32 N 39.06 E
Novorossijsk, Russia 40 I10 44.43 N 37.45 E
Novorybnoe, Russia 50 B10 72.49 N 105.49 E
Novoržev, Russia 26 C12 57.02 N 29.20 E
Novošahtinsk, Russia 40 H11 47.47 N 39.53 E
Novosaratovka, Russia 183a 59.50 N 30.32 E
Novoščerbinovskaja, Russia 38 G17 46.27 N 38.39 E
Novosele, Russia 183a 59.48 N 30.05 E
Novoselivka, Ukr. 38 D16 49.04 N 37.42 E
Novoselivs'ke, Ukr. 38 H12 45.26 N 33.36 E
Novosëlki, Russia 26 D16 56.01 N 33.36 E
Novosëlki, Russia 183a 59.42 N 30.17 E
Novosel'nyj, Kaz. 40 F19 50.00 N 54.38 E
Novoselovo, Russia 48 C16 56.03 N 39.03 E
Novoselovo, Russia 50 E7 55.00 N 90.58 E
Novoselytsia, Ukr. 38 D4 49.47 N 25.03 E
Novoselytsia, Ukr. 38 E5 48.13 N 26.17 E
Novosergievka, Russia 40 E18 52.04 N 53.39 E
Novosergijevka, Russia 183a 59.54 N 30.34 E
Novosibirsk, Russia 48 C14 55.01 N 82.52 E
Novosibirskie ostrova, is., Russia 50 A18 75.00 N 142.00 E
Novosibirskoe vodohranilišče, res., Russia 48 D14 54.35 N 82.35 E
Novosil', Russia 26 H20 52.58 N 37.03 E
Novosil's'ke, Ukr. 38 H7 45.19 N 28.35 E
Novosokol'niki, Russia 26 D13 56.21 N 30.10 E
Novostroevo, Russia 26 F4 54.27 N 21.50 E
Novotavoložanka, Russia 38 C15 50.22 N 36.50 E
Novotroick, Russia 48 D9 51.12 N 58.19 E
Novotroickoe, Kaz. 48 F12 43.40 N 73.45 E
Novotroïts'ke, Ukr. 38 G13 46.21 N 34.21 E
Novotulka, Russia 40 E15 50.50 N 47.32 E
Novoukolovo, Russia 38 B17 51.01 N 38.26 E
Novoukraïnka, Ukr. 38 E10 48.19 N 31.32 E
Novouzensk, Russia 40 F16 50.29 N 48.09 E
Novovasylivka, Ukr. 38 G14 46.49 N 35.44 E
Novovasylivka, Ukr. 38 G15 46.50 N 36.47 E
Novovjatsk, Russia 40 B16 58.29 N 49.43 E
Novovolyns'k, Ukr. 38 C3 50.44 N 24.07 E
Novovoronežskij, Russia 40 F11 51.17 N 39.12 E
Novovorontsovka, Ukr. 38 F12 47.29 N 33.55 E
Novovoskresens'ke, Ukr. 38 F12 47.21 N 33.37 E
Novozaharkino, Russia 40 E16 52.11 N 48.29 E
Novozavidovskij, Russia 26 D19 56.33 N 36.26 E
Novožilovskaja, Russia 12 D24 64.48 N 51.21 E
Novozybkov, Russia 26 H14 52.32 N 31.56 E
Novska, Cro. 30 E13 45.20 N 16.59 E
Nový Bohumín, Czech Rep. 24 G14 49.55 N 18.20 E
Nový Bor, Czech Rep. 24 F10 50.45 N 14.33 E
Novy Dvor, Bela. 26 H7 52.49 N 24.20 E
Novyi Buh, Ukr. 38 F11 47.40 N 32.30 E
Novyi Bykiv, Ukr. 38 C10 50.36 N 31.40 E
Novyi Yarychiv, Ukr. 38 D3 49.54 N 24.18 E
Novyja Dzjanisavičy, Bela. 26 F12 54.11 N 29.13 E
Novyja Valosavičy, Bela. 26 F11 54.45 N 28.51 E
Novyj Bor, Russia 12 C24 66.43 N 52.16 E
Novyj Bujan, Russia 40 E17 53.40 N 50.01 E
Nový Jičín, Czech Rep. 24 G13 49.36 N 18.00 E
Novyj Nekouz, Russia 26 C20 57.54 N 38.03 E
Novyj Oskol, Russia 40 F10 50.46 N 37.53 E
Novyj Port, Russia 48 A12 67.41 N 72.53 E
Novyj Ropsk, Russia 26 H15 52.18 N 32.19 E
Novyj Uzen', Kaz. 48 F8 43.18 N 52.47 E
Novyj Vasjugan, Russia 48 C13 58.35 N 76.29 E
Novy Pahost, Bela. 26 E10 55.30 N 27.29 E
Nowa Dęba, Pol. 24 F17 50.26 N 21.46 E
Nowa Ruda, Pol. 24 F12 50.35 N 16.30 E
Nowa Sól, Pol. 24 E11 51.47 N 15.42 E
Nowata, Ok., U.S. 130 H2 36.42 N 95.38 W
Nowater Creek, stm., Wy., U.S. 140 D5 43.55 N 108.03 W
Nowbarān, Iran 74 C11 35.12 N 49.26 E
Nowe, Pol. 24 C14 53.38 N 18.44 E
Nowe Miasto Lubawskie, Pol. 24 C15 53.27 N 19.35 E
Nowe Miasto nad Pilicą, Pol. 24 E16 51.37 N 20.35 E
Nowendoc, Austl. 98 H8 31.31 S 151.42 E
Nowe Warpno, Pol. 24 C10 53.43 N 14.17 E
Nowfel low Shātow, Iran 74 C12 34.27 N 50.53 E
Nowgong, India 70 F7 25.04 N 79.27 E
Nowingi, Austl. 98 J4 34.36 S 142.14 E
Nowitna, stm., Ak., U.S. 109 D9 65.55 N 154.17 W
Nowogard, Pol. 24 C11 53.40 N 15.07 E
Nowogród, Pol. 24 C17 53.13 N 21.56 E
Nowogrodziec, Pol. 24 E11 51.11 N 15.23 E
Nowood, stm., Wy., U.S. 140 C5 44.16 N 107.58 W
Nowra, Austl. 98 J8 34.53 S 150.36 E
Nowrangapur, India 69 B6 19.12 N 82.33 E
Nowshāk, mtn., Asia 62 A3 36.26 N 71.50 E
Nowshera, Pak. 62 B3 34.01 N 71.58 E
Nowshera, Pak. 70 B4 34.01 N 71.59 E
Nowy Dwór Gdański, Pol. 24 B15 54.12 N 19.07 E
Nowy Dwór Mazowiecki, Pol. 24 D17 52.25 N 20.43 E
Nowy Sącz, Pol. 24 G16 49.37 N 20.41 E
Nowy Staw, Pol. 24 B15 54.08 N 18.59 E
Nowy Targ, Pol. 24 G15 49.27 N 20.02 E
Nowy Tomyśl, Pol. 24 D12 52.19 N 16.06 E
Noxapater, Ms., U.S. 134 E9 32.59 N 89.03 W
Noxen, Pa., U.S. 124 C9 41.26 N 76.03 W
Noxon, Mt., U.S. 146 B11 47.59 N 115.49 W
Noxubee, stm., U.S. 134 D10 32.50 N 88.10 W
Noy, stm., Laos 64 D7 17.05 N 105.02 E
Noya see Noia, Spain 28 B2 42.47 N 8.53 W
Noyant, Fr. 20 G9 47.30 N 0.08 E
Noyers, Ruisseau des, stm., Qc., Can. 193a 45.21 N 73.22 W
Noyon, Fr. 20 E11 49.34 N 3.00 E
Nozay, Fr. 20 G7 47.33 N 1.37 W
Nozay, Fr. 179 48.40 N 2.14 E
Nozuta, Japan 186 35.35 N 139.27 E
Nsanje, Mwi. 88 D6 16.58 S 35.12 E
Nsawam, Ghana 84 H4 5.50 N 0.20 W
Nsok, Eq. Gui. 84 I7 1.07 N 11.15 E
Nsouélé, Congo 191b 4.12 S 15.11 E
Nsukka, Nig. 84 H6 6.51 N 7.23 E
Nsuta, Ghana 84 H4 5.16 N 1.58 W
Ntui, Cam. 86 D2 4.27 N 11.37 E
Ntwetwe Pan, pl., Bots. 90 B7 20.37 S 25.34 E
Nu (Salween) (Khong) (Thanlwin), stm., Asia 62 C8 16.33 N 97.39 E
Nuanétsi see Mwenezi, stm., Afr. 90 B10 22.38 S 31.44 E
Nuannuan, Tai. 187d 25.06 N 121.44 E
Nuasjärvi, l., Fin. 18 C14 64.10 N 28.05 E
Nūbah, Jibāl an-, mts., Sudan 82 E6 11.06 N 30.24 E
Nubian Desert, des., Sudan 82 C6 20.30 N 33.00 E
Ñuble, stm., Chile 172 H2 36.38 S 72.27 W
Nucet, Rom. 36 C9 46.28 N 22.35 E
Nuchatlitz Inlet, b., B.C., Can. 144 G3 49.45 N 126.56 W
Nucla, Co., U.S. 150 E8 38.16 N 108.32 W
Núcleo Colonial São Bento, Braz. 205a 22.44 S 43.18 W
Nudol'-Šarino, Russia 26 D19 56.05 N 36.30 E
Nudow, Ger. 182a 52.20 N 13.10 E
Nueces, stm., Tx., U.S. 136 F9 27.49 N 97.21 W
Nueces Plains, pl., Tx., U.S. 136 F8 28.30 N 99.15 W
Nueltin Lake, l., Can. 110 C11 60.19 N 99.40 W
Nuestra Señora de Talavera, Arg. 172 B6 25.26 S 63.46 W
Nueva, Isla, i., Chile 166 K3 55.13 S 66.32 W
Nueva Antioquia, Col. 168 E7 6.03 N 69.27 W
Nueva Atzacoalco, ngh., Mex. 204a 19.29 N 99.05 W
Nueva Chicago, ngh., Arg. 206 34.40 S 58.30 W
Nueva Ciudad Guerrero, Mex. 154 B9 26.34 N 99.13 W
Nueva Esparta, state, Ven. 168 B9 11.00 N 64.00 W
Nueva Francia, Arg. 172 D5 28.11 S 64.12 W
Nueva Galia, Arg. 172 G5 35.07 S 65.15 W
Nueva Germania, Para. 172 A9 23.52 S 56.41 W
Nueva Gerona, Cuba 156 B6 21.53 N 82.48 W
Nueva Imperial, Chile 166 G2 38.44 S 72.57 W
Nueva Italia de Ruiz, Mex. 154 F7 19.00 N 102.06 W
Nueva Loja, Ec. 168 G3 0.05 N 76.50 W
Nueva Palmira, Ur. 172 F8 33.52 S 58.23 W
Nueva Pompeya, ngh., Arg. 206 34.39 S 58.25 W
Nueva Rosita, Mex. 154 A8 27.57 N 101.13 W
Nueva San Salvador, El Sal. 156 F3 13.41 N 89.17 W
Nueva Toltén, Chile 166 G2 39.12 S 73.13 W
Nueve, Canal Numero, can., Arg. 172 H8 36.07 S 57.16 W
Nueve de Julio, Arg. 172 G7 35.27 S 60.53 W
Nuevitas, Cuba 156 B9 21.32 N 77.16 W
Nuevo, Bajo, unds., Col. 156 E8 15.54 N 78.34 W
Nuevo, Cayo, i., Mex. 154 E12 21.50 N 92.05 W
Nuevo, Golfo, b., Arg. 166 H4 42.42 S 64.36 W
Nuevo Berlín, Ur. 172 F8 32.59 S 58.03 W
Nuevo Camarón, Mex. 136 G8 27.07 N 99.59 W
Nuevo Casas Grandes, Mex. 120 F9 30.24 N 107.54 W
Nuevo Delicias, Mex. 154 B7 26.14 N 102.48 W
Nuevo Laredo, Mex. 154 B9 27.28 N 99.30 W
Nuevo León, state, Mex. 154 B8 25.40 N 100.00 W
Nuevo Poblado el Oro, Mex. 136 H6 26.50 N 101.19 W

Name Page Map Ref. Latitude Longitude

Nuevo Primero de Mayo, Mex. 136 H9 26.01 N 98.01 W
Nuevo Progreso, Mex. 154 F12 18.36 N 92.17 W
Nuevo Rocafuerte, Ec. 168 H4 0.56 S 75.24 W
Nuevo San Lucas, Mex. 136 F2 28.21 N 105.34 W
Nuevo Saucillo, Mex. 136 G3 27.19 N 104.54 W
Nufcor, S. Afr. 191d 26.17 S 27.44 E
Nugrus, Gebel, mtn., Egypt 74 H4 24.51 N 34.38 E
Nûgssuaq, pen., Grnld. 108 C15 70.25 N 52.30 W
Nugu, res., India 69 F3 11.57 N 76.26 E
Nūh, Rās, c., Pak. 62 C1 25.05 N 62.22 E
Nuha see Şeki, Azer. 42 E12 41.09 N 47.10 E
Nui, at., Tuvalu 94 D8 7.15 S 177.10 E
Nuia, Est. 26 B8 58.04 N 25.33 E
Nuku'alofa, Tonga 100e n14 21.08 S 175.12 W
Nukuhu, Pap. N. Gui. 101a b4 5.34 S 149.20 E
Nukunuku, Tonga 100e n13 21.07 S 175.18 W
Nukus, Uzb. 48 F9 42.28 N 59.35 E
Nul, Vanuatu 101d k17 16.47 S 168.23 E
Nulato, Ak., U.S. 109 D8 64.43 N 158.06 W
Nullagine, Austl. 96 D4 21.53 S 120.07 E
Nullarbor, Austl. 96 F6 31.26 S 130.53 E
Nullarbor Plain, pl., Austl. 96 F5 31.00 S 129.00 E
Numan, Nig. 84 H7 9.27 N 12.01 E
Numancia (Numantia), hist., Spain 28 C8 41.48 N 2.26 W
Numantia see Numancia, hist., Spain 28 C8 41.48 N 2.26 W
Numata, Japan 56 C12 36.38 N 139.03 E
Numazu, Japan 56 D11 35.06 N 138.52 E
Numedalen, val., Nor. 16 G6 60.06 N 9.06 E
Numfoor, Pulau, i., Indon. 60 F10 1.03 S 134.54 E
Numto, Russia 48 B12 63.31 N 71.20 E
Numurkah, Austl. 98 K5 36.05 S 145.26 E
Nunavut, state, Can. 110 B12 70.00 N 95.00 W
Nunda, N.Y., U.S. 124 B7 42.34 N 77.56 W
Nuneaton, Eng., U.K. 10 I11 52.31 N 1.28 W
Núñez, ngh., Arg. 206 34.33 S 58.27 W
Nuñez, Cape, c., S. Geor. 166 J9 54.15 S 37.24 W
Nunivak Island, i., Ak., U.S. 109 D6 60.00 N 166.29 W
Nunjiang, China 52 B10 49.10 N 125.14 E
Nunkun, mtn., India 70 A6 33.59 N 76.01 E
Nunnanen, Fin. 14 D15 68.24 N 24.30 E
Nunnelly, Tn., U.S. 130 I10 35.52 N 87.28 W
Ñuñoa, Chile 204e 33.28 S 70.36 W
Nuomin, stm., China 52 B10 48.13 N 124.31 E
Nuorgam, Fin. 14 B18 70.04 N 27.54 E
Nuoro, Italy 32 D3 40.19 N 9.20 E
Nuorttijoki see Nota, stm., Eur. 14 D20 68.09 N 30.15 E
Nuquí, Col. 168 E3 5.41 N 77.16 W
Nura, Kaz. 48 E12 48.53 N 62.19 E
Nura, stm., Kaz. 48 E12 50.22 N 69.15 E
Nur Dağları, mts., Tur. 76 B7 36.45 N 36.20 E
Nurek, Taj. 48 G11 38.23 N 69.20 E
Nuremberg see Nürnberg, Ger. 24 G6 49.27 N 11.03 E
Nuremburg see Nürnberg, Ger. 24 G6 49.27 N 11.03 E
Nuriootpa, Austl. 98 J2 34.28 S 138.59 E
Nurlat, Russia 40 D17 54.25 N 50.47 E
Nurlaty, Russia 40 D16 55.36 N 48.16 E
Nurmes, Fin. 18 D15 63.33 N 29.02 E
Nurmijärvi, Fin. 18 G11 60.28 N 24.48 E
Nürnberg (Nuremberg), Ger. 24 G6 49.27 N 11.03 E
Nūrpur, India 70 B5 32.18 N 75.54 E
Nursery, Tx., U.S. 136 F10 28.56 N 97.06 W
Nürtingen, Ger. 24 H5 48.37 N 9.20 E
Nusa Tenggara Barat, state, Indon. 66 G10 8.50 S 117.30 E
Nusa Tenggara Timur, state, Indon. 66 H12 9.04 S 120.29 E
Nusaybin, Tur. 42 G9 37.06 N 41.13 E
Nuṣayrīyah, Jabal an-, mts., Syria 76 C7 35.30 N 36.12 E
Nushagak, stm., Ak., U.S. 109 E8 59.03 N 158.24 W
Nu Shan, mts., China 52 F4 27.00 N 99.00 E
Nüshan Hu, l., China 58 E8 32.57 N 118.03 E
Nushki, Pak. 62 C2 29.34 N 66.03 E
Nussdorf, ngh., Aus. 182b 48.15 N 16.22 E
Nutfield, Eng., U.K. 178 51.14 N 0.07 W
Nut Lake Indian Reserve, ind. res., Sk., Can. 142 B10 52.23 N 103.40 W
Nutrioso, Az., U.S. 150 J7 33.56 N 109.10 W
Nut Swamp Brook, stm., N.J., U.S. 194 40.21 N 74.06 W
Nuttby Mountain, hill, N.S., Can. 122 E13 45.33 N 63.13 W
Nutter Fort, W.V., U.S. 124 E5 39.15 N 80.18 W
Nutting Lake, l., Ma., U.S. 201 42.32 N 71.16 W
Nuuk see Godthåb, Grnld. 108 E15 64.11 N 51.44 W
Nuupere, Pointe, c., Fr. Poly. 100h v20 17.35 S 149.49 W
Nuwākot, Nepal 70 D9 28.07 N 83.53 E
Nuweiba, Egypt 76 J5 28.58 N 34.38 E
Nuwerus, S. Afr. 90 G4 31.08 S 18.22 E
Nuweveldberge, mts., S. Afr. 90 H6 32.14 S 21.48 E
Nūzvīd, India 69 C5 16.47 N 80.51 E
Nyabéssan, Cam. 86 D2 2.24 N 10.23 E
Nyabing, Austl. 96 F3 33.32 S 118.08 E
Nyack, N.Y., U.S. 124 C12 41.06 N 73.56 W
Nyack Beach State Park, p.o.i., N.Y., U.S. 194 41.07 N 73.55 W
Nyahanga, Tan. 86 E6 2.26 S 33.32 E
Nyah West, Austl. 98 J4 35.12 S 143.23 E
Nyainqêntanglha Feng, mtn., China 52 E3 30.22 N 90.35 E
Nyainqêntanglha Shan, mts., China 62 C6 30.00 N 90.00 E
Nyainrong, China 62 E3 32.01 N 92.24 E
Nyakanazi, Tan. 86 E6 3.03 S 31.12 E
Nyala, Sudan 82 E5 12.03 N 24.53 E
Nyalam, China 70 D10 28.10 N 85.58 E
Nyamandhlovu, Zimb. 88 D4 19.52 S 28.15 E
Nyamlell, Sudan 82 F5 9.08 N 26.58 E
Nyamtumbo, Tan. 86 G7 10.30 S 36.05 E
Nyang, stm., China 70 D14 29.58 N 92.56 E
Nyanga, stm., Afr. 84 J7 2.58 S 10.18 E
Nyanza-Lac, Bdi. 86 E5 4.19 S 29.37 E
Nyasa, Lake, l., Afr. 88 C5 12.00 S 34.30 E
Nyasaland see Malawi, ctry., Afr. 88 C5 13.30 S 34.00 E
Nyaunglebin, Mya. 64 C3 17.57 N 96.43 E
Nybergsund, Nor. 16 F10 61.16 N 12.19 E
Nyboe Land, reg., Grnld. 108 A14 81.55 N 55.54 W
Nyborg, Den. 16 L8 55.19 N 10.47 E
Nybro, Swe. 16 K13 56.44 N 15.54 E
Nyda, Russia 48 A12 66.37 N 72.56 E
Nyêmo, China 62 C7 29.22 N 90.10 E
Nyeri, Kenya 86 E7 0.25 S 36.56 E
Nyerol, Sudan 82 F6 8.40 N 32.01 E
Nyika Plateau, plat., Mwi. 88 C5 10.40 S 33.50 E
Nyimba, Zam. 88 C5 14.32 S 30.48 E
Nyingchi, China 52 F3 29.33 N 94.30 E
Nyíradony, Hung. 36 B8 47.41 N 21.54 E
Nyírbátor, Hung. 36 B9 47.50 N 22.08 E
Nyíregyháza, Hung. 36 B8 47.57 N 21.43 E
Nykarleby, Fin. 18 D9 63.31 N 22.32 E
Nykøbing, Den. 16 M9 54.46 N 11.52 E
Nykøbing Sjælland, Den. 16 L9 55.55 N 11.40 E
Nyköping, Swe. 16 I14 58.45 N 17.00 E
Nykroppa, Swe. 16 H12 59.37 N 14.18 E
Nyland, Swe. 18 E4 63.00 N 17.45 E
Nyland see Uusimaa, state, Fin. 18 G11 60.30 N 25.00 E
Nylstroom, S. Afr. 90 D9 24.42 S 28.25 E
Nymagee, Austl. 98 I6 32.04 S 146.19 E
Nymboida, stm., Austl. 98 G9 29.39 S 152.30 E
Nymburk, Czech Rep. 24 F11 50.11 N 15.02 E
Nynäshamn, Swe. 16 I15 58.55 N 17.57 E
Nyngan, Austl. 98 H6 31.33 S 147.10 E
Nyoma, India 70 B7 33.11 N 78.38 E
Nyon, Switz. 30 D3 46.23 N 6.13 E
Nyons, Fr. 22 E11 44.21 N 5.07 E
Nyrov, Russia 48 B9 60.42 N 56.42 E
Nýrsko, Czech Rep. 24 G9 49.17 N 13.08 E
Nyrud, Nor. 14 C20 69.09 N 29.13 E
Nyš, Russia 50 F17 51.30 N 142.43 E
Nysa, Pol. 24 F13 50.28 N 17.21 E
Nysa Kłodzka, stm., Pol. 24 F12 50.49 N 17.39 E
Nysa Łużycka (Lausitzer Neisse), stm., Eur. 24 E10 52.04 N 14.45 E
Nyslott see Savonlinna, Fin. 18 F15 61.52 N 28.54 E
Nyssa, Or., U.S. 146 G9 43.53 N 116.59 W
Nystad see Uusikaupunki, Fin. 18 G8 60.48 N 21.25 E
Nysted, Den. 16 M9 54.40 N 11.44 E
Nytva, Russia 40 C19 57.56 N 55.19 E
Nyugati Pályaudvar, trans., Hung. 182c 47.31 N 19.04 E
Nyunzu, D.R.C. 86 F5 5.57 S 28.01 E
Nyuri, India 70 E14 27.42 N 92.13 E
Nyūzen, Japan 56 C10 36.54 N 137.29 E
Nyvrovo, Russia 50 F17 54.18 N 142.37 E
Nyzhankovychi, Ukr. 38 D1 49.40 N 22.49 E
Nyzhnia Duvanka, Ukr. 38 D17 49.35 N 38.10 E
Nyzhnii Rohachyk, Ukr. 38 F13 47.21 N 34.02 E
Nyzhni Sirohozy, Ukr. 38 G13 46.50 N 34.22 E
Nyzhn'ohirs'kyi, Ukr. 38 H13 45.27 N 34.44 E
Nyzy, Ukr. 38 C13 50.47 N 34.49 E
Nzaba, Congo 191b 4.06 S 15.16 E
Nzébéla, Gui. 84 H3 8.04 N 9.05 W
Nzérékoré, Gui. 84 H3 7.45 N 8.49 W
N'zeto, Ang. 88 B1 7.14 S 12.52 E
Nzwani, i., Com. 88 C7 12.15 S 44.25 E

O

Oacoma, S.D., U.S. 140 D13 43.48 N 99.24 W
Oad Street, Eng., U.K. 178 51.20 N 0.41 E
Oahe, Lake, res., U.S. 140 B12 45.28 N 100.20 W
Oahe Dam, dam., S.D., U.S. 140 C12 44.21 N 100.23 W
Oahu, i., Hi., U.S. 100a b4 21.30 N 158.00 W
Oak, stm., Mb., Can. 142 E13 49.50 N 100.29 W
Oakbank, Austl. 98 I3 33.03 S 140.35 E
Oak Bay, B.C., Can. 144 H7 48.26 N 123.17 W
Oak Beach, N.Y., U.S. 194 40.38 N 73.17 W
Oak Bluffs, Ma., U.S. 124 C15 41.27 N 70.34 W
Oak Brook, Il., U.S. 196 41.49 N 87.55 W
Oakbrook Center, shp. cen., Il., U.S. 196 41.52 N 87.57 W
Oakbrook Terrace, Il., U.S. 196 41.52 N 87.58 W
Oakburn, Mb., Can. 142 D13 50.33 N 100.34 W
Oak City, N.C., U.S. 124 I8 35.57 N 77.18 W
Oak City, Ut., U.S. 150 D4 39.22 N 112.20 W
Oak Creek, Co., U.S. 150 C9 40.16 N 106.57 W
Oak Creek, stm., U.S. 140 B12 45.35 N 100.26 W
Oak Creek, stm., Az., U.S. 150 I5 34.40 N 111.56 W
Oak Creek, stm., Co., U.S. 150 C10 40.23 N 106.49 W
Oak Creek, stm., Ks., U.S. 138 B10 39.29 N 98.28 W
Oak Creek, stm., N.D., U.S. 142 F13 48.38 N 100.24 W
Oak Creek, stm., Tx., U.S. 136 C7 31.48 N 100.13 W
Oakdale, Ca., U.S. 148 F5 37.46 N 120.50 W
Oakdale, La., U.S. 134 G6 30.48 N 92.39 W
Oakdale, Ne., U.S. 140 E14 42.03 N 97.58 W
Oakdale, N.J., U.S. 203 39.59 N 74.49 W
Oakdale, Tn., U.S. 130 I13 35.59 N 84.33 W
Oakdale Woods, Il., U.S. 196 41.56 N 87.58 W
Oakes, N.D., U.S. 140 A14 46.08 N 98.05 W
Oakesdale, Wa., U.S. 146 C9 47.07 N 117.14 W
Oakey, Austl. 98 F8 27.25 S 151.43 E
Oakeys Brook, stm., N.J., U.S. 194 40.25 N 74.30 W
Oakfield, Me., U.S. 122 D8 46.06 N 68.09 W
Oakfield, N.Y., U.S. 126 E11 43.04 N 78.15 W
Oakfield, Wi., U.S. 128 H10 43.41 N 88.32 W
Oakgrove, Eng., U.K. 180 53.13 N 2.07 W
Oak Grove, La., U.S. 134 E7 32.51 N 91.23 W
Oak Harbor, Wa., U.S. 146 B4 48.17 N 122.39 W
Oak Hill, De., U.S. 203 39.44 N 75.36 W
Oak Hill, Fl., U.S. 132 H5 28.51 N 80.51 W
Oak Hill, Mi., U.S. 126 D3 44.13 N 86.18 W
Oak Hill, Oh., U.S. 124 F3 38.53 N 82.30 W
Oak Hill, W.V., U.S. 124 G4 37.58 N 81.08 W
Oakhurst, Ca., U.S. 148 F6 37.18 N 119.38 W
Oakhurst, Tx., U.S. 136 D12 30.43 N 95.18 W
Oak Island, i., N.Y., U.S. 194 40.39 N 73.18 W
Oak Knolls, Ca., U.S. 148 I5 34.52 N 120.25 W
Oak Lake, Mb., Can. 142 E13 49.46 N 100.38 W
Oak Lake, l., Mb., Can. 142 E13 49.40 N 100.45 W
Oak Lake, l., On., Can. 128 A5 50.26 N 93.50 W
Oakland, Ca., U.S. 148 F3 37.48 N 122.16 W
Oakland, Ca., U.S. 200 37.48 N 122.16 W
Oakland, Il., U.S. 130 E9 39.38 N 88.02 W
Oakland, Ia., U.S. 130 C2 41.18 N 95.23 W
Oakland, Me., U.S. 122 F7 44.32 N 69.43 W
Oakland, Md., U.S. 124 E6 39.24 N 79.24 W
Oakland, Md., U.S. 202c 38.51 N 76.55 W
Oakland, Ms., U.S. 134 C9 34.03 N 89.54 W
Oakland, Ne., U.S. 130 C1 41.50 N 96.28 W
Oakland, Or., U.S. 146 G3 43.25 N 123.17 W
Oakland, ngh., Pa., U.S. 197b 40.26 N 79.58 W
Oakland-Alameda County Coliseum, p.o.i., Ca., U.S. 200 37.45 N 122.12 W
Oakland Army Base, mil., Ca., U.S. 200 37.49 N 122.19 W
Oakland City, In., U.S. 130 F10 38.20 N 87.21 W
Oakland Gardens, ngh., N.Y., U.S. 194 40.45 N 73.45 W
Oakland Mall, shp. cen., Mi., U.S. 199 42.32 N 83.07 W
Oakland Park, Fl., U.S. 132 J5 26.10 N 80.08 W
Oakland-Pontiac Airport, arpt., Mi., U.S. 199 42.40 N 83.24 W
Oaklands, ngh., S. Afr. 191d 26.09 S 28.04 E
Oakland Southwest Airport, arpt., Mi., U.S. 199 42.30 N 83.37 W
Oakland University, educ., Mi., U.S. 199 42.41 N 83.13 W
Oak Lane Manor, De., U.S. 203 39.47 N 75.32 W
Oak Lawn, Il., U.S. 130 C10 41.43 N 87.44 W
Oaklawn, Ks., U.S. 138 D11 37.36 N 97.17 W
Oaklawn, Md., U.S. 202c 38.47 N 76.57 W
Oakleigh South, Austl. 192b 37.56 S 145.05 E
Oakley, Id., U.S. 146 H13 42.15 N 113.52 W
Oakley, Ks., U.S. 138 B8 39.07 N 100.51 W
Oaklyn, N.J., U.S. 203 39.54 N 75.05 W
Oakman, Al., U.S. 134 D11 33.42 N 87.23 W
Oak Mountain State Park, p.o.i., Al., U.S. 134 D12 33.22 N 86.41 W
Oakmulgee Creek, stm., Al., U.S. 134 E11 32.28 N 87.09 W
Oak Neck, pen., N.Y., U.S. 194 40.54 N 73.34 W
Oak Neck Point, c., N.Y., U.S. 194 40.55 N 73.34 W
Oakohay Creek, stm., Ms., U.S. 134 F9 31.44 N 89.25 W
Oakover, stm., Austl. 96 D4 20.43 S 120.33 E
Oak Park, Austl. 192b 37.43 S 144.55 E
Oak Park, Il., U.S. 130 C10 41.53 N 87.47 W
Oak Park, Pa., U.S. 203 40.15 N 75.18 W
Oak Point, Mb., Can. 142 D15 50.30 N 98.01 W
Oakridge, Or., U.S. 146 G4 43.45 N 122.27 W
Oak Ridge, Tn., U.S. 124 H1 36.01 N 84.14 W
Oak Ridge Lake, N.J., U.S. 194 41.00 N 74.32 W
Oak Ridge National Laboratory, sci., Tn., U.S. 124 H1 36.00 N 84.15 W
Oak Ridge Reservoir, res., N.J., U.S. 194 41.03 N 74.30 W
Oaks, Pa., U.S. 203 40.08 N 81.28 W
Oak Shades, N.J., U.S. 194 40.26 N 74.13 W
Oakton, Va., U.S. 202c 38.52 N 77.18 W
Oaktown, In., U.S. 130 F10 38.52 N 87.26 W
Oak Valley, Va., U.S. 202c 38.54 N 77.18 W
Oak View, Ca., U.S. 148 I6 34.23 N 119.18 W
Oak View, Md., U.S. 202c 39.01 N 76.59 W
Oakview, N.J., U.S. 203 39.51 N 75.09 W
Oakville, Mb., Can. 142 E15 49.56 N 97.58 W
Oakville, On., Can. 126 E10 43.26 N 79.39 W
Oakwood, N.J., U.S. 203 39.52 N 74.50 W
Oakwood, Oh., U.S. 124 C1 41.05 N 84.22 W
Oakwood, Tx., U.S. 136 C12 31.34 N 95.51 W
Oakwood Park, p.o.i., Oh., U.S. 197a 41.26 N 82.06 W
Oamaru, N.Z. 102 G4 45.05 S 170.57 E
Ōana, Japan 186 35.45 N 140.04 E
Oancea, Rom. 36 D15 45.55 N 28.06 E
Ōarai, Japan 56 C13 36.18 N 140.34 E
Oatka Creek, stm., N.Y., U.S. 126 F11 43.01 N 77.43 W
Oatlands, Austl. 99a o13 42.18 S 147.21 E
Oatley, Austl. 192a 33.59 S 151.05 E
Oatley Park, p.o.i., Austl. 192a 33.59 S 151.04 E
Oatman, Az., U.S. 150 H2 35.01 N 114.22 W
Oaxaca, state, Mex. 154 G10 17.00 N 96.30 W
Oaxaca de Juárez, Mex. 154 G10 17.03 N 96.43 W
Ob', stm., Russia 48 A11 66.46 N 68.55 E
Obabika Lake, l., On., Can. 126 A9 47.04 N 80.16 W
Obal', Bela. 26 E12 55.21 N 29.18 E
Obal', stm., Bela. 26 E12 55.21 N 29.14 E
Obala, Cam. 86 D2 4.10 N 11.32 E
Obama, Japan 56 G3 32.42 N 130.13 E
Obama, Japan 56 D8 35.30 N 135.45 E
Oban, Austl. 98 C2 21.14 S 139.06 E
Oban, Scot., U.K. 10 E7 56.24 N 5.28 W
Obanazawa, Japan 56 A13 38.36 N 140.24 E
Obando, Phil. 187f 14.43 N 120.56 E
O Barco de Valdeorras, Spain 28 B4 42.25 N 6.59 W
Ob Bay see Obskaja guba, b., Russia 48 A12 69.00 N 73.00 E
Obbola, Swe. 16 D18 63.41 N 20.18 E
Obed, Ab., Can. 138 C13 53.32 N 117.15 W
Obed, stm., Tn., U.S. 130 H13 36.04 N 84.40 W
Obedjiwan, Réserve indienne, ind. res., Qc., Can. 122 B1 48.40 N 74.56 W
Obeliai, Lith. 26 E8 55.56 N 25.46 E
Oberá, Arg. 172 C10 27.29 S 55.08 W
Oberbauer, Ger. 181 51.17 N 7.26 E
Oberbonsfeld, Ger. 181 51.22 N 7.08 E
Oberbrügge, Ger. 181 51.11 N 7.34 E
Oberelfringhausen, Ger. 181 51.20 N 7.11 E
Oberhaan, Ger. 181 51.13 N 7.02 E
Oberhausen, Ger. 24 E2 51.27 N 6.51 E
Ober-Kassel, ngh., Ger. 181 51.14 N 6.46 E
Oberkirchbach, Aus. 182b 48.17 N 16.12 E
Oberlaa, ngh., Aus. 182b 48.08 N 16.24 E
Oberlaapark, p.o.i., Aus. 182b 48.08 N 16.25 E
Oberlin, Ks., U.S. 138 B8 39.49 N 100.31 W
Oberlin, La., U.S. 134 G6 30.36 N 92.46 W
Oberlin, Oh., U.S. 124 C3 41.17 N 82.12 W
Obernai, Fr. 24 H3 48.27 N 7.29 E
Obernburg am Main, Ger. 24 G5 49.49 N 9.08 E
Oberon, Austl. 98 I7 33.42 S 149.51 E
Oberösterreich, state, Aus. 30 B10 48.15 N 14.00 E
Oberpfälzer Wald see Bohemian Forest, mts., Eur. 24 G8 48.53 N 13.51 E
Oberpullendorf, Aus. 30 C13 47.30 N 16.31 E
Ober Sankt Veit, ngh., Aus. 182b 48.11 N 16.16 E
Oberschöneweide, ngh., Ger. 182a 52.28 N 13.31 E
Obertyn, Ukr. 38 E4 48.42 N 25.10 E
Oberursel, Ger. 24 F4 50.12 N 8.35 E
Obervellach, Aus. 30 D10 46.56 N 13.12 E
Oberviechtach, Ger. 24 G8 49.27 N 12.25 E
Oberwengern, Ger. 181 51.23 N 7.22 E
Obey, East Fork, stm., Tn., U.S. 130 H12 36.27 N 85.08 W
Obey, West Fork, stm., Tn., U.S. 134 A13 36.27 N 85.08 W
Obgruiten, Ger. 181 51.13 N 7.01 E
Obi, Kepulauan, is., Indon. 60 F8 1.27 S 127.38 E
Obi, Pulau, i., Indon. 60 F8 1.30 S 127.45 E
Obi, Selat, strt., Indon. 60 F8 0.57 S 127.29 E
Óbidos, Braz. 164 D6 1.54 S 55.30 W
Obihiro, Japan 54 C15 42.55 N 143.12 E
Obi Islands see Obi, Kepulauan, is., Indon. 60 F8 1.27 S 127.38 E
Obikhody, Ukr. 38 B7 51.02 N 28.59 E
Obing, Ger. 24 H8 48.01 N 12.22 E
Obion, Tn., U.S. 130 H8 36.15 N 89.11 W
Obion, stm., Tn., U.S. 130 H8 35.54 N 89.38 W
Obion, Middle Fork, stm., Tn., U.S. 130 H9 36.12 N 88.56 W
Obion, Rutherford Fork, stm., Tn., U.S. 134 B10 36.16 N 89.01 W
Obion, South Fork, stm., Tn., U.S. 130 H9 36.16 N 89.01 W
Oblačnaja, gora, mtn., Russia 54 C11 43.45 N 134.10 E
Oblivskaja, Russia 40 G13 48.32 N 42.30 E
Oblong, Il., U.S. 130 F10 39.00 N 87.54 W
Obluče, Russia 50 G15 49.00 N 131.03 E
Obninsk, Russia 26 E19 55.05 N 36.37 E
Obnova, Blg. 36 F12 43.26 N 25.00 E
Obo, C.A.R. 86 C5 5.23 N 26.29 E
Obock, Dji. 82 E8 11.58 N 43.15 E
Obojan', Russia 40 F10 51.12 N 36.16 E
Obokote, D.R.C. 86 E5 0.52 S 26.16 E
Oboldino, Russia 183b 55.53 N 37.56 E
Obolon', Ukr. 38 D11 49.36 N 32.53 E
Oborniki, Pol. 24 D12 52.38 N 16.49 E
Obozërskij, Russia 18 D27 63.27 N 40.19 E
Obra, stm., Pol. 24 D11 52.36 N 15.28 E
Obrenovac, Yugo. 36 E7 44.39 N 20.12 E
O'Brien, Or., U.S. 148 A2 42.03 N 123.41 W
O'Brien Coulee, stm., Mt., U.S. 146 B16 48.38 N 110.22 W
Obrovac, Cro. 30 F12 44.11 N 15.40 E
Obša, stm., Russia 26 E16 55.55 N 32.32 E
Obščij syrt, mts., Eur. 40 F17 52.00 N 51.30 E
Observation Peak, mtn., Ca., U.S. 148 C5 40.46 N 120.10 W
Obskaja guba, b., Russia 48 A12 69.00 N 73.00 E
Obtove, Ukr. 38 B12 51.37 N 33.12 E
Obu, ngh., Japan 188 34.44 N 135.09 E
Obuasi, Ghana 84 H4 6.13 N 1.40 W
Óbuda, ngh., Hung. 182c 47.33 N 19.02 E
Óbudai-sziget, i., Hung. 182c 47.33 N 19.04 E
Obudu, Nig. 84 H6 6.39 N 9.09 E
Obuhova, Russia 26 D15 56.05 N 32.22 E
Obukhiv, Ukr. 38 C9 50.07 N 30.37 E
Obukhovychi, Ukr. 38 B8 50.59 N 29.46 E
Obu-tōge, p., Japan 188 34.44 N 135.10 E
Obva, stm., Russia 40 B19 58.32 N 55.27 E
Obvinsk, Russia 40 B19 58.28 N 54.48 E
Obytichna kosa, spit, Ukr. 38 G15 46.35 N 36.15 E
Obytichna zatoka, b., Ukr. 38 G14 46.32 N 35.54 E
Očakovo, ngh., Russia 183b 55.41 N 37.27 E
Ocala, Fl., U.S. 132 G3 29.11 N 82.08 W
Ocallí, Peru 164 E2 6.09 S 78.18 W
Očamčira, Geor. 42 D9 42.42 N 41.28 E
Ocamo, stm., Ven. 168 F9 2.48 N 65.14 W
Ocampo, Mex. 154 B7 27.20 N 102.20 W
Ocampo, Mex. 154 A4 28.11 N 108.23 W
Ocaña, Col. 168 C5 8.14 N 73.21 W
Ocaña, Spain 28 E7 39.57 N 3.30 W
Ocate Creek, stm., N.M., U.S. 138 E4 36.14 N 104.27 W
Occhito, Lago di, res., Italy 32 C8 41.34 N 14.56 E
Occidental, Cordillera, mts., Col. 168 E3 5.00 N 76.00 W
Occidental College, educ., Ca., U.S. 198 34.08 N 118.13 W
Oceana, W.V., U.S. 124 G4 37.41 N 81.37 W
Oceana Naval Air Station, mil., Va., U.S. 124 H10 36.47 N 75.59 W
Ocean Bay Park, N.Y., U.S. 194 40.39 N 73.08 W
Ocean Beach, N.Y., U.S. 194 40.38 N 73.18 W
Ocean Cape, c., Ak., U.S. 109 E12 59.32 N 139.50 W
Ocean City, Md., U.S. 124 F10 38.19 N 75.05 W
Ocean City, N.J., U.S. 124 E11 39.16 N 74.34 W
Ocean Falls, B.C., Can. 144 D3 52.21 N 127.40 W
Ocean Island see Banaba, i., Kir. 94 D7 0.51 S 169.32 E
Ocean Lake, l., Wy., U.S. 140 D4 43.11 N 108.36 W
Oceano, Ca., U.S. 148 H5 35.06 N 120.36 W
Ocean Park, Wa., U.S. 146 D2 46.29 N 124.02 W
Ocean Park, p.o.i., China 189d 22.15 N 114.09 E
Ocean Port, N.J., U.S. 194 40.19 N 74.00 W
Oceanside, Ca., U.S. 148 J8 33.12 N 117.21 W
Ocean Springs, Ms., U.S. 134 G10 30.24 N 88.49 W
Očer, Russia 40 C19 57.53 N 54.43 E
O. C. Fisher Lake, res., Tx., U.S. 136 C7 31.30 N 100.30 W
Ochagavía, Canal, can., Chile 204e 33.30 S 70.49 W
Ochakiv, Ukr. 38 G10 46.37 N 31.33 E
Očhamuri, Geor. 42 E9 41.52 N 41.50 E
Ochanomizu University, educ., Japan 186 35.43 N 139.44 E
Ochapowace Indian Reserve, ind. res., Sk., Can. 142 D11 50.30 N 102.24 W
Ocheyedan, Ia., U.S. 128 H3 43.25 N 95.32 W
Ocheyedan, stm., U.S. 128 H3 43.08 N 95.09 W
Ōchi, Japan 56 E7 34.14 N 134.20 E
Ochiai, ngh., Japan 186 35.43 N 139.42 E
O'Chiese Indian Reserve, ind. res., Ab., Can. 144 D15 52.50 N 115.23 W
Ochlocknee, Ga., U.S. 132 F1 30.58 N 84.03 W
Ochlockonee, stm., U.S. 116 E10 29.58 N 84.26 W
Ochoco Creek, stm., Or., U.S. 146 F6 44.19 N 120.53 W
Ochoco Mountains, mts., Or., U.S. 146 F6 44.30 N 120.35 W
Ocho Rios, Jam. 158d i13 18.23 N 77.06 W
Ochre River, Mb., Can. 142 C14 51.03 N 99.46 W
Ochsenfurt, Ger. 24 G5 49.40 N 10.03 E
Ocilla, Ga., U.S. 132 E2 31.35 N 83.14 W
Ockelbo, Swe. 16 G14 60.53 N 16.43 E
Öckerö, Swe. 16 J9 57.43 N 11.38 E
Ockham, Eng., U.K. 178 51.18 N 0.27 W
Ocmulgee National Monument, p.o.i., Ga., U.S. 132 D2 32.43 N 83.38 W
Ocna Mureș, Rom. 36 C10 46.23 N 23.52 E
Ocnița, Mol. 38 E6 48.24 N 27.31 E
Ocoa, Bahía de, b., Dom. Rep. 156 C12 18.22 N 70.39 W
Ocoee, Fl., U.S. 132 H4 28.34 N 81.32 W
Ocoee (Toccoa), stm., U.S. 134 B14 35.12 N 84.40 W
Ocoña, stm., Peru 164 G3 16.25 S 73.07 W
Oconee, stm., Ga., U.S. 132 D3 31.58 N 82.32 W
Oconee, Lake, res., Ga., U.S. 132 C2 33.28 N 83.16 W
Oconomowoc, Wi., U.S. 130 A9 43.06 N 88.29 W
Oconto, Wi., U.S. 126 D2 44.53 N 87.52 W
Oconto, stm., Wi., U.S. 126 D1 44.53 N 87.49 W
Oconto, North Branch, stm., Wi., U.S. 128 F10 44.59 N 88.22 W
Oconto Falls, Wi., U.S. 126 D1 44.52 N 88.07 W
Ocosingo, Mex. 154 G12 16.54 N 92.06 W
Ocotal, Nic. 156 F4 13.38 N 86.27 W
Ocotes, Cerro, mtn., Mex. 154 B5 25.58 N 106.08 W
Ocotlán, Mex. 154 E7 20.21 N 102.46 W
Ocotlán de Morelos, Mex. 154 G10 16.47 N 96.40 W
Ocozocuautla, Mex. 154 G12 16.46 N 93.21 W
Ocracoke, N.C., U.S. 132 A9 35.06 N 75.59 W
Ocracoke Island, i., N.C., U.S. 132 A10 35.06 N 75.58 W
Ocumare del Tuy, Ven. 168 B8 10.06 N 66.46 W
Oda, Ghana 84 H4 5.56 N 0.58 W
Ōda, Japan 56 D5 35.11 N 132.30 E
Oda, Jabal, mtn., Sudan 82 C7 20.21 N 36.39 E
Ōdaigahara-zan, mtn., Japan 56 E9 34.11 N 136.06 E
Odaka, Japan 56 B14 37.34 N 141.00 E
Ōdate, Japan 54 D14 40.15 N 140.33 E
Odawara, Japan 56 D12 35.15 N 139.10 E
Odayeri, ngh., Tur. 185b 41.14 N 28.51 E
Odda, Nor. 16 G4 60.04 N 6.32 E
Odder, Den. 16 L8 55.58 N 10.09 E
Odebolt, Ia., U.S. 130 B2 42.18 N 95.15 W
Odeleite, stm., Port. 28 G3 37.20 N 7.26 W
Odell, Il., U.S. 130 D9 41.00 N 88.30 W
Odell, Ne., U.S. 138 A12 40.02 N 96.47 W
Odell, Tx., U.S. 138 G9 34.20 N 99.25 W
Odem, Tx., U.S. 136 G10 27.56 N 97.34 W
Odemira, Port. 28 G2 37.35 N 8.38 W
Ödemiş, Tur. 34 E10 38.14 N 27.58 E
Ödenburg see Sopron, Hung. 36 B3 47.41 N 16.36 E
Odendaalsrus, S. Afr. 90 E8 27.52 S 26.41 E
Odense, Den. 16 L8 55.23 N 10.23 E
Odenwald, mts., Ger. 24 G5 49.36 N 8.55 E
Oder (Odra), stm., Eur. 24 D10 53.55 N 14.16 E
Oder, stm., Ger. 20 C19 51.40 N 10.06 E
Oderberg, Ger. 24 D9 52.52 N 14.02 E
Oderbucht see Pomeranian Bay, b., Eur. 24 B10 54.04 N 14.19 E
Oderzo, Italy 30 E9 45.46 N 12.29 E
Odesa, Ukr. 38 G9 46.28 N 30.41 E
Odesa, co., Ukr. 38 G9 47.30 N 30.00 E
Ödeshög, Swe. 16 I12 58.13 N 14.39 E
Odessa, On., Can. 126 D13 44.17 N 76.43 W
Odessa see Odesa, Ukr. 38 G9 46.28 N 30.41 E
Odessa, Mo., U.S. 130 F3 38.59 N 93.57 W
Odessa, Tx., U.S. 136 C5 31.50 N 102.22 W
Odessa, Wa., U.S. 146 C8 47.19 N 118.41 W
Odesskoe, Russia 48 D12 54.12 N 72.58 E
Odet, stm., Fr. 20 F4 47.58 N 4.06 W
Odiel, stm., Spain 28 G4 37.19 N 6.58 W
Odienné, C. Iv. 84 H3 9.29 N 7.33 W
Odin, Mount, mtn., B.C., Can. 144 F12 50.33 N 118.08 W
Odincovo, Russia 26 E20 55.39 N 37.16 E
Odivelas, Port. 184c 38.47 N 9.11 W
Odobești, Rom. 36 D13 45.45 N 27.04 E
Odoev, Russia 26 G19 53.56 N 36.41 E
Odolanów, Pol. 24 E13 51.34 N 17.40 E
Odon, In., U.S. 130 F11 38.50 N 86.59 W
Ŏdŏngk, Camb. 64 G7 11.48 N 104.44 E
O'Donnell, Tx., U.S. 136 B6 32.57 N 101.49 W
Odorheiu Secuiesc, Rom. 36 C12 46.18 N 25.18 E
Odra (Oder), stm., Eur. 24 D10 53.55 N 14.16 E
Odrinhas, Port. 184c 38.53 N 9.22 W
Odrzywół, Pol. 24 E16 51.31 N 20.33 E
Odum, Ga., U.S. 132 E3 31.40 N 82.02 W
Odžaci, Yugo. 36 D6 45.30 N 19.15 E
Oebisfelde, Ger. 24 D6 52.25 N 10.59 E
Oeiras, Braz. 170 D4 7.01 S 42.08 W
Oeiras, Port. 184c 38.41 N 9.21 W
Oella, Md., U.S. 202b 39.16 N 76.47 W
Oels see Oleśnica, Pol. 24 E13 51.12 N 17.23 E
Oelsnitz, Ger. 24 F8 50.24 N 12.10 E
Oelwein, Ia., U.S. 130 B6 42.40 N 91.54 W
Oenpelli, Austl. 96 B6 12.18 S 133.05 E
Oermten, Ger. 181 51.29 N 6.27 E
Oespel, ngh., Ger. 181 51.30 N 7.23 E
Oeste, Canal del, can., Spain 184a 40.32 N 3.42 W
Oeste, Parque del, p.o.i., Spain 184a 40.26 N 3.44 W
Oestrich, Ger. 181 51.22 N 7.38 E
Oestrich, ngh., Ger. 181 51.34 N 7.22 E
Oestrum, ngh., Ger. 181 51.25 N 6.40 E
Oettingen in Bayern, Ger. 24 H6 48.57 N 10.36 E
Oetz, Aus. 30 C7 47.12 N 10.54 E
O'Fallon, Mo., U.S. 130 F7 38.48 N 90.41 W
O'Fallon Creek, stm., Mt., U.S. 140 A8 46.50 N 105.09 W
Ofanto, stm., Italy 32 D9 41.21 N 16.12 E
Ofaqim, Isr. 76 G5 31.17 N 34.36 E
Offa, Nig. 84 H5 8.09 N 4.43 E
Offaly, state, Ire. 10 H5 53.20 N 7.30 W
Offenbach am Main, Ger. 24 F4 50.06 N 8.45 E
Offenburg, Ger. 24 H3 48.28 N 7.56 E
Offerdal, Swe. 16 D12 63.28 N 14.00 E
Offham, Eng., U.K. 178 51.17 N 0.23 E
Officer, Austl. 192b 38.04 S 145.25 E
Offida, Italy 30 H10 42.56 N 13.41 E
Offutt Air Force Base, mil., Ne., U.S. 130 C1 41.08 N 95.56 W
Oficina Alemania, Chile 172 B3 25.11 S 69.49 W
Oficina Chile, Chile 172 B3 25.09 S 69.50 W
Ofin, Nig. 191a 6.33 N 3.30 E
Ofotfjorden, b., Nor. 14 D7 68.25 N 16.51 E
Ofu, i., Am. Sam. 101c h13 14.10 S 169.39 W
Ōfukuroshinden, Japan 186 35.53 N 139.27 E
Ōfuna, Japan 186 35.21 N 139.32 E
Ogaadeen see Ogaden, reg., Afr. 82 F8 8.00 N 44.00 E
Ogaden, reg., Afr. 82 F8 8.00 N 44.00 E
Ōgaki, Japan 56 D9 35.21 N 136.37 E
Ogallala, Ne., U.S. 140 F11 41.07 N 101.43 W
Ogan, stm., Indon. 66 E4 3.01 S 104.44 E
Ogasawara-guntō, is., Japan 44 G18 26.57 N 142.14 E
Ogasawara-shotō, is., Japan 46 G18 26.00 N 142.00 E
Ogatsu, Japan 56 A14 38.31 N 141.28 E
Ogawa, Japan 56 G3 32.35 N 130.41 E
Ogawa, Japan 186 35.44 N 139.28 E
Ogbomosho, Nig. 84 H5 8.08 N 4.15 E
Ogden, Ia., U.S. 130 B3 42.02 N 94.01 W
Ogden, Ks., U.S. 138 B12 39.06 N 96.42 W
Ogden, Ut., U.S. 150 B5 41.14 N 111.57 W
Ogden Reservoir, res., Eng., U.K. 180 53.42 N 2.22 W
Ogdensburg, N.Y., U.S. 126 D14 44.41 N 75.29 W
Ogea Levu, i., Fiji 101e q20 19.08 S 178.24 W
Ogeechee, stm., Ga., U.S. 132 D4 31.50 N 81.04 W
Ogema, Sk., Can. 142 E8 49.34 N 104.54 W
Ogidaki Mountain, hill, On., Can. 126 A6 46.58 N 83.58 W
Ogijo, Nig. 191a 6.42 N 3.31 E
Ogilvie, Mn., U.S. 128 F5 45.49 N 93.25 W
Ogilvie Mountains, mts., Yk., Can. 110 C3 65.02 N 139.28 W
Oglesby, Il., U.S. 130 C8 41.17 N 89.03 W
Oglesby, Tx., U.S. 136 C10 31.25 N 97.31 W
Oglethorpe, Ga., U.S. 132 D1 32.17 N 84.03 W
Ogliastra, reg., Italy 32 E3 39.56 N 9.37 E
Oglio, stm., Italy 30 E6 45.03 N 10.40 E
Ogmore, Austl. 98 D7 22.36 S 149.40 E
Ognon, stm., Fr. 20 G15 47.19 N 5.27 E
Ōgo, ngh., Japan 188 34.49 N 135.06 E
Ōgo, stm., Japan 188 34.47 N 135.03 E
Ogoamas, Bulu, mtn., Indon. 66 C12 0.38 N 120.13 E
Ogoja, Nig. 84 H6 6.39 N 8.47 E
Ogoki, stm., On., Can. 118 E11 51.37 N 85.56 W
Ogoki Lake, l., On., Can. 114 A7 50.50 N 87.10 W
Ogooué, stm., Afr. 84 I7 0.48 S 9.00 E
Ogorelyši, Russia 18 D22 63.01 N 35.41 E
Ogōri, Japan 56 E4 34.05 N 131.24 E
Ogosta, stm., Blg. 36 F10 43.45 N 23.52 E
Ogoyo, Nig. 191a 6.26 N 3.29 E
Ogre, Lat. 26 D7 56.48 N 24.37 E
Ogre, stm., Lat. 26 D8 56.47 N 24.36 E
Ogrodzieniec, Pol. 24 F15 50.27 N 19.31 E

Name	Page	Map Ref.	Latitude	Longitude
O Grove, Spain	28	B2	42.29 N	8.51 W
Ogudu, Nig.	191a		6.34 N	3.24 E
Ogulin, Cro.	30	E12	45.16 N	15.13 E
Ogun Forest Reserve, p.o.i., Nig.	191a		6.37 N	3.26 E
Oguni, Japan	56	A12	38.04 N	139.43 E
Ogunlogun, Nig.	191a		6.41 N	3.28 E
Ogunquit, Me., U.S.	122	G6	43.14 N	70.36 W
Ogurdžaly, ostrov, i., Turkmen.	72	B7	38.56 N	53.02 E
Oğuzeli, Tur.	42	G7	36.57 N	37.30 E
Oha, Russia	50	F17	53.34 N	142.56 E
Ohanet, Alg.	84	D6	28.41 N	8.53 E
Ohansk, Russia	40	C19	57.43 N	55.23 E
Ōhara, Japan	56	D13	35.14 N	140.23 E
Ōharano, ngh., Japan	188		34.58 N	135.40 E
Ōhatake, Japan	186		35.57 N	139.46 E
O'Higgins, Cabo, c., Chile	1001	e30	27.06 S	109.14 W
O'Higgins, Cerro, mtn., Chile	166	I2	48.48 S	73.11 W
O'Higgins, Lago (San Martín, Lago), l., S.A.	166	I2	48.52 S	72.38 W
Ohio, Il., U.S.	130	C8	41.33 N	89.27 W
Ohio, state, U.S.	114	F9	40.15 N	82.45 W
Ohio, stm., U.S.	114	H6	36.58 N	89.08 W
Ohio Canal, can., Oh., U.S.	197a		41.26 N	81.40 W
Ohio Peak, mtn., Co., U.S.	138	C1	38.49 N	107.07 W
Ohiopyle State Park, p.o.i., Pa., U.S.	124	E6	39.50 N	79.28 W
Ohlau see Oława, Pol.	24	F13	50.56 N	17.18 E
Ohligs, ngh., Ger.	181		51.09 N	7.00 E
Ohm, stm., Ger.	20	D17	50.51 N	8.47 E
'Ohonua, Tonga	100e	o15	21.20 S	174.57 W
Ohoopee, stm., Ga., U.S.	132	D3	31.54 N	82.07 W
Ōhori, Japan	186		35.20 N	139.52 E
Ohota, stm., Russia	50	E17	59.19 N	143.04 E
Ohotsk, Russia	50	E17	59.21 N	143.17 E
Ohotskoe more see Okhotsk, Sea of, s., Asia	50	F18	53.00 N	150.00 E
Ohōtuku-kai see Okhotsk, Sea of, s., Asia	50	F18	53.00 N	150.00 E
Ohře, stm., Eur.	24	F9	50.31 N	14.08 E
Ohrid, Mac.	34	B3	41.07 N	20.48 E
Ohrid, Lake, l., Eur.	32	D14	41.02 N	20.43 E
Ohridsko Ezero see Ohrid, Lake, l., Eur.	32	D14	41.02 N	20.43 E
Ohrigstad, S. Afr.	90	D10	24.45 S	30.23 E
Öhringen, Ger.	24	G5	49.12 N	9.30 E
Ohrit, Liqeni i see Ohrid, Lake, l., Eur.	32	D14	41.02 N	20.43 E
Ohta, stm., Russia	183a		59.57 N	30.24 E
Ohtan'jarvi, ozero, l., Russia	18	B17	65.29 N	30.46 E
Ohuira, Bahía de, l., Mex.	154	C4	25.38 N	108.58 W
Ohvat, Russia	26	D15	56.46 N	32.26 E
Ōi, Japan	186		35.51 N	139.30 E
Ōi, ngh., Japan	186		35.35 N	139.45 E
Ōi, stm., Japan	56	E11	34.45 N	138.18 E
Oiapoque, Braz.	164	C7	3.50 N	51.49 W
Oiapoque (Oyapok), stm., S.A.	164	C7	4.09 N	51.37 W
Oies, Île aux, i., Qc., Can.	122	C6	47.06 N	70.30 W
Oikarainen, Fin.	14	F16	66.26 N	26.05 E
Oil Center, N.M., U.S.	136	B4	32.29 N	103.16 W
Oil City, La., U.S.	136	B14	32.44 N	93.58 W
Oil City, Pa., U.S.	124	C6	41.25 N	79.42 W
Oildale, Ca., U.S.	148	H7	35.25 N	119.01 W
Oilmont, Mt., U.S.	146	B15	48.44 N	111.50 W
Oilton, Ok., U.S.	134	A2	36.04 N	96.35 W
Oilton, Tx., U.S.	136	G9	27.27 N	98.57 W
Oil Trough, Ar., U.S.	134	B7	35.37 N	91.27 W
Oinville-sur-Montcient, Fr.	179		49.02 N	1.51 E
Oise, state, Fr.	20	E11	49.30 N	2.30 E
Oise, stm., Eur.	20	E11	48.59 N	2.04 E
Ōiso, Japan	188		34.33 N	135.01 E
Oissery, Fr.	179		49.04 N	2.49 E
Oistins, Barb.	159d	n8	13.04 N	59.32 W
Ōita, Japan	56	F4	33.14 N	131.36 E
Ōita, state, Japan	56	F4	33.15 N	131.20 E
Oiticica, Braz.	170	C5	5.03 S	41.05 W
Oituz, Pasul, p., Rom.	36	C13	46.03 N	26.23 E
Ōiwa, Japan	188		34.53 N	135.33 E
Ojai, Ca., U.S.	148	I6	34.26 N	119.14 W
Öjaren, l., Swe.	18	G3	60.42 N	16.51 E
Ojat', stm., Russia	18	G21	60.30 N	33.01 E
Öje, Swe.	18	G11	60.49 N	13.50 E
Ojinaga, Mex.	154	A6	29.33 N	104.24 W
Ojiya, Japan	56	B11	37.18 N	138.48 E
Ojmjakon, Russia	50	D17	63.28 N	142.49 E
Ojocaliente, Mex.	154	D7	22.33 N	102.12 W
Ojo de la Casa, Mex.	136	C1	31.23 N	106.32 W
Ojo del Carrizo, Mex.	120	G10	29.58 N	105.16 W
Ojo de Liebre, Laguna, b., Mex.	154	B1	27.45 N	114.15 W
Ojos del Salado, Cerro see Ojos del Salado, Nevado, mtn., S.A.	172	C3	27.05 S	68.32 W
Ojos del Salado, Nevado, mtn., S.A.	172	C3	27.05 S	68.32 W
Ojos Negros, Mex.	148	L9	31.53 N	116.16 W
Ojota, Nig.	191a		6.35 N	3.23 E
Oka, stm., Russia	26	F20	56.20 N	43.59 E
Oka, stm., Russia	48	D18	55.16 N	102.17 E
Okaba, Indon.	60	G10	8.03 S	139.40 E
Okahandja, Nmb.	90	B3	21.57 S	16.54 E
Okaihau, N.Z.	102	B5	35.19 S	173.47 E
Okak Islands, is., Nf., Can.	108	F13	57.30 N	61.50 W
Okamoto, Japan	188		34.59 N	135.58 E
Okamoto, ngh., Japan	188		34.44 N	135.16 E
Okanagan (Okanogan), stm., N.A.	144	G11	48.05 N	119.44 W
Okanagan Centre, B.C., Can.	144	F11	50.00 N	119.25 W
Okanagan Falls, B.C., Can.	144	G11	49.20 N	119.34 W
Okanagan Indian Reserve, ind. res., B.C., Can.	144	F11	50.21 N	119.17 W
Okanagan Lake, l., B.C., Can.	144	F11	49.54 N	119.30 W
Okanagan Landing, B.C., Can.	144	F11	50.13 N	119.22 W
Okanagan Mountain Provincial Park, p.o.i., B.C., Can.	144	G11	49.45 N	119.40 W
Okanagan Range, mts., Can.	144	G10	49.00 N	120.00 W
Okanogan, Wa., U.S.	146	B7	48.22 N	119.34 W
Okanogan (Okanagan), stm., N.A.	144	G11	48.05 N	119.44 W
Okanogan Range, mts., Can.	146	A6	49.12 N	120.18 W
Okapilco Creek, stm., Ga., U.S.	132	E2	30.45 N	83.29 W
Okāra, Pak.	70	C4	30.48 N	73.26 E
Okarche, Ok., U.S.	138	F11	35.44 N	97.58 W
Okasaki, Japan	188		34.46 N	135.52 E
Okatibbee Lake, res., Ms., U.S.	134	E9	32.30 N	88.48 W
Okaukuejo, Nmb.	88	D2	19.10 S	15.54 E
Okavango (Cubango), stm., Afr.	88	D2	18.56 S	22.24 E
Okavango Delta, del., Bots.	88	D3	19.28 S	22.31 E
Okavango Swamp see Okavango Delta, del., Bots.	88	D3	19.28 S	22.31 E
Ōkawa, Japan	56	F3	33.12 N	130.23 E
Ōkawado, Japan	186		35.56 N	139.50 E
Okawville, Il., U.S.	130	F8	38.25 N	89.33 W
Okaya, Japan	56	C11	36.03 N	138.02 E
Okayama, Japan	56	E6	34.39 N	133.55 E
Okayama, state, Japan	56	E6	35.00 N	134.00 E
Okazaki, Japan	56	E10	34.56 N	137.09 E
Oke-Aro, Nig.	191a		6.41 N	3.19 E
Okeechobee, Fl., U.S.	132	I5	27.14 N	80.49 W
Okeechobee, Lake, l., Fl., U.S.	132	J5	26.55 N	80.45 W
O'Keefe Centre, bldg., On., Can.	193b		43.37 N	79.22 W
Okeene, Ok., U.S.	138	E10	36.06 N	98.18 W
Okefenokee Swamp, sw., U.S.	132	F3	30.42 N	82.20 W
Okehampton, Eng., U.K.	10	K8	50.45 N	3.59 W
Okemah, Ok., U.S.	134	B2	35.26 N	96.18 W
Okemos, Mi., U.S.	124	B1	42.43 N	84.25 W
Okene, Nig.	84	H6	7.28 N	6.15 E
Oke Ogbe, Nig.	191a		6.24 N	3.23 E
Oker, stm., Ger.	20	B19	52.31 N	10.22 E
Okhaldhunggā, Nepal	70	E11	27.18 N	86.30 E
Okhla, ngh., India	190a		28.34 N	77.18 E
Okhotsk, Sea of, s., Asia	50	F18	53.00 N	150.00 E
Okhotsk Basin, unds.	174	D17	53.00 N	148.00 E
Okhtyrka, Ukr.	38	C13	50.18 N	34.54 E
Okiep, S. Afr.	90	F3	29.39 S	17.53 E
Okinawa, Japan	55a	I18	26.19 N	127.48 E
Okinawa Island see Okinawa-jima, i., Japan	55a	I19	26.31 N	127.59 E
Okinawa-jima, i., Japan	55a	I19	26.31 N	127.59 E
Okinawa-shotō, is., Japan	52	F10	27.14 N	128.01 E
Okino-Erabu-shima, i., Japan	55a	I19	27.22 N	128.35 E
Oki-shotō, is., Japan	56	C6	36.11 N	133.10 E
Okitipupa, Nig.	84	H5	6.29 N	4.47 E
Okkerbil', stm., Russia	183a		59.56 N	30.26 E
Okladnevo, Russia	26	B16	58.36 N	33.39 E
Oklahoma, Pa., U.S.	197b		40.35 N	79.35 W
Oklahoma, state, U.S.	138	F11	35.30 N	98.00 W
Oklahoma City, Ok., U.S.	138	F11	35.28 N	97.30 W
Oklawaha, Fl., U.S.	132	G4	29.02 N	81.55 W
Oklee, Mn., U.S.	128	D3	47.49 N	95.50 W
Okmulgee, Ok., U.S.	134	B3	35.36 N	95.57 W
Okobojo Creek, stm., S.D., U.S.	140	C12	44.33 N	100.31 W
Okollo, Ug.	86	D6	2.40 N	31.08 E
Okolona, Ar., U.S.	134	D5	34.00 N	93.20 W
Okolona, Ky., U.S.	130	F12	38.08 N	85.40 W
Okolona, Ms., U.S.	134	C10	33.59 N	88.45 W
Okombahe, Nmb.	90	B2	21.21 S	15.23 E
Okondja, Gabon	86	E2	0.42 S	13.47 E
Okonek, Pol.	24	C12	53.32 N	16.50 E
Okotoks, Ab., Can.	144	F16	50.44 N	113.59 W
Okoyo, Congo	86	E2	1.28 S	15.04 E
Oksbøl, Den.	16	L6	55.38 N	8.17 E
Øksfjord, Nor.	14	B13	70.14 N	22.21 E
Øksfjordjøkelen, ice, Nor.	14	B12	70.10 N	22.00 E
Oksko-Donskaja ravnina, pl., Russia	40	E12	53.00 N	40.30 E
Oksovskij, Russia	18	E26	62.37 N	39.55 E
Oksskolten, mtn., Nor.	16	A12	66.00 N	14.17 E
Oktiabrs'ke, Ukr.	38	H13	45.17 N	34.08 E
Oktjabr', Russia	26	C20	57.49 N	37.23 E
Oktjabr'sk, Kaz.	48	E9	49.28 N	57.25 E
Oktjabr'sk, Russia	40	E16	53.10 N	48.41 E
Oktjabr'skij, Russia	40	F20	61.04 N	43.12 E
Oktjabr'skij, Russia	14	E25	67.30 N	34.30 E
Oktjabr'skij, Russia	26	F21	54.14 N	38.55 E
Oktjabr'skij, Russia	38	C15	50.25 N	36.21 E
Oktjabr'skij see Oktjabrskij, Russia	38	F18	47.28 N	40.04 E
Oktjabrskij, Russia	38	F18	47.28 N	40.04 E
Oktjabr'skij, Russia	40	G14	47.57 N	43.37 E
Oktjabr'skij, Russia	40	B16	59.27 N	48.54 E
Oktjabr'skij, Russia	40	B14	58.19 N	44.19 E
Oktjabr'skij, Russia	40	C20	56.31 N	57.12 E
Oktjabr'skij, Russia	40	D18	54.28 N	53.29 E
Oktjabr'skij, Russia	48	C17	56.05 N	99.24 E
Oktjabr'skij, Russia	50	F14	53.00 N	128.39 E
Oktjabr'skij, Russia	183b		55.37 N	37.58 E
Oktjabr'skoe, Kaz.	48	D11	52.04 N	65.42 E
Oktjabr'skoe, Russia	40	E19	52.20 N	55.30 E
Oktjabr'skoe, Russia	40	E15	52.52 N	46.28 E
Oktjabr'skoe, Russia	48	B10	62.29 N	65.58 E
Oktwin, Mya.	64	C3	18.49 N	96.24 E
Ōkubo, Japan	186		35.21 N	139.56 E
Ōkubo, Japan	188		34.41 N	134.57 E
Ōkubo, ngh., Japan	186		35.24 N	139.35 E
Ōkuchi, Japan	56	G3	32.03 N	130.37 E
Okulovka, Russia	26	B16	58.22 N	33.18 E
Okunëv Nos, Russia	12	C25	66.16 N	52.26 E
Okusawa, ngh., Japan	186		35.36 N	139.40 E
Okushiri-tō, i., Japan	54	C13	42.10 N	139.27 E
Ōkusu-yama, hill, Japan	186		35.15 N	139.38 E
Okuta, Nig.	84	H5	9.12 N	3.11 E
Okwa, stm., Afr.	90	C6	22.14 S	23.59 E
Ola, Russia	50	E19	59.36 N	151.20 E
Ola, Ar., U.S.	134	B5	35.01 N	93.13 W
Ólafsfjörður, Ice.	12a	j30	66.04 N	18.41 W
Olancha, Ca., U.S.	148	G8	36.16 N	118.00 W
Olancha Peak, mtn., Ca., U.S.	148	G7	36.16 N	118.07 W
Olanchito, Hond.	156	E4	15.28 N	86.34 W
Öland, i., Swe.	16	K14	56.45 N	16.38 E
Olanga, stm., Eur.	14	F20	66.09 N	30.41 E
Olanta, S.C., U.S.	132	C6	33.56 N	79.56 W
Olar, S.C., U.S.	132	C4	33.10 N	81.11 W
Olaria, Braz.	205a		22.41 S	43.08 W
Olaria, ngh., Braz.	205a		22.52 S	43.15 W
Olary, Austl.	98	I3	32.17 S	140.19 E
Olascoaga, Arg.	172	G7	35.14 S	60.37 W
Olasore, Nig.	191a		6.40 N	3.17 E
Olathe, Co., U.S.	150	E8	38.36 N	107.58 W
Olathe, Ks., U.S.	130	F3	38.52 N	94.48 W
Olavarría, Arg.	172	H7	36.53 S	60.19 W
Olavinlinna, hist., Fin.	18	F15	61.52 N	29.00 E
Oława (Ohlau), Pol.	24	F13	50.56 N	17.18 E
Olbia, Italy	32	D3	40.55 N	9.30 E
Olbia, Golfo di, b., Italy	32	D3	40.56 N	9.38 E
Olcott, N.Y., U.S.	126	E11	43.19 N	78.42 W
Old Bahama Channel see Bahama, Canal Viejo de, strt., N.A.	156	A9	22.39 N	78.40 W
Old Bethpage, N.Y., U.S.	194		40.45 N	73.27 W
Old Bethpage Village, hist., N.Y., U.S.	194		40.47 N	73.28 W
Old Bridge, N.J., U.S.	194		40.24 N	74.21 W
Old Brookville, N.Y., U.S.	194		40.49 N	73.36 W
Old Cairo, ngh., Egypt	191c		30.00 N	31.14 E
Old Castille see Castilla la Vieja, hist. reg., Spain	28	C7	41.30 N	4.00 W
Oldcastle, Ire.	10	H5	53.46 N	7.10 W
Old City, The, hist., China	187b		31.13 N	121.29 E
Old Cork, Austl.	98	D3	22.56 S	141.52 E
Old Creek Estates, Va., U.S.	202c		38.50 N	77.16 W
Old Crow, Yk., Can.	109	C12	67.35 N	139.49 W
Old Crow, stm., N.A.	109	C11	67.35 N	139.47 W
Old Economy, hist., Pa., U.S.	197b		40.36 N	80.14 W
Olden, Nor.	16	F4	61.49 N	6.48 E
Olden, Tx., U.S.	136	B9	32.25 N	98.45 W
Oldenburg, Ger.	24	C4	53.08 N	8.13 E
Oldenburg, hist. reg., Ger.	24	C4	53.00 N	8.00 E
Oldenburg in Holstein, Ger.	24	B6	54.17 N	10.53 E
Oldenzaal, Neth.	20	B15	52.18 N	6.56 E
Olderdalen, Nor.	14	C11	69.36 N	20.31 E
Old Faithful Geyser, gysr., Wy., U.S.	146	F16	44.30 N	110.46 W
Old Farm, Md., U.S.	202c		39.03 N	77.09 W
Old Field, N.Y., U.S.	194		40.57 N	73.08 W
Old Field Point, c., N.Y., U.S.	194		40.58 N	73.07 W
Oldfjällen, mts., Swe.	16	D11	63.52 N	13.37 E
Old Forge, N.Y., U.S.	126	E15	43.43 N	74.58 W
Old Forge, Pa., U.S.	124	C10	41.22 N	75.44 W
Old Forge Village, N.J., U.S.	194		40.49 N	74.29 W
Old Fort Bay see Vieux-Fort, Qc., Can.	111a	i22	51.25 N	57.49 W
Old Fort Erie, hist., On., Can.	202a		42.53 N	78.56 W
Old Fort Mountain, mtn., B.C., Can.	144	A4	55.05 N	126.30 W
Old Fort Niagara, hist., N.Y., U.S.	202a		43.16 N	79.03 W
Old Fort Point, c., Bah.	158f	m17	25.03 N	77.29 W
Old Greenwich, Ct., U.S.	194		41.02 N	73.34 W
Oldham, Eng., U.K.	10	H10	53.32 N	2.04 W
Oldham, S.D., U.S.	140	C15	44.13 N	97.18 W
Oldham, mun., Eng., U.K.	180		53.34 N	2.03 W
Oldham, mun., Eng., U.K.	180		53.34 N	2.03 W
Oldham Pines, Ma., U.S.	201		42.05 N	70.50 W
Oldham Pond, l., Ma., U.S.	201		42.03 N	70.51 W
Old Harbor, Ak., U.S.	109	E9	57.12 N	153.22 W
Old Harbour, Jam.	158d	j13	17.55 N	77.07 W
Old Hickory Lake, res., Tn., U.S.	130	H11	36.18 N	86.30 W
Old Malden, ngh., Eng., U.K.	178		51.23 N	0.15 W
Oldman, stm., Ab., Can.	144	G17	49.56 N	111.42 W
Old Manor, N.J., U.S.	194		40.24 N	74.11 W
Old Mkushi, Zam.	88	C4	14.21 S	29.22 E
Old North Bridge, hist., Ma., U.S.	201		42.28 N	71.21 W
Old North Church, rel., Ma., U.S.	201		42.22 N	71.03 W
Old Norwood, Monts.	159a	d3	16.46 N	62.11 W
Old Orchard, shp. cen., Il., U.S.	196		42.04 N	87.45 W
Old Orchard Beach, Me., U.S.	122	G6	43.30 N	70.23 W
Old Place Creek, stm., N.J., U.S.	194		40.38 N	74.12 W
Old Road, Antig.	159b	f4	17.01 N	61.50 W
Old Road Bay, b., Md., U.S.	202b		39.12 N	76.27 W
Old Road Bluff, c., Antig.	159b	g4	17.00 N	61.49 W
Old Road Town, St. K./N.	159a	c2	17.19 N	62.48 W
Olds, Ab., Can.	144	E16	51.47 N	114.05 W
Old Saybrook, Ct., U.S.	124	C13	41.18 N	72.22 W
Old Speck Mountain, mtn., Me., U.S.	122	F5	44.33 N	70.58 W
Old Swamp, stm., Ma., U.S.	201		42.11 N	70.57 W
Old Swedes Church, rel., De., U.S.	203		39.44 N	75.32 W
Old Tappan, N.J., U.S.	194		41.00 N	73.59 W
Old Tate, Bots.	90	B8	21.32 S	27.57 E
Old Town, Me., U.S.	122	F8	44.55 N	68.39 W
Old Trafford Cricket Ground, p.o.i., Eng., U.K.	180		53.28 N	2.17 W
Old Trap, N.C., U.S.	124	H9	36.15 N	76.02 W
Olduvai Gorge, val., Tan.	86	E7	2.58 S	35.22 E
Old Westbury, N.Y., U.S.	194		40.47 N	73.37 W
Old Westbury Gardens, p.o.i., N.Y., U.S.	194		40.46 N	73.36 W
Old Windsor, Eng., U.K.	178		51.28 N	0.35 W
Old Wives Lake, l., Sk., Can.	142	D8	50.06 N	106.00 W
Old Woman Creek, stm., Wy., U.S.	140	D8	43.22 N	104.16 W
Olean, N.Y., U.S.	124	B7	42.04 N	78.25 W
O'Leary, P.E., Can.	122	D12	46.42 N	64.13 W
Olecko, Pol.	24	B18	54.02 N	22.30 E
Olëkma, stm., Russia	50	E13	60.22 N	120.40 E
Olekminsk, Russia	50	D13	60.22 N	120.25 E
Olëkminskij Stanovik, mts., Russia	50	F12	54.30 N	119.57 E
Oleksandriia, Ukr.	38	E12	48.40 N	33.07 E
Oleksandrivka, Ukr.	38	G14	46.32 N	35.29 E
Oleksandrivka, Ukr.	38	F10	47.41 N	31.16 E
Oleksandrivka, Ukr.	38	E11	48.57 N	32.15 E
Oleksandrivka, Ukr.	38	E15	48.43 N	36.55 E
Oleksandrivs'k, Ukr.	38	E18	48.35 N	39.11 E
Oleksiivka, Ukr.	38	F15	47.13 N	36.32 E
Olema, Russia	12	D21	64.30 N	46.08 E
Ølen, Nor.	16	H3	59.36 N	5.48 E
Olenegorsk, Russia	14	D23	68.08 N	33.14 E
Olenëk, Russia	50	C11	68.32 N	112.23 E
Olenëk, stm., Russia	50	C12	73.00 N	119.45 E
Olenëkskij zaliv, b., Russia	50	B13	73.20 N	121.00 E
Olenica, Russia	14	F26	66.27 N	35.21 E
Olenij, ostrov, i., Russia	18	B21	65.45 N	34.50 E
Olenij, ostrov, i., Russia	50	B4	72.25 N	77.45 E
Olenino, Russia	26	D16	56.12 N	33.29 E
Olenivka, Ukr.	38	F16	47.50 N	37.40 E
Olenivka, Ukr.	38	H11	45.22 N	32.32 E
Olenja Rečka, Russia	48	D16	52.47 N	93.14 E
Olenty, Kaz.	40	F17	50.02 N	52.07 E
Oléron, Île d', i., Fr.	22	D4	45.56 N	1.18 W
Oles'ko, Ukr.	38	C4	49.57 N	24.54 E
Oleśnica, Pol.	24	E13	51.12 N	17.23 E
Olesno, Pol.	24	F14	50.53 N	18.25 E
Olevsk, Ukr.	38	B6	51.13 N	27.38 E
Ol'ga, Russia	54	C11	43.44 N	135.17 E
Olga, Mount, mtn., Austl.	96	D6	25.17 S	130.41 E
Olgastretet, strt., Nor.	108	B30	78.30 N	24.00 E
Olgiata, Italy	185a		42.02 N	12.22 E
Ol'gino, ngh., Russia	183a		60.00 N	30.09 E
Ol'ginskaja, Russia	38	H17	45.56 N	38.32 E
Ölgiy, Mong.	48	E16	48.57 N	89.57 E
Ølgod, Den.	16	L6	55.49 N	8.37 E
Olhão, Port.	28	G3	37.01 N	7.50 W
Olho d'Água das Cunhãs, Braz.	170	C3	4.43 S	44.34 W
Olho d'Água das Flores, Braz.	170	E7	9.33 S	37.17 W
Ol'hon, ostrov, i., Russia	50	F10	53.09 N	107.24 E
Ol'hopil', Ukr.	38	E8	48.10 N	29.30 E
Ol'hovatka, Russia	40	F11	50.16 N	39.17 E
Ol'hovka, Russia	40	G14	49.51 N	44.33 E
Ol'hynka, Ukr.	38	F16	47.41 N	37.30 E
Olib, Otok, i., Cro.	30	F11	44.22 N	14.48 E
Oliena, Italy	32	D3	40.16 N	9.24 E
Olifants (Elefantes), stm., Afr.	90	D10	24.06 S	32.38 E
Olifants, stm., S. Afr.	90	H4	31.39 S	18.11 E
Olifants, stm., S. Afr.	90	H6	33.41 S	21.43 E
Olifantshoek, S. Afr.	90	E6	27.57 S	22.44 E
Oliki, Russia	183a		59.46 N	29.55 E
Ólimbos (Olympus), mtn., Cyp.	76	C3	34.56 N	32.51 E
Olimpia, Braz.	170	K1	20.44 S	48.54 W
Olímpico, Estadio, p.o.i., Mex.	204a		19.20 N	99.12 W
Olímpico, Estadio, p.o.i., Spain	184d		41.22 N	2.09 E
Olimpico, Stadio, p.o.i., Italy	185a		41.56 N	12.27 E
Olin, Ia., U.S.	130	B6	41.59 N	91.09 W
Olinalá, Mex.	154	G9	17.50 N	98.51 W
Olinda, Austl.	192b		37.51 S	145.22 E
Olinda, Braz.	170	D8	8.01 S	34.51 W
Olinda, Mount, mtn., Austl.	192b		37.52 S	145.21 E
Olinda Creek, stm., Austl.	192b		37.41 S	145.21 E
Olindina, Braz.	170	F6	11.22 S	38.21 W
Olio, Austl.	98	C4	21.54 S	143.13 E
Olite, Spain	28	B9	42.28 N	1.39 W
Oliva, Arg.	172	F6	32.03 S	63.34 W
Oliva, Spain	28	F10	38.54 N	0.07 W
Oliva de la Frontera, Spain	28	F4	38.16 N	6.54 W
Olivais, ngh., Port.	184c		38.46 N	9.06 E
Olival Basto, Port.	184c		38.47 N	9.10 W
Olivares, Cerro de, mtn., S.A.	172	E3	30.17 S	69.53 W
Olive Branch, Ms., U.S.	134	C9	34.57 N	89.49 W
Olivees Mountain, mtn., St. K./N.	159a	c2	17.20 N	62.45 W
Olive Hill, Ky., U.S.	124	F2	38.17 N	83.10 W
Olivehurst, Ca., U.S.	148	D4	39.05 N	121.33 W
Oliveira, Braz.	170	K3	20.42 S	44.49 W
Oliveira dos Brejinhos, Braz.	170	G4	12.18 S	42.53 W
Olive Mount, ngh., Eng., U.K.	180		53.24 N	2.55 W
Olivença, Moz.	88	C6	11.46 S	35.12 E
Olivenza, Spain	28	F3	38.41 N	7.06 W
Oliver, B.C., Can.	144	G11	49.10 N	119.33 W
Oliver Estates, Va., U.S.	202c		38.59 N	77.18 W
Oliver Springs, Tn., U.S.	130	H13	36.02 N	84.21 W
Olivet, Mi., U.S.	124	B1	42.26 N	84.55 W
Olivet, S.D., U.S.	140	D15	43.14 N	97.40 W
Olivia, Mn., U.S.	128	G3	44.46 N	94.59 W
Olji Moron, stm., China	54	B4	44.10 N	121.29 E
Oljutorskij, mys, c., Russia	50	E23	59.57 N	170.21 E
Oljutorskij zaliv, b., Russia	50	D22	60.15 N	168.30 E
Olla, La., U.S.	134	F6	31.54 N	92.14 W
Ollagüe, Chile	166	D3	21.12 S	68.15 W
Ollagüe, Volcán, vol., S.A.	166	D3	21.18 S	68.10 W
Ollainville, Fr.	179		48.35 N	2.13 E
Ollei, Palau	100b	f8	7.42 N	134.37 E
Ollerton, Eng., U.K.	180		53.17 N	2.20 W
Olmedillo de Roa, Spain	28	C7	41.47 N	3.55 W
Olmedo, Spain	28	C6	41.17 N	4.40 W
Olmos, Peru	164	E2	5.55 S	79.46 W
Olmsted Falls, Oh., U.S.	197a		41.22 N	81.54 W
Olmütz see Olomouc, Czech Rep.	24	G13	49.36 N	17.16 E
Olney, Il., U.S.	130	F9	38.43 N	88.05 W
Olney, Mt., U.S.	146	B12	48.32 N	114.34 W
Olney, Tx., U.S.	138	H10	33.22 N	98.45 W
Olney, ngh., Pa., U.S.	203		40.02 N	75.08 W
Oloči, Russia	50	F12	51.21 N	119.54 E
Olofström, Swe.	16	K12	56.16 N	14.31 E
Olomouc, Czech Rep.	24	G13	49.36 N	17.16 E
Olonec, Russia	18	F20	60.59 N	32.59 E
Olongapo, Phil.	68	C3	14.51 N	120.16 E
Oloron, Gave d', stm., Fr.	28	A10	43.32 N	1.04 W
Oloron-Sainte-Marie, Fr.	22	F5	43.11 N	0.36 W
Olot, Spain	28	B13	42.11 N	2.29 E
Olovgora, gora, mtn., Russia	18	D23	63.23 N	36.59 E
Olovjannaja, Russia	50	F12	50.56 N	115.33 E
Olpe, Ger.	24	E3	51.02 N	7.52 E
Olpe, Ks., U.S.	130	F1	38.15 N	96.10 W
Ol'šanka, Russia	38	B14	51.46 N	35.25 E
Olshammar, Swe.	16	I12	58.45 N	14.48 E
Ol'shana, Ukr.	38	C13	50.48 N	34.01 E
Olsufevo, Russia	26	G16	53.36 N	33.40 E
Olsztyn, Pol.	24	C16	53.46 N	20.28 E
Olsztynek, Pol.	24	C16	53.34 N	20.17 E
Olt, state, Rom.	36	E11	44.20 N	24.30 E
Olt, stm., Rom.	36	D11	43.43 N	24.48 E
Olta, Arg.	172	E4	30.37 S	66.15 W
Oltedal, Nor.	16	I4	58.50 N	6.04 E
Olten, Switz.	30	C4	47.21 N	7.54 E
Olteni, Rom.	36	E12	44.09 N	25.17 E
Oltenița, Rom.	36	E13	44.05 N	26.38 E
Olteț, stm., Rom.	36	E10	44.14 N	24.27 E
Olton, Tx., U.S.	138	G6	34.11 N	102.08 W
Oltu, Tur.	42	E10	40.32 N	42.03 E
Oluan Pi, c., Tai.	58	K9	21.54 N	120.50 E
Olustee, Fl., U.S.	132	F3	30.12 N	82.26 W
Olustee, Ok., U.S.	138	G9	34.33 N	99.24 W
Olustee Creek, stm., Fl., U.S.	132	F3	29.56 N	82.31 W
Olutanga Island, i., Phil.	68	G4	7.22 N	122.52 E
Olute, Nig.	191a		6.28 N	3.16 E
Oluwo, Nig.	191a		6.42 N	3.18 E
Olvera, Spain	28	H5	36.56 N	5.16 W
Olyka, Ukr.	38	C4	50.42 N	25.50 E
Olykhovatka, Ukr.	38	C16	50.11 N	37.30 E
Olym, Russia	38	B17	51.46 N	38.07 E
Olympia, Wa., U.S.	146	C3	47.02 N	122.53 W
Olympiá, hist., Grc.	34	F4	37.38 N	21.41 E
Olympia Park, p.o.i., S. Afr.	191d		26.15 S	28.26 E
Olympia-Stadion, p.o.i., Ger.	182a		52.31 N	13.14 E
Olympic Mountains, mts., Wa., U.S.	146	C3	47.50 N	123.45 W
Olympic National Park, p.o.i., Wa., U.S.	146	C2	47.51 N	123.43 W
Olympic Park, p.o.i., Kor., S.	189b		37.32 N	127.07 E
Olympic Stadium, p.o.i., Grc.	185c		38.02 N	23.48 E
Olympic Stadium, p.o.i., Indon.	187e		6.13 S	106.48 E
Olympic Stadium, p.o.i., Kor., S.	189b		37.31 N	127.04 E
Olympic Stadium, p.o.i., Russia	183b		55.47 N	37.37 E
Olympieion, hist., Grc.	185c		37.58 N	23.44 E
Olympique, Stade, p.o.i., Qc., Can.	193a		45.33 N	73.33 W
Ólympos, Grc.	34	H10	35.44 N	27.11 E
Ólympos (Olympus, Mount), mtn., Grc.	34	C5	40.05 N	22.21 E
Olympus see Ólimbos, mtn., Cyp.	76	C3	34.56 N	32.51 E
Olympus, Mount see Ólympos, mtn., Grc.	34	C5	40.05 N	22.21 E
Olympus, Mount, mtn., Wa., U.S.	146	C3	47.48 N	123.43 W
Olympus, Mount, hill, Ky., U.S.	124	F2	38.03 N	83.39 W
Olyshivka, Ukr.	38	B10	51.13 N	31.20 E
Om', stm., Russia	48	D13	54.58 N	73.22 E
Ōmachi, Japan	56	C10	36.30 N	137.51 E
Ōmachi, Japan	188		34.28 N	135.25 E
Omae-zaki, c., Japan	56	E11	34.36 N	138.14 E
Ōmagari, Japan	54	E14	39.27 N	140.29 E
Omagh, On., Can.	193b		43.30 N	79.49 W
Omagh, N. Ire., U.K.	10	G5	54.36 N	7.17 W
Ōmagi, Japan	186		35.52 N	139.42 E
Omaha, Ne., U.S.	130	C2	41.15 N	95.56 W
Omaha, Tx., U.S.	134	D4	33.11 N	94.44 W
Omaha Indian Reservation, ind. res., Ne., U.S.	114	F2	42.06 N	96.31 W
Omaheke, state, Nmb.	90	E1	21.50 S	19.30 E
Omak, Wa., U.S.	146	B7	48.24 N	119.31 W
Omak Lake, l., Wa., U.S.	146	B7	48.16 N	119.23 W
Oman, ctry., Asia	72	F8	22.00 N	58.00 E
'Omān, Daryā-ye see Oman, Gulf of, b., Asia	72	E8	24.30 N	58.30 E
Oman, Gulf of, b., Asia	72	E8	24.30 N	58.30 E
Omarama, N.Z.	102	G3	44.30 S	169.56 E
Omaruru, Nmb.	90	B3	21.25 S	15.57 E
Omaruru, stm., Nmb.	90	B2	22.06 S	14.15 E
Omatako, mtn., Nmb.	90	B3	21.12 S	16.43 E
Omatako, stm., Nmb.	90	B3	17.57 S	20.28 E
Omate, Peru	164	G3	16.40 S	70.58 W
Ombabika Bay, b., On., Can.	128	A10	50.12 N	88.15 W
Ombo, i., Nor.	16	H4	59.15 N	6.00 E
Ombotozo, mtn., Nmb.	90	B3	21.17 S	16.47 E
Omboué, Gabon	86	E1	1.37 S	9.16 E
Ombrone, stm., Italy	30	H8	42.39 N	11.00 E
Omčak, Russia	50	D18	61.33 N	147.59 E
Omdurman see Umm Durmān, Sudan	82	D6	15.38 N	32.28 E
Ōme, Japan	56	D12	35.47 N	139.15 E
Omega, Ga., U.S.	132	E2	31.20 N	83.35 W
Omegna, Italy	30	E5	45.53 N	8.24 E
Omelianivka, Ukr.	38	H13	45.32 N	34.53 E
Omel'nyk, Ukr.	38	D12	49.12 N	33.32 E
Omemee, On., Can.	126	D11	44.16 N	78.34 W
Omeo, Austl.	98	K6	37.06 S	147.35 E
Ömerköy, Tur.	34	D11	39.48 N	28.04 E
Ömerli Barajı, res., Tur.	34	C12	41.00 N	29.21 E
Ometepe, Isla de, i., Nic.	156	G5	11.30 N	85.35 W
Ometepec, Mex.	154	G9	16.40 N	98.24 W
Ōmi-hachiman, Japan	56	D8	35.08 N	136.06 E
Ōminato see Mutsu, Japan	54	D14	41.17 N	141.10 E
Omineca, stm., B.C., Can.	110	D6	56.06 N	124.27 W
Omineca Mountains, mts., B.C., Can.	110	D5	56.00 N	125.00 W
Omin-ni, ngh., Kor., S.	189b		37.27 N	127.01 E
Ōmino, Japan	188		34.32 N	135.33 E
Omitara, Nmb.	90	C3	22.17 S	18.00 E
Ōmiya, Japan	56	D12	35.54 N	139.38 E
Ōmiya-daichi, plat., Japan	186		35.56 N	139.38 E
Ōmiya Park Race Track, p.o.i., Japan	186		35.55 N	139.38 E
Ommaney, Cape, c., Ak., U.S.	109	E13	56.10 N	134.39 W
Ommanney Bay, b., Nu., Can.	110	A10	73.02 N	100.48 W
Ommen, Neth.	20	B15	52.31 N	6.25 E
Omø, i., Den.	16	L9	55.09 N	11.09 E
Omo, stm., Afr.	82	F7	4.30 N	36.02 E
Omo Botego see Omo, stm., Afr.	82	F7	4.30 N	36.02 E
Omodeo, Lago, res., Italy	32	D2	40.07 N	8.54 E
Omole, Nig.	191a		6.38 N	3.22 E
Omoloj, stm., Russia	50	B15	71.13 N	131.57 E
Omolon, stm., Russia	50	C20	68.42 N	158.43 E
Ōmori, ngh., Japan	186		35.34 N	139.44 E
Omro, Wi., U.S.	128	G10	44.01 N	88.44 W
Omsk, Russia	48	C12	54.57 N	73.23 E
Omsukčan, Russia	50	D20	62.30 N	155.45 E
O-mu, Mya.	64	A4	22.57 N	99.20 E
Ōmuda see Ōmuta, Japan	56	F3	33.00 N	130.26 E
Omul, Vârful, mtn., Rom.	36	D12	45.26 N	25.26 E
Omulew, stm., Pol.	24	C17	53.04 N	21.33 E
Ōmura, Japan	56	G2	32.54 N	129.57 E
Ōmura-wan, b., Japan	56	G2	32.57 N	129.52 E
Ōmuro, Japan	186		35.54 N	139.58 E
Omurtag, Blg.	36	F13	43.07 N	26.26 E
Ōmuta, Japan	56	F3	33.00 N	130.26 E
Omutinskij, Russia	48	C11	56.28 N	67.40 E
Omutninsk, Russia	40	B18	58.39 N	52.11 E
Ona see Birjusa, stm., Russia	48	C17	57.42 N	95.27 E
Onabas, Mex.	154	A4	28.30 N	109.33 W
Onaga, Ks., U.S.	130	E1	39.29 N	96.10 W
Onagawa, Japan	56	A14	38.26 N	141.27 E
Onaman Lake, l., On., Can.	128	B11	49.58 N	87.29 W
Onamia, Mn., U.S.	128	E5	46.04 N	93.40 W
Onancock, Va., U.S.	124	G10	37.42 N	75.45 W
Onangué, Lac, l., Gabon	86	E1	0.58 S	10.05 E
Onaping, stm., On., Can.	126	B8	46.36 N	81.17 W
Onaping Lake, l., On., Can.	126	A8	47.08 N	81.36 W
Onarga, Il., U.S.	130	D10	40.42 N	87.59 W
Ōnari, Japan	186		35.55 N	139.37 E
Onatchiway, Lac, res., Qc., Can.	122	A5	49.02 N	71.03 W
Onawa, Ia., U.S.	130	B1	42.01 N	96.05 W
Onaway, Mi., U.S.	126	C5	45.21 N	84.13 W
Oncativo, Arg.	172	E6	31.55 S	63.41 W
Once, Canal Numero, can., Arg.	172	H8	36.08 S	58.36 W
Onchāi, India	190b		22.57 N	88.19 E
Oncócua, Ang.	88	D1	16.35 S	13.26 E
Onda, Spain	28	E10	39.58 N	0.15 W
Ondangwa, Nmb.	88	D2	17.55 S	16.00 E
Ondas, stm., Braz.	170	G3	12.08 S	45.00 W
Ondava, stm., Slvk.	24	H17	48.27 N	21.49 E
Ondjiva, Ang.	88	D2	17.04 S	15.43 E
Ondo, Japan	56	E5	34.11 N	132.32 E
Ondo, Nig.	84	H5	7.05 N	4.49 E
Öndörhaan, Mong.	52	B7	47.19 N	110.40 E
Ondozero, Russia	18	D20	63.52 N	33.06 E
Ondozero, ozero, l., Russia	18	D20	63.48 N	33.20 E
One Arrow Indian Reserve, ind. res., Sk., Can.	142	B8	52.44 N	106.01 W
Oneco, Fl., U.S.	132	I3	27.25 N	82.32 W
Onega, Russia	18	D25	63.54 N	38.06 E
Onega, stm., Russia	18	D25	63.56 N	37.56 E
Onega, Lake see Onežskoe ozero, l., Russia	18	F22	61.30 N	35.45 E
Onega Bay see Onežskaja guba, b., Russia	18	C23	64.20 N	36.30 E

Name	Page	Map Ref.	Latitude	Longitude
One Hundred and Two, stm., Mo., U.S.	130	D3	39.44 N	94.43 W
One Hundred and Two, West Fork, stm., U.S.	130	D3	40.31 N	94.51 W
One Hundred Fifty Mile House, B.C., Can.	144	D9	52.06 N	121.55 W
One Hundred Mile House, B.C., Can.	144	E9	51.37 N	121.18 W
Oneida, Il., U.S.	130	C7	41.04 N	90.13 W
Oneida, Ky., U.S.	124	G2	37.15 N	83.39 W
Oneida, N.Y., U.S.	126	E14	43.05 N	75.39 W
Oneida, Tn., U.S.	130	H13	36.29 N	84.31 W
Oneida Indian Reservation, ind. res., Wi., U.S.	126	D1	44.30 N	88.10 W
Oneida Lake, l., N.Y., U.S.	126	E14	43.13 N	76.00 W
O'Neill, Ne., U.S.	140	E14	42.27 N	98.38 W
Onekama, Mi., U.S.	126	D3	44.22 N	86.11 W
Onekotan, ostrov, i., Russia	50	G20	49.21 N	154.42 E
Oneonta, Al., U.S.	134	D12	33.56 N	86.28 W
Oneonta, N.Y., U.S.	124	B10	42.27 N	75.03 W
Oneroa, i., Cook Is.	100j	b27	21.15 S	159.43 W
Onești, Rom.	36	C13	46.15 N	26.46 E
One Tree Hill, hill, Austl.	192b		37.52 S	145.19 E
Onevai, i., Tonga	100e	n14	21.05 S	175.07 W
Onežskaja guba (Onega Bay), b., Russia	18	C23	64.20 N	36.30 E
Onežskij poluostrov, pen., Russia	18	C25	64.35 N	38.00 E
Onežskoe ozero (Onega, Lake), l., Russia	18	F22	61.30 N	35.45 E
Ong Con, Cu Lao, i., Viet.	187c		10.45 N	106.50 E
Ongjin-ŭp, Kor., N.	54	F6	37.55 N	125.21 E
Ongniud Qi, China	54	C3	42.56 N	119.01 E
Ongole, India	69	D5	15.29 N	80.02 E
Ongudaj, Russia	48	D15	50.44 N	86.08 E
Oni, Geor.	42	D10	42.36 N	43.27 E
Onida, S.D., U.S.	140	C12	44.42 N	100.04 W
Onilahy, stm., Madag.	88	F7	23.34 S	43.45 E
Onion Creek, stm., Tx., U.S.	136	D10	30.12 N	97.35 W
Onitsha, Nig.	84	H6	6.09 N	6.47 E
Onji, Japan	188		34.37 N	135.38 E
Onkivesi, l., Fin.	18	D13	63.17 N	27.17 E
Ōno, Japan	56	D9	35.59 N	136.29 E
Ōno, Japan	188		34.57 N	135.14 E
Ono, i., Fiji	101e	q19	18.53 S	178.29 E
Onoda, Japan	56	F4	33.58 N	131.11 E
Ono-i-Lau, i., Fiji	94	F9	20.39 S	178.42 W
Onomichi, Japan	56	E6	34.24 N	133.12 E
Onon, Mong.	52	B7	49.07 N	112.40 E
Onondaga Indian Reservation, ind. res., N.Y., U.S.	124	B9	42.56 N	76.09 W
Onon Gol, stm., Asia	50	F11	51.41 N	115.49 E
Onoto, Ven.	168	C9	9.36 N	65.11 W
Onotoa, at., Kir.	94	D8	1.53 S	175.34 E
Onoway, Ab., Can.	144	C16	53.42 N	114.12 W
Ons, Illa de, i., Spain	28	B2	42.22 N	8.55 W
Ons, Isla de see Ons, Illa de, i., Spain	28	B2	42.22 N	8.55 W
Onseepkans, S. Afr.	90	F4	28.44 S	19.16 E
Onset, Ma., U.S.	124	C15	41.44 N	70.41 W
Onslow, Austl.	96	D3	21.39 S	115.06 E
Onslow Bay, b., N.C., U.S.	132	B8	34.20 N	77.20 W
Onslow Village, Eng., U.K.	178		51.14 N	0.36 W
On-take, vol., Japan	56	H3	31.35 N	130.39 E
Ontake-san, vol., Japan	56	D10	35.53 N	137.29 E
Ontario, Ca., U.S.	148	I8	34.04 N	117.39 W
Ontario, Or., U.S.	146	F10	44.01 N	116.57 W
Ontario, state, Can.	110	E13	51.00 N	85.00 W
Ontario, Lake, l., N.A.	126	E11	43.45 N	78.00 W
Ontario Place, p.o.i., On., Can.	193b		43.38 N	79.25 W
Ontario Science Centre, bldg., On., Can.	193b		43.43 N	79.21 W
Ontinyent, Spain	28	F10	38.49 N	0.36 W
Ontojärvi, l., Fin.	18	C15	64.08 N	29.09 E
Ontonagon, Mi., U.S.	128	E9	46.51 N	89.19 W
Ontonagon, stm., Mi., U.S.	128	E9	46.51 N	89.18 W
Ontonagon, East Branch, stm., Mi., U.S.	128	E10	46.41 N	89.08 W
Ontonagon, Middle Branch, stm., Mi., U.S.	128	E9	46.41 N	89.08 W
Ontonagon, West Branch, stm., Mi., U.S.	128	E9	46.41 N	89.11 W
Ontong Java, at., Sol. Is.	94	D7	5.19 S	159.16 E
Onufriivka, Ukr.	38	E12	48.54 N	33.27 E
Ōnuma, Japan	186		35.32 N	139.25 E
Onverwacht, Sur.	164	B6	5.35 N	55.12 W
Ŏnyang, Kor., S.	56	D2	35.34 N	129.07 E
Oodnadatta, Austl.	96	E7	27.32 S	135.26 E
Ooldea, Austl.	96	F6	30.27 S	131.50 E
Oolitic, In., U.S.	130	F11	38.53 N	86.31 W
Oologah, Ok., U.S.	130	H2	36.26 N	95.42 W
Oologah Lake, res., Ok., U.S.	130	H2	36.33 N	95.36 W
Oorlogskloof, stm., S. Afr.	90	G4	31.52 S	19.01 E
Oos-Londen see East London, S. Afr.	90	H8	33.00 S	27.54 E
Oostburg, Wi., U.S.	126	E2	43.37 N	87.47 W
Oostelijk Flevoland, reg., Neth.	20	B14	52.30 N	5.40 E
Oostende, Bel.	20	C11	51.13 N	2.54 E
Oosterhout, Neth.	20	C13	51.38 N	4.50 E
Oosterschelde, est., Neth.	20	C12	51.34 N	3.57 E
Oostpunt, c., Neth. Ant.	158g	p22	12.02 N	68.45 W
Ootsa Lake, B.C., Can.	144	C4	53.48 N	126.02 W
Ootsa Lake, res., B.C., Can.	144	C4	53.49 N	126.18 W
Ootua, mtn., Fr. Poly.	100g	s19	9.46 S	138.57 W
Opaka, Blg.	36	F13	43.27 N	26.10 E
Opala, D.R.C.	86	E4	0.36 S	24.18 E
Opalenica, Pol.	24	D12	52.18 N	16.23 E
Opaliha, Russia	183b		55.49 N	37.15 E
Oparino, Russia	12	G23	59.51 N	48.17 E
Opasatika, stm., On., Can.	114	B9	50.24 N	82.22 W
Opatija, Cro.	30	E11	45.20 N	14.17 E
Opatów, Pol.	24	F17	50.48 N	21.25 E
Opava, Czech Rep.	24	G13	49.56 N	17.54 E
Opava, stm., Eur.	24	F13	49.49 N	18.13 E
Opawica, stm., Qc., Can.	122	A2	49.11 N	74.28 W
Opečenskij Posad, Russia	26	B17	58.16 N	34.05 E
Opeilu, Nig.	191a		6.42 N	3.18 E
Opelika, Al., U.S.	134	E13	32.38 N	85.22 W
Opelousas, La., U.S.	134	G6	30.32 N	92.04 W
Opeongo, stm., On., Can.	126	C12	45.29 N	77.56 W
Opeongo Lake, l., On., Can.	126	C11	45.41 N	78.23 W
Opheim, Mt., U.S.	142	F7	48.51 N	106.25 W
Opherdicke, Ger.	181		51.29 N	7.38 E
Ophir, Ak., U.S.	109	D8	63.10 N	156.31 W
Ophir, Or., U.S.	146	H2	42.34 N	124.21 W
Ophirton, ngh., S. Afr.	191d		26.14 S	28.01 E
Opihikao, Hi., U.S.	100a	d7	19.26 N	154.53 W
Opinaca, stm., Qc., Can.	110	E15	52.14 N	78.00 W
Opiscotéo, Lac, l., Qc., Can.	110	E17	53.09 N	68.13 W
Opishnia, Ukr.	38	D13	49.58 N	34.35 E
Opobo, Nig.	84	I6	4.34 N	7.34 E
Opočka, Russia	26	D11	56.42 N	28.40 E
Opoczno, Pol.	24	E16	51.22 N	20.18 E
Opole, Pol.	24	F13	50.39 N	17.56 E
Opole Lubelskie, Pol.	24	E18	51.08 N	21.58 E
Opolskie, state, Pol.	24	F13	50.30 N	17.45 E
Opon see Lapu-Lapu, Phil.	68	E4	10.18 N	123.57 E
Opornyj, Kaz.	40	H19	46.13 N	54.27 E
Oporto see Porto, Port.	28	C2	41.09 N	8.36 W
Opotiki, N.Z.	102	D7	37.59 S	177.16 E
Opp, Al., U.S.	134	F12	31.16 N	86.15 W
Oppdal, Nor.	16	E7	62.35 N	9.41 E
Oppeln see Opole, Pol.	24	F13	50.39 N	17.56 E
Oppenheim Park, p.o.i., N.Y., U.S.	202a		43.06 N	78.54 W
Oppland, state, Nor.	16	F7	61.10 N	9.40 E
Opportunity, Mt., U.S.	146	D14	46.06 N	112.50 W
Opportunity, Wa., U.S.	146	C9	47.39 N	117.12 W
Oppum, ngh., Ger.	181		51.19 N	6.37 E
Opsa, Bela.	26	E9	55.32 N	26.47 E
Optima Lake, res., Ok., U.S.	138	E7	36.40 N	101.10 W
Opua, N.Z.	102	B6	35.18 S	174.06 E
Opunake, N.Z.	102	D5	39.27 S	173.51 E
Opunohu, Baie d', b., Fr. Poly.	100h	u20	17.29 S	149.51 W
Opuwo, Nmb.	88	D1	18.01 S	13.41 E
Oquawka, Il., U.S.	128	K7	40.55 N	90.56 W
Oquendo, Peru	204d		11.58 S	77.08 W
Or, Côte d', mts., Fr.	20	G13	47.10 N	4.50 E
Or, Étang d', l., Fr.	179		48.38 N	1.51 E
Oracle, Az., U.S.	150	K6	32.37 N	110.45 W
Oradea, Rom.	36	B8	47.03 N	21.55 E
Oradell, N.J., U.S.	194		40.57 N	74.02 W
Oradell Reservoir, res., N.J., U.S.	194		40.58 N	74.01 W
Öræfajökull, ice, Ice.	12a	k31	64.03 N	16.38 W
Orahovica, Cro.	30	E14	45.31 N	17.56 E
Orai, India	70	F7	25.59 N	79.28 E
Oraibi Wash, stm., Az., U.S.	150	H6	35.26 N	110.49 W
Oral see Ural'sk, Kaz.	48	D8	51.13 N	51.21 E
Oran see Wahran, Alg.	84	B4	35.41 N	0.39 W
Oran, Mo., U.S.	130	G8	37.05 N	89.39 W
Orange, Austl.	98	I7	33.17 S	149.05 E
Orange, Fr.	22	E10	44.08 N	4.48 E
Orange, Ma., U.S.	124	B13	42.35 N	72.18 W
Orange, N.J., U.S.	194		40.46 N	74.13 W
Orange, Oh., U.S.	197a		41.26 N	81.29 W
Orange, Tx., U.S.	136	D14	30.05 N	93.44 W
Orange, Va., U.S.	124	F7	38.14 N	78.06 W
Orange (Oranje) (Senqu), stm., Afr.	90	F3	28.35 S	16.28 E
Orange, Cabo, c., Braz.	164	C7	4.22 N	51.32 W
Orangeburg, S.C., U.S.	132	C5	33.29 N	80.51 W
Orange City, Fl., U.S.	132	H4	28.57 N	81.18 W
Orange City, Ia., U.S.	130	A2	43.00 N	96.03 W
Orange Cove, Ca., U.S.	148	G6	36.36 N	119.18 W
Orange Free State see Free State, state, S. Afr.	90	F8	28.30 S	27.00 E
Orange Grove, Tx., U.S.	136	G9	27.57 N	97.56 W
Orange Grove, ngh., S. Afr.	191d		26.10 S	28.05 E
Orange Lake, Fl., U.S.	132	G3	29.24 N	82.12 W
Orange Lake, l., Fl., U.S.	132	G3	29.27 N	82.10 W
Orange Park, Fl., U.S.	132	F4	30.10 N	81.41 W
Orange Park Acres, Ca., U.S.	198		33.48 N	117.47 W
Orange Reservoir, res., N.J., U.S.	194		40.46 N	74.17 W
Orangeville, On., Can.	126	E9	43.55 N	80.05 W
Orangeville, Ut., U.S.	150	D5	39.13 N	111.03 W
Orange Walk, Belize	156	C3	18.05 N	88.32 W
Orango, Ilha de, i., Gui.-B.	84	G1	11.07 N	16.09 W
Orani, Phil.	68	C3	14.48 N	120.31 E
Oranienburg, Ger.	24	D9	52.45 N	13.14 E
Oranje see Orange, stm., Afr.	90	F3	28.35 S	16.28 E
Oranje Gebergte, mts., Sur.	164	C6	3.00 N	55.05 W
Oranjemund, Nmb.	90	F3	28.34 S	16.27 E
Oranjestad, Aruba	158g	o19	12.32 N	70.01 W
Oranjestad, Neth. Ant.	159a	c1	17.29 N	62.59 W
Oranje Vrijstaat see Free State, state, S. Afr.	90	F8	28.30 S	27.00 E
Orăștie, Rom.	36	D10	45.50 N	23.12 E
Orașul Stalin see Brașov, Rom.	36	D12	45.39 N	25.37 E
Orativ, Ukr.	38	D8	49.12 N	29.32 E
Oratório, Ribeirão do, stm., Braz.	205b		23.37 S	46.32 W
Oravainen, Fin.	18	D9	63.17 N	22.23 E
Oravais see Oravainen, Fin.	18	D9	63.17 N	22.23 E
Oravița, Rom.	36	D8	45.02 N	21.41 E
Orb, stm., Fr.	22	F9	43.15 N	3.17 E
Orba, stm., Italy	30	F5	44.52 N	8.37 E
Orba Co, l., China	70	A8	34.31 N	81.02 E
Orbetello, Italy	30	H8	42.26 N	11.13 E
Orbetello, Laguna di, l., Italy	30	H7	42.27 N	11.12 E
Orbieu, stm., Fr.	22	F8	43.13 N	2.53 E
Órbigo, stm., Spain	28	B5	41.57 N	5.39 W
Orbisonia, Pa., U.S.	124	D8	40.15 N	77.53 W
Orbost, Austl.	98	K7	37.42 S	148.27 E
Örbyhus, Swe.	16	G15	60.13 N	17.42 E
Orcadas, sci., Ant.	103	B36	60.45 S	44.43 W
Orcemont, Fr.	179		48.35 N	1.49 E
Orcera, Spain	28	F8	38.19 N	2.39 W
Orchard, Ne., U.S.	140	E14	42.20 N	98.14 W
Orchard City, Co., U.S.	150	E8	38.49 N	107.59 W
Orchard Hills, Austl.	192a		33.47 S	150.43 E
Orchard Hills, Pa., U.S.	197b		40.35 N	79.32 W
Orchard Homes, Mt., U.S.	146	D12	46.53 N	114.02 W
Orchard Lake, l., Mi., U.S.	199		42.35 N	83.22 W
Orchard Lake Village, Mi., U.S.	199		42.35 N	83.21 W
Orchard Mesa, Co., U.S.	150	E8	39.00 N	108.28 W
Orchard Park, N.Y., U.S.	124	B7	42.46 N	78.44 W
Orchard Park Airport, arpt., N.Y., U.S.	202a		42.48 N	78.45 W
Orchards, The, Md., U.S.	202b		39.18 N	76.50 W
Orchard Valley, Wy., U.S.	140	F8	41.06 N	104.48 W
Orchard View, N.J., U.S.	203		40.04 N	74.53 W
Orchyk, stm., Ukr.	38	D14	49.10 N	35.04 E
Orco, stm., Italy	30	E4	45.11 N	7.52 E
Ord, Ne., U.S.	140	F14	41.36 N	98.55 W
Ord, stm., Austl.	96	C5	15.14 S	128.12 E
Ord, Mount, mtn., Austl.	96	C5	17.20 S	125.34 E
Orda, Russia	40	C20	57.11 N	56.54 E
Ordenes see Ordes, Spain	28	A2	43.04 N	8.24 W
Orderville, Ut., U.S.	150	F4	37.16 N	112.38 W
Ordes, Spain	28	A2	43.04 N	8.24 W
Ordesa y Monte Perdido, Parque Nacional de, p.o.i., Spain	28	B10	42.39 N	0.02 E
Ord Mountain, mtn., Ca., U.S.	148	I9	34.41 N	116.48 W
Ordoqui, Arg.	172	G7	35.52 S	61.09 W
Ordos Desert see Mu Us Shamo, des., China	58	B3	38.45 N	109.10 E
Ord River, Austl.	96	C5	17.24 S	128.51 E
Ordu, Tur.	42	E7	40.58 N	37.52 E
Ordu, state, Tur.	42	E7	40.45 N	37.30 E
Ordway, Co., U.S.	138	C5	38.13 N	103.45 W
Ordžhonikidze see Vladikavkaz, Russia	42	D11	43.02 N	44.39 E
Ordzhonikidze, Ukr.	38	F13	47.40 N	34.03 E
Ordžonikidzeabad, Taj.	72	B10	38.32 N	69.01 E
Ordžonikidzevskij, Russia	42	D9	43.53 N	41.53 E
Öreälven, stm., Swe.	16	C16	63.31 N	19.44 E
Örebro, Swe.	16	H13	59.17 N	15.12 E
Örebro, state, Swe.	16	H12	59.30 N	15.00 E
Ore City, Tx., U.S.	136	B13	32.48 N	94.43 W
Oredež, Russia	26	B13	58.49 N	30.20 E
Oredež, stm., Russia	26	A13	58.49 N	29.58 E
Oregon, Il., U.S.	130	B8	42.01 N	89.20 W
Oregon, Mo., U.S.	130	D2	39.59 N	95.08 W
Oregon, Oh., U.S.	124	C2	41.38 N	83.24 W
Oregon, state, U.S.	146	G7	44.00 N	121.00 W
Oregon Caves National Monument, p.o.i., Or., U.S.	148	B2	42.06 N	123.24 W
Oregon City, Or., U.S.	146	E4	45.20 N	122.35 W
Oregon Dunes National Recreation Area, p.o.i., Or., U.S.	146	G2	43.46 N	124.08 W
Öregrund, Swe.	16	G16	60.19 N	18.26 E
Orehovo-Zuevo, Russia	26	E21	55.47 N	38.57 E
Orekhovo-Zuevo, Russia	40	D11	55.47 N	38.57 E
Orel, Russia	26	G18	52.58 N	36.04 E
Orel', ozero, l., Russia	50	F16	53.29 N	139.43 E
Oreland, Pa., U.S.	203		40.07 N	75.10 W
Orellana, Peru	164	E2	6.54 S	75.09 W
Orellana, Embalse de, res., Spain	28	E5	39.00 N	5.24 W
Orem, Ut., U.S.	150	C5	40.16 N	111.40 W
Ore Mountains, mts., Eur.	24	F9	50.37 N	12.53 E
Ören, Tur.	34	F10	37.02 N	27.57 E
Orenburg, Russia	40	F19	51.48 N	55.05 E
Orenburg see Orenburgskaja oblast', co., Russia	40	E19	52.21 N	54.56 E
Orenburgskaja oblast', co., Russia	40	E19	52.21 N	54.56 E
Örencik, Tur.	34	D12	39.15 N	29.32 E
Orense, Arg.	172	I8	38.41 S	59.47 W
Orense see Ourense, Spain	28	B3	42.20 N	7.51 W
Orense see Ourense, co., Spain	28	B3	42.15 N	7.30 W
Oreor, i., Palau	100b	g8	7.20 N	134.29 E
Orestes Pereyra, Mex.	154	B6	26.29 N	105.37 W
Orestiáda, Grc.	34	B9	41.30 N	26.32 E
Öresund see Sound, The, strt., Eur.	16	L10	55.49 N	12.40 E
Øresund see Sound, The, strt., Eur.	16	L10	55.49 N	12.40 E
Orford, Eng., U.K.	180		53.25 N	2.35 W
Orford Ness, c., Eng., U.K.	10	I14	52.05 N	1.33 E
Orfordville, Wi., U.S.	130	B8	42.37 N	89.15 W
Organ Needle, mtn., N.M., U.S.	136	B1	32.21 N	106.33 W
Organ Pipe Cactus National Monument, p.o.i., Az., U.S.	150	K4	32.00 N	112.55 W
Orgaz, Spain	28	E7	39.38 N	3.52 W
Orgelet, Fr.	20	H14	46.31 N	5.36 E
Orgerus, Fr.	179		48.50 N	1.42 E
Orgeval, stm., Fr.	179		49.00 N	1.54 E
Órgiva, Spain	28	H7	36.54 N	3.25 W
Orgosolo, Italy	32	D3	40.12 N	9.21 E
Orgūn, Afg.	72	C10	32.58 N	69.10 E
Orhaneli, Tur.	34	D11	39.54 N	28.59 E
Orhangazi, Tur.	34	C12	40.29 N	29.18 E
Orhei, Mol.	38	F7	47.22 N	28.49 E
Orhej see Orhei, Mol.	38	F7	47.22 N	28.49 E
Orhon, stm., Mong.	52	B5	50.13 N	106.07 E
Oria, stm., Spain	22	F3	43.17 N	2.07 W
Orichuna, stm., Ven.	168	D7	7.27 N	68.58 W
Orick, Ca., U.S.	148	B1	41.18 N	124.01 W
Orient, Ia., U.S.	130	C3	41.12 N	94.24 W
Orient, Wa., U.S.	146	B8	48.53 N	118.12 W
Oriental, N.C., U.S.	132	A9	35.01 N	76.41 W
Oriental, Cordillera, mts., Col.	168	E5	6.00 N	73.00 W
Oriental, Cordillera, mts., Peru	164	E2	7.00 S	76.00 W
Oriental, Pico, mtn., Ven.	204c		10.32 N	66.50 W
Oriente, Arg.	172	I7	38.43 S	60.36 W
Orientos, Austl.	98	G3	28.05 S	141.14 E
Origgio, Italy	184b		45.36 N	9.01 E
Orihuela see Oriola, Spain	28	F10	38.05 N	0.57 W
Orikhiv, Ukr.	38	F14	47.33 N	35.47 E
Oril', stm., Ukr.	38	E13	48.30 N	34.53 E
Orillia, On., Can.	126	D10	44.36 N	79.25 W
Orimattila, Fin.	18	G12	60.48 N	25.46 E
Orinduik, Guy.	168	E11	4.42 N	60.01 W
Orinoco, stm., S.A.	168	C10	8.47 N	60.39 W
Orinoco, Delta del, del., Ven.	168	C11	9.15 N	61.30 W
Oriola, Spain	28	F10	38.05 N	0.57 W
Oriole Park, p.o.i., Md., U.S.	202b		39.18 N	76.37 W
Orion, Il., U.S.	130	C7	41.21 N	90.22 W
Oripää, Fin.	18	G9	60.51 N	22.41 E
Oriskany, N.Y., U.S.	126	E14	43.09 N	75.20 W
Orissa, state, India	62	D5	20.00 N	84.00 E
Orissaare, Est.	26	B6	58.33 N	23.03 E
Oristano, Italy	32	E2	39.54 N	8.35 E
Oristano, Golfo di, b., Italy	32	E2	39.50 N	8.29 E
Orituco, stm., Ven.	168	C8	8.45 N	67.25 W
Orivesi, Fin.	18	F11	61.40 N	24.21 E
Orivesi, l., Fin.	18	E15	62.16 N	29.24 E
Oriximiná, Braz.	164	D6	1.45 S	55.52 W
Orizaba, Mex.	154	F10	18.50 N	97.05 W
Orizona, Braz.	170	I1	17.01 S	48.17 W
Orjahovo, Blg.	36	F10	43.44 N	23.57 E
Ørje, Nor.	16	H9	59.28 N	11.38 E
Orjen, mtn., Yugo.	36	G5	42.34 N	18.32 E
Orkanger, Nor.	16	D7	63.18 N	9.52 E
Orkdalen, val., Nor.	16	D7	63.10 N	9.42 E
Orkelljunga, Swe.	16	K11	56.16 N	13.17 E
Orken, Ger.	181		51.06 N	6.34 E
Orkhey see Orhei, Mol.	38	F7	47.22 N	28.49 E
Orkla, stm., Nor.	16	E7	63.19 N	9.51 E
Orkney, Sk., Can.	142	E5	49.08 N	107.54 W
Orkney, S. Afr.	90	E8	26.58 S	26.40 E
Orkney Islands, is., Scot., U.K.	10	C10	59.00 N	3.00 W
Orland, Ca., U.S.	148	D3	39.44 N	122.11 W
Orlândia, Braz.	170	K1	20.42 S	47.53 W
Orland Lake, l., Il., U.S.	196		41.38 N	87.52 W
Orlando, S. Afr.	191d		26.14 S	27.55 E
Orlando, Fl., U.S.	132	H4	28.32 N	81.22 W
Orlando Dam, res., S. Afr.	191d		26.16 S	27.56 E
Orlando West Extension, S. Afr.	191d		26.15 S	27.54 E
Orland Square, shp. cen., Il., U.S.	196		41.36 N	87.51 W
Orléanais, hist. reg., Fr.	20	F11	47.52 N	2.00 E
Orleans, On., Can.	126	C14	45.28 N	75.30 W
Orléans, Fr.	20	G10	47.54 N	1.54 E
Orleans, Ca., U.S.	148	B2	41.18 N	123.32 W
Orleans, In., U.S.	130	F11	38.39 N	86.27 W
Orleans, Ma., U.S.	124	C15	41.47 N	69.59 W
Orleans, Ne., U.S.	138	A9	40.08 N	99.27 W
Orleans, Vt., U.S.	122	F4	44.48 N	72.12 W
Orléans, Canal d', can., Fr.	20	G11	47.53 N	2.01 E
Orléans, Île d', i., Qc., Can.	122	D6	46.55 N	70.58 W
Orlik, Russia	48	D18	52.27 N	99.53 E
Orlivka, Ukr.	38	H12	45.40 N	33.22 E
Orlivka, Ukr.	38	B11	51.54 N	32.48 E
Orlja, Bela.	26	G7	53.30 N	24.59 E
Orlov, Russia	40	B16	58.32 N	48.53 E
Orlov Gaj, Russia	40	F16	50.56 N	48.12 E
Orlovo, Russia	38	B18	51.45 N	39.35 E
Orlovo, ngh., Russia	183b		55.38 N	37.23 E
Orlovskaja oblast', co., Russia	40	E10	53.00 N	36.20 E
Orlovskij, Russia	40	H13	46.52 N	42.03 E
Orlovskij zaliv, b., Russia	14	E32	67.15 N	41.11 E
Orly, Fr.	20	F11	48.45 N	2.24 E
Orly, Fr.	179		48.45 N	2.24 E
Ormāra, Pak.	62	C1	25.12 N	64.37 E
Orme, Rivière à l', stm., Qc., Can.	193a		45.27 N	73.56 W
Ormiston, Sk., Can.	142	E8	49.44 N	105.23 W
Ormoc, Phil.	68	E5	11.01 N	124.36 E
Ormond, Austl.	192b		37.54 S	145.03 E
Ormond Beach, Fl., U.S.	132	G4	29.16 N	81.03 W
Ormsjön, l., Swe.	16	C14	64.23 N	16.03 E
Ornain, stm., Fr.	20	F13	48.45 N	4.40 E
Ornans, Fr.	20	G15	47.06 N	6.09 E
Orne, state, Fr.	20	F9	48.40 N	0.05 E
Orne, stm., Fr.	20	E14	49.17 N	6.11 E
Orne, stm., Fr.	20	F8	49.16 N	0.14 W
Ørnes, Nor.	14	F4	66.52 N	13.43 E
Orneta, Pol.	24	B16	54.07 N	20.08 E
Ornö, i., Swe.	16	H16	59.04 N	18.26 E
Örnsköldsvik, Swe.	16	D16	63.17 N	18.42 E
Orobie, Alpi, mts., Italy	30	D6	46.00 N	10.00 E
Oročen, Russia	50	E14	58.27 N	125.26 E
Orocovis, P.R.	158a	b3	18.13 N	66.23 W
Orocué, Col.	168	E6	4.48 N	71.19 W
Orofino, Id., U.S.	146	D10	46.29 N	116.14 W
Orog nuur, l., Mong.	52	B5	45.03 N	100.42 E
Oro Grande, Ca., U.S.	148	I8	34.36 N	117.20 W
Orohena, Mont, mtn., Fr. Poly.	100h	v22	17.37 S	149.28 W
Oroluk, at., Micron.	94	C6	7.30 N	155.17 E
Oromocto, N.B., Can.	122	E10	45.50 N	66.28 W
Oromocto Lake, l., N.B., Can.	122	E10	45.36 N	67.00 W
Oron, Nig.	84	I6	4.48 N	8.14 E
Orona, at., Kir.	94	D9	4.29 S	172.10 W
Orono, On., Can.	126	D11	43.59 N	78.36 W
Orono, Me., U.S.	122	F8	44.52 N	68.40 W
Oronsay, i., Scot., U.K.	10	F6	56.01 N	6.14 W
Orontes (Asi) ('Āṣī), stm., Asia	76	B7	36.02 N	35.58 E
Oropuche, stm., Trin.	159f	s12	10.13 N	61.30 W
Oroquieta, Phil.	68	F4	8.29 N	123.48 E
Orós, Braz.	170	D6	6.15 S	38.55 W
Orós, Açude, res., Braz.	170	D6	6.16 S	38.57 W
Orosei, Italy	32	D3	40.23 N	9.41 E
Orosei, Golfo di, b., Italy	32	D3	40.15 N	9.44 E
Orosháza, Hung.	36	C7	46.33 N	20.40 E
Oroszlány, Hung.	36	B5	47.29 N	18.19 E
Orote Peninsula, pen., Guam	100c	j9	13.25 N	144.38 E
Oroville, Ca., U.S.	148	D4	39.30 N	121.33 W
Oroville, Wa., U.S.	146	B7	48.55 N	119.25 W
Oroville, Lake, res., Ca., U.S.	148	D4	39.38 N	121.29 W
Orowoc Creek, stm., N.Y., U.S.	194		40.43 N	73.13 W
Orpheus Island, i., Austl.	98	B6	18.37 S	146.30 E
Orphin, Fr.	179		48.35 N	1.47 E
Orpington, ngh., Eng., U.K.	178		51.23 N	0.06 E
Orreagal see Roncesvalles, Spain	28	A9	43.01 N	1.19 W
Orrefors, Swe.	16	K13	56.50 N	15.45 E
Orrick, Mo., U.S.	130	E3	39.12 N	94.06 W
Orrin, N.D., U.S.	142	F13	48.05 N	100.09 W
Òrrius, Spain	184d		41.33 N	2.21 E
Orroroo, Austl.	98	I2	32.43 S	138.36 E
Orrs Island, Me., U.S.	122	G7	43.46 N	69.57 W
Orrville, Al., U.S.	134	E11	32.19 N	87.15 W
Orrville, Pa., U.S.	197b		40.33 N	79.47 W
Orša, Bela.	26	F13	54.30 N	30.24 E
Orsa, Swe.	16	F12	61.07 N	14.37 E
Orsasjön, l., Swe.	16	F12	61.05 N	14.33 E
Orsett, Eng., U.K.	178		51.31 N	0.22 E
Orsjön, l., Swe.	16	F14	61.34 N	16.22 E
Orsk, Russia	48	D9	51.12 N	58.33 E
Orșova, Rom.	36	E9	44.42 N	22.24 E
Ørsta, Nor.	16	E4	62.12 N	6.08 E
Orta, Tur.	34	C16	40.38 N	33.06 E
Orta, Lago d', l., Italy	30	E5	45.49 N	8.24 E
Ortaca, Tur.	34	G11	36.48 N	28.47 E
Ortakent, Tur.	34	F10	37.03 N	27.21 E
Ortaklar, Tur.	34	F10	37.53 N	27.30 E
Ortaköy, ngh., Tur.	185b		41.03 N	29.01 E
Orta Nova, Italy	32	C9	41.19 N	15.41 E
Ortega, Col.	168	F4	3.56 N	75.13 W
Ortegal, Cabo, c., Spain	28	A2	43.45 N	7.53 W
Orteguaza, stm., Col.	168	G4	0.44 N	75.15 W
Ortelsburg see Szczytno, Pol.	24	C17	53.33 N	21.00 E
Orthez, Fr.	22	F5	43.29 N	0.46 W
Orthon, stm., Bol.	166	B3	10.49 S	66.04 W
Órthrys, Óros, mts., Grc.	34	D5	39.02 N	22.37 E
Ortigueira, Braz.	172	B12	24.11 S	50.57 W
Ortigueira, Spain	28	A3	43.40 N	7.50 W
Orting, Wa., U.S.	146	C4	47.05 N	122.12 W
Ortisei, Italy	30	D8	46.34 N	11.40 E
Ortiz, Mex.	154	A3	28.17 N	110.43 W
Ortiz, Ven.	168	C8	9.37 N	67.15 W
Ortoire, stm., Trin.	159f	s12	10.20 N	61.00 W
Ortolo, stm., Fr.	22	H15	41.30 N	8.55 E
Ortona, Italy	30	H11	42.21 N	14.24 E
Orton Park, p.o.i., On., Can.	193b		43.46 N	79.12 W
Ortonville, Mn., U.S.	118	F2	45.18 N	96.26 W
Örträsk, Swe.	16	C16	64.08 N	18.59 E
Ortúzar, Canal, can., Chile	204e		33.33 S	70.47 W
Ortze, stm., Ger.	20	B19	52.40 N	9.56 E
Oruba, Nig.	191a		6.35 N	3.25 E
Orūmīyeh (Urmia), Iran	74	B9	37.32 N	45.04 E
Orūmīyeh, Daryācheh-ye, l., Iran	42	F11	37.40 N	45.30 E
Oruro, Bol.	164	G4	17.58 S	67.06 W
Orust, i., Swe.	16	I9	58.10 N	11.38 E
Orvieto, Italy	30	H9	42.44 N	12.06 E
Orvilliers, Fr.	179		48.52 N	1.39 E
Orwell, Oh., U.S.	124	C5	41.31 N	80.52 W
Orxon, stm., China	52	B8	48.56 N	117.45 E
Orynyn, Ukr.	38	E5	48.46 N	26.24 E
Oryu-dong, ngh., Kor., S.	189b		37.29 N	126.51 E
Orzhiv, Ukr.	38	C5	50.44 N	26.06 E
Orzhytsia, Ukr.	38	D11	49.47 N	32.42 E
Orzinuovi, Italy	30	E6	45.24 N	9.55 E
Orzyc, stm., Pol.	24	D17	52.46 N	21.13 E
Orzysz, Pol.	24	C17	53.48 N	21.56 E
Oš, Kyrg.	48	F12	40.32 N	72.48 E
Os, Nor.	16	E9	62.30 N	11.12 E
Os see Osøyro, Nor.	16	G3	60.12 N	5.27 E
Osa, Russia	40	C19	57.16 N	55.27 E
Osa, Península de, pen., C.R.	156	H6	8.34 N	83.31 W
Osage, Ia., U.S.	128	H6	43.17 N	92.48 W
Osage, N.J., U.S.	203		39.51 N	75.01 W
Osage, Wy., U.S.	140	D8	43.58 N	104.25 W
Osage, stm., Mo., U.S.	130	F5	38.35 N	91.56 W
Osage Beach, Mo., U.S.	130	F5	38.09 N	92.37 W
Osage City, Ks., U.S.	130	F2	38.38 N	95.48 W
Osage Indian Reservation, ind. res., Ok., U.S.	138	E12	36.30 N	96.15 W
Ōsaka, Japan	56	E8	34.40 N	135.30 E
Ōsaka, Japan	188		34.40 N	135.30 E
Ōsaka, state, Japan	56	E8	34.30 N	135.30 E
Osaka Aquarium, bldg., Japan	188		34.39 N	135.26 E
Osaka Castle, hist., Japan	188		34.41 N	135.32 E
Ōsaka-heiya, pl., Japan	188		34.43 N	135.30 E
Ōsaka International Airport, arpt., Japan	188		34.47 N	135.26 E
Ōsaka-kō, b., Japan	188		34.38 N	135.26 E
Osakarovka, Kaz.	48	D12	50.33 N	72.35 E
Ōsaka-tōge, p., Japan	188		34.56 N	135.18 E
Osaka University, educ., Japan	188		34.42 N	135.30 E
Ōsaka-wan, b., Japan	56	E8	34.30 N	135.18 E
Osakis, Mn., U.S.	128	F3	45.51 N	95.09 W
Osăm, stm., Blg.	36	F11	43.43 N	24.51 E
Osasco, mun., Braz.	205b		23.32 S	46.46 W
Osawatomie, Ks., U.S.	130	F3	38.29 N	94.57 W
Osbaldeston, Eng., U.K.	180		53.47 N	2.32 W
Osborne, Ks., U.S.	138	B10	39.26 N	98.41 W
Osborne, Pa., U.S.	197b		40.32 N	80.10 W
Osburn, Id., U.S.	146	C11	47.29 N	115.59 W
Osby, Swe.	16	K11	56.22 N	13.59 E
Oscar Peak, mtn., B.C., Can.	144	B1	54.51 N	129.07 W
Osceola, Ar., U.S.	134	B8	35.42 N	89.58 W
Osceola, Ia., U.S.	130	C4	41.02 N	93.45 W
Osceola, Mo., U.S.	130	F4	38.02 N	93.40 W
Osceola, Ne., U.S.	140	F15	41.10 N	97.33 W
Osceola, Wi., U.S.	128	F6	45.19 N	92.42 W
Osceola Mills, Pa., U.S.	124	D7	40.51 N	78.16 W
Oschatz, Ger.	24	E9	51.17 N	13.06 E
Oschersleben, Ger.	24	D7	52.02 N	11.14 E
Oscoda, Mi., U.S.	126	D6	44.24 N	83.19 W
Öse, stm., Ger.	181		51.26 N	7.49 E
Osečenka, Russia	26	C17	57.33 N	34.48 E
Osečina, Yugo.	36	E6	44.23 N	19.36 E
Oseevskaja, Russia	183b		55.53 N	38.10 E
Osen, Nor.	16	C8	64.18 N	10.30 E
Osëtr, stm., Russia	26	F21	54.58 N	38.46 E
Osetrovo, Russia	50	E10	56.47 N	105.48 E
Osgood, In., U.S.	130	E12	39.07 N	85.17 W
Oshamambe, Japan	54	C14	42.31 N	140.22 E
Oshawa, On., Can.	126	E11	43.54 N	78.51 W
Oshibe, ngh., Japan	188		34.45 N	135.04 E
Oshika, Japan	56	A14	38.17 N	141.31 E
Oshika-hantō, pen., Japan	56	A14	38.20 N	141.30 E
Ōshima, Japan	56	F2	33.02 N	129.36 E
Ō-shima, i., Japan	56	E12	34.43 N	139.24 E
Oshima-hantō, pen., Japan	54	C14	42.00 N	140.30 E
Oshivre, ngh., India	190c		19.09 N	72.51 E
Oshkosh, Ne., U.S.	140	F10	41.24 N	102.20 W
Oshkosh, Wi., U.S.	128	G10	44.01 N	88.31 W
Oshnovīyeh, Iran	74	B9	37.02 N	45.06 E
Oshodi, Nig.	191a		6.34 N	3.21 E
Oshogbo, Nig.	84	H5	7.46 N	4.33 E
Oshtorān Kūh, mtn., Iran	74	D11	33.20 N	49.16 E
Oshtorīnān, Iran	42	H13	34.01 N	48.33 E
Oshwe, D.R.C.	86	E3	3.21 S	19.30 E
Osica de Jos, Rom.	36	E11	44.15 N	24.18 E
Osiek, Pol.	24	F17	50.31 N	21.28 E
Osijek, Cro.	36	E15	45.33 N	18.42 E
Osilo, Italy	32	D2	40.45 N	8.39 E
Osimo, Italy	30	G10	43.29 N	13.29 E
Osinniki, Russia	48	D15	53.36 N	87.19 E
Osipaonica, Yugo.	36	E8	44.32 N	21.03 E
Osipenko see Berdians'k, Ukr.	38	G15	46.44 N	36.48 E
Osipoviči see Asipovičy, Bela.	26	G11	53.17 N	28.38 E
Osipovo Selo, Russia	26	D13	56.50 N	30.29 E
Osire Süd, Nmb.	90	B3	21.00 S	17.20 E
Osivān, India	70	E4	26.43 N	72.55 E
Oskaloosa, Ia., U.S.	130	C5	41.17 N	92.38 W
Oskaloosa, Ks., U.S.	130	E2	39.12 N	95.20 W
Oskarshamn, Swe.	16	J14	57.15 N	16.28 E
Oskarström, Swe.	16	K10	56.48 N	12.58 E
Oskil (Oskol), stm., Eur.	38	D16	49.05 N	37.27 E
Os'kino, Russia	38	B17	51.14 N	39.02 E
Oskol (Oskil), stm., Eur.	38	D16	49.05 N	37.27 E
Oskolkovo, Russia	12	B26	67.59 N	53.41 E
Oskū, Iran	74	B10	37.56 N	46.00 E
Oskuj, Russia	26	A15	59.15 N	32.04 E
Oskuja, stm., Russia	26	A15	59.14 N	31.54 E
Oslava, stm., Czech Rep.	24	G12	49.05 N	16.22 E
Oslo, Nor.	16	H8	59.55 N	10.45 E
Oslo, state, Nor.	16	G8	60.00 N	10.40 E
Oslofjorden, b., Nor.	16	H8	59.20 N	10.35 E
Os'ma, stm., Russia	26	E16	57.52 N	47.45 E
Osmānābād, India	69	B3	18.10 N	76.02 E
Osmancık, Tur.	34	E6	40.58 N	34.48 E
Osmaneli, Tur.	34	C12	40.22 N	30.01 E
Osmaniye, Tur.	42	G7	37.04 N	36.16 E
Os'mino, Russia	26	A11	59.01 N	29.06 E
Ošmjanskaja vozvyšennost' see Ašmjanskae uzvyšša, plat., Eur.	26	F9	54.22 N	26.08 E
Ösmo, Swe.	16	I15	58.59 N	17.54 E
Osmond, Ne., U.S.	140	E15	42.21 N	97.35 W
Osmoy, Fr.	179		48.52 N	1.43 E
Osmussaar, i., Est.	26	A6	59.17 N	23.23 E
Osnabrück, Ger.	24	D4	52.16 N	8.03 E
Ośno Lubuskie, Pol.	24	D10	52.28 N	14.50 E
Osny, Fr.	179		49.04 N	2.04 E
Osorio, Quebrada, stm., Ven.	204c		10.36 N	66.56 W
Osorno, Chile	166	H2	40.34 S	73.07 W
Osorno, Spain	28	B6	42.24 N	4.22 W
Osorun, Nig.	191a		6.33 N	3.29 E
Osoyoos, B.C., Can.	144	G11	49.01 N	119.28 W
Osoyoos Indian Reserve, ind. res., B.C., Can.	144	G11	49.08 N	119.30 W

Name | Page | Map Ref. | Latitude | Longitude

Osoyoos Lake, l., N.A. 146 A7 48.59 N 119.26 W
Osøyro, Nor. 16 G3 60.12 N 5.27 E
Ospino, Ven. 168 C7 9.17 N 69.27 W
Oss, Neth. 20 C14 51.46 N 5.31 E
Ossa, Mount, mtn., Austl. 99a n13 41.54 S 146.01 E
Ossabaw Island, i., Ga., U.S. 132 E4 31.47 N 81.06 W
Osse, stm., Fr. 22 F6 44.07 N 0.16 E
Ossenberg, Ger. 181 51.34 N 6.35 E
Osseo, Wi., U.S. 128 G7 44.34 N 91.13 W
Ossian, In., U.S. 130 D12 40.52 N 85.10 W
Ossian, Ia., U.S. 130 A6 43.08 N 91.45 W
Ossining, N.Y., U.S. 124 C12 41.09 N 73.51 W
Ossipee, N.H., U.S. 122 G5 43.42 N 71.07 W
Ossjøen, l., Nor. 16 F9 61.13 N 11.52 E
Ossona, Italy 184b 45.30 N 8.54 E
Ossora, Russia 50 E21 59.17 N 163.09 E
Ossum-Bösinghoven, Ger. 181 51.18 N 6.39 E
Ostankino, ngh., Russia 183b 55.49 N 37.37 E
Ostap'ie, Ukr. 38 D12 49.32 N 33.46 E
Ostaškov, Russia 26 C16 57.08 N 33.07 E
Ostašovo, Russia 26 E18 55.51 N 35.53 E
Ostbüren, Ger. 181 51.31 N 7.46 E
Østby, Nor. 16 F10 61.15 N 12.32 E
Oste, stm., Ger. 20 A18 53.23 N 9.05 E
Ostende see Oostende, Bel. 20 C11 51.13 N 2.54 E
Ostër, Russia 26 F15 54.01 N 32.48 E
Oster, Ukr. 38 C9 50.57 N 30.53 E
Ostër (Ascör), stm., Eur. 26 G14 53.47 N 31.46 E
Oster, stm., Ukr. 38 C10 50.56 N 30.51 E
Osterbönen, Ger. 181 51.37 N 7.48 E
Osterburg, Ger. 24 D7 52.47 N 11.45 E
Österbybruk, Swe. 16 G15 60.12 N 17.54 E
Österbymo, Swe. 16 J13 57.49 N 15.16 E
Österdalälven, stm., Swe. 16 F11 60.32 N 15.07 E
Østerdalen, val., Nor. 16 F8 61.18 N 11.13 E
Osterfeld, ngh., Ger. 181 51.30 N 6.53 E
Östergötland, state, Swe. 16 I13 58.25 N 15.45 E
Osterholz-Scharmbeck, Ger. 24 C4 53.13 N 8.47 E
Osterley Park, p.o.i., Eng., U.K. 178 51.30 N 0.21 W
Osterode see Ostróda, Pol. 24 C15 53.41 N 19.59 E
Osterode am Harz, Ger. 24 E6 51.43 N 10.15 E
Osterøyni, i., Nor. 16 G3 60.33 N 5.35 E
Österreich see Austria, ctry., Eur. 30 C11 47.20 N 13.20 E
Östersjön see Baltic Sea, s., Eur. 8 D12 57.00 N 19.00 E
Østersøen see Baltic Sea, s., Eur. 8 D12 57.00 N 19.00 E
Östersund, Swe. 16 E12 63.10 N 14.39 E
Östervåla, Swe. 16 G15 60.11 N 17.11 E
Osterwieck, Ger. 24 E6 51.58 N 10.42 E
Ostfeld, ngh., Ger. 181 51.40 N 7.45 E
Østfold, state, Nor. 16 H9 59.20 N 11.30 E
Ostfriesische Inseln (East Frisian Islands), is., Ger. 24 C3 53.44 N 7.25 E
Ostfriesland, hist. reg., Ger. 24 C3 53.22 N 7.30 E
Østgrønland (Tunu), state, Grnld. 108 C18 69.59 N 35.00 W
Östhammar, Swe. 16 G16 60.15 N 18.22 E
Ostia, Bonifica di, reg., Italy 185a 41.46 N 12.18 E
Oštinskij Pogost, Russia 18 G22 60.52 N 35.30 E
Ostky, Ukr. 38 B6 51.15 N 27.22 E
Östmark, Swe. 16 G10 60.17 N 12.46 E
Ostpreussen, hist. reg., Eur. 26 F4 54.19 N 21.10 E
Östra Kikkejaure, l., Swe. 16 B17 65.33 N 19.53 E
Östra Silen, l., Swe. 16 H10 59.11 N 12.19 E
Ostrau see Ostrava, Czech Rep. 24 G14 49.50 N 18.17 E
Ostrava, Czech Rep. 24 G14 49.50 N 18.17 E
Östrich, Ger. 181 51.40 N 6.55 E
Ostróda, Pol. 24 C15 53.41 N 19.59 E
Ostrogožsk, Russia 40 F11 50.52 N 39.04 E
Ostroh, Ukr. 38 C5 50.19 N 26.32 E
Ostrołęka, Pol. 24 C17 53.04 N 21.34 E
Ostroróg, Pol. 24 D12 52.38 N 16.25 E
Ostrov, Czech Rep. 24 F8 50.18 N 12.56 E
Ostrov, Rom. 36 E14 44.06 N 27.23 E
Ostrov, Russia 18 G24 60.33 N 37.52 E
Ostrov, Russia 26 C11 57.20 N 28.20 E
Ostrov, Russia 183b 55.35 N 37.51 E
Ostrov, i., Slvk. 24 I13 47.55 N 17.35 E
Ostrovki, Russia 183a 59.48 N 30.50 E
Ostrov-Zalit, Russia 26 B11 58.01 N 28.06 E
Ostrowiec Świętokrzyski, Pol. 24 F17 50.56 N 21.23 E
Ostrów Lubelski, Pol. 24 E18 51.29 N 22.53 E
Ostrów Mazowiecka, Pol. 24 D17 52.48 N 21.54 E
Ostrów Wielkopolski, Pol. 24 E13 51.39 N 17.48 E
Ostrzeszów, Pol. 24 E13 51.25 N 17.57 E
Ostsee see Baltic Sea, s., Eur. 8 D12 57.00 N 19.00 E
Ost-Sümmern, Ger. 181 51.26 N 7.44 E
Ostuni, Italy 32 D11 40.44 N 17.33 E
Osuga, Russia 26 D17 56.01 N 34.21 E
Osuga, stm., Russia 26 C17 57.16 N 34.49 E
O'Sullivan Lake, l., On., Can. 128 A11 50.24 N 87.02 W
Osum, stm., Alb. 32 D14 40.49 N 19.52 E
Ōsumi, Japan 188 34.50 N 135.45 E
Ōsumi-hantō, pen., Japan 56 H3 31.20 N 130.55 E
Osumi Islands see Ōsumi-shotō, is., Japan 52 E11 30.28 N 130.38 E
Ōsumi-kaikyō, strt., Japan 54 I9 31.00 N 131.00 E
Ōsumi-shotō, is., Japan 52 E11 30.28 N 130.38 E
Osuna, Spain 28 G5 37.14 N 5.06 W
Oswaldtwistle Moor, for., Eng., U.K. 180 53.43 N 2.23 W
Oswegatchie, stm., N.Y., U.S. 126 D14 44.42 N 75.30 W
Oswegatchie, West Branch, stm., N.Y., U.S. 126 D14 44.17 N 75.20 W
Oswego, Il., U.S. 130 C9 41.40 N 88.20 W
Oswego, Ks., U.S. 130 G2 37.10 N 95.06 W
Oswego, N.Y., U.S. 126 E13 43.27 N 76.30 W
Oswego, stm., N.Y., U.S. 126 E13 43.27 N 76.30 W
Oswestry, Eng., U.K. 10 I9 52.51 N 3.03 W
Oświęcim (Auschwitz), Pol. 24 F15 50.03 N 19.13 E
Osyka, Ms., U.S. 134 F8 31.00 N 90.28 W
Osypenko, Ukr. 38 G15 46.54 N 36.49 E
Ōta, Japan 56 C12 36.17 N 139.22 E
Ōta, ngh., Japan 186 35.34 N 139.43 E
Otaci, Mol. 38 E6 48.25 N 27.47 E
Ōtake, Japan 56 E5 34.12 N 132.13 E
Otaki, N.Z. 102 E6 40.45 S 175.08 E
Otanmäki, Fin. 18 C13 64.07 N 27.03 E
Otaru, Japan 54 C14 43.11 N 140.59 E
Otautau, N.Z. 102 H2 46.08 S 167.59 E
Otava, Fin. 18 F13 61.38 N 27.04 E
Otava, stm., Czech Rep. 24 G9 49.26 N 14.11 E
Otavalo, Ec. 168 G2 0.14 N 78.16 W
Otavi, Nmb. 88 D2 19.38 S 17.20 E
Ōtawara, Japan 56 C12 36.52 N 140.02 E
Otawa-yama, mtn., Japan 188 34.28 N 135.53 E
Otego Creek, stm., N.Y., U.S. 122 G3 42.25 N 75.07 W
Oteotea, Sol. Is. 101b e9 9.04 S 161.10 E
Otepää, Est. 26 B9 58.03 N 26.29 E
Oteros, stm., Mex. 154 B4 27.28 N 108.30 W
Otertinden, mtn., Nor. 14 C11 69.13 N 19.56 E
Otham, Eng., U.K. 178 51.15 N 0.35 E
Othello, Wa., U.S. 146 D7 46.49 N 119.09 W
Othis, Fr. 179 49.04 N 2.41 E
Othonoi, i., Grc. 34 D2 39.50 N 19.26 E
Otinapa, Mex. 154 C6 24.11 N 105.02 W
Otis, Co., U.S. 138 A6 40.09 N 102.58 W
Otis, Ks., U.S. 138 C9 38.32 N 99.03 W
Otish, Monts, mts., Qc., Can. 110 E16 52.18 N 70.37 W
Otjassy, Russia 40 E12 53.14 N 41.38 E
Otjikondo, Nmb. 88 D2 19.50 S 15.27 E
Otjimbingwe, Nmb. 90 C2 22.20 S 16.08 E
Otjinene, Nmb. 90 B4 21.12 S 18.46 E
Otjiwarongo, Nmb. 90 B3 20.26 S 16.38 E
Otjozondjou, stm., Nmb. 90 B5 20.20 S 20.56 E
Otjozondjupa, state, Nmb. 90 B3 20.05 S 17.46 E
Otnes, Nor. 16 F9 61.45 N 11.12 E
Otočac, Cro. 30 F12 44.52 N 15.13 E
Otog Qi, China 58 B3 39.03 N 108.00 E
Ōtori-kita, Japan 188 34.33 N 135.27 E
Otorma, Russia 40 E13 53.32 N 42.32 E
Otoskwin, stm., On., Can. 110 E13 52.10 N 87.44 W
Otowa-yama, mtn., Japan 188 34.58 N 135.51 E
Otra, stm., Nor. 16 I5 58.08 N 8.00 E
Otradnaja, Russia 42 C9 44.22 N 41.31 E
Otradnoe, Russia 183a 59.47 N 30.49 E
Otradnyj, Russia 40 E17 53.21 N 51.19 E
Otradokubanskoe, Russia 40 I12 45.14 N 40.50 E
Otranto, Italy 32 D12 40.08 N 18.28 E
Otranto, Canale di see Otranto, Strait of, strt., Eur. 32 D12 40.00 N 19.00 E
Otranto, Strait of, strt., Eur. 32 D12 40.00 N 19.00 E
Otrokovice, Czech Rep. 24 G13 49.13 N 17.31 E
Otrøya, i., Nor. 16 E4 62.42 N 6.48 E
Ötscher, mtn., Aus. 30 C12 47.52 N 15.12 E
Otse, Bots. 90 D7 25.02 S 25.44 E
Otsego, Mi., U.S. 130 B12 42.27 N 85.41 W
Otselic, stm., N.Y., U.S. 124 B10 42.19 N 75.58 W
Ōtsu, Japan 56 D8 35.00 N 135.52 E
Ōtsu, Japan 186 35.16 N 139.42 E
Ōtsu, stm., Japan 188 34.30 N 135.24 E
Otta, Nor. 16 F7 61.46 N 9.33 E
Otta, stm., Nor. 16 F6 61.46 N 9.32 E
Ottadalen, val., Nor. 16 F5 61.53 N 8.21 E
Ottakring, ngh., Aus. 182b 48.12 N 16.19 E
Ottarnic Pond, l., N.H., U.S. 201 42.46 N 71.25 W
Ottavia, ngh., Italy 185a 41.58 N 12.24 E
Ottawa, On., Can. 126 C14 45.24 N 75.40 W
Ottawa, Il., U.S. 130 C9 41.20 N 88.50 W
Ottawa, Ks., U.S. 130 F2 38.36 N 95.16 W
Ottawa, Oh., U.S. 124 C1 41.01 N 84.02 W
Ottawa (Outaouais), stm., Can. 126 C15 45.20 N 73.58 W
Ottawa Islands, is., Nu., Can. 110 D14 59.30 N 80.10 W
Ottenby, Swe. 16 K14 56.13 N 16.25 E
Otterburne, Mb., Can. 142 E16 49.31 N 97.03 W
Otter Creek, Fl., U.S. 132 G3 29.19 N 82.46 W
Otter Creek, stm., Ia., U.S. 128 J5 41.20 N 93.29 W
Otter Creek, stm., Mo., U.S. 130 E6 39.31 N 91.52 W
Otter Creek, stm., Mt., U.S. 140 B6 45.36 N 106.16 W
Otter Creek, stm., Ut., U.S. 150 E5 38.10 N 112.02 W
Otter Creek, stm., Vt., U.S. 126 D16 44.12 N 73.19 W
Otter Lake, Qc., Can. 126 C13 45.51 N 76.25 W
Otter Lake, Mi., U.S. 126 E6 43.12 N 83.28 W
Otterøya, i., Nor. 16 C8 64.35 N 11.15 E
Ottershaw, Eng., U.K. 178 51.22 N 0.32 W
Otter Tail, stm., Mn., U.S. 128 E2 46.16 N 96.36 W
Otter Tail Lake, l., Mn., U.S. 128 E2 46.22 N 95.41 W
Otterup, Den. 16 L8 55.31 N 10.23 E
Otterville, Mo., U.S. 130 F5 38.42 N 93.00 W
Ottosdal, S. Afr. 90 E7 26.48 S 26.00 E
Ottoshoop, S. Afr. 90 D8 25.45 S 25.59 E
Ottoville, Oh., U.S. 124 D1 40.56 N 84.20 W
Ottsjön, l., Swe. 16 D10 63.12 N 13.02 E
Ottumwa, Ia., U.S. 130 C5 41.00 N 92.24 W
Ottweiler, Ger. 24 G3 49.24 N 7.10 E
Otu see Ōtsu, Japan 56 D8 35.00 N 135.52 E
Otumpa, Arg. 172 C6 27.19 S 62.12 W
Otun, Nig. 191a 6.42 N 3.22 E
Otway, Cape, c., Austl. 98 L4 38.51 S 143.30 E
Otwock, Pol. 24 D17 52.06 N 21.16 E
Otyniia, Ukr. 38 E3 48.44 N 24.51 E
Ötztaler Alpen (Venoste, Alpi), mts., Eur. 30 D7 46.54 N 10.49 E
Ou, stm., China 58 G9 28.01 N 120.37 E
Ou, stm., China 58 I6 20.10 N 113.03 E
Ou, stm., Laos 64 B6 20.03 N 102.12 E
Ouacha, Niger 84 G6 13.21 N 9.17 E
Ouachita, stm., U.S. 134 F7 31.37 N 91.48 W
Ouachita, Lake, res., Ar., U.S. 134 C5 34.36 N 93.22 W
Ouachita Mountains, mts., U.S. 134 C4 34.40 N 94.25 W
Ouaco, N. Cal. 101d m15 20.50 S 164.27 E
Ouadda, C.A.R. 86 C4 8.03 N 22.24 E
Ouadé, Tchabal see Chappal, Waddi, mtn., Afr. 82 F2 7.02 N 11.43 E
Ouagadougou, Burkina 84 G4 12.22 N 1.32 W
Ouahigouya, Burkina 84 G4 13.34 N 2.25 W
Ouahran see Wahran, Alg. 84 B4 35.41 N 0.39 W
Ouaka, stm., C.A.R. 86 C4 4.59 N 19.56 E
Oualâta, Maur. 84 F3 17.17 N 7.01 W
Ouallam, Niger 84 G5 14.19 N 2.05 E
Ouallene, Alg. 84 E5 24.36 N 1.15 E
Ouanary, Fr. Gu. 164 C7 4.13 N 51.40 W
Ouanda Djallé, C.A.R. 86 C4 8.53 N 22.48 E
Ouango, C.A.R. 86 D4 4.19 N 22.33 E
Ouangolodougou, C. Iv. 84 H3 9.56 N 5.09 W
Ouanne, stm., Fr. 20 G12 47.57 N 2.47 E
Ouarâne, reg., Maur. 84 E2 21.00 N 10.30 W
Ouareau, Lac, l., Qc., Can. 126 B15 46.17 N 74.09 W
Ouarkziz, Jbel, mts., Afr. 84 D3 28.31 N 8.57 W
Ouarzazate, Mor. 84 C3 30.55 N 6.53 W
Ouasiemsca, stm., Qc., Can. 122 A4 49.06 N 72.48 W
Oubangui (Ubangi), stm., Afr. 82 F3 0.25 S 17.47 E
Oudenaarde, Bel. 20 D12 50.50 N 3.36 E
Oudjda see Oujda, Mor. 84 C4 34.41 N 1.53 W
Oudon, stm., Fr. 20 G8 47.36 N 0.41 W
Oudtshoorn, S. Afr. 90 H6 33.35 S 22.11 E
Oued Fodda, Alg. 28 H12 36.10 N 1.31 E
Oued-Zem, Mor. 84 C3 32.52 N 6.34 W
Ouellé, C. Iv. 84 H4 7.18 N 4.02 W
Ouémé, stm., Benin 84 H5 6.27 N 2.33 E
Ouen, Île, i., N. Cal. 101d n16 22.25 S 166.47 E
Ouenzé, ngh., Congo 191b 4.14 S 15.17 E
Ouessant, Île d' (Ushant), i., Fr. 20 F3 48.28 N 5.05 W
Ouesso, Congo 86 D3 1.36 N 16.03 E
Ouezzane, Mor. 84 C3 34.48 N 5.34 W
Ouham, stm., Afr. 82 F3 9.17 N 18.16 E
Ouidah, Benin 84 H5 6.20 N 2.05 E
Ouimet Canyon, misc. cult., On., Can. 128 C10 48.49 N 88.45 W
Ouistreham, Fr. 20 E8 49.17 N 0.15 W
Oujda, Mor. 84 C4 34.41 N 1.53 W
Oulainen, Fin. 18 C11 64.16 N 24.49 E
Oulangan kansallispuisto, p.o.i., Fin. 14 F20 66.21 N 29.27 E
Oulankajoki see Olanga, stm., Eur. 14 F20 66.09 N 30.41 E
Oulu (Uleåborg), Fin. 18 B12 65.00 N 25.28 E
Oulu, state, Fin. 12 D12 65.00 N 27.00 E
Oulujärvi, l., Fin. 18 C14 64.17 N 27.08 E
Oulujoki, stm., Fin. 18 C12 65.01 N 25.29 E
Oum-Chalouba, Chad 82 D4 15.47 N 20.46 E
Oumé, C. Iv. 84 H3 6.23 N 5.25 W
Oum er Rbia, Oued, stm., Mor. 8 I7 33.20 N 8.20 W
Oum-Hadjer, Chad 82 E3 13.16 N 19.41 E
Oumiao, China 58 F5 31.56 N 112.11 E
Ounasjoki, stm., Fin. 14 F16 66.30 N 25.44 E
Ounastunturi, mtn., Fin. 14 D14 68.16 N 23.48 E
Ounianga Kébir, Chad 82 D3 19.03 N 20.29 E
Our, stm., Eur. 20 D15 49.52 N 6.17 E
Ouray, Co., U.S. 150 E9 38.01 N 107.39 W
Ouray, Mount, mtn., Co., U.S. 138 C2 38.25 N 106.14 W
Ourcq, stm., Fr. 20 E12 49.00 N 3.01 E
Ourém, Braz. 170 A2 1.32 S 47.06 W
Ourense, Spain 28 B3 42.20 N 7.51 W
Ourense, co., Spain 28 B3 42.15 N 7.30 W
Ouricuri, Braz. 170 D5 7.53 S 40.05 W
Ourinhos, Braz. 166 D7 22.59 S 49.51 W
Ourique, Port. 28 G2 37.38 N 8.13 W
Ouro, Ponta do, c., Moz. 90 E11 26.51 S 32.53 E
Ouro Branco, Braz. 170 D7 6.42 S 36.57 W
Ouro Fino, Braz. 170 L2 22.17 S 46.22 W
Ouro Preto, Braz. 170 K4 20.23 S 43.30 W
Ours, Grande chute à l', wtfl., Qc., Can. 122 B4 48.46 N 72.35 W
Ourthe, stm., Bel. 20 D14 50.36 N 5.37 E
Ōu-sammyaku, mts., Japan 54 F14 38.51 N 140.34 E
Oust, can., Fr. 20 F6 47.38 N 2.05 W
Outaouais (Ottawa), stm., Can. 126 C15 45.20 N 73.58 W
Outardes, stm., Qc., Can. 110 E17 49.02 N 68.29 W
Outardes, Baie aux, b., Qc., Can. 122 A8 49.01 N 68.33 W
Outardes Quatre, Réservoir, res., Qc., Can. 114 B15 49.58 N 69.27 W
Outcalt, N.J., U.S. 194 40.23 N 74.24 W
Outerbridge Crossing, trans., U.S. 194 40.31 N 74.15 W
Outer Hebrides, is., Scot., U.K. 10 D5 57.45 N 7.00 W
Outer Island, i., Wi., U.S. 128 D8 47.03 N 90.25 W
Outer Santa Barbara Passage, strt., Ca., U.S. 148 J7 33.10 N 118.30 W
Outjo, Nmb. 90 B3 20.06 S 16.08 E
Outlane, Eng., U.K. 180 53.39 N 1.53 W
Outlook, Sk., Can. 142 C6 51.30 N 107.03 W
Outlook, Mt., U.S. 142 F9 48.53 N 104.46 W
Outokumpu, Fin. 18 E15 62.43 N 29.03 E
Out Skerries, is., Scot., U.K. 10a n19 60.25 N 0.48 W
Ouvéa, i., N. Cal. 101d m16 20.33 S 166.34 E
Ouvidor, Braz. 170 J2 18.13 S 47.49 W
Ouye, Forêt de l', p.o.i., Fr. 179 48.32 N 2.00 E
Ouyen, Austl. 98 J4 35.04 S 142.19 E
Ovacık, Tur. 34 B15 41.05 N 32.55 E
Ovada, Italy 30 F5 44.38 N 8.38 E
Ovakent, Tur. 34 E11 38.06 N 28.01 E
Oval, The, hist. reg., Eng., U.K. 178 51.29 N 0.07 W
Ovalau, i., Fiji 101e p19 17.40 S 178.48 E
Ovalle, Chile 172 E2 30.36 S 71.12 W
Ovamboland, hist. reg., Nmb. 88 D2 17.45 S 16.30 E
Ovana, Cerro, mtn., Ven. 168 E8 4.41 N 66.46 W
Ovar, Port. 28 D2 40.52 N 8.36 W
Ovcyno, Russia 183a 59.48 N 30.37 E
Ovejas, Col. 168 C4 9.30 N 75.14 W
Ovenden, Eng., U.K. 180 53.44 N 1.53 W
Overberge, Ger. 181 51.37 N 7.41 E
Overbrook, Ks., U.S. 130 F2 38.46 N 95.33 W
Overbrook, ngh., Pa., U.S. 197b 40.24 N 79.59 W
Overbrook, ngh., Pa., U.S. 203 39.58 N 75.16 W
Overflowing, stm., Can. 142 A12 52.59 N 100.52 W
Överkalix, Swe. 14 F13 66.18 N 22.50 E
Overland Park, Ks., U.S. 130 F3 38.58 N 94.40 W
Övermark see Ylimarkku, Fin. 18 E8 62.37 N 21.29 E
Overpeck Creek, stm., N.J., U.S. 194 40.51 N 74.02 W
Overton, Ne., U.S. 140 G13 40.44 N 99.32 W
Overton, Nv., U.S. 150 G2 36.32 N 114.26 W
Overton, Tx., U.S. 136 B12 32.16 N 94.59 W
Overton Arm, b., Nv., U.S. 150 G2 36.22 N 114.22 W
Övertorneå, Swe. 14 F14 66.23 N 23.39 E
Överum, Swe. 16 I14 57.59 N 16.18 E
Överuman, l., Swe. 14 F5 66.04 N 14.50 E
Ovett, Ms., U.S. 134 F9 31.28 N 89.02 W
Ovid, Mi., U.S. 130 A13 42.59 N 84.22 W
Ovid, N.Y., U.S. 124 B9 42.40 N 76.49 W
Ovidiopol', Ukr. 38 G9 46.15 N 30.26 E
Oviedo, Spain 28 A5 43.22 N 5.50 W
Oviken, Swe. 16 D12 62.59 N 14.24 E
Oviksfjällen, mts., Swe. 16 E11 63.02 N 13.51 E
Ovinišče, Russia 26 B20 58.20 N 37.00 E
Ovino, Russia 26 A16 59.40 N 33.10 E
Ovīši, Lat. 26 C4 57.33 N 21.43 E
Ovoot, Mong. 52 B7 45.18 N 113.51 E
Øvre Anárjohka Nasjonalpark, p.o.i., Nor. 14 D15 68.50 N 24.45 E
Øvre Årdal, Nor. 16 F5 61.18 N 7.50 E
Øvre Dividal Nasjonalpark, p.o.i., Nor. 14 D10 68.46 N 20.06 E
Övre Fryken, l., Swe. 16 G11 59.56 N 13.08 E
Øvre Pasvik nasjonalpark, p.o.i., Nor. 14 C19 69.06 N 28.56 E
Øvre Rendal, Nor. 16 F9 61.53 N 11.05 E
Övre Soppero, Swe. 14 D12 68.05 N 21.41 E
Övre Svartlå, Swe. 14 F12 66.01 N 21.09 E
Ovruch, Ukr. 38 B7 51.19 N 28.49 E
Ovsjanka, Russia 50 F14 53.34 N 126.53 E
Ovstug, Russia 26 G16 53.24 N 33.52 E
Ōwada, Japan 186 35.49 N 139.33 E
Owando, Congo 86 E3 0.28 S 15.54 E
Owase, Japan 56 E9 34.04 N 136.12 E
Owasso, Ok., U.S. 130 H2 36.16 N 95.50 W
Owatonna, Mn., U.S. 128 G5 44.05 N 93.13 W
Owbeh, Afg. 72 C9 34.21 N 63.08 E
Owe, India 190c 19.04 N 73.04 E
Owego, N.Y., U.S. 124 B9 42.06 N 76.15 W
Owen, Wi., U.S. 128 G8 44.56 N 90.33 W
Owen, Mount, mtn., N.Z. 102 E5 41.33 S 172.32 E
Owendo, Gabon 86 D1 0.18 N 9.30 E
Owens, stm., Ca., U.S. 148 F7 36.24 N 117.52 W
Owensboro, Ky., U.S. 130 G10 37.45 N 87.06 W
Owens Lake, l., Ca., U.S. 148 G8 36.25 N 117.56 W
Owen Sound, On., Can. 126 D8 44.33 N 80.55 W
Owen Sound, b., On., Can. 126 D9 44.39 N 80.53 W
Owen Stanley Range, mts., Pap. N. Gui. 101a b4 9.20 S 147.55 E
Owensville, In., U.S. 130 F10 38.16 N 87.41 W
Owensville, Mo., U.S. 130 F6 38.20 N 91.30 W
Owenton, Ky., U.S. 130 F13 38.32 N 84.50 W
Owerri, Nig. 84 H6 5.29 N 7.01 E
Owikeno Lake, l., B.C., Can. 144 E3 51.39 N 126.55 W
Owings Mills, Md., U.S. 202b 39.25 N 76.46 W
Owingsville, Ky., U.S. 124 F2 38.08 N 83.45 W
Owl, stm., Ab., Can. 144 B19 55.01 N 111.46 W
Owl, stm., Mb., Can. 110 D12 57.50 N 92.44 W
Owl Creek, stm., U.S. 140 C9 44.40 N 103.28 W
Owl Creek, stm., Mt., U.S. 140 B5 45.18 N 107.21 W
Owl Creek, stm., Wy., U.S. 140 D4 43.41 N 108.10 W
Owl Creek, South Fork, stm., Wy., U.S. 140 D3 43.39 N 108.48 W
Owl Creek Mountains, mts., Wy., U.S. 140 D4 43.33 N 108.37 W
Owo, Nig. 84 H6 7.11 N 5.35 E
Oworonsoki, Nig. 191a 6.33 N 3.24 E
Owosso, Mi., U.S. 130 A13 42.59 N 84.10 W
Owuru, stm., Nig. 191a 6.39 N 3.27 E
Owyhee, Nv., U.S. 148 B9 41.56 N 116.05 W
Owyhee, stm., U.S. 118 F7 43.48 N 117.02 W
Owyhee, Lake, res., Or., U.S. 146 G9 43.28 N 117.20 W
Owyhee, South Fork, stm., U.S. 146 H10 42.00 N 116.40 W
Öxarfjördur, b., Ice. 12a j31 66.15 N 16.45 W
Oxbow, Sk., Can. 142 E11 49.13 N 102.10 W
Oxbow, Mi., U.S. 199 42.38 N 83.28 W
Oxbow Lake, l., Mi., U.S. 199 42.38 N 83.28 W
Ox Creek, stm., N.D., U.S. 142 F14 48.37 N 100.21 W
Oxelösund, Swe. 16 I15 58.40 N 17.08 E
Oxford, N.S., Can. 122 E13 45.42 N 63.52 W
Oxford, N.Z. 102 F5 43.17 S 172.10 E
Oxford, Eng., U.K. 10 J11 51.45 N 1.15 W
Oxford, Al., U.S. 134 D13 33.36 N 85.52 W
Oxford, In., U.S. 130 D10 40.31 N 87.15 W
Oxford, Ia., U.S. 130 C6 41.43 N 91.47 W
Oxford, Ks., U.S. 138 D11 37.16 N 97.10 W
Oxford, Me., U.S. 122 F6 44.08 N 70.29 W
Oxford, Md., U.S. 124 F9 38.41 N 76.10 W
Oxford, Mi., U.S. 124 B2 42.49 N 83.15 W
Oxford, Ms., U.S. 134 C9 34.21 N 89.32 W
Oxford, Ne., U.S. 138 A9 40.15 N 99.37 W
Oxford, N.Y., U.S. 124 B10 42.26 N 75.35 W
Oxford, N.C., U.S. 124 H7 36.18 N 78.35 W
Oxford, Oh., U.S. 130 E13 39.30 N 84.44 W
Oxford, Pa., U.S. 126 I14 39.46 N 75.58 W
Oxford, Wi., U.S. 128 H9 43.46 N 89.34 W
Oxford Falls, Austl. 192a 33.44 S 151.15 E
Oxford Junction, Ia., U.S. 128 J8 41.58 N 90.57 W
Oxford Lake, l., Mb., Can. 110 E11 54.48 N 95.29 W
Oxford Peak, mtn., Id., U.S. 146 H14 42.16 N 112.06 W
Oxford Valley Mall, shp. cen., Pa., U.S. 203 40.11 N 74.53 W
Oxhey, Eng., U.K. 178 51.39 N 0.23 W
Oxkutzcab, Mex. 156 B3 20.18 N 89.25 W
Oxley Downs, Austl. 98 J4 33.12 S 144.06 E
Oxley Wild Rivers National Park, p.o.i., Austl. 98 H8 30.55 S 151.58 E
Oxnard, Ca., U.S. 148 I6 34.11 N 119.10 W
Oxon Hill, Md., U.S. 202c 38.48 N 76.59 W
Oxon Run, stm., Md., U.S. 202b 38.49 N 77.00 W
Ox Pasture Brook, stm., Ma., U.S. 201 42.45 N 70.54 W
Oxshott, Eng., U.K. 178 51.20 N 0.21 W
Oxus see Amu Darya, stm., Asia 46 E10 44.01 N 59.34 E
Oxus see Amu-Darja, stm., Asia 72 A9 44.01 N 59.34 E
Oya, Malay. 66 B7 2.51 N 111.53 E
Oya, stm., Malay. 66 B8 2.52 N 111.52 E
Oyabe, Japan 56 C9 36.40 N 136.52 E
Ōyake-yama, hill, Japan 188 34.48 N 135.51 E
Oyama, B.C., Can. 144 F11 50.06 N 119.23 W
Oyama, Japan 56 C12 36.17 N 139.47 E
Oyama, Japan 186 35.36 N 139.22 E
Ōyamazaki, Japan 188 34.54 N 135.42 E
Oyameyo, Volcán, vol., Mex. 204a 19.10 N 99.11 W
Ōyano, Japan 56 G3 32.35 N 130.25 E
Oyapok (Oiapoque), stm., S.A. 164 C7 4.09 N 51.37 W
Oyem, Gabon 86 D2 1.36 N 11.35 E
Oyen, Ab., Can. 142 C3 51.21 N 110.28 W
Øyeren, l., Nor. 16 H9 59.48 N 11.14 E
Oykel, stm., Scot., U.K. 10 C8 57.56 N 4.25 W
Oyo, Nig. 84 H5 7.50 N 3.55 E
Oyodo, ngh., Japan 188 34.43 N 135.30 E
Ōyodo, stm., Japan 56 H4 31.53 N 131.28 E
Oyón, Peru 164 F2 10.38 S 76.46 W
Oyonnax, Fr. 22 C11 46.15 N 5.39 E
Oyster Bay, b., N.Y., U.S. 194 40.55 N 73.30 W
Oyster Bay Cove, N.Y., U.S. 194 40.52 N 73.31 W
Oyster Bay Harbor, b., N.Y., U.S. 194 40.53 N 73.32 W
Oyster Creek, mth., Tx., U.S. 136 E12 28.58 N 95.16 W
Oyster Point, mtn., Ca., U.S. 200 37.50 N 121.52 W
Oyster Rock, r., India 190c 18.54 N 72.50 E
Øystese, Nor. 16 G4 60.23 N 6.13 E
Øyvatnet, l., Nor. 16 C10 64.43 N 12.20 E
Ozaki, Japan 186 35.59 N 139.51 E
Ozamis, Phil. 68 F4 8.08 N 123.48 E
Ozanne, stm., Fr. 20 F9 48.11 N 1.22 E
Ozark, Al., U.S. 134 F13 31.27 N 85.38 W
Ozark, Ar., U.S. 134 B5 35.29 N 93.49 W
Ozark, Mo., U.S. 130 G4 37.01 N 93.12 W
Ozark Lake, res., Ar., U.S. 134 B4 35.28 N 93.50 W
Ozark National Scenic Riverways, p.o.i., Mo., U.S. 130 G6 37.10 N 91.10 W
Ozark Plateau, plat., U.S. 116 B6 37.00 N 93.00 W
Ozarks, Lake of the, res., Mo., U.S. 130 F5 38.06 N 92.44 W
Ózd, Hung. 36 A7 48.13 N 20.18 E
Ozeblin, mtn., Cro. 30 F12 44.35 N 15.53 E
Ožerele, Russia 26 F21 54.47 N 38.16 E
Ozerišče, Russia 26 F16 54.48 N 33.14 E
Ozerki, Russia 40 E14 52.00 N 45.28 E
Ozerki, Russia 40 F14 51.31 N 45.15 E
Ozerki, Russia 183a 59.54 N 30.44 E
Ozerne, Ukr. 38 C7 50.11 N 28.42 E
Ozërnoe, Russia 40 F17 51.46 N 51.25 E
Ozernovskij, Russia 50 F20 51.29 N 156.30 E
Ozërnyj, Russia 48 D10 51.07 N 60.52 E
Ozërsk, Russia 26 F5 54.24 N 22.00 E
Ozery, Russia 26 F21 54.51 N 38.33 E
Ozette Lake, l., Wa., U.S. 146 B2 48.06 N 124.38 W
Ozieri, Italy 32 D2 40.35 N 8.59 E
Ozimek, Pol. 24 F14 50.40 N 18.13 E
Ozinki, Russia 40 F16 51.11 N 49.42 E
Ozirs'k, Ukr. 38 B5 51.43 N 26.25 E
Ozoir-la-Ferrière, Fr. 179 48.46 N 2.40 E
Ozona, Tx., U.S. 136 D6 30.42 N 101.12 W
Ozone Park, ngh., N.Y., U.S. 194 40.40 N 73.51 W
Ozorków, Pol. 24 E15 51.57 N 19.18 E
Ozouer-le-Voulgis, Fr. 179 48.40 N 2.47 E
Ōzu, Japan 56 G3 32.52 N 130.52 E
Ōzu, Japan 56 F5 33.30 N 132.33 E
Ozuluama, Mex. 154 E9 21.39 N 97.51 W
Ozurgeti, Geor. 42 E10 41.55 N 42.00 E

P

Paagoumène, N. Cal. 101d m14 20.28 S 164.10 E
Paama, i., Vanuatu 101d k17 16.28 S 168.14 E
Paamiut see Frederikshåb, Grnld. 108 E15 62.00 N 49.41 W
Paar, stm., Ger. 30 B8 48.46 N 11.36 E
Paardekraal Monument, hist., S. Afr. 191d 26.06 S 27.47 E
Paaren, Ger. 182a 52.39 N 12.59 E
Paarl, S. Afr. 90 H4 33.43 S 18.57 E
Paasbach, stm., Ger. 181 51.25 N 7.11 E
Paauilo, Hi., U.S. 100a c6 20.02 N 155.22 W
Pabbay, i., Scot., U.K. 10 D5 57.46 N 7.13 W
Pabbi, Pak. 70 B3 33.59 N 71.46 E
Pabbiring, Kepulauan, is., Indon. 66 F11 4.50 S 119.06 E
Pabean, Indon. 66 G9 6.50 S 115.22 E
Pabellón, Ensenada del, b., Mex. 154 C4 24.25 N 107.33 W
Pabianice, Pol. 24 E15 51.39 N 19.21 E
Pablo, Mt., U.S. 146 C12 47.36 N 114.07 W
Pābna, Bngl. 70 G12 24.00 N 89.14 E
Pabradė, Lith. 26 F8 54.58 N 25.46 E
Paca, Indon. 66 H12 8.29 S 120.11 E
Pacaás Novos, Serra dos, mts., Braz. 166 B4 10.36 S 64.37 W
Pacaembú, Estádio do, p.o.i., Braz. 205b 23.33 S 46.39 W
Pacajus, Braz. 170 C6 4.10 S 38.28 W
Pacaraima, Serra see Pakaraima Mountains, mts., S.A. 168 E11 5.05 N 60.39 W
Pacaraima, Sierra de see Pakaraima Mountains, mts., S.A. 168 E11 5.05 N 60.39 W
Pacasmayo, Peru 164 E2 7.23 S 79.32 W
Pacatuba, Braz. 170 C6 3.58 S 38.37 W
Pace, Fl., U.S. 134 G11 30.35 N 87.09 W
Pačelma, Russia 40 E13 53.19 N 43.19 E
Páchi, Grc. 185c 37.59 N 23.22 E
Páchi, i., Grc. 185c 37.58 N 23.22 E
Pachino, Italy 32 H9 36.43 N 15.05 E
Pachitea, stm., Peru 164 E3 8.46 S 74.32 W
Pachkoli, ngh., India 190c 19.08 N 72.54 E
Pachmarhi, India 70 G7 22.27 N 78.26 E
Pacho, Col. 168 E4 5.08 N 74.09 W
Pāchora, India 70 H5 20.40 N 75.21 E
Pachuca de Soto, Mex. 154 E9 20.06 N 98.44 W
Pacific, B.C., Can. 144 B2 54.46 N 128.16 W
Pacific, Mo., U.S. 130 F7 38.28 N 90.44 W
Pacifica, Ca., U.S. 148 F3 37.37 N 122.29 W
Pacific-Antarctic Ridge, unds. 174 P22 62.00 S 157.00 W
Pacific Creek, stm., Wy., U.S. 140 E3 42.08 N 109.23 W
Pacific Grove, Ca., U.S. 148 G4 36.37 N 121.54 W
Pacific Ocean, oc. 174 F20 10.00 S 150.00 W
Pacific Palisades, ngh., Ca., U.S. 198 34.03 N 118.32 W
Pacific Ranges, mts., B.C., Can. 144 E5 51.10 N 125.32 W
Pacific Rim National Park, p.o.i., B.C., Can. 144 H5 48.44 N 125.05 W
Paciran, Indon. 66 G8 6.52 S 112.20 E
Pacitan, Indon. 66 H7 8.12 S 111.07 E
Packanack Lake, l., N.J., U.S. 194 40.56 N 74.15 W
Pacock Brook, stm., N.J., U.S. 194 41.05 N 74.31 W
Paço de Arcos, Port. 184c 38.42 N 9.17 W
Pacoima, ngh., Ca., U.S. 198 34.16 N 118.26 W
Pacolet, stm., S.C., U.S. 132 B4 34.50 N 81.27 W
Pacora, Pan. 168 C2 9.05 N 79.17 W
Pacov, Czech Rep. 24 G11 49.28 N 15.00 E
Pacuí, stm., Braz. 170 I3 16.46 S 45.01 W
Paczków, Pol. 24 F12 50.27 N 17.00 E
Padada, Phil. 68 G5 6.41 N 125.21 E
Padam, India 70 B6 33.29 N 76.50 E
Padamo, stm., Ven. 168 F9 2.54 N 65.17 W
Padampur, India 70 H9 20.59 N 83.04 E
Padang, Indon. 66 D2 0.57 S 100.21 E
Padang, Indon. 66 D6 1.39 S 108.55 E
Padang, Indon. 66 G12 6.14 S 120.27 E
Padang, Indon. 66 B4 2.59 N 105.41 E
Padang, Pulau, i., Indon. 66 C3 1.10 N 102.20 E
Padangbetuah, Indon. 66 E2 3.38 S 102.12 E
Padang Endau, Malay. 64 K6 2.39 N 103.37 E
Padangpanjang, Indon. 66 D2 0.27 S 100.24 E
Padangsidempuan, Indon. 66 C1 1.22 N 99.15 E
Padany, Russia 18 D20 63.17 N 33.25 E
Padas, stm., Malay. 66 A9 5.14 N 115.34 E
Padasjoki, Fin. 18 F12 61.20 N 25.17 E
Padauari, stm., Braz. 168 G9 0.15 S 64.05 W
Paddington, ngh., Eng., U.K. 178 51.31 N 0.10 W
Paddington Station, trans., Eng., U.K. 178 51.31 N 0.11 W
Paddle, stm., Ab., Can. 144 C15 54.05 N 114.14 W
Paddle Prairie, Ab., Can. 110 D7 57.58 N 117.26 W
Padea, Rom. 36 E10 44.01 N 23.52 E
Padeghar, India 190c 18.58 N 73.03 E
Paden City, W.V., U.S. 124 E5 39.36 N 80.51 W
Paderborn, Ger. 24 E4 51.43 N 8.45 E
Paderno Dugnano, Italy 184b 45.34 N 9.10 E
Padghe, India 190c 19.03 N 73.07 E
Padjelanta Nationalpark, p.o.i., Swe. 14 E7 67.28 N 16.41 E
Padle, India 190c 19.09 N 73.03 E
Padloping Island, i., Nu., Can. 108 D13 67.07 N 62.35 W
Padma see Ganges, stm., Asia 70 G13 21.58 N 90.56 E
Pàdova (Padua), Italy 30 E8 45.24 N 11.52 E
Pādra, India 70 G4 22.14 N 73.05 E
Padrauna, India 70 E9 26.54 N 83.58 E

Name	Page	Map Ref.	Latitude	Longitude
Padre Bernardo, Braz.	170	H1	15.18 S	48.10 W
Padre Island, i., Tx., U.S.	136	G10	27.00 N	97.23 W
Padre Island National Seashore, p.o.i., Tx., U.S.	136	G10	27.00 N	97.25 W
Padre Miguel, ngh., Braz.	205a		22.53 S	43.26 W
Padre Paraíso, Braz.	170	I5	17.07 S	41.31 W
Padstow, Austl.	192a		33.57 S	151.02 E
Padstow, Eng., U.K.	10	K8	50.33 N	4.56 W
Padsville, Bela.	26	E10	55.09 N	27.58 E
Padua see Pádova, Italy	30	E8	45.24 N	11.52 E
Paducah, Ky., U.S.	130	G9	37.04 N	88.36 W
Paducah, Tx., U.S.	138	G8	34.01 N	100.18 W
Paea, Fr. Poly.	100h	v21	17.40 S	149.35 W
Paedun, Kor., S.	56	D1	35.03 N	128.21 E
Paektu-san, mtn., Asia	54	D8	41.59 N	128.06 E
Paengnyŏng-do, i., Kor., S.	54	F6	37.57 N	124.40 E
Paerdegat Basin, b., N.Y., U.S.	194		40.37 N	73.54 W
Paestum, hist., Italy	32	D9	40.25 N	14.59 E
Páez, stm., Col.	168	F4	2.28 N	75.33 W
Pafúri, Moz.	90	C10	22.26 S	31.20 E
Pag, Cro.	30	F12	44.27 N	15.03 E
Pag, Otok, i., Cro.	30	F11	44.27 N	15.00 E
Pagadenbaru, Indon.	66	G5	6.27 S	107.48 E
Pagadian, Phil.	68	G4	7.49 N	123.25 E
Pagai Selatan, Pulau, i., Indon.	66	E2	3.00 S	100.20 E
Pagai Utara, Pulau, i., Indon.	66	E2	2.42 S	100.07 E
Pagalu see Annobón, i., Eq. Gui.	84	J6	1.25 S	5.37 E
Pagan, Mya.	64	B2	21.11 N	94.54 E
Pagan, i., N. Mar. Is.	94	B5	18.07 N	145.46 E
Pagancillo, Arg.	172	D3	29.33 S	68.04 W
Pagaralam, Indon.	66	E3	4.02 S	103.15 E
Pagasitikós Kólpos, b., Grc.	34	D5	39.13 N	23.02 E
Pagatan, Indon.	66	E9	3.36 S	115.55 E
Page, Az., U.S.	150	G5	36.54 N	111.28 W
Page, N.D., U.S.	142	G16	47.09 N	97.35 W
Pagėgiai, Lith.	26	E4	55.08 N	21.54 E
Pageland, S.C., U.S.	132	B5	34.46 N	80.23 W
Pagerdewa, Indon.	66	E4	3.46 S	105.17 E
Paget, Mount, mtn., S. Geor.	166	J9	54.26 S	36.33 W
Paglia, stm., Italy	30	H8	42.41 N	12.11 E
Pagliete, Bonifica delle, reg., Italy	185a		41.53 N	12.12 E
Pago Bay, b., Guam	100c	j10	13.25 N	144.47 E
Pagoda Peak, mtn., Co., U.S.	138	A1	40.09 N	107.19 W
Pagoda Point, c., Mya.	64	E2	15.58 N	94.15 E
Pagon, Bukit, mtn., Asia	68	A9	4.18 N	115.19 E
Pago Pago, Am. Sam.	101c	h12	14.16 S	170.42 W
Pagosa Springs, Co., U.S.	138	D1	37.16 N	107.02 W
Pagote, India	190c		18.54 N	72.59 E
Pagsañgahan, Phil.	68	D4	13.13 N	122.33 E
Paguate, N.M., U.S.	150	H9	35.08 N	107.22 W
Pagudpud, Phil.	68	A3	18.33 N	120.47 E
Pagueras, Torrente de, stm., Spain	184d		41.28 N	1.58 E
Pahača, Russia	50	D22	60.34 N	169.02 E
Pahādi, ngh., India	190c		19.10 N	72.51 E
Pahala, Hi., U.S.	100a	d6	19.11 N	155.27 W
Pahang, state, Malay.	64	K6	3.30 N	102.45 E
Pahang, stm., Malay.	64	K6	3.30 N	103.23 E
Pahlād Garhi, India	190a		28.40 N	77.21 E
Pahlavī see Bandar-e Anzalī, Iran	74	B11	37.28 N	49.28 E
Pahlevī see Bandar-e Anzalī, Iran	74	B11	37.28 N	49.28 E
Pahoa, Hi., U.S.	100a	d7	19.30 N	154.56 W
Pahokee, Fl., U.S.	132	J5	26.49 N	80.39 W
Pahost, Bela.	26	H10	52.50 N	27.41 E
Pahost, Bela.	26	G12	53.50 N	29.10 E
Pahraničny, Bela.	26	G6	53.07 N	23.58 E
Pahrump, Nv., U.S.	148	G10	36.12 N	115.58 W
Pahsimeroi, stm., Id., U.S.	146	F13	44.41 N	114.03 W
Pahvant Range, mts., Ut., U.S.	150	E4	38.45 N	112.15 W
Pai, Thai.	64	C4	19.19 N	98.25 E
Pai, stm., Asia	64	C3	19.08 N	97.32 E
Pai, Ilha do, i., Braz.	205a		22.59 S	43.05 W
Paianía, Grc.	185c		37.57 N	23.51 E
Paico, Peru	164	F3	14.02 S	73.38 W
Paide, Est.	26	B8	58.53 N	25.34 E
Paige, Tx., U.S.	136	D10	30.12 N	97.06 W
Paignton, Eng., U.K.	10	K9	50.26 N	3.34 W
Paiguano, Chile	172	E2	30.00 S	70.30 W
Päijänne, l., Fin.	18	F12	61.35 N	25.30 E
Päijänteen kansallispuisto, p.o.i., Fin.	18	F12	61.21 N	25.27 E
Paikü Co, l., China	70	D10	28.53 N	85.36 E
Pailin, Camb.	64	F6	12.51 N	102.36 E
Pailitas, Col.	168	C5	8.57 N	73.37 W
Pailolo Channel, strt., Hi., U.S.	100a	b5	21.05 N	156.42 W
Paimio, Fin.	18	G9	60.28 N	22.41 E
Paimpol, Fr.	20	F5	48.46 N	3.03 W
Painan, Indon.	66	D2	1.20 S	100.34 E
Painesdale, Mi., U.S.	128	D10	47.02 N	88.39 W
Painesville, Oh., U.S.	124	C4	41.43 N	81.14 W
Paint, stm., Mi., U.S.	128	E10	45.58 N	88.15 W
Paint Creek, stm., Mi., U.S.	199		42.06 N	83.36 W
Paint Creek, stm., Oh., U.S.	130	E14	39.17 N	82.56 W
Paint Creek, stm., Tx., U.S.	136	D8	30.18 N	99.54 W
Painted Desert, des., Az., U.S.	150	H5	35.45 N	111.06 W
Painted Rock Reservoir, res., Az., U.S.	150	J3	33.00 N	112.50 W
Paintertown, Pa., U.S.	197b		40.21 N	79.42 W
Paint Rock, Tx., U.S.	136	C8	31.30 N	99.55 W
Paint Rock, stm., Al., U.S.	134	C12	34.28 N	86.28 W
Paintsville, Ky., U.S.	124	G3	37.48 N	82.48 W
Pai Pobre, Morro do, mtn., Braz.	205b		23.40 S	46.55 W
Paisley, Austl.	192b		37.51 S	144.51 E
Paisley, Scot., U.K.	10	F8	55.50 N	4.25 W
Paisley, Or., U.S.	146	H6	42.41 N	120.32 W
Paistunturit, mtn., Fin.	14	C17	69.36 N	26.22 E
Paita, N. Cal.	101d	n16	22.08 S	166.21 E
Paita, Peru	164	E1	5.05 S	81.06 W
Paitan, Telukan, b., Malay.	68	G1	6.45 N	117.20 E
Paiton, Indon.	66	G8	7.42 S	113.30 E
Paittasjärvi, l., Swe.	14	E10	67.52 N	19.08 E
Paiva, stm., Port.	28	D2	41.03 N	8.15 W
Paj, Russia	18	F16	61.13 N	34.26 E
Pajala, Swe.	14	E14	67.13 N	23.23 E
Paján, Ec.	168	H1	1.33 S	80.25 W
Pajares, Puerto de, p., Spain	28	B5	43.00 N	5.45 W
Pajaros Point, c., Br. Vir. Is.	158b	d9	18.30 N	64.19 W
Pajęczno, Pol.	24	E14	51.08 N	18.59 E
Pajer, gora, mtn., Russia	50	C1	66.42 N	64.25 E
Pajeú, stm., Braz.	170	E6	8.38 S	38.35 W
Paj-Hoj, hills, Russia	48	A10	69.00 N	63.00 E
Pak, stm., Laos	64	B6	21.05 N	102.30 E
Paka, Malay.	64	J6	4.37 N	103.26 E
Pākāla, India	69	E4	13.26 N	79.07 E
Pakaljubičy, Bela.	26	H14	52.30 N	31.02 E
Pakaraima Mountains, mts., S.A.	168	E11	5.05 N	60.39 W
Pakashkan Lake, l., On., Can.	128	B8	49.21 N	90.15 W
Pākaur, India	70	F11	24.38 N	87.51 E
Pak Ban, Laos	64	B6	21.14 N	102.28 E
Pak Chong, Thai.	64	E5	14.42 N	101.24 E
Pākhāl, l., India	69	C5	17.56 N	79.59 E
Pákhna, Cyp.	76	D3	34.46 N	32.48 E
Pakhoi see Beihai, China	58	K3	21.27 N	109.05 E
Pākistān see Pakistan, ctry., Asia	62	C2	30.00 N	70.00 E
Pakistan, ctry., Asia	62	C2	30.00 N	70.00 E
Pakistan, East see Bangladesh, ctry., Asia	70	G13	24.00 N	90.00 E
Pak Kong, China	189d		22.23 N	114.15 E
Pak Kret, Thai.	187a		13.55 N	100.30 E
Pak Kwo Chau, i., China	189d		22.16 N	114.20 E
Paklenica Nacionalni Park, p.o.i., Cro.	30	F12	44.20 N	15.30 E
Pakokku, Mya.	64	B2	21.19 N	95.05 E
Pakość, Pol.	24	D14	52.48 N	18.05 E
Pakowki Lake, l., Ab., Can.	142	E3	49.22 N	110.57 W
Pākpattan, Pak.	70	C4	30.20 N	73.23 E
Pak Phanang, Thai.	64	H5	8.21 N	100.12 E
Pak Phayun, Thai.	64	I5	7.19 N	100.19 E
Pak Phraek, Thai.	64	H5	8.12 N	100.11 E
Pakrac, Cro.	30	E14	45.26 N	17.11 E
Pakruojis, Lith.	26	E6	55.58 N	23.50 E
Paks, Hung.	36	C5	46.39 N	18.53 E
Pak Sane see Muang Pakxan, Laos	64	C6	18.24 N	103.39 E
Pak Thong Chai, Thai.	64	E6	14.42 N	102.01 E
Paktīā, state, Afg.	70	B2	33.30 N	69.30 E
Paktīkā, state, Afg.	70	B2	32.30 N	68.45 E
Pakwach, Ug.	86	D6	2.28 N	31.29 E
Pakwash Lake, l., On., Can.	128	A5	50.40 N	93.38 W
Pakxé, Laos	64	E7	15.08 N	105.47 E
Pala, Chad	82	F2	9.21 N	14.54 E
Pala, Mya.	64	F4	12.51 N	98.40 E
Palacca Point, c., Bah.	156	B11	21.13 N	73.23 W
Palacios, Tx., U.S.	136	F11	28.42 N	96.12 W
Palagruža, Otoci, is., Cro.	30	H13	42.24 N	16.15 E
Palai, India	69	G3	9.42 N	76.41 E
Palaikhóri, Cyp.	76	D4	34.55 N	33.05 E
Pala Indian Reservation, ind. res., Ca., U.S.	148	J8	33.21 N	117.04 W
Palaiochóra, Grc.	34	H6	35.14 N	23.40 E
Palaión Fáliron, Grc.	185c		37.55 N	23.41 E
Pālakodu, India	69	C5	16.32 N	81.44 E
Pālam, ngh., India	190a		28.35 N	77.05 E
Palamás, Grc.	34	D5	39.27 N	22.04 E
Palamós, Spain	28	C14	41.51 N	3.07 E
Pālampur, India	70	B6	32.07 N	76.32 E
Palamu National Park, p.o.i., India	70	G10	23.52 N	84.10 E
Palamuse, Est.	26	B9	58.41 N	26.35 E
Palamut, Tur.	34	D10	39.00 N	27.41 E
Palana, Russia	50	E20	59.05 N	159.59 E
Palanan, Mount, mtn., Phil.	68	B4	17.03 N	122.15 E
Palanan Bay, b., Phil.	68	B4	17.10 N	122.26 E
Palanga, Lith.	26	E3	55.54 N	21.04 E
Palangkaraya, Indon.	66	E8	2.10 S	113.53 E
Palani, India	69	F3	10.27 N	77.31 E
Pālanpur, India	70	F4	24.10 N	72.27 E
Palanquinos, Spain	28	B5	42.27 N	5.29 W
Palaoa Point, c., Hi., U.S.	100a	c4	20.44 N	156.57 W
Palapye, Bots.	90	C8	22.34 S	27.06 E
Pālār, stm., India	69	E4	12.28 N	80.07 E
Palas de Rei, Spain	28	B3	42.52 N	7.52 W
Palas de Rey see Palas de Rei, Spain	28	B3	42.52 N	7.52 W
Palatka, Russia	50	D19	60.06 N	150.56 E
Palatka, Fl., U.S.	132	G4	29.39 N	81.38 W
Palau, Italy	32	C3	41.11 N	9.22 E
Palau, Mex.	136	G6	27.53 N	101.25 W
Palau, ctry., Oc.	60	D9	5.00 N	137.00 E
Palauig, Phil.	68	C2	15.25 N	119.55 E
Palau Islands, is., Palau	60	D10	7.23 N	134.28 E
Palauk, Mya.	64	F4	13.16 N	98.36 E
Palaw, Mya.	64	F4	12.58 N	98.38 E
Palawan, i., Phil.	68	F2	9.30 N	118.30 E
Palawan Passage, strt., Phil.	68	F1	10.00 N	118.00 E
Palayan, Phil.	68	C3	15.32 N	121.05 E
Pālayankottai, India	69	G3	8.42 N	77.44 E
Pal'co, Russia	26	G17	53.17 N	34.56 E
Paldiski, Est.	26	A7	59.20 N	24.06 E
Palembang, Indon.	66	E4	2.58 S	104.46 E
Palena, Italy	30	I11	41.59 N	14.08 E
Palena, stm., S.A.	166	H2	43.46 S	72.59 W
Palencia, Spain	28	B6	42.01 N	4.32 W
Palencia, co., Spain	28	B6	42.25 N	4.35 W
Palen Lake, l., Ca., U.S.	150	J1	33.46 N	115.12 W
Palenque, Mex.	154	G13	17.31 N	91.57 W
Palenque, hist., Mex.	154	G12	17.30 N	92.00 W
Palenque, Punta, c., Dom. Rep.	156	C12	18.14 N	70.09 W
Palermo, Col.	168	F4	2.54 N	75.26 W
Palermo, Italy	32	F7	38.07 N	13.21 E
Palermo, Ur.	172	F10	33.47 S	55.57 W
Palermo, ngh., Arg.	206		34.35 S	58.25 W
Palermo, Golfo di, b., Italy	32	F7	38.08 N	13.26 E
Palesse, Bela.	26	G14	53.05 N	31.17 E
Palesse see Pripet Marshes, reg., Eur.	40	E5	52.00 N	27.00 E
Palestina, Mex.	136	E7	29.10 N	100.55 W
Palestine, Ar., U.S.	134	B8	34.59 N	90.54 W
Palestine, Il., U.S.	130	E10	39.00 N	87.36 W
Palestine, Tx., U.S.	136	C12	31.45 N	95.38 W
Palestine, hist. reg., Asia	76	G6	32.00 N	35.15 E
Palestine, Lake, res., Tx., U.S.	136	B12	32.12 N	95.28 W
Palestrina, Italy	30	I9	41.51 N	12.52 E
Paletwa, Mya.	70	H14	21.18 N	92.51 E
Pālghāt, India	69	F3	10.46 N	76.39 E
Palgrave Point, c., Nmb.	88	E1	20.28 S	13.15 E
Palhais, Port.	184c		38.37 N	9.03 W
Palhano, Braz.	170	C6	4.44 S	37.57 W
Palhano, stm., Braz.	170	C6	4.38 S	37.49 W
Pāli, India	70	F4	25.46 N	73.20 E
Palikir, Micron.	100d	m11	6.55 N	158.09 E
Palima, Indon.	66	F12	4.19 S	120.20 E
Palimbang, Phil.	68	G5	6.12 N	124.11 E
Palinuro, Capo, c., Italy	32	D9	40.02 N	15.17 E
Palisade, Co., U.S.	150	D8	39.07 N	108.20 W
Palisade, Ne., U.S.	138	A7	40.20 N	101.06 W
Palisades, Id., U.S.	146	G15	43.21 N	111.13 W
Palisades, N.Y., U.S.	194		41.01 N	73.55 W
Palisades Amusement Park, p.o.i., N.J., U.S.	194		40.50 N	73.59 W
Palisades Park, N.J., U.S.	194		40.50 N	73.59 W
Palisades Reservoir, res., U.S.	146	G15	43.12 N	111.05 W
Pālitāna, India	70	H3	21.31 N	71.49 E
Palivere, Est.	26	A6	58.51 N	23.52 E
Palizada, Mex.	154	F12	18.15 N	92.05 W
Paljakka, hill, Fin.	18	C15	64.41 N	28.04 E
Pälkäne, Fin.	18	F11	61.20 N	24.16 E
Palk Bay, b., Asia	69	G4	9.30 N	79.15 E
Palkino, Russia	26	C10	57.32 N	28.00 E
Palkino, Russia	40	B13	58.15 N	42.56 E
Pālkonda, India	69	B6	18.36 N	83.46 E
Pālkonda Range, mts., India	69	D4	14.05 N	79.05 E
Palk Strait, strt., Asia	69	G4	10.00 N	79.45 E
Pallasovka, Russia	40	F15	50.02 N	46.53 E
Pallastunturi, mtn., Fin.	14	D14	68.06 N	24.00 E
Pallejà, Spain	184d		41.25 N	2.00 E
Pallës, Bishti i, c., Alb.	32	C13	41.24 N	19.24 E
Palling, B.C., Can.	144	B5	54.21 N	125.54 W
Pallíni, Grc.	185c		38.00 N	23.53 E
Palliser, Cape, c., N.Z.	102	E6	41.37 S	175.17 E
Pallu, India	70	D5	28.56 N	74.13 E
Palma, Braz.	170	K4	21.22 S	42.19 W
Palma, Moz.	88	C7	10.46 S	40.28 E
Palma, stm., Braz.	170	G2	12.33 S	47.52 W
Palma, Badia de, b., Spain	28	E13	39.27 N	2.35 E
Palma, Sierra de la, mts., Mex.	136	H6	26.02 N	101.35 W
Palmácia, Braz.	170	C6	4.08 S	38.50 W
Palma del Río, Spain	28	G5	37.42 N	5.17 W
Palma de Mallorca, Spain	28	E13	39.34 N	2.38 E
Palma di Montechiaro, Italy	32	G7	37.11 N	13.46 E
Palmar, stm., Ven.	168	B5	10.11 N	71.51 W
Palmar, Lago Artificial del, res., Ur.	172	F9	33.05 S	57.10 W
Palmar Camp, Belize	156	D3	16.26 N	88.53 W
Palmar de Cariaco, Ven.	204c		10.34 N	66.55 W
Palmarejo, P.R.	158a	b1	18.02 N	67.04 W
Palmares, Braz.	170	E8	8.41 S	35.36 W
Palmares do Sul, Braz.	172	E12	30.16 S	50.31 W
Palmarito, Ven.	168	D6	7.36 N	70.08 W
Palmarola, Isola, i., Italy	32	D6	40.55 N	12.51 E
Palmas, Braz.	170	F1	10.05 S	48.20 W
Palmas, Braz.	172	C12	26.29 S	52.00 W
Palmas, Golfo di, b., Italy	32	F2	39.00 N	8.31 E
Palmas, Ilha das, i., Braz.	205a		23.02 S	43.12 W
Palmas, Ilha das, i., Braz.	205a		23.04 S	43.31 W
Palmas Bellas, Pan.	156	H7	9.13 N	80.04 W
Palmas de Monte Alto, Braz.	170	H4	14.16 S	43.10 W
Palma Soriano, Cuba	156	B9	20.12 N	75.59 W
Palm Bay, Fl., U.S.	132	H5	28.02 N	80.35 W
Palm Beach, Fl., U.S.	132	J5	26.43 N	80.02 W
Palmdale, Ca., U.S.	148	I7	34.35 N	118.06 W
Palm Desert, Ca., U.S.	148	J9	33.43 N	116.23 W
Palmeira, Braz.	172	B13	25.24 S	50.00 W
Palmeira das Missões, Braz.	172	C11	27.54 S	53.18 W
Palmeira dos Índios, Braz.	170	E7	9.25 S	36.37 W
Palmeiras, Braz.	170	G5	12.30 S	41.34 W
Palmeiras, stm., Braz.	170	G2	12.22 S	46.59 W
Palmeirinhas, Ponta das, c., Ang.	88	B1	9.04 S	12.59 E
Palmelo, Braz.	170	I1	17.20 S	48.27 W
Palmer, P.R.	158a	b4	18.22 N	65.46 W
Palmer, Ak., U.S.	109	D10	61.31 N	149.05 W
Palmer, Ma., U.S.	124	B13	42.09 N	72.19 W
Palmer, Ms., U.S.	134	F9	31.16 N	89.15 W
Palmer, Ne., U.S.	140	F14	41.13 N	98.15 W
Palmer, Tn., U.S.	134	B13	35.20 N	85.33 W
Palmer, Tx., U.S.	136	B11	32.26 N	96.40 W
Palmer, sci., Ant.	103	B34	64.46 S	64.03 W
Palmerah, ngh., Indon.	187e		6.12 S	106.47 E
Palmer Lake, Co., U.S.	138	B3	39.07 N	104.54 W
Palmer Land, reg., Ant.	103	C34	71.30 S	64.59 W
Palmer Mill Brook, stm., Ma., U.S.	201		41.58 N	70.52 W
Palmer Park, Md., U.S.	202c		38.55 N	76.52 W
Palmer Park, p.o.i., Mi., U.S.	199		42.26 N	83.07 W
Palmerston, On., Can.	126	E9	43.50 N	80.51 W
Palmerston, N.Z.	102	G4	45.29 S	170.43 E
Palmerston, at., Cook Is.	94	E10	0.05 S	1.10 W
Palmerston, Cape, c., Austl.	98	C7	21.33 S	149.28 E
Palmerston North, N.Z.	102	E6	40.21 S	175.36 E
Palmerton, Pa., U.S.	124	D10	40.48 N	75.37 W
Palmerville, Austl.	96	C8	15.59 S	144.03 E
Palmetto, Ga., U.S.	134	D14	33.31 N	84.40 W
Palmetto, La., U.S.	134	G7	30.43 N	91.54 W
Palmetto Point, c., Antig.	159b	e4	17.35 N	61.51 W
Palmi, Italy	32	F9	38.21 N	15.51 E
Palmira, Col.	168	F3	3.32 N	76.18 W
Palmira, Cuba	156	A7	22.14 N	80.23 W
Palmira, Ec.	168	I2	2.03 S	78.43 W
Palmira, Mex.	136	F7	28.58 N	100.46 W
Palmitas, Ur.	172	F9	33.31 S	57.47 W
Palmitos, Braz.	172	C11	27.04 S	53.09 W
Palmnicken see Jantarnyj, Russia	26	F2	54.52 N	19.57 E
Palms, ngh., Ca., U.S.	198		34.02 N	118.25 W
Palm Springs, Ca., U.S.	148	J9	33.50 N	116.32 W
Palmyra see Tudmur, Syria	76	D9	34.32 N	38.16 E
Palmyra, Il., U.S.	130	E7	39.26 N	89.59 W
Palmyra, Mo., U.S.	130	E6	39.47 N	91.31 W
Palmyra, N.Y., U.S.	124	A8	43.03 N	77.13 W
Palmyra, Pa., U.S.	124	D9	40.18 N	76.35 W
Palmyra, Va., U.S.	124	G7	37.51 N	78.15 W
Palmyra, hist., Syria	76	D9	34.33 N	38.17 E
Palmyra Atoll, at., Oc.	94	C10	5.52 N	162.06 W
Palo Alto, Mex.	136	H8	26.30 N	99.44 W
Palo Alto, Ca., U.S.	148	F3	37.26 N	122.08 W
Palo Alto Airport, arpt., Ca., U.S.	200		37.28 N	122.07 W
Palo Blanco, Mex.	136	H6	26.45 N	101.32 W
Palo Blanco, P.R.	158a	b2	18.25 N	66.38 W
Palo Blanco Creek, stm., Tx., U.S.	136	G9	27.09 N	97.52 W
Palo Duro Canyon State Park, p.o.i., Tx., U.S.	138	G7	34.55 N	101.42 W
Palo Duro Creek, stm., U.S.	138	E7	36.39 N	100.58 W
Palo Duro Creek, stm., Tx., U.S.	138	F6	34.59 N	101.53 W
Palo Flechado Pass, p., N.M., U.S.	138	E3	36.20 N	105.25 W
Paloh, Indon.	66	C6	1.42 N	109.17 E
Paloh, Malay.	66	B7	2.24 N	111.15 E
Paloich, Sudan	82	E6	10.27 N	32.31 E
Palojoensuu, Fin.	14	D13	68.16 N	23.04 E
Palomares Creek, stm., Ca., U.S.	200		37.42 N	122.02 W
Palomar Mountain, mtn., Ca., U.S.	148	J9	33.22 N	116.50 W
Palomar Park, Ca., U.S.	200		37.29 N	122.16 W
Palomas, Mex.	136	F4	28.43 N	103.45 W
Palomas, Mesa de, mtn., Mex.	136	F4	28.46 N	103.41 W
Palominos, Isla, i., P.R.	158a	b4	18.21 N	65.34 W
Palo Pinto, Tx., U.S.	136	B9	32.46 N	98.18 W
Palo Pinto Creek Reservoir, res., Tx., U.S.	136	B9	32.38 N	98.18 W
Palopo, Indon.	66	E12	3.00 S	120.11 E
Palora, stm., Ec.	168	H2	1.51 S	77.50 W
Palos, Cabo de, c., Spain	28	G10	37.37 N	0.41 W
Palo Santo, Arg.	172	B8	25.33 S	59.21 W
Palos Gardens, Il., U.S.	196		41.40 N	87.48 W
Palos Hills, Il., U.S.	196		41.41 N	87.49 W
Palos Hills, p.o.i., Il., U.S.	196		41.42 N	87.53 W
Palos Park, Il., U.S.	196		41.40 N	87.49 W
Palos Verdes Hills, hills, Ca., U.S.	198		33.46 N	118.21 W
Palos Verdes Point, c., Ca., U.S.	148	J7	33.46 N	118.24 W
Palotai-sziget, i., Hung.	182c		47.35 N	19.05 E
Paloúkia, Grc.	185c		37.58 N	23.31 E
Palouse, Wa., U.S.	146	D9	46.53 N	117.04 W
Palouse, stm., U.S.	146	D8	46.35 N	118.13 W
Palouse, South Fork, stm., U.S.	146	D9	46.53 N	117.22 W
Palo Verde, Ca., U.S.	150	J2	33.24 N	114.43 W
Palpa, Peru	164	F2	14.33 S	75.12 W
Palpalá, Arg.	172	B5	24.14 S	65.13 W
Pålsboda, Swe.	16	H13	59.04 N	15.20 E
Paltamo, Fin.	18	C14	64.24 N	27.49 E
Paltenbach, stm., Aus.	30	C11	47.34 N	14.19 E
Palu, Indon.	66	D11	0.54 S	119.51 E
Palu, Tur.	42	F8	38.41 N	39.59 E
Palu, stm., Indon.	66	D11	0.53 S	119.51 E
Palu, Teluk, b., Indon.	66	D11	0.45 S	119.49 E
Paluan, Phil.	68	D3	13.25 N	120.26 E
Paluga, Russia	12	D21	65.15 N	45.14 E
Paluxy, stm., Tx., U.S.	136	B10	32.14 N	97.43 W
Palwal, India	70	D6	28.08 N	77.20 E
Pal-Waukee Airport, arpt., Il., U.S.	196		42.07 N	87.54 W
Pam, N. Cal.	101d	m15	20.15 S	164.18 E
Pama, Burkina	84	G5	11.15 N	0.43 E
Pamaluan, Indon.	66	D10	1.01 S	116.40 E
Pamanukan, Indon.	66	G5	6.17 S	107.49 E
Pāmban Channel, strt., India	69	G4	9.17 N	79.10 E
Pāmban Island, i., India	69	G4	9.15 N	79.20 E
Pamekasan, Indon.	66	G8	7.10 S	113.28 E
Pamenang, Indon.	66	E3	2.07 S	102.31 E
Pameungpeuk, Indon.	66	G5	7.38 S	107.42 E
Pamiers, Fr.	22	F7	43.07 N	1.36 E
Pamir, mts., Asia	72	B11	38.00 N	73.00 E
Pāmīr, Daryā-ye see Pamir, mts., Asia	72	B11	38.00 N	73.00 E
Pamlico, stm., N.C., U.S.	132	A9	35.20 N	76.28 W
Pamlico Sound, strt., N.C., U.S.	116	C14	35.20 N	75.55 W
Pampa, Tx., U.S.	138	F8	35.32 N	100.57 W
Pampã, stm., Braz.	170	I5	17.43 S	40.36 W
Pampa, reg., Arg.	166	G4	35.00 S	63.00 W
Pampa Almirón, Arg.	172	C8	26.43 S	59.07 W
Pampa del Chañar, Arg.	172	E3	30.11 S	68.43 W
Pampa del Indio, Arg.	172	B7	26.02 S	59.57 W
Pampa del Infierno, Arg.	172	C7	26.29 S	61.10 W
Pampa de los Guanacos, Arg.	172	C6	26.14 S	61.51 W
Pampanga, stm., Phil.	68	C3	14.46 N	120.39 E
Pampanua, Indon.	66	F12	4.14 S	120.08 E
Pampas, Peru	164	F3	12.20 S	74.56 W
Pampas, stm., Peru	164	F3	13.24 S	73.13 W
Pampeluna see Pamplona, Spain	28	B9	42.48 N	1.39 W
Pamplico, S.C., U.S.	132	B6	33.59 N	79.34 W
Pamplona, Col.	168	D5	7.22 N	72.37 W
Pamplona, Spain	28	B9	42.48 N	1.39 W
Pamukkale (Hierapolis), hist., Tur.	34	F12	37.58 N	29.19 E
Pamukova, Tur.	34	C13	40.31 N	30.10 E
Pana, Il., U.S.	130	E8	39.23 N	89.04 W
Pana, stm., Russia	14	E26	66.52 N	35.55 E
Panabá, Mex.	156	B3	21.17 N	88.16 W
Panabo, Phil.	68	G5	7.16 N	125.40 E
Panaca, Nv., U.S.	150	F2	37.47 N	114.24 W
Panacea, Fl., U.S.	134	G14	30.02 N	84.23 W
Panadura, Sri L.	69	H4	6.42 N	79.54 E
Panagía, Grc.	34	C8	39.59 N	25.25 E
Panagjurište, Blg.	36	G11	42.30 N	24.11 E
Panahan, Indon.	66	D7	1.45 S	111.46 E
Panaitan, Pulau, i., Indon.	66	G4	6.36 S	105.12 E
Panaji, India	69	D1	15.29 N	73.49 E
Pānākua, India	190b		22.23 N	88.21 E
Panamá, Braz.	170	J1	18.11 S	49.18 W
Panamá, Pan.	156	H8	8.58 N	79.32 W
Panama, Ok., U.S.	134	B4	35.10 N	94.40 W
Panama, ctry., N.A.	152	F9	9.00 N	80.00 W
Panamá see Panama, ctry., N.A.	152	F9	9.00 N	80.00 W
Panamá, Bahía de, b., Pan.	156	H8	8.50 N	79.20 W
Panamá, Canal de (Panama Canal), can., Pan.	156	H8	9.22 N	79.56 W
Panamá, Golfo de, b., Pan.	168	D2	8.00 N	79.30 W
Panama, Gulf of see Panamá, Golfo de, b., Pan.	168	D2	8.00 N	79.30 W
Panama, Isthmus of see Panamá, Istmo de, isth., Pan.	156	H8	9.00 N	80.00 W
Panamá, Istmo de (Panama, Isthmus of), isth., Pan.	156	H8	9.00 N	80.00 W
Panama Basin, unds.	176	H5	5.00 N	83.30 W
Panama Canal see Panamá, Canal de, can., Pan.	156	H8	9.22 N	79.56 W
Panama City, Fl., U.S.	134	G13	30.10 N	85.39 W
Panambi, Braz.	172	D11	28.19 S	53.30 W
Panamint Range, mts., Ca., U.S.	148	G8	36.23 N	117.15 W
Panamint Valley, val., Ca., U.S.	148	G8	36.03 N	117.19 W
Pan'an, China	58	G9	29.05 N	120.24 E
Panao, Peru	164	E2	9.49 S	76.00 W
Panarea, Isola, i., Italy	32	F9	38.38 N	15.04 E
Panaro, stm., Italy	30	F8	44.56 N	11.25 E
Panay, i., Phil.	68	E4	11.15 N	122.30 E
Panay Gulf, b., Phil.	68	E4	10.15 N	122.15 E
Pancas, Port.	184c		38.48 N	8.55 W
Pančevo, Yugo.	36	E7	44.52 N	20.39 E
Pancheve, Ukr.	38	E10	48.44 N	31.52 E
Pānchgharia, India	190b		22.44 N	88.16 E
Panch'iao, Tai.	187d		25.01 N	121.27 E
Pancho Simón, stm., Cuba	204b		23.03 N	82.21 W
Pānchur, India	190b		22.32 N	88.16 E
Pānchuria, India	190b		22.33 N	88.29 E
Panciu, Rom.	36	D14	45.55 N	27.05 E
Panda, Moz.	90	D12	24.03 S	34.44 E
Pandan, Malay.	66	B8	3.10 N	113.21 E
Pandan, Selat, strt., Sing.	189c		1.15 N	103.44 E
Pandan Reservoir, res., Sing.	189c		1.19 N	103.44 E
Pandaria, India	70	G8	22.13 N	81.25 E
Pan de Azúcar, Ur.	172	G10	34.46 S	55.12 W
Pan de Azúcar, Cerro, mtn., Chile	204e		33.19 S	70.42 W
Pandėlys, Lith.	26	D8	56.01 N	25.13 E
Pāndharkawada, India	69	A4	20.01 N	78.33 E
Pandharpur, India	69	C2	17.40 N	75.19 E
Pāndhurna, India	70	H7	21.36 N	78.31 E
Pando, Ur.	172	G10	34.42 S	55.56 W
Panelas, Braz.	170	E8	8.40 S	36.01 W
Panevėžys, Lith.	26	E7	55.44 N	24.22 E
Panfilov, Kaz.	48	F13	44.10 N	79.59 E
Pāng, stm., Mya.	64	B4	20.57 N	98.30 E
Panga, D.R.C.	86	D5	1.49 N	26.24 E
Pangala, Congo	86	E2	3.19 S	14.34 E
Pangandaran, Indon.	66	G6	7.40 S	108.39 E
Pangani, Tan.	86	F7	5.26 S	38.58 E
Pangani, stm., Tan.	86	E7	5.24 S	38.57 E
Pangburn, Ar., U.S.	134	B7	35.25 N	91.50 W
Panghkam, Mya.	62	D8	23.53 N	97.37 E
Pangi, D.R.C.	86	E5	3.10 S	26.37 E
Pangian, Indon.	66	D11	1.08 S	119.24 E
Pangkajene, Indon.	66	F11	4.50 S	119.32 E
Pangkalanbrandan, Indon.	64	J4	4.01 N	98.17 E
Pangkalanbuun, Indon.	66	E7	2.41 S	111.37 E
Pangkalansusu, Indon.	64	J4	4.06 N	98.13 E
Pangkalpinang, Indon.	66	E5	2.08 S	106.06 E
Pangman, Sk., Can.	142	E9	49.38 N	104.37 W
Pangnirtung, Nu., Can.	110	B17	66.07 N	65.43 W
Pango Aluquem, Ang.	88	B1	8.42 S	14.28 E
Pangŏjin, Kor., S.	56	D2	35.29 N	129.25 E
Pangong Tso, l., Asia	70	B7	33.44 N	78.41 E
Pangp'u see Bengbu, China	58	E7	32.56 N	117.21 E
Pangtara, Mya.	64	B3	20.56 N	96.40 E
Panguiranan, Phil.	68	D4	12.04 N	123.18 E
Panguitch, Ut., U.S.	150	F4	37.49 N	112.26 W
Pangururan, Indon.	66	B1	2.36 N	98.41 E
Pangutaran, Phil.	68	G3	6.17 N	120.34 E
Pangutaran Group, is., Phil.	68	G3	6.13 N	120.38 E
Panhandle, Tx., U.S.	138	F7	35.20 N	101.22 W
Pania-Mutombo, D.R.C.	86	F4	5.11 S	23.51 E
Paniau, mtn., Hi., U.S.	100a	b1	21.56 N	160.05 W
Panié, Mont, mtn., N. Cal.	101d	m15	20.36 S	164.46 E
Panino, Russia	26	D17	56.24 N	34.34 E
Panino, Russia	38	B19	51.39 N	40.08 E
Panīpat, India	70	D6	29.23 N	76.58 E
Panitan, Phil.	68	E4	11.27 N	122.46 E
Paniutyne, Ukr.	38	E15	48.56 N	36.17 E
Panj (Pjandž), stm., Asia	72	B11	37.00 N	68.15 E
Panjang, Indon.	66	F4	5.29 S	105.20 E
Panjang, Pulau, i., Indon.	66	B6	2.44 N	108.55 E
Panjang, Selat, strt., Indon.	66	C3	0.45 N	102.38 E
Panje, India	190c		18.54 N	72.57 E
Panjim see Panaji, India	69	D1	15.29 N	73.49 E
Pankakoski, Fin.	18	D17	63.19 N	30.10 E
Panke, stm., Ger.	182a		52.32 N	13.22 E
Pankratovo, Russia	40	B13	59.09 N	43.30 E
Pankshin, Nig.	84	H6	9.19 N	9.25 E
Panlong (Lo), stm., Asia	64	A7	21.17 N	105.26 E
P'anmunjŏm-ni, Kor., N.	54	E7	37.57 N	126.40 E
Panna, India	70	F8	24.43 N	80.11 E
Panna National Park, p.o.i., India	70	F7	24.50 N	79.55 E
Pannawonica, Austl.	96	D3	21.39 S	116.22 E
Pannonhalma, rel., Hung.	36	B4	47.28 N	17.50 E
Panola, U.S.	134	E10	32.57 N	88.16 W
Páno Lévkara, Cyp.	76	D4	34.52 N	33.18 E
Panopah, Indon.	66	D7	1.56 S	111.10 E
Páno Panayiá, Cyp.	76	D3	34.55 N	32.38 E
Panora, Ia., U.S.	130	C3	41.41 N	94.21 W
Panorama, Braz.	166	D6	21.21 S	51.50 W
Panovo, Russia	12	G22	59.46 N	46.28 E
Panovo, Russia	48	C18	58.57 N	101.58 E
Panozero, Russia	14	C19	64.58 N	32.53 E
Panruti, India	69	F4	11.46 N	79.33 E
Panshan, China	54	D4	41.10 N	122.03 E
Panshanger Aerodrome, arpt., Eng., U.K.	178		51.48 N	0.08 W
Pansionat, Russia	183b		55.59 N	37.41 E
Pantanal, reg., S.A.	166	C5	18.00 S	56.00 W
Pantanaw, Mya.	64	D2	16.58 N	95.27 E
Pantar, Pulau, i., Indon.	60	G7	8.25 S	124.07 E
Pantelleria, Italy	32	H5	36.50 N	11.57 E
Pantelleria, Isola di, i., Italy	32	H6	36.47 N	12.00 E
Panteón Nacional, hist., Ven.	204c		10.31 N	66.55 W
Pantheon, hist., Italy	185a		41.55 N	12.29 E
Panther Creek, stm., Id., U.S.	146	E12	45.19 N	114.24 W
Panther Creek, stm., Ky., U.S.	130	G10	37.44 N	87.19 W
Pantitlán, ngh., Mex.	204a		19.25 N	99.05 W
Pantonlabu, Indon.	64	J3	5.07 N	97.27 E
Pantry Brook, stm., Ma., U.S.	201		42.24 N	71.22 W
Pánuco, Mex.	154	E10	22.02 N	98.11 W
Pánuco, stm., Mex.	154	E9	22.15 N	97.46 W
Panuke Lake, l., N.S., Can.	122	F12	44.48 N	64.07 W
Panvel, stm., India	190c		19.01 N	73.04 W
Panvel Creek, stm., India	190c		18.59 N	73.00 E
Panxian, China	52	F5	25.48 N	104.34 E
Panyam, Nig.	84	H6	9.24 N	9.12 E
Panzerstausee, res., Ger.	181		51.11 N	7.16 E
Panzós, Guat.	156	E3	15.23 N	89.39 W
Pao, stm., Thai.	64	D6	16.13 N	103.42 E
Pao, stm., Ven.	168	C9	8.02 N	64.19 W
Pao, stm., Ven.	168	C8	8.32 N	68.01 W
Pão de Açúcar, mtn., Braz.	205a		22.57 S	43.09 W
Paoki see Baoji, China	58	D2	34.23 N	107.08 E
Paola, Italy	32	E9	39.22 N	16.03 E
Paola, Ks., U.S.	130	F3	38.34 N	94.52 W
Paoli, In., U.S.	130	F11	38.33 N	86.28 W
Paonia, Co., U.S.	150	E9	38.52 N	107.35 W
Paopao, Fr. Poly.	100h	v20	17.30 S	149.49 W
Paotow see Baotou, China	58	A4	40.35 N	109.57 E
Pápa, Hung.	36	B4	47.20 N	17.28 E
Papagaio, stm., Braz.	168	I10	1.51 S	62.33 W
Papagaios, Braz.	170	D3	6.00 S	45.21 W
Papagayo, Golfo de, b., C.R.	156	G4	10.42 N	85.50 W
Papago Indian Reservation, ind. res., Az., U.S.	150	K4	32.20 N	112.00 W
Papaikou, Hi., U.S.	100a	d6	19.47 N	155.05 W
Papakating Creek, stm., N.J., U.S.	194		41.11 N	74.38 W
Papantla de Olarte, Mex.	154	E10	20.26 N	97.19 W
Papara, Fr. Poly.	100h	v22	17.43 S	149.20 W
Papara, Sol. Is.	101b	d7	7.08 S	156.51 E
Papa Stour, i., Scot., U.K.	10a	n18	60.20 N	1.42 W
Papawai Point, c., Hi., U.S.	100a	c5	20.47 N	156.32 W
Papeari, Fr. Poly.	100h	w22	17.44 S	149.20 W
Papeete, Fr. Poly.	100h	v21	17.32 S	149.34 W
Papelón, Ven.	204c		10.27 N	66.47 W
Papenburg, Ger.	24	C3	53.05 N	7.24 E
Papenoo, Fr. Poly.	100h	u22	17.30 S	149.25 W
Papenoo, stm., Fr. Poly.	100h	v22	17.30 S	149.25 W
Papetoai, Fr. Poly.	100h	v20	17.29 S	149.52 W

Name Page Map Ref. Latitude Longitude

Papey, i., Ice. 12a k32 64.35 N 14.10 W
Paphos see Néa Páfos, Cyp. 76 D3 34.46 N 32.25 E
Papigochic, stm., Mex. 120 G8 29.31 N 109.14 W
Papilė, Lith. 26 D5 56.09 N 22.48 E
Papillion, Ne., U.S. 130 C1 41.06 N 96.14 W
Papineau, Lac, l., Qc., Can. 126 C15 45.48 N 74.45 W
Paposo, Chile 172 B2 25.01 S 70.27 W
Papua, Gulf of, b., Pap. N. Gui. 94 D5 8.30 S 145.00 E
Papua New Guinea, ctry., Oc. 92 D5 6.00 S 147.00 E
Papudo, Chile 172 F2 32.30 S 71.27 W
Papulovo, Russia 12 F23 60.35 N 48.00 E
Papun, Mya. 64 C3 18.03 N 97.26 E
Papunáua, stm., Col. 168 G6 2.15 N 70.00 W
Papurí (Papurí), stm., S.A. 168 G6 0.36 N 69.11 W
Papurí (Papurí), stm., S.A. 168 G6 0.36 N 69.11 W
Paquetá, Ilha de, i., Braz. 205a 22.46 S 43.06 W
Pará see Belém, Braz. 170 A1 1.26 S 48.28 W
Pará, state, Braz. 164 D7 4.00 S 53.00 W
Pará, stm., Braz. 170 A1 1.28 S 49.03 W
Pará, stm., Braz. 170 J3 19.13 S 45.07 W
Parabel', Russia 48 C14 58.42 N 81.27 E
Paraburdoo, Austl. 96 D3 23.11 S 117.43 E
Paracatu, Braz. 170 I2 17.13 S 46.52 W
Paracatu, stm., Braz. 170 I3 16.35 S 45.06 W
Paracatu, stm., Braz. 170 I3 16.36 S 45.03 W
Paracel Islands see Xisha Qundao, is., China 60 B5 16.30 N 112.15 E
Pārachinār, Pak. 70 B3 33.53 N 70.05 E
Paracho de Verduzco, Mex. 154 F7 19.39 N 102.04 W
Parachute, Co., U.S. 150 D8 39.27 N 108.03 W
Paraćin, Yugo. 36 F8 43.51 N 21.24 E
Paracuellos de Jarama, Spain 184a 40.30 N 3.32 W
Paracuru, Braz. 170 B6 3.24 S 39.02 W
Parád, Hung. 36 B7 47.55 N 20.02 E
Parada, Punta, c., Peru 164 G2 15.22 S 75.10 W
Paradise, Ca., U.S. 148 D4 39.45 N 121.36 W
Paradise, Mt., U.S. 146 C12 47.23 N 114.48 W
Paradise, Nv., U.S. 148 G10 36.07 N 115.10 W
Paradise, Tx., U.S. 136 A10 33.09 N 97.40 W
Paradise Island, i., Bah. 158f m18 25.05 N 77.19 W
Paradise Valley, Az., U.S. 150 J5 33.32 N 111.56 W
Paradise Valley, Nv., U.S. 148 B8 41.29 N 117.31 W
Pāradwīp, India 70 H11 20.16 N 86.41 E
Parafiivka, Ukr. 38 C11 50.52 N 32.38 E
Paragonah, Ut., U.S. 150 F4 37.54 N 112.47 W
Paragould, Ar., U.S. 130 H7 36.03 N 90.29 W
Paraguá, stm., Bol. 166 B4 13.32 S 61.49 W
Paragua, stm., Ven. 168 D10 6.56 N 62.55 W
Paraguaçu, stm., Braz. 170 G6 12.50 S 38.47 W
Paraguai (Paraguay), stm., S.A. 166 D5 27.19 S 58.35 W
Paraguaipoa, Ven. 168 B6 11.21 N 71.58 W
Paraguaná, Península de, pen., Ven. 168 A6 11.55 N 70.02 W
Paraguarí, Para. 172 B9 25.36 S 57.08 W
Paraguarí, state, Para. 172 C9 26.00 S 57.10 W
Paraguay, ctry., S.A. 166 D5 23.00 S 58.00 W
Paraguay (Paraguai), stm., S.A. 166 E5 27.19 S 58.35 W
Parahyba see João Pessoa, Braz. 170 D8 7.07 S 34.52 W
Paraíba see João Pessoa, Braz. 170 D8 7.07 S 34.52 W
Paraíba, state, Braz. 170 D7 7.15 S 36.30 W
Paraíba do Sul, stm., Braz. 170 K4 21.37 S 41.02 W
Paraibano, Braz. 170 D3 6.30 S 44.01 W
Parainen, Fin. 18 G9 60.17 N 22.18 E
Paraíso, Mex. 154 F12 18.22 N 93.13 W
Paraíso, Pan. 156 H8 9.03 N 79.37 W
Parakou, Benin 84 H5 9.19 N 2.37 E
Paralía Asprópyrgou, Grc. 185c 38.02 N 23.35 E
Paralimni, Cyp. 76 C5 35.02 N 33.59 E
Paramakkudi, India 69 G4 9.32 N 78.36 E
Paramaribo, Sur. 164 B6 5.49 N 55.10 W
Parambu, Braz. 170 D5 6.13 S 40.43 W
Paramillo, Parque Nacional, p.o.i., Col. 168 D3 7.15 N 76.15 W
Paramirim, Braz. 170 G4 13.26 S 42.14 W
Paramirim, stm., Braz. 170 F4 11.34 S 43.17 W
Páramo de Masa, Puerto de, p., Spain 28 B7 42.36 N 3.43 W
Paramoti, Braz. 170 C6 4.06 S 39.15 W
Paramušir, ostrov, i., Russia 50 F20 50.25 N 155.50 E
Paramus Park, shp. cen., N.J., U.S. 194 40.57 N 74.04 W
Paramythiá, Grc. 34 D3 39.28 N 20.29 E
Paran, Nahal (Girafi, Wadi), stm. 76 I5 30.24 N 35.09 E
Paraná, Arg. 172 E7 31.44 S 60.30 W
Paranã, Braz. 170 G2 12.33 S 47.52 W
Paraná, state, Braz. 166 D6 24.00 S 51.00 W
Paranã, stm., Braz. 170 G1 12.30 S 48.14 W
Paraná, stm., S.A. 166 F5 33.48 S 59.14 W
Paraná, Pico, mtn., Braz. 172 B13 25.16 S 48.48 W
Paranaguá, Braz. 172 B13 25.31 S 48.30 W
Paranaguá, Baía de, b., Braz. 172 B13 25.26 S 48.22 W
Paranaíba, Braz. 166 C6 19.41 S 51.11 W
Paranaíba, stm., Braz. 166 C6 20.07 S 51.00 W
Paranaidji, Braz. 170 D2 6.31 S 47.23 W
Paranapanema, stm., Braz. 166 D6 22.41 S 53.10 W
Paranapiacaba, Serra do, mts., Braz. 172 B13 24.20 S 49.00 W
Parañaque, Phil. 187f 14.30 N 120.59 E
Paranavaí, Braz. 166 D6 23.04 S 52.28 W
Parang, Phil. 68 H3 5.55 N 120.54 E
Parang, Phil. 68 G5 7.21 N 124.16 E
Parang, Pulau, i., Indon. 66 F7 5.44 S 110.14 E
Parângu Mare, Vârful, mtn., Rom. 36 D10 45.22 N 23.33 E
Paranhos, Braz. 172 A10 23.53 S 55.25 W
Paranoá, Lago do, res., Braz. 170 H2 15.48 S 47.50 W
Paraopeba, Braz. 170 J3 19.17 S 44.24 W
Parapara, Ven. 168 C8 9.44 N 67.16 W
Parapetí, stm., Bol. 166 C4 18.58 S 62.23 W
Parara, Indon. 66 E12 2.37 S 120.13 E
Parás, Mex. 136 H8 26.30 N 99.31 W
Paratinga, Braz. 170 G4 12.42 S 43.11 W
Paratoo, Austl. 98 I2 32.42 S 139.22 E
Paray-le-Monial, Fr. 22 C10 46.26 N 4.07 E
Pārbati, stm., India 70 F6 25.50 N 76.33 E
Pārbatipur, Bngl. 70 F12 25.39 N 88.54 E
Parbhani, India 69 B3 19.15 N 76.46 E
Parbold, Eng., U.K. 180 53.36 N 2.46 W
Parchim, Ger. 24 C7 53.25 N 11.50 E
Parczew, Pol. 24 E18 51.38 N 22.53 E
Pardeeville, Wi., U.S. 128 H9 43.32 N 89.18 W
Pārdi, India 70 H4 20.30 N 72.57 E
Parding, China 70 B12 32.59 N 88.38 E
Pardo, stm., Braz. 166 D6 21.46 S 52.09 W
Pardo, stm., Braz. 170 H5 15.39 S 38.57 W
Pardo, stm., Braz. 170 K1 20.08 S 48.37 W
Pardo, stm., Braz. 170 L1 22.55 S 49.23 W
Pardo, stm., Braz. 172 D11 29.59 S 52.22 W
Pardubice, Czech Rep. 24 F11 50.02 N 15.46 E
Parěčča, Bela. 26 G7 53.53 N 24.08 E
Parecis, Braz. 166 B5 14.09 S 56.56 W
Parede, Port. 184c 38.41 N 9.21 W
Paredón, Mex. 154 C8 25.55 N 100.58 W
Parelhas, Braz. 170 D7 6.41 S 36.39 W
Parempei, i., Micron. 100d I12 7.00 N 158.15 E
Paren', Russia 50 D21 62.25 N 163.07 E
Paren', stm., Russia 50 D21 62.24 N 163.06 E
Parent, Qc., Can. 122 C2 47.55 N 74.36 W
Parentis-en-Born, Fr. 22 E4 44.21 N 1.04 W
Parepare, Indon. 66 E11 4.01 S 119.38 E
Parera, Arg. 172 G5 35.07 S 64.31 W
Parets del Vallès, Spain 184d 41.34 N 2.14 E
Parfenevo, Russia 12 F20 61.21 N 42.45 E
Parfenevo, Russia 40 B13 58.29 N 43.24 E
Parfino, Russia 26 B14 57.58 N 31.35 E
Parforce-Heide, for., Ger. 182a 52.22 N 13.10 E
Párga, Grc. 34 D3 39.17 N 20.24 E
Pārgaon, India 190c 18.59 N 73.05 E
Pargas see Parainen, Fin. 18 G9 60.17 N 22.18 E
Pargey Creek, stm., N.J., U.S. 203 39.49 N 75.18 W
Pargolovo, ngh., Russia 183a 60.04 N 30.18 E
Parham, Antig. 159b f4 17.06 N 61.45 W
Pari, ngh., Braz. 205b 23.32 S 46.37 W
Paria, stm., U.S. 150 G5 36.52 N 111.36 W
Paria, Golfo de see Paria, Gulf of, b. 168 B10 10.20 N 62.00 W
Paria, Gulf of, b. 168 B10 10.20 N 62.00 W
Paria, Península de, pen., Ven. 168 B10 10.40 N 62.10 W
Pariaguán, Ven. 168 C9 8.50 N 64.43 W
Pariaman, Indon. 66 D1 0.38 S 100.07 E
Pariči see Paryčy, Bela. 26 H12 52.48 N 29.25 E
Paricutín, vol., Mex. 154 F7 19.28 N 102.15 W
Pariette Draw, stm., Ut., U.S. 150 C6 40.02 N 109.44 W
Parigi, Indon. 66 D12 0.48 S 120.09 E
Parika, Guy. 164 B6 6.50 N 58.25 W
Parikkala, Fin. 18 F16 61.33 N 29.31 E
Parima, stm., Braz. 168 F10 3.33 N 63.46 W
Parima, Serra (Parima, Sierra), mts., S.A. 168 F9 3.23 N 64.09 W
Parima, Sierra (Parima, Serra), mts., S.A. 168 F9 3.23 N 64.09 W
Parima Tapirapecó, Parque Nacional, p.o.i., Ven. 168 F9 2.30 N 64.30 W
Pariñas, Punta, c., Peru 162 F6 4.40 S 81.20 W
Parintins, Braz. 164 D6 2.37 S 56.45 W
Pariquera-Açu, Braz. 172 B14 24.43 S 47.52 W
Paris, On., Can. 126 E9 43.11 N 80.22 W
Paris, Fr. 20 F11 48.51 N 2.20 E
Paris, Fr. 179 48.52 N 2.20 E
Paris, Ar., U.S. 134 B5 35.17 N 93.43 W
Paris, Id., U.S. 146 H15 42.14 N 111.24 W
Paris, Il., U.S. 130 E10 39.36 N 87.41 W
Paris, Ky., U.S. 124 F1 38.12 N 84.15 W
Paris, Me., U.S. 122 F6 44.15 N 70.30 W
Paris, Mo., U.S. 130 E5 39.28 N 92.00 W
Paris, Tn., U.S. 130 H9 36.18 N 88.19 W
Paris, Tx., U.S. 134 D3 33.40 N 95.33 W
Paris, state, Fr. 179 48.52 N 2.20 E
Paris, Port de, b., Fr. 179 48.57 N 2.17 E
Parisien de Pantin, Cimetière, misc. cult., Fr. 179 48.54 N 2.23 E
Parisienne, Ile, i., On., Can. 126 B5 46.41 N 84.43 W
Paris-le-Bourget, Aéroport de, arpt., Fr. 179 48.58 N 2.26 E
Paris-Orly, Aéroport de, arpt., Fr. 179 48.43 N 2.22 E
Parit, Indon. 66 E4 3.14 S 104.39 E
Parita, Bahía de, b., Pan. 156 H7 8.08 N 80.24 W
Parit Buntar, Malay. 64 J5 5.04 N 100.31 E
Park, stm., N.D., U.S. 142 F16 48.28 N 97.09 W
Park, North Branch, stm., N.D., U.S. 142 F16 48.26 N 97.27 W
Park, South Branch, stm., N.D., U.S. 142 F15 48.25 N 97.27 W
Parkalompolo, Swe. 14 E13 67.43 N 22.51 E
Parkano, Fin. 18 E9 62.01 N 23.04 E
Parkchester, Pa., U.S. 203 40.00 N 75.35 W
Park City, Ks., U.S. 130 D11 37.48 N 97.19 W
Park City, Mt., U.S. 140 B4 45.38 N 108.56 W
Park City, Ut., U.S. 150 C5 40.38 N 111.29 W
Park Creek, stm., Pa., U.S. 203 40.13 N 75.08 W
Parkdale, Or., U.S. 146 E5 45.31 N 121.36 W
Parkdene, S. Afr. 191d 26.14 S 28.16 E
Parker, Az., U.S. 150 I2 34.08 N 114.17 W
Parker, Co., U.S. 138 B4 39.31 N 104.45 W
Parker, Fl., U.S. 134 G13 30.08 N 85.35 W
Parker, S.D., U.S. 140 D15 43.24 N 97.07 W
Parker, Cape, c., Nu., Can. 108 B10 75.00 N 79.43 W
Parker City, In., U.S. 130 D12 40.10 N 85.12 W
Parker Dam, Ca., U.S. 150 I2 34.16 N 114.09 W
Parker Dam, dam, U.S. 150 I2 34.17 N 114.08 W
Parker Ford, Pa., U.S. 203 40.12 N 75.35 W
Parker Peak, mtn., S.D., U.S. 140 D9 43.24 N 103.41 W
Parker River National Wildlife Refuge, ind. res., Ma., U.S. 201 42.45 N 70.48 W
Parkersburg, Il., U.S. 130 F9 38.35 N 88.03 W
Parkersburg, Ia., U.S. 130 B5 42.34 N 92.47 W
Parkersburg, W.V., U.S. 124 E4 39.15 N 81.33 W
Parkers Creek, stm., N.J., U.S. 203 40.00 N 74.53 W
Parkers Prairie, Mn., U.S. 128 E3 46.08 N 95.20 W
Parkes, Austl. 98 I7 33.08 S 148.10 E
Park Falls, Wi., U.S. 128 F8 45.56 N 90.26 W
Park Forest, Il., U.S. 130 C10 41.28 N 87.39 W
Parkgate, Eng., U.K. 180 53.16 N 2.20 W
Parkgate, Eng., U.K. 180 53.18 N 3.05 W
Parkhill, On., Can. 126 E8 43.09 N 81.40 W
Parkhill Gardens, S. Afr. 191d 26.14 S 28.11 E
Parkhomivka, Ukr. 38 C14 50.06 N 35.00 E
Parkin, Ar., U.S. 134 B8 35.15 N 90.33 W
Parkland, Pa., U.S. 203 40.09 N 74.56 W
Parkland, Wa., U.S. 146 C4 47.08 N 122.25 W
Parklawn, Va., U.S. 202c 38.50 N 77.09 W
Parklea, Austl. 192a 33.44 S 150.57 E
Park Meadows, Pa., U.S. 197b 40.18 N 79.44 W
Park Orchards, Austl. 192b 37.46 S 145.13 E
Park Plateau, plat., Co., U.S. 138 D4 37.15 N 104.45 W
Park Range, mts., Co., U.S. 150 C10 40.40 N 106.40 W
Park Rapids, Mn., U.S. 118 E3 46.55 N 95.03 W
Park Ridge, N.J., U.S. 194 41.02 N 74.02 W
Park Ridge Farms, N.J., U.S. 203 40.10 N 74.42 W
Park River, N.D., U.S. 142 F16 48.23 N 97.45 W
Parkrose, Or., U.S. 146 E4 45.33 N 122.32 W
Park Rynie, S. Afr. 90 G10 30.23 S 30.41 E
Parkside, Md., U.S. 202c 39.02 N 77.06 W
Parkside, Pa., U.S. 203 39.52 N 75.23 W
Parksley, Va., U.S. 124 G10 37.46 N 75.39 W
Park Station, trans., S. Afr. 191d 26.12 S 28.03 E
Parkston, S.D., U.S. 140 D14 43.23 N 97.59 W
Parksville, B.C., Can. 144 G6 49.19 N 124.19 W
Parktown, ngh., S. Afr. 191d 26.11 S 28.03 E
Parktown North, ngh., S. Afr. 191d 26.09 S 28.02 E
Parkview, Pa., U.S. 197b 40.30 N 79.56 W
Parkville, Md., U.S. 124 E9 39.23 N 76.33 W
Parkville, Mo., U.S. 130 E3 39.11 N 94.41 W
Parkwood, Md., U.S. 202c 39.01 N 77.05 W
Parla, Spain 28 D7 40.14 N 3.46 W
Parlākimidi, India 69 B7 18.46 N 84.06 E
Pärlälven, stm., Swe. 14 F10 66.36 N 19.29 E
Parle, Lac qui, res., Mn., U.S. 128 F2 45.05 N 95.58 W
Parli, India 69 B3 18.51 N 76.32 E
Parliament, Houses of, bldg., Eng., U.K. 178 51.30 N 0.07 W
Parliament Building, bldg., Indon. 187e 6.13 S 106.48 E
Parma, Italy 30 F7 44.48 N 10.19 E
Parma, Id., U.S. 146 G10 43.47 N 116.56 W
Parma, Mo., U.S. 130 H8 36.36 N 89.49 W
Parma, Oh., U.S. 124 C4 41.23 N 81.42 W
Parma, stm., Italy 30 F7 44.56 N 10.25 E
Parmain, Fr. 179 49.07 N 2.12 E
Parmatown Mall, shp. cen., Oh., U.S. 197a 41.23 N 81.44 W
Parnaguá, Braz. 170 F3 10.13 S 44.38 W
Parnaíba, Braz. 170 B5 2.54 S 41.47 W
Parnaíba, stm., Braz. 164 D9 2.46 S 41.50 W
Parnaibinha, stm., Braz. 170 E2 9.17 S 45.54 W
Parnamirim, Braz. 170 E6 8.05 S 39.34 W
Parnarama, Braz. 170 C4 5.41 S 43.06 W
Parnassós, mtn., Grc. 34 E5 38.32 N 22.35 E
Párnitha, mtn., Grc. 34 E6 38.11 N 23.42 E
Párnitha, mts., Grc. 185c 38.07 N 23.44 E
Párnon, mts., Grc. 34 F5 37.10 N 22.39 E
Pärnu, Est. 26 B7 58.21 N 24.33 E
Pärnu, stm., Est. 26 B7 58.22 N 24.28 E
Pärnu-Jaagupi, Est. 26 B7 58.37 N 24.30 E
Pärnu laht, b., Est. 26 B7 58.15 N 24.25 E
Paro, Bhu. 70 E12 27.26 N 89.25 E
Pārola, India 70 H5 20.52 N 75.06 E
Paromaj, Russia 50 F17 52.30 N 143.06 E
Paroo, stm., Austl. 98 G5 30.23 S 143.59 E
Parorā, India 190b 22.48 N 88.09 E
Páros, Grc. 34 F8 37.04 N 25.08 E
Páros, i., Grc. 34 F8 37.05 N 25.12 E
Parowan, Ut., U.S. 150 F4 37.50 N 112.49 W
Parpaillon, mts., Fr. 22 E12 44.30 N 6.40 E
Parque Nacional da Chapada da Diamantina, p.o.i., Braz. 170 G4 12.47 S 41.25 W
Parral, Chile 172 H2 36.09 S 71.50 W
Parral, stm., Mex. 154 B6 27.39 N 105.07 W
Parramatta, Austl. 98 I8 33.49 S 151.00 E
Parramatta, stm., Austl. 192a 33.51 S 151.14 E
Parramatta Park, p.o.i., Austl. 192a 33.49 S 151.00 E
Parras de la Fuente, Mex. 154 C7 25.26 N 102.10 W
Parrett, stm., Eng., U.K. 10 J10 51.13 N 3.00 W
Parrish, Al., U.S. 134 D11 33.44 N 87.16 W
Parrish, Fl., U.S. 132 I3 27.34 N 82.25 W
Parris Island Marine Corps Recruit Depot, mil., S.C., U.S. 132 D5 32.20 N 80.41 W
Parrsboro, N.S., Can. 122 E12 45.25 N 64.20 W
Parry, Cape, c., N.T., Can. 110 A6 70.08 N 124.24 W
Parry, Mount, mtn., B.C., Can. 144 D2 52.53 N 128.45 W
Parry Bay, b., Nu., Can. 110 B14 68.14 N 81.37 W
Parry Channel, strt., Can. 106 B12 74.20 N 98.00 W
Parry Island, i., On., Can. 126 C9 45.16 N 80.09 W
Parry Peninsula, pen., N.T., Can. 110 B6 69.44 N 124.38 W
Parry Sound, On., Can. 126 C9 45.20 N 80.01 W
Parsberg, Ger. 24 G7 49.09 N 11.43 E
Parsęta, stm., Pol. 24 B11 54.11 N 15.33 E
Parshād, India 70 F4 24.11 N 73.43 E
Parshall, N.D., U.S. 142 G11 47.57 N 102.08 W
Parshallville, Mi., U.S. 199 42.41 N 83.46 W
Paršino, Russia 48 C20 59.14 N 111.51 E
Parsippany, Lake, l., N.J., U.S. 194 40.51 N 74.26 W
Parsnip, stm., B.C., Can. 144 A8 55.09 N 123.01 W
Parsoburan, Indon. 66 B1 2.18 N 99.20 E
Parsonage Island, i., N.Y., U.S. 194 40.37 N 73.37 W
Parsons, Ks., U.S. 130 G2 37.20 N 95.16 W
Parsons, Tn., U.S. 134 B10 35.38 N 88.07 W
Parsons, W.V., U.S. 124 E6 39.05 N 79.41 W
Pärsti, Est. 26 B8 58.25 N 25.32 E
Partanna, Italy 32 G6 37.43 N 12.53 E
Pårtefjällen, mts., Swe. 14 E8 67.12 N 17.39 E
Parthala, India 190a 28.36 N 77.24 E
Parthenay, Fr. 20 H8 46.39 N 0.15 W
Partille, Swe. 16 J10 57.44 N 12.08 E
Partington, Eng., U.K. 180 53.25 N 2.26 W
Partinico, Italy 32 F7 38.03 N 13.07 E
Partizansk, Russia 54 C10 43.07 N 133.07 E
Partizánske, Slvk. 24 H14 48.37 N 18.21 E
Paru, stm., Braz. 164 D7 1.34 S 52.31 W
Parú, stm., Ven. 168 E9 4.25 N 66.16 W
Paru de Oeste, stm., Braz. 164 C6 1.31 S 56.02 W
Parūr, India 69 F3 10.08 N 76.14 E
Parutyne, Ukr. 38 G10 46.42 N 31.53 E
Pārvatīpuram, India 69 B6 18.47 N 83.26 E
Părvomaj, Blg. 36 G12 42.06 N 25.12 E
Paryang, China 70 C9 30.09 N 83.08 E
Paryčy, Bela. 26 H12 52.48 N 29.25 E
Påryd, Swe. 16 K13 56.34 N 15.55 E
Parys, S. Afr. 90 E8 26.54 S 27.27 E
Pas, stm., Spain 22 F2 43.26 N 3.57 W
Paša, stm., Russia 18 G20 60.29 N 32.55 E
Paşabahçe, ngh., Tur. 185b 41.06 N 29.05 E
Pasadena, Ca., U.S. 148 I7 34.08 N 118.08 W
Pasadena, Tx., U.S. 136 E12 29.41 N 95.12 W
Pasado, Cabo, c., Ec. 168 H1 0.23 S 80.28 W
Pasaje, Ec. 164 D2 3.20 S 79.49 W
Pa Sak, stm., Thai. 64 D5 14.20 N 100.35 E
Paşaköy, N. Cyp. 76 C4 35.09 N 33.36 E
Paşalimanı Adası, i., Tur. 34 C10 40.28 N 27.37 E
Pasangkayu, Indon. 66 D11 1.11 S 119.20 E
Pasarbantal, Indon. 66 E2 2.45 S 101.20 E
Pasarseluma, Indon. 66 F3 4.08 S 102.31 E
Pasar Senen Station, trans., Indon. 187e 6.10 S 106.50 E
Pasaunda, India 190a 28.42 N 77.21 E
Pasawng, Mya. 64 C3 18.52 N 97.19 E
Pasay, Phil. 187f 14.33 N 121.00 E
Pascack Brook, stm., U.S. 194 40.59 N 73.59 W
Pascagoula, Ms., U.S. 134 G10 30.22 N 88.31 W
Pascagoula, stm., Ms., U.S. 134 G10 30.21 N 88.36 W
Paşcani, Rom. 36 B13 47.15 N 26.44 E
Pasco, Wa., U.S. 146 D7 46.13 N 119.05 W
Pascoag, R.I., U.S. 124 C14 41.57 N 71.42 W
Pascoe Vale, Austl. 192b 37.44 S 144.56 E
Pascua, Isla de (Easter Island) (Rapa Nui), i., Chile 100l f30 27.07 S 109.22 W
Pas-de-Calais, state, Fr. 20 D11 50.30 N 2.20 E
Pasewalk, Ger. 24 C10 53.30 N 13.59 E
Pasig, stm., Phil. 187f 14.36 N 120.58 E
Pašija, Russia 40 B21 58.26 N 58.15 E
Pasinler, Tur. 42 E9 39.59 N 41.41 E
Pasirganting, Indon. 66 E2 2.02 S 100.53 E
Pasir Gudang, Malay. 189c 1.27 N 103.53 E
Pasir Mas, Malay. 64 J6 6.02 N 102.08 E
Pasir Panjang, Sing. 189c 1.17 N 103.47 E
Pasirpengarayan, Indon. 66 C2 0.52 N 100.17 E
Pasir Puteh, Malay. 64 J6 5.50 N 102.24 E
Pasir Puteh, Malay. 189c 1.26 N 103.56 E
Påskallavik, Swe. 16 J14 57.08 N 16.27 E
Paškovo, Russia 50 G15 48.53 N 130.39 E
Paškovskij, Russia 40 I11 45.01 N 39.06 E
Pasłęk, Pol. 24 B15 54.03 N 19.40 E
Pasłęka, stm., Pol. 24 C16 54.25 N 19.44 E
Pasley Bay, b., Nu., Can. 110 A11 70.40 N 96.27 W
Pašman, Otok, i., Cro. 30 G12 43.58 N 15.21 E
Pasmore, stm., Austl. 98 H2 31.06 S 139.49 E
Pasni, Pak. 62 C1 25.16 N 63.27 E
Paso de Indios, Arg. 166 H3 43.50 S 68.56 W
Paso del Cerro, Ur. 172 E10 31.29 S 55.49 W
Paso de los Libres, Arg. 172 D9 29.41 S 57.08 W
Paso de los Toros, Ur. 172 F9 32.48 S 56.30 W
Paso del Rey, Arg. 206 34.39 S 58.46 W
Paso de Patria, Para. 172 C8 27.13 S 58.34 W
Paso de San Antonio, Mex. 136 E3 29.06 N 103.54 W
Paso Hondo, Mex. 154 H13 15.44 N 91.59 W
Paso Robles, Ca., U.S. 148 H5 35.38 N 120.41 W
Paso Seco, P.R. 158a c3 18.00 N 66.23 W
Pašozero, Russia 18 G21 60.02 N 34.37 E
Pasqua Indian Reserve, ind. res., Sk., Can. 142 D9 50.45 N 104.02 W
Pasquia Hills, hills, Sk., Can. 142 A11 53.15 N 102.30 W
Pasquotank, stm., N.C., U.S. 124 H9 36.09 N 76.00 W
Pasrūr, Pak. 70 B5 32.15 N 74.39 E
Passadumkeag, Me., U.S. 122 E8 45.11 N 68.37 W
Passadumkeag Mountain, hill, Me., U.S. 122 E8 45.10 N 68.20 W
Passagem Franca, Braz. 170 D4 6.10 S 43.47 W
Passage Point, c., N.T., Can. 109 B16 73.28 N 115.17 W
Passage West, Ire. 10 J4 51.52 N 8.20 W
Passaic, N.J., U.S. 126 H15 40.51 N 74.08 W
Passaic, stm., N.J., U.S. 194 40.43 N 74.07 W
Passaic Falls, wtfl., N.J., U.S. 194 40.55 N 74.11 W
Passamaquoddy Bay, b., N.A. 122 E10 45.06 N 66.59 W
Passau, Ger. 24 H9 48.34 N 13.27 E
Pass Creek, stm., S.D., U.S. 140 D11 43.45 N 101.28 W
Passero, Capo, c., Italy 32 H9 36.40 N 15.09 E
Passkij Perevoz, Russia 18 G19 60.23 N 32.59 E
Passo Fundo, Braz. 172 D11 28.14 S 52.24 W
Passo Real, Represa do, res., Braz. 172 D11 28.55 S 53.08 W
Passos, Braz. 170 K2 20.43 S 46.36 W
Passy, ngh., Fr. 179 48.52 N 2.17 E
Pastavy, Bela. 26 E9 55.07 N 26.50 E
Pastaza, state, Ec. 168 H3 1.45 S 76.50 W
Pastaza, stm., S.A. 164 D2 4.54 S 76.24 W
Pastillo, P.R. 158a b3 17.59 N 66.28 W
Pasto, Col. 168 G3 1.12 N 77.15 W
Pastora Peak, mtn., Az., U.S. 150 G7 36.47 N 109.10 W
Pastos Bons, Braz. 170 D3 6.36 S 44.05 W
Pasuruan, Indon. 66 G8 7.38 S 112.53 E
Pasvalys, Lith. 26 D7 56.04 N 24.24 E
Pásztó, Hung. 36 B6 47.55 N 19.42 E
Patacamaya, Bol. 166 C3 17.14 S 67.55 W
Patadkal, hist., India 69 C3 15.55 N 75.49 E
Patagonia, Az., U.S. 150 L6 31.33 N 110.44 W
Patagonia, reg., Arg. 166 I2 44.00 S 68.00 W
Pataha Creek, stm., Wa., U.S. 146 D9 46.30 N 117.59 W
Pātan, India 70 G4 23.50 N 72.07 E
Patapsco, Cooks Branch, stm., Md., U.S. 202b 39.27 N 76.53 W
Patapsco, Davis Branch, stm., Md., U.S. 202b 39.19 N 76.51 W
Patapsco, Rockburn Branch, stm., Md., U.S. 202b 39.14 N 76.43 W
Patapsco, Soapstone Branch, stm., Md., U.S. 202b 39.13 N 76.43 W
Patapsco River Neck, pen., Md., U.S. 202b 39.14 N 76.27 W
Pâtârlagele, Rom. 36 D13 45.19 N 26.22 E
Pataula Creek, stm., Ga., U.S. 134 F14 31.43 N 85.06 W
Patchewollock, Austl. 98 J3 35.22 S 142.11 E
Patchogue, N.Y., U.S. 124 D13 40.45 N 73.00 W
Patchogue Bay, b., N.Y., U.S. 194 40.44 N 73.01 W
Patea, N.Z. 102 D6 39.45 S 174.28 E
Pategi, Nig. 84 H6 8.43 N 5.45 E
Pate Island, i., Kenya 86 E8 2.05 S 41.03 E
Patel Nagar, ngh., India 190a 28.39 N 77.10 E
Patensie, S. Afr. 90 H7 33.46 S 24.49 E
Patéras Óros, mts., Grc. 185c 38.07 N 23.25 E
Paterna, Spain 28 E10 39.30 N 0.26 W
Paternal, ngh., Arg. 206 34.36 S 58.28 W
Paternion, Aus. 30 D10 46.42 N 13.37 E
Paternò, Italy 32 G8 37.34 N 14.54 E
Pateros, Phil. 187f 14.33 N 121.04 E
Pateros, Wa., U.S. 146 B7 48.02 N 119.53 W
Paterson, S. Afr. 90 H8 33.26 S 25.57 E
Paterson, N.J., U.S. 124 D11 40.54 N 74.09 W
Pathānkot, India 70 B5 32.15 N 75.38 E
Pātharghāta, India 190b 22.34 N 88.35 E
Pathein, Mya. 64 D2 16.46 N 94.43 E
Pathein see Bassein, stm., Mya. 64 D2 16.00 N 94.22 E
Pathfinder Reservoir, res., Wy., U.S. 140 E6 42.25 N 106.54 W
Pathiu, Thai. 64 G4 10.42 N 99.19 E
Pathum Thani, Thai. 64 E5 14.01 N 100.32 E
Pati, Indon. 66 D7 0.33 S 111.18 E
Pati, Indon. 66 G7 6.44 S 111.02 E
Patía, Col. 168 F3 2.03 N 77.03 W
Patía, stm., Col. 168 F2 2.12 N 78.39 W
Patiāla, India 70 C6 30.19 N 76.23 E
Pātihāl, India 190b 22.39 N 88.08 E
Patillas, P.R. 158a b3 18.00 N 66.00 W
Patīpāda, India 190c 19.04 N 73.05 E
Pati Point, c., Guam 100c i10 13.35 N 144.57 E
Pativilca, Peru 164 F2 10.40 S 77.48 W
Pātkai Range, mts., Asia 52 F4 27.00 N 96.00 E
Pat Mayse Lake, res., Tx., U.S. 134 D3 33.49 N 95.35 W
Pátmos, i., Grc. 34 F9 37.21 N 26.33 E
Patna, India 70 H11 21.56 N 87.52 E
Patna, India 70 F10 25.36 N 85.06 E
Pātna, India 190b 22.59 N 88.18 E
Patnāgarh, India 70 H9 20.42 N 83.08 E
Patnanongan Island, i., Phil. 68 C4 14.48 N 122.11 E
Pātnoli, India 190c 18.57 N 73.05 E
Patnos, Tur. 42 F10 39.14 N 42.52 E
Pato Branco, Braz. 172 C11 26.13 S 52.41 W
Patoka, Il., U.S. 130 F8 38.44 N 89.05 W
Patoka, stm., In., U.S. 130 F10 38.23 N 87.45 W
Patoka Lake, res., In., U.S. 130 F11 38.25 N 86.39 W
Patom Plateau see Patomskoe nagor'e, plat., Russia 50 E12 59.00 N 114.00 E
Patomskoe nagor'e, plat., Russia 50 E12 59.00 N 114.00 E
Paton, Île, i., Qc., Can. 193a 45.31 N 73.45 W
Patonga, Ug. 86 D6 2.46 N 33.18 E
Patoniva, Fin. 14 C18 69.44 N 27.00 E
Patos, Braz. 170 D7 7.01 S 37.16 W
Patos, stm., Arg. 172 E3 31.15 S 69.23 W
Patos, Lagoa dos, b., Braz. 172 E12 31.06 S 51.15 W
Patos de Minas, Braz. 170 J2 18.35 S 46.30 W
Patquía, Arg. 172 D4 30.02 S 66.52 W
Pátra, Grc. 34 E4 38.14 N 21.44 E
Patrai, Gulf of see Patraïkós Kólpos, b., Grc. 34 E4 38.15 N 21.32 E
Patrai, Gulf of see Patraïkós Kólpos, b., Grc. 34 E4 38.15 N 21.32 E
Patraïkós Kólpos (Patraikós Kólpos), b., Grc. 34 E4 38.15 N 21.32 E
Patraikós Kólpos (Patraïkós Kólpos), b., Grc. 34 E4 38.15 N 21.32 E
Patrakeevka, Russia 18 B27 64.57 N 40.22 E
Patricio Lynch, Isla, i., Chile 166 I1 48.37 S 75.26 W
Patrick Air Force Base, mil., Fl., U.S. 132 H5 28.15 N 80.36 W
Patrocínio, Braz. 170 J2 18.56 S 46.59 W
Patrocínio Paulista, Braz. 170 K2 20.37 S 47.16 W
Patsaliga Creek, stm., Al., U.S. 134 F12 31.22 N 86.31 W
Pattani, Thai. 64 I5 6.51 N 101.15 E
Pattani, stm., Thai. 64 I5 6.53 N 101.15 E
Pattaya, Thai. 64 F5 13.19 N 100.58 E
Patten, Me., U.S. 122 D8 45.59 N 68.27 W
Pattenville, Ma., U.S. 201 42.35 N 71.14 W
Patterson, Ca., U.S. 148 F4 37.28 N 121.07 W
Patterson, Ga., U.S. 132 E3 31.23 N 82.07 W
Patterson, La., U.S. 134 H7 29.41 N 91.18 W
Patterson, stm., Austl. 192b 38.05 S 145.07 E
Patterson, Mount, mtn., Yk., Can. 110 C4 64.04 N 134.39 W
Patterson Creek, stm., W.V., U.S. 124 E7 39.33 N 78.43 W
Patterson Island, i., On., Can. 128 C12 48.39 N 87.00 W
Patterson Park, p.o.i., Md., U.S. 202b 39.17 N 76.35 W
Patti, Italy 32 F8 38.08 N 14.58 E
Patti, Golfo di, b., Italy 32 F8 38.12 N 15.05 E
Pattison, Ms., U.S. 134 F8 31.53 N 90.53 W
Pattoki, Pak. 70 C4 31.01 N 73.51 E
Patton, Pa., U.S. 124 D7 40.37 N 78.38 W
Patton Park, p.o.i., Mi., U.S. 199 42.19 N 83.10 W
Pattonsburg, Mo., U.S. 130 D3 40.02 N 94.08 W
Pattscheid, ngh., Ger. 181 51.05 N 7.03 E
Pattukkottai, India 69 F4 10.25 N 79.19 E
Pattullo, Mount, mtn., B.C., Can. 110 D5 56.14 N 129.39 W
Patuākhāli, Bngl. 70 G13 22.20 N 90.20 E
Patuca, stm., Hond. 156 E5 15.48 N 84.17 W
Patuca, Punta, c., Hond. 156 E5 15.48 N 84.18 W
Pātul, India 190b 22.45 N 88.10 E
Patul, mtn., Ec. 168 I2 2.40 S 79.03 W
Pātūr, India 70 H6 20.27 N 76.56 E
Patusi, Pap. N. Gui. 101a a4 2.10 S 147.10 E
Patuxent, stm., Md., U.S. 124 F9 38.18 N 76.25 W
Patuxent Wildlife Research Center, sci., Md., U.S. 202c 39.03 N 76.48 W
Patvinsuon kansallispuisto, p.o.i., Fin. 18 D17 63.06 N 30.39 E
Patwāri, India 190a 28.35 N 77.27 E
Pátzcuaro, Mex. 154 F8 19.31 N 101.37 W
Pau, Fr. 22 F5 43.18 N 0.22 W
Pau, Gave de, stm., Fr. 22 F5 43.33 N 1.12 W
Pau Brasil, Braz. 170 H6 15.26 S 39.38 W
Pau dos Ferros, Braz. 170 D6 6.07 S 38.10 W
Pauh, Indon. 66 E3 2.07 S 102.48 E
Pauini, Braz. 164 E4 7.39 S 66.57 W
Pauini, stm., Braz. 164 E4 7.47 S 67.05 W
Pauini, stm., Braz. 168 H10 1.42 S 62.48 W
Pauk, Mya. 64 B2 21.26 N 94.28 E
Pauksa Taung, mtn., Mya. 64 C2 19.55 N 94.18 E
Paul, Id., U.S. 146 H13 42.37 N 113.47 W
Paulding, Ms., U.S. 134 E9 32.01 N 89.02 W
Paulding, Oh., U.S. 124 C1 41.07 N 84.34 W
Paulicéia, Braz. 166 D6 21.18 S 51.50 W
Paulina Peak, mtn., Or., U.S. 146 G5 43.41 N 121.15 W
Pauline, Mount, mtn., Can. 144 C11 53.33 N 119.54 W
Paulino Neves, Braz. 170 B4 2.43 S 42.33 W
Paulis see Isiro, D.R.C. 86 D5 2.45 N 27.37 E
Paulistana, Braz. 170 E5 8.09 S 41.09 W
Paulistas, Braz. 170 J4 18.25 S 42.52 W
Paullina, Ia., U.S. 130 B2 42.58 N 95.41 W
Paulo Afonso, Braz. 170 E6 9.21 S 38.14 W
Paulo Afonso, Cachoeira de, wtfl., Braz. 170 E6 9.23 S 38.12 W
Paulo de Faria, Braz. 170 K1 20.01 S 49.24 W
Paulpietersburg, S. Afr. 90 E10 27.29 S 30.49 E
Paul-Sauvé, Parc, p.o.i., Qc., Can. 193a 45.28 N 74.02 W
Pauls Valley, Ok., U.S. 138 G11 34.44 N 97.12 W
Paulton, Pa., U.S. 197b 40.34 N 79.34 W
Pāunān, India 190b 22.57 N 88.17 E
Paung, Mya. 64 D3 16.37 N 97.27 E
Paungde, Mya. 64 C2 18.28 N 95.30 E
Paunggyi, Mya. 64 D3 17.18 N 96.10 E
Pauri, India 70 C7 30.08 N 78.47 E
Pausin, Ger. 182a 52.38 N 13.03 E
Paute, Ec. 168 I2 2.46 S 78.45 W
Paute, stm., Ec. 168 I2 2.45 S 78.18 W
Pauto, stm., Col. 168 E6 5.08 N 70.54 W
Pavai, ngh., India 190c 19.07 N 72.55 E
Pavai Lake, l., India 190c 19.07 N 72.55 E
Pāveh, Iran 74 C10 35.03 N 46.22 E
Pavelec Station, trans., Russia 183b 55.44 N 37.38 E
Pavia, Italy 30 E6 45.12 N 9.09 E
Pavia, Naviglio di, can., Italy 184b 45.27 N 9.11 E

Name	Page	Map Ref.	Latitude	Longitude
Pavilion, B.C., Can.	144	F9	50.52 N	121.50 W
Pavillion, Wy., U.S.	140	D4	43.13 N	108.42 W
Pāvilosta, Lat.	26	D4	56.52 N	21.13 E
Pavino, Russia	40	B15	59.06 N	46.03 E
Pavlikeni, Blg.	36	F12	43.14 N	25.19 E
Pavlivka, Ukr.	38	F16	47.45 N	37.13 E
Pavlivka, Ukr.	38	D17	49.37 N	38.42 E
Pavlodar, Kaz.	48	D13	52.17 N	76.59 E
Pavlof Volcano, vol., Ak., U.S.	109	E7	55.24 N	161.52 W
Pavlohrad, Ukr.	38	E14	48.32 N	35.53 E
Pavlovka, Russia	40	F19	51.53 N	54.46 E
Pavlovka, Russia	40	D20	55.23 N	56.38 E
Pavlovo, Russia	40	D13	55.57 N	43.04 E
Pavlovo, Russia	183a		59.49 N	30.54 E
Pavlovo, Russia	183a		59.56 N	30.40 E
Pavlovsk, Russia	26	A13	59.39 N	30.27 E
Pavlovsk, Russia	40	F12	50.27 N	40.08 E
Pavlovsk, Russia	48	D14	53.18 N	82.59 E
Pavlovskaja, Russia	40	H11	46.08 N	39.47 E
Pavlovskij Posad, Russia	26	E21	55.46 N	38.40 E
Pavlysh, Ukr.	38	E12	48.55 N	33.21 E
Pavne, India	190c		19.05 N	73.01 E
Pavo, Ga., U.S.	132	F2	30.58 N	83.44 W
Pavón, Col.	168	F5	3.36 N	72.17 W
Pavona, Italy	185a		41.43 N	12.37 E
Pavšino, Russia	183b		55.49 N	37.21 E
Pavšozero, Russia	18	G22	60.38 N	35.34 E
Pavullo nel Frignano, Italy	30	F7	44.20 N	10.49 E
Pavuna, Arroio, stm., Braz.	205a		22.58 S	43.23 W
Pavuvu Island, i., Sol. Is.	101b	e8	9.03 S	159.06 E
Pavy, Russia	26	B12	58.03 N	29.30 E
Pawai, Pulau, i., Sing.	189c		1.12 N	103.43 E
Pawan, stm., Indon.	66	D7	1.50 S	109.56 E
Pawhuska, Ok., U.S.	138	E12	36.40 N	96.20 W
Pawn, stm., Mya.	64	C3	18.52 N	97.19 E
Pawnee, Il., U.S.	130	E8	39.35 N	89.34 W
Pawnee, Ok., U.S.	134	A2	36.20 N	96.48 W
Pawnee, stm., Ks., U.S.	138	C9	38.10 N	99.06 W
Pawnee City, Ne., U.S.	130	D1	40.06 N	96.09 W
Pawnee Creek, stm., Co., U.S.	140	G9	40.33 N	103.14 W
Pawnee Rock, Ks., U.S.	138	C9	38.15 N	98.58 W
Pawni, India	70	H7	20.47 N	79.39 E
Pawota, Mya.	64	D3	17.46 N	97.18 E
Paw Paw, Il., U.S.	130	C8	41.41 N	88.58 W
Paw Paw, Mi., U.S.	130	B12	42.12 N	85.53 W
Paw Paw, W.V., U.S.	124	E7	39.31 N	78.26 W
Pawtucket, R.I., U.S.	124	C14	41.52 N	71.22 W
Paxoí, i., Grc.	34	D3	39.12 N	20.10 E
Paxson, Ak., U.S.	109	D10	63.02 N	145.32 W
Paxton, Il., U.S.	130	D9	40.27 N	88.05 W
Paxton, Ne., U.S.	140	F11	41.07 N	101.21 W
Paya, Hond.	156	E5	15.36 N	85.14 W
Payagyi, Mya.	64	D3	17.28 N	96.31 E
Payakumbuh, Indon.	66	D2	0.14 S	100.38 E
Paya Lebar, Sing.	189c		1.22 N	103.53 E
Paya Lebar Airport, arpt., Sing.	189c		1.21 N	103.54 E
Payamlı, Tur.	76	A9	37.01 N	38.35 E
Payas, Cerro, mtn., Hond.	156	E5	15.47 N	84.56 W
Payerne, Switz.	30	D3	46.48 N	6.55 E
Payeti, Indon.	66	H12	9.41 S	120.21 E
Payette, Id., U.S.	146	F10	44.04 N	116.55 W
Payette, stm., Id., U.S.	146	G10	44.05 N	116.56 W
Payette, Middle Fork, stm., Id., U.S.	146	F11	44.05 N	116.06 W
Payette, North Fork, stm., Id., U.S.	146	F10	44.05 N	116.07 W
Payette, South Fork, stm., Id., U.S.	146	F11	44.06 N	115.59 W
Payette Lake, l., Id., U.S.	146	F10	44.57 N	116.05 W
Paylampur, India	190b		22.47 N	88.16 E
Payne, Oh., U.S.	124	C1	41.04 N	84.43 W
Payne, Lac, l., Can.	110	D16	59.27 N	74.14 W
Paynes Find, Austl.	96	E3	29.15 S	117.41 E
Paynesville, S. Afr.	191d		26.14 S	28.28 E
Paynesville, Mn., U.S.	128	F4	45.22 N	94.43 W
Paynton, Sk., Can.	142	A5	53.01 N	108.55 W
Paysandú, Ur.	172	F8	32.19 S	58.04 W
Payson, Az., U.S.	150	I5	34.10 N	111.19 W
Payson, Il., U.S.	130	E6	39.49 N	91.14 W
Payson, Ut., U.S.	150	C5	40.03 N	111.44 W
Payún, Cerro, mtn., Arg.	172	H3	36.24 S	69.12 W
Paz, Cañada de la, stm., Arg.	206		34.53 S	58.38 W
Pazar, Tur.	42	E9	41.10 N	40.52 E
Pazarbaşı Burnu, c., Tur.	34	B13	41.08 N	30.12 E
Pazarcık, Tur.	42	G7	37.29 N	37.18 E
Pazardžik, Blg.	36	G11	42.11 N	24.20 E
Pazarköy, Tur.	34	D10	39.51 N	27.25 E
Pazaryeri, Tur.	34	D12	40.00 N	29.54 E
Paz de Ariporo, Col.	168	E6	5.52 N	71.53 W
Pazin, Cro.	30	E10	45.14 N	13.56 E
Pčevža, Russia	26	A15	59.21 N	32.23 E
Pčevža, stm., Russia	26	A15	59.21 N	31.53 E
Pcič, Bela.	26	H11	52.10 N	28.49 E
Pcič, stm., Bela.	26	G11	52.08 N	28.52 E
Pe, Mya.	64	F4	13.27 N	98.29 E
Pea, Tonga	100e	n13	21.10 S	175.14 W
Pea, stm., U.S.	134	F12	31.01 N	85.51 W
Peabody, Ks., U.S.	138	C11	38.10 N	97.06 W
Peabody, Ma., U.S.	124	B14	42.32 N	70.55 W
Peace, stm., Can.	110	D8	58.59 N	111.24 W
Peace, stm., Fl., U.S.	132	I4	26.57 N	82.01 W
Peace and Friendship Stadium, p.o.i., Grc.	185c		37.56 N	23.40 E
Peace Bridge, trans., N.A.	202a		42.54 N	78.55 W
Peace River, Ab., Can.	110	D7	56.14 N	117.16 W
Peach Creek, stm., Tx., U.S.	136	E10	29.24 N	97.19 W
Peach Creek, stm., Tx., U.S.	136	D12	30.07 N	95.10 W
Peachland, B.C., Can.	144	G11	49.46 N	119.44 W
Peach Orchard, Ga., U.S.	132	C3	33.23 N	82.01 W
Peach Springs, Az., U.S.	150	H3	35.31 N	113.25 W
Pea Hill Branch, stm., Md., U.S.	202c		38.45 N	76.57 W
Peak Dale, Eng., U.K.	180		53.17 N	1.52 W
Peak District National Park, p.o.i., Eng., U.K.	10	H11	53.14 N	1.40 W
Peak Downs, Austl.	98	D7	22.18 S	148.13 E
Peaked Mountain, mtn., Me., U.S.	122	D8	46.34 N	68.49 W
Peak Forest, Eng., U.K.	180		53.19 N	1.50 W
Peak Forest Canal, can., Eng., U.K.	180		53.29 N	2.06 W
Peak Hill, Austl.	96	E3	25.38 S	118.43 E
Peak Hill, Austl.	98	I7	32.43 S	148.11 E
Peakhurst, Austl.	192a		33.58 S	151.04 E
Peäldoajvi, mtn., Fin.	14	C17	69.11 N	26.36 E
Peale, Mount, mtn., Ut., U.S.	150	E7	38.26 N	109.14 W
Peapack Brook, stm., N.J., U.S.	194		40.41 N	74.39 W
Pearce, Az., U.S.	150	L7	31.55 N	109.48 W
Pea Ridge National Military Park, p.o.i., Ar., U.S.	130	H4	36.27 N	94.02 W
Pearisburg, Va., U.S.	124	G5	37.19 N	80.44 W
Pearl, Il., U.S.	130	E7	39.27 N	90.37 W
Pearl, Ms., U.S.	134	E8	32.16 N	90.07 W
Pearl, stm., U.S.	134	G9	30.11 N	89.32 W
Pearl, Lake, l., Ma., U.S.	201		42.04 N	71.21 W
Pearland, Tx., U.S.	136	E12	29.33 N	95.17 W
Pearl Creek, stm., S.D., U.S.	140	C14	44.14 N	98.08 W
Pearl Harbor, b., Hi., U.S.	100a	b3	21.21 N	157.58 W
Pearl Peak, mtn., Nv., U.S.	148	C10	40.14 N	115.32 W
Pearl River, La., U.S.	134	G9	30.22 N	89.45 W
Pearns Point, c., Antig.	159b	f4	17.05 N	61.54 W
Pearsall, Tx., U.S.	136	F8	28.53 N	99.05 W
Pearsoll Peak, mtn., Or., U.S.	148	A2	42.18 N	123.50 W
Pearson, Ga., U.S.	132	E3	31.17 N	82.50 W
Pearston, S. Afr.	90	H7	32.35 S	25.08 E
Peary Channel, strt., Nu., Can.	108	B5	79.40 N	101.30 W
Peary Land, reg., Grnld.	108	A18	83.00 N	35.00 W
Pease, stm., Tx., U.S.	138	G9	34.11 N	99.07 W
Pebane, Moz.	88	D6	17.15 S	38.08 E
Pebas, Peru	164	D3	3.18 S	71.51 W
Pebble Island, i., Falk. Is.	166	J5	51.19 S	59.33 W
Peć, Yugo.	36	G7	42.40 N	20.18 E
Pecan Bayou, stm., Tx., U.S.	136	C9	31.25 N	98.43 W
Pecan Gap, Tx., U.S.	134	D3	33.26 N	95.50 W
Peçanha, Braz.	170	J4	18.32 S	42.33 W
Peças, Ilha das, i., Braz.	172	B13	25.25 S	48.17 W
Pecatonica, Il., U.S.	130	B8	42.18 N	89.21 W
Pecatonica, stm., U.S.	130	B8	42.26 N	89.04 W
Pecatu, Indon.	66	H9	8.50 S	115.07 E
Pécel, Hung.	182c		47.29 N	19.21 E
Pečenga, Russia	14	C22	69.33 N	31.13 E
Pečenga, stm., Russia	14	C21	69.34 N	31.15 E
Peche Island, i., On., Can.	199		42.21 N	82.56 W
Pechenihy, Ukr.	38	D15	49.52 N	36.55 E
Pechenizhyn, Ukr.	38	E3	48.32 N	24.54 E
Pecheniz'ke vodoskhovyshche, res., Ukr.	38	C15	50.04 N	36.48 E
Pechera, Ukr.	38	E7	48.51 N	28.43 E
Pechincha, ngh., Braz.	205a		22.56 S	43.21 W
Pechora see Pečora, stm., Russia	48	B9	67.59 N	53.56 E
Pechora Bay see Pečorskaja guba, b., Russia	48	A8	68.40 N	54.45 E
Pechra-Pokrovskoje, Russia	183b		55.50 N	37.57 E
Pecica, Rom.	36	C8	46.10 N	21.04 E
Peck, Mi., U.S.	126	E7	43.15 N	82.48 W
Peck-Berge, hills, Ger.	182a		52.36 N	13.34 E
Pecket Well, Eng., U.K.	180		53.46 N	2.00 W
Peckman, stm., N.J., U.S.	194		40.53 N	74.13 W
Pečora, Russia	48	A9	65.07 N	57.09 E
Pečora, stm., Russia	48	B9	67.59 N	53.56 E
Pecoraro, Monte, mtn., Italy	32	F10	38.32 N	16.20 E
Pečorskaja guba, b., Russia	48	A8	68.40 N	54.45 E
Pečorskoe more, s., Russia	48	A8	70.00 N	54.00 E
Pečory, Russia	26	C10	57.50 N	27.36 E
Pecos, N.M., U.S.	138	F3	35.34 N	105.40 W
Pecos, Tx., U.S.	136	C4	31.25 N	103.29 W
Pecos, stm., U.S.	120	F11	29.41 N	101.22 W
Pecos National Monument, p.o.i., N.M., U.S.	138	F3	35.26 N	105.56 W
Pecos Plains, pl., N.M., U.S.	120	E10	33.32 N	104.18 W
Pecqueuse, Fr.	179		48.39 N	2.03 E
Pécs, Hung.	36	C5	46.04 N	18.13 E
Pedana, India	69	C5	16.16 N	81.10 E
Pedasí, Pan.	156	I7	7.32 N	80.01 W
Pedder, Lake, res., Austl.	99a	o12	42.54 S	146.12 E
Peddie, S. Afr.	90	H8	33.13 S	27.07 E
Peddocks Island, i., Ma., U.S.	201		42.17 N	70.56 W
Pededze, stm., Eur.	26	C10	56.57 N	26.55 E
Pedernales, Arg.	172	G8	35.16 S	59.36 W
Pedernales, Dom. Rep.	156	C12	18.02 N	71.43 W
Pedernales, Ven.	168	C10	9.57 N	62.14 W
Pedernales, stm., Tx., U.S.	136	D9	30.25 N	98.03 W
Pedernales, Salar de, pl., Chile	172	C3	26.15 S	69.10 W
Pedernales Falls State Park, p.o.i., Tx., U.S.	136	D9	30.20 N	98.14 W
Pedetsi see Pededze, stm., Eur.	26	C10	56.57 N	26.55 E
Pedhoulás, Cyp.	76	D3	34.58 N	32.50 E
Pedja, stm., Est.	26	B9	58.24 N	26.11 E
Pedra Azul, Braz.	170	I5	15.59 S	41.16 W
Pedra Branca, Braz.	170	C6	5.27 S	39.43 W
Pedra Lume, C.V.	85a	k10	16.45 N	22.54 W
Pedras, Rio das, stm., Braz.	205a		22.51 S	43.01 W
Pedras de Fogo, Braz.	170	D8	7.23 S	35.07 W
Pedras Negras, Braz.	166	B4	12.51 S	62.54 W
Pedras Salgadas, Port.	28	C3	41.32 N	7.36 W
Pedraza, Col.	168	B4	10.11 N	74.54 W
Pedregal, Pan.	156	H6	8.22 N	82.26 W
Pedregal, Ven.	168	B6	11.01 N	70.08 W
Pedregulho, Braz.	170	K2	20.14 S	47.28 W
Pedreiras, Braz.	170	C3	4.34 S	44.39 W
Pedriceña, Mex.	154	C7	25.06 N	103.47 W
Pedro, Point, c., Sri L.	69	G5	9.50 N	80.14 E
Pedro Afonso, Braz.	170	E1	8.59 S	48.09 W
Pedro Avelino, Braz.	170	C7	5.31 S	36.23 W
Pedro Cays, is., Jam.	156	D9	17.00 N	77.50 W
Pedrógão Grande, Port.	28	E2	39.54 N	8.09 W
Pedro Gomes, Braz.	166	C6	18.04 S	54.32 W
Pedro II, Braz.	170	C5	4.25 S	41.28 W
Pedro II, Ilha, i., S.A.	168	G8	0.40 N	66.39 W
Pedro II, Isla see Pedro II, Ilha, i., S.A.	168	G8	0.40 N	66.39 W
Pedro Juan Caballero, Para.	166	D5	22.33 S	55.44 W
Pedro Leopoldo, Braz.	170	J3	19.38 S	44.03 W
Pedro Luro, Arg.	166	G4	39.27 S	62.42 W
Pedro Osório, Braz.	172	E11	31.51 S	52.48 W
Pedro R. Fernández, Arg.	172	D8	28.44 S	58.40 W
Pedro Velho, Braz.	170	D8	6.26 S	35.14 W
Peebinga, Austl.	98	J3	34.56 S	140.55 E
Peebles, Scot., U.K.	10	F9	55.39 N	3.11 W
Peebles, Oh., U.S.	124	F2	38.56 N	83.24 W
Pee Dee, stm., U.S.	132	A6	34.42 N	79.52 W
Peekaboo Mountain, hill, Me., U.S.	122	E9	45.45 N	67.56 W
Peekskill, N.Y., U.S.	124	C12	41.17 N	73.55 W
Peel, I. of Man	10	G8	54.13 N	4.41 W
Peel, stm., Can.	110	B4	67.42 N	134.31 W
Pe Ell, Wa., U.S.	146	D3	46.33 N	123.18 W
Peel Point, c., N.T., Can.	109	B17	73.22 N	114.35 W
Peel Sound, strt., Nu., Can.	110	A11	73.15 N	96.30 W
Peene, stm., Ger.	24	C9	54.08 N	13.45 E
Peepeekisis Indian Reserve, ind. res., Sk., Can.	142	D10	50.52 N	103.24 W
Peerless, Mt., U.S.	142	F8	48.46 N	105.49 W
Peers, Ab., Can.	144	C15	53.40 N	116.00 W
Peesane, Sk., Can.	142	B10	52.52 N	103.37 W
Peetz, Co., U.S.	140	G9	40.57 N	103.06 W
Peetzsee, l., Ger.	182a		52.26 N	13.50 E
Pegasus Bay, b., N.Z.	102	F5	43.20 S	173.00 E
Pegnitz, Ger.	24	G7	49.45 N	11.32 E
Pegnitz, stm., Ger.	24	G7	49.29 N	10.59 E
Pegu see Bago, Mya.	64	D3	17.20 N	96.29 E
Pegu, stm., Mya.	64	D3	16.44 N	96.12 E
Peguis Indian Reserve, ind. res., Mb., Can.	142	C16	51.20 N	97.35 W
Pegu Yoma, mts., Mya.	64	C3	19.00 N	95.50 E
Pegyš, Russia	12	E24	63.26 N	50.32 E
Pehčevo, Mac.	34	B5	41.46 N	22.54 E
Pehladpur, ngh., India	190a		28.35 N	77.06 E
Pehlivanköy, Tur.	34	B9	41.21 N	26.55 E
Pehorka, stm., Russia	183b		55.35 N	38.03 E
Pehra-Jakovlevskaja, Russia	183b		55.48 N	37.58 E
Pehuajó, Arg.	172	G7	35.48 S	61.54 W
Pehula, Fin.	18	F9	61.16 N	22.41 E
Peiching see Beijing, China	58	B7	39.55 N	116.22 E
Peigan Indian Reserve, ind. res., Ab., Can.	144	G17	49.35 N	113.40 W
Peikang, Tai.	58	J9	23.34 N	120.18 E
Peine, Ger.	24	D6	52.19 N	10.14 E
Peine, Pointe à, c., Dom.	159c	j6	15.23 N	61.15 W
Peinnechaung, i., Mya.	70	I14	19.48 N	92.49 E
Peipsi järv see Peipus, Lake, l., Eur.	26	B10	58.45 N	27.25 E
Peipus, Lake, l., Eur.	26	B10	58.45 N	27.25 E
Peiraiás (Piraeus), Grc.	34	F6	37.57 N	23.39 E
Peiraiás (Piraeus), Grc.	185c		37.57 N	23.38 E
Peissenberg, Ger.	24	I7	47.48 N	11.04 E
Peit'ou, ngh., Tai.	187d		25.08 N	121.30 E
Peixe, Braz.	170	G1	12.03 S	48.32 W
Peixe, stm., Braz.	166	D6	21.30 S	51.57 W
Peixian, China	58	D7	34.18 N	117.56 E
Peixoto, Represa de, res., Braz.	170	K2	20.04 S	47.22 W
Pejantan, Pulau, i., Indon.	66	C5	0.07 N	107.14 E
Pek, stm., Yugo.	36	E8	44.46 N	21.30 E
Pekalongan, Indon.	66	G6	6.53 S	109.40 E
Pekan, Malay.	64	K6	3.29 N	103.25 E
Pekanbaru, Indon.	66	C2	0.31 N	101.26 E
Pekanheran, Indon.	66	D3	0.21 S	102.26 E
Pekin, Il., U.S.	130	D8	40.33 N	89.38 W
Pekin, In., U.S.	130	F11	38.30 N	86.01 W
Pekin, N.Y., U.S.	202a		43.10 N	78.53 W
Peking see Beijing, China	58	B7	39.55 N	116.22 E
Pekkino, Russia	26	G16	53.32 N	33.31 E
Pekša, stm., Russia	26	D22	56.21 N	39.19 E
Pekul'nej, hrebet, mts., Russia	50	C24	66.00 N	175.00 E
Pelabohan Klang, Malay.	64	K5	3.00 N	101.24 E
Pelabuhandagang, Indon.	66	D3	1.08 S	103.05 E
Pelabuhanratu, Indon.	66	G5	7.00 S	106.34 E
Pelado, Volcán, vol., Mex.	204a		19.09 N	99.13 W
Pelagie, Isole, is., Italy	32	I6	35.40 N	12.40 E
Pelahatchie, Ms., U.S.	134	E9	32.19 N	89.47 W
Pelaihari, Indon.	66	E9	3.47 S	114.45 E
Pelalawan, Indon.	66	C3	0.27 N	102.05 E
Pelat, Mont, mtn., Fr.	22	E12	44.16 N	6.42 E
Pelczyce, Pol.	24	C11	53.03 N	15.18 E
Pelé, Mont, mtn., Gabon	86	E2	3.15 S	11.14 E
Peleduj, Russia	48	C20	59.39 N	112.44 E
Pelée, Montagne, vol., Mart.	159c	k6	14.48 N	61.10 W
Pelee, Point, c., On., Can.	126	G7	41.54 N	82.30 W
Pelee Island, i., On., Can.	126	G7	41.46 N	82.39 W
Pelega, Vârful, mtn., Rom.	36	D9	45.22 N	22.54 E
Peleliu see Beliliou, i., Palau	60	D9	7.00 N	134.14 E
Peleng, Pulau, i., Indon.	60	F7	1.15 S	123.08 E
Pelham, Al., U.S.	134	D12	33.17 N	86.48 W
Pelham, Ga., U.S.	132	E1	31.07 N	84.09 W
Pelham, N.Y., U.S.	194		40.54 N	73.48 W
Pelham Bay, b., N.Y., U.S.	194		40.52 N	73.47 W
Pelham Bay Park, p.o.i., N.Y., U.S.	194		40.52 N	73.49 W
Pelham Manor, N.Y., U.S.	194		40.53 N	73.48 W
Pelhřimov, Czech Rep.	24	G11	49.26 N	15.13 E
Pelican, Ak., U.S.	109	E12	58.00 N	136.15 W
Pelican, stm., Mn., U.S.	128	E2	46.17 N	96.09 W
Pelican, Punta, c., Mex.	150	L3	31.20 N	113.38 W
Pelican Bay, b., Mb., Can.	142	B13	52.50 N	100.22 W
Pelican Lake, Wi., U.S.	128	F9	45.30 N	89.09 W
Pelican Lake, l., Mb., Can.	142	B13	52.30 N	100.20 W
Pelican Lake, l., Mb., Can.	142	E14	49.20 N	99.35 W
Pelican Lake, l., Sk., Can.	142	D8	50.32 N	106.00 W
Pelican Lake, l., Mn., U.S.	128	C5	48.03 N	92.53 W
Pelican Lake, l., S.D., U.S.	140	C15	44.52 N	97.11 W
Pelican Narrows, Sk., Can.	110	D10	55.10 N	102.55 W
Pelican Rapids, Mb., Can.	142	B13	52.43 N	100.42 W
Pelican Rapids, Mn., U.S.	128	E2	46.34 N	96.04 W
Pelinia, Mol.	38	F6	47.52 N	27.50 E
Pelister Nacionalni Park, p.o.i., Mac.	34	C4	40.57 N	21.14 E
Pelješac, Poluotok, pen., Cro.	30	H14	42.58 N	17.20 E
Peljušnja, Russia	26	B15	58.55 N	32.53 E
Pelkosenniemi, Fin.	14	E18	67.07 N	27.28 E
Pelkum, Ger.	181		51.40 N	7.24 E
Pella, Ia., U.S.	130	C5	41.24 N	92.54 W
Pélla, hist., Grc.	34	C5	40.45 N	22.33 E
Pell City, Al., U.S.	134	D12	33.35 N	86.17 W
Pellegrini, Arg.	172	H6	36.15 S	63.10 W
Pellegrini, Lago, l., Arg.	172	I4	38.41 S	67.59 W
Pellegrino, Cozzo del, mtn., Italy	32	E10	39.43 N	16.00 E
Pellendorf, Aus.	182b		48.06 N	16.27 E
Pello, Fin.	12	C11	66.48 N	24.00 E
Pello, Swe.	14	F14	66.48 N	23.59 E
Pellston, Mi., U.S.	126	C5	45.32 N	84.46 W
Pellworm, i., Ger.	24	B4	54.31 N	8.38 E
Pelly, Sk., Can.	142	C12	51.52 N	101.55 W
Pelly, stm., Yk., Can.	110	C4	62.46 N	137.19 W
Pelly Bay, b., Nu., Can.	110	B12	68.53 N	89.51 W
Pelly Crossing, Yk., Can.	110	C3	62.50 N	136.34 W
Pelly Lake, l., Nu., Can.	110	B10	65.52 N	101.06 W
Pelly Mountains, mts., Yk., Can.	110	C4	62.00 N	133.00 W
Peloncillo Mountains, mts., U.S.	150	K8	32.15 N	109.00 W
Pelón de Ñado, mtn., Mex.	154	E9	20.03 N	99.56 W
Peloponnesus see Pelopónnisos, pen., Grc.	34	F5	37.30 N	22.00 E
Pelopónnisos, state, Grc.	34	F5	37.30 N	22.30 E
Pelopónnisos (Peloponnesus), pen., Grc.	34	F5	37.30 N	22.00 E
Peloritani, Monti, mts., Italy	32	F9	38.03 N	15.20 E
Pelotas, Braz.	172	E11	31.45 S	52.19 W
Pelotas, stm., Braz.	172	C12	27.28 S	51.54 W
Pelplin, Pol.	24	C14	53.55 N	18.42 E
Pelque, stm., Arg.	166	J2	51.02 S	70.57 W
Pelusium Bay see Tīna, Khalīg el-, b., Egypt	76	G3	31.08 N	32.40 E
Pemadumcook Lake, l., Me., U.S.	122	E7	45.41 N	68.54 W
Pemalang, Indon.	66	G6	6.53 S	109.23 E
Pemangkat, Indon.	66	C6	1.09 N	108.58 E
Pematang, Indon.	66	D2	0.12 S	102.04 E
Pematangsiantar, Indon.	66	B1	2.56 N	99.03 E
Pemba, Moz.	88	C7	13.01 S	40.31 E
Pemba, Zam.	88	D4	16.31 S	27.20 E
Pemba, i., Tan.	86	F7	5.10 S	39.48 E
Pemberton, Austl.	96	F3	34.27 S	116.00 E
Pemberton, B.C., Can.	144	F8	50.20 N	122.48 W
Pemberton, Eng., U.K.	180		53.32 N	2.41 W
Pemberton Airport, arpt., N.J., U.S.	203		39.59 N	74.41 W
Pemberton Heights, N.J., U.S.	203		39.58 N	74.41 W
Pembina, N.D., U.S.	128	C1	48.57 N	97.15 W
Pembina, stm., Ab., Can.	144	B16	54.45 N	114.17 W
Pembina, stm., N.A.	142	F16	48.57 N	97.14 W
Pembina Hills, hills, N.A.	142	E15	49.22 N	98.34 W
Pembine, Wi., U.S.	126	C2	45.37 N	88.00 W
Pembroke, On., Can.	126	C12	45.49 N	77.06 W
Pembroke, Wales, U.K.	10	J8	51.40 N	4.54 W
Pembroke, Ga., U.S.	132	D4	32.08 N	81.37 W
Pembroke, Ky., U.S.	130	H10	36.46 N	87.21 W
Pembroke, Me., U.S.	122	F9	44.57 N	67.10 W
Pembroke, N.C., U.S.	132	B6	34.40 N	79.11 W
Pembroke, Va., U.S.	124	G5	37.18 N	80.38 W
Pembroke, Cape, c., Nu., Can.	110	C14	62.55 N	81.56 W
Pembroke Pines, Fl., U.S.	132	K5	26.00 N	80.16 W
Pembrokeshire Coast National Park, p.o.i., Wales, U.K.	10	J7	51.45 N	5.06 W
Pembuang, Indon.	66	E7	2.29 S	112.07 E
Pembuang, stm., Indon.	66	D8	3.21 S	112.33 E
Pemigewasset, stm., N.H., U.S.	122	G5	43.26 N	71.39 W
Pemuco, Chile	172	H1	36.58 S	72.06 W
Pemynoos Indian Reserve, ind. res., B.C., Can.	144	F9	50.29 N	121.15 W
Pena, Parque de, p.o.i., Port.	184c		38.47 N	9.23 W
Peñafiel, Port.	28	C2	41.12 N	8.17 W
Peñafiel, Spain	28	C6	41.36 N	4.07 W
Pen'agino, ngh., Russia	183b		55.50 N	37.21 E
Peña Gorda, Cerro, mtn., Mex.	154	E6	20.44 N	104.50 W
Peña Grande, ngh., Spain	184a		40.29 N	3.44 W
Peñalara, Pico de, mtn., Spain	28	D7	40.51 N	3.57 W
Peñalolén, Chile	204e		33.29 S	70.32 W
Penalva, Braz.	170	B3	3.17 S	45.10 W
Penang see George Town, Malay.	64	J5	5.25 N	100.18 E
Peñaranda de Bracamonte, Spain	28	D5	40.54 N	5.12 W
Pen Argyl, Pa., U.S.	124	D10	40.52 N	75.15 W
Peñarroya-Pueblonuevo, Spain	28	F5	38.18 N	5.16 W
Peñas, Cabo de, c., Spain	28	A5	43.39 N	5.51 W
Penas, Golfo de, b., Chile	166	I2	47.22 S	74.50 W
Penasco, N.M., U.S.	138	E3	36.09 N	105.41 W
Peñasco, stm., N.M., U.S.	136	B3	32.45 N	104.19 W
Penataquit Creek, stm., N.Y., U.S.	194		40.43 N	73.14 W
Pencahue, Chile	172	G2	35.24 S	71.46 W
Pen Centre, shp. cen., On., Can.	202a		43.08 N	79.14 W
Penchard, Fr.	179		48.59 N	2.52 E
Pench National Park, p.o.i., India	70	H7	21.35 N	79.14 E
Pendang, Indon.	66	D9	1.31 S	114.51 E
Pend-d'Oreille see Pend Oreille, stm., N.A.	146	B9	49.00 N	117.37 W
Pendelikón Óros, mtn., Grc.	185c		38.06 N	23.54 E
Pendembu, S.L.	84	H2	8.06 N	10.41 W
Pendembu, S.L.	84	H2	9.06 N	12.12 W
Pendências, Braz.	170	C7	5.15 S	36.43 W
Pender, Ne., U.S.	128	I2	42.06 N	96.42 W
Pendhar, India	190c		19.04 N	73.06 E
Pendlebury, Eng., U.K.	180		53.31 N	2.20 W
Pendle Hill, Austl.	192a		33.48 S	150.57 E
Pendleton, In., U.S.	130	E12	39.59 N	85.44 W
Pendleton, N.Y., U.S.	202a		43.05 N	78.44 W
Pendleton, Or., U.S.	146	E8	45.39 N	118.47 W
Pendleton, S.C., U.S.	132	B3	34.39 N	82.46 W
Pendolo, Indon.	66	E12	2.06 S	120.41 E
Pendopo, Indon.	66	E3	3.18 S	103.52 E
Pend Oreille, stm., N.A.	146	B9	49.00 N	117.37 W
Pend Oreille, Lake, l., Id., U.S.	146	B10	48.10 N	116.17 W
Pend Oreille, Mount, mtn., Id., U.S.	146	B10	48.25 N	116.10 W
Pendotiba, stm., Braz.	205a		22.53 S	43.02 W
Pendžikent, Taj.	72	B10	39.29 N	67.36 E
Penebel, Indon.	66	H9	8.25 S	115.08 E
Penedo, Braz.	170	F7	10.15 S	36.34 W
Penetanguishene, On., Can.	126	D9	44.45 N	79.55 W
Peneus see Pineiós, stm., Grc.	34	D5	39.55 N	22.42 E
Penfield, Pa., U.S.	124	C7	41.12 N	78.35 W
Penganga, stm., India	70	H6	19.54 N	79.09 E
Peng Chau, i., China	189d		22.17 N	114.02 E
Penge, S. Afr.	90	D10	24.18 S	30.10 E
Penge, ngh., Eng., U.K.	178		51.25 N	0.04 W
Penghu, China	58	I8	25.22 N	118.09 E
P'enghu Ch'üntao (Pescadores), is., Tai.	58	J8	23.30 N	119.30 E
P'enghu Shuitao, strt., Tai.	58	J8	23.30 N	119.50 E
Pengiki, Pulau, i., Indon.	66	C6	0.15 N	108.03 E
Pengkalan Hulu, Malay.	64	J5	5.41 N	101.01 E
Pengkou, China	58	I7	25.32 N	116.42 E
Penglai, China	58	C9	37.48 N	120.42 E
Pengpu see Bengbu, China	58	E7	32.56 N	117.21 E
Pengshui, China	58	G3	29.17 N	108.09 E
Pengwaluote Shan, mtn., China	70	B11	33.30 N	86.35 E
Pengxi, China	58	F1	30.45 N	105.42 E
Pengxian, China	52	E5	30.59 N	103.56 E
Pengze, China	58	G7	29.53 N	116.33 E
Penha, Braz.	172	C13	26.46 S	48.39 W
Penha, ngh., Braz.	205a		22.49 S	43.17 W
Penha de França, ngh., Braz.	205b		23.32 S	46.32 W
Penhold, Ab., Can.	144	D17	52.07 N	113.52 W
Penhold, Canadian Forces Base, mil., Ab., Can.	144	D16	52.12 N	113.53 W
Penhorn Creek, stm., N.J., U.S.	194		40.45 N	74.05 W
Penhsi see Benxi, China	52	C9	41.18 N	123.45 E
Penibética, Cordillera, mts., Spain	28	G8	37.00 N	4.00 W
Peniche, Port.	28	E1	39.21 N	9.22 W
Penicuik, Scot., U.K.	10	F9	55.49 N	3.13 W
Penida, Nusa, i., Indon.	66	H9	8.44 S	115.32 E
Peningo Neck, pen., N.Y., U.S.	194		40.57 N	73.41 W
Peninjai, Indon.	66	D2	1.26 S	101.50 E
Peninsular Malaysia see Semenanjung Malaysia, hist. reg., Malay.	64	K6	4.00 N	102.00 E
Peninsula State Park, p.o.i., Wi., U.S.	126	C2	45.08 N	87.12 W
Peñíscola, Spain	28	D11	40.22 N	0.24 E
Penitencia Creek, stm., Ca., U.S.	200		37.27 N	121.55 W
Penitente, Serra do, hills, Braz.	170	E2	8.28 S	46.07 W
Penketh, Eng., U.K.	180		53.23 N	2.40 W
Penki see Benxi, China	52	C9	41.18 N	123.45 E
Penllyn, Pa., U.S.	203		40.10 N	75.15 W
Penn, Pa., U.S.	197b		40.20 N	79.38 W
Penn Acres, De., U.S.	203		39.40 N	75.34 W
Pennant Hills, Austl.	192a		33.44 S	151.04 E
Pennant Hills Park, p.o.i., Austl.	192a		33.45 S	151.06 E
Pennant Point, c., N.S., Can.	122	F13	44.26 N	63.38 W
Pennant Station, Sk., Can.	142	D5	50.32 N	108.13 W
Pennask Lake, l., B.C., Can.	144	F10	50.00 N	120.07 W
Pennask Mountain, mtn., B.C., Can.	144	G10	49.53 N	120.07 W
Penn Brook, stm., Ma., U.S.	201		42.44 N	70.59 W
Penndel, Pa., U.S.	203		40.09 N	74.55 W
Penne, Italy	30	H10	42.27 N	13.55 E
Pennel Creek, stm., Mt., U.S.	140	A8	46.33 N	104.51 W
Penneru, stm., India	69	D4	14.34 N	80.10 E
Penn Hills, Pa., U.S.	126	H10	40.28 N	79.51 W
Penn Hills Center, shp. cen., Pa., U.S.	197b		40.28 N	79.50 W
Pennine, Alpi see Pennine Alps, mts., Eur.	30	D4	46.05 N	7.49 E
Pennine Alps, mts., Eur.	30	D4	46.05 N	7.49 E
Pennines, mts., Eng., U.K.	10	G10	54.11 N	2.01 W
Pennington Gap, Va., U.S.	124	H2	36.45 N	83.02 W
Pennsauken Creek, stm., N.J., U.S.	203		39.59 N	75.03 W
Pennsauken Creek, North Branch, stm., N.J., U.S.	203		39.58 N	75.01 W
Pennsauken Creek, South Branch, stm., N.J., U.S.	203		39.58 N	75.01 W
Pennsboro, W.V., U.S.	124	E4	39.16 N	80.58 W
Penns Brook, stm., N.J., U.S.	194		40.43 N	74.32 W
Pennsbury Heights, Pa., U.S.	203		40.12 N	74.49 W
Pennsbury Manor, hist., Pa., U.S.	203		40.08 N	74.46 W
Penns Creek, stm., Pa., U.S.	126	H12	40.48 N	76.51 W
Penns Neck, N.J., U.S.	194		40.20 N	74.38 W
Penns Woods, Pa., U.S.	197b		40.21 N	79.46 W
Pennsylvania, state, U.S.	124	C8	40.45 N	77.30 W
Pennsylvania, University of, educ., Pa., U.S.	203		39.57 N	75.12 W
Pennsylvania Canal, can., Pa., U.S.	203		40.13 N	74.47 W
Pennsylvania Station, trans., N.Y., U.S.	194		40.45 N	74.00 W
Penn Valley, Pa., U.S.	203		40.01 N	75.16 W
Penn Valley Terrace, Pa., U.S.	203		40.11 N	74.47 W
Penn Wynne, Pa., U.S.	203		39.59 N	75.16 W
Penny, B.C., Can.	144	C9	53.49 N	121.16 W
Penn Yan, N.Y., U.S.	124	B8	42.39 N	77.02 W
Penny Hill, De., U.S.	203		39.46 N	75.30 W
Penny Ice Cap, ice, Nu., Can.	110	B17	67.10 N	66.00 W
Pennypack Creek, stm., Pa., U.S.	203		40.02 N	75.00 W
Pennypack Park, p.o.i., Pa., U.S.	203		40.04 N	75.03 W
Pennyrile Forest State Resort Park, p.o.i., Ky., U.S.	130	G10	37.04 N	87.39 W
Penny Strait, strt., Nu., Can.	108	B6	76.30 N	97.00 W
Peno, Russia	26	D15	56.57 N	32.45 E
Penobscot, stm., Me., U.S.	122	F8	44.29 N	68.48 W
Penobscot, East Branch, stm., Me., U.S.	122	D8	45.36 N	68.32 W
Penobscot, West Branch, stm., Me., U.S.	122	D7	45.36 N	68.32 W
Penobscot Bay, b., Me., U.S.	122	F8	44.15 N	68.52 W
Penola, Austl.	98	K3	37.22 S	140.49 E
Peñón de Ifac see Penyal d'Ifac, misc. cult., Spain	28	F11	38.38 N	0.05 E
Penong, Austl.	96	F6	31.55 S	133.00 E
Penonomé, Pan.	156	H7	8.31 N	80.22 W
Penrhyn, at., Cook Is.	94	D11	9.00 S	158.00 W
Penrith, Austl.	98	I8	33.45 S	150.42 E
Penrith, Eng., U.K.	10	G10	54.39 N	2.45 W
Pensacola, Fl., U.S.	134	G11	30.25 N	87.13 W
Pensacola Bay, b., Fl., U.S.	134	G12	30.25 N	87.06 W
Pensacola Mountains, mts., Ant.	103	D36	84.21 S	47.01 W
Pensacola Naval Air Station, mil., Fl., U.S.	134	G11	30.21 N	87.19 W
Pensaukee, stm., Wi., U.S.	126	D1	44.49 N	87.53 W
Pensby, Eng., U.K.	180		53.21 N	3.06 W
Pense, Sk., Can.	142	D9	50.24 N	104.59 W
Pensiangan, Malay.	66	A10	4.32 N	116.18 E
Pensilvania, Col.	168	E4	5.31 N	75.03 W
Pentagon, bldg., Va., U.S.	202c		38.52 N	77.03 W
Pentagon Mountain, mtn., Mt., U.S.	146	C13	47.56 N	113.07 W
Pentecostes, Braz.	170	B6	3.48 S	39.17 W
Pentecost Island see Pentecôte, i., Vanuatu	101d	j17	15.42 S	168.10 E
Pentecôte (Pentecost Island), i., Vanuatu	101d	j17	15.42 S	168.10 E
Pentéli, Grc.	185c		38.03 N	23.52 E
Penticton, B.C., Can.	144	G11	49.29 N	119.34 W
Penticton Indian Reserve, ind. res., B.C., Can.	144	G11	49.25 N	119.40 W
Pentland, Austl.	98	C5	20.31 S	145.23 E
Pentland Firth, strt., Scot., U.K.	10	C9	58.44 N	3.07 W
Pentre Halkyn, Wales, U.K.	180		53.15 N	3.12 W
Pentucket, Lake, l., Ma., U.S.	201		42.47 N	71.05 W
Pentucket Pond, l., Ma., U.S.	201		42.44 N	71.00 W
Pentwater, Mi., U.S.	126	E3	43.46 N	86.25 W
Penuba, Indon.	66	D4	0.19 S	104.27 E
Peñuelas, P.R.	158a	b2	18.03 N	66.43 W
Penuguan, Indon.	66	E4	2.27 S	104.31 E

Name | Page | Map Ref. | Latitude | Longitude

Penukonda, India 69 D3 14.05 N 77.34 E
Pènwègon, Mya. 64 C3 18.13 N 96.34 E
Penwell, Tx., U.S. 136 C5 31.44 N 102.35 W
Peny, Russia 38 B14 51.04 N 35.54 E
Penyagolosa, mtn., Spain 28 D10 40.13 N 0.21 W
Penyal d'Ifac, misc. cult., Spain 28 F11 38.38 N 0.05 E
Penza, Russia 40 E14 53.12 N 45.00 E
Penzance, Eng., U.K. 10 K7 50.07 N 5.33 W
Penzberg, Ger. 24 I7 47.45 N 11.23 E
Penzenskaja oblast', co., Russia 40 E14 53.00 N 45.00 E
Penžina, stm., Russia 50 D22 62.28 N 165.15 E
Penzing, ngh., Aus. 182b 48.12 N 16.18 E
Penzino, Russia 40 E17 52.07 N 50.27 E
Penžinskaja guba, b., Russia 50 D21 61.00 N 162.00 E
Penžinskij hrebet, mts., Russia 50 D22 62.30 N 167.00 E
Peoples Creek, stm., Mt., U.S. 142 F5 48.22 N 108.17 W
People's Democratic Republic of Korea see Korea, North, ctry., Asia 54 D7 40.00 N 127.00 E
Peoria, Az., U.S. 150 J4 33.35 N 112.14 W
Peoria, Il., U.S. 130 D8 40.41 N 89.35 W
Peoria Heights, Il., U.S. 128 K9 40.44 N 89.34 W
Peotone, Il., U.S. 130 C10 41.19 N 87.46 W
Peover Eye, stm., Eng., U.K. 180 53.15 N 2.31 W
Peover Heath, Eng., U.K. 180 53.15 N 2.19 W
Pepaw, stm., Sk., Can. 142 B11 52.39 N 102.23 W
Pepel, S.L. 84 H2 8.35 N 13.03 W
Pepin, Wi., U.S. 128 G6 44.26 N 92.08 W
Pepin, Lake, l., U.S. 128 G7 44.27 N 92.14 W
Pepper Pike, Oh., U.S. 197a 41.28 N 81.27 W
Peqin, Alb. 32 C13 41.03 N 19.45 E
Peqini see Peqin, Alb. 32 C13 41.03 N 19.45 E
Pequannock, stm., N.J., U.S. 194 40.58 N 74.17 W
Pequanticut Brook, stm., Ma., U.S. 201 42.01 N 71.08 W
Pequeñas Antillas see Lesser Antilles, is. 106 H16 15.00 N 61.00 W
Pequeno, stm., Braz. 205a 22.55 S 43.25 W
Pequizeiro, Braz. 170 E1 8.32 S 48.58 W
Pequop Mountains, mts., Nv., U.S. 150 C2 40.42 N 114.38 W
Pequot Lakes, Mn., U.S. 128 E4 46.36 N 94.19 W
Perabumulih, Indon. 66 E4 3.26 S 104.14 E
Perak, state, Malay. 64 J5 5.00 N 101.00 E
Perak, stm., Malay. 64 J5 3.57 N 100.53 E
Perak, Kuala, b., Malay. 64 J5 4.05 N 100.42 E
Perales de Alfambra, Spain 28 D9 40.37 N 1.00 W
Perales del Río, Spain 184a 40.19 N 3.38 W
Peralillo, Chile 172 G2 34.28 S 71.28 W
Peralta, N.M., U.S. 138 G2 34.50 N 106.41 W
Pérama, Grc. 185c 37.58 N 23.34 E
Perambalur, India 69 F4 11.14 N 78.51 E
Peraní, Ákra, c., Grc. 185c 37.54 N 23.31 E
Peräseinäjoki, Fin. 18 E10 62.33 N 23.04 E
Percé, Qc., Can. 122 B12 48.31 N 64.14 W
Perchas, P.R. 158a b2 18.19 N 66.59 W
Perche, Collines du, hills, Fr. 20 F9 48.33 N 0.37 E
Perche Creek, stm., Mo., U.S. 130 E5 38.48 N 92.23 W
Perchtoldsdorf, Aus. 24 H12 48.07 N 16.15 E
Percival Lakes, l., Austl. 96 D4 21.25 S 125.00 E
Percy Isles, is., Austl. 98 C8 21.39 S 150.16 E
Perdasdefogu, Italy 32 E3 39.41 N 9.26 E
Perdices, Arroyo de las, stm., Arg. 206 34.41 S 58.22 W
Perdida, stm., Braz. 170 E2 9.20 S 47.53 W
Perdido, Al., U.S. 134 F11 31.00 N 87.38 W
Perdido, stm., U.S. 134 G11 30.29 N 87.26 W
Perdido, Monte, mtn., Spain 28 B11 42.40 N 0.05 E
Perdido Bay, b., U.S. 134 G11 30.20 N 87.27 W
Perdizes, Braz. 170 J2 19.21 S 47.17 W
Perdreauville, Fr. 179 48.58 N 1.38 E
Perdue, Sk., Can. 142 B6 52.04 N 107.32 W
Perebrody, Ukr. 38 B6 51.43 N 27.00 E
Perechyn, Ukr. 40 G3 48.44 N 22.28 E
Peredel, Russia 26 E18 55.12 N 35.41 E
Peredelkino, ngh., Russia 183b 55.39 N 37.21 E
Peredmistne, Ukr. 38 H13 45.56 N 34.36 E
Pereez'na, Russia 12 G22 59.43 N 48.12 E
Peregino, Russia 26 C14 57.27 N 31.21 E
Perehins'ke, Ukr. 38 E3 48.48 N 24.12 E
Perehonivka, Ukr. 38 E9 48.32 N 30.31 E
Pereiaslav-Khmel'nyts'kyi, Ukr. 38 C10 50.04 N 31.28 E
Pereira, Col. 168 E4 4.49 N 75.41 W
Pereiro, Braz. 170 D6 6.03 S 38.28 W
Perekopivka, Ukr. 38 C12 50.37 N 33.25 E
Père-Lachaise, Cimetière du, misc. cult., Fr. 179 48.51 N 2.25 E
Perelazovskij, Russia 40 G13 49.08 N 42.34 E
Perelazy, Russia 26 G14 53.02 N 31.28 E
Pereleshinskij, Russia 40 F12 51.44 N 40.08 E
Pere Marquette, stm., Mi., U.S. 126 E4 43.56 N 86.26 W
Pere Marquette, Big South Branch, stm., Mi., U.S. 126 E4 43.55 N 86.11 W
Peremyshliany, Ukr. 38 D3 49.40 N 24.34 E
Peremyšl', Russia 26 F19 54.15 N 36.09 E
Pererov, Bela. 38 A7 52.03 N 28.00 E
Pereshchepyne, Ukr. 38 D14 49.01 N 35.22 E
Pereslavl'-Zalesskij, Russia 26 D21 56.44 N 38.51 E
Peretsjyn, Ukr. 24 H18 48.44 N 22.28 E
Perevoz, Russia 183a 59.43 N 30.47 E
Pereyra, Arroyo, stm., Arg. 206 34.47 S 58.08 W
Pérez, Arg. 172 F7 32.59 S 60.45 W
Perg, Aus. 24 H10 48.14 N 14.37 E
Pergamino, Arg. 172 F7 33.54 S 60.34 W
Pergamum, hist., Tur. 34 D10 39.10 N 27.13 E
Pergine Valsugana, Italy 30 D8 46.04 N 11.14 E
Pergola, Italy 30 G9 43.33 N 12.49 E
Perham, Mn., U.S. 128 E3 46.35 N 95.34 W
Perho, Fin. 18 D11 63.13 N 24.25 E
Perhuškovo, Russia 183b 55.41 N 37.10 E
Péribonka, Qc., Can. 122 B4 48.46 N 72.03 W
Péribonka, stm., Qc., Can. 110 F16 48.45 N 72.02 W
Péribonka, Lac, l., Qc., Can. 114 A15 50.02 N 71.13 W
Perico, Arg. 172 B5 24.22 S 65.07 W
Perico, Sierra del, mtn., Mex. 136 F1 28.43 N 106.27 W
Pericos, Mex. 154 C5 25.03 N 107.42 W
Pericumã, stm., Braz. 170 B3 2.15 S 44.45 W
Peridot, Az., U.S. 150 J6 33.17 N 110.26 W
Perigiraja, Indon. 66 D3 0.20 S 103.25 E
Périgord, hist. reg., Fr. 22 D7 45.17 N 0.45 E
Périgueux, Fr. 22 D6 45.10 N 0.43 E
Perijá, Serranía de, mts., S.A. 168 B5 10.00 N 73.00 W
Perijá, Sierra de see Perijá, Serranía de, mts., S.A. 168 B5 10.00 N 73.00 W
Perim see Barīm, i., Yemen 72 G5 12.39 N 43.23 E
Peri-Mirim, Braz. 170 B3 2.38 S 44.54 W
Periprava, Rom. 36 D16 45.22 N 29.34 E
Peristérion, Grc. 185c 38.01 N 23.42 E
Perito Moreno, Arg. 166 I2 46.36 S 70.55 W
Peritoró, Braz. 170 C3 4.20 S 44.18 W
Perivale, ngh., Eng., U.K. 178 51.32 N 0.19 W
Periyār, stm., India 69 F3 10.10 N 76.13 E
Periyar Tiger Reserve, ind. res., India 69 G3 9.28 N 77.05 E
Perkasie, Pa., U.S. 124 D10 40.22 N 75.18 W
Perkins, Ok., U.S. 134 A2 35.58 N 97.02 W
Perkinston, Ms., U.S. 134 G9 30.46 N 89.09 W
Perkiomen Junction, Pa., U.S. 203 40.06 N 75.28 W
Perkiomen Valley Airport, arpt., Pa., U.S. 203 40.12 N 75.25 W
Perlas, Archipiélago de las, is., Pan. 156 H8 8.25 N 79.00 W
Perlas, Laguna de, b., Nic. 156 F6 12.30 N 83.40 W
Perleberg, Ger. 24 C7 53.04 N 11.51 E
Perlëvka, Russia 38 B17 51.51 N 38.51 E
Perlez, Yugo. 36 D7 45.12 N 20.24 E
Perlis, state, Malay. 64 I5 6.30 N 100.15 E
Perm', Russia 40 C20 58.00 N 56.15 E
Permanente Creek, stm., Ca., U.S. 200 37.25 N 122.05 W
Permas, Russia 40 B14 59.20 N 45.36 E
Përmet, Alb. 32 D14 40.14 N 20.21 E
Përmeti see Përmet, Alb. 32 D14 40.14 N 20.21 E
Permskaja oblast', co., Russia 40 C20 57.25 N 56.34 E
Pernambuco see Recife, Braz. 170 E8 8.03 S 34.54 W
Pernambuco, state, Braz. 170 E6 8.00 S 37.00 W
Pernate, Italy 184b 45.27 N 8.41 E
Pernik, Blg. 36 G10 42.37 N 23.02 E
Perniö, Fin. 18 G10 60.12 N 23.07 E
Pero, Italy 184b 45.31 N 9.05 E
Peroba, Ribeirão do, stm., Braz. 205b 23.27 S 46.22 W
Péronne, Fr. 20 E11 49.55 N 2.56 E
Pero Pinheiro, Port. 184c 38.51 N 9.20 W
Perote, Mex. 154 F10 19.33 N 97.15 W
Perotó, Bol. 166 B4 14.54 S 64.36 W
Perovo, ngh., Russia 183b 55.44 N 37.46 E
Perow, B.C., Can. 144 B4 54.31 N 126.26 W
Perpignan, Fr. 22 G8 42.41 N 2.53 E
Perrault Falls, On., Can. 128 A5 50.20 N 93.08 W
Perray, stm., Fr. 179 48.31 N 1.42 E
Perrin, Tx., U.S. 136 A9 33.01 N 98.04 W
Perrine, Fl., U.S. 132 K5 25.35 N 80.21 W
Perris, Ca., U.S. 148 J8 33.47 N 117.13 W
Perris Reservoir, res., Ca., U.S. 148 J8 33.51 N 117.10 W
Perro, Laguna del, l., N.M., U.S. 138 G3 34.38 N 105.57 W
Perro, Punta del, c., Spain 28 H4 36.44 N 6.25 W
Perros, Bahía de, strt., Cuba 156 A8 22.20 N 78.31 W
Perros-Guirec, Fr. 20 F5 48.48 N 3.27 W
Perry, Fl., U.S. 132 F2 30.07 N 83.34 W
Perry, Ga., U.S. 132 D2 32.27 N 83.43 W
Perry, Ia., U.S. 130 C3 41.50 N 94.06 W
Perry, Ks., U.S. 130 E2 39.05 N 95.24 W
Perry, Mi., U.S. 124 B1 42.49 N 84.13 W
Perry, Mo., U.S. 130 E6 39.25 N 91.40 W
Perry, N.Y., U.S. 124 B7 42.42 N 78.00 W
Perry, Ok., U.S. 138 E11 36.17 N 97.17 W
Perry, Ut., U.S. 150 B4 41.28 N 112.02 W
Perry, Kap, c., Grnld. 108 B11 77.02 N 71.11 W
Perry Lake, res., Ks., U.S. 130 E2 39.14 N 95.28 W
Perrymont, Pa., U.S. 197b 40.33 N 80.02 W
Perrysburg, Oh., U.S. 124 C2 41.33 N 83.37 W
Perry's Landing Monument, hist., Japan 186 35.13 N 139.43 E
Perry's Victory and International Peace Memorial, p.o.i., Oh., U.S. 124 C2 41.33 N 82.50 W
Perrysville, Oh., U.S. 124 D3 40.39 N 82.18 W
Perryton, Tx., U.S. 138 E8 36.23 N 100.48 W
Perryville, Ak., U.S. 109 E8 55.54 N 159.10 W
Perryville, Ar., U.S. 134 B6 35.00 N 92.48 W
Perryville, Ky., U.S. 130 G13 37.38 N 84.57 W
Perryville, Mo., U.S. 130 G8 37.43 N 89.51 W
Peršamajski, Bela. 26 G8 53.54 N 25.23 E
Perșani, Munții, mts., Rom. 36 D12 45.48 N 25.21 E
Persberg, Swe. 16 H12 59.44 N 14.14 E
Persepolis see Takht-e Jamshīd, hist., Iran 74 E13 29.57 N 52.52 E
Perseverancia, Bol. 166 B4 14.44 S 62.48 W
Pershotravens'k, Ukr. 38 C6 50.12 N 27.38 E
Pershotravens'k, Ukr. 38 E15 48.20 N 36.24 E
Pershotravneve, Ukr. 38 F16 47.03 N 37.18 E
Pershotravneve, Ukr. 38 B7 51.24 N 28.53 E
Persia, Ia., U.S. 130 C2 41.34 N 95.34 W
Persia see Iran, ctry., Asia 72 C7 32.00 N 53.00 E
Persian Gulf, b., Asia 72 D7 27.00 N 51.00 E
Persimmon Creek, stm., Al., U.S. 134 F12 31.30 N 86.49 W
Perstorp, Swe. 16 K11 56.07 N 13.21 E
Pertek, Tur. 42 F8 38.50 N 39.21 E
Perth, Austl. 96 F3 31.57 S 115.51 E
Perth, On., Can. 126 D13 44.54 N 76.15 W
Perth, Scot., U.K. 10 E9 56.24 N 3.26 W
Perth Amboy, N.J., U.S. 124 D11 40.30 N 74.14 W
Perth-Andover, N.B., Can. 122 D9 46.44 N 67.41 W
Perth Basin, unds. 174 L13 28.29 S 109.57 E
Pertominsk, Russia 18 C25 64.47 N 38.26 E
Pertuis, Fr. 22 F11 43.41 N 5.30 E
Peru, Il., U.S. 130 C8 41.19 N 89.07 W
Peru, In., U.S. 130 D11 40.44 N 86.03 W
Peru, Ne., U.S. 130 D2 40.28 N 95.43 W
Peru, N.Y., U.S. 126 D16 44.34 N 73.30 W
Perú see Peru, ctry., S.A. 164 E2 10.00 S 76.00 W
Peru, ctry., S.A. 164 E2 10.00 S 76.00 W
Peru Basin, unds. 176 J5 15.00 S 85.00 W
Perućac, Jezero, res., Eur. 30 G16 43.54 N 19.11 E
Perućačko jezero see Perućac, Jezero, res., Eur. 30 G16 43.54 N 19.11 E
Peru-Chile Trench, unds. 176 K6 20.00 S 71.44 W
Perugia, Italy 30 G9 43.07 N 12.22 E
Perugorría, Arg. 172 D8 29.19 S 58.36 W
Peruíbe, Braz. 172 B14 24.19 S 47.00 W
Perušić, Cro. 30 F12 44.39 N 15.22 E
Pervari, Tur. 42 G10 37.54 N 42.36 E
Pervoavgustovskij, Russia 26 H18 52.13 N 35.42 E
Pervomais'ke, Ukr. 38 E9 48.02 N 30.50 E
Pervomais'ke, Ukr. 38 H12 45.43 N 33.51 E
Pervomais'kyi, Ukr. 38 D15 49.23 N 36.13 E
Pervomajsk, Russia 40 D13 54.51 N 43.48 E
Pervomajskij, Russia 26 F15 54.04 N 32.28 E
Pervomajskij, Russia 26 F19 51.33 N 55.02 E
Pervomajskij, Russia 40 E19 53.41 N 55.57 E
Pervomajskij, Russia 40 E12 53.14 N 40.18 E
Pervomajskoe, Russia 26 H16 52.54 N 33.37 E
Pervoural'sk, Russia 48 C9 56.54 N 59.56 E
Pervyj Kuril'skij proliv, strt., Russia 50 F20 50.50 N 156.36 E
Perwenitz, Ger. 182a 52.40 N 13.01 E
Pes', Russia 26 B17 58.55 N 34.19 E
Pes', stm., Russia 26 A18 59.09 N 35.17 E
Pesangrohan, stm., Indon. 187e 6.11 S 106.45 E
Pesaro, Italy 30 G9 43.54 N 12.54 E
Pescadores see P'enghu Ch'üntao, is., Tai. 58 J8 23.30 N 119.30 E
Pescadores, Punta, c., Mex. 154 D4 23.48 N 109.42 W
Pescadores Channel see P'enghu Shuitao, strt., Tai. 58 J8 23.30 N 119.50 E
Pesčanoe, Russia 18 E22 62.10 N 35.47 E
Pesčanokopskoe, Russia 40 H12 46.10 N 41.05 E
Pesčanyj, mys, c., Kaz. 42 D14 43.09 N 51.16 E
Pescara, Italy 30 H11 42.28 N 14.12 E
Pescara, stm., Italy 30 H11 42.28 N 14.13 E
Pescasseroli, Italy 32 C7 41.48 N 13.46 E
Pesch, Ger. 181 51.11 N 6.32 E
Pesch, Schloss, hist., Ger. 181 51.18 N 6.39 E
Peschio, Monte, mtn., Italy 185a 41.43 N 12.46 E
Pescia, Italy 30 G7 43.54 N 10.41 E
Pesé, Pan. 168 D1 7.54 N 80.37 W
Pesek, Pulau, i., Sing. 189c 1.17 N 103.41 E
Pesek Kechil, Pulau, i., Sing. 189c 1.17 N 103.41 E
Peshāwar, Pak. 70 B3 33.59 N 71.33 E
Peshkopi, Alb. 32 C14 41.40 N 20.26 E
Peshkopija see Peshkopi, Alb. 32 C14 41.40 N 20.26 E
Peshtigo, Wi., U.S. 126 C2 45.03 N 87.44 W
Peshtigo, stm., Wi., U.S. 128 F10 44.58 N 87.39 W
Pesio, stm., Italy 30 F4 44.28 N 7.52 E
Peski, Bela. 26 G7 53.21 N 24.38 E
Peski, Russia 26 E21 55.13 N 38.46 E
Peskovka, Russia 40 B18 59.02 N 52.21 E
Peškovo, Russia 38 F18 47.01 N 39.24 E
Pesmes, Fr. 20 G14 47.16 N 5.34 E
Pešnoj, poluostrov, i., Kaz. 40 H17 46.51 N 51.40 E
Pesočenskij, Russia 26 F19 54.10 N 36.06 E
Pesočnoe, Russia 26 B22 58.00 N 39.11 E
Pesočnoe, ozero, l., Russia 14 E27 67.11 N 37.12 E
Pesočnyj, Russia 18 G17 60.07 N 30.11 E
Peso da Régua, Port. 28 C3 41.10 N 7.47 W
Pesquería, Mex. 136 I7 25.47 N 100.02 W
Pesquería, stm., Mex. 136 I8 25.53 N 99.18 W
Pessac, Fr. 22 E5 44.48 N 0.38 W
Pest, state, Hung. 36 B6 47.25 N 19.20 E
Pest, ngh., Hung. 182c 47.30 N 19.04 E
Peštera, Blg. 36 G11 42.02 N 24.19 E
Pesterzsébet, ngh., Hung. 182c 47.26 N 19.07 E
Pesthidegkút, ngh., Hung. 182c 47.34 N 18.58 E
Pestimre, ngh., Hung. 182c 47.24 N 19.12 E
Pestlőrinc, ngh., Hung. 182c 47.26 N 19.12 E
Pestovo, Russia 26 B18 58.35 N 35.50 E
Pëstraja Dresva, Russia 50 D20 61.32 N 156.40 E
Pestravka, Russia 40 E16 52.24 N 49.57 E
Pestújhely, ngh., Hung. 182c 47.32 N 19.07 E
Petacalco, Bahía, b., Mex. 154 G7 17.55 N 101.57 W
Petah Tiqwa, Isr. 76 F5 32.06 N 34.53 E
Petäjäskoski, Fin. 14 F16 66.15 N 25.21 E
Petäjävesi, Fin. 18 E12 62.16 N 25.11 E
Petal, Ms., U.S. 134 F9 31.20 N 89.15 W
Petalcingo, Mex. 154 G12 17.17 N 92.27 W
Petalión, Kólpos, b., Grc. 34 E7 37.58 N 24.09 E
Petaluma, Ca., U.S. 148 E3 38.14 N 122.38 W
Petare, Ven. 168 B8 10.29 N 66.49 W
Petatlán, Mex. 154 G8 17.31 N 101.16 W
Petawawa, On., Can. 126 C12 45.54 N 77.16 W
Petawawa, stm., On., Can. 126 C12 45.55 N 77.14 W
Petén Itzá, Lago, l., Guat. 156 D2 16.59 N 89.51 W
Petenwell Lake, res., Wi., U.S. 128 G8 44.07 N 89.57 W
Peter and Paul Fortress, hist., Russia 183a 59.57 N 30.19 E
Peterborough, Austl. 98 I2 32.58 S 138.49 E
Peterborough, On., Can. 126 D11 44.17 N 78.19 W
Peterborough, Eng., U.K. 10 I12 52.34 N 0.15 W
Peterhead, Scot., U.K. 10 D11 57.30 N 1.47 W
Peter I Island, i., Ant. 103 B31 68.47 S 90.34 W
Peter Island, i., Br. Vir. Is. 158b e8 18.21 N 64.35 W
Peter Lake, l., Nu., Can. 110 C12 63.08 N 92.48 W
Peterlee, Eng., U.K. 10 G11 54.46 N 1.19 W
Peter Lougheed Provincial Park, p.o.i., Ab., Can. 144 F15 50.45 N 115.15 W
Peterman, Al., U.S. 134 F11 31.35 N 87.15 W
Petermann Ranges, mts., Austl. 96 D5 25.07 S 129.45 E
Peter Pond Lake, l., Sk., Can. 110 D9 56.06 N 109.05 W
Peters Brook, stm., N.J., U.S. 194 40.33 N 74.37 W
Petersburg, Ak., U.S. 109 E13 56.48 N 132.57 W
Petersburg, Il., U.S. 128 K9 40.00 N 89.50 W
Petersburg, In., U.S. 130 F10 38.29 N 87.16 W
Petersburg, Mi., U.S. 124 C2 41.53 N 83.43 W
Petersburg, Ne., U.S. 140 F14 41.51 N 98.05 W
Petersburg, Tn., U.S. 134 B12 35.18 N 86.38 W
Petersburg, Tx., U.S. 138 H7 33.52 N 101.36 W
Petersburg, Va., U.S. 124 G8 37.13 N 77.24 W
Petersburg, W.V., U.S. 124 F6 38.59 N 79.07 W
Peters Canyon Reservoir, res., Ca., U.S. 198 33.47 N 117.45 W
Peters Creek, stm., Ca., U.S. 200 37.15 N 122.13 W
Peters Creek, stm., Pa., U.S. 197b 40.18 N 79.52 W
Peters Creek, Piney Fork, stm., Pa., U.S. 197b 40.16 N 79.58 W
Petersfield, S. Afr. 191d 26.14 S 28.26 E
Petersfield, Eng., U.K. 10 J12 51.00 N 0.56 W
Petersham, Austl. 192a 33.54 S 151.09 E
Peterson, Ia., U.S. 130 B2 42.55 N 95.21 W
Peterson Air Force Base, mil., Co., U.S. 138 C4 38.49 N 104.42 W
Peters Pond, l., Ma., U.S. 201 42.43 N 71.16 W
Peter the Great Bay see Petra Velikogo, zaliv, b., Russia 54 C9 42.40 N 132.00 E
Peter the Great Monument, hist., Russia 183a 59.56 N 30.18 E
Pétervására, Hung. 36 A7 48.01 N 20.07 E
Petilia Policastro, Italy 32 E10 39.07 N 16.47 E
Pétion-Ville, Haiti 156 C11 18.31 N 72.17 W
Petit, S. Afr. 191d 26.06 S 28.22 E
Petit Bois Island, i., U.S. 134 G10 30.12 N 88.26 W
Petit-Bourg, Guad. 159c h5 16.12 N 61.35 W
Petit-Canal, Guad. 159c h6 16.23 N 61.29 W
Petitcodiac, N.B., Can. 122 E11 45.56 N 65.11 W
Petitcodiac, stm., N.B., Can. 122 D12 45.49 N 64.33 W
Petit Cul-de-Sac Marin, b., Guad. 159c h5 16.12 N 61.33 W
Petite Rivière Noire, Piton de la, mtn., Mrts. 89a i10 20.25 S 57.28 E
Petites-Anses, Guad. 159c i5 15.50 N 61.38 W
Petit-Goâve, Haiti 156 C11 18.25 N 72.51 W
Petit Jean, stm., Ar., U.S. 134 B5 35.10 N 92.55 W
Petit Jean State Park, p.o.i., Ar., U.S. 134 B6 35.06 N 92.57 W
Petit Morin, stm., Fr. 20 F12 48.56 N 3.07 E
Petitot, stm., Can. 110 D6 60.14 N 123.29 W
Petit Piton, vol., St. Luc. 159c m6 13.50 N 61.04 W
Petit Saint-Bernard, Col du see Little Saint Bernard Pass, p., Eur. 30 E3 45.41 N 6.51 E
Petitsikapau Lake, l., Nf., Can. 110 E17 54.43 N 66.28 W
Petkula, Fin. 14 E17 67.41 N 26.46 E
Petlād, India 70 G4 22.28 N 72.48 E
Petlalcingo, Mex. 154 F9 18.04 N 97.56 W
Peto, Mex. 156 B3 20.07 N 88.54 W
Petorca, Chile 172 F2 32.14 S 70.56 W
Petoskey, Mi., U.S. 126 C5 45.22 N 84.57 W
Petra see Al-Baträ', hist., Jord. 76 H6 30.20 N 35.26 E
Petra Velikogo, zaliv (Peter the Great Bay), b., Russia 54 C9 42.40 N 132.00 E
Petre, Point, c., On., Can. 126 E12 43.50 N 77.08 W
Petrič, Blg. 36 H10 41.24 N 23.13 E
Petrified Forest National Park, p.o.i., Az., U.S. 150 I7 34.54 N 109.47 W
Petrila, Rom. 36 D10 45.27 N 23.23 E
Petrinja, Cro. 30 E13 45.26 N 16.16 E
Petriščevo, Russia 26 E19 55.29 N 36.18 E
Petrítis, Ákra, c., Grc. 185c 37.56 N 23.24 E
Petrivka, Ukr. 38 G9 46.54 N 30.43 E
Petrivka, Ukr. 38 E18 48.48 N 39.16 E
Petrivs'ke, Ukr. 38 D15 49.10 N 36.54 E
Petrodvorec, Russia 26 A12 59.53 N 29.51 E
Petrograd see Sankt-Peterburg, Russia 18 H17 59.56 N 30.15 E
Petrokrepost see Šlissel'burg, Russia 26 A13 59.57 N 31.02 E
Petrolândia, Braz. 170 E6 9.05 S 38.18 W
Petrólea, Col. 168 C5 8.30 N 72.34 W
Petrolia, Tx., U.S. 138 G10 34.01 N 98.13 W
Petrolina, Braz. 170 E5 9.24 S 40.30 W
Petrolina de Goiás, Braz. 170 I1 16.06 S 49.20 W
Petrona, Punta, c., P.R. 158a c3 17.56 N 66.23 W
Petronila Creek, stm., Tx., U.S. 136 G10 27.22 N 97.29 W
Petropavl see Petropavlovsk, Kaz. 48 D11 54.52 N 69.08 E
Petropavlivka, Ukr. 38 E15 48.28 N 36.26 E
Petropavlovka, Russia 40 F12 50.05 N 40.53 E
Petropavlovka, Russia 50 F10 50.36 N 105.19 E
Petropavlovsk, Kaz. 48 D11 54.52 N 69.08 E
Petropavlovsk, Russia 40 C20 56.20 N 57.08 E
Petropavlovsk-Kamčatskij, Russia 50 F20 53.01 N 158.40 E
Petropavlovskoe, Russia 40 I14 45.05 N 44.17 E
Petrópolis, Braz. 170 L4 22.31 S 43.10 W
Petros, Tn., U.S. 130 H13 36.05 N 84.26 W
Petroșani, Rom. 36 D10 45.25 N 23.22 E
Petro-Slav'anka, Russia 183a 59.48 N 30.31 E
Petroúpolis, Grc. 185c 38.03 N 23.41 E
Petrovac, Yugo. 36 E8 44.22 N 21.25 E
Petrove, Ukr. 38 E12 48.20 N 33.16 E
Petrovgrad see Zrenjanin, Yugo. 36 D7 45.23 N 20.24 E
Petrovo, Russia 26 B18 58.22 N 35.08 E
Petrovo-Dal'nee, Russia 183b 55.45 N 37.11 E
Petrovsk, Russia 40 E14 52.19 N 45.23 E
Petrovskaja, Russia 38 H16 45.25 N 37.57 E
Petrovskij, Russia 40 C12 56.38 N 40.18 E
Petrovskoe, Russia 26 D22 57.00 N 39.16 E
Petrovskoe, Russia 183b 55.36 N 37.53 E
Petrovsko-Razumovskoe, ngh., Russia 183b 55.50 N 37.34 E
Petrovsk-Zabajkal'skij, Russia 50 F10 51.16 N 108.50 E
Petrov Val, Russia 40 F14 50.08 N 45.12 E
Petrozavodsk, Russia 18 F21 61.47 N 34.21 E
Petrozsény see Petroșani, Rom. 36 D10 45.25 N 23.22 E
Petrusburg, S. Afr. 90 F7 29.08 S 25.27 E
Petrušino, Russia 183a 59.48 N 30.50 E
Petrus Steyn, S. Afr. 90 E9 27.39 S 28.08 E
Petrusville, S. Afr. 90 G7 30.05 S 24.39 E
Petrykau, Bela. 26 H11 52.07 N 28.30 E
Petrykivka, Ukr. 38 E13 48.43 N 34.38 E
Petticoat Creek, stm., On., Can. 193b 43.48 N 79.06 W
Pettus, Tx., U.S. 136 F10 28.37 N 97.48 W
Petty Island, i., N.J., U.S. 203 39.58 N 75.07 W
Petua, India 190b 22.25 N 88.27 E
Petuhovo, Russia 48 C11 55.04 N 67.53 E
Petzow, Ger. 182a 52.21 N 12.56 E
Peuerbach, Aus. 24 H9 48.20 N 13.45 E
Peuetsagoe, Gunung, vol., Indon. 64 J3 4.55 N 96.20 E
Peureulak, Indon. 64 J3 4.48 N 97.53 E
Peusangan, stm., Indon. 64 J3 5.15 N 96.51 E
Pevek, Russia 50 C23 69.40 N 170.21 E
Pews Creek, stm., N.J., U.S. 194 40.27 N 74.06 W
Péyia, Cyp. 76 D3 34.53 N 32.23 E
Peza, stm., Russia 12 D23 65.36 N 44.37 E
Pezawa Taung, mtn., Mya. 64 C2 19.33 N 94.31 E
Pézenas, Fr. 22 F9 43.26 N 3.25 E
Pezinok, Slvk. 24 H13 48.17 N 17.16 E
Pežostrov, ostrov, i., Russia 14 F25 66.16 N 33.53 E
Pezu, Pak. 70 B3 32.19 N 70.43 E
Pfaffenöden, hill, Aus. 182b 48.04 N 16.33 E
Pfaffstätten, Aus. 182b 48.01 N 16.16 E
Pfarrkirchen, Ger. 24 H8 48.26 N 12.56 E
Pfaueninsel, Schloss, hist., Ger. 182a 52.26 N 13.07 E
Pferderennbahn, p.o.i., Ger. 181 51.31 N 7.32 E
Pförten see Brody, Pol. 24 E10 51.46 N 14.48 E
Pforzheim, Ger. 24 H4 48.53 N 8.42 E
Pfronten, Ger. 24 I6 47.34 N 10.33 E
Pfullendorf, Ger. 20 G18 47.55 N 9.14 E
Pfunds, Aus. 30 D7 46.57 N 10.32 E
Pfungstadt, Ger. 24 G4 49.48 N 8.36 E
Pha-an, Mya. 64 D3 16.53 N 97.38 E
Phachi, stm., Thai. 64 F4 13.56 N 99.23 E
Phaëton, Port, b., Fr. Poly. 100h w22 17.44 S 149.19 W
Phagwāra, India 70 C5 31.13 N 75.46 E
Phala, Bots. 90 C8 23.42 S 26.58 E
Phalaborwa, S. Afr. 90 C10 23.54 S 31.13 E
Phālia, Pak. 70 B4 32.26 N 73.35 E
Phalodi, India 70 E4 27.08 N 72.22 E
Phaltan, India 69 C2 17.59 N 74.25 E
Phalti, India 190b 22.46 N 88.34 E
Phan, Thai. 64 C4 19.28 N 99.43 E
Phanat Nikhom, Thai. 64 F5 13.26 N 101.11 E
Phangan, Ko, i., Thai. 64 H5 9.44 N 100.00 E
Phang Hoei, Khao, mtn., Thai. 64 E5 15.14 N 101.27 E
Phangnga, Thai. 64 H4 8.27 N 98.32 E
Phaniang, stm., Thai. 64 D6 16.48 N 102.24 E
Phanom Dong Rak, Thiu Khao see Phanom Dongrak Range, mts., Asia 64 E6 14.25 N 103.30 E
Phanom Dongrak Range, mts., Asia 64 E6 14.25 N 103.30 E
Phanom Thuan, Thai. 64 E4 14.07 N 99.41 E
Phan Rang, Viet. 64 G9 11.33 N 108.59 E
Phan Si Pan see Fan Si Pan, mtn., Viet. 64 A6 22.15 N 103.46 E
Phan Thiet, Viet. 64 G9 10.55 N 108.05 E
Phan Thong, Thai. 64 F5 13.28 N 101.06 E
Pharenda, India 70 E9 27.06 N 83.16 E
Phariāro, Pak. 70 E2 27.13 N 68.59 E
Pharr, Tx., U.S. 136 H9 26.11 N 98.10 W
Phasi Charoen, Thai. 187a 13.43 N 100.26 E
Phasi Charoen, Khlong, can., Thai. 187a 13.44 N 100.30 E
Phat Diem, Viet. 64 B8 20.01 N 106.06 E
Phato, Thai. 64 H4 9.47 N 98.47 E
Phatthalung, Thai. 64 I5 7.37 N 100.05 E
Phayao, Thai. 64 C4 19.10 N 99.55 E
Pheasant Creek, stm., Sk., Can. 142 D10 50.36 N 103.30 W
Pheba, Ms., U.S. 134 D9 33.35 N 88.56 W
Phelps, N.Y., U.S. 124 B8 42.57 N 77.03 W
Phelps, Wi., U.S. 128 E9 46.04 N 89.03 W
Phelps Lake, l., N.C., U.S. 124 I9 35.45 N 76.27 W
Phenix City, Al., U.S. 134 E13 32.28 N 85.01 W
Phepane, stm., S. Afr. 90 E6 25.49 S 22.47 E
Phet Buri, stm., Thai. 64 F4 13.06 N 100.03 E
Phetchabun, Thai. 64 D5 16.24 N 101.09 E
Phetchabun, Thiu Khao, mts., Thai. 64 D5 16.32 N 100.55 E
Phetchaburi, Thai. 64 F4 13.06 N 99.57 E
Phibun Mangsahan, Thai. 64 E7 15.14 N 105.14 E
Phichai, Thai. 64 D5 17.15 N 100.05 E
Phichit, Thai. 64 D5 16.26 N 100.21 E
Philadelphia, Ms., U.S. 134 E9 32.46 N 89.07 W
Philadelphia, N.Y., U.S. 126 D14 44.09 N 75.43 W
Philadelphia, Pa., U.S. 124 E10 39.57 N 75.09 W
Philadelphia, Pa., U.S. 203 39.57 N 75.09 W
Philadelphia, Tn., U.S. 132 A1 35.40 N 84.23 W
Philadelphia, co., Pa., U.S. 203 39.57 N 75.07 W
Philadelphia Museum of Art, bldg., Pa., U.S. 203 39.58 N 75.11 W
Philadelphia Naval Shipyard, mil., Pa., U.S. 203 39.53 N 75.11 W
Philadelphia Park Race Track, p.o.i., Pa., U.S. 203 40.07 N 74.57 W
Philae, hist., Egypt 74 I3 24.01 N 32.53 E
Phil Campbell, Al., U.S. 134 C11 34.21 N 87.42 W
Philip, S.D., U.S. 140 C11 44.02 N 101.39 W
Philipp, Ms., U.S. 134 D8 33.45 N 90.12 W
Philippeville see Skikda, Alg. 84 B6 36.52 N 6.54 E
Philippeville, Bel. 20 D13 50.11 N 4.33 E
Philippi, W.V., U.S. 124 E5 39.08 N 80.02 W
Philippi see Fílippoi, hist., Grc. 34 B7 41.00 N 24.16 E
Philippi, Lake, l., Austl. 98 E2 24.22 S 139.00 E
Philippine Basin, unds. 174 H15 17.00 N 132.00 E
Philippine International Convention Center, p.o.i., Phil. 187f 14.32 N 120.59 E
Philippines, ctry., Asia 44 H16 13.00 N 122.00 E
Philippines, Cultural Center of the, bldg., Phil. 187f 14.33 N 120.59 E
Philippines, University of the, educ., Phil. 187f 14.39 N 121.04 E
Philippine Sea, s. 46 H17 20.00 N 135.00 E
Philippine Trench, unds. 174 I15 9.00 N 127.00 E
Philippolis, S. Afr. 90 G7 30.15 S 25.15 E
Philippopolis see Plovdiv, Blg. 36 G11 42.09 N 24.45 E
Philippsthal, Ger. 182a 52.20 N 13.09 E
Philipsburg, Neth. Ant. 159a a1 18.01 N 63.03 W
Philipsburg, Mt., U.S. 146 D13 46.19 N 113.17 W
Philipsburg, Pa., U.S. 124 D7 40.53 N 78.13 W
Philipsburg Manor, hist., N.Y., U.S. 194 41.05 N 73.52 W
Philipse Manor Hall State Historic Site, hist., N.Y., U.S. 194 40.56 N 73.54 W
Philip Smith Mountains, mts., Ak., U.S. 109 C10 68.30 N 148.00 W
Philipstown, S. Afr. 90 G7 30.25 S 24.28 E
Phillaur, India 70 C5 31.01 N 75.47 E
Phillip Island, i., Austl. 98 L5 38.29 S 145.14 E
Phillips, Me., U.S. 122 F6 44.49 N 70.20 W
Phillips, Tx., U.S. 138 F7 35.41 N 101.21 W
Phillips, Wi., U.S. 128 F8 45.41 N 90.24 W
Phillipsburg, Ga., U.S. 132 E2 31.24 N 83.31 W
Phillipsburg, Ks., U.S. 128 B9 39.45 N 99.19 W
Phillipsburg, N.J., U.S. 124 D10 40.41 N 75.11 W
Philo, Il., U.S. 130 E9 40.00 N 88.09 W
Philo, Oh., U.S. 124 E4 39.51 N 81.54 W
Philomath, Or., U.S. 146 F3 44.32 N 123.21 W
Philpots Island, i., Nu., Can. 108 C10 74.52 N 79.48 W
Phimai, Thai. 64 E6 15.13 N 102.29 E
Phinga, India 190b 22.41 N 88.25 E
Phitsanulok, Thai. 64 D5 16.49 N 100.16 E
Phnom Penh see Phnum Pénh, Camb. 64 G7 11.33 N 104.54 E
Phnum Pénh (Phnom Penh), Camb. 64 G7 11.33 N 104.54 E
Phnum Thbeng Méanchey, Camb. 64 F7 13.47 N 104.58 E
Phoenix, Az., U.S. 150 J4 33.26 N 112.05 W
Phoenix, Il., U.S. 196 41.36 N 87.38 W
Phoenix, N.Y., U.S. 126 E13 43.14 N 76.18 W
Phoenix, Or., U.S. 148 A3 42.17 N 122.48 W
Phoenix Islands, is., Kir. 94 D9 4.00 S 172.00 W
Phoenix Lake, res., Ca., U.S. 200 37.57 N 122.35 W
Phoenix Park, p.o.i., Mi., U.S. 199 42.24 N 83.27 W
Phoenixville, Pa., U.S. 124 D10 40.07 N 75.31 W
Phofung (Sources, Mont-aux-), mtn., Afr. 90 F9 28.46 S 28.52 E
Phon, Thai. 64 E6 15.48 N 102.36 E
Phong, stm., Thai. 64 D6 16.22 N 102.56 E
Phôngsali, Laos 64 B6 21.42 N 102.07 E
Phong Tho, Viet. 64 A6 22.32 N 103.21 E
Phon Phisai, Thai. 64 D6 17.59 N 103.05 E
Phosphate Hill, Austl. 98 C2 21.51 S 139.50 E
Phra Chedi Sam Ong, p., Asia 64 E4 15.18 N 98.22 E
Phrae, Thai. 64 C5 18.08 N 100.09 E
Phra Khanong, ngh., Thai. 187a 13.42 N 100.35 E
Phra Nakhon see Krung Thep, Thai. 64 F5 13.45 N 100.31 E

Name Page Map Ref. Latitude Longitude

Phra Nakhon Si Ayutthaya, Thai. 64 E5 14.20 N 100.34 E
Phran Kratai, Thai. 64 D4 16.39 N 99.35 E
Phrao, Thai. 64 C4 19.21 N 99.12 E
Phra Pradaeng, Thai. 187a 13.40 N 100.32 E
Phra Rop, Khao, mtn., Thai. 64 F4 13.11 N 99.31 E
Phrom Phiram, Thai. 64 D5 17.02 N 100.12 E
Phsar Réam, Camb. 64 G6 10.30 N 103.37 E
Phu Cat, Viet. 64 E9 13.59 N 109.03 E
Phu Huu, Viet. 187c 10.43 N 106.47 E
Phuket, Thai. 64 I4 7.52 N 98.23 E
Phuket, Ko, i., Thai. 64 I4 8.00 N 98.22 E
Phu Loc, Viet. 64 D8 16.16 N 107.53 E
Phu Ly, Viet. 64 B7 20.30 N 105.55 E
Phum Duang, stm., Thai. 64 H4 9.12 N 99.21 E
Phumĭ Bâ Khăm, Camb. 64 F8 13.50 N 107.20 E
Phumĭ Banam, Camb. 64 G7 11.19 N 105.17 E
Phumĭ Bĕng, Camb. 64 F7 13.07 N 104.19 E
Phumĭ Châmbák, Camb. 64 G7 11.14 N 104.48 E
Phumĭ Chăngho Ândêng, Camb. 64 F7 12.38 N 104.33 E
Phumĭ Chhuk, Camb. 64 G7 10.49 N 104.27 E
Phumĭ Chruŏy Slêng, Camb. 64 F7 13.14 N 105.59 E
Phumĭ Dăk Dăm, Camb. 64 F8 12.20 N 107.20 E
Phumĭ Kâmpóng Srâlau, Camb. 64 E8 14.04 N 105.46 E
Phumĭ Kâmpóng Trâbêk, Camb. 64 F7 13.09 N 105.14 E
Phumĭ Kântuŏt Sâmraông, Camb. 64 E7 14.12 N 104.37 E
Phumĭ Kaôh Kért, Camb. 64 F7 13.47 N 104.32 E
Phumĭ Kaôh Kŏng, Camb. 64 G6 11.28 N 103.09 E
Phumĭ Khpôb, Camb. 64 G7 11.01 N 105.12 E
Phumĭ Krêk, Camb. 64 G7 11.46 N 105.56 E
Phumĭ Lvéa Kraôm, Camb. 64 F6 13.21 N 102.54 E
Phumĭ Moŭng, Camb. 64 F6 13.45 N 103.33 E
Phumĭ Narŭng, Camb. 64 F7 13.53 N 105.34 E
Phumĭ Phnum Srâlau, Camb. 64 G6 11.02 N 103.40 E
Phumĭ Prêk Kák, Camb. 64 F7 12.16 N 105.31 E
Phumĭ Prey Toch, Camb. 64 F6 12.52 N 103.20 E
Phumĭ Puŏk Chăs, Camb. 64 F6 13.26 N 103.43 E
Phumĭ Rôluŏs Chăs, Camb. 64 F6 13.19 N 103.59 E
Phumĭ Sâmraông, Camb. 64 E6 14.11 N 103.30 E
Phumĭ Spœ Tbong, Camb. 64 F7 12.19 N 105.19 E
Phumĭ Srê Kôkir, Camb. 64 F8 13.07 N 106.04 E
Phumĭ Srê Rônéam, Camb. 64 F8 12.17 N 106.24 E
Phumĭ Tbêng, Camb. 64 F7 13.32 N 104.52 E
Phumĭ Thalabârĭvăt, Camb. 64 F7 13.33 N 105.56 E
Phumĭ Thmâ Pôk, Camb. 64 E6 13.56 N 103.03 E
Phumĭ Tnaôt, Camb. 64 F7 12.57 N 104.34 E
Phumĭ Tœk Choŭ, Camb. 64 F6 13.36 N 103.24 E
Phu My, Viet. 64 E9 14.10 N 109.03 E
Phung Hiep, Viet. 64 H7 9.48 N 105.49 E
Phuoc Khanh, Viet. 187c 10.40 N 106.48 E
Phuoc Long, Viet. 64 H7 9.28 N 105.27 E
Phuoc Long, Viet. 64 G8 11.48 N 106.58 E
Phuoc Long Xa, Viet. 187c 10.49 N 106.46 E
Phuoc Luong, Viet. 187c 10.45 N 106.48 E
Phu Pan National Park, p.o.i., Thai. 64 D6 17.00 N 103.56 E
Phu Quoc, Viet. 64 G6 10.13 N 103.58 E
Phu Quoc, Dao, i., Viet. 64 G6 10.12 N 104.00 E
Phurphura, India 190b 22.44 N 88.08 E
Phu Tho, Viet. 64 B7 21.25 N 105.13 E
Phu Tho Hoa, Viet. 187c 10.46 N 106.38 E
Phu Tho Race Track, p.o.i., Viet. 187c 10.46 N 106.40 E
Phu Vang, Viet. 64 D8 16.29 N 107.37 E
Phu Yen, Viet. 64 B7 21.15 N 104.40 E
Pi, stm., China 58 F7 32.27 N 116.30 E
Piaçabuçu, Braz. 170 F7 10.24 S 36.24 W
Piacenza, Italy 30 E6 45.03 N 9.42 E
Pialba, Austl. 98 E9 25.17 S 152.50 E
Piāli, stm., India 190b 22.23 N 88.35 E
Piancó, Braz. 170 D7 7.12 S 37.57 W
Pian Creek, stm., Austl. 98 G7 30.02 S 148.12 E
Pianguan, China 58 B4 39.35 N 111.35 E
Pianosa, Isola, i., Italy 30 H12 42.13 N 15.44 E
Pianosa, Isola, i., Italy 30 H7 42.35 N 10.04 E
Piapot, Sk., Can. 142 E4 49.59 N 109.07 W
Piapot Indian Reserve, ind. res., Sk., Can. 142 D9 50.45 N 104.26 W
Piaseczno, Pol. 24 D16 52.03 N 21.02 E
Piaski, Pol. 24 E18 51.08 N 22.52 E
Piatã, Braz. 170 G6 13.09 S 41.47 W
Piatra-Neamț, Rom. 36 B13 46.56 N 26.23 E
Piatra-Olt, Rom. 36 E11 44.24 N 24.16 E
P'iatykhatky, Ukr. 38 E12 48.24 N 33.43 E
Piauí, state, Braz. 170 D4 7.00 S 43.00 W
Piauí, stm., Braz. 170 D4 6.38 S 42.41 W
Piauí, stm., Braz. 170 I5 16.41 S 41.53 W
Piauí, Morro do, mtn., Braz. 170 H2 14.59 S 47.31 W
Piave, stm., Italy 30 E9 45.32 N 12.44 E
Piaxtla, stm., Mex. 154 D5 23.42 N 106.48 W
Piazza Armerina, Italy 32 G8 37.23 N 14.22 E
Pibor Post, Sudan 82 F6 6.47 N 33.07 E
Pibroch, Ab., Can. 144 B17 54.15 N 113.51 W
Pic, stm., On., Can. 128 B12 49.38 N 86.15 W
Pica, Chile 166 D3 20.30 S 69.22 W
Picacho, Az., U.S. 150 K5 32.43 N 111.30 W
Picacho, Cerro del, mtn., Mex. 204a 19.35 N 99.08 W
Picanoc, stm., Qc., Can. 126 C13 46.04 N 76.03 W
Picardie, hist. reg., Fr. 20 E11 49.49 N 2.11 E
Picardy see Picardie, hist. reg., Fr. 20 E11 49.49 N 2.11 E
Picatinny Arsenal, mil., N.J., U.S. 194 40.57 N 74.33 W
Picatinny Lake, l., N.J., U.S. 194 40.57 N 74.33 W
Picayune, Ms., U.S. 134 G9 30.31 N 89.41 W
Piccadilly Station, trans., Eng., U.K. 180 53.28 N 2.14 W
Piccolo San Bernardo, Colle del see Little Saint Bernard Pass, p., Eur. 30 E3 45.41 N 6.51 E
Piccotts End, Eng., U.K. 178 51.46 N 0.28 W
Pic du Paradis, hill, Guad. 159a a1 18.05 N 63.03 W
Piceance Creek, stm., Co., U.S. 150 D9 40.05 N 108.14 W
Pichanal, Arg. 166 D4 23.18 S 64.13 W
Picher, Ok., U.S. 130 H3 36.59 N 94.49 W
Pichilemu, Chile 172 G1 34.23 S 72.00 W
Pichimá, Col. 168 E3 4.24 N 77.21 W
Pichi Mahuida, Arg. 172 I5 38.50 S 64.56 W
Pichincha, state, Ec. 168 H2 0.10 S 78.40 W
Pichucalco, Mex. 154 G12 17.30 N 93.09 W
Pic Island, i., On., Can. 128 C12 48.42 N 86.37 W
Pickardville, Ab., Can. 144 B17 54.03 N 113.53 W
Pickens, Ms., U.S. 134 E9 32.53 N 89.58 W
Pickens, S.C., U.S. 132 B3 34.53 N 82.42 W
Pickens, W.V., U.S. 124 F5 38.38 N 80.12 W
Pickensville, Al., U.S. 134 D10 33.14 N 88.15 W
Pickerel, stm., On., Can. 126 C9 45.56 N 80.51 W
Pickerel Lake, l., Mb., Can. 142 B14 52.34 N 99.30 W
Pickering, Eng., U.K. 10 G12 54.14 N 0.46 W
Pickering Creek, stm., Pa., U.S. 203 40.08 N 75.30 W
Pickering Creek Reservoir, res., Pa., U.S. 203 40.07 N 75.30 W
Pickford, Mi., U.S. 126 B5 46.09 N 84.21 W
Pickle Lake, On., Can. 110 E12 51.30 N 90.04 W
Pickmere, Eng., U.K. 180 53.17 N 2.28 W
Pick Mere, l., Eng., U.K. 180 53.17 N 2.29 W
Pickstown, S.D., U.S. 140 D14 43.04 N 98.31 W
Pickton, Tx., U.S. 136 A12 33.02 N 95.23 W
Pickwick Lake, res., U.S. 134 B10 34.55 N 88.10 W
Picnic Point, c., Austl. 192b 37.57 S 145.00 E
Pico, mtn., C.V. 85a I10 14.57 N 24.21 W
Pico, i., Port. 80 C3 38.28 N 28.20 W
Pico da Neblina, Parque Nacional, p.o.i., Braz. 168 G9 0.30 N 66.00 W
Pico de Orizaba, Parque Nacional, p.o.i., Mex. 154 F10 19.05 N 97.16 W
Pico de Orizaba, Volcán (Citlaltépetl, Volcán), vol., Mex. 154 F10 19.01 N 97.16 W
Picos, Braz. 170 D5 7.05 S 41.28 W
Picquigny, Fr. 20 E11 49.57 N 2.09 E
Picton, Austl. 98 J8 34.11 S 150.36 E
Picton, On., Can. 126 D13 44.00 N 77.08 W
Picton, N.Z. 102 E6 41.17 S 173.59 E
Picton, Eng., U.K. 180 53.14 N 2.51 W
Picton, Isla, i., Chile 166 K3 55.03 S 66.54 W
Pictou, N.S., Can. 122 E14 45.40 N 62.42 W
Pictou Island, i., N.S., Can. 122 E14 45.48 N 62.33 W
Picture Butte, Ab., Can. 144 G18 49.53 N 112.45 W
Pictured Rocks National Lakeshore, p.o.i., Mi., U.S. 126 B3 46.31 N 86.24 W
Picúa, Punta, c., P.R. 158a b4 18.24 N 65.46 W
Picuí, Braz. 170 D7 6.31 S 36.21 W
Picún Leufú, Arg. 166 G3 39.32 S 69.18 W
Picuris Indian Reservation, ind. res., N.M., U.S. 138 E3 36.12 N 105.42 W
Pidálion, Akrotírion, c., Cyp. 76 D5 34.57 N 34.05 E
Pidbyzh see Pidbyzj, Ukr. 24 G19 49.23 N 23.14 E
Pidbyzj, Ukr. 24 G19 49.23 N 23.14 E
Pide Adası, i., Tur. 185b 40.53 N 29.04 E
Pidhaitsi, Ukr. 38 D4 49.15 N 25.08 E
Pidhorodne, Ukr. 38 E9 48.08 N 30.49 E
Pidhorodne, Ukr. 38 E14 48.34 N 35.07 E
Pidkamin', Ukr. 38 D4 49.56 N 25.19 E
Pidlisne, Ukr. 38 E11 48.47 N 32.15 E
Pidurutalagala, mtn., Sri L. 69 H5 6.59 N 80.45 E
Pidvolochys'k, Ukr. 38 D5 49.32 N 26.07 E
Piedade, Braz. 205a 22.41 S 43.05 W
Piedade, ngh., Braz. 205a 22.53 S 43.19 W
Piedade do Baruel, Braz. 205b 23.37 S 46.18 W
Piedecuesta, Col. 168 D5 6.56 N 73.04 W
Piedimonte Matese, Italy 32 C8 41.21 N 14.21 E
Piedmont, Al., U.S. 134 D13 33.55 N 85.36 W
Piedmont, Mo., U.S. 130 G7 37.09 N 90.42 W
Piedmont, S.C., U.S. 132 B3 34.42 N 82.27 W
Piedmont see Piemonte, state, Italy 30 F4 45.00 N 8.00 E
Piedra, stm., Co., U.S. 150 F9 37.00 N 107.24 W
Piedra, Cerro, mtn., Chile 172 H1 37.40 S 73.07 W
Piedra Azul, Quebrada, stm., Ven. 204c 10.36 N 66.57 W
Piedrabuena, Spain 28 E6 39.02 N 4.09 W
Piedra del Águila, Arg. 166 H3 40.03 S 70.03 W
Piedrafita, Puerto de, p., Spain 28 B3 42.43 N 7.00 W
Piedrahita, Spain 28 D5 40.28 N 5.19 W
Piedras, Arroyo de las, stm., Arg. 206 34.43 S 58.19 W
Piedras, Punta, c., Arg. 172 G9 35.26 S 57.07 W
Piedras, Punta, c., Ven. 168 B11 10.40 N 61.40 W
Piedras Blancas, Arg. 172 E8 31.11 S 59.56 W
Piedras Negras, Guat. 156 D2 17.10 N 91.15 W
Piedras Negras, Mex. 154 A8 28.42 N 100.31 W
Piedra Sola, Ur. 172 F9 32.05 S 56.18 W
Pie Island, i., On., Can. 128 C9 48.14 N 89.05 W
Pieksämäki, Fin. 18 E14 62.17 N 27.10 E
Pielach, stm., Aus. 30 C12 48.14 N 15.20 E
Pielavesi, Fin. 18 D13 63.14 N 26.45 E
Pielavesi, l., Fin. 18 D13 63.18 N 26.35 E
Pielinen, l., Fin. 18 D15 63.15 N 29.40 E
Pieljekaise Nationalpark, p.o.i., Swe. 14 F7 66.18 N 16.58 E
Piemonte, state, Italy 30 F4 45.00 N 8.00 E
Pienaarsrivier, S. Afr. 90 D9 25.12 S 28.18 E
Piendamó, Col. 168 F3 2.38 N 76.30 W
Pieniężno, Pol. 24 B16 54.15 N 20.08 E
Pieniński Park Narodowy, p.o.i., Pol. 24 G16 49.25 N 20.25 E
Pieni-Salpausselkä, mts., Fin. 18 G13 61.01 N 28.17 E
Pieńsk, Pol. 24 E11 51.14 N 15.02 E
Pienza, Italy 30 G8 43.05 N 11.40 E
Pierce, Co., U.S. 140 G8 40.38 N 104.45 W
Pierce, Id., U.S. 146 D11 46.30 N 115.48 W
Pierce, Ne., U.S. 140 E15 42.12 N 97.31 W
Pierce City, Mo., U.S. 138 E14 36.57 N 94.00 W
Pierceton, In., U.S. 130 C12 41.11 N 85.41 W
Pierpont, S.D., U.S. 140 B15 45.29 N 97.49 W
Pierre, S.D., U.S. 140 C12 44.22 N 100.20 W
Pierre, Bayou, stm., La., U.S. 134 E5 31.50 N 93.05 W
Pierre, Bayou, stm., Ms., U.S. 134 E8 31.54 N 91.11 W
Pierrefitte-sur-Seine, Fr. 179 48.58 N 2.22 E
Pierrelaye, Fr. 179 49.01 N 2.09 E
Pierre Part, La., U.S. 134 H7 29.57 N 91.12 W
Pierreville, Trin. 159f s13 10.17 N 61.00 W
Pierson, Fl., U.S. 132 G4 29.14 N 81.27 W
Piersonville, N.J., U.S. 203 40.10 N 74.42 W
Pierz, Mn., U.S. 128 F4 45.58 N 94.06 W
Pieskehaure, l., Swe. 14 F7 66.57 N 16.35 E
Piešťany, Slvk. 24 H13 48.35 N 17.49 E
Pietarsaari, Fin. 18 D9 63.40 N 22.42 E
Pietermaritzburg, S. Afr. 90 F10 29.36 S 30.23 E
Pietersburg, S. Afr. 90 C9 23.53 S 29.26 E
Pietrasanta, Italy 30 F7 43.57 N 10.13 E
Piet Retief, S. Afr. 90 E10 27.00 S 30.49 E
Pietrosu, Vârful, mtn., Rom. 36 B11 47.36 N 24.38 E
Pietrosu, Vârful, mtn., Rom. 36 B12 47.08 N 25.11 E
Pieve di Cadore, Italy 30 D9 46.26 N 12.22 E
Pigeon, Mi., U.S. 126 E6 43.49 N 83.15 W
Pigeon, stm., Mb., Can. 142 B17 52.25 N 97.16 W
Pigeon, stm., N.A. 128 C9 48.00 N 89.35 W
Pigeon, stm., U.S. 124 I2 35.49 N 83.04 W
Pigeon, stm., U.S. 130 C12 41.45 N 85.46 W
Pigeon, stm., Mi., U.S. 126 C5 45.26 N 84.33 W
Pigeon, stm., Mi., U.S. 126 E6 43.56 N 83.16 W
Pigeon Creek, stm., Al., U.S. 134 F12 31.20 N 86.42 W
Pigeon Creek, stm., In., U.S. 130 F10 37.58 N 87.35 W
Pigeon Creek, stm., Pa., U.S. 197b 40.12 N 79.55 W
Pigeon Creek, stm., Pa., U.S. 203 40.12 N 75.35 W
Pigeon Forge, Tn., U.S. 124 I2 35.46 N 83.32 W
Pigeon Lake, l., Ab., Can. 144 C17 53.00 N 114.00 W
Pigeon Lake, l., On., Can. 126 D11 44.30 N 78.30 W
Pigeon Run, stm., Pa., U.S. 203 40.06 N 75.35 W
Pigeon Swamp, sw., N.J., U.S. 194 40.23 N 74.29 W
Piggott, Ar., U.S. 130 H7 36.23 N 90.11 W
Piggs Peak, Swaz. 90 E10 25.57 S 31.16 E
Pigs, Bay of see Cochinos, Bahía de, b., Cuba 156 A7 22.07 N 81.10 W
Pigüé, Arg. 172 H6 37.36 S 62.24 W
Piha Passage, strt., Tonga 100e n14 21.06 S 175.02 W
Pihāni, India 70 E8 27.37 N 80.12 E
Pihkva järv see Pskov, Lake, l., Eur. 26 B10 58.00 N 28.00 E
Pihlajavesi, l., Fin. 18 F15 61.45 N 28.50 E
Pihlava, Fin. 18 F8 61.33 N 21.35 E
Pihtipudas, Fin. 18 D12 63.23 N 25.34 E
Piikkiö, Fin. 18 G9 60.26 N 22.31 E
Piippola, Fin. 18 C12 64.10 N 25.58 E
Pijijiapan, Mex. 154 H12 15.41 N 93.12 W
Pijol, Pico, mtn., Hond. 156 E4 15.06 N 87.35 W
Pikalëvo, Russia 26 A17 59.30 N 34.11 E
Pikangikum, On., Can. 118 B19 51.49 N 93.57 W
Pike, stm., Wi., U.S. 126 C2 45.26 N 87.51 W
Pike, North Branch, stm., Wi., U.S. 128 F10 45.29 N 88.00 W
Pike, South Branch, stm., Wi., U.S. 128 F10 45.29 N 87.59 W
Pike Creek, stm., On., Can. 199 42.19 N 82.51 W
Pike Creek, stm., De., U.S. 203 39.42 N 75.42 W
Pike Lowe, hill, Eng., U.K. 180 53.42 N 2.34 W
Pike Run, stm., N.J., U.S. 194 40.25 N 74.38 W
Pikes Peak, mtn., Co., U.S. 138 C3 38.51 N 105.03 W
Pikes Rocks, hill, Pa., U.S. 124 C6 41.56 N 79.24 W
Pikesville, Md., U.S. 124 E9 39.22 N 76.43 W
Piketberg, S. Afr. 90 H4 32.54 S 18.46 E
Piketon, Oh., U.S. 124 E2 39.03 N 83.01 W
Pikeville, Ky., U.S. 124 G3 37.30 N 82.33 W
Pikeville, Tn., U.S. 134 B13 35.36 N 85.11 W
Pikkola, ngh., Russia 183a 59.42 N 30.08 E
Pikou, China 58 B10 39.24 N 122.20 E
Pikounda, Congo 86 D3 0.33 N 16.37 E
Pila, Arg. 172 G8 36.00 S 58.08 W
Piła, Pol. 24 C12 53.09 N 16.44 E
Pilanesberg, hill, S. Afr. 90 D8 25.11 S 27.04 E
Pilanesberg Game Reserve, ind. res., S. Afr. 90 D8 25.15 S 27.05 E
Pilão Arcado, Braz. 170 E4 9.56 S 42.29 W
Pilar, Arg. 172 E7 31.26 S 61.15 W
Pilar, Arg. 172 E6 31.41 S 63.53 W
Pilar, Braz. 170 E8 9.36 S 35.56 W
Pilar, Braz. 205a 22.42 S 43.19 W
Pilar, Para. 172 C8 26.53 S 58.18 W
Pilar, state, Arg. 206 34.28 S 58.52 W
Pilarcitos Creek, stm., Ca., U.S. 200 37.28 N 122.27 W
Pilarcitos Lake, l., Ca., U.S. 200 37.33 N 122.25 W
Pilar de Goiás, Braz. 170 H1 14.42 S 49.27 W
Pilar do Sul, Braz. 172 A14 23.48 S 47.41 W
Pilares, Mex. 136 D3 30.24 N 104.52 W
Pilas Group, is., Phil. 68 G3 6.45 N 121.37 E
Pilawa, Pol. 24 D17 51.58 N 21.31 E
Pilcher Park, p.o.i., Il., U.S. 196 41.32 N 88.01 W
Pilcomayo, stm., S.A. 166 D5 25.16 S 57.39 W
Pilcomayo, Brazo Norte, stm., Para. 172 B8 24.56 S 58.14 W
Pilcomayo, Brazo Sur del, stm., S.A. 172 B8 24.56 S 58.14 W
Pilcomayo, Parque Nacional, p.o.i., Arg. 172 B8 25.10 S 58.00 W
Pil'dozero, Russia 18 B20 65.43 N 33.27 E
Piles Creek, stm., N.J., U.S. 194 40.37 N 74.12 W
Pilger, Ne., U.S. 140 E15 41.59 N 97.03 W
Pilgrim Gardens, Pa., U.S. 203 39.57 N 75.19 W
Pilgrims Hatch, Eng., U.K. 178 51.38 N 0.17 E
Pilgrim's Rest, S. Afr. 90 D10 24.52 S 30.46 E
Pili, Phil. 68 D4 13.32 N 123.17 E
Pīlībhīt, India 70 D7 28.38 N 79.48 E
Pilica, stm., Pol. 24 E16 51.52 N 21.17 E
Pilipinas see Philippines, ctry., Asia 44 H16 13.00 N 122.00 E
Pilis, mts., Hung. 182c 47.37 N 18.59 E
Pilisborosjenő, Hung. 182c 47.36 N 19.00 E
Pillar Point, c., Ca., U.S. 200 37.30 N 122.30 W
Pillau see Baltijsk, Russia 26 F2 54.38 N 19.55 E
Pilliga, Austl. 98 H7 30.21 S 148.54 E
Pillings Pond, l., Ma., U.S. 201 42.32 N 71.02 W
Pillsbury Sound, strt., V.I.U.S. 158b e7 18.20 N 64.49 W
Pillsbury State Park, p.o.i., N.H., U.S. 122 G4 43.15 N 72.04 W
Pilot, The, mtn., Austl. 98 K7 36.45 S 148.12 E
Pilot Butte, Sk., Can. 142 D9 50.29 N 104.25 W
Pilot Grove, Mo., U.S. 130 F5 38.52 N 92.54 W
Pilot Knob, Mo., U.S. 130 G7 37.37 N 90.38 W
Pilot Knob, mtn., Ar., U.S. 134 B5 35.42 N 93.57 W
Pilot Knob, mtn., Id., U.S. 146 E11 45.54 N 115.42 W
Pilot Mound, Mb., Can. 142 E15 49.12 N 98.52 W
Pilot Mountain, N.C., U.S. 124 H5 36.22 N 80.27 W
Pilot Peak, mtn., Nv., U.S. 148 E8 38.20 N 117.58 W
Pilot Peak, mtn., Nv., U.S. 150 B2 41.02 N 114.06 W
Pilot Peak, mtn., Wy., U.S. 146 F17 44.58 N 109.53 W
Pilot Point, Tx., U.S. 138 H12 33.23 N 96.57 W
Pilot Rock, Or., U.S. 146 E8 45.29 N 118.49 W
Pilot Rock, mtn., Az., U.S. 150 H7 35.09 N 109.53 W
Pilottown, La., U.S. 134 H9 29.11 N 89.14 W
Pilsen see Plzeň, Czech Rep. 24 G9 49.44 N 13.22 E
Piltene, Lat. 26 C4 57.12 N 21.40 E
Pilu, stm., Mya. 64 B3 19.32 N 97.24 E
Pilzno, Pol. 24 G17 49.59 N 21.17 E
Pima, Az., U.S. 150 K7 32.53 N 109.49 W
Pimba, Austl. 96 F7 31.15 S 136.47 E
Pimenteira, Vereda, stm., Braz. 170 F4 9.58 S 42.49 W
Pimenteiras, Braz. 170 D5 6.14 S 41.25 W
Pimentel, Braz. 170 B3 3.44 S 45.31 W
Pimlico Race Course, p.o.i., Md., U.S. 202b 39.21 N 76.40 W
Pimmit Hills, Va., U.S. 202c 38.54 N 77.12 W
Pimmit Run, stm., Va., U.S. 202c 38.55 N 77.07 W
Pimville, ngh., S. Afr. 191d 26.16 S 27.54 E
Pina, stm., Bela. 26 H8 52.07 N 26.07 E
Pinang see George Town, Malay. 64 J5 5.25 N 100.18 E
Pinang, Pulau, i., Malay. 64 J5 5.23 N 100.15 E
Pinangah, Malay. 66 A10 5.07 N 116.47 E
Pınarbaşı, Tur. 34 B16 41.35 N 33.05 E
Pınarbaşı, Tur. 42 F7 38.42 N 36.25 E
Pinar del Río, Cuba 156 A6 22.25 N 83.41 W
Pinarello, Fr. 22 H15 41.41 N 9.22 E
Pınarhisar, Tur. 36 B10 41.37 N 27.29 E
Pinas, Arg. 172 E5 31.10 S 65.31 W
Pinatubo, Mount, vol., Phil. 68 C3 15.08 N 120.21 E
Pinazo, Arroyo, stm., Arg. 206 34.24 S 58.48 W
Pincher Creek, Ab., Can. 144 G17 49.29 N 113.56 W
Pinchi Lake, l., B.C., Can. 144 B6 54.35 N 124.20 W
Pinckney, Mi., U.S. 124 B2 42.27 N 83.56 W
Pinckneyville, Il., U.S. 130 F8 38.04 N 89.23 W
Pinconning, Mi., U.S. 126 E5 43.51 N 83.57 W
Pińczów, Pol. 24 F16 50.31 N 20.32 E
Pindale, Mya. 64 B2 21.11 N 95.56 E
Pindamonhangaba, Braz. 170 L3 22.55 S 45.27 W
Pindaré, stm., Braz. 170 B3 3.17 S 44.47 W
Pindaré-Mirim, Braz. 170 B3 3.36 S 45.20 W
Pinders Point, c., Bah. 132 J7 26.29 N 78.43 W
Pindi Gheb, Pak. 70 B4 33.13 N 72.16 E
Pindobaçu, Braz. 170 F5 10.44 S 40.21 W
Pindorama de Goiás, Braz. 170 F2 10.56 S 47.41 W
Píndos Óros (Pindus Mountains), mts., Grc. 34 D4 39.49 N 21.14 E
Pinduši, Russia 18 E21 62.55 N 34.35 E
Pindus Mountains see Píndos Óros, mts., Grc. 34 D4 39.49 N 21.14 E
Pindwāra, India 70 F4 24.48 N 73.04 E
Pine, stm., Mb., Can. 142 C13 52.10 N 99.57 W
Pine, stm., Mi., U.S. 126 E5 43.35 N 84.17 W
Pine, stm., Mi., U.S. 126 D6 44.29 N 83.22 W
Pine, stm., Mi., U.S. 126 B5 46.03 N 84.39 W
Pine, stm., Mi., U.S. 126 D4 44.14 N 85.54 W
Pine, stm., Wi., U.S. 128 F10 45.50 N 88.08 W
Pine, stm., Wi., U.S. 128 H8 43.12 N 90.18 W
Pine Apple, Al., U.S. 134 F11 31.51 N 86.59 W
Pine Banks Park, p.o.i., Ma., U.S. 201 42.26 N 71.04 W
Pine Barrens, reg., N.J., U.S. 124 E11 39.46 N 74.29 W
Pine Bluff, Ar., U.S. 134 C7 34.13 N 92.00 W
Pine Bluff Arsenal, mil., Ar., U.S. 134 C6 34.20 N 92.07 W
Pine Bluffs, Wy., U.S. 140 F8 41.11 N 104.03 W
Pine Brook, N.J., U.S. 194 40.52 N 74.20 W
Pine Brook, stm., U.S. 194 41.04 N 74.05 W
Pine Brook, stm., Ma., U.S. 201 42.00 N 70.47 W
Pine Brook, stm., N.J., U.S. 194 40.19 N 74.20 W
Pine Bush, N.Y., U.S. 124 C11 41.36 N 74.18 W
Pine Castle, Fl., U.S. 132 H4 28.28 N 81.22 W
Pine City, Mn., U.S. 128 F6 45.49 N 92.58 W
Pinecliff Lake, l., N.J., U.S. 194 41.08 N 74.23 W
Pine Creek, Austl. 96 B6 13.48 S 131.49 E
Pine Creek, stm., Ab., Can. 144 B18 54.56 N 112.31 W
Pine Creek, stm., Ca., U.S. 200 37.58 N 122.02 W
Pine Creek, stm., Nv., U.S. 148 C9 40.36 N 116.11 W
Pine Creek, stm., Pa., U.S. 124 C8 41.10 N 77.16 W
Pine Creek, stm., Pa., U.S. 197b 40.30 N 79.57 W
Pine Creek, stm., Pa., U.S. 203 40.05 N 75.37 W
Pine Creek Indian Reserve, ind. res., Mb., Can. 142 B13 52.03 N 100.14 W
Pine Creek Lake, res., Ok., U.S. 134 C3 34.08 N 95.05 W
Pine Creek Point, c., Ct., U.S. 194 41.07 N 73.16 W
Pine Crest Point, c., On., Can. 202a 42.52 N 79.11 W
Pinedale, Wy., U.S. 146 H17 42.52 N 109.52 W
Pine Falls, Mb., Can. 142 D17 50.34 N 96.14 W
Pine Flat Lake, res., Ca., U.S. 148 G6 36.51 N 119.17 W
Pinega, Russia 12 D20 64.43 N 43.23 E
Pinega, stm., Russia 12 D20 64.08 N 41.54 E
Pine Grove, On., Can. 193b 43.48 N 79.35 W
Pine Grove, N.J., U.S. 203 39.53 N 74.52 W
Pine Grove, Pa., U.S. 124 D9 40.32 N 76.23 W
Pine Grove, W.V., U.S. 124 E5 39.33 N 80.41 W
Pine Hill, Austl. 98 D6 23.39 S 146.58 E
Pine Hill, Al., U.S. 134 F11 31.58 N 87.35 W
Pine Hills, Fl., U.S. 132 H4 28.34 N 81.26 W
Pinehouse Lake, l., Sk., Can. 110 D9 55.33 N 106.31 W
Pinehurst, Ga., U.S. 132 D2 32.11 N 83.45 W
Pinehurst, Id., U.S. 146 E10 45.15 N 116.20 W
Pinehurst, N.Y., U.S. 202a 42.44 N 78.57 W
Pinehurst, N.C., U.S. 132 A6 35.11 N 79.28 W
Pinehurst Lake, l., Ab., Can. 144 B19 54.39 N 111.25 W
Pineiós (Peneus), stm., Grc. 34 D5 39.55 N 22.42 E
Pine Island, Mn., U.S. 128 G6 44.12 N 92.38 W
Pine Island, i., Fl., U.S. 132 J3 26.35 N 82.06 W
Pine Island Bay, b., Ant. 103 C30 74.50 S 102.05 W
Pine Island Bayou, stm., Tx., U.S. 136 D13 30.09 N 94.06 W
Pine Island Creek, stm., Ma., U.S. 201 42.47 N 70.48 W
Pine Lake, Ma., U.S. 201 42.23 N 71.27 W
Pine Lake, l., Mi., U.S. 199 42.35 N 83.20 W
Pineland, Tx., U.S. 136 C14 31.14 N 93.58 W
Pinellas Park, Fl., U.S. 132 I3 27.50 N 82.43 W
Pine Marsh, sw., N.Y., U.S. 194 40.37 N 73.34 W
Pine Meadow Lake, l., N.Y., U.S. 194 41.11 N 74.07 W
Pine Mountain, mtn., Ca., U.S. 148 H4 35.41 N 121.05 W
Pine Mountain, mtn., Ca., U.S. 198 34.13 N 117.54 W
Pine Mountain, mtn., Or., U.S. 146 G6 43.49 N 120.56 W
Pine Mountain, mtn., Wy., U.S. 150 B8 41.02 N 109.01 W
Pine Mountain, mts., U.S. 124 G3 36.51 N 83.25 W
Pine Mountain, mts., Ga., U.S. 134 E14 32.51 N 84.47 W
Pine Orchard Meadows, Md., U.S. 202b 39.17 N 76.52 W
Pine Pass, p., B.C., Can. 144 A8 55.22 N 122.38 W
Pine Point, N.T., Can. 110 C8 60.50 N 114.27 W
Pine Point Park, p.o.i., On., Can. 193b 43.43 N 79.33 W
Pine Prairie, La., U.S. 134 G6 30.47 N 92.25 W
Pine Rest, Ma., U.S. 201 42.23 N 71.26 W
Pine Ridge, Pa., U.S. 203 39.55 N 75.22 W
Pine Ridge, S.D., U.S. 140 D10 43.01 N 102.33 W
Pine Ridge, Va., U.S. 202c 38.52 N 77.14 W
Pine Ridge, mts., Ne., U.S. 140 E10 42.40 N 103.00 W
Pine Ridge Estates, N.Y., U.S. 194 41.02 N 73.41 W
Pine Ridge Indian Reservation, ind. res., S.D., U.S. 140 D10 43.25 N 102.21 W
Pine River, Mb., Can. 142 C13 51.47 N 100.31 W
Pine River, Mn., U.S. 128 E4 46.42 N 94.25 W
Pinerolo, Italy 30 F4 44.53 N 7.20 E
Piñeros, Isla, i., P.R. 158a b4 18.15 N 65.35 W
Pine Run, stm., Pa., U.S. 197b 40.37 N 79.35 W
Pines, stm., Ma., U.S. 201 42.27 N 70.58 W
Pines, Isle of see Juventud, Isla de la, i., Cuba 156 B6 21.40 N 82.50 W
Pines, Lake O' The, res., Tx., U.S. 136 B12 32.48 N 94.38 W
Pines, Point of, c., Ma., U.S. 201 42.26 N 70.58 W
Pines Lake, l., N.J., U.S. 194 41.00 N 74.16 W
Pines Run, stm., N.J., U.S. 203 39.50 N 75.05 W
Pine Swamp Knob, mtn., W.V., U.S. 124 E6 39.33 N 79.31 W
Pinetop-Lakeside, Az., U.S. 150 I6 34.07 N 109.56 W
Pinetops, N.C., U.S. 124 I8 35.47 N 77.38 W
Pinetown, S. Afr. 90 F10 29.52 S 30.46 E
Pine Tree Hill, mtn., Malay. 64 K5 3.43 N 101.42 E
Pine Valley, Md., U.S. 202b 39.26 N 76.39 W
Pine Valley, val., Ut., U.S. 150 E3 38.25 N 113.44 W
Pineville, Ky., U.S. 124 H2 36.44 N 83.42 W
Pineville, La., U.S. 134 F6 31.19 N 92.26 W
Pineville, Mo., U.S. 130 H3 36.35 N 94.23 W
Pineville, N.C., U.S. 132 A5 35.05 N 80.53 W
Pineville, W.V., U.S. 124 G4 37.34 N 81.31 W
Pinewood, S.C., U.S. 132 C5 33.44 N 80.27 W
Piney, Fr. 20 F13 48.21 N 4.20 E
Piney, stm., Tn., U.S. 134 B11 35.49 N 87.33 W
Piney Branch, stm., Va., U.S. 202c 38.56 N 77.18 W
Piney Creek, stm., Tx., U.S. 136 C13 31.03 N 94.34 W
Piney Creek, stm., Wy., U.S. 140 C5 44.33 N 106.31 W
Piney Run, stm., Va., U.S. 202c 38.58 N 77.17 W
Piney Woods, Ms., U.S. 134 E8 32.03 N 89.59 W
Pinfold, Eng., U.K. 180 53.36 N 2.55 W
Ping, stm., Thai. 64 E5 15.42 N 100.09 E
Ping'an, China 54 B5 45.20 N 123.40 E
Pingba, China 58 H2 26.22 N 106.09 E
Pingba, China 58 F5 31.19 N 113.17 E
Pingchang, China 58 F2 31.34 N 107.05 E
Pingding, China 58 C5 37.48 N 113.36 E
Pingdingshan, China 58 E5 33.44 N 113.18 E
Pingdu, China 58 C8 36.46 N 119.56 E
Pingelly, Austl. 96 F3 32.32 S 117.05 E
Pingfang, China 189a 39.56 N 116.33 E
Pingguo, China 58 J2 23.17 N 107.39 E
Pinghe, China 64 A6 22.51 N 102.29 E
Pinghu, China 58 F9 30.40 N 121.00 E
Pingjiang, China 58 G5 28.42 N 113.34 E
Pingle, China 58 I2 24.34 N 106.54 E
Pingle, China 58 I4 24.37 N 110.40 E
Pingli, China 58 E3 32.22 N 109.23 E
Pingliang, China 58 D2 35.32 N 106.41 E
Pinglucheng, China 58 B5 39.50 N 112.16 E
Pingluo, China 58 B2 38.54 N 106.32 E
Pingnan, China 58 J4 23.30 N 110.29 E
Pingnan, China 58 H8 26.56 N 119.01 E
Pingquan, China 58 A8 40.58 N 118.39 E
Pingshan, China 58 B6 38.15 N 114.11 E
Ping Shan, China 189d 22.27 N 114.00 E
Pingshi, China 58 I5 25.20 N 113.02 E
Pingtan, China 58 I8 25.31 N 119.47 E
Pingtan Dao, i., China 58 I8 25.33 N 119.48 E
Pingtang, China 58 I2 25.50 N 107.19 E
P'ingtung, Tai. 58 J9 22.40 N 120.29 E
Pingwu, China 52 E5 32.24 N 104.32 E
Pingxiang, China 58 J2 22.07 N 106.44 E
Pingxiang, China 58 H5 27.38 N 113.50 E
Pingyang, China 58 H9 27.40 N 120.34 E
Pingyao, China 58 C5 37.16 N 112.13 E
Pingyi, China 58 D7 35.30 N 117.37 E
Pingyin, China 58 C7 36.16 N 116.25 E
Pingyuan, China 58 I6 24.35 N 115.55 E
Pinhão, Braz. 170 F7 10.35 S 37.43 W
Pinheiro, Braz. 170 B3 2.31 S 45.05 W
Pinheiro de Loures, Port. 184c 38.50 N 9.12 W
Pinheiro Machado, Braz. 172 E11 31.34 S 53.23 W
Pinheiros, Braz. 170 J5 18.24 S 40.12 W
Pinheiros, stm., Braz. 205b 23.32 S 46.44 W
Pinhel, Port. 28 D3 40.46 N 7.04 W
Pini, Pulau, i., Indon. 60 E2 0.08 N 98.40 E
Pinillos, Col. 168 C4 8.55 N 74.27 W
Pinjarra, Austl. 96 F3 32.37 S 115.52 E
Pinjug, Russia 12 F22 60.14 N 47.46 E
Pink Mountain, B.C., Can. 110 D6 57.02 N 122.30 W
Pinlaung, Mya. 64 B3 20.08 N 96.47 E
Pinn, stm., Eng., U.K. 178 51.31 N 0.29 W
Pinnacle, mtn., N.Y., U.S. 126 E15 43.13 N 74.23 W
Pinnacle, mtn., Va., U.S. 124 E7 39.08 N 78.26 W
Pinnacle Buttes, mtn., Wy., U.S. 146 G17 43.44 N 109.57 W
Pinnacles National Monument, p.o.i., Ca., U.S. 148 G4 36.29 N 121.11 W
Pinnaroo, Austl. 98 J3 35.15 S 140.54 E
Pinneberg, Ger. 24 C5 53.40 N 9.47 E
Pinner, ngh., Eng., U.K. 178 51.36 N 0.23 W
Pino, Sierra del, mts., Mex. 136 F4 28.15 N 103.03 W
Pinole Creek, stm., Ca., U.S. 200 38.01 N 122.18 W
Pinole Point, c., Ca., U.S. 200 38.01 N 122.22 W
Pinole Ridge, mtn., Ca., U.S. 200 37.59 N 122.15 W
Pinos, Mex. 154 D8 22.18 N 101.34 W
Pinos, Isla de see Juventud, Isla de la, i., Cuba 156 B6 21.40 N 82.50 W
Pinos, Mount, mtn., Ca., U.S. 148 I6 34.48 N 119.09 W
Pinos Puente, Spain 28 G7 37.15 N 3.44 W
Pinrang, Indon. 66 E11 3.48 S 119.39 E
Pins, Île des, i., N. Cal. 101d n16 22.36 S 167.27 E
Pins, Pointe aux, c., On., Can. 126 F8 42.15 N 81.51 W
Pinsk, Bela. 26 H9 52.07 N 26.06 E
Pinsk Marshes see Pripet Marshes, reg., Eur. 40 E5 52.00 N 27.00 E
Pinson, Al., U.S. 134 D12 33.41 N 86.41 W
Pinta, Isla, i., Ec. 164a h11 0.35 N 90.44 W
Pintada Arroyo, stm., N.M., U.S. 138 G3 34.53 N 104.39 W
Pintados, Chile 166 D3 20.37 S 69.37 W
Pintasan, Malay. 66 A10 5.26 N 117.43 E
Pinteus, Port. 184c 38.52 N 9.09 W
Pintlala Creek, stm., Al., U.S. 134 E12 32.21 N 86.30 W
Pinto, Cerro, mtn., Mex. 136 F1 28.09 N 106.21 W
Pinto Butte, mtn., Sk., Can. 142 E6 49.22 N 107.25 W
Pinto Creek, stm., Ab., Can. 144 C13 53.51 N 117.34 W
Pinto Creek, stm., Sk., Can. 142 E6 49.39 N 106.41 W
Pintoyacu, stm., Ec. 168 H3 2.07 S 76.03 W
Pin Valley National Park, p.o.i., India 70 C6 32.00 N 77.56 E
Pinzgau, val., Aus. 24 I8 47.17 N 12.40 E
Pioche, Nv., U.S. 150 F2 37.56 N 114.25 W
Pio IX, Braz. 170 D5 6.50 S 40.37 W
Piombino, Italy 30 H7 42.55 N 10.31 E
Piombino, Canale di, strt., Italy 30 H7 42.54 N 10.28 E
Pioneer, Oh., U.S. 124 C1 41.40 N 84.32 W
Pioneer Mine, B.C., Can. 144 F8 50.45 N 122.45 W
Pioneer Mountains, mts., Mt., U.S. 146 E14 45.30 N 112.59 W
Pioneer Park, p.o.i., S. Afr. 191d 26.14 S 28.04 E
Pionerskij, Russia 26 F3 54.55 N 20.24 E

Name	Page	Map Ref.	Latitude	Longitude
Pionki, Pol.	24	E17	51.30 N	21.27 E
Pio Pico State Historical Monument, p.o.i., Ca., U.S.	198		33.59 N	118.04 W
Piorini, stm., Braz.	164	D5	3.23 S	63.30 W
Piorini, Lago, l., Braz.	164	D5	3.33 S	63.14 W
Piotrków Trybunalski, Pol.	24	E15	51.24 N	19.41 E
Pio V. Corpuz, Phil.	68	E5	11.53 N	124.03 E
Piove di Sacco, Italy	30	E8	45.18 N	12.01 E
Pio XII, Braz.	170	B3	3.53 S	45.17 W
Pipanaco, Salar de, pl., Arg.	172	D4	28.07 S	66.25 W
Pipār, India	70	E4	26.23 N	73.32 E
Piparia, India	70	G7	22.45 N	78.21 E
Pipar Road, India	70	E4	26.27 N	73.27 E
Pipe Creek, stm., In., U.S.	130	D12	40.44 N	86.12 W
Pipe Spring National Monument, p.o.i., Az., U.S.	150	G4	36.49 N	112.48 W
Pipestem Creek, stm., N.D., U.S.	142	G14	46.54 N	98.43 W
Pipestem State Park, p.o.i., W.V., U.S.	124	G4	37.32 N	81.00 W
Pipestone, Mn., U.S.	128	H2	43.59 N	96.19 W
Pipestone, stm., On., Can.	110	E12	52.54 N	89.14 W
Pipestone Creek, stm., Can.	142	E12	49.40 N	100.48 W
Pipestone National Monument, p.o.i., Mn., U.S.	128	G2	44.00 N	96.18 W
Pipinas, Arg.	172	G9	35.32 S	57.19 W
Piping Brook, stm., U.S.	194		41.08 N	73.37 W
Piplān, Pak.	70	B3	32.17 N	71.22 E
Pipmuacan, Réservoir, res., Qc., Can.	114	B15	49.36 N	70.27 W
Piqua, Oh., U.S.	124	D1	40.09 N	84.15 W
Piquet Carneiro, Braz.	170	C6	5.48 S	39.25 W
Piquiri see Itiquira, stm., Braz.	166	C5	17.18 S	56.43 W
Piquiri, stm., Braz.	172	B11	24.01 S	54.06 W
Piracanjuba, Braz.	170	I1	17.18 S	49.01 W
Piracanjuba, stm., Braz.	170	I1	18.13 S	48.48 W
Piracão, stm., Braz.	205a		23.02 S	43.36 W
Piracicaba, Braz.	170	L2	22.43 S	47.36 W
Piracicaba, stm., Braz.	170	L1	22.37 S	48.19 W
Piracuruca, Braz.	170	B5	3.56 S	41.42 W
Pirae, Fr. Poly.	100h	v21	17.31 S	149.33 W
Piraeus see Peiraiás, Grc.	34	F6	37.57 N	23.39 E
Piraí do Sul, Braz.	172	B12	24.31 S	49.56 W
Piraju, Braz.	170	L1	23.11 S	49.21 W
Pirajuba, Braz.	170	J1	19.53 S	48.43 W
Pirajucara, Ribeirão, stm., Braz.	205b		23.34 S	46.43 W
Pirajuí, Braz.	170	L1	21.59 S	49.27 W
Pirámide de Cuicuilco, hist., Mex.	204a		19.18 N	99.11 W
Pirámide de Santa Cecilia, hist., Mex.	204a		19.33 N	99.09 W
Pirámide de Tenayuca, hist., Mex.	204a		19.32 N	99.11 W
Piram Island, i., India	70	H4	21.36 N	72.41 E
Piran, Slvn.	30	E10	45.31 N	13.34 E
Piraña, Arroyo, stm., Arg.	206		34.24 S	58.30 W
Piranè, Arg.	172	B8	25.43 S	59.05 W
Piranga, Braz.	170	K4	20.41 S	43.17 W
Piranhas, Braz.	166	C6	16.31 S	51.51 W
Piranhas, stm., Braz.	170	D1	5.56 S	48.14 W
Piranhas, stm., Braz.	170	E1	9.38 S	49.07 W
Piranhas, stm., Braz.	170	C7	5.12 S	36.43 W
Piranji, stm., Braz.	170	C7	4.22 S	37.49 W
Pīrān Shahr, Iran	74	B9	36.41 N	45.08 E
Pirapemas, Braz.	170	B3	3.43 S	44.14 W
Pirapora, Braz.	170	I3	17.21 S	44.55 W
Pirapora do Bom Jesus, mun., Braz.	205b		23.24 S	46.56 W
Piraquara, Braz.	172	B13	25.26 S	49.04 W
Piraquê, stm., Braz.	205a		23.01 S	43.37 W
Pirarajá, Ur.	172	F10	33.44 S	54.45 W
Pirassununga, Braz.	170	K2	22.00 S	47.26 W
Pirata, Monte, hill, P.R.	158a	b4	18.06 N	65.33 W
Pirate Creek, stm., Ca., U.S.	200		37.33 N	121.52 W
Piratinga, stm., Braz.	170	H2	15.39 S	46.07 W
Piratini, Braz.	172	E11	31.26 S	53.05 W
Piratini, stm., Braz.	172	D10	28.05 S	55.26 W
Piratininga, Braz.	205a		22.57 S	43.04 W
Piratuba, Braz.	172	C12	27.25 S	51.50 W
Pirbright, Eng., U.K.	178		51.18 N	0.39 W
Pirdop, Blg.	36	G11	42.42 N	24.11 E
Pires, Ribeirão, stm., Braz.	205b		23.43 S	46.25 W
Pires do Rio, Braz.	170	I1	17.18 S	48.16 W
Piriápolis, Ur.	172	G10	34.51 S	55.16 W
Pirin, mts., Blg.	36	H10	41.40 N	23.30 E
Pirin, Parki Narodowe, p.o.i., Blg.	36	H10	41.47 N	23.28 E
Pirinççi, ngh., Tur.	185b		41.10 N	28.50 E
Pirineos see Pyrenees, mts., Eur.	28	B12	42.40 N	1.00 E
Piripiri, Braz.	170	C5	4.16 S	41.47 W
Piritiba, Braz.	170	F5	11.43 S	40.33 W
Píritu, Ven.	168	C7	9.22 N	69.12 W
Pirituba, ngh., Braz.	205b		23.29 S	46.43 W
Pirmasens, Ger.	24	G3	49.12 N	7.36 E
Pirna, Ger.	24	F9	50.57 N	13.56 E
Pirogovskij, Russia	183b		55.59 N	37.44 E
Pirogovskoe vodohranilišče, res., Russia	183b		55.58 N	37.40 E
Pirojpur, Bngl.	70	G12	22.34 N	89.59 E
Pirón, stm., Spain	28	C6	41.23 N	4.31 W
Pirot, Yugo.	36	F9	43.09 N	22.35 E
Pirovano, Arg.	172	H7	36.30 S	61.34 W
Pirovskoe, Russia	48	C16	57.37 N	92.17 E
Pīr Panjāl Range, mts., Asia	70	B5	33.30 N	74.32 E
Pirtleville, Az., U.S.	150	L7	31.22 N	109.33 W
Pirttikoski, Fin.	14	F18	66.20 N	27.08 E
Pirttikylä, Fin.	18	E8	62.42 N	21.37 E
Piru, Indon.	68	F8	3.03 S	128.11 E
Piru Creek, stm., Ca., U.S.	148	I7	34.23 N	118.47 W
Pisa, Italy	30	G7	43.43 N	10.24 E
Pisa, hill, Fin.	18	D15	63.13 N	28.16 E
Pisa, stm., Pol.	24	C17	53.13 N	21.52 E
Pisagua, Chile	166	C2	19.34 S	70.11 W
Pisarevka, Russia	38	D19	49.53 N	40.11 E
Pisarve, India	190c		19.06 N	73.05 E
Pisau, Tanjong, c., Malay.	68	G2	6.00 N	118.00 E
Pişchia, Rom.	36	D8	45.55 N	21.20 E
Pisco, Peru	164	F2	13.42 S	76.12 W
Pişcolt, Rom.	36	B9	47.34 N	22.17 E
Písek, Czech Rep.	24	G10	49.18 N	14.08 E
Pisgah Forest, N.C., U.S.	132	A3	35.15 N	82.41 W
Pishan, China	62	A4	37.36 N	78.16 E
Pishchana, Ukr.	38	E8	48.07 N	29.44 E
Pishchane, Ukr.	38	D10	49.44 N	31.51 E
Pishchanka, Ukr.	38	E7	48.12 N	28.53 E
Pisinemo, Az., U.S.	150	K4	32.02 N	112.18 W
Piskivka, Ukr.	38	C8	50.42 N	29.38 E
Pisky, Ukr.	38	D17	49.27 N	39.00 E
Pisky, Ukr.	38	C12	50.22 N	33.27 E
Pisky-Rad'kivs'ki, Ukr.	38	D16	49.16 N	37.38 E
Pismo Beach, Ca., U.S.	148	H5	35.09 N	120.40 W
Pišnur, Russia	40	C15	57.48 N	47.56 E
Pistajarvi, ozero, l., Russia	18	B17	65.30 N	30.30 E
Pisticci, Italy	32	D10	40.23 N	16.34 E
Pistoia, Italy	30	G7	43.55 N	10.54 E
Pisuerga, stm., Spain	28	B6	41.33 N	4.51 W
Pisz, Pol.	24	C17	53.36 N	21.51 E
Pit, stm., Ca., U.S.	148	B4	40.45 N	122.22 W
Pit, North Fork, stm., Ca., U.S.	148	B5	41.28 N	120.33 W
Pit, South Fork, stm., Ca., U.S.	148	B5	41.28 N	120.33 W
Pita, Gui.	84	G2	11.05 N	12.24 W
Pitalito, Col.	168	G4	1.51 N	76.01 W
Pitampura Kālan, ngh., India	190a		28.42 N	77.08 E
Pitanga, Braz.	172	B12	24.44 S	51.44 W
Pitangui, Braz.	170	J3	19.40 S	44.53 W
Pitcairn, Pa., U.S.	197b		40.24 N	79.46 W
Pitcairn, dep., Pit.	100k	c28	25.04 S	130.05 W
Pitcairn Island, i., Pit.	94	F13	25.04 S	130.06 W
Pitch Place, Eng., U.K.	178		51.16 N	0.36 W
Piteå, Swe.	14	G12	65.19 N	21.28 E
Piteälven, stm., Swe.	14	G12	65.22 N	21.18 E
Pitelino, Russia	40	D12	54.34 N	41.49 E
Pitești, Rom.	36	E11	44.51 N	24.52 E
Pithapuram, India	69	C6	17.07 N	82.15 E
Pithara, Austl.	96	F3	30.23 S	116.40 E
Pithiviers, Fr.	20	F11	48.10 N	2.15 E
Pithom, hist., Egypt	76	H2	30.33 N	32.04 E
Pithorāgarh, India	70	D8	29.35 N	80.13 E
Pitinga, stm., Braz.	168	H12	1.07 S	59.36 W
Pitiquito, Mex.	120	F6	30.41 N	112.02 W
Pitkjaranta, Russia	18	F18	61.34 N	31.29 E
Pitljar, Russia	50	C2	65.50 N	65.54 E
Pitlochry, Scot., U.K.	10	E9	56.41 N	3.42 W
Pitman Airport, arpt., N.J., U.S.	203		39.45 N	75.08 W
Pitomača, Cro.	30	D14	45.58 N	17.13 E
Pitrufquén, Chile	166	G2	38.58 S	72.38 W
Pitsea, Eng., U.K.	178		51.34 N	0.31 E
Pitt, Mount, mtn., Norf. I.	100i	y25	29.01 S	167.56 E
Pitt Island, i., B.C., Can.	110	E5	53.35 N	129.45 W
Pitt Lake, l., B.C., Can.	144	G8	49.25 N	122.32 W
Pittsboro, Ms., U.S.	134	D9	33.56 N	89.20 W
Pittsboro, N.C., U.S.	122	I6	35.43 N	79.10 W
Pittsburg, Ks., U.S.	130	G3	37.24 N	94.42 W
Pittsburg, Tx., U.S.	136	B13	33.00 N	94.58 W
Pittsburgh, Pa., U.S.	124	D6	40.27 N	80.00 W
Pittsburgh, Pa., U.S.	197b		40.26 N	79.59 W
Pittsburgh, University of, educ., Pa., U.S.	197b		40.27 N	79.58 W
Pittsburgh-Monroeville Airport, arpt., Pa., U.S.	197b		40.27 N	79.46 W
Pittsfield, Il., U.S.	130	E7	39.36 N	90.48 W
Pittsfield, Me., U.S.	122	F7	44.47 N	69.23 W
Pittsfield, Ma., U.S.	124	B12	42.26 N	73.15 W
Pittsfield, N.H., U.S.	122	G5	43.18 N	71.19 W
Pittsford, Mi., U.S.	124	C1	41.51 N	84.28 W
Pitt Stadium, p.o.i., Pa., U.S.	197b		40.27 N	79.58 W
Pittston, Pa., U.S.	124	C10	41.19 N	75.46 W
Pittsview, Al., U.S.	134	E13	32.11 N	85.09 W
Pittsworth, Austl.	98	F8	27.43 S	151.38 E
Pituil, Arg.	172	D4	28.34 S	67.26 W
Pium, Braz.	170	F1	10.26 S	49.11 W
Piura, Peru	164	E1	5.11 S	80.37 W
Piute Peak, mtn., Ca., U.S.	148	H7	35.27 N	118.24 W
Piva, stm., Eur.	30	H15	43.20 N	18.50 E
Pivan', Russia	50	F16	50.29 N	137.05 E
Pivdennyy Buh (Pivdennyi Buh) (Southern Bug), stm., Ukr.	38	F10	46.39 N	31.56 E
Pivdennyy Buh (Pivdennyi Buh) (Southern Bug), stm., Ukr.	38	F10	46.39 N	31.56 E
Pivijay, Col.	168	B4	10.27 N	74.36 W
Piwniczna, Pol.	24	G16	49.27 N	20.42 E
Pixley, Ca., U.S.	148	H6	35.58 N	119.17 W
Pizarro, Col.	168	E3	4.58 N	77.21 W
Pižma, stm., Russia	40	C15	57.36 N	49.02 E
Pizzo, Italy	32	F10	38.44 N	16.10 E
Pjakupur, stm., Russia	48	B13	64.55 N	77.44 E
Pjalica, Russia	14	F30	66.12 N	39.34 E
Pjalka, Russia	14	F31	66.43 N	40.59 E
Pjal'ma, Russia	18	E22	62.24 N	35.52 E
Pjandž (Panj), stm., Asia	72	B11	37.00 N	68.15 E
Pjaozero, ozero, l., Russia	18	A17	66.05 N	30.58 E
Pjaršai, Bela.	26	F9	54.02 N	26.42 E
Pjasina, stm., Russia	50	B6	73.51 N	87.09 E
Pjasino, ozero, l., Russia	50	B6	69.44 N	87.45 E
Pjasinskij zaliv, b., Russia	50	B5	74.00 N	86.00 E
Pjatigorsk, Russia	42	C10	44.03 N	43.03 E
Pjatnickoe, Russia	40	F10	50.25 N	37.50 E
Pjatovskij, Russia	26	F19	54.40 N	36.03 E
Pjažel'ka, Russia	18	G22	60.05 N	35.31 E
Pjažieva Sel'ga, Russia	18	F21	61.29 N	34.30 E
Pjuhjajarvi, ozero (Pyhäjärvi), l., Eur.	18	F16	61.53 N	29.57 E
P. K. le Roux dam see Vanderkloof Dam, res., S. Afr.	90	G7	30.12 S	24.54 E
Place Bonaventure, shp. cen., Qc., Can.	193a		45.30 N	73.34 W
Placentia Bay, b., Nf., Can.	111a	j23	47.15 N	54.30 W
Placer, Phil.	60	C7	11.53 N	123.55 E
Placerville, Ca., U.S.	148	E5	38.43 N	120.47 W
Placetas, Cuba	156	A8	22.19 N	79.39 W
Place Versailles, shp. cen., Qc., Can.	193a		45.35 N	73.32 W
Plácido Rosas, Ur.	172	F11	32.44 S	53.43 W
Plačkovica, mts., Mac.	34	B5	41.45 N	22.35 E
Plailly, Fr.	179		49.06 N	2.35 E
Plai Mat, stm., Thai.	64	E6	15.21 N	102.45 E
Plain City, Ut., U.S.	150	B4	41.19 N	112.04 W
Plain Dealing, La., U.S.	136	B14	32.54 N	93.42 W
Plaines, Île aux, i., Qc., Can.	193a		45.21 N	73.50 W
Plainfield, Ct., U.S.	124	C14	41.40 N	71.55 W
Plainfield, In., U.S.	130	E11	39.41 N	86.23 W
Plainfield, N.J., U.S.	124	D11	40.37 N	74.26 W
Plainfield, Wi., U.S.	128	G9	44.12 N	89.29 W
Plains, Ga., U.S.	134	E14	32.02 N	84.23 W
Plains, Ks., U.S.	138	D8	37.15 N	100.35 W
Plains, Mt., U.S.	146	C12	47.27 N	114.53 W
Plains, Tx., U.S.	136	A5	33.11 N	102.50 W
Plainview, Mn., U.S.	128	G6	44.09 N	92.09 W
Plainview, Ne., U.S.	140	E15	42.21 N	97.47 W
Plainview, Tx., U.S.	138	G7	34.11 N	101.42 W
Plainville, In., U.S.	130	F10	38.48 N	87.08 W
Plainville, Ks., U.S.	138	B9	39.14 N	99.17 W
Plainwell, Mi., U.S.	130	B12	42.26 N	85.37 W
Plaisance, Baie de, b., Qc., Can.	122	C15	47.18 N	61.53 W
Plaisir, Fr.	179		48.49 N	1.57 E
Plakhtiivka, Ukr.	38	G8	46.06 N	29.43 E
Plaksino, Russia	26	D13	56.10 N	30.41 E
Plamondon, Ab., Can.	144	B18	54.50 N	112.19 W
Plampang, Indon.	66	H10	8.48 S	117.47 E
Planá, Czech Rep.	24	G8	49.52 N	12.44 E
Plana, Isla see Plana, L'Illa, i., Spain	28	F10	38.09 N	0.28 W
Plana, L'Illa, i., Spain	28	F10	38.09 N	0.28 W
Planada, Ca., U.S.	148	F5	37.17 N	120.18 W
Planalto, Braz.	170	H5	14.40 S	40.29 W
Planalto, Braz.	172	C11	27.20 S	53.03 W
Planchón, Cerro del (El Planchón, Volcán), vol., S.A.	172	G2	35.13 S	70.34 W
Plandome, N.Y., U.S.	194		40.48 N	73.42 W
Plandome Heights, N.Y., U.S.	194		40.48 N	73.42 W
Plandome Manor, N.Y., U.S.	194		40.49 N	73.42 W
Planers'ke, Ukr.	38	I14	44.57 N	35.14 E
Planeta Rica, Col.	168	C4	8.25 N	75.35 W
Plankinton, S.D., U.S.	140	D14	43.42 N	98.29 W
Plano, Il., U.S.	130	C9	41.39 N	88.31 W
Plano, Tx., U.S.	136	A11	33.01 N	96.42 W
Plantagenet, On., Can.	126	C14	45.31 N	75.00 W
Plantation, Fl., U.S.	132	J5	26.06 N	80.13 W
Plant City, Fl., U.S.	132	I3	28.01 N	82.07 W
Plantersville, Al., U.S.	134	E12	32.39 N	86.55 W
Plantersville, Ms., U.S.	134	C10	34.13 N	88.40 W
Planting Fields Arboretum State Park, p.o.i., N.Y., U.S.	194		40.52 N	73.33 W
Plantsite, Az., U.S.	150	J7	33.03 N	109.20 W
Plaquemine, La., U.S.	134	G7	30.17 N	91.14 W
Plasencia, Spain	28	D4	40.02 N	6.05 W
Plaster Rock, N.B., Can.	122	D9	46.55 N	67.24 W
Plastun, Russia	54	B12	44.44 N	136.17 E
Plasy, Czech Rep.	24	G9	49.56 N	13.23 E
Plata, stm., P.R.	158a	b3	18.28 N	66.15 W
Plata, Isla de la, i., Ec.	168	H1	1.16 S	81.03 W
Plátani, stm., Italy	32	G7	37.23 N	13.16 E
Plátanos, Arg.	206		34.47 S	58.11 W
Plátanos, Arroyo, stm., Arg.	206		34.45 S	58.08 W
Plate, Île, i., Qc., Can.	193a		45.22 N	73.48 W
Plateau Creek, stm., Co., U.S.	150	D8	39.10 N	108.17 W
Plato, Col.	168	C4	9.47 N	74.47 W
Platt, Eng., U.K.	178		51.17 N	0.20 E
Platte, S.D., U.S.	140	D14	43.23 N	98.50 W
Platte, stm., U.S.	130	E3	39.15 N	94.50 W
Platte, stm., Mn., U.S.	128	F4	45.48 N	94.19 W
Platte, stm., Ne., U.S.	114	F2	41.03 N	95.53 W
Platte, stm., Wi., U.S.	130	B7	42.36 N	90.40 W
Platte, Île, i., Sey.	89b	k13	5.52 S	55.23 E
Platte Center, Ne., U.S.	140	F15	41.32 N	97.29 W
Platte City, Mo., U.S.	130	E3	39.21 N	94.47 W
Platte Creek, stm., S.D., U.S.	140	D14	43.17 N	99.01 W
Platteville, Co., U.S.	138	A4	40.12 N	104.49 W
Platteville, Wi., U.S.	130	B7	42.44 N	90.28 W
Platt Hall, hist., Eng., U.K.	180		53.27 N	2.13 W
Plattling, Ger.	24	H8	48.47 N	12.52 E
Plattsburg, Mo., U.S.	130	E3	39.33 N	94.27 W
Plattsburgh, N.Y., U.S.	126	D16	44.42 N	73.27 W
Plattsmouth, Ne., U.S.	130	D2	41.00 N	95.53 W
Plau, Ger.	24	C8	53.27 N	12.16 E
Plauen, Ger.	24	F8	50.30 N	12.08 E
Plav, Yugo.	36	G6	42.35 N	19.56 E
Pļaviņas, Lat.	26	D8	56.37 N	25.43 E
Plavsk, Russia	26	G20	53.42 N	37.17 E
Plaxtol, Eng., U.K.	178		51.15 N	0.18 E
Playa Azul, Mex.	154	G7	17.58 N	102.20 W
Playa Baracoa, Cuba	204b		23.03 N	82.34 W
Playa de Fajardo, P.R.	158a	b4	18.20 N	65.38 W
Playa de Guayanés, P.R.	158a	b4	18.03 N	65.49 W
Playa de Guayanilla, P.R.	158a	c2	18.00 N	66.44 W
Playa del Carmen, Mex.	156	B4	20.36 N	87.06 W
Playa del Rey, ngh., Ca., U.S.	198		33.58 N	118.26 W
Playa de Naguabo, P.R.	158a	b4	18.11 N	65.42 W
Playa de Ponce, P.R.	158a	c2	17.59 N	66.37 W
Playa Noriega, Laguna, l., Mex.	154	A3	29.03 N	111.56 W
Playas Lake, l., N.M., U.S.	150	L8	31.54 N	108.35 W
Playa Vicente, Mex.	154	G11	17.48 N	95.49 W
Playgreen Lake, l., Mb., Can.	110	E11	53.54 N	98.13 W
Play Ku, Viet.	64	F8	13.58 N	108.00 E
Playland, p.o.i., N.Y., U.S.	194		40.58 N	73.41 W
Plaza, N.D., U.S.	142	F12	48.01 N	101.57 W
Plaza at Mid Island, shp. cen., N.Y., U.S.	194		40.46 N	73.32 W
Plaza de Mayo, p.o.i., Arg.	206		34.36 S	58.23 W
Plaza de Toros, p.o.i., Spain	184a		40.26 N	3.39 W
Plaza de Toros Las Arenas, p.o.i., Spain	184d		41.23 N	2.09 W
Plaza de Toros Monumental, p.o.i., Spain	184d		41.24 N	2.11 E
Plaza Park, N.J., U.S.	203		40.04 N	74.53 W
Pleasant, On., Can.	193b		43.41 N	79.49 W
Pleasant, Lake, res., Az., U.S.	150	J4	33.52 N	112.16 W
Pleasant, Mount, mtn., Va., U.S.	124	G6	37.44 N	79.10 W
Pleasant, Mount, hill, N.B., Can.	122	E10	45.25 N	66.48 W
Pleasant Bay, N.S., Can.	122	D16	46.49 N	60.49 W
Pleasantdale, Sk., Can.	142	B9	52.34 N	104.29 W
Pleasant Gap, Pa., U.S.	124	D8	40.52 N	77.46 W
Pleasant Grove, Ut., U.S.	150	C5	40.22 N	111.43 W
Pleasant Hill, Il., U.S.	130	E7	39.27 N	90.53 W
Pleasant Hill, La., U.S.	136	C14	31.48 N	93.31 W
Pleasant Hill, Mo., U.S.	130	F3	38.47 N	94.16 W
Pleasant Island see Nauru, i., Nauru	94	D7	0.32 S	166.55 E
Pleasanton, Ks., U.S.	130	F3	38.10 N	94.42 W
Pleasanton, Tx., U.S.	136	F9	28.58 N	98.28 W
Pleasanton Ridge, mtn., Ca., U.S.	200		37.40 N	121.55 W
Pleasant Plains, Il., U.S.	130	E8	39.51 N	89.55 W
Pleasant Ridge, Mi., U.S.	199		42.31 N	83.10 W
Pleasant Valley, Pa., U.S.	197b		40.31 N	75.18 W
Pleasantville, Ia., U.S.	130	C4	41.23 N	93.16 W
Pleasantville, Md., U.S.	202b		39.11 N	76.38 W
Pleasantville, N.J., U.S.	124	E11	39.23 N	74.31 W
Pleasantville, Pa., U.S.	124	C6	41.35 N	79.34 W
Pleasington, Eng., U.K.	180		53.44 N	2.34 W
Pleaux, Fr.	22	D8	45.08 N	2.14 E
Plehanovo, Russia	20	F20	54.14 N	37.33 E
Plehovo, Russia	38	B14	51.07 N	35.19 E
Pleiku see Play Ku, Viet.	64	F8	13.58 N	108.00 E
Plenty, Sk., Can.	142	C5	51.47 N	108.39 W
Plenty, stm., Austl.	192b		37.45 S	145.07 E
Plenty, Bay of, b., N.Z.	102	C7	37.40 S	177.00 E
Plentywood, Mt., U.S.	142	F9	48.46 N	104.31 W
Pleščanicy, Bela.	26	F10	54.25 N	27.50 E
Pleščeevo, ozero, l., Russia	26	D21	56.46 N	38.47 E
Pleseck, Russia	12	E19	62.42 N	40.18 E
Plëso, Russia	18	H22	59.47 N	35.44 E
Pless see Pszczyna, Pol.	24	G14	49.58 N	18.57 E
Plessisville, Qc., Can.	122	D5	46.13 N	71.45 W
Pleszew, Pol.	24	E13	51.53 N	17.46 E
Pletenyi Tashlyk, Ukr.	38	E10	48.29 N	31.40 E
Plétipi, Lac, l., Qc., Can.	110	E16	51.44 N	70.06 W
Plettenbergbaai, S. Afr.	90	I6	34.03 S	23.22 E
Pleven, Blg.	36	F11	43.24 N	24.36 E
Plevna, Mt., U.S.	140	A8	46.25 N	104.31 W
Plintovka, Russia	183a		60.01 N	30.46 E
Plitvička Jezera Nacionalni Park, p.o.i., Cro.	30	F12	44.51 N	15.35 E
Plješevica, mts., Eur.	30	F12	44.41 N	15.50 E
Pljevlja, Yugo.	36	F6	43.21 N	19.21 E
Pljuskovo, Russia	26	H16	52.46 N	33.49 E
Pljussa, Russia	26	B12	58.26 N	29.21 E
Pljussa, stm., Russia	26	A11	59.18 N	28.09 E
Płock, Pol.	24	D15	52.32 N	19.42 E
Pločno, mtn., Bos.	36	F4	43.36 N	17.34 E
Ploërmel, Fr.	20	G6	47.56 N	2.24 W
Ploeşti see Ploieşti, Rom.	36	E12	44.56 N	26.02 E
Ploieşti, Rom.	36	E12	44.56 N	26.02 E
Plomári, Grc.	34	E9	38.59 N	26.22 E
Plomb du Cantal, mtn., Fr.	22	D8	45.04 N	2.45 E
Plomer, Point, c., Austl.	98	H9	31.18 S	152.57 E
Plön, Ger.	24	B6	54.09 N	10.25 E
Płońsk, Pol.	24	D16	52.37 N	20.23 E
Ploskoe, Russia	26	H21	52.45 N	38.21 E
Ploskoš', Russia	26	D14	56.46 N	31.16 E
Plotnica, Bela.	26	H9	52.03 N	26.39 E
Płoty, Pol.	24	C11	53.49 N	15.16 E
Ploudalmézeau, Fr.	20	F4	48.32 N	4.39 W
Plovdiv, Blg.	36	G11	42.09 N	24.45 E
Plovdiv, state, Blg.	36	G11	42.00 N	24.30 E
Plover, stm., Wi., U.S.	128	G9	44.28 N	89.33 W
Pluckemin, N.J., U.S.	194		40.39 N	74.39 W
Plumas, Mb., Can.	142	D14	50.23 N	99.05 W
Plum Brook, stm., Mi., U.S.	199		42.34 N	82.58 W
Plum Creek, stm., Il., U.S.	196		41.33 N	87.29 W
Plum Creek, stm., Ne., U.S.	140	F16	41.52 N	96.44 W
Plum Creek, stm., Oh., U.S.	197a		41.18 N	82.09 W
Plum Creek, stm., Pa., U.S.	197b		40.31 N	79.51 W
Plum Creek, stm., S.D., U.S.	140	C11	44.12 N	100.43 W
Plum Creek, stm., Tx., U.S.	136	E10	29.37 N	97.35 W
Plumerville, Ar., U.S.	134	B6	35.08 N	92.38 W
Plum Grove Estates, Il., U.S.	196		42.04 N	88.02 W
Plum Island, Ma., U.S.	201		42.49 N	70.59 W
Plum Island Airport, arpt., Ma., U.S.	201		42.48 N	70.50 W
Plum Island Sound, strt., Ma., U.S.	201		42.45 N	70.48 W
Plum Island State Park, p.o.i., Ma., U.S.	201		42.42 N	70.47 W
Plumley, Eng., U.K.	180		53.17 N	2.25 W
Plummer, Id., U.S.	146	C10	47.19 N	116.53 W
Plum Point, c., N.Y., U.S.	194		40.50 N	40.43 W
Plumpton, Austl.	192a		33.45 S	150.50 E
Plumridge Lakes, l., Austl.	96	E5	29.27 S	125.15 E
Plum Run, stm., Pa., U.S.	197b		40.15 N	80.13 W
Plumtree, Zimb.	88	E4	20.29 S	27.48 E
Plungė, Lith.	26	E4	55.54 N	21.52 E
Plutarco Elías Calles, Presa, res., Mex.	120	G8	29.08 N	109.40 W
Plymouth, Monts.	159a	d3	16.42 N	62.12 W
Plymouth, Trin.	159f	r13	11.13 N	60.45 W
Plymouth, Eng., U.K.	10	K8	50.23 N	4.09 W
Plymouth, Ca., U.S.	148	E5	38.28 N	120.50 W
Plymouth, Il., U.S.	130	D7	40.17 N	90.54 W
Plymouth, In., U.S.	130	C11	41.20 N	86.18 W
Plymouth, Ma., U.S.	124	C15	41.57 N	70.40 W
Plymouth, Ne., U.S.	138	A11	40.18 N	96.59 W
Plymouth, N.H., U.S.	122	G5	43.45 N	71.41 W
Plymouth, N.C., U.S.	124	I9	35.51 N	76.44 W
Plymouth, Oh., U.S.	124	C3	40.59 N	82.40 W
Plymouth, Pa., U.S.	124	C10	41.14 N	75.57 W
Plymouth, Wi., U.S.	126	E1	43.45 N	87.58 W
Plymouth, stm., Ma., U.S.	201		42.12 N	70.54 W
Plymouth Harbor, b., Ma., U.S.	201		41.58 N	70.39 W
Plymouth Meeting, Pa., U.S.	203		40.06 N	75.16 W
Plymouth Meeting Mall, shp. cen., Pa., U.S.	203		40.07 N	75.17 W
Plymouth Valley, Pa., U.S.	203		40.07 N	75.23 W
Plyskiv, Ukr.	38	D8	49.24 N	29.17 E
Plysky, Ukr.	38	B11	51.06 N	32.26 E
Plzeň, Czech Rep.	24	G9	49.44 N	13.22 E
Pniewy, Pol.	24	D12	52.30 N	16.15 E
Pô, Burkina	84	G4	11.10 N	1.09 W
Po, stm., Italy	30	F8	44.58 N	12.02 E
Po, Foci del, mth., Italy	30	F9	44.54 N	12.32 E
Po, Mouths of the see Po, Foci del, mth., Italy	30	F9	44.54 N	12.32 E
Poá, mun., Braz.	205b		23.31 S	46.20 W
Poá, stm., Braz.	205b		23.37 S	46.45 W
Poarta Orientală, Pasul, p., Rom.	36	D9	45.06 N	22.17 E
Pobè, Benin	84	H5	6.58 N	2.40 E
Pobé, Burkina	84	G4	13.53 N	1.46 W
Pobeda, gora, mtn., Russia	50	C18	65.12 N	146.12 E
Pobedino, Russia	50	G17	49.50 N	142.46 E
Pobedy, pik, mtn., Asia	48	F14	42.02 N	80.05 E
Poblado Cerro Gordo, P.R.	158a	a3	18.29 N	66.20 W
Poblado Jacaguas, P.R.	158a	b2	18.03 N	66.32 W
Poblado Medianía Alta, P.R.	158a	b4	18.25 N	65.50 W
Poblado Sábalos, P.R.	158a	b1	18.10 N	67.08 W
Poblado Santana, P.R.	158a	b2	18.26 N	66.39 W
Pobra de Trives, Spain	28	B3	42.20 N	7.14 W
Pocahontas, Ar., U.S.	130	H6	36.15 N	90.58 W
Pocahontas, Il., U.S.	130	F8	38.48 N	89.32 W
Pocahontas, Ia., U.S.	130	B3	42.44 N	94.39 W
Pocantico Hills, N.Y., U.S.	194		41.06 N	73.50 W
Pocantico Lake, l., N.Y., U.S.	194		41.07 N	73.50 W
Poção, Braz.	170	E7	8.11 S	36.42 W
Pocatalico, stm., W.V., U.S.	124	F4	38.28 N	81.49 W
Pocatello, Id., U.S.	146	H14	42.52 N	112.27 W
Počep, Russia	26	H16	52.54 N	33.28 E
Pochaiv, Ukr.	38	C4	50.00 N	25.30 E
Pöchlarn, Aus.	24	H11	48.12 N	15.14 E
Počinki, Russia	40	D14	54.42 N	44.51 E
Počinnaja Sopka, Russia	26	B17	58.24 N	34.20 E
Počinok, Russia	48	D4	54.24 N	32.27 E
Pocitos, Salar, pl., Arg.	172	B4	24.24 S	67.02 W
Pocoata, Bol.	166	C3	18.42 S	66.09 W
Poço da Cruz, Açude, res., Braz.	170	E7	8.29 S	37.41 W
Poço do Bispo, ngh., Port.	184c		38.44 N	9.06 W
Poções, Braz.	170	H5	14.31 S	40.22 W
Pocola, Ok., U.S.	134	B4	35.13 N	94.28 W
Pocomoke, stm., U.S.	124	F10	37.58 N	75.38 W
Pocomoke City, Md., U.S.	124	F10	38.04 N	75.33 W
Poconé, Braz.	166	C5	16.16 S	56.37 W
Pocono Mountains, hills, Pa., U.S.	124	C10	41.10 N	75.20 W
Pocono Summit, Pa., U.S.	124	C10	41.06 N	75.23 W
Pocopson, Pa., U.S.	203		39.54 N	75.37 W
Pocopson Creek, stm., Pa., U.S.	203		39.54 N	75.37 W
Poço Redondo, Braz.	170	E7	9.49 S	37.41 W
Poços de Caldas, Braz.	170	K2	21.47 S	46.33 W
Pocrane, Braz.	170	J5	19.36 S	41.35 W
Podbereze, Russia	26	D13	56.55 N	30.37 E
Podborove, Russia	26	A18	59.30 N	35.02 E
Podbuže, Russia	26	G17	53.30 N	34.56 E
Poddębice, Pol.	24	E14	51.53 N	18.58 E
Poddolgoe, Russia	26	G21	53.12 N	38.04 E
Poddore, Russia	26	C13	57.28 N	31.05 E
Poděbrady, Czech Rep.	24	F11	50.09 N	15.16 E
Podgorenskij, Russia	38	C18	50.24 N	39.38 E
Podgorica (Titograd), Yugo.	36	G6	42.26 N	19.15 E
Podgornoe, Russia	40	F11	50.26 N	39.38 E
Podgornoe, Russia	48	C14	57.46 N	82.39 E
Podillia, hist. reg., Ukr.	38	E8	48.50 N	27.30 E
Podil's'ka vysochyna, plat., Ukr.	38	D5	49.00 N	27.00 E
Po di Volano, stm., Italy	30	F8	44.47 N	12.16 E
Podjuga, Russia	12	F19	61.05 N	40.53 E
Podkamennaja Tunguska, Russia	48	B16	61.36 N	90.07 E
Podkamennaja Tunguska, stm., Russia	48	B16	61.35 N	90.09 E
Podkarpackie, state, Pol.	24	G18	50.00 N	22.00 E
Podlasie, reg., Pol.	24	D19	52.35 N	23.05 E
Podlaskie, state, Pol.	24	C18	53.15 N	23.00 E
Podlesnoe, Russia	40	F15	51.50 N	47.01 E
Podolia see Podil's'ka vysochyna, plat., Ukr.	38	D5	49.00 N	27.00 E
Podol'sk, Russia	26	E20	55.26 N	37.33 E
Podor, Sen.	84	F2	16.38 N	14.58 W
Podosinovec, Russia	12	F22	60.16 N	47.03 E
Podporože, Russia	18	G21	60.55 N	34.09 E
Podravina, reg., Cro.	30	E15	45.41 N	18.15 E
Podtësovo, Russia	48	C16	58.37 N	92.05 E
Podujevo, Yugo.	36	G8	42.55 N	21.12 E
Poduškino, Russia	183b		55.43 N	37.17 E
Podu Turcului, Rom.	36	C14	46.12 N	27.25 E
Podyvote, Russia	38	A13	52.03 N	34.08 E
Poel, i., Ger.	24	B7	54.00 N	11.26 E
Poelela, Lagoa, l., Moz.	90	D12	24.32 S	35.02 E
Pofadder, S. Afr.	90	F4	29.07 S	19.23 E
Pogamasing Lake, l., On., Can.	126	B8	46.55 N	81.49 W
Pogăniș, stm., Rom.	36	D8	45.41 N	21.20 E
Pogar, Russia	26	H16	52.33 N	33.16 E
Poggibonsi, Italy	30	G8	43.28 N	11.09 E
Pogibi, Russia	50	F17	52.13 N	141.40 E
Pogliano, Italy	184b		45.32 N	8.59 E
Pogoanele, Rom.	36	E13	44.55 N	26.59 E
Pogoniani, Grc.	34	D3	40.00 N	20.25 E
Pogoreloe Gorodišče, Russia	26	D17	56.08 N	34.55 E
Pogožee, Russia	38	B16	51.35 N	37.15 E
Pogradec, Alb.	32	D14	40.53 N	20.40 E
Pogradeci see Pogradec, Alb.	32	D14	40.53 N	20.40 E
Pograničnyj, Russia	54	B9	44.24 N	131.23 E
Pogruznaja, Russia	40	D17	54.13 N	50.26 E
P'ohang, Kor., S.	54	F8	36.02 N	129.22 E
Pohénégamook, Qc., Can.	122	C7	47.30 N	69.18 W
Pohick Creek, stm., Va., U.S.	202c		38.46 N	77.14 W
Pohick Creek, Rabbit Branch, stm., Va., U.S.	202c		38.48 N	77.17 W
Pohick Creek, Sideburn Branch, stm., Va., U.S.	202c		38.48 N	77.17 W
Pohjanlahti see Bothnia, Gulf of, b., Eur.	18	D8	63.00 N	20.00 E
Pohjanmaa, reg., Fin.	18	D11	64.00 N	25.00 E
Pohjois-Karjala, state, Fin.	18	E16	63.00 N	30.00 E
Pohnpei, i., Micron.	100d	I11	6.54 N	158.15 E
Pohořelice, Czech Rep.	24	G12	48.58 N	16.30 E
Pohorje, mts., Slvn.	30	D12	46.27 N	15.19 E
Pohreby, Ukr.	38	D12	49.15 N	33.18 E
Pohrebyshche, Ukr.	38	D8	49.29 N	29.16 E
Pohri, India	70	F6	25.32 N	77.21 E
Pohue Bay, b., Hi., U.S.	100a	e6	19.00 N	155.48 W
Pohvistnevo, Russia	40	E17	53.39 N	52.07 E
Poiana Mare, Rom.	36	F10	43.55 N	23.04 E
Poiana Ruscă, Munții, mts., Rom.	36	D9	45.38 N	22.33 E
Pōide, Est.	26	B6	58.30 N	23.02 E
Poigny-la-Forêt, Fr.	179		48.41 N	1.45 E
Poinsett, Cape, c., Ant.	103	B16	65.48 S	113.10 E
Poinsett, Lake, l., S.D., U.S.	140	C15	44.34 N	97.05 W
Point, Tx., U.S.	136	B12	32.56 N	95.51 W
Point Arena, Ca., U.S.	148	E2	38.54 N	123.41 W
Point Au Fer Island, i., La., U.S.	134	H7	29.15 N	91.15 W
Point Baker, Ak., U.S.	109	E13	56.20 N	133.35 W
Point Blanche, c., Neth. Ant.	159a	a1	18.00 N	63.02 W
Point Comfort, Tx., U.S.	136	F11	28.41 N	96.33 W
Point Cook, Austl.	192b		37.56 S	144.45 E
Pointe-à-la-Frégate, Qc., Can.	122	A11	49.11 N	64.56 W
Pointe-à-la-Garde, Qc., Can.	122	B10	48.05 N	66.32 W
Pointe a la Hache, La., U.S.	134	H9	29.34 N	89.47 W
Pointe-à-Pitre, Guad.	159c	h5	16.14 N	61.31 W
Pointe-à-Pitre-le Raizet, Aéroport de, arpt., Guad.	159c	h5	16.16 N	61.31 W
Pointe-Calumet, Qc., Can.	193a		45.30 N	73.58 W
Pointe-des-Cascades, Qc., Can.	193a		45.20 N	73.58 W
Pointe du Canonnier, c., Guad.	159a	a1	18.03 N	63.08 W
Pointe-du-Moulin, Qc., Can.	193a		45.22 N	73.52 W
Point Edward, On., Can.	126	E7	42.59 N	82.24 W
Pointe-Noire, Congo	86	E2	4.47 S	11.51 E
Pointe-Noire, Guad.	159c	h5	16.14 N	61.46 W
Point Fortin, Trin.	159f	s12	10.11 N	61.38 W
Point Hope, Ak., U.S.	109	C6	68.21 N	166.41 W
Point Imperial, mtn., Az., U.S.	150	G5	36.16 N	112.01 W
Point Jupiter, c., St. Vin.	159e	p11	13.24 N	61.19 W
Point Lake, l., N.T., Can.	106	B8	65.15 N	113.04 W
Point Lookout, N.Y., U.S.	194		40.35 N	73.35 W
Point Marion, Pa., U.S.	124	E6	39.44 N	79.53 W
Point Mugu Naval Air Station, mil., Ca., U.S.	148	I6	34.07 N	119.07 W
Point O'Woods, N.Y., U.S.	194		40.39 N	73.08 W
Point Pelee National Park, p.o.i., On., Can.	126	G7	41.57 N	82.30 W
Point Pleasant, Md., U.S.	202b		39.11 N	76.35 W
Point Pleasant, N.J., U.S.	124	D11	40.05 N	74.03 W
Point Pleasant, W.V., U.S.	124	F3	38.51 N	82.08 W

Name	Page	Map Ref.	Latitude	Longitude
Point Reyes National Seashore, p.o.i., Ca., U.S.	148	E2	38.06 N	122.53 W
Point Roberts, Wa., U.S.	146	B3	48.59 N	123.04 W
Point Salines International Airport, arpt., Gren.	159e	q10	12.00 N	61.47 W
Point Sapin, N.B., Can.	122	D12	46.58 N	64.50 W
Point View Reservoir, res., N.J., U.S.	194		40.58 N	74.15 W
Poison Spider Creek, stm., Wy., U.S.	140	E6	42.46 N	106.31 W
Poisson Blanc, Lac du, res., Qc., Can.	126	B14	45.58 N	75.44 W
Poissy, Fr.	20	F10	48.56 N	2.02 E
Poitiers, Fr.	22	C6	46.34 N	0.20 E
Poitou, hist. reg., Fr.	22	C5	46.45 N	0.30 W
Poivre Atoll, i., Sey.	89b	k12	5.46 S	53.19 E
Pojarkovo, Russia	50	G14	49.37 N	128.39 E
Pojo, Bol.	166	C4	17.45 S	64.49 W
Pojoaque Valley, N.M., U.S.	138	F2	35.53 N	106.02 W
Pojuca, Braz.	170	G6	12.25 S	38.18 W
Pojuca, stm., Braz.	170	G6	12.35 S	38.02 W
Pokaran, India	70	E3	26.55 N	71.55 E
Pokataroo, Austl.	98	G7	29.35 S	148.42 E
Pokateeva, Russia	48	C17	56.58 N	97.24 E
Poke Run, stm., Pa., U.S.	197b		40.30 N	79.33 W
Pokharā, Nepal	70	D10	28.13 N	83.59 E
Pokka, Fin.	14	D16	68.07 N	25.35 E
Poko, D.R.C.	86	D5	3.08 N	26.53 E
Pokrovsk, Russia	50	D14	61.31 N	129.11 E
Pokrovs'ke, Ukr.	38	G10	46.32 N	31.37 E
Pokrovs'ke, Ukr.	38	D17	49.44 N	38.14 E
Pokrovs'ke, Ukr.	38	E15	47.58 N	36.12 E
Pokrovskoe, Russia	18	C25	64.18 N	38.04 E
Pokrovskoe, Russia	26	H19	52.36 N	36.51 E
Pokrovskoe, Russia	38	F17	47.24 N	38.54 E
Pokrovskoe, Russia	183a		59.44 N	30.46 E
Pokrovskoe, ngh., Russia	183b		55.37 N	37.37 E
Pokrovsko-Strešnevo, ngh., Russia	183b		55.49 N	37.29 E
Pola, Russia	26	C14	57.56 N	31.50 E
Pola, stm., Russia	26	C14	58.04 N	31.37 E
Polacca, Az., U.S.	150	H6	35.50 N	110.23 W
Polacca Wash, stm., Az., U.S.	150	H6	35.22 N	110.49 W
Polack, Bela.	26	E11	55.29 N	28.47 E
Pola de Lena, Spain	28	A5	43.10 N	5.49 W
Pola de Siero, Spain	28	A5	43.23 N	5.39 W
Polanco, Ur.	172	F10	33.52 S	55.07 W
Poland, ctry., Eur.	6	E12	52.00 N	19.00 E
Polanów, Pol.	24	B12	54.07 N	16.40 E
Polatlı, Tur.	34	D15	39.35 N	32.09 E
Polba, India	190b		22.57 N	88.18 E
Polcura, Chile	172	H2	37.17 S	71.42 W
Połczyn-Zdrój, Pol.	24	C12	53.45 N	16.05 E
Poldnevica, Russia	40	B15	58.36 N	46.36 E
Polebridge, Mt., U.S.	146	B12	48.46 N	114.16 W
Polecat Creek, stm., Ok., U.S.	134	B2	36.00 N	95.57 W
Pol-e Khomrī, Afg.	72	B10	35.56 N	68.42 E
Pole Moor, Eng., U.K.	180		53.39 N	1.54 W
Polenezköy, ngh., Tur.	185b		41.07 N	29.12 E
Pol-e Safīd, Iran	74	B13	36.07 N	53.04 E
Polesden Lacey, hist., Eng., U.K.	178		51.15 N	0.22 W
Polese see Pripet Marshes, reg., Eur.	40	E5	52.00 N	27.00 E
Polesine, reg., Italy	30	E8	45.02 N	11.43 E
Polessk, Russia	26	F4	54.52 N	21.05 E
Polevaja, Russia	38	B15	51.36 N	36.30 E
Polewali, Indon.	66	E11	3.25 S	119.19 E
Pol-e Žahāb, Iran	74	C9	34.27 N	45.51 E
Polga, Russia	18	D21	63.42 N	34.53 E
Polgár, Hung.	36	B8	47.52 N	21.07 E
Poli, Cam.	86	C2	8.28 N	13.14 E
Poli, China	58	D8	35.41 N	119.46 E
Policastro, Golfo di, b., Italy	32	E9	40.00 N	15.30 E
Police (Pölitz), Pol.	24	C10	53.33 N	14.33 E
Polichnitos, Grc.	34	D9	39.04 N	26.10 E
Polička, Czech Rep.	24	G12	49.43 N	16.15 E
Poligny, Fr.	20	H14	46.49 N	5.42 E
Polillo Island, i., Phil.	68	C3	14.50 N	121.57 E
Polillo Islands, is., Phil.	68	C4	14.50 N	122.05 E
Polillo Strait, strt., Phil.	68	C3	14.44 N	121.51 E
Polinyà de Vallès, Spain	184d		41.33 N	2.10 E
Pólis, Cyp.	76	C3	35.01 N	32.25 E
Polis'ke, Ukr.	38	B8	51.14 N	29.23 E
Polissya see Pripet Marshes, reg., Eur.	40	E5	52.00 N	27.00 E
Polist', stm., Russia	26	C14	58.06 N	31.31 E
Polistena, Italy	32	F10	38.25 N	16.05 E
Politécnico Nacional, Instituto, educ., Mex.	204a		19.30 N	99.08 W
Politotdel'skoe, Russia	38	F18	47.33 N	39.05 E
Pölitz see Police, Pol.	24	C10	53.33 N	14.33 E
Poljarnye Zori, Russia	14	E23	67.20 N	32.27 E
Poljarnyj, Russia	14	C24	69.11 N	33.27 E
Poljarnyj, Russia	50	C24	69.06 N	178.39 E
Poljarnyj Ural, mts., Russia	48	A10	67.06 N	65.29 E
Polk, Ne., U.S.	140	F15	41.04 N	97.47 W
Polk, Pa., U.S.	124	C6	41.21 N	79.55 W
Pol'kino, Russia	50	B8	71.08 N	99.08 E
Polkton, N.C., U.S.	132	A5	35.00 N	80.12 W
Pollāchi, India	69	F3	10.39 N	77.00 E
Pöllau, Aus.	30	C12	47.17 N	15.50 E
Pollino, Monte, mtn., Italy	32	E10	39.55 N	16.11 E
Pollock, La., U.S.	134	F6	31.31 N	92.24 W
Pollock, S.D., U.S.	140	B12	45.53 N	100.17 W
Pollock Run, stm., Pa., U.S.	197b		40.14 N	79.47 W
Polmak, Nor.	14	B19	70.04 N	27.58 E
Polná, Czech Rep.	24	G11	49.30 N	15.43 E
Polnovo-Seliger, Russia	26	C15	57.32 N	32.57 E
Polo, Il., U.S.	130	B8	41.59 N	89.34 W
Polo, Mo., U.S.	130	E3	39.33 N	94.02 W
Polock see Polack, Bela.	26	E11	55.29 N	28.47 E
Polohy, Ukr.	38	F15	47.28 N	36.15 E
Polom, Russia	40	B17	59.11 N	50.49 E
Pölömäki, hill, Fin.	18	D13	63.21 N	27.01 E
Polomet', stm., Russia	26	C15	57.41 N	32.12 E
Polonio, Cabo, c., Ur.	172	G11	34.24 S	53.46 W
Polonnaruwa, Sri L.	69	H5	7.55 N	81.00 E
Polonnaruwa, hist., Sri L.	69	H5	7.56 N	81.00 E
Polonne, Ukr.	38	C6	50.07 N	27.31 E
Polotnjanyj, Russia	26	F19	54.44 N	36.00 E
Polotsk see Polack, Bela.	26	E11	55.29 N	28.47 E
Polovo, Russia	26	C15	57.03 N	32.24 E
Polska see Poland, ctry., Eur.	6	E12	52.00 N	19.00 E
Polski Trămbeš, Blg.	36	F12	43.22 N	25.38 E
Polson, Mt., U.S.	146	C12	47.41 N	114.09 W
Poltava, Ukr.	38	D13	49.35 N	34.31 E
Poltava, co., Ukr.	38	D13	49.45 N	34.00 E
Poltavka, Russia	48	D12	54.21 N	71.45 E
Poltimore, Qc., Can.	126	C14	45.46 N	75.43 W
Põltsamaa, Est.	26	B9	58.38 N	25.58 E
Põltsamaa, stm., Est.	26	B8	58.27 N	26.10 E
Poluj, stm., Russia	48	A11	66.32 N	66.34 E
Polunočnoe, Russia	48	B10	60.52 N	60.25 E
Polur, India	69	E4	12.30 N	79.08 E
Poluškino, Russia	183b		55.41 N	38.05 E
Pol'ustrovo, ngh., Russia	183a		59.58 N	30.25 E
Põlva, Est.	26	B9	58.03 N	27.03 E
Polvijärvi, Fin.	18	E16	62.51 N	29.22 E
Polvilho, Braz.	205b		23.23 S	46.50 W
Polvoranca, Spain	184a		40.19 N	3.48 W
Polýaigos, i., Grc.	34	G7	36.46 N	24.38 E
Polygyros, Grc.	34	C6	40.23 N	23.27 E
Polýkastro, Grc.	34	B5	40.59 N	22.35 E
Polynesia, is., Oc.	174	J22	4.00 S	156.00 W
Polynésie see Polynesia, is., Oc.	174	J22	4.00 S	156.00 W
Polynésie française see French Polynesia, dep., Oc.	174	K24	15.00 S	140.00 W
Polysaevo see Polysajevo, Russia	50	F6	54.35 N	86.14 E
Polysajevo, Russia	50	F6	54.35 N	86.14 E
Pomarkku, Fin.	18	F8	61.41 N	22.01 E
Pomáz, Hung.	182c		47.39 N	19.02 E
Pombais, Ribeira de, stm., Port.	184c		38.48 N	9.07 W
Pombal, Braz.	170	D7	6.46 S	37.47 W
Pombal, Port.	28	E2	39.54 N	8.36 W
Pombia, Italy	184b		45.39 N	8.38 E
Pomene, Moz.	90	C12	22.55 S	35.32 E
Pomerania, hist. reg., Eur.	24	B12	54.30 N	17.40 E
Pomeranian Bay, b., Eur.	24	B10	54.04 N	14.19 E
Pomerene, Az., U.S.	150	K6	32.00 N	110.19 W
Pomerode, Braz.	172	C13	26.44 S	49.10 W
Pomeroy, Ia., U.S.	130	B3	42.33 N	94.40 W
Pomeroy, Oh., U.S.	124	E3	39.02 N	82.01 W
Pomeroy, Wa., U.S.	146	D9	46.28 N	117.35 W
Pomfret, S. Afr.	90	D6	25.50 S	23.31 E
Pomi, Rom.	36	B10	47.42 N	23.19 E
Pomichna, Ukr.	38	E10	48.14 N	31.25 E
Pomme de Terre, stm., Mn., U.S.	128	F3	45.10 N	96.07 W
Pomme de Terre, stm., Mo., U.S.	130	G4	38.13 N	93.25 W
Pomme de Terre Lake, res., Mo., U.S.	130	G4	37.52 N	93.19 W
Pommern see Pomerania, hist. reg., Eur.	24	B12	54.30 N	17.40 E
Pommersche Bucht see Pomeranian Bay, b., Eur.	24	B10	54.04 N	14.19 E
Pomona, Ca., U.S.	148	I8	34.03 N	117.45 W
Pomona, Ks., U.S.	130	F2	38.36 N	95.26 W
Pomona, N.Y., U.S.	194		41.10 N	74.02 W
Pomona College, educ., Ca., U.S.	198		34.06 N	117.44 W
Pomona Estates, S. Afr.	191d		26.06 S	28.15 E
Pomona Lake, res., Ks., U.S.	130	F2	38.40 N	95.35 W
Pomona Park, Fl., U.S.	132	G4	29.28 N	81.32 W
Pomoriany, Ukr.	38	D3	49.38 N	24.56 E
Pomorie, Blg.	36	G14	42.34 N	27.36 E
Pomorska, Zatoka see Pomeranian Bay, b., Eur.	24	B10	54.04 N	14.19 E
Pomorskie, state, Pol.	24	B14	54.13 N	18.36 E
Pomorskij bereg, cst., Russia	18	D23	64.15 N	35.45 E
Pomorskij proliv, strt., Russia	12	B23	68.55 N	51.16 E
Pomorze see Pomerania, hist. reg., Eur.	24	B12	54.30 N	17.40 E
Pompano Beach, Fl., U.S.	132	J5	26.14 N	80.07 W
Pompeevka see Pompejevka, Russia	50	G15	48.21 N	130.47 E
Pompei, hist., Italy	32	D8	40.45 N	14.30 E
Pompejevka, Russia	50	G15	48.21 N	130.47 E
Pompeston Creek, stm., N.J., U.S.	203		40.01 N	75.01 W
Pompéu, Braz.	170	J3	19.13 S	45.00 W
Pomponio Creek, stm., Ca., U.S.	200		37.18 N	122.25 W
Pomponio State Beach, p.o.i., Ca., U.S.	200		37.17 N	122.24 W
Pomponne, Fr.	179		48.53 N	2.41 E
Pompon-yama, mtn., Japan	188		34.56 N	135.37 E
Pompton, stm., N.J., U.S.	194		40.54 N	74.16 W
Pompton Lakes, l., N.J., U.S.	194		41.00 N	74.17 W
Pomquet, N.S., Can.	122	E15	45.39 N	61.49 W
Ponape see Pohnpei, i., Micron.	100d	I11	6.54 N	158.15 E
Ponass Lakes, l., Sk., Can.	142	B9	52.15 N	103.59 W
Ponazyrevo, Russia	40	B15	58.21 N	46.19 E
Ponca, Ne., U.S.	130	B1	42.32 N	96.42 W
Ponca City, Ok., U.S.	128	E11	36.42 N	97.05 W
Ponca Creek, stm., U.S.	140	E14	42.48 N	98.05 W
Ponce, P.R.	158a	b2	18.00 N	66.36 W
Ponce, Aeropuerto, arpt., P.R.	158a	b2	18.01 N	66.34 W
Ponce de Leon, Fl., U.S.	134	G13	30.44 N	85.56 W
Ponce de Leon Inlet, b., Fl., U.S.	132	G5	29.04 N	80.55 W
Poncha Pass, p., Co., U.S.	138	C2	38.25 N	106.06 W
Ponchatoula, La., U.S.	134	G8	30.26 N	90.26 W
Pond, stm., Ky., U.S.	130	G10	37.31 N	87.21 W
Pond Brook, stm., N.J., U.S.	194		41.02 N	74.15 W
Pond Brook, stm., Oh., U.S.	197a		41.17 N	81.24 W
Pond Creek, Ok., U.S.	128	E11	36.39 N	97.48 W
Pond Creek, stm., U.S.	128	E11	36.40 N	97.33 W
Pond Creek, stm., Tx., U.S.	136	D11	31.01 N	96.46 W
Pondera Coulee, stm., Mt., U.S.	146	B15	48.16 N	111.02 W
Ponderay, Id., U.S.	146	B10	48.18 N	116.31 W
Ponders End, ngh., Eng., U.K.	178		51.39 N	0.03 W
Pondicherry (Puduchcheri), India	69	F4	11.55 N	79.49 E
Pondicherry, state, India	69	E5	11.56 N	79.50 E
Pond Inlet, Nu., Can.	110	A15	72.40 N	77.59 W
Pond Inlet, b., Nu., Can.	110	A15	72.46 N	77.00 W
Pondosa, Ca., U.S.	148	B4	41.12 N	121.41 W
Pond Run, stm., N.J., U.S.	203		40.13 N	74.44 W
Ponente, Riviera di, cst., Italy	30	F5	44.10 N	8.20 E
Ponérihouen, N. Cal.	101d	m15	21.05 S	165.23 E
Ponferrada, Spain	28	B4	42.33 N	6.35 W
Pong, Thai.	64	C5	19.10 N	100.17 E
Pongola, stm., S. Afr.	90	E10	26.51 S	32.20 E
Pon'goma, Russia	18	D20	65.21 N	34.23 E
Pon'goma, ozero, l., Russia	18	B19	65.21 N	32.55 E
Poniatowa, Pol.	24	E17	51.11 N	22.05 E
Poniec, Pol.	24	E12	51.45 N	16.48 E
Ponil Creek, stm., N.M., U.S.	138	E3	36.29 N	104.48 W
Poninka, Ukr.	38	C6	50.10 N	27.32 E
Ponizovje, Russia	26	E14	55.15 N	31.04 E
Ponkapoag Pond, l., Ma., U.S.	201		42.12 N	71.06 W
Pŏnley, Camb.	64	F7	12.27 N	104.28 E
Ponnaiyār, stm., India	69	F4	11.46 N	79.45 E
Ponnāni, India	69	F2	10.46 N	75.55 E
Ponnūru Nidubrolu, India	69	C5	16.04 N	80.33 E
Ponoj, Russia	14	C31	67.04 N	41.04 E
Ponoj, stm., Russia	14	E32	66.59 N	41.16 E
Ponoka, Ab., Can.	144	D17	52.40 N	113.34 W
Ponomarëvka, Russia	40	E18	53.19 N	54.08 E
Ponornytsia, Ukr.	38	B11	51.43 N	32.48 E
Ponorogo, Indon.	66	G7	7.52 S	111.27 E
Ponpāj, India	190b		22.56 N	88.15 E
Pons, Fr.	22	D5	45.34 N	0.32 W
Pons see Ponts, Spain	28	C12	41.55 N	1.11 E
Ponsul, stm., Port.	28	E3	39.39 N	7.31 W
Ponta Delgada, Port.	78	C3	37.44 N	25.39 W
Ponta de Pedras, Braz.	170	A1	1.23 S	48.50 W
Ponta Grossa, Braz.	172	B12	25.05 S	50.09 W
Pontalina, Braz.	170	I1	17.31 S	49.26 W
Pontão, Port.	28	E2	39.53 N	8.21 W
Ponta Porã, Braz.	166	D5	22.32 S	55.41 W
Pontarlier, Fr.	20	H15	46.54 N	6.21 E
Pontas de Pedra, Braz.	170	D8	7.40 S	34.50 W
Pontassieve, Italy	30	G8	43.47 N	11.26 E
Pontault-Combault, Fr.	179		48.47 N	2.36 E
Pontcarré, Fr.	179		48.48 N	2.42 E
Pontchartrain, Fr.	179		48.48 N	1.54 E
Pontchartrain, Lake, l., La., U.S.	134	G8	30.10 N	90.10 W
Pontchâteau, Fr.	20	G6	47.26 N	2.05 W
Pont-de-Vaux, Fr.	22	C10	46.26 N	4.56 E
Ponte Alta do Bom Jesus, Braz.	170	G2	12.05 S	46.29 W
Ponte Alta do Norte, Braz.	170	F2	10.44 S	47.33 W
Ponteareas, Spain	28	B2	42.10 N	8.30 W
Ponte-Caldelas, Spain	28	B2	42.23 N	8.30 W
Ponte da Barca, Port.	28	C2	41.48 N	8.24 W
Ponte de Lima, Port.	28	C2	41.46 N	8.35 W
Pontedera, Italy	30	G7	43.40 N	10.37 E
Ponte de Sor, Port.	28	E2	39.15 N	8.01 W
Pontedeume, Spain	28	A2	43.24 N	8.10 W
Ponte do Púngoè, Moz.	90	A12	19.29 S	34.31 E
Ponte Galeria, ngh., Italy	185a		41.49 N	12.21 E
Ponteix, Sk., Can.	142	E6	49.46 N	107.29 W
Ponte Nova, Braz.	170	K4	20.24 S	42.53 W
Ponte Serrada, Braz.	172	C12	26.52 S	51.57 W
Pontevedra, Spain	28	B2	42.25 N	8.38 W
Pontevedra, co., Spain	28	B2	42.30 N	8.40 W
Pontevedra, Ría de, est., Spain	28	B1	42.22 N	8.47 W
Ponte Vedra Beach, Fl., U.S.	132	F4	30.14 N	81.23 W
Ponthévrard, Fr.	179		48.33 N	1.55 E
Ponthierry, Fr.	179		48.32 N	2.33 E
Pontiac, Il., U.S.	130	D9	40.52 N	88.37 W
Pontiac, Mi., U.S.	124	B2	42.38 N	83.17 W
Pontiac Lake, Mi., U.S.	199		42.40 N	83.28 W
Pontiac Lake, l., Mi., U.S.	199		42.40 N	83.28 W
Pontiac Mall, shp. cen., Mi., U.S.	199		42.39 N	83.20 W
Pontiac State Recreation Area, p.o.i., Mi., U.S.	199		42.41 N	83.28 W
Pontianak, Indon.	66	C6	0.00 N	109.20 E
Pontine Islands see Ponziane, Isole, is., Italy	32	D6	40.55 N	12.57 E
Pontinha, ngh., Port.	184c		38.46 N	9.11 W
Pontivy, Fr.	20	F6	48.03 N	2.58 W
Pont-l'Abbé, Fr.	20	G4	47.52 N	4.13 W
Pontoise, Fr.	20	E11	49.02 N	2.05 E
Pontoise-Cormeilles-en-Vexin, Aérodrome, arpt., Fr.	179		49.06 N	2.02 E
Pontonnyj, Russia	183a		59.47 N	30.38 E
Pontorson, Fr.	20	F7	48.33 N	1.30 W
Pontotoc, Ms., U.S.	134	C9	34.14 N	88.59 W
Pontotoc, Tx., U.S.	136	D9	30.54 N	98.58 W
Pontremoli, Italy	30	F6	44.22 N	9.52 E
Pontresina, Switz.	30	D6	46.29 N	9.54 E
Pont-Rouge, Qc., Can.	122	D5	46.45 N	71.41 W
Ponts, Spain	28	C12	41.55 N	1.11 E
Ponts Quentin, Ruisseau des, stm., Fr.	179		48.44 N	1.48 E
Pont-sur-Yonne, Fr.	20	F12	48.17 N	3.12 E
Pontuda, Ilha, i., Braz.	205a		23.02 S	43.18 W
Pontus Mountains see Doğu Karadeniz Dağları, mts., Tur.	72	A5	40.30 N	40.30 E
Pont-Viau, ngh., Qc., Can.	193a		45.34 N	73.41 W
Pontypridd, Wales, U.K.	10	J9	51.36 N	3.20 W
Pony, Mt., U.S.	146	E15	45.39 N	111.53 W
Ponyri, Russia	26	H19	52.18 N	36.18 E
Ponza, i., Italy	32	D6	40.54 N	12.57 E
Ponziane, Isole (Pontine Islands), is., Italy	32	D6	40.55 N	12.57 E
Poochera, Austl.	96	F6	32.43 S	134.49 E
Poole, Eng., U.K.	10	K11	50.43 N	1.58 W
Poole's Cavern, cv., Eng., U.K.	180		53.14 N	1.56 W
Pooley Island, i., B.C., Can.	144	D2	52.44 N	128.14 W
Poolville, Tx., U.S.	136	B10	32.58 N	97.52 W
Poona see Pune, India	69	B1	18.32 N	73.51 E
Pooncarie, Austl.	98	I4	33.23 S	142.34 E
Poopó, Bol.	166	C3	18.23 S	66.58 W
Poopó, Lago, l., Bol.	166	C3	18.47 S	67.05 W
Poor Man Indian Reserve, ind. res., Sk., Can.	142	C9	51.30 N	104.23 W
Poor Meadow Brook, stm., Ma., U.S.	201		42.01 N	70.55 W
Popasna, Ukr.	38	E17	48.38 N	38.23 E
Popasne, Ukr.	38	E14	48.49 N	35.31 E
Popayán, Col.	168	F3	2.27 N	76.36 W
Pope, Ms., U.S.	134	C9	34.12 N	89.56 W
Popeşti, Rom.	36	B9	47.14 N	22.25 E
Popeşti-Leordeni, Rom.	36	E13	44.22 N	26.08 E
Popham Bay, b., Nu., Can.	110	C17	64.14 N	65.14 W
Popigaj, Russia	50	B11	71.53 N	110.47 E
Popigaj, stm., Russia	50	B10	72.56 N	106.09 E
Popil'nia, Ukr.	38	D8	49.57 N	29.27 E
Popiltah Lake, l., Austl.	98	I3	33.10 S	141.43 E
Popinci, Blg.	36	G11	42.25 N	24.16 E
Poplar, Mt., U.S.	142	F8	48.06 N	105.13 W
Poplar, Wi., U.S.	128	E7	46.35 N	91.47 W
Poplar, ngh., Eng., U.K.	178		51.31 N	0.01 W
Poplar, stm., Can.	142	B16	53.01 N	97.27 W
Poplar, stm., N.A.	142	F8	48.04 N	105.10 W
Poplar, stm., Mn., U.S.	128	D2	47.50 N	96.05 W
Poplar, West Fork, stm., N.A.	142	F8	48.31 N	105.21 W
Poplar Bluff, Mo., U.S.	130	H7	36.45 N	90.23 W
Poplar Heights, Va., U.S.	202c		38.53 N	77.12 W
Poplar Hill, On., Can.	110	E12	52.04 N	94.17 W
Poplar Mountain, mtn., Ky., U.S.	130	H12	36.43 N	85.03 W
Poplar Point, Mb., Can.	142	D16	50.03 N	97.57 W
Poplarville, Ms., U.S.	134	G9	30.50 N	89.33 W
Poplevinskij, Russia	40	E11	53.41 N	39.34 E
Popocatépetl, Volcán, vol., Mex.	154	F9	19.01 N	98.37 W
Popoh, Indon.	66	H7	8.15 S	111.48 E
Popokabaka, D.R.C.	86	F3	5.42 S	16.35 E
Popoli, Italy	30	H10	42.10 N	13.49 E
Popondetta, Pap. N. Gui.	101a	b4	8.46 S	148.13 E
Popovka, Russia	12	F18	60.07 N	39.21 E
Popovo, Blg.	36	F13	43.21 N	26.14 E
Popov Porog, Russia	18	D20	63.23 N	34.01 E
Popple, stm., Wi., U.S.	128	F10	45.50 N	88.21 W
Poprad, Slvk.	24	G16	49.03 N	20.18 E
Poprad, stm., Eur.	24	G16	49.35 N	20.38 E
Popricani, Rom.	36	B14	47.18 N	27.32 E
Pŏptong-ŭp, Kor., N.	54	E7	38.59 N	127.05 E
Poquessing Creek, stm., Pa., U.S.	203		40.03 N	74.58 W
Poquoson, Va., U.S.	124	G9	37.07 N	76.23 W
Poquott, N.Y., U.S.	194		40.57 N	73.05 W
Poranga, Braz.	170	C5	4.44 S	40.55 W
Porangatu, Braz.	170	G1	13.25 S	49.11 W
Porazava, Bela.	26	H7	52.56 N	24.22 E
Porbandar, India	70	H2	21.38 N	69.36 E
Porce, stm., Col.	168	D4	7.27 N	74.54 W
Porcher Island, i., B.C., Can.	110	E4	53.57 N	130.30 W
Porcheville, Fr.	179		48.58 N	1.47 E
Porco, Bol.	166	C3	19.47 S	65.59 W
Porcos, stm., Braz.	170	G3	12.42 S	45.07 W
Porcuna, Spain	28	G6	37.52 N	4.11 W
Porcupine, stm., N.A.	110	B3	66.34 N	145.20 W
Porcupine Brook, stm., N.H., U.S.	201		42.46 N	71.13 W
Porcupine Creek, stm., Mt., U.S.	142	F7	48.06 N	106.20 W
Porcupine Creek, Middle Fork, stm., Mt., U.S.	142	F7	48.31 N	106.29 W
Porcupine Creek, West Fork, stm., Mt., U.S.	142	F7	48.31 N	106.29 W
Porcupine Hills, hills, Can.	142	B12	52.30 N	101.45 W
Porcupine Mountains State Park, p.o.i., Mi., U.S.	128	E8	46.46 N	89.45 W
Pordenone, Italy	30	D9	45.57 N	12.39 E
Pordim, Blg.	36	F11	43.23 N	24.51 E
Poreč, Cro.	30	E10	45.13 N	13.36 E
Poreče, Russia	26	E18	55.43 N	35.33 E
Poreče, Russia	26	D13	56.05 N	30.28 E
Poreče-Rybnoe, Russia	26	C22	57.05 N	39.23 E
Poreckoe, Russia	40	D15	55.11 N	46.18 E
Porez, Russia	40	C17	57.39 N	51.10 E
Porhov, Russia	26	C12	57.45 N	29.34 E
Pori (Björneborg), Fin.	18	F8	61.29 N	21.47 E
Poricy Brook, stm., N.J., U.S.	194		40.21 N	74.05 W
Porjaguba, Russia	14	F24	66.46 N	33.45 E
Porjus, Swe.	14	F10	66.55 N	19.49 E
Porkkala, Fin.	18	H11	59.59 N	24.26 E
Porlamar, Ven.	168	B10	10.57 N	63.50 W
Porma, stm., Spain	28	B5	42.29 N	5.27 W
Pornic, Fr.	20	G6	47.07 N	2.06 W
Porog, Russia	18	D25	63.50 N	38.27 E
Porog, Russia	26	A16	59.15 N	33.29 E
Porogi, Russia	183a		59.46 N	30.47 E
Porokylä, Fin.	18	D16	63.31 N	29.10 E
Poronajsk, Russia	50	G17	49.13 N	143.05 E
Poroshkove, Ukr.	38	E1	48.41 N	22.45 E
Porosozero, Russia	18	E19	62.43 N	32.42 E
Porpoise Bay, b., Ant.	103	B17	66.30 S	128.30 E
Porpoise Channel, strt., N.Y., U.S.	194		40.55 N	73.09 W
Porrentruy, Switz.	30	C3	47.25 N	7.04 E
Porretta Terme, Italy	30	F7	44.09 N	10.58 E
Porsangen, b., Nor.	14	B16	70.57 N	26.11 E
Porsangerhalvøya, pen., Nor.	14	B15	70.50 N	24.59 E
Porsea, Indon.	66	B1	2.28 N	99.08 E
Porsgrunn, Nor.	14	H7	59.08 N	9.39 E
Porsuk, stm., Tur.	34	D13	39.41 N	31.59 E
Portachuelo, Bol.	166	C4	17.21 S	63.24 W
Port Adelaide, Austl.	98	J2	34.50 S	138.30 E
Portadown, N. Ire., U.K.	10	G6	54.25 N	6.27 W
Portage, Mi., U.S.	130	B12	42.12 N	85.34 W
Portage, Ut., U.S.	146	I14	41.58 N	112.14 W
Portage, Wi., U.S.	128	H9	43.32 N	89.27 W
Portage, stm., Oh., U.S.	124	C2	41.30 N	83.02 W
Portage Bay, b., Mb., Can.	142	C15	51.33 N	98.50 W
Portage Lake, l., Mi., U.S.	128	D10	47.04 N	88.30 W
Portage la Prairie, Mb., Can.	142	E15	49.57 N	98.17 W
Portage Park, ngh., Il., U.S.	196		41.57 N	87.46 W
Portageville, Mo., U.S.	130	H8	36.26 N	89.42 W
Portal, Ga., U.S.	132	D4	32.32 N	81.55 W
Portal, N.D., U.S.	142	F11	49.00 N	102.32 W
Port Alberni, B.C., Can.	144	G6	49.14 N	124.47 W
Portalegre, Braz.	170	C6	6.02 S	38.00 W
Portalegre, Port.	28	E3	39.16 N	7.25 W
Portalegre, state, Port.	28	E3	39.20 N	7.40 W
Portales, N.M., U.S.	138	G5	34.10 N	103.20 W
Port Alfred, S. Afr.	90	H8	33.35 S	26.53 E
Port Alice, B.C., Can.	144	F3	50.23 N	127.25 W
Port Allegany, Pa., U.S.	124	C7	41.48 N	78.16 W
Port Allen, La., U.S.	134	G7	30.27 N	91.12 W
Port Alma, Austl.	98	D8	23.35 S	150.51 E
Port Angeles, Wa., U.S.	146	B3	48.06 N	123.26 W
Port Antonio, Jam.	158d	i14	18.09 N	76.26 W
Port Aransas, Tx., U.S.	136	G10	27.49 N	97.04 W
Portarlington, Ire.	10	H5	53.09 N	7.12 W
Port Arthur, Austl.	99a	o13	43.08 S	147.50 E
Port Arthur see Lüshun, China	58	B9	38.48 N	121.15 E
Port Arthur, Tx., U.S.	136	E13	29.53 N	93.55 W
Port Askaig, Scot., U.K.	10	F6	55.51 N	6.07 W
Port Augusta, Austl.	96	F7	32.30 S	137.46 E
Port au Port Peninsula, pen., Nf., Can.	122	B17	48.36 N	59.15 W
Port-au-Prince, Haiti	156	C11	18.32 N	72.19 W
Port-au-Prince, Baie de, b., Haiti	156	C11	18.40 N	72.30 W
Port Austin, Mi., U.S.	126	D6	44.02 N	83.00 W
Port Barre, La., U.S.	134	G7	30.33 N	91.57 W
Port Blair, India	62	F7	11.39 N	92.45 E
Port Borden, P.E., Can.	122	D13	46.15 N	63.41 W
Port Byron, Il., U.S.	128	J8	41.36 N	90.19 W
Port Campbell, Austl.	98	L4	38.37 S	142.59 E
Port Canning, India	70	G12	22.18 N	88.40 E
Port-Cartier, Qc., Can.	110	E17	50.01 N	66.52 W
Port Chalmers, N.Z.	102	G4	45.48 S	170.35 E
Port Charlotte, Fl., U.S.	132	J3	26.58 N	82.06 W
Port Chester Harbor, b., U.S.	194		40.59 N	73.40 W
Port Clinton, Oh., U.S.	124	C3	41.30 N	82.57 W
Port Clyde, Me., U.S.	122	G7	43.56 N	69.15 W
Port Colborne, On., Can.	126	F10	42.53 N	79.14 W
Port Coquitlam, B.C., Can.	144	G8	49.16 N	122.46 W
Port Costa, Ca., U.S.	200		38.03 N	122.11 W
Port-de-Paix, Haiti	156	C11	19.55 N	72.49 W
Port Dickson, Malay.	64	K5	2.31 N	101.48 E
Port Dover, On., Can.	126	F9	42.47 N	80.11 W
Porte Crayon, Mount, mtn., W.V., U.S.	124	F6	38.56 N	79.27 W
Port Edward see Weihai, China	58	C10	37.30 N	122.07 E
Port Edward, S. Afr.	90	G10	31.03 S	30.11 E
Port Edwards, Wi., U.S.	128	G9	44.20 N	89.51 W
Porteirinha, Braz.	170	H4	15.45 S	43.02 W
Portel, Braz.	164	D7	1.57 S	50.48 W
Portel, Port.	28	F3	38.18 N	7.42 W
Portela, Aeroporto da, arpt., Port.	184c		38.46 N	9.08 W
Port Elgin, N.B., Can.	122	D12	46.02 N	64.05 W
Port Elgin, On., Can.	124	D8	44.25 N	81.23 W
Port Elizabeth, St. Vin.	159e	o11	13.00 N	61.13 W
Port Elizabeth, S. Afr.	90	H7	33.56 S	25.33 E
Port Ellen, Scot., U.K.	10	F6	55.38 N	6.11 W
Port-en-Bessin, Fr.	20	E8	49.21 N	0.45 W
Porter, Ok., U.S.	130	I2	35.52 N	95.31 W
Porter, Tx., U.S.	136	D12	30.06 N	95.14 W
Porter Creek, stm., Oh., U.S.	197a		41.41 N	81.56 W
Port Erin, I. of Man	10	G8	54.05 N	4.46 W
Porter Point, c., St. Vin.	159e	o11	13.23 N	61.11 W
Porters Run, stm., Pa., U.S.	197b		40.27 N	79.33 W
Porterville, S. Afr.	90	H4	33.00 S	18.59 E
Porterville, Ca., U.S.	148	G7	36.04 N	119.01 W
Porterville, Ms., U.S.	134	E10	32.41 N	88.28 W
Portete, Bahía, b., Col.	168	A6	12.13 N	71.54 W
Port Fairy, Austl.	98	L4	38.22 S	142.13 E
Port-Francqui see Ilebo, D.R.C.	86	E4	4.19 S	20.36 E
Port Gamble, Wa., U.S.	146	C4	47.51 N	122.36 W
Port-Gentil, Gabon	86	E1	0.43 S	8.47 E
Port Gibson, Ms., U.S.	134	F8	31.57 N	90.59 W
Port Graham, Ak., U.S.	109	E9	59.20 N	151.49 W
Port Greville, N.S., Can.	122	E12	45.24 N	64.33 W
Port Hacking, Austl.	192a		34.04 S	151.08 E
Port-Harcourt, Nig.	84	I6	4.46 N	7.00 E
Port Hardy, B.C., Can.	144	F3	50.42 N	127.30 W
Port Hawkesbury, N.S., Can.	122	E15	45.37 N	61.21 W
Port Hedland, Austl.	96	D3	20.18 S	118.35 E
Port Heiden, Ak., U.S.	109	E8	56.55 N	158.41 W
Port Henry, N.Y., U.S.	126	D16	44.02 N	73.27 W
Port Hill, P.E., Can.	122	D13	46.34 N	63.52 W
Porthmadog, Wales, U.K.	10	I8	52.55 N	4.08 W
Port Hood, N.S., Can.	122	D15	46.00 N	61.32 W
Port Hope, On., Can.	126	E11	43.57 N	78.17 W
Port Hope, Mi., U.S.	126	E7	43.56 N	82.42 W
Port Hope Simpson, Nf., Can.	110	E19	52.33 N	56.18 W
Port Huron, Mi., U.S.	124	B3	42.58 N	82.25 W
Port-İliç, Azer.	42	F13	38.52 N	48.48 E
Portimão, Port.	28	G2	37.08 N	8.32 W
Portinho, Rio do, stm., Braz.	205a		23.03 S	43.35 W
Port Isabel, Tx., U.S.	136	H10	26.04 N	97.12 W
Port Jefferson Harbor, b., N.Y., U.S.	194		40.58 N	73.05 W
Port Jervis, N.Y., U.S.	124	C11	41.22 N	74.41 W
Port-Katon, Russia	40	H11	46.52 N	38.45 E
Port Kembla, Austl.	98	J8	34.28 S	150.53 E
Port Kennedy, Pa., U.S.	203		40.06 N	75.25 W
Port Lairge see Waterford, Ire.	10	I5	52.15 N	7.06 W
Portland, Austl.	98	I7	33.21 S	149.58 E
Portland, Austl.	98	L3	38.20 S	141.36 E
Portland, Ar., U.S.	134	D7	33.14 N	91.30 W
Portland, In., U.S.	130	D13	40.25 N	84.58 W
Portland, Me., U.S.	122	G6	43.39 N	70.16 W
Portland, Mi., U.S.	124	B1	42.51 N	84.54 W
Portland, N.D., U.S.	142	G16	47.29 N	97.22 W
Portland, Or., U.S.	146	E4	45.31 N	122.39 W
Portland, Tn., U.S.	130	H11	36.34 N	86.30 W
Portland, Tx., U.S.	136	G10	27.52 N	97.19 W
Portland, Bill of, c., Eng., U.K.	10	K10	50.31 N	2.27 W
Portland, Cape, c., Austl.	99a	n13	40.44 S	147.56 E
Portland, Isle of, i., Eng., U.K.	10	K10	50.33 N	2.27 W
Portland Bay, b., Austl.	98	L3	38.19 S	141.47 E
Portland Bight, b., Jam.	158d	j13	17.50 N	77.05 W
Portland Point, c., Jam.	158d	j13	17.42 N	77.10 W
Portlaoise, Ire.	10	H5	53.02 N	7.18 W
Port Laoise see Portlaoise, Ire.	10	H5	53.02 N	7.18 W
Port Lavaca, Tx., U.S.	136	F11	28.36 N	96.37 W
Port Leyden, N.Y., U.S.	126	E14	43.35 N	75.20 W
Port Lincoln, Austl.	96	F7	34.44 S	135.52 E
Port Loko, S.L.	84	H2	8.46 N	12.47 W
Port-Louis, Guad.	159c	h5	16.25 N	61.31 W
Port Louis, Mrts.	89a	h10	20.10 S	57.30 E
Port-Lyautey see Kénitra, Mor.	84	C3	34.16 N	6.34 W
Port MacDonnell, Austl.	98	L3	38.03 S	140.40 E
Port Macquarie, Austl.	98	H9	31.26 S	152.55 E
Port Maitland, N.S., Can.	122	G10	43.59 N	66.06 W
Port Maria, Jam.	158d	i14	18.22 N	76.54 W
Port McNeill, B.C., Can.	144	F3	50.34 N	127.05 W
Port McNicoll, On., Can.	126	D10	44.44 N	79.47 W
Port Melbourne, Austl.	192b		37.51 S	144.56 E
Port Mellon, B.C., Can.	144	G7	49.31 N	123.30 W
Port-Menier, Qc., Can.	110	F18	49.48 N	64.20 W
Port Moller, Ak., U.S.	109	E7	55.59 N	160.34 W
Port Monmouth, N.J., U.S.	194		40.25 N	74.05 W
Port Morant, Jam.	158d	j14	17.54 N	76.19 W
Portmore, Jam.	158d	j14	17.57 N	76.53 W
Port Moresby, Pap. N. Gui.	101a	b4	9.28 S	147.11 E
Port Morien, N.S., Can.	122	D17	46.08 N	59.53 W
Port Morris, N.J., U.S.	194		40.54 N	74.41 W
Port Mouton, N.S., Can.	122	G12	43.55 N	64.51 W
Port Neches, Tx., U.S.	136	E14	29.59 N	93.56 W
Port Nelson, Mb., Can.	110	D12	57.03 N	92.37 W
Portneuf, stm., Qc., Can.	122	B7	48.38 N	69.05 W
Portneuf, stm., Id., U.S.	146	H14	42.57 N	112.36 W
Portneuf-sur-Mer, Qc., Can.	122	B7	48.37 N	69.07 W
Port Neville, B.C., Can.	144	F4	50.29 N	126.03 W
Port Nolloth, S. Afr.	90	F3	29.15 S	16.52 E
Port Norris, N.J., U.S.	124	E10	39.14 N	75.02 W
Porto, Braz.	170	B4	3.54 S	42.42 W
Porto, Fr.	22	G14	42.16 N	8.42 E
Porto, Port.	28	C2	41.09 N	8.36 W
Porto, state, Port.	28	C2	41.10 N	8.20 W
Porto, Bonifica di, reg., Italy	185a		41.48 N	12.16 E
Porto, Golfe de, b., Fr.	22	G14	42.16 N	8.36 E
Porto Acre, Braz.	164	E4	9.34 S	67.33 W
Porto Alegre, Braz.	172	E12	30.02 S	51.12 W
Porto Alegre, S. Tom./P.	84	J6	0.02 N	6.32 E
Porto Amboim, Ang.	86	C1	10.44 S	13.46 E
Porto Amélia see Pemba, Moz.	88	C7	13.01 S	40.31 E
Porto Belo, Braz.	172	C13	27.09 S	48.35 W
Portobelo, Pan.	156	H8	9.33 N	79.38 W
Porto Calvo, Braz.	170	E8	9.04 S	35.24 W
Port O'Connor, Tx., U.S.	136	F11	28.26 N	96.24 W
Porto de Moz, Braz.	164	D7	1.45 S	52.14 W
Porto de Pedras, Braz.	170	E8	9.09 S	35.17 W
Porto di Traiano, Necropoli del, hist., Italy	185a		41.46 N	12.16 E
Porto dos Gaúchos, Braz.	166	B5	11.22 S	57.22 W
Porto Empedocle, Italy	32	G7	37.17 N	13.32 E
Porto Esperança, Braz.	166	C5	19.35 S	57.27 W
Porto Esperidião, Braz.	166	C5	15.51 S	58.28 W

Name	Page	Map Ref.	Latitude	Longitude
Porto Feliz, Braz.	170	L2	23.13 S	47.31 W
Portoferraio, Italy	30	H7	42.49 N	10.19 E
Porto Ferreira, Braz.	170	K2	21.51 S	47.28 W
Port of Ness, Scot., U.K.	10	C6	58.29 N	6.13 W
Porto Franco, Braz.	170	D2	6.20 S	47.23 W
Port of Spain, Trin.	159f	s12	10.39 N	61.29 W
Porto Grande, Braz.	164	C7	0.43 N	51.24 W
Portogruaro, Italy	30	E9	45.46 N	12.50 E
Portola, Ca., U.S.	148	D5	39.48 N	120.28 W
Pörtom see Pirttikylä, Fin.	18	E8	62.42 N	21.37 E
Portomaggiore, Italy	30	F8	44.41 N	11.48 E
Porto Mendes, Braz.	172	B10	24.29 S	54.25 W
Porto Murtinho, Braz.	166	D5	21.41 S	57.52 W
Porto Nacional, Braz.	170	F1	10.42 S	48.25 W
Porto-Novo, Benin	84	H5	6.28 N	2.37 E
Porto Novo, India	69	F4	11.29 N	79.45 E
Porto Novo Creek, b., Nig.	191a		6.26 N	3.20 E
Port Orange, Fl., U.S.	132	G5	29.10 N	81.01 W
Port Orchard, Wa., U.S.	146	C4	47.32 N	122.38 W
Porto Recanati, Italy	30	G10	43.25 N	13.39 E
Port Orford, Or., U.S.	146	H2	42.45 N	124.28 W
Porto Salvo, Port.	184c		38.43 N	9.18 W
Porto San Giorgio, Italy	30	G10	43.10 N	13.47 E
Porto Santana, Braz.	164	D7	0.01 S	51.11 W
Porto Santo, i., Port.	84	C1	33.04 N	16.20 W
Porto Santo Stefano, ngh., Italy	30	H8	42.26 N	11.07 E
Porto Seguro, Braz.	170	I6	16.25 S	39.04 W
Porto Tolle, Italy	30	F9	44.57 N	12.19 E
Porto Torres, Italy	32	D2	40.50 N	8.24 E
Porto União, Braz.	172	C12	26.14 S	51.03 W
Porto Válter, Braz.	164	E3	8.15 S	72.47 W
Porto-Vecchio, Fr.	22	H15	41.35 N	9.16 E
Porto Velho, Braz.	164	E5	8.46 S	63.54 W
Portoviejo, Ec.	168	H1	1.03 S	80.27 W
Port Patrick, Vanuatu	101d	m17	20.08 S	169.49 E
Port Perry, On., Can.	126	D11	44.06 N	78.56 W
Port Phillip Bay, b., Austl.	98	L5	38.07 S	144.48 E
Port Pirie, Austl.	96	F7	33.12 S	138.00 E
Port Providence, Pa., U.S.	203		40.08 N	75.30 W
Port Reading, N.J., U.S.	194		40.33 N	74.15 W
Portree, Scot., U.K.	10	D6	57.24 N	6.12 W
Port Renfrew, B.C., Can.	144	H6	48.32 N	124.26 W
Port Richey, Fl., U.S.	132	H3	28.16 N	82.43 W
Port Robinson, On., Can.	202a		43.02 N	79.13 W
Port Rowan, On., Can.	126	F9	42.36 N	80.27 W
Port Royal, Jam.	158d	j14	17.56 N	76.49 W
Port Royal, Pa., U.S.	124	D8	40.31 N	77.23 W
Port Royal, S.C., U.S.	132	D5	32.21 N	80.44 W
Port-Royal-des-Champs, Abbaye de, rel., Fr.	179		48.45 N	2.01 E
Port Royal National Historic Park, p.o.i., N.S., Can.	122	F11	44.44 N	65.40 W
Portrush, N. Ire., U.K.	10	F6	55.12 N	6.39 W
Port Said see Bûr Sa'îd, Egypt	76	G3	31.15 N	32.17 E
Port Saint Joe, Fl., U.S.	134	H13	29.48 N	85.17 W
Port Saint Johns, S. Afr.	90	G9	31.36 S	29.32 E
Port Saint Lucie, Fl., U.S.	132	I5	27.19 N	80.19 W
Port Sanilac, Mi., U.S.	126	E7	43.26 N	82.33 W
Port Saunders, Nf., Can.	111a	i22	50.39 N	57.18 W
Portsea, Austl.	98	L5	38.19 S	144.42 E
Port Simpson, B.C., Can.	110	E4	54.33 N	130.25 W
Portsmouth, Dom.	159c	i6	15.34 N	61.27 W
Portsmouth, Eng., U.K.	10	K11	50.48 N	1.05 W
Portsmouth, N.H., U.S.	122	G6	43.04 N	70.45 W
Portsmouth, Oh., U.S.	124	F2	38.44 N	82.59 W
Portsmouth, Va., U.S.	124	H9	36.49 N	76.18 W
Portsmouth Naval Shipyard, mil., Me., U.S.	122	G6	43.05 N	70.45 W
Portsoy, Scot., U.K.	10	D10	57.40 N	2.42 W
Port Stanley, On., Can.	126	F8	42.39 N	81.13 W
Port Stanley see Stanley, Falk. Is.	166	J5	51.42 S	57.49 W
Port Sudan see Bûr Sûdân, Sudan	82	D7	19.37 N	37.12 E
Port Sulphur, La., U.S.	134	H9	29.28 N	89.41 W
Port Sunlight, Eng., U.K.	180		53.21 N	2.59 W
Port Talbot, Wales, U.K.	10	J9	51.36 N	3.49 W
Porttipahdan tekojärvi, l., Fin.	14	D17	68.05 N	26.38 E
Port Townsend, Wa., U.S.	146	B4	48.06 N	122.45 W
Portugal, ctry., Eur.	28	D3	39.30 N	8.00 W
Portugalete, Spain	28	A7	43.19 N	3.01 W
Portuguesa, state, Ven.	168	C7	9.10 N	69.15 W
Portuguesa, stm., Ven.	168	C8	7.56 N	67.32 W
Portuguese Guinea see Guinea-Bissau, ctry., Afr.	84	G1	12.00 N	15.00 W
Portumna, Ire.	10	H4	53.06 N	8.13 W
Port Union, On., Can.	193b		43.47 N	79.08 W
Port-Vendres, Fr.	22	G9	42.31 N	3.06 E
Port Victoria see Victoria, Sey.	89b	j13	4.39 S	55.24 E
Port Vila, Vanuatu	101d	k17	17.44 S	168.19 E
Portville, N.Y., U.S.	124	B7	42.02 N	78.20 W
Port-Vladimir, Russia	14	C24	69.24 N	33.07 E
Port Vue, Pa., U.S.	197b		40.20 N	79.52 W
Port Washington, Wi., U.S.	126	E2	43.23 N	87.52 W
Port Wentworth, Ga., U.S.	132	D4	32.08 N	81.11 W
Port Wing, Wi., U.S.	128	E7	46.46 N	91.23 W
Porum, Ok., U.S.	134	B3	35.21 N	95.15 W
Porus, Jam.	158d	i13	18.02 N	77.25 W
Porvenir, Chile	166	J2	53.17 S	70.21 W
Porvoo (Borgå), Fin.	18	G12	60.23 N	25.40 E
Porzuna, Spain	28	E6	39.09 N	4.09 W
Posad, Russia	18	D26	63.06 N	39.14 E
Posada, stm., Italy	32	D3	40.39 N	9.44 E
Posadas, Arg.	172	C9	27.22 S	55.54 W
Posadas, Spain	28	G5	37.48 N	5.06 W
Posavina, val., Eur.	30	E14	45.10 N	17.20 E
Poschiavo, Switz.	30	D6	46.18 N	10.03 E
Pošehon'e, Russia	26	B22	58.30 N	39.06 E
Poseidonos, Naós toy, hist., Grc.	34	F6	37.40 N	24.00 E
Posëlok, Russia	183a		59.43 N	30.12 E
Posen see Poznań, Pol.	24	D12	52.23 N	16.53 E
Posen, Il., U.S.	196		41.37 N	87.40 W
Posen, Mi., U.S.	126	C6	45.15 N	83.41 W
Posets, mtn., Spain	28	B11	42.39 N	0.25 E
Posio, Fin.	18	A15	66.06 N	28.09 E
Poso, Indon.	66	D12	1.23 S	120.46 E
Poso, Danau, l., Indon.	66	D12	1.52 S	120.35 E
Poso, Teluk, b., Indon.	66	D12	1.14 S	120.54 E
Pospelíha, Russia	48	D14	51.58 N	81.49 E
Posse, Braz.	170	H2	14.05 S	46.21 W
Possession Island, i., Nmb.	90	E2	27.01 S	15.11 E
Pössneck, Ger.	24	F7	50.42 N	11.37 E
Possum Kingdom Lake, res., Tx., U.S.	136	A9	32.53 N	98.27 W
Post, Tx., U.S.	136	A6	33.11 N	101.22 W
Posta de Jihuites, Mex.	136	I2	25.44 N	105.36 W
Postelle, Tn., U.S.	132	A1	35.02 N	84.33 W
Post Falls, Id., U.S.	146	C10	47.42 N	116.56 W
Postmasburg, S. Afr.	90	F6	28.19 S	23.04 E
Postojna, Slvn.	30	E11	45.47 N	14.13 E
Postrervalle, Bol.	166	C4	18.29 S	63.51 W
Poststadion, p.o.i., Ger.	182a		52.32 N	13.21 E
Postville, Ia., U.S.	130	A6	43.04 N	91.34 W
Potake Pond, l., U.S.	194		41.08 N	74.13 W
Potam, Mex.	154	B3	27.35 N	110.23 W
Potanino, Russia	18	G19	60.16 N	32.47 E
Potaro, stm., Guy.	168	E12	5.24 N	59.15 W
Potaro Landing, Guy.	168	E12	5.24 N	59.06 W
Potaro-Siparuni, state, Guy.	168	E12	4.42 N	59.28 W
Potato Creek, stm., Ga., U.S.	132	C1	32.47 N	84.21 W
Potawatomie Woods, p.o.i., Il., U.S.	196		42.08 N	87.53 W
Potawatomi Indian Reservation, ind. res., Ks., U.S.	130	E2	39.20 N	95.50 W
Potchefstroom, S. Afr.	90	E8	26.42 S	27.06 E
Poté, Braz.	170	I5	17.49 S	41.48 W
Poteau, Ok., U.S.	134	B4	35.03 N	94.37 W
Poteau, stm., U.S.	134	B4	35.22 N	94.26 W
Poteet, Tx., U.S.	136	E9	29.02 N	98.34 W
Potengi, stm., Braz.	170	C8	5.47 S	35.15 W
Potenza, Italy	32	D9	40.38 N	15.48 E
Potenza, stm., Italy	30	G10	43.25 N	13.40 E
Potes, Spain	28	A6	43.09 N	4.37 W
Potgietersrus, S. Afr.	90	D9	24.11 S	29.01 E
Poth, Tx., U.S.	136	E9	29.04 N	98.04 W
Potholes Reservoir, res., Wa., U.S.	146	C7	47.01 N	119.19 W
Poti, Geor.	42	D9	42.09 N	41.39 E
Poti, stm., Braz.	170	C5	5.01 S	42.50 W
Potiivka, Ukr.	38	C7	50.37 N	28.58 E
Potiraguá, Braz.	170	H6	15.36 S	39.53 W
Potiskum, Nig.	84	G7	11.43 N	11.04 E
Potlatch, Id., U.S.	146	D10	46.56 N	116.54 W
Potlatch, stm., Id., U.S.	146	D10	46.28 N	116.46 W
Po Toi Island, i., China	189d		22.10 N	114.15 E
Po Toi Island Group, is., China	189d		22.11 N	114.16 E
Potomac, Il., U.S.	130	D10	40.17 N	87.48 W
Potomac, Md., U.S.	202c		39.01 N	77.12 W
Potomac, stm., U.S.	124	F9	37.59 N	76.18 W
Potomac, North Fork South Branch, stm., U.S.	124	F6	38.59 N	79.11 W
Potomac, South Branch, stm., U.S.	124	E7	39.31 N	78.34 W
Potomac, South Fork South Branch, stm., W.V., U.S.	124	F6	39.03 N	78.58 W
Potomac Heights, Md., U.S.	124	F8	38.35 N	77.07 W
Poto-Poto, ngh., Congo	191b		4.15 S	15.18 E
Potosí, Bol.	166	C3	19.35 S	65.45 W
Potosi, Mo., U.S.	130	G7	37.56 N	90.47 W
Potrerillos, Chile	172	C3	26.26 S	69.29 W
Potrero, ngh., Ca., U.S.	200		37.48 N	122.24 W
Potrero, Arroyo del, stm., Mex.	136	E1	29.19 N	105.55 W
Potrero del Llano, Mex.	136	E3	29.12 N	104.26 W
Potro, Cerro del (El Potro, Cerro), mtn., S.A.	172	D3	28.24 S	69.39 W
Potsdam, Ger.	24	D9	52.24 N	13.04 E
Potsdam, N.Y., U.S.	126	D15	44.40 N	74.59 W
Potsdam, Staatsforst, p.o.i., Ger.	182a		52.26 N	13.04 E
Pott, Île, i., N. Cal.	101d	I14	19.35 S	163.35 E
Pottawatomie Creek, stm., Ks., U.S.	130	F2	38.29 N	94.55 W
Potten End, Eng., U.K.	178		51.46 N	0.31 W
Potter, Ne., U.S.	140	F9	41.13 N	103.18 W
Potter Point, c., Austl.	192a		34.03 S	151.13 E
Potter Street, Eng., U.K.	178		51.46 N	0.08 E
Pottersville, N.J., U.S.	194		40.42 N	74.43 W
Potterville, Mi., U.S.	124	B1	42.37 N	84.44 W
Potts Camp, Ms., U.S.	134	C9	34.38 N	89.18 W
Potts Hill Reservoirs, res., Austl.	192a		33.54 S	151.02 E
Pott Shrigley, Eng., U.K.	180		53.19 N	2.05 W
Pottstown, Pa., U.S.	124	D10	40.15 N	75.39 W
Pottstown Landing, Pa., U.S.	203		40.14 N	75.40 W
Pottstown Limerick Airport, arpt., Pa., U.S.	203		40.14 N	75.34 W
Pottstown Municipal Airport, arpt., Pa., U.S.	203		40.16 N	75.40 W
Pottsville, Pa., U.S.	124	D9	40.41 N	76.12 W
Potwin, Ks., U.S.	138	D12	37.56 N	97.01 W
Pötzleinsdorf, ngh., Aus.	182b		48.15 N	16.19 E
Pötzleinsdorfer Park, p.o.i., Aus.	182b		48.14 N	16.18 E
Pouancé, Fr.	20	G7	47.44 N	1.11 W
Pouembout, N. Cal.	101d	m15	21.07 S	164.53 E
Poughkeepsie, N.Y., U.S.	124	C11	41.42 N	73.55 W
Poulain, Étang, l., Fr.	179		48.43 N	1.44 E
Poulan, Ga., U.S.	132	E2	31.30 N	83.48 W
Poulsbo, Wa., U.S.	146	C4	47.44 N	122.38 W
Poulter, Lac, l., Qc., Can.	126	A13	47.05 N	76.45 W
Poultney, Vt., U.S.	126	E16	43.31 N	73.14 W
Poum, N. Cal.	101d	m14	20.15 S	164.03 E
Pound, Va., U.S.	124	G3	37.07 N	82.36 W
Poundmaker Indian Reserve, ind. res., Sk., Can.	142	B4	52.51 N	109.00 W
Pouso Alegre, Braz.	170	L3	22.13 S	45.56 W
Poŭthĭsăt, Camb.	64	F6	12.32 N	103.55 E
Poŭthĭsăt, stm., Camb.	64	F6	12.41 N	104.07 E
Poutini see Westland National Park, p.o.i., N.Z.	102	F3	43.30 S	170.10 E
Poutrincourt, Lac, l., Qc., Can.	122	A2	49.11 N	74.07 W
Pouzauges, Fr.	20	H8	46.47 N	0.50 W
Považská Bystrica, Slvk.	24	G14	49.06 N	18.27 E
Povenec, Russia	18	E21	62.51 N	34.45 E
Poveneckij zaliv, b., Russia	18	E21	62.40 N	35.00 E
Poverennyj, Russia	40	H13	46.45 N	43.12 E
Povljen, mts., Yugo.	36	E6	44.08 N	19.42 E
Póvoa, Mouchão da, i., Port.	184c		38.51 N	9.03 W
Póvoa de Santa Iria, Port.	184c		38.52 N	9.04 W
Póvoa de Santo Adrião, Port.	184c		38.48 N	9.10 W
Póvoa de Varzim, Port.	28	C2	41.22 N	8.45 W
Povorino, Russia	40	F13	51.11 N	42.15 E
Povorotnyj, mys, c., Russia	54	C10	42.40 N	133.02 E
Povorsk, Ukr.	38	B3	51.15 N	25.05 E
Povungnituk, Qc., Can.	110	C15	60.02 N	77.19 W
Povungnituk, stm., Qc., Can.	110	C15	60.00 N	77.22 W
Powassan, On., Can.	126	B10	46.04 N	79.21 W
Poway, Ca., U.S.	148	K9	32.57 N	117.01 W
Powder, stm., U.S.	140	E8	47.44 N	105.26 W
Powder, stm., Or., U.S.	146	F9	44.45 N	117.03 W
Powder, Dry Fork, stm., Wy., U.S.	140	D6	43.47 N	106.15 W
Powder, Middle Fork, stm., Wy., U.S.	140	D5	43.41 N	106.33 W
Powder, North Fork, stm., Wy., U.S.	140	D6	43.41 N	106.33 W
Powder, Red Fork, stm., Wy., U.S.	140	D6	43.39 N	106.47 W
Powder, South Fork, stm., Wy., U.S.	140	D6	43.40 N	106.31 W
Powder Horn Lake, l., Il., U.S.	196		41.38 N	87.32 W
Powderly, Tx., U.S.	134	D3	33.49 N	95.31 W
Powdermaker Ditch, can., Oh., U.S.	197a		41.30 N	82.02 W
Powder Mill Village, Md., U.S.	202c		39.03 N	76.57 W
Powder River Pass, p., Wy., U.S.	140	C5	44.07 N	107.04 W
Powell, Wy., U.S.	140	C4	44.45 N	108.45 W
Powell, stm., U.S.	124	H2	36.29 N	83.42 W
Powell, Lake, res., U.S.	150	F5	37.28 N	110.43 W
Powell, Mount, mtn., Co., U.S.	138	B2	39.46 N	106.20 W
Powell Creek, stm., Austl.	98	E5	25.03 S	143.40 E
Powellhurst, Or., U.S.	146	E4	45.30 N	122.32 W
Powell Lake, l., B.C., Can.	144	F6	50.11 N	124.23 W
Powell River, B.C., Can.	144	G6	49.52 N	124.32 W
Powellton, W.V., U.S.	124	F4	38.06 N	81.22 W
Powers, Mi., U.S.	126	C2	45.41 N	87.31 W
Powers, Or., U.S.	146	H2	42.53 N	124.02 W
Powers Lake, N.D., U.S.	142	F11	48.33 N	102.38 W
Powhatan, La., U.S.	134	F5	31.52 N	93.12 W
Powhatan, Va., U.S.	124	G7	37.31 N	77.55 W
Powhatan Mill, Md., U.S.	202b		39.20 N	76.43 W
Powhatan Point, Oh., U.S.	124	E5	39.51 N	80.50 W
Powissett Brook, stm., Ma., U.S.	201		42.16 N	71.14 W
Poxoréu, Braz.	166	C6	15.50 S	54.23 W
Poya, N. Cal.	101d	m15	21.19 S	165.09 E
Poyang Hu, l., China	58	G7	29.00 N	116.25 E
Poyan Reservoir, res., Sing.	189c		1.23 N	103.40 E
Poyen, Ar., U.S.	134	C6	34.18 N	92.38 W
Poygan, Lake, l., Wi., U.S.	128	G9	44.08 N	88.46 W
Poyle, Eng., U.K.	178		51.28 N	0.31 W
Poynette, Wi., U.S.	128	H9	43.23 N	89.23 W
Poyraz, ngh., Tur.	185b		41.12 N	29.07 E
Poyraz Burnu, c., Tur.	185b		41.12 N	29.08 E
Pöyrisjärvi, l., Fin.	14	D14	68.43 N	23.50 E
Pozantı, Tur.	76	A5	37.25 N	34.52 E
Požarevac, Yugo.	36	E8	44.37 N	21.11 E
Poza Rica de Hidalgo, Mex.	154	E10	20.32 N	97.28 W
Požega, Cro.	30	E14	45.20 N	17.41 E
Požega, Yugo.	36	F7	43.51 N	20.01 E
Poznań, Pol.	24	D12	52.23 N	16.53 E
Pozo Alcón, Spain	28	G8	37.42 N	2.56 W
Pozo Almonte, Chile	166	D3	20.15 S	69.47 W
Pozoblanco, Spain	28	F6	38.22 N	4.50 W
Pozo-Cañada, Spain	28	F9	38.48 N	1.44 W
Pozo del Molle, Arg.	172	F6	32.01 S	62.57 W
Pozo del Tigre, Arg.	172	B7	24.54 S	60.20 W
Pozo Hondo, Arg.	172	C5	27.08 S	64.28 W
Pozos, Punta, c., Arg.	166	I3	47.57 S	65.47 W
Pozsony see Bratislava, Slvk.	24	H13	48.09 N	17.07 E
Pozuelo de Alarcón, Spain	184a		40.26 N	3.49 W
Pozuelos, Ven.	168	B9	10.12 N	64.36 W
Pozzallo, Italy	32	H8	36.43 N	14.50 E
Pozzuoli, Italy	32	D8	40.49 N	14.06 E
Prabuty, Pol.	24	C15	53.44 N	19.13 E
Praça Sêca, ngh., Braz.	205a		22.54 S	43.21 W
Prachatice, Czech Rep.	24	G10	49.00 N	14.00 E
Prachin Buri, Thai.	64	E5	14.03 N	101.22 E
Prachuap Khiri Khan, Thai.	64	G4	11.49 N	99.47 E
Pradera, Col.	168	F3	3.25 N	76.15 W
Prades, Fr.	22	G8	42.37 N	2.26 E
Prado, Braz.	170	I6	17.17 S	39.15 W
Prado, Museo del, bldg., Spain	184a		40.25 N	3.41 W
Prado Dam, dam, Ca., U.S.	198		33.54 N	117.39 W
Prado Flood Control Basin, bas., Ca., U.S.	198		33.54 N	117.38 W
Prados, Braz.	170	K3	21.03 S	44.05 W
Præstø, Den.	16	L10	55.07 N	12.03 E
Prague see Praha, Czech Rep.	24	F10	50.05 N	14.26 E
Prague, Ne., U.S.	140	F16	41.18 N	96.48 W
Prague, Ok., U.S.	134	B2	35.28 N	96.40 W
Praha (Prague), Czech Rep.	24	F10	50.05 N	14.26 E
Praha, mtn., Czech Rep.	24	G9	49.40 N	13.49 E
Prahova, state, Rom.	36	D13	45.00 N	26.00 E
Prahova, stm., Rom.	36	E13	44.43 N	26.27 E
Prahran, Austl.	192b		37.51 S	144.59 E
Praia, C.V.	85a	I10	14.55 N	23.31 W
Praia da Cruz Quebrada, Port.	184c		38.42 N	9.14 W
Praia das Maçãs, Port.	184c		38.50 N	9.28 W
Praia Funda, Ponta da, c., Braz.	205a		23.05 S	43.33 W
Praia Grande, Braz.	172	D13	29.11 S	49.57 W
Prainha, Braz.	164	D7	1.47 S	53.28 W
Prainha Nova, Braz.	164	E5	7.29 S	60.37 W
Prairie, Austl.	98	C5	20.51 S	144.35 E
Prairie, stm., Mi., U.S.	126	G4	41.54 N	85.38 W
Prairie, stm., Mn., U.S.	128	D5	47.13 N	93.30 W
Prairie, stm., Wi., U.S.	128	F9	45.10 N	89.42 W
Prairie City, Il., U.S.	130	D7	40.36 N	90.27 W
Prairie City, Ia., U.S.	130	C4	41.35 N	93.13 W
Prairie City, Or., U.S.	146	F8	44.27 N	118.42 W
Prairie Creek, stm., Il., U.S.	196		41.36 N	87.40 W
Prairie Creek, stm., Ne., U.S.	140	F15	41.21 N	97.33 W
Prairie Dog Creek, stm., Ks., U.S.	138	B8	40.00 N	99.23 W
Prairie du Chien, Wi., U.S.	130	A6	43.03 N	91.08 W
Prairie du Sac, Wi., U.S.	128	H9	43.17 N	89.43 W
Prairie Elk Creek, stm., Mt., U.S.	142	G8	48.00 N	105.51 W
Prairie Grove, Ar., U.S.	130	H3	35.58 N	94.18 W
Prairie River, Sk., Can.	142	B11	52.51 N	102.58 W
Prairies, Coteau des, hills, U.S.	140	C16	44.30 N	96.45 W
Prairies, Lake of the, res., Can.	142	C12	51.05 N	101.25 W
Prairies, Rivière des, stm., Qc., Can.	193a		45.42 N	73.29 W
Prairie View, Il., U.S.	196		42.12 N	87.57 W
Prairie View, Tx., U.S.	136	D12	30.05 N	95.59 W
Prairie Village, Ks., U.S.	138	B14	38.59 N	94.37 W
Prakhon Chai, Thai.	64	E6	14.36 N	103.04 E
Pralls Island, i., N.Y., U.S.	194		40.37 N	74.12 W
Pran Buri, Thai.	64	F4	12.22 N	99.55 E
Pran Buri, stm., Thai.	64	F4	12.24 N	99.59 E
Prangli, i., Est.	26	A8	59.37 N	25.00 E
Prānhita, stm., India	69	B5	18.50 N	79.55 E
Prapa, Khlong, can., Thai.	187a		13.46 N	100.32 E
Prapat, Indon.	66	B1	2.40 N	98.56 E
Praslin, i., Sey.	89b	j13	4.19 S	55.44 E
Prasonísi, Ákra, c., Grc.	34	H10	35.53 N	27.46 E
Praszka, Pol.	24	E14	51.04 N	18.26 E
Prata, Braz.	170	J1	19.16 S	48.54 W
Prata, Braz.	205a		22.45 S	43.25 W
Prata, stm., Braz.	170	I2	17.28 S	46.35 W
Prata, stm., Braz.	170	J1	19.22 S	49.19 W
Prata, Rio da, stm., Braz.	205a		22.56 S	43.34 W
Pratāpgarh, India	70	F5	24.01 N	74.47 E
Pratápolis, Braz.	170	K2	20.45 S	46.52 W
Pratas Island see Tungsha Tao, i., Tai.	58	K7	20.42 N	116.43 E
Prat de Llobregat see El Prat de Llobregat, Spain	28	C13	41.20 N	2.05 E
Prater, p.o.i., Aus.	182b		48.12 N	16.25 E
Prathet Thai see Thailand, ctry., Asia	64	E5	15.00 N	100.00 E
Pratinha, Braz.	170	J2	19.45 S	46.24 W
Prato, Italy	30	G8	43.53 N	11.05 E
Pratt, Ks., U.S.	138	D10	37.38 N	98.44 W
Pratt's Bottom, ngh., Eng., U.K.	178		51.20 N	0.07 E
Prattsburg, N.Y., U.S.	124	B8	42.31 N	77.17 W
Prattville, Al., U.S.	134	E12	32.27 N	86.27 W
Pratudão, stm., Braz.	170	H3	13.56 S	44.55 W
Pravdinsk, Russia	26	F3	54.26 N	21.01 E
Pravdinskij, Russia	26	D20	56.03 N	37.52 E
Pravia, Spain	28	A4	43.30 N	6.06 W
Prawet Buri Rom, Khlong, can., Thai.	187a		13.42 N	100.35 E
Praya, Indon.	66	H10	8.42 S	116.17 E
Preajba, Rom.	36	E12	44.24 N	25.20 E
Preakness Brook, stm., N.J., U.S.	194		40.54 N	74.15 W
Preakness Mountain, mtn., N.J., U.S.	194		40.58 N	74.13 W
Preakness Valley Park, p.o.i., N.J., U.S.	194		40.55 N	74.14 W
Prečistoe, Russia	26	E15	55.30 N	32.21 E
Prečistoe, Russia	26	E17	55.39 N	34.55 E
Prečistoe, Russia	40	B12	58.24 N	40.20 E
Précy-sur-Marne, Fr.	179		48.56 N	2.47 E
Predeal, Rom.	36	D12	45.30 N	25.34 E
Prédecelle, stm., Fr.	179		48.35 N	2.07 E
Predeşti, Rom.	36	E10	44.21 N	23.32 E
Preeceville, Sk., Can.	142	C11	51.57 N	102.39 W
Pré-en-Pail, Fr.	20	F8	48.27 N	0.12 W
Preetz, Ger.	24	B6	54.14 N	10.16 E
Pregarten, Aus.	24	H10	48.20 N	14.32 E
Pregnana, Italy	184b		45.31 N	9.00 E
Pregolja, stm., Russia	26	F3	54.41 N	20.22 E
Pregonero, Ven.	168	D6	8.00 N	71.46 W
Pregradnoe, Russia	40	I12	45.49 N	41.45 E
Preguiças, stm., Braz.	170	B4	2.33 S	42.44 W
Preila, Lith.	26	E4	55.22 N	21.02 E
Preiļi, Lat.	26	D9	56.17 N	26.43 E
Prěk Poŭthĭ, Camb.	64	G7	11.49 N	105.05 E
Prelate, Sk., Can.	142	D4	50.51 N	109.23 W
Přelouč, Czech Rep.	24	F11	50.02 N	15.33 E
Premià de Dalt, Spain	184d		41.31 N	2.21 E
Premià de Mar, Spain	184d		41.29 N	2.21 E
Premnitz, Ger.	24	D8	52.31 N	12.20 E
Premont, Tx., U.S.	136	G9	27.21 N	98.07 W
Premuda, Otok, i., Cro.	30	F11	44.20 N	14.37 E
Prenjasi see Prrenjas, Alb.	32	C14	41.04 N	20.32 E
Prentice, Wi., U.S.	128	F8	45.32 N	90.17 W
Prentiss, Ms., U.S.	134	F9	31.36 N	89.51 W
Prenton, Eng., U.K.	180		53.22 N	3.03 W
Prenzlau, Ger.	24	C9	53.19 N	13.52 E
Prenzlauer Berg, ngh., Ger.	182a		52.32 N	13.26 E
Preobraženie, Russia	54	C10	42.56 N	133.56 E
Preparis Island, i., Mya.	62	F7	14.53 N	93.41 E
Preparis North Channel, strt., Mya.	62	F7	15.32 N	94.05 E
Preparis South Channel, strt., Mya.	62	F7	14.37 N	93.53 E
Přerov, Czech Rep.	24	G13	49.27 N	17.27 E
Prescott, On., Can.	126	D14	44.43 N	75.31 W
Prescott, Az., U.S.	150	I4	34.33 N	112.28 W
Prescott, Ar., U.S.	134	D5	33.48 N	93.23 W
Prescott, Wi., U.S.	128	G6	44.45 N	92.47 W
Prescott Island, i., Nu., Can.	110	A11	73.03 N	96.49 W
Preševo, Yugo.	36	G8	42.17 N	21.39 E
Presho, S.D., U.S.	140	D12	43.54 N	100.03 W
Presidencia de la Plaza, Arg.	172	C8	26.59 S	59.50 W
Presidencia Roca, Arg.	172	C8	26.08 S	59.35 W
Presidencia Roque Sáenz Peña, Arg.	172	C7	26.47 S	60.25 W
Presidente Costa e Silva, Ponte, trans., Braz.	205a		22.53 S	43.10 W
Presidente Dutra, Braz.	170	C3	5.15 S	44.30 W
Presidente Epitácio, Braz.	166	D6	21.46 S	52.07 W
Presidente Hayes, state, Para.	172	B8	24.08 S	58.24 W
Presidente Nicolás Avellaneda, Parque, p.o.i., Arg.	206		34.39 S	58.29 W
Presidente Olegário, Braz.	170	J2	18.24 S	46.24 W
Presidente Prudente, Braz.	166	D6	22.07 S	51.23 W
Presidente Roosevelt, Estação, trans., Braz.	205b		23.33 S	46.36 W
Presidential Heights, Pa., U.S.	197b		40.34 N	80.03 W
Presidio, Tx., U.S.	136	E3	29.34 N	104.23 W
Presidio, stm., Mex.	154	D5	23.05 N	106.17 W
Presles-en-Brie, Fr.	179		48.43 N	2.45 E
Presnogor'kovka, Kaz.	48	D11	54.30 N	65.46 E
Prešov, Slvk.	24	H17	48.59 N	21.14 E
Prespa, Lake, l., Eur.	32	D14	40.54 N	21.02 E
Prespansko Ezero see Prespa, Lake, l., Eur.	32	D14	40.54 N	21.02 E
Prespes se Madhe, Liqeni i see Prespa, Lake, l., Eur.	32	D14	40.54 N	21.02 E
Prespes se Vogel, Liqeni i see Mikrí Préspa, Límni, l., Eur.	32	D15	40.46 N	21.06 E
Presque Isle, Me., U.S.	122	D8	46.41 N	68.00 W
Presque Isle, pen., Pa., U.S.	124	B5	42.09 N	80.05 W
Presque Isle, stm., U.S.	128	E9	46.41 N	89.58 W
Pressburg see Bratislava, Slvk.	24	H13	48.09 N	17.07 E
Prestbury, Eng., U.K.	180		53.17 N	2.09 W
Prestea, Ghana	84	H4	5.26 N	2.08 W
Presteid, Nor.	14	D6	68.05 N	15.38 E
Přeštice, Czech Rep.	24	G9	49.34 N	13.19 E
Presto, Pa., U.S.	197b		40.23 N	80.07 W
Preston, Eng., U.K.	10	H10	53.45 N	2.42 W
Preston, Ga., U.S.	134	E14	32.03 N	84.32 W
Preston, Id., U.S.	146	H15	42.06 N	111.52 W
Preston, Ia., U.S.	130	B7	42.03 N	90.25 W
Preston, Ks., U.S.	138	D10	37.45 N	98.33 W
Preston, Mn., U.S.	128	H6	43.40 N	92.05 W
Preston, mun., Eng., U.K.	180		53.48 N	2.42 W
Preston Airport, arpt., N.J., U.S.	194		40.22 N	74.15 W
Preston Brook, Eng., U.K.	180		53.19 N	2.39 W
Preston Brook Canal Tunnel, trans., Eng., U.K.	180		53.19 N	2.38 W
Preston North End Football Ground, p.o.i., Eng., U.K.	180		53.47 N	2.42 W
Preston Peak, mtn., Ca., U.S.	148	B2	41.50 N	123.37 W
Prestonsburg, Ky., U.S.	124	G3	37.40 N	82.47 W
Prestwick, Scot., U.K.	10	F8	55.29 N	4.37 W
Preto, stm., Braz.	168	I9	1.42 S	63.48 W
Preto, stm., Braz.	170	G1	13.37 S	48.06 W
Preto, stm., Braz.	170	B4	3.31 S	43.46 W
Preto, stm., Braz.	170	F3	11.21 S	43.52 W
Preto, stm., Braz.	170	K1	20.10 S	49.38 W
Preto, stm., Braz.	170	L4	22.14 S	43.06 W
Preto, stm., Braz.	170	I2	17.00 S	46.12 W
Preto do Igapó-açu, stm., Braz.	164	E5	4.25 S	59.48 W
Pretoria, S. Afr.	90	D9	25.45 S	28.11 E
Pretty Prairie, Ks., U.S.	138	D10	37.46 N	98.01 W
Preussisch Eylau see Bagrationovsk, Russia	26	F3	54.23 N	20.38 E
Préveza, Grc.	34	E3	38.57 N	20.45 E
Prey Lvéa, Camb.	64	G7	11.09 N	104.57 E
Prey Nób, Camb.	64	G6	10.38 N	103.47 E
Prey Vêng, Camb.	64	G7	11.29 N	105.19 E
Priadivka, Ukr.	38	E13	48.55 N	34.42 E
Pribilof Islands, is., Ak., U.S.	109	E5	57.00 N	170.00 W
Priboj, Yugo.	36	F6	43.34 N	19.32 E
Příbram, Czech Rep.	24	G10	49.41 N	14.00 E
Pribylovo, Russia	18	G15	60.25 N	28.41 E
Price, Tx., U.S.	136	B13	32.08 N	94.57 W
Price, Ut., U.S.	150	D6	39.35 N	110.48 W
Price, stm., Ut., U.S.	150	D6	39.11 N	110.06 W
Price Bend, b., N.Y., U.S.	194		40.55 N	73.24 W
Price Island, i., B.C., Can.	144	D2	52.22 N	128.40 W
Prichard, Al., U.S.	134	G10	30.44 N	88.04 W
Prickly Pear Cays, is., Anguilla	159a	a1	18.15 N	63.09 W
Prickly Point, c., Gren.	159e	r10	11.59 N	61.45 W
Priddy, Tx., U.S.	136	C9	31.39 N	98.30 W
Priego, Spain	28	D8	40.27 N	2.18 W
Priego de Córdoba, Spain	28	G6	37.26 N	4.11 W
Priekule, Lat.	26	D4	56.26 N	21.35 E
Priekule, Lith.	26	E4	55.33 N	21.19 E
Prienai, Lith.	26	F6	54.38 N	23.56 E
Prieska, S. Afr.	90	F6	29.39 S	22.44 E
Priest, stm., Id., U.S.	146	B10	48.10 N	116.53 W
Priest Lake, res., Id., U.S.	146	B9	48.34 N	116.52 W
Priest River, Id., U.S.	146	B10	48.11 N	116.54 W
Prieta, Peña, mtn., Spain	28	A6	43.01 N	4.44 W
Prieto, stm., P.R.	158a	b2	18.15 N	66.54 W
Prieto Diaz, Phil.	68	D5	13.02 N	124.11 E
Prievidza, Slvk.	24	H14	48.46 N	18.37 E
Prijedor, Bos.	36	E3	44.59 N	16.42 E
Prijepolje, Yugo.	36	F6	43.23 N	19.39 E
Prijutnoe, Russia	40	H13	46.06 N	43.30 E
Prijutovo, Russia	40	E19	53.53 N	53.56 E
Prikaspijskaja nizmennost' see Caspian Depression, pl.	48	E7	48.00 N	52.00 E
Prikumskij, Russia	40	I14	45.15 N	45.48 E
Prilep, Mac.	34	B4	41.21 N	21.33 E
Priluki, Russia	18	D26	63.13 N	39.08 E
Priluki, Russia	26	A22	59.15 N	39.53 E
Prima Porta, ngh., Italy	185a		42.00 N	12.29 E
Primeira Cruz, Braz.	170	B4	2.30 S	43.26 W
Primera, Tx., U.S.	136	H10	26.13 N	97.44 W
Primero, stm., Arg.	172	E6	30.49 S	62.50 W
Primero de Mayo, Mex.	136	G6	27.12 N	101.14 W
Primghar, Ia., U.S.	130	A2	43.05 N	95.37 W
Primore, Russia	26	F2	54.57 N	20.02 E
Primorka, Russia	18	F18	47.16 N	39.02 E
Primorsk, Russia	18	G15	60.21 N	28.37 E
Primorsk, Russia	26	F2	54.44 N	20.00 E
Primorsk, Russia	40	G14	49.16 N	45.02 E
Primorskij, Russia	54	C9	43.07 N	131.37 E
Primorskij hrebet, mts., Russia	50	F10	52.30 N	105.50 E
Primorsko, Blg.	36	G14	42.10 N	27.51 E
Primorsko-Ahtarsk, Russia	40	H10	46.02 N	38.10 E
Primos, Pa., U.S.	203		39.55 N	75.18 W
Primo Tapia, Mex.	148	K9	32.12 N	116.54 W
Primrose, S. Afr.	191d		26.12 S	28.10 E
Primrose, Pa., U.S.	197b		40.21 N	80.16 W
Primrose Brook, stm., N.J., U.S.	194		40.43 N	74.31 W
Primrose Lake, l., Can.	110	E9	54.55 N	109.45 W
Prims, stm., Ger.	20	E15	49.20 N	6.43 E
Prince Albert, Sk., Can.	142	A8	53.12 N	105.45 W
Prince Albert, S. Afr.	90	H6	33.13 S	22.01 E
Prince Albert Sound, strt., N.T., Can.	110	A7	70.27 N	114.49 W
Prince Alfred, Cape, c., N.T., Can.	109	B15	74.20 N	124.46 W
Prince Charles Island, i., Nu., Can.	110	B15	67.46 N	76.06 W
Prince Charles Mountains, mts., Ant.	103	C11	72.00 S	67.00 E
Prince Edward Island, state, Can.	122	D13	46.20 N	63.20 W
Prince Edward Island, i., P.E., Can.	106	E16	46.20 N	63.20 W
Prince Edward Island National Park, p.o.i., P.E., Can.	122	C10	46.29 N	63.25 W
Prince Edward Islands, is., S. Afr.	80	K9	46.33 S	37.44 E
Prince Edward Park, p.o.i., Austl.	192a		34.02 S	151.03 E
Prince Frederick, Md., U.S.	124	F9	38.32 N	76.35 W
Prince George, B.C., Can.	144	C8	53.54 N	122.45 W
Prince George, Va., U.S.	124	G8	37.13 N	77.15 W
Prince Georges Plaza, shp. cen., Md., U.S.	202c		38.58 N	76.57 W
Prince Gustaf Adolf Sea, s., Can.	108	B4	78.09 N	106.11 W
Prince of Wales, Cape, c., Ak., U.S.	109	C6	65.39 N	168.06 W
Prince of Wales Island, i., Austl.	96	B8	10.40 S	142.10 E
Prince of Wales Island, i., Nu., Can.	110	A11	72.40 N	99.00 W
Prince of Wales Island, i., Ak., U.S.	109	E13	55.47 N	132.50 W
Prince of Wales Strait, strt., N.T., Can.	109	B15	73.00 N	117.00 W
Prince Olav Coast, cst., Ant.	103	B9	68.30 S	42.30 E
Prince Patrick Island, i., N.T., Can.	109	A16	76.43 N	119.21 W
Prince Regent Inlet, b., Nu., Can.	110	A12	73.00 N	90.30 W
Prince Rupert, B.C., Can.	110	E4	54.18 N	130.16 W
Prince Rupert Bay, b., Dom.	159c	i5	15.34 N	61.29 W
Prince Rupert Bluff Point, c., Dom.	159c	i5	15.34 N	61.28 W
Princesa Isabel, Braz.	170	D6	7.44 S	38.00 W
Princes Bay, b., N.Y., U.S.	194		40.31 N	74.12 W
Princes Islands see Kızıl Adalar, is., Tur.	34	C11	40.52 N	29.05 E
Princess Anne, Md., U.S.	124	F10	38.12 N	75.41 W

Name / Page / Map Ref. / Latitude / Longitude

Princess Astrid Coast, cst., Ant. 103 C6 70.58 S 13.20 E
Princess Charlotte Bay, b., Austl. 96 B8 14.14 S 143.56 E
Princess Martha Coast, cst., Ant. 103 C4 72.00 S 7.30 W
Princess Ragnhild Coast, cst., Ant. 103 C7 71.01 S 28.48 E
Princess Royal Channel, strt., B.C., Can. 144 C2 53.08 N 128.36 W
Princess Royal Island, i., B.C., Can. 144 C2 52.57 N 128.49 W
Princes Town, Trin. 159f s12 10.16 N 61.22 W
Princeton, B.C., Can. 144 G10 49.27 N 120.30 W
Princeton, Ca., U.S. 148 D3 39.23 N 122.00 W
Princeton, Il., U.S. 130 C8 41.22 N 89.27 W
Princeton, In., U.S. 130 F10 38.21 N 87.34 W
Princeton, Ky., U.S. 130 G10 37.06 N 87.52 W
Princeton, Me., U.S. 122 E9 45.13 N 67.34 W
Princeton, Mi., U.S. 126 B2 46.16 N 87.28 W
Princeton, Mn., U.S. 128 F5 45.34 N 93.34 W
Princeton, Mo., U.S. 130 D4 40.24 N 93.34 W
Princeton, N.J., U.S. 124 D11 40.21 N 74.39 W
Princeton, N.C., U.S. 132 A7 35.28 N 78.10 W
Princeton, W.V., U.S. 124 G4 37.21 N 81.06 W
Princeton, Wi., U.S. 128 H9 43.50 N 89.08 W
Princeton Airfield, arpt., N.J., U.S. 194 40.24 N 74.39 W
Princeton Battlefield Park, hist., N.J., U.S. 194 40.20 N 74.41 W
Princeton Township, N.J., U.S. 194 40.22 N 74.40 W
Princeton University, educ., N.J., U.S. 194 40.21 N 74.39 W
Princeville, Qc., Can. 122 D5 46.10 N 71.53 W
Princeville, Il., U.S. 130 D8 40.55 N 89.45 W
Prince William Sound, strt., Ak., U.S. 109 D10 60.42 N 147.06 W
Príncipe, i., S. Tom./P. 84 I6 1.37 N 7.25 E
Príncipe da Beira, Braz. 166 B4 12.25 S 64.25 W
Prineville, Or., U.S. 146 F6 44.18 N 120.51 W
Prineville Reservoir, res., Or., U.S. 146 F6 44.07 N 120.41 W
Pringsewu, Indon. 66 F4 5.22 S 105.05 E
Pringy, Fr. 179 48.31 N 2.34 E
Prinses Margrietkanaal, can., Neth. 20 B14 52.50 N 5.40 E
Prins Karls Forland, i., Nor. 108 B27 78.32 N 11.10 E
Prinzapolka, Nic. 156 F6 13.23 N 83.34 W
Prinzapolka, stm., Nic. 156 F6 13.24 N 83.34 W
Prior, Cabo, c., Spain 28 A2 43.33 N 8.18 W
Priort, Ger. 182a 52.31 N 12.58 E
Priozërnyj, Kaz. 48 E14 47.39 N 84.17 E
Priozersk, Russia 18 F17 61.02 N 30.08 E
Pripet (Pryp'yat') (Pryp'iat') (Prypjac'), stm., Eur. 38 B3 51.21 N 30.10 E
Pripet Marshes, reg., Eur. 40 E5 52.00 N 27.00 E
Pripjat' see Pripet, stm., Eur. 38 B3 51.21 N 30.10 E
Pripjat' see Pryp'yat', stm., Eur. 38 B3 51.21 N 30.10 E
Pripoljarnyj Ural, mts., Russia 48 A9 65.00 N 60.00 E
Prirečnyj, Russia 14 C21 69.01 N 30.16 E
Prisele, Russia 26 E15 55.09 N 32.48 E
Pristen', Russia 40 F10 51.15 N 36.43 E
Priština, Yugo. 36 G8 42.40 N 21.10 E
Pritchett, Co., U.S. 138 D6 37.22 N 102.51 W
Pritzwalk, Ger. 24 C8 53.09 N 12.10 E
Privas, Fr. 22 E10 44.43 N 4.36 E
Priverno, Italy 32 C7 41.28 N 13.11 E
Privodino, Russia 12 F22 61.04 N 46.30 E
Privol'naja, Russia 38 G17 46.08 N 38.41 E
Privol'noe, Russia 40 F15 50.55 N 46.04 E
Privolže, Russia 40 E16 52.52 N 48.35 E
Privolžskaja vozvyšennost' (Volga Plateau), plat., Russia 40 E15 52.00 N 46.00 E
Privolžskij, Russia 40 F15 51.23 N 46.02 E
Privolžskoe, Russia 40 F15 51.05 N 45.56 E
Prizren, Yugo. 36 G7 42.12 N 20.44 E
Prizzi, Italy 32 G7 37.43 N 13.26 E
Prjamicyno, Russia 40 F10 51.38 N 35.57 E
Prjaža, Russia 18 F20 61.40 N 33.37 E
Prnjavor, Bos. 36 E4 44.52 N 17.40 E
Probolinggo, Indon. 66 G8 7.45 S 113.13 E
Probstzella, Ger. 24 F7 50.31 N 11.22 E
Prochowice, Pol. 24 E12 51.17 N 16.22 E
Procida, Isola di, i., Italy 32 D7 40.45 N 14.00 E
Procter, B.C., Can. 144 G14 49.36 N 116.56 W
Proctor, Mn., U.S. 128 E6 46.44 N 92.13 W
Proctor, Vt., U.S. 122 G3 43.39 N 73.02 W
Proctor Brook, stm., Ma., U.S. 201 42.32 N 70.54 W
Proctor Lake, res., Tx., U.S. 136 C9 32.00 N 98.29 W
Proddatūr, India 69 D4 14.44 N 78.33 E
Proença-a-Nova, Port. 28 E2 39.45 N 7.55 W
Progreso, Mex. 148 K10 32.35 N 115.36 W
Progreso, Mex. 154 B8 27.25 N 100.58 W
Progreso, Mex. 156 B3 21.16 N 89.39 W
Progreso, Ur. 172 G9 34.40 S 56.13 W
Prohladnyj, Russia 42 D11 43.44 N 44.02 E
Prohorkino, Russia 48 C14 59.31 N 79.25 E
Project City, Ca., U.S. 148 C3 40.40 N 122.20 W
Prokletije see North Albanian Alps, mts., Eur. 32 B13 42.27 N 19.47 E
Prokopevsk, Russia 48 D15 53.53 N 86.43 E
Prokuplje, Yugo. 36 F8 43.13 N 21.35 E
Prokuševo, Russia 18 H21 59.55 N 34.56 E
Proletarij, Russia 26 B14 58.25 N 31.41 E
Proletarsk, Russia 40 H12 46.41 N 41.43 E
Proletarskij, Russia 26 E20 55.01 N 37.23 E
Proletarskij, Russia 40 F9 50.48 N 35.46 E
Prolysovo, Russia 26 H17 52.53 N 34.10 E
Prome, Mya. 64 C2 18.49 N 95.13 E
Promyslovka, Russia 40 I15 45.43 N 47.09 E
Pronin, Russia 40 G13 49.12 N 42.12 E
Pronja, stm., Bela. 26 G14 53.27 N 31.01 E
Pronja, stm., Russia 26 F21 54.17 N 38.54 E
Pronsk, Russia 40 D11 54.06 N 39.35 E
Prony, Baie de, b., N. Cal. 101d n16 22.23 S 166.51 E
Prophet, stm., B.C., Can. 110 D6 58.45 N 122.43 W
Prophetstown, Il., U.S. 130 C8 41.39 N 89.56 W
Propriá, Braz. 170 F7 10.13 S 36.49 W
Propriano, Fr. 22 H14 41.41 N 8.54 E
Prorva, Kaz. 40 H18 46.01 N 53.18 E
Proserpine, Austl. 98 C7 20.23 S 148.34 E
Prosiana, Ukr. 38 E15 48.07 N 36.22 E
Prosiane, Ukr. 38 D14 49.43 N 35.50 E
Proskurov see Khmel'nyts'kyi, Ukr. 38 D5 49.25 N 27.00 E
Prosna, stm., Pol. 24 E14 52.08 N 17.40 E
Prosotsáni, Grc. 34 B6 41.10 N 23.58 E
Prospect, Austl. 192a 33.48 S 150.56 E
Prospect, Oh., U.S. 124 D2 40.26 N 83.11 W
Prospect Creek, stm., Austl. 192a 33.55 S 150.59 E
Prospect Heights, Il., U.S. 196 42.05 N 87.56 W
Prospect Hill, hill, Ma., U.S. 201 42.23 N 71.15 W
Prospect Hill Park, p.o.i., Ma., U.S. 201 42.23 N 71.15 W
Prospect Park, N.J., U.S. 194 40.56 N 74.10 W
Prospect Park, Pa., U.S. 203 39.53 N 75.18 W
Prospect Park, p.o.i., N.Y., U.S. 194 40.40 N 73.58 W
Prospect Park Lake, l., N.Y., U.S. 194 40.39 N 73.57 W
Prospect Plains, N.J., U.S. 194 40.19 N 74.28 W
Prospect Point, N.J., U.S. 194 40.58 N 74.38 W
Prospect Point, c., N.Y., U.S. 194 40.52 N 73.43 W
Prospect Reservoir, res., Austl. 192a 33.49 S 150.54 E
Prospectville, Pa., U.S. 203 40.13 N 75.11 W
Prosperi Airport, arpt., Il., U.S. 196 41.33 N 87.47 W
Prosperidad, Phil. 68 F5 8.34 N 125.54 E
Prosser, Wa., U.S. 146 D7 46.12 N 119.45 W
Prostějov, Czech Rep. 24 G13 49.29 N 17.07 E
Prostki, Pol. 24 C18 53.43 N 22.26 E
Proston, Austl. 98 F8 26.09 S 151.36 E
Prošyka, Bela. 26 F12 54.29 N 29.08 E
Proszowice, Pol. 24 F16 50.11 N 20.18 E
Protea, S. Afr. 191d 26.17 S 27.51 E
Protection, Ks., U.S. 138 D9 37.12 N 99.29 W
Protem, S. Afr. 90 I5 34.16 S 20.04 E
Protoka, stm., Russia 40 I10 45.44 N 37.46 E
Protva, stm., Russia 26 F20 54.50 N 37.17 E
Prötzeler Forst, for., Ger. 182a 52.40 N 13.53 E
Proud Lake State Recreation Area, p.o.i., Mi., U.S. 199 42.34 N 83.33 W
Provadija, Blg. 36 F14 43.10 N 27.27 E
Prøven (Kangersuatsiaq), Grnld. 108 C14 72.23 N 55.32 W
Provencal, La., U.S. 134 F5 31.39 N 93.12 W
Provence, hist. reg., Fr. 22 F12 44.00 N 6.00 E
Providence, Ky., U.S. 130 G10 37.23 N 87.45 W
Providence, R.I., U.S. 124 C14 41.50 N 71.24 W
Providence, Ut., U.S. 150 B5 41.43 N 111.49 W
Providence, Atoll de, i., Sey. 89b k12 9.14 S 51.02 E
Providence, Cape, c., N.Z. 102 H2 46.00 S 166.27 E
Providencia, Chile 204e 33.26 S 70.37 W
Providencia, Mex. 136 G4 27.05 N 103.32 W
Providencia, Isla de, i., Col. 156 F7 13.21 N 81.22 W
Providenciales, i., T./C. Is. 156 B11 21.47 N 72.17 W
Providenija, Russia 50 D26 64.23 N 173.18 W
Provincetown, Ma., U.S. 124 B15 42.03 N 70.11 W
Provins, Fr. 20 F12 48.33 N 3.18 E
Provo, Ut., U.S. 150 C5 40.12 N 111.37 W
Provo, stm., Ut., U.S. 150 C5 40.15 N 111.45 W
Provost, Ab., Can. 142 B3 52.21 N 110.15 W
Prozor, Bos. 36 F4 43.48 N 17.36 E
Prrenjas, Alb. 32 C14 41.04 N 20.32 E
Prudentópolis, Braz. 172 B12 25.12 S 50.58 W
Prudhoe Bay, Ak., U.S. 109 B10 70.18 N 148.09 W
Prudhoe Island, i., Austl. 98 C7 21.19 S 149.40 E
Prudianka, Ukr. 38 C15 50.14 N 36.10 E
Prudnik, Pol. 24 F13 50.19 N 17.35 E
Prüm, Ger. 24 F2 50.12 N 6.24 E
Prüm, stm., Ger. 20 D15 49.49 N 6.28 E
Prunay-le-Temple, Fr. 179 48.52 N 1.40 E
Prunay-sous-Ablis, Fr. 179 48.32 N 1.48 E
Pruszków, Pol. 24 D16 52.10 N 20.48 E
Prut, stm., Eur. 36 C15 45.27 N 28.12 E
Pružany, Bela. 26 H7 52.33 N 24.28 E
Pryazovs'ka vysochyna, plat., Ukr. 38 F16 47.30 N 37.30 E
Pryazovs'ke, Ukr. 38 G14 46.43 N 35.37 E
Prychornomors'ka nyzovyna, pl., Ukr. 38 G12 47.00 N 33.00 E
Prydniprovs'ka nyzovyna, pl., Ukr. 38 D12 50.00 N 32.00 E
Prydniprovs'ka vysochyna, plat., Ukr. 38 E9 49.00 N 32.00 E
Prydz Bay, b., Ant. 103 B12 69.00 S 76.00 E
Prykolotne, Ukr. 38 C16 50.08 N 37.22 E
Pryluky, Ukr. 38 C11 50.35 N 32.23 E
Prymors'k, Ukr. 38 G15 46.43 N 36.20 E
Prymors'ke, Ukr. 38 F16 47.11 N 37.42 E
Prymors'kyi, Ukr. 38 H14 45.06 N 35.29 E
Pryor, Ok., U.S. 132 H2 36.19 N 95.19 W
Pryor Creek, stm., Mt., U.S. 140 B4 45.53 N 108.19 W
Pryp'iat', Ukr. 38 B9 51.24 N 30.09 E
Pryp'iat' see Pripet, stm., Eur. 38 B3 51.21 N 30.10 E
Pryp'iat' see Pryp'yat', stm., Eur. 38 B3 51.21 N 30.10 E
Prypjac' see Pripet, stm., Eur. 38 B3 51.21 N 30.10 E
Prypjac' see Pryp'yat', stm., Eur. 38 B3 51.21 N 30.10 E
Pryputni, Ukr. 38 C11 50.57 N 32.14 E
Pryp'yat' (Pripet) (Pryp'iat') (Prypjac'), stm., Eur. 38 B3 51.21 N 30.10 E
Pryshyb, Ukr. 38 F14 47.15 N 35.19 E
Pryvil'ne, Ukr. 38 F11 47.29 N 32.18 E
Pryvitne, Ukr. 38 I13 44.49 N 34.41 E
Przasnysz, Pol. 24 D16 53.01 N 20.53 E
Przedbórz, Pol. 24 E15 51.04 N 19.55 E
Przemków, Pol. 24 E11 51.31 N 15.47 E
Przemyśl, Pol. 24 G18 49.47 N 22.46 E
Prževal'sk see Karakol, Kyrg. 48 F13 42.29 N 78.23 E
Przeworsk, Pol. 24 F18 50.03 N 22.30 E
Przysucha, Pol. 24 E16 51.21 N 20.37 E
Psachná, Grc. 34 E6 38.34 N 23.38 E
Psará, i., Grc. 34 E8 38.35 N 25.35 E
Psebaj, Russia 42 C9 44.06 N 40.47 E
Psël (Ps'ol), stm., Eur. 38 C13 49.01 N 33.33 E
Pselec, Russia 38 B15 51.17 N 36.32 E
Pšiš, gora, mtn., Russia 42 D9 43.24 N 41.12 E
Pskov, Russia 26 C11 57.48 N 28.21 E
Pskov, Lake, l., Eur. 26 B10 58.00 N 28.00 E
Pskovskaja oblast', co., Russia 26 C11 57.00 N 29.00 E
Pskovskoe ozero see Pskov, Lake, l., Eur. 26 B10 58.00 N 28.00 E
Ps'ol (Psël), stm., Eur. 38 C13 49.01 N 33.33 E
Psychikón, Grc. 185c 38.01 N 23.46 E
Psyttáleia, i., Grc. 185c 37.56 N 23.35 E
Pszczyna, Pol. 24 G14 49.58 N 18.57 E
Ptarmigan, Cape, c., N.T., Can. 110 A7 71.01 N 118.18 W
Ptolemaís, Grc. 34 C4 40.31 N 21.42 E
Ptuj, Slvn. 30 D12 46.25 N 15.52 E
Puakatike, Volcán, vol., Chile 100l e30 27.06 S 109.15 W
Puamau, Baie, b., Fr. Poly. 100g r19 9.45 S 138.52 W
Puán, Arg. 172 H6 37.32 S 62.46 W
Pu'apu'a, Samoa 101c g11 13.34 S 172.12 W
Pubnico, N.S., Can. 122 G11 43.42 N 65.46 W
Pucallpa, Peru 164 E3 8.23 S 74.32 W
Pucará, Bol. 166 C4 18.43 S 64.11 W
Puces, stm., On., Can. 199 42.18 N 82.47 W
Pučeveem, stm., Russia 50 C23 68.51 N 170.24 E
Pučež, Russia 40 C13 56.58 N 43.11 E
Pucheng, China 58 H8 27.55 N 118.32 E
Pucheng, China 58 D3 34.57 N 109.34 E
Pucheta, Arg. 172 D9 29.53 S 57.35 W
Púchov, Slvk. 24 G14 49.07 N 18.18 E
Pucioasa, Rom. 36 D12 45.04 N 25.28 E
Pučišća, Cro. 30 G13 43.21 N 16.44 E
Puck, Pol. 24 B14 54.43 N 18.24 E
Pucketa Creek, stm., Pa., U.S. 197b 40.33 N 79.45 W
Pudahuel, Chile 204e 33.26 S 70.46 W
Pudasjärvi, Fin. 18 B13 65.21 N 26.59 E
Puddingstone Reservoir, res., Ca., U.S. 198 34.05 N 117.48 W
Puddington, Eng., U.K. 180 53.15 N 3.00 W
Pudem, Russia 40 B18 58.17 N 52.09 E
Pudož, Russia 18 F23 61.48 N 36.33 E
Puduari, stm., Braz. 168 I11 2.04 S 61.12 W
Puduchcheri see Pondicherry, India 69 F4 11.55 N 79.49 E
Pudukkottai, India 69 F4 10.22 N 78.49 E
Puebla, Mex. 154 F9 19.02 N 98.11 W
Puebla, state, Mex. 154 F10 18.50 N 98.00 W
Puebla de Alcocer, Spain 28 F5 38.59 N 5.15 W
Puebla de Don Fadrique, Spain 28 G8 37.57 N 2.26 W
Puebla de Don Rodrigo, Spain 28 E6 39.05 N 4.37 W
Puebla de Sanabria, Spain 28 B4 42.02 N 6.37 W
Puebla de Trives see Pobra de Trives, Spain 28 B3 42.20 N 7.14 W
Pueblito, Mex. 136 E2 29.06 N 105.06 W
Pueblito de Ponce, P.R. 158a b2 18.26 N 66.57 W
Pueblo, Co., U.S. 138 C4 38.15 N 104.36 W
Pueblo Libre, Peru 204d 12.05 S 77.04 W
Pueblo Mountain, mtn., Or., U.S. 148 A7 42.06 N 118.39 W
Pueblonuevo, Col. 168 C4 8.31 N 75.15 W
Pueblo Nuevo, P.R. 158a b2 18.27 N 66.50 W
Pueblo Nuevo, Ven. 168 B7 11.56 N 69.55 W
Pueblo Nuevo, ngh., Spain 184a 40.26 N 3.39 W
Pueblo of Acoma, N.M., U.S. 150 H9 35.04 N 107.42 W
Pueblo Reservoir, res., Co., U.S. 138 C3 38.16 N 104.45 W
Pueblo Viejo, Laguna, l., Mex. 154 D10 22.10 N 97.53 W
Pueblo Yaqui, Mex. 154 B4 27.21 N 110.02 W
Puelches, Arg. 172 I5 38.09 S 65.55 W
Puenteáreas see Ponteareas, Spain 28 B2 42.10 N 8.30 W
Puente-Caldelas see Ponte-Caldelas, Spain 28 B2 42.23 N 8.30 W
Puente de Arganda, Spain 184a 40.19 N 3.31 W
Puente del Arzobispo, Spain 28 E5 39.48 N 5.10 W
Puentedeume see Pontedeume, Spain 28 A2 43.24 N 8.10 W
Puente Genil, Spain 28 G6 37.23 N 4.47 W
Puente Hills, hills, Ca., U.S. 198 34.00 N 117.55 W
Puente Hills Mall, shp. cen., Ca., U.S. 198 33.59 N 117.56 W
Puente la Reina, Spain 28 B9 42.40 N 1.49 W
Puente Nuevo, Embalse de, res., Spain 28 F5 38.00 N 5.00 W
Puente Piedra, Peru 204d 11.57 S 77.05 W
Pueo Point, c., Hi., U.S. 100a b1 21.54 N 160.05 W
Pu'er, China 64 A5 23.07 N 101.01 E
Puerca, Punta, c., P.R. 158a b4 18.14 N 65.36 W
Puerco, stm., U.S. 150 I7 34.53 N 110.07 W
Puerco, stm., N.M., U.S. 150 I10 34.22 N 106.50 W
Puerto Acosta, Bol. 166 C3 15.32 S 69.14 W
Puerto Adela, Para. 172 B10 24.32 S 54.17 W
Puerto Aisén, Chile 176 I2 45.14 S 72.15 W
Puerto Alegre, Bol. 166 B4 13.53 S 61.36 W
Puerto Ángel, Mex. 154 H10 15.39 N 96.29 W
Puerto Arista, Mex. 156 H12 15.56 N 93.48 W
Puerto Armuelles, Pan. 156 H6 8.17 N 82.52 W
Puerto Asís, Col. 168 G3 0.31 N 76.30 W
Puerto Ayacucho, Ven. 168 E8 5.40 N 67.38 W
Puerto Bahía Negra, Para. 166 D5 20.13 S 58.11 W
Puerto Baquerizo Moreno, Ec. 164a i12 0.54 S 89.36 W
Puerto Barrios, Guat. 156 E3 15.43 N 88.35 W
Puerto Bermúdez, Peru 164 F3 10.20 S 74.54 W
Puerto Berrío, Col. 168 D4 6.28 N 74.25 W
Puerto Bolívar, Col. 168 A5 12.14 N 71.58 W
Puerto Boyacá, Col. 168 E4 5.57 N 74.34 W
Puerto Cabello, Ven. 168 B7 10.28 N 68.00 W
Puerto Cabezas, Nic. 156 F6 14.01 N 83.23 W
Puerto Carreño, Col. 168 D8 6.10 N 67.29 W
Puerto Chicama, Peru 164 E2 7.41 S 79.24 W
Puerto Colombia, Col. 168 B4 10.59 N 74.58 W
Puerto Cortés, Hond. 156 E3 15.50 N 87.56 W
Puerto Cumarebo, Ven. 168 B7 11.29 N 69.21 W
Puerto de la Cruz, Spain 84 D1 28.23 N 16.33 W
Puerto Delicia, Arg. 172 C10 26.11 S 54.36 W
Puerto del Rosario, Spain 84 D2 28.29 N 13.51 W
Puerto de Pollensa see Es Port de Pollença, Spain 28 E14 39.54 N 3.04 E
Puerto Deseado, Arg. 166 I3 47.44 S 65.54 W
Puerto Escondido, Mex. 154 H10 15.51 N 97.04 W
Puerto Escondido, c., Ven. 158g p20 12.09 N 69.58 W
Puerto Esperanza, Arg. 172 B10 26.02 S 54.38 W
Puerto Fonciere, Para. 166 D5 22.21 S 57.48 W
Puerto Francisco de Orellana, Ec. 168 H3 0.27 S 76.57 W
Puerto Guaraní, Para. 166 D5 21.17 S 57.55 W
Puerto Heath, Bol. 166 B3 12.30 S 68.39 W
Puerto Iguazú, Arg. 172 B10 25.34 S 54.34 W
Puerto Ingeniero Ibáñez, Chile 166 I2 46.16 S 71.56 W
Puerto Inírida, Col. 168 F8 3.53 N 67.50 W
Puerto Juárez, Mex. 156 B4 21.10 N 86.48 W
Puerto la Cruz, Ven. 168 B9 10.13 N 64.38 W
Puerto la Plata, Zona Nacional, state, Arg. 206 34.52 S 57.52 W
Puerto Leguízamo, Col. 168 H4 0.11 S 74.46 W
Puerto Libertad, Arg. 172 B10 25.55 S 54.35 W
Puerto Libertad, Mex. 150 G6 29.54 N 112.40 W
Puerto Limón, Col. 168 F5 3.23 N 73.29 W
Puerto Limón, C.R. 156 G6 9.59 N 83.02 W
Puertollano, Spain 28 F6 38.41 N 4.06 W
Puerto Lobos, Arg. 166 H4 42.00 S 65.05 W
Puerto López, Col. 168 E5 4.04 N 72.57 W
Puerto Madero, Mex. 154 H12 14.43 N 92.25 W
Puerto Madryn, Arg. 166 H3 42.46 S 65.03 W
Puerto Maldonado, Peru 164 F4 12.36 S 69.11 W
Puerto Manatí, Cuba 156 B9 21.22 N 76.49 W
Puerto Montt, Chile 166 H2 41.28 S 72.57 W
Puerto Morelos, Mex. 156 B4 20.53 N 86.52 W
Puerto Nariño, Col. 168 E8 4.56 N 67.50 W
Puerto Natales, Chile 166 J2 51.42 S 72.29 W
Puerto Nuevo, Punta, c., P.R. 158a a3 18.29 N 66.23 W
Puerto Padre, Cuba 156 B9 21.11 N 76.35 W
Puerto Páez, Ven. 168 D8 6.13 N 67.27 W
Puerto Palmer, Pico, mtn., Mex. 136 G6 27.08 N 101.47 W
Puerto Peñasco, Mex. 120 F6 31.19 N 113.32 W
Puerto Pinasco, Para. 166 D5 22.37 S 57.49 W
Puerto Pirámides, Arg. 166 H4 42.34 S 64.15 W
Puerto Piray, Arg. 172 C10 26.28 S 54.42 W
Puerto Píritu, Ven. 168 B9 10.02 N 65.01 W
Puerto Plata, Dom. Rep. 156 C12 19.45 N 70.38 W
Puerto Portillo, Peru 164 E3 9.46 S 72.45 W
Puerto Presidente Stroessner see Ciudad del Este, Para. 172 B10 25.29 S 54.38 W
Puerto Princesa, Phil. 68 F2 9.44 N 118.44 E
Puerto Real, P.R. 158a b1 18.05 N 67.11 W
Puerto Real, Spain 28 H4 36.32 N 6.11 W
Puerto Rico, Arg. 172 C10 26.48 S 55.01 W
Puerto Rico, Bol. 166 B3 11.06 S 67.31 W
Puerto Rico, Col. 168 G4 1.54 N 75.09 W
Puerto Rico, dep., U.S. 160 D8 18.15 N 66.30 W
Puerto Rico, i., P.R. 106 H16 18.15 N 66.30 W
Puerto Rico Trench, unds. 176 G7 19.58 N 65.59 W
Puerto Rondón, Col. 168 D6 6.16 N 71.06 W
Puerto San José, Guat. 156 F2 13.55 N 90.49 W
Puerto San Julián, Arg. 166 I3 49.18 S 67.43 W
Puerto Santa Cruz, Arg. 166 J3 50.01 S 68.33 W
Puerto Sastre, Para. 166 D5 22.02 S 58.00 W
Puerto Siles, Bol. 166 B3 12.48 S 65.04 W
Puerto Suárez, Bol. 166 C5 18.57 S 57.51 W
Puerto Tejada, Col. 168 F3 3.14 N 76.24 W
Puerto Tolosa, Col. 168 H4 1.03 S 74.05 W
Puerto Umbría, Col. 168 G3 0.52 N 76.33 W
Puerto Vallarta, Mex. 154 E6 20.36 N 105.14 W
Puerto Varas, Chile 166 H2 41.19 S 72.58 W
Puerto Victoria, Arg. 172 C10 26.19 S 54.38 W
Puerto Victoria, Peru 164 E3 9.51 S 74.59 W
Puerto Viejo, C.R. 156 G5 10.27 N 84.04 W
Puerto Villamil, Ec. 164a i11 0.56 S 91.01 W
Puerto Villamizar, Col. 168 C5 8.19 N 72.26 W
Puerto Visser, Arg. 166 I3 45.24 S 67.08 W
Puerto Wilches, Col. 168 D5 7.20 N 73.54 W
Puerto Ybapobó, Para. 166 D5 23.38 S 57.22 W
Pueyrredón, Lago (Cochrane, Lago), l., S.A. 166 I2 47.20 S 71.56 W
Puffing Billy Railroad Station, trans., Austl. 192b 37.55 S 145.21 E
Pugačov, Russia 40 E16 52.01 N 48.48 E
Puget Sound, strt., Wa., U.S. 146 C4 47.49 N 122.27 W
Pughtown, Pa., U.S. 203 40.10 N 75.40 W
Puglia, state, Italy 32 C11 41.00 N 16.30 E
Pugong-ni, Kor., S. 189b 37.43 N 126.58 E
Pugŏ-ri, Kor., N. 54 D9 42.01 N 129.57 E
Pugwash, N.S., Can. 122 E13 45.50 N 63.39 W
Puhaviči, Bela. 26 G11 53.31 N 28.15 E
Puhi-waero see South West Cape, c., N.Z. 102 H2 47.16 S 167.28 E
Puhja, Est. 26 B9 58.20 N 26.18 E
Puhos, Fin. 18 E16 62.05 N 29.54 E
Puhosjärvi, l., Fin. 18 B14 65.19 N 27.55 E
Puiești, Rom. 36 C14 46.25 N 27.33 E
Puigcerdà, Spain 22 G7 42.26 N 1.55 E
Puigcerdà, Spain 28 B12 42.26 N 1.55 E
Puigmal (Puigmal d' Err), mtn., Eur. 28 B13 42.23 N 2.07 E
Puigmal d' Err (Puigmal), mtn., Eur. 28 B13 42.23 N 2.07 E
Puinān, India 190b 22.56 N 88.13 E
Puisaye, Collines de la, hills, Fr. 20 G12 47.37 N 3.14 E
Puiseux-en-France, Fr. 179 49.03 N 2.29 E
Puiseux-Pontoise, Fr. 179 49.03 N 2.01 E
Pujiang, China 58 G8 29.27 N 119.52 E
Pujilí, Ec. 168 H2 0.57 S 78.41 W
Pujun, Indon. 66 D9 1.21 S 114.21 E
Puka see Pukë, Alb. 32 B13 42.02 N 19.53 E
Pukaki, Lake, l., N.Z. 102 F3 44.07 S 170.10 E
Puk'ansan National Park, p.o.i., Kor., S. 189b 37.40 N 126.59 E
Pukaskwa National Park, p.o.i., On., Can. 114 B7 48.20 N 85.50 W
Pukch'ŏng-ŭp, Kor., N. 54 D8 40.14 N 128.18 E
Pukë, Alb. 32 B13 42.02 N 19.53 E
Pukeashun Mountain, mtn., B.C., Can. 144 E11 51.12 N 119.14 W
Pukekohe, N.Z. 102 C6 37.12 S 174.54 E
Pŭkhan-san, mtn., Kor., S. 189b 37.41 N 127.00 E
Pukhrāyān, India 70 E7 26.14 N 79.51 E
Pukou, China 58 H6 26.15 N 119.36 E
Puksoozero, Russia 12 E19 62.35 N 40.36 E
Pula, Cro. 30 F10 44.52 N 13.51 E
Pula, Italy 32 F3 39.01 N 9.00 E
Pulacayo, Bol. 166 D3 20.22 S 66.41 W
Pulangpisau, Indon. 66 E9 2.46 S 114.15 E
Pulantien see Xinjin, China 58 B9 39.23 N 121.59 E
Pulap, at., Micron. 94 C5 7.34 N 149.24 E
Púlar, Cerro, vol., Chile 172 B3 24.12 S 68.03 W
Pulaski, N.Y., U.S. 126 E13 43.33 N 76.07 W
Pulaski, Tn., U.S. 134 B11 35.12 N 87.01 W
Pulaski, Va., U.S. 124 G5 37.02 N 80.46 W
Pulaski, Wi., U.S. 126 D1 44.39 N 88.14 W
Pulau, stm., Indon. 60 G10 5.42 S 138.24 E
Pulaukida, Indon. 66 E3 2.44 S 102.32 E
Pulaukijang, Indon. 66 D3 0.40 S 103.13 E
Pulau Pinang, state, Malay. 64 J5 5.25 N 100.25 E
Puławy, Pol. 24 E18 51.25 N 21.58 E
Pulgaon, India 70 H7 20.43 N 78.19 E
Puli, Tai. 58 J9 23.58 N 120.58 E
Pulicat, India 69 E5 13.26 N 80.18 E
Pulicat Lake, l., India 69 E5 13.35 N 80.10 E
Puliyangudi, India 69 G3 9.10 N 77.24 E
Pulju, Fin. 14 D15 68.13 N 24.49 E
Pulkau, stm., Aus. 30 B12 48.43 N 16.20 E
Pulkkila, Fin. 18 C12 64.15 N 25.53 E
Pulkovo, ngh., Russia 183a 59.46 N 30.20 E
Pulkovo-2 Airport, arpt., Russia 183a 59.48 N 30.16 E
Pullman, Wa., U.S. 146 D9 46.43 N 117.10 W
Pullman, ngh., Il., U.S. 196 41.43 N 87.36 W
Pul'mo, Ukr. 38 B2 51.30 N 23.48 E
Pulog, Mount, mtn., Phil. 68 B3 16.36 N 120.54 E
Pulogadung, ngh., Indon. 187e 6.11 S 106.54 E
Pulon'ga, Russia 14 F31 66.16 N 39.59 E
Pulonga, stm., Russia 14 F30 66.15 N 39.58 E
Pulozero, Russia 14 D24 68.21 N 33.18 E
Pulsano, Italy 32 D11 40.23 N 17.22 E
Pułtusk, Pol. 24 D17 52.42 N 21.05 E
Pülümür, Tur. 42 F8 39.29 N 39.54 E
Puma Yumco, l., China 52 F3 28.32 N 90.24 E
Pumei, China 64 A7 23.29 N 105.16 E
Pumphrey, Md., U.S. 202b 39.13 N 76.38 W
Pumpkin Buttes, mtn., Wy., U.S. 140 D7 43.44 N 105.54 W
Pumpkin Creek, stm., Mt., U.S. 140 B7 46.15 N 105.45 W
Pumpkin Creek, stm., Ne., U.S. 140 F10 41.31 N 102.41 W
Puná, Isla, i., Ec. 164 D1 2.47 S 80.08 W
Punaauia, Fr. Poly. 100h v21 17.37 S 149.36 W
Punakha, Bhu. 70 E12 27.37 N 89.52 E
Punan, Indon. 66 C9 1.20 N 115.34 E
Punan, Indon. 66 B10 3.24 N 116.16 E
Punata, Bol. 166 C3 17.32 S 65.50 W
Pūnch, India 70 B5 33.46 N 74.05 E
Punchaw, B.C., Can. 144 C7 53.27 N 123.13 W
Punchbowl, Austl. 192a 33.56 S 151.03 E
Punda Milia, S. Afr. 90 C10 22.40 S 31.05 E
Pune (Poona), India 69 B1 18.32 N 73.51 E
P'ungam-ni, Kor., S. 56 B1 37.42 N 128.11 E
Punganūru, India 69 E4 13.21 N 78.34 E
Pungești, Rom. 36 C14 46.42 N 27.20 E
Punggol, Sing. 189c 1.25 N 103.55 E
Punggol, stm., Sing. 189c 1.25 N 103.54 E
Pungo, stm., N.C., U.S. 132 A9 35.21 N 76.34 W
P'ungsan-ŭp, Kor., N. 54 D7 40.47 N 128.09 E
Pungué, stm., Afr. 90 A12 19.49 S 34.44 E
Pungwe see Pungué, stm., Afr. 90 A12 19.49 S 34.44 E
Punia, D.R.C. 86 E5 1.28 S 26.26 E
Punilla, Sierra de la, mts., Arg. 172 D3 28.48 S 69.01 W
Punitaqui, Chile 172 E2 30.50 S 71.16 W
Punjab, state, India 70 C5 31.00 N 75.30 E
Punjab, state, Pak. 70 C4 31.00 N 72.00 E
Punkaharju, misc. cult., Fin. 18 F16 61.47 N 29.20 E
Punkalaidun, Fin. 18 F10 61.06 N 23.07 E
Punnichy, Sk., Can. 142 C9 51.22 N 104.17 W
Puno, Peru 164 G3 15.50 S 70.01 W
Punta, Castillo de la, hist., Cuba 204b 23.09 N 82.21 W
Punta, Cerro de, mtn., P.R. 158a b2 18.10 N 66.36 W
Punta Alta, Arg. 172 I6 38.53 S 62.04 W
Punta Arenas, Chile 166 J2 53.09 S 70.55 W
Punta Banda, Cabo, c., Mex. 120 F4 31.44 N 116.42 W
Punta Brava, ngh., Cuba 204b 23.01 N 82.30 W
Punta Cardón, Ven. 168 B6 11.37 N 70.12 W
Punta Colnett, Mex. 120 F4 31.04 N 116.12 W
Punta de Agua Creek (Tramperos Creek), stm., U.S. 138 E5 35.32 N 102.27 W
Punta de Díaz, Chile 172 C2 28.02 S 70.36 W
Punta del Cobre, Chile 172 C2 27.30 S 70.15 W
Punta del Este, Ur. 172 G10 34.58 S 54.56 W
Punta Delgada, Arg. 166 H4 42.45 S 63.39 W
Punta de los Llanos, Arg. 172 E4 30.09 S 66.33 W
Punta de Mata, Ven. 168 C10 9.42 N 63.37 W
Punta de Piedras, Ven. 168 B10 10.54 N 64.06 W
Punta Gorda, Belize 156 D3 16.06 N 88.48 W
Punta Gorda, Nic. 156 G6 11.31 N 83.47 W
Punta Gorda, Fl., U.S. 132 J3 26.55 N 82.03 W
Punta Gorda, Bahía de, b., Nic. 156 G6 11.15 N 83.45 W
Punta Negra, Salar de, pl., Chile 172 B3 24.48 S 68.56 W
Punta Prieta, Mex. 154 A1 28.59 N 114.11 W
Puntarenas, C.R. 156 G5 9.58 N 84.50 W
Punta Santiago, P.R. 158a b4 18.09 N 65.45 W
Puntas del Sauce, Ur. 172 F9 33.53 S 57.01 W
Punto Fijo, Ven. 168 B6 11.42 N 70.11 W
Puntzi Lake, l., B.C., Can. 144 D6 52.12 N 124.02 W
Punung, Indon. 66 H7 8.08 S 111.01 E
Punxsutawney, Pa., U.S. 124 D7 40.56 N 78.57 W
Puolanka, Fin. 18 C14 64.52 N 27.40 E
Puolo Point, c., Hi., U.S. 100a b2 21.54 N 159.36 W
Puper, Indon. 60 F9 0.10 S 131.17 E
Puppy's Point, c., Norf. I. 100i y24 29.01 S 167.55 E
Pup'yŏng, Kor., S. 189b 37.30 N 126.43 E
Puqi, China 58 G9 28.09 N 121.00 E
Puqi, China 58 G5 29.43 N 113.53 E
Puqian, China 58 L4 20.01 N 110.35 E
Puquio, Peru 164 F3 14.42 S 74.08 W
Pur, stm., Russia 48 A13 67.21 N 77.55 E
Puracé, Volcán, vol., Col. 168 F3 2.17 N 76.23 W
Pūranpur, India 70 D7 28.30 N 80.08 E
Purcell, Ok., U.S. 138 F11 35.01 N 97.22 W
Purcell Mountains, mts., N.A. 144 G15 49.28 N 116.13 W
Purcellville, Va., U.S. 124 E8 39.08 N 77.43 W
Purchase, N.Y., U.S. 194 41.02 N 73.43 W
Purchena, Spain 28 G8 37.21 N 2.22 W
Purdy, Mo., U.S. 130 H4 36.49 N 93.55 W
Purdy Islands see Mwilitau Islands, is., Pap. N. Gui. 101a a4 2.50 S 146.20 E
Puré (Purui), stm., S.A. 168 I6 1.39 S 68.08 W
Purgatoire, stm., Co., U.S. 138 D5 38.04 N 103.10 W
Purgatory Brook, stm., Ma., U.S. 201 42.11 N 71.11 W
Puri, India 70 I10 19.48 N 85.51 E
Purificación, Col. 168 F4 3.51 N 74.54 W
Purificación, Mex. 154 F6 19.42 N 104.36 W
Purificación, stm., Mex. 154 C9 23.57 N 98.40 W
Purikari neem, c., Est. 26 A8 59.39 N 25.41 E
Purísima, Mex. 136 E7 29.11 N 100.47 W
Purísima, Sierra de la, mts., Mex. 136 H6 26.29 N 101.47 W
Purisima Creek, stm., Ca., U.S. 200 37.24 N 122.26 W
Purleigh, Eng., U.K. 178 51.41 N 0.40 E
Purley, ngh., Eng., U.K. 178 51.20 N 0.07 W
Purmerend, Neth. 20 B13 52.31 N 4.57 E
Pūrna, stm., India 70 H5 19.06 N 77.01 E
Pūrna, stm., India 70 H6 21.05 N 76.00 E
Purnac, stm., Russia 14 F30 67.02 N 40.12 E
Purnea see Pūrnia, India 70 F11 25.46 N 87.28 E
Purnema, Russia 18 C24 64.23 N 37.27 E
Pūrnia, India 70 F11 25.46 N 87.28 E
Puronga, Russia 12 F19 60.08 N 40.53 E
Pursat see Poŭthĭsăt, Camb. 64 F6 12.32 N 103.55 E
Purui (Puré), stm., S.A. 168 I6 1.39 S 68.08 W
Purukcahu, Indon. 66 D9 0.37 S 114.33 E
Puruliya, India 70 G11 23.20 N 86.22 E
Puruni, stm., Guy. 168 D12 6.00 N 59.12 W
Purús (Purus), stm., S.A. 164 F3 3.40 S 61.28 W
Purus (Purús), stm., S.A. 164 E4 3.40 S 61.28 W
Puruvesi, l., Fin. 18 F16 61.50 N 29.24 E
Purvis, Ms., U.S. 134 F9 31.08 N 89.24 W
Purwakarta, Indon. 66 G5 6.33 S 107.25 E
Purwodadi, Indon. 66 G7 7.04 S 110.54 E
Purwodadi, Indon. 66 G6 7.48 S 109.59 E
Purwokerto, Indon. 66 G6 7.25 S 109.13 E
Purworejo, Indon. 66 G6 7.42 S 110.00 E
Pusa, Malay. 66 C7 1.36 N 111.17 E
Pusad, India 69 B3 19.54 N 77.34 E
Pusa Institute, sci., India 190a 28.38 N 77.10 E
Pusan (Fusan), Kor., S. 54 G8 35.05 N 129.02 E
Pusan-jikhalsi, state, Kor., S. 56 D2 35.10 N 129.05 E
Pusat Gayo, Pegunungan, mts., Indon. 64 J3 4.15 N 97.05 E
Pushkar, India 70 E5 26.30 N 74.33 E
Pushkarivka, Ukr. 38 E13 48.40 N 34.15 E

Name	Page	Map Ref.	Latitude	Longitude
Pushkin Airport, arpt., Russia	183a		59.41 N	30.21 E
Pushkin Drama Theatre, bldg., Russia	183a		59.56 N	30.21 E
Puškin, Russia	26	A13	59.42 N	30.25 E
Puškino, Russia	26	D20	56.00 N	37.50 E
Puškino, Russia	40	F15	51.13 N	46.58 E
Puškinskie Gory, Russia	26	D11	57.01 N	28.55 E
Puškinskij, Russia	183a		59.43 N	30.18 E
Puskwaskau, stm., Ab., Can.	144	A13	55.16 N	117.36 W
Pušlahta, Russia	18	C23	64.48 N	36.35 E
Pušnoj, Russia	18	C21	64.23 N	34.08 E
Püspökladány, Hung.	36	B8	47.19 N	21.07 E
Püssi, Est.	26	A10	59.21 N	27.03 E
Pustin', Russia	18	H22	59.52 N	35.34 E
Pustomyty, Ukr.	38	D2	49.42 N	23.55 E
Pustoška, Russia	26	D12	56.20 N	29.21 E
Pustozersk, Russia	12	C25	67.31 N	52.29 E
Puszczykowo, Pol.	24	D12	52.18 N	16.52 E
Putaendo, Chile	172	F2	32.37 S	70.44 W
Putah Creek, stm., Ca., U.S.	148	E4	38.31 N	121.47 W
Putang, stm., Indon.	187e		6.13 S	106.54 E
Putao, Mya.	62	C8	27.21 N	97.24 E
Puteaux, Fr.	179		48.53 N	2.14 E
Putfontein Landbouhoewes, S. Afr.	191d		26.08 S	28.24 E
Puth Kalān, ngh., India	190a		28.43 N	77.05 E
Putian, China	58	G6	29.16 N	114.58 E
Putian, China	58	I8	25.25 N	119.00 E
Putignano, Italy	32	D11	40.50 N	17.06 E
Putilkovo, Russia	183b		55.52 N	37.23 E
Puting, Tanjung, c., Indon.	66	E7	3.31 S	111.48 E
Putjatino, Russia	40	D12	54.10 N	41.07 E
Putla de Guerrero, Mex.	152	D5	17.00 N	97.54 W
Putnam, Ct., U.S.	124	C14	41.54 N	71.54 W
Putnam, Tx., U.S.	136	B8	32.22 N	99.12 W
Putnam Lake, l., Ct., U.S.	194		41.05 N	73.38 W
Putnamville Reservoir, res., Ma., U.S.	201		42.36 N	70.57 W
Putney, Ga., U.S.	132	E1	31.29 N	84.07 W
Putney, Vt., U.S.	124	B13	42.58 N	72.31 W
Putney, ngh., Eng., U.K.	178		51.28 N	0.13 W
Putorana, plato, plat., Russia	50	C7	69.00 N	95.00 E
Putri Narrows, strt., Asia	189c		1.27 N	103.42 E
Putsonderwater, S. Afr.	90	F5	29.09 S	21.51 E
Pütt, Ger.	181		51.11 N	6.59 E
Puttalam, Sri L.	69	G4	8.01 N	79.50 E
Puttalam Lagoon, b., Sri L.	69	G4	8.07 N	79.47 E
Puttgarden, Ger.	24	B7	54.29 N	11.12 E
Puttūr, India	69	E4	13.25 N	79.32 E
Putú, Chile	172	G1	35.13 S	72.17 W
Putumayo, state, Col.	168	G4	0.30 N	76.00 W
Putumayo (Içá), stm., S.A.	164	D3	3.06 S	67.56 W
Putuo, China	58	F10	29.58 N	122.17 E
Putussibau, Indon.	66	C8	0.50 N	112.54 E
Putyla, Ukr.	38	F4	48.00 N	25.02 E
Putyvl', Ukr.	38	B12	51.20 N	33.53 E
Pu'uhonua o Honaunau National Historical Park, p.o.i., Hi., U.S.	100a	d6	19.25 N	155.54 W
Puukohola Heiau National Historic Site, p.o.i., Hi., U.S.	100a	c5	20.01 N	155.48 W
Puu Kukui, mtn., Hi., U.S.	100a	c5	20.54 N	156.35 W
Puula, l., Fin.	18	F13	61.50 N	26.42 E
Puumala, Fin.	18	F15	61.31 N	28.11 E
Puurmani, Est.	26	B9	58.35 N	26.17 E
Puxico, Mo., U.S.	130	H7	36.57 N	90.09 W
Puyallup, Wa., U.S.	146	C4	47.11 N	122.17 W
Puyallup, stm., Wa., U.S.	146	C4	47.11 N	122.15 W
Puyang, China	58	D6	35.42 N	115.00 E
Puy-de-Dôme, state, Fr.	22	D9	45.45 N	3.05 E
Puylaurens, Fr.	28	A13	43.33 N	2.00 E
Puy-l'Évêque, Fr.	22	E7	44.30 N	1.08 E
Puymorens, Col de, p., Fr.	22	G7	42.30 N	1.49 E
Puyo, Ec.	168	H3	1.28 S	77.58 W
Pweto, D.R.C.	86	F5	8.28 S	28.54 E
Pwinbyu, Mya.	64	B2	20.13 N	94.45 E
Pwllheli, Wales, U.K.	10	I8	52.54 N	4.24 W
Pyalo, Mya.	64	C2	19.09 N	95.11 E
Pyapon, Mya.	64	D2	16.17 N	95.41 E
Pyawbwe, Mya.	64	B3	20.35 N	96.04 E
Pyaye, Mya.	64	C2	19.15 N	95.06 E
Pyčas, Russia	40	C18	56.30 N	52.27 E
Pyè see Prome, Mya.	64	C2	18.49 N	95.13 E
Pyhäjärvi (Pjuhjajarvi, ozero), l., Eur.	18	F16	61.53 N	29.57 E
Pyhäjärvi, l., Fin.	18	F8	61.00 N	22.18 E
Pyhäjärvi, l., Fin.	18	D12	63.35 N	25.57 E
Pyhäjärvi, l., Fin.	18	E11	62.43 N	25.29 E
Pyhäjärvi, l., Fin.	18	F10	61.26 N	23.31 E
Pyhäjoki, Fin.	18	C11	64.28 N	24.15 E
Pyhäjoki, stm., Fin.	18	D12	64.28 N	24.13 E
Pyhämaa, l., Fin.	18	G8	60.58 N	21.17 E
Pyhän-Häkin kansallispuisto, p.o.i., Fin.	18	E12	62.52 N	25.30 E
Pyhäsalmi, Fin.	18	D12	63.41 N	25.58 E
Pyhäselkä, Fin.	18	E16	62.27 N	29.58 E
Pyhäselkä, l., Fin.	18	E16	62.28 N	29.46 E
Pyhätunturi, mtn., Fin.	14	E18	67.01 N	27.09 E
Pyhätunturin kansallispuisto, p.o.i., Fin.	14	F18	67.01 N	27.10 E
Pyhtää, Fin.	18	G13	60.30 N	26.32 E
Pyinbongyi, Mya.	64	D3	17.34 N	96.33 E
Pyinkayaing, Mya.	64	E2	15.59 N	94.23 E
Pyinmana, Mya.	64	C3	19.44 N	96.12 E
Pýlos, Grc.	34	G4	36.55 N	21.43 E
Pymatuning Reservoir, res., U.S.	124	C5	41.37 N	80.30 W
Pymatuning State Park, p.o.i., Pa., U.S.	124	C5	41.30 N	80.27 W
Pymble, Austl.	192a		33.45 S	151.09 E
Pyŏktong-ŭp, Kor., N.	54	D6	40.34 N	125.19 E
P'yŏngch'ang, Kor., S.	56	B1	37.23 N	128.22 E
P'yonghae, Kor., S.	56	C2	36.45 N	129.26 E
P'yŏngt'aek, Kor., S.	54	F7	37.00 N	127.05 E
P'yŏngyang, Kor., N.	54	E6	39.01 N	125.44 E
Pyote, Tx., U.S.	136	C4	31.32 N	103.08 W
Pyramid Lake, l., Nv., U.S.	148	D6	40.01 N	119.35 W
Pyramid Lake, res., Ca., U.S.	120	D3	34.39 N	118.46 W
Pyramid Lake Indian Reservation, ind. res., Nv., U.S.	148	C6	40.12 N	119.36 W
Pyramid Peak, mtn., Wy., U.S.	146	G16	43.27 N	110.28 W
Pyrenees, mts., Eur.	28	B12	42.40 N	1.00 E
Pyrénées-Atlantiques, state, Fr.	22	F5	43.15 N	0.50 W
Pyrénées Occident, Parc National des, p.o.i., Fr.	22	G5	42.51 N	0.14 W
Pyrénées-Orientales, state, Fr.	22	G8	42.30 N	2.20 E
Pyrford, Eng., U.K.	178		51.19 N	0.30 W
Pýrgos, Grc.	34	F4	37.40 N	21.26 E
Pyriatyn, Ukr.	38	C11	50.14 N	32.31 E
Pyritz see Pyrzyce, Pol.	24	C10	53.09 N	14.53 E
Pyrohivka, Ukr.	38	B12	51.54 N	33.17 E
Pyrzyce, Pol.	24	C10	53.09 N	14.53 E
Pytalovo, Russia	26	C10	57.03 N	27.54 E
Pythonga, Lac, l., Qc., Can.	126	B13	46.23 N	76.25 W
Pyttegga, mtn., Nor.	16	E5	62.18 N	7.42 E
Pyttis see Pyhtää, Fin.	18	G13	60.30 N	26.32 E
Pyu, Mya.	64	C3	18.28 N	96.26 E
Pyuntaza, Mya.	64	D3	17.52 N	96.42 E
Pyūthān, Nepal	70	D9	28.07 N	82.54 E
Pyvėsa, stm., Lith.	26	E7	56.04 N	24.25 E
Pyzdry, Pol.	24	D13	52.10 N	17.43 E
Q				
Qaanaaq see Thule, Grnld.	108	B12	76.40 N	68.50 W
Qabbāsīn, Syria	76	B8	36.25 N	37.34 E
Qabırrı see Iori, stm., Asia	42	E11	41.02 N	46.27 E
Qacentina (Constantine), Alg.	84	B6	36.21 N	6.36 E
Qaddis Antwân, Deir el- (Saint Anthony, Monastery of), rel., Egypt	76	J3	28.55 N	32.21 E
Qāderābād, Iran	74	E13	30.17 N	53.16 E
Qā'emshahr, Iran	74	B13	36.27 N	52.51 E
Qā'en, Iran	72	C8	33.43 N	59.10 E
Qagan Moron, stm., China	54	C3	43.13 N	119.03 E
Qagan Nur, l., China	52	C7	43.24 N	114.50 E
Qahar Youyi Zhongqi, China	58	A5	41.16 N	112.37 E
Qaidam, stm., China	52	D4	36.51 N	95.57 E
Qaidam Pendi, bas., China	52	D3	37.00 N	95.00 E
Qalāt, Afg.	72	C10	32.06 N	66.53 E
Qal'at al-Mu'azzam, Sau. Ar.	74	G5	27.44 N	37.30 E
Qal'at ash-Shaqīf (Beaufort Castle), hist., Leb.	76	E6	33.19 N	35.32 E
Qal'at Bīshah, Sau. Ar.	72	E5	19.59 N	42.36 E
Qal'at Şāliḩ, Iraq	74	E10	31.31 N	47.19 E
Qal'at Sukkar, Iraq	74	E10	31.51 N	46.05 E
Qal'eh-ye Now, Afg.	72	C9	34.59 N	63.07 E
Qalībah, Wādī al-, stm., Sau. Ar.	76	J8	28.31 N	37.37 E
Qalīb ash-Shuyūkh, Kuw.	74	F10	29.09 N	47.59 E
Qallābāt, Sudan	82	E7	12.57 N	36.08 E
Qalyūb, Egypt	76	H2	30.10 N	31.12 E
Qalyûb, Egypt	191c		30.11 N	31.12 E
Qamar, Ghubbat al-, b., Yemen	72	F7	16.00 N	52.30 E
Qamdo, China	52	E4	31.10 N	97.08 E
Qamea, i., Fiji	101e	p20	16.46 S	179.46 W
Qamīnis, Libya	82	A3	31.39 N	20.00 E
Qamr-ud-dīn Kārez, Pak.	70	C2	31.39 N	68.24 E
Qamşar, Iran	74	D12	33.45 N	51.28 E
Qanā, Leb.	76	E6	33.12 N	35.18 E
Qanā, Sau. Ar.	74	G7	27.46 N	41.26 E
Qandahār, Afg.	72	C10	31.36 N	65.42 E
Qandala, Som.	86	B9	11.27 N	49.52 E
Qaqortoq see Julianehåb, Grnld.	108	E16	60.43 N	46.01 W
Qarabağlar, Azer.	42	F11	39.25 N	45.12 E
Qārah, Sau. Ar.	74	F7	29.52 N	40.13 E
Qārah, Syria	76	D7	34.09 N	36.44 E
Qarazhal see Karažal, Kaz.	48	E12	48.01 N	70.49 E
Qardho, Som.	86	C9	9.30 N	49.05 E
Qareh, stm., Iran	74	C12	34.37 N	51.44 E
Qareh Sū, stm., Iran	74	A10	39.26 N	47.22 E
Qarqan, stm., China	48	G15	39.26 N	88.22 E
Qartabā, Leb.	76	D6	34.06 N	35.51 E
Qārūn, Birket (Moeris, Lake), l., Egypt	76	I1	29.28 N	30.38 E
Qarwāw, Ra's, c., Oman	72	F8	17.55 N	56.21 E
Qashqeh, Kūh-e, mtn., Iran	74	F14	28.23 N	55.18 E
Qasigiannguit see Christianshåb, Grnld.	108	D15	68.50 N	51.12 W
Qaşr al-Azraq, hist., Jord.	76	G7	31.53 N	36.49 E
Qaşr al-Kharānah, hist., Jord.	76	G7	31.44 N	36.28 E
Qaşr al-Mushattá, hist., Jord.	76	G7	31.44 N	36.01 E
Qaşr aṭ-Ṭūbah, hist., Jord.	76	G7	31.20 N	36.34 E
Qaşr Dab'ah, hist., Jord.	76	G7	31.36 N	36.03 E
Qaşr-e Fīrūzeh, Iran	185d		35.40 N	51.32 E
Qaşr-e Shīrīn, Iran	74	C9	34.30 N	45.35 E
Qasr Farâfra, Egypt	82	B5	27.03 N	27.58 E
Qatanā, Syria	76	E7	33.26 N	36.05 E
Qatar, ctry., Asia	74	H12	25.00 N	51.10 E
Qaṭar see Qatar, ctry., Asia	74	H12	25.00 N	51.10 E
Qatmah, Syria	76	B7	36.35 N	36.57 E
Qatrani, Gebel, hill, Egypt	76	I1	29.41 N	30.35 E
Qattâra, Munkhafad el- (Qattara Depression), depr., Egypt	82	B5	30.00 N	27.30 E
Qattara Depression see Qattâra, Munkhafad el-, depr., Egypt	82	B5	30.00 N	27.30 E
Qaţţīnah, Buḩayrat, res., Syria	76	D7	34.39 N	36.34 E
Qawz Rajab, Sudan	82	D7	16.03 N	35.35 E
Qax, Azer.	42	E11	41.26 N	46.55 E
Qāzigund, India	70	B5	33.37 N	75.07 E
Qazımämmäd, Azer.	42	E13	40.02 N	48.56 E
Qazvīn, Iran	74	B11	36.16 N	49.58 E
Qena, Egypt	74	G3	26.10 N	32.43 E
Qena, Wadi, stm., Egypt	76	K3	26.12 N	32.44 E
Qeqertarsuaq see Godhavn, Grnld.	108	D15	69.15 N	53.33 W
Qesari, Horbat (Caesarea), hist., Isr.	76	F5	32.29 N	34.54 E
Qeshm, Iran	74	G15	26.57 N	56.15 E
Qeshm, Jazīreh-ye, i., Iran	74	G14	26.45 N	55.45 E
Qetura, Isr.	76	I5	29.58 N	35.03 E
Qeydār, Iran	74	B11	36.07 N	48.35 E
Qezel Owzan, stm., Iran	74	B11	36.46 N	49.08 E
Qi, stm., China	58	D6	35.29 N	114.16 E
Qian, stm., China	58	J3	23.24 N	110.05 E
Qian'an, China	54	B6	45.00 N	124.02 E
Qian Gorlos, China	52	B9	45.06 N	124.49 E
Qianjiang, China	58	J3	23.37 N	108.58 E
Qianning, China	52	E5	30.28 N	101.30 E
Qianpai, China	58	J4	22.23 N	111.14 E
Qianshan, China	58	F7	30.42 N	116.36 E
Qianwei, China	52	F5	29.12 N	103.57 E
Qianxi, China	58	H2	26.56 N	106.07 E
Qianyang, China	58	H3	27.11 N	110.02 E
Qiaojiang, China	187b		31.15 N	121.19 E
Qiaolima, China	70	A8	34.31 N	80.58 E
Qiaomu, China	58	B6	39.34 N	114.27 E
Qiaowan, China	52	C4	40.35 N	96.40 E
Qiaoxu, China	58	J3	22.50 N	109.51 E
Qidong, China	58	F9	26.44 N	112.04 E
Qiemo, China	48	G15	38.09 N	85.29 E
Qieshikou, China	189a		39.59 N	116.24 E
Qift, Egypt	74	G3	26.00 N	32.49 E
Qigong, China	52	F5	28.38 N	100.38 E
Qijiang, China	58	G2	29.02 N	106.39 E
Qilaguganni Shan, mtn., China	70	D11	28.46 N	87.38 E
Qila Lādgasht, Pak.	62	C1	27.54 N	62.55 E
Qila Saifullāh, Pak.	70	C2	30.44 N	68.15 E
Qilian Shan, mtn., China	52	D4	39.12 N	98.35 E
Qilian Shan, mts., China	52	D4	39.06 N	98.40 E
Qilimiao, China	58	D3	34.19 N	108.27 E
Qimen, China	58	G7	29.50 N	117.42 E
Qin, stm., China	58	D5	35.01 N	113.24 E
Qing, stm., China	58	F4	30.23 N	111.26 E
Qingcheng, China	58	C7	37.11 N	117.40 E
Qingchengzi, China	54	D5	40.43 N	123.36 E
Qingdao (Tsingtao), China	58	C9	36.05 N	120.20 E
Qingfeng, China	58	D6	35.54 N	115.06 E
Qinggang, China	52	B10	46.41 N	126.06 E
Qinghai, state, China	52	D4	36.00 N	96.00 E
Qinghai Hu, l., China	52	D5	36.48 N	100.06 E
Qingjian, China	58	C4	37.07 N	110.05 E
Qingjiang, China	58	G6	28.05 N	115.29 E
Qingjiang, China	58	E8	33.36 N	119.00 E
Qinglong, China	58	F6	25.46 N	105.08 E
Qinglonggang, China	58	F9	31.52 N	121.13 E
Qingshan, China	54	I3	30.36 N	119.41 E
Qingshen, China	52	F5	29.50 N	103.51 E
Qingshui, China	52	D4	39.21 N	99.00 E
Qingshui, China	58	D2	34.42 N	106.21 E
Qingshui, stm., China	52	C2	37.28 N	105.31 E
Qingshui, stm., China	58	H3	27.08 N	109.36 E
Qingtang, China	58	I5	24.12 N	113.51 E
Qingtongxia, China	52	C1	37.54 N	105.57 E
Qingyang, China	54	B8	45.20 N	128.47 E
Qingyang, China	58	F7	30.37 N	117.51 E
Qingyang, China	58	C2	36.00 N	107.52 E
Qingyuan, China	54	C6	42.07 N	124.57 E
Qingyuan, China	58	J5	23.42 N	113.02 E
Qingyuan, China	58	H8	27.37 N	119.05 E
Qingyuan, China	58	I3	24.35 N	108.45 E
Qingyuan see Baoding, China	58	B6	38.51 N	115.29 E
Qing Zang Gaoyuan (Tibet, Plateau of), plat., China	62	B6	33.00 N	92.00 E
Qingzhen, China	58	H2	26.27 N	106.21 E
Qinhuangdao, China	58	B8	39.56 N	119.36 E
Qin Ling, mts., China	58	E4	34.00 N	108.00 E
Qinshihuang Mausoleum (Terra Cotta Army), hist., China	58	D3	34.19 N	109.09 E
Qinshui, China	58	D5	35.41 N	112.13 E
Qinxian, China	58	C5	36.46 N	112.41 E
Qinyang, China	58	D5	35.05 N	112.56 E
Qinyuan, China	58	C5	36.30 N	112.19 E
Qinzhou, China	58	J3	21.57 N	108.37 E
Qionghai, China	58	L4	19.15 N	110.28 E
Qionglai, China	58	E5	30.24 N	103.27 E
Qionglaishan, mts., China	52	E5	31.08 N	102.45 E
Qiongzhong, China	58	L3	19.02 N	109.47 E
Qiongzhou Haixia, strt., China	58	K3	20.10 N	110.15 E
Qiqian, China	50	F13	52.09 N	120.47 E
Qiqihar, China	52	B9	47.19 N	123.57 E
Qira, China	62	A5	37.00 N	80.47 E
Qiryat Ata, Isr.	76	F6	32.48 N	35.06 E
Qiryat Gat, Isr.	76	G5	31.36 N	34.46 E
Qiryat Shemona, Isr.	76	E6	33.12 N	35.34 E
Qishn, Yemen	72	F7	15.24 N	51.40 E
Qişrāyā, Syria	76	D7	34.53 N	36.26 E
Qiţā' Ghazzah see Gaza Strip, dep., Asia	76	G5	31.25 N	34.23 E
Qitai, China	52	C2	44.01 N	89.35 E
Qitaihe, China	52	B11	45.48 N	130.52 E
Qitamu, China	54	B7	44.21 N	126.20 E
Qixia, China	58	C9	37.16 N	120.48 E
Qixian, China	58	D6	34.33 N	114.47 E
Qiyang, China	58	H4	26.29 N	111.43 E
Qiying, China	58	C2	36.29 N	106.09 E
Qīzān see Jīzān, Sau. Ar.	72	F5	16.54 N	42.36 E
Qizhou, China	58	F6	30.04 N	115.21 E
Qızılağaç körfäzi, b., Azer.	42	F13	39.09 N	49.03 E
Qizil Jilga, China	70	A7	35.20 N	78.52 E
Qizil Langar, China	70	A7	35.13 N	77.59 E
Qogir Feng see K2, mtn., Asia	62	A4	35.53 N	76.30 E
Qolhak, ngh., Iran	185d		35.47 N	51.26 E
Qom, Iran	74	C12	34.38 N	50.53 E
Qom, stm., Iran	74	C12	34.47 N	51.02 E
Qomolangma Feng see Everest, Mount, mtn., Asia	70	D11	27.59 N	86.56 E
Qomsheh, Iran	74	D12	32.00 N	51.51 E
Qondūz see Kondūz, Afg.	72	B10	36.44 N	68.51 E
Qonggyai, China	70	D13	29.10 N	91.47 E
Qôrnoq, Grnld.	108	E15	64.32 N	51.06 W
Qorveh, Iran	74	C10	35.10 N	47.48 E
Qostanay see Kustanaj, Kaz.	48	D10	53.12 N	63.37 E
Qotbābād, Iran	74	F13	28.45 N	53.34 E
Qotūr, Iran	74	A9	38.29 N	44.25 E
Qowowuyag (Chopu), mtn., Asia	70	D11	28.06 N	86.39 E
Qu, stm., China	58	G8	29.11 N	119.27 E
Qu, stm., China	58	F2	30.02 N	106.19 E
Quabbin Reservoir, res., Ma., U.S.	124	B13	42.22 N	72.18 W
Quadra Island, i., B.C., Can.	144	F5	50.11 N	125.15 W
Quadraro, ngh., Italy	185a		41.51 N	12.33 E
Quadros, Lagoa dos, l., Braz.	172	D12	29.42 S	50.05 W
Quakenbrück, Ger.	24	D3	52.40 N	7.57 E
Qualicum Beach, B.C., Can.	144	G6	49.21 N	124.27 W
Quambatook, Austl.	98	J4	35.51 S	143.31 E
Quanah, Tx., U.S.	138	G9	34.18 N	99.44 W
Quanbao Shan, mtn., China	58	D4	34.09 N	111.29 E
Quang Ngai, Viet.	64	E9	15.07 N	108.47 E
Quang Trach, Viet.	64	D8	17.45 N	106.26 E
Quan Long see Ca Mau, Viet.	64	H7	9.10 N	105.09 E
Quannapowitt, Lake, l., Ma., U.S.	201		42.31 N	71.05 W
Quantico, Va., U.S.	124	F8	38.31 N	77.17 W
Quantico Marine Corps Air Station, mil., Va., U.S.	124	F8	38.32 N	77.26 W
Quantou, China	54	C6	42.51 N	124.09 E
Quanyang, China	54	C7	42.17 N	127.35 E
Quanzhou, China	58	I4	25.50 N	111.02 E
Quanzhou, China	58	I8	24.54 N	118.34 E
Qu'Appelle, Sk., Can.	142	D10	50.32 N	103.50 W
Qu'Appelle, stm., Can.	142	D12	50.26 N	101.19 W
Qu'Appelle Dam, dam., Sk., Can.	142	D7	51.00 N	106.25 W
Quaraí, Braz.	172	E9	30.22 S	56.27 W
Quaraí (Cuareim), stm., S.A.	172	E9	30.11 S	57.36 W
Quarles, Pegunungan, mts., Indon.	66	E11	2.55 S	119.06 E
Quarry Heights, N.Y., U.S.	194		41.04 N	73.45 W
Quarryville, Pa., U.S.	124	E9	39.53 N	76.10 W
Quartier d'Orléans, Guad.	159a	a1	18.04 N	63.02 W
Quartu Sant'Elena, Italy	32	E3	39.14 N	9.11 E
Quartz Hill, Ca., U.S.	148	I7	34.39 N	118.13 W
Quartz Lake, l., Nu., Can.	110	A14	70.56 N	80.40 W
Quartz Mountain, mtn., Or., U.S.	146	G4	43.10 N	122.40 W
Quartzsite, Az., U.S.	150	J2	33.39 N	114.11 W
Quatre, Isle à, i., St. Vin.	159e	p11	12.57 N	61.15 W
Quatsino Sound, strt., B.C., Can.	144	F2	50.25 N	127.59 W
Quba, Azer.	42	E13	41.21 N	48.30 E
Qūchān, Iran	72	B8	37.06 N	58.30 E
Quchijie, China	58	G4	28.02 N	111.54 E
Qudaym, Syria	76	C9	35.03 N	38.25 E
Qudsia Gardens, p.o.i., India	190a		28.40 N	77.13 E
Queanbeyan, Austl.	98	J7	35.21 S	149.13 E
Québec, Qc., Can.	122	D5	46.48 N	71.13 W
Québec, state, Can.	110	E16	52.00 N	72.00 W
Quebec see Québec, state, Can.	110	E16	52.00 N	72.00 W
Quebec House, hist., Eng., U.K.	178		51.14 N	0.05 E
Quebeck, Tn., U.S.	130	I12	35.49 N	85.34 W
Quebra-Anzol, stm., Braz.	170	J2	19.09 S	47.38 W
Quebracho, Ur.	172	E9	31.55 S	57.54 W
Quebrada Seca, P.R.	158a	b4	18.14 N	65.39 W
Quebradillas, P.R.	158a	b2	18.28 N	66.56 W
Quebrângulo, Braz.	170	E7	9.20 S	36.29 W
Quedal, Cabo, c., Chile	166	H2	40.58 S	73.55 W
Quedlinburg, Ger.	24	E7	51.47 N	11.08 E
Queen, Cape, c., Nu., Can.	110	C15	64.42 N	78.18 W
Queen Anne Creek, stm., Pa., U.S.	203		40.08 N	74.53 W
Queen Bess, Mount, mtn., B.C., Can.	144	E6	51.17 N	124.35 W
Queen Charlotte Islands, is., B.C., Can.	110	E4	53.00 N	132.00 W
Queen Charlotte Sound, strt., B.C., Can.	144	E2	51.19 N	128.21 W
Queen Charlotte Strait, strt., B.C., Can.	144	F3	50.50 N	127.25 W
Queen City, Mo., U.S.	130	D5	40.24 N	92.34 W
Queen City, Tx., U.S.	134	D4	33.09 N	94.09 W
Queen Elizabeth II Reservoir, res., Eng., U.K.	178		51.23 N	0.24 W
Queen Elizabeth Islands, is., Can.	106	B12	78.00 N	95.00 W
Queen Mary, bldg., Ca., U.S.	198		33.45 N	118.12 W
Queen Mary Coast, cst., Ant.	103	B14	67.00 S	96.00 E
Queen Mary Reservoir, res., Eng., U.K.	178		51.25 N	0.28 W
Queen Maud Gulf, b., Nu., Can.	110	B10	68.25 N	102.30 W
Queen Maud Land, reg., Ant.	103	C4	74.59 S	15.51 E
Queen Maud Mountains, mts., Ant.	103	D23	86.00 S	160.00 W
Queens, ngh., N.Y., U.S.	194		40.44 N	73.54 W
Queenscliff, Austl.	98	L5	38.16 S	144.38 E
Queensland, state, Austl.	96	D8	22.00 S	145.00 E
Queens Park, p.o.i., Austl.	192a		33.54 S	151.16 E
Queens Park, p.o.i., On., Can.	193b		43.40 N	79.24 W
Queens Park, p.o.i., Eng., U.K.	180		53.35 N	2.27 W
Queen's Park, p.o.i., Eng., U.K.	180		53.44 N	2.28 W
Queensport, N.S., Can.	122	E15	45.20 N	61.16 W
Queens Sound, strt., B.C., Can.	144	E2	51.56 N	128.19 W
Queenston, On., Can.	202a		43.10 N	79.03 W
Queenston Chippawa Power Canal, can., On., Can.	202a		43.08 N	79.03 W
Queenstown, Austl.	99a	o12	42.04 S	145.33 E
Queenstown see Cobh, Ire.	10	J4	51.51 N	8.17 W
Queenstown, N.Z.	102	G3	45.01 S	168.39 E
Queenstown, S. Afr.	90	G8	31.53 S	26.52 E
Queen Victoria Park, p.o.i., On., Can.	202a		43.05 N	79.05 W
Queets, stm., Wa., U.S.	146	C2	47.32 N	124.21 W
Queguay Grande, stm., Ur.	172	F9	32.08 S	58.08 W
Queimada Nova, Braz.	170	E5	8.35 S	41.25 W
Queimadas, Braz.	170	F6	10.58 S	39.38 W
Queimados, Braz.	170	L4	22.42 S	43.32 W
Quela, Ang.	88	B2	9.16 S	17.03 E
Quelelevu, i., Fiji	101e	p20	16.05 S	179.09 W
Quelimane, Moz.	88	D6	17.52 S	36.53 E
Quellón, Chile	166	H2	43.07 S	73.37 W
Quelpart Island see Cheju-do, i., Kor., S.	54	H7	33.22 N	126.29 E
Queluz, Port.	184c		38.45 N	9.15 W
Quemado, N.M., U.S.	150	I8	34.20 N	108.30 W
Quemado, Tx., U.S.	136	F7	28.55 N	100.38 W
Quemado, Punta de, c., Cuba	156	B10	20.12 N	74.08 W
Quemoy see Chinmen Tao, i., Tai.	58	I8	24.27 N	118.23 E
Quemú Quemú, Arg.	172	H6	36.02 S	63.33 W
Quequén, Arg.	172	I8	38.32 S	58.43 W
Querary, stm., Col.	168	G6	1.03 N	69.50 W
Quercy, hist. reg., Fr.	22	E7	44.35 N	1.31 E
Querenburg, ngh., Ger.	181		51.27 N	7.16 E
Querétaro, Mex.	154	E8	20.35 N	100.22 W
Querétaro, state, Mex.	154	E8	21.00 N	99.55 W
Querobabi, Mex.	120	F7	30.03 N	111.01 W
Quesada, C.R.	152	E8	10.19 N	84.25 W
Quesada, Spain	28	G7	37.51 N	3.03 W
Queset Brook, stm., Ma., U.S.	201		42.02 N	71.04 W
Queshan, China	58	E5	32.47 N	114.01 E
Quesnel, B.C., Can.	144	C8	52.58 N	122.28 W
Quesnel, stm., B.C., Can.	144	D8	52.58 N	122.30 W
Quesnel Lake, l., B.C., Can.	144	D9	52.32 N	121.05 W
Que Son, Viet.	64	E9	15.40 N	108.13 E
Questa, N.M., U.S.	138	E3	36.43 N	105.36 W
Quetico Lake, l., On., Can.	128	C7	48.33 N	91.51 W
Quetico Provincial Park, p.o.i., On., Can.	128	C7	48.26 N	91.36 W
Quetta, Pak.	62	B2	30.12 N	67.01 E
Quettehou, Fr.	20	E7	49.36 N	1.18 W
Quetzaltenango, Guat.	156	E2	14.50 N	91.30 W
Quevedo, Ec.	168	H2	1.01 S	79.26 W
Quezon City, Phil.	68	C3	14.38 N	121.03 E
Quezon Memorial, hist., Phil.	187f		14.39 N	121.03 E
Qufu, China	58	D7	35.36 N	117.02 E
Quibala, Ang.	88	C2	10.43 S	14.58 E
Quibaxe, Ang.	88	B1	8.30 S	14.31 E
Quibdó, Col.	168	E3	5.41 N	76.39 W
Quiberon, Fr.	20	G5	47.29 N	3.07 W
Quíbor, Ven.	168	C7	9.55 N	69.37 W
Quibray Bay, b., Austl.	192a		34.01 S	151.11 E
Quibú, stm., Cuba	204b		23.05 N	82.27 W
Quiçama, Parque Nacional da, p.o.i., Ang.	88	B1	9.45 S	13.30 E
Quiculungo, Ang.	88	B2	8.31 S	15.18 E
Quiindy, Para.	172	B9	25.58 S	57.14 W
Quila, Mex.	154	C5	24.25 N	107.13 W
Quilcene, Wa., U.S.	146	C4	47.49 N	122.52 W
Quilengues, Ang.	88	C1	14.04 S	14.04 E
Quilicura, Chile	204e		33.22 S	70.45 W
Quilimarí, Chile	172	F2	32.05 S	71.30 W
Quilino, Arg.	172	E5	30.13 S	64.29 W
Quillabamba, Peru	164	F3	12.49 S	72.42 W
Quillacollo, Bol.	166	C3	17.26 S	66.17 W
Quillan, Fr.	22	G8	42.52 N	2.10 E
Quill Lake, Sk., Can.	142	B9	52.02 N	104.14 W
Quillota, Chile	172	F2	32.51 S	71.13 W
Quilmes, state, Arg.	206		34.44 S	58.16 W
Quilmes, Aeródromo, arpt., Arg.	206		34.42 S	58.15 W
Quilon, India	69	G3	8.52 N	76.35 E
Quilotosa Wash, stm., Az., U.S.	150	K4	32.59 N	112.46 W
Quilpie, Austl.	98	F5	26.37 S	144.15 E
Quilpué, Chile	172	F2	33.03 S	71.27 W
Quimarí, Alto de, mtn., Col.	168	C3	8.07 N	76.23 W
Quimaria, Ang.	88	B1	6.48 S	13.18 E
Quimby, Ia., U.S.	130	B2	42.37 N	95.38 W
Quimilí, Arg.	172	C6	27.38 S	62.24 W
Quimper (Kemper), Fr.	20	F5	48.00 N	4.06 W
Quimperlé, Fr.	20	G5	47.52 N	3.32 W
Quinalasag Island, i., Phil.	68	C4	13.56 N	123.38 E
Quinault, stm., Wa., U.S.	146	C3	47.20 N	124.18 W
Quinault Indian Reservation, ind. res., Wa., U.S.	146	C2	47.24 N	124.10 W
Quince Mil, Peru	164	F3	13.15 S	70.36 W
Quincy, Ca., U.S.	148	D4	39.56 N	120.56 W
Quincy, Fl., U.S.	134	G14	30.35 N	84.34 W
Quincy, Il., U.S.	130	E6	39.55 N	91.23 W
Quincy, Ma., U.S.	124	B14	42.14 N	71.02 W
Quincy, Mi., U.S.	124	C1	41.56 N	84.53 W
Quincy, Wa., U.S.	146	C7	47.13 N	119.50 W
Quincy Bay, b., Ma., U.S.	201		42.17 N	70.58 W
Quincy-sous-Sénart, Fr.	179		48.40 N	2.33 E
Quincy-Voisins, Fr.	179		48.54 N	2.53 E
Quindío, state, Col.	168	E4	4.30 N	75.40 W
Quines, Arg.	172	F5	32.14 S	65.47 W
Quingyi, stm., China	58	F8	31.18 N	118.28 E
Quinhagak, Ak., U.S.	109	E7	59.45 N	161.43 W
Quinlan, Tx., U.S.	136	B11	32.55 N	96.08 W
Quinn, stm., Nv., U.S.	148	B7	40.52 N	119.03 W
Quiñones, Arroyo de los, stm., Spain	184a		40.33 N	3.34 W
Quinta da Boa Vista, p.o.i., Braz.	205a		22.54 S	43.15 W
Quintanar de la Orden, Spain	28	E7	39.35 N	3.02 W
Quintana Roo, state, Mex.	156	C3	19.40 N	88.30 W
Quinta Normal, Chile	204e		33.27 S	70.42 W
Quinta Normal de Agricultura, educ., Chile	204e		33.27 S	70.42 W
Quinte, Bay of, b., On., Can.	126	D12	44.09 N	77.15 W
Quinter, Ks., U.S.	138	B8	39.04 N	100.13 W
Quintero, Chile	172	F2	32.47 S	71.32 W
Quintette Mountain, mtn., B.C., Can.	144	B10	54.52 N	120.53 W
Quintino Sella, Canale, can., Italy	184b		45.29 N	8.38 E
Quinto, Spain	28	C10	41.25 N	0.30 W
Quinto, stm., Arg.	172	G5	34.14 S	64.12 W
Quinton, Ok., U.S.	134	B3	35.07 N	95.22 W
Quinto Romano, ngh., Italy	184b		45.29 N	9.05 E
Quipapá, Braz.	170	E7	8.50 S	36.02 W
Quipar, stm., Spain	28	F9	38.14 N	1.35 W
Quirauk Mountain, mtn., Md., U.S.	124	E8	39.42 N	77.31 W
Quiriguá, hist., Guat.	156	E3	15.17 N	89.04 W
Quirihue, Chile	172	H1	36.16 S	72.32 W
Quirindi, Austl.	98	H8	31.31 S	150.40 E
Quirinópolis, Braz.	166	C6	18.31 S	50.31 W
Quiriquire, Ven.	168	C10	9.58 N	63.13 W
Quiroga, Mex.	154	F8	19.40 N	101.32 W
Quiroga, Spain	28	B3	42.28 N	7.15 W
Quirós, Arg.	172	D5	28.47 S	65.07 W
Quiros, Cap, c., Vanuatu	101d	j16	14.55 S	167.00 E
Quissanga, Moz.	88	C7	12.26 S	40.28 E
Quissico, Moz.	90	D12	24.42 S	34.44 E
Quitaque, Tx., U.S.	138	G7	34.22 N	101.04 W
Quitasueño, unds., Col.	156	E7	14.20 N	81.15 W
Quitasueño, Banco see Quitasueño, unds., Col.	156	E7	14.20 N	81.15 W
Quita Sueno Bank see Quitasueño, unds., Col.	156	E7	14.20 N	81.15 W
Quiterajo, Moz.	88	C7	11.45 S	40.25 E
Quitilipi, Arg.	172	C7	26.51 S	60.13 W
Quitman, Ga., U.S.	132	F2	30.47 N	83.33 W
Quitman, Ms., U.S.	134	E10	32.02 N	88.43 W
Quitman, Tx., U.S.	136	B12	32.48 N	95.26 W
Quito, Ec.	168	H2	0.12 S	78.29 W
Quixadá, Braz.	170	C6	4.58 S	39.01 W
Quixeramobim, Braz.	170	C6	5.12 S	39.17 W
Qujiadian, China	54	C5	43.13 N	123.53 E
Qujiang, China	58	I5	24.46 N	113.16 E
Qujing, China	52	F5	25.34 N	103.49 E
Qujiu, China	58	J2	22.31 N	107.35 E
Qulay'ah, Ra's al-, c., Kuw.	74	F11	28.52 N	48.16 E
Qulin, Mo., U.S.	130	H7	36.36 N	90.15 W
Qum see Qom, Iran	74	C12	34.38 N	50.53 E
Qumarlêb, China	52	E4	34.29 N	95.21 E
Qumbu, S. Afr.	90	G9	31.09 S	28.52 E
Qumrān, Khirbat, hist., W.B.	76	G6	31.44 N	35.27 E
Qunayfidhah, Nafūd, sand, Sau. Ar.	74	H9	24.34 N	45.55 E
Qungtag, China	70	C11	29.58 N	87.37 E
Quoich, stm., Nu., Can.	110	C12	64.00 N	93.29 W
Quorn, Austl.	96	F7	32.20 S	138.02 E
Quoxo, stm., Bots.	90	C7	22.13 S	24.01 E
Qurdūd, Sudan	82	E5	10.17 N	29.55 E
Qus, Egypt	74	H3	25.55 N	32.45 E
Quseir, Egypt	74	G4	26.06 N	34.16 E
Qūshchī, Iran	74	A9	38.02 N	45.08 E
Qutbapur, ngh., India	190a		28.35 N	77.01 E
Qutb Minar, rel., India	190a		28.32 N	77.11 E
Qutdligssat, Grnld.	108	C15	70.04 N	53.01 W
Quthing, Leso.	90	G8	30.24 S	27.42 E
Quweisna, Egypt	76	H2	30.33 N	31.09 E
Quxian, China	58	F2	30.51 N	106.58 E
Quxian see Quzhou, China	58	G8	28.57 N	118.51 E
Qüxü, China	70	D13	29.21 N	90.43 E
Quyang, China	58	B6	38.37 N	114.41 E
Quy Chau, Viet.	64	C7	19.33 N	105.06 E
Quy Nhon, Viet.	64	F9	13.46 N	109.14 E

Name Page Map Ref. Latitude Longitude

Quyon, Qc., Can. 126 C13 45.31 N 76.14 W
Quyquyó, Para. 172 C9 26.14 S 56.59 W
Quzhou, China 58 C6 36.46 N 114.57 E
Quzhou, China 58 G8 28.57 N 118.51 E
Qyzylorda see Kzyl-Orda, Kaz. 48 F11 44.51 N 65.30 E

R

Raab see Győr, Hung. 36 B4 47.40 N 17.38 E
Raab (Rába), stm., Eur. 30 D12 47.44 N 17.47 E
Raadt, ngh., Ger. 181 51.24 N 6.56 E
Raahe, Fin. 18 C11 64.40 N 24.30 E
Rääkkylä, Fin. 18 E16 62.20 N 29.37 E
Råaktjoentjahke, mtn., Nor. 16 B12 65.24 N 14.22 E
Raalte, Neth. 20 B15 52.23 N 6.16 E
Ra'anana, Isr. 76 F5 32.09 N 34.52 E
Raas, Pulau, i., Indon. 66 G9 7.09 S 114.32 E
Raasay, i., Scot., U.K. 10 D6 57.22 N 6.03 W
Raasay, Sound of, strt., Scot., U.K. 10 D6 57.27 N 6.06 W
Raasdorf, Aus. 182b 48.15 N 16.34 E
Raasiku, Est. 26 A8 59.22 N 25.11 E
Raattama, Fin. 14 D15 68.08 N 24.12 E
Rab, Cro. 30 F11 44.45 N 14.45 E
Rab, Otok, i., Cro. 30 F11 44.47 N 14.45 E
Raba, Indon. 66 H11 8.29 S 118.45 E
Rába (Raab), stm., Eur. 30 D12 47.44 N 17.47 E
Raba, stm., Pol. 24 G16 50.08 N 20.30 E
Rabaçal, stm., Port. 28 C3 41.30 N 7.11 W
Rábade, Spain 28 A3 43.07 N 7.37 W
Rabak, Sudan 82 E6 13.09 N 32.44 E
Rabal, Indon. 60 G10 6.21 S 134.50 E
Rabat, Malta 32 I8 35.52 N 14.25 E
Rabat, Malta 32 H8 36.02 N 14.14 E
Rabat, Mor. 84 C3 34.00 N 6.50 W
Rabaul, Pap. N. Gui. 101a a5 4.12 S 152.10 E
Rabbit Creek, stm., S.D., U.S. 140 B10 45.12 N 102.11 W
Rabbit Ears Pass, p., Co., U.S. 150 C10 40.24 N 106.37 W
Rabbit Lake, res., On., Can. 126 A10 46.58 N 79.39 W
Rábca, stm., Hung. 30 C14 47.41 N 17.38 E
Rabeira, Ponta da, c., Braz. 205a 22.49 S 43.10 W
Rabette, Ruisseau la, stm., Fr. 179 48.35 N 2.00 E
Rabi, i., Fiji 101e p20 16.30 S 179.57 W
Rābi', Ash-Shallāl ar- (Fourth Cataract), wtfl., Sudan 82 D6 18.43 N 32.03 E
Rābigh, Sau. Ar. 72 E4 22.47 N 39.02 E
Rabindra Sarobar, p.o.i., India 190b 22.31 N 88.21 E
Rabka, Pol. 24 G15 49.36 N 19.56 E
Rabkavi Banhatti, India 69 C2 16.28 N 75.06 E
Rābnița, Mol. 38 F8 47.45 N 29.01 E
Rabnitz see Répce, stm., Eur. 30 C14 47.41 N 17.03 E
Rabočeostrovsk, Russia 18 B22 64.59 N 34.45 E
Rabun Bald, mtn., Ga., U.S. 132 B2 34.58 N 83.18 W
Rabwāh, Pak. 70 C4 31.49 N 72.51 E
Raby, Eng., U.K. 180 53.19 N 3.02 W
Rabyānah, Ramlat, des., Libya 82 C4 24.30 N 21.00 E
Răcari, Rom. 36 E12 44.37 N 25.45 E
Raccoon, stm., Ia., U.S. 130 C4 41.34 N 93.36 W
Raccoon Creek, stm., Oh., U.S. 130 E15 39.04 N 82.21 W
Raccoon Creek, South Branch, stm., N.J., U.S. 203 39.44 N 75.15 W
Raccoon Island, i., N.J., U.S. 203 39.49 N 75.22 W
Race, Cape, c., Nf., Can. 111a j23 46.39 N 53.06 W
Raceland, La., U.S. 134 H8 29.43 N 90.36 W
Race Point, c., Ma., U.S. 124 B15 42.04 N 70.14 W
Raceview, S. Afr. 191d 26.17 S 28.08 E
Rach Gia, Viet. 64 G7 10.00 N 105.05 E
Rach Gia, Vinh, b., Viet. 64 H7 10.00 N 105.00 E
Raciąż, Pol. 24 D16 52.46 N 20.06 E
Racibórz, Pol. 24 F14 50.05 N 18.13 E
Racine, Wi., U.S. 130 B10 42.43 N 87.46 W
Ráckeve, Hung. 36 B5 47.10 N 18.59 E
Ráckevei-Duna, mth., Hung. 182c 47.19 N 19.02 E
Radaškovičy, Bela. 26 F10 54.09 N 27.14 E
Rădăuți, Rom. 36 B12 47.50 N 25.55 E
Radčenskoe, Russia 40 G12 49.48 N 40.29 E
Radcliff, Ky., U.S. 130 G12 37.50 N 85.56 W
Råde, Nor. 16 H8 59.21 N 10.50 E
Radebaugh, Pa., U.S. 197b 40.19 N 79.35 W
Radeberg, Ger. 24 E9 51.07 N 13.55 E
Radebeul, Ger. 24 E9 51.05 N 13.39 E
Radeče, Slvn. 30 D12 46.05 N 15.10 E
Radekhiv, Ukr. 38 C3 50.17 N 24.38 E
Radford, Va., U.S. 124 G5 37.07 N 80.35 W
Rādhānagar, India 190b 22.27 N 88.28 E
Rādhanpur, India 70 G3 23.49 N 71.36 E
Rădinești, Rom. 36 E10 44.48 N 23.45 E
Radisson, Sk., Can. 142 B6 52.28 N 107.21 W
Radium Hot Springs, B.C., Can. 144 F14 50.38 N 116.03 W
Rad'kovka, Russia 38 B15 51.06 N 36.58 E
Radlett Aerodrome, arpt., Eng., U.K. 178 51.43 N 0.19 W
Radley Run, stm., Pa., U.S. 203 39.54 N 75.37 W
Radnevo, Blg. 36 G12 42.17 N 25.56 E
Radnice, Czech Rep. 24 G9 49.51 N 13.36 E
Radnor, Pa., U.S. 203 40.02 N 75.21 W
Radnor Mere, l., Eng., U.K. 180 53.17 N 2.14 W
Rădoaia, Mol. 38 F7 47.44 N 28.10 E
Radofinnikovo, Russia 26 A13 59.08 N 30.52 E
Radogošča, Russia 18 H21 59.46 N 34.50 E
Radolfzell, Ger. 20 G17 47.44 N 8.58 E
Radom, Pol. 24 E17 51.24 N 21.09 E
Radomir, Blg. 36 G9 42.33 N 22.58 E
Radomka, Ukr. 38 B11 51.55 N 32.33 E
Radomka, stm., Pol. 24 E16 51.42 N 21.27 E
Radomsko, Pol. 24 E15 51.04 N 19.26 E
Radomyshl', Ukr. 38 C8 50.30 N 29.15 E
Radomyśl Wielki, Pol. 24 F17 50.12 N 21.16 E
Radotín, Czech Rep. 24 G10 49.59 N 14.21 E
Radoviš, Mac. 34 B5 41.38 N 22.28 E
Radstadt, Aus. 30 C10 47.23 N 13.27 E
Radul', Ukr. 38 B9 51.49 N 30.42 E
Radun', Bela. 26 F7 54.03 N 25.00 E
Radushne, Ukr. 38 F12 47.49 N 33.30 E
Radutino, Russia 26 H17 52.39 N 33.58 E
Radvaň nad Laborcom, Slvk. 24 G17 49.06 N 21.58 E
Radviliškis, Lith. 26 E6 55.48 N 23.32 E
Radville, Sk., Can. 142 E9 49.27 N 104.17 W
Radway, Ab., Can. 144 B18 54.04 N 112.57 W
Radykovskoe, Russia 40 I13 45.56 N 41.57 E
Radymno, Pol. 24 G18 49.57 N 22.48 E
Radyvyliv, Ukr. 38 C4 50.07 N 25.16 E
Radziejów, Pol. 24 D14 52.37 N 18.32 E
Radzyń Chełmiński, Pol. 24 C14 53.23 N 18.55 E
Radzyń Podlaski, Pol. 24 E18 51.47 N 22.36 E
Rae, N.T., Can. 110 C7 62.50 N 116.01 W
Rae, stm., Nu., Can. 110 B7 67.54 N 115.45 W
Rāe Bareli, India 70 E8 26.13 N 81.14 E
Raeford, N.C., U.S. 132 B6 34.58 N 79.15 W
Rae Isthmus, isth., Nu., Can. 110 B13 66.55 N 86.10 W
Rae Strait, strt., Nu., Can. 110 B12 68.44 N 94.57 W
Raetihi, N.Z. 102 D6 39.26 S 175.17 E
Raevskij, Russia 40 D19 54.04 N 54.57 E
Rafaela, Arg. 172 E7 31.15 S 61.29 W
Rafael Castillo, Arg. 206 34.43 S 58.37 W
Rafael Freyre, Cuba 156 B10 21.01 N 75.59 W
Rafah, Gaza 76 G5 31.17 N 34.15 E
Rafalivka, Ukr. 38 B5 51.18 N 26.00 E
Raffelberg, Rennbahn, p.o.i., Ger. 181 51.26 N 6.50 E
Rafhā', Sau. Ar. 72 D5 29.40 N 43.27 E
Rafsanjān, Iran 74 E14 30.24 N 55.58 E
Raft, stm., U.S. 146 H13 42.06 N 113.19 W
Raft River Mountains, mts., Ut., U.S. 150 B3 41.55 N 113.25 W
Raga, Sudan 82 F5 8.27 N 25.40 E
Ragay Gulf, b., Phil. 68 D4 13.30 N 122.45 E
Ragged Island, i., Bah. 156 A10 22.13 N 75.43 W
Ragged Island Range, is., Bah. 156 A10 22.34 N 75.52 W
Ragged Top Mountain, mtn., Wy., U.S. 140 F7 41.27 N 105.20 W
Raghabpur, India 190b 22.25 N 88.21 E
Ragland, Al., U.S. 134 D12 33.44 N 86.09 W
Ragnozero, ozero, l., Russia 18 E23 62.07 N 36.32 E
Rago Nasjonalpark, p.o.i., Nor. 14 E6 67.29 N 15.57 E
Ragow, Ger. 182a 52.17 N 13.33 E
Ragusa, Italy 84 B7 36.54 N 14.44 E
Raguva, Lith. 26 E7 55.33 N 24.37 E
Rahačoŭ, Bela. 26 G12 53.04 N 30.03 E
Rahad al-Bardī, Sudan 82 E4 11.17 N 23.53 E
Rahat, Harrat, lav., Sau. Ar. 74 H6 24.22 N 39.55 E
Rāhatgarh, India 70 G7 23.46 N 78.23 E
Rahbah, Leb. 76 D7 34.30 N 36.09 E
Rahimatpur, India 69 C1 17.36 N 74.10 E
Rahīm Ki Bāzār, Pak. 70 F2 24.18 N 69.09 E
Rahīmyār Khān, Pak. 70 D3 28.25 N 70.18 E
Rahja, Russia 18 G17 60.05 N 30.50 E
Rahm, Ger. 181 51.26 N 6.26 E
Rahm, ngh., Ger. 181 51.21 N 6.47 E
Rahm, ngh., Ger. 181 51.32 N 7.23 E
Rahmanovka, Russia 40 F16 51.57 N 49.27 E
Rahmede, stm., Ger. 181 51.17 N 7.41 E
Rahmersee, l., Ger. 182a 52.45 N 13.25 E
Rahns, Pa., U.S. 203 40.12 N 75.27 W
Rahnsdorf, ngh., Ger. 182a 52.26 N 13.42 E
Råholt, Nor. 16 G9 60.16 N 11.10 E
Rahway, stm., N.J., U.S. 194 40.35 N 74.12 W
Rahway, East Branch, stm., N.J., U.S. 194 40.42 N 74.18 W
Rahway, Robinsons Branch, stm., N.J., U.S. 194 40.37 N 74.17 W
Rahway, South Branch, stm., N.J., U.S. 194 40.36 N 74.17 W
Rahway, West Branch, stm., N.J., U.S. 194 40.42 N 74.18 W
Rahway River Parkway, p.o.i., N.J., U.S. 194 40.41 N 74.19 W
Rāichūr, India 69 C3 16.12 N 77.21 E
Raiford, Fl., U.S. 132 F3 30.04 N 82.13 W
Raiganj, India 70 F12 25.37 N 88.07 E
Raigarh, India 70 H9 21.53 N 83.24 E
Rāikot, India 70 C5 30.38 N 75.36 E
Railroad Valley, val., Nv., U.S. 148 E10 38.25 N 115.40 W
Railton, Austl. 99a n13 41.21 S 146.25 E
Rainbow Bridge, trans., N.A. 202a 43.05 N 79.04 W
Rainbow Bridge National Monument, p.o.i., Ut., U.S. 150 F6 37.06 N 110.57 W
Rainbow Falls, wtfl., B.C., Can. 144 D11 52.22 N 119.58 W
Rainbow Lakes, N.J., U.S. 194 40.52 N 74.28 W
Rainbow Park, p.o.i., Il., U.S. 196 41.46 N 87.33 W
Rainelle, W.V., U.S. 124 G5 37.56 N 80.48 W
Rainham, ngh., Eng., U.K. 178 51.31 N 0.12 E
Rainhill, Eng., U.K. 180 53.26 N 2.46 W
Rainhill Stoops, Eng., U.K. 180 53.24 N 2.45 W
Rainier, Mount, vol., Wa., U.S. 146 D5 46.51 N 121.45 W
Rainow, Eng., U.K. 180 53.17 N 2.04 W
Rainsford Island, i., Ma., U.S. 201 42.18 N 70.57 W
Rainy, stm., N.A. 128 C4 48.52 N 94.40 W
Rainy, stm., Mi., U.S. 126 C5 45.28 N 84.17 W
Rainy Lake, l., N.A. 128 C5 48.38 N 93.16 W
Rainy River, On., Can. 128 C4 48.43 N 94.34 W
Raipur, India 70 H8 21.14 N 81.38 E
Raipur, India 190a 28.32 N 77.20 E
Raipur, India 190b 22.24 N 88.09 E
Raipur Uplands, plat., India 70 H9 21.00 N 82.20 E
Rairākhol, India 70 H10 21.16 N 84.14 E
Räisduottarháldi, mtn., Nor. 14 C12 69.19 N 21.16 E
Raisen, India 70 G6 23.19 N 77.47 E
Raisin, stm., On., Can. 126 C15 45.07 N 74.26 W
Raisin, stm., Mi., U.S. 130 B13 41.53 N 83.20 W
Raivavae, i., Fr. Poly. 94 F12 23.52 S 147.40 W
Raizeux, Fr. 179 48.37 N 1.41 E
Raja, Ujung, c., Indon. 64 K3 3.44 N 96.32 E
Rajabasa, Indon. 66 F4 5.31 S 104.13 E
Rājahmundry, India 69 C5 17.00 N 81.47 E
Raja-Jooseppi, Fin. 14 D19 68.28 N 28.25 E
Rājaldesar, India 70 E5 28.01 N 74.28 E
Rajamäki, Fin. 18 G11 60.31 N 24.45 E
Rājāmpet, India 69 D4 14.11 N 79.09 E
Rajang, stm., Malay. 66 B7 2.09 N 111.21 E
Rājanpur, Pak. 70 D3 29.06 N 70.19 E
Rājapālaiyam, India 69 G3 9.27 N 77.33 E
Rājāpur, India 69 C1 16.39 N 73.30 E
Rājāpur, India 190b 22.39 N 88.11 E
Rājāpur Canal, can., India 190b 22.30 N 88.07 E
Rājasthān, state, India 70 E5 27.00 N 74.00 E
Rajbari, Bngl. 70 G12 23.46 N 89.39 E
Raj Bhavan, bldg., India 190b 22.34 N 88.21 E
Rajčihinsk, Russia 50 G14 49.48 N 129.24 E
Rāj Gangpur, India 70 G10 22.11 N 84.35 E
Rājgarh, India 70 D5 28.38 N 75.22 E
Rājgarh, India 70 E6 27.14 N 76.36 E
Rājgarh, India 70 G6 23.54 N 76.54 E
Rajghat, rel., India 190a 28.39 N 77.15 E
Rajgorodok, Kaz. 40 G18 48.46 N 52.53 E
Rajgród, Pol. 24 C18 53.44 N 22.42 E
Rājhāt, India 190b 22.56 N 88.21 E
Rājibpur, India 190b 22.49 N 88.34 E
Rajik, Indon. 66 E4 2.35 S 105.54 E
Rajka, Hung. 36 B4 47.59 N 17.11 E
Rājkot, India 70 G3 22.18 N 70.47 E
Rajkuzi, Russia 183a 59.47 N 29.57 E
Rāj Nāndgaon, India 70 H8 21.06 N 81.02 E
Rajokri, ngh., India 190a 28.31 N 77.07 E
Rājpipla, India 70 H4 21.53 N 73.31 E
Rājpur, India 70 G5 21.58 N 75.04 E
Rājpur, India 190a 28.44 N 77.22 E
Rājpur, ngh., India 190a 28.41 N 77.12 E
Rājpura, India 70 C6 30.28 N 76.35 E
Rājshāhi, Bngl. 70 F12 24.22 N 88.36 E
Rājshāhi, state, Bngl. 70 F12 25.15 N 89.15 E
Rājula, India 70 H3 21.02 N 71.27 E
Raka, stm., China 70 D11 29.22 N 87.57 E
Rakamaz, Hung. 36 A8 48.07 N 21.27 E
Rakaposhi, mtn., Pak. 62 A3 36.10 N 74.30 E
Rakata, Pulau (Krakatoa), i., Indon. 66 G4 6.10 S 105.26 E
Rakhine, state, Mya. 64 C1 19.30 N 93.55 E
Rakhiv, Ukr. 38 E3 48.02 N 24.12 E
Rakhmanivka, Ukr. 38 F12 47.48 N 33.13 E
Rakhni, Pak. 70 C2 30.01 N 69.56 E
Rakhny-Lisovi, Ukr. 38 E7 48.47 N 28.29 E
Rakhshān, stm., Pak. 62 C1 27.04 N 63.30 E
Rakiraki, Fiji 101e p19 17.23 S 178.09 E
Rakitnoe, Russia 38 C14 50.51 N 35.52 E
Rakitnoe see Rakitnoje, Russia 52 B11 45.35 N 134.16 E
Rakitnoje, Russia 52 B11 45.35 N 134.16 E
Rakiura see Stewart Island, i., N.Z. 102 H3 47.00 S 167.50 E
Rakke, Est. 26 B9 58.59 N 26.15 E
Rakkestad, Nor. 16 H9 59.25 N 11.21 E
Rakoniewice, Pol. 24 D12 52.09 N 16.15 E
Rakops, Bots. 90 B7 21.01 S 24.24 E
Rákoscsaba, ngh., Hung. 182c 47.29 N 19.17 E
Rákoshegy, ngh., Hung. 182c 47.28 N 19.14 E
Rákoskeresztúr, ngh., Hung. 182c 47.29 N 19.15 E
Rákoskert, ngh., Hung. 182c 47.28 N 19.19 E
Rákosliget, ngh., Hung. 182c 47.30 N 19.16 E
Rákospalota, ngh., Hung. 182c 47.34 N 19.08 E
Rákos-patak, stm., Hung. 182c 47.33 N 19.04 E
Rákosszentmihály, ngh., Hung. 182c 47.32 N 19.11 E
Rakovník, Czech Rep. 24 F9 50.06 N 13.44 E
Rakovski, Blg. 36 G11 42.17 N 24.58 E
Rakušečnyj, mys, c., Kaz. 42 D14 42.49 N 51.55 E
Råkvågen, Nor. 16 D8 63.46 N 10.05 E
Rakvere, Est. 26 A9 59.20 N 26.22 E
Raleigh, Ms., U.S. 134 E9 32.02 N 89.31 W
Raleigh, N.C., U.S. 124 I7 35.47 N 78.38 W
Ralik Islands, is., Marsh. Is. 94 C7 8.00 N 167.00 E
Ralls, Tx., U.S. 138 H7 33.40 N 101.23 W
Ralston, Ne., U.S. 130 C1 41.12 N 96.02 W
Ralston, Pa., U.S. 124 C9 41.30 N 76.57 W
Ram, stm., Ab., Can. 144 D15 52.22 N 115.25 W
Ramah, N.M., U.S. 150 H8 35.07 N 108.31 W
Ramah Indian Reservation, ind. res., N.M., U.S. 150 I8 34.50 N 108.25 W
Ramales de la Victoria, Spain 28 A7 43.15 N 3.27 W
Rām Allāh, W.B. 76 G6 31.54 N 35.12 E
Rāmanagaram, India 69 E3 12.42 N 77.16 E
Rāmanāthapuram, India 69 G4 9.21 N 78.50 E
Ramanāthpur, India 190b 22.41 N 88.14 E
Ramanbāti, India 190b 22.47 N 88.08 E
Rāmānuj Ganj, India 70 G9 23.46 N 83.41 E
Ramapo, N.Y., U.S. 194 41.08 N 74.10 W
Ramapo, stm., U.S. 194 40.58 N 74.17 W
Ramapo Lake, l., N.J., U.S. 194 41.02 N 74.16 W
Ramapo Mountains, mts., U.S. 194 41.08 N 74.12 W
Ramas, Cape, c., India 69 D1 15.07 N 73.55 E
Ramasuha, Russia 26 H16 52.45 N 33.32 E
Ramat Gan, Isr. 76 F5 32.05 N 34.49 E
Ramat HaSharon, Isr. 76 F5 32.08 N 34.50 E
Ramatlabama, Bots. 90 D7 25.40 S 25.35 E
Rama VI Bridge, trans., Thai. 187a 13.48 N 100.31 E
Ramberg, Nor. 14 D4 68.06 N 13.14 E
Rambervillers, Fr. 20 F15 48.20 N 6.37 E
Ramblewood, N.J., U.S. 203 39.55 N 74.56 W
Rambouillet, Fr. 20 F10 48.39 N 1.50 E
Rambouillet, Château de, hist., Fr. 179 48.39 N 1.49 E
Rambouillet, Forêt de, p.o.i., Fr. 179 48.40 N 1.50 E
Rambutyo Island, i., Pap. N. Gui. 101a a4 2.17 S 147.48 E
Rām Dās, India 70 B5 31.57 N 74.54 E
Rāmdurg, India 69 C2 15.58 N 75.19 E
Ramea, Nf., Can. 111a j22 47.31 N 57.24 W
Rāmechhāp, Nepal 70 E11 27.19 N 86.05 E
Ramene, Russia 12 F20 60.17 N 43.46 E
Ramenka, ngh., Russia 183b 55.41 N 37.30 E
Ramenskoe, Russia 26 E21 55.33 N 38.13 E
Ramer, Al., U.S. 134 E12 32.03 N 86.13 W
Rameški, Russia 26 C18 57.20 N 36.03 E
Rāmeswaram, India 69 G4 9.16 N 79.19 E
Rāmgarh, Bngl. 70 G13 22.59 N 91.44 E
Rāmgarh, India 70 E3 27.22 N 70.30 E
Rāmgarh, India 70 E5 27.15 N 75.11 E
Rāmgarh, India 70 G10 23.37 N 85.30 E
Ram Head, c., V.I.U.S. 158b e8 18.18 N 64.42 W
Rāmhormoz, Iran 74 E11 31.16 N 49.36 E
Ramírez, Mex. 136 I10 25.56 N 97.47 W
Ramírez, Mex. 136 G7 27.20 N 100.58 W
Ramkhamhaeng University, educ., Thai. 187a 13.45 N 100.37 E
Ramla, Isr. 76 G5 31.55 N 34.51 E
Ramlu, mtn., Afr. 82 E8 13.24 N 41.45 E
Ramm, Jabal, mtn., Jord. 76 I6 29.35 N 35.24 E
Râmna, stm., Rom. 36 D13 45.39 N 27.19 E
Rāmnagar, India 70 F9 25.16 N 83.02 E
Rāmnagar, India 70 D7 29.23 N 79.07 E
Rāmnagar, India 190b 22.23 N 88.19 E
Ramnäs, Swe. 16 H14 59.46 N 16.12 E
Râmnicu Sărat, Rom. 36 D14 45.22 N 27.03 E
Râmnicu Vâlcea, Rom. 36 D11 45.06 N 24.23 E
Ramon, Har, mtn., Isr. 76 H5 30.30 N 34.38 E
Ramona, Ca., U.S. 148 J9 33.02 N 116.51 W
Ramona, Ok., U.S. 130 H2 36.32 N 95.55 W
Ramona, S.D., U.S. 140 C15 44.07 N 97.13 W
Ramos, Mex. 154 D8 22.50 N 101.55 W
Ramos, ngh., Braz. 205a 22.51 S 43.15 W
Ramos, stm., Mex. 154 C6 25.32 N 105.09 W
Ramotswa, Bots. 90 D7 24.54 S 25.48 E
Rampart, Ak., U.S. 109 C9 65.30 N 150.08 W
Ramparts, stm., N.T., Can. 110 B4 66.11 N 129.02 W
Rāmpur, India 70 D7 28.48 N 79.01 E
Rāmpur, India 70 C6 31.25 N 77.37 E
Rāmpura, India 70 F5 24.28 N 75.26 E
Rampur Boalia see Rājshāhi, Bngl. 70 F12 24.22 N 88.36 E
Rāmpur Hāt, India 70 F11 24.10 N 87.47 E
Ramrath, Ger. 181 51.06 N 6.41 E
Ramree Island, i., Mya. 64 C1 19.06 N 93.48 E
Ramsden Bellhouse, Eng., U.K. 178 51.37 N 0.29 E
Ramsden Heath, Eng., U.K. 178 51.38 N 0.28 E
Ramsele, Swe. 16 D14 63.32 N 16.28 E
Ramseur, N.C., U.S. 124 I6 35.44 N 79.39 W
Ramsey, I. of Man 10 G8 54.19 N 4.23 W
Ramsey, Il., U.S. 130 E8 39.08 N 89.06 W
Ramsey Brook, stm., N.J., U.S. 194 41.02 N 74.08 W
Ramsey Lake, l., On., Can. 126 A7 47.05 N 82.16 W
Ramsgate, Austl. 192a 33.59 S 151.08 E
Ramsgate, Eng., U.K. 10 J14 51.20 N 1.24 E
Rāmshīr, Iran 74 E11 30.53 N 49.24 E
Ramshorn Peak, mtn., Mt., U.S. 146 E15 45.09 N 111.06 W
Ramsjö, Swe. 16 E13 62.11 N 15.38 E
Rāmtek, India 70 H7 21.23 N 79.20 E
Rāmu, Bngl. 70 H14 21.25 N 92.06 E
Ramu, Kenya 86 D8 3.54 N 41.12 E
Ramu, stm., Pap. N. Gui. 101a a3 4.02 S 144.39 E
Ramuševo, Russia 26 C14 57.49 N 31.37 E
Ramvik, Swe. 16 E15 62.49 N 17.51 E
Ramville, Îlet, i., Mart. 159c k7 14.41 N 60.53 W
Ramygala, Lith. 26 E7 55.31 N 24.18 E
Ramzaj, Russia 40 E14 53.18 N 44.45 E
Ranafjorden, b., Nor. 14 F3 66.14 N 13.28 E
Rānāghāt, India 70 G12 23.10 N 88.34 E
Rana Kao, Volcán, vol., Chile 100l f29 27.11 S 109.25 W
Rāna Pratāp Sāgar, res., India 70 F5 24.50 N 75.36 E
Ranau, Malay. 68 H1 5.56 N 116.40 E
Ranau, Danau, l., Indon. 66 F3 4.50 S 103.55 E
Ranburne, Al., U.S. 134 D13 33.31 N 85.20 W
Rancagua, Chile 172 G2 34.10 S 70.43 W
Rancah, Indon. 66 G6 7.12 S 108.30 E
Rancevo, Russia 26 D16 56.39 N 33.01 E
Rancevo, Russia 26 D16 56.56 N 34.02 E
Rancharia, Braz. 166 D6 22.13 S 50.52 W
Rancheria, stm., Col. 168 B5 11.33 N 72.54 W
Rancheria Rock, mtn., Or., U.S. 146 F6 44.53 N 120.08 W
Ranchester, Wy., U.S. 140 C5 44.55 N 107.12 W
Rānchi, India 70 G10 23.20 N 85.19 E
Ranchillos, Arg. 172 C5 26.56 S 65.02 W
Ranch Lake, l., Sk., Can. 142 B9 52.30 N 104.46 W
Rancho Colorado, Presa de, res., Mex. 204a 19.29 N 99.17 W
Rancho Cordova, Ca., U.S. 148 E4 38.35 N 121.17 W
Rancho Nuevo, Mex. 136 H8 26.21 N 99.53 W
Ranchos, Arg. 172 G8 35.31 S 58.18 W
Ranchos de Taos, N.M., U.S. 138 E3 36.20 N 105.38 W
Ranco, Lago, l., Chile 166 H2 40.13 S 72.24 W
Rancocas Creek, stm., N.J., U.S. 203 40.02 N 74.59 W
Rancocas Creek, Southwest Branch, stm., N.J., U.S. 203 39.57 N 74.48 W
Rancocas Heights, N.J., U.S. 203 39.59 N 74.51 W
Rancocas State Park, p.o.i., N.J., U.S. 203 40.00 N 74.50 W
Rancocas Woods, N.J., U.S. 203 39.59 N 74.51 W
Rancul, Arg. 172 G5 35.04 S 64.42 W
Rand, Austl. 98 J6 35.35 S 146.34 E
Rand (Germiston) Airport, arpt., S. Afr. 191d 26.15 S 28.09 E
Randaberg, Nor. 16 H3 59.00 N 5.35 E
Randall Park Mall, shp. cen., Oh., U.S. 197a 41.26 N 81.32 W
Randalls Island, i., N.Y., U.S. 194 40.48 N 73.55 W
Randallstown, Md., U.S. 202b 39.22 N 76.48 W
Randazzo, Italy 32 G8 37.53 N 14.57 E
Randburg, S. Afr. 191d 26.06 S 27.59 E
Randers, Den. 16 K8 56.28 N 10.02 E
Randfontein, state, S. Afr. 191d 26.13 S 27.40 E
Randgate, S. Afr. 191d 26.11 S 27.41 E
Randhurst, shp. cen., Il., U.S. 196 42.05 N 87.56 W
Randijaur, Swe. 14 F10 66.45 N 19.15 E
Randijaur, l., Swe. 14 F10 66.42 N 19.18 E
Randleman, N.C., U.S. 124 I6 35.49 N 79.48 W
Randlett, Ok., U.S. 138 G10 34.10 N 98.27 W
Randolph, Az., U.S. 150 K5 32.55 N 111.32 W
Randolph, Me., U.S. 122 F7 44.13 N 69.45 W
Randolph, Ne., U.S. 140 E15 42.22 N 97.21 W
Randolph, N.Y., U.S. 124 B7 42.09 N 78.58 W
Randolph, Ut., U.S. 150 B5 41.40 N 111.11 W
Randolph, Vt., U.S. 122 G4 43.55 N 72.40 W
Randolph, Wi., U.S. 128 H10 43.32 N 89.00 W
Randolph Air Force Base, mil., Tx., U.S. 136 E9 29.32 N 98.16 W
Randolph Hills, Md., U.S. 202c 39.03 N 77.05 W
Randolph Village, Md., U.S. 202c 38.53 N 76.52 W
Random Lake, Wi., U.S. 126 E2 43.33 N 87.57 W
Randse Afrikaanse Universiteit, educ., S. Afr. 191d 26.11 S 27.50 E
Randsfjorden, l., Nor. 16 G7 60.25 N 10.24 E
Rand Stadium, p.o.i., S. Afr. 191d 26.14 S 28.03 E
Randwick Racecourse, p.o.i., Austl. 192a 33.54 S 151.14 E
Råneå, Swe. 14 G13 65.52 N 22.18 E
Råneälven, stm., Swe. 14 F11 65.52 N 22.20 E
Ranemsletta, Nor. 16 C9 64.29 N 11.57 E
Rāner, India 70 D4 28.53 N 73.17 E
Ranfurly, N.Z. 102 G4 45.07 S 170.04 E
Rāngāmāti, Bngl. 70 G13 22.42 N 92.08 E
Rangantemiang, Indon. 66 D8 0.34 S 113.20 E
Rangas, Tanjung, c., Indon. 66 E11 2.38 S 118.49 E
Rangasa, Tanjung, c., Indon. 66 E11 3.33 S 118.56 E
Rangaunu Bay, b., N.Z. 102 B5 34.49 S 173.13 E
Range Creek, stm., Ut., U.S. 150 D6 39.18 N 110.02 W
Range Indian Reserve, ind. res., B.C., Can. 144 G11 49.09 N 119.50 W
Rangeley, Me., U.S. 122 E6 44.58 N 70.39 W
Rangely, Co., U.S. 150 C8 40.06 N 108.49 W
Range Ponds State Park, p.o.i., Me., U.S. 122 F6 44.03 N 70.18 W
Ranger, Tx., U.S. 136 B9 32.28 N 98.40 W
Ranger Lake, l., On., Can. 126 B6 46.54 N 83.35 W
Rangia, India 70 E13 26.26 N 91.36 E
Rangitaiki, stm., N.Z. 102 D7 37.54 S 176.52 E
Rangitata, stm., N.Z. 102 F4 44.11 S 171.30 E
Rangitikei, stm., N.Z. 102 D6 40.16 S 175.14 E
Rangkasbitung, Indon. 66 G5 6.20 S 106.15 E
Rangoon see Yangon, Mya. 64 D2 16.46 N 96.11 E
Rangoon, stm., Mya. 64 D3 16.33 N 96.15 E
Rangpo, India 70 E12 27.10 N 88.32 E
Rangpur, Bngl. 70 F12 25.44 N 89.15 E
Rangpur, Pak. 70 C3 30.30 N 71.32 E
Rangpuri, hist., India 190a 28.33 N 77.08 E
Rangsang, Pulau, i., Indon. 66 C3 1.00 N 102.55 E
Rangsdorfer See, l., Ger. 182a 52.17 N 13.24 E
Ranholas, Port. 184c 38.47 N 9.22 W
Rānībennur, India 69 D2 14.40 N 75.32 E
Rānīganj, India 70 G11 23.36 N 87.07 E
Rānīkhet, India 70 D7 29.39 N 79.25 E
Rānīwāra, India 70 F4 24.45 N 72.12 E
Rāniyah, Iraq 74 B9 36.15 N 44.53 E
Rankamhaeng National Park, p.o.i., Thai. 64 D4 16.52 N 99.39 E
Ranken, stm., Austl. 96 D7 20.31 S 137.36 E
Ranken Store, Austl. 96 C7 19.36 S 136.56 E
Rankin, Il., U.S. 130 D10 40.27 N 87.54 W
Rankin, Pa., U.S. 197b 40.24 N 79.52 W
Rankin, Tx., U.S. 136 C6 31.13 N 101.56 W
Rankin Inlet, Nu., Can. 110 C12 62.49 N 92.09 W
Rankins Springs, Austl. 98 I6 33.50 S 146.16 E
Ranlo, N.C., U.S. 132 A4 35.16 N 81.07 W
Rannee, Russia 40 F18 51.29 N 52.36 E
Rannersdorf, Aus. 182b 48.08 N 16.28 E
Rannoch, Loch, l., Scot., U.K. 10 E8 56.41 N 4.15 W
Rann of Kutch see Kutch, Rann of, reg., Asia 70 F2 24.15 N 70.46 E
Ranohira, Madag. 88 E8 22.33 S 45.25 E
Ranong, Thai. 64 H4 9.57 N 98.39 E
Ranongga Island, i., Sol. Is. 101b e7 8.05 S 156.34 E
Ranot, Thai. 64 I5 7.46 N 100.18 E
Rānsai, India 190c 18.53 N 73.05 E
Ransäter, Swe. 16 H11 59.46 N 13.27 E
Ransiki, Indon. 60 F9 1.28 S 134.12 E
Ransom, Ks., U.S. 138 C8 38.38 N 99.56 W
Ransom Creek, stm., N.Y., U.S. 202a 43.04 N 78.45 W
Ranson, W.V., U.S. 124 E8 39.17 N 77.51 W
Rantabe, Madag. 88 D8 15.42 S 49.38 E
Rantasalmi, Fin. 18 E15 62.04 N 28.18 E
Rantau, Indon. 66 E9 2.56 S 115.09 E
Rantaukampar, Indon. 66 C2 1.25 N 100.59 E
Rantaupanjang, Indon. 66 D2 1.17 S 101.48 E
Rantaupanjang, Indon. 66 D3 1.51 S 102.17 E
Rantauprapat, Indon. 66 B1 2.06 N 99.49 E
Rantekombola, Bulu, mtn., Indon. 66 E12 3.23 S 120.01 E
Rantepao, Indon. 66 E11 2.58 S 119.54 E
Rantoul, Il., U.S. 130 D9 40.18 N 88.09 W
Rantsila, Fin. 18 C12 64.30 N 25.40 E
Ranua, Fin. 18 B13 65.55 N 26.32 E
Rānvād, India 190c 18.53 N 72.55 E
Råö, Swe. 16 J9 57.23 N 11.56 E
Raohe, China 52 B11 46.47 N 134.00 E
Raoping, China 58 J7 23.41 N 117.00 E
Raoul, Ga., U.S. 132 B2 34.26 N 83.36 W
Raoul-Blanchard, Mont, mtn., Qc., Can. 122 C6 47.17 N 70.50 W
Raoul Island, i., N.Z. 94 F9 29.16 S 177.54 W
Rapa, i., Fr. Poly. 94 F12 27.36 S 144.20 W
Rapa, Ponta do, c., Braz. 172 C13 27.23 S 48.25 W
Rapallo, Italy 30 F6 44.21 N 9.14 E
Rapang, Indon. 66 E11 3.50 S 119.49 E
Rapa Nui see Pascua, Isla de, i., Chile 100l f30 27.07 S 109.22 W
Rāpar, India 70 G3 23.34 N 70.38 E
Rapel, stm., Chile 172 F2 33.53 S 71.49 W
Rapel, Embalse, res., Chile 172 G2 34.08 S 71.29 W
Rapelli, Arg. 172 C5 26.23 S 64.29 W
Raper, Cape, c., Nu., Can. 110 B17 69.43 N 67.07 W
Rāpi, mtn., Swe. 14 D12 68.26 N 21.23 E
Rapid, stm., Mi., U.S. 126 B2 45.55 N 86.58 W
Rapid, stm., Mn., U.S. 128 C4 48.41 N 94.26 W
Rapidan, stm., Va., U.S. 124 F7 38.21 N 77.37 W
Rapid Bay, Austl. 98 J2 35.31 S 138.10 E
Rapid City, Mb., Can. 142 D13 50.07 N 100.03 W
Rapid City, Mi., U.S. 126 D4 44.50 N 85.16 W
Rapid City, S.D., U.S. 140 C9 44.04 N 103.13 W
Rapid Creek, stm., S.D., U.S. 140 D10 43.54 N 102.37 W
Rapide-Blanc, Qc., Can. 122 C4 47.48 N 72.58 W
Rapide-Blanc-Station, Qc., Can. 122 C3 47.41 N 73.03 W
Rapid River, Mi., U.S. 126 C2 45.53 N 86.59 W
Rāpina, Est. 26 B10 58.06 N 27.27 E
Rapla, Est. 26 A7 59.00 N 24.47 E
Raposo, hill, Port. 184c 38.40 N 9.11 W
Rappahannock, stm., Va., U.S. 124 G9 37.34 N 76.17 W
Rapperswil, Switz. 24 I4 47.14 N 8.49 E
Rāpti, stm., Asia 70 E9 26.17 N 83.40 E
Rapu Rapu Island, i., Phil. 68 D5 13.12 N 124.09 E
Raqaba, Khasm el-, hill, Egypt 76 J2 28.14 N 31.46 E
Raraka, at., Fr. Poly. 94 E12 16.10 S 144.54 W
Rarotonga, i., Cook Is. 100j a26 21.13 S 159.46 W
Rarotonga International Airport, arpt., Cook Is. 100j a26 21.11 S 159.48 W
Rasa, Ilha, i., Braz. 205a 23.04 S 43.09 W
Rasa, Punta, c., Arg. 166 H4 40.51 S 62.19 W
Rasa, Punta, c., Arg. 172 H9 36.18 S 56.46 W
Ra's al-'Ayn, Syria 74 B7 36.49 N 40.03 E
Ra's al-Khaymah, U.A.E. 74 H14 25.46 N 55.57 E
Ra's an-Naqb, Jord. 76 I6 29.59 N 35.29 E
Ra's Ba'labakk, Leb. 76 D7 34.15 N 36.24 E
Râșcani, Mol. 38 F6 47.57 N 27.34 E
Rașcov, Mol. 38 F7 47.57 N 28.52 E
Ras Dashen Terara, mtn., Eth. 82 E7 13.16 N 38.24 E
Ras Djebel, Tun. 32 G4 37.13 N 10.09 E
Raseborg, Fin. 18 H10 59.59 N 23.39 E
Raseiniai, Lith. 26 E6 55.22 N 23.08 E
Rās el-Barr, Egypt 76 G2 31.30 N 31.49 E
Rashād, Sudan 82 E6 11.51 N 31.03 E
Rashid (Rosetta), Egypt 76 G1 31.23 N 30.24 E
Rashid, Masabb (Rosetta Mouth), mth., Egypt 76 G1 31.29 N 30.20 E
Rashin see Najin, Kor., N. 54 C9 42.15 N 130.18 E
Rashivka, Ukr. 38 C12 50.13 N 33.53 E
Rashkov see Rașcov, Mol. 38 F7 47.57 N 28.52 E
Rasht, Iran 74 B11 37.16 N 49.35 E
Rashtrapati Bhawan, bldg., India 190a 28.37 N 77.12 E
Rasina, stm., Yugo. 36 F8 43.37 N 21.21 E
Rasi Salai, Thai. 64 E7 15.20 N 104.09 E
Raška, Yugo. 36 F7 43.17 N 20.36 E
Rās Koh, mtn., Pak. 62 C2 28.50 N 65.12 E
Rasm al-Arwām, Sabkhat, l., Syria 76 C8 35.33 N 37.40 E
Rasna, Bela. 26 F14 54.00 N 31.11 E
Râșnov, Rom. 36 D12 45.35 N 25.27 E
Raso, Cabo, c., Port. 184c 38.43 N 9.29 W
Rasony, Bela. 26 E11 55.54 N 28.49 E
Raspberry Mountain, mtn., Ar., U.S. 134 C5 34.22 N 94.00 W
Rasra, India 70 F9 25.51 N 83.51 E
Rasskazovka, Russia 183b 55.38 N 37.20 E
Rasskazovo, Russia 40 E12 52.39 N 41.52 E
Rasšua, ostrov, i., Russia 50 G19 47.45 N 153.01 E
Rassypnaja, Russia 40 F18 51.36 N 53.37 E

Name	Page	Map Ref.	Latitude	Longitude
Rast, Rom.	36	F10	43.53 N	23.17 E
Rasta, stm., Bela.	26	G13	53.36 N	30.55 E
Råstajavri see Råstojaure, l., Eur.	14	D11	68.45 N	20.28 E
Ra's Tannūrah, Sau. Ar.	74	G12	26.42 N	50.06 E
Ras Tanura see Ra's Tannūrah, Sau. Ar.	74	G12	26.42 N	50.06 E
Rastatt, Ger.	24	H4	48.51 N	8.12 E
Rastede, Ger.	24	C4	53.14 N	8.11 E
Rastenburg see Kętrzyn, Pol.	24	B17	54.04 N	21.23 E
Råstojaure, l., Eur.	14	D11	68.45 N	20.28 E
Rásttigáisá, mtn., Nor.	14	B17	70.00 N	26.18 E
Rasūl, Pak.	70	B4	32.41 N	73.33 E
Rasulpur, India	190a		28.37 N	77.22 E
Rasulpur, ngh., India	190a		28.42 N	77.01 E
Rat, stm., Mb., Can.	142	E17	49.35 N	97.08 W
Ratak Islands, is., Marsh. Is.	94	B8	9.00 N	171.00 E
Ratamka, Bela.	26	G10	53.55 N	27.20 E
Ratangarh, India	70	D5	28.04 N	74.37 E
Ratanpur, India	190b		22.50 N	88.14 E
Rätansbyn, Swe.	16	E12	62.28 N	14.31 E
Rat Burana, Thai.	187a		13.41 N	100.30 E
Rat Buri, Thai.	64	F4	13.32 N	99.49 E
Rāth, India	70	F7	25.35 N	79.34 E
Rath, ngh., Ger.	181		51.17 N	6.49 E
Rathbun Lake, res., Ia., U.S.	130	D4	40.51 N	92.58 W
Rathdrum, Ire.	10	I6	52.56 N	6.14 W
Rathdrum, Id., U.S.	146	C9	47.48 N	116.53 W
Rathenow, Ger.	24	D8	52.36 N	12.20 E
Rathkeale, Ire.	10	I4	52.32 N	8.56 W
Rathlin Island, i., N. Ire., U.K.	10	F6	55.18 N	6.13 W
Ráth Luirc, Ire.	10	I4	52.22 N	8.41 W
Rathmecke, Ger.	181		51.15 N	7.38 E
Rathwell, Mb., Can.	142	E15	49.39 N	98.32 W
Ratibor see Racibórz, Pol.	24	F14	50.05 N	18.13 E
Rätische Alpen see Rhaetian Alps, mts., Eur.	30	D7	46.29 N	10.00 E
Rat Island, i., Ak., U.S.	109a	g22	51.47 N	178.19 E
Rat Islands, is., Ak., U.S.	109a	g22	52.00 N	178.00 E
Ratlām, India	70	G5	23.20 N	75.02 E
Ratmanova, ostrov, i., Russia	50	C27	65.47 N	169.04 W
Ratnāgiri, India	69	C1	16.59 N	73.17 E
Ratnapura, Sri L.	69	H5	6.40 N	80.23 E
Ratne, Ukr.	38	B3	51.40 N	24.31 E
Ratodero, Pak.	70	E2	27.48 N	68.18 E
Raton, N.M., U.S.	138	E4	36.54 N	104.25 W
Raton Pass, p., N.M., U.S.	138	E4	36.59 N	104.28 W
Rats, stm., Qc., Can.	122	A4	49.16 N	72.19 W
Rattanaburi, Thai.	64	E6	15.19 N	103.51 E
Rattaphum, Thai.	64	I5	7.08 N	100.17 E
Rattlesnake, Mt., U.S.	146	D13	46.56 N	113.59 W
Rattlesnake Creek, stm., Ks., U.S.	138	D10	38.13 N	98.22 W
Rattlesnake Creek, stm., Or., U.S.	146	H9	42.44 N	117.47 W
Rattlesnake Peak, mtn., Ca., U.S.	198		34.16 N	117.47 W
Rattling Run, stm., Pa., U.S.	197b		40.33 N	79.32 W
Rattosjärvi, Fin.	14	F15	66.50 N	24.53 E
Rättvik, Swe.	16	G13	60.53 N	15.07 E
Ratz, Mount, mtn., B.C., Can.	110	D4	57.23 N	132.19 W
Ratzeburg, Ger.	24	C6	53.41 N	10.47 E
Rau, Indon.	66	C2	0.33 N	100.01 E
Raub, Malay.	64	K5	3.47 N	101.51 E
Rauch, Arg.	172	H8	36.47 S	59.05 W
Rauchenwarth, Aus.	182b		48.05 N	16.32 E
Raudanjoki, stm., Fin.	14	F17	66.27 N	26.04 E
Raudeberg, Nor.	16	E2	61.59 N	5.08 E
Raudlia, Nor.	16	B11	65.54 N	14.26 E
Raufarhöfn, Ice.	12a	j32	66.28 N	15.57 W
Raufoss, Nor.	16	G8	60.43 N	10.37 E
Raukumara Range, mts., N.Z.	102	C7	37.58 S	177.53 E
Raul Soares, Braz.	170	K4	20.06 S	42.27 W
Rauma, Fin.	18	F8	61.07 N	21.30 E
Rauma, stm., Nor.	16	E5	62.33 N	7.43 E
Rauna, Lat.	26	C8	57.20 N	25.39 E
Raung, Gunung, vol., Indon.	66	H9	8.07 S	114.03 E
Raurkela, India	70	G10	22.13 N	84.51 E
Răut, stm., Mol.	38	F6	47.15 N	29.08 E
Rautalampi, Fin.	18	E13	62.37 N	26.47 E
Rāutara, India	190b		22.51 N	88.28 E
Rautavaara, Fin.	18	D15	63.30 N	28.20 E
Ravalgaon, India	70	H5	20.38 N	74.25 E
Ravanica, Manastir, rel., Yugo.	36	F8	43.58 N	21.26 E
Ravānsar, Iran	74	C10	34.42 N	46.39 E
Ravanusa, Italy	32	G7	37.16 N	13.58 E
Rava-Rus'ka, Ukr.	38	C2	50.13 N	23.37 E
Raven, Va., U.S.	124	G4	37.05 N	81.48 W
Ravena, N.Y., U.S.	124	B12	42.28 N	73.49 W
Ravenna, Italy	30	F9	44.25 N	12.12 E
Ravenna, Ky., U.S.	124	G2	37.40 N	83.57 W
Ravenna, Mi., U.S.	130	A11	43.11 N	85.56 W
Ravenna, Ne., U.S.	140	F13	41.01 N	98.54 W
Ravenna, Oh., U.S.	126	G8	41.09 N	81.15 W
Ravensburg, Ger.	24	I5	47.47 N	9.36 E
Ravenscrag, Sk., Can.	142	E4	49.29 N	109.05 W
Ravenshoe, Austl.	98	A5	17.36 S	145.28 E
Ravensthorpe, Austl.	96	F4	33.34 S	120.03 E
Ravenswood, S. Afr.	191d		26.11 S	28.15 E
Ravenswood, W.V., U.S.	124	F4	38.57 N	81.45 W
Ravenswood Park, p.o.i., Ma., U.S.	201		42.36 N	70.42 W
Ravenswood Point, c., Ca., U.S.	200		37.30 N	122.08 W
Ravensworth, Va., U.S.	202c		38.48 N	77.13 W
Rāvi, stm., Asia	70	C4	30.37 N	71.52 E
Ravine Lake, res., N.J., U.S.	194		40.43 N	74.38 W
Ravinia Park, p.o.i., Il., U.S.	196		42.09 N	87.46 W
Ravnina, Turkmen.	72	B9	37.57 N	62.40 E
Rāwah, Iraq	74	C7	34.30 N	41.54 E
Rawaki, at., Kir.	94	D9	3.43 S	170.43 W
Rāwalpindi, Pak.	70	B4	33.36 N	73.04 E
Rawa Mazowiecka, Pol.	24	E16	51.46 N	20.16 E
Rawandoz, Iraq	74	B9	36.37 N	44.34 E
Rawas, stm., Indon.	66	E3	2.42 S	103.24 E
Rawdah, l., Syria	74	C7	35.15 N	41.04 E
Rawdah, Wādī ar-, stm., Syria	76	D8	34.24 N	37.29 E
Rawd el-Farag, ngh., Egypt	191c		30.05 N	31.14 E
Rawdon, Qc., Can.	126	B16	46.02 N	73.42 W
Rawhide Creek, stm., Wy., U.S.	140	E8	42.06 N	104.20 W
Rawhide Lake, l., On., Can.	126	B7	46.39 N	82.37 W
Rawhide Mountain, mtn., Nv., U.S.	148	E9	38.17 N	116.25 W
Rawi, Indon.	66	E8	2.05 S	113.54 E
Rawicz, Pol.	24	E12	51.36 N	16.51 E
Rawlinna, Austl.	96	F4	31.02 S	125.18 E
Rawlins, Wy., U.S.	150	B9	41.47 N	107.14 W
Rawreth, Eng., U.K.	178		51.37 N	0.35 E
Rawson, Arg.	166	H4	43.19 S	65.05 W
Rawson, Arg.	172	G7	34.36 S	60.05 W
Raxāul, India	70	E10	26.58 N	84.49 E
Ray, N.D., U.S.	142	F10	48.19 N	103.12 W
Ray, Cape, c., Nf., Can.	122	C17	47.38 N	59.18 W
Raya, Indon.	66	C11	1.03 N	118.31 E
Raya, Bukit, mtn., Indon.	66	D8	0.40 S	112.41 E
Rāyachoti, India	69	D4	14.02 N	78.45 E
Rāyadurg, India	69	D3	14.41 N	76.50 E
Rāyagarha, India	69	B6	19.10 N	83.24 E
Rayen, Ger.	181		51.28 N	6.32 E
Ray Hubbard, Lake, res., Tx., U.S.	136	B11	32.54 N	96.30 W
Rāyikhah, l., Sau. Ar.	74	G5	26.10 N	36.23 E
Raymond, Ab., Can.	144	G18	49.27 N	112.38 W
Raymond, Il., U.S.	130	E8	39.18 N	89.34 W
Raymond, Mn., U.S.	128	F3	45.00 N	95.14 W
Raymond, Ms., U.S.	134	E8	32.15 N	90.25 W
Raymond, Wa., U.S.	146	D3	46.41 N	123.43 W
Raymond Terrace, Austl.	98	I8	32.45 S	151.44 E
Raymondville, Tx., U.S.	136	H10	26.29 N	97.46 W
Raymore, Sk., Can.	142	C9	51.24 N	104.31 W
Rayne, La., U.S.	134	G6	30.14 N	92.16 W
Raynham Greyhound Park, p.o.i., Ma., U.S.	201		41.59 N	71.04 W
Rayón, Mex.	120	G7	29.42 N	110.34 W
Rayones, Mex.	154	C8	25.01 N	100.05 W
Rayong, Thai.	64	F5	12.41 N	101.16 E
Rāypur, India	190b		22.25 N	88.31 E
Rayside-Balfour, On., Can.	126	B8	46.37 N	81.13 W
Raytown, Mo., U.S.	130	E3	38.59 N	94.28 W
Rayville, La., U.S.	134	E7	32.29 N	91.45 W
Raz, Pointe du, c., Fr.	20	F4	48.02 N	4.44 W
Razan, Iran	74	C11	35.22 N	49.04 E
Ražanj, Yugo.	36	F8	43.41 N	21.33 E
Razbegaj, Russia	183a		59.47 N	29.56 E
Războieni, Rom.	36	B13	47.03 N	26.34 E
Razdan see Hrazdan, Arm.	42	E11	40.29 N	44.45 E
Razdolinsk, Russia	48	C16	58.25 N	94.36 E
Razdol'noe, Russia	54	C9	43.30 N	131.49 E
Razdory, Russia	183b		55.45 N	37.18 E
Răzeni, Mol.	38	G7	46.45 N	28.54 E
Razgrad, Blg.	36	F13	43.32 N	26.31 E
Razim, Lacul, l., Rom.	36	E15	44.54 N	28.57 E
Razlog, Blg.	36	H10	41.53 N	23.29 E
Razmitelevo, Russia	183a		59.54 N	30.41 E
Rāznas ezers, l., Lat.	26	D10	56.20 N	27.27 E
Raznomojka, Russia	40	E19	52.28 N	55.52 E
Razorback Mountain, mtn., B.C., Can.	144	E6	51.35 N	124.42 W
Răzvani, Rom.	36	E13	44.24 N	26.53 E
Ré, Île de, i., Fr.	22	C4	46.11 N	1.23 W
Read, Eng., U.K.	180		53.49 N	2.21 W
Reading, Eng., U.K.	10	J12	51.28 N	0.59 W
Reading, Ks., U.S.	138	C12	38.31 N	95.57 W
Reading, Mi., U.S.	124	C1	41.49 N	84.44 W
Reading, Oh., U.S.	124	E1	39.13 N	84.26 W
Reading, Pa., U.S.	124	D9	40.20 N	75.56 W
Reading Station, trans., Pa., U.S.	203		39.57 N	75.10 W
Readlyn, Ia., U.S.	130	B5	42.42 N	92.13 W
Readstown, Wi., U.S.	128	H6	43.26 N	90.45 W
Real, stm., Braz.	170	F6	11.26 S	37.22 W
Real, Cordillera, mts., S.A.	164	G4	16.50 S	66.34 W
Real del Castillo, Mex.	148	L9	31.55 N	116.18 W
Real del Padre, Arg.	172	G4	34.50 S	67.46 W
Real Felipe, Museo Histórico del, hist., Peru	204d		12.04 S	77.09 W
Realicó, Arg.	172	G5	35.02 S	64.14 W
Realitos, Tx., U.S.	136	G9	27.26 N	98.31 W
Réalmont, Fr.	22	F8	43.47 N	2.11 E
Reardan, Wa., U.S.	146	C9	47.40 N	117.52 W
Reata, Mex.	154	B8	26.08 N	101.04 W
Réau, Fr.	179		48.37 N	2.38 E
Reay, Scot., U.K.	10	C9	58.33 N	3.47 W
Rebbenesøya, i., Nor.	14	B9	70.03 N	18.47 E
Rebecca, Lake, l., Austl.	96	F4	29.53 S	122.10 E
Rebel Hill, Pa., U.S.	203		40.04 N	75.20 W
Rebi, Indon.	60	G9	6.21 S	134.07 E
Rebiana Sand Sea see Rabyānah, Ramlat, des., Libya	82	C4	24.30 N	21.00 E
Rebild Bakker, misc. cult., Den.	16	K7	56.50 N	9.51 E
Reboly, Russia	18	D17	63.48 N	30.48 E
Rebouças, Braz.	172	B12	25.37 S	50.42 W
Rebouças, Túnel, trans., Braz.	205a		22.56 S	43.14 W
Rebun-tō, i., Japan	54	B14	45.23 N	141.02 E
Recalde, Arg.	172	H7	36.38 S	61.05 W
Recanati, Italy	30	G10	43.24 N	13.33 E
Rečane, Russia	26	D14	56.24 N	31.38 E
Recherche, Archipelago of the, is., Austl.	96	F4	34.05 S	122.45 E
Recherche, Cape, c., Sol. Is.	101b	f9	10.11 S	161.19 E
Rečica see Rèčyca, Bela.	26	H13	52.21 N	30.24 E
Recife, Braz.	170	E8	8.03 S	34.54 W
Recinto, Chile	172	H2	36.48 S	71.43 W
Recklinghausen, Ger.	24	E3	51.36 N	7.11 E
Recknitz, stm., Ger.	24	C8	54.15 N	12.26 E
Recoleta, Chile	204e		33.23 S	70.38 W
Reconquista, Arg.	172	D8	29.09 S	59.37 W
Reconquista, stm., Arg.	206		34.25 S	58.35 W
Recreio, Braz.	170	K4	21.31 S	42.28 W
Recreo, Arg.	172	D5	29.17 S	65.04 W
Rector, Ar., U.S.	130	H7	36.15 N	90.17 W
Recuay, Peru	164	E2	9.43 S	77.28 W
Rèčyca, Bela.	26	H13	52.21 N	30.24 E
Rèčyca, Bela.	38	B5	51.51 N	26.48 E
Recz, Pol.	24	C11	53.16 N	15.33 E
Red (Hong, Song) (Yuan), stm., Asia	62	D9	20.18 N	106.32 E
Red, stm., N.A.	128	A1	50.24 N	96.47 W
Red, stm., U.S.	116	E7	29.49 N	91.22 W
Red, stm., U.S.	130	H10	36.31 N	87.21 W
Red, stm., Ky., U.S.	124	G2	37.49 N	84.05 W
Red, stm., N.M., U.S.	138	E3	36.39 N	105.41 W
Red, stm., Wi., U.S.	128	G10	44.49 N	88.37 W
Red, Elm Fork, stm., U.S.	138	F8	34.52 N	99.19 W
Red, North Fork, stm., U.S.	138	F8	34.23 N	99.16 W
Red, Prairie Dog Town Fork, stm., U.S.	134	H7	34.34 N	99.57 W
Red, Salt Fork, stm., U.S.	138	G9	34.27 N	99.22 W
Red, South Fork, stm., U.S.	130	H11	36.40 N	86.55 W
Red, West Fork, stm., U.S.	130	H10	36.32 N	87.20 W
Reda, Pol.	24	B14	54.36 N	18.21 E
Redang, Pulau, i., Malay.	64	J6	5.46 N	103.00 E
Red Bank, N.J., U.S.	124	D11	40.20 N	74.04 W
Red Bank, Tn., U.S.	134	B13	35.06 N	85.16 W
Red Bank Battle Monument, hist., Pa., U.S.	203		39.52 N	75.11 W
Redbank Creek, stm., Pa., U.S.	124	C6	40.58 N	79.32 W
Red Banks, Ms., U.S.	134	C9	34.49 N	89.34 W
Red Bay, Nf., Can.	111a	I22	51.44 N	56.24 W
Red Bay, Al., U.S.	134	C10	34.26 N	88.07 W
Redbay, Fl., U.S.	134	G12	30.35 N	85.56 W
Redberry Lake, l., Sk., Can.	142	B6	52.40 N	107.10 W
Red Bluff, Ca., U.S.	148	C3	40.11 N	122.14 W
Red Bluff Reservoir, res., U.S.	136	B4	31.57 N	103.56 W
Red Boiling Springs, Tn., U.S.	130	H12	36.31 N	85.50 W
Red Bud, Il., U.S.	130	F7	38.12 N	89.59 W
Red Canyon, val., S.D., U.S.	140	D9	43.18 N	103.49 W
Redcar, Eng., U.K.	10	G11	54.36 N	1.03 W
Red Cedar, stm., Mi., U.S.	130	B13	42.42 N	84.31 W
Red Cedar, stm., Wi., U.S.	128	G7	44.42 N	91.52 W
Red Cedar Lake, l., On., Can.	126	B9	46.44 N	79.54 W
Red Clay Creek, stm., U.S.	203		39.43 N	75.39 W
Red Clay Creek, East Branch, stm., Pa., U.S.	203		39.49 N	75.42 W
Red Clay Creek, West Branch, stm., Pa., U.S.	203		39.49 N	75.42 W
Redcliff, Ab., Can.	142	D3	50.05 N	110.47 W
Redcliff see Red Cliff, Co., U.S.	138	B2	39.30 N	106.22 W
Red Cliff, Co., U.S.	138	B2	39.30 N	106.22 W
Redcliffe, Austl.	98	F9	27.14 S	153.06 E
Redcliffe, Mount, mtn., Austl.	96	E4	28.25 S	121.32 E
Red Cliff Indian Reservation, ind. res., Wi., U.S.	128	E7	46.55 N	90.48 W
Red Cliffs, Austl.	98	J4	34.18 S	142.11 E
Red Cloud, Ne., U.S.	138	A10	40.05 N	98.31 W
Red Creek, stm., Ms., U.S.	134	G10	30.38 N	88.38 W
Red Deer, Ab., Can.	144	D17	52.15 N	113.48 W
Red Deer, stm., Can.	118	B10	50.55 N	109.53 W
Red Deer, stm., Can.	142	B12	52.59 N	100.52 W
Red Deer Creek, stm., Tx., U.S.	138	F8	35.56 N	100.24 W
Red Deer Lake, l., Ab., Can.	144	D17	52.44 N	113.06 W
Red Deer Lake, l., Mb., Can.	142	B12	52.56 N	101.20 W
Reddersburg, S. Afr.	90	F8	29.38 S	26.10 E
Red Devil, Ak., U.S.	109	D8	61.46 N	157.18 W
Redding, Ca., U.S.	148	C3	40.35 N	122.22 W
Reddish, Eng., U.K.	180		53.26 N	2.09 W
Redditch, Eng., U.K.	10	I10	52.18 N	1.56 W
Rede, stm., Eng., U.K.	10	F10	55.07 N	2.13 W
Redenção, Braz.	170	C6	4.13 S	38.43 W
Redes Mere, l., Eng., U.K.	180		53.15 N	2.14 W
Redeye, stm., Mn., U.S.	128	E3	46.25 N	94.49 W
Redfield, Ia., U.S.	130	C3	41.35 N	94.10 W
Redfield, S.D., U.S.	140	C14	44.52 N	98.30 W
Redfish Lake, l., Id., U.S.	146	F12	44.07 N	114.56 W
Redford, Tx., U.S.	136	E3	29.26 N	104.10 W
Redford, ngh., Mi., U.S.	199		42.25 N	83.16 W
Red Fox Forest, Va., U.S.	202c		38.49 N	77.15 W
Redhead, Trin.	159f	s13	10.47 N	60.57 W
Redhill, Austl.	98	F7	33.32 S	138.14 E
Red Hill, Ca., U.S.	198		33.45 N	117.48 W
Redhill Aerodrome, arpt., Eng., U.K.	178		51.12 N	0.07 W
Red Hill Branch, stm., Md., U.S.	202b		39.14 N	76.51 W
Red Hook, N.Y., U.S.	124	C12	41.59 N	73.52 W
Redhouse Creek, stm., Md., U.S.	202b		39.18 N	76.31 W
Redja, stm., Russia	26	C14	58.05 N	31.33 E
Redkey, In., U.S.	130	D12	40.20 N	85.08 W
Redkino, Russia	26	D19	56.38 N	36.18 E
Red Lake, On., Can.	118	D13	51.00 N	93.49 W
Redlake, Mn., U.S.	128	D3	47.51 N	95.00 W
Red Lake, l., On., Can.	118	B18	51.01 N	94.05 W
Red Lake, l., Az., U.S.	150	H2	35.40 N	114.04 W
Red Lake, l., S.D., U.S.	140	D13	43.43 N	99.13 W
Red Lake, stm., Mn., U.S.	128	D2	47.55 N	97.01 W
Red Lake Falls, Mn., U.S.	128	D2	47.52 N	96.16 W
Red Lake Indian Reservation, ind. res., Mn., U.S.	128	B3	48.02 N	94.58 W
Red Lake Road, On., Can.	128	B5	49.59 N	93.22 W
Redlands, Ca., U.S.	148	I8	34.02 N	117.11 W
Redlands, Co., U.S.	150	D8	39.05 N	108.37 W
Red Level, Al., U.S.	134	F12	31.24 N	86.36 W
Red Lick, Ms., U.S.	134	F8	31.47 N	90.58 W
Red Lion, Pa., U.S.	124	E9	39.54 N	76.36 W
Red Lion, Pa., U.S.	203		39.53 N	75.41 W
Red Lion Airport, arpt., N.J., U.S.	203		39.54 N	74.45 W
Red Lodge, Mt., U.S.	140	B3	45.11 N	109.15 W
Redmond, Or., U.S.	146	F5	44.16 N	121.10 W
Redmond, Ut., U.S.	150	D5	39.00 N	111.51 W
Redmond, Wa., U.S.	146	C4	47.40 N	122.06 W
Red Mountain, mtn., Ca., U.S.	148	B2	41.35 N	123.06 W
Red Mountain, mtn., Mt., U.S.	146	C14	47.07 N	112.44 W
Red Mountain Pass, p., Co., U.S.	150	F9	37.53 N	107.42 W
Red Oak, Ia., U.S.	130	D2	41.00 N	95.14 W
Red Oak, Ok., U.S.	134	C3	34.57 N	95.04 W
Redon, Fr.	20	G6	47.39 N	2.05 W
Redonda, i., Antig.	159a	d3	16.56 N	62.20 W
Redonda, Isla, i., Ven.	159f	t12	9.54 N	61.28 W
Redonda Islands, is., B.C., Can.	144	F6	50.13 N	124.48 W
Redondela, Spain	28	B2	42.17 N	8.35 W
Redondo, Port.	28	F3	38.38 N	7.32 W
Redondo Beach, Ca., U.S.	148	J7	33.50 N	118.23 W
Redondo Beach State Park, p.o.i., Ca., U.S.	198		33.50 N	118.24 W
Redoubt Volcano, vol., Ak., U.S.	109	D9	60.29 N	152.45 W
Red Pass, B.C., Can.	144	D11	52.59 N	119.00 W
Red Pheasant Indian Reserve, ind. res., Sk., Can.	142	B5	52.30 N	108.07 W
Red Rock, B.C., Can.	144	C8	53.41 N	122.40 W
Red Rock, On., Can.	128	C10	48.58 N	88.18 W
Red Rock, i., Ca., U.S.	200		37.56 N	122.26 W
Red Rock, stm., Mt., U.S.	146	F14	44.59 N	112.53 W
Red Rock, Lake, res., Ia., U.S.	130	C4	41.25 N	93.06 W
Red Rock Creek, stm., Ok., U.S.	138	E11	36.27 N	96.58 W
Red Root Creek, stm., N.J., U.S.	194		40.30 N	74.19 W
Red Run, stm., Md., U.S.	202b		39.24 N	76.47 W
Red Run, stm., Mi., U.S.	199		42.34 N	82.58 W
Redruth, Eng., U.K.	10	K7	50.14 N	5.14 W
Red Sea, s.	82	C7	20.00 N	38.00 E
Red Springs, N.C., U.S.	132	B6	34.49 N	79.10 W
Redstone, B.C., Can.	144	D7	52.07 N	123.40 W
Redstone Arsenal, mil., Al., U.S.	134	C12	34.35 N	86.39 W
Redstone Creek, stm., S.D., U.S.	140	C15	44.03 N	98.05 W
Redstone Lake, l., On., Can.	126	C11	45.11 N	78.32 W
Reduction, Pa., U.S.	197b		40.11 N	79.46 W
Redvers, Sk., Can.	142	E12	49.35 N	101.41 W
Redwater, Ab., Can.	144	C17	53.57 N	113.06 W
Redwater, stm., Mt., U.S.	142	G8	48.03 N	105.12 W
Redwillow, stm., Can.	144	A11	55.01 N	119.18 W
Red Willow Creek, stm., Ne., U.S.	140	G12	40.13 N	100.29 W
Red Wing, Mn., U.S.	128	G6	44.33 N	92.31 W
Redwood, stm., Mn., U.S.	128	G3	44.34 N	95.06 W
Redwood Creek, stm., Ca., U.S.	148	C2	41.17 N	124.05 W
Redwood Creek, stm., Ca., U.S.	200		37.52 N	122.35 W
Redwood Creek, stm., Ca., U.S.	200		37.31 N	122.12 W
Redwood Falls, Mn., U.S.	128	G3	44.32 N	95.06 W
Redwood National Park, p.o.i., Ca., U.S.	148	B1	41.20 N	124.02 W
Redwood Point, c., Ca., U.S.	200		37.32 N	122.12 W
Redwood Regional Park, p.o.i., Ca., U.S.	200		37.38 N	122.10 W
Redwood Terrace, Ca., U.S.	200		37.19 N	122.18 W
Redwood Valley, Ca., U.S.	148	D2	39.15 N	123.12 W
Ree, Lough, l., Ire.	10	H5	53.35 N	8.00 W
Reed City, Mi., U.S.	126	E4	43.53 N	85.32 W
Reeder, N.D., U.S.	140	A10	46.06 N	102.57 W
Reed Lake, l., Sk., Can.	142	D6	50.24 N	107.05 W
Reedley, Ca., U.S.	148	G6	36.35 N	119.26 W
Reedsburg, Wi., U.S.	128	H8	43.31 N	89.59 W
Reeds Peak, mtn., N.M., U.S.	150	J9	33.09 N	107.51 W
Reedsport, Or., U.S.	146	G2	43.41 N	124.05 W
Reedsville, Wi., U.S.	126	D2	44.08 N	87.57 W
Reefton, N.Z.	102	F4	42.06 S	171.50 E
Reelfoot Lake, l., Tn., U.S.	130	H8	36.24 N	89.21 W
Rees, Ger.	24	E2	51.46 N	6.24 E
Reese, Mi., U.S.	126	E6	43.27 N	83.41 W
Reese, stm., Nv., U.S.	148	D8	40.39 N	116.55 W
Reese Air Force Base, mil., Tx., U.S.	138	H6	33.36 N	102.02 W
Reeseville, Wi., U.S.	128	H10	43.17 N	88.50 W
Reform, Al., U.S.	134	D11	33.22 N	88.00 W
Refuge Cove, B.C., Can.	144	F6	50.07 N	124.49 W
Refugio, Tx., U.S.	136	F10	28.18 N	97.16 W
Refugio Creek, stm., Ca., U.S.	200		38.01 N	122.17 W
Rega, stm., Pol.	24	C11	54.08 N	15.17 E
Regen, Ger.	24	H9	48.58 N	13.07 E
Regen, stm., Ger.	24	G8	49.01 N	12.07 E
Regência, Braz.	170	J6	19.38 S	39.50 W
Regency Estates, Md., U.S.	202c		39.03 N	77.10 W
Regeneração, Braz.	170	D4	6.15 S	42.41 W
Regensburg, Ger.	24	H8	49.01 N	12.05 E
Regent, Austl.	192b		37.44 S	145.00 E
Regent, N.D., U.S.	140	A10	46.24 N	102.34 W
Regent Park, Md., U.S.	202c		39.03 N	77.10 W
Regents Park, Austl.	192a		33.53 S	151.02 E
Regents Park, ngh., S. Afr.	191d		26.15 S	28.04 E
Regent's Park, p.o.i., Eng., U.K.	178		51.32 N	0.09 W
Regentville, Austl.	192a		33.47 S	150.40 E
Reggâne, Alg.	84	D5	26.42 N	0.10 E
Reggio di Calabria, Italy	32	F9	38.07 N	15.39 E
Reggio nell'Emilia, Italy	30	F7	44.42 N	10.38 E
Reghin, Rom.	36	C11	46.46 N	24.42 E
Regina, Sk., Can.	142	D9	50.26 N	104.38 W
Regina Beach, Sk., Can.	142	D8	50.47 N	105.00 W
Regina Elena, Canale, can., Italy	184b		45.41 N	8.39 E
Región Metropolitana, state, Chile	172	F2	33.30 S	70.30 W
Registan see Rīgestān, reg., Afg.	72	C9	31.00 N	65.00 E
Registro, Braz.	172	B14	24.29 S	47.50 W
Regla, ngh., Cuba	204b		23.08 N	82.20 W
Rego Park, ngh., N.Y., U.S.	194		40.44 N	73.52 W
Regozero, Russia	18	B18	65.27 N	31.13 E
Reguengos de Monsaraz, Port.	28	F3	38.25 N	7.32 W
Rehau, Ger.	24	F7	50.14 N	12.02 E
Rehberge, hill, Ger.	182a		52.35 N	13.11 E
Rehberge, Volkspark, p.o.i., Ger.	182a		52.33 N	13.20 E
Rehoboth, Nmb.	90	C3	23.19 S	17.05 E
Rehoboth Beach, De., U.S.	124	F10	38.43 N	75.04 W
Reḥovot, Isr.	76	G5	31.53 N	34.48 E
Reiche Liesing, stm., Aus.	182b		48.08 N	16.16 E
Reichenbach, Ger.	24	F8	50.37 N	12.18 E
Reichenbach see Dzierżoniów, Pol.	24	F12	50.43 N	16.39 E
Reichsbrücke, trans., Aus.	182b		48.14 N	16.25 E
Reid, Mont, hill, Qc., Can.	114	A12	50.45 N	76.50 W
Reid Lake, l., Sk., Can.	142	D5	50.02 N	108.05 W
Reidsville, Ga., U.S.	132	D3	32.04 N	82.06 W
Reidsville, N.C., U.S.	132	H6	36.21 N	79.40 W
Reigate, Eng., U.K.	10	J12	51.14 N	0.13 W
Reigate and Banstead, mun., Eng., U.K.	178		51.17 N	0.12 W
Reihoku, Japan	56	G2	32.30 N	130.02 E
Reims (Rheims), Fr.	20	E12	49.15 N	4.02 E
Rein Anteriur (Vorderrhein), stm., Switz.	30	D5	46.49 N	9.24 E
Reinbeck, Ia., U.S.	130	B5	42.19 N	92.35 W
Reindeer, stm., Sk., Can.	110	D10	55.34 N	103.09 W
Reindeer Island, i., Mb., Can.	142	B15	52.25 N	98.00 W
Reindeer Lake, l., Can.	110	D10	57.15 N	102.15 W
Reine, Nor.	14	E4	67.56 N	13.03 E
Reineskarvet, mts., Nor.	16	G6	60.47 N	8.13 E
Reinga, Cape, c., N.Z.	102	B5	34.25 S	172.40 E
Reinheimen, reg., Nor.	16	F6	62.02 N	8.28 E
Reinickendorf, ngh., Ger.	182a		52.35 N	13.21 E
Reinosa, Spain	28	A6	42.59 N	4.08 W
Reinøya, i., Nor.	14	C10	69.56 N	19.42 E
Reinøya, i., Nor.	14	B16	70.16 N	25.18 E
Reinshagen, ngh., Ger.	181		51.10 N	7.09 E
Reisaelva, stm., Nor.	14	C12	69.46 N	21.00 E
Reisafjorden, b., Nor.	14	C11	69.53 N	21.00 E
Reisa Nasjonalpark, p.o.i., Nor.	14	C13	69.13 N	22.00 E
Reisdorf, Camp, mil., D.R.C.	191b		4.21 S	15.15 E
Reisduoddar-hal'di see Haltiatunturi, mtn., Eur.	14	C12	69.18 N	21.16 E
Reisholz, ngh., Ger.	181		51.11 N	6.52 E
Reisjärvi, Fin.	18	D11	63.37 N	24.56 E
Reisterstown, Md., U.S.	124	E9	39.28 N	76.49 W
Reisterstown Road Plaza, shp. cen., Md., U.S.	202b		39.02 N	76.42 W
Reitdiep, stm., Neth.	20	A15	53.21 N	6.10 E
Reitz, S. Afr.	90	E9	27.48 S	28.26 E
Reivilo, S. Afr.	90	E7	27.34 S	24.11 E
Rejmyra, Swe.	16	I13	58.50 N	15.55 E
Rejowiec Fabryczny, Pol.	24	E19	51.07 N	23.13 E
Rekjoāni, India	190b		22.37 N	88.28 E
Reliance, N.T., Can.	110	C9	62.43 N	109.07 W
Reliance, Wy., U.S.	150	B7	41.40 N	109.11 W
Rellinghausen, ngh., Ger.	181		51.25 N	7.04 E
Remada, Tun.	84	C7	32.18 N	10.23 E
Remagen, Ger.	24	F3	50.34 N	7.13 E
Remanso, Braz.	170	E4	9.37 S	42.07 W
Remarde, stm., Fr.	179		48.35 N	2.15 E
Rembang, Indon.	66	G7	6.43 S	111.20 E
Remedios, Col.	168	D4	7.00 N	74.42 W
Remedios, Pan.	156	H7	8.13 N	81.49 W
Remedios, Punta, c., El Sal.	156	F2	13.31 N	89.48 W
Remedios, Santuario de los, rel., Mex.	204a		19.28 N	99.15 W
Remer, Mn., U.S.	128	D5	47.02 N	93.56 W
Remich Airport, arpt., Pa., U.S.	197b		40.36 N	79.49 W
Remington, In., U.S.	130	D10	40.45 N	87.08 W
Remington, Va., U.S.	124	F8	38.31 N	77.47 W
Rémiré, Fr. Gu.	164	C7	4.53 N	52.17 W
Remiremont, Fr.	20	G15	48.00 N	6.35 E
Remolà, Estany del, b., Spain	184d		41.17 N	2.04 E
Remoulins, Fr.	22	F10	43.56 N	4.33 E
Rempang, Pulau, i., Indon.	66	C4	0.51 N	104.10 E
Rems, stm., Ger.	30	B6	48.52 N	9.16 E
Remscheid, Ger.	24	E3	51.11 N	7.11 E
Remscheider-Stausee, res., Ger.	181		51.10 N	7.14 E
Remsen, Ia., U.S.	130	B1	42.48 N	96.00 W
Remus, Mi., U.S.	126	E4	43.35 N	85.09 W
Rena, Nor.	16	F9	61.08 N	11.20 E
Renaix see Ronse, Bel.	20	D12	50.44 N	3.36 E
Renata, B.C., Can.	144	G12	49.25 N	118.06 W
Renca, Chile	204e		33.24 S	70.44 W
Renca, Cerro, mtn., Chile	204e		33.23 S	70.43 W
Renceni, Lat.	26	C8	57.44 N	25.25 E
Renda, Lat.	26	C5	57.09 N	22.22 E
Rende, Italy	32	E10	39.19 N	16.11 E
Rend Lake, res., Il., U.S.	130	F8	38.05 N	88.58 W
Rendova Island, i., Sol. Is.	101b	e7	8.32 S	157.20 E
Rendsburg, Ger.	24	B5	54.18 N	9.40 E
Renfrew, On., Can.	126	C13	45.28 N	76.41 W
Rengat, Indon.	66	D3	0.25 S	102.35 E
Rengel, Indon.	66	G8	7.04 S	112.00 E
Rengen, l., Eur.	16	C11	64.05 N	14.03 E
Rengkang, Indon.	66	C8	1.07 N	112.10 E
Rengo, Chile	172	G2	34.28 S	70.53 W
Reng Tlāng, mtn., Asia	70	H14	21.59 N	92.36 E
Renheji, China	58	F6	31.56 N	115.07 E
Renhuai, China	58	H2	27.48 N	106.19 E
Reni, Ukr.	38	H7	45.27 N	28.17 E
Renick, W.V., U.S.	124	F5	37.59 N	80.21 W
Renju, China	58	I6	24.51 N	115.54 E
Renko, Fin.	18	G11	60.54 N	24.18 E
Renland, reg., Grnld.	108	C20	71.12 N	26.45 W
Renmark, Austl.	98	J3	34.11 S	140.45 E
Rennell, i., Sol. Is.	94	E7	11.33 S	160.04 E
Rennell, Islas, is., Chile	166	J2	52.00 S	74.00 W
Rennell and Bellona, state, Sol. Is.	101b	f9	10.45 S	160.08 E
Rennerdale, Pa., U.S.	197b		40.24 N	80.08 W
Rennes, Fr.	20	F7	48.06 N	1.40 W
Rennesøy, i., Nor.	16	H3	59.06 N	5.43 E
Rennie, Mb., Can.	142	E18	49.51 N	95.33 W
Rennie's Mill, China	189d		22.18 N	114.15 E
Reno, Nv., U.S.	148	D6	39.31 N	119.48 W
Reno, stm., Italy	30	F8	44.36 N	12.16 E
Reno Hill, mtn., Wy., U.S.	140	E6	42.35 N	106.03 W
Renoster, stm., S. Afr.	90	G5	31.20 S	20.17 E
Renous, N.B., Can.	122	D11	46.49 N	65.48 W
Renous, stm., N.B., Can.	122	D10	46.49 N	65.47 W
Renovo, Pa., U.S.	124	C8	41.19 N	77.45 W
Rensjön, Swe.	14	D10	68.04 N	19.48 E
Rensselaer, In., U.S.	130	D10	40.56 N	87.08 W
Rensselaer, N.Y., U.S.	124	B12	42.39 N	73.44 W
Rentería, Spain	28	A9	43.18 N	1.52 W
Rentfort, ngh., Ger.	181		51.35 N	6.57 E
Renton, Wa., U.S.	146	C4	47.29 N	122.10 W
Renville, Mn., U.S.	128	G3	44.47 N	95.13 W
Renwick, Ia., U.S.	130	B4	42.49 N	93.58 W
Renziehausen Park, p.o.i., Pa., U.S.	197b		40.21 N	79.50 W
Reo, Indon.	66	H12	8.18 S	120.28 E
Reola, ngh., India	190a		28.34 N	76.59 E
Repaupo, N.J., U.S.	203		39.48 N	75.18 W
Répce, stm., Eur.	30	C14	47.41 N	17.03 E
Repetek, Turkmen.	72	B9	38.34 N	63.11 E
Repëvka, Russia	38	B17	51.05 N	38.39 E
Repino, Russia	18	G16	60.10 N	29.52 E
Repojoki, stm., Fin.	14	D16	68.24 N	26.02 E
Repolka, Russia	26	A12	59.16 N	29.34 E
Reposaari, Fin.	18	F8	61.37 N	21.27 E
Reppin see Rzepin, Pol.	24	D10	52.20 N	14.49 E
Repton, Al., U.S.	134	F11	31.24 N	87.14 W
Republic, Ks., U.S.	138	B11	39.55 N	97.49 W
Republic, Mi., U.S.	126	B1	46.23 N	88.00 W
Republic, Mo., U.S.	130	G4	37.07 N	93.28 W
Republic, Wa., U.S.	146	B8	48.38 N	118.43 W
República Dominicana see Dominican Republic, ctry., N.A.	152	D10	19.00 N	70.40 W
Republic Airport, arpt., N.Y., U.S.	194		40.44 N	73.25 W
Republican, stm., U.S.	138	B11	39.03 N	96.48 W
Republican, North Fork, stm., U.S.	138	A6	40.09 N	102.02 W
Republican, South Fork, stm., U.S.	138	B7	40.03 N	101.30 W
Republic Observatory, sci., S. Afr.	191d		26.11 S	28.05 E
Republic of Korea see Korea, South, ctry., Asia	54	G8	36.30 N	128.00 E
Republic Steel Corporation, sci., Oh., U.S.	197a		41.28 N	81.40 W
République centrafricaine see Central African Republic, ctry., Afr.	82	F4	7.00 N	21.00 E
Repuebelo de Oriente, Mex.	136	I8	25.50 N	99.38 W
Repulse Bay, Nu., Can.	110	B13	66.31 N	86.13 W
Repulse Bay, b., Austl.	98	C7	20.36 S	148.43 E
Repvåg, Nor.	14	B16	70.44 N	25.40 E
Requena, Peru	164	D3	5.05 S	73.52 W
Requena, Spain	28	E9	39.29 N	1.06 W
Réquista, Fr.	22	E8	44.02 N	2.32 E
Reriutaba, Braz.	170	C5	4.10 S	40.35 W
Reşadiye, ngh., Tur.	185b		41.05 N	29.15 E
Reşadiye Yarımadası, pen., Tur.	34	G10	36.42 N	27.29 E
Resang, Tanjong, c., Malay.	64	K6	2.34 N	103.49 E
Rescalda, Italy	184b		45.38 N	8.56 E

Name	Page	Map Ref.	Latitude	Longitude
Rescaldina, Italy	184b		45.37 N	8.57 E
Reschenpass (Resia, Passo di), p., Eur.	30	D7	46.50 N	10.30 E
Reschenscheideck see Reschenpass, p., Eur.	30	D7	46.50 N	10.30 E
Reschenscheideck see Resia, Passo di, p., Eur.	30	D7	46.50 N	10.30 E
Research, Austl.	192b		37.42 S	145.11 E
Reseda, ngh., Ca., U.S.	198		34.12 N	118.31 W
Resen, Mac.	34	B4	41.05 N	21.00 E
Reserva, Braz.	172	B12	24.38 S	50.50 W
Reserva, Parque de la, p.o.i., Peru	204d		12.04 S	77.02 W
Reserve, La., U.S.	134	G8	30.03 N	90.33 W
Reserve, N.M., U.S.	150	J8	33.43 N	108.46 W
Reserve Township, Pa., U.S.	197b		40.29 N	79.59 W
Reservoir, Austl.	192b		37.43 S	145.00 E
Reservoir Pond, l., Ma., U.S.	201		42.10 N	71.07 W
Rešetnikovo, Russia	26	D19	56.27 N	36.34 E
Reshetylivka, Ukr.	38	D13	49.34 N	34.05 E
Resht see Rasht, Iran	74	B11	37.16 N	49.35 E
Resia, Passo di (Reschenpass), p., Eur.	30	D7	46.50 N	10.30 E
Resina see Ercolano, Italy	32	D8	40.48 N	14.20 E
Resistencia, Arg.	172	C8	27.26 S	59.00 W
Reşiţa, Rom.	36	D8	45.17 N	21.53 E
Resko, Pol.	24	C11	53.46 N	15.25 E
Resolute (Kaujuitoq), Nu., Can.	108	C7	74.41 N	94.53 W
Resolution Island, i., Nu., Can.	108	E12	61.30 N	65.00 W
Resolution Island, i., N.Z.	102	G2	45.40 S	166.40 E
Rešoty, Russia	26	C11	57.08 N	28.31 E
Resplandes, Braz.	170	D3	6.16 S	45.11 W
Resplendor, Braz.	170	J5	19.20 S	41.15 W
Ressa, stm., Russia	26	F18	54.44 N	35.12 E
Ressaca, Ribeirão da, stm., Braz.	205b		23.38 S	46.51 W
Resse, ngh., Ger.	181		51.34 N	7.07 E
Resseta, stm., Russia	26	G18	53.48 N	35.15 E
Restigouche, stm., Can.	122	C9	48.01 N	66.12 W
Restinga Seca, Braz.	172	D11	29.48 S	53.22 W
Reston, Mb., Can.	124	E12	49.33 N	101.05 W
Restoule Lake, l., On., Can.	126	B10	46.03 N	79.47 W
Restrepo, Col.	168	E5	4.16 N	73.31 W
Retalhuleu, Guat.	156	E2	14.32 N	91.41 W
Retamosa, Ur.	172	F10	33.35 S	54.44 W
Retezat, Munții, mts., Rom.	36	D10	45.20 N	22.45 E
Retezat, Parcul Național, p.o.i., Rom.	36	D9	45.21 N	22.50 E
Rethel, Fr.	20	E13	49.30 N	4.22 E
Réthymno, Grc.	34	H7	35.21 N	24.29 E
Retiche, Alpi see Rhaetian Alps, mts., Eur.	30	D7	46.29 N	10.00 E
Retiro, Estacion, trans., Arg.	206		34.36 S	58.22 W
Retiro, Parque del, p.o.i., Spain	184a		40.25 N	3.41 W
Rettendon, Eng., U.K.	178		51.39 N	0.33 E
Rettendon Place, Eng., U.K.	178		51.38 N	0.34 E
Rettihovka, Russia	54	B10	44.08 N	132.46 E
Reunion, dep., Afr.	89a	i10	21.06 S	55.36 E
Réunion see Reunion, dep., Afr.	89a	i10	21.06 S	55.36 E
Réunion, i., Reu.	80	I11	21.06 S	55.36 E
Reus, Spain	28	C12	41.09 N	1.06 E
Reuschenberg, Ger.	181		51.10 N	6.42 E
Reuss, stm., Switz.	30	C5	47.29 N	8.13 E
Reuterstadt Stavenhagen, Ger.	24	C8	53.41 N	12.54 E
Reutlingen, Ger.	24	H5	48.29 N	9.11 E
Reval see Tallinn, Est.	26	A7	59.25 N	24.48 E
Revda, Russia	14	E25	67.57 N	34.34 E
Réveillon, Ruisseau le, stm., Fr.	179		48.42 N	2.30 E
Revelstoke, B.C., Can.	144	F12	50.59 N	118.11 W
Revelstoke, Lake, res., B.C., Can.	144	E12	51.30 N	118.30 W
Reventazón, Peru	164	E1	6.08 S	80.57 W
Revere Beach, cst., Ma., U.S.	201		42.25 N	70.59 W
Revesby, Austl.	192a		33.57 S	151.01 E
Revigna, Rom.	36	E14	44.41 N	27.06 E
Revilla del Campo, Spain	28	B7	42.13 N	3.32 W
Revillagigedo, Islas, is., Mex.	152	D2	18.48 N	112.05 W
Revillagigedo Island, i., Ak., U.S.	109	E13	55.38 N	131.25 W
Revillagigedo Islands see Revillagigedo, Islas, is., Mex.	152	D2	18.48 N	112.05 W
Revillo, S.D., U.S.	128	F2	45.00 N	96.34 W
Revin, Fr.	20	E13	49.56 N	4.39 E
Revjakino, Russia	26	F20	54.21 N	37.40 E
Revolución, Mex.	136	H2	26.12 N	105.05 W
Revolution, Museum of the, bldg., Russia	183b		55.46 N	37.36 E
Revsbotn, b., Nor.	14	B14	70.43 N	24.22 E
Revsundssjön, l., Swe.	16	E13	62.48 N	15.19 E
Rewa, India	70	F8	24.31 N	81.17 E
Rewāri, India	70	D6	28.11 N	76.36 E
Rexburg, Id., U.S.	146	G15	43.49 N	111.47 W
Rexdale, ngh., On., Can.	193b		43.43 N	79.35 W
Rexford, Ks., U.S.	138	B8	39.28 N	100.44 W
Rexford, Mt., U.S.	146	B11	48.53 N	115.09 W
Rexhame, Ma., U.S.	201		42.06 N	70.40 W
Rexton, N.B., Can.	122	D12	46.38 N	64.52 W
Rey, Arroyo del, stm., Arg.	206		34.46 S	58.27 W
Rey, Embalse del, res., Spain	184a		40.18 N	3.32 W
Rey, Isla del, i., Pan.	156	H8	8.22 N	78.55 W
Rey, Laguna del, l., Mex.	154	B7	27.01 N	103.24 W
Reyes, Bol.	166	B3	14.18 S	67.22 W
Reyes, Point, c., Ca., U.S.	148	F2	38.00 N	123.01 W
Reyhanlı, Tur.	42	G7	36.16 N	36.34 E
Reykjanes, pen., Ice.	108	E21	63.49 N	22.43 W
Reykjanes Ridge, unds.	176	C10	62.00 N	27.00 W
Reykjavík, Ice.	12a	k28	64.08 N	21.56 W
Reyno, Ar., U.S.	130	H7	36.22 N	90.45 W
Reynolds, Ga., U.S.	132	D1	32.33 N	84.05 W
Reynolds, N.D., U.S.	142	G16	47.57 N	97.45 W
Reynolds Channel, strt., N.Y., U.S.	194		40.36 N	73.40 W
Reynoldsville, Pa., U.S.	124	C7	41.05 N	78.52 W
Reynosa, Mex.	154	B9	26.04 N	98.17 W
Reẓā'īyeh see Orūmīyeh, Iran	74	B9	37.32 N	45.04 E
Rezé, Fr.	20	G7	47.11 N	1.32 W
Rēzekne, Lat.	26	D10	56.30 N	27.19 E
Rēzekne, stm., Lat.	26	D10	56.47 N	26.57 E
Rezeny see Răzeni, Mol.	38	G7	46.45 N	28.54 E
Rezina, Mol.	38	F7	47.44 N	28.54 E
Rezovo, Blg.	36	G15	41.59 N	28.01 E
Rezovska (Mutlu), stm., Eur.	36	G14	41.59 N	28.01 E
Reẕvānshahr, Iran	74	B11	37.33 N	49.08 E
Rhadeswood Reservoir, res., Eng., U.K.	180		53.29 N	1.56 W
Rhaetian Alps, mts., Eur.	30	D7	46.29 N	10.00 E
Rhame, N.D., U.S.	140	A9	46.13 N	103.39 W
Rhea Creek, stm., Or., U.S.	146	E7	45.29 N	119.46 W
Rheda-Wiedenbrück, Ger.	24	E4	51.50 N	8.18 E
Rheims see Reims, Fr.	20	E12	49.15 N	4.02 E
Rhein, Sk., Can.	142	C11	51.21 N	102.11 W
Rhein see Rhine, stm., Eur.	20	C15	51.52 N	6.02 E
Rheinbrücke, trans., Ger.	181		51.12 N	6.44 E
Rheine, Ger.	24	D3	52.17 N	7.26 E
Rheinen, Ger.	181		51.27 N	7.38 E
Rheinfelden, Ger.	20	G16	47.33 N	7.46 E
Rhein-Herne-Kanal, can., Ger.	181		51.27 N	6.47 E
Rheinland-Pfalz, state, Ger.	24	G3	50.00 N	7.00 E
Rheinstadion, p.o.i., Ger.	181		51.16 N	6.44 E
Rheydt, Schloss, hist., Ger.	181		51.11 N	6.29 E
Rhin see Rhine, stm., Eur.	20	F16	51.52 N	6.02 E
Rhine, Ga., U.S.	132	E2	31.59 N	83.11 W
Rhine (Rhein) (Rhin), stm., Eur.	20	C15	51.52 N	6.02 E
Rhinebeck, N.Y., U.S.	124	C12	41.55 N	73.54 W
Rhinelander, Wi., U.S.	128	F9	45.37 N	89.24 W
Rhineland-Palatinate see Rheinland-Pfalz, state, Ger.	24	G3	50.00 N	7.00 E
Rhinns Point, c., Scot., U.K.	10	F6	55.40 N	6.30 W
Rhir, Cap, c., Mor.	84	C2	30.37 N	9.53 W
Rho, Italy	30	E5	45.31 N	9.02 E
Rhode Island, state, U.S.	124	C14	41.40 N	71.30 W
Rhode Island Sound, strt., U.S.	124	C14	41.25 N	71.15 W
Rhodes, Austl.	192a		33.50 S	151.05 E
Rhodes see Ródos, Grc.	34	G11	36.26 N	28.13 E
Rhodes, Eng., U.K.	180		53.33 N	2.14 W
Rhodes see Ródos, i., Grc.	34	G10	36.10 N	28.00 E
Rhodesia see Zimbabwe, ctry., Afr.	88	D4	20.00 S	30.00 E
Rhodes Matopos National Park, p.o.i., Zimb.	90	B9	20.33 S	28.20 E
Rhodes Park, p.o.i., S. Afr.	191d		26.12 S	28.06 E
Rhodes Peak, mtn., Id., U.S.	146	D12	46.40 N	114.47 W
Rhodes' Tomb, hist., Zimb.	88	E4	20.30 S	28.30 E
Rhodon, Fr.	179		48.43 N	2.04 E
Rhodon, Ruisseau le, stm., Fr.	179		48.42 N	2.04 E
Rhodope Mountains, mts., Eur.	36	H11	41.30 N	24.30 E
Rhön, mts., Ger.	24	F6	50.43 N	9.58 E
Rhondda, Wales, U.K.	10	J9	51.39 N	3.28 W
Rhône, state, Fr.	22	D10	45.55 N	4.40 E
Rhône, stm., Eur.	22	F10	43.52 N	4.38 E
Rhosesmor, Wales, U.K.	180		53.12 N	3.10 W
Rhue, stm., Fr.	22	D8	45.22 N	2.28 E
Rhyl, Wales, U.K.	10	H9	53.19 N	3.28 W
Riachão, Braz.	170	D2	7.21 S	46.39 W
Riachão do Jacuípe, Braz.	170	F6	11.49 S	39.21 W
Riacho de Santana, Braz.	170	G4	13.38 S	42.55 W
Riachos, Islas de los, is., Arg.	166	H4	40.10 S	62.08 W
Riachuelo, stm., Arg.	206		34.38 S	58.22 W
Riamkanan, Waduk, res., Indon.	66	E9	3.31 S	115.06 E
Rianápolis, Braz.	170	H1	15.29 S	49.28 W
Riāng, India	70	E14	27.31 N	92.56 E
Riaño, Spain	28	A6	42.59 N	4.59 W
Riánsares, stm., Spain	28	E7	39.30 N	3.18 W
Riāsi, India	70	B5	33.03 N	74.48 E
Riasnopil', Ukr.	38	F10	47.04 N	31.11 E
Riau, state, Indon.	66	D2	1.00 N	102.00 E
Riau, Kepulauan, is., Indon.	66	C4	1.00 N	104.30 E
Riaza, Spain	28	C7	41.16 N	3.28 W
Riaza, stm., Spain	28	C7	41.42 N	3.54 W
Ribadavia, Spain	28	B2	42.17 N	8.08 W
Ribadeo, Spain	28	A3	43.32 N	7.02 W
Ribadesella, Spain	28	A5	43.27 N	5.04 W
Ribas de Jarama, Spain	184a		40.23 N	3.31 W
Ribas do Rio Pardo, Braz.	166	D6	20.27 S	53.45 W
Ribáuè, Moz.	88	C6	14.54 S	38.18 E
Ribble, stm., Eng., U.K.	10	H10	53.44 N	2.49 W
Ribbleton, Eng., U.K.	180		53.46 N	2.40 W
Ribble Valley, mun., Eng., U.K.	180		53.48 N	2.31 W
Ribchester, Eng., U.K.	180		53.49 N	2.32 W
Ribe, Den.	16	L6	55.19 N	8.46 E
Ribe, state, Den.	16	L6	55.35 N	8.50 E
Ribeauvillé, Fr.	24	H3	48.11 N	7.19 E
Ribeira, Braz.	172	B13	24.39 S	49.00 W
Ribeira do Pombal, Braz.	170	F6	10.50 S	38.31 W
Ribeira Grande, C.V.	85a	k9	17.10 N	25.04 W
Ribeirão, Braz.	170	E8	8.31 S	35.23 W
Ribeirão Pires, mun., Braz.	205b		23.43 S	46.21 W
Ribeirão Preto, Braz.	170	K2	21.10 S	47.48 W
Ribeirão Vermelho, Braz.	170	K3	21.11 S	45.03 W
Ribeiro Gonçalves, Braz.	170	D3	7.33 S	45.14 W
Ribera, Italy	32	G7	37.30 N	13.16 E
Riberalta, Bol.	166	B3	11.00 S	66.05 W
Rib Lake, Wi., U.S.	128	F8	45.19 N	90.12 W
Ribnica, Slvn.	30	E11	45.44 N	14.44 E
Ribnitz-Damgarten, Ger.	24	B8	54.14 N	12.25 E
Ribstone Creek, stm., Ab., Can.	144	D19	52.51 N	110.04 W
Ricarda, Estany de la, b., Spain	184d		41.18 N	2.07 E
Ricardo Flores Magón, Mex.	120	F9	29.56 N	106.57 W
Ricaurte, Col.	168	G2	1.13 N	77.59 W
Riccia, Italy	32	C8	41.29 N	14.50 E
Riccione, Italy	30	F9	44.00 N	12.39 E
Rice, Tx., U.S.	136	B11	32.15 N	96.30 W
Rice Lake, Wi., U.S.	128	F7	45.30 N	91.44 W
Rice Lake, l., On., Can.	126	D11	44.08 N	78.13 W
Riceville, Ia., U.S.	128	H6	43.21 N	92.33 W
Riceville, Tn., U.S.	134	B14	35.23 N	84.41 W
Richan, On., Can.	126	B6	49.59 N	92.50 W
Richard B. Russell Lake, res., U.S.	132	B3	34.05 N	82.39 W
Richard Collinson Inlet, b., N.T., Can.	109	B17	72.45 N	113.45 W
Richards, Tx., U.S.	136	D12	30.32 N	95.51 W
Richards Bay, S. Afr.	90	F11	28.47 S	32.04 E
Richards Bay, b., S. Afr.	90	F11	28.48 S	32.02 E
Richards Island, i., N.T., Can.	109	C13	69.20 N	134.30 W
Richardson, Tx., U.S.	136	B11	32.57 N	96.44 W
Richardson, Wa., U.S.	146	B4	48.27 N	122.54 W
Richardson Bay, b., Ca., U.S.	200		37.52 N	122.29 W
Richardson Mountains, mts., Can.	110	B3	67.22 N	136.03 W
Richardson Park, De., U.S.	203		39.44 N	75.35 W
Richard Toll, Sen.	84	F1	16.27 N	15.41 W
Richardton, N.D., U.S.	140	A10	46.52 N	102.20 W
Riche, Pointe, c., Nf., Can.	111a	i22	50.42 N	57.25 W
Richebourg, Fr.	179		48.49 N	1.38 E
Richelieu, Fr.	20	G9	47.01 N	0.19 E
Richelieu, stm., Qc., Can.	126	C16	46.04 N	73.06 W
Richer, Mb., Can.	142	E17	49.39 N	96.28 W
Richey, Mt., U.S.	142	G8	47.38 N	105.04 W
Richfield, Id., U.S.	146	G12	43.03 N	114.09 W
Richfield, Mn., U.S.	128	G5	44.53 N	93.16 W
Richfield, Pa., U.S.	124	D8	40.41 N	77.06 W
Richfield, Ut., U.S.	150	E4	38.46 N	112.05 W
Richfield Springs, N.Y., U.S.	124	B11	42.51 N	74.59 W
Richford, Vt., U.S.	122	F4	44.59 N	72.40 W
Rich Hill, Mo., U.S.	130	F3	38.06 N	94.21 W
Richibucto, N.B., Can.	122	D12	46.41 N	64.53 W
Richky, Ukr.	38	B13	51.07 N	34.30 E
Richland, Ga., U.S.	134	E14	32.05 N	84.39 W
Richland, Mi., U.S.	130	B12	42.22 N	85.27 W
Richland, Mo., U.S.	130	G5	37.51 N	92.24 W
Richland, Mt., U.S.	142	F7	48.49 N	106.03 W
Richland, Tx., U.S.	136	C11	31.54 N	96.26 W
Richland, Wa., U.S.	146	D7	46.16 N	119.16 W
Richland Center, Wi., U.S.	128	H8	43.20 N	90.23 W
Richland Creek, stm., Tn., U.S.	134	B11	35.01 N	86.55 W
Richland Creek, stm., Tx., U.S.	136	C11	31.57 N	96.03 W
Richlands, N.C., U.S.	132	B8	34.53 N	77.32 W
Richlands, Va., U.S.	124	G4	37.05 N	81.46 W
Richland Springs, Tx., U.S.	136	C9	31.16 N	98.57 W
Richmond, Austl.	98	I8	33.36 S	150.45 E
Richmond, Austl.	98	C4	20.43 S	143.07 E
Richmond, Austl.	192b		37.49 S	145.00 E
Richmond, B.C., Can.	144	G7	49.09 N	123.10 W
Richmond, On., Can.	126	C14	45.11 N	75.49 W
Richmond, Qc., Can.	122	E4	45.39 N	72.08 W
Richmond, N.Z.	102	E5	41.21 S	173.10 E
Richmond, S. Afr.	90	F10	29.54 S	30.06 E
Richmond, S. Afr.	90	G6	31.24 S	23.56 E
Richmond, Eng., U.K.	10	G11	54.24 N	1.44 W
Richmond, Ca., U.S.	148	F3	37.56 N	122.20 W
Richmond, In., U.S.	130	E13	39.49 N	84.53 W
Richmond, Ks., U.S.	130	F2	38.24 N	95.15 W
Richmond, Ky., U.S.	124	G1	37.44 N	84.18 W
Richmond, Me., U.S.	122	F7	44.05 N	69.47 W
Richmond, Mi., U.S.	124	B3	42.48 N	82.44 W
Richmond, Mn., U.S.	128	F4	45.26 N	94.31 W
Richmond, Mo., U.S.	130	E4	39.16 N	93.58 W
Richmond, Tx., U.S.	136	E12	29.34 N	95.45 W
Richmond, Ut., U.S.	146	I15	41.56 N	111.48 W
Richmond, Vt., U.S.	126	D16	44.24 N	72.59 W
Richmond, Va., U.S.	126	G8	37.33 N	77.26 W
Richmond, ngh., Ca., U.S.	200		37.46 N	122.29 W
Richmond, ngh., Pa., U.S.	203		39.59 N	75.06 W
Richmond, Point, c., Ca., U.S.	200		37.55 N	122.23 W
Richmond Creek, stm., N.Y., U.S.	194		40.34 N	74.11 W
Richmond Heights, Fl., U.S.	132	K5	25.37 N	80.24 W
Richmond Highlands, Wa., U.S.	146	C4	47.45 N	122.20 W
Richmond Hill, On., Can.	126	E10	43.52 N	79.25 W
Richmond Hill, Ga., U.S.	132	E4	31.56 N	81.18 W
Richmond Hill, ngh., N.Y., U.S.	194		40.42 N	73.49 W
Richmond Mall, shp. cen., Oh., U.S.	197a		41.32 N	81.30 W
Richmond Park, p.o.i., Eng., U.K.	178		51.26 N	0.16 W
Richmond Peak, mtn., St. Vin.	159e	o11	13.17 N	61.12 W
Richmond-San Rafael Bridge, trans., Ca., U.S.	200		37.56 N	122.27 W
Richmondtown Restoration, hist., N.Y., U.S.	194		40.34 N	74.09 W
Richmond Valley, ngh., N.Y., U.S.	194		40.31 N	74.13 W
Richmondville, N.Y., U.S.	124	B11	42.38 N	74.34 W
Richrath, Ger.	181		51.08 N	6.56 E
Rich Square, N.C., U.S.	124	H8	36.16 N	77.16 W
Rich Stadium, p.o.i., N.Y., U.S.	202a		42.57 N	78.47 W
Richton, Ms., U.S.	134	F10	31.20 N	88.56 W
Richwood, N.J., U.S.	203		39.43 N	75.10 W
Richwood, Oh., U.S.	124	D2	40.25 N	83.17 W
Richwood, W.V., U.S.	124	F5	38.13 N	80.33 W
Ricketts Glen State Park, p.o.i., Pa., U.S.	124	C9	41.20 N	76.18 W
Ricketts Point, c., Austl.	192b		38.00 S	145.02 E
Rickleån, stm., Swe.	16	C18	64.05 N	20.56 E
Rico, Co., U.S.	150	F9	37.41 N	108.00 W
Ricobayo, Embalse de, res., Spain	28	C4	41.38 N	5.54 W
Riddle, Or., U.S.	146	H3	42.57 N	123.21 W
Riddle Mountain, mtn., Or., U.S.	146	G8	43.07 N	118.30 W
Riddlewood, Pa., U.S.	203		39.54 N	75.26 W
Rideau, stm., On., Can.	126	D14	45.26 N	75.42 W
Ridge, Eng., U.K.	178		51.41 N	0.15 W
Ridge Acres, N.J., U.S.	194		40.41 N	74.32 W
Ridgecrest, Ca., U.S.	148	H8	35.37 N	117.40 W
Ridgedale, Sk., Can.	142	A9	53.03 N	104.08 W
Ridgefield Park, N.J., U.S.	194		40.51 N	74.01 W
Ridgeland, Ms., U.S.	134	E8	32.25 N	90.08 W
Ridgeland, S.C., U.S.	132	D4	32.29 N	80.58 W
Ridgely, Tn., U.S.	130	H8	36.15 N	89.29 W
Ridgetown, On., Can.	126	F8	42.26 N	81.52 W
Ridgeville, Mb., Can.	142	E16	49.04 N	97.01 W
Ridgeville, S.C., U.S.	132	C5	33.05 N	80.18 W
Ridgeway, On., Can.	202a		42.53 N	79.03 W
Ridgeway, Mo., U.S.	130	D4	40.22 N	93.56 W
Ridgeway, Wi., U.S.	130	A8	42.59 N	89.58 W
Ridgeway Ditch, can., Oh., U.S.	197a		41.25 N	82.05 W
Ridgewood, ngh., N.Y., U.S.	194		40.42 N	73.53 W
Ridgewood Farm, Pa., U.S.	203		39.57 N	75.34 W
Ridgewood Reservoir, res., N.Y., U.S.	194		40.41 N	73.53 W
Ridgway, Co., U.S.	150	E9	38.09 N	107.47 W
Ridgway, Il., U.S.	130	G9	37.47 N	88.15 W
Ridgway, Pa., U.S.	124	C7	41.25 N	78.43 W
Riding Mountain, mts., Mb., Can.	142	D14	50.43 N	99.51 W
Riding Mountain National Park, p.o.i., Mb., Can.	142	D13	50.55 N	100.25 W
Ridley Creek, stm., Pa., U.S.	203		39.51 N	75.21 W
Ridley Creek State Park, p.o.i., Pa., U.S.	203		39.57 N	75.27 W
Ridley Park, Pa., U.S.	203		39.52 N	75.19 W
Riebnesjaure, l., Swe.	14	F7	66.30 N	17.08 E
Ried im Innkreis, Aus.	30	B10	48.12 N	13.29 E
Riegelwood, N.C., U.S.	132	B7	34.20 N	78.13 W
Riehppegáisá, mtn., Nor.	14	C12	69.44 N	21.31 E
Riemke, ngh., Ger.	181		51.30 N	7.13 E
Rienzi, Ms., U.S.	134	C10	34.45 N	88.31 W
Riesa, Ger.	24	E9	51.18 N	13.17 E
Riesco, Isla, i., Chile	166	J2	53.00 S	72.29 W
Riesi, Italy	32	G8	37.17 N	14.05 E
Riet, stm., S. Afr.	90	F7	29.00 S	23.53 E
Riet, stm., S. Afr.	90	H5	31.36 S	20.37 E
Rietavas, Lith.	26	E4	55.43 N	21.56 E
Rietfontein, Nmb.	90	B5	21.55 S	20.53 E
Rietfontein (Buitsivango), stm., Afr.	90	B4	22.25 S	22.13 E
Rieti, Italy	30	H9	42.24 N	12.51 E
Rietspruit, stm., S. Afr.	191d		26.19 S	28.18 E
Rietspruit, stm., S. Afr.	191d		26.06 S	27.39 E
Rif, mts., Mor.	84	C4	35.00 N	4.00 W
Riffe Lake, res., Wa., U.S.	146	D4	46.30 N	122.20 W
Rifflart, D.R.C.	191b		4.25 S	15.21 E
Rifle, Co., U.S.	150	D9	39.32 N	107.46 W
Rifle, stm., Mi., U.S.	126	D5	43.59 N	83.49 W
Rifstangi, c., Ice.	12a	j31	66.31 N	16.09 W
Rift Valley, val., Afr.	80	F9	3.00 S	29.00 E
Rīga, Lat.	26	D7	56.57 N	24.06 E
Riga, Gulf of, b., Eur.	26	C6	57.30 N	23.35 E
Rigaih, Indon.	64	J2	4.39 N	95.33 E
Rīgas jūras līcis see Riga, Gulf of, b., Eur.	26	C6	57.30 N	23.35 E
Rīga Station, trans., Russia	183b		55.48 N	37.38 E
Rigby, Id., U.S.	146	G15	43.40 N	111.56 W
Rīgestān, reg., Afg.	72	C9	31.00 N	65.00 E
Riggins, Id., U.S.	146	E10	45.25 N	116.19 W
Rigi, mtn., Switz.	30	C5	47.05 N	8.30 E
Rigo, Pap. N. Gui.	101a	b4	9.48 S	147.34 E
Rig-Rig, Chad	82	E2	14.16 N	14.21 E
Riguldi, Est.	26	A6	59.07 N	23.33 E
Riihimäki, Fin.	18	G11	60.44 N	24.47 E
Riiser-Larsen Peninsula, pen., Ant.	103	B8	68.55 S	33.59 E
Riisitunturin kansallispuisto, p.o.i., Fin.	14	F19	66.14 N	28.28 E
Riječki Zaljev, b., Cro.	30	E11	45.13 N	14.24 E
Rijeka (Fiume), Cro.	30	E11	45.20 N	14.27 E
Rijn see Rhine, stm., Eur.	20	C15	51.52 N	6.02 E
Rijssen, Neth.	24	D2	52.18 N	6.31 E
Rikers Island, i., N.Y., U.S.	194		40.47 N	73.53 W
Rikers Island Channel, strt., N.Y., U.S.	194		40.47 N	73.52 W
Rila, mts., Blg.	36	G10	42.08 N	23.33 E
Riley, Ks., U.S.	138	B12	39.18 N	96.49 W
Riley, Mount, mtn., N.M., U.S.	150	L9	31.56 N	107.12 W
Rillito, Az., U.S.	150	K5	32.25 N	111.08 W
Rilski manastir, rel., Blg.	36	G10	42.09 N	23.20 E
Rímac, Peru	204d		12.03 S	77.03 W
Rimatara, i., Fr. Poly.	94	F11	22.38 S	152.51 W
Rimavská Sobota, Slvk.	24	H15	48.23 N	20.04 E
Rimbey, Ab., Can.	144	D16	52.36 N	114.13 W
Rimbo, Swe.	16	H16	59.44 N	18.22 E
Rimersburg, Pa., U.S.	124	C6	41.02 N	79.30 W
Rimforsa, Swe.	16	I13	58.08 N	15.42 E
Rimini, Italy	30	F9	44.04 N	12.34 E
Rimouski, Qc., Can.	122	B8	48.26 N	68.32 W
Rimouski, stm., Qc., Can.	122	B8	48.27 N	68.32 W
Rimrock Lake, res., Wa., U.S.	146	D5	46.38 N	121.11 W
Rinbung, China	62	C7	29.18 N	89.58 E
Rinca, Pulau, i., Indon.	66	H11	8.42 S	119.40 E
Rincón, P.R.	158a	b1	18.20 N	67.14 W
Rincon, Ga., U.S.	132	D4	32.17 N	81.14 W
Rincon, N.M., U.S.	150	K9	32.42 N	107.03 W
Rincón, Bahía de, b., P.R.	158a	c3	17.58 N	66.20 W
Rinconada, Arg.	166	D3	22.26 S	66.10 W
Rinconada, Hipódromo de la, p.o.i., Ven.	204c		10.26 N	66.56 W
Rincón del Bonete, Lago Artificial de, res., Ur.	172	F9	32.43 S	56.01 W
Rincón de Romos, Mex.	154	D7	22.14 N	102.18 W
Rindal, Nor.	16	D7	63.03 N	9.13 E
Rīngas, India	70	E5	27.21 N	75.34 E
Ringdove, Vanuatu	101d	k16	16.38 S	168.08 E
Ringe, Den.	16	L8	55.14 N	10.29 E
Ringebu, Nor.	16	F8	61.31 N	10.10 E
Ringertown, Pa., U.S.	197b		40.25 N	79.36 W
Ringgold, Ga., U.S.	134	C13	34.54 N	85.06 W
Ringgold, La., U.S.	134	E5	32.19 N	93.17 W
Ringim, Nig.	84	G6	12.09 N	9.09 E
Ringkøbing, Den.	16	K6	56.05 N	8.15 E
Ringkøbing, state, Den.	16	K6	56.10 N	8.50 E
Ringkøbing Fjord, b., Den.	16	L6	56.00 N	8.15 E
Ringling, Ok., U.S.	138	G11	34.09 N	97.35 W
Rings Island, Ma., U.S.	201		42.49 N	70.52 W
Ringsted, Den.	16	L9	55.27 N	11.49 E
Ringsted, Ia., U.S.	128	H4	43.17 N	94.30 W
Ringvassøya, i., Nor.	14	C10	69.55 N	19.15 E
Ringwood Manor, hist., N.J., U.S.	194		41.08 N	74.15 W
Ringwood North, Austl.	192b		37.48 S	145.14 E
Rinjani, Gunung, vol., Indon.	66	H10	8.23 S	116.28 E
Rinteln, Ger.	24	D5	52.11 N	9.04 E
Rio, Wi., U.S.	128	H9	43.26 N	89.13 W
Rio Azul, Braz.	172	B12	25.43 S	50.47 W
Riobamba, Ec.	168	H2	1.40 S	78.38 W
Río Blanco, Chile	172	F2	32.55 S	70.19 W
Rio Blanco, stm., Co., U.S.	138	D2	37.07 N	107.02 W
Rio Bonito, ngh., Braz.	205b		23.43 S	46.41 W
Rio Branco, Braz.	166	A3	9.58 S	67.48 W
Río Branco, Ur.	172	F11	32.35 S	53.23 W
Río Bravo, Mex.	136	F7	28.17 N	100.55 W
Río Bravo, Mex.	154	C9	25.58 N	98.05 W
Río Bravo, Parque Internacional del, p.o.i., Mex.	136	F5	29.00 N	102.40 W
Rio Brilhante, Braz.	166	D6	21.48 S	54.32 W
Río Bueno, Chile	166	H2	40.18 S	72.58 W
Río Caribe, Ven.	168	B10	10.41 N	63.06 W
Rio Casca, Braz.	170	K4	20.13 S	42.38 W
Río Ceballos, Arg.	172	E5	31.10 S	64.21 W
Río Chico, Ven.	168	B9	10.18 N	65.59 W
Rio Claro, Braz.	170	L2	22.25 S	47.33 W
Rio Claro, Trin.	159f	s12	10.18 N	61.09 W
Río Colorado, Arg.	172	I5	38.59 S	64.07 W
Rio Comprido, ngh., Braz.	205a		22.55 S	43.12 W
Río Cuarto, Arg.	172	F5	33.08 S	64.21 W
Rio das Contas, Braz.	170	G5	13.35 S	41.48 W
Rio das Pedras, Moz.	90	C12	23.11 S	35.23 E
Rio de Janeiro, Braz.	170	L4	22.54 S	43.14 W
Rio de Janeiro, Braz.	205a		22.54 S	43.14 W
Rio de Janeiro, state, Braz.	170	L4	22.00 S	42.30 W
Rio de Janeiro, mun., Braz.	205a		22.55 S	43.30 W
Rio Dell, Ca., U.S.	148	C1	40.30 N	124.05 W
Rio de Mouro, Port.	184c		38.46 N	9.20 W
Río de Oro, Col.	168	C5	8.17 N	73.24 W
Rio do Prado, Braz.	170	I5	16.36 S	40.34 W
Rio do Sul, Braz.	172	C13	27.13 S	49.39 W
Rio Douro, Braz.	205a		22.39 S	43.32 W
Rio Espera, Braz.	170	K4	20.51 S	43.28 W
Rio Felix, stm., N.M., U.S.	138	H3	33.09 N	104.18 W
Río Gallegos, Arg.	166	J3	51.38 S	69.13 W
Río Grande, Arg.	166	J3	53.48 S	67.47 W
Rio Grande, Braz.	172	F11	32.02 S	52.05 W
Río Grande, Mex.	154	D7	23.50 N	103.02 W
Río Grande, Nic.	156	F4	12.53 N	86.33 W
Río Grande, P.R.	158a	b4	18.22 N	65.48 W
Río Grande, Ven.	204c		10.35 N	66.57 W
Rio Grande (Bravo) (Grande, Río), stm., N.A.	120	H13	25.56 N	97.08 W
Rio Grande, Ponte do, trans., Braz.	205b		23.46 S	46.31 W
Rio Grande City, Tx., U.S.	136	H9	26.23 N	98.48 W
Rio Grande da Serra, Braz.	205b		23.44 S	46.24 W
Rio Grande da Serra, mun., Braz.	205b		23.45 S	46.23 W
Río Grande de Loiza, Embalse, res., P.R.	158a	b3	18.17 N	66.01 W
Rio Grande do Norte, state, Braz.	164	E10	5.45 S	36.00 W
Rio Grande do Sul see Rio Grande, Braz.	172	F11	32.02 S	52.05 W
Rio Grande do Sul, state, Braz.	172	D11	30.00 S	54.00 W
Ríohacha, Col.	168	B5	11.32 N	72.54 W
Río Hato, Pan.	156	H7	8.23 N	80.10 W
Río Hondo, Mex.	204a		19.25 N	99.16 W
Rio Hondo, Tx., U.S.	136	H10	26.14 N	97.34 W
Rio Hondo, stm., N.M., U.S.	138	H3	33.22 N	104.24 W
Rio Hondo, Embalse, res., Arg.	172	C5	27.33 S	65.01 W
Río Jueyes, P.R.	158a	b3	18.01 N	66.20 W
Río Lagartos, Mex.	156	B3	21.34 N	88.10 W
Riolândia, Braz.	166	D6	19.58 S	49.41 W
Rio Largo, Braz.	170	E8	9.29 S	35.51 W
Riom, Fr.	22	D9	45.53 N	3.07 E
Río Mayo, Arg.	166	I2	45.41 S	70.14 W
Río Mulatos, Bol.	166	C3	19.42 S	66.46 W
Riondel, B.C., Can.	144	G14	49.45 N	116.50 W
Rio Negro, Braz.	172	C13	26.05 S	49.47 W
Rionegro, Col.	168	D5	7.16 N	73.10 W
Río Negro, state, Arg.	166	G3	40.00 S	67.00 W
Rio Negro, Pantanal do, sw., Braz.	166	C5	19.00 S	56.00 W
Rionero in Vulture, Italy	32	D9	40.55 N	15.40 E
Riópar, Spain	28	F8	38.30 N	2.27 W
Rio Pardo, Braz.	172	E11	29.58 S	52.21 W
Rio Pardo de Minas, Braz.	170	H4	15.37 S	42.33 W
Río Piedras, Arg.	172	B5	25.18 S	64.53 W
Río Piedras, P.R.	158a	b3	18.24 N	66.03 W
Rio Piracicaba, Braz.	170	J4	19.56 S	43.12 W
Rio Pomba, Braz.	170	K4	21.16 S	43.10 W
Rio Preto, Braz.	170	L4	22.05 S	43.49 W
Rio Rancho, N.M., U.S.	138	F2	35.14 N	106.38 W
Rio Real, Braz.	170	F6	11.28 S	37.55 W
Río Segundo, Arg.	172	E5	31.38 S	63.56 W
Ríosucio, Col.	168	E4	5.25 N	75.42 W
Ríosucio, Col.	168	D3	7.25 N	77.05 W
Río Tercero, Arg.	172	F5	32.10 S	64.06 W
Rio Tinto, Braz.	170	D8	6.48 S	35.05 W
Rio Tuba, Phil.	68	F1	8.30 N	117.24 E
Rio Verde, Braz.	166	C6	17.46 S	50.55 W
Ríoverde, Mex.	154	E8	21.56 N	99.59 W
Rio Verde de Mato Grosso, Braz.	166	C6	18.56 S	54.52 W
Rio Vermelho, Braz.	170	J4	18.18 S	43.00 W
Rio Vista, Ca., U.S.	148	E4	38.09 N	121.41 W
Rioz, Fr.	20	G15	47.25 N	6.04 E
Riozinho, stm., Braz.	164	D4	2.53 S	66.57 W
Riozinho, stm., Braz.	170	E3	8.23 S	45.42 W
Ripky, Ukr.	38	B10	51.47 N	31.05 E
Ripley, Eng., U.K.	178		51.18 N	0.29 W
Ripley, Ms., U.S.	134	C10	34.44 N	88.57 W
Ripley, N.Y., U.S.	124	B6	42.15 N	79.42 W
Ripley, Oh., U.S.	124	F2	38.44 N	83.50 W
Ripley, Tn., U.S.	134	B9	35.44 N	89.32 W
Ripley, W.V., U.S.	124	F4	38.48 N	81.43 W
Ripoll, Spain	28	B13	42.12 N	2.12 E
Ripoll, stm., Spain	184d		41.29 N	2.12 E
Ripollet, Spain	184d		41.30 N	2.10 E
Ripon, Qc., Can.	126	C14	45.47 N	75.06 W
Ripon, Eng., U.K.	10	G11	54.08 N	1.31 W
Ripon, Ca., U.S.	148	F4	37.44 N	121.07 W
Ripon, Wi., U.S.	128	H10	43.50 N	88.49 W
Riposto, Italy	32	G9	37.44 N	15.12 E
Rippling Ridge, Md., U.S.	202b		39.11 N	76.37 W
Rippowam, stm., Ct., U.S.	194		41.03 N	73.33 W
Ririe, Id., U.S.	146	G15	43.39 N	111.47 W
Risaralda, state, Col.	168	E3	5.00 N	76.00 W
Risbäck, Swe.	16	C13	64.42 N	15.32 E
Rishā', Wādī ar-, stm., Sau. Ar.	74	H9	25.06 N	44.08 E
Rīshahr, Iran	74	F12	28.55 N	50.50 E
Rishīkesh, India	70	C7	30.06 N	78.18 E
Rishiri-suidō, strt., Japan	54	B14	45.10 N	141.25 E
Rishiri-tō, i., Japan	54	B14	45.11 N	141.14 E
Rishon LeẔiyyon, Isr.	76	G5	31.57 N	34.48 E
Rishra, India	190b		22.43 N	88.21 E
Rishton, Eng., U.K.	180		53.46 N	2.25 W
Rishworth, Eng., U.K.	180		53.40 N	1.57 W
Rishworth Moor, for., Eng., U.K.	180		53.39 N	2.01 W
Rising Star, Tx., U.S.	136	B9	32.06 N	98.58 W
Rising Sun, In., U.S.	130	F13	38.56 N	84.51 W
Rising Sun, Md., U.S.	124	E9	39.41 N	76.03 W
Risle, stm., Fr.	20	E9	49.26 N	0.22 E
Risnjak, mtn., Cro.	30	E11	45.26 N	14.37 E
Rison, Ar., U.S.	134	D6	33.57 N	92.11 W
Risør, Nor.	16	I7	58.43 N	9.14 E
Risøyhamn, Nor.	14	C6	68.58 N	15.37 E
Riss, stm., Ger.	20	F18	48.17 N	9.49 E
Risti, Est.	26	A7	58.59 N	24.02 E
Ristigouche see Restigouche, stm., Can.	122	C9	48.01 N	66.12 W
Ristiina, Fin.	18	F14	61.30 N	27.15 E
Ristijärvi, Fin.	18	C15	64.29 N	28.13 E
Ristna, Est.	26	B5	58.55 N	22.06 E
Rita Blanca Creek, stm., Tx., U.S.	138	F6	35.40 N	102.29 W
Ritchie, S. Afr.	90	F7	29.02 S	24.36 E
Ritchie, Md., U.S.	202c		38.52 N	76.52 W
Ritchie Branch, stm., Md., U.S.	202c		38.53 N	76.52 W
Rithāla, ngh., India	190a		28.43 N	77.06 E
Ritidian Point, c., Guam	100c	i10	13.38 N	144.51 E
Ritsumeikan University, educ., Japan	188		35.01 N	135.46 E
Ritter, Mount, mtn., Ca., U.S.	148	F6	37.42 N	119.12 W
Rittman, Oh., U.S.	124	D4	40.58 N	81.46 W
Ritzville, Wa., U.S.	146	C8	47.07 N	118.22 W
Rivadavia, Arg.	172	B6	24.11 S	62.53 W
Rivadavia, Arg.	172	E3	31.33 S	68.36 W
Rivadavia, Arg.	172	G6	35.29 S	62.58 W
Rivadavia, Chile	172	D2	29.58 S	70.34 W
Riva del Garda, Italy	30	E7	45.53 N	10.50 E
Rivanna, stm., Va., U.S.	124	G7	37.44 N	78.10 W
Rivas, Nic.	156	G5	11.27 N	85.51 W
Rivasdale, S. Afr.	191d		26.17 S	27.56 E
Rivas-Vaciamadrid, Spain	184a		40.20 N	3.31 W
Rive, Île de la, i., D.R.C.	191b		4.21 S	15.26 E
Rive-de-Gier, Fr.	22	D10	45.32 N	4.37 E
Rivera, Arg.	172	H6	37.09 S	63.15 W
Rivera, Ur.	172	E10	30.54 S	55.33 W
Riverbank, Ca., U.S.	148	F5	37.44 N	120.55 W

Name	Page	Map Ref.	Latitude	Longitude
River Cess, Lib.	84	H3	5.30 N	9.36 W
Riverdale, Ca., U.S.	148	G6	36.25 N	119.51 W
Riverdale, Il., U.S.	196		41.38 N	87.37 W
Riverdale, Md., U.S.	202c		38.57 N	76.55 W
Riverdale, N.J., U.S.	194		40.59 N	74.18 W
Riverdale, N.D., U.S.	142	G12	47.29 N	101.20 W
Riverdale, ngh., N.Y., U.S.	194		40.54 N	73.54 W
Riverdale Heights, Md., U.S.	202c		38.58 N	76.55 W
Riverdale Park, p.o.i., On., Can.	193b		43.40 N	79.21 W
River Edge, N.J., U.S.	194		40.55 N	74.02 W
River Edge, Oh., U.S.	197a		41.25 N	81.51 W
River Falls, Al., U.S.	134	F12	31.21 N	86.32 W
River Falls, Wi., U.S.	128	G6	44.51 N	92.37 W
River Forest, Il., U.S.	196		41.53 N	87.48 W
River Grove, Il., U.S.	196		41.55 N	87.50 W
Riverhead, Eng., U.K.	178		51.17 N	0.10 E
Riverhead, N.Y., U.S.	124	D13	40.55 N	72.39 W
River Hebert, N.S., Can.	122	E12	45.41 N	64.22 W
River Hill, Pa., U.S.	197b		40.12 N	79.54 W
Riverhurst, Sk., Can.	142	D7	50.54 N	106.52 W
Riverina, reg., Austl.	98	J6	35.30 S	145.30 E
River John, N.S., Can.	122	E13	45.45 N	63.03 W
River Jordan, B.C., Can.	144	H6	48.25 N	124.02 W
River Lea Navigation, can., Eng., U.K.	178		51.32 N	0.02 W
River Meadow Brook, stm., Ma., U.S.	201		42.38 N	71.17 W
Rivermont, N.C., U.S.	132	A8	35.13 N	77.38 W
River Oaks, Va., U.S.	202c		38.57 N	77.11 W
River Ridge Estates, Md., U.S.	202c		38.47 N	77.00 W
River Road, Or., U.S.	146	F3	44.05 N	123.06 W
River Rouge Park, p.o.i., Mi., U.S.	199		42.22 N	83.15 W
Rivers, Mb., Can.	142	D13	50.02 N	100.13 W
Rivers, Lake of the, l., Sk., Can.	142	E8	49.48 N	105.44 W
Riversdale, S. Afr.	90	I5	34.05 S	21.15 E
Riverside, Ca., U.S.	148	J8	33.58 N	117.21 W
Riverside, Ct., U.S.	194		41.02 N	73.35 W
Riverside, Il., U.S.	196		41.50 N	87.49 W
Riverside, Ia., U.S.	130	C6	41.28 N	91.34 W
Riverside, Tx., U.S.	136	D12	30.51 N	95.24 W
Riverside, Wa., U.S.	146	B7	48.30 N	119.30 W
Riverside, ngh., On., Can.	199		42.20 N	82.57 W
Riverside Manors, N.Y., U.S.	202a		43.11 N	79.03 W
Riverside Park, p.o.i., Mi., U.S.	199		42.22 N	83.26 W
Riverside Park, p.o.i., N.Y., U.S.	202a		42.57 N	78.54 W
Rivers Inlet, B.C., Can.	144	E3	51.41 N	127.14 W
Rivers Inlet, b., B.C., Can.	144	E3	51.37 N	127.29 W
Riversleigh, Austl.	96	C7	19.01 S	138.44 E
Riverton, Austl.	98	J2	34.08 S	138.44 E
Riverton, Mb., Can.	142	C16	50.58 N	96.59 W
Riverton, N.Z.	102	H2	46.21 S	168.01 E
Riverton, Il., U.S.	130	E8	39.50 N	89.32 W
Riverton, Ne., U.S.	138	A10	40.05 N	98.46 W
Riverton, Ut., U.S.	150	C4	40.31 N	111.56 W
Riverton, Va., U.S.	124	F7	38.56 N	78.11 W
Riverton, Wy., U.S.	140	D4	43.01 N	108.23 W
Riverton Heights, Wa., U.S.	146	C4	47.28 N	122.17 W
River Vale, N.J., U.S.	194		40.59 N	74.00 W
River View, Al., U.S.	134	E13	32.42 N	85.08 W
Riverview, Ks., U.S.	138	D11	37.47 N	97.21 W
Riverview Park, p.o.i., Pa., U.S.	197b		40.29 N	80.01 W
Riverwood, Austl.	192a		33.57 S	151.03 E
Riverwoods, Il., U.S.	196		42.10 N	87.54 W
Rives, Tn., U.S.	130	H8	36.21 N	89.02 W
Rivesaltes, Fr.	22	G8	42.45 N	2.52 E
Rive Sud, Canal de la, can., Qc., Can.	193a		45.25 N	73.41 W
Rivesville, W.V., U.S.	124	E5	39.31 N	80.08 W
Riviera, Tx., U.S.	136	G10	27.17 N	97.48 W
Riviera Beach, Fl., U.S.	132	J5	26.46 N	80.03 W
Rivière-à-Claude, Qc., Can.	122	A11	49.12 N	65.53 W
Rivière-à-Pierre, Qc., Can.	122	C5	46.59 N	72.11 W
Rivière-Bleue, Qc., Can.	122	C7	47.26 N	69.03 W
Rivière-de-la-Chaloupe, Qc., Can.	122	A14	49.08 N	62.32 W
Rivière-des-Prairies, ngh., Qc., Can.	193a		45.39 N	73.33 W
Rivière-du-Loup, Qc., Can.	122	C7	47.49 N	69.31 W
Rivière-Matane, Qc., Can.	122	B9	48.49 N	67.19 W
Rivière-Matawin, Qc., Can.	126	B16	46.55 N	72.56 W
Rivière-Pentecôte, Qc., Can.	114	B17	49.47 N	67.10 W
Rivière-Pilote, Mart.	159c	I7	14.29 N	60.54 W
Rivière-Salée, Mart.	159c	k7	14.31 N	60.59 W
Rivière-Verte, N.B., Can.	122	C8	47.19 N	68.09 W
Rivington, Eng., U.K.	180		53.37 N	2.34 W
Rivington Reservoirs, res., Eng., U.K.	180		53.37 N	2.34 W
Rivne, Ukr.	38	C5	50.37 N	26.14 E
Rivne, Ukr.	38	E10	48.14 N	31.45 E
Rivne, co., Ukr.	38	B5	51.00 N	26.30 E
Rivoli, Italy	30	E4	45.04 N	7.29 E
Rivoli Bay, b., Austl.	98	K2	37.32 S	140.04 E
Riyadh see Ar-Riyāḍ, Sau. Ar.	72	E6	24.38 N	46.43 E
Riyāq, Leb.	76	E7	33.51 N	36.00 E
Rīz see Zarrīn Shahr, Iran	74	D12	32.23 N	51.28 E
Rizal see Pasay, Phil.	187l		14.33 N	121.00 E
Rizal Memorial Stadium, p.o.i., Phil.	187l		14.34 N	120.59 E
Rizal Park, p.o.i., Phil.	187l		14.35 N	120.59 E
Rize, Tur.	42	E9	41.01 N	40.31 E
Rize, state, Tur.	42	E9	40.55 N	40.55 E
Rizzuto, Capo, c., Italy	32	F11	38.54 N	17.06 E
Rjabcevo, Russia	26	F15	54.38 N	32.17 E
Rjad, Russia	26	C18	57.56 N	35.04 E
Rjapusovskij Pogost, Russia	18	F25	62.00 N	38.17 E
Rjazan', Russia	40	D11	54.38 N	39.44 E
Rjazancevo, Russia	26	D22	56.42 N	39.13 E
Rjazanskaja oblast', co., Russia	40	D12	54.30 N	40.30 E
Rjažsk, Russia	40	E12	53.42 N	40.04 E
Rjukan, Nor.	16	H6	59.52 N	8.34 E
Rjuven, mtn., Nor.	16	H5	59.14 N	7.15 E
Ro, N. Cal.	101d	m16	21.23 S	167.51 E
Roa, Nor.	16	G8	60.17 N	10.37 E
Roa, Spain	28	C7	41.41 N	3.55 W
Roachdale, In., U.S.	130	E11	39.50 N	86.48 W
Road Town, Br. Vir. Is.	158b	e8	18.26 N	64.37 W
Roan Cliffs, clf., U.S.	150	D7	39.16 N	109.26 W
Roan Creek, stm., Co., U.S.	150	D8	39.19 N	108.12 W
Roan Mountain, Tn., U.S.	124	H3	36.12 N	82.04 W
Roanne, Fr.	22	C9	46.02 N	4.04 E
Roanoke, Al., U.S.	134	D13	33.09 N	85.22 W
Roanoke, Il., U.S.	130	D8	40.47 N	89.11 W
Roanoke, In., U.S.	130	D12	40.57 N	85.21 W
Roanoke, Va., U.S.	124	G6	37.16 N	79.56 W
Roanoke, stm., U.S.	124	H8	35.57 N	76.42 W
Roanoke Island, i., N.C., U.S.	124	I10	35.53 N	75.39 W
Roanoke Rapids, N.C., U.S.	124	H8	36.27 N	77.39 W
Roanoke Rapids Lake Dam, dam., N.C., U.S.	124	H8	36.28 N	77.38 W
Roan Plateau, plat., U.S.	150	D7	39.30 N	109.40 W
Roaring Fork, stm., Co., U.S.	138	B2	39.33 N	107.20 W
Roaring River Slough, stm., Ca., U.S.	200		38.05 N	121.55 W
Roaring River State Park, p.o.i., Mo., U.S.	130	H4	36.35 N	93.48 W
Roaring Run, stm., Pa., U.S.	197b		40.33 N	79.32 W
Roaring Spring, Pa., U.S.	124	D7	40.19 N	78.23 W
Roaring Springs, Tx., U.S.	138	H8	33.53 N	100.50 W
Roaringwater Bay, b., Ire.	10	J3	51.31 N	9.26 W
Roatán, Hond.	156	D4	16.19 N	86.31 W
Roatán, Isla de, i., Hond.	156	D4	16.21 N	86.29 W
Robāt Karīm, Iran	74	C12	35.28 N	51.05 E
Robbers Cave State Park, p.o.i., Ok., U.S.	134	B3	35.01 N	95.27 W
Robbins, N.C., U.S.	132	A6	35.25 N	79.35 W
Robbins, Tn., U.S.	130	H13	36.21 N	84.35 W
Robbins Airport, arpt., Ma., U.S.	201		42.34 N	70.58 W
Robbins Island, i., Austl.	99a	n12	40.42 S	144.54 E
Robbins Pond, l., Ma., U.S.	201		42.00 N	70.55 W
Robbins Rest, N.Y., U.S.	194		40.39 N	73.10 W
Robbinsville, N.C., U.S.	132	A2	35.19 N	83.48 W
Robe, Austl.	98	K2	37.10 S	139.44 E
Robe, stm., Ire.	10	H3	53.38 N	9.16 W
Robe, Mount, hill, Austl.	98	H3	31.40 S	141.20 E
Robecchetto con Induno, Italy	184b		45.32 N	8.46 E
Robecco sul Naviglio, Italy	184b		45.26 N	8.53 E
Röbel, Ger.	24	C8	53.22 N	12.36 E
Robeline, La., U.S.	134	F5	31.41 N	93.18 W
Robersonville, N.C., U.S.	124	I8	35.49 N	77.15 W
Robert, Havre du, b., Mart.	159c	k7	14.40 N	60.55 W
Roberta, Ga., U.S.	132	D1	32.43 N	84.02 W
Roberta Mills, N.C., U.S.	132	A5	35.21 N	80.38 W
Robert E. Lee Memorial Park, p.o.i., Md., U.S.	202b		39.23 N	76.39 W
Robert F. Kennedy Memorial Stadium, p.o.i., D.C., U.S.	202c		38.53 N	76.58 W
Robert Lee, Tx., U.S.	136	C7	31.54 N	100.28 W
Robert Louis Stevenson's Tomb, hist., Samoa	101c	g12	13.51 S	171.45 W
Robert Morse College, educ., Pa., U.S.	197b		40.31 N	80.12 W
Roberts, Id., U.S.	146	G14	43.43 N	112.10 W
Roberts, Mt., U.S.	140	B3	45.21 N	109.10 W
Roberts Canyon, val., Ca., U.S.	198		34.11 N	117.54 W
Roberts Creek Mountain, mtn., Nv., U.S.	148	D9	39.52 N	116.18 W
Robertsdale, Al., U.S.	134	G11	30.33 N	87.42 W
Robertsdale, Pa., U.S.	124	D7	40.11 N	78.06 W
Robertsfors, Swe.	16	C18	64.11 N	20.51 E
Robertsham, ngh., S. Afr.	191d		26.15 S	28.00 E
Robert S. Kerr Lake, res., Ok., U.S.	134	B3	35.24 N	94.58 W
Robertson, S. Afr.	90	H4	33.48 S	19.50 E
Roberts Park, Il., U.S.	196		41.44 N	87.49 W
Roberts Peak, mtn., B.C., Can.	144	D10	52.57 N	120.32 W
Roberts Port, Lib.	84	H2	6.44 N	11.21 W
Robertstown, Austl.	98	I2	33.59 S	139.04 E
Roberval, Qc., Can.	122	B4	48.31 N	72.13 W
Robeson Channel, strt., N.A.	108	A13	82.03 N	60.40 W
Robins Air Force Base, mil., Ga., U.S.	132	D2	32.38 N	83.35 W
Robinson, Il., U.S.	130	E10	39.00 N	87.44 W
Robinson, Tx., U.S.	136	C10	31.28 N	97.06 W
Robinson, Lake, res., S.C., U.S.	132	B5	34.26 N	80.09 W
Robinson Brook, stm., Ma., U.S.	201		43.02 N	71.13 W
Róbinson Crusoe, Isla, i., Chile	162	I7	33.38 S	78.52 W
Robinson Lake Aerodrome, arpt., S. Afr.	191d		26.08 S	27.42 E
Robinson Pond, l., N.H., U.S.	201		42.48 N	71.23 W
Robinson Run, stm., Pa., U.S.	197b		40.23 N	80.06 W
Robinson Run, North Branch, stm., Pa., U.S.	197b		40.23 N	80.11 W
Robinvale, Austl.	98	J4	34.36 S	142.46 E
Robleda, Spain	28	D4	40.23 N	6.36 W
Robledo, Spain	28	F8	38.45 N	2.27 W
Roblin, Mb., Can.	142	C12	51.14 N	101.23 W
Roboré, Bol.	166	C5	18.20 S	59.45 W
Rob Roy Island, i., Sol. Is.	101b	d7	7.24 S	157.35 E
Robson, Mount, mtn., B.C., Can.	144	C11	53.07 N	119.09 W
Robstown, Tx., U.S.	136	G10	27.47 N	97.40 W
Roby, Eng., U.K.	180		53.25 N	2.51 W
Roby, Tx., U.S.	136	B7	32.44 N	100.22 W
Roby Mill, Eng., U.K.	180		53.34 N	2.44 W
Roca, Cabo da, c., Port.	28	F1	38.46 N	9.29 W
Roçado, Braz.	170	D3	6.40 S	44.19 W
Rocafuerte, Ec.	168	H1	0.55 S	80.27 W
Rocanville, Sk., Can.	142	D12	50.24 N	101.43 W
Roca Partida, Isla, i., Mex.	154	F2	19.00 N	112.04 W
Roca Partida, Punta, c., Mex.	154	F11	18.41 N	95.12 W
Rocas, Atol das, at., Braz.	162	F11	3.51 S	33.49 W
Rocca Priora, Italy	185a		41.48 N	12.45 E
Rocciamelone, mtn., Italy	30	E4	45.12 N	7.05 E
Ročegda, Russia	12	E20	62.39 N	43.26 E
Rocha, Ur.	172	G10	34.29 S	54.18 W
Rocha Miranda, ngh., Braz.	205a		22.52 S	43.22 W
Rocha Sobrinho, Braz.	205a		22.47 S	43.25 W
Rochdale, Eng., U.K.	10	H10	53.37 N	2.09 W
Rochdale, mun., Eng., U.K.	180		53.37 N	2.08 W
Rochdale, mun., Eng., U.K.	180		53.37 N	2.08 W
Rochdale Canal, can., Eng., U.K.	180		53.43 N	1.54 W
Rochechouart, Fr.	22	D6	45.50 N	0.50 E
Rochefort, Bel.	20	D14	50.09 N	5.13 E
Rochefort, Fr.	22	D5	45.57 N	0.58 W
Rochelle, Ga., U.S.	132	E2	31.56 N	83.26 W
Rochelle, Il., U.S.	130	C8	41.55 N	89.03 W
Rochelle, Tx., U.S.	136	C8	31.13 N	99.12 W
Rochelle Park, N.J., U.S.	194		40.54 N	74.04 W
Roche-Percée, Sk., Can.	142	E10	49.03 N	102.53 W
Rocher Fendu, Rapides du, wtfl., Qc., Can.	193a		45.19 N	73.57 W
Rochester, Austl.	98	K5	36.21 S	144.41 E
Rochester, In., U.S.	130	C11	41.03 N	86.11 W
Rochester, Mi., U.S.	124	B2	42.40 N	83.07 W
Rochester, Mn., U.S.	128	G6	44.01 N	92.28 W
Rochester, N.H., U.S.	122	G5	43.18 N	70.58 W
Rochester, N.Y., U.S.	126	E12	43.09 N	77.36 W
Rochester, Tx., U.S.	138	H9	33.19 N	99.51 W
Rochester City Airport, arpt., Eng., U.K.	178		51.21 N	0.30 E
Rochford, mun., Eng., U.K.	178		51.36 N	0.39 E
Rochlitz, Ger.	24	E8	51.03 N	12.47 E
Rock, Mi., U.S.	126	B2	46.03 N	87.10 W
Rock, stm., U.S.	128	H2	43.03 N	96.28 W
Rock, stm., U.S.	128	J8	41.28 N	90.37 W
Rockall, i., Scot., U.K.	8	D6	57.35 N	13.48 W
Rockall Rise, unds.	176	C12	59.00 N	14.00 W
Rockaway Inlet, b., N.Y., U.S.	194		40.34 N	73.55 W
Rockaway Neck, N.J., U.S.	194		40.51 N	74.21 W
Rockaway Park, ngh., N.Y., U.S.	194		40.35 N	73.50 W
Rockaway Point, ngh., N.Y., U.S.	194		40.33 N	73.55 W
Rockaway Point, c., N.Y., U.S.	194		40.33 N	73.56 W
Rockaways' Playland, p.o.i., N.Y., U.S.	194		40.35 N	73.49 W
Rockbank, Austl.	192b		37.43 S	144.39 E
Rock Bay, B.C., Can.	144	F5	50.19 N	125.29 W
Rock Brook, stm., N.J., U.S.	194		40.25 N	74.40 W
Rockcastle, stm., Ky., U.S.	130	G13	36.57 N	84.21 W
Rock Creek, B.C., Can.	144	G11	49.04 N	119.00 W
Rock Creek, stm., N.A.	142	F7	48.23 N	107.05 W
Rock Creek, stm., U.S.	202c		38.54 N	77.04 W
Rock Creek, stm., Co., U.S.	140	G10	40.19 N	102.32 W
Rock Creek, stm., Mt., U.S.	140	B3	45.31 N	108.49 W
Rock Creek, stm., Mt., U.S.	146	D13	46.42 N	113.41 W
Rock Creek, stm., Nv., U.S.	148	C9	40.39 N	116.54 W
Rock Creek, stm., Or., U.S.	146	E6	45.34 N	120.23 W
Rock Creek, stm., Or., U.S.	146	H7	42.39 N	119.08 W
Rock Creek, stm., S.D., U.S.	140	C15	43.43 N	97.58 W
Rock Creek, stm., Ut., U.S.	150	C6	40.17 N	110.30 W
Rock Creek, stm., Wa., U.S.	146	D8	46.54 N	117.55 W
Rock Creek, stm., Wy., U.S.	140	F6	41.54 N	106.08 W
Rock Creek Butte, mtn., Or., U.S.	146	F8	44.49 N	118.07 W
Rock Creek Hills, Md., U.S.	202c		39.01 N	77.04 W
Rock Creek Park, p.o.i., D.C., U.S.	202c		38.58 N	77.03 W
Rockdale, Il., U.S.	130	C9	41.30 N	88.06 W
Rockdale, Md., U.S.	202b		39.21 N	76.45 W
Rockdale, Pa., U.S.	203		39.53 N	75.26 W
Rockdale, Tx., U.S.	136	D11	30.39 N	97.00 W
Rockefeller Center, bldg., N.Y., U.S.	194		40.45 N	74.00 W
Rockefeller Park, p.o.i., Oh., U.S.	197a		41.32 N	81.38 W
Rockefeller Plateau, plat., Ant.	103	D27	80.00 S	135.00 W
Rockenhausen, Ger.	24	G3	49.38 N	7.49 E
Rock Falls, Il., U.S.	130	C8	41.46 N	89.41 W
Rock Ferry, Eng., U.K.	180		53.22 N	3.00 W
Rockford, Al., U.S.	134	E12	32.53 N	86.13 W
Rockford, Il., U.S.	130	B8	42.16 N	89.05 W
Rockford, Ia., U.S.	130	A5	43.03 N	92.57 W
Rockford, Mi., U.S.	130	A12	43.07 N	85.33 W
Rockford, Oh., U.S.	124	D1	40.41 N	84.38 W
Rockford, Tn., U.S.	134	B15	35.48 N	83.57 W
Rockglen, Sk., Can.	142	E8	49.10 N	105.57 W
Rock Hall, Md., U.S.	124	E9	39.08 N	76.14 W
Rockhampton, Austl.	98	D8	23.22 S	150.31 E
Rockhampton Downs, Austl.	96	C7	18.57 S	135.10 E
Rock Hill, S.C., U.S.	132	B4	34.56 N	81.02 W
Rockingham, N.C., U.S.	132	B6	34.56 N	79.46 W
Rockingham Bay, b., Austl.	98	B6	18.10 S	146.05 E
Rockingham Park, p.o.i., N.H., U.S.	201		42.47 N	71.14 W
Rockingham State Historic Site, hist., N.J., U.S.	194		40.24 N	74.37 W
Rock Island, Il., U.S.	130	C7	41.29 N	90.34 W
Rocklake, N.D., U.S.	142	F14	48.46 N	99.13 W
Rock Lake, l., Mb., Can.	142	E14	49.12 N	99.10 W
Rock Lake, l., Il., U.S.	196		41.40 N	88.03 W
Rock Lake, l., N.D., U.S.	142	F14	48.49 N	99.12 W
Rockland, On., Can.	126	C14	45.33 N	75.17 W
Rockland, De., U.S.	203		39.47 N	75.34 W
Rockland, Id., U.S.	146	H14	42.35 N	112.52 W
Rockland, Me., U.S.	122	F7	44.06 N	69.06 W
Rockland, Ma., U.S.	124	B15	42.08 N	70.54 W
Rockland, Mi., U.S.	128	E9	46.42 N	89.12 W
Rockland Lake, N.Y., U.S.	194		41.09 N	73.55 W
Rockland Lake, l., N.Y., U.S.	194		41.08 N	73.55 W
Rockland Lake State Park, p.o.i., N.Y., U.S.	194		41.08 N	73.55 W
Rocklands Reservoir, l., Austl.	98	K3	37.15 S	142.00 E
Rockledge, Fl., U.S.	132	H5	28.20 N	80.44 W
Rockledge, Pa., U.S.	203		40.03 N	75.05 W
Rockleigh, N.J., U.S.	194		41.00 N	73.55 W
Rocklin, Ca., U.S.	148	E4	38.47 N	121.14 W
Rockmart, Ga., U.S.	134	D13	34.00 N	85.02 W
Rock Meadow Brook, stm., Ma., U.S.	201		42.16 N	71.13 W
Rock Pond, l., Ma., U.S.	201		42.44 N	71.00 W
Rockport, In., U.S.	130	G10	37.52 N	87.02 W
Rockport, Ky., U.S.	130	G11	37.19 N	87.00 W
Rockport, Me., U.S.	122	F7	44.11 N	69.05 W
Rockport, Ma., U.S.	124	B15	42.39 N	70.37 W
Rock Port, Mo., U.S.	130	D2	40.24 N	95.31 W
Rockport, Tx., U.S.	136	F10	28.01 N	97.03 W
Rock Rapids, Ia., U.S.	128	H2	43.26 N	96.09 W
Rock River, Wy., U.S.	140	F6	41.44 N	105.59 W
Rock Run, stm., Md., U.S.	202c		38.58 N	77.11 W
Rock Sound, Bah.	132	L9	24.52 N	76.09 W
Rocksprings, Tx., U.S.	136	E8	30.01 N	100.12 W
Rock Springs, Wy., U.S.	150	B7	41.35 N	109.13 W
Rockstone, Guy.	164	B6	5.59 N	58.32 W
Rock Tombs see Speos, hist., Egypt	76	K1	27.54 N	30.52 E
Rockton, Il., U.S.	130	B8	42.27 N	89.04 W
Rock Valley, Ia., U.S.	128	H2	43.12 N	96.17 W
Rockville, In., U.S.	130	E10	39.45 N	87.13 W
Rockville, Md., U.S.	124	E8	39.05 N	77.09 W
Rockville, Ma., U.S.	201		42.08 N	71.21 W
Rockwall, Tx., U.S.	136	B11	32.55 N	96.27 W
Rockwell, Ia., U.S.	130	B4	42.59 N	93.11 W
Rockwell, N.C., U.S.	132	A5	35.33 N	80.24 W
Rockwell City, Ia., U.S.	130	B3	42.23 N	94.37 W
Rockwell International Corporation, sci., Ca., U.S.	198		33.52 N	117.51 W
Rockwood, Me., U.S.	122	E7	45.40 N	69.44 W
Rockwood, Pa., U.S.	126	I10	39.54 N	79.08 W
Rockwood, Tn., U.S.	130	I13	35.52 N	84.41 W
Rockwood Lake, l., Ct., U.S.	194		41.06 N	73.38 W
Rockwood Lake Brook, stm., Ct., U.S.	194		41.03 N	73.36 W
Rocky, Ok., U.S.	138	F9	35.09 N	99.03 W
Rocky, stm., Ab., Can.	144	C13	53.08 N	117.58 W
Rocky, stm., N.C., U.S.	132	A6	35.36 N	79.09 W
Rocky, East Branch, stm., Oh., U.S.	197a		41.24 N	81.53 W
Rocky Arroyo, stm., N.M., U.S.	136	B3	32.32 N	104.21 W
Rocky Boy's Indian Reservation, ind. res., Mt., U.S.	146	B17	48.17 N	109.50 W
Rocky Branch, stm., Va., U.S.	202c		38.53 N	77.19 W
Rocky Cape National Park, p.o.i., Austl.	99a	n12	40.53 S	145.29 E
Rocky Comfort Creek, stm., Ga., U.S.	132	C3	32.59 N	82.25 W
Rocky Coulee, stm., Wa., U.S.	146	C8	47.11 N	119.10 W
Rockyford, Ab., Can.	144	E17	51.13 N	113.08 W
Rocky Ford, Co., U.S.	138	C5	38.03 N	103.42 W
Rocky Harbour, b., China	189d		22.20 N	114.19 E
Rocky Hill, N.J., U.S.	194		40.24 N	74.38 W
Rocky Island Lake, res., On., Can.	126	B7	46.56 N	82.56 W
Rocky Mount, N.C., U.S.	124	I8	35.56 N	77.47 W
Rocky Mount, Va., U.S.	124	H6	37.00 N	79.53 W
Rocky Mountain, mtn., Mt., U.S.	146	C14	47.49 N	112.49 W
Rocky Mountain House, Ab., Can.	144	D16	52.22 N	114.56 W
Rocky Mountain National Park, p.o.i., Co., U.S.	140	G7	40.19 N	105.42 W
Rocky Mountains, mts., N.A.	106	D11	48.00 N	116.00 W
Rocky Mountain Trench, val., N.A.	144	G15	48.40 N	114.48 W
Rocky Point, c., Bah.	132	K8	25.59 N	77.23 W
Rocky Point, c., Norf. I.	100i	y24	29.03 S	167.55 E
Rocky Point, c., N.Y., U.S.	194		40.55 N	73.32 W
Rocky Ridge, mtn., Ca., U.S.	200		37.48 N	122.03 W
Rocky River Reservation, p.o.i., Oh., U.S.	197a		41.27 N	81.50 W
Rocky Run, stm., N.D., U.S.	142	G14	47.37 N	99.03 W
Rocky Run, stm., Pa., U.S.	203		39.54 N	75.28 W
Rocky Run, stm., Va., U.S.	202c		38.58 N	77.15 W
Rocky Top, mtn., Or., U.S.	146	F4	44.47 N	122.17 W
Rocquencourt, Fr.	179		48.50 N	2.07 E
Rôda, Gezîret el-, i., Egypt	191c		30.01 N	31.13 E
Rodalben, Ger.	24	G3	49.13 N	7.38 E
Rodaun, ngh., Aus.	182b		48.08 N	16.16 E
Rødberg, Nor.	16	G7	60.16 N	8.58 E
Rødby, Den.	16	M9	54.41 N	11.23 E
Rødbyhavn, Den.	16	M9	54.39 N	11.21 E
Roddickton, Nf., Can.	111a	i22	50.52 N	56.07 W
Rødekro, Den.	16	L7	55.04 N	9.21 E
Rodeo, Arg.	172	E3	30.12 S	69.06 W
Rodeo, Mex.	154	C6	25.11 N	104.34 W
Rodeo, N.M., U.S.	150	L7	31.51 N	109.01 W
Rodeo Lagoon, b., Ca., U.S.	200		37.50 N	122.31 W
Roderick Island, i., B.C., Can.	144	D2	52.38 N	128.21 W
Rodewisch, Ger.	24	F8	50.32 N	12.24 E
Rodez, Fr.	22	E8	44.20 N	2.33 E
Rodi Garganico, Italy	30	I12	41.55 N	15.52 E
Roding, Ger.	24	G8	49.11 N	12.31 E
Roding, stm., Eng., U.K.	20	C9	51.31 N	0.05 E
Rodino, Russia	40	B14	58.57 N	44.59 E
Rodionovo-Nesvetajskaja, Russia	38	F18	47.36 N	39.41 E
Rodnei, Munții, mts., Rom.	36	B11	47.31 N	24.47 E
Rodney, On., Can.	126	F8	42.33 N	81.40 W
Rodney, Cape, c., Ak., U.S.	109	D6	64.39 N	166.22 W
Rodney Bay, b., St. Luc.	159c	I6	14.05 N	60.58 W
Rodniki, Russia	40	C12	57.06 N	41.44 E
Rodniki, Russia	183b		55.39 N	38.04 E
Rodnja, Russia	26	D17	56.22 N	34.54 E
Rodonit, Kepi i, c., Alb.	32	C13	41.35 N	19.27 E
Rodopi see Rhodope Mountains, mts., Eur.	36	H11	41.30 N	24.30 E
Rodópi, Oroseirá see Rhodope Mountains, mts., Eur.	36	H11	41.30 N	24.30 E
Ródos (Rhodes), Grc.	34	G11	36.26 N	28.13 E
Ródos (Rhodes), i., Grc.	34	G10	36.10 N	28.00 E
Rødøy, i., Nor.	14	F3	66.40 N	13.03 E
Rodrigo de Freitas, Lagoa, b., Braz.	205a		22.58 S	43.13 W
Rodrigues, i., Mrts.	174	K9	19.42 S	63.25 E
Rodríguez, Mex.	136	G7	27.10 N	100.01 W
Rodríguez, Arroyo, stm., Arg.	206		34.52 S	58.02 W
Rødven, Nor.	16	E5	62.37 N	7.29 E
Roebourne, Austl.	96	D3	20.45 S	117.09 E
Roebuck Bay, b., Austl.	96	C4	18.04 S	122.17 E
Roehampton, ngh., Eng., U.K.	178		51.27 N	0.14 W
Roe Island, i., Ca., U.S.	200		38.04 N	122.02 W
Roeland Park, Ks., U.S.	130	E3	39.02 N	94.36 W
Roer see Rur, stm., Eur.	20	C15	51.11 N	5.58 E
Roermond, Neth.	20	C14	51.11 N	5.59 E
Roeselare, Bel.	20	D12	50.56 N	3.07 E
Roes Welcome Sound, strt., Nu., Can.	110	C13	64.00 N	88.00 W
Roff, Ok., U.S.	134	C2	34.38 N	96.50 W
Rogačevo, Russia	26	D20	56.25 N	37.10 E
Rogačovka, Russia	40	F11	51.30 N	39.32 E
Rogagua, Laguna, l., Bol.	166	B3	13.41 S	67.07 W
Rogaguado, Laguna, l., Bol.	166	B3	12.52 S	65.43 W
Rogaland, state, Nor.	16	H4	59.00 N	6.15 E
Rogans Hill, Austl.	192a		33.44 S	151.01 E
Rogaška Slatina, Slvn.	30	D12	46.14 N	15.39 E
Rogatica, Bos.	36	F6	43.48 N	19.00 E
Rogen, l., Eur.	16	E10	62.19 N	12.22 E
Roger Island, i., Ma., U.S.	201		42.43 N	70.50 W
Rogers, Ar., U.S.	130	H3	36.20 N	94.07 W
Rogers, Tx., U.S.	136	D10	30.55 N	97.13 W
Rogers, Mount, mtn., Va., U.S.	124	H4	36.39 N	81.33 W
Rogers City, Mi., U.S.	126	C6	45.24 N	83.49 W
Rogers Lake, l., Ca., U.S.	148	I8	34.52 N	117.51 W
Rogers Park, ngh., Il., U.S.	196		42.01 N	87.40 W
Rogers Pass, p., B.C., Can.	144	E13	51.20 N	117.27 W
Rogersville, N.B., Can.	122	D11	46.43 N	65.25 W
Rogersville, Al., U.S.	134	C11	34.49 N	87.17 W
Rogersville, Tn., U.S.	124	H3	36.24 N	83.00 W
Roggeveldberge, clf., S. Afr.	90	H5	32.07 S	20.12 E
Roggewein, Cabo, c., Chile	100l	e30	27.07 S	109.14 W
Rogliano, Fr.	22	G15	42.57 N	9.25 E
Rognan, Nor.	14	E6	67.04 N	15.22 E
Rognedino, Russia	26	G16	53.48 N	33.33 E
Rogovatoe, Russia	38	B17	51.13 N	38.22 E
Rogovskaja, Russia	38	H17	45.43 N	38.43 E
Rogoźno, Pol.	24	D12	52.45 N	16.59 E
Rogue, stm., Mi., U.S.	126	E4	43.03 N	85.34 W
Rogue, stm., Or., U.S.	146	H2	42.25 N	124.25 W
Rogue River, Or., U.S.	148	A2	42.26 N	123.09 W
Rohan', Ukr.	38	D15	49.54 N	36.29 E
Rohatyn, Ukr.	38	D3	49.25 N	24.37 E
Rohdenhaus, Ger.	181		51.18 N	7.01 E
Rohinjan, India	190c		19.06 N	73.04 E
Röhlinghausen, ngh., Ger.	181		51.30 N	7.10 E
Rohmojva, gora, mtn., Russia	14	F20	66.54 N	29.15 E
Rohoziv, Ukr.	38	C10	50.13 N	31.03 E
Rohrbeck, Ger.	182a		52.32 N	13.02 E
Rohri, Pak.	70	E2	27.40 N	68.55 E
Rohtak, India	70	D6	28.53 N	76.35 E
Roia see Roya, stm., Eur.	30	F4	43.47 N	7.36 E
Roi Et, Thai.	64	E6	16.02 N	103.39 E
Roi George, Îles du, is., Fr. Poly.	94	E12	14.32 S	145.08 W
Roilianka, Ukr.	38	G8	46.17 N	29.47 E
Roine, l., Fin.	18	F10	61.24 N	24.06 E
Roinville, Fr.	179		48.32 N	2.03 E
Roissy, Fr.	179		48.47 N	2.39 E
Roissy-en-France, Fr.	179		49.00 N	2.31 E
Roja, Lat.	26	C5	57.30 N	22.48 E
Rojas, Arg.	172	G7	34.12 S	60.44 W
Rojo, Cabo, c., Mex.	154	E10	21.33 N	97.20 W
Rojo, Cabo, c., P.R.	158a	c1	17.56 N	67.11 W
Rokan, Indon.	66	C2	0.33 N	100.25 E
Rokan, stm., Indon.	66	C2	1.50 N	100.55 E
Rokel, stm., S.L.	84	H2	8.33 N	12.55 W
Rokiškis, Lith.	26	E8	55.57 N	25.35 E
Rokkō-sanchi, mts., Japan	188		34.45 N	135.13 E
Rokugō, ngh., Japan	186		35.33 N	139.43 E
Rokycany, Czech Rep.	24	G9	49.44 N	13.35 E
Rokytne, Ukr.	38	B6	51.16 N	27.13 E
Rokytne, Ukr.	38	D9	49.43 N	30.28 E
Roland, Mb., Can.	142	E16	49.21 N	97.56 W
Roland, Ar., U.S.	134	C6	34.54 N	92.30 W
Roland, Ia., U.S.	130	B4	42.09 N	93.30 W
Roland, Lake, res., Md., U.S.	202b		39.23 N	76.38 W
Rolândia, Braz.	166	D6	23.18 S	51.22 W
Roland Park, ngh., Md., U.S.	202b		39.22 N	76.39 W
Roland Run, stm., Md., U.S.	202b		39.23 N	76.39 W
Røldal, Nor.	16	H4	59.50 N	6.48 E
Roldanillo, Col.	168	E3	4.24 N	76.09 W
Rolette, N.D., U.S.	142	F14	48.39 N	99.50 W
Rolfe, Ia., U.S.	130	B3	42.48 N	94.31 W
Roll, Az., U.S.	150	K2	32.44 N	113.59 W
Rolla, Ks., U.S.	138	D7	37.07 N	101.36 W
Rolla, Mo., U.S.	130	G6	37.57 N	91.46 W
Rolla, N.D., U.S.	142	F14	48.51 N	99.36 W
Rolla, i., Nor.	14	D8	68.47 N	17.02 E
Rolleboise, Fr.	179		49.01 N	1.36 E
Rolleston, Austl.	98	E7	24.27 S	148.37 E
Rolling Acres, Md., U.S.	202b		39.17 N	76.52 W
Rolling Fork, Ms., U.S.	134	E8	32.54 N	90.52 W
Rolling Fork, stm., Ky., U.S.	130	G12	37.55 N	85.50 W
Rolling Hills, Ca., U.S.	198		33.46 N	118.21 W
Rolling Hills Estates, Ca., U.S.	198		33.47 N	118.21 W
Rolling River Indian Reserve, ind. res., Mb., Can.	142	D14	50.28 N	100.02 W
Rollingstone, Austl.	98	B6	19.03 S	146.24 E
Rollingwood, Ca., U.S.	200		37.57 N	122.20 W
Rollins, Mt., U.S.	146	C12	47.55 N	114.11 W
Rolvøysundet, strt., Nor.	14	B14	70.55 N	24.10 E
Rolvsøya, i., Nor.	14	A14	71.00 N	24.00 E
Roma, Austl.	98	F7	26.34 S	148.47 E
Roma (Rome), Italy	30	I9	41.54 N	12.29 E
Roma (Rome), Italy	185a		41.54 N	12.29 E
Roma, Leso.	90	F8	29.30 S	27.53 E
Roma, Tx., U.S.	136	H8	26.24 N	99.00 W
Romagna, hist. reg., Italy	30	F9	44.19 N	12.09 E
Romain, Cape, c., S.C., U.S.	132	D6	33.01 N	79.25 W
Romainville, Fr.	179		48.53 N	2.26 E
Romakloster, Swe.	16	J16	57.31 N	18.28 E
Roman, Rom.	36	C13	46.55 N	26.56 E
Romanche, stm., Fr.	22	D12	45.05 N	5.43 E
Romanche Gap, unds.	176	I12	0.10 S	18.15 W
Romang, Pulau, i., Indon.	60	G8	7.33 S	127.25 E
Românî, Egypt	76	G3	31.00 N	32.39 E
Romania, ctry., Eur.	36	D11	46.00 N	25.30 E
România see Romania, ctry., Eur.	36	D11	46.00 N	25.30 E
Roman-Kosh, hora, mtn., Ukr.	38	I13	44.37 N	34.15 E
Roman-Kosj, hora, mtn., Ukr.	40	I9	44.37 N	34.15 E
Roman Nose Mountain, mtn., Or., U.S.	146	G3	43.55 N	123.44 W
Romano, Cape, c., Fl., U.S.	132	K4	25.50 N	81.41 W
Romano, Cayo, i., Cuba	156	A9	22.04 N	77.50 W
Romano Banco, Italy	184b		45.25 N	9.06 E
Romanovka, Russia	40	F13	51.44 N	42.46 E
Romanovka, Russia	50	F11	53.12 N	112.45 E
Romanovka, Russia	183a		60.03 N	30.42 E
Romans-sur-Isère, Fr.	22	D11	45.03 N	5.02 E
Romansville, Pa., U.S.	203		39.57 N	75.45 W
Romanzof, Cape, c., Ak., U.S.	109	D6	61.48 N	166.05 W
Romanzof Mountains, mts., Ak., U.S.	109	C11	69.00 N	144.00 W
Romaškovo, Russia	183b		55.44 N	37.20 E
Romblon, Phil.	68	D4	12.34 N	122.15 E
Rome see Roma, Italy	30	I9	41.54 N	12.29 E
Rome, Ga., U.S.	134	C13	34.15 N	85.09 W
Rome, Il., U.S.	128	K9	40.53 N	89.29 W
Rome, N.Y., U.S.	126	E14	43.13 N	75.27 W
Romeo, Mi., U.S.	124	B2	42.48 N	83.00 W
Romford, ngh., Eng., U.K.	178		51.35 N	0.11 E
Romiley, Eng., U.K.	180		53.25 N	2.05 W
Romilly-sur-Seine, Fr.	20	F12	48.31 N	3.43 E
Romitorio, Italy	185a		42.01 N	12.39 E
Romney, W.V., U.S.	124	E7	39.20 N	78.46 W
Romny, Ukr.	38	C12	50.44 N	33.28 E
Rømø, i., Den.	16	L6	55.08 N	8.31 E
Romodan, Ukr.	38	C12	49.59 N	33.20 E
Romodanovo, Russia	40	D14	54.25 N	45.20 E
Romont, Switz.	30	D3	46.41 N	6.54 E
Romorantin-Lanthenay, Fr.	20	G10	47.21 N	1.44 E
Rompin, stm., Malay.	64	K6	2.49 N	103.29 E
Romsdal, reg., Nor.	16	E5	62.44 N	7.38 E
Romsdalen, val., Nor.	16	E6	62.11 N	8.32 E
Romsdalsfjorden, b., Nor.	16	E4	62.39 N	7.15 E
Romsey, Eng., U.K.	10	J11	50.59 N	1.30 W
Røn, Nor.	16	F7	61.02 N	9.01 E
Ron, Mui, c., Viet.	64	C8	18.06 N	106.25 E
Rona, i., Scot., U.K.	10	D7	57.33 N	5.58 W
Rona, i., Scot., U.K.	10	B7	59.07 N	5.49 W
Ronan, Mt., U.S.	146	C12	47.31 N	114.06 W
Roncador, Banco see Roncador, Cayos de, unds., Col.	156	F7	13.31 N	80.06 W
Roncador, Cayos de, unds., Col.	156	F7	13.31 N	80.06 W

Name	Page	Map Ref.	Latitude	Longitude
Roncador, Serra do, plat., Braz.	166	B6	12.00 S	52.00 W
Roncador Bank see Roncador, Cayos de, unds., Col.	156	F7	13.31 N	80.06 W
Roncesvalles, Spain	28	A9	43.01 N	1.19 W
Ronceverte, W.V., U.S.	124	G5	37.44 N	80.28 W
Ronda, Spain	28	H5	36.44 N	5.09 W
Ronda, Serranía de, mts., Spain	28	H5	36.44 N	5.03 W
Rondane, mts., Nor.	16	F7	61.56 N	9.45 E
Rondane Nasjonalpark, p.o.i., Nor.	16	E8	61.50 N	9.50 E
Rønde, Den.	16	K8	56.17 N	10.28 E
Ronde, Pointe, c., Dom.	159c	i5	15.32 N	61.28 W
Rondeau Provincial Park, p.o.i., On., Can.	126	F8	42.16 N	81.51 W
Rondebult, S. Afr.	191d		26.18 S	28.14 E
Ronde Island, i., Gren.	159e	q10	12.18 N	61.35 W
Rondônia, state, Braz.	164	F5	11.00 S	63.00 W
Rondonópolis, Braz.	166	C6	16.28 S	54.38 W
Rondout, Il., U.S.	196		42.17 N	87.53 W
Ronehamn, Swe.	16	J16	57.09 N	18.28 E
Rong, stm., China	58	I3	24.32 N	109.15 E
Rong'an, China	58	I3	25.08 N	109.23 E
Rongcheng, China	58	C10	37.09 N	122.24 E
Ronge, Lac la, l., Sk., Can.	110	D10	55.10 N	105.00 W
Rongelap, at., Marsh. Is.	94	B7	11.20 N	166.50 E
Rongjiang, China	58	I3	25.51 N	108.35 E
Rongkop, Indon.	66	H7	8.09 S	110.45 E
Rongshui, China	58	I3	25.06 N	109.15 E
Rõngu, Est.	26	B9	58.09 N	26.15 E
Rongxian, China	58	J4	22.51 N	110.33 E
Ronkiti Harbor, b., Micron.	100d	m11	6.47 N	158.09 E
Ronkonkoma, N.Y., U.S.	194		40.48 N	73.06 W
Ronkonkoma, Lake, l., N.Y., U.S.	194		40.50 N	73.07 W
Rønne, Den.	16	L12	55.06 N	14.42 E
Ronneby, Swe.	16	K13	56.12 N	15.17 E
Ronne Ice Shelf, ice, Ant.	103	C34	78.27 S	61.08 W
Rönsahl, Ger.	181		51.07 N	7.30 E
Ronsdorf, ngh., Ger.	181		51.14 N	7.12 E
Ronse, Bel.	20	D12	50.44 N	3.36 E
Röntgenmuseum, bldg., Ger.	181		51.12 N	7.16 E
Ronui, Mont, mtn., Fr. Poly.	100h	w23	17.49 S	149.12 W
Ronuro, stm., Braz.	166	B6	11.55 S	53.32 W
Roodepoort, state, S. Afr.	191d		26.10 S	27.52 E
Roodhouse, Il., U.S.	130	E7	39.29 N	90.22 W
Roof Butte, mtn., Az., U.S.	150	G7	36.28 N	109.05 W
Rooiboklaagte, stm., Nmb.	90	B5	20.51 S	20.57 E
Rookwood Cemetery, misc. cult., Austl.	192a		33.53 S	151.04 E
Roorkee, India	70	D6	29.51 N	77.53 E
Roosendaal, Neth.	20	C13	51.32 N	4.28 E
Roosevelt, Az., U.S.	150	J5	33.40 N	111.11 W
Roosevelt, Mn., U.S.	128	C3	48.48 N	95.06 W
Roosevelt, N.Y., U.S.	194		40.40 N	73.35 W
Roosevelt, Ok., U.S.	138	G9	34.51 N	99.01 W
Roosevelt, Ut., U.S.	150	C6	40.18 N	109.59 W
Roosevelt, stm., Braz.	164	E5	7.34 S	60.40 W
Roosevelt Campobello International Park, p.o.i., N.B., Can.	122	F10	44.52 N	66.58 W
Roosevelt Field, shp. cen., N.Y., U.S.	194		40.45 N	73.37 W
Roosevelt Island, i., Ant.	103	C24	79.30 S	161.59 W
Roosevelt Park, p.o.i., N.J., U.S.	194		40.33 N	74.21 W
Roosevelt Roads Naval Station, mil., P.R.	158a	b4	18.15 N	65.38 W
Root, stm., Mn., U.S.	128	H7	43.45 N	91.14 W
Root, stm., Wi., U.S.	130	B9	42.43 N	87.46 W
Root, North Branch, stm., Mn., U.S.	128	H6	43.48 N	92.09 W
Root, South Branch, stm., Mn., U.S.	128	H6	43.44 N	91.57 W
Ropaži, Lat.	26	C7	57.08 N	24.30 E
Ropczyce, Pol.	24	F17	50.03 N	21.37 E
Roper, N.C., U.S.	124	I9	35.52 N	76.37 W
Roper, stm., Austl.	96	B6	14.44 S	135.23 E
Roper Valley, Austl.	96	B6	14.54 S	134.00 E
Ropes Creek, stm., Austl.	192a		33.43 S	150.47 E
Ropesville, Tx., U.S.	138	H6	33.25 N	102.09 W
Ropša, Russia	183a		59.44 N	29.52 E
Roque, Braz.	170	B3	3.01 S	45.24 W
Roquefort, Fr.	22	E5	44.02 N	0.19 W
Roque Pérez, Arg.	172	G8	35.24 S	59.20 W
Roraima, state, Braz.	164	C5	1.00 N	61.00 W
Roraima, Monte see Roraima, Mount, mtn., S.A.	168	E11	5.12 N	60.43 W
Roraima, Mount, mtn., S.A.	168	E11	5.12 N	60.43 W
Rörbäcksnäs, Swe.	16	F9	61.07 N	12.49 E
Rorketon, Mb., Can.	142	C14	51.25 N	99.36 W
Røros, Nor.	16	E9	62.34 N	11.22 E
Rørvik, Nor.	16	C9	64.51 N	11.12 E
Rørvik, Nor.	16	D8	63.31 N	10.09 E
Ros', Bela.	26	G7	53.17 N	24.25 E
Ros', stm., Ukr.	38	D9	49.41 N	31.36 E
Rosa, Cap, c., Alg.	32	H2	36.56 N	8.12 E
Rosa, Lake, l., Bah.	156	B11	21.01 N	73.30 W
Rosairinho, Port.	184c		38.40 N	9.01 W
Rosales, Mex.	154	A6	28.12 N	105.33 W
Rosalia, Wa., U.S.	146	C9	47.14 N	117.22 W
Rosamond, Ca., U.S.	148	I7	34.51 N	118.09 W
Rosamond Lake, l., Ca., U.S.	148	I7	34.50 N	118.04 W
Rosamorada, Mex.	154	D6	22.08 N	105.12 W
Rosanna, Austl.	192b		37.45 S	145.04 E
Rosário, Arg.	172	F7	32.57 S	60.40 W
Rosário, Braz.	170	B3	2.57 S	44.14 W
Rosário, Mex.	154	D6	23.00 N	105.52 W
Rosario, Mex.	154	B4	27.37 N	109.16 W
Rosário, Para.	172	B9	24.24 S	57.06 W
Rosario, Ur.	172	G9	34.19 S	57.20 W
Rosario, stm., Arg.	172	B5	25.05 S	65.23 W
Rosario, Bahía del, b., Mex.	120	G4	29.52 N	115.43 W
Rosario, Islas del, is., Col.	168	B4	10.10 N	75.46 W
Rosario de Arriba, Mex.	120	F5	30.04 N	115.43 W
Rosario de la Frontera, Arg.	172	B5	25.48 S	64.57 W
Rosario de Lerma, Arg.	172	B5	24.59 S	65.35 W
Rosario del Tala, Arg.	172	F8	32.17 S	59.08 W
Rosário do Sul, Braz.	172	E10	30.15 S	54.55 W
Rosário Oeste, Braz.	166	B5	14.50 S	56.25 W
Rosarito, Mex.	148	K8	32.20 N	117.03 W
Rosarito, Mex.	154	B3	26.27 N	111.37 W
Rosarito, Mex.	154	A2	28.35 N	114.08 W
Rosarito, Embalse de, res., Spain	28	D5	40.05 N	5.17 W
Rosarno, Italy	32	F9	38.29 N	15.59 E
Rosas, Mex.	136	H4	26.08 N	103.26 W
Roščino, Russia	18	G16	60.15 N	29.37 E
Roscoe, S.D., U.S.	140	B13	45.25 N	99.20 W
Roscoe, Tx., U.S.	136	B7	32.26 N	100.32 W
Roscommon, Ire.	10	H4	53.38 N	8.11 W
Roscommon, Mi., U.S.	126	D5	44.29 N	84.35 W
Roscommon, state, Ire.	10	H4	53.45 N	8.15 W
Roscrea, Ire.	10	I5	52.57 N	7.47 W
Rose, Mount, mtn., Nv., U.S.	148	D6	39.21 N	119.55 W
Roseau, Dom.	159c	j6	15.17 N	61.23 W
Roseau, Mn., U.S.	128	C3	48.50 N	95.45 W
Roseau, stm., Dom.	159c	j6	15.18 N	61.23 W
Roseau, stm., N.A.	128	C2	49.08 N	97.15 W
Roseau, stm., St. Luc.	159c	m6	13.57 N	61.01 W
Rosebank, ngh., S. Afr.	191d		26.09 S	28.02 E
Rosebank Station, On., Can.	193b		43.47 N	79.07 W
Roseberth, Austl.	98	E2	25.47 S	139.37 E
Rosebery, Austl.	99a	n12	41.47 S	145.31 E
Rosebery, ngh., Austl.	192a		33.55 S	151.12 E
Roseboro, N.C., U.S.	132	B7	34.57 N	78.30 W
Rose Bowl, p.o.i., Ca., U.S.	198		34.10 N	118.09 W
Rosebud, Mt., U.S.	140	A6	46.16 N	106.29 W
Rosebud, S.D., U.S.	140	D12	43.13 N	100.51 W
Rosebud, Tx., U.S.	136	C11	31.04 N	96.58 W
Rosebud, stm., Ab., Can.	144	E17	51.25 N	112.37 W
Rosebud Creek, stm., Mt., U.S.	140	B6	46.16 N	106.29 W
Rosebud Indian Reservation, ind. res., S.D., U.S.	140	D12	43.07 N	100.32 W
Roseburg, Or., U.S.	146	G3	43.13 N	123.19 W
Rosebush, Mi., U.S.	126	E5	43.42 N	84.45 W
Rose City, Mi., U.S.	126	D5	44.25 N	84.07 W
Rose Creek, stm., U.S.	138	A11	40.06 N	97.09 W
Rosecroft Raceway, p.o.i., Md., U.S.	202c		38.48 N	76.58 W
Rosedale, Austl.	98	E8	24.37 S	151.55 E
Rosedale, Ab., Can.	144	E18	51.25 N	112.38 W
Rosedale, In., U.S.	130	E10	39.37 N	87.17 W
Rosedale, La., U.S.	134	G7	30.26 N	91.27 W
Rosedale, Md., U.S.	202b		39.19 N	76.30 W
Rosedale, Ms., U.S.	134	D7	33.51 N	91.01 W
Rosedale, ngh., On., Can.	193b		43.41 N	79.22 W
Rosedale, ngh., N.Y., U.S.	194		40.39 N	73.45 W
Rosedale Estates, Md., U.S.	202c		38.47 N	76.58 W
Rose Hill, N.C., U.S.	132	B7	34.49 N	78.01 W
Rose Hill, Va., U.S.	124	H2	36.39 N	83.21 W
Rosehill Cemetery, misc. cult., Il., U.S.	196		41.59 N	87.41 W
Rosehill Racecourse, p.o.i., Austl.	192a		33.49 S	151.02 E
Rose Hills Memorial Park, misc. cult., Ca., U.S.	198		34.01 N	118.02 W
Rose Island, i., Bah.	132	K8	25.05 N	77.09 W
Rose Lake, B.C., Can.	144	B4	54.25 N	126.01 W
Roseland, La., U.S.	134	G8	30.45 N	90.31 W
Roseland, N.J., U.S.	194		40.49 N	74.17 W
Roseland, ngh., Il., U.S.	196		41.42 N	87.38 W
Roselle, N.J., U.S.	194		40.39 N	74.15 W
Roselle Field, arpt., Il., U.S.	196		41.59 N	88.06 W
Rosellen, Ger.	181		51.08 N	6.43 E
Roselle Park, N.J., U.S.	194		40.39 N	74.15 W
Rosellerheide, Ger.	181		51.07 N	6.44 E
Rosemary, Ab., Can.	144	F18	50.46 N	112.05 W
Rosemary Brook, stm., Ma., U.S.	201		42.19 N	71.15 W
Rosemead, Ca., U.S.	198		34.04 N	118.04 W
Rosemont, Il., U.S.	196		41.59 N	87.52 W
Rosemont, Pa., U.S.	203		40.01 N	75.19 W
Rosemont Horizon, p.o.i., Il., U.S.	196		42.00 N	87.53 W
Rosenberg, Tx., U.S.	136	E12	29.33 N	95.48 W
Rosendal, Nor.	16	H4	59.59 N	6.01 E
Roseneath, S. Afr.	191d		26.17 S	28.11 E
Rosenheim, Ger.	24	I8	47.51 N	12.08 E
Rosenhügel, ngh., Ger.	181		51.10 N	7.12 E
Rosenthal, ngh., Ger.	182a		52.36 N	13.23 E
Rose Peak, mtn., Az., U.S.	150	J7	33.39 N	109.21 W
Rosepine, La., U.S.	134	G5	30.55 N	93.17 W
Roses, Golf de, b., Spain	28	B14	42.10 N	3.09 E
Roses, Golfo de see Roses, Golf de, b., Spain	28	B14	42.10 N	3.09 E
Roseto degli Abruzzi, Italy	30	H11	42.40 N	14.00 E
Rosetown, Sk., Can.	142	C6	51.31 N	108.00 W
Rose Tree, Pa., U.S.	203		39.56 N	75.23 W
Rose Tree Park, p.o.i., Pa., U.S.	203		39.56 N	75.24 W
Rosetta see Rashid, Egypt	76	G1	31.23 N	30.24 E
Rosetta Mouth see Rashid, Masabb, mth., Egypt	76	G1	31.29 N	30.20 E
Rosettenville, ngh., S. Afr.	191d		26.15 S	28.03 E
Rose Valley, Sk., Can.	142	B10	52.18 N	103.47 W
Rose Valley, Pa., U.S.	203		39.53 N	75.23 W
Rose Valley, Pa., U.S.	203		40.10 N	75.13 W
Roseville, Austl.	192a		33.47 S	151.11 E
Roseville, Il., U.S.	130	D7	40.43 N	90.39 W
Roseville, Mi., U.S.	126	F7	42.30 N	82.56 W
Roseville, Mn., U.S.	128	F5	45.01 N	93.09 W
Roseville, Oh., U.S.	124	E3	39.48 N	82.04 W
Roseville Park, De., U.S.	203		39.42 N	75.43 W
Rosewood, Austl.	98	F9	27.38 S	152.35 E
Roshage, c., Den.	16	J6	57.07 N	8.38 E
Roshanara Gardens, p.o.i., India	186		28.40 N	77.12 E
Rosherville Dam, res., S. Afr.	191d		26.14 S	28.07 E
Rosholt, S.D., U.S.	128	F2	45.51 N	96.44 W
Rosholt, Wi., U.S.	128	G9	44.37 N	89.17 W
Rosica, stm., Blg.	36	F12	43.15 N	25.41 E
Rosiclare, Il., U.S.	130	G9	37.25 N	88.20 W
Rosignano Marittimo, Italy	30	G7	43.25 N	10.28 E
Rosignol, Guy.	164	B6	6.16 N	57.32 W
Roșiori de Vede, Rom.	36	E12	44.07 N	24.59 E
Roskilde, Den.	16	L10	55.38 N	12.05 E
Roskilde, state, Den.	16	L10	55.30 N	12.05 E
Roslavl', Russia	26	G15	53.57 N	32.51 E
Roslev, Den.	16	K6	56.42 N	8.59 E
Roslindale, ngh., Ma., U.S.	201		42.18 N	71.07 W
Rosljakovo, Russia	14	C23	69.00 N	33.08 E
Roslyn, N.Y., U.S.	194		40.48 N	73.39 W
Roslyn, Pa., U.S.	203		39.57 N	75.36 W
Roslyn, Wa., U.S.	146	C6	47.13 N	121.00 W
Roslyn Estates, N.Y., U.S.	194		40.47 N	73.40 W
Roslyn Harbor, N.Y., U.S.	194		40.49 N	73.38 W
Roslyn Heights, N.Y., U.S.	194		40.47 N	73.38 W
Rosman, N.C., U.S.	132	A3	35.08 N	82.49 W
Rosmead, S. Afr.	90	G7	31.28 S	25.06 E
Ros Mhic Thriúin see New Ross, Ire.	10	I6	52.23 N	6.56 W
Rosne, Ruisseau le, stm., Fr.	179		48.58 N	2.25 E
Rosny-sous-Bois, Fr.	179		48.53 N	2.29 E
Ross, Austl.	99a	o13	42.02 S	147.29 E
Ross, N.Z.	102	F4	42.52 S	170.49 E
Ross, In., U.S.	196		41.32 N	87.23 W
Ross, stm., Yk., Can.	110	C4	61.59 N	132.26 W
Ross, Point, c., Norf. I.	100i	y25	29.03 S	167.56 E
Ross, Pointe, c., Qc., Can.	193a		45.21 N	73.48 W
Røssåga, stm., Nor.	14	G4	66.09 N	13.47 E
Rossano, Italy	32	E10	39.35 N	16.39 E
Rossasna, Bela.	26	F13	54.39 N	30.53 E
Rossburn, Mb., Can.	142	D13	50.40 N	100.49 W
Rosscott Manor, De., U.S.	203		39.39 N	75.44 W
Rosseau, Lake, l., On., Can.	126	C10	45.10 N	79.34 W
Rossel, Cap, c., N. Cal.	101d	m16	20.23 S	166.35 E
Rossel Island see Yela Island, i., Pap. N. Gui.	96	B10	11.21 S	154.09 E
Rossell y Rius, Ur.	172	F10	33.10 S	55.40 W
Rossendale, mun., Eng., U.K.	180		53.43 N	2.14 W
Rossford, Oh., U.S.	124	C2	41.36 N	83.33 W
Ross Fork Creek, stm., Mt., U.S.	146	D17	47.04 N	109.43 W
Ross Ice Shelf, ice, Ant.	103	D23	81.30 S	175.00 W
Rossignol, Lake, l., N.S., Can.	122	F11	44.11 N	65.08 W
Rossija see Russia, ctry., Eur.	48	B9	60.00 N	100.00 E
Rossio, Estação do, trans., Port.	184c		38.43 N	9.09 W
Ross Island, i., Ant.	103	C22	77.29 S	167.45 E
Rossiter, Pa., U.S.	124	D7	40.53 N	78.55 W
Rossitten see Rybačij, Russia	26	E3	55.09 N	20.50 E
Ross Lake, res., N.A.	146	B5	48.53 N	121.02 W
Ross Lake National Recreation Area, p.o.i., Wa., U.S.	146	B6	48.46 N	121.01 W
Rossland, B.C., Can.	144	G13	49.04 N	117.47 W
Rosslare, Ire.	10	I6	52.16 N	6.24 W
Rosslau, Ger.	24	E8	51.53 N	12.14 E
Rosslyn Farms, Pa., U.S.	197b		40.26 N	80.05 W
Rossmoor, Ca., U.S.	198		33.47 N	118.05 W
Rossmore, Austl.	192a		33.57 S	150.46 E
Rosso, Maur.	84	F1	16.30 N	15.48 W
Rossön, Swe.	16	D14	63.55 N	16.21 E
Ross-on-Wye, Eng., U.K.	10	J10	51.55 N	2.35 W
Rossoš', Russia	38	B17	51.06 N	38.29 E
Rossoš', Russia	40	F11	50.12 N	39.34 E
Ross R. Barnett Reservoir, res., Ms., U.S.	134	E9	32.26 N	90.01 W
Ross River, Yk., Can.	110	C4	62.00 N	132.25 W
Ross Sea, s., Ant.	103	C23	76.00 S	175.00 W
Ross Township, Pa., U.S.	197b		40.32 N	80.01 W
Rossu, Capu, c., Fr.	22	G14	42.14 N	8.33 E
Røssvassholmen, i., Nor.	16	B11	65.41 N	14.00 E
Røssvatnet, l., Nor.	16	B11	65.45 N	14.00 E
Rossville, Ga., U.S.	134	C13	34.59 N	85.17 W
Rossville, Il., U.S.	130	D10	40.22 N	87.39 W
Rossville, In., U.S.	130	D11	40.24 N	86.35 W
Rossville, Ks., U.S.	130	E2	39.08 N	95.57 W
Rossville, Md., U.S.	202b		39.20 N	76.29 W
Røst, is., Nor.	12	C4	67.28 N	12.01 E
Rostavytsia, stm., Ukr.	38	D8	49.44 N	30.01 E
Røsthavet, strt., Nor.	14	E3	67.35 N	12.21 E
Rosthern, Sk., Can.	142	B7	52.40 N	106.20 W
Rostherne, Eng., U.K.	180		53.21 N	2.23 W
Rostherne Mere, l., Eng., U.K.	180		53.21 N	2.23 W
Roštkala, Taj.	72	B11	37.16 N	71.49 E
Rostock, Ger.	24	B8	54.05 N	12.07 E
Rostov, Russia	26	C22	57.11 N	39.25 E
Rostov-na-Donu, Russia	40	H11	47.13 N	39.42 E
Rostovskaja oblast', co., Russia	40	H12	47.00 N	41.00 E
Rostraver Airport, arpt., Pa., U.S.	197b		40.13 N	79.50 W
Rosvinskoe, Russia	12	C25	66.31 N	52.24 E
Roswell, Ga., U.S.	132	B1	34.01 N	84.21 W
Roswell, N.M., U.S.	138	H4	33.23 N	104.31 W
Rota, i., N. Mar. Is.	94	B5	14.10 N	145.12 E
Rotan, Tx., U.S.	136	B7	32.51 N	100.27 W
Rotary Island, i., N.J., U.S.	203		40.14 N	74.49 W
Rotbach, stm., Ger.	181		51.34 N	6.41 E
Rotberg, Ger.	182a		52.21 N	13.31 E
Rote-Erde, Stadion, p.o.i., Ger.	181		51.30 N	7.27 E
Rotenburg, Ger.	24	C5	53.06 N	9.24 E
Rotenburg an der Fulda, Ger.	20	D18	50.59 N	9.44 E
Roth, Ger.	24	G7	49.14 N	11.05 E
Rothaargebirge, mts., Ger.	24	E4	51.10 N	8.20 E
Rothenburg ob der Tauber, Ger.	24	G6	49.22 N	10.10 E
Rothenstein, hill, Ger.	181		51.07 N	7.41 E
Rother, stm., Eng., U.K.	10	J13	50.57 N	0.44 E
Rothera, sci., Ant.	103	B34	67.34 S	68.08 W
Rotherham, Eng., U.K.	10	H11	53.25 N	1.23 W
Rothes, Scot., U.K.	10	D9	57.31 N	3.12 W
Rothesay, N.B., Can.	122	E11	45.23 N	66.00 W
Rothesay, Scot., U.K.	10	F7	55.50 N	5.03 W
Rothneusiedl, ngh., Aus.	182b		48.08 N	16.23 E
Rothsay, Mn., U.S.	128	E2	46.28 N	96.17 W
Rothschild, Wi., U.S.	128	G9	44.51 N	89.37 W
Rothwell, N.B., Can.	122	D10	46.04 N	66.02 W
Roti, Pulau, i., Indon.	60	H7	10.45 S	123.10 E
Roto, Austl.	98	I5	33.03 S	145.28 E
Rotondella, Italy	32	D10	40.10 N	16.32 E
Rotondo, Monte, mtn., Fr.	22	G14	42.13 N	9.03 E
Rotorua, N.Z.	102	D7	38.08 S	176.14 E
Rott, stm., Ger.	30	B10	48.27 N	13.25 E
Rott am Inn, Ger.	24	I8	47.59 N	12.08 E
Rottenburg, Ger.	24	H4	48.28 N	8.56 E
Rottenburg am Neckar, Ger.	20	F17	48.28 N	8.56 E
Rottenburg an der Laaber, Ger.	24	H8	48.42 N	12.02 E
Rottenmann, Aus.	24	I10	47.31 N	14.22 E
Rotterdam, Neth.	20	C13	51.55 N	4.28 E
Rotterdam, N.Y., U.S.	124	B11	42.49 N	74.00 W
Rotthausen, ngh., Ger.	181		51.30 N	7.05 E
Rottneros, Swe.	16	H11	59.47 N	13.07 E
Rottum, Ger.	181		51.36 N	7.42 E
Rottweil, Ger.	24	H4	48.10 N	8.37 E
Rotuma, i., Fiji	94	E8	12.30 S	177.05 E
Roubaix, Fr.	20	D12	50.41 N	3.10 E
Roubideau Creek, stm., Co., U.S.	150	E8	38.45 N	108.15 W
Roubidoux Creek, stm., Mo., U.S.	130	G5	37.51 N	92.12 W
Roubion, stm., Fr.	22	E11	44.33 N	4.42 E
Roudnice nad Labem, Czech Rep.	24	F10	50.25 N	14.15 E
Rouen, Fr.	20	E10	49.26 N	1.06 E
Rouge, stm., Qc., Can.	122	E2	45.38 N	74.41 W
Rouge, Bell Branch, stm., Mi., U.S.	199		42.23 N	83.16 W
Rouge, River, stm., Mi., U.S.	199		42.17 N	83.06 W
Rougeau, Forêt de, p.o.i., Fr.	179		48.35 N	2.30 E
Rough, stm., Ky., U.S.	130	G11	37.28 N	87.07 W
Rough River Lake, res., Ky., U.S.	130	G11	37.35 N	86.29 W
Rouillac, Fr.	22	D5	45.46 N	0.04 W
Rouillon, Fr.	179		48.33 N	2.00 E
Rouleau, Sk., Can.	142	D9	50.11 N	104.55 W
Roulers see Roeselare, Bel.	20	D12	50.56 N	3.07 E
Roulette, Pa., U.S.	124	C7	41.46 N	78.09 W
Round Hill Head, c., Austl.	98	E8	24.10 S	151.53 E
Round Hill Regional Park, p.o.i., Pa., U.S.	197b		40.15 N	79.51 W
Round Lake, Il., U.S.	196		42.21 N	88.05 W
Round Lake, Mn., U.S.	128	H3	43.32 N	95.28 W
Round Lake, l., On., Can.	126	C12	45.38 N	77.32 W
Round Lake, l., Sk., Can.	142	D11	50.32 N	102.24 W
Round Lake, l., Il., U.S.	196		42.22 N	88.05 W
Round Mound, hill, Ks., U.S.	138	C9	38.42 N	99.40 W
Round Mountain, Nv., U.S.	148	E8	38.42 N	117.04 W
Round Mountain, mtn., Austl.	98	H9	30.27 S	152.14 E
Round Pond, l., Ma., U.S.	201		42.36 N	70.49 W
Round Rock, Tx., U.S.	136	D10	30.30 N	97.40 W
Round Top Regional Park, p.o.i., Ca., U.S.	200		37.51 N	122.12 W
Roundup, Mt., U.S.	140	A4	46.26 N	108.32 W
Round Valley Indian Reservation, ind. res., Ca., U.S.	148	D2	39.48 N	123.21 W
Rourkela see Raurkela, India	70	G10	22.13 N	84.51 E
Rousay, i., Scot., U.K.	10	B9	59.10 N	3.04 W
Rouse Hill, Austl.	192a		33.41 S	150.56 E
Rouses Point, N.Y., U.S.	126	C16	45.00 N	73.22 W
Roussigny, Fr.	179		48.39 N	2.06 E
Roussillon, hist. reg., Fr.	22	G8	42.30 N	2.30 E
Routhierville, Qc., Can.	122	B9	48.10 N	67.09 W
Rouxville, S. Afr.	90	G8	30.24 S	26.50 E
Rouyn-Noranda, Qc., Can.	114	B11	48.14 N	79.01 W
Rovaniemi, Fin.	14	F16	66.29 N	25.42 E
Roven'ki, Russia	38	D17	49.55 N	38.55 E
Roven'ky, Ukr.	38	E18	48.05 N	39.23 E
Rovenskaja Slabada, Bela.	26	H13	52.13 N	30.19 E
Rovereto, Italy	30	E8	45.53 N	11.02 E
Roversi, Arg.	172	C6	27.34 S	61.56 W
Roverud, Nor.	16	G10	60.14 N	12.03 E
Rovigo, Italy	30	E8	45.04 N	11.47 E
Rovinj, Cro.	30	E10	45.05 N	13.38 E
Rovnoe, Russia	40	F15	50.46 N	46.03 E
Rovuma (Ruvuma), stm., Afr.	86	G8	10.30 S	40.23 E
Rowan Lake, l., On., Can.	128	B5	49.18 N	93.32 W
Rowena, Austl.	98	G7	29.48 S	148.55 E
Rowena, Tx., U.S.	136	C7	31.39 N	100.02 W
Rowe Park, p.o.i., Nig.	191a		6.30 N	3.23 E
Rowhill, S. Afr.	191d		26.14 S	28.26 E
Rowland, N.C., U.S.	132	B6	34.32 N	79.17 W
Rowland Heights, Ca., U.S.	198		33.58 N	117.54 W
Rowley, stm., Nu., Can.	110	A15	70.16 N	77.44 W
Rowley, stm., Ma., U.S.	201		42.43 N	70.49 W
Rowley Island, i., Nu., Can.	110	B14	69.05 N	78.51 W
Rowntree Mill Park, p.o.i., On., Can.	193b		43.45 N	79.35 W
Rowville, Austl.	192b		37.56 S	145.14 E
Roxas, Phil.	68	E4	11.35 N	122.45 E
Roxboro, Qc., Can.	193a		45.31 N	73.48 W
Roxboro, N.C., U.S.	124	H7	36.23 N	78.58 W
Roxborough, Trin.	159f	r13	11.14 N	60.34 W
Roxborough, ngh., Pa., U.S.	203		40.02 N	75.13 W
Roxburgh, N.Z.	102	G3	45.32 S	169.17 E
Roxbury, ngh., Ma., U.S.	201		42.20 N	71.06 W
Roxbury, ngh., N.Y., U.S.	194		40.34 N	73.54 W
Roxen, l., Swe.	16	I13	58.30 N	15.41 E
Roxie, Ms., U.S.	134	F7	31.30 N	91.04 W
Roxo, Cabo see Roxo, Cap, c., Afr.	84	G1	12.19 N	16.43 W
Roxo, Cap, c., Afr.	84	G1	12.19 N	16.43 W
Roxton, Tx., U.S.	134	D3	33.33 N	95.43 W
Roxwell, Eng., U.K.	178		51.45 N	0.23 E
Roy, N.M., U.S.	138	F4	35.56 N	104.11 W
Roy, Ut., U.S.	150	B4	41.10 N	112.01 W
Roy, Wa., U.S.	146	C4	47.00 N	122.32 W
Roya, stm., Eur.	30	F4	43.47 N	7.36 E
Royal, Ia., U.S.	130	A2	43.03 N	95.17 W
Royal, Mount, hill, On., Can.	128	B10	49.55 N	88.48 W
Royal, Mount, hill, St. Vin.	159e	p11	12.43 N	61.19 W
Royal Air Force Museum, bldg., Eng., U.K.	178		51.36 N	0.14 W
Royal Albert Hall, bldg., Eng., U.K.	178		51.30 N	0.11 W
Royal Bangkok Sports Club, p.o.i., Thai.	187a		13.44 N	100.33 E
Royal Bardiyā Wild Life Reserve, ind. res., India	70	D8	28.28 N	81.28 E
Royal Botanic Gardens, p.o.i., Austl.	192a		33.52 S	151.13 E
Royal Botanic Gardens, p.o.i., Austl.	192b		37.50 S	144.59 E
Royal Canal, can., Ire.	10	H5	53.21 N	6.14 W
Royal Center, In., U.S.	130	D11	40.51 N	86.30 W
Royal Chitwan National Park, p.o.i., Nepal	70	E10	27.30 N	84.30 E
Royal City, Wa., U.S.	146	D7	46.54 N	119.38 W
Royale, Isle, i., Mi., U.S.	128	D10	48.00 N	89.00 W
Royal Gorge, val., Co., U.S.	138	C3	38.27 N	105.21 W
Royal Island, i., Bah.	132	K9	25.31 N	76.51 W
Royal Leamington Spa, Eng., U.K.	10	I11	52.17 N	1.31 W
Royal Natal National Park, p.o.i., S. Afr.	90	F9	28.45 S	28.57 E
Royal Naval College, mil., Eng., U.K.	178		51.29 N	0.01 W
Royal Oak, Mi., U.S.	124	B2	42.30 N	83.08 W
Royal Oak Township, Mi., U.S.	199		42.27 N	83.10 W
Royal Ontario Museum, bldg., On., Can.	193b		43.40 N	79.24 W
Royal Palms State Beach, p.o.i., Ca., U.S.	198		33.44 N	118.19 W
Royal Park, p.o.i., Austl.	192b		37.47 S	144.57 E
Royalton, Mn., U.S.	128	F4	45.49 N	94.17 W
Royal Tunbridge Wells, Eng., U.K.	10	J13	51.08 N	0.15 E
Royal Turf Club, p.o.i., Thai.	187a		13.46 N	100.32 E
Royan, Fr.	22	D5	45.37 N	1.01 W
Royce Brook, stm., N.J., U.S.	194		40.32 N	70.35 W
Roye, Fr.	20	E11	49.41 N	2.47 E
Røyken, Nor.	16	H8	59.45 N	10.24 E
Røyrvik, Nor.	16	C11	64.54 N	13.34 E
Royse City, Tx., U.S.	136	A11	32.58 N	96.20 W
Royston, Eng., U.K.	10	I12	52.03 N	0.01 W
Royston, Ga., U.S.	132	B2	34.17 N	83.06 W
Rožaj, Yugo.	36	G7	42.50 N	20.09 E
Różan, Pol.	24	D17	52.53 N	21.24 E
Roždestveno, Russia	26	D19	56.51 N	36.34 E
Roždestveno, Russia	26	C20	57.44 N	37.56 E
Roždestvo, Russia	26	C16	57.35 N	33.48 E
Rozdil'na, Ukr.	38	G9	46.51 N	30.05 E
Rozdol'ne, Ukr.	38	H12	45.47 N	33.29 E
Rozdory, Ukr.	38	E14	48.20 N	35.42 E
Rozelle, Austl.	192a		33.52 S	151.10 E
Rozewie, Przylądek, c., Pol.	24	B14	54.50 N	18.19 E
Rozhniativ, Ukr.	38	E3	48.56 N	24.09 E
Rozhyshche, Ukr.	38	C4	50.54 N	25.16 E
Rozivka, Ukr.	38	F16	47.23 N	37.04 E
Rožňava, Slvk.	24	H16	48.39 N	20.32 E
Roznov, Rom.	36	C13	46.49 N	26.33 E
Rožnov pod Radhoštěm, Czech Rep.	24	G14	49.27 N	18.09 E
Rożnów, Pol.	24	G16	49.46 N	20.42 E
Roztochchya see Roztocze, hills, Eur.	24	F18	50.28 N	23.16 E
Roztocze, hills, Eur.	24	F18	50.28 N	23.16 E
Roztoky, Czech Rep.	24	F10	50.09 N	14.23 E
Rrëshen, Alb.	32	C13	41.46 N	19.53 E
Rrogozhina see Rrogozhinë, Alb.	32	C13	41.04 N	19.40 E
Rrogozhinë, Alb.	32	C13	41.04 N	19.40 E
Rtiščevo, Russia	40	E13	52.15 N	43.47 E
Ru, stm., China	58	E6	32.36 N	115.11 E
Ruacaná, Quedas do see Ruacana Falls, wtfl., Afr.	88	D1	17.23 S	14.13 E
Ruacana Falls, wtfl., Afr.	88	D1	17.23 S	14.13 E
Ruahine Range, mts., N.Z.	102	E6	40.05 S	176.04 E
Ruapehu, Mount, vol., N.Z.	102	D6	39.17 S	175.34 E
Ruapuke Island, i., N.Z.	102	H3	46.47 S	168.30 E
Rub'al-Khāli see Ar-Rub' al-Khālī, des., Asia	72	E6	20.00 N	51.00 E
Rubanivka, Ukr.	38	F13	46.59 N	34.10 E
Rubbestadneset, Nor.	16	H3	59.49 N	5.17 E
Rubcovsk, Russia	48	D14	51.30 N	81.11 E
Rubel', Bela.	38	B6	51.57 N	27.05 E
Rubelles, Fr.	179		48.34 N	2.41 E
Rubí, Spain	184d		41.29 N	2.02 E
Rubi, stm., D.R.C.	86	D5	2.48 N	23.53 E
Rubí, stm., Spain	184d		41.26 N	2.00 E
Rubicon, stm., Ca., U.S.	148	E5	39.00 N	120.44 W
Rubim, Braz.	170	I5	16.22 S	40.32 W
Rubio, Ven.	168	D5	7.41 N	72.21 W
Rubio Woods, p.o.i., Il., U.S.	196		41.38 N	87.46 W
Rubizhne, Ukr.	38	E17	49.01 N	38.23 E
Rublëvo, Russia	183b		55.47 N	37.21 E
Rubondo Island, i., Tan.	86	E6	2.20 S	31.52 E
Ruby, Ak., U.S.	109	D8	64.44 N	155.30 W
Ruby, stm., Mt., U.S.	146	E14	45.30 N	112.21 W
Ruby Dome, mtn., Nv., U.S.	148	C10	40.37 N	115.28 W
Ruby Lake, sw., Nv., U.S.	148	C10	40.08 N	115.29 W
Ruby Mountains, mts., Nv., U.S.	148	C10	40.24 N	115.30 W
Ruby Valley, val., Nv., U.S.	148	C10	40.30 N	115.17 W
Rucava, Lat.	26	D4	56.08 N	21.09 E
Ruche, Fr.	179		49.02 N	2.27 E
Rucheng, China	58	I5	25.33 N	113.40 E
Ruciane-Nida, Pol.	24	C17	53.39 N	21.35 E
Ručji, ngh., Russia	183a		60.01 N	30.24 E
Ruda Śląska, Pol.	24	F14	50.18 N	18.51 E
Rudauli, India	70	E8	26.45 N	81.45 E
Ruḍaymat al-Liwā', Syria	76	E7	33.01 N	36.35 E
Rūdbār, Afg.	72	C9	30.09 N	62.34 E
Rūdbār, Iran	74	B11	36.49 N	49.27 E
Rüdersdorf, Ger.	24	D9	52.28 N	13.47 E
Rüdersdorf, Forst, for., Ger.	182a		52.26 N	13.50 E
Rudeville, N.J., U.S.	194		41.09 N	74.33 W
Rudge Ramos, Braz.	205b		23.41 S	46.34 W
Rūdiškės, Lith.	26	F7	54.31 N	24.50 E
Rudkino, Russia	38	B18	51.27 N	39.01 E
Rudkøbing, Den.	16	M8	54.56 N	10.43 E
Rudky, Ukr.	38	D2	49.39 N	23.29 E
Rudnaja Pristan', Russia	54	B11	44.21 N	135.48 E
Rudnevka, stm., Russia	183b		55.43 N	37.56 E
Rudnik, Pol.	24	F18	50.26 N	22.15 E
Rudnja, Russia	26	F14	54.57 N	31.06 E
Rudnyj, Kaz.	48	D10	52.58 N	63.07 E
Rudnyj, Russia	54	B11	44.21 N	134.58 E
Rudnytsia, Ukr.	38	E7	48.15 N	28.57 E
Rūdnyy see Rudnyj, Kaz.	48	D10	52.58 N	63.07 E
Rudo, Bos.	36	F6	43.37 N	19.22 E
Rudolf, Lake (Turkana, Lake), l., Afr.	86	D7	3.30 N	36.00 E
Rudolf Häyk' see Rudolf, Lake, l., Afr.	86	D7	3.30 N	36.00 E
Rudolstadt, Ger.	24	F7	50.43 N	11.20 E
Rudong, China	58	K4	21.36 N	111.26 E
Rudong, China	58	E9	32.19 N	121.10 E
Rudozem, Blg.	36	H11	41.29 N	24.51 E
Rudrón, stm., Spain	28	B7	42.47 N	3.46 W
Rūdsar, Iran	74	B12	37.08 N	50.17 E
Rudyard, Mi., U.S.	126	B5	46.13 N	84.35 W
Rudyard, Mt., U.S.	146	B16	48.34 N	110.33 W
Rudzensk, Bela.	26	G10	53.35 N	27.52 E
Rue, Fr.	20	D10	50.16 N	1.40 E
Ruecas, stm., Spain	28	E5	38.59 N	5.54 W
Rueil-Malmaison, Fr.	179		48.53 N	2.11 E
Ruen, mtn., Eur.	36	G9	42.10 N	22.31 E
Rufā'ah, Sudan	82	E6	14.45 N	33.22 E
Ruffec, Fr.	22	C6	46.01 N	0.12 E
Ruffin, S.C., U.S.	132	C5	33.00 N	80.49 W
Ruffle Bar, i., N.Y., U.S.	194		40.36 N	46.51 W
Rufford, Eng., U.K.	180		53.38 N	2.49 W
Rufford Old Hall, hist., Eng., U.K.	180		53.38 N	2.49 W
Ruffs Dale, Pa., U.S.	197b		40.10 N	79.37 W
Rufiji, stm., Tan.	86	F7	7.58 S	39.25 E
Rufino, Arg.	172	G6	34.16 S	62.42 W
Rufisque, Sen.	84	G1	14.44 N	17.16 W
Rufunsa, Zam.	88	D4	15.04 S	29.38 E
Rufus, Or., U.S.	146	E6	45.41 N	120.44 W
Rugāji, Lat.	26	D10	57.00 N	27.06 E
Rugao, China	58	E9	32.23 N	120.33 E
Rugby, Eng., U.K.	10	I11	52.22 N	1.16 W
Rugby, N.D., U.S.	142	F14	48.22 N	99.59 W
Rügen, i., Ger.	24	B9	54.25 N	13.24 E
Rügenwalde see Darłowo, Pol.	24	B12	54.25 N	16.24 E
Rüggeberg, Ger.	181		51.16 N	7.22 E
Rugged Mountain, mtn., B.C., Can.	144	F4	50.02 N	126.41 W
Ruguj, Russia	26	A15	59.27 N	32.50 E
Ruhan', Russia	26	G15	53.33 N	32.48 E
Ruhea, Bngl.	70	E12	26.10 N	88.25 E
Ruhengeri, Rw.	86	E5	1.30 S	29.38 E
Ruhlsdorf, Ger.	182a		52.23 N	13.16 E
Ruhnu saar, i., Est.	26	C6	57.48 N	23.15 E
Ruhpolding, Ger.	24	I8	47.45 N	12.38 E
Ruhrort, ngh., Ger.	181		51.26 N	6.45 E
Ruhr-Universität, educ., Ger.	181		51.27 N	7.16 E
Ruhunu National Park, p.o.i., Sri L.	69	H5	6.30 N	81.30 E
Rui'an, China	58	H9	27.50 N	120.35 E
Ruicheng, China	58	D4	34.45 N	110.45 E
Ruidoso, N.M., U.S.	138	H3	33.20 N	105.41 W
Ruidoso, stm., N.M., U.S.	138	H3	33.23 N	105.16 W
Ruidoso Downs, N.M., U.S.	138	H3	33.20 N	105.34 W

Name | Page | Map Ref. | Latitude | Longitude

Ruihong, China 58 G7 28.45 N 116.23 E
Ruijin, China 58 I6 25.51 N 116.00 E
Ruislip, ngh., Eng., U.K. 178 51.34 N 0.25 W
Ruiz, Mex. 154 D6 21.57 N 105.09 W
Ruiz, Nevado del, vol., Col. 168 E4 4.52 N 75.19 W
Ruiz de Montoya, Arg. 172 C10 26.58 S 55.01 W
Rūjiena, Lat. 26 C8 57.53 N 25.20 E
Rukatunturi, hill, Fin. 18 A16 66.08 N 29.10 E
Ruki, stm., D.R.C. 86 E3 0.04 N 18.17 E
Rukwa, Lake, l., Tan. 86 F6 8.00 S 32.25 E
Rule, Tx., U.S. 136 A8 33.11 N 99.53 W
Rule Creek, stm., Co., U.S. 138 D5 38.04 N 103.00 W
Ruleville, Ms., U.S. 134 D8 33.43 N 90.33 W
Rulo, Ne., U.S. 130 D2 40.03 N 95.26 W
Rùm, i., Scot., U.K. 10 D6 57.00 N 6.22 W
Rum, stm., Mn., U.S. 128 F5 45.11 N 93.24 W
Ruma, Yugo. 36 D6 45.00 N 19.49 E
Rumāh, Sau. Ar. 74 H10 25.34 N 47.09 E
Rumbek, Sudan 82 F5 6.48 N 29.41 E
Rum Cay, i., Bah. 152 C10 23.40 N 74.53 W
Rumelifeneri, ngh., Tur. 185b 41.14 N 29.06 E
Rumelihisarı, ngh., Tur. 185b 41.05 N 29.03 E
Rumelihisarı, hist., Tur. 185b 41.05 N 29.02 E
Rumelikavağı, ngh., Tur. 185b 41.11 N 29.04 E
Rumford, Me., U.S. 122 F6 44.33 N 70.33 W
Rumford, stm., Ma., U.S. 201 41.58 N 71.11 W
Rumia, Pol. 24 B14 54.34 N 18.23 E
Rumigny, Fr. 20 E13 49.48 N 4.15 E
Rumjancevo, Russia 183b 55.38 N 37.26 E
Rum Jungle, Austl. 96 B6 13.00 S 130.58 E
R'umki, Russia 183a 59.47 N 30.02 E
Rummah, Wādī ar-, stm., Sau. Ar. 74 H8 26.12 N 44.03 E
Rummelsburg, ngh., Ger. 182a 52.30 N 13.29 E
Rummenohl, ngh., Ger. 181 51.17 N 7.32 E
Rumoi, Japan 54 B14 43.56 N 141.39 E
Rumphi, Mwi. 88 C5 11.00 S 33.51 E
Rump Mountain, mtn., Me., U.S. 122 E5 45.12 N 71.04 W
Runan, China 58 E6 33.00 N 114.20 E
Runanga, N.Z. 102 F4 42.23 S 171.15 E
Runaway, Cape, c., N.Z. 102 C7 37.32 S 177.59 E
Runde, stm., Zimb. 90 B10 20.33 S 30.30 E
Rundeng, Indon. 64 K3 2.39 N 97.50 E
Rundēni, Lat. 26 D10 56.16 N 27.50 E
Rundu, Nmb. 88 D2 17.54 S 19.45 E
Rundvik, Swe. 16 D17 63.32 N 19.26 E
Rŭng, Kaôh, i., Camb. 64 G6 10.44 N 103.14 E
Runge, Tx., U.S. 136 F10 28.52 N 97.42 W
Rungis, Fr. 179 48.45 N 2.21 E
Rungis-Halles, Marché de, bldg., Fr. 179 48.46 N 2.21 E
Rungwa, Tan. 86 F6 6.56 S 33.31 E
Rungwa, stm., Tan. 86 F6 7.36 S 31.49 E
Runmarö, i., Swe. 16 H16 59.17 N 18.46 E
Runn, l., Swe. 16 G13 60.32 N 15.42 E
Runnemede, N.J., U.S. 203 39.51 N 75.04 W
Running Water Draw, stm., U.S. 138 G6 33.58 N 101.30 W
Runnymede, mun., Eng., U.K. 178 51.24 N 0.32 W
Rünthe, Ger. 181 51.39 N 7.39 E
Runwell, Eng., U.K. 178 51.37 N 0.32 E
Ruo, stm., China 52 C4 41.03 N 100.20 E
Ruokolahti, Fin. 18 F15 61.17 N 28.50 E
Ruoqiang, China 52 D2 39.01 N 88.10 E
Ruovesi, Fin. 18 F11 61.58 N 24.04 E
Ruoxi, China 58 G6 29.20 N 115.19 E
Rupat, Pulau, i., Indon. 66 C2 1.50 N 101.35 E
Rupea, Rom. 36 C12 46.02 N 25.13 E
Rupert, Id., U.S. 144 H13 42.37 N 113.40 W
Rupert, W.V., U.S. 124 G5 37.57 N 80.41 W
Rupert, stm., Qc., Can. 110 E15 51.29 N 78.48 W
Rupert Creek, stm., Austl. 98 C4 20.51 S 142.21 E
Rupununi, stm., Guy. 168 F12 3.43 N 59.22 W
Rur, stm., Eur. 20 C15 51.11 N 5.58 E
Rural Hall, N.C., U.S. 124 H5 36.14 N 80.17 W
Rural Retreat, Va., U.S. 124 H4 36.53 N 81.16 W
Rural Ridge, Pa., U.S. 197b 40.35 N 79.50 W
Rurrenabaque, Bol. 166 B3 14.27 S 67.30 W
Rurutu, i., Fr. Poly. 94 F11 22.26 S 151.20 W
Rusaniv, Ukr. 38 C10 50.30 N 31.10 E
Rusanivka, Ukr. 38 C12 50.30 N 33.45 E
Rusape, Zimb. 88 D5 18.32 S 32.07 E
Rusavkina-Popovščina, Russia 183b 55.42 N 38.04 E
Ruṣayriṣ, Khazzān ar-, res., Afr. 82 E6 11.34 N 34.27 E
Ruschuk see Ruse, Blg. 36 F12 43.50 N 25.56 E
Ruse, Blg. 36 F12 43.50 N 25.56 E
Ruse, state, Blg. 36 F13 43.40 N 26.30 E
Rusera, India 70 F11 25.45 N 86.03 E
Rush, stm., N.D., U.S. 142 H16 46.59 N 96.54 W
Rush, stm., Wi., U.S. 128 G6 44.32 N 92.19 W
Rushan, China 58 C9 36.53 N 121.28 E
Rush Center, Ks., U.S. 128 C9 38.27 N 99.17 W
Rush City, Mn., U.S. 128 F5 45.41 N 92.57 W
Rush Creek, stm., Co., U.S. 128 C5 38.22 N 102.32 W
Rush Creek, stm., Ne., U.S. 140 F10 41.27 N 102.31 W
Rush Creek, stm., N.Y., U.S. 202a 42.00 N 78.52 W
Rush Creek, stm., Ok., U.S. 138 G11 34.41 N 97.10 W
Rushford, Mn., U.S. 128 H7 43.48 N 91.46 W
Rush Lake, l., Wi., U.S. 128 H10 43.55 N 88.47 W
Rushland, Pa., U.S. 203 40.15 N 75.02 W
Rushmore, Mn., U.S. 128 H3 43.37 N 95.47 W
Rusholme, ngh., Eng., U.K. 180 53.27 N 2.12 W
Rush Springs, Ok., U.S. 138 G11 34.46 N 97.57 W
Rushville, Il., U.S. 130 D7 40.07 N 90.33 W
Rushville, In., U.S. 130 E12 39.36 N 85.27 W
Rushville, Ne., U.S. 140 E10 42.43 N 102.27 W
Rusinga Island, i., Kenya 86 E6 0.24 S 34.10 E
Rusizi, stm., Afr. 86 E5 3.20 S 29.16 E
Rusk, Tx., U.S. 136 C12 31.47 N 95.09 W
Ruskeala, Russia 18 F17 61.55 N 30.36 E
Rusken, l., Swe. 16 J12 57.17 N 14.20 E
Ruskin, Fl., U.S. 132 I3 27.43 N 82.25 W
Rusnė, Lith. 26 E4 55.17 N 21.22 E
Rušons, l., Lat. 26 D10 56.11 N 27.02 E
Russa, India 190b 22.29 N 88.21 E
Russas, Braz. 170 C6 4.56 S 37.58 W
Russell, Mb., Can. 142 D12 50.46 N 101.14 W
Russell, On., Can. 126 C14 45.15 N 75.21 W
Russell, Ia., U.S. 130 D4 40.59 N 93.11 W
Russell, Ks., U.S. 138 C10 38.49 N 98.49 W
Russell, Ky., U.S. 124 F3 38.31 N 82.41 W
Russell, Mn., U.S. 128 G3 44.18 N 95.57 W
Russell, Cape, c., N.T., Can. 109 A16 75.14 N 117.38 W
Russell Cave National Monument, p.o.i., Al., U.S. 134 C13 34.57 N 85.47 W
Russell Creek, stm., Ky., U.S. 130 G12 37.13 N 85.31 W
Russell Gardens, N.Y., U.S. 194 40.47 N 73.43 W
Russell Islands, is., Sol. Is. 101b e8 9.04 S 159.12 E
Russellkonda, India 70 I10 19.55 N 84.34 E
Russell Range, mts., Austl. 96 F4 33.23 S 123.33 E
Russells Point, Oh., U.S. 124 D2 40.27 N 83.53 W
Russell Springs, Ky., U.S. 130 G12 37.03 N 85.05 W
Russellville, Al., U.S. 134 C11 34.30 N 87.43 W
Russellville, Ar., U.S. 134 B5 35.16 N 93.08 W
Russellville, Ky., U.S. 130 H11 36.50 N 86.53 W
Russellville, Mo., U.S. 130 F5 38.30 N 92.26 W
Rüsselsheim, Ger. 24 G4 49.59 N 8.24 E
Russia, ctry., Eur. 48 B9 60.00 N 100.00 E
Russian, stm., Ca., U.S. 148 E2 38.26 N 123.08 W
Russiaville, In., U.S. 130 D11 40.24 N 86.15 W
Russka, Russia 26 A11 59.00 N 28.29 E
Russkaja Bujlovka, Russia 38 C19 50.21 N 40.04 E
Russkaja Žuravka, Russia 40 F12 50.21 N 40.33 E
Russkij, Russia 54 C9 43.04 N 131.50 E
Russkij Brod, Russia 26 H20 52.35 N 37.23 E
Russko-Vysockoe, Russia 183a 59.42 N 29.56 E
Rust, Aus. 30 C13 47.47 N 16.40 E
Rustajskij, Russia 40 C14 56.30 N 44.48 E
Rustavi, Geor. 42 E11 41.32 N 45.01 E
Rustburg, Va., U.S. 124 G6 37.16 N 79.06 W
Rustenburg, S. Afr. 90 D8 25.39 S 27.14 E
Rustic Canyon, val., Ca., U.S. 198 34.04 N 118.31 W
Ruston, La., U.S. 134 E6 32.32 N 92.38 W
Rusville, S. Afr. 191d 26.10 S 28.18 E
Rutana, Bdi. 86 E6 3.55 S 29.58 E
Rute, Spain 28 G6 37.19 N 4.22 W
Ruteng, Indon. 66 H12 8.35 S 120.28 E
Rutenga, Zimb. 88 E5 21.15 S 30.42 E
Rutgers University, educ., N.J., U.S. 194 40.30 N 74.27 W
Rutgers University (Newark), educ., N.J., U.S. 194 40.44 N 74.10 W
Rutgers University (Camden), educ., N.J., U.S. 203 39.56 N 75.07 W
Ruth, Ms., U.S. 134 F8 31.22 N 90.18 W
Ruth, Nv., U.S. 148 D10 39.16 N 114.59 W
Rutherford, Tn., U.S. 130 H8 36.07 N 88.59 W
Rutherfordton, N.C., U.S. 132 A3 35.21 N 81.57 W
Ruthin, Wales, U.K. 10 H9 53.06 N 3.18 W
Ruthton, Mn., U.S. 128 G2 44.10 N 96.06 W
Ruthven, Ia., U.S. 128 H4 43.07 N 94.53 W
Rutland, B.C., Can. 144 G11 49.53 N 119.23 W
Rutland, N.D., U.S. 140 A15 46.03 N 97.30 W
Rutland, Vt., U.S. 122 G4 43.37 N 72.58 W
Rutland Island, i., India 62 F7 11.25 N 92.40 E
Rutledge, Ga., U.S. 132 C2 33.37 N 83.36 W
Rutledge, Pa., U.S. 203 39.54 N 75.20 W
Rutledge, Tn., U.S. 124 H2 36.16 N 83.30 W
Rutog, China 70 B7 33.26 N 79.42 E
Rutshuru, D.R.C. 86 E5 1.11 S 29.27 E
Rüttenscheid, ngh., Ger. 181 51.26 N 7.00 E
Rutter, On., Can. 126 B9 46.06 N 80.39 W
Ruukki, Fin. 18 C11 64.40 N 25.06 E
Ruvinvaara, gora, hill, Russia 18 C17 64.42 N 30.42 E
Ruvuma (Rovuma), stm., Afr. 86 G8 10.30 S 40.23 E
Ruwenzori, mts., Afr. 86 D6 0.20 N 29.53 E
Ruwenzori Range see Ruwenzori, mts., Afr. 86 D6 0.20 N 29.53 E
Ruy Barbosa, Braz. 170 G5 12.17 S 40.26 W
Ruza, Russia 26 E19 55.41 N 36.12 E
Ruza, stm., Russia 26 E18 55.37 N 36.17 E
Ruzaevka, Russia 40 D14 54.04 N 44.56 E
Ružany, Bela. 26 H7 52.51 N 24.53 E
Ruzhychanka, Ukr. 38 D5 49.23 N 26.57 E
Ruzhyn, Ukr. 38 D8 49.43 N 29.12 E
Ruzizi see Rusizi, stm., Afr. 86 E5 3.20 S 29.16 E
Ružomberok, Slvk. 24 G15 49.04 N 19.18 E
Rwanda, ctry., Afr. 86 E6 2.00 S 30.00 E
Ryal Fold, Eng., U.K. 180 53.41 N 2.30 W
Ryan, Ok., U.S. 138 G11 34.01 N 97.58 W
Ryan, stm., B.C., Can. 144 F7 50.22 N 122.51 W
Ryan, Loch, b., Scot., U.K. 10 F7 54.58 N 5.02 W
Ryan Field, p.o.i., Il., U.S. 196 42.04 N 87.41 W
Ryan Peak, mtn., Id., U.S. 146 G12 43.54 N 114.25 W
Ryarsh, Eng., U.K. 178 51.19 N 0.24 E
Rybače, Kaz. 48 E14 46.26 N 81.28 E
Rybače see Issyk-Kul', Kyrg. 48 F13 42.27 N 76.11 E
Rybačij, Russia 26 E3 55.09 N 20.50 E
Rybačij, poluostrov, pen., Russia 14 C23 69.42 N 32.36 E
Rybackaja, ngh., Russia 183a 60.00 N 30.30 E
Rybackoe, ngh., Russia 183a 59.50 N 30.30 E
Rybakivka, Ukr. 38 G10 46.37 N 31.19 E
Rybinsk, Russia 26 B21 58.03 N 38.52 E
Rybinskie Budy, Russia 38 B14 51.13 N 35.57 E
Rybinskoe vodohranilišče (Rybinsk Reservoir), res., Russia 26 B21 58.28 N 38.16 E
Rybinsk Reservoir see Rybinskoe vodohranilišče, res., Russia 26 B21 58.28 N 38.16 E
Rybkino, Russia 40 D13 54.15 N 43.45 E
Rybnaja Sloboda, Russia 40 D16 55.27 N 50.07 E
Rybnica see Rîbniţa, Mol. 38 F8 47.45 N 29.01 E
Rybnik, Pol. 24 F14 50.05 N 18.33 E
Rybnitsa see Rîbniţa, Mol. 38 F8 47.45 N 29.01 E
Rybnoe, Russia 40 D11 54.43 N 39.30 E
Rybnoe see Rybnoje, Russia 50 E7 58.08 N 94.30 E
Rybnoje, Russia 50 E7 58.08 N 94.30 E
Rybreka, Russia 18 F22 61.16 N 35.32 E
Ryburn, stm., Eng., U.K. 180 53.43 N 1.54 W
Rychwał, Pol. 24 D14 52.04 N 18.10 E
Ryd, Swe. 16 K12 56.27 N 14.41 E
Rydaholm, Swe. 16 J12 56.59 N 14.17 E
Rydal, Pa., U.S. 203 40.06 N 75.06 W
Rydalmere, Austl. 192a 33.49 S 151.02 E
Ryde, Eng., U.K. 10 K11 50.43 N 1.10 W
Ryder, N.D., U.S. 142 G12 47.55 N 101.40 W
Ryderwood, Wa., U.S. 146 D3 46.22 N 123.02 W
Rydzyna, Pol. 24 E12 51.47 N 16.39 E
Rye, Eng., U.K. 10 K13 50.57 N 0.43 E
Rye, stm., Eng., U.K. 10 G12 54.10 N 0.45 W
Ryegate, Mt., U.S. 140 A3 46.18 N 109.13 W
Rye Hills-Rye Brook, N.Y., U.S. 194 41.00 N 73.41 W
Rye Lake, l., N.Y., U.S. 194 41.04 N 73.43 W
Ryeosu see Yŏsu, Kor., S. 54 G7 34.46 N 127.44 E
Rye Patch Reservoir, res., Nv., U.S. 148 C7 40.39 N 118.19 W
Ryer Island, i., Ca., U.S. 200 38.05 N 122.01 W
Ryfoss, Nor. 16 F6 61.07 N 8.48 E
Ryfylke, reg., Nor. 16 H3 59.35 N 6.09 E
Rygnestad, Nor. 16 H5 59.16 N 7.29 E
Ryker Lake, l., N.J., U.S. 194 41.03 N 74.33 W
Ryki, Pol. 24 E17 51.38 N 21.56 E
Rykovec, Russia 18 H23 59.33 N 36.35 E
Ryley, Ab., Can. 144 C18 53.17 N 112.26 W
Rylovići, Russia 26 H15 52.31 N 32.04 E
Ryl'sk, Russia 40 F9 51.34 N 34.42 E
Rymanów, Pol. 24 G17 49.34 N 21.52 E
Rýmařov, Czech Rep. 24 G13 49.55 N 17.15 E
Rynda, stm., Russia 14 D27 68.54 N 36.49 E
Rynfield, S. Afr. 191d 26.09 S 28.20 E
Ryn-Peski, des., Kaz. 40 G16 48.24 N 49.00 E
Ryō, Japan 188 34.44 N 135.55 E
Ryōhaku-sanchi, mts., Japan 56 D9 36.09 N 136.45 E
Ryojun see Lüshun, China 58 B9 38.48 N 121.15 E
Ryōke, Japan 186 35.58 N 139.33 E
Ryōtsu, Japan 56 A11 38.05 N 138.25 E
Rypin, Pol. 24 C15 53.04 N 19.25 E
Ryshnivka, Ukr. 38 D6 49.48 N 27.33 E
Rysy, mtn., Eur. 24 G15 49.10 N 20.03 E
Ryūgasaki, Japan 56 D13 35.54 N 140.11 E
Ryukyu Islands see Nansei-shotō, is., Japan 52 F10 25.44 N 126.57 E
Ryukyu Trench, unds. 174 G15 23.59 N 127.01 E
Ryūmon-dake, mtn., Japan 188 34.26 N 135.53 E
Ryūsen, Japan 188 34.28 N 135.37 E
Ržaksa, Russia 40 E13 52.08 N 42.01 E
Ržanica, Russia 26 G16 53.26 N 33.55 E
Ržava, Russia 38 B15 51.14 N 36.42 E
Rzepin, Pol. 24 D10 52.20 N 14.49 E
Rzeszów, Pol. 24 F18 50.02 N 22.00 E
Ržev, Russia 26 D17 56.16 N 34.19 E
Rzhyshchiv, Ukr. 38 D9 49.58 N 31.03 E
Ržovka, ngh., Russia 183a 59.58 N 30.30 E

S

Sa, Thai. 64 C5 18.33 N 100.44 E
Sa'ādatābād, Iran 74 E13 30.06 N 53.08 E
Sääksjärvi, l., Fin. 18 F9 61.24 N 22.24 E
Saale, stm., Ger. 24 E7 51.57 N 11.55 E
Saales, Fr. 24 H3 48.21 N 7.07 E
Saalfeld, Ger. 24 F7 50.39 N 11.22 E
Saar see Saarland, state, Ger. 24 G2 49.20 N 7.00 E
Saar (Sarre), stm., Eur. 20 E15 49.42 N 6.34 E
Saarbrücken, Ger. 24 G2 49.13 N 6.59 E
Saarburg, Ger. 24 G2 49.36 N 6.33 E
Sääre, Est. 26 C5 57.56 N 22.04 E
Saaremaa, i., Est. 26 B5 58.25 N 22.30 E
Saarijärvi, Fin. 18 E12 62.42 N 25.15 E
Saaristomeren kansallispuisto, p.o.i., Fin. 18 H8 59.48 N 21.51 E
Saarland, state, Ger. 24 G2 49.20 N 7.00 E
Saarlouis, Ger. 24 G2 49.19 N 6.45 E
Saarmund, Ger. 182a 52.19 N 13.07 E
Saarn, ngh., Ger. 181 51.24 N 6.53 E
Saarnberg, ngh., Ger. 181 51.25 N 6.53 E
Saatlı, Azer. 42 F13 39.55 N 48.22 E
Saavedra, Arg. 172 H6 37.46 S 62.21 W
Saba, i., Neth. Ant. 159a b1 17.38 N 63.13 W
Saba, stm., Russia 26 B12 59.07 N 29.00 E
Sab 'Ābār, Syria 76 E8 33.49 N 37.52 E
Šabac, Yugo. 36 E6 44.45 N 19.41 E
Sabadell, Spain 28 C13 41.32 N 2.06 E
Sabae, Japan 56 D9 35.57 N 136.11 E
Sabah, state, Malay. 68 H1 5.04 N 117.28 E
Sabah, hist. reg., Malay. 60 D6 5.20 N 117.10 E
Sabak, Malay. 64 K5 3.46 N 100.59 E
Sabalān, mtn., Iran 74 A10 38.15 N 47.48 E
Sabalana, Kepulauan, is., Indon. 66 G11 6.45 S 118.50 E
Sabana, P.R. 158a b4 18.20 N 65.44 W
Sabana, Archipiélago de, is., Cuba 156 A7 22.46 N 79.24 W
Sabana de la Mar, Dom. Rep. 156 C13 19.03 N 69.23 W
Sabana de Mendoza, Ven. 168 C6 9.25 N 70.48 W
Sabanagrande, Hond. 156 F4 13.48 N 87.16 W
Sabana Grande, P.R. 158a b1 18.05 N 66.57 W
Sabanalarga, Col. 168 B4 10.38 N 74.55 W
Sabana Llana, P.R. 158a b3 18.01 N 66.14 W
Sabancuy, Mex. 156 C2 18.58 N 91.11 W
Sabang, Indon. 64 J2 5.52 N 95.20 E
Sabang, Indon. 66 C11 0.12 N 119.52 E
Sabarei, Kenya 86 D7 4.20 N 36.55 E
Sābari, stm., India 69 C5 17.34 N 81.16 E
Sābarmati, stm., India 70 G4 22.19 N 72.23 E
Sab'atayn, Ramlat as-, sand, Yemen 72 F6 15.30 N 46.10 E
Sabatini, Monti, mts., Italy 30 H9 42.10 N 12.15 E
Sabaudia, Italy 32 C6 41.18 N 13.01 E
Sabaudia, Lago di, l., Italy 32 C6 41.16 N 13.02 E
Sabaya, Bol. 166 C3 19.00 S 68.22 W
Sabbioneta, Italy 30 F7 44.59 N 10.28 E
Sabe, India 190c 19.11 N 73.02 E
Šabel'sk, Russia 38 G17 46.50 N 38.28 E
Sāberī, Hāmūn-e, l., Asia 62 B1 31.30 N 61.20 E
Sabetha, Ks., U.S. 130 E2 39.54 N 95.48 W
Sabhā, Libya 82 B2 27.00 N 14.27 E
Sabi see Save, stm., Afr. 88 E5 20.57 S 35.03 E
Sabicy, Russia 26 B12 58.50 N 29.18 E
Sabīdana, Jabal, mtn., Sudan 82 D7 18.04 N 36.50 E
Sabie, S. Afr. 90 D10 25.10 S 30.48 E
Sabie, stm., Afr. 90 D10 25.19 S 32.18 E
Sabile, Lat. 26 C5 57.02 N 22.35 E
Sabina, Oh., U.S. 124 E2 39.29 N 83.38 W
Sabina, hist. reg., Italy 30 H9 42.15 N 12.42 E
Sabinal, Tx., U.S. 136 E8 29.19 N 99.27 W
Sabinal, stm., Tx., U.S. 136 E8 29.05 N 99.26 W
Sabinal, Cayo, i., Cuba 156 B9 21.40 N 77.18 W
Sabiñánigo, Spain 28 B10 42.31 N 0.22 W
Sabinas, Mex. 154 B8 27.51 N 101.06 W
Sabinas, stm., Mex. 154 B9 26.50 N 99.34 W
Sabinas, stm., Mex. 154 B8 27.28 N 100.40 W
Sabinas Hidalgo, Mex. 154 B8 26.30 N 100.10 W
Sabine, stm., U.S. 136 D14 30.00 N 93.46 W
Sabine Bay, b., Can. 109 A17 75.35 N 109.30 W
Sabine Lake, l., U.S. 136 E13 29.53 N 93.48 W
Sabine Pass, strt., U.S. 136 E14 29.44 N 93.52 W
Sabini, Monti, mts., Italy 30 H9 42.13 N 12.50 E
Sabinópolis, Braz. 170 J4 18.39 S 43.04 W
Sabinov, Slvk. 24 G17 49.06 N 21.08 E
Sabiote, Spain 28 F7 38.04 N 3.18 W
Sabirabad, Azer. 42 E13 40.00 N 48.28 E
Šabla, Blg. 36 F15 43.33 N 28.32 E
Sable, Anse au, b., Qc., Can. 193a 45.21 N 73.56 W
Sable, Cape, c., N.S., Can. 122 G11 43.24 N 65.37 W
Sable, Cape, pen., Fl., U.S. 132 K4 25.12 N 81.05 W
Sable Island, i., N.S., Can. 122 G16 43.56 N 59.55 W
Sables, stm., On., Can. 126 B7 46.12 N 82.03 W
Sablé-sur-Sarthe, Fr. 20 G8 47.50 N 0.19 W
Sablūkah, Ash-Shallāl as- (Sixth Cataract), wtfl., Sudan 80 E9 16.18 N 32.41 E
Sablūkah, Shallāl as- see Sablūkah, Shallāl as-, wtfl., Sudan 82 D6 16.18 N 32.41 E
Sablūkah, Shallāl as- (Sixth Cataract), wtfl., Sudan 82 D6 16.18 N 32.41 E
Šablykino, Russia 26 H18 52.50 N 35.12 E
Saboeiro, Braz. 170 D5 6.32 S 39.54 W
Sāboli, ngh., India 190a 28.43 N 77.18 E
Sabor, stm., Port. 28 C4 41.10 N 7.06 W
Sabou, Burkina 84 G4 12.03 N 2.14 W
Sabres, Fr. 22 E5 44.09 N 0.44 W
Sabrina Coast, cst., Ant. 103 B16 67.19 S 118.03 E
Sabugo, Port. 184c 38.49 N 9.18 W
Sabuka, D.R.C. 191b 4.27 S 15.10 E
Sabula, Ia., U.S. 130 B7 42.05 N 90.10 W
Saburovo, Russia 183b 55.53 N 37.16 E
Saburovo, ngh., Russia 183b 55.38 N 37.42 E
Şabyā, Sau. Ar. 72 F5 17.09 N 42.39 E
Sabyin, Mya. 64 C2 19.06 N 94.11 E
Sabzevār, Iran 72 B8 36.12 N 57.40 E
Sac, stm., Mo., U.S. 130 G4 38.00 N 93.44 W
Sacagawea, stm., Mt., U.S. 142 G5 47.25 N 107.55 W
Sacajawea Peak, mtn., Or., U.S. 146 E9 45.15 N 117.17 W
Sac and Fox, ind. res., Mo., U.S. 130 C5 41.58 N 92.39 W
Sacaton, Az., U.S. 150 J5 33.05 N 111.43 W
Sacavém, Port. 184c 38.47 N 9.06 W
Sac City, Ia., U.S. 130 B3 42.25 N 94.59 W
Sacco, stm., Italy 32 C7 41.31 N 13.32 E
Săcele, Rom. 36 D12 45.36 N 25.42 E
Sachayoj, Arg. 172 C7 26.41 S 61.48 W
Sachsen, state, Ger. 24 F9 51.00 N 13.00 E
Sachsen (Saxony), hist. reg., Ger. 24 D4 52.45 N 9.30 E
Sachsen-Anhalt, state, Ger. 24 D7 52.00 N 11.30 E
Sachs Harbour, N.T., Can. 109 B14 71.59 N 125.15 W
Šack, Bela. 26 G10 53.26 N 27.41 E
Šack, Russia 40 D12 54.01 N 41.43 E
Sackets Harbor, N.Y., U.S. 126 E13 43.56 N 76.07 W
Sackville, N.B., Can. 122 E12 45.53 N 64.21 W
Saclay, Fr. 179 48.44 N 2.10 E
Saclay, Étang de, l., Fr. 179 48.45 N 2.10 E
Saco, Me., U.S. 122 G6 43.30 N 70.26 W
Saco, Mt., U.S. 142 F6 48.27 N 107.20 W
Saco, stm., U.S. 122 F5 43.27 N 70.22 W
Saco Bay, b., Me., U.S. 122 G6 43.30 N 70.15 W
Sacotes, Port. 184c 38.48 N 9.20 W
Sacra, Isola, i., Italy 185a 41.45 N 12.15 E
Sacramento, Braz. 170 J2 19.52 S 47.24 W
Sacramento, Ca., U.S. 148 E4 38.34 N 121.28 W
Sacramento, stm., Mex. 136 F1 28.39 N 106.03 W
Sacramento, stm., Ca., U.S. 148 E4 38.03 N 121.52 W
Sacramento, stm., N.M., U.S. 136 B2 32.20 N 105.30 W
Sacramento Mountains, mts., N.M., U.S. 120 E10 32.41 N 105.36 W
Sacramento Valley, val., Ca., U.S. 148 D4 39.15 N 122.00 W
Sacramento Wash, stm., Az., U.S. 150 I2 34.43 N 114.29 W
Sacré-Cœur, rel., Fr. 179 48.53 N 2.21 E
Sacred Heart, Mn., U.S. 128 G3 44.47 N 95.21 W
Sacro Monte, rel., Italy 30 E5 45.49 N 8.15 E
Sacrow, ngh., Ger. 182a 52.26 N 13.06 E
Sacrower-Paretzer Kanal, can., Ger. 182a 52.28 N 12.55 E
Sacrower See, l., Ger. 182a 52.27 N 13.06 E
Săcueni, Rom. 36 B9 47.21 N 22.06 E
Sacupana, Ven. 168 C11 8.32 N 61.35 W
Sádaba, Spain 28 B9 42.16 N 1.16 W
Sa'dābād, Iran 42 H14 34.51 N 50.36 E
Sa'dābād, Iran 74 F12 29.22 N 51.07 E
Sadad, Syria 76 D7 34.18 N 36.55 E
Şa'dah, Yemen 72 F5 16.48 N 43.47 E
Sadaik Taung, mtn., Mya. 64 E4 15.09 N 98.12 E
Sada-misaki, c., Japan 56 F4 33.20 N 132.01 E
Sada-misaki-hantō, pen., Japan 56 F5 33.26 N 132.13 E
Sadang, stm., Indon. 66 E11 3.41 S 119.27 E
Sa Dao, Thai. 64 I5 6.37 N 100.25 E
Sādarpur, India 190a 28.33 N 77.21 E
Sadda, Pak. 70 B3 33.42 N 70.19 E
Saddle, stm., U.S. 194 40.52 N 74.07 W
Saddle Brook, N.J., U.S. 194 40.54 N 74.06 W
Saddle Hill, hill, St. K./N. 159a c2 17.06 N 62.34 W
Saddle Lake Indian Reserve, ind. res., Ab., Can. 144 B18 53.58 N 111.43 W
Saddle Mountain, mtn., Co., U.S. 138 C3 38.50 N 105.28 W
Saddle Mountain, mtn., Or., U.S. 146 E3 45.58 N 123.41 W
Saddle Mountains, mts., Wa., U.S. 146 D7 46.47 N 119.51 W
Saddle Peak, mtn., India 62 F7 13.09 N 93.01 E
Saddle River, N.J., U.S. 194 40.54 N 74.05 W
Saddle Rock, N.Y., U.S. 194 40.48 N 73.45 W
Saddleworth, Eng., U.K. 180 53.33 N 1.59 W
Saddleworth Moor, for., Eng., U.K. 180 53.33 N 1.57 W
Sa Dec, Viet. 64 G7 10.17 N 105.46 E
Sadêng, China 52 E3 31.13 N 94.29 E
Sādiqābād, Pak. 70 D3 28.18 N 70.08 E
Sadiya, India 62 C8 27.50 N 95.40 E
Sadlers, St. K./N. 159a c1 17.24 N 62.47 W
Sado, i., Japan 56 A11 38.00 N 138.25 E
Sado, stm., Port. 28 F2 38.24 N 8.37 W
Sado-kaikyō, strt., Japan 56 B11 37.50 N 138.40 E
Sadovoe, Russia 40 H14 47.45 N 44.30 E
Sadowara, Japan 56 G4 32.02 N 131.28 E
Sādri, India 70 F4 25.11 N 73.27 E
Šadrino, Russia 26 E7 55.52 N 91.06 E
Šadrinsk, Russia 48 C10 56.05 N 63.38 E
Sädvajaure, l., Swe. 14 F7 66.27 N 16.33 E
Sädvaluspen, Swe. 14 F7 66.26 N 16.42 E
Saeby, Den. 16 J8 57.19 N 10.31 E
Saegertown, Pa., U.S. 124 C5 41.43 N 80.09 W
Saeki, Japan 56 E7 34.51 N 134.07 E
Saeki see Saiki, Japan 56 G4 32.57 N 131.54 E
Saerluojia Hu, l., China 70 B11 33.50 N 86.59 E
Saesnuten, mtn., Nor. 16 H5 59.40 N 7.24 E
Safad see Ẕefat, Isr. 76 F6 32.57 N 35.30 E
Safāga, Egypt 74 G3 26.45 N 33.56 E
Safāga, Gezîret, i., Egypt 74 G3 26.45 N 33.59 E
Šafárikovo, Slvk. 24 H16 48.25 N 20.19 E
Safdar Jang Airport, arpt., India 190a 28.37 N 77.13 E
Safdar Jang's Tomb, hist., India 190a 28.36 N 77.13 E
Säffle, Swe. 16 H10 59.08 N 12.56 E
Safford, Az., U.S. 150 K7 32.49 N 109.42 W
Saffron Walden, Eng., U.K. 10 I13 52.01 N 0.14 E
Safi, Mor. 84 C3 32.18 N 9.12 W
Safīd Kūh, Selseleh-ye, mts., Afg. 72 C9 34.30 N 63.30 E
Şāfītā, Syria 76 D7 34.49 N 36.07 E
Safonovo, Russia 12 D22 65.42 N 47.39 E
Safonovo, Russia 26 E16 55.06 N 33.14 E
Safrakköyü, ngh., Tur. 185b 41.00 N 28.47 E
Safranbolu, Tur. 34 B15 41.14 N 32.42 E
Saft el-Laban, Egypt 191c 30.02 N 31.10 E
Safwān, Iraq 74 E10 30.07 N 47.43 E
Saga, China 70 D10 29.28 N 85.08 E
Saga, Japan 56 F3 33.15 N 130.18 E
Saga, Kaz. 40 G19 49.26 N 55.16 E
Saga, state, Japan 56 F3 33.15 N 130.15 E
Sagae, Japan 56 A13 38.22 N 140.17 E
Sagaing, Mya. 64 B2 21.52 N 95.58 E
Sagaing, state, Mya. 64 A2 22.31 N 95.25 E
Sagamihara, Japan 56 D12 35.34 N 139.22 E
Sagamihara-daichi, plat., Japan 186 35.27 N 139.27 E
Sagami-nada, b., Japan 56 D12 34.59 N 139.29 E
Sagamore Hill National Historic Site, hist., N.Y., U.S. 194 40.53 N 73.30 W
Sagamore Hills, Oh., U.S. 197a 41.02 N 81.26 W
Sagan see Żagań, Pol. 24 E11 51.36 N 15.18 E
Saganaga Lake, l., N.A. 128 C8 48.14 N 90.52 W
Saganashkee Slough, stm., Il., U.S. 196 41.41 N 87.53 W
Saganoseki, Japan 56 F4 33.14 N 131.53 E
Saganthit Kyun, i., Mya. 64 G4 11.56 N 98.29 E
Sagaon, India 190c 19.12 N 73.06 E
Sāgar, India 69 D2 14.09 N 75.01 E
Sāgar, India 70 G7 23.50 N 78.45 E
Sagara, Japan 56 E11 34.40 N 138.11 E
Sagaranten, Indon. 66 G5 7.13 S 106.52 E
Sagarmāthā see Everest, Mount, mtn., Asia 70 D11 27.59 N 86.56 E
Sagavanirktok, stm., Ak., U.S. 109 C10 70.21 N 148.10 W
Sagay, Phil. 68 E4 10.55 N 123.26 E
Sage Creek, stm., N.A. 142 E3 48.57 N 110.06 W
Sage Creek, stm., U.S. 140 B4 44.50 N 108.22 W
Sage Creek, stm., Mt., U.S. 146 C17 47.16 N 109.43 W
Sage Creek, stm., Mt., U.S. 146 B16 48.19 N 110.03 W
Sagemace Bay, b., Mb., Can. 142 C13 51.49 N 100.03 W
Sage Mountain, mtn., Br. Vir. Is. 158b e8 18.25 N 64.39 W
Sagerton, Tx., U.S. 136 A8 33.04 N 99.57 W
Saggat, l., Swe. 14 F8 66.53 N 17.52 E
Saginaw, Mi., U.S. 126 E6 43.25 N 83.57 W
Saginaw, stm., Mi., U.S. 126 E5 43.38 N 83.50 W
Saginaw Bay, b., Mi., U.S. 126 E6 43.50 N 83.40 W
Sagiz, Kaz. 48 E8 48.13 N 54.52 E
Sağkaya, Tur. 76 A6 37.11 N 35.41 E
Sagleipie, Lib. 84 H3 6.57 N 8.50 W
Saglek Bay, b., Nf., Can. 108 F13 58.32 N 62.52 W
Sagonar, Russia 48 D16 51.32 N 92.48 E
Sagone, Golfe de, b., Fr. 22 G14 42.04 N 8.39 E
Sagra, mtn., Spain 28 G8 37.57 N 2.34 W
Sagres, Port. 28 H2 37.00 N 8.56 W
Şagu, Rom. 36 C8 46.03 N 21.16 E
Saguache, Co., U.S. 138 C2 38.06 N 106.09 W
Saguache Creek, stm., Co., U.S. 138 C2 37.52 N 105.51 W
Sagua de Tánamo, Cuba 156 B10 20.35 N 75.13 W
Sagua la Grande, Cuba 156 A7 22.48 N 80.04 W
Saguaro National Park, p.o.i., Az., U.S. 150 K5 32.16 N 111.12 W
Saguenay, stm., Qc., Can. 122 B7 48.07 N 69.41 W
Saguenay, Parc de conservation du, ind. res., Qc., Can. 122 B6 48.17 N 70.17 W
Saguna, India 190b 22.59 N 88.29 E
Sagunt, Spain 28 E10 39.41 N 0.16 W
Sagunto see Sagunt, Spain 28 E10 39.41 N 0.16 W
Saguny, Russia 38 C18 50.35 N 39.43 E
Sagutevo, Russia 26 H16 52.27 N 33.28 E
Sāgwāra, India 70 G4 23.40 N 74.02 E
Sagy, Fr. 179 49.03 N 1.57 E
Sa'gya, China 70 D12 28.53 N 88.03 E
Sagyz, stm., Kaz. 40 G18 48.12 N 53.47 E
Sahagún, Col. 168 C4 8.57 N 75.27 W
Sahagún, Spain 28 B5 42.23 N 5.01 W
Sahalin, ostrov, i., Russia 46 D18 51.00 N 143.00 E
Sahalinskij zaliv, b., Russia 50 F17 53.45 N 141.30 E
Sahand, Kūh-e, mtn., Iran 74 B10 37.44 N 46.27 E
Sahara, des., Afr. 80 E6 26.00 N 13.00 E
Sahāranpur, India 70 C6 29.57 N 77.32 E
Saharsa, India 70 F11 25.52 N 86.35 E
Şahbuz, Azer. 42 F11 39.25 N 45.34 E
Sahel see Sudan, reg., Afr. 80 E7 12.00 N 17.00 E
Sāhibābād, India 190a 28.40 N 77.22 E
Sāhibābād, ngh., India 190a 28.45 N 77.05 E
Sāhibganj, India 70 F11 25.14 N 87.37 E
Sāhil see Sudan, reg., Afr. 80 E7 12.00 N 17.00 E
Sāhīwāl, Pak. 70 C4 30.40 N 73.06 E
Sāhīwāl, Pak. 70 C4 31.58 N 72.20 E
Şahneh, Iran 74 C10 34.29 N 47.41 E
Šahovskaja, Russia 26 D18 56.01 N 35.30 E
Şaḩrā' see Sahara, des., Afr. 80 E6 26.00 N 13.00 E
Šahrisabz, Uzb. 48 G11 39.03 N 66.50 E
Šahterskij, Russia 50 D24 64.43 N 177.42 E
Šahtinsk, Kaz. 48 E12 49.40 N 72.35 E
Šahtjorsk, Russia 50 G17 49.10 N 142.07 E
Šahty, Russia 40 H12 47.42 N 40.12 E
Sahuaripa, Mex. 154 A4 29.02 N 109.14 W
Sahuarita, Az., U.S. 150 L5 31.58 N 110.57 W
Sahuayo de José María Morelos, Mex. 154 E7 20.04 N 102.43 W
Šahunivka, Ukr. 38 D11 49.17 N 32.22 E
Šahunja, Russia 40 C15 57.40 N 46.37 E
Sa Huynh, Viet. 64 E9 14.42 N 109.02 E
Šahy, Slvk. 24 H14 48.04 N 18.57 E
Sai Buri, Thai. 64 I5 6.42 N 101.37 E
Sai Buri, stm., Thai. 64 I5 6.42 N 101.38 E
Sa'īdābād, Iran 185d 35.40 N 51.11 E
Sa'īdīyeh, Iran 74 B11 36.25 N 48.47 E
Saido, Japan 186 35.52 N 139.41 E
Saidor, Pap. N. Gui. 101a b4 5.38 S 146.28 E
Saidpur, Bngl. 70 F12 25.47 N 88.54 E
Saidu, Pak. 62 B3 34.45 N 72.20 E
Saigō, Japan 56 C6 36.12 N 133.20 E
Saigon see Thanh Pho Ho Chi Minh, Viet. 64 G8 10.45 N 106.40 E
Saigon see Thanh Pho Ho Chi Minh, Viet. 187c 10.45 N 106.40 E
Sai Gon, stm., Viet. 187c 10.45 N 106.45 E
Saija, Fin. 14 E19 67.04 N 28.52 E
Saijō, Japan 56 F6 33.54 N 133.11 E
Sai Keng, China 189d 22.26 N 114.16 E
Saiki, Japan 56 G4 32.57 N 131.54 E
Sai Kung, China 189d 22.23 N 114.15 E
Sailly, Fr. 179 49.02 N 1.48 E
Sailmouille, Ruisseau, stm., Fr. 179 48.37 N 2.17 E
Sailor Creek, stm., Id., U.S. 146 H11 42.56 N 115.29 W
Saim, Russia 48 B10 60.20 N 64.10 E
Saimaa, l., Fin. 18 F15 61.15 N 28.15 E
Saimbeyli, Tur. 42 F6 37.59 N 36.05 E
Saín Alto, Mex. 154 D7 23.35 N 103.13 W
Şā'īn Dezh, Iran 74 B10 36.40 N 46.33 E
Saint Abb's Head, c., Scot., U.K. 10 F10 55.55 N 2.08 W
Saint-Affrique, Fr. 22 F8 43.57 N 2.53 E
Sainte Agathe, Mb., Can. 142 E16 49.34 N 97.11 W

Name	Page	Map Ref.	Latitude	Longitude
Saint-Agathe-des-Monts, Qc., Can.	126	B15	46.03 N	74.16 W
Saint-Agrève, Fr.	22	D10	45.01 N	4.24 E
Saint Alban's, Nf., Can.	111a	j22	47.53 N	55.51 W
Saint Albans, Eng., U.K.	10	J12	51.45 N	0.20 W
Saint Albans, Vt., U.S.	126	D16	44.48 N	73.04 W
Saint Albans, W.V., U.S.	124	F4	38.22 N	81.49 W
Saint Albans, mun., Eng., U.K.	178		51.45 N	0.20 W
Saint Albans, ngh., N.Y., U.S.	194		40.42 N	73.46 W
Saint Albans Cathedral, rel., Eng., U.K.	178		51.45 N	0.20 W
Saint Albert, Ab., Can.	144	C17	53.38 N	113.37 W
Saint Aldhelm's Head, c., Eng., U.K.	10	K10	50.35 N	2.03 W
Saint-Alexandre-de-Kamouraska, Qc., Can.	122	C7	47.41 N	69.38 W
Saint-Alexis-des-Monts, Qc., Can.	126	B16	46.28 N	73.08 W
Saint-Amable, Qc., Can.	193a		45.39 N	73.18 W
Saint-Amand-Mont-Rond, Fr.	20	H11	46.43 N	2.30 E
Sainte-Amélie, Mb., Can.	142	D14	50.59 N	99.24 W
Saint-André, Cap see Vilanandro, Tanjona, c., Madag.	88	D7	16.12 S	44.28 E
Saint-André, Ruisseau, stm., Qc., Can.	193a		45.22 N	73.29 W
Saint-André-Avellin, Qc., Can.	126	C14	45.43 N	75.02 W
Saint Andrew, Barb.	159d	n8	13.15 N	59.33 W
Saint Andrew, Mount, mtn., St. Vin.	159e	o11	13.11 N	61.13 W
Saint Andrews, N.B., Can.	122	E9	45.05 N	67.04 W
Saint Andrews, Scot., U.K.	10	E10	56.20 N	2.47 W
Saint Andrews, S.C., U.S.	132	D5	32.47 N	79.59 W
Saint Andrew's Cathedral, rel., Sing.	189c		1.18 N	103.51 E
Saint Andrews Channel, strt., N.S., Can.	122	D16	46.03 N	60.39 W
Sainte-Anne, Guad.	159c	h6	16.14 N	61.22 W
Saint Anne, Guern.	20	E6	49.43 N	2.12 W
Sainte-Anne, Mart.	159c	l7	14.26 N	60.53 W
Saint Anne, Il., U.S.	130	C10	41.01 N	87.42 W
Sainte-Anne, stm., Qc., Can.	122	C6	47.01 N	70.52 W
Saint Anne, Cathedral of, rel., D.R.C.	191b		4.18 S	15.19 E
Sainte Anne, Lac, l., Ab., Can.	144	C16	53.43 N	114.27 W
Sainte-Anne-de-Beaupré, Qc., Can.	122	C5	47.02 N	70.56 W
Sainte-Anne-de-Bellevue, Qc., Can.	193a		45.24 N	73.57 W
Sainte-Anne-de-Madawaska, N.B., Can.	122	C8	47.15 N	68.02 W
Sainte-Anne-des-Chênes, Mb., Can.	142	E17	49.40 N	96.38 W
Sainte-Anne-des-Monts, Qc., Can.	122	A10	49.06 N	66.32 W
Sainte-Anne-du-Lac, Qc., Can.	126	B14	46.53 N	75.20 W
Saint Anne of the Congo, rel., Congo	191b		4.16 S	15.17 E
Saint Ann's Bay, Jam.	158d	i13	18.25 N	77.11 W
Saint Anns Bay, b., N.S., Can.	122	D16	46.22 N	60.29 W
Saint-Anselme, Qc., Can.	122	D6	46.37 N	70.57 W
Saint Ansgar, Ia., U.S.	128	H6	43.22 N	92.54 W
Saint Anthony, Nf., Can.	111a	i22	51.21 N	55.36 W
Saint Anthony, Id., U.S.	146	G15	43.58 N	111.41 W
Saint Anthony, Monastery of see Qaddis Antwān, Deir el-, rel., Egypt	76	J3	28.55 N	32.21 E
Saint Anthony's Peak, hill, St. K./N.	159a	c2	17.14 N	62.38 W
Saint-Antoine, N.B., Can.	122	D12	46.22 N	64.45 W
Saint Arnaud, Austl.	98	K4	36.37 S	143.15 E
Saint-Arnoult, Forêt de, p.o.i., Fr.	179		48.35 N	1.55 E
Saint Augustin, Qc., Can.	111a	i22	51.13 N	58.38 W
St.-Augustin, Qc., Can.	193a		45.38 N	73.59 W
Saint Augustine, Fl., U.S.	132	G4	29.53 N	81.18 W
Saint Austell, Eng., U.K.	10	K8	50.20 N	4.48 W
Saint-Avold, Fr.	20	E15	49.06 N	6.42 E
Saint Barnabas Chapel, rel., Norf. I.	100i	y24	29.02 S	167.55 E
Saint-Barthélemy, i., Guad.	159a	b2	17.54 N	62.50 W
Saint-Basile, N.B., Can.	122	C8	47.21 N	68.14 W
Saint Bathans, Mount, mtn., N.Z.	102	G3	44.44 S	169.46 E
Saint-Béat, Fr.	22	G6	42.54 N	0.40 E
Saint Bees Head, c., Eng., U.K.	10	G9	54.30 N	3.38 W
Saint-Benoît, Fr.	179		48.40 N	1.55 E
Saint-Bernard, Île, i., Qc., Can.	193a		45.23 N	73.45 W
Saint-Boniface-de-Shawinigan, Qc., Can.	122	D4	46.30 N	72.49 W
Saint-Bonnet, Fr.	22	E11	44.40 N	6.04 E
Saint-Brice-sous-Forêt, Fr.	179		49.00 N	2.21 E
Saint Bride, Mount, mtn., Ab., Can.	144	E15	51.31 N	115.57 W
Saint Brides Bay, b., Wales, U.K.	10	J7	51.49 N	5.17 W
Saint-Brieuc, Fr.	20	F6	48.30 N	2.45 W
Saint-Brieuc, Baie de, b., Fr.	20	F6	48.39 N	2.43 W
Saint Brieux, Sk., Can.	142	B9	52.38 N	104.52 W
Saint-Bruno, Mont, hill, Qc., Can.	193a		45.33 N	73.19 W
Saint-Calais, Fr.	20	G9	47.55 N	0.44 E
Saint Catharines, On., Can.	126	E10	43.10 N	79.13 W
Saint Catharines Airport, arpt., On., Can.	202a		43.11 N	79.10 W
Saint Catherine, Monastery of, rel., Egypt	74	F3	28.28 N	33.59 E
Saint Catherine, Mount, vol., Gren.	159e	q10	12.10 N	61.40 W
Saint Catherines Island, i., Ga., U.S.	132	E4	31.38 N	81.10 W
Saint Catherine's Point, c., Eng., U.K.	10	K11	50.35 N	1.17 W
Saint-Céré, Fr.	22	E7	44.51 N	1.53 E
Saint-Chamond, Fr.	22	D10	45.28 N	4.30 E
Saint Charles, Ar., U.S.	134	C7	34.22 N	91.08 W
Saint Charles, Id., U.S.	146	H15	42.07 N	111.23 W
Saint Charles, Il., U.S.	130	C9	41.54 N	88.18 W
Saint Charles, Mi., U.S.	126	E5	43.17 N	84.08 W
Saint Charles, Mn., U.S.	128	H6	43.58 N	92.03 W
Saint Charles, Mo., U.S.	130	F7	38.47 N	90.29 W
Saint-Charles, stm., Qc., Can.	193a		45.40 N	73.27 W
Saint Charles Mesa, Co., U.S.	138	C4	38.14 N	104.32 W
Saint-Chély-d'Apcher, Fr.	22	E9	44.48 N	3.17 E
Saint-Chéron, Fr.	179		48.33 N	2.07 E
Saint Christopher (Saint Kitts), i., St. K./N.	159a	c2	17.20 N	62.45 W
Saint Christopher and Nevis see Saint Kitts and Nevis, ctry., N.A.	159a	c2	17.20 N	62.45 W
Saint Clair, Mi., U.S.	124	B3	42.49 N	82.29 W
Saint Clair, Mo., U.S.	130	F7	38.20 N	90.58 W
Saint Clair, Pa., U.S.	197b		40.16 N	79.33 W
Saint Clair, stm., N.A.	124	B3	42.29 N	82.30 W
Saint Clair Beach, On., Can.	199		42.19 N	82.51 W
Saint Clair Flats, pl., Mi., U.S.	199		42.35 N	82.36 W
Saint Clair Flats State Wildlife Area, ind. res., Mi., U.S.	199		42.36 N	82.40 W
Saint Clair Shores, Mi., U.S.	124	B3	42.30 N	82.54 W
Saint Clairsville, Oh., U.S.	124	D5	40.04 N	80.53 W
Saint-Claud, Fr.	22	D6	45.53 N	0.23 E
Saint Claude, Mb., Can.	142	E15	49.39 N	98.22 W
Saint-Claude, Fr.	22	C11	46.23 N	5.50 E
Saint-Claude, Guad.	159c	h5	16.01 N	61.41 W
Saint-Claude, Ruisseau, stm., Qc., Can.	193a		45.25 N	73.28 W
Saint Cloud, Fl., U.S.	132	H4	28.15 N	81.17 W
Saint Cloud, Mn., U.S.	128	F4	45.34 N	94.10 W
Saint-Cloud, Parc de, p.o.i., Fr.	179		48.50 N	2.13 E
Sainte-Croix, Qc., Can.	122	D5	46.37 N	71.43 W
Saint Croix, i., V.I.U.S.	158c	g10	17.45 N	64.45 W
Saint Croix, stm., N.A.	122	E9	45.09 N	67.09 W
Saint Croix, stm., U.S.	128	G6	44.44 N	92.47 W
Saint Croix Falls, Wi., U.S.	128	F6	45.23 N	92.37 W
Saint Croix Indian Reservation, ind. res., Wi., U.S.	128	F6	45.48 N	92.12 W
Saint Croix Island National Monument, p.o.i., Me., U.S.	122	E9	45.08 N	67.08 W
Saint Croix National Scenic Riverway, p.o.i., U.S.	128	F6	46.00 N	92.25 W
Saint Croix State Park, p.o.i., Mn., U.S.	128	F6	45.57 N	92.37 W
Saint-Cyr, stm., Qc., Can.	122	A1	49.07 N	75.22 W
Saint-Cyr-l'École, Aérodrome de, arpt., Fr.	179		48.49 N	2.04 E
Sainte-Cyr-sous-Dourdan, Fr.	179		48.34 N	2.02 E
Saint David, Az., U.S.	150	L6	31.54 N	110.12 W
Saint David, Il., U.S.	130	D7	40.29 N	90.02 W
Saint Davids, On., Can.	202a		43.10 N	79.06 W
Saint David's, Wales, U.K.	10	J7	51.53 N	5.15 W
Saint Davids, Pa., U.S.	203		40.02 N	75.22 W
Saint David's Head, c., Wales, U.K.	10	J7	51.54 N	5.18 W
Saint David's Island, i., Ber.	158e	k16	32.22 N	64.39 W
Saint-Denis, Fr.	20	F11	48.56 N	2.21 E
Saint-Denis, Reu.	89a	i10	20.52 S	55.28 E
Saint-Denis, Basilique, rel., Fr.	179		48.56 N	2.22 E
Saint-Dié, Fr.	20	F15	48.17 N	6.57 E
Saint-Dizier, Fr.	20	F13	48.38 N	4.57 E
Saint-Donat-de-Montcalm, Qc., Can.	126	B15	46.19 N	74.13 W
Sainte-Dorothée, ngh., Qc., Can.	193a		45.32 N	73.49 W
Saint Edward, Ne., U.S.	140	F15	41.34 N	97.51 W
Saint Elias, Cape, c., Ak., U.S.	109	E11	59.48 N	144.35 W
Saint Elias, Mount, mtn., N.A.	109	D11	60.18 N	140.55 W
Saint Elias Mountains, mts., N.A.	109	D12	60.46 N	139.53 W
Saint-Élie, Fr. Gu.	164	C7	4.50 N	53.17 W
Saint Elmo, Il., U.S.	130	E9	39.01 N	88.51 W
Saint-Éloi, Qc., Can.	122	B7	48.02 N	69.17 W
Sainte-Énimie, Fr.	22	E9	44.22 N	3.26 E
Saint-Étienne, Fr.	22	D10	45.26 N	4.23 E
Saint-Étienne-du-Rouvray, Fr.	20	E10	49.21 N	1.06 E
Saint-Eugène, Qc., Can.	122	B4	48.59 N	72.17 W
Saint-Eustache, Qc., Can.	126	C16	45.33 N	73.52 W
Saint-Fabien, Qc., Can.	122	B8	48.18 N	68.52 W
Saint-Fargeau-Ponthierry, Fr.	179		48.33 N	2.32 E
Saint-Félicien, Qc., Can.	122	B4	48.39 N	72.26 W
Sainte-Félicité, Qc., Can.	122	B9	48.53 N	67.20 W
Saint-Félix-de-Valois, Qc., Can.	126	B16	46.10 N	73.26 W
Saint-Florent, Fr.	22	G15	42.40 N	9.18 E
Saint-Florent, Golfe de, b., Fr.	22	G15	42.44 N	9.16 E
Saint-Florentin, Fr.	20	F12	47.59 N	3.43 E
Saint-Florent-sur-Cher, Fr.	20	G11	46.59 N	2.15 E
Saint-Flour, Fr.	22	D9	45.02 N	3.05 E
Sainte-Foy, Qc., Can.	122	D5	46.46 N	71.17 W
Sainte-Foy-la-Grande, Fr.	22	E6	44.50 N	0.13 E
Saint Francis, Ks., U.S.	138	B7	39.46 N	101.48 W
Saint Francis, S.D., U.S.	140	D12	43.08 N	100.54 W
Saint Francis, Wi., U.S.	128	I11	42.58 N	87.52 W
Saint Francis, stm., N.A.	122	C7	47.10 N	68.53 W
Saint Francis, stm., U.S.	134	A8	36.24 N	90.03 W
Saint Francis, Cape, c., S. Afr.	90	I7	34.11 S	24.49 E
Saint Francis, Lake see Saint-François, Lac, l., Can.	126	C15	45.08 N	74.25 W
Saint Francis Bay, b., S. Afr.	90	I7	34.04 S	25.02 E
Saint Francisville, Il., U.S.	130	F10	38.35 N	87.38 W
Saint Francisville, La., U.S.	134	G7	30.46 N	91.22 W
Saint-François, Guad.	159c	h6	16.15 N	61.16 W
Saint-François, stm., Qc., Can.	122	D4	46.07 N	72.55 W
Saint-François see Saint Francis, stm., N.A.	122	C7	47.10 N	68.53 W
Saint-François, Lac, l., Can.	126	C15	45.08 N	74.25 W
Saint-François, Lac, res., Qc., Can.	122	E5	45.55 N	71.09 W
Saint-François-de-Laval, ngh., Qc., Can.	193a		45.40 N	73.34 W
Saint Francois Mountains, hills, Mo., U.S.	130	G7	37.30 N	90.35 W
Saint Francois State Park, p.o.i., Mo., U.S.	130	F7	37.59 N	90.31 W
Saint-Gabriel, Can.	122	B8	48.25 N	68.09 W
Saint-Gabriel, Qc., Can.	126	B16	46.17 N	73.22 W
Saint-Gabriel-de-Gaspé, Qc., Can.	122	B12	48.32 N	64.33 W
Saint-Gabriel-de-Rimouski see Saint-Gabriel, Qc., Can.	122	B8	48.25 N	68.09 W
Saint-Gall see Sankt Gallen, Switz.	30	C6	47.25 N	9.22 E
Saint-Gaudens, Fr.	22	F6	43.06 N	0.44 E
Sainte-Geneviève, Qc., Can.	193a		45.29 N	73.52 W
Sainte Genevieve, Mo., U.S.	130	G7	37.59 N	90.03 W
Saint George, Austl.	98	G7	28.02 S	148.34 E
Saint George, Ber.	158e	k16	32.23 N	64.40 W
Saint George, N.B., Can.	122	E10	45.07 N	66.49 W
Saint George, On., Can.	126	E9	43.13 N	80.15 W
Saint George, S.C., U.S.	132	C5	33.11 N	80.34 W
Saint George, Ut., U.S.	150	F3	37.06 N	113.34 W
Saint George, ngh., N.Y., U.S.	194		40.39 N	74.05 W
Saint George, Cape, c., Nf., Can.	122	B17	48.28 N	59.15 W
Saint George, Cape, c., Fl., U.S.	134	H13	29.35 N	85.04 W
Saint George, Point, c., Ca., U.S.	148	B1	41.46 N	124.13 W
Saint George Island, i., Ak., U.S.	109	E6	56.35 N	169.35 W
Saint George Island, i., Fl., U.S.	134	H14	29.39 N	84.53 W
Saint-Georges, Qc., Can.	122	D6	46.07 N	70.40 W
Saint-Georges, Qc., Can.	122	D4	46.37 N	72.39 W
Saint-Georges, Fr. Gu.	164	C7	3.56 N	51.47 W
Saint George's, Gren.	159e	q10	12.03 N	61.44 W
Saint George's Bay, b., Nf., Can.	111a	j22	48.20 N	59.00 W
Saint Georges Bay, b., N.S., Can.	122	E15	45.50 N	61.45 W
Saint George's Channel, strt., Eur.	10	I7	52.00 N	6.00 W
Saint George's Channel, strt., Pap. N. Gui.	101a	a5	4.40 S	152.27 E
Saint George's Island, i., Ber.	158e	k16	32.23 N	64.41 W
Saint George Sound, strt., Fl., U.S.	134	H14	29.47 N	84.42 W
Saint-Germain, Forêt de, p.o.i., Fr.	179		48.55 N	2.05 E
Saint-Germain-en-Laye, Château de, hist., Fr.	179		48.54 N	2.06 E
Saint-Germain-Laxis, Fr.	179		48.35 N	2.43 E
Saint-Germain-lès-Corbeil, Fr.	179		48.37 N	2.29 E
Saint-Germain-sur-Morin, Fr.	179		48.53 N	2.51 E
Saint-Gervais-d'Auvergne, Fr.	22	C8	46.02 N	2.49 E
Saint-Gilles-Croix-de-Vie, Fr.	20	H6	46.42 N	1.57 W
Saint-Girons, Fr.	22	F7	42.58 N	1.08 E
San Gotthard Pass see San Gottardo, Passo del, p., Switz.	30	D5	46.33 N	8.33 E
Saint-Gratien, Fr.	179		48.58 N	2.17 E
Saint Helena, Ca., U.S.	148	E3	38.30 N	122.28 W
Saint Helena, dep., Afr.	78	H5	15.57 S	5.42 W
Saint Helena, i., St. Hel.	80	H5	15.57 S	5.43 W
Saint Helena Bay see Sint Helenabaai, b., S. Afr.	90	I3	32.41 S	18.07 E
Saint Helena Sound, strt., S.C., U.S.	132	D5	32.27 N	80.25 W
Sainte-Hélène, Île, i., Qc., Can.	193a		45.31 N	73.32 W
Saint Helens, Austl.	99a	n14	41.19 S	148.14 E
Saint Helens, Eng., U.K.	10	H10	53.27 N	2.44 W
Saint Helens, Or., U.S.	146	E4	45.51 N	122.48 W
Saint Helens, mun., Eng., U.K.	180		53.28 N	2.45 W
Saint Helens, mun., Eng., U.K.	180		53.28 N	2.45 W
Saint Helens, Mount, vol., Wa., U.S.	146	D4	46.12 N	122.11 W
Saint Helens Canal, can., Eng., U.K.	180		53.27 N	2.42 W
Saint Helier, Jersey	20	E6	49.11 N	2.06 W
Saint-Hilaire-du-Harcouët, Fr.	20	F7	48.35 N	1.06 W
Saint-Hilarion, Fr.	179		48.37 N	1.44 E
Saint-Hubert, Étang de, l., Fr.	179		48.43 N	1.51 E
Saint-Hubert-le-Roi, Fr.	179		48.43 N	1.52 E
Saint-Hyacinthe, Qc., Can.	126	C17	45.37 N	72.56 W
Saint-Ignace, N.B., Can.	122	D11	46.42 N	65.03 W
Saint Ignace, Mi., U.S.	126	C5	45.51 N	84.43 W
Saint Ignace Island, i., On., Can.	128	C11	48.48 N	87.56 W
Saint Ignatius, Guy.	168	F12	3.20 N	59.47 W
Saint Ignatius, Mt., U.S.	146	C12	47.17 N	114.05 W
Saint-Isidore, N.B., Can.	122	C11	47.33 N	65.03 W
Saint-Isidore-de-Laprairie, Qc., Can.	193a		45.18 N	73.41 W
Saint Ives, Austl.	192a		33.44 S	151.10 E
Saint Ives, Eng., U.K.	10	K7	50.12 N	5.29 W
Saint-Jacques, stm., Qc., Can.	193a		45.26 N	73.29 W
Saint James, Mi., U.S.	126	C4	45.44 N	85.31 W
Saint James, Mn., U.S.	128	G4	43.58 N	94.37 W
Saint James, Mo., U.S.	130	G6	37.59 N	91.37 W
Saint James, Cape, c., B.C., Can.	110	E4	51.56 N	131.01 W
Saint James Islands, is., V.I.U.S.	158b	e7	18.19 N	64.50 W
Saint-Janvier, Qc., Can.	193a		45.43 N	73.56 W
Saint-Jean, Guad.	159a	b2	17.54 N	62.50 W
Saint-Jean, stm., Qc., Can.	122	B12	48.42 N	64.09 W
Saint-Jean, Île, i., Qc., Can.	193a		45.41 N	73.39 W
Saint-Jean, Lac, res., Qc., Can.	122	B4	48.35 N	72.05 W
Saint-Jean, Rapides de, wtfl., Qc., Can.	193a		45.19 N	73.15 W
Saint-Jean Airport, arpt., Qc., Can.	193a		45.18 N	73.17 W
Saint Jean Baptiste, Mb., Can.	142	E16	49.15 N	97.20 W
Saint-Jean-d'Angély, Fr.	22	C5	45.57 N	0.31 W
Saint-Jean-de-Luz, Fr.	22	F4	43.23 N	1.39 W
Saint-Jean-de-Maurienne, Fr.	22	D12	45.16 N	6.19 E
Saint-Jean-de-Monts, Fr.	20	H6	46.47 N	2.02 W
Saint-Jean-du-Gard, Fr.	22	E9	44.06 N	3.53 E
Saint-Jean-Pied-de-Port, Fr.	22	F4	43.10 N	1.14 W
Saint-Jean-Port-Joli, Qc., Can.	122	C6	47.13 N	70.16 W
Saint-Jean-sur-Richelieu, Qc., Can.	126	C16	45.18 N	73.15 W
Saint-Jérôme, Qc., Can.	126	C16	45.46 N	74.00 W
Saint Jo, Tx., U.S.	138	H11	33.41 N	97.31 W
Saint Joe, stm., Id., U.S.	146	C11	47.21 N	116.42 W
Saint John, N.B., Can.	122	E11	45.16 N	66.04 W
Saint John, Ks., U.S.	138	C10	38.00 N	98.45 W
Saint John, N.D., U.S.	142	F14	48.56 N	99.42 W
Saint John, Wa., U.S.	146	C9	47.06 N	117.35 W
Saint John, i., V.I.U.S.	158b	e8	18.20 N	64.45 W
Saint John, stm., N.A.	122	E10	45.15 N	66.03 W
Saint John, Cape, c., Nf., Can.	110	E19	49.59 N	55.31 W
Saint John's, Antig.	159b	f4	17.07 N	61.50 W
Saint John's, Nf., Can.	111a	j23	47.33 N	52.43 W
Saint Johns, Az., U.S.	150	I7	34.30 N	109.22 W
Saint Johns, Mi., U.S.	130	B13	42.59 N	84.33 W
Saint Johns, stm., Fl., U.S.	132	G4	30.24 N	81.23 W
Saint Johnsbury, Vt., U.S.	122	F4	44.25 N	72.00 W
Saint John's Jerusalem, hist., Eng., U.K.	178		51.25 N	0.14 E
Saint John's University, educ., N.Y., U.S.	194		40.43 N	73.48 W
Saint Joseph, Dom.	159c	j6	15.24 N	61.25 W
Saint-Joseph, Mart.	159c	k6	14.40 N	61.02 W
Saint-Joseph, N. Cal.	101d	m16	20.25 S	166.35 E
Saint Joseph, Il., U.S.	130	D9	40.06 N	88.02 W
Saint Joseph, La., U.S.	134	F7	31.54 N	91.14 W
Saint Joseph, Mi., U.S.	130	B11	42.05 N	86.28 W
Saint Joseph, Mn., U.S.	128	F4	45.34 N	94.18 W
Saint Joseph, Mo., U.S.	130	E3	39.46 N	94.50 W
Saint Joseph, Tn., U.S.	134	B11	35.02 N	87.30 W
Saint Joseph, stm., U.S.	130	C13	41.04 N	85.07 W
Saint Joseph, stm., U.S.	130	C12	42.06 N	86.28 W
Saint-Joseph, Île, i., Qc., Can.	193a		45.41 N	73.42 W
Saint Joseph, Lake, l., On., Can.	110	E12	51.03 N	90.52 W
Saint Joseph Bay, b., Fl., U.S.	134	H13	29.47 N	85.21 W
Saint Joseph Channel, strt., On., Can.	126	B6	46.15 N	83.46 W
Saint-Joseph-de-Beauce, Qc., Can.	122	D6	46.18 N	70.52 W
Saint-Joseph-du-Lac, Qc., Can.	193a		45.32 N	74.00 W
Saint Joseph Island, i., On., Can.	126	B6	46.13 N	83.57 W
Saint Joseph's University, educ., Pa., U.S.	203		40.00 N	75.14 W
Saint-Jovite, Qc., Can.	126	B15	46.07 N	74.35 W
Saint-Julien-en-Born, Fr.	22	E4	44.03 N	1.14 W
Sainte-Julienne, Qc., Can.	126	C16	45.58 N	73.43 W
Saint-Junien, Fr.	22	D6	45.53 N	0.54 E
Saint Just, P.R.	158a	b4	18.23 N	65.59 W
Saint Kilda, i., Scot., U.K.	10	D4	57.49 N	8.36 W
Saint Kitts see Saint Christopher, i., St. K./N.	159a	c2	17.20 N	62.45 W
Saint Kitts and Nevis, ctry., N.A.	159a	c2	17.20 N	62.45 W
Saint-Lambert, Qc., Can.	126	C16	45.30 N	73.29 W
Saint-Lambert, Fr.	179		48.44 N	2.01 E
Saint Landry, La., U.S.	134	G6	30.50 N	92.15 W
Saint Laurent, Mb., Can.	142	D16	50.24 N	97.55 W
Saint-Laurent see Saint Lawrence, stm., N.A.	114	B16	49.14 N	67.01 W
Saint-Laurent, Golfe du see Saint Lawrence, Gulf of, b., Can.	110	F18	48.00 N	62.00 W
Saint-Laurent du Maroni, Fr. Gu.	164	B7	5.28 N	54.02 W
Saint-Laurent-et-Benon, Fr.	22	D5	45.09 N	0.49 W
Saint Lawrence, Austl.	98	D7	22.21 S	149.32 E
Saint Lawrence (Saint-Laurent), stm., N.A.	114	B16	49.14 N	67.01 W
Saint Lawrence, Cape, c., N.S., Can.	122	C16	47.02 N	60.36 W
Saint Lawrence, Gulf of, b., Can.	110	F18	48.00 N	62.00 W
Saint Lawrence Island, i., Ak., U.S.	109	D5	63.30 N	170.30 W
Saint Lawrence Islands National Park, p.o.i., On., Can.	114	D12	44.18 N	76.08 W
Saint Lawrence Seaway, can., N.A.	193a		45.43 N	73.25 W
Saint Lazare, Mb., Can.	142	D12	50.26 N	101.16 W
Saint-Lazare, Gare, trans., Fr.	179		48.53 N	2.20 E
Saint-Léandre, Qc., Can.	122	B9	48.43 N	67.36 W
Saint-Léonard, N.B., Can.	122	C9	47.10 N	67.55 W
Saint-Léonard-d'Aston, Qc., Can.	122	D4	46.06 N	72.21 W
Saint-Lô, Fr.	20	E7	49.07 N	1.06 W
Saint Louis, Sk., Can.	142	B8	52.54 N	105.47 W
Saint-Louis, Guad.	159c	i6	15.57 N	61.18 W
Saint-Louis, Sen.	84	F1	16.01 N	16.29 W
Saint Louis, Mi., U.S.	126	E5	43.24 N	84.36 W
Saint Louis, Mo., U.S.	130	F7	38.37 N	90.14 W
Saint-Louis, stm., Qc., Can.	193a		45.19 N	73.53 W
Saint Louis, stm., U.S.	128	E6	46.41 N	92.01 W
Saint-Louis, Lac, l., Qc., Can.	126	C16	45.24 N	73.48 W
Saint-Louis de Kent, N.B., Can.	122	D12	46.43 N	64.58 W
Saint Louis Park, Mn., U.S.	128	G5	44.56 N	93.21 W
Saint-Loup-sur-Semouse, Fr.	20	G15	47.53 N	6.15 E
Sainte-Luce, Mart.	159c	l7	14.27 N	60.55 W
Saint Lucia, ctry., N.A.	159c	m6	13.53 N	60.58 W
Saint Lucia, Cape, c., S. Afr.	90	F11	28.25 S	32.25 E
Saint Lucia, Lake, l., S. Afr.	90	E11	28.04 S	32.28 E
Saint Lucia Channel, strt., N.A.	159c	l6	14.09 N	60.57 W
Saint Lucia Game Reserve, ind. res., S. Afr.	90	F11	28.10 S	32.28 E
Sainte-Lucie, Canal de see Saint Lucia Channel, strt., N.A.	159c	l6	14.09 N	60.57 W
Saint Lucie Canal, can., Fl., U.S.	132	J5	27.07 N	80.16 W
Saint Lucie Inlet, b., Fl., U.S.	132	I5	27.10 N	80.10 W
Saint-Lucien, Fr.	179		48.39 N	1.38 E
Saint Magnus Bay, b., Scot., U.K.	10a	n18	60.24 N	1.36 W
Saint-Malo, Fr.	20	F7	48.39 N	2.00 W
Saint-Malo, Golfe de, b., Fr.	20	F6	48.45 N	2.00 W
Saint-Mandé, Fr.	179		48.50 N	2.25 E
Saint-Marc, Haiti	156	C11	19.06 N	72.40 W
Saint-Marc, Canal de, strt., Haiti	156	C11	18.50 N	72.45 W
Saint-Marc-des-Carrières, Qc., Can.	122	D4	46.40 N	72.02 W
Saint-Marcellin, Fr.	22	D11	45.09 N	5.18 E
Saint-Marc-sur-Richelieu, Qc., Can.	193a		45.41 N	73.12 W
Saint-Mard, Fr.	179		49.02 N	2.42 E
Saint Margarets Bay, b., N.S., Can.	122	F13	44.36 N	64.00 W
Saint Margaret's Hope, Scot., U.K.	10	C10	58.49 N	2.57 W
Sainte-Marie, Mart.	159c	k7	14.46 N	61.00 W
Sainte-Marie, Cap see Vohimena, Tanjona, c., Madag.	88	F8	25.35 S	45.08 E
Sainte Marie, Nosy, i., Madag.	88	D9	16.50 S	49.56 E
Saint Maries, Id., U.S.	146	C10	47.18 N	116.34 W
Saint Maries, stm., Id., U.S.	146	C10	47.18 N	116.33 W
Saint Marks, Fl., U.S.	132	F1	30.09 N	84.12 W
Saint Marks, stm., Fl., U.S.	132	F1	30.08 N	84.12 W
Sainte-Marthe-sur-le-Lac, Qc., Can.	193a		45.32 N	73.56 W
Saint-Martin (Sint Maarten), i., N.A.	159a	a1	18.04 N	63.04 W
Saint-Martin, Cap, c., Mart.	159c	k6	14.51 N	61.12 W
Saint Martin, Lake, l., Mb., Can.	142	C15	51.37 N	98.29 W
Saint-Martin-de-Bréthencourt, Fr.	179		48.31 N	1.56 E
Saint-Martin-de-Nigelles, Fr.	179		48.37 N	1.37 E
Saint-Martin-des-Champs, Fr.	179		48.53 N	1.43 E
Saint-Martin-du-Tertre, Fr.	179		49.06 N	2.21 E
Saint-Martin-la-Garenne, Fr.	179		49.02 N	1.41 E
Saint Martins, N.B., Can.	122	E11	45.20 N	65.33 W
Saint Martinville, La., U.S.	134	G7	30.07 N	91.49 W
Saint Mary, Mo., U.S.	130	G8	37.52 N	89.57 W
Saint Mary, stm., B.C., Can.	144	G14	49.37 N	115.37 W
Saint Mary, stm., N.A.	144	G18	49.34 N	112.50 W
Saint Mary Cray, ngh., Eng., U.K.	178		51.23 N	0.07 E
Saint Mary Lake, l., Mt., U.S.	146	B13	48.41 N	113.30 W
Saint Marylebone, ngh., Eng., U.K.	178		51.31 N	0.10 W
Saint Mary of the Lake Seminary, educ., Il., U.S.	196		42.17 N	88.00 W
Saint Mary Peak, mtn., Austl.	98	H2	31.30 S	138.33 E
Saint Mary Reservoir, res., Ab., Can.	144	G17	49.19 N	113.12 W
Saint Marys, Austl.	99a	n14	41.35 S	148.10 E
Saint Mary's, On., Can.	126	E8	43.15 N	81.07 W
Saint Marys, Ak., U.S.	109	D7	62.04 N	163.10 W
Saint Marys, Ga., U.S.	132	F4	30.44 N	81.32 W
Saint Marys, Ks., U.S.	130	E1	39.11 N	96.03 W
Saint Marys, Oh., U.S.	124	D1	40.32 N	84.23 W
Saint Marys, Pa., U.S.	124	C7	41.25 N	78.34 W
Saint Marys, W.V., U.S.	124	E4	39.23 N	81.12 W
Saint Mary's, i., Eng., U.K.	10	L6	49.55 N	6.18 W
Saint Marys, stm., N.S., Can.	122	E14	45.08 N	61.59 W
Saint Marys, stm., N.A.	126	B5	46.57 N	83.52 W
Saint Marys, stm., U.S.	130	D13	41.02 N	85.09 W
Saint Marys, stm., U.S.	132	F4	30.42 N	81.27 W
Saint Marys, Cape, c., N.S., Can.	122	F10	44.05 N	66.12 W
Saint Marys, South Prong, stm., Fl., U.S.	132	F3	30.21 N	82.06 W
Saint Mary's Bay, b., Nf., Can.	111a	j23	46.50 N	53.47 W
Saint Marys Bay, b., N.S., Can.	122	F10	44.23 N	66.07 W
Saint Marys City, Md., U.S.	124	F9	38.11 N	76.26 W
Saint Mary's Hoo, Eng., U.K.	178		51.28 N	0.36 E
Saint Marys Lake, l., Il., U.S.	196		42.17 N	87.59 W
Saint Mary's Marshes, sw., Eng., U.K.	178		51.28 N	0.35 E
Saint-Mathieu, Fr.	22	D6	45.42 N	0.45 E
Saint-Mathieu, Pointe de, c., Fr.	20	F4	48.20 N	4.46 W
Saint-Mathieu-de-Laprairie, Qc., Can.	193a		45.19 N	73.31 W
Saint Matthew Island, i., Ak., U.S.	109	D5	60.28 N	172.53 W
Saint Matthews, Ky., U.S.	130	F12	38.15 N	85.39 W
Saint Matthews, S.C., U.S.	132	C5	33.40 N	80.46 W
Sainte-Maure-de-Touraine, Fr.	20	G9	47.06 N	0.37 E
Saint-Maurice, Fr.	179		48.49 N	2.25 E
Saint-Maurice, stm., Qc., Can.	122	D4	46.20 N	72.30 W
Saint-Maurice-Montcouronne, Fr.	179		48.35 N	2.07 E
Sainte-Maxime, Fr.	22	F12	43.19 N	6.38 E
Saint Meinrad, In., U.S.	130	F11	38.10 N	86.48 W
Sainte-Menehould, Fr.	20	E13	49.05 N	4.53 E
Saint-Méry, Fr.	179		48.35 N	2.50 E
Sainte-Mesme, Fr.	179		48.32 N	1.58 E
Sainte-Mesmes, Fr.	179		48.59 N	2.42 E
Saint-Méthode, Qc., Can.	122	B4	48.44 N	72.25 W
Saint Michael, Ak., U.S.	109	D7	63.29 N	162.02 W
Saint Michaels, Md., U.S.	124	F9	38.47 N	76.13 W
Saint-Michel, ngh., Qc., Can.	193a		45.35 N	73.35 W
Saint-Michel-des-Saints, Qc., Can.	126	B16	46.40 N	73.55 W
Saint-Michel-sur-Orge, Fr.	179		48.38 N	2.18 E
Saint-Mihiel, Fr.	20	F14	48.54 N	5.32 E
Saint Moritz see Sankt Moritz, Switz.	30	D6	46.29 N	9.49 E
Saint-Moritz see Sankt Moritz, Switz.	30	D6	46.29 N	9.49 E
Saint-Nazaire, Fr.	20	G6	47.16 N	2.12 W
Saint Nazianz, Wi., U.S.	126	D2	44.00 N	87.55 W
Saint-Nicolas see Sint-Niklaas, Bel.	20	C13	51.10 N	4.08 E
Saint-Nom-la-Bretèche, Fr.	179		48.51 N	2.01 E
Saint-Omer, Fr.	20	D11	50.45 N	2.15 E
Saintonge, hist. reg., Fr.	22	D5	45.38 N	0.42 W
Saint-Ouen, Fr.	179		48.54 N	2.20 E
Saint-Pacôme, Qc., Can.	122	C7	47.24 N	69.57 W
Saint-Pamphile, Qc., Can.	122	D7	46.57 N	69.46 W
Saint Pancras, ngh., Eng., U.K.	178		51.32 N	0.07 W
Saint Paris, Oh., U.S.	124	D2	40.07 N	83.57 W
Saint-Pascal, Qc., Can.	122	C7	47.34 N	69.45 W
Saint-Pathus, Fr.	179		49.04 N	2.48 E
Saint-Patrice, Lac, l., Qc., Can.	126	B12	46.21 N	77.18 W
Saint Paul, Ab., Can.	144	B19	53.59 N	111.16 W
Saint-Paul, Reu.	89a	i10	21.00 S	55.16 E
Saint Paul, In., U.S.	130	E12	39.25 N	85.38 W
Saint Paul, Ks., U.S.	130	G2	37.30 N	95.10 W
Saint Paul, Mn., U.S.	128	G5	44.57 N	93.05 W
Saint Paul, Ne., U.S.	140	F14	41.13 N	98.27 W
Saint Paul, Va., U.S.	124	H3	36.54 N	82.19 W
Saint Paul, stm., Lib.	84	H2	6.25 N	10.43 W
Saint-Paul, Île, i., Afr.	174	M10	38.43 S	77.29 E
Saint Paul, Monastery of see Bolos, Deir Mar, rel., Egypt	76	J3	28.52 N	32.33 E
Saint Paul Island, i., N.S., Can.	122	C16	47.12 N	60.09 W
Saint Paul Island, i., Ak., U.S.	109	E6	57.10 N	170.15 W
Saint Paul's, St. K./N.	159a	c2	17.24 N	62.49 W
Saint Pauls, N.C., U.S.	132	B7	34.48 N	78.58 W

Name	Page	Map Ref.	Latitude	Longitude
Saint Paul's Cathedral, rel., Eng., U.K.	178		51.31 N	0.06 W
Saint Paul's Cray, ngh., Eng., U.K.	178		51.24 N	0.07 E
Saint Paul's Point, c., Pit.	100k	c28	25.04 S	130.05 W
Saint Peter, Mn., U.S.	128	G4	44.19 N	93.58 W
Saint Peter Port, Guern.	20	E6	49.27 N	2.33 W
Saint Peters, N.S., Can.	122	E16	45.40 N	60.53 W
Saint Peters, Pa., U.S.	203		40.11 N	75.44 W
Saint Peters Bay, P.E., Can.	122	D14	46.24 N	62.34 W
Saint Petersburg see Sankt-Peterburg, Russia	18	H17	59.56 N	30.15 E
Saint Petersburg, Fl., U.S.	132	I3	27.46 N	82.39 W
Saint Peter's College, educ., N.J., U.S.	194		40.44 N	74.05 W
Saint-Philippe-de-Laprairie, Qc., Can.	193a		45.21 N	73.28 W
Saint-Pierre, Qc., Can.	193a		45.27 N	73.39 W
Saint-Pierre, Mart.	159c	k6	14.44 N	61.10 W
Saint-Pierre, Reu.	89a	i10	21.19 S	55.29 E
Saint-Pierre, St. P./M.	111a	j22	46.46 N	56.11 W
Saint-Pierre, St. P./M.	111a	j22	46.46 N	56.11 W
Saint Pierre, i., Sey.	89b	k12	9.19 S	50.43 E
Saint-Pierre, stm., Qc., Can.	193a		45.23 N	73.34 W
Saint-Pierre, Lac, l., Qc., Can.	122	D4	46.10 N	72.51 W
Saint Pierre and Miquelon, dep., N.A.	111a	j22	46.55 N	56.20 W
Saint-Pierre-et-Miquelon see Saint Pierre and Miquelon, dep., N.A.	111a	j22	46.55 N	56.20 W
Saint Pierre-Jolys, Mb., Can.	142	E16	49.27 N	96.59 W
Saint-Pierre-le-Moûtier, Fr.	20	H12	46.47 N	3.06 E
Saint-Pierre-sur-Dives, Fr.	20	E8	49.01 N	0.01 W
Saint-Pol-de-Léon, Fr.	20	F5	48.41 N	3.59 W
Saint-Pol-sur-Ternoise, Fr.	20	D11	50.23 N	2.20 E
Saint-Pons-de-Thomières, Fr.	22	F8	43.29 N	2.46 E
Saint-Pourçain-sur-Sioule, Fr.	22	C9	46.18 N	3.17 E
Saint-Prime, Qc., Can.	122	B4	48.35 N	72.20 W
Saint-Prix, Fr.	179		49.01 N	2.16 E
Saint-Prosper-de-Dorchester, Qc., Can.	122	D6	46.13 N	70.28 W
Saint-Quentin, N.B., Can.	122	C9	47.28 N	67.23 W
Saint-Quentin, Fr.	20	E12	49.50 N	3.17 E
Saint-Quentin, Étang de, l., Fr.	179		48.47 N	2.01 E
Saint-Raphaël, Fr.	22	F12	43.25 N	6.46 E
Saint-Raymond, Qc., Can.	122	D5	46.53 N	71.49 W
Saint Regis, Mt., U.S.	146	C11	47.17 N	115.05 W
Saint-Régis, stm., Qc., Can.	193a		45.24 N	73.34 W
Saint Regis, stm., N.A.	122	F2	45.00 N	74.39 W
Saint-Régis, stm., N.A.	126	D15	45.00 N	74.39 W
Saint Regis, stm., Mt., U.S.	146	C11	47.17 N	115.05 W
Saint Regis, West Branch, stm., N.Y., U.S.	126	D15	44.47 N	74.47 W
Saint Regis Falls, N.Y., U.S.	126	D15	44.40 N	74.32 W
Saint Regis Indian Reservation, ind. res., N.Y., U.S.	126	D15	44.59 N	74.37 W
Saint-Rémi-d'Amherst, Qc., Can.	126	C15	46.01 N	74.46 W
Saint-Rémy-de-Provence, Fr.	22	F10	43.47 N	4.50 E
Saint-Rémy-l'Honoré, Fr.	179		48.45 N	1.53 E
Saint-Renan, Fr.	20	F4	48.26 N	4.37 W
Saint Robert, Mo., U.S.	130	G5	37.50 N	92.10 W
Saint-Roch-de-Mékinac, Qc., Can.	126	B17	46.49 N	72.46 W
Saint-Romuald, Qc., Can.	122	D5	46.45 N	71.14 W
Sainte-Rose, Guad.	159c	h5	16.19 N	61.42 W
Sainte-Rose, ngh., Qc., Can.	193a		45.36 N	73.47 W
Sainte-Rose-du-dégelis see Dégelis, Can.	122	C8	47.32 N	68.38 W
Sainte Rose Du Lac, Mb., Can.	142	C14	51.03 N	99.31 W
Saintry-sur-Seine, Fr.	179		48.36 N	2.30 E
Saintes, Fr.	22	D5	45.45 N	0.38 W
Saint-Savin, Fr.	20	H9	46.33 N	0.52 E
Saint Sebastian Bay, b., S. Afr.	90	I5	34.25 S	21.00 E
Saint-Siméon, Qc., Can.	122	C6	47.48 N	69.53 W
Saint Simons Island, Ga., U.S.	132	E4	31.09 N	81.23 W
Saint Simons Island, i., Ga., U.S.	132	E4	31.14 N	81.21 W
Saintes-Maries-de-la-Mer, Fr.	22	F10	43.27 N	4.25 E
Saint-Soupplets, Fr.	179		49.02 N	2.48 E
Saint Stephen, N.B., Can.	122	E9	45.12 N	67.17 W
Saint Stephen, S.C., U.S.	132	C6	33.24 N	79.55 W
Saint-Sulpice-de-Favières, Fr.	179		48.33 N	2.11 E
Saint-Symphorien, Fr.	22	E5	44.25 N	0.29 W
Saint-Symphorien, Fr.	179		48.31 N	1.46 E
Sainte-Thérèse, Île, i., Qc., Can.	193a		45.22 N	73.15 W
Sainte-Thérèse, Île, i., Qc., Can.	193a		45.41 N	73.28 W
Sainte-Thérèse-de-Blainville, Qc., Can.	126	C16	45.38 N	73.49 W
Saint-Thibault-des-Vignes, Fr.	179		48.52 N	2.41 E
Saint Thomas, On., Can.	126	F8	42.46 N	81.11 W
Saint Thomas, N.D., U.S.	142	F16	48.36 N	97.25 W
Saint Thomas, i., V.I.U.S.	158b	e7	18.21 N	64.55 W
Saint-Tite, Qc., Can.	122	D4	46.43 N	72.33 W
Saint-Tite-des-Caps, Qc., Can.	122	C6	47.08 N	70.46 W
Saint-Trond see Sint-Truiden, Bel.	20	D14	50.49 N	5.11 E
Saint-Tropez, Fr.	22	F12	43.16 N	6.38 E
Saint-Ubald see Saint-Ubalde, Qc., Can.	122	D4	46.44 N	72.16 W
Saint-Ubalde, Qc., Can.	122	D4	46.44 N	72.16 W
Saint-Urbain-de-Charlevoix, Qc., Can.	122	C6	47.33 N	70.32 W
Saint-Valéry-en-Caux, Fr.	20	E9	49.52 N	0.42 E
Saint-Valéry-sur-Somme, Fr.	20	D10	50.11 N	1.37 E
Saint-Vallier, Fr.	22	D10	45.10 N	4.51 E
Sainte-Véronique, Qc., Can.	126	B14	46.31 N	74.59 W
Saint-Vincent, Italy	30	E4	45.45 N	7.38 E
Saint Vincent, Mn., U.S.	128	C1	48.57 N	97.12 W
Saint Vincent, i., St. Vin.	159e	o11	13.15 N	61.12 W
Saint-Vincent, Baie de, b., N. Cal.	101d	n15	22.00 S	166.05 E
Saint-Vincent, Cap see Ankaboa, Tanjona, c., Madag.	88	E7	21.54 S	43.17 E
Saint Vincent, Cape, c., Austl.	99a	o12	43.18 S	145.51 E
Saint Vincent, Gulf, b., Austl.	98	J2	34.54 S	138.04 E
Saint Vincent and the Grenadines, ctry., N.A.	159e	p11	13.15 N	61.12 W
Saint-Vincent-de-Paul, ngh., Qc., Can.	193a		45.37 N	73.39 W
Saint Vincent Passage, strt., N.A.	152a	i15	13.30 N	61.00 W
Saint-Vith, Bel.	20	D15	50.16 N	6.07 E
Saint-Vivien-de-Médoc, Fr.	22	D4	45.25 N	1.01 W
Saint-Vrain, Fr.	179		48.33 N	2.20 E
Saint Walburg, Sk., Can.	110	E9	53.39 N	109.12 W
Saint-Witz, Fr.	179		49.05 N	2.34 E
Saint-Yrieix-la-Perche, Fr.	22	D7	45.31 N	1.12 E
Saint-Yvon, Qc., Can.	122	A12	49.08 N	64.48 W
Saint-Zénon, Qc., Can.	126	B16	46.33 N	73.49 W
Saipan, i., N. Mar. Is.	94	B5	15.12 N	145.45 E
Saiqi, China	58	H8	27.00 N	119.43 E
Saitama, state, Japan	56	C12	36.00 N	139.30 E
Saitama University, educ., Japan	186		35.52 N	139.36 E
Saito, Japan	56	G4	32.06 N	131.24 E
Saiwai, ngh., Japan	186		35.33 N	139.41 E
Saiyidān, ngh., India	190a		28.40 N	77.05 E
Sai Yok, Thai.	64	E4	14.06 N	99.08 E
Sai Yok National Park, p.o.i., Thai.	64	E4	14.28 N	98.48 E
Sajak, Kaz.	48	E13	47.00 N	77.23 E
Sajama, Nevado, mtn., Bol.	166	C3	18.06 S	68.54 W
Sajan Mountains, mts., Asia	46	D13	53.32 N	94.50 E
Sajanogorsk, Russia	48	D16	53.05 N	91.23 E
Sajany see Sajan Mountains, mts., Asia	46	D13	53.32 N	94.50 E
Sajany see Sayan Mountains, mts., Asia	48	D17	53.32 N	94.50 E
Sajat, Turkmen.	72	B9	38.46 N	63.54 E
Šajman, Taj.	72	B11	37.31 N	74.49 E
Sajó (Slaná), stm., Eur.	24	H16	47.58 N	21.02 E
Sajószentpéter, Hung.	36	A7	48.13 N	20.43 E
Sājūr (Bağırsak), stm., Asia	76	B8	36.40 N	38.06 E
Saj-Utes, Kaz.	40	I18	44.20 N	53.32 E
Sak, stm., S. Afr.	90	G5	30.05 S	20.42 E
Sa Kaeo, Thai.	64	F6	13.48 N	102.03 E
Sakai, Japan	56	E8	34.34 N	135.28 E
Sakai, Japan	186		35.25 N	139.22 E
Sakaide, Japan	56	E6	34.18 N	133.51 E
Sakaiminato, Japan	56	D6	35.32 N	133.14 E
Sakākah, Sau. Ar.	74	F7	29.58 N	40.12 E
Sakakawea, Lake, res., N.D., U.S.	142	F11	47.44 N	102.17 W
Sakala, Pulau, i., Indon.	66	G10	6.56 S	116.14 E
Sakami, stm., Qc., Can.	110	E15	53.40 N	76.34 W
Sakami, Lac, l., Qc., Can.	110	E15	53.15 N	76.45 W
Sakania, D.R.C.	86	G5	12.45 S	28.34 E
Sakar, mts., Blg.	36	H13	41.59 N	26.16 E
Sakaraha, Madag.	88	E7	22.55 S	44.32 E
Sakart'velo see Georgia, ctry., Asia	42	D11	42.00 N	44.00 E
Sakarya, Tur.	34	C13	40.47 N	30.24 E
Sakarya, state, Tur.	34	C13	40.45 N	30.35 E
Sakarya (Sangarius), stm., Tur.	34	B13	41.07 N	30.39 E
Sakata, Japan	56	A12	38.54 N	139.50 E
Sakawa, Japan	56	F6	33.30 N	133.18 E
Sakchu-ŭp, Kor., N.	56	D4	40.23 N	125.01 E
Sakété, Benin	84	H5	6.43 N	2.40 E
Sakha see Jakutija, state, Russia	50	D14	67.00 N	125.00 E
Sakhalin see Sahalin, ostrov, i., Russia	46	D18	51.00 N	143.00 E
Sakhnin, Isr.	76	F6	32.51 N	35.17 E
Sakhnovshchyna, Ukr.	38	D14	49.08 N	35.52 E
Sakht Sar, Iran	74	B12	36.53 N	50.41 E
Sāki, ngh., India	190c		19.06 N	72.53 E
Šakiai, Lith.	26	E6	54.58 N	23.04 E
Sakiet Sidi Youssef, Tun.	32	H2	36.13 N	8.22 E
Sakijang Bendera, Pulau, i., Sing.	189c		1.13 N	103.51 E
Sakijang Pelepah, Pulau, i., Sing.	189c		1.13 N	103.52 E
Sakishima-shotō, is., Japan	52	G9	24.32 N	124.26 E
Sakito, Japan	56	F2	33.00 N	129.34 E
Sakkara see Saqqâra, Egypt	76	I2	29.51 N	31.14 E
Sakmara, stm., Russia	40	E19	51.54 N	56.21 E
Sako, Japan	188		34.53 N	135.47 E
Sakon Nakhon, Thai.	64	D6	17.09 N	104.09 E
Sakra, Pulau, i., Sing.	189c		1.16 N	103.42 E
Sakrand, Pak.	70	E2	26.07 N	68.16 E
Sakrivier, S. Afr.	90	G5	30.52 S	20.26 E
Saks, Al., U.S.	134	D13	33.42 N	85.51 W
Saksahan', stm., Ukr.	38	E12	47.53 N	33.21 E
Sakskøbing, Den.	16	M9	54.47 N	11.38 E
Sakti, India	70	H9	22.01 N	82.58 E
Saku, Japan	56	C11	36.09 N	138.28 E
Sakuma, Japan	56	D10	35.05 N	137.48 E
Sakurai, Japan	56	E8	34.30 N	135.51 E
Sakura-tōge, p., Japan	188		34.36 N	135.53 E
Saky, Ukr.	38	H12	45.08 N	33.36 E
Säkylä, Fin.	18	F9	61.03 N	22.22 E
Sakyō, ngh., Japan	188		35.02 N	135.48 E
Sal, i., C.V.	85a	k10	16.48 N	22.56 W
Sal, stm., Russia	40	H12	47.30 N	40.43 E
Sal, Ponta do, c., Port.	184c		38.41 N	9.22 W
Šal'a, Slvk.	24	H13	48.09 N	17.53 E
Sala, Swe.	16	H14	59.55 N	16.36 E
Salaberry-de-Valleyfield, Qc., Can.	126	C15	45.15 N	74.07 W
Salaca, stm., Lat.	26	C7	57.45 N	24.26 E
Salacgrīva, Lat.	26	C7	57.44 N	24.21 E
Sala Consilina, Italy	32	D9	40.24 N	15.34 E
Salada, Laguna, l., Mex.	120	E5	32.20 N	115.40 W
Saladas, Arg.	172	D8	28.14 S	58.38 W
Saladillo, Arg.	172	G8	35.38 S	59.46 W
Saladillo, stm., Arg.	172	D6	29.06 S	63.22 W
Saladillo Dulce, Arroyo, stm., Arg.	172	E7	31.00 S	60.19 W
Salado, stm., Arg.	172	G4	38.49 S	64.59 W
Salado, stm., Arg.	172	D4	29.12 S	66.33 W
Salado, stm., Arg.	172	D6	31.40 S	60.43 W
Salado, stm., Arg.	172	G8	35.44 S	57.23 W
Salado, stm., Cuba	156	B9	20.36 N	76.56 W
Salado, stm., Mex.	154	B9	26.52 N	99.18 W
Salado, stm., N.M., U.S.	150	I9	34.16 N	106.51 W
Salado Creek, stm., Tx., U.S.	136	E9	29.13 N	98.24 W
Salaga, Ghana	84	H4	8.32 N	0.31 W
Salāh ad-Dīn, state, Iraq	74	D8	34.35 N	43.45 E
Salairskij krjaž, mts., Russia	48	D14	54.11 N	85.08 E
Sălaj, state, Rom.	36	B10	47.15 N	23.00 E
Salakas, Lith.	26	E9	55.34 N	26.07 E
Salakuša, Russia	12	E19	62.16 N	40.16 E
Salal, Chad	82	E3	14.54 N	17.17 E
Salala, Chile	172	E2	30.38 S	71.30 W
Salālah, Oman	72	F7	17.00 N	54.06 E
Salālah, Sudan	82	C7	21.19 N	36.15 E
Salamá, Hond.	156	E4	14.49 N	86.34 W
Salamajärven kansallispuisto, p.o.i., Fin.	18	D11	63.20 N	24.40 E
Salamanca, Chile	172	E2	31.46 S	70.58 W
Salamanca, Mex.	154	E8	20.34 N	101.12 W
Salamanca, Peru	204d		12.05 S	77.00 W
Salamanca, Spain	28	D5	40.57 N	5.39 W
Salamanca, N.Y., U.S.	126	F11	42.09 N	78.42 W
Salamanca, co., Spain	28	D4	40.45 N	6.00 W
Salamanga, Moz.	90	E11	26.28 S	32.38 E
Salamanperän luonnonpuisto, ind. res., Fin.	18	D11	63.10 N	24.56 E
Salamat, Bahr, stm., Chad	82	F3	9.27 N	18.06 E
Salamina, Col.	168	E4	5.25 N	75.29 W
Salamína, Grc.	34	F6	37.57 N	23.31 E
Salamína, Grc.	185c		37.58 N	23.29 E
Salamína, i., Grc.	34	F6	37.55 N	23.29 E
Salamínos, Órmos, b., Grc.	185c		37.56 N	23.27 E
Salamis, hist., N. Cyp.	76	C4	35.10 N	33.54 E
Salamīyah, Syria	76	C8	35.01 N	37.03 E
Salamonie, stm., In., U.S.	130	D12	40.49 N	85.42 W
Salani, Samoa	101c	h12	14.01 S	171.36 W
Salantai, Lith.	26	D4	56.03 N	21.32 E
Salaquí, Col.	168	D3	7.19 N	77.35 W
Salaquí, stm., Col.	168	D3	7.25 N	77.07 W
Sălard, Rom.	36	B9	47.13 N	22.02 E
Salarëvo, Russia	183b		55.37 N	37.26 E
Salas, Peru	164	E2	6.16 S	79.36 W
Salas de los Infantes, Spain	28	B7	42.01 N	3.17 W
Salat, stm., Fr.	22	G7	43.09 N	0.58 E
Salatiga, Indon.	66	G7	7.19 S	110.30 E
Salavat, Russia	40	E19	53.22 N	55.55 E
Salaverry, Peru	164	E2	8.13 S	78.58 W
Salavina, Arg.	172	D6	28.48 S	63.25 W
Salawati, i., Indon.	60	F9	1.07 S	130.52 E
Salay, Phil.	68	F5	8.52 N	124.47 E
Salāya, India	70	G2	22.18 N	69.36 E
Sala y Gómez, Isla, i., Chile	174	L28	26.25 S	105.26 W
Sala y Gomez Ridge, unds.	174	L29	25.00 S	98.00 W
Salbani, India	70	G11	22.37 N	87.21 E
Salcia, Rom.	36	F11	43.57 N	24.54 E
Šalčininkai, Lith.	26	F8	54.18 N	25.23 E
Salcombe, Eng., U.K.	10	K9	50.14 N	3.46 W
Šaldaj, Kaz.	48	D13	51.55 N	78.49 E
Saldaña, Spain	28	B6	42.31 N	4.43 W
Saldaña, stm., Col.	168	F4	4.00 N	74.51 W
Saldanha, S. Afr.	90	H3	32.59 S	17.56 E
Saldungaray, Arg.	172	I7	38.12 S	61.46 W
Saldus, Lat.	26	D5	56.39 N	22.30 E
Sale, Austl.	98	L6	38.06 S	147.04 E
Salé, Mor.	84	C3	34.03 N	6.48 W
Sale Creek, Tn., U.S.	134	B13	35.22 N	85.06 W
Salée, Rivière, strt., Guad.	159c	h5	16.17 N	61.33 W
Saleh, Teluk, b., Indon.	66	H10	8.35 S	117.53 E
Salehard, Russia	48	A11	66.32 N	66.37 E
Salem, India	69	F4	11.39 N	78.09 E
Salem, Monts.	159a	d3	16.44 N	62.13 W
Salem, Ar., U.S.	130	H6	36.22 N	91.50 W
Salem, Il., U.S.	130	F9	38.36 N	88.56 W
Salem, In., U.S.	130	F11	38.36 N	86.06 W
Salem, Ia., U.S.	130	D6	40.51 N	91.37 W
Salem, Ky., U.S.	130	G9	37.16 N	88.14 W
Salem, Ma., U.S.	124	B15	42.31 N	70.53 W
Salem, Mi., U.S.	199		42.24 N	83.34 W
Salem, Mo., U.S.	130	G6	37.38 N	91.32 W
Salem, N.H., U.S.	124	B14	42.47 N	71.13 W
Salem, N.J., U.S.	124	E10	39.34 N	75.27 W
Salem, N.Y., U.S.	126	E16	43.10 N	73.19 W
Salem, Oh., U.S.	124	D5	40.54 N	80.50 W
Salem, Or., U.S.	146	F3	44.56 N	123.01 W
Salem, S.D., U.S.	140	D15	43.43 N	97.23 W
Salem, Ut., U.S.	150	C5	40.04 N	111.40 W
Salem, Va., U.S.	124	G5	37.17 N	80.03 W
Salem, W.V., U.S.	124	E5	39.16 N	80.33 W
Salem Airfield, arpt., Mi., U.S.	199		42.25 N	83.34 W
Salem Canal, can., N.J., U.S.	203		39.41 N	75.31 W
Salem Depot, N.H., U.S.	201		42.47 N	71.12 W
Salem Harbor, b., Ma., U.S.	201		42.31 N	70.53 W
Salemi, Italy	32	G6	37.49 N	12.48 E
Salem State College, educ., Ma., U.S.	201		42.30 N	70.54 W
Salem Upland, plat., Mo., U.S.	130	G6	37.25 N	91.30 W
Sälen, Swe.	16	F11	61.10 N	13.16 E
Salentina, Penisola, pen., Italy	32	D12	40.16 N	18.07 E
Salerno, Italy	32	D8	40.40 N	14.46 E
Salerno, Golfo di, b., Italy	32	D8	40.32 N	14.42 E
Salers, Fr.	22	D8	45.08 N	2.30 E
Salesbury, Eng., U.K.	180		53.47 N	2.30 W
Salford, mun., Eng., U.K.	180		53.28 N	2.23 W
Salford, mun., Eng., U.K.	180		53.29 N	2.22 W
Salfords, Eng., U.K.	178		51.12 N	0.10 W
Šalgačova, Russia	18	E26	62.19 N	39.33 E
Salgar, Col.	168	D4	5.58 N	75.59 W
Salgótarján, Hung.	36	A6	48.06 N	19.49 E
Šalgovaara, Russia	18	D20	63.31 N	33.12 E
Salgueiro, Braz.	170	E6	8.04 S	39.06 W
Salher, mtn., India	70	H4	20.43 N	73.56 E
Salhus, Nor.	16	G3	60.29 N	5.16 E
Sali, Cro.	30	G12	43.56 N	15.09 E
Šali, Russia	40	D16	55.40 N	49.38 E
Salida, Co., U.S.	138	C3	38.32 N	105.59 W
Salies-de-Béarn, Fr.	22	F4	43.29 N	0.55 W
Salihli, Tur.	34	E11	38.29 N	28.07 E
Salihorsk, Bela.	26	H10	52.48 N	27.32 E
Salima, Mwi.	88	C5	13.45 S	34.26 E
Salimbatu, Indon.	66	B10	2.56 N	117.20 E
Salimgarh Fort, hist., India	190a		28.40 N	77.14 E
Salin, Mya.	64	B2	20.34 N	94.39 E
Salina, Ks., U.S.	138	C11	38.50 N	97.36 W
Salina, Ok., U.S.	130	H2	36.17 N	95.09 W
Salina, Ut., U.S.	150	E5	38.57 N	111.51 W
Salina, Isola, i., Italy	32	F8	38.34 N	14.50 E
Salina Cruz, Mex.	154	G11	16.11 N	95.11 W
Salina Point, c., Bah.	156	A10	22.10 N	74.17 W
Salinas, Braz.	170	I4	16.09 S	42.17 W
Salinas, Ec.	168	I1	2.13 S	80.57 W
Salinas, Mex.	136	G5	27.38 N	102.24 W
Salinas, P.R.	158a	c3	17.58 N	66.17 W
Salinas, Ca., U.S.	148	G4	36.40 N	121.39 W
Salinas, stm., Braz.	170	I4	16.37 S	42.18 W
Salinas, stm., N.A.	156	D2	16.27 N	90.32 W
Salinas, stm., Ca., U.S.	148	G4	36.45 N	121.48 W
Salinas, Pampa de las, pl., Arg.	172	E4	31.58 S	66.42 W
Salinas, Ponta das, c., Ang.	88	C1	12.50 S	12.56 E
Salinas de Hidalgo, Mex.	154	D8	22.38 N	101.43 W
Salinas Pueblo Missions National Monument, p.o.i., N.M., U.S.	138	G3	34.05 N	106.14 W
Salinas Victoria, Mex.	136	I7	25.53 N	100.19 W
Saline, La., U.S.	134	E5	32.09 N	92.58 W
Saline, Mi., U.S.	124	B2	42.09 N	83.46 W
Saline, stm., Ar., U.S.	134	D6	33.09 N	92.08 W
Saline, stm., Ar., U.S.	134	C4	33.38 N	93.52 W
Saline, stm., Il., U.S.	130	G9	37.34 N	88.07 W
Saline, stm., Ks., U.S.	138	C11	38.52 N	97.30 W
Saline, North Fork, stm., Il., U.S.	130	G9	37.43 N	88.19 W
Saline Bay, b., Trin.	159f	s12	10.38 N	61.01 W
Saline Bayou, stm., La., U.S.	134	E6	31.44 N	92.58 W
Saline Lake, l., La., U.S.	134	F6	31.53 N	92.54 W
Salines, Cap de ses, c., Spain	28	E14	39.15 N	3.03 E
Salines, Point, c., Gren.	159e	r10	12.00 N	61.47 W
Salines, Pointe des, c., Mart.	159c	l7	14.24 N	60.53 W
Salingyi, Mya.	64	B2	21.58 N	95.05 E
Salinópolis, Braz.	164	D8	0.37 S	47.19 W
Salipolo, Indon.	66	E11	3.45 S	119.29 E
Salisbury, Austl.	98	J2	34.46 S	138.37 E
Salisbury, Dom.	159c	j6	15.25 N	61.26 W
Salisbury, Eng., U.K.	10	J11	51.05 N	1.48 W
Salisbury, Md., U.S.	124	F10	38.21 N	75.35 W
Salisbury, Mo., U.S.	130	E5	39.25 N	92.47 W
Salisbury, N.C., U.S.	124	I5	35.40 N	80.28 W
Salisbury, Pa., U.S.	124	E6	39.45 N	79.04 W
Salisbury see Harare, Zimb.	88	D5	17.50 S	31.03 E
Salisbury Hall, hist., Eng., U.K.	178		51.43 N	0.16 W
Salisbury Island, i., Nu., Can.	110	C15	63.30 N	77.00 W
Salisbury Plain, pl., Eng., U.K.	10	J11	51.12 N	1.55 W
Salisbury Plain, stm., Ma., U.S.	201		42.02 N	70.58 W
Salish Mountains, mts., Mt., U.S.	146	B12	48.15 N	114.45 W
Salitpa, Al., U.S.	134	F10	31.37 N	88.01 W
Salitpa Creek, stm., Al., U.S.	134	F11	31.39 N	88.05 W
Salitre, stm., Braz.	170	E5	9.29 S	40.39 W
Šalja, Russia	40	C21	57.14 N	58.43 E
Šalkar, ozero, l., Kaz.	40	F17	50.33 N	51.40 E
Salkehatchie, stm., S.C., U.S.	132	C4	32.48 N	80.53 W
Salkhad, Syria	76	F7	32.29 N	36.42 E
Salkhia, India	190b		22.35 N	88.21 E
Salla, Fin.	14	F19	66.50 N	28.39 E
Salles-Curan, Fr.	22	E8	44.11 N	2.47 E
Salling, pen., Den.	16	K6	56.38 N	8.52 E
Sallisaw, Ok., U.S.	134	B4	35.28 N	94.47 W
Sallisaw Creek, stm., Ok., U.S.	134	B4	35.21 N	94.51 W
Salluit, Qc., Can.	110	C15	62.13 N	75.36 W
Sallūm, Sudan	82	D7	19.23 N	37.06 E
Salmās, Iran	74	A9	38.11 N	44.46 E
Salme, Est.	26	B5	58.09 N	22.14 E
Salmi, Russia	18	F18	61.22 N	31.52 E
Salmivaara, Fin.	14	F19	66.48 N	28.23 E
Salmo, B.C., Can.	144	G13	49.11 N	117.17 W
Salmon, Id., U.S.	146	E13	45.10 N	113.54 W
Salmon, stm., B.C., Can.	144	B8	54.03 N	122.33 W
Salmon, stm., N.B., Can.	122	D11	46.04 N	65.55 W
Salmon, stm., N.A.	126	D15	45.02 N	74.30 W
Salmon, stm., Id., U.S.	146	E10	45.51 N	116.47 W
Salmon, stm., N.Y., U.S.	126	E14	43.34 N	76.11 W
Salmon, stm., Or., U.S.	146	E5	45.22 N	122.01 W
Salmon, East Fork, stm., Id., U.S.	146	F12	44.16 N	114.19 W
Salmon, Middle Fork, stm., Id., U.S.	146	E12	45.18 N	114.36 W
Salmon, South Fork, stm., Id., U.S.	146	E11	45.23 N	115.31 W
Salmon Arm, B.C., Can.	144	F11	50.41 N	119.19 W
Salmon Falls Creek, stm., U.S.	146	H12	42.43 N	114.51 W
Salmon Falls Creek Reservoir, res., Id., U.S.	148	A10	42.07 N	114.44 W
Salmon Gums, Austl.	96	F4	32.58 S	121.38 E
Salmon Mountain, mtn., N.A.	122	E5	45.14 N	71.08 W
Salmon Mountains, mts., Ca., U.S.	148	B2	41.00 N	123.00 W
Salmon Peak, mtn., Tx., U.S.	136	E7	29.28 N	100.10 W
Salmon River Mountains, mts., Id., U.S.	146	F12	44.57 N	114.52 W
Salmon Valley, B.C., Can.	144	B8	54.04 N	122.42 W
Salmyš, stm., Russia	40	E19	52.00 N	55.22 E
Sal'nyja, Ukr.	38	D7	49.44 N	28.01 E
Salo, Fin.	18	G10	60.23 N	23.07 E
Salò, Italy	30	E7	45.36 N	10.30 E
Salome, Az., U.S.	150	J3	33.46 N	113.36 W
Salomon, Cap, c., Mart.	159c	l6	14.30 N	61.06 W
Salomone, Monte, mtn., Italy	185a		41.47 N	12.44 E
Salon, stm., Fr.	20	G14	47.32 N	5.40 E
Salon-de-Provence, Fr.	22	F11	43.38 N	5.05 E
Salonga, Parc National de la, p.o.i., D.R.C.	86	E4	1.51 S	21.53 E
Salonika see Thessaloníki, Grc.	34	C6	40.37 N	22.58 E
Salonika, Gulf of see Thermaikós Kólpos, b., Grc.	34	C6	39.50 N	23.10 E
Salonjarvi, ozero, l., Russia	18	E18	62.10 N	32.13 E
Salonta, Rom.	36	C8	46.48 N	21.40 E
Salor, stm., Spain	28	E4	39.39 N	7.03 W
Saloslovo, Russia	183b		55.42 N	37.09 E
Šalovka, stm., Russia	183b		55.47 N	38.12 E
Salpausselkä, mts., Eur.	18	F13	61.00 N	26.31 E
Salqīn, Syria	76	B7	36.08 N	36.27 E
Sal Rei, C.V.	85a	k10	16.10 N	22.54 W
Salsacate, Arg.	172	E5	31.20 S	65.04 W
Salsbruket, Nor.	16	C9	64.48 N	11.50 E
Salsette Island, i., India	190c		19.10 N	72.53 E
Salsipuedes, Canal, strt., Mex.	154	A2	28.38 N	113.00 W
Salsipuedes, Punta, c., Mex.	120	E4	32.04 N	116.52 W
Sal'sk, Russia	40	H12	46.28 N	41.32 E
Šal'skij, Russia	18	F22	61.48 N	35.59 E
Salso, stm., Italy	32	G7	37.05 N	13.57 E
Salsomaggiore Terme, Italy	30	F6	44.49 N	9.59 E
Salsvatnet, l., Nor.	16	C9	64.43 N	11.40 E
Salt, stm., U.S.	146	H16	43.10 N	111.03 W
Salt, stm., Az., U.S.	150	J4	33.22 N	112.17 W
Salt, stm., Ky., U.S.	130	F12	38.00 N	85.57 W
Salt, stm., Mi., U.S.	199		42.39 N	82.47 W
Salt, stm., Mo., U.S.	130	E6	39.27 N	91.03 W
Salt, Elk Fork, stm., Mo., U.S.	130	E5	39.28 N	91.53 W
Salt, Middle Fork, stm., Mo., U.S.	130	E5	39.28 N	91.48 W
Salt, North Fork, stm., Mo., U.S.	130	E5	39.29 N	91.46 W
Salt, South Fork, stm., Mo., U.S.	130	E6	39.29 N	91.46 W
Salta, Arg.	172	B5	24.47 S	65.24 W
Salta, state, Arg.	166	D4	25.00 S	64.30 W
Saltaire, N.Y., U.S.	194		40.39 N	73.12 W
Saltanovka, Russia	26	H17	52.45 N	34.21 E
Saltash, Eng., U.K.	10	K8	50.25 N	4.14 W
Salt Basin, l., Tx., U.S.	136	C2	31.44 N	104.59 W
Salt Cay, i., Bah.	158f	m18	25.05 N	77.16 W
Saltcoats, Sk., Can.	142	C11	51.03 N	102.10 W
Salt Creek, stm., On., Can.	193b		43.48 N	79.42 W
Salt Creek, stm., Il., U.S.	130	D8	40.07 N	89.49 W
Salt Creek, stm., Il., U.S.	196		41.49 N	87.50 W
Salt Creek, stm., Ks., U.S.	138	B11	39.03 N	97.41 W
Salt Creek, stm., N.M., U.S.	138	H4	33.35 N	104.23 W
Salt Creek, stm., Ok., U.S.	138	E12	36.32 N	96.43 W
Salt Creek, stm., Or., U.S.	146	G4	43.43 N	122.26 W
Salt Creek, stm., Wy., U.S.	140	D6	43.41 N	106.19 W
Salt Creek, West Branch, stm., Il., U.S.	196		42.02 N	88.01 W
Salt Draw, stm., Tx., U.S.	136	C4	31.19 N	103.26 W
Saltee Islands, is., Ire.	10	I6	52.07 N	6.36 W
Saltelva, stm., Nor.	14	F6	67.06 N	15.26 E
Salten, pen., Nor.	14	E6	67.24 N	15.01 E
Saltfjellet, mts., Nor.	14	F6	66.38 N	15.06 E
Saltfjellet Svartisen Nasjonalpark, p.o.i., Nor.	14	F5	66.38 N	14.35 E
Saltfjorden, b., Nor.	14	E5	67.13 N	14.20 E
Salt Fork State Park, p.o.i., Oh., U.S.	124	D4	40.06 N	81.29 W
Saltholm, i., Den.	16	L10	55.38 N	12.46 E
Saltillo, Mex.	154	C8	25.25 N	101.00 W
Saltillo, Ms., U.S.	134	C10	34.22 N	88.40 W
Saltillo, Tn., U.S.	134	B10	35.22 N	88.12 W
Salt Island, i., Br. Vir. Is.	158b	e8	18.22 N	64.31 W
Salt Lake, l., N.M., U.S.	138	G5	34.05 N	103.05 W
Salt Lake City, Ut., U.S.	150	C4	40.46 N	111.54 W
Salto, Arg.	172	G7	34.18 S	60.14 W
Salto, Ur.	172	E9	31.23 S	57.57 W
Salto, stm., Italy	30	H10	42.23 N	12.53 E
Salto da Divisa, Braz.	170	I6	16.00 S	39.57 W
Salto del Fraile, c., Peru	204d		12.11 S	77.03 W
Salto del Guairá, Para.	172	A10	24.01 S	54.20 W
Salto Grande, Embalse, res., S.A.	172	E8	30.55 S	57.53 W
Salto Grande, Embalse de see Salto Grande, Embalse, res., S.A.	172	E8	30.55 S	57.53 W
Saltoluokta, Swe.	14	E9	67.23 N	18.31 E
Salton City, Ca., U.S.	148	J9	33.19 N	115.59 W
Salton Sea, l., Ca., U.S.	148	J10	33.19 N	115.50 W
Salton Sea State Recreation Area, p.o.i., Ca., U.S.	148	J10	33.26 N	115.50 W
Saltonstall, Lake, l., Ma., U.S.	201		42.47 N	71.04 W
Salto Santiago, Represa de, res., Braz.	172	B11	25.41 S	52.25 W
Salt Pan Creek, stm., Austl.	192a		33.59 S	151.02 E
Saltpeter Creek, b., Md., U.S.	202b		39.20 N	76.22 W
Salt River Indian Reservation, ind. res., Az., U.S.	150	J5	33.31 N	111.48 W
Saltsjöbaden, Swe.	16	H16	59.17 N	18.18 E
Saltspring Island, i., B.C., Can.	144	H7	48.47 N	123.27 W
Saltville, Va., U.S.	124	H4	36.52 N	81.45 W
Salt Wells Creek, stm., Wy., U.S.	150	B8	41.39 N	108.57 W
Saltykovka, Russia	40	E14	52.07 N	44.05 E
Saltykovka, Russia	183b		55.46 N	37.55 E
Saluda, S.C., U.S.	132	B4	34.00 N	81.46 W
Saluda, Va., U.S.	124	G9	37.36 N	76.35 W
Saluda, stm., S.C., U.S.	132	C5	34.00 N	81.04 W
Salûm, Egypt	82	A5	31.34 N	25.08 E
Sālūmbar, India	70	F5	24.08 N	74.03 E
Salūq 'Afiq, Syria	76	B10	36.35 N	39.08 E
Sālūr, India	69	B6	18.31 N	83.12 E
Saluzzo, Italy	30	F4	44.38 N	7.28 E
Salvado, Mount, mtn., Austl.	96	E4	25.15 S	121.01 E
Salvador, Braz.	170	G6	12.59 S	38.30 W
Salvador, El see El Salvador, ctry., N.A.	156	F3	13.50 N	88.55 W
Salvador, Lake, l., La., U.S.	134	H8	29.45 N	90.15 W
Salvatierra, Mex.	154	E8	20.13 N	100.54 W
Salviac, Fr.	22	E7	44.41 N	1.16 E
Salwā, Dawhat as-, b., Asia	74	H12	25.30 N	50.40 E
Salween (Nu) (Khong) (Thanlwin), stm., Asia	62	E8	16.33 N	97.39 E
Salyan, Azer.	42	F13	39.35 N	48.58 E
Salyān, Nepal	70	D9	28.22 N	82.09 E
Salyer, Ca., U.S.	148	C2	40.54 N	123.34 W
Salyersville, Ky., U.S.	124	G2	37.43 N	83.04 W
Salza, stm., Aus.	30	C12	47.40 N	14.42 E
Salzach, stm., Eur.	30	B9	48.12 N	12.55 E
Salzburg, Aus.	30	C10	47.48 N	13.02 E
Salzburg, state, Aus.	30	C10	47.25 N	13.15 E
Salzgitter, Ger.	24	D6	52.08 N	10.26 E
Salzkammergut, reg., Aus.	30	C10	47.40 N	13.34 E
Salzwedel, Ger.	24	D7	52.51 N	11.09 E
Sām, India	70	E3	26.49 N	70.30 E
Samā, Jord.	76	F7	32.28 N	36.14 E
Sam A. Baker State Park, p.o.i., Mo., U.S.	130	G7	37.16 N	90.31 W
Samacá, Col.	168	E5	5.27 N	73.26 W
Samacěvičy, Bela.	26	G14	53.12 N	31.50 E
Sama de Langreo see Langreo, Spain	28	A5	43.18 N	5.41 W
Samagaltaj, Russia	48	D16	50.36 N	95.00 E
Samah, Libya	82	B3	28.00 N	19.30 E
Samāika, ngh., India	190a		28.32 N	77.05 E
Samaipata, Bol.	166	C4	18.10 S	63.52 W
Samalanga, Indon.	64	J3	5.12 N	96.21 E
Samalayuca, Mex.	120	F9	31.21 N	106.28 W
Samales Group, is., Phil.	68	G3	6.03 N	121.46 E
Samalga Pass, strt., Ak., U.S.	109a	g25	52.54 N	169.25 W
Samal Island, i., Phil.	68	G5	7.03 N	125.44 E
Sāmalkot, India	69	C6	17.03 N	82.10 E
Samālût, Egypt	82	J1	28.18 N	30.42 E
Samaná, Dom. Rep.	156	C13	19.12 N	69.18 W
Samāna, India	70	C6	30.09 N	76.12 E
Samaná, Bahía de, b., Dom. Rep.	156	C13	19.10 N	69.25 W
Samaná, Cabo, c., Dom. Rep.	156	C13	19.18 N	69.09 W
Samana Cay, i., Bah.	156	A11	23.05 N	73.44 W
Samandağı, Tur.	42	G6	36.05 N	35.59 E
Samandıra, stm., Tur.	185b		40.59 N	29.15 E
Samaniego, Col.	168	G3	1.20 N	77.35 W
Samanlı Dağları, mts., Tur.	34	C13	40.35 N	29.38 E

Name	Page	Map Ref.	Latitude	Longitude
Samaqua, stm., Qc., Can.	122	A4	49.17 N	72.29 W
Samar, i., Phil.	68	E5	12.00 N	125.00 E
Samara (Kujbyšev), Russia	40	E16	53.11 N	50.06 E
Samara, stm., Russia	40	E17	53.10 N	50.04 E
Samara, stm., Ukr.	38	E14	48.27 N	35.06 E
Samarai, Pap. N. Gui.	101a	c5	10.35 S	150.42 E
Samaria, Id., U.S.	146	H14	42.07 N	112.20 W
Samaria Gorge see Samariás, Farángi, val., Grc.	34	H6	35.18 N	23.51 E
Samariapo, Ven.	168	E8	5.17 N	67.48 W
Samariás, Farángi (Samaria Gorge), val., Grc.	34	H6	35.18 N	23.51 E
Samarinda, Indon.	66	D10	0.30 S	117.09 E
Samarka, Russia	54	B11	44.44 N	134.13 E
Samarkand, Uzb.	48	G11	39.39 N	66.56 E
Sāmarrā', Iraq	74	C8	34.11 N	43.52 E
Samarskaja oblast', co., Russia	40	E17	53.30 N	50.30 E
Samarskoe, Russia	40	H11	46.56 N	39.41 E
Šamary, Russia	40	C21	57.20 N	58.13 E
Samastīpur, India	70	F10	25.51 N	85.47 E
Samatya, ngh., Tur.	185b		41.00 N	28.56 E
Samaúna, Braz.	164	E5	7.55 S	60.01 W
Şamaxi, Azer.	48	F7	40.37 N	48.38 E
Samba, D.R.C.	86	E5	4.38 S	26.21 E
Samba, India	70	B5	32.33 N	75.07 E
Samba Caju, Ang.	88	B2	8.45 S	15.24 E
Sambaíba, Braz.	170	D3	7.08 S	45.21 W
Sambalpur, India	70	H9	21.27 N	83.59 E
Sambar, Tanjung, c., Indon.	66	E7	3.00 S	110.17 E
Sambas, Indon.	66	C6	1.18 N	109.16 E
Sambava, Madag.	88	C9	14.15 S	50.09 E
Şambayat, Tur.	76	A9	37.40 N	38.05 E
Sambāža, Pak.	70	C2	31.48 N	69.22 E
Sambhal, India	70	D7	28.35 N	78.33 E
Sāmbhar, India	70	E5	26.54 N	75.13 E
Sāmbhar Lake, l., India	70	E5	26.57 N	75.02 E
Sambir, Ukr.	38	D2	49.31 N	23.12 E
Sambit, Pulau, i., Indon.	66	C11	1.46 N	119.03 E
Sambito, stm., Braz.	170	D4	5.38 S	42.09 W
Samboja, Indon.	66	D10	1.01 S	117.01 E
Sâmbor, Camb.	64	F7	12.46 N	105.58 E
Samborombón, stm., Arg.	172	G9	35.43 S	57.20 W
Samborombón, Bahía, b., Arg.	172	G9	36.00 S	57.12 W
Samborondón, Ec.	168	H2	1.56 S	79.43 W
Sambre, stm., Eur.	20	D12	50.27 N	4.52 E
Sambre à l'Oise, Canal de la, can., Fr.	20	E12	49.26 N	2.51 E
Sambriāl, Pak.	70	B5	32.28 N	74.20 E
Sambú, stm., Pan.	168	C2	8.04 N	78.16 W
Samburg, Russia	48	A13	66.58 N	78.15 E
Samch'ŏk, Kor., S.	54	F8	37.27 N	129.10 E
Sam Chom, Khao, mtn., Thai.	64	H4	8.07 N	99.26 E
Same, Tan.	86	E7	4.04 S	37.44 E
Sāmen, Iran	74	C11	34.08 N	48.32 E
Sam Ford Fiord, b., Nu., Can.	110	A16	70.40 N	70.49 W
Samfya, Zam.	88	C4	11.21 S	29.30 E
Saminka, stm., Russia	183b		55.45 N	37.17 E
Samka, Mya.	64	B3	20.11 N	96.56 E
Şämkir, Azer.	42	E11	40.49 N	46.01 E
Samlesbury, Eng., U.K.	180		53.46 N	2.38 W
Samlesbury Aerodrome, arpt., Eng., U.K.	180		53.47 N	2.34 W
Samlesbury Bottoms, Eng., U.K.	180		53.45 N	2.34 W
Samlesbury Higher Hall, hist., Eng., U.K.	180		53.46 N	2.34 W
Şamlı, Tur.	34	D10	39.48 N	27.51 E
Samnangjin, Kor., S.	56	D1	35.22 N	128.49 E
Sam Ngao, Thai.	64	D4	17.14 N	99.01 E
Samoa, ctry., Oc.	101c	g12	13.55 S	172.00 W
Samoa i Sisifo see Samoa, ctry., Oc.	101c	g12	13.55 S	172.00 W
Samoa Islands, is., Oc.	101c	h12	14.00 S	171.00 W
Samo Alto, Chile	172	E2	30.24 S	70.58 W
Samobor, Cro.	30	E12	45.49 N	15.42 E
Samoded, Russia	12	E19	63.37 N	40.30 E
Samofalovka, Russia	40	G14	48.57 N	44.13 E
Samokov, Blg.	36	G10	42.20 N	23.34 E
Samora, stm., Port.	184c		38.50 N	8.57 W
Sámos, Grc.	34	F9	37.44 N	26.58 E
Sámos, i., Grc.	34	F9	37.42 N	26.49 E
Samoset, Fl., U.S.	132	I3	27.28 N	82.32 W
Samosir, Pulau, i., Indon.	66	B1	2.35 N	98.50 E
Samothrace see Samothráki, i., Grc.	34	C8	40.28 N	25.36 E
Samothráki, Grc.	34	C8	40.28 N	25.31 E
Samothráki (Samothrace), i., Grc.	34	C8	40.28 N	25.36 E
Samouco, Port.	184c		38.43 N	9.00 W
Sampacho, Arg.	172	F5	33.23 S	64.43 W
Sampaga, Indon.	66	E11	2.20 S	119.07 E
Sampanahan, Indon.	66	E10	2.39 S	116.10 E
Sampang, Indon.	66	G8	7.12 S	113.16 E
Sampawams Creek, stm., N.Y., U.S.	194		40.41 N	73.19 W
Sampit, Indon.	66	E8	2.33 S	112.57 E
Sampit, stm., Indon.	66	E8	2.55 S	113.00 E
Sampit, Teluk, b., Indon.	66	E8	3.05 S	113.03 E
Sampson, Pa., U.S.	197b		40.10 N	79.53 W
Sampués, Col.	168	C4	9.10 N	75.22 W
Sampwe, D.R.C.	86	F5	9.21 S	27.25 E
Sam Rayburn Reservoir, res., Tx., U.S.	136	C13	31.12 N	94.17 W
Samro, ozero, l., Russia	26	B11	58.57 N	28.48 E
Samrong, Khlong, can., Thai.	187a		13.39 N	100.34 E
Samsang, China	70	C9	30.31 N	82.33 E
Samsø, i., Den.	16	L8	55.52 N	10.37 E
Samsø Bælt, strt., Den.	16	L8	55.48 N	10.47 E
Samson, Al., U.S.	134	F12	31.06 N	86.02 W
Sam Son, Viet.	64	C7	19.44 N	105.53 E
Samson Indian Reserve, ind. res., Ab., Can.	144	D17	52.47 N	113.22 W
Samsun, Tur.	42	E7	41.17 N	36.19 E
Samsun, state, Tur.	42	E6	41.15 N	36.00 E
Samsun Körfezi, b., Tur.	42	E7	41.22 N	36.21 E
Samsu-ŭp, Kor., N.	54	D7	41.19 N	127.58 E
Samtown, La., U.S.	134	F6	31.16 N	92.26 W
Samtredia, Geor.	42	D10	42.10 N	42.20 E
Samu, Indon.	66	D10	2.01 S	115.56 E
Samuel, Mount, hill, Austl.	96	C6	19.41 S	134.09 E
Samuhú, Arg.	172	C7	27.31 S	60.24 W
Samui, Ko, i., Thai.	64	H5	9.31 N	100.00 E
Samundri, Pak.	70	C4	31.03 N	72.57 E
Samut Prakan, Thai.	64	F5	13.34 N	100.35 E
Samut Prakan, state, Thai.	187a		13.35 N	100.35 E
Samut Sakhon, Thai.	64	F5	13.32 N	100.17 E
Samut Songkhram, Thai.	64	F5	13.23 N	99.59 E
San, Mali	84	G3	13.17 N	4.54 W
San (Xan), stm., Asia	64	F8	13.32 N	106.01 E
San, stm., China	58	E8	32.53 N	119.21 E
San (Syan), stm., Eur.	24	F18	50.44 N	21.51 E
Saña, Peru	164	E2	6.53 S	79.33 W
San'ā', Yemen	72	F5	15.21 N	44.12 E
Sana, stm., Bos.	36	E3	45.03 N	16.23 E
Sanaa see San'ā', Yemen	72	F5	15.21 N	44.12 E
Sanaba, Burkina	84	G4	12.23 N	3.49 W
Sanabu, Egypt	76	K1	27.29 N	30.47 E
Sanāfir, i., Sau. Ar.	74	G4	27.56 N	34.42 E
Sanaga, stm., Cam.	86	D2	3.33 N	9.39 E
San Agustín, Arg.	172	I8	38.00 S	58.21 W
San Agustín, Arg.	172	E5	32.00 S	64.23 W
San Agustín, Col.	168	G3	1.52 N	76.15 W
San Agustín, Mex.	136	C1	31.35 N	106.16 W
San Agustin, Cape, c., Phil.	68	G6	6.17 N	126.11 E
San Agustin, Plains of, pl., N.M., U.S.	150	J8	33.53 N	107.57 W
San Agustín de Valle Fértil, Arg.	172	E4	30.38 S	67.27 W
Sanak Islands, is., Ak., U.S.	109	F7	54.25 N	162.35 W
San Alberto, Mex.	136	G6	27.30 N	101.20 W
San Ambrosio, Isla, i., Chile	162	H7	26.21 S	79.54 W
Sanam Chai, Khlong, can., Thai.	187a		13.38 N	100.27 E
Sanana, Pulau, i., Indon.	60	F8	2.12 S	125.55 E
Sānand, India	70	G4	22.59 N	72.23 E
Sanandaj, Iran	74	C10	35.19 N	47.00 E
San Andreas, Ca., U.S.	148	E5	38.11 N	120.40 W
San Andreas Lake, l., Ca., U.S.	200		37.36 N	122.26 W
San Andrés, Col.	156	F7	12.33 N	81.42 W
San Andrés, Mex.	154	B1	27.14 N	114.14 W
San Andrés, Isla de, i., Col.	156	F7	12.33 N	81.42 W
San Andres Mountains, mts., N.M., U.S.	138	I2	33.22 N	106.36 W
San Andrés Sajcabajá, Guat.	156	E2	15.13 N	90.55 W
San Andrés Totoltepec, ngh., Mex.	204a		19.15 N	99.10 W
San Andrés Tuxtla, Mex.	154	F11	18.26 N	95.12 W
San Andrés y Providencia, state, Col.	156	F7	12.30 N	81.45 W
Sananduva, Braz.	172	C12	27.57 S	51.48 W
San Angel see Álvaro Obregón, ngh., Mex.	204a		19.21 N	99.12 W
San Angelo, Tx., U.S.	136	C7	31.27 N	100.26 W
San Antero, Col.	168	C4	9.23 N	75.46 W
San Antonio, Arg.	172	B5	24.21 S	65.19 W
San Antonio, Arg.	172	D5	28.56 S	65.06 W
San Antonio, Belize	154	A10	16.14 N	89.03 W
San Antonio, Chile	172	F2	33.36 S	71.36 W
San Antonio, Chile	172	C2	27.53 S	70.03 W
San Antonio, Col.	168	F4	3.55 N	75.28 W
San Antonio, P.R.	158a	b1	18.29 N	67.06 W
San Antonio, N.M., U.S.	138	F2	35.06 N	106.22 W
San Antonio, N.M., U.S.	138	H2	33.55 N	106.51 W
San Antonio, Tx., U.S.	136	E9	29.25 N	98.29 W
San Antonio, Ur.	172	E9	31.21 S	57.47 W
San Antonio, mun., Cuba	204b		22.55 N	82.29 W
San Antonio, stm., Mex.	136	F4	29.10 N	103.42 W
San Antonio, stm., U.S.	138	E2	37.11 N	105.54 W
San Antonio, stm., Tx., U.S.	136	F10	28.30 N	96.53 W
San Antonio, mth., Arg.	206		34.24 S	58.31 W
San Antonio, Cabo, pen., Arg.	172	H9	36.40 S	56.42 W
San Antonio, Cabo de, c., Cuba	156	B5	21.52 N	84.57 W
San Antonio, Lake, res., Ca., U.S.	148	H4	35.53 N	121.02 W
San Antonio, Mount, mtn., Ca., U.S.	148	I8	34.17 N	117.39 W
San Antonio, Punta, c., Mex.	120	G4	29.46 N	115.42 W
San Antonio, Punta, c., Mex.	154	B3	26.32 N	111.27 W
San Antonio Abad see Sant Antoni de Portmany, Spain	28	F12	38.58 N	1.18 E
San Antonio Bay, b., Tx., U.S.	136	F11	28.20 N	96.45 W
San Antonio Canyon, val., Ca., U.S.	198		34.12 N	117.40 W
San Antonio Dam, dam., Ca., U.S.	198		34.09 N	117.41 W
San Antonio de Bravo, Mex.	120	F10	30.10 N	104.42 W
San Antonio de Galipán, Ven.	204c		10.33 N	66.53 W
San Antonio de La Paz see San Antonio, Arg.	172	D5	28.56 S	65.06 W
San Antonio de los Baños, Cuba	156	A6	22.53 N	82.29 W
San Antonio de los Cobres, Arg.	172	B4	24.13 S	66.19 W
San Antonio del Táchira, Ven.	168	D5	7.48 N	72.25 W
San Antonio de Tamanaco, Ven.	168	C8	9.41 N	66.03 W
San Antonio el Grande, Mex.	136	F2	28.37 N	105.49 W
San Antonio Mountain, mtn., N.M., U.S.	138	E2	36.52 N	106.02 W
San Antonio Oeste, Arg.	166	H4	40.45 S	64.58 W
San Antonio Someyucan, Mex.	204a		19.27 N	99.16 W
San Antonio Tecómitl, ngh., Mex.	204a		19.13 N	98.59 W
San Antonio Ticino, Italy	184b		45.35 N	8.46 E
Sanatoga, Pa., U.S.	203		40.15 N	75.36 W
Sanatoga Creek, stm., Pa., U.S.	203		40.14 N	75.36 W
Sanatorium, Ms., U.S.	134	F9	31.53 N	89.46 W
San Augustine, Tx., U.S.	136	C14	31.31 N	94.06 W
San Augustin Pass, p., N.M., U.S.	136	B1	32.26 N	106.34 W
Sanāw, Yemen	72	F7	17.49 N	51.01 E
Sanāwad, India	70	G6	22.10 N	76.03 E
San Bartolomeo in Galdo, Italy	32	C9	41.25 N	15.01 E
San Benedetto del Tronto, Italy	30	H10	42.57 N	13.52 E
San Benedetto Po, Italy	30	F7	45.02 N	10.55 E
San Benedicto, Isla, i., Mex.	154	F3	19.18 N	110.49 W
San Benito, Tx., U.S.	136	H10	26.07 N	97.37 W
San Benito, stm., Ca., U.S.	148	G4	36.53 N	121.35 W
San Benito Mountain, mtn., Ca., U.S.	148	G5	36.22 N	120.38 W
San Bernard, stm., Tx., U.S.	136	E12	28.51 N	95.26 W
San Bernardino, Ca., U.S.	148	I8	34.06 N	117.17 W
San Bernardino Mountains, mts., Ca., U.S.	148	I9	34.10 N	116.45 W
San Bernardino National Forest, p.o.i., Ca., U.S.	198		34.12 N	117.38 W
San Bernardino Strait, strt., Phil.	68	D5	12.32 N	124.10 E
San Bernardo, Arg.	172	C7	27.17 S	60.42 W
San Bernardo, Chile	172	F2	33.36 S	70.41 W
San Bernardo, Mex.	154	B6	25.59 N	105.31 W
San Bernardo, Islas de, is., Col.	168	C4	9.45 N	75.50 W
San Bernardo del Viento, Col.	168	C3	9.21 N	75.57 W
Sanbe-yama, vol., Japan	56	D5	35.08 N	132.37 E
San Blas, Mex.	154	E6	21.32 N	105.17 W
San Blas, Mex.	154	B4	26.05 N	108.45 W
San Blas, Cape, c., Fl., U.S.	134	H13	29.40 N	85.22 W
San Blas, Golfo de, b., Pan.	156	H8	9.30 N	79.00 W
San Blas, Serranía de, mts., Pan.	156	H8	9.15 N	78.29 W
San Borja, Bol.	166	B3	14.49 S	66.51 W
Sanborn, Ia., U.S.	128	H3	43.11 N	95.39 W
Sanborn, N.D., U.S.	142	H15	46.56 N	98.13 W
San Bovio, Italy	184b		45.28 N	9.19 E
San Bruno, Ca., U.S.	148	F3	37.37 N	122.24 W
San Bruno, Point, c., Ca., U.S.	200		37.39 N	122.22 W
San Bruno Mountain, mtn., Ca., U.S.	200		37.42 N	122.25 W
San Buenaventura, Bol.	166	B3	14.27 S	67.33 W
San Buenaventura, Mex.	154	B8	27.03 N	101.32 W
San Buenaventura see Ventura, Ca., U.S.	148	I6	34.16 N	119.17 W
San Carlos, Arg.	172	B4	25.56 S	65.56 W
San Carlos, Chile	172	H2	36.25 S	71.57 W
San Carlos, Chile	204e		33.36 S	70.35 W
San Carlos, Mex.	154	C9	24.35 N	98.56 W
San Carlos, Mex.	154	A8	29.01 N	100.51 W
San Carlos, Nic.	156	G5	11.07 N	84.46 W
San Carlos, Pan.	156	H8	8.29 N	79.57 W
San Carlos, Phil.	68	C3	15.55 N	120.21 E
San Carlos, Phil.	68	E4	10.30 N	123.25 E
San Carlos, Az., U.S.	150	J6	33.20 N	110.26 W
San Carlos, Ca., U.S.	148	F3	37.30 N	122.15 W
San Carlos, Ur.	172	G10	34.47 S	54.54 W
San Carlos, Ven.	168	C7	9.40 N	68.35 W
San Carlos, stm., C.R.	156	G5	10.46 N	84.11 W
San Carlos, stm., Az., U.S.	150	J6	33.14 N	110.26 W
San Carlos, stm., Ven.	168	C7	8.57 N	68.16 W
San Carlos Airport, arpt., Ca., U.S.	200		37.31 N	122.15 W
San Carlos Centro, Arg.	172	E7	31.43 S	61.05 W
San Carlos de Bariloche, Arg.	166	H2	41.09 S	71.17 W
San Carlos de Bolívar, Arg.	172	H7	36.13 S	61.06 W
San Carlos de Chena, Chile	204e		33.35 S	70.44 W
San Carlos de Guaroa, Col.	168	F5	3.46 N	73.13 W
San Carlos del Zulia, Ven.	168	C6	9.02 N	71.56 W
San Carlos de Río Negro, Ven.	168	G8	1.55 N	67.03 W
San Carlos Indian Reservation, ind. res., Az., U.S.	150	J7	33.23 N	110.09 W
San Carlos Reservoir, res., Az., U.S.	150	J6	33.11 N	110.27 W
San Carlos Viejo, Canal, can., Chile	204e		33.25 S	70.38 W
San Cataldo, Italy	32	G7	37.29 N	13.59 E
San Cayetano, Arg.	172	I8	38.20 S	59.36 W
Sancerre, Fr.	20	G11	47.19 N	2.50 E
Sancerrois, Collines du, hills, Fr.	20	G11	47.21 N	2.40 E
Sancha, stm., China	58	H1	26.26 N	106.04 E
Sanchahe, China	54	B7	44.59 N	126.02 E
Sanchenglong, China	54	B4	44.02 N	120.58 E
Sanchung, Tai.	187d		25.04 N	121.30 E
Sanch'ungch'iao, Tai.	187d		25.12 N	121.35 E
San Ciro de Acosta, Mex.	154	E9	21.39 N	99.49 W
San Clemente, Spain	28	E8	39.24 N	2.25 W
San Clemente, Ca., U.S.	148	J8	33.25 N	117.36 W
San Clemente, Arroyo de, stm., Spain	184d		41.20 N	2.00 E
San Clemente Island, i., Ca., U.S.	148	K7	32.54 N	118.29 W
Sancoins, Fr.	20	H11	46.49 N	2.54 E
San Cosme, Arg.	172	C8	27.22 S	58.33 W
San Cristóbal, Arg.	172	E7	30.18 S	61.13 W
San Cristóbal, Dom. Rep.	156	C12	18.25 N	70.06 W
San Cristóbal, Ven.	168	D5	7.45 N	72.13 W
San Cristobal, i., Sol. Is.	101b	f9	10.36 S	161.45 E
San Cristóbal, Bahía, b., Mex.	154	B1	27.23 N	114.34 W
San Cristóbal, Cerro, mtn., Chile	204e		33.25 S	70.39 W
San Cristóbal, Cerro, mtn., Peru	204d		12.02 S	77.01 W
San Cristóbal, Isla, i., Ec.	164a	i12	0.49 S	89.26 W
San Cristóbal, Volcán, vol., Nic.	156	F4	12.42 N	87.01 W
San Cristóbal de las Casas, Mex.	154	G12	16.44 N	92.38 W
San Cristobal Wash, stm., Az., U.S.	150	K3	32.47 N	113.45 W
Sancti Spíritus, Cuba	156	A8	21.56 N	79.26 W
San Cugat, Riera de, stm., Spain	184d		41.29 N	2.11 E
Sančursk, Russia	40	C15	56.57 N	47.16 E
Sancy, Puy de, mtn., Fr.	22	D8	45.32 N	2.49 E
Sand, Nor.	16	H4	59.29 N	6.15 E
Sand, stm., Ab., Can.	144	B19	54.55 N	111.08 W
Sand, stm., S. Afr.	90	C9	22.18 S	30.07 E
Sand, stm., S. Afr.	90	F8	28.05 S	26.25 E
Sanda, Japan	186		35.28 N	139.21 E
Sandai, Indon.	66	D7	1.15 S	110.32 E
Sandakan, Malay.	68	H2	5.51 N	118.06 E
Sandal, ozero, l., Russia	18	E21	62.24 N	34.06 E
Sândân, Camb.	64	F8	12.41 N	106.01 E
Sandane, Nor.	16	F4	61.46 N	6.14 E
Sandanski, Blg.	36	H10	41.34 N	23.17 E
Sandaré, Mali	84	G2	14.42 N	10.18 W
Sandared, Swe.	16	J10	57.43 N	12.46 E
Sandarne, Swe.	16	F15	61.15 N	17.09 E
Sand Arroyo, stm., U.S.	138	D7	37.29 N	101.29 W
Sanday, i., Scot., U.K.	10	B10	59.15 N	2.35 W
Sanday Sound, b., Scot., U.K.	10	B10	59.11 N	2.35 W
Sandbochum, ngh., Ger.	181		51.40 N	7.41 E
Sand Coulee, Mt., U.S.	146	C15	47.24 N	111.09 W
Sand Coulee Creek, stm., Mt., U.S.	146	C15	47.26 N	111.18 W
Sand Creek, stm., U.S.	140	G7	41.13 N	105.43 W
Sand Creek, stm., In., U.S.	130	E12	39.03 N	85.51 W
Sand Creek, stm., Ks., U.S.	138	D10	37.26 N	98.12 W
Sand Creek, stm., Mn., U.S.	128	E6	45.55 N	92.37 W
Sand Creek, stm., Mt., U.S.	142	G7	47.18 N	106.45 W
Sand Creek, stm., S.D., U.S.	140	C14	44.01 N	98.06 W
Sand Creek, stm., Wy., U.S.	140	C5	44.15 N	107.54 W
Sand Creek, stm., Wy., U.S.	140	D7	43.27 N	105.27 W
Sand Creek, stm., Wy., U.S.	150	B8	41.01 N	107.52 W
Sanddøla, stm., Nor.	16	C10	64.27 N	12.18 E
Sande, Nor.	16	H8	59.35 N	10.13 E
Sandefjord, Nor.	16	H8	59.07 N	10.14 E
Sandeid, Nor.	16	H3	59.33 N	5.51 E
Sanders, Az., U.S.	150	H7	35.14 N	109.20 W
Sanderson, Tx., U.S.	136	D5	30.08 N	102.23 W
Sanderstead, ngh., Eng., U.K.	178		51.20 N	0.05 W
Sandersville, Ga., U.S.	132	D3	32.59 N	82.48 W
Sandersville, Ms., U.S.	134	F9	31.47 N	89.01 W
Sandfjellet, mtn., Nor.	14	B18	70.50 N	28.02 E
Sand Fork, W.V., U.S.	124	F5	38.55 N	80.45 W
Sandgate, Austl.	98	F9	27.19 S	153.04 E
Sandhammaren, c., Swe.	16	L12	55.23 N	14.12 E
Sandhamn, Swe.	16	H16	59.17 N	18.55 E
Sandhill, On., Can.	193b		43.50 N	79.49 W
Sand Hill, stm., Mn., U.S.	128	D2	47.36 N	96.52 W
Sand Hills, hills, Ne., U.S.	140	F11	42.00 N	101.00 W
Sandhornøya, i., Nor.	14	E4	67.06 N	14.09 E
Sāndi, India	70	E8	27.17 N	79.57 E
Sandia, Peru	164	F4	14.16 S	69.27 W
Sandia Crest, mtn., N.M., U.S.	138	F2	35.13 N	106.27 W
Sandia Indian Reservation, ind. res., N.M., U.S.	138	F2	35.15 N	106.30 W
San Diego, Ca., U.S.	148	K8	32.43 N	117.08 W
San Diego, Tx., U.S.	136	G9	27.45 N	98.14 W
San Diego, stm., Ca., U.S.	148	K9	32.45 N	117.15 W
San Diego, Cabo, c., Arg.	166	J3	54.39 S	65.07 W
San Diego Aqueduct, aq., Ca., U.S.	148	J8	32.55 N	116.55 W
San Diego Creek, stm., Tx., U.S.	136	G9	27.47 N	98.03 W
San Diego de la Unión, Mex.	154	E8	21.28 N	100.52 W
Sandies Creek, stm., Tx., U.S.	136	E10	29.06 N	97.19 W
Sandıklı, Tur.	34	E13	38.28 N	30.17 E
Sandīla, India	70	E8	27.04 N	80.30 E
Sandilands Village, Bah.	158f	m18	25.02 N	77.18 W
San Dimas Canyon, val., Ca. U.S.	198		34.10 N	117.46 W
San Dimas Reservoir, res., Ca., U.S.	198		34.09 N	117.43 W
Sand in Taufers see Campo Túres, Italy	30	D8	46.55 N	11.58 E
Sandiway, Eng., U.K.	180		53.14 N	2.36 W
Sand Key, i., Fl., U.S.	132	I3	27.53 N	82.51 W
Sand Lake, l., On., Can.	128	A4	50.05 N	94.39 W
Sandnes, Nor.	16	I3	58.51 N	5.44 E
Sandnessjøen, Nor.	16	A10	66.00 N	12.38 E
Sandoa, D.R.C.	86	F4	9.42 S	22.52 E
Sandomierz, Pol.	24	F17	50.40 N	21.46 E
San Domino, Isola, i., Italy	30	H12	42.07 N	15.29 E
Sandon, Eng., U.K.	178		51.43 N	0.32 E
Sandoná, Col.	168	G3	1.17 N	77.28 W
San Donà di Piave, Italy	30	E9	45.38 N	12.34 E
Sandoval, Il., U.S.	130	F8	38.36 N	89.06 W
Sandovo, Russia	26	B19	58.28 N	36.24 E
Sandoway, Mya.	64	C2	18.27 N	94.22 E
Sandown, Eng., U.K.	12	K11	50.39 N	1.09 W
Sandown Park Racecourse, p.o.i., Austl.	192b		37.57 S	145.10 E
Sandown Park Race Course, p.o.i., Eng., U.K.	178		51.22 N	0.22 W
Sandoy, i., Far. Is.	12b	n34	61.50 N	6.45 W
Sand Point, Ak., U.S.	109	E7	55.20 N	160.29 W
Sandpoint, Id., U.S.	146	B10	48.16 N	116.33 W
Sandrancourt, Fr.	179		49.02 N	1.39 E
Sandridge, Eng., U.K.	178		51.47 N	0.18 W
Sandringham, Austl.	98	E2	24.04 S	139.04 E
Sandringham, ngh., S. Afr.	191d		26.09 S	28.07 E
Sandslån, Swe.	16	D15	63.01 N	17.48 E
Sandspit, B.C., Can.	110	E4	53.13 N	131.50 W
Sands Point, N.Y., U.S.	194		40.51 N	73.43 W
Sands Point, c., N.Y., U.S.	194		40.52 N	73.44 W
Sand Springs, Ok., U.S.	134	A2	36.08 N	96.06 W
Sand Springs, Tx., U.S.	136	B6	32.16 N	101.21 W
Sandspruit, stm., S. Afr.	191d		26.07 S	28.04 E
Sandstone, Austl.	96	E3	27.59 S	119.17 E
Sandstone, Mn., U.S.	128	E6	46.07 N	92.52 W
Sandu, China	58	H3	25.59 N	107.52 E
Sandu Ao, b., China	58	H8	26.35 N	119.50 E
Sandusky, Mi., U.S.	126	E7	43.25 N	82.49 W
Sandusky, Oh., U.S.	126	C3	41.26 N	82.42 W
Sandusky, stm., Oh., U.S.	124	C2	41.26 N	83.00 W
Sandværet, is., Nor.	16	B9	65.20 N	12.00 E
Sandvig, Den.	16	L12	55.17 N	14.47 E
Sandvika, Nor.	16	H8	59.53 N	10.33 E
Sandvika, Nor.	16	C11	64.28 N	13.37 E
Sandviken, Swe.	16	G14	60.37 N	16.46 E
Sandwich, Eng., U.K.	10	J14	51.16 N	1.19 E
Sandwich, Il., U.S.	130	C9	41.39 N	88.36 W
Sandwich Bay, b., Nmb.	90	C2	23.22 S	14.29 E
Sandwick, B.C., Can.	144	G5	49.42 N	124.59 W
Sandwip Island, i., Bngl.	70	G13	22.30 N	91.25 E
Sandy, Or., U.S.	146	E4	45.23 N	122.14 W
Sandy, Ut., U.S.	150	C5	40.37 N	111.53 W
Sandy, stm., Me., U.S.	122	F6	44.45 N	69.53 W
Sandy, stm., Or., U.S.	146	E4	45.33 N	122.21 W
Sandy, stm., Va., U.S.	124	H6	36.35 N	79.25 W
Sandy Bay, b., Ma., U.S.	201		42.40 N	70.37 W
Sandy Bay Indian Reserve, ind. res., Mb., Can.	142	D15	50.33 N	98.40 W
Sandy Bay Mountain, mtn., Me., U.S.	122	E6	45.47 N	70.25 W
Sandy Branch, stm., Md., U.S.	202c		39.03 N	77.16 W
Sandy Cape, c., Austl.	98	E9	24.42 S	153.17 E
Sandy Cape, c., Austl.	99a	n12	41.25 S	144.44 E
Sandy Creek, stm., Austl.	98	I5	32.04 S	144.08 E
Sandy Creek, stm., U.S.	138	E10	36.46 N	98.12 W
Sandy Creek, stm., U.S.	138	G9	34.24 N	99.35 W
Sandy Creek, stm., N.Y., U.S.	126	E13	43.43 N	76.12 W
Sandy Creek, stm., Tx., U.S.	136	D9	30.34 N	98.24 W
Sandy Creek, stm., Tx., U.S.	136	E11	29.01 N	96.33 W
Sandy Hook, Ky., U.S.	124	F2	38.04 N	83.10 W
Sandy Hook, Ms., U.S.	134	F9	31.02 N	89.48 W
Sandy Hook, spit, N.J., U.S.	124	D12	40.27 N	74.00 W
Sandy Hook Bay, b., N.J., U.S.	194		40.26 N	74.03 W
Sandykači, Turkmen.	72	B9	36.33 N	62.33 E
Sandy Lake, l., On., Can.	110	E12	53.02 N	93.00 W
Sandy Point, c., Trin.	159f	r13	11.09 N	60.50 W
Sandy Point Town, St. K./N.	159a	c2	17.22 N	62.51 W
Sandy Springs, Ga., U.S.	132	C1	33.55 N	84.24 W
Sandžak, reg., Yugo.	36	F6	43.10 N	19.30 E
San Elizario, Tx., U.S.	136	C1	31.35 N	106.13 W
San Enrique, Arg.	172	G7	35.47 S	60.21 W
San Estanislao, Para.	172	B9	24.39 S	56.29 W
San Esteban, Isla, i., Mex.	154	A2	28.42 N	112.34 W
San Esteban de Gormaz, Spain	28	C7	41.35 N	3.12 W
San Felipe, Chile	172	F2	32.44 S	70.42 W
San Felipe, Col.	168	G8	1.55 N	67.06 W
San Felipe, Mex.	120	F5	31.01 N	114.50 W
San Felipe, Mex.	154	E8	21.28 N	101.12 W
San Felipe, Phil.	68	C2	15.04 N	120.04 E
San Felipe, Ven.	168	B7	10.20 N	68.44 W
San Felipe, Castillo de, hist., Guat.	156	E3	15.39 N	89.01 W
San Felipe, Cayos de, is., Cuba	156	B6	21.58 N	83.30 W
San Felipe Creek, stm., Ca., U.S.	148	J9	33.09 N	115.49 W
San Felipe Indian Reservation, ind. res., N.M., U.S.	138	F2	35.26 N	106.26 W
San Felipe Nuevo Mercurio, Mex.	154	C7	24.21 N	102.05 W
San Felipe Pueblo, N.M., U.S.	138	F2	35.26 N	106.27 W
San Felíu de Guíxols see Sant Feliu de Guíxols, Spain	28	C14	41.47 N	3.01 E
San Félix, Isla, i., Chile	162	H6	26.16 S	80.05 W
San Fermín, Mex.	136	H3	26.20 N	104.49 W
San Fernando, Chile	172	G2	34.35 S	70.59 W
San Fernando, Mex.	136	F7	28.32 N	100.54 W
San Fernando, Mex.	150	L6	31.16 N	110.36 W
San Fernando, Mex.	154	C9	24.50 N	98.09 W
San Fernando, Phil.	68	C3	15.01 N	120.41 E
San Fernando, Phil.	68	B3	16.36 N	120.19 E
San Fernando, Spain	28	H4	36.28 N	6.11 W
San Fernando, Trin.	159f	s12	10.17 N	61.27 W
San Fernando, Ca., U.S.	148	I7	34.16 N	118.26 W
San Fernando, state, Arg.	206		34.28 S	58.34 W
San Fernando, Aeródromo, arpt., Arg.	206		34.27 S	58.35 W
San Fernando Airport, arpt., Ca., U.S.	198		34.17 N	118.25 W
San Fernando Creek, stm., Tx., U.S.	136	G10	27.27 N	97.46 W
San Fernando de Apure, Ven.	168	D8	7.52 N	67.27 W
San Fernando de Atabapo, Ven.	168	E8	4.01 N	67.41 W
San Fernando de Henares, Spain	184a		40.26 N	3.32 W
San Fernando del Valle de Catamarca, Arg.	172	D4	28.27 S	65.46 W
San Fernando Mission, rel., Ca., U.S.	198		34.16 N	118.28 W
San Fernando Valley, val., Ca., U.S.	198		34.13 N	118.27 W
Sånfjället, mtn., Swe.	16	E11	62.17 N	13.32 E
Sånfjällets Nationalpark, p.o.i., Swe.	16	E11	62.18 N	13.37 E
Sanford, Co., U.S.	138	D3	37.15 N	105.54 W
Sanford, Fl., U.S.	132	H4	28.47 N	81.16 W
Sanford, Me., U.S.	122	G6	43.27 N	70.46 W
Sanford, Mi., U.S.	126	E5	43.40 N	84.23 W
Sanford, N.C., U.S.	132	A6	35.28 N	79.10 W
Sanford, Tx., U.S.	138	F7	35.42 N	101.32 W
Sanford, stm., Austl.	96	E3	27.22 S	115.53 E
Sanford, Mount, vol., Ak., U.S.	109	D11	62.13 N	144.09 W
San Francesco, Convento, rel., Italy	185a		42.03 N	12.46 E
San Francisco, Arg.	172	E6	31.25 S	62.05 W
San Francisco, Col.	168	G3	1.11 N	76.55 W
San Francisco, El Sal.	156	F3	13.42 N	88.06 W
San Francisco, Ca., U.S.	148	F3	37.47 N	122.25 W
San Francisco, Ca., U.S.	200		37.46 N	122.25 W
San Francisco, stm., Arg.	172	B5	23.57 S	64.43 W
San Francisco, stm., U.S.	150	J8	32.58 N	109.21 W
San Francisco, Arroyo, stm., Arg.	206		34.43 S	58.19 W
San Francisco, Paso de, p., S.A.	172	C3	26.52 S	68.19 W
San Francisco, University of, educ., Ca., U.S.	200		37.46 N	122.26 W
San Francisco Bay, b., Ca., U.S.	148	F3	37.39 N	122.18 W
San Francisco Creek, stm., Tx., U.S.	136	E5	29.53 N	102.19 W
San Francisco Culhuacán, ngh., Mex.	204a		19.20 N	99.08 W
San Francisco de Borja, Mex.	154	B5	27.53 N	106.41 W
San Francisco de Conchos, Mex.	136	G2	27.35 N	105.20 W
San Francisco de Horizonte, Mex.	136	I4	25.56 N	103.26 W
San Francisco del Chañar, Arg.	172	D5	29.47 S	63.56 W
San Francisco del Monte de Oro, Arg.	172	F4	32.36 S	66.07 W
San Francisco del Oro, Mex.	154	B5	26.52 N	105.51 W
San Francisco del Rincón, Mex.	154	E8	21.01 N	101.51 W
San Francisco de Macorís, Dom. Rep.	156	C12	19.18 N	70.15 W
San Francisco de Mostazal, Chile	172	F2	33.56 S	70.42 W
San Francisco el Grande, Iglesia de, rel., Spain	184a		40.25 N	3.43 W
San Francisco Maritime National Historical Park, p.o.i., Ca., U.S.	200		37.48 N	122.27 W
San Francisco-Oakland Bay Bridge, trans., Ca., U.S.	200		37.48 N	122.22 W
San Francisco State Fish and Game Refuge, ind. res., Ca., U.S.	200		37.35 N	122.25 W
San Francisco State University, educ., Ca., U.S.	200		37.43 N	122.28 W
San Francisco Tlaltenco, ngh., Mex.	204a		19.17 N	99.01 W
San Francisco Zoological Gardens, p.o.i., Ca., U.S.	200		37.44 N	122.30 W
San Francisquito Creek, stm., Ca., U.S.	200		37.28 N	122.07 W
San Gabriel, Ec.	168	G3	0.35 N	77.49 W
San Gabriel, stm., Ca., U.S.	198		33.45 N	118.07 W
San Gabriel, stm., Tx., U.S.	136	D10	30.45 N	97.01 W
San Gabriel, North Fork, stm., Ca., U.S.	198		34.15 N	117.52 W
San Gabriel, North Fork, stm., Tx., U.S.	136	D10	30.38 N	97.40 W
San Gabriel, South Fork, stm., Tx., U.S.	136	D10	30.38 N	97.40 W
San Gabriel Arcangel, Mission, rel., Ca., U.S.	198		34.06 N	118.06 W
San Gabriel Chilac, Mex.	154	F10	18.19 N	97.20 W

Name	Page	Map Ref.	Latitude	Longitude
San Gabriel Dam, dam., Ca., U.S.	198		34.13 N	117.52 W
San Gabriel Mountains, mts., Ca., U.S.	148	I8	34.20 N	118.00 W
San Gabriel Peak, mtn., Ca., U.S.	198		34.15 N	118.06 W
Šangaly, Russia	12	F20	61.07 N	43.19 E
Sangamankanda Point, c., Sri L.	69	H5	7.01 N	81.52 E
Sangamner, India	69	B2	19.34 N	74.13 E
Sangamon, stm., Il., U.S.	130	D7	40.01 N	90.26 W
Sangar, Russia	50	D14	63.55 N	127.28 E
Sangarius see Sakarya, stm., Tur.	34	B13	41.07 N	30.39 E
Sangasanga-dalam, Indon.	66	D10	0.39 S	117.14 E
San Gavino Monreale, Italy	32	E2	39.33 N	8.48 E
Sangay, vol., Ec.	168	I2	2.00 S	78.20 W
Sangay, Parque Nacional, p.o.i., Ec.	168	H3	1.50 S	78.20 W
Sangbé, Cam.	86	C2	6.02 N	12.28 E
Sangchris Lake, l., Il., U.S.	130	E8	39.35 N	89.30 W
Sange, D.R.C.	86	F5	7.02 S	28.21 E
Sangeang, Pulau, i., Indon.	66	H11	8.12 S	119.04 E
Sangenjaya, ngh., Japan	186		35.38 N	139.40 E
Sanger, Ca., U.S.	148	G6	36.42 N	119.32 W
Sanger, Tx., U.S.	138	H11	33.22 N	97.10 W
Sângera, Mol.	38	F7	47.38 N	28.09 E
Sangerhausen, Ger.	24	E7	51.28 N	11.17 E
San Germán, P.R.	158a	b1	18.05 N	67.02 W
Sangerville, Me., U.S.	122	E7	45.11 N	69.23 W
Sanggan, stm., China	58	A6	40.20 N	115.25 E
Sanggau, Indon.	66	C7	0.06 N	110.34 E
Sangge-ri, ngh., Kor., S.	189b		37.41 N	127.05 E
Sanggin Dalai, China	58	B1	38.11 N	105.17 E
Sangha, stm., Afr.	86	E3	1.12 S	16.50 E
Sanghar, Pak.	70	E2	26.02 N	68.57 E
Sangihe, Kepulauan, is., Indon.	60	E7	3.00 N	125.30 E
Sangihe, Pulau, i., Indon.	60	E8	3.35 N	125.32 E
San Gil, Col.	168	D5	6.33 N	73.07 W
Sangilen, hrebet, mts., Russia	48	D17	50.10 N	96.22 E
San Gimignano, Italy	30	G7	43.28 N	11.02 E
San Giorgio su Legnano, Italy	184b		45.34 N	8.55 E
San Giovanni in Fiore, Italy	32	E10	39.15 N	16.42 E
San Giovanni in Laterano, rel., Italy	185a		41.53 N	12.30 E
San Giovanni in Persiceto, Italy	30	F8	44.38 N	11.11 E
San Giovanni Rotondo, Italy	32	C9	41.42 N	15.43 E
San Giovanni Valdarno, Italy	30	G8	43.34 N	11.32 E
San Giuliano Milanese, Italy	184b		45.24 N	9.17 E
Sangiyn Dalay nuur, l., Mong.	52	B4	49.17 N	99.00 E
Sangju, Kor., S.	54	F8	36.24 N	128.09 E
Sangkapura, Indon.	66	F8	5.50 S	112.38 E
Sângkê, stm., Camb.	64	F6	13.12 N	103.41 E
Sangkhai, Thai.	64	E6	14.38 N	103.51 E
Sangkulirang, Indon.	66	C10	1.00 N	117.57 E
Sangley Point, c., Phil.	187f		14.30 N	120.55 E
Sāngli, India	69	C2	16.51 N	74.34 E
Sangmélima, Cam.	86	D2	2.56 N	11.59 E
Sangngagqoiling, China	70	D14	28.31 N	92.55 E
Sango, Japan	188		34.36 N	135.42 E
Sāngole, India	69	C2	17.26 N	75.12 E
Sangolquí, Ec.	168	H2	0.19 S	78.27 W
San Gorgonio Mountain, mtn., Ca., U.S.	148	I9	34.06 N	116.50 W
San Gottardo, Passo del, p., Switz.	30	D5	46.33 N	8.33 E
Sangre de Cristo Mountains, mts., U.S.	138	E3	37.31 N	105.21 W
San Gregorio, Arg.	172	G6	34.20 S	62.02 W
San Gregorio, ngh., Mex.	204a		19.15 N	99.03 W
San Gregorio Creek, stm., Ca., U.S.	200		37.19 N	122.25 W
San Gregorio State Beach, p.o.i., Ca., U.S.	200		37.19 N	122.24 W
Sangre Grande, Trin.	159f	s12	10.35 N	61.07 W
Sangro, stm., Italy	30	H11	42.14 N	14.32 E
Sangrūr, India	70	C5	30.14 N	75.50 E
Sangsang, China	70	D11	29.26 N	86.35 E
Sangsues, Lac aux, l., Qc., Can.	126	B12	46.29 N	77.57 W
Sangudo, Ab., Can.	144	C16	53.54 N	114.55 W
Sangue, stm., Braz.	164	F6	10.57 S	58.20 W
Sangüesa, Spain	28	B9	42.34 N	1.16 W
Sāngurli, India	190c		18.56 N	73.07 E
Sangutane, stm., Moz.	90	C11	24.06 S	33.47 E
Sangya, China	70	C13	30.52 N	91.38 E
Sanhechang, China	58	F2	31.22 N	106.48 E
San Hipólito, Punta, c., Mex.	154	B1	26.58 N	113.59 W
Sanhu, China	58	H6	27.56 N	115.23 E
Sānhūr, Egypt	76	I1	29.24 N	30.46 E
Sanibel Island, i., Fl., U.S.	132	J3	26.27 N	82.08 W
San Ignacio, Arg.	172	C10	27.15 S	55.32 W
San Ignacio, Mex.	154	D8	23.12 N	100.12 W
San Ignacio, Mex.	154	B2	27.17 N	112.53 W
San Ignacio, Para.	172	C9	26.53 S	56.55 W
San Ignacio, Isla, i., Mex.	154	C4	25.25 N	108.54 W
San Ignacio, Laguna, b., Mex.	154	B2	26.52 N	113.10 W
San Ignacio de Moxo, Bol.	166	B3	14.56 S	65.36 W
San Ignacio de Velasco, Bol.	166	C4	16.22 S	60.57 W
San Ildefonso, Cape, c., Phil.	68	C4	16.02 N	122.00 E
San Ildefonso, Cerro, mtn., Hond.	156	E3	15.31 N	88.17 W
San Ildefonso Indian Reservation, ind. res., N.M., U.S.	138	F2	35.53 N	106.08 W
Sanino, Russia	183a		59.50 N	29.54 E
San Isidro, Arg.	172	D5	28.26 S	65.43 W
San Isidro, Arg.	172	G8	34.28 S	58.30 W
San Isidro, Peru	204d		12.07 S	77.03 W
San Isidro, Tx., U.S.	136	H9	26.43 N	98.27 W
San Isidro, state, Arg.	206		34.29 S	58.33 W
San Isidro de Curuguaty, Para.	172	B10	24.30 S	55.44 W
San Isidro del General, C.R.	156	H6	9.22 N	83.42 W
San Isidro el Real, Catedral de, rel., Spain	184a		40.25 N	3.42 W
Sanīyah, Iraq	74	D8	33.49 N	42.42 E
San Jacinto, Col.	168	C4	9.49 N	75.07 W
San Jacinto, Ca., U.S.	148	J9	33.47 N	116.57 W
San Jacinto, East Fork, stm., Tx., U.S.	136	D12	30.04 N	95.09 W
San Jacinto, West Fork, stm., Tx., U.S.	136	D12	30.00 N	95.07 W
San Jacinto Peak, mtn., Ca., U.S.	148	J9	33.49 N	116.46 W
San Jaime, Arg.	172	E8	30.20 S	58.18 W
San Javier, Arg.	172	E8	30.34 S	59.55 W
San Javier, Arg.	172	C10	27.52 S	55.08 W
San Javier, Bol.	166	C4	16.20 S	62.38 W
San Javier, Bol.	166	B4	14.38 S	64.48 W
San Javier, Chile	172	G2	35.35 S	71.43 W
San Javier, Mex.	136	H8	26.15 N	99.25 W
San Javier, Ur.	172	F8	32.40 S	58.07 W
San Javier, stm., Arg.	172	E8	31.31 S	60.19 W
San Javier, Cerro, mtn., Mex.	136	H2	26.06 N	105.11 W
Sanjāwi, Pak.	70	C2	30.15 N	68.20 E
Sanjay National Park, p.o.i., India	70	G8	23.42 N	82.08 E
San Jerónimo, Guat.	156	E2	15.04 N	90.13 W
Sanjiang, China	58	I3	25.40 N	109.27 E
Sanjō, Japan	56	B11	37.37 N	138.57 E
San Joaquín, Bol.	166	B4	13.04 S	64.49 W
San Joaquín, Chile	204e		33.30 S	70.37 W
San Joaquín, Para.	172	B9	24.57 S	56.06 W
San Joaquín, stm., Bol.	166	B4	13.08 S	63.41 W
San Joaquin, stm., Ca., U.S.	148	E4	38.02 N	121.52 W
San Joaquín de Omaguas, Peru	164	D3	4.10 S	73.21 W
San Joaquin Valley, val., Ca., U.S.	148	F5	36.55 N	120.29 W
San Jon, N.M., U.S.	138	F5	35.05 N	103.21 W
San Jorge, Arg.	172	E7	31.54 S	61.51 W
San Jorge, stm., Col.	168	C4	9.07 N	74.43 W
San Jorge, Bahía de, b., Mex.	120	F6	31.09 N	113.13 W
San Jorge, Golfo, b., Arg.	166	I3	46.00 S	67.00 W
San Jorge Island, i., Sol. Is.	101b	e8	8.27 S	159.35 E
San José, Arg.	172	C10	27.46 S	55.46 W
San José, C.R.	156	H5	9.55 N	84.05 W
San José, Mex.	136	F7	28.15 N	100.15 W
San Jose, Phil.	68	C3	15.48 N	120.59 E
San Jose, Phil.	68	E3	10.45 N	121.57 E
San Jose, Ca., U.S.	148	F4	37.20 N	121.53 W
San Jose, Ca., U.S.	200		37.20 N	121.53 W
San Jose, Il., U.S.	130	D8	40.17 N	89.35 W
San Jose, N.M., U.S.	138	F3	35.23 N	105.28 W
San José, Ven.	158g	q19	11.59 N	70.07 W
San José, Ven.	204c		10.34 N	66.57 W
San José, mun., Cuba	204b		22.57 N	82.14 W
San Jose, stm., B.C., Can.	144	E9	52.09 N	122.16 W
San Jose, stm., N.M., U.S.	150	I9	34.52 N	107.01 W
San Jose, Arroyo, stm., Ca., U.S.	200		38.03 N	122.30 W
San José, Cerro, mtn., Mex.	136	H2	26.17 N	105.30 W
San José, Isla, i., Mex.	154	C3	25.00 N	110.37 W
San José, Isla, i., Pan.	156	H8	8.15 N	79.07 W
San José, Laguna, b., P.R.	158a	b3	18.25 N	66.01 W
San Jose, Mission, rel., Ca., U.S.	200		37.32 N	121.55 W
San Jose Arena, p.o.i., Ca., U.S.	200		37.20 N	121.54 W
San Jose Creek, stm., Ca., U.S.	198		34.01 N	118.03 W
San José de Aura, Mex.	136	G6	27.34 N	101.22 W
San José de Bácum, Mex.	154	B3	27.32 N	110.09 W
San José de Batuc, Mex.	154	A4	29.15 N	109.45 W
San José de Chiquitos, Bol.	166	C4	17.50 S	60.43 W
San José de Feliciano, Arg.	172	E8	30.23 S	58.45 W
San José de Galipán, Ven.	204c		10.35 N	66.54 W
San José de Galipán, Quebrada, stm., Ven.	204c		10.37 N	66.54 W
San José de Guanipa, Ven.	168	C10	8.53 N	64.09 W
San José de Jáchal, Arg.	172	E3	30.13 S	68.44 W
San José de la Popa, Mex.	136	H7	26.10 N	100.49 W
San José de las Lajas, Cuba	156	A6	22.58 N	82.09 W
San José del Cabo, Mex.	154	D4	23.03 N	109.41 W
San José del Guaviare, Col.	168	F5	2.33 N	72.38 W
San José de Mayo, Ur.	172	G9	34.21 S	56.42 W
San José de Ocuné, Col.	168	E6	4.13 N	70.20 W
San José de Raíces, Mex.	154	C8	24.34 N	100.14 W
San José de Tiznados, Ven.	168	C8	9.23 N	67.33 W
San Jose Hills, hills, Ca., U.S.	198		34.04 N	117.49 W
San Jose Island, i., Tx., U.S.	136	G11	28.02 N	96.54 W
San Jose State University, educ., Ca., U.S.	200		37.20 N	121.53 W
San Juan, Arg.	172	E3	31.32 S	68.31 W
San Juan, Mex.	136	E3	29.34 N	104.35 W
San Juan, Peru	164	G2	15.20 S	75.08 W
San Juan, P.R.	158a	b3	18.28 N	66.07 W
San Juan, state, Arg.	172	E3	31.00 S	69.00 W
San Juan, stm., Arg.	172	F4	32.17 S	67.22 W
San Juan, stm., Col.	168	E3	4.11 N	77.26 W
San Juan, stm., Mex.	136	H8	26.03 N	99.05 W
San Juan, stm., N.A.	156	G5	10.56 N	83.42 W
San Juan, stm., Phil.	187f		14.35 N	121.01 E
San Juan, stm., S.A.	168	G2	1.11 N	78.32 W
San Juan, stm., U.S.	150	F6	37.10 N	110.42 W
San Juan, stm., Ven.	168	B10	10.09 N	62.36 W
San Juan, Bahía de, b., P.R.	158a	a3	18.27 N	66.07 W
San Juan, Cabezas de, c., P.R.	158a	b4	18.23 N	65.37 W
San Juan, Cabo, c., Arg.	166	J4	54.43 S	63.49 W
San Juan, Embalse de, res., Spain	28	D6	40.23 N	4.19 W
San Juan, Pasaje de, strt., P.R.	158a	b4	18.23 N	65.36 W
San Juan, Pico, mtn., Cuba	156	B7	21.59 N	80.09 W
San Juan, Punta, c., Chile	100l	e29	27.04 S	109.21 W
San Juan Basin, bas., N.M., U.S.	150	G8	36.34 N	108.35 W
San Juan Bautista, Mex.	136	H6	26.58 N	101.23 W
San Juan Bautista, Para.	172	C9	26.52 S	57.01 W
San Juan Bautista see Sant Joan de Labritja, Spain	28	E12	39.05 N	1.30 E
San Juan Bautista, Ca., U.S.	148	G4	36.50 N	121.32 W
San Juan Creek, stm., Ca., U.S.	148	H5	35.39 N	120.22 W
San Juan de Abajo, Mex.	154	E6	20.48 N	105.13 W
San Juan de Aragón, Bosque, p.o.i., Mex.	204a		19.28 N	99.04 W
San Juan de Aragón, Zoológico de, p.o.i., Mex.	204a		19.28 N	99.05 W
San Juan de Colón, Ven.	168	C5	8.02 N	72.15 W
San Juan de Dios, Ven.	204c		10.35 N	66.55 W
San Juan de Guadalupe, Mex.	154	C7	24.37 N	102.46 W
San Juan de la Maguana, Dom. Rep.	156	C12	18.48 N	71.13 W
San Juan del César, Col.	168	B5	10.46 N	72.59 W
San Juan del Monte, Phil.	187f		14.36 N	121.02 E
San Juan del Norte, Nic.	156	G6	10.55 N	83.42 W
San Juan de los Cayos, Ven.	168	B7	11.10 N	68.25 W
San Juan de los Morros, Ven.	168	B8	9.54 N	67.20 W
San Juan del Río, Mex.	154	E8	20.22 N	100.00 W
San Juan del Río, Mex.	154	C6	24.47 N	104.27 W
San Juan del Sur, Nic.	156	G4	11.14 N	85.51 W
San Juan de Lurigancho, Peru	204d		11.59 S	77.01 W
San Juan de Micay, stm., Col.	168	F3	3.04 N	77.32 W
San Juan de Miraflores, Peru	204d		12.11 S	76.57 W
San Juan de Payara, Ven.	168	D8	7.38 N	67.36 W
San Juan de Sabinas, Mex.	136	G6	27.55 N	101.18 W
San Juan Evangelista, Mex.	154	G11	17.53 N	95.07 W
San Juanico, Mex.	154	B2	26.15 N	112.29 W
San Juan Indian Reservation, ind. res., N.M., U.S.	138	E2	36.03 N	106.04 W
San Juan Islands, is., Wa., U.S.	146	B3	48.36 N	123.06 W
San Juanito, Isla, i., Mex.	154	E5	21.46 N	106.40 W
San Juan Ixtayopan, ngh., Mex.	204a		19.14 N	99.00 W
San Juan Mountains, mts., Co., U.S.	120	C9	37.31 N	107.31 W
San Juan Nepomuceno, Col.	168	C4	9.57 N	75.05 W
San Juan Nepomuceno, Para.	172	C9	26.05 S	55.58 W
San Julián, Quebrada, stm., Ven.	204c		10.37 N	66.51 W
San Justo, Arg.	172	E7	30.47 S	60.35 W
San Justo, Aeródromo, arpt., Arg.	206		34.44 S	58.36 W
Sankarani, stm., Afr.	84	G3	11.59 N	8.17 W
Sankarpur, India	190b		22.51 N	88.27 E
Sankeshwar, India	69	C2	16.15 N	74.28 E
Sankey Brook, stm., Eng., U.K.	180		53.22 N	2.38 W
Sankh, stm., India	70	G10	22.14 N	84.48 E
Sankheda, India	70	G4	22.11 N	73.35 E
Sankosh, stm., Asia	70	E13	25.58 N	89.50 E
Sānkra, India	70	H9	21.17 N	82.39 E
Sānkrāil, India	190b		22.34 N	88.14 E
Sankt Aegyd am Neuwalde, Aus.	24	I11	47.51 N	15.34 E
Sankt Anton am Arlberg, Aus.	30	C7	47.08 N	10.15 E
Sankt Gallen, Aus.	24	I10	47.42 N	14.38 E
Sankt Gallen, Switz.	30	C6	47.25 N	9.22 E
Sankt Gilgen, Aus.	24	I9	47.46 N	13.22 E
Sankt Goar, Ger.	24	F3	50.08 N	7.42 E
Sankt Goarshausen, Ger.	24	F3	50.09 N	7.44 E
Sankt Ingbert, Ger.	24	G3	49.16 N	7.07 E
Sankt Johann im Pongau, Aus.	24	I8	47.21 N	13.12 E
Sankt Johann in Tirol, Aus.	24	I8	47.31 N	12.25 E
Sankt Michel see Mikkeli, Fin.	18	F14	61.41 N	27.16 E
Sankt Moritz, Switz.	30	D6	46.29 N	9.49 E
Sankt Peter, rel., Ger.	181		51.37 N	7.12 E
Sankt-Peterburg (Saint Petersburg), Russia	18	H17	59.56 N	30.15 E
Sankt-Peterburg (Saint Petersburg), Russia	183a		59.55 N	30.15 E
Sankt-Peterburg, Gorod, mun., Russia	183a		59.55 N	30.15 E
Sankt Peter-Ording, Ger.	24	B4	54.18 N	8.38 E
Sankt Pölten, Aus.	30	B12	48.12 N	15.37 E
Sankt-Quirinus-Dom, rel., Ger.	181		51.12 N	6.42 E
Sankt Ulrich see Ortisei, Italy	30	D8	46.34 N	11.40 E
Sankt Valentin, Aus.	24	H10	48.09 N	14.31 E
Sankt Veit an der Glan, Aus.	30	D11	46.46 N	14.21 E
Sankt-Viktors-Dom, rel., Ger.	181		51.40 N	6.27 E
Sankt-Vith see Saint-Vith, Bel.	20	D15	50.16 N	6.07 E
Sankt Wendel, Ger.	24	G3	49.28 N	7.09 E
Sankt-Willibrodi-Dom, rel., Ger.	181		51.40 N	6.37 E
Sankuru, stm., D.R.C.	86	E4	4.17 S	20.24 E
San Lázaro, Cabo, c., Mex.	154	C2	24.48 N	112.17 W
San Lazaro Race Track, p.o.i., Phil.	187f		14.37 N	120.59 E
San Leandro, Ca., U.S.	148	F3	37.43 N	122.09 W
San Leandro Creek, stm., Ca., U.S.	200		37.45 N	122.12 W
San Leonardo, Mex.	136	G3	27.28 N	104.55 W
Şanlıurfa, Tur.	42	G8	37.09 N	38.47 E
Şanlıurfa, state, Tur.	42	G8	37.20 N	39.15 E
San Lope, Col.	168	D5	6.11 N	71.57 W
San Lorenzo, Arg.	172	D8	28.07 S	58.46 W
San Lorenzo, Arg.	172	F7	32.44 S	60.45 W
San Lorenzo, Bol.	166	D4	21.26 S	64.46 W
San Lorenzo, Ec.	168	G2	1.15 N	78.49 W
San Lorenzo, Mex.	154	C7	25.30 N	102.11 W
San Lorenzo, P.R.	158a	b4	18.12 N	65.57 W
San Lorenzo, Ven.	158g	p19	12.07 N	70.00 W
San Lorenzo, stm., Mex.	154	C5	24.17 N	107.24 W
San Lorenzo, Cabo, c., Ec.	168	H1	1.03 S	80.53 W
San Lorenzo, Isla, i., Mex.	154	A2	28.35 N	112.46 W
San Lorenzo, Monte (Cochrane, Cerro), mtn., S.A.	166	I2	47.37 S	72.19 W
San Lorenzo Creek, stm., Ca., U.S.	200		37.39 N	122.09 W
San Lorenzo de El Escorial, Spain	28	D6	40.35 N	4.08 W
San Lorenzo de la Parrilla, Spain	28	E8	39.51 N	2.22 W
San Lorenzo Tezonco, ngh., Mex.	204a		19.18 N	99.04 W
Sanlúcar de Barrameda, Spain	28	H4	36.47 N	6.21 W
San Lucas, Bol.	166	D3	20.06 S	65.08 W
San Lucas, Mex.	154	D3	22.53 N	109.54 W
San Lucas, Cabo, c., Mex.	154	D4	22.52 N	109.53 W
San Luis, Arg.	172	F4	33.18 S	66.21 W
San Luis, Cuba	156	B10	20.11 N	75.50 W
San Luis, Guat.	156	D3	16.13 N	89.26 W
San Luis, Peru	204d		12.04 S	77.00 W
San Luis, Az., U.S.	150	K5	32.04 N	111.57 W
San Luis, Co., U.S.	138	D3	37.13 N	105.26 W
San Luis, Ven.	168	B7	11.07 N	69.42 W
San Luis, state, Arg.	172	F4	34.00 S	66.00 W
San Luis, ngh., Cuba	204b		23.05 N	82.20 W
San Luis, Laguna, l., Bol.	166	B4	13.45 S	64.00 W
San Luis, Sierra de, mts., Arg.	172	F5	32.50 S	65.55 W
San Luis Creek, stm., Co., U.S.	138	C3	37.40 N	105.44 W
San Luis de la Paz, Mex.	154	E8	21.17 N	100.31 W
San Luis Gonzaga, Mex.	154	C3	24.55 N	111.16 W
San Luis Gonzaga, Bahía, b., Mex.	120	G5	29.47 N	114.21 W
San Luis Jilotepeque, Guat.	156	E3	14.38 N	89.43 W
San Luis Obispo, Ca., U.S.	148	H5	35.17 N	120.39 W
San Luis Peak, mtn., Co., U.S.	138	D2	37.59 N	106.56 W
San Luis Potosí, Mex.	154	D8	22.09 N	100.58 W
San Luis Potosí, state, Mex.	154	D8	22.30 N	100.30 W
San Luis Reservoir, res., Ca., U.S.	148	F4	37.03 N	121.08 W
San Luis Rey, stm., Ca., U.S.	148	J9	33.12 N	117.23 W
San Luis Río Colorado, Mex.	120	E5	32.28 N	114.46 W
San Luis Valley, val., Co., U.S.	138	D3	37.25 N	106.00 W
Sanluri, Italy	32	E2	39.34 N	8.54 E
San Macario, Italy	184b		45.36 N	8.47 E
Sanmaiden, Japan	188		34.34 N	135.51 E
San Manuel, Arg.	172	H8	37.47 S	58.50 W
San Manuel, Az., U.S.	150	K6	32.36 N	110.37 W
San Marcial, stm., Mex.	154	A3	28.02 N	110.43 W
San Marcos, Chile	172	E2	30.56 S	71.04 W
San Marcos, Col.	168	C4	8.39 N	75.08 W
San Marcos, Mex.	136	F2	28.05 N	105.18 W
San Marcos, Mex.	154	G9	16.48 N	99.22 W
San Marcos, Tx., U.S.	136	E10	29.52 N	97.56 W
San Marcos, stm., Tx., U.S.	136	E10	29.29 N	97.28 W
San Marcos, Isla, i., Mex.	154	B2	27.13 N	112.04 W
San Marcos, Universidad Nacional de, educ., Peru	204d		12.04 S	77.05 W
San Marino, S. Mar.	30	G9	43.56 N	12.26 E
San Marino, Ca., U.S.	198		34.07 N	118.06 W
San Marino, ctry., Eur.	30	G9	43.56 N	12.25 E
San Martín, Arg.	172	D5	29.14 S	65.46 W
San Martín, Arg.	172	F3	33.05 S	68.28 W
San Martín, Col.	168	F5	3.42 N	73.41 W
San Martín, stm., Bol.	166	B4	13.07 S	63.46 W
San Martín, sci., Ant.	103	B34	68.07 S	67.08 W
San Martín, Lago (O'Higgins, Lago), l., S.A.	166	I2	48.52 S	72.38 W
San Martín de los Andes, Arg.	166	H2	40.09 S	71.21 W
San Martín de Porras, Peru	204d		12.04 S	77.04 W
San Martín de Valdeiglesias, Spain	28	D6	40.21 N	4.24 W
San Martino di Castrozza, ngh., Italy	30	D8	46.16 N	11.47 E
San Mateo, Mex.	136	G1	27.04 N	106.20 W
San Mateo, Phil.	187f		14.42 N	121.07 E
San Mateo see Sant Mateu del Maestrat, Spain	28	D11	40.28 N	0.10 E
San Mateo, Ca., U.S.	148	F3	37.33 N	122.19 W
San Mateo, Fl., U.S.	132	G4	29.35 N	81.35 W
San Mateo, N.M., U.S.	150	H9	35.19 N	107.38 W
San Mateo, Ven.	168	C9	9.44 N	64.32 W
San Mateo Bridge, trans., Ca., U.S.	200		37.36 N	122.13 W
San Mateo Creek, stm., Ca., U.S.	200		37.34 N	122.18 W
San Mateo Memorial Park, p.o.i., Ca., U.S.	200		37.17 N	122.18 W
San Mateo Tecoloapan, Mex.	204a		19.34 N	99.14 W
San Matías, Bol.	166	C5	16.22 S	58.24 W
San Matías, Golfo, b., Arg.	166	H4	41.30 S	64.15 W
San Medi, Arroyo de, stm., Spain	184d		41.28 N	2.06 E
Sanmen, China	58	G9	29.06 N	121.23 E
Sanmenxia, China	58	D4	34.46 N	111.11 E
San Miguel, Arg.	172	C9	27.59 S	57.35 W
San Miguel, Chile	204e		33.30 S	70.40 W
San Miguel, Ec.	168	H2	1.46 S	79.02 W
San Miguel, El Sal.	156	F3	13.27 N	88.10 W
San Miguel, Mex.	154	A8	29.10 N	101.28 W
San Miguel, Pan.	156	H8	8.27 N	78.56 W
San Miguel, Peru	204d		12.06 S	77.07 W
San Miguel, Ca., U.S.	148	H5	35.45 N	120.42 W
San Miguel, stm., Bol.	166	B4	13.52 S	63.53 W
San Miguel, stm., S.A.	168	G3	0.08 N	75.51 W
San Miguel, stm., Co., U.S.	150	E8	38.23 N	108.48 W
San Miguel, Golfo de, b., Pan.	156	H8	8.22 N	78.17 W
San Miguel Creek, stm., Tx., U.S.	136	F9	28.30 N	98.25 W
San Miguel de Allende, Mex.	154	E8	20.54 N	100.44 W
San Miguel de Cruces, Mex.	154	C6	24.25 N	105.50 W
San Miguel del Monte, Arg.	172	G8	35.26 S	58.48 W
San Miguel de Salcedo, Ec.	168	H2	1.03 S	78.35 W
San Miguel de Tucumán, Arg.	172	C5	26.49 S	65.13 W
San Miguel Island, i., Ca., U.S.	148	I5	34.02 N	120.22 W
Sanming, China	58	H7	26.14 N	117.36 E
San Miniato, Italy	30	G7	43.40 N	10.51 E
San Murezzan see Sankt Moritz, Switz.	30	D6	46.29 N	9.49 E
Sannār, Sudan	82	E6	13.33 N	33.32 E
Sannicandro Garganico, Italy	30	I12	41.50 N	15.33 E
San Nicolás, Peru	164	G2	15.14 S	75.12 W
San Nicolas, Phil.	68	A3	18.10 N	120.35 E
San Nicolás, stm., Mex.	154	F6	19.38 N	105.13 W
San Nicolás, Canal de, strt., N.A.	156	A8	22.43 N	78.53 W
San Nicolás de los Arroyos, Arg.	172	F7	33.19 S	60.13 W
San Nicolás de los Garza, Mex.	154	C8	25.45 N	100.18 W
San Nicolas Island, i., Ca., U.S.	148	J6	33.15 N	119.31 W
Sânnicolau Mare, Rom.	36	D7	46.04 N	20.38 E
Sannieshof, S. Afr.	90	E7	26.31 S	25.48 E
Sannikova, proliv, strt., Russia	50	B16	74.30 N	140.00 E
Sannois, Fr.	179		48.58 N	2.15 E
Sano, Japan	56	C12	36.18 N	139.35 E
Sañogasta, Arg.	172	D4	29.18 S	67.35 W
Sanok, Pol.	24	G18	49.33 N	22.13 E
Sânon, stm., Fr.	20	F15	48.37 N	6.21 E
San Onofre, Col.	168	C4	9.44 N	75.32 W
San Pablo, Phil.	68	C3	14.04 N	121.19 E
San Pablo, ngh., Mex.	204a		19.11 N	99.04 W
San Pablo, Point, c., Ca., U.S.	200		37.58 N	122.26 W
San Pablo Bay, b., Ca., U.S.	148	E3	38.05 N	122.22 W
San Pablo Creek, stm., Ca., U.S.	200		37.58 N	122.30 W
San Pablo Reservoir, res., Ca., U.S.	200		37.56 N	122.15 W
San Pablo Ridge, mtn., Ca., U.S.	200		37.55 N	122.15 W
San Pablo Strait, strt., Ca., U.S.	200		37.58 N	122.26 W
Sanpāda, India	190c		19.04 N	73.01 E
San Pasqual, Punta, c., Mex.	154	C3	25.30 N	111.01 W
San Pedro, Arg.	172	F8	33.40 S	59.41 W
San Pedro, Arg.	172	C5	27.57 S	65.09 W
San Pedro, Arg.	172	B5	24.14 S	64.51 W
San Pedro, Belize	156	D4	17.58 N	87.57 W
San Pedro, Chile	172	F2	33.54 S	71.26 W
San Pedro, Col.	168	C4	9.24 N	75.04 W
San-Pédro, C. Iv.	84	I3	4.44 N	6.37 W
San Pedro, Neth. Ant.	159a	a1	18.03 N	63.03 W
San Pedro, Ven.	168	C6	8.49 N	71.58 W
San Pedro, state, Para.	172	B9	24.18 S	56.34 W
San Pedro, stm., Mex.	120	F8	30.56 N	108.08 W
San Pedro, stm., Mex.	136	G2	28.00 N	105.43 W
San Pedro, stm., N.A.	150	K6	32.58 N	110.46 W
San Pedro, stm., N.A.	156	D2	17.45 N	91.24 W
San Pedro, stm., Ven.	204c		10.35 N	66.48 W
San Pedro, Point, c., Ca., U.S.	200		37.35 N	122.31 W
San Pedro, Point, c., Ca., U.S.	200		37.59 N	122.27 W
San Pedro, Punta, c., Chile	172	B2	25.31 S	70.37 W
San Pedro, Volcán, vol., Chile	166	D3	21.53 S	68.25 W
San Pedro Breakwater, trans., Ca., U.S.	198		33.42 N	118.16 W
San Pedro Carchá, Guat.	156	E2	15.28 N	90.18 W
San Pedro Channel, strt., Ca., U.S.	148	J7	33.35 N	118.25 W
San Pedro Creek, stm., Ca., U.S.	200		37.36 N	122.30 W
San Pedro de Jujuy see San Pedro, Arg.	172	B5	24.14 S	64.51 W
San Pedro de las Colonias, Mex.	154	C7	25.45 N	102.58 W
San Pedro del Gallo, Mex.	154	C6	25.33 N	104.17 W
San Pedro del Paraná, Para.	172	C9	26.45 S	56.17 W
San Pedro de Macorís, Dom. Rep.	156	C13	18.27 N	69.18 W
San Pedro de Ycuamandiyú, Para.	172	B9	24.05 S	57.07 W
San Pedro Mártir, ngh., Mex.	204a		19.16 N	99.10 W
San Pedro Mártir, Sierra, mts., Mex.	120	F5	30.58 N	115.29 W
San Pedro Peaks, mtn., N.M., U.S.	138	E2	36.07 N	106.49 W
San Pedro Pochutla, Mex.	154	H10	15.43 N	96.28 W
San Pedro Sula, Hond.	156	E3	15.29 N	88.01 W
San Pedro Tabasco, Mex.	156	D2	17.46 N	91.09 W
San Pedro Xalostoc, Mex.	204a		19.32 N	99.05 W
San Pelayo, Col.	168	C4	8.58 N	75.50 W
San Pellegrino Terme, Italy	30	E6	45.49 N	9.39 E
San Pietro, Isola di, i., Italy	32	E2	39.08 N	8.16 E
San Pietro in Vaticano, rel., Vat.	185a		41.54 N	12.28 E
San Pitch, stm., Ut., U.S.	150	D5	39.01 N	111.50 W
Sanpoil, stm., Wa., U.S.	146	B8	47.56 N	118.40 W
San Quentin, Ca., U.S.	200		37.56 N	122.29 W
San Quentin State Prison, bldg., Ca., U.S.	200		37.56 N	122.28 W
Sanquhar, Scot., U.K.	10	F9	55.22 N	3.55 W
Sanquianga, Parque Nacional, p.o.i., Col.	168	F2	2.30 N	78.15 W
San Quintín, Cabo, c., Mex.	120	F4	30.22 N	115.59 W
San Rafael, Arg.	172	G3	34.37 S	68.20 W
San Rafael, Chile	172	G2	35.18 S	71.32 W
San Rafael, Mex.	154	C8	25.01 N	100.33 W
San Rafael, Ca., U.S.	148	E3	37.58 N	122.31 W
San Rafael, N.M., U.S.	150	H9	35.06 N	107.53 W
San Rafael, Ven.	168	B6	10.57 N	71.43 W
San Rafael, stm., Bol.	166	C5	18.47 S	58.46 W
San Rafael, stm., Mex.	120	F5	30.58 N	116.16 W
San Rafael, stm., Ut., U.S.	150	E6	38.46 N	110.06 W
San Rafael Bay, b., Ca., U.S.	200		37.58 N	122.28 W
San Rafael de las Tortillas, Mex.	136	H8	26.54 N	99.38 W
San Rafael del Norte, Nic.	156	F4	13.12 N	86.06 W
San Rafael Desert, des., Ut., U.S.	150	E6	38.37 N	110.28 W
San Rafael Hills, hills, Ca., U.S.	198		34.10 N	118.12 W
San Rafael Mountains, mts., Ca., U.S.	148	I6	34.45 N	119.50 W
San Rafael Swell, plat., Ut., U.S.	150	E6	38.56 N	110.47 W
San Ramón, Arg.	172	C5	27.41 S	64.17 W
San Ramón, Bol.	166	B4	13.17 S	64.43 W
San Ramón, Peru	164	F2	11.07 S	75.19 W
San Ramon, Ca., U.S.	200		37.47 N	121.59 W
San Ramon Creek, stm., Ca., U.S.	200		37.54 N	122.03 W
San Ramón de la Nueva Orán, Arg.	166	D4	23.08 S	64.19 W
San Ramon Valley, val., Ca., U.S.	200		37.46 N	121.58 W
San Remo, Italy	30	G4	43.49 N	7.46 E
San Rodrigo, stm., Mex.	136	F6	28.54 N	100.37 W
San Román, Cabo, c., Ven.	168	A7	12.11 N	70.00 W
San Roque, Arg.	172	D8	28.34 S	58.42 W
San Roque, Arg.	172	E3	30.17 S	68.41 W
San Roque, Phil.	187f		14.29 N	120.54 E
San Roque, Punta, c., Mex.	154	B1	27.10 N	114.25 W
San Saba, Tx., U.S.	136	C9	31.11 N	98.43 W
San Saba, stm., Tx., U.S.	136	C9	31.15 N	98.35 W
San Saep, Khlong, can., Thai.	187a		13.45 N	100.36 E
San Salvador, Arg.	172	E8	31.37 S	58.30 W
San Salvador, El Sal.	156	F3	13.40 N	89.13 W
San Salvador, i., Bah.	152	C10	24.02 N	74.27 W
San Salvador, Isla see Santiago, Isla, i., Ec.	164a	i11	0.14 S	90.45 W
San Salvador de Jujuy, Arg.	172	A5	24.11 S	65.17 W
Sansanné-Mango, Togo	84	G5	10.21 N	0.28 E
Sans Bois Creek, stm., Ok., U.S.	134	B3	35.20 N	94.49 W
San Sebastián, P.R.	158a	b1	18.20 N	66.59 W
San Sebastián see Donostia, Spain	6	G8	43.18 N	1.59 W
San Sebastián, Bahía, b., Arg.	166	J3	53.11 S	68.19 W
San Sebastián de los Reyes, Spain	184a		40.33 N	3.38 W
Sansepolcro, Italy	30	G9	43.34 N	12.08 E
San Severo, Italy	30	I12	41.41 N	15.23 E
Sansha, China	58	H9	26.56 N	120.11 E

Name Page Map Ref. Latitude Longitude

Sanshengchang, China 54 B4 44.51 N 120.21 E
San Simon, Az., U.S. 150 K7 32.16 N 109.13 W
San Simon, stm., Az., U.S. 150 K7 32.51 N 109.32 W
San Simon Wash, stm., Az., U.S. 150 K4 31.46 N 112.25 W
San Siro, ngh., Italy 184b 45.29 N 9.07 E
San Siro, Ippodromo di, p.o.i., Italy 184b 45.28 N 9.07 E
Sanski Most, Bos. 36 E3 44.46 N 16.40 E
San Solano, Arg. 172 E4 33.59 S 65.55 W
Sans Souci, Austl. 192a 33.59 S 151.08 E
Sans-Souci, hist., Haiti 156 C12 19.37 N 72.12 W
San Stefano Ticino, Italy 184b 45.29 N 8.55 E
Santa, stm., Peru 164 E2 9.00 S 78.38 W
Santa Adélia, Braz. 170 K1 21.14 S 48.47 W
Santa Amalia, Spain 28 E4 39.01 N 6.01 W
Santa Ana, Arg. 172 C10 27.21 S 55.35 W
Santa Ana, Bol. 166 B3 13.45 S 65.34 W
Santa Ana, Ec. 168 H1 1.13 S 80.22 W
Santa Ana, El Sal. 156 E3 13.59 N 89.34 W
Santa Ana, Mex. 120 F7 30.32 N 111.07 W
Santa Ana, Mex. 154 C8 24.04 N 100.30 W
Santa Ana, Ca., U.S. 148 J8 33.44 N 117.53 W
Santa Ana, Ven. 168 C9 9.18 N 64.39 W
Santa Ana, stm., Cuba 204b 23.04 N 82.32 W
Santa Ana, Cuchilla de (Santana, Coxilha de), hills, S.A. 172 E10 31.15 S 55.15 W
Santa Ana Canyon, val., Ca., U.S. 198 33.53 N 117.43 W
Santa Ana de Chena, Chile 204e 33.34 S 70.47 W
Santa Ana del Alto Beni, Bol. 166 C3 15.30 S 67.29 W
Santa Ana Indian Reservation, ind. res., N.M., U.S. 138 F2 35.28 N 106.37 W
Santa Ana Island, i., Sol. Is. 101b f10 10.50 S 162.28 E
Santa Ana Race Track, p.o.i., Phil. 187f 14.35 N 121.01 E
Santa Ana Tlacotenco, ngh., Mex. 204a 19.10 N 98.59 W
Santa Anita Canyon, val., Ca., U.S. 198 34.12 N 118.01 W
Santa Anita Park, p.o.i., Ca., U.S. 198 34.08 N 118.03 W
Santa Anna, Tx., U.S. 136 C8 31.44 N 99.19 W
Santa Bárbara, Chile 172 H2 37.40 S 72.00 W
Santa Barbara, Col. 168 E4 5.52 N 75.33 W
Santa Bárbara, Hond. 156 E3 14.55 N 88.14 W
Santa Bárbara, Mex. 154 B6 26.49 N 105.47 W
Santa Barbara, Ca., U.S. 148 I6 34.25 N 119.41 W
Santa Bárbara, Ven. 168 D6 7.48 N 71.10 W
Santa Bárbara, Ven. 168 F8 3.56 N 67.03 W
Santa Bárbara, stm., Mex. 136 G2 27.02 N 105.01 W
Santa Bárbara, Morro de, mtn., Braz. 205a 22.57 S 43.28 W
Santa Bárbara, Túnel, trans., Braz. 205a 22.56 S 43.12 W
Santa Barbara Channel, strt., Ca., U.S. 148 I5 34.15 N 119.55 W
Santa Barbara Island, i., Ca., U.S. 148 J7 33.28 N 119.02 W
Santa Catalina, Arg. 166 D3 21.57 S 66.04 W
Santa Catalina, Arroyo, stm., Arg. 206 34.46 S 58.27 W
Santa Catalina, Gulf of, b., Ca., U.S. 148 J7 33.20 N 117.45 W
Santa Catalina, Isla, i., Mex. 154 C3 25.38 N 110.49 W
Santa Catalina, Laguna, l., Arg. 206 34.46 S 58.27 W
Santa Catalina Island, i., Ca., U.S. 148 J7 33.23 N 118.24 W
Santa Catarina, Mex. 148 L10 31.41 N 115.49 W
Santa Catarina, Mex. 154 C8 25.41 N 100.28 W
Santa Catarina, state, Braz. 172 C13 27.00 S 50.00 W
Santa Catarina, Ilha de, i., Braz. 172 C13 27.36 S 48.30 W
Santa Cecília, Braz. 172 C12 26.57 S 50.25 W
Santa Cesarea Terme, Italy 32 D12 40.02 N 18.27 E
Santa Clara, Col. 168 I7 2.43 S 69.42 W
Santa Clara, Cuba 156 A8 22.24 N 79.57 W
Santa Clara, Mex. 154 A5 29.17 N 107.01 W
Santa Clara, Mex. 204a 19.34 N 99.04 W
Santa Clara, Ca., U.S. 148 F3 37.21 N 121.55 W
Santa Clara, Ut., U.S. 150 F3 37.07 N 113.39 W
Santa Clara, stm., Ca., U.S. 148 I7 34.14 N 119.15 W
Santa Clara, stm., Ut., U.S. 150 F3 37.04 N 113.34 W
Santa Clara, University of, educ., Ca., U.S. 200 37.21 N 121.56 W
Santa Clara de Olimar, Ur. 172 F10 32.54 S 54.57 W
Santa Clara Indian Reservation, ind. res., N.M., U.S. 138 F2 35.59 N 106.10 W
Santa Clarita, Peru 204d 12.00 S 77.01 W
Santa Clarita, Ca., U.S. 148 I7 34.23 N 118.33 W
Santa Clotilde, Peru 164 D3 2.32 S 73.43 W
Santa Coloma de Cervelló, Spain 184d 41.22 N 2.01 E
Santa Coloma de Farners, Spain 28 C13 41.52 N 2.40 E
Santa Coloma de Farnés see Santa Coloma de Farners, Spain 28 C13 41.52 N 2.40 E
Santa Coloma de Gramanet, Spain 184d 41.27 N 2.13 E
Santa Comba, Spain 28 A2 43.02 N 8.49 W
Santa Comba Dão, Port. 28 D2 40.24 N 8.07 W
Santa Cruz, Braz. 170 J5 19.58 S 40.09 W
Santa Cruz, Braz. 170 D8 6.13 S 36.01 W
Santa Cruz, Chile 172 G2 34.37 S 71.20 W
Santa Cruz, C.R. 156 G5 10.15 N 85.35 W
Santa Cruz, Mex. 150 L6 31.14 N 110.36 W
Santa Cruz, Phil. 68 D4 13.29 N 122.01 E
Santa Cruz, Phil. 68 C2 15.44 N 119.55 E
Santa Cruz, Phil. 68 C3 14.17 N 121.24 E
Santa Cruz, Ca., U.S. 148 G3 36.58 N 122.01 W
Santa Cruz, Ven. 204c 10.26 N 67.01 W
Santa Cruz, state, Arg. 166 I2 49.00 S 70.00 W
Santa Cruz, ngh., India 190c 19.05 N 72.50 E
Santa Cruz, stm., Arg. 166 J3 50.08 S 68.20 W
Santa Cruz, stm., Cuba 204b 23.04 N 82.29 W
Santa Cruz, stm., N.A. 150 J4 33.15 N 112.11 W
Santa Cruz, Ilha, i., Braz. 205a 22.52 S 43.07 W
Santa Cruz, Isla, i., Ec. 164a i11 0.38 S 90.23 W
Santa Cruz Cabrália, Braz. 170 I6 16.17 S 39.02 W
Santa Cruz de la Palma, Spain 84 D1 28.41 N 17.45 W
Santa Cruz de la Sierra, Bol. 166 C4 17.48 S 63.10 W
Santa Cruz de la Zarza, Spain 28 E7 39.58 N 3.10 W
Santa Cruz del Quiché, Guat. 156 E2 15.02 N 91.08 W
Santa Cruz del Sur, Cuba 156 B9 20.42 N 77.59 W
Santa Cruz de Mudela, Spain 28 F7 38.38 N 3.27 W
Santa Cruz de Tenerife, Spain 84 D1 28.28 N 16.15 W
Santa Cruz do Capibaribe, Braz. 170 D7 7.57 S 36.12 W
Santa Cruz do Piauí, Braz. 170 D5 7.09 S 41.48 W
Santa Cruz do Rio Pardo, Braz. 170 L1 22.55 S 49.37 W
Santa Cruz do Sul, Braz. 172 D11 29.43 S 52.26 W
Santa Cruz International Airport, arpt., India 190c 19.05 N 72.52 E
Santa Cruz Island, i., Ca., U.S. 148 J6 34.01 N 119.45 W
Santa Cruz Islands, is., Sol. Is. 94 E7 11.00 S 166.15 E
Santa Cruz Meyehualco, ngh., Mex. 204a 19.20 N 99.03 W
Sant Adrià de Besòs, Spain 184d 41.25 N 2.14 E
Santa Elena, Arg. 172 E8 30.56 S 59.47 W
Santa Elena, Ec. 168 I1 2.14 S 80.51 W
Santa Elena, Mex. 154 B7 27.28 N 102.31 W
Santa Elena, Bahía de, b., Ec. 168 H1 1.59 S 80.50 W
Santa Elena, Cabo, c., C.R. 156 G4 10.53 N 85.56 W
Santa Elena, Punta, c., Ec. 168 I1 2.11 S 81.00 W
Santa Elena del Gomero, Chile 204e 33.29 S 70.46 W
Santa Elena de Uairén, Ven. 168 E11 4.38 N 61.07 W
Santa Eufemia, Spain 28 F6 38.35 N 4.54 W
Santa Eugenia see Santa Uxía, Spain 28 B1 42.33 N 8.59 W
Santa Eulalia, Spain 28 D9 40.34 N 1.18 W
Santa Eulalia del Río see Santa Eulària del Riu, Spain 28 E12 38.59 N 1.32 E
Santa Eulària del Riu, Spain 28 E12 38.59 N 1.32 E
Santa Fe, Arg. 172 E7 31.37 S 60.42 W
Santa Fe, Spain 28 G7 37.11 N 3.42 W
Santa Fe, N.M., U.S. 138 F3 35.41 N 105.56 W
Santa Fe, state, Arg. 172 D7 31.00 S 61.00 W
Santa Fé, ngh., Cuba 204b 23.05 N 82.31 W
Santa Fe, stm., Fl., U.S. 132 G3 29.53 N 82.53 W
Santa Fe, stm., N.M., U.S. 138 F2 35.36 N 106.20 W
Santa Fé, Aeropuerto, arpt., Cuba 204b 23.04 N 82.28 W
Santa Fé, Ribeirão, stm., Braz. 205b 23.24 S 46.48 W
Santa Fe Baldy, mtn., N.M., U.S. 138 F3 35.50 N 105.46 W
Santa Fe Dam, dam., Ca., U.S. 198 34.07 N 117.58 W
Santa Fe de Bogotá, Col. 168 E5 4.36 N 74.05 W
Santa Fe de Minas, Braz. 170 I3 16.41 S 45.25 W
Santa Fé do Sul, Braz. 166 D6 20.12 S 50.56 W
Santa Fe Flood Control Basin, bas., Ca., U.S. 198 34.07 N 117.58 W
Santa Fe Springs, Ca., U.S. 198 33.56 N 118.04 W
Santa Filomena, Braz. 170 E3 9.07 S 45.54 W
Sant'Agata di Militello, Italy 32 F8 38.04 N 14.38 E
Santa Gertrudis, Mex. 136 H9 26.08 N 98.44 W
Santa Gertrudis, Mex. 136 G2 27.47 N 105.44 W
Santa Helena, Braz. 170 B3 2.13 S 45.17 W
Santa Helena de Goiás, Braz. 166 C6 17.43 S 50.35 W
Santai, China 58 F1 31.08 N 105.00 E
Santa Inês, Braz. 170 G6 13.17 S 39.49 W
Santa Inés, Bahía, b., Mex. 154 B3 26.59 N 111.58 W
Santa Inés, Isla, i., Chile 166 J2 53.46 S 72.44 W
Santa Iria de Azóia, Port. 184c 38.51 N 9.05 W
Santa Isabel, Arg. 172 H4 36.14 S 66.56 W
Santa Isabel see Malabo, Eq. Gui. 84 I6 3.44 N 8.46 E
Santa Isabel, P.R. 158a c3 17.57 N 66.23 W
Santa Isabel, i., Sol. Is. 101b e8 8.00 S 159.00 E
Santa Isabel, stm., Mex. 136 F1 28.02 N 106.07 W
Santa Isabel, Pico de, mtn., Eq. Gui. 84 I6 3.35 N 8.46 E
Santa Isabel Creek, stm., Tx., U.S. 136 G8 27.38 N 99.37 W
Santa Isabel do Araguaia, Braz. 170 C1 6.05 S 48.19 W
Santa Julia, Chile 204e 33.30 S 70.38 W
Santa Juliana, Braz. 170 J2 19.19 S 47.32 W
Santal, Baie du, b., N. Cal. 101d m16 20.50 S 167.03 E
Sāntalpur, India 62 G3 23.45 N 71.09 E
Santa Lucía, Arg. 172 D8 28.59 S 59.06 W
Santa Lucía, Ur. 172 G9 34.28 S 56.23 W
Santa Lucía, Ven. 168 C7 8.07 N 69.46 W
Santa Lucia Range, mts., Ca., U.S. 148 H4 36.00 N 121.20 W
Santaluz, Braz. 170 F6 11.14 S 39.21 W
Santa Luzia, Braz. 170 D7 6.53 S 36.56 W
Santa Luzia, Port. 28 G2 37.44 N 8.24 W
Santa Magdalena, Arg. 172 G6 34.31 S 63.56 W
Santa Magdalena, Isla, i., Mex. 154 C2 24.53 N 112.12 W
Santa Margarita, Ca., U.S. 148 H5 35.23 N 120.36 W
Santa Margarita, Isla, i., Mex. 154 C3 24.27 N 111.50 W
Santa Margherita Ligure, Italy 30 F6 44.19 N 9.12 E
Santa María, Arg. 172 C4 26.38 S 66.01 W
Santa Maria, Braz. 172 D10 29.40 S 53.48 W
Santa María, Mex. 136 F6 27.58 N 101.25 W
Santa María, P.R. 158a b5 18.09 N 65.25 W
Santa Maria, Ca., U.S. 148 I5 34.57 N 120.26 W
Santa Maria, i., Vanuatu 101d j16 14.14 S 167.27 E
Santa Maria, stm., Braz. 172 E10 29.48 S 54.55 W
Santa María, stm., Mex. 154 F9 31.02 N 107.14 W
Santa María, stm., Mex. 154 E8 21.47 N 99.10 W
Santa Maria, stm., Az., U.S. 150 I3 34.19 N 113.31 W
Santa María, Bahía, b., Mex. 154 C4 25.04 N 108.06 W
Santa María, Cabo, c., Ur. 172 G10 34.40 S 54.08 W
Santa Maria, Cabo de, c., Ang. 88 C1 13.24 S 12.32 E
Santa Maria, Cabo de, c., Moz. 86 G2 26.05 S 32.57 E
Santa Maria, Cabo de, c., Port. 28 H3 36.57 N 7.54 W
Santa María, Cerro, mtn., Peru 204d 11.56 S 76.57 W
Santa María, Isla, i., Chile 172 H1 37.02 S 73.31 W
Santa María, Isla, i., Ec. 164a i11 1.17 S 90.26 W
Santa María, Laguna de, l., Mex. 120 F9 31.08 N 107.17 W
Santa María Asunción Tlaxiaco, Mex. 154 G10 17.16 N 97.41 W
Santa Maria Capua Vetere, Italy 32 C8 41.05 N 14.15 E
Santa María Colotepec, Mex. 154 H10 15.52 N 96.55 W
Santa Maria da Boa Vista, Braz. 170 E6 8.49 S 39.49 W
Santa Maria da Vitória, Braz. 170 G3 13.23 S 44.11 W
Santa María de Ipire, Ven. 168 C9 8.48 N 65.19 W
Santa Maria de Itabira, Braz. 170 J4 19.26 S 43.06 W
Santa Maria delle Grazie, rel., Italy 184b 45.27 N 9.10 E
Santa María del Oro, Mex. 154 C6 25.56 N 105.22 W
Santa María del Río, Mex. 154 E8 21.48 N 100.44 W
Santa Mariá de Mohovano, Mex. 154 B7 26.42 N 103.37 W
Santa Maria di Galeria, ngh., Italy 185a 42.01 N 12.19 E
Santa Maria di Leuca, Capo, c., Italy 32 E12 39.47 N 18.21 E
Santa Maria do Suaçuí, Braz. 170 J4 18.11 S 42.25 W
Santa María la Real de Nieva, Spain 28 C6 41.04 N 4.24 W
Santa Maria Madalena, Braz. 170 K5 21.57 S 42.00 W
Santa Maria Maggiore, rel., Italy 185a 41.53 N 12.30 E
Santa María Tulpetlac, Mex. 204a 19.34 N 99.03 W
Santa Marinella, Italy 30 H8 42.02 N 11.51 E
Santa Marta, Col. 168 B4 11.14 N 74.11 W
Santa Marta, Cabo de, c., Ang. 88 C1 13.52 S 12.25 E
Santa Marta, Cerro, mtn., Mex. 154 F11 18.19 N 94.52 W
Santa Marta, Ciénaga Grande, b., Col. 168 B4 10.50 N 74.25 W
Santa Marta Grande, Cabo de, c., Braz. 172 D13 28.33 S 48.47 W
Santa Mónica, Mex. 136 F7 28.10 N 100.40 W
Santa Monica, Ca., U.S. 148 I7 34.00 N 118.28 W
Santa Mónica, ngh., Ven. 204c 10.29 N 66.53 W
Santa Monica Bay, b., Ca., U.S. 148 J7 33.56 N 118.33 W
Santa Monica Beach State Park, p.o.i., Ca., U.S. 198 34.01 N 118.30 W
Santa Monica Municipal Airport, arpt., Ca., U.S. 198 34.01 N 118.27 W
Santan, Indon. 66 D10 0.04 S 117.28 E
Santana, Braz. 170 G3 12.58 S 44.03 W
Sântana, Rom. 36 C8 46.20 N 21.30 E
Santana, ngh., Braz. 205b 23.29 S 46.38 W
Santana, Coxilha de (Santa Ana, Cuchilla de), hills, S.A. 172 E10 31.15 S 55.15 W
Santana, Ilha de, i., Braz. 170 B4 2.46 S 42.08 W
Santana da Boa Vista, Braz. 172 E11 30.52 S 53.06 W
Santana de Parnaíba, mun., Braz. 205b 23.27 S 46.54 W
Santana do Ipanema, Braz. 170 E7 9.22 S 37.14 W
Santana do Livramento, Braz. 172 E10 30.52 S 55.30 W
Santander, Col. 168 F3 3.02 N 76.28 W
Santander, Phil. 68 F4 9.25 N 123.19 E
Santander, Spain 28 A7 43.28 N 3.48 W
Santander, state, Col. 168 D5 7.00 N 73.15 W
Santander see Cantabria, state, Spain 28 A6 43.15 N 4.00 W
Santander Jiménez, Mex. 154 C9 24.13 N 98.28 W
Sant'Andrea, Isola, i., Italy 32 D11 40.02 N 17.56 E
Sant Andreu de la Barca, Spain 184d 41.27 N 1.59 E
Sant'Angelo, Castel, hist., Italy 185a 41.55 N 12.28 E
Sant'Angelo, Monte, mtn., Italy 185a 41.56 N 12.49 E
Sant'Angelo Romano, Italy 185a 42.02 N 12.42 E
Santanghu, China 52 C3 44.15 N 93.21 E
Santanilla, Islas, is., Hond. 156 D6 17.25 N 83.55 W
Sant'Antine, Nuraghe, hist., Italy 32 D2 40.29 N 8.46 E
Sant'Antioco, Italy 32 E2 39.04 N 8.27 E
Sant'Antioco, Isola di, i., Italy 32 E2 39.02 N 8.25 E
Sant Antoni de Portmany, Spain 28 F12 38.58 N 1.18 E
Santañy see Santanyí, Spain 28 E14 39.21 N 3.07 E
Santanyí, Spain 28 E14 39.21 N 3.07 E
Santa Paula, Ca., U.S. 148 I6 34.21 N 119.03 W
Santa Perpètua de Mogoda, Spain 184d 41.32 N 2.11 E
Santapogue Creek, stm., N.Y., U.S. 194 40.40 N 73.21 W
Santa Pola, Cap de, c., Spain 28 F10 38.12 N 0.31 W
Sant'Apollinare in Classe, rel., Italy 30 F9 44.22 N 12.15 E
Santaquin, Ut., U.S. 150 D5 39.58 N 111.47 W
Santa Quitéria, Braz. 170 C5 4.20 S 40.10 W
Santa Quitéria do Maranhão, Braz. 170 B4 3.31 S 42.32 W
Sant'Arcangelo, Italy 32 D10 40.15 N 16.16 E
Santarcangelo di Romagna, Italy 30 F9 44.04 N 12.26 E
Santarém, Braz. 164 D7 2.26 S 54.42 W
Santarém, Port. 28 E2 39.13 N 8.40 W
Santarém, state, Port. 28 E2 39.15 N 8.30 W
Santarém, state, Port. 184c 38.50 N 8.56 W
Santaren Channel, strt., Bah. 152 C9 24.00 N 79.30 W
Santa Rita, Braz. 170 D8 7.08 S 34.58 W
Santa Rita, Braz. 205a 22.41 S 43.28 W
Santa Rita, Col. 168 G5 0.33 N 73.43 W
Santa Rita, Hond. 156 E4 15.10 N 87.53 W
Santa Rita, Mex. 136 G7 27.29 N 100.32 W
Santa Rita, Mex. 154 A3 28.34 N 111.42 W
Santa Rita, Mt., U.S. 146 B14 48.42 N 112.19 W
Santa Rita, Ven. 158g p20 12.02 N 69.51 W
Santa Rita, Ven. 168 B6 10.33 N 71.30 W
Santa Rosa, Arg. 172 H5 36.37 S 64.16 W
Santa Rosa, Braz. 170 H2 15.04 S 47.11 W
Santa Rosa, Braz. 172 C10 27.52 S 54.26 W
Santa Rosa, Col. 168 F7 2.31 N 68.12 W
Santa Rosa, Ec. 164 D2 3.27 S 79.58 W
Santa Rosa, Para. 172 C9 26.53 S 56.50 W
Santa Rosa, Ca., U.S. 148 E3 38.25 N 122.43 W
Santa Rosa, N.M., U.S. 138 G4 34.56 N 104.40 W
Santa Rosa, Tx., U.S. 136 H10 26.15 N 97.49 W
Santa Rosa, Ven. 168 C7 8.24 N 69.38 W
Santa Rosa, Ven. 168 D7 7.03 N 68.28 W
Santa Rosa, Ven. 204c 10.30 N 66.46 W
Santa Rosa, Mount, hill, Guam 100c i10 13.32 N 144.54 E
Santa Rosa Beach, Fl., U.S. 134 G12 30.22 N 86.13 W
Santa Rosa de Amanadona, Ven. 168 G8 1.29 N 66.55 W
Santa Rosa de Copán, Hond. 156 E3 14.45 N 88.46 W
Santa Rosa de Huechuraba, Chile 204e 33.21 S 70.41 W
Santa Rosa del Conlara, Arg. 172 F5 32.20 S 65.11 W
Santa Rosa de Leales, Arg. 172 C5 27.09 S 65.15 W
Santa Rosa de Locobe, Chile 204e 33.26 S 70.33 W
Santa Rosa de Osos, Col. 168 D4 6.39 N 75.28 W
Santa Rosa de Río Primero, Arg. 172 E6 31.09 S 63.24 W
Santa Rosa de Sucumbíos, Ec. 168 G3 0.21 N 77.08 W
Santa Rosa de Viterbo, Col. 168 E5 5.53 N 73.00 W
Santa Rosa Island, i., Ca., U.S. 148 J5 33.58 N 120.06 W
Santa Rosa Island, i., Fl., U.S. 134 G12 30.22 N 86.55 W
Santa Rosalía, Mex. 136 H9 26.05 N 98.57 W
Santa Rosalía, Mex. 154 B2 27.20 N 112.17 W
Santa Rosalía, Ven. 168 C7 9.01 N 69.01 W
Santa Rosa Range, mts., Nv., U.S. 148 B8 41.35 N 117.40 W
Santa Rosa Wash, stm., Az., U.S. 150 K5 33.04 N 112.01 W
Santa Rosita, Peru 204d 12.03 S 76.59 W
Šantarskie ostrova, is., Russia 50 E16 54.53 N 137.33 E
Santa Sylvina, Arg. 172 C7 27.50 S 61.08 W
Santa Teresa, Braz. 170 J5 19.55 S 40.36 W
Santa Teresa, Braz. 170 G1 13.38 S 49.01 W
Santa Teresa, Mex. 136 E3 29.34 N 104.39 W
Santa Teresa, Mex. 154 C9 25.16 N 97.52 W
Santa Teresa, stm., Braz. 170 G1 11.47 S 48.37 W
Santa Teresa, Embalse de, res., Spain 28 D5 40.37 N 5.33 W
Santa Teresa, Fortaleza de, hist., Ur. 172 F11 33.59 S 53.32 W
Santa Teresa de lo Ovalle, Chile 204e 33.23 S 70.47 W
Santa Teresa Gallura, Italy 32 C3 41.14 N 9.11 E
Santa Uxía, Spain 28 B1 42.33 N 8.59 W
Santa Vitória do Palmar, Braz. 172 F11 33.31 S 53.21 W
Santa Ynez, stm., Ca., U.S. 148 I5 34.41 N 120.36 W
Santa Ynez Canyon, val., Ca., U.S. 198 34.04 N 118.34 W
Santa Ynez Mountains, mts., Ca., U.S. 148 I6 34.32 N 119.59 W
Sant Bartomeu de la Quadra, Spain 184d 41.26 N 2.02 E
Sant Boi de Llobregat, Spain 184d 41.21 N 2.03 E
Sant Climent de Llobregat, Spain 184d 41.20 N 2.00 E
Sant Cugat del Vallès, Spain 184d 41.28 N 2.05 E
Santee, Ca., U.S. 148 K8 32.50 N 116.57 W
Santee, stm., S.C., U.S. 132 C6 33.14 N 79.27 W
Santee Dam, dam., S.C., U.S. 132 C5 33.27 N 80.09 W
Santee Indian Reservation, ind. res., Ne., U.S. 140 E15 42.45 N 97.50 W
Santeny, Fr. 179 48.43 N 2.34 E
Santerno, stm., Italy 30 F8 44.34 N 11.57 E
Sant'Eufemia, Golfo di, b., Italy 32 F9 38.49 N 16.06 E
Sant Feliu de Guíxols, Spain 28 C14 41.47 N 3.01 E
Sant Feliu de Llobregat, Spain 184d 41.23 N 2.03 E
Sant Fost de Campsentelles, Spain 184d 41.31 N 2.14 E
Santhià, Italy 30 E5 45.22 N 8.09 E
Santiago, Braz. 172 D10 29.11 S 54.52 W
Santiago, Chile 172 F2 33.27 S 70.40 W
Santiago, Chile 204e 33.27 S 70.40 W
Santiago, Mex. 154 D4 23.28 N 109.43 W
Santiago, Pan. 156 H7 8.06 N 80.58 W
Santiago, Para. 172 C9 27.09 S 56.47 W
Santiago, i., C.V. 85a I10 15.02 N 23.38 W
Santiago, stm., Arg. 206 34.50 S 57.57 W
Santiago, stm., Mex. 154 C6 25.10 N 105.26 W
Santiago, stm., S.A. 164 D2 4.26 S 77.38 W
Santiago, Cerro, mtn., Pan. 156 H7 8.33 N 81.44 W
Santiago, Isla, i., Arg. 206 34.50 S 57.53 W
Santiago, Isla, i., Ec. 164a i11 0.14 S 90.45 W
Santiago, Serranía de, mts., Bol. 166 C5 18.14 S 59.45 W
Santiago Dam, dam., Ca., U.S. 198 33.47 N 117.43 W
Santiago de Compostela, Spain 28 B2 42.52 N 8.32 W
Santiago de Cuba, Cuba 156 C10 20.01 N 75.49 W
Santiago de las Vegas, ngh., Cuba 204b 22.58 N 82.23 W
Santiago del Estero, Arg. 172 C5 27.47 S 64.16 W
Santiago del Estero, state, Arg. 172 C6 28.00 S 63.30 W
Santiago de los Caballeros, Dom. Rep. 156 C12 19.27 N 70.42 W
Santiago de Méndez, Ec. 168 I2 2.43 S 78.19 W
Santiago de Surco, Peru 204d 12.09 S 77.01 W
Santiago do Cacém, Port. 28 F2 38.00 N 8.41 W
Santiago Island, i., Phil. 68 B2 16.24 N 119.56 E
Santiago Ixcuintla, Mex. 154 E6 21.49 N 105.11 W
Santiago Jamiltepec, Mex. 154 G10 16.17 N 97.50 W
Santiago Larre, Arg. 172 G8 35.35 S 59.10 W
Santiago Papasquiaro, Mex. 154 C6 25.02 N 105.25 W
Santiago Peak, mtn., Ca., U.S. 148 J8 33.42 N 117.32 W
Santiago Peak, mtn., Tx., U.S. 136 E4 29.47 N 103.25 W
Santiago Tepalcatlapan, ngh., Mex. 204a 19.15 N 99.08 W
Santiaguillo, Laguna, l., Mex. 154 C6 24.45 N 104.48 W
Santiam Pass, p., Or., U.S. 146 F5 44.25 N 121.51 W
San Timoteo, Ven. 168 C6 9.47 N 71.03 W
Säntis, mtn., Switz. 30 C6 47.15 N 9.21 E
Santíssimo, ngh., Braz. 205a 22.53 S 43.31 W
Santisteban del Puerto, Spain 28 F7 38.15 N 3.12 W
Sant Joan de Labritja, Spain 28 E12 39.05 N 1.30 E
Sant Joan Despí, Spain 184d 41.22 N 2.04 E
Sant Jordi, Golf de, b., Spain 28 D11 40.54 N 0.56 E
Sant Just Desvern, Spain 184d 41.23 N 2.05 E
Sant Mateu del Maestrat, Spain 28 D11 40.28 N 0.10 E
Santo, Tx., U.S. 136 B9 32.36 N 98.13 W
Santo Amaro, Braz. 170 B4 2.33 S 43.14 W
Santo Amaro, Braz. 170 G6 12.32 S 38.42 W
Santo Amaro, ngh., Braz. 205b 23.39 S 46.42 W
Santo Amaro da Imperatriz, Braz. 172 C13 27.41 S 48.46 W
Santo André, Braz. 170 L2 23.39 S 46.31 W
Santo André, mun., Braz. 205b 23.45 S 46.29 W
Santo Ângelo, Braz. 172 D10 28.16 S 54.15 W
Santo Antão, i., C.V. 85a k10 17.03 N 25.07 W
Santo Antônio, Braz. 170 D8 6.18 S 35.27 W
Santo António, S. Tom./P. 84 I6 1.39 N 7.26 E
Santo Antônio, stm., Braz. 170 F1 11.31 S 48.37 W
Santo Antônio, stm., Braz. 170 I3 17.30 S 45.37 W
Santo Antônio, stm., Braz. 205a 22.42 S 43.37 W
Santo António, Ilha de see Benguerua, Ilha, i., Moz. 90 B12 21.53 S 35.26 E
Santo António da Charneca, Port. 184c 38.37 N 9.02 W
Santo Antônio da Patrulha, Braz. 172 D12 29.49 S 50.31 W
Santo Antônio de Jesus, Braz. 170 G6 12.57 S 39.14 W
Santo Antônio de Pádua, Braz. 170 K4 21.32 S 42.10 W
Santo Antônio do Amparo, Braz. 170 K3 20.57 S 44.54 W
Santo Antônio do Içá, Braz. 164 D4 3.04 S 67.56 W
Santo Antônio do Rio Verde, Braz. 170 I2 17.57 S 47.27 W
Santo Augusto, Braz. 172 C11 27.49 S 53.46 W
Santo Domingo, Cuba 152 C8 22.35 N 80.14 W
Santo Domingo, Dom. Rep. 156 C13 18.29 N 69.53 W
Santo Domingo, Mex. 136 I3 25.47 N 104.28 W
Santo Domingo, Mex. 154 C2 25.30 N 111.56 W
Santo Domingo, Mex. 154 D8 23.20 N 101.44 W
Santo Domingo, Nic. 156 F5 12.16 N 85.05 W
Santo Domingo, Ven. 168 D5 7.35 N 72.04 W
Santo Domingo see Hispaniola, i., N.A. 152 D10 19.00 N 71.00 W
Santo Domingo de la Calzada, Spain 28 B8 42.26 N 2.57 W
Santo Domingo de los Colorados, Ec. 168 H2 0.14 S 79.09 W
Santo Domingo Indian Reservation, ind. res., N.M., U.S. 138 F2 35.34 N 106.26 W
Santo Domingo Pueblo, N.M., U.S. 138 F2 35.30 N 106.21 W
Santo Domingo Tehuantepec, Mex. 154 G11 16.18 N 95.14 W
Santo Domingo Zanatepec, Mex. 154 G11 16.27 N 94.22 W
Santo Estêvão, Braz. 170 G6 12.26 S 39.14 W
Santolea, Embalse de, res., Spain 28 D10 40.45 N 0.19 W
San Tomé, Ven. 168 C9 8.56 N 64.07 W
Sant' Onofrio, ngh., Italy 185a 41.56 N 12.25 E
Santo Onofre, stm., Braz. 170 G4 12.34 S 43.12 W
Santop, Pic, mtn., Vanuatu 101d I17 18.39 S 169.03 E
Santorini see Thíra, i., Grc. 34 G8 36.25 N 25.26 E
Santos, Braz. 170 L2 23.56 S 46.19 W
Santos Dumont, Braz. 170 K4 21.28 S 43.33 W
Santoshpur, India 190b 22.40 N 88.10 E
Santo Tirso, Port. 28 C2 41.20 N 8.28 W
Santo Tomás, Mex. 120 F4 31.33 N 116.23 W
Santo Tomás, Nic. 156 F5 12.03 N 85.06 W
Santo Tomás, Peru 164 F3 14.27 S 72.05 W
Santo Tomás, stm., Mex. 148 L9 31.31 N 116.39 W
Santo Tomás, Punta, c., Mex. 120 F4 31.33 N 116.40 W
Santo Tomas, University of, educ., Phil. 187f 14.37 N 120.59 E
Santo Tomé, Arg. 172 D9 28.33 S 56.02 W
Santo Tomé, Arg. 172 E7 31.40 S 60.46 W
Santo Tomé de Guayana see Ciudad Guayana, Ven. 168 C10 8.21 N 62.39 W
Sant Quirze de la Serra, Spain 184d 41.32 N 2.05 E
Santu Lussurgiu, Italy 32 D2 40.07 N 8.38 E
Sant Vicenç dels Horts, Spain 184d 41.24 N 2.01 E
Sanuki, Japan 186 35.16 N 139.53 E
Sanuki-sammyaku, mts., Japan 56 E7 34.09 N 134.11 E
San Vicente, state, Arg. 206 34.56 S 58.24 W
San Vicente Creek, stm., Ca., U.S. 200 37.32 N 122.31 W
San Vicente de Alcántara, Spain 28 E3 39.21 N 7.07 W
San Vicente de Baracaldo see Barakaldo, Spain 28 A8 43.18 N 2.59 W
San Vicente de la Barquera, Spain 28 A6 43.22 N 4.28 W
San Vicente del Caguán, Col. 168 F4 2.06 N 74.46 W
San Vicente Mountain, mtn., Ca., U.S. 198 34.08 N 118.31 W
San Vincente, Arg. 172 D5 28.27 S 64.08 W
San Vincenzo, Italy 30 G7 43.05 N 10.32 E
San Vito, Italy 32 E3 39.27 N 9.32 E
San Vito, Capo, c., Italy 32 F6 38.11 N 12.43 E
San Xavier Indian Reservation, ind. res., Az., U.S. 150 K5 32.02 N 111.07 W
Sanya, China 58 L3 18.14 N 109.30 E
Sanyati, stm., Zimb. 88 D4 16.49 S 28.45 E
San Ygnacio, Tx., U.S. 136 G8 27.02 N 99.24 W
Sanyō, Japan 56 E4 34.03 N 131.10 E
Sanyuan, China 58 D3 34.36 N 108.55 E
Sanzao Dao, i., China 58 K5 22.03 N 113.21 E
Sanza Pombo, Ang. 88 B2 7.19 S 15.59 E
São Benedito, Braz. 170 C5 4.03 S 40.53 W
São Benedito do Rio Preto, Braz. 170 B4 3.20 S 43.35 W
São Bento, Braz. 170 B3 2.42 S 44.50 W
São Bento, Mosteiro de, rel., Braz. 205a 22.54 S 43.11 W
São Bento do Norte, Braz. 170 C7 5.04 S 36.02 W
São Bento do Sul, Braz. 172 C13 26.15 S 49.22 W
São Bento do Una, Braz. 170 E7 8.32 S 36.22 W
São Bernardino, Braz. 205a 22.40 S 43.26 W
São Bernardo, Braz. 170 B4 3.24 S 42.26 W
São Bernardo do Campo, mun., Braz. 205b 23.44 S 46.33 W
São Borja, Braz. 172 D10 28.38 S 56.00 W
São Caetano do Sul, Braz. 170 L2 23.36 S 46.34 W
São Caetano do Sul, mun., Braz. 205b 23.37 S 46.33 W
São Carlos, Braz. 170 L2 22.01 S 47.53 W
São Cristóvão, Braz. 170 F7 11.01 S 37.12 W
São Cristóvão, ngh., Braz. 205a 22.54 S 43.14 W
São Domingos, Braz. 170 G2 13.24 S 46.20 W
São Domingos, Braz. 172 C11 26.35 S 52.28 W
São Domingos, Gui.-B. 84 G1 12.24 N 16.12 W
São Domingos do Capim, Braz. 170 A2 1.41 S 47.47 W
São Domingos do Maranhão, Braz. 170 C3 5.42 S 44.22 W
São Felipe, Braz. 170 H5 14.53 S 41.28 W
São Félix de Balsas, Braz. 170 D3 7.08 S 44.52 W
São Félix do Piauí, Braz. 170 C4 5.56 S 42.07 W
São Francisco, Braz. 170 H3 15.57 S 44.51 W
São Francisco, stm., Braz. 170 E6 10.30 S 36.24 W

Name | Page | Map Ref. | Latitude | Longitude

São Francisco, stm., Braz. 170 H5 16.09 S 40.39 W
São Francisco, stm., Braz. 205a 22.57 S 43.20 W
São Francisco, Baía de, b., Braz. 172 C13 26.15 S 48.44 W
São Francisco, Ilha de, i., Braz. 172 C13 26.18 S 48.37 W
São Francisco de Assis, Braz. 172 D10 29.33 S 55.07 W
São Francisco de Goiás, Braz. 170 H1 15.54 S 49.15 W
São Francisco de Paula, Braz. 172 D12 29.26 S 50.34 W
São Francisco do Croará, Braz. 205a 22.42 S 43.08 W
São Francisco do Maranhão, Braz. 170 D4 6.15 S 42.52 W
São Francisco do Piauí, Braz. 170 D4 7.15 S 42.32 W
São Francisco do Sul, Braz. 172 C13 26.15 S 48.37 W
São Gabriel, Braz. 170 F5 11.14 S 41.52 W
São Gabriel, Braz. 172 E10 30.20 S 54.19 W
São Gabriel da Palha, Braz. 170 J5 18.57 S 40.31 W
São Gabriel de Goiás, Braz. 170 H2 15.11 S 47.34 W
São Gonçalo, mun., Braz. 205a 22.48 S 43.01 W
São Gonçalo do Abaeté, Braz. 170 J3 18.20 S 45.49 W
São Gonçalo do Sapucaí, Braz. 170 K3 21.55 S 45.34 W
São Gonçalo dos Campos, Braz. 170 G6 12.25 S 38.56 W
Sao Hill, Tan. 86 F7 8.15 S 35.14 E
São Jerônimo, Braz. 172 E12 29.58 S 51.43 W
São Jerônimo, Serra de, plat., Braz. 166 C6 16.29 S 54.55 W
São Jerônimo da Serra, Braz. 172 A12 23.43 S 50.44 W
São João da Aliança, Braz. 170 H2 14.44 S 47.31 W
São João da Barra, Braz. 170 K5 21.37 S 41.01 W
São João da Boa Vista, Braz. 170 L2 21.58 S 46.47 W
São João da Ponte, Braz. 170 H3 15.56 S 44.01 W
São João das Lampas, Port. 184c 38.52 N 9.24 W
São João de Cortês, Braz. 170 B3 2.12 S 44.32 W
São João Del Rei, Braz. 170 K3 21.07 S 44.14 W
São João de Meriti, mun., Braz. 205a 22.48 S 43.21 W
São João de Meriti, stm., Braz. 205a 22.48 S 43.18 W
São João do Araguaia, Braz. 170 C1 5.20 S 48.47 W
São João do Jaguaribe, Braz. 170 C6 5.16 S 38.16 W
São João do Paraíso, Braz. 170 H5 15.19 S 42.01 W
São João do Piauí, Braz. 170 E4 8.21 S 42.15 W
São João dos Patos, Braz. 170 D4 6.30 S 43.42 W
São João Evangelista, Braz. 170 J4 18.33 S 42.46 W
São Joaquim, Braz. 172 D12 28.18 S 49.56 W
São Joaquim, Parque Nacional de, p.o.i., Braz. 172 D12 28.14 S 49.33 W
São Joaquim da Barra, Braz. 170 K1 20.34 S 47.52 W
São Jorge, Castelo de, hist., Port. 184c 38.43 N 9.08 W
São José, Braz. 172 C13 27.38 S 48.39 W
São José, stm., Braz. 170 J5 19.10 S 40.12 W
São José, stm., Braz. 205a 22.39 S 43.27 W
São José da Laje, Braz. 170 E7 9.01 S 36.03 W
São José das Piranhas, Braz. 170 D6 7.07 S 38.30 W
São José de Anauá, Braz. 168 G11 0.59 N 61.24 W
São José do Belmonte, Braz. 170 D6 7.52 S 38.46 W
São José do Cedro, Braz. 172 C11 26.30 S 53.30 W
São José do Egito, Braz. 170 D7 7.28 S 37.16 W
São José do Gurupi, Braz. 170 A2 1.35 S 46.12 W
São José do Mipibu, Braz. 170 D8 6.05 S 35.15 W
São José do Norte, Braz. 172 E12 31.59 S 52.02 W
São José do Peixe, Braz. 170 D4 7.24 S 42.34 W
São José do Rio Preto, Braz. 170 K1 20.49 S 49.23 W
São José dos Campos, Braz. 170 L3 23.11 S 45.52 W
São José dos Pinhais, Braz. 172 B13 25.31 S 49.13 W
São Julião da Barra, Port. 184c 38.40 N 9.21 W
São Julião do Tojal, Port. 184c 38.51 N 9.08 W
São Leopoldo, Braz. 172 D12 29.46 S 51.08 W
São Lourenço, Braz. 170 L3 22.07 S 45.03 W
São Lourenço, Pantanal de, sw., Braz. 166 C5 17.30 S 56.30 W
São Lourenço do Sul, Braz. 172 E12 31.22 S 51.58 W
São Luís, Braz. 170 B3 2.31 S 44.16 W
São Luís do Curu, Braz. 170 B6 3.40 S 39.14 W
São Luís do Quitunde, Braz. 170 E8 9.20 S 35.33 W
São Luís Gonzaga, Braz. 172 D10 28.24 S 54.56 W
São Mamede, Braz. 170 D7 6.56 S 37.06 W
São Manuel, Braz. 170 L1 22.43 S 48.33 W
São Manuel, stm., Braz. 164 E6 7.21 S 58.08 W
São Marcos, stm., Braz. 170 I2 18.15 S 47.37 W
São Marcos, Baía de, b., Braz. 170 B3 2.30 S 44.17 W
São Mateus, Braz. 170 J6 18.43 S 39.51 W
São Mateus, Braço Norte, stm., Braz. 170 J5 18.35 S 39.44 W
São Mateus do Sul, Braz. 172 B12 25.51 S 50.23 W
São Miguel, Braz. 170 D6 6.13 S 38.30 W
São Miguel, i., Port. 80 C3 37.47 N 25.30 W
São Miguel, stm., Braz. 170 I5 16.26 S 41.00 W
São Miguel do Araguaia, Braz. 166 B6 13.19 S 50.13 W
São Miguel d'Oeste, Braz. 172 C11 26.43 S 53.30 W
São Miguel do Guamá, Braz. 170 A2 1.36 S 47.27 W
São Miguel dos Campos, Braz. 170 E7 9.47 S 36.05 W
São Miguel dos Macacos, Braz. 164 D7 1.09 S 50.29 W
São Miguel do Tapuio, Braz. 170 C5 5.30 S 41.20 W
Saona, Isla, i., Dom. Rep. 156 C13 18.09 N 68.40 W
Saône, stm., Fr. 22 C10 45.43 N 4.49 E
Saône-et-Loire, state, Fr. 22 C10 46.42 N 4.45 E
Saonek, Indon. 101a a1 0.24 S 130.53 E
Saoner, India 70 H7 21.23 N 78.55 E
São Nicolau, i., C.V. 85a k10 16.35 N 24.10 W
São Nicolau, stm., Braz. 170 C5 5.44 S 42.05 W
São Paulo, Braz. 170 L2 23.32 S 46.37 W
São Paulo, Braz. 205b 23.32 S 46.37 W
São Paulo, state, Braz. 166 D7 22.00 S 49.00 W
São Paulo, mun., Braz. 205b 23.33 S 46.38 W
São Paulo de Olivença, Braz. 164 D4 3.27 S 68.56 W
São Paulo do Potengi, Braz. 170 C8 5.55 S 35.45 W
São Pedro, stm., Braz. 170 I5 16.30 S 41.17 W
São Pedro do Estoril, Port. 184c 38.42 N 9.22 W
São Pedro do Piauí, Braz. 170 C4 5.56 S 42.43 W
São Pedro do Sul, Braz. 172 D10 29.36 S 54.10 W
São Pedro do Sul, Port. 28 D3 40.45 N 8.04 W
São Raimundo das Mangabeiras, Braz. 170 D3 7.01 S 45.29 W
São Raimundo Nonato, Braz. 170 E4 9.01 S 42.42 W
São Romão, Braz. 170 I3 16.22 S 45.04 W
São Roque, Braz. 170 L2 23.32 S 47.08 W
São Roque, Cabo de, c., Braz. 170 C8 5.29 S 35.16 W
São Salvador see Salvador, Braz. 170 G6 12.59 S 38.30 W
São Sebastião, Braz. 170 L3 23.48 S 45.24 W
São Sebastião, Ilha de, i., Braz. 170 L3 23.51 S 45.20 W
São Sebastião, Ponta, c., Moz. 90 C12 22.07 S 35.28 E
São Sebastião do Maranhão, Braz. 170 I4 18.05 S 42.35 W
São Sebastião do Paraíso, Braz. 170 K2 20.55 S 46.59 W
São Sepé, Braz. 172 E11 30.09 S 53.34 W
São Simão, Braz. 170 K2 21.28 S 47.33 W
São Simão, Represa de, res., Braz. 166 C7 18.36 S 49.58 W
São Timóteo, Braz. 170 G4 13.50 S 42.09 W
São Tomé, Braz. 170 C7 5.58 S 36.04 W
São Tomé, S. Tom./P. 84 I6 0.20 N 6.44 E
São Tomé, i., S. Tom./P. 84 I6 0.11 N 6.36 E
São Tomé, Cabo de, c., Braz. 170 L5 21.59 S 40.59 W
São Tomé, Pico de, mtn., S. Tom./P. 84 I6 0.16 N 6.33 E
Sao Tome and Principe, ctry., Afr. 84 I6 1.00 N 7.00 E
São Tomé e Príncipe see Sao Tome and Principe, ctry., Afr. 84 I6 1.00 N 7.00 E
Saoura, Oued, stm., Alg. 84 D4 29.00 N 0.56 W
São Valério, stm., Braz. 170 F1 11.20 S 48.28 W
São Vicente, Braz. 170 M3 23.57 S 46.22 W
São Vicente, i., C.V. 85a k9 16.48 N 24.55 W
São Vicente, Cabo de, c., Port. 28 G1 37.01 N 8.59 W
São Vicente de Minas, Braz. 170 K3 21.41 S 44.26 W
Sa Pa, Viet. 64 A6 22.21 N 103.48 E
Sapanca, Tur. 34 C13 40.41 N 30.16 E
Sapang Baho, stm., Phil. 187f 14.33 N 121.06 E
Sapão, stm., Braz. 170 F2 11.01 S 45.32 W
Sapé, stm., Braz. 205a 22.52 S 43.02 W
Sape, Selat, strt., Indon. 66 H11 8.36 S 119.15 E
Sapele, Nig. 84 H6 5.53 N 5.40 E
Sapello, stm., N.M., U.S. 138 F3 35.47 N 104.59 W
Sapelo Island, i., Ga., U.S. 132 E4 31.28 N 81.15 W
Sapërnaja, Russia 183a 59.46 N 30.41 E
Sápes, Grc. 34 B8 41.00 N 25.42 E
Şaphane, Tur. 34 D12 39.00 N 29.12 E
Sapitwa, mtn., Mwi. 88 D6 15.57 S 35.36 E
Šapki, Russia 26 A14 59.35 N 31.12 E
Šapkina, stm., Russia 12 C26 67.43 N 55.40 E
Šapkovo, Russia 26 E16 55.46 N 33.17 E
Sapockin, Bela. 26 G6 53.49 N 23.39 E
Sappa Creek, stm., U.S. 138 A9 40.07 N 99.37 W
Sappa Creek, Middle Fork, stm., Ks., U.S. 138 B7 39.40 N 100.51 W
Sappa Creek, North Fork, stm., Ks., U.S. 138 B8 39.47 N 100.35 W
Sappa Creek, South Fork, stm., Ks., U.S. 138 B7 39.59 N 99.58 W
Sapphire Mountains, mts., Mt., U.S. 146 D13 46.15 N 113.50 W
Sappho, Wa., U.S. 146 B2 48.04 N 124.15 W
Sapporo, Japan 54 C14 43.03 N 141.21 E
Sapri, Italy 32 D9 40.04 N 15.38 E
Šapša, Russia 18 G21 60.33 N 34.02 E
Sap Songkhla, Thale, l., Thai. 64 I5 7.11 N 100.29 E
Šapsugskaja, Russia 38 I17 44.45 N 38.05 E
Saptakośī, stm., Nepal 70 E11 26.31 N 86.55 E
Sapta-ri, Kor., S. 189b 37.43 N 126.44 E
Sapudi, Pulau, i., Indon. 66 G9 7.06 S 114.20 E
Sapulpa, Ok., U.S. 134 A2 36.00 N 96.06 W
Sapwe, D.R.C. 86 G5 10.58 S 28.10 E
Sāq, Jabal, hill, Sau. Ar. 74 G8 26.17 N 43.16 E
Sāqiyat Makkī, Egypt 191c 30.00 N 31.13 E
Saqqâra, Egypt 76 I2 29.51 N 31.14 E
Saqqâra, Egypt 191c 29.51 N 31.13 E
Saqqâra, Pyramides de (Step Pyramid), hist., Egypt 76 I1 29.52 N 31.13 E
Saqqâra, Pyramids of (Step Pyramid), hist., Egypt 191c 29.52 N 31.13 E
Saqqez, Iran 74 B10 36.13 N 46.17 E
Saquish Neck, pen., Ma., U.S. 201 42.00 N 70.37 W
Saraana, Baie, b., Qc., Can. 122 B1 48.26 N 75.16 W
Sarāb, Iran 74 B10 37.56 N 47.31 E
Saraburi, Thai. 64 E5 14.30 N 100.54 E
Saracura, stm., Braz. 170 G5 12.18 S 40.07 W
Saracuruna, stm., Braz. 205a 22.41 S 43.13 W
Sarafére, Mali 84 F4 15.49 N 3.42 W
Saragosa, Tx., U.S. 136 C4 31.01 N 103.39 W
Saragossa see Zaragoza, Spain 28 C10 41.39 N 0.53 W
Saraguay, ngh., Qc., Can. 193a 45.31 N 73.45 W
Saraguro, Ec. 164 D2 3.37 S 79.12 W
Sarāi Naurang, Pak. 70 B3 32.49 N 70.46 E
Saraipāli, India 70 H9 21.18 N 83.00 E
Säräisniemi, Fin. 18 C13 64.20 N 26.52 E
Sarajas de Madrid, ngh., Spain 184a 40.28 N 3.35 W
Sarajevo, Bos. 36 F5 43.51 N 18.25 E
Saraj-Gir, Russia 40 E18 53.35 N 53.22 E
Saraji, Austl. 98 D7 22.23 S 148.14 E
Sarakhs, Iran 72 B9 36.31 N 61.09 E
Saraktaš, Russia 40 F20 51.47 N 56.21 E
Saraland, Al., U.S. 134 G10 30.48 N 88.05 W
Saran', Kaz. 48 E12 49.46 N 72.52 E
Saran, Gunung, mtn., Indon. 66 D7 0.25 S 111.18 E
Saranac, Mi., U.S. 130 B12 42.55 N 85.12 W
Saranac, stm., N.Y., U.S. 126 D16 44.42 N 73.26 W
Saranac Lake, N.Y., U.S. 126 D15 44.19 N 74.07 W
Saranap, Ca., U.S. 200 37.53 N 122.06 W
Saranda see Sarandë, Alb. 32 E13 39.52 N 20.00 E
Sarandë, Alb. 32 E13 39.52 N 20.00 E
Sarandí, Braz. 172 C11 27.54 S 53.01 W
Sarandí del Yi, Ur. 172 F10 33.21 S 55.36 W
Sarandí Grande, Ur. 172 F9 33.44 S 56.20 W
Šaranga, Russia 40 C15 57.10 N 46.32 E
Sarangani Bay, b., Phil. 68 H5 5.57 N 125.11 E
Sarangani Island, i., Phil. 60 D8 5.27 N 125.28 E
Sarangani Islands, is., Phil. 68 H5 5.25 N 125.26 E
Sarangani Strait, strt., Phil. 68 H5 5.31 N 125.23 E
Sārangarh, India 70 H9 21.35 N 83.05 E
Sārangpur, India 70 G6 23.33 N 76.28 E
Saranpaul', Russia 48 B10 64.15 N 60.53 E
Saransk, Russia 40 D14 54.10 N 45.09 E
Sarantapótamos, stm., Grc. 185c 38.03 N 23.34 E
Saraphi, Thai. 64 C4 18.42 N 99.02 E
Sarapó, stm., Braz. 205a 22.46 S 43.37 W
Sarapuí, stm., Braz. 205a 22.46 S 43.24 W
Sarapuí, Canal de, can., Braz. 205a 22.44 S 43.16 W
Sarapul, Russia 40 C18 56.28 N 53.47 E
Sarapul'skoe, Russia 50 G16 48.50 N 135.57 E
Sarāqib, Syria 76 C7 35.52 N 36.48 E
Sarare, Ven. 168 C7 9.47 N 69.09 W
Sarare, stm., Ven. 168 D6 7.17 N 70.41 W
Sarasota, Fl., U.S. 132 I3 27.19 N 82.32 W
Šarašova, Bela. 26 H7 52.33 N 24.13 E
Saraswati, stm., India 190b 22.59 N 88.22 E
Sarata, Ukr. 38 G8 46.01 N 29.40 E
Saratoga, Ca., U.S. 148 F3 37.15 N 122.00 W
Saratoga, Tx., U.S. 136 D13 30.17 N 94.31 W
Saratoga, Wy., U.S. 150 B10 41.27 N 106.48 W
Saratoga Creek, stm., Ca., U.S. 200 37.25 N 121.58 W
Saratoga National Historical Park, p.o.i., N.Y., U.S. 124 B12 43.00 N 73.38 W
Saratoga Springs, N.Y., U.S. 126 E16 43.04 N 73.47 W
Saratok, Malay. 66 C7 1.44 N 111.20 E
Saratov, Russia 40 F15 51.33 N 45.59 E
Saratovka, Russia 40 F19 51.10 N 55.00 E
Saratov Reservoir see Saratovskoe vodohranilišče, res., Russia 40 E15 52.47 N 48.26 E
Saratovskaja oblast', co., Russia 40 F15 51.30 N 47.00 E
Saratovskoe vodohranilišče, res., Russia 40 E15 52.47 N 48.26 E
Saraurcu, mtn., Ec. 168 H3 0.06 S 77.55 W
Sarāvān, Iran 72 D9 27.22 N 62.19 E
Saravan, Laos 64 E8 15.42 N 106.25 E
Saravena, Col. 168 D6 6.58 N 71.51 W
Sarawak, state, Malay. 66 B8 2.30 N 113.30 E
Sarawak, hist. reg., Malay. 60 E5 2.30 N 113.30 E
Saray, Tur. 34 B10 41.26 N 27.56 E
Saraya, Gui. 84 G2 10.46 N 10.23 W
Sarā-ye Ahmadī, Iran 74 G15 27.56 N 56.42 E
Sarayevo see Sarajevo, Bos. 36 F5 43.51 N 18.25 E
Sarayköy, Tur. 34 F11 37.54 N 28.57 E
Sarayönü, Tur. 34 E15 38.16 N 32.25 E
Sarbāz, Iran 72 D9 26.39 N 61.14 E
Sárbogárd, Hung. 36 C5 46.53 N 18.37 E
Sarca, stm., Italy 30 D7 45.44 N 10.45 E
Sarcee Indian Reserve, ind. res., Ab., Can. 144 E16 50.57 N 114.19 W
Sarcelle, Passe de la, strt., N. Cal. 101d n16 22.28 S 167.13 E
Sarcidano, reg., Italy 32 E2 39.50 N 9.09 E
Sarcoxie, Mo., U.S. 130 G3 37.04 N 94.06 W
Sārda (Mahākālī), stm., Asia 70 D8 27.23 N 81.19 E
Sardah, Bngl. 70 F12 24.18 N 88.44 E
Sardārpur, India 70 G5 22.39 N 74.59 E
Sardārshahr, India 70 D5 28.26 N 74.29 E
Sar Dasht, Iran 74 B9 36.09 N 45.28 E
Sar Dasht, Iran 74 D11 32.32 N 48.52 E
Sardegna, state, Italy 32 D4 40.00 N 9.00 E
Sardegna (Sardinia), i., Italy 32 D2 40.00 N 9.00 E
Sardeh Band, Afg. 70 B2 33.17 N 68.37 E
Sardinas, Mex. 136 H2 26.05 N 105.33 W
Sardinata, Col. 156 H11 8.02 N 72.47 W
Sardinata see Tarra, stm., S.A. 168 C5 9.03 N 72.29 W
Sardinia see Sardegna, state, Italy 32 D4 40.00 N 9.00 E
Sardinia see Sardegna, i., Italy 32 D2 40.00 N 9.00 E
Sardis, Al., U.S. 134 E12 32.17 N 86.59 W
Sardis, Ga., U.S. 134 D2 32.58 N 81.44 W
Sardis, Ms., U.S. 134 C9 34.26 N 89.55 W
Sardis, Pa., U.S. 197b 40.29 N 79.42 W
Sardis, Tn., U.S. 134 B10 35.26 N 88.17 W
Sardis, hist., Tur. 34 E10 38.26 N 28.00 E
Sardis Lake, res., Ms., U.S. 134 C9 34.27 N 89.43 W
Sardis Lake, res., Ok., U.S. 134 C3 34.42 N 95.21 W
Šardonem', Russia 12 E21 63.55 N 44.34 E
Šardozero, ozero, l., Russia 18 E25 62.55 N 38.42 E
Sarek, mtn., Swe. 14 E8 67.25 N 17.46 E
Sareks Nationalpark, p.o.i., Swe. 14 E8 67.15 N 17.30 E
Sārenga, India 190b 22.31 N 88.13 E
Sar-e Pol, Afg. 72 B10 36.12 N 65.56 E
Sarepta, La., U.S. 134 E5 32.54 N 93.26 W
Sargatskoe, Russia 48 C12 55.36 N 73.29 E
Sargent, Ga., U.S. 134 D14 33.25 N 84.52 W
Sargent, Ne., U.S. 140 F13 41.38 N 99.22 W
Sargodha, Pak. 70 B4 32.04 N 72.40 E
Sarh, Chad 82 F3 9.09 N 18.23 E
Sārī, Iran 74 B13 36.34 N 53.04 E
Saria, i., Grc. 34 H10 35.51 N 27.13 E
Saric, Mex. 120 F7 31.06 N 111.23 W
Sarıgazi, ngh., Tur. 185b 41.01 N 29.12 E
Sarıgöl, Tur. 34 E11 38.14 N 28.41 E
Sarıkamış, Tur. 42 E10 40.19 N 42.36 E
Sarıkaya, Tur. 34 E15 38.47 N 32.15 E
Sarikei, Malay. 66 B7 2.07 N 111.31 E
Sarıköy, Tur. 34 C10 40.12 N 27.36 E
Sarilhos Grandes, Port. 184c 38.41 N 8.58 W
Sarilhos Pequenos, Port. 184c 38.41 N 8.59 W
Sarimbun, Pulau, i., Sing. 189c 1.26 N 103.41 E
Sarina, Austl. 98 C7 21.25 S 149.14 E
Sarine, stm., Switz. 30 D4 46.54 N 7.13 E
Sariñena, Spain 28 C10 41.47 N 0.09 W
Sarīr, Libya 82 B4 27.36 N 22.32 E
Sariska Tiger Reserve, ind. res., India 70 E6 27.25 N 76.15 E
Sarita, Tx., U.S. 136 G10 27.13 N 97.47 W
Sariwŏn, Kor., N. 54 E6 38.30 N 125.45 E
Sarıyar Barajı, res., Tur. 34 D14 40.01 N 31.38 E
Šarja, Russia 40 B14 58.22 N 45.30 E
Sark, i., Guern. 20 E6 49.26 N 2.22 W
Sarkad, Hung. 36 C8 46.43 N 21.23 E
Šarkand, Kaz. 48 E13 45.24 N 79.54 E
Šarkaušcyna, Bela. 10 E10 55.22 N 27.25 E
Şarkikaraağaç, Tur. 34 E14 38.04 N 31.22 E
Şarkışla, Tur. 42 F7 39.21 N 36.26 E
Şarköy, Tur. 34 C10 40.37 N 27.07 E
Sarlat-la-Canéda, Fr. 22 E7 44.53 N 1.13 E
Sarles, N.D., U.S. 142 F15 48.56 N 98.59 W
Šarlyk, Russia 40 E19 52.55 N 54.44 E
Sarmi, Indon. 60 F10 1.50 S 138.42 E
Sarmiento, Arg. 166 I3 45.35 S 69.05 W
Sarmiento, stm., Arg. 206 34.25 S 58.35 W
Sarmitunturi, mtn., Fin. 14 D19 68.42 N 28.25 E
Särna, Swe. 16 F11 61.41 N 13.08 E
Sărnena Gora, mts., Blg. 34 A8 42.27 N 25.33 E
Sărnena Gora, mts., Blg. 36 G12 42.35 N 25.10 E
Sarnia, On., Can. 126 F7 42.58 N 82.23 W
Sarno, Italy 32 D8 40.49 N 14.36 E
Sarnowa, Pol. 24 E12 51.37 N 16.54 E
Sarny, Ukr. 38 B5 51.20 N 26.36 E
Sarolangun, Indon. 66 E3 2.18 S 102.42 E
Saronic Gulf see Saronikós Kólpos, b., Grc. 34 F6 37.49 N 23.17 E
Saronikós Kólpos, b., Grc. 34 F6 37.49 N 23.17 E
Saronno, Italy 30 E6 45.38 N 9.02 E
Saros Körfezi, b., Tur. 34 C8 40.30 N 26.20 E
Sárospatak, Hung. 36 A8 48.19 N 21.34 E
Sarowbī, Afg. 72 C10 34.37 N 69.42 E
Sarpa, Russia 40 H14 47.06 N 45.28 E
Sarpa, ozero, l., Russia 40 H14 47.19 N 45.16 E
Šar-planina, mts., Eur. 36 G7 42.05 N 20.50 E
Sarpsborg, Nor. 16 H9 59.16 N 11.08 E
Sarpy Creek, stm., Mt., U.S. 140 A5 46.15 N 107.08 W
Sarralbe, Fr. 20 E15 49.00 N 7.01 E
Sarratt, Eng., U.K. 178 51.41 N 0.29 W
Sarre (Saar), stm., Eur. 20 F16 49.42 N 6.34 E
Sarrebourg, Fr. 20 F16 48.44 N 7.03 E
Sarrebruck see Saarbrücken, Ger. 24 G2 49.13 N 6.59 E
Sarreguemines, Fr. 20 E16 49.06 N 7.04 E
Sarre-Union, Fr. 24 H3 48.57 N 7.06 E
Sarria, Spain 28 B3 42.46 N 7.24 W
Sarriá, ngh., Spain 184d 41.24 N 2.08 E
Sars, Russia 40 C20 56.33 N 57.08 E
Šarscin, Bela. 26 H14 52.39 N 31.03 E
Sarsol, India 190c 19.02 N 73.01 E
Sarsuna, India 190b 22.28 N 88.18 E
Sartana, Ukr. 38 F16 47.10 N 37.41 E
Sartang, stm., Russia 50 C15 67.27 N 133.14 E
Sartell, Mn., U.S. 128 F4 45.37 N 94.12 W
Sartène, Fr. 22 H14 41.37 N 8.56 E
Sarthe, state, Fr. 20 G9 48.00 N 0.05 E
Sarthe, stm., Fr. 20 G8 47.29 N 0.31 W
Sartrouville, Fr. 179 48.57 N 2.10 E
Saruhanlı, Tur. 34 E10 38.44 N 27.34 E
Sarus see Seyhan, stm., Tur. 42 G6 36.43 N 34.55 E
Saru-shima, i., Japan 186 35.17 N 139.42 E
Sárvár, Hung. 36 B3 47.15 N 16.56 E
Sarvestān, Iran 74 F13 29.16 N 53.13 E
Sárvíz, can., Hung. 36 C5 46.23 N 18.40 E
Sarych, mys, c., Ukr. 40 I8 44.24 N 33.45 E
Saryg-Sep, Russia 48 D17 51.29 N 95.33 E
Sarykamyšskoe ozero, l., Asia 72 A8 41.56 N 57.25 E
Sarykopa, ozero, l., Kaz. 48 E10 50.22 N 64.08 E
Saryozek, Kaz. 48 F13 44.21 N 77.58 E
Šarypovo, Russia 48 C15 55.32 N 89.12 E
Sarysu, stm., Kaz. 48 E11 45.10 N 66.39 E
Sary-Taš, Kyrg. 48 G12 39.43 N 73.14 E
Sarytsj, mys, c., Ukr. 42 C5 44.24 N 33.45 E
Sarzana, Italy 30 F6 44.07 N 9.57 E
Sasabe, Az., U.S. 150 L5 31.28 N 111.31 W
Sasabeneh, Eth. 82 F8 7.56 N 43.38 E
Sasaginnigak Lake, l., Mb., Can. 142 C18 51.35 N 95.40 W
Sasak, Indon. 66 D1 0.01 S 99.43 E
Sasakwa, Ok., U.S. 134 C2 34.57 N 96.31 W
Sasamungga, Sol. Is. 101b d7 7.02 S 156.45 E
Sasao, Japan 188 34.57 N 135.20 E
Sasar, Tanjung, c., Indon. 66 H11 9.17 S 119.56 E
Sāsarām, India 70 F9 24.56 N 84.01 E
Sasayama, Japan 56 D8 35.04 N 135.13 E
Sasco Brook, stm., Ct., U.S. 194 41.07 N 73.18 W
Sásd, Hung. 36 C5 46.15 N 18.06 E
Sasebo, Japan 56 F2 33.09 N 129.43 E
Saseginaga, Lac, l., Qc., Can. 126 A11 47.06 N 78.35 W
Sashalom, ngh., Hung. 182c 47.31 N 19.11 E
Sas-hegy, hill, Hung. 182c 47.23 N 19.18 E
Saskatchewan, state, Can. 110 E9 54.00 N 105.00 W
Saskatchewan, stm., Can. 110 E10 53.15 N 98.50 W
Saskatchewan Landing Provincial Park, p.o.i., Sk., Can. 142 D5 50.36 N 107.52 W
Saskatoon, Sk., Can. 142 B7 52.08 N 106.38 W
Saskylah, Russia 50 B11 71.52 N 114.06 E
Saslaya, Cerro, mtn., Nic. 156 F5 13.45 N 85.03 W
Sasnovy Bor, Bela. 26 H12 52.31 N 29.36 E
Sasolburg, S. Afr. 90 E8 26.49 S 27.50 E
Sasovo, Russia 40 D13 54.20 N 41.57 E
Saspamco, Tx., U.S. 136 E9 29.14 N 98.18 W
Sassafras, Austl. 192b 37.52 S 145.21 E
Sassafras, Ky., U.S. 124 G2 37.12 N 83.08 W
Sassafras Mountain, mtn., U.S. 132 A3 35.03 N 82.48 W
Sassandra, C. Iv. 84 I3 4.57 N 6.05 W
Sassandra, stm., C. Iv. 84 I3 4.57 N 6.04 W
Sassari, Italy 32 D2 40.43 N 8.33 E
Sassnitz, Ger. 24 B9 54.31 N 13.38 E
Sasso Marconi, Italy 30 F8 44.23 N 11.13 E
Sassuolo, Italy 30 F7 44.32 N 10.46 E
Sastre, Arg. 172 E7 31.46 S 61.49 W
Sasyk, ozero, l., Ukr. 38 H8 45.40 N 29.40 E
Sasyk, ozero, l., Ukr. 38 H12 45.10 N 33.31 E
Sasykkol', ozero, l., Kaz. 48 E14 46.35 N 81.00 E
Satadougou, Mali 84 G2 12.32 N 11.23 W
Satah Mountain, vol., B.C., Can. 144 D6 52.29 N 124.41 W
Satakunta, reg., Fin. 18 F9 61.35 N 22.50 E
Šatalovka, Russia 40 F11 51.08 N 38.16 E
Šatalovo, Russia 26 F15 54.19 N 32.27 E
Sata-misaki, c., Japan 56 H3 30.59 N 130.39 E
Satāna, India 70 H5 20.35 N 74.11 E
Sataniv, Ukr. 38 D5 49.15 N 26.16 E
Satanta, Ks., U.S. 138 D7 37.26 N 100.59 W
Sátão, Port. 28 D3 40.44 N 7.44 W
Sātāra, India 69 C1 17.41 N 74.00 E
Satara Ruskamp, S. Afr. 90 D10 24.28 S 31.46 E
Sātbāria, India 190b 22.25 N 88.33 E
Satélite, Mex. 120 F9 31.44 N 106.25 W
Satellite Beach, Fl., U.S. 132 H5 28.11 N 80.36 W
Satengar, Pulau, i., Indon. 66 G10 7.32 S 117.18 E
Säter, Swe. 16 G13 60.20 N 15.44 E
Satevó, Mex. 136 G1 27.58 N 106.06 W
Satevó, stm., Mex. 136 G1 27.55 N 106.01 W
Sātghara, India 190b 22.44 N 88.21 E
Satihaure, l., Swe. 14 E9 67.28 N 18.43 E
Satilla, stm., Ga., U.S. 132 E4 30.58 N 81.28 W
Satipo, Peru 164 F3 11.11 S 74.36 W
Sátiro Dias, Braz. 170 F6 11.36 S 38.35 W
Satīt (Tekezē), stm., Afr. 82 E7 14.20 N 35.50 E
Satkānia, Bngl. 70 G13 22.05 N 92.02 E
Šatki, Russia 40 D14 55.12 N 44.07 E
Satluj see Sutlej, stm., Asia 70 C5 29.20 N 71.02 E
Satna, India 70 F8 24.34 N 80.49 E
Sato, Cañada de, stm., Arg. 206 34.35 S 58.38 W
Sátoraljaújhely, Hung. 36 A8 48.24 N 21.40 E
Sātpura Range, mts., India 70 H5 22.00 N 78.00 E
Satsuma, Al., U.S. 134 G10 30.49 N 88.04 W
Satsuma-hantō, pen., Japan 56 H3 31.25 N 130.25 E
Satsunan-shotō, is., Japan 55a k19 29.00 N 130.00 E
Sattahip, Thai. 64 F5 12.40 N 100.53 E
Satthwa, Mya. 64 D2 17.46 N 94.30 E
Satui, Indon. 66 E9 3.47 S 115.26 E
Sātuli, India 190b 22.33 N 88.34 E
Satu Mare, Rom. 36 B9 47.47 N 22.53 E
Satu Mare, state, Rom. 36 B10 47.40 N 23.00 E
Satun, Thai. 64 I4 6.37 N 100.04 E
Šatura, Russia 40 D11 55.34 N 39.32 E
Saturnino M. Laspiur, Arg. 172 E6 31.41 S 62.29 W
Satus Creek, stm., Wa., U.S. 146 D6 46.15 N 120.06 W
Satyamangalam, India 69 F3 11.30 N 77.14 E
Satzkorn, Ger. 182a 52.29 N 12.59 E
Sau, stm., Viet. 187c 10.46 N 106.48 E
Sauce, Arg. 172 E8 30.05 S 58.47 W
Sauce, Arroyo del, stm., Arg. 206 34.41 S 58.50 W
Sauce Corto, Arroyo, stm., Arg. 172 H7 36.59 S 61.45 W
Saucier, Ms., U.S. 134 G9 30.37 N 89.08 W
Saucillo, Mex. 154 A6 28.01 N 105.16 W
Sauda, Nor. 16 H4 59.39 N 6.20 E
Sauđárkrókur, Ice. 12a k30 65.44 N 19.40 W
Saúde, Braz. 170 F5 10.57 S 40.23 W
Saúde, ngh., Braz. 205b 23.37 S 46.37 W
Saudi Arabia, ctry., Asia 72 E5 25.00 N 45.00 E
Sauer, stm., Eur. 20 E15 49.42 N 6.30 E
Sauerkohl-Berge, hill, Ger. 182a 52.20 N 13.45 E
Sauerland, reg., Ger. 24 E3 51.21 N 8.02 E
Saueruiná, stm., Braz. 166 B5 11.55 S 58.26 W
Saugatuck, Ct., U.S. 194 41.08 N 73.23 W
Saugatuck, Mi., U.S. 130 B11 42.39 N 86.11 W
Saugatuck, stm., Ct., U.S. 194 41.07 N 73.22 W
Saugeen, stm., On., Can. 126 D8 44.29 N 81.22 W
Saugerties, N.Y., U.S. 124 B12 42.04 N 73.57 W
Saughall, Eng., U.K. 180 53.13 N 2.58 W
Saugor see Sāgar, India 70 G7 23.50 N 78.45 E
Saugstad, Mount, mtn., B.C., Can. 144 D4 52.15 N 126.31 W
Saugus, stm., Ma., U.S. 201 42.28 N 70.58 W
Saugus Iron Works National Historic Site, hist., Ma., U.S. 201 42.28 N 71.01 W
Saujbulagh see Mahābād, Iran 74 B9 36.45 N 45.43 E
Saujil, Arg. 172 D4 28.11 S 66.14 W
Sauk, stm., Mn., U.S. 128 F4 45.35 N 94.11 W
Sauk, stm., Wa., U.S. 146 B5 48.28 N 121.36 W
Sauk Centre, Mn., U.S. 128 F3 45.44 N 94.57 W
Sauk City, Wi., U.S. 128 H9 43.16 N 89.43 W
Sauk Rapids, Mn., U.S. 128 F4 45.35 N 94.10 W
Saukville, Wi., U.S. 126 E1 43.23 N 87.56 W
Saül, Fr. Gu. 164 C7 3.37 N 53.11 W
Sauldre, stm., Fr. 20 G10 47.16 N 1.31 E
Sauldre, Canal de la, can., Fr. 22 B8 47.35 N 2.04 E
Saulgau, Ger. 24 I5 48.00 N 9.30 E
Saulieu, Fr. 20 G13 47.17 N 4.13 E
Saulkrasti, Lat. 26 C7 57.19 N 24.26 E
Sault-au-Mouton, Qc., Can. 122 B7 48.32 N 69.16 W
Sault au Récollet, ngh., Qc., Can. 193a 45.34 N 73.39 W
Sault aux Cochons, stm., Qc., Can. 122 B7 48.43 N 69.03 W
Sault-de-Vaucluse, Fr. 22 E11 44.05 N 5.25 E
Saulteaux, stm., Ab., Can. 144 B16 55.15 N 114.19 W
Saulteaux Indian Reserve, ind. res., Sk., Can. 142 A5 53.08 N 108.18 W
Sault Sainte Marie, On., Can. 126 B5 46.31 N 84.19 W
Sault Sainte Marie, Mi., U.S. 126 B5 46.29 N 84.21 W
Saulx, stm., Fr. 179 48.41 N 2.19 E
Saulx-les-Chartreux, Fr. 179 48.42 N 2.16 E
Saumarez Reef, rf., Austl. 98 C9 21.49 S 153.26 E
Saumlaki, Indon. 60 G9 7.59 S 131.18 E
Saumon, stm., Qc., Can. 122 E5 45.41 N 71.27 W
Saumons see Salmon, stm., N.A. 126 D15 45.02 N 74.30 W
Saumur, Fr. 20 G8 47.16 N 0.05 W
Saundatti, India 69 D2 15.46 N 75.07 E
Saunders Island, i., Falk. Is. 166 J4 51.22 S 60.13 W
Saunders Island, i., S. Geor. 103 A2 57.47 S 26.27 W
Sauquoit, N.Y., U.S. 124 B10 43.00 N 75.15 W
Saurimo, Ang. 88 B3 9.40 S 20.23 E
Sausar, India 70 H7 21.39 N 78.48 E
Sausu, Indon. 66 D12 1.00 S 120.30 E
Sautar, Ang. 88 C2 11.10 S 18.25 E
Sauteurs, Gren. 159e q10 12.12 N 61.38 W
Sauveterre-de-Béarn, Fr. 22 F4 43.24 N 0.57 W
Sauveterre-de-Guyenne, Fr. 22 E5 44.41 N 0.04 W
Sauvo, Fin. 18 G9 60.20 N 22.41 E
Sauwald, for., Aus. 30 B10 48.28 N 13.40 E
Sauzal, Mex. 136 C1 31.41 N 106.20 W
Sava, stm., Eur. 30 F16 44.50 N 20.27 E
Savage, Mt., U.S. 142 G9 47.27 N 104.21 W
Savai'i, i., Samoa 101c g11 13.35 S 172.25 W
Savalen, l., Nor. 16 E8 62.15 N 10.29 E
Savalou, Benin 84 H5 7.55 N 1.58 E
Savanna, Il., U.S. 130 B7 42.05 N 90.08 W
Savanna, Ok., U.S. 134 C3 34.49 N 95.50 W
Savannah, Ga., U.S. 132 D4 32.04 N 81.07 W
Savannah, Mo., U.S. 130 E3 39.56 N 94.50 W
Savannah, Tn., U.S. 134 B10 35.13 N 88.14 W
Savannah, stm., U.S. 132 D4 32.01 N 80.53 W
Savannah River Plant, sci., S.C., U.S. 132 C4 33.15 N 81.40 W
Savannah Sound, Bah. 132 K9 25.06 N 76.08 W
Savannakhét, Laos 64 D7 16.34 N 104.45 E
Savanna-la-Mar, Jam. 158d i12 18.13 N 78.08 W
Savanna Portage State Park, p.o.i., Mn., U.S. 128 E5 46.51 N 93.10 W
Savant Lake, On., Can. 128 A8 50.13 N 90.42 W
Savant Lake, l., On., Can. 128 A8 50.30 N 90.25 W
Sāvantvādi, India 69 D1 15.54 N 73.49 E
Savanūr, India 69 D2 14.58 N 75.24 E
Sävar, Swe. 16 D18 63.54 N 20.34 E
Săvârșin, Rom. 36 D9 46.00 N 22.18 E
Savaştepe, Tur. 34 D10 39.23 N 27.40 E
Savcılıbüyükoba, Tur. 42 F5 39.14 N 33.41 E
Savè, Benin 84 H5 8.01 N 2.25 E
Save, stm., Afr. 88 E5 20.57 S 35.03 E
Save, stm., Fr. 22 F7 43.47 N 1.17 E

Name	Page	Map Ref.	Latitude	Longitude
Sāveh, Iran	74	C12	35.01 N	50.21 E
Savelugu, Ghana	84	H4	9.37 N	0.49 W
Savenay, Fr.	20	G7	47.22 N	1.57 W
Săveni, Rom.	36	B13	47.57 N	26.51 E
Saverdun, Fr.	22	F7	43.13 N	1.34 E
Saverne, Fr.	24	H3	48.44 N	7.21 E
Savery Creek, stm., Wy., U.S.	150	B9	41.00 N	107.27 W
Savick Brook, stm., Eng., U.K.	180		53.45 N	2.47 W
Savičy, Bela.	26	H11	52.24 N	29.01 E
Savigliano, Italy	30	F4	44.39 N	7.40 E
Savigny-le-Temple, Fr.	179		48.35 N	2.35 E
Savill Gardens, p.o.i., Eng., U.K.	178		51.27 N	0.36 W
Savinka, Russia	40	F15	50.04 N	47.06 E
Savino-Borisovskaja, Russia	12	E21	62.36 N	44.27 E
Savinskij, Russia	18	E27	62.55 N	40.08 E
Savissik, Grnld.	108	B13	76.01 N	65.05 W
Savitaipale, Fin.	18	F14	61.12 N	27.42 E
Šavnik, Yugo.	36	G6	42.57 N	19.05 E
Savoie, state, Fr.	22	D12	45.30 N	6.25 E
Savoie, hist. reg., Fr.	22	D12	45.55 N	6.30 E
Savo Island, i., Sol. Is.	101b	e8	9.08 S	159.49 E
Sav'olovo Station, trans., Russia	183b		55.48 N	37.35 E
Savona, B.C., Can.	144	F10	50.45 N	120.50 W
Savona, Italy	30	F5	44.19 N	8.28 E
Savonet, Neth. Ant.	158g	p21	12.21 N	69.06 W
Savonlinna, Fin.	18	F15	61.52 N	28.54 E
Savonranta, Fin.	18	E16	62.10 N	29.12 E
Savoy, Tx., U.S.	134	D2	33.35 N	96.19 W
Savoy see Savoie, hist. reg., Fr.	22	D12	45.55 N	6.30 E
Savran', Ukr.	38	E9	48.07 N	30.05 E
Sävsjö, Swe.	16	J12	57.24 N	14.40 E
Savukoski, Fin.	14	E19	67.17 N	28.11 E
Savusavu, Fiji	101e	p19	16.47 S	179.21 E
Savusavu Bay, b., Fiji	101e	p19	16.45 S	179.15 E
Savu Sea see Sawu, Laut, s., Indon.	60	G7	9.40 S	122.00 E
Savuto, stm., Italy	32	E10	39.02 N	16.06 E
Savyntsi, Ukr.	38	D16	49.24 N	37.04 E
Sawah, Indon.	66	B9	2.24 N	115.14 E
Sawahlunto, Indon.	66	D2	0.40 S	100.45 E
Sawāi Mādhopur, India	70	E6	25.59 N	76.21 E
Sawākin, Sudan	82	D7	19.06 N	37.19 E
Sawang, Indon.	66	C3	0.43 N	103.22 E
Sawankhalok, Thai.	64	D4	17.18 N	99.50 E
Sawara, Japan	56	D13	35.53 N	140.30 E
Sawata, Japan	56	A11	38.00 N	138.16 E
Sawatch Range, mts., Co., U.S.	138	C2	39.10 N	106.25 W
Sawdā', Jabal, mtn., Sau. Ar.	72	F5	18.18 N	42.22 E
Sawdā', Jabal as-, hills, Libya	82	A4	28.48 N	15.39 E
Sawdā', Qurnat as-, mtn., Leb.	76	D7	34.18 N	36.07 E
Sawdirī, Sudan	82	E5	14.23 N	29.06 E
Sawel Mountain, mtn., N. Ire., U.K.	10	G6	54.49 N	7.02 W
Sawi, Thai.	64	G4	10.14 N	99.06 E
Saw Log Creek, stm., Ks., U.S.	138	D9	38.07 N	99.42 W
Saw Mill, stm., N.Y., U.S.	194		40.56 N	73.53 W
Sawmill Brook, stm., Ma., U.S.	201		42.34 N	70.46 W
Sawmill Brook, stm., N.J., U.S.	194		40.28 N	74.26 W
Sawmill Creek, stm., N.J., U.S.	194		40.46 N	74.05 W
Sawmill Creek, stm., Pa., U.S.	197b		40.10 N	79.58 W
Sawmill Pond Brook, stm., N.J., U.S.	194		41.10 N	74.23 W
Sawmill Run, stm., Pa., U.S.	203		40.07 N	75.21 W
Şawqirah, Oman	72	F8	18.07 N	56.31 E
Şawqirah, Dawhat, b., Oman	72	F8	18.35 N	57.00 E
Sawridge Indian Reserve, ind. res., Ab., Can.	144	A16	55.17 N	114.54 W
Sawtooth National Recreation Area, p.o.i., Id., U.S.	146	F12	44.00 N	114.55 W
Sawu, Laut (Savu Sea), s., Indon.	60	G7	9.40 S	122.00 E
Sawu, Pulau, i., Indon.	60	H7	10.30 S	121.54 E
Sawyer, Mi., U.S.	130	C11	41.52 N	86.35 W
Sawyer, N.D., U.S.	142	F12	48.05 N	101.04 W
Saxby, stm., Austl.	98	B3	18.24 S	140.51 E
Saxike, China	58	C11	30.44 N	86.25 E
Saxis, Va., U.S.	124	G10	37.55 N	75.43 W
Saxnäs, Swe.	16	C13	64.58 N	15.19 E
Saxon, Wi., U.S.	128	E8	46.29 N	90.24 W
Saxon Woods Park, p.o.i., N.Y., U.S.	194		40.59 N	73.45 W
Saxony see Sachsen, state, Ger.	24	F9	51.00 N	13.00 E
Saxony see Sachsen, hist. reg., Ger.	24	D4	52.45 N	9.30 E
Saxony-Anhalt see Sachsen-Anhalt, state, Ger.	24	D7	52.00 N	11.30 E
Saxton, Pa., U.S.	124	D7	40.12 N	78.14 W
Say, Niger	84	G5	13.06 N	2.20 E
Sayama, Japan	188		34.31 N	135.34 E
Sayama-kyūryō, hills, Japan	186		35.47 N	139.24 E
Sayán, Peru	164	F2	11.07 S	77.11 W
Sayan Mountains, mts., Asia	48	D17	53.32 N	94.50 E
Sayaxché, Guat.	156	D2	16.31 N	90.09 W
Saybrook, Il., U.S.	130	D9	40.25 N	88.31 W
Şaydā (Sidon), Leb.	76	E6	33.33 N	35.22 E
Şaydā, state, Leb.	76	E6	33.15 N	35.15 E
Sayhūt, Yemen	72	F7	15.12 N	51.13 E
Sayil, hist., Mex.	156	B3	20.12 N	89.41 W
Saylac, Som.	86	B8	11.20 N	43.28 E
Saylorville Lake, res., Ia., U.S.	130	C4	41.44 N	93.42 W
Saylūn, Khirbat (Shiloh), hist., W.B.	76	F6	32.03 N	35.17 E
Säynätsalo, Fin.	18	E12	62.08 N	25.44 E
Saynshand, Mong.	52	C7	44.55 N	110.08 E
Sayram Hu, l., China	48	F14	44.36 N	81.06 E
Sayre, Ok., U.S.	138	F9	35.18 N	99.37 W
Sayre, Pa., U.S.	124	C9	41.58 N	76.31 W
Sayreville, N.J., U.S.	124	D11	40.28 N	74.21 W
Sayward, B.C., Can.	144	F5	50.20 N	125.55 W
Saywūn, Yemen	72	F6	15.56 N	48.45 E
Saza, Japan	56	F2	33.14 N	129.39 E
Sazan, i., Alb.	32	D13	40.30 N	19.17 E
Sažino, Russia	40	C21	56.19 N	58.11 E
Sazlijka, stm., Blg.	36	G12	42.02 N	25.52 E
Sazonovo, Russia	26	A18	59.05 N	35.14 E
Sba, Alg.	84	D4	28.14 N	0.10 W
Ščadryn, Bela.	26	H12	52.53 N	29.33 E
Scaër, Fr.	20	F5	48.02 N	3.42 W
Scafell Pike, mtn., Eng., U.K.	10	G9	54.27 N	3.12 W
Scafell Pikes see Scafell Pike, mtn., Eng., U.K.	10	G9	54.27 N	3.12 W
Scajaquada Creek, stm., N.Y., U.S.	202a		42.56 N	78.53 W
Scala, Teatro alla, bldg., Italy	184b		45.28 N	9.11 E
Scalea, Italy	32	E9	39.49 N	15.48 E
Scalpay, i., Scot., U.K.	10	D7	57.17 N	5.58 W
Scammon, Ks., U.S.	130	G3	37.16 N	94.48 W
Scammon Bay, Ak., U.S.	109	D6	61.53 N	165.38 W
Scammonden Water, res., Eng., U.K.	180		53.38 N	1.56 W
Scandia, Ks., U.S.	138	B11	39.47 N	97.47 W
Scandinavia, reg., Eur.	8	C11	62.30 N	15.00 E
Scanlon, Mn., U.S.	128	E6	46.42 N	92.25 W
Scansano, Italy	30	H8	42.41 N	11.20 E
Scapa, Ab., Can.	144	E19	51.52 N	111.58 W
Scapa Flow, b., Scot., U.K.	10	C9	58.52 N	3.06 W
Scapegoat Mountain, mtn., Mt., U.S.	146	C14	47.19 N	112.50 W
Ščapino, Russia	50	E20	55.20 N	159.26 E
Scappoose, Or., U.S.	146	E4	45.45 N	122.52 W
Ščara, stm., Bela.	26	G8	53.26 N	24.44 E
Scarborough, St. K./N.	159a	c2	17.11 N	62.34 W
Scarborough, Trin.	159f	r13	11.10 N	60.44 W
Scarborough, Eng., U.K.	10	G12	54.16 N	0.25 W
Scarborough, ngh., On., Can.	126	E10	43.44 N	79.16 W
Scarborough Centre, shp. cen., On., Can.	193b		43.47 N	79.16 W
Scarisbrick, Eng., U.K.	180		53.37 N	2.56 W
Scărişoara, Rom.	36	F11	44.00 N	24.35 E
Scarp, i., Scot., U.K.	10	C5	58.01 N	7.07 W
Scarper Peak, mtn., Ca., U.S.	200		37.32 N	122.26 W
Scarth Hill, Eng., U.K.	180		53.33 N	2.52 W
Scatarie Island, i., N.S., Can.	122	D17	46.01 N	59.45 W
Scawfell Island, i., Austl.	98	C7	20.52 S	149.36 E
Sceaux, Château de, hist., Fr.	179		48.46 N	2.18 E
Ščedro, Otok, i., Cro.	30	G13	43.05 N	16.42 E
Ščeglovo, Russia	183a		60.02 N	30.46 E
Ščekino, Russia	26	F20	54.00 N	37.30 E
Ščëkino, Russia	26	F20	54.27 N	37.00 E
Ščelkovo, Russia	26	E20	55.54 N	38.01 E
Ščelkovo, Russia	183b		55.55 N	38.00 E
Ščemilovo, Russia	183b		55.48 N	38.05 E
Sceptre, Sk., Can.	142	D4	50.51 N	109.15 W
Ščerbakovo, Russia	50	C21	65.12 N	160.34 E
Ščerbakty, Kaz.	48	D13	52.29 N	78.10 E
Ščerbinka, Russia	26	E20	55.31 N	37.34 E
Schaalsee, l., Ger.	20	A19	53.34 N	11.08 E
Schaephuysen, Ger.	181		51.26 N	6.29 E
Schäferberg, hill, Ger.	182a		52.25 N	13.08 E
Schaffhausen, Switz.	30	C5	47.42 N	8.38 E
Schaffhouse see Schaffhausen, Switz.	30	C5	47.42 N	8.38 E
Schalke, ngh., Ger.	181		51.31 N	7.05 E
Schälker Heide, for., Ger.	181		51.24 N	7.36 E
Schaller, Ia., U.S.	130	B2	42.30 N	95.17 W
Schardenberg, hill, Ger.	181		51.27 N	6.28 E
Schärding, Aus.	30	B10	48.27 N	13.26 E
Scharnhorst, ngh., Ger.	181		51.32 N	7.32 E
Schässburg see Sighişoara, Rom.	36	C11	46.13 N	24.48 E
Schefferville, Qc., Can.	110	E17	54.48 N	66.50 W
Scheibbs, Aus.	30	B12	48.00 N	15.09 E
Scheiblingstein, Aus.	182b		48.16 N	16.13 E
Scheinfeld, Ger.	24	G6	49.40 N	10.27 E
Schelde, stm., Eur.	20	C13	51.21 N	4.15 E
Schell Creek Range, mts., Nv., U.S.	150	D2	39.06 N	114.40 W
Schelsen, ngh., Ger.	181		51.09 N	6.31 E
Schenectady, N.Y., U.S.	124	B11	42.47 N	73.56 W
Schenevus Creek, stm., N.Y., U.S.	124	B11	42.29 N	74.59 W
Schenkendorf, Ger.	182a		52.16 N	13.35 E
Schenkenhorst, Ger.	182a		52.20 N	13.12 E
Schenley Park, p.o.i., Pa., U.S.	197b		40.26 N	79.56 W
Scherlebeck, Ger.	181		51.37 N	7.08 E
Schertz, Tx., U.S.	136	E9	29.33 N	98.16 W
Schesslitz, Ger.	24	F7	49.59 N	11.01 E
Schevelinger-Stausee, res., Ger.	181		51.08 N	7.26 E
Schiedam, Neth.	20	C13	51.55 N	4.23 E
Schiermonnikoog, i., Neth.	24	C2	53.29 N	6.10 E
Schiffshebewerk, trans., Ger.	181		51.37 N	7.19 E
Schiltigheim, Fr.	20	F16	48.35 N	7.44 E
Schio, Italy	30	E8	45.42 N	11.20 E
Schiza, i., Grc.	34	G4	36.44 N	21.46 E
Schkeuditz, Ger.	24	E8	51.24 N	12.13 E
Schladming, Aus.	30	C10	47.23 N	13.40 E
Schlänitz-see, l., Ger.	182a		52.27 N	12.57 E
Schlater, Ms., U.S.	134	D8	33.38 N	90.20 W
Schlegel Lake, l., N.J., U.S.	194		40.59 N	74.03 W
Schlei, l., Ger.	16	M7	54.36 N	9.45 E
Schleiden, Ger.	24	F2	50.31 N	6.28 E
Schleswig, Ger.	24	B5	54.31 N	9.33 E
Schleswig, Ia., U.S.	130	B2	42.10 N	95.25 W
Schleswig-Holstein, state, Ger.	24	B6	54.03 N	10.09 E
Schlinge, stm., Eur.	20	C15	51.55 N	6.19 E
Schlitz, Ger.	24	F5	50.40 N	9.33 E
Schlüchtern, Ger.	24	F5	50.20 N	9.31 E
Schmachtendorf, ngh., Ger.	181		51.32 N	6.49 E
Schmidmühlen, Ger.	24	G7	49.15 N	11.55 E
Schmöckwitz, ngh., Ger.	182a		52.23 N	13.39 E
Schmölln, Ger.	24	F8	50.53 N	12.20 E
Schneeberg, Ger.	24	F8	50.36 N	12.38 E
Schneeberg, mtn., Aus.	30	C12	47.47 N	15.47 E
Schneeberg, mtn., Ger.	24	F7	50.03 N	11.51 E
Schneidemühl see Piła, Pol.	24	C12	53.09 N	16.44 E
Schneverdingen, Ger.	24	C5	53.07 N	9.47 E
Schœlcher, Mart.	159c	k6	14.36 N	61.06 W
Schoen Lake Provincial Park, p.o.i., B.C., Can.	144	F4	50.10 N	126.15 W
Schofield, Wi., U.S.	128	G9	44.53 N	89.36 W
Schofields, Austl.	192a		33.42 S	150.52 E
Schoharie, N.Y., U.S.	124	B11	42.40 N	74.18 W
Schoharie Creek, stm., N.Y., U.S.	124	B11	42.56 N	74.17 W
Schöller, ngh., Ger.	181		51.14 N	7.01 E
Scholven, ngh., Ger.	181		51.36 N	7.03 E
Schönbrunn, Schloss, bldg., Aus.	182b		48.11 N	16.19 E
Schönbrunner Schlosspark, p.o.i., Aus.	182b		48.11 N	16.19 E
Schönebeck, Ger.	24	D7	52.01 N	11.44 E
Schönebeck, ngh., Ger.	181		51.28 N	6.56 E
Schöneberg, ngh., Ger.	182a		52.29 N	13.21 E
Schönefeld, Ger.	182a		52.23 N	13.30 E
Schönerlinde, Ger.	182a		52.39 N	13.27 E
Schönfeld, Ger.	182a		52.41 N	13.44 E
Schönfliess, Ger.	182a		52.39 N	13.20 E
Schongau, Ger.	24	I6	47.49 N	10.54 E
Schönhausen, Ger.	181		51.37 N	7.38 E
Schonnebeck, ngh., Ger.	181		51.29 N	7.04 E
Schoolcraft, Mi., U.S.	130	B12	42.06 N	85.37 W
Schoolhouse Run, stm., Pa., U.S.	203		40.13 N	75.27 W
Schopfheim, Ger.	24	I3	47.39 N	7.49 E
Schorndorf, Ger.	24	H5	48.48 N	9.31 E
Schouten, Kepulauan, is., Indon.	60	F10	0.55 S	135.55 E
Schouten Island, i., Austl.	99a	o14	42.19 S	148.17 E
Schouten Islands, is., Pap. N. Gui.	101a	a3	3.26 S	144.29 E
Schramberg, Ger.	24	H4	48.13 N	8.23 E
Schreiber, On., Can.	128	C11	48.47 N	87.15 W
Schriever, La., U.S.	134	H8	29.44 N	90.48 W
Schrobenhausen, Ger.	24	H7	48.33 N	11.15 E
Schroffenstein, mtn., Nmb.	90	E4	27.11 S	18.44 E
Schroon, stm., N.Y., U.S.	126	E16	43.29 N	73.48 W
Schroon Lake, l., N.Y., U.S.	126	E16	43.46 N	73.46 W
Schulenburg, Tx., U.S.	136	E11	29.40 N	96.54 W
Schuls see Scuol, Switz.	30	D7	46.48 N	10.18 E
Schultz Lake, l., Nu., Can.	110	C11	64.45 N	97.30 W
Schulzenhöhe, Ger.	182a		52.29 N	13.47 E
Schüren, ngh., Ger.	181		51.30 N	7.32 E
Schuyler, Ne., U.S.	140	F15	41.27 N	97.03 W
Schuyler, Va., U.S.	124	G7	37.46 N	78.42 W
Schuylkill, stm., Pa., U.S.	124	D10	39.52 N	75.11 W
Schuylkill Canal, can., Pa., U.S.	203		40.14 N	75.42 W
Schuylkill Haven, Pa., U.S.	124	D9	40.38 N	76.10 W
Schwabach, Ger.	24	G7	49.19 N	11.01 E
Schwaben, hist. reg., Ger.	24	H5	48.10 N	9.25 E
Schwäbische Alb, mts., Ger.	24	H5	48.25 N	9.30 E
Schwäbisch Gmünd, Ger.	24	H5	48.48 N	9.47 E
Schwäbisch Hall, Ger.	24	G5	49.06 N	9.44 E
Schwabmünchen, Ger.	24	H6	48.10 N	10.45 E
Schwafheim, Ger.	181		51.25 N	6.39 E
Schwandorf in Bayern, Ger.	24	G8	49.19 N	12.06 E
Schwanenwerder, ngh., Ger.	182a		52.27 N	13.10 E
Schwaner, Pegunungan, mts., Indon.	66	D8	0.40 S	112.40 E
Schwante, Ger.	182a		52.44 N	13.05 E
Schwarza, stm., Aus.	24	I11	47.44 N	16.13 E
Schwarzach im Pongau, Aus.	30	C10	47.19 N	13.11 E
Schwarzbach, stm., Ger.	181		51.19 N	6.44 E
Schwarzenberg, ngh., Ger.	181		51.24 N	6.42 E
Schwarzenberg Park, p.o.i., Aus.	182b		48.14 N	16.15 E
Schwarzer Berg, hill, Ger.	181		51.41 N	7.12 E
Schwarzrand, plat., Nmb.	90	D3	25.38 S	16.57 E
Schwarzwald (Black Forest), mts., Ger.	24	H4	48.20 N	8.10 E
Schwatka Mountains, mts., Ak., U.S.	109	C8	67.25 N	157.00 W
Schwaz, Aus.	30	C8	47.20 N	11.42 E
Schwechat, Aus.	30	B13	48.08 N	16.29 E
Schwedt, Ger.	24	C10	53.03 N	14.16 E
Schweflinghausen, Ger.	181		51.16 N	7.25 E
Schweidnitz see Świdnica, Pol.	24	F12	50.50 N	16.29 E
Schweinfurt, Ger.	24	F6	50.03 N	10.13 E
Schweiz see Switzerland, ctry., Eur.	30	D5	47.00 N	8.00 E
Schweizer National Park see Schweizer Nationalpark, p.o.i., Switz.	30	D7	46.38 N	10.11 E
Schweizer Nationalpark, p.o.i., Switz.	30	D7	46.38 N	10.11 E
Schweizer-Reineke, S. Afr.	90	E7	27.11 S	25.19 E
Schwenke, Ger.	181		51.11 N	7.26 E
Schwenksville, Pa., U.S.	203		40.16 N	75.28 W
Schwerin, Ger.	24	C7	53.38 N	11.25 E
Schwerin, Ger.	181		51.33 N	7.20 E
Schwerin see Skwierzyna, Pol.	24	D11	52.35 N	15.30 E
Schweriner See, l., Ger.	24	C7	53.41 N	11.27 E
Schwiebus see Świebodzin, Pol.	24	D11	52.14 N	15.31 E
Schwielowsee, l., Ger.	182a		52.20 N	12.57 E
Schwitten, Ger.	181		51.27 N	7.48 E
Schwyz, Switz.	30	C5	47.02 N	8.40 E
Sciacca, Italy	32	G7	37.31 N	13.03 E
Scicli, Italy	32	H8	36.47 N	14.42 E
Science and Industry, Museum of, bldg., Il., U.S.	196		41.47 N	87.35 W
Ščigry, Russia	40	F10	51.52 N	36.55 E
Scilly, Isles of, is., Eng., U.K.	10	L6	49.55 N	6.20 W
Ścinawa, Pol.	24	E12	51.24 N	16.25 E
Scio, Oh., U.S.	124	D4	40.23 N	81.04 W
Scio, Or., U.S.	146	F4	44.41 N	122.51 W
Scioto, stm., Oh., U.S.	124	E3	38.43 N	83.01 W
Scipio, Ut., U.S.	150	D4	39.14 N	112.08 W
Ščit, mtn., Bos.	36	E4	44.02 N	17.47 E
Scobey, Mt., U.S.	142	F8	48.47 N	105.24 W
Scone, Austl.	98	I8	32.03 S	150.52 E
Scooba, Ms., U.S.	134	E10	32.49 N	88.28 W
Scordia, Italy	32	G8	37.18 N	14.51 E
Scoresby, Austl.	192b		37.54 S	145.14 E
Scoresby Land, reg., Grnld.	108	C21	71.45 N	24.30 W
Scoresbysund (Ittoqqortoormiit), Grnld.	108	C21	70.29 N	21.58 W
Scoresby Sund, strt., Grnld.	108	C21	70.43 N	25.07 W
Scorff, stm., Fr.	20	F5	47.43 N	3.20 W
Scotia, Ne., U.S.	140	F14	41.27 N	98.42 W
Scotia, N.Y., U.S.	124	B12	42.50 N	73.57 W
Scotia Lake, l., On., Can.	126	A8	47.05 N	81.22 W
Scotia Ridge, unds.	176	N8	54.00 S	49.59 W
Scotia Sea, s.	162	K10	56.00 S	40.00 W
Scotland, On., Can.	126	E9	43.00 N	80.23 W
Scotland, S.D., U.S.	140	D15	43.08 N	97.43 W
Scotland, Tx., U.S.	138	H10	33.40 N	98.28 W
Scotland, state, U.K.	10	E8	56.30 N	3.42 W
Scotland Neck, N.C., U.S.	124	H8	36.07 N	77.25 W
Scotland Run, stm., N.J., U.S.	203		39.39 N	75.03 W
Scotlandville, La., U.S.	134	G7	30.31 N	91.10 W
Scotsburn, N.S., Can.	122	E14	45.38 N	62.51 W
Scott, Sk., Can.	142	B5	52.21 N	108.49 W
Scott, Ms., U.S.	134	D7	33.35 N	91.04 W
Scott, stm., Ca., U.S.	148	B3	41.47 N	123.02 W
Scott, Cape, c., B.C., Can.	144	F2	50.46 N	128.25 W
Scott, Mount, mtn., Ok., U.S.	138	G10	34.44 N	98.32 W
Scott, Mount, mtn., Or., U.S.	146	H4	42.56 N	122.01 W
Scott Air Force Base, mil., Il., U.S.	130	F8	38.32 N	89.50 W
Scott Base, sci., Ant.	103	C22	77.50 S	166.25 E
Scottburgh, S. Afr.	90	G10	30.18 S	30.39 E
Scott City, Ks., U.S.	138	C8	38.28 N	100.54 W
Scott City, Mo., U.S.	130	G8	37.13 N	89.31 W
Scott Cove, b., Ct., U.S.	194		41.03 N	73.28 W
Scottdale, Pa., U.S.	124	D6	40.05 N	79.35 W
Scott Haven, Pa., U.S.	197b		40.15 N	79.47 W
Scott Island, i., Ant.	103	B23	67.24 S	179.55 W
Scott Islands, is., B.C., Can.	144	F2	50.48 N	128.40 W
Scott Mountain, mtn., Id., U.S.	146	F11	44.11 N	115.47 W
Scott Peak, mtn., Id., U.S.	146	F14	44.21 N	112.50 W
Scott Reef, rf., Austl.	96	B4	14.07 S	121.50 E
Scott Run, stm., Va., U.S.	202c		38.58 N	77.12 W
Scottsbluff, Ne., U.S.	140	F9	41.52 N	103.39 W
Scotts Bluff National Monument, p.o.i., Ne., U.S.	140	F9	41.49 N	103.41 W
Scottsboro, Al., U.S.	134	C12	34.40 N	86.01 W
Scottsburg, In., U.S.	130	F12	38.41 N	85.46 W
Scottsdale, Austl.	99a	n13	41.10 S	147.31 E
Scottsdale, Az., U.S.	150	J5	33.30 N	111.54 W
Scotts Head, c., Dom.	159c	j6	15.12 N	61.22 W
Scotts Hill, Tn., U.S.	134	B10	35.30 N	88.14 W
Scotts Level Branch, stm., Md., U.S.	202b		39.22 N	76.45 W
Scottsville, Ky., U.S.	130	H11	36.45 N	86.11 W
Scott Township, Pa., U.S.	197b		40.32 N	80.11 W
Scottville, Mi., U.S.	126	E3	43.57 N	86.17 W
Scourie, Scot., U.K.	10	C7	58.20 N	5.09 W
Scout Lake, Sk., Can.	142	E8	49.20 N	106.01 W
Scranton, Ia., U.S.	130	B3	42.01 N	94.32 W
Scranton, N.D., U.S.	140	A9	46.08 N	103.08 W
Scranton, Pa., U.S.	124	C10	41.26 N	75.39 W
Screven, Ga., U.S.	132	E3	31.29 N	82.00 W
Scribner, Ne., U.S.	128	J2	41.39 N	96.40 W
Scridain, Loch, b., Scot., U.K.	10	E6	56.21 N	6.07 W
Scrivia, stm., Italy	30	F5	45.03 N	8.54 E
Scrub Island, i., Anguilla	159a	a2	18.18 N	62.57 W
Scrub Island, i., Br. Vir. Is.	158b	e8	18.28 N	64.30 W
Ščuče, Russia	48	C10	55.16 N	62.48 E
Ščuče Ozero, Russia	40	C20	56.28 N	56.38 E
Ščučinsk, Kaz.	48	D12	52.55 N	70.10 E
Ščuč'ja, stm., Russia	50	C2	66.48 N	68.22 E
Ščučyn, Bela.	26	G7	53.36 N	24.45 E
Scugog, Lake, l., On., Can.	126	D11	44.09 N	78.49 W
Scunthorpe, Eng., U.K.	10	H12	53.35 N	0.39 W
Scuol, Switz.	30	D7	46.48 N	10.18 E
Scurry, Tx., U.S.	136	B11	32.31 N	96.23 W
Scutari see Shkodër, Alb.	32	B13	42.04 N	19.31 E
Scutari, Lake, l., Eur.	30	H16	42.12 N	19.18 E
Scviha see Stviga, stm., Eur.	38	B6	52.04 N	27.54 E
Ščytkavičy, Bela.	26	G10	53.13 N	27.59 E
Sé, ngh., Braz.	205b		23.33 S	46.37 W
Seabird Island Indian Reserve, ind. res., B.C., Can.	144	G9	49.17 N	121.42 W
Sea Bright, N.J., U.S.	194		40.21 N	73.58 W
Seabrook, Md., U.S.	202c		38.58 N	76.50 W
Seabrook, Lake, l., Austl.	96	F3	30.53 S	119.39 E
Seacombe, Eng., U.K.	180		53.25 N	3.01 W
Sea Dog Island, i., N.Y., U.S.	194		40.36 N	73.35 W
Seaford, De., U.S.	124	F10	38.38 N	75.36 W
Seaford, N.Y., U.S.	194		40.39 N	73.29 W
Seaford Creek, stm., N.Y., U.S.	194		40.38 N	73.29 W
Seaforth, Austl.	192a		33.48 S	151.15 E
Seaforth, On., Can.	126	E8	43.33 N	81.24 W
Seaforth, Eng., U.K.	180		53.28 N	3.01 W
Seagraves, Tx., U.S.	136	B5	32.56 N	102.33 W
Seaholme, Austl.	192b		37.52 S	144.50 E
Seahorse Point, c., Nu., Can.	110	C15	63.45 N	80.09 W
Sea Islands, is., U.S.	132	E5	31.20 N	81.20 W
Sea Isle City, N.J., U.S.	124	E11	39.09 N	74.41 W
Seal, Eng., U.K.	178		51.17 N	0.14 E
Seal, stm., Mb., Can.	110	D11	59.04 N	94.46 W
Seal, Cape, c., S. Afr.	90	I6	34.06 S	23.24 E
Sea Lake, Austl.	98	J4	35.30 S	142.51 E
Sealand, Wales, U.K.	180		53.12 N	2.58 W
Sealark Channel, strt., Sol. Is.	101b	e9	9.19 S	160.23 E
Seal Beach National Wildlife Refuge, ind. res., Ca., U.S.	198		33.45 N	118.03 W
Seal Cays, is., T./C. Is.	156	B12	21.10 N	71.38 W
Sealdah Railroad Station, trans., India	190b		22.34 N	88.23 E
Seale, Al., U.S.	134	E13	32.17 N	85.10 W
Sealevel, N.C., U.S.	132	B9	34.52 N	76.24 W
Seal Island, i., N.S., Can.	122	G10	43.25 N	66.01 W
Seal Islands, is., Ca., U.S.	200		38.03 N	122.03 W
Seal Rocks, r., Ca., U.S.	200		37.47 N	122.31 W
Sealy, Tx., U.S.	136	E11	29.46 N	96.09 W
Seara, Braz.	172	C11	27.08 S	52.18 W
Searchlight, Nv., U.S.	150	H2	35.27 N	114.55 W
Searcy, Ar., U.S.	134	B7	35.15 N	91.44 W
Searles Lake, l., Ca., U.S.	148	H8	35.43 N	117.20 W
Searles Lake, l., Mi., U.S.	199		42.35 N	83.39 W
Searsport, Me., U.S.	122	F8	44.27 N	68.55 W
Sears Tower, bldg., Il., U.S.	196		41.53 N	87.38 W
Searsville Lake, l., Ca., U.S.	200		37.24 N	122.14 W
Seaside, Ca., U.S.	148	G4	36.36 N	121.50 W
Seaside, Or., U.S.	146	D3	45.59 N	123.55 W
Seaside Park, N.J., U.S.	124	E11	39.54 N	74.04 W
Seaside Park, p.o.i., Ct., U.S.	194		41.10 N	73.12 W
Seat Pleasant, Md., U.S.	202c		38.53 N	76.54 W
Seattle, Wa., U.S.	146	C4	47.36 N	122.19 W
Seatuck National Wildlife Refuge, ind. res., N.Y., U.S.	194		40.43 N	73.13 W
Sea View, Ma., U.S.	201		42.08 N	70.42 W
Seaview, N.Y., U.S.	194		40.39 N	73.09 W
Seba, Indon.	96	B4	10.29 S	121.51 E
Sébaco, Nic.	156	F4	12.50 N	86.05 W
Sebago Lake, l., Me., U.S.	122	G6	43.50 N	70.35 W
Se Bai, stm., Thai.	64	E7	15.14 N	104.46 E
Sebakung, Indon.	66	D10	1.37 S	116.26 E
Šebalin, Russia	40	H13	47.22 N	43.36 E
Sebanga, Indon.	66	C2	1.24 N	101.10 E
Sebangan, Teluk, b., Indon.	66	E8	3.15 S	113.30 E
Sebangka, Pulau, i., Indon.	66	C4	0.07 N	104.36 E
Sébaou, Oued, stm., Alg.	28	H14	36.46 N	4.04 E
Sebarok, Pulau, i., Sing.	189c		1.13 N	103.48 E
Sebastian, Tx., U.S.	136	H10	26.20 N	97.46 W
Sebastian, Cape, c., Or., U.S.	148	A1	42.19 N	124.24 W
Sebastián Vizcaíno, Bahía, b., Mex.	154	A1	28.00 N	114.30 W
Sebastopol, Ca., U.S.	148	E3	38.23 N	122.49 W
Sebastopol, Ms., U.S.	134	E9	32.34 N	89.20 W
Sebec Lake, l., Me., U.S.	122	E7	45.16 N	69.18 W
Sebeka, Mn., U.S.	128	E3	46.38 N	95.05 W
Šebekino, Russia	40	F10	50.25 N	36.55 E
Seben, Tur.	34	C14	40.24 N	31.32 E
Seberi, Braz.	172	C11	27.29 S	53.24 W
Seberida, Indon.	66	D3	0.44 S	102.30 E
Sebeș, Rom.	36	D10	45.57 N	23.34 E
Sebes Körös (Crișul Repede), stm., Eur.	36	B8	46.55 N	20.58 E
Sebewaing, Mi., U.S.	126	E6	43.44 N	83.26 W
Sebež, Russia	26	D11	56.17 N	28.28 E
Sebille Manor, Mi., U.S.	199		42.39 N	82.49 W
Şebinkarahisar, Tur.	42	E8	40.17 N	38.26 E
Sebino see Iseo, Lago d', l., Italy	30	E6	45.44 N	10.04 E
Sebiș, Rom.	36	C9	46.22 N	22.08 E
Sebnitz, Ger.	24	F10	50.58 N	14.16 E
Sebree, Ky., U.S.	130	G10	37.36 N	87.31 W
Sebring, Fl., U.S.	132	I4	27.30 N	81.26 W
Sebuku, Indon.	66	A10	4.00 N	117.01 E
Sebuku, Pulau, i., Indon.	66	E10	3.30 S	116.22 E
Sebuku, Teluk, b., Indon.	66	B10	4.04 N	117.43 E
Šebunino, Russia	52	B13	46.26 N	141.51 E
Sebuyau, Malay.	66	C7	1.30 N	110.49 E
Seca, Ilha, i., Braz.	205a		22.50 S	43.11 W
Secane, Pa., U.S.	203		39.55 N	75.18 W
Secaucus, N.J., U.S.	194		40.47 N	74.03 W
Secchia, stm., Italy	30	F7	45.04 N	10.59 E
Secesh, stm., Id., U.S.	146	E11	45.02 N	115.43 W
Sechelt, B.C., Can.	144	G7	49.28 N	123.45 W
Sechura, Peru	164	E1	5.33 S	80.49 W
Sechura, Desierto de, des., Peru	164	E1	5.50 S	80.40 W
Seclantás, Arg.	172	B4	25.17 S	66.14 W
Seco, stm., Spain	184d		41.30 N	2.09 E
Seco, Arroyo, stm., Ca., U.S.	148	G4	36.25 N	121.20 W
Seco, Arroyo, stm., Ca., U.S.	198		34.05 N	118.13 W
Seco Creek, stm., N.M., U.S.	150	K9	32.59 N	107.18 W
Seco Creek, stm., Tx., U.S.	136	E8	29.01 N	99.08 W
Second, stm., N.J., U.S.	194		40.47 N	74.09 W
Second Cliff, clf., Ma., U.S.	201		42.12 N	70.43 W
Second Herring Brook, stm., Ma., U.S.	201		42.09 N	70.47 W
Second Watchung Mountain, mtn., N.J., U.S.	194		40.55 N	74.13 W
Sečovce, Slvk.	24	H17	48.42 N	21.39 E
Sečovská Polianka, Slvk.	24	H17	48.47 N	21.42 E
Section, Al., U.S.	134	C13	34.34 N	85.59 W
Security, Co., U.S.	138	C4	38.45 N	104.44 W
Security Square, shp. cen., Md., U.S.	202b		39.19 N	76.45 W
Séd, stm., Hung.	30	C15	46.59 N	18.30 E
Seda, China	52	E5	32.20 N	100.41 E
Seda, Lat.	26	C8	57.39 N	25.47 E
Seda, Lith.	26	D5	56.10 N	22.05 E
Seda, stm., Lat.	26	C8	57.45 N	25.14 E
Sedah, Indon.	96	B4	10.46 S	123.10 E
Sedalia, Ab., Can.	142	C3	51.41 N	110.39 W
Sedalia, Mo., U.S.	130	F4	38.42 N	93.13 W
Sedan, Fr.	20	E13	49.42 N	4.56 E
Sedan, Ks., U.S.	138	D12	37.07 N	96.11 W
Sedano, Spain	28	B7	42.43 N	3.44 W
Sedanovo, Russia	48	C18	56.57 N	101.20 E
Sedayu, Indon.	66	G8	6.59 S	112.32 E
Sedbergh, Eng., U.K.	10	G10	54.19 N	2.31 W
Seddin-Berg, hill, Ger.	182a		52.24 N	13.40 E
Seddinsee, l., Ger.	182a		52.23 N	13.41 E
Seddon, Kap, c., Grnld.	108	B14	75.21 N	58.41 W
Seddonville, N.Z.	102	E4	41.32 S	171.58 E
Sedel'nikovo, Russia	48	C13	56.56 N	75.18 E
Séderon, Fr.	22	E11	44.12 N	5.32 E
Sedgefield, N.J., U.S.	194		40.51 N	74.28 W
Sedge Island, i., N.J., U.S.	194		40.21 N	73.59 W
Sedgewick, Ab., Can.	144	D19	52.47 N	111.41 W
Sedgwick, Co., U.S.	140	G10	40.55 N	102.31 W
Sedgwick, Ks., U.S.	138	D11	37.55 N	97.25 W
Sedgwick, Mount, mtn., N.M., U.S.	150	H8	35.11 N	108.06 W
Sédhiou, Sen.	84	G1	12.42 N	15.34 W
Sedini, Italy	32	D2	40.50 N	8.48 E
Sedlčany, Czech Rep.	24	G10	49.39 N	14.25 E
Sedniv, Ukr.	38	B10	51.39 N	31.34 E
Šedok, Russia	42	C9	44.12 N	40.51 E
Sedom (Sodom), hist., Isr.	76	G6	31.04 N	35.23 E
Sedona, Az., U.S.	150	I5	34.50 N	111.47 W
Sedro Woolley, Wa., U.S.	146	B4	48.30 N	122.13 W
Šeduva, Lith.	26	E6	55.45 N	23.46 E
Sée, stm., Fr.	20	F7	48.40 N	1.24 W
Seeberg, Ger.	182a		52.33 N	13.41 E
Seeburg, Ger.	182a		52.31 N	13.07 E
Seefeld in Tirol, Aus.	24	I7	47.20 N	11.10 E
Seegefeld, Ger.	182a		52.33 N	13.05 E
Seehausen, Ger.	24	D7	52.53 N	11.45 E
Seeheim, Nmb.	90	E3	26.49 S	17.49 E
Seehof, Ger.	182a		52.24 N	13.17 E
Seeis, Nmb.	90	C3	22.26 S	17.35 E
Seekoei, stm., S. Afr.	90	G7	30.17 S	25.01 E
Seeley Lake, Mt., U.S.	146	C13	47.10 N	113.29 W
Seelow, Ger.	24	D10	52.31 N	14.22 E
Seelyville, In., U.S.	130	E10	39.29 N	87.15 W
Seemore Downs, Austl.	96	F5	30.44 S	125.16 E
Seer Green, Eng., U.K.	178		51.37 N	0.36 W
Sées, Fr.	20	F9	48.36 N	0.10 E
Seesen, Ger.	24	E6	51.53 N	10.10 E
Sefadu, S.L.	84	H2	8.40 N	11.01 W
Seferihisar, Tur.	34	E9	38.11 N	26.50 E
Sefīd, stm., Iran	74	B11	37.26 N	49.55 E
Sefton, Eng., U.K.	180		53.30 N	2.58 W
Sefton, mun., Eng., U.K.	180		53.31 N	3.02 W
Sefton, mun., Eng., U.K.	180		53.31 N	3.02 W
Sefton Park, p.o.i., Eng., U.K.	180		53.23 N	2.56 W
Segama, stm., Malay.	66	A11	5.30 N	118.48 E
Segamat, Malay.	64	K6	2.30 N	102.49 E
Şegarcea, Rom.	36	E10	44.06 N	23.45 E
Šegarka, stm., Russia	48	C14	57.15 N	84.03 E
Ségbana, Benin	84	G5	10.55 N	3.41 E
Segeri, Indon.	66	F11	4.38 S	119.33 E
Segesta, hist., Italy	32	G6	37.56 N	12.50 E
Segesvár see Sighișoara, Rom.	36	C11	46.13 N	24.48 E
Segeža, Russia	18	D21	63.44 N	34.18 E
Šegmas, Russia	12	D23	64.44 N	49.18 E
Segorbe, Spain	28	E10	39.50 N	0.28 W
Ségou, Mali	84	G3	13.26 N	6.16 W
Segovary, Russia	12	E20	62.21 N	42.57 E
Segovia, Col.	168	D4	7.05 N	74.42 W
Segovia, Spain	28	D6	40.56 N	4.07 W
Segovia, co., Spain	28	C6	41.15 N	4.00 W
Segozero, ozero, l., Russia	18	D20	63.18 N	33.45 E

Name	Page	Map Ref.	Latitude	Longitude
Segrate, Italy	184b		45.29 N	9.19 E
Segré, Fr.	20	G8	47.41 N	0.52 W
Segre, stm., Eur.	28	C11	41.22 N	0.18 E
Seguam Island, i., Ak., U.S.	109a	g24	52.17 N	172.30 W
Séguédine, Niger	84	E7	20.12 N	12.59 E
Séguéla, C. Iv.	84	H3	7.57 N	6.40 W
Seguí, Arg.	172	E7	31.57 S	60.08 W
Seguin, Tx., U.S.	136	E10	29.34 N	97.57 W
Seguine Point, c., N.Y., U.S.	194		40.31 N	74.12 W
Segundo, Co., U.S.	138	D4	37.06 N	104.44 W
Segundo, stm., Arg.	172	E6	31.22 S	62.56 W
Seguntur, Indon.	66	C10	1.54 N	117.47 E
Segura, Port.	28	E3	39.50 N	6.58 W
Segura, stm., Spain	28	F10	38.06 N	0.38 W
Segura, Sierra de, mts., Spain	28	G8	38.00 N	2.43 W
Sehāni Kalān, India	190a		28.41 N	77.25 E
Sehāni Khurd, India	190a		28.42 N	77.25 E
Sehithwa, Bots.	90	B6	20.27 S	22.42 E
Sehore, India	70	G6	23.12 N	77.05 E
Sehwān, Pak.	62	C2	26.27 N	67.51 E
Seia, Port.	28	D3	40.25 N	7.42 W
Seibert, Co., U.S.	138	B6	39.18 N	102.52 W
Seibu, Japan	186		35.50 N	139.22 E
Seigneurial, Lac, l., Qc., Can.	193a		45.33 N	73.20 W
Seika, Japan	188		34.46 N	135.48 E
Seikpyu, Mya.	64	B2	20.54 N	94.47 E
Seiland, i., Nor.	14	B14	70.25 N	23.15 E
Seilandsjøkelen, ice, Nor.	14	B14	70.24 N	23.16 E
Seilhac, Fr.	22	D7	45.22 N	1.42 E
Seiling, Ok., U.S.	138	E10	36.08 N	98.57 W
Seim see Seim', stm., Eur.	38	B12	51.27 N	32.35 E
Seim see Sejm, stm., Eur.	38	B12	51.27 N	32.35 E
Seim' (Sejm), stm., Eur.	38	B12	51.27 N	32.35 E
Seinäjoki, Fin.	18	E9	62.47 N	22.50 E
Seine, stm., Mb., Can.	142	E17	49.54 N	97.07 W
Seine, stm., On., Can.	128	C6	48.38 N	92.58 W
Seine, stm., Fr.	20	E9	49.28 N	0.28 E
Seine, Baie de la, b., Fr.	20	E8	49.30 N	0.30 W
Seine, Bay of the see Seine, Baie de la, b., Fr.	20	E8	49.30 N	0.30 W
Seine-et-Marne, state, Fr.	20	F12	48.30 N	3.00 E
Seine-Maritime, state, Fr.	20	E9	49.45 N	1.00 E
Seine-Saint-Denis, state, Fr.	179		48.55 N	2.30 E
Seishin see Ch'ŏngjin, Kor., N.	54	D8	41.46 N	129.48 E
Seitevare, Swe.	14	F9	66.58 N	18.34 E
Seitovka, Russia	40	H16	46.46 N	48.01 E
Seitsemisen kansallispuisto, p.o.i., Fin.	18	F10	61.58 N	23.20 E
Seixal, Port.	28	F1	38.38 N	9.06 W
Seixas, Ponta do, c., Braz.	170	D8	7.09 S	34.47 W
Sejaka, Indon.	66	E10	3.33 S	116.12 E
Sejerø, i., Den.	16	L9	55.53 N	11.09 E
Sejerø Bugt, b., Den.	16	L8	55.50 N	11.15 E
Sejm (Seim'), stm., Eur.	38	B12	51.27 N	32.35 E
Sejmčan, Russia	50	D19	62.54 N	152.24 E
Sejny, Pol.	24	B19	54.06 N	23.20 E
Sekadau, Indon.	66	C7	0.00 N	110.53 E
Sekayam, stm., Indon.	66	C7	0.08 N	110.37 E
Sekayu, Indon.	66	E3	2.52 S	103.49 E
Sekeladi, Indon.	66	E3	2.38 S	102.14 E
Šeki, Azer.	42	E12	41.09 N	47.10 E
Seki, Japan	56	D9	35.29 N	136.55 E
Sekima, Indon.	66	D7	1.42 S	111.27 E
Sekiu, Wa., U.S.	146	B2	48.15 N	124.18 W
Sekiya, Japan	188		34.27 N	135.42 E
Sekoma, Bots.	90	D6	24.31 S	23.57 E
Sekondi see Sekondi-Takoradi, Ghana	84	I4	4.59 N	1.43 W
Sekondi-Takoradi, Ghana	84	I4	4.59 N	1.43 W
Sek'ot'a, Eth.	82	E7	12.37 N	39.02 E
Sekretaris, stm., Indon.	187e		6.10 S	106.47 E
Šeksna, Russia	26	A21	59.12 N	38.31 E
Šelagskij, mys, c., Russia	50	B23	70.06 N	170.29 E
Selah, Wa., U.S.	146	D6	46.38 N	120.31 W
Selama, Malay.	64	J5	5.13 N	100.40 E
Selangor, state, Malay.	64	K5	3.20 N	101.30 E
Selaön, i., Swe.	16	H15	59.24 N	17.12 E
Selaphum, Thai.	64	D6	16.01 N	103.56 E
Selaru, Pulau, i., Indon.	60	G9	8.10 S	130.59 E
Selatan, Tanjung, c., Indon.	66	F9	4.10 S	114.38 E
Selatpanjang, Indon.	66	C3	0.59 N	102.42 E
Selawik, Ak., U.S.	109	C8	66.39 N	160.07 W
Selawik Lake, l., Ak., U.S.	109	C7	66.30 N	160.40 W
Selayar, Pulau, i., Indon.	66	F12	6.05 S	120.30 E
Selayar, Selat, strt., Indon.	66	F12	5.42 S	120.28 E
Selb, Ger.	24	F8	50.10 N	12.08 E
Selbeck, ngh., Ger.	181		51.22 N	6.52 E
Selbecke, ngh., Ger.	181		51.20 N	7.28 E
Selbjørnsfjorden, b., Nor.	16	H2	59.56 N	5.08 E
Selbusjøen, l., Nor.	16	D9	63.14 N	10.53 E
Selby, Austl.	192b		37.55 S	145.22 E
Selby, Eng., U.K.	10	H11	53.47 N	1.04 W
Selby, S.D., U.S.	140	B12	45.30 N	100.02 W
Selby, ngh., S. Afr.	191d		26.13 S	28.02 E
Selbyville, De., U.S.	124	F10	38.26 N	75.13 W
Selchow, Ger.	182a		52.21 N	13.28 E
Sel'co, Russia	12	E19	63.18 N	41.22 E
Sel'co, Russia	26	G17	53.21 N	34.07 E
Selcourt, S. Afr.	191d		26.18 S	28.27 E
Selçuk, Tur.	34	F10	37.56 N	27.21 E
Sel'cy, Russia	26	C18	57.57 N	35.59 E
Sel'cy, Russia	183a		59.57 N	30.43 E
Selden, Ks., U.S.	138	B8	39.33 N	100.34 W
Seldovia, Ak., U.S.	109	E9	59.26 N	151.42 W
Sele, stm., Italy	32	D9	40.29 N	14.56 E
Selebi-Phikwe, Bots.	90	C9	21.59 S	27.50 E
Selec, Russia	26	H16	52.32 N	33.36 E
Seleckoe, ozero, l., Russia	18	D19	63.12 N	33.09 E
Selečnja, Russia	26	H17	52.23 N	34.22 E
Selection Park, S. Afr.	191d		26.18 S	28.27 E
Šelehov, Russia	48	D18	52.12 N	104.05 E
Selemadeg, Indon.	66	H9	8.30 S	115.01 E
Selembao, D.R.C.	191b		4.22 S	15.17 E
Selemdža, stm., Russia	50	F14	51.43 N	128.53 E
Selemdžinsk, Russia	50	F15	52.36 N	131.10 E
Selendi, Tur.	34	E11	38.45 N	28.53 E
Selenduma, Russia	50	F10	50.54 N	106.13 E
Selenga (Selenge), stm., Asia	50	F10	52.16 N	106.15 E
Selenge, D.R.C.	86	E3	1.58 S	18.10 E
Selenge (Selenga), stm., Asia	50	G9	52.16 N	106.15 E
Selenica see Selenicë, Alb.	32	D13	40.33 N	19.38 E
Selenicë, Alb.	32	D13	40.33 N	19.38 E
Selennjah, stm., Russia	50	C16	67.50 N	144.52 E
Sélestat, Fr.	20	F16	48.15 N	7.27 E
Seletar, stm., Sing.	189c		1.25 N	103.52 E
Seletar, Pulau, i., Sing.	189c		1.27 N	103.52 E
Seletar Airport, arpt., Sing.	189c		1.16 N	103.53 E
Seletar Hills, Sing.	189c		1.23 N	103.53 E
Selezenëvo, Russia	40	B12	59.12 N	42.16 E
Seleznëvo, Russia	18	G15	60.44 N	28.37 E
Selezni, Russia	26	E14	55.38 N	31.29 E
Selezni, Russia	40	E12	52.48 N	41.13 E
Self Defense Fleet Headquarters, mil., Japan	186		35.18 N	139.38 E
Selfoss, Ice.	12a	I29	63.56 N	20.58 W
Selfridge, N.D., U.S.	140	A12	46.02 N	100.55 W
Selfridge Air National Guard Base, mil., Mi., U.S.	199		42.36 N	82.49 W
Selghar, India	190c		18.57 N	73.02 E
Sel'gi, Russia	18	D20	63.08 N	33.11 E
Sel'gon, Russia	50	G16	49.35 N	135.23 E
Seliatyn, Ukr.	38	F4	47.53 N	25.12 E
Sélibabi, Maur.	84	F2	15.10 N	12.11 W
Seliger, ozero, l., Russia	26	C16	57.13 N	33.02 E
Seligman, Az., U.S.	150	H4	35.19 N	112.53 W
Seligman, Mo., U.S.	130	H3	36.31 N	93.56 W
Šelihova, zaliv, b., Russia	50	D20	60.00 N	158.00 E
Selimbau, Indon.	66	C8	0.36 N	112.08 E
Selimiye, Tur.	34	F10	37.23 N	27.39 E
Selimiye Mosque, rel., Tur.	185b		41.00 N	29.01 E
Selínia, Grc.	185c		37.56 N	23.32 E
Selinsgrove, Pa., U.S.	124	D9	40.48 N	76.51 W
Selinunte, hist., Italy	32	G6	37.35 N	12.49 E
Selišče, Russia	12	D22	64.57 N	46.18 E
Selišče, Russia	26	D16	56.53 N	33.16 E
Seližarovo, Russia	26	D16	56.51 N	33.28 E
Selje, Nor.	16	E3	62.02 N	5.22 E
Seljord, Nor.	16	H6	59.29 N	8.37 E
Selkirk, Mb., Can.	142	D17	50.09 N	96.52 W
Selkirk, Scot., U.K.	10	F10	55.33 N	2.50 W
Selkirk Mountains, mts., N.A.	144	F13	51.00 N	117.40 W
Šelkovskaja, Russia	42	D12	43.31 N	46.20 E
Sellers, S.C., U.S.	132	B6	34.17 N	79.27 W
Sellersburg, In., U.S.	130	F12	38.23 N	85.45 W
Selles-sur-Cher, Fr.	20	G10	47.16 N	1.33 E
Sells, Az., U.S.	150	L5	31.55 N	111.53 W
Selm, Ger.	24	E3	51.41 N	7.28 E
Selma, Al., U.S.	134	E11	32.24 N	87.01 W
Selma, Ca., U.S.	148	G6	36.34 N	119.37 W
Selma, N.C., U.S.	132	A7	35.32 N	78.17 W
Selmer, Tn., U.S.	134	B10	35.10 N	88.35 W
Selmigerheide, ngh., Ger.	181		51.38 N	7.47 E
Selmont, Al., U.S.	134	E11	32.22 N	87.01 W
Šelon', stm., Russia	26	B13	58.12 N	30.45 E
Selong, Indon.	66	H10	8.39 S	116.31 E
Selsdon, ngh., Eng., U.K.	178		51.21 N	0.04 W
Selty, Russia	40	C18	57.18 N	52.07 E
Seltz, Fr.	24	H4	48.53 N	8.05 E
Sélune, stm., Fr.	20	F7	48.38 N	1.21 W
Selva, Arg.	172	D6	29.46 S	62.03 W
Selvagens, Ilhas, is., Port.	84	C1	30.08 N	15.52 W
Selvas, for., Braz.	162	F8	5.00 S	68.00 W
Selway, stm., Id., U.S.	146	D11	46.07 N	115.35 W
Selwyn, Austl.	98	C3	21.32 S	140.30 E
Selwyn, Passage, strt., Vanuatu	101d	k16	16.02 S	168.12 E
Selwyn Lake, l., Can.	110	D10	59.54 N	104.21 W
Selwyn Mountains, mts., Can.	110	C4	63.10 N	130.20 W
Selwyn Range, mts., Austl.	98	C3	21.35 S	140.35 E
Selydove, Ukr.	38	E16	48.08 N	37.17 E
Semakau, Pulau, i., Sing.	189c		1.12 N	103.46 E
Seman, stm., Alb.	32	D13	40.50 N	19.25 E
Semangka, Teluk, b., Indon.	66	F4	5.36 S	104.42 E
Semans, Sk., Can.	142	C9	51.24 N	104.42 W
Semara, W. Sah.	84	D2	26.44 N	11.40 W
Semarang, Indon.	66	G7	6.58 S	110.24 E
Sematan, Malay.	66	C6	1.48 N	109.45 E
Semayang, Kenohan, l., Indon.	66	D10	0.14 S	116.28 E
Sembakung, stm., Indon.	66	B10	3.45 N	117.28 E
Sembawang, Sing.	189c		1.27 N	103.50 E
Sembé, Congo	86	D2	1.38 N	14.36 E
Semberong, stm., Malay.	66	B3	2.25 N	103.38 E
Semča, stm., Russia	18	E20	62.31 N	33.33 E
Semcy, Russia	26	H16	52.50 N	33.29 E
Şemdinli, Tur.	42	G11	37.18 N	44.35 E
Semeliškės, Lith.	26	F7	54.40 N	24.40 E
Semenanjung Malaysia, hist. reg., Malay.	64	K6	4.00 N	102.00 E
Semenicului, Munţii, mts., Rom.	36	D9	45.05 N	22.05 E
Semenivka, Ukr.	38	A11	52.10 N	32.35 E
Semenivka, Ukr.	40	G8	49.36 N	33.10 E
Semenov, Russia	40	C14	56.47 N	44.29 E
Semeru, Gunung, vol., Indon.	66	H8	8.05 S	112.55 E
Semey see Semipalatinsk, Kaz.	48	D13	50.24 N	80.13 E
Semežava, Bela.	26	H10	52.57 N	27.00 E
Semibalki, Russia	38	F17	47.00 N	39.02 E
Semibratovo, Russia	26	C22	57.18 N	39.31 E
Semichi Islands, is., Ak., U.S.	109a	g21	52.47 N	173.57 E
Semidesjatnoe, Russia	38	B17	51.21 N	38.44 E
Semikarakorsk, Russia	40	H12	47.30 N	40.48 E
Semiluki, Russia	40	F11	51.41 N	39.02 E
Semily, Czech Rep.	24	F11	50.35 N	15.20 E
Seminary, Ms., U.S.	134	F9	31.33 N	89.29 W
Seminoe Reservoir, res., Wy., U.S.	150	A9	42.02 N	106.51 W
Seminoe State Park, p.o.i., Wy., U.S.	150	A9	42.05 N	106.55 W
Seminole, Ok., U.S.	134	B2	35.13 N	96.40 W
Seminole, Tx., U.S.	134	B5	32.43 N	102.38 W
Seminole, Lake, res., U.S.	134	G13	30.46 N	84.50 W
Seminole Draw, stm., U.S.	136	B5	32.27 N	102.20 W
Semiozërnoe, Kaz.	48	D10	52.21 N	64.08 E
Semipalatinsk, Kaz.	48	D13	50.24 N	80.13 E
Semitau, Indon.	66	C7	0.32 N	111.58 E
Semizbuga, Kaz.	48	D13	50.11 N	74.51 E
Semlëvo, Russia	26	E17	55.03 N	33.58 E
Semliki, stm., Afr.	86	D6	1.12 N	30.30 E
Semnān, Iran	74	C13	35.34 N	53.23 E
Semnān, state, Iran	74	C14	35.30 N	54.00 E
Semois, stm., Eur.	20	E13	49.52 N	4.44 E
Šemonaiha, Kaz.	48	D14	50.38 N	81.54 E
Sempang Mangayau, Tanjong, c., Malay.	68	G1	7.00 N	116.45 E
Semporna, Malay.	66	A11	4.28 N	118.36 E
Semuda, Indon.	66	E8	2.51 S	112.56 E
Semur-en-Auxois, Fr.	20	G13	47.29 N	4.20 E
Semypolky, Ukr.	40	F7	50.43 N	30.56 E
Semža, Russia	12	C21	66.08 N	44.08 E
Sên, stm., Camb.	64	F7	12.31 N	104.28 E
Sena, Bol.	166	B3	11.31 S	67.15 W
Sena see Vila de Sena, Moz.	88	D5	17.26 S	35.01 E
Senador Canedo, Braz.	170	I1	16.42 S	49.05 W
Senador Firmino, Braz.	170	K4	20.55 S	43.06 W
Senador Pompeu, Braz.	170	C6	5.35 S	39.22 W
Senago, Italy	184b		45.35 N	9.07 E
Senainville, Fr.	179		48.30 N	1.37 E
Senaja, Malay.	68	G1	6.43 N	117.02 E
Senaki, Geor.	42	D10	42.16 N	42.03 E
Sena Madureira, Braz.	164	E4	9.04 S	68.40 W
Senanayake Samudra, res., Sri L.	69	H5	7.11 N	81.29 E
Senang, Pulau, i., Sing.	189c		1.11 N	103.44 E
Senanga, Zam.	88	D3	16.07 S	23.17 E
Sénart, Forêt de, p.o.i., Fr.	179		48.40 N	2.30 E
Senate, Sk., Can.	142	E4	49.15 N	109.39 W
Senath, Mo., U.S.	130	H7	36.08 N	90.10 W
Senatobia, Ms., U.S.	134	C8	34.37 N	89.57 W
Šenber, Kaz.	48	E11	49.47 N	66.08 E
Sencha, Ukr.	38	C12	50.15 N	33.21 E
Send, Eng., U.K.	178		51.17 N	0.31 W
Sendai, Japan	56	H3	31.48 N	130.18 E
Sendai, Japan	56	A13	38.15 N	140.53 E
Sendai, stm., Japan	56	H3	31.49 N	130.14 E
Sendai-heiya, pl., Japan	56	A14	38.34 N	141.09 E
Sendelingsdrif, Nmb.	90	F3	28.10 S	16.52 E
Sendhwa, India	70	H5	21.40 N	75.05 E
Sêndo, China	52	E4	31.32 N	95.16 E
Sendurjana, India	70	H7	21.31 N	78.17 E
Senduruhan, Indon.	66	D7	0.59 S	110.46 E
Senebui, Tanjung, c., Indon.	66	B2	2.17 N	101.03 E
Senec, Slvk.	24	H13	48.13 N	17.24 E
Seneca, Il., U.S.	130	C9	41.18 N	88.36 W
Seneca, Ks., U.S.	130	E1	39.50 N	96.03 W
Seneca, Md., U.S.	202c		39.04 N	77.17 W
Seneca, Mo., U.S.	130	H3	36.50 N	94.36 W
Seneca, Or., U.S.	146	F8	44.08 N	118.58 W
Seneca, S.C., U.S.	132	B3	34.41 N	82.56 W
Seneca, Mount, mtn., N.Y., U.S.	124	B7	42.02 N	78.49 W
Seneca Creek, b., Md., U.S.	202b		39.19 N	76.22 W
Seneca Creek, stm., U.S.	138	E5	36.36 N	102.52 W
Seneca Falls, N.Y., U.S.	124	B9	42.54 N	76.48 W
Seneca Lake, l., N.Y., U.S.	124	B9	42.40 N	76.54 W
Seneca Mall, shp. cen., N.Y., U.S.	202a		42.50 N	78.47 W
Senecaville Lake, res., Oh., U.S.	124	E4	39.55 N	81.25 W
Senegal, ctry., Afr.	84	G2	14.00 N	14.00 W
Sénégal see Senegal, ctry., Afr.	84	G2	14.00 N	14.00 W
Sénégal, stm., Afr.	84	F2	15.48 N	16.32 W
Senekal, S. Afr.	90	F8	28.19 S	27.37 E
Senetosa, Capu di (Senetosa, Punta di), c., Fr.	22	H14	41.33 N	8.47 E
Senetosa, Punta di see Senetosa, Capu di, c., Fr.	22	H14	41.33 N	8.47 E
Senftenberg, Ger.	24	E10	51.31 N	14.00 E
Sengbachstausee, res., Ger.	181		51.08 N	7.09 E
Sengejskij, ostrov, i., Russia	12	B24	68.27 N	51.05 E
Sengés, Braz.	172	B13	24.07 S	49.28 W
Sênggê, stm., China	70	B8	32.29 N	79.41 E
Sengilej, Russia	40	E16	53.57 N	48.47 E
Senhor do Bonfim, Braz.	170	F5	10.26 S	40.11 W
Senica, Slvk.	24	H13	48.40 N	17.22 E
Senigallia, Italy	30	G10	43.43 N	13.12 E
Senirkent, Tur.	34	E13	38.06 N	30.34 E
Senise, Italy	32	D10	40.08 N	16.17 E
Senj, Cro.	30	F11	44.59 N	14.54 E
Senja, i., Nor.	14	C8	69.20 N	17.30 E
Senkaku-shotō, is., Japan	52	F9	25.45 N	124.00 E
Senkevychivka, Ukr.	38	C4	50.31 N	25.01 E
Sen'kove, Ukr.	38	D16	49.31 N	37.40 E
Şenköy, Tur.	76	B7	36.00 N	36.10 E
Šenkursk, Russia	12	E20	62.07 N	42.53 E
Senlac, Sk., Can.	142	B4	52.29 N	109.41 W
Şenlikköy, ngh., Tur.	185b		40.59 N	28.47 E
Senlis, Fr.	20	E11	49.12 N	2.35 E
Senlisse, Fr.	179		48.41 N	1.59 E
Senmonorom, Camb.	64	F8	12.26 N	107.14 E
Sennaja, Russia	38	H16	45.17 N	36.59 E
Senneterre, Qc., Can.	114	B12	48.23 N	77.14 W
Senneville, Qc., Can.	193a		45.27 N	73.57 W
Sennoj, Russia	40	E15	52.09 N	46.58 E
Sennokura-yama, mtn., Japan	56	C11	36.49 N	138.50 E
Senoia, Ga., U.S.	134	D14	33.18 N	84.33 W
Senorbì, Italy	32	E3	39.32 N	9.07 E
Şenpazar, Tur.	34	B16	41.48 N	33.16 E
Senqu see Orange, stm., Afr.	90	F3	28.35 S	16.28 E
Senriyama, Japan	188		34.47 N	135.30 E
Sens, Fr.	20	F12	48.11 N	3.16 E
Senta, Yugo.	36	D7	45.55 N	20.05 E
Sentarum, Danau, l., Indon.	66	C7	0.51 N	112.06 E
Sentinel, Ok., U.S.	138	F9	35.09 N	99.10 W
Sentinel Butte, mtn., N.D., U.S.	140	A9	46.53 N	103.50 W
Sentinel Peak, mtn., B.C., Can.	144	B8	54.54 N	121.57 W
Sentosa, i., Sing.	189c		1.15 N	103.50 E
Sento Sé, Braz.	170	E5	9.47 S	41.53 W
Senyavin Islands, is., Micron.	94	C6	6.53 N	158.03 E
Senzu-dake, mtn., Japan	188		34.57 N	135.52 E
Seo de Urgel see La Seu d'Urgell, Spain	28	B12	42.21 N	1.27 E
Seonāth, stm., India	70	H8	21.43 N	82.28 E
Seoni, India	70	G7	22.05 N	79.33 E
Seoni Mālwa, India	70	G6	22.26 N	77.27 E
Seorīnārāyan, India	70	H9	21.44 N	82.35 E
Seoul see Sŏul, Kor., S.	54	F7	37.33 N	127.00 E
Seoul Arts Center, bldg., Kor., S.	189b		37.29 N	127.01 E
Seoul National University, educ., Kor., S.	189b		37.28 N	126.57 E
Seoul Sports Complex, p.o.i., Kor., S.	189b		37.31 N	127.04 E
Seoul Station, trans., Kor., S.	189b		37.34 N	126.58 E
Seoul Tower, bldg., Kor., S.	189b		37.34 N	126.59 E
Sepanjang, Pulau, i., Indon.	66	G9	7.10 S	115.50 E
Separation Creek, stm., Wy., U.S.	150	B9	41.59 N	107.28 W
Sepasu, Indon.	66	C10	0.42 N	117.34 E
Sepetiba, Baía de, b., Braz.	170	L3	23.00 S	43.48 W
Sepi, Sol. Is.	101b	e8	8.33 S	159.51 E
Sepik, stm., Pap. N. Gui.	101a	a3	3.53 S	144.28 E
Sępólno Krajeńskie, Pol.	24	C13	53.27 N	17.32 E
Sépone see Muang Xépôn, Laos	64	D8	16.42 N	106.12 E
Sępopol, Pol.	24	B17	54.16 N	21.01 E
Septemvri, Blg.	36	G11	42.12 N	24.08 E
Septeuil, Fr.	179		48.54 N	1.41 E
Sept-Îles, Qc., Can.	110	E17	50.12 N	66.22 W
Sepulga, stm., Al., U.S.	134	F12	31.11 N	86.46 W
Sepúlveda, Spain	28	C7	41.18 N	3.45 W
Sepulveda, ngh., Ca., U.S.	198		34.13 N	118.28 W
Sepulveda Dam, dam., Ca., U.S.	198		34.10 N	118.29 W
Seputih, stm., Indon.	66	F4	4.39 S	105.51 E
Sequatchie, stm., Tn., U.S.	134	B13	35.01 N	85.38 W
Sequeros, Spain	28	D4	40.31 N	6.01 W
Sequillo, stm., Spain	28	C5	41.44 N	5.30 W
Sequim, Wa., U.S.	146	B3	48.04 N	123.06 W
Sequoia National Park, p.o.i., Ca., U.S.	148	G7	36.30 N	118.33 W
Šerabad, Uzb.	72	B10	37.40 N	67.01 E
Serafettin Dağları, mts., Tur.	48	G6	39.05 N	41.10 E
Serafimovič, Russia	40	G13	49.34 N	42.44 E
Serafimovskoe, Russia	40	I13	45.12 N	43.54 E
Seraing, Bel.	20	D14	50.36 N	5.31 E
Serakhovychi, Ukr.	38	B3	51.24 N	24.41 E
Seram (Ceram), i., Indon.	60	F8	3.00 S	129.00 E
Seram, Laut (Ceram Sea), s., Indon.	60	F8	2.30 S	128.00 E
Serang, Indon.	66	G5	6.07 S	106.09 E
Serangoon, Sing.	189c		1.22 N	103.54 E
Serangoon, stm., Sing.	189c		1.24 N	103.56 E
Serangoon, Pulau, i., Sing.	189c		1.25 N	103.56 E
Serangoon Harbour, b., Sing.	189c		1.23 N	103.57 E
Serasan, Pulau, i., Indon.	66	B6	2.30 N	109.03 E
Serasan, Selat, strt., Indon.	66	B6	2.20 N	109.00 E
Seraya, Pulau, i., Sing.	189c		1.16 N	103.43 E
Serayevo see Sarajevo, Bos.	36	F5	43.51 N	18.25 E
Serbeulangit, Pegunungan, mts., Indon.	64	K3	3.45 N	97.50 E
Serbia see Srbija, state, Yugo.	36	E8	44.00 N	21.00 E
Serchio, stm., Italy	30	G7	43.47 N	10.16 E
Serdež, Russia	40	C16	57.17 N	48.18 E
Serdo, Eth.	82	E8	11.57 N	41.18 E
Serdobsk, Russia	40	E14	52.27 N	44.12 E
Séré'ama, Mont, mtn., Vanuatu	101d	i16	13.47 S	167.29 E
Serebr'anka, Russia	183b		55.45 N	37.55 E
Serebr'anka, stm., Russia	183b		55.47 N	37.42 E
Serebr'anyj Bor, ngh., Russia	183b		55.48 N	37.25 E
Serebrjansk, Kaz.	48	E14	49.43 N	83.19 E
Serebrjanye Prudy, Russia	26	F21	54.28 N	38.44 E
Sered', Slvk.	24	H13	48.17 N	17.45 E
Sereda, Russia	26	E18	55.54 N	35.31 E
Seredejskij, Russia	26	F18	54.03 N	35.14 E
Serediči, Russia	26	G18	53.35 N	35.50 E
Serëdka, Russia	26	B11	58.11 N	28.11 E
Serednëvo, Russia	183b		55.35 N	37.18 E
Serednikovo, Russia	183b		55.56 N	37.14 E
Seredyna-Buda, Ukr.	38	A13	52.10 N	34.02 E
Seredžius, Lith.	26	E6	55.05 N	23.25 E
Şereflikoçhisar, Tur.	42	F5	38.56 N	33.33 E
Seremban, Malay.	64	K5	2.43 N	101.56 E
Seremetevo-1 Airport, arpt., Russia	183b		55.59 N	37.23 E
Seremetevo-2 Airport, arpt., Russia	183b		55.59 N	37.24 E
Serengeti National Park, p.o.i., Tan.	86	E6	2.20 S	34.50 E
Serengeti Plain, pl., Tan.	86	E6	2.50 S	35.00 E
Serengka, Indon.	66	D7	1.46 S	110.42 E
Serenje, Zam.	88	C5	13.13 S	30.13 E
Seret (Siret), stm., Eur.	36	A12	45.24 N	28.01 E
Seret, stm., Ukr.	38	D4	48.37 N	25.51 E
Ser'ga, Russia	40	C20	57.47 N	56.53 E
Sergač, Russia	40	D14	55.31 N	45.29 E
Sergeant Bluff, Ia., U.S.	130	B1	42.24 N	96.21 W
Sergeevka, Kaz.	48	D11	53.52 N	67.25 E
Sergeevka, Russia	54	C10	43.20 N	133.21 E
Sergeevka, Russia	54	B9	44.19 N	131.39 E
Sergeja Kirova, ostrova, is., Russia	50	A6	77.11 N	88.59 E
Sergen, Tur.	34	B10	41.42 N	27.42 E
Sergievo, Russia	18	E23	62.53 N	36.01 E
Sergiev Posad, Russia	26	D21	56.18 N	38.09 E
Serginskij, Russia	48	B10	62.30 N	65.35 E
Sergipe, state, Braz.	170	F7	10.30 S	37.30 W
Sergozero, ozero, l., Russia	14	F27	66.45 N	36.41 E
Seria, Bru.	66	A9	4.36 N	114.20 E
Serian, Malay.	66	C7	1.10 N	110.33 E
Seribudolok, Indon.	66	B1	2.48 N	99.01 E
Seribudolok, Indon.	66	B1	2.56 N	98.36 E
Seridó, stm., Braz.	170	D7	6.12 S	37.10 W
Sérifos, Grc.	34	F7	37.09 N	24.30 E
Sérifos, i., Grc.	34	F7	37.11 N	24.31 E
Serik, Tur.	34	G14	36.55 N	31.06 E
Seringat, Pulau, i., Sing.	189c		1.14 N	103.51 E
Serinyol, Tur.	76	B7	36.23 N	36.14 E
Serio, stm., Italy	30	E6	45.15 N	9.41 E
Serkovo, Russia	48	A15	54.27 N	38.46 E
Šerlovaja Gora, Russia	50	F12	50.32 N	116.18 E
Serm, ngh., Ger.	181		51.21 N	6.42 E
Sermaise, Fr.	179		48.32 N	2.05 E
Šerna, stm., Russia	26	D21	55.50 N	38.34 E
Sernambetiba, Pontal de, c., Braz.	205a		23.02 S	43.27 W
Sernambitiba, Braz.	205a		22.41 S	42.59 W
Sernovodsk, Russia	40	E17	53.55 N	51.14 E
Sernur, Russia	40	C16	56.55 N	49.09 E
Sernyky, Ukr.	38	B5	51.49 N	26.14 E
Serodino, Arg.	172	F7	32.37 S	60.57 W
Serov, Russia	48	C10	59.36 N	60.35 E
Serowe, Bots.	90	C8	22.23 S	26.42 E
Serpa, Port.	28	G3	37.56 N	7.36 W
Serpeddì, Punta, mtn., Italy	32	E3	39.22 N	9.18 E
Serpejsk, Russia	26	F17	54.20 N	34.59 E
Serpentine Lakes, l., Austl.	96	E5	28.43 S	129.05 E
Serpents Mouth, strt.	168	C11	10.00 N	62.00 W
Serpiente, Boca de la see Serpents Mouth, strt.	168	C11	10.00 N	62.00 W
Serpis, stm., Spain	28	F10	38.59 N	0.08 W
Serpneve, Ukr.	38	G8	46.19 N	29.02 E
Serpuhov, Russia	26	F20	54.54 N	37.25 E
Serra, Braz.	170	K5	20.06 S	40.17 W
Serra Branca, Braz.	170	D7	7.29 S	36.40 W
Serra da Canastra, Parque Nacional da, p.o.i., Braz.	170	K2	20.08 S	46.47 W
Serra da Capivara, Parque Nacional da, p.o.i., Braz.	170	E4	8.40 S	42.15 W
Serra de Outes, Spain	28	B2	42.49 N	8.54 W
Serra do Navio, Braz.	164	C7	0.55 N	52.00 W
Serra dos Aimorés, Braz.	170	I5	17.46 S	40.15 W
Serra do Salitre, Braz.	170	J2	19.06 S	46.40 W
Serra dos Órgãos, Parque Nacional da, p.o.i., Braz.	170	L4	22.26 S	43.02 W
Serramonte Center, shp. cen., Ca., U.S.	200		37.40 N	122.28 W
Serrana, Braz.	170	K2	21.12 S	47.37 W
Serrana, Cayo de, unds., Col.	156	E7	14.23 N	80.12 W
Serrana Bank see Serrana, Cayo de, unds., Col.	156	E7	14.23 N	80.12 W
Serrania, Braz.	170	K2	21.33 S	46.02 W
Serranía de la Neblina, Parque Nacional, p.o.i., Ven.	168	G9	1.30 N	66.02 W
Serranilla, Banco see Serranilla, Cayo de, unds., Col.	156	E8	15.50 N	79.50 W
Serranilla, Cayo de, unds., Col.	156	E8	15.50 N	79.50 W
Serranilla Bank see Serranilla, Cayo de, unds., Col.	156	E8	15.50 N	79.50 W
Serrano, Banco see Serrana, Cayo de, unds., Col.	156	E7	14.23 N	80.12 W
Serra San Bruno, Italy	32	F10	38.35 N	16.20 E
Serrat, Cap, c., Tun.	32	G3	37.14 N	9.13 E
Serra Talhada, Braz.	170	E6	7.59 S	38.18 W
Serre, stm., Fr.	20	E12	49.39 N	3.22 E
Serres, Fr.	22	E11	44.25 N	5.41 E
Sérres, Grc.	34	B6	41.05 N	23.33 E
Serrezuela, Arg.	172	E5	30.38 S	65.23 W
Serrinha, Braz.	170	F6	11.39 S	39.00 W
Serris, Fr.	179		48.51 N	2.47 E
Serrita, Braz.	170	D6	7.56 S	39.19 W
Serro, Braz.	170	J4	18.36 S	43.23 W
Sertã, Port.	28	E2	39.48 N	8.06 W
Sertânia, Braz.	170	E7	8.05 S	37.16 W
Sertãozinho, Braz.	170	K1	21.08 S	47.59 W
Serui, Indon.	60	F10	1.52 S	136.16 E
Serule, Bots.	90	B8	21.56 S	27.18 E
Serutu, Pulau, i., Indon.	66	D6	1.42 S	108.45 E
Seruwai, Indon.	64	J4	4.21 N	98.10 E
Sérvia, Grc.	34	C5	40.11 N	22.00 E
Servon, Fr.	179		48.43 N	2.35 E
Sêrxü, China	52	E4	33.07 N	97.55 E
Seryševo, Russia	50	F14	51.05 N	128.23 E
Şes, Munţii, mts., Rom.	36	B10	47.01 N	22.42 E
Sesayap, stm., Indon.	66	B10	3.36 N	117.14 E
Sesayap Lama, Indon.	66	B10	3.34 N	116.59 E
Sešča, Russia	26	G16	53.44 N	33.20 E
Seseganaga Lake, l., On., Can.	128	A8	50.04 N	90.25 W
Sese Islands, is., Ug.	86	E6	0.20 S	32.20 E
Seseke, stm., Ger.	181		51.37 N	7.32 E
Sesfontein, Nmb.	88	D1	19.08 S	13.36 E
Sesheke, Zam.	88	D3	17.28 S	24.18 E
Sesia, stm., Italy	30	E5	45.07 N	8.35 E
Sesibu, Indon.	66	A10	4.00 N	116.31 E
Sesimbra, Port.	28	F1	38.26 N	9.05 W
Seskar, ostrov, i., Russia	18	G15	60.01 N	28.23 E
Seskarö, Swe.	14	G14	65.44 N	23.44 E
Šešma, stm., Russia	40	D17	55.21 N	51.08 E
Sespe Creek, stm., Ca., U.S.	148	I6	34.23 N	118.56 W
Sessa Aurunca, Italy	32	C7	41.14 N	13.55 E
Sessøya, i., Nor.	14	C9	69.44 N	18.12 E
Sestao, Spain	28	A7	43.18 N	3.00 W
Sestra, stm., Russia	26	D19	56.43 N	37.13 E
Sestriere, Italy	30	F3	44.57 N	6.53 E
Sestri Levante, Italy	30	F6	44.16 N	9.24 E
Sestroreck, Russia	18	G16	60.06 N	29.57 E
Sestroreckij Razliv, ozero, l., Russia	183a		60.04 N	30.00 E
Šešupe (Šešupė), stm., Eur.	26	F5	55.03 N	22.12 E
Šešupė (Šešupe), stm., Eur.	26	F5	55.03 N	22.12 E
Šešuvis, stm., Lith.	26	E5	55.13 N	22.15 E
Seta, Japan	188		34.58 N	135.55 E
Šeta, Lith.	26	E7	55.17 N	24.15 E
Seta, stm., Japan	188		34.56 N	135.54 E
Setagaya, ngh., Japan	186		35.39 N	139.40 E
Sète, Fr.	22	F9	43.24 N	3.41 E
Sete Barras, Braz.	172	B13	24.23 S	47.55 W
Sete Cidades, Parque Nacional de, p.o.i., Braz.	170	C5	4.04 S	41.39 W
Sete Lagoas, Braz.	170	J3	19.28 S	44.14 W
Sete Quedas, Parque Nacional de, p.o.i., Braz.	172	A11	24.02 S	54.12 W
Sete Quedas, Salto das (Guairá, Salto del), wtfl., S.A.	172	B10	24.02 S	54.14 W
Seterdalen, val., Nor.	16	B11	65.15 N	13.28 E
Sete Rios, ngh., Port.	184c		38.45 N	9.10 W
Setermoen, Nor.	14	D9	68.51 N	18.19 E
Setesdal, val., Nor.	16	H5	59.25 N	7.25 E
Seth Ward, Tx., U.S.	138	G7	34.13 N	101.42 W
Setlagole, S. Afr.	90	E7	26.16 S	25.06 E
Seto, Japan	56	D10	35.12 N	137.05 E
Seto-naikai (Inland Sea), s., Japan	56	E5	34.21 N	133.36 E
Seton Hall University, educ., N.J., U.S.	194		40.45 N	74.15 W
Seton Lake, l., B.C., Can.	144	F8	50.41 N	122.08 W
Seton Portage, B.C., Can.	144	F8	50.42 N	122.17 W
Šetpe, Kaz.	42	C15	44.09 N	52.10 E
Settat, Mor.	84	C3	32.59 N	7.36 W
Setté Cama, Gabon	86	E1	2.31 S	9.46 E
Settecamini, ngh., Italy	185a		41.56 N	12.37 E
Sette-Daban, hrebet, mts., Russia	50	D16	62.00 N	138.00 E
Settimo Milanese, Italy	184b		45.29 N	9.03 E
Settlers, S. Afr.	90	D9	25.01 S	28.28 E
Settlers Cabin Regional Park, p.o.i., Pa., U.S.	197b		40.26 N	80.10 W
Setúbal, Port.	28	F2	38.31 N	8.52 W
Setúbal, state, Port.	28	F2	38.37 N	9.00 W
Setúbal, state, Port.	184c		38.37 N	9.00 W
Setúbal, Baía de, b., Port.	28	F1	38.17 N	9.04 W
Setun', stm., Russia	183b		55.44 N	37.33 E
Seugne, stm., Fr.	22	D5	45.42 N	0.32 W
Seui, Italy	32	E3	39.50 N	9.20 E
Seul, Lac, l., On., Can.	110	E12	50.35 N	91.49 W
Seul Choix Point, c., Mi., U.S.	126	C4	45.56 N	85.55 W
Seulimeum, Indon.	64	J2	5.19 N	95.34 E
Seurre, Fr.	20	H14	46.59 N	5.08 E
Sev, stm., Russia	38	A13	52.18 N	34.14 E
Sevan, Arm.	42	E11	40.32 N	44.57 E
Sevan, Lake see Sevana Lich, l., Arm.	42	E11	40.17 N	45.18 E
Sevan, ozero see Sevana Lich, l., Arm.	42	E11	40.17 N	45.18 E
Sevana Lich (Sevan, Lake), l., Arm.	42	E11	40.17 N	45.18 E
Sevastopol', Ukr.	38	I12	44.35 N	33.32 E
Ševčenko see Aktau, Kaz.	48	F8	43.38 N	51.10 E
Ševelevskaja, Russia	12	F20	60.51 N	44.10 E
Seven Hills, Austl.	192a		33.46 S	150.57 E
Seven Kings, ngh., Eng., U.K.	178		51.34 N	0.05 E
Sevenoaks, mun., Eng., U.K.	178		51.18 N	0.10 E
Sevenoaks Weald, Eng., U.K.	178		51.14 N	0.12 E
Seven Persons, Ab., Can.	142	E3	49.52 N	110.54 W
Seven Sisters Peaks, mtn., B.C., Can.	144	B2	54.58 N	128.10 W

Name Page Map Ref. Latitude Longitude

Seventy Mile House, B.C., Can. 144 E9 51.17 N 121.22 W
Sévérac-le-Château, Fr. 22 E9 44.19 N 3.04 E
Severance Center, shp. cen., Oh., U.S. 197a 41.31 N 81.33 W
Severn, stm., On., Can. 110 E12 55.59 N 87.36 W
Severn, stm., U.K. 10 J10 51.49 N 2.22 W
Severnaja Dvina (Northern Dvina), stm., Russia 12 D20 64.40 N 39.51 E
Severnaja Osetija, state, Russia 42 D11 43.00 N 44.15 E
Severnaja Sos'va, stm., Russia 48 B10 64.10 N 65.26 E
Severnaja Zemlja, is., Russia 46 B13 79.30 N 98.00 E
Severna Park, Md., U.S. 124 E9 39.04 N 76.33 W
Severnoe, Russia 48 C13 56.20 N 78.22 E
Severnye uvaly, hills, Russia 48 C7 59.28 N 48.13 E
Severnyj, Russia 18 C19 64.04 N 32.47 E
Severnyj, ngh., Russia 183b 55.56 N 37.33 E
Severnyj Kommunar, Russia 40 B19 58.22 N 54.00 E
Severnyj Ural, mts., Russia 48 B9 63.00 N 59.00 E
Severodvinsk (Molotovsk), Russia 18 C26 64.34 N 39.50 E
Severo-Enisejskij, Russia 48 B16 60.22 N 93.01 E
Severo-Kuril'sk, Russia 50 F20 50.41 N 156.06 E
Severomorsk, Russia 14 C24 69.04 N 33.28 E
Severo-Sibirskaja nizmennost' (North Siberian Lowland), pl., Russia 50 B6 73.00 N 100.00 E
Severoural'sk, Russia 48 B10 60.09 N 59.57 E
Severo-Zadonsk, Russia 26 F21 54.01 N 38.24 E
Severskij Donec see Northern Donets, stm., Eur. 40 G10 47.35 N 40.54 E
Severy, Ks., U.S. 138 D12 37.37 N 96.13 W
Seveso, stm., Italy 184b 45.30 N 9.12 E
Sevettijärvi, Fin. 14 C19 69.28 N 28.46 E
Sevier, stm., Ut., U.S. 150 D4 39.01 N 113.06 W
Sevier, East Fork, stm., Ut., U.S. 150 F4 38.14 N 112.11 W
Sevier Bridge Reservoir, res., Ut., U.S. 150 D5 39.20 N 111.56 W
Sevier Desert, des., Ut., U.S. 150 D4 39.25 N 112.50 W
Sevier Lake, l., Ut., U.S. 120 B6 38.55 N 113.08 W
Sevierville, Tn., U.S. 124 I2 35.51 N 83.33 W
Sevilla, Col. 168 E4 4.15 N 75.55 W
Sevilla (Seville), Spain 28 G5 37.22 N 5.58 W
Sevilla, co., Spain 28 G5 37.25 N 5.35 W
Seville see Sevilla, Spain 28 G5 37.22 N 5.58 W
Seville, Fl., U.S. 132 G4 29.19 N 81.29 W
Sevlievo, Blg. 36 F12 43.01 N 25.06 E
Sevsk, Russia 40 E9 52.08 N 34.30 E
Sewanee, Tn., U.S. 134 B13 35.12 N 85.55 W
Sewāni, India 70 D5 28.54 N 75.37 E
Seward, Ak., U.S. 109 D10 60.07 N 149.26 W
Seward, Ne., U.S. 140 G15 40.54 N 97.06 W
Seward, Pa., U.S. 124 D7 40.24 N 79.01 W
Seward Peninsula, pen., Ak., U.S. 109 C7 65.00 N 164.00 W
Sewaren, N.J., U.S. 194 40.33 N 74.15 W
Sewickley Creek, stm., Pa., U.S. 197b 40.14 N 79.47 W
Sewickley Heights, Pa., U.S. 197b 40.33 N 80.09 W
Sewickley Hills, Pa., U.S. 197b 40.34 N 80.08 W
Sewri, ngh., India 190c 19.00 N 72.51 E
Sexsmith, Ab., Can. 144 A12 55.20 N 118.48 W
Sextín, stm., Mex. 154 B6 25.42 N 105.06 W
Sexton Island, i., N.Y., U.S. 194 40.39 N 73.14 W
Seya, ngh., Japan 186 35.29 N 139.29 E
Seya, ngh., Japan 186 35.27 N 139.30 E
Seybaplaya, Mex. 156 C2 19.40 N 90.39 W
Seychelles, ctry., Afr. 89b k12 4.35 S 55.40 E
Seychelles, is., Sey. 89b k13 4.35 S 55.40 E
Seydişehir, Tur. 34 F14 37.25 N 31.50 E
Seydisfjördur, Ice. 12a k32 65.15 N 14.01 W
Seyhan, stm., Tur. 42 G6 36.43 N 34.55 E
Seyhan Barajı, res., Tur. 76 A6 37.05 N 35.15 E
Seyitgazi, Tur. 34 D13 39.27 N 30.42 E
Seymour, Austl. 98 K5 37.01 S 145.08 E
Seymour, S. Afr. 90 H8 32.32 S 26.46 E
Seymour, Ct., U.S. 124 C12 41.23 N 73.04 W
Seymour, In., U.S. 130 F12 38.57 N 85.53 W
Seymour, Ia., U.S. 128 K5 40.41 N 93.07 W
Seymour, Mo., U.S. 130 G5 37.09 N 92.45 W
Seymour, Tx., U.S. 138 H9 33.35 N 99.16 W
Seymour, Wi., U.S. 126 D1 44.30 N 88.19 W
Seymour, stm., B.C., Can. 144 E4 51.11 N 126.40 W
Seymour Inlet, b., B.C., Can. 144 E3 51.02 N 127.09 W
Seymour Johnson Air Force Base, mil., N.C., U.S. 132 A8 35.20 N 77.57 W
Seymourville, La., U.S. 134 G7 30.27 N 91.29 W
Seyring, Aus. 182b 48.20 N 16.29 E
Şeytan, stm., Tur. 185b 41.06 N 28.59 E
Sežana, Slvn. 30 E10 45.42 N 13.52 E
Sézanne, Fr. 20 F12 48.43 N 3.43 E
Sezela, S. Afr. 90 G10 30.28 S 30.37 E
Sezimovo Ústí, Czech Rep. 24 G10 49.23 N 14.42 E
Sfákia, Grc. 34 H7 35.12 N 24.09 E
Sfântu Gheorghe, Rom. 36 D12 45.51 N 25.48 E
Sfântu Gheorghe, Braţul, stm., Rom. 36 E16 44.54 N 29.35 E
Sfântu Gheorghe, Ostrovul, i., Rom. 36 D16 45.07 N 29.22 E
Sfax, Tun. 84 C7 34.44 N 10.45 E
Sforzesco, Castello, hist., Italy 184b 45.28 N 9.11 E
's-Gravenhage (The Hague), Neth. 20 B13 52.05 N 4.17 E
Sha, stm., China 58 H7 26.34 N 118.01 E
Sha, stm., China 58 E6 33.37 N 114.37 E
Shaanxi, state, China 58 E3 35.00 N 109.00 E
Shabakunk Creek, stm., N.J., U.S. 203 40.15 N 74.43 W
Shabeelle (Shebelē Wenz, Wabē), stm., Afr. 82 G9 0.10 N 42.45 E
Shabel'kivka, Ukr. 38 E16 48.45 N 37.30 E
Shabestar, Iran 74 A9 38.10 N 45.41 E
Shabo, Ukr. 38 G9 46.07 N 30.23 E
Shabramant, Egypt 191c 29.56 N 31.12 E
Shabunda, D.R.C. 86 E5 2.41 S 27.20 E
Shabwah, Yemen 72 F6 15.22 N 47.01 E
Shache, China 48 G13 38.24 N 77.14 E
Shackan Indian Reserve, ind. res., B.C., Can. 144 F9 50.17 N 121.12 W
Shackleton Ice Shelf, ice, Ant. 103 B14 66.00 S 100.00 E
Shackleton Range, mts., Ant. 103 D2 80.40 S 26.00 W
Shādegān, Iran 74 E11 30.39 N 48.42 E
Shadehill Reservoir, res., S.D., U.S. 140 B10 45.43 N 102.15 W
Shadow Lake, l., Ma., U.S. 201 42.50 N 71.14 W
Shadow Lake, l., N.J., U.S. 194 40.21 N 74.06 W
Shadwān, Gezîret, i., Egypt 76 K4 27.30 N 33.59 E
Shady Cove, Or., U.S. 148 A3 42.04 N 122.36 W
Shady Grove, Fl., U.S. 132 F2 30.15 N 83.36 W
Shadyside, Oh., U.S. 124 E5 39.58 N 80.45 W
Shafer Butte, mtn., Id., U.S. 146 G10 43.47 N 116.05 W
Shaft, Iran 42 G13 37.12 N 49.24 E
Shafter, Ca., U.S. 148 H6 35.29 N 119.15 W
Shaftesbury, Eng., U.K. 10 K11 51.00 N 2.11 W
Shafton, Pa., U.S. 197b 40.20 N 79.42 W
Shageluk, Ak., U.S. 109 D8 62.36 N 159.32 W
Shag Rocks, r., S. Geor. 166 J8 53.33 S 42.02 W
Shāhābād, India 69 C3 17.08 N 76.56 E
Shāhābād, India 70 E7 27.38 N 79.56 E
Shāhābād, India 70 C6 30.09 N 76.52 E
Shāhābād, India 190c 19.01 N 73.02 E
Shāhābād, Iran 74 B15 37.31 N 56.53 E
Shāhābād, Iran 185d 35.47 N 51.31 E
Shāhāda, India 70 H5 21.30 N 74.21 E
Shah Alam, Malay. 64 K5 3.03 N 101.33 E
Shahany, ozero, l., Ukr. 38 H9 45.43 N 29.52 E
Shāhdādpur, Pak. 70 F2 25.55 N 68.38 E
Shāhdara, India 190a 28.30 N 77.25 E
Shāhdara, ngh., India 190a 28.40 N 77.18 E
Shahdol, India 70 G8 23.18 N 81.21 E
Shahe, China 58 J3 22.04 N 109.41 E
Shahezhen, China 58 A7 40.07 N 116.15 E
Shāhgarh, India 70 E2 27.07 N 69.54 E
Shāhī see Qā'emshahr, Iran 74 B13 36.27 N 52.51 E
Shāhjahānpur, India 70 E7 27.52 N 79.54 E
Shāh Kot, Pak. 70 C4 31.34 N 73.29 E
Shāhpur, India 69 C3 16.42 N 76.50 E
Shāhpur, Pak. 70 D2 28.43 N 68.24 E
Shāhpura, India 70 G8 23.11 N 80.42 E
Shāhpura, India 70 E5 27.23 N 75.58 E
Shāhpura, India 70 F5 25.37 N 74.56 E
Shāhpur Chākar, Pak. 70 E2 26.09 N 68.39 E
Shahrak, Afg. 72 C9 34.06 N 64.18 E
Shahr-e Bābak, Iran 74 E14 30.07 N 55.09 E
Shahr-e Kord, Iran 74 D12 32.19 N 50.51 E
Shāhrūd see Emāmshahr, Iran 74 B14 36.25 N 54.59 E
Shāhrūd, stm., Iran 74 B12 36.40 N 49.25 E
Shahryār, Iran 42 H14 35.37 N 50.59 E
Shaighālu, Pak. 70 C2 31.10 N 68.57 E
Shājāpur, India 70 G6 23.25 N 76.17 E
Shajingzi, China 58 C1 37.42 N 105.10 E
Shakarpura, India 190a 28.46 N 77.21 E
Shakarpur Khās, ngh., India 190a 28.38 N 77.17 E
Shakawe, Bots. 88 D3 18.22 S 21.50 E
Shaker Heights, Oh., U.S. 126 G8 41.29 N 81.36 W
Shaker Heights Park, p.o.i., Oh., U.S. 197a 41.29 N 81.33 W
Shakespeare Island, i., On., Can. 128 B10 49.38 N 88.25 W
Shakhtars'k, Ukr. 38 E17 48.03 N 38.28 E
Shaki, Nig. 84 H5 8.39 N 3.23 E
Shakopee, Mn., U.S. 128 G5 44.47 N 93.31 W
Shakotan-hantō, pen., Japan 54 C14 43.20 N 140.30 E
Shaktoolik, Ak., U.S. 109 D7 64.20 N 161.09 W
Shakujii, ngh., Japan 186 35.45 N 139.37 E
Shakūrpur, ngh., India 190a 28.41 N 77.09 E
Shala, Lake see Shala Hāyk', l., Eth. 82 F7 7.27 N 38.31 E
Shala Hāyk', l., Eth. 82 F7 7.27 N 38.31 E
Shalalth, B.C., Can. 144 F8 50.44 N 122.12 W
Shaler Mountains, mts., Can. 110 A8 72.29 N 110.22 W
Shalford, Eng., U.K. 178 51.13 N 0.34 W
Shalimar Railroad Station, trans., India 190b 22.33 N 88.19 E
Shallotte, N.C., U.S. 132 C7 33.58 N 78.23 W
Shallowater, Tx., U.S. 138 H6 33.41 N 101.59 W
Shallow Brook, stm., N.J., U.S. 194 40.21 N 74.35 W
Shaluli Shan, mts., China 52 E4 30.11 N 99.30 E
Shalyhyne, Ukr. 38 B13 51.34 N 34.06 E
Shām, Bādiyat ash- see Syrian Desert, des., Asia 74 D6 32.00 N 40.00 E
Shām, Jabal ash-, mtn., Oman 72 E8 23.13 N 57.16 E
Shamattawa, Mb., Can. 110 D12 55.51 N 92.02 W
Shambe, Sudan 82 F6 7.06 N 30.46 E
Shambu, Eth. 82 F7 9.36 N 37.02 E
Shamepūr, ngh., India 190a 28.45 N 77.09 E
Shāmli, India 70 D6 29.26 N 77.18 E
Shamokin, Pa., U.S. 124 D9 40.47 N 76.35 W
Shamona Creek, stm., Pa., U.S. 203 40.02 N 75.43 W
Shamraïvka, Ukr. 38 D8 49.46 N 29.52 E
Shamrock, Fl., U.S. 132 G2 29.38 N 83.08 W
Shamrock, Tx., U.S. 138 F8 35.13 N 100.15 W
Shamsher, India 190a 28.44 N 77.24 E
Shamva, Zimb. 88 D5 17.18 S 31.33 E
Shan, state, Mya. 64 B4 21.34 N 98.35 E
Shancheng, China 58 C2 37.00 N 106.59 E
Shandan, China 52 D5 38.46 N 101.07 E
Shandatgyi, Mya. 64 C2 19.37 N 94.43 E
Shandī, Sudan 82 D6 16.41 N 33.26 E
Shandong, state, China 58 C7 36.00 N 118.00 E
Shandong Bandao (Shantung Peninsula), pen., China 58 C9 37.00 N 121.00 E
Shandrivka, Ukr. 38 E14 48.56 N 35.47 E
Shand uul, mtn., Mong. 52 C5 43.28 N 104.02 E
Shaner, Pa., U.S. 197b 40.17 N 79.47 W
Shangani, Zimb. 90 A9 19.47 S 29.22 E
Shangani, stm., Zimb. 88 D4 18.30 S 27.12 E
Shangbahe, China 58 F6 30.39 N 115.06 E
Shangcheng, China 58 F6 31.47 N 115.24 E
Shangchuan Dao, i., China 58 K5 21.42 N 112.47 E
Shangdu, China 52 C7 41.34 N 113.31 E
Shangfu, China 58 G6 28.40 N 114.59 E
Shanghai, China 58 F9 31.14 N 121.28 E
Shanghai, China 187b 31.14 N 121.28 E
Shanghai, state, China 52 E9 31.10 N 121.30 E
Shanghai (Hongqiao) International Airport, arpt., China 187b 31.12 N 121.20 E
Shanghai Art Museum, bldg., China 187b 31.14 N 121.28 E
Shanghai Exhibition Centre, bldg., China 187b 31.13 N 121.26 E
Shanghai Normal University, educ., China 187b 31.10 N 121.24 E
Shanghai Shih see Shanghai, state, China 52 E9 31.10 N 121.30 E
Shanghai Station, trans., China 187b 31.15 N 121.28 E
Shanghang, China 58 I7 25.06 N 116.25 E
Shanghe, China 58 C7 37.17 N 117.07 E
Shangjin, China 58 E4 33.09 N 110.03 E
Shangkasa, China 70 B8 33.42 N 80.11 E
Shanglin, China 58 J3 23.29 N 108.31 E
Shangnan, China 58 E4 33.33 N 110.44 E
Shangqing, China 58 I8 25.53 N 118.36 E
Shangqiu, China 58 D6 34.22 N 115.36 E
Shangqiu, China 58 D6 34.26 N 115.38 E
Shangrao, China 58 G7 28.26 N 117.58 E
Shangshe, China 58 B5 38.16 N 113.19 E
Shangshui, China 58 E6 33.33 N 114.33 E
Shangsi, China 58 J2 22.09 N 107.56 E
Shangxian, China 58 E3 33.52 N 109.55 E
Shangyi, China 58 A6 41.06 N 113.59 E
Shangying, China 54 B7 44.09 N 127.14 E
Shangyou Shuiku, res., China 58 I6 25.50 N 114.22 E
Shangyu, China 58 F9 30.01 N 120.54 E
Shangyun, China 64 A4 23.01 N 99.49 E
Shangzhi, China 52 B10 45.13 N 127.59 E
Shanhaiguan, China 58 A8 40.00 N 119.45 E
Shanhaikwan see Shanhaiguan, China 58 A8 40.00 N 119.45 E
Shanhetun, China 54 B7 44.42 N 127.13 E
Shankou, China 58 K3 21.38 N 109.43 E
Shannon, Ga., U.S. 134 C13 34.20 N 85.04 W
Shannon, Il., U.S. 130 B8 42.09 N 89.44 W
Shannon, Ms., U.S. 134 C10 34.06 N 88.42 W
Shannon, stm., Ire. 10 I3 52.34 N 9.40 W
Shannon, Mouth of the, strt., Ire. 10 I2 52.29 N 9.51 W
Shannon Ø, i., Grnld. 108 B22 75.10 N 18.20 W
Shannontown, S.C., U.S. 132 C5 33.52 N 80.21 W
Shanshan, China 52 C3 42.52 N 90.10 E
Shansi see Shanxi, state, China 58 B5 37.00 N 112.00 E
Shantar Islands see Šantarskie ostrova, is., Russia 50 E16 54.53 N 137.33 E
Shāntipur, India 70 G12 23.14 N 88.26 E
Shantou, China 58 J7 23.21 N 116.40 E
Shantung see Shandong, state, China 58 C7 36.00 N 118.00 E
Shantung Peninsula see Shandong Bandao, pen., China 58 C9 37.00 N 121.00 E
Shanwei, China 58 J6 22.46 N 115.21 E
Shanxi, state, China 58 B5 37.00 N 112.00 E
Shanxian, China 58 D7 34.47 N 116.04 E
Shanxu, China 58 J2 22.25 N 107.58 E
Shanyang, China 58 E3 33.31 N 109.52 E
Shanyin, China 58 B5 39.31 N 112.49 E
Shaoguan, China 58 I5 24.48 N 113.35 E
Shaohing see Shaoxing, China 58 G9 29.58 N 120.34 E
Shaoleng, stm., China 54 C2 43.14 N 119.27 E
Shaowu, China 58 H7 27.19 N 117.29 E
Shaoxing, China 58 G9 29.58 N 120.34 E
Shaoyang, China 58 H4 26.59 N 111.16 E
Shaoyang, China 58 H4 27.15 N 111.28 E
Shapinsay, i., Scot., U.K. 10 B10 59.02 N 2.53 W
Shāpūr, stm., Iran 74 F12 29.19 N 51.06 E
Shaq'ah, Ra's ash-, c., Leb. 76 D6 34.18 N 35.41 E
Shaqqā, Syria 76 F7 32.53 N 36.42 E
Shaqrā', Sau. Ar. 72 D6 25.14 N 45.15 E
Shaqrā', Yemen 72 G6 13.22 N 45.42 E
Shara, gora, mtn., Asia 42 D10 43.00 N 43.06 E
Sharafābād, India 190a 28.36 N 77.23 E
Sharafkhāneh, Iran 42 F11 38.09 N 45.31 E
Sharan Jogīzai, Pak. 70 C2 31.01 N 68.32 E
Sharbot Lake, On., Can. 126 D13 44.46 N 76.41 W
Sharhorod, Ukr. 38 E7 48.44 N 28.05 E
Shari-dake, mtn., Japan 54 C16 43.46 N 144.43 E
Sharīn Gol, Mong. 52 B6 49.15 N 106.25 E
Sharītah, Ra's, c., Oman 74 G15 26.21 N 56.22 E
Sharivka, Ukr. 38 C14 50.00 N 35.31 E
Sharjah see Ash-Shāriqah, U.A.E. 74 H14 25.22 N 55.24 E
Shark Bay, b., Austl. 96 E2 25.30 S 113.30 E
Shark Point, c., Austl. 192a 33.55 S 151.17 E
Sharktooth Mountain, mtn., B.C., Can. 110 D5 58.35 N 127.57 W
Sharm el Sheik see Sharm el-Sheikh, Egypt 76 K5 27.51 N 34.16 E
Sharm el-Sheikh, Egypt 76 K5 27.51 N 34.16 E
Sharon, N.D., U.S. 142 G16 47.35 N 97.53 W
Sharon, Pa., U.S. 124 C5 41.13 N 80.30 W
Sharon, Tn., U.S. 130 H9 36.13 N 88.49 W
Sharon, Wi., U.S. 130 B9 42.30 N 88.43 W
Sharon Hill, Pa., U.S. 203 39.54 N 75.16 W
Sharon Springs, Ks., U.S. 138 C7 38.53 N 101.45 W
Sharpe, Lake, res., S.D., U.S. 140 C12 44.09 N 99.54 W
Sharp Island, i., China 189d 22.22 N 114.17 E
Sharpley, De., U.S. 203 39.48 N 75.33 W
Sharp Park, p.o.i., Ca., U.S. 200 37.37 N 122.29 W
Sharpsburg, Pa., U.S. 197b 40.29 N 79.55 W
Sharps Hill, Pa., U.S. 197b 40.30 N 79.56 W
Sharps Run, stm., N.J., U.S. 203 39.54 N 74.49 W
Sharptown, N.J., U.S. 203 39.39 N 75.21 W
Sharqī, Al-Jabal ash- see Anti-Lebanon, mts., Asia 76 E7 34.00 N 36.30 E
Shashe, stm., Afr. 90 B9 22.10 S 29.20 E
Shashemenē, Eth. 82 F7 7.12 N 38.35 E
Shashi, China 58 F5 30.19 N 112.14 E
Shashibu, China 58 I6 25.48 N 114.58 E
Shasi see Shashi, China 58 F5 30.19 N 112.14 E
Shasta, Ca., U.S. 148 C3 40.35 N 122.29 W
Shasta, stm., Ca., U.S. 148 B3 41.49 N 122.36 W
Shasta, Mount, vol., Ca., U.S. 148 B3 41.24 N 122.12 W
Shasta Lake, res., Ca., U.S. 148 C3 40.46 N 122.22 W
Shāṭi', Wādī ash-, stm., Libya 82 B2 27.30 N 13.15 E
Sha Tin, China 189d 22.23 N 114.11 E
Shats'k, Ukr. 38 B2 51.30 N 23.58 E
Shats'kyi Pryrodnyi Natsional'nyi Park, p.o.i., Ukr. 38 B2 51.30 N 23.55 E
Shattuck, Ok., U.S. 138 E9 36.16 N 99.52 W
Shaunavon, Sk., Can. 142 E5 49.38 N 108.24 W
Shavers Fork, stm., W.V., U.S. 124 F6 39.05 N 79.41 W
Shaw, Ms., U.S. 134 D8 33.36 N 90.46 W
Shaw Air Force Base, mil., S.C., U.S. 132 C5 33.58 N 80.29 W
Shawan, China 52 C2 44.20 N 85.34 E
Shawanaga Inlet, b., On., Can. 126 C9 45.32 N 80.24 W
Shawano, Wi., U.S. 128 G10 44.46 N 88.36 W
Shaw Creek, stm., S.C., U.S. 132 C4 33.34 N 81.30 W
Shawforth, Eng., U.K. 180 53.41 N 2.10 W
Shawinigan, Qc., Can. 126 B17 46.32 N 72.45 W
Shawinigan-Sud, Qc., Can. 126 B17 46.31 N 72.45 W
Shawnee, Ks., U.S. 130 E3 39.01 N 94.43 W
Shawnee, Oh., U.S. 124 E3 39.37 N 82.11 W
Shawnee, Ok., U.S. 134 B2 35.19 N 96.55 W
Shawnee, Lake, l., N.J., U.S. 194 40.58 N 74.35 W
Shawneetown, Il., U.S. 130 G9 37.42 N 88.11 W
Shawsheen, stm., Ma., U.S. 201 42.42 N 71.08 W
Shawsheen Village, Ma., U.S. 201 42.40 N 71.09 W
Shawtown, Pa., U.S. 197b 40.20 N 79.42 W
Shawville, Qc., Can. 126 C13 45.36 N 76.29 W
Shaxian, China 58 H7 26.23 N 117.47 E
Shayang, China 58 F5 30.41 N 112.32 E
Shaybārā, i., Sau. Ar. 74 H5 25.25 N 36.50 E
Shay Gap, Austl. 96 D4 20.30 S 120.04 E
Shāyib el-Banat, Gebel, mtn., Egypt 76 K4 26.59 N 33.29 E
Shaykh, Jabal ash- see Hermon, Mount, mtn., Asia 76 E6 33.25 N 35.51 E
Shaykh Al-Hadīd, Syria 76 B7 36.30 N 36.35 E
Shaykh Miskīn, Syria 76 F7 32.49 N 36.09 E
Shaykh Sa'd, Iraq 74 D10 32.32 N 46.16 E
Shaykh 'Uthmān, Yemen 72 G6 12.51 N 45.00 E
Shchastia, Ukr. 38 E18 48.44 N 39.14 E
Shchors, Ukr. 38 B10 51.49 N 31.57 E
Shchors'k, Ukr. 38 E13 48.21 N 34.07 E
Shchūchinsk see Ščučinsk, Kaz. 48 D12 52.55 N 70.10 E
She, stm., China 58 F6 30.41 N 114.30 E
Shea Island, i., Ct., U.S. 194 41.03 N 73.24 W
Shea Stadium, p.o.i., N.Y., U.S. 194 40.45 N 73.51 W
Shebelē Wenz, Wabē (Shabeelle), stm., Afr. 86 C8 0.10 N 42.45 E
Shebelynka, Ukr. 38 D15 49.27 N 36.30 E
Sheberghān, Afg. 72 B10 36.40 N 65.44 E
Sheboygan, Wi., U.S. 126 E2 43.45 N 87.43 W
Sheboygan, stm., Wi., U.S. 126 E1 43.44 N 87.41 W
Sheboygan Falls, Wi., U.S. 126 E2 43.43 N 87.48 W
Shechem, hist., W.B. 76 F6 32.13 N 35.15 E
Shecheng, China 58 C5 37.13 N 112.58 E
Shediac, N.B., Can. 122 D12 46.12 N 64.34 W
Shedin Peak, mtn., B.C., Can. 110 D5 55.55 N 127.32 W
Sheelin, Lough, l., Ire. 10 H5 53.47 N 7.21 W
Sheenjek, stm., Ak., U.S. 109 C11 66.44 N 144.33 W
Sheep, stm., Ab., Can. 144 F16 50.44 N 113.51 W
Sheep Creek, stm., Ab., Can. 144 B11 54.03 N 119.00 W
Sheep Creek, stm., U.S. 146 H11 42.16 N 115.48 W
Sheep Creek, stm., Ut., U.S. 150 C7 40.54 N 109.35 W
Sheep Creek, stm., Wy., U.S. 140 E7 42.02 N 106.04 W
Sheep Haven, b., Ire. 10 F4 55.12 N 7.54 W
Sheep Mountain, mtn., Az., U.S. 150 K2 32.29 N 114.13 W
Sheep Mountain, mtn., Wy., U.S. 146 G16 43.33 N 110.32 W
Sheep Peak, mtn., Tx., U.S. 136 C2 31.14 N 104.59 W
Sheep Range, mts., Nv., U.S. 148 G10 36.45 N 115.07 W
Sheepshead Bay, ngh., N.Y., U.S. 194 40.35 N 73.56 W
Sheerness, Eng., U.K. 10 J13 51.26 N 0.44 E
Sheet Harbour, N.S., Can. 122 F14 44.55 N 62.32 W
Sheffield, N.Z. 102 F4 43.22 S 172.01 E
Sheffield, Eng., U.K. 10 H11 53.23 N 1.28 W
Sheffield, Al., U.S. 134 C11 34.45 N 87.41 W
Sheffield, Il., U.S. 128 J9 41.21 N 89.43 W
Sheffield, Ia., U.S. 130 B4 42.53 N 93.13 W
Sheffield, Pa., U.S. 124 C6 41.41 N 79.01 W
Sheffield, Tx., U.S. 136 D6 30.41 N 101.49 W
Sheffield Island, i., Ct., U.S. 194 41.03 N 73.25 W
Sheffield Island Harbor, b., Ct., U.S. 194 41.03 N 73.25 W
Shegaon, India 70 H6 20.47 N 76.41 E
Sheho, Sk., Can. 142 C10 51.35 N 103.12 W
Shehong, China 58 F1 30.55 N 105.20 E
Shehuen see Chalía, stm., Arg. 166 I2 49.34 S 69.30 W
Sheikhpura, India 70 F10 25.08 N 85.51 E
Shekhūpura, Pak. 70 C5 31.42 N 73.59 E
Shek Kong, China 189d 22.26 N 114.06 E
Shek Kong Airfield, arpt., China 189d 22.27 N 114.05 E
Shek Kwu Chau, i., China 189d 22.12 N 113.59 E
Shek Uk Shan, mtn., China 189d 22.27 N 114.18 E
Shelagyote Peak, mtn., B.C., Can. 110 D5 55.58 N 127.12 W
Shelbina, Mo., U.S. 130 E5 39.41 N 92.02 W
Shelburn, In., U.S. 130 E10 39.10 N 87.23 W
Shelburne, N.S., Can. 122 G11 43.46 N 65.19 W
Shelburne, On., Can. 126 D9 44.04 N 80.11 W
Shelburne Falls, Ma., U.S. 124 B13 42.36 N 72.44 W
Shelby, Ia., U.S. 130 C2 41.31 N 95.27 W
Shelby, Mi., U.S. 126 E3 43.36 N 86.21 W
Shelby, Ms., U.S. 134 D8 33.57 N 90.45 W
Shelby, Mt., U.S. 146 B15 48.30 N 111.51 W
Shelby, Ne., U.S. 140 F15 41.11 N 97.25 W
Shelby, N.C., U.S. 132 A4 35.17 N 81.32 W
Shelby, Oh., U.S. 124 D3 40.52 N 82.39 W
Shelby Village, Mi., U.S. 199 42.38 N 83.04 W
Shelbyville, Il., U.S. 130 E9 39.24 N 88.47 W
Shelbyville, In., U.S. 130 E12 39.30 N 85.45 W
Shelbyville, Ky., U.S. 130 F12 38.12 N 85.13 W
Shelbyville, Mo., U.S. 130 E5 39.48 N 92.02 W
Shelbyville, Tn., U.S. 134 B12 35.29 N 86.27 W
Shelbyville, Lake, res., Il., U.S. 130 E9 39.30 N 88.42 W
Sheldon, Ia., U.S. 128 H3 43.10 N 95.51 W
Sheldon, Mo., U.S. 130 G3 37.39 N 94.17 W
Sheldon Brook, stm., N.Y., U.S. 194 41.03 N 73.52 W
Sheldon Point, Ak., U.S. 109 D6 62.32 N 164.52 W
Sheldonville, Ma., U.S. 201 42.02 N 71.23 W
Sheldrake, stm., N.Y., U.S. 194 40.57 N 73.44 W
Sheldrake Lake, l., N.Y., U.S. 194 40.57 N 73.46 W
Shelek see Čilik, Kaz. 48 F13 43.35 N 78.15 E
Shelekhov, Gulf of see Šelihova, zaliv, b., Russia 50 D20 60.00 N 158.00 E
Shelikof Strait, strt., Ak., U.S. 109 E9 57.17 N 155.41 W
Shell, stm., Mb., Can. 142 C12 50.57 N 101.24 W
Shellbrook, Sk., Can. 142 A7 53.13 N 106.22 W
Shell Creek, stm., U.S. 150 C8 40.55 N 108.37 W
Shell Creek, stm., Ne., U.S. 140 F15 41.30 N 96.54 W
Shell Creek, stm., N.D., U.S. 142 F11 47.47 N 102.20 W
Shell Creek, stm., Wy., U.S. 140 C5 44.30 N 108.03 W
Shelley, B.C., Can. 144 C8 53.59 N 122.36 W
Shelley, Id., U.S. 146 G14 43.22 N 112.07 W
Shellharbour, Austl. 98 J8 34.35 S 150.52 E
Shell Lake, Wi., U.S. 128 F7 45.44 N 91.55 W
Shellman, Ga., U.S. 134 F14 31.45 N 84.36 W
Shellmouth Dam, dam., Mb., Can. 142 D12 50.58 N 101.25 W
Shellow Bowells, Eng., U.K. 178 51.45 N 0.20 E
Shell Rock, Ia., U.S. 130 B5 42.42 N 92.34 W
Shell Rock, stm., U.S. 128 I6 42.38 N 92.30 W
Shellsburg, Ia., U.S. 130 B6 42.05 N 91.52 W
Shelter, Port, b., China 189d 22.21 N 114.17 E
Shelter Island, i., China 189d 22.20 N 114.17 E
Shelton, Ct., U.S. 124 C12 41.18 N 73.05 W
Shelton, Ne., U.S. 140 G14 40.47 N 98.43 W
Shelton, Wa., U.S. 146 C3 47.12 N 123.06 W
Shemogue, N.B., Can. 122 D12 46.09 N 64.10 W
Shemonaikha see Šemonaiha, Kaz. 48 D14 50.38 N 81.54 E
Shenandoah, Ia., U.S. 130 D2 40.45 N 95.22 W
Shenandoah, Va., U.S. 124 F7 38.29 N 78.37 W
Shenandoah, stm., U.S. 124 F7 39.19 N 77.43 W
Shenandoah, North Fork, stm., Va., U.S. 124 F7 38.56 N 78.11 W
Shenandoah, South Fork, stm., Va., U.S. 124 F7 38.56 N 78.11 W
Shenandoah National Park, p.o.i., Va., U.S. 124 F7 38.34 N 78.20 W
Shenchi, China 58 B5 39.05 N 112.09 E
Shencottah, India 69 G3 8.58 N 77.17 E
Shendam, Nig. 84 H6 8.54 N 9.28 E
Shenfield, Eng., U.K. 178 51.38 N 0.19 E
Shenge, S.L. 84 H2 7.54 N 12.55 W
Shengsi Liedao, is., China 54 I5 30.45 N 122.31 E
Shengxian, China 58 G9 29.35 N 120.49 E
Shengze, China 58 F9 30.54 N 120.38 E
Shenjing, China 58 J5 22.00 N 112.27 E
Shenk'eng, Tai. 187d 25.00 N 121.36 E
Shenley, Eng., U.K. 178 51.41 N 0.17 W
Shenmu, China 58 B4 38.49 N 110.28 E
Shenqiu, China 58 E6 33.23 N 115.04 E
Shensi see Shaanxi, state, China 58 E3 35.00 N 109.00 E
Shenton, Mount, mtn., Austl. 96 E4 28.00 S 123.22 E
Shenxian, China 58 C6 36.14 N 115.39 E
Shenyang, China 52 C9 41.48 N 123.24 E
Shenzhen, China 58 J6 22.34 N 114.06 E
Sheoganj, India 70 F4 25.09 N 73.05 E
Sheopur, India 70 F6 25.40 N 76.41 E
Shepard, Ab., Can. 144 E17 50.57 N 113.53 W
Shepards Brook, stm., Ma., U.S. 201 42.08 N 71.25 W
Shepetivka, Ukr. 38 C5 50.11 N 27.04 E
Shepherd, Mi., U.S. 126 E5 43.31 N 84.41 W
Shepherd, Tx., U.S. 136 D13 30.30 N 94.59 W
Shepherd, Îles, is., Vanuatu 101d k17 16.59 S 168.28 E
Shepherdstown, W.V., U.S. 124 E8 39.25 N 77.48 W
Shepherdsville, Ky., U.S. 130 F12 37.59 N 85.42 W
Sheppard Air Force Base, mil., Tx., U.S. 138 H10 33.58 N 98.30 W
Sheppard Pond, l., N.J., U.S. 194 41.08 N 74.13 W
Shepparton, Austl. 98 K5 36.23 S 145.24 E
Shepperton, Eng., U.K. 178 51.24 N 0.27 W
Sheppey, Isle of, i., Eng., U.K. 10 J13 51.24 N 0.50 E
Sheppler Hill, hill, Pa., U.S. 197b 40.09 N 79.49 W
Shepway, Eng., U.K. 178 51.15 N 0.33 E
Sheqi, China 58 E5 33.02 N 112.56 E
Sheraden, ngh., Pa., U.S. 197b 40.28 N 80.05 W
Sherard, Cape, c., Nu., Can. 108 C10 74.36 N 80.25 W
Sherard Osburn Fjord, b., Grnld. 108 A14 82.10 N 51.22 W
Sherborn, Ma., U.S. 201 42.14 N 71.22 W
Sherborne, Eng., U.K. 10 K10 50.57 N 2.31 W
Sherbro Island, i., S.L. 84 H2 7.34 N 12.42 W
Sherbrooke, N.S., Can. 122 E14 45.08 N 62.00 W
Sherbrooke, Qc., Can. 122 E5 45.24 N 71.53 W
Sherbrooke Lake, l., N.S., Can. 122 F12 44.41 N 64.36 W
Sherburn, Mn., U.S. 128 H4 43.39 N 94.43 W
Sherburne, N.Y., U.S. 124 B10 42.41 N 75.30 W
Shere, Eng., U.K. 178 51.13 N 0.28 W
Sheridan, Ar., U.S. 134 C6 34.18 N 92.24 W
Sheridan, In., U.S. 130 D11 40.08 N 86.12 W
Sheridan, Mt., U.S. 146 E14 45.27 N 112.11 W
Sheridan, Or., U.S. 146 E3 45.05 N 123.22 W
Sheridan, Tx., U.S. 136 E11 29.29 N 96.40 W
Sheridan, Wy., U.S. 140 C6 44.48 N 106.57 W
Sheridan, Mount, mtn., Wy., U.S. 146 F16 44.16 N 110.32 W
Sheridan Park, p.o.i., N.Y., U.S. 202a 42.59 N 78.54 W
Sheringham, Eng., U.K. 10 I14 52.56 N 1.12 E
Sherkston, On., Can. 202a 42.53 N 79.08 W
Sherman, Ms., U.S. 134 C10 34.21 N 88.50 W
Sherman, N.Y., U.S. 124 B6 42.09 N 79.35 W
Sherman, Tx., U.S. 134 D2 33.39 N 96.36 W
Sherman Mills, Me., U.S. 122 E8 45.52 N 68.23 W
Sherman Mountain, mtn., Ar., U.S. 130 H4 36.01 N 93.17 W
Sherman Oaks, ngh., Ca., U.S. 198 34.09 N 118.26 W
Sherman Reservoir, res., Ne., U.S. 140 F14 41.20 N 98.55 W
Sherman Station, Me., U.S. 122 E8 45.53 N 68.25 W
Sherpur, Bngl. 70 F12 24.40 N 89.24 E
Sherpur, Bngl. 70 F13 25.01 N 90.02 E
Sherrard, Il., U.S. 130 C7 41.19 N 90.31 W
Sherridon, Mb., Can. 110 E10 55.06 N 101.05 W
Sherrill, N.Y., U.S. 126 E14 43.04 N 75.36 W
Shertallai, India 69 G3 9.41 N 76.19 E
's-Hertogenbosch, Neth. 20 C14 51.41 N 5.19 E
Sherway Centre, shp. cen., On., Can. 193b 43.37 N 79.33 W
Sherwood, On., Can. 193b 43.50 N 79.31 W
Sherwood, Ar., U.S. 134 C6 34.48 N 92.13 W
Sherwood, N.D., U.S. 142 F12 48.57 N 101.37 W
Sherwood, Oh., U.S. 124 C1 41.16 N 84.33 W
Sherwood, Tn., U.S. 134 B12 35.04 N 85.55 W
Sherwood, Lake, l., Mi., U.S. 199 42.36 N 83.33 W
Sherwood Forest, Md., U.S. 202c 39.05 N 77.01 W
Sherwood Island State Park, p.o.i., Ct., U.S. 194 41.07 N 73.20 W
Sherwood Park, Ab., Can. 144 C17 53.31 N 113.18 W
Sherwood Park, De., U.S. 203 39.44 N 75.39 W
Sherwood Park, p.o.i., On., Can. 193b 43.43 N 79.24 W
Sherwood Point, c., Ct., U.S. 194 41.07 N 73.20 W
Sherwood Shores, Tx., U.S. 136 D9 30.34 N 98.22 W
Shesh Gāv, Afg. 70 B2 33.44 N 68.33 E
Shestakivka, Ukr. 38 E10 48.31 N 31.57 E
Shestirnia, Ukr. 38 F12 47.32 N 33.17 E
Shet Bandar, India 190c 18.58 N 72.56 E
Shetek, Lake, l., Mn., U.S. 128 G2 44.07 N 95.41 W
Shetland Islands, is., Scot., U.K. 10 n18 60.25 N 1.39 W
Shetrunji, stm., India 70 H3 21.19 N 72.04 E
Sheva, India 190c 18.56 N 72.57 E
Sheva Nhava, India 190c 18.58 N 72.58 E
Shevaroy Hills, hills, India 69 F4 11.50 N 78.16 E

Name	Page	Map Ref.	Latitude	Longitude
Shevchenkove, Ukr.	38	H8	45.33 N	29.20 E
Shevchenkove, Ukr.	38	D16	49.42 N	37.10 E
Shevington, Eng., U.K.	180		53.34 N	2.42 W
Shevington Moor, Eng., U.K.	180		53.35 N	2.41 W
Shexian, China	58	G8	29.53 N	118.26 E
Sheyang, China	58	E9	33.46 N	120.15 E
Sheyenne, N.D., U.S.	142	G14	47.49 N	99.07 W
Sheyenne, stm., N.D., U.S.	142	H16	47.01 N	96.49 W
Sheykhābād, Afg.	70	A2	34.03 N	68.44 E
Shherbakov see Rybinsk, Russia	26	B21	58.03 N	38.52 E
Shi, stm., China	58	E6	32.16 N	114.29 E
Shiant Islands, is., Scot., U.K.	10	D6	57.53 N	6.22 W
Shiba, stm., Japan	186		35.47 N	139.44 E
Shibadu, China	58	H4	28.01 N	110.51 E
Shibām, Yemen	72	F6	15.54 N	48.40 E
Shibasaki, Japan	186		35.39 N	139.34 E
Shibata, Japan	56	B12	37.56 N	139.19 E
Shibden Hall, hist., Eng., U.K.	180		53.44 N	1.51 W
Shibîn el-Kôm, Egypt	76	H1	30.33 N	31.00 E
Shibing, China	58	H2	26.49 N	108.04 E
Shibogama Lake, On., Can.	110	E13	53.35 N	88.15 W
Shibukawa, Japan	56	C12	36.29 N	139.00 E
Shibure-yama, mtn., Japan	188		34.45 N	135.05 E
Shibushi, Japan	56	H4	31.27 N	131.05 E
Shibuya, ngh., Japan	186		35.40 N	139.42 E
Shicheng, China	58	H7	26.22 N	116.22 E
Shickley, Ne., U.S.	140	G15	40.25 N	97.43 W
Shickshinny, Pa., U.S.	124	C9	41.09 N	76.09 W
Shidai, China	58	F7	30.20 N	117.56 E
Shidao, China	58	C10	36.54 N	122.24 E
Shidler, Ok., U.S.	138	E12	36.46 N	96.39 W
Shiel, Loch, l., Scot., U.K.	10	E7	56.47 N	5.35 W
Shields, stm., Mt., U.S.	146	E16	45.43 N	110.27 W
Shifang, China	58	I7	25.01 N	116.14 E
Shiga, state, Japan	56	D9	35.15 N	136.00 E
Shigangmen, China	187b		31.21 N	121.17 E
Shigezhuang, China	58	B7	38.57 N	116.19 E
Shigouyi, China	58	C2	37.43 N	106.24 E
Shiguaigou, China	58	A4	40.40 N	110.14 E
Shihkiachwang see Shijiazhuang, China	58	C6	38.02 N	114.29 E
Shihlin, ngh., Tai.	187d		25.06 N	121.31 E
Shihti, Tai.	187d		25.02 N	121.44 E
Shihting, Tai.	187d		24.59 N	121.39 E
Shihuajie, China	58	E4	32.20 N	111.25 E
Shijiaba, China	58	F1	30.18 N	104.45 E
Shijiazhai, China	187b		31.23 N	121.30 E
Shijiazhuang, China	58	C6	38.02 N	114.29 E
Shijiu Hu, l., China	58	F8	31.28 N	118.53 E
Shijōnawate, Japan	188		34.45 N	135.39 E
Shikami-yama, mtn., Japan	188		34.47 N	135.10 E
Shikārpur, India	69	D2	14.15 N	75.21 E
Shikārpur, Pak.	70	E2	27.57 N	68.38 E
Shikengkong, mtn., China	58	I5	24.56 N	113.00 E
Shikewusumiao, China	58	A3	40.10 N	108.50 E
Shikohābād, India	70	E7	27.06 N	78.34 E
Shikoku, i., Japan	56	F6	33.45 N	133.30 E
Shikoku-sanchi, mts., Japan	56	F6	33.47 N	133.29 E
Shikoma, Japan	186		35.11 N	139.56 E
Shikotan-tō see Šikotan, ostrov, i., Russia	54	C17	43.47 N	146.45 E
Shikotsu-ko, l., Japan	54	C14	42.45 N	141.20 E
Shil, India	190c		19.09 N	73.03 E
Shilabo, Eth.	82	F8	6.05 N	44.45 E
Shiliguri, India	70	E12	26.43 N	88.25 E
Shillelagh, Ire.	10	I6	52.44 N	6.32 W
Shillington, Pa., U.S.	126	H13	40.18 N	75.57 W
Shillong, India	70	F13	25.34 N	91.53 E
Shiloh, Oh., U.S.	130	E13	39.49 N	84.15 W
Shiloh see Saylūn, Khirbat, hist., W.B.	76	F6	32.03 N	35.17 E
Shiloh National Military Park, p.o.i., Tn., U.S.	134	B10	35.08 N	88.21 W
Shilong, China	58	J5	23.05 N	113.50 E
Shilong, China	58	F2	30.15 N	106.32 E
Shima, Japan	56	E9	34.16 N	136.47 E
Shima, Japan	188		34.59 N	135.20 E
Shimabara, Japan	56	G3	32.46 N	130.22 E
Shimada, Japan	56	E11	34.49 N	138.10 E
Shimada, Japan	186		35.59 N	139.25 E
Shimane, state, Japan	56	D5	35.00 N	132.30 E
Shimanto, stm., Japan	56	F5	32.56 N	132.58 E
Shimber Berris see Shimbiris, mtn., Som.	86	B9	10.44 N	47.15 E
Shimbiris, mtn., Som.	86	B9	10.44 N	47.15 E
Shimen, China	58	G4	29.28 N	111.17 E
Shimian, China	52	F5	29.15 N	102.17 E
Shimizu, Japan	56	D11	35.01 N	138.29 E
Shimizu see Tosa-shimizu, Japan	56	G5	32.46 N	132.58 E
Shimla, India	70	C6	31.06 N	77.09 E
Shimminato, Japan	56	C10	36.46 N	137.05 E
Shimoda, Japan	56	E11	34.40 N	138.57 E
Shimodate, Japan	56	C13	36.18 N	139.58 E
Shimofusa-daichi, plat., Japan	186		35.45 N	139.58 E
Shimofusa Naval Air Base, mil., Japan	186		35.48 N	140.01 E
Shimoga, India	69	E2	13.55 N	75.34 E
Shimogawara, Japan	186		35.56 N	139.21 E
Shimogōri, Japan	186		35.21 N	140.03 E
Shimogyō, ngh., Japan	188		34.59 N	135.45 E
Shimohōya, Japan	186		35.45 N	139.34 E
Shimoigusa, ngh., Japan	186		35.43 N	139.37 E
Shimomatsu, Japan	188		34.27 N	135.23 E
Shimomizo, Japan	186		35.31 N	139.23 E
Shimoniikura, Japan	186		35.47 N	139.38 E
Shimonoseki, Japan	56	F3	33.57 N	130.56 E
Shimono-shima, i., Japan	56	E2	34.12 N	129.15 E
Shimookudomi, Japan	186		35.53 N	139.26 E
Shimosakamoto, Japan	188		35.03 N	135.53 E
Shimotajiri, Japan	188		34.57 N	135.28 E
Shimotomi, Japan	186		35.50 N	139.29 E
Shimotsuchidana, Japan	186		35.24 N	139.27 E
Shimotsuruma, Japan	186		35.29 N	139.28 E
Shimoya, Japan	186		35.23 N	139.21 E
Shimoyugi, Japan	186		35.38 N	139.23 E
Shimura, ngh., Japan	186		35.46 N	139.41 E
Shin, Loch, l., Scot., U.K.	10	C8	58.06 N	4.33 W
Shinagawa, ngh., Japan	186		35.37 N	139.45 E
Shinan, China	58	J3	22.44 N	109.52 E
Shinano, stm., Japan	56	C11	37.56 N	139.04 E
Shinbâri, Egypt	191c		30.07 N	31.09 E
Shīndand, Afg.	72	C9	33.17 N	62.08 E
Shindenbaru-kichi, Kōkū-jieitai-, mil., Japan	56	G4	32.04 N	131.30 E
Shindo, Japan	186		35.21 N	139.21 E
Shiner, Tx., U.S.	136	E10	29.25 N	97.10 W
Shingbwiyang, Mya.	62	C8	26.43 N	96.11 E
Shingishū see Sinŭiju, Kor., N.	54	D6	40.05 N	124.23 E
Shing Mun Reservoir, res., China	189d		22.23 N	114.08 E
Shingū, Japan	56	F9	33.43 N	136.00 E
Shingū, Japan	56	E7	34.55 N	134.33 E
Shingwidzi, S. Afr.	90	C10	23.06 S	31.26 E
Shingwidzi (Singuédeze), stm., Afr.	90	C10	23.05 S	31.24 E
Shining Tor, mtn., Eng., U.K.	180		53.16 N	2.01 W
Shinji-ko, l., Japan	56	D5	35.27 N	132.58 E
Shinjō, Japan	56	A13	38.46 N	140.18 E
Shinjō, Japan	188		34.30 N	135.44 E
Shinjuku, ngh., Japan	186		35.41 N	139.42 E
Shinminato, stm., Japan	188		34.38 N	135.09 E
Shinsai-bashi, ngh., Japan	188		34.40 N	135.31 E
Shinshār, Syria	76	D7	34.36 N	36.44 E
Shinyanga, Tan.	86	E6	3.39 S	33.25 E
Shin-yōdo, mth., Japan	188		34.41 N	135.26 E
Shiocton, Wi., U.S.	128	G10	44.26 N	88.34 W
Shiogama, Japan	56	A14	38.19 N	141.01 E
Shiojiri, Japan	56	C10	36.06 N	137.57 E
Shiono-misaki, c., Japan	56	F8	33.26 N	135.45 E
Shioya, ngh., Japan	188		34.38 N	135.06 E
Shioya-zaki, c., Japan	56	C13	36.59 N	140.58 E
Shipbourne, Eng., U.K.	178		51.15 N	0.17 E
Shiping, China	52	G5	23.43 N	102.28 E
Shiping, China	58	G2	28.20 N	107.42 E
Shipka Pass see Šipčenski Prohod, p., Blg.	36	G12	42.47 N	25.18 E
Shipman, Va., U.S.	124	G7	37.42 N	78.51 W
Shippan Point, c., Ct., U.S.	194		41.01 N	73.32 W
Shippegan, N.B., Can.	122	C12	47.44 N	64.43 W
Shippensburg, Pa., U.S.	124	D8	40.02 N	77.31 W
Shiprock, N.M., U.S.	150	G8	36.47 N	108.41 W
Ship Rock, mtn., N.M., U.S.	150	G8	36.42 N	108.50 W
Shipshaw, stm., Qc., Can.	122	B5	48.27 N	71.13 W
Shipu, China	58	G9	29.12 N	121.55 E
Shiqian, China	58	H3	27.31 N	108.20 E
Shiqizhen see Zhongshan, China	58	J5	22.31 N	113.22 E
Shiquan, China	58	E3	33.02 N	108.14 E
Shirahama, Japan	56	F8	33.40 N	135.21 E
Shirakawa, Japan	56	B13	37.06 N	140.13 E
Shirakawa-tōge, hill, Japan	188		34.42 N	135.07 E
Shiraone, India	190c		19.03 N	73.01 E
Shīrāz, Iran	74	F13	29.36 N	52.32 E
Shirbîn, Egypt	76	G2	31.11 N	31.31 E
Shirdley Hill, Eng., U.K.	180		53.36 N	2.58 W
Shire, stm., Afr.	88	D5	17.41 S	35.19 E
Shiretoko-misaki, c., Japan	54	B16	44.20 N	145.20 E
Shīr Kūh, mtn., Iran	74	E13	31.37 N	54.04 E
Shirley, In., U.S.	130	E12	39.53 N	85.35 W
Shiroishi, Japan	56	A13	38.00 N	140.37 E
Shirone, Japan	56	B11	37.45 N	139.00 E
Shiro-yama, mtn., Japan	188		34.38 N	135.53 E
Shirpur, India	70	H5	21.21 N	74.53 E
Shīrvān, Iran	72	B8	37.24 N	57.55 E
Shisanzhan, China	50	F14	51.18 N	125.45 E
Shisha Hai, l., China	189a		39.57 N	116.22 E
Shishaldin Volcano, vol., Ak., U.S.	109	F7	54.45 N	163.57 W
Shishi, China	58	I8	24.47 N	118.35 E
Shishmaref, Ak., U.S.	109	C6	66.14 N	166.05 W
Shishou, China	58	G5	29.43 N	112.19 E
Shisler Point, c., On., Can.	202a		42.52 N	79.08 W
Shitai, China	58	F7	30.13 N	117.26 E
Shitang, China	58	I4	25.38 N	110.50 E
Shitara, Japan	56	D10	35.05 N	137.33 E
Shithāthah, Iraq	74	D8	32.34 N	43.29 E
Shiv, India	70	E3	26.11 N	71.15 E
Shively, Ky., U.S.	120	F12	38.12 N	85.48 W
Shivpuri, India	70	F6	25.25 N	77.39 E
Shivta, Horvot (Subeita), hist., Isr.	76	H5	30.53 N	34.38 E
Shivwits Plateau, plat., Az., U.S.	150	G3	36.07 N	113.36 W
Shiwan, China	58	C3	37.35 N	109.00 E
Shiwu, China	54	C6	43.50 N	124.12 E
Shixi, China	58	G7	28.15 N	117.46 E
Shiyan, China	58	E4	32.42 N	110.45 E
Shiyangchang, China	58	G1	29.56 N	105.37 E
Shizhu, China	58	G8	28.50 N	120.05 E
Shizhu, China	58	G3	29.56 N	108.09 E
Shizugawa, Japan	56	A14	38.40 N	141.27 E
Shizui, China	54	C6	43.08 N	126.06 E
Shizunai, Japan	54	C15	42.20 N	142.22 E
Shizuoka, Japan	56	E11	34.58 N	138.23 E
Shizuoka, state, Japan	56	E11	35.00 N	138.00 E
Shkodër, Alb.	32	B13	42.04 N	19.31 E
Shkodra see Shkodër, Alb.	32	B13	42.04 N	19.31 E
Shkodres, Liqeni i see Scutari, Lake, l., Eur.	30	H16	42.12 N	19.18 E
Shkumbin, stm., Alb.	32	C14	41.00 N	19.26 E
Shō, stm., Japan	56	C10	36.47 N	137.04 E
Shoal, stm., Fl., U.S.	134	G12	30.41 N	86.39 W
Shoal Creek, stm., U.S.	130	D5	40.29 N	92.41 W
Shoal Creek, stm., U.S.	130	H3	37.03 N	94.42 W
Shoal Creek, stm., Il., U.S.	130	F8	38.28 N	89.34 W
Shoal Creek, stm., Mo., U.S.	130	E4	39.44 N	93.32 W
Shoalhaven, stm., Austl.	98	J8	34.52 S	150.36 E
Shoal Lake, Mb., Can.	112	D13	50.26 N	100.35 W
Shoal Lake, l., Can.	128	B3	49.32 N	95.00 W
Shoal Point, c., Ct., U.S.	194		41.08 N	73.15 W
Shoals, In., U.S.	130	F11	38.39 N	86.47 W
Shoalwater Bay, b., Austl.	98	D8	22.19 S	150.20 E
Shōbara, Japan	56	E6	34.51 N	133.01 E
Shōdai, Japan	188		34.51 N	135.42 E
Shodnja, Russia	183b		55.57 N	37.18 E
Shodnja, stm., Russia	183b		55.50 N	37.25 E
Shōdo-shima, i., Japan	56	E7	34.30 N	134.17 E
Shogunle, Nig.	191a		6.35 N	3.21 E
Sholingnur, India	69	E4	13.06 N	79.25 E
Shomolu, Nig.	191a		6.32 N	3.23 E
Shōnan, Japan	186		35.50 N	140.02 E
Shongum, N.J., U.S.	194		40.50 N	74.33 W
Shongum Lake, l., N.J., U.S.	194		40.51 N	74.32 W
Shooters Island, i., U.S.	194		40.39 N	74.10 W
Shoranūr, India	69	F3	10.45 N	76.16 E
Shorāpur, India	69	C3	16.31 N	76.45 E
Shoreacres, B.C., Can.	144	G13	49.26 N	117.30 W
Shoreditch, ngh., Eng., U.K.	178		51.32 N	0.05 W
Shoreham, Eng., U.K.	178		51.20 N	0.11 E
Shorewood, Wi., U.S.	130	A10	43.04 N	87.52 W
Shorkot, Pak.	70	C3	30.49 N	72.04 E
Shorne, Eng., U.K.	178		51.25 N	0.26 E
Shortland Island, i., Sol. Is.	101b	d6	7.03 S	155.42 E
Shortland Islands, is., Sol. Is.	101b	d6	7.01 S	155.40 E
Short Mountain, mtn., Tn., U.S.	124	H2	36.23 N	83.10 W
Shoshone, Id., U.S.	146	H12	42.56 N	114.24 W
Shoshone, stm., Wy., U.S.	140	C4	44.51 N	108.11 W
Shoshone, North Fork, stm., Wy., U.S.	140	C3	44.29 N	109.12 W
Shoshone, South Fork, stm., Wy., U.S.	146	F17	44.29 N	109.12 W
Shoshone Basin, bas., Wy., U.S.	140	D4	43.05 N	108.05 W
Shoshone Lake, l., Wy., U.S.	146	F15	44.22 N	110.42 W
Shoshone Mountains, mts., Nv., U.S.	148	D8	38.58 N	117.33 W
Shoshone Peak, mtn., Nv., U.S.	148	G9	36.56 N	116.16 W
Shoshone Range, mts., Nv., U.S.	148	C9	40.11 N	116.59 W
Shoshong, Bots.	90	C8	23.00 S	26.26 E
Shoshoni, Wy., U.S.	140	D4	43.14 N	108.06 W
Shostka, Ukr.	38	B12	51.51 N	33.29 E
Shotton, Wales, U.K.	180		53.12 N	3.02 W
Shotwick, Eng., U.K.	180		53.14 N	2.59 W
Shouchang, China	58	G8	29.21 N	119.14 E
Shouguang, China	58	C8	36.52 N	118.44 E
Shouning, China	58	H8	27.27 N	119.30 E
Shouxian, China	58	E7	32.34 N	116.46 E
Shouyang, China	58	C5	37.52 N	113.10 E
Show Low, Az., U.S.	150	I6	34.15 N	110.02 W
Shpola, Ukr.	38	D10	49.00 N	31.23 E
Shpykiv, Ukr.	38	E7	48.47 N	28.33 E
Shqipëria see Albania, ctry., Eur.	32	C14	41.00 N	20.00 E
Shqiptare, Alpet see North Albanian Alps, mts., Eur.	32	B13	42.27 N	19.47 E
Shramkivka, Ukr.	38	C11	50.11 N	32.05 E
Shreve, Oh., U.S.	124	D4	40.40 N	82.01 W
Shreveport, La., U.S.	136	B14	32.30 N	93.45 W
Shrevewood, Va., U.S.	202c		38.53 N	77.13 W
Shrewsbury, Eng., U.K.	10	I10	52.43 N	2.45 W
Shrewsbury River, b., N.J., U.S.	194		40.21 N	74.00 W
Shri Dūngargarh, India	70	D4	28.05 N	74.00 E
Shri Mohangarh, India	70	E3	27.17 N	71.14 E
Shropshire Union Canal, can., Eng., U.K.	180		53.17 N	2.53 W
Shū see Šu, Kaz.	48	F12	43.35 N	73.44 E
Shū see Ču, stm., Asia	48	F11	45.00 N	67.44 E
Shu, stm., China	58	D8	34.07 N	118.30 E
Shuajingsi, China	62	B9	32.00 N	103.16 E
Shuang, stm., Tai.	187d		25.00 N	121.31 E
Shuangcheng, China	52	B10	45.21 N	126.19 E
Shuangfeng, China	58	H5	27.26 N	112.04 E
Shuanggang, China	54	B5	45.06 N	122.55 E
Shuanggou, China	58	E5	32.11 N	112.22 E
Shuanggou, China	58	D7	34.02 N	117.34 E
Shuang-hsi, Tai.	187d		25.01 N	121.39 E
Shuangji, stm., China	58	D5	34.09 N	114.18 E
Shuangjiang, China	52	G4	23.37 N	99.42 E
Shuangliao, China	52	C9	43.30 N	123.30 E
Shuangpai, China	58	I4	25.57 N	111.32 E
Shuangshutai, China	54	C4	43.48 N	121.13 E
Shuangyang, China	52	C10	43.31 N	125.41 E
Shuangyashan, China	52	B11	46.35 N	131.18 E
Shubenacadie, stm., N.S., Can.	122	F13	45.20 N	63.30 W
Shubrâ el-Kheima, Egypt	76	H2	30.06 N	31.14 E
Shubrâ el-Kheima, Egypt	191c		30.06 N	31.15 E
Shubuta, Ms., U.S.	134	F10	31.51 N	88.41 W
Shucheng, China	58	F7	31.26 N	116.56 E
Shugudali, China	50	F13	52.49 N	124.03 E
Shuibatang, China	58	G2	28.39 N	107.03 E
Shuicheng see Lupanshui, China	52	F5	26.37 N	104.47 E
Shuifeng Shuiku see Supung Reservoir, res., Asia	54	D6	40.30 N	125.02 E
Shuiji, China	58	H8	27.25 N	118.20 E
Shuijingtang, China	58	G3	28.50 N	108.11 E
Shuikouguan, China	58	J2	22.27 N	106.35 E
Shuikoushan, China	58	H5	26.30 N	112.30 E
Shuitou, China	58	I8	24.41 N	118.24 E
Shuiye, China	58	C6	36.07 N	114.06 E
Shujāābād, Pak.	70	D3	29.52 N	71.17 E
Shujālpur, India	70	G6	23.23 N	76.42 E
Shuksan, Mount, mtn., Wa., U.S.	146	B5	48.50 N	121.36 W
Shulan, China	52	C10	44.24 N	126.57 E
Shulaps Peak, mtn., B.C., Can.	144	F8	50.57 N	122.31 W
Shule, China	48	G13	39.21 N	76.05 E
Shule, stm., China	52	C4	40.21 N	93.29 E
Shul'hynka, Ukr.	38	D17	49.08 N	38.55 E
Shullsburg, Wi., U.S.	130	B7	42.34 N	90.13 W
Shumagin Islands, is., Ak., U.S.	109	F7	55.06 N	159.43 W
Shumatuscacant, stm., Ma., U.S.	201		42.03 N	70.51 W
Shums'k, Ukr.	38	C5	50.05 N	26.08 E
Shunchang, China	58	H7	26.50 N	117.48 E
Shunde, China	58	J5	22.50 N	113.14 E
Shungnak, Ak., U.S.	109	C8	66.55 N	157.07 W
Shunyi, China	58	A7	40.07 N	116.38 E
Shupiyan, India	70	B5	33.42 N	74.47 E
Shuqayyiqah, Nafūd, sand, Sau. Ar.	74	H9	25.45 N	43.55 E
Shuqualak, Ms., U.S.	134	E10	32.58 N	88.34 W
Shūr, stm., Iran	74	C12	34.42 N	51.46 E
Shūr, stm., Iran	74	E14	31.54 N	55.09 E
Shūr, stm., Iran	74	B15	35.24 N	56.00 E
Shurkhua, Mya.	64	A1	22.14 N	93.37 E
Shurugwi, Zimb.	88	D5	19.39 S	30.01 E
Shūsh, Iran	74	D11	32.11 N	48.16 E
Shūshtar, Iran	74	D11	32.03 N	48.51 E
Shuswap, stm., B.C., Can.	144	F12	50.49 N	119.03 W
Shuswap Lake, l., B.C., Can.	144	E12	50.57 N	119.15 W
Shutlingsloe, mtn., Eng., U.K.	180		53.13 N	2.02 W
Shuwak, Sudan	82	E7	14.24 N	35.52 E
Shuyak Island, i., Ak., U.S.	109	E9	58.31 N	152.30 W
Shuyang, China	58	D8	34.07 N	118.47 E
Shuyūkh Fawqānī, Syria	76	B9	36.45 N	38.02 E
Shwangliao see Liaoyuan, China	52	C10	42.54 N	125.08 E
Shwebo, Mya.	64	A2	22.34 N	95.42 E
Shwegun, Mya.	64	D3	17.09 N	97.39 E
Shwegyin, Mya.	64	D3	17.55 N	96.53 E
Shwenyaung, Mya.	64	B3	20.45 N	96.55 E
Shymkent see Šymkent, Kaz.	48	F11	42.18 N	69.35 E
Shyok, India	70	A7	34.09 N	78.10 E
Shyok, stm., Asia	62	B4	35.14 N	75.55 E
Shypuvate, Ukr.	38	D16	49.56 N	37.24 E
Shyriaieve, Ukr.	38	F9	47.23 N	30.11 E
Shyrmivka, Ukr.	38	D8	49.34 N	29.06 E
Shyroke, Ukr.	38	E13	48.07 N	34.49 E
Shyroke, Ukr.	38	F12	47.41 N	33.14 E
Shyrokolanivka, Ukr.	38	F10	47.10 N	31.26 E
Shyshaky, Ukr.	38	D13	49.52 N	34.00 E
Si, stm., China	58	D7	35.14 N	116.39 E
Sia, Indon.	60	G9	6.48 S	134.19 E
Siabu, Indon.	66	C1	1.01 N	99.29 E
Siāhān Range, mts., Pak.	72	D10	27.17 N	64.19 E
Siāh Kūh, Kavīr-e, pl., Iran	74	D14	32.40 N	53.52 E
Siak, stm., Indon.	66	C2	1.13 N	102.10 E
Siak Sri Indrapura, Indon.	66	C3	0.46 N	102.04 E
Siālkot, Pak.	70	B5	32.31 N	74.32 E
Sialsūk, India	70	G14	23.24 N	92.45 E
Siam see Thailand, ctry., Asia	64	E5	15.00 N	100.00 E
Siam, Gulf of see Thailand, Gulf of, b., Asia	64	G5	10.00 N	101.00 E
Sian see Xi'an, China	58	D3	34.15 N	108.52 E
Siangtan see Xiangtan, China	58	H5	27.51 N	112.54 E
Sianhala, C. Iv.	84	G3	10.02 N	6.51 W
Sianów, Pol.	24	B12	54.15 N	16.17 E
Siari, Pak.	70	A6	34.55 N	76.44 E
Siasconset, Ma., U.S.	124	C15	41.16 N	69.58 W
Siasi, Phil.	68	H3	5.33 N	120.49 E
Siasi Island, i., Phil.	68	H3	5.33 N	120.51 E
Šiaškotan, ostrov, i., Russia	50	G19	48.51 N	154.09 E
Siátista, Grc.	34	C4	40.15 N	21.33 E
Siau, Pulau, i., Indon.	60	E7	2.45 N	125.22 E
Šiauliai, Lith.	26	E6	55.55 N	23.19 E
Sibâ'i, Gebel el-, mtn., Egypt	74	H4	25.41 N	34.09 E
Sibaj, Russia	48	D9	52.42 N	58.40 E
Sibayi, Lake, l., S. Afr.	90	E11	27.21 S	32.42 E
Sibbald, Ab., Can.	142	C3	51.23 N	110.07 W
Sibbo, Fin.	18	G12	60.22 N	25.12 E
Šibenik, Cro.	30	G12	43.44 N	15.53 E
Siberia see Sibir', reg., Russia	50	D9	65.00 N	110.00 E
Siberut, Pulau, i., Indon.	66	D1	1.20 S	98.55 E
Sibi, Pak.	62	C2	29.32 N	67.52 E
Sibigo, Indon.	64	K2	2.49 N	95.54 E
Sibir', reg., Russia	50	D9	65.00 N	110.00 E
Sibircevo, Russia	54	B10	44.12 N	132.27 E
Sibirjakova, ostrov, i., Russia	50	B4	72.50 N	79.00 E
Sibiti, Congo	86	E2	3.41 S	13.21 E
Sibiu, Rom.	36	D11	45.47 N	24.09 E
Sibiu, state, Rom.	36	D11	46.00 N	24.15 E
Sibley, Ia., U.S.	128	H3	43.24 N	95.44 W
Sibley, La., U.S.	134	E5	32.32 N	93.18 W
Sibley, Ms., U.S.	134	F7	31.22 N	91.23 W
Sibley Peninsula, pen., On., Can.	128	C10	48.29 N	88.46 W
Siboa, Indon.	66	C12	0.25 N	120.00 E
Sibolga, Indon.	66	C1	1.45 N	98.47 E
Sibpur, India	190b		22.24 N	88.33 E
Sibpur, India	190b		22.34 N	88.19 E
Sibsāgar, India	62	C7	26.59 N	94.38 E
Sibu, Malay.	66	B7	2.18 N	111.49 E
Sibu, Pulau, i., Malay.	64	K7	2.13 N	104.04 E
Sibuguey Bay, b., Phil.	68	G4	7.30 N	122.40 E
Sibut, C.A.R.	86	C3	5.43 N	19.04 E
Sibutu Island, i., Phil.	68	H2	4.46 N	119.29 E
Sibutu Passage, strt., Asia	68	H2	4.50 N	119.35 E
Sibuyan Island, i., Phil.	68	D4	12.26 N	122.34 E
Sibuyan Sea, s., Phil.	68	D4	12.50 N	122.40 E
Sicamous, B.C., Can.	144	F12	50.49 N	119.00 W
Sicapoo, Mount, mtn., Phil.	68	B3	18.01 N	120.56 E
Siccus, stm., Austl.	98	H2	31.27 S	139.29 E
Sichang see Xichang, China	52	F5	27.54 N	102.16 E
Si Chon, Thai.	64	H4	9.00 N	99.53 E
Sichuan, state, China	52	E5	31.00 N	105.00 E
Sichuan Pendi, bas., China	52	E5	30.00 N	105.00 E
Sichuanzhai, China	64	A5	23.00 N	101.45 E
Sicié, Cap, c., Fr.	22	F11	43.03 N	5.51 E
Sicilia, state, Italy	32	F8	37.30 N	14.00 E
Sicilia (Sicily), i., Italy	32	G8	37.30 N	14.00 E
Sicilia, Canale di see Sicily, Strait of, strt.	32	G5	37.09 N	11.36 E
Sicily see Sicilia, state, Italy	32	F8	37.30 N	14.00 E
Sicily see Sicilia, i., Italy	32	G8	37.30 N	14.00 E
Sicily, Strait of, strt.	32	G5	37.09 N	11.36 E
Sicily Island, La., U.S.	134	F7	31.50 N	91.39 W
Sico Tinto, stm., Hond.	156	E5	15.50 N	85.03 W
Sicuani, Peru	164	F3	14.16 S	71.13 W
Šid, Yugo.	36	D6	45.07 N	19.14 E
Sidao, China	189a		39.51 N	116.26 E
Sidareja, Indon.	66	G6	7.29 S	108.47 E
Sidas, Indon.	66	C6	0.24 N	109.45 E
Sidasjav'ri see Sitasjaure, l., Eur.	14	E8	68.00 N	17.24 E
Sidcup, ngh., Eng., U.K.	178		51.25 N	0.06 E
Siddhapur, India	70	G4	23.55 N	72.22 E
Siddinghausen, Ger.	181		51.32 N	7.48 E
Siddington, Eng., U.K.	180		53.14 N	2.14 W
Siddipet, India	69	B4	18.06 N	78.51 E
Sid el- Ha'âm, Gebel, mtn., Egypt	76	I2	29.46 N	31.43 E
Sidéradougou, Burkina	84	G4	10.40 N	4.15 W
Siderno, Italy	32	F10	38.16 N	16.18 E
Siderópolis, Braz.	172	D13	28.35 S	49.25 W
Síderos, Ákra, c., Grc.	34	H9	35.18 N	26.18 E
Sidhauli, India	70	E8	27.16 N	80.50 E
Sidhi, India	70	F8	24.24 N	81.52 E
Sidi Akacha, Alg.	28	H12	36.28 N	1.17 E
Sīdi Barrâni, Egypt	82	A5	31.36 N	25.55 E
Sidi bel Abbès, Alg.	84	B4	35.12 N	0.11 W
Sidi-Ifni, Mor.	84	D2	29.22 N	10.10 W
Sidikalang, Indon.	64	K4	2.44 N	98.19 E
Siding Spring Mountain, mtn., Austl.	98	H7	31.20 S	149.03 E
Sidirókastro, Grc.	34	B6	41.14 N	23.23 E
Sidi Sâlim, Egypt	76	G1	31.16 N	30.46 E
Sidlaghatta, India	69	E3	13.23 N	77.51 E
Sidley, Mount, mtn., Ant.	103	C28	77.02 S	125.59 W
Sidmouth, Eng., U.K.	10	K9	50.41 N	3.14 W
Sidnaw, Mi., U.S.	128	E10	46.30 N	88.43 W
Sidney, B.C., Can.	144	H7	48.39 N	123.23 W
Sidney, Il., U.S.	130	D9	40.01 N	88.04 W
Sidney, Ia., U.S.	130	D2	40.44 N	95.39 W
Sidney, Mt., U.S.	142	G9	47.42 N	104.09 W
Sidney, Ne., U.S.	140	F10	41.08 N	102.59 W
Sidney, N.Y., U.S.	124	B10	42.18 N	75.23 W
Sidney, Oh., U.S.	124	D1	40.17 N	84.09 W
Sidney Lanier, Lake, res., Ga., U.S.	132	B2	34.15 N	83.57 W
Sidoan, Indon.	66	C12	0.16 N	120.12 E
Sidon see Sayda, Leb.	76	E6	33.33 N	35.22 E
Sidon, Ms., U.S.	134	D8	33.25 N	90.12 W
Sidorovsk, Russia	48	A14	66.34 N	82.17 E
Sidra, Gulf of see Surt, Khalīj, b., Libya	82	A3	31.30 N	18.00 E
Sidrolândia, Braz.	166	D6	20.55 S	54.57 W
Siedlce, Pol.	24	D18	52.09 N	22.16 E
Siedove, Ukr.	38	F17	47.03 N	38.09 E
Siegburg, Ger.	24	F3	50.47 N	7.12 E
Siegen, Ger.	24	F4	50.52 N	8.01 E
Siegenfeld, Aus.	182b		48.02 N	16.10 E
Siemensstadt, ngh., Ger.	182a		52.32 N	13.17 E
Siemianowice Śląskie, Pol.	24	F15	50.19 N	19.01 E
Siemiatycze, Pol.	24	D18	52.25 N	22.52 E
Siěmpang, Camb.	64	E8	14.07 N	106.23 E
Siěmréab, Camb.	64	F6	13.21 N	103.51 E
Siena, Italy	30	G8	43.18 N	11.19 E
Sieniawa, Pol.	24	F18	50.10 N	22.36 E
Sienyang see Xianyang, China	58	D3	34.20 N	108.42 E
Sieppijärvi, Fin.	14	E15	67.09 N	23.58 E
Sieradz, Pol.	24	E14	51.36 N	18.45 E
Sieraków, Pol.	24	D12	52.37 N	16.05 E
Sierpc, Pol.	24	D15	52.51 N	19.39 E
Sierra Blanca, Tx., U.S.	136	C2	31.10 N	105.21 W
Sierra Blanca Peak, mtn., N.M., U.S.	138	H3	33.23 N	105.48 W
Sierra Chica, Arg.	172	H7	36.50 S	60.13 W
Sierra Colorada, Arg.	166	H3	40.35 S	67.44 W
Sierra de Agua, Belize	156	D3	17.32 N	88.54 W
Sierra de Outes see Serra de Outes, Spain	28	B2	42.49 N	8.54 W
Sierra Gorda, Chile	166	D3	22.54 S	69.20 W
Sierra Leone, ctry., Afr.	84	H2	8.30 N	11.30 W
Sierra Mojada, Mex.	136	G4	27.17 N	103.41 W
Sierra Nevada, Parque Nacional, p.o.i., Ven.	168	C6	8.33 N	70.49 W
Sierra Peak, mtn., Ca., U.S.	198		33.51 N	117.39 W
Sierras Bayas, Arg.	172	H7	36.56 S	60.08 W
Sierra Vista, Az., U.S.	150	L6	31.34 N	110.17 W
Sierre, Switz.	30	D4	46.17 N	7.31 E
Siesta Key, Fl., U.S.	132	I3	27.16 N	82.33 W
Siethen, Ger.	182a		52.17 N	13.13 E
Siethener See, l., Ger.	182a		52.17 N	13.12 E
Sievering, ngh., Aus.	182b		48.15 N	16.20 E
Sieverodonets'k, Ukr.	38	D17	48.57 N	38.29 E
Sífnos, i., Grc.	34	F7	36.58 N	24.40 E
Sitón Villanueva, Mex.	136	G7	27.16 N	100.17 W
Sifton, Mb., Can.	142	C13	51.21 N	100.07 W
Sig, Russia	18	B21	65.35 N	34.11 E
Sigatoka, Fiji	101e	q18	18.08 S	177.30 E
Sigean, Fr.	22	F8	43.01 N	2.57 E
Sigep, Indon.	66	D1	1.03 S	98.47 E
Sighetu Marmației, Rom.	36	B10	47.55 N	23.55 E
Sighișoara, Rom.	36	C11	46.13 N	24.48 E
Sigiriya, Sri L.	69	H5	7.56 N	80.49 E
Siglan, Russia	50	E19	59.04 N	152.20 E
Sigli, Indon.	64	J2	5.22 N	95.56 E
Siglufjördur, Ice.	12a	j30	66.09 N	18.55 W
Sigmaringen, Ger.	24	H5	48.04 N	9.13 E
Signal Hill, Ca., U.S.	198		33.47 N	118.09 W
Signal Mountain, Tn., U.S.	134	B13	35.07 N	85.20 W
Signal Mountain, mtn., Vt., U.S.	122	F4	44.12 N	72.20 W
Signal Peak, mtn., Ut., U.S.	150	F3	37.19 N	113.29 W
Signy, sci., Ant.	103	B36	60.43 S	45.36 W
Sigourney, Ia., U.S.	130	C5	41.20 N	92.12 W
Sigsig, Ec.	164	D2	3.00 S	78.47 W
Sigtuna, Swe.	16	H15	59.37 N	17.43 E
Siguanea, Ensenada de la, b., Cuba	156	B6	21.38 N	83.05 W
Siguatepeque, Hond.	156	E3	14.35 N	87.50 W
Sigüenza, Spain	28	C8	41.04 N	2.38 W
Sigüés, Spain	28	B10	42.39 N	1.01 W
Siguiri, Gui.	84	G3	11.25 N	9.10 W
Sigulda, Lat.	26	C7	57.09 N	24.52 E
Sigurd, Ut., U.S.	150	E5	38.50 N	111.57 W
Siguri Falls, wtfl., Tan.	86	F7	8.32 S	37.22 E
Sihabuhabu, Dolok, mtn., Indon.	66	B1	2.10 N	99.21 E
Sihala see Sri Lanka, ctry., Asia	69	G5	7.00 N	81.00 E
Sihanoukville see Kâmpóng Saôm, Camb.	64	G6	10.37 N	103.30 E
Šihany, Russia	40	E15	52.07 N	47.13 E
Sihor, India	70	H3	21.42 N	71.56 E
Sihorā, India	70	G8	23.29 N	80.07 E
Sihote-Alin', mts., Russia	46	E17	48.00 N	138.00 E
Šihtovo, Russia	26	E15	55.42 N	32.17 E
Sihui, China	58	J5	23.21 N	112.40 E
Sihŭng, ngh., Kor., S.	189b		37.28 N	126.54 E
Siikajoki, stm., Fin.	18	C12	64.50 N	24.44 E
Siilinjärvi, Fin.	18	D14	63.04 N	27.39 E
Siirt, Tur.	42	G9	37.56 N	41.57 E
Siirt, state, Tur.	42	G10	38.00 N	42.00 E
Sija, Russia	12	E19	63.37 N	41.36 E
Sijiazi, China	54	D4	41.46 N	120.02 E
Sijunjung, Indon.	66	D2	0.40 S	100.57 E
Sikandarābād, India	70	D6	28.26 N	77.41 E
Sikandarpur, India	190a		28.42 N	77.21 E
Sikandarpur, India	190b		22.57 N	88.12 E
Sikanni Chief, stm., B.C., Can.	110	D6	58.17 N	121.44 W
Sikao, Thai.	64	I4	7.32 N	99.19 E
Sikar, India	70	E5	27.36 N	75.08 E
Sikarpur, India	190b		22.36 N	88.32 E
Sikasso, Mali	84	G3	11.18 N	5.39 W
Sikeston, Mo., U.S.	130	H8	36.52 N	89.35 W
Si Khiu, Thai.	64	E5	14.55 N	101.41 E
Sikhote-Alin Mountains see Sihote-Alin', mts., Russia	46	E17	48.00 N	138.00 E
Sikinos, Grc.	34	G8	36.40 N	25.05 E
Síkinos, i., Grc.	34	G8	36.39 N	25.05 E
Sikkim, state, India	70	E12	27.35 N	88.35 E
Siklós, hist., Hung.	36	D5	45.50 N	18.18 E
Sikonge, Tan.	86	F6	5.36 S	32.46 E
Šikotan, ostrov (Shikotan-tō), i., Russia	54	C17	43.47 N	146.45 E
Sikrod, India	190a		28.43 N	77.11 E
Siktjah, Russia	50	B13	69.55 N	125.05 E
Sikuati, Malay.	68	G1	6.52 N	116.40 E
Sikutu, Indon.	66	C12	0.52 N	120.37 E
Sikyón, hist., Grc.	34	F5	37.59 N	22.44 E
Sil, stm., Spain	28	B3	42.27 N	7.44 W
Šila, Russia	50	E7	56.32 N	93.02 E
Silacayoapan, Mex.	154	G9	17.30 N	98.09 W
Sila Grande, mts., Italy	32	E10	39.22 N	16.30 E
Šilalė, Lith.	26	E5	55.28 N	22.12 E
Silāmpur, ngh., India	190a		28.40 N	77.16 E
Silao, Mex.	154	E8	20.56 N	101.25 W
Silas, Al., U.S.	134	F10	31.45 N	88.19 W
Silat, Indon.	66	C7	0.20 N	111.47 E
Silaut, Indon.	66	E2	2.25 S	101.09 E
Silay, Phil.	68	E4	10.48 N	122.59 E
Silba, Cro.	30	F11	44.22 N	14.41 E
Silchar, India	70	F14	24.49 N	92.48 E
Silda, i., Nor.	14	B12	70.20 N	21.44 E
Sildegapet, b., Nor.	16	E2	62.03 N	5.10 E
Sile, Tur.	34	B12	41.11 N	29.36 E
Šilega, Russia	12	D20	64.01 N	44.00 E
Siler City, N.C., U.S.	124	I6	35.43 N	79.27 W
Sileru, stm., India	69	C5	17.48 N	81.24 E
Silesia, hist. reg., Eur.	24	F13	50.33 N	18.00 E
Silet, Alg.	84	E5	22.41 N	4.38 E
Sileti, stm., Kaz.	48	D12	53.06 N	73.24 E
Siletyteniz, ozero, l., Kaz.	48	D12	53.15 N	73.15 E
Siletz, Or., U.S.	146	F3	44.43 N	123.55 W
Siletz, stm., Or., U.S.	146	F3	44.55 N	124.01 W
Siligadhī, Nepal	70	D8	29.13 N	80.59 E
Silghāt, India	70	E14	26.36 N	92.55 E
Silhouette, i., Sey.	89b	j13	4.29 S	55.14 E
Siliana, Tun.	32	H3	36.04 N	9.22 E
Siliana, Oued, stm., Tun.	32	I3	36.33 N	9.25 E

Name	Page	Map Ref.	Latitude	Longitude
Silifke, Tur.	42	G5	36.22 N	33.56 E
Siliguri see Shiliguri, India	70	E12	26.43 N	88.25 E
Siling Co, l., China	52	E2	31.47 N	89.00 E
Silistra, Blg.	36	E14	44.07 N	27.16 E
Silivri, Tur.	34	B11	41.05 N	28.12 E
Šiljak, mtn., Yugo.	36	F8	43.45 N	21.50 E
Siljan, l., Swe.	16	G12	60.50 N	14.45 E
Siljansnäs, Swe.	16	G12	60.46 N	14.53 E
Šilka, Russia	50	F12	51.51 N	116.02 E
Šilka, stm., Russia	50	F12	53.20 N	121.26 E
Silkeborg, Den.	16	K7	56.10 N	9.32 E
Sill, stm., Aus.	30	C8	47.17 N	11.24 E
Sillamäe, Est.	26	A10	59.23 N	27.46 E
Sillaro, stm., Italy	30	F8	44.34 N	11.51 E
Sillem Island, i., Nu., Can.	110	A16	70.57 N	71.44 W
Sillian, Aus.	30	D9	46.44 N	12.25 E
Sillon de Talbert, pen., Fr.	20	F5	48.53 N	3.05 W
Silly-le-Long, Fr.	179		49.06 N	2.48 E
Šil'naja Balka, Kaz.	40	F16	50.34 N	48.59 E
Siloam Springs, Ar., U.S.	130	H3	36.11 N	94.32 W
Silogui, Indon.	66	D1	1.13 S	98.59 E
Šiloviči, Russia	26	E15	55.24 N	32.33 E
Šilovo, Russia	26	F16	54.59 N	33.44 E
Šilovo, Russia	40	D12	54.18 N	40.52 E
Silsbee, Tx., U.S.	136	D13	30.20 N	94.10 W
Silschede, Ger.	181		51.21 N	7.19 E
Silton, Sk., Can.	142	D9	50.48 N	104.54 W
Siluas, Indon.	66	C6	1.16 N	109.50 E
Šilute, Lith.	26	E4	55.20 N	21.28 E
Silvan, Tur.	42	F9	38.09 N	41.00 E
Silvāneh, Iran	74	B9	37.25 N	44.51 E
Silvânia, Braz.	170	I1	16.41 S	48.37 W
Silvassa, India	70	H4	20.17 N	73.01 E
Silver, Tx., U.S.	136	B7	32.04 N	100.39 W
Silver Bank Passage, strt., N.A.	156	B12	20.52 N	70.17 W
Silver Bay, Mn., U.S.	128	D7	47.17 N	91.15 W
Silver Bell, Az., U.S.	150	K5	32.23 N	111.32 W
Silver City, N.M., U.S.	150	K8	32.46 N	108.16 W
Silver City, N.C., U.S.	132	B6	34.59 N	79.14 W
Silver Creek, Ms., U.S.	134	F9	31.35 N	89.59 W
Silver Creek, Ne., U.S.	140	F15	41.18 N	97.39 W
Silver Creek, N.Y., U.S.	124	B6	42.32 N	79.10 W
Silver Creek, stm., Az., U.S.	150	I6	34.44 N	110.02 W
Silver Creek, stm., Il., U.S.	130	F8	38.19 N	89.52 W
Silver Creek, stm., Il., U.S.	196		41.54 N	87.50 W
Silver Creek, stm., Mi., U.S.	199		42.06 N	83.17 E
Silver Creek, stm., Or., U.S.	146	G7	43.16 N	119.13 W
Silverdale, Wa., U.S.	146	C4	47.38 N	122.41 W
Silverdalen, Swe.	16	J13	57.31 N	15.46 E
Silverdome, p.o.i., Mi., U.S.	199		42.39 N	83.15 W
Silver Falls State Park, p.o.i., Or., U.S.	146	F4	44.48 N	122.50 W
Silverfields, S. Afr.	191d		26.07 S	27.49 E
Silver Hill, Md., U.S.	202c		38.50 N	76.56 W
Silver Lake, Ks., U.S.	130	E2	39.06 N	95.51 W
Silver Lake, Mn., U.S.	128	G4	44.54 N	94.11 W
Silver Lake, Or., U.S.	146	G5	43.07 N	121.02 W
Silver Lake, Wi., U.S.	130	B9	42.33 N	88.09 W
Silver Lake, l., Ma., U.S.	201		42.01 N	70.48 W
Silver Lake, l., N.Y., U.S.	194		41.03 N	73.45 W
Silver Lake, l., Or., U.S.	146	G5	43.06 N	120.53 W
Silver Lake, l., Or., U.S.	146	G7	43.22 N	119.24 W
Silver Lake Park, p.o.i., N.Y., U.S.	194		41.03 N	73.45 W
Silver Lake Reservoir, res., Ca., U.S.	198		34.06 N	118.16 W
Silver Lake Reservoir, res., N.Y., U.S.	194		40.37 N	74.06 W
Silvermine, stm., U.S.	194		41.08 N	73.26 W
Silver Mine Bay, b., China	189d		22.16 N	114.00 E
Silvermine Brook, stm., Ct., U.S.	194		41.08 N	73.27 W
Silver Mountain, mtn., Ca., U.S.	198		34.12 N	117.52 W
Silver Peak Range, mts., U.S.	148	F8	37.41 N	117.52 W
Silver Spring, Md., U.S.	124	E8	39.00 N	77.01 W
Silver Star Mountain, mtn., Wa., U.S.	146	B6	48.33 N	120.35 W
Silver Star Provincial Park, p.o.i., B.C., Can.	144	F12	50.22 N	119.05 W
Silverthrone Mountain, vol., B.C., Can.	144	E4	51.31 N	126.06 W
Silvertip Mountain, mtn., Mt., U.S.	146	C13	47.47 N	113.15 W
Silverton, Austl.	98	H3	31.53 S	141.13 E
Silverton, B.C., Can.	144	G13	49.57 N	117.21 W
Silverton, Co., U.S.	150	F9	37.48 N	107.39 W
Silverton, Or., U.S.	146	E4	45.00 N	122.46 W
Silverton, Tx., U.S.	138	G7	34.28 N	101.18 W
Silves, Port.	28	G2	37.11 N	8.26 W
Silvi, Italy	30	H11	42.34 N	14.05 E
Silvia, Col.	168	F3	2.37 N	76.18 W
Silvies, stm., Or., U.S.	146	G7	43.26 N	118.51 W
Silview, De., U.S.	203		39.42 N	75.37 W
Silwa Bahari, Egypt	74	H3	24.44 N	32.56 E
Sim, Russia	40	D20	54.59 N	57.42 E
Simanavičy, Bela.	26	G11	53.04 N	28.37 E
Simaničy, Bela.	38	B7	51.53 N	28.05 E
Šimanovsk, Russia	50	F14	52.00 N	127.41 E
Simao, China	52	G5	22.46 N	100.58 E
Simão Dias, Braz.	170	F7	10.43 S	37.47 W
Simard, Lac, l., Qc., Can.	114	C11	47.37 N	78.41 W
Simatang, Pulau, i., Indon.	66	C12	1.03 N	120.23 E
Simav, Tur.	34	D11	39.05 N	28.58 E
Simav, stm., Tur.	34	D11	40.24 N	28.30 E
Simba, D.R.C.	86	D4	0.41 N	22.53 E
Simbach, Ger.	24	H8	48.33 N	12.44 E
Simbirsk see Uljanovsk, Russia	40	D16	54.19 N	48.22 E
Simbo Island, i., Sol. Is.	101b	e7	8.16 S	156.31 E
Simcoe, On., Can.	126	F9	42.50 N	80.18 W
Simcoe, Lake, l., On., Can.	126	D10	44.27 N	79.19 W
Simcoe Point, c., On., Can.	193b		43.49 N	79.01 W
Simdega, India	70	G10	22.36 N	84.30 E
Simeonovgrad, Blg.	36	G12	42.01 N	25.50 E
Simeria, Rom.	36	D10	45.51 N	23.01 E
Simeto, stm., Italy	32	G8	37.24 N	15.05 E
Simeulue, Pulau, i., Indon.	64	K2	2.36 N	96.04 E
Simferopol', Ukr.	38	I13	44.57 N	34.05 E
Simikot, Nepal	70	C9	29.57 N	81.47 E
Similkameen, stm., N.A.	144	G10	48.54 N	119.25 W
Simití, Col.	168	D4	7.56 N	73.56 W
Simi Valley, Ca., U.S.	148	I7	34.16 N	118.46 W
Simizu see Shimizu, Japan	56	D11	35.01 N	138.29 E
Simla see Shimla, India	70	C6	31.06 N	77.09 E
Simla, India	190b		22.47 N	88.16 E
Simla, India	190b		22.54 N	88.22 E
Simla, Co., U.S.	138	B4	39.08 N	104.05 W
Simla, ngh., India	190b		22.35 N	88.22 E
Şimleu Silvaniei, Rom.	36	B9	47.14 N	22.48 E
Simmering, ngh., Aus.	182b		48.11 N	16.25 E
Simmern, Ger.	24	G3	49.59 N	7.31 E
Simmesport, La., U.S.	134	G7	30.58 N	91.48 W
Simmie, Sk., Can.	142	E5	49.56 N	108.06 W
Simmons Island, i., Ca., U.S.	200		38.06 N	121.58 W
Simmons Point, c., Ca., U.S.	200		38.03 N	121.56 W
Simmonswood Moss, for., Eng., U.K.	180		53.30 N	2.50 W
Simms, Mt., U.S.	146	C15	47.29 N	111.54 W
Simnas, Lith.	26	F6	54.21 N	23.39 E
Simoca, Arg.	172	C5	27.16 S	65.21 W
Simões, Braz.	170	D5	7.36 S	40.49 W
Simojärvi, l., Fin.	18	A13	66.03 N	27.14 E
Simojovel, Mex.	154	G12	17.07 N	92.38 W
Simon, Lac, l., Qc., Can.	126	C14	45.58 N	75.05 W
Simón Bolívar, Aeropuerto Internacional, arpt., Ven.	204c		10.37 N	66.59 W
Simonette, stm., Ab., Can.	144	A12	55.09 N	118.15 W
Simonoseki see Shimonoseki, Japan	56	F3	33.57 N	130.56 E
Simonson Brook, stm., N.J., U.S.	194		40.26 N	74.37 W
Simonstad see Simon's Town, S. Afr.	90	I4	34.15 S	18.27 E
Simonstone, Eng., U.K.	180		53.48 N	2.20 W
Simon's Town, S. Afr.	90	I4	34.15 S	18.27 E
Simoom Sound, B.C., Can.	144	F4	50.45 N	126.26 W
Simpang, Indon.	66	C3	0.09 N	103.15 E
Simpang, Indon.	66	D6	1.01 S	110.06 E
Simpang, Indon.	66	D3	1.16 S	104.01 E
Simpang-kiri, stm., Indon.	64	K3	2.14 N	97.46 E
Simpele, Fin.	18	F16	61.27 N	29.23 E
Simplício Mendes, Braz.	170	D4	7.51 S	41.54 W
Simplon Pass, p., Switz.	30	D4	46.15 N	8.00 E
Simpson, La., U.S.	134	F6	31.15 N	93.00 W
Simpson Desert, des., Austl.	96	D7	25.00 S	137.00 E
Simpson Island, i., On., Can.	128	C11	48.47 N	87.41 W
Simpson Peninsula, pen., Nu., Can.	110	B13	68.34 N	88.45 W
Simpson Strait, strt., Nu., Can.	110	B11	68.24 N	96.54 W
Simpsonville, S.C., U.S.	132	B3	34.45 N	82.15 W
Simrishamn, Swe.	16	L12	55.33 N	14.20 E
Šimsk, Russia	26	B13	58.12 N	30.42 E
Simsonbaai, Neth. Ant.	159a	a1	18.02 N	63.05 W
Simunjan, Malay.	66	C7	1.23 N	110.45 E
Simušir, ostrov, i., Russia	50	G19	46.58 N	152.02 E
Sīna, stm., India	69	B2	17.23 N	75.53 E
Sinabang, Indon.	64	K3	2.26 N	96.22 E
Sinabung, Gunung, vol., Indon.	64	K4	3.10 N	98.24 E
Sinai (Sinai Peninsula), pen., Egypt	76	J4	29.30 N	34.00 E
Sinai, Mount see Mûsa, Gebel, mtn., Egypt	76	J5	28.32 N	33.59 E
Sinai, Mount, vol., Gren.	159e	q10	12.04 N	61.42 W
Sinaia, Rom.	36	D12	45.21 N	25.33 E
Sinai Peninsula see Sinai, pen., Egypt	76	J4	29.30 N	34.00 E
Sinaja see Sinjaja, stm., Eur.	26	D11	57.09 N	28.32 E
Sinajana, Guam	100c	j9	13.26 N	144.45 E
Sinaloa, state, Mex.	154	C5	25.00 N	107.30 W
Sinaloa, stm., Mex.	154	C5	25.17 N	108.30 W
Sinamaica, Ven.	168	B6	11.05 N	71.51 W
Sinan, China	58	H3	27.55 N	108.14 E
Sinanpaşa, Tur.	34	E13	38.45 N	30.15 E
Sīnāwin, Libya	82	A2	31.02 N	10.36 E
Sinbad Creek, stm., Ca., U.S.	200		37.35 N	121.53 W
Sinbaungwe, Mya.	64	C2	19.43 N	95.09 E
Sincan, Tur.	34	D15	39.57 N	32.36 E
Sincé, Col.	164	B2	9.15 N	75.09 W
Sincelejo, Col.	168	C4	9.18 N	75.23 W
Sinch'ang-ŭp, Kor., N.	54	D8	40.06 N	128.26 E
Sin-ch'on, Kor., N.	54	E6	38.21 N	125.29 E
Sinch'ŏn-ni, Kor., S.	189b		37.27 N	126.48 E
Sinclair, Wy., U.S.	150	B9	41.46 N	107.06 W
Sinclair, Lake, res., Ga., U.S.	132	C2	33.11 N	83.16 W
Sinclair Mills, B.C., Can.	144	B9	54.01 N	121.40 W
Sind, state, Pak.	70	F2	25.37 N	69.27 E
Sind, stm., India	70	F6	26.26 N	79.12 E
Sindal, Den.	16	J8	57.27 N	10.12 E
Sindañgan, Phil.	68	F4	8.14 N	123.00 E
Sindangbarang, Indon.	66	G5	7.27 S	107.09 E
Sindara, Gabon	86	E2	1.02 S	10.38 E
Sindari, India	70	F3	25.34 N	71.56 E
Sindelfingen, Ger.	24	H5	48.42 N	9.01 E
Sindhnūr, India	69	D3	15.46 N	76.45 E
Sindhulī Mādi, Nepal	70	E10	27.12 N	85.53 E
Sindi, Est.	26	B7	58.24 N	24.41 E
Sindingale, Mya.	64	C2	18.16 N	94.23 E
Sındırgı, Tur.	34	D11	39.14 N	28.10 E
Sindor, Russia	48	B8	62.51 N	51.53 E
Sinekli, Tur.	34	B11	41.12 N	28.12 E
Sines, Port.	28	G2	37.57 N	8.51 W
Sines, Cabo de, c., Port.	28	G1	37.57 N	8.53 W
Sinettä, Fin.	14	F16	66.38 N	25.24 E
Sinezërki, Russia	26	G17	52.59 N	34.28 E
Sinfra, C. Iv.	84	H3	6.37 N	5.55 W
Singako, Chad	82	F3	9.50 N	19.28 E
Singalamwe, Nmb.	88	D3	17.40 S	23.26 E
Singapore, Sing.	66	C3	1.18 N	103.49 E
Singapore, Sing.	189c		1.17 N	103.51 E
Singapore, i., Sing.	189c		1.23 N	103.48 E
Singapore, stm., Sing.	189c		1.17 N	103.51 E
Singapore, National University of, educ., Sing.	189c		1.18 N	103.46 E
Singapore, Selat see Singapore Strait of, strt., Asia	64	L6	1.15 N	104.00 E
Singapore, Strait of, strt., Asia	64	L6	1.15 N	104.00 E
Singapore Science Centre, bldg., Sing.	189c		1.20 N	103.44 E
Singapore Station, trans., Sing.	189c		1.17 N	103.50 E
Singapura, Selat see Singapore, Strait of, strt., Asia	64	L6	1.15 N	104.00 E
Singaraja, Indon.	66	H9	8.06 S	115.05 E
Singarka, stm., Russia	183a		59.53 N	29.54 E
Sing Buri, Thai.	64	E5	14.53 N	100.23 E
Singe, India	190b		22.57 N	88.26 E
Singen, Ger.	24	I4	47.45 N	8.51 E
Singer, La., U.S.	134	G5	30.39 N	93.24 W
Singida, Tan.	86	E6	4.48 S	34.44 E
Singitic Gulf see Agíou Órous, Kólpos, b., Grc.	34	C6	40.12 N	24.03 E
Singkaling Hkāmti, Mya.	62	C8	26.00 N	95.42 E
Singkang, Indon.	66	F11	4.08 S	120.01 E
Singkawang, Indon.	66	C6	0.54 N	108.59 E
Singkep, Pulau, i., Indon.	66	D4	0.30 S	104.25 E
Singkil, Indon.	66	C1	2.17 N	97.47 E
Singkuang, Indon.	66	C1	1.04 N	98.55 E
Singleton, Austl.	98	I8	32.34 S	151.10 E
Singleton, Mount, mtn., Austl.	96	D6	22.00 S	130.46 E
Singleton, Mount, mtn., Austl.	96	E3	29.28 S	117.18 E
Singlewell or Ifield, Eng., U.K.	178		51.25 N	0.23 E
Singö, i., Swe.	16	G16	60.11 N	18.46 E
Singora see Songkhla, Thai.	64	I5	7.11 N	100.36 E
Singpāra, India	190b		22.40 N	88.31 E
Singuédeze (Shingwidzi), stm., Afr.	90	C10	23.05 S	31.24 E
Sin Ho, Viet.	64	A6	22.22 N	103.14 E
Siničkа, stm., Russia	183b		55.50 N	37.19 E
Sinie Lipjagi, Russia	38	B17	51.22 N	38.28 E
Sining see Xining, China	52	D5	36.37 N	101.49 E
Siniscola, Italy	32	D3	40.34 N	9.41 E
Sinivuoren luonnonpuisto, ind. res., Fin.	18	F11	61.33 N	24.35 E
Sinj, Cro.	30	G13	43.42 N	16.38 E
Sinjah, Sudan	82	E6	13.07 N	33.54 E
Sinjai, Indon.	66	F12	5.07 S	120.15 E
Sinjaja, stm., Eur.	26	D11	57.09 N	28.32 E
Sinjaja, stm., Russia	50	D14	61.06 N	126.52 E
Sinjār, Iraq	74	B7	36.19 N	41.52 E
Sinjaukа, Bela.	26	H9	52.58 N	26.29 E
Sinjavka, Russia	38	F18	47.16 N	39.16 E
Sinjuga, Russia	50	E12	57.44 N	115.14 E
Sinkāt, Sudan	82	D7	18.50 N	36.50 E
Sinkiang see Xinjiang, state, China	62	A5	40.00 N	85.00 E
Sin'kok-ni, Kor., S.	189b		37.37 N	126.46 E
Šinkovo, Russia	26	D14	56.03 N	31.31 E
Sinks Canyon State Park, p.o.i., Wy., U.S.	140	E4	42.45 N	108.50 W
Sinn, stm., Ger.	20	D18	50.03 N	9.41 E
Sinnamahoning, Pa., U.S.	124	C7	41.19 N	78.05 W
Sinnamary, Fr. Gu.	164	B7	5.22 N	52.57 W
Sinnar, India	69	B2	19.50 N	74.00 E
Sinnes, Nor.	16	I4	58.56 N	6.50 E
Sinni, stm., Italy	32	D10	40.09 N	16.41 E
Sinnūris, Egypt	76	I1	29.25 N	30.52 E
Sinnyŏng, Kor., S.	56	C1	36.04 N	128.46 E
Sinoie, Lacul, l., Rom.	36	E15	44.38 N	28.53 E
Sinop, Tur.	42	E6	42.01 N	35.09 E
Sinop, state, Tur.	42	E6	41.40 N	34.50 E
Sinp'a-ŭp, Kor., N.	54	D7	41.24 N	127.46 E
Sinsen, Ger.	181		51.40 N	7.11 E
Sinsheim, Ger.	24	G4	49.15 N	8.52 E
Sinsiang see Xinxiang, China	58	D5	35.18 N	113.51 E
Sinskoe, Russia	50	D14	61.08 N	126.46 E
Sintang, Indon.	66	C7	0.04 N	111.29 E
Sint Christoffelberg, hill, Neth. Ant.	158g	p21	12.20 N	69.08 W
Sint Eustatius, i., Neth. Ant.	159a	b1	17.30 N	62.59 W
Sint Helenabaai, b., S. Afr.	90	H3	32.41 S	18.07 E
Sint Kruis, Neth. Ant.	158g	p21	12.18 N	69.08 W
Sint Maarten see Saint-Martin, i., N.A.	159a	a1	18.04 N	63.04 W
Sint Nicolaas, Aruba	158g	p20	12.26 N	69.54 W
Sint-Niklaas, Bel.	20	C13	51.10 N	4.08 E
Sinton, Tx., U.S.	136	F10	28.02 N	97.30 W
Sintra, Port.	28	F1	38.47 N	9.22 W
Sintra, Serra de, hills, Port.	184c		38.47 N	9.25 W
Sintra Granjo do Marquez, Aeroporto, arpt., Port.	184c		38.49 N	9.20 W
Sint-Truiden, Bel.	20	D14	50.49 N	5.11 E
Sinú, stm., Col.	168	D3	9.23 N	75.55 W
Sinŭiju, Kor., N.	54	D6	40.05 N	124.23 E
Sió, stm., Hung.	36	C5	46.20 N	18.54 E
Siocon, Phil.	68	G4	7.42 N	122.08 E
Siófok, Hung.	36	C5	46.54 N	18.03 E
Sion, Switz.	30	D4	46.13 N	7.21 E
Siorapaluk, Grnld.	108	B12	77.47 N	70.45 W
Sioux Center, Ia., U.S.	128	H2	43.04 N	96.10 W
Sioux City, Ia., U.S.	130	B1	42.29 N	96.22 W
Sioux Falls, S.D., U.S.	128	H2	43.33 N	96.42 W
Sioux Lookout, On., Can.	128	A6	50.06 N	91.55 W
Sioux Narrows, On., Can.	128	B4	49.25 N	94.05 W
Sioux Rapids, Ia., U.S.	130	B2	42.53 N	95.08 W
Sipalay, Phil.	68	F4	9.44 N	122.25 E
Šipan, Otok, i., Cro.	30	H14	42.43 N	17.54 E
Sipapo, stm., Ven.	168	E8	5.03 N	67.47 W
Siparia, Trin.	159f	s12	10.08 N	61.30 W
Šipčenski Prohod (Shipka Pass), p., Blg.	36	G12	42.47 N	25.18 E
Šipicyno, Russia	12	F22	61.16 N	46.30 E
Siping, China	52	C9	43.09 N	124.22 E
Sipitang, Malay.	66	A9	5.03 N	115.32 E
Sipiwesk, Mb., Can.	110	D11	55.27 N	97.23 W
Sipiwesk Lake, l., Mb., Can.	110	D11	55.05 N	97.35 W
Siple, Mount, mtn., Ant.	103	C28	73.15 S	126.05 W
Şipoteni, Mol.	38	F7	47.17 N	28.11 E
Si Prachan, Thai.	64	E5	14.38 N	100.08 E
Sipsey, stm., Al., U.S.	134	D10	33.00 N	88.10 W
Sipsey Creek, stm., U.S.	134	C10	33.53 N	88.17 W
Šipunskij, mys, c., Russia	50	F21	53.06 N	160.01 E
Sipura, Pulau, i., Indon.	66	E1	2.12 S	99.40 E
Siqueira Campos, Braz.	172	A12	23.41 S	49.51 W
Siquia, stm., Nic.	156	F5	12.11 N	84.16 W
Siquijor, Phil.	68	F4	9.11 N	123.30 E
Siquijor Island, i., Phil.	68	F4	9.11 N	123.34 E
Siquirres, C.R.	156	G6	10.05 N	83.30 W
Siquisique, Ven.	168	B7	10.32 N	69.43 W
Sīra, India	69	E3	13.45 N	76.59 E
Sira, Nor.	16	I4	58.25 N	6.38 E
Šira, Russia	48	D16	54.29 N	89.57 E
Sira, stm., Nor.	16	I4	58.16 N	6.23 E
Si Racha, Thai.	64	F5	13.09 N	100.56 E
Siracusa, Italy	32	G9	37.04 N	15.17 E
Sir Adam Beck II Reservoir, res., On., Can.	202a		43.08 N	79.04 W
Sirāhā, Nepal	70	E11	26.39 N	86.12 E
Sirājganj, Bngl.	70	F12	24.26 N	89.41 E
Sir Alexander, Mount, mtn., B.C., Can.	144	C10	53.56 N	120.23 W
Siraway, Phil.	68	G4	7.34 N	122.09 E
Sīr Banī Yās, i., U.A.E.	74	H13	24.19 N	52.37 E
Sirdalen, val., Nor.	16	I4	58.47 N	6.45 E
Sirdalsvatnet, l., Nor.	16	I4	58.32 N	6.42 E
Sirdān, Iran	74	B11	36.38 N	49.11 E
Sirdar, B.C., Can.	144	G14	49.14 N	116.37 W
Sir Douglas, Mount, mtn., Can.	144	F15	50.44 N	115.20 W
Sir Edward Pellew Group, is., Austl.	96	C7	15.40 S	136.48 E
Siret, Rom.	36	B13	47.57 N	26.04 E
Siret (Seret), stm., Eur.	36	A12	45.24 N	28.01 E
Sirevåg, Nor.	16	I3	58.29 N	5.47 E
Sir Francis Drake, Mount, mtn., B.C., Can.	144	F6	50.48 N	124.47 W
Sir Francis Drake Channel, strt., Br. Vir. Is.	158b	e8	18.25 N	64.30 W
Sirhān, Wādī as-, val., Sau. Ar.	74	E5	30.58 N	37.40 E
Sirik, Tanjong, c., Malay.	66	B7	2.46 N	111.19 E
Sirikit Reservoir, res., Thai.	64	D5	17.52 N	100.27 E
Sirino, Monte, mtn., Italy	32	D9	40.08 N	15.50 E
Sir James MacBrien, Mount, mtn., N.T., Can.	110	C4	62.07 N	127.41 W
Sīrjān, Iran	74	F14	29.27 N	55.40 E
Sirkeli, Tur.	34	C15	40.09 N	32.52 E
Sirkka, Fin.	14	E15	67.48 N	24.48 E
Sirmione, Italy	30	E7	45.30 N	10.36 E
Şırnak, Tur.	42	G10	37.31 N	42.27 E
Şırnak, state, Tur.	42	G10	37.30 N	42.30 E
Sirocina, Bela.	26	E12	55.22 N	29.37 E
Sirohi, India	70	F4	24.53 N	72.51 E
Širokaja Pad', Russia	50	F17	50.14 N	142.10 E
Širokovo, Russia	48	C17	55.25 N	99.24 E
Sirombu, Indon.	64	L3	0.57 N	97.24 E
Sironj, India	70	F6	24.05 N	77.41 E
Sırpsındığı, Tur.	34	B9	41.46 N	26.29 E
Sīrrī, Jazīreh-ye, i., Iran	74	H14	25.54 N	54.31 E
Sirsa, India	70	D5	29.31 N	75.02 E
Sir Sandford, Mount, mtn., B.C., Can.	144	E13	51.40 N	117.52 W
Sirsi, India	69	D2	14.38 N	74.51 E
Sirsilla, India	69	B4	18.24 N	78.48 E
Sirte, Gulf of see Surt, Khalīj, b., Libya	82	A3	31.30 N	18.00 E
Sir Thomas, Mount, mtn., Austl.	96	E6	27.10 S	129.45 E
Sir Timothy's Hill, hill, St. K./N.	159a	c2	17.16 N	62.41 W
Sirupa, stm., Mex.	120	G8	29.09 N	108.35 W
Sīrvān (Diyālā), stm., Asia	74	C9	33.13 N	44.30 E
Širvintos, Lith.	26	E7	55.03 N	24.57 E
Sir Wilfrid Laurier, Mount, mtn., B.C., Can.	144	D11	52.47 N	119.45 W
Sir Wilfrid Laurier's Birthplace National Historic Site, p.o.i., Qc., Can.	126	C16	45.51 N	73.45 W
Sisaba, mtn., Tan.	86	F6	6.09 S	29.48 E
Sisak, Cro.	30	E13	45.29 N	16.22 E
Si Sa Ket, Thai.	64	E7	15.07 N	104.19 E
Si Satchanalai, Thai.	64	D4	17.31 N	99.46 E
Šiševka, Russia	26	B21	58.51 N	38.51 E
Sishen, S. Afr.	90	E6	27.50 S	22.59 E
Sishilijie, China	58	G7	29.07 N	116.45 E
Sishui, China	58	D7	35.39 N	117.16 E
Sisib Lake, l., Mb., Can.	142	B14	52.35 N	99.22 W
Sisimiut see Holsteinsborg, Grnld.	108	D15	66.55 N	53.40 W
Siskiyou Mountains, mts., U.S.	148	B3	42.04 N	123.02 W
Siskiyou Pass, p., Or., U.S.	148	A3	42.02 N	122.36 W
Şişli, ngh., Tur.	185b		41.04 N	28.59 E
Sisŏphŏn, Camb.	64	F6	13.34 N	102.58 E
Sisquoc, stm., Ca., U.S.	148	I5	34.54 N	120.18 W
Sissach, Switz.	24	I3	47.27 N	7.48 E
Sisseton, S.D., U.S.	128	F1	45.40 N	97.03 W
Sisson Branch Reservoir, res., N.B., Can.	122	C9	47.17 N	67.15 W
Sissonville, W.V., U.S.	124	F4	38.31 N	81.39 W
Sīstān, reg., Asia	62	B1	30.36 N	61.28 E
Sister Bay, Wi., U.S.	126	C2	45.11 N	87.07 W
Sisteron, Fr.	22	E11	44.12 N	5.56 E
Sisters, Or., U.S.	146	F5	44.17 N	121.32 W
Sistersville, W.V., U.S.	124	E5	39.33 N	80.59 W
Sistranda, Nor.	16	D6	63.43 N	8.50 E
Sit', stm., Russia	26	B20	58.25 N	37.58 E
Sītāmarhi, India	70	E10	26.36 N	85.29 E
Sitangkai, Phil.	68	H2	4.40 N	119.24 E
Sītāpur, India	70	E8	27.34 N	80.40 E
Sitasjaure, l., Eur.	14	E8	68.00 N	17.24 E
Siteía, Grc.	34	H9	35.12 N	26.06 E
Siteki, Swaz.	90	E10	26.29 S	31.56 E
Si Thep, hist., Thai.	64	E5	15.30 N	101.10 E
Sithonía, pen., Grc.	34	C6	40.10 N	23.47 E
Sitidgi Lake, l., N.T., Can.	110	B4	68.32 N	132.42 W
Sítio d'Abadia, Braz.	170	H2	14.48 S	46.16 W
Sítio Novo, Braz.	170	C2	5.49 S	46.42 W
Sitka, Ak., U.S.	109	E12	57.03 N	135.18 W
Sitkalidak Island, i., Ak., U.S.	109	E9	57.06 N	153.14 W
Sitna, stm., Rom.	36	B13	47.36 N	27.07 E
Sitnica, stm., Yugo.	36	G7	42.53 N	20.53 E
Sittard, Neth.	20	C15	50.59 N	5.52 E
Sitten see Sion, Switz.	30	D4	46.13 N	7.21 E
Sittendorf, Aus.	182b		48.05 N	16.10 E
Sittoung, stm., Mya.	64	C3	17.22 N	96.52 E
Sittwe, Mya.	70	H14	20.08 N	92.53 E
Siulakderas, Indon.	66	D2	1.55 S	101.18 E
Siu Lek Yuen, China	189d		22.23 N	114.12 E
Siu Mo To, i., China	189d		22.20 N	113.58 E
Siuna, Nic.	156	F5	13.41 N	84.50 W
Siuri, India	70	G11	23.53 N	87.33 E
Siuslaw, stm., Or., U.S.	146	G3	44.01 N	124.08 W
Sivaganga, India	69	G4	9.51 N	78.28 E
Sivakāsi, India	69	G3	9.26 N	77.48 E
Sivaki, Russia	50	F14	52.37 N	126.44 E
Sīvand, stm., Iran	74	E13	29.51 N	52.46 E
Sivas, Tur.	42	F7	39.44 N	37.01 E
Sivas, state, Tur.	42	F7	39.30 N	37.15 E
Sivaslı, Tur.	34	E12	38.29 N	29.40 E
Šiveluč, vulkan, vol., Russia	50	E21	56.39 N	161.18 E
Siverek, Tur.	42	G8	37.45 N	39.19 E
Siverskij, Russia	26	A13	59.21 N	30.04 E
Sivers'kyi Donets' see Northern Donets, stm., Eur.	40	G10	47.35 N	40.54 E
Sivers'kyi Donets'-Donbas, kanal, can., Ukr.	38	E16	48.53 N	37.45 E
Sivri Ada, i., Tur.	185b		40.54 N	28.59 E
Sivrihisar, Tur.	34	D14	39.27 N	31.32 E
Sivry-Courtry, Fr.	179		48.32 N	2.45 E
Siwa, Egypt	82	B5	29.12 N	25.31 E
Siwalik Range, mts., India	70	C6	31.00 N	78.00 E
Siwān, India	70	E10	26.13 N	84.22 E
Sixian, China	58	E7	33.28 N	117.52 E
Six Mile Creek, stm., On., Can.	202a		43.15 N	79.10 W
Sixmile Creek, stm., N.Y., U.S.	202a		43.17 N	78.58 W
Sixmile Run, stm., N.J., U.S.	194		40.28 N	74.35 W
Sixshooter Draw, stm., Tx., U.S.	136	D5	30.51 N	102.33 W
Sixteen Mile Creek, stm., On., Can.	193b		43.27 N	79.40 W
Sixteenmile Creek, stm., Mt., U.S.	146	D16	46.05 N	111.24 W
Sixth Cataract see Sablūkah, Shallāl as-, wtfl., Sudan	82	D6	16.18 N	32.41 E
Siyang, China	58	E8	33.42 N	118.40 E
Si Yat, stm., Thai.	64	F5	13.41 N	101.26 E
Siyäzän, Azer.	42	E13	41.04 N	49.06 E
Siz'ma, Russia	18	H25	59.25 N	38.42 E
Sizuoka see Shizuoka, Japan	56	E11	34.58 N	138.23 E
Sjælland, i., Den.	16	L9	55.30 N	11.45 E
Sjalec, Bela.	26	G13	53.22 N	30.22 E
Själevad, Swe.	16	D16	63.17 N	18.35 E
Sjamozero, Russia	18	F20	61.52 N	33.18 E
Sjamozero, ozero, l., Russia	18	E20	61.55 N	33.10 E
Sjamža, Russia	12	F19	60.01 N	41.06 E
Sjanno, Bela.	26	F12	54.48 N	29.42 E
Sjarheevičy, Bela.	26	G10	53.30 N	27.45 E
Sjas', stm., Russia	18	H20	60.09 N	32.30 E
Sjas'stroj, Russia	18	G19	60.09 N	32.34 E
Sjava, Russia	40	C15	58.00 N	46.19 E
Sjenica, Yugo.	36	F7	43.16 N	20.00 E
Sjeništa, mtn., Bos.	36	F5	43.42 N	18.37 E
Sjoa, stm., Nor.	16	F7	61.40 N	9.32 E
Sjöbo, Swe.	16	L11	55.37 N	13.41 E
Sjøholt, Nor.	16	E4	62.29 N	6.49 E
Sjona, b., Nor.	14	F4	66.18 N	13.15 E
Sjøvegan, Nor.	14	D8	68.52 N	17.51 E
Sjun', stm., Russia	40	D19	55.43 N	54.17 E
Sjurab, Taj.	72	A11	40.02 N	70.32 E
Sjus'ma, Russia	18	C26	64.41 N	39.00 E
Sjuzikozero, Russia	18	F24	61.48 N	37.22 E
Skaby, Ger.	182a		52.19 N	13.51 E
Skaby-Berge, hill, Ger.	182a		52.19 N	13.49 E
Skäckerfjällen, mts., Swe.	16	D10	63.50 N	12.43 E
Skadarsko jezero see Scutari, Lake, l., Eur.	30	H16	42.12 N	19.18 E
Skadovs'k, Ukr.	38	G11	46.07 N	32.55 E
Skælskør, Den.	16	L9	55.15 N	11.17 E
Skærbæk, Den.	16	L6	55.09 N	8.46 E
Skærfjorden, b., Grnld.	108	B22	77.29 N	20.00 W
Skaftafell Nasjonalpark, p.o.i., Ice.	12a	k31	64.15 N	17.00 W
Skaftung, Fin.	18	E8	62.07 N	21.22 E
Skagafjörđur, b., Ice.	12a	j30	65.55 N	19.35 W
Skagastølstindane, mtn., Nor.	16	F5	61.27 N	7.51 E
Skagen, Den.	16	J8	57.43 N	10.34 E
Skagern, l., Swe.	16	H12	58.59 N	14.17 E
Skagerrak, strt., Eur.	16	J6	57.45 N	9.00 E
Skaget, mtn., Nor.	16	F7	61.19 N	9.13 E
Skagit, stm., N.A.	144	H8	48.21 N	122.28 W
Skagit Valley Provincial Recreation Area, p.o.i., B.C., Can.	144	G9	49.03 N	121.09 W
Skagway, Ak., U.S.	109	E12	59.28 N	135.18 W
Skáidi, Nor.	14	B15	70.26 N	24.27 E
Skaistkalne, Lat.	26	D7	56.23 N	24.39 E
Skåland, Nor.	12	B7	58.25 N	6.33 E
Skala-Podil's'ka, Ukr.	38	E5	48.51 N	26.12 E
Skalbmierz, Pol.	24	F16	50.19 N	20.24 E
Skälderviken, b., Swe.	16	K10	56.18 N	12.38 E
Skålevik, Nor.	16	I6	58.04 N	8.01 E
Skalica, Slvk.	24	H13	48.50 N	17.14 E
Skalino, Russia	40	B12	58.31 N	40.13 E
Skalistyj Golec, gora, mtn., Russia	50	E12	56.24 N	119.12 E
Skalka, l., Swe.	14	F9	66.52 N	18.42 E
Skal'nyj, Russia	40	B20	58.21 N	57.57 E
Skanderborg, Den.	16	K7	56.02 N	9.56 E
Skåne, state, Swe.	16	K11	56.00 N	13.30 E
Skåne, hist. reg., Swe.	16	L11	55.59 N	13.30 E
Skånevik, Nor.	16	H3	59.44 N	5.59 E
Skänninge, Swe.	16	I12	58.24 N	15.05 E
Skara, Swe.	16	I11	58.23 N	13.27 E
Skaramagás, Grc.	185c		38.01 N	23.36 E
Skärblacka, Swe.	16	I13	58.34 N	15.54 E
Skarđ, Ice.	12a	k29	64.02 N	19.50 W
Skardberget, Nor.	14	D7	68.14 N	16.12 E
Skardsøya, i., Nor.	16	D6	63.21 N	8.35 E
Skardtind, mtn., Nor.	16	E6	62.01 N	8.35 E
Skārdu, Pak.	62	A4	35.18 N	75.37 E
Skärhamn, Swe.	16	I9	58.00 N	11.33 E
Skarnes, Nor.	16	G9	60.15 N	11.41 E
Skarodnae, Bela.	38	B7	51.37 N	28.49 E
Skarsvåg, Nor.	14	A16	71.06 N	25.49 E
Skarszewy, Pol.	24	B14	54.04 N	18.27 E
Skarvsjö, Swe.	16	C15	64.59 N	17.05 E
Skaryszew, Pol.	24	E17	51.19 N	21.15 E
Skarżysko-Kamienna, Pol.	24	E16	51.07 N	20.53 E
Skaudvilė, Lith.	26	E5	55.24 N	22.35 E
Skaulen, mtn., Nor.	16	H4	59.38 N	6.34 E
Skaulo, Swe.	14	E12	67.24 N	21.08 E
Skaw, The see Grenen, c., Den.	16	J8	57.44 N	10.39 E
Skawina, Pol.	24	F15	49.58 N	19.48 E
Skee, Swe.	16	I9	58.53 N	11.17 E
Skeena, stm., B.C., Can.	110	E5	54.08 N	130.06 W
Skeena Crossing, B.C., Can.	144	A3	55.06 N	127.49 W
Skeena Mountains, mts., B.C., Can.	110	D5	56.34 N	128.40 W
Skegness, Eng., U.K.	10	H13	53.09 N	0.20 E
Skei, Nor.	16	F4	61.37 N	6.31 E
Skei, Nor.	16	B9	65.06 N	11.43 E
Skeleton Coast, cst., Nmb.	90	C1	22.18 S	14.11 E
Skeleton Creek, stm., Ok., U.S.	138	E11	35.58 N	97.25 W
Skellefteå, Swe.	16	C19	64.45 N	20.58 E
Skellefteälven, stm., Swe.	16	C18	64.42 N	21.08 E
Skelleftehamn, Swe.	16	C19	64.41 N	21.14 E
Skellytown, Tx., U.S.	138	F7	35.34 N	101.10 W
Skene, Swe.	16	J10	57.28 N	12.37 E
Skerryvore, r., Scot., U.K.	10	E5	56.19 N	7.07 W
Ski, Nor.	16	H8	59.43 N	10.51 E
Skíathos, Grc.	34	D6	39.10 N	23.28 E
Skíathos, i., Grc.	34	D6	39.10 N	23.28 E
Skiatook, Ok., U.S.	130	H1	36.22 N	96.00 W
Skibbereen, Ire.	10	J3	51.32 N	9.16 W
Skibotn, Nor.	14	C11	69.22 N	20.16 E
Skibotndalen, val., Nor.	14	C11	69.16 N	20.31 E
Skidal', Bela.	26	G7	53.34 N	24.15 E
Skiddaw, mtn., Eng., U.K.	10	G9	54.38 N	3.07 W
Skidegate, B.C., Can.	110	E4	53.15 N	132.00 W
Skidmore, Tx., U.S.	136	F10	28.15 N	97.41 W
Skien, Nor.	16	H7	59.12 N	9.36 E
Skierniewice, Pol.	24	E16	51.57 N	20.09 E
Skiftet, strt., Fin.	18	G7	60.15 N	21.05 E
Skihist Mountain, mtn., B.C., Can.	144	F9	50.11 N	121.54 W
Skikda, Alg.	84	B6	36.52 N	6.54 E
Skilak Lake, l., Ak., U.S.	109	D9	60.26 N	150.25 W
Skillet Fork, stm., Il., U.S.	130	F9	38.07 N	88.07 W
Skillingaryd, Swe.	16	J12	57.26 N	14.05 E
Skillman, N.J., U.S.	194		40.25 N	74.42 W
Skinnastađir, Ice.	12a	j31	66.03 N	16.27 W
Skinnskatteberg, Swe.	16	H13	59.49 N	15.41 E
Skippack, Pa., U.S.	203		40.14 N	75.24 W
Skippack Creek, stm., Pa., U.S.	203		40.09 N	75.27 W
Skippack Creek, West Branch, stm., Pa., U.S.	203		40.14 N	75.23 W
Skipton, Austl.	98	K4	37.41 S	143.21 E
Skipton, Eng., U.K.	10	H10	53.57 N	2.00 W
Skiptvet, Nor.	16	H9	59.26 N	11.09 E

Name	Page	Map Ref.	Latitude	Longitude
Skive, Den.	16	K7	56.34 N	9.02 E
Skjærhollen, Nor.	16	H9	59.01 N	11.02 E
Skjálfandafljót, stm., Ice.	12a	k31	65.58 N	17.36 W
Skjeberg, Nor.	16	H9	59.12 N	11.11 E
Skjern, Den.	16	L6	55.57 N	8.30 E
Skjernøy, i., Nor.	16	J5	57.59 N	7.31 E
Skjerstadfjorden, b., Nor.	14	E5	67.14 N	15.13 E
Skjervøy, Nor.	14	B11	70.02 N	20.57 E
Sklad, Russia	50	B13	71.54 N	123.31 E
Sklinna, is., Nor.	16	B8	65.12 N	10.59 E
Škloŭ, Bela.	26	F13	54.13 N	30.18 E
Škofja Loka, Slvn.	30	D11	46.10 N	14.18 E
Skoganvarre, Nor.	14	C15	69.47 N	25.05 E
Skogfoss, Nor.	14	C20	69.23 N	29.40 E
Skoghall, Swe.	16	H11	59.19 N	13.28 E
Skogn, Nor.	16	D9	63.41 N	11.12 E
Skogshorn, mtn., Nor.	16	G6	60.53 N	8.44 E
Skogsøya, i., Nor.	14	D5	68.54 N	14.55 E
Skoki, Pol.	24	D13	52.40 N	17.10 E
Skokie, Il., U.S.	130	B10	42.01 N	87.45 W
Skokie Lagoons, b., Il., U.S.	196		42.07 N	87.47 W
Skokloster, hist., Swe.	16	H15	59.42 N	17.37 E
Skole, Ukr.	38	D2	49.01 N	23.29 E
Skomoroshky, Ukr.	38	D8	49.20 N	29.26 E
Skŏn, Camb.	64	F7	12.03 N	105.03 E
Skópelos, Grc.	34	D6	39.07 N	23.43 E
Skópelos, i., Grc.	34	D6	39.10 N	23.40 E
Skopin, Russia	40	E11	53.49 N	39.32 E
Skopje, Mac.	34	A4	42.00 N	21.27 E
Skoplje see Skopje, Mac.	34	A4	42.00 N	21.27 E
Skórcz, Pol.	24	C14	53.47 N	18.31 E
Skorovatn, Nor.	16	C11	64.38 N	13.07 E
Skorpa, i., Nor.	16	F2	61.36 N	4.51 E
Skørping, Den.	16	K7	56.50 N	9.53 E
Skotfoss, Nor.	16	H7	59.12 N	9.29 E
Skotselv, Nor.	16	H7	59.50 N	9.53 E
Skotterud, Nor.	16	G10	59.59 N	12.08 E
Skövde, Swe.	16	I11	58.24 N	13.51 E
Skovorodino, Russia	44	D16	53.58 N	123.56 E
Skowhegan, Me., U.S.	122	F7	44.46 N	69.43 W
Skownan, Mb., Can.	142	C14	51.57 N	99.36 W
Skradin, Cro.	30	G12	43.49 N	15.55 E
Skreia, Nor.	16	G8	60.39 N	10.56 E
Skridulaupen, mtn., Nor.	16	F5	61.56 N	7.37 E
Skriplivka, Russia	26	C13	57.32 N	30.38 E
Skrīveri, Lat.	26	D8	56.38 N	25.08 E
Skromberga, Swe.	16	L11	55.59 N	12.59 E
Skrudaliena, Lat.	26	E9	55.49 N	26.43 E
Skrunda, Lat.	26	D4	56.40 N	21.59 E
Skruv, Swe.	16	K13	56.40 N	15.23 E
Skudenesfjorden, strt., Nor.	16	H2	59.06 N	5.19 E
Skudeneshavn, Nor.	16	H3	59.09 N	5.17 E
Skukuza, S. Afr.	90	D10	25.01 S	31.38 E
Skuleberget, hill, Swe.	16	D16	63.05 N	18.21 E
Skulgammen, Nor.	14	C9	69.47 N	19.04 E
Skull, Ire.	10	J3	51.32 N	9.33 W
Skull Valley, Az., U.S.	150	I4	34.30 N	112.41 W
Skull Valley Indian Reservation, ind. res., Ut., U.S.	150	C4	40.24 N	112.45 W
Skuløya, i., Nor.	16	E4	62.40 N	6.19 E
Skultorp, Swe.	16	I11	58.20 N	13.49 E
Skuna, can., Ms., U.S.	134	D9	33.54 N	89.39 W
Skunk, stm., Ia., U.S.	130	D6	40.41 N	91.06 W
Šķunovka, Russia	40	F19	50.45 N	55.23 E
Skuodas, Lith.	26	D4	56.16 N	21.32 E
Skuratovskij, Russia	26	F20	54.06 N	37.35 E
Skurinskaja, Russia	38	G18	46.35 N	39.21 E
Skurup, Swe.	16	L11	55.29 N	13.29 E
Skutskär, Swe.	16	G15	60.37 N	17.25 E
Skutvika, Nor.	14	D8	68.01 N	15.19 E
Skvyra, Ukr.	38	D8	49.43 N	29.40 E
Skwentna, Ak., U.S.	109	D9	61.57 N	151.09 W
Skwierzyna, Pol.	24	D11	52.35 N	15.30 E
Skye, Island of, i., Scot., U.K.	10	D6	57.25 N	6.27 W
Sky Harbor Airport, arpt., Il., U.S.	196		42.09 N	87.51 W
Skykomish, stm., Wa., U.S.	146	C5	47.49 N	122.02 W
Skykomish, South Fork, stm., Wa., U.S.	146	C5	47.48 N	121.33 W
Skyland, N.C., U.S.	132	A3	35.29 N	82.32 W
Skyline, Md., U.S.	202c		38.50 N	76.54 W
Skyline Lakes, l., N.J., U.S.	194		41.04 N	74.16 W
Skyring, Peninsula, pen., Chile	166	I1	45.58 S	74.53 W
Skyring, Seno, strt., Chile	166	J2	52.36 S	72.06 W
Skýros, Grc.	34	E7	38.54 N	24.33 E
Skýros, i., Grc.	34	E7	38.53 N	24.32 E
Sky Sailing Airport, arpt., Ca., U.S.	200		37.30 N	121.58 W
Slabada, Bela.	26	G11	53.58 N	28.06 E
Slabodka, Bela.	26	E10	55.41 N	27.11 E
Slackhall, Eng., U.K.	180		53.20 N	1.53 W
Slade Green, ngh., Eng., U.K.	178		51.28 N	0.12 E
Slagelse, Den.	16	L9	55.24 N	11.20 E
Slagnäs, Swe.	16	B16	65.35 N	18.09 E
Slagoviŝči, Russia	26	G18	53.57 N	35.54 E
Slaithwaite, Eng., U.K.	180		53.37 N	1.53 W
Slamet, Gunung, vol., Indon.	66	G6	7.14 S	109.12 E
Slaná (Sajó), stm., Eur.	24	H16	47.58 N	21.02 E
Slancy, Russia	26	A11	59.06 N	28.05 E
Slaney, stm., Ire.	10	I6	52.21 N	6.30 W
Slănic, Rom.	36	D12	45.15 N	25.57 E
Slănic Moldova, Rom.	36	C13	46.12 N	26.27 E
Slano, Cro.	30	H14	42.47 N	17.53 E
Slanské vrchy, mts., Slvk.	24	H17	48.50 N	21.30 E
Slaný, Czech Rep.	24	F10	50.14 N	14.05 E
Šlapanice, Czech Rep.	24	G12	49.09 N	16.43 E
Slaščevskaja, Russia	40	G13	49.52 N	42.20 E
Śląsk see Silesia, hist. reg., Eur.	24	F13	50.33 N	18.00 E
Śląskie, state, Pol.	24	F14	50.30 N	19.00 E
Slate Bottom Creek, stm., N.Y., U.S.	202a		42.53 N	78.45 W
Slate Creek, stm., Ks., U.S.	138	D11	37.08 N	97.09 W
Slate Creek, stm., Pa., U.S.	197b		40.28 N	79.32 W
Slater, Ia., U.S.	130	C4	41.52 N	93.41 W
Slater, Mo., U.S.	130	E4	39.13 N	93.04 W
Slater Creek, stm., Co., U.S.	150	C9	40.59 N	107.23 W
Slatina, Cro.	30	E14	45.42 N	17.42 E
Slatina, Rom.	36	E11	44.26 N	24.22 E
Slaton, Tx., U.S.	138	H7	33.26 N	101.38 W
Slattocks, Eng., U.K.	180		53.35 N	2.10 W
Slatyne, Ukr.	38	C15	50.12 N	36.09 E
Slaughter, La., U.S.	134	G7	30.42 N	91.08 W
Slaŭharad, Bela.	26	G13	53.26 N	31.00 E
Slaŭnae, Bela.	26	F12	54.18 N	29.27 E
Slautnoe, Russia	50	D22	63.09 N	167.59 E
Slav'anka, stm., Russia	183a		59.50 N	30.32 E
Slave, stm., Can.	110	C8	61.16 N	113.35 W
Slavečna, stm., Eur.	38	B8	51.40 N	29.42 E
Slave Coast, cst., Afr.	84	H5	6.21 N	3.00 E
Slave Lake, Ab., Can.	144	A16	55.16 N	114.47 W
Slavgorod, Russia	48	D13	53.00 N	78.38 E
Slavhorod, Ukr.	38	E14	48.06 N	35.31 E
Slavhorod, Ukr.	38	C14	50.35 N	35.21 E
Slavjanka, Russia	54	C9	42.52 N	131.20 E
Slavjansk-na-Kubani, Russia	40	I10	45.15 N	38.07 E
Slavkoviči, Russia	26	C12	57.39 N	29.03 E
Slavkov u Brna, Czech Rep.	24	G12	49.09 N	16.52 E
Slavonia see Slavonija, hist. reg., Cro.	30	E14	45.00 N	18.00 E
Slavonice, Czech Rep.	24	H11	49.00 N	15.21 E
Slavonija, hist. reg., Cro.	30	E14	45.00 N	18.00 E
Slavonski Brod, Cro.	30	E15	45.09 N	18.00 E
Slavsk, Russia	26	E4	55.03 N	21.41 E
Slavs'ke, Ukr.	38	E2	48.49 N	23.23 E
Slavuta, Ukr.	38	C5	50.17 N	26.51 E
Sława, Pol.	24	E12	51.52 N	16.04 E
Sławno, Pol.	24	B12	54.21 N	16.41 E
Slayton, Mn., U.S.	128	G3	43.59 N	95.45 W
Sleaford, Eng., U.K.	10	H12	53.00 N	0.24 W
Sleat, Sound of, strt., Scot., U.K.	10	E7	57.06 N	5.49 W
Sledge, Ms., U.S.	134	C8	34.26 N	90.13 W
Sledzjuki, Bela.	26	G13	53.34 N	30.21 E
Sleeper Islands, is., Nu., Can.	110	D14	57.30 N	79.45 W
Sleeping Bear Dunes National Lakeshore, p.o.i., Mi., U.S.	126	D3	44.50 N	86.02 W
Sleeping Giant Provincial Park, p.o.i., On., Can.	128	C10	48.25 N	88.49 W
Sleepy Eye, Mn., U.S.	128	G4	44.17 N	94.43 W
Sleepy Hollow, Ca., U.S.	198		33.57 N	117.47 W
Slepino, Russia	26	A11	59.10 N	29.04 E
Ślesin, Pol.	24	D14	52.22 N	18.18 E
Slettefjellet, mts., Nor.	16	F6	61.13 N	8.45 E
Slezsko see Silesia, hist. reg., Eur.	24	F13	50.33 N	18.00 E
Slidell, La., U.S.	134	G9	30.16 N	89.46 W
Slide Mountain, mtn., N.Y., U.S.	124	B11	42.00 N	74.24 W
Sliderock Mountain, mtn., Mt., U.S.	146	D13	46.35 N	113.33 W
Sliema, Malta	32	I8	35.55 N	14.30 E
Slievekimalta, mtn., Ire.	10	I4	52.45 N	8.16 W
Sligeach see Sligo, Ire.	10	G4	54.16 N	8.28 W
Sligo, Ire.	10	G4	54.16 N	8.28 W
Sligo, Pa., U.S.	124	C6	41.06 N	79.29 W
Sligo, state, Ire.	10	G4	54.10 N	8.40 W
Sligo Bay, b., Ire.	10	G4	54.18 N	8.41 W
Sligo Creek, stm., Va., U.S.	202c		38.57 N	76.58 W
Slingebeek see Schlinge, stm., Eur.	20	C15	51.55 N	6.19 E
Slinger, Wi., U.S.	128	H10	43.19 N	88.16 W
Šlino, ozero, l., Russia	26	C16	57.40 N	33.23 E
Slippery Rock, Pa., U.S.	124	C5	41.03 N	80.03 W
Šlissel'burg, Russia	26	A13	59.57 N	31.02 E
Šlissel'burg, Russia	183a		59.57 N	31.02 E
Slite, Swe.	16	J16	57.42 N	18.48 E
Slīteres Rezervāts, ind. res., Lat.	26	C5	57.38 N	22.25 E
Sliven, Blg.	36	G13	42.40 N	26.20 E
Slivnica, Blg.	36	G10	42.50 N	23.01 E
Sljudjanka, Russia	48	D18	51.39 N	103.42 E
Sloan, Ia., U.S.	130	B1	42.13 N	96.15 W
Sloan, Nv., U.S.	148	H10	35.56 N	115.11 W
Slobidka, Ukr.	38	F8	47.53 N	29.21 E
Sloboda, Russia	26	E14	55.30 N	31.51 E
Sloboda, Ukr.	38	B12	51.11 N	33.36 E
Slobodskoj, Russia	40	B17	58.43 N	50.11 E
Slobozia, Mol.	38	G8	46.44 N	29.42 E
Slobozia, Rom.	36	E14	44.34 N	27.22 E
Slobozia, Rom.	36	F12	43.51 N	25.53 E
Slobozia Mare, Mol.	38	H7	45.34 N	28.10 E
Slocan, B.C., Can.	144	G13	49.45 N	117.28 W
Slocan Lake, l., B.C., Can.	144	G13	49.56 N	117.23 W
Slocomb, Al., U.S.	134	F13	31.06 N	85.35 W
Słomniki, Pol.	24	F16	50.15 N	20.05 E
Slonim, Bela.	26	G8	53.05 N	25.19 E
Slonovka, Russia	38	C16	50.39 N	37.46 E
Sloop Channel, strt., N.Y., U.S.	194		40.36 N	73.31 W
Sloping Hills, N.J., U.S.	194		40.42 N	74.34 W
Slosh Indian Reserve, ind. res., B.C., Can.	144	F8	50.43 N	122.12 W
Slough, Eng., U.K.	10	J12	51.30 N	0.36 W
Slough, mun., Eng., U.K.	178		51.32 N	0.35 W
Slough, mun., Eng., U.K.	178		51.31 N	0.36 W
Slough Brook, stm., N.J., U.S.	194		40.45 N	74.21 W
Slovakia, ctry., Eur.	24	H15	48.30 N	20.00 E
Slovechna see Slavečna, stm., Eur.	38	B8	51.40 N	29.42 E
Slovechne, Ukr.	38	B7	51.23 N	28.21 E
Slovečna see Slavečna, stm., Eur.	38	B8	51.40 N	29.42 E
Slovenia, ctry., Eur.	30	E12	46.15 N	15.10 E
Slovenija see Slovenia, ctry., Eur.	30	E12	46.15 N	15.10 E
Slovenska Bistrica, Slvn.	30	D12	46.23 N	15.33 E
Slovenské rudohorie, mts., Slvk.	24	H16	48.44 N	20.09 E
Slovensko see Slovakia, ctry., Eur.	24	H15	48.30 N	20.00 E
Slov'ianka, Ukr.	38	E15	48.24 N	36.43 E
Slov'ians'k, Ukr.	38	E16	48.51 N	37.36 E
Slovinka, Russia	40	B13	58.01 N	43.08 E
Słowiński Park Narodowy, p.o.i., Pol.	24	B13	54.41 N	17.23 E
Słubice, Pol.	24	D10	52.21 N	14.34 E
Sluč, stm., Bela.	26	H10	52.08 N	27.31 E
Sluch, stm., Ukr.	38	D5	51.38 N	26.38 E
Sluck, Bela.	26	G10	53.01 N	27.33 E
Sludy, Russia	26	B19	58.52 N	36.52 E
Sluice, The, can., Eng., U.K.	180		53.41 N	2.57 W
Šluknov, Czech Rep.	24	E10	51.00 N	14.27 E
Slunj, Cro.	30	E12	45.07 N	15.33 E
Słupca, Pol.	24	D13	52.18 N	17.51 E
Słupia, stm., Pol.	24	B13	54.34 N	16.49 E
Słupsk (Stolp), Pol.	24	B13	54.27 N	17.02 E
Slurry, S. Afr.	90	D7	25.49 S	25.52 E
Smackover, Ar., U.S.	134	D6	33.22 N	92.43 W
Smackover Creek, stm., Ar., U.S.	134	D6	33.21 N	92.33 W
Smålandsfarvandet, b., Den.	16	L9	55.05 N	11.20 E
Smålandsstenar, Swe.	16	J11	57.10 N	13.26 E
Smalininkai, Lith.	26	E5	55.04 N	22.34 E
Smaljany, Bela.	26	F13	54.35 N	30.02 E
Smaljavičy, Bela.	26	F10	54.01 N	28.05 E
Smallbridge, Eng., U.K.	180		53.38 N	2.08 W
Smalleytown, N.J., U.S.	194		40.39 N	74.28 W
Smallwood Reservoir, res., Nf., Can.	106	D16	54.08 N	64.24 W
Smaloŭka, Bela.	26	E13	55.32 N	30.12 E
Smarhon', Bela.	26	F9	54.28 N	26.24 E
Smederevo, Yugo.	36	E7	44.39 N	20.55 E
Smederevska Palanka, Yugo.	36	E7	44.22 N	20.58 E
Smedjebacken, Swe.	16	G13	60.08 N	15.25 E
Šmelëvka, Russia	40	D16	54.47 N	49.11 E
Smelt Brook, stm., Ma., U.S.	201		42.00 N	70.43 W
Smelt Brook, stm., Ma., U.S.	201		42.13 N	70.58 W
Smelt Pond, l., Ma., U.S.	201		41.58 N	70.43 W
Smeralda, Costa, cst., Italy	32	C3	41.05 N	9.32 E
Smethport, Pa., U.S.	124	C7	41.49 N	78.27 W
Smidovič, Russia	50	G15	48.36 N	133.49 E
Šmidta, poluostrov, pen., Russia	50	F17	54.10 N	142.40 E
Śmigiel, Pol.	24	D12	52.00 N	16.31 E
Smila, Ukr.	38	D10	49.13 N	31.52 E
Smilavičy, Bela.	26	G11	53.45 N	28.00 E
Smile, Ukr.	38	C12	50.55 N	33.35 E
Smiley, Sk., Can.	142	C4	51.37 N	109.29 W
Smiley, Tx., U.S.	136	E10	29.16 N	97.38 W
Smiltene, Lat.	26	C8	57.25 N	25.54 E
Smirnyh, Russia	50	G17	49.44 N	142.50 E
Smith, Ab., Can.	144	A16	55.09 N	114.02 W
Smith, stm., U.S.	124	H5	36.28 N	79.45 W
Smith, stm., Ca., U.S.	148	B2	41.56 N	124.12 W
Smith, stm., Mt., U.S.	146	C15	47.25 N	111.29 W
Smith, stm., Or., U.S.	146	G2	43.42 N	124.05 W
Smith, Cape, c., On., Can.	126	C8	45.47 N	81.34 W
Smith Arm, b., N.T., Can.	110	B6	66.15 N	124.00 W
Smith Bay, b., Nu., Can.	108	B10	77.10 N	78.23 W
Smith Bay, b., Ak., U.S.	109	B9	70.53 N	154.17 W
Smith Canyon, val., Co., U.S.	138	D5	37.33 N	103.24 W
Smith Center, Ks., U.S.	138	B10	39.46 N	98.47 W
Smithdale, Pa., U.S.	197b		40.14 N	79.48 W
Smithers, B.C., Can.	144	B3	54.47 N	127.11 W
Smithfield, Austl.	192a		33.51 S	150.57 E
Smithfield, S. Afr.	90	G8	30.12 S	26.32 E
Smithfield, N.C., U.S.	132	A7	35.30 N	78.20 W
Smithfield, Ut., U.S.	146	I15	41.50 N	111.50 W
Smithfield, Va., U.S.	124	G9	36.58 N	76.37 W
Smith Haven Mall, shp. cen., N.Y., U.S.	194		40.52 N	73.08 W
Smithills Hall, hist., Eng., U.K.	180		53.36 N	2.27 W
Smith Island see Sumisu-jima, i., Japan	52	E13	31.27 N	140.03 E
Smith Island, i., N.C., U.S.	132	C8	33.52 N	77.58 W
Smithland, Ky., U.S.	130	G9	37.08 N	88.24 W
Smith Mountain, mtn., Ca., U.S.	198		34.17 N	117.52 W
Smith Mountain Lake, res., Va., U.S.	124	G6	37.07 N	79.39 W
Smith Peak, mtn., Id., U.S.	146	B10	48.50 N	116.39 W
Smith Point, c., N.S., Can.	122	E13	45.51 N	63.25 W
Smith River, Ca., U.S.	148	B1	41.55 N	124.08 W
Smiths, Al., U.S.	134	E13	32.32 N	85.05 W
Smiths Falls, On., Can.	126	D13	44.54 N	76.01 W
Smiths Fork, stm., Wy., U.S.	150	B6	41.23 N	110.12 W
Smiths Grove, Ky., U.S.	130	G11	37.03 N	86.12 W
Smiths Mills, N.J., U.S.	194		41.01 N	74.22 W
Smith Sound, strt., B.C., Can.	144	E3	51.18 N	127.48 W
Smithton, Austl.	99a	n12	40.51 S	145.07 E
Smithton, Mo., U.S.	130	F4	38.41 N	93.05 W
Smithton, Pa., U.S.	197b		40.09 N	79.44 W
Smithtown Bay, b., N.Y., U.S.	194		40.57 N	73.12 W
Smithville, Ga., U.S.	132	E1	31.54 N	84.15 W
Smithville, Ms., U.S.	134	C10	34.04 N	88.23 W
Smithville, Mo., U.S.	130	E3	39.23 N	94.35 W
Smithville, N.J., U.S.	203		39.29 N	74.27 W
Smithville, Tn., U.S.	130	I12	35.56 N	85.49 W
Smithville, Tx., U.S.	136	D10	30.00 N	97.09 W
Smithville Lake, res., Mo., U.S.	130	E3	39.25 N	94.31 W
Smoke Creek, stm., Mt., U.S.	142	F9	48.18 N	104.41 W
Smoke Creek, stm., N.Y., U.S.	202a		42.49 N	78.52 W
Smoke Creek, South Branch, stm., N.Y., U.S.	202a		42.49 N	78.49 W
Smoke Creek Desert, des., Nv., U.S.	148	C6	40.31 N	119.47 W
Smokey, Cape, c., N.S., Can.	122	D16	46.37 N	60.21 W
Smoky, stm., Ab., Can.	110	E7	56.11 N	117.19 W
Smoky Cape, c., Austl.	98	H9	30.55 S	153.03 E
Smoky Dome, mtn., Id., U.S.	146	G12	43.29 N	114.56 W
Smoky Hill, stm., U.S.	138	B12	39.03 N	96.48 W
Smoky Hill, North Fork, stm., U.S.	138	B7	38.55 N	101.17 W
Smoky Lake, Ab., Can.	144	B18	54.06 N	112.27 W
Smøla, i., Nor.	16	D5	63.24 N	8.00 E
Smolensk, Russia	26	F15	54.47 N	32.03 E
Smolenskaja-Moskovskaja vozvyšennost', plat., Eur.	26	F15	54.30 N	33.00 E
Smolenskaja oblast', co., Russia	26	F15	55.00 N	33.00 E
Smolensk-Moscow Upland see Smolenskaja-Moskovskaja vozvyšennost', plat., Eur.	26	F15	54.30 N	33.00 E
Smólikas, mtn., Grc.	34	C3	40.06 N	20.52 E
Smoljan, Blg.	36	H11	41.34 N	24.42 E
Smolny, bldg., Russia	183a		59.57 N	30.24 E
Smolovka see Smaloŭka, Bela.	26	E13	55.32 N	30.12 E
Smoot, Wy., U.S.	146	H16	42.37 N	110.54 W
Smooth Rock Falls, On., Can.	114	B10	49.17 N	81.38 W
Smoothrock Lake, l., On., Can.	128	A9	50.30 N	89.30 W
Smorodovka, Russia	26	C12	57.07 N	29.53 E
Smotrych, Ukr.	38	E5	48.56 N	26.34 E
Smotrych, stm., Ukr.	38	D5	48.33 N	26.38 E
Smrčiny see Fichtelgebirge, mts., Eur.	24	F7	50.01 N	11.55 E
Smygehuk, c., Swe.	16	L11	55.21 N	13.23 E
Smyrna see İzmir, Tur.	34	E10	38.26 N	27.09 E
Smyrna, De., U.S.	124	E10	39.18 N	75.36 W
Smyrna, Ga., U.S.	134	D14	33.54 N	84.28 W
Smyrna, Tn., U.S.	130	I11	35.59 N	86.31 W
Smythe, Mount, mtn., B.C., Can.	110	D6	57.54 N	124.53 W
Smythe Park, p.o.i., On., Can.	193b		43.41 N	79.30 W
Snæfell, mtn., Ice.	12a	k32	64.48 N	15.32 W
Snaefell, mtn., I. of Man	10	G8	54.16 N	4.27 W
Snæfellsnes, pen., Ice.	12a	k28	64.50 N	23.00 W
Snag, Yk., Can.	110	C3	62.22 N	140.24 W
Snagost', Russia	38	B13	51.20 N	34.54 E
Snake, stm., Yk., Can.	110	B4	65.59 N	134.11 W
Snake, stm., U.S.	146	D8	46.11 N	119.01 W
Snake, stm., Mn., U.S.	128	E5	45.49 N	92.45 W
Snake, stm., Mn., U.S.	128	C2	48.25 N	97.07 W
Snake, stm., Ne., U.S.	140	E11	42.46 N	100.48 W
Snake Brook, stm., Ma., U.S.	201		42.18 N	71.22 W
Snake Creek, stm., Mt., U.S.	142	F4	48.32 N	108.52 W
Snake Creek, stm., Ne., U.S.	140	E9	42.01 N	102.45 W
Snake Creek, stm., S.D., U.S.	140	B14	44.57 N	98.29 W
Snake Creek, South Fork, stm., S.D., U.S.	140	B14	45.01 N	98.33 W
Snake Indian, stm., Ab., Can.	144	C12	53.11 N	117.58 W
Snake Range, mts., Nv., U.S.	150	E2	39.00 N	114.15 W
Snake River Plain, pl., Id., U.S.	146	G14	43.00 N	113.00 W
Snake Valley, val., U.S.	150	D3	39.20 N	113.55 W
Snares Islands, is., N.Z.	102	H2	48.00 S	166.30 E
Snåsa, Nor.	16	C10	64.15 N	12.21 E
Snåsahögarna, mtn., Swe.	16	D10	63.13 N	12.21 E
Snåsavatnet, l., Nor.	16	C9	64.10 N	11.58 E
Snay Pôl, Camb.	64	G7	11.39 N	105.13 E
Sneads, Fl., U.S.	134	G14	30.42 N	84.55 W
Snedsted, Den.	16	K6	56.54 N	8.32 E
Sneedville, Tn., U.S.	124	H2	36.31 N	83.14 W
Sneek, Neth.	20	A14	53.02 N	5.40 E
Snelgrove, On., Can.	193b		43.44 N	79.49 W
Snelling, Ca., U.S.	148	F5	37.31 N	120.26 W
Sněžka, mtn., Czech Rep.	24	F11	50.43 N	15.43 E
Sneżnik, mtn., Slvn.	30	E11	45.35 N	14.27 E
Śniardwy, Jezioro, l., Pol.	24	C17	53.45 N	21.43 E
Sniardwy Lake see Śniardwy, Jezioro, l., Pol.	24	C17	53.45 N	21.43 E
Sniatyn, Ukr.	38	E4	48.27 N	25.34 E
Snihurivka, Ukr.	38	F11	47.04 N	32.48 E
Snina, Slvk.	24	G18	48.59 N	22.09 E
Snipe Lake, l., Ab., Can.	144	A14	55.07 N	116.46 W
Snizhne, Ukr.	38	F17	48.01 N	38.46 E
Snizort, Loch, b., Scot., U.K.	10	D6	57.33 N	6.28 W
Snjadin, Bela.	26	H11	52.03 N	28.21 E
Snøfjelltind, mtn., Nor.	16	B10	65.36 N	12.42 E
Snøhetta, mtn., Nor.	16	E7	62.20 N	9.17 E
Snohomish, Wa., U.S.	146	C4	47.55 N	122.05 W
Snønipa, mtn., Nor.	16	F4	61.42 N	6.41 E
Snønuten, mtn., Nor.	16	H4	59.31 N	6.53 E
Snoqualmie Pass, p., Wa., U.S.	146	C5	47.24 N	121.24 W
Snota, mtn., Nor.	16	E6	62.54 N	8.51 E
Snøtinden, mtn., Nor.	14	F4	66.38 N	14.00 E
Snoŭ, Bela.	26	G9	53.12 N	26.25 E
Snov, stm., Eur.	40	F7	51.32 N	31.32 E
Snover, Mi., U.S.	126	E7	43.27 N	82.59 W
Snowbird Lake, l., N.T., Can.	110	C10	60.41 N	103.00 W
Snow Canyon State Park, p.o.i., Ut., U.S.	150	F3	37.13 N	113.38 W
Snowden, Pa., U.S.	197b		40.16 N	79.58 W
Snowden Oaks, Md., U.S.	202c		39.04 N	76.52 W
Snowdenville, Pa., U.S.	203		40.11 N	75.36 W
Snowdon, mtn., Wales, U.K.	10	H8	53.04 N	4.05 W
Snowdonia National Park, p.o.i., Wales, U.K.	10	I9	52.53 N	3.54 W
Snowdoun, Al., U.S.	134	E12	32.14 N	86.17 W
Snowdrift see Łutselk'e, N.T., Can.	110	C8	62.22 N	110.55 W
Snowflake, Az., U.S.	150	I6	34.30 N	110.05 W
Snow Hill, Md., U.S.	124	F10	38.10 N	75.23 W
Snow Hill, N.C., U.S.	132	A8	35.27 N	77.41 W
Snow Lake, Mb., Can.	110	E10	54.53 N	100.01 W
Snowmass Mountain, mtn., Co., U.S.	138	B1	39.07 N	107.04 W
Snow Mountain, mtn., Ca., U.S.	148	D3	39.23 N	122.45 W
Snow Peak, mtn., Wa., U.S.	146	B8	48.35 N	118.29 W
Snows Brook, stm., U.S.	201		42.47 N	71.06 W
Snowshoe Peak, mtn., Mt., U.S.	146	B11	48.13 N	115.41 W
Snowtown, Austl.	98	I2	33.46 S	138.12 E
Snow Water Lake, l., Nv., U.S.	150	C2	40.46 N	114.56 W
Snowy, stm., Austl.	98	K7	37.48 S	148.32 E
Snowy Mountain, mtn., N.Y., U.S.	126	E15	43.42 N	74.23 W
Snowy Mountains, mts., Austl.	98	K7	36.15 S	148.18 E
Snowy River National Park, p.o.i., Austl.	98	K6	37.12 S	148.24 E
Snowyside Peak, mtn., Id., U.S.	146	G12	43.57 N	114.58 W
Snuŏl, Camb.	64	F8	12.03 N	106.25 E
Snyder, Ok., U.S.	138	G10	34.40 N	98.56 W
Snyder, Tx., U.S.	136	B7	32.43 N	100.55 W
Soacha, Col.	168	E4	4.34 N	74.12 W
Soalala, Madag.	88	D8	16.05 S	45.20 E
Soap Creek, stm., Ia., U.S.	128	K6	40.53 N	92.12 W
Soap Lake, Wa., U.S.	146	C7	47.23 N	119.29 W
Soar, stm., Eng., U.K.	10	I11	52.52 N	1.17 W
Soatá, Col.	168	D5	6.19 N	72.40 W
Soavinandriana, Madag.	88	D8	19.10 S	46.44 E
Sob, stm., Ukr.	38	E8	48.40 N	29.17 E
Sobaek-sanmaek, mts., Kor., S.	56	C1	36.51 N	128.28 E
Sobernheim, Ger.	24	G3	49.47 N	7.39 E
Soběslav, Czech Rep.	24	G10	49.15 N	14.44 E
Sobinka, Russia	40	D11	55.58 N	40.01 E
Sobolev, Russia	40	F17	51.56 N	51.41 E
Sobolivka, Ukr.	38	E8	48.37 N	29.29 E
Sobótka, Pol.	24	F12	50.55 N	16.45 E
Sobradinho, Braz.	172	D11	29.24 S	53.01 W
Sobradinho, Represa de, res., Braz.	170	E5	9.40 S	42.00 W
Sobral, Braz.	170	B5	3.42 S	40.21 W
Sobrance, Slvk.	24	H18	48.45 N	22.11 E
Sobrante Ridge, mtn., Ca., U.S.	200		37.58 N	122.15 W
Sobrarbe, hist. reg., Spain	28	B10	42.16 N	0.06 E
Sobych, Ukr.	38	C12	51.51 N	33.15 E
Soča see Isonzo, stm., Eur.	30	E10	45.43 N	13.33 E
Socaire, Chile	172	A4	23.34 S	67.52 W
Socgorodok, Russia	40	F11	50.10 N	38.09 E
Sochaczew, Pol.	24	D16	52.13 N	20.14 E
Soči, Russia	42	D8	43.35 N	39.43 E
Social Circle, Ga., U.S.	132	C2	33.39 N	83.43 W
Social Security Administration, bldg., Md., U.S.	202b		39.19 N	76.44 W
Sociedade Hípica Paulista, p.o.i., Braz.	205b		23.36 S	46.41 W
Société, Archipel de la (Society Islands), is., Fr. Poly.	94	E11	17.00 S	150.00 W
Society Hill, S.C., U.S.	132	B6	34.31 N	79.51 W
Society Islands see Société, Archipel de la, is., Fr. Poly.	94	E11	17.00 S	150.00 W
Soco, stm., Dom. Rep.	156	C13	18.27 N	69.12 W
Socompa, Paso (Socompa, Portezuelo de), p., S.A.	172	B3	24.27 S	68.18 W
Socompa, Portezuelo de (Socompa, Paso), p., S.A.	172	B3	24.27 S	68.18 W
Soconusco, Sierra de see Madre de Chiapas, Sierra, mts., N.A.	154	G12	16.01 N	93.08 W
Socorro, Col.	168	D5	6.29 N	73.16 W
Socorro, N.M., U.S.	138	G2	34.03 N	106.53 W
Socorro, Tx., U.S.	136	C1	31.39 N	106.16 W
Socorro, ngh., Braz.	205b		23.39 S	46.42 W
Socorro, Isla, i., Mex.	154	F3	18.45 N	110.58 W
Socotra see Suquṭrā, i., Yemen	72	G7	12.30 N	53.53 E
Soc Trang, Viet.	64	H7	9.36 N	105.58 E
Socuéllamos, Spain	28	E8	39.17 N	2.47 W
Soda Creek, B.C., Can.	144	D8	52.21 N	122.18 W
Soda Lake, l., Ca., U.S.	148	H9	35.08 N	116.04 W
Sodankylä, Fin.	14	E17	67.25 N	26.34 E
Soda Springs, Id., U.S.	146	H15	42.39 N	111.35 W
Soddy-Daisy, Tn., U.S.	134	B13	35.16 N	85.10 W
Söderälgen, l., Swe.	16	H12	59.43 N	14.37 E
Söderfors, Swe.	16	G15	60.23 N	17.14 E
Söderhamn, Swe.	16	F15	61.18 N	17.05 E
Söderköping, Swe.	16	I14	58.28 N	16.20 E
Södermanland, state, Swe.	16	H14	59.15 N	16.40 E
Södertälje, Swe.	16	H15	59.12 N	17.37 E
Södertörn, pen., Swe.	16	I15	59.05 N	18.00 E
Sodingen, ngh., Ger.	181		51.32 N	7.15 E
Sodo, Eth.	82	F7	6.51 N	37.46 E
Sodom see Sedom, hist., Isr.	76	G6	31.04 N	35.23 E
Sodpur, India	190b		22.39 N	88.23 E
Södra Kvarken (Ahvenanrauma), strt., Eur.	16	G17	60.15 N	19.05 E
Södra Storfjället, mtn., Swe.	16	B12	65.38 N	14.48 E
Södra Vi, Swe.	16	J13	57.44 N	15.48 E
Sodus, N.Y., U.S.	126	E12	43.14 N	77.03 W
Sodwana Bay National Park, p.o.i., S. Afr.	90	E11	27.30 S	32.39 E
Soe, Indon.	60	G7	9.52 S	124.16 E
Soe, mys, c., Turkmen.	42	E15	41.46 N	52.26 E
Soekmekaar, S. Afr.	90	C9	23.29 S	29.55 E
Soela väin, strt., Est.	26	B5	58.39 N	22.32 E
Soerabaja see Surabaya, Indon.	66	G8	7.14 S	112.44 E
Soest, Ger.	24	E4	51.34 N	8.06 E
Soest, Neth.	20	B14	52.09 N	5.18 E
Soeurs, Île des, i., Qc., Can.	193a		45.28 N	73.33 W
Sofádes, Grc.	34	D5	39.20 N	22.05 E
Sofala, Moz.	90	B12	20.09 S	34.44 E
Sofala, state, Moz.	90	B12	20.08 S	34.10 E
Sofia see Sofija, Blg.	36	G10	42.42 N	23.19 E
Sofiïvka, Ukr.	38	G13	46.33 N	34.03 E
Sofiïvka, Ukr.	38	E12	48.02 N	33.52 E
Sofija (Sofia), Blg.	36	G10	42.42 N	23.19 E
Sofija, state, Blg.	36	G10	42.20 N	23.20 E
Sofijsk, Russia	50	F16	51.34 N	139.49 E
Sofijsk, Russia	50	F15	52.15 N	133.58 E
Sofjanga, Russia	18	B18	65.51 N	31.14 E
Sofporog, Russia	18	B18	65.48 N	31.25 E
Sofrino, Russia	26	D20	56.09 N	37.57 E
Sofronovo, Russia	18	H23	59.48 N	36.54 E
Sogamoso, Col.	168	E5	5.43 N	72.56 W
Sogamoso, stm., Col.	168	D5	7.12 N	73.55 W
Soğanlı, stm., Tur.	34	B16	40.58 N	32.59 E
Soğanlıköy, ngh., Tur.	185b		40.55 N	29.12 E
Sogcho see Sokch'o, Kor., S.	54	E8	38.11 N	128.34 E
Sogda, Russia	50	F15	50.22 N	132.16 E
Sogndalsfjøra, Nor.	16	F5	61.14 N	7.03 E
Søgne, Nor.	16	I5	58.05 N	7.49 E
Sognefjorden, b., Nor.	16	F3	61.06 N	5.09 E
Sognesjøen, b., Nor.	16	G2	61.04 N	5.00 E
Sogn og Fjordane, state, Nor.	16	F4	61.30 N	6.50 E
Sogod, Phil.	68	E5	10.23 N	124.59 E
Sogo Nur, l., China	52	C5	42.17 N	101.14 E
Sogoža, stm., Russia	26	B22	58.25 N	38.34 E
Soğuksu Milli Parkı, p.o.i., Tur.	34	C15	40.34 N	32.34 E
Söğüt, Tur.	34	D13	40.01 N	30.11 E
Söğüt Gölü, l., Tur.	34	F12	37.03 N	29.53 E
Söğütlü, Tur.	34	C13	40.54 N	30.29 E
Sog Xian, China	52	E3	31.49 N	93.46 E
Sohāgpur, India	70	G7	22.42 N	78.11 E
Soharkha, India	190a		28.35 N	77.24 E
Sohna, India	70	D6	28.14 N	77.04 E
Sohor, gora, mtn., Russia	50	F10	51.18 N	105.15 E
Sŏhwa-ri, Kor., S.	56	A1	38.15 N	128.13 E
Soignies, Bel.	20	D13	50.34 N	4.04 E
Soignolles-en-Brie, Fr.	179		48.39 N	2.42 E
Soindres, Fr.	179		48.57 N	1.40 E
Soini, Fin.	18	E11	62.52 N	24.15 E
Sointula, B.C., Can.	144	F4	50.38 N	127.00 W
Soira, mtn., Erit.	82	E7	14.45 N	39.32 E
Soisalo, mts., Fin.	18	E15	62.27 N	28.04 E
Soissons, Fr.	20	E12	49.22 N	3.19 E
Soisy-sous-Montmorency, Fr.	179		48.59 N	2.18 E
Soisy-sur-Seine, Fr.	179		48.39 N	2.27 E
Sojana, Russia	12	D20	65.46 N	43.23 E
Sojat, India	70	F4	25.55 N	73.40 E
Šojda, Russia	18	F24	61.11 N	37.41 E
Šojda, stm., Russia	18	F24	61.05 N	37.37 E
Sōjiji Temple, rel., Japan	186		35.31 N	139.41 E
Šojna, Russia	12	C20	67.50 N	44.09 E
Sŏjosŏn-man, b., Kor., N.	54	E6	39.20 N	124.50 E
Sok, stm., Russia	40	E17	53.24 N	50.07 E
Soka, Kor., S.	189b		37.30 N	126.48 E
Sokal', Ukr.	38	C3	50.28 N	24.17 E
Sokch'o, Kor., S.	54	E8	38.11 N	128.34 E
Söke, Tur.	34	F10	37.45 N	27.24 E
Sokehs Passage, strt., Micron.	100d	I11	7.01 N	158.10 E
Sokele, D.R.C.	86	F4	9.55 S	24.36 E
Sokna, Nor.	16	G7	60.15 N	9.55 E
Sokodé, Togo	84	H5	8.59 N	1.08 E
Sokol, Russia	40	B12	59.27 N	40.07 E
Sokol, Russia	50	B14	72.23 N	126.48 E
Sokółka, Pol.	24	C19	53.24 N	23.30 E
Sokol'niki, ngh., Russia	183b		55.48 N	37.41 E
Sokolniki Park, p.o.i., Russia	183b		55.48 N	37.41 E
Sokolo, Mali	84	G3	14.44 N	6.07 W
Sokolohirne, Ukr.	38	G13	46.29 N	34.56 E

Name	Page	Map Ref.	Latitude	Longitude
Sokolov, Czech Rep.	24	F8	50.10 N	12.39 E
Sokolova Hora, Ukr.	38	C7	50.17 N	28.37 E
Sokolovo, Russia	26	H17	52.55 N	34.39 E
Sokolovo-Kundrjučenskij, Russia	38	F18	47.49 N	39.56 E
Sokołów Małopolski, Pol.	24	F18	50.13 N	22.07 E
Sokołów Podlaski, Pol.	24	D18	52.24 N	22.15 E
Sokone, Sen.	84	G1	13.53 N	16.22 W
Sokosti, mtn., Fin.	14	D19	68.12 N	28.13 E
Sokoto, Nig.	84	G5	13.03 N	5.14 E
Sokoto, stm., Nig.	84	G5	11.24 N	4.07 E
Šokša, Russia	18	F22	61.26 N	34.58 E
Sokyriany, Ukr.	38	E6	48.27 N	27.26 E
Sokyryntsi, Ukr.	38	C11	50.42 N	32.47 E
Sol, Costa del, cst., Spain	28	H5	36.43 N	4.05 W
Sola, Nor.	16	I3	58.53 N	5.36 E
Sola, Vanuatu	101d	i16	13.52 S	167.32 E
Søla, l., Nor.	16	B9	65.40 N	11.43 E
Soła, stm., Pol.	24	G15	50.04 N	19.13 E
Solacolu, Rom.	36	E13	44.23 N	26.33 E
Solai, Kenya	86	D7	0.01 N	36.09 E
Šolaksaj, Kaz.	48	D10	51.45 N	64.46 E
Solan, India	70	C6	30.54 N	77.06 E
Solana, Fl., U.S.	132	J3	26.56 N	82.01 W
Solander, Cape, c., Austl.	192a		34.01 S	151.14 E
Solânea, Braz.	170	D8	6.45 S	35.39 W
Solangāri, India	190b		22.36 N	88.27 E
Solano, Phil.	68	B3	16.31 N	121.11 E
Solāpur, India	69	C2	17.40 N	75.54 E
Solar, Morro, hill, Peru	204d		12.11 S	77.02 W
Solaro, Italy	184b		45.37 N	9.05 E
Solbad Hall in Tirol see Hall in Tirol, Aus.	30	C8	47.17 N	11.30 E
Solberg, Swe.	16	D15	63.47 N	17.38 E
Solbergfjorden, b., Nor.	14	C8	69.08 N	17.45 E
Solbiate Olona, Italy	184b		45.39 N	8.53 E
Solca, Arg.	172	E4	30.46 S	66.28 W
Solca, Rom.	36	B12	47.42 N	25.51 E
Sol'cy, Russia	26	B13	58.07 N	30.19 E
Solda Gölü, l., Tur.	34	F12	37.31 N	29.40 E
Sölde, ngh., Ger.	181		51.31 N	7.35 E
Sol de Julio, Arg.	172	D6	29.33 S	63.27 W
Sölderholz, ngh., Ger.	181		51.29 N	7.35 E
Soldier Creek, stm., Ks., U.S.	130	E2	39.04 N	95.39 W
Soldier Field, p.o.i., Il., U.S.	196		41.52 N	87.37 W
Soldier Point, c., Antig.	159b	f4	17.02 N	61.41 W
Soldier Pond, Me., U.S.	122	C8	47.09 N	68.35 W
Soldiers Grove, Wi., U.S.	128	H6	43.23 N	90.46 W
Soldotna, Ak., U.S.	109	D9	60.28 N	151.03 W
Sol Duc, stm., Wa., U.S.	146	C3	47.54 N	124.38 W
Solec Kujawski, Pol.	24	C14	53.04 N	18.14 E
Soledad, Col.	168	B4	10.55 N	74.46 W
Soledad, Ca., U.S.	148	G4	36.27 N	121.21 W
Soledad, Ven.	168	C10	8.10 N	63.33 W
Soledad, Cerro, mtn., Mex.	136	H4	26.29 N	103.23 W
Soledad, Picacho, mtn., Mex.	154	B5	26.32 N	107.17 W
Soledad Díez Gutiérrez, Mex.	154	D8	22.11 N	100.56 W
Soledade, Braz.	172	D11	28.49 S	52.30 W
Soledad Pass, p., Ca., U.S.	148	I7	34.29 N	118.07 W
Soledar, Ukr.	38	E17	48.40 N	38.06 E
Solen, N.D., U.S.	140	A12	46.23 N	100.47 W
Sølen, mtn., Nor.	16	F9	61.55 N	11.30 E
Solenoe, Russia	40	H13	46.13 N	42.32 E
Sølensjøen, l., Nor.	16	F9	61.55 N	11.36 E
Solenzara, Fr.	22	H15	41.51 N	9.23 E
Solers, Fr.	179		48.40 N	2.43 E
Soleure see Solothurn, Switz.	30	C4	47.12 N	7.32 E
Solginskij, Russia	12	F19	61.02 N	41.20 E
Solheim, Nor.	16	G3	60.53 N	5.27 E
Solheim, S. Afr.	191d		26.11 S	28.10 E
Solihull, Eng., U.K.	10	I11	52.25 N	1.46 W
Solikamsk, Russia	48	C9	59.39 N	56.45 E
Sol'-Ileck, Russia	40	F19	51.09 N	55.00 E
Sol-Iletsk see Sol'-Ileck, Russia	40	F19	51.09 N	55.00 E
Soliman, Tun.	32	H4	36.42 N	10.30 E
Solimões see Amazon, stm., S.A.	164	D7	0.03 S	49.15 W
Solingen, Ger.	24	E3	51.09 N	7.05 E
Solís de Mataojo, Ur.	172	G10	34.35 S	55.27 W
Sollefteå, Swe.	16	D15	63.10 N	17.16 E
Sollentuna, Swe.	16	H15	59.27 N	17.54 E
Sóller, Spain	28	E13	39.45 N	2.42 E
Sollerön, i., Swe.	16	G12	60.55 N	14.37 E
Sollom, Eng., U.K.	180		53.40 N	2.50 W
Solna, Swe.	16	H15	59.21 N	17.59 E
Solncedar, Russia	38	I16	44.34 N	38.00 E
Solncevo, ngh., Russia	183b		55.39 N	37.24 E
Solnečnodol'sk, Russia	40	I12	45.17 N	41.29 E
Solnečnogorsk, Russia	26	D19	56.11 N	36.59 E
Solo see Surakarta, Indon.	66	G7	7.34 S	110.49 E
Solodniki, Russia	40	G14	48.24 N	45.16 E
Sologne, reg., Fr.	20	G10	47.20 N	2.00 E
Šologoncy, Russia	50	C11	66.13 N	114.12 E
Šolohovskij, Russia	40	G12	48.17 N	41.03 E
Solok, Indon.	66	D2	0.48 S	100.39 E
Solomennoe, Russia	18	F21	61.52 N	34.15 E
Solomon, Az., U.S.	150	K7	32.48 N	109.37 W
Solomon, Ks., U.S.	138	C11	38.55 N	97.22 W
Solomon, stm., Ks., U.S.	138	B11	38.54 N	97.22 W
Solomon, North Fork, stm., Ks., U.S.	138	B10	39.29 N	98.26 W
Solomon, South Fork, stm., Ks., U.S.	138	B10	39.29 N	98.26 W
Solomon Basin, unds.	174	J18	7.00 S	152.00 E
Solomon Islands, ctry., Oc.	101b	e7	8.00 S	159.00 E
Solomon Islands, is., Oc.	94	D6	8.00 S	159.00 E
Solomon Sea, s., Oc.	94	D6	8.00 S	155.00 E
Solomon's Pools see Sulaymān, Birak, hist., W.B.	76	G5	31.41 N	35.10 E
Solon, China	52	B9	46.36 N	121.13 E
Solon, Ia., U.S.	130	C6	41.49 N	91.30 W
Solon, Me., U.S.	122	F7	44.57 N	69.51 W
Solone, Ukr.	38	E13	48.12 N	34.53 E
Solone Ozero, Ukr.	38	H13	45.53 N	34.27 E
Solonka, Russia	40	F12	50.11 N	41.27 E
Solonópole, Braz.	170	C6	5.44 S	39.01 W
Solon Springs, Wi., U.S.	128	E7	46.21 N	91.49 W
Solothurn, Switz.	30	C4	47.12 N	7.32 E
Solotvyn, Ukr.	38	E3	48.42 N	24.25 E
Solotvyna, Ukr.	38	F2	47.57 N	23.52 E
Soloveckie, Russia	18	B22	65.01 N	35.44 E
Soloveckie, ostrov, i., Russia	18	B22	65.04 N	35.41 E
Soloveckie ostrova, is., Russia	18	B22	65.07 N	35.53 E
Solovëvka, Russia	18	G17	60.46 N	30.09 E
Solov'evsk, Russia	50	F13	54.13 N	124.26 E
Solov'evsk, Russia	50	F12	49.55 N	115.42 E
Solozero, ozero, l., Russia	18	C25	64.16 N	38.44 E
Solsona, Spain	28	C12	41.59 N	1.31 E
Solt, Hung.	36	C6	46.48 N	19.00 E
Šolta, Otok, i., Cro.	30	G13	43.23 N	16.15 E
Soltānābād, Iran	72	B8	36.24 N	58.01 E
Soltau, Ger.	24	C5	52.59 N	9.49 E
Solvang, Ca., U.S.	148	I5	34.37 N	120.04 W
Solvay, N.Y., U.S.	124	A9	43.03 N	76.13 W
Sölvesborg, Swe.	16	K12	56.02 N	14.35 E
Sol'vyčegodsk, Russia	12	F22	61.19 N	46.54 E
Solway Firth, b., U.K.	10	G9	54.50 N	3.35 W
Solwezi, Zam.	88	C4	12.10 S	26.19 E
Soly, Bela.	26	F9	54.31 N	26.11 E
Solymár, Hung.	182c		47.36 N	18.56 E
Solza, Russia	18	C26	64.32 N	39.32 E
Solza, stm., Russia	18	C25	64.32 N	39.33 E
Sōma, Japan	56	B13	37.48 N	140.57 E
Soma, Tur.	34	D10	39.10 N	27.34 E
Somabhula, Zimb.	88	D4	19.41 S	29.39 E
Somalia, ctry., Afr.	86	D9	6.00 N	48.00 E
Somali Basin, unds.	174	I8	5.00 N	53.00 E
Somaliland see Somalia, ctry., Afr.	86	D9	6.00 N	48.00 E
Somali Republic see Somalia, ctry., Afr.	86	D9	6.00 N	48.00 E
Sombo, Ang.	88	B3	8.45 S	20.59 E
Sombor, Yugo.	36	D6	45.46 N	19.07 E
Sombrerete, Mex.	154	D7	23.40 N	103.38 W
Sombreretillo, Mex.	136	H8	26.19 N	99.55 W
Sombrero Channel, strt., India	62	G7	7.44 N	93.33 E
Sombrio, Braz.	172	D13	29.07 S	49.40 W
Sombrio, Lagoa do, l., Braz.	172	D13	29.10 S	49.41 W
Şomcuta Mare, Rom.	36	B10	47.30 N	23.28 E
Somdari, India	70	F4	25.50 N	72.34 E
Somero, Fin.	18	G10	60.38 N	23.31 E
Sõmerpalu, Est.	26	C9	57.50 N	26.49 E
Somers, Mt., U.S.	146	B12	48.05 N	114.13 W
Somerset, Austl.	99a	n12	41.02 S	145.49 E
Somerset, Mb., Can.	142	E15	49.24 N	98.39 W
Somerset, Co., U.S.	150	E9	38.55 N	107.28 W
Somerset, Ky., U.S.	130	G13	37.05 N	84.36 W
Somerset, Md., U.S.	202c		38.58 N	77.05 W
Somerset, Oh., U.S.	124	E3	39.48 N	82.17 W
Somerset, Pa., U.S.	124	D6	40.00 N	79.04 W
Somerset, Tx., U.S.	136	E9	29.13 N	98.39 W
Somerset Airport, arpt., N.J., U.S.	194		40.37 N	74.40 W
Somerset East, S. Afr.	90	H7	32.43 S	25.35 E
Somerset Hills Airport, arpt., N.J., U.S.	194		40.41 N	74.32 W
Somerset Island, i., Ber.	158e	k15	32.17 N	64.52 W
Somerset Island, i., Nu., Can.	110	A12	73.15 N	93.30 W
Somerset West, S. Afr.	90	I4	34.04 S	18.50 E
Somers Point, N.J., U.S.	124	E11	39.18 N	74.35 W
Somersworth, N.H., U.S.	122	G5	43.15 N	70.52 W
Somerton, Az., U.S.	150	K2	32.35 N	114.42 W
Somerton, ngh., Pa., U.S.	203		40.06 N	75.01 W
Somerville, N.J., U.S.	124	D11	40.35 N	74.36 W
Somerville, Tn., U.S.	134	B9	35.14 N	89.21 W
Somerville, Tx., U.S.	136	D11	30.20 N	96.32 W
Somerville Lake, res., Tx., U.S.	136	D11	30.17 N	96.38 W
Someș (Szamos), stm., Eur.	36	B9	48.06 N	22.21 E
Someșu Cald, stm., Rom.	36	C10	46.44 N	23.21 E
Someșu Mare, stm., Rom.	36	B11	47.11 N	24.12 E
Someșu Mic, stm., Rom.	36	C10	47.09 N	23.55 E
Somino, Russia	26	A17	59.20 N	34.51 E
Somma Lombardo, Italy	184b		45.41 N	8.42 E
Sommariva, Austl.	98	F6	26.25 S	146.35 E
Somme, state, Fr.	20	D11	49.55 N	2.30 E
Somme, stm., Fr.	20	E11	50.10 N	1.39 E
Somme, Baie de la, b., Fr.	20	D10	50.13 N	1.35 E
Sommen, l., Swe.	16	J13	58.00 N	15.13 E
Sommerberg, ngh., Ger.	181		51.27 N	7.32 E
Sömmerda, Ger.	24	E7	51.09 N	11.07 E
Sommerfeld see Lubsko, Pol.	24	E10	51.47 N	14.58 E
Somme Woods, p.o.i., Il., U.S.	196		42.09 N	87.49 W
Sømna, pen., Nor.	16	B10	65.24 N	12.20 E
Somnitel'nyj, Russia	50	F16	52.12 N	139.11 E
Somo, stm., Wi., U.S.	128	F9	45.28 N	89.49 W
Somogy, state, Hung.	36	C4	46.25 N	17.35 E
Somosierra, Puerto de, p., Spain	28	C7	41.08 N	3.35 W
Somosomo, Fiji	101e	p20	16.46 S	179.57 W
Somosomo Strait, strt., Fiji	101e	r19	16.47 S	179.58 E
Somoto, Nic.	156	F4	13.28 N	86.35 W
Somovo, Russia	26	H17	52.51 N	34.57 E
Somovo, Russia	38	B18	51.44 N	39.21 E
Sompion luonnonpuisto, ind. res., Fin.	14	D18	68.10 N	27.20 E
Sompolno, Pol.	24	D14	52.23 N	18.30 E
Somport, Col du (Somport, Puerto de), p., Eur.	28	B10	42.47 N	0.31 W
Somport, Puerto de (Somport, Col du), p., Eur.	28	B10	42.47 N	0.31 W
Sompuis, Fr.	20	F13	48.41 N	4.22 E
Somuncurá, Meseta de, plat., Arg.	166	H3	41.30 S	67.30 W
Son, stm., India	70	F10	25.42 N	84.52 E
Soná, Pan.	156	H7	8.00 N	81.18 W
Sonāmarg, India	70	A5	34.18 N	75.18 E
Sonāmukhi, India	70	G11	23.18 N	87.25 E
Sonari, India	190c		18.52 N	72.59 E
Sonarpur, India	190b		22.26 N	88.25 E
Sonātikri, India	190b		22.57 N	88.20 E
Sonchamp, Fr.	179		48.35 N	1.53 E
Sŏnch'ŏn-ŭp, Kor., N.	54	E6	39.47 N	124.55 E
Sønderborg, Den.	16	M7	54.54 N	9.48 E
Sønderjylland, state, Den.	16	L7	55.10 N	9.15 E
Sønder Omme, Den.	16	L6	55.50 N	8.54 E
Sondershausen, Ger.	24	E6	51.22 N	10.51 E
Søndre Strømfjord, Grnld.	108	D15	67.01 N	50.40 W
Sondrio, Italy	30	D6	46.10 N	9.52 E
Sonduga, Russia	12	F20	60.07 N	41.56 E
Sonepur, India	70	H9	20.49 N	83.54 E
Song, Malay.	66	C8	1.59 N	112.33 E
Song, Nig.	84	H7	9.50 N	12.38 E
Song, Thai.	64	C5	18.27 N	100.11 E
Songa, stm., Nor.	16	H5	59.47 N	7.43 E
Songavatnet, l., Nor.	16	H5	59.51 N	7.34 E
Song Bay Hap, Cua, b., Viet.	64	H7	8.46 N	104.52 E
Song Cau, Viet.	64	F9	13.28 N	109.13 E
Song Da see Black, stm., Asia	64	B7	21.14 N	105.21 E
Songe, Nor.	16	I6	58.41 N	9.00 E
Songea, Tan.	86	G7	10.41 S	35.39 E
Songhua, stm., China	52	B11	47.42 N	132.31 E
Songhua Hu, res., China	52	C10	43.25 N	127.10 E
Songjiang, China	58	F9	31.01 N	121.14 E
Sŏngjin see Kimch'aek, Kor., N.	54	D8	40.40 N	129.12 E
Songjŏng, Kor., S.	54	G7	35.08 N	126.46 E
Sŏngju, Kor., S.	56	D1	35.55 N	128.16 E
Songkan, China	58	G2	28.27 N	106.50 E
Songkhla, Thai.	64	I5	7.11 N	100.36 E
Songkhram, stm., Thai.	64	C6	17.39 N	104.28 E
Songlinba, China	58	I7	23.57 N	115.58 E
Sŏngnam, Kor., S.	54	F7	37.26 N	127.08 E
Songnim, Kor., N.	54	E6	38.44 N	125.38 E
Songololo, D.R.C.	86	F2	5.41 S	14.02 E
Songpan, China	52	E5	32.40 N	103.24 E
Song Phi Nong, Thai.	64	E4	14.13 N	100.02 E
Sŏngsa-ri, Kor., S.	189b		37.38 N	126.52 E
Songtao, China	58	G3	28.05 N	109.10 E
Šonguj, Russia	14	D23	68.47 N	33.05 E
Songxi, China	58	H8	27.31 N	118.46 E
Songxian, China	58	D4	34.10 N	112.05 E
Son Ha, Viet.	64	E9	15.04 N	108.33 E
Sonid Youqi, China	52	C7	42.44 N	112.39 E
Sonid Zuoqi, China	52	C7	43.58 N	113.59 E
Sonīpat, India	70	D6	28.59 N	77.00 E
Sonkël', ozero, l., Kyrg.	48	F13	41.50 N	75.08 E
Sonkovo, Russia	26	C20	57.47 N	37.09 E
Son La, Viet.	64	B6	21.19 N	103.55 E
Sonmiāni, Pak.	62	C2	25.25 N	66.37 E
Sonmiāni Bay, b., Pak.	62	C2	25.15 N	66.30 E
Sonnberg, mtn., Aus.	182b		48.20 N	16.15 E
Sonneberg, Ger.	24	F7	50.21 N	11.10 E
Sonningdale, Sk., Can.	142	B6	52.24 N	107.40 W
Sono, Japan	188		34.48 N	135.55 E
Sono, stm., Braz.	170	F2	8.58 S	48.10 W
Sono, stm., Braz.	170	I3	17.02 S	45.32 W
Sonoita Creek, stm., Az., U.S.	150	L6	31.29 N	110.59 W
Sonoma, Ca., U.S.	148	E3	38.17 N	122.27 W
Sonoma Peak, mtn., Nv., U.S.	148	C10	40.52 N	117.36 W
Sonora, Ca., U.S.	148	F5	37.59 N	120.22 W
Sonora, Tx., U.S.	136	D7	30.33 N	100.38 W
Sonora, state, Mex.	152	B2	29.20 N	110.40 W
Sonora, stm., Mex.	120	G7	29.04 N	110.54 W
Sonora, Desierto de, des., N.A.	152	A2	30.00 N	113.00 W
Sonoran Desert see Sonora, Desierto de, des., N.A.	152	A2	30.00 N	113.00 W
Sonostrov, Russia	14	F25	66.08 N	34.10 E
Sonoyta, Mex.	120	F6	31.51 N	112.51 W
Sonoyta, stm., Mex.	150	L3	31.15 N	113.19 W
Sonqor, Iran	74	C10	34.47 N	47.36 E
Sŏnsan, Kor., S.	56	C1	36.14 N	128.18 E
Sonseca, Spain	28	E6	39.40 N	3.58 W
Sonsón, Col.	168	E4	5.43 N	75.18 W
Sonsonate, El Sal.	156	F3	13.43 N	89.43 W
Sonsorol Islands, is., Palau	60	D9	5.20 N	132.13 E
Sonstraal, S. Afr.	90	E6	27.07 S	22.27 E
Sontag, Ms., U.S.	134	F8	31.38 N	90.12 W
Son Tay, Viet.	64	B7	21.07 N	105.30 E
Sonthofen, Ger.	24	I6	47.31 N	10.17 E
Soochow see Suzhou, China	58	F9	31.18 N	120.37 E
Sooke, B.C., Can.	144	H7	48.22 N	123.44 W
Soomaaliya see Somalia, ctry., Afr.	86	D9	6.00 N	48.00 E
Soome laht see Finland, Gulf of, b., Eur.	18	H10	60.00 N	27.00 E
Sooner Lake, res., Ok., U.S.	134	A1	36.26 N	97.02 W
Soongshil University, educ., Kor., S.	189b		37.30 N	126.58 E
Sopchoppy, Fl., U.S.	134	G14	30.04 N	84.31 W
Soperton, Ga., U.S.	132	D3	32.22 N	82.35 W
Sop Hao, Laos	64	B7	20.33 N	104.26 E
Sophia, W.V., U.S.	124	G4	37.42 N	81.14 W
Sopki, Russia	26	C13	57.05 N	30.55 E
Sopot, Pol.	24	B14	54.28 N	18.32 E
Sop Pong, Laos	64	A6	22.04 N	102.03 E
Sop Prap, Thai.	64	D4	17.53 N	99.20 E
Sopron, Hung.	36	B3	47.41 N	16.36 E
Sopur, India	70	A5	34.16 N	74.28 E
Sor, Ribeira de, stm., Port.	28	E2	38.59 N	8.16 W
Sora, Italy	30	I10	41.43 N	13.36 E
Sorada, India	70	I10	19.46 N	84.26 E
Sorae-san, mtn., Kor., S.	189b		37.27 N	126.47 E
Söråker, Swe.	16	E15	62.30 N	17.31 E
Sorata, Bol.	166	C3	15.47 S	68.40 W
Sorbas, Spain	28	G8	37.07 N	2.07 W
Sorbhog, India	70	E13	26.30 N	90.52 E
Sorbonne, educ., Fr.	179		48.51 N	2.21 E
Sore, Fr.	22	E5	44.20 N	0.35 W
Sorel, Qc., Can.	126	B16	46.02 N	73.05 W
Sorell, Austl.	99a	o13	42.46 S	147.33 E
Sorell, Cape, c., Austl.	99a	o12	42.11 S	145.10 E
Sørfold, Nor.	14	E6	67.27 N	15.16 E
Sørfolda, b., Nor.	14	E6	67.28 N	15.30 E
Sörforsa, Swe.	16	F15	61.40 N	17.00 E
Sórgono, Italy	30	D3	40.01 N	9.05 E
Sorgues, Fr.	22	E10	44.00 N	4.51 E
Soria, Spain	28	C8	41.46 N	2.28 W
Soria, co., Spain	28	C8	41.35 N	2.35 W
Soriano, Ur.	172	F8	33.24 S	58.19 W
Sørli, Nor.	16	C11	64.15 N	13.45 E
Sorø, Den.	16	L9	55.26 N	11.34 E
Soro, India	70	H11	21.17 N	86.42 E
Soro, Monte, mtn., Italy	32	G8	37.56 N	14.42 E
Soroca, Mol.	38	E7	48.09 N	28.17 E
Sorocaba, Braz.	170	L2	23.29 S	47.27 W
Soročinsk, Russia	40	E18	52.26 N	53.10 E
Soroco, P.R.	158a	b4	18.23 N	65.37 W
Soroka see Soroca, Mol.	38	E7	48.09 N	28.17 E
Soroksár, ngh., Hung.	182c		47.24 N	19.07 E
Sorol, at., Micron.	94	C5	8.06 N	140.22 E
Sorong, Indon.	60	F9	0.52 S	131.15 E
Sororó, stm., Braz.	170	C1	5.23 S	49.08 W
Sorot', stm., Russia	26	C12	57.04 N	28.49 E
Soroti, Ug.	86	D6	1.43 N	33.36 E
Sørøya, i., Nor.	14	B13	70.33 N	22.21 E
Sørøyane, is., Nor.	16	E3	62.18 N	5.43 E
Sørøysundet, strt., Nor.	14	B13	70.37 N	23.15 E
Sorraia, stm., Port.	28	F2	38.55 N	9.00 W
Sørreisa, Nor.	14	C9	69.09 N	18.09 E
Sorrento, Italy	32	D8	40.37 N	14.22 E
Sorrento, La., U.S.	134	G8	30.10 N	90.51 W
Sorris-Sorris, Nmb.	90	B2	20.56 S	14.47 E
Sor Rondane Mountains, mts., Ant.	103	C7	72.00 S	25.00 E
Sorsakoski, Fin.	18	E14	62.27 N	27.40 E
Sorsatunturi, mtn., Fin.	14	E20	67.24 N	29.38 E
Sorsele, Swe.	16	B15	65.32 N	17.32 E
Sorsk, Russia	48	D16	54.00 N	90.14 E
Sorso, Italy	32	D2	40.47 N	8.34 E
Sorsogon, Phil.	68	D4	12.59 N	124.00 E
Sort, Spain	28	B12	42.25 N	1.08 E
Sortandy, Kaz.	48	D12	51.42 N	71.00 E
Sortavala, Russia	18	F17	61.41 N	30.40 E
Sortland, Nor.	14	D6	68.42 N	15.23 E
Sortlandsundet, b., Nor.	14	D5	68.38 N	15.20 E
Sør-Trøndelag, state, Nor.	16	D8	63.00 N	10.40 E
Sørumsand, Nor.	16	H9	59.58 N	11.15 E
Sørvær, Nor.	14	B12	70.38 N	21.59 E
Sörve neem, c., Est.	26	C4	57.54 N	22.03 E
Sosa, Kor., S.	189b		37.29 N	126.47 E
Šoša, stm., Russia	26	D18	56.31 N	36.10 E
Sos del Rey Católico, Spain	28	B10	42.29 N	1.13 W
Sosedka, Russia	40	E13	53.13 N	42.40 E
Sosedno, Russia	26	B11	58.13 N	28.42 E
Sosenka, stm., Russia	183b		55.47 N	37.42 E
Sosenka, stm., Russia	183b		55.35 N	37.23 E
Soshigaya, ngh., Japan	186		35.39 N	139.36 E
Sösjöfjällen, mts., Swe.	16	D11	63.55 N	13.13 E
Soskovo, Russia	26	H18	52.44 N	35.22 E
Sosna, stm., Russia	40	E11	52.41 N	38.54 E
Sosneado, Cerro, mtn., Arg.	172	G3	34.44 S	69.58 W
Sosnicy, Russia	26	C13	57.37 N	30.25 E
Sosnogorsk, Russia	48	B8	63.36 N	53.52 E
Sosnovaja Pol'ana, ngh., Russia	183a		59.50 N	30.09 E
Sosnove, Ukr.	38	C5	50.49 N	27.00 E
Sosnovec, Russia	18	C21	64.25 N	34.26 E
Sosnovka, Kaz.	48	D13	51.26 N	79.28 E
Sosnovka, Russia	14	F31	66.28 N	40.31 E
Sosnovka, Russia	40	E13	52.24 N	43.29 E
Sosnovka, Russia	40	C17	56.15 N	51.17 E
Sosnovka, Russia	40	E12	53.14 N	41.22 E
Sosnovka, Russia	50	F10	54.09 N	109.35 E
Sosnovka, stm., Russia	14	F31	66.30 N	40.35 E
Sosnovo, Russia	18	G17	60.32 N	30.12 E
Sosnovoborsk, Russia	40	E14	53.18 N	46.14 E
Sosnovo-Ozërskoe, Russia	50	F11	52.31 N	111.32 E
Sosnovskoe, Russia	40	D13	55.47 N	43.10 E
Sosnovyj, Russia	18	A19	66.00 N	32.21 E
Sosnovyj Bor, Russia	26	A11	59.53 N	29.06 E
Sosnovyj Bor, Russia	40	C19	57.06 N	55.03 E
Sosnowiec, Pol.	24	F15	50.18 N	19.08 E
Sosnytsia, Ukr.	38	B11	51.31 N	32.30 E
Soso, Ms., U.S.	134	F9	31.45 N	89.16 W
Sosok, Indon.	66	C7	0.17 N	110.14 E
Sos'va, Russia	48	B10	63.36 N	61.55 E
Sosyka, stm., Russia	40	H11	46.35 N	39.04 E
Sotkamo, Fin.	18	C15	64.07 N	28.23 E
Sotla (Sutla), stm., Eur.	30	D12	45.52 N	15.40 E
Soto, Mex.	136	F1	28.18 N	106.08 W
Soto, Neth. Ant.	158g	p21	12.15 N	69.05 W
Soto de Aldovea, Spain	184a		40.26 N	3.27 W
Soto de Pajares, Spain	184a		40.17 N	3.32 W
Soto la Marina, Mex.	154	D9	23.46 N	98.13 W
Soto la Marina, Barra, i., Mex.	154	C10	24.09 N	97.43 W
Sotonera, Embalse de, res., Spain	28	B10	42.07 N	0.40 W
Sotouboua, Togo	84	H5	8.34 N	0.58 E
Šotozero, ozero, l., Russia	18	F19	61.47 N	33.00 E
Sottern, l., Swe.	16	I13	59.02 N	15.29 E
Sotteville-lès-Rouen, Fr.	20	E10	49.25 N	1.04 E
Sottunga, i., Fin.	18	G7	60.08 N	20.40 E
Souanké, Congo	86	D2	2.06 N	14.03 E
Soubré, C. Iv.	84	H3	5.47 N	6.35 W
Soudan, Austl.	96	D7	20.03 S	137.00 E
Souderton, Pa., U.S.	124	D10	40.18 N	75.19 W
Souflí, Grc.	34	B9	41.12 N	26.18 E
Soufrière, St. Luc.	159c	m6	13.51 N	61.03 W
Soufrière, vol., Guad.	159c	h5	16.04 N	61.40 W
Soufrière, vol., St. Vin.	159e	o11	13.20 N	61.11 W
Soufrière Bay, b., Dom.	159c	j6	15.13 N	61.22 W
Soufrière Bay, b., St. Luc.	159c	m6	13.50 N	61.04 W
Sougahatchee Creek, stm., Al., U.S.	134	E13	32.36 N	85.53 W
Souhegan, stm., N.H., U.S.	122	H5	42.51 N	71.29 W
Souillac, Fr.	22	E7	44.53 N	1.28 E
Souilly, Fr.	20	E14	49.01 N	5.17 E
Sŏul (Seoul), Kor., S.	54	F7	37.33 N	127.00 E
Sŏul (Seoul), Kor., S.	189b		37.33 N	126.58 E
Soulac-sur-Mer, Fr.	22	D4	45.31 N	1.07 W
Soulanges, Canal de, can., Qc., Can.	193a		45.20 N	73.58 W
Sound, The, strt., Eur.	16	L10	55.49 N	12.40 E
Sounding Creek, stm., Ab., Can.	144	E19	52.06 N	110.28 W
Sounding Lake, l., Ab., Can.	142	B3	52.10 N	110.28 W
Sound View Park, p.o.i., N.Y., U.S.	194		40.49 N	73.52 W
Soúnio, Ákra, c., Grc.	34	F7	37.40 N	24.01 E
Sources, Mont-aux- (Phofung), mtn., Afr.	90	F9	28.46 S	28.52 E
Soure, Braz.	164	D8	0.43 S	48.30 W
Soure, Port.	28	D2	40.02 N	8.37 W
Sour el Ghozlane, Alg.	28	H14	36.08 N	3.41 E
Souris, Mb., Can.	122	E13	49.37 N	100.16 W
Souris, P.E., Can.	122	D14	46.21 N	62.14 W
Souris, stm., N.A.	122	E13	49.39 N	99.34 W
Sourlake, Tx., U.S.	136	D13	30.07 N	94.24 W
Sourland Mountain, hill, N.J., U.S.	124	D11	40.29 N	74.43 W
Sousa, Braz.	170	D6	6.45 S	38.14 W
Sousel, Port.	28	F3	38.57 N	7.40 W
Sousse, Tun.	84	B7	35.49 N	10.38 E
Sout, stm., S. Afr.	90	F5	28.55 S	20.39 E
Sout, stm., S. Afr.	90	G4	31.34 S	18.23 E
Sout, stm., S. Afr.	90	H6	33.01 S	23.27 E
South, stm., Ia., U.S.	130	C4	41.29 N	93.20 W
South, stm., Ma., U.S.	201		42.10 N	70.43 W
South, stm., N.C., U.S.	132	B7	34.37 N	78.16 W
South, stm., Va., U.S.	124	G6	37.45 N	79.24 W
South Africa, ctry., Afr.	90	F8	30.00 S	26.00 E
Southall, ngh., Eng., U.K.	178		51.31 N	0.23 W
South America, cont.	4	H9	15.00 S	60.00 W
Southampton, N.S., Can.	122	E12	45.35 N	64.15 W
Southampton, On., Can.	122	D8	44.29 N	81.21 W
Southampton, Eng., U.K.	10	K11	50.54 N	1.24 W
Southampton, N.Y., U.S.	124	D13	40.52 N	72.23 W
Southampton, Pa., U.S.	203		40.10 N	75.02 W
Southampton, Cape, c., Nu., Can.	110	C13	62.09 N	83.41 W
Southampton Island, i., Nu., Can.	110	C14	64.20 N	84.40 W
South Andaman, i., India	62	F7	11.47 N	92.43 E
South Anna, stm., Va., U.S.	124	G8	37.48 N	77.24 W
South Antler Creek see Antler, stm., N.A.	142	E12	49.07 N	101.00 W
Southards Pond, l., N.Y., U.S.	194		40.43 N	73.20 W
South Australia, state, Austl.	96	E6	30.00 S	135.00 E
South Australian Basin, unds.	174	M15	38.00 S	126.00 E
Southaven, Ms., U.S.	134	B8	34.59 N	90.02 W
South Bald Mountain, mtn., Co., U.S.	140	G7	40.45 N	105.41 W
South Baldy, mtn., N.M., U.S.	150	J9	33.59 N	107.11 W
Southbank, B.C., Can.	144	C5	54.01 N	125.47 W
South Barrington, Il., U.S.	196		42.06 N	88.07 W
South Bay, Fl., U.S.	132	J5	26.39 N	80.43 W
South Bay, b., Nu., Can.	110	C14	63.59 N	83.31 W
South Bay, b., On., Can.	126	C8	45.38 N	81.52 W
South Baymouth, On., Can.	126	C7	45.33 N	82.01 W
South Beach, p.o.i., N.Y., U.S.	194		40.35 N	74.05 W
South Beloit, Il., U.S.	128	I9	42.29 N	89.02 W
South Bend, In., U.S.	130	C11	41.40 N	86.14 W
South Bend, Wa., U.S.	146	D3	46.39 N	123.46 W
South Bentinck Arm, b., B.C., Can.	144	D4	52.11 N	126.54 W
South Borneo see Kalimantan Selatan, state, Indon.	66	E9	2.30 S	115.30 E
South Boston, Va., U.S.	124	H6	36.41 N	78.54 W
South Boston, ngh., Ma., U.S.	201		42.20 N	71.03 W
South Bound Brook, N.J., U.S.	194		40.33 N	74.32 W
South Branch, N.J., U.S.	194		40.33 N	74.42 W
Southbridge, N.Z.	102	F5	43.51 S	172.15 E
Southbridge, Ma., U.S.	124	B13	42.04 N	72.02 W
South Brook, stm., Pa., U.S.	203		39.52 N	75.44 W
South Brookfield, N.S., Can.	122	F11	44.23 N	64.58 W
South Brooklyn, ngh., N.Y., U.S.	194		40.41 N	73.59 W
South Bruny Island, i., Austl.	99a	o13	43.23 S	147.17 E
South Bucks, mun., Eng., U.K.	178		51.34 N	0.35 W
South Burlington, Vt., U.S.	126	D16	44.28 N	73.10 W
South Byfield, Ma., U.S.	201		42.44 N	70.54 W
South Carolina, state, U.S.	132	C5	34.00 N	81.00 W
South Celebes see Sulawesi Selatan, state, Indon.	66	E11	3.43 S	119.58 E
South Chagrin Reservation, p.o.i., Oh., U.S.	197a		41.25 N	81.25 W
South Channel, strt., Mi., U.S.	126	C5	45.41 N	84.30 W
South Channel, mth., N.A.	199		42.32 N	82.40 W
South Charleston, W.V., U.S.	124	F4	38.21 N	81.44 W
South Chelmsford, Ma., U.S.	201		42.34 N	71.23 W
South Chicago, ngh., Il., U.S.	196		41.44 N	87.33 W
South China Basin, unds.	174	H14	15.00 N	115.00 E
South China Sea, s., Asia	46	I15	10.00 N	113.00 E
South Coast Botanic Garden, p.o.i., Ca., U.S.	198		33.47 N	118.21 W
South Coffeyville, Ok., U.S.	130	H2	36.59 N	95.37 W
South Concho, stm., Tx., U.S.	136	C7	31.21 N	100.28 W
South Crest, S. Afr.	191d		26.15 S	28.07 E
South Dakota, state, U.S.	140	C13	44.15 N	100.00 W
South Darenth, Eng., U.K.	178		51.24 N	0.15 E
South Downs, hills, Eng., U.K.	10	K12	50.53 N	0.20 W
South East, state, Bots.	90	D7	25.00 S	25.45 E
South East Cape, c., Austl.	99a	o13	43.37 S	146.51 E
Southeast Pacific Basin, unds.	174	P25	60.00 S	115.00 W
South East Point, c., Austl.	98	L6	39.07 S	146.25 E
South El Monte, Ca., U.S.	198		34.03 N	118.02 W
Southend-on-Sea, Eng., U.K.	10	J13	51.32 N	0.45 E
Southend-on-Sea, mun., Eng., U.K.	178		51.33 N	0.41 E
Southend Pier, trans., Eng., U.K.	178		51.31 N	0.44 E
South English, stm., Ia., U.S.	130	C5	41.30 N	91.55 W
Southern, state, Bots.	90	D7	24.45 S	24.00 E
Southern see HaDarom, state, Isr.	76	H5	30.40 N	34.50 E
Southern Alps, mts., N.Z.	102	F4	43.30 S	170.30 E
Southern Bug see Pivdennyi Buh, stm., Ukr.	38	F10	46.39 N	31.56 E
Southern Bug see Pivdennyy Buh, stm., Ukr.	38	F10	46.39 N	31.56 E
Southern California, University of, educ., Ca., U.S.	198		34.02 N	118.17 W
Southern Cook Islands, is., Cook Is.	94	E10	20.00 S	159.00 W
Southern Cross, Austl.	96	F3	31.13 S	119.19 E
Southern Ghāts, mts., India	69	G3	9.30 N	77.00 E
Southern Indian Lake, l., Mb., Can.	110	D10	57.13 N	98.21 W
Southern Ocean, oc.	174	N13	50.00 S	135.00 E
Southern Pines, N.C., U.S.	132	A6	35.10 N	79.23 W
Southern Uplands, mts., Scot., U.K.	10	F9	55.30 N	3.30 W
Southern Ute Indian Reservation, ind. res., Co., U.S.	150	F9	37.05 N	107.45 W
South Esk, stm., Austl.	99a	n13	41.25 S	147.08 E
South Esk, stm., Scot., U.K.	10	E10	56.43 N	2.33 W
Southey, Sk., Can.	142	D9	50.56 N	104.29 W
South Fabius, stm., Mo., U.S.	130	E6	39.53 N	91.27 W
South Fallsburg, N.Y., U.S.	124	C11	41.42 N	74.38 W
South Farmbridge, Eng., U.K.	178		51.38 N	0.41 E
South Farmingdale, N.Y., U.S.	194		40.43 N	73.26 W
Southfield, Mi., U.S.	124	B2	42.27 N	83.17 W
South Fiji Basin, unds.	174	L20	26.00 S	175.00 E
Southfleet, Eng., U.K.	178		51.25 N	0.19 E
South Floral Park, N.Y., U.S.	194		40.43 N	73.42 W
South Foreland, c., Eng., U.K.	10	J14	51.09 N	1.22 E
South Fork, Co., U.S.	138	D2	37.40 N	106.39 W
South Fox Island, i., Mi., U.S.	126	C4	45.24 N	85.50 W
South Fulton, Tn., U.S.	136	H9	36.29 N	88.53 W
Southgate, Mi., U.S.	124	B2	42.12 N	83.11 W
Southgate, ngh., Eng., U.K.	178		51.38 N	0.08 W
Southgate U.S.A., shp. cen., Oh., U.S.	197a		41.25 N	81.32 W
South Georgia, i., S. Geor.	166	J9	54.15 S	36.45 W
South Georgia and the South Sandwich Islands, dep., S.A.	160	K11	54.00 S	38.00 W
South Grand, stm., Mo., U.S.	130	F3	38.18 N	93.28 W
South Grand Island Bridge, trans., N.Y., U.S.	202a		43.00 N	78.56 W
South Green, Eng., U.K.	178		51.37 N	0.26 E
South Hackensack, N.J., U.S.	194		40.51 N	74.02 W
South Hanningfield, Eng., U.K.	178		51.39 N	0.31 E
South Hanover, Ma., U.S.	201		42.05 N	70.51 W
South Harbor, b., Phil.	187l		14.33 N	120.58 E
South Hātia Island, i., Bngl.	70	G13	22.19 N	91.07 E

Name	Page	Map Ref.	Latitude	Longitude
South Haven, Ks., U.S.	138	D11	37.03 N	97.24 W
South Haven, Mi., U.S.	130	B11	42.23 N	86.15 W
South Head, c., Austl.	192a		33.50 S	151.17 E
South Heights, Pa., U.S.	197b		40.35 N	80.14 W
South Hempstead, N.Y., U.S.	194		40.41 N	73.37 W
South Henderson, N.C., U.S.	124	H7	36.16 N	78.24 W
South Henik Lake, l., Nu., Can.	110	C11	61.30 N	97.27 W
South Hero, Vt., U.S.	126	D16	44.38 N	73.18 W
South Hill, Va., U.S.	124	H7	36.43 N	78.07 W
South Hills, ngh., S. Afr.	191d		26.15 S	28.05 E
South Hills Village, shp. cen., Pa., U.S.	197b		40.21 N	80.03 W
South Hill Village, Anguilla	159a	a1	18.12 N	63.05 W
South Holston Lake, res., U.S.	124	H3	36.32 N	82.03 W
South Honshu Ridge, unds.	174	G16	24.00 N	142.00 E
South Horr, Kenya	86	D7	2.06 N	36.55 E
South Houston, Tx., U.S.	136	E12	29.39 N	95.14 W
South Huntington, N.Y., U.S.	194		40.49 N	73.23 W
South Indian Basin, unds.	174	O12	60.00 S	120.00 E
South Indian Lake, Mb., Can.	110	D11	56.47 N	98.56 W
South International Falls, Mn., U.S.	128	C5	48.36 N	93.24 W
South Island, i., N.Z.	102	G5	43.00 S	171.00 E
South Konkan Hills, hills, India	69	C1	17.29 N	73.22 E
South Korea see Korea, South, ctry., Asia	54	G8	36.30 N	128.00 E
South Ladder Creek, stm., U.S.	138	C7	38.41 N	101.34 W
South Lake Tahoe, Ca., U.S.	148	E5	38.57 N	119.56 W
Southland, Tx., U.S.	138	H7	33.21 N	101.33 W
Southland, shp. cen., Ca., U.S.	200		37.39 N	122.06 W
South Laurel, Md., U.S.	202c		39.05 N	76.52 W
Southlawn, Il., U.S.	130	E8	39.45 N	89.36 W
Southlawn, Md., U.S.	202c		38.48 N	76.59 W
South Layhill, Md., U.S.	202c		39.04 N	77.03 W
South Line Island, i., N.Y., U.S.	194		40.37 N	73.30 W
South Llano, stm., Tx., U.S.	136	D8	30.29 N	99.45 W
South Lockport, N.Y., U.S.	202a		43.09 N	78.42 W
South Lorain, Oh., U.S.	197a		41.27 N	82.08 W
South Loup, stm., Ne., U.S.	140	F13	41.04 N	98.39 W
South Lynnfield, Ma., U.S.	201		42.31 N	71.00 W
South Lyon, Mi., U.S.	130	B14	42.27 N	83.38 W
South Magnetic Pole, misc. cult.	103	B18	65.18 S	139.30 E
South Manitou Island, i., Mi., U.S.	126	D3	45.01 N	86.06 W
South Media, Pa., U.S.	203		39.54 N	75.23 W
South Melbourne, Austl.	192b		37.50 S	144.57 E
South Miami, Fl., U.S.	132	K5	25.42 N	80.16 W
South Mills, N.C., U.S.	124	H9	36.27 N	76.19 W
South Milwaukee, Wi., U.S.	130	B10	42.54 N	87.51 W
South Mimms, Eng., U.K.	178		51.42 N	0.14 W
South Molton, Eng., U.K.	10	J9	51.01 N	3.50 W
South Mountain, mtn., Id., U.S.	146	H10	42.44 N	116.54 W
South Mountain Reservation, p.o.i., N.J., U.S.	194		40.45 N	74.18 W
South Nahanni, stm., N.T., Can.	110	C5	61.03 N	123.20 W
South Nation, stm., On., Can.	126	C14	45.34 N	75.06 W
South Negril Point, c., Jam.	158d	i12	18.15 N	78.21 W
South Norwalk Reservoir, res., Ct., U.S.	194		41.11 N	73.27 W
South Norwood, ngh., Eng., U.K.	178		51.24 N	0.04 W
South Nutfield, Eng., U.K.	178		51.14 N	0.08 W
South Nyack, N.Y., U.S.	194		41.04 N	73.55 W
South Ogden, Ut., U.S.	150	B5	41.12 N	111.58 W
South Orange, N.J., U.S.	194		40.47 N	74.15 W
South Orkney Islands, is., Ant.	103	B36	60.35 S	44.06 W
Southowram, Eng., U.K.	180		53.43 N	1.50 W
South Oxhey, Eng., U.K.	178		51.38 N	0.23 W
South Oyster Bay, b., N.Y., U.S.	194		40.38 N	73.28 W
South Palo Duro Creek, stm., Tx., U.S.	138	E7	36.06 N	101.28 W
South Paris, Me., U.S.	122	F6	44.13 N	70.31 W
South Park, p.o.i., N.Y., U.S.	202a		42.50 N	78.50 W
South Park, p.o.i., Pa., U.S.	197b		40.19 N	80.01 W
South Pasadena, Ca., U.S.	198		34.06 N	118.08 W
South Pass, p., Wy., U.S.	140	E4	42.22 N	108.54 W
South Pekin, Il., U.S.	130	D8	40.30 N	89.38 W
South Philadelphia, ngh., Pa., U.S.	203		39.56 N	75.10 W
South Pittsburg, Tn., U.S.	134	B13	35.00 N	85.43 W
South Platte, stm., U.S.	118	G14	41.07 N	100.41 W
South Platte, North Fork, stm., Co., U.S.	138	B3	39.24 N	105.09 W
South Point, c., Barb.	159d	n8	13.02 N	59.30 W
South Pole, misc. cult., Ant.	103	D1	90.00 S	0.00 W
Southport (Gold Coast), Austl.	98	F9	27.57 S	153.24 E
Southport, Austl.	99a	o13	43.24 S	146.57 E
Southport, Eng., U.K.	10	H9	53.38 N	3.00 W
Southport, Fl., U.S.	134	G13	30.17 N	85.38 W
Southport, In., U.S.	130	E11	39.39 N	86.07 W
Southport, N.C., U.S.	132	C7	33.55 N	78.01 W
South Portland, Me., U.S.	122	G6	43.38 N	70.15 W
South Range, Mi., U.S.	128	D10	47.05 N	88.40 W
South Reservoir, res., Ma., U.S.	201		42.27 N	71.07 W
South Ribble, mun., Eng., U.K.	180		53.45 N	2.42 W
South River, On., Can.	126	C10	45.49 N	79.22 W
South Rockwood, Mi., U.S.	124	B2	42.03 N	83.16 W
South Ronaldsay, i., Scot., U.K.	10	C10	58.46 N	2.57 W
South Sandwich Islands, is., S. Geor.	103	A2	57.30 S	26.36 W
South Sandwich Trench, unds.	176	N11	56.30 S	25.00 W
South San Gabriel, Ca., U.S.	198		34.03 N	118.05 W
South San Jose Hills, Ca., U.S.	198		34.01 N	117.55 W
South San Ramon Creek, stm., Ca., U.S.	200		37.42 N	121.55 W
South Santiam, stm., Or., U.S.	146	F4	44.40 N	122.56 W
South Saskatchewan, stm., Can.	142	A8	53.13 N	105.04 W
South Saugeen, stm., On., Can.	126	D9	44.07 N	81.01 W
South Shetland Islands, is., Ant.	103	B35	62.00 S	58.00 W
South Shore, ngh., Il., U.S.	196		41.46 N	87.35 W
South Shore Mall, shp. cen., N.Y., U.S.	194		40.44 N	73.15 W
South Shore Plaza, shp. cen., Ma., U.S.	201		42.13 N	71.01 W
South Side, ngh., Pa., U.S.	197b		40.26 N	79.58 W
South Sioux City, Ne., U.S.	128	I2	42.28 N	96.24 W
South Skunk, stm., Ia., U.S.	130	C5	41.14 N	92.01 W
South Slocan, B.C., Can.	144	G13	49.27 N	117.31 W
South Spicer Island, i., Nu., Can.	110	B15	68.17 N	79.04 W
South Station, trans., Ma., U.S.	201		42.21 N	71.04 W
South Stony Brook, N.Y., U.S.	194		40.53 N	73.07 W
South Sulphur, stm., Tx., U.S.	134	D3	33.23 N	95.21 W
South Sumatra see Sumatera Selatan, state, Indon.	66	E3	3.00 S	104.00 E
South Sunday Creek, stm., Mt., U.S.	140	A6	46.29 N	105.45 W
South Taranaki Bight, b., N.Z.	102	D6	39.40 S	174.14 E
South Tasman Rise, unds.	174	N17	47.37 S	147.58 E
South Thompson, stm., B.C., Can.	144	F11	50.40 N	120.19 W
South Torrington, Wy., U.S.	140	E8	42.03 N	104.11 W
South Tucson, Az., U.S.	150	K6	32.10 N	110.58 W
South Uist, i., Scot., U.K.	10	D5	57.15 N	7.22 W
South Umpqua, stm., Or., U.S.	146	G3	43.15 N	123.27 W
South Valley Hills, hills, Pa., U.S.	203		40.00 N	75.40 W
South Valley Stream, N.Y., U.S.	194		40.38 N	73.44 W
South Ventana Cone, mtn., Ca., U.S.	148	G4	36.17 N	121.38 W
South Vietnam see Vietnam, ctry., Asia	64	E9	16.00 N	108.00 E
Southview Apartments, Md., U.S.	202c		38.50 N	77.00 W
South Walpole, Ma., U.S.	201		42.06 N	71.15 W
Southwark, ngh., Eng., U.K.	178		51.30 N	0.06 W
South Weald, Eng., U.K.	178		51.37 N	0.16 E
South West Africa see Namibia, ctry., Afr.	88	E2	22.00 S	17.00 E
Southwest Bay, b., Bah.	158f	n18	24.59 N	77.29 W
Southwest Branch, stm., Md., U.S.	202c		38.53 N	76.48 W
South Westbury, N.Y., U.S.	194		40.45 N	73.35 W
South West Cape, c., Austl.	99a	o12	43.32 S	146.03 E
South West Cape, c., N.Z.	102	H2	47.16 S	167.28 E
South West City, Mo., U.S.	130	H3	36.30 N	94.36 W
Southwest Harbor, Me., U.S.	122	F8	44.17 N	68.20 W
Southwest Indian Ridge, unds.	174	M8	30.00 S	60.00 E
Southwest Miramichi, stm., N.B., Can.	122	D10	46.58 N	65.34 W
Southwest Museum, bldg., Ca., U.S.	198		34.06 N	118.13 W
Southwest National Park, p.o.i., Austl.	99a	o12	43.04 S	146.08 E
Southwest Pacific Basin, unds.	174	M23	40.00 S	150.00 W
Southwest Point, c., Bah.	158f	K8	25.51 N	77.12 W
Southwest Point, c., Gren.	159e	q10	12.26 N	61.29 W
South Weymouth, Ma., U.S.	201		42.10 N	70.57 W
South Weymouth Naval Air Station, mil., Ma., U.S.	124	B15	42.09 N	70.57 W
South Whitley, In., U.S.	130	C12	41.04 N	85.37 W
South Whittier, Ca., U.S.	198		33.57 N	118.02 W
South Wichita, stm., Tx., U.S.	138	H9	33.43 N	99.30 W
South Windham, Me., U.S.	122	G6	43.44 N	70.25 W
Southwold, Eng., U.K.	10	I14	52.19 N	1.40 E
South Yadkin, stm., N.C., U.S.	124	I5	35.44 N	80.27 W
South Yarra, Austl.	192b		37.51 S	145.00 E
Soutpansberg, mts., S. Afr.	90	C9	23.01 S	29.25 E
Souvigny, Fr.	22	C9	46.32 N	3.11 E
Souzy-la-Briche, Fr.	179		48.32 N	2.09 E
Sovata, Rom.	36	C12	46.35 N	25.05 E
Sovdozero, Russia	18	E19	62.47 N	33.08 E
Soverato, Italy	32	F10	38.41 N	16.33 E
Sovetsk, Russia	26	E4	55.04 N	21.53 E
Sovetsk, Russia	26	G20	53.55 N	37.38 E
Sovetsk, Russia	40	C16	57.35 N	48.58 E
Sovetskaja, Russia	42	C9	44.46 N	41.10 E
Sovetskaja Gavan', Russia	50	G17	48.58 N	140.17 E
Sovetskij, Russia	18	G15	60.32 N	28.42 E
Sovetskij, Russia	40	F20	51.06 N	56.28 E
Sovetskoe, Russia	38	C18	50.20 N	39.00 E
Sovetskoe, Russia	42	D11	42.52 N	45.41 E
Sovico, Italy	184b		45.39 N	9.16 E
Soviets'kyi, Ukr.	38	H13	45.20 N	34.56 E
Søvik, Nor.	16	E4	62.32 N	6.17 E
Sovpole, Russia	12	D20	65.17 N	43.54 E
Sowa Pan, pl., Bots.	90	B7	20.47 S	25.54 E
Sowek, Indon.	60	F10	0.48 S	135.31 E
Sowerby, Eng., U.K.	180		53.42 N	1.56 W
Soweto, S. Afr.	90	E8	26.16 S	27.51 E
Sowjetisches Ehrenmal, hist., Ger.	182a		52.29 N	13.28 E
Sōya-kaikyō see La Perouse Strait, strt., Asia	52	B13	45.45 N	142.00 E
Sōya-misaki, c., Japan	54	B14	45.29 N	141.55 E
Soyang-chŏsuji, res., Kor., S.	54	E8	37.56 N	127.53 E
Soyland Moor, for., Eng., U.K.	180		53.40 N	2.02 W
Soyo, Ang.	88	B1	6.07 S	12.18 E
Sož, stm., Eur.	40	E7	51.57 N	30.50 E
Sozh see Sož, stm., Eur.	40	E7	51.57 N	30.50 E
Sozimskij, Russia	48	C8	59.44 N	52.15 E
Šožma, Russia	12	F18	61.56 N	40.15 E
Sozopol, Blg.	36	G14	42.25 N	27.42 E
Sozzago, Italy	184b		45.24 N	8.43 E
Spa, Bel.	20	D14	50.29 N	5.51 E
Space Obelisk, hist., Russia	183b		55.49 N	37.38 E
Spain, ctry., Eur.	28	E7	40.00 N	4.00 W
Spalding, Austl.	98	I2	33.30 S	138.36 E
Spalding, Sk., Can.	142	B9	52.20 N	104.29 W
Spalding, Eng., U.K.	10	I12	52.47 N	0.09 W
Spalding, Ne., U.S.	140	F14	41.40 N	98.21 W
Spandau, Berliner Forst, for., Ger.	182a		52.35 N	13.11 E
Spanish, On., Can.	126	B7	46.11 N	82.20 W
Spanish, stm., On., Can.	126	B8	46.10 N	82.13 W
Spanish Fork, Ut., U.S.	150	C5	40.07 N	111.38 W
Spanish Peak, mtn., Or., U.S.	146	F7	44.24 N	119.46 W
Spanish Point, c., Antig.	159b	e4	17.32 N	61.44 W
Spanish Point, c., Ber.	158e	k15	32.18 N	64.48 W
Spanish Sahara see Western Sahara, dep., Afr.	84	E2	24.30 N	13.00 W
Spanish Town, Br. Vir. Is.	158b	e9	18.26 N	64.26 W
Spanish Town, Jam.	158d	i13	17.59 N	76.57 W
Spánta, Ákra, c., Grc.	34	H6	35.40 N	23.44 E
Sparbach, Aus.	182b		48.04 N	16.11 E
Sparbu, Nor.	16	D9	63.54 N	11.26 E
Spargi, Isola, i., Italy	32	C3	41.14 N	9.20 E
Sparkill, N.Y., U.S.	194		41.02 N	73.56 W
Sparkman, Ar., U.S.	134	D6	33.54 N	92.51 W
Sparks, Ga., U.S.	132	E2	31.10 N	83.26 W
Sparks, Nv., U.S.	148	D6	39.32 N	119.44 W
Sparland, Il., U.S.	130	C8	41.01 N	89.26 W
Sparlingville, Mi., U.S.	130	B15	42.57 N	82.29 W
Sparreholm, Swe.	16	H14	59.04 N	16.50 E
Sparrowpit, Eng., U.K.	180		53.19 N	1.52 W
Sparrows Point, Md., U.S.	124	E9	39.12 N	76.28 W
Sparrows Point, c., Md., U.S.	202b		39.12 N	76.30 W
Sparta see Spárti, Grc.	34	F5	37.05 N	22.25 E
Sparta, Ga., U.S.	132	C3	33.16 N	82.58 W
Sparta, Il., U.S.	130	F8	38.07 N	89.42 W
Sparta, Ky., U.S.	130	F13	38.40 N	84.54 W
Sparta, Mi., U.S.	130	A12	43.09 N	85.41 W
Sparta, N.J., U.S.	124	C11	41.01 N	74.38 W
Sparta, N.C., U.S.	124	H4	36.29 N	81.06 W
Sparta, Tn., U.S.	130	I12	35.55 N	85.27 W
Sparta, Wi., U.S.	128	H8	43.56 N	90.48 W
Sparta Brook, stm., N.Y., U.S.	194		41.08 N	73.52 W
Spartak Garden, p.o.i., Russia	183a		59.51 N	30.30 E
Spartanburg, S.C., U.S.	132	B4	34.56 N	81.56 W
Spárti, Grc.	34	F5	37.05 N	22.25 E
Spartivento, Capo, c., Italy	32	G10	37.55 N	16.04 E
Spartivento, Capo, c., Italy	32	F2	38.53 N	8.50 E
Spas-Demensk, Russia	26	F16	54.24 N	34.02 E
Spas-Klepiki, Russia	40	D12	55.07 N	40.11 E
Spasskaja Guba, Russia	18	E20	62.06 N	33.56 E
Spassk-Dal'nij, Russia	54	B10	44.35 N	132.49 E
Spasskoe, Russia	26	G19	53.06 N	36.24 E
Spassk-Rjazanskij, Russia	40	D12	54.25 N	40.23 E
Spáta, Grc.	185c		37.48 N	23.55 E
Spatha, Cape see Spánta, Ákra, c., Grc.	34	H6	35.40 N	23.44 E
Spearfish, S.D., U.S.	140	C9	44.29 N	103.51 W
Spearman, Tx., U.S.	138	E7	36.11 N	101.11 W
Spearville, Ks., U.S.	138	D9	37.51 N	99.45 W
Spectacle Island, i., Ma., U.S.	201		42.19 N	70.59 W
Spectrum, p.o.i., Pa., U.S.	203		39.54 N	75.10 W
Spednic Lake, l., N.A.	122	E9	45.35 N	67.30 W
Speedway, In., U.S.	130	E11	39.47 N	86.15 W
Speightstown, Barb.	159d	n8	13.14 N	59.38 W
Speikkogel, mtn., Aus.	30	C12	47.14 N	15.03 E
Speising, ngh., Aus.	182b		48.10 N	16.17 E
Speke, ngh., Eng., U.K.	180		53.21 N	2.51 W
Speke Gulf, b., Tan.	86	E6	2.20 S	33.15 E
Speke Hall, hist., Eng., U.K.	180		53.20 N	2.52 W
Speldorf, ngh., Ger.	181		51.25 N	6.52 E
Spellen, Ger.	181		51.37 N	6.37 E
Spelthorne, mun., Eng., U.K.	178		51.25 N	0.28 W
Spence Bay see Taloyoak, Nu., Can.	110	B12	69.32 N	93.31 W
Spencer, In., U.S.	130	E11	39.17 N	86.46 W
Spencer, Ia., U.S.	128	H3	43.08 N	95.09 W
Spencer, Ne., U.S.	140	E14	42.51 N	98.41 W
Spencer, N.C., U.S.	124	I5	35.41 N	80.26 W
Spencer, Tn., U.S.	134	B13	35.44 N	85.27 W
Spencer, W.V., U.S.	124	F4	38.47 N	81.22 W
Spencer, Wi., U.S.	128	G8	44.45 N	90.17 W
Spencer, Cape, c., Austl.	96	G7	35.17 S	136.53 E
Spencer, Cape, c., N.B., Can.	122	E11	45.12 N	65.54 W
Spencer Brook, stm., Ma., U.S.	201		42.28 N	71.22 W
Spencer Field, arpt., Mi., U.S.	199		42.31 N	83.33 W
Spencer Gulf, b., Austl.	96	F7	34.00 S	137.00 E
Spencerville, Oh., U.S.	124	D1	40.42 N	84.21 W
Spences Bridge, B.C., Can.	144	F9	50.25 N	121.21 W
Spenser Mountains, mts., N.Z.	102	F5	42.15 S	172.30 E
Speos (Rock Tombs), hist., Egypt	76	K1	27.54 N	30.52 E
Sperillen, l., Nor.	16	G7	60.28 N	10.03 E
Spermaceti Cove, b., N.J., U.S.	194		40.26 N	73.59 W
Sperrin Mountains, mts., N. Ire., U.K.	10	G6	54.50 N	7.05 W
Sperry Creek, stm., Oh., U.S.	197a		41.29 N	81.53 W
Sperry Rand Corporation, sci., N.Y., U.S.	194		40.45 N	73.42 W
Sperryville, Va., U.S.	124	F7	38.38 N	78.14 W
Spétses, i., Grc.	34	F6	37.16 N	23.08 E
Spey, stm., Scot., U.K.	10	D9	57.39 N	3.05 W
Spey Bay, b., Scot., U.K.	10	D9	57.41 N	3.05 W
Speyer, Ger.	24	G4	49.19 N	8.25 E
Spezia see La Spezia, Italy	30	F6	44.07 N	9.49 E
Spezzano Albanese, Italy	32	E10	39.40 N	16.19 E
Sphinx see Abū el-Hul, hist., Egypt	76	I1	29.59 N	31.08 E
Sphinx (Abū el-Hul), hist., Egypt	191c		29.59 N	31.08 E
Spicer, Mn., U.S.	128	F4	45.13 N	94.56 W
Spicer Creek, stm., N.Y., U.S.	202a		43.02 N	78.53 W
Spickard, Mo., U.S.	130	D4	40.13 N	93.35 W
Spicket, stm., U.S.	201		42.42 N	71.09 W
Spiekeroog, i., Ger.	24	C3	53.46 N	7.42 E
Spiez, Switz.	30	D4	46.41 N	7.39 E
Spildra, i., Nor.	14	B12	70.01 N	21.37 E
Spilimbergo, Italy	30	D9	46.07 N	12.54 E
Spillimacheen, stm., B.C., Can.	144	E14	50.54 N	116.23 W
Spillville, Ia., U.S.	130	A6	43.12 N	91.57 W
Spinazzola, Italy	32	D10	40.58 N	16.04 E
Spindale, N.C., U.S.	132	A4	35.21 N	81.55 W
Spipskjølen, mtn., Nor.	14	B20	70.22 N	29.31 E
Spires see Speyer, Ger.	24	G4	49.19 N	8.25 E
Spirit Lake, Id., U.S.	146	B10	47.58 N	116.52 W
Spirit Lake, Ia., U.S.	128	H3	43.25 N	95.06 W
Spirit River, Ab., Can.	110	D7	55.47 N	118.50 W
Spiro, Ok., U.S.	134	B4	35.13 N	94.38 W
Spirovo, Russia	26	C17	57.25 N	34.59 E
Spišská Nová Ves, Slvk.	24	H16	48.56 N	20.34 E
Spitsbergen, i., Nor.	106	B24	78.45 N	16.00 E
Spitsbergen Bank, unds.	174	B5	76.00 N	23.00 E
Spittal an der Drau, Aus.	30	D10	46.47 N	13.29 E
Spitz, Aus.	24	H11	48.22 N	15.25 E
Spitzer Berg, hill, Ger.	182a		52.38 N	13.35 E
Spivakivka, Ukr.	38	D17	49.02 N	38.55 E
Spjelkavik, Nor.	16	E4	62.27 N	6.21 E
Split, Cro.	30	G13	43.30 N	16.26 E
Split, Cape, c., N.S., Can.	122	E12	45.19 N	64.29 W
Split Lake, res., Mb., Can.	110	D11	56.08 N	96.15 W
Splitrock Reservoir, res., N.J., U.S.	194		40.58 N	74.27 W
Spofford, Tx., U.S.	136	E7	29.11 N	100.24 W
Špogi, Lat.	26	D9	56.04 N	26.44 E
Spokane, Wa., U.S.	146	C9	47.39 N	117.24 W
Spokane, stm., U.S.	146	C8	47.53 N	118.20 W
Spokane, Mount, mtn., Wa., U.S.	146	C9	47.55 N	117.07 W
Spokane Indian Reservation, ind. res., Wa., U.S.	146	C8	47.55 N	118.00 W
Spoleto, Italy	30	H9	42.44 N	12.44 E
Sponds Hill, hill, Eng., U.K.	180		53.19 N	2.03 W
Spóng, Camb.	64	F7	13.27 N	105.33 E
Spoon, stm., Il., U.S.	130	D7	40.18 N	90.03 W
Spooner, Wi., U.S.	128	F7	45.49 N	91.53 W
Sporava, Bela.	26	H8	52.25 N	25.20 E
Spornoe, Russia	50	D19	62.20 N	151.05 E
Sportforum, p.o.i., Ger.	182a		52.33 N	13.29 E
Sports and Show Palace, bldg., Russia	183a		59.52 N	30.21 E
Sportsman's Park Race Track, p.o.i., Il., U.S.	196		41.50 N	87.46 W
Spot Pond, l., Ma., U.S.	201		42.27 N	71.06 W
Spotswood, Austl.	192b		37.50 S	144.53 E
Spotsylvania, Va., U.S.	124	F8	38.11 N	77.35 W
Sprague, Mb., Can.	142	E18	49.01 N	95.38 W
Sprague, Wa., U.S.	146	C9	47.17 N	117.57 W
Sprague, stm., Or., U.S.	146	H5	42.34 N	121.52 W
Sprague, North Fork, stm., Or., U.S.	146	H5	42.27 N	121.06 W
Sprague, South Fork, stm., Or., U.S.	148	A5	42.26 N	121.06 W
Sprain Ridge Park, p.o.i., N.Y., U.S.	194		40.59 N	73.51 W
Spratly Islands, is., Asia	60	D5	10.00 N	114.00 E
Spray, Or., U.S.	146	F7	44.50 N	119.47 W
Spray Lakes Reservoir, res., Ab., Can.	144	F15	50.55 N	115.20 W
Spreča, stm., Bos.	36	E5	44.44 N	18.05 E
Spremberg, Ger.	24	E10	51.34 N	14.22 E
Spring, stm., U.S.	130	H3	36.48 N	94.45 W
Spring, stm., Ar., U.S.	130	H6	36.06 N	91.04 W
Spring, North Fork, stm., Mo., U.S.	138	D14	37.17 N	94.21 W
Spring, South Fork, stm., U.S.	130	H6	36.19 N	91.30 W
Spring Bay, b., Ut., U.S.	150	B4	41.40 N	112.50 W
Springbok, S. Afr.	90	F3	29.43 S	17.55 E
Spring Branch, stm., Md., U.S.	202b		39.26 N	76.35 W
Springbrook, On., Can.	193b		43.39 N	79.47 W
Springbrook, Md., U.S.	202c		39.03 N	77.00 W
Spring Brook, stm., Il., U.S.	196		41.58 N	87.59 W
Springbrook Forest, Md., U.S.	202c		39.03 N	77.01 W
Spring City, Tn., U.S.	134	B14	35.41 N	84.51 W
Spring City, Ut., U.S.	150	D5	39.28 N	111.29 W
Spring Coulee, stm., N.D., U.S.	142	F12	48.31 N	100.54 W
Spring Creek, stm., Austl.	98	D3	24.15 S	140.58 E
Spring Creek, stm., U.S.	140	G11	40.30 N	101.20 W
Spring Creek, stm., Ga., U.S.	134	F14	30.46 N	84.47 W
Spring Creek, stm., Il., U.S.	196		41.32 N	88.04 W
Spring Creek, stm., N.D., U.S.	142	G11	47.14 N	101.48 W
Spring Creek, stm., S.D., U.S.	140	B13	45.51 N	100.22 W
Spring Creek, stm., S.D., U.S.	148	C8	40.00 N	117.44 W
Spring Creek, stm., Tx., U.S.	136	D12	30.01 N	95.16 W
Springdale, Nf., Can.	111a	j22	49.31 N	56.04 W
Springdale, Ar., U.S.	130	H3	36.11 N	94.07 W
Springdale, Ut., U.S.	150	F4	37.12 N	112.59 W
Springdale, Wa., U.S.	146	B9	48.03 N	117.44 W
Spring Dale, W.V., U.S.	124	G5	37.53 N	80.49 W
Springe, Ger.	24	D5	52.12 N	9.34 E
Springer, N.M., U.S.	138	E4	36.22 N	104.36 W
Springers Brook, stm., N.J., U.S.	203		39.44 N	74.41 W
Springerville, Az., U.S.	150	I7	34.06 N	109.17 W
Springfield, N.S., Can.	122	F12	44.38 N	64.53 W
Springfield, Co., U.S.	138	D6	37.24 N	102.36 W
Springfield, Fl., U.S.	134	G13	30.12 N	85.37 W
Springfield, Ga., U.S.	132	D4	32.22 N	81.18 W
Springfield, Il., U.S.	130	E8	39.47 N	89.38 W
Springfield, Ky., U.S.	130	G12	37.41 N	85.13 W
Springfield, Ma., U.S.	124	B13	42.07 N	72.35 W
Springfield, Mn., U.S.	128	G4	44.14 N	94.59 W
Springfield, Mo., U.S.	130	G4	37.12 N	93.17 W
Springfield, N.J., U.S.	194		40.43 N	74.18 W
Springfield, Oh., U.S.	124	E2	39.55 N	83.48 W
Springfield, Or., U.S.	146	F3	44.03 N	123.00 W
Springfield, Pa., U.S.	203		39.55 N	75.19 W
Springfield, S.C., U.S.	132	C4	33.29 N	81.16 W
Springfield, S.D., U.S.	140	E15	42.51 N	97.53 W
Springfield, Tn., U.S.	130	H11	36.30 N	86.53 W
Springfield, Vt., U.S.	122	G4	43.17 N	72.28 W
Springfield, Va., U.S.	202c		38.45 N	77.13 W
Springfield, Lake, res., Il., U.S.	130	E8	39.44 N	89.36 W
Springfield Estates, Va., U.S.	202c		38.47 N	77.11 W
Springfield Lake, l., Pa., U.S.	203		40.11 N	75.00 W
Springfield Mall, shp. cen., Va., U.S.	202c		38.46 N	77.11 W
Springfield Plateau, plat., Mo., U.S.	130	G5	37.10 N	93.30 W
Springfontein, S. Afr.	90	G7	30.16 S	25.42 E
Spring Garden Brook, stm., N.J., U.S.	194		40.46 N	74.23 W
Spring Glen, Ut., U.S.	150	D6	39.38 N	110.51 W
Spring Green, Wi., U.S.	130	A7	43.10 N	90.04 W
Spring Grove, Mn., U.S.	128	H7	43.33 N	91.38 W
Springhill, N.S., Can.	122	E12	45.39 N	64.03 W
Springhill, La., U.S.	134	D5	33.00 N	93.27 W
Spring Hill, Tn., U.S.	134	B12	35.45 N	86.55 W
Spring Hope, N.C., U.S.	124	I7	35.56 N	78.06 W
Springhouse, B.C., Can.	144	E8	51.55 N	122.07 W
Spring House, Pa., U.S.	203		40.11 N	75.14 W
Spring Lake, N.C., U.S.	132	A7	35.10 N	78.59 W
Spring Lake, l., N.J., U.S.	194		40.35 N	74.25 W
Spring Mill, Pa., U.S.	203		40.04 N	75.17 W
Spring Mill Reservoir, res., Eng., U.K.	180		53.39 N	2.13 W
Spring Mill State Park, p.o.i., In., U.S.	130	F11	38.43 N	86.24 W
Spring Mountains, mts., Nv., U.S.	148	G10	36.19 N	115.43 W
Spring Pond, l., Ma., U.S.	201		42.30 N	70.57 W
Springs, S. Afr.	90	E9	26.15 S	28.26 E
Springs, state, S. Afr.	191d		26.14 S	28.30 E
Springs Aerodrome, arpt., S. Afr.	191d		26.15 S	28.24 E
Springside, N.J., U.S.	203		40.04 N	74.51 W
Springsure, Austl.	98	E7	24.07 S	148.05 E
Springtown, Tx., U.S.	136	A10	32.57 N	97.40 W
Springvale, Austl.	98	D3	23.33 S	140.42 E
Springvale, Me., U.S.	122	G6	43.28 N	70.48 W
Springvale South, Austl.	192b		37.58 S	145.09 E
Spring Valley, Ca., U.S.	148	K9	32.44 N	116.58 W
Spring Valley, Il., U.S.	128	J9	41.19 N	89.11 W
Spring Valley, Mn., U.S.	128	H6	43.41 N	92.24 W
Spring Valley, N.Y., U.S.	124	C11	41.06 N	74.03 W
Spring Valley, Wi., U.S.	128	G6	44.50 N	92.14 W
Spring Valley, val., Nv., U.S.	150	E2	39.15 N	114.25 W
Spring Valley Creek, stm., Nv., U.S.	150	D2	39.20 N	114.26 W
Springview, Ne., U.S.	140	E13	42.48 N	99.44 W
Springville, Al., U.S.	134	D12	33.46 N	86.30 W
Springville, Ca., U.S.	148	G7	36.08 N	118.49 W
Springville, Ia., U.S.	130	B6	42.03 N	91.26 W
Springville, N.J., U.S.	203		39.56 N	74.52 W
Springville, Ut., U.S.	150	C5	40.10 N	111.36 W
Sproat Lake, l., B.C., Can.	144	G5	49.16 N	125.02 W
Sprogels Run, stm., Pa., U.S.	203		40.14 N	75.37 W
Sprout Brook, stm., N.J., U.S.	194		40.54 N	74.05 W
Spruce Grove, Ab., Can.	144	C17	53.32 N	113.55 W
Spruce Knob, mtn., W.V., U.S.	124	F6	38.42 N	79.32 W
Spruce Knob-Seneca Rocks National Recreation Area, p.o.i., W.V., U.S.	124	F6	38.50 N	79.20 W
Spruce Mountain, mtn., Az., U.S.	150	I4	34.28 N	112.23 W
Spruce Mountain, mtn., Nv., U.S.	148	C11	40.33 N	114.49 W
Spruce Pine, Al., U.S.	134	C11	34.23 N	87.44 W
Spruce Pine, N.C., U.S.	124	I3	35.55 N	82.04 W
Spruce Woods Provincial Park, p.o.i., Mb., Can.	142	E14	49.40 N	99.08 W
Spulico, Capo, c., Italy	32	E10	39.57 N	16.37 E
Spur, Tx., U.S.	138	H8	33.28 N	100.51 W
Spurfield, Ab., Can.	144	A16	55.12 N	114.15 W
Spurger, Tx., U.S.	136	D13	30.42 N	94.11 W
Spurn Head, c., Eng., U.K.	10	H13	53.34 N	0.06 E
Sputendorf, Ger.	182a		52.20 N	13.13 E
Spuzzum, B.C., Can.	144	G9	49.39 N	121.25 W
Spy Hill, Sk., Can.	142	D12	50.36 N	101.41 W
Spy Pond, l., Ma., U.S.	201		42.24 N	71.09 W
Squamish, B.C., Can.	144	G7	49.42 N	123.08 W
Squamish, stm., B.C., Can.	144	F7	49.39 N	123.14 W
Squam Lake, l., N.H., U.S.	122	G5	43.45 N	71.32 W
Square Butte Creek, stm., N.D., U.S.	142	H12	46.58 N	100.56 W
Square Lake, l., Me., U.S.	122	D8	47.03 N	68.20 W
Squatec, Qc., Can.	122	C8	47.52 N	68.44 W
Squaw Cap Mountain, mtn., N.B., Can.	122	C10	47.52 N	66.52 W
Squaw Creek, stm., Id., U.S.	146	F10	43.56 N	116.21 W
Squaw Creek, stm., Il., U.S.	196		42.21 N	88.07 W
Squaw Creek, stm., Or., U.S.	146	F5	44.27 N	121.20 W
Squaw Hill, mtn., Wy., U.S.	140	F8	41.48 N	105.02 W
Squaw Island, i., N.Y., U.S.	202a		42.56 N	78.54 W
Squaw Peak, mtn., Mt., U.S.	146	C12	47.10 N	114.21 W
Squaw Run, stm., Pa., U.S.	197b		40.29 N	79.52 W
Squilax, B.C., Can.	144	F11	50.52 N	119.35 W
Squillace, Italy	32	F10	38.47 N	16.31 E
Squillace, Golfo di, b., Italy	32	F10	38.50 N	16.50 E
Squinzano, Italy	32	D12	40.25 N	18.02 E
Squires, Mount, mtn., Austl.	96	E5	26.12 S	127.28 E
Squirrel Hill, ngh., Pa., U.S.	197b		40.26 N	79.55 W
Squirrel Hill Tunnel, trans., Pa., U.S.	197b		40.26 N	79.55 W
Squirrel's Heath, ngh., Eng., U.K.	178		51.35 N	0.13 E
Sragen, Indon.	66	G7	7.25 S	111.02 E
Srbija (Serbia), state, Yugo.	36	E8	44.00 N	21.00 E
Srbobran, Yugo.	36	D6	45.33 N	19.47 E
Srê Âmbĕl, Camb.	64	G6	11.08 N	103.46 E
Sredec, Blg.	36	G14	42.21 N	27.11 E
Sredinnyj hrebet, mts., Russia	50	E20	56.00 N	158.00 E
Sredna Gora, mts., Blg.	36	G11	42.33 N	24.24 E
Srednee Kujto, ozero, l., Russia	18	B19	65.08 N	31.15 E
Srednegore, Russia	18	G16	60.34 N	29.26 E
Srednekolymsk, Russia	50	C19	67.27 N	153.40 E
Srednerusskaja vozvyšennost' (Central Russian Upland), plat., Russia	40	F11	52.00 N	38.00 E
Srednesibirskoe ploskogor'e (Central Siberian Uplands), plat., Russia	50	C10	65.00 N	105.00 E
Srednij Egorlyk, Russia	40	H12	46.21 N	40.49 E
Srednij Ural, mts., Russia	48	C9	58.00 N	59.00 E
Srednij Vasjugan, Russia	48	C13	59.13 N	78.15 E
Srednjaja Olëkma, Russia	50	E13	55.25 N	120.33 E
Srednogorie, Blg.	36	G11	42.44 N	24.10 E
Srê Khtŭm, Camb.	64	F8	12.12 N	106.52 E
Śrem, Pol.	24	D13	52.04 N	17.01 E
Srê Moăt, Camb.	64	F8	13.17 N	107.09 E
Sremska Mitrovica, Yugo.	36	E6	44.58 N	19.36 E
Sremski Karlovci, Yugo.	36	D6	45.12 N	19.56 E
Srêng, stm., Camb.	64	F6	13.20 N	103.31 E
Srêpôk, stm., Camb.	64	F8	13.32 N	106.17 E
Sretensk, Russia	50	F12	52.14 N	117.42 E
Sri Aman, Malay.	66	C7	1.13 N	111.27 E
Sri Jayawardenepura (Kotte), Sri L.	69	H4	6.53 N	79.54 E
Srīkākulam, India	69	B6	18.17 N	83.54 E
Sri Kālahasti, India	69	E4	13.45 N	79.42 E
Sri Lanka, ctry., Asia	69	G5	7.00 N	81.00 E
Sri Lanka, i., Sri L.	4	F18	7.00 N	81.00 E
Srīnagar, India	70	A5	34.05 N	74.48 E
Srīpur, Bngl.	70	F13	24.12 N	90.28 E
Srīrampur, India	69	B2	19.35 N	74.30 E
Srirāmpur, India	190b		22.49 N	88.29 E
Srīrangam, India	69	F4	10.51 N	78.42 E
Srīvardhan, India	69	B1	18.03 N	73.01 E
Srīvilliputtūr, India	69	G3	9.30 N	77.38 E
Środa Śląska, Pol.	24	E12	51.10 N	16.36 E
Środa Wielkopolska, Pol.	24	D13	52.13 N	17.17 E
Srpska Crnja, Yugo.	36	D7	45.43 N	20.42 E
Ssangmun-ni, ngh., Kor., S.	189b		37.39 N	127.02 E
Staaten, stm., Austl.	96	C8	16.23 S	141.18 E
Stabbursdalen Nasjonalpark, p.o.i., Nor.	14	B14	70.06 N	24.30 E
Stacksteads, Eng., U.K.	180		53.41 N	2.13 W

Name	Page	Map Ref.	Latitude	Longitude
Stacyville, Ia., U.S.	128	H6	43.26 N	92.46 W
Stade, Ger.	24	C5	53.36 N	9.28 E
Stadhavet, strt., Nor.	16	E2	62.14 N	5.03 E
Stadil Fjord, l., Den.	16	K6	56.10 N	8.13 E
Stadion am Zoo, p.o.i., Ger.	181		51.14 N	7.07 E
Städjan, mtn., Swe.	16	F10	61.55 N	12.52 E
Stadlandet, pen., Nor.	16	E3	62.07 N	5.18 E
Stadlau, ngh., Aus.	182b		48.14 N	16.28 E
Stadl-Paura, Aus.	30	B10	48.04 N	13.52 E
Stadoličy, Bela.	38	B7	51.43 N	28.28 E
Stadskanaal, Neth.	20	A16	52.59 N	6.57 E
Stadtallendorf, Ger.	24	F5	50.50 N	9.01 E
Städtische Rahmede, Ger.	181		51.17 N	7.40 E
Stadtoldendorf, Ger.	24	E5	51.52 N	9.37 E
Staffelde, Ger.	182a		52.44 N	13.00 E
Staffelsee, l., Ger.	30	C7	47.41 N	11.10 E
Staffelstein, Ger.	24	F7	50.06 N	11.00 E
Stafford, Eng., U.K.	10	I10	52.48 N	2.07 W
Stafford, Ks., U.S.	138	D10	37.57 N	98.36 W
Stafford, Va., U.S.	124	F8	38.25 N	77.24 W
Stafford Springs, Ct., U.S.	124	C13	41.57 N	72.18 W
Staffordsville, Ky., U.S.	130	G15	37.49 N	82.50 W
Stagen, Indon.	66	E10	3.18 S	116.10 E
Stag Pond, l., N.J., U.S.	194		40.59 N	74.42 W
Stahl-Berg, hill, Ger.	182a		52.21 N	13.46 E
Staicele, Lat.	26	C7	57.49 N	24.45 E
Staiky, Ukr.	38	C9	50.04 N	30.54 E
Staines, Eng., U.K.	10	J12	51.26 N	0.31 W
Staines Reservoirs, res., Eng., U.K.	178		51.27 N	0.30 W
Stainland, Eng., U.K.	180		53.40 N	1.53 W
Stains, Fr.	179		48.57 N	2.23 E
Staked Plain see Estacado, Llano, pl., U.S.	138	H6	33.30 N	102.40 W
Stakhanov, Ukr.	38	E17	48.34 N	38.40 E
Stalać, Yugo.	36	F8	43.39 N	21.23 E
Stalin see Kuçovë, Alb.	32	D13	40.47 N	19.55 E
Stalin see Varna, Blg.	36	F14	43.13 N	27.54 E
Stalin see Brașov, Rom.	36	D12	45.39 N	25.37 E
Stalin see Donets'k, Ukr.	38	F16	47.59 N	37.47 E
Stalinabad see Dušanbe, Taj.	72	B10	38.34 N	68.46 E
Stalingrad see Volgograd, Russia	40	G14	48.44 N	44.25 E
Stalino see Donets'k, Ukr.	38	F16	47.59 N	37.47 E
Stalinogorsk see Novomoskovsk, Russia	26	F21	54.05 N	38.12 E
Stalinsk see Novokuzneck, Russia	48	D15	53.44 N	87.07 E
Ställdalen, Swe.	16	H12	59.56 N	14.57 E
Stallworthy, Cape, c., Nu., Can.	108	A7	81.23 N	93.30 W
Stalowa Wola, Pol.	24	F18	50.35 N	22.03 E
Stambaugh, Mi., U.S.	128	E10	46.04 N	88.37 W
Stamford, Austl.	98	C4	21.15 S	143.49 E
Stamford, Eng., U.K.	10	I12	52.39 N	0.29 W
Stamford, Ct., U.S.	124	C12	41.03 N	73.32 W
Stamford, N.Y., U.S.	124	B11	42.24 N	74.37 W
Stamford, Tx., U.S.	136	B8	32.55 N	99.48 W
Stamford, Lake, res., Tx., U.S.	136	A8	33.02 N	99.36 W
Stamford Brige Stadium, p.o.i., Eng., U.K.	178		51.29 N	0.11 W
Stamford Harbor, b., Ct., U.S.	194		41.02 N	73.32 W
Stamford Museum, bldg., Ct., U.S.	194		41.07 N	73.33 W
Stammersdorf, ngh., Aus.	182b		48.18 N	16.25 E
Stampriet, Nmb.	90	D4	24.20 S	18.20 E
Stamps, Ar., U.S.	134	D5	33.22 N	93.29 W
Stamsund, Nor.	14	D4	68.08 N	13.51 E
Stanaford, W.V., U.S.	124	G4	37.49 N	81.09 W
Stanardsville, Va., U.S.	124	F7	38.17 N	78.26 W
Stanberry, Mo., U.S.	130	D3	40.13 N	94.32 W
Stanborough, Eng., U.K.	178		51.47 N	0.13 W
Stancionno-Ojašinskij, Russia	48	C14	55.28 N	83.48 E
Standard, Ab., Can.	144	E18	51.06 N	112.58 W
Standard Oil Company Refinery, sci., Ca., U.S.	200		37.57 N	122.24 W
Standard Shaft, Pa., U.S.	197b		40.10 N	79.32 W
Standedge Canal Tunnel, trans., Eng., U.K.	180		53.34 N	2.00 W
Standedge Railway Tunnel, trans., Eng., U.K.	180		53.34 N	2.00 W
Standerton, S. Afr.	90	E9	26.57 S	29.14 E
Standing Rock Indian Reservation, ind. res., U.S.	140	B11	45.50 N	101.10 W
Standing Stone State Park, p.o.i., Tn., U.S.	130	H12	36.26 N	85.24 W
Standish, Mi., U.S.	126	E6	43.58 N	83.57 W
Standish Monument, hist., Ma., U.S.	201		42.01 N	70.41 W
Stanfield, Az., U.S.	150	K5	32.52 N	111.56 W
Stanfield, Or., U.S.	146	E7	45.45 N	119.11 W
Stanford, Ky., U.S.	130	G13	37.31 N	84.40 W
Stanford, Mt., U.S.	146	C16	47.09 N	110.13 W
Stanford Center, shp. cen., Ca., U.S.	200		37.27 N	122.10 W
Stanford Linear Accelerator, sci., Ca., U.S.	200		37.25 N	122.12 W
Stanford Rivers, Eng., U.K.	178		51.41 N	0.13 E
Stanford University, educ., Ca., U.S.	200		37.26 N	122.10 W
Stånga, Swe.	16	J16	57.15 N	18.28 E
Stange, Nor.	16	G9	60.43 N	11.11 E
Stanger, S. Afr.	90	F10	29.25 S	31.14 E
Stanhope, Ia., U.S.	130	B4	42.17 N	93.47 W
Stanislaus, stm., Ca., U.S.	148	F5	37.39 N	121.14 W
Stanislaus, Middle Fork, stm., Ca., U.S.	148	E6	38.09 N	120.21 W
Stanislaus, North Fork, stm., Ca., U.S.	148	E5	38.09 N	120.21 W
Stanislav, Ukr.	38	G11	46.34 N	32.08 E
Stanislav see Ivano-Frankivs'k, Ukr.	38	E3	48.55 N	24.43 E
Stanislavchyk, Ukr.	38	E7	48.58 N	28.06 E
Stanisławów see Ivano-Frankivs'k, Ukr.	38	E3	48.55 N	24.43 E
Stânișoara, Munții, mts., Rom.	36	B13	47.11 N	25.57 E
Stanley, Austl.	99a	n12	40.45 S	145.16 E
Stanley, N.B., Can.	122	D10	46.17 N	66.43 W
Stanley, China	189d		22.13 N	114.12 E
Stanley, Falk. Is.	166	J5	51.42 S	57.49 W
Stanley, N.C., U.S.	132	A4	35.21 N	81.05 W
Stanley, N.D., U.S.	142	F11	48.19 N	102.23 W
Stanley, Va., U.S.	124	F7	38.33 N	78.31 W
Stanley, Wi., U.S.	128	G8	44.57 N	90.55 W
Stanley, Mont, hill, D.R.C.	191b		4.19 S	15.15 E
Stanley Bay, b., China	189d		22.12 N	114.12 E
Stanley Falls, wtfl., D.R.C.	86	D4	0.28 N	25.13 E
Stanley Mills, On., Can.	193b		43.46 N	79.44 W
Stanley Mound, mtn., China	189d		22.14 N	114.12 E
Stanley Park, p.o.i., Eng., U.K.	180		53.49 N	3.02 W
Stanley Park, p.o.i., Eng., U.K.	180		53.26 N	2.57 W
Stanley Reservoir, res., India	69	F3	11.53 N	77.51 E
Stanleyville see Kisangani, D.R.C.	86	D5	0.31 N	25.11 E
Stanmore, ngh., Eng., U.K.	178		51.37 N	0.19 W
Stanovoe nagor'e, mts., Russia	50	E11	56.00 N	114.00 E
Stanovoj hrebet, mts., Russia	50	E14	55.48 N	125.34 E
Stanovoj Kolodez', Russia	26	H19	52.50 N	36.14 E
Stanovoy Mountains see Stanovoe nagor'e, mts., Russia	50	E11	56.00 N	114.00 E
Stansted, Eng., U.K.	178		51.20 N	0.18 E
Stanthorpe, Austl.	98	G8	28.39 S	151.55 E
Stanton, Ia., U.S.	130	D2	40.59 N	95.08 W
Stanton, Ky., U.S.	124	G2	37.50 N	83.54 W
Stanton, Mi., U.S.	126	E4	43.17 N	85.04 W
Stanton, Ne., U.S.	140	F15	41.57 N	97.13 W
Stanton, N.D., U.S.	142	G12	47.19 N	101.23 W
Stanton, Tn., U.S.	134	B9	35.28 N	89.24 W
Stanton, Tx., U.S.	136	B6	32.07 N	101.47 W
Stantonsburg, N.C., U.S.	132	A8	35.36 N	77.49 W
Stanwell, Eng., U.K.	178		51.27 N	0.29 W
Stanwell Moor, Eng., U.K.	178		51.28 N	0.30 W
Stanwood, Wa., U.S.	146	B4	48.14 N	122.22 W
Stanwyck Estates, De., U.S.	203		39.42 N	75.33 W
Stanychno-Luhans'ke, Ukr.	38	E18	48.39 N	39.29 E
Stapleford Abbotts, Eng., U.K.	178		51.38 N	0.10 E
Stapleford Aerodrome, arpt., Eng., U.K.	178		51.39 N	0.08 E
Stapleford Tawney, Eng., U.K.	178		51.40 N	0.11 E
Staples, Mn., U.S.	128	E4	46.21 N	94.48 W
Stapleton, Al., U.S.	134	G11	30.44 N	87.47 W
Stapleton, Ne., U.S.	140	F12	41.29 N	100.30 W
Staporków, Pol.	24	E16	51.09 N	20.33 E
Star', Russia	26	G17	53.36 N	34.09 E
Star, Ms., U.S.	134	E8	32.05 N	90.02 W
Star, N.C., U.S.	132	A6	35.24 N	79.46 W
Stará Boleslav see Brandýs nad Labem-Stará Boleslav, Czech Rep.	24	F10	50.11 N	14.39 E
Starachowice, Pol.	24	E17	51.03 N	21.04 E
Staraja, Russia	183a		59.55 N	30.38 E
Staraja Belica, Bela.	26	F12	54.42 N	29.38 E
Staraja Belica, Russia	40	F9	51.59 N	35.13 E
Staraja Derevn'a, ngh., Russia	183a		59.59 N	30.15 E
Staraja Majna, Russia	40	D16	54.35 N	48.55 E
Staraja Rudnja, Bela.	26	H13	52.50 N	30.17 E
Staraja Russa, Russia	26	B14	57.59 N	31.21 E
Staraja Toropa, Russia	26	D14	56.17 N	31.39 E
Staraja Veduga, Russia	38	B17	51.48 N	38.29 E
Stara Maiachka, Ukr.	38	G12	46.31 N	33.10 E
Stara Pazova, Yugo.	36	D7	44.59 N	20.10 E
Stara Planina see Balkan Mountains, mts., Eur.	36	F10	42.45 N	25.00 E
Stara Syniava, Ukr.	38	D6	49.36 N	27.37 E
Stara Ushytsia, Ukr.	38	E6	48.34 N	27.08 E
Stara Vyzhivka, Ukr.	38	B3	51.26 N	24.26 E
Stara Zagora, Blg.	36	G12	42.25 N	25.38 E
Starbeevo, Russia	183b		55.58 N	37.28 E
Starbuck, Mb., Can.	142	E16	49.45 N	97.37 W
Starbuck, Mn., U.S.	128	F3	45.36 N	95.31 W
Starbuck, Wa., U.S.	146	D8	46.30 N	118.07 W
Starbuck, i., Kir.	94	D11	5.37 S	155.53 W
Starchenkove, Ukr.	38	F16	47.16 N	36.58 E
Star City, Sk., Can.	142	B9	52.52 N	104.19 W
Star City, Ar., U.S.	134	D7	33.56 N	91.50 W
Star City, In., U.S.	126	H3	40.58 N	86.33 W
Stargard in Pommern see Stargard Szczeciński, Pol.	24	C11	53.19 N	15.02 E
Stargard Szczeciński, Pol.	24	C11	53.19 N	15.02 E
Stargo, Az., U.S.	150	J7	33.03 N	109.22 W
Star Harbour, b., Sol. Is.	101b	f10	10.47 S	162.18 E
Starica, Russia	26	D17	56.30 N	34.55 E
Starica, Russia	26	A12	59.03 N	29.29 E
Stari Grad, Cro.	30	G13	43.11 N	16.36 E
Starij Rjad, Russia	26	B17	58.05 N	34.54 E
Stari Popyliukhy, Ukr.	38	E17	48.17 N	28.55 E
Stari Sanzhary, Ukr.	38	D13	49.24 N	34.28 E
Stari Vlah, reg., Yugo.	36	F6	43.35 N	20.15 E
Starke, Fl., U.S.	132	G3	29.57 N	82.06 W
Starkville, Ms., U.S.	134	D10	33.27 N	88.49 W
Starnberg, Ger.	24	H7	47.59 N	11.20 E
Starnberger See, l., Ger.	24	I7	47.54 N	11.18 E
Starobaltačevo, Russia	40	C19	56.00 N	55.56 E
Starobesheve, Ukr.	38	F17	47.44 N	38.01 E
Starobil's'k, Ukr.	38	D17	49.16 N	38.55 E
Starobin, Bela.	26	H10	52.42 N	27.27 E
Starodub, Russia	26	H15	52.35 N	32.46 E
Staroe Drožžanoe, Russia	40	D15	54.43 N	47.32 E
Staroe Rahino, Russia	26	B15	58.07 N	32.39 E
Starogard Gdański, Pol.	24	C14	53.58 N	18.32 E
Staroje Sjalo, Bela.	26	E13	55.13 N	29.53 E
Starokostiantyniv, Ukr.	38	D6	49.45 N	27.13 E
Starokozache, Ukr.	38	G8	46.20 N	29.59 E
Staromar'evka, Russia	40	I13	45.05 N	42.11 E
Starominskaja, Russia	40	H11	46.31 N	39.02 E
Staromlynivka, Ukr.	38	F15	47.41 N	36.49 E
Starošcerbinovskaja, Russia	38	G17	46.37 N	38.40 E
Starosubhangulovo, Russia	40	E20	53.06 N	57.26 E
Starotimoškino, Russia	40	E15	53.42 N	47.30 E
Staroutkinsk, Russia	40	C21	57.13 N	59.20 E
Starovirivka, Ukr.	38	D14	49.33 N	35.41 E
Star Peak, mtn., Nv., U.S.	148	C7	40.32 N	118.10 W
Start Point, c., Eng., U.K.	10	K9	50.13 N	3.39 W
Starvation Reservoir, res., Ut., U.S.	150	C6	40.12 N	110.27 W
Staryi Chortoryis'k, Ukr.	38	B4	51.13 N	25.53 E
Staryi Krym, Ukr.	38	I14	45.01 N	35.05 E
Staryi Krym, Ukr.	38	F16	47.09 N	37.32 E
Staryi Sambir, Ukr.	38	D2	49.26 N	23.00 E
Staryja Darohi, Bela.	26	H11	53.03 N	28.15 E
Staryj Birjuzjak, Russia	42	I15	44.48 N	46.55 E
Staryj Bol'ševik, Russia	183b		55.57 N	37.47 E
Staryj Lesken, Russia	42	D11	43.21 N	43.59 E
Staryj Medved', Russia	26	B13	58.17 N	30.29 E
Staryj Oskol, Russia	40	F10	51.18 N	37.50 E
Starý Plzenec, Czech Rep.	24	G9	49.41 N	13.28 E
Stary Sącz, Pol.	24	G16	49.33 N	20.38 E
Stassfurt, Ger.	24	E7	51.51 N	11.35 E
Staszów, Pol.	24	F17	50.34 N	21.19 E
State Art Gallery, bldg., Russia	183b		55.44 N	37.36 E
State Center, Ia., U.S.	130	C4	42.01 N	93.09 W
State College, Pa., U.S.	124	D8	40.47 N	77.51 W
State Fair Grounds, p.o.i., Md., U.S.	202b		39.27 N	76.38 W
State Line, Ms., U.S.	134	F10	31.26 N	88.28 W
Stateline, Nv., U.S.	148	E6	38.57 N	119.56 W
Staten Island see Estados, Isla de los, i., Arg.	166	J4	54.48 S	64.32 W
Staten Island, i., N.Y., U.S.	194		40.35 N	74.09 W
Staten Island Mall, shp. cen., N.Y., U.S.	194		40.35 N	74.10 W
Statenville, Ga., U.S.	132	F2	30.42 N	83.01 W
State Road, N.C., U.S.	124	H5	36.19 N	80.51 W
Statesboro, Ga., U.S.	132	D4	32.26 N	81.47 W
Statesville, N.C., U.S.	124	I5	35.46 N	80.53 W
Stateville Correctional Center, bldg., Il., U.S.	196		41.35 N	88.06 W
Statue Park Museum, bldg., Hung.	182c		47.25 N	18.59 E
Staŭbun, Bela.	26	H14	52.48 N	31.25 E
Staunton, Il., U.S.	130	E8	39.00 N	89.47 W
Staunton, Va., U.S.	124	F6	38.09 N	79.04 W
Staunton see Roanoke, stm., U.S.	124	H8	35.57 N	76.42 W
Stavanger, Nor.	16	I3	58.58 N	5.45 E
Stave Lake, l., B.C., Can.	144	G8	49.22 N	122.17 W
Stavely, Ab., Can.	144	F17	50.09 N	113.39 W
Staveren, Neth.	20	B14	52.53 N	5.22 E
Stavern, Nor.	16	I8	58.59 N	10.01 E
Stavne, Ukr.	24	G18	49.00 N	22.39 E
Stavropol see Tol'jatti, Russia	40	E16	53.32 N	49.25 E
Stavropol', Russia	40	I12	45.02 N	41.59 E
Stavropol'skaja vozvyšennost', mts., Russia	42	C10	44.58 N	42.54 E
Stavropol'skij kraj, co., Russia	42	C10	44.30 N	43.30 E
Stavyshche, Ukr.	38	D9	49.23 N	30.11 E
Stawell, Austl.	98	K4	37.03 S	142.45 E
Stawell, stm., Austl.	98	C4	20.38 S	142.55 E
Stawiski, Pol.	24	C18	53.23 N	22.09 E
Stawiszyn, Pol.	24	E14	51.55 N	18.06 E
Stayner, On., Can.	126	D9	44.24 N	80.04 W
Stayton, Or., U.S.	146	F4	44.47 N	122.47 W
Steamboat Mountain, mtn., Wy., U.S.	150	A8	41.58 N	108.58 W
Steamboat Springs, Co., U.S.	150	C10	40.29 N	106.50 W
Stearns, Ky., U.S.	130	H13	36.41 N	84.28 W
Stearns Pond, l., Ma., U.S.	201		42.37 N	71.04 W
Stębark, Pol.	24	C16	53.30 N	20.08 E
Steel, stm., On., Can.	128	B12	48.46 N	86.53 W
Steele, Mo., U.S.	130	H8	36.05 N	89.50 W
Steele, N.D., U.S.	142	H14	46.51 N	99.54 W
Steele, ngh., Ger.	181		51.27 N	7.05 E
Steele, Mount, mtn., Wy., U.S.	150	B9	41.50 N	107.00 W
Steeles Corners, On., Can.	193b		43.48 N	79.25 W
Steeleville, Il., U.S.	130	G8	38.00 N	89.39 W
Steels Point, c., Norf. I.	100i	y25	29.01 S	167.59 E
Steels Run, stm., Pa., U.S.	197b		40.25 N	79.38 W
Steelton, N.Y., U.S.	202a		42.47 N	78.49 W
Steelville, Mo., U.S.	130	G6	37.58 N	91.22 W
Steensby Inlet, b., Nu., Can.	110	A15	70.15 N	78.35 W
Steens Mountain, mts., Or., U.S.	146	H8	42.35 N	118.40 W
Steenwijk, Neth.	20	B15	52.47 N	6.07 E
Steep Rock, Mb., Can.	142	C15	51.26 N	98.48 W
Stefanie, Lake, l., Afr.	82	G7	4.40 N	36.50 E
Stefansson Island, i., Nu., Can.	110	A9	73.20 N	105.45 W
Ștefan Vodă, Rom.	36	E14	44.18 N	27.19 E
Stegalovka, Russia	26	H21	52.24 N	38.19 E
Stege, Den.	16	M10	54.59 N	12.17 E
Stegeborg, Swe.	16	I14	58.26 N	16.34 E
Steglitz, ngh., Ger.	182a		52.28 N	13.19 E
Stehekin, Wa., U.S.	146	B6	48.18 N	120.39 W
Ștei, Rom.	36	C9	46.32 N	22.28 E
Steiermark, state, Aus.	30	C12	47.10 N	15.10 E
Steinach, Aus.	30	C8	47.05 N	11.28 E
Steinamanger see Szombathely, Hung.	36	B3	47.14 N	16.38 E
Steinbach, Mb., Can.	142	E17	49.31 N	96.41 W
Steinberg, hill, Ger.	181		51.05 N	7.27 E
Steinberger Slough, stm., Ca., U.S.	200		37.33 N	122.13 W
Steinfjellet, mtn., Nor.	16	B11	65.01 N	13.24 E
Steinfurth, Ger.	181		51.09 N	6.32 E
Steinfurt, Ger.	24	D3	52.09 N	7.20 E
Steinhatchee, stm., Fl., U.S.	132	G2	29.40 N	83.24 W
Steinhausen, Nmb.	90	B4	21.48 S	18.17 E
Steinkjer, Nor.	16	C9	64.01 N	11.28 E
Steinkopf, S. Afr.	90	F3	29.18 S	17.43 E
Steinshamn, Nor.	16	E4	62.46 N	6.28 E
Steinstücken, ngh., Ger.	182a		52.23 N	13.08 E
Steklino, Russia	26	D15	56.51 N	32.09 E
Stekljanka, Russia	40	B12	59.07 N	41.36 E
Stella, S. Afr.	90	E7	26.33 S	24.52 E
Stella, Ne., U.S.	128	K3	40.13 N	95.46 W
Stellaquo Indian Reserve, ind. res., B.C., Can.	144	C6	54.03 N	124.55 W
Stellarton, N.S., Can.	122	E14	45.33 N	62.39 W
Stellenbosch, S. Afr.	90	H4	33.55 S	18.51 E
Stelvio, Parco Nazionale dello, p.o.i., Italy	30	D7	46.30 N	10.36 E
Stelvio, Passo dello, p., Italy	30	D7	46.32 N	10.27 E
Stenay, Fr.	20	E14	49.29 N	5.11 E
Stendal, Ger.	24	D7	52.36 N	11.51 E
Stende, Lat.	26	C5	57.08 N	22.32 E
Stenden, Ger.	181		51.25 N	6.27 E
Stenó, Grc.	185c		37.58 N	23.25 E
Stenón Návstathmou, strt., Grc.	185c		37.58 N	23.33 E
Stensele, Swe.	16	B15	65.04 N	17.08 E
Stenstorp, Swe.	16	I11	58.16 N	13.43 E
Stenstrup, Den.	16	L8	55.07 N	10.30 E
Stentrop, Ger.	181		51.30 N	7.49 E
Stenungsund, Swe.	16	I9	58.04 N	11.49 E
Step', Ukr.	38	B5	51.08 N	26.19 E
Stepanakert see Xankändi, Azer.	42	F12	39.48 N	46.45 E
Stepanavan, Arm.	42	E11	40.59 N	44.23 E
Stepancevo, Russia	40	C12	56.08 N	41.42 E
Stepanivka, Ukr.	38	C13	50.58 N	34.37 E
Stepanovskoe, Russia	183b		55.47 N	37.10 E
Stephans-Dom, rel., Aus.	182b		48.12 N	16.23 E
Stephen, Mn., U.S.	128	C2	48.26 N	96.52 W
Stephens, Ar., U.S.	134	D5	33.25 N	93.04 W
Stephens, Port, b., Austl.	98	I9	32.43 S	152.05 E
Stephens City, Va., U.S.	124	E7	39.05 N	78.13 W
Stephens Creek, Austl.	98	H3	31.50 S	141.30 E
Stephens Knob, hill, Ky., U.S.	124	H1	36.37 N	84.20 W
Stephens Lake, res., Mb., Can.	110	D11	56.26 N	95.07 W
Stephenson, Mi., U.S.	126	C2	45.25 N	87.36 W
Stephenville, Nf., Can.	111a	j22	48.33 N	58.36 W
Stephenville, Tx., U.S.	136	B9	32.13 N	98.12 W
Stepney, ngh., Eng., U.K.	178		51.31 N	0.02 W
Stepnjak, Kaz.	48	D12	52.49 N	70.47 E
Stepnoe, Russia	42	C11	44.16 N	44.34 E
Step Pyramid see Saqqâra, Pyramides de, hist., Egypt	76	I1	29.52 N	31.13 E
Step Pyramid see Saqqâra, Pyramids of, hist., Egypt	191c		29.52 N	31.13 E
Steptoe Valley, val., Nv., U.S.	150	D2	39.29 N	114.47 W
Stepurino, Russia	26	D18	56.22 N	35.17 E
Sterdyń, Pol.	24	D18	52.35 N	22.18 E
Steréa Elláda, state, Grc.	34	E5	38.30 N	23.00 E
Sterkrade, ngh., Ger.	181		51.31 N	6.51 E
Sterkstroom, S. Afr.	90	G8	31.32 S	26.33 E
Sterlibaševo, Russia	40	E19	53.26 N	55.15 E
Sterling, Co., U.S.	140	G9	40.37 N	103.12 W
Sterling, Il., U.S.	130	C8	41.47 N	89.41 W
Sterling, Ks., U.S.	138	C10	38.12 N	98.11 W
Sterling, Mi., U.S.	126	D5	44.02 N	84.01 W
Sterling, Ne., U.S.	130	D1	40.27 N	96.23 W
Sterling, Ok., U.S.	138	G10	34.44 N	98.10 W
Sterling City, Tx., U.S.	136	C7	31.50 N	101.00 W
Sterling Forest Lake, l., N.Y., U.S.	194		41.10 N	74.16 W
Sterling Park, Ca., U.S.	200		37.41 N	122.26 W
Sterlington, La., U.S.	134	E6	32.41 N	92.04 W
Sterlitamak, Russia	40	E19	53.36 N	55.57 E
Šternberk, Czech Rep.	24	G13	49.44 N	17.17 E
Sterzing see Vipiteno, Italy	30	D8	46.54 N	11.26 E
Stęszew, Pol.	24	D12	52.16 N	16.41 E
Stetson Pond, l., Ma., U.S.	201		42.02 N	70.50 W
Stettin see Szczecin, Pol.	24	C10	53.26 N	14.32 E
Stettiner Haff see Stettin Lagoon, b., Eur.	24	C10	53.47 N	14.22 E
Stettin Lagoon, b., Eur.	24	C10	53.47 N	14.22 E
Stettler, Ab., Can.	144	D18	52.19 N	112.43 W
Steubenville, Oh., U.S.	124	D5	40.22 N	80.37 W
Stevenage, Eng., U.K.	10	J12	51.54 N	0.13 W
Stevens, N.J., U.S.	203		40.05 N	74.49 W
Stevens Creek, stm., Ca., U.S.	200		37.26 N	122.05 W
Stevens Creek, stm., S.C., U.S.	132	C3	33.34 N	82.03 W
Stevens Creek Park, p.o.i., Ca., U.S.	200		37.17 N	122.04 W
Stevens Creek Reservoir, res., Ca., U.S.	200		37.17 N	122.05 W
Stevens Institute of Technology, educ., N.J., U.S.	194		40.44 N	74.02 W
Stevenson, Al., U.S.	134	C13	34.52 N	85.50 W
Stevenson, Md., U.S.	202b		39.25 N	76.43 W
Stevenson, Wa., U.S.	146	E5	45.42 N	121.53 W
Stevenson Entrance, strt., Ak., U.S.	109	E9	58.44 N	152.14 W
Stevens Pass, p., Wa., U.S.	146	C5	47.45 N	121.04 W
Stevens Peak, mtn., Id., U.S.	146	C11	47.27 N	115.46 W
Stevens Point, Wi., U.S.	128	G9	44.31 N	89.34 W
Stevensville, On., Can.	202a		42.57 N	79.04 W
Stevensville, Mi., U.S.	130	B11	42.00 N	86.30 W
Stevensville, Mt., U.S.	146	D12	46.30 N	114.05 W
Stevns Klint, clf., Den.	16	L10	55.18 N	12.27 E
Stewardson, Il., U.S.	130	E9	39.15 N	88.37 W
Stewart, B.C., Can.	110	D4	55.55 N	129.57 W
Stewart, Mn., U.S.	128	G4	44.43 N	94.29 W
Stewart, stm., Yk., Can.	110	C3	63.17 N	139.23 W
Stewart, Isla, i., Chile	166	J2	54.51 S	71.12 W
Stewart, Mount, mtn., Austl.	98	C5	20.12 S	145.29 E
Stewart Island, i., N.Z.	102	H3	47.00 S	167.50 E
Stewart Manor, N.Y., U.S.	194		40.43 N	73.41 W
Stewartstown, Pa., U.S.	124	E9	39.45 N	76.35 W
Stewartsville, Mo., U.S.	130	E3	39.45 N	94.29 W
Stewartsville, Pa., U.S.	197b		40.21 N	79.46 W
Stewart Valley, Sk., Can.	142	D6	50.36 N	107.50 W
Stewartville, Mn., U.S.	128	H6	43.51 N	92.30 W
Stewiacke, N.S., Can.	122	E13	45.08 N	63.22 W
Steynsburg, S. Afr.	90	G7	31.16 S	25.50 E
Steyr, Aus.	30	B11	48.02 N	14.25 E
Steyr, stm., Aus.	30	C11	48.02 N	14.25 E
Steytlerville, S. Afr.	90	H7	33.20 S	24.20 E
Štiavnické vrchy, mts., Slvk.	24	H14	48.28 N	18.50 E
Stickle Pond, l., N.J., U.S.	194		40.59 N	74.25 W
Stickney, S.D., U.S.	140	D14	43.35 N	98.26 W
Stiene, Lat.	26	C7	57.26 N	24.34 E
Stienitzfliess, stm., Ger.	182a		52.33 N	13.43 E
Stienitzsee, l., Ger.	182a		52.30 N	13.49 E
Stiepel, ngh., Ger.	181		51.25 N	7.15 E
Stif, Alg.	84	B6	36.11 N	5.24 E
Stiftskirche, rel., Ger.	181		51.23 N	7.00 E
Stigler, Ok., U.S.	134	B3	35.15 N	95.07 W
Stigliano, Italy	32	D10	40.23 N	16.14 E
Stigtomta, Swe.	16	I14	58.48 N	16.47 E
Stih, hora, mtn., Ukr.	38	E2	48.37 N	23.11 E
Stikine, stm., N.A.	110	D4	56.41 N	132.14 W
Stikine Ranges, mts., B.C., Can.	110	D4	58.43 N	130.00 W
Stilbaai, S. Afr.	90	I5	34.22 S	21.24 E
Stiles Pond, l., Ma., U.S.	201		42.41 N	71.02 W
Stilfontein, S. Afr.	90	E8	26.50 S	26.48 E
Stillhouse Hollow Lake, res., Tx., U.S.	136	D10	31.01 N	97.35 W
Stillmore, Ga., U.S.	132	D3	32.26 N	82.12 W
Still Run, stm., N.J., U.S.	203		39.49 N	75.18 W
Stillwater, B.C., Can.	144	G6	49.46 N	124.18 W
Stillwater, Mn., U.S.	128	F6	45.03 N	92.48 W
Stillwater, Ok., U.S.	134	A1	36.07 N	97.04 W
Stillwater, stm., Mt., U.S.	140	B3	45.38 N	109.17 W
Stillwater Range, mts., Nv., U.S.	148	D7	39.52 N	118.06 W
Stillwell, Ok., U.S.	130	I3	35.49 N	94.37 W
Stilo, Punta, c., Italy	32	F10	38.27 N	16.34 E
Stimberg, hill, Ger.	181		51.40 N	7.15 E
Stimson, Mount, mtn., Mt., U.S.	146	B13	48.31 N	113.36 W
Stînca-Costești, Lacul, res., Eur.	36	A13	47.53 N	27.13 E
Stine Mountain, mtn., Mt., U.S.	146	E13	45.44 N	113.07 W
Stinking Water Creek, stm., Ne., U.S.	140	G11	40.22 N	101.06 W
Stinnett, Tx., U.S.	138	F7	35.49 N	101.26 W
Stintonville, S. Afr.	191d		26.14 S	28.13 E
Štip, Mac.	34	B5	41.44 N	22.11 E
Stirling, Austl.	96	D6	21.44 S	133.45 E
Stirling, Austl.	96	F3	31.53 S	115.47 E
Stirling, Ab., Can.	144	G18	49.30 N	112.30 W
Stirling, On., Can.	126	D12	44.17 N	77.33 W
Stirling, Scot., U.K.	10	E9	56.07 N	3.55 W
Stirling City, Ca., U.S.	148	D4	39.54 N	121.31 W
Stirrat, W.V., U.S.	130	G15	37.43 N	82.00 W
Stittsville, On., Can.	126	C14	45.14 N	75.54 W
Stjernøya, i., Nor.	14	B13	70.18 N	22.45 E
Stjernsundet, strt., Nor.	14	B13	70.14 N	22.40 E
Stjørdalshalsen, Nor.	16	D8	63.28 N	10.55 E
Stobi, hist., Mac.	34	B4	41.32 N	21.57 E
Stock, Eng., U.K.	178		51.40 N	0.27 E
Stockach, Ger.	24	I5	47.50 N	9.00 E
Stockbridge, Ga., U.S.	132	C1	33.32 N	84.13 W
Stockbridge, Mi., U.S.	124	B1	42.26 N	84.10 W
Stockbridge Indian Reservation, ind. res., Wi., U.S.	128	G9	44.54 N	88.52 W
Stockbury, Eng., U.K.	178		51.20 N	0.39 E
Stockdale, Tx., U.S.	136	E9	29.13 N	97.57 W
Stockerau, Aus.	30	B13	48.23 N	16.12 E
Stockett, Mt., U.S.	146	C15	47.21 N	111.08 W
Stockholm, Swe.	16	H15	59.20 N	18.03 E
Stockholm, Me., U.S.	122	C8	47.03 N	68.09 W
Stockholm, state, Swe.	16	H16	59.30 N	18.20 E
Stockholm, Lake, l., N.J., U.S.	194		41.04 N	74.32 W
Stockport, Eng., U.K.	10	H10	53.25 N	2.10 W
Stockport, mun., Eng., U.K.	180		53.23 N	2.08 W
Stockport, mun., Eng., U.K.	180		53.23 N	2.08 W
Stockton, Al., U.S.	134	G11	30.59 N	87.51 W
Stockton, Ca., U.S.	148	F4	37.57 N	121.16 W
Stockton, Il., U.S.	130	B8	42.20 N	90.00 W
Stockton, Ks., U.S.	138	B9	39.25 N	99.16 W
Stockton, Mo., U.S.	130	G4	37.41 N	93.48 W
Stockton, Ut., U.S.	150	C4	40.27 N	112.22 W
Stockton Heath, Eng., U.K.	180		53.22 N	2.34 W
Stockton-on-Tees, Eng., U.K.	10	G11	54.34 N	1.18 W
Stockton Plateau, plat., Tx., U.S.	136	D5	30.30 N	102.30 W
Stockton Reservoir, res., Mo., U.S.	130	G4	37.38 N	93.45 W
Stockton Springs, Me., U.S.	122	F8	44.29 N	68.51 W
Stockum, Ger.	181		51.28 N	7.22 E
Stockum, Ger.	181		51.32 N	7.47 E
Stockum, Ger.	181		51.36 N	6.39 E
Stockum, ngh., Ger.	181		51.16 N	6.44 E
Stockville, Ne., U.S.	140	G12	40.32 N	100.23 W
Stockwell, Lake, l., N.J., U.S.	203		39.51 N	74.47 W
Stoczek Łukowski, Pol.	24	D18	51.57 N	21.58 E
Stod, Nor.	16	C9	64.04 N	11.40 E
Stöde, Swe.	16	E14	62.25 N	16.35 E
Stødi, Nor.	14	F6	66.33 N	15.20 E
Stodolišče, Russia	26	F15	54.11 N	32.39 E
Stœng Tréng, Camb.	64	F8	13.31 N	105.58 E
Stoffberg, S. Afr.	90	D9	25.25 S	29.50 E
Stojba, Russia	50	F15	52.48 N	131.42 E
Stoke, Eng., U.K.	178		51.27 N	0.37 E
Stoke D'Abernon, Eng., U.K.	178		51.19 N	0.23 W
Stoke Newington, ngh., Eng., U.K.	178		51.34 N	0.05 W
Stoke-on-Trent, Eng., U.K.	10	I10	52.59 N	2.09 W
Stoke Poges, Eng., U.K.	178		51.33 N	0.35 W
Stokes Point, c., Austl.	99a	n11	40.09 S	143.55 E
Stokhid, stm., Ukr.	38	B4	51.51 N	25.38 E
Stokkøya, i., Nor.	16	C7	64.03 N	9.58 E
Stokksnes, c., Ice.	12a	k32	64.15 N	15.03 W
Stokkvågen, Nor.	14	F3	66.20 N	13.00 E
Stokmarknes, Nor.	14	D5	68.34 N	14.53 E
Stol, mtn., Yugo.	36	E9	44.13 N	22.14 E
Stolac, Bos.	36	F4	43.05 N	17.57 E
Stolberg, Ger.	24	F2	50.46 N	6.13 E
Stolbovo, Russia	26	H17	52.38 N	34.47 E
Stolbovoj, ostrov, i., Russia	50	B16	74.05 N	136.00 E
Stolbovoy see Stolbovoj, ostrov, i., Russia	50	B16	74.05 N	136.00 E
Stolin, Bela.	38	B5	51.53 N	26.51 E
Stöllet, Swe.	16	G11	60.23 N	13.18 E
Stol'ne, Ukr.	38	B10	51.31 N	31.55 E
Stolp see Słupsk, Pol.	24	B13	54.27 N	17.02 E
Stolpe, Ger.	182a		52.40 N	13.16 E
Stolper Heide, for., Ger.	182a		52.39 N	13.14 E
Ston, Cro.	30	H14	42.49 N	17.41 E
Stondon Massey, Eng., U.K.	178		51.41 N	0.18 E
Stone, Eng., U.K.	178		51.27 N	0.16 E
Stoneboro, Pa., U.S.	124	C5	41.20 N	80.06 W
Stone Canyon Reservoir, res., Ca., U.S.	198		34.07 N	118.28 W
Stonecutters Island, i., China	189d		22.19 N	114.08 E
Stonefort, Il., U.S.	130	G9	37.36 N	88.42 W
Stoneham, Ma., U.S.	201		42.28 N	71.06 W
Stone Harbor, N.J., U.S.	124	E11	39.03 N	74.45 W
Stonehaven, Scot., U.K.	10	E10	56.57 N	2.13 W
Stonehenge, Austl.	98	E4	24.21 S	143.18 E
Stonehenge, hist., Eng., U.K.	10	J11	51.10 N	1.50 W
Stonehill College, educ., Ma., U.S.	201		42.03 N	71.05 W
Stone Indian Reserve, ind. res., B.C., Can.	144	E7	51.55 N	123.08 W
Stone Mountain, Ga., U.S.	132	C1	33.48 N	84.10 W
Stone Mountain, mtn., Vt., U.S.	122	F5	44.34 N	71.40 W
Stone Mountain Memorial State Park, p.o.i., Ga., U.S.	132	C1	33.49 N	84.06 W
Stone Park, Il., U.S.	196		41.54 N	87.53 W
Stoner, B.C., Can.	144	C8	53.35 N	122.39 W
Stones, East Fork, stm., Tn., U.S.	130	I11	35.59 N	86.27 W
Stones, West Fork, stm., Tn., U.S.	130	I11	35.59 N	86.27 W
Stones River National Battlefield, p.o.i., Tn., U.S.	130	I11	35.52 N	86.26 W
Stonestown, shp. cen., Ca., U.S.	200		37.44 N	122.28 W
Stonevilla, Pa., U.S.	197b		40.18 N	79.31 W
Stoneville, N.C., U.S.	124	H6	36.27 N	79.54 W
Stonewall, Mb., Can.	142	D16	50.08 N	97.19 W
Stonewall, La., U.S.	136	B14	32.16 N	93.50 W
Stonewall, Ms., U.S.	134	E10	32.07 N	88.47 W
Stonewall, Ok., U.S.	134	C2	34.38 N	96.31 W
Stonewall Manor, Va., U.S.	202c		38.53 N	77.14 W
Stoney Creek, On., Can.	126	E10	43.13 N	79.46 W
Stoney Indian Reserve, ind. res., Ab., Can.	144	E16	51.10 N	114.55 W
Stonington, Il., U.S.	130	E8	39.37 N	89.11 W
Stonington, Me., U.S.	122	F8	44.09 N	68.40 W
Stony, stm., Ak., U.S.	109	D8	61.47 N	156.40 W
Stony, stm., Mn., U.S.	128	D7	47.44 N	91.47 W
Stony Brook, stm., Ct., U.S.	194		41.04 N	73.28 W
Stony Brook, stm., Ct., U.S.	194		41.08 N	73.22 W
Stony Brook, stm., Ma., U.S.	201		42.22 N	71.16 W
Stony Brook, stm., Ma., U.S.	201		42.38 N	71.22 W
Stony Brook, stm., N.J., U.S.	194		40.56 N	74.26 W
Stony Brook, stm., N.J., U.S.	194		40.19 N	74.41 W

Name	Page	Map Ref.	Latitude	Longitude
Stony Brook Harbor, b., N.Y., U.S.	194		40.54 N	73.10 W
Stony Brook Reservation, p.o.i., Ma., U.S.	201		42.16 N	71.09 W
Stony Creek, stm., Ca., U.S.	148	D3	39.40 N	121.58 W
Stony Creek, stm., Il., U.S.	196		41.41 N	87.51 W
Stony Creek, stm., Pa., U.S.	203		40.07 N	75.21 W
Stony Creek Indian Reserve, ind. res., B.C., Can.	144	C6	53.56 N	124.05 W
Stony Island, i., Mi., U.S.	199		42.07 N	83.08 W
Stony Lake, l., Mb., Can.	110	D11	58.51 N	98.35 W
Stony Lake, l., On., Can.	126	D11	44.34 N	78.04 W
Stony Plain, Ab., Can.	144	C16	53.32 N	114.00 W
Stony Plain Indian Reserve, ind. res., Ab., Can.	144	C16	53.27 N	113.43 W
Stony Point, Mi., U.S.	124	C2	41.56 N	83.15 W
Stony Point, N.C., U.S.	124	I4	35.51 N	81.02 W
Stony Point, c., N.Y., U.S.	202a		42.50 N	78.52 W
Stony Rapids, Sk., Can.	110	D9	59.14 N	105.50 W
Stony River, Ak., U.S.	109	D8	61.46 N	156.40 W
Stony Run, Md., U.S.	202b		39.11 N	76.42 W
Stony Run, stm., Pa., U.S.	203		40.09 N	75.32 W
Stop, stm., Ma., U.S.	201		42.10 N	71.19 W
Stopnica, Pol.	24	F16	50.26 N	20.56 E
Stoppenberg, ngh., Ger.	181		51.29 N	7.02 E
Storå, Swe.	16	H13	59.42 N	15.09 E
Storå, stm., Den.	16	K6	56.19 N	8.19 E
Stora Alvaret, pl., Swe.	16	K14	56.29 N	16.31 E
Stora Gla, l., Swe.	16	H10	59.30 N	12.30 E
Stora Le, l., Eur.	16	H9	59.05 N	11.53 E
Stora Luleälven, stm., Swe.	14	F11	66.26 N	20.39 E
Stora Lulevatten, l., Swe.	14	E9	67.09 N	19.24 E
Storavan, l., Swe.	14	G9	65.42 N	18.13 E
Stor-Blåsjön, l., Swe.	16	C11	64.48 N	14.11 E
Storby, Fin.	18	G6	60.13 N	19.34 E
Stord, i., Nor.	16	H3	59.53 N	5.25 E
Stordalen, Nor.	16	E5	62.23 N	6.59 E
Storebælt, strt., Den.	16	L8	55.30 N	11.00 E
Store Heddinge, Den.	16	L10	55.19 N	12.23 E
Store Koldewey, i., Grnld.	108	B22	76.22 N	18.51 W
Støren, Nor.	16	D8	63.02 N	10.17 E
Storeskrekken, hill, Nor.	16	G5	60.13 N	7.48 E
Store Sotra, i., Nor.	16	G2	60.18 N	5.05 E
Store Tamsøya, i., Nor.	14	B16	70.41 N	25.50 E
Storeton, Eng., U.K.	180		53.21 N	3.03 W
Storfjärden, l., Swe.	18	G4	60.30 N	17.23 E
Storfjellet, mtn., Nor.	14	E6	67.00 N	15.33 E
Storfjorden, b., Nor.	16	E4	62.25 N	6.30 E
Storfors, Swe.	16	H12	59.32 N	14.16 E
Storforshei, Nor.	14	F5	66.24 N	14.31 E
Storglomvatnet, l., Nor.	14	F4	66.42 N	14.09 E
Störitzsee, l., Ger.	182a		52.23 N	13.51 E
Storjord, Nor.	14	F6	66.48 N	15.24 E
Storjuktan, l., Swe.	16	B14	65.25 N	17.04 E
Storkerson Bay, b., N.T., Can.	109	B14	72.57 N	124.47 W
Storkerson Peninsula, pen., Nu., Can.	110	A9	72.30 N	106.30 W
Storlien, Swe.	16	D10	63.19 N	12.05 E
Storm Bay, b., Austl.	99a	o13	43.10 S	147.32 E
Storm Lake, Ia., U.S.	130	B2	42.38 N	95.12 W
Stormolla, i., Nor.	14	D5	68.16 N	14.52 E
Stormsrivier, S. Afr.	90	H6	33.58 S	23.51 E
Stornorrfors, Swe.	16	D17	63.52 N	20.03 E
Stornoway, Scot., U.K.	10	C6	58.12 N	6.23 W
Storozhynets', Ukr.	38	E4	48.09 N	25.44 E
Stor-Rensjön, l., Swe.	16	D10	63.38 N	12.34 E
Storrs, Ct., U.S.	124	C13	41.48 N	72.14 W
Storsjøen, l., Nor.	16	G9	60.21 N	11.41 E
Storsjøen, l., Nor.	16	F9	61.35 N	11.12 E
Storsjön, l., Swe.	16	G14	60.34 N	16.44 E
Storsjön, l., Swe.	16	E11	62.48 N	13.07 E
Storsjön, l., Swe.	16	D11	63.12 N	14.18 E
Storsjouten, l., Swe.	16	C12	64.35 N	14.59 E
Storskarhøi, mtn., Nor.	16	E6	62.30 N	8.45 E
Storskrymten, mtn., Nor.	16	E7	62.23 N	9.04 E
Storslett, Nor.	14	C11	69.46 N	21.02 E
Storsølnkletten, mtn., Nor.	16	F8	61.58 N	10.21 E
Storsteinnes, Nor.	14	C10	69.15 N	19.13 E
Storsteinsfjellet, mtn., Nor.	14	D8	68.14 N	17.52 E
Storstrøm, state, Den.	16	M9	54.58 N	11.55 E
Storstrømmen, strt., Den.	24	A7	54.58 N	11.55 E
Storsund, Swe.	16	B18	65.34 N	20.39 E
Stort, stm., Eng., U.K.	178		51.46 N	0.01 E
Storthoaks, Sk., Can.	142	E12	49.24 N	101.36 W
Storuman, Swe.	16	B14	65.04 N	17.04 E
Storuman, l., Swe.	16	B13	65.14 N	16.48 E
Storvätteshågna, mtn., Swe.	16	E10	62.07 N	12.27 E
Storvik, Swe.	16	G14	60.35 N	16.32 E
Storvindeln, l., Swe.	16	B14	65.43 N	17.05 E
Storvreta, Swe.	16	H15	59.57 N	17.42 E
Story, Wy., U.S.	140	C6	44.34 N	106.53 W
Story City, Ia., U.S.	130	B4	42.11 N	93.36 W
Stosch, Isla, i., Chile	166	I1	49.09 S	75.26 W
Støttvær, is., Nor.	14	F4	66.55 N	13.25 E
Stoubcy, Bela.	26	G9	53.28 N	26.45 E
Stough Park, p.o.i., Ca., U.S.	198		34.12 N	118.18 W
Stoughton, Sk., Can.	142	E10	49.41 N	103.03 W
Stoughton, Eng., U.K.	178		51.15 N	0.35 W
Stoughton, Ma., U.S.	124	B14	42.07 N	71.06 W
Stoughton, Wi., U.S.	130	B8	42.55 N	89.13 W
Stoŭng, stm., Camb.	64	F7	12.50 N	104.18 E
Stour, stm., Eng., U.K.	10	K10	50.44 N	1.47 W
Stour, stm., Eng., U.K.	10	J13	51.57 N	1.16 E
Stover, Mo., U.S.	130	F4	38.26 N	92.59 W
Stow, Oh., U.S.	124	C4	41.09 N	81.26 W
Stowe, Vt., U.S.	122	F4	44.27 N	72.41 W
Stowell, Tx., U.S.	136	E13	29.47 N	94.23 W
Stowe Township, Pa., U.S.	197b		40.29 N	80.04 W
Stow Maries, Eng., U.K.	178		51.40 N	0.39 E
Stowmarket, Eng., U.K.	10	I14	52.11 N	0.59 E
Stoyoma Mountain, mtn., B.C., Can.	144	G9	49.59 N	121.13 W
Strabane, N. Ire., U.K.	10	G5	54.49 N	7.27 W
Straberg, Ger.	181		51.05 N	6.45 E
Stradella, Italy	30	E6	45.05 N	9.18 E
Stradzečy, Bela.	26	I6	51.56 N	23.40 E
Strahan, Austl.	99a	o12	42.09 S	145.19 E
Strakonice, Czech Rep.	24	G9	49.15 N	13.54 E
Stralsund, Ger.	24	B9	54.18 N	13.05 E
Strand, S. Afr.	90	I4	34.06 S	18.49 E
Stranda, Nor.	16	E4	62.18 N	6.54 E
Strandža see Yıldız Dağları, mts., Eur.	36	H14	41.50 N	27.30 E
Stranger Creek, stm., Ks., U.S.	138	B13	39.00 N	95.01 W
Strangford Lough, b., N. Ire., U.K.	10	G7	54.28 N	5.35 W
Strängnäs, Swe.	16	H15	59.22 N	17.01 E
Stranraer, Scot., U.K.	10	G8	54.54 N	5.01 W
Strasbourg, Sk., Can.	142	C9	51.04 N	104.57 W
Strasbourg, Fr.	20	F16	48.34 N	7.44 E
Strasburg, Ger.	24	C9	53.30 N	13.44 E
Strasburg, Co., U.S.	138	B4	39.44 N	104.20 W
Strasburg, N.D., U.S.	140	A12	46.07 N	100.09 W
Strasburg, Oh., U.S.	124	D4	40.35 N	81.31 W
Strasburg, Pa., U.S.	124	E9	39.58 N	76.10 W
Strasburg, Va., U.S.	124	F7	38.59 N	78.21 W
Străşeni, Mol.	38	F7	47.08 N	28.37 E
Straševiči, Russia	26	D17	56.49 N	34.35 E
Strässa, Swe.	16	H13	59.44 N	15.12 E
Stratford, On., Can.	126	E8	43.21 N	80.58 W
Stratford, N.Z.	102	D6	39.20 S	174.17 E
Stratford, Ca., U.S.	148	G6	36.11 N	119.49 W
Stratford, Ct., U.S.	124	C12	41.12 N	73.08 W
Stratford, De., U.S.	203		39.40 N	75.38 W
Stratford, Ia., U.S.	130	B4	42.16 N	93.55 W
Stratford, Ok., U.S.	134	C2	34.47 N	96.58 W
Stratford, Tx., U.S.	138	E6	36.20 N	102.04 W
Stratford, Wi., U.S.	128	G8	44.47 N	90.04 W
Stratford Point, c., Ct., U.S.	194		41.09 N	73.06 W
Stratford Square, shp. cen., Il., U.S.	196		41.57 N	88.07 W
Stratford-upon-Avon, Eng., U.K.	10	I11	52.11 N	1.42 W
Strathalbyn, Austl.	98	J2	35.15 S	138.53 E
Strathclair, Mb., Can.	142	D13	50.25 N	100.23 W
Strathcona Provincial Park, p.o.i., B.C., Can.	144	G5	49.40 N	125.50 W
Strathgordon, Austl.	99a	o12	42.46 S	146.03 E
Strathlorne, N.S., Can.	122	D15	46.11 N	61.17 W
Strathmoor, ngh., Mi., U.S.	199		42.23 N	83.11 W
Strathmore, Ab., Can.	144	E17	51.03 N	113.23 W
Strathmore, Ca., U.S.	148	G6	36.08 N	119.03 W
Strathmore, N.J., U.S.	194		40.24 N	74.13 W
Strathmore, val., Scot., U.K.	10	E9	56.40 N	3.04 W
Strathroy, On., Can.	126	F8	42.57 N	81.36 W
Strathy Point, c., Scot., U.K.	10	C8	58.36 N	4.01 W
Stratton, Co., U.S.	138	B6	39.18 N	102.36 W
Stratton, Me., U.S.	122	E6	45.08 N	70.27 W
Stratton, Ne., U.S.	138	A7	40.08 N	101.14 W
Stratton Mountain, mtn., Vt., U.S.	122	G4	43.05 N	72.56 W
Straubing, Ger.	24	H8	48.52 N	12.34 E
Strauch, Ger.	181		51.09 N	6.56 E
Straumen, Nor.	16	D9	63.52 N	11.18 E
Straumsjøen, Nor.	14	D5	68.41 N	14.30 E
Strausberg, Ger.	24	D9	52.34 N	13.52 E
Straus-Berger Stadtforst, p.o.i., Ger.	182a		52.34 N	13.52 E
Strausberg-Vorstadt, Ger.	182a		52.32 N	13.51 E
Straussee, l., Ger.	182a		52.35 N	13.53 E
Strawberry, stm., Ar., U.S.	130	H6	35.53 N	91.13 W
Strawberry, stm., Ut., U.S.	150	C6	40.10 N	110.24 W
Strawberry Island, i., N.Y., U.S.	202a		42.57 N	78.55 W
Strawberry Mountain, mtn., Or., U.S.	146	F8	44.19 N	118.43 W
Strawberry Point, Ca., U.S.	200		37.54 N	122.31 W
Strawberry Point, Ia., U.S.	130	B6	42.40 N	91.32 W
Strawberry Point, c., Ma., U.S.	201		42.15 N	70.46 W
Strawberry Reservoir, res., Ut., U.S.	150	C5	40.11 N	111.08 W
Strawbridge Lake, l., N.J., U.S.	203		39.57 N	74.57 W
Strawn, Tx., U.S.	136	B9	32.33 N	98.29 W
Straw Pump, Pa., U.S.	197b		40.19 N	79.40 W
Strážnice, Czech Rep.	24	H13	48.53 N	17.19 E
Strážske, Slvk.	24	H17	48.52 N	21.50 E
Streaky Bay, b., Austl.	96	F6	32.36 S	134.08 E
Streatham, B.C., Can.	144	C4	53.49 N	126.14 W
Streatham, ngh., Eng., U.K.	178		51.26 N	0.08 W
Streator, Il., U.S.	130	C9	41.07 N	88.49 W
Strebersdorf, ngh., Aus.	182b		48.18 N	16.23 E
Stredoslovenský, state, Slvk.	24	H15	48.50 N	19.10 E
Streeter, N.D., U.S.	140	A13	46.39 N	99.21 W
Streetman, Tx., U.S.	136	C11	31.52 N	96.19 W
Streetsboro, Oh., U.S.	124	C4	41.14 N	81.19 W
Streets Run, stm., Pa., U.S.	197b		40.23 N	79.56 W
Streetsville, On., Can.	126	E10	43.34 N	79.42 W
Strehaia, Rom.	36	E10	44.37 N	23.12 E
Strelica, Russia	38	B17	51.38 N	38.56 E
Strelka, Russia	48	C16	58.04 N	93.01 E
Strelka, stm., Russia	183a		59.52 N	30.03 E
Strelka-Čunja, Russia	48	B18	61.43 N	102.47 E
Strel'na, Russia	14	F29	66.04 N	38.38 E
Strel'na, Russia	18	H17	59.50 N	30.02 E
Strel'na, stm., Russia	14	F29	66.03 N	38.37 E
Strel'skaja, Russia	40	B15	59.27 N	47.45 E
Strenči, Lat.	26	C8	57.37 N	25.39 E
Stresa, Italy	30	E5	45.53 N	8.32 E
Strešin see Strėšyn, Bela.	26	H13	52.43 N	30.07 E
Strėšyn, Bela.	26	H13	52.43 N	30.07 E
Streymoy, i., Far. Is.	12b	m34	62.08 N	7.00 W
Striberg, Swe.	16	H12	59.33 N	14.56 E
Stříbro, Czech Rep.	24	G8	49.45 N	12.59 E
Strickherdicke, Ger.	181		51.29 N	7.43 E
Strickland, stm., Pap. N. Gui.	101a	b3	7.34 S	141.23 E
Strilkove, Ukr.	38	H13	45.54 N	34.53 E
Strimasund, Swe.	16	A12	66.02 N	14.53 E
Strimon, Gulf of see Strymonikós Kólpos, b., Grc.	34	C6	40.40 N	23.50 E
Strjama, stm., Blg.	36	G11	42.10 N	24.56 E
Strobel, Arg.	172	E7	31.57 S	60.39 W
Stroeder, Arg.	166	H4	40.11 S	62.37 W
Strofádes, is., Grc.	34	F3	37.15 N	21.00 E
Strogino, ngh., Russia	183b		55.49 N	37.25 E
Stroitel', Russia	38	C15	50.47 N	36.28 E
Stromboli, Isola, i., Italy	32	F9	38.47 N	15.13 E
Strome, Ab., Can.	144	D18	52.48 N	112.02 W
Stromeferry, Scot., U.K.	10	D7	57.21 N	5.32 W
Stromness, Scot., U.K.	10	C9	58.57 N	3.18 W
Strömsbruk, Swe.	16	F15	61.52 N	17.19 E
Stromsburg, Ne., U.S.	140	F15	41.07 N	97.35 W
Strömsnäsbruk, Swe.	16	K11	56.32 N	13.43 E
Strömstad, Swe.	16	I9	58.56 N	11.11 E
Strömsund, Swe.	16	D13	63.51 N	15.35 E
Strömsvattudal, l., Swe.	16	C12	63.56 N	15.28 E
Strong, Ar., U.S.	134	D6	33.06 N	92.22 W
Strong, stm., Ms., U.S.	134	F8	31.51 N	90.08 W
Strong City, Ks., U.S.	138	C12	38.24 N	96.32 W
Stronghurst, Il., U.S.	130	D7	40.44 N	90.54 W
Strongoli, Italy	32	E11	39.15 N	17.03 E
Strongs Creek, stm., N.Y., U.S.	194		40.40 N	73.22 W
Strongs Neck, pen., N.Y., U.S.	194		40.58 N	73.07 W
Strongsville Airport, arpt., Oh., U.S.	197a		41.19 N	81.52 W
Stronsay, i., Scot., U.K.	10	B10	59.06 N	2.35 W
Stropkov, Slvk.	24	G17	49.12 N	21.39 E
Stroud, Austl.	98	I8	32.20 S	151.55 E
Stroud, Eng., U.K.	10	J10	51.45 N	2.13 W
Stroud, Ok., U.S.	134	B2	35.45 N	96.39 W
Stroudsburg, Pa., U.S.	124	D10	40.59 N	75.11 W
Strubenvale, S. Afr.	191d		26.16 S	28.28 E
Struer, Den.	16	K6	56.29 N	8.37 E
Struga, Mac.	34	B3	41.11 N	20.41 E
Strugi-Krasnye, Russia	26	B11	58.16 N	29.06 E
Struisbult, S. Afr.	191d		26.19 S	28.29 E
Strule, stm., N. Ire., U.K.	10	G5	54.43 N	7.21 W
Strum, Wi., U.S.	128	G7	44.32 N	91.23 W
Struma (Strymónas), stm., Eur.	34	B6	41.42 N	23.09 E
Strumble Head, c., Wales, U.K.	10	I7	52.02 N	5.04 W
Strumica, Mac.	34	B5	41.26 N	22.37 E
Strümp, Ger.	181		51.17 N	6.40 E
Strunino, Russia	26	D21	56.22 N	38.35 E
Struthers, Oh., U.S.	124	C5	41.03 N	80.36 W
Strydenburg, S. Afr.	90	F6	29.56 S	23.40 E
Stryi, Ukr.	38	D2	49.15 N	23.51 E
Stryi, stm., Ukr.	38	D2	49.24 N	24.13 E
Stryker, Mt., U.S.	146	B12	48.40 N	114.46 W
Stryker, Oh., U.S.	130	C13	41.30 N	84.23 W
Stryków, Pol.	24	E15	51.54 N	19.36 E
Strymón (Struma), stm., Eur.	34	C6	40.57 N	23.49 E
Strymonikós Kólpos (Strimon, Gulf of), b., Grc.	34	C6	40.40 N	23.50 E
Stryn, Nor.	16	F4	61.54 N	6.43 E
Strypa, stm., Ukr.	24	D4	48.52 N	25.25 E
Stryzhavka, Ukr.	38	D7	49.18 N	28.28 E
Strzegom, Pol.	24	F12	50.57 N	16.21 E
Strzegowo-Osada, Pol.	24	D16	52.54 N	20.17 E
Strzelce Krajeńskie, Pol.	24	D11	52.52 N	15.31 E
Strzelce Opolskie, Pol.	24	F14	50.31 N	18.18 E
Strzelecki Creek, stm., Austl.	98	G3	29.21 S	139.48 E
Strzelecki Desert, des., Austl.	98	G3	28.00 S	140.10 E
Strzelecki National Park, p.o.i., Austl.	99a	n13	40.14 S	148.06 E
Strzelin, Pol.	24	F13	50.47 N	17.04 E
Strzelno, Pol.	24	D14	52.37 N	18.10 E
Strzyżów, Pol.	24	G17	49.53 N	21.49 E
Stuart, Fl., U.S.	132	I5	27.11 N	80.15 W
Stuart, Ia., U.S.	130	C3	41.30 N	94.19 W
Stuart, Ne., U.S.	140	E13	42.35 N	99.08 W
Stuart, Va., U.S.	124	H5	36.38 N	80.16 W
Stuart, stm., B.C., Can.	144	B7	53.59 N	123.32 W
Stuart, Mount, mtn., Wa., U.S.	146	C6	47.29 N	120.54 W
Stuart Island, i., Ak., U.S.	109	D7	63.35 N	162.31 W
Stuart Lake, l., B.C., Can.	144	B5	54.32 N	124.35 W
Stuarts Draft, Va., U.S.	124	G6	38.01 N	79.02 W
Stübbecken, Ger.	181		51.23 N	7.36 E
Stubbekøbing, Den.	16	M10	54.53 N	12.02 E
Stubbins, Eng., U.K.	180		53.39 N	2.19 W
Stubla, stm., Ukr.	38	C4	50.50 N	26.04 E
Studenica, Manastir, rel., Yugo.	36	F7	43.31 N	20.31 E
Studen Kladenec, Jazovir, res., Blg.	36	H12	41.38 N	25.29 E
Studenok, Ukr.	38	B13	51.42 N	34.07 E
Studi, Università degli, educ., Italy	184b		45.28 N	9.14 E
Studsvik, Swe.	16	I15	58.45 N	17.23 E
Stugudalen, Nor.	16	E9	62.54 N	11.52 E
Stugun, Swe.	16	D13	63.10 N	15.37 E
Stuhlweissenburg see Székesfehérvár, Hung.	36	B5	47.12 N	18.24 E
Stuie, B.C., Can.	144	D4	52.22 N	126.02 W
Stump Creek, stm., N.J., U.S.	194		40.28 N	74.16 W
Stumpf, Ger.	181		51.06 N	7.13 E
Stump Lake, l., N.D., U.S.	142	G15	47.53 N	98.22 W
Stuorajávri, l., Nor.	14	C13	69.08 N	22.47 E
Stuorre Tjåure, mtn., Swe.	16	C11	63.56 N	13.30 E
Stupino, Russia	26	F20	54.53 N	38.04 E
Stura di Demonte, stm., Italy	30	F4	44.39 N	7.52 E
Sturge Island, i., Ant.	103	B21	67.31 S	164.38 E
Sturgeon, Mo., U.S.	130	E5	39.14 N	92.17 W
Sturgeon, Pa., U.S.	197b		40.23 N	80.13 W
Sturgeon, stm., On., Can.	126	B9	46.30 N	80.04 W
Sturgeon, stm., Mi., U.S.	126	C5	45.23 N	84.37 W
Sturgeon, stm., Mi., U.S.	126	B3	45.49 N	86.40 W
Sturgeon, stm., Mi., U.S.	128	E10	47.01 N	88.28 W
Sturgeon Bay, Wi., U.S.	126	D2	44.50 N	87.21 W
Sturgeon Bay, b., Mb., Can.	142	B16	52.00 N	97.50 W
Sturgeon Falls, On., Can.	126	B10	46.21 N	79.54 W
Sturgeon Lake, l., Ab., Can.	144	A13	55.06 N	117.30 W
Sturgeon Lake, l., On., Can.	126	D11	44.27 N	78.42 W
Sturgeon Lake, l., On., Can.	128	A8	50.03 N	90.44 W
Sturgeon Lake Indian Reserve, ind. res., Ab., Can.	144	B13	55.03 N	117.29 W
Sturgis, Sk., Can.	142	C11	51.55 N	102.32 W
Sturgis, Ky., U.S.	130	G10	37.32 N	87.58 W
Sturgis, Mi., U.S.	130	C12	41.48 N	85.25 W
Sturgis, Ms., U.S.	134	D9	33.20 N	89.02 W
Sturgis, S.D., U.S.	140	C9	44.24 N	103.30 W
Štúrovo, Slvk.	24	I14	47.48 N	18.44 E
Sturt, Mount, mtn., Austl.	98	G3	29.33 S	141.42 E
Sturt Creek, stm., Austl.	96	C5	20.07 S	127.24 E
Sturtevant, Wi., U.S.	130	B10	42.41 N	87.53 W
Sturt National Park, p.o.i., Austl.	98	G3	29.04 S	141.23 E
Sturt Stony Desert, des., Austl.	98	G3	28.30 S	141.00 E
Stürzelberg, Ger.	181		51.08 N	6.49 E
Stutterheim, S. Afr.	90	H8	32.34 S	27.25 E
Stuttgart, Ger.	24	H5	48.48 N	9.11 E
Stuttgart, Ar., U.S.	134	C7	34.30 N	91.33 W
Stviga (Scviha) (Stvyha), stm., Eur.	38	B6	52.04 N	27.54 E
Stvyha see Stviga, stm., Eur.	38	B6	52.04 N	27.54 E
Styal, Eng., U.K.	180		53.21 N	2.15 W
Stykkishólmur, Ice.	12a	k28	65.03 N	22.44 W
Stylís, Grc.	34	E5	38.55 N	22.36 E
Styr, stm., Eur.	38	B4	52.06 N	26.35 E
Styria see Steiermark, state, Aus.	30	C12	47.10 N	15.10 E
Styrum, ngh., Ger.	181		51.27 N	6.51 E
Styx, stm., Al., U.S.	134	G11	30.31 N	87.27 W
Šu, Kaz.	48	F12	43.35 N	73.44 E
Suaçuí Grande, stm., Braz.	170	J4	18.50 S	41.46 W
Suai, Malay.	66	B8	3.47 N	113.38 E
Suaita, Col.	168	D5	6.04 N	73.25 W
Suapure, stm., Ven.	168	D8	6.48 N	67.02 W
Suaqui Grande, Mex.	154	A4	28.24 N	109.54 W
Šubač, Russia	18	G25	60.22 N	38.10 E
Subačius, Lith.	26	E7	55.45 N	24.46 E
Subah, Indon.	66	G6	6.58 S	109.52 E
Subang, Indon.	66	G5	6.34 S	107.45 E
Subansiri, stm., Asia	70	D14	28.20 N	93.40 E
Šubarkuduk, Kaz.	48	E9	49.11 N	56.34 E
Subar Laut, Pulau, i., Sing.	189c		1.13 N	103.50 E
Subarnapur, India	190b		22.58 N	88.34 E
Subarnarekha, stm., India	70	G11	21.33 N	87.23 E
Sūbāṭ, stm., Sudan	82	F6	9.21 N	31.32 E
Subata see Subate, Lat.	26	D8	56.00 N	25.56 E
Subate, Lat.	26	D8	56.00 N	25.56 E
Subei, China	52	D3	39.27 N	95.02 E
Subeita see Shivta, Ḥorvot, hist., Isr.	76	H5	30.53 N	34.38 E
Subhepur, India	190a		28.45 N	77.16 E
Subi, Pulau, i., Indon.	66	B6	2.55 N	108.50 E
Subiaco, Italy	30	I10	41.55 N	13.05 E
Subipur, India	190b		22.54 N	88.08 E
Sublette, Ks., U.S.	138	D8	37.28 N	100.50 W
Sublett Range, mts., Id., U.S.	146	H14	42.21 N	112.55 W
Subotica, Yugo.	36	C6	46.05 N	19.40 E
Suburban Airport, arpt., Md., U.S.	202c		39.05 N	76.50 W
Suburban Village, Pa., U.S.	203		39.58 N	75.34 W
Sucarnoochee, stm., U.S.	134	E10	32.25 N	88.02 W
Succor Creek, stm., U.S.	146	G9	43.38 N	116.56 W
Succotah, hist., Egypt	76	H3	30.33 N	32.07 E
Suceava, Rom.	36	B13	47.40 N	26.16 E
Suceava, state, Rom.	36	B12	47.30 N	25.45 E
Suceava, stm., Rom.	36	B13	47.31 N	26.33 E
Sucha Beskidzka, Pol.	24	G15	49.45 N	19.36 E
Suchań, Pol.	24	C11	53.17 N	15.19 E
Suchedniów, Pol.	24	E16	51.03 N	20.50 E
Suchiapa, stm., Mex.	154	G12	16.35 N	93.00 W
Súchil, Mex.	154	D6	23.39 N	103.57 W
Süchow see Xuzhou, China	58	D7	34.16 N	117.11 E
Sucio, stm., Col.	168	D3	7.25 N	77.06 W
Sucre, Bol.	166	C3	19.02 S	65.15 W
Sucre, Col.	168	C4	8.48 N	74.43 W
Sucre, state, Col.	168	C4	9.00 N	75.00 W
Sucre, state, Ven.	168	B10	10.25 N	63.30 W
Sucre, state, Ven.	204c		10.25 N	66.50 W
Sucúa, Ec.	168	I2	2.28 S	78.10 W
Sucuaro, Col.	168	E7	4.34 N	68.50 W
Sucumbíos, state, Ec.	168	H3	0.06 N	76.52 W
Sucuriju, Braz.	164	C8	1.39 N	49.57 W
Sucuriú, stm., Braz.	166	C6	20.44 S	51.37 W
Sud, state, N. Cal.	101d	m16	21.58 S	166.32 E
Sud, Canal du, strt., Haiti	156	C11	18.40 N	73.05 W
Suda, Russia	26	A20	59.09 N	37.33 E
Suda, stm., Russia	18	H23	59.11 N	37.25 E
Sudaj, Russia	40	B13	58.57 N	43.07 E
Sudak, Ukr.	38	I13	44.51 N	34.58 E
Sudan, Tx., U.S.	138	G6	34.04 N	102.31 W
Sudan, ctry., Afr.	82	E5	15.00 N	30.00 E
Sudan, reg., Afr.	80	E7	12.00 N	17.00 E
Sudarsan, India	190b		22.59 N	88.17 E
Südbahnhof, trans., Aus.	182b		48.11 N	16.23 E
Sudberg, ngh., Ger.	181		51.11 N	7.08 E
Sudbišči, Russia	26	H20	52.56 N	37.39 E
Sudbury, On., Can.	126	B8	46.28 N	80.59 W
Sudbury, Eng., U.K.	10	I13	52.02 N	0.43 E
Sudbury, stm., Ma., U.S.	201		42.28 N	71.22 W
Sudbury Center, Ma., U.S.	201		42.23 N	71.24 W
Sudd see As-Sudd, reg., Sudan	82	F6	8.00 N	31.00 E
Suddie, Guy.	164	B6	7.07 N	58.29 W
Sude, stm., Ger.	24	C6	53.21 N	10.43 E
Suderwich, Ger.	181		51.37 N	7.15 E
Sudeten see Sudetes, mts., Eur.	24	F12	50.36 N	15.52 E
Sudetes, mts., Eur.	24	F12	50.36 N	15.52 E
Sudety see Sudetes, mts., Eur.	24	F12	50.36 N	15.52 E
Südkamen, Ger.	181		51.35 N	7.39 E
Sudogda, Russia	40	D12	55.57 N	40.51 E
Sudomskaja vozvyšennost', plat., Russia	26	C12	57.25 N	29.25 E
Sudong, Pulau, i., Sing.	189c		1.13 N	103.44 E
Sudost', stm., Eur.	26	H16	52.19 N	33.23 E
Sud-Ouest, Pointe du, c., Qc., Can.	122	A13	49.23 N	63.35 W
Sudova Vyshnia, Ukr.	38	D2	49.47 N	23.22 E
Südradde, stm., Ger.	20	B16	52.41 N	7.34 E
Südtirol see Trentino-Alto Adige, state, Italy	30	D8	46.30 N	11.20 E
Suðuroy, i., Far. Is.	12b	n34	61.32 N	6.50 W
Sudža, Russia	40	F9	51.11 N	35.17 E
Sue, stm., Sudan	82	F5	7.39 N	28.02 E
Sueca, Spain	28	E10	39.12 N	0.18 W
Sue Creek, b., Md., U.S.	202b		39.17 N	76.24 W
Šuereckoe, Russia	18	C21	64.44 N	34.43 E
Suez see El-Suweis, Egypt	76	I3	29.58 N	32.33 E
Suez, Gulf of see Suweis, Khalîg el-, b., Egypt	76	J4	29.00 N	32.50 E
Suez Canal see Suweis, Qanâ el-, can., Egypt	76	H3	29.56 N	32.34 E
Suffern Park, N.Y., U.S.	194		41.07 N	74.07 W
Suffield, Ab., Can.	142	D2	50.13 N	111.09 W
Suffield, Canadian Forces Base, mil., Ab., Can.	142	D2	50.15 N	111.10 W
Suffolk, Va., U.S.	124	H9	36.43 N	76.35 W
Şūfīān, Iran	74	A10	38.16 N	45.59 E
Sugandha, India	190b		22.54 N	88.20 E
Sugano, Japan	186		35.44 N	139.56 E
Sugar, stm., U.S.	130	B8	42.26 N	89.11 W
Sugar, stm., N.H., U.S.	122	G4	43.24 N	72.24 W
Sugar City, Id., U.S.	146	G15	43.52 N	111.44 W
Sugar Creek, stm., U.S.	130	D10	40.46 N	87.44 W
Sugar Creek, stm., Il., U.S.	130	D8	40.08 N	89.37 W
Sugar Creek, stm., Mi., U.S.	199		42.06 N	83.36 W
Sugar Creek, stm., Ok., U.S.	138	F10	35.05 N	98.10 W
Sugar Grove, Va., U.S.	124	H4	36.46 N	81.25 W
Sugar Hill, Ga., U.S.	132	B1	34.06 N	84.01 W
Sugar Island, i., Mi., U.S.	126	B5	46.25 N	84.12 W
Sugar Land, Tx., U.S.	136	E12	29.37 N	95.38 W
Sugarloaf, hill, Oh., U.S.	124	C4	41.24 N	81.06 W
Sugarloaf Hill, hill, Austl.	192b		37.58 S	145.19 E
Sugarloaf Mountain, mtn., Me., U.S.	122	E6	45.01 N	70.22 W
Sugar Loaf Mountain, mtn., Ok., U.S.	134	C4	35.02 N	94.28 W
Sugarloaf Peak, mtn., Ca., U.S.	198		34.14 N	117.38 W
Sugarloaf Point, c., Austl.	98	I9	32.26 S	152.31 E
Sugar Loaf Point, c., On., Can.	202a		42.52 N	79.17 W
Sugartown, Pa., U.S.	203		40.00 N	75.31 W
Suginami, ngh., Japan	186		35.42 N	139.38 E
Sugita, ngh., Japan	186		35.23 N	139.38 E
Suğla Gölü, l., Tur.	34	F14	37.20 N	32.02 E
Sugoj, stm., Russia	50	D20	64.14 N	154.29 E
Šugozero, Russia	18	H21	59.55 N	34.10 E
Sugut, stm., Malay.	68	G1	6.26 N	117.43 E
Suhag, Egypt	74	G2	26.32 N	31.41 E
Suhai Hu, l., China	48	G16	38.52 N	93.53 E
Suhaja, stm., Russia	14	E28	67.43 N	38.38 E
Suhana, Russia	50	C12	68.45 N	118.01 E
Şuḥār, Oman	72	E8	24.19 N	56.44 E
Sühbaatar, Mong.	52	A6	50.13 N	106.12 E
Suhindol, Blg.	36	F12	43.11 N	25.10 E
Suhiniči, Russia	26	F18	54.06 N	35.21 E
Suhl, Ger.	24	F6	50.36 N	10.41 E
Suhobezvodnoe, Russia	40	C14	57.02 N	44.52 E
Suhoborka, Russia	40	B16	59.06 N	49.58 E
Suhodol'skij, Russia	26	G21	53.43 N	38.17 E
Suhoj, Russia	40	H12	47.06 N	41.21 E
Suhona, stm., Russia	12	F21	60.45 N	46.17 E
Suhoverkovo, Russia	26	D18	56.37 N	35.35 E
Suhumi, Geor.	42	D9	43.00 N	41.00 E
Şuhut, Tur.	34	E13	38.31 N	30.32 E
Sūi, Pak.	70	D2	28.35 N	69.19 E
Suiá-Miçu, stm., Braz.	166	B6	11.12 S	53.14 W
Suiattle, stm., Wa., U.S.	146	B5	48.19 N	121.32 W
Suichuan, China	58	H6	26.26 N	114.32 E
Suid-Afrika see South Africa, ctry., Afr.	90	F8	30.00 S	26.00 E
Suide, China	58	C4	37.30 N	110.14 E
Suido-suigenchi, res., Japan	188		34.54 N	135.17 E
Suihua, China	52	B10	46.38 N	126.58 E
Suijiang, China	52	F5	28.35 N	104.05 E
Suileng, China	52	B10	47.14 N	127.06 E
Suining, China	58	H4	26.21 N	110.00 E
Suining, China	58	E7	33.53 N	117.57 E
Suining, China	58	F1	30.30 N	105.34 E
Suipacha, Arg.	172	G8	34.46 S	59.41 W
Suiping, China	58	E5	33.08 N	113.58 E
Suippe, stm., Fr.	20	E13	49.25 N	3.57 E
Suippes, Fr.	20	E13	49.07 N	4.32 E
Suir, stm., Ire.	10	I5	52.16 N	7.00 W
Suisse see Switzerland, ctry., Eur.	30	D5	47.00 N	8.00 E
Suitland, Md., U.S.	202c		38.50 N	76.55 W
Suixi, China	58	K4	21.22 N	110.15 E
Suixi, China	58	E7	33.54 N	116.46 E
Suixian see Suizhou, China	58	F5	31.42 N	113.22 E
Suiyang, China	54	B9	44.24 N	130.53 E
Suiyang, China	58	H2	27.56 N	107.18 E
Suiyangdian, China	58	E5	32.02 N	112.54 E
Suizhong, China	58	A9	40.19 N	120.20 E
Suizhou, China	58	F5	31.42 N	113.22 E
Šuja, Russia	18	F21	61.55 N	34.15 E
Šuja, Russia	40	C12	56.51 N	41.22 E
Šuja, stm., Russia	18	F19	61.54 N	34.15 E
Sujāngarh, India	70	E5	27.42 N	74.28 E
Sujāwal, Pak.	70	F2	24.36 N	68.05 E
Šujostrov, ostrov, i., Russia	18	C22	64.44 N	34.55 E
Šujskoe, Russia	40	B12	59.21 N	40.59 E
Sujutkina Kosa, mys, c., Russia	42	C12	44.11 N	47.12 E
Sukabumi, Indon.	66	G5	6.55 S	106.55 E
Sukadana, Indon.	66	D6	1.14 S	109.58 E
Sukadana, Indon.	66	F4	5.04 S	105.32 E
Sukadana, Teluk, b., Indon.	66	D6	1.24 S	109.50 E
Sukagawa, Japan	56	B13	37.17 N	140.23 E
Sukamara, Indon.	66	E7	2.42 S	111.09 E
Sukanegara, Indon.	66	G5	7.05 S	107.07 E
Sukaraja, Indon.	66	E7	2.21 S	110.37 E
Sukarnapura see Jayapura, Indon.	60	F11	2.32 S	140.42 E
Sukarno, Pegunungan see Jaya, Puncak, mtn., Indon.	60	F10	4.05 S	137.11 E
Sukau, Malay.	66	A11	5.32 N	118.16 E
Sukchar, India	190b		22.42 N	88.22 E
Sukematsu, Japan	188		34.31 N	135.26 E
Sukeva, Fin.	18	D14	63.51 N	27.24 E
Sukhothai, Thai.	64	D4	17.01 N	99.49 E
Sukhumi see Suhumi, Geor.	42	D9	43.00 N	41.00 E
Sukhyi Torets', stm., Ukr.	38	E16	48.49 N	37.36 E
Sukkertoppen (Maniitsoq), Grnld.	108	D15	65.25 N	52.56 W
Sukkozero, Russia	18	D19	63.14 N	32.17 E
Sukkozero, ozero, l., Russia	18	D18	63.11 N	32.15 E
Sukkur, Pak.	70	E2	27.42 N	68.52 E
Sukoharjo, Indon.	66	G7	7.41 S	110.50 E
Sukromlja, Russia	26	D17	56.53 N	34.44 E
Sukses, Nmb.	90	B3	21.02 S	16.49 E
Suksun, Russia	40	C20	57.08 N	57.23 E
Sukumo, Japan	56	G5	32.56 N	132.43 E
Sukunka, stm., B.C., Can.	144	A9	55.17 N	121.39 W
Sul, Baía, b., Braz.	172	C13	27.40 S	48.35 W
Sula, i., Nor.	16	E4	62.25 N	6.12 E
Sula, i., Nor.	16	F2	61.08 N	4.55 E
Sula, stm., Russia	12	C23	67.12 N	52.10 E
Sula, stm., Ukr.	38	C13	49.37 N	32.43 E
Sula, Kepulauan (Sula Islands), is., Indon.	60	F8	1.52 S	125.22 E
Sula, ozero, l., Russia	18	D18	63.31 N	31.11 E
Sulaimaniya see As-Sulaymānīyah, Iraq	74	C9	35.33 N	45.26 E
Sulaimān Range, mts., Pak.	70	C3	30.30 N	70.10 E
Sula Islands see Sula, Kepulauan, is., Indon.	60	F8	1.52 S	125.22 E
Sulanheer, Mong.	52	C6	42.41 N	109.20 E
Sulawesi (Celebes), i., Indon.	60	F7	2.00 S	121.00 E
Sulawesi, Laut see Celebes Sea, s., Asia	60	E7	3.00 N	122.00 E
Sulawesi Selatan, state, Indon.	66	E11	3.43 S	119.58 E
Sulawesi Tengah, state, Indon.	66	D12	1.11 S	120.12 E
Sulawesi Tenggara, state, Indon.	66	E12	3.40 S	120.54 E
Sulaymān, Birak (Solomon's Pools), hist., W.B.	76	G5	31.41 N	35.10 E
Sulcis, reg., Italy	32	E2	39.04 N	8.41 E
Suldalsvatnet, l., Nor.	16	H4	59.35 N	6.44 E
Sūldeh, Iran	74	B12	36.34 N	52.01 E
Sulechów, Pol.	24	D11	52.05 N	15.37 E
Sulęcin, Pol.	24	D11	52.26 N	15.06 E
Sulejów, Pol.	24	E15	51.22 N	19.53 E
Sulejówek, Pol.	24	D17	52.14 N	21.16 E
Sulen, Mount, mtn., Pap. N. Gui.	101a	a3	3.24 S	142.16 E
Suleymaniye Mosque, rel., Tur.	185b		41.00 N	28.57 E
Suliki, Indon.	66	D2	0.05 S	100.28 E
Sulina, Rom.	36	D16	45.09 N	29.40 E
Sulina, Bratul, stm., Rom.	36	D15	45.10 N	29.41 E
Sulingen, Ger.	24	D4	52.40 N	8.48 E
Sulitelma, mtn., Eur.	12	C7	67.08 N	16.24 E
Sulitjelma, Nor.	14	E6	67.07 N	16.05 E
Sulitjelma see Sulitelma, mtn., Eur.	12	C7	67.08 N	16.24 E
Sulitjelmaisen, ice, Nor.	14	E6	67.09 N	16.18 E
Suljukta, Kyrg.	72	B10	39.55 N	69.36 E
Sulkava, Fin.	18	F15	61.47 N	28.22 E
Sullana, Peru	164	D1	4.53 S	80.41 W
Sulligent, Al., U.S.	134	D10	33.54 N	88.08 W
Sullivan, Il., U.S.	130	E9	39.35 N	88.37 W
Sullivan, In., U.S.	130	E10	39.05 N	87.24 W
Sullivan, Mo., U.S.	130	F6	38.12 N	91.10 W

Name Page Map Ref. Latitude Longitude
Sullivan Canyon, val., Ca., U.S. 198 34.03 N 118.30 W
Sullivan Lake, l., Ab., Can. 144 E18 52.00 N 112.00 W
Sully-sur-Loire, Fr. 20 G11 47.45 N 2.22 E
Sulmona, Italy 30 H10 42.04 N 13.54 E
Sulphur, La., U.S. 134 G5 30.13 N 93.22 W
Sulphur, Ok., U.S. 134 C2 34.30 N 96.58 W
Sulphur, stm., Ab., Can. 144 C12 53.50 N 119.10 W
Sulphur, stm., U.S. 134 D5 33.05 N 93.51 W
Sulphur Creek, stm., S.D., U.S. 140 C10 44.46 N 102.24 W
Sulphur Draw, stm., Tx., U.S. 138 H6 33.13 N 102.20 W
Sulphur Springs, Tx., U.S. 134 D3 33.08 N 95.36 W
Sulphur Springs Draw, stm., U.S. 138 H6 32.12 N 101.36 W
Sulphur Springs Valley, val., Az., U.S. 150 L7 31.50 N 109.50 W
Sultan, Wa., U.S. 146 C5 47.51 N 121.50 W
Sultanabad see Arāk, Iran 74 C11 34.05 N 49.41 E
Sultanahmet Mosque, rel., Tur. 185b 41.00 N 28.58 E
Sultan Alonto, Lake, l., Phil. 68 G5 7.53 N 124.15 E
Sultanatābād, ngh., Iran 185d 35.46 N 51.28 E
Sultançiftliği, ngh., Tur. 185b 41.02 N 29.13 E
Sultandağı, Tur. 34 E14 38.32 N 31.13 E
Sultan Dağı, mtn., Tur. 34 E10 38.58 N 27.26 E
Sultan Hassan's Mosque, rel., Egypt 191c 30.02 N 31.15 E
Sultanhisar, Tur. 34 F11 37.53 N 28.09 E
Sultan Kudarat, Phil. 68 G5 7.16 N 124.15 E
Sultan Mosque, rel., Sing. 189c 1.18 N 103.52 E
Sultānpur, India 70 E8 26.15 N 82.04 E
Sultānpur Dabās, ngh., India 190a 28.46 N 77.03 E
Sulu, Laut see Sulu Sea, s., Asia 68 F2 8.00 N 120.00 E
Sulu Archipelago, is., Phil. 68 H3 6.00 N 121.00 E
Suluca see Suluova, Tur. 42 E6 40.46 N 35.42 E
Sulu Chi, l., China 70 C11 30.17 N 86.24 E
Sülüklü, Tur. 34 D13 39.05 N 30.58 E
Suluova, Tur. 42 E6 40.46 N 35.42 E
Sulūq, Libya 82 A4 31.40 N 20.15 E
Sulu Sea, s., Asia 68 F2 8.00 N 120.00 E
Sulzbach-Rosenberg, Ger. 24 G7 49.30 N 11.44 E
Šum, Russia 26 A14 59.52 N 31.46 E
Suma, ngh., Japan 188 34.39 N 135.08 E
Suma, stm., Russia 18 D22 64.17 N 35.24 E
Šumadija, reg., Yugo. 36 E7 44.10 N 20.50 E
Sumampa, Arg. 172 D6 29.23 S 63.27 W
Sumangat, Tanjong, c., Malay. 68 G1 6.35 N 117.30 E
Sūmār, Iran 74 D9 33.52 N 45.38 E
Sumarokovo, Russia 48 B15 55.46 N 35.54 E
Sumas, Wa., U.S. 146 B4 48.59 N 122.15 W
Sumatera (Sumatra), i., Indon. 60 E3 0.05 S 102.00 E
Sumatera Barat, state, Indon. 66 D2 1.01 S 101.20 E
Sumatera Selatan, state, Indon. 66 E3 3.00 S 104.00 E
Sumatera Utara, state, Indon. 64 K4 2.24 N 99.53 E
Sumatra see Sumatera, i., Indon. 60 E3 0.05 S 102.00 E
Šumava see Bohemian Forest, mts., Eur. 24 G8 48.53 N 13.51 E
Sumba, Far. Is. 12b n34 61.24 N 6.42 W
Sumba, i., Indon. 66 H11 10.00 S 120.00 E
Sumba, Selat, strt., Indon. 66 H11 9.03 S 120.01 E
Sumbar, stm., Turkmen. 74 A14 37.59 N 55.16 E
Sumbawa, i., Indon. 66 H10 8.48 S 117.56 E
Sumbawa Besar, Indon. 66 H10 8.29 S 117.24 E
Sumbawanga, Tan. 86 F6 7.59 S 31.37 E
Sumbe, Ang. 88 C1 11.14 S 13.51 E
Sumburgh Head, c., Scot., U.K. 10 B11 59.51 N 1.17 W
Sumburgh Roost, strt., Scot., U.K. 10 B11 59.50 N 1.17 W
Sumdo, China 70 A7 35.01 N 78.42 E
Sumé, Braz. 170 D7 7.39 S 36.55 W
Sumedang, Indon. 66 G5 6.50 S 107.55 E
Sümeg, Hung. 36 B4 46.59 N 17.17 E
Šumen, Blg. 36 F13 43.16 N 26.56 E
Sumenep, Indon. 66 G8 7.00 S 113.51 E
Šumeriči, Russia 18 D21 63.20 N 34.20 E
Šumerlja, Russia 40 D15 55.29 N 46.24 E
Sumgait see Sumqayıt, Azer. 42 E13 40.35 N 49.37 E
Sumgait see Sumqayıt, stm., Azer. 42 E13 40.37 N 49.37 E
Sumida, ngh., Japan 186 35.42 N 139.48 E
Sumida, stm., Japan 186 35.40 N 139.47 E
Šumilina, Bela. 26 E12 55.18 N 29.37 E
Suminoe, ngh., Japan 188 34.36 N 135.28 E
Sumisu-jima (Smith Island), i., Japan 52 E13 31.27 N 140.03 E
Sumiyoshi, ngh., Japan 188 34.36 N 135.31 E
Šumjači, Russia 26 G15 53.51 N 32.26 E
Sumkino, Russia 48 C11 58.06 N 68.20 E
Summerfield, Fl., U.S. 132 G3 29.00 N 82.02 W
Summerfield, N.C., U.S. 124 H6 36.12 N 79.55 W
Summer Island, i., Mi., U.S. 126 C3 45.33 N 86.38 W
Summer Lake, l., Or., U.S. 146 H6 42.50 N 120.45 W
Summerland, B.C., Can. 144 G11 49.36 N 119.40 W
Summer Palace, bldg., Russia 183a 59.53 N 29.55 E
Summerseat, Eng., U.K. 180 53.38 N 2.19 W
Summerside, P.E., Can. 122 D13 46.23 N 63.47 W
Summersville, Mo., U.S. 130 G6 37.10 N 91.39 W
Summersville, W.V., U.S. 124 F5 38.15 N 80.51 W
Summerton, S.C., U.S. 132 C5 33.36 N 80.21 W
Summerville, On., Can. 193b 43.37 N 79.34 W
Summerville, Ga., U.S. 134 C13 34.28 N 85.20 W
Summerville, S.C., U.S. 132 C5 33.00 N 80.10 W
Summit, Eng., U.K. 180 53.40 N 2.05 W
Summit, Ms., U.S. 134 F8 31.17 N 90.28 W
Summit, S.D., U.S. 128 F1 45.18 N 97.02 W
Summit Farms, Md., U.S. 202b 39.19 N 76.32 W
Summit Lake, B.C., Can. 144 B8 54.16 N 122.37 W
Summit Mountain, mtn., Nv., U.S. 148 D9 39.23 N 116.28 W
Summit Park, N.Y., U.S. 194 41.09 N 74.03 W
Summit Park Mall, shp. cen., N.Y., U.S. 202a 43.05 N 78.56 W
Summit Peak, mtn., Co., U.S. 138 D2 37.21 N 106.42 W
Summt, Ger. 182a 52.41 N 13.22 E
Summter See, l., Ger. 182a 52.42 N 13.23 E
Sumner, Ia., U.S. 130 B5 42.50 N 92.06 W
Sumner, Ms., U.S. 134 D8 33.58 N 90.22 W
Sumner, Wa., U.S. 146 C4 47.11 N 122.13 W
Sumner, Lake, res., N.M., U.S. 138 G4 34.38 N 104.25 W
Sumner Lake State Park, p.o.i., N.M., U.S. 138 G4 34.38 N 104.24 W
Sumostrov, ostrov, i., Russia 18 C22 64.23 N 35.16 E
Sumoto, Japan 56 E7 34.20 N 134.53 E
Sumozero, ozero, l., Russia 18 C22 63.58 N 35.10 E
Sumozero, ozero, l., Russia 18 F23 61.57 N 36.39 E
Sumpangbinangae, Indon. 66 F11 4.24 S 119.36 E
Šumperk, Czech Rep. 24 G13 49.57 N 16.59 E
Sumpiuh, Indon. 66 G6 7.36 S 109.22 E
Sumpter, Mi., U.S. 199 42.10 N 83.29 W
Sumqayıt, Azer. 42 E13 40.35 N 49.37 E
Sumqayıt, stm., Azer. 42 E13 40.37 N 49.37 E
Sumrall, Ms., U.S. 134 F9 31.24 N 89.32 W
Sumskij Posad, Russia 18 C22 64.15 N 35.26 E
Šumšu, ostrov, i., Russia 50 F20 50.45 N 156.20 E
Sumter, S.C., U.S. 132 C5 33.55 N 80.21 W
Sumusta el-Waqf, Egypt 76 J1 28.55 N 30.51 E
Sumy, Ukr. 38 C13 50.55 N 34.48 E
Sumy, co., Ukr. 38 B13 51.00 N 34.00 E
Sumzom, China 52 F4 29.43 N 96.07 E
Sun, stm., Mt., U.S. 146 C14 47.30 N 111.19 W
Suna, Russia 40 C17 57.50 N 50.04 E
Suna, stm., Russia 18 E20 62.06 N 34.18 E
Sunāmganj, Bngl. 70 F13 25.04 N 91.24 E
Sunart, Loch, b., Scot., U.K. 10 E7 56.40 N 5.53 W
Sunashinden, Japan 186 35.53 N 139.30 E
Sunaysilah, sw., Iraq 74 C7 35.35 N 41.53 E
Sunbright, Tn., U.S. 130 H13 36.15 N 84.39 W
Sunburst, Mt., U.S. 146 B15 48.52 N 111.54 W
Sunbury, Austl. 98 K5 37.34 S 144.45 E
Sunbury, Eng., U.K. 178 51.25 N 0.26 W
Sunbury, N.C., U.S. 124 H9 36.26 N 76.36 W
Sunbury, Oh., U.S. 124 D3 40.14 N 82.52 W
Sunbury, Pa., U.S. 124 D9 40.51 N 76.47 W
Sunchales, Arg. 172 E7 30.56 S 61.33 W
Sunchild Indian Reserve, ind. res., Ab., Can. 144 D15 52.41 N 115.20 W
Suncho Corral, Arg. 172 C6 27.55 S 63.25 W
Sunch'ŏn, Kor., S. 54 G7 34.56 N 127.29 E
Sunch'ŏn-ŭp, Kor., N. 54 E6 39.25 N 125.56 E
Sun City, Az., U.S. 150 J4 33.35 N 112.17 W
Suncook, N.H., U.S. 122 G5 43.07 N 71.26 W
Suncook, stm., N.H., U.S. 122 G5 43.07 N 71.28 W
Sunda, Selat (Sunda Strait), strt., Indon. 66 G4 6.00 S 105.46 E
Sundance, Wy., U.S. 140 C8 44.23 N 104.22 W
Sundar, Malay. 66 A9 4.54 N 115.12 E
Sundarbans, reg., Asia 70 H12 22.00 N 89.00 E
Sundargarh, India 70 G9 22.07 N 84.02 E
Sunda Shelf, unds. 174 I13 4.52 N 107.00 E
Sunda Strait see Sunda, Selat, strt., Indon. 66 G4 6.00 S 105.46 E
Sundays, stm., S. Afr. 90 H7 33.42 S 25.50 E
Sundbyberg, Swe. 16 H15 59.22 N 17.57 E
Sunde, Nor. 16 H3 59.50 N 5.43 E
Sunderland, Eng., U.K. 10 G11 54.54 N 1.23 W
Sundown, Austl. 96 E6 26.13 S 133.09 E
Sundown, Tx., U.S. 138 H6 33.27 N 102.29 W
Sundra, S. Afr. 191d 26.11 S 28.33 E
Sundre, Ab., Can. 144 E16 51.48 N 114.38 W
Sundridge, On., Can. 126 C10 45.45 N 79.23 W
Sundridge, Eng., U.K. 178 51.17 N 0.08 E
Sundsbruk, Swe. 16 E15 62.26 N 17.21 E
Sundsvall, Swe. 16 E15 62.23 N 17.19 E
Sundwig, Ger. 181 51.23 N 7.47 E
Suneori, Japan 186 35.56 N 139.24 E
Sunflower, Ms., U.S. 134 D8 33.32 N 90.32 W
Sunflower, Mount, mtn., Ks., U.S. 138 B7 39.04 N 102.01 W
Šun'ga, Russia 18 E21 62.35 N 34.58 E
Sungaianyar, Indon. 66 E10 2.56 S 116.18 E
Sungaibatu, Indon. 66 C7 0.49 N 110.44 E
Sungaibuntu, Indon. 66 F5 6.03 S 107.23 E
Sungaidareh, Indon. 66 D2 0.58 S 101.30 E
Sungaigerong, Indon. 66 E4 2.59 S 104.50 E
Sungaiguntung, Indon. 66 C3 0.17 N 103.37 E
Sungaikakap, Indon. 66 D6 0.03 S 109.10 E
Sungai Kolok, Thai. 64 J5 6.01 N 101.57 E
Sungailangsat, Indon. 66 D2 0.53 S 101.17 E
Sungailiat, Indon. 66 D5 1.51 S 106.06 E
Sungailimau, Indon. 66 D1 0.31 S 100.03 E
Sungaipenuh, Indon. 66 E2 2.03 S 101.23 E
Sungaipenyu, Indon. 66 C6 0.16 N 109.04 E
Sungai Petani, Malay. 64 J5 5.38 N 100.29 E
Sungaipinang, Indon. 66 D8 0.48 S 114.04 E
Sungairotan, Indon. 66 D3 1.42 S 102.50 E
Sungairotan, Indon. 66 E4 3.06 S 104.16 E
Sungaisalak, Indon. 66 D3 0.29 S 102.59 E
Sungaiselan, Indon. 66 E5 2.23 S 105.59 E
Sungaitiram, Indon. 66 D10 0.47 S 117.12 E
Sungari see Songhua, stm., China 52 B11 47.42 N 132.31 E
Sungari Reservoir see Songhua Hu, res., China 52 C10 43.25 N 127.10 E
Sungguminasa, Indon. 66 F11 5.12 S 119.27 E
Sung Kong, i., China 189d 22.11 N 114.17 E
Sung Noen, Thai. 64 E5 14.56 N 101.45 E
Sungsang, Indon. 66 E4 2.27 S 104.52 E
Sungshan Airport (Domestic), arpt., Tai. 187d 25.04 N 121.33 E
Sunland, ngh., Ca., U.S. 198 34.16 N 118.19 W
Sunland Park, N.M., U.S. 136 C1 31.47 N 106.31 W
Sunlight Creek, stm., Wy., U.S. 146 F17 44.47 N 109.23 W
Sunndalsfjorden, b., Nor. 16 E5 62.45 N 8.25 E
Sunndalsøra, Nor. 16 E6 62.40 N 8.35 E
Sunne, Swe. 16 H11 59.50 N 13.09 E
Sunnedalen, val., Nor. 16 E6 62.38 N 8.48 E
Sunnersta, Swe. 16 H15 59.47 N 17.39 E
Sunnfjord, reg., Nor. 16 F3 61.25 N 5.22 E
Sunnhordland, hist. reg., Nor. 16 H3 59.44 N 6.04 E
Sunningdale, Eng., U.K. 178 51.24 N 0.38 W
Sunnmøre, reg., Nor. 16 E4 62.14 N 6.16 E
Sunnybrae, N.S., Can. 122 E14 45.24 N 62.29 W
Sunny Crest, Il., U.S. 196 41.33 N 87.42 W
Sunnynook, Ab., Can. 144 E19 51.17 N 111.39 W
Sunnyridge, S. Afr. 191d 26.10 S 28.11 E
Sunnyside, Ut., U.S. 150 D6 39.33 N 110.22 W
Sunnyside, Wa., U.S. 146 D7 46.19 N 120.00 W
Sunnyside, hist., N.Y., U.S. 194 41.03 N 73.52 W
Sunnyslope, Ab., Can. 144 E17 51.38 N 113.34 W
Sunnyvale, Ca., U.S. 148 F3 37.22 N 122.01 W
Sunol, Ca., U.S. 200 37.36 N 121.53 W
Sunol Ridge, mtn., Ca., U.S. 200 37.38 N 121.56 W
Sun Prairie, Wi., U.S. 130 A8 43.10 N 89.12 W
Sunray, Tx., U.S. 138 E7 36.01 N 101.49 W
Sunrise, Fl., U.S. 132 J5 26.08 N 80.16 W
Sunrise, Wy., U.S. 140 E8 42.19 N 104.41 W
Sunrise Mall, shp. cen., N.Y., U.S. 194 40.41 N 73.26 W
Sunrise Manor, Nv., U.S. 150 G1 36.11 N 115.03 W
Sunset, La., U.S. 134 G6 30.24 N 92.04 W
Sunset, Tx., U.S. 138 H11 33.27 N 97.45 W
Sunset, ngh., Ca., U.S. 200 37.45 N 122.30 W
Sunset Beach, Ca., U.S. 198 33.43 N 118.04 W
Sunset Country, reg., Austl. 98 J3 35.02 S 141.19 E
Sunset Crater National Monument, p.o.i., Az., U.S. 150 H5 35.21 N 111.31 W
Sunset Heights, Tx., U.S. 136 C5 31.53 N 102.23 W
Sunset Hill, N.J., U.S. 194 40.26 N 74.35 W
Sunset Hills, Pa., U.S. 197b 40.35 N 80.15 W
Sunset Peak, mtn., Ca., U.S. 198 34.13 N 117.42 W
Sunshine, Austl. 98 K5 37.47 S 144.49 E
Sunshine Island, i., China 189d 22.16 N 114.03 E
Sunshine Point, c., Mi., U.S. 199 42.36 N 82.47 W
Suntar, Russia 50 D12 62.09 N 117.38 E
Suntar-Hajata, hrebet, mts., Russia 50 D17 62.00 N 143.00 E
Suntaug Lake, l., Ma., U.S. 201 42.32 N 71.00 W
Sun Temple, rel., Egypt 191c 29.55 N 31.11 E
Sunter, ngh., Indon. 187e 6.09 S 106.50 E
Sunter, Kali, can., Indon. 187e 6.07 S 106.50 E
Sunti, stm., India 190b 22.37 N 88.34 E
Sun Valley, Id., U.S. 146 G12 43.42 N 114.22 W
Sun Valley, ngh., Ca., U.S. 198 34.14 N 118.21 W
SunValley Center, shp. cen., Ca., U.S. 200 37.58 N 122.03 W
Sunwapta, stm., Ab., Can. 144 D13 52.31 N 117.41 W
Sunwu, China 52 B10 49.25 N 127.19 E
Sunyani, Ghana 84 H4 7.20 N 2.20 W
Sunža, stm., Russia 42 D11 43.26 N 46.08 E
Suojarvi, Russia 18 E19 62.04 N 32.22 E
Suojarvi, ozero, l., Russia 18 E19 62.11 N 32.23 E
Suolahti, Fin. 18 E12 62.33 N 25.51 E
Suomenlahti see Finland, Gulf of, b., Eur. 18 H10 60.00 N 27.00 E
Suomenselkä, mts., Fin. 18 C14 63.59 N 27.00 E
Suomi see Finland, ctry., Eur. 12 C12 64.00 N 26.00 E
Suomussalmi, Fin. 18 C16 64.53 N 29.01 E
Suomutunturi, hill, Fin. 14 F18 66.32 N 27.59 E
Suō-nada, s., Japan 56 F4 33.50 N 131.30 E
Suonenjoki, Fin. 18 E14 62.37 N 27.07 E
Suontee, l., Fin. 18 F13 61.39 N 26.31 E
Suordah, Russia 50 C15 66.43 N 131.40 E
Suorva, Swe. 14 E9 67.32 N 18.13 E
Supamo, stm., Ven. 168 D10 6.42 N 61.58 W
Supaul, India 70 E11 26.06 N 86.35 E
Superí see La Merced, Arg. 172 D5 28.09 S 65.38 W
Superior, Az., U.S. 150 J5 33.17 N 111.06 W
Superior, Mt., U.S. 146 C12 47.11 N 114.53 W
Superior, Ne., U.S. 138 A10 40.01 N 98.04 W
Superior, Wi., U.S. 128 E6 46.43 N 92.06 W
Superior, Wy., U.S. 150 B7 41.45 N 108.57 W
Superior, Laguna, b., Mex. 154 G11 16.21 N 94.54 W
Superior, Lake, l., N.A. 114 C7 48.00 N 88.00 W
Supetar, Cro. 30 G13 43.23 N 16.33 E
Suphan Buri, Thai. 64 E4 14.27 N 100.07 E
Suphan Buri, stm., Thai. 64 E5 13.31 N 100.16 E
Süphan Dağı, vol., Tur. 42 G8 38.56 N 42.50 E
Supij, stm., Ukr. 38 D10 49.37 N 31.48 E
Suponevo, Russia 26 G17 53.11 N 34.18 E
Supraśl, Pol. 24 C19 53.13 N 23.22 E
Supraśl, stm., Pol. 24 C19 53.10 N 22.58 E
Sup'ung-ho see Supung Reservoir, res., Asia 54 D6 40.30 N 125.02 E
Supung Reservoir, res., Asia 54 D6 40.30 N 125.02 E
Sūq ash-Shuyūkh, Iraq 74 E10 30.52 N 46.28 E
Suqian, China 58 E8 33.56 N 118.17 E
Sūq Suwayq, Sau. Ar. 72 E4 24.21 N 38.28 E
Suquṭrā (Socotra), i., Yemen 72 G7 12.30 N 53.53 E
Şūr (Tyre), Leb. 76 E6 33.16 N 35.13 E
Şūr, Oman 72 E8 22.34 N 59.30 E
Sur, Cabo, c., Chile 100l f29 27.11 S 109.25 W
Sur, Canal, strt., Arg. 206 34.37 S 58.15 W
Sur, Point, c., Ca., U.S. 148 G4 36.18 N 121.53 W
Sura, Russia 40 E14 53.53 N 45.45 E
Sura, ngh., India 190b 22.33 N 88.25 E
Sura, stm., Russia 40 D14 55.37 N 46.01 E
Šurab see Sjurab, Taj. 72 A11 40.02 N 70.32 E
Surabaja see Surabaya, Indon. 66 G8 7.14 S 112.44 E
Surabaya, Indon. 66 G8 7.14 S 112.44 E
Surag-san, mtn., Kor., S. 189b 37.42 N 127.04 E
Surahammar, Swe. 16 H14 59.42 N 16.13 E
Surakarta, Indon. 66 G7 7.34 S 110.49 E
Suramana, Indon. 66 D11 0.47 S 119.39 E
Şūrān, Syria 76 C7 35.17 N 36.45 E
Şūrān, Syria 76 B8 36.34 N 37.13 E
Šurany, Slvk. 24 H14 48.05 N 18.11 E
Surat, Austl. 98 F7 27.09 S 149.04 E
Sūrat, India 70 H4 21.11 N 72.49 E
Sūratgarh, India 70 D4 29.19 N 73.54 E
Surat Thani, Thai. 64 H4 9.06 N 99.18 E
Surava, Russia 40 E12 52.57 N 41.18 E
Suraž, Bela. 40 D7 55.25 N 30.42 E
Suraž, Pol. 24 D19 52.57 N 22.57 E
Suraž, Russia 26 G15 53.00 N 32.24 E
Surazj, Bela. 12 I14 55.25 N 30.42 E
Surbiton, ngh., Eng., U.K. 178 51.24 N 0.18 W
Surco, stm., Peru 204d 12.13 S 77.03 W
Surdulica, Yugo. 36 G9 42.40 N 22.09 E
Sûre see Sauer, stm., Eur. 20 E15 49.42 N 6.30 E
Şureanu, Munţii, mts., Rom. 36 D10 45.33 N 23.28 E
Surendranagar, India 70 G3 22.43 N 71.37 E
Suresnes, Fr. 179 48.52 N 2.14 E
Surf City, N.J., U.S. 124 E11 39.39 N 74.09 W
Surfers Paradise, Austl. 98 G10 27.59 S 153.25 E
Surgères, Fr. 22 C5 46.06 N 0.44 W
Surgoinsville, Tn., U.S. 124 H3 36.28 N 82.51 W
Surgut, Russia 48 B12 61.15 N 73.12 E
Suri, Pap. N. Gui. 101a b3 7.11 S 143.55 E
Suria, India 190b 22.51 N 88.33 E
Suriāpet, India 69 C4 17.08 N 79.37 E
Surigao, Phil. 68 F5 9.46 N 125.29 E
Surigao Strait, strt., Phil. 68 E5 10.15 N 125.23 E
Surin, Thai. 64 E6 14.53 N 103.29 E
Suriname, ctry., S.A. 164 C6 4.00 N 56.00 W
Suring, Wi., U.S. 128 D1 44.59 N 88.22 W
Sūrīyah see Syria, ctry., Asia 74 C6 35.00 N 38.00 E
Šurma, Russia 40 C17 56.58 N 50.20 E
Sūrmaq, Iran 74 E13 31.04 N 52.48 E
Surna, stm., Nor. 16 E6 62.58 N 8.40 E
Surnadalsøra, Nor. 16 E6 62.58 N 8.40 E
Surovikino, Russia 40 G13 48.36 N 42.51 E
Surovo, Russia 48 C19 55.37 N 105.37 E
Surprise, Az., U.S. 150 J4 33.37 N 112.19 W
Surprise Valley, val., U.S. 148 B5 41.35 N 120.05 W
Surquillo, Peru 204d 12.07 S 77.02 W
Surrency, Ga., U.S. 132 E3 31.43 N 82.11 W
Surrey, N.D., U.S. 142 F12 48.14 N 101.07 W
Surrey, University of, educ., Eng., U.K. 178 51.14 N 0.36 W
Surrey Heath, mun., Eng., U.K. 178 51.23 N 0.35 W
Surry, Va., U.S. 124 G9 37.07 N 76.49 W
Sursee, Switz. 30 C5 47.10 N 8.06 E
Sursk, Russia 40 E14 53.04 N 45.42 E
Surskoe, Russia 40 D15 54.28 N 46.42 E
Surt, Libya 82 A3 31.12 N 16.35 E
Surt, Khalīj (Sidra, Gulf of), b., Libya 82 A3 31.30 N 18.00 E
Surtanāhu, Pak. 70 E2 26.21 N 70.00 E
Surte, Swe. 16 J9 57.50 N 12.01 E
Surtsey, i., Ice. 12a l29 63.18 N 20.34 W
Suru, Pap. N. Gui. 101a b3 6.50 S 144.45 E
Sürüç, Tur. 42 G8 36.58 N 38.26 E
Surud, Raas, c., Som. 86 B9 11.10 N 47.30 E
Suruga-wan, b., Japan 56 E11 34.51 N 138.33 E
Surui, stm., Braz. 205a 22.42 S 43.07 W
Surulangun, Indon. 66 E3 2.37 S 102.45 E
Suru-Lere, ngh., Nig. 191a 6.31 N 3.22 E
Surumu, stm., Braz. 168 F11 3.22 N 60.18 W
Surveyor Creek, stm., Co., U.S. 138 A6 40.20 N 102.38 W
Survilliers, Fr. 179 49.06 N 2.33 E
Šuryškary, Russia 48 A10 65.53 N 65.23 E
Susa see Shūsh, Iran 74 D11 32.11 N 48.16 E
Susa, Italy 30 E4 45.08 N 7.03 E
Susa, Japan 56 E4 34.37 N 131.36 E
Sušac, Otok, i., Cro. 30 H13 42.46 N 16.30 E
Sūsah, Libya 82 A4 32.53 N 21.56 E
Susak, Otok, i., Cro. 30 F11 44.30 N 14.17 E
Susaki, Japan 56 F6 33.23 N 133.17 E
Sūsangerd, Iran 74 E11 31.33 N 48.11 E
Susanino, Russia 26 A13 59.30 N 30.19 E
Susanino, Russia 40 B12 58.08 N 41.36 E
Susanino, Russia 50 F17 52.47 N 140.06 E
Susano, mun., Braz. 205b 23.35 S 46.18 W
Susanville, Ca., U.S. 148 C5 40.25 N 120.38 W
Šušary, Russia 183a 59.46 N 30.21 E
Šušary, Russia 183a 59.48 N 30.23 E
Suşehri, Tur. 42 E8 40.09 N 38.05 E
Šušenskoe, Russia 48 D16 53.19 N 91.56 E
Sušice, Czech Rep. 24 G9 49.14 N 13.31 E
Susitna, stm., Ak., U.S. 109 D9 61.13 N 150.35 W
Susleni, Mol. 38 F8 47.25 N 28.59 E
Suslonger, Russia 40 C16 56.19 N 48.15 E
Susoh, Indon. 64 K3 3.41 N 96.52 E
Susong, China 58 F7 30.09 N 116.07 E
Suspiro del Moro, Puerto, p., Spain 28 G7 37.02 N 3.39 W
Susquehanna, Pa., U.S. 124 C10 41.56 N 75.35 W
Susquehanna, stm., U.S. 124 D9 39.32 N 76.04 W
Susquehanna, West Branch, stm., Pa., U.S. 124 C9 40.53 N 76.48 W
Susques, Arg. 166 D3 23.24 S 66.30 W
Süssenbrunn, ngh., Aus. 182b 48.17 N 16.30 E
Sussex, N.B., Can. 122 E11 45.43 N 65.30 W
Sussex, N.J., U.S. 124 C11 41.12 N 74.36 W
Sussex, Va., U.S. 124 H8 36.54 N 77.16 W
Susubona, Sol. Is. 101b e8 8.18 S 159.27 E
Susul, Malay. 66 A10 4.55 N 116.41 E
Susuman, Russia 50 D18 62.46 N 148.10 E
Susurluk, Tur. 34 D11 39.55 N 28.09 E
Susuzmüsellim, Tur. 34 B9 41.06 N 27.05 E
Šušvė, stm., Lith. 26 E6 55.10 N 23.50 E
Susz, Pol. 24 C15 53.43 N 19.20 E
Sutak, India 70 B6 33.10 N 77.26 E
Sütçüler, Tur. 34 F13 37.30 N 30.59 E
Suthat, Wat, rel., Thai. 187a 13.45 N 100.30 E
Sutherland, S. Afr. 90 H5 32.24 S 20.40 E
Sutherland, Ia., U.S. 130 A2 42.58 N 95.30 W
Sutherland, Ne., U.S. 140 F11 41.09 N 101.07 W
Sutherland, stm., B.C., Can. 144 B5 54.29 N 125.10 W
Sutherlin, Or., U.S. 146 G3 43.23 N 123.18 W
Suthiāna, India 190a 28.31 N 77.26 E
Sutjeska Nacionalni Park, p.o.i., Bos. 36 F5 43.17 N 18.41 E
Sutla (Sotla), stm., Eur. 30 D12 45.52 N 15.40 E
Sutlej (Langqên) (Satluj), stm., Asia 70 D3 29.20 N 71.02 E
Sutter, Ca., U.S. 148 D4 39.10 N 121.45 W
Sutter Buttes, mtn., Ca., U.S. 148 D4 39.12 N 121.49 W
Sutter Creek, Ca., U.S. 148 E5 38.23 N 120.47 W
Sutton, Eng., U.K. 178 51.12 N 0.26 W
Sutton, Ak., U.S. 109 D10 61.42 N 148.52 W
Sutton, Ne., U.S. 140 G15 40.36 N 97.51 W
Sutton, W.V., U.S. 124 F5 38.39 N 80.44 W
Sutton, Monts see Green Mountains, mts., N.A. 122 F4 43.45 N 72.45 W
Sutton-at-Home, Eng., U.K. 178 51.25 N 0.14 E
Sutton in Ashfield, Eng., U.K. 10 H11 53.07 N 1.16 W
Sutton Lake, res., W.V., U.S. 124 F5 38.39 N 80.38 W
Sutton Lane Ends, Eng., U.K. 180 53.14 N 2.08 W
Sutton Leach, Eng., U.K. 180 53.26 N 2.42 W
Sutton Park, N.J., U.S. 194 40.49 N 74.42 W
Sutton Place, hist., Eng., U.K. 178 51.16 N 0.33 W
Suttons Bay, Mi., U.S. 126 C4 44.58 N 85.39 W
Sutton Weaver, Eng., U.K. 180 53.18 N 2.41 W
Sutton West, On., Can. 126 D10 44.17 N 79.20 W
Suttor, stm., Austl. 98 C6 20.36 S 147.01 E
Sutwik Island, i., Ak., U.S. 109 E8 56.33 N 157.10 W
Suure-Jaani, Est. 26 B8 58.32 N 25.28 E
Suur Munamägi, hill, Est. 26 C9 57.43 N 27.05 E
Suur Pakri, i., Est. 26 A6 59.20 N 23.53 E
Suva, Fiji 101e q19 18.07 S 178.26 E
Suvadiva Atoll, at., Mald. 62a i12 0.30 N 73.15 E
Suvainiškis, Lith. 26 D8 56.10 N 25.17 E
Suvalovo Ozërki, ngh., Russia 183a 60.02 N 30.18 E
Suva Planina, mts., Yugo. 36 F9 43.10 N 22.10 E
Suvarlı, Tur. 76 A8 37.32 N 37.38 E
Suvasvesi, l., Fin. 18 E14 62.39 N 28.12 E
Suvorov, Russia 26 F19 54.06 N 36.30 E
Suvorove, Ukr. 38 H8 45.34 N 29.00 E
Suwa, Japan 56 C11 36.02 N 138.08 E
Suwałki, Pol. 24 B18 54.06 N 22.56 E
Suwannaphum, Thai. 64 E6 15.34 N 103.49 E
Suwannee, stm., U.S. 132 G2 29.18 N 83.09 W
Suwanose-jima, i., Japan 55a k19 29.38 N 129.43 E
Suwarrow, at., Cook Is. 94 E10 13.15 S 163.05 W
Suweis, Khalîg el- (Suez, Gulf of), b., Egypt 76 J4 29.00 N 32.50 E
Suweis, Qanâ el- (Suez Canal), can., Egypt 76 H3 29.56 N 32.34 E
Suwŏn, Kor., S. 54 F7 37.16 N 127.00 E
Suxian see Suzhou, China 58 E7 33.38 N 116.58 E
Suzak, Kaz. 48 F11 44.08 N 68.28 E
Suzaka, Japan 56 C11 36.38 N 138.19 E
Suzdal', Russia 40 C12 56.25 N 40.26 E
Suze, stm., Switz. 30 C3 47.08 N 7.13 E
Suzëmka, Russia 26 H16 52.19 N 34.04 E
Suzhou, China 58 E7 33.38 N 116.58 E
Suzhou, China 58 F9 31.18 N 120.37 E
Suzigou, China 58 A10 40.23 N 123.25 E
Suzu, Japan 56 B10 37.25 N 137.14 E
Suzuka, Japan 56 E9 34.52 N 136.34 E
Suzuka-sammyaku, mts., Japan 56 D9 34.59 N 136.24 E
Suzuki, Japan 186 35.43 N 139.31 E
Suzu-misaki, c., Japan 56 B10 37.30 N 137.20 E
Suzun, Russia 48 D14 53.46 N 82.19 E
Suzzara, Italy 30 F7 44.59 N 10.44 E
Sværtholthalvøya, pen., Nor. 14 B17 70.34 N 26.14 E
Svalbard, dep., Eur. 104 B24 78.00 N 17.00 E
Svaliava, Ukr. 38 E2 48.33 N 23.00 E
Svalöv, Swe. 16 L11 55.54 N 13.06 E
Svaneke, Den. 16 L13 55.08 N 15.08 E
Svängsta, Swe. 16 K12 56.15 N 14.46 E
Svanøyna, i., Nor. 16 F2 61.29 N 5.06 E
Svanskog, Swe. 16 H10 59.11 N 12.34 E
Svanstein, Swe. 14 F14 66.38 N 23.50 E
Svapa, stm., Russia 40 F9 51.44 N 34.57 E
Svappavaara, Swe. 14 E12 67.38 N 21.03 E
Svärdsjö, Swe. 16 G13 60.44 N 15.54 E
Svartå, Swe. 16 H12 59.08 N 14.31 E
Svartån, stm., Swe. 16 H14 59.36 N 16.33 E
Svartbyn, Swe. 14 F13 66.16 N 22.50 E
Svartenhuk, pen., Grnld. 108 C15 71.45 N 54.31 W
Svartisen, ice, Nor. 14 F4 66.39 N 13.59 E
Svataj, Russia 50 C19 68.00 N 151.48 E
Svatove, Ukr. 38 D17 49.24 N 38.09 E
Svay Chék, Camb. 64 F6 13.48 N 102.58 E
Svay Riĕng, Camb. 64 G7 11.04 N 105.49 E
Svedala, Swe. 16 L11 55.30 N 13.13 E
Svėdasai, Lith. 26 E8 55.40 N 25.22 E
Sveg, Swe. 16 E12 62.01 N 14.22 E
Svegssjön, l., Swe. 16 E11 62.00 N 14.14 E
Sveindal, Nor. 16 I5 58.30 N 7.28 E
Švėkšna, Lith. 26 E4 55.30 N 21.37 E
Svelgen, Nor. 16 F3 61.46 N 5.18 E
Svelvik, Nor. 16 H8 59.37 N 10.24 E
Sven', Russia 26 G17 53.08 N 34.22 E
Švenčionėliai, Lith. 26 E8 55.09 N 26.00 E
Švenčionys, Lith. 26 E9 55.07 N 26.10 E
Svendborg, Den. 16 L8 55.03 N 10.36 E
Svenljunga, Swe. 16 J11 57.30 N 13.07 E
Svensbu, Nor. 14 C10 69.39 N 19.50 E
Svenstrup, Den. 16 K7 56.59 N 9.52 E
Šventoji, Lith. 26 D4 56.01 N 21.06 E
Šventoji, stm., Lith. 26 E7 55.05 N 24.21 E
Sverdlovsk see Ekaterinburg, Russia 48 C10 56.50 N 60.36 E
Sverdlovs'k, Ukr. 38 E18 48.04 N 39.39 E
Sverdlovskaja oblast', co., Russia 40 C21 56.34 N 59.03 E
Sverdrup, ostrov, i., Russia 50 B4 74.34 N 79.24 E
Sverdrup Channel, strt., Nu., Can. 108 A6 80.02 N 97.40 W
Sverdrup Islands, is., Nu., Can. 108 B5 79.00 N 96.00 W
Sverige see Sweden, ctry., Eur. 12 E6 62.00 N 15.00 E
Svesa, Ukr. 38 B12 51.56 N 33.53 E
Svetac, i., Cro. 30 G12 43.01 N 15.45 E
Sveti Arhandjel Mihajlo, rel., Mac. 34 A4 42.07 N 21.28 E
Sveti Jovan Bigorski, rel., Mac. 34 B3 41.38 N 20.37 E
Sveti Nikole, Mac. 34 B4 41.52 N 21.57 E
Svetlahorsk, Bela. 26 H12 52.37 N 29.45 E
Svetlaja, Russia 52 B12 46.34 N 138.19 E
Světlá nad Sázavou, Czech Rep. 24 G11 49.40 N 15.25 E
Svetlogorsk, Russia 26 F3 54.57 N 20.10 E
Svetlograd, Russia 40 I13 45.20 N 42.50 E
Svetlyj, Russia 26 F3 54.41 N 20.08 E
Svetlyj, Russia 48 D10 50.49 N 60.52 E
Svetlyj, Russia 50 E12 58.28 N 116.06 E
Svetogorsk, Russia 18 F15 61.06 N 28.52 E
Svetozarevo, Yugo. 36 F8 43.58 N 21.15 E
Svid', stm., Russia 18 G25 61.11 N 38.46 E
Svidník, Slvk. 24 G17 49.19 N 21.34 E
Svijaga, stm., Russia 40 D16 55.38 N 48.25 E
Svilajnac, Yugo. 36 E8 44.14 N 21.13 E
Svilengrad, Blg. 36 H13 41.46 N 26.12 E
Svinecea Mare, Vârful, mtn., Rom. 36 E9 44.48 N 22.09 E
Svinesund, Swe. 16 H9 59.05 N 11.16 E
Svínoy, i., Far. Is. 12b m34 62.16 N 6.22 W
Svir, Bela. 26 F9 54.51 N 26.24 E
Svir', stm., Russia 18 G20 60.30 N 32.48 E
Svirica, Russia 18 G19 60.28 N 32.52 E
Svirsk, Russia 48 D18 53.04 N 103.20 E
Svir'stroj, Russia 18 G20 60.48 N 33.44 E
Sviščovka, Russia 40 E13 52.50 N 43.43 E
Svislač, Bela. 26 G7 53.01 N 24.06 E
Svislač, stm., Bela. 26 G11 53.26 N 28.57 E
Svištov, Blg. 36 F12 43.37 N 25.20 E
Svit, Slvk. 24 G16 49.03 N 20.11 E
Svitava, stm., Czech Rep. 24 G12 49.08 N 16.38 E
Svitávka, Czech Rep. 24 G12 49.29 N 16.36 E
Svitavy, Czech Rep. 24 G12 49.45 N 16.27 E
Svitlovods'k, Ukr. 38 D12 49.03 N 33.15 E
Svizzera see Switzerland, ctry., Eur. 30 D5 47.00 N 8.00 E
Svjacilavičy, Bela. 26 H14 52.48 N 31.19 E
Svjatoj Nos, mys, c., Russia 14 D30 68.08 N 39.45 E
Svjatoj Nos, mys, c., Russia 50 B17 72.52 N 140.46 E
Svjatonosskij zaliv, b., Russia 14 D30 68.05 N 39.38 E
Svjatoslavka, Russia 40 F13 51.19 N 43.26 E
Svobodnyy port, Ukr. 38 G10 46.20 N 31.20 E
Svoboda, Russia 38 A15 51.58 N 36.19 E
Svobodnyj, Russia 50 F14 51.22 N 128.08 E
Svoge, Blg. 36 G10 42.58 N 23.21 E
Svol'na, stm., Bela. 26 E11 55.43 N 28.02 E
Svolvær, Nor. 14 D5 68.15 N 14.32 E
Svorkmo, Nor. 16 D7 63.10 N 9.46 E
Svratka, stm., Czech Rep. 24 G12 49.08 N 16.37 E
Svullrya, Nor. 16 G10 60.25 N 12.25 E
Swabia see Schwaben, hist. reg., Ger. 24 H5 48.10 N 9.25 E
Swain Reefs, rf., Austl. 98 C9 21.40 S 152.15 E
Swainsboro, Ga., U.S. 132 D3 32.36 N 82.20 W
Swains Island, at., Am. Sam. 94 E9 11.03 S 171.04 W
Swakop, stm., Nmb. 90 C2 22.40 S 14.31 E
Swakopmund, Nmb. 90 C2 22.40 S 14.32 E
Swale, mun., Eng., U.K. 178 51.21 N 0.41 E
Swale, stm., Eng., U.K. 10 G11 54.05 N 1.20 W
Swan, stm., Can. 142 B11 52.33 N 100.45 W
Swan, stm., Ab., Can. 144 A15 55.11 N 115.18 W
Swan, stm., Mn., U.S. 128 D5 47.00 N 93.16 W
Swan, stm., Mt., U.S. 146 C13 48.03 N 114.04 W
Swan Acres, Pa., U.S. 197b 40.33 N 80.02 W
Swanage, Eng., U.K. 10 K11 50.37 N 1.58 W
Swan Creek, stm., S.D., U.S. 140 B12 45.17 N 100.18 W
Swan Creek, North Branch, stm., Mi., U.S. 199 42.06 N 83.23 W

Name	Page	Map Ref.	Latitude	Longitude

Swan Creek Point, c., Mi., U.S. 199 42.40 N 82.39 W
Swanee see Suwannee, stm., U.S. 132 G2 29.18 N 83.09 W
Swan Hill, Austl. 98 J4 35.20 S 143.33 E
Swan Hills, Ab., Can. 144 B15 54.42 N 115.24 W
Swan Hills, hills, Ab., Can. 144 B15 54.48 N 115.52 W
Swan Islands see Santanilla, Islas, is., Hond. 156 D6 17.25 N 83.55 W
Swan Lake, Mb., Can. 142 E15 49.24 N 98.46 W
Swan Lake, Mt., U.S. 146 C13 47.55 N 113.50 W
Swan Lake, l., Mb., Can. 142 B12 52.30 N 100.45 W
Swan Lake, l., Mn., U.S. 128 G4 44.18 N 94.15 W
Swannanoa, N.C., U.S. 124 I3 35.35 N 82.24 W
Swannanoa, Lake, l., N.J., U.S. 194 41.01 N 74.31 W
Swan Peak, mtn., Mt., U.S. 146 C13 47.43 N 113.38 W
Swanquarter, N.C., U.S. 132 A9 35.24 N 76.20 W
Swan Range, mts., Mt., U.S. 146 C13 47.50 N 113.40 W
Swan Reach, Austl. 98 J2 34.33 S 139.36 E
Swan River, Mb., Can. 142 B12 52.05 N 101.15 W
Swan River Indian Reserve, ind. res., Ab., Can. 144 A15 55.16 N 115.19 W
Swansboro, N.C., U.S. 132 B8 34.41 N 77.03 W
Swanscombe, Eng., U.K. 178 51.26 N 0.18 E
Swansea, Austl. 99a o13 42.08 S 148.04 E
Swansea, Wales, U.K. 10 J8 51.37 N 3.57 W
Swansea, S.C., U.S. 132 C4 33.44 N 81.05 W
Swansea, ngh., On., Can. 193b 43.38 N 79.28 W
Swans Island, i., Me., U.S. 122 F8 44.09 N 68.26 W
Swanson Lake, res., Ne., U.S. 138 A7 40.09 N 101.05 W
Swanton, Vt., U.S. 126 D16 44.55 N 73.07 W
Swanville, Mn., U.S. 128 F4 45.54 N 94.38 W
Swarthmore College, educ., Pa., U.S. 203 39.54 N 75.21 W
Swart-Mfolozi, stm., S. Afr. 90 F10 28.20 S 31.58 E
Swartruggens, S. Afr. 90 D8 25.38 S 26.41 E
Swartz Creek, Mi., U.S. 130 B14 42.57 N 83.50 W
Swarzędz, Pol. 24 D13 52.24 N 17.04 E
Swasey Peak, mtn., Ut., U.S. 150 D3 39.23 N 113.19 W
Swasey Wash, stm., Ut., U.S. 150 D3 39.15 N 112.52 W
Swāt, stm., Pak. 70 A3 34.31 N 71.28 E
Swatow see Shantou, China 58 J7 23.21 N 116.40 E
Swaziland, ctry., Afr. 90 E10 26.30 S 31.30 E
Swea City, Ia., U.S. 128 H4 43.23 N 94.18 W
Swede Hill, Pa., U.S. 197b 40.17 N 79.34 W
Swedeland, Pa., U.S. 203 40.05 N 75.20 W
Sweden, ctry., Eur. 12 E6 62.00 N 15.00 E
Swede Run, stm., N.J., U.S. 203 40.02 N 74.58 W
Swedesburg, Pa., U.S. 203 40.06 N 75.20 W
Swedish Knoll, mtn., Ut., U.S. 150 D5 39.16 N 111.26 W
Swedru, Ghana 84 H4 5.31 N 0.41 W
Sweeney Plan, Pa., U.S. 197b 40.11 N 79.48 W
Sweeny, Tx., U.S. 136 E12 29.02 N 95.41 W
Sweeny Park, p.o.i., N.Y., U.S. 202a 43.02 N 78.52 W
Sweet Briar, Va., U.S. 124 G6 37.32 N 79.04 W
Sweetgrass, Mt., U.S. 146 A15 48.59 N 111.57 W
Sweet Grass Creek, stm., Mt., U.S. 146 D17 45.47 N 109.47 W
Sweet Grass Hills, hills, Mt., U.S. 146 B15 48.55 N 111.30 W
Sweet Grass Indian Reserve, ind. res., Sk., Can. 142 B5 52.44 N 108.45 W
Sweet Home, Or., U.S. 146 F4 44.24 N 122.43 W
Sweet Home, Tx., U.S. 136 E10 29.21 N 97.04 W
Sweet Springs, Mo., U.S. 130 F4 38.57 N 93.25 W
Sweetwater, Tn., U.S. 132 A1 35.36 N 84.27 W
Sweetwater, Tx., U.S. 136 B7 32.28 N 100.24 W
Sweetwater, stm., Wy., U.S. 140 E5 42.27 N 106.54 W
Sweetwater Creek, stm., U.S. 138 F9 35.18 N 99.57 W
Sweetwater Creek, stm., Tx., U.S. 136 B7 32.40 N 100.06 W
Swellendam, S. Afr. 90 H5 34.01 S 20.26 E
Świdnica, Pol. 24 F12 50.50 N 16.29 E
Świdnik, Pol. 24 E18 51.13 N 22.40 E
Świdwin, Pol. 24 C11 53.47 N 15.47 E
Świebodzice, Pol. 24 F12 50.51 N 16.20 E
Świebodzin, Pol. 24 D11 52.14 N 15.31 E
Świecie, Pol. 24 C14 53.24 N 18.26 E
Świerzawa, Pol. 24 E11 51.00 N 15.53 E
Świętokrzyskie, state, Pol. 24 F16 50.45 N 20.45 E
Świętokrzyskie, Góry, mts., Pol. 24 E16 50.56 N 20.54 E
Świętokrzyski Park Narodowy, p.o.i., Pol. 24 F16 50.55 N 21.00 E
Swift Creek, stm., Al., U.S. 134 E12 32.25 N 86.38 W
Swift Creek, stm., N.C., U.S. 124 H8 35.56 N 77.35 W
Swift Creek, stm., N.C., U.S. 132 A8 35.11 N 77.06 W
Swift Current, Sk., Can. 142 D6 50.16 N 107.47 W
Swift Current Creek, stm., Sk., Can. 142 D6 50.39 N 107.44 W
Swifton, Ar., U.S. 134 B7 35.49 N 91.07 W
Swilly, Lough, b., Ire. 10 F5 55.09 N 7.31 W
Swimming, stm., N.J., U.S. 194 40.21 N 74.05 W
Swimming River Reservoir, res., N.J., U.S. 194 40.19 N 74.07 W
Swinburne, Cape, c., Nu., Can. 110 A11 71.19 N 98.35 W
Swinden Reservoirs, res., Eng., U.K. 180 53.48 N 2.10 W
Swindle Island, i., B.C., Can. 144 D2 52.31 N 128.35 W
Swindon, Eng., U.K. 10 J11 51.34 N 1.46 W
Swinemünde see Świnoujście, Pol. 24 C10 53.54 N 14.14 E
Swinford, Ire. 10 H4 53.56 N 8.57 W
Świnoujście (Swinemünde), Pol. 24 C10 53.54 N 14.14 E
Swinton, Eng., U.K. 180 53.31 N 2.20 W
Swissvale, Pa., U.S. 197b 40.25 N 79.52 W
Switzerland, ctry., Eur. 30 D5 47.00 N 8.00 E
Swords, Ire. 10 H6 53.27 N 6.13 W
Swormville, N.Y., U.S. 202a 43.02 N 78.42 W
Sworton Heath, Eng., U.K. 180 53.21 N 2.28 W
Syalah, Russia 50 C13 66.12 N 124.02 E
Syampur, India 190b 22.29 N 88.13 E
Syan (San), stm., Eur. 24 F18 50.44 N 21.51 E
Sybille Creek, stm., Wy., U.S. 140 F7 42.06 N 105.05 W
Syburg, ngh., Ger. 181 51.25 N 7.29 E
Sycamore, Ga., U.S. 132 E2 31.39 N 83.37 W
Sycamore, Il., U.S. 130 C9 41.58 N 88.41 W
Sycamore, Oh., U.S. 124 D2 40.56 N 83.11 W
Sycamore Creek, stm., Az., U.S. 150 J5 33.38 N 111.40 W
Sycamore Creek, stm., Tx., U.S. 136 E7 29.14 N 100.47 W
Sycamore Gardens, De., U.S. 203 39.42 N 75.42 W
Sycamore Island, i., Pa., U.S. 197b 40.29 N 79.52 W
Sycan, stm., Or., U.S. 146 H5 42.27 N 121.17 W
Syčovka, Russia 26 E17 55.49 N 34.17 E
Syców, Pol. 24 E13 51.18 N 17.43 E
Sydenham, Austl. 192b 37.42 S 144.46 E
Sydenham, On., Can. 126 D13 44.24 N 76.35 W
Sydenham, ngh., S. Afr. 191d 26.09 S 28.06 E
Sydenham, ngh., Eng., U.K. 178 51.26 N 0.03 W
Sydenham, stm., On., Can. 126 F7 42.35 N 82.22 W
Sydenham West, Austl. 192b 37.41 S 144.39 E
Sydney, Austl. 98 I8 33.52 S 151.12 E
Sydney, Austl. 192a 33.52 S 151.13 E
Sydney, N.S., Can. 122 D16 46.08 N 60.11 W
Sydney, University of, educ., Austl. 192a 33.53 S 151.11 E
Sydney Bay, b., Norf. I. 100i y25 29.03 S 167.56 E
Sydney Lake, l., On., Can. 128 A4 50.36 N 94.20 W
Sydney Mines, N.S., Can. 122 D16 46.15 N 60.14 W
Sygan, Pa., U.S. 197b 40.21 N 80.08 W
Šyičy, Bela. 26 H12 52.14 N 29.14 E
Syke, Ger. 24 D4 52.54 N 8.49 E
Sykesville, Pa., U.S. 124 C7 41.02 N 78.49 W
Sykiá, Grc. 34 C6 40.02 N 23.56 E
Sykkylven, Nor. 16 E4 62.23 N 6.35 E
Syktyvkar, Russia 48 B8 61.39 N 50.49 E
Sylacauga, Al., U.S. 134 D12 33.10 N 86.15 W
Sylane see Sylarna, mtn., Eur. 16 D10 63.02 N 12.13 E
Sylarna, mtn., Eur. 16 D10 63.02 N 12.13 E
Sylhet, Bngl. 70 F13 24.54 N 91.52 E
Sylling, Nor. 16 H8 59.53 N 10.18 E
Syloga, Russia 12 E20 63.49 N 43.39 E
Sylt, i., Ger. 16 M6 54.54 N 8.20 E
Syltefjordelva, stm., Nor. 14 B20 70.31 N 29.58 E
Sylva, N.C., U.S. 132 A2 35.22 N 83.13 W
Sylva, stm., Russia 40 C20 58.06 N 56.37 E
Sylvan Glen, N.J., U.S. 203 40.11 N 75.42 W
Sylvan Grove, Ks., U.S. 138 C10 39.00 N 98.23 W
Sylvan Hills, Ar., U.S. 134 C6 34.50 N 92.13 W
Sylvania, Austl. 192a 34.01 S 151.07 E
Sylvania, Ga., U.S. 132 D4 32.44 N 81.37 W
Sylvania, Oh., U.S. 124 C2 41.41 N 83.41 W
Sylvania Heights, Austl. 192a 34.02 S 151.06 E
Sylvan Lake, Ab., Can. 144 D16 52.18 N 114.06 W
Sylvan Lake, Il., U.S. 196 42.15 N 88.03 W
Sylvan Lake, Mi., U.S. 199 42.37 N 83.20 W
Sylvan Lake, l., Ab., Can. 144 D16 52.22 N 114.11 W
Sylvan Lake, l., Mi., U.S. 199 42.37 N 83.20 W
Sylvan Pass, p., Wy., U.S. 146 F16 44.28 N 110.09 W
Sylvester, Ga., U.S. 132 E2 31.31 N 83.50 W
Sylvester, Tx., U.S. 136 B7 32.43 N 100.15 W
Sylvia, Ks., U.S. 138 D10 37.57 N 98.23 W
Sym, Russia 48 B15 60.20 N 88.23 E
Sym, stm., Russia 48 B15 60.17 N 90.04 E
Syme see Sými, i., Grc. 34 G10 36.34 N 27.50 E
Sými, Grc. 34 G10 36.36 N 27.50 E
Sými, i., Grc. 34 G10 36.34 N 27.50 E
Šymkent, Kaz. 48 F11 42.18 N 69.35 E
Symmes Creek, stm., Oh., U.S. 130 F15 38.25 N 82.27 W
Syndal, Austl. 192b 37.53 S 145.09 E
Synel'nykove, Ukr. 38 E14 48.19 N 35.32 E
Synevir, Ukr. 38 A8 48.30 N 23.39 E
Syniukha, stm., Ukr. 38 E9 48.03 N 30.50 E
Synivka, Ukr. 38 C13 50.32 N 34.06 E
Synnfjell, mts., Nor. 16 F7 61.05 N 9.45 E
Syon House, hist., Eng., U.K. 178 51.29 N 0.19 W
Syowa, sci., Ant. 103 C9 69.00 S 39.35 E
Syracuse, In., U.S. 130 C12 41.25 N 85.44 W
Syracuse, Ks., U.S. 138 C7 37.58 N 101.44 W
Syracuse, Ne., U.S. 130 D1 40.39 N 96.11 W
Syracuse, N.Y., U.S. 126 E13 43.03 N 76.08 W
Syrdarja, Uzb. 72 A10 40.52 N 68.39 E
Syrdar'ja see Syr Darya, stm., Asia 48 F11 46.06 N 60.47 E
Syr-Darija (Naryn), stm., Asia 72 A10 46.06 N 60.47 E
Syrdar'ja see Naryn, stm., Asia 72 A11 46.06 N 60.47 E
Syrdar'ja see Syr-Darija, stm., Asia 72 A10 46.06 N 60.47 E
Syr Darya (Syrdar'ja), stm., Asia 48 F11 46.06 N 60.47 E
Syria, ctry., Asia 74 C6 35.00 N 38.00 E
Syriam, Mya. 64 D3 16.45 N 96.14 E
Syrian Desert (Shām, Bādiyat ash-), des., Asia 74 D6 32.00 N 40.00 E
Sýrna, i., Grc. 34 G9 36.20 N 26.41 E
Sýros, i., Grc. 34 F7 37.25 N 24.55 E
Šyšćycy, Bela. 26 G10 53.13 N 27.33 E
Sysmä, Fin. 18 F12 61.30 N 25.41 E
Sysoevo, Russia 18 H23 59.12 N 36.12 E
Sysola, stm., Russia 48 B8 61.41 N 50.52 E
Sysslebäck, Swe. 16 G10 60.44 N 12.53 E
Systyg-Hem, Russia 48 D17 52.40 N 95.31 E
Sytkivtsi, Ukr. 38 E8 48.54 N 29.12 E
Syt'kovo, Russia 26 D16 56.32 N 33.57 E
Syukunoshō, Japan 188 34.50 N 135.32 E
Syväjärvi, Fin. 14 E16 67.18 N 25.54 E
Syväri, l., Fin. 18 D15 63.16 N 28.06 E
Syvash, zatoka, strt., Ukr. 38 H14 45.56 N 34.41 E
Syvas'ke, Ukr. 38 G13 46.23 N 34.34 E
Syvtuga, stm., Russia 18 D25 63.35 N 38.34 E
Syzran', Russia 40 E16 53.08 N 48.25 E
Szabadka see Subotica, Yugo. 36 C6 46.05 N 19.40 E
Szabolcs-Szatmár-Bereg, state, Hung. 36 A9 48.00 N 22.10 E
Szada, Hung. 182c 47.38 N 19.19 E
Szamocin, Pol. 24 C13 53.01 N 17.07 E
Szamos (Someș), stm., Eur. 36 B9 48.06 N 22.21 E
Szamotuły, Pol. 24 D12 52.36 N 16.35 E
Szarvas, Hung. 36 C7 46.52 N 20.34 E
Szatmárnémeti see Satu Mare, Rom. 36 B9 47.47 N 22.53 E
Százhalombatta, Hung. 182c 47.20 N 18.56 E
Szczawnica, Pol. 24 G16 49.25 N 20.29 E
Szczecin (Stettin), Pol. 24 C10 53.26 N 14.32 E
Szczecinek, Pol. 24 C12 53.42 N 16.42 E
Szczeciński, Zalew see Stettin Lagoon, b., Eur. 24 C10 53.47 N 14.22 E
Szczekociny, Pol. 24 F15 50.38 N 19.50 E
Szczuczyn, Pol. 24 C18 53.33 N 22.16 E
Szczytno, Pol. 24 C17 53.33 N 21.00 E
Szechwan see Sichuan, state, China 52 E5 31.00 N 105.00 E
Szechwan Basin see Sichuan Pendi, bas., China 52 E5 30.00 N 105.00 E
Szécsény, Hung. 36 A6 48.04 N 19.32 E
Szeged, Hung. 36 C7 46.15 N 20.10 E
Szeghalom, Hung. 36 B8 47.01 N 21.10 E
Székesfehérvár, Hung. 36 B5 47.12 N 18.24 E
Szekszárd, Hung. 36 C5 46.20 N 18.42 E
Szentendre, Hung. 36 B5 47.40 N 19.03 E
Szentendrei-Duna, mth., Hung. 182c 47.36 N 19.05 E
Szentendrei-sziget, i., Hung. 182c 47.39 N 19.07 E
Szentes, Hung. 36 C7 46.39 N 20.16 E
Szentgotthárd, Hung. 36 C3 46.56 N 16.12 E
Szeping see Siping, China 52 C9 43.09 N 124.22 E
Szépművészeti Museum, bldg., Hung. 182c 47.31 N 19.05 E
Szerencs, Hung. 36 A8 48.09 N 21.12 E
Szeszupa see Šešupė, stm., Eur. 26 F5 55.03 N 22.12 E
Szeszupa see Šešupe, stm., Eur. 26 F5 55.03 N 22.12 E
Szigethalom, Hung. 182c 47.20 N 19.00 E
Szigetszentmiklós, Hung. 182c 47.21 N 19.03 E
Szigetvár, Hung. 30 D14 46.03 N 17.48 E
Szilas-patak, stm., Hung. 182c 47.36 N 19.06 E
Szlichtyngowa, Pol. 24 E12 51.43 N 16.14 E
Szob, Hung. 36 B5 47.49 N 18.52 E
Szolnok, Hung. 36 B7 47.10 N 20.12 E
Szombathely, Hung. 36 B3 47.14 N 16.38 E
Szprotawa, Pol. 24 E11 51.33 N 15.33 E
Sztum, Pol. 24 C15 53.56 N 19.01 E
Szubin, Pol. 24 C13 53.00 N 17.44 E
Szydłowiec, Pol. 24 E16 51.13 N 20.52 E
Szypliszki, Pol. 24 B19 54.15 N 23.05 E

T

Taal, Lake, l., Phil. 68 C3 13.59 N 121.01 E
Taalintehdas, Fin. 18 G9 60.01 N 22.30 E
Taaoa, Baie, b., Fr. Poly. 100g s18 9.50 S 139.02 W
Taavetti, Fin. 18 G14 60.55 N 27.34 E
Tabacal, Quebrada, stm., Ven. 204c 10.31 N 67.02 W
Ṭābah, Sau. Ar. 74 G8 27.02 N 42.10 E
Tábara, Spain 28 C5 41.49 N 5.57 W
Tabar Islands, is., Pap. N. Gui. 101a a5 2.45 S 151.57 E
Tabarka, Tun. 32 H2 36.57 N 8.45 E
Tabasco, state, Mex. 152 D6 18.15 N 93.00 W
Tabatinga, stm., Braz. 170 I4 17.30 S 43.29 W
Tabayin, Mya. 64 A2 22.42 N 95.17 E
Tabelbala, Alg. 84 D4 29.23 N 3.14 W
Taber, Ab., Can. 144 G18 49.47 N 112.08 W
Taberg, Swe. 16 J12 57.40 N 14.06 E
Tabernacle, St. K./N. 159a c2 17.23 N 62.46 W
Tabernacle, N.J., U.S. 203 39.50 N 74.42 W
Tabernes de Valldigna see Tavernes de la Valldigna, Spain 28 E10 39.04 N 0.15 W
Tabira, Braz. 170 D7 7.35 S 37.33 W
Tabla, Cerro de la, mtn., P.R. 158a b3 18.03 N 66.08 W
Tablada, Arg. 206 34.42 S 58.32 W
Tablas, Cabo, c., Chile 172 E2 31.51 S 71.34 W
Tablas de Daimiel, Parque Nacional de las, p.o.i., Spain 28 E7 39.07 N 3.36 W
Tablas Island, i., Phil. 68 D4 12.23 N 122.01 E
Tablas Strait, strt., Phil. 68 D3 12.40 N 121.48 E
Tablat, Alg. 28 H14 36.24 N 3.19 E
Table Mountain, mtn., Nf., Can. 122 C17 47.43 N 59.13 W
Table Mountain, mtn., Az., U.S. 150 K6 32.49 N 110.31 W
Table Rock, Ne., U.S. 130 D1 40.10 N 96.06 W
Table Rock Lake, res., U.S. 130 H4 36.35 N 93.30 W
Table Top, mtn., Az., U.S. 150 K4 32.46 N 112.07 W
Tabley Mere, l., Eng., U.K. 180 53.17 N 2.25 W
Tablones, P.R. 158a b4 18.14 N 65.44 W
Taboão, Ribeirão do, stm., Braz. 205b 23.40 S 46.28 W
Tabor, Mount, hill, St. Vin. 159e p11 12.35 N 61.26 W
Tábor, Czech Rep. 24 G10 49.25 N 14.40 E
Tabor, Russia 50 B19 71.15 N 150.17 E
Tabor, Ia., U.S. 130 D2 40.53 N 95.39 W
Tabor, N.J., U.S. 194 40.52 N 74.29 W
Tabor, S.D., U.S. 140 E15 42.55 N 97.38 W
Tabor, Mount see Tavor, Har, mtn., Isr. 76 F6 32.41 N 35.23 E
Tabora, Tan. 86 E6 5.01 S 32.49 E
Tabor City, N.C., U.S. 132 B7 34.08 N 78.52 W
Tabou, C. Iv. 84 I3 4.25 N 7.21 W
Tabrīz, Iran 74 A10 38.05 N 46.16 E
Tábua, Riacho da, stm., Braz. 170 E3 9.12 S 44.25 W
Tabuaço, Port. 28 C3 41.07 N 7.34 W
Tabuaeran, at., Kir. 94 C11 3.51 N 159.18 W
Tabu-dong, Kor., S. 56 C1 36.02 N 128.31 E
Tabuk, Phil. 68 B3 17.24 N 121.25 E
Tabūk, Sau. Ar. 72 D4 28.23 N 36.34 E
Tabuleiro do Norte, Braz. 170 C6 5.15 S 38.07 W
Tabwémasana, Mont, mtn., Vanuatu 101d j16 15.20 S 166.44 E
Täby, Swe. 16 H16 59.29 N 18.04 E
Tacagua, Quebrada, stm., Ven. 204c 10.37 N 67.02 W
Tacámbaro de Codallos, Mex. 154 F8 19.14 N 101.28 W
Tacaná, Volcán, vol., N.A. 154 H12 15.08 N 92.06 W
Tacañitas, Arg. 172 D6 28.37 S 62.36 W
Tacaratu, Braz. 170 E6 9.06 S 38.10 W
Taché, Lac, l., N.T., Can. 110 C7 64.00 N 120.00 W
Tacheng, China 52 B1 46.44 N 82.58 E
Tachia, stm., Tai. 58 I9 24.20 N 120.33 E
Tachichitte, Isla de, i., Mex. 154 C4 24.58 N 108.05 W
Tachie, stm., B.C., Can. 144 B6 54.39 N 124.46 W
Tachikawa Air Base, mil., Japan 186 35.43 N 139.25 E
Táchira, state, Ven. 168 D6 7.50 N 72.05 W
Tachoshui, Tai. 58 I9 24.19 N 121.45 E
Tachov, Czech Rep. 24 G8 49.48 N 12.38 E
Tacima, Braz. 170 D8 6.30 S 35.39 W
Tacloban, Phil. 68 E5 11.14 N 124.59 E
Taclobo, Phil. 68 D4 12.18 N 122.35 E
Tacna, Peru 164 G3 18.01 S 70.15 W
Tacna, Az., U.S. 150 K3 32.41 N 114.00 W
Tacoignières, Fr. 179 48.50 N 1.40 E
Tacoma, Wa., U.S. 146 C4 47.14 N 122.26 W
Taconic Range, mts., U.S. 124 B12 42.30 N 73.20 W
Tacony, ngh., Pa., U.S. 203 40.02 N 75.03 W
Tacony Creek, stm., Pa., U.S. 203 40.01 N 75.06 W
Tacony Creek Park, p.o.i., Pa., U.S. 203 40.02 N 75.07 W
Taco Pozo, Arg. 172 B6 25.36 S 63.15 W
Tacotalpa, stm., Mex. 154 G12 17.48 N 92.51 W
Tacuarembó, Ur. 172 E9 31.42 S 55.59 W
Tacuarembó, stm., Ur. 172 E10 32.25 S 55.28 W
Tacuarí, stm., Ur. 172 F10 32.48 S 53.09 W
Tacuba, ngh., Mex. 204a 19.28 N 99.12 W
Tacubaya, ngh., Mex. 204a 19.25 N 99.12 W
Tacutu (Takutu), stm., S.A. 168 F11 3.02 N 60.29 W
Tadain, Japan 188 34.52 N 135.24 E
Tadami, Japan 56 B12 37.21 N 139.19 E
Tadaoka, Japan 188 34.29 N 135.24 E
Tademaït, Plateau du, plat., Alg. 84 D5 28.20 N 2.47 E
Tādepallegūdem, India 69 C5 16.48 N 81.31 E
Tadine, N. Cal. 101d m16 21.32 S 167.52 E
Tadjemout, Alg. 84 D5 25.26 N 3.40 E
Tadjeraouine, Tun. 32 I2 35.55 N 8.33 E
Tadjoura, Dji. 82 E8 11.47 N 42.53 E
Tadotsu, Japan 56 E6 34.15 N 133.45 E
Tadoule Lake, l., Mb., Can. 110 D11 58.38 N 98.20 W
Tadoussac, Qc., Can. 122 B7 48.10 N 69.41 W
Tādpatri, India 69 D4 14.54 N 78.00 E
Tadžikistan see Tajikistan, ctry., Asia 72 B11 39.00 N 71.00 E
T'aean, Kor., S. 54 F7 36.45 N 126.17 E
T'aebaek-san, mtn., Kor., S. 56 B1 37.06 N 128.55 E
T'aebaek-sanmaek, mts., Asia 54 E8 37.29 N 128.30 E
Taech'ŏn, Kor., S. 54 F7 36.24 N 126.32 E
Taedong-gang, stm., Kor., N. 54 E6 38.43 N 125.07 E
Taegu, Kor., S. 54 G8 35.52 N 128.35 E
Taehan-min'guk see Korea, South, ctry., Asia 54 G8 36.30 N 128.00 E
Taehwajŏn, Kor., S. 189b 37.36 N 126.52 E
Taejin, Kor., S. 56 C2 36.34 N 129.24 E
Taejŏn, Kor., S. 54 F7 36.20 N 127.26 E
Tælavåg, Nor. 16 G2 60.16 N 4.59 E
T'aemo-san, mtn., Kor., S. 189b 37.27 N 127.04 E
Taeng, stm., Thai. 64 C4 19.06 N 98.57 E
Taf, stm., Wales, U.K. 10 J9 51.47 N 4.28 W
Tafahi, i., Tonga 94 E9 15.57 S 173.43 W
Tafalla, Spain 28 B9 42.31 N 1.40 W
Tafanlieh, Tai. 58 J9 21.58 N 120.44 E
Tafassasset, Oued, stm., Afr. 82 C1 21.51 N 9.58 E
Tafassâsset, Oued, stm., Afr. 84 E6 21.51 N 9.58 E
Tafassasset, Ténéré du, des., Niger 84 E7 21.00 N 11.00 E
Tafelberg, hill, Neth. Ant. 158g p22 12.04 N 68.49 W
Tafermaar, Indon. 60 G9 6.49 S 134.07 E
Tafí Viejo, Arg. 172 C5 26.44 S 65.15 W
Tafo, Ghana 84 H4 6.13 N 0.22 W
Taft, Iran 74 E14 31.45 N 54.13 E
Taft, Ca., U.S. 148 H6 35.08 N 119.26 W
Taft, Ok., U.S. 134 B3 35.45 N 95.32 W
Taft, Tx., U.S. 136 F10 27.58 N 97.23 W
Taftān, Kūh-e, vol., Iran 72 D9 28.36 N 61.08 E
Taga, Japan 188 34.49 N 135.49 E
Taga, Samoa 101c g11 13.47 S 172.28 W
Tagajō, Japan 56 A14 38.20 N 141.00 E
Taganrog, Russia 40 H11 47.14 N 38.54 E
Taganrog, Gulf of, b., Eur. 38 G16 47.00 N 38.23 E
Taganrogskij zaliv, b., Eur. 40 H10 47.00 N 38.23 E
Tagânt, reg., Maur. 84 F2 18.00 N 12.00 W
Tagarete, Cerro, mtn., Mex. 154 B6 26.31 N 105.56 W
Tagawa, Japan 56 F3 33.38 N 130.49 E
Tagaytay, Phil. 68 C3 14.05 N 120.56 E
Tagbilaran, Phil. 68 F4 9.39 N 123.52 E
Tagdempt see Tihert, Alg. 84 B5 35.28 N 1.21 E
Tage, Pap. N. Gui. 101a b3 6.21 S 143.18 E
Tagig, stm., Phil. 187f 14.31 N 121.05 E
Tagish Lake, l., Can. 110 C3 59.45 N 134.14 W
Tagliamento, stm., Italy 30 E9 45.39 N 13.05 E
Taglio di Po, Italy 30 E9 45.00 N 12.12 E
Tagnin nuruu see Tannu-Ola, hrebet, mts., Asia 48 D16 51.00 N 94.00 E
Tagnin nuruu see Tannu-Ola Mountains, mts., Asia 50 F7 51.00 N 94.00 E
Tagounit, Mor. 84 D3 29.58 N 5.36 W
Taguatinga, Braz. 170 G2 12.24 S 46.27 W
Taguig, Phil. 187f 14.32 N 121.04 E
Taguke, China 70 B10 32.05 N 84.43 E
Tagula Island, i., Pap. N. Gui. 96 B10 11.30 S 153.30 E
Tagum, Phil. 68 G5 7.26 N 125.48 E
Tagus (Tajo) (Tejo), stm., Eur. 28 E2 38.50 N 8.56 W
Tahakopa, N.Z. 102 H3 46.31 S 169.23 E
Tahan, Gunong, mtn., Malay. 64 J6 4.38 N 102.14 E
Tahanroz'ka zatoka see Taganrog, Gulf of, b., Eur. 38 G16 47.00 N 38.23 E
Tahanroz'ka zatoka see Taganrogskij zaliv, b., Eur. 40 H10 47.00 N 38.23 E
Tahat, mtn., Alg. 84 E6 23.17 N 5.31 E
Tāherī, Iran 74 G13 27.40 N 52.19 E
Tahiataš, Uzb. 48 F9 42.22 N 59.35 E
Tahifet, Alg. 84 E6 23.00 N 6.00 E
Tahiryuak Lake, l., N.T., Can. 110 A8 70.58 N 112.08 W
Tahiti, i., Fr. Poly. 100h v23 17.37 S 149.27 W
Tahiti-Faaa, Aéroport International de, arpt., Fr. Poly. 100h v21 17.33 S 149.36 W
Tahkuna nina, c., Est. 26 A5 59.04 N 22.35 E
Tahlequah, Ok., U.S. 130 I3 35.54 N 94.58 W
Tahoe, Lake, l., U.S. 148 D5 39.07 N 120.03 W
Tahoe City, Ca., U.S. 148 D5 39.10 N 120.08 W
Tahoe Lake, l., Nu., Can. 110 A8 70.01 N 108.53 W
Tahoka, Tx., U.S. 136 A6 33.10 N 101.47 W
Tahoua, Niger 84 F5 14.53 N 5.15 E
Tahquamenon, stm., Mi., U.S. 126 B4 46.33 N 85.02 W
Tahquamenon Falls State Park, p.o.i., Mi., U.S. 126 B4 46.33 N 85.09 W
Tahsis, B.C., Can. 144 G4 49.55 N 126.38 W
Tahta, Egypt 76 L2 26.46 N 31.30 E
Tahta, Russia 48 E6 45.54 N 42.07 E
Tahta-Bazar, Turkmen. 72 B9 35.57 N 62.54 E
Tahtabrod, Kaz. 48 D11 52.37 N 67.34 E
Tahtaköprü, Tur. 34 D12 39.56 N 29.38 E
Tahtamygda, Russia 50 F13 54.06 N 123.34 E
Tahtsa Lake, res., B.C., Can. 144 C3 53.42 N 127.26 W
Tahtsa Peak, mtn., B.C., Can. 144 C3 53.33 N 127.47 W
Tahuamanu, stm., S.A. 164 F4 11.06 S 67.32 W
Tahuata, i., Fr. Poly. 100g s18 9.57 S 139.05 W
Tahulandang, Pulau, i., Indon. 60 E7 2.20 N 125.25 E
Tahuna, Indon. 60 E8 3.36 N 125.30 E
Taï, C. Iv. 84 H3 5.52 N 7.26 W
Tai, Japan 188 34.31 N 135.26 E
Tai, ngh., Japan 188 34.45 N 135.00 E
Tai'an, China 58 C7 36.10 N 117.06 E
Taiarapu, Presqu'île de, pen., Fr. Poly. 100h w22 17.47 S 149.14 W
Taibai, China 58 D2 34.00 N 107.18 E
Taibai Shan, mtn., China 58 E2 33.54 N 107.46 E
Taibai Shan, mtn., China 58 B6 39.19 N 114.11 E
Taibilla, Sierra de, mts., Spain 28 F8 38.06 N 2.12 W
Taibus Qi, China 52 C8 41.52 N 115.17 E
Taicang, China 58 F9 31.26 N 121.07 E
Taichu see T'aichung, Tai. 58 I9 24.09 N 120.41 E
T'aichung, Tai. 58 I9 24.09 N 120.41 E
Taiden see Taejŏn, Kor., S. 54 F7 36.20 N 127.26 E
Taieri, stm., N.Z. 102 G4 46.02 S 170.10 E
Taif see At-Tā'if, Sau. Ar. 72 E5 21.16 N 40.24 E
Taigu, China 58 C5 37.25 N 112.33 E
Tai Hang, China 189d 22.17 N 114.11 E
Taihang Shan, mts., China 58 C5 38.00 N 114.00 E
Taihape, N.Z. 102 D6 39.40 S 175.48 E
Taihe, China 58 H6 26.48 N 114.54 E
Taihe, China 58 E6 33.11 N 115.36 E
Taihezhen, China 54 B5 44.47 N 123.29 E
Taihoku see T'aipei, Tai. 58 I9 25.03 N 121.30 E
T'aihsien see Taizhou, China 58 E8 32.29 N 119.54 E
Taihu, China 58 F7 30.25 N 116.16 E
Tai Hu, l., China 58 F9 31.12 N 120.10 E
Taikang see Dorbod, China 52 B9 46.50 N 124.24 E
Taikang, China 58 D6 34.03 N 114.51 E
Taikkyi, Mya. 64 D2 17.18 N 95.57 E
Taikou, China 58 F4 31.53 N 111.07 E
Taikyu see Taegu, Kor., S. 54 G8 35.52 N 128.35 E
Tailai, China 52 B9 46.22 N 123.24 E
Tai Lake see Tai Hu, l., China 58 F9 31.12 N 120.10 E
Tai Lam Chung, China 189d 22.22 N 114.01 E
Tai Lam Chung Reservoir, res., China 189d 22.23 N 114.01 E
Tailem Bend, Austl. 98 J2 35.16 S 139.27 E
Tai Long, China 189d 22.13 N 113.59 E
Tai Long, China 189d 22.25 N 114.22 E
Tai Long Wan, b., China 189d 22.24 N 114.24 E
Taimba, Russia 48 B17 60.18 N 98.58 E
Tai Mong Tsai, China 189d 22.24 N 114.18 E
Tai Mo Shan, mtn., China 189d 22.25 N 114.07 E
Tain, Scot., U.K. 10 D8 57.48 N 4.02 W
Tainaka, Japan 188 34.36 N 135.37 E
T'ainan, Tai. 58 J9 23.00 N 120.12 E
Taínaro, Ákra, c., Grc. 34 G5 36.24 N 22.29 E
Taining, China 58 H7 26.54 N 117.09 E
Taiobeiras, Braz. 170 H4 15.49 S 42.12 W
T'aipei, Tai. 58 I9 25.03 N 121.30 E
T'aipei, Tai. 187d 25.03 N 121.30 E
T'aipei, co., Tai. 187d 25.00 N 121.40 E
Taipei Bridge, trans., Tai. 187d 25.04 N 121.30 E
T'aipeihsien, Tai. 58 I9 24.58 N 121.25 E
Taipei Institute of Technology, educ., Tai. 187d 25.02 N 121.32 E
Taipei New Park, p.o.i., Tai. 187d 25.03 N 121.31 E
T'aipei Shih, mun., Tai. 187d 25.05 N 121.33 E
Taiping, China 58 J2 22.38 N 107.06 E
Taiping, Malay. 64 J5 4.51 N 100.43 E
Taipingchuan, China 54 B5 44.23 N 123.11 E
Taipingdian, China 58 E4 32.08 N 111.45 E
Taipingzhen, China 58 D2 35.44 N 107.38 E
Tai Po Hoi, b., China 189d 22.26 N 114.12 E
Tai Po Tsai, China 189d 22.21 N 114.15 E
Taipu, Braz. 170 C8 5.37 S 35.36 W
Taira see Iwaki, Japan 56 B13 37.03 N 140.55 E
Tais, Indon. 66 F3 4.04 S 102.34 E
Taisha, Japan 56 D5 35.23 N 132.41 E
Taishaku-zan, mtn., Japan 188 34.47 N 135.07 E
Taishan, China 58 J5 22.15 N 112.46 E
Tai Shan see Yuhuang Ding, mtn., China 58 C9 36.50 N 121.21 E
Taishi, Japan 188 34.31 N 135.39 E
Taishō, ngh., Japan 188 34.38 N 135.27 E
Tai Shui Hang, China 189d 22.25 N 114.13 E
Taishun, China 58 H8 27.33 N 119.43 E
Tai Tam Bay, b., China 189d 22.13 N 114.13 E
Taitao, Peninsula de, pen., Chile 166 I2 46.30 S 74.25 W
Taitō, ngh., Japan 186 35.43 N 139.47 E
Tai Tong, China 189d 22.25 N 114.01 E
T'aitung, Tai. 58 J9 22.45 N 121.08 E
Taivalkoski, Fin. 18 B15 65.34 N 28.16 E
Tai Wan, China 189d 22.10 N 114.15 E
Taiwan, ctry., Asia 52 G9 23.30 N 121.00 E
Taiwan, i., Tai. 46 G16 23.26 N 121.00 E
Taiwan Haixia see Taiwan Strait, strt., Asia 58 I8 24.00 N 119.00 E
Taiwan Strait, strt., Asia 58 I8 24.00 N 119.00 E
Tai Wan Tau, China 189d 22.18 N 114.17 E
Taixian, China 58 E9 32.30 N 120.08 E
Taixing, China 58 E9 32.10 N 120.00 E
Taiyang, China 58 F8 30.11 N 119.16 E
Taiyanggong, China 189a 39.58 N 116.25 E
Taiyiba, Isr. 76 F6 32.16 N 35.01 E
Taiyibe see Taiyiba, Isr. 76 F6 32.16 N 35.01 E
Taiyuan, China 58 C5 37.52 N 112.33 E
Taizhao, China 52 E3 30.01 N 92.57 E
Taizhou, China 58 E8 32.29 N 119.54 E
Taizi, stm., China 54 D5 41.00 N 122.26 E
Ta'izz, Yemen 82 E8 13.34 N 44.01 E
Tajarhī, Libya 82 C2 24.21 N 14.28 E
Tajbola, Russia 14 D24 68.27 N 33.14 E
Tajga, Russia 48 C15 56.03 N 85.36 E
Tajgonos, mys, c., Russia 50 D21 60.34 N 160.09 E
Tajgonos, poluostrov, pen., Russia 50 D21 61.20 N 161.00 E
Tajikistan, ctry., Asia 72 B11 39.00 N 71.00 E
Tajima, Japan 56 B12 37.12 N 139.46 E
Tajimi, Japan 56 D10 35.19 N 137.08 E
Tajique, N.M., U.S. 138 G2 34.44 N 106.17 W
Tajiri, Japan 188 34.24 N 135.18 E
Tajitos, Mex. 120 F6 30.57 N 112.21 W
Tāj Mahal, hist., India 70 E7 27.10 N 78.03 E
Tajmura, stm., Russia 48 B18 63.45 N 98.06 E
Tajmyr, ozero, l., Russia 50 B9 74.35 N 102.24 E
Tajmyr, poluostrov, pen., Russia 50 B7 76.00 N 104.00 E
Tajninka, Russia 183b 55.54 N 37.45 E
Tajo see Tagus, stm., Eur. 28 E5 38.50 N 8.56 W
Tājpur, India 190b 22.44 N 88.16 E
Tajpur Khurd, ngh., India 190a 28.35 N 77.03 E
Tajšet, Russia 48 C17 55.55 N 98.00 E
Tajsojgan, Kaz. 40 G18 48.19 N 53.29 E
Tajumulco, Volcán, vol., Guat. 156 E2 15.02 N 91.55 W
Tajuña, stm., Spain 28 D7 40.07 N 3.35 W
Tak, Thai. 64 D4 16.52 N 99.08 E
Takāb, Iran 74 B10 36.24 N 47.07 E
Takachiho, Japan 56 G4 32.42 N 131.18 E
Takachu, Bots. 90 C5 22.40 S 21.54 E
Takada see Bungo-takada, Japan 56 F4 33.33 N 131.27 E
Takagi, Japan 186 35.56 N 139.35 E
Takahagi, Japan 56 C13 36.43 N 140.43 E

Name	Page	Map Ref.	Latitude	Longitude
Takahashi, Japan	56	E6	34.48 N	133.37 E
Takahe, Mount, mtn., Ant.	103	C29	76.16 S	112.13 W
Takaido, ngh., Japan	186		35.40 N	139.37 E
Takaka, N.Z.	102	E5	40.51 S	172.48 E
Takakkaw Falls, wtfl., B.C., Can.	144	E14	51.30 N	116.29 W
Takalar, Indon.	66	F11	5.28 S	119.25 E
Takamatsu, Japan	56	E7	34.20 N	134.02 E
Takanabe, Japan	56	G4	32.07 N	131.31 E
Takao see Kaohsiung, Tai.	58	J8	22.38 N	120.17 E
Takaoka, Japan	56	C9	36.44 N	137.01 E
Takao-san, mtn., Japan	188		34.49 N	135.51 E
Takara-jima, i., Japan	55a	k19	29.09 N	129.13 E
Takarazuka, Japan	188		34.49 N	135.21 E
Takasago, Japan	56	E7	34.44 N	134.48 E
Takasaki, Japan	56	C11	36.19 N	139.00 E
Takashima, Japan	56	G2	32.39 N	129.45 E
Takata see Joetsu, Japan	56	B11	37.09 N	138.14 E
Takatori-yama, hill, Japan	186		35.18 N	139.37 E
Takatsuki, Japan	56	E8	34.50 N	135.37 E
Ta-kaw, Mya.	64	B4	21.36 N	98.56 E
Takayama, Japan	56	C10	36.08 N	137.15 E
Takayama, Japan	188		34.45 N	135.44 E
Takayanagi, Japan	186		35.25 N	139.57 E
Takefu, Japan	56	D9	35.54 N	136.10 E
Takenake, China	70	A8	34.11 N	81.20 E
Takengon, Indon.	64	J3	4.37 N	96.50 E
Takenotsuka, ngh., Japan	186		35.48 N	139.48 E
Takeo, Japan	56	F3	33.12 N	130.01 E
Takeoka, Japan	186		35.12 N	139.51 E
Take-shima (Tok-to), is., Asia	56	B4	37.15 N	131.50 E
Tākestān, Iran	74	B11	36.03 N	49.42 E
Taketa, Japan	56	G4	32.56 N	131.22 E
Takêv, Camb.	64	G7	10.59 N	104.45 E
Take-yama, hill, Japan	186		35.13 N	139.39 E
Takhādīd, well, Iraq	74	F9	29.59 N	44.30 E
Takhatpur, India	70	G8	22.08 N	81.52 E
Takhli, Thai.	64	E5	15.16 N	100.20 E
Takht-e Jamshīd (Persepolis), hist., Iran	74	E13	29.57 N	52.52 E
Taki, Pap. N. Gui.	101b	d6	6.28 S	155.51 E
Takijuq Lake, l., Nu., Can.	110	B8	66.15 N	113.05 W
Takikawa, Japan	54	C14	43.33 N	141.54 E
Takla Lake, l., B.C., Can.	110	D5	55.25 N	125.53 W
Takla Landing, B.C., Can.	110	D5	55.29 N	125.58 W
Takla Makan Desert see Taklimakan Shamo, des., China	48	G14	39.00 N	83.00 E
Taklimakan Shamo (Takla Makan Desert), des., China	48	G14	39.00 N	83.00 E
Takolekaju, Pegunungan, mts., Indon.	66	E11	2.00 S	121.00 E
Takoma Park, Md., U.S.	202c		38.58 N	77.00 W
Taksimo, Russia	50	F10	51.01 N	107.46 E
Taksony, Hung.	182c		47.20 N	19.04 E
Taku, Japan	56	F3	33.17 N	130.08 E
Takuan, Mount, vol., Pap. N. Gui.	101b	d6	6.29 S	155.36 E
Takua Pa, Thai.	64	H4	8.52 N	98.22 E
Takum, Nig.	84	H7	7.15 N	9.58 E
Takutea, i., Cook Is.	94	E11	19.49 S	158.18 W
Takutu (Tacutu), stm., S.A.	168	F11	3.01 N	60.29 W
Takysie Lake, B.C., Can.	144	C5	53.53 N	125.53 W
Talačyn, Bela.	26	F12	54.24 N	29.42 E
Talagang, Pak.	70	B4	32.55 N	72.25 E
Talagante, Chile	172	F2	33.39 S	70.54 W
Ta Lai, Viet.	64	G8	11.23 N	107.22 E
Talaimannar, Sri L.	69	G4	9.05 N	79.43 E
Talāja, India	70	H4	21.21 N	72.02 E
Talak, reg., Niger	84	F6	18.20 N	6.00 E
Tālāla, India	70	H3	21.03 N	70.32 E
Talalaivka, Ukr.	38	C12	50.50 N	33.08 E
Talamanca, Cordillera de, mts., C.R.	156	H6	9.30 N	83.29 W
Talang, Gunung, vol., Indon.	66	D2	0.59 S	100.39 E
Talangbatu, Indon.	66	F4	4.05 S	105.27 E
Talangbetutu, Indon.	66	E4	2.53 S	104.43 E
Talangpadang, Indon.	66	F4	5.21 S	104.47 E
Talangrimbo, Indon.	66	E4	3.29 S	105.25 E
Talara, Peru	164	D1	4.34 S	81.16 W
Talarrubias, Spain	28	E5	39.02 N	5.13 W
Talas, Kyrg.	48	F12	42.31 N	72.14 E
Talasea, Pap. N. Gui.	101a	b4	5.18 S	150.02 E
Tal'at al-Jamā'ah, Rujm, mtn., Jord.	76	H6	30.23 N	35.30 E
Talata Mafara, Nig.	84	G6	12.34 N	6.04 E
Talaud, Kepulauan (Talaud Islands), is., Indon.	60	E8	4.20 N	126.50 E
Talaud Islands see Talaud, Kepulauan, is., Indon.	60	E8	4.20 N	126.50 E
Talavera de la Reina, Spain	28	D6	39.57 N	4.49 W
Talawanta, Austl.	98	B3	18.37 S	140.15 E
Talawdī, Sudan	82	E6	10.39 N	30.23 E
Talayan, Phil.	68	G5	6.53 N	124.23 E
Talbotton, Ga., U.S.	134	E14	32.40 N	84.32 W
Talbragar, stm., Austl.	98	I7	32.11 S	148.36 E
Talca, Chile	172	G2	35.25 S	71.39 W
Talcahuano, Chile	172	H1	36.41 S	73.07 W
Tālcher, India	70	H10	20.57 N	85.13 E
Talco, Tx., U.S.	134	D3	33.21 N	95.05 W
Taldan, Russia	50	F13	53.41 N	124.49 E
Taldom, Russia	26	D20	56.43 N	37.32 E
Taldykorgan, Kaz.	48	F13	45.01 N	78.22 E
Taldyqorghan see Taldykorgan, Kaz.	48	F13	45.01 N	78.22 E
Talence, Fr.	22	E5	44.49 N	0.35 E
Talent, Or., U.S.	148	A3	42.14 N	122.47 W
Tālesh, Iran	74	B11	37.47 N	48.54 E
Talgar, Kaz.	48	F13	43.18 N	77.14 E
Talghar see Talgar, Kaz.	48	F13	43.18 N	77.14 E
Talhār, Pak.	70	F2	24.52 N	68.51 E
Tali, Pointe de, c., Guad.	159c	i6	15.56 N	61.12 W
Taliabu, Pulau, i., Indon.	60	F7	1.49 S	124.47 E
Talibon, Phil.	68	E5	10.07 N	124.19 E
Talibong, Ko, i., Thai.	64	I4	7.14 N	99.23 E
Talica, Russia	40	B17	58.00 N	51.29 E
Talica, Russia	48	C10	57.00 N	63.43 E
Talihina, Ok., U.S.	134	C3	34.44 N	95.02 W
Tālikota, India	69	C3	16.27 N	76.18 E
Taling Chan, Thai.	187a		13.46 N	100.27 E
Taliparamba, India	69	E2	12.01 N	75.21 E
Talisay, Phil.	68	E4	10.44 N	122.58 E
Taliş dağları see Talish Mountains, mts., Asia	74	B11	37.56 N	48.41 E
Talish Mountains, mts., Asia	74	B11	37.56 N	48.41 E
Taliwang, Indon.	66	H10	8.45 S	116.51 E
Talkeetna, Ak., U.S.	109	D9	62.20 N	150.07 W
Talkeetna Mountains, mts., Ak., U.S.	109	D10	62.10 N	148.15 W
Talkheh, stm., Iran	74	A10	37.52 N	45.53 E
Talla, Egypt	76	J1	28.05 N	30.44 E
Talladega, Al., U.S.	134	D12	33.26 N	86.06 W
Tall 'Afar, Iraq	74	B8	36.22 N	42.27 E
Tallahaga Creek, stm., Ms., U.S.	134	E10	32.55 N	88.58 W
Tallahala Creek, stm., Ms., U.S.	134	F9	31.12 N	89.05 W
Tallahassee, Fl., U.S.	134	G14	30.26 N	84.17 W
Tallahatchie, stm., Ms., U.S.	134	D8	33.31 N	90.10 W
Tall al-Abyaḍ, Syria	76	B9	36.41 N	38.57 E
Tall al-Muqayyar (Ur), hist., Iraq	74	E9	30.57 N	46.09 E
Tallangatta, Austl.	98	K6	36.13 S	147.10 E
Tallapoosa, Ga., U.S.	134	D13	33.45 N	85.17 W
Tallapoosa, stm., U.S.	134	E12	32.30 N	86.16 W
Tallard, Fr.	22	E11	44.28 N	6.03 E
Tallassee, Al., U.S.	134	E13	32.32 N	85.54 W
Tall as-Sulṭān, hist., Gaza	76	G6	31.52 N	35.27 E
Tällberg, Swe.	16	G13	60.49 N	14.59 E
Tall Bīsah, Syria	76	D7	34.50 N	36.44 E
Tall-e Khosrow-ye Soflā, Iran	74	E12	30.36 N	51.35 E
Tallinn, Est.	26	A7	59.25 N	24.48 E
Tall Kalakh, Syria	76	D7	34.40 N	36.15 E
Tall Kayf, Iraq	74	B8	36.29 N	43.08 E
Tall Kūjik, Syria	74	B7	36.48 N	42.04 E
Tallmadge, Oh., U.S.	124	C4	41.06 N	81.26 W
Tallman, N.Y., U.S.	194		41.07 N	74.06 W
Tallman Mountain State Park, p.o.i., N.Y., U.S.	194		41.01 N	73.54 W
Tall Rif'at, Syria	76	B8	36.28 N	37.06 E
Tall Salḥab, Syria	76	C7	35.16 N	36.25 E
Tall Tamir, Syria	74	B7	36.39 N	40.22 E
Tallula, Il., U.S.	130	E8	39.56 N	89.56 W
Tallulah, La., U.S.	134	E7	32.25 N	91.11 W
Tally, Russia	40	E18	53.08 N	53.04 E
Tally Ho, Austl.	192b		37.52 S	145.09 E
Talmage, Ca., U.S.	148	D2	39.05 N	123.10 W
Talmage, Ne., U.S.	128	K2	40.31 N	96.01 W
Talmaz, Mol.	38	G8	46.38 N	29.40 E
Tal'menka, Russia	48	D14	53.49 N	83.34 E
Talnah, Russia	50	C6	69.30 N	88.11 E
Tal'ne, Ukr.	38	E9	48.53 N	30.43 E
Taloda, India	70	H5	21.34 N	74.12 E
Talofofo, Guam	100c	j10	13.20 N	144.45 E
Talofofo Bay, b., Guam	100c	j10	13.20 N	144.46 E
Taloga, Ok., U.S.	138	E10	36.02 N	98.57 W
Taloje Budrukh, India	190c		19.05 N	73.05 E
Talok, Indon.	66	C11	1.03 N	118.49 E
Talon, Lake, l., On., Can.	126	B10	46.18 N	79.02 W
Tāloqān, Afg.	72	B10	36.42 N	69.36 E
Talovaja, Russia	40	F12	51.07 N	40.44 E
Talovka, Russia	48	F7	44.13 N	46.36 E
Talovka, Russia	48	C16	57.10 N	93.09 E
Taloyoak, Nu., Can.	110	B12	69.32 N	93.31 W
Talpa, Tx., U.S.	136	C8	31.46 N	99.42 W
Talquin, Lake, res., Fl., U.S.	134	G14	30.26 N	84.33 W
Tālsa, India	190b		22.49 N	88.33 E
Talsi, Lat.	26	C5	57.14 N	22.36 E
Taltal, Chile	172	B2	25.24 S	70.28 W
Taltapin Lake, l., B.C., Can.	144	B5	54.19 N	125.20 W
Taltson, stm., N.T., Can.	110	C8	61.23 N	112.45 W
Talu, Indon.	66	C1	0.13 N	99.59 E
Taluk, Indon.	66	D2	0.32 S	101.33 E
Talumphuk, Laem, c., Thai.	64	H5	8.30 N	100.09 E
Talvikjulja, Russia	14	D20	68.45 N	29.19 E
Talwood, Austl.	98	G7	28.30 S	149.30 E
Tama, Arg.	172	E4	30.30 S	66.31 W
Tama, Ia., U.S.	130	C5	41.58 N	92.34 W
Tama Cemetery, misc. cult., Japan	186		35.41 N	139.31 E
Tamacuarí, Pico, mtn., S.A.	168	G9	1.15 N	64.45 W
Tamagawa, ngh., Japan	186		35.37 N	139.39 E
Tamagawa-josui, stm., Japan	186		35.42 N	139.35 E
Tama-kyūryō, hills, Japan	186		35.35 N	139.30 E
Tamala, Austl.	96	E2	26.42 S	113.43 E
Tamalameque, Col.	168	C5	8.51 N	73.49 W
Tamale, Ghana	84	H4	9.24 N	0.50 W
Tamalea, Indon.	66	E11	2.31 S	119.18 E
Tamalpais, Mount, mtn., Ca., U.S.	148	F3	37.56 N	122.35 W
Taman', Russia	38	H15	45.12 N	36.42 E
Tamana, Japan	56	G3	32.55 N	130.33 E
Tamaná, Cerro, mtn., Col.	168	E3	5.03 N	76.12 W
Tamana, Mount, hill, Trin.	159f	s12	10.28 N	61.12 W
Tamanaco, stm., Ven.	168	C9	9.28 N	65.12 W
Tamanduateí, stm., Braz.	205b		23.36 S	46.35 W
Tamaniquá, Braz.	168	I9	2.39 S	65.44 W
Taman Negara, p.o.i., Malay.	64	J6	4.43 N	102.23 E
Tamano, Japan	56	E6	34.28 N	133.56 E
Tamanquaré, Ilha, i., Braz.	168	H9	0.28 S	64.55 W
Tamanskij zaliv, b., Russia	38	H15	45.17 N	36.44 E
Tamapatz, Mex.	154	E9	21.35 N	99.09 W
Tamar, stm., Austl.	99a	n13	41.04 S	146.47 E
Tamar, stm., Eng., U.K.	10	K8	50.25 N	4.12 W
Támara, Col.	168	E5	5.50 N	72.10 W
Tamarac, stm., Mn., U.S.	128	C2	48.29 N	97.08 W
Tamarite de Litera, Spain	28	C11	41.52 N	0.24 E
Tamaroa, Il., U.S.	130	F8	38.08 N	89.14 W
Tamarugal, Pampa del, pl., Chile	166	C3	20.14 S	69.37 W
Tamási, Hung.	36	C5	46.37 N	18.17 E
Tamaulipas, state, Mex.	154	C9	24.00 N	98.45 W
Tama Zoological Park, p.o.i., Japan	186		35.39 N	139.24 E
Tamazula, Mex.	154	C5	24.57 N	106.56 W
Tamazulapan del Progreso, Mex.	154	G10	17.41 N	97.34 W
Tamazunchale, Mex.	154	E9	21.16 N	98.47 W
Tambacounda, Sen.	84	G2	13.47 N	13.40 W
Tambak, Indon.	66	F8	5.44 S	112.38 E
Tambakboyo, Indon.	66	G7	6.47 S	111.53 E
Tamba-kōchi, plat., Japan	56	D8	35.20 N	135.30 E
Tambalan, Indon.	66	B9	3.11 N	115.42 E
Tambangsawah, Indon.	66	E3	3.02 S	102.10 E
Tambara, Moz.	88	D5	16.43 S	34.15 E
Tambaram, India	69	E5	12.55 N	80.06 E
Tambault, Île à, i., Qc., Can.	193a		45.20 N	73.51 W
Tambej, Russia	50	B3	71.29 N	71.49 E
Tambelan, Kepulauan, is., Indon.	66	C5	1.00 N	107.30 E
Tambelan Besar, Pulau, i., Indon.	66	C5	0.59 N	107.35 E
Tamberías, Arg.	172	E3	31.28 S	69.25 W
Tambo, Austl.	98	E6	24.53 S	146.15 E
Tambo, stm., Austl.	98	K6	37.51 S	147.48 E
Tambo, stm., Peru	164	G3	17.09 S	71.49 W
Tambohorano, Madag.	88	D7	17.30 S	43.57 E
Tambolongang, Pulau, i., Indon.	66	G12	6.36 S	120.25 E
Tambora, Gunung, vol., Indon.	66	H10	8.13 S	117.55 E
Tamboril, Braz.	170	C5	4.50 S	40.20 W
Tamboritha, Mount, mtn., Austl.	98	K6	37.28 S	146.41 E
Tamboryacu, stm., Peru	168	H4	2.30 S	73.39 W
Tambov, Russia	40	E12	52.43 N	41.24 E
Tambovka, Russia	40	H15	47.18 N	47.22 E
Tambovskaja oblast', co., Russia	40	E13	52.45 N	41.30 E
Tambre, stm., Spain	28	B2	42.49 N	8.53 W
Tambu, Indon.	66	D11	0.04 S	119.51 E
Tambu, Teluk, b., Indon.	66	C11	0.02 N	119.45 E
Tambunan, Malay.	68	H1	5.41 N	116.23 E
Tambura, Sudan	82	F5	5.35 N	27.27 E
Tâmchekket, Maur.	84	F2	17.15 N	10.40 W
Tam Chuak, Laem, c., Thai.	64	H4	8.34 N	98.12 E
Tame, Col.	168	D6	6.28 N	71.43 W
Tame, stm., Eng., U.K.	180		53.25 N	2.09 W
Tameapa, Mex.	154	C5	25.39 N	107.22 W
Tâmega, stm., Port.	28	C2	41.04 N	8.17 W
Tamel Aike, Arg.	166	I2	48.20 S	70.58 W
Tamenghest, Alg.	84	E6	22.48 N	5.31 E
Tamenghest, Oued, stm., Alg.	84	E5	22.12 N	0.19 E
Tamenuen, Indon.	60	G11	6.27 S	139.48 E
Tameside, mun., Eng., U.K.	180		53.29 N	2.03 W
Tameside, mun., Eng., U.K.	180		53.29 N	2.03 W
Tamga, Russia	54	B10	45.34 N	133.37 E
Tamgak, Adrar, mtn., Niger	84	F6	19.11 N	8.42 E
Tamiahua, Mex.	154	E10	21.16 N	97.27 W
Tamiahua, Laguna de, l., Mex.	154	E10	21.35 N	97.35 W
Tamiami Canal, can., Fl., U.S.	132	K4	25.46 N	80.11 W
Tamica, Russia	18	C24	64.10 N	37.59 E
Tamil Nādu, state, India	69	F4	11.00 N	78.15 E
Tamiš (Timiș), stm., Eur.	36	E7	44.51 N	20.37 E
Tâmîya, Egypt	76	I1	29.28 N	30.58 E
Tamkūhi, India	70	E10	26.40 N	84.11 E
Tam Ky, Viet.	64	E9	15.33 N	108.29 E
Tammaro, stm., Italy	32	C8	41.08 N	14.49 E
Tammerfors see Tampere, Fin.	18	F10	61.29 N	23.45 E
Tammisaaren saariston kansallispuisto, p.o.i., Fin.	18	H10	59.50 N	23.25 E
Tammisaari, Fin.	18	H10	59.58 N	23.26 E
Tamms, Il., U.S.	130	G8	37.14 N	89.16 W
Tammûh, Egypt	191c		29.56 N	31.16 E
Tämnaren, l., Swe.	16	G15	60.10 N	17.20 E
Tamon, ngh., Japan	188		34.39 N	135.04 E
Tampa, Fl., U.S.	132	I3	27.58 N	82.27 W
Tampa Bay, b., Fl., U.S.	132	I3	27.45 N	82.35 W
Tampang, Indon.	66	F4	5.54 S	104.42 E
Tampaon, stm., Mex.	154	E9	21.58 N	98.34 W
Tampere (Tammerfors), Fin.	18	F10	61.29 N	23.45 E
Tampico, Mex.	154	D10	22.13 N	97.51 W
Tampico, Il., U.S.	130	C8	41.37 N	89.47 W
Tampin, Malay.	64	K6	2.28 N	102.13 E
Tam Quan, Viet.	64	E9	14.33 N	109.03 E
Tamsagbulag, Mong.	52	B8	47.14 N	117.20 E
Tamsalu, Est.	26	A9	59.09 N	26.06 E
Tamshiyacu, Peru	164	D3	4.00 S	73.07 W
Tamsweg, Aus.	30	C10	47.07 N	13.48 E
Tamu, Mya.	62	D7	24.13 N	94.18 E
Tamuning, Guam	100c	i9	13.29 N	144.46 E
Tamura, Japan	186		35.22 N	139.22 E
Tamworth, Austl.	98	H8	31.05 S	150.55 E
Tamworth, Eng., U.K.	10	I11	52.38 N	1.41 W
Tana (Teno), stm., Eur.	14	B19	70.25 N	28.16 E
Tana, stm., Kenya	86	D8	2.31 S	40.30 E
Tana, Lake see T'ana Hāyk', l., Eth.	82	E7	11.56 N	37.17 E
Tanabe, Japan	56	F8	33.43 N	135.23 E
Tanabi, Braz.	170	K1	20.38 S	49.39 W
Tana bru, Nor.	14	B18	70.25 N	28.17 E
Tanacross, Ak., U.S.	109	D11	63.20 N	143.19 W
Tanafjorden, b., Nor.	14	B19	70.54 N	28.40 E
Tanaga Island, i., Ak., U.S.	109a	g23	51.50 N	178.00 W
Tanagro, stm., Italy	32	D9	40.38 N	15.13 E
Tanaguarena, Ven.	204c		10.37 N	66.49 W
T'ana Hāyk', l., Eth.	82	E7	11.56 N	37.17 E
Tanahbala, Pulau, i., Indon.	60	F2	0.25 S	98.25 E
Tanahgrogot, Indon.	66	D10	1.53 S	116.11 E
Tanahjampea, Pulau, i., Indon.	66	G12	7.05 S	120.42 E
Tanahmasa, Pulau, i., Indon.	60	F2	0.12 S	98.27 E
Tanahmerah, Indon.	60	G10	6.05 S	140.17 E
Tanahmerah, Indon.	66	B10	3.41 N	117.31 E
Tanah Merah, Malay.	64	J6	5.47 N	102.08 E
Tanahputih, Indon.	66	C2	1.41 N	101.03 E
Tanaka, ngh., Japan	188		34.42 N	134.59 E
Tanakeke, Pulau, i., Indon.	66	F11	5.31 S	119.16 E
Tanakpur, India	70	D7	29.04 N	80.06 E
Tanami, Austl.	96	D5	19.57 S	129.41 E
Tanami Desert, des., Austl.	96	C5	20.00 S	129.30 E
Tan An, Viet.	64	H7	8.44 N	105.11 E
Tan An, Viet.	64	G8	10.32 N	106.25 E
Tanana, Ak., U.S.	109	C9	65.10 N	152.04 W
Tanana, stm., Ak., U.S.	109	D10	65.08 N	152.04 W
Tananarive see Antananarivo, Madag.	88	D8	18.55 S	47.31 E
Tanbar, Austl.	98	E3	25.50 S	141.55 E
Tan Binh, Viet.	187c		10.48 N	106.40 E
Tanbu, China	58	G6	28.08 N	114.12 E
Tan Chau, Viet.	64	G7	10.47 N	105.14 E
Tanch'ŏn-ŭp, Kor., N.	54	D8	40.27 N	128.54 E
Tancítaro, Pico de, mtn., Mex.	154	F7	19.23 N	102.13 W
Tanda, Egypt	76	K1	27.40 N	30.45 E
Tānda, India	70	E9	26.33 N	82.39 E
Tānda, India	70	C5	31.40 N	75.38 E
Tandag, Phil.	68	F6	9.04 N	126.12 E
Tandaltī, Sudan	82	E6	13.00 N	31.51 E
Ţăndărei, Rom.	36	E14	44.38 N	27.40 E
Tandil, Arg.	172	H8	37.19 S	59.08 W
Tando Ādam, Pak.	70	F2	25.45 N	68.39 E
Tando Allāhyār, Pak.	70	F2	25.27 N	68.43 E
Tando Bāgo, Pak.	70	F2	24.47 N	68.58 E
Tando Muhammad Khān, Pak.	62	C2	25.08 N	68.32 E
Tandou Lake, l., Austl.	98	I3	32.36 S	142.04 E
Tandridge, Eng., U.K.	178		51.14 N	0.02 W
Tandridge, mun., Eng., U.K.	178		51.17 N	0.05 W
Tandula Tank, res., India	70	H8	20.40 N	81.10 E
Tandun, Indon.	66	C2	0.35 N	100.39 E
Tāndūr, India	69	C3	17.15 N	77.34 E
Tanega-shima, i., Japan	54	I9	30.40 N	131.00 E
Tanete, Indon.	66	F11	4.31 S	119.35 E
Tanew, stm., Pol.	24	F18	50.29 N	22.15 E
Tanezrouft, des., Afr.	84	E4	24.00 N	0.45 W
Tanforan Park, shp. cen., Ca., U.S.	200		37.38 N	122.25 W
Tang, stm., China	58	E5	32.10 N	112.20 E
Tang, stm., China	58	E7	33.18 N	117.46 E
Tang, stm., China	58	B6	38.45 N	115.33 E
Tanga, Russia	50	F11	50.59 N	111.32 E
Tanga, Tan.	86	F7	5.04 S	39.06 E
Tangail, Bngl.	70	F12	24.15 N	89.55 E
Tanga Islands, is., Pap. N. Gui.	101a	a5	3.28 S	153.13 E
Tanga Langua, c., Gren.	159e	q10	12.14 N	61.39 W
Tangalla, Sri L.	69	H5	6.01 N	80.47 E
Tanganika, Lac see Tanganyika, Lake, l., Afr.	86	F6	6.00 S	29.30 E
Tanganyika see Tanzania, ctry., Afr.	86	F6	6.00 S	35.00 E
Tanganyika, Lac see Tanganyika, Lake, l., Afr.	86	F6	6.00 S	29.30 E
Tanganyika, Lake, l., Afr.	86	F6	6.00 S	29.30 E
Tangarana, stm., Peru	168	I4	2.55 S	75.03 W
Tangarare, Sol. Is.	101b	e8	9.34 S	159.39 E
Tanger (Tangier), Mor.	84	B3	35.46 N	5.48 W
Tangerang, Indon.	66	G5	6.10 S	106.37 E
Tangerhütte, Ger.	24	D7	52.26 N	11.48 E
Tangermünde, Ger.	24	D7	52.32 N	11.58 E
Tanggu, China	58	B7	39.01 N	117.39 E
Tanggulashan, China	52	E3	34.12 N	92.23 E
Tanggula Shan, mts., China	52	E3	33.00 N	92.00 E
Tanggula Shankou, p., China	52	E3	32.55 N	91.56 E
Tanghe, China	58	E5	32.41 N	112.50 E
Tangi, Pak.	70	A3	34.17 N	71.38 E
Tangier, N.S., Can.	122	F14	44.49 N	62.44 W
Tangier see Tanger, Mor.	84	B3	35.46 N	5.48 W
Tangier, Va., U.S.	124	G10	37.49 N	75.59 W
Tangipahoa, stm., U.S.	134	G8	30.19 N	90.16 W
Tangjiagou, China	58	F7	30.47 N	117.26 E
Tangkahan, Indon.	66	D8	1.32 S	113.51 E
Tangkou, China	58	F8	30.05 N	118.11 E
Tanglad, Indon.	66	H9	8.46 S	115.35 E
Tangmai, China	52	E4	30.06 N	95.04 E
Tang Nhon Phu, Viet.	187c		10.50 N	106.47 E
Tango-hantō, pen., Japan	56	D8	35.40 N	135.10 E
Tangra Yumco, l., China	70	C11	31.01 N	86.33 E
Tangse, Indon.	64	J2	5.01 N	95.55 E
Tangshan, China	58	B8	39.36 N	118.11 E
Tangtou, China	58	D8	35.15 N	118.29 E
Tangtse, India	70	A7	34.02 N	78.11 E
Tanguiéta, Benin	84	G5	10.37 N	1.15 E
Tangyan, Mya.	64	A4	22.30 N	98.23 E
Tangyin, China	58	D6	35.54 N	114.21 E
Tangyuan, China	52	B10	46.41 N	129.53 E
Tanhoj, Russia	50	F10	51.33 N	105.07 E
Taniantaweng Shan, mts., China	52	F4	30.00 N	98.00 E
Tanigami, ngh., Japan	188		34.46 N	135.10 E
Tanigawa-dake, mtn., Japan	56	C11	36.50 N	138.56 E
Tanimbar, Kepulauan, is., Indon.	60	G9	7.30 S	131.30 E
Tanintharyi, state, Mya.	64	F3	12.00 N	99.00 E
Tanis, hist., Egypt	76	H2	30.57 N	31.53 E
Tanishpa, mtn., Pak.	70	C2	31.10 N	68.24 E
Tanjay, Phil.	68	F4	9.30 N	123.10 E
Tanjore see Thanjāvūr, India	69	F4	10.47 N	79.08 E
Tanjung, Indon.	66	E9	2.08 S	115.23 E
Tanjung, Indon.	66	H10	8.22 S	116.09 E
Tanjungbalai, Indon.	66	B1	2.58 N	99.48 E
Tanjungbatu, Indon.	66	C10	0.46 N	117.26 E
Tanjungbatu, Indon.	66	B11	2.17 N	118.03 E
Tanjungbatu, Indon.	66	C3	0.39 N	103.27 E
Tanjungenim, Indon.	66	E3	3.44 S	103.48 E
Tanjungkarang-Telukbetung, Indon.	66	F4	5.26 S	105.16 E
Tanjunglabu, Indon.	66	E5	2.57 S	106.54 E
Tanjungmengedar, Indon.	66	B2	2.39 N	100.01 E
Tanjungpandan, Indon.	66	E5	2.44 S	107.38 E
Tanjungpinang, Indon.	66	C4	0.54 N	104.28 E
Tanjungpriok, ngh., Indon.	187e		6.06 S	106.53 E
Tanjungpura, Indon.	64	K4	3.54 N	98.24 E
Tanjungpusu, Indon.	66	D8	0.05 S	113.29 E
Tanjungraja, Indon.	66	E4	3.20 S	104.45 E
Tanjungredep, Indon.	66	B10	2.08 N	117.29 E
Tanjungselor, Indon.	66	B10	2.49 N	117.21 E
Tanjunguban, Indon.	66	C4	1.04 N	104.13 E
Tānk, Pak.	70	B3	32.12 N	70.23 E
Tan Kien, Viet.	187c		10.42 N	106.35 E
Tankwa, stm., S. Afr.	90	H5	32.18 S	19.33 E
Tan My, Viet.	64	G9	11.43 N	108.48 E
Tanna, i., Vanuatu	101d	I17	19.30 S	169.20 E
Tännäs, Swe.	16	E10	62.26 N	12.41 E
Tannenberg see Stębark, Pol.	24	C16	53.30 N	20.08 E
Tanner, Al., U.S.	134	C11	34.43 N	86.58 W
Tanner, Mount, mtn., B.C., Can.	144	G12	49.40 N	118.34 W
Tännforsen, wtfl., Swe.	16	D10	63.27 N	12.44 E
Tannila, Fin.	18	B13	65.28 N	25.59 E
Tannis Bugt, b., Den.	16	J8	57.40 N	10.15 E
Tannu-Ola, hrebet, mts., Asia	48	D16	51.00 N	94.00 E
Tannu-Ola Mountains, mts., Asia	50	F7	51.00 N	94.00 E
Tannūrah, Ra's, c., Sau. Ar.	72	D7	26.38 N	50.09 E
Tano, Japan	188		34.57 N	135.36 E
Tanon Strait, strt., Phil.	68	E4	10.20 N	123.30 E
Tanout, Niger	84	F6	14.58 N	8.53 E
Tanque Grande, Ribeirão, stm., Braz.	205b		23.25 S	46.28 W
Tan Qui Dong, Viet.	187c		10.44 N	106.42 E
Tanquinho, Braz.	170	G6	11.59 S	39.06 W
Tansboro, N.J., U.S.	203		39.46 N	74.55 W
Tanshui, Tai.	58	I9	25.09 N	121.25 E
Tan Son Nhut Airport, arpt., Viet.	187c		10.49 N	106.40 E
Tanta, Egypt	76	H2	30.46 N	31.00 E
Tan-Tan, Mor.	84	D2	28.26 N	11.05 W
Tan Thoi Nhut, Viet.	187c		10.50 N	106.36 E
Tan Thuan Dong, Viet.	187c		10.45 N	106.44 E
Tantoyuca, Mex.	154	E9	21.20 N	98.13 W
Tanuku, India	69	C5	16.45 N	81.41 E
Tanumshede, Swe.	16	I9	58.43 N	11.20 E
Tanvald, Czech Rep.	24	F11	50.45 N	15.19 E
Tanyang, Kor., S.	56	C1	36.56 N	128.20 E
Tanzania, ctry., Afr.	86	F6	6.00 S	35.00 E
Tao, Ko, i., Thai.	64	G4	10.04 N	99.50 E
Taochuan, China	58	I4	25.07 N	111.06 E
Tao'er, stm., China	54	B5	45.22 N	123.06 E
Taohuazhen, China	58	A6	40.03 N	114.59 E
Taolakepa, China	70	B10	32.05 N	85.21 E
Taole, China	58	B2	38.46 N	106.39 E
Taonan, China	54	B5	45.20 N	122.46 E
Taongi, at., Marsh. Is.	94	B7	14.37 N	168.58 E
Taormina, Italy	32	G9	37.51 N	15.17 E
Taos, Mo., U.S.	130	F5	38.30 N	92.04 W
Taos, N.M., U.S.	138	E3	36.24 N	105.34 W
Taos Pueblo, N.M., U.S.	138	E3	36.25 N	105.34 W
Taoudenni, Mali	84	E4	22.40 N	3.58 W
Taounate, Mor.	84	C4	34.32 N	4.38 W
Taourirt, Mor.	84	C4	34.19 N	2.49 W
Taoyuan, China	58	G4	28.46 N	111.21 E
Taoyüan, Tai.	58	I9	24.58 N	121.18 E
Tapa, Est.	26	A9	59.15 N	25.58 E
Tapachula, Mex.	154	H12	14.54 N	92.16 W
Tapaga, Cape, c., Samoa	101c	h12	14.02 S	171.25 W
Tapah, Malay.	64	J5	4.12 N	101.15 E
Tapaje, stm., Col.	168	F2	2.32 N	78.05 W
Tapajós, stm., Braz.	164	D6	2.27 S	54.38 W
Tapaktuan, Indon.	64	K3	3.16 N	97.11 E
Tapalqué, Arg.	172	H7	36.21 S	60.01 W
Tapan, Indon.	66	E2	2.09 S	101.04 E
Tapauá, Braz.	164	E5	5.38 S	63.12 W
Tapauá, stm., Braz.	164	E4	5.46 S	64.23 W
Tapejara, Braz.	172	D12	28.04 S	52.01 W
Taperoá, Braz.	170	D7	7.12 S	36.49 W
Taperoá, Braz.	170	G6	13.30 S	39.06 W
Tapes, Braz.	172	E12	30.40 S	51.23 W
Tapeta, Lib.	84	H3	6.29 N	8.51 W
Taphan Hin, Thai.	64	D5	16.13 N	100.26 E
Taphoen, stm., Thai.	64	E4	14.06 N	99.23 E
Tāpi, stm., India	70	H6	21.08 N	72.43 E
Ta Pi, stm., Thai.	64	H4	9.05 N	99.13 E
Tapiales, Arg.	206		34.42 S	58.31 W
Tapiche, stm., Peru	164	E3	5.03 S	73.51 W
Tapini, Pap. N. Gui.	101a	b4	8.21 S	146.59 E
Tapiraí, Braz.	170	J2	19.53 S	46.00 W
Tapis, Gunong, mtn., Malay.	64	J6	4.00 N	102.54 E
Taplan National Park, p.o.i., Thai.	64	E5	14.19 N	101.54 E
Tāplejungg, Nepal	70	E11	27.21 N	87.39 E
Tapolca, Hung.	36	C4	46.53 N	17.26 E
Tappahannock, Va., U.S.	124	G8	37.55 N	76.51 W
Tappan, Lake, res., U.S.	194		41.01 N	73.59 W
Tappan Zee, b., N.Y., U.S.	194		41.06 N	73.53 W
Tappan Zee Bridge, trans., N.Y., U.S.	194		41.04 N	73.54 W
Tappen, N.D., U.S.	142	H14	46.52 N	99.38 W
Tapsiā, ngh., India	190b		22.32 N	88.22 E
Tapuae-o-Uenuku, mtn., N.Z.	102	E5	42.00 S	173.40 E
Tapuio, stm., Braz.	170	C3	3.41 S	44.16 W
Tapul Group, is., Phil.	68	H3	5.37 N	120.55 E
Tapun, Mya.	64	C2	18.22 N	95.27 E
Tapuruquara, Braz.	168	H9	0.23 S	65.05 W
Taputapu, Cape, c., Am. Sam.	101c	h12	14.19 S	170.50 W
Taqātu' Hayyā, Sudan	82	D7	18.20 N	36.22 E
Ṭaqṭaq, Iraq	74	C9	35.53 N	44.37 E
Taquara, Braz.	172	D12	29.39 S	50.46 W
Taquara, ngh., Braz.	205a		22.55 S	43.21 W
Taquaras, Ponta das, c., Braz.	172	C13	27.01 S	48.35 W
Taquari, stm., Braz.	172	D12	29.57 S	51.43 W
Taquari Novo, stm., Braz.	166	C5	19.14 S	57.13 W
Taquaritinga, Braz.	170	K1	21.23 S	48.27 W
Tar, stm., N.C., U.S.	116	C14	35.32 N	77.06 W
Tara, Austl.	98	F8	27.17 S	150.27 E
Tara, Russia	48	C12	56.53 N	74.21 E
Tara, mts., Yugo.	36	F6	43.55 N	19.25 E
Tara, stm., Eur.	30	G16	43.20 N	18.50 E
Tara, stm., Russia	48	C13	56.41 N	74.36 E
Taraba, stm., Nig.	84	H7	8.33 N	10.14 E
Tarabuco, Bol.	166	C3	19.10 S	64.57 W
Ṭarābulus (Tripoli), Leb.	76	D6	34.26 N	35.51 E
Ṭarābulus (Tripoli), Libya	82	A2	32.52 N	13.10 E
Ṭarābulus (Tripolitania), hist. reg., Libya	82	A2	31.00 N	15.00 E
Tarabusi Creek, stm., Mi., U.S.	199		42.24 N	83.19 W
Tarabya, ngh., Tur.	185b		41.08 N	29.03 E
Taraclia, Mol.	38	H7	45.54 N	28.41 E
Taraclia, Mol.	38	G8	46.34 N	29.07 E
Tarāghin, Libya	82	B2	25.59 N	14.33 E
Tarago, Austl.	98	J7	35.04 S	149.39 E
Tara Hills, Ca., U.S.	200		38.00 N	122.19 W
Taraira (Traíra), stm., S.A.	168	H7	1.04 S	69.25 W
Tårajaur, Swe.	14	F10	66.25 N	19.42 E
Taraju, Indon.	66	G6	7.27 S	107.59 E
Tarakan, Indon.	66	B10	3.19 N	117.35 E
Tarakan, Pulau, i., Indon.	66	B10	3.21 N	117.36 E
Taraklı, Tur.	34	C13	40.24 N	30.29 E
Tarakliya see Taraclia, Mol.	38	H7	45.54 N	28.41 E
Taralga, Austl.	98	J7	34.24 S	149.49 E
Tara Nacionalni Park, p.o.i., Yugo.	36	F6	44.55 N	19.30 E
Tārānagar, India	70	D5	28.40 N	75.02 E
Taranaki, Mount (Egmont, Mount), vol., N.Z.	102	D6	39.17 S	174.03 E
Tarancón, Spain	28	D8	40.00 N	3.00 W
Tarango, Presa, res., Mex.	204a		19.22 N	99.13 W
Taransay, i., Scot., U.K.	10	D5	57.54 N	7.01 W
Taranto, Italy	32	D11	40.28 N	17.14 E
Taranto, Golfo di, b., Italy	32	E11	40.10 N	17.20 E
Tarapacá, Col.	168	I7	2.53 S	69.43 W
Tarapoto, Peru	164	E2	6.29 S	76.23 W
Taraquá, Braz.	168	G7	0.06 N	68.23 W
Tarare, Fr.	22	D10	45.54 N	4.26 E
Tarariras, Ur.	172	G9	34.16 S	57.36 W
Tararua Range, mts., N.Z.	102	E6	40.46 S	175.23 E
Tarāsa Dwīp, i., India	62	G7	8.15 N	93.06 E
Tarascon, Fr.	22	F10	43.48 N	4.39 E
Tarascon-sur-Ariège, Fr.	22	G7	42.51 N	1.36 E
Tarashcha, Ukr.	38	D9	49.33 N	30.30 E
Tarasht, ngh., Iran	185d		35.42 N	51.21 E
Tarasjoki, stm., Russia	18	E19	62.11 N	32.37 E
Tarasovka, Russia	183b		55.58 N	37.50 E
Tarasovo, Russia	12	E19	62.49 N	41.09 E
Tarasovo, Russia	12	C22	66.13 N	46.42 E
Tarasovo, Russia	48	C19	55.52 N	107.51 E
Tarasovskij, Russia	40	G12	48.44 N	40.22 E
Tarat, Alg.	84	D6	26.10 N	9.21 E
Tarata, Bol.	166	C3	17.37 S	66.01 W
Taratakbuluh, Indon.	66	C2	0.22 N	101.25 E
Tarauacá, stm., Braz.	164	E3	7.28 S	70.04 W
Taravao, Baie de, b., Fr. Poly.	100h	v22	17.43 S	149.17 W
Taravao, Isthme de, isth., Fr. Poly.	100h	v22	17.43 S	149.18 W
Taravo, stm., Fr.	22	H15	41.43 N	8.49 E
Tarawa, at., Kir.	94	C8	1.21 N	173.07 E
Tarawera, N.Z.	102	D7	39.02 S	176.35 E
Tarazona, Spain	28	C9	41.54 N	1.43 W
Tarbagataj, hrebet, mts., Asia	48	E14	47.12 N	83.00 E
Tarbagatay Shan see Tarbagataj, hrebet, mts., Asia	48	E14	47.12 N	83.00 E
Tarbela Reservoir, res., Pak.	70	A4	34.08 N	72.48 E
Tarbert, Scot., U.K.	10	D6	57.54 N	6.49 W
Tarbert, Scot., U.K.	10	F7	55.51 N	5.25 W
Tarbes, Fr.	22	F6	43.14 N	0.04 E
Tarbock Green, Eng., U.K.	180		53.23 N	2.49 W
Tarboro, N.C., U.S.	124	I8	35.53 N	77.32 W
Tarbū, Libya	82	B3	26.00 N	15.10 E
Tarcăului, Munții, mts., Rom.	36	C13	46.38 N	26.10 E
Tarcoola, Austl.	96	F6	30.41 S	134.33 E
Tarcoon, Austl.	98	H6	30.15 S	146.43 E
Tārdah, India	190b		22.27 N	88.31 E

Name	Page	Map Ref.	Latitude	Longitude
Tardajos, Spain	28	B7	42.21 N	3.49 W
Tardoki-Jani, gora, mtn., Russia	50	G16	48.55 N	138.04 E
Taredo, ngh., India	190c		19.58 N	72.49 E
Taree, Austl.	98	H9	31.54 S	152.27 E
Tareja, Russia	50	B7	73.16 N	90.37 E
Tärendö, Swe.	14	E13	67.10 N	22.38 E
Tarentum, Pa., U.S.	124	D6	40.35 N	79.45 W
Tarfa, Wadi el-, stm., Egypt	76	J2	28.24 N	30.49 E
Tarfaya, Mor.	84	D2	27.56 N	12.54 W
Target Rock National Wildlife Refuge, ind. res., N.Y., U.S.	194		40.56 N	73.26 W
Targhee Pass, p., U.S.	146	F15	44.41 N	111.17 W
Targon, Fr.	22	E5	44.43 N	0.15 W
Târgovište, Blg.	36	F13	43.15 N	26.34 E
Târgoviște, Rom.	36	E12	44.55 N	25.27 E
Târgu Bujor, Rom.	36	D14	45.52 N	27.55 E
Târgu Cărbunești, Rom.	36	E10	44.57 N	23.31 E
Târgu Frumos, Rom.	36	B14	47.12 N	27.01 E
Târgu Jiu, Rom.	36	D10	45.01 N	23.18 E
Târgu Lăpuș, Rom.	36	B10	47.27 N	23.52 E
Târgu Mureș, Rom.	36	C11	46.32 N	24.34 E
Târgu-Neamț, Rom.	36	B13	47.12 N	26.21 E
Târgu Ocna, Rom.	36	C13	46.16 N	26.37 E
Târgu Secuiesc, Rom.	36	D12	46.00 N	26.08 E
Târgușor, Rom.	36	E15	44.28 N	28.25 E
Tarhov Holm, gora, hill, Russia	26	C21	57.05 N	38.36 E
Tarhovka, Russia	183a		60.04 N	29.58 E
Tarifa, Spain	28	H5	36.01 N	5.36 W
Tarifa, Punta de, c., Spain	28	H5	36.01 N	5.36 W
Tarija, Bol.	166	D4	21.32 S	64.43 W
Tarikere, India	69	E2	13.42 N	75.48 E
Tarim, stm., China	48	F14	39.31 N	88.26 E
Tarim Pendi, bas., China	48	F12	39.00 N	83.00 E
Taritatu, stm., Indon.	60	F10	2.54 S	138.28 E
Tarjannevesi, l., Fin.	18	E10	62.08 N	24.02 E
Tarkastad, S. Afr.	90	G8	32.00 S	26.15 E
Tarkhankut, mys, c., Ukr.	38	H11	45.21 N	32.30 E
Tarkhūrān, Iran	74	C11	34.40 N	50.03 E
Tarkio, Mo., U.S.	130	D2	40.26 N	95.23 W
Tarkio, stm., U.S.	130	D2	40.09 N	95.27 W
Tarko-Sale, Russia	48	B13	64.55 N	77.47 E
Tarkwa, Ghana	84	H4	5.18 N	2.00 W
Tarlac, Phil.	68	C3	15.29 N	120.35 E
T'arlevo, Russia	183a		59.42 N	30.27 E
Tarlscough, Eng., U.K.	180		53.37 N	2.52 W
Tarm, Den.	16	L6	55.55 N	8.32 E
Tarma, Peru	164	F2	11.23 S	75.43 W
Tarn, state, Fr.	22	F8	43.50 N	2.00 E
Tarn, stm., Fr.	22	F7	44.05 N	1.02 E
Tarn, stm., Hung.	36	B7	47.30 N	19.58 E
Tärnaby, Swe.	16	B13	65.43 N	15.14 E
Tarnak, stm., Afg.	70	B1	32.51 N	67.55 E
Țarna Mare, Rom.	36	A10	48.05 N	23.12 E
Tärnasjön, l., Swe.	16	B13	66.00 N	15.28 E
Târnava Mare, stm., Rom.	36	C11	46.09 N	23.42 E
Târnava Mică, stm., Rom.	36	C11	46.11 N	23.54 E
Târnăveni, Rom.	36	C11	46.19 N	24.17 E
Tarneit, Austl.	192b		37.52 S	144.41 E
Tarn-et-Garonne, state, Fr.	22	F7	44.05 N	1.20 E
Tarnobrzeg, Pol.	24	F17	50.35 N	21.42 E
Tarnogród, Pol.	24	F18	50.22 N	22.44 E
Tarnogskij Gorodok, Russia	12	F20	60.30 N	43.32 E
Tarnopol see Ternopil', Ukr.	38	D4	49.33 N	25.36 E
Târnova, Mol.	38	E6	48.10 N	27.40 E
Tarnów, Pol.	24	G16	50.00 N	21.00 E
Tarnowskie Góry, Pol.	24	F14	50.27 N	18.52 E
Tärnsjö, Swe.	16	G14	60.09 N	16.56 E
Taro, Sol. Is.	101b	d7	6.46 S	156.28 E
Taro, stm., Italy	30	F7	45.00 N	10.15 E
Taron, Pap. N. Gui.	101a	a5	4.26 S	153.01 E
Tarong, Austl.	98	F8	26.45 S	151.54 E
Taronga Zoo, p.o.i., Austl.	192a		33.51 S	151.15 E
Taroom, Austl.	98	E7	25.38 S	149.47 E
Tarouca, Port.	28	C3	41.00 N	7.42 W
Taroudannt, Mor.	84	C3	30.28 N	8.53 W
Ta Roun, Co, mtn., Viet.	64	D8	17.17 N	106.18 E
Tarpon Springs, Fl., U.S.	132	H3	28.08 N	82.45 W
Tarqui, Peru	164	D2	1.34 S	75.13 W
Tarquinia, Italy	30	H8	42.15 N	11.44 E
Tarra, stm., S.A.	168	C5	9.03 N	72.29 W
Tarrafal, C.V.	85a	k10	15.16 N	23.45 W
Tarragona, Spain	28	C12	41.07 N	1.14 E
Tarragona, co., Spain	28	D11	41.00 N	0.45 E
Tarraleah, Austl.	99a	o13	42.17 S	146.26 E
Tarrant City, Al., U.S.	134	D12	33.34 N	86.46 W
Tarrasa see Terrassa, Spain	28	C13	41.34 N	2.00 E
Tàrrega, Spain	28	C12	41.39 N	1.08 E
Tarryall Creek, stm., Co., U.S.	138	B3	39.05 N	105.19 W
Tarrytown Reservoir, res., N.Y., U.S.	194		41.05 N	73.51 W
Tarsus, Tur.	42	G6	36.54 N	34.54 E
Tartagal, Arg.	166	D4	22.33 S	63.49 W
Tartagal, Arg.	172	D8	28.39 S	59.50 W
Tartu, Est.	26	B9	58.22 N	26.42 E
Țarțūs, Syria	76	D6	34.53 N	35.53 E
Țarțūs, state, Syria	76	D7	35.00 N	36.00 E
Tarum, stm., Indon.	66	G5	5.56 S	107.01 E
Tarumi, ngh., Japan	188		34.38 N	135.03 E
Tarumirim, Braz.	170	J5	19.15 S	41.58 W
Tarumizu, Japan	56	H3	31.29 N	130.42 E
Tarusa, Russia	26	F20	54.43 N	37.10 E
Tarutao, Ko, i., Thai.	64	I4	6.35 N	99.40 E
Tarutao National Park, p.o.i., Thai.	64	I4	6.35 N	99.38 E
Tarutino, Russia	26	E19	55.07 N	36.57 E
Tarutung, Indon.	66	B1	2.01 N	98.58 E
Tarva, is., Nor.	16	D7	63.48 N	9.25 E
Tarvisio, Italy	30	D10	46.30 N	13.35 E
Tarza, Russia	12	E19	62.30 N	40.26 E
Tarzan, Tx., U.S.	136	B6	32.18 N	101.58 W
Tarzana, ngh., Ca., U.S.	198		34.10 N	118.32 W
Taşağıl, Tur.	76	B2	36.55 N	31.13 E
Tašanta, Russia	48	E15	49.43 N	89.10 E
Tasāwah, Libya	82	B2	25.58 N	13.29 E
Tasbuget, Kaz.	48	F11	44.46 N	65.32 E
Taseeva, stm., Russia	48	C16	58.05 N	94.00 E
Taseevo, Russia	48	C17	57.12 N	94.54 E
Taseko, stm., B.C., Can.	144	E7	52.00 N	123.40 W
Taseko Lakes, l., B.C., Can.	144	E7	51.15 N	123.35 W
Taseko Mountain, mtn., B.C., Can.	144	E7	51.14 N	123.28 W
Tāsgaon, India	69	C2	17.01 N	74.35 E
Tashi Gang Dzong, Bhu.	70	E13	27.19 N	91.34 E
Tashk, Daryācheh-ye, l., Iran	74	F13	29.45 N	53.30 E
Tāshkurghān see Kholm, Afg.	72	B10	36.41 N	67.41 E
Tashuik'u, Tai.	187d		25.13 N	121.30 E
Tasikmalaya, Indon.	66	G6	7.20 S	108.13 E
Tåsinge, i., Den.	16	L8	55.00 N	10.35 E
Tåsjö, Swe.	16	C13	64.13 N	15.54 E
Tåsjön, l., Swe.	16	C13	64.14 N	15.47 E
Taşkent, Tur.	34	G15	36.54 N	32.31 E
Taškent, Uzb.	48	F11	41.19 N	69.17 E
Taškepri, Turkmen.	72	B9	36.17 N	62.37 E
Taš-Kumyr, Kyrg.	48	F12	41.21 N	72.13 E
Tašla, Russia	40	F18	51.46 N	52.44 E
Taşlı, stm., Tur.	185b		41.03 N	28.56 E
Tasman Basin, unds.	174	N18	43.00 S	158.00 E
Tasman Bay, b., N.Z.	102	E5	41.00 S	173.20 E
Tasmania, state, Austl.	97a	i13	43.00 S	147.00 E
Tasmania, i., Austl.	99a	o13	42.00 S	147.00 E
Tasman Peninsula, pen., Austl.	99a	o14	43.05 S	147.50 E
Tasman Sea, s., Oc.	94	G7	40.00 S	163.00 E
Tășnad, Rom.	36	B9	47.28 N	22.35 E
Tasoba, Kaz.	40	G16	49.46 N	49.51 E
Tassajara Creek, stm., Ca., U.S.	200		37.41 N	121.53 W
Tassdorf, Ger.	182a		52.30 N	13.47 E
Tassialouc, Lac, l., Qc., Can.	110	D16	59.03 N	74.00 W
Taštagol, Russia	48	D15	52.46 N	87.53 E
Tastiota, Mex.	154	A3	28.22 N	111.23 W
Taşucu, Tur.	76	B4	36.19 N	33.53 E
Tata, Hung.	36	B5	47.38 N	18.20 E
Tata, Mor.	84	D3	29.44 N	7.57 W
Tataa, c., Fr. Poly.	100h	v21	17.34 S	149.37 W
Tatabánya, Hung.	36	B5	47.33 N	18.25 E
Tata Mailau, mtn., Indon.	60	G8	8.55 S	125.30 E
Tata Raphael, Camp, mil., D.R.C.	191b		4.18 S	15.17 E
Tatarbunary, Ukr.	38	H8	45.50 N	29.37 E
Tatarija, state, Russia	40	D17	55.00 N	51.00 E
Tatarinka, Russia	26	E16	55.58 N	33.57 E
Tatarino, Russia	38	C18	50.35 N	39.08 E
Tatarka, Bela.	26	G11	53.15 N	28.48 E
Tatarovo, ngh., Russia	183b		55.46 N	37.26 E
Tātārpur, ngh., India	190a		28.39 N	77.07 E
Tatarsk, Russia	48	C13	55.13 N	75.58 E
Tatarskij proliv, strt., Russia	50	G17	50.00 N	141.15 E
Tatarskoe-Maklakovo, Russia	40	D14	55.48 N	45.34 E
Tatarstan see Tatarija, state, Russia	40	D17	55.00 N	51.00 E
Tatar Strait see Tatarskij proliv, strt., Russia	50	G17	50.00 N	141.15 E
Tatau, stm., Malay.	66	B8	3.04 N	112.48 E
Tate, Ga., U.S.	132	B1	34.25 N	84.23 W
Tate, stm., Austl.	98	A4	17.21 S	143.43 E
Tate Gallery, bldg., Eng., U.K.	178		51.29 N	0.08 W
Tateyama, Japan	56	E12	34.59 N	139.52 E
Tate-yama, vol., Japan	56	C10	36.35 N	137.37 E
Tathlina Lake, l., N.T., Can.	110	C7	60.32 N	117.32 W
Tathong Channel, strt., China	189d		22.15 N	114.15 E
Tathong Point, c., China	189d		22.14 N	114.17 E
Tathra, Austl.	98	K8	36.43 S	149.58 E
Tatiščevo, Russia	40	F14	51.40 N	45.36 E
Tatla Lake, B.C., Can.	144	E6	51.54 N	124.35 W
Tatla Lake, l., B.C., Can.	144	E6	51.57 N	124.27 W
Tatlayoko Lake, B.C., Can.	144	E6	51.40 N	124.23 W
Tatlayoko Lake, l., B.C., Can.	144	E6	51.30 N	124.25 W
Tatlow, Mount, mtn., B.C., Can.	144	E7	51.23 N	123.52 W
Tatnam, Cape, c., Mb., Can.	110	D12	57.14 N	90.54 W
Tatrang, China	48	G15	38.26 N	85.38 E
Tatranský Narodny Park, p.o.i., Slvk.	24	G15	49.09 N	20.10 E
Tatry, mts., Eur.	24	G15	49.11 N	20.08 E
Tatrzański Park Narodowy, p.o.i., Pol.	24	G15	49.15 N	19.59 E
Tatsfield, Eng., U.K.	178		51.18 N	0.02 E
Tatsuno, Japan	56	E7	34.51 N	134.33 E
Tatsuno, Japan	56	D10	35.58 N	137.59 E
Tatton Hall, hist., Eng., U.K.	180		53.20 N	2.23 W
Tatton Mere, l., Eng., U.K.	180		53.19 N	2.22 W
Tatton Park, p.o.i., Eng., U.K.	180		53.20 N	2.22 W
Tatuapé, ngh., Braz.	205b		23.32 S	46.34 W
Tatui, Braz.	170	L2	23.21 S	47.49 W
Tatuk Lake, l., B.C., Can.	144	C6	53.31 N	124.14 W
Tatum, N.M., U.S.	138	H5	33.15 N	103.19 W
Tatum, Tx., U.S.	136	B13	32.19 N	94.31 W
Tat'un Shan, mtn., Tai.	187d		25.11 N	121.31 E
Tatvan, Tur.	42	F10	38.30 N	42.17 E
Tau, Am. Sam.	101c	h13	14.13 S	169.30 W
Tau, Kaz.	40	G15	49.40 N	47.16 E
Tau, Nor.	16	H3	59.04 N	5.54 E
Tau, i., Am. Sam.	101c	h13	14.15 S	169.29 W
Tauá, Braz.	170	C5	6.01 S	40.26 W
Taubaté, Braz.	170	L3	23.01 S	45.33 W
Tauber, stm., Ger.	24	G5	49.44 N	9.30 E
Tauberbischofsheim, Ger.	24	G5	49.37 N	9.40 E
Taučik, Kaz.	48	F8	44.18 N	51.23 E
Taujskaja guba, b., Russia	50	E18	59.20 N	150.20 E
Taulihawā, Nepal	70	E9	27.32 N	83.03 E
Taumarunui, N.Z.	102	D6	38.52 S	175.18 E
Taumaturgo, Braz.	164	E3	8.57 S	72.48 W
Taum Sauk Mountain, mtn., Mo., U.S.	130	G7	37.34 N	90.44 W
Taunay, Cascatinha, wtfl., Braz.	205a		22.57 S	43.17 W
Taung, S. Afr.	90	E7	27.27 S	24.46 E
Taungbon, Mya.	64	E3	15.25 N	97.49 E
Taungdwingyi, Mya.	64	B2	20.00 N	95.32 E
Taunggyi, Mya.	64	B3	20.47 N	97.02 E
Taungnyo Range, mts., Mya.	64	E4	15.38 N	97.56 E
Taungup, Mya.	64	C2	18.51 N	94.15 E
Taungup Pass, p., Mya.	64	C2	18.39 N	94.46 E
Taunsa, Pak.	70	C3	30.42 N	70.39 E
Taunton, Eng., U.K.	10	J9	51.01 N	3.06 W
Taunton, Ma., U.S.	124	C14	41.54 N	71.05 W
Taunton Lake, l., N.J., U.S.	203		39.51 N	74.51 W
Taunton Lakes, N.J., U.S.	203		39.51 N	74.51 W
Taupo, N.Z.	102	D6	38.41 S	176.05 E
Taupo, Lake, l., N.Z.	102	D6	38.49 S	175.55 E
Tauragė, Lith.	26	E5	55.15 N	22.17 E
Tauranga, N.Z.	102	C7	37.41 S	176.09 E
Taurianova, Italy	32	F9	38.21 N	16.01 E
Taurisano, Italy	32	E12	39.57 N	18.13 E
Tauroa Point, c., N.Z.	102	B5	35.10 S	173.04 E
Taurus Mountains see Toros Dağları, mts., Tur.	42	G5	37.00 N	33.00 E
Tautira, Fr. Poly.	100h	w23	17.45 S	149.09 W
Tavajza, Russia	54	B12	45.12 N	136.46 E
Tavālesh, Kūhhā-ye see Talish Mountains, mts., Asia	74	B11	37.56 N	48.41 E
Tavan Bogd see Tavan-Bogdo-Ula, gora, mtn., Asia	48	E15	49.08 N	87.48 E
Tavan-Bogdo-Ula, gora, mtn., Asia	48	E15	49.08 N	87.48 E
Tavares, Braz.	170	D7	7.38 S	37.54 W
Tavares, Fl., U.S.	132	H4	28.49 N	81.42 W
Tavares, Ilha dos, i., Braz.	205a		22.49 S	43.06 W
Tavas, Tur.	34	F12	37.34 N	29.04 E
Tavastehus see Hämeenlinna, Fin.	18	G11	60.58 N	24.30 E
Tavda, Russia	48	C11	58.02 N	65.15 E
Tavda, stm., Russia	48	C11	57.47 N	67.15 E
Tavern Creek, stm., Mo., U.S.	130	F5	38.18 N	92.16 W
Tavernes de la Valldigna, Spain	28	E10	39.04 N	0.15 W
Tavernier, Fl., U.S.	132	K5	25.00 N	80.31 W
Taveta, Kenya	86	E7	3.23 S	37.39 E
Taveuni, i., Fiji	101e	p20	16.51 S	179.58 W
Taviano, Italy	32	E12	39.59 N	18.05 E
Tavignano, stm., Fr.	22	G15	42.06 N	9.31 E
Tavira, Port.	28	G3	37.07 N	7.39 W
Tavistock, On., Can.	126	E9	43.18 N	80.50 W
Tavistock, Eng., U.K.	10	K8	50.33 N	4.09 W
Tavolara, Isola, i., Italy	32	D3	40.54 N	9.42 E
Tavoliere, reg., Italy	32	C9	41.35 N	15.25 E
Tavolžan, Kaz.	48	D13	52.42 N	77.27 E
Tavor, Har, mtn., Isr.	76	F6	32.41 N	35.23 E
Tavoy see Dawei, Mya.	64	E4	14.05 N	98.12 E
Tavoy Point, c., Mya.	64	F3	13.32 N	98.10 E
Tavričanka, Russia	54	C9	43.19 N	131.52 E
Tavry, Russia	183a		59.55 N	30.42 E
Tavşanlı, Tur.	34	D12	39.32 N	29.28 E
Tavua, Fiji	101e	p18	17.27 S	177.51 E
Taw, stm., Eng., U.K.	10	K9	51.04 N	4.04 W
Tawaeli, Indon.	66	D11	0.44 S	119.52 E
Tawakoni, Lake, res., Tx., U.S.	136	A12	32.53 N	95.59 W
Tawara, Japan	188		34.27 N	135.57 E
Tawarada, Japan	186		35.19 N	140.04 E
Tawas City, Mi., U.S.	126	D6	44.15 N	83.31 W
Tawau, Malay.	66	A10	4.15 N	117.53 E
Tawd, stm., Eng., U.K.	180		53.36 N	2.48 W
Tawīla, Gezīra, is., Egypt	76	K4	27.35 N	33.46 E
Tawitawi Group, is., Phil.	68	H3	5.14 N	120.04 E
Tawitawi Island, i., Phil.	68	H2	5.10 N	120.00 E
Ṭawkar, Sudan	82	D7	18.25 N	37.43 E
Tawu, Tai.	58	J9	22.22 N	120.53 E
Tāwūq, Iraq	74	C9	35.08 N	44.27 E
Taxco de Alarcón, Mex.	154	F9	18.33 N	99.36 W
Taxkorgan Tajik Zizhixian, China	48	G13	37.46 N	75.13 E
Tay, stm., Scot., U.K.	10	E9	56.22 N	3.21 W
Tay, Firth of, b., Scot., U.K.	10	E9	56.26 N	3.00 W
Tay, Loch, l., Scot., U.K.	10	E8	56.31 N	4.09 W
Tayabamba, Peru	164	E2	8.17 S	77.16 W
Tayabas Bay, b., Phil.	68	D3	13.45 N	121.45 E
Tayan, Indon.	66	C7	0.02 S	110.07 E
Táygetos Óros, mts., Grc.	34	F5	37.00 N	22.20 E
Taylor, Az., U.S.	150	I6	34.27 N	110.05 W
Taylor, Ar., U.S.	134	D5	33.06 N	93.27 W
Taylor, Ne., U.S.	140	F13	41.45 N	99.22 W
Taylor, Tx., U.S.	136	D10	30.33 N	97.24 W
Taylor, stm., Co., U.S.	138	C2	38.39 N	106.50 W
Taylor, Mount, mtn., N.M., U.S.	150	H9	35.14 N	107.37 W
Taylor Creek, stm., On., Can.	193b		43.42 N	79.20 W
Taylor Mountain, mtn., Id., U.S.	146	F12	44.53 N	114.13 W
Taylor Run, stm., Pa., U.S.	203		39.57 N	75.39 W
Taylors, S.C., U.S.	132	B3	34.54 N	82.19 W
Taylors Bush Park, p.o.i., On., Can.	193b		43.42 N	79.19 W
Taylors Run, stm., Pa., U.S.	197b		40.11 N	79.57 W
Taylorsville, In., U.S.	130	E12	39.17 N	85.56 W
Taylorsville, Ky., U.S.	130	F12	38.02 N	85.20 W
Taylorsville, Ms., U.S.	134	F9	31.49 N	89.26 W
Taylorsville, N.C., U.S.	124	I4	35.55 N	81.10 W
Taylortown, N.J., U.S.	194		40.56 N	74.24 W
Taylortown Reservoir, res., N.J., U.S.	194		40.58 N	74.22 W
Taylorville, Il., U.S.	130	E8	39.32 N	89.17 W
Taymā', Sau. Ar.	72	D4	27.37 N	38.33 E
Taymouth, N.B., Can.	122	D10	46.10 N	66.36 W
Taymyr Peninsula see Tajmyr, poluostrov, pen., Russia	50	B7	76.00 N	104.00 E
Tay Ninh, Viet.	64	G8	11.17 N	106.07 E
Tayoltita, Mex.	154	C6	24.05 N	105.56 W
Tayros, Grc.	185c		37.58 N	23.42 E
Taytay, Phil.	68	E2	10.49 N	119.31 E
Tayu, Indon.	66	G7	6.33 S	111.02 E
Tayuan, China	50	F13	51.27 N	124.16 E
Taz, stm., Russia	48	A14	67.30 N	78.43 E
Taza, Mor.	84	C4	34.14 N	4.00 W
Tazewell, Tn., U.S.	124	H2	36.27 N	83.34 W
Tazewell, Va., U.S.	124	G4	37.07 N	81.31 W
Tazin, stm., Can.	110	C8	60.26 N	110.45 W
Tazin Lake, l., Sk., Can.	110	D9	59.47 N	109.13 W
Tazovskaja guba, b., Russia	48	A13	69.05 N	76.00 E
Tazovskij, Russia	48	A13	67.29 N	78.41 E
Tazovskij poluostrov, pen., Russia	50	C4	68.35 N	76.00 E
Tbessa, Alg.	84	B6	35.24 N	8.07 E
Tbilisi, Geor.	42	E11	41.43 N	44.47 E
Tchad see Chad, ctry., Afr.	82	E3	15.00 N	19.00 E
Tchad, Lac see Chad, Lake, l., Afr.	82	E2	13.20 N	14.00 E
Tchamba, Togo	84	H5	9.01 N	1.25 E
Tchaourou, Benin	84	H5	8.53 N	2.36 E
Tchefuncta, stm., La., U.S.	134	G8	30.24 N	90.09 W
Tchentlo Lake, l., B.C., Can.	144	A5	55.11 N	125.00 W
Tchesinkut Lake, l., B.C., Can.	144	B5	54.05 N	125.38 W
Tchibanga, Gabon	86	E2	2.51 S	11.01 E
Tcholliré, Cam.	86	C2	8.24 N	14.10 E
Tchula, Ms., U.S.	134	D8	33.11 N	90.13 W
Tczew, Pol.	24	B14	54.05 N	18.47 E
Té, stm., Camb.	64	F8	12.26 N	106.01 E
Te, Kinh, can., Viet.	187c		10.45 N	106.42 E
Teá, stm., Braz.	168	H9	0.26 S	65.09 W
Teaca, Rom.	36	C11	46.55 N	24.31 E
Teacapan, Mex.	154	D6	22.32 N	105.44 W
Teak Creek, stm., On., Can.	202a		43.02 N	79.06 W
Teaehoa, c., Fr. Poly.	100g	s18	9.51 S	139.02 W
Teague, Tx., U.S.	136	C11	31.37 N	96.16 W
Teahupoo, Fr. Poly.	100h	w22	17.50 S	149.16 W
Te Anau, N.Z.	102	G2	45.25 S	167.43 E
Te Anau, Lake, l., N.Z.	102	G2	45.12 S	167.45 E
Teano, Italy	32	C8	41.15 N	14.03 E
Teapa, Mex.	154	G12	17.34 N	92.57 W
Te Atukura, mtn., Cook Is.	100j	a26	21.14 S	159.45 W
Te Awamutu, N.Z.	102	C6	38.00 S	175.19 E
Teba, Indon.	60	F10	1.29 S	137.54 E
Teba, Spain	28	H6	36.58 N	4.56 W
Tebakang, Malay.	66	C7	1.05 N	110.29 E
Teberda, Russia	42	D9	43.27 N	41.44 E
Tebicuary, stm., Para.	172	C9	26.38 S	58.11 W
Tebicuary-mí, stm., Para.	172	C9	26.32 S	56.50 W
Tebingbulan, Indon.	66	E3	3.04 S	103.45 E
Tebingtinggi, Indon.	66	C2	0.39 N	101.37 E
Tebingtinggi, Indon.	66	B1	3.19 N	99.09 E
Tebingtinggi, Indon.	66	E3	3.36 S	103.05 E
Tebingtinggi, Pulau, i., Indon.	66	C3	0.54 N	102.45 E
Tébourba, Tun.	32	H3	36.49 N	9.50 E
Téboursouk, Tun.	32	H3	36.27 N	9.15 E
Téboursouk, Monts de, mts., Tun.	32	H3	36.30 N	9.10 E
Tebra, stm., Lat.	26	D4	56.50 N	21.13 E
Tecalitlán, Mex.	154	F7	19.28 N	103.17 W
Tecate, Mex.	120	E4	32.34 N	116.37 W
Tech, stm., Fr.	22	G8	42.36 N	3.02 E
Teche, Bayou, stm., La., U.S.	134	H7	29.43 N	91.13 W
Techirghiol, Rom.	36	E15	44.04 N	28.35 E
Techlé, W. Sah.	84	E2	21.36 N	14.59 W
Tecka, Arg.	166	H2	43.27 S	70.49 W
Tecka, stm., Arg.	166	H2	42.36 S	70.22 W
Tecklenburg, Ger.	24	D3	52.13 N	7.49 E
Tecolote Creek, stm., N.M., U.S.	138	F3	35.14 N	105.09 W
Tecomán, Mex.	154	F7	18.55 N	103.52 W
Tecopa, Ca., U.S.	148	H9	35.51 N	116.13 W
Tecpan de Galeana, Mex.	154	G8	17.12 N	100.36 W
Tecuala, Mex.	154	D6	22.23 N	105.27 W
Tecuautzi, Cerro, mtn., Mex.	204a		19.19 N	99.00 W
Tecuci, Rom.	36	D14	45.50 N	27.25 E
Tecumseh, Ne., U.S.	130	D1	40.22 N	96.11 W
Tecumseh, Ok., U.S.	134	B2	35.15 N	96.56 W
Teddington, ngh., Eng., U.K.	178		51.25 N	0.20 W
Tedžen, Turkmen.	72	B9	37.22 N	60.31 E
Tedžen (Harīrūd), stm., Asia	72	B9	37.23 N	60.30 E
Teec Nos Pos, Az., U.S.	150	G7	36.54 N	109.33 W
Teeli, Russia	48	D15	51.00 N	90.12 E
Teerijärvi, Fin.	18	D10	63.32 N	23.30 E
Tees, stm., Eng., U.K.	10	G11	54.35 N	1.15 W
Tees Bay, b., Eng., U.K.	10	G11	54.39 N	1.08 W
Teeswater, On., Can.	126	D8	44.00 N	81.16 W
Tefé, Braz.	164	D5	3.22 S	64.43 W
Tefé, stm., Braz.	164	D4	3.30 S	64.57 W
Tefenni, Tur.	34	F12	37.17 N	29.46 E
Tegal, Indon.	66	G6	6.51 S	109.07 E
Tégama, reg., Niger	84	F6	15.37 N	8.07 E
Tega-numa, l., Japan	186		35.51 N	140.04 E
Tegéa, hist., Grc.	34	F5	37.28 N	22.22 E
Tegel, Berliner Forst, for., Ger.	182a		52.37 N	13.16 E
Tegel, Schloss, hist., Ger.	182a		52.36 N	13.16 E
Tegeler See, l., Ger.	182a		52.35 N	13.15 E
Tegernsee, Ger.	24	I7	47.43 N	11.45 E
Tegina, Nig.	84	G6	10.03 N	6.11 E
Tegineneng, Indon.	66	F4	5.12 S	105.10 E
Tégua, i., Vanuatu	101d	i16	13.15 S	166.36 E
Tegucigalpa, Hond.	156	E4	14.05 N	87.12 W
Tegul'det, Russia	48	C15	57.18 N	88.10 E
Tehachapi, Ca., U.S.	148	H7	35.08 N	118.26 W
Tehachapi Mountains, mts., Ca., U.S.	148	I7	35.04 N	118.35 W
Tehachapi Pass, p., Ca., U.S.	148	H7	35.06 N	118.17 W
Tehar, ngh., India	190a		28.38 N	77.07 E
Tehata, India	70	G12	23.43 N	88.32 E
Tehek Lake, l., Nu., Can.	110	C11	64.56 N	95.37 W
Teheran see Tehrān, Iran	74	C12	35.40 N	51.24 E
Te Hope O Te Keho, Cap, c., Fr. Poly.	100g	t18	10.01 S	139.06 W
Tehrān (Teheran), Iran	74	C12	35.40 N	51.24 E
Tehrān, Iran	185d		35.40 N	51.26 E
Tehrān, state, Iran	74	C12	35.30 N	51.30 E
Tehrān, University of, educ., Iran	185d		35.42 N	51.24 E
Tehrān Pārs, ngh., Iran	185d		35.44 N	51.32 E
Tehrathum, Nepal	70	E11	27.06 N	87.33 E
Tehuacán, Mex.	154	F10	18.27 N	97.23 W
Tehuacana Creek, stm., Tx., U.S.	136	C11	31.52 N	95.59 W
Tehuantepec, Golfo de, b., Mex.	154	H11	16.00 N	94.50 W
Tehuantepec, Gulf of see Tehuantepec, Golfo de, b., Mex.	154	H11	16.00 N	94.50 W
Tehuantepec, Isthmus of see Tehuantepec, Istmo de, isth., Mex.	154	G11	17.00 N	95.00 W
Tehuantepec, Istmo de, isth., Mex.	154	G11	17.00 N	95.00 W
Teià, Spain	184d		41.30 N	2.19 E
Teide, Pico del, mtn., Spain	84	D1	28.15 N	16.38 W
Teignmouth, Eng., U.K.	10	K9	50.33 N	3.29 W
Teise, stm., Eng., U.K.	178		51.13 N	0.25 E
Teixeira, Braz.	170	D7	7.13 S	37.15 W
Teixeira Pinto, Gui.-B.	84	G1	12.03 N	16.16 W
Teixeira Soares, Braz.	172	B12	25.21 S	50.27 W
Teixeiro, Spain	28	A2	43.06 N	8.02 W
Tejakula, Indon.	66	H9	8.07 S	115.20 E
Tejamén, Mex.	154	C6	24.48 N	105.08 W
Tejkovo, Russia	40	C12	56.51 N	40.32 E
Tejo see Tagus, stm., Eur.	28	F1	38.50 N	8.56 W
Tejon Pass, p., Ca., U.S.	148	I7	34.48 N	118.52 W
Tejupan, Punta, c., Mex.	154	F7	18.20 N	103.30 W
Tejupilco de Hidalgo, Mex.	154	F8	18.54 N	100.09 W
Tékakwitha, Île, i., Qc., Can.	193a		45.25 N	73.42 W
Tekamah, Ne., U.S.	130	C1	41.46 N	96.13 W
Tekapo, Lake, l., N.Z.	102	F4	43.53 S	170.31 E
Tekax, Mex.	156	B3	20.12 N	89.16 W
Teke, Tur.	34	B12	41.04 N	29.39 E
Teke Burnu, c., Tur.	34	E9	38.07 N	26.36 E
Tekeli, Kaz.	48	F13	44.48 N	78.51 E
Tekezē (Satīt), stm., Afr.	82	E7	14.20 N	35.50 E
Tekirdağ, Tur.	34	C10	40.59 N	27.31 E
Tekirdağ, state, Tur.	34	B10	41.00 N	27.30 E
Tekkali, India	69	B7	18.36 N	84.14 E
Tekke Burnu, c., Tur.	34	C9	40.03 N	26.11 E
Tekoa, Wa., U.S.	146	C9	47.13 N	117.04 W
Tekong, Pulau, i., Sing.	189c		1.24 N	104.03 E
Tekong Kechil, Pulau, i., Sing.	189c		1.25 N	104.01 E
Tekonsha, Mi., U.S.	124	B1	42.05 N	84.58 W
Tekstil'ščiki, ngh., Russia	183b		55.42 N	37.44 E
Te Kuiti, N.Z.	102	D6	38.19 S	175.10 E
Tekukor, Pulau, i., Sing.	189c		1.14 N	103.50 E
Tel, stm., India	69	A6	20.25 N	83.33 E
Tela, Hond.	156	E4	15.46 N	87.27 W
Tela, India	190a		28.44 N	77.20 E
Telaopengsha Shan, mtn., China	70	C11	30.32 N	86.31 E
Telavi, Geor.	42	E11	41.55 N	45.28 E
Tel Aviv-Jaffa see Tel Aviv-Yafo, Isr.	76	F5	32.03 N	34.46 E
Tel Aviv-Yafo, Isr.	76	F5	32.03 N	34.46 E
Telč, Czech Rep.	24	G11	49.10 N	15.27 E
Tel'če, Russia	26	G19	53.20 N	36.20 E
Tele (Telle), stm., Afr.	90	G8	30.24 S	27.34 E
Teleckoe, ozero, l., Russia	48	D15	51.37 N	87.39 E
Telefomin, Pap. N. Gui.	101a	b3	5.10 S	141.35 E
Telegapulang, Indon.	66	E8	2.53 S	112.16 E
Telegrafo, Pizzo, mtn., Italy	32	G7	37.37 N	13.10 E
Telegraph Canyon, val., Ca., U.S.	198		33.55 N	117.45 W
Telegraph Cove, B.C., Can.	144	F4	50.32 N	126.49 W
Telegraph Creek, B.C., Can.	110	D4	57.55 N	131.10 W
Telêmaco Borba, Braz.	172	B12	24.20 S	50.37 W
Telemark, state, Nor.	16	H6	59.30 N	8.40 E
Telembí, stm., Col.	168	G2	1.50 N	78.16 W
Telén, Arg.	172	H5	36.15 S	65.30 W
Telen, stm., Indon.	66	C10	0.08 S	116.41 E
Teleneshty see Telenești, Mol.	38	F7	47.29 N	28.22 E
Telenești, Mol.	38	F7	47.29 N	28.22 E
Teleno, mtn., Spain	28	B4	42.21 N	6.23 W
Teleorman, state, Rom.	36	E12	44.00 N	25.15 E
Teleorman, stm., Rom.	36	E11	43.52 N	25.25 E
Téléphone, Île du, i., D.R.C.	191b		4.20 S	15.12 E
Telerig, Blg.	36	F14	43.51 N	27.40 E
Telescope Peak, mtn., Ca., U.S.	148	G8	36.10 N	117.05 W
Telescope Point, c., Gren.	159e	q10	12.08 N	61.36 W
Telese, Italy	32	C8	41.13 N	14.31 E
Telesterion, hist., Grc.	185c		38.02 N	23.32 E
Telford, Eng., U.K.	10	I10	52.40 N	2.26 W
Telfs, Aus.	24	I7	47.18 N	11.03 E
Télimélé, Gui.	84	G2	10.53 N	13.02 W
Telire, stm., C.R.	156	H6	9.34 N	82.53 W
Telizi, Russia	183a		59.42 N	29.59 E
Teljo, Jabal, mtn., Sudan	82	E5	14.42 N	25.56 E
Telkwa, B.C., Can.	144	B3	54.41 N	127.02 W
Telkwa, stm., B.C., Can.	144	B3	54.41 N	127.02 W
Tellaro, stm., Italy	32	H8	36.50 N	15.06 E
Tell Atlas see Atlas Tellien, mts., Alg.	80	C6	36.00 N	3.00 E
Tell Basta, hist., Egypt	76	H2	30.34 N	31.31 E
Tell City, In., U.S.	130	G11	37.57 N	86.45 W
Telle (Tele), stm., Afr.	90	G8	30.24 S	27.34 E
Tell El-Amarna, hist., Egypt	76	K1	27.38 N	30.54 E
Tellel Rub, hist., Egypt	76	H2	30.58 N	31.31 E
Teller, Ak., U.S.	109	C6	65.14 N	166.20 W
Tellicherry, India	69	F2	11.44 N	75.29 E
Tellico, stm., U.S.	132	A1	35.36 N	84.13 W
Tellico Plains, Tn., U.S.	132	A1	35.21 N	84.18 W
Tellier, Arg.	166	I3	47.37 S	66.02 W
Tello, Col.	168	F4	3.03 N	75.08 W
Telluride, Co., U.S.	150	F9	37.56 N	107.47 W
Tel'manove, Ukr.	38	F17	47.24 N	38.01 E
Tel Megiddo, hist., Isr.	76	F6	32.35 N	35.11 E
Telmen nuur, l., Mong.	52	B4	48.50 N	97.18 E
Telogia Creek, stm., Fl., U.S.	134	G14	30.16 N	84.44 W
Teloloapan, Mex.	154	F9	18.21 N	99.51 W
Telos see Tílos, i., Grc.	34	G10	36.23 N	27.24 E
Telsen, Arg.	166	H3	42.26 S	66.58 W
Telšiai, Lith.	26	E5	55.59 N	22.15 E
Teltow, Ger.	24	D9	52.23 N	13.15 E
Teltow, reg., Ger.	182a		52.18 N	13.25 E
Teltower Hochfläche, plat., Ger.	182a		52.22 N	13.20 E
Teltowkanal, can., Ger.	182a		52.26 N	13.35 E
Telukbatang, Indon.	66	D6	0.58 S	109.45 E
Telukbayur, Indon.	66	D2	1.00 S	100.22 E
Telukbayur, Indon.	66	B10	2.09 N	117.25 E
Telukbutun, Indon.	66	A6	4.12 N	108.13 E
Telukdalem, Indon.	64	L3	0.34 N	97.48 E
Teluk Intan, Malay.	64	K5	4.01 N	101.01 E
Teluklanjut, Indon.	66	C3	0.08 N	103.29 E
Teluk Punggur, Ujung, c., Indon.	66	E2	3.53 S	102.17 E
Telumengtang Shan, mtn., China	70	C11	30.47 N	87.52 E
Tema, Ghana	84	H5	5.38 N	0.01 E
Temae, Fr. Poly.	100h	u20	17.29 S	149.46 W
Temagami, Lake, l., On., Can.	126	B9	47.00 N	80.05 W
Temaju, Pulau, i., Indon.	66	C6	0.29 N	108.52 E
Temali Bendi, dam., Tur.	185b		41.04 N	29.06 E
Te Manga, mtn., Cook Is.	100j	a26	21.13 S	159.45 W
Temangga, Indon.	66	C7	0.27 N	111.21 E
Tematangi, at., Fr. Poly.	94	F12	21.41 S	140.40 W
Temax, Mex.	156	B3	21.09 N	88.56 W
Tembakul, Pulau, i., Sing.	189c		1.14 N	103.52 E
Tembeling, stm., Malay.	64	J6	4.05 N	102.19 E
Tembenči, stm., Russia	48	A17	64.36 N	99.55 E
Tembesi, stm., Indon.	66	E3	1.42 S	103.05 E
Tembilahan, Indon.	66	D3	0.15 S	103.13 E
Temblador, Ven.	168	C10	8.59 N	62.37 W
Tembleque, Spain	28	E7	39.42 N	3.30 W
Temblor Range, mts., Ca., U.S.	148	H6	35.24 N	119.53 W
Teme, stm., Eng., U.K.	10	I10	52.10 N	2.13 W
Temecula, Ca., U.S.	148	J8	33.29 N	117.08 W
Temelli, Tur.	34	D15	39.44 N	32.20 E
Temengor, Tasik, res., Malay.	64	J5	5.31 N	101.21 E
Temerin, Yugo.	36	D6	45.24 N	19.54 E
Temescal Canyon, val., Ca., U.S.	198		34.04 N	118.32 W
Temesvár see Timișoara, Rom.	36	D8	45.45 N	21.13 E
Temetiu, mtn., Fr. Poly.	100g	s18	9.49 S	139.03 W
Temiang, Pulau, i., Indon.	66	C4	0.19 N	104.23 E
Temir, Kaz.	48	E9	49.08 N	57.07 E
Temirtau, Kaz.	48	D12	50.02 N	72.57 E
Témiscaming, Qc., Can.	126	B10	46.43 N	79.05 W
Témiscamingue, Lac (Timiskaming, Lake), res., Can.	126	B10	47.10 N	79.08 W
Témiscouata, Lac, l., Qc., Can.	122	C8	47.39 N	68.48 W
Těmkino, Russia	26	E17	55.05 N	35.01 E
Temnikovo, Russia	183b		55.43 N	38.01 E
Temo, stm., Italy	32	D2	40.18 N	8.29 E
Temora, Austl.	98	J6	34.26 S	147.32 E
Temosachic, Mex.	154	A5	28.57 N	107.50 W
Tempe, Az., U.S.	150	J5	33.25 N	111.55 W
Tempe, Danau, l., Indon.	66	F12	4.06 S	119.57 E
Tempelfelde, Ger.	182a		52.43 N	13.43 E
Tempelhof, ngh., Ger.	182a		52.28 N	13.23 E
Tempilang, Indon.	66	E4	2.06 S	105.39 E
Tempino, Indon.	66	D3	1.47 S	103.30 E
Tempio Pausania, Italy	32	D3	40.54 N	9.05 E
Temple, Ok., U.S.	138	G10	34.16 N	98.14 W
Temple, Tx., U.S.	136	C10	31.05 N	97.20 W
Temple Hills Park, Md., U.S.	202c		38.48 N	76.57 W
Templemore, Ire.	10	I5	52.47 N	7.50 W
Temple University, educ., Pa., U.S.	203		39.59 N	75.09 W

Name Page Map Ref. Latitude Longitude

Templi, Valle dei, hist., Italy 32 G7 37.17 N 13.35 E
Templin, Ger. 24 C9 53.07 N 13.30 E
Templiner See, l., Ger. 182a 52.22 N 13.01 E
Tempoal, stm., Mex. 154 E9 21.46 N 98.27 W
Tempoal de Sánchez, Mex. 154 E9 21.31 N 98.23 W
Tempy, Russia 26 D20 56.38 N 37.19 E
Temrjuk, Russia 40 I10 45.16 N 37.22 E
Temrjukskij zaliv, b., Russia 40 I10 45.28 N 37.19 E
Temuco, Chile 166 G2 38.44 S 72.35 W
Temwen, i., Micron. 100d m12 6.50 N 158.19 E
Tena, Ec. 168 H3 0.58 S 77.48 W
Tenabo, Mex. 156 B2 20.03 N 90.13 W
Tenaha, Tx., U.S. 136 C13 31.56 N 94.14 W
Tenakill Brook, stm., N.J., U.S. 194 40.59 N 73.58 W
Tena Kourou, mtn., Burkina 84 G4 10.45 N 5.25 W
Tenāli, India 69 C5 16.14 N 80.34 E
Tenantongo, Presa, res., Mex. 204a 19.28 N 99.16 W
Tenasserim, Mya. 64 F4 12.04 N 99.01 E
Tendaho, Eth. 82 E8 11.42 N 40.56 E
Tendai-san, mtn., Japan 188 34.55 N 135.28 E
Tende, Fr. 22 E13 44.05 N 7.35 E
Tende, Col de, p., Eur. 30 F4 44.09 N 7.33 E
Ten Degree Channel, strt., India 62 G7 10.00 N 93.00 E
Tendō, Japan 56 A13 38.21 N 140.22 E
Tendrivs'ka Kosa, ostriv, spit, Ukr. 38 G10 46.12 N 31.50 E
Tendrivs'ka zatoka, b., Ukr. 38 G10 46.15 N 31.55 E
Ténenkou, Mali 84 G3 14.26 N 4.55 W
Tenente Portela, Braz. 172 C11 27.22 S 53.45 W
Ténéré, des., Niger 84 F7 18.42 N 10.51 E
Ténéré, Erg du, sand, Niger 84 F7 17.35 N 10.55 E
Tenerife, i., Spain 84 D1 28.19 N 16.34 W
Ténès, Alg. 28 H12 36.30 N 1.17 E
Ténès, Cap, c., Alg. 28 H12 36.33 N 1.21 E
Teng, stm., Mya. 64 B3 19.51 N 97.44 E
Tengah, Kepulauan, is., Indon. 66 G10 7.30 S 117.30 E
Tengchong, China 52 G4 25.01 N 98.30 E
Tengeh Reservoir, res., Sing. 189c 1.21 N 103.39 E
Tenggara, Nusa (Lesser Sunda Islands), is., Indon. 60 G6 9.00 S 120.00 E
Tenggara Celebes see Sulawesi Tenggara, state, Indon. 66 E12 3.40 S 120.54 E
Tenggarong, Indon. 66 D10 0.23 S 116.58 E
Tengger Shamo, des., China 52 D5 38.28 N 104.29 E
Tenggul, Pulau, i., Malay. 64 J6 4.48 N 103.41 E
Tenghilan, Malay. 68 G1 6.13 N 116.18 E
Tengiz, ozero, l., Kaz. 48 D11 50.21 N 68.56 E
Tengqiao, China 58 L3 18.24 N 109.45 E
Tengra, India 190b 22.48 N 88.32 E
Tengréla, C. Iv. 84 G3 10.28 N 6.24 W
Tengtiao (Na), stm., Asia 64 A6 22.40 N 102.58 E
Ten'guševo, Russia 40 D13 54.45 N 42.43 E
Tengxian, China 58 J4 23.20 N 110.52 E
Tengxian, China 58 D7 35.04 N 117.09 E
Tenino, Wa., U.S. 146 D4 46.51 N 122.50 W
Tenjo, Mount, hill, Guam 100c j9 13.24 N 144.41 E
Tenkāsi, India 69 G3 8.56 N 77.19 E
Tenke, D.R.C. 86 G5 10.35 S 26.07 E
Tenkeli, Russia 50 B17 70.00 N 140.57 E
Tenkiller Ferry Lake, res., Ok., U.S. 134 B3 35.41 N 94.57 W
Tenkodogo, Burkina 84 G4 11.46 N 0.21 W
Tenmile, stm., Ma., U.S. 201 41.58 N 71.20 W
Ten Mile Creek, stm., On., Can. 202a 43.07 N 79.11 W
Tenmile Run, stm., N.J., U.S. 194 40.27 N 74.35 W
Tenmile Wash, stm., Az., U.S. 150 K3 32.52 N 113.31 W
Tenna, stm., Italy 30 G10 43.14 N 13.46 E
Tennant Creek, Austl. 96 C6 19.39 S 134.10 E
Tennent Pond, l., N.J., U.S. 194 40.26 N 74.20 W
Tennessee, state, U.S. 116 C10 35.50 N 85.30 W
Tennessee, stm., U.S. 116 C8 37.04 N 88.34 W
Tennevollen, Nor. 14 D8 68.44 N 17.49 E
Tenniöjoki see Tenniöjoki, stm., Eur. 14 E19 67.16 N 28.18 E
Tennille, Ga., U.S. 132 D3 32.56 N 82.48 W
Tenniöjoki, stm., Eur. 14 E19 67.16 N 28.18 E
Tennōji, ngh., Japan 188 34.39 N 135.31 E
Teno, Chile 172 G2 34.53 S 71.11 W
Teno (Tana), stm., Eur. 14 B19 70.25 N 28.16 E
Tenom, Malay. 66 A9 5.07 N 115.56 E
Tenos see Tínos, Grc. 34 F8 37.32 N 25.09 E
Tenos see Tínos, i., Grc. 34 F8 37.35 N 25.09 E
Ténos, Pointe, c., Mart. 159c k7 14.48 N 61.00 W
Tenosique, Mex. 156 D2 17.28 N 91.25 W
Tenryū, Japan 56 E10 34.52 N 137.49 E
Tenryū, stm., Japan 56 D11 34.40 N 137.47 E
Tensas, stm., La., U.S. 134 F7 31.37 N 91.48 W
Tensed, Id., U.S. 146 C10 47.09 N 116.56 W
Ten Sleep, Wy., U.S. 140 C5 44.03 N 107.27 W
Tente, ngh., Ger. 181 51.18 N 7.14 E
Tentena, Indon. 66 D12 1.44 S 120.39 E
Tenterfield, Austl. 98 G8 29.03 S 152.01 E
Ten Thousand Islands, is., Fl., U.S. 132 K4 25.50 N 81.33 W
Tentolomatinan, Gunung, mtn., Indon. 60 E7 0.54 N 121.43 E
Tentulia, India 190b 22.50 N 88.28 E
Teocaltiche, Mex. 154 E7 21.26 N 102.34 W
Teodelina, Arg. 172 G7 34.10 S 61.32 W
Teófilo Cunha, Braz. 205a 22.39 S 43.34 W
Teófilo Otoni, Braz. 170 I5 17.52 S 41.30 W
Teofipol', Ukr. 38 D5 49.50 N 26.25 E
Teo Lakes, l., Sk., Can. 142 C4 51.30 N 109.21 W
Teotihuacán, hist., Mex. 154 F9 19.44 N 98.50 W
Tepa, Indon. 60 G8 7.50 S 129.36 E
Tepalcatepec, Mex. 154 F7 19.11 N 102.51 W
Tepebaşı, Tur. 76 B3 36.40 N 32.45 E
Tepehuanes, Mex. 154 C6 25.21 N 105.44 W
Tepehuanes, stm., Mex. 154 C6 25.10 N 105.26 W
Tepeji de Ocampo, Mex. 154 F9 19.54 N 99.21 W
Tepelena see Tepelenë, Alb. 32 D13 40.18 N 20.01 E
Tepelenë, Alb. 32 D13 40.18 N 20.01 E
Tepepan, ngh., Mex. 204a 19.16 N 99.08 W
Tepe Safi, Iran 185d 35.36 N 51.18 E
Tepic, Mex. 154 E6 21.30 N 104.53 W
Teplice, Czech Rep. 24 F9 50.38 N 13.49 E
Teplitz see Teplice, Czech Rep. 24 F9 50.38 N 13.49 E
Tëploe, Russia 26 G20 53.36 N 37.35 E
Tëploe, Russia 40 E11 53.13 N 38.53 E
Tëplyj Stan, ngh., Russia 183b 55.37 N 37.30 E
Teplyk, Ukr. 38 E8 48.39 N 29.45 E
Tepoca, Bahía de, b., Mex. 120 F6 30.11 N 112.47 W
Tepoca, Punta, c., Mex. 120 G6 29.54 N 112.43 W
Tepopa, Cabo, c., Mex. 120 G6 29.22 N 112.24 W
Tepostete, Cerro, mtn., Mex. 136 H2 26.53 N 105.28 W
Tepsa, Fin. 14 E16 67.33 N 25.40 E
Ter, stm., Spain 28 B14 42.02 N 3.07 E
Téra, Niger 84 G5 14.00 N 0.45 E
Tera, stm., Spain 28 C4 41.54 N 5.44 W
Teradomari, Japan 56 B11 37.37 N 138.46 E
Teraina, i., Kir. 94 C11 4.42 N 160.45 W
Teramo, Italy 30 H10 42.39 N 13.42 E
Terang, Austl. 98 L4 38.14 S 142.55 E
Teratak, Indon. 66 D7 0.46 S 110.32 E
Terbuny, Russia 26 H21 52.09 N 38.18 E
Terceira, i., Port. 80 C3 38.43 N 24.13 W
Tercero, stm., Arg. 172 F6 32.55 S 62.19 W
Tercero de Febrero, Parque, p.o.i., Arg. 206 34.34 S 58.25 W
Terdal, India 69 C2 16.29 N 75.05 E
Terdoppio, Torrente, stm., Italy 184b 45.23 N 8.50 E
Terebovlia, Ukr. 38 D4 49.17 N 25.42 E
Terebutinec, Russia 26 A16 59.01 N 33.39 E
Terek, stm., Russia 42 D12 43.44 N 46.33 E
Terempa, Indon. 66 B5 3.12 N 106.12 E
Terence Bay, N.S., Can. 122 F13 44.28 N 63.39 W
Terengganu, state, Malay. 64 J6 5.00 N 103.00 E
Terengganu, stm., Malay. 64 J6 5.19 N 103.06 E
Terenino, Russia 26 F16 54.31 N 33.35 E
Terenos, Braz. 166 D6 20.26 S 54.52 W
Teresina, Braz. 170 C4 5.05 S 42.49 W
Tereška, stm., Russia 40 E15 51.49 N 46.31 E
Teresópolis, Braz. 170 L4 22.25 S 42.59 W
Terespol, Pol. 24 D19 52.04 N 23.37 E
Teresva, Ukr. 38 E2 48.00 N 23.41 E
Terevaka, Cerro, mtn., Chile 100l e29 27.05 S 109.23 W
Tergüün Bogd uul, mtn., Mong. 52 C5 44.57 N 100.15 E
Teriang, stm., Malay. 64 K6 3.19 N 102.30 E
Teriberka, Russia 14 C26 69.07 N 35.07 E
Teriberka, stm., Russia 14 D25 69.07 N 35.08 E
Teriberskij, mys, c., Russia 14 C26 69.14 N 35.09 E
Terihi, i., Fr. Poly. 100g t19 10.01 S 138.48 W
Terjärv see Teerijärvi, Fin. 18 D10 63.32 N 23.30 E
Terlingua, Tx., U.S. 136 E4 29.19 N 103.37 W
Terlingua Creek, stm., Tx., U.S. 136 E4 29.09 N 103.36 W
Termas del Arapey, Ur. 172 E9 30.56 S 57.30 W
Termas de Río Hondo, Arg. 172 C5 27.29 S 64.51 W
Terme, Tur. 42 E7 41.12 N 36.59 E
Termez, Uzb. 72 B10 37.14 N 67.16 E
Terminal Island, i., Ca., U.S. 198 33.45 N 118.15 W
Terminal Island Coast Guard Base, mil., Ca., U.S. 198 33.43 N 118.17 W
Termini Imerese, Italy 32 G7 37.59 N 13.42 E
Termini Imerese, Golfo di, b., Italy 32 F7 38.01 N 13.45 E
Terminillo, Monte, mtn., Italy 30 H9 42.28 N 13.00 E
Términos, Laguna de, b., Mex. 152 D6 18.36 N 91.33 W
Termoli, Italy 30 H11 42.00 N 14.59 E
Termonde see Dendermonde, Bel. 20 C12 51.01 N 4.06 E
Termsdorf, Ger. 182a 52.16 N 13.07 E
Tern, stm., Eng., U.K. 10 I10 52.47 N 2.32 W
Ternberg, Aus. 22 I10 47.56 N 14.21 E
Ternej, Russia 54 B12 45.02 N 136.36 E
Terneuzen, Neth. 20 C12 51.20 N 3.50 E
Terni, Italy 30 H9 42.33 N 12.38 E
Ternitz, Aus. 30 C13 47.43 N 16.02 E
Ternivka, Ukr. 38 F11 47.02 N 32.01 E
Ternivka, Ukr. 38 E8 48.32 N 29.57 E
Ternopil', Ukr. 38 D4 49.33 N 25.36 E
Ternopil', co., Ukr. 38 D4 49.30 N 25.30 E
Ternopol' see Ternopil', Ukr. 38 D4 49.33 N 25.36 E
Ternuvate, Ukr. 38 F15 47.49 N 36.07 E
Terny, Ukr. 38 C12 50.59 N 33.58 E
Terny, Ukr. 38 E12 48.06 N 33.33 E
Terpenija, mys, c., Russia 50 G17 48.39 N 144.43 E
Terpenija, zaliv, b., Russia 50 G17 49.00 N 143.30 E
Terra Alta, W.V., U.S. 124 E6 39.26 N 79.31 W
Terra Bella, Ca., U.S. 148 H6 35.58 N 119.03 W
Terrace, B.C., Can. 144 B2 54.31 N 128.34 W
Terrace Bay, On., Can. 128 C11 48.46 N 87.07 W
Terracina, Italy 32 C7 41.17 N 13.14 E
Terra Cotta Army (Qinshihuang Mausoleum), hist., China 58 D3 34.19 N 109.09 E
Terråk, Nor. 16 B10 65.04 N 12.21 E
Terral, Ok., U.S. 138 H11 33.53 N 97.56 W
Terralba, Italy 32 E2 39.43 N 8.37 E
Terra Linda, Ca., U.S. 200 38.01 N 122.32 W
Terranova di Sicilia see Gela, Italy 32 G8 37.04 N 14.15 E
Terra Roxa, Braz. 172 B10 24.10 S 54.05 W
Terras, Pinhal do, for., Port. 184c 38.39 N 9.02 W
Terra Santa, Braz. 164 D6 2.06 S 56.29 W
Terrassa, Spain 28 C13 41.34 N 2.00 E
Terrebonne Bay, b., La., U.S. 134 H8 29.09 N 90.35 W
Terre-de-Bas, Guad. 159c i5 15.51 N 61.37 W
Terre-de-Bas, i., Guad. 159c i5 15.51 N 61.37 W
Terre-de-Haut, Guad. 159c i5 15.52 N 61.34 W
Terre-de-Haut, i., Guad. 159c i5 15.52 N 61.34 W
Terre des Hommes, p.o.i., Qc., Can. 193a 45.31 N 73.32 W
Terre Haute, In., U.S. 130 E10 39.28 N 87.24 W
Terrell, Tx., U.S. 136 B11 32.44 N 96.16 W
Terrell Hills, Tx., U.S. 136 E9 29.28 N 98.26 W
Terre-Neuve see Newfoundland, state, Can. 110 E19 48.16 N 59.28 W
Terre Noire Creek, stm., Ar., U.S. 134 D5 33.49 N 92.55 W
Terre Rouge Creek, stm., Ar., U.S. 134 D5 33.48 N 93.11 W
Territoire du Yukon see Yukon, state, Can. 110 B3 64.00 N 135.00 W
Territoires du Nord-Ouest see Northwest Territories, state, Can. 110 C6 65.00 N 120.00 W
Terrugem, Port. 184c 38.51 N 9.20 W
Terry, Ms., U.S. 134 E8 32.06 N 90.18 W
Terry, Mt., U.S. 140 A7 46.47 N 105.18 W
Terry Peak, mtn., S.D., U.S. 140 C9 44.19 N 103.50 W
Tersa, stm., Russia 40 F13 50.45 N 44.39 E
Terschelling, i., Neth. 20 A14 53.24 N 5.20 E
Terskej-Alatau, hrebet, mts., Kyrg. 48 F13 41.55 N 77.00 E
Terskij bereg, cst., Russia 14 F31 66.20 N 40.00 E
Teruel, Col. 168 F4 2.45 N 75.32 W
Teruel, Spain 28 D9 40.20 N 1.06 W
Teruel, co., Spain 28 D10 40.35 N 0.45 W
Terujak, Indon. 64 J3 4.26 N 97.29 E
Tervakoski, Fin. 18 G11 60.48 N 24.38 E
Tervel, Blg. 36 F14 43.45 N 27.25 E
Tervola, Fin. 18 A11 66.05 N 24.48 E
Terzaghi Dam, dam., B.C., Can. 144 F8 50.49 N 122.12 W
Tes, stm., Asia 48 D16 50.29 N 93.03 E
Teša, Russia 40 D13 55.30 N 42.48 E
Tesalia, Col. 168 F4 2.28 N 75.41 W
Tescott, Ks., U.S. 138 B11 39.00 N 97.52 W
Teseney, Erit. 82 D7 15.07 N 36.42 E
Teshekpuk Lake, l., Ak., U.S. 109 B9 70.35 N 153.30 W
Tes-Hem see Tes, stm., Asia 48 D16 50.29 N 93.03 E
Teshio, Japan 54 B14 44.53 N 141.45 E
Teshio, stm., Japan 54 B15 44.52 N 141.44 E
Teslić, Bos. 36 E4 44.35 N 17.48 E
Teslin, Yk., Can. 110 C4 60.10 N 132.43 W
Teslin, stm., Can. 110 C4 61.34 N 134.53 W
Teslin Lake, l., Can. 110 C4 60.15 N 132.57 W
Tësovo, Russia 26 E17 55.36 N 34.30 E
Tësovo-Netyl'skij, Russia 26 B13 58.57 N 31.05 E
Tësovskij, Russia 26 B13 58.48 N 30.52 E
Tessa, Oued, stm., Tun. 32 H2 36.34 N 8.53 E
Tessalit, Mali 84 E5 20.12 N 1.00 E
Tessancourt-sur-Aubette, Fr. 179 49.02 N 1.55 E
Tessaoua, Niger 84 G6 13.45 N 7.59 E
Tessiner Alpen see Lepontine Alps, mts., Eur. 30 D6 46.25 N 8.40 E
Test, stm., Eng., U.K. 10 J11 50.55 N 1.28 W
Testa, Capo, c., Italy 32 C3 41.14 N 9.08 E
Teston, On., Can. 193b 43.52 N 79.32 W
Teston, Eng., U.K. 178 51.15 N 0.26 E
Testour, Tun. 32 H3 36.33 N 9.26 E
Tesuque, N.M., U.S. 138 F3 35.45 N 105.56 W
Têt, stm., Fr. 22 G8 42.44 N 3.02 E
Tetachuck Lake, res., B.C., Can. 144 C4 53.20 N 125.50 W
Tetagouche, stm., N.B., Can. 122 C11 47.37 N 65.38 W
Tetas, Punta, c., Chile 172 A2 23.30 S 70.36 W
Tete, Moz. 88 D5 16.08 S 33.36 E
Tête Jaune Cache, B.C., Can. 144 D11 52.57 N 119.23 W
Tetepare Island, i., Sol. Is. 101b e7 8.43 S 157.33 E
Teterboro, N.J., U.S. 194 40.52 N 74.03 W
Teterboro Airport, arpt., N.J., U.S. 194 40.51 N 74.04 W
Teteriv, stm., Ukr. 38 C8 51.02 N 30.11 E
Teterow, Ger. 24 C8 53.46 N 12.34 E
Teteven, Blg. 36 G11 42.55 N 24.16 E
Tetica, mtn., Spain 28 G8 37.15 N 2.25 W
Tetiïv, Ukr. 38 D8 49.22 N 29.41 E
Tetilla, Cerro la, mtn., Mex. 154 E6 20.21 N 104.59 W
Tetjuši, Russia 40 D16 54.56 N 48.49 E
Tëtkino, Russia 38 B13 51.16 N 34.16 E
Teton, Id., U.S. 146 G15 43.53 N 111.40 W
Teton, stm., Id., U.S. 146 G15 43.53 N 111.50 W
Teton, stm., Mt., U.S. 146 C15 47.56 N 110.31 W
Tetonia, Id., U.S. 146 G15 43.49 N 111.09 W
Teton Range, mts., Wy., U.S. 146 G16 43.44 N 110.54 W
Tetouan, Mor. 84 B4 35.34 N 5.21 W
Tetovo, Mac. 34 A4 42.00 N 20.58 E
Tétreauville, ngh., Qc., Can. 193a 45.36 N 73.32 W
Tetschen see Děčín, Czech Rep. 24 F10 50.46 N 14.13 E
Tetufera, Mont, mtn., Fr. Poly. 100h v22 17.40 S 149.26 W
Teuco, stm., Arg. 166 D4 25.39 S 60.10 W
Teuhtli, Volcán, vol., Mex. 204a 19.14 N 99.01 W
Teulada, Italy 32 F2 38.58 N 8.46 E
Teulada, Capo, c., Italy 32 F2 38.52 N 8.38 E
Téul de González Ortega, Mex. 154 E7 21.28 N 103.29 W
Tėuli, Bela. 26 H7 52.22 N 24.17 E
Teulon, Mb., Can. 142 D16 50.23 N 97.16 W
Teunom, stm., Indon. 64 J2 4.26 N 95.48 E
Teurajärvi, Swe. 14 F13 66.47 N 22.57 E
Teutoburger Wald, hills, Ger. 24 D4 52.06 N 8.11 E
Teuva, Fin. 18 E8 62.28 N 21.44 E
Teverya, Isr. 76 F6 32.47 N 35.32 E
Tevriz, Russia 48 C12 57.30 N 72.24 E
Te Waewae Bay, b., N.Z. 102 H2 46.15 S 167.30 E
Tewah, Indon. 66 D8 1.03 S 113.43 E
Tewantin-Noosa, Austl. 98 F9 26.24 S 153.04 E
Tewkesbury, Eng., U.K. 10 I11 51.59 N 2.09 W
Tew-Mac Airport, arpt., Ma., U.S. 201 42.36 N 71.12 W
Têwo, China 52 E5 33.55 N 103.01 E
Texada Island, i., B.C., Can. 144 G6 49.40 N 124.24 W
Texana, Lake, res., Tx., U.S. 136 F11 28.58 N 96.32 W
Texarkana, Ar., U.S. 134 D4 33.26 N 94.02 W
Texarkana, Tx., U.S. 134 D4 33.25 N 94.03 W
Texas, Austl. 98 G8 28.51 S 151.10 E
Texas, state, U.S. 112 E8 31.30 N 99.00 W
Texas City, Tx., U.S. 136 E13 29.23 N 94.54 W
Texel, i., Neth. 20 A13 53.05 N 4.49 E
Texhoma, Ok., U.S. 138 E7 36.30 N 101.46 W
Texico, N.M., U.S. 138 G5 34.23 N 103.03 W
Texline, Tx., U.S. 138 E5 36.22 N 103.01 W
Texoma, Lake, res., U.S. 138 G12 33.53 N 96.37 W
Teyateyaneng, Leso. 90 F8 29.09 S 27.45 E
Teywarah, Afg. 72 C9 33.28 N 64.20 E
Teziutlán, Mex. 154 F10 19.49 N 97.21 W
Tezpur, India 70 E14 26.37 N 92.48 E
Tezzeron Lake, l., B.C., Can. 144 B6 54.41 N 124.25 W
Tha, stm., Laos 64 B5 20.06 N 100.35 E
Tha-anne, stm., Nu., Can. 110 C11 60.29 N 94.39 W
Thabana-Ntlenyana, mtn., Leso. 90 F9 29.28 S 29.16 E
Thabaung, Mya. 64 D2 17.02 N 94.47 E
Thabawleikkyi, Mya. 64 G4 12.00 N 99.11 E
Thabazimbi, S. Afr. 90 D8 24.37 S 27.24 E
Thabyu, Mya. 64 E4 15.35 N 98.28 E
Thach An, Viet. 64 A8 22.26 N 106.31 E
Thādiq, Sau. Ar. 74 H9 25.17 N 45.52 E
Thagyettaw, Mya. 64 F3 13.45 N 98.09 E
Thai Binh, Viet. 64 B8 20.27 N 106.20 E
Thai Lan, Vinh see Thailand, Gulf of, b., Asia 64 G5 10.00 N 101.00 E
Thailand, ctry., Asia 64 E5 15.00 N 100.00 E
Thailand, Gulf of, b., Asia 64 G5 10.00 N 101.00 E
Thai Muang, Thai. 64 H4 8.24 N 98.16 E
Thai Nguyen, Viet. 64 B7 21.36 N 105.50 E
Thak, Pak. 70 C3 30.32 N 70.13 E
Thakhek see Muang Khammouan, Laos 64 D7 17.24 N 104.49 E
Thākurdwāri, India 190b 22.34 N 88.28 E
Thākurpukur, India 190b 22.28 N 88.19 E
Thākurvādi, India 190c 18.54 N 73.04 E
Thal, Pak. 70 B3 33.21 N 70.33 E
Thala, Tun. 32 I2 35.35 N 8.40 E
Thalang, Thai. 64 H4 8.01 N 98.19 E
Thal Desert, des., Pak. 70 C3 31.40 N 71.28 E
Thalfang, Ger. 24 G2 49.44 N 6.59 E
Tha Li, Thai. 64 D5 17.38 N 101.21 E
Thalia, Tx., U.S. 138 H9 33.58 N 99.32 W
Thālith, Ash-Shallāl ath- (Third Cataract), wtfl., Sudan 82 D6 19.48 N 30.19 E
Thallon, Austl. 98 G7 28.38 S 148.52 E
Thalwil, Switz. 30 C5 47.17 N 8.34 E
Thames, N.Z. 102 C6 37.08 S 175.33 E
Thames, stm., On., Can. 126 F8 42.18 N 82.26 W
Thames, stm., Eng., U.K. 10 J13 51.27 N 0.20 E
Thames, Firth of, b., N.Z. 102 C6 37.00 S 175.25 E
Thames Barrier, dam., Eng., U.K. 178 51.29 N 0.03 E
Thames Ditton, Eng., U.K. 178 51.23 N 0.21 W
Thames Estuary, est., Eng., U.K. 178 51.30 N 0.40 W
Thamesford, On., Can. 126 E8 43.04 N 80.59 W
Thames Haven, Eng., U.K. 178 51.30 N 0.31 E
Thamesville, On., Can. 126 F7 42.32 N 81.57 W
Thammasat University, educ., Thai. 187a 13.45 N 100.30 E
Thāna, India 69 B1 19.13 N 72.59 E
Thāna Creek, b., India 190c 19.00 N 72.57 E
Thandaung, Mya. 64 C3 19.03 N 96.42 E
Thang Binh, Viet. 64 E9 15.44 N 108.22 E
Thangoo, Austl. 96 C4 18.10 S 122.23 E
Thangool, Austl. 98 E8 24.29 S 150.35 E
Thanh Hoa, Viet. 64 C7 19.48 N 105.46 E
Thanh My Tay, Viet. 187c 10.49 N 106.46 E
Thanh Pho Ho Chi Minh (Ho Chi Minh City) (Saigon), Viet. 64 G8 10.45 N 106.40 E
Thanh Pho Ho Chi Minh (Saigon), Viet. 187c 10.45 N 106.40 E
Thanjāvūr, India 69 F4 10.47 N 79.08 E
Thanlwin see Nu, stm., Asia 62 C8 16.33 N 97.39 E
Thanlwin see Salween, stm., Asia 62 C8 16.33 N 97.39 E
Thann, Fr. 22 B12 47.49 N 7.05 E
Than Uyen, Viet. 64 A7 21.59 N 103.54 E
Tha Pla, Thai. 64 D5 17.48 N 100.29 E
Thap Than, stm., Thai. 64 E6 15.20 N 104.05 E
Tharabwin West, Mya. 64 F4 12.18 N 99.02 E
Tharād, India 70 F3 24.23 N 71.37 E
Thar Desert (Great Indian Desert), des., Asia 70 E3 27.00 N 71.00 E
Thargomindah, Austl. 98 F5 28.00 S 143.49 E
Tharrawaddy, Mya. 64 D2 17.38 N 95.46 E
Tharrawaw, Mya. 64 D2 17.42 N 95.29 E
Tharthār, Buḩayrat ath-, res., Iraq 74 C8 33.52 N 43.20 E
Tharthār, Wādī ath-, stm., Iraq 74 C8 34.27 N 43.04 E
Tha Sala, Thai. 64 H4 8.39 N 99.56 E
Thásos, Grc. 34 C7 40.46 N 24.41 E
Thásos, i., Grc. 34 C7 40.39 N 24.40 E
Thásos, hist., Grc. 34 C7 40.45 N 24.42 E
Tha Tako, Thai. 64 E5 15.38 N 100.29 E
Thatch Cay, i., V.I.U.S. 158b e7 18.22 N 64.52 W
Thatcher, Az., U.S. 150 K7 32.50 N 109.45 W
Thatch Island, i., N.Y., U.S. 194 40.38 N 73.23 W
Thaton, Mya. 64 D3 16.55 N 97.22 E
That Phanom, Thai. 64 D7 16.56 N 104.43 E
Thatto Heath, Eng., U.K. 180 53.26 N 2.45 W
Tha Tum, Thai. 64 E6 15.18 N 103.40 E
Thau, Bassin de, l., Fr. 22 F9 43.23 N 3.35 E
Thaungyin (Moei), stm., Asia 64 D3 17.49 N 97.41 E
Tha Uthen, Thai. 64 D7 17.33 N 104.34 E
Thaya (Dyje), stm., Eur. 24 H12 48.36 N 16.56 E
Thayawthadangyi Kyun, i., Mya. 64 F3 12.20 N 98.00 E
Thayer, Ks., U.S. 130 G2 37.29 N 95.27 W
Thayer, Mo., U.S. 130 H6 36.31 N 91.32 W
Thayetchaung, Mya. 64 F4 13.50 N 98.16 E
Thayetmyo, Mya. 64 C2 19.19 N 95.11 E
Thazi, Mya. 64 B3 20.50 N 96.03 E
Thebes see Thíva, Grc. 34 E6 38.20 N 23.19 E
Thebes, Il., U.S. 130 G8 37.12 N 89.27 W
Thebes, hist., Egypt 74 H3 25.41 N 32.38 E
The Bottom, Neth. Ant. 159a b1 17.37 N 63.14 W
The Cheviot, mtn., Eng., U.K. 10 F10 55.28 N 2.09 W
The Citadel, hist., Egypt 191c 30.02 N 31.15 E
The Citadel, hist., Hung. 182c 47.29 N 19.03 E
The Coteau, hills, Sk., Can. 142 C6 51.10 N 107.30 W
The Dalles, Or., U.S. 146 E5 45.35 N 121.10 W
Thedford, Ne., U.S. 140 E12 41.59 N 100.33 W
Theebine, Austl. 98 E9 25.57 S 152.32 E
The Father see Ulawun, Mount, vol., Pap. N. Gui. 101a b5 5.03 S 151.20 E
The Fens, reg., Eng., U.K. 10 I12 52.36 N 0.12 W
The Fishing Lakes, l., Sk., Can. 142 D10 50.46 N 103.49 W
The Flat Tops, mts., Co., U.S. 138 B1 39.55 N 107.17 W
Thègon, Mya. 64 C2 18.39 N 95.25 E
The Granites, Austl. 96 D6 20.33 S 130.21 E
The Granites, hill, Austl. 96 D6 20.36 S 130.18 E
The Hague see 's-Gravenhage, Neth. 20 B13 52.05 N 4.17 E
The Heads, c., Or., U.S. 146 H2 42.45 N 124.30 W
The Hermitage, bldg., Russia 183a 59.56 N 30.20 E
Theinkun, Mya. 64 G4 11.51 N 99.08 E
The Key Indian Reserve, ind. res., Sk., Can. 142 C11 51.45 N 102.08 W
The Lakes National Park, p.o.i., Austl. 98 L7 37.58 S 147.43 E
The Little Minch, strt., Scot., U.K. 10 D6 57.35 N 6.55 W
Thelon, stm., Can. 110 C11 64.16 N 96.07 W
Thelwall, Eng., U.K. 180 53.23 N 2.32 W
The Lynd, Austl. 98 B5 18.54 S 144.28 E
Thémericourt, Fr. 179 49.05 N 1.54 E
The Minch, strt., Scot., U.K. 10 C7 58.10 N 5.50 W
The Naze, c., Eng., U.K. 10 J14 51.52 N 1.16 E
Thenia, Alg. 28 H14 36.43 N 3.32 E
Theodore, Austl. 98 E8 24.57 S 150.04 E
Theodore, Sk., Can. 142 C10 51.25 N 102.54 W
Theodore, Al., U.S. 134 G10 30.33 N 88.11 W
Theodore Roosevelt Inaugural National Historic Site, hist., N.Y., U.S. 202a 42.54 N 78.52 W
Theodore Roosevelt Island, i., D.C., U.S. 202c 38.54 N 77.03 W
Theodor-Heuss-Brücke, trans., Ger. 181 51.15 N 6.45 E
Theológos, Grc. 34 C7 40.39 N 24.41 E
The Pas, Mb., Can. 110 E10 53.49 N 101.13 W
The Peak, mtn., N.C., U.S. 124 H4 36.24 N 81.39 W
Thepha, Thai. 64 I5 6.50 N 100.57 E
The Pinnacle, hill, Mo., U.S. 130 E7 39.22 N 90.55 W
The Rajah, mtn., Ab., Can. 144 C12 53.15 N 118.31 W
The Rand see Witwatersrand, mts., S. Afr. 90 D8 26.00 S 27.00 E
Theresa, N.Y., U.S. 126 D14 44.12 N 75.48 W
Theresa Creek, stm., Austl. 98 D6 23.26 S 148.18 E
Theresa Park, Austl. 192a 34.01 S 150.39 E
The Rhins, pen., Scot., U.K. 10 G7 54.48 N 4.58 W
Thermaïkós Kólpos (Salonika, Gulf of), b., Grc. 34 C6 39.50 N 23.10 E
Thermopolis, Wy., U.S. 140 D4 43.38 N 108.12 W
Thermopylae see Thermopýles, hist., Grc. 34 E5 38.48 N 22.33 E
Thermopýles (Thermopylae), hist., Grc. 34 E5 38.48 N 22.33 E
The Rock, Austl. 98 J6 35.16 S 147.06 E
The Rockies, mtn., Wa., U.S. 146 D4 46.39 N 122.22 W
The Rope, clf., Pit. 100k c28 25.04 S 130.05 W
Thesiger Bay, b., N.T., Can. 109 B15 71.30 N 124.05 W
The Slot see New Georgia Sound, strt., Sol. Is. 101b d8 8.00 S 158.10 E
The Snares see Snares Islands, is., N.Z. 102 H2 48.00 S 166.30 E
The Solent, strt., Eng., U.K. 10 K11 50.45 N 1.22 W
Thessalía, state, Grc. 34 D5 39.30 N 22.30 E
Thessalía, hist. reg., Grc. 34 D5 39.30 N 22.15 E
Thessalon, On., Can. 126 B6 46.15 N 83.33 W
Thessaloníki (Salonika), Grc. 34 C6 40.37 N 22.58 E
Thessaly see Thessalía, hist. reg., Grc. 34 D5 39.30 N 22.15 E
The Tauride Palace, bldg., Russia 183a 59.57 N 30.23 E
Thetford, Eng., U.K. 10 I13 52.25 N 0.45 E
Thetford Mines, Qc., Can. 122 D5 46.05 N 71.18 W
Theunissen, S. Afr. 90 F8 28.24 S 26.43 E
The Valley, Anguilla 159a a1 18.13 N 63.04 W
The Village, Ok., U.S. 138 F11 35.33 N 97.33 W
The Wash, b., Eng., U.K. 10 I13 52.55 N 0.16 E
The Weald, reg., Eng., U.K. 10 J12 51.04 N 0.02 E
Theydon Bois, Eng., U.K. 178 51.40 N 0.06 E
Thiais, Fr. 179 48.46 N 2.23 E
Thibaudeau, Pointe, c., Qc., Can. 193a 45.19 N 73.53 W
Thibodaux, La., U.S. 134 H8 29.47 N 90.49 W
Thief, stm., Mn., U.S. 128 C2 48.07 N 96.10 W
Thief Lake, l., Mn., U.S. 128 C3 48.30 N 95.55 W
Thief River Falls, Mn., U.S. 128 C2 48.07 N 96.10 W
Thielsen, Mount, mtn., Or., U.S. 146 G4 43.09 N 122.04 W
Thiene, Italy 30 E8 45.42 N 11.28 E
Thiers, Fr. 22 D9 45.51 N 3.31 E
Thiès, Sen. 84 G1 14.48 N 16.55 W
Thiesi, Italy 32 D2 40.31 N 8.43 E
Thieux, Fr. 179 49.01 N 2.40 E
Thieveley Pike, hill, Eng., U.K. 180 53.45 N 2.12 W
Thika, Kenya 86 E7 1.02 S 37.04 E
Thilmet, Mersa, b., Egypt 76 I3 29.03 N 32.38 E
Thimphu, Bhu. 70 E12 27.28 N 89.39 E
Thingvallavatn, l., Ice. 12a k29 64.12 N 21.10 W
Thingvellir, Ice. 12a k29 64.15 N 21.07 W
Thingvellir Nasjonalpark, p.o.i., Ice. 12a k29 64.19 N 21.04 W
Thio, N. Cal. 101d m16 21.37 S 166.13 E
Thionville, Fr. 20 E15 49.21 N 6.09 E
Thira, Grc. 34 G8 36.25 N 25.26 E
Thíra (Santorini), i., Grc. 34 G8 36.25 N 25.26 E
Third, stm., N.J., U.S. 194 40.49 N 74.08 W
Third Cataract see Thālith, Ash-Shallāl ath-, wtfl., Sudan 82 D6 19.48 N 30.19 E
Third Cliff, clf., Ma., U.S. 201 42.11 N 70.43 W
Third Creek, stm., N.C., U.S. 132 A5 35.44 N 80.55 W
Third Herring Brook, stm., Ma., U.S. 201 42.07 N 70.48 W
Third Street Station, trans., Ca., U.S. 200 37.46 N 122.23 W
Thirsk, Eng., U.K. 10 G11 54.14 N 1.20 W
Thirtieth Street Station, trans., Pa., U.S. 203 39.57 N 75.11 W
Thirtymile Creek, stm., N.D., U.S. 140 A10 46.21 N 102.03 W
Thiruvananthapuram see Trivandrum, India 69 G3 8.30 N 76.57 E
Thiruvārūr, India 69 F4 10.46 N 79.38 E
Thiseion, hist., Grc. 185c 37.58 N 23.43 E
Thisted, Den. 16 K6 56.57 N 8.42 E
Thistilfjörður, b., Ice. 12a j32 66.20 N 15.25 W
Thistledown Race Track, p.o.i., Oh., U.S. 197a 41.26 N 81.32 W
Thistletown, ngh., On., Can. 193b 43.44 N 79.33 W
Thíva, Grc. 34 E6 38.20 N 23.19 E
Thiverval-Grignon, Fr. 179 48.51 N 1.55 E
Thiviers, Fr. 22 D6 45.25 N 0.56 E
Thjórsá, stm., Ice. 12a k30 63.53 N 20.39 W
Tho Chu, Dao, i., Viet. 64 H6 9.18 N 103.28 E
Thoen, Thai. 64 D4 17.38 N 99.14 E
Thohoyandou, S. Afr. 90 C10 23.00 S 30.34 E
Thoi Binh, Viet. 64 H7 9.20 N 105.05 E
Thoiry, Fr. 179 48.52 N 1.48 E
Thomas, Ok., U.S. 138 F10 35.45 N 98.44 W
Thomas, Pa., U.S. 197b 40.15 N 80.06 W
Thomas, W.V., U.S. 124 E6 39.08 N 79.30 W
Thomasboro, Il., U.S. 130 D9 40.15 N 88.10 W
Thomas Creek, stm., Or., U.S. 146 F4 44.40 N 122.57 W
Thomas Hill Reservoir, res., Mo., U.S. 130 E5 39.37 N 92.37 W
Thomas J. O'Brien Lock and Dam, trans., Il., U.S. 196 41.39 N 87.35 W
Thomaston, Al., U.S. 134 E11 32.15 N 87.37 W
Thomaston, Ga., U.S. 132 D1 32.53 N 84.19 W
Thomaston, Me., U.S. 122 F7 44.05 N 69.11 W
Thomaston, N.Y., U.S. 194 40.47 N 73.43 W
Thomastown, Austl. 192b 37.41 S 145.01 E
Thomasville, Al., U.S. 134 F11 31.54 N 87.44 W
Thomasville, Ga., U.S. 132 F2 30.50 N 83.58 W
Thomasville, N.C., U.S. 124 I5 35.52 N 80.04 W
Thomes Creek, stm., Ca., U.S. 148 D3 39.59 N 122.06 W
Thompson, Mb., Can. 110 D11 55.44 N 97.50 W
Thompson, Ia., U.S. 128 H5 43.22 N 93.46 W
Thompson, N.D., U.S. 128 D1 47.45 N 97.06 W
Thompson, stm., B.C., Can. 144 F9 50.14 N 121.34 W

Name	Page	Map Ref.	Latitude	Longitude
Thompson, stm., U.S.	130	D4	39.45 N	93.36 W
Thompson Creek, stm., U.S.	140	B8	45.04 N	104.25 W
Thompson Creek, stm., Ms., U.S.	134	F10	31.10 N	88.54 W
Thompson Falls, Mt., U.S.	146	C11	47.35 N	115.20 W
Thompson Island, i., Ma., U.S.	201		42.23 N	71.01 W
Thompson Peak, mtn., Ca., U.S.	148	B3	41.00 N	123.03 W
Thompson Run, stm., Pa., U.S.	197b		40.24 N	79.50 W
Thompsons Creek, stm., On., Can.	202a		43.03 N	79.08 W
Thompsonville, Mi., U.S.	126	D4	44.31 N	85.56 W
Thomsen, stm., N.T., Can.	109	B16	74.05 N	119.46 W
Thomson, Ga., U.S.	132	C3	33.27 N	82.30 W
Thomson, Il., U.S.	130	C7	41.58 N	90.06 W
Thomson, stm., Austl.	98	E4	25.11 S	142.50 E
Thomson Lake, l., Sk., Can.	142	E7	49.45 N	106.35 W
Thon Buri, Thai.	64	F5	13.42 N	100.27 E
Thong, Eng., U.K.	178		51.24 N	0.24 E
Thong Hoe, Sing.	189c		1.25 N	103.42 E
Thong Tay Hoi, Viet.	187c		10.50 N	106.39 E
Thongwa, Mya.	64	D3	16.45 N	96.31 E
Thonon-les-Bains, Fr.	22	C12	46.22 N	6.28 E
Thonotosassa, Fl., U.S.	132	H3	28.03 N	82.18 W
Thonze, Mya.	64	D2	17.36 N	95.47 E
Thoreau, N.M., U.S.	150	H8	35.25 N	108.18 W
Thorhild, Ab., Can.	144	B17	54.10 N	113.07 W
Thorigny-sur-Marne, Fr.	179		48.53 N	2.42 E
Thórisvatn, l., Ice.	12a	k30	64.16 N	18.52 W
Thorlákshöfn, Ice.	12a	l28	63.51 N	21.23 W
Thorn see Toruń, Pol.	24	C14	53.01 N	18.36 E
Thornaby-on-Tees, Eng., U.K.	10	G11	54.33 N	1.18 W
Thornapple, stm., Wi., U.S.	128	F8	45.27 N	91.14 W
Thornburg, Pa., U.S.	197b		40.26 N	80.05 W
Thornbury, Austl.	192b		37.45 S	145.00 E
Thornbury, On., Can.	126	D9	44.33 N	80.26 W
Thorn Creek, stm., Il., U.S.	196		41.36 N	87.35 W
Thorndale, Tx., U.S.	136	D10	30.36 N	97.12 W
Thornhill, On., Can.	193b		43.48 N	79.25 W
Thornhill, S. Afr.	191d		26.07 S	28.09 E
Thornhill, Scot., U.K.	10	F9	55.14 N	3.46 W
Thornleigh, Austl.	192a		33.44 S	151.05 E
Thornton, Eng., U.K.	180		53.30 N	3.00 W
Thornton, Eng., U.K.	180		53.47 N	1.51 W
Thornton, Ar., U.S.	134	D6	33.46 N	92.29 W
Thornton, Co., U.S.	138	B4	39.52 N	104.57 W
Thornton, Il., U.S.	196		41.35 N	87.37 W
Thornton, Pa., U.S.	203		39.54 N	75.32 W
Thornton, Tx., U.S.	136	C11	31.24 N	96.34 W
Thornton Beach, p.o.i., Ca., U.S.	200		37.42 N	122.30 W
Thornton Hough, Eng., U.K.	180		53.19 N	3.03 W
Thornton-le-Moors, Eng., U.K.	180		53.16 N	2.50 W
Thornton Moor Reservoir, res., Eng., U.K.	180		53.47 N	1.55 W
Thorntonville, Tx., U.S.	136	C4	31.34 N	102.56 W
Thornwood Common, Eng., U.K.	178		51.43 N	0.08 E
Thorny Mountain, hill, Mo., U.S.	130	G6	37.06 N	91.10 W
Thorofare, N.J., U.S.	203		39.50 N	75.11 W
Thorold South, On., Can.	202a		43.06 N	79.12 W
Thorp, Wi., U.S.	128	G8	44.57 N	90.47 W
Thorpe, Eng., U.K.	178		51.24 N	0.32 W
Thorsby, Ab., Can.	144	C16	53.13 N	114.04 W
Thorsby, Al., U.S.	134	E12	32.54 N	86.42 W
Thorshavn see Tórshavn, Far. Is.	12b	n34	62.00 N	6.46 W
Thórshöfn, Ice.	12a	j32	66.11 N	15.18 W
Thot Not, Viet.	64	G7	10.15 N	105.31 E
Thouars, Fr.	20	H8	46.59 N	0.12 W
Thoune see Thun, Switz.	30	D4	46.45 N	7.37 E
Thourout see Torhout, Bel.	20	C12	51.04 N	3.05 E
Thousand Hills State Park, p.o.i., Mo., U.S.	130	D5	40.11 N	92.40 W
Thousand Lake Mountain, mtn., Ut., U.S.	150	E5	38.25 N	111.29 W
Thousand Oaks, Ca., U.S.	148	I7	34.09 N	118.49 W
Thousand Ships Bay, b., Sol. Is.	101b	e8	8.28 S	159.41 E
Thousand Springs Creek, stm., U.S.	150	B2	41.17 N	113.51 W
Thrace, hist. reg., Eur.	8	G14	41.20 N	26.45 E
Thrákí see Thrace, hist. reg., Eur.	8	G14	41.20 N	26.45 E
Thrakikó Pélagos, s., Grc.	34	C8	40.15 N	24.28 E
Three Fathoms Cove, b., China	189d		22.26 N	114.17 E
Three Fingered Jack, mtn., Or., U.S.	146	F5	44.29 N	121.50 W
Three Forks, Mt., U.S.	146	E15	45.53 N	111.33 W
Three Gorges Dam, dam., China	58	F4	30.57 N	110.46 E
Three Hills, Ab., Can.	144	E17	51.42 N	113.15 W
Three Hummock Island, i., Austl.	99a	n12	40.26 S	144.55 E
Three Kings Islands, is., N.Z.	102	B5	34.10 S	172.05 E
Three Lakes, Wi., U.S.	128	F9	45.47 N	89.07 W
Three M Airport, arpt., Pa., U.S.	203		40.08 N	74.51 W
Three Mile Plains, N.S., Can.	122	F12	44.58 N	64.06 W
Three Pagodas Pass see Phra Chedi Sam Ong, p., Asia	64	E4	15.18 N	98.22 E
Three Points, Cape, c., Ghana	84	I4	4.44 N	2.05 W
Three Rivers, Mi., U.S.	130	C12	41.56 N	85.37 W
Three Rivers, Tx., U.S.	136	F9	28.27 N	98.10 W
Three Rivers, mun., Eng., U.K.	178		51.40 N	0.27 W
Three Sisters, mtn., Or., U.S.	146	F5	44.10 N	121.46 W
Three Sisters Islands, is., Sol. Is.	101b	f10	10.09 S	162.00 E
Three Springs, Austl.	96	E3	29.31 S	115.45 E
Thrissur see Trichūr, India	69	F3	10.30 N	76.12 E
Throckmorton, Tx., U.S.	136	A8	33.10 N	99.10 W
Throgs Neck, ngh., N.Y., U.S.	194		40.49 N	73.49 W
Throgs Neck Bridge, trans., N.Y., U.S.	194		40.48 N	73.48 W
Throgs Point, c., N.Y., U.S.	194		40.48 N	73.48 W
Throssel, Lake, l., Austl.	96	E4	27.33 S	124.11 E
Thruway Mall, shp. cen., N.Y., U.S.	202a		42.55 N	78.46 W
Thu, Cu Lao, i., Viet.	64	G9	10.31 N	108.56 E
Thuan Chau, Viet.	64	B6	21.25 N	103.45 E
Thu Dau Mot, Viet.	64	G8	10.58 N	106.39 E
Thu Duc, Viet.	187c		10.51 N	106.45 E
Thuin, Bel.	20	D13	50.20 N	4.16 E
Thul, Pak.	70	D2	28.17 N	68.47 E
Thule (Qaanaaq), Grnld.	108	B12	76.40 N	68.50 W
Thuli, stm., Zimb.	90	B9	21.47 S	29.03 E
Thun, Switz.	30	D4	46.45 N	7.37 E
Thun Chang, Thai.	64	C5	19.25 N	100.53 E
Thunder Bay, On., Can.	128	C9	48.24 N	89.15 W
Thunder Bay, b., On., Can.	128	C9	48.24 N	89.00 W
Thunder Bay, b., Mi., U.S.	126	D6	44.59 N	83.22 W
Thunder Bay, stm., Mi., U.S.	126	C6	45.03 N	83.25 W
Thunder Bay, North Branch, stm., Mi., U.S.	126	C6	45.07 N	83.35 W
Thunderbird, Lake, res., Ok., U.S.	138	F11	35.13 N	97.17 W
Thunderbolt, Ga., U.S.	132	D4	32.01 N	81.03 W
Thunder Butte, mtn., S.D., U.S.	140	B11	45.19 N	101.53 W
Thunder Butte Creek, stm., S.D., U.S.	140	B10	45.13 N	101.41 W
Thunder Creek, stm., Sk., Can.	142	D7	50.23 N	105.30 W
Thundersley, Eng., U.K.	178		51.34 N	0.35 E
Thuner See, l., Switz.	30	D4	46.40 N	7.45 E
Thung Salaeng Luang National Park, p.o.i., Thai.	64	D5	16.50 N	100.50 E
Thung Song, Thai.	64	H4	8.10 N	99.41 E
Thung Wa, Thai.	64	I4	7.01 N	99.41 E
Thüringen, state, Ger.	24	F7	51.00 N	11.00 E
Thüringer Wald, mts., Ger.	24	F7	50.38 N	10.41 E
Thuringia see Thüringen, state, Ger.	24	F7	51.00 N	11.00 E
Thurles, Ire.	10	I5	52.41 N	7.49 W
Thurmont, Md., U.S.	124	E8	39.37 N	77.24 W
Thurnham, Eng., U.K.	178		51.17 N	0.36 E
Thurrock, mun., Eng., U.K.	178		51.30 N	0.21 E
Thurrock, mun., Eng., U.K.	178		51.30 N	0.21 E
Thursday Island, Austl.	96	B8	10.36 S	142.15 E
Thurso, Scot., U.K.	10	C9	58.35 N	3.31 W
Thurso, stm., Scot., U.K.	10	C9	58.36 N	3.30 W
Thurstaston, Eng., U.K.	180		53.21 N	3.08 W
Thurston Island, i., Ant.	103	C31	72.20 S	98.59 W
Thusis, Switz.	30	D6	46.41 N	9.26 E
Thy, reg., Den.	16	K6	57.00 N	8.30 E
Thyborøn, Den.	16	K6	56.42 N	8.13 E
Thylungra, Austl.	98	F4	26.05 S	143.25 E
Thyolo, Mwi.	88	D5	16.02 S	35.11 E
Thysville see Mbanza-Ngungu, D.R.C.	86	F3	5.14 S	14.52 E
Tiachiv, Ukr.	38	E2	48.01 N	23.33 E
Tiahynka, Ukr.	38	G12	46.46 N	33.03 E
Tía Juana, Ven.	168	B6	10.17 N	71.22 W
Tiana, Spain	184d		44.29 N	2.16 E
Tian'anmen Square, hist., China	189a		39.55 N	116.23 E
Tianbao, China	58	I7	24.34 N	117.34 E
Tianchang, China	58	E8	32.41 N	118.59 E
Tiandeng, China	58	J2	23.08 N	107.10 E
Tiandong, China	58	J2	23.35 N	107.08 E
Tian'e, China	58	I2	25.01 N	107.20 E
Tianeti, Geor.	42	D11	42.06 N	44.57 E
Tianfanjie, China	58	G7	29.21 N	116.52 E
Tiangang, China	54	C7	43.55 N	127.00 E
Tianguá, Braz.	170	B5	3.44 S	40.59 W
Tianjiaba, China	58	E3	32.08 N	110.03 E
Tianjin (Tientsin), China	58	B7	39.07 N	117.11 E
Tianjin, state, China	58	B7	39.30 N	117.15 E
Tianjun, China	52	D4	37.19 N	98.57 E
Tianlin, China	58	I2	24.15 N	106.02 E
Tian Ling, mtn., China	54	B8	44.22 N	129.52 E
Tianmen, China	58	F5	30.38 N	113.10 E
Tianqiaoling, China	54	C8	43.25 N	129.38 E
Tianshifu, China	54	D6	41.17 N	124.21 E
Tianshui, China	58	D1	34.32 N	105.54 E
Tiantai, China	58	G9	29.08 N	121.00 E
Tiantang, China	58	J4	22.33 N	111.51 E
Tianwangsi, China	58	F8	31.44 N	119.11 E
Tianyang, China	58	J2	23.45 N	106.56 E
Tianyar, Indon.	66	H9	8.12 S	115.30 E
Tianzhen, China	58	A6	40.28 N	114.05 E
Tianzhu, China	52	D5	36.59 N	103.06 E
Tianzhu, China	58	H3	26.49 N	109.00 E
Tiarei, Fr. Poly.	100h	v22	17.32 S	149.20 W
Tiaro, Austl.	98	E9	25.43 S	152.34 E
Tiasmyn, stm., Ukr.	38	D11	49.03 N	32.48 E
Tiassalé, C. Iv.	84	H4	5.53 N	4.48 W
Ti'avea, Samoa	101c	g12	13.58 S	171.26 W
Tīb (Meymeh), stm., Asia	74	D10	32.01 N	47.14 E
Tiba see Chiba, Japan	56	D13	35.35 N	140.07 E
Tibagi, Braz.	172	B12	24.30 S	50.26 W
Tibaji, stm., Braz.	172	A12	22.47 S	50.58 W
Tibal-og, Phil.	68	G5	7.30 N	125.37 E
Tibasti, Sarīr, des., Libya	82	C3	24.00 N	17.00 E
Tibati, Cam.	86	C2	6.26 N	12.37 E
Tibbie, Al., U.S.	134	F10	31.21 N	88.14 W
Tibé, Pic de, mtn., Gui.	84	H3	8.52 N	8.54 W
Tiber see Tevere, stm., Italy	30	H9	41.44 N	12.14 E
Tiberias see Teverya, Isr.	76	F6	32.47 N	35.32 E
Tiberias, Lake see Kinneret, Yam, l., Isr.	76	F6	32.48 N	35.35 E
Tibesti, mts., Afr.	82	C3	21.30 N	17.30 E
Tibet see Xizang, state, China	62	B5	32.00 N	88.00 E
Tibet, Plateau of see Qing Zang Gaoyuan, plat., China	62	B6	33.00 N	92.00 E
Tibiao, Phil.	68	E3	11.16 N	122.03 E
Tibidabo, mtn., Spain	184d		41.25 N	2.07 E
Tiblawan, Phil.	68	G6	6.29 N	126.06 E
Tibnah, Syria	76	E7	32.58 N	36.14 E
Tibnīn, Leb.	76	E6	33.11 N	35.24 E
Tibooburra, Austl.	98	G4	29.26 S	142.01 E
Tibro, Swe.	16	I12	58.25 N	14.11 E
Tiburón, Cabo, c.	156	H9	8.40 N	77.21 W
Tiburón, Isla, i., Mex.	120	G6	29.00 N	112.23 W
Tiburon Peninsula, pen., Ca., U.S.	200		37.53 N	122.28 W
Tiča, Jazovir, res., Blg.	36	F13	43.02 N	26.42 E
Ticao Island, i., Phil.	68	D4	12.31 N	123.42 E
Tice, Fl., U.S.	132	J4	26.40 N	81.48 W
Tice Creek, stm., Ca., U.S.	200		37.53 N	122.03 W
Tichît, Maur.	84	F3	18.28 N	9.27 W
Ticino, stm., Eur.	30	E5	45.09 N	9.13 E
Tickfaw, stm., U.S.	134	G8	30.21 N	90.28 W
Ticomán, ngh., Mex.	204a		19.31 N	99.08 W
Ticonderoga, N.Y., U.S.	126	E16	43.51 N	73.25 W
Ticul, Mex.	156	B3	20.24 N	89.32 W
Tidaholm, Swe.	16	I11	58.11 N	13.57 E
Tiddim, Mya.	52	G3	23.22 N	93.39 E
Tide Lake, l., Ab., Can.	142	D2	50.33 N	111.20 W
Tidioute, Pa., U.S.	124	C6	41.41 N	79.23 W
Tidiquin, Jbel, mtn., Mor.	84	C4	34.50 N	4.30 W
Tidjikja, Maur.	84	F2	18.33 N	11.25 W
Tiébissou, C. Iv.	84	H3	7.09 N	5.13 W
Tiefenbroich, Ger.	181		51.18 N	6.49 E
Tiel, Neth.	20	C14	51.53 N	5.26 E
Tieli, China	52	B10	46.59 N	128.04 E
Tieling, China	54	C5	42.17 N	123.50 E
Tielt, Bel.	20	C12	51.00 N	3.19 E
Tiémé, C. Iv.	84	H3	9.33 N	7.19 W
Tien Giang see Mekong, stm., Asia	64	G7	10.33 N	105.26 E
Tien Shan, mts., Asia	48	F13	42.00 N	80.00 E
Tientsin see Tianjin, China	58	B7	39.07 N	117.11 E
Tientsin see Tianjin, state, China	58	B7	39.30 N	117.15 E
Tien Yen, Viet.	64	B8	21.19 N	107.22 E
Tie Plant, Ms., U.S.	134	D9	33.44 N	89.47 W
Tierga, Spain	28	C9	41.36 N	1.36 W
Tiergarten, ngh., Ger.	182a		52.31 N	13.21 E
Tiergarten, p.o.i., Ger.	182a		52.31 N	13.21 E
Tieroko, Tarso, mtn., Chad	82	C3	20.45 N	17.52 E
Tierp, Swe.	16	G15	60.19 N	17.30 E
Tierpark, p.o.i., Ger.	182a		52.30 N	13.32 E
Tierra Amarilla, Chile	172	C2	27.28 S	70.15 W
Tierra Amarilla, N.M., U.S.	138	E2	36.40 N	106.35 W
Tierra Blanca, Mex.	136	G3	27.12 N	104.53 W
Tierra Blanca, Mex.	154	F10	18.26 N	96.21 W
Tierra Blanca Creek, stm., U.S.	138	G6	34.59 N	101.53 W
Tierra de Campos, reg., Spain	28	B6	42.10 N	4.50 W
Tierra del Fuego, mun., Arg.	166	J3	54.00 S	68.00 W
Tierra del Fuego, i., S.A.	166	J3	54.00 S	69.00 W
Tierralta, Col.	168	C3	8.11 N	76.03 W
Tiétar, stm., Spain	28	E5	39.50 N	6.00 W
Tietê, Braz.	170	L2	23.07 S	47.42 W
Tietê, stm., Braz.	166	D6	20.37 S	51.34 W
Tiéti, N. Cal.	101d	m15	20.56 S	165.17 E
Tieton, stm., Wa., U.S.	146	D5	46.44 N	120.47 W
Tietzow, Ger.	182a		52.43 N	12.56 E
Tiffany Mountain, mtn., Wa., U.S.	146	B7	48.40 N	119.56 W
Tiffin, Oh., U.S.	124	C2	41.06 N	83.10 W
Tifton, Ga., U.S.	132	E2	31.27 N	83.29 W
Tiga, Île, i., N. Cal.	101d	m16	21.07 S	167.48 E
Tigalda Island, i., Ak., U.S.	109	F7	54.05 N	164.58 W
Tigapuluh, Pegunungan, mts., Indon.	66	D3	1.05 S	102.30 E
Tigasaki see Chigasaki, Japan	56	D12	35.18 N	139.24 E
Tigeaux, Fr.	179		48.50 N	2.54 E
Tiger Stadium, p.o.i., Mi., U.S.	199		42.20 N	83.04 W
Tigery, Fr.	179		48.38 N	2.31 E
Tighina, Mol.	38	G8	46.50 N	29.28 E
Tigil', Russia	50	E20	57.46 N	158.41 E
Tignall, Ga., U.S.	132	C3	33.52 N	82.44 W
Tignish, P.E., Can.	122	D12	46.57 N	64.01 W
Tigoda, stm., Russia	26	A14	59.22 N	31.53 E
Tigre, Col.	168	F7	2.27 N	68.13 W
Tigre, state, Arg.	206		34.24 S	58.37 W
Tigre, stm., Arg.	206		34.25 S	58.35 W
Tigre, stm., Peru	164	D2	4.28 S	74.04 W
Tigre, stm., Ven.	168	C10	9.20 N	62.28 W
Tigris (Dicle) (Dijlah), stm., Asia	74	E10	30.59 N	47.26 E
Tiguabos, Cuba	156	B10	20.14 N	75.21 W
Tiguentourine, Alg.	84	D6	27.51 N	9.11 E
Tigzirt, Alg.	28	H15	36.53 N	4.06 E
Tīh, Gebel el-, plat., Egypt	76	I4	29.33 N	33.54 E
Tihany, hist., Hung.	36	C4	46.54 N	17.53 E
Tihert, Alg.	84	B5	35.28 N	1.21 E
Tihmenevo, Russia	26	C21	57.59 N	38.36 E
Tihon, Russia	40	B15	59.23 N	46.38 E
Tihookeanskij, Russia	54	C10	42.58 N	132.25 E
Tihoreck, Russia	40	I12	45.51 N	40.07 E
Tihtozero, Russia	18	B17	65.35 N	30.31 E
Tihuatlán, Mex.	154	E10	20.43 N	97.33 W
Tihvin, Russia	26	A16	59.38 N	33.31 E
Tihvinskaja grjada, mts., Russia	18	H21	59.23 N	34.33 E
Tiilikkajärven kansallispuisto, p.o.i., Fin.	18	D15	63.38 N	28.20 E
Tijuana, Mex.	120	E4	32.32 N	117.01 W
Tijuana, stm., N.A.	148	K9	32.33 N	117.08 W
Tijuca, ngh., Braz.	205a		22.56 S	43.14 W
Tijuca, Barra da, strt., Braz.	205a		23.01 S	43.18 W
Tijuca, Lagoa da, b., Braz.	205a		22.59 S	43.20 W
Tijuca, Parque Nacional da, p.o.i., Braz.	205a		22.58 S	43.15 W
Tijuca, Pico da, mtn., Braz.	205a		22.56 S	43.17 W
Tijucas, Braz.	172	C13	27.14 S	48.38 W
Tijucas do Sul, Braz.	172	B13	25.55 S	49.09 W
Tijuco, stm., Braz.	170	J1	19.16 S	48.27 W
Tikal, hist., Guat.	156	D3	17.20 N	89.39 W
Tikal, Parque Nacional, p.o.i., Guat.	156	D3	17.14 N	89.38 W
Tikhand, ngh., India	190a		28.31 N	77.17 E
Tikrīt, Iraq	74	C8	34.36 N	43.41 E
Tikša, Russia	18	C19	64.07 N	32.23 E
Tikšeozero, ozero, l., Russia	14	F22	66.16 N	31.53 E
Tiksi, Russia	50	B14	71.38 N	128.48 E
Tiku, Indon.	66	D1	0.23 S	99.55 E
Tiladummati Atoll, at., Mald.	62a	h12	6.50 N	73.05 E
Tilburg, Neth.	20	C14	51.34 N	5.05 E
Tilbury, On., Can.	126	F7	42.15 N	82.25 W
Tilcha, Austl.	98	G3	29.36 S	140.53 E
Tilden, Il., U.S.	130	F8	38.12 N	89.40 W
Tilden, Ne., U.S.	140	E15	42.02 N	97.50 W
Tilden, Tx., U.S.	136	F9	28.28 N	98.33 W
Tilden Woods, Md., U.S.	202c		39.03 N	77.09 W
Tilhar, India	70	D7	27.57 N	79.44 E
Tilimsen, Alg.	84	C4	34.53 N	1.18 W
Tilin, Mya.	64	B2	21.41 N	94.05 E
Tilisarao, Arg.	172	F5	32.43 S	65.16 W
Tillabéri, Niger	84	G5	14.12 N	1.27 E
Tillamook, Or., U.S.	146	E3	45.27 N	123.50 W
Tillberga, Swe.	16	H14	59.41 N	16.37 E
Tillery, Lake, res., N.C., U.S.	132	A5	35.16 N	80.05 W
Tilley, Ab., Can.	144	F19	50.27 N	111.38 W
Tillia, Niger	84	F5	16.08 N	4.47 E
Tilling Bourne, stm., Eng., U.K.	178		51.13 N	0.34 W
Tillmans Corner, Al., U.S.	134	G10	30.38 N	88.11 W
Tillson, N.Y., U.S.	124	C11	41.49 N	74.04 W
Tillsonburg, On., Can.	126	F9	42.51 N	80.43 W
Tílos, i., Grc.	34	G10	36.23 N	27.24 E
Tilpa, Austl.	98	H5	30.57 S	144.24 E
Tilsit see Sovetsk, Russia	26	E4	55.04 N	21.53 E
Tilton, Il., U.S.	130	D10	40.05 N	87.38 W
Tilton, N.H., U.S.	122	G5	43.27 N	71.35 W
Tiltonsville, Oh., U.S.	124	D5	40.10 N	80.42 W
Tim, Russia	38	B16	51.38 N	37.06 E
Tim, stm., Russia	38	B16	51.45 N	37.11 E
Tima, Egypt	76	L2	26.54 N	31.26 E
Timah, Bukit, hill, Sing.	189c		1.21 N	103.47 E
Timaná, Col.	168	G3	1.58 N	75.55 W
Timanskij krjaž, hills, Russia	48	B8	65.00 N	51.00 E
Timariha, Russia	40	C14	57.33 N	44.48 E
Timaru, N.Z.	102	G4	44.23 S	171.13 E
Timaševo, Russia	40	E17	53.20 N	51.09 E
Timaševsk, Russia	40	I11	45.37 N	38.56 E
Timbalier Bay, b., La., U.S.	134	H8	29.10 N	90.20 W
Timbaúba, Braz.	170	D8	7.31 S	35.19 W
Timbavati Game Reserve, ind. res., S. Afr.	90	D10	24.27 S	31.27 E
Timbedgha, Maur.	84	F3	16.15 N	8.10 W
Timber Creek, stm., S.D., U.S.	140	B14	44.47 N	98.18 W
Timber Lake, Il., U.S.	196		42.14 N	88.07 W
Timber Lake, S.D., U.S.	140	B11	45.26 N	101.04 W
Timber Run, stm., Md., U.S.	202b		39.27 N	76.52 W
Timber Trails, Il., U.S.	196		41.52 N	87.57 W
Timberview, Md., U.S.	202b		39.13 N	76.45 W
Timbío, Col.	168	F3	2.20 N	76.40 W
Timbiras, Braz.	170	C4	4.15 S	43.57 W
Timbó, Braz.	172	C13	26.50 S	49.16 W
Timbo, Lib.	84	H3	5.36 N	9.41 W
Timbó, stm., Braz.	205a		22.52 S	43.16 W
Timboon, Austl.	98	L4	38.29 S	142.58 E
Timbuctoo, N.J., U.S.	203		40.00 N	74.49 W
Timbuktu see Tombouctou, Mali	84	F4	16.46 N	3.00 W
Timbun Mata, Pulau, i., Malay.	66	A11	4.38 N	118.27 E
Times Square, hist., N.Y., U.S.	194		40.45 N	74.00 W
Timétrine, Mali	84	F4	19.27 N	0.26 W
Timétrine, mts., Mali	84	F4	19.20 N	0.42 W
Timeu Creek, stm., Ab., Can.	144	B16	54.27 N	114.26 W
Timimoun, Alg.	84	D5	29.14 N	0.16 E
Timirist, Râs, c., Maur.	84	F1	19.23 N	16.32 W
Timirjazevo, Kaz.	48	D11	53.44 N	66.31 E
Timirjazevo, Russia	26	E4	55.05 N	21.36 E
Timiș, state, Rom.	36	D8	45.40 N	21.20 E
Timiș (Tamiš), stm., Eur.	36	E7	44.51 N	20.37 E
Timiskaming, Lake (Témiscamingue, Lac), res., Can.	126	B10	47.10 N	79.25 W
Timișoara, Rom.	36	D8	45.45 N	21.13 E
Timitis Crack, c., Pit.	100k	c28	25.04 S	130.06 W
Timmendorfer Strand, Ger.	24	B6	53.59 N	10.47 E
Timmernabben, Swe.	16	K14	56.59 N	16.25 E
Timmins, On., Can.	114	B10	48.29 N	81.20 W
Timmonsville, S.C., U.S.	132	B6	34.08 N	79.56 W
Timms Hill, mtn., Wi., U.S.	128	F8	45.27 N	90.09 W
Timna' see Mikhrot Timna', hist., Isr.	76	I5	29.45 N	34.56 E
Timohino, Russia	18	H22	59.35 N	36.04 E
Timok, stm., Eur.	36	E9	44.12 N	22.40 E
Timon, Braz.	170	C4	5.06 S	42.49 W
Timor, i., Indon.	60	G8	9.00 S	125.00 E
Timor, Laut see Timor Sea, s.	46	K16	11.00 S	128.00 E
Timor Sea, s.	46	K16	11.00 S	128.00 E
Timošino, Russia	18	G23	60.05 N	36.10 E
Timošino, Russia	40	C14	57.49 N	44.25 E
Timotes, Ven.	168	C6	8.59 N	70.44 W
Timpanogos Cave National Monument, p.o.i., Ut., U.S.	150	C5	40.25 N	111.43 W
Timpas Creek, stm., Co., U.S.	138	D5	38.02 N	103.38 W
Timperley, Eng., U.K.	180		53.24 N	2.19 W
Timpson, Tx., U.S.	136	C13	31.53 N	94.24 W
Timpton, stm., Russia	50	E14	58.44 N	127.10 E
Timrå, Swe.	16	E15	62.28 N	17.19 E
Timšer, Russia	48	B9	62.06 N	54.40 E
Tims Ford Lake, res., Tn., U.S.	134	B12	35.12 N	86.13 W
Tina, stm., S. Afr.	90	G9	31.17 S	29.12 E
Tīna, Khalīg el- (Pelusium Bay), b., Egypt	76	G3	31.08 N	32.40 E
Tinaca Point, c., Phil.	68	H5	5.34 N	125.20 E
Tinaco, Ven.	168	C7	9.42 N	68.26 W
Tinambung, Indon.	66	E11	3.30 S	119.01 E
Tinapagee, Austl.	98	G5	29.28 S	144.23 E
Tinaquillo, Ven.	168	C7	9.54 N	68.18 W
Tindari see Tyndaris, hist., Italy	32	F8	38.09 N	15.03 E
Tindivanam, India	69	E4	12.14 N	79.39 E
Tindouf, Alg.	84	D3	27.48 N	8.07 W
Tineba, Pegunungan, mts., Indon.	66	D12	1.42 S	120.24 E
Tinée, stm., Fr.	30	F4	43.55 N	7.10 E
Tineg, stm., Phil.	68	B3	17.31 N	120.24 E
Tineo, Spain	28	A4	43.20 N	6.24 W
Ting, stm., China	58	I7	24.24 N	116.34 E
Tinggi, Pulau, i., Malay.	64	K7	2.18 N	104.07 E
Tingha, Austl.	98	G8	29.57 S	151.12 E
Tinghert, Hamādat (Tinghert, Plateau du), plat., Afr.	82	B2	29.00 N	9.00 E
Tinghert, Plateau du (Tinghert, Hamādat), plat., Afr.	82	B1	29.00 N	9.00 E
Ting Kau, China	189d		22.22 N	114.05 E
Tinglev, Den.	16	M7	54.56 N	9.15 E
Tingo María, Peru	164	E2	9.09 S	75.55 W
Tingri, China	70	D11	28.37 N	87.10 E
Tingri see Dingyê, China	70	D11	28.34 N	86.37 E
Tingsryd, Swe.	16	K12	56.31 N	14.58 E
Tingstäde, Swe.	16	J16	57.44 N	18.37 E
Tinguiririca, Volcán, vol., Chile	172	G2	34.49 S	70.21 W
Tingvoll, Nor.	16	E6	62.55 N	8.12 E
Tingzhou see Changting, China	58	I7	25.50 N	116.21 E
Tinharé, Ilha de, i., Braz.	170	G6	13.29 S	38.56 W
Tinh Bien, Viet.	64	G7	10.36 N	104.57 E
Tinian, i., N. Mar. Is.	94	B5	15.00 N	145.38 E
Tinjar, stm., Malay.	66	B9	4.03 N	114.17 E
Tinker Air Force Base, mil., Ok., U.S.	138	F11	35.25 N	97.24 W
Tinkers Creek, stm., Md., U.S.	202c		38.46 N	76.57 W
Tinkertown, Ma., U.S.	201		42.01 N	70.44 W
Tinley Creek, stm., Il., U.S.	196		41.39 N	87.45 W
Tinley Creek Woods, p.o.i., Il., U.S.	196		41.39 N	87.47 W
Tinniswood, Mount, mtn., B.C., Can.	144	F7	50.19 N	123.50 W
Tinnoset, Nor.	16	H6	59.43 N	9.02 E
Tinnsjå, l., Nor.	16	H6	59.54 N	8.55 E
Tinogasta, Arg.	172	D4	28.03 S	67.34 W
Tinos, Grc.	34	F8	37.32 N	25.09 E
Tinos, i., Grc.	34	F8	37.35 N	25.09 E
Tinrhert, Hamada de see Tinghert, Hamādat, plat., Afr.	82	B2	29.00 N	9.00 E
Tinrhert, Hamada de see Tinghert, Plateau du, plat., Afr.	82	B2	29.00 N	9.00 E
Tin Sam, China	189d		22.22 N	114.11 E
Tinsley, Ms., U.S.	134	E8	32.44 N	90.27 W
Tinsukia, India	62	C8	27.30 N	95.21 E
Tintagel, B.C., Can.	144	B5	54.12 N	125.33 W
Tintas, Rio das, stm., Braz.	205a		22.52 S	43.28 W
Tintina, Arg.	172	C6	27.02 S	62.42 W
Tintinara, Austl.	98	J3	35.53 S	140.02 E
Tinto, stm., Spain	28	G4	37.17 N	6.50 W
Tinton Falls, N.J., U.S.	194		40.19 N	74.04 W
Tintwistle, Eng., U.K.	180		53.28 N	1.58 W
Tio, Erit.	82	E8	14.40 N	40.56 E
Tiobrad Árann see Tipperary, Ire.	10	I4	52.28 N	8.10 W
Tioga, N.D., U.S.	142	F11	48.24 N	102.55 W
Tioga, Pa., U.S.	124	C8	41.55 N	77.07 W
Tioga, ngh., Pa., U.S.	203		40.00 N	75.10 W
Tiojala, Fin.	12	F10	61.09 N	23.51 E
Tioman, Pulau, i., Malay.	64	K7	2.48 N	104.10 E
Tione di Trento, Italy	30	D7	46.02 N	10.43 E
Tionesta, Pa., U.S.	124	C6	41.29 N	79.26 W
Tionesta Creek, stm., Pa., U.S.	126	G10	41.28 N	79.22 W
Tioughnioga, stm., N.Y., U.S.	126	F13	42.14 N	75.51 W
Tioughnioga, East Branch, stm., N.Y., U.S.	124	B10	42.36 N	76.09 W
Tipasa, Alg.	28	H13	36.35 N	2.25 E
Tipitapa, Nic.	156	F4	12.12 N	86.06 W
Tippecanoe, stm., In., U.S.	130	D11	40.30 N	86.47 W
Tipperary, Austl.	96	B6	13.43 S	131.02 E
Tipperary, Ire.	10	I4	52.28 N	8.10 W
Tipperary, state, Ire.	10	I5	52.40 N	8.00 W
Tipton, Ca., U.S.	148	G6	36.03 N	119.18 W
Tipton, In., U.S.	130	D11	40.16 N	86.01 W
Tipton, Ia., U.S.	130	C6	41.46 N	91.08 W
Tipton, Mo., U.S.	130	F5	38.39 N	92.46 W
Tipton, Ok., U.S.	138	G9	34.30 N	99.08 W
Tipton, Mount, mtn., Az., U.S.	150	H2	35.32 N	114.12 W
Tiptonville, Tn., U.S.	130	H8	36.22 N	89.28 W
Tip Top Mountain, mtn., On., Can.	114	B8	48.16 N	85.59 W
Tiptūr, India	69	E3	13.15 N	76.28 E
Tiputini, stm., Ec.	168	H4	0.48 S	75.32 W
Tira, Isr.	76	F5	32.13 N	34.57 E
Tīrān, i., Sau. Ar.	74	G4	27.56 N	34.32 E
Tīrān, Madīq see Tiran, Strait of, strt.	76	K5	27.58 N	34.28 E
Tīrān, Madīq see Tiran, Strait of, strt.	76	K5	27.58 N	34.28 E
Tiran, Strait of, strt.	76	K5	27.58 N	34.28 E
Tirana see Tiranë, Alb.	32	C13	41.20 N	19.50 E
Tiranë, Alb.	32	C13	41.20 N	19.50 E
Tirano, Italy	30	D7	46.13 N	10.10 E
Tiraspol' see Tiraspol, Mol.	38	G8	46.51 N	29.38 E
Tiraspol, Mol.	38	G8	46.51 N	29.38 E
Tirat Karmel, Isr.	74	D4	32.46 N	34.59 E
Tire, Tur.	34	E10	38.05 N	27.43 E
Tiree, i., Scot., U.K.	10	E6	56.30 N	6.55 W
Tires, Port.	184c		38.43 N	9.21 W
Tîrgoviște see Târgoviște, Rom.	36	E12	44.55 N	25.27 E
Tîrgu Mureș see Târgu Mureș, Rom.	36	C11	46.32 N	24.34 E
Tirich Mīr, mtn., Pak.	62	A3	36.15 N	71.50 E
Tirma, stm., India	69	B3	18.04 N	76.57 E
Tirnovo see Veliko Tărnovo, Blg.	36	F12	43.04 N	25.38 E
Tirodi, India	70	H7	21.41 N	79.43 E
Tirol, state, Aus.	30	D9	47.15 N	11.20 E
Tiroler Ache (Gross Ache), stm., Eur.	30	C9	47.51 N	12.31 E
Tiros, Braz.	170	J3	18.59 S	45.58 W
Tirreno, Mar see Tyrrhenian Sea, s., Eur.	8	G11	40.00 N	12.00 E
Tirsā, Egypt	191c		29.58 N	31.12 E
Tirschenreuth, Ger.	24	G8	49.53 N	12.20 E
Tirso, stm., Italy	32	E2	39.53 N	8.32 E
Tirthahalli, India	69	E2	13.41 N	75.14 E
Tiruchchirāppalli, India	69	F4	10.48 N	78.41 E
Tiruchengodu, India	69	F3	11.22 N	77.54 E
Tirukkalukkunram, India	69	E5	12.36 N	80.03 E
Tirukkovilūr, India	69	F4	11.56 N	79.12 E
Tirunelveli, India	69	G3	8.43 N	77.41 E
Tirupati, India	69	E4	13.37 N	79.25 E
Tiruppattūr, India	69	E4	12.29 N	78.34 E
Tiruppur, India	69	F3	11.05 N	77.21 E
Tirūr, India	69	F2	10.55 N	75.54 E
Tiruturaippūndi, India	69	F4	10.32 N	79.39 E
Tiruvalla, India	69	G3	9.22 N	76.36 E
Tiruvannāmalai, India	69	E4	12.13 N	79.04 E
Tiruvottiyūr, India	69	E5	13.10 N	80.17 E
Tiruvur, India	69	C5	17.06 N	80.37 E
Tisa (Tisza) (Tysa), stm., Eur.	36	D7	45.07 N	20.17 E
Tisaiyanvilai, India	69	G3	8.19 N	77.52 E
Tisdale, Sk., Can.	142	B9	52.50 N	104.03 W
Tishomingo, Ms., U.S.	134	C10	34.38 N	88.12 W
Tishomingo, Ok., U.S.	134	C2	34.13 N	96.40 W
Tisīyah, Syria	76	F7	32.24 N	36.27 E
Tisjön, l., Swe.	16	G11	60.55 N	12.57 E
Tiskilwa, Il., U.S.	130	C8	41.17 N	89.30 W
Tisnaren, l., Swe.	16	I13	58.57 N	15.57 E
Tišnov, Czech Rep.	24	G12	49.21 N	16.25 E
Tisovec, Slvk.	24	H15	48.42 N	19.57 E
Tissø, l., Den.	16	L9	55.34 N	11.17 E
Tista, stm., Asia	70	F12	25.30 N	89.41 E
Tisul', Russia	48	C15	55.45 N	88.18 E
Tisza (Tisa) (Tysa), stm., Eur.	36	D7	45.07 N	20.17 E
Tiszaföldvár, Hung.	36	C7	46.58 N	20.15 E
Tiszafüred, Hung.	36	B7	47.37 N	20.49 E
Tiszaújváros, Hung.	36	B7	47.55 N	21.02 E
Tiszavasvári, Hung.	36	A8	47.57 N	21.22 E
Titaf, Alg.	84	D4	27.26 N	0.13 W
Tit-Ary, Russia	50	B14	71.58 N	127.02 E
Titicaca, Lago see Titicaca, Lake, l., S.A.	166	C3	15.50 S	69.20 W
Titicaca, Lake, l., S.A.	166	C3	15.50 S	69.20 W
Titikaveka, Cook Is.	100j	b26	21.15 S	159.45 W
Titilāgarh, India	70	H9	20.17 N	83.09 E
Titograd see Podgorica, Yugo.	36	G6	42.26 N	19.15 E
Titonka, Ia., U.S.	128	H4	43.14 N	94.02 W
Titovo Velenje, Slvn.	30	D12	46.21 N	15.05 E
Titov Veles, Mac.	34	B4	41.43 N	21.47 E
Titov vrh, mtn., Mac.	34	B3	42.00 N	20.51 E
Titran, Nor.	16	D6	63.40 N	8.18 E
Tittabawassee, stm., Mi., U.S.	126	E5	43.22 N	83.58 W
Tittling, Ger.	24	H9	48.43 N	13.22 E
Tittmoning, Ger.	24	H8	48.04 N	12.46 E
Titu, Rom.	36	E12	44.39 N	25.32 E
Titule, D.R.C.	86	D5	3.17 N	25.30 E
Titusville, Fl., U.S.	132	H5	28.36 N	80.48 W
Titusville, Pa., U.S.	124	C6	41.38 N	79.40 W
Tiu Chung Chau, i., China	189d		22.20 N	114.19 E
Tiuni, India	70	C6	30.57 N	77.50 E

Name	Page	Map Ref.	Latitude	Longitude
Tivaouane, Sen.	84	F1	14.57 N	16.49 W
Tiveden, hills, Swe.	16	I12	58.45 N	14.40 E
Tiverton, Eng., U.K.	10	K9	50.54 N	3.29 W
Tivoli, Gren.	159e	q10	12.10 N	61.37 W
Tivoli, Italy	30	I9	41.57 N	12.47 E
Tivoli, Tx., U.S.	136	F11	28.27 N	96.53 W
Tīwī, Oman	72	E8	22.49 N	59.15 E
Tiyās, Syria	76	D8	34.33 N	37.40 E
Tizapán, ngh., Mex.	204a		19.20 N	99.13 W
Tizimín, Mex.	156	B3	21.09 N	88.09 W
Tizi-Ouzou, Alg.	84	B5	36.48 N	4.02 E
Tizmant el-Zawâya, Egypt	76	I1	29.02 N	31.03 E
Tiznados, stm., Ven.	168	C8	8.23 N	67.53 W
Tiznit, Mor.	84	D3	29.41 N	9.43 W
Tjaktjajaure, l., Swe.	14	E9	67.03 N	18.26 E
Tjåmotis, Swe.	14	F9	66.55 N	18.35 E
Tjan'-Šan' see Tien Shan, mts., Asia	48	F13	42.00 N	80.00 E
Tjeggelvas, l., Swe.	14	F8	66.35 N	17.40 E
Tjeldøya, i., Nor.	14	D7	68.29 N	16.20 E
Tjidtjak, mtn., Swe.	14	F7	66.35 N	16.32 E
Tjilatjap see Cilacap, Indon.	66	G6	7.44 S	109.00 E
Tjirebon see Cirebon, Indon.	66	G6	6.44 S	108.33 E
Tjøme, i., Nor.	16	H8	59.07 N	10.24 E
Tjorbufjellet, mtn., Nor.	16	H6	59.30 N	8.52 E
Tjörn, i., Swe.	16	J9	58.00 N	11.38 E
Tjuhtet, Russia	48	C15	56.32 N	89.19 E
Tjukalinsk, Russia	48	C12	55.52 N	72.12 E
Tjulen'i, ostrova, is., Kaz.	40	I17	44.55 N	50.10 E
Tjulenij, ostrov, i., Russia	42	C12	44.28 N	47.32 E
Tjul'gan, Russia	40	E20	52.24 N	56.13 E
Tjumen', Russia	48	C10	57.09 N	65.32 E
Tjumjati see Sklad, Russia	50	B13	71.54 N	123.31 E
Tjung, stm., Russia	50	D13	63.46 N	121.31 E
Tjurtojva, gora, mtn., Russia	14	F22	66.50 N	31.08 E
Tjuva-Guba, Russia	14	C24	69.08 N	33.37 E
Tkvarčeli, Geor.	42	D9	42.50 N	41.41 E
Tlacotalpan, Mex.	154	F11	18.37 N	95.40 W
Tlacotepec, Mex.	154	G9	17.46 N	99.59 W
Tláhuac, ngh., Mex.	204a		19.16 N	99.00 W
Tlahualilo de Zaragoza, Mex.	154	B7	26.06 N	103.26 W
Tlalixtaquilla, Mex.	154	G9	17.21 N	98.28 W
Tlalnepantla, Mex.	154	F9	19.32 N	99.12 W
Tlalnepantla, stm., Mex.	204a		19.31 N	99.16 W
Tlalpan, ngh., Mex.	204a		19.17 N	99.10 W
Tlaltenango de Sánchez Román, Mex.	154	E7	21.46 N	103.17 W
Tlapaneco, stm., Mex.	154	G9	18.03 N	98.47 W
Tlaquepaque, Mex.	154	E7	20.39 N	103.19 W
Tlaxcala, state, Mex.	154	F9	19.25 N	98.10 W
Tlaxcala de Xicohténcatl, Mex.	154	F9	19.19 N	98.14 W
Tlētē Ouāte Gharbī, Jabal, mtn., Syria	74	C6	35.20 N	39.13 E
Tlumach, Ukr.	38	E4	48.51 N	25.00 E
Tłuszcz, Pol.	24	D17	52.25 N	21.26 E
Tmassah, Libya	82	B3	26.21 N	15.48 E
Tnâot, stm., Camb.	64	G7	11.29 N	104.57 E
Toa Alta, P.R.	158a	b3	18.25 N	66.14 W
Toa Baja, P.R.	158a	b3	18.27 N	66.15 W
Toachi, stm., Ec.	168	H2	0.07 S	79.15 W
Toahayana, Mex.	154	B5	26.08 N	107.43 W
Toamasina, Madag.	88	D8	18.09 S	49.24 E
Toan, Kor., N.	54	D7	40.33 N	127.35 E
Toano, Va., U.S.	124	G9	37.22 N	76.48 W
Toano Draw, stm., Nv., U.S.	150	B2	41.27 N	114.34 W
Toano Range, mts., Nv., U.S.	150	C2	40.56 N	114.17 W
Toa Vaca, Embalse, res., P.R.	158a	b3	18.06 N	66.28 W
Toay, Arg.	172	H5	36.40 S	64.23 W
Toba, Japan	56	E9	34.28 N	136.50 E
Toba, stm., B.C., Can.	144	F6	50.30 N	124.19 W
Toba, Danau, l., Indon.	64	K4	2.43 N	98.41 E
Tobacco Plains Indian Reserve, ind. res., B.C., Can.	144	G15	49.02 N	115.08 W
Tobacco Root Mountains, mts., Mt., U.S.	146	E14	45.35 N	112.00 W
Tobago, i., Trin.	159f	r13	11.15 N	60.40 W
Toba Inlet, b., B.C., Can.	144	F6	50.18 N	124.47 W
Toba Kākar Range, mts., Pak.	62	B2	31.15 N	68.00 E
Tobalaba Eulogio Sánchez, Aeródromo, arpt., Chile	204e		33.27 S	70.33 W
Tobarra, Spain	28	F9	38.35 N	1.41 W
Tobas, Arg.	172	D6	28.07 S	62.42 W
Toba Tek Singh, Pak.	70	C4	30.57 N	72.28 E
Tobejuba, Isla, i., Ven.	168	C11	9.20 N	60.52 W
Tobekuduk, Kaz.	40	G18	49.51 N	54.15 E
Tobermorey, Austl.	96	D7	22.16 S	137.58 E
Tobermory, Austl.	98	F4	27.17 S	143.41 E
Tobermory, On., Can.	126	C8	45.14 N	81.39 W
Tobermory, Scot., U.K.	10	E6	56.36 N	6.02 W
Tobias, Ne., U.S.	140	G15	40.25 N	97.20 W
Tobias Barreto, Braz.	170	F6	11.10 S	37.59 W
Tobin, Mount, mtn., Nv., U.S.	148	C8	40.22 N	117.32 W
Tobique, stm., N.B., Can.	122	C9	46.45 N	67.42 W
Toblach see Dobbiaco, Italy	30	D9	46.43 N	12.13 E
Toboali, Indon.	66	E5	3.00 S	106.26 E
Tobol, Kaz.	48	D10	52.41 N	62.35 E
Tobol, stm., Asia	48	C11	58.09 N	68.13 E
Toboli, Indon.	66	D12	0.43 S	120.05 E
Tobol'sk, Russia	48	C11	58.11 N	68.15 E
Tobong-san, mtn., Kor., S.	189b		37.42 N	127.01 E
Toboso, Phil.	68	E4	10.43 N	123.30 E
Tobruk see Tubruq, Libya	82	A4	32.04 N	23.56 E
Tobseda, Russia	12	B25	68.35 N	52.20 E
Tobyhanna, Pa., U.S.	124	C10	41.10 N	75.25 W
Tobyš, stm., Russia	12	C24	65.29 N	51.01 E
Toca Grande, Morro da, mtn., Braz.	205a		22.58 S	43.31 W
Tocantínia, Braz.	170	E1	9.32 S	48.21 W
Tocantinópolis, Braz.	170	D2	6.18 S	47.25 W
Tocantins, state, Braz.	164	F8	10.00 S	48.00 W
Tocantins, stm., Braz.	164	D8	1.45 S	49.11 W
Tocantins, stm., Braz.	170	F1	5.23 S	56.05 W
Tocantinzinho, stm., Braz.	170	H1	13.56 S	48.19 W
Toccoa, Ga., U.S.	132	B2	34.34 N	83.19 W
Toccoa (Ocoee), stm., U.S.	134	B14	35.12 N	84.40 W
Toce, stm., Italy	30	D5	45.52 N	8.34 E
Tochcha Lake, l., B.C., Can.	144	B5	54.56 N	125.54 W
Tochigi, Japan	56	C12	36.22 N	139.44 E
Tochigi, state, Japan	56	C12	36.45 N	139.45 E
Tochio, Japan	56	B12	37.28 N	139.00 E
Tockholes, Eng., U.K.	180		53.42 N	2.31 W
Töcksfors, Swe.	16	H9	59.30 N	11.50 E
Toco, Trin.	159f	s13	10.49 N	60.57 W
Tocoa, Hond.	156	E5	15.38 N	86.01 W
Tócome, stm., Ven.	204c		10.29 N	66.49 W
Toconao, Chile	166	D3	23.10 S	67.59 W
Tocopilla, Chile	166	D2	22.06 S	70.11 W
Tocuco, stm., Ven.	168	C5	9.24 N	72.22 W
Tocumwal, Austl.	98	J5	35.48 S	145.34 E
Tocuyo, stm., Ven.	168	B7	11.03 N	68.20 W
Tocuyo de la Costa, Ven.	168	B7	11.01 N	68.22 W
Todaiji Temple, rel., Japan	188		34.42 N	135.51 E
Todang-ni, Kor., S.	189b		37.37 N	126.50 E
Toda Räisingh, India	70	E5	26.01 N	75.29 E
Todd Estates, De., U.S.	203		39.40 N	75.43 W
Todd Point, c., Md., U.S.	202b		39.15 N	76.27 W
Todi, Italy	30	H9	42.47 N	12.23 E
Todoromi, Japan	188		34.53 N	135.28 E
Todos os Santos, Baía de, b., Braz.	170	G6	12.50 S	38.36 W
Todos Santos, Bol.	166	C3	16.48 S	65.08 W
Todos Santos, Mex.	154	D3	23.27 N	110.13 W
Todos Santos, Bahía de, b., Mex.	120	F4	31.48 N	116.42 W
Todtnau, Ger.	24	I3	47.50 N	7.58 E
Toemoek Hoemak Gebergte see Tumuc-Humac Mountains, mts., S.A.	164	C6	2.18 N	54.35 W
Tofield, Ab., Can.	144	C18	53.21 N	112.40 W
Tofino, B.C., Can.	144	G5	49.08 N	125.54 W
Töfsingdalens Nationalpark, p.o.i., Swe.	16	E10	62.09 N	12.30 E
Toga, i., Vanuatu	101d	i16	13.25 S	166.41 E
Toganas, Kaz.	40	F18	50.49 N	52.02 E
Togi, Japan	56	B9	37.08 N	136.44 E
Togiak, Ak., U.S.	109	F7	59.04 N	160.24 W
Togian, Kepulauan, is., Indon.	60	F7	0.20 S	122.00 E
Togliatti see Toljatti, Russia	40	E16	53.32 N	49.25 E
Togo, ctry., Afr.	84	H5	8.00 N	1.10 E
Togtoh, China	58	A4	40.16 N	111.09 E
Togučin, Russia	48	C14	55.13 N	84.23 E
Togur, Russia	48	C14	58.22 N	82.51 E
Togwotee Pass, p., Wy., U.S.	146	G16	43.45 N	110.04 W
Togyz, Kaz.	48	E10	47.34 N	60.32 E
Tōhaku, Japan	56	D6	35.30 N	133.40 E
Tohakum Peak, mtn., Nv., U.S.	148	C6	40.11 N	119.27 W
Tohiea, Mont, mtn., Fr. Poly.	100h	v20	17.33 S	149.49 W
Tohma, stm., Tur.	42	F7	38.30 N	38.26 E
Toholampi, Fin.	18	D11	63.45 N	24.15 E
Tohopekaliga, Lake, l., Fl., U.S.	132	H4	28.12 N	81.23 W
Tohta, Russia	12	E23	62.14 N	48.49 E
Tohtamyš, Taj.	72	B11	37.50 N	74.39 E
Toijala, Fin.	18	F10	61.10 N	23.52 E
Toi-misaki, c., Japan	56	H4	31.21 N	131.19 E
Toi Sar, Pak.	70	C2	31.06 N	69.54 E
Toiyabe Range, mts., Nv., U.S.	148	D8	39.10 N	117.10 W
Tōjō, Japan	56	E6	34.53 N	133.16 E
Tōjō, Japan	188		34.55 N	135.04 E
Tojtepa, Uzb.	48	F11	41.04 N	69.20 E
Tok, Ak., U.S.	109	D11	63.19 N	143.00 W
Tok, stm., Russia	40	E18	52.45 N	52.22 E
Tokachi, stm., Japan	54	C15	42.43 N	143.42 E
Tokachi-dake, vol., Japan	54	C15	43.25 N	142.41 E
Tōkagi, Japan	186		35.42 N	139.56 E
Tokaj, Hung.	36	A8	48.06 N	21.25 E
Tōkamachi, Japan	56	B11	37.08 N	138.46 E
Tokanui, N.Z.	102	H3	46.33 S	168.54 E
Tokara-kaikyō, strt., Japan	55a	j20	30.10 N	130.10 E
Tokara-rettō, is., Japan	55a	k19	29.36 N	129.43 E
Tokarëvka, Russia	40	F12	51.59 N	41.10 E
Tokarëvo, Russia	26	E18	55.18 N	35.06 E
Tokarëvo, Russia	183b		55.38 N	37.55 E
Tokari, Russia	18	F21	61.04 N	34.21 E
Tokat, Tur.	42	E7	40.19 N	36.34 E
Tokat, state, Tur.	42	E7	40.25 N	36.30 E
Tŏkchŏk-kundo, is., Kor., S.	54	F6	37.06 N	126.05 E
Tokelau, dep., Oc.	92	D9	9.00 S	171.45 W
Tokelau Islands, is., Tok.	94	D9	9.00 S	171.45 W
Tokeneke Brook, stm., Ct., U.S.	194		41.03 N	73.28 W
Tokiwadaira, Japan	186		35.48 N	139.57 E
Tokke, l., Nor.	16	H7	58.59 N	9.15 E
Tokke, stm., Nor.	16	H6	59.27 N	7.57 E
Tokko, Russia	50	D12	59.59 N	119.51 E
Tokma, Russia	48	C19	58.16 N	105.53 E
Tokmak, Kyrg.	48	F13	42.49 N	75.18 E
Tokmak, Ukr.	38	F14	47.15 N	35.42 E
Tokmak, mys, c., Kaz.	42	D15	42.47 N	52.17 E
Tököl, Hung.	182c		47.19 N	18.58 E
Tokoro, stm., Japan	54	C15	44.07 N	144.04 E
Tokoroa, N.Z.	102	D6	38.13 S	175.51 E
Tokovs'ke, Ukr.	38	F12	47.37 N	33.57 E
Tokša, stm., Russia	18	E24	62.17 N	38.17 E
Toksovo, Russia	18	G17	60.09 N	30.31 E
Tok-to (Take-shima), is., Asia	56	B4	37.15 N	131.50 E
Toktogul, Kyrg.	48	F12	41.52 N	72.53 E
Tokung, Indon.	66	D9	0.18 S	114.28 E
Tokuno-shima, i., Japan	55a	I19	27.45 N	128.58 E
Tokur, Russia	50	F15	53.08 N	132.53 E
Tokura, Japan	188		34.58 N	135.18 E
Tokushima, Japan	56	E7	34.04 N	134.34 E
Tokushima, state, Japan	56	F7	33.50 N	134.20 E
Tokuyama, Japan	56	E4	34.02 N	131.48 E
Tokwe, stm., Zimb.	90	B10	20.37 S	30.40 E
Tōkyō, Japan	56	D12	35.41 N	139.46 E
Tōkyō, Japan	186		35.42 N	139.46 E
Tōkyō, state, Japan	56	D12	35.40 N	139.30 E
Tokyo (Haneda) International Airport, arpt., Japan	186		35.33 N	139.46 E
Tokyo Bay see Tōkyō-wan, b., Japan	56	D12	35.26 N	139.41 E
Tōkyō-daigaku-uchūkūkan-kenkyūsho, sci., Japan	56	H4	31.17 N	131.04 E
Tokyo Disneyland, p.o.i., Japan	186		35.37 N	139.53 E
Tokyo Dome, p.o.i., Japan	186		35.43 N	139.45 E
Tōkyō-kō, b., Japan	186		35.37 N	139.47 E
Tokyo Station, trans., Japan	186		35.41 N	139.46 E
Tokyo Tower, bldg., Japan	186		35.39 N	139.45 E
Tokyo University, educ., Japan	186		35.42 N	139.46 E
Tokyo University, educ., Japan	186		35.39 N	139.41 E
Tokyo University of Education, educ., Japan	186		35.43 N	139.44 E
Tōkyō-wan, b., Japan	56	D12	35.26 N	139.41 E
Tolala, Indon.	66	E12	2.58 S	121.05 E
Tôlañaro, Madag.	88	F8	25.02 S	47.00 E
Tolbo, Mong.	52	B3	48.21 N	90.22 E
Toledo, Braz.	172	B11	24.43 S	53.44 W
Toledo, Col.	168	D5	7.17 N	72.28 W
Toledo, Phil.	68	E4	10.22 N	123.39 E
Toledo, Spain	28	E6	39.52 N	4.02 W
Toledo, Il., U.S.	130	E9	39.15 N	88.14 W
Toledo, Ia., U.S.	130	B5	41.59 N	92.34 W
Toledo, Oh., U.S.	124	C2	41.39 N	83.32 W
Toledo, Or., U.S.	146	F3	44.37 N	123.55 W
Toledo, co., Spain	28	E6	39.45 N	4.00 W
Toledo, Montes de, mts., Spain	28	E6	39.33 N	4.20 W
Toledo Bend Reservoir, res., U.S.	136	C14	31.30 N	93.45 W
Tolentino, Italy	30	G10	43.12 N	13.16 E
Tolga, Nor.	16	E8	62.25 N	11.00 E
Toli, China	52	B1	45.56 N	83.36 E
Toliara, Madag.	88	E7	23.21 S	43.39 E
Tolima, state, Col.	168	E4	3.45 N	75.15 W
Tolima, Nevado del, vol., Col.	168	E4	4.40 N	75.19 W
Tolitoli, Indon.	66	C12	1.02 N	120.49 E
Toljatti, Russia	40	E16	53.32 N	49.25 E
Tol'ka, Russia	48	B14	64.02 N	81.56 E
Tolkmicko, Pol.	24	B15	54.18 N	19.30 E
Tollarp, Swe.	16	L11	55.55 N	13.58 E
Tolleson, Az., U.S.	150	J4	33.27 N	112.16 W
Tolloche, Arg.	172	B6	25.30 S	63.30 W
Tølløse, Den.	16	L9	55.37 N	11.45 E
Tollygunge, ngh., India	190b		22.30 N	88.21 E
Tolmači, Russia	26	C18	57.25 N	35.41 E
Tolmačovo, Russia	26	B12	58.50 N	29.52 E
Tolmezzo, Italy	30	D10	46.24 N	13.00 E
Tolmin, Slvn.	30	D10	46.11 N	13.44 E
Tolna, Hung.	36	C5	46.25 N	18.47 E
Tolna, state, Hung.	36	C5	46.30 N	18.35 E
Tolo, D.R.C.	86	E3	2.55 S	18.34 E
Tolo, Teluk, b., Indon.	60	F7	2.00 S	122.30 E
Toloa, Houma, c., Tonga	100e	o14	21.15 S	175.08 W
Tolono, Il., U.S.	130	E9	39.58 N	88.15 W
Tolosa, Spain	28	A8	43.08 N	2.04 W
Tolosa, Aeródromo, arpt., Arg.	206		34.53 S	57.58 W
Tolstoj, mys, c., Russia	50	E20	59.11 N	155.08 E
Tolstopal'cevo, Russia	183b		55.38 N	37.13 E
Tolstoy Museum, bldg., Russia	183b		55.44 N	37.35 E
Tolti, Pak.	70	A6	35.02 N	76.03 E
Tolú, Col.	168	C4	9.30 N	75.33 W
Toluca, Mex.	154	F9	19.17 N	99.38 W
Toluca, Il., U.S.	130	D8	41.00 N	89.07 W
Toluca, Nevado de, vol., Mex.	154	F9	19.04 N	99.44 W
Tolvajarvi, Russia	18	E18	62.16 N	31.27 E
Tolvant, ozero, l., Russia	14	F22	66.53 N	31.05 E
Tolvuja, Russia	18	E22	62.30 N	35.16 E
Tolworth, ngh., Eng., U.K.	178		51.23 N	0.17 W
Tolybaj, Kaz.	48	D10	50.32 N	62.16 E
Tom', stm., Russia	48	C14	56.52 N	84.27 E
Tomah, Wi., U.S.	128	H8	43.59 N	90.30 W
Tomahawk, Wi., U.S.	128	F9	45.27 N	89.43 W
Tomakivka, Ukr.	38	F13	47.48 N	34.44 E
Tomakomai, Japan	54	C14	42.37 N	141.35 E
Tomani, Malay.	66	A9	4.51 N	115.53 E
Tomanivi, mtn., Fiji	101e	p19	17.37 S	178.01 E
Tomar, Port.	28	E2	39.36 N	8.25 W
Tomari, Russia	50	G17	47.45 N	142.04 E
Tomarovka, Russia	40	F9	50.41 N	36.14 E
Tomás Gomensoro, Ur.	172	E9	30.23 S	57.28 W
Tomashhorod, Ukr.	38	B6	51.18 N	27.01 E
Tomashpil', Ukr.	38	F11	48.32 N	28.31 E
Tomasine, stm., Qc., Can.	126	B13	46.38 N	76.15 W
Tomaszów Lubelski, Pol.	24	F19	50.27 N	23.25 E
Tomaszów Mazowiecki, Pol.	24	E15	51.32 N	20.01 E
Tomatlán, Mex.	154	F6	19.55 N	105.13 W
Tomba di Nerone, ngh., Italy	185a		41.57 N	12.27 E
Tombador, Serra do, plat., Braz.	164	F6	12.00 S	57.40 W
Tomball, Tx., U.S.	136	D12	30.05 N	95.37 W
Tombe, Sudan	82	F6	5.48 N	31.40 E
Tombigbee, stm., U.S.	134	F10	31.04 N	87.58 W
Tombos, Braz.	170	K5	20.56 S	42.01 W
Tombouctou (Timbuktu), Mali	84	F4	16.46 N	3.00 W
Tombs of the Caliphs, hist., Egypt	191c		30.03 N	31.17 E
Tombstone, Az., U.S.	150	L6	31.42 N	110.04 W
Tombstone Mountain, mtn., Yk., Can.	110	C3	64.25 N	138.30 W
Tombua, Ang.	88	D1	15.48 S	11.48 E
Tom Burke, S. Afr.	90	C9	23.04 S	28.00 E
Tomé, Chile	172	H1	36.36 S	72.57 W
Tomé-Açu, Braz.	170	B1	2.26 S	48.08 W
Tömek, Tur.	34	E15	38.00 N	32.43 E
Tomelilla, Swe.	16	L11	55.33 N	13.57 E
Tomelloso, Spain	28	E8	39.09 N	3.01 W
Tomichi Creek, stm., Co., U.S.	138	C2	38.30 N	106.57 W
Tomiko Lake, l., On., Can.	126	B10	46.31 N	79.48 W
Tomilino, Russia	183b		55.39 N	37.57 E
Tomini, Indon.	66	C12	0.32 N	120.31 E
Tomini, Gulf of see Tomini, Teluk, b., Indon.	60	F7	0.20 S	121.00 E
Tomini, Teluk (Tomini, Gulf of), b., Indon.	60	F7	0.20 S	121.00 E
Tomio, stm., Japan	188		34.35 N	135.44 E
Tomioka, Japan	56	C11	36.15 N	138.53 E
Tomkinson Ranges, mts., Austl.	96	E5	26.11 S	129.05 E
Tomma, i., Nor.	14	F3	66.15 N	12.48 E
Tommot, Russia	50	E14	58.57 N	126.18 E
Tomo, stm., Col.	168	E6	5.19 N	67.50 W
Tompa, Russia	50	E10	55.08 N	109.45 E
Tompkins, Nf., Can.	122	C17	47.47 N	59.14 W
Tompkins, Sk., Can.	142	D5	50.04 N	108.47 W
Tompkinsville, Ky., U.S.	130	H12	36.42 N	85.41 W
Tompo, Indon.	66	C12	0.53 N	120.19 E
Tom Price, Austl.	96	D3	22.41 S	117.47 E
Tomptokan, Russia	50	E15	57.06 N	133.59 E
Tomra, Nor.	16	E4	62.34 N	6.55 E
Toms, stm., N.J., U.S.	132	I15	39.55 N	74.06 W
Tomsk, Russia	48	C15	56.30 N	84.58 E
Toms River, N.J., U.S.	124	E11	39.56 N	74.11 W
Tom Steed Reservoir, res., Ok., U.S.	138	G9	34.45 N	99.00 W
Tomtabacken, hill, Swe.	16	J12	57.30 N	14.28 E
Tömük, Tur.	76	B5	36.41 N	34.22 E
Tonalá, Mex.	154	G12	16.04 N	93.44 W
Tonami, Japan	56	C9	36.38 N	136.57 E
Tonantins, Braz.	168	I8	2.53 S	67.48 W
Tonantins, stm., Braz.	168	I7	2.54 S	67.46 W
Tonasket, Wa., U.S.	146	B7	48.42 N	119.25 W
Tonate, Fr. Gu.	164	C7	4.55 N	52.22 W
Tonawanda, N.Y., U.S.	124	B6	42.59 N	78.52 W
Tonawanda Channel, mth., N.Y., U.S.	202a		43.04 N	79.00 W
Tonawanda Island, i., N.Y., U.S.	202a		43.02 N	78.53 W
Tonbo, Mya.	64	C2	18.31 N	95.05 E
Tonbridge, Eng., U.K.	10	J13	51.12 N	0.16 E
Tonbridge and Malling, mun., Eng., U.K.	178		51.16 N	0.20 E
Tonda, Japan	188		34.50 N	135.36 E
Tondano, Indon.	60	E8	1.17 N	124.55 E
Tønder, Den.	16	M6	54.56 N	8.52 E
Tondhre, India	190c		19.05 N	73.08 E
Tondi, India	69	G4	9.44 N	79.01 E
Tone, stm., Japan	56	D13	35.44 N	140.51 E
Tonekābon, Iran	74	B12	36.48 N	50.52 E
Tone-unga, can., Japan	186		35.54 N	139.53 E
Tonež, Bela.	38	B6	51.49 N	27.48 E
Tonga, ctry., Oc.	92	E9	20.00 S	175.00 W
Tongaat, S. Afr.	90	F10	29.38 S	31.04 E
Tonga Islands, is., Tonga	94	E9	20.00 S	175.00 W
Tong'an, China	58	I8	24.43 N	118.09 E
Tonganoxie, Ks., U.S.	130	E2	39.06 N	95.05 W
Tonga Ridge, unds.	174	K21	21.00 S	175.00 W
Tongariro National Park, p.o.i., N.Z.	102	D6	39.15 S	175.30 E
Tongatapu, i., Tonga	100e	n13	21.10 S	175.10 W
Tonga Trench, unds.	174	L21	20.00 S	173.00 W
Tongbai, China	58	E5	32.21 N	113.23 E
Tongbai Shan, mtn., China	58	E5	32.20 N	113.14 E
Tongbai Shan, mts., China	58	E5	32.20 N	113.15 E
Tongbei, China	52	B10	47.45 N	126.46 E
Tongcheng, China	58	F7	31.03 N	116.56 E
Tongchuan, China	58	D3	35.04 N	109.04 E
Tongdaemun Stadium, p.o.i., Kor., S.	189b		37.35 N	127.02 E
Tongdao, China	58	H3	26.23 N	109.25 E
Tongde, China	52	D5	35.17 N	100.37 E
Tongeren, Bel.	20	D14	50.47 N	5.28 E
Tongguan, China	58	G5	28.27 N	112.48 E
Tongguan, China	58	D4	34.36 N	110.16 E
Tonghai, China	52	G5	24.07 N	102.47 E
Tonghe, China	52	B10	45.57 N	128.45 E
Tonghua, China	52	C10	41.43 N	125.56 E
Tonghui, stm., China	189a		39.53 N	116.41 E
Tongjiang, China	52	B11	47.38 N	132.29 E
Tongjiang, China	58	F2	31.55 N	107.13 E
Tongji University, educ., China	187b		31.17 N	121.29 E
Tongjosŏn-man, b., Kor., N.	54	E7	39.30 N	128.00 E
Tongliang, China	58	G1	29.50 N	106.03 E
Tongliao, China	52	C9	43.36 N	122.16 E
Tongling, China	58	J3	23.30 N	109.38 E
Tongling, China	58	F7	30.53 N	117.45 E
Tonglu, China	58	G8	29.48 N	119.39 E
Tongmu, China	58	I3	24.09 N	109.58 E
Tongnae, Kor., S.	54	G8	35.12 N	129.05 E
Tongnan, China	58	F1	30.10 N	105.48 E
Tongo, Austl.	98	H4	30.30 S	143.45 E
Tongoa, i., Vanuatu	101d	k17	16.54 S	168.34 E
Tongoy, Chile	172	E2	30.15 S	71.29 W
Tongren, China	52	D5	35.30 N	102.00 E
Tongren, China	58	H3	27.42 N	109.11 E
Tongres see Tongeren, Bel.	20	D14	50.47 N	5.28 E
Tongsa Dzong, Bhu.	70	E13	27.31 N	90.30 E
Tongsan-ni, Kor., S.	189b		37.38 N	126.53 E
Tongta, Mya.	64	B4	21.20 N	99.15 E
Tongtian, stm., China	52	E4	33.33 N	96.40 E
Tongue, Scot., U.K.	10	C8	58.28 N	4.25 W
Tongue, stm., U.S.	140	A7	46.24 N	105.52 W
Tongue, stm., N.D., U.S.	142	F16	48.56 N	97.18 W
Tongue, stm., Tx., U.S.	138	H8	34.07 N	100.23 W
Tongue of the Ocean, unds.	152	C9	24.30 N	77.30 W
Tongue River Reservoir, res., Mt., U.S.	140	B5	45.06 N	106.47 W
Tongwei, China	58	D1	35.11 N	105.16 E
Tongxian, China	58	B7	39.54 N	116.39 E
Tongxin, China	58	C1	36.58 N	105.54 E
Tongxu, China	58	D6	34.28 N	114.27 E
Tongyu, China	52	C9	44.48 N	123.05 E
Tongzi, China	58	G2	28.08 N	106.49 E
Tonica, Il., U.S.	130	C8	41.12 N	89.04 W
Tönisberg, Ger.	181		51.25 N	6.30 E
Tönisheide, Ger.	181		51.19 N	7.03 E
Tonj, Sudan	82	F5	7.16 N	28.44 E
Tonk, India	70	E5	26.09 N	75.47 E
Tonkawa, Ok., U.S.	138	E11	36.41 N	97.18 W
Tonkin see Tonking, hist. reg., Viet.	46	G14	22.00 N	105.00 E
Tonkin see Bac Phan, hist. reg., Viet.	64	A7	22.00 N	105.00 E
Tonkin, Gulf of, b., Asia	52	G6	20.00 N	108.00 E
Tonking, hist. reg., Viet.	46	G14	22.00 N	105.00 E
Tonkino, Russia	40	C15	57.22 N	46.27 E
Tônlé Sab, Bœng, l., Camb.	64	F6	13.00 N	104.00 E
Tonle Sap see Tônlé Sab, Bœng, l., Camb.	64	F6	13.00 N	104.00 E
Tonneins, Fr.	22	E6	44.23 N	0.19 E
Tonner Canyon, val., Ca., U.S.	198		33.58 N	117.48 W
Tonnes, Nor.	14	F4	66.30 N	13.00 E
Tönning, Ger.	24	B4	54.19 N	8.57 E
Tonogaya, Japan	186		35.46 N	139.22 E
Tonopah, Nv., U.S.	148	E8	38.04 N	117.12 W
Tonoshō, Japan	56	E7	34.29 N	134.12 E
Tonosí, Pan.	168	D1	7.24 N	80.26 W
Tonotha, Bots.	90	B8	21.26 S	27.29 E
Tonquish Creek, stm., Mi., U.S.	199		42.21 N	83.22 W
Tons, stm., India	70	F8	25.19 N	82.05 E
Tønsberg, Nor.	16	H8	59.16 N	10.25 E
Tönsholt, Ger.	181		51.38 N	6.58 E
Tonstad, Nor.	16	I4	58.40 N	6.43 E
Tonto Creek, stm., Az., U.S.	150	I5	33.46 N	111.15 W
Tonto National Monument, p.o.i., Az., U.S.	150	J5	33.34 N	111.02 W
Tonya, Tur.	42	E8	40.53 N	39.16 E
Toobeah, Austl.	98	G7	28.25 S	149.52 E
Toodyay, Austl.	96	F3	31.32 S	116.27 E
Tooele, Ut., U.S.	150	C4	40.32 N	112.18 W
Toogoolawah, Austl.	98	F9	27.05 S	152.22 E
Toompine, Austl.	98	F5	27.13 S	144.22 E
Toomsboro, Ga., U.S.	132	D2	32.49 N	83.06 W
Toongabbie, Austl.	192a		33.47 S	150.57 E
Toora-Hem, Russia	48	D17	52.27 N	96.10 E
Toorak, Austl.	192b		37.51 S	145.01 E
Toosey Indian Reserve, ind. res., B.C., Can.	144	E8	51.56 N	122.29 W
Toot Hill, Eng., U.K.	178		51.42 N	0.12 E
Tootsi, Est.	26	B7	58.33 N	24.47 E
Toowoomba, Austl.	98	F8	27.34 S	151.56 E
Topanga Canyon, val., Ca., U.S.	198		34.05 N	118.36 W
Topanga State Park, p.o.i., Ca., U.S.	198		34.06 N	118.33 W
Topawa, Az., U.S.	150	L5	31.48 N	111.51 W
Topeka, Ks., U.S.	130	E2	39.02 N	95.41 W
Top Hill, hill, Gren.	159e	q11	12.28 N	61.26 W
Topia, Mex.	154	C5	25.13 N	106.34 W
Topilejo, ngh., Mex.	204a		19.12 N	99.09 W
Topkapı, ngh., Tur.	185b		41.02 N	28.54 E
Topkapı Palace, hist., Tur.	185b		41.00 N	28.59 E
Topki, Russia	48	C15	55.17 N	85.38 E
Topko, gora, mtn., Russia	50	E16	57.08 N	137.24 E
Topl'a, stm., Slvk.	24	H17	48.44 N	21.46 E
Topley, B.C., Can.	144	B4	54.30 N	126.17 W
Toplica, stm., Yugo.	36	F8	43.12 N	21.50 E
Toplița, Rom.	36	C12	46.55 N	25.22 E
Topo, stm., Ven.	204c		10.33 N	67.00 W
Topocalma, Punta, c., Chile	172	G1	34.07 S	72.00 W
Top of Hebers, Eng., U.K.	180		53.34 N	2.12 W
Topo Infiernito, mtn., Ven.	204c		10.33 N	66.55 W
Topol'čany, Slvk.	24	H14	48.33 N	18.10 E
Topolobampo, Mex.	154	C4	25.36 N	109.03 W
Topolog, Rom.	36	E15	44.53 N	28.23 E
Topolovățu Mare, Rom.	36	D8	45.46 N	21.38 E
Topolovgrad, Blg.	36	G13	42.04 N	26.21 E
Toporok, Russia	26	B16	58.32 N	33.28 E
Topozero, ozero, l., Russia	18	B18	65.40 N	32.00 E
Toppenish, Wa., U.S.	146	D6	46.22 N	120.18 W
Toppenish Creek, stm., Wa., U.S.	146	D6	46.19 N	120.10 W
Toppings, Eng., U.K.	180		53.37 N	2.25 W
Toprakkale, Tur.	76	A7	37.05 N	36.09 E
Topsa, Russia	12	E20	62.35 N	43.39 E
Topsham, Me., U.S.	122	G6	43.55 N	69.57 W
Top Springs, Austl.	96	C6	16.33 S	131.48 E
Toquima Range, mts., Nv., U.S.	148	E9	39.00 N	117.00 W
Toquop Wash, stm., Nv., U.S.	150	F2	36.45 N	114.11 W
Tor, Eth.	82	F6	7.50 N	33.34 E
Toraya, Peru	164	F3	14.02 S	73.19 W
Torbalı, Tur.	34	E10	38.10 N	27.21 E
Torbat-e Heydarīyeh, Iran	72	B8	35.16 N	59.13 E
Torbat-e Jām, Iran	72	B9	35.14 N	60.37 E
Torbay see Torquay, Eng., U.K.	10	K9	50.28 N	3.31 W
Torbert, Mount, mtn., Ak., U.S.	109	D9	61.25 N	152.24 W
Torbino, Russia	26	B15	58.35 N	32.53 E
Torbrook, N.S., Can.	122	F12	44.54 N	64.58 W
Torch Lake, l., Mi., U.S.	126	D4	45.03 N	85.19 W
Torchyn, Ukr.	38	C4	50.46 N	24.59 E
Torcy, Fr.	179		48.51 N	2.39 E
Torda see Turda, Rom.	36	C10	46.33 N	23.47 E
Tordera, stm., Spain	28	C13	41.41 N	2.43 E
Tordesillas, Spain	28	C5	41.30 N	5.00 W
Tordino, stm., Italy	30	H10	42.43 N	13.57 E
Tor di Quinto, ngh., Italy	185a		41.56 N	12.28 E
Töre, Swe.	14	G13	65.54 N	22.39 E
Töreboda, Swe.	16	I12	58.42 N	14.07 E
Torekov, Swe.	16	K10	56.25 N	12.38 E
Toreno, Spain	28	B4	42.42 N	6.30 W
Torez, Ukr.	38	E17	48.01 N	38.37 E
Torfou, Fr.	179		48.32 N	2.14 E
Torgau, Ger.	24	E8	51.33 N	13.00 E
Torget, i., Nor.	16	B9	65.25 N	12.05 E
Torhamn, Swe.	16	K13	56.05 N	15.50 E
Torhout, Bel.	20	C12	51.04 N	3.05 E
Toribulu, Indon.	66	D11	0.18 S	120.00 E
Toriido, Japan	188		34.25 N	135.43 E
Toriki, ngh., Russia	183a		59.47 N	30.07 E
Torino (Turin), Italy	30	E4	45.03 N	7.40 E
Torío, stm., Spain	28	B5	42.35 N	5.34 W
Torit, Sudan	82	G6	4.24 N	32.33 E
Torkoviči, Russia	26	B13	58.51 N	30.19 E
Törmänen, Fin.	14	D18	68.35 N	27.30 E
Tormentine, Cape, c., N.B., Can.	122	D13	46.06 N	63.47 W
Tormes, stm., Spain	28	C5	41.17 N	6.27 W
Tormey, Ca., U.S.	200		38.03 N	122.15 W
Tormosin, Russia	40	G13	48.10 N	42.40 E
Torna, Russia	12	B20	68.02 N	44.15 E
Torna, mtn., India	69	B1	18.16 N	73.37 E
Tornado Mountain, mtn., Can.	144	G16	49.58 N	114.39 W
Torneälven (Tornionjoki), stm., Eur.	14	E14	65.49 N	24.09 E
Torne Brook, stm., N.Y., U.S.	194		41.08 N	74.10 W
Torneträsk, l., Swe.	14	D10	68.20 N	19.23 E
Torngat Mountains, mts., Can.	108	F13	59.00 N	64.00 W
Tornillo, Tx., U.S.	136	C1	31.27 N	106.05 W
Tornillo Creek, stm., Tx., U.S.	136	E4	29.10 N	102.59 W
Tornio, Fin.	18	B11	65.51 N	24.10 E
Tornionjoki (Torneälven), stm., Eur.	14	E14	65.49 N	24.09 E
Tornquist, Arg.	172	I6	38.05 S	62.13 W
Toro, Spain	28	C5	41.31 N	5.23 W
Toro, mtn., Mex.	154	F6	19.07 N	104.23 W
Torö, i., Swe.	16	I15	58.49 N	17.50 E
Toro, Arroyo, stm., Arg.	206		34.27 S	58.52 W
Toro, Lago del, l., Chile	166	J2	51.13 S	72.47 W
Toro, Punta, c., Chile	172	F1	33.46 S	71.47 W
Törökszentmiklós, Hung.	36	B7	47.10 N	20.25 E
Torom, Russia	50	F16	54.31 N	135.49 E
Toronto, On., Can.	126	E10	43.38 N	79.24 W
Toronto, On., Can.	193b		43.39 N	79.23 W
Toronto, Ks., U.S.	130	G1	37.48 N	95.57 W
Toronto, Oh., U.S.	124	D5	40.27 N	80.36 W
Toronto, S.D., U.S.	128	G2	44.33 N	96.40 W
Toronto, co., On., Can.	193b		43.44 N	79.24 W
Toronto, University of, educ., On., Can.	193b		43.40 N	79.24 W
Toronto Harbour, b., On., Can.	193b		43.38 N	79.22 W
Toronto Island Airport, arpt., On., Can.	193b		43.38 N	79.24 W
Toronto Lake, res., Ks., U.S.	130	G2	37.46 N	95.57 W
Toronto Zoo, Metro, p.o.i., On., Can.	193b		43.49 N	79.11 W
Toro Peak, mtn., Ca., U.S.	148	J9	33.32 N	116.25 W
Toropec, Russia	26	D14	56.30 N	31.39 E
Tororo, Ug.	86	D6	0.41 N	34.10 E
Toros (Acho), Plaza de, p.o.i., Peru	204d		12.02 S	77.02 W
Toros Dağları (Taurus Mountains), mts., Tur.	42	G5	37.00 N	33.00 E
Torošino, Russia	26	C11	57.56 N	28.34 E
Torosozero, Russia	18	E25	62.31 N	38.11 E
Toroume, hill, Cook Is.	100j	b26	21.15 S	159.45 W
Torpa, hist., Swe.	16	J11	57.39 N	13.16 E
Tor Pignatara, ngh., Italy	185a		41.52 N	12.32 E
Torpo, Nor.	16	G6	60.40 N	8.43 E
Torpy, stm., B.C., Can.	144	C9	53.43 N	120.53 W
Torquay, Sk., Can.	142	E11	49.08 N	103.30 W
Torquay (Torbay), Eng., U.K.	10	K9	50.28 N	3.31 W
Torquemada, Spain	28	B6	42.02 N	4.19 W
Torrance, Ca., U.S.	148	J7	33.51 N	118.20 W
Torrance Municipal Airport, arpt., Ca., U.S.	198		33.48 N	118.20 W
Torrão, Port.	28	F2	38.17 N	8.12 W
Torrebaja, Spain	28	D9	40.07 N	1.15 W
Torreblanca, Spain	28	D11	40.13 N	0.11 E
Torrecilla, mtn., Spain	28	H6	36.41 N	4.59 W

Name	Page	Map Ref.	Latitude	Longitude
Torrecilla en Cameros, Spain	28	B8	42.15 N	2.37 W
Torre del Greco, Italy	32	D8	40.47 N	14.22 E
Torre de Moncorvo, Port.	28	C3	41.10 N	7.02 W
Torredonjimeno, Spain	28	G6	37.45 N	3.57 W
Torre Gaia, ngh., Italy	185a		41.51 N	12.39 E
Torrejon Air Base, mil., Spain	184a		40.28 N	3.28 W
Torrejoncillo, Spain	28	E4	39.54 N	6.28 W
Torrejón de Ardoz, Spain	28	D7	40.27 N	3.28 W
Torrejón-Tiétar, Embalse de, res., Spain	28	E5	39.48 N	5.54 W
Torrelaguna, Spain	28	D7	40.49 N	3.31 W
Torrelavega, Spain	28	A6	43.21 N	4.02 W
Torrellas, Riera de, stm., Spain	184d		41.23 N	2.01 E
Torrelles de Llobregat, Spain	184d		41.21 N	1.59 E
Torrelletes, Spain	184d		41.21 N	1.57 E
Torremolinos, Spain	28	H6	36.37 N	4.30 W
Torrens, Lake, l., Austl.	96	F7	31.03 S	137.51 E
Torrens Creek, Austl.	98	C5	20.46 S	145.02 E
Torrens Creek, stm., Austl.	98	D5	22.22 S	145.09 E
Torrent, Arg.	172	D9	28.50 S	56.28 W
Torrent, Spain	28	E10	39.25 N	0.27 W
Torrente see Torrent, Spain	28	E10	39.25 N	0.27 W
Torrenueva, Spain	28	F7	38.38 N	3.21 W
Torreón, Mex.	154	C7	25.33 N	103.26 W
Torre Pellice, Italy	30	F4	44.49 N	7.13 E
Torreperojil, Spain	28	F7	38.02 N	3.16 W
Torres, Braz.	172	D13	29.19 S	49.46 W
Torres, Arroyo, stm., Arg.	206		34.39 S	58.45 W
Torres, Îles, is., Vanuatu	101d	i16	13.10 S	167.07 E
Torresdale, ngh., Pa., U.S.	203		40.03 N	75.00 W
Torres Islands see Torres, Îles, is., Vanuatu	101d	i16	13.10 S	167.07 E
Torres Martinez Indian Reservation, ind. res., Ca., U.S.	148	J9	33.24 N	116.02 W
Torres Novas, Port.	28	E2	39.28 N	8.32 W
Torres Strait, strt., Oc.	101a	b3	10.25 S	142.10 E
Torres Vedras, Port.	28	E1	39.04 N	9.14 W
Torrevella, Spain	28	G10	37.58 N	0.40 W
Torrevieja see Torrevella, Spain	28	G10	37.58 N	0.40 W
Torridge, stm., Eng., U.K.	10	K8	51.02 N	4.12 W
Torridon, Scot., U.K.	10	D7	57.32 N	5.30 W
Torridon, Loch, b., Scot., U.K.	10	D7	57.35 N	5.46 W
Torriglia, Italy	30	F6	44.31 N	9.08 E
Torrijos, Spain	28	D6	39.59 N	4.17 W
Torrimpietra, ngh., Italy	185a		41.56 N	12.13 E
Torrington, Ct., U.S.	124	C12	41.48 N	73.07 W
Torrington, Wy., U.S.	140	E8	42.04 N	104.11 W
Torrinha, Braz.	170	L1	22.25 S	48.09 W
Torröjen, l., Swe.	16	D10	63.55 N	12.56 E
Torronsuon kansallispuisto, p.o.i., Fin.	18	G10	60.43 N	23.37 E
Torsa (Amo), stm., Asia	70	E12	26.15 N	89.35 E
Tor Sapienza, ngh., Italy	185a		41.54 N	12.35 E
Torsås, Swe.	16	K13	56.24 N	16.00 E
Torsburgen, hist., Swe.	16	J16	57.25 N	18.43 E
Torsby, Swe.	16	G10	60.08 N	13.00 E
Torshälla, Swe.	16	H14	59.25 N	16.28 E
Tórshavn (Thorshavn), Far. Is.	12b	n34	62.00 N	6.46 W
Torside Reservoir, res., Eng., U.K.	180		53.29 N	1.54 W
Torsö, i., Swe.	16	I11	58.48 N	13.50 E
Torto, stm., Italy	32	G7	37.58 N	13.46 E
Tortola, i., Br. Vir. Is.	158b	e8	18.27 N	64.36 W
Tórtolas, Cerro de las (Las Tórtolas, Cerro), mtn., S.A.	172	D2	29.56 S	69.53 W
Tortolì, Italy	32	E3	39.55 N	9.39 E
Tortona, Italy	30	F5	44.54 N	8.51 E
Tortorici, Italy	32	F8	38.02 N	14.49 E
Tortosa, Spain	28	D11	40.48 N	0.31 E
Tortosa, Cap de, c., Spain	28	D11	40.43 N	0.53 E
Tortue, Île de la, i., Haiti	156	B11	20.03 N	72.47 W
Tortuga Island see Tortue, Île de la, i., Haiti	156	B11	20.03 N	72.47 W
Tortuguero, Laguna, b., P.R.	158a	b2	18.28 N	66.26 W
Tortuguitas, Arg.	206		34.28 S	58.46 W
Torue, Indon.	66	D12	0.57 S	120.17 E
Toruń, Pol.	24	C14	53.01 N	18.36 E
Torup, Swe.	16	K11	56.57 N	13.05 E
Tõrva, Est.	26	B8	58.00 N	25.55 E
Tory Island, i., Ire.	10	F4	55.16 N	8.14 W
Torysa, stm., Slvk.	24	G16	48.39 N	21.21 E
Toržok, Russia	26	C17	57.02 N	34.57 E
Torzym, Pol.	24	D11	52.18 N	15.03 E
Tosa, Japan	56	F6	33.29 N	133.25 E
Tosa-shimizu, Japan	56	G5	32.46 N	132.58 E
Tosa-wan, b., Japan	56	F6	33.20 N	133.40 E
Tosca, S. Afr.	90	D6	25.52 S	23.57 E
Toscana, state, Italy	30	G8	43.30 N	11.00 E
Toscano, stm., Mex.	154	F7	18.01 N	102.33 W
Tosen, Nor.	16	B10	65.16 N	12.47 E
Tosen, b., Nor.	16	B10	65.12 N	12.43 E
Toses, Collada de, p., Spain	28	B12	42.19 N	1.58 E
Toshima, ngh., Japan	186		35.44 N	139.43 E
To-shima, i., Japan	56	E12	34.31 N	139.17 E
Tosi, Indon.	66	H11	9.34 S	118.57 E
Tosna, stm., Russia	26	A13	59.46 N	30.46 E
Tosno, Russia	26	A13	59.33 N	30.52 E
Toson Hu, l., China	52	D4	35.16 N	98.35 E
Tosontsengel, Mong.	52	B4	48.45 N	98.16 E
Tostado, Arg.	172	D7	29.13 S	61.45 W
Tõstamaa, Est.	26	B6	58.20 N	23.59 E
Tosu, Japan	56	F3	33.21 N	130.31 E
Tosya, Tur.	42	E5	40.59 N	34.04 E
Totagatic, stm., Wi., U.S.	128	E7	46.05 N	92.09 W
Totak, l., Nor.	16	H5	59.42 N	7.57 E
Totana, Spain	28	G9	37.46 N	1.29 W
Toteng, Bots.	90	B6	20.21 S	22.57 E
Tôtes, Fr.	20	E9	49.40 N	1.02 E
Totes Gebirge, mts., Aus.	30	C11	47.39 N	14.01 E
Totiyas, Som.	86	D8	3.56 N	43.58 E
Tot'ma, Russia	12	F20	59.58 N	42.45 E
Totness, Sur.	164	B6	5.53 N	56.19 W
Totoras, Arg.	172	F7	32.36 S	61.10 W
Totoya, i., Fiji	101e	q20	18.56 S	179.51 W
Totsuka, ngh., Japan	186		35.24 N	139.32 E
Tottenham, Austl.	98	I6	32.14 S	147.21 E
Tottenham, On., Can.	126	D10	44.01 N	79.49 W
Tottenham, ngh., Eng., U.K.	178		51.35 N	0.04 W
Tottenham Hotspur Football Ground, p.o.i., Eng., U.K.	178		51.36 N	0.04 W
Tottenville, ngh., N.Y., U.S.	194		40.31 N	74.15 W
Totteridge, ngh., Eng., U.K.	178		51.38 N	0.12 W
Tottori, Japan	56	D7	35.30 N	134.14 E
Tottori, state, Japan	56	D6	35.30 N	134.00 E
Touba, C. Iv.	84	H3	8.16 N	7.41 W
Toubkal, Jebel, mtn., Mor.	84	C3	31.05 N	7.55 W
Touchet, stm., Wa., U.S.	146	D8	46.02 N	118.41 W
Touchwood Hills, plat., Sk., Can.	142	C9	51.25 N	104.16 W
Touchwood Lake, l., Ab., Can.	144	B19	54.50 N	111.23 W
Toudao, stm., China	54	C7	42.37 N	127.09 E
Touggourt, Alg.	84	C6	33.06 N	6.04 E
Toughkenamon, Pa., U.S.	203		39.50 N	75.46 W
Touho, N. Cal.	101d	m15	20.47 S	165.13 E
Toul, Fr.	20	F14	48.40 N	5.53 E
Touléplei, C. Iv.	84	H3	6.34 N	8.25 W
Touliu, Tai.	58	J9	23.42 N	120.31 E
Toulon, Fr.	22	F11	43.07 N	5.56 E
Toulon, Il., U.S.	130	C8	41.05 N	89.51 W
Toulon Lake, l., Nv., U.S.	148	C7	40.01 N	118.39 W
Toulon-sur-Arroux, Fr.	20	H13	46.42 N	4.08 E
Toulourenc, stm., Fr.	22	E11	44.14 N	5.09 E
Toulouse, Fr.	22	F7	43.36 N	1.26 E
Toumodi, C. Iv.	84	H3	6.33 N	5.01 W
Tounassine, Hamada, des., Alg.	84	D3	28.30 N	5.00 W
Toungo, Nig.	84	H7	8.06 N	12.01 E
Toungoo, Mya.	64	C3	18.56 N	96.26 E
Touques, stm., Fr.	20	E9	49.22 N	0.04 E
Tour, Étang de la, l., Fr.	179		48.40 N	1.53 E
Touraine, hist. reg., Fr.	20	G9	47.12 N	0.40 E
Tourakom, Laos	64	C6	18.25 N	102.32 E
Tourane see Da Nang, Viet.	64	D9	16.03 N	108.11 E
Tourcoing, Fr.	20	D12	50.43 N	3.08 E
Touriñan, Cabo, c., Spain	28	A1	43.03 N	9.17 W
Tournai, Bel.	20	D12	50.36 N	3.23 E
Tournon, Fr.	22	D10	45.04 N	4.50 E
Tournus, Fr.	20	H13	46.34 N	4.53 E
Touros, Braz.	170	C8	5.12 S	35.28 W
Tours, Fr.	20	G9	47.23 N	0.42 E
Toussidé, Pic, vol., Chad	82	C3	21.02 N	16.27 E
Toussus-le-Noble, Fr.	179		48.45 N	2.07 E
Toussus-le-Noble, Aéroport de, arpt., Fr.	179		48.45 N	2.06 E
Toutle, stm., Wa., U.S.	146	D4	46.18 N	122.54 W
Toutle, South Fork, stm., Wa., U.S.	146	D4	46.19 N	122.43 W
Touws, stm., S. Afr.	90	H5	33.44 S	21.10 E
Touwsrivier, S. Afr.	90	H5	33.20 S	20.01 E
Toužim, Czech Rep.	24	F9	50.03 N	12.58 E
Tova, Russia	14	G31	65.46 N	40.26 E
Tovar, Ven.	168	C6	8.19 N	71.45 W
Tovarkovskij, Russia	26	G21	53.39 N	38.13 E
Tovdalselva, stm., Nor.	16	I6	58.15 N	8.09 E
Tovste, Ukr.	38	E4	48.50 N	25.43 E
Tovtry, plat., Ukr.	38	E5	48.56 N	26.29 E
Tovuz, Azer.	42	E11	40.59 N	45.37 E
Tow, Tx., U.S.	136	D9	30.53 N	98.28 W
Towada, Japan	54	D14	40.37 N	141.12 E
Towamencin Creek, stm., Pa., U.S.	203		40.13 N	75.23 W
Towanda, Ks., U.S.	138	D12	37.48 N	96.59 W
Towanda, Pa., U.S.	124	C9	41.46 N	76.27 W
Towanda Creek, stm., Pa., U.S.	126	G13	41.44 N	76.26 W
Tower, Mn., U.S.	128	D6	47.48 N	92.16 W
Tower City, N.D., U.S.	142	H16	46.55 N	97.40 W
Tower City, Pa., U.S.	124	D9	40.34 N	76.34 W
Tower Hamlets, ngh., Eng., U.K.	178		51.32 N	0.03 W
Tower Hill, Austl.	98	D5	22.05 S	144.35 E
Tower Hill, Il., U.S.	130	E9	39.22 N	88.57 W
Towerhill Creek, stm., Austl.	98	C5	22.28 S	144.34 E
Tower of London, hist., Eng., U.K.	178		51.30 N	0.05 W
Towers of Silence, rel., India	190c		18.58 N	72.48 E
Tower Soudan State Park, p.o.i., Mn., U.S.	128	D6	47.49 N	92.15 W
Towla, Mount, mtn., Zimb.	90	B9	21.22 S	29.52 E
Town, stm., Ma., U.S.	201		42.00 N	70.57 W
Town and Country, Wa., U.S.	146	C9	47.41 N	117.24 W
Town Creek, stm., Al., U.S.	134	C13	34.24 N	86.13 W
Town Creek, stm., Al., U.S.	134	C11	34.47 N	87.25 W
Towneley Hall, hist., Eng., U.K.	180		53.46 N	2.13 W
Towner, N.D., U.S.	142	F13	48.20 N	100.24 W
Town Estates, N.J., U.S.	203		40.04 N	74.52 W
Town Hill, hill, Ber.	158e	k16	32.19 N	64.44 W
Townline Tunnel, trans., On., Can.	202a		42.57 N	79.15 W
Town of Niagara, N.Y., U.S.	202a		43.06 N	78.59 W
Townsend, Mt., U.S.	146	D15	46.19 N	111.31 W
Townsend Island, i., N.Y., U.S.	194		40.38 N	73.26 W
Townshend Island, i., Austl.	98	D8	22.15 S	150.30 E
Township Line Run, stm., Pa., U.S.	197b		40.13 N	79.33 W
Townsville, Austl.	98	B6	19.16 S	146.48 E
Towra Point, c., Austl.	192a		34.00 S	151.10 E
Towson, Md., U.S.	124	E9	39.23 N	76.35 W
Towson State College, educ., Md., U.S.	202b		39.24 N	76.37 W
Towuti, Danau, l., Indon.	60	F7	2.45 S	121.32 E
Toxkan see Ak-Saj, stm., Asia	48	F13	40.56 N	78.09 E
Toyah, Tx., U.S.	136	C4	31.19 N	103.47 W
Toyah Creek, stm., Tx., U.S.	136	D4	31.18 N	103.26 W
Toyama, Japan	56	C10	36.41 N	137.13 E
Toyama, state, Japan	56	C10	36.30 N	137.30 E
Toyama-heiya, pl., Japan	56	C10	36.40 N	137.15 E
Toyama-wan, b., Japan	56	C10	36.50 N	137.10 E
Tōyō, Japan	56	F7	33.30 N	134.15 E
Tōyo, Japan	56	F6	33.54 N	133.05 E
Toyoda, Japan	186		35.39 N	139.23 E
Toyofuta, Japan	186		35.53 N	139.57 E
Toyohashi, Japan	56	E10	34.45 N	137.22 E
Toyokawa, Japan	56	E10	34.49 N	137.23 E
Toyonaka, Japan	56	E8	34.47 N	135.28 E
Toyooka, Japan	56	D7	35.31 N	134.49 E
Toyooka, Japan	186		35.11 N	139.58 E
Toyosaka, Japan	56	B12	37.56 N	139.13 E
Toyota, Japan	56	D10	35.05 N	137.09 E
Toyoura, Japan	56	E3	34.09 N	130.56 E
Toy's Hill, Eng., U.K.	178		51.14 N	0.06 E
Tozer, Mount, mtn., Austl.	96	B8	12.45 S	143.13 E
Tozeur, Tun.	84	C6	33.55 N	8.08 E
Tpig, Russia	42	E12	41.47 N	47.36 E
Traar, ngh., Ger.	181		51.23 N	6.36 E
Trabiju, Braz.	170	K1	22.02 S	48.18 W
Trabzon, Tur.	42	E8	40.59 N	39.43 E
Trabzon, state, Tur.	42	E8	40.50 N	39.50 E
Tracadie, N.B., Can.	122	C12	47.30 N	64.54 W
Tra Cu, Viet.	64	H8	9.43 N	106.15 E
Tracy, Qc., Can.	126	C16	46.00 N	73.08 W
Tracy, Ca., U.S.	148	F4	37.44 N	121.25 W
Tracy, Mn., U.S.	128	G3	44.14 N	95.37 W
Tracy City, Tn., U.S.	134	B13	35.15 N	85.44 W
Tradewater, stm., Ky., U.S.	130	G10	37.30 N	88.03 W
Traer, Ia., U.S.	130	B5	42.11 N	92.28 W
Trafalgar, On., Can.	193b		43.29 N	79.43 W
Trafalgar, Cabo, c., Spain	28	H4	36.11 N	6.01 W
Trafaria, Port.	184c		38.40 N	9.14 W
Trafford, mun., Eng., U.K.	180		53.24 N	2.21 W
Trafford, mun., Eng., U.K.	180		53.24 N	2.21 W
Trafford Park, Eng., U.K.	180		53.28 N	2.20 W
Tragacete, Spain	28	D9	40.21 N	1.51 W
Tragliata, ngh., Italy	185a		41.58 N	12.15 E
Traição, Córrego, stm., Braz.	205b		23.36 S	46.41 W
Traíd, Spain	28	D9	40.40 N	1.49 W
Tráighlí see Tralee, Ire.	10	I3	52.16 N	9.42 W
Traiguén, Chile	172	I1	38.14 S	72.40 W
Trail, B.C., Can.	144	G13	49.06 N	117.42 W
Traill Ø, i., Grnld.	108	C21	72.32 N	23.10 W
Trail of Tears State Park, p.o.i., Mo., U.S.	130	G8	37.27 N	89.29 W
Trail Ridge, mts., U.S.	132	F3	30.35 N	82.05 W
Trainer, Pa., U.S.	203		39.50 N	75.25 W
Traipu, Braz.	170	E7	9.58 S	37.01 W
Traíra (Taraira), stm., S.A.	168	H7	1.04 S	69.25 W
Traíras, stm., Braz.	170	H1	14.07 S	48.31 W
Trairi, Braz.	170	B6	3.17 S	39.15 W
Traîtres, Baie des see Taaoa, Baie, b., Fr. Poly.	100g	s18	9.50 S	139.02 W
Trajouce, Port.	184c		38.44 N	9.20 W
Trakai, Lith.	26	F7	54.37 N	24.55 E
Trakija see Thrace, hist. reg., Eur.	8	G14	41.20 N	26.45 E
Tralee, Ire.	10	I3	52.16 N	9.42 W
Tralee Bay, b., Ire.	10	I3	52.15 N	9.58 W
Trá Lí see Tralee, Ire.	10	I3	52.16 N	9.42 W
Trammel, Va., U.S.	124	G3	37.00 N	82.17 W
Trammel Creek, stm., U.S.	130	H11	36.52 N	86.22 W
Tramore, Ire.	10	I5	52.09 N	7.09 W
Tramperos Creek (Punta de Agua Creek), stm., U.S.	138	E5	35.32 N	102.27 W
Tramping Lake, l., Sk., Can.	142	B5	52.07 N	108.48 W
Tra My, Viet.	64	E9	15.20 N	108.13 E
Trăn, Blg.	36	G9	42.50 N	22.38 E
Tranås, Swe.	16	I12	58.03 N	14.59 E
Trancão, stm., Port.	184c		38.48 N	9.06 W
Trancas, Arg.	172	C5	26.13 S	65.17 W
Tranco de Beas, Embalse de, res., Spain	28	F8	38.10 N	2.46 W
Trancoso, Port.	28	D3	40.47 N	7.21 W
Tranebjerg, Den.	16	L8	55.50 N	10.36 E
Tranemo, Swe.	16	J11	57.29 N	13.22 E
Trang, Thai.	64	I4	7.32 N	99.36 E
Trangan, Pulau, i., Indon.	60	G9	6.35 S	134.20 E
Trang Dinh, Viet.	64	A8	22.14 N	106.29 E
Trangie, Austl.	98	I6	32.02 S	147.59 E
Trängletsjön, l., Swe.	16	F11	61.32 N	13.26 E
Trängslet, Swe.	16	F11	61.25 N	13.40 E
Trani, Italy	32	C10	41.16 N	16.25 E
Tranmere, Eng., U.K.	180		53.23 N	3.01 W
Tranøya, Nor.	14	D6	68.11 N	15.38 E
Tranqueras, Ur.	172	E10	31.11 S	55.46 W
Transantarctic Mountains, mts., Ant.	103	D30	85.00 S	175.00 W
Transit Airpark, arpt., N.Y., U.S.	202a		43.06 N	78.44 W
Transkei, hist. reg., S. Afr.	90	G8	31.12 S	28.44 E
Transtrand, Swe.	16	F11	61.04 N	13.19 E
Transtrandsfjällen, mts., Swe.	16	G11	61.10 N	13.06 E
Transylvania, hist. reg., Rom.	36	C10	46.44 N	23.37 E
Transylvanian Alps see Carpații Meridionali, mts., Rom.	36	D10	45.25 N	23.32 E
Tranters Creek, stm., N.C., U.S.	132	A8	35.34 N	77.04 W
Trapani, Italy	32	F6	38.01 N	12.31 E
Traphole Brook, stm., Ma., U.S.	201		42.10 N	71.11 W
Trapper Peak, mtn., Mt., U.S.	146	E12	45.54 N	114.18 W
Trapuá, stm., Braz.	205b		23.36 S	46.17 W
Traralgon, Austl.	98	L6	38.12 S	146.32 E
Trârza, reg., Maur.	84	F1	18.00 N	15.00 W
Trascău, Munții, mts., Rom.	36	C10	46.16 N	23.24 E
Trasimeno, Lago, l., Italy	30	G9	43.08 N	12.06 E
Träslövsläge, Swe.	16	J10	57.04 N	12.17 E
Trás-os-Montes, hist. reg., Port.	28	C3	41.30 N	7.15 W
Trăstenik, Blg.	36	F11	43.31 N	24.28 E
Trat, Thai.	64	F6	12.14 N	102.30 E
Traun, Aus.	30	B11	48.12 N	14.14 E
Traun, stm., Aus.	30	B11	48.16 N	14.22 E
Traun, stm., Ger.	30	B9	48.00 N	12.32 E
Traunsee, l., Aus.	30	C10	47.51 N	13.48 E
Traunstein, Ger.	24	I8	47.52 N	12.38 E
Travellers Lake, l., Austl.	98	I4	33.18 S	142.00 E
Travers, Mount, mtn., N.Z.	102	E5	42.01 S	172.44 E
Traverse, Lake, res., U.S.	128	F2	45.42 N	96.43 W
Traverse Bay, b., Mb., Can.	142	D17	50.40 N	96.25 W
Traverse City, Mi., U.S.	126	D4	44.45 N	85.36 W
Travers Reservoir, res., Ab., Can.	144	F18	50.13 N	112.51 W
Tra Vinh, Viet.	64	H8	9.56 N	106.20 E
Travis, Lake, l., Tx., U.S.	136	D10	30.24 N	97.56 W
Travis Air Force Base, mil., Ca., U.S.	148	E4	38.16 N	121.58 W
Travnik, Bos.	36	E4	44.13 N	17.39 E
Travo, stm., Fr.	22	H15	41.55 N	9.24 E
Trayning, Austl.	96	F3	31.07 S	117.47 E
Trbovlje, Slvn.	30	D12	46.09 N	15.03 E
Treales, Eng., U.K.	180		53.47 N	2.51 W
Treasure Island Naval Station, mil., Ca., U.S.	200		37.49 N	122.22 W
Trebbia, stm., Italy	30	F6	45.04 N	9.41 E
Třebechovice pod Orebem, Czech Rep.	24	F12	50.12 N	16.00 E
Třebíč, Czech Rep.	24	G11	49.12 N	15.51 E
Trebinje, Bos.	36	G5	42.42 N	18.23 E
Trebisacce, Italy	32	E10	39.52 N	16.32 E
Trebišov, Slvk.	24	H17	48.38 N	21.43 E
Trebizond see Trabzon, Tur.	42	E8	40.59 N	39.43 E
Treblinka, Pol.	24	D18	52.39 N	22.02 E
Třeboň, Czech Rep.	24	G10	49.00 N	14.45 E
Trece Martires, Phil.	68	C3	14.16 N	120.51 E
Treene, stm., Ger.	24	B5	54.22 N	9.05 E
Trees Mills, Pa., U.S.	197b		40.23 N	80.13 W
Tregosse Islets, is., Austl.	98	A8	17.41 S	150.43 E
Tregubovo, Russia	26	B14	58.58 N	31.32 E
Tréguier, Fr.	20	F5	48.47 N	3.14 W
Treherne, Mb., Can.	142	E15	49.38 N	98.41 W
Trehörningsjö, Swe.	16	D16	63.42 N	18.52 E
Treinta y Tres, Ur.	172	F10	33.13 S	54.22 W
Trélazé, Fr.	20	G8	47.27 N	0.28 W
Trelew, Arg.	166	H3	43.15 S	65.18 W
Trelleborg, Swe.	16	L11	55.22 N	13.10 E
Tremadog Bay, b., Wales, U.K.	10	I8	52.52 N	4.12 W
Tremblant, Mont, mtn., Qc., Can.	126	B15	46.16 N	74.35 W
Tremblay, Hippodrome du, p.o.i., Fr.	179		48.50 N	2.29 E
Tremblay-lès-Gonesse, Fr.	179		48.59 N	2.34 E
Trembleur Lake, l., B.C., Can.	144	B5	54.51 N	125.03 W
Tremedal, Braz.	170	H5	14.55 S	41.26 W
Tremiti, Isole, is., Italy	30	H12	42.06 N	15.29 E
Tremont, Il., U.S.	128	K9	40.31 N	89.29 W
Tremont, ngh., N.Y., U.S.	194		40.51 N	73.55 W
Tremonton, Ut., U.S.	150	B4	41.43 N	112.09 W
Tremp, Spain	28	B11	42.09 N	0.53 E
Trempealeau, Wi., U.S.	128	G7	44.00 N	91.25 W
Trempealeau, stm., Wi., U.S.	128	G7	44.01 N	91.33 W
Trena, Eth.	86	B8	10.45 N	40.39 E
Trenche, stm., Qc., Can.	122	B4	47.45 N	72.53 W
Trenčín, Slvk.	24	H14	48.53 N	18.03 E
Trenel, Arg.	172	G5	35.41 S	64.11 W
Trêng, Camb.	64	F6	12.50 N	102.54 E
Trenggalek, Indon.	66	H7	8.03 S	111.42 E
Trenque Lauquen, Arg.	172	G6	35.58 S	62.44 W
Trent see Trento, Italy	30	D8	46.03 N	11.07 E
Trent, stm., On., Can.	126	D12	44.05 N	77.33 W
Trent, stm., Eng., U.K.	10	H12	53.42 N	0.42 W
Trent, stm., N.C., U.S.	132	A8	35.06 N	77.01 W
Trent and Mersey Canal, can., Eng., U.K.	180		53.19 N	2.39 W
Trente et Un Milles, Lac des, l., Qc., Can.	126	B13	46.09 N	75.48 W
Trentino-Alto Adige, state, Italy	30	D8	46.30 N	11.20 E
Trento (Trent), Italy	30	D8	46.03 N	11.07 E
Trenton, N.S., Can.	122	E14	45.36 N	62.38 W
Trenton, On., Can.	126	D12	44.05 N	77.35 W
Trenton, Fl., U.S.	132	G3	29.37 N	82.49 W
Trenton, Ga., U.S.	134	C13	34.52 N	85.30 W
Trenton, Ky., U.S.	130	H10	36.43 N	87.15 W
Trenton, Mo., U.S.	130	D4	40.04 N	93.37 W
Trenton, Ne., U.S.	138	A8	40.10 N	101.01 W
Trenton, N.J., U.S.	124	D11	40.13 N	74.44 W
Trenton, N.C., U.S.	132	A8	35.03 N	77.21 W
Trenton, Tn., U.S.	130	I8	35.58 N	88.56 W
Trenton, Tx., U.S.	134	D2	33.26 N	96.19 W
Trenton, Canadian Forces Base, mil., On., Can.	126	D12	44.07 N	77.33 W
Trenton Channel, mth., Mi., U.S.	199		42.06 N	83.11 W
Trentwood, Wa., U.S.	146	C9	47.43 N	117.10 W
Trepassey, Nf., Can.	111a	j23	46.44 N	53.22 W
Tres Algarrobos, Arg.	172	G6	35.58 S	62.48 W
Tres Árboles, Ur.	166	F5	32.23 S	56.42 W
Tres Arroyos, Arg.	172	I7	38.21 S	60.16 W
Três Corações, Braz.	170	K3	21.41 S	45.15 W
Três Coroas, Braz.	172	D12	29.34 S	50.47 W
Tres de Febrero, state, Arg.	206		34.36 S	58.35 W
Três de Maio, Braz.	172	C10	27.46 S	54.14 W
Tres Esquinas, Col.	168	G4	0.43 N	75.14 W
Tres Isletas, Arg.	172	C7	26.20 S	60.25 W
Três Lagoas, Braz.	166	D6	20.47 S	51.42 W
Tres Lagos, Arg.	166	I2	49.36 S	71.29 W
Tres Lomas, Arg.	172	H6	36.27 S	62.52 W
Três Marias, Braz.	170	J3	18.12 S	45.13 W
Tres Marías, Islas, is., Mex.	154	E5	21.32 N	106.31 W
Três Marias, Represa de, res., Braz.	170	J3	18.14 S	45.15 W
Tres Montes, Península, pen., Chile	166	I1	46.50 S	75.30 W
Tres Montosas, mtn., N.M., U.S.	150	I9	34.06 N	107.28 W
Tres Morros, Alto de, mtn., Col.	168	D3	7.08 N	76.11 W
Tres Padres, Pico, mtn., Mex.	204a		19.35 N	99.08 W
Tres Palacios, stm., Tx., U.S.	136	E11	28.45 N	96.08 W
Tres Palos, Laguna, l., Mex.	154	G9	16.46 N	99.44 W
Três Passos, Braz.	172	C11	27.27 S	53.55 W
Tres Picos, Cerro, mtn., Arg.	172	I6	38.09 S	61.57 W
Três Pontas, Braz.	170	K3	21.22 S	45.30 W
Tres Puntas, Cabo, c., Arg.	166	I3	47.06 S	65.53 W
Três Ranchos, Braz.	170	J2	18.22 S	47.46 W
Três Rios, Braz.	170	L4	22.06 S	43.12 W
Tressancourt, Fr.	179		48.55 N	2.00 E
Třešť, Czech Rep.	24	G11	49.17 N	15.28 E
Tres Vírgenes, Volcán de las, vol., Mex.	154	B2	27.27 N	112.34 W
Tres Zapotes, hist., Mex.	154	F11	18.28 N	95.24 W
Tret'akovskaja Galereja, bldg., Russia	183b		55.45 N	37.37 E
Tretten, Nor.	16	F8	61.18 N	10.18 E
Treuchtlingen, Ger.	24	H6	48.57 N	10.54 E
Treuenbrietzen, Ger.	24	D8	52.05 N	12.52 E
Trèves see Trier, Ger.	24	G2	49.45 N	6.38 E
Treviglio, Italy	30	E6	45.31 N	9.35 E
Treviño, Spain	28	B8	42.44 N	2.44 W
Treviso, Italy	30	E9	45.40 N	12.14 E
Trevorton, Pa., U.S.	124	D9	40.46 N	76.40 W
Trevose Head, c., Eng., U.K.	10	K7	50.32 N	5.02 W
Trevose Heights, Pa., U.S.	203		40.09 N	74.59 W
Trezevant, Tn., U.S.	130	H9	36.01 N	88.37 W
Trezzano sul Naviglio, Italy	184b		45.25 N	9.04 E
Trgovište, Yugo.	36	G9	42.22 N	22.05 E
Trhové Sviny, Czech Rep.	24	H10	48.51 N	14.38 E
Triabunna, Austl.	99a	o13	42.30 S	147.55 E
Triangle, Eng., U.K.	180		53.42 N	1.56 W
Triánta, Grc.	34	G11	36.25 N	28.08 E
Triberg, Ger.	24	H4	48.07 N	8.14 E
Tribobó, Braz.	205a		22.52 S	43.01 W
Triborough Bridge, trans., N.Y., U.S.	194		40.47 N	73.55 W
Tribugá, Ensenada de, b., Col.	168	E3	5.47 N	77.23 W
Tribune, Sk., Can.	142	E10	49.14 N	103.49 W
Tribune, Ks., U.S.	138	C7	38.27 N	101.44 W
Tribune Channel, strt., B.C., Can.	144	F4	50.50 N	126.16 W
Tribuswinkel, Aus.	182b		48.00 N	16.16 E
Tricarico, Italy	32	D10	40.37 N	16.08 E
Tricase, Italy	32	E13	39.56 N	18.22 E
Trichinopoly see Tiruchchirāppalli, India	69	F4	10.48 N	78.41 E
Trichonida, Límni, l., Grc.	34	E4	38.34 N	21.30 E
Trichūr, India	69	F3	10.30 N	76.12 E
Tri County Supply Canal, can., Ne., U.S.	140	G12	40.51 N	100.10 W
Trida, Austl.	98	I5	33.01 S	145.00 E
Trident Peak, mtn., Nv., U.S.	148	B7	41.54 N	118.25 W
Trieben, Aus.	24	I10	47.29 N	14.28 E
Triel-sur-Seine, Fr.	179		48.59 N	2.00 E
Trier, Ger.	24	G2	49.45 N	6.38 E
Triest see Trieste, Italy	30	E10	45.40 N	13.45 E
Trieste (Trst), Italy	30	E10	45.40 N	13.45 E
Trieste, Golfo di see Trieste, Gulf of, b., Eur.	30	E10	45.38 N	13.28 E
Trieste, Gulf of, b., Eur.	30	E10	45.38 N	13.28 E
Trieux, stm., Fr.	20	F5	48.49 N	3.05 W
Triglav, mtn., Slvn.	30	D10	46.23 N	13.50 E
Triglavski narodni park, p.o.i., Slvn.	30	D10	45.27 N	14.37 E
Trigueros, Spain	28	G4	37.23 N	6.50 W
Tríkala, Grc.	34	D4	39.33 N	21.46 E
Trikora, Puncak, mtn., Indon.	60	F10	4.17 S	138.39 E
Trilbardou, Fr.	179		48.57 N	2.48 E
Trilby, Fl., U.S.	132	H3	28.27 N	82.11 W
Trim, Ire.	10	H6	53.33 N	6.48 W
Trimān, Pak.	70	D2	29.37 N	69.05 E
Trimont, Mn., U.S.	128	H4	43.45 N	94.43 W
Trinchera Creek, stm., Co., U.S.	138	D3	37.19 N	105.44 W
Trincheras, Mex.	120	F7	30.23 N	111.31 W
Trincomalee, Sri L.	69	G5	8.34 N	81.14 E
Trindade, Braz.	170	I1	16.39 S	49.29 W
Trindade, i., Braz.	162	H12	20.30 S	29.19 W
Třinec, Czech Rep.	24	G14	49.41 N	18.40 E
Trinidad, Bol.	166	B3	14.48 S	64.53 W
Trinidad, Col.	168	E6	5.24 N	71.39 W
Trinidad, Cuba	156	B8	21.48 N	79.59 W
Trinidad, Co., U.S.	138	D4	37.10 N	104.30 W
Trinidad, Tx., U.S.	136	B11	32.09 N	96.05 W
Trinidad, Ur.	172	F9	33.32 S	56.53 W
Trinidad, i., Trin.	159f	s13	10.30 N	61.15 W
Trinidad, Isla, i., Arg.	172	I7	39.00 S	61.31 W
Trinidad and Tobago, ctry., N.A.	168	B11	11.00 N	61.00 W
Trinité, Havre de la, b., Mart.	159c	k7	14.44 N	60.57 W
Trinity, Tx., U.S.	136	D12	30.55 N	95.22 W
Trinity, stm., Ca., U.S.	148	C3	41.11 N	123.42 W
Trinity, stm., Tx., U.S.	136	C12	29.45 N	94.41 W
Trinity, Clear Fork, stm., Tx., U.S.	136	B10	32.45 N	97.20 W
Trinity, Elm Fork, stm., Tx., U.S.	138	H11	32.47 N	96.53 W
Trinity, South Fork, stm., Ca., U.S.	148	C2	40.53 N	123.35 W
Trinity, West Fork, stm., Tx., U.S.	138	H11	32.47 N	96.53 W
Trinity Bay, b., Nf., Can.	111a	j23	47.59 N	53.31 W
Trinity Bay, b., Tx., U.S.	136	E13	29.40 N	94.45 W
Trinity Islands, is., Ak., U.S.	109	E9	56.31 N	154.23 W
Trinity Mountain, mtn., Id., U.S.	146	G11	43.36 N	115.26 W
Trinity Mountains, mts., Ca., U.S.	148	B3	40.52 N	122.33 W
Trinity Park, p.o.i., On., Can.	193b		43.39 N	79.25 W
Trinity Peak, mtn., Nv., U.S.	148	C7	40.14 N	118.45 W
Trinity Site, hist., N.M., U.S.	138	H2	33.41 N	106.28 W
Trino, Italy	30	E5	45.12 N	8.18 E
Triolo, stm., Italy	32	C9	41.39 N	15.33 E
Trion, Ga., U.S.	134	C13	34.32 N	85.18 W
Trionto, stm., Italy	32	E10	39.37 N	16.45 E
Triora, Italy	30	G4	43.59 N	7.46 E
Tripa, stm., Indon.	64	J3	3.53 N	96.21 E
Trípoli, Grc.	34	F5	37.30 N	22.22 E
Tripoli see Tarābulus, Leb.	76	D6	34.26 N	35.51 E
Tripoli see Tarābulus, Libya	82	A2	32.52 N	13.10 E
Tripoli, Ia., U.S.	128	I6	42.48 N	92.15 W
Tripolis, hist., Tur.	34	F12	37.58 N	28.59 E
Tripolitania see Ṭarābulus, hist. reg., Libya	82	A2	31.00 N	15.00 E
Tripp, S.D., U.S.	140	D15	43.13 N	97.57 W
Trips Subdivision, Mi., U.S.	199		42.34 N	83.25 W
Tripura, state, India	70	G13	24.00 N	92.00 E
Trisanna, stm., Aus.	30	C7	47.07 N	10.29 E
Tristan da Cunha Group, is., St. Hel.	80	J4	37.15 S	12.30 W
Tristao, Îles, is., Gui.	84	G2	10.53 N	14.58 W
Tristate Village, Il., U.S.	196		41.44 N	87.57 W
Triste, Spain	28	B10	42.24 N	0.43 W
Triste, Golfo, b., Ven.	168	B7	10.40 N	68.10 W
Tri Ton, Viet.	64	G7	10.25 N	105.00 E
Triuggio, Italy	184b		45.40 N	9.16 E
Triumph, La., U.S.	134	H9	29.19 N	89.28 W
Trivandrum, India	69	G3	8.30 N	76.57 E
Trivento, Italy	30	I11	41.47 N	14.32 E
Trnava, Slvk.	24	H13	48.22 N	17.35 E
Trnovo see Veliko Tărnovo, Blg.	36	F12	43.04 N	25.38 E
Trobriand Islands see Kiriwina Islands, is., Pap. N. Gui.	101a	b5	8.35 S	151.05 E
Trochu, Ab., Can.	144	E17	51.49 N	113.13 W
Troekurovo, Russia	40	E11	53.24 N	39.42 E
Trofa, Arroyo de, stm., Spain	184a		40.30 N	3.45 W
Trofors, Nor.	16	B11	65.32 N	13.22 E
Trogir, Cro.	30	G13	43.31 N	16.14 E
Troia, Italy	32	C9	41.22 N	15.18 E
Troianiv, Ukr.	38	C7	50.06 N	28.32 E
Troianivka, Ukr.	38	B4	51.20 N	25.17 E
Troice-Lykovo, ngh., Russia	183b		55.47 N	37.24 E
Troick, Russia	48	D10	54.05 N	61.32 E
Troick, Russia	48	C16	57.24 N	94.48 E
Troickaja, Russia	38	H17	45.07 N	38.07 E
Troickij, Russia	40	F13	50.14 N	43.03 E
Troickij, Russia	40	F19	50.42 N	54.36 E
Troickij Sungur, Russia	40	E15	53.16 N	47.36 E
Troickoe, Russia	40	H14	46.25 N	44.15 E
Troickoe, Russia	40	E20	52.19 N	56.18 E
Troickoe, Russia	40	E18	53.05 N	52.30 E
Troickoe, Russia	48	D15	52.58 N	84.40 E
Troickoe, Russia	50	G16	49.26 N	136.33 E
Troicko-Pečorsk, Russia	48	B9	62.42 N	56.12 E
Troina, Italy	32	G8	37.47 N	14.36 E
Troisdorf, Ger.	24	F3	50.49 N	7.07 E
Trois-Pistoles, Qc., Can.	122	B7	48.06 N	69.11 W
Trois Pitons, Morne, vol., Dom.	159c	j6	15.22 N	61.20 W
Trois-Rivières, Qc., Can.	122	D4	46.21 N	72.33 W
Trois-Rivières, Guad.	159c	i5	15.58 N	61.37 W
Troitsk see Troick, Russia	48	D10	54.05 N	61.32 E
Troïts'ke, Ukr.	38	F9	47.37 N	30.18 E
Troïts'ke, Ukr.	38	D17	49.55 N	38.18 E
Trojan, Blg.	36	G11	42.51 N	24.43 E
Trojanova Tabla, hist., Yugo.	36	E9	44.37 N	22.20 E
Trollhättan, Swe.	16	I10	58.16 N	12.17 E
Trollheta, mtn., Nor.	16	E6	62.55 N	9.09 E
Trolltindane, mtn., Nor.	16	E5	62.28 N	7.42 E
Trombay, ngh., India	190c		19.02 N	72.57 E

Name	Page	Map Ref.	Latitude	Longitude
Trombetas, stm., Braz.	164	C6	1.54 S	55.36 W
Tromelin, Île, i., Reu.	80	H11	15.53 S	54.31 E
Tromøy, i., Nor.	16	I6	58.27 N	8.51 E
Trompsburg, S. Afr.	90	G7	30.01 S	25.45 E
Troms, state, Nor.	14	C10	69.15 N	19.40 E
Tromsø, Nor.	14	C9	69.39 N	18.56 E
Tron, mtn., Nor.	16	E8	62.11 N	10.40 E
Trona, Ca., U.S.	148	H8	35.45 N	117.22 W
Tronador, Cerro, mtn., S.A.	166	H2	41.10 S	71.54 W
Tronador, Monte see Tronador, Cerro, mtn., S.A.	166	H2	41.10 S	71.54 W
Troncoso, Mex.	154	D7	22.44 N	102.22 W
Trondheim, Nor.	16	D8	63.26 N	10.24 E
Trondheimsfjorden, b., Nor.	16	D8	63.30 N	10.16 E
Trondheimsleia, strt., Nor.	16	D6	63.30 N	9.00 E
Tronto, stm., Italy	30	H10	42.53 N	13.54 E
Troödos, Cyp.	76	D3	34.55 N	32.54 E
Troodos Mountains, mts., Cyp.	76	D4	34.55 N	33.00 E
Troon, Scot., U.K.	10	F8	55.32 N	4.39 W
Trooper, Pa., U.S.	203		40.09 N	75.24 W
Troparëvo, ngh., Russia	183b		55.39 N	37.29 E
Tropea, Italy	32	F9	38.40 N	15.54 E
Trophy Mountain, vol., B.C., Can.	144	E11	51.47 N	119.48 W
Tropic, Ut., U.S.	150	F4	37.38 N	112.05 W
Tropojë, Alb.	32	B14	42.24 N	20.10 E
Troppau see Opava, Czech Rep.	24	G13	49.56 N	17.54 E
Trosa, Swe.	16	I15	58.53 N	17.33 E
Troškūnai, Lith.	26	E7	55.35 N	24.52 E
Trosna, Russia	26	H18	52.26 N	35.47 E
Trostianets', Ukr.	38	E8	48.30 N	29.14 E
Trostianets', Ukr.	38	C13	50.28 N	34.57 E
Trottiscliffe, Eng., U.K.	178		51.19 N	0.21 E
Trotuş, stm., Rom.	36	C13	46.03 N	27.14 E
Troup, Tx., U.S.	136	B12	32.09 N	95.07 W
Trout, La., U.S.	134	F6	31.41 N	92.10 W
Trout, stm., N.T., Can.	110	C6	61.19 N	119.51 W
Trout Brook, stm., Ma., U.S.	201		42.16 N	71.18 W
Trout Brook, stm., Ma., U.S.	201		42.39 N	71.16 W
Trout Creek, Mi., U.S.	128	E9	46.29 N	89.01 W
Trout Creek, Mt., U.S.	146	C11	47.50 N	115.36 W
Trout Creek, stm., Az., U.S.	150	H3	34.55 N	113.37 W
Trout Creek, stm., Or., U.S.	146	F6	44.49 N	121.05 W
Trout Creek, stm., Or., U.S.	148	A7	42.22 N	118.36 W
Trout Creek, stm., Pa., U.S.	203		40.07 N	75.24 W
Trout Creek Pass, p., Co., U.S.	138	C3	38.55 N	106.00 W
Trout Lake, l., B.C., Can.	144	F13	50.35 N	117.26 W
Trout Lake, l., N.T., Can.	110	C6	60.35 N	121.10 W
Trout Lake, l., On., Can.	118	B19	51.13 N	93.20 W
Trout Lake, l., On., Can.	126	B9	46.13 N	80.35 W
Trout Lake, l., On., Can.	126	B10	46.18 N	79.21 W
Trout Peak, mtn., Wy., U.S.	140	C3	44.36 N	109.32 W
Troutville, Va., U.S.	124	G6	37.25 N	79.52 W
Trouville-sur-Mer, Fr.	20	E9	49.21 N	0.05 E
Trowbridge, Eng., U.K.	10	J10	51.19 N	2.13 W
Troy, Al., U.S.	134	F13	31.48 N	85.58 W
Troy, Id., U.S.	146	D10	46.43 N	116.45 W
Troy, In., U.S.	130	F11	37.59 N	86.47 W
Troy, Ks., U.S.	130	E2	39.46 N	95.05 W
Troy, Mo., U.S.	130	F7	38.58 N	90.58 W
Troy, Mt., U.S.	146	B11	48.29 N	115.54 W
Troy, N.H., U.S.	124	B13	42.49 N	72.10 W
Troy, N.Y., U.S.	124	B12	42.43 N	73.41 W
Troy, N.C., U.S.	132	A6	35.21 N	79.54 W
Troy, Oh., U.S.	124	D1	40.02 N	84.12 W
Troy, Pa., U.S.	124	C9	41.46 N	76.47 W
Troy, Tn., U.S.	130	H8	36.20 N	89.09 W
Troy, Tx., U.S.	136	C10	31.12 N	97.17 W
Troy see Truva, hist., Tur.	34	D9	39.57 N	26.15 E
Troy Brook, stm., N.J., U.S.	194		40.50 N	74.22 W
Troyes, Fr.	20	F13	48.18 N	4.04 E
Troy Lake, l., Ca., U.S.	148	I9	34.49 N	116.33 W
Troy Meadows, sw., N.J., U.S.	194		40.50 N	74.22 W
Troy Peak, mtn., Nv., U.S.	148	E10	38.19 N	115.30 W
Trpanj, Cro.	30	G14	42.59 N	17.17 E
Tršćanski zaljev see Trieste, Gulf of, b., Eur.	30	E10	45.38 N	13.28 E
Trst see Trieste, Italy	30	E10	45.40 N	13.45 E
Trstená, Slvk.	24	G15	49.21 N	19.36 E
Trstenik, Yugo.	36	F7	43.37 N	20.59 E
Truax, Sk., Can.	142	E8	49.54 N	104.57 W
Trubčevsk, Russia	26	H16	52.34 N	33.47 E
Truchas, N.M., U.S.	138	E3	36.02 N	105.48 W
Truchas Peak, mtn., N.M., U.S.	138	E3	35.58 N	105.39 W
Trucial States see United Arab Emirates, ctry., Asia	72	E7	24.00 N	54.00 E
Truckee, Ca., U.S.	148	D5	39.19 N	120.10 W
Truckee, stm., U.S.	148	D6	39.51 N	119.27 W
Trud, Russia	26	C16	57.36 N	33.58 E
Trudfront, Russia	40	I15	45.55 N	47.40 E
Trues Creek, stm., N.Y., U.S.	194		40.41 N	73.17 W
Truganina, Austl.	192b		37.49 S	144.43 E
Trujillo, Col.	168	E3	4.09 N	76.18 W
Trujillo, Hond.	156	E4	15.54 N	85.57 W
Trujillo, Peru	164	E2	8.06 S	79.02 W
Trujillo, Spain	28	E5	39.27 N	5.52 W
Trujillo, Ven.	168	C6	9.21 N	70.26 W
Trujillo, state, Ven.	168	C6	9.25 N	70.30 W
Trujillo Alto, P.R.	158a	b4	18.21 N	65.59 W
Trujillo Creek, stm., U.S.	138	G5	35.22 N	103.23 W
Truk Islands see Chuuk, is., Micron.	94	C6	7.16 N	151.44 E
Trull Brook, stm., Ma., U.S.	201		42.39 N	71.15 W
Truman, Mn., U.S.	128	H4	43.49 N	94.26 W
Trumann, Ar., U.S.	134	B8	35.40 N	90.31 W
Trumansburg, N.Y., U.S.	124	B9	42.32 N	76.39 W
Trumbull, Ct., U.S.	124	C12	41.15 N	73.12 W
Trumbull, Mount, mtn., Az., U.S.	150	G3	36.25 N	113.10 W
Trumon, Indon.	64	K3	2.49 N	97.38 E
Trundle, Austl.	98	I6	32.54 S	147.42 E
Trung Phan (Annam), hist. reg., Viet.	64	D8	15.00 N	108.00 E
Truro, Austl.	98	J2	34.24 S	139.06 E
Truro, N.S., Can.	122	E13	45.21 N	63.16 W
Truro, Eng., U.K.	10	K7	50.16 N	5.02 W
Trusan, stm., Malay.	66	A9	4.57 N	115.11 E
Truscott, Tx., U.S.	138	H9	33.44 N	99.48 W
Truşeni, Mol.	38	F7	47.04 N	28.41 E
Truşeşti, Rom.	36	B14	47.46 N	27.01 E
Truskavets', Ukr.	38	D2	49.16 N	23.33 E
Trus Madi, Gunong, mtn., Malay.	66	A10	5.33 N	116.31 E
Truth or Consequences, N.M., U.S.	150	J9	33.08 N	107.15 W
Trutnov, Czech Rep.	24	F11	50.33 N	15.54 E
Truva (Troy), hist., Tur.	34	D9	39.57 N	26.15 E
Truxall, Pa., U.S.	197b		40.33 N	79.33 W
Truxton Wash, stm., Az., U.S.	150	H3	35.37 N	114.03 W
Truyère, stm., Fr.	22	E8	44.38 N	2.33 E
Tryduby, Ukr.	38	E9	48.04 N	30.25 E
Trylisy, Ukr.	38	C9	49.59 N	29.50 E
Tryon, Ne., U.S.	140	F12	41.32 N	100.57 W
Tryon, N.C., U.S.	132	A3	35.12 N	82.14 W
Trypillia, Ukr.	38	C9	50.07 N	30.46 E
Trysil, reg., Nor.	16	F10	61.23 N	12.28 E
Trysilelva (Klarälven), stm., Eur.	16	F9	59.19 N	13.28 E
Trysilfjellet, mtn., Nor.	16	F10	61.18 N	12.13 E
Tryškiai, Lith.	26	D5	56.04 N	22.35 E
Tržaški zaliv see Trieste, Gulf of, b., Eur.	30	E10	45.38 N	13.28 E
Trzcianka, Pol.	24	C12	53.02 N	16.28 E
Trzciel, Pol.	24	D11	52.22 N	15.52 E
Trzcińsko-Zdrój, Pol.	24	C10	52.57 N	14.35 E
Trzebiatów, Pol.	24	B11	54.03 N	15.15 E
Trzebież, Pol.	24	C10	53.39 N	14.30 E
Trzebinia, Pol.	24	F15	50.09 N	19.28 E
Trzebnica, Pol.	24	E13	51.18 N	17.03 E
Trzemeszno, Pol.	24	D13	52.33 N	17.50 E
Tsacha Lake, l., B.C., Can.	144	C6	53.02 N	124.49 W
Tsagaannuur, Mong.	48	E16	49.31 N	89.46 E
Tsaidam Basin see Qaidam Pendi, bas., China	52	D3	37.00 N	95.00 E
Tsåktso, mtn., Swe.	14	D11	68.28 N	20.25 E
Tsala Apopka Lake, l., Fl., U.S.	132	H3	28.53 N	82.20 W
Ts'anghsien see Cangzhou, China	58	B7	38.18 N	116.51 E
Tsaratanana, Madag.	88	D8	16.46 S	47.37 E
Tsaratanana, mts., Madag.	88	C8	14.00 S	49.00 E
Tsaratanana, Massif du see Tsaratanana, mts., Madag.	88	C8	14.00 S	49.00 E
Tsau, Bots.	88	E3	20.13 S	22.20 E
Tsavo, Kenya	86	E7	2.59 S	38.27 E
Tsaydaychuz Peak, mtn., B.C., Can.	144	C4	53.02 N	126.35 W
Tschenstochau see Częstochowa, Pol.	24	F15	50.48 N	19.07 E
Tschida, Lake, res., N.D., U.S.	140	A11	46.36 N	101.53 W
Tsebrykove, Ukr.	38	F9	47.08 N	30.06 E
Tsenke, stm., D.R.C.	191b		4.24 S	15.26 E
Tses, Nmb.	90	D4	25.54 S	18.07 E
Tsetserleg, Mong.	52	B5	47.27 N	101.27 E
Tsévié, Togo	84	H5	6.25 N	1.13 E
Tshabong, Bots.	90	D6	26.01 S	22.24 E
Tshane, Bots.	90	D5	24.01 S	21.52 E
Tshangu, stm., D.R.C.	191b		4.25 S	15.23 E
Tshela, D.R.C.	86	E2	4.58 S	12.56 E
Tshidilamolomo, S. Afr.	90	D7	25.50 S	24.41 E
Tshikapa, D.R.C.	86	F4	6.24 S	20.47 E
Tshikapa see Chicapa, stm., Afr.	86	F4	6.24 S	20.47 E
Tshofa, D.R.C.	86	F5	5.14 S	25.14 E
Tshootsha, Bots.	90	C5	22.07 S	20.51 E
Tshuapa, stm., D.R.C.	86	E4	0.16 S	20.45 E
Tshumbe (Chiumbe), stm., Afr.	86	F4	6.59 S	21.11 E
Tsiafajavona, vol., Madag.	88	D8	19.20 S	47.14 E
Tsiémé, stm., Congo	191b		4.15 S	15.18 E
Tsiigehtchic, N.T., Can.	110	B4	67.27 N	133.34 W
Tsimlyansk Reservoir see Cimljanskoe vodohranilišče, res., Russia	40	G13	48.00 N	43.00 E
Tsinan see Jinan, China	58	C7	36.39 N	116.58 E
Tsineng, S. Afr.	90	E6	27.05 S	23.04 E
Tsinghai see Qinghai, state, China	52	D4	36.00 N	96.00 E
Tsingkiang see Qingjiang, China	58	E8	33.36 N	119.00 E
Tsingtao see Qingdao, China	58	C9	36.05 N	120.20 E
Tsing Yi, i., China	189d		22.21 N	114.05 E
Tsining see Jining, China	58	D7	35.23 N	116.34 E
Tsintsabis, Nmb.	88	D2	18.44 S	17.57 E
Tsiombe, Madag.	88	F8	25.19 S	45.29 E
Tsiribihina, stm., Madag.	88	D7	19.50 S	44.27 E
Tsiroanomandidy, Madag.	88	D8	18.46 S	46.02 E
Tsitsutl Peak, mtn., B.C., Can.	144	D5	52.44 N	125.47 W
Tsiurupyns'k, Ukr.	38	G11	46.37 N	32.42 E
Tsjop, Ukr.	36	A9	48.26 N	22.13 E
Tsjynadijeve, Ukr.	36	A9	48.30 N	22.50 E
Tskhinvali see Chinvali, Geor.	42	D10	42.11 N	43.58 E
Tsöh Gol see Cöch, stm., Asia	52	B6	51.02 N	106.38 E
Tsolo, S. Afr.	90	G9	31.18 S	28.45 E
Tsomo, stm., S. Afr.	90	H8	32.23 S	27.49 E
Tsomog, Mong.	52	B6	45.59 N	108.50 E
Tsu, Japan	56	E9	34.43 N	136.31 E
Tsubame, Japan	56	B11	37.39 N	138.56 E
Tsuboro-suigenchi, res., Japan	188		34.24 N	135.54 E
Tsuchiura, Japan	56	C13	36.04 N	140.12 E
Tsuda, Japan	188		34.49 N	135.43 E
Tsuen Wan, China	189d		22.22 N	114.07 E
Tsugaru-kaikyō, strt., Japan	54	D14	41.35 N	141.00 E
Tsujidō, Japan	186		35.20 N	139.27 E
Tsukahara, Japan	186		35.18 N	139.58 E
Tsukumi, Japan	56	F3	33.03 N	131.51 E
Tsukumono, ngh., Japan	188		34.50 N	135.11 E
Tsukushi-sanchi, mts., Japan	56	F3	33.30 N	130.30 E
Tsuman', Ukr.	38	C4	50.49 N	25.53 E
Tsumeb, Nmb.	88	D2	19.15 S	17.42 E
Tsumkwe, Nmb.	88	D3	19.36 S	20.30 E
Tsunashima, ngh., Japan	186		35.32 N	139.38 E
Tsuruga, Japan	56	D9	35.39 N	136.04 E
Tsurugaoka-hachimangu Shrine, rel., Japan	186		35.19 N	139.33 E
Tsurugashima, Japan	186		35.56 N	139.24 E
Tsurugi-san, mtn., Japan	56	F7	33.51 N	134.06 E
Tsuruhara, Japan	188		34.26 N	135.20 E
Tsuruma, Japan	186		35.51 N	139.33 E
Tsurumi, ngh., Japan	186		35.30 N	139.41 E
Tsuruoka, Japan	56	A12	38.43 N	139.49 E
Tsushima, is., Japan	56	E2	34.30 N	129.22 E
Tsushima-kaikyō (Eastern Channel), strt., Japan	56	E2	34.00 N	129.00 E
Tsuwano, Japan	56	E4	34.28 N	131.47 E
Tsuyama, Japan	56	D7	35.03 N	134.00 E
Tsvitkove, Ukr.	38	D10	49.09 N	31.32 E
Tsvitne, Ukr.	38	E11	48.56 N	32.29 E
Tswaane, Bots.	90	C6	22.28 S	22.03 E
Tsybuliv, Ukr.	38	D8	49.04 N	29.50 E
Ttruchchendūr, India	69	G4	8.29 N	78.07 E
Tu see Tsu, Japan	56	E9	34.43 N	136.31 E
Tua, D.R.C.	86	E3	3.38 S	16.39 E
Tua, stm., Port.	28	C3	41.12 N	7.25 W
Tua, Tanjung, c., Indon.	66	F4	5.53 S	105.43 E
Tua Chua, Viet.	64	B6	21.53 N	103.20 E
Tuaim see Tuam, Ire.	10	H4	53.31 N	8.51 W
Tual, Indon.	60	G9	5.39 S	132.43 E
Tualatin, stm., Or., U.S.	146	E4	45.20 N	122.39 W
Tuam, Ire.	10	H4	53.31 N	8.51 W
Tuamotu, Îles, is., Fr. Poly.	94	E12	19.00 S	142.00 W
Tuamotu Archipelago see Tuamotu, Îles, is., Fr. Poly.	94	E12	19.00 S	142.00 W
Tuamotu Ridge, unds.	174	K24	17.00 S	145.00 W
Tuanan, Indon.	66	E9	2.11 S	114.25 E
Tuan Giao, Viet.	64	B6	21.35 N	103.25 E
Tuangku, Pulau, i., Indon.	64	K3	2.10 N	97.16 E
Tuanshantzu see Raohe, China	52	B11	46.47 N	134.00 E
Tuanxi, China	58	H2	27.28 N	107.08 E
Tuapse, Russia	42	C8	44.06 N	39.04 E
Tuasivi, Cape, c., Samoa	101c	g11	13.39 S	172.10 W
Tuba, Russia	48	C18	57.24 N	102.52 E
Tuba, stm., Russia	48	D16	53.56 N	91.29 E
Tubac, Az., U.S.	150	L5	31.37 N	111.03 W
Tuba City, Az., U.S.	150	G5	36.08 N	111.15 W
Tuban, Indon.	66	G8	6.53 S	112.04 E
Tubarão, Braz.	172	D13	28.28 S	49.03 W
Ṭūbās, W.B.	76	F6	32.19 N	35.22 E
Tubau, Malay.	66	B8	3.08 N	113.42 E
Tubbs Island, i., Ca., U.S.	200		38.08 N	122.26 W
Tübingen, Ger.	24	H5	48.31 N	9.03 E
Tubruq, Libya	82	A4	32.04 N	23.56 E
Tubuai, i., Fr. Poly.	94	F12	23.18 S	149.30 W
Tucacas, Ven.	168	B7	10.47 N	68.19 W
Tucacas, Punta, c., Ven.	168	B7	10.52 N	68.14 W
Tucannon, stm., Wa., U.S.	146	D9	46.33 N	118.11 W
Tucano, Braz.	170	F6	10.58 S	38.46 W
Tucheng, China	58	G2	28.13 N	106.01 E
T'uch'eng, Tai.	187d		24.59 N	121.26 E
Tuchola, Pol.	24	C13	53.35 N	17.51 E
Tuchów, Pol.	24	G17	49.53 N	21.04 E
Tuckahoe, N.Y., U.S.	194		40.57 N	73.49 W
Tuckanarra, Austl.	96	E3	27.07 S	118.06 E
Tuckerman, Ar., U.S.	134	B7	35.44 N	91.12 W
Tuckerton, N.J., U.S.	124	E11	39.36 N	74.20 W
Tučkovo, Russia	26	E19	55.35 N	36.29 E
Tucson, Az., U.S.	150	K5	32.12 N	110.58 W
Tucumán see San Miguel de Tucumán, Arg.	172	C5	26.49 S	65.13 W
Tucumán, state, Arg.	172	C5	27.00 S	65.30 W
Tucumcari, N.M., U.S.	138	F5	35.10 N	103.43 W
Tucumcari Mountain, mtn., N.M., U.S.	138	F5	35.08 N	103.42 W
Tucunuco, Arg.	172	E3	30.37 S	68.37 W
Tucupido, Ven.	168	C9	9.16 N	65.46 W
Tucupita, Ven.	168	C11	9.02 N	62.02 W
Tucuruí, Braz.	164	D8	3.43 S	49.43 W
Tucuruí, Represa de, res., Braz.	164	D8	4.32 S	49.31 W
Tucuruvi, ngh., Braz.	205b		23.28 S	46.35 W
Tuczna, Pol.	24	E19	51.53 N	23.25 E
Tudcum, Arg.	172	E3	30.14 S	69.15 W
Tudela, Phil.	68	F4	8.15 N	123.50 E
Tudela, Spain	28	B9	42.03 N	1.36 W
Tudmur (Palmyra), Syria	76	D9	34.32 N	38.16 E
Tudmur see Palmyra, hist., Syria	76	D9	34.33 N	38.17 E
Tudu, Est.	26	A9	59.11 N	26.51 E
Tuela, stm., Port.	28	C3	41.30 N	7.11 W
Tuen Mun, China	189d		22.24 N	113.58 E
Tufānganj, India	70	E12	26.18 N	89.41 E
Tufi, Pap. N. Gui.	101a	b4	9.04 S	149.19 E
Tufts University, educ., Ma., U.S.	201		42.24 N	71.07 W
Tugaske, Sk., Can.	142	D7	50.53 N	106.16 W
Tugela, stm., S. Afr.	90	F10	29.13 S	31.29 E
Tug Fork, stm., U.S.	124	G3	38.06 N	82.36 W
Tuggerah Lake, b., Austl.	98	I8	33.18 S	151.30 E
Tughlakābād, ngh., India	190a		28.31 N	77.16 E
Tughlakabad Fort, hist., India	190a		28.31 N	77.16 E
Tuguegarao City, Phil.	68	B3	17.37 N	121.42 E
Tugur, Russia	50	F16	53.46 N	136.50 E
Tuhai, stm., China	58	C7	37.54 N	118.04 E
Tuhkala, Russia	18	B17	65.42 N	30.44 E
Tuhuangba, China	58	F3	31.41 N	108.20 E
Tui, Spain	28	B2	42.03 N	8.38 W
Tuibo, China	54	C8	44.00 N	127.46 E
Tuira, stm., Pan.	168	D3	8.20 N	78.04 W
Tujmazy, Russia	40	D18	54.35 N	53.43 E
Tujunga, ngh., Ca., U.S.	198		34.15 N	118.17 W
Tujunga Valley, val., Ca., U.S.	198		34.17 N	118.20 W
Tujunga Wash, val., Ca., U.S.	198		34.09 N	118.24 W
Tukan, Russia	40	E20	53.50 N	57.27 E
Tukangbesi, Kepulauan, is., Indon.	60	G7	5.40 S	123.50 E
Tukituki, stm., N.Z.	102	D7	39.35 S	176.56 E
Tuk Mèas, Camb.	64	G7	10.40 N	104.33 E
Tukosméra, Mont, mtn., Vanuatu	101d	I17	19.35 S	169.22 E
Tūkrah, Libya	82	A4	32.32 N	20.34 E
Tuktoyaktuk, N.T., Can.	110	B4	69.26 N	133.01 W
Tukums, Lat.	26	D6	56.57 N	23.10 E
Tukuringra, hrebet, mts., Russia	50	F14	54.20 N	126.20 E
Tukuyu, Tan.	86	F6	9.12 S	33.38 E
T'uk'u Yüeh, mtn., Tai.	187d		25.02 N	121.38 E
Tula, Mex.	154	D9	23.00 N	99.42 W
Tula, Russia	26	F20	54.12 N	37.37 E
Tulach Mhór see Tullamore, Ire.	10	H5	53.16 N	7.29 W
Tulaghi, Sol. Is.	101b	e9	9.06 S	160.09 E
Tulancingo, Mex.	154	E9	20.05 N	98.22 W
Tulangbawang, stm., Indon.	66	F4	4.24 S	105.50 E
Tulare, Ca., U.S.	148	G6	36.12 N	119.20 W
Tulare, S.D., U.S.	140	C14	44.44 N	98.30 W
Tulare Lake Bed, reg., Ca., U.S.	148	G6	36.03 N	119.49 W
Tulare Lake Canal, can., Ca., U.S.	148	G6	36.02 N	119.37 W
Tularosa, N.M., U.S.	138	H2	33.05 N	106.02 W
Tularosa, stm., N.M., U.S.	150	J8	33.41 N	108.44 W
Tularosa Valley, bas., N.M., U.S.	120	E9	32.45 N	106.10 W
Tulbagh, S. Afr.	90	H4	33.18 S	19.07 E
Tulbing, Aus.	182b		48.18 N	16.09 E
Tulbinger Kogel, hill, Aus.	182b		48.17 N	16.09 E
Tulcán, Ec.	168	G3	0.48 N	77.43 W
Tulcea, Rom.	36	D15	45.10 N	28.48 E
Tulcea, state, Rom.	36	D15	45.00 N	29.00 E
Tul'chyn, Ukr.	38	E7	48.40 N	28.52 E
Tule Creek, stm., Tx., U.S.	138	G7	34.40 N	101.13 W
Tulelake, Ca., U.S.	148	B4	41.57 N	121.29 W
Tule Lake, l., Ca., U.S.	148	B4	41.54 N	121.32 W
Tulemalu Lake, l., Nu., Can.	110	C11	62.58 N	99.25 W
Tule River Indian Reservation, ind. res., Ca., U.S.	148	G7	36.02 N	118.42 W
Tule Valley, val., Ut., U.S.	150	D3	39.14 N	113.31 W
Tuli, Zimb.	88	E4	21.55 S	29.12 E
Tulia, Tx., U.S.	138	G7	34.32 N	101.45 W
Tulianan, stm., Phil.	187f		14.41 N	120.58 E
Tuliszków, Pol.	24	D14	52.05 N	18.17 E
Tulita, N.T., Can.	110	C5	64.54 N	125.33 W
Tūlkarm, W.B.	76	F6	32.19 N	35.02 E
Tullahoma, Tn., U.S.	134	B12	35.21 N	86.12 W
Tullamarine, Austl.	192b		37.41 S	144.52 E
Tullamarine International Airport, arpt., Austl.	192b		37.40 S	144.50 E
Tullamore, Austl.	98	I6	32.36 S	147.33 E
Tullamore, On., Can.	193b		43.47 N	79.46 W
Tullamore, Ire.	10	H5	53.16 N	7.29 W
Tulle, Fr.	22	D7	45.16 N	1.46 E
Tullibigeal, Austl.	98	I6	33.25 S	146.43 E
Tulln, Aus.	30	B13	48.20 N	16.04 E
Tullner Feld, reg., Aus.	182b		48.19 N	16.10 E
Tullock Creek, stm., Mt., U.S.	140	B5	46.07 N	107.28 W
Tullos, La., U.S.	134	F6	31.49 N	92.19 W
Tullow, Ire.	10	I6	52.48 N	6.44 W
Tullus, Sudan	82	E4	11.03 N	24.32 E
Tully, Austl.	98	A5	17.56 S	145.55 E
Tuloma, stm., Russia	14	D23	69.02 N	33.03 E
Tulos, ozero, l., Russia	18	D17	63.34 N	30.33 E
Tulppio, Fin.	14	E20	67.49 N	29.21 E
Tulsa, Ok., U.S.	138	E12	36.09 N	95.59 W
Tulsequah, B.C., Can.	110	D4	58.36 N	133.35 W
Tulsī Lake, l., India	190c		19.11 N	72.55 E
Tul'skaja oblast', co., Russia	40	E10	54.00 N	37.30 E
Tultitlán, Mex.	204a		19.39 N	99.09 W
Tuluá, Col.	168	E3	4.05 N	76.11 W
Tulum, Mex.	156	B4	20.13 N	87.27 W
Tulum, hist., Mex.	156	B4	20.12 N	87.26 W
Tulun, Russia	48	D18	54.34 N	100.34 E
Tulungagung, Indon.	66	H7	8.04 S	111.54 E
Tulungselapan, Indon.	66	E4	3.14 S	105.18 E
Tulyehualco, ngh., Mex.	204a		19.15 N	99.01 W
Tuma, stm., Nic.	156	F5	13.03 N	84.44 W
Tumacacori National Historical Park, p.o.i., Az., U.S.	150	L5	31.25 N	111.01 W
Tumaco, Col.	168	G2	1.47 N	78.47 W
Tumaco, Rada de, b., Col.	168	G2	1.55 N	78.45 W
Tuman-gang (Tumen), stm., Asia	54	C9	42.17 N	130.40 E
Tumannyj, Russia	14	D26	68.50 N	35.38 E
Tumanovo, Russia	26	E17	55.24 N	34.39 E
Tumanskij, Russia	50	D24	63.58 N	178.23 E
Tumany, Russia	50	D20	60.56 N	155.55 E
Tumatumari, Guy.	164	B6	5.20 N	59.00 W
Tumba, Swe.	16	H15	59.11 N	17.49 E
Tumba, stm., Russia	18	D18	63.23 N	32.44 E
Tumbarumba, Austl.	98	J6	35.46 S	148.00 E
Tumbes, Peru	164	D1	3.33 S	80.27 W
Tumbes, Punta, c., Chile	172	H1	36.37 S	73.06 W
Tumble Mountain, mtn., Mt., U.S.	146	E16	45.19 N	110.02 W
Tumbler Ridge, B.C., Can.	144	A10	55.07 N	120.57 W
Tumča (Tuntsajoki), stm., Eur.	14	E20	66.36 N	30.48 E
Tumčaozero, ozero, l., Russia	14	F21	66.31 N	30.58 E
Tŭmch'on-ni, ngh., Kor., S.	189b		37.34 N	126.51 E
Tumen, China	52	C10	42.57 N	129.50 E
Tumen (Tuman-gang), stm., Asia	54	C9	42.17 N	130.40 E
Tumeremo, Ven.	168	D11	7.19 N	61.28 W
Tumiritinga, Braz.	170	J5	18.59 S	41.39 W
Tumkūr, India	69	E3	13.20 N	77.06 E
Tummo see Bi'r al Waʻr, Libya	82	C2	22.31 N	14.08 E
Tumon Bay, b., Guam	100c	i9	13.30 N	144.47 E
Tumoteqi, China	58	A4	40.49 N	111.36 E
Tumpat, Malay.	64	I6	6.11 N	102.10 E
Tumsar, India	70	H7	21.23 N	79.45 E
Tumtum, Wa., U.S.	146	C9	47.53 N	117.40 W
Tumu, Ghana	84	G4	10.52 N	1.59 W
Tumuc-Humac, Massif des see Tumuc-Humac Mountains, mts., S.A.	164	C6	2.18 N	54.35 W
Tumuc-Humac Mountains, mts., S.A.	164	C6	2.18 N	54.35 W
Tumucumaque, Serra see Tumuc-Humac Mountains, mts., S.A.	164	C6	2.18 N	54.35 W
Tumut, Austl.	98	J7	35.18 S	148.13 E
Tumwater, Wa., U.S.	146	C3	47.00 N	122.54 W
Tumyn'czjan see Tuman-gang, stm., Asia	54	C9	42.17 N	130.40 E
Tumyn'czjan see Tumen, stm., Asia	54	C9	42.17 N	130.40 E
Tun, stm., Thai.	64	D4	17.25 N	98.41 E
Tuna Canyon, val., Ca., U.S.	198		34.03 N	118.36 W
Tunapuna, Trin.	159f	s12	10.37 N	61.24 W
Tunari, Cerro, mtn., Bol.	166	C3	17.16 S	66.22 W
Tunas Creek, stm., Tx., U.S.	136	D5	31.02 N	102.13 W
Tunas de Zaza, Cuba	156	B8	21.38 N	79.33 W
Tunbridge Wells see Royal Tunbridge Wells, Eng., U.K.	10	J13	51.08 N	0.15 E
Tunca see Tundža, stm., Eur.	36	G13	41.40 N	26.32 E
Tunçbilek, Tur.	34	D12	39.37 N	29.27 E
Tunceli, Tur.	42	F8	39.06 N	39.32 E
Tunceli, state, Tur.	42	F8	39.10 N	39.30 E
Tunchang, China	58	L3	19.26 N	110.08 E
Tunduru, Tan.	86	G7	11.05 S	37.21 E
Tundža, stm., Eur.	36	G13	41.40 N	26.32 E
Tunga, Nig.	84	H6	8.04 N	9.22 E
Tungabhadra, stm., India	69	C3	15.58 N	78.15 E
Tungabhadra Reservoir, res., India	69	D2	15.11 N	76.08 E
Tungaru, Sudan	82	E6	10.09 N	30.43 E
T'ungchou see Tongxian, China	58	B7	39.54 N	116.39 E
Tunghwa see Tonghua, China	52	C10	41.43 N	125.56 E
Tungkal, stm., Indon.	66	D3	0.48 S	103.27 E
Tungku, Malay.	66	A11	5.00 N	118.51 E
Tungla, Nic.	156	F5	13.19 N	84.26 W
Tung Lung Island, i., China	189d		22.15 N	114.17 E
Tung O, China	189d		22.12 N	114.08 E
Tungokočen, Russia	50	F12	53.32 N	115.36 E
Tungozero, Russia	18	B18	65.45 N	31.14 E
Tungsha Tao (Pratas Island), i., Tai.	58	K7	20.42 N	116.43 E
Tungshih, Tai.	58	I9	24.15 N	120.49 E
Tungsten, N.T., Can.	110	C5	61.57 N	128.16 W
Tungudskoe, ozero, l., Russia	18	C20	64.21 N	33.10 E
Tungurahua, state, Ec.	168	H2	1.15 S	78.35 W
Tungurahua, vol., Ec.	168	H2	1.27 S	78.26 W
Tunhovdfjorden, l., Nor.	16	G6	60.25 N	8.50 E
Tuni, India	69	C6	17.21 N	82.33 E
Tunia, stm., Col.	168	G5	1.11 N	72.43 W
Tunica, Ms., U.S.	134	C8	34.41 N	90.23 W
Tunis, Tun.	84	B6	36.48 N	10.11 E
Tunis see Tunisia, ctry., Afr.	84	C6	34.00 N	9.00 E
Tunis, Golfe de, b., Tun.	84	B7	37.00 N	10.30 E
Tunis, Gulf of see Tunis, Golfe de, b., Tun.	84	B7	37.00 N	10.30 E
Tunisia, ctry., Afr.	84	C6	34.00 N	9.00 E
Tunisie see Tunisia, ctry., Afr.	84	C6	34.00 N	9.00 E
Tunitas Creek, stm., Ca., U.S.	200		37.21 N	122.24 W
Tunja, Col.	168	E5	5.30 N	73.22 W
Tunkhannock, Pa., U.S.	124	C9	41.32 N	75.57 W
Tunliu, China	58	C5	36.19 N	112.54 E
Tunnel Hill, Ga., U.S.	134	C13	34.50 N	85.01 W
Tunnelton, W.V., U.S.	124	E6	39.22 N	79.45 W
Tunnsjøen, l., Nor.	16	C10	64.43 N	13.24 E
Tunø, i., Den.	16	L8	55.57 N	10.26 E
Tuntsajoki (Tumča), stm., Eur.	14	E20	66.36 N	30.48 E
Tuntum, Braz.	170	C3	5.14 S	44.39 W
Tunu see Østgrønland, state, Grnld.	108	C18	69.59 N	35.00 W
Tununak, Ak., U.S.	109	D6	60.35 N	165.16 W
Tunuyán, Arg.	172	F3	33.33 S	69.00 W
Tunuyán, stm., Arg.	172	F4	33.55 S	66.49 W
Tunxi, China	58	G8	29.43 N	118.17 E
Tuo, stm., China	58	G1	29.03 N	105.15 E
Tuo, stm., China	58	E7	33.16 N	117.45 E
Tuobalage, China	70	C12	31.37 N	88.10 E
Tuobuja, Russia	50	D13	61.59 N	122.02 E
Tuoj-Haja, Russia	48	B20	62.32 N	111.18 E
Tuokedingling, China	70	B10	32.45 N	84.55 E
Tuokusidawan Ling, mtn., China	62	A6	37.14 N	85.47 E
Tuolumne, Ca., U.S.	148	F5	37.57 N	120.14 W
Tuolumne, stm., Ca., U.S.	148	F5	37.36 N	121.10 W
Tuong Duong, Viet.	64	C7	19.16 N	104.25 E
Tuotuo, stm., China	52	E3	34.05 N	92.58 E
Tupã, Braz.	166	D6	21.55 S	50.31 W
Tupaciguara, Braz.	170	J1	18.36 S	48.40 W
Tupanciretã, Braz.	172	D10	29.05 S	53.50 W
Tuparro, stm., Col.	168	E7	5.13 N	67.49 W
Tupelo, Ms., U.S.	134	C10	34.15 N	88.42 W
Tupelo, Ok., U.S.	134	C2	34.35 N	96.26 W
Tupelo National Battlefield, p.o.i., Ms., U.S.	134	C10	34.13 N	88.44 W
Tupik, Russia	50	F13	54.25 N	119.58 E
Tupinambarana, Ilha, i., Braz.	164	D6	3.00 S	58.00 W
Tupiraçaba, Braz.	170	H1	14.31 S	48.32 W
Tupiza, Bol.	166	D3	21.25 S	65.43 W
Tuplice, Pol.	24	E10	51.39 N	14.50 E
Tupper Lake, N.Y., U.S.	126	D15	44.13 N	74.27 W
Tupungato, Arg.	172	F3	33.21 S	69.07 W
Tupungato, Cerro, mtn., S.A.	172	F3	33.25 S	69.44 W
Tupychiv, Ukr.	38	B10	51.46 N	31.26 E
Tuquan, China	52	B9	45.22 N	121.32 E
Túquerres, Col.	168	G3	1.03 N	77.35 W
Tura, Egypt	191c		29.56 N	31.16 E
Tura, India	70	F13	25.31 N	90.13 E
Tura, Russia	48	B18	64.17 N	100.14 E
Tura, stm., Russia	48	C11	57.12 N	66.57 E
Turabah, Sau. Ar.	72	E5	21.13 N	41.39 E
Turabah, well, Sau. Ar.	74	F8	28.15 N	42.55 E
Turaiyūr, India	69	F4	11.08 N	78.35 E
Turambhe, India	190c		19.04 N	73.01 E
Turan, Russia	48	D16	52.08 N	93.55 E
Turan lowland (Turanskaja nizmennost'), pl., Asia	48	F10	42.15 N	60.48 E
Turano, stm., Italy	30	H9	42.23 N	12.51 E
Turanskaja nizmennost' see Turan lowland, pl., Asia	48	F10	42.15 N	60.48 E
Turāq al-ʻIlab, hills, Syria	76	E9	33.55 N	38.18 E
Turate, Italy	184b		45.39 N	9.00 E
Turaŭ, Bela.	26	H10	52.04 N	27.43 E
Turayf, Sau. Ar.	76	E6	31.40 N	38.40 E
Turbaco, Col.	168	B4	10.20 N	75.24 W
Turbacz, mtn., Pol.	24	G16	49.33 N	20.08 E
Turbat, Pak.	62	C1	25.59 N	63.03 E
Turbiv, Ukr.	38	D7	49.22 N	28.43 E
Turbo, Col.	168	C3	8.06 N	76.43 W
Turčasovo, Russia	18	D26	63.06 N	39.15 E
Turčiansky Svätý Martin see Martin, Slvk.	24	G14	49.04 N	18.55 E
Turda, Rom.	36	C10	46.33 N	23.47 E
Turdej, Russia	26	G20	53.21 N	38.00 E
Turek, Pol.	24	D14	52.01 N	18.29 E
Turenki, Fin.	18	G11	60.55 N	24.38 E
Turfan see Turpan, China	52	C2	42.58 N	89.13 E
Turfan Depression see Turpan Pendi, depr., China	52	C2	42.40 N	89.10 E
Turffontein, ngh., S. Afr.	191d		26.15 S	28.02 E
Turffontein Race Course, p.o.i., S. Afr.	191d		26.14 S	28.03 E
Turgaj, Kaz.	48	E10	49.37 N	63.30 E
Turgaj, stm., Kaz.	48	E10	48.02 N	62.34 E
Turgajskaja ložbina, reg., Kaz.	48	D10	52.30 N	64.00 E
Turgajskoe plato, plat., Kaz.	48	D10	51.00 N	64.00 E
Turgay see Turgaj, stm., Kaz.	48	E10	48.02 N	62.34 E
Turginovo, Russia	26	D18	56.30 N	36.04 E
Turgoš, Russia	26	A18	59.17 N	35.10 E
Turgut, Tur.	34	E14	38.37 N	31.48 E
Turgutlu, Tur.	34	E10	38.30 N	27.42 E
Turhal, Tur.	42	E7	40.22 N	36.05 E
Türi, Est.	26	B8	58.48 N	25.25 E
Turia (Túria), stm., Spain	28	D9	39.27 N	0.19 W
Túria (Turia), stm., Spain	28	D9	39.27 N	0.19 W
Turiaçu, Braz.	170	A3	1.42 S	45.22 W
Turiaçu, stm., Braz.	170	B3	1.44 S	45.16 W
Turiia, stm., Ukr.	38	B3	51.47 N	24.51 E
Turiis'k, Ukr.	38	B3	51.05 N	24.32 E
Turij, mys, c., Russia	14	F25	66.32 N	34.29 E
Turij Rog, Russia	54	B10	45.13 N	131.57 E
Turimetta Head, c., Austl.	192a		33.42 S	151.19 E
Turimiquire, Cerro, mtn., Ven.	168	B10	10.07 N	63.53 W
Turin, Ab., Can.	144	F18	49.58 N	112.30 W
Turin see Torino, Italy	30	E4	45.03 N	7.40 E
Turinsk, Russia	50	C10	58.02 N	63.42 E
Turka, Russia	50	F10	52.55 N	108.13 E
Turka, Ukr.	38	D1	49.09 N	23.02 E
Turkana, Lake see Rudolf, Lake, l., Afr.	86	D7	3.30 N	36.00 E
Türkeli Adası, i., Tur.	34	C10	40.30 N	27.30 E
Turkestan, Kaz.	48	F11	43.18 N	68.16 E

Name	Page	Map Ref.	Latitude	Longitude
Turkestanskij hrebet, mts., Asia	72	B10	39.35 N	69.15 E
Túrkeve, Hung.	36	B7	47.06 N	20.44 E
Turkey, Tx., U.S.	138	G8	34.23 N	100.53 W
Turkey, ctry., Asia	42	F8	39.00 N	35.00 E
Turkey, stm., Ia., U.S.	128	I7	42.41 N	90.56 W
Turkey Branch, stm., Md., U.S.	202c		38.52 N	76.48 W
Turkey Creek, stm., On., Can.	199		42.14 N	83.06 W
Turkey Creek, stm., U.S.	130	D1	39.57 N	96.02 W
Turkey Creek, stm., In., U.S.	196		41.31 N	87.18 W
Turkey Creek, stm., Ks., U.S.	138	C11	38.52 N	97.15 W
Turkey Creek, stm., Ne., U.S.	128	K2	40.22 N	96.53 W
Turkey Creek, stm., Ok., U.S.	138	E11	35.58 N	97.56 W
Turkey Island, i., Md., U.S.	202c		38.58 N	77.12 W
Turkey Run State Park, p.o.i., In., U.S.	130	E10	39.54 N	87.13 W
Turkeytown, Pa., U.S.	197b		40.12 N	79.44 W
Turki, Russia	40	E13	51.58 N	43.16 E
Turkish Republic of Northern Cyprus see Cyprus, North, ctry., Asia	76	C4	35.15 N	33.40 E
Türkiye see Turkey, ctry., Asia	42	F8	39.00 N	35.00 E
Turkmān Deh, Iran	185d		35.40 N	51.36 E
Turkmenbaši, Turkmen.	48	F8	40.01 N	53.02 E
Turkmenbaši, Turkmen.	72	B7	40.00 N	52.57 E
Turkmenia see Turkmenistan, ctry., Asia	72	B8	40.00 N	60.00 E
Turkmenija see Turkmenistan, ctry., Asia	72	B8	40.00 N	60.00 E
Turkmenistan, ctry., Asia	72	B8	40.00 N	60.00 E
Turkmenskij zaliv, b., Turkmen.	42	F15	38.53 N	53.30 E
Türkoğlu, Tur.	76	A7	37.23 N	36.53 E
Turks and Caicos Islands, dep., N.A.	152	C10	21.45 N	71.35 W
Turks Island Passage, strt., T./C. Is.	156	B12	21.25 N	71.17 W
Turks Islands, is., T./C. Is.	156	B12	21.24 N	71.07 W
Turku (Åbo), Fin.	18	G9	60.27 N	22.16 E
Turku ja Pori, state, Fin.	18	G9	61.20 N	22.30 E
Turkwel, stm., Kenya	86	D7	3.06 N	36.06 E
Turley, Ok., U.S.	130	H2	36.14 N	95.58 W
Turlock, Ca., U.S.	148	F5	37.29 N	120.51 W
Turmalina, Braz.	170	I4	17.17 S	42.44 W
Turmantas, Lith.	26	E9	55.41 N	26.28 E
Turmerito, Quebrada, stm., Ven.	204c		10.26 N	66.55 W
Turnagain, stm., B.C., Can.	110	D5	59.09 N	127.35 W
Turnbull, Mount, mtn., Az., U.S.	150	J6	33.04 N	110.16 W
Turneffe Islands, is., Belize	156	D4	17.22 N	87.51 W
Turner, Austl.	96	C5	17.50 S	128.18 E
Turner, Mt., U.S.	142	F5	48.50 N	108.24 W
Turner, Or., U.S.	146	F4	44.50 N	122.56 W
Turner Field, arpt., Pa., U.S.	203		40.13 N	75.13 W
Turners Falls, Ma., U.S.	124	B13	42.36 N	72.33 W
Turnersville, N.J., U.S.	203		39.46 N	75.03 W
Turner Valley, Ab., Can.	144	F16	50.40 N	114.17 W
Turnhout, Bel.	20	C13	51.19 N	4.56 E
Türnitz, Aus.	24	I11	47.56 N	15.29 E
Turnov, Czech Rep.	24	F11	50.35 N	15.09 E
Turnpike Lake, l., Ma., U.S.	201		42.01 N	71.19 W
Turnu Măgurele, Rom.	36	F11	43.45 N	24.53 E
Turnu Roşu, Pasul, p., Rom.	36	D11	45.30 N	24.14 E
Turnu-Severin see Drobeta-Turnu Severin, Rom.	36	E9	44.38 N	22.39 E
Turobin, Pol.	24	F18	50.50 N	22.46 E
Turočak, Russia	48	D15	52.16 N	87.07 E
Turon, Ks., U.S.	138	D10	37.48 N	98.25 W
Turopolje, pl., Cro.	30	E13	45.40 N	16.05 E
Turopyn, Ukr.	38	B3	50.59 N	24.29 E
Turpan, China	52	C2	42.58 N	89.13 E
Turpan Pendi (Turfan Depression), depr., China	52	C2	42.40 N	89.10 E
Turquino, Pico, mtn., Cuba	156	C9	19.59 N	76.50 W
Turramurra, Austl.	192a		33.44 S	151.08 E
Turrell, Ar., U.S.	134	B8	35.23 N	90.15 W
Turret Peak, mtn., Az., U.S.	150	I5	34.15 N	111.53 W
Turriff, Scot., U.K.	10	D10	57.32 N	2.28 W
Turtle, stm., Mb., Can.	142	D14	51.10 N	99.42 W
Turtle, stm., On., Can.	128	B6	48.53 N	92.38 W
Turtle, North Branch, stm., N.D., U.S.	142	G16	47.56 N	97.35 W
Turtle Creek, N.B., Can.	122	E12	45.57 N	64.53 W
Turtle Creek, stm., Pa., U.S.	197b		40.23 N	79.51 W
Turtle Creek, stm., S.D., U.S.	140	C14	44.54 N	98.30 W
Turtle Creek, stm., Wi., U.S.	130	B9	42.29 N	89.02 W
Turtle-Flambeau Flowage, res., Wi., U.S.	128	E8	46.05 N	90.11 W
Turtle Islands, is., S.L.	84	H2	7.37 N	13.00 W
Turtle Lake, N.D., U.S.	142	G13	47.31 N	100.53 W
Turtle Lake, Wi., U.S.	128	F6	45.23 N	92.08 W
Turtle Mountain, hill, Mb., Can.	142	F13	49.00 N	100.15 W
Turtle Mountain Indian Reservation, ind. res., N.D., U.S.	142	F14	48.51 N	99.45 W
Turtle Mountain Provincial Park, p.o.i., Mb., Can.	142	E13	49.03 N	100.15 W
Turtola, Fin.	14	F14	66.39 N	23.53 E
Turton and Entwistle Reservoir, res., Eng., U.K.	180		53.39 N	2.25 W
Turton Bottoms, Eng., U.K.	180		53.38 N	2.24 W
Turton Moor, for., Eng., U.K.	180		53.40 N	2.29 W
Turton Tower, bldg., Eng., U.K.	180		53.38 N	2.25 W
Turu, stm., Russia	48	B18	64.47 N	101.38 E
Turuhan, stm., Russia	48	A14	65.48 N	87.49 E
Turuhansk, Russia	50	C6	65.48 N	87.54 E
Turvo, Braz.	172	D13	28.54 S	49.42 W
Turvo, stm., Braz.	170	K1	20.50 S	48.55 W
Turwi, stm., Zimb.	90	B10	20.27 S	32.05 E
Turzovka, Slvk.	24	G14	49.24 N	18.39 E
Tusas, stm., N.M., U.S.	138	E2	36.23 N	106.02 W
Tuscaloosa, Al., U.S.	134	D11	33.12 N	87.34 W
Tuscaloosa, Lake, res., Al., U.S.	134	D11	33.21 N	87.35 W
Tuscany see Toscana, state, Italy	30	G8	43.30 N	11.00 E
Tuscarora Mountain, mts., Pa., U.S.	124	D8	40.11 N	77.46 W
Tuscarora Mountains, mts., Nv., U.S.	148	C9	41.00 N	116.20 W
Tuscola, Il., U.S.	130	E9	39.47 N	88.16 W
Tuscola, Tx., U.S.	136	B8	32.12 N	99.47 W
Tuscolo, hist., Italy	185a		41.48 N	12.42 E
Tuscumbia, Al., U.S.	134	C11	34.44 N	87.43 W
Tuscumbia, Mo., U.S.	130	F5	38.14 N	92.27 W
Tušino, ngh., Russia	183b		55.50 N	37.26 E
Tuskegee, Al., U.S.	134	E13	32.25 N	85.42 W
Tussøya, i., Nor.	14	C8	69.39 N	18.07 E
Tustin Marine Corps Air Station (Helicopter), mil., Ca., U.S.	198		33.43 N	117.50 W
Tustna, i., Nor.	16	D5	63.11 N	8.06 E
Tustumena Lake, l., Ak., U.S.	109	D9	60.10 N	150.50 W
Tuszyn, Pol.	24	E15	51.36 N	19.33 E
Tutaev, Russia	26	C22	57.53 N	39.33 E
Tutak, Tur.	42	F10	39.32 N	42.44 E
Tuthills Creek, stm., N.Y., U.S.	194		40.45 N	73.02 W
Tuticorin, India	69	G4	8.48 N	78.08 E
Tutin, Yugo.	36	F7	42.59 N	20.20 E
Tutóia, Braz.	170	B4	2.47 S	42.17 W
Tutoko, Mount, mtn., N.Z.	102	G3	44.36 S	168.00 E
Tutong, Bru.	66	A9	4.48 N	114.39 E
Tutova, stm., Rom.	36	C14	46.06 N	27.32 E
Tutrakan, Blg.	36	E13	44.03 N	26.37 E
Tuttle, N.D., U.S.	142	G14	47.08 N	100.00 W
Tuttle, Ok., U.S.	138	F11	35.17 N	97.49 W
Tuttle Creek Lake, res., Ks., U.S.	138	B12	39.21 N	96.41 W
Tuttlingen, Ger.	20	G17	47.59 N	8.49 E
Tutuala, Indon.	60	G8	8.24 S	127.15 E
Tutuban Station, trans., Phil.	187f		14.37 N	120.58 E
Tutuila, i., Am. Sam.	101c	h12	14.18 S	170.42 W
Tutupaca, Volcán, vol., Peru	164	G3	17.01 S	70.22 W
Tutwiler, Ms., U.S.	134	C8	34.01 N	90.26 W
Tutzing, Ger.	24	I7	47.54 N	11.16 E
Tuul, stm., Mong.	52	B6	48.56 N	104.47 E
Tuupovaara, Fin.	18	E17	62.29 N	30.36 E
Tuusniemi, Fin.	18	E15	62.48 N	28.30 E
Tuutapu, Cerro, mtn., Chile	100l	e29	27.08 S	109.24 W
Tuva, state, Russia	48	D16	52.00 N	95.00 E
Tuvalu, ctry., Oc.	92	D8	8.00 S	178.00 E
Tuvalu, is., Tuvalu	94	D8	8.00 S	178.00 E
Tuvuca, i., Fiji	101e	p20	17.40 S	178.48 W
Tuwayq, Jabal, mts., Sau. Ar.	72	E6	23.00 N	46.00 E
Tuxedo Park, De., U.S.	203		39.43 N	75.37 W
Tuxford, Sk., Can.	142	D8	50.34 N	105.33 W
Tuxpan, Mex.	154	E6	21.56 N	105.17 W
Tuxpan de Rodríguez Cano, Mex.	154	E10	20.58 N	97.24 W
Tuxtepec, Mex.	154	F10	18.05 N	96.06 W
Tuxtla Gutiérrez, Mex.	154	G12	16.45 N	93.06 W
Túy see Tui, Spain	28	B2	42.03 N	8.38 W
Tuy, stm., Ven.	168	B8	10.23 N	65.59 W
Tuy An, Viet.	64	F9	13.17 N	109.14 E
Tuyen Hoa, Viet.	64	D8	17.50 N	106.11 E
Tuyen Quang, Viet.	64	B7	21.50 N	105.11 E
Tuy Hoa, Viet.	64	F9	13.04 N	109.18 E
Tüysarkān, Iran	74	C11	34.33 N	48.27 E
Tuyūr, Burj at-, hill, Sudan	82	C5	20.47 N	27.37 E
Tuz, Iraq	74	C9	34.52 N	44.38 E
Tuža, Russia	40	C15	57.36 N	47.56 E
Tuz Gölü, l., Tur.	42	F5	38.45 N	33.25 E
Tuzigoot National Monument, p.o.i., Az., U.S.	150	I4	34.49 N	112.01 W
Tuzla, Bos.	36	E5	44.32 N	18.39 E
Tuzla, Tur.	76	B6	36.42 N	35.06 E
Tuzlov, stm., Russia	38	F18	47.26 N	39.36 E
Tuzluca, Tur.	42	E10	40.03 N	43.37 E
Tuzly, Ukr.	38	H9	45.52 N	30.05 E
Tvărdica, Blg.	36	G12	42.42 N	25.54 E
Tvardiţa, Mol.	38	G8	46.08 N	28.59 E
Tvedestrand, Nor.	16	I6	58.37 N	8.55 E
Tveitsund, Nor.	16	H6	59.01 N	8.33 E
Tver' (Kalinin), Russia	26	D18	56.52 N	35.54 E
Tverca, stm., Russia	26	D18	56.51 N	35.55 E
Tverskaja oblast', co., Russia	26	D16	57.00 N	34.00 E
Twardogóra, Pol.	24	E13	51.22 N	17.28 E
Tweed, On., Can.	126	D12	44.28 N	77.18 W
Tweed, stm., U.K.	10	F10	55.46 N	1.59 W
Tweed Heads, Austl.	98	G9	28.11 S	153.32 E
Tweedsmuir Provincial Park, p.o.i., B.C., Can.	144	C4	52.55 N	126.05 W
Tweedy Mountain, mtn., Mt., U.S.	146	E13	45.29 N	112.58 W
Tweeling, S. Afr.	90	E9	27.38 S	28.30 E
Twee Rivieren, S. Afr.	90	E5	26.25 S	20.37 E
Twelvemile Island, i., Pa., U.S.	197b		40.32 N	79.51 W
Twelve Mile Lake, l., Sk., Can.	142	E7	49.29 N	106.14 W
Twenthekanaal, can., Neth.	20	B15	52.10 N	6.11 E
Twentieth Century Fox Studios, sci., Ca., U.S.	198		34.03 N	118.25 W
Twentynine Palms, Ca., U.S.	148	I9	34.08 N	116.03 W
Twentynine Palms Marine Corps Base, mil., Ca., U.S.	148	I9	34.27 N	115.59 W
Twickenham, ngh., Eng., U.K.	178		51.27 N	0.20 W
Twin Bridge Farm, Pa., U.S.	203		39.57 N	75.33 W
Twin Bridges, Mt., U.S.	146	E14	45.33 N	112.20 W
Twin Butte Creek, stm., Ks., U.S.	138	C7	38.46 N	100.56 W
Twin Buttes, mtn., Or., U.S.	146	F4	44.20 N	122.15 W
Twin Buttes Reservoir, res., Tx., U.S.	136	C7	31.19 N	100.33 W
Twin City, Ga., U.S.	132	D3	32.35 N	82.09 W
Twin Falls, Id., U.S.	146	H12	42.34 N	114.27 W
Twin Lakes, Ga., U.S.	132	F2	30.42 N	83.12 W
Twin Lakes, Wi., U.S.	130	B9	42.31 N	88.14 W
Twin Peaks, mtn., Id., U.S.	146	F12	44.35 N	114.29 W
Twin Peaks, mts., Ca., U.S.	200		37.45 N	122.27 W
Twinsburg, Oh., U.S.	124	C4	41.18 N	81.27 W
Twin Valley, Mn., U.S.	128	D2	47.15 N	96.15 W
Twisp, Wa., U.S.	146	B6	48.21 N	120.07 W
Twiss Green, Eng., U.K.	180		53.27 N	2.32 W
Twitchell Reservoir, res., Ca., U.S.	148	H5	35.02 N	120.19 W
Twitya, stm., N.T., Can.	110	C5	64.10 N	128.11 W
Two Butte Creek, stm., Co., U.S.	138	D6	38.02 N	102.08 W
Twofold Bay, b., Austl.	98	K7	37.05 S	149.54 E
Two Harbors, Mn., U.S.	128	D7	47.01 N	91.40 W
Two Hills, Ab., Can.	144	C19	53.42 N	111.44 W
Two Medicine, stm., Mt., U.S.	146	B13	48.29 N	112.13 W
Two Mile Creek, stm., On., Can.	202a		43.16 N	79.06 W
Twomile Creek, stm., N.Y., U.S.	202a		43.01 N	78.55 W
Two Penny Run, stm., N.J., U.S.	203		39.41 N	75.26 W
Two Rivers, Wi., U.S.	126	D2	44.09 N	87.34 W
Two Rivers Reservoir, res., N.M., U.S.	138	H3	33.17 N	104.45 W
Tybee Island, Ga., U.S.	132	D5	32.00 N	80.51 W
Tychy, Pol.	24	F14	50.07 N	19.01 E
Tyczyn, Pol.	24	G18	49.58 N	22.02 E
Tydal, Nor.	16	D9	63.03 N	11.33 E
Tye, Tx., U.S.	136	B8	32.27 N	99.51 W
Tyende Creek, stm., Az., U.S.	150	G7	36.49 N	109.42 W
Tygarts Creek, stm., Ky., U.S.	130	F14	38.43 N	82.57 W
Tygda, Russia	50	F14	53.06 N	126.19 E
Tygh Valley, Or., U.S.	146	E5	45.14 N	121.09 W
Tyin, l., Nor.	16	F6	61.17 N	8.13 E
Tykhonovychi, Ukr.	38	B11	51.56 N	32.09 E
Tyler, Mn., U.S.	128	G2	44.16 N	96.08 W
Tyler, Tx., U.S.	136	B12	32.21 N	95.18 W
Tyler Park, Va., U.S.	202c		38.52 N	77.12 W
Tylertown, Ms., U.S.	134	F8	31.06 N	90.08 W
Tylihul, stm., Ukr.	38	F9	47.09 N	30.58 E
Tylihul's'kyi lyman, l., Ukr.	38	G10	46.46 N	31.10 E
Tylösand, Swe.	16	K10	56.38 N	12.44 E
Tylöskog, hills, Swe.	16	I13	58.48 N	15.15 E
Tym, stm., Russia	48	C14	59.25 N	80.00 E
Tymovskoe, Russia	50	F17	50.50 N	142.38 E
Tympáki, Grc.	34	H7	35.04 N	24.46 E
Tynda, Russia	50	E13	55.09 N	124.43 E
Tyndall, S.D., U.S.	140	D15	42.59 N	97.52 W
Tyndall Air Force Base, mil., Fl., U.S.	134	G13	30.04 N	85.35 W
Tyndaris, hist., Italy	32	F8	38.09 N	15.03 E
Tynemouth, Eng., U.K.	10	F11	55.01 N	1.25 W
Tyngsboro, Ma., U.S.	201		42.40 N	71.25 W
Tynset, Nor.	16	E8	62.17 N	10.46 E
Tynytsia, Ukr.	38	B11	51.08 N	32.55 E
Tyre see Şūr, Leb.	76	E6	33.16 N	35.13 E
Tyrifjorden, l., Nor.	16	G7	60.02 N	10.08 E
Tyringe, Swe.	16	K11	56.09 N	13.36 E
Tyrka, Russia	48	D19	54.29 N	107.09 E
Tyrma, Russia	50	F15	50.02 N	132.10 E
Tyrma, stm., Russia	50	F15	50.27 N	131.17 E
Tyrnavos, Grc.	34	D5	39.44 N	22.17 E
Tyrone, Ok., U.S.	138	E7	36.57 N	101.03 W
Tyrone, Pa., U.S.	124	D7	40.40 N	78.14 W
Tyrone Lake, l., Mi., U.S.	199		42.42 N	83.43 W
Tyrrell, Lake, l., Austl.	98	J4	35.20 S	142.49 E
Tyrrhenian Sea, s., Eur.	8	G11	40.00 N	12.00 E
Tyrrhénienne, Mer see Tyrrhenian Sea, s., Eur.	8	G11	40.00 N	12.00 E
Tyruliai, Lith.	26	E6	55.46 N	23.21 E
Tysa (Tisa) (Tisza), stm., Eur.	36	D7	45.07 N	20.17 E
Tysfjorden, b., Nor.	14	D7	68.09 N	16.10 E
Tyshkivka, Ukr.	38	E9	48.29 N	30.56 E
Tysmenytsia, Ukr.	38	E3	48.53 N	24.51 E
Tysnesøya, i., Nor.	16	H3	59.57 N	5.33 E
Tysons Corner, Va., U.S.	202c		38.55 N	77.14 W
Tysons Corner Center, shp. cen., Va., U.S.	202c		38.55 N	77.13 W
Tysons Green, Va., U.S.	202c		38.55 N	77.15 W
Tysse, Nor.	16	G3	60.22 N	5.45 E
Tyssedal, Nor.	16	G4	60.05 N	6.33 E
Tytherington, Eng., U.K.	180		53.17 N	2.08 W
Tytuvėnai, Lith.	26	E6	55.36 N	23.12 E
Ty Ty, Ga., U.S.	132	E2	31.28 N	83.40 W
Tyva see Tuva, state, Russia	48	D16	52.00 N	95.00 E
Tyvriv, Ukr.	38	D7	49.00 N	28.30 E
Tywyn, Wales, U.K.	10	I8	52.35 N	4.05 W
Tzaneen, S. Afr.	90	C10	23.49 S	30.10 E
Tzekung see Zigong, China	52	F5	29.21 N	104.46 E
Tzeliutsing see Zigong, China	52	F5	29.21 N	104.46 E
Tzucacab, Mex.	156	B3	20.03 N	89.02 W
Tzupo see Boshan, China	58	C7	36.29 N	117.50 E

U

Name	Page	Map Ref.	Latitude	Longitude
Uamba see Wamba, stm., Afr.	86	F3	3.56 S	17.12 E
Uatumã, stm., Braz.	164	D6	2.24 S	57.33 W
Uauá, Braz.	170	E6	9.50 S	39.28 W
Uaupés, Braz.	168	H8	0.03 S	67.05 W
Uaupés (Vaupés), stm., S.A.	168	G7	0.01 N	67.15 W
Uaxactún, hist., Guat.	156	D3	17.24 N	89.39 W
Ubá, Braz.	170	K4	21.07 S	42.56 W
Ubagan, stm., Kaz.	48	D10	54.24 N	64.45 E
Ubaidullaganj, India	70	G6	22.59 N	77.35 E
Ubaitaba, Braz.	170	H6	14.19 S	39.17 W
Ubajara, Braz.	170	B5	3.51 S	40.56 W
Ubajara, Parque Nacional de, p.o.i., Braz.	170	B5	3.47 S	40.56 W
Ubangi (Oubangui), stm., Afr.	82	G3	0.25 S	17.47 E
Ubarc' (Ubort'), stm., Eur.	38	B6	52.06 N	28.28 E
Ubatã, Braz.	170	H6	14.12 S	39.31 W
Ubaté, Col.	168	E5	5.19 N	73.49 W
Ubatuba, Braz.	170	L3	23.26 S	45.04 W
Ubauro, Pak.	70	D2	28.09 N	69.43 E
Ubayyid, Wādī al-, stm., Asia	74	D7	32.35 N	43.46 E
Ube, Japan	56	F4	33.56 N	131.15 E
Úbeda, Spain	28	F7	38.01 N	3.22 W
Uberaba, Braz.	170	J2	19.45 S	47.55 W
Uberaba, stm., Braz.	170	J1	20.08 S	48.32 W
Uberlândia, Braz.	170	J1	18.54 S	48.14 W
Überlingen, Ger.	24	I5	47.46 N	9.10 E
Ubid', stm., Ukr.	38	B11	51.31 N	32.34 E
Ubin, Pulau, i., Sing.	189c		1.24 N	103.58 E
Ubiña, Peña, mtn., Spain	28	B4	43.00 N	5.57 W
Ubl'a, Slvk.	24	H18	48.53 N	22.24 E
Ubly, Mi., U.S.	126	E7	43.43 N	82.55 W
Uboldo, Italy	184b		45.37 N	9.00 E
Ubombo, S. Afr.	90	E11	27.32 S	32.04 E
Ubon Ratchathani, Thai.	64	E7	15.14 N	104.51 E
Ubort' (Ubarc'), stm., Eur.	38	B6	52.06 N	28.28 E
Ubrique, Spain	28	H5	36.41 N	5.27 W
Ubundu, D.R.C.	86	E5	0.21 S	25.25 E
Uča, stm., Russia	183b		55.56 N	37.57 E
Ucacha, Arg.	172	F6	33.02 S	63.31 W
Učaly, Russia	48	D9	54.17 N	59.26 E
Učami, Russia	48	B17	63.50 N	96.29 E
Ucar, Azer.	42	E12	40.30 N	47.38 E
Učaral, Kaz.	48	E14	46.09 N	80.56 E
Ucayali, stm., Peru	164	D3	4.29 S	73.29 W
Ucero, stm., Spain	22	H2	41.30 N	3.04 W
Uch, Pak.	70	D3	29.12 N	71.02 E
Uchee Creek, stm., Al., U.S.	134	E13	32.18 N	84.57 W
Uchihata, Japan	188		34.25 N	135.27 E
Uchinoura, Japan	56	H4	31.15 N	131.04 E
Uchiura-wan, b., Japan	54	C14	42.20 N	140.40 E
Uchiza, Peru	164	E2	8.25 S	76.24 W
Uchoa, Braz.	170	K1	20.57 S	49.10 W
Ückendorf, ngh., Ger.	181		51.30 N	7.07 E
Uckermark, reg., Ger.	24	C9	53.10 N	13.35 E
Ucluelet, B.C., Can.	144	H5	48.57 N	125.32 W
Ucon, Id., U.S.	146	G15	43.36 N	111.59 W
Üçpınar, Tur.	76	A3	37.07 N	32.14 E
Učur, stm., Russia	50	E15	58.47 N	130.35 E
Uda, stm., Russia	48	C17	56.02 N	99.37 E
Uda, stm., Russia	50	F15	54.42 N	135.18 E
Udagamandalam, India	69	F3	11.24 N	76.42 E
Udai, stm., Ukr.	38	C11	50.04 N	33.07 E
Udaipur, India	70	F4	24.34 N	73.41 E
Udalguri, India	70	E13	26.48 N	92.06 E
Udall, Ks., U.S.	138	D11	37.23 N	97.06 W
Udamalpet, India	69	F3	10.34 N	77.15 E
Udankudi, India	69	G4	8.27 N	78.00 E
Udaquiola, Arg.	172	H8	36.33 S	58.32 W
Udaypur, Nepal	70	E11	26.55 N	86.30 E
Udbina, Cro.	30	F12	44.32 N	15.46 E
Uddeholm, Swe.	16	G11	60.01 N	13.37 E
Uddevalla, Swe.	16	I9	58.20 N	11.55 E
Uddjaur, l., Swe.	14	G9	65.55 N	17.49 E
Udel'naja, ngh., Russia	183a		60.01 N	30.19 E
Udelnyy Park, p.o.i., Russia	183a		60.01 N	30.19 E
Udgīr, India	69	B3	18.23 N	77.06 E
Udhampur, India	70	B5	32.55 N	75.08 E
Udimskij, Russia	12	F21	61.08 N	45.55 E
Udine, Italy	30	D10	46.04 N	13.14 E
Udmurtia see Udmurtija, state, Russia	40	C18	57.00 N	53.00 E
Udmurtija, state, Russia	40	C18	57.00 N	53.00 E
Udokan, hrebet, mts., Russia	50	E12	56.20 N	118.10 E
Udomlja, Russia	26	C17	57.53 N	35.00 E
Udono, Japan	56	F9	33.44 N	136.00 E
Udon Thani, Thai.	64	D6	17.24 N	102.47 E
Udskaja guba, b., Russia	50	F16	54.50 N	135.45 E
Udskoe, Russia	50	F15	54.30 N	134.24 E
Udupi, India	69	E2	13.20 N	74.44 E
Udu Point, c., Fiji	101e	p20	16.08 S	179.57 W
Udy, Ukr.	38	C14	50.23 N	36.03 E
Udyl', ozero, l., Russia	50	F16	52.04 N	139.47 E
Udža, Russia	50	B12	71.15 N	117.06 E
Ueckermünde, Ger.	24	C10	53.44 N	14.02 E
Ueda, Japan	56	C11	36.23 N	138.15 E
Uedesheim, Ger.	181		51.10 N	6.48 E
Uegō, Japan	186		35.13 N	139.56 E
Uele, stm., D.R.C.	86	D4	4.07 N	22.26 E
Uelen, Russia	50	C26	66.08 N	169.48 W
Uel'kal', Russia	50	C25	65.31 N	179.17 W
Uelzen, Ger.	24	C6	52.58 N	10.33 E
Uelzen, Ger.	181		51.33 N	7.44 E
Uemskij, Russia	12	D19	64.29 N	40.49 E
Ueno, Japan	56	E9	34.45 N	136.08 E
Ueno, Japan	188		34.53 N	135.14 E
Ueno Park, p.o.i., Japan	186		35.43 N	139.46 E
Uenoshiba, Japan	188		34.33 N	135.28 E
Uerdingen, ngh., Ger.	181		51.21 N	6.39 E
Uere, stm., D.R.C.	86	D5	3.33 N	25.15 E
Uetersen, Ger.	24	C5	53.41 N	9.40 E
Uetz, Ger.	182a		52.28 N	12.56 E
Ufa, Russia	40	D19	54.42 N	55.57 E
Ufa, stm., Russia	48	C9	54.41 N	56.02 E
Uffenheim, Ger.	24	G6	49.32 N	10.14 E
Ufita, stm., Italy	32	C8	41.08 N	14.54 E
Ugab, stm., Nmb.	88	E2	21.11 S	13.37 E
Ugāle, Lat.	26	C4	57.16 N	22.02 E
Uganda, ctry., Afr.	82	G6	1.00 N	32.00 E
Ugărčin, Blg.	36	F11	43.06 N	24.25 E
Ugarit, hist., Syria	76	C6	35.35 N	35.45 E
Ugashik, Ak., U.S.	109	E8	57.32 N	157.25 W
Ugie, S. Afr.	90	G9	31.11 S	28.13 E
Ugíjar, Spain	28	H7	36.57 N	3.03 W
Uglegorsk, Russia	50	G17	49.03 N	142.02 E
Uglekamensk, Russia	54	C10	43.12 N	133.13 E
Uglič, Russia	26	C21	57.31 N	38.19 E
Ugljan, Otok, i., Cro.	30	F12	44.05 N	15.10 E
Uglovka, Russia	26	B16	58.14 N	33.30 E
Ugodiči, Russia	26	C22	57.10 N	39.29 E
Ugodskij Zavod, Russia	26	E19	55.01 N	36.44 E
Ugra, Russia	26	F17	54.47 N	34.19 E
Ugra, stm., Russia	26	F18	54.30 N	36.07 E
Uh (Uzh), stm., Eur.	24	H18	48.36 N	22.00 E
Uherské Hradiště, Czech Rep.	24	G13	49.04 N	17.27 E
Uherský Brod, Czech Rep.	24	H13	49.01 N	17.39 E
Uhlenhorst, Nmb.	90	C3	23.41 S	17.58 E
Uhma, guba, b., Russia	18	C24	64.24 N	37.42 E
Uhniv, Ukr.	38	C2	50.22 N	23.44 E
Uhra, stm., Russia	26	B22	58.15 N	39.08 E
Uhroïdi, Ukr.	38	C14	50.52 N	35.16 E
Uhta, Russia	18	F25	61.12 N	38.32 E
Uhta, Russia	48	B8	63.33 N	53.43 E
Uhtoma, Russia	18	G25	60.10 N	38.02 E
Uig, Scot., U.K.	10	D6	57.35 N	6.22 W
Uíge, Ang.	88	B1	7.37 S	15.03 E
Uil, Kaz.	48	E8	49.05 N	54.40 E
Uil, stm., Kaz.	40	G18	48.32 N	52.25 E
Uilpata, gora, mtn., Russia	42	D10	42.48 N	43.48 E
Uimaharju, Fin.	18	E17	62.55 N	30.15 E
Uina see Vina, stm., Cam.	86	C2	7.51 N	15.46 E
Uinebona, stm., Ven.	168	E10	5.11 N	63.01 W
Uinskoe, Russia	40	C20	56.53 N	56.35 E
Uinta, stm., Ut., U.S.	150	C6	40.26 N	109.55 W
Uintah and Ouray Indian Reservation, ind. res., Ut., U.S.	150	D7	40.20 N	110.20 W
Uinta Mountains, mts., Ut., U.S.	150	C6	40.43 N	110.46 W
Uiraúna, Braz.	170	D6	6.31 S	38.25 W
Uis, Nmb.	90	B2	21.08 S	14.50 E
Ŭisŏng, Kor., S.	56	C1	36.21 N	128.41 E
Uitenhage, S. Afr.	90	H7	33.39 S	25.26 E
Uithuizermeeden, Neth.	20	A15	53.24 N	6.45 E
Uj, stm., Asia	48	D10	54.16 N	63.58 E
Ujandina, stm., Russia	50	C17	68.23 N	145.51 E
Ujar, Russia	48	C16	55.48 N	94.19 E
Ujelang, at., Marsh. Is.	94	C7	9.46 N	160.58 E
Újfehértó, Hung.	36	B8	47.47 N	21.41 E
Ujhāni, India	70	D7	27.59 N	79.00 E
Uji, Japan	56	E8	34.53 N	135.48 E
Uji-guntō, is., Japan	56	H2	31.11 N	129.27 E
Ujiji, Tan.	86	E5	4.54 S	29.40 E
Uji-yamada see Ise, Japan	56	E9	34.29 N	136.42 E
Ujjain, India	70	G5	23.10 N	75.46 E
Újpest, ngh., Hung.	182c		47.34 N	19.06 E
Ujście, Pol.	24	C12	53.02 N	16.45 E
Ujung, Indon.	66	G12	7.06 S	120.45 E
Ujunggading, Indon.	66	C1	0.15 N	99.34 E
Ujunggenteng, Indon.	66	G5	7.21 S	106.24 E
Ujungkulon National Park, p.o.i., Indon.	66	G4	6.41 S	105.21 E
Ujunglamuru, Indon.	66	F11	4.47 S	119.58 E
Ujungpandang (Makasar), Indon.	66	F11	5.08 S	119.24 E
Újvidék see Novi Sad, Yugo.	36	D6	45.14 N	19.49 E
Uk, Russia	48	C17	55.04 N	98.50 E
Uka, Russia	50	E21	57.50 N	162.06 E
Ukara Island, i., Tan.	86	E6	1.50 S	33.03 E
Ukerewe Island, i., Tan.	86	E6	2.03 S	33.00 E
Ukiah, Ca., U.S.	148	D2	39.08 N	123.12 W
Ukiah, Or., U.S.	146	E7	45.08 N	118.56 W
Uki Island see Uki Ni Masi Island, i., Sol. Is.	101b	f9	10.15 S	161.45 E
Uki Ni Masi Island, i., Sol. Is.	101b	f9	10.15 S	161.45 E
Ukmergė, Lith.	26	E7	55.15 N	24.46 E
Ukraïna see Ukraine, ctry., Eur.	6	F15	49.00 N	32.00 E
Ukraine, ctry., Eur.	6	F15	49.00 N	32.00 E
Uksunioki, stm., Russia	18	F18	61.29 N	31.36 E
Uktym, Russia	12	E23	62.36 N	48.53 E
Ukui, Indon.	66	D3	0.09 S	102.10 E
Ukyō, ngh., Japan	188		35.03 N	135.42 E
Ukyr, Russia	50	G10	49.28 N	108.52 E
Ula, Bela.	26	E12	55.13 N	29.14 E
Ula, India	190b		22.43 N	88.33 E
Ula, Tur.	34	F11	37.06 N	28.24 E
Ula, stm., Bela.	26	E12	55.14 N	29.14 E
Ūla, stm., Bela.	26	F7	54.10 N	24.20 E
Ulaanbaatar, Mong.	52	B6	47.55 N	106.55 E
Ulaangom, Mong.	48	E16	49.58 N	92.04 E
Ulaanjirem, Mong.	52	B6	45.03 N	105.35 E
Ulan, Austl.	98	I7	32.17 S	149.44 E
Ulan Bator see Ulaanbaatar, Mong.	52	B6	47.55 N	106.55 E
Ulan Buh Shamo, des., China	58	A2	40.00 N	106.30 E
Ulan-Burgasy, hrebet, mts., Russia	50	F10	52.27 N	108.14 E
Ulan-Erge, Russia	40	H14	46.18 N	44.51 E
Ulanhad see Chifeng, China	52	C8	42.15 N	118.57 E
Ulan Hol, Russia	40	I15	45.26 N	46.51 E
Ulanhot see Horqin Youyi Qianqi, China	52	B9	46.04 N	122.03 E
Ulaniv, Ukr.	38	D7	49.41 N	28.08 E
Ulanove, Ukr.	38	B13	51.45 N	34.17 E
Ulanów, Pol.	24	F18	50.28 N	22.19 E
Ulansuhai Nur, l., China	58	A3	40.54 N	108.48 E
Ulan-Ude, Russia	50	F10	51.49 N	107.36 E
Ular, Pulau, i., Sing.	189c		1.14 N	103.45 E
Ulawa Island, i., Sol. Is.	101b	e9	9.46 S	161.57 E
Ulawun, Mount, vol., Pap. N. Gui.	101a	b5	5.03 S	151.20 E
Ułazów, Pol.	24	F18	50.16 N	23.00 E
Ulchin, Kor., S.	54	F8	36.59 N	129.23 E
Ulcinj, Yugo.	36	H6	41.56 N	19.13 E
Ulco, S. Afr.	90	F7	28.20 S	24.16 E
Ulcombe, Eng., U.K.	178		51.12 N	0.39 E
Uldz, stm., Asia	52	B8	49.55 N	115.33 E
Uldza see Uldz, stm., Asia	52	B8	49.55 N	115.33 E
Uleåborg see Oulu, Fin.	18	C12	65.00 N	25.28 E
Ulefoss, Nor.	16	H7	59.17 N	9.16 E
Ulen, Mn., U.S.	128	D2	47.04 N	96.15 W
Ulety, Russia	50	F11	51.21 N	112.29 E
Ulëz, Alb.	32	C13	41.42 N	19.54 E
Ulfborg, Den.	16	K6	56.16 N	8.20 E
Ulgueira, Port.	184c		38.47 N	9.28 W
Ulhās, stm., India	190c		19.13 N	73.01 E
Ulhāsnagar, India	69	B1	19.13 N	73.07 E
Ulianivka, Ukr.	38	C13	50.58 N	34.17 E
Ul'ianovka, Ukr.	38	E9	48.19 N	30.15 E
Uliastay, Mong.	52	B4	47.44 N	96.51 E
Ulimang, Palau	100b	f8	7.37 N	134.39 E
Ulindi, stm., D.R.C.	86	E5	1.40 S	25.52 E
Ulithi, at., Micron.	60	D10	9.55 N	139.42 E
Ulja, Russia	50	E17	58.51 N	141.49 E
Uljanovka, Russia	26	A13	59.38 N	30.46 E
Uljanovo, Russia	26	G18	53.43 N	35.32 E
Uljanovsk, Russia	40	D16	54.19 N	48.22 E
Ul'janovskaja oblast', co., Russia	40	D15	53.30 N	47.30 E
Ul'janovskij, Kaz.	48	D12	50.03 N	73.43 E
Ul'kan, Russia	48	C19	57.14 N	107.22 E
Ulla, stm., Spain	28	B2	42.39 N	8.44 W
Ulladulla, Austl.	98	J8	35.21 S	150.28 E
Ullapool, Scot., U.K.	10	D7	57.53 N	5.09 W
Ullastrell, Spain	184d		41.31 N	1.58 E
Ullatti, Swe.	14	E12	67.01 N	21.49 E
Üllendahl, ngh., Ger.	181		51.17 N	7.11 E
Ullin, Il., U.S.	130	G8	37.17 N	89.11 W
Üllő, Hung.	182c		47.23 N	19.21 E
Ullsfjorden, b., Nor.	14	C10	69.53 N	19.54 E
Ullswater, l., Eng., U.K.	10	G10	54.34 N	2.53 W
Ullŭng-do, i., Kor., S.	54	F9	37.29 N	130.52 E
Ullvettern, l., Swe.	16	H11	59.26 N	14.16 E
Ulm, Ger.	24	H5	48.24 N	9.59 E
Ulm, Mt., U.S.	146	C15	47.26 N	111.30 W
Ulmarra, Austl.	98	G9	29.37 S	153.02 E
Ulmeni, Rom.	36	D13	45.04 N	26.38 E
Ulónguè, Moz.	88	C5	14.37 S	34.19 E
Uløya, i., Nor.	14	C11	69.51 N	20.36 E
Ulricehamn, Swe.	16	J11	57.48 N	13.25 E
Ulrum, Neth.	24	C2	53.22 N	6.20 E
Ulsan, Kor., S.	54	G8	35.32 N	129.19 E
Ulster, hist. reg., Eur.	10	G5	54.35 N	7.00 W
Ulster, stm., Ger.	20	D18	50.50 N	9.59 E
Ulster Canal, can., Eur.	10	G5	54.08 N	7.21 W
Ulsvåg, Nor.	14	D6	68.07 N	15.51 E
Ultevis, mtn., Swe.	14	E9	67.13 N	18.36 E
Ultraoriental, Cordillera see Divisor, Serra do, plat., S.A.	164	E3	8.20 S	73.30 W
Ulu, Indon.	60	E8	2.42 N	125.22 E
Ulu, Russia	50	D14	60.18 N	127.29 E
Ulúa, stm., Hond.	156	E3	15.52 N	87.44 W
Ulubat Gölü, l., Tur.	34	C11	40.10 N	28.36 E
Ulubey, Tur.	34	E12	38.25 N	29.18 E
Uluborlu, Tur.	34	E13	38.04 N	30.28 E
Uluçınar, Tur.	76	B6	36.25 N	35.55 E
Uludağ, mtn., Tur.	34	C12	40.04 N	29.13 E
Uludağ Yarımdası Milli Parkı, p.o.i., Tur.	34	C12	40.12 N	29.14 E
Uludāngar, India	190b		22.51 N	88.31 E
Uludere, Tur.	42	G10	37.27 N	42.52 E
Ulugqat, China	48	G12	39.50 N	74.19 E
Ulukışla, Tur.	42	G6	37.33 N	34.32 E
Ulul, i., Micron.	94	C5	8.35 N	149.39 E
Ulu Laho, Bukit, mtn., Malay.	64	J5	5.44 N	101.31 E
Ulundi, S. Afr.	88	F5	28.17 S	31.25 E
Ulunga, Russia	52	B12	46.31 N	136.56 E
Ulungur, stm., China	52	B2	46.58 N	87.25 E
Ulungur Hu, l., China	52	B2	47.12 N	87.16 E
Ulunhan, Russia	50	F11	54.51 N	111.02 E
Uluru (Ayers Rock), mtn., Austl.	96	E6	25.19 S	130.59 E
Ulus, Tur.	34	B15	41.35 N	32.38 E

Name	Page	Map Ref.	Latitude	Longitude
Ulutau, gory, mts., Kaz.	48	E11	49.00 N	67.00 E
Ulva, India	190c		18.59 N	73.02 E
Ulva, i., Scot., U.K.	10	E6	56.28 N	6.12 W
Ulverston, Eng., U.K.	10	G9	54.11 N	3.05 W
Ulverstone, Austl.	99a	n12	41.09 S	146.10 E
Ulvik, Nor.	16	G4	60.34 N	6.54 E
Ulysses, Ks., U.S.	138	D7	37.34 N	101.21 W
Ulysses, Ne., U.S.	140	F15	41.04 N	97.12 W
Uma, China	50	F13	52.35 N	120.38 E
Umag, Cro.	30	E10	45.24 N	13.31 E
Umán, Mex.	156	B3	20.53 N	89.45 W
Uman', Ukr.	38	E9	48.44 N	30.14 E
'Umān see Oman, ctry., Asia	72	F8	22.00 N	58.00 E
'Umān, Khalīj see Oman, Gulf of, b., Asia	72	E8	24.30 N	58.30 E
Umanak, Grnld.	108	C15	70.40 N	52.07 W
Umanak Fjord, b., Grnld.	108	C15	70.55 N	53.00 W
Umargãon, India	70	H4	20.13 N	72.46 E
Umari, Braz.	170	D6	6.38 S	38.42 W
Umaria, India	70	G8	23.31 N	80.50 E
Umarizal, Braz.	170	D7	5.59 S	37.49 W
Umarkot, Pak.	70	F2	25.21 N	69.44 E
Umatac, Guam	100c	j9	13.16 N	144.39 E
Umatilla, Fl., U.S.	132	H4	28.56 N	81.40 W
Umatilla, Or., U.S.	146	E7	45.54 N	119.20 W
Umatilla, stm., Or., U.S.	146	E7	45.55 N	119.20 W
Umatilla, Lake, res., U.S.	146	E4	45.38 N	121.56 W
Umatilla Indian Reservation, ind. res., Or., U.S.	146	E8	45.41 N	118.31 W
Umaze, Japan	188		34.57 N	135.03 E
Umba, Russia	14	F25	66.40 N	34.17 E
Umba, stm., Russia	14	E25	67.06 N	34.03 E
Umbaúba, Braz.	170	F7	11.23 S	37.29 W
Umbertide, Italy	30	G9	43.18 N	12.19 E
Umboi Island, i., Pap. N. Gui.	101a	b4	5.35 S	147.52 E
Umbria, state, Italy	30	G9	43.00 N	12.30 E
Umbroli, India	190c		19.11 N	73.06 E
Umbukul, Pap. N. Gui.	101a	a4	2.30 S	149.59 E
Umbuzero, ozero, l., Russia	14	E25	67.43 N	34.25 E
Umeå, Swe.	16	D18	63.49 N	20.16 E
Umeälven, stm., Swe.	16	C17	63.47 N	20.19 E
Umedani, Japan	188		34.44 N	135.51 E
Umët, Russia	40	E13	52.31 N	42.58 E
Umët, Russia	40	D13	54.06 N	42.41 E
Umfolozi Game Reserve, ind. res., S. Afr.	90	F10	28.19 S	31.50 E
Umfors, Swe.	16	B12	65.56 N	15.01 E
Umfreville Lake, res., On., Can.	128	A3	50.18 N	94.45 W
Umirzak, Kaz.	42	D14	43.37 N	51.13 E
Umkomaas, S. Afr.	90	G10	30.12 S	30.47 E
Umm 'Agārim, sand, Egypt	76	H3	30.53 N	32.51 E
Umm al-'Abīd, Libya	82	B3	27.30 N	15.02 E
Umm al-Arānib, Libya	82	B2	26.08 N	14.44 E
Umm al-Jimāl, Khirbat, hist., Jord.	76	F7	32.20 N	36.22 E
Umm al-Qaywayn, U.A.E.	74	H14	25.35 N	55.34 E
Umm al-Qittayn, Jord.	76	F7	32.19 N	36.38 E
Umm as-Sa'd, hist., Syria	76	E7	33.16 N	36.47 E
Umm Bel, Sudan	82	E5	13.31 N	28.04 E
Umm Durmān (Omdurman), Sudan	82	D6	15.38 N	32.28 E
Umm el Fahm, Isr.	76	F6	32.31 N	35.09 E
Umm el-Hawâra, Gebel, mtn., Egypt	76	J2	28.42 N	31.08 E
Umm el-Qûsur, Egypt	76	K1	27.23 N	30.54 E
Umm Kaddādah, Sudan	86	B5	13.35 N	26.40 E
Umm Khunān, Egypt	191c		29.55 N	31.15 E
Umm Lajj, Sau. Ar.	72	D4	25.07 N	37.15 E
Umm Mitmam, sand, Egypt	76	H3	30.41 N	32.28 E
Umm Omeiyid, Râs, mtn., Egypt	76	K3	27.52 N	32.19 E
Umm Qasr, Iraq	74	F10	30.02 N	47.56 E
Umm Ruwābah, Sudan	82	E6	12.54 N	31.12 E
Umm Sayyālah, Sudan	82	E6	14.23 N	31.09 E
Umm Urūmah, i., Sau. Ar.	74	H5	25.45 N	36.32 E
Umnak Island, i., Ak., U.S.	109a	g25	53.25 N	168.10 W
Umnäs, Swe.	16	B14	65.25 N	16.11 E
Umpqua, stm., Or., U.S.	146	G3	43.42 N	124.04 W
Umpulo, Ang.	88	C2	12.42 S	17.41 E
'Umrān, Yemen	72	F5	15.58 N	43.57 E
Umraniye, Tur.	34	D14	39.11 N	31.13 E
Umraniye, ngh., Tur.	185b		41.01 N	29.05 E
Umred, India	70	H7	20.51 N	79.19 E
Umreth, India	70	G4	22.42 N	73.07 E
Umstead State Park, p.o.i., N.C., U.S.	124	I7	35.52 N	78.47 W
Umtata, S. Afr.	90	G9	31.35 S	28.47 E
Umuarama, Braz.	172	A11	23.46 S	53.18 W
Umurbey, Tur.	34	C9	40.14 N	26.36 E
Umzimkulu, S. Afr.	90	G9	30.15 S	29.56 E
Umzingwani, stm., Zimb.	90	B9	22.10 S	29.55 E
Umzinto, S. Afr.	90	G10	30.23 S	30.32 E
Una, Braz.	170	H6	15.17 S	39.04 W
Una, India	70	H3	20.49 N	71.02 E
Una, stm., Eur.	30	E13	45.15 N	16.54 E
Una, Ribeirão, stm., Braz.	205b		23.31 S	46.18 W
Unac, stm., Bos.	36	E3	44.30 N	16.08 E
Uña de Gato, Mex.	136	I8	25.58 N	99.41 W
Unadilla, Ga., U.S.	132	D2	32.15 N	83.43 W
Unadilla, N.Y., U.S.	124	B10	42.19 N	75.19 W
Unadilla, stm., N.Y., U.S.	124	B10	42.19 N	75.24 W
Unaí, Braz.	170	I2	16.21 S	46.54 W
Unalakleet, Ak., U.S.	109	D7	63.53 N	160.47 W
Unalaska, Ak., U.S.	109	F6	53.52 N	166.32 W
Unalaska Island, i., Ak., U.S.	109	F6	53.45 N	166.45 W
Unare, stm., Ven.	168	C9	10.04 N	65.10 W
Unari, Fin.	14	E16	67.09 N	25.40 E
Unayyir, Harrat al-, lav., Sau. Ar.	74	H5	25.20 N	37.45 E
'Unayzah, Sau. Ar.	72	D5	26.05 N	43.59 E
'Unāzah, Jabal, mtn., Asia	76	F10	32.12 N	39.18 E
Uncia, Bol.	166	C3	18.25 S	66.34 W
Uncompahgre, stm., Co., U.S.	150	E9	38.45 N	108.05 W
Uncompahgre Peak, mtn., Co., U.S.	150	E9	38.04 N	107.28 W
Uncompahgre Plateau, plat., Co., U.S.	150	E8	38.30 N	108.25 W
Unden, l., Swe.	16	I11	58.47 N	14.26 E
Underberg, S. Afr.	90	F9	29.47 S	29.30 E
Under River, Eng., U.K.	178		51.15 N	0.14 E
Underwood, N.D., U.S.	142	G12	47.26 N	101.08 W
Undoža, stm., Russia	18	E25	62.09 N	38.10 E
Undva nina, c., Est.	26	B4	58.30 N	21.56 E
Uneča, Russia	26	H15	52.50 N	32.41 E
Uneča, stm., Russia	26	H15	52.50 N	31.57 E
Uneiuxi, stm., Braz.	168	H9	0.32 S	64.55 W
Unežma, Russia	18	D23	63.46 N	36.42 E
Unga Island, i., Ak., U.S.	109	E7	55.15 N	160.41 W
Ungarie, Austl.	98	I6	33.38 S	146.57 E
Ungava, Baie d' see Ungava Bay, b., Can.	110	D17	59.30 N	67.30 W
Ungava, Péninsule d', pen., Qc., Can.	110	D16	60.00 N	74.00 W
Ungava Bay, b., Can.	110	D17	59.30 N	67.30 W
Ungava Peninsula see Ungava, Péninsule d', pen., Qc., Can.	110	D16	60.00 N	74.00 W
Ungch'ŏn, Kor., S.	56	D1	35.06 N	128.43 E
Ungeny see Ungheni, Mol.	38	F6	47.13 N	27.48 E
Unggi-ŭp, Kor., N.	54	C9	42.20 N	130.24 E
Ungheni, Mol.	38	F6	47.13 N	27.48 E
Ungvár see Užhorod, Ukr.	36	A9	48.37 N	22.18 E
Ungvár see Uzhhorod, Ukr.	40	G3	48.37 N	22.18 E
Unhos, Port.	184c		38.50 N	9.07 W
Uni, Russia	40	C17	57.45 N	51.30 E
União, Braz.	170	C4	4.35 S	42.52 W
União dos Palmares, Braz.	170	E7	9.10 S	36.02 W
Unica, Russia	18	E21	62.37 N	34.27 E
Unicoi, Tn., U.S.	124	H3	36.11 N	82.20 W
Unidad Santa Fe, ngh., Mex.	204a		19.23 N	99.15 W
Uniejów, Pol.	24	D15	51.58 N	18.48 E
Unije, Otok, i., Cro.	30	F11	44.38 N	14.15 E
Unimak Island, i., Ak., U.S.	109	F7	54.43 N	164.27 W
Unimak Pass, strt., Ak., U.S.	109	F6	54.23 N	164.58 W
Unini, stm., Braz.	168	H11	1.41 S	61.31 W
Unión, Arg.	172	G5	35.08 S	65.55 W
Unión, Para.	172	B9	24.48 S	56.33 W
Union, Ia., U.S.	130	B4	42.14 N	93.03 W
Union, La., U.S.	134	G8	30.05 N	90.54 W
Union, Ms., U.S.	134	E9	32.34 N	89.07 W
Union, Mo., U.S.	130	F6	38.26 N	91.00 W
Union, N.J., U.S.	124	D11	40.41 N	74.16 W
Union, Or., U.S.	146	E9	45.12 N	117.51 W
Union, S.C., U.S.	132	B4	34.43 N	81.36 W
Union, Wa., U.S.	146	C3	47.20 N	123.05 W
Union, W.V., U.S.	124	G5	37.35 N	80.32 W
Union Bay, B.C., Can.	144	G6	49.34 N	124.53 W
Union City, Ga., U.S.	134	D14	33.36 N	84.32 W
Union City, In., U.S.	130	D12	40.11 N	85.00 W
Union City, Mi., U.S.	130	B12	42.04 N	85.09 W
Union City, N.J., U.S.	194		40.46 N	74.01 W
Union City, Oh., U.S.	124	D1	40.11 N	84.48 W
Union City, Pa., U.S.	124	C6	41.53 N	79.50 W
Union City, Tn., U.S.	130	H8	36.25 N	89.03 W
Uniondale, S. Afr.	90	H6	33.39 S	23.07 E
Uniondale, N.Y., U.S.	194		40.42 N	73.35 W
Unión de Reyes, Cuba	156	A7	22.48 N	81.32 W
Unión de Tula, Mex.	154	E7	19.57 N	104.16 W
Union Flat Creek, stm., U.S.	146	D9	46.49 N	117.59 W
Union Gap, Wa., U.S.	146	D6	46.32 N	120.28 W
Union Grove, Wi., U.S.	130	B9	42.41 N	88.03 W
Union Island, i., St. Vin.	159e	p11	12.36 N	61.26 W
Union Islands see Tokelau Islands, is., Tok.	94	D9	9.00 S	171.45 W
Union Lake, l., Mi., U.S.	199		42.37 N	83.26 W
Union Point, Ga., U.S.	132	C2	33.37 N	83.04 W
Union Springs, Al., U.S.	134	E13	32.08 N	85.42 W
Union Springs, N.Y., U.S.	124	B9	42.50 N	76.41 W
Union Station, trans., On., Can.	193b		43.39 N	79.23 W
Union Station, trans., Ca., U.S.	198		34.04 N	118.14 W
Union Station, trans., D.C., U.S.	202c		38.54 N	77.00 W
Union Station, trans., Il., U.S.	196		41.53 N	87.38 W
Uniontown, Al., U.S.	134	E11	32.27 N	87.30 W
Uniontown, Ky., U.S.	130	G10	37.46 N	87.56 W
Uniontown, Pa., U.S.	124	E6	39.53 N	79.43 W
Unionville, On., Can.	193b		43.52 N	79.18 W
Unionville, Mi., U.S.	126	E6	43.39 N	83.28 W
Unionville, Mo., U.S.	130	D4	40.28 N	93.00 W
Unionville, N.J., U.S.	203		40.01 N	74.46 W
Unionville, Pa., U.S.	203		39.54 N	75.44 W
United, Pa., U.S.	124	D6	40.13 N	79.29 W
United Arab Emirates, ctry., Asia	72	E7	24.00 N	54.00 E
United Arab Republic see Egypt, ctry., Afr.	82	B5	27.00 N	30.00 E
United Center, p.o.i., Il., U.S.	196		41.53 N	87.40 W
United Kingdom, ctry., Eur.	6	D8	54.00 N	2.00 W
United Kingdom Sovereign Base Area, mil., Cyp.	76	D4	34.59 N	33.45 E
United Nations Headquarters, bldg., N.Y., U.S.	194		40.45 N	73.58 W
United States, ctry., N.A.	104	E12	38.00 N	97.00 W
United States Air Force Academy, mil., Co., U.S.	138	B4	38.59 N	104.51 W
United States Merchant Marine Academy, educ., N.Y., U.S.	194		40.48 N	73.46 W
United States Military Academy, mil., N.Y., U.S.	124	C12	41.23 N	74.00 W
United States Naval Academy, mil., Md., U.S.	124	E9	38.59 N	76.30 W
United States Steel Corporation (Lorain Plant), sci., Oh., U.S.	197a		41.27 N	82.07 W
United States Steel Corporation, sci., Pa., U.S.	197b		40.20 N	79.54 W
United States Steel Corporation Fairless Works, sci., Pa., U.S.	203		40.09 N	74.45 W
Unity, Sk., Can.	142	B4	52.26 N	109.06 W
Unity Reservoir, res., Pa., U.S.	197b		40.17 N	79.30 W
Universal City, Tx., U.S.	136	E9	29.33 N	98.18 W
Universal City, sci., Ca., U.S.	198		34.09 N	118.21 W
Universal Mall, shp. cen., Mi., U.S.	199		42.30 N	83.05 W
Universitaria, Ciudad, educ., Spain	184d		41.23 N	2.08 E
University, Ms., U.S.	134	C9	34.21 N	89.35 W
University City, Mo., U.S.	130	F7	38.39 N	90.18 W
University Gardens, N.Y., U.S.	194		40.46 N	73.43 W
University Heights, Ca., U.S.	200		37.26 N	122.12 W
University Heights, Oh., U.S.	197a		41.29 N	81.32 W
University Park, Md., U.S.	202c		38.58 N	76.57 W
University Park, N.M., U.S.	150	K10	32.17 N	106.44 W
University Park, Tx., U.S.	136	B11	32.51 N	96.47 W
Unjha, India	70	G4	23.47 N	72.24 E
Unna, Ger.	20	C16	51.32 N	7.41 E
Unnão, India	70	E8	26.33 N	80.29 E
Uno, Canal Numero, can., Arg.	172	H8	36.16 S	57.06 W
UNO-City, bldg., Aus.	182b		48.14 N	16.25 E
Unqua Point, c., N.Y., U.S.	194		40.39 N	73.26 W
Unquillo, Arg.	172	E5	31.14 S	64.18 W
Unskaja guba, b., Russia	18	C25	64.45 N	38.15 E
Unst, i., Scot., U.K.	10a	n19	60.45 N	0.52 W
Unstrut, stm., Ger.	24	E7	51.10 N	11.48 E
Unterbach, Ger.	181		51.12 N	6.54 E
Untergrüne, Ger.	181		51.22 N	7.39 E
Unterlaa, ngh., Aus.	182b		48.08 N	16.25 E
Untermauerbach, Aus.	182b		48.14 N	16.12 E
Unterrath, ngh., Ger.	181		51.16 N	6.47 E
Unuli Horog, China	52	E3	35.10 N	91.51 E
Ünye, Tur.	42	E7	41.07 N	37.16 E
Unža, stm., Russia	40	B14	57.39 N	43.39 E
Unzen-dake, vol., Japan	56	G3	32.45 N	130.17 E
Uong Bi, Viet.	64	B8	21.02 N	106.47 E
Uozu, Japan	56	C10	36.48 N	137.24 E
Upa, stm., Russia	26	G20	54.01 N	36.20 E
Upanema, Braz.	170	C7	5.38 S	37.15 W
Upano, stm., Ec.	168	I2	2.45 S	78.17 W
Upata, Ven.	168	C10	8.01 N	62.24 W
Upatoi Creek, stm., Ga., U.S.	134	E14	32.22 N	84.58 W
Upchurch, Eng., U.K.	178		51.23 N	0.39 E
Upemba, Lac, l., D.R.C.	86	F5	8.36 S	26.26 E
Upernavik, Grnld.	108	C14	72.45 N	56.07 W
Upham, N.D., U.S.	142	F13	48.34 N	100.44 W
Up Holland, Eng., U.K.	180		53.33 N	2.44 W
Upía, stm., Col.	168	E5	4.17 N	72.45 W
Upington, S. Afr.	90	F5	28.27 S	21.13 E
Upire, stm., Ven.	168	B7	11.26 N	68.58 W
Upland, Ne., U.S.	138	A10	40.19 N	98.54 W
Upland, Pa., U.S.	203		39.51 N	75.23 W
Upleta, India	70	H3	21.44 N	70.16 E
Upolokša, Russia	14	E22	67.32 N	31.52 E
Upolu, i., Samoa	101c	h11	13.55 S	171.45 W
Upolu Point, c., Hi., U.S.	100a	c6	20.16 N	155.51 W
Upper Arlington, Oh., U.S.	124	D2	40.00 N	83.03 W
Upper Arrow Lake, l., B.C., Can.	144	F12	50.31 N	117.55 W
Upper Artichoke Reservoir, res., Ma., U.S.	201		42.48 N	70.57 W
Upper Austria see Oberösterreich, state, Aus.	30	B10	48.15 N	14.00 E
Upper Bay, b., U.S.	194		40.41 N	74.03 W
Upper Beaconsfield, Austl.	192b		38.01 S	145.25 E
Upper Berkshire Valley, N.J., U.S.	194		40.56 N	74.35 W
Upper Blackville, N.B., Can.	122	D11	46.38 N	65.51 W
Upper Brookville, N.Y., U.S.	194		40.51 N	73.34 W
Upper Castlereagh, Austl.	192a		33.43 S	150.40 E
Upper Crystal Springs Reservoir, res., Ca., U.S.	200		37.30 N	122.20 W
Upper Darby, Pa., U.S.	124	E10	39.55 N	75.16 W
Upper Des Lacs Lake, l., N.A.	142	F11	48.49 N	102.07 W
Upper Egypt see El-Sa'îd, hist. reg., Egypt	74	G2	27.06 N	30.55 E
Upper End, Eng., U.K.	180		53.17 N	1.52 W
Upper Erskine Lake, l., N.J., U.S.	194		41.06 N	74.15 W
Upper Falls, Md., U.S.	202b		39.26 N	76.24 W
Upper Ferntree Gully, Austl.	192b		37.54 S	145.19 E
Upper Fraser, B.C., Can.	144	B8	54.08 N	121.58 W
Upper Ganga Canal, can., India	70	D6	29.57 N	78.10 E
Upper Ganges Canal see Upper Ganga Canal, can., India	70	D6	29.57 N	78.10 E
Upper Greenwood Lake, N.J., U.S.	194		41.10 N	74.22 W
Upper Greenwood Lake, l., N.J., U.S.	194		41.11 N	74.23 W
Upper Hat Creek, B.C., Can.	144	F9	50.38 N	121.33 W
Upper Iowa, stm., U.S.	128	H7	43.29 N	91.13 W
Upper Kapuas Mountains, mts., Asia	66	C8	1.15 N	113.30 E
Upper Keechi Creek, stm., Tx., U.S.	136	C12	31.22 N	95.41 W
Upper Klamath Lake, l., Or., U.S.	146	H5	42.24 N	121.53 W
Upper Lake, Ca., U.S.	148	D3	39.09 N	122.54 W
Upper Lake, l., Ca., U.S.	148	B5	41.44 N	120.08 W
Upper Manitou Lake, l., On., Can.	128	B5	49.24 N	92.48 W
Upper Missouri Wild and Scenic River, p.o.i., Mt., U.S.	146	C16	47.46 N	109.58 W
Upper Musquodoboit, N.S., Can.	122	E14	45.08 N	62.56 W
Upper Mystic Lake, l., Ma., U.S.	201		42.27 N	71.09 W
Upper Peirce Reservoir, res., Sing.	189c		1.22 N	103.48 E
Upper Red Lake, l., Mn., U.S.	128	C4	48.10 N	94.40 W
Upper River Rouge, stm., Mi., U.S.	199		42.23 N	83.16 W
Upper Saddle River, N.J., U.S.	194		41.03 N	74.05 W
Upper Saint Clair, Pa., U.S.	197b		40.21 N	80.05 W
Upper Sandusky, Oh., U.S.	124	D2	40.49 N	83.16 W
Upper Seletar Reservoir, res., Sing.	189c		1.24 N	103.48 E
Upper Straits Lake, l., Mi., U.S.	199		42.35 N	83.24 W
Upper Takutu-Upper Essequibo, state, Guy.	168	F12	2.33 N	59.30 W
Upper Tooting, ngh., Eng., U.K.	178		51.26 N	0.10 W
Upper Trajan's Wall, misc. cult., Mol.	38	G7	46.35 N	29.00 E
Upper Volta see Burkina Faso, ctry., Afr.	84	G4	13.00 N	1.30 W
Upplands-Väsby, Swe.	16	H15	59.31 N	17.53 E
Uppsala, Swe.	16	H15	59.52 N	17.38 E
Uppsala, state, Swe.	16	G15	60.00 N	17.45 E
Upsala see Uppsala, Swe.	16	H15	59.52 N	17.38 E
Upshi, India	70	B6	33.49 N	77.49 E
Upstart, Cape, c., Austl.	98	B6	19.43 S	147.46 E
Upton, Eng., U.K.	178		51.30 N	0.35 W
Upton, Eng., U.K.	180		53.23 N	3.06 W
Upton, Ky., U.S.	130	G12	37.27 N	85.53 W
Upton, Wy., U.S.	140	C8	44.05 N	104.38 W
Uptown, ngh., Il., U.S.	196		41.58 N	87.40 W
Upwey, Austl.	192b		37.54 S	145.20 E
'Uqlat aṣ-Ṣuqūr, Sau. Ar.	74	H7	25.50 N	42.12 E
Uquía, Cerro, mtn., Ven.	168	E10	4.22 N	63.46 W
Ur see Tall al-Muqayyar, hist., Iraq	74	E9	30.57 N	46.09 E
Urabá, Golfo de, b., Col.	168	C3	8.25 N	76.53 W
Uracoa, Ven.	168	C10	8.59 N	62.20 W
Urad Zhonghou Lianheqi, China	52	C6	41.42 N	108.49 E
Uraga, Japan	186		35.15 N	139.43 E
Uraga-kō, b., Japan	186		35.14 N	139.44 E
Uraguba, Russia	14	C23	69.16 N	32.48 E
Uraj, Russia	32	B10	60.07 N	64.46 E
Urakawa, Japan	54	C15	42.10 N	142.47 E
Ural, stm.	48	E8	46.50 N	51.32 E
Uralla, Austl.	98	H8	30.39 S	151.30 E
Ural Mountains see Ural'skie gory, mts., Russia	48	C9	60.00 N	60.00 E
Uralovo, Ukr.	38	A12	52.10 N	33.33 E
Ural'sk, Kaz.	48	D8	51.13 N	51.21 E
Ural'sk see Zapadno-Kazahstan, state, Kaz.	40	G17	50.00 N	51.00 E
Ural'skie gory (Ural Mountains), mts., Russia	48	C9	60.00 N	60.00 E
Uran, India	190c		18.52 N	72.56 E
Urana, Austl.	98	J6	35.20 S	146.16 E
Urandangi, Austl.	96	D7	21.37 S	138.19 E
Urandi, Braz.	170	H4	14.46 S	42.39 W
Urangan, Austl.	98	E9	25.17 S	152.54 E
Urania, La., U.S.	134	F6	31.51 N	92.17 W
Uranium City, Sk., Can.	110	D9	59.34 N	108.35 W
Uraricaá, stm., Braz.	168	F10	3.19 N	61.55 W
Uraricoera, Braz.	168	F11	3.27 N	60.58 W
Uraricoera, stm., Braz.	168	F11	3.02 N	60.29 W
Ura-Tjube, Taj.	72	B10	39.54 N	69.00 E
Uravakonda, India	69	D3	14.55 N	77.15 E
Uravan, Co., U.S.	150	E8	38.22 N	108.43 W
Urawa, Japan	56	D12	35.51 N	139.39 E
Urazmetovo, Russia	40	E19	53.48 N	55.24 E
Urazovo, Russia	38	C17	50.07 N	38.04 E
Urbana, Ar., U.S.	134	D6	33.09 N	92.26 W
Urbana, Il., U.S.	130	D9	40.06 N	88.12 W
Urbana, Mo., U.S.	130	G4	37.50 N	93.10 W
Urbana, Oh., U.S.	124	D2	40.06 N	83.45 W
Urbandale, Ia., U.S.	130	C4	41.37 N	93.42 W
Urbania, Italy	30	G9	43.40 N	12.31 E
Urbano Santos, Braz.	170	B4	3.12 S	43.23 W
Urbe, Aeroporto dell', arpt., Italy	185a		41.57 N	12.30 E
Urbino, Italy	30	G9	43.44 N	12.38 E
Urbino, Étang d', l., Fr.	22	G15	42.03 N	9.28 E
Urcos, Peru	164	F3	13.41 S	71.37 W
Urda, Kaz.	40	G15	48.46 N	47.25 E
Urdenbach, ngh., Ger.	181		51.09 N	6.53 E
Urdevárri, hill, Nor.	14	D13	68.44 N	22.31 E
Urdinarrain, Arg.	172	F8	32.40 S	58.53 W
Urdoma, Russia	12	F23	61.45 N	48.33 E
Urdžar, Kaz.	48	E14	47.05 N	81.37 E
Urê, Col.	168	D4	7.45 N	75.33 W
Ure, stm., Eng., U.K.	10	G11	54.01 N	1.13 W
Urèčča, Bela.	26	H10	52.56 N	27.53 E
Ureče see Urèčča, Bela.	26	H10	52.56 N	27.53 E
Uren', Russia	40	C14	57.27 N	45.47 E
Ureña, Ven.	168	D5	7.55 N	72.28 W
Urengoj, Russia	48	A13	65.56 N	78.17 E
Uréparapara, i., Vanuatu	101d	i16	13.31 S	167.19 E
Ures, Mex.	120	G7	29.25 N	110.23 W
Ureshino, Japan	56	F2	33.06 N	129.59 E
Urewera National Park, p.o.i., N.Z.	102	D7	38.40 S	177.00 E
Urfa see Şanlıurfa, Tur.	42	G8	37.09 N	38.47 E
Urfa see Şanlıurfa, state, Tur.	42	G8	37.20 N	39.15 E
Urgenč, Uzb.	48	F10	41.33 N	60.38 E
Ürgüp, Tur.	42	F6	38.38 N	34.55 E
Urho Kekkosen kansallispuisto, p.o.i., Fin.	14	D19	68.10 N	28.30 E
Uri, India	70	A4	34.05 N	74.02 E
Uriah, Al., U.S.	134	F11	31.17 N	87.30 W
Uriah, Mount, mtn., N.Z.	102	E4	42.02 S	171.34 E
Uribante, stm., Ven.	168	D6	7.17 N	70.42 W
Uribe, Col.	168	F4	3.13 N	74.23 W
Uribia, Col.	168	B5	11.43 N	72.17 W
Urich, Mo., U.S.	130	F4	38.27 N	93.59 W
Urick, ngh., Russia	183a		59.50 N	30.11 E
Urickij, Kaz.	48	D11	53.18 N	65.32 E
Urión, mth., Arg.	206		34.24 S	58.31 W
Urique, Mex.	154	B4	27.13 N	107.54 W
Urique, stm., Mex.	154	B5	26.55 N	107.56 W
Urjala, Fin.	18	F10	61.05 N	23.32 E
Urjung-Haja, Russia	50	B11	72.52 N	113.27 E
Urjupinsk, Russia	40	F13	50.47 N	42.00 E
Urla, Tur.	34	E9	38.18 N	26.45 E
Urlați, Rom.	36	D13	44.57 N	26.13 E
Urlings, Antig.	159b	f4	17.01 N	61.52 W
Urman, Russia	40	D20	54.52 N	56.51 E
Urmary, Russia	40	D15	55.40 N	47.55 E
Urmia see Orūmīyeh, Iran	74	B9	37.32 N	45.04 E
Urmia, Lake see Orūmīyeh, Daryācheh-ye, l., Iran	42	F11	37.40 N	45.30 E
Urnes, Nor.	16	F5	61.17 N	7.20 E
Üröm, Hung.	182c		47.36 N	19.01 E
Uromi, Nig.	84	H6	6.43 N	6.19 E
Uroševac, Yugo.	36	G8	42.22 N	21.09 E
Uroyán, Montañas de, mts., P.R.	158a	b2	18.10 N	66.58 W
Urrao, Col.	168	D3	6.20 N	76.07 W
Ursa, Il., U.S.	130	D6	40.03 N	91.21 W
Uruaçu, Braz.	170	H1	14.31 S	49.08 W
Uruana, Braz.	166	C7	15.29 S	49.41 W
Uruapan, Mex.	148	L9	31.37 N	116.27 W
Uruapan del Progreso, Mex.	154	F8	19.25 N	102.04 W
Urubamba, Peru	164	F3	13.17 S	72.07 W
Urubamba, stm., Peru	164	F3	10.43 S	73.44 W
Urubaxi, stm., Braz.	168	H9	0.31 S	64.50 W
Urubu, stm., Braz.	164	D6	2.58 S	58.28 W
Urubu, stm., Braz.	170	F1	10.42 S	49.07 W
Uruburetama, Braz.	170	B6	3.38 S	39.30 W
Uruçanga, Braz.	172	D13	28.31 S	49.19 W
Urucará, Braz.	164	D6	2.31 S	57.44 W
Urucu, stm., Braz.	164	D5	4.06 S	63.27 W
Uruçuca, Braz.	170	H6	14.35 S	39.16 W
Uruçuí, Serra da, hills, Braz.	170	E3	9.00 S	44.45 W
Urucuia, stm., Braz.	170	I3	16.08 S	45.05 W
Uruçuí-preto, stm., Braz.	170	E3	7.19 S	44.37 W
Uruguai (Uruguay), stm., S.A.	172	F8	34.10 S	58.17 W
Uruguaiana, Braz.	172	D9	29.45 S	57.04 W
Uruguay, ctry., S.A.	172	F10	33.00 S	56.00 W
Uruguay (Uruguai), stm., S.A.	172	F8	34.10 S	58.17 W
Urumchi see Ürümqi, China	52	C2	43.48 N	87.35 E
Ürümqi, China	52	C2	43.48 N	87.35 E
Urundi see Burundi, ctry., Afr.	86	E6	3.15 S	30.00 E
Uruoca, Braz.	170	B5	3.20 S	40.32 W
Urup, stm., Russia	42	C9	44.59 N	41.10 E
Urup, gora, mtn., Russia	42	D9	43.38 N	41.30 E
Urup, ostrov, i., Russia	50	G19	46.00 N	150.00 E
Urupês, Braz.	172	D1	21.11 S	49.16 W
Uruša, Russia	50	F13	54.03 N	122.52 E
Urussu, Russia	40	D18	54.35 N	53.27 E
Urutaí, Braz.	170	I1	17.27 S	48.11 W
Urutaú, Arg.	172	B6	25.42 S	63.02 W
Uruwira, Tan.	86	F6	6.27 S	31.20 E
Uryū-yama, mtn., Japan	188		35.03 N	135.48 E
Uryv, Russia	40	F11	51.07 N	39.09 E
Urziceni, Rom.	36	E13	44.42 N	26.39 E
Uržum, Russia	40	C16	57.06 N	50.01 E
Us, Fr.	179		49.06 N	1.58 E
Usa, Japan	56	F4	33.33 N	131.22 E
Uša, stm., Bela.	26	G11	53.59 N	28.55 E
Usa, stm., Russia	48	A9	65.57 N	56.56 E
Ušača, stm., Bela.	26	E11	55.31 N	28.30 E
Ušačy, Bela.	26	E11	55.11 N	28.37 E
Uşak, Tur.	34	E12	38.40 N	29.24 E
Uşak, state, Tur.	34	E12	38.35 N	29.20 E
Ušaki, Russia	26	A13	59.29 N	30.59 E
Usakos, Nmb.	90	B2	21.59 S	15.35 E
Usangu Flats, pl., Tan.	88	B5	8.30 S	34.15 E
Usborne, Mount, mtn., Falk. Is.	166	J5	51.41 S	58.50 W
Ušće, Yugo.	36	F7	43.28 N	20.37 E
Uščerpe, Russia	26	H14	52.42 N	31.53 E
Usedom, i., Eur.	24	B10	54.00 N	14.00 E
Ushant see Ouessant, Île d', i., Fr.	20	F3	48.28 N	5.05 W
Ushashi, Tan.	86	E6	2.01 S	33.54 E
Ushibuka, Japan	56	G2	32.11 N	130.00 E
Ushtobe see Uštobe, Kaz.	48	E13	45.14 N	77.57 E
Ushuaia, Arg.	166	J3	54.47 S	68.18 W
Ushytsia, stm., Ukr.	38	D6	48.34 N	27.09 E
Usingen, Ger.	24	F4	50.19 N	8.31 E
Usinsk, Russia	48	A9	65.57 N	57.23 E
Usk, B.C., Can.	144	B2	54.38 N	128.24 W
Usk, Wa., U.S.	146	B9	48.18 N	117.16 W
Usk, stm., Wales, U.K.	10	J9	51.34 N	2.59 W
Uskovo, Russia	183b		55.56 N	37.19 E
Üsküb see Skopje, Mac.	34	A4	42.00 N	21.27 E
Uskumru, ngh., Tur.	185b		41.12 N	29.01 E
Uslar, Ger.	24	E5	51.39 N	9.38 E
Usman', Russia	40	E11	52.03 N	39.44 E
Usmānpur, ngh., India	190a		28.41 N	77.15 E
Usmas ezers, l., Lat.	26	C4	57.10 N	22.11 E
Usmyn', Russia	26	E14	55.50 N	31.10 E
Usoke, Tan.	86	F6	5.05 S	32.20 E
Usole, Russia	48	C9	59.25 N	56.40 E
Usole-Sibirskoe, Russia	48	D18	52.45 N	103.38 E
Usovo, Russia	183b		55.44 N	37.13 E
Uspallata, Arg.	172	F3	32.35 S	69.20 W
Uspanapa, stm., Mex.	154	G11	17.56 N	94.27 W
Ussaymir, Wādī el-, val., Egypt	191c		30.04 N	31.23 E
Ussel, Fr.	22	D8	45.33 N	2.18 E
Usshers Creek, stm., On., Can.	202a		43.03 N	79.02 W
Ussuri (Wusuli), stm., Asia	52	C11	48.27 N	135.04 E
Ussurijsk, Russia	54	C10	43.48 N	131.58 E
Ust'-Ajsk, Russia	40	C20	56.07 N	57.40 E
Ustaoset, Nor.	16	G6	60.30 N	8.04 E
Ust'-Barguzin, Russia	50	F10	53.24 N	109.01 E
Ust'-Belaja, Russia	50	C23	65.29 N	173.15 E
Ust'-Bol'šereck, Russia	50	F20	52.49 N	156.17 E
Ust'-Čaun, Russia	50	C23	68.48 N	170.24 E
Ust'-Chorna, Ukr.	38	E2	48.17 N	23.56 E
Ust'-Cil'ma, Russia	12	D25	65.25 N	52.05 E
Ust'-Dolyssy, Russia	26	D12	56.07 N	29.39 E
Ust'-Džegutinskaja, Russia	42	C9	44.04 N	41.58 E
Uste, Russia	18	G19	60.49 N	32.50 E
Uste, Russia	26	C22	57.44 N	39.48 E
Uste, Russia	40	B11	59.38 N	39.43 E
Uste-Kirovskoe, Russia	26	B18	58.44 N	35.54 E
Uster, Switz.	30	C5	47.21 N	8.43 E
Ustevatnet, l., Nor.	16	G5	60.29 N	7.57 E
Ust'-Grjaznuha, Russia	40	F14	50.28 N	45.26 E
Ustica, Isola di, i., Italy	32	F7	38.42 N	13.10 E
Ust'-Ilimsk, Russia	48	C18	58.00 N	102.40 E
Ust'-Ilimskoe vodohranilišče, res., Russia	48	C18	57.20 N	102.20 E
Ústí nad Labem, Czech Rep.	24	F10	50.39 N	14.02 E
Ústí nad Orlicí, Czech Rep.	24	G12	49.58 N	16.24 E
Ustinov see Iževsk, Russia	40	C18	56.50 N	53.11 E
Ust'-Išim, Russia	48	C12	57.41 N	71.10 E
Ust'-Ižora, Russia	183a		59.48 N	30.36 E
Ustja, stm., Russia	12	F21	61.31 N	42.35 E
Ust'-Javron'ga, Russia	12	E21	63.23 N	44.20 E
Ustjuckoe, Russia	26	B18	58.30 N	35.21 E
Ustjurt, plato see Ust-Urt Plateau, plat., Asia	48	F9	43.00 N	56.00 E
Ustjužna, Russia	26	B19	58.50 N	36.28 E
Ustka, Pol.	24	B12	54.34 N	16.51 E
Ust'-Kamčatsk, Russia	50	E21	56.13 N	162.29 E
Ust'-Kamenogorsk, Kaz.	48	E14	49.56 N	82.37 E
Ust'-Karsk, Russia	50	F12	52.42 N	118.48 E
Ust'-Katav, Russia	40	D20	54.56 N	58.10 E
Ust'-Kišert', Russia	40	C20	57.22 N	57.15 E
Ust'-Koksa, Russia	48	D15	50.17 N	85.37 E
Ust'-Koža, Russia	18	D25	63.36 N	38.33 E
Ust'-Kujda, Russia	50	B16	69.59 N	135.35 E
Ust'-Kulom, Russia	48	B8	61.41 N	53.41 E
Ust'-Kut, Russia	48	C18	56.46 N	105.42 E
Ust'-Labinsk, Russia	40	I11	45.13 N	39.41 E
Ust'-Luga, Russia	26	A11	59.39 N	28.17 E
Ust'-Lyža, Russia	48	A9	65.43 N	56.29 E
Ust'-Maja, Russia	50	D15	60.24 N	134.29 E
Ust'-Man'ja, Russia	48	B10	62.11 N	60.20 E
Ust'-Nera, Russia	50	D17	64.33 N	143.17 E
Ust'-Njukža, Russia	50	E13	56.33 N	121.36 E
Uštobe, Kaz.	48	E13	45.14 N	77.57 E
Ust'-Omčug, Russia	50	D18	61.07 N	149.37 E
Ust'-Ordynskij, Russia	48	D18	52.48 N	104.45 E
Ust'-Ozërnoe, Russia	48	C15	58.53 N	87.45 E
Ust'-Paden'ga, Russia	12	F20	61.53 N	42.38 E
Ust'-Pinega, Russia	12	D19	64.08 N	41.57 E
Ust'-Pit, Russia	48	C16	58.57 N	91.47 E
Ust'-Reka, Russia	18	F24	61.45 N	37.44 E
Ustreka, Russia	26	B17	58.37 N	34.33 E
Ust'-Reki, Russia	12	E22	62.11 N	46.47 E
Ustroń, Pol.	24	G14	49.43 N	18.49 E
Ustrzyki Dolne, Pol.	24	G18	49.25 N	22.36 E
Ust'-Sara, Russia	18	G21	60.14 N	33.58 E
Ust'-Slavjanka, ngh., Russia	183a		59.50 N	30.32 E
Ust'-Šonoša, Russia	12	F19	61.10 N	41.18 E
Ust'-Sumy, Russia	48	D14	54.48 N	80.27 E
Ust'-Tym, Russia	6	D24	59.26 N	79.58 E
Ust'-Uda, Russia	48	D18	54.10 N	103.01 E
Ust'-Ulagan, Russia	48	D15	50.37 N	87.57 E
Ust'-Umal'ta, Russia	50	F15	51.39 N	133.18 E
Ust'-Urgal, Russia	50	F15	51.17 N	132.30 E
Ust-Urt Plateau, plat., Asia	48	F9	43.00 N	56.00 E
Ust'-Uza, Russia	48	D7	52.59 N	45.17 E
Ust'-Vyjskaja, Russia	12	E22	62.56 N	46.41 E
Ustylyh, Ukr.	38	C3	50.52 N	24.10 E
Ustynivka, Ukr.	38	F11	47.57 N	32.32 E
Usu, China	52	C1	44.26 N	84.40 E
Usuki, Japan	56	F4	33.06 N	131.48 E
Usulután, El Sal.	156	F3	13.20 N	88.26 W
Usumacinta, stm., N.A.	152	D6	18.23 N	92.39 W
Usumbura see Bujumbura, Bdi.	86	E5	3.23 S	29.22 E
Usumun, Russia	50	F14	52.47 N	126.32 E
Usutu see Maputo, stm., Afr.	90	E11	26.10 S	32.41 E
Usvjaty, Russia	26	E13	55.43 N	30.44 E

Name	Page	Map Ref.	Latitude	Longitude
Utah, state, U.S.	150	D5	39.30 N	111.30 W
Utah Lake, l., Ut., U.S.	150	C4	40.13 N	111.49 W
Utajärvi, Fin.	18	C13	64.46 N	26.26 E
Utan, Indon.	66	H10	8.25 S	117.09 E
Utata, Russia	48	D18	50.49 N	102.46 E
Ute, Ia., U.S.	130	B2	42.02 N	95.42 W
Ute Creek, stm., N.M., U.S.	138	F5	35.22 N	103.30 W
Utegi, Tan.	86	E6	1.18 S	34.12 E
Ute Mountain Indian Reservation, ind. res., U.S.	150	F7	37.10 N	108.35 W
Utena, Lith.	26	E8	55.29 N	25.36 E
Ute Reservoir, res., N.M., U.S.	138	F5	35.20 N	103.32 W
Utersum, Ger.	24	B4	54.43 N	8.24 E
Utete, Tan.	86	F7	7.59 S	38.47 E
Utevka, Russia	40	E17	52.57 N	51.02 E
Utfort, Ger.	181		51.28 N	6.38 E
Uthai Thani, Thai.	64	E4	15.22 N	100.01 E
Uthal, Pak.	62	C2	25.48 N	66.38 E
U Thong, Thai.	64	E4	14.22 N	99.53 E
Uthumphon Phisai, Thai.	64	E6	15.07 N	104.08 E
Utiariti, Braz.	166	B5	13.02 S	58.17 W
Utica, Ks., U.S.	138	C8	38.38 N	100.10 W
Utica, Mi., U.S.	126	F6	42.37 N	83.02 W
Utica, Ms., U.S.	134	E8	32.06 N	90.37 W
Utica, Ne., U.S.	140	G15	40.53 N	97.21 W
Utica, N.Y., U.S.	126	E14	43.06 N	75.14 W
Utica, Oh., U.S.	124	D3	40.14 N	82.27 W
Utica see Utique, hist., Tun.	32	G3	37.03 N	10.03 E
Utiel, Spain	28	E9	39.34 N	1.12 W
Utila, Hond.	156	D4	16.06 N	86.54 W
Utila, Isla de, i., Hond.	156	D4	16.06 N	86.56 W
Utinga, Braz.	205b		23.38 S	46.32 W
Utinga, stm., Braz.	170	G5	12.34 S	41.20 W
Utique (Utica), hist., Tun.	32	G3	37.03 N	10.03 E
Utlängan, i., Swe.	16	L14	56.01 N	15.48 E
Utliuts'kyi lyman, est., Ukr.	38	G14	46.17 N	35.09 E
Uto, Japan	56	G3	32.41 N	130.40 E
Utö, i., Swe.	16	I16	58.56 N	18.16 E
Utopia, Austl.	96	D6	22.13 S	134.33 E
Utopia, Tx., U.S.	136	E8	29.37 N	99.32 W
Utorgoš, Russia	26	B13	58.16 N	30.15 E
Utraula, India	70	E9	27.19 N	82.25 E
Utrecht, Neth.	20	B14	52.05 N	5.08 E
Utrecht, S. Afr.	90	E10	27.39 S	30.19 E
Utrera, Spain	28	G5	37.11 N	5.46 W
Utrik, at., Marsh. Is.	94	B7	11.10 N	169.43 E
Utroja, stm., Eur.	26	D10	57.22 N	28.11 E
Utsjoki, Fin.	14	C17	69.53 N	26.57 E
Utsjoki, stm., Fin.	14	C17	69.54 N	27.02 E
Utsunomiya, Japan	56	C12	36.33 N	139.53 E
Utta, Russia	40	H15	46.22 N	46.00 E
Uttamapālaiyam, India	69	G3	9.47 N	77.20 E
Uttaradit, Thai.	64	D5	17.37 N	100.05 E
Uttarkāshi, India	70	C7	30.44 N	78.26 E
Uttarpara-Kotrung, India	190b		22.40 N	88.21 E
Uttar Pradesh, state, India	70	E8	27.00 N	80.00 E
Ütterlingsen, Ger.	181		51.15 N	7.45 E
Uttlesford, mun., Eng., U.K.	178		51.47 N	0.19 E
Utuado, P.R.	158a	b2	18.15 N	66.41 W
Utukok, stm., Ak., U.S.	109	C7	70.04 N	162.22 W
Utunomiya see Utsunomiya, Japan	56	C12	36.33 N	139.53 E
Utupua, i., Sol. Is.	94	E7	11.14 S	166.28 E
Uulu, Est.	26	B7	58.17 N	24.35 E
Uurainen, Fin.	18	E12	62.30 N	25.26 E
Üüreg nuur, l., Mong.	48	D16	50.10 N	91.00 E
Uusikaarlepyy see Nykarleby, Fin.	18	D9	63.31 N	22.32 E
Uusikaupunki, Fin.	18	G8	60.48 N	21.25 E
Uusimaa, state, Fin.	18	G11	60.30 N	25.00 E
Uusimaa, reg., Fin.	18	G12	60.36 N	24.59 E
Uva, Russia	40	C18	56.58 N	52.12 E
Uvá, stm., Col.	168	F7	3.55 N	68.33 W
Uvalda, Ga., U.S.	132	D3	32.01 N	82.30 W
Uvalde, Tx., U.S.	136	E8	29.12 N	99.47 W
Uvaravičy, Bela.	26	H13	52.35 N	30.44 E
Uvaroviči see Uvaravičy, Bela.	26	H13	52.35 N	30.44 E
Uvarovka, Russia	26	E18	55.31 N	35.37 E
Uvarovo, Russia	40	F13	51.59 N	42.16 E
Uvdal, Nor.	16	G6	60.17 N	8.43 E
Uvinza, Tan.	86	F6	5.06 S	30.23 E
Uvira, D.R.C.	86	E5	3.22 S	29.08 E
Uvs, l., Asia	48	D16	50.20 N	92.45 E
Uvs Lake see Uvs, l., Asia	48	D16	50.20 N	92.45 E
Uvs Lake see Uvs nuur, l., Asia	50	F7	50.20 N	92.45 E
Uvs nuur, l., Asia	50	F7	50.20 N	92.45 E
Uvworé, c., Vanuatu	101d	I17	18.46 S	169.16 E
Uwa, Japan	56	F5	33.21 N	132.31 E
Uwajima, Japan	56	F5	33.12 N	132.34 E
Uwayl, Sudan	82	F5	8.46 N	27.24 E
'Uwaynāt, Syria	76	C6	35.43 N	36.05 E
'Uwayriḍ, Harrat al-, lav., Sau. Ar.	74	G5	27.00 N	37.30 E
Uwchland, Pa., U.S.	203		40.05 N	75.42 W
Uwi, Pulau, i., Indon.	66	C5	1.05 N	107.24 E
Uxbridge, On., Can.	126	D10	44.05 N	79.07 W
Uxbridge, ngh., Eng., U.K.	178		51.33 N	0.29 W
Uxmal, hist., Mex.	156	B3	20.22 N	89.46 W
Uyama, Japan	188		34.50 N	135.41 E
U-yin, Mya.	64	A2	23.01 N	95.03 E
Uyo, Nig.	84	H6	5.01 N	7.55 E
Uyuni, Bol.	166	D3	20.27 S	66.50 W
Uyuni, Salar de, pl., Bol.	166	D3	20.17 S	68.06 W
Uza, stm., Russia	26	C12	57.48 N	29.30 E
Uza, stm., Russia	40	E14	53.00 N	45.17 E
Užava, Lat.	26	C4	57.13 N	21.29 E
'Uzaym, Nahr al-, stm., Iraq	74	C9	34.00 N	44.18 E
Uzbekistan, ctry., Asia	44	E10	41.00 N	64.00 E
Uzbekiston see Uzbekistan, ctry., Asia	44	E10	41.00 N	64.00 E
Uzda, Bela.	26	G10	53.27 N	27.13 E
Uzdin, Yugo.	36	D7	45.12 N	20.38 E
Uzerche, Fr.	22	D7	45.26 N	1.34 E
Uzès, Fr.	22	E10	44.01 N	4.24 E
Uzgen, Kyrg.	48	F12	40.46 N	73.18 E
Užgorod see Uzjhorod, Ukr.	36	A9	48.37 N	22.18 E
Užgorod see Uzhhorod, Ukr.	40	G3	48.37 N	22.18 E
Uzh (Uh), stm., Eur.	24	H18	48.36 N	22.00 E
Uzh, stm., Ukr.	38	B9	51.15 N	30.15 E
Uzhhorod, Ukr.	40	G3	48.37 N	22.18 E
Užice, Yugo.	36	F6	43.51 N	19.50 E
Uzjhorod, Ukr.	36	A9	48.37 N	22.18 E
Uzkoe, ngh., Russia	183b		55.37 N	37.32 E
Uzlovaja, Russia	26	F21	53.58 N	38.10 E
Uzmore, Russia	40	F14	51.15 N	45.56 E
Uznam see Usedom, i., Eur.	24	B10	54.00 N	14.00 E
Üzümlü, Tur.	34	G12	36.43 N	29.14 E
Üzümlü, Tur.	34	F14	37.33 N	31.38 E
Uzun Ada, i., Tur.	34	E9	38.29 N	26.43 E
Uzunca, stm., Tur.	185b		40.58 N	28.50 E
Uzunköprü, Tur.	34	B9	41.16 N	26.41 E
Uzunkuduk, Uzb.	48	F11	40.34 N	67.09 E
Užur, Russia	48	C16	55.18 N	89.48 E
Užventis, Lith.	26	E5	55.47 N	22.39 E
Uzyn, Ukr.	38	D9	49.49 N	30.25 E

V

Name	Page	Map Ref.	Latitude	Longitude
Vä, Swe.	16	L12	55.59 N	14.06 E
Vaajakoski, Fin.	18	E12	62.16 N	25.53 E
Vääksy, Fin.	18	F12	61.10 N	25.32 E
Vaal, stm., S. Afr.	90	F7	29.04 S	23.38 E
Vaala, Fin.	18	C13	64.34 N	26.48 E
Vaaldam, res., S. Afr.	90	E8	26.55 S	28.12 E
Vaalkop, mtn., S. Afr.	90	G8	31.21 S	26.32 E
Vaalwater, S. Afr.	90	D8	24.17 S	28.06 E
Vaasa (Vasa), Fin.	18	D8	63.05 N	21.36 E
Vaasa, state, Fin.	18	D9	63.00 N	23.00 E
Vabalninkas, Lith.	26	D7	55.58 N	24.45 E
Vác, Hung.	36	B6	47.47 N	19.07 E
Vača, Russia	18	D20	63.58 N	33.28 E
Vacacaí, stm., Braz.	172	D11	29.56 S	53.04 W
Vacaria, Braz.	172	D12	28.30 S	50.56 W
Vacaria, stm., Braz.	170	I4	16.38 S	42.24 W
Vacaville, Ca., U.S.	148	E4	38.21 N	121.59 W
Vaccarès, Étang de, l., Fr.	22	F10	43.32 N	4.34 E
Vache, Île à, i., Haiti	156	C11	18.04 N	73.37 W
Vaches, Île aux, i., Qc., Can.	193a		45.41 N	73.40 W
Vacía Talega, Punta, c., P.R.	158a	b4	18.27 N	65.54 W
Vad, Russia	40	D14	55.32 N	44.12 E
Vad, stm., Russia	40	E13	54.30 N	42.30 E
Vadakara see Badagara, India	69	F2	11.37 N	75.34 E
Väddö, i., Swe.	16	G16	60.01 N	18.49 E
Vădeni, Rom.	36	D14	45.22 N	27.56 E
Vadheim, Nor.	16	F3	61.13 N	5.49 E
Vādi, India	190c		18.56 N	73.06 E
Vadino, Russia	26	E16	55.15 N	33.16 E
Vadinsk, Russia	40	E13	53.41 N	43.03 E
Vadnagar, India	70	G4	23.47 N	72.38 E
Vado, N.M., U.S.	136	B1	32.04 N	106.37 W
Vadodara (Baroda), India	70	G4	22.18 N	73.11 E
Vado de Cedillos, Mex.	136	C2	31.05 N	105.38 W
Vado Ligure, Italy	30	F5	44.16 N	8.26 E
Vadsø, Nor.	14	B20	70.04 N	29.45 E
Vadstena, Swe.	16	I12	58.27 N	14.54 E
Vaduz, Liech.	30	C6	47.08 N	9.31 E
Værlandet, i., Nor.	16	F2	61.17 N	4.43 E
Værøy, i., Nor.	14	E3	67.40 N	12.39 E
Vaga, stm., Russia	12	F20	62.48 N	42.53 E
Vågåmo, Nor.	16	F7	61.52 N	9.09 E
Vágar, i., Far. Is.	12b	m34	62.05 N	7.16 W
Vagårshel, Nor.	16	I6	58.46 N	8.51 E
Vågåvatnet, l., Nor.	16	F6	61.51 N	8.51 E
Vaggeryd, Swe.	16	J12	57.29 N	14.07 E
Vaghena Island, i., Sol. Is.	101b	d7	7.26 S	157.46 E
Vågsfjorden, b., Nor.	14	D7	68.54 N	16.50 E
Vågsøy, i., Nor.	16	F2	61.58 N	5.05 E
Vah, stm., Russia	48	B13	60.48 N	76.48 E
Váh, stm., Slvk.	24	H13	47.44 N	18.09 E
Vahsel, Cape, c., S. Geor.	166	J9	54.45 S	35.47 W
Vahtan, Russia	40	C15	57.57 N	46.41 E
Vaiden, Ms., U.S.	134	D9	33.19 N	89.44 W
Vaigai, stm., India	69	G4	9.19 N	79.00 E
Vaigat, strt., Grnld.	108	C15	70.11 N	53.00 W
Vaijāpur, India	69	B2	19.55 N	74.43 E
Vaikam, India	69	G3	9.45 N	76.24 E
Väike-Maarja, Est.	26	A9	59.08 N	26.15 E
Väike Pakri, i., Est.	26	A6	59.20 N	23.59 E
Vail, Co., U.S.	138	B2	39.38 N	106.21 W
Vail, Ia., U.S.	130	B2	42.03 N	95.12 W
Vaimali, Vanuatu	101d	k17	16.35 S	168.10 E
Vaiņode, Lat.	26	D4	56.24 N	21.49 E
Vaippār, stm., India	69	G4	9.01 N	78.15 E
Vairao, Fr. Poly.	100h	w22	17.48 S	149.17 W
Vaires-sur-Marne, Fr.	179		48.52 N	2.39 E
Vaisaluokta, Swe.	14	E8	67.41 N	17.15 E
Vaison-la-Romaine, Fr.	22	E11	44.14 N	5.04 E
Vaitahu, Fr. Poly.	100g	s18	9.56 S	139.06 W
Vajdaguba, Russia	14	C23	69.55 N	31.59 E
Vākhān, hist. reg., Afg.	72	B11	37.00 N	73.00 E
Vaklan, India	190c		19.07 N	73.06 E
Vaksdal, Nor.	16	G3	60.29 N	5.44 E
Valaam, Russia	18	F17	61.22 N	30.57 E
Vålådalen, Swe.	16	D10	63.10 N	12.57 E
Valadeces, Mex.	136	H9	26.13 N	98.40 W
Valamaz, Russia	40	C18	57.32 N	52.05 E
Valandovo, Mac.	34	B5	41.19 N	22.33 E
Valap, India	190c		19.03 N	73.08 E
Valašské Klobouky, Czech Rep.	24	G13	49.07 N	18.00 E
Valašské Meziříčí, Czech Rep.	24	G13	49.28 N	17.58 E
Valatie, N.Y., U.S.	124	B12	42.24 N	73.40 W
Vala Ull, India	190c		19.02 N	73.07 E
Vålberg, Swe.	16	H11	59.24 N	13.12 E
Valbo, Swe.	16	G15	60.39 N	17.04 E
Valcanuta, ngh., Italy	185a		41.53 N	12.25 E
Vâlcea, state, Rom.	36	E11	45.19 N	24.00 E
Vălčedrăm, Blg.	36	F10	43.41 N	23.27 E
Valcheta, Arg.	166	H3	40.42 S	66.09 W
Valchetta, stm., Italy	185a		41.58 N	12.30 E
Valdagno, Italy	30	E8	45.38 N	11.17 E
Valdai Hills see Valdajskaja vozvyšennost', hills, Russia	26	C15	57.00 N	33.30 E
Valdaj, Russia	18	D22	63.25 N	35.32 E
Valdaj, Russia	26	B16	57.58 N	33.14 E
Valdajskaja vozvyšennost' (Valdai Hills), hills, Russia	26	C15	57.00 N	33.30 E
Valdarno, val., Italy	30	G8	43.35 N	11.30 E
Valdavia, stm., Spain	28	B6	42.23 N	4.16 W
Valdebeba, Arroyo de, stm., Spain	184a		41.23 N	2.10 E
Val-de-Cães, Braz.	170	A1	1.31 S	48.40 W
Valdecañas, Embalse de, res., Spain	28	E5	39.48 N	5.25 W
Val-de-Marne, state, Fr.	179		48.47 N	2.29 E
Valdemārpils, Lat.	26	C5	57.21 N	22.30 E
Valdemarsvik, Swe.	16	I14	58.12 N	16.35 E
Valdepeñas, Spain	28	F7	38.45 N	3.23 W
Valderaduey, stm., Spain	28	C5	41.32 N	5.42 W
Valderrobres, Spain	28	D11	40.53 N	0.08 E
Valders, Wi., U.S.	126	D2	44.03 N	87.52 W
Valdés, Península, pen., Arg.	166	H4	42.30 S	64.00 W
Val-des-Bois, Qc., Can.	126	C14	45.53 N	75.36 W
Valdéz, Ec.	168	G2	1.15 N	78.59 W
Valdez, Ak., U.S.	109	D10	61.08 N	146.20 W
Val-d'Isère, Fr.	22	D12	45.27 N	6.58 E
Valdivia, Chile	166	G2	39.49 S	73.12 W
Valdivia, Col.	168	D4	7.11 N	75.27 W
Valdobbiadene, Italy	30	E8	45.54 N	12.00 E
Val-d'Oise, state, Fr.	20	E10	49.10 N	2.10 E
Val-d'Or, Qc., Can.	114	B12	48.06 N	77.46 W
Valdosta, Ga., U.S.	132	F2	30.50 N	83.17 W
Valdoviño see Aviño, Spain	28	A2	43.36 N	8.08 W
Valdres, val., Nor.	16	F6	60.58 N	9.14 E
Vale, Or., U.S.	146	G9	43.59 N	117.14 W
Valea lui Mihai, Rom.	36	B9	47.31 N	22.08 E
Vale de Lobos, Port.	184c		38.49 N	9.17 W
Valehouse Reservoir, res., Eng., U.K.	180		53.29 N	1.57 W
Valemount, B.C., Can.	144	D11	52.50 N	119.15 W
Valença, Braz.	170	G6	13.22 S	39.05 W
Valença, Braz.	170	L4	22.15 S	43.42 W
Valença, Port.	28	B2	42.01 N	8.38 W
Valença do Piauí, Braz.	170	D5	6.24 S	41.45 W
Valençay, Fr.	20	G10	47.09 N	1.34 E
Valence, Fr.	22	E10	44.56 N	4.53 E
Valencia, Phil.	68	F5	7.56 N	125.05 E
València, Spain	28	E10	39.28 N	0.22 W
Valencia, Ven.	168	B7	10.11 N	68.00 W
València, state, Spain	28	E9	39.20 N	0.50 W
Valencia see València, state, Spain	28	E9	39.20 N	0.50 W
València, co., Spain	28	E10	39.30 N	0.45 W
Valencia see València, co., Spain	28	E10	39.30 N	0.45 W
València, Golf de, b., Spain	28	E10	39.50 N	0.30 E
Valencia, Golfo de see València, Golf de, b., Spain	28	E10	39.50 N	0.30 E
Valencia, Gulf of see València, Golf de, b., Spain	28	E10	39.50 N	0.30 E
Valencia, Lago de, l., Ven.	168	B8	10.10 N	67.43 W
Valencia, Quebrada, stm., Ven.	204c		10.30 N	66.46 W
Valencia de Alcántara, Spain	28	E3	39.24 N	7.13 W
Valencia de Don Juan, Spain	28	B5	42.17 N	5.30 W
Valencia Island, i., Ire.	10	J2	51.54 N	10.21 W
Valenciennes, Fr.	20	D12	50.21 N	3.31 E
Vălenii de Munte, Rom.	36	D13	45.12 N	26.03 E
Valente, Braz.	170	F6	11.34 S	39.27 W
Valentin, Russia	54	C11	43.07 N	134.17 E
Valentín Alsina, ngh., Arg.	206		34.40 S	58.25 W
Valentine, Ne., U.S.	140	E12	42.52 N	100.33 W
Valentine, Tx., U.S.	136	D3	30.33 N	104.27 W
Valentinovka, Russia	183b		55.55 N	37.56 E
Valenton, Fr.	179		48.45 N	2.28 E
Valenza, Italy	30	F5	45.01 N	8.38 E
Valenzuela, Phil.	187f		14.42 N	120.58 E
Våler, Nor.	16	G9	60.40 N	11.50 E
Valera, Ven.	168	C6	9.19 N	70.37 W
Valérien, Mont, hill, Fr.	179		48.53 N	2.13 E
Vale Royal, mun., Eng., U.K.	180		53.17 N	2.37 W
Valga, Est.	26	C9	57.46 N	26.03 E
Valge, stm., Est.	26	A8	59.35 N	25.42 E
Valhalla, Lake, l., N.J., U.S.	194		40.56 N	74.22 W
Valhalla Provincial Park, p.o.i., B.C., Can.	144	F13	49.50 N	117.40 W
Valiente, Península, pen., Pan.	156	H7	9.05 N	81.51 W
Valier, Mt., U.S.	146	B14	48.18 N	112.14 W
Valili, mtn., Fiji	101e	p19	16.39 S	179.10 E
Valinco, Golfe de, b., Fr.	22	H14	41.40 N	8.49 E
Valinda, Ca., U.S.	198		34.02 N	117.56 W
Valira, stm., Eur.	22	G7	42.20 N	1.26 E
Valjevo, Yugo.	36	E6	44.16 N	19.53 E
Valka, Lat.	26	C8	57.45 N	25.58 E
Valkeakoski, Fin.	18	F11	61.16 N	24.01 E
Valkenswaard, Neth.	20	C14	51.21 N	5.27 E
Valkininkas, Lith.	26	F7	54.20 N	24.51 E
Valky, Ukr.	38	D14	49.50 N	35.37 E
Valladares, Mex.	136	H7	26.53 N	100.38 W
Valladolid, Mex.	156	B3	20.41 N	88.12 W
Valladolid, Spain	28	C6	41.39 N	4.43 W
Valladolid, co., Spain	28	C6	41.40 N	4.50 W
Vallco Fashion Park, shp. cen., Ca., U.S.	200		37.19 N	122.01 W
Vall de Uxó see La Vall d'Uixó, Spain	28	E10	39.49 N	0.14 W
Valldoreix, Spain	184d		41.28 N	2.04 E
Valle, Lat.	26	D7	56.30 N	24.44 E
Valle, Spain	28	A6	43.13 N	4.18 W
Vallecas, ngh., Spain	184a		40.23 N	3.37 W
Vallecillo, Mex.	136	H7	26.39 N	99.59 W
Vallecitos, N.M., U.S.	138	E2	36.33 N	106.10 W
Vallecitos Creek, stm., Ca., U.S.	200		37.36 N	121.53 W
Valle d'Aosta, state, Italy	30	E4	45.45 N	7.25 E
Valle de Allende, Mex.	136	H2	26.56 N	105.23 W
Valle de Guanape, Ven.	168	C9	9.54 N	65.41 W
Valle de la Pascua, Ven.	168	C8	9.13 N	66.00 W
Valle del Cauca, state, Col.	168	F3	3.45 N	76.30 W
Valle del Rosario, Mex.	136	G1	27.19 N	106.18 W
Valle de Olivos, Mex.	154	B5	27.11 N	106.16 W
Valle de Santiago, Mex.	154	E8	20.23 N	101.11 W
Valle de Zaragoza, Mex.	154	B6	27.28 N	105.49 W
Valledupar, Col.	168	B5	10.28 N	73.15 W
Vallée d'Aoste see Valle d'Aosta, state, Italy	30	E4	45.45 N	7.25 E
Valle Edén, Ur.	172	E9	31.49 S	56.10 W
Vallegrande, Bol.	166	C4	18.29 S	64.06 W
Valle Hermoso, Mex.	154	C10	25.39 N	97.49 W
Vallejo, Ca., U.S.	148	E3	38.06 N	122.15 W
Vällen, l., Swe.	18	G5	60.03 N	18.20 E
Vallenar, Chile	172	D2	28.34 S	70.46 W
Vallentuna, Swe.	16	H16	59.32 N	18.04 E
Valle Redondo, Mex.	148	K9	32.31 N	116.46 W
Valles Caldera, crat., N.M., U.S.	138	F2	35.52 N	106.33 W
Valletta, Malta	32	I8	35.54 N	14.31 E
Valley, Al., U.S.	134	E13	32.50 N	85.11 W
Valley, Ne., U.S.	130	C1	41.19 N	96.20 W
Valley, Wa., U.S.	146	B9	48.10 N	117.43 W
Valley, stm., Mb., Can.	142	C13	51.22 N	99.54 W
Valley Bend, W.V., U.S.	124	F6	38.45 N	79.55 W
Valley Center, Ks., U.S.	138	D11	37.50 N	97.22 W
Valley City, N.D., U.S.	142	H16	46.55 N	98.00 W
Valley Creek, stm., Pa., U.S.	203		40.06 N	75.28 W
Valley Creek, stm., Pa., U.S.	203		39.58 N	75.40 W
Valley Creek, stm., Tx., U.S.	136	C7	31.43 N	100.02 W
Valleydale, Ca., U.S.	198		34.06 N	117.56 W
Valley East, On., Can.	126	B8	46.41 N	81.03 W
Valley Falls, Ks., U.S.	130	E2	39.20 N	95.27 W
Valley Farms, Az., U.S.	150	K5	32.59 N	111.26 W
Valley Forge Estates, Pa., U.S.	203		40.05 N	75.26 W
Valley Forge National Historical Park, p.o.i., Pa., U.S.	124	D10	40.06 N	75.27 W
Valley Head, Al., U.S.	134	C13	34.34 N	85.37 W
Valley Head, W.V., U.S.	124	F5	38.31 N	80.02 W
Valley Mede, Md., U.S.	202b		39.17 N	76.50 W
Valley Mills, Tx., U.S.	136	C10	31.39 N	97.28 W
Valley of Fire State Park, p.o.i., Nv., U.S.	150	G2	36.26 N	114.33 W
Valley of the Kings, hist., Egypt	74	H3	25.45 N	32.37 E
Valley Plaza, shp. cen., Ca., U.S.	198		34.11 N	118.24 W
Valley Springs, S.D., U.S.	128	H2	43.34 N	96.28 W
Valley Station, Ky., U.S.	130	F12	38.06 N	85.51 W
Valley Stream, stm., N.Y., U.S.	194		40.39 N	73.45 W
Valley Stream State Park, p.o.i., N.Y., U.S.	194		40.41 N	73.42 W
Valleyview, Ab., Can.	144	A13	55.04 N	117.17 W
Valley View, Oh., U.S.	197a		41.23 N	81.37 W
Valley View, Tx., U.S.	138	H11	33.29 N	97.09 W
Vallgrund, i., Fin.	18	D8	63.12 N	21.15 E
Valliant, Ok., U.S.	134	D4	34.00 N	95.05 W
Vallimanca, Arroyo, stm., Arg.	172	G7	35.43 S	60.08 W
Vallirana, Spain	184d		41.23 N	1.56 E
Vallo della Lucania, Italy	32	D9	40.14 N	15.15 E
Vallorbe, Switz.	30	D3	46.42 N	6.22 E
Vallromanes, Spain	184d		41.32 N	2.18 E
Valls, Spain	28	C12	41.16 N	1.14 E
Vallvidrera, ngh., Spain	184d		41.25 N	2.07 E
Vallvidrera, Riera de, stm., Spain	184d		41.25 N	2.01 E
Val Marie, Sk., Can.	142	E6	49.14 N	107.44 W
Valmeyer, Il., U.S.	130	F7	38.17 N	90.19 W
Valmiera, Lat.	26	C8	57.32 N	25.25 E
Valmondois, Fr.	179		49.06 N	2.12 E
Valognes, Fr.	20	E7	49.30 N	1.28 W
Valois, Baie de, b., Qc., Can.	193a		45.26 N	73.47 W
Valok, Ukr.	38	H13	45.47 N	34.57 E
Valona see Vlorë, Alb.	32	D13	40.28 N	19.29 E
Valoria la Buena, Spain	28	C6	41.48 N	4.32 W
Valožyn, Bela.	26	F9	54.05 N	26.32 E
Vālpārai, India	69	F3	10.19 N	76.53 E
Valparaíso, Chile	172	F2	33.02 S	71.37 W
Valparaíso, Mex.	154	D7	22.46 N	103.34 W
Valparaiso, Fl., U.S.	134	G12	30.30 N	86.30 W
Valparaiso, In., U.S.	130	C10	41.28 N	87.02 W
Valparaiso, Ne., U.S.	140	F16	41.04 N	96.50 W
Valparaíso, state, Chile	172	F2	32.34 S	71.08 W
Valpovo, Cro.	30	E15	45.39 N	18.24 E
Valréas, Fr.	22	E10	44.23 N	4.59 E
Vals, stm., S. Afr.	90	E8	27.23 S	26.31 E
Vals, Tanjung, c., Indon.	60	G10	8.24 S	137.37 E
Valsbaai see False Bay, b., S. Afr.	90	I4	34.12 S	18.40 E
Valset, Swe.	16	D7	63.38 N	9.43 E
Valsjöbyn, Swe.	16	C12	64.04 N	14.08 E
Valtimo, Fin.	18	D15	63.41 N	28.48 E
Valuec, Russia	26	H16	52.45 N	33.24 E
Valuevo, Russia	183b		55.35 N	37.21 E
Valujki, Russia	40	F11	50.11 N	38.08 E
Valverde del Camino, Spain	28	G4	37.34 N	6.45 W
Valyncy, Bela.	26	E11	55.43 N	28.12 E
Våmhus, Swe.	16	F12	61.07 N	14.28 E
Vammala, Fin.	18	F9	61.19 N	22.55 E
Vamori Wash, stm., Az., U.S.	150	L5	31.57 N	112.19 W
Van, Tur.	42	F10	38.29 N	43.24 E
Van, Tx., U.S.	136	B12	32.32 N	95.38 W
Van, state, Tur.	42	F10	39.00 N	43.45 E
Van, Lake see Van Gölü, l., Tur.	42	F10	38.33 N	42.46 E
Vanadzor, Arm.	42	E11	40.48 N	44.29 E
Vanajavesi, l., Fin.	18	F10	61.09 N	24.15 E
Vanak, ngh., Iran	185d		35.45 N	51.23 E
Van Alstyne, Tx., U.S.	134	D2	33.25 N	96.34 W
Vananda, B.C., Can.	144	G6	49.45 N	124.33 W
Vanavara, Russia	48	B18	60.20 N	102.15 E
Van Bruyssel, Qc., Can.	122	C4	47.56 N	72.09 W
Van Buren, Ar., U.S.	134	B4	35.26 N	94.21 W
Van Buren, Me., U.S.	122	C8	47.10 N	67.56 W
Van Buren, Mo., U.S.	130	G7	36.59 N	91.01 W
Vance Air Force Base, mil., Ok., U.S.	138	E10	36.21 N	97.55 W
Vanceboro, Me., U.S.	122	E9	45.33 N	67.26 W
Vanceburg, Ky., U.S.	124	F2	38.35 N	83.19 W
Van Chan, Viet.	64	B7	21.36 N	104.31 E
Vancleave, Ms., U.S.	134	G10	30.32 N	88.41 W
Van Cortlandt Park, p.o.i., N.Y., U.S.	194		40.54 N	73.53 W
Vancouver, B.C., Can.	144	G7	49.16 N	123.07 W
Vancouver, Wa., U.S.	146	E4	45.38 N	122.39 W
Vancouver Island, i., B.C., Can.	144	G4	49.45 N	126.00 W
Vancouver Island Ranges, mts., B.C., Can.	144	G5	49.25 N	125.25 W
Vanda see Vantaa, Fin.	18	G12	60.16 N	25.02 E
Vandalia, Il., U.S.	130	F8	38.57 N	89.05 W
Vandalia, Mo., U.S.	130	E6	39.18 N	91.29 W
Vandalia, Oh., U.S.	124	E1	39.53 N	84.12 W
Vandavāsi, India	69	E4	12.30 N	79.37 E
Vandenberg Air Force Base, mil., Ca., U.S.	148	I5	34.43 N	120.33 W
Vanderbijlpark, S. Afr.	90	E8	26.41 S	27.49 E
Vanderbilt, Mi., U.S.	126	C5	45.08 N	84.40 W
Vanderbilt, Tx., U.S.	136	F11	28.49 N	96.37 W
Vanderbilt Museum, bldg., N.Y., U.S.	194		40.54 N	73.22 W
Vanderhoof, B.C., Can.	144	B6	54.01 N	124.06 W
Vanderkloof Dam, res., S. Afr.	90	G7	30.12 S	24.54 E
Vanderlin Island, i., Austl.	96	C7	15.44 S	137.02 E
Vandervoort, Ar., U.S.	134	C4	34.23 N	94.21 W
Van Diemen, Cape, c., Austl.	96	B6	11.10 S	130.23 E
Van Diemen Gulf, b., Austl.	96	B6	11.50 S	132.00 E
Vändra, Est.	26	B8	58.39 N	25.01 E
Vandry, Qc., Can.	122	C3	47.52 N	73.34 W
Van Duzen, stm., Ca., U.S.	148	C2	40.32 N	124.08 W
Vandykpark, S. Afr.	191d		26.16 S	28.19 E
Vandžiogala, Lith.	26	E6	55.07 N	23.58 E
Vanegas, Mex.	154	D8	23.53 N	100.56 W
Vänern, l., Swe.	16	I11	58.55 N	13.30 E
Vänersborg, Swe.	16	I10	58.22 N	12.18 E
Vangaindrano, Madag.	88	E8	23.21 S	47.36 E
Vängelälven, stm., Swe.	16	D14	63.40 N	16.25 E
Van Gölü, l., Tur.	42	F10	38.33 N	42.46 E
Vangsnes, Nor.	16	F4	61.09 N	6.39 E
Vangsvika, Nor.	14	C8	69.10 N	17.43 E
Vanguard, Sk., Can.	142	E6	49.55 N	107.19 W
Vangunu, Mount, mtn., Sol. Is.	101b	e7	8.42 S	158.00 E
Vangunu Island, i., Sol. Is.	101b	e8	8.38 S	158.00 E
Van Hook Arm, b., N.D., U.S.	142	G11	47.54 N	102.21 W
Van Horn, Tx., U.S.	136	C3	31.02 N	104.49 W
Van Horne, Ia., U.S.	130	B5	42.00 N	92.05 W
Vanier, On., Can.	126	C14	45.25 N	75.38 W
Vanikolo, i., Sol. Is.	94	E7	11.37 S	166.51 E
Vaniköy, ngh., Tur.	185b		41.04 N	29.04 E
Vanimo, Pap. N. Gui.	101a	a3	2.43 S	141.20 E
Vanino, Russia	50	G17	49.06 N	140.16 E
Vānīvilāsa Sāgara, res., India	69	E3	13.51 N	76.27 E
Vāniyambādi, India	69	E4	12.40 N	78.37 E
Vânju Mare, Rom.	36	E9	44.25 N	22.52 E
Vankarem, Russia	50	C25	67.50 N	175.50 W
Van Kleef Aquarium, p.o.i., Sing.	189c		1.18 N	103.51 E
Vankleek Hill, On., Can.	126	C15	45.32 N	74.37 W
Van Lear, Ky., U.S.	124	G3	37.46 N	82.48 W
Vanna, i., Nor.	14	B10	70.09 N	19.50 E
Vännäs, Swe.	16	D17	63.55 N	19.45 E
Vanndale, Ar., U.S.	134	B8	35.18 N	90.46 W
Vanne, stm., Fr.	20	F12	48.11 N	3.16 E
Vanne et du Loing, Aqueduc de, aq., Fr.	179		48.36 N	2.26 E
Vannes, Fr.	20	G6	47.39 N	2.45 W
Van Ninh, Viet.	64	F9	12.42 N	109.13 E
Vannsundet, strt., Nor.	14	B10	70.01 N	19.44 E
Van Nuys Airport, arpt., Ca., U.S.	198		34.12 N	118.29 W
Van Nuys-Sherman Oaks War Memorial Park, p.o.i., Ca., U.S.	198		34.10 N	118.27 W
Vanoise, Massif de la, mts., Fr.	22	D12	45.16 N	6.37 E
Van Phong, Vung, b., Viet.	64	F9	12.33 N	109.18 E
Van Phong Bay see Van Phong, Vung, b., Viet.	64	F9	12.33 N	109.18 E
Van Reenen, S. Afr.	90	F9	28.23 S	29.24 E
Van Rees, Pegunungan, mts., Indon.	60	F10	2.35 S	138.15 E
Vanrhynsdorp, S. Afr.	90	G4	31.35 S	18.44 E
Vanryndam, res., S. Afr.	191d		26.09 S	28.21 E
Vansant, Va., U.S.	124	G3	37.13 N	82.05 W
Van Saun Mill Brook, stm., N.J., U.S.	194		40.55 N	74.03 W
Vansbro, Swe.	16	G12	60.31 N	14.13 E
Van Sciver Lake, l., Pa., U.S.	203		40.09 N	74.48 W
Van Sickle Island, i., Ca., U.S.	200		38.04 N	121.53 W
Vansittart Island, i., Nu., Can.	110	B14	65.50 N	84.00 W
Vanskoe, Russia	26	B19	58.56 N	36.51 E
Van Stadensrus, S. Afr.	90	F8	29.58 S	27.00 E
Vantaa (Vanda), Fin.	18	G12	60.16 N	25.02 E
Vanthali, India	70	H3	21.28 N	70.20 E
Vanua Balavu, i., Fiji	101e	p20	17.13 S	178.56 W
Vanua Lava, i., Vanuatu	101d	i16	13.44 S	167.27 E
Vanua Levu, i., Fiji	101e	p19	16.33 S	179.15 E
Vanuatu, ctry., Oc.	92	E7	16.00 S	167.00 E
Vanves, Fr.	179		48.50 N	2.18 E
Van Vleck, Tx., U.S.	136	E12	29.01 N	95.53 W
Van Voorhis, Pa., U.S.	197b		40.10 N	79.58 W
Van Wert, Oh., U.S.	124	D1	40.51 N	84.34 W
Van Wyksdorp, S. Afr.	90	H5	33.44 S	21.27 E
Vanwyksvlei, S. Afr.	90	G5	30.20 S	21.50 E
Vanzaghello, Italy	184b		45.35 N	8.47 E
Vanzago, Italy	184b		45.32 N	9.00 E
Van Zylsrus, S. Afr.	90	E6	26.52 S	22.03 E
Vao, N. Cal.	101d	n16	22.40 S	167.28 E
Vapniarka, Ukr.	38	E7	48.32 N	28.43 E
Var, state, Fr.	22	F12	43.30 N	6.20 E
Var, stm., Fr.	22	E12	43.39 N	7.11 E
Vara, stm., Italy	30	F6	44.09 N	9.53 E
Varada, stm., India	69	D2	14.55 N	75.40 E
Varakļāni, Lat.	26	D9	56.36 N	26.45 E
Varaldsøy, i., Nor.	16	G3	60.07 N	6.00 E
Varallo, Italy	30	E5	45.49 N	8.14 E
Varallo, Italy	184b		45.40 N	8.38 E
Varāmīn, Iran	74	C12	35.20 N	51.39 E
Vārānasi (Benares), India	70	F9	25.20 N	82.59 E
Varandej, Russia	48	A9	68.48 N	58.00 E
Varangerbotn, Nor.	14	B19	70.10 N	28.33 E
Varangerfjorden, b., Nor.	14	B20	70.00 N	30.00 E
Varangerhalvøya, pen., Nor.	14	B20	70.25 N	29.30 E
Varano, Lago di, l., Italy	30	I12	41.53 N	15.45 E
Varapaeva, Bela.	26	E10	55.08 N	27.12 E
Varaždin, Cro.	30	D13	46.18 N	16.20 E
Varazze, Italy	30	F5	44.21 N	8.34 E
Varberg, Swe.	16	J10	57.06 N	12.15 E
Vardak, state, Afg.	70	A2	34.16 N	68.24 E
Vardaman, Ms., U.S.	134	D9	33.52 N	89.10 W
Vardar (Axiós), stm., Eur.	34	B5	40.31 N	22.43 E
Varde, Den.	16	L6	55.38 N	8.29 E
Vardø, Nor.	14	B22	70.21 N	31.00 E
Vardoúsia Óri, mts., Grc.	34	E5	38.44 N	22.07 E
Varedo, Italy	184b		45.36 N	9.09 E
Varegovo, Russia	26	C22	57.47 N	39.17 E
Varel, Ger.	24	C4	53.23 N	8.08 E
Varela, Arg.	172	G4	34.07 S	66.27 W
Varėna, Lith.	26	F7	54.12 N	24.35 E
Varenikovskaja, Russia	40	I10	45.07 N	37.38 E
Varennes, Îles de, is., Qc., Can.	193a		45.40 N	73.27 W
Varennes-Jarcy, Fr.	179		48.41 N	2.34 E
Varennes-sur-Allier, Fr.	22	C9	46.19 N	3.23 E
Vareš, Bos.	36	E5	44.08 N	18.19 E
Varese, Italy	30	E5	45.49 N	8.49 E
Varese, Lago di, l., Italy	30	E5	45.49 N	8.45 E
Vârfurile, Rom.	36	C9	46.18 N	22.32 E
Vårgårda, Swe.	16	I10	58.02 N	12.49 E
Vargas, state, Ven.	204c		10.34 N	66.52 W
Vargaši, Russia	48	C11	55.22 N	65.48 E
Vargem, Riacho da, stm., Braz.	170	E6	8.42 S	39.09 W
Vargem Grande, Braz.	170	B3	3.33 S	43.56 W
Vargem Grande, ngh., Braz.	205a		22.59 S	43.29 W
Varginha, Braz.	170	K3	21.33 S	45.25 W
Vargsundet, strt., Nor.	14	B14	70.22 N	23.30 E
Varhaug, Nor.	16	I3	58.37 N	5.39 E
Väringen, l., Swe.	16	H13	59.25 N	15.22 E
Varkallai, India	69	G3	8.37 N	76.47 E
Varkaus, Fin.	18	E14	62.18 N	27.54 E
Värmeln, l., Swe.	16	H10	59.32 N	12.55 E
Värmland, state, Swe.	16	H11	59.45 N	13.15 E
Värmlandsnäs, pen., Swe.	16	I11	59.00 N	13.10 E
Varna, Blg.	36	F14	43.13 N	27.54 E
Varna, Russia	48	D10	53.22 N	60.59 E
Varna, state, Blg.	36	F14	43.20 N	27.30 E
Värnamo, Swe.	16	J12	57.11 N	14.03 E
Varnavino, Russia	40	C14	57.24 N	45.05 E
Varnenski Zaliv, b., Blg.	36	F14	43.11 N	27.56 E
Varniai, Lith.	26	E5	55.45 N	22.22 E
Varnjany, Bela.	26	F9	54.43 N	26.01 E
Varnsdorf, Czech Rep.	24	F10	50.54 N	14.37 E
Varnville, S.C., U.S.	132	D4	32.50 N	81.04 W
Värö bruk, Swe.	16	J10	57.15 N	12.10 E
Városliget, p.o.i., Hung.	182c		47.31 N	19.06 E
Varpaisjärvi, Fin.	18	D14	63.22 N	27.46 E
Várpalota, Hung.	36	B5	47.12 N	18.08 E
Varresbeck, ngh., Ger.	181		51.15 N	7.06 E

Name	Page	Map Ref.	Latitude	Longitude
Värriöjoki, stm., Fin.	14	E19	67.27 N	28.22 E
Värriötunturit, mtn., Fin.	14	E20	67.41 N	29.32 E
Varšec, Blg.	36	F10	43.12 N	23.17 E
Värska, Est.	26	C10	57.57 N	27.38 E
Vârtopu, Rom.	36	E10	44.12 N	23.20 E
Varva, Ukr.	38	C11	50.30 N	32.43 E
Varvarin, Yugo.	36	F8	43.43 N	21.21 E
Varvarivka, Ukr.	38	E14	48.42 N	36.00 E
Varvarivka, Ukr.	38	D14	49.32 N	35.12 E
Várzea, stm., Braz.	172	C11	27.13 S	53.19 W
Várzea Alegre, Braz.	170	D6	6.47 S	39.17 W
Várzea da Palma, Braz.	170	I3	17.36 S	44.44 W
Varzea de Sintra, Port.	184c		38.49 N	9.24 W
Várzea Grande, Braz.	166	C5	15.39 S	56.08 W
Varzeão, Braz.	172	B13	24.32 S	49.26 W
Varzi, Italy	30	F6	44.49 N	9.12 E
Varzi, Russia	40	C18	56.02 N	52.50 E
Varzino, Russia	14	D29	68.19 N	38.20 E
Varzuga, stm., Russia	14	F26	66.16 N	36.55 E
Varzy, Fr.	20	G12	47.21 N	3.22 E
Vas, state, Hung.	36	B3	47.05 N	16.45 E
Vasa see Vaasa, Fin.	18	D8	63.05 N	21.36 E
Vasa see Vaasa, state, Fin.	18	D9	63.00 N	23.00 E
Vasai, India	62	E3	19.21 N	72.48 E
Vasalemma, Est.	26	A7	59.13 N	24.17 E
Vasar, India	190c		19.11 N	73.09 E
Vascão, stm., Port.	28	G3	37.31 N	7.30 W
Vașcău, Rom.	36	C9	46.28 N	22.28 E
Vasco, País see Euskal Herriko, state, Spain	28	A8	43.00 N	2.30 W
Vāshi, India	190c		19.04 N	72.59 E
Vashkivtsi, Ukr.	38	E4	48.23 N	25.32 E
Vashkivtsi, Ukr.	38	E6	48.25 N	27.08 E
Vashon Island, i., Wa., U.S.	146	C4	47.25 N	122.28 W
Vasil'euka, Bela.	26	H14	52.14 N	31.30 E
Vasilevičy, Bela.	26	H12	52.14 N	29.49 E
Vasilevo, Russia	18	G25	60.46 N	38.56 E
Vasilevskij, ostrov, i., Russia	183a		59.56 N	30.15 E
Vasilevskij Moh, Russia	26	C18	57.01 N	35.55 E
Vasilevskoe, Russia	40	C14	56.30 N	45.49 E
Vasiliká, Grc.	34	C6	40.28 N	23.08 E
Vasilišķi, Bela.	26	G7	53.47 N	24.51 E
Vasjugan, stm., Russia	48	C13	59.07 N	80.46 E
Vaška, stm., Russia	12	D21	64.54 N	45.42 E
Vaskelovo, Russia	18	G17	60.22 N	30.22 E
Vaskijärven luonnonpuisto, ind. res., Fin.	18	G9	60.50 N	22.13 E
Vaskojoki, stm., Fin.	14	D17	68.54 N	26.38 E
Vaslui, Rom.	36	C14	46.38 N	27.44 E
Vaslui, state, Rom.	36	C14	46.30 N	27.45 E
Väsman, l., Swe.	16	G12	60.11 N	15.02 E
Vass, N.C., U.S.	132	A6	35.15 N	79.16 W
Vassar, Mi., U.S.	126	E6	43.22 N	83.35 W
Vastenjaure, l., Swe.	14	E7	67.28 N	16.30 E
Västerås, Swe.	16	H14	59.37 N	16.33 E
Västerbotten, state, Swe.	18	D8	64.00 N	17.30 E
Västerdalälven, stm., Swe.	16	G11	60.32 N	15.07 E
Västerfjäll, Swe.	14	F8	66.42 N	17.25 E
Västerhaninge, Swe.	16	H16	59.07 N	18.06 E
Västernorrland, state, Swe.	16	D15	63.00 N	17.30 E
Västervik, Swe.	16	J14	57.45 N	16.38 E
Västmanland, state, Swe.	16	H14	59.45 N	16.20 E
Vasto, Italy	30	H11	42.06 N	14.42 E
Västra Götaland, state, Swe.	16	I10	58.15 N	13.05 E
Västra Kikkejaure, l., Swe.	14	G9	65.43 N	18.56 E
Västra Silen, l., Swe.	16	H10	59.15 N	12.08 E
Vastseliina, Est.	26	C10	57.43 N	27.20 E
Vašutino, Russia	183b		55.56 N	37.26 E
Vasvár, Hung.	36	B3	47.03 N	16.47 E
Vasylivka, Ukr.	38	F14	47.26 N	35.17 E
Vasyl'kiv, Ukr.	38	C9	50.10 N	30.19 E
Vasyl'kivka, Ukr.	38	E15	48.12 N	36.01 E
Vața de Jos, Rom.	36	C9	46.10 N	22.35 E
Vatan, Fr.	20	G10	47.05 N	1.48 E
Vatican see Vatican City, ctry., Eur.	30	I9	41.54 N	12.27 E
Vatican (Cité du) see Vatican City, ctry., Eur.	185a		41.54 N	12.27 E
Vatican City, ctry., Eur.	30	I9	41.54 N	12.27 E
Vatican City (Città del Vaticano), ctry., Eur.	185a		41.54 N	12.27 E
Vaticano, Capo, c., Italy	32	F9	38.38 N	15.50 E
Vaticano, Città del see Vatican City, ctry., Eur.	30	I9	41.54 N	12.27 E
Vatnajökull, ice, Ice.	12a	k31	64.25 N	16.50 W
Vatneyri, Ice.	12a	k27	65.35 N	23.58 W
Vatomandry, Madag.	88	D8	19.20 S	48.57 E
Vatra Dornei, Rom.	36	B12	47.20 N	25.22 E
Vättern, l., Swe.	16	I12	58.24 N	14.36 E
Vatu-i-ra Channel, strt., Fiji	101e	p19	17.17 S	178.31 E
Vatukoula, Fiji	101e	p18	17.31 S	177.51 E
Vatulele, i., Fiji	101e	q18	18.31 S	177.37 E
Vatutine, Ukr.	38	D9	49.00 N	31.03 E
Vauclin, Montagne du, mtn., Mart.	159c	k7	14.33 N	60.53 W
Vaucluse, Austl.	192a		33.51 S	151.17 E
Vaucluse, state, Fr.	22	F11	44.00 N	5.10 E
Vaucouleurs, Fr.	20	F14	48.36 N	5.41 E
Vaucouleurs, stm., Fr.	179		48.59 N	1.44 E
Vaudherland, Fr.	179		49.00 N	2.29 E
Vaudreuil, Baie de, b., Qc., Can.	193a		45.24 N	74.00 W
Vaughan, On., Can.	126	E10	43.47 N	79.35 W
Vaughn, N.M., U.S.	138	G3	34.35 N	105.14 W
Vaugrigneuse, Fr.	179		48.36 N	2.07 E
Vauhallan, Fr.	179		48.44 N	2.12 E
Vaujours, Fr.	179		48.56 N	2.35 E
Vaukavysk, Bela.	26	G7	53.09 N	24.27 E
Vaupés, state, Col.	168	G6	0.45 N	70.30 W
Vaupés (Uaupés), stm., S.A.	168	G7	0.01 N	67.15 W
Vauréal, Fr.	179		49.02 N	2.02 E
Vauvise, stm., Fr.	20	G11	47.16 N	2.53 E
Vaux, Ru des, stm., Fr.	179		48.42 N	2.00 E
Vauxhall, Ab., Can.	144	F18	50.03 N	112.05 W
Vaux-le-Pénil, Fr.	179		48.32 N	2.41 E
Vaux-sur-Seine, Fr.	179		49.00 N	1.58 E
Vava'u, i., Tonga	94	E9	18.36 S	174.00 W
Vavoua, C. Iv.	84	H3	7.22 N	6.27 W
Vavuniya, Sri L.	69	G5	8.45 N	80.30 E
Växjö, Swe.	16	K12	56.53 N	14.48 E
Vaza-barris, stm., Braz.	170	E6	11.06 S	37.09 W
Vazante, Braz.	170	J2	17.59 S	46.53 W
Važgort, Russia	12	E22	64.01 N	47.01 E
Važinka, stm., Russia	18	F20	60.57 N	34.01 E
Vazuza, stm., Russia	26	E17	55.50 N	34.19 E
Vazuzskoe vodohranilišče, res., Russia	26	E17	55.58 N	34.27 E
Veado, Ilha do, i., Braz.	205a		22.57 S	43.06 W
Veazie, Me., U.S.	122	F8	44.50 N	68.42 W
Veblen, S.D., U.S.	140	B15	45.51 N	97.17 W
Vecht (Vechte), stm., Eur.	20	B15	52.33 N	6.06 E
Vechta, Ger.	24	D4	52.43 N	8.17 E
Vechte (Vecht), stm., Eur.	20	B15	52.33 N	6.06 E
Vecpiebalga, Lat.	26	C8	57.08 N	25.50 E
Vecsés, Hung.	36	B6	47.24 N	19.17 E
Vecumnieki, Lat.	26	D7	56.35 N	24.32 E
Vedado, ngh., Cuba	204b		23.08 N	82.24 W
Vedano al Lambro, Italy	184b		45.37 N	9.16 E
Vedavågen, Nor.	16	H3	59.18 N	5.13 E
Veddige, Swe.	16	J10	57.15 N	12.20 E
Vedea, Rom.	36	E11	44.47 N	24.36 E
Vedea, stm., Rom.	36	F12	43.42 N	25.33 E
Vedeno, Russia	42	D12	42.58 N	46.06 E
Vedia, Arg.	172	G7	34.29 S	61.33 W
Vedlozero, ozero, l., Russia	18	F19	61.33 N	32.43 E
Vednoe, Russia	26	C19	57.07 N	36.10 E
Vedøya, i., Nor.	14	E2	67.28 N	12.00 E
Veedersburg, In., U.S.	130	D10	40.06 N	87.15 W
Veen, Ger.	181		51.37 N	6.27 E
Veendam, Neth.	20	A15	53.06 N	6.52 E
Veenendaal, Neth.	20	C14	52.01 N	5.33 E
Vefsna, stm., Nor.	16	B11	65.49 N	13.12 E
Vefsnfjorden, strt., Nor.	16	B10	65.58 N	12.52 E
Vega, Tx., U.S.	138	F6	35.15 N	102.26 W
Vega, i., Nor.	16	B9	65.39 N	11.50 E
Vega, Arroyo de la, stm., Spain	184a		40.31 N	3.33 W
Vega Alta, P.R.	158a	b3	18.25 N	66.19 W
Vega Baja, P.R.	158a	b3	18.27 N	66.22 W
Vegår, l., Nor.	16	I6	58.48 N	8.48 E
Vegreville, Ab., Can.	144	C18	53.30 N	112.03 W
Veguita, N.M., U.S.	138	G2	34.31 N	106.47 W
Vehār Lake, l., India	190c		19.09 N	72.55 E
Vehlefanz, Ger.	182a		52.43 N	13.06 E
Veinticinco de Mayo, Arg.	172	G3	34.34 S	68.32 W
Veinticinco de Mayo, Arg.	172	G7	35.25 S	60.11 W
Veiros, Braz.	164	D7	2.04 S	52.09 W
Veisiejai, Lith.	26	F6	54.06 N	23.42 E
Vejdelevka, Russia	38	C17	50.09 N	38.27 E
Vejen, Den.	16	L7	55.28 N	9.08 E
Vejer de la Frontera, Spain	28	H5	36.15 N	5.58 W
Vejle, Den.	16	L7	55.42 N	9.31 E
Vejle, state, Den.	16	L7	55.45 N	9.30 E
Vela Luka, Cro.	30	H13	42.57 N	16.43 E
Velapāda, India	190c		18.59 N	73.04 E
Velas, Cabo, c., C.R.	156	G4	10.21 N	85.52 W
Velázquez, Ur.	172	G10	34.02 S	54.17 W
Velddrif, S. Afr.	90	H4	32.47 S	18.11 E
Velden, Aus.	30	D11	46.36 N	14.02 E
Velden, Ger.	24	H8	48.22 N	12.16 E
Veldozero, Russia	18	F19	61.35 N	32.50 E
Velebit, mts., Cro.	30	F12	44.38 N	15.03 E
Velebitski Kanal, strt., Cro.	30	F11	44.58 N	14.50 E
Veleka, stm.	36	G14	42.04 N	27.58 E
Velencei-tó, l., Hung.	30	C15	47.13 N	18.37 E
Velesa, stm., Russia	26	D15	56.03 N	31.59 E
Velestino, Grc.	34	D5	39.23 N	22.45 E
Veleuščina, Bela.	26	F11	54.43 N	28.36 E
Vélez, Col.	168	D5	6.00 N	73.43 W
Vélez-Málaga, Spain	28	H7	36.47 N	4.06 W
Vélez-Rubio, Spain	28	G9	37.38 N	2.05 W
Velfjorden, b., Nor.	16	B10	65.29 N	12.28 E
Vel'gija, Russia	26	B17	58.23 N	33.59 E
Velhas, stm., Braz.	170	I3	17.13 S	44.49 W
Velhas, Canal do, can., Braz.	205a		22.42 S	43.22 W
Veličaevskoe, Russia	40	I14	44.57 N	45.07 E
Velikaja, Russia	40	B16	59.10 N	49.06 E
Velikaja, stm., Russia	26	C11	57.51 N	28.09 E
Velikaja, stm., Russia	50	D23	64.34 N	176.12 E
Velikaja Guba, Russia	18	E22	62.15 N	35.03 E
Velikaja Kema, Russia	54	B12	45.28 N	137.14 E
Velika Kapela, mts., Cro.	30	E12	45.13 N	15.04 E
Velika Kikinda see Kikinda, Yugo.	36	D7	45.49 N	20.28 E
Velika Morava, stm., Yugo.	36	E8	44.43 N	21.02 E
Velika Plana, Yugo.	36	E8	44.20 N	21.03 E
Veliki Bečkerek see Zrenjanin, Yugo.	36	D7	45.23 N	20.24 E
Velikie Luki, Russia	26	D13	56.20 N	30.33 E
Velikij, ostrov, i., Russia	14	F24	66.33 N	33.18 E
Velikij Ustjug, Russia	12	F22	60.45 N	46.19 E
Veliki Vitorog, mtn., Bos.	36	E4	44.07 N	17.03 E
Velikoe, Russia	18	H24	59.33 N	36.58 E
Velikoe, ozero, l., Russia	26	C19	57.02 N	36.34 E
Veliko Gradište, Yugo.	36	E8	44.46 N	21.30 E
Velikonda Hills, hills, India	69	D4	14.45 N	79.10 E
Velikooktjabr'skij, Russia	26	C16	57.26 N	33.49 E
Veliko Tărnovo, Blg.	36	F12	43.04 N	25.38 E
Velikovisočnoe, Russia	12	C25	67.16 N	51.59 E
Velilla de San Antonio, Spain	184a		40.22 N	3.29 W
Veli Lošinj, Cro.	30	F11	44.31 N	14.30 E
Vélingara, Sen.	84	G2	13.08 N	14.06 W
Velingrad, Blg.	36	G10	42.01 N	24.00 E
Velino, stm., Italy	30	H10	42.33 N	12.42 E
Velino, Monte, mtn., Italy	30	H10	42.09 N	13.23 E
Veliž, Russia	26	E14	55.36 N	31.11 E
Vélizy-Villacoublay, Fr.	179		48.47 N	2.10 E
Velká Bíteš, Czech Rep.	24	G12	49.17 N	16.13 E
Veľké Kapušany, Slvk.	24	H18	48.33 N	22.05 E
Velké Meziříčí, Czech Rep.	24	G12	49.21 N	16.00 E
Vel'kyj Milič (Nagy-Milic), mtn., Eur.	24	H17	48.35 N	21.28 E
Vella Gulf, strt., Sol. Is.	101b	d7	8.00 S	156.50 E
Vella Lavella, i., Sol. Is.	101b	d7	7.45 S	156.40 E
Vellār, stm., India	69	F4	11.28 N	79.45 E
Velletri, Italy	30	I9	41.41 N	12.46 E
Vellinge, Swe.	16	L10	55.28 N	13.01 E
Vellore, On., Can.	193b		43.50 N	79.34 W
Vellore, India	69	E4	12.54 N	79.08 E
Velm, Aus.	182b		48.03 N	16.27 E
Velma, Ok., U.S.	138	G11	34.27 N	97.40 W
Vel'sk, Russia	12	F20	61.04 N	42.06 E
Vel't, Russia	12	B23	68.02 N	49.54 E
Velten, Ger.	24	D9	52.41 N	13.10 E
Velva, N.D., U.S.	142	F13	48.03 N	100.56 W
Velyka Bahachka, Ukr.	38	D12	49.47 N	33.43 E
Velyka Bilozerka, Ukr.	38	F13	47.16 N	34.40 E
Velyka Blahovishchenka, Ukr.	38	G13	46.52 N	34.04 E
Velyka Chernihivka, Ukr.	38	E18	48.57 N	39.25 E
Velyka Danylivka, Ukr.	38	C15	50.07 N	36.23 E
Velyka Dymerka, Ukr.	38	C9	50.35 N	30.54 E
Velyka Hlusha, Ukr.	38	B4	51.48 N	25.01 E
Velyka Korenykha, Ukr.	38	G10	46.56 N	31.54 E
Velyka Koshnytsia, Ukr.	38	E7	48.07 N	28.29 E
Velyka Lepetykha, Ukr.	38	F12	47.10 N	33.56 E
Velyka Mykhailivka, Ukr.	38	F8	47.04 N	29.52 E
Velyka Novosilka, Ukr.	38	F15	47.49 N	36.49 E
Velyka Oleksandrivka, Ukr.	38	F12	47.18 N	33.16 E
Velyka Rublivka, Ukr.	38	D13	49.54 N	34.48 E
Velyki Dederkaly, Ukr.	38	C4	50.02 N	26.07 E
Velyki Kopani, Ukr.	38	G11	46.29 N	32.58 E
Velyki Korovyntsi, Ukr.	38	C7	49.58 N	28.17 E
Velyki Krynky, Ukr.	38	D12	49.27 N	33.29 E
Velyki Luchky see Velyki Lutsjky, Ukr.	24	H18	48.26 N	22.35 E
Velyki Lutsjky, Ukr.	24	H18	48.26 N	22.35 E
Velyki Mosty, Ukr.	38	C3	50.13 N	24.07 E
Velyki Sorochyntsi, Ukr.	38	C12	50.01 N	33.56 E
Velykodolyns'ke, Ukr.	38	G9	46.20 N	30.35 E
Velykoplos'ke, Ukr.	38	F8	47.00 N	29.41 E
Velykyi Bereznyi, Ukr.	24	H18	48.53 N	22.27 E
Velykyi Burluk, Ukr.	38	C16	50.04 N	37.24 E
Velykyi Bychkiv, Ukr.	38	F3	47.58 N	24.00 E
Velykyi Hlybochok, Ukr.	38	D4	49.36 N	25.33 E
Velykyi Khutir, Ukr.	38	D11	49.51 N	32.06 E
Velykyj Kuial'nyk, stm., Ukr.	38	F9	46.47 N	30.36 E
Velykyi Vys', stm., Ukr.	38	E10	48.45 N	30.54 E
Velykyi Zhvanchyk, Ukr.	38	E5	48.45 N	26.58 E
Velykyj Kuialnyk, stm., Ukr.	36	B17	46.47 N	30.36 E
Velymche, Ukr.	38	B3	51.36 N	24.44 E
Vémars, Fr.	179		49.04 N	2.34 E
Vemdalen, Swe.	16	E11	62.26 N	13.52 E
Venadillo, Col.	168	E4	4.43 N	74.55 W
Venado Tuerto, Arg.	172	F7	33.45 S	61.58 W
Venafro, Italy	32	C8	41.29 N	14.02 E
Venâncio Aires, Braz.	172	D11	29.36 S	52.11 W
Venant, Fr.	179		48.30 N	2.06 E
Vence, Fr.	22	F13	43.43 N	7.07 E
Venda, hist. reg., S. Afr.	90	C10	23.00 S	30.30 E
Venda Nova, Port.	28	C3	41.40 N	7.58 W
Vendas Novas, Port.	28	F2	38.39 N	8.27 W
Vendée, state, Fr.	22	C4	46.40 N	1.20 W
Vendéen, Bocage, reg., Fr.	22	C4	46.40 N	1.30 W
Vendôme, Fr.	20	G10	47.47 N	1.04 E
Vendrell see El Vendrell, Spain	28	C12	41.13 N	1.32 E
Vendsyssel, reg., Den.	16	J8	57.19 N	9.44 E
Vendychany, Ukr.	38	E6	48.37 N	27.48 E
Venecia, C.R.	156	G5	10.22 N	84.17 W
Veneta, Laguna, b., Italy	30	E9	45.21 N	12.16 E
Venetia see Veneto, state, Italy	30	E8	45.30 N	11.45 E
Venetie, Ak., U.S.	109	C10	67.01 N	146.23 W
Veneto, state, Italy	30	E8	45.30 N	11.45 E
Venev, Russia	26	F21	54.20 N	38.16 E
Venézia (Venice), Italy	30	E9	45.26 N	12.19 E
Venezia, Golfo di see Venice, Gulf of, b., Eur.	30	E9	45.15 N	13.00 E
Venezuela, ctry., S.A.	164	B4	8.00 N	66.00 W
Venezuela, Golfo de, b., S.A.	168	B6	11.30 N	71.00 W
Venezuela, Gulf of see Venezuela, Golfo de, b., S.A.	168	B6	11.30 N	71.00 W
Venezuelan Basin, unds.	176	G7	15.00 N	68.00 W
Vengerovo, Russia	48	C13	55.40 N	76.45 E
Vengsøya, i., Nor.	14	C9	69.50 N	18.30 E
Vengurla, India	69	D1	15.51 N	73.38 E
Veniaminof, Mount, vol., Ak., U.S.	109	E8	56.13 N	159.18 W
Venice see Venézia, Italy	30	E9	45.26 N	12.19 E
Venice, Fl., U.S.	132	I3	27.05 N	82.27 W
Venice, La., U.S.	134	H9	29.16 N	89.22 W
Venice, Pa., U.S.	197b		40.19 N	80.14 W
Venice, Gulf of, b., Eur.	30	E9	45.15 N	13.00 E
Vénissieux, Fr.	22	D10	45.41 N	4.53 E
Venjan, Swe.	16	G11	60.57 N	13.53 E
Venjansjön, l., Swe.	16	G11	60.54 N	14.02 E
Venkatagiri, India	69	E4	13.57 N	79.35 E
Venlo, Neth.	20	C15	51.22 N	6.10 E
Vennesla, Nor.	16	I5	58.15 N	7.58 E
Vennesund, Nor.	16	B10	65.13 N	12.03 E
Vennhausen, ngh., Ger.	181		51.13 N	6.51 E
Venosa, Italy	32	D9	40.57 N	15.49 E
Venoste, Alpi (Ötztaler Alpen), mts., Eur.	30	D7	46.54 N	10.49 E
Venray, Neth.	20	C15	51.31 N	6.00 E
Venta, stm., Eur.	26	C4	57.23 N	21.33 E
Ventanas, Ec.	168	H2	1.15 S	79.22 W
Ventersburg, S. Afr.	90	F8	28.05 S	27.08 E
Ventersdorp, S. Afr.	90	E8	26.19 S	26.50 E
Venterspos, S. Afr.	191d		26.18 S	27.39 E
Venterstad, S. Afr.	90	G7	30.46 S	25.47 E
Ventimiglia, Italy	30	G4	43.48 N	7.35 E
Ventotene, Isola, i., Italy	32	D7	40.47 N	13.25 E
Ventspils, Lat.	26	C4	57.23 N	21.34 E
Ventuari, stm., Ven.	168	E8	3.58 N	67.03 W
Ventura, Ca., U.S.	148	I6	34.16 N	119.17 W
Venturia, N.D., U.S.	140	B13	45.59 N	99.32 W
Venus, Fl., U.S.	132	I4	27.04 N	81.21 W
Vénus, Pointe, c., Fr. Poly.	100h	u22	17.30 S	149.29 W
Venustiano Carranza, Mex.	154	G12	16.21 N	92.33 W
Venustiano Carranza, Presa, res., Mex.	154	B8	27.29 N	100.37 W
Vepryk, Ukr.	38	C13	50.22 N	34.11 E
Vepsovskaja vozvyšennost', plat., Russia	18	G21	60.20 N	35.15 E
Vera, Arg.	172	D7	29.28 S	60.13 W
Vera, Spain	28	G9	37.14 N	1.52 W
Vera, Cape, c., Nu., Can.	108	B8	76.14 N	89.11 W
Veracruz, Mex.	154	F10	19.11 N	96.08 W
Veracruz, state, Mex.	154	F10	19.20 N	96.40 W
Veramejki, Bela.	26	G14	53.46 N	31.15 E
Verano Brianza, Italy	184b		45.41 N	9.14 E
Veranópolis, Braz.	172	D12	28.55 S	51.32 W
Verāval, India	70	H3	20.54 N	70.21 E
Verba, Ukr.	38	C4	50.16 N	25.37 E
Verbania, Italy	30	E5	45.56 N	8.33 E
Verbano see Maggiore, Lago, l., Eur.	30	D5	45.55 N	8.35 E
Verbeek, Pegunungan, mts., Indon.	66	E12	2.14 S	121.01 E
Verberg, ngh., Ger.	181		51.22 N	6.36 E
Verbilki, Russia	26	D20	56.31 N	37.35 E
Verbliuzhka, Ukr.	38	E11	48.22 N	32.53 E
Vercelli, Italy	30	E5	45.19 N	8.25 E
Vercors, reg., Fr.	22	E11	44.57 N	5.25 E
Verdalsøra, Nor.	16	D9	63.47 N	11.28 E
Verde, stm., Braz.	166	D4	21.11 S	51.52 W
Verde, stm., Braz.	166	B5	11.44 S	55.43 W
Verde, stm., Braz.	170	I2	17.05 S	46.05 W
Verde, stm., Braz.	170	J1	19.32 S	48.53 W
Verde, stm., Braz.	170	H1	15.07 S	48.40 W
Verde, stm., Braz.	170	F4	10.27 S	42.16 W
Verde, stm., Mex.	154	E7	20.44 N	103.16 W
Verde, stm., Az., U.S.	150	J5	33.32 N	111.40 W
Verde, Cape, c., Bah.	156	A10	22.54 N	74.50 W
Verde Grande, stm., Braz.	170	H4	14.35 S	43.53 W
Verden, Ger.	24	D5	52.55 N	9.14 E
Verden, Ok., U.S.	138	F10	35.03 N	98.05 W
Verde Pequeno, stm., Braz.	170	H4	14.48 S	43.31 W
Verdesela, Pinhal da, p.o.i., Port.	184c		38.37 N	9.08 W
Verdi, Nv., U.S.	148	D5	39.30 N	119.59 W
Verdigre, Ne., U.S.	140	E14	42.35 N	98.02 W
Verdigre Creek, stm., Ne., U.S.	140	E14	42.42 N	98.03 W
Verdigris, stm., U.S.	138	E13	35.48 N	95.19 W
Verdon, Ne., U.S.	130	D2	40.08 N	95.42 W
Verdon, stm., Fr.	22	F12	43.44 N	5.45 E
Verduga, Russia	26	B12	58.46 N	29.12 E
Verdugo Mountains, mts., Ca., U.S.	198		34.13 N	118.18 W
Verdun, Qc., Can.	126	C16	45.27 N	73.34 W
Verdun-sur-Garonne, Fr.	22	F7	43.50 N	1.13 E
Verdun-sur-Meuse, Fr.	20	E14	49.09 N	5.23 E
Vereb'ě, Russia	26	B15	58.41 N	32.42 E
Vereeniging, S. Afr.	90	E9	26.40 S	27.56 E
Veregin, Sk., Can.	142	C11	51.35 N	102.04 W
Vereja, Russia	26	E19	55.20 N	36.11 E
Vereja, Russia	183b		55.37 N	38.02 E
Vereščagino, Russia	40	B19	58.04 N	54.38 E
Vereščagino, Russia	48	B15	64.13 N	87.36 E
Veresegyház, Hung.	182c		47.39 N	19.17 E
Veresoch, Ukr.	38	B10	51.20 N	31.51 E
Verga, N.J., U.S.	203		39.52 N	75.10 W
Vergara see Bergara, Spain	22	F3	43.07 N	2.24 W
Vergara, Ur.	172	F11	32.56 S	53.57 W
Vergemont Creek, stm., Austl.	98	D4	24.16 S	143.16 E
Vergennes, Vt., U.S.	126	D16	44.10 N	73.14 W
Verhnebakanskij, Russia	38	I16	44.50 N	37.39 E
Verhnedneprovskij, Russia	26	E16	54.59 N	33.21 E
Verhnee Kujto, ozero, l., Russia	18	B17	65.02 N	30.45 E
Verhnee Kumozero, ozero, l., Russia	18	B19	65.34 N	32.56 E
Verhnee Ondomozero, ozero, l., Russia	14	F29	66.22 N	38.15 E
Verhnee Talyzino, Russia	40	D14	55.05 N	45.49 E
Verhnee Volozero, ozero, l., Russia	18	E22	62.50 N	35.22 E
Verhnee Zolotica, Russia	14	G31	65.41 N	40.22 E
Verhneimbatsk, Russia	48	B15	63.09 N	87.58 E
Verhnemulomskoe vodohranilišče, res., Russia	14	D21	68.30 N	31.05 E
Verhne-Svirskoe vodohranilišče, res., Russia	18	F22	61.08 N	34.52 E
Verhnetulomskij, Russia	14	D22	68.37 N	31.47 E
Verhneural'sk, Russia	48	D9	53.53 N	59.13 E
Verhnevilujsk, Russia	50	D13	63.26 N	120.18 E
Verhnie Kigi, Russia	40	D21	55.24 N	58.36 E
Verhnie Lipki, Russia	40	G13	49.36 N	43.52 E
Verhnie Tatyšly, Russia	40	C19	56.17 N	55.51 E
Verhnie Važiny, Russia	18	F20	61.22 N	33.41 E
Verhnij Avzjan, Russia	40	E20	53.31 N	57.32 E
Verhnij Baskunčak, Russia	40	G15	48.13 N	46.43 E
Verhnij Ikorec, Russia	38	B18	51.11 N	39.47 E
Verhnij Lebjažinskij, Russia	40	H15	46.43 N	47.48 E
Verhnij Mamon, Russia	40	F12	50.09 N	40.22 E
Verhnij Most, Russia	26	C11	57.29 N	28.52 E
Verhnij Ufalej, Russia	48	C10	56.03 N	60.14 E
Verhnjadzvinsk, Bela.	26	E10	55.47 N	27.56 E
Verhnjaja Amga, Russia	50	E14	59.37 N	127.06 E
Verhnjaja Angara, stm., Russia	50	E11	55.45 N	109.53 E
Verhnjaja Grajvoronka, Russia	38	B16	51.40 N	37.47 E
Verhnjaja Inta, Russia	48	A10	65.59 N	60.19 E
Verhnjaja Salda, Russia	48	C10	58.02 N	60.33 E
Verhnjaja Tajmyra, stm., Russia	50	B8	74.20 N	99.55 E
Verhnjaja Tojma, Russia	12	E21	62.13 N	45.02 E
Verhnjaja Troica, Russia	26	C20	57.15 N	37.10 E
Verhnye Nikuljasy, Russia	18	G17	60.25 N	30.45 E
Verhojansk, Russia	50	C15	67.31 N	133.24 E
Verhojanskij hrebet (Verkhoyansk Mountains), mts., Russia	50	C14	67.00 N	129.00 E
Verhopuja, Russia	12	F19	61.34 N	41.28 E
Verhovaže, Russia	12	F20	60.43 N	42.00 E
Verhove, Russia	26	H20	52.49 N	37.14 E
Verigin see Veregin, Sk., Can.	142	C11	51.35 N	102.04 W
Verín, Spain	28	C3	41.56 N	7.25 W
Veriora, Est.	26	B10	58.00 N	27.20 E
Veríssimo, Braz.	170	J1	19.42 S	48.16 W
Verkhivtseve, Ukr.	38	E13	48.29 N	34.15 E
Verkhnia Khortytsia, Ukr.	38	F13	47.51 N	35.02 E
Verkhne Syn'ovydne, Ukr.	38	D2	49.05 N	23.36 E
Verkhniachka, Ukr.	38	E9	48.49 N	30.02 E
Verkhnieduvannyi, Ukr.	38	E18	48.20 N	39.48 E
Verkhnii Rohachyk, Ukr.	38	F13	47.14 N	34.21 E
Verkhn'odniprovs'k, Ukr.	38	E13	48.39 N	34.20 E
Verkhn'osadove, Ukr.	38	I12	44.41 N	33.42 E
Verkhovyna, Ukr.	38	E3	48.09 N	24.46 E
Verkhoyansk Mountains see Verhojanskij hrebet, mts., Russia	50	C14	67.00 N	129.00 E
Vermejo, stm., N.M., U.S.	138	E4	36.30 N	104.33 W
Vermelho, stm., Braz.	170	E2	7.43 S	47.16 W
Vermenton, Fr.	20	G12	47.39 N	3.43 E
Vermezzo, Italy	184b		45.24 N	8.59 E
Vermilion, Oh., U.S.	124	C3	41.25 N	82.21 W
Vermilion, stm., Ab., Can.	144	C19	53.28 N	111.22 W
Vermilion, stm., On., Can.	126	B8	46.15 N	81.41 W
Vermilion, stm., Il., U.S.	130	C9	41.18 N	89.03 W
Vermilion, stm., Mn., U.S.	128	C6	48.16 N	92.28 W
Vermilion Bay, On., Can.	128	B5	49.51 N	93.24 W
Vermilion Bay, b., La., U.S.	134	H7	29.40 N	92.00 W
Vermilion Lake, l., On., Can.	128	A6	50.03 N	92.13 W
Vermilion Lake, l., Mn., U.S.	128	D6	47.53 N	92.25 W
Vermilion Pass, p., Can.	144	E14	51.13 N	116.04 W
Vermillion, S.D., U.S.	140	E16	42.46 N	96.55 W
Vermillion, stm., S.D., U.S.	140	E15	42.43 N	96.53 W
Vermillion, East Fork, stm., S.D., U.S.	140	C15	43.24 N	97.04 W
Vermillion, West Fork, stm., S.D., U.S.	140	D15	43.23 N	97.04 W
Vermillion Bluffs, clf., Co., U.S.	150	C8	40.50 N	108.30 W
Vermillion Creek, stm., U.S.	150	B8	40.45 N	108.53 W
Vermillion Creek, stm., Ks., U.S.	130	E1	39.12 N	96.13 W
Vermillon, stm., Qc., Can.	122	C3	47.38 N	72.56 W
Vermont, Austl.	192b		37.50 S	145.12 E
Vermont, Il., U.S.	130	D7	40.17 N	90.25 W
Vermont, state, U.S.	122	F4	43.50 N	72.45 W
Vernadsky, sci., Ant.	160	L8	65.15 S	64.15 W
Vernal, Ut., U.S.	150	C7	40.27 N	109.32 W
Verndale, Mn., U.S.	128	E3	46.23 N	95.01 W
Verner, On., Can.	126	B9	46.24 N	80.06 W
Verneuil, Fr.	20	F9	48.44 N	0.55 E
Verneuil-L'Étang, Fr.	179		48.39 N	2.50 E
Verneuil-sur-Seine, Fr.	179		48.59 N	1.59 E
Vernon, B.C., Can.	144	F11	50.15 N	119.15 W
Vernon, Fr.	20	E10	49.05 N	1.28 E
Vernon, Al., U.S.	134	D10	33.45 N	88.07 W
Vernon, Ca., U.S.	198		34.01 N	118.13 W
Vernon, Ct., U.S.	124	C13	41.51 N	72.28 W
Vernon, Fl., U.S.	134	G13	30.37 N	85.42 W
Vernon, In., U.S.	130	F12	38.59 N	85.36 W
Vernon, Tx., U.S.	138	G9	34.09 N	99.17 W
Vernon, Ut., U.S.	150	C4	40.06 N	112.25 W
Vernonia, Or., U.S.	146	E3	45.51 N	123.12 W
Vernon Lake, res., La., U.S.	134	F5	31.11 N	93.21 W
Vernon River, P.E., Can.	122	D14	46.12 N	62.50 W
Vernouillet, Fr.	179		48.58 N	1.59 E
Verny, Fr.	24	G2	49.01 N	6.12 E
Vero, stm., Spain	28	B11	41.59 N	0.10 E
Vero Beach, Fl., U.S.	132	I5	27.37 N	80.24 W
Véroia, Grc.	34	C5	40.32 N	22.12 E
Verona, On., Can.	126	D13	44.28 N	76.42 W
Verona, Italy	30	E8	45.26 N	10.59 E
Verona, Ms., U.S.	134	C10	34.12 N	88.42 W
Verona, N.J., U.S.	194		40.49 N	74.14 W
Verona, Pa., U.S.	197b		40.30 N	79.50 W
Verona, Wi., U.S.	130	B8	42.59 N	89.32 W
Verónica, Arg.	172	G9	35.23 S	57.20 W
Verperluda, ostrov, i., Russia	183a		59.59 N	30.01 E
Verrières, Bois de, p.o.i., Fr.	179		48.45 N	2.15 E
Verrières-le-Buisson, Fr.	179		48.45 N	2.16 E
Versailles, Fr.	20	F11	48.48 N	2.08 E
Versailles, Il., U.S.	130	E7	39.52 N	90.39 W
Versailles, In., U.S.	130	E12	39.03 N	85.15 W
Versailles, Ky., U.S.	130	F13	38.02 N	84.44 W
Versailles, Mo., U.S.	130	F5	38.25 N	92.50 W
Versailles, Oh., U.S.	124	D1	40.13 N	84.29 W
Versailles, Pa., U.S.	197b		40.21 N	79.51 W
Versailles, Château de, hist., Fr.	179		48.48 N	2.07 E
Versailles, Parc de, p.o.i., Fr.	179		48.49 N	2.06 E
Verse, stm., Ger.	181		51.15 N	7.46 E
Versec see Vršac, Yugo.	36	D8	45.07 N	21.18 E
Versetausee, res., Ger.	181		51.11 N	7.41 E
Veršino-Darasunskij, Russia	50	F12	52.21 N	115.31 E
Veršino-Šahtaminskij, Russia	50	F12	51.17 N	117.52 E
Ver-sur-Launette, Fr.	179		49.06 N	2.41 E
Vert, Fr.	179		48.57 N	1.41 E
Vert, Cap, c., Sen.	80	E4	14.43 N	17.29 W
Verte, Île, i., Qc., Can.	122	B7	48.02 N	69.26 W
Verte, Île, i., Qc., Can.	193a		45.34 N	73.30 W
Vertedero, P.R.	158a	b3	18.04 N	66.13 W
Vertientes, Cuba	156	B8	21.15 N	78.09 W
Vertiivka, Ukr.	38	B10	51.09 N	31.51 E
Vert-le-Grand, Fr.	179		48.34 N	2.22 E
Vert-le-Petit, Fr.	179		48.33 N	2.22 E
Vert-Saint-Denis, Fr.	179		48.34 N	2.37 E
Verulam, S. Afr.	90	F10	29.45 S	31.02 E
Verviers, Bel.	20	D14	50.35 N	5.52 E
Verwoerd Reservoir see Gariep Dam, res., S. Afr.	90	G7	30.40 S	25.40 E
Vesanto, Fin.	18	E13	62.56 N	26.25 E
Vesava, ngh., India	190c		19.08 N	72.48 E
Vescovato, Fr.	22	G15	42.30 N	9.26 E
Vesegonsk, Russia	26	B20	58.40 N	37.16 E
Vesele, Ukr.	38	G14	47.01 N	34.55 E
Veselí nad Lužnicí, Czech Rep.	24	G10	49.11 N	14.41 E
Veselí nad Moravou, Czech Rep.	24	H13	48.57 N	17.24 E
Veselovskoe vodohranilišče, res., Russia	40	H12	47.00 N	41.18 E
Vesëlyj Jar, Russia	54	C11	43.57 N	135.27 E
Vesëlyj Posëlok, ngh., Russia	183a		59.54 N	30.28 E
Veselynove, Ukr.	38	F10	47.21 N	31.14 E
Vešenskaja, Russia	40	G12	49.37 N	41.44 E
Vesijärvi, l., Fin.	18	F12	61.08 N	25.29 E
Veškajma, Russia	40	D15	54.02 N	47.07 E
Veški, Russia	183b		55.56 N	37.37 E
Vesle, stm., Fr.	20	E12	49.23 N	3.28 E
Vešnjaki, ngh., Russia	183b		55.44 N	37.49 E
Vesole, Monte, mtn., Italy	32	D9	40.24 N	15.09 E
Vesoul, Fr.	20	G15	47.37 N	6.09 E
Vespasiano, Braz.	170	J4	19.41 S	43.55 W
Vesta, C.R.	156	H6	9.43 N	83.03 W
Vest-Agder, state, Nor.	16	I5	58.30 N	7.10 E
Vestavia Hills, Al., U.S.	134	D12	33.26 N	86.46 W
Vestbygd, Nor.	16	I4	58.06 N	6.35 E
Vesterålen, is., Nor.	14	C6	68.40 N	15.33 E
Vesterålsfjorden, b., Nor.	14	D4	68.27 N	14.07 E
Vesterhavet see North Sea, s., Eur.	8	D9	56.00 N	3.00 E
Vesterø Havn, Den.	16	J8	57.17 N	10.56 E
Vestfjorden, b., Nor.	14	E4	68.08 N	15.00 E
Vestfold, state, Nor.	16	H8	59.15 N	10.10 E
Vestgrønland (Kitaa), state, Grnld.	108	D16	65.01 N	45.04 W
Vestmanna, Far. Is.	12b	m34	62.09 N	7.10 W
Vestmannaeyjar, Ice.	12a	l29	63.25 N	20.16 W
Vestnes, Nor.	16	E5	62.38 N	7.04 E
Vestre Jakobselv, Nor.	14	B20	70.07 N	29.19 E
Vestsjælland, state, Den.	16	L9	55.35 N	11.30 E
Vestvågøya, i., Nor.	14	D4	68.12 N	13.42 E
Vesuvio (Vesuvius), vol., Italy	32	D8	40.49 N	14.26 E
Vesuvius see Vesuvio, vol., Italy	32	D8	40.49 N	14.26 E
Veszprém, Hung.	36	B4	47.05 N	17.54 E
Veszprém, state, Hung.	36	B4	47.10 N	17.40 E
Vésztő, Hung.	36	C8	46.55 N	21.15 E
Vet, stm., S. Afr.	90	F8	27.40 S	25.38 E
Vetapālem, India	69	D5	15.47 N	80.19 E
Veterans Stadium, p.o.i., Pa., U.S.	203		39.54 N	75.10 W
Vetju, Russia	12	E24	62.56 N	50.47 E
Vetka, Bela.	26	H14	52.33 N	31.11 E
Vetlanda, Swe.	16	J13	57.25 N	15.05 E
Vetluga, Russia	40	C14	57.51 N	45.47 E
Vetluga, stm., Russia	40	C14	56.47 N	45.32 E
Vetlužskij, Russia	40	C14	57.10 N	45.06 E
Vetlužskij, Russia	40	B14	58.23 N	45.28 E
Vetovo, Blg.	36	F13	43.42 N	26.15 E
Vetrenyj pojas, krjaž, hills, Russia	18	D23	63.15 N	37.30 E
Vetrișoaia, Rom.	36	C15	46.26 N	28.13 E
Vetryna, Bela.	26	E11	55.26 N	28.27 E
Vetschau, Ger.	24	E9	51.47 N	14.05 E
Vettifoss, wtfl., Nor.	16	F6	61.27 N	8.00 E
Vettore, Monte, mtn., Italy	30	H10	42.49 N	13.16 E
Veurne, Bel.	20	C11	51.04 N	2.40 E
Vevay, In., U.S.	130	F12	38.45 N	85.04 W
Vevey, Switz.	30	D3	46.27 N	6.50 E
Veynes, Fr.	22	E11	44.32 N	5.49 E
Vézère, stm., Fr.	22	D7	44.52 N	0.53 E
Vezirköprü, Tur.	42	E6	41.08 N	35.29 E
Viacha, Bol.	166	C3	16.39 S	68.17 W
Viadana, Italy	30	F7	44.56 N	10.31 E
Viadutos, Braz.	172	C11	27.33 S	52.01 W
Viale, Arg.	172	E8	31.52 S	60.00 W
Vialonga, Port.	184c		38.52 N	9.05 W
Viamão, Braz.	172	E12	30.05 S	51.02 W
Viamonte, Arg.	172	F6	33.44 S	63.06 W
Vian, Ok., U.S.	134	B4	35.30 N	94.58 W
Viana, Braz.	170	B3	3.12 S	45.00 W
Viana, Ilha do, i., Braz.	205a		22.52 S	43.08 W

Name	Page	Map Ref.	Latitude	Longitude
Viana del Bollo see Viana do Bolo, Spain	28	B3	42.11 N	7.05 W
Viana do Bolo, Spain	28	B3	42.11 N	7.05 W
Viana do Castelo, Port.	28	C2	41.41 N	8.49 W
Viana do Castelo, state, Port.	28	C2	41.50 N	8.40 W
Viangchan (Vientiane), Laos	64	D6	17.57 N	102.36 E
Viangphoukha, Laos	64	B5	20.40 N	101.04 E
Viar, stm., Spain	28	G5	37.36 N	5.49 W
Viareggio, Italy	30	G7	43.52 N	10.14 E
Viaur, stm., Fr.	22	E8	44.09 N	1.58 E
V'iazivok, Ukr.	38	D10	49.10 N	31.24 E
Vibank, Sk., Can.	142	D10	50.20 N	103.55 W
Viborg, Den.	16	K7	56.26 N	9.24 E
Viborg, S.D., U.S.	140	D15	43.10 N	97.04 W
Viborg, state, Den.	16	K6	56.18 N	9.27 E
Vibo Valentia, Italy	32	F10	38.40 N	16.06 E
Viburnum, Mo., U.S.	130	G6	37.43 N	91.08 W
Vic, Spain	28	C13	41.56 N	2.15 E
Vicálvaro, ngh., Spain	184a		40.24 N	3.36 W
Vicam, Mex.	154	B3	27.36 N	110.19 W
Vicebsk, Bela.	26	E13	55.11 N	30.12 E
Vicebsk, state, Bela.	26	E11	55.20 N	29.00 E
Vic-en-Bigorre, Fr.	28	A10	43.23 N	0.03 E
Vicente, Point, c., Ca., U.S.	198		33.44 N	118.25 W
Vicente Guerrero, Mex.	154	D7	23.43 N	103.57 W
Vicente Guerrero, Presa, res., Mex.	154	D9	23.57 N	98.45 W
Vicente López, state, Arg.	206		34.32 S	58.30 W
Vicenza, Italy	30	E8	45.32 N	11.32 E
Viceroy, Sk., Can.	142	E8	49.27 N	105.22 W
Vich see Vic, Spain	28	C13	41.56 N	2.15 E
Vichada, state, Col.	168	E7	5.00 N	69.30 W
Vichada, stm., Col.	168	E7	4.55 N	67.49 W
Vichadero, Ur.	172	E10	31.48 S	54.42 W
Vichigasta, Arg.	172	D4	29.29 S	67.31 W
Vichra, stm., Eur.	26	F14	54.00 N	31.50 E
Vichuquén, Chile	172	G1	34.50 S	72.00 W
Vichy, Fr.	22	C9	46.07 N	3.26 E
Vici, Ok., U.S.	138	E9	36.09 N	99.17 W
Vicksburg, Mi., U.S.	130	B12	42.07 N	85.32 W
Vicksburg, Ms., U.S.	134	E8	32.21 N	90.52 W
Vicksburg National Military Park, p.o.i., Ms., U.S.	134	E8	32.24 N	90.52 W
Vico, Lago di, l., Italy	30	H9	42.19 N	12.10 E
Viçosa, Braz.	170	K4	20.45 S	42.52 W
Viçosa do Ceará, Braz.	170	B5	3.34 S	41.05 W
Vicq, Fr.	179		48.49 N	1.50 E
Vic-sur-Cère, Fr.	22	E8	44.59 N	2.37 E
Victor, Id., U.S.	146	G15	43.36 N	111.06 W
Victor, Ia., U.S.	130	C5	41.43 N	92.17 W
Victor, Mt., U.S.	146	D12	46.25 N	114.08 W
Victor Harbor, Austl.	98	J2	35.33 S	138.36 E
Victoria, Arg.	172	F7	32.36 S	60.09 W
Victoria see Vitória, Braz.	170	K5	20.18 S	40.20 W
Victoria see Limbe, Cam.	86	D1	4.01 N	9.12 E
Victoria, B.C., Can.	144	H7	48.26 N	123.21 W
Victoria, P.E., Can.	122	D13	46.14 N	63.30 W
Victoria, Chile	172	I1	38.14 S	72.20 W
Victoria see Xianggang, China	58	J6	22.15 N	114.10 E
Victoria see Xianggang, China	189d		22.17 N	114.09 E
Victoria, Gren.	159e	q10	12.11 N	61.41 W
Victoria, Gui.	84	G2	10.50 N	14.32 W
Victoria see Labuan, Malay.	66	A9	5.17 N	115.15 E
Victoria see Rabat, Malta	32	H8	36.02 N	14.14 E
Victoria, Rom.	36	D11	45.45 N	24.41 E
Victoria, Sey.	89b	j13	4.39 S	55.24 E
Victoria, Ks., U.S.	138	C9	38.50 N	99.10 W
Victoria, Tx., U.S.	136	F11	28.48 N	97.00 W
Victoria, Va., U.S.	124	G7	36.58 N	78.13 W
Victoria, state, Austl.	98	K5	38.00 S	145.00 E
Victoria, ngh., Arg.	206		34.28 S	58.31 W
Victoria, stm., Austl.	96	C6	15.07 S	129.39 E
Victoria, Lake, l., Afr.	86	E6	1.00 S	33.00 E
Victoria, Lake, l., Austl.	98	I3	34.00 S	141.16 E
Victoria, Mount, mtn., Mya.	64	B1	21.14 N	93.55 E
Victoria, Mount, mtn., Pap. N. Gui.	101a	b4	8.53 S	147.32 E
Victoria, Pont, trans., Qc., Can.	193a		45.29 N	73.32 W
Victoria and Albert Museum, bldg., India	190c		18.59 N	72.50 E
Victoria Beach, Mb., Can.	142	D17	50.42 N	96.32 W
Victoria Beach, cst., Nig.	191a		6.25 N	3.25 E
Victoria Falls, wtfl., Afr.	88	D4	17.54 S	25.50 E
Victoria Fjord, b., Grnld.	108	A16	82.10 N	46.00 W
Victoria Gardens, p.o.i., India	190c		18.59 N	72.50 E
Victoria Harbour, On., Can.	126	D10	44.44 N	79.45 W
Victoria Harbour, b., China	189d		22.17 N	114.10 E
Victoria Island, i., Can.	110	A8	71.00 N	110.00 W
Victoria Island, i., Nig.	191a		6.26 N	3.26 E
Victoria Lake, l., S. Afr.	191d		26.14 S	28.09 E
Victoria Land, reg., Ant.	103	C20	75.00 S	163.00 E
Victoria Lawn Tennis Association Courts, p.o.i., Austl.	192b		37.51 S	145.02 E
Victoria Memorial Hall, bldg., Sing.	189c		1.17 N	103.51 E
Victoria Memorial Museum, bldg., India	190b		22.33 N	88.21 E
Victoria Nile, stm., Ug.	86	D6	2.14 N	31.26 E
Victoria Park, p.o.i., China	189d		22.17 N	114.11 E
Victoria Park, p.o.i., Eng., U.K.	180		53.23 N	2.34 W
Victoria Peak, mtn., Belize	156	D3	16.48 N	88.37 W
Victoria Peak, mtn., B.C., Can.	144	F4	50.03 N	126.06 W
Victoria Peak, mtn., China	189d		22.17 N	114.08 E
Victoria Peaks, mtn., Phil.	68	F2	9.22 N	118.20 E
Victoria River Downs, Austl.	96	C6	16.23 S	131.00 E
Victorias, Phil.	68	E4	10.54 N	123.05 E
Victoria State Car Club Race Circuit, p.o.i., Austl.	192b		37.45 S	145.11 E
Victoria Station, trans., Eng., U.K.	180		53.29 N	2.15 W
Victoria Strait, strt., Nu., Can.	110	B10	69.15 N	100.30 W
Victoria Terminus, trans., India	190c		18.57 N	72.50 E
Victoria University of Manchester, educ., Eng., U.K.	180		53.28 N	2.14 W
Victoriaville, Qc., Can.	122	D5	46.03 N	71.56 W
Victoria West, S. Afr.	90	G6	31.23 S	23.06 E
Victorica, Arg.	172	H5	36.12 S	65.26 W
Victorino, Ven.	168	F8	2.49 N	67.50 W
Victorino de la Plaza, Arg.	172	H6	36.37 S	62.39 W
Victorville, Ca., U.S.	148	I8	34.32 N	117.17 W
Victory Gardens, N.J., U.S.	194		40.52 N	74.32 W
Victory Hills, Pa., U.S.	197b		40.11 N	79.53 W
Victory Monument, hist., Thai.	187a		13.46 N	100.33 E
Vičuga, Russia	40	C12	57.12 N	41.54 E
Vicuña, Chile	172	E2	30.00 S	70.47 W
Vicuña Mackenna, Arg.	172	F5	33.54 S	64.24 W
Vidalia, Ga., U.S.	132	D3	32.13 N	82.24 W
Vidalia, La., U.S.	134	F7	31.33 N	91.26 W
Vidal Ramos, Braz.	172	C13	27.22 S	49.20 W
Videbæk, Den.	16	K6	56.05 N	8.38 E
Videira, Braz.	172	C12	27.00 S	51.08 W
Videle, Rom.	36	E12	44.16 N	25.32 E
Vidigueira, Port.	28	F3	38.12 N	7.47 W
Vidin, Blg.	36	E9	43.59 N	22.52 E
Vidisha, India	70	G6	23.31 N	77.48 E
Vidlica, Russia	18	F19	61.11 N	32.24 E
Vidor, Tx., U.S.	136	D13	30.07 N	94.00 W
Vidos, stm., Tur.	185b		40.58 N	28.53 E
Vidöstern, l., Swe.	16	J11	57.04 N	14.01 E
Vidoy, i., Far. Is.	12b	m34	62.21 N	6.32 W
Vidra, Rom.	36	E13	44.15 N	26.11 E
Vidra, Rom.	36	D13	45.54 N	26.54 E
Vidsel, Swe.	14	G11	65.51 N	20.25 E
Vidzeme, hist. reg., Lat.	26	C8	57.10 N	25.45 E
Vidzy, Bela.	26	E9	55.24 N	26.38 E
Viechtach, Ger.	24	G8	49.04 N	12.53 E
Viedma, Arg.	166	H4	40.49 S	62.59 W
Viedma, Lago, l., Arg.	166	I2	49.35 S	72.35 W
Vieille Case, Dom.	159c	i6	15.36 N	61.24 W
Viejo, Cerro, mtn., Peru	164	D2	4.46 S	79.26 W
Viekšniai, Lith.	26	D5	56.15 N	22.30 E
Viella, Spain	28	B11	42.42 N	0.47 E
Vielle-Eglise-en-Yvelines, Fr.	179		48.40 N	1.53 E
Vienna see Wien, Aus.	30	B13	48.13 N	16.20 E
Vienna, Ga., U.S.	132	D2	32.05 N	83.47 W
Vienna, Il., U.S.	130	G9	37.24 N	88.53 W
Vienna, Md., U.S.	124	F10	38.28 N	75.49 W
Vienna, Mo., U.S.	130	F5	38.11 N	91.57 W
Vienna, S.D., U.S.	140	C15	44.42 N	97.30 W
Vienna, W.V., U.S.	124	E4	39.19 N	81.32 W
Vienna see Wien, state, Aus.	30	B13	48.12 N	16.22 E
Vienna Woods see Wienerwald, mts., Aus.	30	B13	48.15 N	16.00 E
Vienne, Fr.	22	D10	45.31 N	4.52 E
Vienne, state, Fr.	22	C6	46.35 N	0.30 E
Vienne, stm., Fr.	22	C6	47.12 N	0.05 E
Vienne-en-Arthies, Fr.	179		49.04 N	1.44 E
Vientiane see Viangchan, Laos	64	D6	17.57 N	102.36 E
Vieques, P.R.	158a	b5	18.09 N	65.26 W
Vieques, Aeropuerto, arpt., P.R.	158a	b5	18.07 N	65.30 W
Vieques, Isla de, i., P.R.	158a	b5	18.08 N	65.25 W
Vieques, Pasaje de, strt., P.R.	158a	b4	18.11 N	65.37 W
Vieques, Sonda de, strt., P.R.	158a	b5	18.15 N	65.23 W
Vieremä, Fin.	18	D13	63.45 N	26.58 E
Vieringhausen, ngh., Ger.	181		51.11 N	7.10 E
Viersen, Ger.	20	C15	51.15 N	6.23 E
Vierumäki, Fin.	18	F12	61.07 N	25.57 E
Vierwaldstätter See (Lucerne, Lake of), l., Switz.	30	D5	46.59 N	8.20 E
Vierzehnheiligen, rel., Ger.	24	F7	50.07 N	11.03 E
Vierzon, Fr.	20	G11	47.12 N	2.04 E
Viesca, Mex.	154	C7	25.20 N	102.47 W
Viesīte, Lat.	26	D8	56.21 N	25.33 E
Vieste, Italy	30	I13	41.53 N	16.10 E
Viet Nam see Vietnam, ctry., Asia	64	E9	16.00 N	108.00 E
Vietnam, ctry., Asia	64	E9	16.00 N	108.00 E
Vietnam Veterans Memorial, hist., D.C., U.S.	202c		38.53 N	77.03 W
Viet Tri, Viet.	64	B7	21.18 N	105.25 E
Vietz see Witnica, Pol.	24	D10	52.40 N	14.53 E
Vieux-Fort, Qc., Can.	111a	i22	51.25 N	57.49 W
Vieux-Fort, Guad.	159c	i5	15.57 N	61.41 W
Vieux-Fort, St. Luc.	159c	m7	13.43 N	60.57 W
Vieux-Fort, Pointe du, c., Guad.	159c	i5	15.57 N	61.41 W
Vieux Fort Bay, b., St. Luc.	159c	m7	13.43 N	60.57 W
Vieux-Habitants, Guad.	159c	h5	16.04 N	61.45 W
Vievis, Lith.	26	F7	54.46 N	24.48 E
View Park, Ca., U.S.	198		34.00 N	118.20 W
Vieytes, Arg.	172	G9	35.16 S	57.34 W
Vigala, Est.	26	B7	58.43 N	24.23 E
Vigan, Phil.	68	B3	17.34 N	120.23 E
Vigeland, Nor.	16	I5	58.05 N	7.18 E
Vigentino, ngh., Italy	184b		45.25 N	9.11 E
Vigésima Quinta de Abril, Ponte, trans., Port.	184c		38.41 N	9.11 W
Vigevano, Italy	30	E5	45.19 N	8.51 E
Vigia, Cerro el, mtn., Mex.	154	E6	21.19 N	104.03 W
Vigie Airport, arpt., St. Luc.	159c	l6	14.01 N	60.59 W
Vignale, Italy	184b		45.29 N	8.36 E
Vigneux-sur-Seine, Fr.	179		48.42 N	2.25 E
Vignola, Italy	30	F7	44.28 N	11.00 E
Vigny, Fr.	179		49.05 N	1.56 E
Vigo, Spain	28	B2	42.14 N	8.43 W
Vigo, Ría de, est., Spain	28	B1	42.12 N	8.50 W
Vigra, i., Nor.	16	E3	62.33 N	6.04 E
Vigrestad, Nor.	16	I3	58.34 N	5.42 E
Vihanti, Fin.	18	C11	64.29 N	24.58 E
Vihāri, Pak.	70	D4	30.02 N	72.21 E
Vihiers, Fr.	20	G8	47.09 N	0.32 W
Vihorevka, Russia	48	C18	56.06 N	101.11 E
Vihowa, Pak.	70	C3	31.07 N	70.30 E
Vihren, mtn., Blg.	36	H10	41.46 N	23.24 E
Vihti, Fin.	18	G11	60.24 N	24.18 E
Viiala, Fin.	18	F10	61.12 N	23.49 E
Viinijärvi, Fin.	18	E16	62.39 N	29.12 E
Viinijärvi, l., Fin.	18	E16	62.44 N	29.16 E
Viipuri see Vyborg, Russia	18	G15	60.42 N	28.45 E
Viişoara, Mol.	38	G7	46.20 N	28.26 E
Viitasaari, Fin.	18	D12	63.04 N	25.50 E
Viivikonna, Est.	26	A10	59.18 N	27.41 E
Vijāpur, India	70	G4	23.33 N	72.44 E
Vijayawāda, India	69	C5	16.30 N	80.37 E
Vikajärvi, Fin.	14	F17	66.37 N	26.12 E
Vikārābād, India	69	C3	17.20 N	77.54 E
Vikbolandet, pen., Swe.	16	I14	58.32 N	16.40 E
Viken, Swe.	16	K10	56.08 N	12.35 E
Viken, l., Swe.	16	I12	58.39 N	14.20 E
Vikersund, Nor.	16	H7	59.59 N	10.02 E
Vikhroli, ngh., India	190c		19.07 N	72.56 E
Viking, Ab., Can.	144	C19	53.06 N	111.46 W
Vikmanshyttan, Swe.	16	G13	60.17 N	15.49 E
Vikna, Nor.	12	D4	64.52 N	10.56 E
Vikna, i., Nor.	16	C8	64.57 N	10.58 E
Vikno, Ukr.	38	E4	48.34 N	25.58 E
Vikøyri, Nor.	16	F4	61.05 N	6.36 E
Vikramasingapuram, India	69	G3	8.43 N	77.25 E
Vikulovo, Russia	48	C12	56.49 N	70.36 E
Vila Augusta, Braz.	205b		23.28 S	46.32 W
Vila Babi, Braz.	205a		22.42 S	43.23 W
Vila Boacaya, ngh., Braz.	205b		23.29 S	46.44 W
Vila Cabral see Lichinga, Moz.	88	C6	13.16 S	35.14 E
Vila Coutinho see Ulónguè, Moz.	88	C5	14.37 S	34.19 E
Vila da Ribeira Brava, C.V.	85a	k10	16.36 N	24.18 W
Viladecans, Spain	184d		41.19 N	2.00 E
Viladecavalls del Vallès, Spain	184d		41.33 N	1.58 E
Vila de Rei, Port.	28	E2	39.40 N	8.09 W
Vila de Sena, Moz.	88	D5	17.26 S	35.01 E
Vila Dirce, Braz.	205b		23.35 S	46.48 W
Vila do Bispo, Port.	28	G2	37.04 N	8.54 W
Vila do Conde, Port.	28	C2	41.21 N	8.44 W
Vila Flor, Port.	28	C3	41.18 N	7.08 W
Vila Fontes, Moz.	88	D6	17.49 S	35.21 E
Vila Formosa, ngh., Braz.	205b		23.34 S	46.33 W
Vilafranca del Panadés see Vilafranca del Penedès, Spain	28	C12	41.21 N	1.41 E
Vilafranca del Penedès, Spain	28	C12	41.21 N	1.41 E
Vila Franca de Xira, Port.	28	F2	38.56 N	8.59 W
Vila Galvão, Braz.	205b		23.27 S	46.33 W
Vila Gamito, Moz.	88	C5	14.08 S	32.58 E
Vilagarcía de Arousa, Spain	28	B2	42.35 N	8.45 W
Vila Guilherme, ngh., Braz.	205b		23.30 S	46.36 W
Vilaine, stm., Fr.	20	G7	47.30 N	2.28 W
Vila Isabel, ngh., Braz.	205a		22.55 S	43.15 W
Vila Jaguára, ngh., Braz.	205b		23.31 S	46.45 W
Viļaka, Lat.	26	C10	57.11 N	27.41 E
Vilalba, Spain	28	A3	43.17 N	7.40 W
Vila Madalena, ngh., Braz.	205b		23.33 S	46.42 W
Vila Maria, ngh., Braz.	205b		23.31 S	46.34 W
Vila Mariana, ngh., Braz.	205b		23.35 S	46.38 W
Vila Matilde, ngh., Braz.	205b		23.32 S	46.31 W
Vilanandro, Tanjona, c., Madag.	88	D7	16.12 S	44.28 E
Viļāni, Lat.	26	D9	56.34 N	26.57 E
Vilankulo, Moz.	90	B12	21.59 S	35.19 E
Vila Nova de Famalicão, Port.	28	C2	41.24 N	8.30 W
Vila Nova de Gaia, Port.	28	C2	41.08 N	8.37 W
Vilanova de la Roca, Spain	184d		41.33 N	2.17 E
Vilanova i la Geltrú, Spain	28	C12	41.13 N	1.45 E
Vila Pery see Chimoio, Moz.	88	D5	19.09 S	33.29 E
Vila Progresso, Braz.	205a		22.55 S	43.03 W
Vila Prudente, ngh., Braz.	205b		23.35 S	46.33 W
Vila Real, Port.	28	C3	41.17 N	7.44 W
Vila-Real, Spain	28	E10	39.56 N	0.06 W
Vila Real, state, Port.	28	C3	41.30 N	7.30 W
Vilar Formoso, Port.	28	D4	40.37 N	6.50 W
Vilassar de Dalt, Spain	184d		41.31 N	2.22 E
Vilassar de Mar, Spain	184d		41.30 N	2.24 E
Vila Velha, Braz.	164	C7	3.13 N	51.13 W
Vila Velha, Braz.	170	K5	20.20 S	40.17 W
Vila Velha de Ródão, Port.	28	E3	39.38 N	7.40 W
Vila Verde, Port.	28	C2	41.38 N	8.26 W
Vila Verde, Port.	184c		38.50 N	9.22 W
Vila Viçosa, Port.	28	F2	38.47 N	8.13 W
Vilcabamba, Cordillera de, mts., Peru	164	F3	13.07 S	73.07 W
Vil'cha, Ukr.	38	B1	51.21 N	29.25 E
Vil'che, Ukr.	38	D1	49.13 N	22.54 E
Vildbjerg, Den.	16	K6	56.12 N	8.46 E
Vilejka, Bela.	26	F9	54.29 N	26.54 E
Vilelas, Arg.	172	C6	27.57 S	62.36 W
Vilhelmina, Swe.	16	C14	64.37 N	16.39 E
Vilhena, Braz.	166	B4	12.43 S	60.07 W
Vilija (Neris), stm., Eur.	26	F6	54.53 N	23.52 E
Viljandi, Est.	26	B8	58.22 N	25.36 E
Viljuj, stm., Russia	50	D13	64.23 N	126.26 E
Viljujsk, Russia	50	D13	63.44 N	121.36 E
Viljujskoe vodohranilišče, res., Russia	48	B20	62.34 N	111.12 E
Vilkaviškis, Lith.	26	F6	54.39 N	23.02 E
Vil'kickogo, ostrov, i., Russia	50	A19	75.43 N	152.30 E
Vil'kickogo, proliv, strt., Russia	50	A9	77.55 N	102.59 E
Vilkija, Lith.	26	E6	55.02 N	23.35 E
Villa Abecia, Bol.	166	D3	21.00 S	65.21 W
Villa Aberastain, Arg.	172	E3	31.40 S	68.35 W
Villa Ada, p.o.i., Italy	185a		41.56 N	12.30 E
Villa Adelina, ngh., Arg.	206		34.31 S	58.32 W
Villa Ana, Arg.	172	D8	28.30 S	59.36 W
Villa Ángela, Arg.	172	C7	27.34 S	60.42 W
Villa Atamisqui, Arg.	172	D6	28.29 S	63.47 W
Villa Atuel, Arg.	172	G3	34.50 S	67.55 W
Villabé, Fr.	179		48.35 N	2.27 E
Villa Bella, Bol.	166	B3	10.25 S	65.24 W
Villa Berthet, Arg.	172	C7	27.17 S	60.24 W
Villablino, Spain	28	B4	42.56 N	6.18 W
Villa Borghese, bldg., Italy	185a		41.55 N	12.29 E
Villa Bosch, ngh., Arg.	206		34.35 S	58.34 W
Villa Bruzual, Ven.	168	C7	9.19 N	69.06 W
Villa Cañás, Arg.	172	G7	34.00 S	61.36 W
Villacañas, Spain	28	E7	39.37 N	3.20 W
Villa Carlos Paz, Arg.	172	E5	31.25 S	64.29 W
Villacarriedo, Spain	28	A7	43.14 N	3.48 W
Villacarrillo, Spain	28	F7	38.06 N	3.04 W
Villa Castelli, Arg.	172	D3	29.00 S	68.13 W
Villacastín, Spain	28	D6	40.47 N	4.25 W
Villach, Aus.	30	D10	46.36 N	13.50 E
Villacidro, Italy	32	E2	39.27 N	8.45 E
Villa Clara, Arg.	172	E8	31.47 S	58.45 W
Villa Concepción del Tío, Arg.	172	E6	31.18 S	62.48 W
Villa Constitución, Arg.	172	F7	33.14 S	60.19 W
Villa Cortese, Italy	184b		45.34 N	8.53 E
Villacoublay, Aérodrome de, arpt., Fr.	179		48.45 N	2.10 E
Villada, Spain	28	B6	42.15 N	4.58 W
Villa de Arista, Mex.	154	D8	22.38 N	100.50 W
Villa de Arriaga, Mex.	154	E8	21.55 N	101.22 W
Villa de Cos, Mex.	154	D7	23.17 N	102.21 W
Villa de Cura, Ven.	168	B8	10.02 N	67.29 W
Villa del Carmen, Arg.	172	F5	32.56 S	65.02 W
Villa del Carmen, Ur.	172	F9	33.15 S	56.00 W
Villa del Río, Spain	28	G6	37.58 N	4.17 W
Villa del Rosario, Arg.	172	E6	31.32 S	63.32 W
Villa del Rosario, Arg.	172	E8	30.47 S	57.55 W
Villa del Rosario, Ven.	168	B5	10.19 N	72.19 W
Villa de María, Arg.	172	D6	29.54 S	63.43 W
Villa de Soto, Arg.	172	E5	30.51 S	64.58 W
Villa d'Este, hist., Italy	185a		41.57 N	12.48 E
Villa Devoto, ngh., Arg.	206		34.36 S	58.31 W
Villa Diamante, ngh., Arg.	206		34.41 S	58.26 W
Villadiego, Spain	28	B7	42.31 N	4.00 W
Villa Dolores, Arg.	172	E5	31.56 S	65.11 W
Villa Doria Pamphili, p.o.i., Italy	185a		41.53 N	12.26 E
Villa Elisa, Arg.	172	F8	32.09 S	58.23 W
Villa Flores, Mex.	154	G12	16.14 N	93.14 W
Villa Florida, Para.	172	C9	26.24 S	57.07 W
Villafranca del Bierzo, Spain	28	B4	42.36 N	6.48 W
Villafranca de los Barros, Spain	28	F4	38.33 N	6.20 W
Villafranca di Verona, Italy	30	E7	45.21 N	10.50 E
Villagarcía de Arosa see Vilagarcía de Arousa, Spain	28	B2	42.35 N	8.45 W
Village see The Village, Ok., U.S.	138	F11	35.33 N	97.33 W
Village Creek, stm., Ar., U.S.	134	B7	35.32 N	91.18 W
Village Green, Pa., U.S.	203		39.52 N	75.26 W
Villa General Roca, Arg.	172	F4	32.39 S	66.27 W
Village of Drummond Hill, De., U.S.	203		39.43 N	75.42 W
Village of the Branch, N.Y., U.S.	194		40.51 N	73.11 W
Villa Gesell, Arg.	172	H9	37.14 S	56.57 W
Villa Giambruno, Arg.	206		34.48 S	58.13 W
Villagrán, Mex.	154	C9	24.28 N	99.29 W
Villa Grove, Il., U.S.	130	E9	39.51 N	88.09 W
Villaguay, Arg.	172	E8	31.51 S	59.01 W
Villa Guerrero, Mex.	154	F9	18.57 N	99.38 W
Villa Guillermina, Arg.	172	D8	28.14 S	59.27 W
Villa Hayes, Para.	172	B9	25.04 S	57.33 W
Villahermosa, Mex.	154	G12	17.59 N	92.55 W
Villa Hidalgo, Mex.	136	H3	26.15 N	104.54 W
Villa Hidalgo, Mex.	154	E7	21.40 N	102.36 W
Villa Huidobro, Arg.	172	G5	34.50 S	64.35 W
Villa Insurgentes, Mex.	154	C3	25.15 N	111.47 W
Villa Iris, Arg.	172	I6	38.10 S	63.13 W
Villa José L. Suárez, ngh., Arg.	206		34.32 S	58.35 W
Villajoyosa see La Vila Joiosa, Spain	28	F10	38.30 N	0.14 W
Villa Juárez, Mex.	154	B4	27.09 N	109.50 W
Villa Krause, Arg.	172	E3	31.34 S	68.32 W
Villalba, P.R.	158a	b3	18.08 N	66.30 W
Villalba see Vilalba, Spain	28	A3	43.17 N	7.40 W
Villaldama, Mex.	154	B8	26.29 N	100.25 W
Villalon, Phil.	68	E5	11.30 N	124.22 E
Villalón de Campos, Spain	28	B5	42.05 N	5.06 W
Villalonga, Arg.	166	G4	39.55 S	62.38 W
Villalpando, Spain	28	C5	41.52 N	5.24 W
Villa Lugano, ngh., Arg.	206		34.41 S	58.28 W
Villa Lynch see Lynch, ngh., Arg.	206		34.36 S	58.31 W
Villa Madero, Arg.	206		34.42 S	58.30 W
Villa Mainero, Mex.	154	C9	24.33 N	99.36 W
Villa María, Arg.	172	F6	32.24 S	63.14 W
Villa María del Triunfo, Peru	204d		12.10 S	76.56 W
Villamartín, Spain	28	H5	36.52 N	5.38 W
Villa Matamoros, Mex.	136	H2	26.45 N	105.35 W
Villa Matoque, Arg.	172	B6	25.50 S	63.48 W
Villa Mazán, Arg.	172	D4	28.39 S	66.33 W
Villa Media Agua, Arg.	172	E3	31.59 S	68.25 W
Villa Mercedes, Arg.	172	F5	33.40 S	65.27 W
Villa Montes, Bol.	166	D4	21.15 S	63.28 W
Villandraut, Fr.	22	E5	44.27 N	0.22 W
Villa Nova, Md., U.S.	202b		39.21 N	76.44 W
Villanova University, educ., Pa., U.S.	203		40.02 N	75.21 W
Villa Nueva, Arg.	172	F6	32.26 S	63.14 W
Villanueva, Col.	168	B5	10.36 N	72.58 W
Villanueva, Mex.	154	D7	22.20 N	102.52 W
Villanueva, N.M., U.S.	138	F3	35.16 N	105.21 W
Villanueva de Córdoba, Spain	28	F6	38.19 N	4.37 W
Villanueva de la Serena, Spain	28	E5	38.58 N	5.48 W
Villanueva de la Sierra, Spain	28	D4	40.13 N	6.23 W
Villanueva de los Infantes, Spain	28	F8	38.44 N	2.59 W
Villanueva del Río y Minas, Spain	28	G5	37.38 N	5.42 W
Villanueva y Geltrú see Vilanova i la Geltrú, Spain	28	C12	41.13 N	1.45 E
Villa Numancia, Arg.	206		34.55 S	58.24 W
Villa Ocampo, Arg.	172	D8	28.29 S	59.21 W
Villa Ocampo, Mex.	136	H2	26.27 N	105.32 W
Villa Ojo de Agua, Arg.	172	D6	29.30 S	63.42 W
Villa Oliva, Para.	172	B9	26.00 S	57.51 W
Villa Papale, bldg., Italy	185a		41.45 N	12.39 E
Villa Park, Il., U.S.	196		41.53 N	87.59 W
Villa Park Dam, dam., Ca., U.S.	198		33.48 N	117.46 W
Villa Pérez, P.R.	158a	b2	18.11 N	66.46 W
Villapinzón, Col.	168	E5	5.13 N	73.35 W
Villa Quintilio Varo, hist., Italy	185a		41.58 N	12.47 E
Villarcayo, Spain	28	B7	42.56 N	3.33 W
Villardefrades, Spain	28	C5	41.43 N	5.15 W
Villar del Arzobispo, Spain	28	E10	39.44 N	0.49 W
Villa Real, ngh., Arg.	206		34.37 S	58.31 W
Villa Regina, Arg.	166	G3	39.06 S	67.05 W
Villa Reynolds, Arg.	172	F5	33.42 S	65.23 W
Villa Rica, Ga., U.S.	134	D14	33.44 N	84.55 W
Villaroche, Fr.	179		48.37 N	2.39 E
Villaroche, mil., Fr.	179		48.37 N	2.40 E
Villarreal see Vila-Real, Spain	28	E10	39.56 N	0.06 W
Villarrica, Col.	168	F4	3.57 N	74.36 W
Villarrica, Para.	172	B9	25.45 S	56.27 W
Villarrobledo, Spain	28	E8	39.16 N	2.36 W
Villarrubia de los Ojos, Spain	28	E7	39.13 N	3.36 W
Villas, N.J., U.S.	124	E11	39.01 N	74.56 W
Villa Sáenz Peña, ngh., Arg.	206		34.36 S	58.31 W
Villa San Andrés, ngh., Arg.	206		34.33 S	58.32 W
Villa San Giovanni, Italy	32	F9	38.13 N	15.38 E
Villa San Martín, Arg.	172	D5	28.17 S	64.10 W
Villa Santa Rita de Catuna, Arg.	172	E4	30.57 S	66.13 W
Villa Santos Lugares, ngh., Arg.	206		34.36 S	58.32 W
Villasayas, Spain	28	C8	41.21 N	2.36 W
Villa Serrano, Bol.	166	C4	19.06 S	64.18 W
Villasimius, Italy	32	E3	39.09 N	9.31 E
Villasis, Phil.	68	C3	15.55 N	120.34 E
Villa Tunari, Bol.	166	C3	16.55 S	65.22 W
Villa Turdera, ngh., Arg.	206		34.48 S	58.25 W
Villa Unión, Arg.	172	D3	29.19 S	68.13 W
Villa Unión, Arg.	172	D6	29.24 S	62.47 W
Villa Unión, Mex.	154	D5	23.10 N	106.12 W
Villa Unión, Mex.	154	A8	28.13 N	100.43 W
Villa Valeria, Arg.	172	G5	34.20 S	64.55 W
Villaverde, ngh., Spain	184a		40.21 N	3.42 W
Villavicencio, Col.	168	E5	4.09 N	73.38 W
Villaviciosa, Spain	28	A5	43.29 N	5.26 W
Villaviciosa de Córdoba, Spain	28	F5	38.04 N	5.01 W
Villazón, Bol.	166	D3	22.04 S	65.35 W
Villa Zorraquín, Arg.	172	E8	31.19 S	58.00 W
Villé, Fr.	24	H3	48.20 N	7.18 E
Villebois, Qc., Can.	114	B11	49.06 N	79.09 W
Villebon-sur-Yvette, Fr.	179		48.42 N	2.15 E
Villeconin, Fr.	179		48.31 N	2.08 E
Villecresnes, Fr.	179		48.43 N	2.32 E
Ville-d'Avray, Fr.	179		48.50 N	2.11 E
Villedieu, Fr.	20	F7	48.50 N	1.13 W
Villefranche-de-Rouergue, Fr.	22	E8	44.21 N	2.02 E
Villefranche-sur-Saône, Fr.	22	C10	45.59 N	4.43 E
Villejust, Fr.	179		48.41 N	2.14 E
Villemoisson-sur-Orge, Fr.	179		48.40 N	2.19 E
Villemomble, Fr.	179		48.53 N	2.31 E
Villena, Spain	28	F10	38.37 N	0.51 W
Villeneuve-la-Garenne, Fr.	179		48.56 N	2.20 E
Villeneuve-le-Comte, Fr.	179		48.49 N	2.50 E
Villeneuve-Saint-Denis, Fr.	179		48.49 N	2.48 E
Villeneuve-sous-Dammartin, Fr.	179		49.02 N	2.39 E
Villeneuve-sur-Lot, Fr.	22	E6	44.25 N	0.42 E
Villeneuve-sur-Yonne, Fr.	20	F12	48.05 N	3.17 E
Villennes-sur-Seine, Fr.	179		48.56 N	2.00 E
Villepinte, Fr.	179		48.58 N	2.32 E
Ville Platte, La., U.S.	134	G6	30.41 N	92.16 W
Villepreux, Fr.	179		48.50 N	2.01 E
Villeron, Fr.	179		49.03 N	2.33 E
Villers-Cotterêts, Fr.	20	E12	49.14 N	3.05 E
Villers-en-Arthies, Fr.	179		49.05 N	1.44 E
Villerupt, Fr.	20	E14	49.28 N	5.53 E
Villeta, Col.	168	E4	4.59 N	74.29 W
Villeurbanne, Fr.	22	D10	45.45 N	4.51 E
Villevaudé, Fr.	179		48.55 N	2.39 E
Villeziers, Fr.	179		48.40 N	2.10 E
Villiers, S. Afr.	90	E9	27.01 S	28.36 E
Villiers-Adam, Fr.	179		49.04 N	2.14 E
Villiers-le-Bâcle, Fr.	179		48.44 N	2.08 E
Villiers-le-Bel, Fr.	179		49.00 N	2.23 E
Villiers-le-Sec, Fr.	179		49.04 N	2.23 E
Villiers-Saint-Frédéric, Fr.	179		48.49 N	1.54 E
Villiers-sur-Marne, Fr.	179		48.50 N	2.33 E
Villiers-sur-Morin, Fr.	179		48.52 N	2.53 E
Villigst, Ger.	181		51.26 N	7.35 E
Villingen-Schwenningen, Ger.	24	H4	48.03 N	8.27 E
Villisca, Ia., U.S.	130	D3	40.55 N	94.58 W
Villmanstrand see Lappeenranta, Fin.	18	F15	61.03 N	28.12 E
Villoresi, Canale, can., Italy	184b		45.33 N	9.19 E
Vilna, Ab., Can.	144	B19	54.07 N	111.55 W
Vilna see Vilnius, Lith.	26	F8	54.40 N	25.17 E
Vilnius, Lith.	26	F8	54.40 N	25.17 E
Vil'nohirs'k, Ukr.	38	E13	48.29 N	34.01 E
Vilppula, Fin.	18	F11	62.01 N	24.30 E
Vils, stm., Ger.	30	B10	48.38 N	13.11 E
Vilsandi saar, i., Est.	26	B4	58.23 N	21.49 E
Vilsbiburg, Ger.	24	H8	48.26 N	12.21 E
Vil'shana, Ukr.	38	D10	49.12 N	31.13 E
Vil'shanka, Ukr.	38	E9	48.14 N	30.52 E
Vil'shany, Ukr.	38	D16	49.47 N	37.45 E
Vil'shany, Ukr.	38	C14	50.03 N	35.53 E
Vilshofen, Ger.	24	H9	48.38 N	13.11 E
Viluppuram, India	69	E4	11.56 N	79.30 E
Vil'va, Russia	40	B20	58.37 N	56.57 E
Vilvoorde, Bel.	20	D13	50.56 N	4.26 E
Vilvorde see Vilvoorde, Bel.	20	D13	50.56 N	4.26 E
Vimianzo, Spain	28	A1	43.06 N	9.01 W
Vimmerby, Swe.	16	J13	57.40 N	15.52 E
Vimodrone, Italy	184b		45.31 N	9.17 E
Vimoutiers, Fr.	20	F9	48.55 N	0.12 E
Vimpeli, Fin.	18	D10	63.09 N	23.49 E
Vimperk, Czech Rep.	24	G9	49.02 N	13.46 E
Vina, Ca., U.S.	148	D3	39.56 N	122.02 W
Vina, stm., Cam.	86	C2	7.51 N	15.46 E
Viña del Mar, Chile	172	F2	33.01 S	71.33 W
Vinalhaven, Me., U.S.	122	F8	44.02 N	68.49 W
Vinalhaven Island, i., Me., U.S.	122	G8	44.05 N	68.51 W
Vinantes, Fr.	179		49.01 N	2.44 E
Vina Roni, Mount, mtn., Sol. Is.	101b	d7	8.06 S	157.29 E
Vinarós, Spain	28	D11	40.28 N	0.27 E
Vinaroz see Vinarós, Spain	28	D11	40.28 N	0.27 E
Vincennes, In., U.S.	130	F10	38.40 N	87.31 W
Vincennes, Bois de, p.o.i., Fr.	179		48.50 N	2.25 E
Vincennes, Château de, hist., Fr.	179		48.51 N	2.26 E
Vincennes, Étang de, l., Fr.	179		48.47 N	2.45 E
Vincennes Bay, b., Ant.	103	B15	66.17 S	108.48 E
Vincent, Al., U.S.	134	D12	33.22 N	86.22 W
Vincent, Point, c., Norf. I.	100i	x24	29.00 S	167.55 E
Vinces, Ec.	168	H2	1.33 S	79.44 W
Vinchina, Arg.	172	D3	28.46 S	68.10 W
Vindelälven, stm., Swe.	16	C17	63.55 N	19.51 E
Vindelgransele, Swe.	16	B16	65.06 N	18.18 E
Vindeln, Swe.	16	C17	64.11 N	19.43 E
Vinderup, Den.	16	K6	56.29 N	8.47 E
Vindhya Range, mts., India	70	G7	23.00 N	77.00 E
Vine Brook, stm., Ma., U.S.	201		42.27 N	71.13 W
Vinegar Hill, mtn., Or., U.S.	146	F8	44.43 N	118.34 W
Vine Grove, Ky., U.S.	130	G11	37.48 N	85.58 W
Vine Hill, Ca., U.S.	200		38.00 N	122.06 W
Vineland, N.J., U.S.	124	E10	39.29 N	75.01 W
Vinemont, Al., U.S.	134	C12	34.14 N	86.51 W
Vineyard Haven, Ma., U.S.	124	C15	41.27 N	70.36 W
Vineyard Sound, strt., Ma., U.S.	124	C15	41.25 N	70.46 W
Vingåker, Swe.	16	H13	59.03 N	15.53 E
Vingeanne, stm., Fr.	20	G14	47.22 N	5.29 E
Ving Ngün, Mya.	64	A4	22.38 N	99.15 E
Vinh, Viet.	64	C7	18.40 N	105.40 E
Vinhais, Port.	28	C4	41.50 N	7.00 W
Vinhas, Ribeira das, stm., Port.	184c		38.42 N	9.25 W
Vinh Chau, Viet.	64	H8	9.19 N	105.58 E
Vinh Loc, Viet.	187c		10.49 N	106.34 E
Vinh Long, Viet.	64	G8	10.14 N	105.58 E
Vinh Yen, Viet.	64	B7	21.18 N	105.35 E
Vinica, Slvn.	30	E12	45.27 N	15.15 E
Vinita, Ok., U.S.	130	H2	36.38 N	95.09 W
Vin'kivtsi, Ukr.	38	D6	49.02 N	27.14 E
Vinkovci, Cro.	30	E15	45.17 N	18.48 E
Vinnica see Vinnytsia, Ukr.	38	D7	49.14 N	28.31 E
Vinnicy, Russia	18	G21	60.38 N	34.46 E
Vinnum, Ger.	181		51.41 N	7.24 E
Vinnytsia, Ukr.	38	D7	49.14 N	28.31 E
Vinnytsia, co., Ukr.	38	E8	49.00 N	28.45 E
Vinogradovo, ngh., Russia	183b		55.57 N	37.32 E
Vinogrobol', Russia	38	B15	51.50 N	36.25 E
Vinslöv, Swe.	16	K11	56.06 N	13.55 E
Vinson Massif, mtn., Ant.	103	C32	78.31 S	85.14 W
Vinstra, Nor.	16	F7	61.35 N	9.44 E
Vinstra, stm., Nor.	16	F7	61.35 N	9.44 E
Vinstri, l., Nor.	16	F6	61.18 N	8.57 E
Vintilă Vodă, Rom.	36	D13	45.27 N	26.47 E
Vinton, Ia., U.S.	130	B5	42.10 N	92.01 W

Name	Page	Map Ref.	Latitude	Longitude
Vinton, La., U.S.	136	D14	30.11 N	93.34 W
Vinton, Va., U.S.	124	G6	37.16 N	79.53 W
Viñuelas, Arroyo de, stm., Spain	184a		40.33 N	3.33 W
Viny, Russia	26	B15	58.22 N	32.13 E
Viola, Il., U.S.	130	C7	41.11 N	90.34 W
Viola, N.Y., U.S.	194		41.08 N	74.05 W
Viola, Wi., U.S.	128	H8	43.30 N	90.40 W
Vioolsdrif, S. Afr.	90	F3	28.50 S	17.39 E
Vipiteno, Italy	30	D8	46.54 N	11.26 E
Vir, Otok, i., Cro.	30	F11	44.18 N	15.04 E
Virac, Phil.	68	D5	13.35 N	124.14 E
Viramgām, India	70	G3	23.07 N	72.02 E
Virandozero, Russia	18	C22	64.02 N	35.54 E
Viranşehir, Tur.	42	G8	37.13 N	39.46 E
Virarājendrapet, India	69	E2	12.11 N	75.48 E
Virbalis, Lith.	26	F5	54.37 N	22.49 E
Virden, Mb., Can.	142	E13	49.49 N	100.54 W
Virden, Il., U.S.	130	E8	39.30 N	89.45 W
Virden, N.M., U.S.	150	K8	32.41 N	109.00 W
Vire, Fr.	20	F8	48.50 N	0.52 W
Vire, stm., Fr.	20	E7	49.19 N	1.07 W
Virgem da Lapa, Braz.	170	I4	16.49 S	42.21 W
Virgen, Pasaje de la see Virgin Passage, strt., N.A.	158a	b5	18.16 N	65.09 W
Virgen del San Cristóbal, rel., Chile	204e		33.26 S	70.39 W
Vírgenes, Cabo, c., S.A.	166	J3	52.21 S	68.19 W
Virgil, On., Can.	202a		43.13 N	79.08 W
Virgil, Ks., U.S.	138	C13	37.59 N	96.00 W
Virgilina, Va., U.S.	124	H7	36.32 N	78.50 W
Virgin, stm., U.S.	150	G2	36.31 N	114.20 W
Virgin, North Fork, stm., Ut., U.S.	150	F4	37.09 N	113.00 W
Virgin Gorda, i., Br. Vir. Is.	158b	e9	18.30 N	64.24 W
Virgin Gorda Peak, mtn., Br. Vir. Is.	158b	e9	18.30 N	64.24 W
Virginia, S. Afr.	90	F8	28.05 S	26.52 E
Virginia, Il., U.S.	130	E7	39.56 N	90.12 W
Virginia, Mn., U.S.	128	D6	47.31 N	92.32 W
Virginia, state, U.S.	124	G7	37.30 N	78.45 W
Virginia Beach, Va., U.S.	124	H10	36.51 N	75.59 W
Virginia City, Mt., U.S.	146	E14	45.18 N	111.57 W
Virginia City, Nv., U.S.	148	D6	39.18 N	119.38 W
Virginia Falls, wtfl., N.T., Can.	110	C5	61.36 N	125.44 W
Virginia Peak, mtn., Nv., U.S.	148	D6	39.45 N	119.28 W
Virginia Water, Eng., U.K.	178		51.24 N	0.34 W
Virginia Water, res., Eng., U.K.	178		51.24 N	0.37 W
Virgin Islands, dep., N.A.	158b	e7	18.20 N	64.50 W
Virgin Islands, is., N.A.	158b	e7	18.00 N	64.40 W
Virgin Islands National Park, p.o.i., V.I.U.S.	158b	e7	18.20 N	64.44 W
Virgin Passage, strt., N.A.	158a	b5	18.16 N	65.09 W
Virgolândia, Braz.	170	J4	18.27 S	42.16 W
Virihaure, l., Swe.	14	E7	67.22 N	16.37 E
Virje, Cro.	30	D13	46.03 N	17.01 E
Virkkala, Fin.	18	G10	60.12 N	24.01 E
Virôchey, Camb.	64	F8	13.58 N	106.48 E
Virojoki, Fin.	18	G14	60.35 N	27.42 E
Viron, Grc.	185c		37.57 N	23.45 E
Viroqua, Wi., U.S.	128	H8	43.33 N	90.53 W
Virovitica, Cro.	30	E14	45.50 N	17.23 E
Virpazar, Yugo.	36	G5	42.10 N	19.00 E
Virrat, Fin.	18	E10	62.14 N	23.44 E
Virsbo, Swe.	16	H14	59.52 N	16.03 E
Virserum, Swe.	16	J13	57.18 N	15.35 E
Virtaniemi, Fin.	14	D19	68.53 N	28.26 E
Virton, Bel.	20	E14	49.34 N	5.32 E
Virtsu, Est.	26	B6	58.34 N	23.31 E
Virú, Peru	164	E2	8.25 S	78.47 W
Virudunagar, India	69	G3	9.34 N	77.57 E
Viru-Jaagupi, Est.	26	A9	59.15 N	26.28 E
Virulento, Mex.	136	F3	28.52 N	104.21 W
Virunga, Parc National de, p.o.i., D.R.C.	86	D5	0.21 N	29.34 E
Viru-Nigula, Est.	26	A9	59.27 N	26.41 E
Virvytė, stm., Lith.	26	D5	56.14 N	22.33 E
Vis, Cro.	30	G13	43.03 N	16.11 E
Vis, stm., Fr.	22	F9	43.56 N	3.40 E
Vis see Fish, stm., Nmb.	90	E3	28.05 S	17.10 E
Vis, stm., S. Afr.	90	G5	30.55 S	20.22 E
Vis, Otok, i., Cro.	30	G13	43.02 N	16.11 E
Visale, Sol. Is.	101b	e8	9.15 S	159.40 E
Visalia, Ca., U.S.	148	G6	36.19 N	119.17 W
Visayan Islands, is., Phil.	68	E4	10.39 N	123.05 E
Visayan Sea, s., Phil.	68	E4	11.35 N	123.51 E
Visby, Swe.	16	J16	57.38 N	18.18 E
Viscount, Sk., Can.	142	C8	51.57 N	105.37 W
Viscount Melville Sound, strt., Can.	106	B11	74.10 N	108.00 W
Višegrad, Bos.	36	F6	43.47 N	19.17 E
Višera, stm., Russia	26	B14	58.33 N	31.24 E
Viseu, Port.	28	D3	40.39 N	7.54 W
Viseu, state, Port.	28	D3	40.45 N	7.45 W
Vişeu, stm., Rom.	38	E3	47.55 N	24.09 E
Vişeu de Sus, Rom.	36	B11	47.43 N	24.23 E
Vishākhapatnam, India	69	C6	17.42 N	83.18 E
Visim, Russia	40	C21	57.39 N	59.30 E
Visingsö, i., Swe.	16	I12	58.02 N	14.20 E
Visitation, Île de la, i., Qc., Can.	193a		45.35 N	73.40 W
Viskafors, Swe.	16	J10	57.38 N	12.52 E
Viskan, stm., Swe.	16	J10	57.13 N	12.13 E
Vislanda, Swe.	16	K12	56.47 N	14.28 E
Visnagar, India	70	G4	23.42 N	72.33 E
Visnes, Nor.	16	H3	59.22 N	5.16 E
Višneva, Bela.	26	F9	54.08 N	26.14 E
Višnëvka, Kaz.	48	D12	50.49 N	72.11 E
Višnjaki, Russia	183b		55.47 N	37.54 E
Višnjakovo, Russia	183b		55.45 N	38.10 E
Viso, Monte see Monviso, mtn., Italy	30	F4	44.40 N	7.07 E
Visoki Dečani, Manastir, rel., Yugo.	36	G7	42.34 N	20.15 E
Visoko, Bos.	36	E5	43.59 N	18.11 E
Visokoi Island, i., S. Geor.	103	A2	56.42 S	27.11 W
Visp, Switz.	30	D4	46.17 N	7.52 E
Vissefjärda, Swe.	16	K13	56.32 N	15.36 E
Visselhövede, Ger.	24	C5	52.59 N	9.35 E
Vista, Ca., U.S.	148	J8	33.11 N	117.14 W
Vista Alegre, Chile	204e		33.30 S	70.43 W
Vista Alegre, Peru	204d		12.09 S	77.00 W
Vista Flores, Arg.	172	F3	33.39 S	69.07 W
Vistheden, Swe.	14	G11	65.41 N	20.39 E
Vistina, Russia	26	A11	59.45 N	28.28 E
Vistula see Wisła, stm., Pol.	24	B14	54.20 N	18.56 E
Vistula Lagoon, b., Eur.	24	B16	54.26 N	19.41 E
Vita, Mb., Can.	142	E17	49.07 N	96.32 W
Vita, stm., Col.	168	E7	6.09 N	67.30 W
Vitacura, Chile	204e		33.24 S	70.36 W
Vitali, Phil.	68	G4	7.22 N	122.17 E
Vitarte, Peru	164	F2	12.02 S	76.56 W
Vite, India	69	C2	17.16 N	74.31 E
Vitebsk see Vicebsk, Bela.	26	E13	55.11 N	30.12 E
Vitebsk see Vicebsk, state, Bela.	26	E11	55.20 N	29.00 E
Vitebsk Station, trans., Russia	183a		59.55 N	30.21 E
Viterbo, Italy	30	H9	42.25 N	12.05 E
Viti see Fiji, ctry., Oc.	92	E8	18.00 S	178.00 E
Vitiaz Strait, strt., Pap. N. Gui.	101a	b4	5.50 S	147.20 E
Vitigudino, Spain	28	C4	41.01 N	6.26 W
Viti Levu, i., Fiji	101e	p19	18.00 S	178.00 E
Vitim, Russia	50	E11	59.27 N	112.33 E
Vitim, stm., Russia	50	E12	59.27 N	112.34 E
Vitimskij, Russia	50	E11	58.13 N	113.15 E
Vitimskoe ploskogor'e, plat., Russia	50	F11	54.00 N	113.30 E
Vitinia, ngh., Italy	185a		41.47 N	12.24 E
Vitinja, p., Blg.	36	G10	42.46 N	23.48 E
Vítkov, Czech Rep.	24	G13	49.46 N	17.45 E
Vitória, Braz.	164	D7	2.53 S	52.00 W
Vitória, Braz.	170	K5	20.18 S	40.20 W
Vitoria see Gasteiz, Spain	28	B8	42.51 N	2.40 W
Vitória da Conquista, Braz.	170	H5	14.51 S	40.50 W
Vitória de Santo Antão, Braz.	170	E8	8.07 S	35.18 W
Vitória do Mearim, Braz.	170	B3	3.28 S	44.53 W
Vitorino Freire, Braz.	170	C3	4.03 S	45.11 W
Vitré, Fr.	20	F7	48.07 N	1.12 W
Vitry-le-François, Fr.	20	F13	48.43 N	4.35 E
Vittangi, Swe.	14	E12	67.40 N	21.38 E
Vitteaux, Fr.	20	G13	47.24 N	4.32 E
Vittel, Fr.	20	F14	48.11 N	5.56 E
Vittoria, Italy	32	H8	36.57 N	14.32 E
Vittorio Veneto, Italy	30	E9	45.59 N	12.17 E
Vitvattnet, Swe.	14	F14	66.03 N	23.14 E
Vivarais, Monts du, plat., Fr.	22	E10	44.55 N	4.15 E
Viveiro, Spain	28	A3	43.40 N	7.35 W
Vivekananda Bridge, trans., India	190b		22.39 N	88.21 E
Viver, Spain	28	E10	39.55 N	0.36 W
Vivero see Viveiro, Spain	28	A3	43.40 N	7.35 W
Vivi, stm., Russia	50	D8	63.53 N	97.48 E
Vivian, La., U.S.	136	B13	32.52 N	93.58 W
Viviers, Fr.	22	E10	44.29 N	4.40 E
Vivoratá, Arg.	172	H9	37.40 S	57.40 W
Vizagapatam see Vishākhapatnam, India	69	C6	17.42 N	83.18 E
Vizcaíno, Desierto de, des., Mex.	154	B2	27.33 N	113.38 W
Vizcaya see Bizkaiko, co., Spain	28	A8	43.20 N	2.45 W
Vizcaya, Golfo de see Biscay, Bay of, b., Eur.	8	G8	44.00 N	4.00 W
Vize, Tur.	34	B10	41.34 N	27.46 E
Vizianagaram, India	69	B6	18.07 N	83.25 E
Vizille, Fr.	22	D11	45.04 N	5.45 E
Vizinga, Russia	48	B7	61.04 N	50.05 E
Vizzola, Italy	184b		45.38 N	8.42 E
Vjala, stm., Russia	14	F25	66.39 N	34.18 E
Vjalikaja Berastavica, Bela.	26	G7	53.11 N	24.01 E
Vjalikaja Maščanica, Bela.	26	G12	53.57 N	29.38 E
Vjaliki Bor, Bela.	38	A8	52.02 N	29.56 E
Vjalikija Aucjuki, Bela.	26	H12	52.04 N	29.32 E
Vjalikija Radvaničy, Bela.	26	I7	52.01 N	24.00 E
Vjalozero, ozero, l., Russia	14	F26	66.51 N	35.07 E
Vjartsilja, Russia	18	E17	62.10 N	30.38 E
Vjaseja, Bela.	26	G10	53.03 N	27.41 E
Vjatčyn, Bela.	26	H11	52.26 N	28.09 E
Vjatka, stm., Russia	48	C8	55.34 N	51.28 E
Vjatskie Poljany, Russia	40	C17	56.13 N	51.04 E
Vjazemskij, Russia	50	G15	47.32 N	134.45 E
Vjaz'ma, Russia	26	E17	55.12 N	34.17 E
Vjaz'ma, stm., Russia	26	E16	55.28 N	33.34 E
Vjazniki, Russia	40	C12	56.14 N	42.07 E
Vjazovka, Russia	40	G14	48.19 N	45.36 E
Vjazovka, Russia	40	F14	50.52 N	43.57 E
Vjazovoe, Russia	38	B15	51.54 N	36.58 E
Vjazyn', Bela.	26	F10	54.24 N	27.11 E
Vjosës (Aóös), stm., Eur.	32	D13	40.39 N	19.19 E
Vjunka, stm., Russia	183b		55.42 N	38.01 E
Vlaardingen, Neth.	20	C13	51.54 N	4.19 E
Vlădeasa, Vârful, mtn., Rom.	36	C9	46.45 N	22.48 E
Vlădeni, Rom.	36	B14	47.24 N	27.19 E
Vladičin Han, Yugo.	36	G8	42.42 N	22.03 E
Vladikavkaz (Dzaudzhikau), Russia	42	D11	43.02 N	44.39 E
Vladikavkaz see Ordzhonikidze, Ukr.	38	F13	47.40 N	34.03 E
Vladimir, Russia	40	C12	56.08 N	40.24 E
Vladimirovka, Kaz.	48	D10	53.27 N	64.02 E
Vladimirskaja oblast', co., Russia	40	D12	56.00 N	40.30 E
Vladimirskij Tupik, Russia	26	E16	55.40 N	33.15 E
Vladivostok, Russia	54	C9	43.08 N	131.55 E
Vladyčnoe, Russia	26	B22	58.48 N	39.28 E
Vladykino, ngh., Russia	183b		55.52 N	37.36 E
Vlasenica, Bos.	36	E5	44.11 N	18.56 E
Vlašim, Czech Rep.	24	G10	49.42 N	14.53 E
Vlasotince, Yugo.	36	G9	42.58 N	22.07 E
Vlasovo, Russia	50	B16	70.47 N	134.51 E
Vlazoviči, Russia	26	G15	53.01 N	32.18 E
Vlieland, i., Neth.	20	A13	53.15 N	4.57 E
Vlissingen, Neth.	20	C12	51.27 N	3.35 E
Vlonë see Vlorë, Alb.	32	D13	40.28 N	19.29 E
Vlora see Vlorë, Alb.	32	D13	40.28 N	19.29 E
Vlorë, Alb.	32	D13	40.28 N	19.29 E
Vlorës, Gjiri i, b., Alb.	32	D13	40.25 N	19.25 E
Vltava (Moldau), stm., Czech Rep.	24	F10	50.20 N	14.28 E
Vnukovo, Russia	26	E20	55.36 N	37.16 E
Vnukovo Airport, arpt., Russia	183b		55.37 N	37.17 E
Voca, Tx., U.S.	136	D8	31.00 N	99.11 W
Vöcklabruck, Aus.	30	C10	48.00 N	13.39 E
Vo Dat, Viet.	64	G8	11.08 N	107.30 E
Vodla, Russia	18	E24	62.05 N	37.27 E
Vodla, stm., Russia	18	F24	61.47 N	36.05 E
Vodlozero, ozero, l., Russia	18	E23	62.20 N	36.55 E
Vodnjan, Cro.	30	F10	44.57 N	13.50 E
Vodosalma, Russia	18	C17	64.28 N	30.44 E
Vodzimonie, Russia	40	C17	56.48 N	51.37 E
Voël, stm., S. Afr.	90	H7	33.07 S	25.07 E
Voerde, Ger.	181		51.18 N	7.24 E
Vogelheim, ngh., Ger.	181		51.29 N	6.59 E
Vogel Peak see Dimlang, mtn., Nig.	84	H7	8.24 N	11.47 E
Vogelsberg, mts., Ger.	24	F5	50.31 N	9.06 E
Vogesen see Vosges, mts., Fr.	20	F16	48.12 N	7.01 E
Voghera, Italy	30	E4	44.59 N	9.01 E
Vognema, Russia	18	H25	59.58 N	38.10 E
Voh, N. Cal.	101d	m15	20.57 S	164.41 E
Vohémar see Iharaña, Madag.	88	C9	13.21 S	50.00 E
Vohenstrauss, Ger.	24	G8	49.37 N	12.20 E
Vohimena, Tanjona, c., Madag.	88	F8	25.35 S	45.08 E
Vohipeno, Madag.	88	E8	22.20 S	47.50 E
Võhma, Est.	26	B8	58.38 N	25.34 E
Vohtoga, Russia	40	B12	58.49 N	41.02 E
Vohwinkel, ngh., Ger.	181		51.14 N	7.09 E
Voi, Kenya	86	E7	3.23 S	38.34 E
Voikkaa, Fin.	18	G13	60.57 N	26.36 E
Voikove, Ukr.	38	H12	45.30 N	33.52 E
Voikovs'kyi, Ukr.	38	F17	47.46 N	38.20 E
Voineşti, Rom.	36	B14	47.05 N	27.26 E
Voinjama, Lib.	84	H3	8.25 N	9.44 W
Voïnka, Ukr.	38	H13	45.52 N	33.59 E
Voinyliv, Ukr.	38	D3	49.08 N	24.30 E
Voiron, Fr.	22	D11	45.21 N	5.34 E
Voisenon, Fr.	179		48.34 N	2.40 E
Voitsberg, Aus.	30	C12	47.02 N	15.09 E
Vojens, Den.	16	L7	55.15 N	9.19 E
Vojmsjön, l., Swe.	16	B13	64.56 N	16.29 E
Vojnić, Cro.	30	E12	45.19 N	15.42 E
Vojnica, Russia	18	B17	65.12 N	30.15 E
Vojvodina, co., Yugo.	36	D7	45.00 N	20.00 E
Voknavolok, Russia	18	C17	64.56 N	30.29 E
Volary, Czech Rep.	24	H9	48.54 N	13.53 E
Volcán, Arg.	172	A5	23.51 S	65.28 W
Volcán, Pan.	156	H6	8.45 N	82.38 W
Volcano, Hi., U.S.	100a	d6	19.26 N	155.13 W
Volcano Islands see Kazan-rettō, is., Japan	46	G18	25.00 N	141.00 E
Volčiha, Russia	48	D14	52.01 N	80.22 E
Volčij Nos, mys, c., Russia	18	G19	60.31 N	32.35 E
Volčki, Russia	40	E12	52.29 N	40.41 E
Volda, Nor.	16	E3	62.09 N	6.04 E
Voldozero, Russia	18	D20	63.41 N	34.00 E
Volga, Russia	26	C21	57.57 N	38.23 E
Volga, Ia., U.S.	130	B6	42.48 N	91.32 W
Volga, S.D., U.S.	128	G2	44.18 N	96.56 W
Volga, stm., Russia	40	I15	45.45 N	47.56 E
Volga, stm., Ia., U.S.	130	B6	42.45 N	91.15 W
Volga-Baltic Canal see Volgo-Baltijskij kanal, can., Russia	18	H25	59.06 N	37.52 E
Volga Plateau see Privolžskaja vozvyšennost', plat., Russia	40	E15	52.00 N	46.00 E
Volgino, Russia	26	B16	58.27 N	33.52 E
Volgo, ozero, l., Russia	26	D16	56.55 N	33.09 E
Volgo-Baltijskij kanal, can., Russia	18	H25	59.06 N	37.52 E
Volgodonsk, Russia	40	H12	47.31 N	42.08 E
Volgograd (Stalingrad), Russia	40	G14	48.44 N	44.25 E
Volgograd Reservoir see Volgogradskoe vodohranilišče, res., Russia	40	F15	50.17 N	45.49 E
Volgogradskaja oblast', co., Russia	40	G14	49.30 N	44.00 E
Volgogradskoe vodohranilišče, res., Russia	40	F15	50.17 N	45.49 E
Volhonka-Zil, ngh., Russia	183b		55.40 N	37.37 E
Volhov, Russia	26	A15	59.54 N	32.19 E
Volhov, stm., Russia	12	G15	60.06 N	32.18 E
Volintiri, Mol.	38	G8	46.26 N	29.37 E
Volissós, Grc.	34	E8	38.28 N	25.56 E
Völkermarkt, Aus.	30	D11	46.39 N	14.38 E
Völklingen, Ger.	24	G2	49.15 N	6.51 E
Volkovo Cemetery, misc. cult., Russia	183a		59.54 N	30.22 E
Volksrust, S. Afr.	90	E9	27.21 S	29.53 E
Vollme, Ger.	181		51.10 N	7.36 E
Volma, stm., Bela.	26	G11	53.34 N	28.18 E
Volme, stm., Ger.	181		51.24 N	7.27 E
Volmerswerth, ngh., Ger.	181		51.11 N	6.46 E
Vol'naja Gorka, Russia	26	B13	58.43 N	30.51 E
Volnovakha, Ukr.	38	F16	47.35 N	37.29 E
Vol'nyj, ostrov, i., Russia	183a		59.58 N	30.14 E
Voločanka, Russia	50	B7	70.59 N	94.31 E
Volochys'k, Ukr.	38	D5	49.31 N	26.14 E
Volockaja, Russia	12	F20	60.16 N	42.58 E
Volodarka, Ukr.	38	D8	49.31 N	29.55 E
Volodars'ke, Ukr.	38	F16	47.12 N	37.19 E
Volodarskij, Russia	40	H16	46.23 N	48.31 E
Volodarskij, ngh., Russia	183a		59.49 N	30.05 E
Volodarskoe, Kaz.	48	D11	53.17 N	68.06 E
Volodars'k-Volyns'kyi, Ukr.	38	C7	50.35 N	28.25 E
Volodymyrets', Ukr.	38	B5	51.25 N	26.08 E
Volodymyrivka, Ukr.	38	F11	47.31 N	32.55 E
Volodymyr-Volyns'kyi, Ukr.	38	C3	50.51 N	24.19 E
Voloe, Russia	26	F17	54.09 N	34.35 E
Vologda, Russia	26	A22	59.13 N	39.54 E
Vologda, stm., Russia	26	A22	59.17 N	40.08 E
Vologodskaja oblast', co., Russia	12	G19	60.00 N	40.00 E
Volokolamsk, Russia	26	D18	56.01 N	35.57 E
Volokonovka, Russia	38	C16	50.29 N	37.52 E
Volokovaja, Russia	12	C23	66.28 N	48.10 E
Voloma, Russia	18	D18	63.44 N	31.53 E
Volonga, Russia	12	C22	67.07 N	47.46 E
Volonne, Fr.	22	E11	44.06 N	6.00 E
Vólos, Grc.	34	D5	39.22 N	22.56 E
Volos, Gulf of see Pagasitikós Kólpos, b., Grc.	34	D5	39.13 N	23.02 E
Vološka, Russia	12	F19	61.20 N	40.05 E
Vološka, stm., Russia	18	F26	61.27 N	39.25 E
Vološno, Russia	26	B11	58.28 N	28.28 E
Volosovo, Russia	26	A12	59.26 N	29.30 E
Volot, Russia	26	C13	57.55 N	30.41 E
Volovets', Ukr.	38	E2	48.43 N	23.11 E
Volovo, Russia	26	G21	53.33 N	38.00 E
Voložin see Valožyn, Bela.	26	F9	54.05 N	26.32 E
Volšepahk, gora, mtn., Russia	14	D24	68.28 N	33.49 E
Vol'sk, Russia	40	F15	52.02 N	47.21 E
Volta, stm., Ghana	84	H5	5.46 N	0.40 E
Volta, Lake, res., Ghana	84	H4	7.29 N	0.07 E
Volta Blanche (White Volta), stm., Afr.	84	G4	8.56 N	1.09 W
Volta Noire (Black Volta) (Mouhoun), stm., Afr.	84	G4	8.40 N	0.59 W
Volta Redonda, Braz.	170	L3	22.32 S	44.06 W
Volterra, Italy	30	G7	43.23 N	10.51 E
Vol'teva, Russia	12	D21	64.29 N	44.08 E
Voltri, ngh., Italy	30	F5	44.26 N	8.44 E
Volturino, Monte, mtn., Italy	32	D9	40.25 N	15.49 E
Volturno, stm., Italy	32	C8	41.01 N	13.54 E
Vólvi, Límni, l., Grc.	34	C6	40.40 N	23.30 E
Volyn', co., Ukr.	38	B4	51.00 N	25.00 E
Volyn', hist. reg., Ukr.	38	C7	50.50 N	27.00 E
Volyně, Czech Rep.	24	G9	49.10 N	13.53 E
Volynka, Ukr.	38	B11	51.36 N	32.21 E
Volyns'ka vysochyna, plat., Ukr.	38	C4	50.30 N	25.30 E
Volžsk, Russia	40	D16	55.51 N	48.20 E
Volžskij, Russia	40	G14	48.49 N	44.45 E
Vomano, stm., Italy	30	H10	42.39 N	14.01 E
Vombsjön, l., Swe.	16	L11	55.41 N	13.36 E
Vonavona Island, i., Sol. Is.	101b	e7	8.15 S	157.05 E
Vonda, Sk., Can.	142	B7	52.18 N	106.05 W
Vondanka, Russia	40	B15	59.06 N	47.48 E
Vondrozo, Madag.	88	E8	22.49 S	47.20 E
Von Frank Mountain, mtn., Ak., U.S.	109	D8	63.33 N	154.20 W
Von'ga, stm., Russia	18	B20	65.25 N	34.28 E
Võnnu, Est.	26	B10	58.17 N	27.02 E
Vonozero, Russia	18	G21	60.22 N	34.25 E
Vop', stm., Russia	26	E15	54.56 N	32.44 E
Vopnafjörður, Ice.	12a	k32	65.44 N	14.52 W
Vopnafjörður, b., Ice.	12a	k32	65.52 N	14.40 W
Vörå see Vöyri, Fin.	18	D9	63.09 N	22.15 E
Voranava, Bela.	26	F8	54.09 N	25.19 E
Vorarlberg, state, Aus.	30	C6	47.15 N	9.55 E
Vorau, Aus.	30	C12	47.25 N	15.54 E
Vorderrhein see Rein Anteriur, stm., Switz.	30	D5	46.49 N	9.24 E
Vordingborg, Den.	16	L9	55.00 N	11.54 E
Vóreio Aigaío, state, Grc.	34	D8	38.30 N	26.00 E
Vóreioi Sporades, is., Grc.	34	D6	39.15 N	23.55 E
Vóreios Evvoïkós, b., Grc.	34	E6	38.45 N	23.08 E
Vorga, Russia	26	G15	53.45 N	32.45 E
Vorhalle, ngh., Ger.	181		51.23 N	7.28 E
Vøringsfossen, wtfl., Nor.	16	G5	60.26 N	7.16 E
Vorja, stm., Russia	26	E18	54.53 N	35.00 E
Vorkuta, Russia	48	A10	67.29 N	64.02 E
Vorma, stm., Nor.	16	G9	60.08 N	11.28 E
Vormholz, Ger.	181		51.24 N	7.18 E
Vormsi, i., Est.	26	A6	59.00 N	23.15 E
Vorobevo, Russia	48	C13	56.07 N	76.32 E
Vorobiove, Ukr.	38	H12	45.20 N	33.15 E
Vorokhta, Ukr.	38	E3	48.17 N	24.34 E
Vorona, stm., Russia	40	E13	51.20 N	42.02 E
Voroncov, Mol.	38	F8	47.43 N	29.08 E
Voroncovka, Russia	50	E11	58.51 N	112.54 E
Voroncovo, Russia	26	C11	57.17 N	28.43 E
Voronë, Russia	14	D26	68.26 N	35.23 E
Voronež, Russia	40	F11	51.40 N	39.09 E
Voronež see Voronežskaja oblast', co., Russia	40	F12	51.00 N	40.00 E
Voronež, stm., Russia	40	E11	51.32 N	39.05 E
Voronežskaja oblast', co., Russia	40	F12	51.00 N	40.00 E
Voronizh, Ukr.	38	B12	51.46 N	33.28 E
Voronja, stm., Russia	14	D26	69.00 N	35.42 E
Voron'ky, Ukr.	38	C11	50.13 N	33.02 E
Voronok, Russia	26	H15	52.21 N	32.40 E
Voronov, mys, c., Russia	18	G18	60.15 N	32.05 E
Voronovkova Niva, Russia	26	C12	57.05 N	29.14 E
Voronovo, Russia	50	E5	56.00 N	83.48 E
Voronovytsia, Ukr.	38	D7	49.06 N	28.41 E
Vorontsivka, Ukr.	38	H12	45.50 N	33.47 E
Vorošilovgrad see Luhans'k, Ukr.	38	E18	48.33 N	39.20 E
Vorotynec, Russia	40	C14	56.03 N	45.51 E
Vorozhba, Ukr.	38	B13	51.11 N	34.14 E
Vorpommern, hist. reg., Ger.	24	C9	53.40 N	13.45 E
Vorskla, stm., Eur.	38	E13	48.56 N	34.10 E
Vorsma, Russia	40	C13	55.59 N	43.17 E
Vørterkaka Nunatak, mtn., Ant.	103	C8	72.20 S	27.29 E
Võrtsjärv, l., Est.	26	B8	58.16 N	26.03 E
Võru, Est.	26	C10	57.50 N	27.01 E
Vorzel', Ukr.	38	C9	50.33 N	30.09 E
Vosburg, S. Afr.	90	G6	30.32 S	22.52 E
Vosges, state, Fr.	20	F15	48.10 N	6.20 E
Vosges, mts., Fr.	20	F16	48.12 N	7.01 E
Voskresenovskoe, Russia	183a		59.43 N	30.47 E
Voskresensk, Russia	26	E21	55.19 N	38.42 E
Voskresens'ke, Ukr.	38	F11	47.01 N	32.08 E
Voskresenskoe, Russia	26	A20	59.25 N	37.55 E
Voskresenskoe, Russia	26	C20	57.49 N	37.40 E
Voskresenskoe, Russia	26	B21	58.54 N	38.36 E
Voskresenskoe, Russia	40	E19	53.07 N	56.09 E
Voss, Nor.	16	G4	60.38 N	6.25 E
Vosso, stm., Nor.	16	G4	60.39 N	6.04 E
Vostočnaja Kambal'nica, Russia	12	B22	68.18 N	45.56 E
Vostočnaja Lica, stm., Russia	14	D28	68.37 N	37.44 E
Vostočnoe Munozero, Russia	14	E25	67.04 N	34.44 E
Vostočno-Kounradskij, Kaz.	48	E13	47.01 N	75.08 E
Vostočno-Sibirskoe more, s., Russia	46	B20	74.00 N	166.00 E
Vostočnyj, Russia	50	G17	48.16 N	142.37 E
Vostočnyj Sajan, mts., Russia	48	D17	53.00 N	97.00 E
Vostok, i., Kir.	94	E11	10.06 S	152.23 W
Vostok, sci., Ant.	103	C15	78.30 S	106.50 E
Vosves, Fr.	179		48.31 N	2.36 E
Votice, Czech Rep.	24	G10	49.38 N	14.38 E
Votkinsk, Russia	40	C18	57.03 N	53.59 E
Votkinskoe vodohranilišče, res., Russia	40	C19	56.59 N	54.15 E
Votkinsk Reservoir see Votkinskoe vodohranilišče, res., Russia	40	C19	56.59 N	54.15 E
Votuporanga, Braz.	166	D7	20.26 S	49.58 W
Vouga, stm., Port.	28	D2	40.41 N	8.39 W
Vouillé, Fr.	20	H9	46.38 N	0.09 E
Voulangis, Fr.	179		48.51 N	2.54 E
Vouziers, Fr.	20	E13	49.23 N	4.42 E
Vovcha, stm., Ukr.	38	E15	48.38 N	35.42 E
Vovchans'k, Ukr.	38	C15	50.16 N	36.56 E
Voves, Fr.	20	F10	48.16 N	1.37 E
Vovkovyntsi, Ukr.	38	D6	49.12 N	27.40 E
Voxnan, stm., Swe.	16	F12	61.19 N	16.27 E
Voyageurs National Park, p.o.i., Mn., U.S.	128	C6	48.30 N	93.00 W
Vöyri, Fin.	18	D9	63.09 N	22.15 E
Vozdvyzhivka, Ukr.	38	F15	47.41 N	36.05 E
Vože, ozero, l., Russia	18	G26	60.36 N	39.00 E
Vožega, Russia	12	F19	60.28 N	40.12 E
Vožgaly, Russia	40	B17	58.08 N	50.11 E
Vožgora, Russia	12	D23	64.32 N	48.25 E
Voznesene, Russia	18	G22	60.59 N	35.28 E
Voznesenka, Ukr.	38	G14	46.51 N	35.27 E
Voznesens'k, Ukr.	38	F10	47.34 N	31.20 E
Voznesenskoe, Russia	40	D13	54.53 N	42.45 E
Vozroždenie, Russia	40	E15	52.41 N	48.11 E
Vozroždenija, ostrov, i., Asia	48	E9	45.13 N	59.07 E
Vozsiiats'ke, Ukr.	38	F11	47.40 N	32.06 E
Vrå, Den.	16	J7	57.21 N	9.57 E
Vráble, Slvk.	24	H14	48.14 N	18.19 E
Vraca, Blg.	36	F10	43.12 N	23.33 E
Vrådal, Nor.	16	H6	59.20 N	8.25 E
Vradyïvka, Ukr.	38	F9	47.51 N	30.36 E
Vrancea, state, Rom.	36	D13	45.45 N	27.00 E
Vrancei, Munții, mts., Rom.	36	D13	45.44 N	26.24 E
Vrangelja, ostrov (Wrangel Island), i., Russia	50	B24	71.14 N	179.21 W
Vranje, Yugo.	36	G8	42.33 N	21.54 E
Vranov nad Toplou, Czech Rep.	24	H11	48.53 N	15.48 E
Vrbas, Yugo.	36	D6	45.34 N	19.38 E
Vrbas, stm., Bos.	36	E4	45.06 N	17.30 E
Vrbovec, Cro.	30	E13	45.54 N	16.25 E
Vrbovsko, Cro.	30	E12	45.23 N	15.05 E
Vrchlabí, Czech Rep.	24	F11	50.37 N	15.37 E
Vrede, S. Afr.	90	E9	27.25 S	29.09 E
Vredefort, S. Afr.	90	E8	27.00 S	27.22 E
Vredenburg, S. Afr.	90	H3	32.54 S	17.59 E
Vredenburgh, Al., U.S.	134	F11	31.49 N	87.19 W
Vredenburg-Saldanha see Vredenburg, S. Afr.	90	H3	32.54 S	17.59 E
Vredendal, S. Afr.	90	G4	31.38 S	18.31 E
Vrena, Swe.	16	I14	58.52 N	16.41 E
Vriddhāchalam, India	69	F4	11.30 N	79.20 E
Vrigstad, Swe.	16	J12	57.21 N	14.29 E
Vrilíssia, Grc.	185c		38.02 N	23.50 E
Vrindāvan, India	70	E6	27.34 N	77.41 E
Vrnograč, Bos.	36	D2	45.10 N	15.57 E
Vršac, Yugo.	36	D8	45.07 N	21.18 E
Vrútky, Slvk.	24	G14	49.07 N	18.54 E
Vryburg, S. Afr.	90	E7	26.57 S	24.44 E
Vryheid, S. Afr.	90	E10	27.46 S	30.47 E
Vselug, ozero, l., Russia	26	C15	57.03 N	32.42 E
Vsetín, Czech Rep.	24	G13	49.20 N	18.00 E
Vsevidof, Mount, mtn., Ak., U.S.	109	F6	53.08 N	168.37 W
Vsevoložsk, Russia	18	G17	60.01 N	30.39 E
Vsevoložsk, Russia	183a		60.01 N	30.40 E
Vshody, Russia	26	F17	54.40 N	34.05 E
Vtoroe Potapovo, Russia	183b		55.56 N	37.58 E
Vtorye Levye Lamki, Russia	40	E12	53.15 N	41.03 E
Vučitrn, Yugo.	36	G7	42.49 N	20.58 E
Vuhlehirs'k, Ukr.	38	E17	48.18 N	38.17 E
Vuhle-Zavod, Ukr.	38	A11	52.11 N	32.53 E
Vukovar, Cro.	30	E16	45.20 N	19.00 E
Vulcan, Ab., Can.	144	F17	50.23 N	113.14 W
Vulcan, Rom.	36	D10	45.22 N	23.18 E
Vulcan, Mi., U.S.	126	C2	45.47 N	87.54 W
Vulcănești, Mol.	38	H7	45.41 N	28.24 E
Vulcano, Isola, i., Italy	32	F8	38.24 N	14.58 E
Vulkanichnyy khrebet, mts., Eur.	24	H18	48.26 N	23.07 E
Vulsino see Bolsena, Lago di, l., Italy	30	H9	42.36 N	11.56 E
Vung Tau, Viet.	64	G8	10.21 N	107.04 E
Vunidawa, Fiji	101e	p19	17.49 S	178.19 E
Vunisea, Fiji	101e	q19	19.03 S	178.09 E
Vuoggatjålme, Swe.	14	F7	66.37 N	16.18 E
Vuohijärvi, Fin.	18	F13	61.05 N	26.49 E
Vuohijärvi, l., Fin.	18	F12	61.12 N	26.41 E
Vuoksa, stm., Eur.	18	F15	61.03 N	30.11 E
Vuoksa, ozero, l., Russia	18	G16	60.40 N	29.53 E
Vuoksenniska, Fin.	18	F15	61.13 N	28.49 E
Vuoksi see Vuoksa, stm., Eur.	18	F15	61.03 N	30.11 E
Vuollerim, Swe.	14	F11	66.25 N	20.38 E
Vuolvojaure, l., Swe.	14	F9	66.25 N	18.29 E
Vuotso, Fin.	14	D17	68.08 N	27.08 E
Vuva, stm., Russia	14	D22	68.05 N	30.45 E
Vuyyūru, India	69	C5	16.22 N	80.51 E
Vyāra, India	70	H4	21.07 N	73.24 E
Vyborg (Viipuri), Russia	18	G15	60.42 N	28.45 E
Vyborgskij zaliv, b., Russia	18	G15	60.35 N	28.26 E
Vyčegda, stm., Russia	48	B7	61.16 N	46.36 E
Vyčegodskij, Russia	12	F22	61.14 N	46.54 E
Východoslovenský, state, Slvk.	24	H16	49.00 N	21.15 E
Vydrino, Russia	48	C17	56.50 N	99.02 E
Vyg, stm., Russia	18	D22	63.20 N	35.17 E
Vygoniči, Russia	26	G17	53.07 N	34.08 E
Vygozero, ozero, l., Russia	18	D21	63.35 N	34.42 E
Vyhanaščy, Bela.	26	H8	52.37 N	25.55 E
Vyhino, ngh., Russia	183b		55.43 N	37.48 E
Vyhoda, Ukr.	38	E2	48.55 N	23.54 E
Vyksa, Russia	40	D13	55.18 N	42.11 E
Vylkove, Ukr.	38	H8	45.24 N	29.37 E
Vym', stm., Russia	48	B8	62.12 N	50.23 E
Vynnyky, Ukr.	38	D3	49.48 N	24.09 E
Vynohradiv, Ukr.	38	E2	48.08 N	23.02 E
Vypolzovo, Russia	26	C16	57.52 N	33.42 E
Vyrica, Russia	26	A13	59.23 N	30.20 E
Vyša, Russia	40	E13	53.52 N	42.24 E
Vyšgorodok, Russia	26	C11	57.02 N	28.01 E
Vyshcha Dubechnia, Ukr.	38	C9	50.44 N	30.40 E
Vyshkivs'kï, pereval, p., Ukr.	38	E2	48.50 N	23.30 E
Vyshneve, Ukr.	38	E12	48.26 N	33.55 E
Vyshnivets', Ukr.	38	D4	49.54 N	25.45 E
Vyška, Russia	26	C18	57.31 N	35.58 E
Vyskod', Russia	26	C13	57.45 N	30.06 E
Vyškov, Czech Rep.	24	G12	49.16 N	16.59 E
Vyškov, Russia	26	H14	52.28 N	31.41 E
Vyšneol'šanoe, Russia	26	H20	52.08 N	37.39 E
Vyšnevolockoe vodohranilišče, res., Russia	26	C16	57.35 N	34.28 E
Vyšnij Voločok, Russia	26	C17	57.35 N	34.34 E
Vysock, Russia	18	G15	60.37 N	28.32 E
Vysokae, Bela.	26	H6	52.21 N	23.22 E
Vysoké Mýto, Czech Rep.	24	G12	49.57 N	16.09 E
Vysokiniči, Russia	26	F19	54.54 N	36.55 E
Vysokoe, Russia	26	D17	56.42 N	34.55 E
Vysokoe, Russia	26	F16	54.01 N	33.46 E
Vysokoe, Russia	183b		55.59 N	37.09 E
Vysokogornyj, Russia	50	G16	50.05 N	139.08 E
Vysokopillia, Ukr.	38	F12	47.29 N	33.32 E
Vysokovsk, Russia	26	D19	56.19 N	36.34 E
Vysots'k, Ukr.	38	B5	51.43 N	26.39 E
Vyšší Brod, Czech Rep.	24	H10	48.37 N	14.18 E
Vystupovychi, Ukr.	38	B8	51.34 N	29.05 E
Vysun', stm., Ukr.	38	F11	47.07 N	32.54 E
Vytebet', stm., Russia	26	G18	53.52 N	35.39 E
Vytegra, Russia	18	F23	61.00 N	36.27 E
Vytiazivka, Ukr.	38	F11	48.00 N	31.54 E
Vyzhivka, stm., Ukr.	38	B3	51.41 N	24.35 E
Vyzhnytsia, Ukr.	38	E4	48.14 N	25.11 E
Vzvad, Russia	26	B14	58.09 N	31.27 E

W

Name	Page	Map Ref.	Latitude	Longitude
Wa, Ghana	84	G4	10.03 N	2.29 W
Waackaack Creek, stm., N.J., U.S.	194		40.27 N	74.08 W
Waajid, Som.	86	D8	3.48 N	43.09 E
Waal, stm., Neth.	20	C14	51.49 N	5.00 E
Waalwijk, Neth.	20	C14	51.41 N	5.04 E
Wabag, Pap. N. Gui.	101a	b3	5.30 S	143.43 E
Wabakimi Lake, l., On., Can.	128	A8	50.40 N	89.59 W
Wabakimi Provincial Park, p.o.i., On., Can.	128	A9	50.32 N	89.39 W

Name	Page	Map Ref.	Latitude	Longitude
Wabamun, Ab., Can.	144	C16	53.33 N	114.31 W
Wabamun Indian Reserve, ind. res., Ab., Can.	144	C16	53.30 N	114.25 W
Wabamun Lake, l., Ab., Can.	144	C16	53.33 N	114.35 W
Waban, Ma., U.S.	201		42.20 N	71.14 W
Waban, Lake, l., Ma., U.S.	201		42.17 N	71.17 W
Wabana, Nf., Can.	111a	j23	47.38 N	52.57 W
Wabasca, stm., Ab., Can.	110	D7	58.21 N	115.20 W
Wabasca-Desmarais, Ab., Can.	110	D8	55.57 N	113.51 W
Wabash, In., U.S.	130	D12	40.47 N	85.48 W
Wabash, stm., U.S.	130	F9	37.47 N	88.01 W
Wabasha, Mn., U.S.	128	G6	44.22 N	92.02 W
Wabasso, Fl., U.S.	132	I5	27.45 N	80.26 W
Wabasso, Mn., U.S.	128	G3	44.23 N	95.15 W
Wabeno, Wi., U.S.	128	F10	45.27 N	88.39 W
Wabera, Eth.	82	F8	6.25 N	40.45 E
Wabigoon Lake, l., On., Can.	128	B6	49.46 N	92.40 W
Wabowden, Mb., Can.	110	E11	54.54 N	98.36 W
Wabrah, well, Sau. Ar.	74	G10	27.26 N	47.22 E
Wąbrzeźno, Pol.	24	C14	53.16 N	18.57 E
Wabu Hu, l., China	58	E7	32.23 N	116.54 E
Waccamaw, stm., U.S.	132	C6	33.36 N	79.06 W
Waccamaw, Lake, l., N.C., U.S.	132	B7	34.17 N	78.30 W
Waccasassa Bay, b., Fl., U.S.	132	G3	29.06 N	82.52 W
Wachapreague, Va., U.S.	124	G10	37.36 N	75.41 W
Wachau, reg., Aus.	30	B12	48.18 N	15.24 E
Wachock, Klasztory, rel., Pol.	24	E17	51.05 N	21.01 E
Wachusett Mountain, mtn., Ma., U.S.	124	B14	42.29 N	71.53 W
Wacissa, Fl., U.S.	132	F2	30.21 N	83.59 W
Waco, Tx., U.S.	136	C10	31.33 N	97.09 W
Waco Lake, res., Tx., U.S.	136	C10	31.34 N	97.13 W
Waconda Lake, res., Ks., U.S.	138	B10	39.30 N	98.24 W
Waconia, Mn., U.S.	128	G5	44.50 N	93.47 W
Wada, Japan	186		35.12 N	139.38 E
Wada, Japan	188		34.33 N	135.55 E
Wadayama, Japan	56	D7	35.19 N	134.52 E
Wad Bandah, Sudan	82	E5	13.06 N	27.56 E
Wadbilliga National Park, p.o.i., Austl.	98	K7	36.22 S	149.36 E
Waddān, Libya	82	B3	29.10 N	16.09 E
Waddeneilanden see West Friese Eilanden, is., Neth.	20	A14	53.26 N	5.30 E
Waddenzee, strt., Neth.	20	A14	53.15 N	5.15 E
Waddington, N.Y., U.S.	126	D14	44.51 N	75.11 W
Waddington, Mount, mtn., B.C., Can.	144	E5	51.22 N	125.16 W
Wadena, Sk., Can.	142	C10	51.55 N	103.47 W
Wadena, Mn., U.S.	128	E3	46.26 N	95.08 W
Wädenswil, Switz.	24	I4	47.14 N	8.40 E
Wadesboro, N.C., U.S.	132	B5	34.58 N	80.04 W
Wadeville, S. Afr.	191d		26.16 S	28.11 E
Wadhams, B.C., Can.	144	E3	51.29 N	127.30 W
Wādī as-Sīr, Jord.	76	G6	31.57 N	35.49 E
Wādī Gimāl, Gezîret, i., Egypt	74	H4	24.39 N	35.09 E
Wādī Halfā', Sudan	82	C6	21.47 N	31.20 E
Wading, stm., Ma., U.S.	201		41.56 N	71.13 W
Wadley, Al., U.S.	134	D13	33.07 N	85.34 W
Wadley, Ga., U.S.	132	D3	32.51 N	82.24 W
Wad Madanī, Sudan	82	E6	14.23 N	33.31 E
Wadowice, Pol.	24	G15	49.53 N	19.29 E
Wadsworth, Nv., U.S.	148	D6	39.38 N	119.17 W
Wadsworth, Oh., U.S.	124	C4	41.01 N	81.43 W
Wadsworth Moor, for., Eng., U.K.	180		53.48 N	2.02 W
Waegwan, Kor., S.	56	D1	35.59 N	128.24 E
Waelder, Tx., U.S.	136	E10	29.42 N	97.18 W
Wafangdian, China	58	B9	39.37 N	122.00 E
Wafrah, Kuw.	74	F10	28.33 N	48.02 E
Wagadugu see Ouagadougou, Burkina	84	G4	12.22 N	1.32 W
Wageningen, Neth.	20	C14	51.58 N	5.40 E
Wager Bay, b., Nu., Can.	110	B13	65.26 N	88.40 W
Waggaman Heights, Md., U.S.	202c		38.49 N	76.57 W
Wagga Wagga, Austl.	98	J6	35.07 S	147.21 E
Wagin, Austl.	96	F3	33.18 S	117.20 E
Waging am See, Ger.	24	I8	47.56 N	12.43 E
Waginger See, l., Ger.	30	C9	47.56 N	12.47 E
Waglan Island, i., China	189d		22.11 N	114.18 E
Wagner, S.D., U.S.	140	D14	43.04 N	98.17 W
Wagner College, educ., N.Y., U.S.	194		40.37 N	74.07 W
Wagoner, Ok., U.S.	130	I2	35.58 N	95.23 W
Wagon Mound, N.M., U.S.	138	F4	36.00 N	104.42 W
Wagontire Mountain, mtn., Or., U.S.	146	G7	43.21 N	119.53 W
Wagrien, reg., Ger.	24	B6	54.16 N	10.52 E
Wągrowiec, Pol.	24	D13	52.48 N	17.13 E
Waha, Libya	82	B4	28.16 N	19.54 E
Wahai, Indon.	60	F8	2.48 S	129.31 E
Wāh Cantonment, Pak.	70	B4	33.47 N	72.40 E
Wahiawa, Hi., U.S.	100a	b3	21.30 N	158.01 W
Wahoo, Ne., U.S.	128	J2	41.12 N	96.37 W
Wahpeton, N.D., U.S.	128	E2	46.15 N	96.35 W
Wahran (Oran), Alg.	84	B4	35.41 N	0.39 W
Währing, ngh., Aus.	182b		48.14 N	16.21 E
Wahroonga, Austl.	192a		33.43 S	151.07 E
Wahweap Creek, stm., Ut., U.S.	150	F5	37.00 N	111.27 W
Wai, India	69	B1	17.58 N	73.54 E
Waialeale, mtn., Hi., U.S.	100a	a2	22.04 N	159.30 W
Waialua, Hi., U.S.	100a	b3	21.34 N	158.08 W
Waianae, Hi., U.S.	100a	b3	21.26 N	158.11 W
Waiau, N.Z.	102	F5	42.39 S	173.03 E
Waiau, stm., N.Z.	102	F5	42.35 S	172.51 E
Waiau, stm., N.Z.	102	G2	46.08 S	167.40 E
Waiblingen, Ger.	24	H5	48.49 N	9.18 E
Waidhān, India	70	F9	24.04 N	82.39 E
Waidhofen an der Thaya, Aus.	30	B12	48.48 N	15.17 E
Waidhofen an der Ybbs, Aus.	30	C11	47.57 N	14.46 E
Waidmannslust, ngh., Ger.	182a		52.36 N	13.20 E
Waigeo, Pulau, i., Indon.	60	E9	0.10 S	130.55 E
Waihi, N.Z.	102	C6	37.23 S	175.50 E
Waikabubak, Indon.	66	H11	9.37 S	119.25 E
Waikato, stm., N.Z.	102	C6	37.22 S	174.43 E
Waikelo, Indon.	66	H11	9.25 S	119.14 E
Waikerie, Austl.	98	J2	34.11 S	139.59 E
Wailuku, Hi., U.S.	100a	c5	20.53 N	156.30 W
Waimangura, Indon.	66	H11	9.30 S	119.13 E
Waimate, N.Z.	102	G4	44.44 S	171.01 E
Waimea, Hi., U.S.	100a	a2	21.58 N	159.40 W
Waimea see Kamuela, Hi., U.S.	100a	d6	20.01 N	155.39 W
Wainganga, stm., India	70	H7	20.39 N	79.46 E
Waingapu, Indon.	66	H12	9.39 S	120.16 E
Waini, stm., Guy.	168	D12	8.20 N	59.44 W
Wainscott, Eng., U.K.	178		51.25 N	0.31 E
Wainstalls, Eng., U.K.	180		53.45 N	1.56 W
Wainunu Bay, b., Fiji	101e	p19	16.55 S	178.53 E
Wainwright, Ab., Can.	142	B3	52.50 N	110.50 W
Wainwright, Ak., U.S.	109	B7	70.38 N	159.59 W
Waipara, N.Z.	102	F5	43.03 S	172.44 E
Waipukurau, N.Z.	102	E7	39.59 S	176.34 E
Wairarapa, Lake, l., N.Z.	102	E6	41.13 S	175.15 E
Wairau, stm., N.Z.	102	E5	41.26 S	174.01 E
Wairoa, N.Z.	102	D7	39.01 S	177.24 E
Wairoa, stm., N.Z.	102	D7	39.03 S	177.26 E
Wairoa, stm., N.Z.	102	B6	36.06 S	173.57 E
Waisisi, Vanuatu	101d	I17	19.29 S	169.24 E
Waitaki, stm., N.Z.	102	G4	44.56 S	171.08 E
Waitara, Austl.	192a		33.43 S	151.07 E
Waitara, N.Z.	102	D6	39.00 S	174.13 E
Waitemata, N.Z.	102	C6	36.55 S	174.40 E
Waite Park, Mn., U.S.	128	F4	45.33 N	94.13 W
Waitotara, N.Z.	102	D6	39.48 S	174.43 E
Waitsburg, Wa., U.S.	146	D8	46.16 N	118.08 W
Waitzen see Vác, Hung.	36	B6	47.47 N	19.07 E
Waiuku, N.Z.	102	C6	37.15 S	174.43 E
Waiwo, Indon.	60	F9	0.56 S	131.02 E
Wajima, Japan	56	B9	37.23 N	136.54 E
Wajir, Kenya	86	D8	1.45 N	40.04 E
Waka, D.R.C.	86	D4	1.02 N	20.13 E
Waka, Eth.	82	F7	7.10 N	37.21 E
Waka, Tx., U.S.	138	E7	36.17 N	101.03 W
Wakakusa-yama, hill, Japan	188		34.42 N	135.52 E
Wakamatsu see Aizu-wakamatsu, Japan	56	B12	37.29 N	139.55 E
Wakarusa, In., U.S.	130	C11	41.31 N	86.03 W
Wakarusa, stm., Ks., U.S.	130	F2	38.57 N	95.05 W
Wakasa-wan, b., Japan	56	D8	35.45 N	135.40 E
Wakatipu, Lake, l., N.Z.	102	G3	45.05 S	168.34 E
Wakaw, Sk., Can.	142	B8	52.39 N	105.44 W
Wakaw Lake, l., Sk., Can.	142	B8	52.40 N	105.35 W
Wakayama, Japan	56	E8	34.13 N	135.10 E
Wakayama, state, Japan	56	F8	34.00 N	135.20 E
Wakayanagi, Japan	56	A14	38.46 N	141.08 E
WaKeeney, Ks., U.S.	138	B9	39.01 N	99.53 W
Wakefield, Eng., U.K.	10	H11	53.40 N	1.29 W
Wakefield, Ks., U.S.	138	B11	39.12 N	97.01 W
Wakefield, Ne., U.S.	140	E16	42.16 N	96.51 W
Wakefield, R.I., U.S.	124	C14	41.26 N	71.30 W
Wakefield, Va., U.S.	124	H8	36.58 N	76.59 W
Wakefield Forest, Va., U.S.	202c		38.50 N	77.14 W
Wake Forest, N.C., U.S.	124	I7	35.58 N	78.30 W
Wake Island, dep., Oc.	92	B7	19.17 N	166.36 E
Wake Island, at., Wake I.	94	B7	19.18 N	166.38 E
Wakema, Mya.	64	D2	16.36 N	95.11 E
Wakeman, stm., B.C., Can.	144	E4	51.13 N	126.31 W
Wakenda Creek, stm., Mo., U.S.	130	E4	39.18 N	93.16 W
Wake Village, Tx., U.S.	134	D4	33.25 N	94.06 W
Wakhān see Vākhān, hist. reg., Afg.	72	B11	37.00 N	73.00 E
Waki, Japan	56	E7	34.04 N	134.09 E
Wakis, Pap. N. Gui.	101a	b5	6.13 S	150.17 E
Wakita, Ok., U.S.	138	E11	36.53 N	97.55 W
Wakkanai, Japan	54	B14	45.24 N	141.40 E
Wakkerstroom, S. Afr.	90	E10	27.19 S	30.08 E
Wakō, Japan	186		35.47 N	139.37 E
Wakomata Lake, l., On., Can.	126	B6	46.34 N	83.22 W
Wakonassin, stm., On., Can.	126	B7	46.27 N	81.51 W
Wakonda, S.D., U.S.	140	E15	43.00 N	97.05 W
Waku Kungo, Ang.	88	C2	11.23 S	15.08 E
Walachia, hist. reg., Rom.	36	E11	44.00 N	25.00 E
Walanae, stm., Indon.	66	F12	4.07 S	119.58 E
Walawe, stm., Sri L.	66	F5	6.07 N	81.01 E
Wałbrzych, Pol.	24	F12	50.46 N	16.17 E
Walcha, Austl.	98	H8	30.59 S	151.35 E
Walchensee, l., Ger.	30	C8	47.35 N	11.20 E
Walcott, B.C., Can.	144	B4	54.31 N	126.51 W
Walcott, Ia., U.S.	130	C7	41.35 N	90.46 W
Walcott, N.D., U.S.	128	E1	46.33 N	96.56 W
Walcott, Lake, res., Id., U.S.	146	H13	42.40 N	113.22 W
Wałcz, Pol.	24	C12	53.16 N	16.28 E
Wald, ngh., Ger.	181		51.11 N	7.03 E
Waldbauer, ngh., Ger.	181		51.18 N	7.28 E
Waldbröl, Ger.	24	F3	50.52 N	7.37 E
Walden, On., Can.	126	B8	46.23 N	81.23 W
Walden, Co., U.S.	150	C10	40.43 N	106.17 W
Walden, N.Y., U.S.	124	C11	41.33 N	74.11 W
Walden, Lake, l., Mi., U.S.	199		42.39 N	83.46 W
Waldenburg see Wałbrzych, Pol.	24	F12	50.46 N	16.17 E
Walden Pond, l., Ma., U.S.	201		42.28 N	71.00 W
Walden Pond, l., Ma., U.S.	201		42.26 N	71.20 W
Walden Ridge, mts., Tn., U.S.	134	B13	35.31 N	85.13 W
Walderslade, Eng., U.K.	178		51.21 N	0.32 E
Waldheim, Sk., Can.	142	B7	52.37 N	106.38 W
Waldkirchen, Ger.	24	H9	48.44 N	13.37 E
Waldkraiburg, Ger.	30	B9	48.12 N	12.26 E
Waldmünchen, Ger.	24	G8	49.22 N	12.42 E
Waldo, B.C., Can.	144	G15	49.11 N	115.11 W
Waldo, Ar., U.S.	134	D5	33.21 N	93.18 W
Waldoboro, Me., U.S.	122	F7	44.06 N	69.23 W
Waldo Lake, l., Ma., U.S.	201		42.07 N	71.03 W
Waldo Lake, l., Or., U.S.	146	G5	43.44 N	122.03 W
Waldorf, Md., U.S.	124	F9	38.37 N	76.54 W
Waldport, Or., U.S.	146	F2	44.25 N	124.03 W
Waldron, Sk., Can.	142	D11	50.51 N	102.29 W
Waldron, Ar., U.S.	134	C4	34.53 N	94.05 W
Waldron, In., U.S.	130	E12	39.27 N	85.39 W
Waldron, Mi., U.S.	124	C1	41.43 N	84.24 W
Waldshut-Tiengen, Ger.	24	I4	47.37 N	8.12 E
Waldviertel, reg., Aus.	30	B11	48.40 N	15.15 E
Waldwick, N.J., U.S.	194		41.00 N	74.07 W
Walenstadt, Switz.	24	I5	47.07 N	9.18 E
Wales, Ak., U.S.	109	C6	65.36 N	168.03 W
Wales, state, U.K.	10	I9	52.30 N	3.30 W
Wales Island, i., Nu., Can.	110	B13	68.00 N	86.43 W
Walewale, Ghana	84	G4	10.21 N	0.48 W
Walgett, Austl.	98	G6	30.01 S	148.06 E
Walgreen Coast, cst., Ant.	103	C30	75.35 S	101.21 W
Walhachin, B.C., Can.	144	F10	50.45 N	120.59 W
Walhalla, N.D., U.S.	142	F15	48.55 N	97.55 W
Walhalla, S.C., U.S.	132	B2	34.46 N	83.03 W
Walhalla, hist., Ger.	24	G8	49.03 N	12.15 E
Walikale, D.R.C.	86	E5	1.25 S	28.03 E
Walker, Ia., U.S.	130	B6	42.17 N	91.46 W
Walker, Mn., U.S.	128	D4	47.05 N	94.34 W
Walker, stm., Nv., U.S.	148	D7	38.49 N	118.45 W
Walker Bay, b., S. Afr.	90	I4	34.30 S	19.17 E
Walker Creek, stm., Az., U.S.	150	G7	36.57 N	109.41 W
Walker Creek, stm., Ma., U.S.	201		42.38 N	70.44 W
Walker Creek, stm., Wy., U.S.	140	D8	43.08 N	104.52 W
Walker Lake, l., Nv., U.S.	148	E7	38.44 N	118.43 W
Walkers Mill, Pa., U.S.	197b		40.24 N	80.08 W
Walkerton, On., Can.	126	D8	44.07 N	81.08 W
Walkerton, In., U.S.	130	C11	41.28 N	86.28 W
Walkertown, N.C., U.S.	124	H5	36.10 N	80.09 W
Walkerville, Mt., U.S.	146	D14	46.02 N	112.31 W
Walk Mill, Eng., U.K.	180		53.46 N	2.12 W
Wall, Pa., U.S.	197b		40.24 N	79.47 W
Wall, S.D., U.S.	140	D10	43.59 N	102.13 W
Wallace, Id., U.S.	146	C11	47.28 N	115.55 W
Wallace, Ne., U.S.	140	G11	40.49 N	101.09 W
Wallace, N.C., U.S.	132	B7	34.44 N	77.59 W
Wallaceburg, On., Can.	126	F7	42.35 N	82.22 W
Wallace Lake, l., Oh., U.S.	197a		41.22 N	81.52 W
Wallace Lake, res., La., U.S.	134	E5	32.20 N	93.45 W
Wallach, Ger.	181		51.35 N	6.34 E
Wallal Downs, Austl.	96	C4	19.47 S	120.40 E
Wallam Creek, stm., Austl.	98	G6	28.48 S	147.16 E
Wallangarra, Austl.	98	G8	28.55 S	151.55 E
Wallaroo, Austl.	96	F7	33.56 S	137.37 E
Wallasey, Eng., U.K.	10	H9	53.25 N	3.03 W
Walla Walla, Wa., U.S.	146	D8	46.04 N	118.19 W
Walled Lake, l., Mi., U.S.	199		42.31 N	83.29 W
Wallend, Eng., U.K.	178		51.27 N	0.42 E
Waller, Tx., U.S.	136	D12	30.03 N	95.55 W
Wallgrove, Austl.	192a		33.47 S	150.51 E
Wallhead Airport, arpt., Oh., U.S.	197a		41.21 N	82.09 W
Wallingford, Ct., U.S.	124	C13	41.27 N	72.49 W
Wallingford, Pa., U.S.	203		39.54 N	75.22 W
Wallingford, Vt., U.S.	122	G4	43.28 N	72.58 W
Wallington, N.J., U.S.	194		40.51 N	74.06 W
Wallington, ngh., Eng., U.K.	178		51.21 N	0.09 W
Wallis, Tx., U.S.	136	E11	29.37 N	96.03 W
Wallis, Îles, is., Wal./F.	94	E9	13.18 S	176.10 W
Wallis and Futuna, dep., Oc.	92	E9	14.00 S	177.00 W
Walliser Alpen see Pennine Alps, mts., Eur.	30	D4	46.05 N	7.49 E
Wallis et Futuna see Wallis and Futuna, dep., Oc.	92	E9	14.00 S	177.00 W
Wallisville Lake, res., Tx., U.S.	136	E13	29.50 N	94.45 W
Wallkill, stm., U.S.	194		41.11 N	74.35 W
Wallkill, Wildcat Branch, stm., N.J., U.S.	194		41.07 N	74.36 W
Wall Lake, Ia., U.S.	128	I3	42.16 N	95.05 W
Wallmer Bridge, Eng., U.K.	180		53.43 N	2.48 W
Wallowa, Or., U.S.	146	E9	45.34 N	117.31 W
Wallowa, stm., Or., U.S.	146	E9	45.43 N	117.47 W
Wallowa Mountains, mts., Or., U.S.	146	E9	45.16 N	117.20 W
Walls, Ms., U.S.	134	C8	34.57 N	90.09 W
Walls of Jericho National Park, p.o.i., Austl.	99a	n13	41.45 S	146.18 E
Walmersley, Eng., U.K.	180		53.37 N	2.18 W
Walnut, Il., U.S.	130	C8	41.33 N	89.34 W
Walnut, Ia., U.S.	130	C2	41.28 N	95.13 W
Walnut, Ks., U.S.	130	G2	37.36 N	95.04 W
Walnut, Ms., U.S.	134	C10	34.56 N	88.53 W
Walnut, N.C., U.S.	124	I3	35.51 N	82.44 W
Walnut, stm., Ks., U.S.	138	D11	37.02 N	97.00 W
Walnut Canyon National Monument, p.o.i., Az., U.S.	150	H5	35.10 N	111.31 W
Walnut Canyon Reservoir, res., Ca., U.S.	198		33.50 N	117.45 W
Walnut Cove, N.C., U.S.	124	H5	36.17 N	80.08 W
Walnut Creek, stm., Ca., U.S.	198		34.03 N	118.01 W
Walnut Creek, stm., Ca., U.S.	200		37.54 N	122.03 W
Walnut Creek, stm., Ks., U.S.	138	C9	38.21 N	98.41 W
Walnut Creek, stm., Oh., U.S.	130	E15	39.40 N	82.59 W
Walnut Creek, Middle Fork, stm., Ks., U.S.	138	C8	38.31 N	100.08 W
Walnut Creek, South Fork, stm., Ks., U.S.	138	C8	38.25 N	99.53 W
Walnut Grove, Mn., U.S.	128	G3	44.13 N	95.28 W
Walnut Grove, Ms., U.S.	134	E9	32.35 N	89.28 W
Walnut Heights, Ca., U.S.	200		37.53 N	122.08 W
Walnut Lake, Mi., U.S.	199		42.33 N	83.19 W
Walnut Lake, l., Mi., U.S.	199		42.33 N	83.20 W
Walnut Park, Ca., U.S.	198		33.58 N	118.13 W
Walnut Ridge, Ar., U.S.	130	H7	36.03 N	90.57 W
Walnut Springs, Tx., U.S.	136	B10	32.03 N	97.45 W
Walpert Ridge, mtn., Ca., U.S.	200		37.38 N	122.00 W
Walpeup, Austl.	98	J3	35.08 S	142.01 E
Walpole, Austl.	96	G3	34.58 S	116.44 E
Walpole, N.H., U.S.	122	G4	43.05 N	72.25 W
Walsall, Eng., U.K.	10	I11	52.35 N	1.58 W
Walsden, Eng., U.K.	180		53.42 N	2.06 W
Walsenburg, Co., U.S.	138	D4	37.37 N	104.46 W
Walsh, Austl.	96	C8	16.39 S	143.54 E
Walsh, Ab., Can.	142	E3	49.57 N	110.03 W
Walsh, Co., U.S.	138	D6	37.23 N	102.16 W
Walsh, stm., Austl.	98	A5	17.06 S	145.00 E
Walshaw Dean Reservoirs, res., Eng., U.K.	180		53.48 N	2.03 W
Walsingham, Cape, c., Nu., Can.	108	D13	66.02 N	61.58 W
Walsrode, Ger.	24	D5	52.51 N	9.35 E
Walterboro, S.C., U.S.	132	D5	32.54 N	80.40 W
Walter Reed Army Medical Center, bldg., D.C., U.S.	202c		38.58 N	77.02 W
Walters, Ok., U.S.	138	G10	34.21 N	98.18 W
Waltersdorf, Ger.	182a		52.22 N	13.35 E
Waltershausen, Ger.	24	F6	50.54 N	10.33 E
Waltersville, Ms., U.S.	134	E8	32.22 N	90.52 W
Walthall, Ms., U.S.	134	D9	33.36 N	89.16 W
Walthamstow, ngh., Eng., U.K.	178		51.35 N	0.01 W
Walthill, Ne., U.S.	130	B1	42.08 N	96.28 W
Walton, N.S., Can.	122	E13	45.13 N	64.00 W
Walton, In., U.S.	130	D11	40.39 N	86.14 W
Walton, Ky., U.S.	124	F1	38.52 N	84.36 W
Walton, N.Y., U.S.	124	B10	42.10 N	75.08 W
Walton on the Hill, Eng., U.K.	178		51.17 N	0.15 W
Walton Run, stm., Pa., U.S.	203		40.05 N	74.59 W
Walt Whitman Bridge, trans., U.S.	203		39.54 N	75.08 W
Walt Whitman Homes, N.J., U.S.	203		39.52 N	75.11 W
Walt Whitman House State Historic Site, hist., N.Y., U.S.	194		40.49 N	73.25 W
Walt Whitman Mall, shp. cen., N.Y., U.S.	194		40.50 N	73.25 W
Walvisbaai see Walvis Bay, Nmb.	90	C2	22.57 S	14.31 E
Walvis Bay (Walvisbaai), Nmb.	90	C2	22.57 S	14.31 E
Walvis Bay, b., Nmb.	90	C2	22.51 S	14.29 E
Walvis Ridge, unds.	176	K14	28.00 S	3.00 E
Walwen, Wales, U.K.	180		53.14 N	3.15 W
Walworth, Wi., U.S.	130	B9	42.31 N	88.36 W
Walze, Ger.	181		51.16 N	7.31 E
Wamba, D.R.C.	86	D5	2.08 N	28.00 E
Wamba, Nig.	84	H6	8.57 N	8.37 E
Wamba (Uamba), stm., Afr.	86	F3	3.56 S	17.12 E
Wambel, ngh., Ger.	181		51.32 N	7.32 E
Wamego, Ks., U.S.	130	E1	39.12 N	96.18 W
Wamesit, Ma., U.S.	201		42.37 N	71.15 W
Wamma, stm., Indon.	60	F10	3.22 S	135.09 E
Wampsville, N.Y., U.S.	124	A10	43.04 N	75.42 W
Wampú, Hond.	156	E5	14.58 N	84.57 W
Wampú, stm., Hond.	156	E5	14.57 N	84.58 W
Wampum, Pa., U.S.	124	D5	40.53 N	80.20 W
Wampus, stm., N.Y., U.S.	194		41.07 N	73.43 W
Wampus Lake Reservoir, res., N.Y., U.S.	194		41.09 N	73.43 W
Wamsutter, Wy., U.S.	150	B9	41.40 N	107.58 W
Wanaaring, Austl.	98	G4	29.42 S	144.09 E
Wanaka, N.Z.	102	G3	44.42 S	169.07 E
Wanaka, Lake, l., N.Z.	102	G3	44.30 S	169.08 E
Wanamingo, Mn., U.S.	128	G6	44.18 N	92.48 W
Wan'an, China	58	H6	26.30 N	114.49 E
Wanapa, Neth. Ant.	158g	p23	12.06 N	68.14 W
Wanapitei, stm., On., Can.	126	B9	46.07 N	80.47 W
Wanapitei Lake, l., On., Can.	126	B9	46.45 N	80.45 W
Wanaque, stm., N.J., U.S.	194		40.58 N	74.17 W
Wanbaoshan, China	54	B6	44.12 N	125.11 E
Wanbi, Austl.	98	J3	34.46 S	140.19 E
Wanblee, S.D., U.S.	140	D11	43.32 N	101.40 W
Wanchese, N.C., U.S.	124	I10	35.50 N	75.38 W
Wandel Hav, s., Grnld.	108	A22	82.15 N	17.00 W
Wandering, stm., Ab., Can.	144	A18	55.13 N	112.26 W
Wandhofen, Ger.	181		51.26 N	7.33 E
Wandlitzer See, l., Ger.	182a		52.46 N	13.27 E
Wandoan, Austl.	98	F7	26.07 S	149.57 E
Wanette, Ok., U.S.	138	G11	34.57 N	97.01 W
Wanfoxia, China	52	C4	40.05 N	95.55 E
Wang, stm., Thai.	64	D4	17.07 N	99.04 E
Wanganui, N.Z.	102	D6	39.56 S	175.01 E
Wanganui, stm., N.Z.	102	D6	39.57 S	175.00 E
Wangaratta, Austl.	98	K6	36.21 S	146.19 E
Wang Chin, Thai.	64	D4	17.53 N	99.36 E
Wangcun, China	58	C7	36.40 N	117.40 E
Wangdu Phodrang, Bhu.	70	E12	27.28 N	89.55 E
Wangen im Allgäu, Ger.	20	G18	47.41 N	9.50 E
Wangerooge, i., Ger.	24	C3	53.47 N	7.53 E
Wanggao, China	58	I4	24.39 N	111.23 E
Wanggil-li, Kor., S.	189b		37.36 N	126.39 E
Wang Hin, Khlong, can., Thai.	187a		13.48 N	100.35 E
Wangiwangi, Pulau, i., Indon.	60	G7	5.20 S	123.35 E
Wang Noi, Thai.	64	E5	14.12 N	100.39 E
Wangpan Yang, b., China	58	F9	30.30 N	121.46 E
Wangqing, China	52	C10	43.18 N	129.47 E
Wang Saphung, Thai.	64	D5	17.18 N	101.46 E
Wangsim-ni, ngh., Kor., S.	189b		37.36 N	127.03 E
Wangtai, China	58	H7	26.39 N	117.58 E
Wangzhuangbu, China	58	B5	39.26 N	113.54 E
Wanhedian, China	58	E5	32.16 N	113.14 E
Wanheimerort, ngh., Ger.	181		51.24 N	6.46 E
Wani, India	69	A4	20.03 N	78.57 E
Wanie-Rukula, D.R.C.	86	D5	0.15 N	25.29 E
Wanigela, Pap. N. Gui.	101a	b4	9.20 S	149.10 E
Wanipigow, stm., Can.	142	C18	51.04 N	95.34 W
Wānkāner, India	70	G3	22.37 N	70.57 E
Wanli, Tai.	187d		25.11 N	121.41 E
Wān Namton, Mya.	64	A4	22.02 N	99.33 E
Wanneroo, Austl.	96	F3	31.45 S	115.48 E
Wannian, China	58	G7	28.42 N	117.05 E
Wanning, China	58	L4	18.48 N	110.23 E
Wanon Niwat, Thai.	64	D6	17.38 N	103.45 E
Wanparti, India	69	C4	16.21 N	78.04 E
Wansdorf, Ger.	182a		52.38 N	13.05 E
Wanstead, ngh., Eng., U.K.	178		51.34 N	0.02 E
Wantan, China	58	F4	30.02 N	110.17 E
Wantirna, Austl.	192b		37.51 S	145.14 E
Wantirna South, Austl.	192b		37.52 S	145.14 E
Wanxian, China	58	F3	30.48 N	108.22 E
Wanyuan, China	58	E3	32.03 N	108.02 E
Wanzai, China	58	G6	28.05 N	114.27 E
Wanzleben, Ger.	24	D7	52.03 N	11.27 E
Wapakoneta, Oh., U.S.	124	D1	40.34 N	84.11 W
Wapanucka, Ok., U.S.	134	C2	34.22 N	96.25 W
Wapato, Wa., U.S.	146	D6	46.26 N	120.24 W
Wapella, Sk., Can.	142	D11	50.15 N	102.00 W
Wapello, Ia., U.S.	130	C6	41.10 N	91.11 W
Wapesi Lake, l., On., Can.	128	A6	50.34 N	92.21 W
Wāpi, India	70	H4	20.22 N	72.54 E
Wapiti, stm., Can.	144	A12	55.08 N	118.18 W
Wappingers Falls, N.Y., U.S.	124	C12	41.36 N	73.55 W
Wapsipinicon, stm., U.S.	128	J8	41.43 N	90.18 W
War, W.V., U.S.	124	G4	37.17 N	81.42 W
Warangal, India	69	B4	18.00 N	79.35 E
Wārāseoni, India	70	H7	21.45 N	80.03 E
Waratah, Austl.	99a	n12	41.27 S	145.32 E
Waratah Bay, b., Austl.	98	L5	38.51 S	146.04 E
Warbreccan, Austl.	98	E4	24.19 S	142.50 E
Warburg, Ger.	24	E5	51.29 N	9.08 E
Warburton, Austl.	98	K5	37.45 S	145.41 E
Warburton, Eng., U.K.	180		53.24 N	2.27 W
Warburton Bay, b., N.T., Can.	110	C8	64.02 N	110.21 W
Ward, Pa., U.S.	203		39.53 N	75.31 W
Ward, stm., Austl.	98	E6	26.25 S	146.05 E
Warden, S. Afr.	90	E9	27.51 S	28.58 E
Warden, Wa., U.S.	146	C8	46.58 N	119.02 W
Wardha, India	70	H7	20.44 N	78.36 E
Wardha, stm., India	70	H7	19.36 N	79.46 E
Ward Hill, hill, Scot., U.K.	10	C9	58.53 N	3.22 W
Wardlow, Ab., Can.	144	F19	50.55 N	111.33 W
Ward Mountain, mtn., Mt., U.S.	146	D12	46.10 N	114.17 W
Wardner, B.C., Can.	144	G15	49.25 N	115.26 W
Wards Chapel, Md., U.S.	202b		39.24 N	76.52 W
Wards Island, i., N.Y., U.S.	194		40.47 N	73.56 W
Wardswell Draw, stm., U.S.	136	B5	32.39 N	102.35 W
Ware, stm., Ma., U.S.	124	B13	42.11 N	72.21 W
War Eagle Creek, stm., Ar., U.S.	134	A5	36.14 N	94.00 W
Wareham, Ma., U.S.	124	C15	41.45 N	70.43 W
Waremme, Bel.	20	D14	50.41 N	5.16 E
Waren, Ger.	24	C8	53.31 N	12.40 E
Waren, Indon.	60	F10	2.16 S	136.21 E
Warenai, stm., Indon.	60	F10	2.52 S	135.56 E
Warenda, Austl.	98	D3	22.37 S	140.32 E
Warendorf, Ger.	24	E3	51.57 N	7.59 E
Ware Shoals, S.C., U.S.	132	B3	34.23 N	82.14 W
Wargla, Alg.	84	C6	31.55 N	5.22 E
Warialda, Austl.	98	G8	29.32 S	150.34 E
Warinanco Park, p.o.i., N.J., U.S.	194		40.39 N	74.14 W
Warin Chamrap, Thai.	64	E7	15.11 N	104.52 E
Warka, Pol.	24	E17	51.47 N	21.12 E
Warkworth, On., Can.	126	D11	44.12 N	77.52 W
Warland, Eng., U.K.	180		53.41 N	2.05 W
Warland Reservoir, res., Eng., U.K.	180		53.41 N	2.04 W
Warley Moor Reservoir, res., Eng., U.K.	180		53.47 N	1.57 W
Warman, Sk., Can.	142	B7	52.18 N	106.34 W
Warmandi, Indon.	101a	a1	0.21 S	132.38 E
Warmbad, Nmb.	90	F4	28.26 S	18.45 E
Warmbad, S. Afr.	90	D9	24.53 S	28.18 E
Warm Baths see Warmbad, S. Afr.	90	D9	24.53 S	28.18 E
Warmińsko-Mazurskie, state, Pol.	24	C16	53.45 N	21.00 E
Warminster, Eng., U.K.	10	J10	51.12 N	2.11 W
Warminster, Pa., U.S.	124	D10	40.12 N	75.06 W
Warminster Naval Air Development Center, mil., Pa., U.S.	203		40.12 N	75.09 W
Warm Springs, Ga., U.S.	134	E14	32.53 N	84.40 W
Warm Springs, Mt., U.S.	146	D14	46.10 N	112.48 W
Warm Springs, Or., U.S.	146	F5	44.45 N	121.16 W
Warm Springs, Va., U.S.	124	F6	38.02 N	79.47 W
Warm Springs, stm., Or., U.S.	146	F5	44.51 N	121.04 W
Warm Springs Indian Reservation, ind. res., Or., U.S.	146	F5	44.52 N	121.23 W
Warm Springs Reservoir, res., Or., U.S.	146	G8	43.37 N	118.14 W
Warnemünde, ngh., Ger.	24	B7	54.10 N	12.04 E
Warner, Ab., Can.	144	G18	49.17 N	112.11 W
Warner, N.H., U.S.	122	G5	43.16 N	71.49 W
Warner, Ok., U.S.	134	B3	35.30 N	95.20 W
Warner Lakes, l., Or., U.S.	146	H6	42.24 N	119.49 W
Warner Mountains, mts., U.S.	148	B5	41.32 N	120.15 W
Warner Peak, mtn., Or., U.S.	148	A6	42.27 N	119.44 W
Warner Robins, Ga., U.S.	132	D2	32.37 N	83.35 W
Warners Pond, l., Ma., U.S.	201		42.28 N	71.24 W
Warnes, Arg.	172	G7	34.53 S	60.32 W
Warnes Brook, stm., N.Y., U.S.	194		40.25 N	74.18 W
Warnicken see Primore, Russia	26	F2	54.57 N	20.02 E
Warnow, stm., Ger.	24	B8	54.05 N	12.09 E
Warpath, stm., Mb., Can.	142	B15	52.20 N	98.25 W
Warra, Austl.	98	F8	26.56 S	150.55 E
Warracknabeal, Austl.	98	K4	36.15 S	142.23 E
Warragul, Austl.	98	L5	38.09 S	145.55 E
Warrandyte, Austl.	192b		37.45 S	145.13 E
Warrandyte South, Austl.	192b		37.46 S	145.14 E
Warrâq el-Arab, Egypt	191c		30.06 N	31.12 E
Warrâq el-Hadar, Gezîret, i., Egypt	191c		30.07 N	31.13 E
Warrâq el-Hadar Ambûbah Mit el-Nasâra, Egypt	191c		30.06 N	31.13 E
Warrawagine, Austl.	96	D4	20.51 S	120.43 E
Warrawee, Austl.	192a		33.44 S	151.07 E
Warrego, stm., Austl.	98	G5	30.24 S	145.21 E
Warrego Range, mts., Austl.	98	E6	24.50 S	146.32 E
Warren, Austl.	98	H6	31.42 S	147.49 E
Warren, Eng., U.K.	180		53.14 N	2.10 W
Warren, Ar., U.S.	134	D6	33.37 N	92.04 W
Warren, Il., U.S.	130	B8	42.29 N	89.59 W
Warren, In., U.S.	130	D12	40.40 N	85.24 W
Warren, Mi., U.S.	124	B2	42.30 N	83.01 W
Warren, Mn., U.S.	128	C2	48.11 N	96.47 W
Warren, N.J., U.S.	194		40.37 N	74.30 W
Warren, Oh., U.S.	124	C5	41.13 N	80.48 W
Warren, Pa., U.S.	124	C6	41.50 N	79.08 W
Warren H. Manning State Park, p.o.i., Ma., U.S.	201		42.34 N	71.18 W
Warren Peaks, mtn., Wy., U.S.	140	C8	44.30 N	104.27 W
Warrenpoint, N. Ire., U.K.	10	G6	54.06 N	6.15 W
Warrens, Wi., U.S.	128	G8	44.07 N	90.30 W
Warrensburg, Mo., U.S.	130	F4	38.45 N	93.44 W
Warrensburg, N.Y., U.S.	126	E16	43.29 N	73.46 W
Warrenton, S. Afr.	90	F7	28.07 S	24.50 E
Warrenton, Ga., U.S.	132	C3	33.24 N	82.39 W
Warrenton, Mo., U.S.	130	F6	38.48 N	91.08 W
Warrenton, N.C., U.S.	124	H7	36.23 N	78.09 W
Warrenton, Or., U.S.	146	D2	46.09 N	123.55 W
Warrenton, Va., U.S.	124	F8	38.42 N	77.47 W
Warri, Nig.	84	H6	5.30 N	5.45 E
Warriewood, Austl.	192a		33.42 S	151.18 E
Warrington, Eng., U.K.	10	H10	53.23 N	2.36 W
Warrington, Fl., U.S.	134	G11	30.23 N	87.16 W
Warrington, Pa., U.S.	203		40.15 N	75.08 W
Warrington, mun., Eng., U.K.	180		53.24 N	2.33 W
Warrington, mun., Eng., U.K.	180		53.24 N	2.33 W
Warrington Airport, arpt., Pa., U.S.	203		40.16 N	75.09 W
Warrior, Al., U.S.	134	D12	33.49 N	86.49 W
Warrior Creek, stm., Ga., U.S.	132	E2	31.15 N	83.34 W
Warrnambool, Austl.	98	L4	38.23 S	142.29 E
Warroad, Mn., U.S.	128	C3	48.54 N	95.18 W
Warrumbungle National Park, p.o.i., Austl.	98	H7	31.18 S	148.58 E
Warsaw see Warszawa, Pol.	24	D16	52.15 N	21.00 E
Warsaw, Il., U.S.	130	D6	40.21 N	91.25 W
Warsaw, In., U.S.	130	C12	41.14 N	85.50 W
Warsaw, Ky., U.S.	130	F13	38.46 N	84.54 W
Warsaw, Mo., U.S.	130	F4	38.14 N	93.22 W
Warsaw, N.Y., U.S.	124	B7	42.44 N	78.07 W
Warsaw, N.C., U.S.	132	A8	34.59 N	78.05 W
Warsaw, Oh., U.S.	124	D4	40.19 N	82.00 W
Warsaw, Va., U.S.	124	G9	37.57 N	76.45 W
Warsaw Station, trans., Russia	183a		59.54 N	30.19 E
Warspite, Ab., Can.	144	B18	54.06 N	112.37 W
Warszawa (Warsaw), Pol.	24	D16	52.15 N	21.00 E
Warta, Pol.	24	E14	51.41 N	18.39 E
Warta, stm., Pol.	24	D10	52.35 N	14.36 E
Wartburg, Tn., U.S.	130	H13	36.05 N	84.35 W
Wartburg, hist., Ger.	24	F6	50.57 N	10.18 E
Wartenberg, ngh., Ger.	182a		52.34 N	13.31 E
Warthe see Warta, stm., Pol.	24	D10	52.35 N	14.36 E
Warton Aerodrome, arpt., Eng., U.K.	180		53.45 N	2.54 W
Wartrace, Tn., U.S.	134	B12	35.31 N	86.19 W
Wartsberg, hill, Ger.	181		51.25 N	6.29 E
Warud, India	70	H7	21.28 N	78.16 E
Warwick, Austl.	98	G9	28.13 S	152.01 E
Warwick, Qc., Can.	122	E5	45.56 N	71.58 W
Warwick, Eng., U.K.	10	I11	52.17 N	1.38 W
Warwick, R.I., U.S.	124	C14	41.43 N	71.22 W
Warwick Channel, strt., Austl.	96	B7	13.59 S	136.18 E
Warwick Farm Racecourse and Motor Race Track, p.o.i., Austl.	192a		33.55 S	150.57 E

Name	Page	Map Ref.	Latitude	Longitude
Wasaga Beach, On., Can.	126	D10	44.30 N	80.00 W
Wasagu, Nig.	84	G6	11.22 N	5.48 E
Wasatch Plateau, plat., Ut., U.S.	150	D5	39.14 N	111.21 W
Wasatch Range, mts., Ut., U.S.	150	C5	40.36 N	111.42 W
Wasbank, S. Afr.	90	F10	28.18 S	30.06 E
Wascana Creek, stm., Sk., Can.	142	D9	50.38 N	104.54 W
Wasco, Ca., U.S.	148	H6	35.35 N	119.19 W
Wasco, Or., U.S.	146	E6	45.34 N	120.41 W
Waseca, Mn., U.S.	128	G5	44.04 N	93.30 W
Waseda University, educ., Japan	186		35.42 N	139.43 E
Wasgomuwa National Park, p.o.i., Sri L.	69	H5	7.41 N	80.52 E
Washademoak Lake, l., N.B., Can.	122	E11	45.48 N	65.58 W
Washburn, Il., U.S.	130	D8	40.55 N	89.17 W
Washburn, Me., U.S.	122	D8	46.47 N	68.09 W
Washburn, N.D., U.S.	142	G12	47.17 N	101.01 W
Washburn, Wi., U.S.	128	E7	46.40 N	90.53 W
Washburn, Mount, mtn., Wy., U.S.	146	F16	44.48 N	110.25 W
Washburn Lake, l., Nu., Can.	110	A9	70.04 N	107.30 W
Wāshīm, India	70	H6	20.07 N	77.07 E
Washington, D.C., U.S.	124	F9	38.53 N	77.01 W
Washington, D.C., U.S.	202c		38.53 N	77.02 W
Washington, Ga., U.S.	132	C3	33.44 N	82.44 W
Washington, Il., U.S.	130	D8	40.41 N	89.24 W
Washington, In., U.S.	130	F10	38.39 N	87.10 W
Washington, Ia., U.S.	130	C6	41.17 N	91.41 W
Washington, Ks., U.S.	138	B11	39.49 N	97.03 W
Washington, Ky., U.S.	124	F2	38.36 N	83.48 W
Washington, La., U.S.	134	G6	30.36 N	92.03 W
Washington, Mo., U.S.	130	F6	38.33 N	91.00 W
Washington, N.C., U.S.	132	A8	35.33 N	77.03 W
Washington, Pa., U.S.	124	D5	40.10 N	80.15 W
Washington, Tx., U.S.	136	D11	30.20 N	96.10 W
Washington, Ut., U.S.	150	F3	37.07 N	113.30 W
Washington, Va., U.S.	124	F7	38.42 N	78.09 W
Washington, state, U.S.	146	C5	47.30 N	120.30 W
Washington, Mount, mtn., N.H., U.S.	122	F5	44.15 N	71.17 W
Washington Court House, Oh., U.S.	124	E2	39.31 N	83.26 W
Washington Heights, ngh., N.Y., U.S.	194		40.52 N	73.56 W
Washington Island, Wi., U.S.	126	C3	45.23 N	86.55 W
Washington Island see Teraina, i., Kir.	94	C11	4.42 N	160.45 W
Washington Island, i., Wi., U.S.	126	C3	45.22 N	86.54 W
Washington Land, reg., Grnld.	108	A12	80.15 N	66.00 W
Washington Memorial Chapel, rel., Pa., U.S.	203		40.06 N	75.26 W
Washington Monument, p.o.i., D.C., U.S.	202c		38.53 N	77.03 W
Washington Park, p.o.i., Il., U.S.	196		41.48 N	87.37 W
Washington Park, p.o.i., Oh., U.S.	197a		41.27 N	81.40 W
Washington Rock State Park, p.o.i., N.J., U.S.	194		40.37 N	74.28 W
Washington's Headquarters, hist., Pa., U.S.	203		40.06 N	75.28 W
Washington Terrace, Ut., U.S.	150	B5	41.10 N	111.59 W
Washington Township, N.J., U.S.	194		40.54 N	74.00 W
Washington Valley, N.J., U.S.	194		40.48 N	74.32 W
Washington Valley Reservoir, res., N.J., U.S.	194		40.36 N	74.34 W
Washita, stm., U.S.	138	G12	34.08 N	96.36 W
Washoe Lake, l., Nv., U.S.	148	D6	39.16 N	119.48 W
Washow Bay, b., Mb., Can.	142	C17	51.22 N	96.47 W
Washpool National Park, p.o.i., Austl.	98	G9	29.22 S	152.20 E
Washtucna, Wa., U.S.	146	D8	46.45 N	118.17 W
Wāshuk, Pak.	62	C1	27.43 N	64.47 E
Wasian, Indon.	60	F9	1.55 S	133.17 E
Wasilków, Pol.	24	C19	53.11 N	23.12 E
Wasior, Indon.	60	F9	2.43 S	134.31 E
Wāsit, state, Iraq	74	D9	32.45 N	45.25 E
Waskada, Mb., Can.	142	E13	49.06 N	100.48 W
Waskaganish, Qc., Can.	110	E15	51.28 N	78.44 W
Waskahigan, stm., Ab., Can.	144	B13	54.45 N	117.11 W
Waskatenau, Ab., Can.	144	B18	54.05 N	112.46 W
Waskom, Tx., U.S.	136	B13	32.29 N	94.03 W
Wąsosz, Pol.	24	E12	51.33 N	16.41 E
Waspam, Nic.	156	E5	14.43 N	83.58 W
Waspán see Waspam, Nic.	156	E5	14.43 N	83.58 W
Wassenaar, Neth.	20	B13	52.07 N	4.22 E
Wasseralfingen, Ger.	24	H6	48.52 N	10.06 E
Wasserburg am Inn, Ger.	24	H8	48.03 N	12.13 E
Wasserkuppe, mtn., Ger.	24	F5	50.30 N	9.56 E
Wasserkurl, Ger.	181		51.33 N	7.38 E
Wassmannsdorf, Ger.	182a		52.22 N	13.28 E
Wassy, Fr.	20	F13	48.30 N	4.57 E
Wasum, Pap. N. Gui.	101a	b4	6.03 S	149.21 E
Waswanipi, Lac, l., Qc., Can.	114	B13	49.34 N	76.25 W
Watampone, Indon.	66	F12	4.32 S	120.19 E
Watansopeng, Indon.	66	F11	4.19 S	119.52 E
Watatic, Mount, mtn., Ma., U.S.	124	B14	42.42 N	71.53 W
Watchung, N.J., U.S.	194		40.38 N	74.27 W
Watchung Reservation, p.o.i., N.J., U.S.	194		40.41 N	74.23 W
Water, Eng., U.K.	180		53.44 N	2.14 W
Waterberge, mts., S. Afr.	90	D8	24.27 S	27.58 E
Waterberg Plateau Park, ind. res., Nmb.	90	B3	20.30 S	17.00 E
Waterbury, Ct., U.S.	124	C12	41.33 N	73.02 W
Waterbury, Vt., U.S.	122	F4	44.20 N	72.45 W
Wateree, stm., S.C., U.S.	116	C12	33.44 N	80.37 W
Wateree Lake, res., S.C., U.S.	132	B5	34.25 N	80.50 W
Waterend, Eng., U.K.	178		51.47 N	0.30 W
Water End, Eng., U.K.	180		53.41 N	2.15 W
Waterford, On., Can.	126	F9	42.56 N	80.17 W
Waterford (Port Lairge), Ire.	10	I5	52.15 N	7.06 W
Waterford, Ca., U.S.	148	F5	37.38 N	120.45 W
Waterford, Pa., U.S.	124	C6	41.56 N	79.59 W
Waterford, Wi., U.S.	130	B9	42.45 N	88.13 W
Waterford, state, Ire.	10	I5	52.10 N	7.40 W
Waterford Harbour, b., Ire.	10	I5	52.10 N	6.55 W
Watergrove Reservoir, res., Eng., U.K.	180		53.39 N	2.08 W
Waterhen Lake, l., Mb., Can.	142	B14	52.06 N	99.34 W
Wateringbury, Eng., U.K.	178		51.15 N	0.25 E
Water Island, N.Y., U.S.	194		40.41 N	73.02 W
Waterloo, Austl.	96	C5	16.37 S	129.15 E
Waterloo, Bel.	20	D13	50.43 N	4.24 E
Waterloo, On., Can.	126	E9	43.27 N	80.29 W
Waterloo, Qc., Can.	122	E4	45.20 N	72.30 W
Waterloo, Al., U.S.	134	C10	34.55 N	88.04 W
Waterloo, Il., U.S.	130	F7	38.19 N	90.09 W
Waterloo, Ia., U.S.	130	B5	42.29 N	92.21 W
Waterloo, N.Y., U.S.	124	B9	42.54 N	76.52 W
Waterloo, Wi., U.S.	130	A9	43.10 N	88.59 W
Waterman, Il., U.S.	130	C9	41.46 N	88.46 W
Waterman Wash, stm., Az., U.S.	150	J4	33.21 N	112.31 W
Waterproof, La., U.S.	134	F7	31.48 N	91.23 W
Waterside Park, N.Y., U.S.	194		40.56 N	73.20 W
Watersmeet, Mi., U.S.	128	E9	46.17 N	89.13 W
Waterton, stm., N.A.	144	G17	49.31 N	113.17 W
Waterton-Glacier International Peace Park, p.o.i., N.A.	146	B13	48.47 N	113.45 W
Waterton Lakes National Park, p.o.i., Ab., Can.	118	C8	49.05 N	114.00 W
Watertown, N.Y., U.S.	126	E14	43.58 N	75.54 W
Watertown, S.D., U.S.	140	C15	44.54 N	97.06 W
Watertown, Wi., U.S.	130	A9	43.11 N	88.42 W
Waterval Boven, S. Afr.	90	D10	25.39 S	30.16 E
Water Valley, Ms., U.S.	134	C9	34.09 N	89.37 W
Water Valley, N.Y., U.S.	202a		42.42 N	78.51 W
Waterville, N.S., Can.	122	E12	45.03 N	64.40 W
Waterville, Ks., U.S.	138	B12	39.41 N	96.44 W
Waterville, Me., U.S.	122	F7	44.33 N	69.37 W
Waterville, Mn., U.S.	128	G5	44.13 N	93.34 W
Waterville, Oh., U.S.	124	C2	41.30 N	83.43 W
Waterville, Wa., U.S.	146	C6	47.38 N	120.04 W
Watervliet, N.Y., U.S.	124	B12	42.44 N	73.42 W
Watford, On., Can.	126	F8	42.56 N	81.52 W
Watford, Eng., U.K.	10	J12	51.39 N	0.24 W
Watford, mun., Eng., U.K.	178		51.40 N	0.25 W
Watford City, N.D., U.S.	142	G10	47.48 N	103.17 W
Wathena, Ks., U.S.	130	E2	39.45 N	94.57 W
Watheroo, Austl.	96	F3	30.18 S	116.03 E
Watkins Glen, N.Y., U.S.	124	B9	42.22 N	76.52 W
Watkins Glen State Park, p.o.i., N.Y., U.S.	124	B8	42.22 N	76.55 W
Watkins Island, i., Md., U.S.	202c		39.02 N	77.17 W
Watkins Lake, l., Mi., U.S.	199		42.40 N	83.22 W
Watkinsville, Ga., U.S.	132	C2	33.51 N	83.24 W
Watling Island see San Salvador, i., Bah.	152	C10	24.02 N	74.27 W
Watoga State Park, p.o.i., W.V., U.S.	124	F5	38.05 N	80.08 W
Watonga, Ok., U.S.	138	F10	35.50 N	98.24 W
Watonwan, stm., Mn., U.S.	128	G4	44.04 N	94.08 W
Wat Phai Tan, Khlong, can., Thai.	187a		13.48 N	100.33 E
Watrous, Sk., Can.	142	C8	51.40 N	105.27 W
Watrous, N.M., U.S.	138	F4	35.47 N	104.58 W
Watsa, D.R.C.	86	D5	3.02 N	29.32 E
Watseka, Il., U.S.	130	D10	40.46 N	87.43 W
Watsikengo, D.R.C.	86	E4	0.45 S	20.30 E
Watson, Sk., Can.	142	B9	52.07 N	104.32 W
Watsonia, Austl.	192b		37.43 S	145.05 E
Watson Lake, Yk., Can.	110	C5	60.04 N	128.43 W
Watsons Bay, Austl.	192a		33.51 S	151.17 E
Watsons Creek, Austl.	192b		37.40 S	145.13 E
Watsons Creek, stm., Austl.	192b		37.43 S	145.16 E
Watsonville, Ca., U.S.	148	G4	36.54 N	121.45 W
Wattle Glen, Austl.	192b		37.40 S	145.11 E
Wattle Park, p.o.i., Austl.	192b		37.50 S	145.07 E
Watt Mountain, vol., Dom.	159c	j6	15.19 N	61.19 W
Watts, ngh., Ca., U.S.	198		33.56 N	118.15 W
Watts Bar Lake, res., Tn., U.S.	134	B14	35.47 N	84.39 W
Watts Branch, stm., Md., U.S.	202c		39.03 N	77.15 W
Watts Mills, S.C., U.S.	132	B4	34.30 N	81.59 W
Wattville, S. Afr.	191d		26.13 S	28.18 E
Wattwil, Switz.	30	C6	47.18 N	9.05 E
Watubela, Kepulauan, is., Indon.	60	F9	4.35 S	131.40 E
Watzmann, mtn., Ger.	24	I8	47.33 N	12.55 E
Waubay, S.D., U.S.	140	B15	45.19 N	97.18 W
Waubay Lake, l., S.D., U.S.	140	B15	45.24 N	97.23 W
Wauchope, Austl.	96	D6	20.37 S	134.11 E
Wauchope, Austl.	98	H9	31.27 S	152.44 E
Wauchula, Fl., U.S.	132	I4	27.32 N	81.48 W
Wauconda, Wa., U.S.	146	B7	48.43 N	119.01 W
Waugh, Mb., Can.	128	B3	49.39 N	95.12 W
Waugh Mountain, mtn., Id., U.S.	146	E12	45.29 N	114.47 W
Waukara, Bukit, mtn., Indon.	66	D11	1.10 S	119.47 E
Waukaringa, Austl.	98	I2	32.18 S	139.26 E
Waukarlycarly, Lake, l., Austl.	96	D4	21.16 S	121.51 E
Waukegan, Il., U.S.	130	B10	42.21 N	87.50 W
Waukesha, Wi., U.S.	130	A9	43.00 N	88.13 W
Waukomis, Ok., U.S.	138	E11	36.16 N	97.53 W
Waukon, Ia., U.S.	128	H7	43.16 N	91.29 W
Waunakee, Wi., U.S.	130	A8	43.11 N	89.26 W
Wauneta, Ne., U.S.	140	G11	40.24 N	101.21 W
Waupaca, Wi., U.S.	128	G9	44.21 N	89.05 W
Waupun, Wi., U.S.	128	H10	43.37 N	88.43 W
Waurika, Ok., U.S.	138	G11	34.09 N	97.59 W
Waurika Lake, res., Ok., U.S.	138	G10	34.18 N	98.05 W
Wausa, Ne., U.S.	140	E15	42.30 N	97.32 W
Wausau, Wi., U.S.	128	G9	44.57 N	89.36 W
Wausaukee, Wi., U.S.	126	C1	45.22 N	87.58 W
Wauseon, Oh., U.S.	124	C1	41.32 N	84.08 W
Waushakum Pond, l., Ma., U.S.	201		42.16 N	71.26 W
Wautoma, Wi., U.S.	128	G9	44.04 N	89.17 W
Wauwatosa, Wi., U.S.	130	A9	43.02 N	88.00 W
Wauzeka, Wi., U.S.	130	A7	43.05 N	90.52 W
Wave Hill, Austl.	96	C6	17.23 S	130.56 E
Waveland, Ma., U.S.	201		42.17 N	70.53 W
Waveland, Ms., U.S.	134	G9	30.17 N	89.22 W
Waveney, stm., Eng., U.K.	10	I14	52.28 N	1.44 E
Waverley, Austl.	192a		33.54 S	151.16 E
Waverley, Ma., U.S.	201		42.23 N	71.11 W
Waverley, ngh., S. Afr.	191d		26.08 S	28.04 E
Waverly, Al., U.S.	134	E13	32.44 N	85.35 W
Waverly, Ia., U.S.	130	B5	42.43 N	92.28 W
Waverly, Ks., U.S.	130	F2	38.23 N	95.36 W
Waverly, Mo., U.S.	130	E4	39.12 N	93.31 W
Waverly, Ne., U.S.	130	D1	40.55 N	96.31 W
Waverly, N.Y., U.S.	124	B9	42.00 N	76.31 W
Waverly, Oh., U.S.	124	E2	39.07 N	82.59 W
Waverly, Tn., U.S.	130	H10	36.05 N	87.47 W
Waverly, Va., U.S.	124	G8	37.01 N	77.05 W
Waverly Hall, Ga., U.S.	134	E14	32.41 N	84.44 W
Wāw, Sudan	82	F5	7.41 N	27.59 E
Wawa, On., Can.	114	B8	47.59 N	84.46 W
Wawa, Nig.	84	H5	9.54 N	4.25 E
Wawa, stm., Nic.	156	E5	13.52 N	83.27 W
Wāw al-Kabīr, Libya	82	B3	25.19 N	16.43 E
Wawanesa, Mb., Can.	142	E14	49.35 N	99.41 W
Wawayanda State Park, p.o.i., N.J., U.S.	194		41.11 N	74.26 W
Wawiag, stm., On., Can.	128	C8	48.22 N	91.12 W
Wawota, Sk., Can.	142	E11	49.54 N	102.01 W
Waxahachie, Tx., U.S.	136	B11	32.24 N	96.50 W
Waxhaw, N.C., U.S.	132	B5	34.55 N	80.44 W
Way, Lake, l., Austl.	96	E4	26.47 S	120.21 E
Waya, i., Fiji	101e	p18	17.18 S	177.08 E
Waycross, Ga., U.S.	132	E3	31.12 N	82.21 W
Wayland, Ia., U.S.	130	C6	41.08 N	91.39 W
Wayland, Ky., U.S.	124	G3	37.25 N	82.48 W
Wayland, Ma., U.S.	201		42.21 N	71.21 W
Wayland, Mi., U.S.	130	B12	42.40 N	85.38 W
Wayland, N.Y., U.S.	124	B8	42.33 N	77.35 W
Waylyn, S.C., U.S.	132	D6	32.50 N	79.57 W
Wayne, Ab., Can.	144	E18	51.23 N	112.39 W
Wayne, Mi., U.S.	124	B2	42.16 N	83.22 W
Wayne, Ne., U.S.	140	E15	42.14 N	97.01 W
Wayne, N.J., U.S.	124	D11	40.55 N	74.16 W
Wayne, Ok., U.S.	138	G11	34.55 N	97.18 W
Wayne, W.V., U.S.	124	F3	38.12 N	82.27 W
Wayne City, Il., U.S.	130	F9	38.20 N	88.35 W
Waynesboro, Ga., U.S.	132	C3	33.05 N	82.01 W
Waynesboro, Ms., U.S.	134	F10	31.40 N	88.38 W
Waynesboro, Tn., U.S.	134	B11	35.19 N	87.45 W
Waynesboro, Va., U.S.	124	F6	38.04 N	78.53 W
Wayne State University, educ., Mi., U.S.	199		42.21 N	83.04 W
Waynesville, Il., U.S.	130	D8	40.15 N	89.08 W
Waynesville, Mo., U.S.	130	G5	37.50 N	92.12 W
Waynesville, N.C., U.S.	132	A3	35.29 N	82.59 W
Waynoka, Ok., U.S.	138	E10	36.35 N	98.52 W
Wayoh Reservoir, res., Eng., U.K.	180		53.39 N	2.24 W
Waza, Cam.	86	B2	11.23 N	14.34 E
Wazah, Afg.	70	B2	33.22 N	69.26 E
Wāzah Khwāh, Afg.	70	B2	32.04 N	68.19 E
Wazīrābād, Pak.	70	B5	32.26 N	74.06 E
Wazīrābād, ngh., India	190a		28.43 N	77.14 E
Wazīrpur, ngh., India	190a		28.41 N	77.10 E
Wazuka, stm., Japan	188		34.45 N	135.53 E
Wda, stm., Pol.	24	C14	53.24 N	18.29 E
Wé, N. Cal.	101d	m16	20.54 S	167.16 E
We, Pulau, i., Indon.	64	J2	5.51 N	95.18 E
Weald Park, p.o.i., Eng., U.K.	178		51.38 N	0.14 E
Wealdstone, ngh., Eng., U.K.	178		51.36 N	0.20 W
Weatherford, Ok., U.S.	138	F10	35.31 N	98.42 W
Weatherford, Tx., U.S.	136	B10	32.45 N	97.47 W
Weatherly, Pa., U.S.	124	D10	40.56 N	75.50 W
Weaubleau, Mo., U.S.	130	G4	37.53 N	93.32 W
Weaver, Al., U.S.	134	D13	33.45 N	85.48 W
Weaver, stm., Eng., U.K.	10	H10	53.18 N	2.45 W
Weaver Lake, l., Mb., Can.	142	B17	52.45 N	96.35 W
Weavertown, Pa., U.S.	197b		40.16 N	80.11 W
Weaverville, Ca., U.S.	148	C3	40.44 N	122.55 W
Weaverville, N.C., U.S.	124	I3	35.41 N	82.35 W
Webb, Sk., Can.	142	D5	50.12 N	108.12 W
Webb, Ms., U.S.	134	D8	33.56 N	90.20 W
Webb Brook, stm., Ma., U.S.	201		42.32 N	71.14 W
Webb City, Mo., U.S.	130	G3	37.08 N	94.27 W
Webbwood, On., Can.	126	B7	46.16 N	81.53 W
Weber, stm., Ut., U.S.	150	B5	41.14 N	112.06 W
Weber City, Va., U.S.	124	H3	36.37 N	82.33 W
Webster, Ab., Can.	144	A12	55.27 N	118.40 W
Webster, Fl., U.S.	132	H3	28.36 N	82.03 W
Webster, Ma., U.S.	124	B14	42.03 N	71.52 W
Webster, S.D., U.S.	140	B15	45.19 N	97.31 W
Webster, Wi., U.S.	128	F6	45.52 N	92.22 W
Webster City, Ia., U.S.	130	B4	42.28 N	93.48 W
Websters Corners, N.Y., U.S.	202a		41.47 N	78.45 W
Webster Springs, W.V., U.S.	124	F5	38.28 N	80.24 W
Weda, Indon.	60	E8	0.20 N	127.51 E
Wedau, ngh., Ger.	181		51.24 N	6.48 E
Wedau, Sportpark, p.o.i., Ger.	181		51.25 N	6.47 E
Weddell Island, i., Falk. Is.	166	J4	51.52 S	61.04 W
Weddell Sea, s., Ant.	103	C36	72.00 S	45.00 W
Wedderburn, Austl.	98	K4	36.25 S	143.36 E
Weddinghofen, Ger.	181		51.36 N	7.37 E
Wedge Mountain, mtn., B.C., Can.	144	F8	50.09 N	122.42 W
Wedgeport, N.S., Can.	122	G11	43.45 N	65.59 W
Wedowee, Al., U.S.	134	D13	33.18 N	85.29 W
Weed, Ca., U.S.	148	B3	41.25 N	122.23 W
Weedsport, N.Y., U.S.	126	E13	43.03 N	76.33 W
Weehawken, N.J., U.S.	194		40.46 N	74.01 W
Weeks Point, c., N.Y., U.S.	194		40.53 N	73.39 W
Weems, Va., U.S.	124	G9	37.38 N	76.27 W
Weenen, S. Afr.	90	F10	28.51 S	30.04 E
Weeney Bay, b., Austl.	192a		34.01 S	151.10 E
Weeping Water, Ne., U.S.	130	D2	40.52 N	96.08 W
Weequahic Lake, l., N.J., U.S.	194		40.42 N	74.12 W
Weert, Neth.	20	C14	51.15 N	5.42 E
Weesow, Ger.	182a		52.39 N	13.43 E
Weetfeld, ngh., Ger.	181		51.38 N	7.49 E
Weethalle, Austl.	98	I6	33.52 S	146.37 E
Weeton, Eng., U.K.	180		53.48 N	2.56 W
Wee Waa, Austl.	98	H7	30.13 S	149.26 E
Wegendorf, Ger.	182a		52.36 N	13.45 E
Węgliniec, Pol.	24	E11	51.17 N	15.11 E
Węgorzewo, Pol.	24	B17	54.13 N	21.44 E
Węgorzyno, Pol.	24	C11	53.33 N	15.31 E
Węgrów, Pol.	24	D17	52.24 N	22.03 E
Wegscheid, Ger.	24	H9	48.36 N	13.47 E
Wehofen, ngh., Ger.	181		51.32 N	6.46 E
Wehringhausen, ngh., Ger.	181		51.21 N	7.27 E
Wei, stm., China	58	D3	34.21 N	107.37 E
Wei, stm., China	56	C6	36.49 N	115.40 E
Wei, stm., China	58	C8	37.08 N	119.29 E
Weichang, China	52	C8	42.00 N	117.40 E
Weichuan, China	58	D6	34.17 N	113.59 E
Weida, Ger.	24	F8	50.46 N	12.04 E
Weiden in der Oberpfalz, Ger.	24	G8	49.40 N	12.09 E
Weidling, Aus.	182b		48.17 N	16.19 E
Weidlingau, ngh., Aus.	182b		48.13 N	16.13 E
Weidlingbach, Aus.	182b		48.16 N	16.15 E
Weidlingerbach, stm., Aus.	182b		48.18 N	16.20 E
Weifang, China	58	C8	36.42 N	119.05 E
Weihai, China	58	C10	37.30 N	122.07 E
Weihe, China	54	B8	44.55 N	128.23 E
Weilburg, Ger.	24	F4	50.28 N	8.16 E
Weilheim, Ger.	24	I7	47.50 N	11.09 E
Weilmoringle, Austl.	98	G6	29.15 S	146.51 E
Weimar, Ger.	24	E7	50.59 N	11.19 E
Weimar, Tx., U.S.	136	E11	29.42 N	96.46 W
Weinan, China	58	D3	34.29 N	109.29 E
Weinel Cross Roads, Pa., U.S.	197b		40.37 N	79.37 W
Weiner, Ar., U.S.	134	B8	35.37 N	90.53 W
Weingarten, Ger.	20	G18	47.48 N	9.37 E
Weinheim, Ger.	24	G4	49.33 N	8.39 E
Weining, China	52	F5	26.52 N	104.17 E
Weipa, Austl.	96	B8	12.42 S	141.56 E
Weippe, Id., U.S.	146	D11	46.22 N	115.56 W
Weir, Ks., U.S.	138	D14	37.18 N	94.46 W
Weir, Ms., U.S.	134	D9	33.15 N	89.17 W
Weir, stm., Austl.	98	F8	28.50 S	149.06 E
Weir, stm., Ma., U.S.	201		42.16 N	70.53 W
Weir, Lake, l., Fl., U.S.	132	G4	29.00 N	81.57 W
Weirsdale, Fl., U.S.	132	H4	28.59 N	81.55 W
Weirton, W.V., U.S.	124	D5	40.24 N	80.34 W
Weisburd, Arg.	172	C6	27.18 S	62.35 W
Weiser, Id., U.S.	146	F10	44.15 N	116.58 W
Weiser, stm., Id., U.S.	146	F10	44.14 N	116.58 W
Weishan Hu, l., China	58	D7	34.36 N	117.09 E
Weishi, China	58	D6	34.24 N	114.11 E
Weisner Mountain, mtn., Al., U.S.	134	C13	34.02 N	85.40 W
Weissenbach, Aus.	182b		48.05 N	16.13 E
Weissenburg in Bayern, Ger.	24	G7	49.01 N	10.58 E
Weissenfels, Ger.	24	E7	51.12 N	11.58 E
Weissensee, ngh., Ger.	182a		52.33 N	13.27 E
Weiss Lake, res., U.S.	134	C13	34.12 N	85.37 W
Weisswasser, Ger.	24	E10	51.30 N	14.38 E
Weitmar, ngh., Ger.	181		51.27 N	7.12 E
Weitra, Aus.	30	B11	48.41 N	14.53 E
Weixi, China	52	F4	27.10 N	99.16 E
Weixian, China	58	C6	36.58 N	115.15 E
Weiyuan, stm., China	64	A5	22.55 N	100.41 E
Weiz, Aus.	30	C12	47.13 N	15.37 E
Weizhou Dao, i., China	58	K3	21.03 N	109.06 E
Wejherowo, Pol.	24	B14	54.36 N	18.14 E
Wekoewa Punt, c., Neth. Ant.	158g	p23	12.08 N	68.15 W
Welaka, Fl., U.S.	132	G4	29.28 N	81.40 W
Welbourn Hill, Austl.	96	E6	27.21 S	134.04 E
Welch, Ok., U.S.	130	H2	36.51 N	95.06 W
Welch, Tx., U.S.	136	B5	32.56 N	102.07 W
Welch, W.V., U.S.	124	G4	37.25 N	81.35 W
Welch Creek, stm., Ca., U.S.	200		37.32 N	121.51 W
Welcome, Mn., U.S.	128	H4	43.40 N	94.37 W
Welcome Monument, hist., Indon.	187e		6.11 S	106.49 E
Weldiya, Eth.	82	E7	11.49 N	39.35 E
Weldon, Sk., Can.	142	A8	53.00 N	105.08 W
Weldon, Il., U.S.	130	D9	40.07 N	88.44 W
Weldon, stm., U.S.	130	D4	40.06 N	93.39 W
Weldona, Co., U.S.	140	G9	40.20 N	103.58 W
Weldon Brook, stm., N.J., U.S.	194		40.58 N	74.35 W
Weleetka, Ok., U.S.	134	B2	35.20 N	96.08 W
Welel, Tulu, mtn., Eth.	82	F7	8.53 N	34.47 E
Welfare Island, i., N.Y., U.S.	194		40.45 N	73.57 W
Welgedag, S. Afr.	191d		26.12 S	28.30 E
Welhamgreen, Eng., U.K.	178		51.44 N	0.13 W
Welheim, ngh., Ger.	181		51.32 N	6.59 E
Weligama, Sri L.	69	I5	5.58 N	80.24 E
Welk'īte, Eth.	82	F7	8.16 N	37.46 E
Welkom, S. Afr.	90	E8	27.58 S	26.44 E
Welland, On., Can.	126	F10	42.59 N	79.15 W
Welland, stm., On., Can.	126	E10	43.03 N	79.02 W
Welland, stm., Eng., U.K.	10	I12	52.53 N	0.00 W
Welland Junction, On., Can.	202a		42.57 N	79.14 W
Wellborn, Fl., U.S.	132	F3	30.13 N	82.49 W
Wellborn, Tx., U.S.	136	D11	30.32 N	96.18 W
Wellers Creek, stm., Il., U.S.	196		42.03 N	87.53 W
Wellesley College, educ., Ma., U.S.	201		42.18 N	71.19 W
Wellesley Hills, Ma., U.S.	201		42.19 N	71.17 W
Wellesley Islands, is., Austl.	94	E4	16.42 S	139.30 E
Wellfleet, Ma., U.S.	124	C15	41.56 N	70.01 W
Well Hill, Eng., U.K.	178		51.21 N	0.09 E
Welling, ngh., Eng., U.K.	178		51.28 N	0.07 E
Wellingborough, Eng., U.K.	10	I12	52.18 N	0.42 W
Wellinghofen, ngh., Ger.	181		51.28 N	7.29 E
Wellington, Austl.	98	I7	32.33 S	148.56 E
Wellington, On., Can.	126	E12	43.57 N	77.20 W
Wellington, N.Z.	102	E6	41.17 S	174.46 E
Wellington, S. Afr.	90	H4	33.38 S	18.59 E
Wellington, Eng., U.K.	10	K9	50.58 N	3.13 W
Wellington, Co., U.S.	140	G7	40.41 N	104.59 W
Wellington, Ks., U.S.	138	D11	37.16 N	97.23 W
Wellington, Mo., U.S.	130	E4	39.07 N	93.59 W
Wellington, Oh., U.S.	124	C3	41.09 N	82.13 W
Wellington, Tx., U.S.	138	G8	34.51 N	100.12 W
Wellington, Ut., U.S.	150	D6	39.32 N	110.44 W
Wellington, Isla, i., Chile	166	I2	49.20 S	74.40 W
Wellington Bay, b., Nu., Can.	110	B9	69.21 N	106.38 W
Wellington Channel, strt., Nu., Can.	108	B7	75.00 N	93.00 W
Wellington Station, P.E., Can.	122	D12	46.27 N	64.00 W
Wellman, Ia., U.S.	130	C6	41.28 N	91.49 W
Wellman, Tx., U.S.	136	A5	33.03 N	102.26 W
Wells, B.C., Can.	144	C9	53.06 N	121.32 W
Wells, Eng., U.K.	10	J10	51.13 N	2.39 W
Wells, Mi., U.S.	126	C2	45.46 N	87.04 W
Wells, Mn., U.S.	128	H5	43.44 N	93.43 W
Wells, Nv., U.S.	148	B11	41.06 N	114.57 W
Wells, N.Y., U.S.	126	E15	43.24 N	74.17 W
Wells, Tx., U.S.	136	C13	31.29 N	94.56 W
Wells, Lake, l., Austl.	96	E4	26.41 S	123.10 E
Wells, Mount, hill, Austl.	96	C5	17.25 S	127.12 E
Wellsboro, Pa., U.S.	124	C8	41.44 N	77.17 W
Wellsburg, Ia., U.S.	130	B4	42.26 N	92.55 W
Wellsburg, W.V., U.S.	124	D5	40.16 N	80.36 W
Wellsford, N.Z.	102	C6	36.18 S	174.31 E
Wells Gray Provincial Park, p.o.i., B.C., Can.	144	D11	52.20 N	119.53 W
Wells-next-the-Sea, Eng., U.K.	10	H13	52.57 N	0.50 E
Wells Point, c., Md., U.S.	202b		39.17 N	76.23 W
Wellston, Oh., U.S.	124	E3	39.06 N	82.32 W
Wellston, Ok., U.S.	134	B1	35.41 N	97.03 W
Wellsville, Ks., U.S.	138	C13	38.43 N	95.04 W
Wellsville, Mo., U.S.	130	E6	39.04 N	91.34 W
Wellsville, N.Y., U.S.	124	B8	42.07 N	77.56 W
Wellsville, Oh., U.S.	124	D5	40.36 N	80.39 W
Wellsville, Ut., U.S.	150	B5	41.38 N	111.56 W
Wellton, Az., U.S.	150	K2	32.39 N	114.09 W
Welmen, Ger.	181		51.39 N	6.41 E
Welper, Ger.	181		51.25 N	7.12 E
Wels, Aus.	30	B10	48.09 N	14.01 E
Welsford, N.B., Can.	122	E10	45.27 N	66.20 W
Welsh, La., U.S.	134	G6	30.14 N	92.49 W
Welshpool, Wales, U.K.	10	I9	52.39 N	3.08 W
Welwyn Garden City, Eng., U.K.	10	J12	51.48 N	0.12 W
Welwyn Hatfield, mun., Eng., U.K.	178		51.47 N	0.12 W
Wembley, Ab., Can.	144	A11	55.08 N	119.09 W
Wembley, ngh., Eng., U.K.	178		51.33 N	0.18 W
Wembley Stadium, p.o.i., S. Afr.	191d		26.14 S	28.03 E
Wembley Stadium, p.o.i., Eng., U.K.	178		51.33 N	0.17 W
Wena, D.R.C.	86	E4	0.24 S	21.39 E
Wenatchee, Wa., U.S.	146	C6	47.25 N	120.18 W
Wenatchee, stm., Wa., U.S.	146	C6	47.27 N	120.18 W
Wenatchee Mountains, mts., Wa., U.S.	146	C6	47.20 N	120.45 W
Wenceslau Braz, Braz.	170	L1	23.53 S	49.48 W
Wenchang, China	58	L4	19.33 N	110.44 E
Wencheng, China	58	H8	27.48 N	120.05 E
Wenchi, Ghana	84	H4	7.41 N	2.06 W
Wenchow, China	58	G9	28.00 N	120.37 E
Wendel, Pa., U.S.	197b		40.18 N	79.41 W
Wendell, Id., U.S.	146	H12	42.46 N	114.42 W
Wendelville, N.Y., U.S.	202a		43.04 N	78.47 W
Wenden, Az., U.S.	150	J3	33.49 N	113.32 W
Wendeng, China	58	C10	37.11 N	122.03 E
Wendover, Ut., U.S.	150	C2	40.44 N	114.02 W
Wenebegon, stm., On., Can.	126	B6	47.09 N	83.07 W
Weng, stm., China	58	I5	24.10 N	113.24 E
Weng'an, China	58	H2	26.53 N	107.22 E
Wengbo, China	70	C11	31.22 N	86.38 E
Wengern, Ger.	181		51.24 N	7.21 E
Wenham Lake, l., Ma., U.S.	201		42.35 N	70.53 W
Wenham Swamp, sw., Ma., U.S.	201		42.37 N	70.55 W
Wenling, China	58	G9	28.21 N	121.22 E
Wenlock, Austl.	96	B8	13.05 S	142.58 E
Wenlock, stm., Austl.	96	B8	12.15 S	141.56 E
Wennington, ngh., Eng., U.K.	178		51.30 N	0.13 E
Wenona, Il., U.S.	130	C8	41.03 N	89.02 W
Wenquan, China	48	E14	44.59 N	81.04 E
Wenshan, China	52	G5	23.29 N	104.28 E
Wenshang, China	58	D7	35.43 N	116.28 E
Wenshui, China	58	G2	28.28 N	106.30 E
Wenshui, China	58	C4	37.26 N	112.00 E
Wensickendorf, Ger.	182a		52.45 N	13.23 E
Wensleydale, val., Eng., U.K.	10	G10	54.19 N	2.00 W
Wensu, China	48	F14	41.15 N	80.14 E
Wentworth, Austl.	98	J3	34.06 S	141.54 E
Wentworth, S.D., U.S.	128	G2	43.59 N	96.58 W
Wentworth Park, S. Afr.	191d		26.07 S	27.48 E
Wentworthville, Austl.	192a		33.48 S	150.58 E
Wenxi, China	58	D4	35.26 N	111.09 E
Wenxian, China	58	D5	34.56 N	113.04 E
Wenzhou, China	52	F9	28.00 N	120.37 E
Wepener, S. Afr.	90	F8	29.44 S	27.02 E
Werda, Bots.	90	D6	25.17 S	23.13 E
Werdau, Ger.	24	F8	50.43 N	12.23 E
Werden, ngh., Ger.	181		51.23 N	7.00 E
Werdēr, Eth.	82	F9	6.58 N	45.20 E
Werder, Ger.	24	D8	52.22 N	12.56 E
Wernadinga, Austl.	98	B2	18.07 S	139.58 E
Werne, ngh., Ger.	181		51.29 N	7.18 E
Wernigerode, Ger.	24	E6	51.50 N	10.46 E
Wernitz, Ger.	182a		52.34 N	12.55 E
Wernsdorf, Ger.	182a		52.22 N	13.43 E
Wernsdorfer See, l., Ger.	182a		52.23 N	13.42 E
Werra, stm., Ger.	24	E5	51.25 N	9.38 E
Werribee, Austl.	98	K5	37.53 S	144.40 E
Werrikimbe National Park, p.o.i., Austl.	98	H9	31.15 S	152.13 E
Werrington, Austl.	192a		33.45 S	150.46 E
Werris Creek, Austl.	98	H8	31.20 S	150.39 E
Wersten, ngh., Ger.	181		51.11 N	6.49 E
Wertach, stm., Ger.	30	B7	48.24 N	10.53 E
Wertheim, Ger.	24	G5	49.45 N	9.31 E
Wertingen, Ger.	24	H6	48.34 N	10.41 E
Wervin, Eng., U.K.	180		53.15 N	2.52 W
Wesel, Ger.	24	E2	51.40 N	6.38 E
Wesel-Datteln-Kanal, can., Ger.	20	C15	51.38 N	6.36 E
Wesendahl, Ger.	182a		52.36 N	13.49 E
Weser, stm., Ger.	24	D5	53.32 N	8.34 E
Weser-Elbe-Kanal see Mittellandkanal, can., Ger.	24	D5	52.14 N	11.42 E
Wesermünde see Bremerhaven, Ger.	24	C4	53.31 N	8.35 E
Wesham, Eng., U.K.	180		53.48 N	2.53 W
Wesickaman Creek, stm., N.J., U.S.	203		39.44 N	74.43 W
Weskan, Ks., U.S.	138	C7	38.52 N	101.57 W
Weslaco, Tx., U.S.	136	H10	26.09 N	97.59 W
Weslemkoon Lake, l., On., Can.	126	C12	45.02 N	77.25 W
Wesley, Dom.	159c	I6	15.33 N	61.19 W
Wesley, Ia., U.S.	130	A3	43.05 N	93.58 W
Wesleyville, Pa., U.S.	124	B5	42.07 N	80.02 W
Wessel, Cape, c., Austl.	96	B7	11.02 S	136.45 E
Wessel Islands, is., Austl.	96	B7	11.30 S	136.25 E
Wesselsbron, S. Afr.	90	E7	27.50 S	25.23 E
Wessington, S.D., U.S.	140	C14	44.27 N	98.41 W
Wessington Springs, S.D., U.S.	140	C14	44.04 N	98.34 W
Wesson, Ms., U.S.	134	F8	31.41 N	90.24 W
West, Ms., U.S.	134	D9	33.12 N	89.47 W
West, Tx., U.S.	136	C10	31.47 N	97.05 W
West, stm., Vt., U.S.	122	G4	42.51 N	72.33 W
West Allis, Wi., U.S.	130	B10	43.00 N	88.00 W
West Amityville, N.Y., U.S.	194		40.41 N	73.26 W
West Antarctica, reg., Ant.	103	D30	79.00 S	105.00 W
West Athens, Ca., U.S.	198		33.55 N	118.18 W
Westbahnhof, trans., Aus.	182b		48.11 N	16.20 E
Westbank, B.C., Can.	144	G11	49.50 N	119.36 W
West Bank, dep., Asia	76	F6	31.40 N	35.15 E
West Bay, N.S., Can.	122	E15	45.43 N	61.11 W
West Bay, Fl., U.S.	134	G13	30.17 N	85.52 W
West Bay, b., Fl., U.S.	134	G13	30.16 N	85.47 W
West Bay, b., Tx., U.S.	136	E12	29.15 N	94.57 W
West Bay Shore, N.Y., U.S.	194		40.42 N	73.16 W
West Bend, Ia., U.S.	130	B3	42.56 N	94.26 W
West Bend, Wi., U.S.	126	E1	43.25 N	88.10 W
West Bengal, state, India	70	G11	24.00 N	88.00 E
West Bijou Creek, stm., Co., U.S.	138	B4	39.51 N	104.07 W
West Billerica, Ma., U.S.	201		42.33 N	71.19 W
West Blocton, Al., U.S.	134	D11	33.07 N	87.07 W
West Borneo see Kalimantan Barat, state, Indon.	66	D7	0.30 N	110.00 E
Westbourne, Mb., Can.	142	D15	50.07 N	98.33 W
West Bow Creek, stm., Ne., U.S.	140	E15	42.46 N	97.08 W
West Boxford, Ma., U.S.	201		42.42 N	71.04 W
West Branch, Ia., U.S.	130	C6	41.40 N	91.20 W
West Branch, Mi., U.S.	126	D5	44.16 N	84.13 W

Name — Page — Map Ref. — Latitude — Longitude

Westbridge, B.C., Can. 144 G11 49.09 N 118.59 W
West Bristol, Pa., U.S. 203 40.06 N 74.53 W
West Bromwich, Eng., U.K. 10 I11 52.31 N 1.55 W
Westbrook, Me., U.S. 122 G6 43.41 N 70.21 W
Westbrook, Mn., U.S. 128 G3 44.02 N 95.26 W
Westbrook, Tx., U.S. 136 B6 32.21 N 101.01 W
West Brook, stm., N.J., U.S. 194 41.04 N 74.18 W
West Burlington, Ia., U.S. 130 D6 40.49 N 91.09 W
West Burra, i., Scot., U.K. 10 A11 60.05 N 1.21 W
Westbury, N.Y., U.S. 194 40.45 N 73.35 W
West Butte, mtn., Mt., U.S. 146 B15 48.57 N 111.32 W
Westby, Austl. 98 J6 35.29 S 147.24 E
Westby, Mt., U.S. 142 F9 48.52 N 104.03 W
Westby, Wi., U.S. 128 H8 43.38 N 90.51 W
West Cache Creek, stm., Ok., U.S. 138 G10 34.11 N 98.18 W
West Caicos, i., T./C. Is. 156 B11 21.39 N 72.28 W
West Caldwell, N.J., U.S. 194 40.50 N 74.18 W
West Canada Creek, stm., N.Y., U.S. 126 E15 43.01 N 74.58 W
West Cape, c., N.Z. 102 G2 45.54 S 166.25 E
West Cape Howe, c., Austl. 96 G3 35.06 S 117.36 E
West Carlisle, Tx., U.S. 138 H7 33.34 N 101.56 W
West Caroline Basin, unds. 174 I16 4.00 N 138.00 E
West Carson, Ca., U.S. 198 33.57 N 118.23 W
West Chelmsford, Ma., U.S. 201 42.37 N 71.23 W
West Chester, Pa., U.S. 124 E10 39.57 N 75.36 W
Westchester, Va., U.S. 202c 38.51 N 77.16 W
Westchester, ngh., Ca., U.S. 198 33.55 N 118.25 W
Westchester, ngh., N.Y., U.S. 194 40.51 N 73.52 W
West Chester Airport, arpt., Pa., U.S. 203 39.59 N 75.35 W
Westchester Creek, stm., N.Y., U.S. 194 40.48 N 73.51 W
Westchester Estates, Md., U.S. 202c 38.47 N 76.55 W
Westchester Station, N.S., Can. 122 E13 45.38 N 63.38 W
West Chester University of Pennsylvania, educ., Pa., U.S. 203 39.57 N 75.36 W
West Clandon, Eng., U.K. 178 51.15 N 0.30 W
West Clear Creek, stm., Az., U.S. 150 I5 34.34 N 111.51 W
Westcliffe, Co., U.S. 138 C3 38.08 N 105.28 W
Westcliffe, ngh., S. Afr. 191d 26.11 S 28.02 E
Westcliff-on-Sea, Eng., U.K. 178 51.32 N 0.41 E
West Collingswood Heights, N.J., U.S. 203 39.59 N 75.07 W
West Columbia, S.C., U.S. 132 B4 33.59 N 81.04 W
West Columbia, Tx., U.S. 136 E12 29.08 N 95.38 W
West Conshohocken, Pa., U.S. 203 40.04 N 75.19 W
West Cote Blanche Bay, b., La., U.S. 134 H7 29.40 N 91.45 W
Westcott, Eng., U.K. 178 51.13 N 0.22 W
Westcott Cove, b., Ct., U.S. 194 41.02 N 73.30 W
Westdale, Ma., U.S. 201 42.01 N 70.59 W
West Deane Park, p.o.i., On., Can. 193b 43.40 N 79.34 W
Westdene, ngh., S. Afr. 191d 26.11 S 27.59 E
West Derby, ngh., Eng., U.K. 180 53.26 N 2.54 W
West Des Moines, Ia., U.S. 130 C4 41.34 N 93.42 W
West Ditch, can., N.J., U.S. 194 40.56 N 74.19 W
West Dolores, stm., Co., U.S. 150 F8 37.35 N 108.20 W
West Drayton, ngh., Eng., U.K. 178 51.30 N 0.29 W
West Duxbury, Ma., U.S. 201 42.03 N 70.47 W
West Edmondale, Md., U.S. 202b 39.18 N 76.43 W
West Elizabeth, Pa., U.S. 197b 40.17 N 79.54 W
West Elk Mountains, mts., Co., U.S. 150 E9 38.40 N 107.15 W
West Elk Peak, mtn., Co., U.S. 138 C1 38.43 N 107.13 W
West End, Bah. 132 J7 26.41 N 78.58 W
West End, Eng., U.K. 178 51.44 N 0.04 W
West End, Eng., U.K. 178 51.20 N 0.38 W
West End, Ar., U.S. 134 C6 34.13 N 92.03 W
West End, N.C., U.S. 132 A6 35.14 N 79.34 W
West End, ngh., Eng., U.K. 178 51.32 N 0.24 W
West End, ngh., Pa., U.S. 197b 40.27 N 80.02 W
Westende, Ger. 181 51.25 N 7.24 E
Westenfeld, ngh., Ger. 181 51.28 N 7.09 E
Westerbauer, ngh., Ger. 181 51.20 N 7.23 E
Westerbönen, Ger. 181 51.36 N 7.46 E
Westerholz, for., Ger. 181 51.32 N 7.28 E
Westerland, Ger. 24 B4 54.54 N 8.18 E
Westerly, R.I., U.S. 124 C14 41.22 N 71.49 W
Western, Ne., U.S. 140 G15 40.23 N 97.11 W
Western, state, Sol. Is. 101b e7 8.50 S 157.02 E
Western, stm., Austl. 98 D4 22.20 S 142.24 E
Western Australia, state, Austl. 96 D4 25.00 S 122.00 E
Western Branch, stm., Md., U.S. 202c 38.55 N 76.48 W
Western Cape, state, S. Afr. 90 H5 33.30 S 20.00 E
Western Channel, strt., Asia 56 E2 34.16 N 128.30 E
Western Desert, des., Egypt 82 B5 27.00 N 27.00 E
Western Division, state, Fiji 101e p18 17.09 S 177.46 E
Western Dvina (Daugava) (Zahodnjaja Dzvina) (Zapadnaja Dvina), stm., Eur. 26 D7 57.03 N 24.02 E
Western Ghāts, mts., India 62 E3 14.00 N 75.00 E
Westernport, Md., U.S. 124 E6 39.29 N 79.02 W
Western Sahara, dep., Afr. 84 E2 24.30 N 13.00 W
Western Samoa see Samoa, ctry., Oc. 101c g12 13.55 S 172.00 W
Western Sayans see Zapadnyj Sajan, mts., Russia 48 D16 53.00 N 94.00 E
Western Shore, N.S., Can. 122 F12 44.32 N 64.20 W
Western Springs, Il., U.S. 196 41.48 N 87.54 W
Westerschelde, est., Neth. 20 C12 51.22 N 3.44 E
Westerstede, Ger. 24 C3 53.15 N 7.55 E
Westerville, Oh., U.S. 124 D3 40.07 N 82.54 W
Westerwald, mts., Ger. 24 F4 50.40 N 7.55 E
West European Basin, unds. 176 D12 47.00 N 14.58 W
Westfalenhalle, bldg., Ger. 181 51.30 N 7.27 E
West Falkland, i., Falk. Is. 166 J4 51.49 S 59.59 W
West Fargo, N.D., U.S. 128 E1 46.52 N 96.53 W
West Farleigh, Eng., U.K. 178 51.15 N 0.27 E
Westfield, Il., U.S. 130 E9 39.26 N 88.00 W
Westfield, In., U.S. 130 D11 40.02 N 86.07 W
Westfield, Ma., U.S. 122 H4 42.07 N 72.44 W
Westfield, N.J., U.S. 124 D11 40.39 N 74.20 W
Westfield, N.Y., U.S. 124 B6 42.19 N 79.34 W
Westfield, Pa., U.S. 124 C8 41.55 N 77.32 W
Westfield, Wi., U.S. 128 H9 43.53 N 89.29 W
Westford, Ma., U.S. 201 42.34 N 71.26 W
West Fork, Ar., U.S. 130 I3 35.55 N 94.11 W
West Foxboro, Ma., U.S. 201 42.05 N 71.17 W
West Frankfort, Il., U.S. 130 G9 37.53 N 88.56 W
West Friese Eilanden, is., Neth. 20 A14 53.26 N 5.30 E
West Frisian Islands see West Friese Eilanden, is., Neth. 20 A14 53.26 N 5.30 E
Westgate, Austl. 98 F6 26.35 S 146.12 E
West Gilgo Beach, N.Y., U.S. 194 40.37 N 73.25 W
West Glacier, Mt., U.S. 146 B13 48.29 N 113.58 W
West Grand Lake, res., Me., U.S. 122 E8 45.14 N 67.51 W
West Ham, ngh., Eng., U.K. 178 51.31 N 0.01 E
West Ham Football Club, p.o.i., Eng., U.K. 178 51.32 N 0.02 E
West Hamlin, W.V., U.S. 124 F3 38.16 N 82.12 W
Westhampton, Va., U.S. 202c 38.54 N 77.11 W
West Hanningfield, Eng., U.K. 178 51.40 N 0.30 E
West Hanover, Ma., U.S. 201 42.07 N 70.53 W
West Harbor, b., N.Y., U.S. 194 40.54 N 73.32 W
West Hartford, Ct., U.S. 124 C13 41.45 N 72.44 W
Westhaven, Ca., U.S. 148 B1 41.02 N 124.05 W
West Haven, Ct., U.S. 124 C13 41.16 N 72.57 W
Westhaven, Il., U.S. 196 41.35 N 87.51 W
Westhead, Eng., U.K. 180 53.34 N 2.51 W
West Heidelberg, Austl. 192b 37.45 S 145.02 E
West Helena, Ar., U.S. 134 C8 34.32 N 90.39 W
Westhemmerde, Ger. 181 51.33 N 7.47 E
West Hempstead, N.Y., U.S. 194 40.42 N 73.39 W
West Hill, ngh., On., Can. 193b 43.46 N 79.11 W
Westhofen, Ger. 181 51.25 N 7.31 E
Westhoff, Tx., U.S. 136 E10 29.12 N 97.28 W
West Homestead, Pa., U.S. 197b 40.24 N 79.55 W
Westhope, N.D., U.S. 142 F12 48.54 N 101.00 W
West Horndon, Eng., U.K. 178 51.34 N 0.21 E
West Horsley, Eng., U.K. 178 51.16 N 0.27 W
Westhoughton, Eng., U.K. 180 53.33 N 2.32 W
West Hoxton, Austl. 192a 33.55 S 150.49 E
West Humble, Eng., U.K. 178 51.15 N 0.20 W
West Huntington, N.Y., U.S. 194 40.49 N 73.26 W
West Hyde, Eng., U.K. 178 51.37 N 0.30 W
West Ice Shelf, ice, Ant. 103 B13 67.00 S 85.00 E
Westick, Ger. 181 51.35 N 7.38 E
Westig, Ger. 181 51.22 N 7.45 E
West Indies, is. 106 G15 19.00 N 70.00 W
West Java see Jawa Barat, state, Indon. 66 G5 7.00 S 107.00 E
West Jefferson, N.C., U.S. 124 H4 36.23 N 81.28 W
West Jordan, Ut., U.S. 150 C4 40.37 N 111.56 W
West Keansburg, N.J., U.S. 194 40.27 N 74.09 W
West Kettle, stm., B.C., Can. 144 G12 49.10 N 118.58 W
West Kingston, R.I., U.S. 124 C14 41.28 N 71.33 W
West Lafayette, In., U.S. 130 D11 40.25 N 86.54 W
West Lafayette, Oh., U.S. 124 D4 40.16 N 81.45 W
Westlake, La., U.S. 134 G5 30.14 N 93.15 W
West Lake, l., N.J., U.S. 194 40.58 N 74.22 W
West Lamma Channel, strt., China 189d 22.13 N 114.04 E
West Lancashire, mun., Eng., U.K. 180 53.35 N 2.50 W
Westland Center, shp. cen., Mi., U.S. 199 42.20 N 83.23 W
Westland National Park, p.o.i., N.Z. 102 F3 43.30 S 170.10 E
West Lanham Hills, Md., U.S. 202c 38.57 N 76.53 W
West Laramie, Wy., U.S. 140 F7 41.18 N 105.37 W
West Lawn, Va., U.S. 202c 38.52 N 77.11 W
West Lebanon, In., U.S. 130 D10 40.15 N 87.24 W
Westleigh, Eng., U.K. 180 53.30 N 2.31 W
West Liberty, Ia., U.S. 130 C6 41.34 N 91.15 W
West Liberty, Ky., U.S. 124 G2 37.55 N 83.15 W
West Liberty, Oh., U.S. 124 D2 40.14 N 83.46 W
West Liberty, ngh., Pa., U.S. 197b 40.24 N 80.01 W
West Little Owyhee, stm., Or., U.S. 148 A8 42.29 N 117.12 W
Westlock, Ab., Can. 144 B17 54.09 N 113.52 W
West Lorne, On., Can. 126 F8 42.36 N 81.36 W
West Los Angeles, ngh., Ca., U.S. 198 34.03 N 118.28 W
West Malling Aerodrome, arpt., Eng., U.K. 178 51.16 N 0.24 E
West Manayunk, Pa., U.S. 203 40.01 N 75.14 W
Westmeath, state, Ire. 10 H5 53.30 N 7.30 W
West Memphis, Ar., U.S. 134 B8 35.09 N 90.10 W
Westminster, Co., U.S. 138 B3 39.51 N 105.03 W
Westminster, Md., U.S. 124 E9 39.33 N 76.59 W
Westminster, S.C., U.S. 132 B2 34.40 N 83.05 W
Westminster, ngh., Eng., U.K. 178 51.30 N 0.09 W
Westminster Abbey, rel., Eng., U.K. 178 51.30 N 0.07 W
Westminster Mall, shp. cen., Ca., U.S. 198 33.45 N 118.01 W
West Monroe, La., U.S. 134 E6 32.30 N 92.08 W
Westmont, Ca., U.S. 198 33.56 N 118.18 W
Westmont, Il., U.S. 196 41.47 N 87.58 W
Westmont, N.J., U.S. 203 39.54 N 75.02 W
Westmoreland, Ks., U.S. 138 B12 39.23 N 96.24 W
Westmoreland, Tn., U.S. 130 H11 36.32 N 86.14 W
Westmorland, Ca., U.S. 148 J10 33.03 N 115.36 W
West Mountain, mtn., N.Y., U.S. 126 E15 43.51 N 74.43 W
West Nab, mtn., Eng., U.K. 180 53.35 N 1.53 W
West Newton, Ma., U.S. 201 42.21 N 71.14 W
West New York, N.J., U.S. 194 40.47 N 74.00 W
West Nicholson, Zimb. 88 E4 21.05 S 29.24 E
West Nishnabotna, stm., Ia., U.S. 130 C2 40.30 N 95.41 W
West Nodaway, stm., Ia., U.S. 130 C3 40.38 N 95.01 W
West Norwood, ngh., Eng., U.K. 178 51.26 N 0.06 W
West Nueces, stm., Tx., U.S. 136 E7 29.16 N 99.56 W
West Nusa Tenggara see Nusa Tenggara Barat, state, Indon. 66 G10 8.50 S 117.30 E
Weston, Malay. 66 A9 5.12 N 115.36 E
Weston, Eng., U.K. 180 53.19 N 2.44 W
Weston, Co., U.S. 138 D4 37.07 N 104.50 W
Weston, Id., U.S. 146 H14 42.03 N 111.58 W
Weston, Mo., U.S. 130 E3 39.24 N 94.54 W
Weston, Ne., U.S. 128 J2 41.11 N 96.45 W
Weston, Oh., U.S. 124 C2 41.20 N 83.47 W
Weston, Or., U.S. 146 E8 45.48 N 118.25 W
Weston, W.V., U.S. 124 E5 39.01 N 80.28 W
Weston, mun., On., Can. 193b 43.43 N 79.31 W
Westonaria, S. Afr. 191d 26.19 S 27.39 E
Weston Reservoir, res., Ma., U.S. 201 42.21 N 71.18 W
Westons Mill Pond, l., N.J., U.S. 194 40.28 N 74.25 W
Weston-super-Mare, Eng., U.K. 10 J9 51.20 N 2.58 W
West Orange, N.J., U.S. 194 40.47 N 74.14 W
West Orange, Tx., U.S. 136 D14 30.05 N 93.46 W
Westover, Tn., U.S. 134 B10 35.36 N 88.52 W
Westover, W.V., U.S. 124 E5 39.37 N 79.58 W
Westover Air Force Base, mil., Ma., U.S. 124 B13 42.12 N 72.33 W
Westowne, Md., U.S. 202b 39.17 N 76.43 W
West Palm Beach, Fl., U.S. 132 J5 26.40 N 80.05 W
West Palm Beach Canal, can., Fl., U.S. 132 J5 26.38 N 80.02 W
West Paris, Me., U.S. 122 F6 44.19 N 70.33 W
West Paterson, N.J., U.S. 194 40.53 N 74.11 W
West Peckham, Eng., U.K. 178 51.15 N 0.22 E
West Pensacola, Fl., U.S. 134 G11 30.25 N 87.15 W
Westphalia, Ks., U.S. 130 F2 38.11 N 95.29 W
West Plains, Mo., U.S. 130 H6 36.43 N 91.51 W
West Point, Ca., U.S. 148 E5 38.23 N 120.31 W
West Point, Ga., U.S. 134 E13 32.54 N 85.09 W
West Point, Ia., U.S. 130 D6 40.43 N 91.27 W
West Point, Ky., U.S. 130 F12 37.59 N 85.57 W
West Point, Ms., U.S. 134 D10 33.36 N 88.39 W
West Point, Ne., U.S. 128 J2 41.50 N 96.42 W
West Point, N.Y., U.S. 124 C11 41.24 N 73.58 W
West Point, Pa., U.S. 203 40.12 N 75.18 W
West Point, Va., U.S. 124 G9 37.32 N 76.47 W
West Point, c., P.E., Can. 122 D12 46.37 N 64.23 W
West Point Lake, res., U.S. 134 D14 32.59 N 85.11 W
West Pond, l., N.Y., U.S. 194 40.53 N 73.38 W
West Poplar see Poplar, West Fork, stm., N.A. 142 F8 48.31 N 105.21 W
Westport, N.S., Can. 122 F10 44.15 N 66.21 W
Westport, On., Can. 126 D13 44.40 N 76.24 W
Westport, Ire. 10 H3 53.47 N 9.31 W
Westport, N.Z. 102 E4 41.45 S 171.35 E
Westport, Ct., U.S. 124 C12 41.08 N 73.21 W
Westport, In., U.S. 130 E12 39.10 N 85.34 W
Westport, Or., U.S. 146 D3 46.07 N 123.22 W
Westport, Wa., U.S. 146 D2 46.53 N 124.06 W
West Portsmouth, Oh., U.S. 124 F2 38.45 N 83.02 W
West Prairie, stm., Ab., Can. 144 A14 55.02 N 116.17 W
West Puente Valley, Ca., U.S. 198 34.04 N 117.59 W
West Pullman, ngh., Il., U.S. 196 41.41 N 87.39 W
Westpunt, c., Aruba 158g o19 12.37 N 70.03 W
West Pymble, Austl. 192a 33.46 S 151.08 E
West Quoddy Head, c., Me., U.S. 122 F10 44.48 N 66.57 W
West Rand, S. Afr. 191d 26.07 S 27.45 E
Westray, i., Scot., U.K. 10 B9 59.18 N 3.00 W
Westray Firth, strt., Scot., U.K. 10 B10 59.12 N 2.55 W
West Richland, Wa., U.S. 146 D7 46.17 N 119.22 W
West Road, stm., B.C., Can. 144 C7 53.18 N 122.52 W
West Rosebud Creek, stm., Mt., U.S. 146 E17 45.29 N 109.27 W
West Roxbury, ngh., Ma., U.S. 201 42.17 N 71.09 W
West Rutland, Vt., U.S. 122 G3 43.36 N 73.03 W
West Ryde, Austl. 192a 33.48 S 151.05 E
West Saint Marys, stm., N.S., Can. 122 E14 45.15 N 62.04 W
West Salem, Il., U.S. 130 F9 38.30 N 88.00 W
West Salem, Oh., U.S. 124 D3 40.57 N 82.07 W
West Salem, Wi., U.S. 128 H7 43.53 N 91.04 W
West Salt Creek, stm., Co., U.S. 150 D8 39.13 N 108.54 W
West Sayville, N.Y., U.S. 194 40.43 N 73.05 W
West Sayville County Park, p.o.i., N.Y., U.S. 194 40.43 N 73.06 W
West Shoal Lake, l., Mb., Can. 142 D16 50.20 N 97.41 W
West Siberian Plain see Zapadno-Sibirskaja ravnina, pl., Russia 48 B12 60.00 N 75.00 E
West Side Tennis Club, p.o.i., N.Y., U.S. 194 40.43 N 73.51 W
West Slovakia see Západoslovenský, state, Slvk. 24 H14 48.20 N 18.00 E
West Spanish Peak, mtn., Co., U.S. 138 D4 37.23 N 104.59 W
West Sumatra see Sumatera Barat, state, Indon. 66 D2 1.01 S 101.20 E
West Terre Haute, In., U.S. 130 E10 39.27 N 87.26 W
West Thurrock, Eng., U.K. 178 51.29 N 0.16 E
West Tilbury, Eng., U.K. 178 51.29 N 0.24 E
Westtown, Pa., U.S. 203 39.56 N 75.33 W
West Turffontein, ngh., S. Afr. 191d 26.16 S 28.02 E
West Union, Ia., U.S. 130 B6 42.57 N 91.48 W
West Union, Oh., U.S. 124 F2 38.47 N 83.32 W
West Union, W.V., U.S. 124 E5 39.17 N 80.45 W
West Union Creek, stm., Ca., U.S. 200 37.25 N 122.16 W
West Unity, Oh., U.S. 124 C1 41.35 N 84.26 W
West Valley City, Ut., U.S. 150 C4 40.41 N 111.58 W
West Vancouver, B.C., Can. 144 G7 49.19 N 123.08 W
West View Amusement Park, p.o.i., Pa., U.S. 197b 40.31 N 80.02 W
Westville, N.S., Can. 122 E14 45.33 N 62.42 W
Westville, In., U.S. 130 C11 41.32 N 86.53 W
Westville, N.J., U.S. 203 39.52 N 75.07 W
Westville, Ok., U.S. 130 H3 35.59 N 94.34 W
Westville Grove, N.J., U.S. 203 39.51 N 75.07 W
Westville Oaks, N.J., U.S. 203 39.51 N 75.08 W
West Virginia, state, U.S. 124 F5 38.45 N 80.30 W
West Walker, stm., U.S. 148 E6 38.53 N 119.10 W
West Warwick, R.I., U.S. 124 C14 41.42 N 71.31 W
West Webster, N.Y., U.S. 126 E12 43.10 N 77.29 W
West Whittier, Ca., U.S. 198 33.59 N 118.03 W
West Wickham, ngh., Eng., U.K. 178 51.22 N 0.01 W
Westwold, B.C., Can. 144 F11 50.28 N 119.44 W
Westwood, Ca., U.S. 148 C5 40.18 N 121.00 W
Westwood, ngh., Ca., U.S. 198 34.04 N 118.27 W
Westwood Lakes, Fl., U.S. 132 K5 25.44 N 80.22 W
West Wyalong, Austl. 98 I6 33.55 S 147.11 E
West Yellow Creek, stm., Mo., U.S. 130 E4 39.38 N 93.03 W
West Yellowstone, Mt., U.S. 146 F15 44.39 N 111.03 W
West Yorkshire, co., Eng., U.K. 180 53.43 N 1.58 W
West Yorkshire, hist. reg., Eng., U.K. 180 53.43 N 1.58 W
Wetar, Pulau, i., Indon. 60 G8 7.48 S 126.18 E
Wetar, Selat, strt., Indon. 60 G8 8.20 S 126.30 E
Wetaskiwin, Ab., Can. 144 C17 52.58 N 113.22 W
Wete, Tan. 86 E7 5.02 S 39.43 E
Wetherill Park, Austl. 192a 33.51 S 150.54 E
Wethersfield, Ct., U.S. 124 C13 41.41 N 72.39 W
Wethmar, Ger. 181 51.37 N 7.33 E
Wetmore, Ks., U.S. 130 E2 39.38 N 95.48 W
Wet Mountains, mts., Co., U.S. 138 C3 38.03 N 105.11 W
Wettigan, Mya. 64 C2 18.57 N 95.21 E
Wetumka, Ok., U.S. 134 B2 35.14 N 96.14 W
Wetumpka, Al., U.S. 134 E12 32.32 N 86.12 W
Wetzlar, Ger. 24 F4 50.33 N 8.29 E
Wewahitchka, Fl., U.S. 134 G13 30.06 N 85.12 W
Wewak, Pap. N. Gui. 101a a3 3.34 S 143.38 E
Wewoka, Ok., U.S. 134 B2 35.09 N 96.29 W
Wexford, Ire. 10 I6 52.19 N 6.27 W
Wexford, state, Ire. 10 I6 52.20 N 6.40 W
Wexford, ngh., On., Can. 193b 43.45 N 79.18 W
Wexford Harbour, b., Ire. 10 I6 52.20 N 6.24 W
Wey, stm., Eng., U.K. 10 J12 51.22 N 0.27 W
Weyanoke, Va., U.S. 202c 38.48 N 77.09 W
Weyauwega, Wi., U.S. 128 G10 44.18 N 88.56 W
Weyburn, Sk., Can. 142 E10 49.40 N 103.51 W
Weyer, ngh., Ger. 181 51.10 N 7.01 E
Weyer Markt, Aus. 24 I10 47.51 N 14.38 E
Weymontachie, Qc., Can. 122 C3 47.54 N 73.47 W
Weymouth, N.S., Can. 122 F10 44.25 N 66.00 W
Weymouth, Eng., U.K. 10 K10 50.36 N 2.28 W
Weymouth, Ma., U.S. 124 B15 42.13 N 70.56 W
Weymouth Back, stm., Ma., U.S. 201 42.15 N 70.55 W
Weymouth Fore, stm., Ma., U.S. 201 42.16 N 70.56 W
Weymouth Great Pond, l., Ma., U.S. 201 42.12 N 71.02 W
Whakatane, N.Z. 102 C7 37.58 S 176.59 E
Whalan, Austl. 192a 33.45 S 150.49 E
Whale Creek, stm., N.J., U.S. 194 40.27 N 74.13 W
Whalsay, i., Scot., U.K. 10a n19 60.21 N 0.59 W
Whangarei, N.Z. 102 B6 35.43 S 174.19 E
Whapmagoostui, Qc., Can. 110 D15 55.17 N 77.44 W
Wharfe, stm., Eng., U.K. 10 H11 53.50 N 1.08 W
Wharles, Eng., U.K. 180 53.49 N 2.50 W
Wharton, Tx., U.S. 136 E11 29.18 N 96.05 W
Wharton, W.V., U.S. 124 G4 37.54 N 81.41 W
Wharton Basin, unds. 174 K12 21.00 S 100.00 E
Wharton Lake, l., Nu., Can. 110 C10 64.00 N 99.51 W
Wharton State Forest, p.o.i., N.J., U.S. 203 39.45 N 74.40 W
Whataroa, N.Z. 102 F4 43.14 S 170.20 E
What Cheer, Ia., U.S. 130 C5 41.24 N 92.21 W
Whatley, Al., U.S. 134 F11 31.39 N 87.42 W
Whatshan Lake, l., B.C., Can. 144 F12 50.01 N 118.06 W
Wheatland, Ca., U.S. 148 D4 39.00 N 121.25 W
Wheatland, Ia., U.S. 130 C7 41.49 N 90.49 W
Wheatland, Wy., U.S. 140 E8 42.03 N 104.57 W
Wheatland Reservoir, res., Wy., U.S. 140 F7 41.52 N 105.36 W
Wheatley, On., Can. 126 F7 42.06 N 82.27 W
Wheatley, Ar., U.S. 134 C7 34.55 N 91.06 W
Wheaton, Il., U.S. 130 C9 41.51 N 88.06 W
Wheaton, Md., U.S. 124 E8 39.02 N 77.03 W
Wheaton, Mn., U.S. 128 F2 45.48 N 96.29 W
Wheaton Plaza, shp. cen., Md., U.S. 202c 39.02 N 77.03 W
Wheaton Regional Park, p.o.i., Md., U.S. 202c 39.03 N 77.02 W
Wheat Ridge, Co., U.S. 138 B3 39.48 N 105.05 W
Wheelbarrow Peak, mtn., Nv., U.S. 148 F9 37.27 N 116.05 W
Wheeler, Ms., U.S. 134 C10 34.34 N 88.36 W
Wheeler, Tx., U.S. 138 F8 35.26 N 100.16 W
Wheeler, stm., Qc., Can. 110 D17 57.04 N 67.09 W
Wheeler Dam, dam., N.H., U.S. 201 42.48 N 71.12 W
Wheeler Island, i., Ca., U.S. 200 38.05 N 121.56 W
Wheeler Lake, res., Al., U.S. 134 C12 34.40 N 87.05 W
Wheeler Peak, mtn., Ca., U.S. 148 E6 38.25 N 119.17 W
Wheeler Peak, mtn., Nv., U.S. 150 D2 38.59 N 114.19 W
Wheeler Peak, mtn., N.M., U.S. 138 E3 36.34 N 105.25 W
Wheelers Hill, Austl. 192b 37.55 S 145.11 E
Wheeling, W.V., U.S. 124 D5 40.03 N 80.40 W
Whelton, Eng., U.K. 180 53.41 N 2.36 W
Wheelwright, Arg. 172 F7 33.47 S 61.13 W
Wheelwright, Ky., U.S. 124 G3 37.19 N 82.43 W
Wheelwright Park, p.o.i., Ma., U.S. 201 42.15 N 70.49 W
Whelpleyhill, Eng., U.K. 178 51.44 N 0.33 W
Whidbey Island, i., Wa., U.S. 146 B4 48.16 N 122.42 W
Whigham, Ga., U.S. 134 G14 30.52 N 84.18 W
Whippany, stm., N.J., U.S. 194 40.51 N 74.21 W
Whirlpool, The, stm., N.A. 202a 43.07 N 79.04 W
Whiskey Peak, mtn., Wy., U.S. 140 E5 42.18 N 107.35 W
Whiskeytown-Shasta-Trinity National Recreation Area, p.o.i., Ca., U.S. 148 C2 40.51 N 122.45 W
Whisky Chitto Creek, stm., La., U.S. 134 G5 30.30 N 92.54 W
Whistler, B.C., Can. 144 F8 50.06 N 123.00 W
Whiston, Eng., U.K. 180 53.25 N 2.50 W
Whitaker, Pa., U.S. 197b 40.24 N 79.53 W
Whitakers, N.C., U.S. 124 H8 36.06 N 77.42 W
Whitby, On., Can. 126 E11 43.52 N 78.55 W
Whitby, Eng., U.K. 10 G12 54.29 N 0.37 W
Whitby, Eng., U.K. 180 53.17 N 2.54 W
Whitchurch, Eng., U.K. 10 H10 52.58 N 2.41 W
Whitchurch-Stouffville, On., Can. 126 E10 43.57 N 79.15 W
White, Ga., U.S. 134 C14 34.16 N 84.44 W
White, S.D., U.S. 128 G2 44.25 N 96.39 W
White, stm., B.C., Can. 144 F15 50.21 N 115.37 W
White, stm., N.A. 109 D11 63.10 N 139.34 W
White, stm., U.S. 116 C7 33.52 N 91.03 W
White, stm., U.S. 140 D13 43.42 N 99.27 W
White, stm., U.S. 150 C7 40.04 N 109.41 W
White, stm., Az., U.S. 150 J6 33.44 N 110.13 W
White, stm., In., U.S. 130 F10 38.24 N 87.44 W
White, stm., Mi., U.S. 126 E3 43.21 N 86.24 W
White, stm., Nv., U.S. 150 F1 37.42 N 115.10 W
White, stm., Or., U.S. 146 E5 45.13 N 121.03 W
White, stm., Tx., U.S. 138 H7 33.14 N 100.56 W
White, stm., Vt., U.S. 122 G4 43.39 N 72.18 W
White, stm., Wa., U.S. 146 C6 47.50 N 120.49 W
White, stm., Wa., U.S. 146 C5 47.15 N 122.25 W
White, stm., Wi., U.S. 128 E7 46.35 N 90.41 W
White, East Fork, stm., Az., U.S. 150 J7 33.47 N 109.59 W
White, East Fork, stm., In., U.S. 130 F10 38.32 N 87.14 W
White, Lake, l., Austl. 96 D5 21.06 S 128.59 E
White, North Fork, stm., Az., U.S. 150 J7 33.47 N 109.59 W
White, North Fork, stm., Co., U.S. 150 C9 39.58 N 107.38 W
White, South Fork, stm., Co., U.S. 150 D9 39.58 N 107.38 W
White Bay, b., Nf., Can. 111a i22 50.07 N 56.27 W
White Bear Indian Reserve, ind. res., Sk., Can. 142 E11 49.45 N 102.15 W
White Bear Lake, Mn., U.S. 128 F6 45.03 N 93.00 W
Whitebear Lake, l., Sk., Can. 142 C5 51.05 N 108.05 W
White Bluff, Tn., U.S. 130 H10 36.06 N 87.13 W
White Breast Creek, stm., Ia., U.S. 128 J5 41.24 N 93.03 W
White Butte, mtn., N.D., U.S. 140 A9 46.23 N 103.19 W
White Cap Mountain, mtn., Me., U.S. 122 E7 45.32 N 69.18 W
White Castle, La., U.S. 134 G7 30.09 N 91.08 W
White City, Ks., U.S. 138 C12 38.47 N 96.44 W
White City Stadium, p.o.i., Eng., U.K. 178 51.31 N 0.14 W
White Clay Creek, stm., U.S. 140 E10 43.12 N 102.49 W
White Clay Creek, stm., U.S. 203 39.42 N 75.37 W
White Cliffs, Austl. 96 E4 28.25 S 122.55 E
White Cliffs, Austl. 98 H4 30.51 S 143.05 E
White Cloud, Mi., U.S. 126 E4 43.33 N 85.45 W
Whitecourt, Ab., Can. 144 B15 54.08 N 115.43 W
White Deer, Tx., U.S. 138 F7 35.26 N 101.10 W
White Earth, stm., N.D., U.S. 142 F11 48.05 N 102.44 W
White Earth Indian Reservation, ind. res., Mn., U.S. 128 D3 47.18 N 95.50 W
Whiteface, Tx., U.S. 138 H6 33.36 N 102.37 W
Whiteface, stm., Mn., U.S. 128 D6 46.58 N 92.47 W
Whiteface Mountain, mtn., N.Y., U.S. 126 D16 44.22 N 73.54 W
Whitefield, N.H., U.S. 122 F5 44.22 N 71.36 W
Whitefish, Mt., U.S. 146 B12 48.24 N 114.20 W
Whitefish, stm., Mi., U.S. 126 B3 45.55 N 86.57 W
Whitefish Bay, Wi., U.S. 130 A10 43.05 N 87.53 W
Whitefish Bay, b., On., Can. 128 B4 49.26 N 94.14 W
Whitefish Bay, b., N.A. 126 B5 46.40 N 84.50 W
Whitefish Lake, l., Ab., Can. 144 B18 54.22 N 111.55 W
Whitefish Lake, l., N.T., Can. 110 C9 62.41 N 106.48 W
Whitefish Lake, l., Mt., U.S. 146 B12 48.26 N 114.22 W
White Fish Lake Indian Reserve, ind. res., Ab., Can. 144 B18 54.19 N 111.49 W
Whitefish Point, Mi., U.S. 126 B4 46.45 N 84.58 W
Whitefish Point, c., Mi., U.S. 126 B4 46.45 N 84.59 W
Whitefish Range, mts., Mt., U.S. 146 B12 48.40 N 114.26 W
White Hall, Ar., U.S. 134 C6 34.16 N 92.06 W
White Hall, Il., U.S. 130 E7 39.26 N 90.24 W
Whitehall, Mi., U.S. 126 E3 43.23 N 86.20 W
Whitehall, Mt., U.S. 146 E14 45.52 N 112.06 W
Whitehall, N.Y., U.S. 126 E16 43.33 N 73.24 W
Whitehall, Wi., U.S. 128 G7 44.21 N 91.18 W
Whitehaven, Eng., U.K. 10 G9 54.32 N 3.34 W
White Haven, Pa., U.S. 124 C10 41.03 N 75.47 W
White Holme Reservoir, res., Eng., U.K. 180 53.41 N 2.02 W
Whitehorse, Yk., Can. 110 C4 60.43 N 135.07 W
White House, Tn., U.S. 130 H11 36.31 N 86.38 W
Whitehouse, Tx., U.S. 136 B12 32.13 N 95.12 W
White House, bldg., D.C., U.S. 202c 38.54 N 77.02 W
White Island, i., Nu., Can. 110 B13 65.50 N 84.50 W
White Island, i., N.Z. 102 C7 37.31 S 177.10 E
White Lake, Mi., U.S. 199 42.41 N 83.33 W
White Lake, S.D., U.S. 140 D14 43.43 N 98.42 W
White Lake, Wi., U.S. 128 F10 45.10 N 88.44 W
White Lake, l., On., Can. 126 C13 45.17 N 76.31 W
White Lake, l., La., U.S. 134 H6 29.43 N 92.28 W
White Lake, l., Mi., U.S. 199 42.40 N 83.34 W
Whiteley Village, Eng., U.K. 178 51.21 N 0.26 W
Whiteman Air Force Base, mil., Mo., U.S. 130 F4 38.44 N 93.36 W
Whiteman Airpark, arpt., Ca., U.S. 198 34.15 N 118.25 W
Whitemark, Austl. 99a n13 40.06 S 148.01 E
White Marsh, Md., U.S. 202b 39.23 N 76.26 W
Whitemarsh Run, stm., Md., U.S. 202b 39.22 N 76.25 W
White Meadow Lake, l., N.J., U.S. 194 40.55 N 74.31 W
White Mountain, Ak., U.S. 109 D7 64.41 N 163.24 W
White Mountain Peak, mtn., Ca., U.S. 148 F7 37.37 N 118.16 W
White Mountains, mts., U.S. 148 F7 37.33 N 118.13 W
White Mountains, mts., Az., U.S. 150 J7 33.55 N 109.33 W
White Mountains, mts., N.H., U.S. 122 F5 44.10 N 71.35 W
Whitemouth, Mb., Can. 142 E17 49.57 N 95.59 W
Whitemouth, stm., Mb., Can. 142 E18 50.07 N 96.01 W
Whitemouth Lake, l., Mb., Can. 142 E18 49.14 N 95.40 W
Whitemud, stm., Mb., Can. 142 D15 50.20 N 98.30 W
White Nile (Abyad, Al-Bahr al-), stm., Sudan 82 E6 15.38 N 32.31 E
White Oak, Md., U.S. 202c 39.02 N 77.00 W
White Oak, Pa., U.S. 197b 40.20 N 79.48 W
White Oak, Tx., U.S. 136 B13 32.32 N 94.51 W
White Oak, stm., N.C., U.S. 132 B8 34.40 N 77.06 W
White Oak Creek, stm., Tx., U.S. 134 D3 33.15 N 94.39 W
White Oak Lake, res., Ar., U.S. 134 D5 33.40 N 93.05 W
White Oak Regional Park, p.o.i., Pa., U.S. 197a 40.21 N 79.47 W
White Otter Lake, l., On., Can. 128 B6 49.07 N 91.52 W
White Pigeon, Mi., U.S. 130 C12 41.47 N 85.38 W
White Pine, Mi., U.S. 128 E9 46.44 N 89.35 W
Whitepine, Mt., U.S. 146 C11 47.45 N 115.29 W
White Pine, Tn., U.S. 124 H2 36.06 N 83.17 W
White Pines, Il., U.S. 196 41.57 N 87.57 W
White Plains, N.Y., U.S. 124 C12 41.02 N 73.45 W
White Plains, N.C., U.S. 124 H5 36.26 N 80.37 W
White Pond, l., Ma., U.S. 201 42.26 N 71.23 W
Whiteriver, Az., U.S. 150 J6 33.49 N 109.57 W
White River, S.D., U.S. 140 D12 43.34 N 100.44 W
White River Junction, Vt., U.S. 122 G4 43.39 N 72.19 W
White Rock, B.C., Can. 144 G8 49.01 N 122.48 W

Name	Page	Map Ref.	Latitude	Longitude
White Rock Creek, stm., Ks., U.S.	138	B10	39.55 N	97.52 W
White Rock Creek, stm., Tx., U.S.	136	C12	30.53 N	95.15 W
White Rocks, mtn., U.S.	124	H2	36.40 N	83.27 W
Whiterocks, stm., Ut., U.S.	150	C7	40.26 N	109.55 W
White Roding, Eng., U.K.	178		51.48 N	0.16 E
White Russia see Belarus, ctry., Eur.	40	E5	53.50 N	28.00 E
Whitesail Lake, res., B.C., Can.	144	C4	53.30 N	127.00 W
White Salmon, Wa., U.S.	146	E5	45.43 N	121.28 W
White Salmon, stm., Wa., U.S.	146	E5	45.43 N	121.31 W
Whitesand, stm., Sk., Can.	142	C11	51.33 N	101.56 W
White Sands Missile Range, mil., N.M., U.S.	138	H2	33.17 N	106.27 W
White Sands National Monument, p.o.i., N.M., U.S.	136	B1	32.46 N	106.20 W
Whitesboro, Tx., U.S.	134	D2	33.40 N	96.54 W
Whitesburg, Ky., U.S.	124	G3	37.07 N	82.49 W
White Sea see Beloe more, s., Russia	14	G27	65.36 N	37.52 E
White Sea-Baltic Canal see Belomorsko-Baltijskij kanal, can., Russia	18	D22	62.48 N	34.48 E
White Settlement, Tx., U.S.	136	B10	32.46 N	97.27 W
Whiteshell Provincial Park, p.o.i., Mb., Can.	128	B3	50.03 N	95.29 W
White Springs, Fl., U.S.	132	F3	30.19 N	82.45 W
Whitestone, ngh., N.Y., U.S.	194		40.47 N	73.49 W
White Sulphur Springs, Mt., U.S.	146	D16	46.32 N	110.54 W
White Sulphur Springs, W.V., U.S.	124	G5	37.47 N	80.17 W
Whitesville, Ky., U.S.	130	G11	37.41 N	86.52 W
Whiteville, N.C., U.S.	132	B7	34.19 N	78.42 W
Whiteville, Tn., U.S.	134	B9	35.19 N	89.08 W
White Volta (Volta Blanche), stm., Afr.	84	G4	8.56 N	1.09 W
Whitewater, Ks., U.S.	138	D11	37.58 N	97.09 W
Whitewater, Mt., U.S.	142	F6	48.45 N	107.37 W
Whitewater, Wi., U.S.	130	B9	42.50 N	88.43 W
Whitewater, stm., U.S.	130	E13	39.09 N	84.47 W
Whitewater, stm., Ca., U.S.	148	J9	33.30 N	116.03 W
Whitewater, stm., Mo., U.S.	130	G8	36.56 N	89.42 W
Whitewater Baldy, mtn., N.M., U.S.	150	J8	33.20 N	108.39 W
Whitewater Bay, b., Fl., U.S.	132	K4	25.16 N	81.00 W
Whitewater Creek, stm., N.A.	142	F6	48.32 N	107.24 W
Whitewater Creek, stm., Ga., U.S.	134	E14	32.20 N	84.02 W
Whitewater Lake, l., Mb., Can.	142	E13	49.15 N	100.20 W
White Woman Creek, stm., U.S.	138	C7	38.25 N	100.54 W
Whitewood, Austl.	98	C4	21.28 S	143.36 E
Whitewood, Sk., Can.	142	D11	50.20 N	102.15 W
Whitewood, S.D., U.S.	140	C9	44.27 N	103.38 W
Whitewood, Lake, l., S.D., U.S.	140	C15	44.20 N	97.17 W
Whitewright, Tx., U.S.	134	D2	33.30 N	96.23 W
Whithorn, Jam.	158d	i12	18.15 N	78.01 W
Whithorn, Scot., U.K.	10	G8	54.43 N	4.25 W
Whiting, Ia., U.S.	130	B1	42.08 N	96.10 W
Whiting, Ks., U.S.	130	E2	39.35 N	95.36 W
Whiting, Wi., U.S.	128	G9	44.29 N	89.32 W
Whiting Field Naval Air Station, mil., Fl., U.S.	134	G11	30.43 N	87.02 W
Whitley City, Ky., U.S.	130	H13	36.43 N	84.28 W
Whitley Row, Eng., U.K.	178		51.15 N	0.09 E
Whitman, Ma., U.S.	124	B15	42.04 N	70.56 W
Whitman Mission National Historic Site, p.o.i., Wa., U.S.	146	E8	46.01 N	118.30 W
Whitmans Pond, l., Ma., U.S.	201		42.12 N	70.57 W
Whitmire, S.C., U.S.	132	B4	34.30 N	81.36 W
Whitmore Lake, l., Mi., U.S.	199		42.26 N	83.45 W
Whitmore Mountains, mts., Ant.	103	D31	82.35 S	104.30 W
Whitney, On., Can.	126	C11	45.29 N	78.14 W
Whitney, Tx., U.S.	136	C10	31.57 N	97.19 W
Whitney, Lake, res., Tx., U.S.	136	C10	31.55 N	97.25 W
Whitney, Mount, mtn., Ca., U.S.	148	G7	36.35 N	118.18 W
Whitney Point, N.Y., U.S.	124	B10	42.18 N	75.56 W
Whitney Woods Reservation, p.o.i., Ma., U.S.	201		42.13 N	70.51 W
Whitsunday Island, i., Austl.	98	C7	20.15 S	148.58 E
Whittemore, Ia., U.S.	130	A3	43.04 N	94.26 W
Whittemore, Mi., U.S.	126	D6	44.14 N	83.48 W
Whittier, Ak., U.S.	109	D10	60.46 N	148.45 W
Whittier Narrows Dam, dam., Ca., U.S.	198		34.01 N	118.04 W
Whittier Narrows Flood Control Basin, res., Ca., U.S.	198		34.02 N	118.04 W
Whittle, Cap, c., Qc., Can.	111a	i22	50.11 N	60.09 W
Whittle Hill, hill, Eng., U.K.	180		53.40 N	2.16 W
Whittle-le-Woods, Eng., U.K.	180		53.41 N	2.38 W
Whittlesea, Austl.	98	K5	37.30 S	145.07 E
Whittlesea, S. Afr.	90	H8	32.10 S	26.49 E
Whittlesey, Mount, hill, Wi., U.S.	128	E8	46.18 N	90.37 W
Whitwell, Tn., U.S.	134	B13	35.12 N	85.31 W
Wholdaia Lake, l., N.T., Can.	110	C9	60.40 N	104.17 W
Whyalla, Austl.	96	F7	33.02 S	137.34 E
Whycocomagh, N.S., Can.	122	E15	45.59 N	61.08 W
Whymper, Mount, mtn., B.C., Can.	144	H6	48.57 N	124.10 W
Wiang Pa Pao, Thai.	64	C4	19.21 N	99.30 E
Wiang Phan, Thai.	64	B4	20.25 N	99.53 E
Wiarton, On., Can.	126	D8	44.44 N	81.08 W
Wiązów, Pol.	24	F13	50.49 N	17.11 E
Wibaux, Mt., U.S.	142	H9	46.59 N	104.11 W
Wiblingwerde, Ger.	181		51.18 N	7.37 E
Wichian Buri, Thai.	64	E5	15.39 N	101.06 E
Wichita, Ks., U.S.	138	D11	37.40 N	97.17 W
Wichita, stm., Tx., U.S.	138	G10	34.06 N	98.10 W
Wichita Falls, Tx., U.S.	138	H10	33.54 N	98.29 W
Wichita Mountains, mts., Ok., U.S.	138	G10	34.45 N	98.40 W
Wichlinghofen, ngh., Ger.	181		51.27 N	7.30 E
Wick, Scot., U.K.	10	C9	58.26 N	3.05 W
Wick, stm., Scot., U.K.	10	C9	58.26 N	3.05 W
Wickatunk, N.J., U.S.	194		40.21 N	74.14 W
Wickede, ngh., Ger.	181		51.32 N	7.37 E
Wickenburg, Az., U.S.	150	J4	33.58 N	112.43 W
Wickepin, Austl.	96	F3	32.46 S	117.30 E
Wicker Memorial Park, p.o.i., In., U.S.	196		41.34 N	87.28 W
Wickett, Tx., U.S.	136	C5	31.33 N	102.59 W
Wickham, Austl.	96	D3	20.41 S	117.09 E
Wickham, Cape, c., Austl.	98	L4	39.34 S	143.56 E
Wickham Bishops, Eng., U.K.	178		51.47 N	0.40 E
Wickiup Reservoir, res., Or., U.S.	146	G5	43.41 N	121.42 W
Wickliffe, Ky., U.S.	130	H8	36.58 N	89.05 W
Wicklow, Ire.	10	H6	52.59 N	6.03 W
Wicklow, state, Ire.	10	H7	53.00 N	6.30 W
Wicklow Head, c., Ire.	10	I7	52.57 N	6.00 W
Wicklow Mountains, mts., Ire.	10	H6	53.02 N	6.24 W
Wicksteed Lake, l., On., Can.	126	B10	46.45 N	79.40 W
Wid, stm., Eng., U.K.	178		51.45 N	0.27 E
Widdert, ngh., Ger.	181		51.08 N	7.04 E
Widdop Reservoir, res., Eng., U.K.	180		53.48 N	2.06 W
Widen, W.V., U.S.	124	F5	38.27 N	80.51 W
Widener College, educ., Pa., U.S.	203		39.52 N	75.21 W
Wide Ruin Wash, stm., Az., U.S.	150	H7	35.12 N	109.54 W
Widford, Eng., U.K.	178		51.43 N	0.27 E
Widgeegoara Creek, stm., Austl.	98	G6	27.24 S	145.54 E
Widgiemooltha, Austl.	96	F4	31.31 S	121.36 E
Widur, Nepal	70	E10	27.54 N	85.09 E
Więcbork, Pol.	24	C13	53.22 N	17.30 E
Wiek, Ger.	24	B9	54.37 N	13.17 E
Wieleń, Pol.	24	D12	52.53 N	16.11 E
Wielichowo, Pol.	24	D12	52.07 N	16.20 E
Wieliczka, Pol.	24	F16	49.59 N	20.03 E
Wielkopolska, reg., Pol.	24	E14	51.50 N	17.20 E
Wielkopolskie, state, Pol.	24	D12	52.30 N	17.00 E
Wielkopolski Park Narodowy, p.o.i., Pol.	24	D12	52.15 N	16.50 E
Wieluń, Pol.	24	E14	51.13 N	18.34 E
Wiemelhausen, ngh., Ger.	181		51.28 N	7.13 E
Wien (Vienna), Aus.	30	B13	48.13 N	16.20 E
Wien (Vienna), Aus.	182b		48.13 N	16.20 E
Wien, stm., Aus.	182b		48.13 N	16.23 E
Wien, Universität, educ., Aus.	182b		48.13 N	16.22 E
Wiener Berg, hills, Aus.	182b		48.10 N	16.22 E
Wienerherberg, Aus.	182b		48.03 N	16.33 E
Wiener Neustadt, Aus.	30	C13	47.48 N	16.14 E
Wienerwald, mts., Aus.	30	B13	48.15 N	16.00 E
Wieprz, stm., Pol.	24	E18	51.32 N	21.50 E
Wieprza, stm., Pol.	24	B12	54.26 N	16.23 E
Wieprz-Krzna, Kanał, can., Pol.	24	E19	51.58 N	22.46 E
Wierden, Neth.	24	D2	52.21 N	6.35 E
Wiergate, Tx., U.S.	136	D14	30.59 N	93.42 W
Wieruszów, Pol.	24	E14	51.17 N	18.10 E
Wierzyca, stm., Pol.	24	B14	53.49 N	18.50 E
Wiesbaden, Ger.	24	F4	50.04 N	8.14 E
Wiescheid, ngh., Ger.	181		51.08 N	6.59 E
Wiescherhöfen, ngh., Ger.	181		51.39 N	7.46 E
Wieselburg, Aus.	24	H11	48.08 N	15.08 E
Wiesloch, Ger.	24	G4	49.18 N	8.41 E
Wietze, Ger.	24	D5	52.39 N	9.50 E
Wigan, Eng., U.K.	10	H10	53.33 N	2.38 W
Wigan, mun., Eng., U.K.	180		53.32 N	2.35 W
Wigan, mun., Eng., U.K.	180		53.32 N	2.35 W
Wiggington, Eng., U.K.	178		51.47 N	0.38 W
Wiggins, Co., U.S.	138	A4	40.14 N	104.04 W
Wiggins, Ms., U.S.	134	G9	30.51 N	89.08 W
Wiggins Fork, stm., Wy., U.S.	140	D3	43.27 N	109.27 W
Wight, Isle of, i., Eng., U.K.	10	K11	50.40 N	1.20 W
Wigmore, Eng., U.K.	178		51.21 N	0.35 E
Wigtown, Scot., U.K.	10	G8	54.51 N	4.27 W
Wigtown Bay, b., Scot., U.K.	10	G8	54.47 N	4.17 W
Wijalpurā, Nepal	70	E10	26.54 N	85.52 E
Wilber, Ne., U.S.	140	G15	40.28 N	96.58 W
Wilbur, Wa., U.S.	146	C8	47.45 N	118.42 W
Wilburton, Ok., U.S.	134	C3	34.55 N	95.18 W
Wilcannia, Austl.	98	H4	31.33 S	143.22 E
Wilcox, Sk., Can.	142	D9	50.05 N	104.45 W
Wilcox, Ne., U.S.	138	A9	40.22 N	99.09 W
Wilcox, Pa., U.S.	124	C7	41.34 N	78.41 W
Wildboarclough, Eng., U.K.	180		53.13 N	2.02 W
Wildcat Canyon Regional Park, p.o.i., Ca., U.S.	200		37.56 N	122.17 W
Wildcat Creek, stm., Ca., U.S.	200		37.57 N	122.23 W
Wildcat Creek, stm., In., U.S.	130	D11	40.27 N	86.51 W
Wildcat Hill, mtn., Sk., Can.	142	A11	53.17 N	102.30 W
Wild Coast, cst., S. Afr.	90	H9	31.55 S	29.15 E
Wilde, ngh., Arg.	206		34.42 S	58.20 W
Wildenbruch, Ger.	182a		52.17 N	13.04 E
Wilder, Id., U.S.	146	G10	43.41 N	116.54 W
Wilderness of Judaea (Midbar Yehuda), des., Asia	76	G6	31.30 N	35.18 E
Wilderness State Park, p.o.i., Mi., U.S.	126	C4	45.42 N	84.57 W
Wildersville, Tn., U.S.	134	B10	35.47 N	88.21 W
Wildhay, stm., Ab., Can.	144	C13	53.59 N	117.17 W
Wildhorse Creek, stm., U.S.	140	G10	40.28 N	101.43 W
Wildhorse Creek, stm., Ok., U.S.	138	G11	34.31 N	97.09 W
Wild Horse Creek, stm., Wy., U.S.	140	C7	44.38 N	106.08 W
Wild Horse Draw, stm., Tx., U.S.	136	D3	31.50 N	104.28 W
Wild Horse Lake, l., Mt., U.S.	146	B17	48.57 N	110.01 W
Wild Rice, stm., Mn., U.S.	128	D2	47.19 N	96.50 W
Wild Rice, stm., N.D., U.S.	142	H17	46.46 N	96.47 W
Wild Rice, South Branch, stm., Mn., U.S.	128	D2	47.12 N	96.38 W
Wildrose, N.D., U.S.	142	F10	48.38 N	103.11 W
Wild Rose, Wi., U.S.	128	G9	44.10 N	89.15 W
Wildspitze, mtn., Aus.	30	D7	46.53 N	10.52 E
Wildwood, Ab., Can.	144	C15	53.36 N	115.15 W
Wildwood, N.J., U.S.	124	F11	38.59 N	74.48 W
Wildwood, Lake, l., N.J., U.S.	194		41.09 N	74.32 W
Wild Wood Beach, Md., U.S.	202b		39.15 N	76.25 W
Wildwood Canyon Park, p.o.i., Ca., U.S.	198		34.13 N	118.17 W
Wilge, stm., S. Afr.	90	E9	27.02 S	28.21 E
Wilgespruit, stm., S. Afr.	191d		26.07 S	27.52 E
Wilhelm, Mount, mtn., Pap. N. Gui.	101a	b3	5.46 S	145.00 E
Wilhelmina Gebergte, mts., Sur.	164	C6	3.45 N	56.30 W
Wilhelmina Peak see Trikora, Puncak, mtn., Indon.	60	F10	4.17 S	138.39 E
Wilhelm-Pieck-Stadt see Guben, Ger.	24	E10	51.57 N	14.42 E
Wilhelmshaven, Ger.	24	C4	53.31 N	8.06 E
Wilhelmstadt, ngh., Ger.	182a		52.31 N	13.11 E
Wilhelmstal, Nmb.	90	B3	21.54 S	16.19 E
Wilkerson Pass, p., Co., U.S.	138	B3	39.01 N	105.25 W
Wilkes-Barre, Pa., U.S.	124	C10	41.14 N	75.52 W
Wilkesboro, N.C., U.S.	124	H4	36.08 N	81.09 W
Wilkes Land, reg., Ant.	103	C16	69.00 S	120.00 E
Wilket Creek, stm., On., Can.	193b		43.43 N	79.21 W
Wilket Creek Park, p.o.i., On., Can.	193b		43.43 N	79.21 W
Wilkie, Sk., Can.	142	B5	52.25 N	108.40 W
Wilkins Township, Pa., U.S.	197b		40.25 N	79.50 W
Willacoochee, Ga., U.S.	132	E2	31.20 N	83.02 W
Willamette, stm., Or., U.S.	146	E4	45.39 N	122.45 W
Willamette, Middle Fork, stm., Or., U.S.	146	G4	44.01 N	123.00 W
Willamina, Or., U.S.	146	E3	45.04 N	123.29 W
Willandra Billabong Creek, stm., Austl.	98	I5	33.06 S	144.06 E
Willandra National Park, p.o.i., Austl.	98	I5	33.14 S	145.04 E
Willapa, stm., Wa., U.S.	146	D3	46.42 N	123.52 W
Willapa Bay, b., Wa., U.S.	146	D2	46.37 N	124.00 W
Willard, Mo., U.S.	130	G4	37.18 N	93.26 W
Willard, N.M., U.S.	138	G2	34.35 N	106.03 W
Willard, Oh., U.S.	124	C3	41.03 N	82.43 W
Willard, Ut., U.S.	150	B4	41.25 N	112.02 W
Willard, Punta, c., Mex.	154	A2	28.52 N	112.34 W
Willaston, Eng., U.K.	180		53.18 N	3.00 W
Willcox, Az., U.S.	150	K7	32.15 N	109.50 W
Willcox Playa, l., Az., U.S.	150	K7	32.08 N	109.51 W
Willemstad, Neth. Ant.	158g	p22	12.06 N	68.55 W
Willerburn Acres, Md., U.S.	202c		39.03 N	77.10 W
Willeroo, Austl.	96	C6	15.16 S	131.35 E
Willesden, ngh., Eng., U.K.	178		51.33 N	0.14 W
Willett Pond, l., Ma., U.S.	201		42.11 N	71.14 W
Willey Creek, stm., Oh., U.S.	197a		41.25 N	81.25 W
William, Mount, mtn., Austl.	98	K4	37.17 S	142.36 E
William Bill Dannelly Reservoir, res., Al., U.S.	134	E11	32.02 N	87.17 W
William Boyce Regional Park, p.o.i., Pa., U.S.	197b		40.28 N	79.45 W
William Girling Reservoir, res., Eng., U.K.	178		51.37 N	0.02 W
William Patterson College, educ., N.J., U.S.	194		40.56 N	74.12 W
William P. Gleason Park, p.o.i., In., U.S.	196		41.33 N	87.21 W
Williams, Az., U.S.	150	H4	35.15 N	112.11 W
Williams, Ca., U.S.	148	D3	39.08 N	122.08 W
Williams, Ia., U.S.	128	I5	42.29 N	93.32 W
Williams, Mn., U.S.	128	C4	48.44 N	94.53 W
Williams, stm., Austl.	98	C3	20.04 S	141.10 E
Williams Bay, Wi., U.S.	128	I10	42.34 N	88.32 W
Williamsburg, Ia., U.S.	130	C5	41.39 N	92.00 W
Williamsburg, Ky., U.S.	124	H1	36.44 N	84.09 W
Williamsburg, Va., U.S.	124	G9	37.16 N	76.42 W
Williamsburg, ngh., N.Y., U.S.	194		40.42 N	73.57 W
Williamsburg Bridge, trans., N.Y., U.S.	194		40.43 N	73.58 W
Williams Creek, stm., Austl.	192a		33.57 S	150.58 E
Williams Fork, stm., Co., U.S.	150	C9	40.27 N	107.38 W
Williams Lake, B.C., Can.	144	D8	52.07 N	122.08 W
Williams Lake Indian Reserve, ind. res., B.C., Can.	144	D9	52.07 N	122.00 W
Williams Mountain, mtn., Ok., U.S.	134	C4	34.14 N	94.33 W
Williamson, N.Y., U.S.	126	E12	43.13 N	77.10 W
Williamson, W.V., U.S.	124	G3	37.40 N	82.17 W
Williamson, stm., Or., U.S.	146	H5	42.27 N	121.58 W
Williamson, Mount, mtn., Ca., U.S.	148	G7	36.38 N	118.19 W
Williamsport, In., U.S.	130	D10	40.16 N	87.17 W
Williamsport, Pa., U.S.	124	C8	41.14 N	77.00 W
Williamston, Mi., U.S.	130	B13	42.41 N	84.16 W
Williamston, S.C., U.S.	132	B3	34.36 N	82.29 W
Williamstown, Ky., U.S.	124	F1	38.38 N	84.34 W
Williamstown, N.J., U.S.	124	E11	39.41 N	74.59 W
Williamstown, Vt., U.S.	122	F4	44.07 N	72.30 W
Williamstown, W.V., U.S.	124	E4	39.23 N	81.27 W
Williamstown Junction, N.J., U.S.	203		39.45 N	74.56 W
Williamsville, Il., U.S.	128	L9	39.57 N	89.32 W
Willikies, Antig.	159b	f4	17.05 N	61.42 W
Willimantic, Ct., U.S.	124	C13	41.42 N	72.12 W
Willingale, Eng., U.K.	178		51.44 N	0.19 E
Willingboro, N.J., U.S.	124	D11	40.02 N	74.53 W
Willingdon, Ab., Can.	144	C18	53.50 N	112.06 W
Willingdon, Mount, mtn., Ab., Can.	144	E14	51.45 N	116.15 W
Willis, Tx., U.S.	136	D12	30.25 N	95.29 W
Willis, stm., Va., U.S.	124	G7	37.40 N	78.06 W
Willis Group, is., Austl.	96	C10	16.18 S	150.00 E
Williston, S. Afr.	90	G5	31.20 S	20.53 E
Williston, Fl., U.S.	132	G3	29.23 N	82.26 W
Williston, N.D., U.S.	142	F10	48.08 N	103.37 W
Williston, S.C., U.S.	132	C4	33.24 N	81.25 W
Williston Lake, res., B.C., Can.	110	D6	56.00 N	123.53 W
Williston Park, N.Y., U.S.	194		40.45 N	73.38 W
Willisville, Il., U.S.	130	G8	37.58 N	89.35 W
Willits, Ca., U.S.	148	D2	39.24 N	123.21 W
Willmar, Mn., U.S.	128	F3	45.07 N	95.03 W
Willmersdorf, Ger.	182a		52.40 N	13.41 E
Willmore Wilderness Provincial Park, p.o.i., Ab., Can.	144	C12	53.45 N	119.00 W
Willoughby, Oh., U.S.	124	C4	41.38 N	81.24 W
Willoughby, Cape, c., Austl.	98	J2	35.51 S	138.07 E
Willoughby Bay, b., Antig.	159b	f4	17.02 N	61.44 W
Willow, Ak., U.S.	109	D10	61.45 N	150.03 W
Willow, stm., B.C., Can.	144	C8	54.05 N	122.30 W
Willow, stm., Mn., U.S.	128	E5	46.40 N	93.36 W
Willow, stm., Wi., U.S.	128	F6	44.58 N	92.45 W
Willowbrook, Sk., Can.	142	C11	51.12 N	102.48 W
Willow Brook, Ca., U.S.	198		33.54 N	118.13 W
Willowbrook, Il., U.S.	196		41.46 N	87.56 W
Willowbrook, Md., U.S.	202c		39.02 N	77.11 W
Willow Brook, stm., N.J., U.S.	194		40.20 N	74.10 W
Willowbrook Mall, shp. cen., N.J., U.S.	194		40.53 N	74.15 W
Willowbrook Park, p.o.i., N.Y., U.S.	194		40.36 N	74.09 W
Willow Bunch, Sk., Can.	142	E8	49.24 N	105.37 W
Willow Bunch Lake, l., Sk., Can.	142	E8	49.27 N	105.28 W
Willow City, N.D., U.S.	142	F13	48.35 N	100.17 W
Willow Creek, Ca., U.S.	148	C2	40.55 N	123.39 W
Willow Creek, Mt., U.S.	146	E15	45.50 N	111.40 W
Willow Creek, stm., Ab., Can.	144	F17	49.46 N	113.21 W
Willow Creek, stm., Mi., U.S.	199		42.20 N	83.25 W
Willow Creek, stm., Mt., U.S.	142	H5	46.27 N	108.26 W
Willow Creek, stm., Mt., U.S.	142	F7	48.09 N	106.35 W
Willow Creek, stm., Mt., U.S.	146	B15	48.22 N	111.11 W
Willow Creek, stm., Nv., U.S.	148	E9	38.08 N	116.35 W
Willow Creek, stm., N.D., U.S.	142	F13	48.34 N	100.32 W
Willow Creek, stm., Oh., U.S.	197a		41.20 N	82.03 W
Willow Creek, stm., Or., U.S.	146	E7	45.48 N	120.01 W
Willow Creek, stm., Or., U.S.	146	F9	43.59 N	117.13 W
Willowdale, ngh., On., Can.	193b		43.47 N	79.26 W
Willowdale State Forest, p.o.i., Ma., U.S.	201		42.40 N	70.54 W
Willowdene, S. Afr.	191d		26.18 S	27.56 E
Willow Glen, ngh., Ca., U.S.	200		37.18 N	121.53 W
Willow Grove Park, p.o.i., Pa., U.S.	203		40.08 N	75.08 W
Willow Lake, S.D., U.S.	140	C15	44.37 N	97.38 W
Willow Lake, l., N.T., Can.	110	C7	62.11 N	119.10 W
Willow Lake, l., N.Y., U.S.	194		40.43 N	73.50 W
Willow Metropolitan Park, p.o.i., Mi., U.S.	199		42.08 N	83.22 W
Willowmore, S. Afr.	90	H6	33.17 S	23.28 E
Willowra, Austl.	96	D6	21.14 S	132.36 E
Willow Reservoir, res., Wi., U.S.	128	F9	45.42 N	89.52 W
Willow Ridge Estates, N.Y., U.S.	202a		43.01 N	78.49 W
Willow River, B.C., Can.	144	B8	54.04 N	122.29 W
Willow Run, De., U.S.	203		39.44 N	75.36 W
Willow Run, Va., U.S.	202c		38.49 N	77.10 W
Willow Run Airport, arpt., Mi., U.S.	199		42.14 N	83.32 W
Willows, Ca., U.S.	148	D3	39.31 N	122.11 W
Willow Springs, Il., U.S.	196		41.44 N	87.51 W
Willow Springs, Mo., U.S.	130	H6	36.59 N	91.58 W
Willow Springs, Pa., U.S.	197b		40.19 N	79.44 W
Willowvale, S. Afr.	90	H9	32.16 S	28.30 E
Willow Woods, Va., U.S.	202c		38.50 N	77.16 W
Will Rogers Beach State Park, p.o.i., Ca., U.S.	198		34.01 N	118.30 W
Will Rogers State Park, p.o.i., Ca., U.S.	198		34.03 N	118.31 W
Wills Creek, stm., Austl.	98	D2	22.43 S	140.02 E
Willshire, Oh., U.S.	124	D1	40.44 N	84.47 W
Wills Point, Tx., U.S.	136	B11	32.42 N	96.00 W
Willston, Va., U.S.	202c		38.52 N	77.08 W
Willunga, Austl.	98	J2	35.16 S	138.32 E
Wilmar, Ar., U.S.	134	D7	33.38 N	91.55 W
Wilmer, Al., U.S.	134	G10	30.49 N	88.21 W
Wilmer, Pa., U.S.	203		40.07 N	75.32 W
Wilmer, Tx., U.S.	136	B11	32.35 N	96.40 W
Wilmerding, Pa., U.S.	197b		40.23 N	79.48 W
Wilmersdorf, ngh., Ger.	182a		52.30 N	13.19 E
Wilmette, Il., U.S.	130	B10	42.04 N	87.42 W
Wilmington, Eng., U.K.	178		51.26 N	0.12 E
Wilmington, De., U.S.	124	E10	39.44 N	75.32 W
Wilmington, Il., U.S.	130	C9	41.18 N	88.08 W
Wilmington, N.C., U.S.	132	B7	34.14 N	77.57 W
Wilmington, Oh., U.S.	124	E2	39.26 N	83.50 W
Wilmington, Vt., U.S.	122	H4	42.52 N	72.52 W
Wilmington, ngh., Ca., U.S.	198		33.47 N	118.16 W
Wilmington Manor, De., U.S.	203		39.41 N	75.35 W
Wilmington Manor Gardens, De., U.S.	203		39.40 N	75.34 W
Wilmore, Ky., U.S.	130	G13	37.45 N	84.37 W
Wilmot, Ar., U.S.	134	D7	33.03 N	91.34 W
Wilmot, S.D., U.S.	128	F2	45.24 N	96.51 W
Wilmot Woods, p.o.i., Il., U.S.	196		42.18 N	87.56 W
Wilna see Vilnius, Lith.	26	F8	54.40 N	25.17 E
Wilpattu National Park, p.o.i., Sri L.	69	G4	8.20 N	80.00 E
Wilpshire, Eng., U.K.	180		53.47 N	2.28 W
Wilsall, Mt., U.S.	146	D16	45.59 N	110.41 W
Wilson, Austl.	98	H2	31.59 S	138.20 E
Wilson, Ar., U.S.	134	B8	35.34 N	90.02 W
Wilson, Il., U.S.	196		42.21 N	87.54 W
Wilson, Ks., U.S.	138	C10	38.49 N	98.28 W
Wilson, La., U.S.	134	G7	30.55 N	91.06 W
Wilson, N.Y., U.S.	126	E11	43.18 N	78.49 W
Wilson, N.C., U.S.	124	I8	35.43 N	77.54 W
Wilson, Ok., U.S.	138	G11	34.09 N	97.25 W
Wilson, Tx., U.S.	138	H7	33.19 N	101.43 W
Wilson, stm., Austl.	98	F4	27.46 S	142.12 E
Wilson, stm., Or., U.S.	146	E3	45.29 N	123.53 W
Wilson, Cape, c., Nu., Can.	110	B14	67.00 N	81.30 W
Wilson, Mount, mtn., Az., U.S.	150	H2	35.59 N	114.37 W
Wilson, Mount, mtn., Ca., U.S.	148	I7	34.13 N	118.03 W
Wilson, Mount, mtn., Ca., U.S.	198		34.13 N	118.04 W
Wilson, Mount, mtn., Co., U.S.	150	F8	37.51 N	107.59 W
Wilson, Mount, mtn., Nv., U.S.	150	E2	38.15 N	114.23 W
Wilson, Mount, mtn., Or., U.S.	146	E5	45.04 N	121.39 W
Wilson Creek, stm., Wa., U.S.	146	C8	47.24 N	119.07 W
Wilson Lake, res., Al., U.S.	134	C11	34.48 N	87.24 W
Wilson Lake, res., Ks., U.S.	138	C10	38.57 N	98.40 W
Wilson Run, stm., De., U.S.	203		39.48 N	75.35 W
Wilson Run, stm., Pa., U.S.	197b		40.13 N	79.37 W
Wilsons Beach, N.B., Can.	122	F10	44.56 N	66.56 W
Wilson's Creek National Battlefield, p.o.i., Mo., U.S.	130	H4	37.06 N	93.27 W
Wilsons Promontory, pen., Austl.	98	L6	38.55 S	146.20 E
Wilsons Promontory National Park, p.o.i., Austl.	98	L6	38.58 S	146.21 E
Wilsonville, Ne., U.S.	138	A8	40.07 N	100.06 W
Wilton, Eng., U.K.	10	J11	51.05 N	1.52 W
Wilton, Me., U.S.	122	F6	44.35 N	70.14 W
Wilton, N.H., U.S.	124	B14	42.50 N	71.44 W
Wilton, N.D., U.S.	142	G13	47.09 N	100.47 W
Wilton, Wi., U.S.	128	H8	43.48 N	90.31 W
Wilton, stm., Austl.	96	B6	14.43 S	134.33 E
Wilton Farm Acres, Md., U.S.	202b		39.18 N	76.50 W
Wiluna, Austl.	96	E4	26.36 S	120.13 E
Wimauma, Fl., U.S.	132	I3	27.43 N	82.18 W
Wimberley, Tx., U.S.	136	D9	29.59 N	98.06 W
Wimbledon, N.D., U.S.	142	G15	47.09 N	98.27 W
Wimbledon, ngh., Eng., U.K.	178		51.25 N	0.12 W
Wimbledon Common, p.o.i., Eng., U.K.	178		51.26 N	0.14 W
Winamac, In., U.S.	130	C11	41.03 N	86.36 W
Winburg, S. Afr.	90	F8	28.31 S	27.00 E
Wincham, Eng., U.K.	180		53.16 N	2.29 W
Winchendon, Ma., U.S.	124	B13	42.41 N	72.03 W
Winchester, On., Can.	126	C14	45.05 N	75.21 W
Winchester, Eng., U.K.	10	J11	51.04 N	1.19 W
Winchester, Id., U.S.	146	D10	46.14 N	116.37 W
Winchester, Il., U.S.	130	E7	39.37 N	90.27 W
Winchester, In., U.S.	130	D13	40.09 N	84.58 W
Winchester, Ky., U.S.	124	G1	37.59 N	84.10 W
Winchester, Ma., U.S.	201		42.27 N	71.08 W
Winchester, Tn., U.S.	134	B12	35.11 N	86.06 W
Winchester, Va., U.S.	124	E7	39.10 N	78.10 W
Winchmore Hill, Eng., U.K.	178		51.39 N	0.39 W
Winchmore Hill, ngh., Eng., U.K.	178		51.38 N	0.06 W
Wind, stm., Yk., Can.	110	B3	65.50 N	135.17 W
Wind, stm., Wa., U.S.	146	E5	45.42 N	121.47 W
Wind, stm., Wy., U.S.	140	D4	43.35 N	108.11 W
Windau see Ventspils, Lat.	26	C4	57.23 N	21.34 E
Wind Cave National Park, p.o.i., S.D., U.S.	140	D9	43.33 N	103.28 W
Winder, Ga., U.S.	132	B2	34.00 N	83.42 W
Windera, Austl.	98	E9	26.02 S	151.50 E
Windermere, B.C., Can.	144	F15	50.29 N	115.59 W
Windermere, Eng., U.K.	10	G10	54.22 N	2.54 W
Windermere, l., Eng., U.K.	10	G10	54.20 N	2.56 W
Windermere Lake, l., On., Can.	114	B9	47.56 N	83.44 W
Winder Village, Pa., U.S.	203		40.06 N	74.52 W
Windfall, Ab., Can.	144	B14	54.11 N	116.14 W
Windham, N.H., U.S.	201		42.48 N	71.18 W
Windham Manor, Md., U.S.	202c		39.04 N	77.00 W
Windhoek, Nmb.	90	C3	22.33 S	17.05 E
Windigo, stm., Qc., Can.	122	C3	47.46 N	73.19 W
Windischgarsten, Aus.	30	C11	47.43 N	14.19 E
Wind Lake, Wi., U.S.	130	B9	42.49 N	88.09 W
Windlass Run, stm., Md., U.S.	202b		39.24 N	76.24 W
Windlesham, Eng., U.K.	178		51.22 N	0.40 W
Windmill Point, c., On., Can.	202a		42.52 N	79.01 W
Windmill Point, c., Mi., U.S.	199		42.22 N	82.55 W
Windom, Mn., U.S.	128	H3	43.52 N	95.07 W
Windom Peak, mtn., Co., U.S.	150	F9	37.37 N	107.35 W
Windorah, Austl.	98	E4	25.25 S	142.38 E
Window Rock, Az., U.S.	150	H7	35.40 N	109.05 W
Wind River Indian Reservation, ind. res., Wy., U.S.	140	D4	43.26 N	109.00 W
Wind River Peak, mtn., Wy., U.S.	140	E3	42.42 N	109.07 W
Wind River Range, mts., Wy., U.S.	140	E4	43.05 N	109.25 W
Windsor, Austl.	98	I8	33.37 S	150.49 E
Windsor, N.S., Can.	122	E13	44.59 N	64.08 W
Windsor, On., Can.	126	F6	42.18 N	83.02 W
Windsor, On., Can.	199		42.18 N	83.01 W
Windsor, Qc., Can.	122	E5	45.34 N	72.00 W
Windsor, Eng., U.K.	10	J12	51.28 N	0.36 W
Windsor, Ca., U.S.	148	E3	38.33 N	122.49 W
Windsor, Co., U.S.	140	G8	40.28 N	104.53 W
Windsor, Ct., U.S.	124	C13	41.50 N	72.39 W
Windsor, Il., U.S.	130	E9	39.25 N	88.36 W
Windsor, Mo., U.S.	130	F4	38.32 N	93.31 W
Windsor, N.C., U.S.	124	I9	35.59 N	76.57 W
Windsor, Vt., U.S.	122	G4	43.28 N	72.22 W
Windsor, Va., U.S.	124	H9	36.48 N	76.44 W
Windsor, Gare, trans., Qc., Can.	193a		45.30 N	73.34 W
Windsor, University of, educ., On., Can.	199		42.18 N	83.04 W
Windsor and Maidenhead, mun., Eng., U.K.	178		51.28 N	0.37 W
Windsor and Maidenhead, mun., Eng., U.K.	178		51.28 N	0.37 W
Windsor Forest, Ga., U.S.	132	E5	31.55 N	81.10 W
Windsor Great Park, p.o.i., Eng., U.K.	178		51.27 N	0.37 W
Windsor Hills, Ca., U.S.	198		33.59 N	118.21 W
Windsor Locks, Ct., U.S.	124	C13	41.55 N	72.38 W
Windsor Race Course, p.o.i., Eng., U.K.	178		51.29 N	0.39 W
Windsor Raceway, p.o.i., On., Can.	199		42.15 N	83.05 W
Windsor Terrace, Md., U.S.	202b		39.19 N	76.43 W
Windthorst, Tx., U.S.	138	H10	33.34 N	98.26 W
Windward, Gren.	159e	p11	12.30 N	61.25 W
Windward Islands, is., N.A.	152a	i15	13.00 N	61.00 W
Windward Passage, strt., N.A.	156	B11	19.56 N	73.52 W
Windy Hills, De., U.S.	203		39.48 N	75.35 W
Windy Peak, mtn., Co., U.S.	138	C2	38.21 N	106.16 W
Windy Peak, mtn., Wa., U.S.	146	B7	48.56 N	119.58 W
Windy Run, stm., Va., U.S.	202c		38.54 N	77.05 W
Winfield, Ab., Can.	144	D16	52.57 N	114.26 W
Winfield, Al., U.S.	134	D11	33.55 N	87.49 W
Winfield, Ia., U.S.	128	J7	41.07 N	91.26 W
Winfield, Ks., U.S.	138	D12	37.14 N	96.59 W
Winfield, Mo., U.S.	130	E7	38.59 N	90.44 W
Winfield, N.J., U.S.	194		40.38 N	74.17 W
Winfield, W.V., U.S.	124	F4	38.31 N	81.53 W
Wing, N.D., U.S.	142	G13	47.08 N	100.17 W
Wing, stm., Mn., U.S.	128	E3	46.28 N	94.59 W
Wingate, N.C., U.S.	132	B5	34.59 N	80.26 W
Wingates, Eng., U.K.	180		53.34 N	2.32 W
Wingham, Austl.	98	H9	31.52 S	152.22 E
Wingham, On., Can.	126	E8	43.53 N	81.18 W
Wing Lake Shores, Mi., U.S.	199		42.33 N	83.17 W
Wingo, Ky., U.S.	130	H9	36.38 N	88.44 W
Wings Field, arpt., Pa., U.S.	203		40.08 N	75.16 W
Winhole Channel, strt., N.Y., U.S.	194		43.37 N	73.48 W
Winifred, Mt., U.S.	146	C17	47.33 N	109.23 W
Winifreda, Arg.	172	H5	36.13 S	64.14 W
Winisk, On., Can.	110	D13	55.15 N	85.13 W
Winisk, stm., On., Can.	110	E13	55.15 N	85.07 W
Winisk Lake, l., On., Can.	110	E13	52.54 N	87.21 W
Wink, Tx., U.S.	136	C4	31.45 N	103.08 W
Winkana, Mya.	64	E4	15.44 N	98.01 E
Winkelman, Az., U.S.	150	K6	33.00 N	110.45 W
Winkler, Mb., Can.	142	E16	49.10 N	97.56 W
Winklern, Aus.	30	D9	46.52 N	12.52 E
Winlaw, B.C., Can.	144	G13	49.35 N	117.34 W
Winlock, Wa., U.S.	146	D3	46.29 N	122.55 W

Name	Page	Map Ref.	Latitude	Longitude
Winneba, Ghana	84	H4	5.21 N	0.37 W
Winnebago, Il., U.S.	128	I9	42.15 N	89.14 W
Winnebago, Mn., U.S.	128	H4	43.46 N	94.10 W
Winnebago, Ne., U.S.	130	B1	42.13 N	96.28 W
Winnebago, stm., Ia., U.S.	128	H5	43.02 N	92.57 W
Winnebago, Lake, l., Wi., U.S.	128	G10	44.00 N	88.25 W
Winnebago Indian Reservation, ind. res., Ne., U.S.	128	I2	42.15 N	96.31 W
Winnebago Indian Reservation, ind. res., Wi., U.S.	128	G8	44.15 N	90.38 W
Winneconne, Wi., U.S.	128	G10	44.06 N	88.42 W
Winneconnet, Ma., U.S.	201		41.59 N	71.08 W
Winneconnet Pond, l., Ma., U.S.	201		41.58 N	71.08 W
Winnekenni Park, p.o.i., Ma., U.S.	201		42.47 N	71.04 W
Winnemucca, Nv., U.S.	148	B8	40.58 N	117.44 W
Winnemucca Lake, l., Nv., U.S.	148	C6	40.09 N	119.20 W
Winner, S.D., U.S.	140	D13	43.22 N	99.51 W
Winnetka, Il., U.S.	130	B10	42.06 N	87.43 W
Winnetka, ngh., Ca., U.S.	198		34.13 N	118.35 W
Winnett, Mt., U.S.	142	H5	47.00 N	108.21 W
Winnfield, La., U.S.	134	F6	31.55 N	92.38 W
Winnibigoshish, Lake, res., Mn., U.S.	128	D4	47.27 N	94.12 W
Winnie, Tx., U.S.	136	E13	29.49 N	94.23 W
Winning, Austl.	96	D2	23.09 S	114.32 E
Winnipeg, Mb., Can.	142	E16	49.53 N	97.09 W
Winnipeg, stm., Can.	118	B18	50.41 N	96.24 W
Winnipeg, Lake, l., Mb., Can.	110	E11	52.00 N	97.00 W
Winnipeg Beach, Mb., Can.	142	D17	50.30 N	96.58 W
Winnipegosis, Mb., Can.	142	C13	51.38 N	99.56 W
Winnipegosis, Lake, l., Mb., Can.	142	B13	52.30 N	99.58 W
Winnipesaukee, Lake, l., N.H., U.S.	122	G5	43.35 N	71.20 W
Winnsboro, La., U.S.	134	E7	32.10 N	91.43 W
Winnsboro, S.C., U.S.	132	B4	34.23 N	81.04 W
Winnsboro, Tx., U.S.	136	B12	32.57 N	95.17 W
Winnsboro Mills, S.C., U.S.	132	B4	34.21 N	81.04 W
Winona, Ks., U.S.	138	B7	39.03 N	101.14 W
Winona, Mi., U.S.	128	E10	46.52 N	88.55 W
Winona, Mn., U.S.	128	G7	44.02 N	91.38 W
Winona, Ms., U.S.	134	D9	33.28 N	89.43 W
Winona, Mo., U.S.	130	G6	37.00 N	91.19 W
Winooski, stm., Vt., U.S.	122	F4	44.31 N	73.15 W
Winooski, North Branch, stm., Vt., U.S.	122	F4	44.15 N	72.34 W
Winschoten, Neth.	20	A15	53.08 N	7.02 E
Winschoterdiep, can., Neth.	20	A15	53.13 N	6.36 E
Winsen, Ger.	24	C6	53.21 N	10.12 E
Winside, Ne., U.S.	140	E15	42.10 N	97.11 W
Winslow, Az., U.S.	150	H6	35.01 N	110.42 W
Winslow, In., U.S.	130	F10	38.22 N	87.12 W
Winslow, Me., U.S.	122	F7	44.32 N	69.37 W
Winslow, N.J., U.S.	203		39.39 N	74.52 W
Winslow State Park, p.o.i., N.H., U.S.	122	G5	43.22 N	71.52 W
Winsted, Ct., U.S.	124	C12	41.55 N	73.04 W
Winsted, Mn., U.S.	128	G4	44.57 N	94.03 W
Winston, Fl., U.S.	132	H3	28.02 N	82.01 W
Winston, Or., U.S.	146	G3	43.05 N	123.25 W
Winston-Salem, N.C., U.S.	124	H5	36.05 N	80.14 W
Winter, Wi., U.S.	128	F8	45.49 N	91.00 W
Winterberg, Ger.	181		51.17 N	7.18 E
Winterberg, hill, Ger.	181		51.20 N	7.13 E
Winterberge, mts., S. Afr.	90	H8	32.20 S	26.05 E
Winter Creek, stm., Ca., U.S.	198		34.12 N	118.02 W
Winter Garden, Fl., U.S.	132	H4	28.33 N	81.35 W
Winter Harbor, Me., U.S.	122	F8	44.23 N	68.04 W
Winter Harbour, B.C., Can.	144	F2	50.31 N	128.02 W
Winterhaven, Ca., U.S.	150	K2	32.45 N	114.40 W
Winter Haven, Fl., U.S.	132	I4	28.01 N	81.44 W
Winter Hill, hill, Eng., U.K.	180		53.38 N	2.31 W
Wintering, stm., N.D., U.S.	142	G13	48.11 N	100.34 W
Winter Island, i., Nu., Can.	110	B14	66.14 N	83.04 W
Winter Island, i., Ca., U.S.	200		38.03 N	121.51 W
Winter Island, i., Ma., U.S.	201		42.32 N	70.52 W
Winter Park, Fl., U.S.	132	H4	28.36 N	81.19 W
Winterport, Me., U.S.	122	F8	44.38 N	68.51 W
Winters, Ca., U.S.	148	E3	38.31 N	121.58 W
Winters, Tx., U.S.	136	C8	31.57 N	99.57 W
Winterset, Ia., U.S.	130	C4	41.20 N	94.00 W
Winterswijk, Neth.	20	B15	51.58 N	6.43 E
Winterthur, Switz.	30	C5	47.29 N	8.43 E
Winterthur, De., U.S.	203		39.48 N	75.35 W
Winterthur Museum, bldg., De., U.S.	203		39.48 N	75.36 W
Winterville, Ga., U.S.	132	C2	33.58 N	83.16 W
Winterville, Ms., U.S.	134	D7	33.30 N	91.03 W
Winterville, N.C., U.S.	132	A8	35.31 N	77.24 W
Winthrop, Me., U.S.	122	F7	44.18 N	69.58 W
Winthrop, Ma., U.S.	201		42.22 N	70.59 W
Winthrop, Mn., U.S.	128	G4	44.32 N	94.21 W
Winthrop, Wa., U.S.	146	B6	48.28 N	120.11 W
Winthrop, Lake, l., Ma., U.S.	201		42.11 N	71.25 W
Winthrop Harbor, Il., U.S.	130	B10	42.28 N	87.48 W
Wintinna, Austl.	96	E6	27.46 S	134.01 E
Winton, Austl.	98	D4	22.22 S	143.01 E
Winton, N.Z.	102	H3	46.08 S	168.18 E
Winton, N.C., U.S.	124	H9	36.23 N	76.56 W
Winwick, Eng., U.K.	180		53.26 N	2.36 W
Winz, Ger.	181		51.23 N	7.09 E
Winzenberg, Ger.	181		51.06 N	7.38 E
Winzermark, Ger.	181		51.23 N	7.08 E
Wipper, stm., Ger.	20	C19	51.23 N	10.46 E
Wipper, stm., Ger.	181		51.07 N	7.24 E
Wipperfeld, Ger.	181		51.05 N	7.19 E
Wirātnagar, Nepal	70	E11	26.27 N	87.16 E
Wireton, Il., U.S.	196		41.40 N	87.42 W
Wireton, Pa., U.S.	197b		40.34 N	80.14 W
Wirgañj, Nepal	70	E10	27.01 N	84.52 E
Wirral, mun., Eng., U.K.	180		53.22 N	3.05 W
Wirral, mun., Eng., U.K.	180		53.22 N	3.05 W
Wisbech, Eng., U.K.	10	I13	52.40 N	0.09 E
Wisby see Visby, Swe.	16	J16	57.38 N	18.18 E
Wiscasset, Me., U.S.	122	G7	44.00 N	69.40 W
Wisconsin, state, U.S.	128	G9	44.45 N	89.30 W
Wisconsin, stm., Wi., U.S.	128	I7	42.59 N	91.08 W
Wisconsin Dells, Wi., U.S.	128	H9	43.37 N	89.45 W
Wisconsin Dells, misc. cult., Wi., U.S.	128	H9	43.41 N	89.47 W
Wisconsin Rapids, Wi., U.S.	128	G9	44.23 N	89.48 W
Wisdom, Mt., U.S.	146	E13	45.37 N	113.26 W
Wise, Va., U.S.	124	G3	36.58 N	82.35 W
Wise, stm., Mt., U.S.	146	E13	45.48 N	112.57 W
Wiseman, Ak., U.S.	109	C9	67.24 N	150.09 W
Wishart, Sk., Can.	142	C10	51.32 N	103.57 W
Wishek, N.D., U.S.	140	A13	46.15 N	99.33 W
Wishram, Wa., U.S.	146	E6	45.39 N	120.57 W
Wisła, Pol.	24	G14	49.39 N	18.51 E
Wisła (Vistula), stm., Pol.	24	B14	54.20 N	18.56 E
Wiślany, Mierzeja, spit, Eur.	24	B15	54.25 N	19.34 E
Wiślany, Zalew see Vistula Lagoon, b., Eur.	24	B16	54.26 N	19.41 E
Wisley Aerodrome, arpt., Eng., U.K.	178		51.18 N	0.28 W
Wisley Gardens, p.o.i., Eng., U.K.	178		51.19 N	0.29 W
Wisłok, stm., Pol.	24	F18	50.12 N	22.32 E
Wisłoka, stm., Pol.	24	F17	50.26 N	21.23 E
Wismar, Ger.	24	C7	53.53 N	11.28 E
Wisner, La., U.S.	134	F7	31.58 N	91.39 W
Wisner, Ne., U.S.	140	F16	41.59 N	96.55 W
Wissahickon Creek, stm., Pa., U.S.	203		40.01 N	75.12 W
Wissembourg, Fr.	20	E16	49.01 N	7.57 E
Wissinoming, ngh., Pa., U.S.	203		40.01 N	75.04 W
Wissous, Fr.	179		48.44 N	2.20 E
Wister, Ok., U.S.	134	C4	34.58 N	94.43 W
Wisznice, Pol.	24	E19	51.48 N	23.12 E
Witbank, S. Afr.	90	D9	25.53 S	29.14 E
Witbooisvlei, Nmb.	90	D4	25.04 S	18.27 E
Witfield, S. Afr.	191d		26.11 S	28.12 E
Witham, stm., Eng., U.K.	10	H12	52.55 N	0.04 E
Withens Clough Reservoir, res., Eng., U.K.	180		53.42 N	2.02 W
Withernsea, Eng., U.K.	10	H13	53.44 N	0.01 E
Withington, ngh., Eng., U.K.	180		53.26 N	2.14 W
Withington Green, Eng., U.K.	180		53.14 N	2.18 W
Withlacoochee, stm., U.S.	132	F2	30.23 N	83.10 W
Withnell, Eng., U.K.	180		53.42 N	2.34 W
Withokspruit, stm., S. Afr.	191d		26.19 S	28.21 E
Witkowo, Pol.	24	D13	52.26 N	17.46 E
Wit-Mfolozi, stm., S. Afr.	90	F10	28.22 S	31.58 E
Witney, Eng., U.K.	10	J11	51.47 N	1.28 W
Witnica, Pol.	24	D10	52.40 N	14.53 E
Wit Nossob, stm., Nmb.	90	C4	23.06 S	18.40 E
Witsand, S. Afr.	90	I5	34.23 S	20.49 E
Witt, Il., U.S.	130	E8	39.15 N	89.21 W
Witten, Ger.	20	C16	51.25 N	7.20 E
Wittenau, ngh., Ger.	182a		52.35 N	13.20 E
Wittenberg, Wi., U.S.	128	G9	44.49 N	89.09 W
Wittenberge, Ger.	24	C8	52.59 N	11.45 E
Wittenburg, Ger.	24	C6	53.30 N	11.05 E
Wittenoom, Austl.	96	D3	22.15 S	118.23 E
Wittingen, Ger.	24	D6	52.43 N	10.44 E
Wittlich, Ger.	24	G2	49.59 N	6.53 E
Wittmund, Ger.	24	C3	53.34 N	7.47 E
Witton Park, p.o.i., Eng., U.K.	180		53.45 N	2.31 W
Wittstock, Ger.	24	C8	53.09 N	12.29 E
Witu Islands, is., Pap. N. Gui.	101a	a5	4.45 S	149.18 E
Witvlei, Nmb.	90	C4	22.24 S	18.29 E
Witwatersrand, mts., S. Afr.	90	D8	26.00 S	27.00 E
Witwatersrand, University of the, educ., S. Afr.	191d		26.12 S	28.02 E
Witwatersrand Gold Mine, mine, S. Afr.	191d		26.12 S	28.11 E
Witzenhausen, Ger.	24	E5	51.20 N	9.51 E
Witzhelden, Ger.	181		51.07 N	7.06 E
Wiwa Creek, stm., Sk., Can.	142	D7	50.02 N	106.30 W
Wizajny, Pol.	24	B18	54.21 N	22.55 E
W. Kerr Scott Reservoir, res., N.C., U.S.	124	H4	36.07 N	81.16 W
Wkra, stm., Pol.	24	C15	52.26 N	20.45 E
Władysławowo, Pol.	24	B14	54.47 N	18.24 E
Wleń, Pol.	24	E11	51.00 N	15.40 E
Włocławek, Pol.	24	D15	52.39 N	19.04 E
Włodawa, Pol.	24	E19	51.33 N	23.33 E
Włoszczowa, Pol.	24	F15	50.51 N	19.58 E
Woburn, Ma., U.S.	124	B14	42.28 N	71.09 W
Woburn, ngh., On., Can.	193b		43.46 N	79.13 W
Wodonga, Austl.	98	K6	36.08 S	146.53 E
Wodzisław Śląski, Pol.	24	F14	50.01 N	18.28 E
Wojcieszów, Pol.	24	F11	50.58 N	15.56 E
Wokam, Pulau, i., Indon.	60	G10	5.37 S	134.30 E
Woking, Eng., U.K.	10	J12	51.19 N	0.33 W
Woking, mun., Eng., U.K.	178		51.19 N	0.32 W
Wokingham Creek, stm., Austl.	98	C4	22.19 S	142.30 E
Wolbach, Ne., U.S.	140	F14	41.23 N	98.23 W
Wolbrom, Pol.	24	F15	50.23 N	19.46 E
Wolcott, In., U.S.	130	D10	40.45 N	87.01 W
Wolcott, N.Y., U.S.	126	E13	43.12 N	76.48 W
Wolcottville, In., U.S.	130	C12	41.31 N	85.21 W
Wolczyn, Pol.	24	E13	51.01 N	18.03 E
Woldingham, Eng., U.K.	178		51.17 N	0.02 W
Woleai, at., Micron.	94	C5	7.20 N	143.53 E
Woleu see Mbini, stm., Afr.	84	I6	1.34 N	9.37 E
Wolf, stm., On., Can.	128	B10	48.48 N	88.31 W
Wolf, stm., U.S.	134	B9	35.08 N	90.03 W
Wolf, stm., Ms., U.S.	134	G9	30.21 N	89.18 W
Wolf, stm., Wi., U.S.	128	G10	44.13 N	88.50 W
Wolf, Volcán, vol., Ec.	164a	h11	0.00 N	91.20 W
Wolfach, Ger.	24	H4	48.17 N	8.13 E
Wolf Creek, Mt., U.S.	146	C14	47.00 N	112.05 W
Wolf Creek, Or., U.S.	146	H3	42.41 N	123.24 W
Wolf Creek, stm., U.S.	138	E9	36.35 N	99.30 W
Wolf Creek, stm., Co., U.S.	150	C8	40.11 N	108.28 W
Wolf Creek, stm., Ia., U.S.	130	B5	42.19 N	92.09 W
Wolf Creek, stm., Mt., U.S.	142	F8	48.03 N	105.39 W
Wolf Creek, stm., Mt., U.S.	146	C17	47.36 N	109.38 W
Wolf Creek, stm., S.D., U.S.	140	D15	43.20 N	97.37 W
Wolf Creek, stm., S.D., U.S.	140	C14	44.42 N	98.40 W
Wolf Creek Pass, p., Co., U.S.	138	D2	37.37 N	106.44 W
Wolf Creek Reservoir, res., Ks., U.S.	130	F2	38.14 N	95.42 W
Wolfeboro, N.H., U.S.	122	G5	43.35 N	71.12 W
Wolfe City, Tx., U.S.	134	D2	33.22 N	96.04 W
Wolfe Island, i., On., Can.	126	D13	44.10 N	76.23 W
Wolfen, Ger.	24	E8	51.39 N	12.16 E
Wolfenbüttel, Ger.	24	D6	52.10 N	10.32 E
Wolfenden, Mount, mtn., B.C., Can.	144	F3	50.26 N	127.33 W
Wolfforth, Tx., U.S.	138	H6	33.30 N	102.01 W
Wolfhagen, Ger.	24	E5	51.19 N	9.10 E
Wolf Lake, Mi., U.S.	126	E3	43.14 N	86.05 W
Wolf Lake, l., Ab., Can.	144	B20	54.42 N	110.59 W
Wolf Lake, l., U.S.	196		41.40 N	87.31 W
Wolf Lake, l., N.J., U.S.	194		40.57 N	74.42 W
Wolfpassing, Aus.	182b		48.19 N	16.11 E
Wolf Point, Mt., U.S.	142	F8	48.05 N	105.37 W
Wolfratshausen, Ger.	24	I7	47.53 N	11.25 E
Wolf Rock, r., Eng., U.K.	10	L7	49.57 N	5.49 W
Wolfsberg, Aus.	30	D11	46.50 N	14.50 E
Wolfsberg, hill, Ger.	181		51.38 N	6.27 E
Wolfsburg, Ger.	24	D6	52.25 N	10.47 E
Wolftrap Creek, stm., Va., U.S.	202c		38.58 N	77.17 W
Wolf Trap Farms for the Performing Arts, p.o.i., Va., U.S.	202c		38.56 N	77.16 W
Wolfville, N.S., Can.	122	E12	45.05 N	64.22 W
Wolgast, Ger.	24	B9	54.03 N	13.46 E
Wolin, Pol.	24	C10	53.50 N	14.36 E
Woliński Park Narodowy, p.o.i., Pol.	24	C10	53.53 N	14.26 E
Wollaston Beach, cst., Ma., U.S.	201		42.17 N	71.01 W
Wollaston Lake, l., Sk., Can.	110	D10	58.15 N	103.20 W
Wollaston Peninsula, pen., Can.	110	B7	70.00 N	115.00 W
Wollemi National Park, p.o.i., Austl.	98	I7	32.50 S	150.30 E
Wollin see Wolin, Pol.	24	C10	53.50 N	14.36 E
Wollongong, Austl.	98	J8	34.24 S	150.53 E
Wolmaransstad, S. Afr.	90	E8	27.12 S	25.58 E
Wołomin, Pol.	24	D17	52.20 N	21.14 E
Wołów, Pol.	24	E12	51.20 N	16.38 E
Wolseley, Sk., Can.	142	D10	50.25 N	103.16 W
Wolsey, S.D., U.S.	140	C14	44.23 N	98.28 W
Wolsztyn, Pol.	24	D12	52.07 N	16.05 E
Wolverhampton, Eng., U.K.	10	I10	52.35 N	2.08 W
Wolverine, Mi., U.S.	126	C5	45.16 N	84.36 W
Wolverine Lake, Mi., U.S.	199		42.33 N	83.29 W
Wolverine Loon Lake, l., Mi., U.S.	199		42.33 N	83.30 W
Wolverton, Eng., U.K.	10	I12	52.03 N	0.49 W
Wompatuck State Park, p.o.i., Ma., U.S.	201		42.13 N	70.51 W
Wonarah, Austl.	96	C7	19.54 S	136.22 E
Wondai, Austl.	98	F8	26.19 S	151.52 E
Wonderfonteinspruit, stm., S. Afr.	191d		26.16 S	27.42 E
Wonderland, Ca., U.S.	148	C4	40.24 N	121.18 W
Wonderland Center, shp. cen., Mi., U.S.	199		42.22 N	83.20 W
Wondinong, Austl.	96	E3	27.51 S	118.24 E
Wonersh, Eng., U.K.	178		51.12 N	0.33 W
Wonewoc, Wi., U.S.	128	H8	43.39 N	90.12 W
Wonga Park, Austl.	192b		37.44 S	145.16 E
Wong Ka Wai, China	189d		22.24 N	113.58 E
Wongwianyai Railway Station, trans., Thai.	187a		13.43 N	100.30 E
Wŏnju, Kor., S.	54	F7	37.20 N	127.57 E
Wonogiri, Indon.	66	G7	7.48 S	110.55 E
Wonosari, Indon.	66	H7	7.57 S	110.35 E
Wonosobo, Indon.	66	G6	7.21 S	109.54 E
Wŏnsan, Kor., N.	54	E7	39.09 N	127.26 E
Wonthaggi, Austl.	98	L5	38.36 S	145.35 E
Wood, S.D., U.S.	140	D12	43.29 N	100.28 W
Wood, stm., B.C., Can.	144	D12	52.08 N	118.26 W
Wood, stm., Sk., Can.	142	D7	50.08 N	106.16 W
Wood, stm., Ne., U.S.	140	G13	41.01 N	98.04 W
Wood, stm., Wy., U.S.	140	D3	44.06 N	108.57 W
Wood, Mount, mtn., Mt., U.S.	146	E17	45.17 N	109.49 W
Woodall Mountain, hill, Ms., U.S.	134	C10	34.45 N	88.11 W
Woodberry Forest, Md., U.S.	202c		38.48 N	76.56 W
Woodbine, Ga., U.S.	132	F4	30.57 N	81.43 W
Woodbine, Ia., U.S.	130	C2	41.44 N	95.42 W
Woodbine, N.J., U.S.	124	E11	39.14 N	74.48 W
Woodbourne, Pa., U.S.	203		40.12 N	74.53 W
Woodbridge, Eng., U.K.	10	I14	52.06 N	1.18 E
Woodbridge, Va., U.S.	124	F8	38.39 N	77.15 W
Woodbridge Center, shp. cen., N.J., U.S.	194		40.33 N	74.18 W
Woodbridge Creek, stm., N.J., U.S.	194		40.32 N	74.15 W
Woodbridge Island, i., Ma., U.S.	201		42.48 N	70.50 W
Woodburn, Or., U.S.	146	E4	45.08 N	122.50 W
Woodbury, Ga., U.S.	134	E14	32.59 N	84.34 W
Woodbury, N.J., U.S.	124	E10	39.50 N	75.09 W
Woodbury, N.Y., U.S.	194		40.49 N	73.28 W
Woodbury, Tn., U.S.	130	I11	35.49 N	86.03 W
Woodbury Creek, stm., N.J., U.S.	203		39.52 N	75.11 W
Woodbury Heights, N.J., U.S.	203		39.49 N	75.09 W
Woodcliff Lake, N.J., U.S.	194		41.01 N	74.04 W
Woodcliff Lake, l., N.J., U.S.	194		41.01 N	74.03 W
Woodcrest, Pa., U.S.	203		39.59 N	75.35 W
Wood Dale, Il., U.S.	196		41.57 N	87.58 W
Woodenbong, Austl.	98	G9	28.23 S	152.36 E
Woodfibre, B.C., Can.	144	G7	49.39 N	123.15 W
Woodfield, shp. cen., Il., U.S.	196		42.03 N	88.03 W
Woodford, Eng., U.K.	180		53.21 N	2.10 W
Woodford, ngh., Eng., U.K.	178		51.36 N	0.02 E
Woodford Aerodrome, arpt., Eng., U.K.	180		53.20 N	2.09 W
Woodford Bridge, ngh., Eng., U.K.	178		51.36 N	0.04 E
Wood Green, ngh., Eng., U.K.	178		51.36 N	0.07 W
Woodham, Eng., U.K.	178		51.21 N	0.30 W
Woodham Ferrers, Eng., U.K.	178		51.40 N	0.36 E
Woodham Mortimer, Eng., U.K.	178		51.43 N	0.37 E
Woodham Walter, Eng., U.K.	178		51.44 N	0.37 E
Woodhaven, ngh., N.Y., U.S.	194		40.41 N	73.51 W
Woodhead Reservoir, res., Eng., U.K.	180		53.30 N	1.52 W
Woodhill, On., Can.	193b		43.45 N	79.41 W
Wood Hill, hill, Ma., U.S.	201		42.39 N	71.13 W
Woodhull, Il., U.S.	130	C7	41.10 N	90.18 W
Wood Islands, P.E., Can.	122	E14	45.57 N	62.46 W
Woodlake, Ca., U.S.	148	G6	36.24 N	119.06 W
Wood Lake, Ne., U.S.	140	E12	42.37 N	100.15 W
Woodland, Ca., U.S.	148	E4	38.40 N	121.46 W
Woodland, Ga., U.S.	134	E14	32.47 N	84.33 W
Woodland, Me., U.S.	122	E9	45.08 N	67.23 W
Woodland, N.C., U.S.	124	H8	36.19 N	77.12 W
Woodland Caribou Provincial Park, p.o.i., On., Can.	128	A4	50.35 N	94.40 W
Woodland Hills, ngh., Ca., U.S.	198		34.11 N	118.35 W
Woodland Hills Park, p.o.i., Oh., U.S.	197a		41.28 N	81.36 W
Woodland Park, Co., U.S.	138	C3	38.59 N	105.02 W
Woodlands, Sing.	189c		1.27 N	103.46 E
Woodlands, N.Y., U.S.	194		41.01 N	73.50 W
Woodlawn, Md., U.S.	202b		39.19 N	76.43 W
Woodlawn, Md., U.S.	202c		38.57 N	76.53 W
Woodlawn, ngh., Il., U.S.	196		41.47 N	87.36 W
Woodlawn Heights, Md., U.S.	202b		39.11 N	76.39 W
Woodlyn, Pa., U.S.	203		39.52 N	75.20 W
Woodlynne, N.J., U.S.	203		39.55 N	75.05 W
Woodmansterne, Eng., U.K.	178		51.19 N	0.10 W
Woodmere, Oh., U.S.	197a		41.28 N	81.29 W
Woodmoor, Md., U.S.	202b		39.20 N	76.44 W
Wood Mountain, mtn., Sk., Can.	142	E7	49.15 N	106.20 W
Wood Mountain Indian Reserve, ind. res., Sk., Can.	142	E7	49.19 N	106.26 W
Woodplumpton, Eng., U.K.	180		53.48 N	2.47 W
Woodport, N.J., U.S.	194		40.59 N	74.36 W
Woodridge, Mb., Can.	142	E17	49.16 N	96.09 W
Wood-Ridge, N.J., U.S.	194		40.50 N	74.05 W
Wood River, Il., U.S.	130	F8	38.51 N	90.05 W
Wood River, Ne., U.S.	140	G14	40.49 N	98.36 W
Woodroffe, Mount, mtn., Austl.	96	E6	26.20 S	131.45 E
Woodrow, N.C., U.S.	132	A8	35.06 N	77.04 W
Woodruff, Az., U.S.	150	I6	34.47 N	110.02 W
Woodruff, S.C., U.S.	132	B3	34.45 N	82.02 W
Woodruff, Wi., U.S.	128	F9	45.54 N	89.39 W
Woodruff Creek, stm., Mi., U.S.	199		42.21 N	83.43 W
Woods, Lake, l., Austl.	96	C6	17.50 S	133.30 E
Woods, Lake of the, l., N.A.	128	B4	49.15 N	94.45 W
Woodsboro, Tx., U.S.	136	F10	28.14 N	97.19 W
Woodsburgh, N.Y., U.S.	194		40.37 N	73.42 W
Woods Creek, stm., N.Y., U.S.	194		40.39 N	73.24 W
Woods Creek, stm., N.Y., U.S.	202a		43.04 N	78.58 W
Woodsfield, Oh., U.S.	124	E4	39.45 N	81.06 W
Woods Hole, Ma., U.S.	124	C15	41.31 N	70.40 W
Woodside, Austl.	98	L6	38.31 S	146.52 E
Woodside, Eng., U.K.	178		51.45 N	0.11 W
Woodside, Pa., U.S.	203		40.13 N	74.53 W
Woodside, ngh., N.Y., U.S.	194		40.45 N	73.55 W
Woodson, Tx., U.S.	136	A8	33.00 N	99.03 W
Woods Reservoir, res., Tn., U.S.	134	B12	35.18 N	86.04 W
Woodstock, Austl.	98	D3	22.15 S	141.57 E
Woodstock, N.B., Can.	122	D9	46.08 N	67.34 W
Woodstock, On., Can.	126	E9	43.07 N	80.45 W
Woodstock, Eng., U.K.	10	J11	51.51 N	1.21 W
Woodstock, Il., U.S.	130	B9	42.18 N	88.26 W
Woodstock, Md., U.S.	202b		39.19 N	76.52 W
Woodstock, N.Y., U.S.	124	B11	42.02 N	74.07 W
Woodstock, Vt., U.S.	122	G4	43.37 N	72.31 W
Woodstock, Va., U.S.	124	F7	38.52 N	78.30 W
Wood Street, Eng., U.K.	178		51.15 N	0.38 W
Woodsville, N.H., U.S.	122	F4	44.08 N	72.02 W
Woodvale Airfield, arpt., Eng., U.K.	180		53.35 N	3.03 W
Woodville, N.Z.	102	E6	40.20 S	175.52 E
Woodville, Al., U.S.	134	C12	34.37 N	86.17 W
Woodville, Fl., U.S.	132	F1	30.19 N	84.15 W
Woodville, Ga., U.S.	132	C2	33.40 N	83.06 W
Woodville, Ms., U.S.	134	F7	31.06 N	91.17 W
Woodville, Oh., U.S.	130	C14	41.27 N	83.21 W
Woodville, Tx., U.S.	136	D13	30.46 N	94.25 W
Woodward, Ia., U.S.	130	C4	41.51 N	93.55 W
Woodward, Ok., U.S.	138	E9	36.26 N	99.23 W
Woodward Reservoir, res., Ca., U.S.	148	F5	37.51 N	120.52 W
Woody, stm., Can.	142	B13	52.33 N	100.44 W
Woody Creek, stm., Mt., U.S.	142	G7	47.26 N	106.21 W
Woody Head, c., Austl.	98	G9	29.22 S	153.22 E
Woolgoolga, Austl.	98	H9	30.07 S	153.11 E
Woollahra, Austl.	192a		33.53 S	151.15 E
Woolmarket, Ms., U.S.	134	G9	30.28 N	88.59 W
Woolooware Bay, b., Austl.	192a		34.02 S	151.09 E
Woolsey Peak, mtn., Az., U.S.	150	J4	33.10 N	112.53 W
Woolston, Eng., U.K.	180		53.24 N	2.32 W
Woolton, ngh., Eng., U.K.	180		53.23 N	2.52 W
Woolwich, ngh., Eng., U.K.	178		51.29 N	0.04 E
Woomera, Austl.	96	F7	31.12 S	136.49 E
Woonsocket, R.I., U.S.	124	B14	42.00 N	71.30 W
Woonsocket, S.D., U.S.	140	C14	44.03 N	98.16 W
Woorabinda, Austl.	98	E7	24.08 S	149.28 E
Wooramel, Austl.	96	E2	25.44 S	114.17 E
Wooramel, stm., Austl.	96	E2	25.50 S	114.15 E
Wooster, Oh., U.S.	124	D3	40.47 N	81.55 W
Worcester, S. Afr.	90	H4	33.38 S	19.26 E
Worcester, Eng., U.K.	10	I10	52.11 N	2.13 W
Worcester, Ma., U.S.	124	B14	42.16 N	71.48 W
Worcester, Pa., U.S.	203		40.12 N	75.21 W
Worden, Mt., U.S.	140	A4	45.57 N	108.12 W
Wörgl, Aus.	30	C9	47.29 N	12.03 E
Workers' Stadium, p.o.i., China	189a		39.55 N	116.27 E
Workington, Eng., U.K.	10	G9	54.38 N	3.33 W
Worksop, Eng., U.K.	10	H11	53.18 N	1.07 W
Worland, Wy., U.S.	140	C5	44.01 N	107.57 W
World End Pond, l., N.H., U.S.	201		42.45 N	71.12 W
World Trade Centre, bldg., Sing.	189c		1.16 N	103.49 E
Worli, ngh., India	190c		19.01 N	72.50 E
Wormley, Eng., U.K.	178		51.44 N	0.01 W
Worms, Ger.	24	G4	49.37 N	8.21 E
Wormshill, Eng., U.K.	178		51.17 N	0.42 E
Wörnitz, stm., Ger.	30	B7	48.52 N	10.34 E
Woronora, Austl.	192a		34.01 S	151.03 E
Woronora, stm., Austl.	192a		34.00 S	151.04 E
Worplesdon, Eng., U.K.	178		51.16 N	0.37 W
Worsley, Eng., U.K.	180		53.30 N	2.23 W
Worsthorne, Eng., U.K.	180		53.47 N	2.11 W
Worth, Ger.	181		51.13 N	7.39 E
Wortham, Tx., U.S.	136	C11	31.47 N	96.28 W
Wörther See, l., Aus.	30	D11	46.37 N	14.08 E
Worthing, Eng., U.K.	10	K12	50.49 N	0.22 W
Worthington, In., U.S.	130	E11	39.06 N	86.58 W
Worthington, Md., U.S.	202b		39.14 N	76.47 W
Worthington, Mn., U.S.	128	H3	43.37 N	95.35 W
Worthington, N.Y., U.S.	194		41.02 N	73.50 W
Worthington, Oh., U.S.	124	D3	40.05 N	83.01 W
Worthington Peak, mtn., Nv., U.S.	148	F10	37.54 N	115.36 W
Wosu, Indon.	60	F7	2.21 S	121.50 E
Wotho, at., Marsh. Is.	94	B7	10.05 N	166.01 E
Wotton, Eng., U.K.	178		51.13 N	0.23 W
Wotu, Indon.	66	E12	2.36 S	120.48 E
Wouhnta, Nic.	156	F6	13.32 N	83.32 W
Wouldham, Eng., U.K.	178		51.21 N	0.28 E
Wounded Knee, S.D., U.S.	140	D10	43.08 N	102.22 W
Wounded Knee Creek, stm., S.D., U.S.	140	D10	43.26 N	102.33 W
Wour, Chad	82	C3	21.21 N	15.57 E
Wowan, Austl.	98	D8	23.53 S	150.11 E
Wowoni, Pulau, i., Indon.	60	F7	4.08 S	123.06 E
Woy Woy, Austl.	98	I8	33.29 S	151.19 E
Wrangel Island see Vrangelja, ostrov, i., Russia	50	B24	71.14 N	179.21 W
Wrangell, Ak., U.S.	109	E13	56.28 N	132.21 W
Wrangell, Cape, c., Ak., U.S.	109a	g21	52.55 N	172.29 E
Wrangell Mountains, mts., Ak., U.S.	109	D11	62.00 N	143.00 W
Wrath, Cape, c., Scot., U.K.	10	C8	58.37 N	4.59 W
Wray, Co., U.S.	138	A6	40.04 N	102.13 W
Wraysbury, Eng., U.K.	178		51.27 N	0.33 W
Wrea Green, Eng., U.K.	180		53.46 N	2.55 W
Wrens, Ga., U.S.	132	C3	33.11 N	82.20 W
Wrentham, Ab., Can.	144	G18	49.31 N	112.11 W
Wrentham State Forest, p.o.i., Ma., U.S.	201		42.02 N	71.20 W
Wrexham, Wales, U.K.	10	H10	53.02 N	2.59 W
Wright, Mount, mtn., Austl.	98	H4	31.12 S	142.26 E
Wright, Mount, mtn., Mt., U.S.	146	B14	47.58 N	112.49 W
Wright Brothers National Memorial, p.o.i., N.C., U.S.	124	H10	36.00 N	75.39 W
Wright City, Mo., U.S.	130	F6	38.49 N	91.01 W
Wright City, Ok., U.S.	134	C4	34.04 N	95.00 W
Wrightington Bar, Eng., U.K.	180		53.37 N	2.42 W
Wright Patman Lake, res., Tx., U.S.	134	D4	33.16 N	94.14 W
Wright-Patterson Air Force Base, mil., Oh., U.S.	124	E2	39.49 N	84.03 W
Wright Peak, mtn., Ca., U.S.	148	E3	38.58 N	122.46 W
Wrightson, Mount, mtn., Az., U.S.	150	L6	31.42 N	110.50 W
Wrightstown, Wi., U.S.	126	D1	44.19 N	88.09 W
Wrightsville, Ga., U.S.	132	D3	32.43 N	82.43 W
Wrightsville Beach, N.C., U.S.	132	B8	34.15 N	77.46 W
Wrightwood, Ca., U.S.	148	I8	34.21 N	117.37 W
Wrigley, N.T., Can.	110	C6	63.15 N	123.37 W
Wrigley, Tn., U.S.	130	I10	35.53 N	87.20 W
Wrigley Field, p.o.i., Il., U.S.	196		41.57 N	87.39 W
Wrocław (Breslau), Pol.	24	E13	51.06 N	17.01 E
Wrong Lake, l., Mb., Can.	142	B17	52.37 N	96.11 W
Wronki, Pol.	24	D12	52.41 N	16.24 E
Wrotham Heath, Eng., U.K.	178		51.18 N	0.21 E
Wrottesley, Cape, c., N.T., Can.	109	B15	74.33 N	121.32 W
Wroxton, Sk., Can.	142	C12	51.14 N	101.53 W
Września, Pol.	24	D13	52.19 N	17.35 E
Wschowa, Pol.	24	E12	51.48 N	16.19 E
Wu, stm., China	58	I5	24.48 N	113.35 E
Wu, stm., China	58	G2	29.43 N	107.24 E
Wu, stm., China	58	G7	28.54 N	116.43 E
Wu, stm., China	58	H3	27.11 N	109.48 E
Wu, stm., China	58	H4	27.07 N	110.00 E
Wu, stm., China	58	D8	34.23 N	117.53 E
Wubu, China	52	C4	37.27 N	110.39 E
Wuchang, China	52	C10	44.54 N	127.09 E
Wuchang see Wuhan, China	58	F6	30.34 N	114.16 E
Wuchang Hu, l., China	58	F7	30.17 N	116.47 E
Wuchow see Wuzhou, China	58	J4	23.30 N	111.20 E
Wuchuan, China	58	K4	21.22 N	110.41 E
Wuchuan, China	58	A4	41.05 N	111.26 E
Wuda, China	58	B2	39.29 N	106.46 E
Wudaoliang, China	52	D3	35.12 N	93.04 E
Wudi, China	58	C7	37.43 N	117.36 E
Wuding, China	52	F5	25.32 N	102.23 E
Wuding, stm., China	58	C4	37.02 N	110.25 E
Wudu, China	52	E5	33.25 N	104.50 E
Wuduhe, China	58	F4	31.03 N	111.03 E
Wufeng, China	58	F4	30.08 N	110.32 E
Wugang, China	58	H4	26.44 N	110.38 E
Wugong, China	58	D2	34.19 N	108.05 E
Wugong Shan, mtn., China	58	H6	27.35 N	114.18 E
Wugong Shan, mts., China	58	H6	27.21 N	113.50 E
Wuhai, China	58	B2	39.39 N	106.47 E
Wuhan (Hankow), China	58	F6	30.34 N	114.16 E
Wuhe, China	58	I6	24.25 N	115.26 E
Wuhle, stm., Ger.	182a		52.29 N	13.34 E
Wuhu, China	58	F8	31.20 N	118.22 E
Wuhua, China	58	J6	23.56 N	115.46 E
Wuhuanchi, China	54	C4	42.18 N	121.55 E
Wuhudongmiao, China	58	B2	38.18 N	107.19 E
Wujiang, China	70	B7	33.36 N	79.47 E
Wujia, stm., China	58	A3	40.56 N	108.49 E
Wujiangdu, China	58	H2	27.19 N	106.44 E
Wukang, China	58	F8	30.32 N	119.57 E
Wukari, Nig.	84	H6	7.52 N	9.46 E
Wukeshu, China	54	B7	44.47 N	126.09 E
Wulasitai, China	54	C4	43.19 N	121.23 E
Wulateqianqi, China	58	A3	40.37 N	109.05 E
Wuleidao Wan, b., China	58	C9	36.56 N	122.00 E
Wuliang Shan, mts., China	52	G5	24.29 N	100.38 E
Wulichuan, China	58	E4	33.49 N	111.08 E
Wulong, China	58	G2	29.19 N	107.43 E
Wuluhan, Indon.	66	H8	8.19 S	113.33 E
Wuluo, China	58	H3	26.09 N	108.15 E
Wulu Station, trans., China	189a		39.56 N	116.16 E
Wuming, China	58	J3	23.10 N	108.17 E
Wundwin, Mya.	64	B2	21.05 N	96.02 E
Wunnummin Lake, l., On., Can.	110	E13	52.55 N	89.09 W
Wunstorf, Ger.	24	D5	52.25 N	9.26 E
Wuntho, Mya.	62	D8	23.54 N	95.41 E
Wupatki National Monument, p.o.i., Az., U.S.	150	H5	35.31 N	111.25 W
Wupper, stm., Ger.	181		51.05 N	7.00 E
Wuppertal, Ger.	24	E3	51.16 N	7.10 E
Wuppertal, Ger.	181		51.16 N	7.11 E
Wuppertal, S. Afr.	90	H4	32.15 S	19.14 E
Wuqi, China	58	C3	36.54 N	108.10 E
Wuqia, China	48	G13	39.41 N	75.08 E
Wuqiang, China	58	B6	38.02 N	115.57 E
Wurno, Nig.	84	G6	13.17 N	5.24 E
Würzburg, Ger.	24	G5	49.47 N	9.55 E
Wurzen, Ger.	24	E8	51.22 N	12.45 E
Wushan, China	58	F3	31.04 N	109.53 E
Wusheng, China	58	F2	30.20 N	106.17 E
Wushenqi, China	58	B3	38.58 N	109.01 E
Wushi, China	58	J4	22.12 N	110.13 E
Wusi, Vanuatu	101d	j16	15.22 S	166.38 E
Wusih see Wuxi, China	58	F9	31.35 N	120.18 E
Wusuli (Ussuri), stm., Asia	52	B11	48.27 N	135.04 E
Wutai, China	58	B5	38.43 N	113.21 E
Wutai Shan, mtn., China	58	B5	39.04 N	113.35 E
Wutai Shan, mts., China	58	B5	39.13 N	113.45 E
Wutan, China	58	G4	28.29 N	111.40 E
Wutong, China	58	I3	25.18 N	110.01 E
Wutonghaolai, China	54	C3	42.55 N	120.15 E
Wutongqiao, China	52	F5	29.24 N	103.48 E
Wutsin see Changzhou, China	58	F8	31.46 N	119.56 E
Wutungkiao see Wutongqiao, China	52	F5	29.24 N	103.48 E
Wuvulu Island, i., Pap. N. Gui.	101a	a3	1.45 S	142.50 E

Name	Page	Map Ref.	Latitude	Longitude
Wuwei, China	52	D5	37.55 N	102.37 E
Wuwei, China	58	F7	31.18 N	117.54 E
Wuxi, China	58	F3	31.23 N	109.37 E
Wuxi, China	58	F9	31.35 N	120.18 E
Wuxiang, China	58	C5	36.50 N	112.51 E
Wuxing see Huzhou, China	58	F9	30.51 N	120.05 E
Wuxuan, China	58	J3	23.35 N	109.38 E
Wuyang, China	58	H4	26.41 N	110.20 E
Wuyi, China	58	G8	28.53 N	119.48 E
Wuying, China	52	B10	48.07 N	129.14 E
Wuyi Shan, mts., China	58	H7	27.42 N	117.09 E
Wuyuan, China	58	G7	29.15 N	117.50 E
Wuyuan, China	58	A3	41.03 N	108.21 E
Wuzhai, China	58	B4	38.54 N	111.49 E
Wuzhi Shan, mtn., China	62	E10	18.57 N	109.43 E
Wuzhong, China	58	C2	37.59 N	106.12 E
Wuzhou, China	58	J4	23.30 N	111.20 E
Wyaconda, Mo., U.S.	130	D6	40.23 N	91.55 W
Wyaconda, stm., Mo., U.S.	130	D6	40.02 N	91.29 W
Wyalusing, Pa., U.S.	124	C9	41.40 N	76.15 W
Wyandanch, N.Y., U.S.	194		40.45 N	73.21 W
Wyandotte, Mi., U.S.	124	B2	42.12 N	83.08 W
Wyandotte National Wildlife Refuge, ind. res., Mi., U.S.	199		42.14 N	83.08 W
Wyandra, Austl.	98	F5	27.15 S	145.58 E
Wyangala, Lake, res., Austl.	98	I7	33.56 S	149.00 E
Wyatt, Mo., U.S.	130	H8	36.54 N	89.14 W
Wycheproof, Austl.	98	K4	36.04 S	143.13 E
Wychwood, S. Afr.	191d		26.12 S	28.08 E
Wy-Dit-Joli-Village, Fr.	179		49.06 N	1.50 E
Wye, stm., U.K.	10	J10	51.37 N	2.39 W
Wyeville, Wi., U.S.	128	G8	44.01 N	90.22 W
Wyk, Ger.	24	B4	54.41 N	8.33 E
Wykoff, Mn., U.S.	128	H6	43.42 N	92.17 W
Wylandville, Pa., U.S.	197b		40.12 N	80.08 W
Wyleswood Lake, l., Oh., U.S.	197a		41.20 N	81.55 W
Wylie, Pa., U.S.	197b		40.27 N	79.59 W
Wylie, Tx., U.S.	136	A11	33.01 N	96.32 W
Wylie, Lake, res., U.S.	132	A4	35.04 N	81.03 W
Wymark, Sk., Can.	142	D6	50.07 N	107.44 W
Wymondham, Eng., U.K.	10	I13	52.34 N	1.06 E
Wymore, Ne., U.S.	128	K2	40.07 N	96.39 W
Wyncote, Pa., U.S.	203		40.05 N	75.08 W
Wyndham, Austl.	96	C5	15.28 S	128.06 E
Wyndmere, N.D., U.S.	128	E1	46.14 N	97.09 W
Wyndmoor, Pa., U.S.	203		40.04 N	75.11 W
Wynndel, B.C., Can.	144	G14	49.10 N	116.32 W
Wynne, Ar., U.S.	134	B8	35.13 N	90.47 W
Wynnewood, Ok., U.S.	138	G11	34.39 N	97.10 W
Wynnewood, Pa., U.S.	203		40.00 N	75.16 W
Wynniatt Bay, b., Can.	110	A8	72.46 N	110.49 W
Wynona, Ok., U.S.	138	E12	36.32 N	96.20 W
Wynoochee, stm., Wa., U.S.	146	C3	46.58 N	123.36 W
Wynoochee Lake, res., Wa., U.S.	146	C3	47.25 N	123.35 W
Wynot, Ne., U.S.	140	E15	42.44 N	97.10 W
Wynyard, Austl.	99a	n12	40.59 S	145.42 E
Wynyard, Sk., Can.	142	G9	51.47 N	104.10 W
Wyocena, Wi., U.S.	128	H9	43.29 N	89.18 W
Wyodak, Wy., U.S.	140	C7	44.17 N	105.22 W
Wyoming, On., Can.	126	F7	42.57 N	82.07 W
Wyoming, Il., U.S.	130	C8	41.03 N	89.46 W
Wyoming, Ia., U.S.	130	B6	42.03 N	91.00 W
Wyoming, Mi., U.S.	130	B12	42.54 N	85.42 W
Wyoming, state, U.S.	140	E5	43.00 N	107.30 W
Wyoming Peak, mtn., Wy., U.S.	146	H16	42.36 N	110.37 W
Wyong, Austl.	98	I8	33.16 S	151.24 E
Wyperfield National Park, p.o.i., Austl.	98	J3	35.30 S	142.00 E
Wyrzysk, Pol.	24	C13	53.09 N	17.13 E
Wyśmierzyce, Pol.	24	E16	51.37 N	20.50 E
Wysoka, Pol.	24	C12	53.10 N	17.05 E
Wysokie Mazowieckie, Pol.	24	D18	52.54 N	22.30 E
Wyszków, Pol.	24	D17	52.35 N	21.27 E
Wyszogród, Pol.	24	D16	52.23 N	20.12 E
Wythenshawe, ngh., Eng., U.K.	180		53.24 N	2.17 W
Wythenshawe Hall, hist., Eng., U.K.	180		53.24 N	2.17 W
Wytheville, Va., U.S.	124	H4	36.56 N	81.05 W
X				
Xaafuun, Som.	86	B10	10.25 N	51.16 E
Xaafuun, Raas, c., Som.	86	B10	10.26 N	51.23 E
Xàbia, Spain	28	F11	38.47 N	0.10 E
Xabregas, ngh., Port.	184c		38.44 N	9.07 W
Xaidulla, China	62	A4	36.26 N	77.58 E
Xainza, China	70	C12	30.55 N	88.40 E
Xai-Xai, Moz.	90	D11	25.03 S	33.38 E
Xalapa (Jalapa), Mex.	154	F10	19.31 N	96.54 W
Xalin, Som.	86	C9	9.04 N	48.36 E
Xallas, stm., Spain	28	B2	42.54 N	9.07 W
Xam (Chu), stm., Asia	64	B7	19.53 N	105.45 E
Xambioá, Braz.	170	D1	6.27 S	48.35 W
Xambrê, stm., Braz.	172	A11	24.01 S	53.58 W
Xam Nua, Laos	64	B7	20.25 N	104.02 E
Xá-Muteba, Ang.	88	B2	9.30 S	17.48 E
Xan (San), stm., Asia	64	F8	13.32 N	106.01 E
Xang, stm., China	70	D12	29.18 N	89.05 E
Xangongo, Ang.	88	D2	16.43 S	14.58 E
Xankändi, Azer.	42	F12	39.48 N	46.45 E
Xanten, Ger.	20	C15	51.39 N	6.27 E
Xánthi, Grc.	34	B7	41.08 N	24.53 E
Xanxerê, Braz.	172	C11	26.52 S	52.25 W
Xapecó, stm., Braz.	172	C11	27.06 S	53.01 W
Xapuri, Braz.	166	B3	10.39 S	68.31 W
Xarardheere, Som.	86	D9	4.38 N	47.52 E
Xar Moron, stm., China	52	C8	43.25 N	120.45 E
Xarrama, stm., Port.	28	F2	38.14 N	8.19 W
Xàtiva, Spain	28	F10	38.59 N	0.31 W
Xau, Lake, pl., Bots.	90	B7	21.18 S	24.43 E
Xaudum see Nhoma, stm., Afr.	88	D2	19.23 S	22.11 E
Xavantina, Braz.	166	D6	21.16 S	52.49 W
Xaxim, Braz.	172	C11	26.57 S	52.32 W
Xäzär, Dänizi see Caspian Sea, s.	48	F7	41.18 N	50.59 E
Xcalak, Mex.	156	C4	18.16 N	87.50 W
X-Can, Mex.	156	B4	20.53 N	87.38 W
Xelva, Spain	28	E9	39.45 N	0.59 W
Xenia, Il., U.S.	130	F9	38.38 N	88.38 W
Xenia, Oh., U.S.	124	E2	39.40 N	83.56 W
Xènô, Laos	64	D7	16.40 N	104.51 E
Xepenehe, N. Cal.	101d	m16	20.46 S	167.07 E
Xercavins, Arroyo de, stm., Spain	184d		41.30 N	2.02 E
Xéré, N. Cal.	101d	n16	22.15 S	166.59 E
Xeres see Jerez de la Frontera, Spain	28	H4	36.41 N	6.08 W
Xhumo, Bots.	90	B7	21.07 S	24.42 E
Xi, stm., China	58	J5	22.20 N	113.18 E
Xi, stm., China	58	F6	30.20 N	115.06 E
Xiachengzi, China	52	C11	44.41 N	130.27 E
Xiachuan Dao, i., China	58	K5	21.40 N	112.37 E
Xiagaixin, China	64	A5	22.36 N	99.59 E
Xiaguan see Dali, China	52	F5	25.35 N	100.12 E
Xiamaguan, China	58	C2	37.13 N	106.25 E
Xiamen (Amoy), China	58	I7	24.27 N	118.06 E
Xi'an (Sian), China	58	D3	34.15 N	108.52 E
Xianfeng, China	58	G3	29.41 N	109.09 E
Xiang, stm., China	58	G5	28.27 N	112.47 E
Xiangcheng, China	58	E5	33.50 N	113.28 E
Xiangfan, China	58	F4	32.01 N	112.08 E
Xianggang (Hong Kong), China	58	J6	22.15 N	114.10 E
Xianggang (Hong Kong), China	189d		22.17 N	114.09 E
Xianggang, state, China	52	G7	22.15 N	114.10 E
Xiangkhoang, Laos	64	C6	19.20 N	103.22 E
Xiangkhoang, Plateau de, plat., Laos	64	C6	19.30 N	103.10 E
Xiangning, China	54	D4	36.01 N	110.45 E
Xiangride, China	52	D4	35.59 N	97.59 E
Xiangshan, China	58	G9	29.27 N	121.51 E
Xiangshui, China	58	J6	23.15 N	114.10 E
Xiangtan, China	58	H5	27.51 N	112.54 E
Xiangxiang, China	58	H5	27.43 N	112.27 E
Xiangyin, China	58	G5	28.39 N	112.55 E
Xiangyuan, China	58	C5	36.32 N	113.02 E
Xiangzhou, China	58	J3	23.58 N	109.43 E
Xianju, China	58	G9	28.50 N	120.43 E
Xiannongtan Stadium, p.o.i., China	189a		39.52 N	116.23 E
Xianru, China	54	C8	43.11 N	128.01 E
Xianshui, stm., China	62	B9	30.04 N	111.03 E
Xiantao, China	58	F5	30.22 N	113.27 E
Xianyang, China	58	G8	28.02 N	118.30 E
Xianyang, China	58	D3	34.20 N	108.42 E
Xianyou, China	58	I8	25.22 N	118.40 E
Xiao, stm., China	58	G8	28.09 N	120.13 E
Xiaoazhang, China	64	A7	23.43 N	104.57 E
Xiaochengzi, China	54	C5	42.56 N	123.12 E
Xiaodong, China	58	J3	22.13 N	108.37 E
Xiaogan, China	58	F5	30.55 N	113.54 E
Xiaoguai, China	52	B1	45.10 N	85.02 E
Xiaohekou, China	58	E2	33.19 N	107.25 E
Xiao Hinggan Ling (Lesser Khingan Range), mts., China	52	B10	48.45 N	127.00 E
Xiaohongmen, China	189a		39.49 N	116.26 E
Xiaojin, China	52	E5	30.59 N	102.22 E
Xiaojiu, China	54	B7	45.15 N	127.47 E
Xiaoling, China	54	B7	45.20 N	127.18 E
Xiaoluan, stm., China	54	D2	41.34 N	117.04 E
Xiaopingyang, China	58	J3	23.24 N	109.09 E
Xiaoqiao, China	58	H8	26.57 N	118.30 E
Xiaoshan, China	58	F9	30.09 N	120.15 E
Xiaoxian, China	58	D7	34.11 N	116.56 E
Xiaoxintian, China	189a		39.58 N	116.22 E
Xiaoyi, China	58	C4	37.07 N	111.48 E
Xiapu, China	58	H9	26.52 N	120.01 E
Xiawa, China	52	C9	42.37 N	120.37 E
Xiaxian, China	54	D4	35.11 N	111.15 E
Xibaxa see Subansiri, stm., Asia	70	D14	28.20 N	93.40 E
Xibo, stm., China	54	D3	42.19 N	118.58 E
Xichang, China	52	F5	27.54 N	102.16 E
Xichong, China	58	F1	31.00 N	105.52 E
Xicoténcatl, Mex.	154	D9	23.00 N	98.55 W
Xictle, Volcán, vol., Mex.	204a		19.14 N	99.14 W
Xié, stm., Braz.	168	G8	0.53 N	67.11 W
Xielipuke, China	70	C9	31.30 N	82.46 E
Xifei, stm., China	58	E7	32.41 N	116.41 E
Xifeng, China	52	C9	42.44 N	124.43 E
Xifeng, China	58	H2	27.01 N	106.36 E
Xigazê, China	70	D12	29.16 N	88.54 E
Xihan, stm., China	58	D1	33.26 N	106.02 E
Xihe, China	58	F5	31.39 N	113.25 E
Xiheying, China	58	B6	39.57 N	114.45 E
Xihua, China	58	E6	33.47 N	114.32 E
Xiji, China	58	D1	35.58 N	105.43 E
Xijialong, China	64	A6	23.31 N	103.51 E
Xi Jiao Airfield, arpt., China	189a		39.58 N	116.15 E
Xiliao, stm., China	52	C9	43.34 N	123.29 E
Xilin, China	70	D11	28.27 N	87.37 E
Xilinhot, China	58	C8	43.56 N	116.02 E
Xilintuo, China	70	C12	30.06 N	88.05 E
Xiluga, stm., China	54	C3	42.17 N	118.39 E
Ximakou, China	58	F5	30.33 N	113.48 E
Ximalin, China	58	A6	40.48 N	114.29 E
Ximiao, China	52	C5	41.06 N	100.17 E
Ximucheng, China	58	A10	40.41 N	122.54 E
Xin, stm., China	58	G7	28.37 N	116.40 E
Xin'an, China	54	C6	43.48 N	125.41 E
Xin'anjiang Shuiku, res., China	58	G8	29.32 N	118.56 E
Xin'ansuo, China	64	A6	23.16 N	103.27 E
Xinavane, Moz.	90	D11	25.02 S	32.47 E
Xin Barag Youqi, China	52	B8	48.40 N	116.49 E
Xin Barag Zuoqi, China	52	B8	48.12 N	118.16 E
Xinbin, China	54	D6	41.43 N	125.01 E
Xincai, China	58	E6	32.44 N	114.59 E
Xinchang, China	58	G9	29.30 N	120.52 E
Xincheng, China	58	G6	24.04 N	108.46 E
Xincheng, China	58	B6	39.20 N	115.50 E
Xindian, China	58	C8	37.29 N	118.29 E
Xindu, China	58	I4	23.59 N	111.42 E
Xinfeng, China	58	I6	25.24 N	114.56 E
Xinfeng Shuiku, res., China	58	J6	23.52 N	114.30 E
Xing'an, China	58	I4	25.37 N	110.31 E
Xingcheng, China	58	A9	40.36 N	120.42 E
Xingguo, China	58	H6	26.19 N	115.20 E
Xinghai, China	52	D4	35.31 N	99.36 E
Xinghe, China	58	A5	40.52 N	113.52 E
Xinghua, China	58	E8	32.55 N	119.49 E
Xingkai Hu see Khanka, Lake, l., Asia	54	B10	45.11 N	132.25 E
Xinglong, China	58	D1	35.36 N	106.02 E
Xingou, China	58	F5	30.41 N	113.57 E
Xingren, China	58	F6	25.26 N	105.10 E
Xingrenbu, China	58	C1	37.06 N	105.13 E
Xingshanbao, China	54	B6	45.30 N	125.45 E
Xingtai, China	58	C6	37.03 N	114.29 E
Xingtang, China	58	B6	38.25 N	114.33 E
Xingu, stm., Braz.	164	D7	1.29 S	51.49 W
Xingxian, China	58	B4	38.36 N	111.15 E
Xingyi, China	52	F5	25.04 N	104.53 E
Xinhe, China	58	C6	37.31 N	115.14 E
Xinhua, China	58	H4	27.37 N	111.02 E
Xinhui, China	58	J5	22.31 N	113.01 E
Xining, China	52	D5	36.37 N	101.49 E
Xinji, China	58	C6	37.54 N	115.12 E
Xinjiang, China	58	D4	35.37 N	111.13 E
Xinjiang, state, China	62	A5	40.00 N	85.00 E
Xinjiang Weiwuer Zizhiqu see Xinjiang, state, China	62	A5	40.00 N	85.00 E
Xinjin, China	52	E5	30.25 N	103.49 E
Xinjin, China	58	B9	39.23 N	121.59 E
Xinjiulong (New Kowloon), China	58	J6	22.20 N	114.09 E
Xinjiulong (New Kowloon), China	189d		22.20 N	114.10 E
Xinkai, stm., China	54	C5	43.34 N	123.30 E
Xinli, China	54	B7	44.40 N	126.44 E
Xinlitun, China	54	D5	42.00 N	122.10 E
Xinmin, China	54	C5	41.59 N	122.49 E
Xinning, China	58	H4	26.19 N	110.45 E
Xinpu, China	58	I7	24.29 N	116.11 E
Xinpu see Lianyungang, China	58	D8	34.36 N	119.10 E
Xinshao, China	58	H4	27.17 N	111.27 E
Xintian, China	58	I5	25.53 N	112.05 E
Xinwen, China	58	D7	35.52 N	117.40 E
Xinxian, China	58	B5	38.24 N	112.44 E
Xinxian, China	58	F6	31.37 N	114.51 E
Xinxiang, China	58	D5	35.18 N	113.51 E
Xinxing, China	54	C8	43.14 N	129.51 E
Xinxing, China	58	L3	19.56 N	109.32 E
Xinyang, China	58	E6	32.07 N	114.03 E
Xinye, China	58	E5	32.33 N	112.21 E
Xinyi, China	58	J4	22.13 N	110.52 E
Xinyi, China	58	D8	34.22 N	118.20 E
Xinyu, China	58	H6	27.48 N	114.57 E
Xinzhou, China	58	L3	19.44 N	109.17 E
Xinzhuang, China	189a		39.56 N	116.31 E
Xinzo de Limia, Spain	28	B3	42.03 N	7.42 W
Xiongyuecheng, China	58	A9	40.10 N	122.08 E
Xiping, China	58	E6	33.22 N	114.01 E
Xiping, China	58	G8	28.26 N	119.29 E
Xiqing Shan, mts., China	52	E5	35.11 N	101.05 E
Xique-Xique, Braz.	170	F4	10.50 S	42.42 W
Xırdalan, Azer.	42	E13	40.27 N	49.45 E
Xishanqiao, China	58	F8	31.57 N	118.42 E
Xisha Qundao (Paracel Islands), is., China	60	B5	16.30 N	112.15 E
Xishu, China	58	C5	36.41 N	113.48 E
Xishui, China	58	F6	30.27 N	115.15 E
Xiti, China	70	B9	33.27 N	82.48 E
Xitianmu Shan, mtn., China	58	F8	30.21 N	119.25 E
Xiu, stm., China	58	G6	29.02 N	115.47 E
Xi Ujimqin Qi, China	54	B2	44.34 N	117.36 E
Xiushan, China	58	G3	28.31 N	108.52 E
Xiushui, China	58	G6	29.03 N	114.33 E
Xiuyan, China	58	A10	40.16 N	123.17 E
Xiva, Spain	28	E10	39.28 N	0.43 W
Xixabangma Feng, mtn., China	70	D10	28.22 N	85.50 E
Xixi, China	58	H8	26.45 N	118.42 E
Xixia, China	58	E4	33.17 N	111.28 E
Xixian, China	58	E6	32.21 N	114.44 E
Xixiang, China	58	E2	32.58 N	107.45 E
Xixona, Spain	28	F10	38.31 N	0.31 W
Xiyang, China	58	I7	25.49 N	117.25 E
Xiyang, China	58	C5	37.36 N	113.41 E
Xizang (Tibet), state, China	62	B5	32.00 N	88.00 E
Xizhimen Station, trans., China	189a		39.56 N	116.21 E
Xizi, China	54	D3	41.49 N	119.20 E
Xochicalco, hist., Mex.	154	F9	18.48 N	99.19 W
Xochimilco, ngh., Mex.	204a		19.16 N	99.06 W
Xochimilco, Lago de, l., Mex.	204a		19.16 N	99.06 W
Xochistlahuaca, Mex.	154	G9	16.47 N	98.15 W
Xom Binh Phuoc, Viet.	187c		10.40 N	106.47 E
Xom Xoai Minh, Viet.	187c		10.42 N	106.50 E
Xongka see Ca, stm., Asia	64	C7	18.44 N	105.44 E
Xu, stm., China	58	H7	28.00 N	116.20 E
Xuancheng, China	58	F8	30.56 N	118.45 E
Xuan'en, China	58	F3	30.00 N	109.19 E
Xuang, stm., Laos	64	B6	19.58 N	102.15 E
Xuanhan, China	58	F2	31.21 N	107.45 E
Xuanhua, China	58	A6	40.35 N	115.02 E
Xuan Loc, Viet.	64	G8	10.55 N	107.14 E
Xuan Thoi Thuong, Viet.	187c		10.52 N	106.34 E
Xuanwei, China	52	F5	26.06 N	104.05 E
Xuchang, China	58	D5	34.01 N	113.48 E
Xueshan Zhang, mtn., China	58	I5	24.24 N	113.37 E
Xuguit Qi see Yakeshi, China	52	B9	49.16 N	120.43 E
Xujiazhai, China	187b		31.23 N	121.17 E
Xun, stm., China	58	J4	23.26 N	111.29 E
Xungru, China	70	D10	29.15 N	84.48 E
Xunle, China	58	I3	25.17 N	108.12 E
Xunwu, China	58	I6	24.56 N	115.38 E
Xupu, China	58	H4	27.52 N	110.22 E
Xúquer see Júcar, stm., Spain	28	E10	39.09 N	0.14 W
Xuwen, China	58	K4	20.19 N	110.10 E
Xuyi, China	58	E8	33.01 N	118.29 E
Xuyong, China	58	G1	28.10 N	105.25 E
Xuzhou, China	58	D7	34.16 N	117.11 E
Xylókastro, Grc.	34	E5	38.04 N	22.37 E
Y				
Yaak, Mt., U.S.	146	B11	48.49 N	115.41 W
Yaan, China	52	E5	30.01 N	103.03 E
Yaapeet, Austl.	98	J3	35.47 S	142.02 E
Yaba, ngh., Nig.	191a		6.30 N	3.23 E
Yaba College of Technology, educ., Nig.	191a		6.32 N	3.23 E
Yablis, Nic.	156	E6	14.08 N	83.47 W
Yablonovy Range see Jablonovyj hrebet, mts., Russia	50	F11	53.30 N	115.00 E
Yabluniv, Ukr.	38	E4	48.24 N	25.01 E
Yablychne, Ukr.	38	C14	50.18 N	35.14 E
Yabrīn, Sau. Ar.	72	E6	23.17 N	48.58 E
Yabrūd, Syria	76	E7	33.59 N	36.39 E
Yabucoa, P.R.	158a	b4	18.02 N	65.52 W
Yabuli, China	52	C10	44.55 N	128.33 E
Yacambu, Parque Nacional, p.o.i., Ven.	168	C7	9.40 N	69.42 W
Yacata, i., Fiji	101e	p20	17.15 S	179.30 W
Yacheng, China	58	L3	18.23 N	109.10 E
Yachi, stm., China	58	H2	27.14 N	107.07 E
Yaco (Iaco), stm., S.A.	164	F4	9.01 S	68.35 W
Yacuiba, Bol.	166	D4	22.01 S	63.42 W
Yacyretá, Isla, i., Para.	172	C9	27.25 S	56.30 W
Yādgīr, India	69	C3	16.45 N	77.08 E
Yadkin, stm., N.C., U.S.	124	H4	36.13 N	81.00 W
Yadkinville, N.C., U.S.	124	H5	36.08 N	80.39 W
Yadong, China	70	E12	27.29 N	88.54 E
Yadua, i., Fiji	101e	p19	16.49 S	178.18 E
Yaduty, Ukr.	38	B11	51.22 N	32.19 E
Yafran, Libya	82	A2	32.04 N	12.30 E
Yaftābād, Iran	185d		35.39 N	51.19 E
Yagasa Cluster, i., Fiji	101e	q20	18.56 S	178.26 W
Yağcılar, Tur.	34	D11	39.25 N	28.23 E
Yagoona, Austl.	192a		33.55 S	151.02 E
Yagoua, Cam.	86	B3	10.20 N	15.13 E
Yagradagzê Shan, mtn., China	52	D4	35.22 N	95.46 E
Yaguajay, Cuba	156	A8	22.19 N	79.14 W
Yaguarón (Jaguarão), stm., S.A.	172	F11	32.42 S	53.06 W
Yaguas, stm., S.A.	168	I6	2.45 S	70.04 W
Yahara, stm., Wi., U.S.	128	I9	42.47 N	89.06 W
Yahata see Kitakyūshū, Japan	56	F3	33.53 N	130.50 E
Yahe, China	54	B9	45.22 N	130.18 E
Yahk, B.C., Can.	144	G14	49.05 N	116.05 W
Yaho, Japan	186		35.41 N	139.27 E
Yahorlyts'kyi lyman, b., Ukr.	38	G10	46.24 N	31.50 E
Yahotyn, Ukr.	38	C10	50.17 N	31.46 E
Yahualica, Mex.	154	E7	21.08 N	102.50 W
Yahuas see Yaguas, stm., S.A.	168	I6	2.45 S	70.04 W
Yahyalı, Tur.	42	F6	38.05 N	35.22 E
Yai, Khao, mtn., Asia	64	F4	12.27 N	99.26 E
Yai, Khao, mtn., Thai.	64	E4	15.25 N	99.20 E
Yainax Butte, mtn., Or., U.S.	148	A4	42.20 N	121.16 W
Yaita, Japan	56	C12	36.48 N	139.56 E
Yaita, Japan	186		35.57 N	140.03 E
Yaitopya see Ethiopia, ctry., Afr.	82	F7	9.00 N	39.00 E
Yaizu, Japan	56	E11	34.52 N	138.19 E
Yajiang, China	52	E5	30.03 N	101.01 E
Yakacık, Tur.	76	B7	36.46 N	36.13 E
Yakacık, ngh., Tur.	185b		40.55 N	29.13 E
Yakapınar, Tur.	76	B6	36.59 N	35.42 E
Yakeshi, China	52	B9	49.16 N	120.43 E
Yakhnyky, Ukr.	38	C12	50.26 N	33.10 E
Yakima, Wa., U.S.	146	D6	46.35 N	120.29 W
Yakima, stm., Wa., U.S.	146	D7	46.14 N	119.13 W
Yakima Indian Reservation, ind. res., Wa., U.S.	146	D5	46.16 N	121.03 W
Yakmach, Pak.	72	D9	28.45 N	63.51 E
Yako, Burkina	84	G4	12.57 N	2.15 W
Yakō, ngh., Japan	186		35.32 N	139.41 E
Yakoma, D.R.C.	86	D4	4.04 N	22.25 E
Yakuendai, Japan	186		35.43 N	140.03 E
Yakumo, Japan	54	C14	42.15 N	140.16 E
Yaku-shima, i., Japan	54	I9	30.20 N	130.30 E
Yakutat, Ak., U.S.	109	E12	59.32 N	139.43 W
Yakutat Bay, b., Ak., U.S.	109	E11	59.40 N	140.00 W
Yakutia see Jakutija, state, Russia	50	D14	67.00 N	125.00 E
Yakymivka, Ukr.	38	G14	46.41 N	35.09 E
Yala, Thai.	64	I5	6.32 N	101.17 E
Yalahau, Laguna de, b., Mex.	156	B4	21.27 N	87.17 W
Yalding, Eng., U.K.	178		51.13 N	0.26 E
Yale, B.C., Can.	144	G9	49.34 N	121.25 W
Yale, Mi., U.S.	126	E7	43.08 N	82.48 W
Yale, Ok., U.S.	134	A2	36.07 N	96.42 W
Yale, Lake, l., Fl., U.S.	132	H4	28.55 N	81.44 W
Yale, Mount, mtn., Co., U.S.	138	C2	38.51 N	106.18 W
Yalgoo, Austl.	96	E3	28.21 S	116.40 E
Yalinga, C.A.R.	86	C4	6.30 N	23.15 E
Yalleroi, Austl.	98	E5	24.04 S	145.45 E
Yalobusha, stm., Ms., U.S.	134	D9	33.33 N	90.10 W
Yalong, stm., China	52	E5	26.36 N	101.47 E
Yalova, Tur.	34	C12	40.39 N	29.15 E
Yalpuh see Ialpug, stm., Eur.	36	C15	45.41 N	28.35 E
Yalpuh, ozero, l., Ukr.	38	H7	45.26 N	28.38 E
Yalta, Ukr.	38	I13	44.30 N	34.10 E
Yalta, Ukr.	38	G16	46.57 N	37.16 E
Yaltushkiv, Ukr.	38	E6	48.58 N	27.29 E
Yalu (Amnok-kang), stm., Asia	54	D6	39.57 N	124.21 E
Yalvaç, Tur.	34	E14	38.17 N	31.09 E
Yamada, Japan	188		34.31 N	135.39 E
Yamada, Japan	188		34.48 N	135.32 E
Yamada, stm., Japan	188		34.47 N	135.04 E
Yamaga, Japan	56	F3	33.00 N	130.41 E
Yamagata, Japan	56	A13	38.15 N	140.20 E
Yamagata, state, Japan	56	A13	38.37 N	140.06 E
Yamagawa, Japan	56	H3	31.11 N	130.37 E
Yamaguchi, Japan	56	E4	34.10 N	131.28 E
Yamaguchi, Japan	188		34.50 N	135.15 E
Yamaguchi, state, Japan	56	E4	34.20 N	131.30 E
Yamaguchi-chosuichi, res., Japan	186		35.46 N	139.25 E
Yamal Peninsula see Jamal, poluostrov, pen., Russia	50	B2	70.00 N	70.00 E
Yamamoto, Japan	188		34.38 N	135.38 E
Yamanaka, Japan	56	C9	36.15 N	136.22 E
Yamanashi, state, Japan	56	D11	35.30 N	138.30 E
Yamasaki, Japan	56	D7	34.59 N	134.33 E
Yamashina, ngh., Japan	188		34.58 N	135.49 E
Yamaska, stm., Qc., Can.	122	E4	46.06 N	72.56 W
Yamate, Japan	188		34.30 N	135.27 E
Yamatengwumulu, China	52	D4	38.34 N	97.02 E
Yamazaki, Japan	186		35.56 N	139.54 E
Yamba, Austl.	98	G9	29.26 S	153.21 E
Yambio, Sudan	82	G5	4.34 N	28.24 E
Yamdena, Pulau, i., Indon.	60	G9	7.36 S	131.25 E
Yame, Japan	56	F3	33.12 N	130.33 E
Ya Men, b., China	58	J5	22.09 N	113.05 E
Yamenying, China	54	C5	43.23 N	122.12 E
Yamethin, Mya.	64	B3	20.28 N	96.09 E
Yamma Yamma, Lake, l., Austl.	98	F3	26.20 S	141.25 E
Yamoussoukro, C. Iv.	84	H4	6.49 N	5.17 W
Yampa, Co., U.S.	138	A2	40.09 N	106.54 W
Yampa, stm., Co., U.S.	150	C8	40.31 N	108.59 W
Yampa Plateau, plat., U.S.	150	C8	40.25 N	109.00 W
Yampil', Ukr.	38	E7	48.14 N	28.17 E
Yampil', Ukr.	38	D5	49.57 N	26.14 E
Yampil', Ukr.	38	B12	51.56 N	33.47 E
Yamsay Mountain, mtn., Or., U.S.	146	H5	42.56 N	121.22 W
Yamuna, stm., India	70	F8	25.25 N	81.53 E
Yamuna Bridge, trans., India	190a		28.40 N	77.14 E
Yamunānagar, India	72	C12	30.07 N	77.16 E
Yamzho Yumco, l., China	52	F3	28.58 N	90.45 E
Yan, stm., China	58	C3	36.23 N	110.28 E
Yan, stm., Sri L.	69	G5	8.54 N	81.00 E
Yanac, Austl.	98	K3	36.08 S	141.25 E
Yanagawa, Japan	56	F3	33.09 N	130.24 E
Yanagi, Japan	188		34.25 N	135.56 E
Yanagimoto, Japan	188		34.34 N	135.51 E
Yanai, Japan	56	F5	33.57 N	132.06 E
Yanaka, Japan	186		35.24 N	140.01 E
Yanam, India	69	C6	16.43 N	82.15 E
Yan'an, China	58	C3	36.34 N	109.29 E
Yanbu' al-Bahr, Sau. Ar.	72	E4	24.04 N	38.05 E
Yanceyville, N.C., U.S.	124	H6	36.24 N	79.20 W
Yanchang, China	58	C3	36.35 N	110.00 E
Yancheng, China	58	E9	33.24 N	120.09 E
Yanchi, China	58	C2	37.47 N	107.23 E
Yanchuan, China	58	C3	36.54 N	110.10 E
Yanco, Austl.	98	J6	34.36 S	146.24 E
Yanco Creek, stm., Austl.	98	J5	35.17 S	145.15 E
Yanda Creek, stm., Austl.	98	H5	30.19 S	145.34 E
Yandama Creek, stm., Austl.	98	G3	29.59 S	140.09 E
Yandé, Île, i., N. Cal.	101d	m14	20.03 S	163.48 E
Yandina, Sol. Is.	101b	e8	9.06 S	159.12 E
Yandoon, Mya.	64	D2	17.02 N	95.38 E
Yandu Bridge, trans., China	187b		31.15 N	121.32 E
Yanfolila, Mali	84	G3	11.09 N	8.09 W
Yang, stm., China	58	A6	40.21 N	115.24 E
Yang, stm., Thai.	64	D7	15.48 N	104.00 E
Yangambi, D.R.C.	86	D4	0.46 N	24.26 E
Yan'gang, China	58	I7	26.01 N	116.21 E
Yangbajain, China	52	E3	30.07 N	90.33 E
Yangcheng, China	58	D5	35.28 N	112.25 E
Yangch'ŏn, ngh., Kor., S.	189b		37.34 N	126.51 E
Yangchow see Yangzhou, China	58	E8	32.23 N	119.25 E
Yangchun, China	58	J4	22.10 N	111.47 E
Yangcun, China	58	J6	23.25 N	114.28 E
Yangdachengzi, China	54	B6	43.57 N	124.21 E
Yanggao, China	58	A5	40.23 N	113.45 E
Yanggong-ni, Kor., S.	189b		37.39 N	126.37 E
Yanghexi, China	58	G3	29.39 N	108.44 E
Yanghwa Bridge, trans., Kor., S.	189b		37.33 N	126.54 E
Yangjiang, China	58	K4	21.52 N	111.58 E
Yangliuqing, China	58	B7	39.08 N	117.01 E
Yanglousi, China	58	G5	29.30 N	113.38 E
Yangmingshan, ngh., Tai.	187d		25.09 N	121.33 E
Yangming Shan, mtn., China	58	H4	26.03 N	111.56 E
Yangmingshan National Park, p.o.i., Tai.	187d		25.12 N	121.32 E
Yangon (Rangoon), Mya.	64	D2	16.46 N	96.11 E
Yangon, state, Mya.	64	D3	16.50 N	96.10 E
Yangpingguan, China	58	E1	32.50 N	105.54 E
Yangquan, China	58	C5	37.51 N	113.34 E
Yangriwan, China	58	F4	31.41 N	110.46 E
Yangsan, Kor., S.	56	D2	35.21 N	129.03 E
Yangshan, China	58	I5	24.28 N	112.38 E
Yangshuo, China	58	I4	24.46 N	110.28 E
Yangtze see Chang, stm., China	52	E8	31.24 N	121.53 E
Yangtze see Jinsha, stm., China	52	F5	31.24 N	121.53 E
Yangxian, China	58	E2	33.06 N	107.48 E
Yangxiaodian, China	58	F7	31.46 N	116.44 E
Yangxin, China	58	G6	29.49 N	115.13 E
Yangxiudian, China	189a		39.44 N	116.32 E
Yangyang, Kor., S.	56	A1	38.04 N	128.36 E
Yangyuan, China	58	A5	40.05 N	114.09 E
Yangzhou, China	58	E8	32.23 N	119.25 E
Yanhe, China	58	G3	28.37 N	108.35 E
Yanji, China	52	C10	42.53 N	129.29 E
Yanji, China	54	C8	42.46 N	129.25 E
Yanjiadian, China	58	B9	39.48 N	121.48 E
Yankee Stadium, p.o.i., N.Y., U.S.	194		40.50 N	73.56 W
Yankeetown, Fl., U.S.	132	G3	29.02 N	82.43 W
Yankton, S.D., U.S.	140	E15	42.52 N	97.23 W
Yankton Indian Reservation, ind. res., S.D., U.S.	140	D14	43.10 N	98.22 W
Yanna, Austl.	98	F6	26.56 S	146.03 E
Yanqi, China	52	C2	42.03 N	86.33 E
Yanqing, China	58	A6	40.27 N	115.58 E
Yanshan, China	64	A7	23.37 N	104.20 E
Yanshou, China	52	B10	45.26 N	128.21 E
Yantabulla, Austl.	98	G5	29.21 S	145.00 E
Yantai, China	58	C9	37.32 N	121.21 E
Yantan, China	58	G9	28.28 N	120.44 E
Yanting, China	58	F1	31.19 N	105.18 E
Yantongshan, China	54	C6	43.17 N	126.01 E
Yanxi, China	58	I7	24.43 N	117.45 E
Yanyuan, China	52	F5	27.28 N	101.31 E
Yanzhou, China	58	D7	35.33 N	116.49 E
Yao, Chad	82	E3	12.51 N	17.33 E
Yao Airport, arpt., Japan	188		34.36 N	135.36 E
Yaoundé, Cam.	86	D2	3.52 N	11.31 E
Yaoxian, China	58	D3	34.54 N	108.58 E
Yao Yai, Ko, i., Thai.	64	I4	8.02 N	98.35 E
Yap, i., Micron.	94	C4	9.31 N	138.06 E
Yapacana, Parque Nacional, p.o.i., Ven.	168	F8	3.51 N	66.44 W
Yapacani, Bol.	166	C4	16.45 S	64.18 W
Yapen, Pulau, i., Indon.	60	F10	1.45 S	136.15 E
Yapen, Selat, strt., Indon.	60	F10	1.30 S	136.10 E
Yapeyú, Arg.	172	D9	29.24 S	56.50 W
Yappar, stm., Austl.	98	B4	18.22 S	141.16 E
Yaque del Norte, stm., Dom. Rep.	156	C12	19.50 N	71.41 W
Yaqui, stm., Mex.	120	G8	27.40 N	110.37 W
Yaquina, stm., Or., U.S.	146	F3	44.37 N	124.04 W
Yaracuy, state, Ven.	168	B7	10.20 N	69.10 W
Yaraka, Austl.	98	E5	24.53 S	144.04 E
Yardımcı, Tur.	76	A10	37.00 N	39.00 E
Yardımcı Burnu, c., Tur.	34	G13	36.13 N	30.24 E
Yare, stm., Eng., U.K.	10	I14	52.34 N	1.43 E
Yaremcha, Ukr.	38	E3	48.26 N	24.33 E
Yarí, stm., Col.	168	G4	0.19 S	72.20 W
Yariga-take, mtn., Japan	56	C10	36.20 N	137.39 E
Yarim, Yemen	72	G5	14.18 N	44.23 E
Yaring, Thai.	64	I5	6.52 N	101.22 E
Yaritagua, Ven.	168	B7	10.04 N	69.07 W
Yarkand see Yarkant, stm., China	48	G13	40.27 N	80.51 E
Yarkant see Shache, China	48	G13	38.24 N	77.14 E
Yarkant, stm., China	48	G13	40.27 N	80.51 E
Yarloop, Austl.	96	F3	32.57 S	115.54 E
Yarlung see Brahmaputra, stm., Asia	62	C7	24.01 N	91.00 E
Yarma, Tur.	76	A3	37.48 N	32.53 E
Yarmolyntsi, Ukr.	38	D5	49.11 N	26.51 E
Yarmouth, N.S., Can.	122	G10	43.50 N	66.06 W
Yarmouth see Great Yarmouth, Eng., U.K.	10	I14	52.37 N	1.43 E
Yarmouth, Me., U.S.	122	G6	43.48 N	70.11 W
Yarmu, Pap. N. Gui.	101a	a3	4.18 S	142.15 E
Yaroslavets', Ukr.	38	B12	51.32 N	33.39 E
Yarova, Ukr.	38	D16	49.03 N	37.38 E
Yarra Bend Park, p.o.i., Austl.	192b		37.48 S	145.01 E
Yarraloola, Austl.	96	D3	21.32 S	115.51 E
Yarram, Austl.	98	L6	38.33 S	146.40 E
Yarraman, Austl.	98	F9	26.50 S	151.58 E
Yarraville, Austl.	192b		37.49 S	144.53 E
Yarrawonga, Austl.	98	K6	36.01 S	146.00 E
Yarrow, stm., Eng., U.K.	180		53.40 N	2.49 W
Yarrow Reservoir, res., Eng., U.K.	180		53.38 N	2.34 W
Yarumal, Col.	168	D4	6.58 N	75.24 W
Yasawa, i., Fiji	101e	p18	16.47 S	177.31 E
Yasawa Group, is., Fiji	101e	p18	16.36 S	177.29 E
Yashio, Japan	186		35.49 N	139.51 E
Yashiro-jima, i., Japan	56	F5	33.55 N	132.15 E
Yasinia, Ukr.	38	E3	48.16 N	24.22 E
Yasnozir'ia, Ukr.	38	D10	49.29 N	31.35 E
Yasothon, Thai.	64	E7	15.46 N	104.10 E

Name	Page	Map Ref.	Latitude	Longitude
Yass, Austl.	98	J7	34.50 S	148.54 E
Yassıada, i., Tur.	185b		40.51 N	29.00 E
Yassy see Iaşi, Rom.	36	B14	47.10 N	27.35 E
Yasugi, Japan	56	D6	35.26 N	133.15 E
Yāsūj, Iran	74	E12	30.39 N	51.35 E
Yasun Burnu, c., Tur.	42	E7	41.06 N	37.40 E
Yasuní, stm., Ec.	168	H3	0.56 S	75.22 W
Yasuní, Parque Nacional, p.o.i., Ec.	168	H4	1.00 S	75.48 W
Yasynuvata, Ukr.	38	E16	48.08 N	37.51 E
Yata, Bol.	166	B3	13.21 S	66.35 W
Yata, stm., Bol.	166	B3	10.28 S	65.26 W
Yatağan, Tur.	34	F11	37.20 N	28.08 E
Yatate-yama, mtn., Japan	56	E2	34.10 N	129.13 E
Yaté, N. Cal.	101d	n16	22.10 S	166.54 E
Yates Center, Ks., U.S.	130	G2	37.53 N	95.43 W
Yates City, Il., U.S.	130	D7	40.46 N	90.00 W
Yathkyed Lake, l., Nu., Can.	110	C11	62.41 N	98.00 W
Yating, China	58	I2	25.03 N	106.05 E
Yatsuga-take, mtn., Japan	56	D11	35.59 N	138.23 E
Yatsuo, Japan	56	C10	36.34 N	137.08 E
Yatsushiro, Japan	56	G3	32.30 N	130.36 E
Yatsushiro-kai, b., Japan	56	G3	32.20 N	130.25 E
Yatuá, stm., Ven.	168	G8	1.28 N	66.29 W
Yatusiro see Yatsushiro, Japan	56	G3	32.30 N	130.36 E
Yauca, Peru	164	G3	15.40 S	74.32 W
Yauco, P.R.	158a	b2	18.02 N	66.50 W
Yauco, stm., P.R.	158a	b2	17.58 N	66.48 W
Yauco, Embalse de, res., P.R.	158a	b2	18.05 N	66.52 W
Yaundé see Yaoundé, Cam.	86	D2	3.52 N	11.31 E
Yaupi, Ec.	168	I3	2.49 S	77.54 W
Yautepec, Mex.	154	F9	18.52 N	99.02 W
Yau Tong, China	189d		22.18 N	114.13 E
Yāval, India	70	H5	21.10 N	75.41 E
Yavarí (Javari), stm., S.A.	164	D3	4.21 S	70.02 W
Yavaros, Mex.	154	B4	26.42 N	109.32 W
Yavatmāl, India	70	H7	20.23 N	78.08 E
Yaví, Cerro, mtn., Ven.	168	E9	5.32 N	65.59 W
Yavita, Ven.	168	F8	2.55 N	67.26 W
Yaviza, Pan.	156	H9	8.10 N	77.40 W
Yavkine, Ukr.	38	F11	47.16 N	32.36 E
Yavoriv, Ukr.	38	D2	49.56 N	23.24 E
Yavuzeli, Tur.	76	A8	37.20 N	37.34 E
Yaw, stm., Mya.	64	B2	20.54 N	94.48 E
Yawahara, Japan	186		35.59 N	140.01 E
Yawata see Kitakyūshū, Japan	56	F3	33.53 N	130.50 E
Yawata, Japan	186		35.32 N	140.08 E
Yawatahama, Japan	56	F5	33.27 N	132.26 E
Yaxchilán, hist., Mex.	156	D2	16.54 N	90.58 W
Yaxi, China	58	H2	27.30 N	106.44 E
Yaxian see Sanya, China	58	L3	18.14 N	109.30 E
Yayladağı, Tur.	76	C7	35.54 N	36.02 E
Yaylak, Tur.	76	A9	37.22 N	38.20 E
Yayuan, China	54	D7	41.46 N	126.12 E
Yazd, Iran	74	E14	31.53 N	54.21 E
Yazd, state, Iran	74	D14	32.00 N	54.30 E
Yazmān, Pak.	70	D3	29.07 N	71.44 E
Yazoo, stm., Ms., U.S.	134	E8	32.22 N	91.00 W
Yazoo City, Ms., U.S.	134	E8	32.51 N	90.24 W
Ybbs, stm., Aus.	24	H10	48.10 N	15.06 E
Ybbs an der Donau, Aus.	30	B12	48.10 N	15.04 E
Yding Skovhøj, hill, Den.	16	L7	56.00 N	9.48 E
Ýdra, Grc.	34	F6	37.20 N	23.29 E
Ýdra (Hydra), i., Grc.	34	F6	37.20 N	23.29 E
Ye, Mya.	64	E3	15.15 N	97.51 E
Yeading, ngh., Eng., U.K.	178		51.32 N	0.24 W
Yeadon, Pa., U.S.	203		39.56 N	75.15 W
Yebawgyi, Mya.	64	C2	18.40 N	94.35 E
Yèbles, Fr.	179		48.38 N	2.46 E
Yebyu, Mya.	64	E4	14.16 N	98.11 E
Yecheng, China	48	G13	37.53 N	77.25 E
Yech'ŏn, Kor., S.	56	C1	36.38 N	128.27 E
Yecla, Spain	28	F9	38.36 N	1.06 W
Yécora, Mex.	154	A4	28.20 N	108.58 W
Yedashe, Mya.	64	C3	19.10 N	96.20 E
Yedigöller Milli Parkı, p.o.i., Tur.	34	B14	41.15 N	31.44 E
Yedikule, ngh., Tur.	185b		40.59 N	28.55 E
Yedikule, hist., Tur.	185b		40.59 N	28.55 E
Yedseram, stm., Nig.	84	G7	12.27 N	14.05 E
Yeeda, Austl.	96	C4	17.36 S	123.38 E
Yeghegnador, Arm.	42	F11	39.45 N	45.21 E
Yegros, Para.	172	C9	26.27 S	56.24 W
Yegua Creek, stm., Tx., U.S.	136	D11	30.22 N	96.18 W
Yeguas, stm., Spain	28	G6	37.22 N	4.44 W
Yehliu, Tai.	187d		25.12 N	121.41 E
Yehliu Chia, c., Tai.	187d		25.13 N	121.42 E
Yei, Sudan	82	G6	4.06 N	30.40 E
Yeji, China	58	F6	31.50 N	115.53 E
Yekaterinodar see Krasnodar, Russia	40	I11	45.02 N	38.59 E
Ye Kyun, i., Mya.	64	C1	18.37 N	93.47 E
Yela Island, i., Pap. N. Gui.	96	B10	11.21 S	154.09 E
Yelanets', Ukr.	38	F10	47.42 N	31.51 E
Yelarbon, Austl.	98	G8	28.34 S	150.45 E
Yelizarove, Ukr.	38	E13	48.11 N	34.35 E
Yelizavethradka, Ukr.	38	E11	48.48 N	32.24 E
Yell, i., Scot., U.K.	10a	n18	60.36 N	1.10 W
Yellandu, India	69	C5	17.35 N	80.19 E
Yellow see Huang, stm., China	52	D8	37.48 N	118.53 E
Yellow, stm., U.S.	134	G12	30.33 N	87.00 W
Yellow, stm., In., U.S.	130	C11	41.16 N	86.48 W
Yellow, stm., Ia., U.S.	130	A6	43.04 N	91.10 W
Yellow, stm., Wi., U.S.	128	F6	46.00 N	92.21 W
Yellow, stm., Wi., U.S.	128	F7	44.57 N	91.19 W
Yellow, stm., Wi., U.S.	128	G8	43.55 N	90.01 W
Yellow Creek, stm., U.S.	134	D10	33.34 N	88.20 W
Yellow Creek, stm., Co., U.S.	150	C8	40.10 N	108.24 W
Yellow Creek, stm., Tn., U.S.	134	A11	36.25 N	87.34 W
Yellow Grass, Sk., Can.	142	E9	49.47 N	104.08 W
Yellowhead Pass, p., Can.	144	D12	52.53 N	118.22 W
Yellow House Draw, stm., Tx., U.S.	138	H7	33.36 N	101.50 W
Yellowknife, N.T., Can.	110	C8	62.27 N	114.21 W
Yellowknife, stm., N.T., Can.	110	C8	62.26 N	114.19 W
Yellow Medicine, stm., Mn., U.S.	128	G3	44.44 N	95.25 W
Yellow Mountain, mtn., Austl.	98	I6	32.30 S	146.51 E
Yellow Sea, s., Asia	54	G5	36.00 N	123.00 E
Yellowstone, stm., U.S.	118	D13	47.58 N	103.59 W
Yellowstone, Clarks Fork, stm., U.S.	140	C3	45.38 N	108.43 W
Yellowstone Falls, wtfl., Wy., U.S.	146	F16	44.43 N	110.30 W
Yellowstone Lake, l., Wy., U.S.	146	F16	44.27 N	110.23 W
Yellowstone National Park, Wy., U.S.	146	F16	44.58 N	110.42 W
Yellowstone National Park, p.o.i., U.S.	146	F16	44.30 N	110.35 W
Yellowtail Dam, dam., Mt., U.S.	140	B4	45.12 N	107.57 W
Yell Sound, strt., Scot., U.K.	10a	n18	60.32 N	1.15 W
Yellville, Ar., U.S.	130	H5	36.13 N	92.41 W
Yelverton Bay, b., Nu., Can.	108	A9	82.24 N	82.30 W
Yelyseivka, Ukr.	38	F15	47.01 N	36.23 E
Yemassee, S.C., U.S.	132	D5	32.41 N	80.50 W
Yemen, ctry., Asia	72	F6	15.00 N	44.00 E
Yemil'chyne, Ukr.	38	C6	50.52 N	27.48 E
Yenagoa, Nig.	84	H6	4.54 N	6.17 E
Yenakiieve, Ukr.	38	E17	48.14 N	38.14 E
Yenangyaung, Mya.	64	B2	20.27 N	94.52 E
Yenanma, Mya.	64	C2	19.46 N	94.48 E
Yen Bai, Viet.	64	B7	21.42 N	104.52 E
Yen Chau, Viet.	64	B7	21.03 N	104.20 E
Yenda, Austl.	98	J6	34.15 S	146.11 E
Yendéré, Burkina	84	G4	10.12 N	4.58 W
Yendi, Ghana	84	H4	9.26 N	0.00 W
Ye-ngan, Mya.	64	B3	21.09 N	96.27 E
Yengisar, China	48	G13	38.56 N	76.09 E
Yengo National Park, p.o.i., Austl.	98	I8	33.06 S	150.56 E
Yeniçağa, Tur.	34	C14	40.46 N	32.00 E
Yenice, Tur.	34	D10	39.56 N	27.18 E
Yenice, Tur.	76	A6	36.58 N	35.05 E
Yenice, stm., Tur.	34	B15	41.19 N	32.10 E
Yenice see Zamantı, stm., Tur.	42	F7	37.36 N	35.35 E
Yenicekale, Tur.	76	A7	37.37 N	36.37 E
Yeniceoba, Tur.	34	E15	38.52 N	32.47 E
Yenierenköy, N. Cyp.	76	C5	35.32 N	34.11 E
Yenifoça, Tur.	34	E9	38.44 N	26.49 E
Yenikapı, ngh., Tur.	185b		41.00 N	28.57 E
Yeniköy, ngh., Tur.	185b		40.59 N	28.53 E
Yenimehmetli, Tur.	34	D15	39.26 N	32.08 E
Yenipazar, Tur.	34	F11	37.49 N	28.11 E
Yenipazar, Tur.	34	D11	40.11 N	30.30 E
Yenişehir, Tur.	34	C12	40.16 N	29.39 E
Yenisey see Enisej, stm., Russia	50	C6	71.53 N	82.20 E
Yennora, Austl.	192a		33.52 S	150.58 E
Yenshuichen, Tai.	58	J9	23.20 N	120.16 E
Yeo, stm., Eng., U.K.	10	K9	50.45 N	3.33 W
Yeola, India	70	H5	20.02 N	74.29 E
Yeo Lake, l., Austl.	96	E4	27.58 S	124.24 E
Yeoval, Austl.	98	I7	32.44 S	148.39 E
Yeovil, Eng., U.K.	10	K10	50.56 N	2.38 W
Yeoville, ngh., S. Afr.	191d		26.12 S	28.04 E
Yepachic, Mex.	154	A4	28.24 N	108.22 W
Yeppoon, Austl.	98	D8	23.07 S	150.44 E
Yerba Buena Island, i., Ca., U.S.	200		37.48 N	122.22 W
Yerevan (Erivan), Arm.	42	E11	40.11 N	44.30 E
Yering, Austl.	192b		37.41 S	145.23 E
Yerington, Nv., U.S.	148	E6	38.58 N	119.09 W
Yerkes, Pa., U.S.	203		40.10 N	75.27 W
Yerkesik, Tur.	34	F11	37.07 N	28.16 E
Yerköy, Tur.	42	F6	39.38 N	34.29 E
Yerky, Ukr.	38	E10	48.59 N	30.59 E
Yerlisu, Tur.	34	C9	40.43 N	26.44 E
Yermasóyia, Cyp.	76	D4	34.43 N	33.05 E
Yermenonville, Fr.	179		48.33 N	1.37 E
Yermo, Ca., U.S.	148	I9	34.54 N	116.49 W
Yerupajá, Nevado, mtn., Peru	164	F2	10.16 S	76.54 W
Yerushalayim (Jerusalem), Isr.	76	G6	31.46 N	35.13 E
Yesa, Embalse de, res., Spain	28	B9	42.36 N	1.07 W
Yeshiva University, educ., N.Y., U.S.	194		40.51 N	73.55 W
Yeshvi, India	190c		18.55 N	73.03 E
Yeşil, stm., Tur.	8	G16	41.21 N	36.39 E
Yeşildere, Tur.	76	A4	37.09 N	33.31 E
Yeşilhisar, Tur.	42	F6	38.21 N	35.05 E
Yeşilkent, Tur.	76	B7	36.57 N	36.12 E
Yeşilköy, Tur.	34	C11	40.58 N	28.49 E
Yeşilköy Burnu, c., Tur.	185b		40.57 N	28.50 E
Yeşilova, Tur.	34	F12	37.30 N	29.46 E
Yeşiltepe, Tur.	76	A3	37.12 N	33.01 E
Yeso, N.M., U.S.	138	G4	34.25 N	104.36 W
Yeso Creek, stm., N.M., U.S.	138	G4	34.13 N	104.14 W
Yeste, Spain	28	F8	38.22 N	2.18 W
Yetman, Austl.	98	G8	28.54 S	150.46 E
Yetti, reg., Afr.	84	D3	26.10 N	7.50 W
Ye-u, Mya.	64	A2	22.46 N	95.26 E
Yeu, Île d', i., Fr.	20	H6	46.42 N	2.20 W
Yevlax, Azer.	42	E12	40.36 N	47.08 E
Yevpatoriia, Ukr.	38	H12	45.12 N	33.22 E
Yevsuh, Ukr.	38	D18	49.12 N	39.18 E
Yexian, China	58	E5	33.37 N	113.20 E
Yexian, China	58	C8	37.10 N	119.56 E
Yeywa, Mya.	64	B3	21.40 N	96.23 E
Yezd see Yazd, Iran	74	E14	31.53 N	54.21 E
Ygatimí, Para.	172	B10	24.05 S	55.24 W
Ygnacio Canal, can., Ca., U.S.	200		37.55 N	122.03 W
Yguazú, stm., Para.	172	B10	25.21 S	54.56 W
Yhú, Para.	172	B10	24.59 S	55.59 W
Yi, stm., China	58	D8	34.09 N	118.09 E
Yi, stm., China	58	D5	34.40 N	112.46 E
Yi, stm., China	58	B6	39.13 N	115.44 E
Yi, stm., Ur.	172	F10	33.07 S	57.06 W
Yi'allaq, Gebel, mtn., Egypt	76	H4	30.21 N	33.32 E
Yi'an, China	52	B10	47.52 N	125.18 E
Yibin, China	52	F5	28.46 N	104.37 E
Yibug Caka, l., China	70	B11	32.58 N	86.45 E
Yichang, China	58	F4	30.42 N	111.17 E
Yicheng, China	58	F5	31.42 N	112.15 E
Yichuan, China	58	D5	34.25 N	112.25 E
Yichuan, China	58	C4	36.02 N	110.08 E
Yichun, China	52	B10	47.43 N	128.54 E
Yichun, China	58	H6	27.47 N	114.22 E
Yidan, China	54	C6	43.24 N	125.25 E
Yidie, China	58	C4	37.00 N	110.27 E
Yidu, China	58	F4	30.24 N	111.26 E
Yidu, China	58	C8	36.41 N	118.28 E
Yidun, China	62	B8	30.18 N	99.22 E
Yiewsley, ngh., Eng., U.K.	178		51.31 N	0.28 W
Yifeng, China	58	G6	28.23 N	114.46 E
Yığılca, Tur.	34	C14	40.58 N	31.27 E
Yijun, China	58	D3	35.23 N	109.06 E
Yilan, China	52	B10	46.18 N	129.31 E
Yilaxi, China	54	C7	43.47 N	126.08 E
Yıldız Dağları, mts., Eur.	36	H14	41.50 N	27.30 E
Yıldızeli, Tur.	42	F7	39.51 N	36.36 E
Yiliang, China	52	F5	24.56 N	103.07 E
Yilläs, mtn., Fin.	14	E15	67.38 N	24.03 E
Yilong, China	58	F2	31.34 N	106.19 E
Yimianpo, China	54	B7	45.04 N	128.03 E
Yin, stm., China	54	C3	42.18 N	118.39 E
Yin, stm., Mya.	64	B2	20.02 N	95.00 E
Yinbaing, Mya.	64	D3	17.25 N	97.46 E
Yinchuan, China	58	B2	38.27 N	106.16 E
Ying, stm., China	58	E6	32.30 N	116.30 E
Yingcheng, China	58	F5	30.56 N	113.34 E
Yingchengzi, China	54	B6	44.08 N	125.56 E
Yingde, China	58	I5	24.10 N	113.25 E
Yinggehai, China	58	L3	18.31 N	108.48 E
Yingjin, stm., China	54	C3	42.18 N	119.23 E
Yingkoshih, stm., Tai.	187d		25.06 N	121.43 E
Yingkou, China	58	A10	40.37 N	122.30 E
Yingkou, China	58	A10	40.39 N	122.14 E
Yingpan, China	58	I2	25.48 N	106.18 E
Yingshan, China	58	F2	31.01 N	106.31 E
Yingshang, China	58	E7	32.38 N	116.15 E
Yingshouyingzi, China	58	A7	40.31 N	117.37 E
Yingtan, China	58	G7	28.14 N	117.02 E
Yining, China	48	F14	43.54 N	81.18 E
Yinjiang, China	58	G3	28.00 N	108.26 E
Yinkeng, China	58	H6	26.14 N	115.34 E
Yinmabin, Mya.	64	A2	22.04 N	94.54 E
Yinmatu, stm., China	54	D2	41.17 N	117.42 E
Yinnyein, Mya.	64	D3	16.48 N	97.23 E
Yin Shan, mts., China	52	C6	41.32 N	108.56 E
Yio Chu Kang, Sing.	189c		1.23 N	103.51 E
Yi'ong, stm., China	52	E3	29.52 N	95.07 E
Yi Pak, China	189d		22.19 N	114.00 E
Yirga 'Alem, Eth.	82	F7	6.51 N	38.24 E
Yirol, Sudan	82	F6	6.33 N	30.30 E
Yirrkala, Austl.	96	B7	12.13 S	136.50 E
Yirshi, China	52	B8	47.20 N	119.45 E
Yishan, China	58	I3	24.38 N	108.34 E
Yishui, China	58	D8	35.47 N	118.38 E
Yishun, Sing.	189c		1.26 N	103.50 E
Yisra'el see Israel, ctry., Asia	76	G5	31.30 N	34.45 E
Yisuhe, China	58	H5	27.46 N	112.54 E
Yitong, stm., China	54	C6	42.39 N	126.02 E
Yitulihe, China	52	A9	50.37 N	121.33 E
Yiwu, China	58	G8	29.18 N	120.04 E
Yiwu, China	64	A5	22.00 N	101.27 E
Yixian, China	54	D4	41.32 N	121.15 E
Yixing, China	58	F8	31.22 N	119.48 E
Yixun, stm., China	54	C2	40.57 N	117.44 E
Yiyang, China	58	G7	28.23 N	117.26 E
Yiyang, China	58	D5	34.30 N	112.10 E
Yiyang, China	58	G5	28.35 N	112.19 E
Yiyuan, China	58	C8	36.10 N	118.06 E
Yizhang, China	58	I5	25.25 N	112.57 E
Ylakiai, Lith.	26	D4	56.17 N	21.51 E
Yläne, Fin.	18	G9	60.54 N	22.25 E
Ylihärmä, Fin.	18	D9	63.08 N	22.48 E
Yli-Kitka, l., Fin.	18	A15	66.11 N	28.42 E
Ylimarkku, Fin.	18	E8	62.37 N	21.29 E
Ylistaro, Fin.	18	E9	62.57 N	22.31 E
Ylitornio, Fin.	14	F14	66.17 N	23.41 E
Ylivieska, Fin.	18	C11	64.04 N	24.34 E
Ylöjärvi, Fin.	18	F10	61.34 N	23.33 E
Ymeray, Fr.	179		48.31 N	1.42 E
Ymer Ø, i., Grnld.	108	C21	73.09 N	24.20 W
Ymir, B.C., Can.	144	G13	49.16 N	117.13 W
Ymittós, Grc.	185c		37.57 N	23.45 E
Ymittós Óros, mts., Grc.	185c		37.55 N	23.47 E
Yngaren, l., Swe.	16	I14	58.52 N	16.35 E
Yngen, l., Swe.	16	H12	59.44 N	14.18 E
Ynykčanskij, Russia	50	D16	60.15 N	137.41 E
Yoakum, Tx., U.S.	136	E10	29.17 N	97.09 W
Yockanookany, stm., Ms., U.S.	134	D9	32.39 N	89.40 W
Yocona, stm., Ms., U.S.	134	C9	34.10 N	90.12 W
Yōda, Japan	186		35.24 N	139.25 E
Yodogawa, ngh., Japan	188		34.42 N	135.28 E
Yōga, ngh., Japan	186		35.38 N	139.38 E
Yog Point, c., Phil.	68	C5	14.05 N	124.12 E
Yoğuntaş, Tur.	34	B9	41.50 N	27.04 E
Yogyakarta, Indon.	66	G7	7.47 S	110.22 E
Yogyakarta, state, Indon.	66	H7	7.45 S	110.30 E
Yoho National Park, p.o.i., B.C., Can.	144	E14	51.26 N	116.30 W
Yōka, Japan	56	D7	35.24 N	134.46 E
Yokadouma, Cam.	86	D2	3.31 N	15.03 E
Yōkaichi, Japan	56	D9	35.06 N	136.12 E
Yokkaichi, Japan	56	D9	34.58 N	136.38 E
Yoko, Cam.	86	C2	5.32 N	12.18 E
Yokoate-jima, i., Japan	55a	k19	28.48 N	129.00 E
Yokohama, Japan	56	D12	35.27 N	139.36 E
Yokohama, Japan	186		35.27 N	139.39 E
Yokohama, Japan	186		35.27 N	139.39 E
Yokohama-kō, b., Japan	186		35.27 N	139.39 E
Yokohama National University, educ., Japan	186		35.25 N	139.36 E
Yokohama Park Baseball Ground, p.o.i., Japan	186		35.26 N	139.39 E
Yokonuma, Japan	186		35.58 N	139.27 E
Yokosuka, Japan	56	D12	35.16 N	139.40 E
Yokosuka District Naval Headquarters, mil., Japan	186		35.17 N	139.39 E
Yokosuka-kō, b., Japan	186		35.18 N	139.39 E
Yokota, Japan	186		35.23 N	140.01 E
Yokota, Japan	188		34.40 N	135.55 E
Yokota Air Base, mil., Japan	186		35.45 N	139.21 E
Yokote, Japan	54	E14	39.18 N	140.34 E
Yola, Nig.	84	H7	9.11 N	12.29 E
Yolo, stm., D.R.C.	191b		4.19 S	15.20 E
Yolombo, D.R.C.	86	E4	1.32 S	23.15 E
Yom, stm., Thai.	64	D5	15.52 N	100.16 E
Yona, Guam	100c	j10	13.24 N	144.46 E
Yonago, Japan	56	D6	35.26 N	133.20 E
Yoncalla, Or., U.S.	146	G3	43.33 N	123.17 W
Yŏnch'on, ngh., Kor., S.	189b		37.38 N	127.04 E
Yonezawa, Japan	56	B13	37.55 N	140.07 E
Yong'an, China	58	I7	25.58 N	117.21 E
Yongchang, China	52	D5	38.14 N	101.58 E
Yongcheng, China	58	D7	33.55 N	116.21 E
Yŏngch'ŏn, Kor., S.	54	G8	35.57 N	128.55 E
Yongchuan, China	58	G1	29.21 N	105.54 E
Yongding, China	58	I7	24.43 N	116.43 E
Yongding, stm., China	58	A6	39.15 N	117.03 E
Yongdingmen Station, trans., China	189a		39.52 N	116.23 E
Yŏngdŏk, Kor., S.	54	F8	36.26 N	129.23 E
Yŏngdong, Kor., S.	54	F7	36.10 N	127.46 E
Yŏngdŭngp'o, ngh., Kor., S.	189b		37.32 N	126.54 E
Yongfeng, China	58	H6	27.19 N	115.24 E
Yongfeng, China	58	G7	29.44 N	116.50 E
Yonggi, Kor., S.	56	C1	36.22 N	128.24 E
Yonghe, China	58	G5	28.16 N	113.50 E
Yongi, China	54	C7	43.40 N	126.30 E
Yŏngil-man, b., Kor., S.	56	C2	36.02 N	129.26 E
Yongji, China	58	D4	34.51 N	110.28 E
Yŏngju, Kor., S.	54	F8	36.50 N	128.37 E
Yongkang, China	58	G9	28.53 N	120.02 E
Yongle, stm., China	58	H5	26.53 N	113.12 E
Yongnian, China	58	C6	36.47 N	114.28 E
Yongning, China	58	J3	22.44 N	108.28 E
Yongning, China	58	B2	38.20 N	106.16 E
Yongping, China	52	F4	25.24 N	99.29 E
Yongren, China	52	F5	26.05 N	101.48 E
Yongshan, China	52	F5	28.09 N	103.31 E
Yongshou, China	58	D2	34.43 N	108.06 E
Yongshun, China	58	G3	29.00 N	109.51 E
Yongtai, China	58	I8	25.52 N	118.57 E
Yŏngwŏl, Kor., S.	56	B1	37.10 N	128.28 E
Yongxing, China	58	H5	26.07 N	113.06 E
Yongxing, China	58	B4	39.08 N	110.31 E
Yongxiu, China	58	G6	29.03 N	115.49 E
Yŏngyang, Kor., S.	56	C2	36.39 N	129.06 E
Yongzhou, China	58	H4	26.13 N	111.37 E
Yŏnhŭi-ri, Kor., S.	189b		37.33 N	126.41 E
Yŏnhwa-san, mtn., Kor., N.	54	D7	40.46 N	127.23 E
Yonibana, S.L.	84	H2	8.27 N	12.12 W
Yonkers, N.Y., U.S.	124	D12	40.55 N	73.54 W
Yonkers Raceway, p.o.i., N.Y., U.S.	194		40.55 N	73.52 W
Yonne, state, Fr.	20	G12	47.55 N	3.45 E
Yonne, stm., Fr.	20	F12	48.23 N	2.57 E
Yonsei University, educ., Kor., S.	189b		37.34 N	126.56 E
Yopal, Col.	168	E5	5.21 N	72.23 W
Yopurga, China	48	G13	39.14 N	76.45 E
York, Austl.	96	F3	31.53 S	116.45 E
York, Eng., U.K.	10	H11	53.57 N	1.04 W
York, Al., U.S.	134	E10	32.29 N	88.18 W
York, Ne., U.S.	140	G15	40.52 N	97.35 W
York, N.D., U.S.	142	F14	48.18 N	99.35 W
York, Pa., U.S.	124	E9	39.57 N	76.43 W
York, S.C., U.S.	132	A4	34.59 N	81.14 W
York, stm., On., Can.	126	C12	45.20 N	77.34 W
York, stm., Qc., Can.	122	B11	48.49 N	64.28 W
York, stm., Va., U.S.	124	G9	37.14 N	76.24 W
York, Cape, c., Austl.	96	B8	10.42 S	142.32 E
York, Kap, c., Grnld.	108	B12	75.55 N	66.30 W
York Center, Il., U.S.	196		41.52 N	87.59 W
Yorkdale Centre, shp. cen., On., Can.	193b		43.44 N	79.27 W
Yorke Peninsula, pen., Austl.	96	F7	34.14 S	137.42 E
Yorketown, Austl.	96	G7	35.01 S	137.36 E
York Factory, Mb., Can.	110	D12	57.03 N	92.15 W
Yorkfield, Il., U.S.	196		41.52 N	87.56 W
Yorklyn, De., U.S.	203		39.48 N	75.40 W
Yorkshire Dales National Park, p.o.i., Eng., U.K.	10	G10	54.15 N	2.15 W
York Sound, strt., Austl.	96	B4	14.50 S	125.05 E
Yorkton, Sk., Can.	142	C11	51.13 N	102.28 W
Yorktown, Tx., U.S.	136	E10	28.58 N	97.29 W
Yorktown, Va., U.S.	124	G9	37.13 N	76.30 W
Yorktown, shp. cen., Il., U.S.	196		41.51 N	88.01 W
York Township Airport, arpt., Il., U.S.	196		41.51 N	88.02 W
York University, educ., On., Can.	193b		43.47 N	79.30 W
Yorkville, Il., U.S.	128	J10	41.38 N	88.26 W
Yorkville, N.Y., U.S.	126	E14	43.06 N	75.16 W
Yorkville, ngh., On., Can.	193b		43.40 N	79.24 W
Yoro, Hond.	156	E4	15.08 N	87.07 W
Yoron-jima, i., Japan	55a	I19	27.02 N	128.26 E
Yosemite National Park, Ca., U.S.	148	F6	37.42 N	119.36 W
Yosemite National Park, p.o.i., Ca., U.S.	148	F6	37.56 N	119.36 W
Yosemite Village see Yosemite National Park, Ca., U.S.	148	F6	37.42 N	119.36 W
Yoshii, Japan	188		34.53 N	135.03 E
Yoshii, stm., Japan	56	D7	34.36 N	134.02 E
Yoshikawa, Japan	188		34.55 N	135.28 E
Yoshino, stm., Japan	56	E6	34.04 N	134.36 E
Yösöbulag see Altay, Mong.	52	B4	46.23 N	96.15 E
Yos Sudarso, Pulau, i., Indon.	60	G10	7.50 S	138.30 E
Yŏsu, Kor., S.	54	G7	34.46 N	127.44 E
Yotaú, Bol.	166	C4	16.03 S	63.03 W
Yotvata, Isr.	76	I5	29.52 N	35.02 E
You, stm., China	52	G6	22.50 N	108.06 E
You, stm., China	58	I8	26.23 N	118.27 E
You, stm., China	58	G4	28.26 N	110.22 E
Youanmi, Austl.	96	E3	28.37 S	118.49 E
Youbou, B.C., Can.	144	H6	48.53 N	124.13 W
Youghal, Ire.	10	J5	51.56 N	7.51 W
Youghal Bay, b., Ire.	10	J5	51.54 N	7.51 W
Young, Austl.	98	J7	34.18 S	148.17 E
Young, Sk., Can.	142	C8	51.46 N	105.44 W
Young, Az., U.S.	150	I5	34.06 N	110.57 W
Young, Ur.	172	F9	32.42 S	57.37 W
Younghusband Peninsula, pen., Austl.	98	K2	36.03 S	139.33 E
Youngs Rock, r., Pit.	100k	c28	25.03 S	130.07 W
Youngstown, Ab., Can.	142	C2	51.32 N	111.12 W
Youngstown, Fl., U.S.	134	G13	30.21 N	85.26 W
Youngstown, N.Y., U.S.	126	E10	43.14 N	79.02 W
Youngstown, Oh., U.S.	124	C5	41.06 N	80.38 W
Youngsville, La., U.S.	134	G6	30.05 N	91.59 W
Youngsville, N.C., U.S.	124	H7	36.01 N	78.28 W
Youngsville, Pa., U.S.	124	C6	41.51 N	79.18 W
Youngwood Park, p.o.i., Pa., U.S.	197b		40.14 N	79.36 W
Yountville, Ca., U.S.	148	E3	38.24 N	122.21 W
Youssoufia, Mor.	84	C3	32.14 N	8.31 W
Youville, ngh., Qc., Can.	193a		45.33 N	73.39 W
Youxian, China	58	H5	26.59 N	113.20 E
Youyang, China	58	G3	28.58 N	108.41 E
Youyi Feng see Tavan-Bogdo-Ula, gora, mtn., Asia	48	E15	49.08 N	87.48 E
Youyu, China	58	A5	40.10 N	112.20 E
Yŏyang-ni, Kor., S.	56	B1	37.30 N	128.43 E
Yoyogi Stadium, p.o.i., Japan	186		35.40 N	139.42 E
Yozgat, Tur.	42	F6	39.49 N	34.48 E
Yozgat, state, Tur.	42	F6	39.40 N	35.10 E
Ypé Jhú, Para.	172	A10	23.52 S	55.27 W
Ypres see Ieper, Bel.	20	D11	50.51 N	2.52 E
Ypsilanti, Mi., U.S.	124	B2	42.14 N	83.36 W
Yreka, Ca., U.S.	148	B3	41.44 N	122.37 W
Ysabel Channel, strt., Pap. N. Gui.	101a	a4	2.00 S	150.00 E
Yser see IJzer, stm., Eur.	20	C11	51.09 N	2.44 E
Ysieux, Ruisseau l', stm., Fr.	179		49.09 N	2.22 E
Yssingeaux, Fr.	22	D10	45.08 N	4.06 E
Ystad, Swe.	16	L11	55.25 N	13.49 E
Ystwyth, stm., Wales, U.K.	10	I8	52.24 N	4.05 W
Ytambey, stm., Para.	172	B10	24.43 S	54.21 W
Ythan, stm., Scot., U.K.	10	D10	57.21 N	2.01 W
Ytre Sula, i., Nor.	16	F2	61.02 N	4.41 E
Ytterhogdal, Swe.	16	E12	62.10 N	14.55 E
Ytterøya, i., Nor.	16	D9	63.47 N	11.05 E
Yu, stm., China	58	J3	23.23 N	110.05 E
Yuam, stm., Thai.	64	C3	17.46 N	97.44 E
Yuan see Red, stm., Asia	62	D9	20.18 N	106.32 E
Yuan, stm., China	58	H6	28.03 N	115.28 E
Yuan, stm., China	58	G4	28.44 N	111.20 E
Yuan'an, China	58	F4	31.04 N	111.24 E
Yuanling, China	58	G4	28.20 N	110.16 E
Yuanmou, China	52	F5	25.43 N	101.51 E
Yuantan, China	58	J5	23.39 N	113.11 E
Yuanyang, China	58	D5	35.03 N	113.57 E
Yuasa, Japan	56	E8	34.02 N	135.11 E
Yuba, stm., Ca., U.S.	148	D4	39.07 N	121.35 W
Yuba City, Ca., U.S.	148	D4	39.08 N	121.36 W
Yūbari, Japan	54	C15	43.03 N	141.59 E
Yucaipa, Ca., U.S.	148	I8	34.02 N	117.02 W
Yucatán, state, Mex.	152	C7	20.50 N	89.00 W
Yucatán, Canal de see Yucatan Channel, strt., N.A.	156	A4	21.42 N	86.04 W
Yucatán, Península de (Yucatan Peninsula), pen., N.A.	156	C3	19.30 N	89.00 W
Yucatan Channel, strt., N.A.	156	A4	21.42 N	86.04 W
Yucatan Peninsula see Yucatán, Península de, pen., N.A.	156	C3	19.30 N	89.00 W
Yucca, Az., U.S.	150	I2	34.53 N	114.10 W
Yucca Lake, l., Nv., U.S.	148	G10	36.57 N	116.01 W
Yucca Mountain, mtn., Nv., U.S.	148	G9	36.56 N	116.29 W
Yucca Valley, Ca., U.S.	148	I9	34.07 N	116.25 W
Yucheng, China	58	C7	36.55 N	116.37 E
Yuci, China	58	C5	37.40 N	112.44 E
Yudu, China	58	I6	25.57 N	115.26 E
Yuechi, China	58	F2	30.30 N	106.26 E
Yuen Long, China	189d		22.26 N	114.02 E
Yueqing, China	58	G9	28.07 N	120.57 E
Yuexi, China	52	F5	28.40 N	102.30 E
Yueyang, China	58	G5	29.22 N	113.06 E
Yufa, China	58	B7	39.31 N	116.18 E
Yugan, China	58	G7	28.41 N	116.40 E
Yugoslavia, ctry., Eur.	36	F8	44.00 N	21.00 E
Yuguo, China	54	D5	41.52 N	123.15 E
Yuhebu, China	58	C3	37.59 N	109.50 E
Yuhuan Dao, i., China	58	G9	28.08 N	121.12 E
Yuhuang Ding, mtn., China	58	C9	36.50 N	121.21 E
Yukarıdudullu, ngh., Tur.	185b		41.02 N	29.09 E
Yukon, Ok., U.S.	138	F11	35.30 N	97.45 W
Yukon, state, Can.	110	B3	64.00 N	135.00 W
Yukon, stm., N.A.	109	D7	62.35 N	164.49 W
Yukon Flats, sw., Ak., U.S.	109	C11	66.30 N	146.00 W
Yukuhashi, Japan	56	F3	33.43 N	130.58 E
Yulao, China	58	J4	23.30 N	111.44 E
Yuli, China	48	F15	37.00 N	121.21 E
Yüli, Tai.	58	J9	23.20 N	121.18 E
Yuliangpu, China	54	C4	43.26 N	121.55 E
Yulin, China	58	L3	18.14 N	109.32 E
Yulin, China	58	J4	22.38 N	110.07 E
Yulin, China	58	B3	38.17 N	109.44 E
Yuma, Az., U.S.	150	K2	32.43 N	114.37 W
Yuma, Co., U.S.	138	A6	40.07 N	102.43 W
Yuma, Bahía de, b., Dom. Rep.	156	C13	18.21 N	68.35 W
Yuma Marine Corps Air Station, mil., Az., U.S.	150	K2	32.40 N	114.38 W
Yuma Proving Ground, mil., Az., U.S.	150	J2	33.05 N	114.25 W
Yumare, Ven.	168	B7	10.37 N	68.40 W
Yumbel, Chile	172	H1	37.07 S	72.32 W
Yumbi, D.R.C.	86	E3	1.50 S	16.37 E
Yumbo, Col.	168	F3	3.35 N	76.28 W
Yumen, China	52	D4	39.50 N	97.34 E
Yumt uul, mtn., Mong.	52	C4	44.38 N	97.00 E
Yumurtalık, Tur.	76	B6	36.47 N	35.47 E
Yun, stm., China	58	F5	30.41 N	113.56 E
Yuna, stm., Dom. Rep.	156	C13	19.12 N	69.37 W
Yunak, Tur.	34	E14	38.48 N	31.44 E
Yunan, China	58	J4	23.13 N	111.30 E
Yunaska Island, i., Ak., U.S.	109a	g24	52.37 N	170.40 W
Yuncheng, China	58	D4	35.01 N	110.59 E
Yuncheng, China	58	D6	35.35 N	115.56 E
Yungay, Chile	172	H2	37.07 S	72.01 W
Yungho, Tai.	187d		25.01 N	121.31 E
Yung Shue Wan, China	189d		22.14 N	114.06 E
Yunkai Dashan, mts., China	58	J4	22.38 N	110.43 E
Yun Ling, mts., China	52	F4	27.12 N	99.24 E
Yunnan, state, China	52	G5	24.00 N	101.00 E
Yunta, Austl.	98	I2	32.35 S	139.33 E
Yunwu Shan, mtn., China	58	A7	41.05 N	116.41 E
Yunxi, China	58	E4	32.49 N	110.13 E
Yunxian, China	52	G5	24.31 N	100.02 E
Yunxian, China	58	E4	32.48 N	110.49 E
Yunxiao, China	58	I7	24.04 N	117.19 E
Yunyang, China	58	F3	30.56 N	108.41 E
Yunyang see Yunxian, China	58	E4	32.48 N	110.49 E
Yunzalin, stm., Mya.	64	D3	17.22 N	97.40 E
Yuping, China	58	H3	27.10 N	108.48 E
Yuqing, China	58	H2	27.09 N	107.54 E
Yurimaguas, Peru	164	E2	5.54 S	76.05 W
Yuriria, Laguna de, l., Mex.	154	E8	20.15 N	101.06 W
Yur'ivka, Ukr.	38	E14	48.44 N	36.01 E
Yurok Indian Reservation, ind. res., Ca., U.S.	148	B2	41.20 N	123.50 W
Yurove, Ukr.	38	B6	51.21 N	27.50 E
Yuruá see Juruá, stm., S.A.	164	D4	2.34 S	65.47 W
Yuruarí, stm., Ven.	168	D11	6.45 N	61.40 W
Yurubi, Parque Nacional, p.o.i., Ven.	168	B7	10.25 N	68.42 W
Yürük, Tur.	34	C10	40.54 N	27.05 E
Yurumanguí, stm., Col.	168	F3	3.23 N	77.21 W
Yurungkax, stm., China	62	A5	38.01 N	80.32 E
Yuşa Tepesi, hill, Tur.	185b		41.09 N	29.05 E
Yuscarán, Hond.	156	F4	13.56 N	86.49 W
Yûsef, Bahr, can., Egypt	76	K1	29.18 N	30.50 E
Yushan, China	58	G8	28.40 N	118.15 E
Yü Shan, mtn., Tai.	58	J9	23.28 N	120.57 E
Yushanzhen, China	58	G3	29.37 N	108.20 E
Yushu, China	52	E4	33.00 N	97.00 E
Yushu, China	52	C10	44.49 N	126.33 E
Yūsofābād, ngh., Iran	185d		35.44 N	51.25 E
Yuste, Monasterio de, rel., Spain	28	D5	40.08 N	5.45 W
Yutian, China	58	B7	39.52 N	117.44 E
Yutian, China	62	A5	36.51 N	81.40 E
Yuty, Para.	172	C9	26.37 S	56.11 W
Yūwan-dake, mtn., Japan	55a	k19	28.17 N	129.19 E
Yuxian, China	58	D5	34.09 N	113.27 E
Yuxian, China	58	B6	39.50 N	114.34 E
Yuxian, China	58	B5	38.05 N	113.23 E
Yuyao, China	58	F9	30.03 N	121.09 E
Yuyuan Tan, l., China	189a		39.55 N	116.18 E
Yuzawa, Japan	54	E14	39.10 N	140.30 E
Yvelines, state, Fr.	20	F10	48.50 N	1.50 E
Yvelines, Forêt des, p.o.i., Fr.	179		48.40 N	1.55 E
Yverdon-les-Bains, Switz.	30	D3	46.47 N	6.38 E
Yvette, Fr.	179		48.43 N	1.55 E
Ywamun, Mya.	64	B2	20.31 N	95.25 E
Ywathagyi, Mya.	64	A2	22.19 N	95.48 E

Name	Page	Map Ref.	Latitude	Longitude
Ywathit, Mya.	64	C3	19.09 N	97.30 E
Z				
Zābala, stm., Rom.	36	D13	45.51 N	26.46 E
Zabalac', Bela.	26	G7	53.55 N	24.47 E
Zabalocce, Bela.	26	H11	52.40 N	28.34 E
Zăbalț, Rom.	36	C8	46.00 N	21.57 E
Žabasak, Kaz.	48	D10	50.21 N	61.40 E
Zāb-e Kūchek see Little Zab, stm., Asia	74	B9	35.14 N	43.25 E
Zabīd, Yemen	72	G5	14.11 N	43.18 E
Žabinka, Bela.	26	H7	52.11 N	24.01 E
Ząbkowice Śląskie, Pol.	24	F12	50.35 N	16.49 E
Žabljak, Yugo.	36	F6	43.09 N	19.07 E
Zabłudów, Pol.	24	C19	53.00 N	23.20 E
Žabno, Pol.	24	F16	50.09 N	20.54 E
Zābol, Iran	72	C9	31.02 N	61.29 E
Zābol, state, Afg.	70	C1	32.00 N	67.57 E
Zāboli, Iran	72	D9	27.14 N	61.42 E
Zabolotiv, Ukr.	38	E4	48.28 N	25.17 E
Zabolottya, Ukr.	38	B3	51.38 N	24.16 E
Zabor"e, Bela.	26	E12	55.55 N	29.19 E
Zabore, Russia	26	G14	53.06 N	31.42 E
Zabore, Russia	26	F15	54.51 N	32.41 E
Zabore, Russia	26	E14	55.23 N	31.34 E
Zabory, Russia	26	E15	55.57 N	32.19 E
Zábřeh, Czech Rep.	24	G12	49.53 N	16.52 E
Zabrze, Pol.	24	F14	50.18 N	18.46 E
Zaburun'e, Kaz.	40	H17	46.45 N	50.08 E
Zabyčanne, Bela.	26	G14	53.25 N	31.52 E
Zabzugu, Ghana	84	H5	9.17 N	0.22 E
Zacapa, Guat.	156	E3	14.57 N	89.32 W
Zacapu, Mex.	154	F8	19.48 N	101.47 W
Zacatecas, Mex.	154	D7	22.46 N	102.33 W
Zacatecas, state, Mex.	154	D7	23.00 N	103.00 W
Zacatlán, Mex.	154	F10	19.56 N	97.58 W
Zacharias Creek, stm., Pa., U.S.	203		40.11 N	75.23 W
Zachary, La., U.S.	134	G7	30.38 N	91.09 W
Zachepylivka, Ukr.	38	D14	49.12 N	35.14 E
Zachodnio-Pomorskie, state, Pol.	24	C11	53.37 N	16.25 E
Zacks Bay, b., N.Y., U.S.	194		40.36 N	73.29 W
Zacoalco de Torres, Mex.	154	E7	20.13 N	103.33 W
Zacualtipan, Mex.	154	E9	20.38 N	98.39 W
Začysce, Bela.	26	F11	54.24 N	28.44 E
Zadar (Zara), Cro.	30	F12	44.06 N	15.14 E
Zadetkale Kyun, i., Mya.	64	G4	10.08 N	98.12 E
Zadetkyi Kyun, i., Mya.	64	H3	9.58 N	98.13 E
Zadoi, China	62	B8	33.10 N	95.05 E
Zadorra, stm., Spain	28	B8	42.40 N	2.53 W
Zaerap, Russia	26	A19	59.17 N	36.37 E
Za'farâna, well, Egypt	76	I3	29.07 N	32.33 E
Zafer Burnu, c., N. Cyp.	76	C5	35.41 N	34.34 E
Zafirovo, Blg.	36	F14	44.00 N	26.50 E
Zafra, Spain	28	F4	38.25 N	6.24 W
Żagań, Pol.	24	E11	51.36 N	15.18 E
Žagare, Lith.	26	D6	56.21 N	23.14 E
Zagazig, Egypt	76	H2	30.35 N	31.31 E
Zaghouan, Tun.	32	H4	36.24 N	10.09 E
Zaghouan, Jebel, mtn., Tun.	32	H4	36.21 N	10.06 E
Zagora, Mor.	84	C3	30.19 N	5.51 W
Zagora, mts., Cro.	30	G13	43.40 N	16.15 E
Zagor'anskij, Russia	183b		55.55 N	37.55 E
Zagórów, Pol.	24	D13	52.10 N	17.56 E
Zagorsk see Sergiev Posad, Russia	26	D21	56.18 N	38.09 E
Zagórz, Pol.	24	G18	49.31 N	22.17 E
Zagreb, Cro.	30	E12	45.48 N	15.58 E
Zāgros, Kūhhā-ye (Zagros Mountains), mts., Iran	74	D11	33.03 N	48.33 E
Zagros Mountains see Zāgros, Kūhhā-ye, mts., Iran	74	D11	33.03 N	48.33 E
Žagubica, Yugo.	36	E8	44.12 N	21.44 E
Za'gya, stm., China	70	B13	31.56 N	88.59 E
Zagyva, stm., Hung.	36	B7	47.10 N	20.12 E
Zaharkovo, Russia	183b		55.47 N	37.19 E
Zaharovo, Russia	40	D11	54.22 N	39.17 E
Zāhedān, Iran	72	D9	29.29 N	60.51 E
Zahīrābād, India	69	C3	17.40 N	77.37 E
Zahlah, Leb.	76	E6	33.50 N	35.54 E
Zahnitkiv, Ukr.	38	E7	48.02 N	28.53 E
Zahns Airport, arpt., N.Y., U.S.	194		40.42 N	73.24 W
Zahodnjaja Dzvina see Western Dvina, stm., Eur.	26	D7	57.03 N	24.02 E
Záhony, Hung.	36	A9	48.24 N	22.12 E
Zahože, Russia	183a		59.44 N	30.51 E
Zahrebetnoe, Russia	14	C27	69.01 N	36.25 E
Zăicani, Mol.	38	E6	47.58 N	27.22 E
Žailma, Kaz.	48	D10	51.32 N	61.38 E
Zaimokuza, Japan	186		35.18 N	139.33 E
Zainsk, Russia	40	D18	55.19 N	52.03 E
Zaïre see Congo, Democratic Republic of the, ctry., Afr.	86	E4	4.00 S	25.00 E
Zaire see Congo, Democratic Republic of the, ctry., Afr.	86	E4	4.00 S	25.00 E
Zaïre see Congo, stm., Afr.	86	F2	5.58 S	12.44 E
Zaire see Congo, stm., Afr.	86	F2	5.58 S	12.44 E
Zaj, stm., Russia	40	D17	55.35 N	51.38 E
Zajarsk, Russia	48	C18	56.11 N	102.51 E
Zajcevo, Russia	183b		55.39 N	37.11 E
Zaječar, Yugo.	36	F9	43.54 N	22.17 E
Zajsan, Kaz.	48	E14	47.27 N	84.52 E
Zajsan, ozero, l., Kaz.	48	E14	48.00 N	84.00 E
Zaka, Zimb.	90	B10	20.20 S	31.27 E
Zakamensk, Russia	50	F9	50.23 N	103.16 E
Zakarpattia, co., Ukr.	36	A10	48.21 N	23.33 E
Zakhidne, Ukr.	38	B10	51.28 N	31.15 E
Zakhidnyi Buh (Bug) (Buh), stm., Eur.	40	F3	50.54 N	24.12 E
Zakhidnyy Buh (Bug) (Zakhidnyi Buh), stm., Eur.	38	D3	49.54 N	25.00 E
Zakho, Iraq	74	B8	37.08 N	42.42 E
Zakliczyn, Pol.	24	G16	49.51 N	20.48 E
Zaklików, Pol.	24	F18	50.46 N	22.06 E
Zakopane, Pol.	24	G16	49.18 N	19.57 E
Zakouma, Chad	82	E3	10.55 N	19.49 E
Zakroczym, Pol.	24	D16	52.26 N	20.37 E
Zákynthos, Grc.	34	F3	37.47 N	20.54 E
Zákynthos, i., Grc.	34	F3	37.43 N	20.49 E
Zákynthou, Porthmós, strt., Grc.	34	F3	37.50 N	21.00 E
Zala, state, Hung.	36	C3	46.45 N	16.50 E
Zala, stm., Hung.	36	C4	46.42 N	17.17 E
Zalaegerszeg, Hung.	36	C3	46.51 N	16.50 E
Zalalövő, Hung.	36	C3	46.51 N	16.35 E
Zalamea de la Serena, Spain	28	F5	38.39 N	5.39 W
Zalantun, China	52	B9	47.59 N	122.44 E
Zalari, Russia	48	D18	53.33 N	102.30 E
Zalaszentgrót, Hung.	36	C4	46.56 N	17.05 E
Zalău, Rom.	36	B10	47.10 N	23.04 E
Zaldívar, Laguna, l., Cuba	204b		22.58 N	82.27 W
Zalegošč', Russia	26	H19	52.53 N	36.54 E
Zalese, Russia	26	F4	54.50 N	21.31 E
Zalese, Russia	26	B19	58.42 N	36.09 E
Zalim, Sau. Ar.	72	E5	22.43 N	42.10 E
Zalingei, Sudan	82	E4	12.54 N	23.29 E
Zalishchyky, Ukr.	38	E4	48.38 N	25.46 E
Zaliznychne, Ukr.	38	F12	47.52 N	33.28 E
Žalon', stm., Eur.	38	B8	51.33 N	29.50 E
Zalozhtsi, Ukr.	38	D4	49.48 N	25.23 E
Žaltyr, Kaz.	48	D12	51.37 N	69.50 E
Žaltyr, ozero, l., Kaz.	40	H17	47.24 N	51.02 E
Zaluče, Russia	26	C14	57.38 N	31.45 E
Žaludok, Bela.	26	G7	53.35 N	24.58 E
Zalun, Mya.	64	D2	17.29 N	95.34 E
Zal'vjanka, stm., Bela.	26	G7	53.23 N	24.32 E
Zama, Japan	186		35.29 N	139.24 E
Zama, Ms., U.S.	134	E9	32.58 N	89.22 W
Zama, Camp, mil., Japan	186		35.30 N	139.24 E
Zama-iriya, Japan	186		35.29 N	139.24 E
Zamakh, Yemen	72	F6	16.30 N	47.35 E
Zamālik, Gezīret el-, i., Egypt	191c		30.03 N	31.13 E
Žamanajrakty, gora, hill, Kaz.	40	I19	45.02 N	54.26 E
Žamankak, Kaz.	40	G16	48.57 N	48.45 E
Zamantı, stm., Tur.	42	F7	37.36 N	35.35 E
Žamberk, Czech Rep.	24	F12	50.05 N	16.27 E
Zambeze, stm., Afr.	86	G4	18.48 S	36.15 E
Zambezi, Zam.	88	C3	13.32 S	23.06 E
Zambezi (Zambeze), stm., Afr.	88	D5	18.48 S	36.15 E
Zambezi Escarpment, clf., Zimb.	88	D4	16.25 S	30.12 E
Zambia, ctry., Afr.	88	C4	14.30 S	27.30 E
Zamboanga, Phil.	68	G3	6.54 N	122.04 E
Zamboanga Peninsula, pen., Phil.	68	G3	7.32 N	122.16 E
Zambrów, Pol.	24	C18	52.58 N	22.15 E
Zâmbuè, Moz.	88	D5	15.09 S	30.47 E
Zambujal, Port.	184c		38.52 N	9.07 W
Žambyl, Kaz.	48	F12	42.54 N	71.21 E
Žambyl, Kaz.	48	E12	47.11 N	71.44 E
Zamch, Pol.	24	F18	50.20 N	23.00 E
Zameznaja, Russia	12	D24	65.01 N	51.56 E
Zamhlaiy, Ukr.	38	B10	51.49 N	31.13 E
Zami, stm., Mya.	64	D3	16.09 N	97.58 E
Žamkavaja, hara, hill, Bela.	26	G8	53.30 N	25.43 E
Zamora, Ec.	164	D2	4.04 S	78.57 W
Zamora, Spain	28	C5	41.30 N	5.44 W
Zamora, co., Spain	28	C5	41.45 N	6.00 W
Zamora de Hidalgo, Mex.	154	F7	19.59 N	102.16 W
Zamość, Pol.	24	F19	50.43 N	23.15 E
Zamuro, Punta, c., Ven.	168	B7	11.25 N	68.49 W
Zamzor, Russia	48	C17	55.22 N	98.38 E
Zanaga, Congo	86	E2	2.51 S	13.49 E
Žanatas, Kaz.	48	F11	43.33 N	69.44 E
Záncara, stm., Spain	28	E8	39.18 N	3.17 W
Zanda, China	70	C7	31.29 N	79.49 E
Zanesville, Oh., U.S.	124	E3	39.56 N	82.00 W
Zanevka, Russia	183a		59.56 N	30.31 E
Zanjān, Iran	74	B11	36.40 N	48.28 E
Zanjān, state, Iran	74	B11	36.30 N	49.00 E
Zanjān, stm., Iran	74	B11	37.07 N	47.47 E
Zanjón, Arg.	172	C5	27.55 S	64.15 W
Žannetty, ostrov, i., Russia	50	A20	76.43 N	158.00 E
Zannone, Isola, i., Italy	32	D7	40.58 N	13.03 E
Zante see Zákynthos, i., Grc.	34	F3	37.43 N	20.49 E
Žanterek, Kaz.	40	H19	47.57 N	54.18 E
Zanthus, Austl.	96	F4	31.02 S	123.34 E
Zanzibar, Tan.	86	F7	6.10 S	39.12 E
Zanzibar, i., Tan.	86	F7	6.10 S	39.20 E
Zanzibar Channel, strt., Tan.	86	F7	6.00 S	39.00 E
Zaokskij, Russia	26	F20	54.44 N	37.24 E
Zaonežskij zaliv, b., Russia	18	E22	62.25 N	35.45 E
Zaostrove, Russia	18	G20	60.37 N	33.15 E
Zaostrove, Russia	18	G17	60.51 N	30.24 E
Zaō-zan, vol., Japan	56	A13	38.08 N	140.25 E
Zaozere, Russia	26	C21	57.11 N	38.15 E
Zaozere, Russia	183b		55.34 N	38.02 E
Zaozërnyj, Russia	48	C16	55.57 N	94.41 E
Zaozhuang, China	58	D7	34.52 N	117.33 E
Zap, N.D., U.S.	142	G12	47.16 N	101.55 W
Zapadnaja Dvina, Russia	26	D15	56.15 N	32.06 E
Zapadnaja Dvina see Western Dvina, stm., Eur.	26	D7	57.03 N	24.02 E
Zapadnaja Lica, stm., Russia	14	C22	69.10 N	31.56 E
Zapadna Morava, stm., Yugo.	36	F8	43.42 N	21.24 E
Zapadno-Karel'skaja vozvyšennost', plat., Russia	18	D19	63.41 N	31.53 E
Zapadno-Kazahstan, state, Kaz.	40	G17	50.00 N	51.00 E
Zapadno-Sibirskaja ravnina (West Siberian Plain), pl., Russia	48	B12	60.00 N	75.00 E
Zapadnyj hrebet, mts., Russia	50	F17	48.51 N	142.23 E
Zapadnyj Sajan, mts., Russia	48	D16	53.00 N	94.00 E
Západoslovenský, state, Slvk.	24	H14	48.20 N	18.00 E
Zapala, Arg.	166	G2	38.54 S	70.03 W
Zapardiel, stm., Spain	28	C6	41.29 N	5.02 W
Zapata, Tx., U.S.	136	H8	26.55 N	99.16 W
Zapata, Península de, pen., Cuba	156	A7	22.20 N	81.35 W
Zapatoca, Col.	168	D5	6.48 N	73.16 W
Zapatosa, Ciénaga de, l., Col.	168	C5	9.05 N	73.50 W
Zapljuse, Russia	26	B12	58.25 N	29.44 E
Zapole, Russia	26	B12	58.22 N	29.41 E
Zapoljarnyj, Russia	14	C21	69.25 N	30.50 E
Zapopan, Mex.	154	E7	20.43 N	103.24 W
Zaporizhzhia, Ukr.	38	F14	47.51 N	35.09 E
Zaporizhzhia, co., Ukr.	38	F14	47.30 N	35.30 E
Zaporože see Zaporizhzhia, Ukr.	38	F14	47.51 N	35.09 E
Zaporožskaja, Russia	38	H15	45.22 N	36.51 E
Zapovednoe, Russia	26	E4	55.04 N	21.24 E
Zapovednyj, Russia	54	C10	42.49 N	133.43 E
Zaprudnja, Russia	26	D20	56.33 N	37.27 E
Zaqatala, Azer.	42	E12	41.38 N	46.40 E
Zara see Zadar, Cro.	30	F12	44.06 N	15.14 E
Zara, Tur.	42	F7	39.53 N	37.46 E
Zaragoza, Col.	168	D4	7.30 N	74.52 W
Zaragoza, Mex.	120	F9	31.43 N	106.22 W
Zaragoza, Mex.	154	D9	23.56 N	99.46 W
Zaragoza, Mex.	154	A8	28.29 N	100.55 W
Zaragoza (Saragossa), Spain	28	C10	41.39 N	0.53 W
Zaragoza, co., Spain	28	C9	41.45 N	1.15 W
Zarajsk, Russia	26	F21	54.45 N	38.53 E
Zarand, Munții, mts., Rom.	36	C9	46.08 N	22.14 E
Zarand-e Kohneh, Iran	74	C12	35.16 N	50.33 E
Zaranj, Afg.	72	C9	31.06 N	61.52 E
Zarasai, Lith.	26	E9	55.43 N	26.15 E
Zárate, Arg.	172	G8	34.05 S	59.01 W
Zarautz, Spain	28	A8	43.17 N	2.09 W
Zarauz see Zarautz, Spain	28	A8	43.17 N	2.09 W
Zaraza, Ven.	168	C9	9.21 N	65.19 W
Zard Kūh, mtn., Iran	74	D11	32.22 N	50.04 E
Zareče, Russia	12	E21	63.08 N	44.43 E
Zareče, Russia	26	D16	56.51 N	33.48 E
Zareče, Russia	26	B22	58.55 N	39.40 E
Zareče, Russia	183b		55.41 N	37.23 E
Zarečensk, Russia	14	F22	66.40 N	31.20 E
Zarephath, N.J., U.S.	194		40.32 N	74.35 W
Zargān, Iran	74	F13	29.47 N	52.43 E
Zarghūn Shahr, Afg.	72	C10	32.51 N	68.27 E
Zaria, Nig.	84	G6	11.06 N	7.43 E
Zarichne, Ukr.	38	B5	51.47 N	26.07 E
Žarkamys, Kaz.	48	E9	47.55 N	56.27 E
Żarki, Pol.	24	F15	50.38 N	19.22 E
Žarkovskij, Russia	26	E15	55.51 N	32.17 E
Žarma, Kaz.	48	E14	48.47 N	80.51 E
Zarnān, Iran	185d		35.41 N	51.09 E
Zărnești, Rom.	36	D12	45.34 N	25.19 E
Zarrīneh, stm., Iran	74	B10	37.15 N	45.42 E
Zarrīn Shahr, Iran	74	D12	32.23 N	51.28 E
Žarsuat, Kaz.	48	E12	46.28 N	80.49 E
Zarubino, Russia	26	B16	58.44 N	33.26 E
Zarubino, Russia	54	C9	42.38 N	131.04 E
Zarumilla, Peru	164	D1	3.30 S	80.16 W
Żary, Pol.	24	E11	51.38 N	15.08 E
Žaryn', Russia	26	G16	53.47 N	33.01 E
Zarzaïtine, Alg.	84	D6	28.05 N	9.42 E
Zarzal, Col.	168	E4	4.23 N	76.03 W
Zarzuela, Arroyo de la, stm., Spain	184a		40.29 N	3.45 W
Zarzuela, Hipódromo de la, p.o.i., Spain	184a		40.28 N	3.45 W
Zasa, Lat.	26	D8	56.17 N	25.58 E
Zašeek, Russia	14	E23	67.25 N	32.30 E
Zašeek, Russia	14	F22	66.15 N	31.06 E
Zāskār, stm., India	70	B6	34.10 N	77.20 E
Zāskār Mountains, mts., Asia	70	B6	33.00 N	78.00 E
Zaslaue, Bela.	26	F10	54.00 N	27.17 E
Zaslauskae vadashovišča, l., Bela.	26	G10	53.58 N	27.22 E
Zasosna, Russia	38	C17	50.37 N	38.23 E
Zastava, Russia	40	B15	59.11 N	46.41 E
Zastavna, Ukr.	38	E4	48.31 N	25.51 E
Zastron, S. Afr.	90	G8	30.17 S	27.05 E
Zasule, Russia	12	D22	64.41 N	47.46 E
Zasulle, Bela.	26	G9	53.34 N	26.49 E
Žatec, Czech Rep.	24	F9	50.19 N	13.32 E
Zatyshshya, Ukr.	38	F8	47.20 N	29.53 E
Zavalla, Tx., U.S.	136	C13	31.08 N	94.25 W
Zavallia, Ukr.	38	E9	48.12 N	30.01 E
Zave, Zimb.	88	D5	17.12 S	30.02 E
Zavet, Blg.	36	F13	43.45 N	26.41 E
Zavidovići, Bos.	36	E5	44.27 N	18.08 E
Zavodoukovsk, Russia	48	C11	56.30 N	66.34 E
Zavodovski Island, i., S. Geor.	103	A2	56.20 S	27.35 W
Zavolžsk, Russia	40	C13	57.30 N	42.06 E
Zawadzkie, Pol.	24	F14	50.37 N	18.29 E
Zawichost, Pol.	24	F17	50.48 N	21.52 E
Zawiercie, Pol.	24	F15	50.29 N	19.25 E
Zāwiyat al-Mukhaylá, Libya	82	A4	32.10 N	22.18 E
Zāwiyat Masūs, Libya	82	A4	31.34 N	21.00 E
Zawr, Ra's az-, c., Kuw.	74	F11	28.43 N	48.22 E
Zawr, Ra's az-, c., Sau. Ar.	74	G11	27.27 N	49.17 E
Zāwyet Abū Musallam, Egypt	191c		29.56 N	31.10 E
Zāwyet el-Naggar, Egypt	191c		30.11 N	31.17 E
Zāwyet Nābit, Egypt	191c		30.07 N	31.09 E
Zāyandeh, stm., Iran	74	D13	32.15 N	52.53 E
Zaysan see Zajsan, Kaz.	48	E14	47.27 N	84.52 E
Zaysan, Lake see Zajsan, ozero, l., Kaz.	48	E14	48.00 N	84.00 E
Zayü, stm., China	62	C8	28.27 N	97.03 E
Zayzan see Zajsan, Kaz.	48	E14	47.27 N	84.52 E
Zaza, stm., Cuba	156	B8	21.39 N	79.32 W
Zaza, Presa, res., Cuba	156	B8	21.50 N	79.23 W
Zbarazh, Ukr.	38	D4	49.40 N	25.47 E
Zbąszyń, Pol.	24	D11	52.15 N	15.54 E
Zbąszynek, Pol.	24	D11	52.15 N	15.54 E
Zbiroh, Czech Rep.	24	G9	49.52 N	13.47 E
Zboriv, Ukr.	38	D4	49.40 N	25.09 E
Zbraslav, Czech Rep.	24	G10	49.59 N	14.24 E
Zbruch, stm., Ukr.	38	D5	48.32 N	26.26 E
Ždanov see Mariupol', Ukr.	38	F16	47.06 N	37.34 E
Ždanova, Russia	48	C15	58.39 N	88.54 E
Žd'ár nad Sazavou, Czech Rep.	24	G11	49.34 N	15.56 E
Ždiar, Slvk.	24	G16	49.16 N	20.15 E
Zdolbuniv, Ukr.	38	C5	50.31 N	26.15 E
Zduńska Wola, Pol.	24	E14	51.36 N	18.57 E
Zduny, Pol.	24	E13	51.39 N	17.23 E
Zdvyzh, stm., Ukr.	38	C9	51.00 N	30.04 E
Zealandia, Sk., Can.	142	C6	51.37 N	107.45 W
Zearing, Ia., U.S.	130	B4	42.09 N	93.18 W
Zeballos, B.C., Can.	144	G4	49.58 N	126.49 W
Zebedelia, S. Afr.	90	D9	24.19 S	29.18 E
Zebulon, Ga., U.S.	132	C1	33.06 N	84.20 W
Zebulon, N.C., U.S.	132	I7	35.49 N	78.18 W
Zedang, China	70	D13	29.16 N	91.50 E
Zeebrugge, Bel.	20	C11	51.20 N	3.13 E
Zeehan, Austl.	99a	n12	41.53 S	145.20 E
Zeeland, Mi., U.S.	130	B11	42.49 N	86.00 W
Zeeland, N.D., U.S.	140	B13	45.57 N	99.47 W
Zeerust, S. Afr.	90	D7	25.33 S	26.06 E
Zeesener See, l., Ger.	182a		52.17 N	13.39 E
Zeestow, Ger.	182a		52.34 N	12.58 E
Ẓefat, Isr.	76	F6	32.57 N	35.30 E
Žegalovo, Russia	183b		55.54 N	37.59 E
Zehden see Cedynia, Pol.	24	D10	52.51 N	14.11 E
Zehdenick, Ger.	24	D9	52.59 N	13.20 E
Zeil, Mount, mtn., Austl.	96	D6	23.24 S	132.23 E
Zeiselmauer, Aus.	182b		48.20 N	16.11 E
Zeist, Neth.	20	B14	52.05 N	5.15 E
Zeitz, Ger.	24	E8	51.03 N	12.07 E
Zeja, Russia	50	F14	53.43 N	127.15 E
Zeja, stm., Russia	50	F14	50.14 N	127.35 E
Zejskoe vodohranilišče, res., Russia	50	F14	54.28 N	127.45 E
Zekeriyaköy, ngh., Tur.	185b		41.11 N	29.01 E
Želča, stm., Russia	26	B11	58.18 N	27.40 E
Żelechów, Pol.	24	E17	51.49 N	21.54 E
Zelee, Cape, c., Sol. Is.	101b	e9	9.46 S	161.32 E
Zelënaja Rošča, Russia	18	G15	60.10 N	29.08 E
Zelënaja Rošča, Russia	40	D17	54.28 N	52.03 E
Zelenčukskaja, Russia	42	D9	43.51 N	41.35 E
Zelene, Ukr.	38	F12	47.42 N	33.09 E
Zelengora, mts., Bos.	36	F5	43.22 N	18.30 E
Zelenivka, Ukr.	38	G15	46.58 N	36.13 E
Zelenoborskij, Russia	14	F23	66.49 N	32.22 E
Zelenodol'sk, Russia	40	D16	55.50 N	48.31 E
Zelënoe, Kaz.	40	G17	48.07 N	51.31 E
Zelenogorsk, Russia	18	G16	60.12 N	29.42 E
Zelenograd, Russia	26	D20	56.00 N	37.12 E
Zelenogradsk, Russia	26	F3	54.57 N	20.29 E
Zelenokumsk, Russia	42	C10	44.26 N	43.51 E
Zeletin, stm., Rom.	36	C14	45.59 N	27.28 E
Železinka, Kaz.	48	D13	53.31 N	75.18 E
Železnik, Yugo.	36	E7	44.43 N	20.23 E
Železnodorožnyj, Russia	26	F4	54.22 N	21.19 E
Železnodorožnyj, Russia	48	B8	62.35 N	50.51 E
Železnogorsk, Russia	26	H18	52.19 N	35.22 E
Železnogorsk-Ilimskij, Russia	48	C18	56.34 N	104.07 E
Zelienople, Pa., U.S.	124	D5	40.47 N	80.07 W
Zelina, Cro.	36	C3	45.58 N	16.14 E
Željabino, Russia	183b		55.52 N	37.11 E
Zell, Ger.	24	F3	50.01 N	7.11 E
Zella-Mehlis, Ger.	24	F6	50.39 N	10.40 E
Zell am See, Aus.	30	C9	47.19 N	12.46 E
Zell am Ziller, Aus.	30	C8	47.14 N	11.52 E
Želon' see Žalon', stm., Eur.	38	B8	51.33 N	29.50 E
Zelo Surrigone, Italy	184b		45.23 N	8.59 E
Zelów, Pol.	24	E15	51.28 N	19.13 E
Zel'va, Bela.	26	G7	53.08 N	24.49 E
Želva, Lith.	26	E8	55.13 N	25.06 E
Žemaičių Naumiestis, Lith.	26	E4	55.21 N	21.42 E
Žemaitijos nacionalnis parkas, p.o.i., Lith.	26	D4	56.05 N	21.57 E
Zembin, Bela.	26	F11	54.21 N	28.13 E
Zembra, Île, i., Tun.	32	G4	37.08 N	10.48 E
Zemcy, Russia	26	D15	56.14 N	32.23 E
Zemetčino, Russia	40	E13	53.29 N	42.37 E
Zémio, C.A.R.	86	C4	5.02 N	25.08 E
Zempoala, hist., Mex.	154	F10	19.27 N	96.23 W
Zemun, Yugo.	36	E7	44.50 N	20.24 E
Zeneta, Sk., Can.	142	D12	50.44 N	102.02 W
Zeng, stm., China	58	J5	23.09 N	113.46 E
Zenica, Bos.	36	E4	44.12 N	17.54 E
Zenon Park, Sk., Can.	142	A10	53.03 N	103.45 W
Zentral-Friedhof, misc. cult., Aus.	182b		48.09 N	16.27 E
Zentsūji, Japan	56	E6	34.13 N	133.47 E
Zenza do Itombe, Ang.	88	B1	9.16 S	14.13 E
Zephyr, Tx., U.S.	136	C9	31.40 N	98.47 W
Zephyrhills, Fl., U.S.	132	H3	28.13 N	82.11 W
Zepu, China	48	G13	38.12 N	77.15 E
Zeravšan, stm., Asia	72	B10	39.20 N	63.46 E
Zeravšanskij hrebet, mts., Asia	72	B10	39.15 N	68.30 E
Zerbst, Ger.	24	D8	51.57 N	12.05 E
Žerdevka, Russia	40	F12	51.51 N	41.28 E
Zereh, Gowd-e, depr., Afg.	62	C1	29.45 N	61.50 E
Zergenta, Russia	40	H14	47.42 N	45.12 E
Zerind, Rom.	36	C8	46.37 N	21.31 E
Żerków, Pol.	24	D13	52.04 N	17.35 E
Zermatt, Switz.	30	D4	46.02 N	7.44 E
Zernograd, Russia	40	H12	46.50 N	40.18 E
Zerqan, Alb.	32	C14	41.31 N	20.21 E
Žešart, Russia	12	E23	62.03 N	49.33 E
Žetybaj, Kaz.	40	G16	48.55 N	48.04 E
Žetybaj, Kaz.	42	D15	43.35 N	52.05 E
Zeulenroda, Ger.	24	F7	50.38 N	11.59 E
Zeuthener See, l., Ger.	182a		52.21 N	13.39 E
Zeven, Ger.	24	C5	53.17 N	9.17 E
Zevenaar, Neth.	24	E2	51.56 N	6.04 E
Zeyādah Kot, India	190b		22.27 N	88.20 E
Zeyawadi, Mya.	64	C3	18.32 N	96.25 E
Zeydābād, Afg.	70	A2	34.19 N	69.08 E
Zeytinbaği, Tur.	34	C11	40.22 N	28.45 E
Zeytinburnu, ngh., Tur.	185b		40.59 N	28.54 E
Zeytindağ, Tur.	34	E10	38.58 N	27.04 E
Žezdy, Kaz.	48	E11	48.03 N	67.03 E
Zeze, Japan	188		35.00 N	135.54 E
Zêzere, stm., Port.	28	E2	39.28 N	8.20 W
Žezkazgan, Kaz.	48	E11	47.46 N	67.40 E
Zghartā, Leb.	76	D6	34.24 N	35.54 E
Zgierz, Pol.	24	E15	51.51 N	19.24 E
Zgorzelec, Pol.	24	E11	51.08 N	15.00 E
Zhabuchaka Hu, l., China	70	C9	31.20 N	84.00 E
Zhadove, Ukr.	38	A11	52.03 N	32.41 E
Zhakou, China	58	F5	30.00 N	112.15 E
Zhalun, China	70	B8	32.25 N	81.35 E
Zhaluomude, China	50	G13	49.13 N	120.24 E
Zhambyl see Žambyl, Kaz.	48	F12	42.54 N	71.21 E
Zhang, stm., China	58	I6	25.50 N	114.56 E
Zhang, stm., China	58	C5	36.28 N	115.16 E
Zhang, stm., China	58	F5	31.01 N	113.36 E
Zhangaōzen see Novyj Uzen', Kaz.	48	F8	43.18 N	52.47 E
Zhangaqazaly see Novokazalinsk, Kaz.	48	F10	45.51 N	62.07 E
Zhangbei, China	58	A6	41.09 N	114.41 E
Zhangdian see Zibo, China	58	C8	36.47 N	118.02 E
Zhangguangcai Ling, mts., China	52	C10	45.25 N	129.20 E
Zhanghuang, China	58	K3	22.00 N	109.27 E
Zhangjiakou, China	58	A6	40.49 N	114.52 E
Zhangping, China	58	I7	25.17 N	117.25 E
Zhangpu, China	58	I7	24.08 N	117.35 E
Zhangqiu, China	58	C7	36.43 N	117.30 E
Zhangsanta, China	58	B4	39.37 N	110.14 E
Zhangshuping, China	58	F4	31.20 N	111.02 E
Zhangwu, China	52	C9	42.22 N	122.31 E
Zhangye, China	52	D5	38.56 N	100.27 E
Zhangzhou, China	58	I7	24.31 N	117.39 E
Zhanjiang, China	58	K4	21.12 N	110.22 E
Zhanyu, China	54	B5	44.30 N	122.39 E
Zhao'an, China	58	J7	23.43 N	117.09 E
Zhaodong, China	58	B10	46.03 N	125.59 E
Zhaojue, China	62	C9	28.07 N	102.59 E
Zhaoping, China	58	I4	24.03 N	110.52 E
Zhaoqing, China	58	J5	23.03 N	112.27 E
Zhaotong, China	52	F5	27.20 N	103.43 E
Zhaoxing, China	52	B11	47.42 N	131.19 E
Zhaoyuan, China	58	B10	45.31 N	125.09 E
Zhari Namco, l., China	70	C10	30.54 N	85.30 E
Zharma see Žarma, Kaz.	48	E14	48.47 N	80.51 E
Zhashkiv, Ukr.	38	D9	49.14 N	30.07 E
Zhashui, China	58	E3	33.40 N	109.06 E
Zhaxi Co, l., China	70	B10	32.11 N	85.07 E
Zhaxigang, China	70	B7	32.30 N	79.40 E
Zhayyq see Ural, stm.	48	E8	46.50 N	51.32 E
Zhdany, Ukr.	38	C12	50.12 N	33.13 E
Zhecheng, China	58	D6	34.04 N	115.17 E
Zhegu, China	70	D13	28.43 N	91.43 E
Zhejiang, state, China	52	F8	29.00 N	120.00 E
Zhelin, China	58	F9	30.49 N	121.28 E
Zhem see Emba, stm., Kaz.	48	E9	46.43 N	53.08 E
Zhen, stm., China	58	I5	24.55 N	113.44 E
Zhen'an, China	58	E3	33.25 N	109.08 E
Zhenbeikou, China	58	B2	39.14 N	106.20 E
Zheng'an, China	58	G2	28.31 N	107.29 E
Zhengding, China	58	B6	38.08 N	114.33 E
Zhenghe, China	58	H8	27.22 N	118.49 E
Zhengjiawu, China	58	G8	29.30 N	120.05 E
Zhenglan Qi, China	52	C8	42.16 N	115.42 E
Zhengning, China	58	D3	35.30 N	108.26 E
Zhen'guosi, China	189a		39.51 N	116.21 E
Zhengyang, China	58	E6	32.36 N	114.22 E
Zhengzhou, China	58	D5	34.45 N	113.38 E
Zhenhai, China	58	K5	21.53 N	112.25 E
Zhenhai, China	58	G9	29.57 N	121.43 E
Zhenjiang, China	58	E8	32.12 N	119.25 E
Zhenlai, China	52	B9	45.50 N	123.12 E
Zhenning, China	58	H1	26.04 N	105.46 E
Zhenping, China	58	E5	33.08 N	112.19 E
Zhentou, stm., China	58	E6	32.55 N	114.22 E
Zhenxiong, China	52	F5	27.26 N	104.52 E
Zhenyu, China	58	H9	27.06 N	120.19 E
Zhenyuan, China	58	H3	26.51 N	108.18 E
Zhenyuan, China	58	D2	35.45 N	107.06 E
Zheriv, stm., Ukr.	38	B7	51.11 N	29.05 E
Zherong, China	58	H8	27.14 N	119.54 E
Zhetiqara see Džetygara, Kaz.	48	D10	52.11 N	61.12 E
Zhidan, China	58	C3	36.48 N	108.47 E
Zhijiang, China	58	H3	27.26 N	109.40 E
Zhixia, China	58	G8	29.41 N	119.36 E
Zhmerynka, Ukr.	38	D6	49.02 N	28.06 E
Zhob, Pak.	70	C2	31.20 N	69.26 E
Zhob, stm., Pak.	62	B2	32.02 N	69.48 E
Zhongba, China	62	C5	29.54 N	83.40 E
Zhongba, China	70	D10	29.36 N	84.11 E
Zhongdian, China	52	F4	27.49 N	99.42 E
Zhongguo see China, ctry., Asia	44	F14	35.00 N	105.00 E
Zhongning, China	58	C1	37.27 N	105.38 E
Zhongpingchang, China	58	F3	31.15 N	110.10 E
Zhongshan, China	58	I4	24.32 N	111.17 E
Zhongshan, China	58	J5	22.31 N	113.22 E
Zhongshan, sci., Ant.	103	B12	69.22 S	76.23 E
Zhongshan Park, p.o.i., China	187b		31.13 N	121.25 E
Zhongtiao Shan, mts., China	58	D4	35.12 N	111.35 E
Zhongwei, China	58	C1	37.30 N	105.11 E
Zhongxian, China	58	F3	30.28 N	108.05 E
Zhongxiang, China	58	F5	31.09 N	112.35 E
Zhongxin, China	58	I6	24.13 N	114.43 E
Zhongyaozhan, China	50	F14	50.46 N	125.53 E
Zhoucun, China	58	C7	36.47 N	117.50 E
Zhouning, China	58	H8	27.16 N	119.12 E
Zhoushan Dao, i., China	58	F9	30.03 N	122.07 E
Zhoushan Qundao, is., China	58	F10	30.21 N	122.21 E
Zhouzhi, China	58	D3	34.10 N	108.13 E
Zhovkva, Ukr.	38	C3	50.03 N	23.58 E
Zhovnyne, Ukr.	38	D11	49.23 N	32.41 E
Zhovte, Ukr.	38	E12	48.29 N	33.31 E
Zhovte, Ukr.	38	F12	47.47 N	33.50 E
Zhovten', Ukr.	38	F9	47.14 N	30.19 E
Zhovti Vody, Ukr.	38	E12	48.21 N	33.30 E
Zhovtneve, Ukr.	38	E11	48.39 N	33.04 E
Zhovtneve, Ukr.	38	B7	51.14 N	28.09 E
Zhovtneve, Ukr.	38	C13	50.56 N	34.22 E
Zhovtneve, Ukr.	38	G11	46.52 N	32.01 E
Zhovtneve, Ukr.	38	D13	49.39 N	34.09 E
Zhuanghe, China	58	B10	39.42 N	122.58 E
Zhuanglang, China	58	D1	34.58 N	106.07 E
Zhucang, China	58	H2	27.19 N	107.28 E
Zhucheng, China	58	D8	36.00 N	119.24 E
Zhudi, China	187b		31.12 N	121.18 E
Zhugan, stm., China	58	F6	32.16 N	114.42 E
Zhuhe, China	58	G5	29.44 N	113.07 E
Zhuji, China	58	G9	29.42 N	120.14 E
Zhuji see Shangqiu, China	58	D6	34.26 N	115.38 E
Zhujia Jian, i., China	58	G10	29.54 N	122.24 E
Zhujiang Kou, est., Asia	58	J5	22.36 N	113.44 E
Zhulong, stm., China	58	B6	38.46 N	115.55 E
Zhumadian, China	58	E5	32.58 N	114.01 E
Zhuolu, China	58	A6	40.22 N	115.12 E
Zhuozhou, China	58	B6	39.29 N	115.58 E
Zhuozi, China	58	A5	40.56 N	112.51 E
Zhuravychi, Ukr.	38	C4	50.59 N	25.43 E
Zhurivka, Ukr.	38	C10	50.30 N	31.46 E
Zhushan, China	58	E4	32.10 N	110.19 E
Zhusigang, China	58	F8	31.13 N	118.23 E
Zhuxi, China	58	E3	32.16 N	109.44 E
Zhuyangzhen, China	58	D4	34.20 N	110.44 E
Zhuzhou, China	58	H5	27.50 N	113.08 E
Zhydachiv, Ukr.	38	D3	49.23 N	24.08 E
Zhyhailivka, Ukr.	38	C14	50.37 N	35.06 E
Zhytomyr, Ukr.	38	C7	50.15 N	28.41 E
Zhytomyr, co., Ukr.	38	C7	50.30 N	28.30 E
Zi, stm., China	58	G4	28.43 N	112.32 E
Zi, stm., China	58	C8	37.10 N	118.33 E
Zia Indian Reservation, ind. res., N.M., U.S.	138	F2	35.29 N	106.43 W
Ziārat, Pak.	62	B2	30.22 N	67.47 E
Žiar nad Hronom, Slvk.	24	H14	48.35 N	18.52 E
Zibo, China	58	C8	36.47 N	118.02 E
Zicavo, Fr.	22	H15	41.52 N	9.05 E
Zichang, China	58	C3	37.07 N	109.39 E
Žičicy, Russia	26	E14	55.06 N	31.18 E
Ziębice, Pol.	24	F13	50.36 N	17.03 E
Ziebingen see Cybinka, Pol.	24	D10	52.11 N	14.47 E
Ziegenhain, Ger.	24	F5	50.54 N	9.14 E
Ziegenhals, Ger.	182a		52.21 N	13.40 E
Ziegenort see Trzebież, Pol.	24	C10	53.39 N	14.30 E
Zielona Góra, Pol.	24	E11	51.56 N	15.30 E
Zierikzee, Neth.	20	C12	51.39 N	3.54 E
Ziesar, Ger.	24	D8	52.15 N	12.17 E
Žiežmariai, Lith.	26	F7	54.48 N	24.27 E
Zifta, Egypt	76	H2	30.42 N	31.14 E
Žigalovo, Russia	48	D19	54.48 N	105.09 E
Žigansk, Russia	50	C13	66.47 N	123.21 E
Zigazinskij, Russia	40	E20	53.50 N	57.19 E
Zigong, China	52	F5	29.21 N	104.46 E
Zigui, China	58	F4	31.01 N	110.32 E
Ziguinchor, Sen.	84	G1	12.34 N	16.16 W
Žigulevsk, Russia	40	E16	53.25 N	49.27 E
Zig Zag, Cerro, hill, Peru	204d		12.12 S	76.59 W
Zihuatanejo, Mex.	154	G8	17.38 N	101.32 W
Ziiyang, China	58	E3	32.36 N	108.43 E
Zijančurino, Russia	40	F20	51.33 N	56.53 E
Zijin, China	58	J6	23.38 N	115.11 E
Zikeevo, Russia	26	G17	53.44 N	34.52 E
Zikhron Ya'aqov, Isr.	76	F5	32.34 N	34.57 E
Zikoufang, China	58	H7	26.22 N	117.24 E
Žilaja Kosa, Kaz.	40	H18	46.48 N	53.11 E
Žilaja Tambica, Russia	18	E23	62.30 N	36.04 E
Zile, Tur.	42	E6	40.18 N	35.54 E
Žilëvo, Russia	26	E21	54.59 N	38.02 E
Žilina, Slvk.	24	G14	49.13 N	18.44 E
Žilino, Russia	26	F4	54.54 N	21.57 E
Zillah, Libya	82	B3	28.34 N	17.33 E
Zillah, Wa., U.S.	146	D6	46.24 N	120.15 W
Ziller, stm., Aus.	30	C8	47.24 N	11.50 E

Name	Page	Map Ref.	Latitude	Longitude
Zillertaler Alpen (Aurine, Alpi), mts., Eur.	30	C8	46.54 N	11.49 E
Žiloj Bor, Russia	26	A17	59.05 N	34.37 E
Zilupe, Lat.	26	D11	56.23 N	28.06 E
Zilwaukee, Mi., U.S.	126	E6	43.28 N	83.55 W
Zima, Russia	48	D18	53.54 N	102.03 E
Zimapán, Mex.	154	E9	20.44 N	99.22 W
Zimba, Zam.	88	D4	17.19 S	26.13 E
Zimbabwe, ctry., Afr.	88	D4	20.00 S	30.00 E
Zimbabwe Ruins, p.o.i., Zimb.	88	E5	20.17 S	30.57 E
Zimbor, Rom.	36	B10	47.00 N	23.16 E
Zimi, S.L.	84	H2	7.19 N	11.17 W
Zimnicea, Rom.	36	F12	43.39 N	25.22 E
Zimnij bereg, cst., Russia	14	G31	65.53 N	40.42 E
Zimonino, Russia	26	G14	53.46 N	31.49 E
Zimovniki, Russia	40	H13	47.08 N	42.28 E
Zinder, Niger	84	G6	13.48 N	8.58 E
Zinga Mulike, Tan.	86	F7	9.02 S	38.46 E
Zinkgruvan, Swe.	16	I12	58.49 N	15.05 E
Zin'kiv, Ukr.	38	C13	50.12 N	34.22 E
Zin'kiv, Ukr.	38	D6	49.05 N	27.04 E
Zinnik see Soignies, Bel.	20	D13	50.34 N	4.04 E
Zinnowitz, Ger.	24	B9	54.04 N	13.54 E
Zion, Il., U.S.	130	B10	42.26 N	87.48 W
Zion National Park, p.o.i., Ut., U.S.	150	F4	37.17 N	113.01 W
Zionsville, In., U.S.	130	E11	39.57 N	86.16 W
Zipaquirá, Col.	168	E5	5.00 N	74.01 W
Zirbitzkogel, mtn., Aus.	30	C11	47.04 N	14.34 E
Zirgan, Russia	40	E19	53.12 N	55.54 E
Žirjatino, Russia	26	G16	53.14 N	33.43 E
Žirje, Otok, i., Cro.	30	G12	43.39 N	15.38 E
Žirnovsk, Russia	40	F14	50.59 N	44.46 E
Ziro, India	70	E14	27.38 N	93.42 E
Žirovnice, Czech Rep.	24	G11	49.15 N	15.10 E
Zitadelle, hist., Ger.	182a		52.33 N	13.13 E
Žiteli, Russia	12	D22	65.04 N	47.26 E
Žitkovo, Russia	18	G16	60.42 N	29.20 E
Zitong, China	58	F1	31.37 N	105.09 E
Zittau, Ger.	24	F10	50.54 N	14.48 E
Zitundo, Moz.	90	E11	26.45 S	32.49 E
Ziway, Lake see Ziway Hāyk', l., Eth.	82	F7	7.58 N	38.50 E
Ziway Hāyk', l., Eth.	82	F7	7.58 N	38.50 E
Zixi, China	58	G7	28.01 N	117.46 E
Ziya, stm., China	58	B7	39.09 N	117.10 E
Ziyamet, N. Cyp.	76	C5	35.27 N	34.08 E
Ziyuan, China	58	I4	26.01 N	110.31 E
Žizdra, Russia	26	G17	53.44 N	34.44 E
Žizdra, stm., Russia	26	F19	54.13 N	36.12 E
Žižginskij, ostrov, i., Russia	18	B23	65.11 N	36.48 E
Zizhong, China	58	G1	29.47 N	104.50 E
Zizhou, China	58	C3	37.37 N	109.41 E
Žižica, Russia	26	D14	56.17 N	31.22 E
Žižickoe, ozero, l., Russia	26	D14	56.14 N	31.15 E
Zjalëny Bor, Bela.	26	G11	54.00 N	28.27 E
Zlaté Moravce, Slvk.	24	H14	48.22 N	18.23 E
Zlatograd, Blg.	36	H12	41.23 N	25.06 E
Zlatoust, Russia	48	C9	55.10 N	59.40 E
Zlatoustovsk, Russia	50	F15	52.57 N	133.36 E
Zlín, Czech Rep.	24	G13	49.13 N	17.40 E
Zlīṭan, Libya	82	A2	32.28 N	14.34 E
Žlobin, Bela.	26	H13	52.54 N	30.03 E
Złocieniec, Pol.	24	C11	53.33 N	16.03 E
Złoczew, Pol.	24	E14	51.25 N	18.36 E
Złotoryja, Pol.	24	E11	51.07 N	15.54 E
Złotów, Pol.	24	C13	53.21 N	17.02 E
Žlutice, Czech Rep.	24	F9	50.05 N	13.08 E
Zlynka, Russia	26	H14	52.25 N	31.44 E
Zlynka, Ukr.	38	E10	48.29 N	31.32 E
Zmeinogorsk, Russia	48	D14	51.09 N	82.11 E
Zmiev see Zmiïv, Ukr.	38	D15	49.40 N	36.20 E
Zmiëvka, Russia	26	H19	52.40 N	36.22 E
Żmigród, Pol.	24	E12	51.28 N	16.54 E
Zmiïnyi, ostriv, i., Ukr.	38	H9	45.12 N	30.10 E
Zmiïv, Ukr.	38	D15	49.40 N	36.20 E
Žminj, Cro.	30	E10	45.09 N	13.55 E
Znaim see Znojmo, Czech Rep.	24	H12	48.51 N	16.03 E
Znamenka, Russia	26	F17	54.53 N	34.35 E
Znamenka, Russia	40	E12	52.24 N	41.26 E
Znamenka, Russia	48	D18	54.41 N	104.50 E
Znamensk, Russia	26	F4	54.37 N	21.13 E
Znamenskoe, Russia	26	G18	53.16 N	35.41 E
Znamenskoe, Russia	48	C12	57.07 N	73.50 E
Znamenskoe, Russia	183b		55.45 N	37.09 E
Znam'ianka, Ukr.	38	E11	48.42 N	32.39 E
Znam'ianka Druha, Ukr.	38	E11	48.42 N	32.35 E
Żnin, Pol.	24	D13	52.50 N	17.43 E
Znob-Novhorods'ke, Ukr.	38	A12	52.15 N	33.36 E
Znojmo, Czech Rep.	24	H12	48.51 N	16.03 E
Zoar, S. Afr.	90	H5	33.28 S	21.27 E
Žodino see Žodzina, Bela.	26	F11	54.06 N	28.21 E
Žodzina, Bela.	26	F11	54.06 N	28.21 E
Žodziški, Bela.	26	F9	54.37 N	26.30 E
Zoétélé, Cam.	86	D2	3.14 N	11.53 E
Zogang, China	52	F4	29.39 N	97.53 E
Zográfos, Grc.	185c		37.59 N	23.46 E
Žohova, ostrov, i., Russia	50	A19	76.08 N	152.47 E
Zohreh, stm., Iran	74	E11	30.04 N	49.30 E
Zolfo Springs, Fl., U.S.	132	I4	27.29 N	81.48 W
Żółkiewka, Pol.	24	F18	50.54 N	22.49 E
Zolochiv, Ukr.	38	D3	49.48 N	24.54 E
Zolochiv, Ukr.	38	C14	50.16 N	35.59 E
Zolotaja Gora, Russia	50	F14	54.16 N	126.37 E
Zolota Lypa, stm., Ukr.	38	D4	48.58 N	25.04 E
Zolotarëvka, Russia	40	E14	53.04 N	45.19 E
Zolote, Ukr.	38	E17	48.40 N	38.32 E
Zolotkovo, Russia	40	D12	55.31 N	41.05 E
Zolotnyky, Ukr.	38	D4	49.17 N	25.22 E
Zolotonosha, Ukr.	38	D11	49.40 N	32.02 E
Zolotuhino, Russia	40	E10	52.05 N	36.22 E
Zolotyi Potik, Ukr.	38	E4	48.54 N	25.20 E
Žolymbet, Kaz.	48	D12	51.45 N	71.43 E
Zomba, Mwi.	88	D6	15.23 S	35.19 E
Zongjiaxiang, China	187b		31.12 N	121.22 E
Zonguldak, Tur.	34	B14	41.27 N	31.48 E
Zonguldak, state, Tur.	34	B15	41.30 N	32.15 E
Zonza, Fr.	22	H15	41.45 N	9.10 E
Zoo, Bahnhof, trans., Ger.	182a		52.30 N	13.20 E
Zoppot see Sopot, Pol.	24	B14	54.28 N	18.32 E
Zopui, Bngl.	70	G14	23.39 N	92.14 E
Zorita, Spain	28	E5	39.16 N	5.42 W
Zornica, Blg.	36	G13	42.23 N	26.56 E
Zorra, Arroyo de la, stm., Mex.	136	E6	29.31 N	101.15 W
Zorritos, Peru	164	D1	3.41 S	80.39 W
Zouar, Chad	82	C3	20.27 N	16.32 E
Zouérat, Maur.	84	E2	22.40 N	12.26 W
Zoug see Zug, Switz.	30	C5	47.10 N	8.31 E
Zouxian, China	58	D7	35.23 N	116.56 E
Zovka, Russia	26	B11	58.26 N	28.52 E
Zozaya, Picacho de, mtn., Mex.	136	G5	27.10 N	102.34 W
Zoziv, Ukr.	38	D8	49.18 N	29.01 E
Zrenjanin, Yugo.	36	D7	45.23 N	20.24 E
Zrmanja, stm., Cro.	30	F12	44.12 N	15.35 E
Zruč nad Sázavou, Czech Rep.	24	G11	49.44 N	15.07 E
Žuantobe, Kaz.	48	F11	44.45 N	68.49 E
Zuata, stm., Ven.	168	C9	7.52 N	65.20 W
Zubaydīyah, Jabal az-, mtn., Syria	76	E8	33.48 N	37.02 E
Zubcov, Russia	26	D17	56.09 N	34.34 E
Zubkovychi, Ukr.	38	C6	51.00 N	27.42 E
Zubova Poljana, Russia	40	D13	54.04 N	42.50 E
Zubovo, Russia	18	G23	60.18 N	36.56 E
Zubovo, Russia	26	F18	54.33 N	35.29 E
Zuckerhütl, mtn., Aus.	30	C8	46.58 N	11.09 E
Zudáñez, Bol.	166	C4	19.06 S	64.44 W
Zuera, Spain	28	C10	41.52 N	0.47 W
Zuevka, Russia	40	B17	58.24 N	51.08 E
Ẓufar (Dhofar), reg., Oman	72	F7	17.01 N	54.06 E
Zug, Switz.	30	C5	47.10 N	8.31 E
Zugdidi, Geor.	42	D9	42.30 N	41.51 E
Zugersee see Zuger See, l., Switz.	30	C5	47.08 N	8.28 E
Zuger See, l., Switz.	30	C5	47.08 N	8.28 E
Zug Island, i., Mi., U.S.	199		42.17 N	83.07 W
Zugló, ngh., Hung.	182c		47.31 N	19.08 E
Zugspitze, mtn., Eur.	24	I6	47.25 N	10.59 E
Zühlsdorf, Ger.	182a		52.44 N	13.24 E
Zui, Russia	26	C14	57.06 N	31.36 E
Zuia, Ukr.	38	H13	45.03 N	34.19 E
Žuja, stm., Russia	50	E12	58.45 N	118.07 E
Zújar, stm., Spain	28	F5	39.00 N	5.46 W
Zújar, Embalse de, res., Spain	28	F5	38.56 N	5.27 W
Žukopa, Russia	26	D15	56.33 N	32.41 E
Žukopa, stm., Russia	26	D15	56.56 N	32.45 E
Žukovka, Russia	26	G16	53.31 N	33.44 E
Žukovka, Russia	183b		55.44 N	37.15 E
Žukovskij, Russia	26	E21	55.35 N	38.09 E
Żukowo, Pol.	24	B14	54.20 N	18.22 E
Žuldyz, Kaz.	40	G16	49.14 N	49.28 E
Žulebino, Russia	183b		55.42 N	37.51 E
Zuli, stm., China	58	D1	35.46 N	104.55 E
Zulia, state, Ven.	168	C5	10.00 N	72.10 W
Zulia, stm., S.A.	168	C5	9.03 N	72.17 W
Züllichau see Sulechów, Pol.	24	D11	52.05 N	15.37 E
Zululand, hist. reg., S. Afr.	90	F10	28.10 S	32.00 E
Zumar, Turat el-, can., Egypt	191c		29.58 N	31.15 E
Zumbo, Moz.	88	D5	15.36 S	30.26 E
Zumbro, stm., Mn., U.S.	128	G6	44.17 N	91.54 W
Zumbro, North Fork, stm., Mn., U.S.	128	G6	44.15 N	92.28 W
Zumbro, South Fork, stm., Mn., U.S.	128	H6	44.15 N	92.28 W
Zumbrota, Mn., U.S.	128	G6	44.17 N	92.41 W
Zungeru, Nig.	84	H6	9.49 N	6.08 E
Zunhua, China	58	A7	40.10 N	117.57 E
Zuni, stm., U.S.	150	I7	34.38 N	109.40 W
Zuni Indian Reservation, ind. res., N.M., U.S.	150	I7	35.01 N	109.07 W
Zuni Pueblo, N.M., U.S.	150	H8	35.03 N	108.51 W
Zunyi, China	58	H2	27.42 N	106.56 E
Zuo, stm., China	52	G6	22.50 N	108.06 E
Zuodeng, China	58	J2	23.27 N	107.00 E
Zuomuchedong Hu, l., China	70	D12	28.24 N	88.13 E
Zuoyun, China	58	A5	40.04 N	112.45 E
Županja, Cro.	30	E15	45.04 N	18.41 E
Zūrābād, Iran	74	A9	38.49 N	44.35 E
Žuravičy, Bela.	26	G13	53.15 N	30.33 E
Zurayghiṭ, Sau. Ar.	74	G7	26.29 N	40.33 E
Zurich, On., Can.	126	E8	43.26 N	81.37 W
Zürich (Zurigo), Switz.	30	C5	47.22 N	8.32 E
Zurich, Lake see Zürichsee, l., Switz.	30	C5	47.13 N	8.45 E
Zurich, Lake, l., Il., U.S.	196		42.12 N	88.06 W
Zürichsee, l., Switz.	30	C5	47.13 N	8.45 E
Zurigo see Zürich, Switz.	30	C5	47.22 N	8.32 E
Zurmi, Nig.	84	G6	12.46 N	6.46 E
Żuromin, Pol.	24	C15	53.04 N	19.57 E
Zuru, Nig.	84	G6	11.26 N	5.13 E
Zuša, stm., Russia	26	G20	53.26 N	36.23 E
Zusam, stm., Ger.	30	B7	48.42 N	10.47 E
Žut, Otok, i., Cro.	30	G12	43.52 N	15.19 E
Zutphen, Neth.	20	B15	52.08 N	6.11 E
Zuwārah, Libya	82	A2	32.55 N	12.05 E
Zuwayzā, Jord.	76	G6	31.42 N	35.57 E
Z'uzino, Russia	183b		55.40 N	38.07 E
Z'uzino, ngh., Russia	183b		55.39 N	37.35 E
Zv'agino, Russia	183b		55.59 N	37.48 E
Zvannoe, Russia	38	B13	51.22 N	34.32 E
Zvenigorod, Russia	26	E19	55.43 N	36.52 E
Zvenyhorodka, Ukr.	38	D9	49.04 N	30.58 E
Zverinogolovskoe, Russia	48	D10	54.27 N	64.51 E
Zvezdec, Blg.	36	G14	42.07 N	27.26 E
Zvezdnyj, Russia	48	C19	56.44 N	106.31 E
Zvishavane, Zimb.	88	E4	20.19 S	30.02 E
Zvolen, Slvk.	24	H15	48.34 N	19.07 E
Zvornik, Bos.	36	E6	44.23 N	19.06 E
Zweckel, ngh., Ger.	181		51.36 N	6.59 E
Zwedru, Lib.	84	H3	6.04 N	8.07 W
Zweibrücken, Ger.	24	G3	49.15 N	7.21 E
Zweisimmen, Switz.	30	D4	46.33 N	7.21 E
Zwettl, Aus.	30	B12	48.36 N	15.10 E
Zwickau, Ger.	24	F8	50.43 N	12.29 E
Zwierzyniec, Pol.	24	F18	50.37 N	22.58 E
Zwiesel, Ger.	24	G9	49.00 N	13.13 E
Zwoleń, Pol.	24	E17	51.21 N	21.35 E
Zwölfaxing, Aus.	182b		48.06 N	16.28 E
Zwolle, Neth.	20	B14	52.31 N	6.05 E
Zwolle, La., U.S.	136	C14	31.38 N	93.39 W
Żychlin, Pol.	24	D15	52.15 N	19.37 E
Zymoetz, stm., B.C., Can.	144	B2	54.32 N	128.29 W
Zymohir'ia, Ukr.	38	E17	48.35 N	38.56 E
Żyrardów, Pol.	24	D16	52.03 N	20.27 E
Zyrjanka, Russia	50	C19	65.44 N	150.50 E
Zyrjanovsk, Kaz.	48	E14	49.44 N	84.18 E
Zyrjanskoe, Russia	48	C15	56.49 N	86.36 E
Zyryan see Zyrjanovsk, Kaz.	48	E14	49.44 N	84.18 E
Żyrzyn, Pol.	24	E18	51.29 N	22.07 E
Žytkavičy, Bela.	26	H10	52.12 N	27.51 E
Żywiec, Pol.	24	G15	49.41 N	19.12 E
Žyžma, stm., Bela.	26	F8	53.54 N	25.36 E

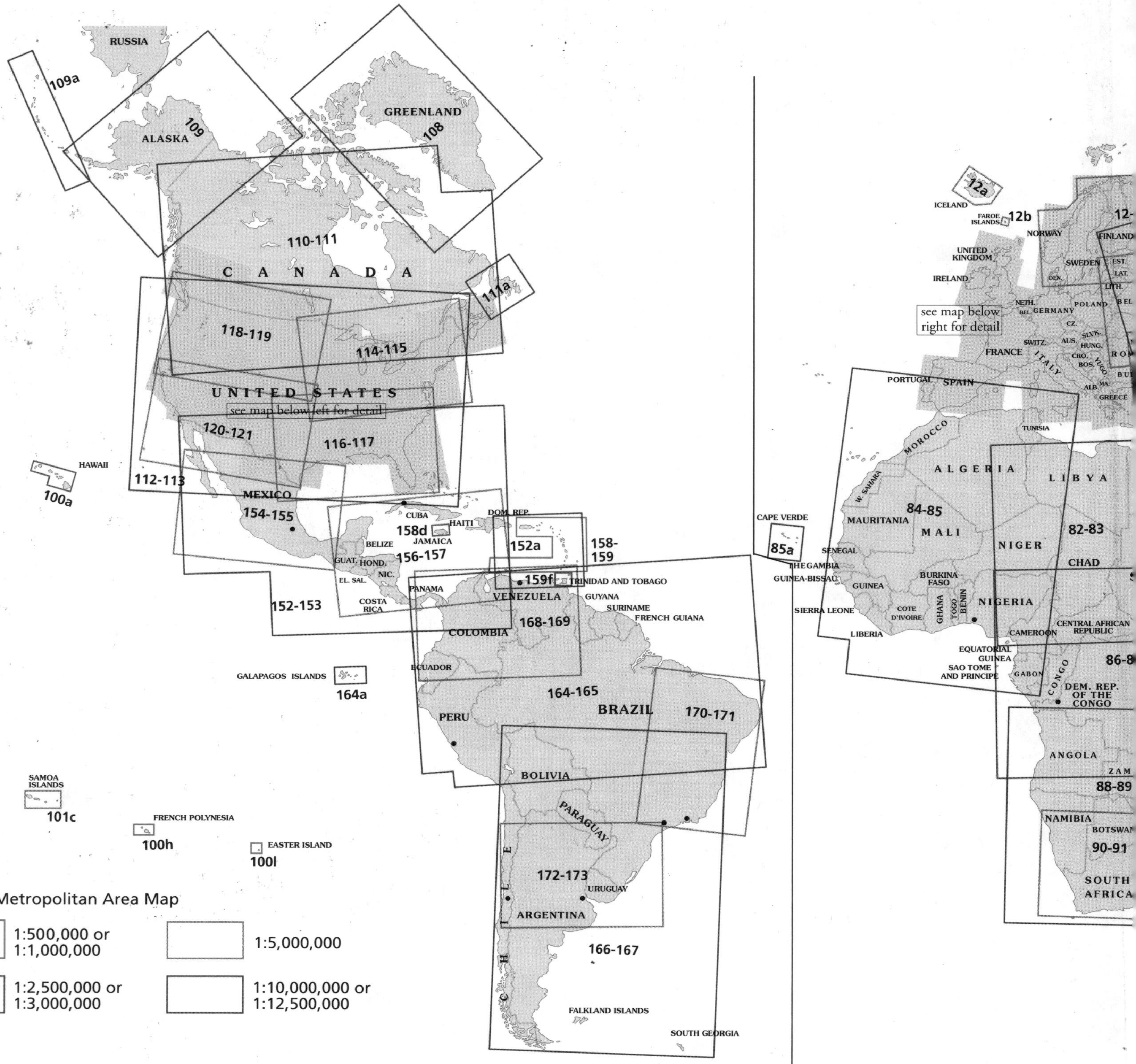

RUSSIA
109a
109
ALASKA
GREENLAND
108
110-111
CANADA
111a
118-119
114-115
UNITED STATES
see map below left for detail
120-121
116-117
HAWAII
100a
112-113
MEXICO
154-155
CUBA
158d
HAITI
DOM. REP.
JAMAICA
BELIZE
156-157
152a
158-159
GUAT.
HOND.
EL SAL.
NIC.
COSTA RICA
PANAMA
159f
TRINIDAD AND TOBAGO
VENEZUELA
GUYANA
SURINAME
FRENCH GUIANA
152-153
COLOMBIA
168-169
ECUADOR
GALAPAGOS ISLANDS
164a
164-165
BRAZIL
170-171
PERU
BOLIVIA
PARAGUAY
SAMOA ISLANDS
101c
FRENCH POLYNESIA
100h
EASTER ISLAND
100l
172-173
URUGUAY
ARGENTINA
CHILE
166-167
FALKLAND ISLANDS
SOUTH GEORGIA
ICELAND
12a
FAROE ISLANDS
12b
NORWAY
UNITED KINGDOM
IRELAND
SWEDEN
FINLAND
EST.
LAT.
LITH.
DEN.
NETH.
BEL.
GERMANY
POLAND
CZ.
SLVK.
AUS.
HUNG.
SWITZ.
FRANCE
ITALY
CRO.
BOS.
ALB.
GREECE
see map below right for detail
PORTUGAL
SPAIN
TUNISIA
MOROCCO
ALGERIA
LIBYA
W. SAHARA
84-85
MAURITANIA
MALI
82-83
NIGER
CHAD
CAPE VERDE
85a
SENEGAL
THE GAMBIA
GUINEA-BISSAU
GUINEA
BURKINA FASO
SIERRA LEONE
COTE D'IVOIRE
GHANA
TOGO
BENIN
NIGERIA
LIBERIA
CAMEROON
CENTRAL AFRICAN REPUBLIC
EQUATORIAL GUINEA
SAO TOME AND PRINCIPE
GABON
CONGO
DEM. REP. OF THE CONGO
ANGOLA
88-89
NAMIBIA
BOTSWANA
90-91
SOUTH AFRICA

• Metropolitan Area Map

1:500,000 or 1:1,000,000

1:5,000,000

1:2,500,000 or 1:3,000,000

1:10,000,000 or 1:12,500,000

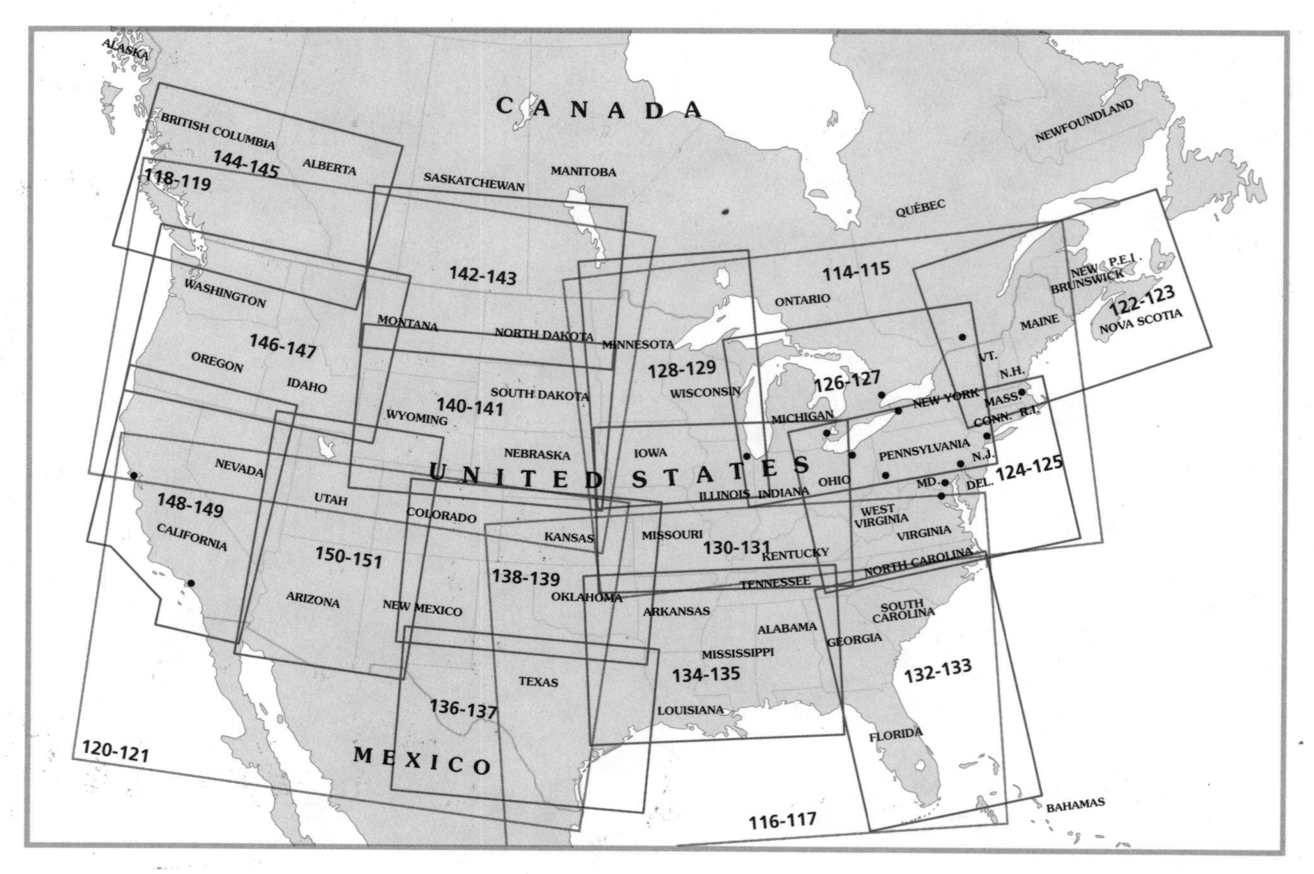